Magdalen College Library
Class No. Magd.

D1460104

Gift of Professor Sir Guenter Treitel
2006.

305918004U

THE COMMON LAW LIBRARY

SALE OF GOODS

WITHDRAWN
From Magdalen College Library

OTHER VOLUMES IN THE COMMON LAW LIBRARY

Chitty on Contracts

Clerk & Lindsell on Torts

Chitty & Jacob's Queen's Bench Forms

Bullen & Leake & Jacob's Precedents of Pleadings

Charlesworth and Percy on Negligence

Bowstead & Reynolds on Agency

Gatley on Libel and Slander

McGregor on Damages

Phipson on Evidence

Jackson & Powell on Professional Negligence

Goff & Jones, The Law of Restitution

Arlidge, Eady & Smith on Contempt

AUSTRALIA
Law Book Co.
Sydney

CANADA and USA
Carswell
Toronto

HONG KONG
Sweet & Maxwell Asia

NEW ZEALAND
Brookers
Wellington

SINGAPORE AND MALAYSIA
Sweet & Maxwell Asia
Singapore and Kuala Lumpur

THE COMMON LAW LIBRARY

BENJAMIN'S SALE OF GOODS

SEVENTH EDITION

LONDON
SWEET & MAXWELL
2006

MAGDALEN COLLEGE LIBRARY

BENJAMIN'S TREATISE ON THE LAW OF SALE OF PERSONAL PROPERTY WITH REFERENCES TO THE FRENCH CODE AND CIVIL LAW

First Edition	(1868)	Judah Philip Benjamin
Second Edition	(1873)	" " "
Third Edition	(1883)	A. B. Pearson and H. F. Boyd
Fourth Edition	(1888)	A. B. Pearson-Gee and H. F. Boyd
Fifth Edition	(1906)	W. C. A. Ker and A. R. Butterworth
Sixth Edition	(1920)	W. C. A. Ker
Seventh Edition	(1931)	His Hon. Judge A. R. Kennedy, K.C.
Eighth Edition	(1950)	The Hon. Sir Donald Leslie Finnemore and Arthur E. James

BENJAMIN'S SALE OF GOODS

First Edition	(1974)	General Editor A. G. Guest
Second Edition	(1981)	" " "
Third Edition	(1987)	" " "
Fourth Edition	(1992)	" " "
Fifth Edition	(1997)	" " "
Sixth Edition	(2002)	" " "
Seventh Edition	(2006)	" " "

Published in 2006 by
Sweet & Maxwell Limited of
100 Avenue Road, Swiss Cottage,
London, NW3 3PF
Typeset by
LBJ Typesetting of Kingsclere
Printed and bound in Great Britain by
William Clowes Ltd, Beccles, Suffolk

©
Sweet & Maxwell
2006

060901
MAGDALEN COLLEGE LIBRARY

GENERAL EDITOR

A. G. GUEST, C.B.E., Q.C., M.A.(OXON.), F.B.A.
Bencher of Gray's Inn; formerly Professor of English Law in the University of London; Fellow of the Chartered Institute of Arbitrators

EDITORS

E. P. ELLINGER, M.JUR.(JER.), D.PHIL.(OXON.)
Advocate and Solicitor, Singapore;
Emeritus Professor, National University of Singapore

D. R. HARRIS, Q.C., B.A., LL.M.(N.Z.), B.C.L., M.A.(OXON.)
Of the Inner Temple, Barrister; Barrister of the High Court of New Zealand; Emeritus Fellow of Balliol College, Oxford

EVA LOMNICKA, M.A., LL.B.(CANTAB.)
Of the Middle Temple, Barrister; Professor of Law in the University of London

C. J. MILLER, B.A., LL.M.(NOTTINGHAM)
Of Lincoln's Inn, Barrister; Emeritus Professor of Law in the University of Birmingham

C. G. J. MORSE, B.C.L., M.A.(OXON.)
Of the Middle Temple, Barrister; Professor of Law in the University of London

F. M. B. REYNOLDS, Q.C., D.C.L.(OXON.), F.B.A.
Honorary Bencher of the Inner Temple;
Emeritus Fellow of Worcester College and
Professor of Law Emeritus in the University of Oxford

L. S. SEALY, M.A., LL.M.(N.Z.), PH.D.(CANTAB.)
Barrister and Solicitor of the High Court of New Zealand;
Fellow of Gonville and Caius College and S. J. Berwin Professor Emeritus of Corporate Law in the University of Cambridge

SIR GUENTER TREITEL, Q.C., D.C.L.(OXON.), F.B.A.
Honorary Bencher of Gray's Inn; formerly Vinerian Professor of English Law in the University of Oxford

A CIP catalogue record for this book is available from the British Library

ISBN-10 0-421-88830-X
ISBN-13 978-0-421-8830-2

All rights reserved. Crown Copyright material is reproduced with the permission of the Controller of HMSO and the Queen's Printer for Scotland. No part of this publication may be reproduced or transmitted in any form or by any means, or stored in any retrieval system of any nature without prior written permission, except for permitted fair dealing under the Copyright, Designs and Patents Act 1988, or in accordance with the terms of a licence issued by the Copyright Licensing Agency in respect of photocopying and/or reprographic reproduction. Application for permission for other use of copyright material including permission to reproduce extracts in other published works shall be made to the publishers. Full acknowledgment of author, publisher and source must be given.

Judah P Benjamin

(The image of Judah P Benjamin is reproduced by kind permission of Special Collections of the University of Virginia Library)

JUDAH PHILIP BENJAMIN, 1811-1884

Judah Philip Benjamin was born on August 6, 1811. His parents were British subjects who in 1807 had emigrated from England, settling at first in the island of St Croix in the West Indies (now part of the US Virgin Islands, but at that time British), where Judah Philip Benjamin was born. Benjamin was, therefore, both a native-born British subject and an Englishman by descent. This status was recognised when he was called to the Bar in England.

Within a few years the Benjamin family moved to the mainland and eventually settled in Charleston, South Carolina. When only fourteen the son became a student at Yale College (now Yale University), where he had an outstanding scholastic record but left after a couple of years without completing his degree; at the age of twenty-one he entered the legal profession at New Orleans, being called to the Bar on December 16, 1832. Benjamin's professional success in America began, as later in England, with the production of a book (a codification of a branch of the law of Louisiana). At this time he married Natalie St Martin, the daughter of an aristocratic Creole family. From 1842-1844 he served in the State legislature and in 1852 was elected to the US Senate and re-elected in 1857. Meantime, as well as pursuing his legal career, he had established a sugar plantation and worked on an ambitious but eventually unfulfilled project to promote railroad expansion from the southern States through Mexico to the Pacific. In 1852, the President offered him a nomination to the Supreme Court of the United States, but he declined, preferring to stay in politics; he also turned down an appointment as ambassador to Spain.

Benjamin made a great impression in the Senate as a speaker, his language being admired both for its eloquence and its restraint. The *Dictionary of National Biography* describes him as follows: "His figure was short, square and sturdy, his face firm and resolute, his eyes piercing, and his voice clear and silvery." Throughout his life, and despite heavy workloads and, at times, grave adversities, his contemporaries record his genial temperament and cheerful optimism–the half-smile that seemed never to leave his face. In his marriage, however, he was rather less happy. Natalie, after a brief stay in Washington, left to live permanently in Paris. Benjamin built a fine mansion for her there and for the rest of his life made an annual visit whenever he was able to.

When the Southern States seceded from the Union, Benjamin withdrew from the Senate and took his stand by his State of Louisiana, becoming successively Jefferson Davis's Attorney-General, Secretary of War, and Secretary of State. As in all his endeavours, he worked tirelessly and for long hours, remembered since as "the brains of the Confederacy". Upon the surrender of General Lee all his property was confiscated and his life was in danger. He escaped Federal capture, leaving the Florida coast in an open boat to the Bahamas. He sailed from there in a ship laden with sponges which was wrecked on the way, and was then picked up by a British warship and taken to St Thomas. From there he started for England in a steamer which caught fire and had to return for a refit. Benjamin arrived in England almost penniless but, true to his character, determined to make a fresh start in a new land.

On January 13, 1866, he was admitted a student of Lincoln's Inn and, by special dispensation, was called to the Bar in June of the same year, at the age of 55. He joined the Northern Circuit. At the outset he had little work; his small remaining capital was lost in the crash of Overend, Gurney & Co and for a time he had to eke out a living by journalism.

In August, 1868, Benjamin published his well-known book on the Contract of Sale. Success was immediate, both in England and America. His reputation and practice thereafter increased rapidly. He received a patent of precedence dating from July 29, 1872, and soon afterwards was appointed Queen's Counsel. In 1875 he became a Bencher of Lincoln's Inn. In his later years he confined his work principally to the House of Lords, the Court of Appeal, and in particular to colonial appeals before the Judicial Committee of the Privy Council, where his knowledge of civil law systems and fluency in foreign languages stood him in good stead. The cases for which he is best known include the *Franconia* prosecution (on the court's criminal jurisdiction within coastal waters) and the *Tichborne* appeal to the House of Lords.

In February, 1883, he retired from practice for reasons of health. On June 30, 1883, a farewell banquet was given to him in the Inner Temple Hall. He retired to Paris and died there on May 6, 1884, survived by his wife and only daughter, Ninette. He is buried in the Cimitière du Père-Lachaise, Paris.

Benjamin's *Treatise on the Law of Sale of Personal Property, with Reference to the American Decisions, to the French Code and Civil Law* (more usually known as "*Benjamin on Sale*") was published in 1868 and a second edition in 1873. A third, written with the aid of co-authors, was only partly revised when his health failed in 1883. Successive editors kept the book in print until an eighth edition in 1950 (although its authority in the United States had fallen away as reforms based on the Uniform Sales Act took effect) but by then, like many nineteenth-century classics, it was showing its age and had begun to lose touch with modern developments in commercial trade and practice.

So, some twenty years later, at the invitation of the publishers, a team of editors undertook a total rewriting of the book, and the new work, re-titled *Benjamin's Sale of Goods*—which drew on the original *Benjamin* rather more for inspiration than for substance–was published in 1974. Six of the original seven editors have been associated with all the editions since. It is our wish that by including this brief biography in the current edition the extraordinary contribution made by Judah Philip Benjamin in so many fields should not be forgotten.

L.S.S.

PREFACE

THE last edition of this book was published in 2002. The editorial team has remained the same for this edition.

The major legislative development has been the making of the Sale and Supply of Goods to Consumers Regulations 2002 which came into force in March 2003. The Regulations gave effect to the important changes that were required to be made to comply with Directive 1999/44/EC on certain aspects of the sale of consumer goods and associated guarantees. These changes were the subject of a Special Supplement to the sixth edition and they are reflected in the coverage of this new edition. Also encountered in this new edition are the changes made by the Consumer Credit Act 2006 (still to be brought into force) to the ambit of the Consumer Credit Act 1974, as well as many other less far reaching enactments. New case law has been duly incorporated. The volume of new cases has been especially great in relation to overseas sales.

In Part One (Nature and Formation of the Contract of Sale) continuing developments in consumer law are noted: in particular the Consumer Credit Act 2006 and the EC Directive 2005/29/EC on Unfair Commercial Practices. These are examined more extensively in later chapters. Attention is drawn to new legislation and other developments in the field of electronic commerce (for example, the Electronic Signatures Regulations 2002) and to a number of recent statutes (the Licensing Act 2003, the Human Tissue Act 2004, the Gambling Act 2005, the Mental Capacity Act 2005, and also the Company Law Reform Bill 2005), which in different ways have a bearing on the law of sale of goods. Among the newest cases, two decisions on the effect of mistake in the law of contract are discussed in detail: *Shogun Finance Ltd v Hudson* (2004) on mistake of identity, and *The Great Peace* (2003), which appears to have laid to rest the notion, debated since the early 1950s, that there is room in the law of contract for a doctrine of "mistake in equity", separate from the established principles of the common law.

In Part Two (Property and Risk) the effect on retention of title clauses of administration orders made under Schedule B1 to the Insolvency Act 1986 (inserted by the Enterprise Act 2002) and the severe curtailment of the power of a floating charge holder to appoint a receiver (also effected by the 2002 Act by an amendment of the 1986 Act) are noted. In Chapter 5 it is submitted that the new section 32(4) of the Sale of Goods Act 1979 which was inserted by the Sale and Supply of Goods to Consumers Regulations 2002, referred to above, and which provides that delivery of goods to a carrier is not delivery of goods to a buyer who deals as consumer, does not affect the rule as to passing of property contained in section 18, rule 5 (2), of the 1979 Act. But the effect of the new section 32 (4) and of the new section 20 (4) (also inserted by the Regulations) on the passing of risk in consumer transactions is fully discussed in Chapter 6. In Chapter 7 (Transfer of Title by Non-Owners) the changes made by the Proceeds of Crime Act 2002, the Criminal Justice Act 2003 and the Courts Act 2003 have been taken into account, as has the decision in *Powell v Wiltshire* on estoppel by judgment.

In Part Three (Performance of the Contract) the case of *South Caribbean Trading Ltd v Trafigura Beheer BV* has been noted concerning variation, waiver and estoppel in relation to the time of delivery and there has been a modest expansion of the discussion of payment in internet sales.

In Part Four (Defective Goods) the historical account of the statutory changes and developments in the implied terms as to description and quality since the original Sale of Goods Act of 1893, contained in Chapter 11, has been shortened, and parts omitted altogether, in an attempt to concentrate on the law now operative in England and Wales. Old cases will doubtless remain useful as examples if no more. The main change however is the introduction into Chapter 12, on Remedies in Respect of Defects, of an account of the new consumer remedies provided by the new Part 5A of the 1979 Act, which were introduced by the Sale and Supply of Goods to Consumers Regulations 2002. The co-existence of these remedies with those already operative at common law creates extreme difficulties of analysis, and is likely to make the lot of an adviser on a fairly simple consumer dispute an unenviable one.The problems caused in attempting to superimpose on a regime with particular (and justifiable) techniques an alien regime with other (doubtless also justifiable) techniques provide a good introduction to the dangers of attempting to harmonise laws. The main changes in Chapter 13, on Exemption Clauses, have been a shortening of the account given of the doctrine of fundamental breach, and an extended discussion of the notion of "dealing as consumer" made necessary by the use of such wording in the new Part 5A. An attempt has also been made to continue the accumulation of the available authority on the notion of reasonableness, though not all the cases concern sale of goods.

Part Five (Consumer Protection) has been extensively revised to reflect the many changes which have taken place over the past four years. Some of these are relatively minor, but others are much more substantial. As in the previous edition, many of the changes (although by no means all) have been necessary to give effect to developments emanating from the European Union and its predecessors—in particular, the Sale and Supply of Goods to Consumers Regulations 2002 (referred to above). Although the details of those Regulations are to be found mainly in Part Four (Defective Goods), the present chapter discusses their background and, in particular, an important free-standing provision which affects consumer or manufacturers' guarantees. In a somewhat different area the General Product Safety Regulations 2005 have been enacted to implement Directive 2001/95/EC on general product safety. Although these provisions build on earlier legislation, they go beyond it in a number of important respects, most notably in introducing a limited power to require the recall of dangerous goods which are already on the market and which are posing a serious risk to the safety of consumers. A further important provision, the Supply of Extended Warranties on Domestic Electrical Goods Order 2005, is not linked to a Community Directive but is linked, rather, to a report of the Competition Commission. It attempts to deal with the long-standing problem of extended warranties which have frequently accompanied the sale of domestic electrical goods and have often been very costly when compared with the limited benefits which they provide. In the area of administrative protection the Enterprise Act 2002 replaces previous provisions (most notably, Part III of the Fair Trading Act 1973 and the Stop Now Orders (EC Directive) Regulations 2001) and introduces new Part 8 procedures whereby enforcement agencies may seek injunctions against persons who are in breach of obligations imposed by domestic or Community law. The principal role is again reserved for the Office of Fair Trading. In the same broad area changes will be required within the lifetime of the new edition to give effect to the controversial provisions contained in Directive 2005/29/EC concerning unfair business-to-consumer commercial practices (the "Unfair Commercial Practices Directive"). Finally, in the context of legislative changes, reference is made to the Consumer Credit Act 2006 which, when brought into force, will amend important parts of the 1974 Act. When compared with the substantial areas of actual or forthcoming legislative change there have been relatively few reported decisions which are of special importance. Given the main driving forces behind developments in the broad area of consumer law, it is not surprising that such decisions include those of the European Court of Justice. Examples to which attention is drawn include *easyCar (UK) Ltd v Office of Fair Trading* (2005) (distance selling) and *O'Byrne v Aventis Pasteur MSD Ltd* (2006) (product liability). In the domestic context the decision of the Court of Appeal in *Office of Fair Trading v Lloyds TSB Bank plc* (2006) is important for its ruling on the scope of section 75 of the Consumer Credit Act 1974 (liability of creditor for breaches by supplier). Overall, as in previous editions, this Part purports to be no more than a general, and necessarily truncated, survey of an increasingly complex and diverse area which has its own specialist literature.

In Part Six (Remedies) references to the new remedies for consumers under Part 5A of the 1979 Act have been integrated into the treatment of the traditional remedies, such as the action for the price, claims for damages and for specific performance. Part Six also contains new sections on the relevance of the claimant's impecuniosity on his ability to mitigate his loss caused by breach; on damages for "loss of a chance"; and on the concept of protecting the "performance interest" of the claimant in a sale of goods case.

In Part Seven (Overseas Sales) the most important change in Chapters 18 to 21 is that relating to the common law concept of a document of title to goods. No topic is more central than this concept to the law of overseas sales; and the decision of the House of Lords in *The Rafaela S* (though strictly concerned only with the meaning of the phrase "document of title" in a statutory context) has led to a considerable restructuring and expansion of the discussion of the topic in Chapter 18; and these changes have had further repercussions in the following three Chapters. The status of straight bills of lading, and the distinction between such documents and sea waybills, has also called for a considerably expanded discussion.

Among the nearly 50 other new cases discussed in this group of Chapters, special reference may here be made to the following: the decision of the House of Lords in *Standard Chartered Bank v Pakistan National Shipping Corp*, on liability for false statements in bills of lading; the decisions of the Court of Appeal in *East West Corp v DKBS*, on the liability of a carrier of goods by sea in bailment, particularly on the shipper's right to sue the carrier in bailment after the shipper has, in consequence of the operation of the Carriage of Goods by Sea Act 1992, lost his right to sue the carrier in contract; in *The Devon* and *Kronos Worldwide v Sempra Oil*, on responsibility, as between c.i.f. or f.o.b. buyer and seller, for demurrage which becomes due to the carrier; and in the *Amiri Flight* case, on the interpretation of section 26 of the Unfair Contract Terms Act 1977; and the decisions at first instance in *The David Agmashenebeli* and *The Ythan*, on the receipt function of bills of lading and on many points arising under the Carriage of Goods by Sea Act 1992; and in *The Azur Gaz* on the effect in c.i.f. contracts of "laycan" provisions and of stipulations as to the estimated time of arrival. The text also takes account of a number of decisions from other jurisdictions. Among these are two Singapore cases: *Voss v APL,* on whether straight bills of lading must be produced to the carrier of goods, shipped in pursuance of a contract of sale, by a person claiming delivery of the goods from the carrier; and *Keppel Tatlee Bank v Bandung Shipping,* on dealings with blank endorsed bills and loss of rights of suit under the Singapore equivalent of the Carriage of Goods by Sea Act 1992; and the Australian case of *El Greco v Mediterranean Shipping*, on the effects on containerised cargo of the Hague Rules package or unit limitation.

The most significant legislative changes considered in these Chapters are the provisions added to the Sale of Goods Act 1979 in 2003: in particular, sections 20(4), 32(4) and Part 5A, all of which apply where the buyer deals as consumer. For reasons given in paragraph 18–259 of the text, the possibility that a buyer in an overseas sale may so deal can no longer be ignored; and where such a buyer does so deal, these provisions give rise to many problems in relation to overseas sales on c.i.f., f.o.b. and other standard terms. The text accordingly discusses (*inter alia*) the questions when, in overseas sales on such terms, the goods are "delivered" to the consumer for the purposes of these provisions; what is the "time of delivery" at which goods so sold must conform to the contract for the purposes of the consumer's "additional rights" under Part 5A; and, where the sale is on such terms, what is the relationship between, on the one hand, the new remedies available to the consumer in respect of non-conformity under Part 5A and, on the other, the remedies for defective delivery available to the buyer under the previous (and surviving) law. Other legislative changes affect, or will affect, the discussion in Chapter 21 of certain carriage documents. The discussion of international air carriage documents takes account of the Carriage by Air Acts (Application of Provisions) Order 2004 and the Railways (Convention on International Carriage by Rail) Regulations 2005.

Chapters 22 and 23 have been brought up to date. A new revision of the UCP is currently in progress, but, as the text has not been finalized, the discussion of documentary letters of credit continues to focus on UCP500. It is possible that some banks will continue to adhere to UCP500 even after the new revision is promulgated.

Chapter 24 on Export Credit Guarantees has been revised and updated, noting recent developments in the measures available both from the ECGD and the private sector that support exports.

Part Eight (Conflict of Laws) has been revised to take account of new decisions, particularly on the Rome Convention. On the legislative front, material has been added dealing with the Sale and Supply of Goods to

Consumers Regulations 2002 and the Electronic Commerce (EC Directive) Regulations 2002.

The Tables and Index are the responsibility of the publishers. We are especially grateful to the copy editor and other members of their editorial staff for the work involved in preparing copy for press and dealing with the proofs. Eva Lomnicka would like to thank Simon Jones of Clyde & Co. and Rene Mul of Atradius for advice on the Atradius policies available.

The law is stated as at April 14, 2006.

A.G.G.

London, June 1, 2006

CONTENTS

Judah Philip Benjamin	ix
Preface	xi
Table of Cases	xxv
Table of Statutes	ccxi
Table of Statutory Instruments	ccli
Table of European Communities Legislation	cclxv
Table of International Conventions	cclxxi
Table of Foreign Legislation	cclxxvii

Part One

NATURE AND FORMATION OF THE CONTRACT OF SALE

		Para.
1. THE CONTRACT OF SALE OF GOODS	*L. S. Sealy*	1–001
1. The Sale of Goods Acts		1–001
2. Related Statutes		1–016
3. The Contract of Sale		1–025
4. Subject-matter of the Contract		1–078
2. FORMATION OF THE CONTRACT	*L. S. Sealy*	2–001
1. Agreement		2–001
2. Formalities		2–021
3. Parties		2–026
4. The Price		2–044
3. APPLICATION OF GENERAL CONTRACTUAL PRINCIPLES	*L. S. Sealy*	3–001
1. Agency		3–002
2. Fraud and Misrepresentation		3–008
3. Duress and Undue Influence		3–010
4. Mistake		3–011
5. Illegality		3–027
6. Assignment		3–043
7. Bankruptcy, Insolvency and Death		3–045

Para.

Part Two

PROPERTY AND RISK

4. THE TITLE OF THE SELLER *A. G. Guest* 4–001
   1. The Seller's Right to Sell the Goods 4–002
   2. Freedom from Encumbrances and Quiet Possession 4–023
   3. Sale of a Limited Title 4–032
   4. Analogous Provisions 4–035

5. PASSING OF PROPERTY *A. G. Guest* 5–001
   1. Effects of the Passing of Property 5–003
   2. Specific Goods 5–016
   3. Goods Delivered on Approval or on Sale or Return 5–040
   4. Unascertained Goods 5–059
   5. Undivided Shares in Goods Forming Part of a Bulk 5–109
   6. Reservation of the Right of Disposal 5–131

6. RISK AND FRUSTRATION *A. G. Guest* 6–001
   1. Risk 6–002
   2. Frustration 6–034

7. TRANSFER OF TITLE BY NON-OWNERS *A. G. Guest* 7–001
   1. In General 7–001
   2. Estoppel 7–008
   3. Sale in Market Overt 7–020
   4. Sale under a Voidable Title 7–021
   5. Mercantile Agents 7–031
   6. Seller in Possession 7–055
   7. Buyer in Possession 7–069
   8. Motor Vehicles Subject to a Hire-Purchase or Conditional Sale Agreement 7–087
   9. Miscellaneous Provisions 7–109
   10. Limitation 7–115

Part Three

PERFORMANCE OF THE CONTRACT

8. DELIVERY *A. G. Guest* 8–001
   1. In General 8–001
   2. Methods of Delivery 8–007
   3. Place of Delivery 8–018

8. DELIVERY—*cont.*

Para.

4. Time of Delivery 8–025
5. Quantity of Goods Delivered 8–045
6. Delivery by Instalments 8–064
7. Clauses Excusing Delivery 8–088

9. ACCEPTANCE AND PAYMENT *A. G. Guest* 9–001
1. Acceptance 9–002
2. Payment 9–021

Part Four

DEFECTIVE GOODS

10. CLASSIFICATION OF STATEMENTS AS TO GOODS *F. M. B. Reynolds* 10–001
1. Introduction 10–001
2. Puffs and Statements of Opinion or Intention 10–005
3. Misrepresentations Inducing the Contract 10–008
4. Collateral Contracts 10–012
5. Warranties 10–015
6. Conditions 10–024
7. Intermediate Terms 10–033
8. Other Classifications 10–039

11. TERMS AS TO DESCRIPTION AND QUALITY IMPLIED BY THE SALE OF GOODS ACT *F. M. B. Reynolds* 11–001
1. Correspondence with Description 11–001
2. Quality and Fitness for Purpose 11–024
3. Sale by Sample 11–073
4. Other Implied Terms 11–088

12. REMEDIES IN RESPECT OF DEFECTS *F. M. B. Reynolds* 12–001
1. Misrepresentation 12–002
2. Breach of Contractual Term 12–017
3. Additional Rights of Buyer in Consumer Cases 12–071
4. Misrepresentations Subsequently Incorporated into the Contract 12–119
5. Tort Liability in Respect of Goods 12–121
6. Mistake as to the Subject-matter of Contract 12–128
7. Vienna Convention 12–129

Para.

13. EXEMPTION CLAUSES — *F. M. B. Reynolds* — 13–001
   1. Introduction — 13–001
   2. Basic Principles of Formation of Contract applied to Exemption Clauses — 13–012
   3. Interpretation of Exemption Clauses — 13–020
   4. Doctrine of Fundamental Breach — 13–040
   5. Control of Exemption Clauses by Statute — 13–052

Part Five

CONSUMER PROTECTION

14. CONSUMER PROTECTION — *C. J. Miller* — 14–001
   1. Introduction — 14–001
   2. Rights Under the Civil Law — 14–004
   3. The Consumer's Remedies — 14–098
   4. Criminal Law — 14–108
   5. Administrative Protection — 14–125
   6. Indirect Protection — 14–140
   7. Consumer Credit Transactions — 14–143

Part Six

REMEDIES

15. THE SELLER'S REMEDIES AFFECTING THE GOODS — *D. R. Harris* — 15–001
   1. Introduction — 15–001
   2. Lien — 15–028
   3. Stoppage in Transit — 15–061
   4. Sub-sales and Other Subsequent Transactions — 15–092
   5. Resale — 15–101

16. OTHER REMEDIES OF THE SELLER — *D. R. Harris* — 16–001
   1. The Claim for the Price — 16–001
   2. General Rules on Damages — 16–031
   3. The Seller's Claim for Damages — 16–060
   4. Miscellaneous Remedies — 16–089

Para.

17. THE REMEDIES OF THE BUYER — *D. R. Harris* — 17–001
   1. Damages for Non-delivery — 17–001
   2. Damages for Delay in Delivery — 17–038
   3. Damages for Defective Quality — 17–047
   4. Other Claims for Damages — 17–086
   5. Repayment of the Price or Advance Payments — 17–090
   6. Remedies Other than Claims to Money — 17–093

Part Seven

OVERSEAS SALES

18. OVERSEAS SALES IN GENERAL — *Sir Guenter Treitel* — 18–001
   1. Preliminary — 18–001
   2. Documents of Title to Goods — 18–006
   3. Passing of Property — 18–208
   4. Loss or Deterioration in Transit — 18–243
   5. Implied Terms — 18–265
   6. Bulk Shipments — 18–285
   7. Export and Import Licences — 18–308
   8. Supervening Prohibition of Export or Import — 18–333

19. C.I.F. CONTRACTS — *Sir Guenter Treitel* — 19–001
   1. Nature of a C.I.F. Contract — 19–001
   2. Duties of the Seller — 19–010
   3. Duties of the Buyer — 19–075
   4. Contractual Relations with Carrier — 19–090
   5. Passing of Property — 19–098
   6. Risk — 19–110
   7. Frustration — 19–124
   8. Remedies of the Buyer — 19–144
   9. Remedies of the Seller — 19–207

20. F.O.B. CONTRACTS — *Sir Guenter Treitel* — 20–001
   1. Definition and Classifcation — 20–001
   2. Duties of the Seller — 20–011
   3. Duties of the Buyer — 20–041
   4. Contractual Relations with Carrier — 20–059
   5. Passing of Property — 20–070
   6. Risk — 20–087
   7. Frustration — 20–095
   8. Remedies of the Buyer — 20–105
   9. Remedies of the Seller — 20–123

		Para.
21. OTHER SPECIAL TERMS AND PROVISIONS IN OVERSEAS SALES	*Sir Guenter Treitel*	21–001
1. Ex Works or Ex Store Contracts		21–002
2. F.A.S. Contracts		21–010
3. C. & F. Contracts		21–012
4. Ex Ship and Arrival Contracts		21–014
5. Sale of a Cargo		21–032
6. F.O.R. and F.O.T. Contracts		21–042
7. Conventions on International Carriage of Goods		21–047
8. Container Transport		21–072
22. NEGOTIABLE INSTRUMENTS IN OVERSEAS SALES	*E. P. Ellinger*	22–001
1. Introduction		22–001
2. Direct Payment by Banker		22–006
3. Payment by Use of Bill of Exchange		22–031
4. Discount and Collection of Bills of Exchange		22–067
5. The Banker's Lien		22–139
23. DOCUMENTARY CREDITS AND FINANCE BY MERCANTILE HOUSES	*E. P. Ellinger*	23–001
1. Practice and Classification		23–001
2. Contract of Buyer and Seller		23–083
3. Contract of Issuing Banker and Buyer		23–113
4. Contract of Issuing Banker and Seller		23–134
5. The Correspondent Banker		23–173
6. Position of Holders of Seller's Draft		23–186
7. The Tender of Documents		23–196
8. Standby Credits and Performance Bonds		23–237
9. Confirming Houses and Financing by Merchants		23–307
24. EXPORT CREDIT GUARANTEES	*Eva Lomnicka*	24–001
1. Introduction		24–001
2. Export and Investment Guarantees Act 1991		24–007
3. Supplier's Credit Policies		24–011
4. Guarantees		24–031
5. Other ECGD Facilities		24–045
6. Overseas Investment Policies		24–047
7. International Aspects		24–050

Para.

Part Eight

CONFLICT OF LAWS

25. CONFLICT OF LAWS *C. G. J. Morse* 25–001
1. Preliminary Considerations 25–001
2. Common Law: The Proper Law Doctrine 25–005
3. The Rome Convention 25–015
4. Contracts Ancillary to Contract of Sale 25–069
5. Formation and Validity of the Contract of Sale 25–078
6. Property 25–121
7. Risk 25–154
8. Performance of the Contract of Sale 25–156
9. Discharge of Obligations Under a Contract of Sale 25–173
10. Remedies of the Seller 25–178
11. Remedies of the Buyer 25–196
12. Procedure 25–203

APPENDIX
The Sale of Goods Act 1979 A—001

INDEX *page* 2335

TABLE OF CASES

References are to paragraph numbers

A. (Minors) (Abduction; Habitual Residence), Re; *sub nom.* A (Abduction: Habitual Residence), Re [1996] 1 W.L.R. 25; [1996] 1 All E.R. 24; [1996] 1 F.L.R. 1; [1995] 3 F.C.R. 635; [1996] Fam. Law 71, Fam Div 25–056
A v. Leeds Teaching Hospital NHS Trust; sub nom. AB v. Leeds Teaching Hospital NHS Trust; Organ Retention Group Litigation, Re [2004] EWHC 644; [2005] Q.B. 506; [2005] 2 W.L.R. 358; [2004] 2 F.L.R. 365; [2004] 3 F.C.R. 324; [2005] Lloyd's Rep. Med. 1; (2004) 77 B.M.L.R. 145; [2004] Fam. Law 501; (2004) 101(16) L.S.G. 28; (2004) 154 N.L.J. 497; *The Times*, April 12, 2004, QBD 1–090
A. v. National Blood Authority; *sub nom.* Hepatitis C Litigation, Re [2001] 3 All E.R. 289; [2001] Lloyd's Rep. Med. 187; (2001) 60 B.M.L.R. 1; *The Times*, April 4, 2001; *The Daily Telegraph*, April 3, 2001, QBD 1–089, 14–081, 14–082, 14–086, 14–089
A.B. v. South West Water Services; *sub nom.* Gibbons v. South West Water Services [1993] Q.B. 507; [1993] 2 W.L.R. 507; [1993] 1 All E.R. 609; [1993] P.I.Q.R. P167; [1992] N.P.C. 146; (1993) 143 N.L.J. 235; *The Independent*, November 18, 1992; *The Times*, November 26, 1992, CA 14–082
A.B.D. (Metals and Waste) Ltd v. Anglo Chemical and Ore Co. Ltd [1955] 2 Lloyd's Rep. 456 .... 16–052, 16–063, 16–064, 16–066, 17–008, 17–026
A.C. Daniels & Co. Ltd v. Jungwoo Logic, unreported, April 14, 2000, QBD 12–056
AEG (International) Ltd v. Logic Resources Ltd [1996] C.L.C. 265 .... 13–013, 13–088, 13–090
AEG U.K. Ltd v. Lewis (1993) 137 S.J.L.B. 24; *The Times*, December 29, 1992, CA 22–060
AGL Victoria Pty Ltd v. Lockwood (2004) 22 A.C.L.C. 237 1–085
AIC Ltd v. ITS Testing Services (UK) Ltd [2005] EWHC 2122; [2006] 1 Lloyd's Rep. 1; [2005] 2 C.L.C. 490, QBD 19–076
AMB Imballaggi Plastici SrL v. Pacflex Ltd [1999] 2 All E.R. (Comm) 249; [1999] C.L.C. 1391; [2000] E.C.C. 381; [1999] Eu. L.R. 930; (1999) 18Tr. L.R. 153; (1999) 96(27) L.S.G. 34; *The Times*, July 8, 1999, CA; affirming (1999) 17 Tr. L.R. 557, QBD (Merc Ct) 18–232
AMF Head Sports Wear Inc. v. Scott's (Ray) All American Sports Club 448 F.Supp. 222 (1978) 23–027, 23–051, 23–136, 23–139, 23–201
A/S Awilco of Oslo v. Fulvia SpA di Navigazione of Cagliari (The Chikuma) [1981] 1 W.L.R. 314; (1981) 125 S.J. 184; [1981] 1 All E.R. 652; [1981] 1 Lloyd's Rep. 371; [1981] Com. L.R. 64 9–038
A/S Hansens Tangens Redric III v. Total Transport Corp. (The Sagona) [1984] 1 Lloyd's Rep. 194 18–063
A/S Iverans Rederei v. KG MS Holstencruiser Seeschiffahrtsgesellschaft MbH & Co. (The Holstencruiser) [1992] 2 Lloyd's Rep. 378 .... 18–029, 18–163, 21–076
A/S Reidar v. Arcos Ltd [1927] 1 K.B. 352 13–036
Aaron's Reefs v. Twiss [1896] A.C. 273; 65 L.J.P.C. 54; 74 L.T. 794 .... 12–006, 12–009
Aaronson Bros. Ltd v. Mederera del Tropico SA 111 S.J. 499; [1967] 2 Lloyd's Rep. 159, CA 6–057
Abbey National Building Society v. Cann [1991] 1 A.C. 56; [1990] 2 W.L.R. 833; [1990] 1 All E.R. 1085; [1990] 2 F.L.R. 122; [1990] 22 H.L.R. 360; (1990) 60 P. & C.R. 278; (1990) 140 N.L.J. 477; [1990] L.S.Gaz. May 9, 32; *The Times*, March 30, 1990, HL 5–134, 5–158, 5–161
Abbott & Co. v. Wolsey [1895] 2 Q.B. 97; 64 L.J.Q.B. 587; 72 LT 581; 59 JP 500; 43 W.R. 513 1–002
Abigail v. Lapin [1934] A.C. 491; [1934] All E.R.Rep. 720; 103 L.J.P.C. 105; 151 L.T. 429, PC 7–013
Abouzaid v. Mothercare (U.K.) Ltd [2000] All E.R. (D) 2436; *The Times*, February 20, 2001, CA 14–076, 14–086, 14–089

Table of Cases

Abrahams v. Herbert Reiach Ltd [1922] 1 K.B. 477 17–002
Abram Steamship Co. Ltd v. Westville Shipping Co. Ltd [1923] A.C. 773; [1923] All E.R.Rep. 645; 93 L.J.P.C. 38; 130 L.T. 67 1–009
Abrey v. Crux (1869) L.R. 5 C.P. 37, 39 L.J.C.P. 9; 21 L.T. 327; 18 W.P. 63 22–118
Acada Chemicals Ltd v. Empresa Nacional Pesquera SA [1994] 1 Lloyd's Rep. 428 19–089
Academy of Health & Fitness Property Ltd v. Power [1973] V.R. 254 ..... 10–040, 12–003, 12–119
Accurate Bailiffs & Collection Agency Ltd v. I.T.M. Industries Ltd (1993) 78 B.C.L.R. (2d) 1 1–044
Acebal v. Levy (1834) 10 Bing. 376; 4 MAS & S. 217; 3 L.J.C.P. 98; 131 E.R. 949 2–047
Acetylene Co. of G.B. v. Canada Carbide Co. (1921) 6 Ll.L.R. 410; (1922) 8 Ll.L.R. 456, CA 6–041, 6–049, 19–009, 19–125, 19–133, 19–142
Ackerman v. Protim Services [1988] 2 E.G.L.R. 259 14–064
Acme Import Pty. Ltd v. Companhia de Navegaceo Lloyd Brasiliero (The Esmarelda) [1988] 1 Lloyd's Rep. 207 21–086
Acme Wood Flooring Co. v. Sutherland Innes Co. (1904) 9 Com.Cas. 170 ... 8–005, 19–031
Acraman v. Morrice (1849) 8 C.B. 449; 19 L.J.C.P. 57; 14 L.T.O.S. 292; 14 Jur. 69, 137 E.R. 584 .... 5–023, 5–030, 5–033
Adair (J.F.) & Co. Ltd v. Birnbaum [1939] 2 K.B. 149; [1938] 4 All E.R. 775; 108 L.J.K.B. 452; 160 L.T. 244 16–037
Adams v. Broughton (1737) 2 Str. 1078 1–072
—— v. Cape Industries plc [1990] Ch. 433; [1990] 2 W.L.R. 657; [1991] 1 All E.R. 929; [1990] B.C.C. 786; [1990] B.C.L.C. 479, CA; affirming *The Times*, June 23, 1988; *The Independent*, June 21, 1988, Ch D 25–064
—— v. Lindsell (1818) 1 B. & Ald. 681; 106 E.R. 250 2–015
—— v. National Bank of Greece SA [1961] A.C. 255; [1960] 3 W.L.R. 8; 104 S.J. 489; [1960] 2 All E.R. 421 25–177
—— v. Richardson and Starling Ltd [1969] 1 W.L.R. 1645; 113 S.J. 282; [1969] 2 All E.R. 1221 14–067
Addax Ltd v. Arcadia Petroleum Ltd [2000] 1 Lloyd's Rep. 493, QBD (Comm Ct) 17–038, 20–139
Addis v. Gramophone Co. Ltd [1909] A.C. 488; [1908–10] All E.R.Rep. 1; 78 L.J.K.B. 1122; 101 L.T. 466 16–047
Addison v. Brown [1954] 1 W.L.R. 779; [1954] 2 All E.R. 213; 98 S.J. 338, QBD 25–119
Addy v. Blake (1887) 19 Q.B.D. 478; 56 L.T. 711; 51 J.P. 599; 35 W.R. 719; 3 T.L.R. 564 5–080
Adelaide Electricity Supply Co. Ltd v. Prudential Assurance Co. Ltd [1934] A.C. 122; [1933] All E.R.Rep. 82, 103 L.J.Ch. 85; 150 L.T. 281; 50 T.L.R. 147; 77 Sol.Jo. 913; 39 Com.Cas. 119 .... 25–165, 25–167
Adriatic, The [1931] P. 241; 100 L.J.P. 138; 145 L.T. 580; 47 T.L.R. 638; 18 Asp.M.L.C. 259 .... 25–010, 25–070
Advent Systems Ltd v. Unisys Corporation 925 F. 2d 670 (1991) 1–086
Aegean Sea Traders Corp. v. Repsol Petroleo SA (The Aegean Sea) [1998] 2 Lloyd's Rep. 39; [1998] C.L.C. 1090, QBD (Comm Ct) 18–016, 18–063, 18–104, 18–105, 18–125, 18–126, 18–127, 18–128
Aeolian Shipping SA v. ISS Machinery Services Ltd (The Aeolian); *sub nom.* ISS Machinery Services Ltd v. Aeolian Shipping SA (The Aeolian) [2001] EWCA Civ 1162; [2001] 2 Lloyd's Rep. 641; [2001] C.L.C. 1708, CA 25–019, 25–020, 25–030, 25–035, 25–060
Aerial Advertising v. Batchelor's Peas Ltd (Manchester) [1938] 2 All E.R. 788; 82 Sol. Jo. 567 17–069
Afovos Shipping Co. v. Pagnan (R.) and Lli (F.) (The Aforos) [1983] 1 W.L.R. 195; (1983) 127 S.J. 98; [1983] 1 All E.R. 449; [1983] Com. L.R. 83; [1983] 1 Lloyd's Rep. 335; [1984] 2 LM.C.L.Q. 189 8–006, 8–033, 8–078, 8–079, 9–010, 9–038, 9–054, 12–021
Agip (Africa) v. Jackson [1991] Ch. 547; [1991] 3 W.L.R. 116; [1992] 4 All E.R. 451; (1991) 135 S.J. 117; *The Times*, January 9, 1991; *Financial Times*, January 18, 1991, CA 7–003, 22–090, 22–118
Agius v. Great Western Colliery Co. [1899] 1 Q.B. 413; 68 L.J.Q.B. 312; 80 L.T. 140; 47 W.R. 403 .... 17–036, 17–045
Agra and Masterman's *ex p.* Asiatic Banking Corporation, *Re* (1867) L.R. 2 Ch.App. 391; 36 L.J.Ch. 222; 16 L.T. 162; 15 W.R. 414 23–063

Agra and Masterman's v. Leighton (1866) L.R. 2 Ex. 56; 4 H & C 656; 36 L.J.Ex 33 22–064
Agra Bank, *ex p.* Tondeur, *Re* (1867) L.R. 5 Eq. 160; 37 L.J.Ch. 121; 16 W.R. 270 .. 23–100
Agricultores Federados Argentines Soc. Coperativa Lda. v. Ampro SA Commerciale Industrielle et Financiere [1965] 2 Lloyd's Rep. 757 .... 12–031, 18–274, 20–031, 20–043, 20–051, 20–052
"Agroexport" Entreprise D'Etat pour le Commerce Exterieur v. N.V. Goorden Import Cy. SA [1956] 1 Lloyd's Rep. 319 .... 11–079, 12–063, 13–033, 13–040
Agroexport State Enterprise for Foreign Trade v. Compagnie Europeene de Cereales [1974] 1 Lloyd's Rep. 499 .... 18–321, 18–345
Agrokor AG v. Tradigrain SA [2000] 1 Lloyd's Rep. 497, QBD (Comm Ct) 8–091, 18–342, 18–344, 18–345, 19–141, 19–142, 20–103
Agrosin Pty Ltd v. Highway Shipping Co. Ltd (The Mata K) [1998] 2 Lloyd's Rep. 614; [1998] C.L.C. 1300, QBD (Comm Ct) 18–034, 18–036, 18–053
Ahmad v. Mitsui O.K. Lines Ltd (ARBN 008 311 831) [2005] F.C.A. 731 18–105
Ahrens Ltd v. Cohen (George), Sons and Co. Ltd (1934) 50 T.L.R. 411 ...... 7–058, 7–062, 7–063, 7–064, 7–077, 7–079
Aiken v. Stewart Wrightson Members Agency [1995] 1 W.L.R. 1281; [1995] 3 All E.R. 449; [1995] 2 Lloyd's Rep. 618; *The Times*, March 8, 1995 12–121
Ailsa Craig Shipping Co. Ltd v. Malvern Fishing Co. and Securicor (Scotland) [1983] 1 W.L.R. 964; (1983) 127 S.J. 508; [1983] 1 All E.R. 101; (1983) 80 L.S.Gaz. 2516, HL 13–019, 13–036, 13–047, 13–051, 18–276
Air Foyle Ltd v, Center Capital Ltd [2002] EWHC 2535; [2003] 2 Lloyd's Rep. 753; [2004] I.L.Pr. 15, QBD 25–121, 25–130
Aircool Installations v. British Telecommunications [1995] C.L.Y. 821 (Cty.Ct.) 5–157, 5–159
Aitchison v. Page Motors Ltd (1935) 154 L.T. 128; [1935] All E.R.Rep. 594; 52 T.L.R. 137 .... 5–057, 6–030
Aitken, Campbell & Co. Ltd v. Boullen and Gattenby, 1908 S.C. 490 11–079
Ajayi v. Briscoe (R.T.) (Nigeria) Ltd [1964] 1 W.L.R. 1326; 108 S.J. 857; [1964] 3 All E.R. 556 .... 9–024, 12–036
Ajello v. Worsley [1898] 1 Ch. 274; [1895–99] All E.R.Rep. 1222; 67 L.J.Ch. 172; 77 L.T. 783; 47 W.R. 245 1–103
Ajit v. Sammy [1967] 1 A.C. 255; [1966] 3 W.L.R. 983; 110 S.J. 790, PC (BG) 8–026
Akrokerii (Atlantic) Mines Ltd v. Economic Bank [1904] 2 K.B. 465; 73 L.J.K.B. 742; 91 L.T. 175; 52 W.R. 670; 20 T.L.R. 564 .... 22–073, 22–075
Akron Tyre Co. Property Ltd v. Kittson (1951) 82 C.L.R. 477 .... 5–149, 5–167
Aktieselskab August Freuchen v. Steen Hansen (1919) 1 Ll. L. Rep. 393, KBD (Comm Ct) 25–070
Aktieselskabet de Danske Sukkerfabrikker v. Bajmar Compania Naviera SA (The Torrenia) [1983] 2 Lloyd's Rep. 210 18–051
Aktieselskabet Reidar v. Arcos Ltd [1927] 1 K.B. 352 16–033
Aktion Maritime Cpn. of Liberia v. Kasmas (S.) & Brothers (The Aktion) [1987] 1 Lloyd's Rep. 283 .... 8–078, 10–037
Al Battani, The [1993] 2 Lloyd's Rep. 219 .... 18–048, 18–051, 18–110
Al Kishtaini v. Shansal [2001] EWCA Civ 264; [2001] 2 All E.R. (Comm) 601; [2001] Lloyd's Rep. Bank. 174; (2001) 98(17) L.S.G. 38; *The Times*, March 8, 2001, CA; reversing *The Times*, June 16, 1999, QBD 25–119
Alamo Savings Association v. Forward Construction Corp. 746 S.W. 2d 897 (1988) .. 23–153
Alan (W.J.) & Co. v. El Nasr Export & Import Co. Ltd [1972] 2 Q.B. 189; [1972] 2 W.L.R. 800; 116 S.J. 139; [1972] 2 All E.R. 127; [1972] 1 Lloyd's Rep. 313, CA 8–030, 9–028, 12–035, 15–021, 16–019, 20–025, 20–057, 23–096, 23–097, 23–098, 23–105, 25–006, 25–007, 25–165, 25–174
Albracruz (Cargo Owners) v. Albazero (owners) [1977] A.C. 774 ... 5–009, 18–002, 18–034, 18–114, 18–116, 18–117, 18–119, 18–209, 19–007, 19–099, 19–103
Albazero, The. *See* Albacruz (Cargo Owners) v. Albazero (Owners).
Albeko Schuhmaschinen A.G. v. Kamborian Shoe Machine Co. Ltd (1961) 111 L.J. 519 .... 18–281, 25–073, 25–079
Albemarle Supply Co. Ltd v. Hind & Co. [1928] 1 K.B. 307; [1927] All E.R.Rep. 401; 97 L.J.K.B. 25; 138 L.T. 102; 43 T.L.R. 783 15–038
Alberta Ltd 876267, Re [2003] 10 W.W.R. 690 1–095

Albright & Wilson UK Ltd v. Biachem Ltd [2002] UKHL 37; [2002] 2 All E.R. (Comm) 753; [2003] 1 C.L.C. 637; (2002) 146 S.J.L.B. 241, HL; reversing in part [2001] EWCA Civ 301; [2001] 2 All E.R. (Comm) 537; [2001] C.L.C. 1023, CA 11–030, 11–039, 11–057
Alcoa Minerals of Jamaica Inc. v. Broderik [2000] 3 W.L.R. 23; [2000] B.L.R. 279; (2000) 2 T.C.L.R. 850; [2000] Env. L.R. 734; (2000) 144 S.J.L.B. 182; *The Times*, March 22, 2000, PC (Jam) 16–053
Alcock v. Smith [1892] 1 Ch. 238; 61 L.J.Ch. 161; 66 L.T. 126; 8 T.L.R. 222; 36 Sol.Jo. 199 .... 25–121, 25–131
Alder v. Moore [1961] 2 Q.B. 57; [1961] 2 W.L.R. 426; 105 S.J. 280; [1961] 1 All E.R. 1; [1960] 2 Lloyd's Rep. 325 .... 16–032, 16–035
Alderslade v. Hendon Laundry Ltd [1945] K.B. 189; [1945] 1 All E.R. 244; 114 L.J.K.B. 196; 172 L.T. 153; 61 T.L.R. 216 13–022
Aldridge v. Johnson (1857) 7 E. & B. 885; 26 L.J.Q.B. 296; 3 J.W.N.S. 913; 5 W.R. 703; 119 E.R. 1476 .... 1–036, 1–037, 5–005, 5–068, 5–079, 5–081, 5–086
Alewyn v. Prior (1826) Ry. & Mood. 406; 171 E.R. 1065 21–030
Alexander v. Gardner (1835) 1 Bing. N.C. 671, 1 Hodg. 147; 1 Scott 630; 4 L.J.C.P. 223; 131 E.R. 1276 .... 5–038, 5–076, 9–056
—— v. Glenbroome Ltd [1957] 1 Lloyd's Rep. 157 5–041
—— v. Railway Executive [1951] 2 K.B. 882; [1951] 2 T.L.R. 69; 95 S.J. 369; [1951] 2 All E.R. 442 .... 13–013, 13–042, 13–052
—— v. Steinhardt, Walker & Co. [1903] 2 K.B. 208; 72 L.J.K.B. 490; 8 Com.Cas. 209; 10 Mans 258 2–015
—— v. Vanderzee (1872) L.R. 7 C.P. 530; 20 W.R. 871 18–267
Alexandria Cotton and Trading Co. (Sudan) Ltd v. Cotton Co. of Ethiopia Ltd [1963] 1 Lloyd's Rep. 576 .... 16–037, 19–013
Alexiadi v. Robinson (1861) 2 F. & F. 679 8–036
Alfred McAlpine Construction Ltd v. Panatown Ltd (No.1); *sub nom*. Panatown Ltd v. Alfred McAlpine Construction Ltd [2001] 1 A.C. 518; [2000] 3 W.L.R. 946; [2000] 4 All E.R. 97; [2000] C.L.C. 1604; [2000] B.L.R. 331; (2000) 2 T.C.L.R. 547; 71 Con. L.R. 1; [2000] E.G.C.S. 102; (2000) 97(38) L.S.G. 43; (2000) 150 N.L.J. 1299; (2000) 144 S.J.L.B. 240; [2000] N.P.C. 89; *The Times*, August 15, 2000, HL; reversing [1998] C.L.C. 636; 88 B.L.R. 67; 58 Con. L.R. 46; (1998) 14 Const. L.J. 267; [1998] E.G.C.S. 19; [1998] N.P.C. 17; *The Times*, February 11, 1998, CA 14–020, 17–07, 18–114
Alfred McAlpine plc v. BAI (Run-off) Ltd [2000] 1 All E.R. (Comm) 545; [2000] 1 Lloyd's Rep. 437; [2000] C.L.C. 812; (2001) 3 T.C.L.R. 5; 69 Con. L.R. 87; [2000] Lloyd's Rep. I.R. 352, CA; affirming [1998] 2 Lloyd's Rep. 694; [1998] C.L.C. 1145; (1999) 1 T.C.L.R. 92; 66 Con. L.R. 57, QBD (Comm Ct) 18–357, 19–064
Alicia Hosiery Ltd v. Brown, Shipley & Co. Ltd [1970] 1 Q.B. 195; [1969] 2 W.L.R. 1268; 113 S.J. 466; [1969] 2 All E.R. 504 .... 8–016, 18–173, 18–174, 18–193
Alimport v. Soubert Shipping Co Ltd [2000] 2 Lloyd's Rep. 447, QBD 18–047
All Russian Co-operative Society Ltd v. Benjamin Smith & Sons (1923) 14 Ll.L.R. 351 20–029
All Trades Distributors Ltd v.Agencies Kaufman Ltd (1969) 113 S.J. 995 .... 9–032, 17–050, 22–064
All Service Exportacao SA v. Banco Bamerindus do Brazil SA 921 F2d 32 (2nd Ct. 1990) 23–139
Allan v. Gripper (1832) 2 C. & J. 218; 149 E.R. 94 15–070
Allan (J.M.) (Merchandising) Ltd v. Cloke [1963] 2 Q.B. 340; [1963] 2 W.L.R. 899; 107 S.J. 213; [1963] 2 All E.R. 258; 61 L.G.R. 304 3–029
Allard & Co. (Rubber) Ltd v. R.J. Hawkins & Co. (Dudley) Ltd [1958] 1 Lloyd's Rep. 184 12–065
Allen v. Edmundson (1848) 2 Exch. 719; 17 L.J.Ex 291; 154 E.R. 680 ...... 22–125, 22–131
—— v. Hopkins (1844) 13 M. & W. 94; 13 L.J.Ex 316; 3 L.T.O.S. 204; 153 E.R. 39 16–019
—— v. Robles [1969] 1 W.L.R. 1193; [1969] 3 All E.R. 154; [1969] 2 Lloyd's Rep. 61; (1969) 113 S.J. 484, CA 12–009, 14–047
—— Royal Bank of Canada (1925) 95 L.J.P.C. 17; 134 L.T. 194; 41 T.L.R. 625 9–030
Allester (David) Ltd, *Re* [1922] 2 Ch. 211; [1922] All E.R.Rep. 589; 91 L.J.Ch. 797; 127 L.T. 434; 38 T.L.R. 611 .... 5–153, 7–031, 18–238

Allgemeine Gold- und Silberschcideananstalt v. Customs & Excise Commissioners [1980] Q.B. 390 1–084
Alliance Bank v. Broom (1864) 2 Dr. & Sm. 289; 5 New Rep. 69; 34 L.J.Ch. 256; 11 L.T. 332; 10 Jur. N.S. 1121 .... 18–067, 23–137
Allied Bank International v. Banco Credito Agricola 757 F 2d 516 (1985) 22–015
Allied Maples Group Ltd v. Simmons & Simmons [1995] 1 W.L.R. 1602; [1995] 4 All E.R. 907; [1996] C.L.C. 153; 46 Con. L.R. 134; [1955–95] P.N.L.R. 701; (1995) 145 N.L.J. 1646; [1995] N.P.C. 83; (1995) 70 P. & C.R. D14, CA 16–050
Allied Marine Transport Ltd v. Vale do Rio Doce Navegacao SA [1985] 1 W.L.R. 925; (1985) 129 S.J. 431; [1985] 2 All E.R. 796; [1985] 2 Lloyd's Rep. 18; (1985) 82 L.S.Gaz. 2160 .... 8–030, 8–039
Alimport v. Soubert Shipping Co. Ltd [2000] 2 Lloyd's Rep. 447, QBD (Comm Ct) 18–029, 18–054
Allison v. Bristol Marine Insurance Co. Ltd (1876) 1 App.Cas. 209, 34 L.T. 809; 24 W.R. 1039; 3 Asp.M.L.C. 178 .... 5–027, 5–084
Allseas International Management Ltd v. Panroy Bulk Transport SA [1985] 1 Lloyd's Rep. 370 17–099
Alma Shipping Corp. v. Union of India (The Astaea) [1971] 2 Lloyd's Rep. 494 12–037
Aluminium Industrie Vaassen B.V. v. Romalpa Aluminium [1976] 1 W.L.R. 676; 120 S.J. 95; [1976] 2 All E.R. 552; [1976] 1 Lloyd's Rep. 443, CA ... 1–009, 1–048, 1–060, 1–062, 1–108, 3–004, 5–005, 5–141, 5–144, 5–145, 5–146, 5–147, 5–151, 5–152, 5–153, 5–156, 5–160, 5–170, 18–212, 18–235, 18–240, 25–003, 25–134
Alves v. Hodgson (1797) 7 T.R. 241 25–086
Amalgamated Investment & Property Co. Ltd v. Walker (John) & Sons Ltd [1977] 1 W.L.R. 164; (1976) 32 P. & C.R. 278 3–022
Amalgamated Investments & Property Co. Ltd v. Texas Commerce International Bank Ltd [1982] Q.B. 84; [1981] 3 W.L.R. 565; (1981) 125 S.J. 623; [1981] 3 All E.R. 577; [1981] Com.L.R. 236 7–012
Amar Singh v. Kulubya [1964] A.C. 142; [1963] 3 W.L.R. 513; 107 S.J. 616; [1963] 3 All E.R. 499 3–030
Amazona and Yayamaria. The. *See* Government of Sierra Leone v. Marmaro Shipping Co.
Amazonia, The. *See* Furness Withy (Australia) v. Metal Distributors (U.K.) (The Amazonia).
Amco Enterprises Property Ltd v. Wade [1968] Qd.R. 445 1–098
American Accord, The. *See* United City Merchants (Investments) Ltd v. Royal Bank of Canada (The American Accord)
American Bank and Trust Co. v. National City Bank of New York 6 F. 762 (1925) .. 23–054
American Bell International Inc. v. Islamic Republic of Iran 474 F.Supp. 420 (1979) 23–149, 23–241, 23–244
American Can Co. v. Stewart (1915) 50 I.L.T. 132 11–019
American Commerce Co. Ltd v. Frederick Boehm Ltd (1919) 35 T.L.R. 224 19–085
American National Bank and Trust Co. v. Hamilton Industries Inc. 583 F.Supp. 1148 (1983) 23–244
American Steel Co. v. Irving National Bank 266 F. 41 (1920) 23–054
American Sugar Refining Co. v. Page 16 F. 2d 662 (1927) 19–004
Amin Rasheed Shipping Corp. v. Kuwait Insurance Co. [1984] A.C. 50; [1983] 3 W.L.R. 241; (1983) 2 All E.R. 884; [1983] 2 Lloyd's Rep. 365 ...... 25–005, 25–007, 25–008, 25–010, 25–014, 25–028, 25–030, 25–031, 25–032, 25–065, 25–074, 25–089, 25–092, 25–156, 25–190, 25–191
American Motorists Insurance Co (AMICO) v. Cellstar Corp [2003] EWCA Civ 206; [2003] 2 C.L.C. 599; [2003] I.L.Pr. 22; [2003] Lloyd's Rep. I.R. 295; (2003) 100(18) L.S.G. 35; *The Times*, April 1, 2003, CA ... 25–001, 25–030, 25–031, 25–033, 25–057
Amiri Flight Authority v. BAE Systems Plc [2003] EWCA Civ 1447; [2004] 1 All E.R. (Comm) 385; [2003] 2 Lloyd's Rep. 767; [2003] 2 C.L.C. 662, CA ... 13–099, 18–281, 25–090
Amixco Asia (Pte) Ltd v. Bank Bumiputra Malaysia Brhd [1992] 2 S.L.R. 943 (Sup. Ct of Singapore) 23–160, 23–203
Amoco Australia Property Ltd v. Rocca Bros. Motor Engineering Property Ltd [1975] A.C. 561; [1975] 2 W.L.R. 779; 119 S.J. 301; [1975] 1 All E.R. 968 .... 3–036, 3–038, 8–061

Amos and Wood Ltd v. Kaprow (1948) W.N. 71; 64 T.L.R. 110; 92 S.J. 153 .. 8–004, 8–080, 9–023
Amstrad plc v. Seagate Technology Inc. 86 B.L.R. 34; [1998] Masons C.L.R. Rep. 1, QBD 17–068
Amtorg Trading Corp. v. Miehle Printing Co. (of Delaware) 206 F. 2d 103 (1953) .. 20–102
Anchor Line (Henderson Bros.) Ltd, *Re* [1937] Ch. 1; 106 L.J.Ch. 211; 156 L.T. 481; 53 T.L.R. 806 .... 5–016, 5–018, 5–026, 5–027, 25–144
Anchor Line Ltd v. Rowell (Keith) Ltd (The Hazelmoor) [1980] 2 Lloyd's Rep. 351 8–078, 9–010, 9–051
Ancien Maison Marcel Bauche (SA) v. Woodhouse Drake & Carey (Sugar) Ltd [1982] 2 Lloyd's Rep. 516 3–028
Ancona v. Rogers (1876) 1 Ex.D. 285; 46 L.J.Q.B. 121; 35 L.T. 115; 24 W.R. 1000 ... 8–008
Anders Maersk, The [1986] 1 Lloyd's Rep. 483 18–268
Anders Utkilens Rederi A/S v. O/Y Louisa Spevedorung Co. A/B (The Golfstraum) [1985] 2 All E.R. 669; [1985] S.T.C. 301 17–100
Anderson v. Anderson [1895] 1 Q.B. 749; 64 L.J.Q.B. 457; 72 L.T. 3B, 43 W.R. 322; 11 T.L.R. 253 8–089
—— v. Carlisle Horse Clothing Co. (1870) 21 L.T. 760 9–063
—— v. Clark (1824) 2 Bing. 20; 130 E.R. 211 .... 18–097, 18–229, 18–233
—— v. Equitable Life Assurance Society of the U.S. (1926) 134 L.T. 557; [1928] All E.R.Rep. 93; 42 T.L.R. 302; (1926) 45 T.L.R. 468 25–166
—— v. Hillies (1852) 12 C.B. 499; 21 L.J.C.P. 150; 19 L.T.O.S. 92; 16 Jur. 819; 138 E.R. 1002 9–031
Anderson v. Morice (1876) 1 App.Cas. 713; (1875) L.R. 10 C.P. 609 .. 5–012, 5–031, 5–039, 5–079, 5–086, 6–003, 6–012, 6–020, 20–039, 21–013
—— v. Ryan [1967] I.R. 34 .... 4–004, 5–032
Anderson v. Scrutton [1934] SAS.R. 10 11–019
Anderson Ltd v. Daniel [1924] 1 K.B. 138; [1923] All E.R.Rep. Ext. 783; 93 L.J.K.B. 97; 130 L.T. 418; 88 J.P. 53 .... 3–028, 3–029, 14–097
Andrabell Ltd, *Re* [1984] 3 All E.R. 407 .... 5–144, 5–147, 5–148, 5–151, 5–152
André et Cie v. Cook Industries Inc. [1987] 2 Lloyd's Rep. 463; CA; reversing [1986] 2 Lloyd's Rep. 200 .... 8–101, 12–036, 18–319, 19–155
André & Cie SA v. Etablissements Michel Blanc et Fils [1979] 2 Lloyd's Rep. 427 ... 8–091, 8–092, 10–008, 10–009, 18–349
—— v. Marine Transocean Ltd [1981] Q.B. 694; [1981] 3 W.L.R. 43; (1981) 125 S.J. 395; [1981] 2 All E.R. 993; [1981] Com.L.R. 95; [1981] 2 Lloyd's Rep. 29 8–031
André & Cie SA v. Tradax Export SA [1983] 1 Lloyd's Rep. 254; [1983] Com.L.R. 2; [1981] 2 Lloyd's Rep 8–092, 18–312, 18–313, 19–141
Andrews v. Hopkinson [1957] 1 Q.B. 229; [1956] 3 W.L.R. 732; 100 S.J. 768; [1956] 3 All E.R. 422 1–054, 2–027, 10–002, 10–005, 10–013, 12–073, 14–044, 14–060, 17–071
Andrews Bros. (Bournemouth) Ltd v. Singer & Co. Ltd [1934] 1 K.B. 17; [1933] All E.R.Rep. 479; 103 L.J.K.B. 90; 150 L.T. 172; 50 T.L.R. 33 .. 11–002, 11–004, 11–019, 13–026, 13–031, 13–051
Andy Marine Inc. v. Ziddell Inc. 812 F. 2d 534 (9th C. 1987) 23–139
Aneco Reinsurance Underwriting Ltd v. Johnson & Higgins Ltd; *sub nom.* Aneco Reinsurance Undrwriting Ltd v. Johnson & Higgs Ltd [2001] UKHL 51; [2001] 2 All E.R. (Comm) 929; [2002] 1 Lloyd's Rep. 157; [2002] C.L.C. 181; [2002] Lloyd's Rep. I.R. 91; [2002] P.N.L.R. 8, HL; affirming [2000] 1 All E.R. (Comm) 129; [1999] C.L.C. 1918; [2000] Lloyd's Rep. I.R. 12; [2000] Lloyd's Rep. P.N. 1; [2000] P.N.L.R. 152, CA; affirming in part [1998] 1 Lloyd's Rep. 565; *The Times*, November 14, 1997, QBD (Comm Ct) 19–202
Anemone, The. *See* Clipper Maritime v. Shirlstar Container Transport (The Anemone)
Angel v. Jay [1911] 1 K.B. 666; [1908–10] All E.R.Rep. 470; 80 L.J.K.B. 458; 103 L.T. 809; 55 Sol.Jo. 140 12–005
Anglesey, *Re* [1901] 2 Ch. 548 16–007
Anglia Television Ltd v. Reed [1972] 1 Q.B. 60 ..... 6–060, 16–031, 16–086, 17–064, 17–070
Anglo-African Shipping Co. of New York Inc. v. Mortner Ltd [1962] 1 Lloyd's Rep. 610, C.A.; reversing [1962] 1 Lloyd's Rep. 81 3–004, 8–082, 16–022, 16–059, 18–232, 21–010, 23–116, 23–308, 23–309, 23–312, 23–313
Anglo-Austrian Bank (Vogel's Application), Re [1920] 1 Ch. 69, Ch D 25–073

Anglo Celtic Shipping Co Ltd v. Elliot and Jeffery (1926) 42 T.L.R. 297 14–061
Anglo-Continental Holidays Ltd v. Typaldos Lines (London) Ltd 111 S.J. 599; [1967] 2 Lloyd's Rep. 61 13–046
Anglo-Egyptian Navigation Co. v. Rennie (1875) L.R. 10 C.P. 271; 44 L.J.C.P. 130; 32 L.T. 467; 23 W.R. 626 .... 1–043, 5–093
Anglo-Iranian Oil Co. Ltd v. Jaffrate (The Jaffrate) [1953] 1 W.L.R. 246; 97 S.J. 81 .... 1–087, 1–097
Anglo-Irish Asset Finance v. D.S.G. Financial Services [1995] C.L.Y. 4491 .... 7–036, 7–057
Anglo Overseas Transport Ltd v. Titan Industrial Corp. [1959] 2 Lloyd's Rep. 152 18–047
Anglo-Russian Merchant Traders Ltd and John Batt & Co. (London) Ltd, *Re*. [1917] 2 K.B. 679; 86 L.J.K.B. 1360; 116 L.T. 805; 61 Sol. Jo. 591 .... 6–047, 8–091, 18–311, 18–314, 18–316, 18–320, 18–329, 18–337, 19–013
Anglo-South American Trust Co. v. Uhe, 184 N.E. 741 (1933) 23–205
Angus v. McLachlan (1883) 23 Ch.D. 330; 52 L.J.Ch. 587; 48 L.T. 863; 31 W.R. 641 15–031
Annand & Thompson Pty Ltd v. Trade Practices Commission (1979) 25 A.L.R. 91 11–019
Annie Johnson, The Kronprinsessan Margareta [1918] P. 154; 87 L.J.P. 127; 118 L.T. 721; 14 Asp.M.L.C. 301 5–015
Anns v. Merton L.B.C. [1978] A.C. 728; [1977] 2 W.L.R. 1024; (1977) 121 S.J. 377; (1977) 75 L.G.R. 535; [1977] J.P.L. 514; (1977) 243 E.G. 523 12–126
Anonima Petroli Italiana Sp A and Neste Oy v. Marlucidez Armadora SA: Filiatra Legacy, The [1991] 2 Lloyd's Rep. 337, C.A.; reversing [1990] 1 Lloyd's Rep. 354; *The Times*, November 21, 1989 .... 5–009, 5–137, 18–023, 18–150, 18–209, 18–218, 18–219, 19–099, 19–104, 19–106
Anselme Dewavrin v. Wilsons and N.E. Railway Shipping Co. Ltd (1931) 39 Ll.L.R. 289 .... 25–070, 25–195
Anspach & Co. Ltd v. C.N.R. [1950] 3 D.L.R. 26 .... 25–081, 25–202
Ant. Jurgens Margarinefabrieken v. Louis Dreyfus & Co. [1914] 3 K.B. 40; 83 L.J.K.B. 1344; 111 L.T. 248; 19 Com.Cas. 333 .... 5–065, 5–122, 7–034, 7–072, 7–077, 7–085, 8–013, 15–097, 18–197
Antares (Nos. 1 & 2), The. *See* Kenya Railways v. Antares Pte. (The Antares Nos. 1 & 2).
Anthony v. Halstead (1877) 37 L.T. 433 .... 10–005, 11–012
Antonelli v. Secretary of State for Trade and Industry [1998] Q.B. 948; [1998] 2 W.L.R. 826; [1998] 1 All E.R. 997; [1998] Admin. L.R. 75; [1998] 1 E.G.L.R. 9; [1998] 14 E.G. 133; [1998] C.O.D. 178; (1997) 94(35) L.S.G. 35; (1997) 141 S.J.L.B. 198; [1997] N.P.C. 123; *The Times*, October 3, 1997; *The Independent*, October 14, 1997, CA; affirming [1996] 2 E.G.L.R. 229; [1995] C.O.D. 334; [1995] N.P.C. 68, QBD 14–138
Anziani, *Re* Herbert v. Christopherson [1930] 1 Ch. 407; 99 L.J.Ch. 215, 142 L.T. 520 25–121
Apex Supply Co. Ltd, *Re* [1942] 1 Ch. 108; [1941] 3 All E.R. 473; 111 L.J.Ch. 89; 166 L.T. 264; 86 Sol.Jo. 27 1–066
Apioil Ltd v. Kuwait Petroleum Italia SpA [1995] 1 Lloyd's Rep. 124 ...... 13–040, 19–056
Apple Corps Ltd v. Apple Computer Inc [2004] EWHC 768; [2004] 2 C.L.C. 720; [2004] I.L.Pr. 34, Ch D 25–019, 25–020, 25–021, 25–065
Appleby v. Myers (1867) L.R. 2 C.P. 651; [1861–73] All E.R.Rep. 452; 36 L.J.C.P. 331; 16 L.T. 669 .... 1–043, 6–040, 6–051, 6–055, 6–063
—— v. Sleep [1968] 1 W.L.R. 948; 112 S.J. 380; [1968] 2 All E.R. 265; 66 L.G.R. 555 .... 1–071, 2–026
Aquitaine S.A.R.L. v. Laporte Materials (Barrow) Ltd *See* Clef Aquitaine S.A.R.L. v. Laporte Materials (Barrow) Ltd
Arab Bank Ltd v. Barclays Bank [1954] A.C. 495; [1954] 2 W.L.R. 1022; 98 S.J. 350; [1954] 2 All E.R. 226 .... 6–044, 22–013, 25–176
Arab Bank Ltd v. Ross [1952] 2 Q.B. 216; [1952] 1 T.L.R. 811; 96 S.J. 229; [1952] 1 All E.R. 709 .... 22–026, 22–061
Arab Banking Corp. BSC v. First Union National Bank 200 Folio 1298, QBD (Comm Ct) 25–076
Aramis, The [1989] 1 Lloyd's Rep. 213, CA 5–060, 5–061, 18–045, 18–084, 18–100, 18–139, 18–141, 18–142, 19–006

Arbitration, An, between Reinhold & Co. and Hansloh, *Re* (1896) 12 T.L.R. 442 ... 18–286, 19–033, 23–235
Arbitration between Skipton, Anderson & Co. and Harrison Bros & Co. [1915] 3 K.B. 676 ... 5–025
Arbuthnot v. Streckheisen (1866) 35 L.J.C.P. 305 ... 8–054
Archbolds (Freightage) Ltd v. Spanglett (S.), Randali (Third Party) Ltd [1961] 1 Q.B. 374; [1961] 2 W.L.R. 170; 105 S.J. 149; [1961] 1 All E.R. 417 ... 3–028
Archer v. Bamford (1822) 3 Stark. 175 ... 22–064
Archer v. Brown [1985] Q.B. 401; [1984] 3 W.L.R. 350; (1984) 128 S.J. 532; [1984] 2 All E.R. 267; (1984) 134 New L.J. 235; (1984) 81 L.S.Gaz. 2770 ... 12–012
Archivent Sales and Developments Ltd v. Strathclyde R.C. (1984) 24 Build. L.R. 98 ... 5–156, 5–157, 7–055, 7–072, 7–077, 7–081
Arcona v. Marks (1862) 31 L.J.Ex. 163 ... 22–059
Arcos Ltd v. Ronaasen (E.A.) & Son [1933] A.C. 470; [1933] All E.R.Rep. 646; 102 L.J.K.B. 346; 149 L.T. 98; 49 T.L.R. 231; 77 Sol.Jo. 99 ... 8–050, 10–034, 11–016, 11–018, 18–231, 19–146, 19–159
Ardennes (S.S.) (Owner of Cargo) v. Ardennes (S.S.) (Owners) [1951] 1 K.B. 55; 66 T.L.R. (Pt. 2) 312; [1950] 2 All E.R. 517 ... 18–047, 18–048, 18–051, 18–088, 18–106, 19–096, 20–043
Arenson v. Arenson. *See* Arenson v. Casson, Beckman Rutley & Co.
—— v. Casson Beckman Rutley & Co. [1977] A.C. 405; [1975] 3 W.L.R. 815; 119 S.J. 810; [1975] 3 All E.R. 901; [1976] 1 Lloyd's Rep. 179 ... 2–051, 2–052, 13–040
Argentina, The (1867) L.R.I.A. & E. 370; 16 L.T. 743; 2 Mar.L.C. 529 ... 5–137, 18–086, 18–216
Aristoc Industries Property Ltd v. R.A. Wenham (Builders) Pty Ltd [1965] N.S.W.R. 581 ... 1–043
Ark Therapeutics Plc v. True North Capital Ltd [2005] EWHC 1585; [2006] 1 All E.R. (Comm) 138, QBD ... 25–060
Armagas v. Mundogas SA (The Ocean Frost) [1986] 2 W.L.R. 1063, H.L.; affirming [1986] A.C. 717; [1985] 3 W.L.R. 640; (1984) 129 S.J. 362; [1985] 3 All E.R. 795; [1985] 1 Lloyd's Rep. 1; (1984) 82 L.S.Gaz. 2169, CA ... 18–030
Armaghdown Motors Ltd v. Gray Motors Ltd [1963] N.Z.L.R. 5 ... 5–019, 11–019, 12–038, 12–051
Armanac Industries Ltd v. Citytrust, 525 A. 2d. 77 (Conn. 1987) ... 23–245
Armar Shipping Co. Ltd v. Caisse Algerienne D'Assurance et de Reassurance (The Armar) [1981] 1 W.L.R. 207; [1981] 1 All E.R. 498; [1980] 2 Lloyd's Rep. 450 ... 25–006
Armitage v. Insole (1850) 14 Q.B. 728; 19 L.J.Q.B. 202; 14 L.T.O.S. 439; 14 Jur. 619; 117 E.R. 280 ... 20–042
Armitage v. John Haigh & Sons (1893) 9 T.L.R. 287 ... 5–066, 5–091
Armitage v. Nurse [1998] Ch. 241; [1997] 2 All E.R. 705; *The Times*, March 31, 1997, CA ... 13–015, 19–075, 19–192, 19–200
Armour v. Thyssen Edelstahlwerke A.G. [1991] 2 A.C. 339; [1990] 3 W.L.R. 810; (1990) 134 S.J. 1337; [1990] 3 All E.R. 481; [1991] 1 Lloyd's Rep. 395; [1991] B.C.L.C. 28; [1990] B.C.C. 925; *The Times*, October 25, 1990, HL ... 1–065, 5–146, 5–149, 15–001, 15–113, 16–028, 16–029, 25–141, 25–142, 25–143
Armory v. Delamirie (1722) 1 Sta. 505; 93 E.R. 664 ... 5–010
Armour & Co. Ltd v. Leopold Walford (London) Ltd [1921] 3 K.B. 473; 91 L.J.K.B. 26; 125 L.T. 860; 15 Asp.M.L.C. 415; 27 Com.Cas. 37 ... 18–047
Armstrong v. Allen Bros. (1892) 67 L.T. 738; 9 T.L.R. 38, 7 Asp.M.L.C. 293; 4 R 107 5–135
—— v. Christiani (1848) 5 C.B. 687; 17 L.J.C.P. 181; 10 L.T.O.S. 418; 136 E.R. 1048 ... 22–124
Armstrong v. Jackson [1917] 2 K.B. 822; [1916–17] All E.R.Rep. 1117; 86 L.J.K.B. 1375; 117 L.T. 47a; 33 T.L.R. 444; 61 Sol.Jo. 631 ... 12–007, 12–059
—— v. Stokes (1872) L.R. 7 Q.B. 598 ... 25–081
—— v. Strain [1952] 1 K.B. 232; [1952] 1 T.L.R. 82; [1952] 1 All E.R. 139 ... 10–006
Arnhold Karberg & Co. v. Blythe Green Jourdain & Co. *See* Karberg (Arnhold) & Co. v. Blythe, Green Jourdain & Co.
Arnot v. Stewart (1817) 5 Dow.App.Cas. 274; 3 E.R. 1327 ... 18–246
Arnott v. Redfern (1926) 3 Bing. 353 ... 25–073
Aron (J.) & Co. v. Comptoir Wegimont [1921] 3 K.B. 435; 90 L.J.K.B. 1233; 37 T.L.R. 879; 26 Com.Cas. 303 ... 5–100, 11–018, 13–033, 18–028, 18–267, 18–268, 18–271, 18–276, 18–277, 18–284, 19–144

Aron (J.) & Co. (Inc) v. Miall (1928) 98 L.J.K.B. 204) [1928] All E.R.Rep. 655; 139 L.T. 562; 34 Com.Cas. 18 .... 19–052, 21–017
Aronson v. Mologa Holzindustrie A/G (1927) 138 L.T. 470; (1927) 32 Com.Cas. 276 17–009
Arpad, The [1934] P. 189; [1934] All E.R.Rep. 326; 103 L.J.P. 129; 152 L.T. 521; 50 T.L.R. 505; 78 Sol.Jo. 534 16–063, 16–070, 17–021, 17–022, 17–028, 17–029, 17–031, 17–032, 17–105, 18–285, 18–290, 18–306, 19–100
Art Direction Ltd v. U.P.S. Needham (N.Z.) Ltd [1977] 2 N.Z.L.R. 12 1–046
Aruna Mills Ltd v. Dhanrajmal Gobindram [1968] 1 Q.B. 655; [1968] 2 W.L.R. 101; [1968] 1 All E.R. 113; [1968] 1 Lloyd's Rep. 304 .... 8–024, 16–043, 16–046, 17–046, 18–267
Aryeh v. Lawrence Kostoris & Son Ltd [1967] 1 Lloyd's Rep. 63 ... 16–074, 17–004, 17–018, 17–029, 17–038, 17–051, 19–216
Asamera Oil Corp. Ltd v. Sea Oil & General Corp. (1978) 89 D.L.R. (3d) 1, Can. Sup. Ct 16–053
Asbury Park and Ocean Grove Bank v. National City Bank of New York 35 N. Y.S. 2d 985 (1942) affd. 52 N.Y.S. 2d 583 (1944) 23–054, 23–175
Asfar & Co. v. Blundell [1896] 1 Q.B. 123; 65 L.J.Q.B. 138; 73 L.T. 648; 44 W.R. 130; 12 T.L.R. 29; 40 Sol. Jo. 66; 8 Asp.M.L.C. 106 .... 1–128, 6–035, 15–126, 18–128, 19–113
Ashburn Anstalt v. W.J. Arnold & Co. (No.1) [1989] Ch. 1; [1988] 2 All E.R. 147; (1988) 55 P. & C.R. 137; (1987) 284 E.G. 1375; (1988) 132 S.J. 416; *The Times*, November 9, 1987, CA; affirming (1988) 55 P. & C.R. 13, Ch D 8–022
Ashby v. James (1843) 11 M. & W. 542; 12 L.J.Ex. 295; 152 E.R. 920 9–041
Ashford Shire Council v. Dependable Motors Property Ltd [1961] A.C. 336; [1960] 3 W.L.R. 999; 104 S.J. 1055; [1961] 1 All E.R. 96 .... 11–057, 11–063
Ashforth v. Redford (1873) L.R. 9 C.P. 20; *sub nom.* Ashworth v. Redford 43 L.J.C.P. 57 9–062
Ashington Piggeries Ltd v. Christopher Hill Ltd; *sub nom.* Christopher Hill Ltd v. Ashington Piggeries Ltd; Christopher Hill Ltd v. Fur Farm Supplies Ltd, Norsildmel (Third Parties) [1972] A.C. 441; [1971] 2 W.L.R. 1051; [1971] 1 All E.R. 847; [1971] 1 Lloyd's Rep. 245; 115 S.J. 223, HL 1–003, 1–047, 10–017, 11–005, 11–013, 11–014, 11–015, 11–016, 11–017, 11–018, 11–020, 11–025, 11–027, 11–047, 11–055, 11–060, 11–079, 13–032, 13–033, 14–017, 16–043, 17–066, 17–074, 18–273, 19–146
Ashmore & Son v. C.S. Cox & Co. [1899] 1 Q.B. 436; 68 L.J.Q.B. 72; 15 T.L.R. 55; 4 Com. Cas 48 .... 6–049, 8–066, 8–093, 12–031, 18–270, 19–131
Ashmore, Benson, Pease & Co. Ltd v. Dawson (A.V.) Ltd [1973] 1 W.L.R. 828; 117 S.J. 203; [1973] 2 All E.R. 856; [1973] 2 Lloyd's Rep. 21; [1973] R.T.R. 473 ... 3–029
Ashworth v. Wells (1898) 78 L.T. 136; (1898) 14 T.L.R. 227 .... 17–054, 17–066
Asia Oil & Minerals Ltd; *Re* (1986) 10 A.C.L.R. 333 1–050
Askey v. Golden Wine Co. Ltd 64 T.L.R. 379; 92 S.J. 411; [1948] 2 All E.R. 35 17–065
Associacion de Azucareros de Guatamala v. United States National Bank 423 F. 2d. 638 (1970) 23–183
Associated Alloys Pty Ltd v. CAN 001 452 106 Pty Ltd (2002) 202 C.L.R. 558; (2002) 74 A.L.J.R. 862, High Ct (Australia) 5–153
Associated Japanese Bank (International) Ltd v. Credit du Nord SA [1989] 1 W.L.R. 255; (1989) 133 S.J. 81; [1988] 3 All E.R. 902; [1989] F.L.R. 117 ...... 3–020, 3–022, 12–128
Assunzione, The [1954] P. 150; [1954] 2 W.L.R. 234; 98 S.J. 107; [1954] 1 All E.R. 278; [1953] 2 Lloyd's Rep. 716 .... 25–010, 25–070, 25–071
Astilleros Canaries SA v. Cape Hatteras Shipping Co. SA [1982] 1 Lloyd's Rep. 518 7–012
Astley v. Austrust Ltd [1999] Lloyd's Rep. P.N. 758, HC (Bar) 16–051
Astley Industrial Trust Ltd v. Grimley [1963] 1 W.L.R. 584; 107 S.J. 474; [1963] 2 All E.R. 33 .... 13–044, 13–051
—— v. Miller [1968] 2 All E.R. 36 .... 1–083, 4–013, 5–049, 7–002, 7–038, 7–044, 7–046, 7–059, 7–070, 7–105
Astra Trust Ltd v. Adams & Williams [1969] 1 Lloyd's Rep. 81 2–016
Astraea, The. *See* Alma Shipping Cpn. v. Union of India (The Astraea).
Astro Amo Compania Naviera SA v. Elf Union SA (The "Zographia M.") [1976] 2 Lloyd's Rep. 382 22–118

Astro Exito Navegacion SA v. Chase Manhattan Bank (The "Messiniaki Tolmi") [1986] 1 Lloyd's Rep. 455; affd. [1988] 2 Lloyd's Rep. 217 . . . 23–196, 23–213, 23–235
—— v. Southland Enterprise Co. (No. 2) [1983] 2 A.C. 787; [1983] 3 W.L.R. 130; (1983) 127 S.J. 461; [1983] 2 All E.R. 725; [1983] Com.L.R. 217; (1983) 80 L.S.Gaz. 3083, H.L.; [1982] Q.B. 1248; [1982] 3 W.L.R. 296; [1982] 3 All E.R. 335 . . . 17–103, 23–112
Astro Venturoso Compania Naviera v. Hellenic Shipyards SA (The Mariannina) [1983] 1 Lloyd's Rep. 12 . . . 25–006, 25–079
Aswan Engineering Establishment Co. v. Lupdine (Thurger Bolle, third party). *See* M/S Aswan Engineering Establishing Co. v. Lupdine (Thurger Bolle, third party).
Atack v. Lee [2005] 1 W.L.R. 2643 . . . 14–005
Atari Corporation (UK) Ltd v. Electronics Boutique Stores (UK) Ltd [1998] Q.B. 539; [1998] 2 W.L.R. 66; [1998] 1 All E.R. 1010; (1997) 16 Tr. L.R. 529; (1997) 94(33) L.S.G. 27; (1997) 141 S.J.L.B. 168; *The Times*, July 25, 1997, CA . . . 1–056, 5–041, 5–044, 5–052, 5–053
Athenasia Comninos and George Chr. Lemos, The (1979) [1990] 1 Lloyd's Rep. 277 . . . 18–053, 18–125, 18–133, 18–134, 18–141, 18–143, 19–091, 20–067
Athens Cape Naviera SA v. Deutsche Dampfschiffahrtgesellschaft "Hansa" Aktiengesellschaft (The Barenbels) [1985] 1 Lloyd's Rep. 528; (1985) 82 L.S.Gaz. 1256 . . . 4–023
Atisa SA v. Aztec A.G. [1983] 2 Lloyd's Rep. 579 . . . 6–041, 18–309, 18–317, 18–339, 18–340, 19–130, 19–140, 20–098
Atkinson v. Bell (1828) 8 B. & C. 277; Dan. & Ll. 93; 2 Man. & Ry. K.B. 292; 6 L.J.O.S. K.B. 258; 108 E.R. 1046 . . . 5–005, 5–077, 5–080, 5–091, 16–021
—— v. Denby (1862) 6 H. & N. 934; 31 L.J.Ex. 362; 8 Jur. N.S. 1012; 10 W.R. 389 . . 3–032
—— v. Newcastle & Gateshead Waterworks Co. (1877) 2 Ex.D. 441; [1874–80] All E.R.Rep. 757; 46 L.J.Ex. 775; 36 L.T. 761; 25 W.R. 794 . . . 1–071
Atlantic Concrete Ltd v. LeVatte Construction Co. Ltd (1975) 62 D.L.R. (3d) 663 . . . 1–098
Atlantic Lines and Navigation Co. Inc. v. Hallam Ltd (The Lucy) [1983] 1 Lloyd's Rep. 188 . . . 12–004, 12–007, 12–120
Atlantic Maritime Co. Inc. v. Gibbon [1954] 1 Q.B. 105; [1953] 3 W.L.R. 714; 97 S.J. 760; [1953] 2 All E.R. 1086; [1958] 2 Lloyd's Rep. 294, CA; affirming [1954] 1 Q.B. 88; [1953] 2 W.L.R. 725; 97 S.J. 248; [1953] 1 All E.R. 893; [1953] 1 Lloyd's Rep. 278 . . . 6–045, 6–046, 18–336
Atlantic Mutual Insurance v. Poseidon Schiffahrt 313 F. 2d. 872 (1963) . . . 21–091
Atlantic Paper Stock Ltd v. St. Anne-Nackawic Pulp & Paper Co. (1975) 56 D.L.R. (3d) 409 . . . 6–055, 8–099
Atlantic Shipping and Trading Co. Ltd v. Louis Dreyfus & Co. [1922] 2 A.C. 250; [1922] All E.R.Rep. 559; 91 L.J.K.B. 513; 127 L.T. 411; 38 T.L.R. 534; 66 Sol.Jo. 437 . . . 13–036, 13–038, 13–041
Atlantic Telecom GmbH, Noter, 2004 S.L.T. 1031; 2004 G.W.D. 30–623, OH . . . 25–019, 25–024, 25–076
Atlantic Underwriting Agencies Ltd v. Compagnia di Assicuiazione di Milano SpA [1979] 2 Lloyd's Rep. 240 . . . 25–007, 25–073, 25–074
Atlas Express v. Kafco (Importers and Distribution) [1989] Q.B. 833; [1989] 3 W.L.R. 389; (1989) 133 S.J. 977; [1989] 1 All E.R. 641; (1990) 9 Tr.L.R. 56; (1989) 139 N.L.J. 111 . . . 3–010
Atlas Shipping Agency (UK) Ltd v. Suisse Atlantique Societe d'Armement Maritime SA (The Gulf Grain and The El Amaan) [1995] 2 Lloyd's Rep. 188; [1995] I.L.Pr. 600; *The Times*, May 4, 1995, QBD (Comm Ct) . . . 25–082
Attenborough v. London & St. Katherine's Docks (1878) 3 C.P.D. 450; 26 W.R. 583 . . . 7–028
—— v. Solomon [1913] A.C. 76; [1911–13] All E.R.Rep. 155; 82 L.J.Ch. 173; 107 L.T. 833; 29 T.L.R. 79; 57 Sol.Jo. 76 . . . 7–110
Attica Sea Carriers Corporation v. Ferrostaal Poseidon Bulk Reederei GmbH (The Puerto Buitrago) [1976] 1 Lloyd's Rep. 250 . . . 16–059, 19–214, 20–126
Attock Cement Co. Ltd v. Romanian Bank for Foreign Trade [1989] 1 W.L.R. 1147; (1989) 133 S.J. 1298; [1989] 1 All E.R. 1189; [1989] 1 Lloyd's Rep. 572 . . . 22–013, 25–076, 25–161
Att.-Gen. v. Barker [1976] 2 N.Z.L.R. 495 . . . 2–017

Att.-Gen. v. Blake [2001] 1 A.C. 268; [2000] 3 W.L.R. 625; [2000] 4 All E.R. 385; [2000] 2 All E.R. (Comm) 487; [2001] I.R.L.R. 36; [2001] Emp. L.R. 329; [2000] E.M.L.R. 949; (2000) 23(12) I.P.D. 23098; (2000) 97(32) L.S.G. 37; (2000) 150 N.L.J. 1230; (2000) 144 S.J.L.B. 242; *The Times*, August 3, 2000; *Independent*, November 6, 2000 (C.S), HL 16–031
—— v. Leopold Walford (London) Ltd (1923) 14 Ll.L.R. 359 .... 20–018, 20–054
—— v. Morgan [1891] 1 Ch. 432; 60 L.J.Ch. 126; 64 L.T. 403; 39 W.R. 324;7 T.L.R. 209 1–097
—— v. Nathan (L.D.) & Co. Ltd [1990] 1 N.Z.L.R. 129 1–033
—— v. Pritchard (1928) 97 L.J.K.B. 561; 44 T.L.R. 490 .... 5–021, 5–146, 15–114, 16–015
—— v. Stewards Ltd (1901) 18 T.L.R. 131 8–059
Att.-Gen. for Australia v. Adelaide S.S. Co. Ltd [1913] A.C. 781 .... 3–035, 3–038, 3–039
Att.-Gen of Ceylon v. Scindia Steam Navigation Co. of India [1962] A.C. 60; [1961] 3 W.L.R. 936; [1961] 32 All E.R. 684; [1961] 2 Lloyd's Rep. 173; 105 S.J. 865, PC (Cey) 18–036
Att.-Gen. of the Republic of Ghana and Ghana National Petroleum Corp. v. Texaco Overseas Tank Ships; Texaco Melbourne, The [1994] 1 Lloyd's Rep. 473; *The Times*, February 16, 1994; Lloyd's List, March 18, 1994, HL; affirming [1993] 2 Lloyd's Rep. 471, CA; reversing [1992] 1 Lloyd's Rep. 303 .... 19–186, 25–193, 25–200
Att.-Gen.'s Reference (No. 5 of 1980), *Re* [1981] 1 W.L.R. 88; (1980) 124 S.J. 827; [1980] 3 All E.R. 816; (1980) 72 Cr.App.R. 71; [1981] Crim.L.R. 45 1–078
Attwood v. Emery (1856) 1 C.B. (N.S.) 110; 26 L.J.C.P. 73; 5 W.R. 19; 140 E.R. 45 8–036
Auckland Corporation v. Alliance Assurance Co. Ltd [1937] A.C. 587; [1937] 1 All E.R. 645; 106 L.J.P.C. 40; 156 L.T. 367; 81 Sol.Jo. 96 .... 25–158, 25–167
Aure v. Van Cauwenberghe & Fils [1938] 2 All E.R. 300 .... 6–021, 19–019
Austen v. Craven (1812) 4 Taunt. 644; 128 E.R. 483 5–060
Austin, Baldwin & Co. v. Wilfred Turner & Co. Ltd (1920) 36 T.L.R. 769 .... 18–309, 18–313, 18–335, 20–016
Australian Conference Association Ltd v. Mainline Construction Property Ltd (1978) 53 A.L.J.R. 63 .... 23–274, 23–289
Australian Knitting Mills Ltd v. Grant *See* Grant v. Australian Knitting Mills Ltd
Automobile and General Finance Corporation Ltd v. Morris (1929) 73 S.J. 451 1–066
Avco Corp. v. Borgal and Brandon v. Leckie (1972) 29 D.L.R. (3d) 633 7–082
Avery v. Bowden (1856) 6 E. & B. 953, 962; 26 L.J.Q.B. 3; 28 L.T.O.S. 145; 3 Jur. N.S. 239 .... 8–006, 9–018, 12–021, 15–111, 17–015, 18–347, 18–349
Avery Dennison Corp v. Home Trust and Savings Bank [2003] U.S. Dist., Lexis 204/3 .... 23–284, 23–285
Avimex SA v. Dewulf & Cie [1979] 2 Lloyd's Rep. 57 .... 8–091, 8–092, 8–095, 8–099, 8–101, 12–035, 12–036, 12–037, 18–346, 18–349, 18–350, 18–357, 18–358, 19–139, 19–151, 19–181
Avon Insurance plc v. Swire Fraser Ltd [2000] 1 All E.R. (Comm) 573; [2000] C.L.C. 665; [2000] Lloyd's Rep. I.R. 535, QBD (Comm Ct) 12–015
Awaroa Holdings Ltd v. Commercial Securities and Finance Ltd [1976] 1 N.Z.L.R. 19 10–009
Ayers v. S. Australian Banking Co. (1871) L.R. 3 P.C. 548; 7 Moo.P.C.C. 432; 19 W.R. 860; 17 E.R. 163 2–043
Ayres v. Moore [1940] 1 K.B. 278; 109 L.J.K.B. 91; 163 L.T. 337; 56 T.L.R. 145; 84 Sol.Jo. 96 22–047
Ayscough v. Sheed, Thomson & Co. Ltd (1924) 19 Ll.L.R. 104; (1924) 93 L.J.K.B. 924; 131 L.T. 610; 40 T.L.R. 707; 3; Com.Cas. 23 .... 13–037, 13–041
Axa Assurances Inc. v. Chase Manhattan Bank (2001) 339 N.J. Super 22 23–067
Axel Johnson Petroleum A.B. v. M.G. Mineral Group [1992] 1 W.L.R. 270; [1992] 2 All E.R. 163; 135 S.J.L.B. 60, CA 17–049
Azémar v. Casella (1867) L.R. 2 C.P. 677; 36 L.J.C.P. 263; 16 L.T. 571; 15 W.R. 998 .... 11–004, 11–022, 11–078, 13–023
Aziz v. Knightsbridge Gaming and Catering Services and Supplies (1982) 79 L.S.Gaz. 1412 22–116
Azov Shipping Co. v. Baltic Shipping Co. (No.3) [1999] 2 All E.R. (Comm) 453; [1999] 2 Lloyd's Rep. 159; [1999] C.L.C. 1425, QBD (Comm Ct) 18–030

B (A Child) v. McDonald's Restaurants Ltd [2002] EWHC 490, QBD 14–086

B. and B. Viennese Fashions v. Losane [1952] 1 T.L.R. 750; [1952] 1 All E.R. 909 .. 14–097
B. & H. Constructions Property Ltd v. Campbell [1963] N.S.W.R. 333 5–091
B. & P. Wholesale Distributors v. Marko Ltd, *The Times*, February 20, 1953 11–061
B. & S. Contracts & Designs Ltd v. Victor Green Publications Ltd [1984] I.C.R. 419 .... 8–090, 8–091, 8–097, 8–099
B.B.M.M. Finance (H.K.) Ltd v. Eda Holdings Ltd [1990] 1 W.L.R. 409; (1990) 134 S.J. 425; [1991] 2 All E.R. 129 .... 7–002, 17–106
B.C. Fruit Market Ltd v. National Fruit Co. (1921) 59 D.L.R. 87 8–015
B.H.P. Petroleum Ltd v. British Steel plc [2000] 2 All E.R. (Comm) 133; [2000] 2 Lloyd's Rep. 277; [2000] C.L.C. 1162; 74 Con. L.R. 63, CA; affirming [1999] 2 All E.R. (Comm) 544; [1999] 2 Lloyd's Rep. 583, QBD (Comm Ct) 13–037, 13–065
B.I.C.C. plc v. Burndy Corporation [1985] Ch. 232; [1985] 2 W.L.R. 132; (1984) 128 S.J. 750; [1985] 1 All E.R. 417; (1984) 81 L.S.Gaz. 3011 .... 15–134, 16–038, 17–049, 17–100
B.O.C. Group plc v. Centeon LLC [1999] 1 All E.R. (Comm) 970; 63 Con. L.R. 104, CA; affirming [1999] 1 All E.R. (Comm) 53; [1999] C.L.C. 497, QBD (Comm Ct) 13–039
B. S. Brown & Son Ltd v. Craiks Ltd [1970] 1 W.L.R. 752; [1970] 1 All E.R. 823; 1970 S.C. (H.L.) 51; 1970 S.L.T. 141; 114 S.J. 282, HL 11–032
B.S. & N. Ltd (BVI) v. Micado Shipping Ltd (Malta) (The Seaflower) (No.1) [2001] 1 All E.R. (Comm) 240; [2001] 1 Lloyd's Rep. 341; [2001] C.L.C. 421; CA 18–357
B.S. & N. Ltd (BVI) v. Micado Shipping Ltd (Malta) (The Seaflower) (No.2) [2000] 2 All E.R. (Comm) 169; [2000] 2 Lloyd's Rep. 37; [2000] C.L.C. 802, QBD (Comm Ct) 9–020, 10–037, 18–313, 19–166
B.T.P. Tioxide Ltd v. Pioneer Shipping Ltd (The Nema). *See* Pioneer Shipping v. B.T.P. Tioxide.
B.V. Oliehandel Jonglarid v. Coastal International Ltd [1983] 2 Lloyd's Rep. 463 .... 9–019, 9–061, 18–002
Baarn (No. 1), The [1933] P. 251; 102 L.J.P. 120; 150 L.T. 50; 49 T.L.R. 554; 18 Asp.M.L.C. 434 25–174
Baarn (No. 2), The [1934] P. 171; 103 L.J.P. 149; 152 L.T. 439; 18 Asp.M.L.C 506 .. 25–174
Babcock v. Lawson (1880) 5 Q.B.D. 284; 49 L.J.Q.B. 408; 42 L.T. 289; 28 W.R. 591 .... 7–022, 7–028
Baber v. Kenwood Manufacturing Co. Ltd [1978] 1 Lloyd's Rep. 175; (1977) 121 S.J. 606 2–051
Bacardi-Martini Beverages Ltd v. Messer U.K. Ltd *See* Bacardi-Martini Beverages Ltd v. Thomas Hardy Packaging Ltd
Bacardi-Martini Beverages Ltd v. Thomas Hardy Packaging Ltd; *sub nom.* Messer UK Ltd v. Bacardi-Martini Beverages Ltd; Messer UK Ltd v. Thomas Hardy Packaging Ltd [2002] EWCA Civ 549; [2002] 2 All E.R. (Comm) 335; [2002] 2 Lloyd's Rep. 379, CA 1–087, 12–12–122, 13–037, 13–090
Bache & Co. (London) Ltd v. Banque Vernes et Commerciale de Paris SA (1973) 117 S.J. 483; [1973] 2 Lloyd's Rep. 437 23–278
Bache and Vig v. Montague L. Meyer (1921) 7 Ll.L.R. 63 20–103
Bacon v. Cooper (Metals) Ltd [1982] 1 All E.R. 397 .... 16–007, 16–055, 17–023
Badham v. Lambs Ltd [1946] K.B. 45 14–088
Badische Anilin und Soda Fabrik v. Basle Chemical Works [1898] A.C. 200; 67 L.J.Ch. 141; 77 L.T. 573; 46 W.R. 255 ... 5–088, 5–013, 5–098, 5–101, 8–014, 15–046, 18–211, 20–012, 25–133
—— v. Hickson [1906] A.C. 419; 75 L.J. Ch. 621; 95 C.T. 68; 22 T.L.R. 641; 23 R.P.C. 149 .... 5–013, 5–018, 5–060, 5–088
Badische Co. Ltd, *Re* [1921] 2 Ch. 331; 91 L.J.Ch. 133; 169 L.T. 466 6–041, 6–042, 18–299, 19–136, 19–142, 20–101
Baetjer v. New England Alcohol Co., 66 N.E. 2d 798 (1946) 20–100
Baglehole v. Walters (1811) 3 Camp. 154; 170 E.R. 1338 13–028
Bagueley v. Hawley (1867) L.R. 2 C.P. 625; 36 L.J.C.P. 328; 17 L.T. 116 ...... 4–001, 4–032
Bailey v. Bullock [1950] W.N. 482; 66 T.L.R. (Pt. 2) 791; 94 S.J. 689; [1950] 2 All E.R. 1167 16–047
—— v. Gouldsmith (1791) Peake 78 .... 5–040, 5–050
—— v. Porter (1845) 14 M. & W. 44 .... 22–110, 22–124

Bailey v. United Chinese Bank Ltd (1953) 37 Hong Kong L.R. 102 .... 23–221, 23–222
Baily v. Merrell (1615) 3 Bulst. 94 10–019
Bain v. Brand (1876) 1 App. Cas. 762 1–095
—— v. Fothergill (1874) L.R. 7 H.L. 158; 43 L.J.Ex. 243; 31 C.T. 387; 39 J.P. 228; 23 W.R. 261 1–100
—— v. Gregory (1866) 14 L.T. 601; 14 W.R. 845 22–124
Bain (D.H.) v. Field & Co. (1920) 5 Ll.L.R. 16 .... 18–312, 20–028, 25–165, 25–193
Bainbridge v. Hemingway (1865) 12 L.T. 74 22–065
Baindail v. Baindail [1946] P. 122, CA 25–084
Baines v. National Provincial Bank (1927) 96 L.J.K.B. 801; 137 L.T. 631; 32 Cam.Cas. 216 22–099
Baird Textile Holdings Ltd v. Marks & Spencer Plc; *sub nom.* Baird Textiles Holdings Ltd v. Marks & Spencer Plc [2001] EWCA Civ 274; [2002] 1 All E.R. (Comm) 737; [2001] C.L.C. 999, CA 2–016, 2–017, 2–021, 18–045
Bairstow Eves London Central Ltd v. Smith [2004] EWHC 263; [2004] 2 E.G.L.R. 25; [2004] 29 E.G. 118, QBD 14–034
Baker v. Birch (1811) 3 Camp. 107 22–116
—— v. Efford (1873) 4 A.J.R. 161 (Aust.) 22–043
—— v. Gray (1856) 17 C.B. 462; 25 L.J.C.P. 161; 2 Jur.(N.S.) 400; 4 W.R. 297, 139 E.R. 1154 5–093
—— v. Lipton Ltd (1899) 15 T.L.R. 435 9–042
—— v. National Boulevard Bank, 399 F.Supp. 1021 (1975) 23–239
Baker v. Wait (1869–70) L.R. 9 Eq. 103, Ct of Chancery 5–098
—— v. Walker (1845) 14 M. & W. 465; 3 Dow & L 4b; 14 L.J.Ex. 371; 153 E.R. 558 9–030
Baker Perkins Ltd v. Thompson [1960] N.S.W.R. 488 10–020
Baker (Roland M.) Co. v. Brown 100 N.E. 1025 (1913) 25–139
Bakker v. Bowness Auto Parts Co. Ltd (1977) 68 D.L.R. 173 11–020
Baldey v. Parker (1823) 2 B & C. 37; 3 Dow & Ry K.B. 220; 1 L.J.O.S.K.B. 229; 10; 7 E.R. 297 15–050
Baldry v. Marshall [1925] 1 K.B. 260; [1924] all E.R. Rep. 155; 94 L.J.K.B. 208; 132 L.T. 326 .... 11–065, 13–025
Baldwin v. Richardson (1823) 1 B. & C. 245; 2 Dow & Ry. K.B. 285; 107 E.R. 91 .. 22–130
Balfour Beatty Construction (Scotland) v. Scottish Power 1994 S.L.T. 807, HL 16–043
Ballantine & Co. v. Cramp & Bosman (1923) 129 L.T. 502; [1923] All E.R. Rep. 579; 16 Asp.M.L.C. 224 .... 8–065, 8–068, 8–074, 8–076, 11–018
Ballard (Kent) Ltd v. Oliver Ashworth (Holdings) Ltd; *sub nom.* Oliver Ashworth (Holdings) Ltd v. Ballard (Kent) Ltd [2000] Ch. 12; [1999] 3 W.L.R. 57; [1999] 2 All E.R. 791; [1999] L. & T.R. 400; [1999] 2 E.G.L.R. 23; [1999] 19 E.G. 161; (1999) 96(16) L.S.G. 36; (1999) 149 N.L.J. 521; [1999] N.P.C. 36; *The Times*, April 1, 1999; *The Independent*, March 26, 1999, CA; reversing [1998] 3 E.G.L.R. 60; [1998] 46 E.G. 190, Ch D 18–358, 19–150
Balmoral Supermarket Ltd v. Bank of New Zealand [1974] 2 Lloyd's Rep. 164; [1974] 2 N.Z.L.R. 155 22–118
"Baltimex" Baltic Import and Export Co. Ltd v. Metallo Chemical Refining Co. Ltd [1956] 1 Lloyd's Rep. 450, CA; affirming [1955] 2 Lloyd's Rep. 438 23–093
Baltic Shipping Co. v. Dillon (1993) 176 C.L.R. 344 4–006
Bamberski v. Krombach (Case C-7/98); *sub nom.* Krombach v. Bamberski (Case C-7/98) [2001] Q.B. 709; [2001] 3 W.L.R. 488; [2001] All E.R. (EC) 584; [2000] E.C.R. 1–1935; [2001] I.L.Pr. 36; *The Times*, March 30, 2000, ECJ; [1998] I.L.Pr. 681, BGH (Ger) 25–043
Banbury and Cheltenham Direct Railway v. Daniel (1884) 54 L.J.Ch. 265; 33 W.R. 321 5–093
Banca Popolare di Novara (Co-operative Society with Limited Liability) v. Livanos (John) & Sons Ltd [1965] 2 Lloyd's Rep. 149, *The Times*, June 22, 1973, CA 22–103
Banco Atlantico SA v. British Bank of the Middle East [1990] 2 Lloyd's Rep. 504; *Financial Times*, June 5, 1990, CA 22–052
Banco de Portugal v. Waterlow & Sons Ltd [1932] A.C. 452; [1932] All E.R. Rep. 181; 101 L.J.K.B. 417; 147 L.T. 101; 48 T.L.R. 404; 76 Sol.Jo. 327 .... 16–030, 16–050, 17–026
Banco Espanol de Credito v. State Street Bank and Trust Co. 226 F.Supp. 106 (1967); 385 F.2d 230 (1967); 409 F.2d 711 (1969) 23–129, 23–141, 23–196, 23–235

Banco Nacional de Cuba v. Sabbationo 376 U.S. 398 (1964) 22–015
Banco Nacional Ultramarino v. First National Bank of Boston 289 F. 169 (1923) ... 23–061, 23–063, 23–187, 23–188
Banco Santander SA v. Banque Paribas *See* Banco Santander SA v. Bayfern Ltd
Banco Santander SA v. Bayfern Ltd; *sub nom.* Banco Santander SA v. Banque Paribas [2000] 1 All E.R. (Comm) 776; [2000] Lloyd's Rep. Bank. 165; [2000] C.L.C. 906, CA; affirming [1999] 2 All E.R. (Comm) 18; [1999] Lloyd's Rep. Bank. 239; [1999] C.L.C. 1321; (1999) 96(26) L.S.G. 27; *The Times*, June 29, 1999, QBD (Comm Ct) 23–062, 23–069, 23–146, 23–170
Banco Tornquist SA v. American Bank and Trust Co., 337 N.Y.S. 2d 489 (1972) ... 23–210, 23–239
Bangkok Bank Ltd v. Cheng [1990] 2 M.L.J. 5 23–285
Bangladesh Chemical Industrial Corp. v. Henry Stephens Shipping Co. Ltd (The S.L.S Everest) [1981] Com.L.R. 176; [1982] 2 Lloyd's Rep. 389 ...... 18–046, 25–071
Bangladesh Export Import Co. v. Sucden Kerry SA [1995] 2 Lloyd's Rep. 1, CA ... 18–309, 18–304, 18–322, 18–331, 18–335, 19–008, 19–137
Bank fúr Gemeinwirtschaft Actiengesellschaft v. City of London Garages Ltd [1971] 1 W.L.R. 149; 114 S.J. 970; [1971] 1 All E.R. 541, CA 22–061
Bank Leumi Le Israel BM v. Cablefast Ltd (unreported, October 19, 1988, CA) 23–164
Bank Line Ltd v. Arthur Capel & Co. [1919] A.C. 435; [1918–19] All E.R.Rep. 504; S.P. L.J.K.B. 211; 120 L.T. 129; 35 T.L.R. 150 .... 6–034, 6–045, 6–050, 6–056, 18–336, 18–341, 18–354
Bank Melli Iran v. Barclays Bank D.C.O. [1951] 2 T.L.R. 1057; [1951] 2 Lloyd's Rep. 367 .... 23–160, 23–174, 23–196, 23–214, 23–232, 23–235
Bank Negara Indonesia v. Lariza (Singapore) Pte Ltd [1988] A.C. 583, [1988] 2 W.L.R. 374; (1988) 132 S.J. 125, [1986] 1 M.L.J. 287 23–076
Bank of Africal Ltd v. Salisbury Gold Mining Co. Ltd [1892] A.C. 281; 61 L.J.P.C. 34; 66 L.T. 237; 41 W.R. 47; 8 T.L.R. 322 15–058
Bank of America v. Whitney-Central National Bank, 291 F. 929 (1923) 23–186
Bank of Australasia v. Clan Line Steamers Ltd [1916] 1 K.B. 39; 84 L.J.K.B. 1250; 113 L.T. 261; 13 Asp.M.L.C. 909; 21 Com.Cas. 13 13–038
Bank of Baroda v. Vysya Bank Ltd [1994] 2 Lloyd's Rep. 87; [1994] 3 Bank L.R. 216, QBD 23–140, 25–020, 25–065, 25–066, 25–073, 25–076, 25–161
Bank of Boston Connecticut v. European Grain & Shipping Ltd (The Dominique) [1989] A.C. 1056; [1989] 2 W.L.R. 440; (1989) 133 S.J. 219; [1989] 1 All E.R. 545; [1989] 1 Lloyd's Rep. 431 .... 19–075, 19–166
Bank of Canton v. Republic National Bank, 509 F.Supp. 1310 (1980), affd. 636 F. 2d. 30 (1980) 23–235
Bank of China v. Standard Chartered Bank of Australia Ltd (unreported decision July 16, 1991) 23–154
Bank of China, Japan and The Straits v. American Trading Co [1984] A.C. 266; 63 L.J.P.C. 92; 70 & 849; 6R 494 9–017
Bank of Credit and Commerce Hong Kong v. Sonali Bank [1995] 1 Lloyd's Rep. 227; *The Independent*, October 20, 1994 .... 23–140, 25–076, 25–161
Bank of Credit and Commerce International (Overseas) Ltd v. Price Waterhouse Ltd (No.2) [1998] Lloyd's Rep. Bank. 85; [1998] B.C.C. 617; [1998] E.C.C. 410; [1998] P.N.L.R. 564; (1998) 95(15) L.S.G. 32; (1998) 142 S.J.L.B. 86; *The Times*, March 4, 1998, CA; reversing [1997] B.C.C. 585; *The Times*, February 10, 1997, Ch D 12–013
Bank of Credit and Commerce International SA v. Dawson and Wright [1987] F.L.R. 342 22–061
Bank of Credit and Commerce International SA (In Liquidation) (No.8), Re; *sub nom.* Morris v. Rayners Enterprises Inc; Morris v. Agrichemicals Ltd [1998] A.C. 214; [1997] 3 W.L.R. 909; [1997] 4 All E.R. 568; [1998] Lloyd's Rep. Bank. 48; [1997] B.C.C. 965; [1998] 1 B.C.L.C. 68; [1998] B.P.I.R. 211; (1997) 94(44) L.S.G. 35; (1997) 147 N.L.J. 1653; (1997) 141 S.J.L.B. 229; *The Times*, November 13, 1997, HL; affirming [1996] Ch. 245; [1996] 2 W.L.R. 631; [1996] 2 All E.R. 121; [1996] B.C.C. 204; [1996] 2 B.C.L.C. 254; (1996) 140 S.J.L.B. 36; *The Times*, January 8, 1996, CA; affirming [1995] Ch. 46; [1994] 3 W.L.R. 911; [1994] 3 All E.R. 565; [1994] 1 B.C.L.C. 758; *The Times*, March 22, 1994, Ch D 22–144, 23–105

Bank of Credit and Commerce International SA (In Liquidation) (No.11), Re [1997] Ch. 213; [1997] 2 W.L.R. 172; [1996] 4 All E.R. 796; [1996] B.C.C. 980; [1997] 1 B.C.L.C. 80; *The Times*, October 8, 1996, Ch D 25–191
Bank of Cyprus (London) Ltd v. Jones (1984) 134 N.L.J. 522 22–061
Bank of East Asia Ltd v. Pang 240 P.1060 (1926) 23–163
Bank of England v. Vagliano Brothers [1891] A.C. 107; [1891–4] All E.R.Rep. 93; 60 L.J.Q.B. 145; 64 L.T. 353; 38 W.R. 657 .... 1–002, 15–007, 22–033
Bank of Ireland v. Evans' Trustees (1855) 5 H.L.C. 389; 25 L.T.O.S. 272; 3 W.R. 573; 3 C.L.R. 1060; 10 E.R. 950 7–016
Bank of Montreal v. Dezcan Industries Ltd (1983) 5 W.W.R. 83 22–045
—— v. Federal National Bank, 622 F.Supp. 6 (1986) 23–197
Bank of New South Wales v. Commonwealth Steel Co. Ltd [1983] 1 N.S.W.L.R. 69 .... 23–054, 23–137
—— v. Palmer [1970] 2 N.S.W.R. 532 .... 7–063, 7–077
—— v. Ross, Stuckey and Morawa [1974] 2 Lloyd's Rep. 110 .... 22–140, 22–143
Bank of New York and Trust Co. v. Atterbury Bros. Inc., 234 N.Y.S. 442 (1929) affd. 171 N.E. 786 (1930) 23–205
Bank of North Carolina v. Rock Island Bank, 570 F. 2d 202 (1978) 23–196
Bank of Nova Scotia v. Hellenic War Risk Association (Bermuda) (The Good Luck) [1992] 1 A.C. 233; [1991] 2 W.L.R. 1279; [1991] 3 All E.R. 1; [1991] 2 Lloyd's Rep. 191; (1991) 141 W.L.J. 779; *The Times*, May 17, 1991; *Financial Times*, May 21, 1991; *The Independent*, May 31, 1991, HL; reversing [1990] 1 Q.B. 818; [1990] 2 W.L.R. 547; [1989] 3 All E.R. 628; [1989] 2 Lloyd's Rep. 238; [1990] L.S.Gaz. March 14, 34, CA; reversing [1988] 1 Lloyd's Rep. 514 .... 16–051, 18–059, 18–276, 19–066, 20–022
Bank of Scotland v. Alfred Truman (A Firm) [2005] EWHC 583; [2005] C.C.L.R. 3, QBD 14–154
Bank of Scotland v. Dominion Bank [1891] A.C. 592 .... 22–087, 22–091
—— v. Gardiner (1907) 15 S.L.T. 229 7–042
Bank of Taiwan Ltd v. Union National Bank, 1 F.2d 65 (1924) 23–203
Bank of United States v. Seltzer 251 N.Y.S. 637 (1931) 23–099, 23–126
Bank of Van Diemen's Land v. Bank of Victoria (1871) L.R. 3 P.C. 526; 7 Nos. P.C.N.S. 501; 40 L.J.P.C. 28; 19 W.R. 857 .... 22–058, 22–087, 22–100, 22–105
Bank Polski v. Mulder (K.J.) & Co. [1941] 2 K.B. 266; [1942] 1 K.B. 497; 111 L.J.K.B. 431; 166 L.T. 259; 58 T.L.R. 178 .... 22–104, 22–110
Bank Russo-Iran v. Gordon, Woodroffe & Co. Ltd 1972 (unrep.) 23–164, 25–191
Bank Tejarat v. Hong Kong and Shanghai Banking Corp. [1995] 1 Lloyd's Rep. 239 23–168
Bank voor Scheepvart N.V. v. Slatford [1954] A.C. 584; [1954] 2 W.L.R. 867; 98 S.J. 301; [1954] 1 All E.R. 969; [1954] T.R. 115; 47 R. & I.T. 373; 35 T.C. 311; 33 A.T.C. 102 25–114
Bankamerica Finance Ltd v. Nock [1988] A.C. 1002; [1987] 3 W.L.R. 1191; [1988] 1 All E.R. 81; (1988) 85(2) L.S.G. 34; (1987) 137 N.L.J. 1158; (1987) 131 S.J. 1699, HL 4–017
Bankart v. Bowers (1866) L.R. 1 C.P. 484 8–004
Bankers Insurance Co. Ltd v. South [2003] EWHC 380; [2004] Lloyd's Rep. I.R. 1; [2003] P.I.Q.R. P28, QBD 14–032
Bankers Trust Co. v. State Bank of India [1991] 1 Lloyd's Rep. 587 .... 23–018, 23–157, 23–159, 23–203, 23–216
Bankes, Re [1902] 2 Ch. 333 25–086
Banner, *ex p. See* Tappenbeck, *Re, ex p.* Banner.
Banner v. Johnston (1871) L.R. 5 H.L. 157; 40 L.J.Ch. 730 5–140
Bannerman v. White (1861) 10 C.B. (N.S.) 844; 31 L.J.C.P. 28; 4 L.T. 740; 8 Jur. N.S. 282; 9 W.R. 784 .... 10–026, 12–063
Banque Belge pour 1'Etranger v. Hambrouck [1921] 1 K.B. 321; 90 L.J.K.B. 322; 37 T.L.R. 76; 65 Sol.Jo. 74; 26 Com.Cas. 72, CA 7–005, 22–091
Banque de L'Indochine et de Suez SA v. Rayner (J.H.) (Mincing Lane) Ltd [1983] Q.B. 711; [1983] 2 W.L.R. 841; (1983) 127 S.J. 361; [1983] 1 All E.R. 1137, [1983] 1 Lloyd's Rep. 228 .... 23–166, 23–206, 23–215, 23–223
Banque des Marchands de Moscow, *Re*, Royal Exchange Assurance v. The Liquidator [1952] W.N. 151; [1952] 1 T.L.R. 739 [1952] 1 All E.R. 1269 15–106

Banque Financière de la Cité SA v. Westgate Insurance Co. [1991] 2 A.C. 249; [1990] 3 W.L.R. 364; [1990] 2 All E.R. 947; [1990] 2 Lloyd's Rep. 377; 134 S.J. 1265; 140 N.L.J. 1074; [1990] L.S.Gaz., October 3, 36, HL; affirming [1990] 1 Q.B. 665; [1989] 3 W.L.R. 25; [1988] 2 Lloyd's Rep. 513; [1989] 2 All E.R. 952; 133 S.J. 817; 1989 Fin.L.R. 1, CA 16–049
Banque Keyser Ullmann SA v. Skandia (U.K.) Insurance Co. Ltd *See* Banque Financière de la cité SA v. Westgate Insurance Co.
Banque Nationale de Paris v. Credit Agricole [2001] 2 S.L.R. 1 (Singapore CA) 23–062, 23–063
Banque Nationale de Paris plc v. International Bank Commodities (unreported, February 7, 992) 22–060, 22–069
Banque Paribas v. Cargil International SA [1992] 2 Lloyd's Rep. 19, CA; affirming [1992] 1 Lloyd's Rep. 96 2–012
Banque Saudi Fransi v. Lear Siegler Services Inc [2006] Lloyd's Rep. 272 .. 23–274, 23–276, 23–282
Barbe v. Parker (1789) 1 H.Bl. 283 .... 1–034, 1–039
Barbee v. Rogers 425 S.W. (2d) 342 (1968) 1–046
Barber v. Inland Truck Sales Ltd (1970) 11 D.L.R. (3d) 469 12–065
—— v. Meyerstein (1870) L.R. 4 H.L. 317 .... 18–016, 18–080, 18–084, 18–091, 18–092, 18–094, 18–113
—— v. NWS Bank plc [1996] 1 W.L.R. 641; [1996] 1 All E.R. 906; [1996] R.T.R. 388; [1996] C.C.L.R. 30; (1995) 145 N.L.J. 1814; *The Times*, November 27, 1995; *The Independent*, December 1, 1995, CA 4–004, 4–005, 4–006, 4–008, 4–021, 7–106, 17–090
—— v. Richards (1851) 6 Exch. 63; 20 L.J.Ex. 135; 135; 16 L.T.O.S. 344; 155 E.R. 455 22–060
—— v. Taylor (1839) 5 M & W 527; (1839) 9 L.J.Ex. 21; 151 E.R. 223 19–066
Barclay v. Bailey (1810) 2 Camp. 527 22–099
Barclays Bank v. Fairclough Building [1995] Q.B. 214; [1994] 3 W.L.R. 1057; [1995] 1 All E.R. 289; [1995] P.I.Q.R. 152; [1995] E.G.C.S. 10; 38 Con.L.R. 86; 68 B.L.R. 1; 11 Const. L.J. 35; 91 (25) L.S.Gaz. 30; 138 S.J.L.B. 118; *The Times*, May 11, 1994, CA 16–051
Barclays Bank v. Glasgow City Council; Kleinwort Benson v. Same; *sub nom.* Kleinwort Benson v. City of Glasgow District Council; Barclays Bank v. Same [1994] Q.B. 404; [1994] 2 W.L.R. 466; [1994] 4 All E.R. 865, CA; affirming in part [1993] Q.B. 429; [1994] 4 All E.R. 865; [1992] 3 W.L.R. 827; (1993) 5 Admin.L.R. 382; *The Times*, March 17, 1992; *Financial Times*, March 4, 1992, QBD. *See also* Kleinwort Benson v. City of Glasgow District Council 25–021
Barclays Bank v. O'Brien [1994] 1 A.C. 180; [1993] 3 W.L.R. 786; [1993] 4 All E.R. 417; [1994] 1 F.L.R. 1; [1994] 1 F.C.R. 357 [1994] Tr.L.R. 165; [1994] Fam.Law 78; [1994] C.C.L.R. 94; [1993] E.G.C.S. 169; [1993] N.P.C. 135; 26 H.L.R. 75; 137 S.J.L.B. 240; *The Times*, October 22, 1993; *The Independent*, October 22, 1993, HL 14–051A
Barclays Bank D.C.O. v. Mercantile National Bank 339 F.Supp. 457 (1972), affirmed 481 F.2d 1224 (1972); [1973] 2 Lloyd's Rep. 541 .... 23–239, 23–241, 23–247, 23–249
Barclays Bank International Ltd v. Levin Brothers (Bradford) Ltd [1977] Q.B. 270; [1976] 3 W.L.R. 852; (1976) 120 S.J. 801; [1976] 3 All E.R. 900; [1977] 1 Lloyd's Rep. 51 .... 25–167, 25–194
Barclays Bank Ltd v. Aschaffenburger Zellstoffwerke A.G. 111 S.J. 350; [1967] 1 Lloyd's Rep. 387; 117 New L.J. 268, CA 9–032, 22–060, 22–069
—— v. Astley Industrial Trust Ltd [1970] 2 Q.B. 527; [1970] 2 W.L.R. 876; [1970] 1 All E.R. 719 .... 22–060, 22–061, 22–075
—— v. Bank of England [1985] 1 All E.R. 385; [1985] F.L.R. 209; (1985) 135 New L.J. 104 22–057
—— v. Commissioners of Customs and Excise [1963] 1 Lloyd's Rep. 81 .... 18–016, 18–063, 18–127
—— v. I.R.C. [1961] A.C. 509; [1960] 3 W.L.R. 280; 104 S.J. 563; [1960] 2 All E.R. 817; [1960] T.R. 185; 39 A.T.C. 141 24–008
—— v. T.O.S.G. Trust Fund Ltd [1984] A.C. 626; [1984] 2 W.L.R. 650; (1984) 128 S.J. 261; [1984] 1 All E.R. 1060; (1984) L.S. Gaz. 1360; (1984) New L.J. 656 .... 2–043, 7–046

Barclays Bank Plc v. Fairclough Building Ltd (No.1) [1995] Q.B. 214; [1994] 3 W.L.R. 1057; [1995] 1 All E.R. 289; 68 B.L.R. 1; 38 Con. L.R. 86; (1995) 11 Const. L.J. 35; [1995] E.G.C.S. 10; (1994) 91(25) L.S.G. 30; (1994) 138 S.J.L.B. 118; *The Times*, May 11, 1994, CA 13–067
Barclays Bank plc v. Tackport Ltd (CA) unreported, April 25, 1991 .... 22–073, 22–076
Baring v. Lyman 1 Story 396; 2 Fed.Cas. 794 (1841) 23–124
Baring Brothers & Co. v. Cunninghame DC [1997] C.L.C. 108; *The Times*, September 30, 1996, OH 25–169
Barker v. Bell [1971] 1 W.L.R. 983; 115 S.J. 364; [1971] 2 All E.R. 867 7–099
—— v. Walker (1845) 14 M. & W. 465 9–030
Barker (George) (Transport) Ltd v. Eynon [1974] 1 W.L.R. 462; (1973) 118 S.J. 240; [1974] 1 All E.R. 900; [1974] 1 Lloyd's Rep. 65 5–161
Barker (W.) (Jr.) & Co. Ltd v. Edward T. Agius Ltd (1927) 43 T.L.R. 751; (1927) 33 Com.Cas. 120 .... 12–030, 13–025
Barkworth v. Young (1856) 4 Drew 1; (1856) 26 L.J.Ch. 153; 28 L.T.O.S. 199; 3 Jur. N.S. 34 6–052
Barley (Y.P.) Producers Ltd v. E.C. Robertson Property Ltd [1927] V.L.R. 194 .... 9–017, 9–020
Barlow & Co. v. Hanslip [1926] N.I. 113n 1–061
Barned's Banking Co., *Re* (1871) 6 Ch.App. 3881; 40 L.J.Ch. 590; (1871) L.R. 5 H.L. 157 23–100
Barned's Banking Co. Ltd, Massey's Case, *Re*, (1870) 39 L.J.Ch. 635; 22 L.T. 853; 18 W.R. 818 23–125
Barnes & Co. v. Toye (1884) 13 Q.B.D. 410; 53 L.J.Q.B. 567, 48 J.P. 664 2–030
Barnett v. Ira L. and A.C. Berk Property Ltd (1952) 52 S.R. (N.S.W.) 268 8–089
—— v. Javeri & Co. [1916] 2 K.B. 390, 85 L.J.K.B. 1703; 115 L.T. 217; 13 Asp.M.L.C. 424; 22 Com.Cas. 5 .... 21–022, 21–026, 21–029, 21–031
—— v. Sanker (1925) 41 T.L.R. 660; 69 Sol.Jo. 824 1–104
Barningham v. Smith (1874) 31 L.T. 540 .... 8–068, 8–084, 8–087
Barr v. Gibson (1838) 3 M. & W. 390; 1 Horn. & H. 70; 7 L.J.Ex. 124; 150 E.R. 1196 .... 1–128, 6–035, 11–003, 11–013
Barre (J.) Johnston & Co. v. Oldham (1895) 11 T.L.R. 401 10–021
Barrett v. Bank of the Manhattan Co. 218 F. 2d 263 (1954) 25–136
Barros Mattos Junior v. MacDaniels Ltd; *sub nom.* Mattos Junior v. MacDaniels Ltd; Barros Mattos Junior v. General Securities & Finance Co Ltd [2004] EWHC 1188; [2005] 1 W.L.R. 247; [2004] 3 All E.R. 299; [2004] 2 All E.R. (Comm) 501; [2004] 2 Lloyd's Rep. 475, Ch D 25–119
Barros Mattos Junior v. MacDaniels Ltd (Amendments) [2005] EWHC 1323; [2005] I.L.Pr. 45, Ch D 25–204
Barrow, *ex p.* (1877) 6 Ch.D. 783 .... 15–078, 15–079
Barrow v. Arnaud (1846) 8 Q.B. 595; 10 Jur. 319; 115 E.R. 1104 ... 16–062, 16–074, 17–004
—— v. Cole (1811) 3 Camp. 92; 170 E.R. 1316 7–086
Barrow Lane & Ballard Ltd v. Phillip Phillips & Co. Ltd [1929] 1 K.B. 574 ... 1–126, 1–127, 1–130, 1–133, 3–023, 6–035, 6–040, 18–112, 19–108, 19–113
Barry v. Davies; *sub nom.* Heathcote Ball & Co. (Commercial Auctions) Ltd v. Barry; Barry v. Heathcote Ball & Co. (Commercial Auctions) Ltd [2001] 1 W.L.R. 1962; [2001] 1 All E.R. 944; [2000] 3 E.G.L.R. 7; [2000] 47 E.G. 178; (2000) 97(39) L.S.G. 41; (2000) 150 N.L.J/1377; (2000) 144 S.J.L.B. 249; *The Times*, August 31, 2000, CA 2–005, 17–004
Barry v. Slade (1920) 20 S.R. (N.S.W.) 121 22–064
Bartlett v. Holmes (1835) 13 C.B. 630; 1 C.L.R. 159; 22 L.J.C.P. 182; 21 L.T.O.S. 104 8–012
—— v. Marcus (Sidney) Ltd [1965] 1 W.L.R. 1013; 109 S.J. 451; [1965] 2 All E.R. 753 .... 11–048, 11–058
Barton, Thompson & Co. v. Vigers Bros. (1906) 19 Com.Cas. 175; N; 19 Com.Cas. 175 .... 18–212, 18–221
Baschet v. London Illustrated Standard Co. [1900] 1 Ch. 73; 69 L.J.Ch. 35; 81 L.T. 509; 48 W.R. 56; 44 S.J. 42 25–190
Base Metal Trading Ltd v. Shamurin [2004] EWCA Civ 1316; [2005] 1 W.L.R. 1157; [2005] 1 All E.R. (Comm) 17; [2005] B.C.C. 325; [2005] 2 B.C.L.C. 171; [2004] 2 C.L.C. 916; (2004) 148 S.J.L.B. 1281; *The Times*, November 1, 2004, CA 25–019, 25–024

Basildon D.C. v. Lesser (J.E.) (Properties) Ltd [1985] Q.B. 839; [1984] 3 W.L.R. 812; [1985] 1 All E.R. 20; (1984) 1 Const. L.J. 57; (1987) 8 Con L.R. 89; (1984) 134 New L.J. 330; (1984) 81 L.S.Gaz. 1437 6–028
Basse and Selve v. Bank of Australasia (1904) 90 L.T. 618; 20 T.L.R. 431 .. 23–128, 23–129, 23–204, 23–235
Bastone or Firminger Ltd v. Nasima Enterprises (Nigeria) Ltd [1996] C.L.C. 1902, QBD 22–092
Bateman v. Green (1867) I.R. 2 C.L. 607 .... 18–084, 18–212, 18–223
Bates (Thomas) & Son v. Wyndham's (Lingeric) [1981] 1 W.L.R. 505; [1980] 125 S.J. 32; [1981] 1 All E.R. 1077; (1980) 257 E.G. 381; (1980) 41 P. & C.R. 345, CA 2–017
Batt (John) & Co. (London) Ltd v. Brooker, Dore & Co. Ltd (1942) 72 W.L.R. 149; 72 Ll.L. Rep. 149 8–099
Battersby [2001] J.B.L. 1 .... 4–001, 5–001
Battley v. Faulkner (1820) 3 B. & A. 288; 106 E.R. 668 12–121
Batty v. Metropolitan Property Realisations Ltd [1978] Q.B. 554; [1978] 2 W.L.R. 500; (1977) 122 S.J. 63; [1978] 2 All E.R. 445; (1977) 245 E.G. 43; (1977) 7 Build. L.R. 1 12–126
Bavins Jnr. & Sims v. London & South Western Bank Ltd [1900] 1 Q.B. 270; 69 L.J.Q.B. 164; 81 L.T. 655; 16 T.L.R. 61; 5 Com.Cas. 1 .... 22–023, 22–041
Bawden v. London, Edinburgh & Glasgow Assurance Co. [1892] 2 Q.B. 534; 61 L.J.Q.B. 792; 57 J.P. 116 10–009
Baxendale v. London Chatham & Dover Railway (1874) L.R. 10 Ex. 35; 44 L.J.Ex. 20; 32 L.T. 330; 23 W.R. 167 17–077
Baxter v. Chapman (1873) 29 L.T. 642; 2 Asp.M.L.C. 170 .... 5–140, 19–035
——v. Ford Motor Co. 12 P. 2d 409 (1934) 14–078
Baxter Fell & Co. Ltd v. Galbraith & Grant Ltd (1941) 70 Ll.L.R. 142 ..... 19–037, 19–099
Bayerische Veriensbank A.G. v. National Bank of Pakistan [1997] 1 Lloyd's Rep. 59 .... 23–203, 23–210
Baynes & Co. v. Lloyd & Sons [1895] 1 Q.B. 820; 64 L.J.Q.B. 787; 73 L.T. 250; 59 J.P. 710; 44 W.R. 328 4–030
Beal v. South Devon Railway (1864) 3 H. & C. 337; [1861–74] All E.R. Rep. 972; 11 L.T. 184; 12 W.R. 1115; 159 E.R. 580 23–176
Beale v. Mouls (1847) 10 Q.B. 976; 5 Ry & Com.Cas. 105; 16 L.J.Q.B. 410; 11 J.W. 345; 116 E.R. 370 5–092
——v. Taylor [1967] 1 W.L.R. 1193; 111 S.J. 668; [1964] 3 All E.R. 253 ...... 1–011, 3–020, 10–018, 11–010, 11–011, 11–012, 11–019, 13–030 13–077, 14–009
Beathard v. Chicago Football Club Inc. 419 F.Supp. 1133 (1976) ... 23–049, 23–135, 23–239, 23–250
Beattie v. Ebury (Cora) (1872) L.R. 7 Ch.App. 777; 41 L.J. Ch 804; 27 L.T. 398; 20 W.R. 994; L.J.J. 10–009
Becher (Kurt A.) GmbH & Co. v. Roplak Enterprises SA (The World Navigator) [1991] 2 Lloyd's Rep. 23 .... 8–039, 8–040, 9–020, 20–033, 21–040
Beck (Ernest) & Co. v. Szymanowski & Co. [1923] 1 K.B. 457; [1924] A. C 43; [1923] All E.R. Rep. 244; 93 L.J.K.B. 25 .... 13–032, 13–034, 13–038, 13–040, 18–279
Becker v. Ricbald (1913) 30 T.L.R. 142 5–159
Beckett v. Tower Assets Co. Ltd [1891] 1 Q.B. 638; 60 L.J.Q.B. 493; 64 L.T. 497; 7 T.L.R. 400; [1891–4] All E.R. Rep. Ext. 2038; 55 J.P. 438; 39 W.R. 438, CA; reversing [1891] 1 Q.B. 1; 60 L.J.Q.B. 56, 7 T.L.R. 21 .... 1–064, 5–167
Beckman Cotton Co. v. First National Bank 34 U.C.C. Rep.Ser. 986 (1982) 23–116
Bedford Insce. Co. Ltd v. Instituto de Resseguros do Brasil [1985] Q.B. 966; [1984] 3 W.L.R. 726; (1984) 128 S.J. 701; [1984] 3 All E.R. 766; [1984] 1 Lloyd's Rep. 210; 1985 F.L.R. 49; [1984] L.M.C.L.Q. 386 3–028
Beebee & Co. v. Turner's Successors (1931) 48 T.L.R. 61 7–113
Beecham Foods Ltd v. North Supplies (Edmonton) Ltd [1959] 1 W.L.R. 643; 103 S.J. 432; [1959] 2 All E.R. 336; L.R. 1 R.P. 262 1–061
Beecham (H.) & Co. Property Ltd v. Francis Howard & Co. Property Ltd [1921] V.L.R. 428 .... 11–010, 11–059
Beeching v. Gower (1816) Holt 313 22–110
Beed v. Blandford (1828) 2 Y. & J. 278; 148 E.R. 924 12–068
Beer v. Bowden [1981] 1 W.L.R. 522; [1981] 1 All E.R. 1071; (1976) 41 P. & C.R. 317 2–017

Beer v. Walker (1877) 46 L.J.Q.B. 677; 37 L.T. 278; 41 J.P. 728; 25 W.R. 880 .... 6–019, 6–022, 11–040, 11–067, 18–255
Beesly v. Hallwood Estates Ltd [1961] Ch. 105; [1961] 2 W.L.R. 36; 105 S.J. 61; [1961] 1 All E.R. 90 9–024
Beevor v. Marler (1898) 14 T.L.R. 259 23–164
Behn v. Burness (1863) 3 B. & S. 751 .... 10–003, 10–023, 18–270
Behnke v. Bede Shipping Company Ltd [1927] 1 K.B. 649; 96 L.J.K.B. 325; 136 L.T. 667; 43 T.L.R. 170; 71 S.J. 105; 32 Com.Cas. 134; 17 Asp.M.L.C. 222 .... 1–082, 17–099, 17–103
Behrend & Co. Ltd v. Produce Brokers Ltd [1920] 3 K.B. 530; 9 L.J.K.B. 143; 124 L.T. 281; 36 T.L.R. 775; 15 Asp. M.L.C. 139; 25 Com.Cas. 286 .... 6–040, 8–046, 8–064, 12–061, 12–069, 17–091
Behzadi v. Shaftesbury Hotels Ltd [1992] Ch. 1; [1991] 2 W.L.R. 1251; [1991] 2 All E.R. 477; (1991) 62 P. & C.R. 163; (1990) 140 N.L.J. 1385; *The Independent*, August 22, 1990, CA 8–026
Bekh v. Page (1859) 5 C.B. (N.S.) 708 8–054
Belding v. Read (1865) 3 H. & C. 955; 6 New Rep. 301; 34 L.J.Ex. 212; 13 L.T. 66; 11 Jur. (O.S.) 547; 13 W.R. 867; 159 E.R. 812 1–105
Belginn Grain and Produce Co. Ltd v. Cox & Co. (France) Ltd [1919] W.N. 308; 1 H.L. Rep. 256; 1 Ll.L. Rep. 256 .... 19–049, 23–171, 23–196, 23–231
Belgische Radio en Televisie v. S.V.SAB.A.M. [1974] 1 E.C.R. 51 3–041
Bell v. Lever Bros. Ltd [1932] A.C. 161 ... 1–130, 1–131, 1–133, 3–018, 3–019, 3–020, 3–022, 10–009
Bell & Co. v. Antwerp, London and Brazil Line [1891] 1 Q.B. 103 .... 9–047, 9–059
Bell Houses Ltd v. City Wall Properties Ltd (1967) 205 E.G. 535; affirming [1966] 2 Q.B. 656; [1966] 2 W.L.R. 1323; 110 S.J. 268; [1966] 2 All E.R. 674; [1965] C.L.Y. 482, CA 2–028
Bell, Rannie & Co. v. White's Trustee (1885) 22 Sc.L.R. 597 5–045
Bellamy v. Davey [1891] 3 Ch. 540; 60 L.J.Ch. 778; 65 L.T. 308; 40 W.R. 118; 7 T.L.R. 725 .... 5–066, 5–091, 15–010
Belle Bonfils Memorial Blood Bank v. Hansen 579 P. 2d. 1158 (1978) 1–089
Bellhouse v. Mellor, Proudman & Mellor (1859) 4 H. & N. 116 8–033
Belmont Finance Corp. Ltd v. Williams Furniture Ltd [1979] Ch. 250; [1978] 3 W.L.R. 712; (1977) 122 S.J. 743; [1979] 1 All E.R. 118 3–032
Belshaw v. Bush (1851) 11 C.B. 191; 22 L.J.C.P. 24; 17 Jur. 67 .... 9–030, 9–044, 22–118
Belsize Motor Supply Co. v. Cox [1914] 1 K.B. 244 .... 1–072, 7–068
Belvoir Finance Co. Ltd v. Cole (Harold G.) Co. Ltd [1969] 1 W.L.R. 1877; [1969] 2 All E.R. 904 .... 7–032, 7–037, 7–038, 7–070, 7–074, 7–090
——v. Stapleton [1971] 1 Q.B. 210; [1970] 3 W.L.R. 530; 114 S.J. 719; [1970] 3 All E.R. 664 .... 3–030, 3–031, 4–013, 7–002, 7–105, 15–118
Bem Dis A Turk Ticaret S/A TR v. International Agri Trade Co. Ltd (The Selda) [1999] 1 All E.R. (Comm.) 619; [1999] 1 Lloyd's Rep. 729; [1999] C.L.C. 813, CA; affirming [1998] 1 Lloyd's Rep. 416; *The Times*, December 13, 1997, QBD (Comm Ct) 16–061, 16–086, 17–052, 19–176, 19–216, 19–218
Benabu & Co. v. Produce Brokers Co. Ltd (1921) 37 T.L.R. 851; *sub nom.* Benabu & Co., Sellers & Produce Brokers Co. Ltd. *Re* 26 Com.Cas. 335 18–271
Benaim & Co. v. L.S. Debono [1924] A.C. 514; 93 L.J.P.C 133; 131 L.T. 1 .... 12–051, 20–012, 20–111, 25–009, 25–011, 25–066, 25–188
Benarty, The, *See* Lister (R.A.) & Co. v. Thomson (E.G.) (Shipping) (The Benarty).
Bence Graphics International Ltd v. Fasson U.K. Ltd [1998] Q.B. 87; [1997] 3 W.L.R. 205; [1997] 1 All E.R. 979; [1997] C.L.C. 373; (1996) 93(40) L.S.G. 24; (1996) 146 N.L.J. 1577 ... 16–046, 16–061, 17–007, 17–017, 17–019, 17–020, 17–028, 17–029, 17–033, 17–039, 17–047, 17–051, 17–052, 17–054, 17–056, 17–058, 17–061, 17–082, 17–083
Benecke v. Haebler 58 N.Y.S. 16 (1899), affd. 60 N.E. 1107 (1901) 23–129
Benincasa v. Dentalkit Srl (Case C–269/95) [1998] All E.R. (EC) 135; [1997] E.C.R. 1–3767; [1997] E.T.M.R. 447; [1997] I.L.pR. 559; *The Times*, October 13, 1997, ECJ (6th Chamber) 25–045
Bennett v. Griffin Finance Ltd [1967] 2 Q.B. 46; [1967] 2 W.L.R. 561 .... 1–066, 4–010
Bennett & White (Calgary) Ltd v. Municipal District of Sugar City No. 5 [1951] A.C. 786, P.C. 5–093

Bennett (H. & J.M.) Europe Ltd v. Angrexco Co. Ltd. unreported, decision April 6, 1990 23–084
Bennett (Sidney) Ltd v. Kreeger (1925) 41 T.L.R. 609 17–077
Bennett-Cohen v. The State (Zimbabwe S.Ct., February 4, 1985) 1–084
Bentall v. Burn (1824) 3 B. & C. 423; 5 Dow. & Ry. K.B. 284; 3 L.J. (O.s.) K.B. 42; 107 E.R. 791 .... 8–012, 8–013
Bentley Bros. v. Metcalfe & Co. [1906] 2 K.B. 548; 75 L.J.K.B. 891; 95 L.T. 596; 22 T.L.R. 676 1–085
Bentley (Dick) Productions Ltd v. Smith (Harold) (Motors) Ltd [1965] 1 W.L.R. 623; 109 S.J. 329; [1965] 2 All E.R. 65 .... 10–017, 10–018, 14–041
Bentsen v. Taylor, Sons & Co. (No. 2) [1893] A.C. 274; 2 Q.B. 274; 63 L.J.Q.B. 15; 69 L.T. 487; 42 W.R. 8; 9 T.L.R. 552; 4 R. 510 .. 8–025, 8–064, 10–003, 10–027, 12–034, 18–267, 18–270
Bentworth Finance Ltd v. Lubert [1968] 1 Q.B. 680; [1967] 3 W.L.R. 378; 111 S.J. 272; [1967] 2 All E.R. 810 .... 1–083, 10–026
——v. White (1962) 112 L.J. 140 3–005
Beoco v. Alfa Laval Co. [1995] Q.B. 137; [1994] 3 W.L.R. 1179; [1994] 4 All E.R. 464; 66 B.L.R. 1; 144 N.L.J. Rep. 233; *The Times*, January 12, 1994, CA 16–049
Berchtold, *Re* [1923] 1 Ch. 192; 92 L.J.Ch. 185; 128 L.T. 591; 67 S.J. 212 25–004
Berg (V.) & Sons Ltd v. Vanden Avenne-lzegem PVBA [1977] 1 Lloyd's Rep. 499 .. 8–101, 12–037, 18–357, 18–353, 19–160
Berger & Co. Inc. v. Gill & Duffus SA *See* Gill & Duffus v. Berger & Co.
Bergerco U.SA v. Vegoil Ltd [1984] 1 Lloyd's Rep. 440 ... 10–037, 18–270, 19–032, 19–033, 19–157
Bergfeldt v. Markell [1921] 1 W.W.R. 453 4–026
Bergheim v. Blaenavon Iron Co. (1875) L.R. 10 Q.B. 319; 44 L.J. Q.B. 92; 32 L.T. 451; 23 W.R. 618 .... 8–067, 8–068
Bergmann v. Kenburn Waste Management Ltd [2002] EWCA Civ 98; [2002] 2 F.S.R. 711, *The Times*, February 4, 2002, CA; affirming *The Times*, July 9, 2001, Ch D 25–019, 25–020, 25–065
Berk v. International Explosives Co. (1901) 7 Com.Cas. 20 8–060
Berk & Co. v. Day and White (1897) 13 T.L.R. 475 .... 8–076, 8–078
Berkshire, The [1974] 1 Lloyd's Rep. 185 19–028
Berndtson v. Strang (1867) 4 Eq. 481; on appeal (1868) L.R. 3 Ch.App. 588 ...... 15–073, 15–082, 15–090, 15–100, 18–085, 20–085, 20–141
Bernstein v. Pamson Motors (Golders Green) Ltd [1987] 2 All E.R. 220; [1987] R.T.R. 384; (1987) 6 T.L.R. 33 .... 11–044, 11–048, 12–055, 12–056, 14–006, 14–020, 14–021
Berridge v. Fitzgerald (1869) L.R. 4 Q.B. 639; 10 B & S. 668, 38 L.J.Q.B. 335; 17 W.R. 917 .... 22–130, 22–131
Berroles v. Ramsay (1815) Holt N.P. 77 2–031
Berry v. Star Brush Co. (1915) 31 T.L.R. 603 5–052
Besseler Waechter Glover & Co. v. South Derwent Coal Co. [1938] 1 Q.B. 408; [1937] 4 All E.R. 552; 107 L.J.K.B. 365; 158 L.T. 12; 54 T.L.R. 140; 43 Com.Cas. 86; 59 Ll.L.Rep. 104 .... 8–030, 8–069, 9–006
Beswick v. Beswick [1968] A.C. 58; [1967] 3 W.L.R. 932; 111 S.J. 540; [1967] 2 All E.R. 1197 .... 1–004, 18–005
Beta Computers (Europe) Ltd v. Adobe Systems (Europe) Ltd 1996 S.L.T. 604 ..... 1–041, 1–086, 2–012, 11–070, 13–012
Bethell, *Re*, Bethell v. Bethell (1887) 34 Ch.D. 561; 56 L.J.Ch. 334; 56 L.T. 92; 35 W.R. 330; 3 T.L.R. 296 22–116
Bethell v. Clark (1888) 20 Q.B.D. 615; 57 L.J.Q.B. 302; 59 L.T. 808; 36 W.R. 611; 6 Asp.M.L.C. 346; 4 T.L.R 401 ...... 15–066, 15–067, 15–068, 15–069, 15–080, 15–085, 15–088
Bevan v. National Bank Ltd (1906) 23 T.L.R. 65 22–073
Beveridge v. Burgis (1812) 3 Camp. 262 22–131
Beverley v. Lincoln Gas Light & Coke Co. (1837) 6 A. & E. 829 ...... 5–040, 5–041, 5–050
Beverley Acceptances Ltd v. Oakley [1982] R.T.R. 417 .... 7–009, 7–013, 7–016, 7–035, 7–036, 7–037, 7–052, 7–075
Beves & Co. Ltd v. Farkas [1953] 1 Lloyd's Rep. 103 .... 6–041, 6–046, 6–047, 6–054, 18–310, 18–321, 18–335, 18–340, 20–095, 25–168

Bevington & Morris v. Dale & Co. Ltd (1902) 7 Com.Cas. 112 .... 5–041, 5–058, 6–003, 6–009, 6–031
Bexwell v. Christie (1776) 1 Cowp. 395 3–009
Beyene v. Irving Trust Co., 762 F. 2d 4 (1985) 23–197, 23–198
Bhatia Shipping Agencies Pvt Ltd v. Alcobex Metals Ltd [2004] EWHC 2322 (Comm); [2005] 2 Lloyd's Rep. 336 21–104
Bhojwani v. Chung Khiaw Bank [1990] 3 M.L.J. 260 23–157
Bianchi v. Nash (1836) 1 M. & W. 545; Tyr. & Gr. 916; 5 L.J.Ex. 252; 150 E.R. 551 .... 5–058, 6–009, 6–031
Bickerdike v. Bollman (1786) 1 T.R. 405 22–132
Biddle Bros v. Clemens (E.) Horst Co *See* Clemens (E.) Horst Co. v. Biddell Bros.
Biddlecombe v. Bond (1835) 4 A. & E. 332; Har. & W. 612; 5 Nev. & M.K.B. 621; 5 L.J.K.B. 47 15–024
Bieber (Ertel & Co.) v. Rio Tinto Co. Ltd *See* Ertel Bieber & Co. v. Rio Tinto Co. Ltd.
Bigge v. Parkinson (1862) 7 H. & N. 955; 31 L.J.Ex. 301; 8 Jur. (N.S.) 1014; 10 W.R. 349; *sub nom.* Smith v. Parkinson 7 L.T. 92 .... 11–064, 11–068
Biggerstaff v. Rowatt's Wharf Ltd [1896] 2 Ch. 93 ... 6–040, 8–045, 12–061, 12–067, 12–069, 17–091
Biggin & Co. Ltd v. Permanite (Wiggins & Co., Third Parties) [1951] K.B. 314; [1951] 2 T.L.R. 159; [1951] 2 All E.R. 191: 95 S.J. 414, CA; reversing in part [1951] 1 K.B. 422; [1950] 2 All E.R. 859; 66 T.L.R. (Pt. 2) 944 ...... 16–036, 16–046, 17–028, 17–029, 17–033, 17–053, 17–059, 17–076, 17–077, 17–078, 17–079, 17–081, 17–082, 17–083
Biggs v. Evans [1894] 1 Q.B. 88; 69 L.T. 723; 58 J.P. 84; 10 T.L.R. 59 7–043
Bignold, *ex p. Re*, Brercton (1836) 1 Deac. 712 22–116
Bigos v. Bousted [1951] 1 All E.R. 92 .... 3–031, 3–033, 18–324
Bill v. Bament (1841) 9 M. & W. 36; 11 L.J.Ex. 81; 152 E.R. 16 15–050
Billson v. Crofts (1873) L.R. 15 Eq. 314; 42 L.J.Ch. 531; 37 J.P. 565; 212 W.R. 504 15–025
Bines v. Sankey [1958] N.Z.L.R. 886 .... 12–068, 15–053, 15–117
Binladen BSB Landscaping Inc. v. N.V. Nedlloyd Rotterdam 759 F. 2d 1006 (1985) 21–085, 21–086
Birckhead and Carlisle v. Brown 5 Hill (N.Y.) 634 (1843) 23–049, 23–236
Bird v. Brown (1850) 4 Exch. 786 .... 15–008, 15–065, 15–083
—— v. Smith (1848) 12 Q.B. 786; 17 L.J.Q.B. 309; 12 L.T. (O.S.) 104; 12 Jur. 916; 116 E.R. 1065 13–040
Bird & Co. v. Thomas Cook & Sons Ltd [1937] 2 All E.R. 227; 156 L.T. 415 ...... 22–046, 22–050
Birkett v. Acorn Business Machines Ltd [1999] 2 All E.R. (Comm) 429; (1999) 96(31) L.S.G. 35; *The Times*, August 25, 1999, CA 3–029
Birkett Sperling & Co. v. Engholm & Co. (1871) 10 M (Ct. of Sess.) 170 .... 19–002, 19–043, 19–066
Birks v. Trippet (1666) 1 Wms. Saund. 32 8–039
Birmingham and District Land Co. v. L. & N.W. Railway (1888) 40 Ch.D. 268 12–035
Bishop v. Crawshay (1824) 3 B. & C. 415; 5 Dow. & Ry. K.B. 279; 3 L.J. (O.S.) K.B. 65; 107 E.R. 787 .... 5–076, 5–091
Bishop v. Shillito (1819) 2 B. & Ald. 329n; 106 E.R 387 .... 5–135, 16–089
Bishop & Baxter Ltd v. Anglo-Eastern Trading Co. Ltd [1944] K.B. 12. 2–016
Bishopsgate Motor Finance Corporation Ltd v. Transport Brakes (Winsor Garage, Third Party) Ltd [1949] 1 K.B. 332; [1949] L.J.R. 741; 65 T.L.R. 66; 93 S.J. 71; [1949] 1 All E.R. 37 .... 7–001, 7–046
Bisley (A.M.) & Co. Ltd v. Thompson [1982] 2 N.Z.L.R. 696 .... 10–012, 13–021
Bissell v. Fox (1885) 53 L.T. 193; 1 T.L.R. 452 22–118
Bissett v. Wilkinson [1927] A.C. 177; 96 L.J.P.C. 12; 136 L.T. 97; 42 T.L.R. 727 .... 10–006, 10–007
Blackburn v. Smith (1848) 2 Exch. 783; 18 L.J.Ex. 187; 154 E.R. 707 12–068
Blackburn Bobbin Co. Ltd v. Allen (T.W.) & Sons Ltd [1918] 2 K.B. 467; 87 L.J.K.B. 1085; 119 L.T. 215; 34 T.L.R. 508, CA; affirming [1918] 1 K.B. 540 ... 1–110, 6–041, 6–054, 17–011, 17–023, 19–128, 19–130, 19–131
Blackpool & Fylde Aero Club Ltd v. Blackpool B.C. [1990] 1 W.L.R. 1195; [1990] 3 All E.R. 25; (1990) 88 L.G.R. 864; (1991) 155 L.G.Rev. 246; (1991) 3 Admin.L.R. 322 .... 2–003, 18–045

Blakeley v. Muller & Co. (1903) TLR 186 ... 3–021
Blakemore v. Bellamy (1983) 147 J.P. 89; [1983] R.T.R. 303 ... 11–028, 14–011, 14–130
Blanckensee v. Blaiberg (1885) 2 T.L.R. 36 ... 5–040, 5–041, 5–047
Blandy Bros & Co. Ltd v. Nello Simoni Ltd [1963] 2 Lloyd's Rep. 393, CA ... 20–054
Blay v. Pollard & Morris [1930] 1 K.B. 628; 99 L.J.K.B. 421; 143 L.T. 92; 74 S.J. 284; [1930] All E.R. 609 ... 7–018
Bligh v. Martin [1968] 1 W.L.R. 804; 112 S.J. 189; [1968] 1 All E.R. 1157; 19 P. & C.R. 442 ... 3–019
Bloomer v. Bernstein (1874) L.R. 9 C.P. 588; 43 L.J.C.P. 375; 31 L.T. 306; 23 W.R. 238 ... 8–078, 9–010, 15–107
Blount v. War Office [1953] 1 W.L.R. 736; 97 S.J. 388; [1953] 1 All E.R. 1071 ... 6–026
Bloxam v. Sanders (1825) 4 B. & C. 941; 7 Dow. & Ry. K.B. 396; 107 E.R. 1309 ... 8–004, 9–009, 15–002, 15–032, 15–034, 15–043, 15–044, 15–063, 15–064, 15–104, 17–105, 17–106
Bloxsome v. Williams (1824) 3 B. & C. 232; 5 Dow. & Ry. K.B. 82; 2 L.J. (O.S.) K.B. 224; 107 E.R. 720 ... 3–029
Blundell-Leigh v. Attenborough [1921] 3 K.B. 235; [1921] All E.R. 525; 90 L.J.K.B. 1005; 125 L.T. 356; 37 T.L.R. 567; 65 S.J. 474 ... 4–010
Blunt v. Heslop (1838) 8 A. & E. 577 ... 8–034
Blyth Shipbuilding and Dry Docks Co. Ltd. *Re* [1926] Ch. 494; 95 L.J. Ch. 350; 134 L.T. 643; ... 1–047, 5–005, 5–069, 5–092, 5–093
Blythe & Co. v. Richards Turpin & Co. (1916) 85 L.J.K.B. 1425; 114 L.T. 753; 13 Asp.M.L.C. 407 ... 8–092, 19–138, 19–140, 19–157
Board of Trade (Minister of Materials) v. Steel Bros & Co. Ltd [1951] 2 Lloyd's Rep. 259. ... 20–007, 20–018
Boardman v. Phipps [1967] 2 A.C. 46; [1966] 3 W.L.R. 1009; 110 S.J. 853; [1966] 3 All E.R. 721. ... 1–080, 5–151
Boardman v. Sill (1808) 1 Camp. 410; 170 E.R. 1003 ... 15–056
Bobbett v. Pinkett (1876) 1 Ex.D. 368; 45 L.J.Ex. 555; 35 L.T. 851; 24 W.R. 711 ... 22–022
Bocotra Construction Pte Ltd v. A.G. [1995] 2 S.L.R. 733, CA ... 23–282
Boddington v. Lawton [1994] I.C.R. 478; *The Times*, February 19, 1994 ... 3–034
Bodger v. Nicholls (1873) 28 L.T. 441; 37 J.P. 597 ... 10–009, 12–077
Bodley Head Ltd v. Flegon [1972] 1 W.L.R. 680; [1972] F.S.R. 21; [1972] R.P.C. 587; (1971) 115 S.J. 909; *The Times*, November 26, 1971, Ch D ... 25–084
Boehm v. Garcias (1808) 1 Camp. 425 ... 22–103
Bog Lead Mining Co. v. Montague (1861) 10 C.B. (N.S.) 481 ... 12–046
Bohtlingk v. Inglis (1803) East 381; 39 Digest (Repl.) 762 ... 25–183
Boileau v. Heath [1898] 2 Ch. 301 ... 1–097
Boissevain v. Weil [1950] A.C. 327; 66 T.L.R. (Pt. 1) 771, 94 S.J. 319; [1950] 1 All E.R. 728 ... 25–006, 25–119, 25–194
Boks & Co. v. Rayner (J.H.) & Co. (1921) 37 T.L.R. 519 ... 20–109
Bolckow Vaughan & Co. v. Compania Minera de Sierra Mineral (1916) 33 T.L.R. 111 ... 6–054
Boldero & Co., *Re* (1812) 19 Ves.Jun. 25; 1 Rose 254 ... 22–092
Bolivinter Oil SA v. Chase Manhattan Bank N.A. [1984] 1 W.L.R. 392; (1984) 128 S.J. 153; [1984] 1 Lloyd's Rep. 251 ... 23–272, 23–276
Bolt and Nut Co. (Tipton) Ltd v. Rowlands Nicholls & Co. Ltd [1964] 2 Q.B. 10; [1964] 2 W.L.R. 98; [1964] 1 All E.R. 137 ... 9–030, 16–017
Bolton v. Lanes and Yorks Railway (1866) L.R. 1 C.P. 431; 35 L.J.C.P. 137; 13 L.T. 764; 12 Jur. (N.S.) 317; 14 W.R. 430 ... 15–046, 15–063, 15–070, 15–077, 15–078, 15–081, 15–084
Bolus & Co. Ltd v. Inglis Bros. Ltd [1924] N.Z.L.R 164 ... 23–308, 23–313
Bonacina, Re; *sub nom.* Le Brasseur v. Bonacina [1912] 2 Ch. 394, CA; reversing [1912] 2 Ch. 68, Ch D ... 25–079
Bond v. Chief Constable of Kent [1983] 1 W.L.R. 40; (1983) 147 J.P. 107; (1982) 126 S.J. 707; [1983] 1 E.R. 456; (1982) 4 Cr.App. R.(S) 324; [1983] Crim. L.R. 166; (1983) 80 L.S. Gaz. 29 ... 14–107
Bonde, The. *See* Richco International v. Alfred C. Toepfer International GmbH; Bonde, The.
Bond Worth Ltd, *Re* [1980] Ch. 228; [1979] 3 W.L.R. 629; (1979) 123 S.J. 216; [1973] 3 All E.R. 919 ... 1–052, 5–134, 5–144, 5–146, 5–147, 5–148, 5–150, 5–152, 5–153, 5–156, 5–158, 5–160, 5–170, 18–238

Bondholders Securities Corp. v. Manville [1933] 4 D.L.R. 699 25–084
Bone v. Ekless (1860) 5 H. & N. 925; 29 L.J.Ex. 438; 157 E.R. 1450 3–033
Bonython v. Commonwealth of Australia [1951] A.C. 201; 66 T.L.R. (Pt. 2) 969; 94 S.J. 821 .... 25–008, 25–010, 25–156, 25–165, 25–174
Boone v. Eyre (1777) 1 H.B1. 273n 10–026
Booth v. Bowron (1892) 8 T.L.R. 641 .... 8–078, 8–085
Booth S.S. Co. Ltd v. Cargo Fleet Iron Co. Ltd [1916] 2 K.B. 570; 85 L.J.K.B. 1577; 115 L.T. 199; 32 T.L.R. 535; 13 Asp.M.L.C. 451; 22 Com.Cas. 9 .... 15–061, 15–064, 15–085, 15–087, 15–088, 15–089, 15–091, 20–141
Borag, The. *See* Compania Financiera Soleada SA, Netherlands Antilles Ships Management Corp. and Dammers and van der Heide's Shipping and Trading Co. v. Hamoor Tanker Corp. Inc. (The Borag).
Borden (U.K.) Ltd v. Scottish Timber Products and McNicol Brownlie Ltd [1981] Ch. 25; [1979] 3 W.L.R. 672; (1979) 123 S.J. 688; [1979] 3 All E.R. 961; [1980] 1 Lloyd's Rep. 160..... 1–060, 5–144, 5–16, 5–147, 5–148, 5–149, 5–150, 5–153, 5–154, 7–004, 18–238
Border National Bank v. American National Bank 282 F. 73 (1922) 23–134
Borealis AB v. Stargas Ltd (The Berge Sisar) [2001] UKHL 17; [2002] 2 A.C. 205, [2001] 2 W.L.R. 1118; [2001] 2 All E.R. 193; [2001] 1 All E.R. (Comm) 673; [2001] 1 Lloyd's Rep. 663; [2001] C.L.C. 1084; (2001) 98(20) L.S.G. 43; (2001) 145 S.J.L.B. 93; *The Times*, March 27, 2001, HL; affirming [1999] Q.B. 863; [1998] 3 W.L.R. 1353; [1998] 4 All E.R. 821; [1998] 2 Lloyd's Rep. 475; [1998] C.L.C. 1589; *The Times*, September 14, 1998, CA: reversing [1997] 1 Lloyd's Rep. 642 (Note), QBD (Comm Ct) 18–011, 18–034, 18–064, 18–065, 18–066, 18–080, 18–082, 18–097, 18–098, 18–100, 18–101, 18–104, 18–113, 18–114, 18–123, 18–125, 18–126, 18–128, 18–129, 18–131, 18–132, 18–149, 18–150, 18–281
Borradaile v. Brunton (1818) 8 Taunt. 535; 2 Moo.C.P. 528 17–074
Borries v. Hutchinson (1865) 18 C.B. (N.S.) 445; 5 New Rep. 281; 34 L.J. C.P. 169; 11 L.T. 771; 11 Jur. (N.S.) 267; 13 W.R. 386 ... 16–067, 17–021, 17–036, 17–038, 17–044
Borrowman v. Drayton (1876) 2 Ex.D. 15; 46 L.J.Q.B. 273; 35 L.T. 727; 25 W.R. 194; 3 Asp. M.L.C. 303, CA 5–086, 8–046, 11–004, 14–027, 21–033, 21–034, 21–036, 21–037, 21–040
Borrowman, Phillips & Co. v. Free and Hollis (1878) 4 Q.B.D. 500; 48 L.J.Q.B. 65; 40 L.T. 25 .... 5–087, 8–065, 12–031, 14–016, 19–021, 19–066, 19–071
Borthwick v. Bank of New Zealand (1900) 17 T.L.R. 2; 6 Com.Cas. 1 ..... 19–043, 23–229, 23–230
Borthwick (Thomas) & Sons (Australasia) Ltd v. South Otago Freezing Co. Ltd [1978] 1 N.Z.L.R. 538 .... 1–008, 1–009, 10–008
Borthwick (Thomas) (Glasgow) Ltd v. Bunge & Co. Ltd [1969] 1 Lloyd's Rep. 17 ... 8–037
—— v. Faure Fairclough Ltd [1968] 1 Lloyd's Rep. 16 .... 8–098, 8–099
Bosanquet v. Forster (1841) 9 C. & P. 659 22–057
Boshali v. Allied Commercial Exporters Ltd (1961) 105 S.J. 987 11–022
Bossier Bank & Trust Company v. Union Planters National Bank 550 F. 2d 1077 (1977) 23–244
Bostel Bros. Ltd v. Hurlock [1949] 1 K.B. 74; [1948] L.J.R. 1846; 64 T.L.R. 495; 92 S.J. 361; [1948] 2 All E.R. 312 3–029
Bostock & Co. Ltd. v. Nicholson & Sons Ltd [1904] 1 K.B. 725; 73 L.J.K.B. 524; 91 L.T. 626; 53 W.R. 155; 20 T.L.R. 342; 9 Com.Cas. 200 ..... 11–020, 12–038, 12–068, 17–047, 17–063, 17–066, 17–074, 17–076, 17–081, 17–090
Boston Deep Sea Fishing and Ice Co. v. Ansell (1888) 39 Ch.D. 339 9–016, 15–110, 19–159
Boswell v. Kilborn and Morrill (1862) 15 Moo.P.C. 309; 6 L.T. 79; 8 Jur. (N.S.) 443; 10 W.R. 517; 15 E.R. 511 .... 5–061, 16–021
Bottomley v. Nuttall (1858) 5 C.B. (N.S.) 122 9–030
Boulter v. Arnott (1833) 1 Cr. & M. 333; 3 Tyr. 267; 2 L.J.Ex. 97; 149 E.R. 427 .... 15–039, 15–050
Boulton v. Jones (1857) 2 H. & N. 564; 27 L.J.Ex. 117; 157 E.R. 232; *sub nom.* Bolton v. Jones 30 L.T. (o.s.) 188; 3 Jur. (N.S.) 1156; 6 W.R. 107 3–012
Bounty Trading Corporation v. S.E.K. Sportswear Ltd. 370 N.Y.S. 2d 4 (1975) 23–205 23–236, 23–245
Bourgeois and Wilson Holgate & Co., *Re* (1920) 25 Com.Cas. 260 .... 16–037, 19–176

Bourne v. Seymour (1855) 16 C.B. 337; 24 L.J.C.P. 202; 25 L.T. (o.s.) 162; 1 Jur. (N.S.) 1001; 3 W.R. 511; 139 E.R. 788 8–054
Bourne (Inspector of Taxes) v. Norwich Crematorium Ltd [1967] 1 W.L.R. 691; 111 S.J. 256; [1967] 2 All E.R. 576; 44 T.C. 164; [1967] T.R. 49; 46 A.T.C. 43 1–089
Bow, McLachlan & Co. Ltd. v. Ship "Camosun" [1909] A.C. 597 17–049
Bow (R. & J.) Ltd v. Hill (1930) Ll.L.R. 46 23–308
Bowdell v. Parsons (1808) 10 East, 359; 103 E.R. 811 .... 8–039, 12–020
Bowden Bros. & Co. Ltd. v. Little (1907) 4 C.L.R. 1364 .... 6–019, 11–067, 18–257, 19–002, 19–110
Bowen v. Paramount Builders (Hamilton) Ltd [1977] 1 N.Z.L.R. 394 12–126
——— v. R.B. Young Products Property Ltd [1967] W.A.R. 97 .... 11–047, 11–060
Bower v. Bantam Investments Ltd [1972] 1 W.L.R. 1120; 116 S.J. 633; [1972] 3 All E.R. 349 17–103
Bowerman v. Association of British Travel Agents, *The Independent*, November 23, 1995; *The Times*, November 24, 1995, CA 14–062
Bowes *Re*, Strathmore v. Vane (1886) 33 Ch.D. 586; 56 L.J.Ch. 143; 55 L.T. 260; 35 W.R. 166 .... 22–140, 22–141
Bowes v. Chaleyer (1923) 32 C.L.R. 159 .... 9–018, 18–267, 20–058
—— v. Howe (1813) 5 Taunt. 30 22–116
—— v. Shand (1877) 2 App.Cas. 455; 46 L.J.Q.B. 561; 36 L.T. 857; 25 W.R. 730; 5 Asp.M.L.C. 461 ...... 8–024, 8–025, 8–043, 11–018, 12–025, 18–028, 18–266, 18–267, 18–284, 19–013, 19–063, 20–038
Bowhill Coal Co. Ltd. v. Tobias (1902) 5 F. (Ct of Sess.) 262 .... 20–018, 20–054
Bowmaker (Commercial) Ltd v. Day (Burt, Third Party and W.H. Perry, Fourth Party) [1965] 1 W.L.R. 1396; 109 S.J. 853; [1965] 1 All E.R. 856 ...... 4–012, 4–016, 4–017, 4–029, 17–084
Bowmakers Ltd v. Barnet Instruments Ltd [1945] K.B. 65 3–031
Bowring & Walker Property Ltd v. Jackson's Corio Meat Packing (1965) Property Ltd [1972] 1 N.S.W.R. 277 19–140
Bowron (John) & Sons Ltd v. Rodema Canned Foods Ltd 116 New L.J. 1686; [1967] 1 Lloyd's Rep. 183 .... 11–022, 11–077
Box v. Midland Bank Ltd [1981] 1 Lloyd's Rep. 434 10–006
Boyd v. Siffkin (1809) 2 Camp. 326; 170 E.R. 1172 21–022
Boyd & Forrest v. Glasgow & S.W. Railway 1915 S.C. (H.L.) 21 ..... 4–022, 6–011, 12–059
Boyd (David T.) & Co. Ltd v. Louis Louca [1973] 1 Lloyd's Rep. 209 ..... 20–014, 20–018, 20–042, 20–045, 20–047
Boyers & Co. v. D. & R. Duke [1905] 2 I.R. 617 2–011
Boys v. Chaplin. *See* Chaplin v. Boys.
—— v. Rice (1908) 27 N.Z.L.R. 1038 .... 10–026, 11–008, 11–012
Boyson v. Coles (1817) 6 M. & S. 14 7–012
Boyter v. Thomson [1995] 2 A.C. 629; [1995] 3 W.L.R. 36; [1995] 3 All E.R. 135; (1995) 145 N.L.J. Rep. 922; (1995) 139 S.J.L.B. 174; *The Times*, June 16, 1995, HL 11–029
Bracegirdle v. Heald; (1818) 1 B. & Ald. 722 8–032
Braconnot (J.) et Cie v. Compagnie des Messageries Maritimes [1975] 1 Lloyd's Rep. 372 25–024
Bradburn v. G.W. Railway (1874) L.R. 10 Ex. 1; 44 L.J.Ex. 9; 31 L.T. 464; 23 W.R. 48 16–056
Bradley & Cohn Ltd v. Ramsay & Co. (1912) 106 L.T. 771; (1911) 28 T.L.R. 13 .... 1–074, 5–041, 5–052
Bradley & Sons v. Colonial Continental Trading Ltd [1964] 2 Lloyd's Rep. 52; 108 S.J. 599 .... 8–036, 8–037, 11–044, 16–069
Bradshaw v. Boothe's Marine Ltd [1973] 2 O.R. 646; 35 D.L.R. (3d) 43 .... 1–087, 11–030
Bragg v. Villanova (1923) 40 T.L.R. 154 .... 12–043, 12–067, 20–109
Brain v. Preece (1843) 11 M. & W. 773; 152 E.R. 1016 22–136
Braithwaite v. Foreign Hardwood Co. Ltd [1905] 2 K.B. 543; 74 L.J.K.B. 688; 92 L.T. 637; 21 T.L.R. 413; 10 Asp.M.L.C. 52; Com.Cas. 189 .... 8–078, 9–010, 9–012, 9–013, 9–017, 9–020, 19–167, 19–168, 19–169, 19–170, 19–171, 19–210, 20–058, 20–112
Bramhill v. Edwards [2004] EWCA Civ 403; [2004] 2 Lloyd's Rep. 653, CA 11–031, 11–042, 11–044, 14–008, 14–014

Bramwell v. Lacy (1879) 10 Ch.D. 691; 48 L.J.Ch. 339; 40 L.T. 361; 27 W.R. 463 . . . 11–028
Brandao v. Barnett (1846) 12 Cl. & Fin. 786; C.B. 519 . . . . . 22–139, 22–140, 22–142, 22–145
Brandt v. Bowlby (1831) 2 B. & Ad. 932; 1 L.J.K.B. 14; 109 E.R. 1389 . . . . . . 5–138, 18–221
—— v. Lawrence (1876) 1 Q.B.D. 344; 46 L.J.Q.B. 237; 24 W.R. 749 . . . . 8–065, 8–066, 8–067, 8–072, 8–073, 8–074, 8–083
—— v. Liverpool Brazil and River Plate Steam Navigation Co. Ltd [1924] 1 K.B. 575; [1923] All E.R. Rep. 656; 93 L.J.K.B. 646; 130 L.T. 392; 16 Asp.M.L.C. 262; 29 Com.Cas. 57 . . . . 5–140, 18–059, 18–089, 18–100, 18–102, 18–108, 18–133, 18–139, 18–140, 18–144, 18–145, 18–147, 18–174, 19–097, 23–132
Brandt (H.O.) & Co. v. H.N. Morris & Co. [1917] 2 K.B. 784; 87 L.J.K.B. 101; 117 L.T. 196 . . . . 18–310, 18–325, 18–327
Brandt's (William) Sons & Co. v. Dunlop Rubber Co. [1905] A.C. 462 18–147
Brantom v. Griffiths [1877] 2 C.P.D. 212; 46 L.J.Q.B. 408; 36 L.T. 4; 41 J.P. 468; 25 W.R. 313 1–100
Branwhite v. Worcester Works Finance Ltd [1969] 1 A.C. 552; [1968] 3 W.L.R. 760; 112 S.J. 758; [1968] 3 All E.R. 104 . . . . 1–054, 3–005
Brauer & Co. (Great Britain) Ltd. v. James Clark (Brush Materials) Ltd [1952] W.N. 422; [1952] 2 T.L.R. 349; 96 S.J. 548; [1952] 2 All E.R. 497; [1952] 2 Lloyd's Rep. 147 . . . . 6–047, 6–054, 6–057, 8–092, 8–099, 18–318, 18–321, 18–327, 25–168
Braun v. Intercontinental Bank, 466 So. 2d 1130 23–241
Brayshaw v. Eaton (1839) 5 Bing. N.C. 231 2–031
Breckwoldt v. Hanna (1963) 5 W.L.R. 356 12–048
Breed v. Cluett [1970] 2 Q.B. 459; [1970] 3 W.L.R. 76; 114 S.J. 453; [1970] 2 All E.R. 662; 68 L.G.R. 604 14–113
Bremer Handelsgesellschaft m.b.H. v. Archer Daniels Midland International SA [1981] 2 Lloyd's Rep. 483 . . . . 18–320, 19–133
—— v. Bunge Cpn. [1983] 1 Lloyd's Rep. 476; [1983] Com.L.R. 103 . . . . 8–092, 8–101, 8–103, 18–350, 18–358, 19–150
—— v. Continental Grain Co. [1983] 1 Lloyd's Rep. 269 . . . . . 8–092, 8–102, 8–103, 18–349, 18–350, 18–353
—— v. Deutsche Conti-Handesgesellschaft m.b.H. [1981] 2 Lloyd's Rep. 1121 12–055
—— v.——(No. 1) [1983] 2 Lloyd's Rep. 45 8–030, 8–097, 12–055, 19–020, 19–150, 19–151 19–152
—— v.——G.m.b.H. (No. 2) [1983] 2 Lloyd's Rep. 689 . . . . . 8–101, 18–150, 18–357, 18–358
—— v.——m.b.H. (No. 3) [1984] 1 Lloyd's Rep. 397 18–350
—— v. Finagrain Compagnie Commerciale Agricole et Financiére SA [1981] 1 Lloyd's Rep. 224; [1981] 2 Lloyd's Rep. 259 . . . . 8–088, 8–101, 12–035, 18–357, 18–358, 19–141, 19–150
Bremer Handelsgesellschaft m.b.H. v. Mackprang (C.) Jr. [1979] 1 Lloyd's Rep. 221 . . . . . . 8–030, 8–091, 8–092, 8–095, 8–101, 8–102, 8–103, 12–035, 12–036, 12–037, 18–345, 18–347, 18–349, 18–350, 18–351, 18–353, 18–358, 19–141, 19–150, 19–151, 19–160, 19–181
—— v. Mackprang (C.) [1981] 1 Lloyd's Rep. 292 . . . . 8–092, 8–101, 8–350
—— v. Raiffeissen [1982] 1 Lloyd's Rep. 210; [1982] 1 Lloyd's Rep. 599 . . . . . 8–029, 8–092, 8–101, 18–349, 19–150
—— v. Rayner (J.H.) & Co. [1979] 2 Lloyd's Rep. 216, CA; reversing [1978] 2 Lloyd's Rep. 73, QBD (Comm Ct) 9–020, 19–165, 20–032, 20–046, 20–052, 20–125
—— v. Toepfer [1980] 2 Lloyd's Rep. 43 . . . . 19–019, 19–146
—— v. Vanden Avenne-Izegem P.V.B.A. [1978] 2 Lloyd's Rep. 109 . . . 8–030, 8–091, 8–092 8–095, 8–099, 8–101, 8–102, 8–103, 10–037, 12–035, 12–036, 17–007, 18–342, 18–347, 18–349, 18–353, 18–357, 18–358, 19–018, 19–064, 19–138, 19–141, 19–150, 19–181
—— v. Westzucker GmbH [1981] 1 Lloyd's Rep. 207 . . . . . . 8–092, 12–036, 18–350, 18–357, 19–150, 19–180
—— v. Westzucker GmbH (No. 2) [1981] 1 Lloyd's Rep. 130; affirming [1981] 1 Lloyd's Rep. 214, CA 8–092, 18–150, 18–349, 19–357
—— v. Westzucker GmbH (No. 3) [1989] 1 Lloyd's Rep. 582, CA; affirming [1989] 1 Lloyd's Rep. 198 . . . . 8–092, 8–101, 18–348, 18–350
Bremer Oeltransport GmbH v. Drewry [1933] 1 K.B. 753; 102 L.J.K.B. 360; 148 L.T. 540; 45 Ll.L.Rep. 133 . . . . 9–047, 9–048
Brenner v. Dean Witter Reynolds Inc. (C318/93) [1995] All E.R. (E.C.) 278, E.C.J. 25–045

Brett, *ex. p. Re* Howe (1871) L.R. 6 Ch.App. 838; 40 L.J. Bey, 54; 25 L.T. 252; 19 W.R. 1101 .... 18–226, 22–104
Brett v. Schneideman Bros. Ltd [1923] N.Z.L.R. 938 .... 9–012, 9–015, 9–017, 9–020
Brewer Street Investments Ltd v. Barclays Woollen Co. Ltd [1954] 1 Q.B. 428; [1953] 3 W.L.R. 869; 97 S.J. 796; [1953] 2 All E.R. 1330 6–060
Bridge v. Campbell Discount Co. [1962] A.C. 600; [1962] 2 W.L.R. 439; [1962] 1 All E.R. 385; 106 S.J. 94, HL reversing, *sub nom.* Campbell Discount Co. v. Bridge [1961] 1 Q.B. 445; [1961] 2 W.L.R. 596; [1961] 2 All E.R. 97; 105 S.J. 232 [1961] C.L.Y. 3908, CA 16–032, 16–035, 16–038, 16–039
—— v. Wain (1816) 1 Stark. 504; 171 E.R. 543 17–051
Bridges v. Berry (1810) 3 Taunt. 130 22–134
Brierly v. Kendall (1852) 17 Q.B. 937; 21 L.J.Q.B. 161; 18 L.T. (o.s.) 254; 16 Jur. 449; 117 E.R. 1540 .... 1–072, 7–002, 17–106
Brighty v. Norton (1862) 3 B. & S. 305; 1 New Rep. 93; 32 L.J.Q.B. 38; 7 L.T. 442; 9 Jur. (N.S.) 495; 11 W.R. 167; 122 E.R. 116 9–059
Brij, The [2001] 1 Lloyd's Rep. 431, CFI (HK) 18–018, 18–070, 18–095
Brikom Investments Ltd v. Carr [1979] Q.B. 467; [1979] 2 W.L.R. 737; (1979) 123 S.J. 182; [1979] 2 All E.R. 753; (1979) 241 E.G. 359; (1979) 38 P. & C.R. 326; [1982] M.L.R. 21 .... 10–014, 12–036
Bril v. Suomen Pankki Finlands Bank 97 N.Y.S. 2d. 22; (1950), affd., 101 N.Y.S. 2d 256 (1950) 23–054, 23–175
Brimnes, The, *See* Tenax Steamship Co. v. The Brimnes (Owners).
Brinsmead v. Harrison (1871) L.R. 6 C.P. 584; 40 L.J.C.P. 281; 24 L.T. 798; 19 W.R. 956 1–072
Bristol and West of England Bank v. Midland Railway [1891] 2 Q.B 653 .... 5–009, 5–140, 18–063, 23–132
Bristol Tramways Carriage Co. Ltd v. Fiat Motors Ltd [1910] 2 K.B. 831 .... 1–002, 11–044, 11–055, 11–057
Bristow v. Sequeville (1850) 5 Exch. 275 25–086
Britain and Overseas Trading (Bristles) Ltd v. Brooks Wharf and Bull Wharf Ltd [1967] 2 Lloyd's Rep. 51 13–014
Britain S.S. Co. Ltd v. Lithgows Ltd 1975 S.L.T. (Notes) 20 11–016
Britannia Distribution Co. Ltd v. Factor Pace Ltd [1998] 2 Lloyd's Rep. 420, DR (Manchester) 21–073
Britannia Hygienic Laundry Co. Ltd v. Thorneycroft (John I.) & Co. Ltd (1925) 94 L.J.K.B. 858; 41 T.L.R. 667 17–075
British Airways Board v. Taylor [1976] 1 W.L.R. 13; (1975) 120 S.J. 7; [1976] 1 All E.R. 65; [1976] 1 Lloyd's Rep. 167; (1975) 62 Cr.App.R. 174; 18 Man.Law. 146 14–113
British American Tobacco Co. v. I.R.C. [1943] 1 All E.R. 13; [1943] A.C. 339; 112 L.J.K.B. 81; 169 L.T. 98; 59 T.L.R. 91; 87 S. & J.7 24–008
British and Beningtons Ltd v. N.W. Cachar Tea Co. [1923] A.C. 48 .... 8–079, 9–013, 9–016, 9–020, 18–277, 19–161, 19–167, 19–168, 19–170, 19–171, 20–049, 20–058
British and Commonwealth Holdings plc v. Quadrex Holdings Inc. [1989] Q.B. 842; [1989] 3 W.L.R. 723; [1989] 3 All E.R. 492; (1989) 86(23) L.S.G. 42; (1989) 133 S.J. 694; *The Times*, March 13, 1989; *The Independent*, March 7, 1989, CA; reversing (1989) 139 N.L.J. 13; *The Times*, December 8, 1988; *The Independent*, December 13, 1988; *The Financial Times*, November 30, 1988, QBD 8–026
British and Foreign Marine Insurance Co. Ltd v. Gaunt [1921] 2 A.C. 41 19–045
British and Foreign Marine Insurance Co. Ltd v. Sanday (Samuel) & Co. [1916] 1 A.C. 650; 85 L.J.K.B. 550; 114 L.T. 521; 32 T.L.R. 266; 60 S.J. 253; 13 Asp.M.L.C. 289; 21 Com.Cas. 154 1–002
British Anzani (Felixstowe) Ltd v. International Marine Management (U.K.) Ltd [1980] Q.B. 637; [1979] 3 W.L.R. 451; (1978) 123 S.J. 64; [1979] 2 All E.R. 1063; (1978) 39 P. & C.R. 189; (1978) 25 E.G. 1183 17–049
British Bank for Foreign Trade Ltd v. Novinex Ltd [1949] 1 K.B. 623 [1949] L.J.R. 658; 93 S.J. 146; [1949] 1 All E.R. 155 .... 2–017, 2–046
—— v. Russian Commercial and Industrial Bank (No. 2) (1921) 38 T.L.R. 65 25–166
British Car Auctions Ltd v. Wright [1972] 1 W.L.R. 1519; 116 S.J. 583; [1972] 3 All E.R. 462; [1972] R.T.R. 540; [1972] Crim.L.R. 562 .... 1–027, 2–002, 2–004
British Columbia, etc. Saw Mill Co. Ltd v. Nettleship (1868) L.R. 3 C.P. 499; 37 L.J.C.P. 235; 18 L.T. 604; 16 W.R. 1046; 3 Mar.L.C. 65 .... 16–046, 17–041

British Controlled Oilfields v. Stagg [1921] W.N. 31; 127 L.T. 209; 66 S.J. (W.R.) 18 .... 25–006, 25–083
British Crane Hire Corp. Ltd v. Ipswich Plant Hire Ltd [1975] Q.B. 303; [1974] 2 W.L.R. 856; (1973) 118 S.J. 387; [1974] 1 All E.R. 1059 ..... 2–012, 13–013, 13–015, 18–047
British Electric Traction Co. v. I.R.C. [1902] 1 K.B. 441; 71 L.J.K.B. 92; 85 L.T. 663; 66 J.P. 83; 50 W.R. 280; 18 T.L.R. 105 1–085
British Electrical & Associated Industries (Cardiff) Ltd v. Patley Pressings Ltd [1953] 1 W.L.R. 280; 97 S.J. 96; [1953] 1 All E.R. 94 .... 2–016, 8–088, 17–104
British Fermentation Products Ltd v. Compair Reavell Ltd (1999) 66 Con.L.R. 1 ... 13–090, 13–095
British Imex Industries Ltd v. Midland Bank Ltd [1958] 1 Q.B. 542; [1958] 2 W.L.R. 103; 102 S.J. 69; [1958] 1 All E.R. 264; [1957] 2 Lloyd's Rep. 591 ... 19–038, 23–127, 23–171, 23–221
British Motor Body Co. Ltd v. Shaw (Thomas) (Dundee) Ltd 1914 S.C. 922 8–037
British Motor Trade Association v. Gilbert [1951] W.N. 454; [1951] 2 T.L.R. 514; 95 S.J. 595; [1951] 2 All E.R. 641 .... 16–069, 17–006
British Movietones v. London and District Cinemas Ltd [1952] A.C. 166; [1951] 2 T.L.R. 571; 95 S.J. 499; [1951] 2 All E.R. 617 6–054
British Nylon Spinners Ltd v. Imperial Chemical Industries Ltd [1953] Ch. 19; [1952] 2 All E.R. 780; [1952] 2 T.L.R. 669; (1952) 69 R.P.C. 288, CA 25–119
British Oil and Cake Co. Ltd v. Burstall (J). & Co. Ltd (1923) 67 S.J. 577; 15 Ll.L.Rep. 46; 39 T.L.R. 406 .... 11–020, 17–059, 17–060, 17–079, 17–083
B.P. Exploration Co. (Libya) v. Hunt [1976] 1 W.L.R. 788; 120 S.J. 469; [1976] 3 All E.R. 879; [1976] 1 Lloyd's Rep. 471 .... 19–160, 25–176
B.P. Exploration Co. (Libya) Ltd. v. Hunt (No. 2) [1983] 2 A.C. 352; [1982] 2 W.L.R. 253; [1982] 1 All E.R. 925, H.L.; affirming [1981] 1 W.L.R. 232; (1980) 125 S.J. 165, C.A.; affirming [1979] 1 W.L.R. 783; (1979) 123 S.J. 455 .... 6–058, 6–059, 6–060, 6–061, 6–062, 6–063, 6–065, 6–606, 6–607, 6–071, 12–037, 16–007, 25–191
British Racing Drivers' Club Ltd v. Hextall Erskine & Co. [1996] 3 All E.R. 667 .... 17–075 17–076, 17–078
British Railway Traffic & Electric Co. v. Kahn [1921] W.N. 52 1–066
—— v. Roper (1939) 162 L.T. 217; 84 S.J. 80 .... 3–005, 7–017
—— v. West (H. A.) & Co. Ltd (1921) Jones and Proudfoot, *Notes on Hire Purchase Law (2nd ed) p.87* 1–066
British Road Services v. Crutchley (A. V.) & Co and Factory Guards (Third Party) Practice Note [1968] 1 All E.R. 811; *sub nom.* British Road Services v. Crutchley (A.V.) & Co. Ltd. Factory Guard (Third Party) [1968] 1 Lloyd's Rep. 271 2–013
British South Africa Co. v. De Beers Consolidated Mines Ltd [1910] 2 Ch. 502; 80 L.J.Ch. 65; 103 L.T. 4; 26 T.L.R. 591; 54 S.J. 679 25–010
British Steel Corp. v. Cleveland Bridge & Engineering Co. Ltd [1984] 1 All E.R. 504; (1983) Build.L.R.; [1982] Com.L.R. 54 2–018
British Sugar plc. v. NE1 Power Project Ltd, *The Times*, February 21, 1997 .... 13–036, 13–037
British United Shoe Machinery Co. Ltd v. Somervell Bros. (1906) 95 L.T. 711 3–037
British Westinghouse Electric and Manufacturing Co. Ltd v. Underground Electric Rys. [1912] A.C. 673; 81 L.J.K.B. 1132; 107 L.T. 325; 56 S.J. 734 .... 16–030, 16–050, 16–056, 16–057, 16–075, 17–020, 17–024, 17–056, 17–062, 17–067
Britten Norman Ltd (In Liquidation) v. State Ownership Fund of Romania [2000] All E.R. (D.) 935; [2000] Lloyd's Rep. Bank. 315; (2000) 97(30) L.S.G. 41; *Times*, August 3, 2000, Ch D 23–281
Britvic Soft Drinks Ltd v. Messer UK Ltd; *sub nom.* Messer UK Ltd v. Britvic Soft Drinks Ltd [2002] EWCA Civ 548; [2002] 2 All E.R. (Comm) 321; [2002] 2 Lloyd's Rep. 368; *The Times*, May 22, 2002, CA (Civ Div); affirming [2002] 1 Lloyd's Rep. 20, QBD 2–016, 11–029, 11–044, 11–047, 11–057, 11–059, 11–060, 13–036, 13–083
Brocket v. DSG Retail Ltd [2004] C.L. Jan 332 1–086
Brogden v. Marriott (1836) 3 Bing N.C. 88; 2 Hodg. 136; 2 Scott 712; 5 L.J.C.P. 302; 132 E.R. 343 2–048

Brogden v. Metropolitan Railway (1877) 2 App.Cas. 666 2–011
Broken Hill Property Co. Ltd v. Hapag-Lloyd Aktiengesellschaft [1980] 2 N.S.W.L.R. 572 13–017
—— v. Theodore Xenakis [1982] Com.L.R. 152; [1983] 2 Lloyd's Rep. 304 25–010, 25–071
Bromage v. Vaughan (1846) 9 Q.B. 608; 16 L.J.Q.B. 10; 10 Jur. 982 22–124
Brooke v. White (1805) 1 B. & P.N.R. 330; 127 E.R. 491 9–063
Brooke Tool Manufacturing Co. Ltd v. Hydraulic Gears Co. Ltd (1920) 89 L.J.K.B. 263; 122 L.T. 126 .... 6–041, 8–025
Brooker Dore & Co. v. Keymer, Son & Co. (1923) 15 Ll.L.R. 23 .... 20–112, 20–129
Brooks v. Beirnstein [1909] 1 K.B. 98; 78 L.J.K.B. 243; 99 L.T. 970 15–114
Brooks Robinson Property Ltd v. Rothfield [1951] V.L.R. 405 .... 1–043, 1–090, 1–096
Brook's Wharf and Bull Wharf v. Goodman Bros. [1936] 3 All E.R. 696; [1937] 1 K.B. 534; 106 L.J.K.B. 437; 156 L.T. 4; 53 T.L.R. 126; 80 S.J. 991; 42 Com.Cas. 99 6–029
Broome v. Pardess Co-operative Society of Orange Growers [1939] 3 All E.R. 978; CA [1940] 1 All E.R. 603, CA 6–019, 11–040, 11–067, 18–252, 18–257, 20–086
—— v. Speak [1903] 1 Ch. 586; 72 L.J. Ch. 251; 88 L.T. 580; 51 W.R. 258; 19 T.L.R. 187; 47 S.J. 238; 10 Mans. 38 19–200
Brown v. Gould [1972] Ch. 53; [1971] 3 W.L.R. 334; 115 S.J. 406; [1971] 2 All E.R. 1505; 22 P. & C.R. 871 2–017
—— v. Hodgson (1809) 2 Camp. 36, N.P. 5–009
—— v. KMR Services; Sword-Daniels v. Pitel [1995] 4 All E.R. 598; [1995] 2 Lloyd's Rep. 1; *The Times*, July 26, 1995; *The Independent*, September 13, 1995, CA 16–043
—— v. Muller (1872) L.R. 7 Ex. 319; 41 L.J.Ex. 214; 27 L.T. 272; 21 W.R. 18 .... 8–087, 16–071, 17–008, 17–016, 20–116
—— v. Raphael [1958] Ch. 636; [1958] 2 W.L.R. 647; 102 S.J. 269; [1958] 2 All E.R. 79 10–006
—— v. Rosenstein (C.) Co. 200 N.Y.S. 491 (1923) 23–128
—— v. Sheen & Richmond Car Sales Ltd [1950] W.N. 316; [1950] 1 All E.R. 1102 .. 1–054, 2–027, 14–043
—— v. United States National Bank 371 N.W. 2d 692 (1985) 23–054
Brown, (A.R.) McFarlane & Co. v. C. Shaw Lovell & Sons and Walter Potts (1921) 7 Ll.L.R. 36 .... 18–165, 18–167, 20–005
Brown & Co. v. Bedford Pantechnicon Co. Ltd (1884) 5 T.L.R. 449 7–032
Brown & Son Ltd v. Craiks Ltd. *See* BS Brown & Son Ltd v. Craiks Ltd
Brown and Gracie Ltd v. Green (F.W.) & Co. Ltd [1960] 1 Lloyd's Rep. 289 .... 23–308, 23–311
Brown, Brough & Co. v. National Bank of India Ltd (1902) 18 T.L.R. 669; 46 S.J. 617 22–025
Brown Jenkinson & Co. Ltd. v. Percy Dalton (London) Ltd [1957] 2 Q.B. 621; [1957] 3 W.L.R. 403; 101 S.J. 610; [1957] 1 All E.R. 844; [1957] 1 Lloyd's Rep. 1 ... 12–012
Brown, Shipley & Co. v. Kough (1885) 29 Ch.D. 848; 54 L.J.Ch. 1024; 52 L.T. 878; 34 W.R. 2; 5 Asp.M.L.C. 433 .... 18–241, 22–042
Brown, Shipley & Co. Ltd v. Alicia Hosiery Ltd [1966] 1 Lloyd's Rep. 668; 116 N.L.J. 1144, CA 9–032
Browne v. Hare (1858) 3 H. & N. 484; (1859) 4 H. & N. 822; 29 L.J.Ex. 6; 7 W.R. 619; 157 E.R. 1067; *sub nom.* Hare v. Browne 33 L.T. (o.s.) 334; 5 Jur. (N.S.) 711 .... 5–131, 5–135, 20–026, 20–075, 20–077, 20–078, 20–088
Browner International Ltd v. Monarch Shipping Co. Ltd (The European Enterprise) [1989] 2 Lloyd's Rep. 185 .. 18–035, 18–067, 21–058, 21–081, 21–086, 21–087, 21–090, 21–092, 21–105
Browning v. Morris (1778) 2 Cowp. 790 3–032
Bruce v. Wait (1837) 3 M. & W. 15; Murph. & H. 339; 7 L.J.Ex. 17; 150 E.R. 1036 18–210
Bruce v. Warwick (1815) 6 Taunt. 118 2–036
Bruner v. Moore [1904] 1 Ch. 305 2–015
Brunwick Glass Co. Ltd v. United Contractors Ltd (1975) 12 N.B.R. (2d) 631 1–043
Brush Aggregates Ltd, Re [1983] B.C.L.C. 320 24–029
Bryan v. Maloney (1995) 182 C.L.R. 609 12–078
Bryans v. Nix (1839) 4 M. & W. 775; 1 Horn, & H. 480; 8 L.J.Ex. 137 .... 5–086, 5–098, 18–012, 18–066

Bryant v. Flight (1839) 5 M & W. 114 2–046
—— v. Richardson (1866) 14 L.T. 24 2–031
Bryce v. Ehrmann (1904) 7 F.5 .... 5–041, 5–042
Bryen & Langley Ltd v. Boston [2005] EWCA Civ 973; [2005] B.L.R. 508, CA (Civ Div); reversing [2004] EWHC 2450; [2005] B.L.R. 28; 98 Con. L.R. 82; [2004] N.P.C. 165, QBD 14–035
Buchan v. Ortho Pharmaceutical (Canada) Ltd (1984) 8 D.L.R. (4th) 373 ... 1–046, 11–039, 11–057, 14–084
Buchanan v. Parnshaw (1788) 2 T.R. 745; 100 E.R. 13–038
Buchanan (James) & Co. Ltd v. Babco Forwarding & Shipping (U.K.) Ltd [1978] A.C. 141; [1977] 3 W.L.R. 907; (1977) 121 S.J.811; [1977] 3 All E.R. 1048; [1978] R.T.R. 59; [1978] 1 Lloyd's Rep. 119; [1978] 1 C.M.L.R. 156 16–070
—— v. Hay's Transport Services Ltd [1972] 2 Lloyd's Rep. 535 .... 5–057, 6–026, 6–029
Buchanan-Jardine v. Hamilink 1983 S.L.T. 149 .... 11–027, 11–044
Buck v. Davis (1814) 2 M. & S. 397 5–065
Buckingham (Inspector of Taxes) v. Securities Properties Ltd (1979) *The Times*, December 7, 1979 1–084
Buckland v. Farmer & Moody [1979] 1 W.L.R. 221; (1978) 122 S.J. 211; [1978] 3 All E.R. 929; (1978) 36 P. & C.R. 330 .... 8–030, 9–055
Buckley v. La Reserve [1959] Crim.L.R. 451 14–071
—— v. Lever Bros. Ltd [1953] 4 D.L.R. 16 1–037
Buckman v. Levi (1813) 3 Camp. 414; 170 E.R. 1429 8–015
Budberg v. Jerwood and Word (1934) 51 T.L.R. 99; 78 S.J. 878 7–030
Budd v. Fairmaner (1831) 8 Bing, 48; 5 C. & P. 78; 1 Moo. & S. 74; 1 L.J.C.P. 16 .. 10–005, 11–012
Budden v. B.P. Oil and Shell Oil (1980) 124 S.J. 376; [1980] J.P.L. 586 14–085
Buddle v. Green (1857) 27 L.J.Ex 33 .... 8–001, 8–012
Bulbruin v. Romanyszyn; *sub nom.* Romanyszyn v. Bulbruin [1994] R.T.R. 273; 92 L.G.R. 208, CA 7–109
Bulk Oil (Zug) A.G. v. Sun International Ltd [1984] 2 C.M.L.R. 91; [1984] 1 Lloyd's Rep. 531 .... 9–015, 9–019, 19–161, 19–170, 19–171, 20–042
Bulk Trading Corp. Ltd v. Zenziper Grains and Feedstuffs; *sub nom.* Zenziper Grains and Feed Stuffs v. Bulk Trading Corp. Ltd [2001] 1 All E.R. (Comm) 385; [2001] 1 Lloyd's Rep. 357; [2001] C.L.C. 496; *The Times*, January 23, 2001, CA 8–020, 20–014, 20–042
Bull v. Parker (1842) 2 Dowl. (N.S.) 345; 12 L.J.Q.B 93; 7 Jur. 282 1–035
—— v. Robison (1854) 10 Exch. 342; 2 C.L.R. 1276; 24 L.J.Ex. 165; 23 L.T. (o.s.) 288; 2 W.R. 623; 156 E.R. 476 .... 6–022, 11–040, 11–067, 18–251, 18–252
—— v. Sibbs (1799) 8 T.R. 327 8–007
Bullen v. Swan Electric Engraving Co. (1907) 23 T.L.R. 258 .... 6–026, 6–029
Buller v. Swan Electric Engraving Co. (1907) 23 T.L.R. 258 .... 6–021, 6–024
Buller & Co. Ltd v. Brooks (T.J.) Ltd (1930) 142 L.T. 576; 46 T.L.R. 233; 74 S.J. 139; 35 Com.Cas. 205 .... 7–035, 7–071
Bunge A.G. v. Fuga A.G. [1980] 2 Lloyd's Rep. 513 .... 12–037, 18–350, 18–357
—— v. Giuseppe Rocca & Figli (The lstros 11) [1973] 2 Lloyd's Rep. 152 19–009
—— v. Sestostrad (The Athos C) [1984] 1 Lloyd's Rep. 687; (1984) 134 New L.J. 705 20–041
Bunge & Co. v. Tradax England Ltd [1975] 2 Lloyd's Rep. 235, QBD (Comm Ct) .. 20–043, 20–046, 20–125
Bunge Corporation v. Vegetable Vitamin Foods (Private) Ltd [1985] 1 Lloyd's Rep. 613; (1984) 134 New L.J. 125 .... 9–015, 9–020, 19–165, 19–170, 19–207, 19–210, 23–054, 23–114
Bunge Corporation, New York v. Tradax Export SA [1981] 1 W.L.R. 711; (1981) 125 S.J. 373; [1981] 2 All E.R. 540; [1981] Lloyd's Rep. 1, HL; affirming [1981] 2 All E.R. 524; [1980] 1 Lloyd's Rep. 294, CA 8–025, 9–005, 10–027, 10–031, 10–032, 10–034, 10–035, 10–037, 11–018, 12–022, 12–025, 14–006, 15–121, 17–002, 18–284, 18–357, 19–063, 20–013, 20–031, 20–033, 20–045, 20–046, 20–125
Bunge G.m.b.H. v. C.C.V. Landbouwbelang G.A. [1978] 1 Lloyd's Rep. 217; affirmed [1980] 1 Lloyd's Rep. 458, CA 8–030, 8–078, 8–101, 19–018, 19–208
Bunge G.m.b.H. v. Toepfer (Alfred C.) [1979] 1 Lloyd's Rep. 554, CA; affirming [1978] 1 Lloyd's Rep. 506 .... 8–099, 8–101, 12–037

Bunge SA v. Compagnie Europeenne des Cereales [1982] 1 Lloyd's Rep. 306 .... 8–101, 12–036, 18–350, 18–358, 19–150
—— v. Deutsche Conti-Handelsgesellschaft [1979] 2 Lloyd's Rep. 435 .... 8–092, 18–349, 18–350, 18–351, 19–141
—— v.——(No. 2) [1980] 1 Lloyd's Rep. 352 .... 13–038, 18–314
—— v. Kruse [1980] 2 Lloyd's Rep. 142; affirming [1979] 1 Lloyd's Rep. 279 8–092, 8–101, 8–102, 18–345, 18–351, 18–357, 19–141
—— v. Schleswig-Holsteinische Landwirtschaptliche Haptgenossenschaft Eingetr G.m.b.H [1978] 1 Lloyd's Rep. 480; affirmed [1980] 1 Lloyd's Rep. 458, CA 8–030, 12–036, 12–037
Bunny v. Hopkinson (1859) 27 Bear. 565 4–029
Bunney v. Poyntz (1833) 4 B. & Ad. 568; 1 Nev. & M.K.B. 229; 2 L.J.K.B. 55; 110 E.R. 569 .... 9–030, 15–020, 15–035, 15–036, 15–041
Bunting v. Tory (1948) 64 T.L.R. 353 .... 17–066, 17–074
Bunyard, *Re* (1880) 16 Ch.D. 330; 50 L.J.Ch. 484; 44 L.T. 232; 29 W.R. 407 .... 22–068, 22–069
Burch v. Scory (1699) 12 Mod. 309; 88 E.R. 1341, P.N. 5–040, 5–050
Burch & Co. v. Corry & Co. [1920] N.Z.L.R. 69 .... 20–042, 20–126
Burden v. Halton (1828) 4 Bing. 454 9–030
Burdick v. Sewell *See* Sewell v. Burdick.
Burgess v. Purchase & Sons (Farms) Ltd [1983] Ch. 216; [1983] 2 W.L.R. 361; [1983] 2 All E.R. 4 2–051
Burgh v. Legge (1839) 5 M. & W. 418; 7 Dowl, 814; 8. L.J.Ex. 258 .... 22–121, 22–131
Burghardt, *Re, ex p.* Trevor (1875) 1 Ch.D. 297; 45 L.J.Bey. 27; 33 L.T. 756; 24 W.R. 301 8–036
Burgos v. Nascimento (1908) 100 L.T. 71; 53 S.J. 60; 11 Asp.M.L.C. 181 ... 15–013, 18–088, 18–089, 18–216
Burke v. Utah National Bank 66 N.W. 295 (1896) 23–164
Burliner v. Royle (1880) 5 C.P.D. 354; 43 L.T. 254; 44 J.P. 831 9–030
Burnett v. Westminster Bank Ltd [1966] 1 Q.B. 742; [1965] 3 W.L.R. 863; 109 S.J 533; [1965] 3 All E.R. 51; [1965] 3 All E.R. 81; [1965] 2 Lloyd's Rep. 218 2–012
Burnley Engineering Products Ltd v. Cambridge Vacuum Engineering Ltd 50 Con. L.R. 10, QBD (OR) 11–049
Burrell v. Harding's Executrix 1931 S.L.T. 76 12–055
Burrough, *Re* (1811) 18 Ves.Jun, 229; 1 Rose 155 22–090
Burrough, *Re, ex p.* Sargeant (1810) 1 Rose 153 22–090
Burroughs Business Machines Ltd v. Feed-Rite Mills (1962) Ltd (1973) 42 D.L.R. (3d) 303 .... 1–086, 12–040, 12–055
Burrows v. Jamaica Private Power Co Ltd [2002] 1 All E.R. (Comm) 374; [2002] C.L.C. 255; [2002] Lloyd's Rep. I.R. 466, QBD 25–020, 25–030
—— v. Rhodes [1899] 1 Q.B. 816 3–029
—— v. Smith (1894) 10 T.L.R 246 .... 6–019, 11–067
Burrows (John) Ltd v. Subsurface Surveys Ltd [1968] 66 D.L.R. (2d) 354; [1968] S.C.R. 607 22–043
Burstall v. Grimsdale (1906) 11 Com.Cas. 280 .... 18–053, 19–024, 19–029, 19–033, 19–043, 19–048, 19–050, 21–094, 21–095
Burton v. G.N. Ry. (1854) 9 Exch. 507; 23 L.J.Ex. 184; 2 W.R. 257; 156 E.R. 216 8–059
—— v. Pinkerton (1867) L.R. 2 Ex. 340; 36 L.J.Ex. 137; 16 L.T. 419; 17 L.T. 15; 31 J.P. 615; 15 W.R. 1139; 2 Mar.L.C. 494 16–047
Business Applications Specialists Ltd v. Nationwide Credit Cpn. Ltd [1988] R.T.R. 332 11–048
Business Computers Ltd v. Anglo-African Leasing Ltd [1977] 1 W.L.R. 578; (1977) 121 S.J. 201; [1979] 2 All E.R. 741 .... 16–007, 23–170
Busk v. Davis (1814) 2 M. & S. 397, 5 Taun. 622; 105 E.R. 429 5–061
—— v. Spence (1815) 4 Comp. 329; 171 E.R. 105 18–268
Busse v. British Manufacturing Stationary Co. Report of the Decision of the Mixed Arbitral Tribunals, Vol. 7, 345 (1927) 25–132, 25–154
Bute (Marquess of) v. Barclays Bank Ltd [1955] 1 Q.B. 202; [1954] 3 W.L.R. 741; 98 S.J. 805; [1954] 3 All E.R. 365 22–023
Butler v. Countryside Finance Ltd [1993] 3 N.Z.L.R. 623 17–099
Butler v. Egg and Egg Pulp Marketing Board (1996) 114 C.L.R. 185 17–106

Butler Machine Tool Co. Ltd v. Ex-Cell-O Corp. (England) Ltd [1979] 1 W.L.R. 401; (1977) 121 S.J. 406; [1979] 1 All E.R. 965 .... 2–013, 13–013, 13–095
Butterfield v. Burroughs (1706) 1 Salk. 211 10–019
Butterworth v. Kingsway Motors Hayton Third Party, Kennedy, Fourth Party, Rudolph, Fifth Party, Ltd [1954] 1 W.L.R. 1286; 98 S.J. 717; [1954] 2 All E.R. 694 .... 4–006, 4–010, 4–011, 4–015, 4–016, 17–084
Buxton v. Bedall (1803) 3 East. 303; 102 E.R. 613 1–043
Buxton v. Jones (1840) 1 Man. & G. 83 22–110
Byrne & Co. v. Van Tienhoven (1880) 5 C.P.D. 344; 44 J.P. 667; 49 L.J.Q.B. 316; 42 L.T. 37 2–015
Bywater v. Richardson (1834) 1 A. & E. 508; 3 Nev. & M.K.B. 748; 3 L.J.K.B. 164 13–038
Byzantion, The (1922) 127 L.T. 756; 38 T.L.R. 744; 16 Asp.M.L.C. 19 25–133

C.C.C. Films (London) Ltd v. Impact Quadrant Films Ltd [1985] Q.B. 16; [1984] 3 W.L.R. 245; (1984) 128 S.J. 297; [1984] 3 All E.R. 298; (1984) 134 New L.J. 657 .... 12–121, 16–031, 17–063, 17–070
CGU International Insurance Plc v. Astrazeneca Insurance Co Ltd [2005] EWHC 2755; [2006] 1 C.L.C. 162, QBD 25–057, 25–176
CGU International Insurance plc v. Szabo [2002] 1 All E.R. (Comm.) 83 ... 25–033, 25–057
C.I.A. Barca de Panama SA v. Wimpey (George) & Co. Ltd [1980] 1 Lloyd's Rep. 598 25–191
C.I.R. v. Morris [1958] N.Z.L.R. 1126 12–036
C.N.A. Mortgage Investors Ltd v. Hamilton National Bank, 540 S.W. 2d 238 (Tenn. 1975) 23–196
C.N. Marine Inc. v. Stena Line A/B (The Stena Nautica) (No. 2) [1982] 2 Com.L.R. 203; [1982] 2 Lloyd's Rep. 336; (1982) 79 L.S.Gaz. 922, CA 17–099
C. & P. Haulage v. Middleton [1983] 1 W.L.R. 1461; (1983) 127 S.J. 730; [1983] 3 All E.R. 94 .... 17–062, 17–070
CP Henderson & Co v. Comptoir d'Escompte de Paris (1873–74) L.R. 5 P.C. 253; (1874) 2 Asp. 98; (1874) 21 W.R. 873; (1874) 42 L.J. P.C. 60; (1874) 29 L.T. 192, PC (HK) 18–067
CPC Consolidated Pool Carriers G.m.b.H. v. CTM CIA Transmediterranean SA; CPC Gallia, The [1994] 1 Lloyd's Rep. 68 2–017
CTN Cash and Carry Ltd v. Gallaher [1994] 4 All E.R. 714, CA 3–010, 14–051A
Cabaret Holdings Ltd v. Meeanee Sports & Rodeo Club Inc. [1982] 1 N.Z.L.R. 673 .. 2–028
Cadogan Finance Ltd v. Lavery & Fox [1982] Com.L.R. 248 .... 1–082, 7–014, 7–015, 7–017
Cadre SA v. Astra Asigurari [2005] EWHC 2504, QBD (Comm) 25–020, 25–031
Cahn and Mayer v. Pockett's Bristol Channel Steam Packet Co. Ltd [1899] 1 Q.B. 643; 68 L.J.Q.B. 515; 80 L.T. 269; 47 W.R. 422; 15 T.L.R. 247; 43 S.J. 331; 8 Asp.M.L.C. 517; 4 Com.Cas. 168 .... 5–138, 5–139, 7–074, 7–076, 7–086, 15–092, 15–097, 18–086, 18–087, 18–216, 18–225
Cain v. Moon [1896] 2 Q.B. 283; 65 L.J.Q.B. 587; 74 L.T. 728; 40 S.J. 500 15–049
Caine v. Coulton (1863) 1 H. & C. 764 9–049
Calaminus v. Dowlais Iron Co. (1878) 47 L.J.Q.B. 575 8–067
Calcutta & Burmah Steam Navigation Co. v. De Mattos (1863) 32 L.J.Q.B. 322; on appeal; (1864) 33 L.J.Q.B. 214 ...... 5–101, 6–020, 16–016, 18–092, 19–003, 19–006, 19–102, 19–119
Calcutta S.S. Co. Ltd v. Andrew Weir & Co. [1910] 1 K.B. 759 .... 18–053, 18–057, 18–111, 18–119
Caldwell v. Sumpters [1972] Ch. 478; [1972] 2 W.L.R. 412; (1971) 116 S.J. 15; [1972] 1 All E.R. 567 15–038
Caledonia North Sea Ltd v. London Bridge Engineering Ltd; *sub nom.* Caledonia North Sea Ltd v. British Telecommunications Plc; Caledonia North Sea Ltd v. BT Plc; Caledonia North Sea Ltd v. Norton (No.2) Ltd (In Liquidation); EE Caledonia Ltd v. London Bridge Engineering Ltd [2002] UKHL 4; [2002] 1 All E.R. (Comm) 321; [2002] 1 Lloyd's Rep. 553; 2002 S.C. (H.L.) 117; 2002 S.L.T. 278; 2002 S.C.L.R. 346; [2002] C.L.C. 741; [2002] B.L.R. 139; [2002] Lloyd's Rep. I.R. 261; 2002 G.W.D. 6–178; *The Times*, February 13, 2002, HL 13–037

Caledonia North Sea Ltd v. London Bridge Engineering Ltd; *sub nom.* Caledonia North Sea Ltd v. British Telecommunications plc; Caledonia North Sea Ltd v. BT plc; Caledonia North Sea Ltd v. Norton (No.2) Ltd [2002] UKHL 4; [2002] 1 All E.R. (Comm) 321; 2002 S.L.T. 278; 2002 G.W.D. 6–178; *The Times*, February 13, 2002, HL; affirming 2000 S.L.T. 1123; [2000] Lloyd's Rep. I.R. 249; 2000 G.W.D. 3–84; *The Times*, February 8, 2000, 1 Div 13–037
Caledonia Subsea Ltd v. Micoperi Srl; *sub nom.* Caledonia Subsea Ltd v. Microperi Srl, 2003 S.C. 70; 2002 S.L.T. 1022; 2003 S.C.L.R. 20; 2002 G.W.D. 25–842; *The Times*, September 6, 2002, IH (1 Div); affirming 2001 S.C. 716; 2001 S.L.T. 1186; 2001 S.C.L.R. 634, OH 10–366, 25–019, 25–060, 25–065
Calico Printers' Association v. Barclays Bank (1931) 145 L.T. 51; 36 Com.Cas. 197; 39 Ll.L.R. 51 .... 22–092, 22–096, 23–185
Callender v. Howard (1850) 10 C.B. 290 9–041
Caltex Oil (Australia) Property Ltd v. The Dredge "Willemstad" (1976) 136 C.L.R. 529 1–058
Camac v. Warriner (1845) 1 C.B. 356; 4 L.T. (o.s.) 397; 9 Jur. 162; 135 E.R. 577 10–020
Cameco Inc. v. S.S. American Legion 514 F. 2d 1291 (1974); [1975] 1 Lloyd's Rep. 295 .... 21–082, 21–086, 21–087
Cameron (R.W.) & Co. v. Slutzkin (L.) Property Ltd (1923) 32 C.L.R. 81 .. 11–022, 11–076, 11–077
Cameron-Head v. Cameron & Co. 1919 S.C. 627 16–032
Camidge v. Allenby (1827) 6B. & C. 373; 9 Dow. & Ry. K.B. 391; 5 L.J.O.S.K.B. 95; 108 E.R. 489 22–134
Cammell v. Sewell (1860) 5 H. & N. 728; 29 L.J.Ex. 350; 2 L.T. 799; 6 Jur. N.S. 918; 8 W.R. 639; 157 E.R. 1371 .... 23–127, 25–114, 25–116, 25–122, 25–123
Cammell Laird & Co. Ltd v. Manganese Bronze & Brass Co. Ltd [1934] A.C. 402 ... 1–047, 11–038, 11–042, 11–055, 11–057, 11–060, 11–068, 13–025, 13–040
Camp v. Corn Exchange National Bank, 132 A. 189 (1926) 23–194, 23–221
Campbell v. Bagley 276 F. 2d 28 (1960) 25–127
—— v. Edwards [1976] 1 W.L.R. 403; (1975) 119 S.J. 845; [1976] 1 All E.R. 785; [1976] 1 Lloyd's Rep. 522 2–051
—— v. Mersey Docks and Harbour Board (1863) 14 C.B. (N.S.) 412; 2 New Rep. 32; 8 L.T. 245; 11 W.R. 596; 143 E.R. 506 .... 5–061, 5–068, 5–083, 5–087
Campbell Connelly & Co. Ltd v. Noble [1963] 1 W.L.R. 252; 107 S.J. 135; [1963] 1 All E.R. 237 25–202
Campbell Discount Co. v. Bridge. *See* Bridge v. Campbell Discount Co.
—— v. Gall [1961] 1 Q.B. 431; [1961] 2 W.L.R. 514; 105 S.J. 232; [1961] 2 All E.R. 104 .... 3–005, 7–011, 7–017, 7–018
Campbell Mostyn (Provisions) Ltd v. Barnett Trading Co. [1954] 1 Lloyd's Rep. 65 .... 16–056, 16–069, 16–074, 16–076, 17–019, 17–020, 17–039, 17–054
Campos v. Kentucky and Indiana Terminal Railroad Co. [1962] 2 Lloyd's Rep. 459; (1962) 106 S.J. 469 25–166
Canada and Dominion Sugar Co. Ltd v. Canadian National (West Indies) Steamship Co. Ltd [1947] A.C. 46; (1947) 80 Ll. L. Rep. 13; 62 T.L.R. 666; [1947] L.J.R. 385, PC (Can) 18–028, 18–164, 19–038
Canada Atlantic Grain Export Co. (Inc.) v. Eilers (1929) 35 Ll.L.R. 206; 35 Com.Cas. 90 .... 11–042, 13–025
Canada Bank Note Engraving & Printing Co. v. Toronto Railway Co. (1895) 22 A.R. 462 1–045
Canada Law Book Co. v. Boston Book Co. (1922) 64 S.C.R. (Can.) 182; 66 D.L.R. 209 (Can.) 11–018
Canada Life Assurance Co. v. Canadian Imperial Bank of Commerce (1979) 98 D.L.R. (3d) 670 22–040
Canada Permanent Trust Co. v. Kowal (1981) 32 O.R. (2d) 37 22–045
Canada Rice Mills Ltd v. Union Marine and General Insurance Co. Ltd [1940] 4 All E.R. 169; 110 L.J.P.C. 1; 164 L.T. 367; 57 T.L.R. 41; 85 Sol.Jo. 92; 46 Com.Cas. 74; 19 Asp. M.L.C. 391; 67 Ll. Rep. 549, PC 8–097
Canada Steamship Lines Ltd v. R. [1952] A.C. 192; [1952] 1 T.L.R. 261; 96 S.J. 72; [1952] 1 All E.R. 305; [1952] 1 Lloyd's Rep. 1 .... 13–019, 13–022
Canadian Laboratories Supplies Ltd v. Engelhard Industries Ltd [1980] 2 S.C.R. 450 7–011

Canal Bank and Trust Co.'s Liquidation, *Re* 152 So. 297 (1933) 23–099
Canaplan Leasing Inc. v. Dominion of Canada General Insurance Co. (1990) 69 D.L.R. (4th) 531 7–009
Candlewood Navigation Cpn. Ltd v. Mitsui O.S.K. Lines Ltd (The Mineral Transporter) [1986] A.C. 1; [1985] 3 W.L.R. 381; (1985) 129 S.J. 506; [1985] 2 All E.R. 935; [1985] 2 Lloyd's Rep. 303; (1985) 82 L.S.Gaz. 2912; (1985) 135 New L.J. 677 .... 5–011, 18–149
Cannon v. Hartley [1949] Ch. 213; [1949] L.J.R. 370; 65 T.L.R. 63; 92 S.J. 719; [1949] 1 All E.R. 50 1–032
Canterbury Seed Co. Ltd v. J.G. Ward Farmers Association (1895) 13 N.Z.L.R. 96 .... 12–043, 12–055, 12–059
Cantiare San Rocco SA v. Clyde Shipbuilding and Engineering Co. Ltd [1924] A.C. 226; 93 L.J.P.C. 86; 130 L.T. 610 .... 6–039, 6–042
Cantiere Meccanico Brindisino v. Janson [1912] 3 K.B. 452; 81 L.J.K.B. 1043; 107 L.T. 281; 28 T.L.R. 564; 57 S.J. 62; 12 Asp.M.L.C. 246; 1 Com.Cas. 332 19–042
Cantieri Navali Riuniti SpA v. N.V. Omne Justitia (The Stolt Marmaro) [1985] 2 Lloyd's Rep. 428 .... 25–006, 25–074
Cantieri Navali Triestina v. Russian Soviet Naphtha Agency [1925] 2 K.B. 172, CA 25–119
Cantrell & Cochrane Ltd v. Neeson [1926] N.I. 107 1–061
Cap Palos, The [1921] P. 458; [1921] All E.R. 249; 91 L.J.P. 11; 126 L.T. 82; 37 T.L.R. 921; 15 Asp.M.L.C. 403 13–052
Caparo Industries v. Dickman [1990] 2 A.C. 605; [1990] 2 W.L.R. 358; [1990] 1 All E.R. 568; (1990) 134 S.J. 494; [1990] B.C.C. 164; [1990] B.C.L.C. 273; [1990] L.S.Gaz. March 28, 42; (1990) 140 New L.J. 248 ..... 7–015, 10–013, 12–013, 18–045, 23–185
Cape Asbestos Co. Ltd v. Lloyd's Bank Ltd [1921] W.N. 274 23–052
Cape SNC v. Idealservice Srl (C541/99); Idealservice MN RE SAS v. OMAI Srl (C542/99) [2002] All E.R. (EC) 657; [2001] E.C.R. I-9049; [2003] 1 C.M.L.R. 42, ECJ 14–011, 14–029, 14–071, 14–131
Capital and Counties Bank Ltd v. Gordon [1903] A.C. 240; 72 L.J.K.B.451; 88 L.T. 574; 51 W.R. 671; 19 T.L.R. 462; 8 Com.Cas. 221 ... 22–019, 22–024, 22–025, 22–073
—— v. Warriner (1896) 12 T.L.R. 216; 1 Com.Cas. 314 5–065, 5–122, 7–014, 7–035, 7–067, 7–072, 7–085, 15–052, 15–097
Capital Finance Co. v. Bray [1964] 1 W.L.R. 323; [1964] 1 All E.R. 603; 108 S.J. 95, C.A. 14–004
Capital Motors Ltd v. Beecham [1975] 1 N.Z.L.R. 576 12–013
Capon, *Re*, Trustee in Bankruptcy v. Knight (R.C.) & Sons [1940] Ch. 442; [1940] 2 All E.R. 135; 109 L.J.Ch. 293; 164 L.T. 124; 56 T.L.R. 532; 84 S.J. 270 5–016
Car & Universal Finance Co. Ltd v. Caldwell [1965] 1 Q.B. 525; [1964] 2 W.L.R. 600; 108 S.J. 15; [1964] 1 All E.R. 290 ...... 3–005, 7–024, 7–076, 12–003, 12–005, 15–118
Carapanayoti v. Comptoir Commercial Andre et Cie SA [1972] 1 Lloyd's Rep. 139; (1971) 116 S.J. 96 .... 8–034, 8–035
Carapanayoti & Co. Ltd v. Green (E.T.) Ltd [1959] 1 Q.B. 131; [1958] 3 W.L.R. 390; 102 S.J. 620; [1958] 3 All E.R. 115; [1958] 2 Lloyd's Rep. 169 .... 6–049, 19–131, 19–132
Cardano Giampieri v. Greek Petroleum Co. [1962] 1 W.L.R. 40 21–020
Carew v. Duckworth (1869) L.R. 4 Ex. 313; 38 L.J.Ex. 149; 20 L.T. 882; 17 W.R. 927 22–131
Carew's Estate Act (No. 2), *Re* (1862) 31 Beav. 39; 54 E.R. 1051 22–073
Cargill Inc. v. Mapro Ltd (The Aegis Progress) [1983] 2 Lloyd's Rep. 570; [1983] Com.L.R. 177 .... 20–018, 20–045
Cargill International SA v. Bangladesh Sugar & Food Industries Corp. [1998] 1 W.L.R. 461; [1998] 2 All E.R. 406; [1998] C.L.C. 399; (1998) 95(3) L.S.G. 25;(1998) 142 S.J.L.B. 14; *The Times*, December 10, 1997, CA; affirming[1996] 4 All E.R. 563; [1996] 2 Lloyd's Rep. 524, QBD (Comm Ct) 19–008, 19–074, 23–289
Cargill U.K. Ltd v. Continental U.K. Ltd [1989] 2 Lloyd's Rep. 290 20–051
Carl Zeiss Stiftung v. Rayner & Keeler Ltd (No.2) [1967] 1 A.C. 853; [1966] 3 W.L.R. 125; [1966] 2 All E.R. 536; [1967] R.P.C. 497; 110 S.J. 425, HL; reversing [1965] Ch. 596; [1965] 2 W.L.R. 277; [1965] 1 All E.R. 300; [1965] R.P.C.141; 109 S.J. 51; *The Times*, December 18, 1964; *The Guardian*, December 18, 1964, CA; reversing [1964] R.P.C. 299, RPC 25–085

Carlill v. Carbolic Smoke Ball Co. [1893] 1 Q.B. 256 ...... 10–005, 14–014, 14–062, 14–066
Carlisle and Cumberland Banking Co. v. Bragg [1911] 1 K.B. 489; [1908–10] All E.R. Ext. 977; 8 L.J.K.B. 472; 104 L.T. 121 7–017
Carlos Federspiel & Co. SA v. Charles Twigg & Co. Ltd [1957] 1 Lloyd's Rep. 240; [1957] J.B.L. 296 .... 5–005, 5–027, 5–070, 5–072, 5–080, 5–081, 5–084, 15–012, 18–185, 20–070, 20–071, 20–072, 20–073
Carlton Lodge Club v. Customs and Excise Commissioners [1975] 1 W.L.R. 66; 118 S.J. 757; [1974] 3 All E.R. 798; [1974] S.T.C. 507 1–121
Carlyle Finance Ltd v. Pallas Industrial Finance [1999] 1 All E.R. (Comm) 659; [1999] R.T.R. 281; [1999] C.C.L.R. 85, CA 1–054, 2–011
Carnegie v. Giessen [2005] EWCA Civ 191; [2005] 1 W.L.R. 2510; [2005] C.P. Rep. 24; [2005] 1 C.L.C. 259; (2005) 102(18) L.S.G. 23; *The Times*, March 14, 2005, CA 25–194
Carnes v. Nesbitt (1862) 7 H. & N. 778 16–033
Carpenters' Co. v. British Mutual Banking Co. [1938] 1 K.B. 511; [1937] 3 All E.R. 811; 107 L.J.K.B. 11; 157 L.T. 329; 53 T.L.R. 1040; 81 S.J. 701; 43 Com.Cas. 38 22–024
Carr v. Acraman (1856) 11 Exch. 566; 25 L.J.Ex. 90; 156 E.R. 956 ...... 5–082, 5–094
—— v. L. & N.W. Railway (1875) L.R. 10 C.P. 307; [1874–80] All E.R. 418; 44 L.J.C.P. 109; 31 L.T. 785; 39 J.P. 279; 23 W.R. 747 ...... 5–065, 7–010, 7–017
Carrington v. Roots (1837) 2 M. & W. 248; Murph. & H. 14; L.J.Ex. 95; 1 Jur. 85; 150 E.R. 748 1–093
Carroll v. Fearon; Barclay v. Dunlop Ltd; Carroll v. Bent [1999] E.C.C. 73; [1998] P.I.Q.R. P416; *The Times*, January 26, 1998, CA 14–058, 14–076
Carruthers v. Payne (1828) 5 Bing. 270; 2 Moo. & P. 429; 7 L.J. (o.s.) C.P. 84; 130 E.R. 1065 5–091
Carse v. Coppen 1951 S.C. 233; 1951 S.L.T. 145, 1 Div 25–085
Carson v. Union S.S. Co. [1922] N.Z.L.R. 778 8–054
Carter v. Carter [1896] 1 Ch. 62 7–064
—— v. Crick (1859) 4 H. & N. 412; 28 L.J.Ex. 238; 33 L.T. (o.s.) 166; 7 W.R. 507; 157 E.R. 899 ...... 11–022, 13–029
—— v. Flower (1847) 16 M. & W. 743; 4 Dow. & L. 529; 16 L.J.Ex. 199; 11 Jur. 313 22–132
—— v. Palmer (1841) 8 Cl. & F. 657 23–180
Carter v. Toussaint (1822) 5 B. & Ald. 855; 1 Dow. & Ry. K.B. 515; 106 E.R. 1404 .. 8–009
—— v. White (1883) 25 Ch.D. 666; 54 L.J.Ch. 138; 50 L.T. 670; 32 W.R. 692 22–133
Cartwright v. MacCormack; Trafalgar Insurance Co. (Third Party) [1963] 1 W.L.R. 18; 106 S.J. 957; [1963] 1 All E.R. 11; [1962] 2 Lloyd's Rep. 328 ...... 8–032, 8–034
Carus-Wilson and Greene, *Re* (1886) 18 Q.B.D. 7 2–052
Carver & Co. and Sasson & Co., *Re* (1911) 17 Com.Cas. 59 8–037
Case of Mines (1567) 1 Plowd. 310 1–097
Casey (a Bankrupt), *Re* (unreported, H.C. Ireland, March 1, 1992) 24–012
Cash v. Giles (1828) 3 C. & P. 407; 172 E.R. 477 12–065
Cassaboglou v. Gibb (1883) 11 Q.B.D. 797 .... 15–013, 15–065, 23–307, 23–308, 23–311
Cassidy (Peter Seed Co. Ltd v. Osuustukkukauppa I.L. [1957] 1 W.L.R. 273; 101 S.J. 149; [1957] 1 All E.R. 484; [1957] 1 Lloyd's Rep. 25 .. 6–047, 6–057, 18–309, 18–310, 18–313, 18–317, 18–318, 18–325, 25–119, 25–168
Cassir, Moore & Co. Ltd v. Eastcheap Dried Fruit Co. [1962] 1 Lloyd's Rep. 400 ... 16–037
Castle v. Playford (1872) L.R. 7 Ex. 98, 41 L.J.Ex. 44; 29 L.T. 315; 20 W.R. 440; 1 Asp.M.L.C. 255, Ex.Ch 2–045, 5–135, 6–001, 6–003, 6–020, 19–095, 21–021
—— v. Sworder (1860) 6 H. & N. 828; 30 L.J.Ex. 310; 4 L.T. 865; 8 Jur. (N.S.) 233; 9 W.R. 697; 158 E.R. 341; Ex.Ch. 8–009
Castle Phillips Finance Co. v. Williams (1986) (unreported C.A.T. No. 284) 14–150
Castrique v. Buttigieg (1855) 10 Moore P.C. 94; 4 W.R. 445 22–070
—— v. Imrie (1870) L.R. 4 H.L. 414; 39 L.J.C.P. 350, 23 L.T. 48; 19 W.R. 1; 3 Mar.L.C. 454 ...... 25–121, 25–130
Caterpillar Financial Services Corp v. SNC Passion [2004] EWHC 569; [2004] 2 Lloyd's Rep. 99, QBD 25–037, 25–038, 25–040, 25–076
Catling, *ex p.* (1873) 29 L.T. 431 15–078
Catt v. Tourle (1869) 4 Ch.App. 654 ...... 3–038, 17–099
Cattle v. Stockton Waterworks Co. (1875) L.R. 10 Q.B. 453 5–011

Cauxell Ltd v. Lloyd's Bank plc. *The Times*, December 26, 1995 .... 23–196, 23–272
Cavalier Insurance Co. Ltd, *Re* [1989] 2 Lloyd's Rep. 430; *The Times*, May 31, 1989 .... 3–028, 3–032
Cave v. Coleman (1828) 3 Man. & Ry. 2; 7 L.J. (o.s.) K.B. 25 10–016
Cavendish-Woodhouse Ltd v. Manley (1984) 148 J.P. 299; [1982] L.G.R. 376; [1984] Crim.L.R. 239, DC 11–011, 13–030, 13–067, 14–142
Cebora S.N.C. v. S.I.P. (Industrial Products) Ltd [1976] 1 Lloyd's Rep. 271 .... 9–032, 17–049, 22–064
Cedar Trading Co. Ltd v. Transworld Oil Ltd; The "Gudermes" [1985] 2 Lloyd's Rep. 623 2–017
Cederberg v. Borries, Craig & Co. (1885) 2 T.L.R. 201 18–072
Cehave N.V. v. Bremer Handelsgesellshaft m.b.H.; Hansa Nord, The [1976] Q.B. 44; [1975] 3 W.L.R. 447; 119 S.J. 678; [1975] 3 All E.R. 739; [1975] 2 Lloyd's Rep. 445 1–002, 8–080, 10–026, 10–029, 10–031, 10–032, 10–033, 10–034, 10–036, 11–031, 11–044, 12–019, 17–053, 18–266, 18–357, 19–145, 19–147
Cellulose Acetate Silk Co. Ltd v. Widnes Foundry (1925) Ltd [1933] A.C. 20 ...... 13–036, 16–032, 16–036
Celthene Property Ltd v. W.K.J. Hauliers Property Ltd [1981] 1 N.S.W.L.R. 606 13–016
Center Optical (Hong Kong) Ltd v. Jardine Transport Services (China) Ltd [2001] 2 Lloyd's Rep. 678, CFI (HK) 18–063, 20–008, 20–082, 21–086
Central Bank, *Re* (1892) 21 O.R. 515 .... 25–133, 25–138
Central London Property Trust Ltd v. High Trees House Ltd [1947] K.B. 130; [1946] 1 All E.R. 256; [1947] L.J.R. 77; 175 L.T. 333; 62 T.L.R. 557 9–024
Central Meat Products Co. Ltd v. McDaniel (J.V.) Ltd [1952] 1 Lloyd's Rep. 562 ... 13–033
Central Newbury Car Auctions Ltd v. Unity Finance Ltd, Mercury Motors (Third Party) [1957] 1 Q.B. 371; [1956] 3 W.L.R. 1068; 100 S.J. 927; [1956] 3 All E.R. 905 .... 7–008, 7–009, 7–010, 7–013, 7–016, 7–036, 7–075
Central Regional Council v. Uponor Ltd 1966 S.L.T. 645 11–059
Centrax Ltd v. Citibank NA [1999] 1 All E.R. (Comm) 557, CA ... 25–021, 25–033, 25–057, 25–076
Centri Force Engineering v. Bank of Scotland 1993 S.L.T. 190 23–138
Centrovincial Estates plc v. Merchant Investors' Assurance Co. Ltd [1983] Com.L.Rep. 158 11–009
Century Credit Corp. v. Richard (1962) 34 D.L.R. 2d 291 .... 25–131, 25–147
Cerealmangimi SpA v. Toepfer; Eurometal, The [1981] 1 Lloyd's Rep. 337; [1981] 3 All E.R. 533; [1981] Com.L.R. 13 ..... 8–025, 8–030, 9–019, 12–037, 12–056, 19–063, 19–150, 19–159
Ceres Orchard Partnership v. Fiatgari Australia Pty Ltd [1995] 1 N.Z.L.R. 112 ...... 7–043, 7–047
Cero Navigation Corp. v. Jean Lion & Cie (The Solon) [2000] 1 All E.R. (Comm) 214; [2000] 1 Lloyd's Rep. 292; [2000] C.L.C. 593, QBD (Comm Ct) 8–088
Ceval Alimentos SA v. Agrimpex Trading Co. Ltd (The Northern Progress) (No. 2) [1996] 2 Lloyd's Rep. 319 .... 19–024, 19–031, 19–073, 19–088
Ceval International Ltd v. Cefetra B.V. [1996] 1 Lloyd's Rep. 464, CA; [1994] 1 Lloyd's Rep. 651 .... 19–027, 20–019, 21–019
Chabbra Cpn. Pte. Ltd v. Jag Shakti (Owners) (The Jag Shakti) [1986] A.C. 337; [1986] 2 W.L.R. 87; (1986) 130 S.J. 51; [1986] 1 All E.R. 480; (1986) 83 L.S.Gaz. 45 .... 5–009, 5–010, 18–055, 20–083
Chaigley Farms Ltd v. Crawford, Kaye & Grayshire Ltd [1996] B.C.C. 957 5–149
Chairmasters Inc. v. Public National Bank and Trust Co., 127 N.Y.S. 2d 806 (1954) 23–235
Chalmers, *ex.p., Re* Edwards (1873) L.R. 8 Ch.App. 289; 42 L.J.Bcy. 37; 28 L.T. 325; 21 W.R. 349; L.C. & L.J.J. 15–010, 15–025, 15–028, 15–029, 15–037, 15–042, 15–043, 15–063
Chalmers v. Harding (1868) 17 L.T. 571 .... 10–005, 11–019
—— v. Paterson (1897) 24 R. 1020; 36 Sc.L.R. 768; 5 S.L.T. 112 12–042
Chambers v. Miller (1862) 32 L.J.C.P. 30 22–118
—— v. Smith (1843) 12 W. & W. 2 8–035
Champanhac & Co. Ltd v. Waller Ltd [1948] 2 All E.R. 724 .... 13–023, 13–028
Champion v. Short (1807) 1 Camp. 53; 170 E.R. 874, N.P. 8–046, 8–049, 8–063
Chandelor v. Lopus (1603) Cro.Jac. 4; 79 E.R. 3; *sub nom.* Lopus v. Chandler, Dyer 75n; Ex.Ch. 10–016

Chandler v. Webster [1904] 1 K.B. 493; 73 L.J.K.B. 401; 90 L.T. 217; 52 W.R. 290; 20 T.L.R. 222; 485 S.J. 245 6–033
Chandris v. Isbrandtsen Moller Co. Inc. [1951] 1 K.B. 240; 66 T.L.R. (Pt. 2) 358; 94 S.J. 534; [1950] 2 All E.R. 618; 84 Ll.L.Rep. 347 .... 8–089, 13–046
Channel Island Ferries Ltd v. Sealink U.K. Ltd [1988] 1 Lloyd's Rep. 323 .... 8–091, 8–092, 8–093, 8–097
Channel Tunnel Group and France Manche SA v. Balfour Beatty Construction [1993] A.C. 334; [1993] 2 W.L.R. 262; [1993] 1 All E.R. 664; [1993] 137 S.J.L.B. 36; [1993] 1 Lloyd's Rep. 291; 61 B.L.R. 1; 32 Con.L.R. 1; [1993] N.P.C. 8; *The Times*, January 25, 1993, HL 2–052
Chanter v. Hopkins (1838) 4 M. & W. 399; 1 Horn. & H. 377; 8 L.J.Ex. 14; 3 Jur. 58; 150 E.R. 1484 .... 10–026, 11–003, 11–065, 13–050
Chantflower v. Priestley (1603) Cro.Eliz. 914; 78 E.R. 1135 4–026
Chapelton v. Barry U.D.C. [1940] 1 K.B. 532 .... 2–002, 2–012, 13–013
Chaplin v. Boys [1971] A.C. 356; [1969] 3 W.L.R. 322; 113 S.J. 608; [1969] 2 All E.R. 1085 .... 25–190, 25–191
—— v. Frewin (Leslie) (Publishers) Ltd [1966] Ch. 71; [1966] 2 W.L.R. 40; 109 S.J. 871; [1965] 3 All E.R. 764 .... 2–028, 2–033, 2–039
—— v. Hicks [1911] 2 K.B. 786; 80 L.J.K.B. 1292; 105 L.T. 285; 27 T.L.R. 458; 55 S.J. 580 14–006
—— v. Rogers (1800) 1 East 192; 102 E.R. 75 8–008
Chapman v. Gwyther (1866) L.R. 1 Q.B. 463; 7 B. & S. 417; 35 L.J.Q.B. 142; 14 L.T. 477; 30 J.P. 582; 12 Jur. (N.S.) 522; 14 W.R. 671 .... 10–021, 13–038
—— v. Morton (1843) 11 M. & W. 534; 12 L.J.Ex. 292; 1 L.T. (O.S.) 148; 152 E.R. 917 .... 12–032, 12–047
—— v. Speller (1850) 14 Q.B. 621, 19 L.J.Q.B. 239; 15 L.T. (O.S.) 158; 14 Jur. 652; 117 E.R. 240 .... 4–001, 4–032
—— v. Withers (1888) 20 Q.B.D. 824; 57 L.J.Q.B. 457; 37 W.R. 29; 4 T.L.R. 465 .... 5–043, 6–010, 12–058
Chapman Bros. v. Verco Bros. & Co. Ltd (1933) 49 C.L.R. 306 1–057
Chappell & Co. Ltd v. Nestlé Co. Ltd [1960] A.C. 87; [1959] 3 W.L.R. 168; 103 S.J. 561; [1959] 2 All E.R. 701 .... 1–037, 14–066
Chapple v. Cooper (1844) 13 M. & W. 252; 13 L.J.Ex. 286; 3 L.T. (O.S.) 340, 153 E.R. 105 2–030
Chaproniere v. Mason (1905) 21 T.L.R. 633 11–030
Charge Card Services Ltd, *Re* [1987] Ch. 150, on appeal [1989] Ch. 497; [1988] F.L.R. 308; (1989) 8 Tr.L. 86 .... 1–084, 2–002, 2–044, 5–097, 9–033, 9–034, 22–144, 23–101, 23–103, 23–106
Chargeurs Réunis Compagnie Francaise de Navigation à Vapeur v. English & American Shipping Co. (1921) 9 Ll.L.R. 464 5–011
Charles v. Blackwell (1877) 2 C.P.D. 151; 46 L.J.C.P. 368; 36 L.T. 195; 25 W.R. 472 .... 22–020, 22–024, 22–026
Charles Rickards Ltd v. Oppenhaim *See* Rickards (Charles) Ltd v. Oppenhaim.
Charlotte, *The* [1908] P. 206 .... 5–011, 5–140, 19–099, 19–103
Charlotte Thirty Ltd v. Croker Ltd (1990) 24 Con.L.R. 46 13–090
Charlson v. Warner (Unreported, December 9, 1999), CC 8–100
Charnock v. Liverpool Corporation [1968] 1 W.L.R. 1498; 112 S.J. 781; [1968] 3 All E.R. 473 .... 14–006, 14–049, 14–052A, 18–117
Charrington & Co. Ltd v. Wooder [1914] A.C. 71; 83 L.J.K.B. 220; 110 L.T. 548; 30 T.L.R. 176; 58 S.J. 152 .... 16–066, 16–070
Charron v. Montreal Trust Co. (1958) 15 D.L.R. (2d) 240 25–084
Charter v. Sullivan [1957] 2 Q.B. 117; [1957] 2 W.L.R. 528; [1957] 1 All E.R. 809 .. 16–052, 16–063, 16–064, 16–065, 16–066, 16–067, 16–075, 16–079, 17–004, 17–005
Chartered Bank of India v. Henderson (1874) L.R. 5 P.C. 501; 30 L.T. 578 18–088
Chartered Mercantile Bank of India v. Netherlands India Steam Navigation Co. (1883) 10 Q.B.D. 521 25–070
Chartered Mercantile Bank of India, London and China v. Dickson (1871) L.R. 3 P.C. 574 22–109
Chartered Trust plc v. Conlay [1998] C.L.Y. 2516 (Cty Ct) 7–091
Charterhouse Credit Co. Ltd v. Tolly [1963] 2 Q.B. 683; [1963] 2 W.L.R. 1168; 107 S.J. 234; [1963] 2 All E.R. 432 .... 2–008, 12–067, 13–042, 13–044, 13–048

Chase Manhattan Bank v. Equibank, 394 F. Supp. 352 (1975); 550 F.2d. 882 (1977) 23–236, 23–239, 23–247
—— v. Israel British Bank (London) Ltd [1981] Ch. 105; [1980] 2 W.L.R. 202; (1979) 124 S.J. 99; [1979] 3 All E.R. 1025 .... 22–090, 25–146
Chatenay v. Brazilian Submarine Telegraph Co. [1891] 1 Q.B. 79; [1886–90] All E.R. 339; 60 L.J.Q.B. 295; 63 L.T. 739 .... 25–009, 25–010, 25–081
Cheetham & Co. v. Thornham Spinning Co. [1964] 2 Lloyd's Rep. 17 .... 5–026, 5–071, 18–071, 19–098, 19–102, 19–106
Cheikh Boutros Selin El-Khoury v. Ceylon Shipping Lines (The Madeleine) [1967] 2 Lloyd's Rep. 224 12–021
Chellaram & Sons (London) Ltd v. Butlers Warehousing & Distribution Ltd [1978] 2 Lloyd's Rep. 412 21–073
Chellaram (P.S.) & Co. Ltd v. China Ocean Shipping Co. (The Zhi Jiang Kou) [1991] 1 Lloyd's Rep. 493, Aust. Ct. 2–012, 18–187, 20–080, 21–076, 21–083, 21–086, 21–094, 21–095
Chelmsford Auctions Ltd v. Poole [1973] Q.B. 542; [1973] 2 W.L.R. 219; (1972) 117 S.J. 219; [1973] 1 All E.R. 810 3–004
Chelsea Yacht & Boat Co. Ltd v. Pope [2000] 1 W.L.R. 1941; [2001] 2 All E.R. 409; (2001) 33 H.L.R. 25; [2000] L. & T.R. 401; [2000] 2 E.G.L.R. 23; [2000] 22 E.G. 139; (2000) 80 P. & C.R. D36; *The Times*, June 7, 2000, CA 1–096
Chemiefarma v. E.C. Commission [1970] E.C.R. 661 3–041
Cherry and McDougall v. Colonial Bank of Australasia (1869) L.R. 3 P.C. 24; 6 Moo.P.C.C. (N.S.) 235; 38 L.J.P.C. 49; 16 E.R. 714 10–009
Chesapeak & O.R. Co. v. State National Bank of Maysville (1939) 133 S.W. 2d 511 18–032
Cheshire v. Bailey [1905] 1 K.B. 237 5–057
Chesmer v. Noyes (1815) 4 Camp. 129 22–136
Chester Grosvenor Hotel Co. Ltd v. Alfred McAlpine Management Ltd 56 B.L.R. 115 13–095
Chesterman v. Lamb (1834) 2 A. & E. 129; 4 Nev. & M.K.B. 12–065
Chesterman's Trust, *Re*, Mott v. Browning [1923] 2 Ch. 466; [1923] All E.R. 705; 93 L.J.Ch. 263; 130 L.T. 109 25–166
Cheverny Consulting Ltd v. Whitehead Mann Ltd [2005] EWHC 2431, Ch D 13–056
Chevron International Oil Co. Ltd v. A/S Sea Team (The T.S. Havprins) [1983] 2 Lloyd's Rep. 356; [1983] Com.L.R. 172 .... 2–012, 25–079
Chichester Journey Ltd v. Mowlem (John) & Co. plc (1987) 42 Build.L.R. 100 2–013
Chidell v. Galsworthy (1859) 6 C.B. (N.S.) 471; 33 L.T. (O.S.) 94; 141 E.R. 541 .... 5–082, 5–094
Chidwick v. Beer [1974] R.T.R. 415; [1974] Crim.L.R. 267 .... 14–107, 14–112
Chilean Nitrate Sale Corp. v. Marine Transportation Co. Ltd [1980] 1 Lloyd's Rep. 638 .... 8–078, 8–080
Chilewich Partners v. MV Alligator Fortune [1994] 2 Lloyd's Rep. 314 18–063
Chilton v. Saga Holidays [1986] 1 All E.R. 841 14–101
Chilvers v. Rayner [1984] 1 W.L.R. 328; (1984) 148 J.P. 50; (1984) 128 S.J. 130; [1984] 1 All E.R. 843; (1984) 78 Cr.App.R. 59; (1984) 81 L.S.Gaz. 741 14–108
China Mutual Trading Co. v. Banque Belge Pour L'Etranger (Extreme Orient) SA (1954) 39 Hong Kong L.R. 144 .... 22–010, 22–012, 22–014
China National Foreign Trade Transportation Corporation v. Evlogia Shipping Co. SA of Panama (The Mihalios Xilas) [1979] 1 W.L.R. 1018 12–037
China-Pacific SA v. Food Corp. of India, (The Winson) [1982] A.C. 939; [1981] 3 W.L.R. 860; (1981) 125 S.J. 808; [1981] 3 All E.R. 688; [1982] 1 Lloyd's Rep. 117 .... 3–006, 6–026, 6–027, 12–065, 15–044, 15–088, 15–106
China Shipbuilding Corp. v. Nippon Yusen Kabukishi Kaisha (The Seta Maru, The Saikyo and The Suma) [2000] 1 Lloyd's Rep. 367; [2000] C.L.C. 566, QBD (Comm Ct) 13–033, 13–052
Chinery v. Viall (1860) 5 H. & N. 288; 29 L.J.Ex. 180; 2 L.T. 466; 8 W.R. 629 .... 1–072, 5–003, 7–002, 15–057, 15–110, 16–015, 17–105, 17–106
Chitral, The *See* International Ait and Sea Cargo GmbH v. Owners of the Chitral.
Christopher Hill Ltd v. Ashington Piggeries Ltd. *See* Ashington Piggeries Ltd v. Christopher Hill Ltd.
Chuan Hiap Seng (1979) Pte. Ltd v. Progress Manufacturing Pte. Ltd [1995] 2 Singapore L.R. 641 12–031

Chubb Cash Ltd v. John Crilley & Son [1983] 1 W.L.R. 599; (1983) 127 S.J. 153; [1983] 2 All E.R. 294; [1983] Com.L.R. 153 ..... 4–013, 7–002, 7–015, 7–105, 17–106
Churchward v. R. (1865) L.R. 1 Q.B. 173 ..... 2–009, 8–058
Cia Portorafti Commerciale SA v. Ultramar Panama Inc (The Captain Gregos) (No.2) [1990] 2 Lloyd's Rep. 395, CA 18–034, 18–066
Ciampa v. British India Steam Navigation Co. Ltd [1915] 2 K.B. 774; 84 L.J.K.B. 1652; 20 Com.Cas. 247 8–091
Cie Commerciale Sucres et Denrees v. C. Czarnikow Ltd; Naxos, The. *See* Compagnie Commerciale Sucres et Denrees v. C. Czarnikow Ltd; Nakos, The.
Cie Continentale d'Importation v. Handelsvertretung der Union der Russian Soviet Republic in Deutschland (1928) 138 L.T. 663 ..... 19–018, 19–019
Cie Continentale d'Importation Zurich SA v. Ispahani Ltd [1962] 1 Lloyd's Rep. 213 20–054
Cie Francaise des Chemins de Fer Paris-Orléans v. Leeston Shipping Co. (1919) 1 Ll.L.R. 235 ..... 1–011, 10–040, 12–071
Cie Francaise d'Importation et Distribution v. Deutsche Continental Handelsgesellschaft [1985] 2 Lloyd's Rep. 592 8–031
Cie General Maritime v. Diakan Spirit SA (The Ymnos) [1982] 2 Lloyd's Rep. 574 10–033
Cinderella Rockerfellas Ltd v. Rudd (Valuation Officer); *sub nom*. Rudd (Valuation Officer) v. Cinderella Rockerfellas Ltd [2003] EWCA Civ 529; [2003] 1 W.L.R. 2423; [2003] 3 All E.R. 219; [2003] R.A. 113; [2003] 17 E.G.C.S. 147; (2003) 147 S.J.L.B. 473; [2003] N.P.C. 52; *The Times*, April 23, 2003; *Independent*, April 16, 2003, CA 1–096
Circle Freight International Ltd v. Medeast Gulf Exports Ltd [1988] 2 Lloyd's Rep. 427 ..... 2–012, 13–014
Citibank N/A v. Brown Shipley & Co.; Midland Bank v. Same [1991] 2 All E.R. 690; [1991] 1 Lloyd's Rep. 576; (1990) 140 N.L.J. 1753 ..... 22–020, 22–057
City and Westminster Properties (1934) Ltd v. Mudd [1959] Ch. 129; [1958] 3 W.L.R. 312; 102 S.J. 582; [1958] 2 All E.R. 733 ..... 10–012, 14–042
City Bank v. Barrow (1880) 5 App.Cas. 664; 43 L.T. 393 ..... 7–032, 25–121, 25–131,
City Fur Manufacturing Co. v. Fureenbond [1937] 1 All E.R. 799 ..... 7–035, 7–057, 7–072
City Index Ltd v. Leslie [1992] Q.B. 98; [1991] 3 W.L.R. 207; [1991] 3 All E.R. 180; [1991] B.C.L.C. 643; (1991) 141 N.L.J. 419; *The Times*, March 21, 1991; *The Independent*, April 5, 1991; *The Financial Times*, March 19, 1991, CA; affirming (1990) 140 N.L.J. 1572; *The Times*, October 3, 1990; *The Independent*, August 3, 1990, DC 1–104
City Motors (1933) Property Ltd v. Southern Aerial Super Service Property Ltd (1961) 106 C.L.R. 477 ..... 5–021, 5–132, 18–226
Clan Line Steamers Ltd v. Liverpool and London War Risks Insurance Assn. Ltd [1943] K.B. 209 8–097
Clapham v. Ives (1904) 91 L.T. 69; 48 S.J. 417 1–066
Clare v. Maynard (1837) 6 A. & E. 519 17–052
Claridge v. Dalton (1815) 4 M. & S. 226; 105 E.R. 818 22–132
Clark v. Bulmer (1843) 11 M. & W. 243; 1 Dow. & L. 367; 12 L.J.Ex. 463; 152 E.R. 793 ..... 1–043, 5–093
—— v. Cox, McEuen & Co. [1921] 1 K.B. 139; 89 L.J.K.B. 59; 122 l.T. 67; 15 Asp.M.L.C. 5; 25 Com.Cas. 94 19–083
—— v. England (1916) 29 D.L.R. 374 4–032
—— v. Perks; Macleod (Inspector of Taxes) v. Perks; Guild (Inspector of Taxes) v. Newrick; *sub nom.* Clark v. Perks (Inspector of Taxes); Perks v. Clark (Inspector of Taxes) [2001] EWCA Civ 1228; [2001] 2 Lloyd's Rep. 431; [2001] S.T.C. 1254; [2001] B.T.C. 336; [2001] S.T.I. 1086; (2001) 98(33) L.S.G. 32; (2001) 145 S.J.L.B. 214; *The Times*, October 2, 2001, CA; reversing [2000] S.T.C. 428; [2000] B.T.C. 133; [2000] S.T.I. 667; (2000) 97(19) L.S.G. 44; *The Times*, May 3, 2000, Ch D 1–082
—— v. Wallis (1866) 35 Beav. 460; 55 E.R. 974 15–115
Clark Taylor & Co. Ltd v. Quality Site Development (Edinburgh) Ltd 1981 S.L.T. 308 5–152
Clarke, *Re* (1887) 36 Ch.D. 348 ..... 1–107, 5–094, 17–099
—— v. Army and Navy Co-operative Society Ltd [1903] 1 K.B. 155; 72 L.J.K.B. 153; 88 L.T. 1; 19 T.L.R. 80 13–024

Clarke v. Burn (1866) 14 L.T. 439; 2 Mar.L.C. 342 .... 8–077, 8–080, 8–085
—— v. Dickson (1858) E. B. & E. 148; 27 L.J.Q.B. 223; 31 L.T. (O.S.) 97; 4 Jur. (N.S.) 832 12–007
—— v. Dunraven (Earl), (The Satanita) [1897] A.C. 59; 66 L.J.P. 1; 75 L.T. 337; 13 T.L.R. 58; Asp.M.L.C. 190 18–142
—— v. Harper and Robinson [1938] N.I. 162 25–011
—— v. Hutchins (1811) 14 East. 475; 104 E.R. 683 8–015
—— v. McMahon [1939] SAS.R. 64 11–014
—— v. Millwall Dock Co. (1886) 17 Q.B.D. 494; 55 L.J.Q.B. 378; 54 L.T. 814; 51 J.P. 5; 34 W.R. 698; 2 T.L.R. 669 5–092
—— v. Mumford (1811) 3 Camp. 67 1–046
—— v. Reilly & Sons (1962) 96 I.L.T.R. 96 .... 1–037, 1–039, 5–017
—— v. Spence (1836) 4 A. & El. 448; 1 Har. & W. 760; 6 Nev. & M.K.B. 399; 5 L.J.K.B. 161; 11 E.R. 855 .... 5–091, 5–092
—— v. West Ham Corporation [1909] 2 K.B. 858 13–016
—— v. Westrope (1856) 18 C.B. 765; 25 L.J.C.P. 287; 20 J.P. 728; 139 E.R. 1572 2–049
Clay v. Yates (1856) 1 H. & N. 73; 25 L.J.Ex. 237; 27 L.T. (O.S.) 126; 2 Jur. (N.S.) 908; 4 W.R. 557; 156 E.R. 1123 .... 1–045, 1–047, 3–029
Claydon v. Bradley [1987] 1 W.L.R. 521; (1987) 131 S.J. 593; [1987] 1 All E.R. 522; [1987] F.L.R. 111; (1987) 84 L.S.Gaz. 1571; (1987) 137 New L.J. 57 22–043
Clayton's Case (1816) Mer. 572 7–003
Clea Shipping Corporation v. Bulk Oil International Ltd (The Alaskan Trader) (No. 2) [1984] 1 All E.R. 129; [1983] 2 Lloyd's Rep. 645; [1984] L.M.C.L.Q. 378 .. 16–059, 19–214, 20–126
Clef Aquitaine S.A.R.L. v. Laporte Materials (Barrow) Ltd; *sub nom.* Clef Aquitaine S.A.R.L. v. Sovereign Chemical Industries Ltd [2001] Q.B. 488; [2000] 3 W.L.R. 1760; [2000] 3 All E.R. 493, CA 4–022, 12–012
Clegg v. Andersson (t/a Nordic Marine) [2003] EWCA Civ 320; [2003] 1 All E.R. (Comm) 721; [2003] 2 Lloyd's Rep. 32; (2003) 100(20) L.S.G. 28; *The Times*, April 14, 2003, CA 12–055, 14–021, 19–154, 20–107
—— v. Baretta (1887) 56 L.T. 775 22–023
—— v. Hands (1890) 44 Ch.D. 503 3–038
—— v. Levy (1812) 3 Camp. 166 25–086
Clegg Parkinson Co. v. Earby Gas Co. [1896] 1 Q.B. 592; 65 L.J.Q.B. 339; 44 W.R. 606; 12 T.L.R. 241 1–071
Clemens (E.) Horst Co. v. Biddell Bros. [1912] A.C. 18; 81 L.J.K.B. 42; 105 L.T. 563; 28 T.L.R. 42; 56 S.J. 50; 12 Asp.M.L.C. 80; 17 Com.Cas. 55 ... 9–061, 9–067, 12–042, 18–006, 19–010, 19–016, 19–053, 19–069, 19–075, 19–076, 19–099, 19–102, 19–110, 19–145, 23–234
Cleveland Manufacturing Co. Ltd v. Muslim Commercial Bank Ltd [1981] 2 Lloyd's Rep. 646; [1981] Com.L.R. 247 23–161
Cleveland Petroleum Co. Ltd v. Dartstone [1969] 1 W.L.R. 116; (1968) 112 S.J. 962; [1968] 1 All E.R. 201; 20 P. & C.R. 235 .... 3–036, 3–038, 8–061
Clifford v. Watts (1870) L.R. 5 C.P. 577 3–022
Clifford Chance v. Silver [1992] N.P.C. 103; *Financial Times*, July 31, 1992; *The Times*, September 11, 1992, CA 22–058
Clifford Harris & Co v. Solland International Ltd (No.2) [2005] EWHC 141; [2005] 2 All E.R. 334; [2005] 3 Costs L.R. 414; (2005) 102(17) L.S.G. 32; *The Times*, March 10, 2005, Ch D 15–058
Clipper Maritime v. Shirlstar Container Transport (The Anemone) [1987] 1 Lloyd's Rep. 546 18–030
Clode v. Bayley (1843) 12 M. & W. 51; 13 L.J.Ex. 17; 7 Jur. 1092 22–128
Close Asset Finance Ltd v. Care Graphics Machinery Ltd [2000] 1 W.L.R. 1509; [2000] 2 All E.R. 620; [2000] C.C.L.R. 18; (2000) 150 N.L.J. 99; *The Times*, March 7, 2000, CA 1–053, 7–068
Clough v. London & North Western Railway Co. (1871) L.R. 7 Ex. 26; 41 L.J.Ex. 17; 25 L.T. 708; 20 W.R. 189 .... 12–006, 12–009
Clough Mill Ltd v. Martin [1985] 1 W.L.R. 111; (1984) 128 S.J. 850; [1984] 3 All E.R. 982; (1985) 82 L.S. Gaz. 116; [1985] L.M.C.L.Q. 15 ..... 5–144, 5–145, 5–146, 5–147, 5–148, 5–149, 5–150, 15–113, 15–115, 16–028
Club Speciality (Overseas) Inc. v. United Marine (1939) Ltd [1971] 1 Lloyd's Rep. 482 21–073

Clugas v. Penaluna (1791) 4 T.R. 466 25–119
Clyde Cycle Co. v. Hargreaves (1898) 78 L.T. 296; 14 T.L.R. 338 2–031
Clydebank Engineering and Shipbuilding Co. Ltd v. Don Jose Ramos Yzquierdoy Castaneda [1905] A.C. 6; 74 L.J.C.P. 1; 91 L.T. 666; 21 T.L.R. 58 16–032
Coast Lines Ltd v. Hudig and Veder Chartering N.V. [1972] 2 Q.B. 34; [1972] 2 W.L.R. 280; (1971) 116 S.J. 119; [1972] 1 All E.R. 451; [1972] 1 Lloyd's Rep. 53 .... 25–008, 25–010, 25–058, 25–071
Coastal (Bermuda) Ltd v. Esso Petroleum Co. Ltd [1984] 1 Lloyd's Rep. 11 13–040
Coastal (Bermuda) Petroleum Ltd v. VTT Vulcan Petroleum SA (The Marine Star) [1993] 1 Lloyd's Rep. 329 .... 16–058, 18–318, 19–021, 19–140
—— v. VTT Vulcan Marine Petroleum SA (The Marine Star) (No.2) [1994] 2 Lloyd's Rep. 629 (revsd. on another point) [1996] 2 Lloyd's Rep. 383 .... 16–060, 17–035, 18–267, 19–176
—— v. VTT Vulcan Petroleum SA; Marine Spar, The, [1996] 2 Lloyd's Rep. 8–099
Coastal Estates Property Ltd v. Melevende [1965] V.R. 433 12–006
Coastal International Trading Ltd v. Maroil A.G. [1988] 1 Lloyd's Rep. 92 .... 17–031, 17–035, 19–176, 19–182
Coates v. Railton (1827) 6 B. & C. 422; 9 Dow. & Ry. K.B. 593; 5 L.J. (o.s.) K.B. 209; 108 E.R. 507 .... 15–068, 15–069
—— v. Wilson (1804) 5 Esp. 152 2–031
Coats v. Chaplin (1842) 3 Q.B. 483; 2 Gal. & Dav. 552; 11 L.J.Q.B. 315; 6 Jur. 1123; 114 E.R. 592 5–009
—— v. I.R.C. [1897] 2 Q.B. 423; 66 L.J.Q.B. 732; 77 L.T. 270; 61 J.P. 693; 46 W.R. 1; 13 T.L.R. 548 1–027
Cobbold v. Caston (1824) 1 Bing. 399; 8 Moore C.P. 456; 2 L.J. (o.s.) X.P. 38; 130 E.R. 161 1–048
Cobec Brazilian Trading and Warehousing Corp. v. Toepfer [1983] 2 Lloyd's Rep. 386 .... 8–046, 8–064, 8–065, 8–076, 19–012, 19–036, 19–150, 19–151
Cochran v. McDonald 161 P.(2d) 305 (1945) (Sup.Ct. of Washington) 14–014
Cochrane v. Moore (1890) 25 Q.B.D. 57 .... 1–032, 1–036, 2–026, 18–088
Cock v. Taylor (1811) 13 East 399; 2 Camp. 587; 104 E.R. 424 18–099
Cockburn v. Alexander (1848) 6 C.B. 791; 18 L.J.C.P. 74; 12 L.T. (o.s.) 349; 13 Jur. 13 17–002
Cocker v. McMullen (1900) 81 L.T. 784; 19 Cox C.C. 429 .... 5–080, 5–088
Cockerton v. Naviera Aznar SA [1960] 2 Lloyd's Rep. 450 .... 2–012, 13–013, 13–017, 14–077
Coddington v. Paleologo (1867) L.R. 2 Ex. 193; 36 L.J.Ex. 73; 15 L.T. 581; 15 W.R. 961 .... 8–025, 8–036, 8–067, 8–077, 8–080
Coffey v. Dickson [1960] N.Z.L.R. 1135 .... 10–012, 10–020
Coggs v. Bernard (1703) 2 Ld. Raym. 909 .... 6–026, 6–028
Cohen v. Foster (1892) 61 L.J.Q.B. 643; 66 I.T. 616; 8 T.L.R. 519 5–135
—— v. Hale (1878) 3 Q.B.D. 371 9–030
—— v. Roche [1927] 1 K.B. 169; 95 L.J.K.B. 945; 136 L.T. 219; 42 T.L.R. 674; 70 S.J. 942 .... 3–009, 15–022, 15–023, 15–116, 17–098, 17–099, 17–100, 17–105
Cohen & Co. v. Ockerby & Co. Ltd (1917) 24 C.L.R. 288 .... 9–017, 9–018, 20–015, 20–058
Cointat v. Myham & Son (1914) 84 L.J.K.B. 2253; 110 L.T. 749; 78 J.P. 193; 30 T.L.R. 282; 12 L.G.R. 274; on appeal [1913] 2 K.B. 220 .... 11–078, 13–013, 17–065, 17–069
Colchester Motor Hire-Purchase Co. Ltd v. Wragge (1923) *Jones & Proud, p. 90* 1–066
Coldunell Ltd v. Gallon [1986] Q.B. 1184; [1986] 2 W.L.R. 466; (1986) 130 S.J. 88; [1986] 1 All E.R. 429; [1986] F.L.R. 183; (1986) 82 L.S.Gaz. 520 14–150
Cole v. North Western Bank (1875) L.R. 10 C.P. 354; 44 L.J.C.P. 233; 32 L.T. 733 .... 7–008, 7–013, 7–032, 7–037, 7–038, 7–069
Coleman v. Harvey [1989] 1 N.Z.L.R. 723 .... 1–058, 5–149
Coles v. Trecothick (1804) 9 Ves. 234; 1 Smith K.B. 233; 32 E.R. 592 17–100
Colin & Shields v. W. Weddel & Co. [1952] W.N. 420; [1952] 2 T.L.R. 185; 96 S.J. 547; [1952] 2 All E.R. 337, [1952] 2 Lloyd's Rep. 9 .... 18–171, 18–172, 18–174, 18–181, 18–291, 19–009, 19–031
Collen v. Wright (1857) 8 E. & B. 647 18–045
Colley v. Overseas Exporters [1921] 3 K.B. 302; 90 L.J.K.B. 1301; 126 L.T. 58; 37 T.L.R. 797; 26 Com.Cas. 325 .... 1–029, 5–065, 8–040, 10–039, 16–001, 16–023, 16–024, 16–026, 16–028, 18–244, 19–213, 20–071, 20–073, 20–088, 20–126, 20–128, 20–135

Collier v. Mason (1858) 25 Beav. 200 2–051
Collin v. Duke of Westminster [1985] Q.B. 581; [1985] 2 W.L.R. 553; (1985) 129 S.J. 116; [1985] 1 All E.R. 463; (1985) 50 P. & C.R. 380; (1984) 17 H.L.R. 246; [1985] 1 E.G.L.R. 109; (1985) 273 E.G. 881; (1984) 25 R.V.R. 4; (1985) 82 L.S.Gaz. 767 8–031
Collinge v. Underwood (1839) 9 A. & E. 633 4–023
Collins v. Howell-Jones (1980) 259 E.G. 331 13–055
Collins Trading Co. Property Ltd v. Maher [1969] V.R. 20 1–043
Collyer v. Isaacs (1881) 19 Ch.D. 342; 51 L.J.Ch. 14; 30 W.R. 70 .... 1–107, 5–094
Colonial Bank v. Cady (1890) 15 App.Cas. 267; 60 L.J.Ch. 131; 63 L.T. 27; 39 W.R. 17; 6 T.L.R. 329 .... 7–008, 7–013
Colonial Cedar Co. v. Royal Wood Products Inc., 448 So. 2d 1218 (1984) 23–245
Colonial Insurance Co. of New Zealand v. Adelaide Marine Insurance Co. (1886) 12 App.Cas. 128 .... 5–086, 5–097, 6–012, 8–046, 8–057, 8–065, 20–039, 20–070, 20–071, 20–074, 20–088, 20–101
Coloniale Import-Export v. Loumidis Sons [1978] 2 Lloyd's Rep. 560 .... 8–098, 18–281, 18–282
Colorado National Bank v. Board of County Commissioners (1981) 634 P. (2d) 32 (colo. 1981) 23–245
Colt Telecom Group Plc, Re. *See* Highberry Ltd v. Colt Telecom Group Plc (No.2)
Columbia Shirt Co., *Re* (1922) 3 C.B.R. 268 .... 25–011, 25–183
Colwill v. Reeves (1811) 2 Camp. 575; 170 E.R. 1257 5–044
Combe v. Combe [1951] 2 K.B. 215; [1951] 1 T.L.R. 811; 95 S.J. 317; [1951] 1 All E.R. 767 9–024
Comber v. Leyland [1898] A.C. 524 .... 9–042, 9–048
Comet Group p.l.c. v. British Sky Broadcasting Ltd (1991) *The Times*, April 26, 1991 1–048
Cominco Ltd v. Westinghouse Canada Ltd (1981) 127 D.L.R. (3d) 544 .... 11–055, 11–057
Commercial Banking Co. of Sydney Ltd v. Jalsard Pty. Ltd [1973] A.C. 279; [1972] 3 W.L.R. 566; 116 S.J. 695; [1972] 2 Lloyd's Rep. 529 .... 23–054, 23–117, 23–121, 23–127, 23–160, 23–235
—— v. Mann [1961] A.C. 1 [1960] 3 W.L.R. 726; 104 S.J. 846; [1960] 3 All E.R. 482 .... 22–019, 22–023
—— v. Patrick Intermarine Acceptances Ltd (1978) 19 A.L.R. 563 23–267
Commercial Fibres (Ireland) Ltd v. Zabaida [1975] 1 Lloyd's Rep. 27 .... 12–043, 20–108
Commerzbank A/G v. Large 1977 S.L.T. 219 25–194
Commission Car Sales (Hastings) Ltd v. Saul [1957] N.Z.L.R. 144 .... 15–112, 15–113, 15–124, 15–132
Commission for New Towns v. Cooper Ltd; *sub nom.* Milton Keynes Development Corp. v. Cooper Ltd [1995] Ch. 259; [1995] 2 W.L.R. 677; [1995] 2 All E.R. 929, CA 12–128
Commission of the European Communities v. France (C52/00) [2002] E.C.R. I-3827, ECJ 14–080
—— v. Greece (C154/00) [2002] E.C.R. I-3879, ECJ 14–080
—— v. Italy (Case 7/68) [1968] E.C.R. 423 3–042
—— v. Italy (C35/96); *sub nom.* Customs Agents, *Re* (C35/96) [1998] E.C.R. 1–3851; [1998] 5 C.M.L.R. 889, ECJ (5th Chamber) 3–041
—— v. Spain (C70/03) [2004] E.C.R. I-7999 25–055
—— v. Sweden (C478/99); *sub nom.* Implementation of the Unfair Consumer Terms Directive, Re (C478/99) [2002] E.C.R. I-4147; [2004] 2 C.M.L.R. 34, ECJ 14–035
—— v. United Kingdom (C300/95); *sub nom.* Product Liability Directive, *Re* [1997] All E.R. (E.C.) 481; [1997] E.C.R. 1–2649; [1997] 3 C.M.L.R. 923; *The Times*, June 23, 1997, ECJ (5th Chamber) 14–089
Commissioners of Crown Lands v. Page [1960] 2 Q.B. 274; [1960] 3 W.L.R. 446; 104 S.J. 642; [1960] 2 All E.R. 726 6–048
Commissioners of Customs and Excise v. Diners Club Ltd. *See* Customs and Excise Commissioners v. Diners Club Ltd. Commissioners of Stamps v. Queensland Meat Export Co. Ltd [1917] A.C. 624; 86 L.J.P.C. 202 5–028
Commissioners of Taxation v. Australia and New Zealand Banking Group Ltd (1979) 53 A.L.J.R. 336 22–142
Commonwealth Petrochemicals Ltd v. S.S. Puerto Rico 455 F. Supp. 310 (1978) 21–086
Commonwealth Portland Cement Co. Ltd v. Weber, Lohmann & Co. Ltd [1905] A.C. 66; 74 L.J.P.C. 25; 91 L.T. 813; 53 W.R. 337; 31 T.L.R. 149; 10 Asp.M.L.C. 27 23–176

Commonwealth Trust v. Akotey [1926] A.C. 72 .... 7–007, 7–013, 7–016
Compania Naviera Vasconzada v. Churchill & Sim; Compania Naviera Vasconzada v. Burton & Co [1906] 1 K.B. 237, KBD 18–049
Compania Portorafti Commerciale SA v. Ultramar Panama Inc (The Captain Gregos) (No.2). *See* Cia Portorafti Commerciale SA v. Ultramar Panama Inc (The Captain Gregos) (No.2)
Compagnie Commerciale Sucres et Denrees v. C. Czarnikow Ltd; Naxos, The [1990] 1 W.L.R. 1337; [1990] 3 All E.R. 641; (1990) 134 S.J. 1301; [1990] 1 Lloyd's Rep. 29 .... 8–025, 8–036, 8–039, 8–040, 9–005, 10–037, 14–006, 18–357, 19–063, 20–020, 20–029, 20–030, 20–032, 20–033, 20–046, 20–047
Compagnie d'Armement Maritime SA v. Compagnie Tunisienne de Navigation SA [1971] A.C. 572; [1970] 3 W.L.R. 389; 11 S.J. 618; [1970] 3 All E.R. 71 ..... 25–005, 25–007, 25–008, 25–010, 25–012, 25–031, 25–065, 25–156
Compagnie de Commerce et Commission S.A.R.L. v. Parkinson Stove Co. [1953] 2 Lloyd's Rep. 487, CA 2–011
Compagnie de Renflouement, etc. v. W. Seymour Plant Sales & Hire Ltd [1981] 2 Lloyd's Rep. 466 .... 15–107, 15–113
Compania Commercial Naviera San Martin SA v. China National Foreign Trade Transportation Corp. (The Costanza M) [1981] 2 Lloyd's Rep. 147 .... 18–052, 18–110, 18–123
Compania Continental del Peru SA v. Evelpis Shipping Corp. (The Agiaskepi) [1992] 2 Lloyd's Rep. 467 18–139
Compania Financiera Soleada SA, Netherlands Antilles Ships Management Corp. and Dammers and van der Heide's Shipping and Trading Co. v. Hamoor Tanker Corp. Inc. (The Borag) [1981] 1 W.L.R. 274; (1981) 125 S.J. 185; [1981] 1 All E.R. 856; [1981] 1 Lloyd's Rep. 483; [1981] Com.L.R. 29 .... 16–007, 16–050
Compania Naviera Maropan S/A v. Bowaters Lloyd Pulp and Paper Mills Ltd [1955] 2 Q.B. 68; [1955] 2 W.L.R. 998; 99 S.J. 336; [1955] 2 All E.R. 241; [1955] 1 Lloyd's Rep. 349 16–049
Compania Naviera Micro SA v. Shipley International Inc. (The Parouth) [1982] 2 Lloyd's Rep. 351, CA 25–079, 25–080
Companis Naviera Vasconzada v. Churchill & Sim [1906] 1 K.B. 237; 75 L.J.K.B. 94; 94 L.T. 59; 54 W.R. 406; 22 T.L.R. 85; 50 S.J. 76; 10 Asp.M.L.C. 177; 11 Com.Cas. 49 .... 18–028, 18–029, 18–030, 18–040
Compania Portorafti Commerciale SA v. Ultramar Panama Inc. (*No. 1*) (The Captain Gregos) [1990] 1 Lloyd's Rep. 310 18–149
—— v.——(*No. 2*) (The Captain Gregos) [1990] 2 Lloyd's Rep. 395 .... 18–029, 18–057, 18–098, 18–113, 18–138, 18–139, 18–142, 18–146, 18–149, 18–209
Company No. 005070 of 1994, A (Mitzebrook Ltd.) *Re* (unreported, October 18, 1994) 22–062
Compaq Computer Ltd v. Abercorn Group Ltd [1991] B.C.C. 484 .... 5–142, 5–151, 5–153, 5–160, 5–161
Comptoir Commercial Anversois v. Power, Son & Co. [1920] 1 K.B. 868; 89 L.J.K.B. 849; 122 L.T. 567; 36 T.L.R. 101 .... 5–140, 8–091, 19–128, 19–134, 19–140
Comptoir d'Achat et de Vente du Boerenbond Belge S/A v. Luis de Ridder Lda (The Julia) [1949] A.C. 293; [1949] L.J.R. 513; 65 T.L.R. 126; 93 S.J. 101; [1949] 1 All E.R. 269; 82 Ll.L.Rep. 270 ... 1–119, 5–101, 6–002, 6–003, 6–005, 8–013, 17–090, 18–170, 18–181, 18–193, 18–286, 18–291, 18–292, 18–302, 18–304, 18–305, 19–002, 19–003, 19–006, 19–007, 19–010, 19–012, 19–036, 19–099, 19–102, 19–110, 19–112, 19–113, 19–136, 19–143, 21–014, 21–016, 21–018, 21–020, 21–021
Compton v. Bagley [1892] 1 Ch. 313; 61 L.J.Ch. 113; 65 L.T. 706 15–123
Computer 2000 Distribution Ltd v. ICM Computer Solutions Plc; *sub nom.* ICM Computer Solutions Plc v. Computer 2000 Distribution Ltd [2004] EWCA Civ 1634; [2005] Info. T.L.R. 147; *The Times*, December 29, 2004, CA 8–023
Concadoro, The [1916] 2 A.C. 199; 85 L.J.P.C. 156; 114 L.T. 962; 32 T.L.R. 465; 13 Asp.M.L.C. 355 8–099
Concordia Trading B.V. v. Richco International Ltd [1991] 1 Lloyd's Rep. 475 .... 19–064, 19–066, 20–022, 20–026, 20–077, 20–114, 20–117
Congimex Companhia Geral, etc., S.A.R.L. v. Tradax Export SA [1983] 1 Lloyd's Rep. 250; CA affirming [1981] 2 Lloyd's Rep. 687 ..... 6–045, 6–046, 6–055, 18–311, 18–315, 18–329, 18–330, 18–335, 18–340, 19–006, 19–008, 19–032, 19–037, 19–137, 20–019, 25–119

Congimex S.A.R.L. (Lisbon) v. Continental Grain Export Corp. (New York) [1979] 2 Lloyd's Rep. 346 .... 18–335, 19–137
Congreve v. Evetts (1854) 10 Exch. 298; 23 L.J.Ex. 273; 24 L.T. (o.s.) 62; 18 Jur. 655; 2 C.I.R. 1253; 156 E.R. 457 .... 5–082, 5–094, 8–010
Connaught Restaurants v. Indoor Leisure [1994] 1 W.L.R. 501; [1994] 4 All E.R. 834; [1993] N.P.C. 118; [1993] E.G.C.S. 143; 46 E.G. 184; 143 N.L.J. 1188; *The Times*, July 27, 1993, CA 17–049
Connecticut General Life Insurance Co. v. Chicago Title & Trust Co., 714 F. 2d 48 (1983) 23–239
Connolly Bros. Ltd (No. 2), *Re* [1912] 2 C.L. 25 .... 5–134, 5–161
Conoca U.K. Ltd v. Limni Maritime Co. Ltd (The Sirina) [1988] 2 Lloyd's Rep. 613 5–009
Conservators of the River Thames v. Smeed, Dean & Co. [1897] 2 Q.B. 334 1–004
Consolidated Oil Ltd v. American Express Bank Ltd [2002] C.L.C. 488, CA 23–276
Consolidated Sales Co. Inc. v. Bank of Hampton Roads 68 S.E. 2d (1952) 23–139
Constantia, The (1807) 6 C.Rob.Adm.R. 321; 165 E.R. 947 .... 15–026, 15–085
Constantine (Joseph) S.S. Line Ltd v. Imperial Smelting Corporation Ltd [1942] A.C. 154 .... 6–034, 6–056, 18–331, 25–205
Consten SA and Grundig-Verkaufs GmbH v. E.C. Commission [1966] C.M.L.R. 418 3–041
Contemporary Cottages (NZ) Ltd v. Margin Traders Ltd [1981] 2 N.Z.L.R. 114 (High Ct of New Zealand) 24–029
Contigroup Companies Inc v. Glencore AG [2004] EWHC 2750; [2005] 1 Lloyd's Rep. 241, QBD 1–087, 17–038, 17–040, 17–045
Continental Contractors Ltd v. Medway Oil and Storage Co. Ltd (1925) 27 Ll.L.R. 124; (1925) 23 Ll.L.R. 55 .... 8–077, 8–078, 8–079, 9–013, 9–020, 19–167, 19–170, 19–207
Continental Enterprises Ltd v. Shandong Zhucheng Foreign Trade Group Co [2005] EWHC 92, QBD 25–024, 25–119
Continental Fertiliser Co. Ltd v. Pionier Shipping Co. Ltd (The Pionier) [1995] 1 Lloyd's Rep. 223, QBD (Comm Ct) 18–054
Continental Grain Co. v. Islamic Republic of Iran Shipping Lines (The Iran Bohonar) [1983] 2 Lloyd's Rep. 620 20–077
Continental Grain Export Corp. v. S.T.M. Grain Ltd [1979] 2 Lloyd's Rep. 460 .... 8–088, 8–091, 8–092, 8–103, 18–345, 18–349, 18–353, 19–141
Continental Illinois National Bank & Trust Co. v. Papanicolaou (The Fedora, the Tatiana and the Eretrea II) [1986] 2 Lloyd's Rep. 441; [1986] Fin. L.R. 373; (1986) 83 L.S.G. 2569; *The Times*, July 15, 1986, CA 13–039
Continental Lines SA v. W.H. Holt & Sons (Chorlton-cum-Hardy) Ltd (1932) 43 Ll.L. Rep. 392, KBD 25–119
Continho Caro & Co., *Re* [1918] 2 Ch. 384 6–042
Contra The Torni [1932] P. 78 25–119
Contronic Distributors Pty. Ltd v. Bank of N.S.W. [1984] 3 N.S.W.R. 110 ... 23–145, 23–277
Cood v. Cood (1863) 33 Beav. 314; 3 New. R. 275; 33 L.J.Ch. 273; 9 Jur. (n.s.) 1335; 55 E.R. 388 25–010
Cook v. Lister (1863) 13 C.B. (n.s.) 543; 32 L.J.C.P. 121 .... 9–025, 9–044, 22–118
—— v. Rodgers (1946) 46 S.R. (N.S.W.) 229 .... 7–037, 7–048
Cook Industries v. Meunerie Liegeois [1981] 1 Lloyd's Rep. 359 ..... 8–030, 8–092, 12–036, 18–349, 18–314, 19–141, 19–150
Cook Industries Inc. v. Tradax Export SA [1983] 1 Lloyd's Rep. 327; affirming [1985] 2 Lloyd's Rep. 454 .... 8–092, 18–350, 18–358, 19–141
Cook (James) Hotel Ltd v. Canx Corporate Services Ltd [1989] 3 N.Z.L.R. 213 9–024
Cooke v. Ludlow (1806) 2 B. & P.N.R. 119; 127 E.R. 569 5–100
—— v. Midland Ry. Co. (1892) 9 T.L.R. 147; 57 J.P. 388 .... 13–017, 14–077
Cooke's Trusts, Re (1887) 3 T.L.R. 558 25–084
Coomber, *Re* Coomber v. Coomber [1911] 1 Ch. 723; 80 L.J.Ch. 399; 104 L.T. 517 ... 5–151
Cooper, *ex p.* (1879) 11 Ch.D. 68 .. 15–027, 15–042, 15–072, 15–077, 15–079, 15–081, 15–084 15–085
Cooper, *Re* [1958] Ch. 922; [1958] 3 W.L.R. 468; 102 S.J. 635; [1958] 3 All E.R. 97 7–111
Cooper v. Bill (1865) 3 H. & C. 722; 34 L.J.Ex. 161; 12 L.T. 466 .... 15–039, 15–049
—— v. Cooper (1888) 13 App. Cas. 88 25–084
—— v. Micklefield Coal & Lime Co. (1912) 107 L.T. 457, 56 S.J. 706 3–044

Cooper v. Phibbs (1867) L.R. 2 H.L. 149 3–019
—— v. Shepherd (1846) 3 C.B. 266 1–072
—— v. Shuttleworth (1856) 25 L.J.Exch. 114 .... 2–049, 2–051
—— v. Stubbs [1925] 2 K.B. 753; [1925] All E.R. 643; 94 L.J.K.B. 903; 133 L.T. 582; 41 T.L.R. 614; 69 S.J. 743; 10 Tax Cas. 44 1–104
Cooper Ewing & Co. v. Hamel and Horley Ltd (1922) 13 Ll.L.R. 446 9–017
Co-operative Centrale Raiffaisen-Boerenleen Bank B.A. v. Sumitomo Bank (The Royan) [1988] 2 Lloyd's Rep. 250, affirming and reversing in part [1987] 1 Lloyd's Rep. 345; [1987] 1 F.T.L.R. 233; [1987] F.L.R. 275 .. 23–018, 23–157, 23–159, 23–149, 23–216
Co-operatieve Vereniging Suiker Unie UA v. Commission of the European Communities (40/73); *sub nom.* European Sugar Cartel (40/73), Re; Suiker Unie v. Commission of the European Communities (40/73) [1975] E.C.R. 1663; [1976] 1 C.M.L.R. 295; [1976] F.S.R. 443; *The Times*, December 23, 1975, ECJ 3–041
Cope v. Doherty (1858) 2 De. G. & J. 614; 27 L.J.Ch. 600; 31 L.T.O.S. 307; 4 Jur. (N.S.) 699; 6 W.R. 695; 44 E.R. 1127 25–191
Coral Petroleum, *Re* 878 F. 2d 830 (5th Cir. 1989) 23–196
Corbett Construction Co. Ltd v. Simplot Chemical Co. Ltd [1971] 2 W.W.R. 332 11–059
Corcoran v. Proser (1873) 22 W.L.R. 222 8–078
Cordery v. Colvin (1863) 14 C.B. (N.S.) 374; 32 L.J.C.P. 210; 9 Jur. (N.S.) 1200; 8 L.J. 245 22–131
Cordew v. Drakeford (1811) 3 Taunt. 382 5–028
Cordova Land Co. Ltd v. Victor Bros. Inc; Cordova Land Co. v. Black Diamond Steamship Corporation [1966] 1 W.L.R. 793; 110 S.J. 290 .... 6–019, 11–040, 18–254, 19–111
Coreck Maritime GmbH v. Handelsveem BV (Case C-387/98) [2000] E.C.R. 1–9337; [2001] C.L.C. 550; [2001] I.L.Pr. 39; *The Times*, December 1, 2000, ECJ (5th Chamber) [1999] I.L.Pr. 721, HR (NL) 25–202
Corfield v. Sevenways Garage Ltd [1985] R.T.R. 109; (1984) 148 J.P. 684; (1985) 4 Tr.L. 172; (1984) 148 J.P.N. 621 .... 11–027, 11–045
—— v. Starr [1981] R.T.R. 380 14–112
Cork v. Greavette Boats Ltd [1940] 4 D.L.R. 202 12–056
Cork Distilleries Co. v. G.S. & W. Railway (1874) L.R. 7 H.L. 269 ... 5–009, 5–098, 15–074
Cornelius v. Banque Franco-Serbe [1942] 1 K.B. 29; [1941] 2 All E.R. 728; 110 L.J.K.B. 573; 165 L.T. 374; 57 T.L.R. 610; 46 Com.Cas. 330 .... 6–045, 22–116
Cornfoot v. Royal Exchange Assurance Cpn. [1904] 1 K.B. 40 8–032
Cornish & Co. v. Kanematsu (1913) 3 S.R. (N.S.W.) 83 19–121
Cornwall v. Henson [1900] 2 Ch. 298 .... 8–080, 15–107, 15–112
Cornwall Properties Ltd v. King [1966] N.Z.L.R. 239 13–029
Coro (Canada) Inc., Re (1997) 360.R. (3d) 563 1–058
Corocraft v. Pan American Airways Inc. [1969] 1 Q.B. 616; [1968] 3 W.L.R. 1273; [1969] 1 All E.R. 82; *sub nom.* Corocraft v. Pan American World Airways Inc. (1968) 112 S.J. 903; *sub nom.* Corocraft and Vendome Jewels v. Pan American Airways Inc. [1968] 2 Lloyd's Rep. 459 21–055
Cort v. Ambergate Railway (1851) 17 Q.B. 127; 20 L.J.K.B. 460; 17 L.T. (O.S.) 179; 15 Jur. 117 E.R. 1229 9–017
Cory v. Thames Ironworks and Shipbuilding Co. Ltd (1868) L.R. 3 Q.B. 181; 37 L.J.Q.B. 68; 17 L.T. 495; 16 W.R. 456 .... 17–039, 17–040, 17–041
Cory (Wm.) & Son Ltd v. I.R.C. [1965] A.C. 1088; [1965] 2 W.L.R. 924; 109 S.J. 254; [1965] 1 All E.R. 917; [1965] 1 Lloyd's Rep. 313; [1965] T.R. 77, 44 A.T.C. 61 .... 1–050, 10–024
—— v. London Corporation [1951] 2 K.B. 476; [1951] 2 T.L.R. 174; 115 J.P. 371; 95 S.J. 465; [1951] 2 All E.R. 85; [1951] 1 Lloyd's Rep. 475 18–341
Cory Bros. & Co. Ltd v. Universe Petroleum Co. Ltd (1933) 46 Ll.L.R. 308 ... 8–058, 8–060
Cosslett (Contractors) Ltd, *Re* [1998] Ch. 495; [1996] 3 W.L.R. 299 5–093
Costello v. Chief Constable of Derbyshire [2001] EWCA Civ 381; [2001] 1 W.L.R. 1437; [2001] 3 All E.R. 150; [2001] 2 Lloyd's Rep. 216, CA 7–006
Cothay v. Tute (1811) 3 Camp. 129; 170 E.R. 1329, N.P. 8–015
Cotronic (U.K.) Ltd v. Dezonie (t/a Wendaland Builders Ltd) [1991] B.C.C. 200; [1991] B.C.L.C. 721; *The Times*, March 8, 1991, CA 18–037
Cottam v. Partridge (1842) 4 M. & G. 271 9–041

Cottee v. Seaton (Douglas) (Used Cars) Ltd [1972] 1 W.L.R. 1408; 116 S.J. 821; [1972] 3 All E.R. 750; [1972] R.T.R. 509; [1972] Crim.L.R. 590 12–012
Cotter v. Luckie [1918] N.Z.L.R. 811 . . . . 11–019, 13–028
Couchman v. Hill [1947] K.B. 554; [1948] L.J.R. 295; 176 L.T. 278; 63 T.L.R. 81; [1947] 1 All E.R. 103 . . . . . . 2–027, 10–012, 10–013, 10–022, 10–037, 11–013, 13–016, 13–024, 13–029, 14–042
Couldery v. Bartrum (1881) 19 Ch.D. 394; 51 L.J.Ch. 265; 45 L.T. 689; 30 W.R. 141 9–024
County Laboratories Ltd v. Mindel (J.) Ltd [1957] Ch. 295; [1957] 2 W.L.R. 541; 101 S.J. 286; [1957] 1 All E.R. 806; L.R. I.R.P.I 3–037
County of Durham Electrical Power Co. v. I.R.C. [1909] 2 K.B. 604; 78 L.J.K.B. 1158; 101 L.T. 51; 73 J.P. 425; 25 T.L.R. 672; 8 L.G.R. 1088 1–085
Coupe v. Guyett [1973] 1 W.L.R. 669; 117 S.J. 415; [1973] 2 All E.R. 1058; 71 L.G.R. 355; [1973] R.T.R. 518; [1973] Crim.L.R. 386 14–108
Coupé Co. v. Maddick [1891] 2 Q.B. 413; 60 L.J.Q.B. 676; 65 L.T. 489; 56 J.P. 39 . . . 5–057, 6–029
Coupland v. Arabian Gulf Oil Co. [1983] 1 W.L.R. 1136; (1983) 127 S.J. 597; [1983] 3 All E.R. 226; (1983) 133 New L.J. 893 25–184
Court Line Ltd v. Dant and Russell Inc. [1939] 3 All E.R. 314; 161 L.T. 35; 83 S.J. 500; 44 Com.Cas. 345; 64 Ll.L.R. 212 6–045
Courtaulds North America v. North Carolina National Bank 528 F. 2d 802 (1975) . . 23–052, 23–116, 23–201, 23–213
Courteen Seed Co. v. Hong Kong and Shanghai Banking Corporation 215 N.Y.S. 525 (1926), affd. 157 N.E. 272 (1927) . . . 23–061, 23–180, 23–182, 23–188, 23–194, 23–195
Courtney & Fairbairn Ltd v. Tolaini Bros. (Hotels) Ltd [1975] 1 W.L.R. 297; (1974) 119 S.J. 134; [1975] All E.R. 716 2–016
Cousins (H.) & Co. Ltd v. D. and C. Carriers Ltd [1971] 2 Q.B. 230; [1971] 2 W.L.R. 85; (1970) 114 S.J. 882; [1971] 1 All E.R. 55; [1970] 2 Lloyd's Rep. 397 16–007
Couston, Thomson & Co. v. Chapman (1872) L.R. 2 Sc. & Div. 250 12–055
Couturier v. Hastie (1856) 5 H.L.C. 673 . . . . 1–126, 1–134, 18–209, 19–008, 19–082, 19–113, 21–032
Covas v. Bingham (1853) 2 E. & B. 836; 2 C.L.R. 212; 23 L.J.Q.B. 26; J.P. 569; 18 Jur. 596; 118 E.R. 980 . . . . 8–056, 13–034, 19–040, 21–035
Coventry v. Gladstone (1868) L.R. 6 Eq. 44; 37 L.J.Ch. 492; 16 W.R. 837 . . . . 8–013, 15–078
Coventry City Council v. Lazarus (1996) 160 J.P. 188; [1996] C.C.L.R. 5, QBD 14–142, 14–154
Coventry, Shepperd & Co. v. G.E. Railway (1883) 11 Q.B.D. 776; 52 L.J.Q.B. 694; 49 L.T. 641 . . . . 7–016, 7–017, 18–016, 18–174
Cowan v. O'Connor (1888) 20 Q.B.D. 640; 57 L.J.Q.B. 401; 58 L.T. 857; 36 W.R. 895 2–015
Cowasjee v. Thompson (1845) 3 Moo.Ind.App. 422; 5 Moo.P.C.C. 165; 18 E.R. 560 . . . . 15–073, 18–168, 20–005, 20–018, 20–141
Cowdenbeath Coal Co. Ltd v. Clydesdale Bank Ltd (1895) 22 R. (Ct. of Sess.) 682 . . . . 18–027, 18–084, 18–080, 20–135
Cowdy v. Thomas (1876) 36 L.T. 22 . . . . 10–016, 10–019, 10–020
Cowern v. Nield [1912] 2 K.B. 419; 81 L.J.K.B. 865; 106 L.T. 984; 28 T.L.R. 423; 56 S.J. 552 . . . . 2–030, 2–031, 2–039, 2–040
Cox v. Bankside [1995] 2 Lloyd's Rep. 437 18–256
—— v. Philips Industries Ltd [1976] I.C.R. 138; [1976] 1 W.L.R. 638; (1975) 119 S.J. 760; [1976] 3 All E.R. 161; [1975] I.R.L.R. 334 14–006
—— v. Prentice (1815) 3 M. & S. 344; 105 E.R. 641 3–023
—— v. Walker (1835) 6 A. & E. 523n 17–052, 17–053
Cox, McEuen & Co. v. Malcolm & Co. [1912] 2 K.B. 107 19–027
Cox, Patterson & Co. v. Bruce & Co. (1886) 18 Q.B.D. 147 . . . . 18–022, 19–033, 19–078, 19–155
Coxe v. Harden (1803) 4 East, 211; 1 Smith K.B. 20; 102 E.R. 911 . . . . 18–088, 18–214
Crage v. Fry (1903) 67 J.P. 240; 1 L.G.R. 253 17–065
Craig v. Columbia Compress and Warehouse Co. 210 So. 2d 645 (1968) 25–129
Cranston v. Mallow and Lien 1912 S.C. 112; 49 S.L.R. 186; [1912] 2 S.L.T. 383 S.L.R. 5–043
Crantrave Ltd (In Liquidation) v. Lloyds Bank Plc [2000] Q.B. 917; [2000] 3 W.L.R. 877; [2000] 4 All E.R. 473; [2000] 2 All E.R. (Comm) 89; [2000] Lloyd's Rep. Bank. 181; [2000] C.L.C. 1194; [2001] B.P.I.R. 57; (2000) 97(20) L.S.G. 42; (2000) 144 S.J.L.B. 219; *The Times*, April 24, 2000, CA 9–044

Craven v. Ryder (1816) 6 Taunt. 433; 2 Marsh 127; 128 E.R. 1103 .. 15–073, 18–199, 20–076
Crawcour v. Salter (1881) 18 Ch.D. 30; 45 L.T. 62 1–066
Crawford v. Kingston [1952] 4 D.L.R. 37 1–057
Crawford & Rowat v. Wilson Sons & Co. (1896) 12 T.L.R. 170; 1 Com.Cas. 154 8–094
Crawshay v. Eades (1823) 1 B. & C. 181; 2 Dow & Ry.K.B. 288; 1 L.J. (o.s.) K.B. 90; 107 E.R. 68 .... 15–070, 15–079
Crears v. Hunter (1887) 19 Q.B.D. 341 23–137
Creative Press Ltd v. Harman [1973] I.R. 313 22–043
Credit Agricole Indosuez v. Credit Suisse [2001] All E.R. 161 .... 23–210, 23–219
—— v. Credit Suisse First Boston (Zurich) [2001] 1 All E.R. (Comm) 1088; [2001] Lloyd's Rep. Bank. 218, QBD 23–219
—— v. Generale Bank (No.2) [1999] 2 All E.R. (Comm) 1016; [2000] 1 Lloyd's Rep. 123; [2000] C.L.C. 205, QBD (Comm Ct) 23–119
—— v. Muslim Commercial Bank Ltd [2000] 1 All E.R. (Comm) 172; [2000] 1 Lloyd's Rep. 275; [2000] Lloyd's Rep. Bank, 1; [2000] C.L.C. 437, CA 23–117, 23–206
Credit Industriel et Commercial v. China Merchants Bank [2002] EWHC 973; [2002] 2 All E.R. (Comm) 427; [2002] C.L.C. 1263, QBD 23–207
Crèdit Lyonnais v. Barnard (P.T.) & Associates Ltd [1976] 1 Lloyd's Rep. 557 3–028
Crèdit Lyonnais v. New Hampshire Insurance Co. Ltd [1997] 2 Lloyd's Rep. 1; [1997] 2 C.M.L.R. 610, CA; affirming [1997] 1 Lloyd's Rep. 191; [1997] 6 Re. L.R. 121, QBD (Comm Ct) 25–001, 25–065, 25–068
Crèdit Lyonnais Bank Nederland v. Export Credit Guarantee Department [1996] 1 Lloyd's Rep. 200 24–033
Credit Suisse First Boston (Europe) Ltd v. Seagate Trading Co Ltd [1999] 1 All E.R. (Comm.) 261; [1999] 1 Lloyd's Rep. 784; [1999] C.L.C. 600, QBD 25–083
Cremdean Properties Ltd v. Nash (1977) 244 E.G. 547 .... 10–006, 12–016, 13–055, 13–059, 13–065, 13–107
Cremer v. General Carriers SA [1974] 1 W.L.R. 341; (1973) 117 S.J. 873; [1974] 1 All E.R. 1, *sub nom.* Cremer (Peter), Westfaelische Central Genossenschaft G.m.b.H. and Intergraan N.V. v. General Carriers SA; (The Dona Mari), [1973] 2 Lloyd's Rep. 366 .... 13–040, 18–060, 18–140, 18–171, 18–172, 18–174, 18–179, 18–183, 18–194, 18–291
Cremer (Peter) v. Brinker's Groudstoffen B.V. [1980] 2 Lloyd's Rep. 605 ... 8–031, 18–287, 18–266, 18–288, 19–002, 19–006, 19–008, 19–070
—— v. Granaria B.V. [1981] 2 Lloyd's Rep. 583 .... 8–030, 12–036, 19–150, 19–151, 19–152
Cripps (R.A.) & Son Ltd v. Wickenden [1973] 1 W.L.R. 944; [1973] 2 All E.R. 606; (1972) 117 S.J. 446, Ch D 9–059
Criss v. Alexander (1928) 28 S.R. (N.S.W.) 297; 45 N.S.W.W.N. 76 13–028
Crist v. J. Henry Schroder Bank and Trust Co. 693 F. Supp. 1429 (SD N.Y. 1988) .. 23–236
Crocker (H.S.) Co. v. McFaddin, 148 Cal.App. 2d 639 (1957) 1–034
Crocker First National Bank v. De Sousa, 27 F. 2d 462 (1928) 23–231, 23–234
Croft v. Alison (1821) 4 B. & Ald. 590 5–010
Crofton v. Colgan (1859) 10 lr.C.L.R. 133; 12 lr.Jur. 36 2–048
Crompton Corp. v. Kellog 831 F. 2d 586 (1988) 23–139
Cromwell v. Commerce and Energy Bank 464 So. 2d 721 (La. 1985) 23–142
Crone (W. Pat) Forgings v. Mooring Acro Industries Inc. 403 N.Y.S. 2d. 399 (1978) 23–210
Cronin v. J.B.E. Olson Corp., 104 Cal.Rptr. 433 (1972) (Cal.Sup.Ct) 14–073
Crooks & Co. v. Allan (1879) 5 Q.B.D. 38; 49 L.J.Q.B. 201; 41 L.T. 800; 28 W.R. 304; 4 Asp.M.L.C. 216 18–047
Crosby v. Wadsworth (1805) 6 East 602; 2 Smith K.B. 559; (1803–13] All E.R. 535; 102 E.R. 1419 1–093
Cross v. Eglin (1831) 2 B. & Ad. 106, 9 L.J. (o.s.) K.B. 145; 109 E.R. 1083 ... 8–054, 8–062
Crosse v. Gardner (1688) Carth, 90; Comb. 142; Holt, K.B. 5; 3 Mod.Rep. 261; 1 Shaw. 68; 90 E.R. 656 .... 4–001, 10–016
Crosse v. Smith (1813) 1 M. & S. 545 22–110
Crossley Bros. Ltd v. Lee [1908] 1 K.B. 86; 77 L.J.Q.B. 199; 97 L.T. 850; 24 T.L.R. 35; 52 S.J. 30 .... 1–095, 5–159
Crouch v. Crédit Foncier of England (1873) L.R. 8 Q.B. 374; 42 L.J.Q.B. 183; 29 L.T. 259; 21 W.R. 946 23–028

Croudace Construction Ltd v. Cawoods Concrete Products Ltd [1978] 2 Lloyd's Rep. 55; [1978] 8 Build.L.R. 20 .... 13–036, 13–037
Crowe v. Clay (1854) 9 Exch. 604 .... 9–030, 22–114
Crowther v. Shannon Motor Co. [1975] 1 W.L.R. 30; [1975] 1 All E.R. 139; [1975] R.T.R. 201; [1975] 1 Lloyd's Rep. 382; *sub nom.* Crowther v. Solent Motor Co., 118 S.J. 714 .... 11–040, 11–048, 11–049
Cubitt v. Gamble (1919) 35 T.L.R. 223; 63 S.J. 287 15–022
Culford Metal Industries v. Export Credits Guarantee Department, *The Times*, March 25, 1981 24–013
Cullinane v. British "Rema" Manufacturing Co. [1954] 1 Q.B. 292; [1953] 3 W.L.R. 923; 97 S.J. 811; [1953] 2 All E.R. 1257 .... 16–030, 17–063, 17–067, 17–070
Cumming & Co. Ltd v. Ince (1982) 28 C.L.R. 508 20–014
Cundy v. Lindsay (1878) 3 App.Cas. 459 .... 3–013, 3–014, 5–046, 7–019, 7–021, 16–090
Cunliffe v. Harrison (1851) 6 Exch. 903; 20 L.J.Ex. 325; 17 L.T. (o.s.) 189; 155 E.R. 813 .... 5–086, 8–049
—— v. Whitehead (1837) 3 Bing, N.C. 828; 6 Dowl. 63; 3 Hodg. 182; 5 Scott 31; 6 L.J.C.P. 255; 132 E.R. 629 22–055
Cunningham v. Dunn (1878) 3 C.P.D. 443; 48 L.J.Q.B. 62; 38 L.T. 631; 3 Asp.M.L.C. 595 25–119
Cunningham (J. & J.) Ltd v. Munro (Robert A.) & Co. Ltd (1922) 28 Com.Cas. 42; 13 Ll.L.Rep. 62 .... 6–005, 6–023, 12–051, 18–215, 20–029, 20–038, 20–043, 20–047, 20–051, 20–083, 20–092, 20–119, 20–133
Curragh Investments Ltd v. Cook [1974] 1 W.L.R. 1559; 118 S.J. 737; [1974] 3 All E.R. 658; 28 P. & C.R. 401 3–029
Currie v. Misa (1875) L.R. 10 Ex. 153 9–030
Curtain Dream plc, *Re* [1990] B.C.C. 341; [1990] B.C.L.C. 925 .... 1–065, 1–066, 5–144, 5–167
Curtice v. London City and Midland Bank Ltd [1908] 1 K.B. 293, CA 7–047
Curtis v. Chemical Cleaning & Dyeing Co. [1951] 1 K.B. 805; [1951] 1 T.L.R. 452; 95 S.J. 253; [1951] 1 All E.R. 631 .... 2–012, 13–016
—— v. Mathews [1919] 1 K.B. 425 8–097
—— v. Maloney [1951] 1 K.B. 736 7–111
Cusack v. Robinson (1861) 1 B. & S. 299; 30 L.J.Q.B. 261; 4 L.T. 506; 7 Jur. (N.S.) 542; 9 W.R. 735; 121 E.R. 726 .... 8–009, 15–040, 15–050
Cushing v. Dupuy (1880) 5 App.Cas. 409; 49 L.J.P.C. 63; 42 L.T. 445 1–064
Customs & Excise Commissioners v. A.p.s. Samex [1983] 1 All E.R. 1042; [1983] 3 C.M.L.R. 194; (1983) 133 New L.J. 281; [1983] Com.L.R. 72 .... 18–233, 21–081, 21–083, 21–096
—— v. Diners Club Ltd [1989] 1 W.L.R. 1196 9–033
—— v. Everwine Ltd; *sub nom.* Everwine Ltd v. Customs and Excise Commissioners [2003] EWCA Civ 953; (2003) 147 S.J.L.B. 870, CA 5–130
—— v. Oliver [1980] 1 All E.R. 353; [1980] S.T.C. 73; [1980] T.R. 423 4–001
Cutelli v. Brain Cotter Motors Ltd (1993) 5 T.C.L.R. 500 1–008
Cuthbert v. Robarts, Lubbock & Co. [1909] 2 Ch. 226; 78 L.J.Ch. 529; 100 L.T. 796; 25 T.L.R. 583; 53 S.J. 559 .... 22–141, 22–145
Cutter v. Powell (1795) 6 T.R. 320; 2 Sm.L.C. 1 .... 6–040, 10–026
Czarnikow (C.) v. Koufos. *See* Koufos v. Czarnikow (C.),
Czarnikow Ltd v. Bunge & Co. Ltd [1987] 1 Lloyds Rep. 202 .... 16–070, 17–007
—— v. Centrala Handlu Zagranicznego Rolimpex [1979] A.C. 351; [1978] 3 W.L.R. 274; (1978) 122 S.J. 506; [1978] 2 All E.R. 1043; [1978] 2 Lloyd's Rep. 305 .... 6–047, 6–048, 6–057, 8–092, 18–309, 18–317, 18–322, 18–335, 18–337, 18–339, 18–340, 18–341
Czarnikow Rionda Sugar Trading Inc. v. Standard Bank of London Ltd [1999] 1 All E.R. (Comm) 890; [1999] 2 Lloyd's Rep. 187; [1999] Lloyd's Rep. Bank. 197; [1999] C.L.C. 1148, QBD (Comm Ct) 23–062, 23–148, 23–281

D. & C. Builders Ltd v. Rees [1966] 2 Q.B. 617; [1966] 2 W.L.R. 288; 109 S.J. 971; [1965] 3 All E.R. 837; [1965] C.L.Y. 1486 .... 9–024, 12–036, 22–118
D. & F. Estates Ltd v. Church Commissioners of England [1989] A.C. 177; [1988] 2 E.G.L.R. 213; (1990) 15 Con.L.R. 35 .... 12–126, 18–149
D. & M. Trailers (Halifax) Ltd v. Stirling [1978] R.T.R. 468; (1978) 122 S.J. 625; (1978) 248 E.G. 597 .... 13–013, 13–028, 13–078

DO Ferguson Associates v. Sohl 62 B.L.R. 95; *The Times*, December 24, 1992, CA 12–068
DSW Silo-und Verwaltungsgesellschaft m.b.H. v. Owners of the Sennar (No. 2) [1985] 1 W.L.R. 490; (1985) 129 S.J. 248; [1985] 2 All E.R. 104; [1985] 1 Lloyd's Rep. 521; (1985) 135 New L.J. 316 19–196
Dacre Son & Hartley Ltd v. North Yorkshire Trading Standards; *sub nom.* Dacre Son & Hartley Ltd v. North Yorkshire CC [2004] EWHC 2783; (2005) 169 J.P. 59; [2005] 1 E.G.L.R. 11; [2005] 03 E.G. 118; (2005) 169 J.P.N. 179; [2004] 45 E.G.C.S. 124, QBD 14–113
Daewoo Australia Pty Ltd v. Suncorp-Metway Ltd (2000) 33 A.C.S.R. 481 ... 1–034, 1–084, 2–044
Daewoo Heavy Industries Ltd v. Klipriver Shipping Ltd (The Kapitan Petko Voivoda) [2003] EWCA Civ 451; [2003] 1 All E.R. (Comm) 801; [2003] 2 Lloyd's Rep. 1; [2003] 1 C.L.C. 1092; *Times*, April 17, 2003, CA (Civ Div); affirming [2002] EWHC 1306; [2002] 2 All E.R. (Comm) 560; *Independent*, October 14, 2002, QBD 18–059, 18–059, 21–090, 21–091, 21–092, 21–093
Dagenham (Thames) Dock Co., *Re* (1873) L.R.8 Ch.App. 1022; 43 L.J.Ch. 261; 38 J.P. 180; 21 W.R. 898 .... 16–038, 16–039
Dakin v. Oxley (1864) 15 C.B. (N.S.) 646; 33 L.J.C.P. 115; 10 L.T. 268; 10 Jur. (N.S.) 655; 12 W.R. 557; 2 Mar.L.C. 6; 143 E.R. 938 15–120
Dakin (H.) v. Lee [1916] 1 K.B. 566; [1914–15] All E.R. 1302; 84 L.J.K.B. 2031; 113 L.T. 903; 59 S.J. 650 11–004
Dale S.S. Co. Ltd v. Northern S.S. Co. Ltd (1918) 34 T.L.R. 271; 62 S.J. 328 6–050
Dalgety & Co. Ltd v. John J. Hilton Property Ltd [1981] 2 N.S.W.L.R. 169 22–045
—— v. Bradfield (T.G.) & Co. Ltd (1930) 46 T.L.R. 274; 35 Com.Cas. 213 19–019
Datec Electronic Holdings Ltd v. United Parcels Ltd [2005] EWCA Civ 1418; [2005] 1 Lloyd's Rep. 279 18–047
D'Almeida (J.) Aruajo Lda. v. Becker (Sir Frederick) & Co. Ltd [1953] 2 Q.B. 329; [1953] 2 All E.R. 288; [1953] 2 Lloyd's Rep. 30; *sub nom.* D'Amaido (J.) Aruajo v. Becker (Sir Frederick) & Co. [1953] 3 W.L.R. 57; 97 S.J. 404 25–191
Dalmia Dairy Industries Ltd v. National Bank of Pakistan [1978] 2 Lloyd's Rep. 223; (1977) 121 S.J. 442 .... 6–047, 18–337, 25–119, 25–175
Daly v. General Steam Navigation Co. Ltd (The "Dragon") [1981] 1 W.L.R. 120; [1980] 3 All E.R. 696; [1980] 2 Lloyd's Rep. 415; (1980) 125 S.J. 100, CA; affirming [1979] 1 Lloyd's Rep. 257 .... 2–012, 13–017, 14–077
Damon Compania Naviera SA v. Hapag-Lloyd International SA; Blankenstein, The [1985] 1 W.L.R. 435; (1985) 129 S.J. 218; (1985) 1 All E.R. 475; [1985] 1 Lloyd's Rep. 93; (1985) 82 L.S.Gaz. 1644 .... 1–051, 9–052, 15–132
Daniel v. Whitfield (1885) 15 Q.B.D. 408; 54 L.J.M.C. 134; 53 L.T. 471; 49 L.P. 694; 33 W.R. 905; 1 T.L.R. 574; 15 Cox C.C. 762 5–088
Daniels and Daniels v. White (R.) & Sons Ltd and Tabard [1938] 4 All E.R. 258; 160 L.T. 128; 82 S.J. 912 .... 11–082, 14–018, 14–061
Danish Dairies Co-operative Society v. Midland Railway (1892) 8 T.L.R. 212 18–192
Dan's and Jordan v. James (1776) 5 Burr 2680 5–009
D'Aquila v. Lambert (1761) 1 Amb. 399; 2 Eden. 75; 27 E.R. 266 15–064
Darbishire v. Warran [1963] 1 W.L.R. 1067; 107 S.J. 631; [1963] 3 All E.R. 310; [1963] 2 Lloyd's Rep. 187 16–052
Darlington v. Wiltshier Northern Ltd [1995] 1 W.L.R. 68 18–114
Darlington Borough Council v. Wiltshier Northern [1995] 1 W.L.R. 68; [1995] 3 All E.R. 895; 11 Const. L.J. 36; 91 (37) L.S.Gaz. 49; 138 S.J.L.B. 161; 69 B.L.R. 1; *The Times*, July 4, 1994; *The Independent*, June 29, 1994, CA 17–072, 18–102
Darlington Futures Ltd v. Delco Australia Property Ltd (1986) 161 C.L.R. 500 .... 13–020, 13–036, 13–049
Darlington (Peter) and Partners Ltd v. Gosho Co. Ltd [1964] 1 Lloyd's Rep. 149 ... 11–021
Dalkia Utilities Services Plc v. Caltech International Ltd [2006] EWHC 63 (Comm); [2006] 1 Lloyd's Rep. 8–026, 8–078, 8–101
Daudruy v. Tropical Products SA [1986] 1 Lloyd's Rep. 535 .... 11–016, 11–085, 13–033
Daulatram Rameshwarlall v. European Grain and Shipping Ltd [1971] 1 Lloyd's Rep. 368 19–018
Davey v. Paine Bros. (Motors) Ltd [1954] N.Z.L.R. 1122 .... 1–037, 1–039, 7–043, 7–046
David Agmashenebeli, The. *See* Owners of Cargo Lately Laden on Board the David Agmashenebeli v. Owners of the David Agmashenebeli

David Securities Pty Ltd v. Commonwealth Bank of Australia (1992) 175 C.L.R. 353; (1992) 66 A.L.J.R. 768 .... 4–006, 6–040, 12–069
Davies v. Burnett [1902] 1 K.B. 666; 71 L.J.K.B. 355; 86 L.T. 565; 46 S.J. 300; 66 J.P. 406; 50 W.R. 391 1–121
—— v. Customs and Excise Commissioners [1975] 1 W.L.R. 204; (1974) 119 S.J. 100; [1975] 1 All E.R. 309; [1975] S.T.C. 28; [1974] T.R. 317 1–034
—— v. Directloans Ltd [1986] 1 W.L.R. 823 14–150
—— v. Leighton (1978) 68 Cr.App.R. 4; (1978) 122 S.J. 641; [1978] Crim.L.R. 575 .. 2–002, 5–013, 5–026, 5–082, 5–101
—— v. McLean (1873) 28 L.T. 113; 37 J.P. 198; 21 W.R. 264 .... 8–020, 21–002
—— v. Rees (1886) 17 Q.B.D. 408 1–016
—— v. Sumner [1984] 1 W.L.R. 1301; [1984] 3 All E.R. 831; [1985] L.G.R. 123; [1985] R.T.R. 95; (1985) 149 J.P. 110; (1985) 149 J.P.N. 11; (1985) 4 Tr.L. 1; (1985) 82 L.S.Gaz. 45, HL 11–045, 13–075, 14–029, 14–112
Davies (A.) & Co. (Shopfitters) Ltd v. William Old Ltd (1969) 113 S.J. 266; (1969) 67 L.G.R. 395 2–013
Davis v. Balfour Kilpatrick Ltd [2002] EWCA Civ 736, CA 14–091
—— v. Bowsher (1794) 5 Term Rep. 488 .... 22–139, 22–140
—— v. Clarke (1844) 6 Q.B. 16; 13 L.J.Q.B. 305; 3 L.T. (o.s.) 159; 8 Jur. 688 22–054
—— v. Collins [1945] 1 All E.R. 247 13–046
Davis v. Hedges (1871) L.R. 6 Q.B. 687; 40 L.J.Q.B. 276; 25 L.T. 155; 20 W.R. 60 17–048, 17–051
—— v. Reilly [1898] 1 Q.B. 1; 66 L.J.Q.B. 844; 46 W.R. 96; 41 S.J. 860 9–030
—— v. Tenco, (Unreported, February 25, 1992) 23–216
Davis (Clifford) Ltd v. W.E.A. Records Ltd [1975] 1 W.L.R. 61; 118 S.J. 775; [1975] 1 All E.R. 237 3–035
Davis & Co. (Wines) Ltd v. Afa-Minerva (E.M.I.) Ltd [1974] 2 Lloyd's Rep. 27 .... 10–011, 12–015
Davis Contractors Ltd v. Fareham U.D.C. [1956] A.C. 696; [1956] 3 W.L.R. 37; 100 S.J. 378; [1956] 2 All E.R. 145; 54 L.G.R. 289 .... 6–041, 6–054, 10–030
Davis O'Brien Lumber Co. Ltd v. Bank of Montreal [1951] 3 D.L.R. 536 .... 23–139, 23–196, 23–210
Davison v. Donaldson (1882) 9 Q.B.D. 623; 47 L.T. 564; 31 W.R. 277; 4 Asp.M.L.C. 601 9–031
Davy Offshore v. Emerald Field Contracting [1992] 2 Lloyd's Rep. 142; *The Financial Times*, March 18, CA 1–082, 5–090, 18–218, 23–110
Dawber Williamson Roofing Ltd v. Humberside C.C. (1979) 14 Build.L.R. 70 .... 5–157, 7–068, 7–077
Dawes v. Peck (1799) 8 Term R. 330; 3 Esp. 12; 101 E.R. 1417 5–009
Dawkes v. Lord De Lorane (1771) 2 Wm.Bl. 782; 3 Wils, K.B. 207 22–041
Dawood (Ebrahim) Ltd v. Heath (Est. 1927) Ltd [1961] 2 Lloyd's Rep. 512 .... 17–090, 18–273
Dawson v. Isle [1906] 1 Ch. 633; 75 L.J.Ch. 338; 95 L.T. 385; 54 W.R. 452 .. 22–073, 22–143
Dawson (G.J.) (Clapham) Ltd v. Dutfield (H. & G.) [1936] 2 All E.R. 232 1–039
Dawsons v. Bonnin [1922] 2 A.C. 413; 91 L.J.P.C. 210; 128 L.T. 1; 38 T.L.R. 836 ... 24–013
Day v. Bate (1979) 41 F.L.R. 222 (Australia) 22–104, 22–116
—— v. Nix (1824) 9 Moore C.P. 159; 2 L.J. (o.s.) C.P. 133 22–062
—— v. Picton (1829) 10 B. & C. 120 9–063
De Bèeche v. South American Stores (Gath & Chaves) Ltd [1935] A.C. 148, HL; affirming [1934] All E.R. Rep. 284, CA 25–119
De Bueger v. Ballantyne (J.) & Co. [1938] 1 All E.R. 701; [1938] A.C. 452; 107 L.J.P.C. 61; 158 L.T. 393; 54 T.L.R. 450; 82 S.J. 311 25–165
De Gorter v. Attenborough & Son (1904) 21 T.L.R. 19 7–043
De Jong Verenigde v. V.I.B. [1985] E.C.R. 2061 8–100
De Lassalle v. Guildford [1901] 2 K.B. 215; 70 L.J.K.B. 533; 84 L.T. 549; 49 W.R. 467; 17 T.L.R. 384 10–016
De Medina v. Norman (1842) 9 M. & W. 820 8–004
De Meza and Stuart v. Apple, Van Straten, Shena and Stone [1975] 1 Lloyd's Rep. 498, CA; affirming [1974] 1 Lloyd's Rep. 508 6–028
De Molestina v. Ponton; *sub nom.* Molestina v. Ponton [2002] 1 Lloyd's Rep. 271; [2002] C.P. Rep. 1; [2001] C.L.C. 1412, QBD (Comm Ct) 12–003

De Monchy v. Phoenix Insurance Co. of Hartford (1928) 33 Com.Cas. 197 19–048
De Oleaga v. West Cumberland Iron and Steel Co. (1879) 4 Q.B.D. 472; 48 L.J.Q.B. 753; 41 L.T. 342; 27 W.R. 870 .... 8–070, 8–084
De Sewhanberg v. Buchanan (1832) 5 C. & P. 343 .... 10–003, 10–006
De Symons v. Minchwich (1795) 1 Esp. 429; 170 E.R. 409, N.P. 16–016
De Wútz v. Hendricks (1824) 2 Bing, 314 25–119
Dean v. Prince [1954] Ch. 409; [1954] 2 W.L.R. 538; 98 S.J. 215; [1954] 1 All E.R. 749; 47 R. & I.T. 494 2–051
Dean (Henry) & Sons (Sydney) Ltd v. O'Day Property Ltd (1927) 39 C.L.R. 330 .... 9–014, 19–054, 19–164, 19–165
Dearle v. Hall (1828) 3 Russ. 1 5-161
Debs v. Sibec Developments Ltd [1990] R.T.R. 91 .... 7–008, 7–015
Debtor, a, *Re* [1908] 1 K.B. 344; 77 L.J.K.B. 409; 98 L.T. 652; 52 S.J. 174; 15 Mans. 1 .... 9–030, 15–020
Debtor a, *Re* (No. 3 of 1926) [1927] 1 Ch. 97 11–028
——(No. 38 of 1938) [1939] Ch. 225 12–055
Decca Radar Co. Ltd v. Caserite Ltd [1961] 2 Lloyd's Rep. 301 11–057
Decker Steel Co. v. Exchange National Bank 330 F. 2d. 82 (1964) 23–136
Decro-Wall International SA v. Practitioners in Marketing Ltd; Same v. Same [1971] 1 W.L.R. 361; *sub nom.* Decro-Wall International SA v. Practitioners in Marketing (1970) 115 S.J. 171; [1971] 2 All E.R. 216 .... 8–080, 8–082, 10–027, 12–019, 15–107, 15–109
Deeny v. Gooda Walker (No. 3) [1995] 1 W.L.R. 1206; [1995] 4 All E.R. 289; *The Times*, May 5, 1995 .... 16–092, 17–036, 17–104
Deep Vein Thrombosis and Air Travel Group Litigation, Re [2005] UKHL 72; [2005] 3 W.L.R. 1320; [2006] 1 All E.R. 786; [2006] 1 All E.R. (Comm) 313; [2006] 1 Lloyd's Rep. 231; [2005] 2 C.L.C. 1083; [2006] P.I.Q.R. P14; (2006) 87 B.M.L.R. 1; (2006) 103(3) L.S.G. 26; (2005) 155 N.L.J. 1925; (2006) 150 S.J.L.B. 29; *The Times*, December 12, 2005; *Independent*, December 13, 2005, HL 18–149
Deepak Fertilisers and Petrochemicals Corp. v. Davy McKee (London) Ltd; *See* Deepak Fertilisers and Petrochemicals Corp. v. ICI Chemicals and Polymers Ltd
Deepak Fertilisers and Petrochemicals Corp. v. ICI Chemicals and Polymers Ltd *sub nom.* Deepak Fertilisers and Petrochemicals Corp. v. Davy McKee (London) Ltd [1999] 1 All E.R. (Comm.) 69; [1999] 1 Lloyd's Rep. 387; [1999] B.L.R. 41; (1999) 1 T.C.L.R. 200; 62 Con. L.R. 86, CA; reversing in part [1998] 2 Lloyd's Rep. 139, QBD (Comm Ct) 13–017, 13–037, 13–056
Definitely Maybe (Touring) Ltd v. Marek Lieberberg Konzertagentur GmbH (No.2) [2001] 1 W.L.R. 1745; [2001] 4 All E.R. 283; [2001] 2 All E.R. (Comm) 1; [2001] 2 Lloyd's Rep. 455; [2002] I.L.Pr. 9; *The Daily Telegraph*, April 10, 2001, QBD (Comm Ct) 25–001, 25–019, 25–020, 25–060, 25–065
Defries (J.) & Sons Ltd. *Re*, Eichholz v. Depries (J.) & Sons Ltd [1909] 2 Ch. 423; 78 L.J.Ch. 720; 101 L.T. 486; 25 T.L.R. 752; 53 S.J. 697; 16 Mans. 308 15–036
Deichland, The [1990] 1 Q.B. 361; [1989] 3 W.L.R. 478; [1989] 2 All E.R. 1066; [1989] 2 Lloyd's Rep. 113; [1991] I.L.Pr. 135; (1989) 86(24) L.S.G. 36; (1989) 133 S.J. 596; *The Times*, April 27, 1989, CA; reversing [1988] 2 Lloyd's Rep. 454, QBD (Adm Ct)
Dekor by Nikkei International Inc. v. Federal Republic of Nigeria 647 F. 2d. 300 (1981) 23–135
Delaurier & Co. v. Wyllie (James) and Co. (1889) 17 R. (Ct. of Sess.) 167; 27 Sc.L.R. 148 .... 18–040, 19–102
Delbrueck & Co. v. Barclays Bank International Ltd. *See* Momm v. Barclays Bank International Ltd.
—— v. Barclays Bank International Ltd [1976] 2 Lloyd's Rep. 341; 120 S.J. 486 9–038
Delimitis v. Henniger Bräu [1991] 1 E.C.R. 935 .... 3–040, 3–041
Dell v. Quilty [1924] N.Z.L.R. 1270 11–019
Delos (Cargo Owners) v. Delos Shipping Ltd [2001] 1 All E.R. (Comm) 763; [2001] 1 Lloyd's Rep. 703, QBD (Comm Ct) 18–084
Demby Hamilton & Co. Ltd v. Barden [1949] W.N. 73; [1949] 1 All E.R. 435 .... 6–023, 6–024, 6–025, 6–027, 19–117, 20–071

Demerara Turf Club Ltd v. Wight [1918] A.C. 605 2–004
Democritos, The [1975] 1 Lloyd's Rep. 386 12–035
Dempster (R. & J.) Ltd v. Motherwell Bridge & Engineering Co. Ltd 1964 S.L.T. 353 2–017
Denbigh Cowan & Co. and R. Atcherley & Co., *Re* (1921) 90 L.J.K.B. 836; 125 L.T. 388 .... 18–116, 18–305, 19–003, 19–006, 19–024, 21–015, 21–019
Denholm Fishselling Ltd v. Anderson 1991 S.L.T. (Sh.Ct.) 24 13–088
Denmark Productions Ltd v. Boscobel Productions Ltd [1969] 1 Q.B. 699; [1968] 3 W.L.R. 841; 112 S.J. 761; [1968] 3 All E.R. 513 .... 6–034, 9–016
Dennant v. Skinner and Collom [1948] 2 K.B. 164; [1948] L.J.R. 1576; [1948] 2 All E.R. 29 .... 3–012, 5–004, 5–017, 5–018, 5–026, 7–021
Dennis (J.) & Co. Ltd v. Munn [1949] 2 K.B. 327; [1949] L.J.R. 857; 65 T.L.R. 251; 93 S.J. 181; [1949] 1 All E.R. 616 18–324
Denny v. Skelton (1916) 86 L.J.K.B. 280; 115 L.T. 305; 13 Asp.M.L.C. 437 ... 5–003, 5–087, 5–097, 17–105
Denny (E.M.) & Co. Ltd v. Wholesalers (Australia) Property Ltd [1959] 1 Lloyd's Rep. 167 2–007
Denny, Mott and Dickson Ltd v. (B. James) Fraser & Co. Ltd [1944] A.C. 265 6–044
Dent-Brocklehurst v. Lombank, *The Guardian*, March 14, 1962 7–011
Department of the Environment v. Thomas Bates & Son Ltd [1990] 1 A.C. 499; [1990] 3 W.L.R. 457; [1990] 2 All E.R. 943; [1990] 46 E.G. 115; (1990) 134 S.J. 1077; (1990) 50 Build.L.R. 61; (1990) 21 Con.L.R. 54 12–126
Depperman v. Hubbersty (1852) 17 Q.B. 766 18–233
Derfflinger, The (No. 2) (1918) 87 L.J.P.C. 195; 118 L.T. 521; 14 Asp.M.L.C. 267 ... 19–099
Derry v. Peek (1889) 14 App.Cas. 337 .... 10–004, 10–010, 12–012
Design Company, The v. Elizabeth King, unreported, July 7, 1992, CA 8–078
Deta Nominees Property Ltd v. Viscount Plastic Products Property Ltd [1979] V.R. 167 1–047
Deutsche Conti-Handelsgesellschaft m.b.H. v. Deutsche Bremer Handelsgesellschaft m.b.H. [1984] 1 Lloyd's Rep. 447 .... 8–092, 18–350
Deutsche Rúckversicherung A.G. v. Walbrook Insurance Co. Ltd [1994] 4 All E.R. 181; [1995] 1 W.L.R. 1017; [1995] 1 Lloyd's Rep. 153; (1994) 91 (25) L.S.Gaz. 30; (1994) 138 S.J.L.B. 111; *The Times*, May 6, 1994, QBD 23–147, 23–279
Deutz Engines Ltd v. Terex Ltd 1984 S.L.T. 273 .... 5–146, 25–134
Devaux v. Conolly (1849) 8 C.B. 640; 19 L.J.C.P. 71; 14 L.T. (o.s.) 546; 137 E.R. 658 .... 6–040, 8–062, 12–061, 12–069, 17–091
Dever, *ex p.* (1884) 13 Q.B.D. 766; 51 L.T. 437; 33 W.R. 290 18–241
Deverill v. Burnell (1873) L.R. 8 C.P. 475; 42 L.J.C.P. 214; 28 L.T. 874 22–115
Deveze, Re (1873) 9 Ch.App. 27 25–132
Devlin v. Hall [1990] R.T.R. 320; [1990] Crim.L.R. 879; (1991) 155 J.P. 20; [1991] T.L.R. 46; (1990) 154 J.P.N. 676 11–045
Devonald v. Rosser & Sons [1906] 2 K.B. 728; 75 L.J.K.B. 688; 95 L.T. 232; 22 T.L.R. 682; 50 S.J. 616 23–027
Dewar & Webb v. Rank (Joseph) Ltd (1923) 14 Ll.L.R. 393; 13 Ll.L.Rep. 211 ..... 18–286 18–306, 19–013
Dewhurst (W.A.) & Co. Property Ltd v. Cawrse [1960] V.R. 278 2–015
Dexters Ltd v. Hill Crest Oil Co. (Bradford) Ltd [1926] 1 K.B. 348; *sub nom.* Dexters Ltd and Hillcrest Oil Co. (Bradford), *Re* 95 L.J.K.B. 386; 134 L.T. 494; 42 T.L.R. 212; 31 Com.Cas. 161 17–083
Dexters Ltd v. Schenker & Co. (1923) 14 Ll.L.R. 586 .... 23–054, 23–137, 23–171
Dextra Bank & Trust Co. Ltd v. Bank of Jamaica [2002] 1 All E.R. (Comm.) 193 6–060
Diamond, The [1906] P. 282 8–097
Diamond v. Bank of London & Montreal Ltd [1979] Q.B. 333; [1979] 2 W.L.R. 228; (1978) 122 S.J. 814; [1979] 1 All E.R. 561——[1979] 1 Lloyd's Rep. 335 2–015
—— v. British Columbia Thoroughbred Breeders' Society Ltd (1966) 52 D.L.R. (2d) 146 12–056
—— v. Campbell-Jones [1961] Ch. 22; [1960] 2 W.L.R. 568; 104 S.J. 249; [1960] 1 All E.R. 583; [1960] T.R. 131; 53 R. & I.T. 502; 39 A.T.C. 103 16–045
Diamond Alkali Export Corp. v. Fl. Bourgeois [1921] 3 K.B. 443; 91 L.J.K.B. 147; 126 L.T. 379; 15 Asp.M.L.C. 455; 26 Com.Cas. 310 ..... 18–027, 18–033, 18–038, 18–079, 18–103, 19–030, 19–042, 19–043, 19–047, 23–220, 23–230

Diamond Cutting Works Federation Ltd v. Triefus & Co. Ltd [1956] 1 Lloyd's Rep. 216 .... 17–004, 17–023
Dibrell Bros Int. SA v. Banca Nazionale de Livoro 38 F. 3rd 1571 (11th Cir. 1994) 23–057
Dick v. Lumsden (1793) Peake 250 .... 18–016, 18–216
Dickenson v. Naul (1833) 4 B. & Ad. 638; 1 Nev. & M.K.B. 721; 110 E.R. 596 16–020
Dickinson v. Fanshaw (1892) 8 T.L.R. 271 .... 8–080, 9–011
—— v. Valpy (1829) 10 B. & C. 128 7–010
Dickson v. Zizinia (1851) 10 C.B. 602; 20 L.J.C.P. 73; 16 L.T. (O.S.) 366; 15 Jur. 359; 138 E.R. 238 11–067
Didymi Corp. v. Atlantic Lines & Navigation Co. Inc. [1988] 2 Lloyd's Rep. 108 2–017
Diego Cali & Figli Srl v. Servizi Ecologici Porto di Genova SpA (SEPG) (C343/95) [1997] E.C.R. I-1547; [1997] 5 C.M.L.R. 484; [1997] C.E.C. 1183; [1998] Env. L.R. 31, ECJ 3–041
Dies v. British and International Mining and Finance Corporation Ltd [1939] 1 K.B. 724 16–040
Diesen v. Samson 1971 S.L.T. (Sh. Ct.) 49, Sh Ct (Glasgow) 17–071
Diestal v. Stevenson [1906] 2 K.B. 345; 75 L.J.K.B. 797; 96 L.T. 10; 22 T.L.R. 673; 12 Com.Cas. 1 .... 16–032, 16–036
Dillenkofer v. Germany (C178/94); Erdmann v. Germany (C179/94); Schulte v. Germany (C188/94); Heuer v. Germany (C189/94); Knor v. Germany (C190/94) [1997] Q.B. 259; [1997] 2 W.L.R. 253; [1996] All E.R. (EC) 917; [1996] E.C.R. I-4845; [1996] 3 C.M.L.R. 469; [1997] I.R.L.R. 60; *The Times*, October 14, 1996, ECJ 14–008, 14–016
Dilworth, *Re* (1828) Mont. & M. 102 22–090
Dimmock v. Hallett (1866) L.R. 2 Ch.App. 21; 36 L.J.Ch. 146; 15 L.T. 374; 31 J.P. 163; 12 Jur. (N.S.) 953; 15 W.R. 93 10–005
Dimskal Shipping Co. SA v. International Transport Workers Federation (The Evia Luck) (No.2) [1992] 2 A.C. 152; [1991] 3 W.L.R. 875; [1991] 4 All E.R. 871; [1992] 1 Lloyd's Rep. 115; [1992] I.C.R. 37; [1992] I.R.L.R. 78; *The Times*, November 8, 1991; *The Independent*, January 15, 1992; *The Financial Times*, November 12, 1991, HL; affirming [1990] 1 Lloyd's Rep. 319; [1990] I.C.R. 694; [1990] I.R.L.R. 102, CA; reversing [1989] 1 Lloyd's Rep. 166, QBD (Comm Ct) 25–079, 25–080, 25–083
Dingle v. Hare (1859) 7 C.B. (N.S.) 145; 29 L.J.C.P. 143; 1 L.T. 38; 6 Jur. (N.S.) 679; 141 E.R. 770 .... 17–051, 17–052
Diplock, *Re*; Diplock v. Wintle [1948] Ch. 465; [1948] L.J.R. 1670; 92 S.J. 484 7–003
Director General of Fair Trading v. First National Bank plc [2001] UKHL 52; [2002] 1 A.C. 481, [2001] 3 W.L.R. 1297; [2002] 1 All E.R. 97; [2001] 2 All E.R. (Comm) 1000; (2001) 151 N.L.J. 1610; *The Times*, November 1, 2001; *The Daily Telegraph*, October 30, 2001, HL 14–033, 14–035, 16–009
Director General of Fair Trading v. Tobyward [1989] 1 W.L.R. 517; [1989] 2 All E.R. 266; (1989) 133 S.J. 184; (1990) 9 Tr.L.R. 41 14–140
Dirigo, The [1919] P. 204; 88 L.J.P. 192; 121 L.T. 477; 35 T.L.R. 533; 14 Asp. M.L.C. 467 .... 5–015, 18–218, 18–242
Discount Records Ltd v. Barclays Bank Ltd [1975] 1 W.L.R. 315; (1974) 119 S.J. 133; [1975] 1 All E.R. 1071; [1975] 1 Lloyd's Rep. 444 .... 23–145, 23–146, 23–191
Distington Hematitc Iron Co. v. Possehl [1916] 1 K.B. 811 6–042
Distribuidora del Pacifico SA v. Gonzales 88 F.Supp. 538 (1950) 23–054, 23–136, 23–185
District of Columbia v. Upjohn Co. 185 F. 2d. 992 (1950) 25–132
Ditchfield (H.M. Inspector of Taxes) v. Sharp [1983] 3 All E.R. 681; [1983] S.T.C. 590 22–067
Dix v. Grainger (1922) 10 Ll.L.R. 496 23–083
Dixon v. Baldwen (1804) 5 East 175, 102 E.R. 1036 .... 15–068, 18–248
—— v. Clark (1848) 5 C.B. 365; 5 Dow. & L. 155; 16 L.J.C.P. 237 16–017
—— v. Fletcher (1837) 3 M. & W. 146; Murph. & H. 342; 150 E.R. 1092 8–049
—— v. London Small Arms Co. (1876) 1 App.Cas. 632; 46 L.J.Q.B. 617; 35 L.T. 559; 25 W.R. 142 .... 1–044, 1–060
—— v. Yates (1833) 5 B. & Ad. 313; 2 Nev. & M.K.B. 177; 110 E.R. 806 .... 5–017, 5–018, 15–039, 15–041
Dixon, Irmaos & Cia Ltda. v. Chase National Bank, 144 F. 2d 759 (1944) 23–219, 23–223

Dixon Kerly Ltd v. Robinson [1965] 2 Lloyd's Rep. 404 .... 11–060, 12–080
Dixon (Peter) & Sons Ltd v. Henderson Craig & Co. [1919] 2 K.B. 778; 87 L.J.K.B. 683; 118 L.T. 328 .... 8–094, 8–099
Doak v. Bedford [1964] 2 Q.B. 587; [1964] 2 W.L.R. 545; 128 J.P. 230; 108 S.J. 76; [1964] 1 All E.R. 311; 62 L.G.R. 249 1–121
Dobbins v. Buick (Martin) Co. 227 S.W. 2d 620 (1950) 25–127
Dobbs v. National Bank of Australasia (1935) 53 C.L.R. 643 23–278
Dobell & Co. v. Steamship Rossmore Co. [1895] 1 Q.B. 408; 64 L.J.K.B. 777; 73 L.T. 74; 44 W.R. 37; 11 T.L.R. 501; 8 Asp.M.L.C. 33; 14 R. 558 25–028
Dobell (G.C.) & Co. Ltd v. Barber & Garratt [1931] 1 K.B. 219; 100 L.J.K.B. 65; 144 L.T. 266; 47 T.L.R. 66; 74 S.J. 836; 36 Com.Cas. 87 .... 17–059, 17–060, 17–076, 17–079, 17–081
Dobell, Beckett & Co. v. Neilson (1904) 42 Sc.L.R. 279; 12 S.L.T. 543, 7 F. 281 7–047
Dobson v. General Accident Fire and Life Assurance Cpn. plc [1990] 1 Q.B. 274; [1989] 3 W.L.R. 1066; [1989] 3 All E.R. 927; (1989) 133 S.J. 1445; [1989] 2 Lloyd's Rep. 549; [1990] Crim.L.R. 271 ... 5–013, 5–018, 5–046, 7–023, 7–037, 7–074
—— v. North Tyneside Health Authority [1996] 4 All E.R. 474 1–089
Docker v. Hyams [1969] 1 W.L.R. 1060; 113 S.J. 381; [1969] 3 All E.R. 808; [1969] 1 Lloyd's Rep. 487 13–035
Dodd and Dodd v. Wilson & McWilliam [1946] 2 All E.R. 691 .... 1–046, 14–064
Dodds v. Walker [1981] 1 W.L.R. 1027; (1981) 125 S.J. 463; [1981] 2 All E.R. 609; (1981) 42 P. & C.R. 131 .... 8–031, 8–034
—— v. Yorkshire Bank Finance [1992] C.C.L.R. 92, CA 1–066, 7–046, 7–091, 7–099
Dodsley v. Varley (1840) 12 A. & E. 632; Arm. & H. 128; 4 Per. & Dav. 448; 5 Jur. 316; 113 E.R. 954 .... 7–071, 15–049, 15–053
Doe v. Bowater Ltd [1916] W.N. 185 8–054
Doe *d.* Pittman v. Sutton (1849) 9 C. & P. 706 8–036
Doherty v. Allman (1878) 3 App.Cas. 709; 39 L.T. 129; 26 W.R. 513 17–103
Doleman & Sons v. Ossett Corporation [1912] 3 K.B. 257 .... 13–041, 14–100
Dominion Coal Co. Ltd v. Dominion Iron and Steel and National Trust Co. Ltd [1909] A.C. 293; 78 L.J.P.C. 115; 100 L.T. 245; 25 T.L.R. 3091 .... 8–078, 9–010, 12–019, 17–097, 17–100, 17–103
Dominion Motors Ltd v. Grieves [1936] N.Z.L.R. 766 16–070
Donaghy's Rope and Twine Co. Ltd v. Wright Stephenson & Co. Ltd (1906) 25 N.Z.L.R. 641 5–075
Donald (A.B.) Ltd v. Corry [1916] N.Z.L.R. 228 8–068
Donnell v. Bennet (1883) 22 Ch.D. 835; 52 L.J.Ch. 414; 48 L.T. 68; 47 J.P. 342; 31 W.R. 316 17–103
Donoghue v. Stevenson [1932] A.C. 562 .... 12–074, 14–061, 14–076
Donovan v. Northlea Farms Ltd [1976] 1 N.Z.L.R. 180 10–012
Doodeward v. Spence (1908) 6 C.L.R. 406 1–089
Dore v. Dore, *The Times*, March 18, 1953 .... 7–058, 7–059
Dori v. Recreb Sri (Case C-91/92) [1995] All E.R. (E.C.) 1; [1994] E.C.R. 1–3325; [1995] 1 C.M.L.R. 665; *The Times*, August 4, 1994; *The Financial Times*, August 2, 1994, ECJ 14–045
Dougan v. Ley (1946) 71 C.L.R. 142 17–099
Dovenmuehle Inc. v. East Bank of Colorado Springs, 563 P. 2d 24 (Col. 1977) 23–236
Dow Corning Corporation, v. Hollis (1996) 129 D.L.R. (4th) 609 (Can.Sup.Ct.) 14–078
Dow Jones & Co. Inc. v. Gutnick [2002] H.C.A. 56; (2003) 210 C.L.R. 575 25–051
Dower (E.M.) & Co. v. Corrie, Maccoll & Son (1925) 23 Ll.L.R. 100 12–051
Downie Bros. v. Henry Oakley & Sons [1923] N.Z.L.R. 734 23–311
Doyle v. East [1972] 1 W.L.R. 1080; 116 S.J. 395; [1972] 2 All E.R. 1013; 24 P. & C.R. 1 .... 1–027, 1–034
—— v. Olby (Ironmongers) Ltd [1969] 2 Q.B. 158; [1969] 2 W.L.R. 673; 113 S.J. 128; [1969] 2 All E.R. 119 .... 4–022, 12–012, 12–015
Dracachi v. Anglo-Egyptian Navigation Co. (1868) L.R. 3 C.P. 190; 37 L.J.C.P. 71; 17 L.T. 472; 16 W.R. 277; 3 Mar.L.C. 27 .... 18–084, 18–089, 18–215
Draper (C.E.B.) & Son Ltd v. Edward Turner & Son Ltd [1965] 1 Q.B. 424; [1964] 3 W.L.R. 783; 108 S.J. 582; [1964] 3 All E.R. 148; [1964] 2 Lloyd's Rep. 91 ... 11–061, 11–079, 25–171
Drew Brown Ltd v. The "Orient Trader" (1972) 34 D.L.R. (3d) 339 .... 25–089, 25–190

Drexel v. Drexel [1916] 1 Ch. 251; 85 L.J.Ch. 235; 114 L.T. 350; 32 T.L.R. 208 ...... 9–046, 9–047
Dreyfus (Louis) & Cie. v. Parnaso Cia. Naviera SA; Dominator, The [1960] 2 Q.B. 49; [1960] 2 W.L.R. 637; [1960] 1 All E.R. 759; [1960] 1 Lloyd's Rep. 117; 104 S.J. 287, CA; reversing [1959] 1 Q.B. 498; [1959] 2 W.L.R. 405; [1959] 1 All E.R. 502; [1959] 1 Lloyd's Rep. 125; 103 S.J. 221 17–104
Drinc-O-Matic Inc. v. Frank 141 F. 2d. 177 (1944) 23–134
Drummond v. Van Ingen (1887) 12 App.Cas. 284 .... 11–003, 11–025, 11–078, 11–080
Drury v. Buckland (Victor) Ltd [1941] 1 All E.R. 269 14–044
Du Jardin v. Beadman Bros. [1952] 2 Q.B. 712; [1952] 1 T.L.R. 1601; 96 S.J. 414; [1952] 2 All E.R. 160 .... 7–038, 7–070, 7–074
DuPont de Nemours v. S.S. Mormacvega 493 F. 2d. 97 (1974); [1974] 1 Lloyd's Rep. 296 .... 21–087, 21–093
Dubai Electricity Co. v. Islamic Republic of Iran Shipping Lines (The Iran Vojdan) [1984] 2 Lloyd's Rep. 380 .... 25–006, 25–071, 25–079, 25–080
Dublin City Distillery Ltd v. Doherty [1914] A.C. 823; 83 L.J.P.C. 265; 111 L.T. 81; 58 S.J. 413 .... 8–008, 8–009, 8–012, 8–013, 15–077, 18–066, 18–075, 18–193
Duke of Westminster v. Guild [1985] Q.B. 688; [1984] 3 W.L.R. 630; [1984] 3 All E.R. 144; (1984) 48 P. & C.R. 42; (1983) 267 E.G. 762; (1984) 128 S.J. 581, CA 18–071
Dulaney v. Merry & Sons [1901] 1 K.B. 200; 89 L.J.K.B. 364; 123 L.T. 31; [1919] B. & C.R. 287 25–122
Dulien Steel Products Inc. v. Bankers Trust Co. 189 F.Supp. 922 (1960), affd. 280 F. 2d 836 (1962) 23–139, 23–150
Dumenil (Peter) & Co. Ltd v. James Ruddin Ltd [1953] 1 W.L.R. 815; 97 S.J. 437; [1953] 2 All E.R. 294; [1953] 2 Lloyd's Rep. 4 .... 8–012, 8–013, 8–078
Dumont v. Williamson (1867) 17 L.T. 71 22–071
Duncan v. Topham (1849) 8 C.B. 225; 18 L.J.C.P. 310; 13 L.T. (O.S.) 304; 137 E.R. 495 8–036
Duncan & Co., *Re* [1905] 1 Ch. 307; 74 L.J. Ch. 188; 92 L.T. 108; 53 W.R. 299; 12 Mans. 39 16–006
Duncan, Fox & Co. v. North and South Wales Bank (1880) 6 App.Cas. 1 22–049
—— v. Schrempft and Bonke [1915] 3 K.B. 355; 84 L.J.K.B. 2206; 113 L.T. 600; 31 T.L.R. 491; 13 Asp.M.L.C. 131; 20 Com.Cas. 337; 59 S.J. 578, CA; affirming [1915] 1 K.B. 365 .... 6–043, 18–082, 19–008, 19–037, 19–136,
Duncombe v. Porter (1953) 90 C.L.R. 295 13–033
Dunkirk Colliery Co. v. Lever (1878) 9 Ch.D. 20; 39 L.T. 239; 26 W.R. 841 .... 16–052, 16–063, 16–064, 16–068
Dunlop v. Grote (1845) 2 Car. & K. 153 .... 16–025, 16–026
—— v. Lambert (1839) 6 Cl. & F. 600 .... 5–009, 5–098, 5–101, 8–014, 15–046, 18–005, 18–114, 18–116, 18–117, 18–119, 18–120, 18–122
Dunlop Pneumatic Tyre Co. v. A.G. Cudell & Co. [1902] 1 K.B. 342, CA 25–064
Dunlop Pneumatic Tyre Co. v. New Garage and Motor Co. Ltd [1915] A.C. 79; 83 L.J.K.B. 1574; 111 L.T. 862; 30 T.L.R. 625 .... 16–032, 16–033, 16–034.
—— v. Selfridge & Co. Ltd [1915] A.C. 847 .... 3–037, 13–017
Dupont v. British South Africa Co. (1901) 18 T.L.R. 24 .... 6–020, 18–116, 19–006, 19–080, 19–099, 19–119, 21–015
Duppa v. Mayo (1669) 1 Wms. Saund, (6th ed.) 275 1–093
Durham v. Asser (1968) 67 D.L.R. (2d) 574 7–044
Duthie v. Hilton (1868) L.R. 4 C.P. 138; 38 L.J.C.P. 93; 19 L.T. 285; 17 W.R. 55; 3 Mar.L.C. 166 .... 1–128, 6–035, 15–120, 19–109
Dutton v. Bognor Regis U.D.C. [1972] 1 Q.B. 373; [1972] 2 W.L.R. 299; (1971) 116 S.J. 16; 70 L.G.R. 57; *sub nom* Dutton v. Bognor Regis United Building Co. [1972] 1 All E.R. 462; [1972] 1 Lloyd's Rep. 227 12–126
—— v. Solomonson (1803) 3 B. & P. 582; 127 E.R. 314 .... 5–098, 9–062
Duval & Co. Ltd v. Gans [1904] 2 K.B. 685; 73 L.J.K.B. 907; 91 L.T. 308; 20 T.L.R. 705; 53 W.R. 106 .... 9–047, 9–048
Dyal Singh v. Kenyan Insurance Ltd *See* Singh (Dyal) v. Kenyan Insurance.
Dynamics Corporation of America (No. 2), *Re* [1976] 1 W.L.R. 757; 120 S.J. 450; [1976] 2 All E.R. 669 25–194
Dynamics Corporation of America v. Citizens and Southern National Bank 356 F.Supp. 991 (1973) 23–149, 23–235, 23–239, 23–242, 23–243, 23–246

Dynamit AG v. Rio Tinto Co. Ltd *See* Ertel Bieber & Co. v. Rio Tinto Co. Ltd

E. v. Australian Red Cross Society; New South Wales Division (Australian Red Cross Society) Central Sydney Area Health Service [1991] 2 Med. L.R. 303; 105 A.L.R. 53 1–089
E.D. & F. Man Ltd v. Nigerian Sweets & Confectionery & Co. [1977] 2 Lloyd's Rep. 50 .... 16–019, 19–067, 19–206, 20–130, 23–098, 23–101, 23–102
E.E. Caledonia Ltd (Formerly Occidental Petoleum (Caledonia)) v. Orbit Valve Co. Europe plc; *sub nom.* Elf Enterprise, Caledonia Ltd (formerly Occidental Petroleum (Caledonia)) v. Orbit Valve Co. Europe plc [1994] 1 W.L.R. 1515; [1995] 1 All E.R. 174; [1994] 2 Lloyd's Rep. 239; *The Times*, May 30, 1994, CA; affirming [1994] 1 W.L.R. 221; [1993] 4 All E.R. 165; [1993] 2 Lloyd's Rep. 418, QBD (Comm Ct) 13–020
E. Grimstead & Son Ltd v. McGarrigan, unreported, October 27, 1999, CA 13–030, 13–056, 13–060
E. Hobbs (Farms) Ltd v. Baxenden (Chemical Co.) Ltd; Gerber Foods (Holdings) Ltd v. E. Hobbs (Farms) Ltd [1992] 1 Lloyd's Rep. 54, QBD 12–124, 14–084
E.M.I. Records Ltd v. Riley [1981] 1 W.L.R. 923; (1981) 125 S.J. 412; [1981] 2 All E.R. 838; [1981] F.S.R. 503 14–097
E.R.G. Petroli SpA v. Vitol SA: Ballenita and BP Energy, The [1992] 2 Lloyd's Rep. 455 .... 18–002, 18–321, 19–018, 19–021, 19–063, 19–074
Eagle Star Life Assurance Co Ltd v. Griggs [1998] 1 Lloyd's Rep. 256; *Independent*, October 20, 1997 (C.S.), CA 18–071
Eaglehill Ltd v. Needham (J.) Builders Ltd [1973] A.C. 992; [1972] 3 W.L.R. 789; 116 S.J. 861; [1972] 3 All E.R. 895; [1973] 1 Lloyd's Rep. 143 22–126
Eaglesfield v. Marquis of Londonderry (1876) 4 Ch.D. 693; 35 L.T. 822; 25 W.R. 190 10–009
Eakin v. Continental Illinois National Bank 875 F. 2d 114 (7th Cir. 1989) 23–139
Earl of Falmouth v. Thomas (1832) 1 Cr. & M. 89 1–094
Early v. Garrett (1829) 9 B. & C. 928; 4 Man. & Ry. K.B. 687; 8 L.J. (o.s.) K.B. 76 4–001
East v. Maurer [1991] 1 W.L.R. 461; [1991] 2 All E.R. 733, CA 4–022
East v. Smith (1847) 16 L.J. Q.B. 292; 4 Dow. & L. 744; 9 L.T. (o.s.) 130; 11 Jur. 412 22–122
East Asiatic Co. Inc. v. Canada Rice Mills Ltd [1939] 3 D.L.R. 695 11–075
East Ham Corporation v. Sunley (Bernard) & Sons Ltd [1966] A.C. 406; [1965] 3 W.L.R. 1096; 109 S.J. 874; [1965] 3 All E.R. 619; 64 L.G.R. 43; [1965] 2 Lloyd's Rep. 425 .... 16–043, 16–049, 16–053
East West Corp. v. DKBS 1912 *See* Utaniko Ltd v. P. & O. Nedlloyd BV (No. 1)
Eastham v. Leigh London and Provincial Properties [1971] Ch. 871; [1971] 2 W.L.R. 1149; 115 S.J. 266; [1971] 2 All E.R. 887; [1971] T.R. 33; 50 A.T.C. 53; 46 T.C. 687; [1971] J.P.L. 382, CA 1–051
East Midlands Electricity Board v. Grantham [1980] C.L.Y. 271 .... 1–071, 1–085
East River Steamship Corp. v. Transamerica Delavel Inc. 476 U.S. 858 (1986) 14–079
Easterbrook v. Gibb (1887) 3 T.L.R. 401 .... 8–050, 11–018
—— v. Hopkins [1918] N.Z.L.R. 428 .... 10–002, 10–005, 10–006
Eastern Construction Co. Ltd v. National Trust Co. Ltd [1914] A.C. 197; 83 L.J.P.C. 122; 101 L.T. 321 1–072
Eastern Counties Ry. v. Philipson (1855) 16 C.B. 2; 24 L.J.C.P. 140; 25 L.T. (o.s.) 84; 139 E.R. 653 8–05
Eastern Distributors Ltd v. Goldring (Murphy, Third Persons) [1957] 2 Q.B. 600; [1957] 3 W.L.R. 237; 101 S.J. 553; [1957] 2 All E.R. 525 .... 5–065, 7–009, 7–010, 7–011, 7–058
Eastern Supply Co. v. Keir [1974] 1 M.L.J. 10 12–055
Eastgate, *Re., ex p.* Ward [1905] 1 K.B. 465; 74 L.J.K.B. 324; 92 L.T. 207; 21 T.L.R. 198; 12 Mans. 11; *sub nom.* Eastgate, *Re ex p.* Trustee, 53 W.R. 432 .... 7–024, 7–028, 12–003
Eastman Chemical International A.G. v. N.M.T. Trading Ltd [1972] 2 Lloyd's Rep. 25 2–012
Eastwood v. Magnox Electric Plc; McCabe v. Cornwall CC [2004] UKHL 35; [2005] 1 A.C. 503; [2004] 3 W.L.R. 322; [2004] 3 All E.R. 991; [2004] I.C.R. 1064; [2004] I.R.L.R. 733; (2004) 101(32) L.S.G. 36; (2004) 154 N.L.J. 1155; (2004) 148 S.J.L.B. 909; *The Times*, July 16, 2004; *Independent*, October 11, 2004 (C.S), HL 16–047

Eastwood & Holt v. Studer (1926) 31 Com.Cas. 251 . . . . 19–095, 19–098
Easycar (UK) Ltd v. Office of Fair Trading (C336/03) [2005] All E.R. (EC) 834; [2005] E.C.R. I-1947; [2005] 2 C.M.L.R. 2; [2005] C.E.C. 577; *The Times*, March 15, 2005, ECJ 14–055
Ebbw Vale Steel Co. v. Blaina Iron Co. (1901) 6 Com.Cas. 33 . . . . 8–077, 8–085
Eberle's Hotels & Restaurant Co. v. Jones (1887) 18 QBD 459 1–072
Ebrahim Dawood Ltd v. Heath Ltd [1961] 2 Lloyd's Rep. 512 . . . . . . 6–040, 12–061, 12–067, 12–069
Ecay v. Godfrey (1947) 80 Ll.L.R. 286 10–006
Eclipse Motors Property Ltd v. Nixon [1940] V.L.R. 49 16–065
Economic Assurance Society v. Usbome [1902] A.C. 147; 71 L.J.P.C. 34; 85 L.T. 587 16–008
Ed Learn Ford Sales Ltd v. Giovannone (1990) 74 D.L.R. (4th) 761 . . . 4–012, 4–015, 4–029
Eddy v. Niman (1981) 73 Cr.App.R. 237; [1981] Crim. L.R. 502, R. 237 5–013
Eddy (George) Co. Ltd v. Corey [1951] 4 D.L.R. 90 6–041
Edelstein v. Schuler & Co. [1902] 2 K.B. 144; 71 L.J.K.B. 572; 87 L.T. 204; 50 W.R. 493; 7 Com.Cas. 172 22–023
Eden v. Dudfield (1841) 1 Q.B. 302 8–011
Edgcombe v. Rodd (1804) 5 East 294 9–044
Edgington v. Fitzmaurice (1885) 29 Ch.D. 459, 29 S.J. 650; 33 W.R. 911 . . . 10–007, 10–009, 19–192
Edmund Murray v. B.S.P. International Foundations (1992) 33 Con.L.R. 1, CA 11–060, 13–048, 13–086, 13–090, 13–095
Edilson v. Joyce [1917] N.Z.L.R. 648 8–077
Edmondston v. Drake & Mitchel 5 Pet. (30 U.S.) 624 23–236
Edmunds v. Lloyd Italico, l'Ancora Compagnia di Assicurazioni & Riassicurazione, SpA [1986] 1 W.L.R. 492; (1986) 130 S.J. 242; [1986] 2 All E.R. 249; [1986] 1 Lloyd's Rep. 326; (1986) 83 L.S.Gaz. 876 16–007
—— v. Merchants Despatch Co. (1883) 135 Mass, 283 3–014
—— v. Simmonds [2001] 1 W.L.R. 1003; [2001] R.T.R. 24; [2001] P.I.Q.R. P21; *The Times*, November 21, 2000, QBD 25–191
Edmundson v. Longton Corporation (1902) 19 T.L.R. 15 9–042
Edwards, *Re* (1873) L.R. 8 Ch.App. 289 . . . . 8–085, 8–086
Edwards v. Brewer (1837) 2 M. & W. 375; Murph. & H. 132; 6 L.J.Ex. 135; 1 Jur. 432; 150 E.R. 802 15–070
Edwards v. Clinch [1981] Ch. 1; [1981] 3 W.L.R. 707; (1981) 125 S.J. 762; [1981] 3 All E.R. 543; [1981] S.T.C. 617; (1981) T.C. 367; (1981) T.R. 393; (1982) A.C. 845 1–004
—— v. Ddin [1976] 1 W.L.R. 942; 120 S.J. 587, [1976] 3 All E.R. 705; (1976) 63 Cr.App.R. 218; [1976] R.T.R. 508; [1976] Crim.L.R. 580 . . . . 5–013, 5–097
—— v. Society of Graphical and Allied Trades [1971] Ch. 354; [1970] 3 W.L.R. 713; 114 S.J. 618; [1970] 3 All E.R. 689; 8 K.I.R. 1 17–002
—— v. Vaughan (1910) 26 T.L.R. 545 . . . . 5–042, 6–009, 6–037, 7–070, 7–073
Effort Shipping Co. Ltd v. Lundein Management SA (The Giannis NK) [1996] 1 Lloyd's Rep. 580 . . . . 18–096, 18–134
Egekvist Bakeries v. Tizel & Blinick [1950] 1 D.L.R. 585 . . . . 4–004, 4–026
Egmont Box Co. Ltd v. Registrar-General of Lands [1920] N.Z.L.R. 741 1–098
Egon Oldendorff v. Libera Corp (No.1) [1995] 2 Lloyd's Rep. 64; [1996] C.L.C. 482, QBD 25–001, 25–031, 25–079
—— v.——(No. 2) [1996] 1 Lloyd's Rep. 381, QBD 25–001, 25–020, 25–030, 25–031, 25–079
Egyptian International Foreign Trade Co. v. Soplex Wholesale Supplies (The Raffaella) [1984] 1 Lloyd's Rep. 102 . . . . 18–036, 19–035
Ehlers v. Kauffman (1883) 49 L.T. 806 7–113
Eichholz v. Bannister (1864) 17 C.B. (N.S.) 708; 5 New Rep. 87; 34 L.J.C.P. 105; 11 Jur. (N.S.) 15; 13 W.R. 96; 144 E.R. 284; *sub nom.* Eicoltz v. Bannister 12 L.T. 76 . . . . 4–001, 4–006
Eider, The [1893] P. 119; 62 L.J.P. 65; 69 L.T. 622; 9 T.L.R. 312; 7 Asp.M.C.L. 354; 1 R. 593 . . . . 9–047, 15–028
Eimco Corp. v. Tutt Bryant Ltd [1970] 2 N.S.W.R. 249 22–104
Einar Bugge A.S. v. Bowater (W.H.) Ltd (1925) 31 Com.Cas. 1 . . . . 20–029, 20–030
Eisinger v. General Accident Fire and Life Assurance Corporation Ltd [1955] 1 W.L.R. 869; 99 S.J. 511; [1955] 2 All E.R. 897; [1955] 2 Lloyd's Rep. 95 7–028

El Ajou v. Dollar Land Holdings [1994] 2 All E.R. 685; [1994] B.C.C. 143; [1994] 1 B.C.L.C. 464; [1993] N.P.C. 165; *The Times*, January 3, 1994, CA; reversing [1993] 3 All E.R. 717; [1993] B.C.L.C. 735; [1993] B.C.C. 698 .... 22–090, 25–146
El Amria and El Minia, The [1982] 2 Lloyd's Rep. 28; (1982) 126 S.J. 411; [1982] Com.L.R. 121 .... 18–040, 20–003
El Du Pont de Nemours & Co. v. Agnew [1987] 2 Lloyd's Rep. 585; [1987] F.L.R. 376; [1987] 2 F.T.L.R. 487, CA 25–074
El Greco (Australia) Pty Ltd v. Mediterranean Shipping Co SA [2004] 2 Lloyd's Rep. 537, Fed Ct (Aus) 21–087
Elbe Maru, The *See* Nippon Yuseh Kaisha v. International Import & Export Co. Ltd
Elbinger A.G. v. Armstrong (1874) L.R. 9 Q.B. 473; 43 L.J.Q.B. 211; 30 L.T. 871; 38 J.P. 774; 23 W.R. 127 ..... 16–046, 16–067, 17–021, 17–023, 17–036, 17–038, 17–040, 17–042, 17–045
Elder v. Kelly [1919] 2 K.B. 179; 88 L.J.K.B. 1253; 121 L.T. 94; 83 J.P. 166; 35 T.L.R. 391; 17 L.G.R. 413; 26 Cox C.C. 406 3–030
Elder Dempster & Co Ltd v. Paterson Zochonis & Co Ltd. *See* Paterson Zochonis & Co Ltd v. Elder Dempster & Co Ltd
Elder Dempster Lines v. Zaki Ishag (The Lycaon) [1983] 2 Lloyd's Rep. 548 ...... 18–016, 18–021, 18–022, 18–025, 18–038, 18–079, 18–095, 18–209, 18–214, 21–081
Elder Dempster Lines Ltd v. Ionic Shipping Agency Inc. [1968] 1 Lloyd's Rep. 529 23–196
Elder Smith Goldsbrough Mort Ltd v. McBride [1976] 2 N.S.W.L.R. 631 ... 11–019, 13–024, 13–028
Electrical Enterprises Retail Property Ltd v. Rodgers (1988) 15 N.S.W.L.R. 473 ..... 1–010, 10–008
Elektronska Industrija Oour TVA v. Transped Oour Kintinentalna Spedicna [1986] 1 Lloyd's Rep. 49 .... 21–060, 21–073
Elford v. Teed (1813) 1 M. & S. 28 22–099
Elian and Rabbath v. Matsas and Matsas [1966] 2 Lloyd's Rep. 495 23–277
Elitestone Ltd v. Morris; Elitestone Ltd v. Davies [1997] 1 W.L.R. 687; [1997] 2 All E.R. 513; (1998) 30 H.L.R. 266; [1997] 2 E.G.L.R. 115; [1997] 27 E.G. 116; [1997] E.G.C.S. 62; (1997) 94(19) L.S.G. 25; (1997) 147 N.L.J. 721; (1997) 141 S.J.L.B. 113; [1997] N.P.C. 66; *The Times*, May 7, 1997, HL; reversing (1997) 73 P. & C.R. 259; [1995] N.P.C. 142, CA 1–096
Eljay Trs. Inc. v. Rhada Exports 470 N.Y.S. 2d 12 (1984) 23–139
Elkington v. Amery [1936] 2 All E.R. 86; 80 S.J. 465 .... 2–031, 2–034
Ellershaw v. Magniac (1843) 6 Exch. 570n; 155 E.R. 670 .... 5–132, 5–137, 20–077
Elli 2, The. *See* Ilyssia Compania Naviera SA v. Bamadoah.
Elliman Sons & Co. v. Carrington & Son Ltd [1901] 2 Ch. 275; 70 L.J.Ch. 577; 84 L.T. 858; 49 W.R. 532; 45 S.J. 536 3–037
Elliott v. Pierson [1948] 1 All E.R. 939 16–093
—— v. Pybus (1828) 10 Bing. 512; 4 Moo. & S. 389; 3 L.J.C.P. 182; 131 E.R. 993 ... 5–075, 5–076, 5–077, 5–091
—— v. Thomas (1838) 3 M. & W. 170; 1 Horn. & H. 38; 7 L.J.Ex. 129; 150 E.R. 1102 5–049
Elliott (J.W.) & Co. v. Candor Manufacturing Co. (1920) 3 Ll.L.R. 105 19–075
Elliott Steam Tug Co. Ltd v. The Shipping Controller [1922] 1 K.B. 127; 91 L. J.K.B. 294; 126 L.T. 158; 15 Asp.M.L.C. 406 .... 5–011, 16–052
Ellis v. Glover & Hobson Ltd [1908] 1 K.B. 388 5–159
—— v. Hunt (1789) 3 T.R. 464; 100 E.R. 679 .... 8–008, 15–072
—— v. Mortimer (1805) 1 B. & P.N.R. 257; 127 E.R. 460 .... 5–041, 5–052, 5–053
—— v. Steinberg's Trustee [1925] 4 D.L.R. 733 5–048
—— v. Stenning (John) & Son [1932] 2 Ch. 81; [1932] All E.R. 597; 101 L.J.Ch. 401; 147 L.T. 449; 76 S.J. 232 .... 1–072, 4–012
—— v. Thompson (1838) 3 M. & W. 445; 1 Horn. & H. 131; 7 L.J.Ex. 185; 150 E.R. 1219 8–037
Ellis & Co. v. Cross [1915] 2 K.B. 654; 84 L.J.K.B. 1622; 113 L.T. 503; [1915] H.B.R. 239 7–113
Elmore v. Stone (1809) 1 Taunt. 458; 127 E.R. 912 .... 8–008, 8–009
Elmville, The [1904] P. 319 .... 22–126, 22–130

Elphick v. Barnes (1880) 5 C.P.D. 321; 49 L.J.Q.B. 698; 44 J.P. 651; 29 W.R. 139 ... 5–007, 5–040, 5–041, 5–055, 5–056, 12–057
Elphinstone v. Monkland Iron and Coal Co. (1886) 11 App.Cas. 332; 35 W.R. 17 .. 16–032, 16–036
Elsey & Co. Ltd v. Palmer (1924) ... 1–066
Elsner v. Mirams [1975] Crim.L.R. 519 ... 5–013
Elton (John) & Co. Ltd v. Chas. Page & Co. Ltd (1920) 4 Ll.L.R. 226 ..... 20–001, 20–009, 20–015
Elvin and Powell Ltd v. Plummer Roddis Ltd (1933) 50 T.L.R. 158; 78 S.J. 48 6–011
Elwell v. Jackson (1855) 1 T.L.R. 458 ... 9–030
Elwes v. Brigg Gas Co. (1886) 33 Ch.D. 562 ... 1–097
Elwin v. O'Regan and Maxwell [1971] N.Z.L.R. 1124 ... 7–082
Emanuel (Joseph I.) v. Cardia and Savoca [1958] 1 Lloyd's Rep. 121 ...... 20–114, 21–042, 21–045, 21–046
Emanuel (Lewis) & Son Ltd v. Sammut [1959] 2 Lloyd's Rep. 629 .. 6–049, 19–131, 19–132, 20–097
Embiricos v. Anglo-Austrian Bank [1905] 1 K.B. 677; 74 L.J.K.B. 326; 92 L.T. 305; 53 W.R. 306; 10 Com.Cas. 99; 21 T.L.R. 261 ... 22–022, 25–121, 25–131
—— v. Reid (Sydney) & Co. [1914] 3 K.B. 45; 83 L.J.K.B. 1348; 111 L.T. 291; 30 T.L.R. 451; 12 Asp.M.L.C. 513; 19 Com.Cas. 263 ... 6–046, 18–336
Emerald Stainless Steel Ltd v. South Side Distribution Ltd 1983 S.L.T. 162 ... 5–144, 5–146, 25–141
Emilien Marie, The (1875) 44 L.J.Adm. 9; 32 L.T. 435; Asp.M.L.C. 514 ... 18–088
Emmerson v. Heelis (1809) 2 Taunt. 38; 127 E.R. 989 ... 1–093, 2–004
Emmett v. Tottenham (1853) 8 Exch. 884; 22 L.J.Ex. 281; 21 L.T. (o.s.) 240; 17 Jur. 509; 1 W.R. 372; 1 C.L.R. 291; 155 E.R. 1612 ... 22–059
Empresa Cubana de Fletes v. Lagonisi Shipping Co. Ltd [1971] 1 Q.B. 488; [1971] 2 W.L.R. 221; (1970) 114 S.J. 862; [1971] 1 Lloyd's Rep. 7 ... 12–003
Empresa Cubana Importadora De Alimentos v. Octavia Shipping Co. SA (The Kefalonia Wind) [1986] 1 Lloyd's Rep. 273 ... 25–191
Empressa Exportadora de Azucar v. Industria Azucarera Nacional SA (The Playa Larga) [1983] 2 Lloyd's Rep. 171; [1983] Com. L.R. 58 .... 4–026, 4–027, 4–029, 4–030, 6–048, 6–056, 8–092, 18–210, 18–216, 18–337, 18–339, 18–341, 19–002, 19–008, 19–016, 19–023, 19–035, 19–071, 19–073, 19–103, 19–135, 19–142, 19–171, 19–185, 25–028, 25–119
Encyclopedia Britannica v. Hong Kong Producer, The, and Universal Marine Corporation 422 F. 2d 7 (1969) [1969] 2 Loyds's Rep. 536 ... 21–091, 21–093
Engineering Plastics Ltd v. J. Mercer & Sons Ltd [1985] 2 N.Z.L.R. 72 ... 11–075
Engler v. Janus Versand GmbH (C27/02) [2005] E.C.R. I-481; [2005] C.E.C. 187; [2005] I.L.Pr. 8, ECJ ... 25–045
English v. Cliff [1914] 2 Ch. 376; 83 L.J.Ch. 850; 111 L.T. 751; 30 T.L.R. 599; 58 S.J. 687 ... 8–034
—— v. Donnelly 1958 S.C. 494 ... 25–088
English and Scottish Mercantile Investment Co. Ltd v. Brunton [1892] 2 Q.B. 700; 62 L.J.Q.B. 136; 67 L.T. 406; 41 W.R. 133; 8 T.L.R. 772; 4 R. 58 ... 5–161
English Hop Growers v. Dering [1928] 2 K.B. 174 ...... 1–093, 1–094, 3–035, 3–037, 3–038, 3–039, 16–033
English, Scottish and Australian Bank v. Bank of South Africa (1922) 13 Ll.L.R. 21 .... 23–196, 23–210
Enichem v. Commission [1991] 11 E.C.R. 1623 ... 3–041
Enichem Anic SpA v. Ampelos Shipping Co. Ltd. (The Delfini) [1990] 1 Lloyd's Rep. 252, CA; [1988] 2 Lloyd's Rep. 599, QBD (Comm Ct) 5–131, 5–135, 5–137, 18–015, 18–078, 18–090, 18–107, 18–188, 19–005, 19–067, 19–075, 19–085, 19–087, 19–102, 25–071
Ennis v. Klassen (1990) 70 D.L.R. (4th) 321 ... 12–006
Ennstone Building Products Ltd v. Stanger Ltd; *sub nom.* Ennstone Building Products Ltd (formerly Natural Stone Products Ltd) v. Stanger Ltd (formerly TBV Stanger Ltd) (No.2) [2002] EWCA Civ 916; [2002] 1 W.L.R. 3059; [2002] 2 All E.R. (Comm) 479; [2003] 1 C.L.C. 265; [2002] B.L.R. 347; [2002] T.C.L.R. 23; [2002] P.N.L.R. 42; (2002) 99(35) L.S.G. 34; (2002) 146 S.J.L.B. 200; *Independent*, July 4, 2002, CA ... 25–001, 25.019, 25–022, 25–060, 25–064, 25–065

Entores Ltd v. Miles Far East Corporation [1955] 2 Q.B. 327; [1955] 3 W.L.R. 48; 99 S.J. 384; [1955] 2 All E.R. 493; [1955] 1 Lloyd's Rep. 511 .... 2–011, 2–015
Epsilon Rosa, The (No.2) v. Welex AG. *See* Welex AG v. Rosa Maritime Ltd (The Epsilon Rosa) (No.2)
Equitable Trust Co. of New York v. Dawson Partners Ltd (1927) 27 Ll.L.R. 49..... 22–088, 23–017, 23–115, 23–119, 23–126, 23–174, 23–185, 23–196, 23–198, 23–235
Eridania SpA (Formerly Cereol Italia Srl) v. Oetker (The Fjord Wind) 18–053, 18–114, 18–116, 18–142, 18–147, 20–082
Erie County Natural Gas & Fuel Co. v. Carroll [1911] A.C. 105; 80 L.J.P.C. 59; 103 L.T. 678. .... 1–087, 16–056, 16–058, 17–004, 17–019, 17–023, 17–024, 17–056
Eriksson v. Refiners Export Co., 35 N.Y.S. 2d 829 (1942) 23–068, 23–071, 23–082
Erlanger v. New Sombrero Phosphate Co. (1878) 3 App.Cas. 1218 12–007
Ertel Bieber & Co. v. Rio Tinto Co. [1918] A.C. 260 .... 6–042, 6–056, 18–306, 19–142, 25–119
Erven Warnink Besloten Vernootschap v. Townend (J.) & Sons (Hull) Ltd (No. 2) 126 S.J. 465; [1982] 3 All E.R. 312; [1982] Com.L.R. 184; [1982] R.P.C. 511; (1982) 79 L.S.Gaz. 987 16–012
Esal (Commodities) Ltd v. Oriental Credit Ltd [1985] 2 Lloyd's Rep. 546; [1986] F.L.R. 70 .... 23–140, 23–276, 23–284, 23–290
Escalera Silver Lead Mining Co., *Re* (1908) 25 T.L.R. 87 9–046
Escola v. Coca-Cola Bottling Co. 150 P. 2d 436 (1944) 14–078
Esdaile v. Sowerby (1809) 11 East 114 22–116
Esmail v. Rosenthal (J.) & Sons Ltd *See* Rosenthal (J.) & Sons v. Esmail (T/A H.M.H. Esmail & Sons).
Esposito v. Bowden (1857) 7 E. & B. 763 6–043
Esso Petroleum Co. Ltd v. Customs & Excise Commissioners [1976] 1 W.L.R. 1; (1975) 120 S.J. 49; [1976] 1 All E.R. 117 .... 1–033, 1–034, 2–002, 14–047
—— v. Harper's Garage (Stourport) Ltd [1968] A.C. 269; [1967] 2 W.L.R. 871; 111 S.J. 174; [1967] 1 All E.R. 699..... 1–009, 2–045, 3–034, 3–035, 3–036, 3–038, 8–061, 17–099
—— v. Mardon [1976] Q.B. 801; [1976] 2 W.L.R. 583; [1976] 2 All E.R. 5; [1976] 2 Lloyd's Rep. 305; 120 S.J. 131, CA .. 2–027, 10–006, 10–012, 10–013, 10–017, 10–021, 12–011, 12–013, 14–043
—— v. Milton [1997] 1 W.L.R. 938; [1997] 2 All E.R. 593; [1997] C.L.C. 634; (1997) 16 Tr. L.R. 250; *The Times*, February 13, 1997; *The Independent*, February 19, 1997, CA 9–026, 9–039, 13–039, 13–087
—— v. Niad Ltd [2001] All E.R. (D) 324 3–038
Esteve Trading Corp. v. Agropec International (The Golden Rio) [1990] 2 Lloyd's Rep. 273, QBD (Comm Ct) 16–070, 19–171, 20–070, 20–114, 20–115, 20–134
Etablissement Esefka International Anstalt v. Central Bank of Nigeria [1979] 1 Lloyd's Rep. 445 .... 23–144, 23–146, 23–235
Etablissements Chainbaux S.A.R.L. v. Harbormaster Ltd [1955] 1 Lloyd's Rep. 303 .. 8–030 9–016, 20–058, 23–086
Etablissements Soules et Cie. v. International Trade Development Co. Ltd [1980] 1 Lloyd's Rep. 129 19–150
—— v. Intertradex SA [1991] 1 Lloyd's Rep. 379 .... 19–002, 19–008, 19–088, 19–089, 19–166, 19–207, 19–219
Etler v. Kertesz (1960) 26 D.L.R. (2d) 209 25–176
Eurico SpA v. Philipp Brothers (The Epaphus) [1987] 2 Lloyd's Rep. 215, CA, affirming [1986] 2 Lloyd's Rep. 387 .... 19–011, 19–031, 19–032, 19–088, 19–176
Euro-Diam Ltd v. Bathurst [1990] 1 Q.B. 35 .... 3–028, 25–119
European Asian Bank A.G. v. Punjab and Sind Bank (No. 1) [1982] Com.L.R. 76; [1982] 2 Lloyd's Rep. 356, CA; affirming [1981] Com.L.R. 246; [1981] 2 Lloyd's Rep. 651 .... 23–140, 25–076, 25–161
—— v. Punjab and Sind Bank (No. 2) [1983] 1 W.L.R. 642; (1983) 127 S.J. 379; [1983] 2 All E.R. 508; [1983] 1 Lloyd's Rep. 611; [1983] Com.L.R. 128 ...... 22–085, 23–016, 23–064, 23–117, 23–188
European Bank for Reconstruction & Development v. Tekoglu [2004] EWHC 846, QBD (Comm) 25–109, 25–030, 25–076
European Commission v. United Kingdom *See* Commission of the European Communities v. United Kingdom (C300/95)

European Grain & Shipping Ltd v. Cremer (Peter) [1982] 2 Lloyd's Rep. 211 .... 8–046, 18–350
—— v. Geddes (David) (Proteins) Ltd [1977] 2 Lloyd's Rep. 591 ...... 8–007, 8–036, 8–039
—— v. Hall (R. & H.) plc [1990] 2 Lloyd's Rep. 139 19–181
—— v. Rayner (J.H.) & Co. Ltd [1970] 2 Lloyd's Rep. 239 19–140
Europemballage and Continental Can Co. Inc. v. E.C. Commission [1973] E.C.R. 215; [1973] C.M.L.R. 199 3–041
Evanghelinos (M.P.) v. Leslie and Anderson (1920) 3 Ll.L.R. 17 .... 6–019, 11–052, 18–255
Evans v. Nichol (1841) 3 M. & G. 614; 4 Scott N.R. 43; 11 L.J.C.P. 6; 5 Jur. 1110; 133 E.R. 1286 .... 5–098, 18–066
—— v. Ritchie (1964) 44 D.L.R. (2d) 675 7–032
Evans v. Roberts (1826) 5 B. & C. 829 .... 1–091, 1–093
—— v. Triplex Safety Glass Co. Ltd [1936] 1 All E.R. 283 14–061
—— v. Trueman (1830) 1 Moody & R. 10 7–047
Evans (J.) & Son (Portsmouth) Ltd v. Andrea Merzario Ltd [1976] 1 W.L.R. 1078; 120 S.J. 734; [1976] 2 All E.R. 930; [1976] 2 Lloyd's Rep. 165 ..... 2–027, 10–012, 10–013, 21–073, 21–083, 21–089, 21–093
Evans, Sons & Co. v. Cunard S.S. Co. Ltd (1902) 18 T.L.R. 374 .... 18–060, 19–032
Evansville National Bank v. Kaufman 93 N.Y. 273 (1883) 23–049
Everard v. Watson (1853) 1 El. & Bl. 801; 22 L.J. Q.B. 222; 21 L.T. (o.s.) 74; 17 Jur. 762; 1 C.L.R. 424; 118 E.R. 636 22–124
Everett v. Collins (1810) 2 Camp. 515 9–031
Evergreen Marine Corp v. Aldgate Warehouse (Wholesale) Ltd [2003] EWHC 667; [2003] 2 Lloyd's Rep. 597, QBD 18–047, 18–065, 20–008, 20–026, 20–060, 20–082
Excess Insurance Co. Ltd v. Mander [1997] 2 Lloyd's Rep. 119; [1995] L.R.L.R. 358; *Lloyd's List*, May 18, 1995 (I.D.), QBD (Comm Ct) 18–084
Exercise Shipping Co. Ltd v. Bay Maritime Lines Ltd (Fantasy, The) [1992] 1 Lloyd's Rep. 235, CA; affirming (1991) 2 Lloyd's Rep. 391 21–106
Eximenco Handels A.G. v. Partrederiet Oro Chief (The "Oro Chief") [1983] 2 Lloyd's Rep. 509; (1983) 133 New L.J. 642 17–099
Exotic Transfers Far East Buying Office v. Exotic Trading USA Inc. 717 F. Supp. 14170 (1991) 23–201
Experience Hendrix LLC v. PPX Enterprises Inc [2003] EWCA Civ 323; [2003] 1 All E.R. (Comm) 830; [2003] E.M.L.R. 25; [2003] F.S.R. 46; (2003) 26(7) I.P.D. 26046; (2003) 100(22) L.S.G. 29; (2003) 147 S.J.L.B. 509; *The Times*, April 19, 2003, CA 16–031
Expo Fabrics (UK) Ltd v. Martin [2003] EWCA Civ 1165, CA 13–090
Export Credit Guarantees Department v. Davenport (Shoes) Ltd. (CA, unreported, February 3, 1983) 24–015
Export Credits Guarantee Department v. Universal Oil Products Co. & Procon Inc. and Procon (Great Britain) [1983] 1 W.L.R. 399; (1983) 127 S.J. 403; [1983] 2 All E.R. 205; [1983] 2 Lloyd's Rep. 152; (1983) 133 New L.J. 662; [1983] B.L.R. 106 .... 16–035, 24–042
Exportadora de Azucar v. Industrie Azucarera Nacional SA [1983] 2 Lloyd's Rep. 171 6–041
Exportelisa SA v. Giuseppe & Figli Soc. Coll. [1978] 1 Lloyd's Rep. 433 ..... 6–054, 8–092, 18–286, 18–309, 19–140, 20–105
Eyre v. Measday [1986] 1 All E.R. 488; (1986) 136 New L.J. 91, CA 14–051

Faccini Dori v. Recreb Srl (C91/92) [1995] All E.R. (E.C.) 1; [1994] E.C.R. I-3325; [1995] 1 C.M.L.R. 665; *The Times*, August 4, 1994; *Financial Times*, August 2, 1994, ECJ 14–081
Fair Pavilions Inc. v. First National City Bank, 24 A.D. 2d 109; 264 N.Y.S. 2d 255 (1965) 23–246
Fairclough, Dodd & Jones Ltd v. Vantol (J.H.) Ltd *See* Vantol (J.H.) Ltd v. Fairclough, Dodd & Jones Ltd
Fairfax v. Illawarro Steam Navigation Co. (1872) 11 S.C.R. (N.S.W.) 103 15–070
Fal Oil Co Ltd v. Petronas Trading Corp Sdn Bhd (The Devon) [2004] EWCA Civ 822; [2004] 2 All E.R. (Comm) 537; [2004] 2 Lloyd's Rep. 282; [2004] 2 C.L.C. 1062, CA 19–088
Falcke v. Gray (1859) 4 Drew. 651; 29 L.J.Ch. 28; 33 L.T. (o.s.) 297; 5 Jur. (n.s.) 645; 7 W.R. 535; 62 E.R. 250 .... 17–0199, 17–100

Falco Finance Ltd v. Gough (1999) 17 Tr. L.R. 526; [1999] C.C.L.R. 16, CC (Macclesfield) 14–150
Falk, *ex p.* (1880) 14 Ch.D. 446 15–100
Falk v. Fletcher (1865) 18 C.B. (N.S.) 403; 5 New Rep. 272; 34 L.J.C.P. 146; 11 Jur. (N.S.) 176; 13 W.R. 346; 144 E.R. 501 .... 5–131 18–167, 18–168, 18–210, 18–228, 18–232, 20–141
Famouri v. Dialcord Ltd (1983) 133 N.L.J. 153 23–108
Fanshaw v. Peet (1857) 26 L.J.Ex. 314; 2 H. & N. 1; 5 W.R. 489 22–104
Far Eastern Shipping Co. plc v. Scales Trading Ltd [2001] 1 All E.R. (Comm) 319; [2001] Lloyd's Rep. Bank. 29; [2001] C.L.C. 412, PC (NZ) 12–003
Far Eastern Textile Ltd v. City National Bank and Trust Co. 430 F.Supp. 193 (1977) 23–116, 23–196, 23–201, 23–235
Farina v. Home (1846) 16 M. & W. 119; 16 L.J.Ex. 73; 8 L.T. (O.S.) 277; 153 E.R. 1124 .... 8–012, 8–013, 18–193
Farley v. Skinner (No.2); *sub nom.* Skinner v. Farley [2001] UKHL 49; [2002] 2 A.C. 732, [2001] 3 W.L.R. 899; [2001] 4 All E.R. 801; [2002] B.L.R. 1; 79 Con. L.R. 1; [2002] H.L.R. 5; [2002] P.N.L.R. 2; [2001] 49 E.G. 120; [2001] 48 E.G. 131; [2001] 42 E.G.C.S. 139; (2001) 98(40) L.S.G. 41; (2001) 145 S.J.L.B. 230; [2001] N.P.C. 146; *The Times*, October 15, 2001; *The Daily Telegraph*, October 16, 2001, HL: reversing 73 Con. L.R. 70; [2000] Lloyd's Rep. P.N. 516; [2000] P.N.L.R. 441; [2000] 2 E.G.L.R. 125; [2000] E.G.C.S. 52; (2000) 97(15) L.S.G. 41; [2000] N.P.C. 40; *The Times*, April 14, 2000, CA 14–007, 16–047, 16–048, 17–021, 17–071, 17–099
Farley v. Turner (1857) 26 L.J.Ch. 710; 29 L.T. (O.S.) 257; 3 Jur. (N.S.) 532; 5 W.R. 666 23–125
Farley and Grant, *Re* [1936] 1 D.L.R. 57 25–176
Farmeloe v. Bain (1876) 1 C.P.D. 445; 45 L.J.Q.B. 264; 34 L.T. 324 15–029
Farmers and Mechanics' National Bank v. Loftus 19 A, 347 (1890) 25–127
Farmer's and Settler's Co-op Society Ltd, *Re* (1909) 9 S.R. (N.S.W.) 41 7–052
Farnham v. Atkins (1670) 1 Sid. 446 2–036
Farnsworth v. Federal Commissioner of Taxation (1949) 78 C.L.R. 504 1–057
Farnworth Finance Facilities Ltd v. Atlryde [1970] 1 W.L.R. 1053; 114 S.J. 354; [1970] 2 All E.R. 774 .... 11–073, 13–046, 13–051, 14–021, 14–047
Farquharson Bros. & Co. v. King & Co. [1902] A.C. 325 .... 7–008, 7–009, 7–010, 7–016
Farr v. Hain S.S. Co. 121 F. 2d 940 (1941) 18–059
Farrand v. Lazarus [2002] EWHC 226; [2002] 3 All E.R. 175; (2002) 166 J.P. 227, QBD (Admin Ct) 14–112
Farrell v. Alexander [1977] A.C. 59; [1976] 3 W.L.R. 145; [1976] 2 All E.R. 721; (1976) 32 P. & C.R. 292 .... 1–002, 1–004
Farrow's Bank Ltd, *Re* [1923] 1 Ch. 41; 92 L.J.Ch. 153; 128 L.T. 332; 67 S.J. 78; [1925] B. & C.R. 8 22–073
Fastframe Ltd v. Lochinski, unreported March 3, 1993, CA 9–026
Faulkners Ltd, *Re* (1917) 38 D.L.R. 84 11–075
Fawcett v. Smethurst (1914) 84 L.J.K.B. 473; 112 L.T. 309; 31 T.L.R. 85; 59 S.J. 220 2–033
—— v. Star Car Sales Ltd [1960] N.Z.L.R. 406 3–012
Fay v. Miller, Wilkins & Co. [1941] 2 All E.R. 18; [1941] Ch. 360; 110 L.J.Ch. 124; 166 L.T. 33; 57 T.L.R. 423; 85 S.J. 213 2–006
Feast Contractors Ltd v. Vincent (Ray) Ltd [1974] 1 N.Z.L.R. 212 11–061
Federacion Nacional de Empresas de Instrumentacion Cientifica Medica Tecnica y Dental (FENIN) v. Commission of the European Communities (T319/99) [2004] All E.R. (EC) 300; [2003] E.C.R. II-357; [2003] 5 C.M.L.R. 1; (2003) 72 B.M.L.R. 128, CFI I 3–041
Federal Bulk Carriers Inc. v. C. Itoh Ltd (The Federal Bulker) [1989] 1 Lloyd's Rep. 103 18–063
Federal Commerce & Navigation Co. Ltd v. Molena Alpha Inc. (The Nanfri) (The Benfri), (The Lorfri) [1979] A.C. 757; [1978] 3 W.L.R. 991; (1978) 122 S.J. 843; [1979] 1 All E.R. 307; [1979] 1 Lloyd's Rep. 201 .... 8–078, 8–080, 10–035, 12–019, 12–021, 13–052
—— v. SA (The Martha Envoy) [1978] A.C. 1; [1977] 3 W.L.R. 126; 121 S.J. 459; [1977] 2 All E.R. 849; [1977] 2 Lloyd's Rep. 301 .... 25–193, 25–194
Federspiel (Carlos) & Co. SA v. Charles Twigg & Co. Ltd [1957] 1 Lloyd's Rep. 240 .... 18–210, 20–007, 20–008, 21–004

Feinberg (Philip A.) Inc. v. Varig SA 363 N.Y.S. 2d 195 (1974), affirmed 370 N.Y.S. 2d 499 (1975) 23–128
Feise v. Wray (1802) 3 East 93 .... 15–013, 15–017, 15–062, 15–065
Feldarol Foundry Plc v. Hermes Leasing (London) Ltd; *sub nom.* Feldaroll Foundry Plc v. Hermes Leasing (London) Ltd; Feldarol Foundry Plc v. Amari Sant Agata Classics [2004] EWCA Civ 747; (2004) 101(24) L.S.G. 32; (2004) 148 S.J.L.B. 630, CA 13–074, 14–030
Feliciana, The (1915) 59 S.J. 546 15–024
Felthouse v. Bindley (1862) 11 C.B. (N.S.) 869; 6 L.T. 157 2–014
FENIN v. EC Commission. *See* Federacion Nacional de Empresas de Instrumentacion Cientifica Medica Tecnica y Dental (FENIN) v. Commission of the European Communities (T319/99)
Fenton v. Kenny [1969] N.Z.L.R. 552 12–009
Fenwick v. Macdonald, Fraser & Co. (1904) 6 F. (Ct. Sess.) 850; 41 S.L.R. 638; 12 S.L.T. 227 2–005
Fenwick, Stobart & Co. Ltd. *Re* [1902] 1 Ch. 507; 71 L.J.Ch. 321; 86 L.T. 193; 9 Mans. 205 .... 22–121, 22–131
Fercometal S.A.R.L. v. MSC Mediterranean Shipping Co. SA; Simona, The [1989] A.C. 788; [1988] 3 W.L.R. 200; [1988] 2 All E.R. 742; [1988] 2 Lloyd's Rep. 199; (1988) 132 S.J. 966; 138 New L.J. 178 HL; affirming [1987] 2 Lloyd's Rep. 236, CA 8–006, 9–012, 9–015, 9–018, 9–019, 9–020, 12–021, 16–080, 16–082, 17–013, 17–016, 19–161, 19–165, 19–166, 19–170, 19–177, 19–210
Ferens v. O'Brien (1883) 11 Q.B.D. 21; 52 L.J.M.C. 70; 47 J.P. 472; 31 W.R. 643; 15 Cox C.C. 332 1–087
Feret v. Hill (1854) 15 C.B. 207 3–031
Ferguson v. Carrington (1829) 9 B. & C. 59; 7 L.J. (O.S.) K.B. 139; 109 E.R. 22 16–016
Ferguson Shipbuilders Ltd v. Voith Hydro GmbH & Co. KG 2000 S.L.T. 229; 1999 G.W.D. 31–1500, OH 25–034, 25–060, 25–065
Ferran, [1988] C.L.J. 213 5–161
Ferrier, *Re. ex p.* Trustee v. Donald [1944] Ch. 295; 114 L.J.Ch. 15; 60 T.L.R. 295; 88 S.J. 171 .... 5–005, 5–054
Fertico Belg SA v. Phosphate Chemicals Export Assoc. 100 A.D. 2d 165, 473 N.Y.S. 2d 403 (1984) 23–027
Fessard v. Mugnier (1865) 18 C.B. (N.S.) 286; 5 New Rep. 307; 34 L.J.C.P. 126; 11 L.T. 635; 11 Jur. (N.S.) 283; 13 W.R. 388 .... 9–047, 16–016
Feuer Leather Corp. v. Johnstone & Sons [1983] Com.L.R. 12; [1981] Com.L.R. 251 .... 5–156, 7–047
Fibrosa Spolka Akcyjna v. Fairbairn Lawson Combe Barbour Ltd; *sub nom.* Fibrosa Societe Anonyme v. Fairbairn Lawson Combe Barbour Ltd [1943] A.C. 32; [1942] 2 All E.R. 122; (1942) 73 Ll. L. Rep. 45; 144 A.L.R. 1298; HL; reversing [1942] 1 K.B. 12; (1941) 70 Ll. L. Rep. 30, CA 6–035, 6–039, 6–042, 6–043, 6–051, 6–056, 60971, 12–065, 16–040, 17–090, 17–091, 18–336, 19–072, 19–136, 19–142, 19–143, 20–014, 20–022, 25–176
Ficom SA v. Sociedad Cadex Ltda. [1980] 2 Lloyd's Rep. 118 .... 20–027, 23–110
Fidelity Bank v. Lutheran Mutual Life Insurance Co., 465 F. 2d 211 (1972) 23–239, 23–241
Field v. Lelean (1861) 6 H. & N. 617; 30 L.J.Ex. 168; 4 L.T. 121; 7 Jur. (N.S.) 918; 9 W.R. 387; 158 E.R. 255 .... 15–031, 15–034
Fielding & Co. v. Corry [1898] 1 Q.B. 268; 67 L.J.Q.B. 7; 77 L.T. 453; 46 W.R. 97 22–127, 22–128
Fielding & Platt Ltd v. Najjar [1969] 1 W.L.R. 357, 113 S.J. 160; [1969] 2 All E.R. 150 .... 9–032, 22–064, 25–119
Figgis, *Re*; Roberts v. MacLaren [1969] Ch. 123; [1968] 2 W.L.R. 1173; 112 S.J. 156; [1968] 1 All E.R. 999 8–034
Fillmore's Valley Nurseries Ltd v. North American Cyanamid Ltd (1958) 14 D.L.R. (2d) 297 .... 11–057, 13–012
Fina Supply Ltd v. Shell UK Ltd (The Poitu) [1991] 1 Lloyd's Rep. 452 20–020
Finagrain SA Geneva v. P. Kruse Hamburg [1976] 2 Lloyd's Rep. 508 .... 8–025, 8–030, 8–047, 8–101, 12–035, 12–036, 19–012, 19–150
Financings Ltd v. Baldock [1963] 2 Q.B. 104; [1963] 2 W.L.R. 359; 107 S.J. 15; [1963] 1 All E.R. 443 12–021

Financings Ltd v. Stimson [1962] 1 W.L.R. 1184; [1962] 3 All E.R. 386 ...... 1–054, 2–007, 3–005
Finch Motors Ltd v. Quin (No. 2) [1980] 2 N.Z.L.R. 519 .... 11–057, 12–040, 12–056
Fine Art Society Ltd v. Union Bank of London Ltd (1886) 17 Q.B.D. 705; 56 L.J.Q.B. 70; 55 L.T. 536; 51 J.P. 69; 35 W.R. 114 22–023
Finelvet A.G. v. Vinava Shipping Co. [1983] 1 W.L.R. 1469; (1983) 127 S.J. 680; [1983] 2 All E.R. 658; [1983] 1 Lloyd's Rep. 503; [1983] Com.L.R. 126; (1983) L.S.Gaz. 2684 18–336
Finlay v. Liverpool and Great Western S.S. Co. Ltd (1870) 23 L.T. 251 18–085
Finlay v. Metro Toyota Ltd (1977) 82 D.L.R. (3d) 440 12–056
Finlay (James) & Co. Ltd v. N.V. Kwik Hoo Tong H.M. [1929] 1 K.B. 400; [1928] All E.R. Rep. 110; 98 L.J.K.B. 251; 140 L.T. 389; 45 T.L.R. 149; 34 Com.Cas. 143; 17 Asp.M.L.C. 566 .... 16–052, 17–027, 17–028, 17–032, 19–035, 19–056, 19–144, 19–190, 19–191, 19–192, 19–194, 19–196, 19–197, 19–198, 19–202, 21–039
Finnegan v. Allen [1943] K.B. 425; [1943] 1 All E.R. 493; 112 L.J.K.B. 323; 168 L.T. 316 2–051
Finnish Government (Ministry of Food) v. Ford (H.) & Co. Ltd (1921) 6 Ll.L.R. 188 .... 10–037, 18–235, 20–053, 21–030
Fiorentino Comm Giuseppe Srl v. Farnesi [2005] EWHC 160; [2005] 1 W.L.R. 3718; [2005] 2 All E.R. 737; [2005] 1 All E.R. (Comm) 575; [2005] B.C.C. 771; *The Times*, March 3, 2005, Ch D 22–116
First Energy (U.K.) Ltd v. Hungarian International Bank Ltd [1993] 2 Lloyd's Rep. 194; [1993] B.C.C. 533; [1993] B.C.L.C. 1409; [1993] N.P.C. 34; *The Times*, March 4, 1993, CA 7–010
First National Bank pic v. Thompson [1996] 2 W.L.R. 293 4–011
First Sport v. Barclays Bank [1993] 1 W.L.R. 1229; [1993] 3 All E.R. 789; (1993) 12 Tr.L.R. 69; *The Times*, March 11, 1993, CA 9–034
Firth, *Re* (1879) 12 Ch.D. 337, 48 L.J.Bcy. 122; 40 L.T. 823; 27 W.R. 925 .... 22–068, 22–069, 22–073, 22–074, 22–143
Firth v. Midland Railway (1875) L.R. 20 Eq. 100; 44 L.J.Ch. 313; 32 L.T. 219; 23 W.R. 509 2–051
—— v. Thrush (1828) 8 B. & C. 387; 2 Man. & Ry. K.B. 359; 6 L.J. (o.s.) K.B. 355 22–130
Fischel v. Scott (1854) 15 C.B. 69; 139 E.R. 344; *sub nom.* Fitchett v. Scott 2 C.L.R. 1774 21–023
Fischel & Co. v. Knowles (1922) 12 Ll.L.R. 36 19–029
Fisher v. Bell [1961] 1 Q.B. 394; [1960] 3 W.L.R. 919; 125 J.P. 101; 104 S.J. 981; [1960] 3 All E.R. 731 .... 1–027, 2–002, 4–073
—— v. Calvert (1879) 27 W.R. 301 22–041
—— v. Harrods Ltd 110 S.J. 133; [1966] 1 Lloyd's Rep. 500; 116 New L.J. 919 14–063
Fisher Reeves & Co. v. Armour & Co. [1920] 3 K.B. 614; 90 L.J.K.B. 172; 124 L.T. 122; 36 T.L.R. 800; 64 S.J. 698; 15 Asp.M.L.C. 91; 26 Com.Cas. 46 .... 5–089, 8–005, 12–052, 12–055
Fitt v. Cassanet (1842) 4 M. & G. 898; 5 Scott N.R. 902; 12 L.J.C.P. 70; 134 E.R. 369; *sub nom.* Pitt v. Cassanet, 6 Jur. 1125 .... 17–090, 17–106
Fitzroy v. Cave [1905] 2 K.B. 364, CA 23–068
Fitzwilliam v. Parson of Arcsay (1443) Y.B. 21 Hen. 6 1–106
Flagship Cruises Ltd v. New England Merchants National Bank of Boston 569F. 2d. 699 (1978) 23–016, 23–188, 23–196, 23–203, 23–210, 23–236
Flamar Interocean Ltd v. Denmac Ltd (The Flamar Pride) [1990] 1 Lloyd's Rep. 434 .... 13–090, 13–091, 13–095, 13–096, 18–280
Flanagan v. Seaver (1859) 9 Ir.Ch.R. 230 1–093
Fleet Bros. v. Morrison (1854) 16 D. (Ct. of Sess.) 1122; 26 Sc. Jur. 607 ..... 6–021, 18–246
Fleming & Wendeln GmbH & Co v. Sanofi SA/AG [2003] EWHC 561; [2003] 2 Lloyd's Rep. 473; [2003] 2 C.L.C. 774, QBD 8–030, 19–181
Fletcher v. Bowsher (1819) 2 Stark 561; 171 E.R. 736 13–028
—— v. Budgen [1974] 1 W.L.R. 1056; 118 S.J. 498; [1974] 2 All E.R. 1243; [1974] R.T.R. 471; 72 L.G.R. 634; 59 Cr.App.R. 234; [1974] Crim.L.R. 489 14–112
Fletcher v. Taylcur (1855) 17 C.B. 21; 925 L.J.C.P. 65; 26 L.T. (o.s.) 139 E.R. 973 .. 17–038, 17–040

Flippo v. Mode O'Day Frock Shops of Hollywood 449 S.W. 2d 692 (1970) 11–030
Floating Dock Ltd v. Hong Kong and Shanghai Banking Corporation [1986] 1 Lloyd's Rep. 65 . . . . 23–136, 23–203
Floods of Queensferry Ltd v. Shand Construction Ltd (No.3) [2000] B.L.R. 81, QBD (T&CC) 12–010
Florence, *Re, ex p.* Wingfield (1879) 10 Ch.D. 591; 40 L.T. 15; 27 W.R. 246 5–047
Flower v. London & North Western Railway Co. [1894] 2 Q.B. 65 2–033
Flynn v. Mackin & Mahon [1974] I.R. 101 . . . . 1–031, 1–037, 1–039
—— v. Scott 1949 S.C. 442 . . . . 11–055, 12–055
Foakes v. Beer (1884) 9 App.Cas. 605 . . . . 9–024, 12–035
Foaminol Laboratories v. British Artid Plastics [1941] 2 All E.R. 393 17–070
Foley v. Classique Coaches Ltd [1934] 2 K.B. 1 . . . . 2–017, 2–046, 3–038, 17–103
—— v. Hill (1848) 2 H.L.C. 28; 9 E.R. 1002 . . . . 5–152, 22–144
Folkes v. King [1923] 1 K.B. 282 . . . . 7–022, 7–037, 7–038, 7–074
Food Corporation of India v. Antclizo Shipping Corp. (The Antclizo) [1988] 1 W.L.R. 603; (1988) 132 S.J. 752; [1988] 2 All E.R. 513; [1988] 2 Lloyd's Rep. 93; [1988] 2 F.T.L.R. 124; (1988) 138 New L.J. 135 8–031
Fooks v. Smith (1924) 2 K.B. 508; 94 L.J.K.B. 23; 132 L.T. 486; 16 Asp.M.L.C. 435; 30 Com.Cas. 97; 19 Ll.L.R. 297 19–052
Footersville Property Ltd v. Miles (1988) 48 SAS.R., 525 12–047
Foran v. Wight (1989) 168 C.L.R. 385 . . . . 9–018, 9–019
Ford v. Clarksons Holidays Ltd [1971] 1 W.L.R. 1412; 115 S.J. 642; [1971] 3 All E.R. 454 14–100
—— v. Cotesworth (1870) L.R. 5 Q.B. 544; 10 B. & S. 991; 39 L.J.Q.B. 188; 23 L.T. 1169; 3 Mar. L.C. 468 8–040
—— v. Yates (1841) 2 M. & G. 549; Drinkwater 109; 2 Scott N.R. 645; 10 L.J.C.P. 117; 133 E.R. 866 9–057
Ford & Son (Oldham) Ltd v. Henry Leetham & Sons Ltd (1915) 21 Com.Cas. 55 . . . . 18–344, 18–352
Ford (Charles E.) Ltd v. AFEC Inc. [1986] 2 Lloyd's Rep. 307 . . . . 18–273, 19–165
Ford Motor Co. v. Armstrong (1915) 31 T.L.R. 267; 59 S.J. 362 16–034
Ford Motor Credit Co. Ltd v. Harmack [1972] C.L.Y. 1649 . . . . 7–091, 7–101
Fordy v. Harwood, March 30, 1999, CA 10–005
Foreign Venture Limited Partnership v. Chemical Bank, 399 N.Y.S. 2d 714 (1977) 23–244
Foreman and Ellams Ltd v. Blackburn [1928] 2 K.B. 60; [1928] All E.R. 512; 97 L.J.K.B. 355; 139 L.T. 68; 33 Com.Cas. 359; 17 Asp.M.L.C. 461 . . . . 18–270, 18–271, 18–273, 19–034
Forestall Mimosa Ltd v. Oriental Credit Ltd [1986] 1 W.L.R. 631; (1986) 130 S.J. 202; [1986] 2 All E.R. 400; [1986] 1 Lloyd's Rep. 329; [1986] F.L.R. 171; (1986) 83 L.S.Gaz. 779 . . . . 23–026, 23–029, 23–053, 23–131, 23–135
Forestry Commission of N.S.W. v. Stefanetto (1976) 133 C.L.R. 507 16–035
Forget v. Ostigny [1895] A.C. 318; 64 L.J.P.C. 62; 72 L.T. 399; 43 W.R. 590 P.C. 1–104
Forman v. Wright (1851) 11 C.B. 481; 20 L.J.C.P. 145; 15 Jur. 706 22–064
Forman & Co. Property Ltd v. The Ship "Liddesdale" [1900] A.C. 190; 69 L.J.P.C. 44; 82 L.T. 331; 9 Asp.M.L.C. 45 6–040
Formica v. Export Credits Guarantee Department [1995] 1 Lloyd's Rep. 692; *The Times*, October 19, 1994, QBD 24–013
Formula One Autocentres Ltd v. Birmingham City Council (1999) 163 J.P. 234; [1999] R.T.R. 195; *The Times*, December 29, 1998, QBD 14–113
Forrestt & Son Ltd v. Aramayo (1900) 83 L.T. 335; 9 Asp.M.L.C. 134 . . . . . . 8–004, 20–012, 20–014, 20–035, 20–047, 20–049, 20–050
Forsikringsaktieselskabet Scapet Vesta v. Butcher (No. 1) [1989] A.C. 852; [1989] 2 W.L.R. 290; (1989) 133 S.J. 184; [1989] 1 All E.R. 402; [1989] F.L.R. 223; [1989] 1 Lloyd's Rep. 331, HL; affirming [1988] 3 W.L.R. 565; [1988] 132 S.J. 1181; [1988] 2 All E.R. 43; [1988] 1 F.T.L.R. 78; [1988] F.L.R. 67; [1988] 1 Lloyd's Rep. 19, CA; affirming [1986] 2 All E.R. 498; [1986] 2 Lloyd's Rep. 179 . . . . 6–028, 12–073, 16–0151, 25–010
Forslind v. Becheley Crundall, 1922 S.C. (H.L.) 173 8–078
Forster, *Re* (1840) 1 Mont. D. & De G. 10; 4 Jur. 224 22–090
Forsyth v. Jervis (1816) 1 Stark. 437; 171 E.R. 522, N.P. 1–039

Forsythe International (U.K.) v. Silver Shipping Co. and Petroglobe International; Saetta, The [1994] 1 W.L.R. 1334; [1994] 1 All E.R. 851; [1993] 2 Lloyd's Rep. 268 .... 5–148, 5–156, 7–047, 7–057, 7–062, 7–063, 7–072, 7–077, 7–078, 7–081, 7–086
Forthright Finance Ltd v. Carlyle Finance Ltd [1997] 4 All E.R. 90; [1997] C.C.L.R. 84, CA 1–053, 7–070
Forum Craftsman, The [1985] 1 Lloyd's Rep. 291; [1984] 2 Lloyd's Rep. 102 .... 18–002, 18–054, 19–034, 20–090
Foskett v. McKeown [2001] 1 A.C. 102; [2000] 2 W.L.R. 1299; [2000] 3 All E.R. 97; [2000] Lloyd's Rep. I.R. 627; [2000] W.T.L.R. 667; (1999–2000) 21 T.E.L.R. 711; (2000) 97(23) L.S.G. 44; *The Times*, May 24, 2000; *The Independent*, HL; reversing [1998] Ch. 265; [1998] 2 W.L.R. 298; [1997] 3 All E.R. 392; [1997] N.P.C. 83; *The Times*, June 27, 1997, CA 7–003
Foster v. Eades (1860) 2 F. & F. 103 9–063
—— v. Driscoll [1929] 1 K.B. 470, CA 25–119
—— v. Parker (1876) 2 C.P.D. 18; 46 L.J.Q.B. 77; 25 W.R. 321 22–132
Foster (deceased) v. Earl of Derby (1834) 1 A. & E. 783 7–019
Fothergill v. Rowland (1873) L.R. 17 Eq. 132; 43 L.J.Ch. 252; 29 L.T. 414; 38 J.P. 244; 22 W.R. 42 .... 17–099, 17–103
Foundaries du Lion v. International Factors Ltd [1985] I.L.R.M. 66 5–152
Four Point Garage Ltd v. Carter [1985] 3 All E.R. 12 ... 2–026, 5–144, 5–156, 7–072, 7–078, 8–007
Fowler v. Midland Electric Corporation for Power Distribution Ltd [1917] 1 Ch. 656; 86 L.J.Ch. 472; 117 L.T. 97; 33 T.L.R. 322; 61 S.J. 459 9–047
Fox v. Nott (1861) 6 H. & N. 630; 30 L.J.Ex. 259; 7 Jur. (N.S.) 663; 158 E.R. 260 ... 18–134
Foxboro Co. v. Arabian American Oil Co. 805 F. 2d 34 (1986) 23–153
Fragano v. Long (1825) 4 B. & C. 219 .... 5–009, 5–098, 6–020, 9–055, 19–075, 19–081
France v. Parkinson [1954] 1 W.L.R. 581; 98 S.J. 214; [1954] 1 All E.R. 739 5–010
Francis v. Trans-Canada Trailer Sales Ltd (1969) 6 D.L.R. (3d) 705 13–030
Francis & Co. Ltd, *ex p.* (1887) 56 L.T. 577 15–073
Francovich and Bonnifaci v. Italian Republic (joined Cases 6/90 and 9/90) [1991] E.C.R. 1–5357 14–008
Frangopulo v. Lomas & Co. *See* Lomas & Co. v. Barff Ltd. Frangopulo & Co. v. Lomas & Co.
Frank v. Grosvenor Motor Auctions Ltd [1960] V.R. 607 11–042
Frank (A.J.) & Sons Ltd v. Northern Peat Co. Ltd (1963) 39 D.L.R. (2d) 721 ..... 12–043, 12–049
Franklin v. Neate (1844) 13 M. & W. 481; 14 L.J.Ex. 59; 4 L.T. (O.S.) 214; 153 E.R. 200 1–063
Frans Maas (UK) Ltd v. Samsung Electronics (UK) Ltd [2004] EWHC 1502; [2005] 2 All E.R. (Comm) 783; [2004] 2 Lloyd's Rep. 251; [2005] 1 C.L.C. 647, QBD .. 13–16, 13–036, 13–052, 23–284
Frans Maas (UK) Ltd v. Sun Alliance and London Insurance Plc [2003] EWHC 1803; [2004] 1 Lloyd's Rep. 484; [2004] Lloyd's Rep. I.R. 649, QBD 18–063
Fraser (Inspector of Taxes) v. London Sports Car Centre (1985) 129 S.J. 505; (1987) 59 T.C. 63; [1985] S.T.C. 688; (1985) 83 L.S.Gaz. 3086, CA; affirming (1985) 129 S.J. 68; [1985] S.T.C. 75; (1984) 81 L.S.Gaz. 3426 5–051
Fratclli Moretti SpA v. Nidera Handelscompagnie B.V. [1981] 2 Lloyd's Rep. 47 ... 20–046
Frebold & Sturznickel (Trading as Panda O.H.G.) v. Circle Products Ltd [1970] 1 Lloyd's Rep. 499 .... 20–026, 20–037, 20–081, 21–094
Freehold Land Investments Ltd v. Queensland Estates Ltd (1970) 123 C.L.R. 418 .. 25–006
Freeman v. Appleyard (1862) 32 L.J.Ex. 175 7–035
—— v. Baker (1833) 5 B. & Ad. 797; 2 Nev. & M.K.B. 446; 3 L.J.K.B. 17; 110 E.R. 985 13–029
—— v. Birch (1833) 3 Q.B. 492n; 1 Nev. & M.K.B. 420; 114 E.R. 596 5–009
—— v. Cooke (1848) 2 Exch. 654 7–010
—— v. East India Co. (1822) 5 B. & A. 617; 1 Dow. & Ry. K.B. 234; 106 E.R. 1316 25–130
—— v. Jeffries (1869) L.R. 4 Ex. 189; 38 L.J.Ex. 116; 20 L.T. 533 12–068
—— v. Taylor (1831) 8 Bing. 124; 1 Moo. & S. 182; 1 L.J.C.P. 26; 131 E.R. 348 10–030
Freeth v. Burr (1874) L.R. 9 C.P. 208 8–078

Freiburger Kommunalbauten GmbH Baugesellschaft & Co KG v. Hofstetter (C237/02) [2004] E.C.R. I-3403; [2004] 2 C.M.L.R. 13, ECJ 14–034
Friedlander v. Texas, etc, R. Co. (1989) 130 U.S. 416 18–032
Freke v. Carbery (1873) L.R. 16 Eq. 461; 21 W.R. 835 25–004
French v. Gething [1922] 1 K.B. 236 .... 1–017, 2–025, 8–011
—— v. Hoggett [1968] 1 W.L.R. 94; 132 J.P. 91; 111 S.J. 906; [1967] 3 All E.R. 1042; 66 L.G.R. 383 1–121
French Government v. Sanday (S.) & Co. Ltd (1923) 16 Ll.L.R. 238 19–088
Frenkel v. MacAndrews & Co. Ltd [1929] A.C. 545; [1929] All E.R. 260; 98 L.J.K.B. 389; 141 L.T. 33; 45 T.L.R. 311; 17 Asp.M.L.C. 582; 34 Com.Cas. 241 ..... 18–051, 19–032, 23–131
Frewen v. Hays (1912) 106 L.T. 516, PC 2–004
Friends Provident Life & Pensions Ltd v. Sirius International Insurance Corp [2005] EWCA Civ 601; [2005] 2 All E.R. (Comm) 145; [2005] 2 Lloyd's Rep. 517; [2005] 1 C.L.C. 794; [2006] Lloyd's Rep. I.R. 45; *The Times*, June 8, 2005, CA 18–357, 19–064
Friendship Materials v. Michigan Brick Inc. 679 F. 2d 100 (1982) 23–151
Frigoscandia (Contracting) Ltd v. Continental Irish Meat Ltd [1982] I.L.R.M. 396 5–144
Frith v. Forbes (1826) 4 De G.F. & J. 409; 32 L.J.Ch. 10; 7 L.T. 61; 8 Jur. (N.S.) 1115; 11 W.R. 4; 1 Mar.L.C. 253 18–241
Frogley v. Earl of Lovelace (1859) Johns 333 1–097
Frontier International Shipping Corp v. Swissmarine Corp Inc (The Cape Equinox) [2005] EWHC 8; [2005] 1 All E.R. (Comm) 528; [2005] 1 Lloyd's Rep. 390; [2005] 1 C.L.C. 1, QBD 8–089
Frost v. Aylesbury Dairy Co. [1905] 1 K.B. 608; 74 L.J.K.B. 386; 92 L.T. 527; 53 W.R. 354; 21 T.L.R. 300; 49 S.J. 312 ..... 11–030, 11–055, 11–057, 11–064, 14–011, 17–072
Frost v. Knight (1872) L.R. 7 Ex. Ill 9–018, 16–081, 16–082
Fry v. Hill (1817) 7 Taunt, 397 22–098
—— v. Smellie [1912] 3 K.B. 282; 81 L.J.K.B. 1003; 106 L.T. 404 7–013
Fry & Co. v. Raggio (1891) 40 W.R. 120; 8 T.L.R. 95; 36 S.J. 92 .... 9–047, 9–048
Fuentes v. Montis (1868) L.R. 4 C.P. 93; 38 L.J.C.P. 95; 19 L.T. 364; 17 W.R. 208, Ex. Ch 7–031, 7–040
Fuerst Day Lawson Ltd v. Orion Insurance Co. Ltd [1980] 1 Lloyds Rep. 656 21–013
Fuhrmann and Miller, *Re* (1977) 78 D.L.R. (3d) 284 25–131
Fuller v. Glyn, Mills, Currie & Co. [1914] 2 K.B. 168; 83 L.J.K.B. 764; 110 L.T. 318; 30 T.L.R. 162; 58 S.J. 235; 19 Com.Cas. 186 7–013
—— v. Webster 95 A. 335 (1915) 25–130
Furby v. Hoey [1947] 1 All E.R. 236; 63 T.L.R. 196; 111 J.P. 167; 45 L.G.R. 186 .... 5–013, 5–080, 5–081
Furness Bridge, The [1977] 2 Lloyd's Rep. 367; (1977) 121 S.J. 491 .... 18–345, 18–349, 19–129
Furness Withy (Australia) v. Metal Distributors (U.K.) (The Amazonia) [1990] 1 Lloyd's Rep. 236 .... 3–018, 25–072
Furnis v. Leicester (1619) Cro. Jac. 474 4–001
Furniss v. Scholes [1974] R.T.R. 133; [1974] Crim.L.R. 199 .... 14–107, 14–112
Furst (Enrico) & Co. v. Fischer (W.E.) [1960] 2 Lloyd's Rep. 340 ... 9–028, 19–041, 20–021, 20–024, 20–025, 20–123, 23–084, 23–096
Future Express (The) [1993] 2 Lloyd's Rep. 542, CA; affirming [1992] 2 Lloyd's Rep. 79 .... 18–006, 18–066, 18–080, 18–082, 18–098, 18–099, 18–193, 18–209, 18–220, 19–099, 19–100, 23–132
Fyffes Group Ltd v. Reefer Express Line Pty Ltd (The Kriti Rex) [1996] 2 Lloyd's Rep. 171, 188 .... 20–042, 20–089

G. & C. Finance Corporation Ltd v. Brown 1961 S.L.T. 408 1–065
GE Capital Bank Ltd v. Rushton [2005] EWCA Civ 1556; *The Times*, December 21, 2005; *Independent*, January 12, 2006, CA 7–046, 7–092, 7–099, 14–007
GE Commercial Finance v. Gee [2005] EWHC 2056 (Comm); 1 Lloyd's Rep. 337 .. 19–197
GHL Pte Ltd v. Unitrack Building Construction Pte Ltd [1999] 4 S.L.R. 604 .... 23–280, 23–282
G.K.N. Centrax Gears Ltd v. Matbro Ltd 120 S.J. 401; [1976] 2 Lloyd's Rep. 555 ... 16–046, 17–034, 17–043, 17–069

GKN Contractors Ltd v. Lloyd's Bank plc (1985) 30 Build.L.R. 48 .... 23–145, 23–276
G.U.S. Merchandise Corporation Ltd v. Customs & Excise Commissioners [1981] 1 W.L.R. 1309; (1981) 125 S.J. 624; [1981] S.T.C. 569; [1981] T.R. 135 1–033
Gabarron v. Kreeft (1875) L.R. 10 Ex. 274; 44 L.J.Ex. 238; 33 L.T. 365; 24 W.R. 146; 3 Asp.M.L.C. 36 .... 5–132, 20–007, 20–071, 20–077, 20–084
Gabbiano, The [1940] P. 166; 109 L.J.P. 74; 165 L.T. 5; 56 T.L.R. 774; 84 S.J. 394; 45 Com.Cas. 235; 19 Asp.M.L.C. 371 .... 18–116, 19–008, 19–016, 19–099, 19–104, 19–119
Gabriel v. Schlank & Schick GmbH (C96/00); *sub nom.* Gabriel, Re (C96/00); Gabriel v. Schlanck & Schick GmbH (C96/00) [2002] E.C.R. I-6367; [2002] I.L.Pr. 36, ECJ 825–045
Gabriel Wade & English v. Arcos Ltd (1929) 73 S.J. 483; 34 Ll.L.R. 306 8–049
Gagnon v. Geneau [1951] 1 D.L.R. 516 11–070
Gainsford v. Carroll (1824) 2 B. & C. 624; 4 Dow. & Ry. K.B. 161; 2 L.J. (o.s.) K.B. 112; 107 E.R. 516 .... 17–008, 17–009
Galaxy Energy International Ltd (BVI) v. Eurobunker SpA [2001] 2 All E.R. (Comm) 912; [2001] 2 Lloyd's Rep. 725; [2001] C.L.C. 1725, QBD (Comm Ct) 11–096, 13–040, 18–108
Galbraith v. Mitchenall Estates Ltd [1965] 2 Q.B. 473; [1964] 3 W.L.R. 454; 108 S.J. 749; [1964] 2 All E.R. 653 16–039
Galbraith and Grant Ltd v. Block [1922] 2 K.B. 155; 91 L.J.K.B. 649; 127 L.T. 521; 38 T.L.R. 669; 66 S.J. 596 .... 8–014, 8–023
Gale v. New [1937] 4 All E.R. 645; 54 T.L.R. 213; 82 S.J. 14 .... 5–003, 5–016
Gallagher v. Shilcock [1949] 2 K.B. 765; [1949] L.J.R. 1721; 93 S.J. 302; [1949] 1 All E.R. 921 .... 15–117, 15–123, 15–127, 15–130, 15–133, 16–014
Gallaher Ltd v. British Road Services Ltd [1974] 2 Lloyd's Rep. 440 .... 10–013, 21–073
Galley (Michael) Footwear Ltd v. Laboni [1982] 2 All E.R. 200; [1985] 2 Lloyd's Rep. 251 21–104
Gallie v. Lee. *See* Saunders (formerly Gallie) v. Anglia Building Society.
Galloway v. Galloway (1914) 30 T.L.R. 531 3–022
Galoo Ltd v. Bright Grahame Murray [1994] 1 W.L.R. 1360; [1994] 1 All E.R. 16; [1994] B.C.C. 319; *The Times*, January 14, 1994, CA 16–049
Gamerco SA v. I.C.M./Fair Warning (Agency) Ltd [1995] 1 W.L.R. 1126; [1995] 3 E.M.L.R. 263; *The Times*, May 3, 1995 .... 6–060, 18–314, 18–332
Gamer's Motor Centre (Newcastle) Property Ltd v. Natwest Wholesale Australia Property Ltd (1987) 163 C.L.R. 236 .... 7–063, 7–077, 7–081, 8–002, 8–009
Gan Insurance Co. Ltd v. Tai Ping Insurance Co. Ltd; Royal Reinsurance Co. Ltd v. Central Insurance Co. Ltd [1999] 2 All E.R. (Comm) 54; [1999] C.L.C. 1270; [1999] I.L.Pr. 729; *The Independent*, June 30, 1999, CA; affirming [1998] C.L.C. 1072; [1999] Lloyd's Rep. I.R. 229, QBD (Comm Ct) 25–020, 25–030
Gannow Engineering Co. Ltd v. Richardson [1930] N.Z.L.R. 361 1–049
Gaon & Co. v. Societe Interprofessionelle des Oleagineaux Fluides Alimentaires [1960] 2 Q.B. 348; [1960] 2 W.L.R. 869; 104 S.J. 426; [1960] 2 All E.R. 160; [1960] 1 Lloyd's Rep. 349, CA; affirming [1960] 2 Q.B. 334; [1959] 3 W.L.R. 622; 108 S.J. 601; [1959] 2 All E.R. 693; [1959] 2 Lloyd's Rep. 30; [1959] C.L.Y. 540 .... 6–049, 19–131 19–132
Garbett v. Rufford Motor Co. Ltd. *The Guardian*, March 12, 1962 10–005
Garcia v. Chase Manhatten Bank 735, F. 2nd 645 (1984) 22–016
Garcia v. Page & Co. Ltd (1936) 55 Ll.L.R. 391 .... 23–083, 23–086
Gardano and Giampieri v. Greek Petroleum George Mamidakis & Co. [1962] 1 W.L.R. 40; 106 S.J. 76; [1961] 2 Lloyd's Rep. 259 .... 5–015, 6–019, 18–040, 18–114, 19–002, 21–014
Garden Cottage Foods Ltd v. Milk Marketing Board [1984] A.C. 130; [1983] 3 W.L.R. 143; (1983) 127 S.J. 460; [1983] 2 All E.R. 770; [1983] 3 C.M.L.R. 43; [1984] F.S.R. 23; [1983] Com.L.R. 198 3–041
Garden Neptune Shipping v. Occidental Worldwide Investment Corp. and Concord Petroleum Corp. [1990] 1 Lloyd's Rep. 330, CA 12–016
Gardiner v. Gray (1815) 4 Camp. 144; 171 E.R. 46 .... 11–075, 11–076
Garey v. Pyke (1839) 10 Ad. & El. 512; 2 Per. & Dav. 427; 133 E.R. 193 .... 1–034, 1–035, 16–015

Garnac Grain Co. Inc. v. HMF Faure & Fairclough Ltd. *sub nom* Bunge Corp. v. HMF Faure & Fairclough Ltd [1968] A.C. 1130; [1967] 3 W.L.R. 143; [1967] 2 All E.R. 353; [1967] 1 Lloyd's Rep. 495; 111 S.J. 434, HL; affirming [1966] 1 Q.B. 650; [1965] 3 W.L.R. 934; [1965] 3 All E.R. 273; [1965] 2 Lloyd's Rep. 229; 109 S.J. 571, CA; reversing [1965] 2 W.L.R. 696; [1965] 1 All E.R. 47; [1964] 2 Lloyd's Rep. 296; 108 S.J. 693; *The Times*, August 1, 1964, QBD (Comm Ct) 16–067, 16–069, 16–081, 20–116, 20–140

Garnham, Harris and Elton Ltd v. Ellis (Alfred W.) (Transport) Ltd [1967] 1 W.L.R. 940; 111 S.J. 558; [1967] 2 All E.R. 940; [1967] 2 Lloyd's Rep. 22 13–046

Gatewhite Ltd v. lberia Lineas Aereas de Espana Sociedad [1990] 1 Q.B. 326; [1989] 3 W.L.R. 1080; (1989) 133 S.J. 1337; [1989] 1 All E.R. 944; [1989] 1 Lloyd's Rep. 160 18–149

Gatoil International Inc. v. Tradax Petroleum Ltd (The Rio Sun) [1985] 1 Lloyd's Rep. 350 ...... 4–026, 4–029, 6–019, 6–023, 18–244, 18–255, 18–258, 19–002, 19–008, 19–009, 19–010, 19–036, 19–066, 19–073, 19–085, 19–089, 19–121, 19–186, 19–187

Gator Shipping Corp. v. Trans-Asiatic Oil SA and Occidental Shipping Establishment. (The Odenfeld) [1978] 2 Lloyd's Rep. 357 ...... 7–015, 7–017, 8–082, 16–059, 19–164, 19–214, 20–126

Gator Shipping Corp v. Transatlantic Occidental Shipping Establishment. *See* Ocean Marine Navigation Ltd v. Koch Carbon Inc (The Dynamic)

Gattorno v. Adams (1862) 12 C.B. (N.S.) 560; 142 E.R. 1262 .... 18–271, 21–039

Gaunt v. Thompson (1849) 18 L.J.C.P. 125 22–132

Gavin's Trustee v. Fraser 1920 S.C. 674; 57 S.L.R. 595 .... 1–064, 1–065

Geary v. Physic (1826) 5 B. & C. 234; 7 Dow. & Ry. K.B. 653; 4 L.J. (O.S.) K.B. 147 22–050

Gebr. van Weelde Scheepvartkantor B.V. v. Compania Naviera Sea Orient SA [1987] 2 Lloyd's Rep. 223 8–031

Gebruder Metelmann G.m.b.H. & Co. K.G. v. N.B.R. (London) Ltd [1984] 1 Lloyd's Rep. 614; (1984) 81 L.S.Gaz. 515 .... 16–077, 16–081, 19–181, 19–207, 20–133, 20–137

Geddling v. Marsh [1920] 1 K.B. 668; 89 L.J.K.B. 526; 122 L.T. 775; 36 T.L.R. 337 .. 1–061, 11–030, 17–072

Gee v. Lucas (1867) 16 L.T. 357 .... 10–006, 10–016

Gefco UK Ltd v. Mason (No.1) [1998] 2 Lloyd's Rep. 585; [1998] C.L.C. 1468; (1998) 95(31) L.S.G. 35; (1998) 142 S.J.L.B. 206; *The Times*, August 24, 1998, CA .. 21–060

Geipel v. Smith (1872) L.R. 7 Q.B. 404; 41 L.J.Q.B. 153; 26 L.T. 361; 20 W.R. 332; 1 Asp.M.L.C. 268 8–070

Gelder, *Re, ex p.* Sergeant [1881] W.N. 37 1–066

Gelling v. Crispin (1917) 23 C.L.R. 443 6–041

Gelmini v. Moriggia [1913] 2 K.B. 549 17–008

Gencab of Canada Ltd v. Murray-Jensen Manufacturing Co. Ltd (1980) 114 D.L.R. (3d) 92 4–027

General Accident Insurance Co. v. Noel [1902] 1 K.B. 377; 71 L.J.K.B. 236; 86 L.T. 555; 50 W.R. 381; 18 T.L.R. 164 16–033

General and Finance Facilities Ltd v. Cooks Cars (Romford) Ltd [1963] 1 W.L.R. 644; 107 S.J. 294; [1963] 2 All E.R. 314 15–116

—— v. Hughes (1966) 110 S.J. 847 7–018

General Feeds Inc. Panama v. Slobodna Plovidba Yugoslavia (The Krapan J) [1999] 1 Lloyd's Rep. 688, QBD (Comm Ct) 17–078

General International SA v. Bangladesh Sugar and Food Industries Corp. [1996] 2 Lloyd's Rep. 524 23–280

General Motors Acceptance Corp. (U.K.) Ltd v. Inland Revenue Commissioners [1987] S.T.C. 122; 59 T.C. 651; (1987) 84 L.S.G. 577, CA; affirming [1985] S.T.C. 408; [1985] P.C.C. 376; (1985) 82 L.S.G. 2168, DC 5–044, 5–051

General Steam Navigation Co. v. Guillou (1843) 11 M. & W. 877 25–081

General Trading Co. Ltd. and Van Stolk's Commissiehandel, *Re* (1911) 16 Com.Cas. 95 .... 18–266, 18–267, 18–276, 19–147, 19–158

Genn v. Winkel (1912) 107 L.T. 434, 28 T.L.R. 483; 56 S.J. 612; 17 Com.Cas. 323 ... 5–041, 5–047, 5–048, 5–050, 5–054

George v. Revis (1966) 111 S.J. 51; 116 New L.J. 1544 .... 7–043, 7–075

Georgetown Seafoods Ltd v. Usen Fisheries Ltd (1977) 78 D.L.R. (3d) 542 6–019
Geralopulo v. Wieler (1851) 20 L.J.C.P. 105; 10 C.B. 690; 15 Jur. 316 22–137
Gerson (Michael) (Leasing) Ltd v. Wilkinson [2001] Q.B. 514; [2000] 3 W.L.R. 1645; [2001] 1 All E.R. 148; [2000] 2 All E.R. (Comm) 890; [2000] C.L.C. 1720; (2000) 97(35) L.S.G. 37; *The Times*, September 12, 2000, CA . . . 7–057, 7–063, 7–072, 7–077, 8–009, 15–049, 15–070
Getreide-Import-Gesellschaft m.b.H. v. Contimár SA Compania Comercial y Maritima [1953] 1 W.L.R. 793; 97 S.J. 434; [1953] 2 All E.R. 223; [1953] 1 Lloyd's Rep. 572 9–042
—— v. Itoh & Co. (America) Inc. [1979] 1 Lloyd's Rep. 592 . . . . 8–066, 12–031, 19–021
Gian Singh & Co. Ltd v. Banque de L'Indochine [1974] 1 Lloyd's Rep. 56; affirmed [1974] 2 Lloyd's Rep. 1 . . . . 23–028, 23–112, 23–126, 23–127, 23–128, 23–203, 23–235
Gibb v. Mather (1832) 2 Cr. & J. 254; 2 Tyr. 189; 8 Bing 214; 1 Moo. & S. 387; 1 L.J.Ex. 87 22–110
Gibbett v. Forwood Products Ltd [2001] FCA 290 11–055
Gibbon v. Pease [1905] 1 K.B. 810 1–046
Gibbons v. Trap Motors (1970) 9 D.L.R. (3d) 742 12–007
Gibson v. Bray (1817) 1 Moore C.P. 519; Holt N.P. 556; 8 Taunt. 76; 129 E.R. 311 . . 5–040, 5–041, 5–050
—— v. Carruthers (1841) 8 M. & W. 321; 11 L.J.Ex. 138; 151 E.R. 1061 . . . 15–061, 15–063, 20–055, 20–056, 20–077
—— v. Holland (1865) L.R. I.C.P. 1 25–087
Giddens v. Anglo-African Produce Co. Ltd (1923) 14 Ll.L.R. 230 23–085
Gilbert v. Brett (1604) Davis 18 25–160
—— v. Gilbert and Boucher [1928] P. 1; 96 L.J.P. 137; 137 L.T. 619; 43 T.L.R. 589; 71 S.J. 582 1–004
Gilbert Ash (Northern) Ltd v. Modern Engineering (Bristol) Ltd [1974] A.C. 689; [1973] 3 W.L.R. 421; 117 S.J. 745; [1973] 3 All E.R. 195; 72 L.G.R. 1 . . . . 13–038, 16–035
Giles v. Edwards (1797) 7 T.R. 181 12–067
—— v. Grover (1832) 6 Bli. N.S. 277 . . . . 1–063, 7–113
—— v. Perkins (1807) 9 East. 12 . . . . 22–073, 22–090
Gill & Duffus Landauer Ltd v. London Export Corp. G.m.b.H. [1982] 2 Lloyd's Rep. 627 . . . . 2–015, 25–013, 25–066
Gill and Duffus (Liverpool) v. Scruttons [1953] 1 W.L.R. 1407; [1953] 2 All E.R. 977; [1953] 2 Lloyd's Rep. 545; 97 S.J. 814 5–148
Gill & Duffus SA v. Berger Co. Inc. [1984] A.C. 382; [1984] 2 W.L.R. 95; [1984] 1 All E.R. 438; (1984) 128 S.J. 47; [1984] 1 Lloyd's Rep. 227; (1984) 81 L.S.Gaz. 429; [1984] L.M.C.L.Q. 191; HL; reversing [1983] 1 Lloyd's Rep. 622; [1983] Com.L.R. 122, CA; [1981] 2 Lloyd's Rep. 233; [1981] Com.L.R. 253 . . . 8–006, 8–047, 9–010, 9–014, 9–017, 9–020, 11–016, 11–020, 11–079, 11–085, 12–042, 12–046, 12–052, 12–064, 13–033, 13–040, 15–110, 16–019, 16–061, 17–049, 19–054, 19–058, 19–073, 19–077, 19–079, 19–144, 19–149, 19–161, 19–163, 19–164, 19–165, 19–166, 19–170, 19–171, 19–173, 19–207, 20–049, 20–058
—— v. Rionda Futures Ltd [1994] 2 Lloyd's Rep. 67, QBD (Comm Ct) 19–088
—— v. Société pour L'Exportation des Sucres SA [1986] 1 Lloyd's Rep. 322 . . . . 8–036, 10–037, 20–014, 20–045, 20–047, 20–056
Gillard v. Brittan (1841) 1 Dowl. (N.S.) 424; 8 M. & W. 575; 11 L.J.Ex. 133; 151 E.R. 1168 . . . . 7–002, 15–117, 17–099
Gillat v. Sky Television Ltd [2001] 1 All E.R. (Comm) 461 . . . . 2–017, 2–050
Gillespie Bros. & Co. v. Cheney, Eggar & Co. [1896] 2 Q.B. 59; 65 L.J.Q.B. 552; 12 T.L.R. 274; 40 S.J. 354; 1 Com.Cas. 373 . . . . 11–055, 11–065
—— v. Bowles (Roy) Transport Ltd [1973] Q.B. 400; [1972] 3 W.L.R. 1003; 116 S.J. 861; [1973] 1 All E.R. 193; [1973] 1 Lloyd's Rep. 10; [1973] R.T.R. 95 . . . . 2–012, 13–016, 13–017, 13–022
Gillett v. Hill (1834) 2 C. & M. 530; 4 Tyr. 290; 3 L.J.Ex. 145; 149 E.R. 871 . . 5–061, 5–065, 7–014, 17–097
Gillman Spencer & Co. v. Carbutt & Co. (1889) 61 L.T. 281; 37 W.R. 437; 5 T.L.R. 365 7–014
Gillott's Settlement, *Re* [1934] Ch. 97; 102 L.J.Ch. 332; 149 L.T. 419; 77 S.J. 447 5–094

Gilmour v. Supple (1858) 11 Moore P.C. 551; 32 L.T. (o.s.) 1; 6 W.R. 445; 14 E.R. 803 .... 5–017, 5–030, 5–038
Ginner v. King (1890) 7 T.L.R. 140 .... 5–078, 11–075
Ginzberg v. Barrow Haematite Steel Co. Ltd [1966] 1 Lloyd's Rep. 343; 116 New L.J. 752 .... 5–059, 5–135, 18–071, 19–066, 19–098, 19–103, 19–106
Girardot v. Fitzpatrick (1869) 21 L.T. 470 5–091
Girvin, Roper & Co. v. Monteith (1895) 23 R. 129 25–081
Gladwell v. Turner (1870) L.R. 5 Ex. 59; 39 L.J.Ex. 31; 21 L.T. 674; 18 W.R. 317 .. 22–126, 22–130
Glasscock v. Balls (1889) 24 Q.B.D. 13; 59 L.J.Q.B. 51; 62 L.T. 163; 38 W.R. 155 ... 22–118
Glass's Fruit Markets Ltd v. Southwell (A.) & Son (Fruit) Ltd [1969] 2 Lloyd's Rep. 398 .... 11–020, 11–021
Glebe Island Terminals Pty Ltd v. Continental Seagram Pty Ltd (The Antwerpen) [1994] 1 Lloyd's Rep. 213, Sup.Ct. N.S.W. 18–063, 21–083
Glencore Grain Ltd v. Flacker Shipping Ltd (The Happy Day); *sub nom.* Flacker Shipping Ltd v. Glencore Grain Ltd (The Happy Day) [2002] EWCA Civ 1068; [2002] 2 All E.R. (Comm) 896; [2002] 2 Lloyd's Rep. 487; [2003] 1 C.L.C. 537; *The Times*, July 26, 2002, CA 18–358, 19–150
Glencore Grain Rotterdam BV v. Lebanese Organisation for International Commerce (The Lorico) [1997] 4 All E.R. 514; [1997] 2 Lloyd's Rep. 386; [1997] C.L.C. 1274, CA; reversing [1997] 1 Lloyd's Rep. 578, QBD (Comm Ct) 12–037, 19–159, 19–160, 20–020, 20–024, 20–112, 23–096
Glencore International AG v. Bank of China [1996] 1 Lloyd's Rep. 135 ... 23–196, 23–207, 23–216
Glencore International AG v. Metro Trading Inc. (No.2) [2001] 1 All E.R. (Comm) 103; [2001] 1 Lloyd's Rep. 284, QBD (Comm Ct) 1–058, 5–148, 5–149, 7–004, 25–121, 25–122, 25–130, 25–131, 25–132, 25–133, 25–141, 25–142, 25–143, 25–148, 25–155, 25–179
Glendarroch, The [1894] P. 226 8–097
Glengarnock Iron and Steel Co. Ltd v. Cooper (Henry G.) & Co. (1895) 22 R. (Ct. of Sess.) 672; 32 S.L.R. 546; 3 S.L.T. 36 .... 20–018, 20–088
Glengate Properties Ltd v. Norwich Union Fire Insurance Society [1996] 2 All E.R. 487 20–039
Glennie v. Imri (1839) 3 Y. & C. Ex. 436; 3 Jur. 432 22–064
Glenroy, The [1945] A.C. 124; 114 L.J.P.C. 49; 172 L.T. 326; 61 T.L.R. 303; Ll.P.C. (2nd) 191 .... 5–015, 5–138, 18–188, 18–189, 19–103
Glenwood Lumber Co. v. Phillips [1904] A.C. 405; [1904–7] All E.R. 203; 73 L.J.P.C. 62; 90 L.T. 741 5–010
Gluckstein v. Barnes [1900] A.C. 240; 69 L.J.Ch. 385; 82 L.T. 393; 7 Mans. 321 13–015
Glynn v. Margetson & Co. [1893] A.C. 351 .... 18–053, 19–033
Glynn (H.) (Covent Garden) Ltd v. Wittleder [1959] 2 Lloyd's Rep. 409 .... 6–019, 13–040, 18–255, 19–012, 19–053, 19–157, 25–009, 25–010, 25–012, 25–195, 25–199
Glyn Mills Currie & Co. v. East and West India Dock Co. (1882) 7 App.Cas. 591; 52 L.J.Q.B. 146; 47 L.T. 309; 31 W.R. 201; 4 Asp.M.L.C. 580 .... 18–048, 18–090, 18–092, 18–093, 18–094, 21–009, 23–132
Gobind Chunder Sein v. Ryan (1861) 15 Moo.P.C. 231 7–047
Goddard v. O'Brien (1882) 9 Q.B.D. 37 9–024
—— v. Raake O/Y Osakeyhtio (1935) 53 Ll.L.R. 208 8–076
Godfray v. Coulman (1859) 13 Moore P.C. 11; 15 E.R. 5 22–098
Godley v. Perry, Burton & Sons (Bermondsey) (Third Party), Graham (Fourth Party), [1960] 1 W.L.R. 9; 104 S.J. 16; [1960] 1 All E.R. 36 ... 1–076, 2–036, 11–008, 11–040, 11–057, 11–081, 14–020, 14–064, 16–046, 17–072, 17–084
Godts v. Rose (1855) 17 C.B. 229; 25 L.J.C.P. 61; 26 L.T. (o.s.) 240; 1 Jur. (N.S.) 1173; 4 W.R. 129; 139 E.R. 1058 .... 5–071, 5–077, 5–132, 5–135, 8–012, 9–051
Goldcorp Exchange (In Receivership), *Re: sub nom.* Kensington v. Unrepresented Non-Allocated Claimants [1995] 1 A.C. 74; [1994] 3 W.L.R. 199; [1994] 2 All E.R. 806; [1994] 138 (LB) 127; (1994) Tr.L.R. 434; (1994) 144 N.L.J. 792, D.C. 1–059, 1–108, 1–119, 5–064, 5–065, 5–094, 5–113, 5–130, 7–014, 18–209, 18–292
Golden Acres Ltd v. Queensland Estates Ltd [1969] St. R. Qd. 378 25–006

Golden Strait Corp v. Nippon Yusen Kubishika Kaisha (The Golden Victory) [2005] EWCA Civ 1190; [2006] 1 W.L.R. 533; [2006] 1 All E.R. (Comm) 235; [2005] 2 Lloyd's Rep. 747; [2005] 2 C.L.C. 576; (2005) 102(43) L.S.G. 31; *The Times*, October 21, 2005, CA 9–020, 19–161, 19–165, 19–166, 19–173
Goldfarb v. Bartlett and Kremer [1920] 1 K.B. 639; 89 L.J.K.B. 258; 122 L.T. 588; 64 S.J. 210 22–125
Golding Davis & Co. Ltd, *ex p. Re* Knight (1886) 13 Ch.D. 628; 42 L.T. 270; 28 N.R. 481 .... 15–092, 15–100, 18–065, 20–141, 22–104
Goldsborough, Mort & Co. v. Carter (1914) 19 C.L.R. 429 .... 1–133, 1–132, 8–056
Goldsmith v. Rodger [1962] 2 Lloyd's Rep. 249 .... 1–009, 3–008, 10–002, 10–008
Goldsmith's Company v. West Metropolitan Ry. [1904] 1 K.B. 1 8–034
Golodetz (M) & Co. Inc. v. Czarnikow Rionda Inc. (The Galatia) [1980] 1 W.L.R. 495; (1979) 124 S.J. 201; [1980] 1 All E.R. 501; [1980] 1 Lloyd's Rep. 453 ... 19–034, 19–037, 19–038, 19–080, 19–099, 19–107, 19–110, 19–212, 21–012, 23–026, 23–206, 23–221
Gomersall, *Re* (1875) 1 Ch.D. 137; 45 L.J.Bcy. 1; 24 W.R. 257 7–046
Gompertz v. Bartlett (1853) 2 E. & B. 849 12–067
Gonzalez (Thomas P.) Corp. v. Millers Mühle, Müller G.m.b.H. (No. 2) [1980] 1 Lloyd's Rep. 445 .... 8–091, 18–313, 18–346
Gonzalez (Thomas P.) Corp. v. Wanng (F.R.) (International) Pty [1980] 2 Lloyd's Rep. 160, C.A., affirming [1978] 1 Lloyd's Rep. 494 20–046
Good v. Bruce [1917] N.Z.L.R. 514 1–058
Good v. Cheesman (1831) 2 B. & Ad. 328 9–025
Goodall v. Polhill (1845) 14 L.J.C.P. 146; 1 C.B. 233; 9 Jur. 554 22–128
—— v. Skelton (1794) 2 H.B1. 316; 126 E.R. 570 .... 8–009, 15–039
Goodbody & Co. and Balfour Williamson & Co., *Re* (1899) 82 L.T. 484; 9 Asp.M.L.C. 69; 5 Com.Cas. 59 19–032
Goodchild v. Vaclight [1965] C.L.Y. 2669 14–063
Goodfellow (Charles) Lumber Sales v. Verreault, Hovington and Verreault Navigation Inc. [1971] 1 Lloyd's Rep. 185 8–096
Goodwin v. Robarts (1875) L.R. 10 Ex. 337 23–028
Goodyear Tyre & Rubber Co. (G.B.) Ltd v. Lancashire Batteries Ltd [1958] 1 W.L.R. 857; 102 S.J. 581; [1958] 3 All E.R. 7; L.R. 1 R.P. 22 3–037
Gordon v. Strange (1847) 1 Exch. 477 .... 9–027, 9–050
Gordon (J.) Alison & Co. Ltd v. Wallsend Slipway and Engineering Co. Ltd (1927) 43 T.L.R. 323 13–013
Gore v. Van der Lann [1967] 2 Q.B. 31; [1967] 2 W.L.R. 358; 110 S.J. 928; [1967] 1 All E.R. 360; 65 L.G.R. 94 .... 10–014, 13–017
Gorham v. British Telecommunications plc [2000] 1 W.L.R. 2129; [2000] 4 All E.R. 867; [2001] Lloyd's Rep. I.R. 531; [2000] Lloyd's Rep. P.N. 897; [2001] P.N.L.R. 2; [2000] Pens. L.R. 293; (2000) 97(38) L.S.G. 44; (2000) 144 S.J.L.B. 251; *The Times*, August 16, 2000, CA 18–149
Gorringe v. Irwell India Rubber Works (1886) 34 Ch.D. 128; 56 L.J.Ch. 85; 55 L.T. 572; 35 W.R. 86 18–234
Gorrissen v. Perrin (1857) 2 C.B. (N.S.) 681; 27 L.J.C.P. 29; 29 L.T. (O.S.) 227; 3 Jur. (N.S.) 867; 5 W.R. 709; 140 E.R. 583 .... 8–046, 18–271, 21–024
Gorton v. Macintosh & Co. (1883) W.N. 103 .... 11–019, 13–038
Gosforth, The (Commercial Court of Rotterdam, February 20, 1985) discussed in [1986] L.M.C.L.Q. 4 .... 5–014, 5–110
Gosling v. Anderson (1972) 233 E.G. 1743 12–016
—— v. Birnie (1831) 7 Bing. 339 .... 5–065, 7–014
Goss v. Chilcott [1996] A.C. 788; [1996] 3 W.L.R. 180; [1997] 2 All E.R. 110; (1996) 93(22) L.S.G. 26; (1996) 140 S.J.L.B. 176; [1996] N.P.C. 93; *The Times*, June 6, 1996, PC (NZ) 12–069, 17–091
—— v. Quinton (1842) 3 M. & G. 825; 4 Scott N.R. 471; 12 L.J.C.P. 173; 7 Jur. 901; 133 E.R. 1372 5–093
Gotha City v. Sotheby's (No.2); Germany v. Sotheby's (No.2); *The Times*, October 8, 1998, QBD 25–114
Gough v. Everard (1864) 2 H. & C. 1; 2 New Rep. 169; 32 L.J.Ex. 210; 8 L.T. 363; 11 W.R. 702; 159 E.R. 1 8–008
—— v. Wood & Co. [1894] 1 Q.B. 713 5–159

Goulston Discount Co. Ltd v. Sims (1967) 111 S.J. 682 4–017
Government of Sierra Leone v. Marmaro Shipping Co. (The Amazona and The Yayamaria); Sierra Leone v. Margaritis Marine Co. [1989] 2 Lloyd's Rep. 130, CA 25–072
Government of Swaziland Central Transport Administration v. Leila Maritime Co. Ltd (The Leila) [1985] 2 Lloyd's Rep. 172 18–048
Government of Zanzibar v. British Aerospace *See* Zanzibar v. British Aerospace
Governor & Company of Bank of Scotland of the Mound v. Butcher, July 28, 1998, CA 25–057, 25–065
Gower v. Von Dedalzen (1837) 3 Bing. N.C. 717; 3 Hodge 94; 4 Scott 453; 6 L.J.C.P. 198; 1 Jur. 285; 132 E.R. 587 11–030
Gowers v. Lloyd's and National Provincial Foreign Bank Ltd [1938] 1 All E.R. 766; 158 L.T. 467; 54 L.T.R. 550; 82 S.J. 232 22–029
Graanhandel T. Vink B.V. v. European Grain & Shipping Ltd [1989] 2 Lloyd's Rep. 531 12–032
Grace Shipping and Hai Nguan v. Sharp (C.F.) (Malaya) Pte [1987] 1 Lloyd's Rep. 207, P.C. 2–017
Graff v. Evans (1882) 8 Q.B.D. 373; 46 J.P. 262; 51 L.J.M.C. 25; 46 L.T. 347; 30 W.R. 380 .... 1–121, 2–026
Grafton v. Armitage (1845) 2 C.B. 336 1–046
Graham v. Freer (1980) 35 SAS.R. 424 .... 1–008, 1–011, 10–008
—— v. Jackson (1811) 14 East. 498; 104 E.R. 693 8–054
—— v. Johnson (1869) L.R. 8 Eq. 36; 38 L.J.Ch. 374; 21 L.T. 77; 17 W.R. 810 7–028
Graham (Thomas) & Sons Ltd v. Glenrothes Development Cpn. 1968 S.L.T. 2 7–080
Grain Union S./A. Antwerp v. A/S Hans Larson Aalborg [1933] All E.R. 342; 150 L.T. 78; 49 T.L.R. 540; 38 Com.Cas. 260; 18 Asp.M.L.C. 449 19–022
Grainex Canada Ltd, *Re*, (1987) 34 D.L.R. (4th) 646 .... 8–085, 15–042
Grand Trunk Railway of Canada v. Robinson [1915] A.C. 740 13–016
Grant v. Australian Knitting Mills Ltd; *sub nom*. Australian Knitting Mills v. Grant [1936] A.C. 85; (1934) 50 C.L.R. 387, HC (Aus); reversing (1933) 50 C.L.R. 387, Sup Ct (S. Aus) (Sgl Judge) ... 11–008, 11–043, 11–044, 11–057, 11–059, 11–065, 14–058, 16–047, 17–072
—— v. Norway (1851) 10 C.B. 665; 20 L.J.C.P. 93; 16 L.T. (o.s.) 504; 15 Jur. 296 .. 18–029, 18–030, 18–031, 18–032, 18–034, 18–036, 18–037, 18–040, 18–041, 18–042, 18–045, 18–164
Grantham v. Hawley (1615) Hob. 132; 80 E.R. 281 .... 1–106, 5–095
Grant Smith & Co. and McDonnell Ltd v. Seattle Construction and Dry Dock Co. [1920] A.C. 162 8–097
Granville Oil & Chemicals Ltd v. Davies Turner & Co Ltd; *sub nom.* Granville Oils & Chemicals Ltd v. Davis Turner & Co Ltd [2003] EWCA Civ 570; [2003] 1 All E.R. (Comm) 819; [2003] 2 Lloyd's Rep. 356; [2003] 2 C.L.C. 418; (2003) 147 S.J.L.B. 505, CA 18–280
Graumann v. Treitel (1940) 112 L.T. 383 25–167
Graves v. Legg (1854) 9 Exch. 709; 2 C.L.R. 1266; 23 L.J.Ex. 228; 23 L.T. (o.s.) 254; (1857) 2 H. & N. 210, Ex.Ch. 11–004, 19–018, 19–063, 21–025
—— v. Weld (1833) 5 B. & Ad. 105 1–093
Great China Metal Industries Co. Ltd v. Malaysia International Shipping Corp. Bhd (The Bunga Seroja) [1999] 1 Lloyd's Rep. 512; 1999 A.M.C. 427, HC (Aus); affirming [1994] 1 Lloyd's Rep. 455, Sup Ct (NSW) 8–097
Great Eastern Railway v. Lord's Trustee [1909] A.C. 109; 78 L.J.K.B. 160; 100 L.T. 130; 25 T.L.R. 176; 16 Mans. 1 .... 15–028, 15–038, 15–049
Great Northern Railway v. Harrison (1852) 12 C.B. 576; 22 L.J.C.P. 49; 19 L.T. (o.s.) 259; 16 Jur. 565; 138 E.R. 1032, Ex.Ch. 8–039
Great Northern Railway Co. v. Coal Co-operative Society [1896] 1 Ch. 187 1–016
—— v. Witham (1873) L.R. 9 C.P. 16; 43 L.J.C.P. 1; 29 L.T. 471; 22 W.R. 48 .... 2–009, 8–058
Great Peace Shipping Ltd v. Tsavliris Salvage (International) Ltd [2002] EWCA Civ 1407; [2003] Q.B. 679; [2002] 3 W.L.R. 1617; [2002] 4 All E.R. 689; [2002] 2 All E.R. (Comm) 999; [2002] 2 Lloyd's Rep. 653; [2003] 2 C.L.C. 16; (2002) 99(43) L.S.G. 34; (2002) 152 N.L.J. 1616; [2002] N.P.C. 127; *The Times*, October 17, 2002; *Independent*, October 22, 2002, CA .. 3–018, 3–021, 3–026, 12–128
Great Western Insurance Co. v. Cunliffe (1874) L.R. 9 Ch. 525; 43 L.J.Ch. 741; 30 L.T. 661 16–006

Great Western Railway v. Fisher [1905] 1 Ch. 316; 74 L.J.Ch. 241; 92 L.T. 104; 53 W.R. 279 4–029
—— v. London and County Banking Co. [1901] A.C. 414; 70 L.J.K.B. 915; 85 L.T. 152; 50 W.R. 50; 6 Com.Cas. 275 22–023
—— v. Redmayne (1866) L.R. 1 C.P. 329 17–032
Greater Nottingham Co-operative Society Ltd v. Cementation Piling & Foundations Ltd [1989] Q.B. 71 18–129
Greaves v. Ashlin (1813) 3 Camp. 426; 170 E.R. 1433, N.P. 9–005, 9–009
Greaves & Co. Contractors v. Baynham Meikle & Partners [1975] 1 W.L.R. 1095; [1975] 3 All E.R. 99; [1975] 2 Lloyd's Rep. 325; 119 S.J. 372, CA 14–049
—— v. Hepke (1818) 2 B. & Ald. 131; 106 E.R. 315 5–031
Grébert-Borgnis v. Nugent (J. & W.) (1885) 15 Q.B.D. 85; 54 L.J.Q.B. 511; 1 T.L.R. 434 .... 17–022, 17–035, 17–036, 17–078
Green v. Arcos Ltd (1931) 47 T.L.R. 336; 39 Ll.L.Rep. 229 .... 8–062, 11–018
—— v. Baverstock (1863) 14 C.B. (N.S.) 204; 2 New Rep. 128; 32 L.J.C.P. 181; 8 L.T. 360; 10 Jur. (N.S.) 47 3–009
—— v. Greenbank (1816) 2 Marsh. 485 2–037
—— v. Jo-Ann Accessory Shop Ltd (1983) 21 Man.R. (2d) 261 14–014
—— v. Lewis (1867) 26 U.C.Q.B. 618 25–086
—— v. Sevin (1879) 13 Ch.D. 589 8–026
—— v. Sichel (1860) 7 C.B. (N.S.) 747; 29 L.J.C.P. 213; 2 L.T. 745;6 Jur. (N.S.) 827; 8 W.R. 663; 141 E.R. 1009 .... 16–021, 20–020, 20–042, 20–126
—— v. Van Buskirk 7 Wall. 139 (1868) 25–122
Green (Joseph) v. Arcos Ltd (1931) 39 Ll.L.R. 229 .... 11–018, 13–033
Green (R.W.) Ltd v. Cade Bros. Farms [1978] 1 Lloyd's Rep. 602 .... 12–063, 13–020, 13–034, 13–036, 13–089, 18–280
Greenman v. Yuba Power Products Inc. 377 P. 2d. 897 (1962) 14–078
Greenock Corp. v. Caledonian Ry [1917] A.C. 556 8–097
Greenough v. Munroe, 53 F. 2d 362 (1931) 23–098, 23–099, 23–126
Greenwich Marine Inc. v. Federal Commerce and Navigation Ltd (The Mavro Vetranic) [1985] 1 Lloyd's Rep. 580 .... 10–037, 20–032
Greenwood v. Bennett [1973] 1 Q.B. 195; [1972] 3 W.L.R. 691; 116 S.J. 762; [1972] 3 All E.R. 586; [1972] R.T.R. 535 .... 7–005, 14–007, 15–116
Greer v. Downs Supply Co. [1927] 2 K.B. 28; [1926] All E.R. 675; 96 L.J.K.B. 534; 137 L.T. 174 .... 5–034, 7–047
—— v. Poole (1880) 5 Q.B.D. 572 25–074
Gregg v. Wells (1839) 10 A. & E. 90 7–009
Grein v. Imperial Airways Ltd [1937] 1 K.B. 50; [1936] 2 All E.R. 1258; 106 L.J.K.B. 49; 155 L.T. 380; 52 T.L.R. 681; 80 S.J. 735; 42 Com.Cas. 10 16–051
Grenfell v. Meyrowitz (E.B.) Ltd [1936] 2 All E.R. 1313 11–021
Greville v. da Costa (1797) Peake 113 12–067
Grey v. Inland Revenue Commissioners [1960] A.C. 1; [1959] 3 W.L.R. 759; 103 S.J. 896; [1959] 3 All E.R. 603; [1959] T.R. 311 1–004
Grey (Edward) & Co. v. Tolme and Runge (1915) 31 T.L.R. 551 18–335
Grice v. Richardson (1877) L.R. 3 App.Cas. 319; 47 L.J.P.C. 48; 37 L.T. 677; 26 W.R. 358 .... 15–037, 15–039, 15–040
Griffin v. Weatherby (1868) L.R. 3 Q.B. 753; 9 B. & S. 726; 37 L.J.Q.B. 280; 18 L.T. 881; 17 W.R. 8 .... 22–042, 22–108
Griffith v. Brymer (1903) 19 T.L.R. 434; 47 S.J. 493 3–022
Griffiths v. Arch Engineering Co. Ltd [1968] 3 All E.R. 217 14–063
Griffiths v. Conway (Peter) Ltd [1939] 1 All E.R. 685 .... 11–057, 14–010, 14–084
—— v. Owen (1844) 13 M. & W. 58 9–030
—— v. Perry (1859) 1 E. & E. 680; 28 L.J.Q.B. 204; 32 L.T. (O.S.) 315; 5 Jur. (N.S.) 1076; 120 E.R. 1065 .... 9–030, 15–010, 15–028, 15–036, 15–063, 17–003
—— v. Ystradyfodwg School Board (1890) 24 Q.B.D. 307; 59 L.J.Q.B. 116; 62 L.T. 151; 38 W.R. 425 16–017
Grimoldby v. Wells (1875) L.R. 10 C.P. 391; 44 L.J.C.P. 203; 32 L.T. 490; 39 J.P. 535; 23 W.R. 524 .... 12–032, 12–043, 12–065
Grist v. Bailey [1967] Ch. 532; [1966] 3 W.L.R. 618; 110 S.J. 791; [1966] 2 All E.R. 875 12–128
Griswold v. Haven 25 N.Y. 595 (1862) 18–174

Grizewood v. Blane (1851) 11 C.B. 526 1–104
Grob v. Manufacturers Trust Co., 29 N.Y.S. 2d 916 (1941) 23–206
Groom (C.) Ltd v. Barber [1915] 1 K.B. 316; 84 L.J.K.B. 318; 112 L.T. 301; 31 T.L.R. 66; 59 S.J. 129; 12 Asp.M.C.L. 594; 20 Com.Cas. 71 .... 19–016, 19–023, 19–037, 19–042, 19–043, 19–046, 19–080, 19–082, 19–083
Gross v. Jordan 22 A. 250 (1891) 25–133
Grosspillex, *Re* [1964] 2 C.M.L.R. 237 3–041
Grosvenor Hotel Co. v. Hamilton [1894] 2 Q.B. 836 4–029
Grouf v. State National Bank of St. Louis, 40 F. 2d 2 (1930) 23–236
Group Josi Re Co SA v. Walbrook Insurance Co Ltd; *sub nom.* Group Josi Re (formerly Group Josi Reassurance SA) v. Walbrook Insurance Co Ltd; Deutsche Ruckversicherung AG v. Walbrook Insurance Co Ltd [1996] 1 W.L.R. 1152; [1996] 1 All E.R. 791; [1996] 1 Lloyd's Rep. 345; [1996] 5 Re. L.R. 91, CA 23–281
Groupement National D'Achat Des Tourteaux v. Sociedad Industrial Financiera Argentina (The Milton B. Medary) [1962] 2 Lloyd's Rep. 192 11–079
Gruber v. Bay Wa AG (C464/01) [2006] Q.B. 204; [2006] 2 W.L.R. 205; [2005] E.C.R. I-439; [2005] I.L.Pr. 12, ECJ 25–045, 25–046
Grundt v. Great Boulder Property Gold Mines Ltd (1937) 59 C.L.R. 641 12–036
Grymes v. Blofield (1594) Cro.Eliz. 541 9–044
Guarantee Trust of Jersey Ltd v. Gardner (1973) 117 S.J. 564 .... 11–052, 14–047
Guaranty Trust Co. of New York v. Hannay & Co. [1918] 2 K.B. 623 .... 5–140, 18–216, 19–034, 22–042, 22–062, 22–093, 23–002, 23–128, 23–191
— v. Van Den Berghs Ltd (1925) 22 Ll.L.R. 447 .... 18–015, 18–073, 23–126, 23–132, 23–201
Guépratte v. Young (1851) 4 De G. & Sm. 217 25–086
Gulf International Bank BSC v. Albaraka Islamic Bank BSC [2004] EWCA Civ 416; [2003] All E.R. (D) 460, CA 23–193
Gulf Steel Co. Ltd v. Al Khalifa Shipping Co. (The Anwar al Sabar) [1980] 2 Lloyd's Rep. 261 .... 18–030, 18–047
Gullischen v. Stewart (1883–84) L.R. 13 Q.B.D. 317, CA; affirming (1882–83) L.R. 11 Q.B.D. 186, QBD 18–051
Gunn v. Bolckow, Vaughan & Co. (1875) L.R. 10 Ch.App. 491; 44 L.J.Ch. 732; 32 L.T. 781; 23 W.R. 739 .... 7–036, 8–012, 8–013, 9–030, 9–031, 15–002, 15–018, 15–019, 15–020, 15–036, 15–037, 15–040, 15–094, 23–106
Gurney v. Behrend (1854) 3 E. & B. 622; 23 L.J.Q.B. 265; 23 L.T. (o.s.) 89; 18 Jur. 856; 2 W.R. 425; 118 E.R. 1275 .... 18–057, 18–084, 18–085
Gurr v. Cuthbert (1843) 12 L.J.Ex. 309 15–057
Gurtner v. Circuit [1968] 2 Q.B. 587 18–122
Guthing v. Lynn (1831) 2 B. & Ad. 232 2–019
Gwillim v. Daniell (1835) 2 C.M. & R. 61; 1 Gale 143; 5 Tyr. 644; 4 L.J.Ex. 174; 150 E.R. 26 8–056
Gyles v. Hall (1726) 2 P.Wms. 378 9–050
Gyllenhammar & Partners International Ltd v. Sour Brodogradevna Industrija [1989] 2 Lloyd's Rep. 403 8–089

HIH Casualty and General Insurance Ltd v. Chase Manhattan Bank; Chase Manhattan Bank v. HIH Casualty & General Insurance Ltd [2001] EWCA Civ 1250; [2001] 2 Lloyd's Rep. 483; [2001] C.L.C. 1853; [2001] Lloyd's Rep. I.R. 703, CA; reversing in part [2001] 1 All E.R. (Comm) 719; [2001] 1 Lloyd's Rep. 30; [2001] C.L.C. 48; [2001] Lloyd's Rep. I.R. 191; *The Times*, September 19, 2000, QBD (Comm Ct) 13–016
HIH Casualty & General Insurance Ltd v. Chase Manhattan Bank; Chase Manhattan Bank v. HIH Casualty & General Insurance Ltd [2003] UKHL 6; [2003] 1 All E.R. (Comm) 349; [2003] 2 Lloyd's Rep. 61; [2003] 1 C.L.C. 358; [2003] Lloyd's Rep. I.R. 230; (2003) 147 S.J.L.B. 264, HL 13–016, 13–017, 13–036
HSBC Rail (UK) Ltd v. Network Rail Infrastructure Ltd (formerly Railtrack Plc) [2005] EWCA Civ 1437; [2006] 1 W.L.R. 643; [2006] 1 All E.R. 343; [2006] 1 All E.R. (Comm) 345; [2006] 1 Lloyd's Rep. 358; (2006) 103(1) L.S.G. 17; *The Times*, December 23, 2005, CA 5–010, 18–115
Hack v. Hack (1976) 6 Fam. Law 177 25–056

Hackfield v. Castle 198 P. 1041 (1921) 20–021, 20–098
Hackney Borough Council v. Dore [1922] 1 K.B. 431; 91 L.J.K.B. 109; 126 L.T. 375; 86 J.P. 45; 38 T.L.R. 93; 20 L.G.R. 88 .... 8–098, 8–099
Hadley v. Baxendale (1854) 9 Exch. 341; [1843–60] All E.R. Rep. 461; 23 L.J.Ex. 179; 23 L.T.O.S. 69; 18 Jur. 358; 2 W.R. 302; 2 C.L.R. 517; 156 E.R. 145 .... 13–037, 16–007, 16–030, 16–043, 16–046, 16–055, 16–061, 16–085, 17–001, 17–007, 17–041, 17–047, 17–076, 23–107
—— v. Droitwich Construction Co. Ltd [1968] 1 W.L.R. 37; 111 S.J. 849; (1967) 3 K.L.R. 578 17–075
Hadley & Co. Ltd v. Hadley [1898] 2 Ch. 680 9–030
Hadwen v. Mendisabel (1825) 2 C. & P. 20; 10 Moore C.P. 477; 3 L.J.O.S.C.P. 198 .. 9–030
Hain S.S. Co. Ltd v. Tate & Lyle Ltd [1936] 2 All E.R. 597; 155 L.T. 177; 52 T.L.R. 617; 80 Sol.Jo. 687; 19 Asp. M.L.C. 62; 41 Com.Cas. 350; 55 Lloyd Rep. 159 .... 12–034, 13–046, 18–048, 18–059, 18–060, 18–082, 18–110
Halcyon the Great, The [1975] 1 W.L.R. 515; (1974) 119 S.J 10; [1975] 1 All E.R. 882; [1975] 1 C.M.L.R. 267; [1975] 1 Lloyd's Rep. 518 25–194
Hale v. Rawson (1858) 4 C.B.N.S. 85; 27 L.J.C.P. 189; 31 L.T.O.S. 59; 4 Jur. N.S. 363; 6 W.R. 339; 140 E.R. 1013 .... 21–024, 21–027
Haines House Haulage Co. Ltd v. Gamble [1989] 3 N.Z.L.R. 221 8–024
Hair & Skin Trading Co. v. Norman Airfreight Carriers and World Transport Agencies [1974] 1 Lloyd's Rep. 443 21–073
Halesowen Presswork and Assemblies Ltd v. Westminster Bank Ltd. *See* National Westminster Bank v. Halesowen Presswork and Assemblies.
Halfway Garage (Nottingham) v. Lepley, *The Guardian*, February 8, 1964 7–058
Halifax Building Society v. Edell [1992] Ch. 436; [1992] 3 W.L.R. 136; [1992] 3 All E.R. 389; [1992] 1 E.G.L.R. 195; (1993) 12 Tr.L.R. 117; [1992] 18 E.G. 151; [1992] E.G.C.S. 33; [1992] N.P.C. 38; *The Times*, March 11, 1992 18–141
Halifax Union v. Wheelwright (1875) L.R. 10 Ex. 183; 44 L.J.Ex 121; 32 L.T. 802; 39 J.P. 823; 23 W.R. 704 22–024
Hall v. Burnell [1911] 2 Ch. 551; [1911–13] All E.R.Rep. 631; 81 L.J.Ch. 46; 105 L.T. 409; 55 Sol.Jo. 737 15–112
Hall v. Busst (1960) 104 C.L.R. 206 2–047
—— v. Conder (1857) 2 C.B. (N.S.) 22;26 L.J.C.P. 138; 29 L.T.O.S. 108; 3 Jur. N.S. 366; 5 W.R. 491; 140 E.R. 318 9–029
—— v. Queensland Truck Centre Property Ltd [1970] Qd. R. 231 .... 13–030, 13–052
Hall (R. and H.) Ltd and Pim (W.H.) (Junior) & Co.'s Arbitration [1928] All E.R. Rep. 763; 39 L.T. 550; 33 Com.Cas. 324; 30 Ll.L.R. 159 .... 17–017, 17–029, 17–030, 17–031, 17–032, 17–033, 17–035, 17–036, 17–039
Hallen v. Runder (1834) 1 C.M. & R. 266; 3 Tyr. 959; 3 L.J.Ex. 260; 149 E.R. 1080 1–095
Hallett's Estate, *Re* (1880) 13 Ch.D. 696; [1874–80] All E.R.Rep. 793; *sub nom.* Hallett's Estate, *Re*, Knatchbull v. Hallett, Cotterell v. Hallett 49 L.J.Ch. 415; 42 L.T. 421; 28 W.R. 732 .... 5–146, 5–152, 7–003, 22–090
Hallgarten v. Oldham 45 Am.Rep. 433 (1893) 25–136
Halliday v. Holgate (1868) L.R. 3 Ex. 299 7–108
Hallmark Pool Cpn. v. Storey (1983) 144 D.L.R. (3d) 56 10–013
Halpern v. Halpern [2006] EWHC 603, QBD 25–024, 25–027, 25–028, 25–029, 25–057, 25–083
Halstead v. Skelton (1843) 5 Q.B. 86; 1 Dav. & Mer. 664; 13 L.J.Ex. 177; 2 L.T.O.S. 228; 7 Jur. 680; 114 E.R. 1180 22–104
Hamble Fisheries Ltd v. L. Gardner & Sons Ltd (The Rebecca Elaine) [1999] 2 Lloyd's Rep. 1; (1999) 15 Const. L.J. 152; (1999) 96(6) L.S.G. 34; *The Times*, January 5, 1999, CA 12–124, 12–126
Hambro v. Burnand [1904] 2 K.B. 10; [1904–7] All E.R.Rep. Ext. 1568; 73 L.J.K.B. 669; 90 L.T. 803; 52 W.R. 583; 20 T.L.R. 398; 48 Sol.Jo. 369; 9 Com.Cas. 251 7–047
Hamburg Star, The [1994] 1 Lloyd's Rep. 399, QBD 18–149
Hamilton v. Papakura District Council, [2002], UKPC 9, [2003], N.Z.L.R. 308 [2000] 1 N.Z.L.R. 265 .... 1–087, 11–055
Hamilton Bank NA v. Kookmin Bank 245 F. 3rd 82 (2001) 23–159
Hamilton Fraser & Co. v. Pandorf & Co. (1887) 12 App.Cas. 518 8–097

Hamilton Young & Co., *Re* [1905] 2 K.B. 772; 74 L.J.K.B. 905; 93 L.T. 591; 54 W.R. 260; 21 T.L.R. 757; 12 Mans. 365 15–053
Hamlyn & Co. v. Talisker Distillery [1894] A.C. 202; [1891–4] All E.R.Rep. 849; 71 L.T. 1; 58 J.P. 540; 10 T.L.R. 479; 6 R. 188 .... 22–013, 25–007, 25–010, 25–089
—— v. Wood [1891] 2 Q.B. 488; [1891–4] All E.R. Rep. 168; 60 L.J.Q.B. 734; 65 L.T. 286; 40 W.R. 24; 7 T.L.R. 731 .... 8–058, 8–079
Hammer and Barrow v. Coca-Cola [1962] N.Z.L.R. 723 .... 5–085, 12–045, 12–048, 12–049, 12–056
Hammer and Sohne v. H.W.T. Realisations Ltd 1985 S.L.T. (Sh.Ct.) 21 .... 25–141, 25–142, 25–144
Hammertons Cars Ltd v. Redbridge London B.C. [1974] 1 W.L.R. 484; 118 S.J. 240; [1974] 2 All E.R. 216; [1974] Crim.L.R. 241 14–107
Hammond v. Anderson (1803) 1 B. & P.N.R. 69; 127 E.R. 384 ...... 5–031, 8–012, 15–041
Hammond & Co. v. Bussey (1887) 20 Q.B.D. 79; 57 L.J.Q.B. 58; 4 T.L.R. 95 ..... 17–045, 17–059, 17–061, 17–076, 17–077
Hammond and Waterton, *Re* (1890) 62 L.T. 808; 6 T.L.R. 302 2–052
Hammonds v. Barclay (1802) 2 East. 227; 102 E.R. 356 .... 15–028, 15–029
Hamps v. Darby [1948] 2 K.B. 311; [1949] L.J.R. 487; 64 T.L.R. 440; 92 S.J. 541; [1948] 2 All E.R. 474 1–088
Harrison (A.) & Son (London) Ltd v. Martin (S.) Johnson & Co. Ltd [1953] 1 Lloyd's Rep. 553 .... 18–229, 20–017
Handbury v. Nolan (1977) 13 A.L.D. 339 11–019
Handley Page Ltd v. Rockwell Machine Tool Co. Ltd [1971] 2 Lloyd's Rep. 298 22–064
Hands v. Burton (1808) 9 East. 349; 103 E.R. 606 1–039
Hanjin Shipping Co. Ltd v. Procter & Gamble (Philippines) Ltd [1997] 2 Lloyd's Rep. 341, QBD (Comm Ct) 20–003, 20–061
Hanno (Heinrich) & Co. BV v. Fairlight Shipping Co. Ltd (The Kostas K) [1985] 1 Lloyd's Rep. 231 18–054
Hansen v. Craig and Rose (1859) 21 Dunl. 432; 31 Sc.Jur. 236 6–002
—— v. Dixon (1906) 96 L.T. 32; 23 T.L.R. 56 25–191
Hanson v. Meyer (1805) 6 East. 614; 2 Smith K.B. 670; 102 E.R. 1425 ...... 5–035, 5–038
Hanson (W.) (Harrow) Ltd v. Rapid Civil Engineering Ltd (1987) 38 Build.L.R. 106; (1988) 11 Con.L.R. 119 .... 5–156, 5–157, 7–065, 7–079, 7–080, 7–084, 7–086
Hansson v. Hamel & Horley Ltd [1922] 2 A.C. 36; [1922] All E.R.Rep. 237; 91 L.J.K.B. 433; 127 L.T. 74; 38 T.L.R. 466; 66 Sol.Jo. 421; 15 Asp.M.L.C. 546; 27 Com.Cas. 321; 10 Ll.L.R. 199 ..... 18–047, 18–284, 19–027, 19–028, 19–032, 19–033, 19–034, 19–038, 19–095, 19–098, 19–094, 19–097, 19–099, 19–146, 20–083, 23–160
Harbinger UK Ltd v. GE Information Services Ltd [2000] 1 All E.R. (Comm) 166; (2000) 2 T.C.L.R. 463; [2000] 1 T.C.L.R. 501, CA; reversing [1999] Masons C.L.R. 335, QBD (T&CC) 19–151
Harbottle (R.D.) (Mercantile) Ltd v. National Westminster Bank [1978] 1 Q.B. 146; [1977] 3 W.L.R. 752; (1977) 121 S.J. 745; [1977] 2 All E.R. 862 ..... 23–138, 23–275
Harbutt's Plasticine Ltd v. Wayne Tank and Pump Co. Ltd [1970] 1 Q.B. 447; [1970] 2 W.L.R. 198; 114 S.J. 29; [1970] 1 All E.R. 225; [1970] 1 Lloyd's Rep. 15 ... 13–046, 13–048, 16–056, 17–024, 17–074
Harding v. Wealands [2004] EWCA Civ 1735; [2005] 1 W.L.R. 1539; [2005] 1 All E.R. 415; [2005] 2 C.L.C. 411; [2005] R.T.R. 20; (2005) 155 N.L.J. 59; *The Times*, January 5, 2005, CA 25–191
Hardman v. Booth (1863) 1 H. & C. 803; 1 New Rep. 240; 32 L.J.Ex. 105; 7 L.T. 638; 9 Jur. N.S. 81; 11 W.R. 239; 158 E.R. 1107 .... 3–013, 5–046, 7–021
Hardwick Game Farm v. Suffolk Agricultural Poultry Producers Association *See* Kendall (Henry) & Sons v. William Lillico & Sons Ltd
Hardy v. Woodroofe (1818) 2 Stark. 319 22–116
Hardy & Co. v. Hillerns and Fowler [1923] 2 K.B. 490; [1923] All E.R. Rep. 275; 92 L.J.K.B. 930; 129 L.T. 674; 39 T.L.R. 547; 67 Sol.Jo. 618; 29 Com.Cas. 30 ... 12–045, 12–046, 12–047, 12–048, 12–049, 12–051, 19–154, 19–157, 19–174, 20–109
Hardy (M.W.) & Co. Inc. v. Pound (A. V.) & Co. Ltd. *See* Pound (A.V.) & Co. v. Hardy (M.W.) & Co.
Hare v. Gocher [1962] 2 Q.B. 641; [1962] 3 W.L.R. 339; 126 J.P. 395; 106 S.J. 531; [1962] 2 All E.R. 763; 13 P. & C.R. 298; 60 L.G.R. 278 8–034

Hare v. Nicoll [1966] 2 Q.B. 130; [1966] 2 W.L.R. 441 15–122
Hargreaves Transport Ltd v. Lynch [1969] 1 W.L.R. 215; 112 S.J. 54; [1969] 1 All E.R. 455; 20 P. & C.R. 143 .... 8–040, 10–024
Haringey L.B.C. v. Piro Shoes Ltd [1976] Crim.L.R. 462 1–027
Harland & Wolff Ltd v. Burns & Laird Lines 1931 S.C. 722 21–106
—— v. Burstall & Co. (1901) 84 L.T. 324; 17 T.L.R. 338; 9 Asp.M.L.C. 184; 6 Com.Cas. 113 .... 8–046, 8–050, 8–054, 19–012, 19–016, 19–051
Harling v. Eddy [1951] 2 K.B. 739; [1951] 2 T.L.R. 245; 95 S.J. 501; [1951] 2 All E.R. 212 .... 2–027, 10–006, 10–012, 10–020, 10–022, 10–037, 12–067, 12–068, 13–016, 13–024
Harlingdon & Leinster Enterprises Ltd v. Christopher Hull Fine Art [1991] 1 Q.B. 564; [1990] 3 W.L.R. 13; [1990] 1 All E.R. 737; (1991) 10 Tr.L.R. 65; (1990) 140 N.L.J. 90, CA ... 3–020, 5–006, 11–009, 11–011, 11–032, 11–044, 11–055, 14–009, 18–273
Harlow and Jones Ltd v. American Express Bank Ltd [1990] 2 Lloyd's Rep. 343 ... 22–076, 22–077, 22–083, 22–096, 23–027, 23–184, 23–190
—— v. Panex International Ltd [1967] 2 Lloyd's Rep. 509; [1967] 118 New L.J. 88 .. 9–009, 16–052, 16–077, 20–030, 20–035, 20–135, 20–137
—— v. Walker (P.J.) Shipping & Transport Ltd [1986] 2 Lloyd's Rep. 141 .. 18–118, 21–073
Harman v. Anderson (1809) 2 Camp. 243; 170 E.R. 1143 .... 8–012, 15–052
—— v. Reeve (1856) 18 C.B. 587; 25 L.J.C.P. 257; 27 L.T.O.S. 172; 4 W.R. 599; 139 E.R. 1500 1–091
Harmer v. Cornelius (1858) 5 C.B. (N.S.) 236; [1843–60] All E.R. Rep. 624; 28 L.J.C.P. 85; 32 L.T.O.S. 62; 22 J.P. 724; 4 Jur. N.S. 1110; 6 W.R. 749; 141 E.R. 94 1–041
Harmony & Montague Tin and Copper Mining Co., *Re* (1873) L.R. 8 Ch.App. 407; [1861–73] All E.R.Rep. 261; 42 L.J.Ch. 488; 28 L.T. 153; 21 W.R. 306 9–041
Harnor v. Groves (1855) 15 C.B. 667; 3 C.L.R. 406; 24 L.J.C.P. 53; 24 L.T.O.S. 215; 3 W.R. 168; 139 E.R. 587 .... 12–040, 12–047
Harper v. Godsell (1870) L.R. 5 Q.B. 422; 39 L.J.Q.B. 185; 18 W.R. 954 1–063
—— v. Hochstim 278 F. 102 (1921) 19–002
—— v. South Island Holdings Ltd [1959] N.Z.L.R. 629 13–030
Harper (A.C.) & Co. Ltd v. Mackechnie & Co. Ltd [1925] 2 K.B. 423; 95 L.J.K.B. 162; 134 L.T. 90; 31 Com.Cas. 21 19–047
Harpham v. Child (1859) 1 F. & F. 652 22–124
Harrington v. Browne (1917) 23 C.L.R. 297; [1917] S.R.Q. 172 (Australia) 8–025
Harris v. Best, Ryley & Co. [1891–4] All E.R.Rep. 567; 68 L.T. 76; 9 T.L.R. 149; 7 Asp.M.L.C. 272; 4 R. 222 20–018
—— v. Nickerson (1873) L.R. 8 Q.B. 286; 42 L.J.K.B. 171; 28 L.T. 410; 37 J.P. 536; 21 W.R. 635 2–005
—— v. Packer (1833) 6 Tyr. 370n 22–110
Harris & Sons v. Plymouth Varnish & Colour Co. Ltd (1933) 49 T.L.R. 521; 38 Com.Cas. 316 11–088
Harris Corporation v. National Iranian Radio and Television 691 F. 2d 1344 (1982) 23–149
Harris (Oscar), Son & Co. v. Vallerman & Co. [1940] 1 All E.R. 185; 162 L.T. 212; 56 T.L.R. 302; 84 Sol.Jo. 252 22–064
Harrison, *Re* (1858) 2 De G. & J. 194; 27 B.J.Bcy. 5; 30 L.T. (O.S.) 313; 4 Jur. (N.S.) 547; 6 W.R.273 22–090
Harrison v. Allen (1824) 2 Bing. 4; 1 C. & P. 235; 9 Moo.C.P. 28; 2 L.J. (O.S.) C.P. 97; 130 E.R. 205 .... 5–041, 5–050
—— v. Knowles and Foster [1918] 1 K.B. 608; 87 L.J.K.B. 680; 118 L.T. 566; 34 T.L.R. 235; 14 Asp.M.L.C. 249; 23 Com.Cas. 282, CA; affirming [1917] K.B. 606 .... 1–009, 11–012, 11–013, 13–029
—— v. Lia [1951] V.L.R. 470 5–098
—— v. Luke (1845) 14 M. & W. 139; 14 L.J.Ex. 248; 5 L.T. (O.S.) 130; 153 E.R. 423 1–035
—— v. National Coal Board [1951] A.C. 639; [1951] 1 T.L.R. 1079; 95 S.J. 413; [1951] 1 All E.R. 1102; 50 L.G.R. 1 14–095
—— v. Ruscoe (1846) 15 M. & W. 231; 15 L.J.Ex. 110; 10 Jur. 142 22–122
—— v. Tew [1990] 2 A.C. 523; [1990] 2 W.L.R. 210; [1990] 1 All E.R. 321; (1990) 87(8) L.S.G. 44; (1990) 134 S.J. 374, HL; affirming [1989] Q.B. 307; [1988] 2 W.L.R. 1; [1987] 3 All E.R. 865; (1987) 137 N.L.J. 711; (1987) 131 S.J. 1626, CA 9–041

Harrison & Jones Ltd v. Bunten & Lancaster Ltd [1953] 1 Q.B. 646; [1953] 2 W.L.R. 840; 97 S.J. 281; [1953] 1 All E.R. 903; [1953] 1 Lloyd's Rep. 318 ..... 3–020, 12–128
Harrison and Micks, Lambert & Co., *Re* [1917] 1 K.B. 755; *sub nom.* Harrison v. Micks, Lambert & Co., 86 L.J.K.B. 573; 116 L.T. 606; 33 T.L.R. 221; 14 Asp.M.L.C. 76; 22 Com.Cas. 273 .... 8–056, 21–033, 21–035, 21–038, 21–040
Harrison Sons & Co. Ltd v. Cavroy (Jules) (1922) 12 Ll.L.R. 390 25–119
Harrop v. Fisher (1861) 10 C.B. (N.S.) 196; 30 L.J.C.P. 283; 8 Jur. (N.S.) 1058; 9 W.R. 607 22–055
Harse v. Pearl Life Assce. Co. [1904] 1 K.B. 558; 73 L.J.K.B. 373; 90 L.T. 245; 52 W.R. 457; 20 T.L.R. 264 3–032
Hart v. Herwig (1873) L.R. 8 Ch.App. 860; 42 L.J.Ch. 457; 29 L.T. 47; 21 W.R. 663; 2 Asp.M.L.C. 63 .... 17–100, 17–103
—— v. Mills (1846) 15 M. & W. 85; 15 L.J.Ex. 200; 153 E.R. 771 .... 2–008, 8–049
—— v. O'Connor [1985] A.C. 1000; [1985] 1 N.Z.L.R. 159; [1985] 3 W.L.R. 214; (1985) 129 S.J. 484; [1985] 2 All E.R. 880; (1985) 82 L.S.Gaz. 2658 2–041
—— v. Porthgain Harbour Co. Ltd [1903] 1 Ch. 690; 72 L.J.Ch. 426; 88 L.T. 341; 51 W.R. 461 5–093
—— v. Prater (1837) 1 Jur. 623 2–031
Hartley v. Hitchcock (1816) 1 Stark. 408 15–044
—— v. Hymans [1920] 3 K.B. 475 .... 8–025, 8–030, 8–069, 12–034, 15–121, 16–073, 17–012
—— v. Saunders (1962) 33 D.L.R. 638 5–032
Hartog v. Colin & Shields [1939] 3 All E.R. 566 3–016
Hartwells of Oxford Ltd v. British Motor Trade Association [1951] Ch. 50; 66 T.L.R. (Pt. 2) 483; 94 S.J. 505; [1950] 2 All E.R. 705 .... 8–037, 8–089
Harvela Investments Ltd v. Royal Trust Co. of Canada (C.I.) Ltd [1986] A.C. 207; [1985] 3 W.L.R. 276; (1985) 128 S.J. 522; [1985] 2 All E.R. 966; (1985) 135 New L.J. 730; (1985) 82 L.S.Gaz. 3171 .... 2–003, 2–004, 17–100
Harvey v. Ascot Dry Cleaning Co. Ltd [1953] N.Z.L.R. 549 13–013
Harvey v. Facey [1893] A.C. 552 2–002
Harvey Estates Construction Co. v. Dry Dock Savings Bank F.Supp. 271 (1974) 23–054, 23–239
Haseldine v. Daw (C.A.) & Son Ltd [1941] 2 K.B. 343; 3 All E.R. 156; 111 L.J.K.B. 45; 165 L.T. 185; 58 T.L.R. 1 14–063
Hassall v. Lawrence (1887) 4 T.L.R. 23 9–048
Hassell v. Bagot, Shakes and Lewis Ltd (1911) 13 C.L.R. 374 .... 8–054, 17–005
Hastie & Hutchinson v. Campbell & Dunn (1857) 19 D. 557 .... 6–021, 18–246
Hastings v. Pearson [1893] 1 Q.B. 62 7–032
Hatfield v. Phillips (1845) M. & W. 665 7–039
Hathesing v. Laing (1873) L.R. 17 Eq. 92; 43 L.J.Ch. 233; 29 L.T. 734; 2 Asp.M.L.C. 170 .... 18–164, 18–166, 18–229
Haugland Tankers AS v. RMK Marine Gemi Yapim Sanayii ve Deniz Tasimaciligi Isletmesi AS [2005] EWHC 321; [2005] 1 All E.R. (Comm) 679; [2005] 1 Lloyd's Rep. 573; [2005] 1 C.L.C. 271, QBD 9–052
Havering LBC v. Stevenson [1970] 1 W.L.R. 1375; [1970] 3 All E.R. 609; [1971] R.T.R. 58; (1970) 114 S.J. 664, QBD 11–045
Haviland v. Long (Dunn Trust, Third Parties) [1952] 2 Q.B. 80; (1952) 1 T.L.R. 576; 96 S.J. 180; [1952] 1 All E.R. 463 16–056
Hawes v. Humble (1809) 2 Camp. 327n; 170 E.R. 1172, N.P. 21–022
—— v. Watson (1824) 2 B. & C. 540; 4 Dow & Ry. K.B. 22; Ry. & M. 6; 2 L.J. (O.S.) K.B. 83; 107 E.R. 484 .... 5–065, 7–013, 15–052, 15–096
Hawkes v. Salter (1828) 4 Bing. 715; 1 Moo. & P. 750; 6 L.J. (O.S.) C.P. 180 22–127
Hawkes Bay and East Coast Aero Club Inc. v. McLeod [1972] N.Z.L.R. 289 13–022
Hawkins v. Rutt (1793) Peake 248 9–042
Haydenfayre Ltd v. British National Insurance Society Ltd [1984] 2 Lloyd's Rep. 393 19–146
Hayes v. James & Charles Dodd (a firm) [1990] 2 All E.R. 815, C.A. 14–006, 16–047
Hayes Bros Buick Opel Jeep Inc. v. Can. Permanent Trust Co. (1976) 15 N.B.R. (2d) 166 5–081
Hayes-Leger Association Inc. v. M/V. Oriental Knight (1985) 765 F. 2d 1076 21–086
Hayman v. Flewker (1863) 13 C.B. (N.S.) 519 7–032
Hayman & Son v. M'Lintock 1907 S.C. 936 .... 5–005, 5–061, 5–065, 18–080, 18–291, 18–299

Hayn v. Culliford (1879) 4 C.P.D. 182; 48 L.J.Q.B. 372; 40 L.T. 536; 27 W.R. 541; 4 Asp.M.L.C. 128 5–009
Hayward, *ex p.* (1887) 3 T.L.R. 687 22–104
Hayward v. Scougall (1809) 2 Camp. 56; 150 E.R. 1080 8–054
Hayward Bros. Ltd v. Daniel & Son (1904) 91 L.T. 319 1–110
Hazell v. Hammersmith and Fulham L.B.C. [1992] 2 A.C. 1; [1991] 2 W.L.R. 372; [1991] 1 All E.R. 545; 89 L.G.R. 271; [1991] 141 N.L.J. 127; (1991) 155 J.P.N. 527; (1991) 3 Admin.L.R. 549, H.L. 2–028, 2–043
Head v. Tattersall (1871) L.R. 7 Ex. 7; 41 L.J.Ex. 4; 25 L.T. 631; 20 W.R. 115 .... 1–056, 5–043, 6–010, 6–011, 12–058, 12–063, 13–038
Head (Philip) & Sons Ltd v. Showfronts Ltd [1970] 1 Lloyd's Rep. 140; (1969) 113 S.J. 978 .... 1–043, 5–023, 5–068, 14–046
Healing (Sales) Property Ltd v. Inglis Electrix Property Ltd (1968) 121 C.L.R. 584 .... 4–026, 4–027, 4–029, 4–030, 5–003, 15–117
Healy v. Hewlett & Sons [1917] 1 K.B. 337; 86 L.J.K.B. 252; 116 L.T. 591 .... 5–007, 5–061, 5–099, 5–110, 6–002, 6–017, 18–304
Heap v. Motorists' Advisory Agency [1923] 1 K.B. 577 .... 7–011, 7–033, 7–037, 7–038, 7–045, 7–046, 7–047, 7–068, 7–074, 7–086
Heaton v. Axa Equity & Law Life Assurance Society plc [2002] UKHL 15; [2002] 2 A.C. 329, HL 18–005
Heaven and Kesterton Ltd v. Etablissements Francois Albiac & Cie [1956] 2 Lloyd's Rep. 316 .... 16–052, 17–026, 19–184
Hecht, Pfeiffer (London) Ltd v. Sophus Berendsen (London) Ltd (1929) 33 Ll.L.R. 157 .... 20–014, 20–016, 20–018, 20–045
Hector v. Lyons [1988] P. & C.R. 156 3–014
Hector Whaling Ltd, *Re* [1936] Ch. 208 8–035
Hedley Byrne & Co. Ltd v. Heller & Partners Ltd [1964] A.C. 465; [1963] 3 W.L.R. 101; 107 S.J. 454; [1963] 2 All E.R. 575; [1963] 1 Lloyd's Rep. 485 .... 2–027, 10–010, 12–013, 18–045, 23–176, 23–180, 23–182, 23–191, 24–013
Heil v. Hedges [1951] 1 T.L.R. 512; 95 S.J. 140 11–073
Heilbut, Symons & Co. v. Buckleton [1913] A.C. 30 .... 10–003, 10–012, 10–015, 10–016, 10–017, 10–022, 11–056, 18–038
—— v. Harvey, Christie-Miller & Co. (1922) 1 Ll.L.R. 455 .... 18–171, 18–174, 18–179, 18–286
Heilbutt v. Hickson (1872) L.R. 7 C.P. 438; 41 L.J.C.P. 228; 27 L.T. 336; 20 W.R. 1005 .... 5–050, 5–059, 11–003, 11–075, 11–078, 12–040, 12–041, 12–043, 12–048, 12–065, 12–067, 12–068, 20–108
Heisler v. Anglo-Dal Ltd [1954] 1 W.L.R. 1273; 98 S.J. 698; [1954] 2 All E.R. 770; [1954] 2 Lloyd's Rep. 5 .... 19–159, 19–160, 20–040
Helby v. Matthews [1895] A.C. 471 .... 1–050, 1–053, 4–013, 5–044, 7–062, 7–068, 7–077
Helene Knutsen [2003] EWHC 1964 (Comm); [2003] 2 Lloyd's Rep. 686 13–056
Helicopter Sales (Australia) Property Ltd v. Rotor-Work Property Ltd (1974) 48 A.L.J.R. 390; (1974) 132 C.L.R. 1 .... 1–041, 1–043
Hellenic Steel Co. v. Svolamar Shipping Co. (The Komninos S.) [1990] 1 Lloyd's Rep. 541 .... 25–010, 25–072
Heller Factors Property Ltd v. Toy Corporation Property Ltd [1984] 1 N.S.W.L.R. 121 (Australia) 22–061, 22–104
Hellings v. Russell (1875) 33 L.T. 380 7–032
Helmsing Schiffarts GmbH v. Malta Drydocks Corp. [1977] 2 Lloyd's Rep. 444 25–191
Helps v. Winterbottom (1831) 2 B. & Ad. 431; 9 L.J. (o.s.) K.B. 258; 109 E.R. 1203 .... 9–063, 16–018
Henderson v. Merrett Syndicates Ltd (No.1); *sub nom.* McLarnon Deeney v. Gooda Walker Ltd; Gooda Walker Ltd v. Deeny; Hallam-Eames v. Merrett Syndicates Ltd; Hughes v. Merrett Syndicates Ltd; Feltrim Underwriting Agencies Ltd v. Arbuthnott; Deeny v. Gooda Walker Ltd (Duty of Care) [1995] 2 A.C. 145; [1994] 3 W.L.R. 761; [1994] 3 All E.R. 506; [1994] 2 Lloyd's Rep. 468; (1994) 144 N.L.J. 1204; *The Times*, July 26, 1994; *Independent*, August 3, 1994, HL 10–013, 12–073, 12–078, 13–066, 13–107, 16–051, 18–129, 18–149, 18–151
Henderson v. Prosser [1982] C.L.Y. 21 .... 7–038, 7–044
—— v. Williams [1895] 1 Q.B. 521 .... 7–011, 7–014, 15–077
Henderson and Glass v. Radmore & Co. (1922) 10 Ll.L.R. 727 .... 16–024, 20–011, 20–015, 20–016, 20–041, 20–071, 20–126

Henderson and Keay Ltd v. A.M. Carmichael Ltd 1956 S.L.T. (Notes) 58 16–026
Hendrickson v. Mid-City Motors Ltd [1951] 3 D.L.R. 276 .... 7–021, 7–023
Hendy Lennox (Industrial Engines) Ltd v. Grahame Puttick Ltd [1984] 1 W.L.R. 485; (1984) 128 S.J. 220; [1984] 2 All E.R. 152; [1984] 2 Lloyd's Rep. 422; (1984) 81 L.S.Gaz. 585 .... 1–060, 5–023, 5–068, 5–081, 5–142, 5–144, 5–145, 5–147, 5–149, 5–151, 5–152, 5–156
Henkel v. Pape (1870) L.R. 6 Ex. 7; 40 L.J.Ex. 15; 19 W.R. 106; *sub nom.* Henckel v. Pape, 23 L.T. 419 2–015
Henning's Case (1617) Cro. Jac. 432; 79 E.R. 370; *sub nom.* Haul v. Henning 1 Roll. Rep. 285 9–060
Henningsen v. Bloomfield Motors Inc. 161 A. 2d 69 (1960) 14–078
Henry v. Hammond [1913] 2 K.B. 515; [1911–13] All E.R. 1478; 82 L.J.K.B. 575; 108 L.T. 729; 29 T.L.R. 340; 57 S.J. 358; 12 Asp.M.L.C. 332 .... 5–151, 5–152
Henry (D.I.) Ltd v. Wilhelm C. Clasen [1973] 1 Lloyd's Rep. 159 .... 19–009, 19–088, 19–127
Henry Kendall & Sons v. William Lillico & Sons Ltd; *sub nom.* Hardwick Game Farm v. Suffolk Agricultural and Poultry Producers Association Ltd; Holland Colombo Trading Society Ltd v. Grimsdale & Sons Ltd; Grimsdale & Sons Ltd v. Suffolk Agricultural Poultry Producers Association [1969] 2 A.C. 31; [1968] 3 W.L.R. 110; [1968] 2 All E.R. 444; [1968] 1 Lloyd's Rep. 547, HL ... 11–031
Henshaw (Charles) & Sons Ltd v. Antlerport Ltd [1995] C.L.C. 1312 5–159
Henthorn v. Fraser [1892] 2 Ch. 27; 61 L.J.Ch. 373; 66 L.T. 439; 40 W.R. 433 2–015
Hepburn v. Law 1914 S.C. 918 1–065
Hercules v. Commission [1991] 11 E.C.R. 711 3–041
Herkules Piling v. Tilbury Construction (1992) 61 B.L.R. 107; 32 Con.L.R. 112; *The Times*, September 21, 1992 18–234
Herne Bay Steamboat Co. v. Hutton [1903] 2 K.B. 683; 72 L.J.K.B. 879; 89 L.T. 422; 52 W.R. 183; 47 S.J. 768; 19 T.L.R. 680; Asp.M.L.C. 472 6–055
Herschthal v. Stewart and Ardern Ltd [1940] 1 K.B. 155 .... 12–121, 14–063
Heskell v. Continental Express Ltd [1950] W.N. 210; 94 S.J. 339; [1950] 1 All E.R. 1033; 83 Ll.L.Rep. 438 .... 16–049, 16–063, 16–070, 17–041, 18–018, 18–030, 18–031, 18–033, 18–038, 18–040, 18–041, 18–045, 18–047, 18–084, 18–107, 18–152, 19–024, 20–018, 20–043, 20–065, 20–068
Heugh v. L. & N.W. Railway Co. (1870) L.R. 5 Ex. 51; 39 L.J.Ex. 48; 21 L.T. 676 ... 6–011
Hewett v. Court (1983) 57 A.L.J.R. 211; 149 C.L.R. 639 .... 1–010, 1–043, 1–096
Hewison v. Guthrie (1836) 2 Bing.N.C. 755; 2 Hodg. 51; 3 Scott. 248; 5 L.J.C.P. 283 15–036
—— v. Ricketts (1894) 63 L.J.Q.B. 711; 71 L.T. 191; 10 R. 558 ...... 5–021, 5–146, 15–114
Hewitt v. Thomson (1836) 1 M. & Rob. 543 22–130
Hewlings v. Graham (1901) 70 L.J.Ch. 568; 84 L.T. 497 2–030
Heyman and Another v. Darwins Ltd [1942] A.C. 356; [1942] 1 All E.R. 337; 111 L.J.K.B. 241; 166 L.T. 306; 58 T.L.R. 169 ..... 8–080, 9–015, 9–018, 9–019, 12–018, 13–041, 13–046, 15–110, 19–151
Heyward's Case (1595) 2 Co.Rep. 35a 5–079
Heywood v. Wellers [1976] Q.B. 446; [1976] 2 W.L.R. 101; (1975) 120 S.J. 9; [1976] 1 All E.R. 300; [1976] 2 Lloyd's Rep. 88 14–006
Heyworth v. Hutchinson (1867) L.R. 2 Q.B. 447; 36 L.J.Q.B. 270 11–006
Hibbert v. Carter (1787) 1 T.R. 745 .... 18–089, 18–216
—— v. Shee (1807) 1 Camp. 113; 170 E.R. 596 11–073
Hibernia Bank and Trust Co. v. Aron (J.) & Co. Inc. 233 N.Y.S. 486 (1928) 23–164
Hibernian Bank Ltd v. Gysin and Hanson [1939] 1 K.B. 483; [1939] 1 All E.R. 166; 108 L.J.K.B. 214; 106 C.T. 233; 55 T.L.R. 347; 83 S.J. 113; 44 Com.Cas. 115 22–104
Hick v. Raymond & Reid [1893] A.C. 22; 62 L.J.Q.B. 98; 68 L.T. 175; 41 W.R. 384; 37 S.J. 145; 7 Asp.M.L.C. 233; I.R. 125 .... 8–037, 15–023
Hickman v. Haynes (1875) L.R. 10 C.P. 598; 44 L.J.C.P. 358; L.T. 873; 23 W.R. 872 .... 8–069 8–087, 9–006, 16–069
Hickox v. Adams (1876) 34 L.T. 404; 3 Asp.M.L.C. 142 .... 19–042, 19–043
Higgin v. Pumpherston Oil Co. Ltd (1893) 20 R. 532; 30 Sc.L.R. 595 8–075
Highberry Ltd v. Colt Telecom Group Plc (No.2); *sub nom.* Colt Telecom Group Plc (No.2), Re [2002] EWHC 2815; [2003] B.P.I.R. 324, Ch D 25–043
Highway Foods International (In Administrative Receivership), *Re* [1995] B.C.C. 271; [1995] 1 B.C.L.C. 209; (1995) 14 Tr.L.R. 273; *The Times*, November 1, 1994 .. 5–156, 7–048, 7–065, 7–084

Hill v. Arbon (1876) 34 L.T. 125; 40 J.P. 391 2–031
—— v. Crowe (James) (Cases) Ltd [1978] I.C.R. 298; [1978] 1 All E.R. 812; [1977] 2 Lloyd's Rep. 450 .... 14–061, 14–076
—— v. Heap (1823) Dowl. & Ry. N.P. 57 22–116
—— v. Peters [1918] 2 Ch. 273; 87 L.J.Ch. 584; 119 L.T. 613; 62 S.J. 717 5–161
—— v. Showell (1918) 87 L.J.K.B. 1106 .... 16–056, 16–057
Hill and Lichtenstein Ltd v. Export Guarantee General Manager [1972] N.Z.L.R. 802 (S.C.) 24–021
Hill & Sons v. Showell (Edwin) & Sons Ltd (1918) 87 L.J.K.B. 1106; 119 L.T. 651; 62 S.J. 715 .... 1–044, 16–079, 16–085
Hillas & Co. Ltd v. Arcos Ltd [1931] 40 Ll.L.Rep. 307, HL [1932] All E.R. Rep. 494; (1932) 147 L.T. 503; 38 Com.Cas. 23; 43 Ll.L.R. 359 .... 2–017, 2–046
Hillesden Securities Ltd v. Ryjack Ltd [1983] 1 W.L.R. 959; (1983) 127 S.J. 521; [1983] 2 All E.R. 184; [1983] R.T.R. 491; (1983) 37 L.S.Gaz. 2524; (1983) New L.J. 280 7–002
Hillingdon London B.C. v. Cutler [1968] 1 Q.B. 124; [1967] 3 W.L.R. 246; 65 L.G.R. 535 8–036
Hills v. Sughrue (1846) 15 M. & W. 253; 153 E.R. 844; *sub nom.* Mills v. Seybourne 6 L.T.O.S. 414 19–132
Hilti A.G. v. Commission [1994] 1 C.E.C. 590 3–041
Hilton v. Tucker (1888) 39 Ch.D. 669; 57 L.J.Ch. 973; 59 L.T. 172; 36 W.R. 762; 4 T.L.R. 618 8–008
Hinchcliffe v. Barwick (1880) 5 Ex.D. 177; 49 L.J.Q.B. 495; 42 L.T. 492; 44 J.P. 615; 28 W.R. 940 13–038
Hinde v. Liddell (1875) L.R. 10 Q.B. 265; 44 L.J.Q.B. 105; 32 L.T. 449; 23 W.R. 650 .... 16–067, 17–021, 17–024, 17–024
Hinde v. Whitehouse (1806) 7 East. 558; 3 Smith K.B. 528; 103 E.R. 216 .... 5–018, 5–031, 5–038
Hindley & Co. Ltd v. East Indian Produce Co. Ltd [1973] 2 Lloyd's Rep. 515 ...... 18–034, 18–063, 19–008, 19–035, 19–078, 19–144
—— v. General Fibre Co. Ltd [1940] 2 K.B. 517; 109 L.J.K.B. 857; 163 L.T. 424; 56 T.L.R. 904; 84 S.J. 704 .... 6–043, 6–045, 19–089, 19–129
—— v. Tothill, Watson & Co. (1894) 13 N.Z.L.R. 13 .... 23–097, 23–099
Hine v. Allely (1833) 4 B. & Ad. 624; Inev. & M.K.B. 433; 2 L.J.K.B. 105 22–110
Hing Yip Hing Fat Co. Ltd v. Daiwa Bank Ltd [1991] 2 H.K.L.R. 35 ...... 23–159, 23–199, 23–203
Hinton v. Sparkes (1868) L.R. 3 C.P. 161; 37 L.J.C.P. 81; 17 L.T. 600; 16 W.R. 360 15–132
Hiort v. Bott (1874) L.R. 9 Ex. 86; 43 L.J.Ex. 81; 30 L.T. 25; 22 W.R. 414 6–011
—— v. London & North Western Railway Co. (1879) 4 Ex.D. 188; 48 L.J.Q.B. 545; 40 L.T. 674; 27 W.R. 778 1–072
Hirji Mulji v. Cheong Yue S.S. Co. Ltd [1926] A.C. 497; [1926] All E.R. 51; 95 L.J.P.C. 121; 134 L.T. 737; 42 T.L.R. 359; 17 Asp.M.L.C. 8; 31 Com.Cas. 199 18–354
Hirschfield v. Smith (1866) L.R. 1 C.P. 340; Har. & Ruth 284; 35 L.J.C.P. 177; 12 Jur. (N.S.) 523; 14 C.T. 886; 14 W.R. 455 22–126
Hispanica de Petroleos SA v. Vencedora Oceanica Navegacion SA (The Kapetan Markos No. 2) [1987] 2 Lloyd's Rep. 321 .... 5–009, 18–006, 18–065, 18–098, 18–146, 18–150, 18–152
Hispano Americana Mercantil SA v. Central Bank of Nigeria [1979] 2 Lloyd's Rep. 277 23–135
Hitchcock v. Cameron [1977] 1 N.Z.L.R. 85 12–051
—— v. Humfrey (1843) 5 Man. & Gr. 559; 6 Scott W.R. 540; 12 L.J.C.P. 235; 1 L.T. (O.S.) 109; 7 Jur. 423 22–133
Hitchings and Coulthurst Co. v. Northern Leather Co. [1914] 3 K.B. 907; 83 L.J.K.B. 1819; 111 L.T. 1078; 30 T.L.R. 688; 20 Com.Cas. 25 22–064
Hoadly v. McLaine (1834) 10 Bing. 482; 4 Moo. & S. 340; 3 L.J.C.P. 162; 131 E.R. 982 2–047
Hoare v. Dresser (1859) 7 H.L. Cas. 290; 28 L.J.Ch. 611; 33 L.T. (O.S.) 63; 5 Jur. (N.S.) 371; 7 W.R. 374, 11 E.R. 116 .... 18–265, 19–016
—— v. G.W. Railway (1877) 37 L.T. 186; 25 W.R. 631; De Colynar's County Court Cases, 194n 5–087

Hoare v. Rennie (1859) 5 H. & N. 19; 29 L.J.Ex. 73; 1 L.T. 104; 8 W.R. 80; 157 E.R. 1083 .... 8–080, 8–081
Hobbs v. L. & S.W. Railway Co. (1875) L.R. 10 Q.B. 111; 44 L.J.Q.B. 49; 32 L.T. 252; 39 J.P. 693; 23 W.R. 520 .... 13–017, 14–071, 16–047
Hobbs Padgett & Co. (Reinsurance) Ltd v. J.C. Kirkland Ltd (1969) 113 S.J. 832 2–016
Hodgson v. Davies (1810) 2 Camp. 530; 170 E.R. 1241 19–045
—— v. Loy (1797) 7 T.R. 440; 101 E.R. 1065 .... 15–017, 15–062
—— v. Morella Pastoral Co. (1975) 13 S.A.S.R. 51 11–013
Hodson v. Walker (1871–72) L.R. 7 Ex. 55, Ex Ct 7–019
Hoecheong Products Co. Ltd v. Cargill Hong Kong [1995] 1 W.L.R. 404; [1995] 1 Lloyd's Rep. 584; (1995) L.S.Gaz. 39; (1995) 139 S.J.L.B. 59, P.C.; Lloyd's List, March 29, 1995, PC 8–091, 8–092, 8–101, 18–344, 18–346, 19–139, 19–140
Hoenig v. Isaacs [1952] 1 T.L.R. 1360; [1952] 2 All E.R. 176 .... 10–029, 11–004
Hoffman-La Roche v. E.C. Commission (No. 85/76) [1979] E.C.R. 461; [1980] F.S.R. 13; [1979] 3 C.M.L.R. 211 3–041
Höfner & Elser v. Macroton [1991] E.C.R. 1979 3–041
Holbrow v. Wilkins (1822) 1 B. & C. 10; 2 Dow & Ry. K.B. 59; 1 L.J. (O.S.) K.B. 11 22–133
Holden (Richard) Ltd v. Bostock & Co. Ltd (1902) 50 W.R. 323; 18 T.L.R. 317; 46 S.J. 265 .... 17–063, 17–060, 17–068
Holderness v. Shackles (1828) 8 B. & C. 612 .... 8–009, 15–039
Holland Colombo Trading Soc. Ltd v. Alawdeen [1954] 2 Lloyd's Rep. 45 .... 19–002, 19–027
Hollandia, The [1983] 1 A.C. 565; [1982] 3 W.L.R. 1111; (1982) 126 S.J. 819; [1982] 3 All E.R. 1141; *sub nom.* The Morviken [1983] 1 Lloyd's Rep. 1; [1983] Com.L.R. 44 ...... 21–106, 25–006, 25–014, 25–027, 25–040, 25–042, 25–072, 25–195
Holliday v. Morgan (1858) 1 E. & E. 1 10–019
Hollier v. Rambler Motors (AMC) Ltd [1972] 2 Q.B. 71; [1972] 2 W.L.R. 401; (1971) 116 S.J. 158; [1972] 1 All E.R. 399; [1972] R.T.R. 190 ...... 2–012, 13–014, 13–022
Hollin Bros. & Co. Ltd v. White Sea Timber Trust Ltd [1936] 3 All E.R. 895; 80 S.J. 934 .... 19–014, 19–016, 21–022, 21–026
Hollinger, *Re* (1927) 2 C.B.R. 174 25–183
Hollingworth v. Southern Ferries Ltd (The Eagle) [1977] 2 Lloyd's Rep. 70 .... 2–012, 13–015, 13–017, 14–077
—— v. Tooke (1795) 2 Hy.Bl. 501; 126 E.R. 670; Ex.Ch 18–230
Hollins v. Fowler (1875) L.R. 7 H.L. 757 7–008
Hollis Bros & Co. Ltd v. White Sea Timber Trust Ltd [1936] 3 All E.R. 895; (1936) 56 Ll. L. Rep. 78, KBD 10–024
Holman v. Johnson (1775) 1 Cowp. 341 25–119
Holmes v. Burgess [1975] 2 N.Z.L.R. 311 .... 10–006, 12–023
—— v. Twist (1614) Hob. 51; 80 E.R. 200 9–060
Holt v. Payne Shillington, *The Times*, December 22, 1995 18–149
Holroyd v. Marshall (1862) 10 H.L.Cas. 191; 33 L.J.Ch. 193; L.T. 172; 9 Jur. (N.S.) 213; 11 W.R. 171; 11 E.R. 999 .... 1–010, 1–107, 1–108, 5–094
Holwell Securities Ltd v. Hughes [1974] 1 W.L.R. 155; (1973) 117 S.J. 912; [1974] 1 All E.R. 161; (1973) 26 P. & C.R. 544 2–015
Homburg Houtimport BV v. Agrosin Private Ltd (The Starsin); Owners of Cargo Lately Laden on Board the Starsin v. Owners of the Starsin; Hunter Timber Ltd v. Agrosin Private Ltd [2001] EWCA Civ 56; [2001] 1 All E.R. (Comm) 455; [2001] 1 Lloyd's Rep. 437; [2001] C.L.C. 696, CA; reversing in part [1999] 2 All E.R. (Comm) 591; [2000] 1 Lloyd's Rep. 85; [1999] C.L.C. 1769, QBD (Comm Ct) .... 5–009, 18–015, 18–029, 18–054, 18–065, 18–066, 18–127, 18–149, 18–165, , 18–166, 18–181
Honck v. Muller (1881) 7 Q.B.D. 92; 50 L.J.Q.B. 529; 45 L.T. 202; 29 W.R. 330 .... 8–064, 8–080, 8–081, 8–082, 9–010, 15–110
Hone, A Bankrupt, *Re, ex p.* The Trustee v. Kensington Borough Council [1951] Ch. 85; 66 T.L.R. (Pt. 2) 350; 114 J.P. 495; [1950] 2 All E.R. 716 9–030
Hong Guan & Co. Ltd v. Jumabhoy (R.) & Sons Ltd [1960] A.C. 684; [1960] 2 W.L.R. 754; 104 S.J. 367; [1960] 2 All E.R. 100; [1960] 1 Lloyd's Rep. 405 ... 6–041, 6–052, 8–093, 8–100, 16–070, 17–017, 18–353, 19–014, 19–138, 19–139, 21–023, 21–031

Hong Kong and Shanghai Banking Corp. Ltd v. GD Trade Co. Ltd [1998] C.L.C. 238, CA 22–043
Hongkong and Shanghai Banking Corporation v. Kloeckner & Co. A.G. [1990] 2 Q.B. 514; [1990] 3 W.L.R. 634; [1989] 3 All E.R. 13 .... 13–038, 17–049, 23–168, 23–241
Hong Kong Fir Shipping Co. Ltd v. Kawasaki Kisen Kaisha Ltd [1962] 2 Q.B. 26; [1962] 2 W.L.R. 474; 106 S.J. 35; [1962] 1 All E.R. 474; [1961] 2 Lloyd's Rep. 478 .... 8–078, 10–026, 10–027, 10–030, 10–032, 10–033, 10–036, 10–037, 12–023, 12–081
Hong Kong Shipping Ltd v. Cavalry, The [1987] Hong Kong L. Rep. 287 25–088
Hood v. Anchor Line (Henderson Bros.) Ltd [1918] A.C. 837 2–012
Hookway (F.E.) & Co. Ltd v. Isaacs & (Alfred) Son [1954] 1 Lloyd's Rep. 491 11–079
Hooper v. Gumm, Maclellan v. Gumm (1867) 2 Ch.App. 282; 36 L.J.Ch. 605; 16 L.T. 107; 15 W.R. 464; 2 Mar.L.C. 481, L.C. & L.J. 1–082, 25–124
Hope v. Hayley (1856) 5 E. & B. 830; 25 L.J.Q.B. 155; 26 L.T. (O.S.) 199; 2 Jur. (N.S.) 486; 4 W.R. 238; 119 E.R. 690 .... 5–082, 5–094
—— v. Hope (1856) 22 Beav. 351; 27 L.T. (O.S.) 227; 4 W.R. 583; 52 E.R. 1143 15–115
Hopkins v. Hitchcock (1863) 13 C.B. (N.S.) 65; 2 New Rep. 32; 32 L.J.C.P. 154; 8 L.T. 204; 9 Jur. (N.S.) 896; 11 W.R. 597; 143 E.R. 369 11–014
—— v. Tanqueray (1854) 15 C.B. 130 .... 10–006, 10–020
Hopkinson v. Forster (1874) L.R. 19 Eq. 74; 23 W.R. 301 22–047
Hordern House Property Ltd v. Arnold [1989] V.R. 402 2–004
Hore v. Milner (1797) Peake 58n 15–128
Horgan v. Driscoll (1908) 42 I.L.T. 238 1–046
Horn v. Minister of Food [1948] 2 All E.R. 1036; 65 T.L.R. 106 .... 1–128, 6–003, 6–023, 6–028, 6–031, 6–035, 8–040
Horn Linie GmbH & Co v. Panamericana Formas e Impresos SA [2006] EWHC 373, QBD 25–079, 25–089
Horncastle v. Farran (1820) 3 B. & Ald. 497 .... 15–036, 15–056
Horne v. Midland Railway (1873) L.R. 8 C.P. 131; (1872) L.R. 7 C.P. 583 .... 16–046, 17–031, 17–041
Horne-Roberts v. SmithKline Beecham Plc; *sub nom.* MMR/MR Vaccine Litigation; H (A Child) v. Merk & Co Inc; SmithKline Beecham Plc v. H (A Child); H (A Child) v. Merck & Co Inc; H (A Child) v. Smithkline Beecham Plc; Smithkline Beecham v. Horne-Roberts [2001] EWCA Civ 2006; [2002] 1 W.L.R. 1662; [2002] C.P. Rep. 20; (2002) 65 B.M.L.R. 79; (2002) 99(8) L.S.G. 35; (2002) 146 S.J.L.B. 19; *The Times*, January 10, 2002, CA 14–092
Horsfall v. Key (1848) 2 Ex. 778; 17 L.J.Ex. 266; 11 L.T. (O.S.) 271; 154 E.R. 705 1–095
—— v. Thomas (1862) 1 H. & C. 90; 2 F. & F. 785; 31 L.J.Ex. 322; 6 L.T. 462; 8 Jur. (N.S.) 721; 10 W.R. 650; 158 E.R. 813 .... 12–012, 12–077
Hortico (Australia) Property Ltd v. Energy Equipment & (Aust) Property Ltd [1985] 1 N.S.W.R. 545 .... 23–145, 23–274, 23–277
Horton v. Gibbins (1897) 13 T.L.R. 408 7–068
Hotel Plan Ltd v. Tameside MBC [2001] EWHC Admin 154, QBD 14–113
Hotel Services Ltd v. Hilton International Hotels (U.K.) Ltd [2000] 1 All E.R. (Comm) 750; [2000] B.L.R. 235, CA 13–037
Hotmail Corporation v. Van Money Pie Inc. C98–20064 (N.D. Cal., April 20, 1998) 2–012
Houghland v. Low (R.R.) (Luxury Coaches) Ltd [1962] 1 Q.B. 694; [1962] 2 W.L.R. 1015; 106 S.J. 243; [1962] 2 All E.R. 159 .... 5–057, 6–011, 6–026, 6–029, 6–030
Houlder Bros. & Co. Ltd v. Commissioners of Public Works [1908] A.C. 276; 77 L.J.P.C. 58; L.T. 684; 11 Asp.M.L.C. 61 .... 19–006, 19–009, 19–025, 19–088, 19–099, 19–119
Houlditch v. Desanges (1818) 2 Stark 337; 171 E.R. 666 15–059
Houndsditch Warehouse Co. Ltd v. Waltex Ltd [1944] K.B. 579; [1944] 2 All E.R. 518; 113 L.J.K.B. 547; 171 L.T. 275; 60 T.L.R. 517 .... 11–022, 16–052, 17–026
Hounslow London Borough Council v. Twickenham Garden Developments Ltd [1971] Ch. 233; [1970] 3 W.L.R. 538; 114 S.J. 603; 69 L.G.R. 109 .... 16–022, 16–059
Housego v. Cowne (1837) 2 M. & W. 348; Murph. & H. 54; 6 L.J.Ex. 110; 150 E.R. 790 22–125
Household Machines Ltd v. Cosmos Exporters Ltd [1947] K.B. 217; [1947] L.J.R. 578; 176 L.T. 49; 62 T.L.R. 757; [1946] 2 All E.R. 622 .... 8–046, 8–078, 16–092, 17–030, 17–031, 17–035, 17–036, 17–104

Howard v. Harris (1884) Cab. & El. 253 6–011
—— v. Shepherd (1850) 9 C.B. 297; 19 L.J.C.P. 249 .... 18–098, 18–099
Howard Marine and Dredging Co. Ltd v. Ogden (A.) & Sons (Excavations) Ltd [1978] Q.B. 574; [1978] 2 W.L.R. 515; (1977) 122 S.J. 48; [1978] 2 All E.R. 1134; [1978] 1 Lloyd's Rep. 334; (1977) 9 Build.L.R. 34 .... 10–011, 10–012, 10–013, 10–017, 10–020, 10–022, 11–012, 11–013, 12–012, 12–013, 12–014, 13–019, 13–089, 14–042, 17–089
Howcraft v. Laycock (1898) 14 T.L.R. 460; 42 S.J. 572 13–028
Howcraft and Watkins v. Perkins (1900) 16 T.L.R. 217 13–028
Howden Bros. Ltd v. Ulster Bank Ltd [1924] I.R. 117 5–092
Howe, *Re* (1871) L.R. 6 Ch.App. 838; 40 L.J.Bcy. 54; 25 L.T. 252; 19 W.R. 1101 5–140
—— v. Smith (1884) 27 Ch.D. 89; 53 L.J.Ch. 1055; 50 L.T. 573; 48 J.P. 773; 32 W.R. 802 .... 15–112, 15–115, 15–130, 15–132, 16–037
Howe Richardson Scale Co. Ltd v. Polimex-Cekop [1978] 1 Lloyd's Rep. 161 ...... 23–272, 23–275, 23–277
Howell v. Coupland (1876) 1 Q.B.D. 258; 46 L.J.Q.B. 147; 33 L.T. 832; 40 J.P. 276; 24 W.R. 470, C.A.; (1874) L.R. 9 Q.B. 462 ... 1–115 5–095, 6–038, 6–041, 6–045, 6–051, 19–119, 20–097
—— v. Evans (1926) 134 L.T. 570; 42 T.L.R. 310 .... 8–065, 8–083
—— v. Richards (1809) 11 East. 633 4–030
Howes v. Ball (1827) 7 B. & C. 481; 1 Man. & Ry. K.B. 288; 6 L.J. (o.s.) K.B. 106 .. 15–053
—— v. Watson (1824) 2 B. & C. 243 5–039
Howlett v. Haswell (1814) 4 Camp. 118 2–037
Hoyles, *Re* [1911] 1 Ch. 179; 80 L.J.Ch. 274; 103 L.T. 817; 27 T.L.R. 131; 55 S.J. 169 25–004
Huddersfield Banking Co. Ltd v. Henry Lister & Son Ltd [1895] 2 Ch. 273 5–159
Hudson v. Hill (1874) 43 L.J.C.P. 273; 30 L.T. 555; 2 Asp.M.L.C. 278 8–035
Hudson Fashion Shoppe Ltd, *Re, ex p.,* Royal Dress Co. [1926] 1 D.L.R. 515; 58 O.L.R. 298 (Can.) 25–011, 25–133, 25–183
Hudson v. Shogun Finance Ltd *See* Shogun Finance Ltd v. Hudson
Hughes v. Hall (1981) 125 S.J. 255; [1981] R.T.R. 430 ..... 11–011, 13–030, 13–067, 14–142
—— v. Metropolitan Railway Co. (1877) 2 App.Cas. 439 .... 12–035, 20–051
—— v. Pump House Hotel Co. [1902] 2 K.B. 190 5–160
Hughes Hallett v. Indian Mammoth Gold Mines Ltd (1883) 22 Ch.D. 561; 52 L.J.Ch. 418; 48 L.T. 107; 31 W.R. 285 4–023
Hugill v. Masker (1889) 22 Q.B.D. 364; 58 L.J.Q.B. 171; 60 L.T. 774; 37 W.R. 390 .. 7–070, 15–100
Huilerie l'Abeille v. Société des Huileries du Niger, *See* The Kastellon.
Hull Rope Works Co. Ltd v. Adams (1895) 65 L.J.Q.B. 114; 73 L.T. 446; 44 W.R. 108; 40 S.J. 69 .... 7–063, 7–070, 7–077, 7–080
Hulse v. Chambers [2001] 1 W.L.R. 2386 25–191
Hulton v. Hulton [1917] 1 K.B. 813; 86 L.J.K.B. 633; 116 L.T. 551; 33 T.L.R. 197; 61 S.J. 268 12–007
Hulton (E.) Co. Ltd v. Chadwick and Taylor Ltd (1918) 34 T.L.R. 230 .... 6–041, 6–054
Humbertson, *Re* (1846) De. G. 262; 15 L.J.Bcv. 10; 6 L.T. (o.s.) 449, L.C. 15–117, 17–102
Hummingbird Motors Ltd v. Hobbs [1986] R.T.R. 276 10–005
Humphries v. Carvalho (1812) 16 East. 45 .... 5–040, 5–041
Hungerford v. Halliford (1626) 3 Bulst. 323 8–072
Hunt v. Barry (1905) 13 S.L.T. 34 12–047
—— v. Silk (1804) 5 East. 449; 2 Smith K.B. 15; [1803–13] All E.R. 655; 102 E.R. 1142 12–068
Hunter, *ex p.* (1801) 6 Ves.Jun. 94; 31 E.R. 955 15–119
Hunter v. Moss [1994] 1 W.L.R. 452; [1994] 1 All E.R. 215; (1994) 138 S.J.L.B. 25; *The Times*, January 14, 1994, CA 5–153
—— v. Rice (1812) 15 East. 100; 104 E.R. 782 1–068
Hunter Engineering Co. Inc. v. Syncrude Canada Ltd [1989] 1 S.C.R. 426 .... 11–055, 11–060, 13–020, 13–049
Huntoon Co. v. Kolynos (Inc.) [1930] 1 Ch. 528; (1930) 47 T.L.R. 57 19–104
Huntsman, The [1894] P. 214; 70 L.T. 386; 7 Asp.M.L.C. 431; 6 R. 698 9–031
Huntwave Ltd v. Customs & Excise Commissioners [1973] V.A.T.T.R. 72 1–047

Hurley v. Dyke [1979] R.T.R. 265 .... 12–012, 12–123, 13–018, 13–025, 13–068, 13–106
Hurry, v. Mangles (1808) 1 Camp. 452; 170 E.R. 1018 8–009
Hurst v. Bryk [2002] 1 A.C. 185; [2000] 2 W.L.R. 740; [2000] 2 All E.R. 193; [2000] 2 B.C.L.C. 117; [2000] E.G.C.S. 49; (2000) 97(17) L.S.G. 35; (2000) 150 N.L.J. 511; (2000) 144 S.J.L.B. 189; *The Times*, April 4, 2000, HL; affirming [1999] Ch. 1; [1998] 2 W.L.R. 269; [1997] 2 All E.R. 283; *The Times*, March 20, 1997; *The Independent*, February 7, 1997, CA 19–166
Hurst v. Orbell (1838) 8 A. & E. 107; 3 Nev. & P.K.B. 237; 1 Will. Woll. & H. 157; 7 L.J.Q.B. 138; 2 Jur. 840; 112 E.R. 776 5–053
Hurst (M. & T.) Consultants Ltd v. Grange Motors (Brentwood) Ltd (Manchester, October, 1981) 12–055
Hussey v. Eels [1990] 2 Q.B. 227; [1990] 2 W.L.R. 234; [1990] 1 All E.R. 449; (1990) 140 New L.J. 53; [1990] 19 E.G. 77 .... 16–056, 17–056
Huston v. Newgass, 84 N.E. 910 (1908) 23–236
Hutchings v. Humphreys (1885) 54 L.J.Ch. 650 15–115
—— v. Nunes (1863) 1 Moo.P.C. (N.S.) 243; 9 L.T. 125; 10 Jur. (N.S.) 109; 15 E.R. 692 .... 15–008, 15–065
Hutt Valley Energy Board v. Hayman (1988) 4 N.Z.C.L.C. 64 1–085
Huyton SA v. Peter Cremer GmbH & Co. [1999] 1 Lloyd's Rep. 620; [1999] C.L.C. 230, QBD (Comm Ct) 19–103, 19–212, 20–071, 20–076, 20–084, 20–128
Hyams v. Ogden [1905] 1 K.B. 246 15–116
Hydraulic Engineering Co. v. McHaffie Goslett & Co. (1878) 4 Q.B.D. 670; 27 W.R. 221 .... 8–036, 16–046, 17–044, 17–045, 17–046
Hydrotherm Gerätebau GmbH v. Compact de Dott. Ing. Mario Andredi & C.SAS. (No. 170/83) [1984] E.C.R. 2999; [1985] C.M.L.R. 224 3–041
Hyslop v. Shirlaw (1905) 7 F. (et. of Sess.) 875; 42 Sc.L.R. 668; 13 S.L.T. 209 ...... 10–006, 12–055
Hyundai Heavy Industries Co. Ltd v. Papadopoulos [1980] 1 W.L.R. 1129 .... 1–031, 1–041, 1–042, 1–047, 1–082, 16–027, 16–040, 19–166
Hyundai Shipbuilding and Heavy Industries Co. Ltd v. Pournaras [1979] 2 Lloyd's Rep. 502 19–166
Hyundai Merchant Marine Co. Ltd v. Karander Maritime Co. Ltd (The Niizura) [1996] 2 Lloyd's Rep. 66 .... 19–063, 19–071

I.B.L. Ltd v. Coussens [1991] 2 All E.R. 133; *The Financial Times*, July 4, 1990, CA .. 7–002
I.B.M. Co. Ltd v. Shcherban [1925] 1 D.L.R. 864 11–032
I.C.I. Ltd v. E.C. Commission. *See* Imperial Chemical Industries v. E.C. Commission.
I.C.I. New Zealand v. Agnew [1998] 2 N.Z.L.R. 129 .... 1–060, 5–149, 5–150
I.E. Contractors Ltd v. Lloyds Bank plc [1989] 2 Lloyd's Rep. 205 23–285
I.M. Properties plc v. Cape & Dalgleish [1999] Q.B. 297; [1998] 3W.L.R. 457; [1998] 3 All E.R. 203; (1998) 95(31) L.S.G. 34; (1998) 95(24) L.S.G. 34; (1998) 148 N.L.J. 906; (1998) 142 S.J.L.B. 174; *The Times*, May 28, 1998, CA 16–007
ISS Machinery Services Ltd v. Aeolian Shipping SA (The Aeolian). *See* Aeolian Shipping SA v. ISS Machinery Services Ltd (The Aeolian)
Ian Chisholm Textiles v. Griffiths [1994] B.C.C. 96; [1994] 2 B.C.L.C. 291 .... 5–149, 5–161
Ichard v. Frangoulis [1977] 1 W.L.R. 556; (1976) 121 S.J. 287; [1977] 2 All E.R. 461 14–006
Ide and Christie v. Chalmers & White (1900) 5 Com.Cas. 212 .... 19–043, 19–051
Idle v. Thornton (1812) 3 Camp. 274; 170 E.R. 1380 .... 21–022, 21–027, 21–030
Ignazio Messina & Co. v. Polskie Linie Oceaniczne [1995] 2 Lloyd's Rep. 566 2–017
Ikariada, The. *See* Orinoco Navigation Ltd v. Ecotrade SpA (The Ikariada)
Ikimi v. Ikimi (Divorce: Habitual Residence) [2001] EWCA Civ 873; [2002] Fam. 72; [2001] 3 W.L.R. 672; [2001] 2 F.L.R. 1288; [2001] 2 F.C.R. 385; [2001] Fam. Law 660; (2001) 98(27) L.S.G. 38; (2001) 145 S.J.L.B. 163; *The Times*, July 18, 2001; *The Independent*, June 20, 2001, CA; affirming [2001] 1 F.L.R. 913, Fam Div 25–056
Ikin v. Bradley (1818) 8 Taunt. 250 16–007
Illyssia Compania Naviera SA v. Bamaodah; Kition Compania Naviera v. Same; (The Elli 2) [1985] 1 Lloyd's Rep. 107 ... 18–063, 18–140, 18–141, 19–095, 25–071, 25–202
Imperial Bank v. London and St. Katherine Docks Co. (1877) 5 Ch.D. 195; 46 L.J.Ch. 335; 36 L.T. 233 .... 15–013, 15–014, 15–065

Imperial Ottoman Bank v. Cowan; Cowan v. Imperial Ottoman Bank (1874) 31 L.T. 336; Ex.Ch.; (1873) 29 L.T. 52; 21 W.R. 770; 2 Asp.M.L.C. 57 20–038
Imperial Tobacco Co. Ltd v. Parslay [1936] 2 All E.R. 515; 52 T.L.R. 585; 80 S.J. 464 .... 3–037, 16–033
Import Export Metro Ltd v. Compania Sud Americana de Vapores SA [2003] EWHC 11; [2003] 1 All E.R. (Comm) 703; [2003] 1 Lloyd's Rep. 405; [2004] 2 C.L.C. 757, QBD 25–156, 25–157
Ind. Coope & Co. Ltd. Fisher v. Ind., Coope & Co. Ltd. Knox v. Ind., Coope & Co. Ltd. Arnold v. Ind., Coope & Co. Ltd. *Re* [1911] 2 Ch. 223; 80 L.J.Ch. 661; 105 L.T. 356; 55 S.J. 600 5–161
Independent Automatic Sales Ltd v. Knowles and Foster [1962] 1 W.L.R. 974; 106 S.J. 720; [1962] 3 All E.R. 27 .... 5–143, 5–160, 24–029
Independent Broadcasting Authority v. EMI Electronics and B.I.C.C. Construction
Independent Broadcasting Authority v. EMI Electronics and B.I.C.C. Construction (1980) 14 Build. L.R. 1 .... 10–012, 10–017, 14–051
India v. India Steamship Co Ltd (The Indian Endurance and The Indian Grace) (No.1) [1993] A.C. 410; [1993] 2 W.L.R. 461; [1993] 1 All E.R. 998; [1993] 1 Lloyd's Rep. 387; [1994] I.L.Pr. 498, *The Times*, February 22, 1993; *Independent*, March 29, 1993 (C.S.), HL 7–019
India Steamship Co. Ltd v. Louis Dreyfus Sugar Ltd (The Indian Reliance) [1997] 1 Lloyd's Rep. 52; [1997] C.L.C. 11, QBD (Comm Ct) 18–054
Indian Bank v. Union Bank of Swizerland [1944] 2 S.L.R. 121 (CA) 23–016
Indian Oil Corp. Ltd v. Greenstone Shipping SA (Panama) (The Ypatianna) [1988] Q.B. 345; (1987) 131 S.J. 1121; [1987] 3 All E.R. 893; [1987] 2 F.T.L.R. 95; [1987] 2 Lloyd's Rep. 286; [1987] 84 L.S.Gaz. 2768 .... 5–148, 7–004
Industrial Acceptance Corp. Ltd v. Jordan (1969) 6 D.L.R. (3d) 625 25–189
Industrie, The [1894] P. 58; 63 L.J.P. 84; 70 L.T. 791; 42 W.R. 280; 7 Asp.M.L.C. 457; 6 R. 681 .... 25–010, 25–070
Industrial Bank of Korea v. BNP Paribus [2004] Annual Survey of Letter of Credit, Law and Practice 23–062
Inflatable Toy Co. Pty Ltd v. State Bank of N.S.W. (1994) 34 N.S.W.L.R. 243 23–145
Ingham v. Emes [1955] 2 Q.B. 366, [1955] 2 W.L.R. 245; 99 S.J. 490; [1955] 2 All E.R. 740 .... 1–041, 11–057
Inglefield (George) Ltd. *Re* [1933] Ch. 1 1–066
Inglis v. Robertson & Baxter [1898] A.C. 616 ... 7–055, 7–063, 7–071, 7–083, 8–013 18–165, 18–197
Inglis v. Stock; *sub nom.* Stock v. Inglis (1885) 10 App.Cas. 263; 54 L.J.Q.B. 582; 52 L.T. 821; 33 W.R. 877; 5 Asp.M.L.C. 422, HL affirming (1884) 12 Q.B.D. 564, CA 5–099, 5–110, 6–004, 6–018, 18–286, 18–288, 18–301, 18–302, 18–286 18–303, 20–001, 20–020, 20–070, 20–080, 20–085, 20–096
—— v. Usherwood (1801) 1 East. 515; 102 E.R. 198 ...... 25–123, 25–183, 25–186, 25–187
Ingmar GB Ltd v. Eaton Leonard Technologies Inc. (Case C–381/98) [2001] All E.R. (EC) 57; [2001] 1 All E.R. (Comm) 329; [2000] E.C.R. 1–9305; [2001] 1 C.M.L.R. 9; *The Times*, November 16, 2000, ECJ (5th Chamber) [1999] E.C.C. 49; [1999] Eu. L.R. 88; (1999) 18 Tr. L.R. 327, CA 25–040, 25–073
Ingram v. Little [1961] 1 Q.B. 31; [1960] 3 W.L.R. 504; 104 S.J. 704; [1960] 3 All E.R. 332 .... 3–012, 3–014, 5–026, 5–046, 7–035, 16–090
—— v. Shirley (1816) 1 Stark 185 1–035
I.R.C. v. Bibby & Sons Ltd [1945] 1 All E.R. 667; (1945) 61 T.L.R. 430 24–008
I.R.C. v. Harton Coal Co. [1960] Ch. 563; [1960] 3 W.L.R. 414; [1960] 3 All E.R. 48; 53 R. & I.T. 458; 39 T.C. 174; (1960) 39 A.T.C. 259; [1960] T.R. 165; 104 S.J. 642, Ch D 24–008
Inland Revenue Commissioners v. Maple & Co. (Paris) Ltd [1908] A.C. 22; 77 L.J.K.B. 55; 97 L.T. 814; 24 T.L.R. 140; 52 S.J. 92; 14 Mans. 302 1–027
—— v. Marine Steam Turbine Co. Ltd [1920] 1 K.B. 193 11–028
—— v. Ufitex Group Ltd [1977] 3 All E.R. 924; [1977] S.T.C. 363 1–051
Inntrepreneur Estates (CPC) Ltd v. Worth [1996] 1 E.G.L.R. 84; [1996] 11 E.G. 136; [1995] E.G.C.S. 160, Ch D 13–056, 13–060
Inntrepreneur Pub Co. (GL) v. East Crown Ltd *See* Intrepreneur Pub Co. Ltd v. East Crown Ltd
Inntrepreneur Pub Co. Ltd v. East Crown Ltd; *sub nom.* Inntrepreneur Pub Co. (GL) v. East Crown Ltd [2000] 2 Lloyd's Rep. 611; [2000] 3 E.G.L.R. 31; [2000] 41 E.G. 209; [2000] N.P.C. 93; *The Times*, September 5, 2000, Ch.D 13–056

Instone (S.) & Co. Ltd v. Speeding Marshall & Co. (1915) 32 T.L.R. 202 .... 6–054, 8–094, 19–140
Inter American Foods Inc. v. Co-ordinated Caribbean Transport Inc. 313 F.Supp. 1334 (1970) 21–086
Interfoto Picture Library Ltd v. Stiletto Visual Programmes Ltd [1989] Q.B. 433; (1988) 7 Tr. L. 187 .... 2–002, 2–012, 13–012, 14–036, 16–035
International Air and Sea Cargo GmbH v. Owners of the Chitral [2000] 1 All E.R. (Comm) 932; [2000] 1 Lloyd's Rep. 529; [2000] C.L.C. 1021, QBD 18–013, 18–015, 18–018, 18–020, 18–024, 18–046, 18–067, 18–071, 18–083, 18–155
International Banking Corporation v. Barclays Bank Ltd (1925) 5 Legal Decisions Affecting Bankers 1, 4 23–138
—— v. Ferguson Shaw & Son 1910 S.C. 182 5–149
International Banking Corporation v. Irving National Bank, 283 F. 103 (1922) 23–231
International Factors v. Rodriguez [1979] Q.B. 351; [1978] 3 W.L.R. 877; (1978) 122 S.J. 680; [1979] 1 All E.R. 17, CA 7–002
Internationale Handelsgesellschaft v. Einfuhr-und-Vovratsselle [1970] E.C.R. 1125 8–100
International Harvester Co. of Australia Property Ltd v. Carrigan's Hazeldene Pastoral Co. (1958) 100 C.L.R. 644 .... 1–049, 14–061
International Railway Co. v. Niagara Parks Commission [1941] A.C. 328; [1941] 2 All E.R. 456; 111 L.J.P.C. 55; 57 T.L.R. 462 23–116
International Sales and Agencies Ltd v. Marcus [1982] 3 All E.R. 551; [1982] 2 C.M.L.R. 46 2–043
International Sea Tankers Inc. v. Hemisphere Shipping Co. Ltd (The Wenjiang) (No. 2) [1983] 1 Lloyd's Rep. 400; [1983] Com.L.R. 16 18–300
International Sponge Importers v. Watt 1909 S.L.T. 24 7–032
Interoffice Telephones Ltd v. Freeman (Robert) Co. Ltd [1958] 1 Q.B. 190; [1957] 3 W.L.R. 971; 101 S.J. 958; [1957] 3 All E.R. 749 .... 16–005, 16–045, 16–064
Intertradex SA v. Lesieur Tourteaux S.A.R.L. [1978] 2 Lloyd's Rep. 509, C.A.; affirmed [1977] 2 Lloyd's Rep. 146 .... 6–041, 8–099, 8–101, 8–102, 17–023, 18–353, 18–358, 19–130, 19–140, 19–142, 19–160
Interview Ltd, *Re* [1975] I.R. 382 .... 5–156, 5–160, 7–084, 25–144, 25–147
Intraco Ltd v. Notis Shipping Corporation of Liberia (The Bhoja Trader) [1981] Com.L.R. 184; [1981] 2 Lloyd's Rep. 256 .... 23–140, 23–272
Intraworld Industries Inc. v. Girard Trust Bank, 336 A. 2d 316 (Pa. 1975) 23–239, 23–241 23–248
Invercargill C.C. v. Hamlin [1996] A.C. 624, P.C. (N.Z.) 12–121, 12–126
Investitions und Handels-Bank A.G. v. United California Bank International 227 F.Supp. 1006 (1968) 23–176, 23–177
Ipswich Gaslight Co. v. W.B. King & Co. (1886) 3 T.L.R. 100 11–059
Iran Continental Shelf Oil Co v. IRI International Corp [2002] EWCA Civ 1024; [2004] 2 C.L.C. 696, CA 25–019, 25–021, 25–060, 25–064, 25–065
Ireland v. Livingston (1872) L.R. 5 H.L. 395 .... 1–048, 3–004, 15–013, 18–232, 19–001, 19–009, 19–053, 19–069, 23–117, 23–234, 23–307, 23–308
—— v. Merryton Coal Co. (1894) 21 R. 989 8–067
Irish Shipping Ltd v. Commercial Union Assurance Co. plc [1990] 2 W.L.R. 117; [1989] 3 All E.R. 853; [1989] 2 Lloyd's Rep. 144; (1990) 134 S.J. 426 14–103
Irving v. National Provincial Bank [1962] 2 Q.B. 73; [1962] 2 W.L.R. 503; [1962] 1 All E.R. 157; 126 J.P. 76, CA 7–006
Isaacs v. Hardy (1884) Cab. & El. 287 1–047
—— v. Royal Insurance Co. Ltd (1870) L.R. 5 Ex. 296; 39 L.J.Ex. 189; 22 L.T. 681; 18 W.R. 982 8–033
Ishag v. Allied Bank International [1981] 1 Lloyd's Rep. 92 .... 18–027, 18–038, 18–053, 18–095, 18–103, 18–209, 18–214, 19–029, 19–099, 21–081
Isherwood v. Whitmore (1843) 11 M. & W. 347; 12 L.J.Ex. 318; 1 L.T. (o.s.) 81; 7 Jur. 535; 152 E.R. 837 .... 12–039, 12–042
Ispahani v. Bank Melli Iran [1998] Lloyd's Rep. Bank, 133; *The Times*, December 29, 1997, CA 25–119, 25–120
Itek Corporation v. First National Bank of Boston 566 F.Supp. 1210 (1983) 23–149, 23–152 23–153, 23–244
Ivenel v. Schwab (Case 133/81) [1982] E.C.R. 1891; [1983] 1 C.M.L.R. 538, ECJ 25–018

J. (A Minor) (Abduction: Custody Rights), Re; *sub nom.* C. v. S. (Minors) (Abduction: Illegitimate Child) [1990] 2 A.C. 562; [1990] 3 W.L.R. 492; [1990] 2 All E.R. 961; [1990] 2 F.L.R. 442; [1991] F.C.R. 129; [1991] Fam. Law 57; (1990) 154 J.P.N. 674; (1990) 87(35) L.S.G. 39; (1990) 140 N.L.J. 1191; (1990) 134 S.J. 1039; *The Times*, July 31, 1990; *The Independent*, August 1, 1990; *The Guardian*, July 27, 1990; *The Daily Telegraph*, September 18, 1990, HL; affirming [1990] 2 All E.R. 449; (1990) 154 J.P.N. 563, CA 25–056
J. & H. Ritchie Ltd v. Lloyd Ltd 2005 S.C. 155; 2005 S.L.T. 64; 2005 S.C.L.R. 447; 2005 G.W.D. 2–38, IH 12–031, 12–054
J. & J. Cunningham Ltd v. Robert A Munro & Co Ltd (1922) 28 Co. Cas. 42 18–264
J. & K. Plumbing and Heating Co. Inc. v. International Telephone and Telegraph Corp., 51 A.D. 2d 638, 378 N.Y.S. 2d 828 (1976) 23–239, 23–241
J.I. MacWilliam Co Inc v. Mediterranean Shipping Co SA (The Rafaela S) [2005] UKHL 11; [2005] 2 A.C. 423; [2005] 2 W.L.R. 554; [2005] 2 All E.R. 86; [2005] 1 All E.R. (Comm) 393; [2005] 1 Lloyd's Rep. 347; [2005] 1 C.L.C. 172; 2005 A.M.C. 913; *The Times*, February 21, 2005, HL; affirming [2003] EWCA Civ 556; [2004] Q.B. 702; [2004] 2 W.L.R. 283; [2003] 3 All E.R. 369; [2003] 2 All E.R. (Comm) 219; [2003] 2 Lloyd's Rep. 113; [2003] 2 C.L.C. 94; 2003 A.M.C. 2035; (2003) 100(26) L.S.G. 38; *The Times*, May 5, 2003, CA 18–007, 18–009, 18–013, 18–016, 18–018, 18–020, 18–024, 18–035, 18–044, 18–047, 18–048, 18–064, 18–067, 18–068, 18–069, 18–070, 18–071, 18–074, 18–075, 18–076, 18–077, 18–078, 18–084, 18–089, 18–201
JEB Fastners Ltd v. Marks Bloom & Co. [1983] 1 All E.R. 583 10–009
JSC Zestafoni G Nikoladze Ferroalloy Plant v. Ronly Holdings Ltd [2004] EWHC 245; [2004] 2 Lloyd's Rep. 335; [2004] 1 C.L.C. 1146, QBD 2–015, 25.119
Jack v. Roberts and Gibson (1865) 3 M. (Ct of Session) 554 20–055
Jackson v. Chrysler Acceptances Ltd [1978] R.T.R. 474 . . . . 11–056, 11–073, 14–020, 17–053
—— v. Horizon Holidays Ltd [1975] 1 W.L.R. 1468 . . . . 14–006, 14–071
—— v. Nichol (1839) 5 Bing. 508; 2 Arn. 32; 7 Scott. 577; 8 L.J.C.P. 294; 3 Jur. 772; 132 E.R. 1195 . . . . 15–069, 15–075, 15–078, 15–083
Jackson v. Rotax Motor and Cycle Co. [1910] 2 K.B. 937; 80 L.J.K.B. 38; 103 L.T. 411 . . . . . 8–050, 8–065, 8–074, 8–077, 8–082, 8–083, 8–084, 11–037, 11–032, 11–001, 11–049, 12–060
—— v. Royal Bank of Scotland [2005] UKHL 3; [2005] 1 W.L.R. 377; [2005] 2 All E.R. 71; [2005] 1 All E.R. (Comm) 337; [2005] 1 Lloyd's Rep. 366; (2005) 102(11) L.S.G. 29; (2005) 149 S.J.L.B. 146; *The Times*, February 2, 2005, HL 16–046, 16–050, 17–034, 17–043, 17–069
—— v. Union Marine Insurance Co. Ltd (1874) L.R. 10 C.P. 125; [1874–80] All E.R. 317; 44 L.J.C.P. 27; 31 L.T. 789; 23 W.R. 169; 2 Asp.M.L.C. 435, Ex.Ch. 10–030
—— v. Watson & Sons [1909] 2 K.B. 193; 78 L.J.K.B. 587; 100 L.T. 799; 25 T.L.R. 454; 53 S.J. 447 . . . . 11–064, 14–071, 17–071
Jacobs v. Credit Lyonnais (1884) 12 Q.B.D. 589; 53 L.J.Q.B. 156; 50 L.T. 194; 32 W.R. 761 . . . . 6–041, 8–098, 25–156, 25–175
Jacobs v. Harbach (1886) 2 T.L.R. 419 . . . . 5–050, 8–014
—— v. Latour (1828) 5 Bing. 130; 2 Moo. & P. 201; 6 L.J. (o.s.) C.P. 243; 130 E.R. 1010 15–059
—— v. Scott & Co. (1899) 2 F. 70 11–055
Jacobson van den Berg & Co. (U.K.) Ltd v. Biba Ltd (1977) 121 S.J. 333 8–030
Jade International & Steel Stahl und Eisen G.m.b.H. & Co. K.G. v. Nicholas (Robert) (Steels) Ltd [1978] Q.B. 917; [1978] 3 W.L.R. 39; (1978) 122 S.J. 294; [1978] 3 All E.R. 104; [1978] 2 Lloyd's Rep. 13 22–062
Jager v. Tolme and Runge [1916] 1 K.B. 939; 85 L.J.K.B. 1116; 114 L.T. 647; 32 T.L.R. 291 8–005
Jamal v. Moolla Dawood [1916] 1 A.C. 175; 85 L.J.P.C. 29; 114 L.T. 1; 32 T.L.R. 79; 60 S.J. 139 . . . . 16–056, 16–076, 17–020
James v. Griffin (1837) 2 M. & W. 623; 6 L.J.Ex. 241; 150 E.R. 906 15–070
—— v. Isaacs (1852) 12 C.B. 791; 22 L.J.C.P. 73; 17 Jur. 69; 1 W.R. 21 9–043
—— v. The Commonwealth (1939) 62 C.L.R. 339 . . . . 5–098, 18–209, 18–210, 18–216, 18–226, 19–016, 20–080, 20–084, 20–086
—— v. Williams (1845) 13 M. & W. 828 9–030
James McNaughton Paper Group Ltd v. Hicks Anderson & Co. [1991] 2 Q.B. 113; [1991] 2 W.L.R. 641; [1991] 1 All E.R. 134; [1990] B.C.C. 891; [1991] B.C.L.C. 235; [1991] E.C.C. 186; [1955–95] P.N.L.R. 574; (1990) 140 N.L.J. 1311; *The Independent*, September 11, 1990, CA 12–013

James Slater & Hamish Slater (a firm) v. Finning Ltd [1996] C.L.C. 1236 1–043
Jamshed Khodaram Irani v. Burjorjiü Dhonjibhai (1915) 32 T.L.R. 156 8–026
Janesich v. Attenborough (George) & Son (1910) 102 L.T. 605; 26 T.L.R. 278 ...... 5–045, 7–032, 7–043, 7–046, 25–131
Janred Properties Ltd v. Ente Nazionale Italiano per il Turismo [1989] 2 All E.R. 444 25–085
Jansz v. G.M.B. Imports Property Ltd [1979] V.R. 581 1–015
Jarl Tra AB v. Convoys Ltd [2003] EWHC 1488, [2003] 2 Lloyd's Rep 459, [2003] 2 CLC 1072, QBD 18–047, 18–048, 21–042
Jarrett v. Barclays Bank Plc; Jones v. First National Bank Plc; First National Bank Plc v. Peacock [1999] Q.B. 1; [1997] 3 W.L.R. 654; [1997] 2 All E.R. 484; [1997] 6 Bank. L.R. 66; [1997] C.L.C. 391; [1997] I.L.Pr. 531; [1997] C.C.L.R. 32; (1997) 94(6) L.S.G. 27; (1996) 140 S.J.L.B. 252; [1996] N.P.C. 159; *The Times*, November 18, 1996, CA 25–089
Jarvis v. Harris [1996] 2 W.L.R. 226 16–004
—— v. Swans Tours Ltd [1973] Q.B. 233; [1972] 3 W.L.R. 954; 116 S.J. 822; [1973] 1 All E.R. 71 .... 14–006, 17–071
—— v. Williams [1955] 1 W.L.R. 71; 99 S.J. 73; [1955] 1 All E.R. 108 .... 5–003, 5–016
Jayaar Impex Ltd v. Toaken Group Ltd [1996] 2 Lloyd's Rep. 437 2–012
Jebara v. Ottoman Bank [1927] 2 K.B. 254; 96 L.J.K.B. 581; 137 L.T. 101; 43 T.L.R. 369; 32 Com.Cas. 228 15–106
Jebsen v. East and West India Dock Co. (1875) L.R. 10 C.P. 300; 44 L.J.C.P. 181; 32 L.T. 321; 23 W.R. 624; 2 Asp.M.L.C. 505 16–056
Jeffcott v. Andrew Motors Ltd [1960] N.Z.L.R. 721 ... 7–071, 7–080, 7–086, 15–038, 15–055
Jeffreyes v. Agra and Masterman's Bank (1866) L.R. 2 Eq. 674 .... 22–145, 23–170
Jeffries v. G.W. Railway (1856) 5 E. & B. 802; 25 L.J.Q.B. 107; 26 L.T.O.S. 214; 2 Jur. (N.S.) 230; 119 E.R. 680 5–010
Jendwine v. Slade (1797) 2 Esp. 572 10–006
Jenkins v. Horn (Inspector of Taxes) (1979) 123 S.J. 339; [1979] 2 All E.R. 1141; [1979] S.T.C. 446; [1979] T.R. 55 1–084
—— v. Hutchinson (1849) 13 Q.B. 743; 18 L.J.Q.B. 274; 13 L.T. (o.s.) 401; 13 Jur. 763 23–116
—— v. Jones (1882) 9 Q.B.D. 128; 51 L.J.Q.B. 438; 46 L.T. 795; 30 W.R. 668 4–029
—— v. Watford (1918) 87 L.J.K.B. 136 8–089
Jenkyns v. Brown (1849) 14 Q.B. 496; 19 L.J.Q.B. 286; 14 L.T. (o.s.) 395; 14 Jur. 505; 117 E.R. 193 .... 5–137, 18–214, 18–216, 18–226, 18–229
—— v. Usborne (1844) 7 M. & G. 678; 8 Scott N.R. 505; 13 L.J.C.P. 196; 3 L.T. (o.s.) 300; 8 Jur. 1139; 135 E.R. 273 .... 5–061, 7–069, 15–013, 15–065
Jenner v. Smith (1869) L.R. 4 C.P. 270 .... 5–072, 5–077, 5–078
Jenney v. Herle (1723) 2 Ld. Raym. 1361 22–041
Jennings v. Broughton (1854) 5 De G. M. & G. 126 10–009
Jerome v. Bentley & Co. [1952] W.N. 357; [1952] 2 T.L.R. 58; 96 S.J. 463; [1952] 2 All E.R. 114 .... 7–008, 7–009, 7–016
—— v. Clements Motor Sales Ltd (1958) 15 D.L.R. 689 5–032
Jeune v. Ward (1818) 1 B. & A. 653; 106 E.R. 240 .... 22–100, 22–105
Jewelowski v. Propp [1944] K.B. 510; [1944] 1 All E.R. 483; 113 L.J.K.B. 335; 171 L.T. 234; 60 T.L.R. 559 .... 16–052, 16–078
Jewry v. Busk (1814) 5 Taunt. 302 2–046
Jewson Ltd v. Boyhan; *sub nom.* Jewsons Ltd v. Boykan; Jewson Ltd v. Kelly [2003] EWCA Civ 1030; [2004] 1 Lloyd's Rep. 505; [2004] 1 C.L.C. 87; [2004] B.L.R. 31, CA 11–025, 11–044, 11–059, 11–060, 14–008
Jindal Iron & Steel Co Ltd v. Islamic Solidarity Shipping Co Jordan Inc; TCI Trans Commodities AG v. Islamic Solidarity Shipping Co Jordan Inc [2004] UKHL 49; [2005] 1 W.L.R. 1363; [2005] 1 All E.R. 175; [2005] 1 All E.R. (Comm) 1; [2005] 1 Lloyd's Rep. 57; [2004] 2 C.L.C. 1172; 2005 A.M.C. 1; (2004) 148 S.J.L.B. 1405; *The Times*, November 26, 2004, HL; affirming [2003] EWCA Civ 144; [2003] 1 All E.R. (Comm) 747; [2003] 2 Lloyd's Rep. 87; [2003] 1 C.L.C. 885, CA 18–106, 20–089, 21–104
Joachimson v. Swiss Bank Corporation [1921] 3 K.B. 110; 90 L.J.K.B. 973; 125 L.T. 338; 37 T.L.R. 534; 65 S.J. 434; 26 Com.Cas. 196 22–144
Joblin v. Watkins & Roseveare (Motors) Ltd 64 T.L.R. 464; [1949] 1 All E.R. 47 ... 1–065, 7–037, 7–041, 7–051, 7–075

Jobson v. Eppenheim & Co. (1905) 21 T.L.R. 468 15–071
—— v. Johnson [1989] 1 W.L.R. 1026; [1989] 1 All E.R. 621 ...... 15–134, 16–032, 16–038
John Dee Group Ltd v. WMH (21) Ltd [1998] B.C.C. 972, CA; affirming [1997] B.C.C. 518, Ch D 13–039
Johnson, *Re, ex p.* Wright (1908) 99 L.T. 305 15–072
Johnson v. Agnew [1980] A.C. 367; [1979] 2 W.L.R. 487; (1979) 123 S.J. 217; [1979] 1 All E.R. 883; (1979) 38 P. & C.R. 424; (1979) 251 E.G. 1167 .... 8–030, 12–067, 12–095, 12–128, 13–046, 15–110, 16–031, 16–073, 17–011, 17–100, 19–166, 19–183, 19–207
—— v. Credit Lyonnais Co. (1877) 3 C.P.D. 32; 47 L.J.Q.B. 241; 37 L.T. 657; 42 J.P. 548; 26 W.R. 195 .... 7–009, 7–013, 7–016, 7–017, 7–032, 7–055
—— v. Gore Wood & Co; *sub nom.* Johnson v. Gore Woods & Co. [2001] 2 W.L.R. 72; [2001] 1 All E.R. 481; [2001] C.P.L.R. 49; [2001] B.C.C. 820; [2001] 1 B.C.L.C. 313; [2001] P.N.L.R. 18; (2001) 98(1) L.S.G. 24; (2001) 98(8) L.S.G. 46; (2000) 150 N.L.J. 1889; (2001) 145 S.J.L.B. 29; *The Times*, December 22, 2000, HL; reversing in part [1999] C.P.L.R. 155; [1999] B.C.C. 474; [1999] Lloyd's Rep. P.N. 91; [1999] P.N.L.R. 426; [1998] N.P.C. 151, CA 16–047
—— v. Jones [1972] N.Z.L.R. 313 15–132
—— v. Kirkaldy (1840) 4 Jur. Rep. 988 .... 5–040, 5–041, 5–050
—— v. Macdonald (1842) 9 M. & W. 600; 12 L.J.Ex. 99; 6 Jur. 264; 152 E.R. 253 ... 1–111, 21–022, 21–024, 21–027
—— v. Raylton (1881) 7 Q.B.D. 438; 50 L.J.Q.B. 753; 45 L.T. 374; 30 W.R. 350 11–88
—— v. Robarts (1875) L.R. 10 Ch.App. 505; 44 L.J.Ch. 678; 33 L.T. 138; 23 W.R. 763 22–092
—— v. Stear (1863) 15 C.B. (N.S.) 330 .... 7–110, 17–106
—— v. Taylor Bros. [1920] A.C. 144 ...... 9–048, 19–002, 19–008, 19–010, 19–011, 19–069, 21–081, 21–094
—— v. Unisys Ltd [2001] UKHL 13; [2001] 2 W.L.R. 1076; [2001] 2 All E.R. 801; [2001] L.C.R. 480; [2001] I.R.L.R. 279; *The Times*, March 23, 2001; *The Independent*, March 29, 2001, HL; affirming [1999] 1 All E.R. 854; [1999] I.C.R. 809; [1999] I.R.L.R. 90, CA 16–047
Johnson Matthey Bankers Ltd v. State Trading Corp. of India Ltd [1984] 1 Lloyd's Rep. 427 ..... 2–012, 8–030, 8–101, 17–010, 18–325, 18–331, 18–340, 19–142, 19–183, 21–049
Johnston v. Boyes [1899] 2 Ch. 73; 68 L.J.Ch. 425; 80 L.T. 488; 47 W.R. 517; 43 S.J. 457 2–005
—— v. State Bank, 195 N.W. 2d 126 (1972) 23–241
Johnston (SA) Co. v. Ship The Tindefjell Sealion Navigation Co. SA and Concordia Line A/S (The Tindefjell) [1973] 2 Lloyd's Rep. 253 21–086
Johnstone v. Bloomsbury HA [1992] Q.B. 333; [1991] 2 W.L.R. 1362; [1991] 2 All E.R. 293; [1991] I.C.R. 269; [1991] I.R.L.R. 118; [1991] 2 Med. L.R. 139; (1991) 141 N.L.J. 271, CA 13–065, 18–071
Johnstone v. McRae (1907) 26 N.Z.L.R. 299 .... 10–005, 11–012
—— v. Marks (1887) 19 Q.B.D. 509 2–030
—— v. Milling (1886) 16 Q.B.D. 460; 55 L.J.Q.B. 162; 54 L.T. 629; 50 L.J. 694; 34 W.R. 238; 2 T.L.R. 249 .... 8–006, 9–018, 15–110, 15–111
Jombart v. Woollett (1837) 2 My. & C. 390; Donnelly 229; 6 L.J.Ch. 211; 40 E.R. 688 23–125
Jonassohn v. Young (1863) 4 B. & S. 296; 2 New Rep. 390; 32 L.J.Q.B. 385; 10 Jur. (N.S.) 43; 11 W.R. 962; 122 E.R. 470 8–078
Jonathan Wren & Co. Ltd v. Microdec plc (1999) 65 Con. L.R. 157, QBD (T & CC) 11–070
Jones v. Barkley (1781) 2 Doug. 684 9–017
—— v. Barnett [1899] 1 Ch. 611 4–023
—— v. Bowden (1813) 4 Taunt. 847; 128 E.R. 565 11–087
Jones v. Bright (1829) 5 Bing. 533; Dan, & Ll. 304; 3 Moo. & P. 155; 7 L.J. (O.S.) C.P. 213; 130 E.R. 1167 11–025
—— v. Cowley (1825) 4 B. & C. 445 10–019
—— v. De Marchant (1916) 28 D.L.R. 561 .... 1–060, 5–149
—— v. European and General Express Co. Ltd (1920) 90 L.J.K.B. 159; 124 L.T. 276; 15 Asp.M.L.C. 138; (1920) 25 Com.Cas. 296 .... 21–073, 21–097

Jones v. Flint (1839) 10 Ad. & El. 753 1–093
—— v. Gallagher (t/a Gallery Kitchens and Bathrooms); *sub nom.* Jones v. Gallagher (t/a Gallery Kitchens and Bathrooms) [2004] EWCA Civ 10; [2005] 1 Lloyd's Rep. 377, CA 1–1041A, 1–043, 12–055, 14–021
—— v. Gibbons (1853) 8 Exch. 920 .... 8–037, 8–039
—— v. Gordon (1877) 2 App.Cas. 616; 47 L.J.Bcy. 1; 37 L.T. 477; 26 W.R. 172 ..... 7–046, 22–061
—— v. Jones (1841) 8 M. & W. 431; 10 L.J.Ex. 481; 151 E.R. 1107 15–084
—— v. Just (1868) L.R. 3 Q.B. 197; 9 B. & S. 141; 37 L.J.Q.B. 89; 18 L.T. 208; 16 W.R. 643 .... 11–003, 11–006, 11–024, 11–025, 11–054, 11–067, 11–079, 16–052, 17–051, 17–054
—— v. Lavington [1903] 1 K.B. 253 4–026
—— v. Oceanic Steam Navigation Co. [1924] 2 K.B. 730; (1924) 19 Ll. L. Rep. 348, KBD 25–089
—— v. Padgett (1890) 24 Q.B.D. 650; 59 L.J.Q.B. 261; 62 L.T. 934; 38 W.R. 782 .. 11–059, 11–078
—— v. Peppercorne (1858) Johns 430; 28 L.J.Ch. 158; 5 Jur. (N.S.) 140; 7 W.R. 103 .... 22–139, 22–140, 22–141, 22–142, 22–145
—— v. Samios [1985] A.C.L.D. 381 (Queensland) 1–081
—— v. Sherwood Computer Services [1992] 1 W.L.R. 277; [1992] 2 All E.R. 170; *The Times*, December 14, 1989, CA 2–051, 13–040
—— v. Tarleton (1842) 9 M. & W. 674; 1 Dowl. (N.S.) 625; 11 L.J.Ex. 267; 6 Jur. 348 15–057
—— v. The Flying Clipper 116 F.Supp. 386 (1963) 21–091
Jones (David) Ltd v. Willis (1934) 52 C.L.R. 110 .... 11–008, 11–010
Jones (James) & Sons Ltd v. Earl of Tankerville [1909] 2 Ch. 440; 78 L.J.Ch. 674; 101 L.T. 202; 25 T.L.R. 714 .... 1–009, 1–097, 5–024, 8–022, 17–098, 17–103
Jones (R.E.) Ltd v. Waring and Gillow Ltd [1926] A.C. 670 .... 7–008, 7–016, 22–061, 22–068
Jones (Sydney G.) Ltd v. Bencher (Martin) Ltd [1986] 1 Lloyd's Rep. 54 21–073
Jones & Co.'s Trustee v. Allan (1901) 4 F. (Ct. Sess.) 374 1–065
Jones Brothers (Holloway) Ltd v. Woodhouse [1923] 2 K.B. 117; 92 L.J.K.B. 638; 129 L.T. 317; 67 S.J. 518 7–111
Jorden v. Money (1854) 5 H.L.Cas. 185; 23 L.J.Ch. 865; 24 L.T. (O.S.) 160; 10 E.R. 868 18–174
Jordeson & Co. v. Stora Kapparbergs Bergslags Aktiebolag (1931) 41 Ll.L.R. 201 .. 12–047, 12–051, 20–111
Joseph v. Knox (1813) 3 Camp. 320 .... 5–009, 18–114
—— v. Lyons (1884) 15 Q.B.D. 280; 54 L.J.Q.B. 1; 51 L.T. 470; 33 W.R. 145; I.T.L.R. 16 5–034
Joseph (D.) Ltd v. Wood (Ralph) & Co. [1951] W.N. 224; 95 S.J. 319 .... 5–003, 18–208
Joseph l. Emanuel Ltd v. Cardia and Savoca. *See* Emanuel (Joseph I.) v. Cardia and Savoca.
Josling v. Kingsford (1863) 13 C.B. 447; 1 New Rep. 328; 32 L.J.C.P. 94; 7 L.T. 790; 9 Jur. (N.S.) 947; 11 W.R. 377; 143 E.R. 177 .... 11–004, 13–022
Joyce v. Swann (1864) 17 C.B. 84; 144 E.R. 177 18–214
Joyner v. Weeks [1891] 2 Q.B. 31; 60 L.J.Q.B. 510; 65 L.T. 16; 55 J.P. 725; 39 W.R. 583; 7 T.L.R. 509 .... 16–056, 17–019
Juelle v. Trudeau (1968) 7 D.L.R. (3d) 82 6–033
Jugoslavenska Oceanska Plovidba v. Castle Investment Co. Inc. (The Kozara) [1974] Q.B. 292; [1973] 3 W.L.R. 847; [1973] 3 All E.R. 498; [1973] 2 Lloyd's Rep. 1; 117 S.J. 712, CA 25–194
Julia, The. *See* Comptoir d'Achat et de Vente du Boerenbond Belge S/A v. Luis de Ridder Limitada.
Junior Books Ltd v. Veitchi Co. Ltd [1983] 1 A.C. 520; [1982] 3 W.L.R. 477; (1982) 126 S.J. 538; [1982] 3 All E.R. 201; [1982] Com.L.R. 221; (1982) 79 L.S.Gaz. 1413; (1981) 21 Build L.R. 66 .... 14–010, 18–149
Jurgensen v. Hookway (F.E.) & Co. Ltd [1951] 2 Lloyd's Rep. 129 11–081

KBC Bank v. Industrial Steels (UK) Ltd [2001] 1 All E.R. (Comm) 409; [2001] 1 Lloyd's Rep. 370, QBD (Comm Ct) 19–197, 23–144

K.H. Enterprise (Cargo Owners) v. Pioneer Container (Owners); Pioneer Container, The [1994] 2 A.C. 324; [1994] 3 W.L.R. 1; [1994] 2 All E.R. 250; [1994] 1 Lloyd's Rep. 593; (1994) 138 S.J.L.B. 85; *The Times*, March 29, 1994, PC . . . 18–098, 18–115, 18–150, 21–073
KMW International v. Chase Manhattan Bank 609 F. 2d 10 (1979) 23–149
K/S A/S Seateam Co. v. Iraq National Oil Co. (The Sevonia Team) [1983] 2 Lloyd's Rep. 640, QBD (Comm Ct) 18–104, 18–123
Kadel Chajkin v. Mitchell Cotts & Co. (Middle East) Ltd (The Stensby) [1948] L.J.R. 535; 64 T.L.R. 89; 92 S.J. 72; [1947] 2 All E.R. 786, KBD 25–071
Kahler v. Midland Bank [1950] A.C. 24; [1949] L.J.R. 1687; 65 T.L.R. 663; [1949] 2 All E.R. 621 . . . . 22–013, 25–033, 25–081, 25–119, 25–120, 25–187
Kaines (U.K.) v. Oesterreichische Waren handelsgesellschaft Austrowaren Gesellschaft m.b.H. (formerly C.G.L. Handelsgesellschaft m.b.H.) [1993] 2 Lloyd's Rep. 1, CA 16–081, 17–008, 17–013, 17–015, 20–116
Kallis (George) (Manufacturers) Ltd v. Success Insurance Ltd [1985] 2 Lloyd's Rep. 8, PC 18–048
Kaltenbach v. Lewis (1885) 10 App.Cas. 617; (1883) 24 Ch.D. 54 . . . . 7–050, 7–052
Kammins Ballrooms Co. v. Zenith Investments (Torquay) Ltd [1971] A.C. 850; [1970] 3 W.L.R. 287; 114 S.J. 590; [1970] 2 All E.R. 871; 22 P. & C.R. 74; 19–145
Kapur v. Kapur [1985] Fam. Law 22; [1984] F.L.R. 920; (1984) 81 L.S.G. 2543 25–056
Karberg (Arnhold) & Co. v. Blythe, Green, Jourdain & Co.; Schneider (Theodor) & Co. v. Burgett & Newsam [1916] 1 K.B. 495; 85 L.J.K.B. 665; 114 L.T. 152; 32 T.L.R. 186; 60 S.J. 156; 13 Asp.M.L.C. 235; 21 Com.Cas. 174 . . . . 6–043, 18–116, 18–209, 18–082, 19–006, 19–008, 19–037, 19–080, 19–079, 21–015, 23–216
Karflex Ltd v. Poole [1933] 1 K.B. 251 . . . . 4–005, 4–013, 7–062
Karinjee Javinjee & Co. v. William F. Malcolm & Co. (1926) 25 Ll.L.R. 28 . . . . 18–116, 19–006, 19–078
Karlshamns Olje Fabriker v. Eastport Navigation Cpn. (The Elafi) [1982] 1 All E.R. 208; [1981] 2 Lloyd's Rep. 679; [1981] Com.L.R. 149 . . . . 1–015, 5–059, 5–062, 5–063, 5–066, 5–086, 5–104, 5–107, 5–110, 18–114, 18–149, 18–285, 18–286, 18–288, 18–306, 19–102, 19–103, 21–007
Karsales (Harrow) Ltd v. Wallis [1956] 1 W.L.R. 936; 100 S.J. 548; [1956] 2 All E.R. 866 . . . . 13–041, 13–043, 13–044, 13–051
Kasler and Cohen v. Slavouski [1928] 1 K.B. 78; 96 L.J.K.B. 850; 137 L.T. 641 . . . . . . 4–016, 14–061, 17–061, 17–077, 17–081, 17–084
Kastellon, The; Huilerie L'Abeille v. Société des Huileries du Niger [1978] 2 Lloyd's Rep. 203 . . . . 8–092, 8–099, 19–139, 19–140, 19–193, 19–195, 19–197, 19–198, 19–201
Kat v. Diment [1951] 1 Q.B. 34; 66 T.L.R. (Pt. 2) 474; 114 J.P. 472; 94 S.J. 596; [1950] 2 All E.R. 657; 67 R.P.C. 158; 49 L.G.R. 450 11–021
Katy, The [1895] P. 56; 64 L.J.P. 49; 71 L.T. 709; 11 T.L.R. 116; 39 S.J. 165; 7 Asp.M.L.C. 527; 11 R. 638 8–032
Kaukomarkkinat O/Y v. Elbe Transport-Union G.m.b.H. (The Kelo) [1985] 2 Lloyd's Rep. 85 . . . . 18–089, 18–142, 18–147
Kawasaki Steel Corporation v. Sardoil S.p.a. *See* The Zuiho Maru.
Kay S.N. Co. Ltd v. Barnett (W. & R.) Ltd (1932) T.L.R. 440 . . . . 20–111, 21–040
Kayford, *Re* [1975] 1 W.L.R. 279; (1974) 118 S.J. 752; [1975] 1 All E.R. 604 5–064
Kay's Leasing Corporation Pty. Ltd v. Fletcher (1694) 116 L.L.R. 124 . . . . . . 25–006, 25–088
Kearley v. Thomson (1890) 24 Q.B.D. 742 3–033
Kearon v. Pearson (1861) 7 H. & N. 386 6–049
Kearry v. Pattinson [1939] 1 K.B. 471; [1939] 1 All E.R. 65; 180 L.J.K.Q.B. 158; 160 L.T. 101; 55 T.L.R. 300; 82 S.J. 1050 1–088
Keating v. Horwood (1926) 28 Cox C.C. 198 2–002
Keeble v. Combined Lease Finance plc [1996] C.C.L.R. 63, CA 7–091
Keech v. Sandford (1726) Sel.Cas.t.King 61 1–080
Keegan v. Lenzie 135 P. 2d 717 (1943) 25–127
Keen & Keen, ex p. Collins, Re [1902] 1 K.B. 555, KBD 5–093
Keeley v. Guy McDonald Ltd (1984) 134 N.L.J. 706 11–048
Keetley v. Quinton Pty Ltd (1991) 4 W.A.R. 133 15–115
Keever, *Re*, A Bankrupt, *ex p.* Trustee of the Property of the Bankrupt v. Midland Bank [1967] Ch. 182; [1966] 3 W.L.R. 779; 110 S.J. 847; [1966] 3 All E.R. 631 . . . . 22–060, 22–143

Keighley Maxstead & Co. and Bryant, Durant & Co. (No. 2) (1894) 70 L.T. 155; 7 Asp.M.L.C. 418 .... 19–012, 19–036
Keith Prowse & Co. v. National Telephone Co. [1854] 2 Ch. 147 8–036
Kellman v. Watts [1963] V.L.R. 396 16–045
Kellogg Brown & Root Services Corp. v. Aerotech Herman Nelosn Inc. (2004) 238 D.L.R. (4th) 595 12–007
Kelly v. Enderton [1913] A.C. 191; 82 L.J.P.C. 57; 107 L.T. 781 1–049
—— v. First Westroads Bank 840 F. 2d 554 (8th Cir. 1988) 23–245
Kelly, Douglas & Co. Ltd v. Pollock (1958) 14 D.L.R. (2d) 526 6–019
Kemp v. Baerselman [1906] 2 K.B. 604; 75 L.J.K.B. 873; 50 S.J. 615 3–044
—— v. Balls (1854) 10 Exch. 607 9–044
—— v. Dalziel [1956] N.Z.L.R. 1030 13–029
—— v. Falk (1882) L.R. 7 App.Cas. 573; 52 L.J.Ch. 167; 47 L.T. 454; 5 Asp.M.L.C. 1 15–027, 15–037, 15–041, 15–079, 15–084, 15–086, 15–091, 15–099, 15–100, 18–086 ....
—— v. Ismay, Imrie & Co. (1909) 100 L.T. 996; 14 Com.Cas. 202 15–069
—— v. Watt (1846) 15 M. & W. 672 9–031
Kemp (A.B.) Ltd v. Tolland [1956] 2 Lloyd's Rep. 681 ..... 6–019, 11–040, 11–049, 11–067, 16–007, 18–254, 18–255, 18–274
Kempler v. Bravingtons (1925) 133 L.T. 680; 41 T.L.R. 519; 69 S.J. 639 ...... 5–042, 5–045
Kenburn Waste Management Ltd v. Bergmann [2002] EWCA Civ 98; [2002] C.L.C. 644; [2002] I.L.Pr. 33; [2002] F.S.R. 45; *The Times*, February 4, 2002, CA 25–001
Kendall v. Marshall Stevens & Co. (1883) 11 Q.B.D. 356; 52 L.J.Q.B. 313; 48 L.T. 951; 31 W.R. 597 .... 15–061, 15–064, 15–068, 15–069, 15–080, 18–248
Kendall (Henry) & Sons (A Firm) v. Lillico (William) & Sons; Holland Colombo Trading Society v. Grimsdale & Sons; Grimsdale & Sons v. Suffolk Agricultural Poultry Producers' Association; *sub nom.* Hardwick Game Farm v. Suffolk Agricultural and Poultry Producers Association Ltd [1969] 2 A.C. 31; [1968] 3 W.L.R. 110 [1968] 2 All E.R. 444; [1968] 1 Lloyd's Rep. 547, HL; affirming [1966] 1 W.L.R. 287; [1966] 1 All E.R. 309; [1966] 1 Lloyd's Rep. 197; 110 S.J. 11; *The Times*, December 21, 1965, CA; affirming in part [1964] 2 Lloyd's Rep. 227, QBD 2–012, 5–013, 11–039, 11–045, 11–049, 11–055, 11–058, 11–059, 11–061, 11–062, 11–064, 13–013, 13–022, 13–024, 14–011, 14–094, 16–047, 17–066, 17–074, 18–047, 18–274, 19–001, 25–121, 25–132, 25–136, 25–140, 25–156, 25–170, 25–171
Kendall Produce Inc. v. Terminal Warehouse Transfer Co. 145 A. 511 (1929) 18–064
Kendrick v. Sotheby & Co. (1967) 111 S.J. 470 .... 7–032, 7–038
Kennedy v. Panama etc., Mail Co. Ltd (1867) L.R. 2 Q.B. 580; 8 B. & S. 571; 36 L.J.Q.B. 260; 17 L.T. 62; 15 W.R. 1039 .... 11–003, 11–006
Kennedy (F.W.) & Co. v. Leyland (F.) & Co. Ltd (1923) 16 Ll.L.R. 399 20–141
Kennedy's Trustee v. Hamilton and Manson (1897) 25 R. 252 5–039
Kent v. Godts (1855) 26 L.T. (o.s.) 88; 19 J.P.Jo. 725 .... 8–078, 9–010
—— v. Salomon [1910] T.P.D. 637 25–084
Kent & Sussex Sawmills Ltd *Re* [1947] Ch. 177, [1947] L.J.R. 534; 176 L.T. 167; 62 T.L.R. 747; 91 S.J. 12; [1946] 2 All E.R. 638 5–153
Kenya Railways v. Antares Co. Pte. Ltd (The Antares) (No. 2) [1987] 1 Lloyd's Rep. 424 .... 18–059, 21–091, 21–092, 25–072
Kenyon, Son and Craven Ltd v. Baxter Hoare & Co. Ltd [1971] 1 W.L.R. 519; [1971] 2 All E.R. 708; [1971] 1 Lloyd's Rep. 232 13–046
Keppel Tatlee Bank Ltd v. Bandung Shipping Pte Ltd [2003] 1 Lloyd's Rep. 619, CA (Sing) 18–016, 18–103, 18–115, 18–118
Kerford v. Mondel (1859) 28 L.J.Ex. 303; 33 L.T. (o.s.) 289 15–056
Kerr v. Jeston (1842) 1 Dowl. (n.s.) 538 8–033
Kerr-McGee Chemical Corporation v. Federal Deposit Insurance Corporation 872 F. 2d 971 (11th Cir. 1989) 23–156, 23–200
Kerrison v. Glyn, Mills, Currie & Co. (1912) 81 L.J.K.B. 465; 105 L.T. 721; 28 T.L.R. 106; 56 S.J. 139; 17 Com.Cas. 41 22–145
Kershaw v. Ogden (1865) 3 H. & C. 717; 6 New Rep. 125; 34 L.J.Ex. 159; 12 L.T. 575; 11 Jur. (n.s.) 642; 13 W.R. 755; 159 E.R. 713 5–039
Ketley v. Gilbert [2001] 1 W.L.R. 986; [2001] R.T.R. 22; *The Times*, January 17, 2001; *The Independent*, January 19, 2001, CA 9–065

Ketley Ltd v. Scott [1981] I.C.R. 241 14–150
Kettlewell v. Refuge Assce. Co. [1908] 1 K.B. 545; 77 L.J.K.B. 421; 97 L.T. 896; 24 T.L.R. 216; 52 S.J. 158 3–032
Key v. Cotesworth (1852) 7 Ex. 595; 22 L.J.Ex. 4; 19 L.T. (O.S.) 145; 155 E.R. 1085 18–216, 18–221
Key Appliance Inc. v. First National City Bank, 46 A.D. 2d 622, 359 N.Y.S. 2d 866 (1974) 23–239, 23–245
Keys v. Harwood (1846) 2 C.B. 905 .... 1–034, 1–039, 8–078
Kiddle & Son v. Lovett (1885) 16 Q.B.D. 605; 34 W.R. 518 .... 17–075, 17–078
Kidman v. Fisken Bunning & Co. [1907] SAL.R. 101 11–008
—— v. Patterson (1887) 8 N.S.W.L.R. 290 15–049
Kidston & Co. v. Monceau Ironworks Co. Ltd (1902) 86 L.T. 556; 18 T.L.R. 320; 7 Com.Cas. 82 19–086
Kier (J.L.) & Co. v. Whitehead Iron & Steel Co. Ltd [1938] 1 All E.R. 591; 158 L.T. 228; 54 T.L.R. 452; 82 S.J. 235; 60 Ll.L.R. 8–058, 8–060
Killby v. Rochussen (1865) 18 C.B. (N.S.) 357; 144 E.R. 483 22–131
Kilmer (John H.) v. British Columbia Orchard Lanch Ltd [1913] A.C. 319 16–038
Kin Tye Loong v. Seth (1920) 89 L.J. 113 5–021
King v. Brandywine Reinsurance Co (UK) Ltd (formerly Cigna RE Co (UK) Ltd) [2005] EWCA Civ 235; [2005] 2 All E.R. (Comm) 1; [2005] 1 Lloyd's Rep. 655; [2005] 1 C.L.C. 283; [2005] Env. L.R. 33; [2005] Lloyd's Rep. I.R. 509, CA 25–001, 25–074
—— v. Chester & Cole Ltd (1928) 1–066
—— v. King (1833) 1 My. & K. 442; 39 E.R. 749 15–115
—— v. Lewis; *sub nom.* Lewis v. King [2004] EWCA Civ 1329; [2005] I.L.Pr. 16; [2005] E.M.L.R. 4; (2004) 148 S.J.L.B. 1248; *The Times*, October 26, CA 25–051
—— v. Meredith (1811) 2 Camp. 639; 170 E.R. 1278 5–098
—— v. Parker (1876) 34 L.T. 886 6–041
—— v. Reedman (1883) 49 L.T. 473 .... 9–057, 21–042
—— v. Texacally Joint Venture, 690 S.W. 2d 618 (Tex A. App.) 23–239
King Line Ltd v. Westralian Farmers Ltd (1932) 48 T.L.R. 398 25–165
Kingdom v. Cox (1848) 5 C.B. 522; 17 L.J.C.P. 155; 10 L.T. (O.S.) 328; 12 Jur. 336; 136 E.R. 982 8–064
Kingdom of Sweden v. New York Trust Co., 96 N.Y.S. 2d 779 (1949) 23–082, 23–114, 23–139, 23–174, 23–204
King's Motors (Oxford) Ltd v. Lax [1970] 1 W.L.R. 426; 114 S.J. 168; [1969] 3 All E.R. 665 2–017
King's Norton Metal Co. Ltd v. Edridge, Merrett & Co. Ltd (1897) 14 T.L.R. 98 .... 3–013, 3–014, 7–021, 7–023
Kingsbury v. Collins (1827) 4 Bing. 202 1–093
Kingsford v. Merry (1856) 1 H. & N. 503 .... 7–013, 7–022
Kingsley v. Sterling Industrial Securities Ltd [1967] 2 Q.B. 747; [1966] 2 W.L.R. 1265; 110 S.J. 267; [1966] 2 All E.R. 414 .... 1–066, 3–005, 3–030
Kinnear v. J. & D. Brodie (1902) 3 F. 540; 38 Sc.L.R. 336; 8 S.L.T. 475 ..... 6–011, 12–059
Kiriri Cotton Co. Ltd v. Dewani [1960] A.C. 192; [1960] 2 W.L.R. 127; 104 S.J. 49; [1960] 1 All E.R. 177 3–032
Kirkham v. Attenborough [1897] 1 Q.B. 201; 66 L.J.Q.B. 149; 75 L.T. 543; 45 W.R. 213; 13 T.L.R. 41 S.J. 141 .... 5–004, 5–041, 5–044, 5–047, 5–050
—— v. Peel (1880) 43 L.T. 171 5–151
Kirkness v. Hudson (John) & Co. Ltd [1955] A.C. 696; [1955] 2 W.L.R. 1135; 99 S.J. 368; [1955] 2 All E.R. 345; [1955] T.R. 145; 48 R. & I.T. 352; 34 A.T.C. 142 1–070
Kite, The [1933] P. 154; (1933) 46 Ll. L. Rep. 83, PDAD 18–150
Kitto v. Bilbie, Hobson & Co. (1895) 72 L.T. 266; 22 T.L.R. 214; 2 Mans. 122; 15 R. 188 .... 7–064, 7–079
Kleinert v. Abosso Gold Mining Co. (1913) 58 S.J. (P.C.) 45 8–040
Kleinjan & Holst N.V. Rotterdam v. Bremer Handelsgesellschaft m.b.H. [1972] 2 Lloyd's Rep. 11 .... 19–017, 19–019, 19–021, 19–187, 19–191, 19–196
Kleinwort Benson v. City of Glasgow; *sub nom.* Barclays Bank v. Glasgow City Council (Case C-346/93) [1996] Q.B. 57; [1995] 3 W.L.R. 866; [1995] All E.R. (E.C.) 514; [1995] E.C.R. 1–615; *The Times*, April 17, 1995, ECJ 25–022

Kleinwort Benson Ltd v. Glasgow City Council [1996] 2 W.L.R. 655; [1996] 4 All E.R. 733, C.A. 25–176
—— v. Lincoln City Council [1999] 2 A.C. 349; [1998] 3 W.L.R. 1095; [1998] 4 All E.R. 513; [1998] Lloyd's Rep. Bank. 387; [1999] C.L.C. 332; (1999) 1 L.G.L.R. 148; (1999) 11 Admin. L.R. 130; [1998] R.V.R. 315; (1998) 148 N.L.J. 1674; (1998) 142 S.J.L.B. 279; [1998] N.P.C. 145; *The Times*, October 30, 1998; *The Independent*, November 4, 1998, HL 10–009
—— v. Malaysia Mining Corp. Bhd. [1989] 1 W.L.R. 379; (1989) 133 S.J. 262; [1989] 1 All E.R. 785; [1989] 1 Lloyd's Rep. 556; (1989) 139 New L.J. 221 2–019
Kleinwort Sons & Co. v. Ungarische Baumvolle Industrie A.G. [1939] 2 K.B. 678; [1939] All E.R. 38; 108 L.J.K.B. 861; 160 L.T. 615; 55 T.L.R. 814; 83 S.J. 437; 44 Com.Cas. 324 25–119
Knight & McLennan v. National Mortgage & Agency Co. [1920] N.Z.L.R. 748 1–093
Knight Machinery (Holdings) v. Rennie 1995 S.L.T. 166; 1993 S.L.T. (Sh.Ct.) 65 13–083
Knights v. Wiffen (1870) L.R. 5 Q.B. 660 .... 5–065, 7–013, 15–096, 16–024
Knotz v. Fairclough, Dodds and Jones Ltd [1952] 1 Lloyd's Rep. 226 23–083
Knutsen v. Mauritzen [1918] 1 S.L.T. 85 11–040
Koch Marine Inc. v. D'Amica Societa di Navigazione A.R.L. (The Elena D'Amico) [1980] 1 Lloyd's Rep. 75 16–076
Kodros Shipping Corp. of Monrovia v. Empresa Cubana de Fletes of Havana, Cuba (The Evia) No. 2 [1983] 1 A.C. 736; [1982] 3 W.L.R. 637; (1982) 126 S.J. 656; [1982] 3 All E.R. 350; [1982] 2 Lloyd's Rep. 307; [1982] Com.L.R. 199 .... 6–056, 18–336
Kohnke v. Karger [1951] 2 K.B. 670; [1951] 2 T.L.R. 40; 95 S.J. 484; [1951] 2 All E.R. 179 25–191
Kolfor Plant Ltd v. Tilbury Plant Ltd (1977) 121 S.J. 390 12–063
Kollerich & Cie. SA v. State Trading Corporation of India [1980] 2 Lloyd's Rep. 32 .... 13–040, 19–076
Komninos S., The. *See* Hellenic Steel Co. v. Svolamar Shipping Co. (The Komninos S.).
König v. Brandt (1901) 84 L.T. 748; 9 Asp.M.L.C. 199 .... 5–138, 18–216, 18–241
Koninklijke Bunge v. Cie. Continentale d'Importation [1973] 2 Lloyd's Rep. 44 .... 8–092, 19–138, 19–140
Koninklijke Zwavelzuurfabrieken V/H Ketjen N.V. v. D.A. and D.D. Psychoyos, Pireaus, (The Metamorphosis) [1953] 1 W.L.R. 543; [1953] 1 All E.R. 723; *sub nom.* Metamorphosis, The, 97 S.J. 230; [1953] 1 Lloyd's Rep. 196 .... 25–010, 25–071
Koppel v. Koppel (Wide, Claimant) [1966] 1 W.L.R. 802; 110 S.J. 229; [1966] 2 All E.R. 187 .... 1–036, 5–017
Kordas v. Stokes Seeds Ltd (1992) 96 D.L.R. (4th) 129 13–048
Korea Exchange Bank v. Debenhams (Central Buying) Ltd (1979) 123 S.J. 163; [1979] 1 Lloyd's Rep. 548 .... 22–042, 23–002
Korea Industry Co. v. Andoll [1990] 2 Lloyd's Rep. 183 23–145
Kornatzki v. Oppenheimer [1937] 4 All E.R. 133 25–166
Korner v. Witkowitzer. *See* Vitkovice Horni a Hutni Tezirstvo v. Korner.
Korvine's Trust, Levashoff v. Block, [1921] 1 Ch. 343; 90 L.J.Ch. 192; 124 L.T. 500; 65 S.J. 205 25–121
Koskas v. Standard Marine Insurance Company Ltd (1927) 32 Com.Cas. 160 .... 19–047, 19–048
Koufos v. C. Czarnikow Ltd (The Heron 11) [1969] 1 A.C. 350; [1967] 3 W.L.R. 1491; 111 S.J. 848; *sub nom.* Koufos v. Czarnikow (C.). The Heron 11 [1967] 3 All E.R. 686; *sub nom.* Czarnikow (C.) v. Koufos [1967] 2 Lloyd's Rep. 457 .... 11–055, 16–030, 16–043, 16–044, 16–045, 16–046, 16–069, 17–032, 17–038, 17–039, 17–040, 17–064, 17–070, 17–082
Kpohtaror v. Woolwich Building Society [1996] 4 All E.R. 119 16–043
Kraut (Jean) A.G. v. Albany Fabrics Ltd [1977] Q.B. 182 .... 25–186, 25–194
Kredietbank Antwerp v. Midland Bank plc [1998] 2 Lloyd's Rep. 173, affirmed [1999] 1 All E.R. (Comm) 801 .... 23–200, 23–207
Krell v. Henry [1903] 2 K.B. 740; 72 L.J.K.B. 794; 89 L.T. 320; 19 T.L.R. 711; 52 W.R. 246 6–055
Kremezi v. Ridgway 93 S.J. 287; [1949] 1 All E.R. 662 25–191

Kreuger v. Blanck (1870) L.R. 5 Ex. 179; 23 L.T. 128; 18 W.R. 813; 3 Mar.L.C. 470; *sub nom*. Krenger v. Blanck, 39 L.J.Ex. 160 .... 8–049, 21–034, 21–035, 21–037
Krohn & Co. v. Mitsui & Co. Europe GmbH [1978] 2 Lloyd's Rep. 419 .... 8–055, 18–092, 19–006 19–025
Krombach v. Bamberski (Case C-7/98) *See* Bamberski v. Krombach
Kronman & Co. v. Steinberger (1922) 10 Ll.L.R. 39 23–094
Kronman (Samuel) & Co. Inc. v. Public National Bank of New York 218 N.Y.S. 616 (1926) 23–174, 23–185
Kronos Worldwide Ltd v. Sempra Oil Trading Sarl; *sub nom.* Sempra Oil Trading Sarl v. Kronos Worldwide Ltd [2004] EWCA Civ 3; [2004] 1 All E.R. (Comm) 915; [2004] 1 Lloyd's Rep. 260; [2004] 1 C.L.C. 136; *The Times*, January 29, 2004, CA 19–089, 20–019
Kronprinsessan Margareta, The [1921] 1 A.C. 486; 90 L.J.P. 145; 124 L.T. 609; 15 Asp.M.L.C. 170 ..... 5–015, 18–189, 18–213, 19–093, 19–099, 20–080, 20–083, 21–013
Kronprinzessin Cecilie, The (1917) 33 T.L.R. 292 1–049
Kruppstahl A.G. v. Quitmann Products Ltd [1982] 1 L.R.M. 551 ..... 5–148, 5–150, 25–143, 25–144, 25–145
Kubach v. Hollands [1937] 3 All E.R. 907; 53 T.L.R. 1024; 81 S.J. 766 ..... 14–061, 14–070
Kuenigl v. Donnersmarck [1955] 1 Q.B. 515; [1955] 2 W.L.R. 82; 99 S.J. 60; [1955] 1 All E.R. 46 6–042
Kum v. Wah Tat Bank Ltd [1971] 1 Lloyd's Rep. 439, PC (Mal) ... 18–006, 18–066, 18–067, 18–075, 18–076, 18–077, 18–084, 18–164, 18–166, 18–264
Kunglig Jarnvagsstryelsen v. Dexter & Carpenter Inc. 290 F. 991 (1924) 19–047
—— v. National City Bank of New York 20 F. 2d 307 (1927) 23–175, 23–185
Kurkjran (S.N.) (Commodity Brokers) Ltd v. Marketing Exchange for Africa (formerly T.M. Motrain) (U.K.) (No. 2) Ltd [1986] 2 Lloyd's Rep. 618 ...... 12–037, 19–165
Kursell v. Timber Operators & Contractors Ltd [1927] 1 K.B. 298; 95 L.J.K.B. 569; 135 L.T. 223; 42 T.L.R. 435 .... 1–098, 1–100, 5–016, 5–022, 5–024, 5–033, 6–050, 18–290, 25–119, 25–133, 25–154, 25–155
Kurt A. Becker G.m.b.H. & Co. v. Voest Alpine Intertrading G.m.b.H.: Rio Apa, The [1992] 2 Lloyd's Rep. 586 20–046
Kuwait Airways Corp. v. Iraqi Airways Co. (Nos. 4 & 5) [2001] 3 W.L.R. 1117 ..... 7–002, 25–043, 25–119
Kuwait Airways Corp v. Iraqi Airways Co (No.6); *sub nom.* Kuwait Airways Corp v. Iraq Airways Co (No.6); Kuwait Airways Corp v. Iraqi Airways Co (No.5) [2002] UKHL 19; [2002] 2 A.C. 883; [2002] 2 W.L.R. 1353; [2002] 3 All E.R. 209; [2002] 1 All E.R. (Comm) 843; [2003] 1 C.L.C. 183, *The Times*, May 21, 2002, HL 7–002, 7–115, 25–043, 25–119
—— v. Iraq Airways Co. (No.7) [2001] 1 W.L.R. 429; [2001] 1 Lloyd's Rep. 485; (2001) 98(11) L.S.G. 44; (2001) 145 S.J.L.B. 84; *The Times*, February 14, 2001; *The Daily Telegraph*, February 20, 2001, HL; [2001] 3 W.L.R. 1117; [2001] 1 All E.R. (Comm) 557; [2001] 1 Lloyd's Rep. 161; [2001] C.L.C. 262; (2000) 97(48) L.S.G. 37; (2001) 145 S.J.L.B. 5; *The Times*, November 21, 2000; *The Daily Telegraph*, November 21, 2000, CA; reversing in part [2000] 2 All E.R. (Comm) 360; (2000) 97(23) L.S.G. 44; *The Times*, May 31, 2000, QBD (Comm Ct) 7–002
Kuwait Maritime Transport Co. v. Rickmers Linie K.G. (The Danah) [1993] 1 Lloyd's Rep. 351 21–090
Kuwait Oil Tanker Co. SAK v. Al Bader (No.3) [2000] 2 All E.R. (Comm) 271; (2000) 97(23) L.S.G. 44; *The Times*, May 30, 2000, CA; affirming QBD (Comm Ct) 25–191
Kuwait Petroleum Corp. v. I. & D. Oil Carrier's Ltd (The Houda) [1994] 2 Lloyd's Rep. 541 .... 18–063, 18–084
Kuwait Supply Co. v. Oyster Marine Management Inc. (The Safeer) [1994] 1 Lloyd's Rep. 637, Q.B.D. 6–056, 19–142
Kvaerner Singapore Pte Ltd v. Shipbuilding (S.) Pte Ltd [1993] 3 S.L.R. 350 .... 23–280, 23–282

Kwei Tek Chao (Trading as Zung Fu Co.) v. British Traders and Shippers N.V. Handelsmaatschappij J. Smits Import-Export, Third Party. [1954] 2 Q.B. 459; [1954] 2 W.L.R. 365; 98 S.J. 163; *sub nom.* Chao v. British Traders and Shippers [1954] 1 All E.R. 779; [1954] 1 Lloyd's Rep. 16 ..... 5–085, 9–014, 12–028, 12–035, 12–046, 12–047, 12–049, 12–052, 12–064, 12–067, 12–120, 16–068, 16–069, 16–070, 16–074, 17–028, 17–029, 17–035, 17–054, 19–035, 19–079, 19–144, 19–150, 19–151, 19–154, 19–155, 19–156, 19–157, 19–173, 19–174, 19–190, 19–191, 19–196, 19–197, 19–201, 21–094
Kydon Compania Naviera v. National Westminster Bank Ltd (The Lena) [1981] 1 Lloyd's Rep. 68; [1980] Com.L.R. 12 ...... 19–159, 19–160, 23–017, 23–196, 23–203, 23–211, 23–213, 23–236
Kyprianou (Phoebus D.) v. Cyprus Textiles Ltd [1958] 2 Lloyd's Rep. 60 ..... 6–057, 8–040, 18–312

L.T.U. v. Eurocontrol (Case 29/76) [1976] E.C.R. 1541 25–018
Lacane & Co. v. Crédit Lyonnais [1897] 1 Q.B. 148; 66 L.J.Q.B. 226; 75 L.T. 514; 13 T.L.R. 60; 2 Com.Cas. 17 .... 22–022, 22–059
Lacey (William) (Hounslow) Ltd v. Davis [1957] 1 W.L.R. 932; 101 S.J. 629; [1957] 2 All E.R. 712 6–060
Lacey's Footwear (Wholesale) Ltd v. Bowler International Freight Ltd [1997] 2 Lloyd's Rep. 369; *The Times*, May 12, 1997, CA 13–015
Lacis v. Cashmarts [1969] 2 Q.B. 400; [1969] 2 W.L.R. 329; (1968) 112 S.J. 1005 .... 2–002, 5–013, 5–026
Lackington v. Atherton (1844) 7 M. & G. 360; 8 Scott N.R. 38; 13 L.J.C.P. 140; 3 L.T. (o.s.) 57; 8 Jur. 407; 135 E.R. 151 .... 8–012, 8–013
Laconia, The. *See* Mardorf Peach & Co. Ltd v. Attica Sea Carriers Corporation of Liberia.
Ladbroke Leasing Ltd v. Reekie Plant Ltd 1983 S.L.T. 155, OH 1–065
Ladenburg v. Goodwin Ferreira & Co. Ltd [1912] 3 K.B. 275; 8 L.J.K.B. 1174; 107 L.J. 587; 28 T.L.R. 541; 56 S.J. 722; 18 Com.Cas. 16; 19 Mans. 383 ... 5–153, 18–238
Ladup Ltd v. Shaikh [1983] Q.B. 225; [1982] 3 W.L.R. 172; (1982) 126 S.J. 327 22–061
Laemthong International Lines Co Ltd v. Artis (The Laemthong Glory) (No.2); *sub nom.* Laemthong International Lines Co Ltd v. Abdullah Mohammed Fahem & Co [2005] EWCA Civ 519; [2005] 2 All E.R. (Comm) 167; [2005] 1 Lloyd's Rep. 688; [2005] 1 C.L.C. 739, CA 18–016
Laemthong International Lines Co Ltd v. Artis (The Laemthong Glory) (No.3) [2005] EWHC 1595, QBD 25–082
Lagden v. O'Connor; *sub nom.* Clark v. Tull (t/a Ardington Electrical Services); Burdis v. Livsey; Clark v. Ardington Electrical Services; Dennard v. Plant; Sen v. Steelform Engineering Co Ltd [2003] UKHL 64; [2004] 1 A.C. 1067; [2003] 3 W.L.R. 1571; [2004] 1 All E.R. 277; [2004] R.T.R. 24; [2004] Lloyd's Rep. I.R. 315; (2003) 153 N.L.J. 1869; (2003) 147 S.J.L.B. 1430; *The Times*, December 5, 2003, HL 16–055
Laffitte v. Slatter (1830) 6 Bing. 623; 4 Moo. & P. 457; 8 L.J. (o.s.) C.P. 273; 130 E.R. 1421 22–132
Laidler v. Burlinson (1837) 2 M. & W. 602; Murp. & H.109; 6 L.J.Ex. 160; 150 E.R. 898 .... 5–031, 5–091, 5–092
Laing v. Fidgeon (1815) 4 Camp. 169; (1815) 6 Taunt. 108; 128 E.R. 974 .... 2–046, 11–003
Laing (James), Son & Co. (M/C) v. Eastcheap Dried Fruit Co. Ltd [1961] 2 Lloyd's Rep. 277 .... 16–037, 20–042, 20–133
Laing (Sir James) & Sons v. Barclay, Curle & Co. [1908] A.C. 35 ..... 5–066, 5–091, 5–092
Lake v. Simmons [1926] 2 K.B. 51; [1927] A.C. 487 ..... 3–014, 3–015, 5–026, 5–046, 7–037
Lamb v. Attenborough (1862) 1 B. & S. 830 .... 7–013, 7–032
Lamb (W.T.) & Sons v. Goring Brick Co. Ltd [1932] 1 K.B. 710; 101 L.J.K.B. 214; 146 L.T. 318; 48 T.L.R. 160; 37 Com.Cas. 73 .... 1–049, 3–038, 5–045
Lambert v. G. & C. Finance Corporation (1963) 107 S.J. 666 .. 5–016, 5–026, 7–044, 7–075, 7–081, 7–086
Lambert v. H.T.V. Cymru (Wales) Ltd [1998] E.M.L.R. 629; [1998] F.S.R. 874; (1998) 21(8) I.P.D. 21086; (1998) 95(15) L.S.G. 30; (1998) 142 S.J.L.B. 1184; *The Times*, March 17, 1999, CA 2–017

Lambert v. Lewis [1982] A.C. 225; [1981] 2 W.L.R. 713; [1981] 1 All E.R. 1185; [1981] Lloyd's Rep. 17 .... 10–012, 10–013, 10–019, 10–020, 10–021, 11–040, 11–049, 11–057, 12–013, 12–121, 14–020, 14–062, 14–064, 16–049, 16–051, 16–055, 17–059, 17–060, 17–061, 17–067, 17–075, 17–079, 18–255
Lamborn v. Kirkpatrick (Allen) 135 A. 541 (1927) 23–098
—— v. Lake Shore Banking and Trust Co., 188 N.Y.S. 162 (1921) 23–236
—— v. National Bank of Commerce, 276 U.S. 469, 48 S.Ct. 378 (1928) 23–222
—— v. National Park of New York 148 N.E. 664 (1925) 23–054, 23–210
Lamert v. Heath (1846) 15 M. & W. 486; 4 Ry. & Com.Cas. 302; 15 L.J.Ex. 297; 7 L.T. (o.s.) 186; 10 Jur. 481 23–176
Laminated Structures & Holdings Ltd v. Eastern Woodworkers Ltd (1962) 32 D.L.R. (2d) 1 1–043
Lamine v. Dorrell (1705) 2 Ld. Raym. 1216 .... 1–073, 15–104
Lamond v. Davall (1847) 9 Q.B. 1030; 16 L.J.Q.B. 136; 11 Jur. 266; 115 E.R. 1569 15–128, 15–129, 17–106
Lamont (James) & Co. Ltd v. Hyland Ltd (No. 2) [1950] 1 K.B. 585; 66 T.L.R. (Pt. 1) 937; 94 S.J. 179; [1950] 1 All E.R. 341; 83 Ll.L.Rep. 477 .... 17–049, 22–064, 22–065
Lamport & Holt Lines Ltd v. Coubro & Scrutton (M. & I.) and Coubro & Scrutton (Riggers and Shipwrights), The Raphael, [1982] 2 Lloyd's Rep. 42 2–012
Lancaster v. J.F. Turner & Co. Ltd [1924] 2 K.B. 222; 93 L.J.K.B. 1024; 131 L.T. 525; 29 Com.Cas. 207 16–037
Landauer v. Asser [1905] 2 K.B. 184 .... 19–036, 19–050
—— v. Craven & Speeding [1912] 2 K.B. 94; 81 L.J.K.B. 650; 106 L.T. 298; 56 S.J. 274; 17 Com.Cas. 193 .... 19–027, 19–034, 19–037, 23–231
Langen and Wind Ltd v. Bell [1972] Ch. 685; [1972] 2 W.L.R. 170; (1971) 115 S.J. 966 17–100
Langmead v. Thyer Rubber Co. Ltd (1947) S.R. (SA) 29 .... 7–073, 7–081
Langridge v. Levy (1837) 2 M. & W. 519 12–125
Langton v. Higgins (1859) 4 H. & N. 402; 28 L.J.Ex. 252; 33 L.T. (o.s.) 166; 7 W.R. 489; 157 E.R. 896 .... 5–003, 5–072, 5–079, 5–081, 5–086, 5–095, 17–105
—— v. Hughes (1813) 1 M. & S. 593 3–029
Lanitis (N.F.) & Co. Ltd v. Kyoda Shoji (U.K.) Ltd [1956] 2 Lloyd's Rep. 176 ..... 13–035, 13–052
Lanyon v. Toogood (1844) 13 M. & W. 27; 13 L.J.Ex. 273; 3 L.T. (o.s.) 164; 153 E.R. 11 5–028
Larocque v. Beauchemin [1897] A.C. 358; 66 L.J.P.C. 59; 76 L.T. 473; 45 W.R. 639; 4 Mans. 263 9–041
Larsen v. Sylvester [1908] A.C. 295 8–089
Latham v. Atwood (1635) Cro.Car. 515 1–093
—— v. Chartered Bank of India (1873) 17 Eq. 205; 43 L.J.Ch. 612; 29 L.T. 795; 2 Asp.M.L.C. 178 15–090
Laudisi v. American Exchange National Bank 146 N.E. 347 (1924) 23–080, 23–234
Laurelgates Ltd v. Lombard North Central Ltd (1983) 133 N.L.J. 720 .... 12–032, 12–056, 12–065, 14–020, 14–021
Laurie & Morewood v. Dudin & Sons [1926] 1 K.B. 223 ...... 1–002, 5–003, 5–061, 5–065, 5–097, 5–110, 7–014, 7–036, 7–072, 7–077, 17–097, 18–174, 18–193, 18–194
Lauritzen A.S. v. Wijsmuller B.V. (The "Super Servant Two") [1990] 1 Lloyd's Rep. 1 .... 1–125, 6–034, 6–052, 18–306, 18–354
Lavarack v. Woods of Colchester Ltd [1967] 1 Q.B. 278; [1966] 3 W.L.R. 706; 110 S.J. 770; [1966] 3 All E.R. 683; 1 K.I.R. 312 .... 16–056, 16–057, 17–002, 17–014
Lavery v. Pursell (1888) 39 Ch.D. 508; 57 L.J.Ch. 570; 58 L.T. 846; 37 W.R. 163; 4 T.L.R. 353 .... 1–093, 1–096
Law v. Redditch Local Board [1892] 1 Q.B. 127; 61 L.J.Q.B. 172; 66 L.T. 76; 56 J.P. 292; 8 T.L.R. 90; 36 S.J. 90 16–032
Law and Bonar Ltd v. British American Tobacco Co. Ltd [1916] 2 K.B. 605; 85 L.J.K.B. 1714; 115 L.T. 612; 13 Asp.M.L.C. 499; 21 Com.Cas. 350 .... 6–021, 18–218, 19–043, 19–046, 19–080, 19–113, 19–117, 19–119, 21–013
Lawlor v. Nicol (1898) 12 Man.L.R. 224 1–057

Lawrence v. Fox 20 N.Y. 268 (1859) 18–096
Laybutt v. Amoco Australia Ltd (1974) 132 C.L.R. 57 1–050
Lazenby Garages Ltd v. Wright [1976] 1 W.L.R. 459; 120 S.J. 146; [1976] 2 All E.R. 770; [1976] R.T.R. 314; 19 Man.Law 19 .... 16–064, 16–066, 16–077, 16–079
Leaf v. International Galleries [1950] 2 K.B. 86; 66 T.L.R. (Pt. 1) 1031; [1950] 1 All E.R. 693 ...... 1–009, 1–011, 3–020, 5–019, 10–006, 10–008, 10–040, 12–006, 12–009, 12–128
Leary (C.) & Co. v. Francis Briggs & Co. (1904) 6 F. 857; 41 Sc.L.R. 681; 12 S.L.T. 210 13–033
Lease Management Services Ltd v. Purnell Secretarial Services Ltd 91993) 14 Tr L.R. 337 13–090
Leask v. Scott (1877) 2 Q.B.D. 376; 46 L.J.Q.B. 576; 36 L.T. 784; 25 W.R. 654; 3 Asp.M.L.C. 469 18–088
Leason Property Ltd v. Princes Farm Property Ltd [1983] 2 N.S.W.L.R. 381 .... 1–008, 1–011, 12–006
Leather v. Simpson (1871) L.R. 11 Eq. 398; 40 L.J.Ch. 177; 24 L.T. 286; 19 W.R. 431; 1 Asp.M.L.C. 5 .... 5–140, 19–035
Leather's Best Inc. v. The Mormaclynx; Moore-McCormack Lines Inc., Tide water Terminal Inc. and Universal Terminal and Stevedoring Corporation (The Mormaclynx) [1970] 1 Lloyd's Rep. 527 21–086
Leaves v. Wadham Stringer (Cliftons) Ltd [1980] R.T.R. 308 .... 11–044, 11–057
Leavey (J.) & Co. Ltd v. George H. Hirst & Co. Ltd [1944] K.B. 24; [1943] 2 All E.R. 581; 113 L.J.K.B. 229 .... 17–021, 17–035
Lebeaupin v. Crispin & Co. [1920] 2 K.B. 714; 89 L.J.K.B. 1024; 124 L.T. 124; 36 T.L.R. 739; 64 S.J. 625; 25 Com.Cas. 335 .... 1–131, 6–041, 8–099
Le Blanche v. L.N.W. Railway (1876) 1 C.P.D. 286; 45 L.J.Q.B. 521; 34 L.T. 667; 40 C.P. 580; 24 W.R. 808 .... 16–058, 17–023
Lecaan v. Kirkman (1859) 6 Jur. (N.S.) 17; 7 W.R. 499 22–131
Lecky & Co. Ltd v. Ogilvy, Gillanders & Co. (1897) 3 Com.Cas. 29 .... 18–041, 19–038
Leduc v. Ward (1888) 20 Q.B.D. 475, 57 L.J.Q.B. 379; 58 L.T. 908; 36 W.R. 537; 4 T.L.R. 313; 6 Asp.M.L.C. 290 ..... 18–030, 18–048, 18–051, 18–060, 18–097, 18–106, 18–110, 19–096
Lee v. Abdy (1886) 17 Q.B.D. 309, 55 L.T. 297; 34 W.R. 653 25–127
—— v. Butler [1893] 2 Q.B. 318; 62 L.J.Q.B. 591; 69 L.T. 370; 42 W.R. 88; 9 T.L.R. 631; 4 R. 563 .... 1–052, 1–053, 7–070, 7–081
—— v. Gaskell (1876) 1 Q.B.D. 700; 45 L.J.Q.B. 540; 34 L.T. 759; 40 J.P. 725; 24 W.R. 824 1–095
—— v. Griffin (1861) 1 B. & S. 272 .... 1–045, 1–047, 14–046
—— v. Ridson (1816) 7 Taunt. 188; 2 Marsh. 495; 129 E.R. 76 .... 1–095, 9–062
—— v. York Coach and Marine [1977] R.T.R. 35 .... 11–052, 11–061, 11–062, 14–021
Lee Cooper Ltd v. CH Jeakins & Sons Ltd [1967] 2 Q.B. 1; [1965] 3 W.L.R. 753; [1965] 1 All E.R. 280; [1964] 1 Lloyd's Rep. 300; 109 S.J. 794, QBD 5–009
Lee (John) & Sons (Grantham) Ltd v. Railway Executive [1949] W.N. 373; 65 T.L.R. 604; 93 S.J. 587; [1949] 2 All E.R. 581 13–015
Lee (Paula) Ltd v. Robert Zehil & Co. Ltd [1983] 2 All E.R. 390 17–002
Leeds v. Wright (1803) 3 B. & P. 320; 127 E.R. 176 15–068
Leeds Banking Co., *Re* (1865) L.R. 1 Eq. 1; 35 L.J.Ch. 33; 12 L.T. 314; 1 Jur. (N.S.) 920; 14 W.R. 43 22–125
Leeming v. Snaith (1851) 16 Q.B. 275; 20 L.J.Q.B. 164; 16 L.T. (O.S.) 3621; 15 Jur. 988; 117 E.R. 884 8–054
Leeson v. North British Oil and Candle Co. (1874) Ir.R. 8 C.L. 309 ... 8–039, 8–077, 8–078
Leggett v. Taylor (1965) 50 D.L.R. 516 .... 11–011, 11–019
Legione v. Hateley (1983) 152 C.L.R. 406; (1983) 46 A.L.R. 1 .... 12–035, 16–038
Leidemann v. Gray (1857) 26 L.J.Ex. 162; 3 Jur. (N.S.) 219; *sub nom.* Gray v. Leidermann 28 L.T. (O.S.) 341; 5 W.R. 294 .... 8–064, 8–072
Leigh v. Paterson (1818) 8 Taunt. 540; 2 Moore C.P. 588; 129 E.R. 493 .... 16–071, 17–007, 17–011, 17–016
Leigh v. Taylor [1902] A.C. 157; 71 L.J.Ch. 272; 86 L.T. 239; 50 W.R. 623; 18 T.L.R. 293; 46 S.J. 264 1–095

Leigh & Sillavan Ltd v. Aliakmon Shipping Co. Ltd (The Aliakmon) [1986] A.C. 785; [1986] 2 W.L.R. 902; (1986) 130 S.J. 357; [1986] 2 All E.R. 145; [1986] 2 Lloyd's Rep. 1; (1986) 136 New L.J. 415, HL; affirming [1985] Q.B. 350; [1985] 2 All E.R. 44; [1985] 1 Lloyd's Rep. 199; (1985) 82 L.S.G. 203; (1985) 135 N.L.J. 285; (1985) 129 S.J. 69, CA; reversing [1983] 1 Lloyd's Rep. 203, QBD (Comm Ct) 5–011, 5–026, 5–064, 5–094, 5–110, 5–131, 5–134, 5–136, 18–016, 18–028, 18–029, 18–030, 18–036, 18–065, 18–066, 18–089, 18–098, 18–100, 18–104, 18–115, 18–116, 18–120, 18–144, 18–150, 18–213, 18–214, 18–216, 18–217, 18–232, 18–292, 18–296, 19–080, 19–094, 19–101, 19–103, 19–110, 21–006, 21–020
Leitch (William) & Co. Ltd v. Leydon [1931] A.C. 90; 100 L.J.P.C. 10; 144 L.T. 218; 47 T.L.R. 81; 74 S.J. 836 1–061
Leitner v. TUI Deutschland GmbH & Co KG (C-168/00) [2002] All E.R. (EC) 561; [2002] E.C.R. I-2631; [2002] 2 C.M.L.R. 6; [2002] C.E.C. 349, ECJ 14–007
Lem v. Barotto Sports Ltd (1976) 69 D.L.R. 276 11–057
Lemenda Trading Co. Ltd v. African Middle East Petroleum Co. Ltd [1988] Q.B. 448; [1988] 2 W.L.R. 735; [1988] 1 All E.R. 513; [1988] 1 Lloyd's Rep. 361; [1988] 1 F.T.L.R. 123; (1988) 132 S.J. 538, QBD (Comm Ct) 25–112
Leonard (Cyril) & Co. v. Simo Securities Trust [1972] 1 W.L.R. 80 9–016
Lep Air Services v. Rolloswin Investments. *See* Moschi v. Lep Air Services Ltd
Leroux v. Brown (1852) 12 C.B. 801 25–087
Les Affreteurs Reunis SA v. Leopold Walford (London) Ltd [1919] A.C. 801, HL; affirming [1918] 2 K.B. 498, CA 18–056
Leslie v. Bassett 29 N.E. 834 (1892) 23–126
Leslie (J.) Engineering Co. (In Liquidation), *Re* [1976] 1 W.L.R. 292; (1975) 120 S.J. 146; [1976] 2 All E.R. 85 7–003
Leslie Ltd v. Sheill [1914] 3 K.B. 607 2–038
Leslie (R.) Ltd v. Reliable Advertising and Addressing Agency [1915] 1 K.B. 652 ... 17–065
Lesotho Highlands Development Authority v. Impregilo SpA [2005] UKHL 43; [2006] 1 A.C. 221; [2005] 3 W.L.R. 129; [2005] 3 All E.R. 789; [2005] 2 All E.R. (Comm) 265; [2005] 2 Lloyd's Rep. 310; [2005] 2 C.L.C. 1; [2005] B.L.R. 351; 101 Con. L.R. 1; [2005] 27 E.G.C.S. 220; (2005) 155 N.L.J. 1046; *The Times*, July 6, 2005, HL; reversing [2003] EWCA Civ 1159; [2004] 1 All E.R. (Comm) 97; [2003] 2 Lloyd's Rep. 497; [2003] B.L.R. 347; (2003) 100(39) L.S.G. 37; (2003) 153 N.L.J. 1239; *The Times*, September 15, 2003, CA 25–191
Lester v. Garland (1808) 15 Ves.Jun. 248 8–032
Lesters Leather and Skin Co. Ltd v. Home and Overseas Brokers Ltd [1948] W.N. 437; 64 T.L.R. 569; 92 S.J. 646 ...... 16–052, 16–067, 16–068, 19–157, 19–169
L'Estrange v. Graucob (F.) Ltd [1934] 2 K.B. 394 ...... 2–012, 13–012, 13–030
Leuw v. Dudgeon (1867) L.R. 3 C.P. 17; 37 L.J.C.P. 5; 17 L.T. 145; 16 W.R. 80; 3 Mar.L.C. 3 13–036
Levey & Co. v. Goldberg [1922] 1 K.B. 688; 91 L.J.Q.B. 551; 127 L.T. 298; 38 T.L.R. 446; 28 Com.Cas. 244 ...... 8–069, 9–006
Levi & Browse Island Guano Co. Ltd v. Berk & Co. (1886) 2 T.L.R. 898 ...... 21–029, 21–033, 21–035
Levison v. Patent Steam Carpet Cleaning Co. Ltd [1978] Q.B. 69; [1977] 3 W.L.R. 90; (1977) 121 S.J. 406; [1979] 3 All E.R. 498 ...... 13–016, 13–046
Levy v. Assicurazione Generali [1940] A.C. 791; (1940) 67 Ll.L. Rep. 174, PC (Pal) 8–097
Levy v. Green (1859) 1 E. & E. 969; 28 L.J.Q.B. 319; 33 L.T. (O.S.) 241; 5 Jur. (N.S.) 1245; 7 W.R. 486; 120 E.R. 1174; (1857) 8 E. & B. 575 ...... 5–085, 8–049
Lewin v. Barratt Homes Ltd (2000) 164 J.P. 182; [2000] 1 E.G.L.R. 77; [2000] 03 E.G. 132; [2000] Crim. L.R. 323; (2000) 164 J.P.N. 283; [1999] E.G.C.S. 139; (1999) 96(46) L.S.G. 41; (2000) 79 P. & C.R. D20, QBD 14–113
Lewis v. Averay [1972] 1 Q.B. 198; [1971] 3 W.L.R. 603; 115 S.J. 755; [1971] 3 All E.R. 907 ...... 3–012, 3–013, 3–014, 7–021, 7–023
—— v. Lyster (1835) 2 C.M. & R. 704 9–031
—— v. Nicholson (1852) 18 Q.B. 503; 21 L.J.Q.B. 311; 19 L.T. (O.S.) 122; 16 Jur. 1041 23–116
—— v. Thomas [1919] 1 K.B. 319; 88 L.J.K.B. 275; 118 L.T. 639; [1918–19] B. & C.P. 65 7–068

Lewis & Peat (Produce) Ltd v. Alamatu Properties Ltd. *The Times*, May 14, 1992, CA 22–088
Lewis Construction Co. Ltd v. Tichaner SA [1966] V.R. 341 25–012
Lewis Emanuel & Son Ltd v. Sammut. *See* Emanuel (Lewis) & Son v. Sammut.
Leyvand v. Barasch (2000) 97(11) L.S.G. 37; (2000) 144 S.J.L.B. 126; *The Times*, March 23, 2000, Ch D 25–056
Libau Wood Co. v. H. Smith & Sons Ltd (1930) 37 Ll.L.R. 296 12–051
Liberty National Bank and Trust Co. v. Bank of America 116 F. Supp. 233 (1953) .. 23–114, 23–127, 23–201, 23–210, 23–221
Libyan Arab Foreign Bank v. Bankers Trust Co. [1989] Q.B. 728; [1989] 3 W.L.R. 314; [1989] 3 All E.R. 252; [1987] 2 F.T.L.R. 509; [1988] 1 Lloyd's Rep. 259 .... 22–013, 22–014, 25–076, 25–119, 25–167
—— v. Manufacturers Hanover Trust Co. (No. 1) [1988] 2 Lloyd's Rep. 494; *The Financial Times*, August 2, 1988, QBD (Comm Ct) 25–076
—— v. Manufacturers Hanover Trust Co. (No. 2) [1989] 1 Lloyd's Rep. 608 .... 22–013, 22–014, 22–017, 25–076
Lickbarrow v. Mason (1787) 2 T.R. 63; 6 East. 20n 4 ...... 7–007, 15–010, 15–061, 15–063, 15–102, 18–006, 18–007, 18–008, 18–063, 18–066, 18–067, 18–068, 18–075, 18–078, 18–079, 18–080, 18–084, 18–089, 18–193, 21–083
Liddard v. Kain (1824) 2 Bing. 183 10–019
Liford's Case (1614) 11 Co. Rep. 46b; 77 E.R. 1206; *sub nom.* Stampe v. Clinton (alias Liford) 1 Roll. Rep. 95 .... 1–100, 8–022
Lilley v. Doubleday (1881) 7 Q.B.D. 510; 51 L.J.Q.B. 310; 44 L.T. 814; 46 J.P. 708 .. 13–046
Lillywhite v. Devereux (1846) 15 M. & W. 285; 6 L.T. (o.s.) 103; 153 E.R. 857 8–011
Lind (Peter) & Co. Ltd v. Mersey Docks & Harbour Board [1972] 2 Lloyd's Rep. 234 .... 2–013, 2–018
Linden v. National City Bank of New York 208 N.Y.S. 2d 182 (1960) 23–185
Linden Garden Trust v. Lenesta Sludge Disposals Ltd; St Martins Property Corp. Ltd v. Sir Robert McAlpine & Sons Ltd [1994] 1 A.C. 85; [1993] 3 W.L.R. 408; [1993] 3 All E.R. 417; 63 B.L.R. 1; 36 Con.L.R. 1; (1993) 137 S.J. (L.B.) 183; [1993] E.G.C.S. 139; (1993) 143 New L.J. 1152; *The Times*, July 23, 1993; *The Independent*, July 30, 1993, HL 3–043, 5–009, 17–072, 18–114
Linden Tricotagefabrik v. White and Meacham [1975] 1 Lloyd's Rep. 198 8–0236
Linderne Machine Works Co. v. Kuntz Brewery Ltd (1921) 21 O.W.N. 51 25–194
Lindley v. First National Bank of Waterloo, 41 N.W. 381 (1889) 23–236
Lindo v. Unsworth (1811) 2 Camp. 602 22–126
Lindsay (A.E.) & Co. Ltd v. Cook [1953] 1 Lloyd's Rep. 328 .... 23–081, 23–093
Lindsay (W.N.) and Co. Ltd v. European Grain and Shipping Agency Ltd. 107 S.J. 435; [1963] 1 Lloyd's Rep. 737 .... 11–096, 12–063, 13–025, 13–033, 13–040
Lindy v. Lynn 395 F. Supp. 769 (1974) affirmed 515 F. 2d 507 (1975) 23–239
Lines Bros. Ltd, *Re* [1982] 2 W.L.R. 1010; (1982) 126 S.J. 197; [1982] 2 All E.R. 183; [1982] Com.L.R. 81 25–194
Lingen v. Simpson (1824) 1 S.& S. 600 17–099
Linklaters v. HSBC Bank Plc [2003] EWHC 1113; [2003] 2 Lloyd's Rep. 545; [2003] 2 C.L.C. 162, QBD 22–093
Linz v. Electric Wire Co. of Palestine Ltd [1948] A.C. 371; [1948] L.J.R. 1836; 92 S.J. 308; [1948] 1 All E.R. 604 4–006
Lipe v. Leyland Daf [1993] B.C.C. 385; [1994] 1 B.C.L.C. 84; *The Times*, April 2, 1993, C.A. 5–165
Lipkin Gorman v. Karpnale Ltd [1991] 2 A.C. 548; [1991] 3 W.L.R. 10; [1992] 4 All E.R. 512; (1991) 88(26) L.S.G. 31; (1991) 141 N.L.J. 815; (1991) 135 S.J.L.B. 36; *The Times*, June 7, 1991; *The Independent*, June 18, 1991; *The Financial Times*, June 11, 1991; *The Guardian*, June 13, 1991, HL 1–084, 4–008, 7–003, 22–023, 23–029, 23–164
Lipton Ltd v. Ford [1917] 2 K.B. 647; 86 L.J.K.B. 1241; 116 L.T. 632; 33 T.L.R. 459; 15 L.G.R. 699 .... 6–032, 6–041, 6–050
Lister v. Hesley Hall Ltd [2001] UKHL 22; [2002] 1 A.C. 215; [2001] 2 W.L.R. 1311; [2001] 2 All E.R. 769; [2001] I.C.R. 665; [2001] I.R.L.R. 472; [2001] 2 F.L.R. 307; [2001] 2 F.C.R. 97; (2001) 3 L.G.L.R. 49; [2001] E.L.R. 422; [2001] Fam. Law 595; (2001) 98(24) L.S.G. 45; (2001) 151 N.L.J. 728; (2001) 145 S.J.L.B. 126; [2001] N.P.C. 89; *The Times*, May 10, 2001; *The Daily Telegraph*, May 8, 2001, HL; reversing *The Times*, October 13, 1999, CA 18–029

Lister v. Munro [1924] N.Z.L.R. 1137 1–115
—— v. Schulte [1915] V.L.R. 374 22–042
Lister and Biggs v. Barry & Co. (1886) 3 T.L.R. 99 8–062
Litchfield v. Dreyfus [1906] 1 K.B. 584; 75 L.J.K.B. 447; 22 T.L.R. 385; 50 S.J. 391 .. 7–092, 11–028
Litster v. Forth Dry Dock and Engineering Co. Ltd [1990] 1 A.C. 546; [1989] 2 W.L.R. 634; [1989] 1 All E.R. 1134; 1989 S.L.T. 540; [1989] 2 C.M.L.R. 194; [1989] I.C.R. 341; [1989] I.R.L.R. 161; (1989) 86(23) L.S.G. 18; (1989) 139 N.L.J. 400; (1989) 133 S.J. 455, HL; reversing 1988 S.C. 178; 1989 S.L.T. 153, 2 Div 25–109
Litt v. Cowley (1816) Holt N.P. 338; 2 Marsh 457; (1816) 7 Taunt. 169; 129 E.R. 68 .... 15–085, 15–088
Little v. Courage Ltd (1995) 70 P. & C.R. 469; *The Times*, January 6, 1995, CA; reversing (1995) 69 P. & C.R. 447; [1994] N.P.C. 1; *The Times*, January 19, 1994, Ch. D 2–017
Little v. Kingsbury Motors Ltd (1961) 112 L.J. 60 4–012
Liverpool City Council v. Irwin [1977] A.C. 239; (1976) 238 E.G. 879; (1984) 13 H.L.R. 38 11–88
Liverpool Marine Credit Co. v. Hunter (1868) 3 Ch.App. 476 ...... 25–121, 25–130, 25–182
Liverstone v. Roskilly [1992] 3 N.Z.L.R. 230 13–020
Livesley v. Clemens Horst Co. [1925] 1 D.L.R. 159 .... 25–180, 25–189, 25–190, 25–191
Livingstone v. Ross [1901] A.C. 327; 70 L.J.P.C. 58; 85 L.T. 382 5–045
—— v. Whiting (1850) 15 Q.B. 722 9–041
Lloyd v. Fleming (1872) L.R. 7 Q.B. 299; 41 L.J.Q.B. 93; 925 L.T. 824; 20 W.R. 296; 1 Asp.M.L.C. 192 .... 19–008, 19–052
—— v. Guibert (1865) L.R. 1 Q.B. 115; 6 B. & S. 100; 35 L.J.Q.B. 74; 13 L.T. 602; 2 Mar.L.C. 283; 122 E.R. 1134, Ex.Ch 25–010, 25–071
—— v. Howard (1850) 15 Q.B. 995; 15 Q.B. 995; 20 L.J.Q.B. 1; 16 L.T.O.S. 169; 15 Jur. 218; 117 E.R. 735 22–073
—— v. Stanbury [1971] 1 W.L.R. 535; (1970) 115 S.J. 264; [1971] 2 All E.R. 267; 22 P. & C.R. 432 .... 6–060, 17–064
Lloyd del Pacifico v. Board of Trade (1929) 35 Ll.L.R. 217; (1930) 46 T.L.R. 476; 35 Com.Cas. 325 .... 1–082, 11–058, 13–028, 13–029
Lloyds & Scottish Finance v. Cyril Lord Carpets Sales [1992] B.C.L.C. 609, H.L 1–065
—— v. Modern Cars & Caravans (Kingston) Ltd [1966] 1 Q.B. 764; [1964] 3 W.L.R. 859; 108 S.J. 859; [1964] 2 All E.R. 732 .... 4–004, 4–017, 4–029, 4–030, 7–113, 16–058
—— v. Williamson [1965] 1 W.L.R. 404; 109 S.J. 10; [1965] 1 All E.R. 641 ... 7–010, 7–043
Lloyds Bank Ltd v. Bank of America National Trust and Savings Association [1938] 2 K.B. 147; [1938] 2 All E.R. 63; 107 L.J.K.B. 538; 158 L.T. 301; 54 T.L.R. 599; 82 S.J. 312; 43 Com.Cas. 209 .... 7–013, 7–032, 7–033, 7–037, 18–091, 18–237
—— v. Savory & Co. [1933] A.C. 201; 102 L.J.Q.B. 224; 148 L.T. 291;49 T.L.R. 116; 38 Com.Cas. 115; 44 Ll.L.R. 231 22–023
—— v. Swiss Bankverein (1913) 108 L.T. 143; 29 T.L.R. 219; 57 S.J. 243; 18 Com.Cas. 79 8–008
Load v. Green (1846) 15 M. & W. 216 .... 7–021, 7–028
Lobb (Alec.) (Garages) Ltd v. Total Oil (G.B.) Ltd [1985] 1 W.L.R. 173; (1985) 129 S.J. 83; [1985] 1 All E.R. 303; [1985] 1 E.G.L.R. 33; (1985) 273 E.G. 659; (1985) 129 S.J. 83; (1985) 82 L.S.Gaz. 45 .... 3–038, 8–061, 14–052A
Lock v. Bell [1931] 1 Ch. 35 8–026
Lock v. Furze (1866) L.R. 1 C.P. 441 4–029
Lockett v. Charles (A. & M.) Ltd [1938] 4 All E.R. 170; 159 L.T. 547; 55 T.L.R. 22; 82 S.J. 951 .... 1–046, 2–026, 13–016, 14–018, 14–077
—— v. Nicklin (1848) 2 Exch. 93; 19 L.J.Ex. 403; 154 E.R. 419 9–057
Lockhart v. Osman [1981] V.R. 57 .... 11–006, 11–019
Lockie v. Reid (Walter) & Co. Ltd [1916] Q.S.R. 10 8–068
Lockie & Craggs, *Re* (1901) 86 L.T. 388; 9 Asp.M.L.C. 296; 7 Com.Cas. 7 8–095
Lockwood and Manning v. Brownson, 53 Tex. 523 (1880) 23–236
Loder v. Kekule (1857) 3 C.B. (N.S.) 128; 27 L.J.C.P. 27; 30 L.T. (N.S.) 64; 4 Jur. (N.S.) 93; 5 W.R. 884; 140 E.R. 687 .... 17–051, 17–052, 17–054
Loders & Nucoline Ltd v. Bank of New Zealand (1929) 45 T.L.R. 203; 33 Ll.L.R. 70 19–051

Loeschman v. Williams (1815) 4 Camp. 181 5–135
L'Office National du The et du Sucre v. Philippine Sugar Trading (London) Ltd [1983] 1 Lloyd's Rep. 89 19–137
Logan v. Le Mesurier (1847) 6 Moo.P.C. 116; 11 Jur. 1091; 13 E.R. 6281 .... 5–035, 5–039, 6–037, 6–039
Lomas & Co. v. Barff Ltd (1901) 17 T.L.R. 437, *sub nom.* Frangopulo & Co. v. Lomas & Co. (1902) 18 T.L.R. 461 .... 8–049, 8–062
Lombard Banking Ltd v. Central Garage and Engineering Co. Ltd [1963] 1 Q.B. 220; [1962] 3 W.L.R. 1199; 106 S.J. 491; [1962] 2 All E.R. 949 ... 22–124, 22–126, 22–131
Lombard Finance Ltd v. Brookplain Trading Ltd [1991] 2 All E.R. 762 19–035
Lombard North Central plc v. Butterworth [1987] Q.B. 527; [1987] 2 W.L.R. 7; [1987] 1 All E.R. 267; (1987) 6 T.L.R. 65; (1986) 83 L.S.Gaz. 2750 .... 16–005, 16–035
Lombard Tricity Finance Ltd v. Paton [1989] 1 All E.R. 918 .... 2–045, 14–038
Lomi v. Tucker (1829) 4 C. & P. 15; 172 E.R. 586 10–006
London and County Banking Co. v. Ratcliffe (1881) 6 App.Cas. 722; 51 L.J.Ch. 28; 45 9 Ll.L.R. 116 .... 23–211, 23–213
London and Globe Finance Corporation, *Re* [1902] 2 Ch. 416; 71 L.J.Ch. 893; 87 L.T. 49; 18 T.L.R. 679 .... 22–139, 22–140, 22–141
London and Lancashire Fire Insurance Ltd v. Bolands Ltd [1924] A.C. 836 8–097
London and Mediterranean Bank, *ex p.* Birmingham Banking Co., *Re* (1868) L.R. 3 Ch.App. 651; 37 L.J.Ch. 905; 19 L.T. 193; 16 W.R. 1003 22–050
London & North West Railway v. Bartlett (1861) 7 H. & N. 400; 31 L.J.Ex. 92; 5 Western Ry., 8 Jur. (N.S.) 58; 10 W.R. 109 15–074
London and Provincial Leather Processes Ltd v. Hudson [1939] 2 K.B. 724; [1939] 3 All E.R. 857; 109 L.J.K.B. 100; 162 L.T. 140; 55 T.L.R. 1047; 83 S.J. 733; 64 Ll.L.Rep. 352; [1938–9] B. & C.R. 183 25–180
London and South England Building Society v. Stone [1983] 1 W.L.R. 1242; (1983) 127 S.J. 446; [1983] 3 All E.R. 105; (1983) 267 E.G. 69; (1983) L.S.Gaz. 3048 16–052
London Banking Corporation Ltd v. Horsnail (1898) 14 T.L.R. 266; 3 Com.Cas. 105 22–118
London, Chatham and Dover Railway Co. v. South Eastern Railway Co. [1893] A.C. 429; 63 L.J.Ch. 93; 69 L.T. 637; 50 J.P. 36; I.R. 275 .... 16–007, 16–030
London City and Midland Bank v. Gordon [1903] A.C. 240; 72 L.J.K.B. 451; 88 L.T. 574; 51 W.R. 671; 19 T.L.R. 462; 8 Com.Cas. 221 9–038
London Jewellers v. Altenborough [1934] 2 K.B. 206 ... 5–004, 5–041, 5–046, 5–047, 7–070, 7–074
London Joint Stock Bank Ltd v. British Amsterdam Maritime Agency Ltd. (1910) 104 L.T. 143; 11 Asp.M.L.C. 571; 16 Com.Cas. 102 .... 18–080, 20–083, 20–084, 20–84A
—— v. Macmillan [1918] A.C. 777; 119 L.T. 387; 34 T.L.R. 509; 62 S.J. 650 7–008, 16–048
—— v. Simmons [1892] A.C. 201; [1891–4] All E.R. 415; 61 L.J.Ch. 723; 66 L.T. 625; 50 J.P. 644; 41 W.R. 108; 8 T.L.R. 478; 36 S.J. 394 7–047
London Tricotagefabrik v. White and Meacham [1975] 1 Lloyd's Rep. 384 19–042
London Wine Co. (Shippers) Ltd. *Re* [1986] P.C.C. 121 .... 1–108, 1–119, 1–119, 5–060, 5–061, 5–062, 5–064, 5–065, 5–094, 5–097, 5–110, 5–113, 5–130, 5–134, 7–014, 18–020, 18–283, 18–299, 19–101
Long v. Lloyd [1958] 1 W.L.R. 753; 102 S.J. 488; [1958] 2 All E.R. 402 .... 10–008, 10–011, 10–018, 12–006, 14–015
Longbottom & Co. Ltd v. Bass Walker & Co. Ltd [1922] W.N. 245 ... 8–073, 8–074, 8–084, 15–010, 15–042
Longhurst v. Guildford Godalming & District Water Board [1963] A.C. 265; [1961] 3 W.L.R. 915; 105 S.J. 866; [1961] 3 All E.R. 545; 59 L.G.R. 565; [1961] R.V.R. 670 1–087
Lonrho v. Fayed (No. 2) [1992] 1 W.L.R. 1; [1991] 4 All E.R. 961; *The Guardian*, April 16, 1991 10–009
—— v. Shell Petroleum Co. (No. 2) [1982] A.C. 173; [1980] 1 W.L.R. 627; (1980) 124 S.J. 412, H.L.; affirming [1980] Q.B. 358; [1980] 2 W.L.R. 367; (1980) 124 S.J. 205, C.A.; affirming; *The Times*, February 1, 1978 24–008
Lonrho Exports Ltd v. Export Credits Guarantee Department [1999] Ch. 158; [1998] 3 W.L.R. 394; [1996] 4 All E.R. 673; [1996] 2 Lloyd's Rep. 649; [1997] C.L.C. 259, ChD 24–012, 24–015

Lord v. Price (1874) L.R. 9 Ex. 54; 43 L.J.Ex. 49; 30 L.T. 271; 22 W.R. 318 .... 5–003, 17–105
Lord Advocate v. Glasgow Corporation 1958 S.L.T. 2 11–028
Lord Eldon v. Hedley Bros. [1935] 2 K.B. 1 .... 5–016, 5–022, 5–039
Lord Sheffield v. London Joint Stock Bank (1888) 13 App.Cas. 333 7–047
Lord Strathcona S.S. Co. Ltd v. Dominion Coal Co. Ltd [1926] A.C. 108; (1925) 23 Ll.L. Rep. 145, PC (Can) 18–005
Lord's Trustee v. G.E. Railway [1908] 2 K.B. 54; 77 L.J.K.B. 611; 98 L.T. 910; 24 T.L.R. 470; 52 S.J. 394; 15 Mans. 107 .... 15–028, 15–038, 15–043
Lorymer v. Smith (1822) 1B. & C. 1. 1 L.J. (o.s.) K.B. 7; 107 E.R. 1; 2 Dow. & Ry. K.B. 23 12–039
Lotus Cars Ltd v. Southampton Cargo Handling plc (The Rigoletto); Southampton Cargo Handling plc v. Associated British Ports; *sub nom.* Southampton Cargo Handling plc v. Lotus Cars Ltd (The Rigoletto) [2000] 2 All E.R. (Comm) 705; [2000] 2 Lloyd's Rep. 532; [2001] C.L.C. 25, CA 18–150
Louis Dreyfus Trading Ltd v. Reliance Trading Ltd [2004] EWHC 525; [2004] 2 Lloyd's Rep. 243, QBD 4–026, 4–029, 4–030, 17–047, 17–058, 17–081, 17–082
Lough v. Moran Motors Property Ltd [1962] Q.S.R. 466 10–012
Lovatt v. Hamilton (1839) 5 M. & W. 639; 151 E.R. 271 .... 1–111, 6–035, 6–038, 21–022, 21–023, 21–027
Love v. Norman Wright (Builders) Ltd [1944] K.B. 484 1–043
Love and Stewart Ltd v. Rowtor Steamship Co. Ltd [1916] 2 A.C. 527, HL; reversing 1916 S.C. 223, 2 Div 18–053
Loveday v. Renton (No.1) [1989] 1 Med. L.R. 117; *The Times*, March 31, 1988; Guardian, April 2, 1988, QBD 14–091
Lovegrove, *Re* [1935], Ch. 464; [1935] All E.R. Rep. 749; 104 L.J.Ch. 282; [1934–35] B. & C.R. 262; 152 L.T. 480; 79 S.J. 145; 51 T.L.R. 248 1–066
Lovelock v. Franklyn (1846) 8 Q.B. 371; 15 L.J.Q.B. 146; 10 Jur. 246 8–079
Lovelock (E.R.J.) Ltd v. Exportles [1968] 1 Lloyd's Rep. 163 2–016
Low v. Blease (1975) 119 S.J. 695; [1975] Crim.L.R. 513 1–085
—— v. Bouverie [1891] 3 Ch. 82 18–030
Lowe v. Hope [1970] 1 Ch. 94; [1969] 3 W.L.R. 582; 113 S.J. 796; [1969] 3 All E.R. 605; 20 P. & C.R. 857 15–132
—— v. Lombank Ltd [1960] 1 W.L.R. 196; 104 S.J. 210; [1960] 1 All E.R. 611 .... 11–054, 13–030
Lowe (Joe) Food Products Co. Ltd v. J.A. and P. Holland Ltd [1954] 2 Lloyd's Rep. 70 11–079
Lowendahl v. Hessey 296 U.S. 595 (1935) 25–120
Lowenthal, *ex p.* (1874) L.R. 9 Ch.App. 591, 43 L.J. Bey. 83; 30 L.T. 668 .... 22–113, 22–116, 22–121, 22–124
Lowther v. Harris [1927] 1 K.B. 393; 96 L.J.K.B. 170; 136 L.T. 377; 43 T.L.R. 24 .... 7–033, 7–047
Lubbock v. Tribe (1838) 3 M. & W. 607; 1 Horn & H. 160; 7 L.J.Ex. 158 22–115
Lucas v. Bristow (1858) E.B. & E. 907; 27 L.J.Q.B. 364; 31 L.T. (o.s.) 214; 5 Jur. (N.S.) 68; 6 W.R. 685 11–021
—— v. Smith [1926] V.L.R. 400; 48 A.L.T. 66; [1926] Argus L.R. 319 .... 4–010, 4–011
—— v. Wilkinson (1856) 1 H. & N. 420; 26 L.J.Ex. 13; 5 W.R. 197; 156 E.R. 1265 9–044
Lucas (L.) Ltd v. Exports Credits Guarantee Department [1974] 1 W.L.R. 909; 118 S.J. 461; [1974] 2 All E.R. 889; [1974] 2 Lloyd's Rep. 69 .... 24–012, 24–015
Lucas Laureys v. Graham Earl (November 3, 2005) QBD 10–006, 12–013
Luckins v. Highway Motel (Caernarvon) Property Ltd [1975] 133 C.L.R. 164 25–144
Lucy v. Mouflet (1860) 5 H. & N. 229; 29 L.J.Ex. 110; 157 E.R. 1168 12–039
Ludditt v. Ginger Coote Airways Ltd [1947] A.C. 233; [1947] L.J.R. 1067; 177 L.T. 334; 63 T.L.R. 157; [1947] 1 All E.R. 328 13–015
Luis de Ridder SA v. Andre & Cie. SA (Lausanne) [1941] 1 All E.R. 380; 164 L.T. 298; 57 T.L.R. 309; 85 S.J. 367; 46 Cam.Cas. 185 .... 19–019, 19–037
Lukoil-Kalingradmornef plc v. Tata Ltd (No.2) [1999] 2 Lloyd's Rep. 129, CA; affirming [1999] 1 Lloyd's Rep. 365, QBD (Comm. Ct) 21–073
Luna, The [1920] P. 22; 89 L.J.P. 109; 124 L.T. 382; 36 T.L.R. 112; 15 Asp.M.L.C. 152, 2–012

Lunn v. Thornton (1845) 1 C.B. 379; 14 L.J.C.P. 161; 4 L.T. (o.s.) 417; 9 Jur. 350; 135 E.R. 587 5–094
Lupton v. White (1808) 15 Ves.Jun. 432; 33 E.R. 817 5–148
Lusograin Commercio International de Cereas Ltda. v. Bunge A.G. [1986] 2 Lloyd's Rep. 654 .... 20–046, 20–126, 20–129, 20–130
Lutscher v. Comptoir d'Escompte de Paris (1876) 1 Q.B.D. 709; 34 L.T. 798; 3 Asp.M.L.C. 209 .... 5–140, 18–205, 19–205
Luttges v. Sherwood (1895) 11 T.L.R. 233 9–041
Luttges & Co. v. Ormiston and Glass Ltd (1926) Reports of the Decisions of the Mixed Arbitral Tribunals, Vol. 6, 564, 569 25–132
Lutton v. Saville Tractors (Belfast) Ltd [1986] 12 N.I.J.B. 1 .... 13–029, 13–064
Lyle v. Ajax Distributing Agency Proparty Ltd (1975) 11 SAS.R. 9 1–047
Lyle (B.S.) Ltd v. Rosher [1959] 1 W.L.R. 8; 103 S.J. 15; [1958] 3 All E.R. 597 5–161
Lympe Investments Ltd. *Re* [1972] 1 W.L.R. 523 8–034
Lynn v. Bamber [1930] 2 K.B. 72; 99 L.J.K.B. 504; 143 L.T. 231; 46 T.L.R. 367; 74 S.J. 298 12–073
Lynn Storage Warehouse Co. v. Senator 3 F. 2d 558 (1925) 25–136
Lynsey v. Selby (1705) 2 Ld. Raym. 1118 10–020
Lyon v. Van Raden 85 N.W. 727 (1901) 23–063
Lyons v. Hoffnung (1890) 15 App.Cas. 391; 59 L.J.P.C. 79; 63 L.T. 293; 39 W.R. 390; 6 Asp.M.L.C. 551 15–067
Lyons (J.L.) & Co. Ltd v. May and Baker Ltd [1923] 1 K.B. 685; 92 L.J.K.B. 675; 129L.T. 413 .... 12–065, 15–015
Lysaght v. Bryant (1850) 19 L.J.C.P. 160; 9 C.B. 46 22–115

M. (Minors) (Residence Order; Jurisdiction), Re [1993] 1 F.L.R. 495; [1993] 1 F.C.R. 718; [1993] Fam. Law 285; *The Times*, November 6, 1992, CA 25–056
M.B. Pyramid Sound N.V. v. Briese Schiffahrts GmbH (The Ines) [1995] 2 Lloyd's Rep. 144; [1993] 2 Lloyd's Rep. 492 .... 18–063, 18–079, 18–209
M.C.C. Proceeds Inc. v. Lehman Bros International (Europe) [1998] 4 All E.R. 675; [1998] 2 B.C.L.C. 659; (1998) 95(5) L.S.G. 28; (1998) 142 S.J.L.B. 40; *The Times*, January 14, 1998, CA 7–002, 18–149
M.J.B. Enterprises Ltd v. Defence Construction (1951) Ltd (2000) 193 D.L.R. (4th) 1; (1999) 15 Const.L.J. 455 2–003
M.K. International Development Co. Ltd v. Housing Bank, unreported, decision of December 21, 1990, noted in [1991] J.B.L. 279 22–060
M/S Aswan Engineering Establishing Co. v. Lupdine (Thurger Bolle, third party). [1987] 1 W.L.R. 1; [1987] 1 All E.R. 135; (1987) 6 T.L.R. 1; (1986) 130 S.J. 712; [1986] 2 Lloyd's Rep. 347 .... 1–005, 11–042, 11–043, 11–071, 11–075, 18–149
M.S.C. Mediterranean Shipping Co. SA v. B.R.E. Metro Ltd [1985] 2 Lloyd's Rep. 239 .... 8–030, 18–047
Maas v. Pepper [1905] A.C. 102; 74 L.J.K.B. 452; 92 L.T. 371; 53 W.R.513; 21 T.L.R. 304; 12 Mans. 107 1–066
McArthur v. Seaforth (1810) 2 Taunt. 257 17–009
Macaulay v. A. Schroeder Music Publishing Co. Ltd [1974] 1 W.L.R. 1308 13–004
Macauley v. Horgan [1925] 2 J.R. 1 .... 21–042, 21–046
Macbeth v. North and South Wales Bank [1908] A.C. 137; [1908] 1 K.B. 15 22–023
McCall v. Abelesz [1976] Q.B. 585, [1976] 2 W.L.R. 151; (1975) 120 S.J. 81; [1976] 1 All E.R. 727; (1975) 31 P. & C.R. 256 14–006
McCall Bros. v. Hargreaves [1932] 2 K.B. 423; [1932] All E.R. 854; 101 L.J.K.B. 733; 147 L.T. 257; 48 T.L.R. 450; 76 S.J. 433 22–053
M'Callum v. Mason 1956 S.C. 50; 1956 S.L.T. 50 11–055
McCarren & Co. Ltd v. Humber International Transport Ltd (The Vechscroon) [1982] Com.L.R. 11; [1982] 1 Lloyd's Rep. 301 .... 18–035, 21–058, 21–081, 21–085, 21–105, 21–106
McConnell v. Murphy (1873) L.R. 5 P.C. 203; 28 L.T. 713; 21 W.R. 609 8–055
—— v. E. Prill & Co. [1916] 2 Ch. 57; 85 L.J.Ch. 674; 115 L.T. 71; 32 T.L.R. 509; 60 S.J. 556 1–004
McCowan v. Bowes [1923] 3 D.L.R. 765 15–112
McCrone v. Boots Farm Sales Ltd [1981] S.L.T. 103 .... 2–012, 13–014, 13–095
McCullagh v. Lane Fox and Partners Ltd [1996] E.G.L.R. 35; *The Times*, December 22, 1995, C.A 13–065, 13–107, 14–052A

McCutcheon v. McBrayne (David) Ltd [1964] 1 W.L.R. 125 . . . . 2–012, 13–014
McDill v. Hilson [1920] 2 W.W.R. 877; (1920) 53 D.L.R. 228; 30 Man.L.R. 454 . . . . . 5–032, 6–039
McDonald v. Dennys Lascelles Ltd [1983] Argus L.R. 381; 7 A.L.R. 94; 48 C.L.R. 475 (Aus) 16–040, 19–166
—— v. Provan (of Scotland Street) Ltd 1960 S.L.T. 231 . . . . 4–003, 4–023, 5–149
—— v. Western (1888) 15 R. (Ct. of Sess.) 988 1–049
McDougall v. Aeromarine of Emsworth Ltd [1958] 1 W.L.R. 1126; 102 S.J. 860; [1958] 3 All E.R. 431; [1958] 2 Lloyd's Rep. 343 . . . . 1–082, 5–085, 5–092, 5–093, 8–025, 12–031, 12–063, 12–064
McEllistrim v. Ballymacelligott Co-op. Soc. Ltd [1919] A.C. 548 . . . . 3–035, 3–039
McEntire v. Crossley Bros. [1895] A.C. 457; 64 L.J.P.C. 129; 72 C.T. 731; 2 Mans. 334; 11 R. 207 . . . . 1–053, 5–016, 5–021, 5–026, 5–145, 5–167, 16–029, 16–089
M'Ewan & Sons v. Smith (1849) 2 H.L.Cas. 309 . . . . . 7–069, 8–012, 8–013, 15–052, 15–060, 15–092, 18–165
MacFarlane v. Norris (1862) 2 B. & S. 783; 31 L.J.Q.B. 245; 6 L.T. 492; 9 Jur. (N.S.) 74; 121 E.R. 1263 25–191
McFeetridge v. Stewarts and Lloyds Ltd 1913 S.C. 773 25–084
McGrath v. Shah (1987) 57 P & C.R. 452 . . . . 13–056, 13–060
McGruther v. Pitcher [1904] 2 Ch. 306; 73 L.J.Ch. 653; 91 L.T. 678; 53 W.R. 138; 20 T.L.R. 652; 48 S.J. 639 3–037
Mclnerny v. Lloyds Bank Ltd [1974] 1 Lloyd's Rep. 246 . . . . 12–013, 23–052
Macintosh v. Hayden (1826) Ry. & M. 362 22–114
—— v. Trotter (1838) 3 M. & W. 184 1–095
M'lvor v. Michie [1953] S.L.T. (Sh.Ct.) 53 11–019
Mackay v. Dick (1881) 6 App.Cas. 251 . . . . . . 1–051, 8–040, 10–025, 10–039, 16–023, 21–032
Mackender v. Feldia [1967] 2 Q.B. 590; [1967] 2 W.L.R. 119; [1966] 3 All E.R. 847; [1966] 2 Lloyd's Rep. 449; 110 S.J. 811, CA 25–081, 25–083, 25–119
McKenny v. Drummond and Dvoretsky (1926) 29 W.A.R. 6 17–067
Mackenzie v. Royal Bank of Canada [1934] A.C. 468 10–009
McKeown v. Cavalier Yachts 91988) 13 N.S.W.L.R. 303 5–149
Mackersy v. Ramsays, Bonars & Co. (1843) 9 Cl. & Fin. 818 . . . . 22–088, 22–092
Mackinnon v. Donaldson, Lufkin & Jenrette Securities Corporation [1986] Ch. 482; [1986] 2 W.L.R. 453; (1985) 130 S.J. 224; [1986] 1 All E.R. 653; [1987] E.C.C. 139; [1986] F.L.R. 225; (1986) 83 L.S.Gaz. 1226 22–013
Macklin v. Newbury Sanitary Laundry (1919) 63 S.J. 337 . . . . 16–074, 17–018
Maclaine v. Gatty [1921] 1 A.C. 376 9–051
M'Laren's Trustee v. Argylls Ltd 1915 S.L.T. 241 . . . . 5–021, 9–030
McLay & Co. v. Perry & Co. (1881) 44 L.T. 152 8–056
Maclean v. Dunn and Watkins (1828) 4 Bing. 722; 1 Moo. & P. 761; 130 E.R.947; (1826) L.J. (o.s.) C.P. 184 . . . . 15–120, 15–127, 16–001, 16–074
MacLean (R.G.) Ltd v. Canada Vickers Ltd (1971) 5 D.L.R. (3d) 535 . . . . . . 13–036, 13–051
Macleod v. Kerr 1965 S.C. 253; 1965 S.L.T. 358 . . . . 7–021, 7–024
McLeod Savings and Credit Union Ltd v. Perrett [1978] 6 W.W.R. 178 22–045
McManus v. Cooke (1887) 35 Ch.D. 681; 56 L.J.Ch. 662; 56 L.T. 900; 51 J.P. 708; 35 W.R. 754; 3 T.L.R. 662 1–097
—— v. Eastern Ford Sales Ltd (1981) 128 D.L.R. 246 . . . . 7–009, 7–016, 7–038
McManus v. Fortescue [1907] 2 K.B. 1; 76 L.J.K.B. 393; 96 L.T. 444; 23 T.L.R. 392; 51 S.J. 245 2–006
McMaster & Co. v. Cox, McEwen & Co. 1921 S.C. (H.L.) 24; 58 Sc.L.R. 70 . . . . 6–046, 6–055, 18–310, 18–335, 20–071
Macmillan Inc. v. Bishopsgate Investment Trust Plc (No.3) [1996] 1 W.L.R. 387; [1996] 1 All E.R. 585; [1996] B.C.C. 453; (1995) 139 S.J.L.B.225; *The Times*, November 7, 1995, CA; affirming [1995] 1 W.L.R. 978; [1995] 3 All E.R. 747, Ch D. 25–077, 25–122
Macnee v. Gorst (1867) L.R. 4 Eq. 315; 15 W.R. 1197 7–051
McNeill v. Assoc. Car Markets Ltd (1962) 35 D.L.R. (2d) 581 . . . . 4–006, 4–010
McPherson v. Temiskaming Lumber Co. Ltd [1913] A.C. 145; 82 L.J.P.C. 113; 107 L.T. 664; 29 T.L.R. 80 7–113
McPherson, Thom. Kettle & Co. v. Dench Bros. [1921] V.L.R. 437 . . . . 5–027, 6–001
Macpherson, Train & Co. Ltd v. Ross (Howard) & Co. Ltd [1955] 1 W.L.R. 640; 99 S.J. 385; [1955] 2 All E.R. 445; [1955] 1 Lloyd's Rep. 518 . . . 18–269, 18–270, 18–271, 21–014, 21–030

Macpherson, Train & Co. Ltd v. Milhem (J.) & Sons (No.2) [1955] 2 Lloyd's Rep. 396 .... 18–270, 18–271
McRae v. Bandy 115 So. 2d 479 (1959) 25–127
—— v. Commonwealth Disposals Commission (1951) 84 C.L.R. 377 .... 1–123, 1–130, 1–131, 1–132, 1–133, 17–070
MacRobertson Miller Airline Services v. Commissioner of State Taxation (W.A.) (1975) 133 C.L.R. 125 .... 13–017, 13–064, 14–077
Mactavish's Judicial Factor v. Michael's Trustees, 1912 & S.C. 425 22–133
McVicar v. Herman (1958) 13 D.L.R. 419 7–009
Madeline, The. *See* Cheikh Boutros Selim El-Khoury v. Ceylon Shipping Lines.
Madell v. Thomas & Co. [1891] 1 Q.B. 230; 60 L.J.Q.B. 227; 64 L.T. 9;39 W.R. 280; 7 T.L.R. 170 1–066
Magee v. Pennine Insurance Co. Ltd [1969] 2 Q.B. 507; [1969] 2 W.L.R. 1278; 113 S.J. 303; [1969] 2 All E.R. 891; [1969] 2 Lloyd's Rep. 378 3–022
Maheno, The [1977] 1 Lloyd's Rep. 81 ... 18–074, 18–153, 18–201, 21–073, 21–081, 21–083, 21–098
Mahkutai, The [1996] A.C. 650; [1996] 3 W.L.R. 1; [1996] 3 All E.R. 502 .... 14–064, 18–098, 18–150
Mahmoud and Ispahani, *Re* [1921] 2 K.B. 716 .... 3–028, 3–029, 3–030, 18–324
Mahoney v. Lindsay (1980) 55 A.L.J.R. 118 9–019
Mahonia Ltd v. JP Morgan Chase Bank (No.1) [2003] EWHC 1927; [2003] 2 Lloyd's Rep. 911, QBD 23–141, 25–119, 25–120
Mahonia Ltd v. JP Morgan Chase Bank (No.2); Mahonia Ltd v. West LB AG [2004] EWHC 1938, QBD 25–119
Mahony v. Kekule (1854) 14 C.B. 390 18–045
Maillard v. Duke of Argyle (1843) 6 M. & G. 40 9–031
Maine v. Lyons (1913) 15 C.L.R. 671 .... 5–043, 18–335
Maine Spinning Co. v. Sutcliffe & Co. (1917) 87 L.J.K.B. 382; 118 L.T. 351; 34 T.L.R. 154 .... 18–274, 18–294, 18–299, 19–047, 20–010, 20–015, 20–042, 20–102, 20–103
Mainprice v. Westley (1865) 6 B. & S. 420 2–005
Maitland v. Chartered Mercantile Bank (1869) 38 L.J.Ch. 363 23–063
Majid v. TMV Finance Ltd [1999] C.L.Y. 2448 7–091
Makin v. London Rice Mills Co. Ltd (1869) 20 L.J. 705; 17 W.R. 768 11–018
Malaney v. Union Transport Finance Ltd (1957) 75 Sh.Ct.Rep. 91, 1959 S.L.T. (Sh.Ct.) 37 4–006
Malas (Hamzeh) & Sons v. British Imex Industries Ltd [1958] 2 Q.B. 127; [1958] 2 W.L.R. 100; 102 S.J. 68; [1958] 1 All E.R. 262; [1957] 2 Lloyd's Rep. 549 ... 23–054, 23–136, 23–138, 23–139, 23–142, 23–148
Malcolm v. Cross, (1898) 35 Sc.L.R. 794 (1898) 25 R. (Ct. of Sess.) 1089 10–020
Male v. Roberts (1800) 3 Esp. 163 25–084
Malfroot v. Noxal Ltd (1935) 51 T.L.R. 551 14–060
Malik v. B.C.C.I. [1995] 3 All E.R. 545; [1995] I.R.L.R. 375; 145 N.L.J. 593; *The Times*, April 12, 1995; *The Independent*, March 17, 1995, C.A 16–047
Malik v. Narodni Banka Ceskoslovenska, 176 L.T. 136; [1946] 2 All E.R. 663 .... 9–047, 25–161
Malik & Co. v. Central European Trading Agency Ltd [1974] 2 Lloyd's Rep. 279 .... 6–047, 8–091, 18–320, 18–321, 18–341, 18–345
Malmberg v. H. & J. Evans & Co. (1924) 41 T.L.R. 38; 30 Com.Cas. 107 .... 19–008, 19–043, 19–047, 23–230
Malone v. Metropolitan Police Commissioner [1979] Ch. 344; [1979] 2 W.L.R. 700; (1979) 69 Cr.App.R. 168; *sub nom.* Malone v. Commissioner of Police for Metropolis (1979) 123 S.J. 303; *sub nom.* Malone v. Commissioner of Police of the Metropolis (No. 2) [1979] 2 All E.R. 620 .... 1–071, 1–080,
Malozzi v. Carapelli SpA [1976] 1 Lloyd's Rep. 407 .... 19–009, 19–088, 19–190
Maltass v. Siddle (1859) 28 L.J.C.P. 257; 6 C.B. (N.S.) 494; 33 L.T. (O.S.) 124; 5 Jur. (N.S.) 1169; 7 W.R. 449; 141 E.R. 549 22–132
Malzy v. Eichholz [1916] 2 K.B. 308; 85 L.J.K.B. 1132; 115 L.T. 9; 32 T.L.R. 506; 60 S.J. 511 4–026
Mamidoil-Jetoil Green Petroleum Co. SA v. Okta Crude Oil Refinery (No.1) [2001] E.W.C.A. Civ 406; [2001] 2 All E.R. (Comm) 193; [2001] 2 Lloyd's Rep. 76, CA; reversing [2000] 1 Lloyd's Rep. 554, QBD (Comm Ct) 2–017

Mamidoil-Jetoil Greek Petroleum Co SA v. Okta Crude Oil Refinery AD (No.3); *sub nom.* Okta Crude Oil Refinery AD v. Mamidoil-Jetoil Greek Petroleum Co SA (No.3); Okta Crude Oil Refinery AD v. Moil-Coal Trading Co Ltd (No.3) [2003] EWCA Civ 1031; [2003] 2 All E.R. (Comm) 640; [2003] 2 Lloyd's Rep. 635, CA 8–091, 8–092, 8–101
Man (E.D. & F.) Ltd v. Nigerian Sweets & Confectionery Co. Ltd [1977]2 Lloyd's Rep. 50 .... 15–021, 16–017
Management Corporation Strata Title Plan No. 1166 v. Chubb Singapore Pte. Ltd [1999] 3 S.L.R. 540 1–044
Manasy Pinerro v. Chase Manhatten Bank (1980) 433 N.Y.S. 2d. 868 22–015
Manatee Towing Co. v. Oceanbulk Maritime SA [1999] 2 All E.R. (Comm) 306 2–011
Manbré Saccharin Co. v. Corn Products Co. [1919] 1 K.B. 198; 120 L.T. 113; *sub nom.* Mambré Saccharine Co. v. Corn Product's Co., 88 L.J.K.B. 402; 35 T.L.R. 94 11–018, 18–295, 19–001, 19–002, 19–008, 19–037, 19–042, 19–048, 19–059, 19–072, 19–080, 19–082, 19–083, 19–166
Manchester Liners Ltd v. Rea Ltd [1912] 2 A.C. 74 .... 11–055, 11–057, 11–059
Manchester, Sheffield & Lincolnshire Railway v. North Central Wagon Co. (1888) 13 App.Cas. 554; 58 L.J.Ch. 219; 59 L.T. 730; 37 W.R. 305; 4 T.L.R. 728 1–066
Manchester Ship Canal Co. v. Horlock [1914] 2 Ch. 199; 83 L.J.Ch. 637; 111 L.T. 260; 30 T.L.R. 500; 58 S.J. 533; 12 Asp.M.L.C. 516 1–082
Manchester Trust v. Furness [1895] 2 Q.B. 539; 73 L.T. 110; 44 W.R. 178; 8 Asp.M.L.C. 57; 1 Com.Cas. 39; 14 R. 739 .... 5–034, 7–047
Manders v. Williams (1849) 4 Exch. 339; 18 L.J.Ex. 437; 13 L.T. (o.s.) 325; 154 E.R. 1242 .... 1–061, 5–041
Mangles v. Dixon (1852) 3 H.L.C. 702 .... 7–012, 18–097
Manifatture Tessile Laniera Wooltex v. J.B. Ashley Ltd [1979] 2 Lloyd's Rep. 28 ... 12–055
Mann, George & Co. v. Brown (James and Alexander) (1971) 10 L.L.R. 221 ...... 25–119, 25–175
Manners v. Pearson & Son [1898] 1 Ch. 581 25–191
Mannesman Handel A.G. v. Kaunlaran Shipping Corp. [1993] 1 Lloyd's Rep. 89 23–202
Manton v. Moore (1796) 7 T.R. 67 8–011
Mantovani v. Carapelli SpA (1979) 123 S.J. 568; [1980] 1 Lloyd's Rep.375 .... 12–019, 19–148, 20–027, 20–106
Maple Flock Co. Ltd v. Universal Furniture Products Co. Ltd [1934] 1 K.B. 148; [1933] All E.R.Rep. 15; 103 L.J.K.B. 513; 150 L.T. 69; 50 T.L.R. 58; 39 Com.Cas. 89 .... 8–075, 8–078, 8–080, 8–081, 12–019, 12–032
Maran Road Saw Mill v. Austin Taylor & Co. Ltd [1975] 1 Lloyd's Rep. 156 ...... 23–098, 23–101
Marca v. Bertholet [1928] 2 D.L.R. 691; [1928] 1 W.W.R. 843; 37 Man.R. 307 5–032
Marcel (J.) (Furriers) Ltd v. Tapper [1953] 1 W.L.R. 49; 97 S.J. 10; [1953] 1 All E.R. 15 1–047
Marc Rich & Co. A.G. v. Bishop Rock Marine Co. Ltd (The Nicholas H.) [1996] 1 A.C. 211 .... 18–045, 18–149
—— v. Soc. Italiana Impianti SpA (The Atlantic Emperor) [1989] 1 Lloyd's Rep. 548; [1991] I.L. Pr. 562, CA; affirming [1989] E.C.C. 198; *The Times*, November 14, 1988; *The Financial Times*, November 9, 1988, QBD 25–079
Marconi Communications International Ltd v. PT Pan Indonesia Bank TBK; *sub nom.* Marconi Communications International Ltd v. PT Pan Indonesian Bank Ltd [2005] EWCA Civ 422; [2005] 2 All E.R. (Comm) 325; *The Times*, May 18, 2005, CA 25–073, 25–076, 25–161
Mardorf Peach & Co. Ltd v. Attica Sea Carriers Corporation of Liberia (The Laconia) [1977] A.C. 850; [1977] 2 W.L.R. 286; (1977) 121 S.J. 134; [1977] 1 All E.R. 545; [1977] 1 Lloyd's Rep. 315 .... 9–037, 9–054, 16–037, 22–118
Maredalanto Compania Naviera SA v. Bergbau-Handel G.m.b.H. (The Mihalis Angelos) [1971] 1 Q.B. 164; [1970] 3 W.L.R. 601; 114 S.J. 548; [1970] 3 All E.R. 125, [1970] 2 Lloyd's Rep. 43 ..... 8–077, 9–010, 9–016, 9–020, 10–034, 10–037, 16–049, 17–002, 17–014, 18–235, 19–165, 19–151, 20–053
Margarine Union GmbH v. Cambay Prince Steamship Co. Ltd (The Wear Breeze) [1969] 1 Q.B. 219; [1967] 3 W.L.R. 1569; 111 S.J. 943; [1967] 3 All E.R. 775; [1967] 2 Lloyd's Rep. 315 .... 5–009, 8–013, 18–120, 18–149, 18–171, 18–174, 18–194, 18–286, 18–287, 18–291, 18–292, 18–302, 18–303, 18–305, 19–098

Margaronis Navigation Agency Ltd v. Peabody (Henry W.) & Co. of London Ltd [1965] 2 Q.B. 430; [1964] 3 W.L.R. 873; 108 S.J. 562; [1964] 3 All E.R. 333; [1964] 2 Lloyd's Rep. 153 .... 8–050, 11–018
Margetson v. Wright (1831) 7 Bing. 603 10–019
Margolin v. Wright Property Ltd [1959] Arg.L.R. 988 4–006
Mariannina, The *See* Astro Venturoso Compania Naviera v. Hellenic Shipyards SA; Mariannina, The.
Marifortuna Naviera SA v. Govt. of Ceylon [1970] 1 Lloyd's Rep. 247 8–099
Marimpex v. Mineralöl Handelsgesellshaft m.b.H. v. Louis Dreyfus & Cie Mineralöl G.m.b.H. [1995] 1 Lloyd's Rep. 167 .... 11–016, 11–044, 18–209, 18–265, 19–187
Marine Midland Grace Trust Co. v. Banco del Pais SA 261 F. Supp. 884 (1966) 23–026 23–127, 23–141, 23–156, 23–206
Marino Industries Corporation v. Chase Manhattan Bank, 686 F. 2d.112 (1982) 23–235
Maritime National Fish Ltd v. Ocean Trawlers Ltd [1935] A.C. 524; 104 L.J.P.C. 88; 153 L.T. 425; 79 S.J. 320; 18 Asp.M.L.C. 551 .... 6–034, 6–052, 18–304
Mark v. Mark; *sub nom.* Marks v. Marks (Divorce: Jurisdiction) [2005] UKHL 42; [2006] 1 A.C. 98; [2005] 3 W.L.R. 111; [2005] 3 All E.R. 912; [2005] 2 F.L.R. 1193; [2005] 2 F.C.R. 467; [2005] I.N.L.R. 614; [2005] W.T.L.R. 1223; [2005] Fam. Law 857; (2005) 102(28) L.S.G. 32; *The Times*, July 5, 2005, HL 25–056
Maritrans (A.B.) v. Comet Shipping Co. Ltd [1985] 1 Lloyd's Rep. 568 6–028
Markey v. Brunson 286 F. 893 (1923) 25–169
Markham v. Paget [1908] 1 Ch. 697; 77 L.J.Ch. 451; 98 L.T. 605; 24 T.L.R. 426 4–026
Marks v. Hunt Bros. (Sydney) Property Ltd [1958] S.R. 380 .... 11–011, 11–012, 11–019
Markt & Co. Ltd v. Knight SS. Co. Ltd; Sale & Frazer v. Knight SS. Co. [1910] 2 K.B. 1021; 79 L.J.K.B. 939; 103 L.T. 369; 11 Asp.M.L.C. 460 14–103
Marlborough Hill, The [1921] 1 A.C. 444; 90 L.J.P.C. 87; 124 L.T. 645; 37 T.L.R. 190; 15 Asp.M.L.C. 163; 26 Com.Cas. 121; 5 Lloyd L.R. 362 .... 18–027, 18–079
Marleasing SA v. La Comercial International de Aliementacion SA (C–106/89) [1992] C.M.L.R. 305; [1993] B.C.C. 421, E.C.J. 1–005, 25–109
Marleau v. People's Gas Supply Co. [1940] 4 D.L.R. 433 1–087
Marles v. Philip Trant & Sons Ltd [1954] 1 Q.B. 29; [1953] 2 W.L.R. 564; 97 S.J. 189; [1953] 1 All E.R. 651 .... 3–028, 3–029, 3–032, 14–091, 17–065
Marlow v. Pitfeild (1719) 1 P. Wms. 558 2–035
Maronier v. Larmer [2002] EWCA Civ 774; [2003] Q.B. 620; [2002] 3 W.L.R. 1060; [2003] 3 All E.R. 848; [2003] 1 All E.R. (Comm) 225; [2002] C.L.C. 1281; [2002] I.L.Pr. 39; (2002) 99(28) L.S.G. 30; (2002) 146 S.J.L.B. 161; *The Times*, June 13, CA 25–043
Marrache v. Ashton [1943] A.C. 311; [1943] 1 All E.R. 276; 112 L.J.P.C. 13; 59 T.L.R. 142; 87 S.J. 174 .... 25–166, 25–167
Marreco v. Richardson [1908] 2 K.B. 584; [1908–10] All E.R. 655; 77 L.J.K.B. 859; 99 L.T. 486; 24 T.L.R. 624; 52 S.J. 516 9–030
Marsh v. Hughes-Hallett (1900) 16 T.L.R. 376 5–041
—— v. Jones (1889) 40 Ch.D. 563; 60 L.T. 610 16–008
—— v. Pedder (1815) 4 Camp. 257 9–031
Marshall v. Goulston Discount (Northern) Ltd [1967] Ch. 72; [1966] 3 W.L.R. 599; 110 S.J. 604; [1966] 3 All E.R. 994 7–092
—— v. Green (1875) 1 C.P.D. 35; 45 L.J.Q.B. 153; 33, L.T. 404; 24 W.R. 175 ...... 1–093, 1–099, 8–012, 8–022
Marshall & Co. v. Nicoll & Son 1919 S.C. 244; 1919 S.C. 244; 56 S.L.R. 615 .... 16–065, 16–066, 16–067
Marshall (W.E.) & Co. v. Lewis and Peat (Rubber) Ltd [1963] 1 Lloyd's Rep. 562 .. 12–063, 13–033, 13–038, 13–052
Marshall Knott & Barker Ltd v. Arcos Ltd v. Arcos Ltd (1933) 44 Ll.L.Rep. 384 ... 19–004, 19–031
Marson v. Short (1835) 2 Bing (N.S.) 118; Scott 243; 1 Hodg. 260; 4 L.J.C.P. 270; 132 E.R. 47 1–081
Marston v. Phillips (1863) 3 New Rep. 35; 9 L.T. 289; 12 W.R. 8 1–072
Marston Excelsior Ltd v. Arbuckle and Smith & Co. Ltd 115 S.J. 654; [1971] 2 Lloyd's Rep. 306 21–097
Marten v. Whale [1917] 2 K.B. 480; L.J.K.B. 1305; 117 L.T. 137; 33 T.L.R. 330 ..... 1–051, 7–068, 7–073, 7–074

Martin v. Duffy [1985] Northern Ireland Judgment Bulletin 80 7–081
—— v. Gale [1876] 4 Ch.D. 428; 46 L.J.Ch. 84; 36 L.T. 357; 25 W.R. 406 2–035
—— v. Hogan (1917) 24 C.L.R. 234 .... 16–028, 20–009, 20–123
—— v. Puttick [1968] 2 Q.B. 82; [1967] 2 W.L.R. 1131; 131 J.P. 286; 111 S.J. 131; [1967] 1 All E.R. 899; 51 Cr.App.R. 272 2–002
—— v. Reid (1862) 11 C.B. 730; 31 L.J.C.P. 126; 5 L.T. 727; 142 E.R. 982 7–110
—— v. Thorn Ltd [1978] W.A.R. 10 14–061
Martin (John) of London Ltd v. Taylor (A.E) & Co. Ltd [1953] 2 Lloyd's Rep. 589 .... 18–172, 19–042, 19–048, 19–055, 19–216
Martin (W.H.) Ltd v. Feldbinder Spezialfahrzeugwerke GmbH [1998] I.L.Pr. 794, CA 25–060
Martin-Marietta Corp. v. Bendix Corp. 690 F. 2d 558 (1982) 23–151
Martindale v. Smith (1841) 1 Q.B. 389 .... 9–051, 17–106
Martineau v. Kitching (1872) L.R. 7 Q.B. 436; 41 L.J.Q.B. 227; 26 L.T. 836; 20 W.R. 769 .... 2–045, 5–027, 5–039, 5–084, 6–001, 6–002, 6–003, 6–023, 20–080
Martovana v. Morley [1958] C.L.Y. 2943 25–119
Marubeni Hong Kong and South China Ltd v. Mongolia (Jurisdiction); *sub nom.* Marubeni Hong Kong and South China Ltd v. Ministry of Finance of Mongolia [2002] 2 All E.R. (Comm) 873; *Independent*, November 25, 2002 (C.S), QBD 25–020, 25–030, 25–073, 25–082
Marvin v. Wallace (1856) 25 L.J.Q.B. 369; 25 L.J.Q.B. 369; 27 L.T. (o.s.) 182; 2 Jur. (n.s.) 689; 4 W.R. 611; 119 E.R. 1035 8–009
Marzetti v. Williams (1830) 1 B. & Ad. 415; 1 Tyr. 77n; 9 L.J. (o.s.) K.B. 42 17–004
Mash and Murrell Ltd v. Emanuel (Joseph I.) Ltd [1962] 1 W.L.R. 16; 105 S.J. 1007; [1962] 1 All E.R. 77; [1961] 2 Lloyd's Rep. 326 ...... 6–019, 6–022, 11–040, 11–067, 18–113, 18–255, 18–256, 18–274
Mason v. Burningham [1949] 2 K.B. 545; [1949] L.J.R. 1430; 65 T.L.R. 466; 93 S.J. 496; [1949] 2 All E.R. 134 .... 4–026, 4–029, 12–067, 17–090
—— v. Clarke [1955] A.C. 778; [1955] 2 W.L.R. 853; 99 S.J. 274; [1955] 1 All E.R. 914 .... 3–029, 3–032
—— v. Lickbarrow (1790) 1 Hy.Bl. 357; (1793) 6 East. 21n; 4 Bro.Parl.Cas. 57 7–008
—— v. Morley (1865) 34 Beav. 471; 34 L.J.Ch. 422; 12 L.T. 414 (1865) 11 Jur. 459; 13 W.R. 669; 55 E.R. 717 15–055
—— v. Williams and Williams Ltd [1955] 1 W.L.R. 549; 99 S.J. 338; [1955] 1 All E.R. 808 14–061
Mason County Medical Association v. Knebel 563 F. 2d 256 (1977) 23–151
Massey v. Sladen (1868) L.R. 4 Ex. 13; 38 L.J.Ex. 34 .... 7–002, 8–036, 9–059
Masterfoods v. H.B. Ice Cream [2001] All E.R. (EC) 130; [2001] 4 C.M.L.R. 14; *The Times*, February 2, 2001, ECJ 3–040
Matania v. National Provincial Bank Ltd [1936] 2 All E.R. 633; 106 L.J.K.B. 133; 155 L.T. 74; 80 S.J. 532 4–026
Matsoukis v. Priestman & Co. [1915] 1 K.B. 681; 84 L.J.K.B. 967; 113 L.J.K.B. 967; 113 L.T. 48; 113 Asp.M.L.C. 68; 20 Com.Cas. 252 .... 8–095, 8–099
Matsushita Electric Corp. of America v. S.S. Aegis Spirit 414 F.Supp. 894 (1976) [1977] 1 Lloyd's Rep. 894 21–086
Matthew, *Re* (1884) 12 Q.B.D. 506; 51 L.T. 179; 32 W.R. 813; 1 Morr. 46 9–030
Matthews v. Kuwait Bechtel Corporation [1959] 2 Q.B. 57; [1959] 2 W.L.R. 702; 103 S.J. 393; [1959] 2 All E.R. 345 17–075
Maudslay, Sons & Field, Maudslay v. Maudslay, Sons of Field *Re* [1900] Ch. 602; 69 L.J.Ch. 347; 82 L.T. 378; 48 W.R. 568; 16 T.L.R. 228; 8 Mans. 38 25–144
Maurice Desgagnes, The [1977] 1 Lloyd's Rep. 290 21–081
Maurice O'Meara Co. v. National Park Bank of New York 146 N.E. 636 (1925) 23–141, 23–150, 23–171
Mauroux v. Soc. Com. Abel Pereira da Fonseca S.A.R.L. [1972] 1 W.L.R. 962; [1972] 2 All E.R. 1085; 116 S.J. 392, Ch D 25–073
Maxwell v. Brain (1864) 10 L.T. 301; 10 Jur. (n.s.) 777; 12 W.R. 688 22–124
May v. Chapman (1847) 16 M. & W. 355 7–047
May & Butcher Ltd v. The King [1934] 2 K.B. 17n 2–017, 2–045
Mayfield v. Wadsley (1824) 3 B. & C. 357; 5 Dav. & Ry. K.B. 224; 3 L.J. (o.s.) K.B. 31; 107 E.R. 766 1–094
Mayhew Foods Ltd v. Overseas Containers Ltd [1984] 2 L.M.C.Q.L. 202; [1984] 1 Lloyd's Rep. 317; (1983) 133 New L.J. 1103 .... 19–027, 21–076, 21–104

Maynegrain Property Ltd v. Compafina Bank [1982] 2 N.S.W.L.R. 141 .... 1–119, 5–065, 7–085, 18–174, 18–193
Mayson v. Clouet [1924] A.C. 980; 93 L.J.P.C. 237; 131 L.T. 645; 40 T.L.R. 678 16–040
Mead, *Re* [1916] 2 I.R. 285 2–031
Mead v. S.E. Railway Co. (1870) 18 W.R. 735 5–009
Mears v. L. & S.W. Railway (1862) 11 C.B. 850; 31 L.J.C.P. 220; 6 L.T. 190 .... 5–010, 17–105
Measures Bros. Ltd v. Measures [1910] 2 Ch. 248 8–079
Meb Export Co. Inc. v. National City Bank of New York, 131 N.Y.L.J. 4 (1954) ... 23–079, 23–081, 23–082
Mecca, The [1968] P. 95 16–008
Mechan & Sons Ltd v. Bow, M'Lachlan & Co. Ltd 1910 S.C. 758; 47 Sc.L.R. 650; [1910] 1 S.L.T. 406 12–047
Mechan & Sons Ltd v. N.E. Railway 1911 S.C. 1348; 48 Sc.L.R. 987 .... 15–076, 15–078, 15–080, 15–084, 15–088
Mechanical Horse (Australasia) Property Ltd v. Broken Hill Council (1941) 41 S.R. 135 13–031
Mechans Ltd v. Highland Marine Charters Ltd 1964 S.C. 48 .... 12–045, 13–051
Mediana, The [1900] A.C. 113; 69 L.J.P. 35; 82 L.T. 95; 48 W.R. 398; 16 T.L.R. 194; 44 S.J. 259; 9 Asp.M.L.C. 41 17–004
Medina v. Stoughton (1700) 1 Salk, 210; Holt K.B. 208; 1 Ld. Raym. 593; 91 E.R. 188 .... 4–001, 10–016
Mediterranean and Eastern Export Co. Ltd v. Fortress Fabrics (Manchester) Ltd [1948] W.N. 244; [1948] L.J.R. 1536; 64 T.L.R. 337; 92 S.J. 362; [1948] 2 All E.R. 186; 81 Ll.L.Rep. 401 .... 16–004, 19–210
Medway Oil and Storage Ltd v. Silica Gel Cpn. (1928) 33 Com.Cas. 195 11–060
Meggy v. Imperial Discount Co. (1878) 3 Q.B.D. 711; 48 L.J.Q.B. 54; 38 L.T. 309; 26 W.R. 342 7–009
Meher v. Dresser (1864) 16 C.B. 646 25–191
Mehta v. Sutton (1913) 109 L.T. 529; 58 S.J. 29; 30 T.L.R. 17 .... 7–032, 7–037, 7–043, 25–131, 25–133
Melachrino v. Nickoll and Knight [1920] 1 K.B. 693; 89 L.J.K.B. 906, 122 L.T. 545; 36 T.L.R. 143; 25 Com.Cas. 103 ...... 16–056, 16–071, 16–072, 16–081, 17–008, 17–009, 17–014, 17–015, 19–179
Melbourn, *ex p.* (1870) 6 Ch.App. 64; 40 L.J. Bey. 25; 23 L.T. 578; 19 W.R. 83 ..... 25–188, 25–174
Mellersh v. Rippen (1852) 7 Exch. 578; 21 L.J.Ex. 222; 16 Jur. 366 22–124
Melluish (Inspector of Taxes) v. B.M.I. (No. 3) Ltd [1996] 1 A.C. 454; [1995] 3 W.L.R. 630; [1995] 4 All E.R. 453; [1995] S.T.C. 964; (1995) 139 S.J.L.B. 220 (1995) 92 (40) L.S.Gaz. 22; [1995] E.G.C.S. 150; *The Times*, October 16, 1995; *The Independent*, November 6, 1995 (C.S.), HL 1–005, 1–095
Mellor v. Street (1866) 15 L.T. 223 .... 12–063, 12–065
Menashe Business Mercantile Ltd v. William Hill Organisation Ltd [2002] EWCA Civ 1702; [2003] 1 W.L.R. 1462; [2003] 1 All E.R. 279; [2003] R.P.C. 31; (2003) 26(3) I.P.D. 26013; (2003) 100(5) L.S.G. 32; *The Times*, November 30, 2002, CA 25–037, 25–053
Mendala III Transport v. Total Transport Corp., Total International and Addax; Wilomi Tanana, The [1993] 2 Lloyd's Rep. 41 19–196
Mendelson-Zeller Co. Inc. v. T. & C. Providores Pty. Ltd [1981] 1 N.S.W.L.R. 366 .... 25–009, 25–010, 25–013, 25–170
Mendelssohn v. Normand Ltd [1970] 1 Q.B. 177; [1969] 3 W.L.R. 139; (1969) 113 S.J. 263; [1969] 2 All E.R. 1215 .... 10–012, 13–013, 13–0134, 13–016, 13–024, 13–046
Meng Leong Development Property Ltd v. Jip Hong Trading Co. Property Ltd [1985] A.C. 511; [1984] 3 W.L.R. 1263; (1984) 128 S.J. 852; [1985] 1 All E.R. 120; (1984) 81 L.S.Gaz. 3336 17–094
Mercantile Bank of India Ltd v. Central Bank of India Ltd [1938] A.C. 287 .... 7–008, 7–011, 7–013, 7–016
Mercantile Credit Ltd v. F.C. Upton & Sons Property Ltd (1974) 47 A.L.J.R. 301 ... 7–059
—— v. Hamblin [1965] 2 Q.B. 242; [1964] 3 W.L.R. 798; 108 S.J. 674; [1964] 3 All E.R. 592 .... 1–054, 7–008, 7–011, 7–015, 7–016, 7–017, 7–018
—— v. Waugh (1978) 32 Hire Trading (No.2) 16 .... 7–046, 7–099

Mercantile-Safe Deposits and Trust Co. v. Baltimore County, 562, A. 2d 591 (Md. 1987) 23–245
Mercantile Union Guarantee Corp. v. Ball [1937] 2 K.B. 498; [1937] 3 All E.R. 1; 106 L.J.K.B. 621; 157 L.T. 162; 53 T.L.R. 734; 81 S.J. 478 .... 2–031, 2–033
—— v. Wheatley [1938] 1 K.B. 490; [1937] 4 All E.R. 713; 107 L.J.K.B. 158; 158 L.T. 414; 54 T.L.R. 151; 81 S.J. 1002 .... 4–005, 4–006
Mercer v. Craven Grain Storage Ltd [1994] C.L.C. 328 H.L. 1–057, 1–059, 5–113, 5–148
Merchant Banking Co. of London v. Phoenix Bessemer Steel Co. (1877) 5 Ch.D. 205; 46 L.J.Ch. 418; 36 L.T. 395; 25 W.R. 457 ..... 8–013, 8–086, 15–042, 15–073, 15–093, 18–006, 18–075, 18–193
Merchant Shipping Co. Ltd. The v. Armitage (1873) L.R. 9 Q.B. 99; 43 L.J.Q.B. 24; 29 L.T. 809; 2 Asp.M.L.C. 185 16–026
Meredith, *Re* (1930) C.B.R. 405 .... 25–183, 25–185
Meredith Jones, (A.) & Co. Ltd v. Vangemar Shipping Co. Ltd (The Apostolis) (No.2) [2000] 2 Lloyd's Rep. 337; [2000] C.L.C. 1488, CA; reversing [1999] 2 Lloyd's Rep. 292, QBD (Comm Ct) 18–047
Meridian Global Funds Management Asia Ltd v. Securities Commission [1995] 2 A.C. 500; [1995] 3 W.L.R. 413; [1995] 3 All E.R. 918; [1995] B.C.C. 942; [1995] 2 B.C.L.C. 116; (1995) 92(28) L.S.G. 39; (1995) 139 S.J.L.B. 152; *The Times*, June 29, 1995, PC (NZ) 18–038
Meridien BIAO Bank GmbH v. Bank of New York [1997] 1 Lloyd's Rep. 437; [1997] l.L.Pr. 155, CA 25–191
Merit Shipping Co. Inc. v. T.K. Boesen A/S (The Goodpal) [2000] 1 Lloyd's Rep. 638; [2000] C.L.C. 628, QBD (Comm Ct) 18–014
Merry v. Green (1841) 7 M. & W. 623 1–135
Mersey Steel and Iron Co. v. Naylor Benzon & Co. (1882) 9 Q.B.D. 648; (1884), 9 App.Cas. 434 .... 7–028, 8–075, 8–078, 8–080, 8–085, 9–050
Mertens (Edm. J.M.) & Co. P.V.B.A. v. Veevoeder Import Export Vimex B.V. [1979] 2 Lloyd's Rep. 372 .... 12–037, 19–150, 19–181
Mesnard v. Aldridge (1801) 3 Esp. 271 13–037
Mess v. Duffus & Co. (1901) 6 Com.Cas. 165 .... 3–048, 8–086, 15–025, 15–037, 15–108
Messenger v. Greene [1937] 2 D.L.R. 26; 11 M.P.R. 326 .... 1–035, 1–038
Messers Ltd v. Morrison's Export Co. [1939] 1 All E.R. 92; 55 T.L.R. 245; 83 S.J. 75 18–272
Messier-Dowty Ltd v. Sabena SA [2000] 1 W.L.R. 2040; [2001] 1 All E.R. 275; [2000] 1 All E.R. (Comm) 833; [2000] 1 Lloyd's Rep. 428; [2000] C.P. Rep. 72; [2000] C.L.C. 889; [2001] 1 L.Pr. 5; (2000) 97(10) L.S.G. 36; (2000) 144 S.J.L.B. 124; *The Times*, March 14, 2000; *The Independent*, February 29, 2000, CA 16–092, 17–104
Metaalhaulel J.A. Magnus B.V. v. Ardfields Transport Ltd [1988] 1 Lloyd's Rep. 197; [1987] 2 F.T.L.R. 319, D.C. 25–193
Metal Box Co. Ltd v. Currys Ltd [1988] 1 W.L.R. 175; (1988) 132 S.J. 52; [1988] 1 All E.R. 341; (1987) 54 L.S.Gaz. 3657 16–008
Metal Scrap Trade Corp. v. Kate Shipping Co. (No. 2); Gladys, The [1994] 2 Lloyd's Rep. 402 2–017
Metals Ltd v. Diamond [1930] 3 D.L.R. 886 12–051
Metamorphosis, The, *See* Koninklijke Zwavelzuurfabrieken V/H Ketjen N.V. v. D.A. and D.D. Psychoyos, Piraeus, (The Metamorphosis.).
—— v. Richardson (1852) 11 C.B. 1011 22–124
Metro Meat Ltd v. Fares Rural Co. Property Ltd [1985] 2 Lloyd's Rep. 13 8–078
Metro-SB-Grossmarkte GmbH & K.G. v. E.G. Commission (No. 26/76) [1977] E.C.R. 1875; [1978] 2 C.M.L.R. 1; [1978] F.S.R. 400; [1976] E.L.R. 1353 3–041
Metropolitan Electric Supply Co. Ltd v. Ginder [1901] 2 Ch. 799; 70 L.J.Ch. 862; 82 L.T. 818; 65 J.P. 519; 49 W.R. 508; 17 T.L.R. 435; 45 S.J. 467 .... 16–093, 17–103
Metropolitan Police Commissioner v. Charles. *See* R. v. Charles.
Metropolitan Water Board v. Dick, Kerr & Co. Ltd [1918] A.C. 119 .. 6–045, 6–050, 6–056, 6–050, 8–070
Meux v. G.E. Railway [1895] 2 Q.B. 387; [1895–9] All E.R. 710; 64 L.J.Q.B. 657; 73 L.T. 247; 59 J.P. 662; 43 W.R. 680; 11 T.L.R. 517; 39 S.J. 654; 14 R. 620 5–010
Meyer v. Everth (1814) 4 Camp. 22; 171 E.R. 8 11–076
—— v. Sharpe (1813) 3 Taunt. 74; 2 Rose 124 .... 18–004, 18–016, 18–063, 18–086, 18–216

Meyer v. Sullivan 131 P. 847 (1919) 20–015, 20–016
Meyer & Co. Ltd v. Sze Hai Tong Banking and Insurance Co. Ltd [1913] A.C. 847; 83 L.J.P.C. 103; 109 L.T. 691; 57 S.J. 700 22–118
Meyer (H.) & Co. v. Decroix (J.), Verley et Cie [1891] A.C. 520; 61 L.J.Q.B. 205; 65 L.T. 653; 40 W.R. 573 22–104
Meyerstein v. Barber; *sub nom.* Barber v. Meyerstein (1869–70) L.R. 4 H.L. 317, HL 188–080, 18–081
Michael v. Hart & Co. [1902] 1 K.B. 482; 71 L.J.K.B. 265; 86 L.T. 474; 50 W.R. 308; 18 T.L.R. 254 .... 9–018, 15–11
Michael Gerson (Leasing) Ltd v. Wilkinson [2001] Q.B. 514; [2000] 3 W.L.R. 1645; [2001] 1 All E.R. 148; [2000] 2 All E.R. (Comm) 890; [2000] C.L.C. 1720; (2000) 97(35) L.S.G. 37; *The Times*, September 12, 2000, CA 2–002, 7–074
Michel Freres SA v. Kilkenny Woollen Mills (1929) Ltd [1961] I.R. 157 18–268
Michelin Tyre Co. Ltd v. McFarlane (Glasgow) Ltd (1917) 55 Sc.L.R. 35, H.L. 1–049, 5–045, 5–147,
Microbeads A.G. v. Vinhurst Road Markings Ltd [1975] 1 W.L.R. 218; (1977) 119 S.J. 81; [1975] 1 All E.R. 529; *sub nom.* Microbeads A.G. and Ehrismann (Alfred) A.G. v. Vinhurst Road Markings [1975] 1 Lloyd's Rep. 375; [1976] R.P.C. 19 .... 4–025, 4–026, 4–027, 4–030
Mid-America Tire Inc. v. Ptz Trading Ltd 745 N.E. 2d 438 (Ohio, 2001) 23–139
Middleton, *Re* (1864) 3 De G.J. & Sm. 201; 33 L.J.Bcy. 36; 10 L.T. 82; 46 E.R. 614 5–135
Midland Bank v. Brown Shipley & Co. [1991] 2 All E.R. 690; [1991] 1 Lloyd's Rep. 576 .... 3–012, 22–027, 22–029
—— v. Eastcheap Dried Fruit Co. 106 S.J. 351; [1962] 1 Lloyd's Rep. 359 5–140
—— v. Reckitt [1933] A.C. 1; 102 L.J.K.B. 297; 148 L.T. 374; 48 T.L.R. 271; 76 S.J. 165; 37 Com.Cas. 202 22–075
—— v. Seymour [1955] 2 Lloyd's Rep. 147 .... 22–085, 22–115, 23–054, 23–115, 23–116, 23–117, 23–121, 23–126, 23–196, 23–206, 23–210, 23–215
Midland International Trade Services Ltd v. Sudairy, *Financial Times*, May 2, 1990 25–191
Mietz v. Intership Yachting Sneek BV (Case C–99/96) [1999] E.C.R. 1–2277; [1999] I.L.Pr. 541, ECJ 25–045
Miguel Mico (London) Ltd v. Widdop (H.) & Co. [1955] 1 Lloyd's Rep. 491 8–040
Mihalios Xilas, The, *See* China National Foreign Trade Transportation Corporation v. Evlogia Shipping Co. SA of Panama (The Mihalios Xilas).
Mihalis Angelos, The, *See* Maredelanto Companie Naviera SA v. Bergbau-Handel G.m.b.H.
Mildred, Goyeneche & Co. v. Maspons (1883) 8 App.Cas. 874 .... 7–053, 25–081
Miles, *ex p. Re* Isaacs (1885) 15 Q.B.D. 39; 54 L.J.Q.B. 556 .... 15–065, 15–069, 15–080
Miles v. New Zealand Alford Estate Co. (1886) 32 Ch.D. 266; 55 L.J.Ch. 801; 54 L.T. 582; 34 W.R. 669 23–137
Miles v. Vermont Fruit Co. 124 A. 559 (1924) 25–169
Milgate v. Kebble (1841) 3 M. & G. 100; Drinkwater 225; 3 Scott W.R. 358; 10 L.J.C.P. 277; 133 E.R. 1073 .... 8–008, 15–038, 15–039, 15–049
Miliangos v. Frank (George) (Textiles) Ltd [1976] A.C. 443; [1975] 3 W.L.R. 758; 119 S.J. 774; [1975] 3 All E.R. 801; [1975] 2 C.M.L.R. 585; [1976] 1 Lloyd's Rep. 201 .... 2–044, 23–172, 25–194
—— v. Frank (George) (Textiles) Ltd (No. 2) [1976] 3 W.L.R. 477; 120 S.J. 450; [1976] 3 All E.R. 599; [1976] 2 Lloyd's Rep. 434 25–191
Millar (Andrews) & Co. Ltd v. Taylor & Co. Ltd [1916] 1 K.B. 402 ... 6–045, 6–046, 6–040, 18–335, 18–336, 18–345
Millar's Karri and Jarrah Co. v. Weddel Turner & Co. (1908) 100 L.T. 128; 11 Asp.M.L.C. 184; 14 Com.Cas. 25 .... 8–080, 8–081
Millar's Machinery Co. Ltd v. David Way & Son (1935) 40 Com.Cas. 204 .... 12–067, 13–036, 13–037
Millar's of Falkirk Ltd v. Turpie 1966 S.L.T. 66 .... 10–036, 11–031, 11–040, 12–031, 14–021
Miller v. Cannon Hill Estates Ltd [1931] 2 K.B. 113 10–012
—— v. Newman (1842) 4 Man. & G. 646; 11 L.J.C.P. 265; 134 E.R. 266 ..... 1–048, 1–049
Miller, Gibb & Co. Ltd, *Re* [1957] 1 W.L.R. 703; 101 S.J. 392; [1957] 2 All E.R. 266; [1957] 1 Lloyd's Rep. 258 .... 24–012, 24–027

Miller International Schallplatten G.m.b.H. v. E.C. Commission (No. 19/17), [1978] E.C.R. 131; [1978] 2 C.M.L.R. 334; [1978] F.S.R. 524 3–041
Miller (James) and Partners Ltd v. Whitworth Street Estates (Manchester) Ltd [1970] A.C. 583; [1970] 2 W.L.R. 728; 114 S.J. 225; [1970] 1 All E.R. 796; [1970] 1 Lloyd's Rep. 269 .... 25–005, 25–007, 25–008, 25–010, 25–021, 25–032, 25–065
Millett v. Van Heek & Co. [1921] 2 K.B. 369; 90 L.J.K.B. 671; 125 L.T. 51; 37 T.L.R. 411; 65 S.J. 335 .... 16–072, 16–081, 17–009, 17–013, 19–179, 20–116
Millichamp v. Jones [1982] 1 W.L.R. 1422; (1982) 126 S.J. 726; [1983] 1 All E.R. 267; (1983) 45 P. & C.R. 169; (1983) 80 L.S.Gaz. 35; (1983) 133 New L.J. 134 9–051
Mills v. Barber (1836) 1 M. & W. 425; Tyr. & Gr. 835; 5 L.J.Ex. 204 22–064
—— v. Bayley (1863) 2 H. & C. 36 2–052
—— v. Stokman (1967) 41 A.L.J.R. 16; (1967) 116 C.L.R. 61 .... 1–097, 1–098
Milne Construction Ltd v. Expandite Ltd [1984] 2 N.Z.L.R. 163 .... 11–039, 11–057
Milner v. Staffs, Congregational Union (Inc.) [1956] Ch. 275; [1956] 2 W.L.R. 556; 100 S.J. 170; [1956] 1 All E.R. 494 1–027
—— v. Tucker, (1823) 1 C. & P. 15; 171 E.R. 1082 12–055
Milnes v. Huddersfield Corporation (1886) 11 App.Cas. 511; [1886–90] All E.R.Rep. 350; 56 L.J.Q.B. 1; 55 L.T. 617; 50 J.P. 676; 34 W.R. 761; 2 T.L.R. 821 1–071
Milton B. Medary, The, *See* Groupement National D'Achat Des Tourteaux v. Sociedad Industrial Financiera Argentina.
Min Thai Holdings Pte Ltd [1999] S.L.R. 368 23–282
Mineracoas Brasilieras Reunidas v. E.F. Marine SA (The Freights Queen) [1977] 2 Lloyd's Rep. 140, QBD (Comm Ct) 25–071
Minister of Finance v. Kicking Horse Forest Products Ltd (1975) 57 D.L.R. (3d) 220 1–070
Minister of Materials v. Steel Bros. & Co. Ltd [1952] W.N. 114; [1952] 1 T.L.R. 499; [1952] 1 Lloyd's Rep. 87 13–037
Minister of Supply and Development v. Servicemen's Co-op. Joinery Manufacturers' Ltd (1951) 25 A.L.J. 30; (1951) 82 C.L.R. 621 .... 5–018, 8–011, 9–050, 16–028
Ministry of Agriculture v. Kelly [1953] N.I. 151 8–036
Ministry of Housing and Local Government v. Sharp [1970] 2 Q.B. 223; [1970] 2 W.L.R. 802; 114 S.J. 109; [1970] 1 All E.R. 1009; 66 L.G.R. 187; 21 P. & C.R. 166 23–185
Minories Finance Ltd v. Afribank Nigeria Ltd [1995] 1 Lloyd's Rep. 134 ... 22–129, 23–184, 23–190
Minister Trust Ltd v. Traps Tractors Ltd [1954] 1 W.L.R. 963; [1954] 3 All E.R. 136; 98 S.J. 456, QBD 13–040, 17–052, 17–055
Mintz v. Silverton (1920) 36 T.L.R. 399 5–057
Mirabita v. Imperial Ottoman Bank (1878) 3 Ex.D. 164; 47 L.J.Q.B. 418; 38 L.T. 597; 3 Asp.M.L.C. 591 .... 5–003, 5–098, 5–137, 5–138, 5–140, 6–033, 18–226
Miramar Maritime Corporation v. Holborn Oil Trading Ltd (The Mirimar) [1984] A.C. 676; [1984] 3 W.L.R. 10; (1984) 128 S.J. 414; [1984] 2 All E.R. 326; [1984] 2 Lloyd's Rep. 129; (1984) 81 L.S.Gaz. 2000 18–049
Miramichi, The [1915] P. 71; 84 L.J.P. 105; 112 L.T. 349; 31 T.L.R. 72; 59 S.J. 107; 13 Asp.M.L.C. 21; 1 P.Cas. 137 .... 5–140, 18–221, 19–099
Mirchandani v. Somaia HC0005596, Ch D 25–019
Misa v. Currie (1876) 1 App.Cas. 554; 45 L.J.Ex. 852; 35 L.T. 414; 24 W.R. 1049 ... 22–140, 22–143, 22–144
Mischeff v. Springett [1942] 2 K.B. 331; [1942] 2 All E.R. 349; 111 L.J.K.B. 690; 167 L.T. 402; 106 J.P. 279; 58 T.L.R. 385; 40 L.G.R. 264 .... 1–027, 5–013, 5–060
Miserochi & Co. SpA v. Agricultures Federados Argentines [1982] 1 Lloyd's Rep. 202 .... 20–014, 20–018, 20–030, 20–032, 20–041, 20–045, 20–046
Missouri & Pacific R. Co. v. McFadden (1893) 154 U.S. 155 18–032
Missouri Steamship Co. Ltd, *Re* (1889) 42 Ch.D. 321; 58 L.J.Ch. 721; 37 W.R. 696; *sub nom*. Missouri S.S. Co., Monroe's Claim, *Re* 61 L.T. 316; 5 T.L.R. 438; 6 Asp.M.L.C. 423 .... 25–010, 25–089, 25–119
Mitchell v. Ealing London B.C. [1979] Q.B. 1; [1978] 2 W.L.R. 999; (1978) 122 S.J. 213; [1975] 2 All E.R. 779; (1978) 76 L.G.R. 703 .... 5–053, 5–057, 6–026, 6–029
—— v. Ede (1840) 11 Ad. & El. 888 ...... 18–022, 18–015, 18–018, 18–074, 19–091, 20–061
—— v. Jones (1905) 24 N.Z.L.R. 932 .... 7–059, 7–060
Mitchell Cott & Co. (Middle East) Ltd v. Hairco Ltd [1943] 2 All E.R. 552; 169 L.T. 349; 60 T.L.R. 31; 87 S.J. 447 .... 18–309, 18–311, 18–320

Mitchell (George) (Chesterhall) Ltd v. Finney Lock Seeds Ltd [1983] 2 A.C. 803; [1983] 3 W.L.R. 163; [1983] 2 All E.R. 737; [1983] 2 Lloyd's Rep. 272; [1983] Com.L.R. 209 ...... 2–012, 13–020, 13–022, 13–029, 13–036, 13–048, 13–050, 13–089, 17–069, 17–070, 18–276, 18–280, 23–131
Mitchell-Henry v. Norwich Union Life Insurance Society [1918] 1 K.B. 67; 87 L.J.K.B. 695; 119 L.T. 111; 34 T.L.R. 359; 62 S.J. 487 9–041
Mitsubishi Goshi Kaisha v. J. Aron & Co. Inc. 16 F. 2d 185 (1926) 20–021
Mitsui & Co. Ltd v. American Export Lines Inc. 636 F. 2d. 807 (1981) 21–086, 21–093
—— v. Flota Mercante Grancolombiana (The Ciudad de Pasto) [1988] 1 W.L.R. 1145; (1988) 132 S.J. 1182; [1988] 2 Lloyd's Rep. 208 ... 5–009, 5–027, 5–084, 5–136, 5–137 18–114, 18–139, 18–150, 18–209, 18–210, 18–214, 18–218, 18–226, 20–026, 20–070, 20–077, 20–079, 20–080, 20–082, 20–083, 20–084
—— v. Novorossisk Shipping Co. (The Gudermes) [1991] 1 Lloyd's Rep. 456 ...... 18–142, 18–149
Moakes v. Nicolson (1865) 19 C.B. 290; 34 L.J.C.P. 273; 12 L.T. 573; 144 E.R. 798 .... 5–135, 18–223
Mobil North Sea Ltd v. P.J. Pipe and Valve Co. Ltd [2001] EWCA Civ 741; [2001] 2 All E.R. (Comm) 289, CA; affirming HT 99 248, QBD 16–056, 17–020
Mobil Shipping & Transportation Co. v. Shell Eastern Petroleum (Pte) (The Mobil Courage) [1987] 2 F.T.L.R. 366; [1987] 2 Lloyd's Rep. 655 .. 18–018, 18–063, 18–084
Modelboard v. Outer Box (In Liquidation) [1992] B.C.C. 945; [1993] B.C.L.C. 623 .... 1–060, 5–149, 5–150
Modern Fashions Ltd, *Re* (1969) 8 D.L.R. (3d) 590 25–183
Modern Light Cars Ltd v. Seals [1934] 1 K.B. 32; 102 L.J.K.B. 680; 149 L.T. 285; 49 T.L.R. 503; 77 S.J. 420 .... 1–066, 7–068
Modern Transport Co. Ltd v. Ternsturom and Roos (1924) Ll.L.R. 345 20–052
Modiano Bros. & Sons. v. Bailey & Sons Ltd (1933) 50 T.L.R. 43; 77 S.J. 799; 47 Ll.L.R. 134 19–009
Mody v. Gregson (1868) L.R. 4 Ex. 49; 38 L.J.Ex. 49; 38 L.J.Ex. 12; 19 L.T. 458; 17 W.R. 176 Ex.Ch. 11–003, 11–022, 11–080
Mogridge v. Clapp [1892] 3 Ch.D. 383 7–046
Mohamed v. Alaga & Co.; *sub nom.* Mohammed v. Alaga & Co. [2000] 1 W.L.R. 1815; [1999] 3 All E.R. 699; [2000] C.P. Rep. 87; [1999] 2 Costs L.R. 169; *The Times*, July 29, 1999; *The Independent*, July 14, 1999, CA; reversing in part [1998] 2 All E.R. 720; (1998) 95(17) L.S.G. 29; (1998) 142 S.J.L.B. 142; *The Times*, April 2, 1998; *The Independent*, March 27, 1998, Ch.D 3–028
Mohanlal Hargovind of Jubbulpore v. Commissioner of Income Tax [1949] A.C. 521; 93 S.J. 663; [1949] 2 All E.R. 652, [1949] T.R. 289 8–022
Mohar Investment Co. v. Wilkins (1957) 108 L.J. 140 13–024
Mohsin, Abdullah Alesayi v. Brooly Exim Pte Ltd [1993] 3 Singapore L.R. 433 .... 13–029, 13–030, 13–038, 13–051
Molling & Co. v. Dean & Sons Ltd (1901) 18 T.L.R. 217 .... 8–082, 8–084, 12–043, 12–048, 17–062, 17–063, 17–068, 17–070, 19–157, 20–106, 21–102
Molthes R.A. v. Ellerman's Wilson Line Ltd [1927] 1 K.B. 710; [1926] All E.R.Rep. 417; 96 L.J.K.B. 414; 136 L.T. 767; 17 Asp.M.L.C. 219; 32 Com.Cas. 106 18–051
Momm v. Barclays Bank International Ltd [1977] 1 Q.B. 790; [1977] 2 W.L.R. 407; *sub nom.* Delbrueck & Co. v. Barclays Bank International (1976) 120 S.J. 486; [1976] 2 Lloyd's Rep. 341 .... 9–038, 22–118
Mona Oil Equipment and Supply Co. Ltd v. Rhodesia Rys. [1950] W.N. 10; [1949] 2 All E.R. 1014; 83 Ll.L.Rep. 178 8–040
Monarch S.S. Co. Ltd v. A/B Karlshamns Oljefabriker [1949] A.C. 196; [1949] L.J.R. 772; 65 T.L.R. 217; 93 S.J. 117; [1949] 1 All E.R. 1 .... 16–031, 16–045, 16–049, 16–54
Mondel v. Steel (1841) 8 M. & W. 858 .... 17–049, 17–055
Monkland v. Barclay (Jack) Ltd [1951] 2 K.B. 252; [1951] 1 T.L.R. 763; 95 S.J. 236; [1951] 1 All E.R. 714 .... 1–048, 6–041, 8–037, 8–089
Monolithic Building Co. Ltd Tacon v. The Co., *Re* [1915] 1 Ch. 643; [1914–15] All E.R. 249; 84 L.J.Ch. 441; 112 L.T. 619; 59 S.J. 332 5–143
Montage (G. & H.) G.m.b.H. v. Irvani [1988] 1 W.L.R. 1285 ...... 22–051, 22–133, 25–087
Montague L. Meyer Ltd v. Kivisto (1929) 35 Ll.L.R. 265 .... 11–005, 11–015, 13–033, 18–273, 18–276, 18–279

Montague L. Meyer Ltd v. Osakeyhtio Carelia Timber Co. Ltd (1930) 35 Com.Cas. 17 .... 11–018, 13–033, 18–266, 18–267, 18–278, 18–279
—— v. Travaru (1930) 37 Ll.L.R. 204 .... 13–033, 18–267, 18–272, 18–279
—— v. Vigers Bros. Ltd (1939) 63 Ll.L.R. 10 .... 11–018, 11–021, 18–260
Montana, The [1990] 1 Lloyd's Rep. 402 18–209
Montebianco Industrie Tessali SpA v. Carlyle Mills (London) Ltd [1981] 1 Lloyd's Rep. 509 .... 9–032, 22–064
Montecchi v. Shimco (U.K.) Ltd [1979] 1 W.L.R. 1180; (1978) 123 S.J. 551; *sub nom.* Montecchi v. Shimco (U.K.); Domenica v. Same [1980] 1 Lloyd's Rep. 50 .... 9–032, 22–064
Montedison SpA v. Icroma SpA (The Caspian Sea) [1980] 1 W.L.R. 48; (1979) 123 S.J. 551; [1979] 3 All E.R. 378; [1980] 1 Lloyd's Rep. 91 11–020
Montefiore v. O'Connor (1878) 1 S.C.R. (N.S.W.) 227 (Australia) 22–070
Monterosso Shipping Co. v. International Transport Workers Federation (The Rosso) (1982) 126 S.J. 591; [1982] 3 All E.R. 841; [1982] 2 Lloyd's Rep. 120; [1982] 1 R.L.R. 468; [1982] 1 C.R. 675; (1982) 99 L.S.Gaz. 1175; [1982] Com.L.R. 152 .... 25–010, 25–087, 25–190
Montforts v. Marsden [1895] 1 Ch. 11; 64 L.J.Ch. 52; 71 L.T. 620; 12 R. 193 .... 4–003, 4–027
Montreal Light, Heat & Power Co. v. Sedgwick [1910] A.C. 598; 80 L.J.P.C. 1; 103 L.T. 234; 26 T.L.R. 657; 11 Asp.M.L.C. 437 .... 1–128, 6–035
Montrod Ltd v. Grundkotter Fleischvertriebs GmbH [2001] EWCA Civ 1954; [2002] 1 W.L.R. 1975; [2002] 3 All E.R. 697; [2002] 1 All E.R. (Comm) 257; [2002] C.L.C. 499, CA; reversing in part [2001] 1 All E.R. (Comm) 368; [2001] C.L.C. 466, QBD 23–142, 22–235
Moody v. Pall Mall Deposit and Forwarding Co. Ltd (1917) 33 T.L.R. 306 ... 7–032, 7–038, 7–040, 7–046
Moon v. Mayor of Camberwell (1904) 89 L.T. 595; 68 J.P. 57; 20 T.L.R. 43; 2 L.G.R. 309 8–059
Mooney v. Lipka [1926] 4 D.L.R. 647 5–026
Moore & Co. and Landauer & Co., *Re*, [1921] 2 K.B. 519; 90 L.J.K.B. 731; 125 L.T. 372; 37 T.L.R. 452; 26 Com.Cas. 267 .... 11–004, 11–018
Moore v. Campbell (1854) 10 Exch. 323; 2 C.L.R. 1084; 23 L.J.Ex. 310 8–062
—— v. D.E.R. Ltd [1971] 1 W.L.R. 1476; 115 S.J. 528; [1971] 3 All E.R. 517; [1972] R.T.R. 97; *sub nom.* Moore and Moore v. D.E.R. [1971] 2 Lloyd's Rep. 359 17–027
—— v. Harris (1876) 9 App.Cas. 318; 45 L.J.P.C. 55; 34 L.T. 519; 24 W.R. 887; 3 Asp.M.L.C. 173 .... 25–070, 25–202
—— v. Regents of the University of California 51 Cal. 3rd 120 (1990) 1–089
—— v. Shelley (1883) 8 App.Cas. 285; 52 L.J.P.C. 35; 48 L.T. 918 .... 8–036, 9–059
Moore Large & Co Ltd v. Hermes Credit & Guarantee Plc (sued as Credit & Guarantee Insurance Co Plc) [2003] EWHC 26; [2003] 1 Lloyd's Rep. 163; [2003] Lloyd's Rep. I.R. 315, QBD 14–047
Moorgate Mercantile Co. Ltd v. Bowman (1974) 28 Hire Trading (No. 2) 15 7–090
—— v. Twitchings [1977] A.C. 890; [1976] 3 W.L.R. 66; 120 S.J. 470; [1976] 2 All E.R. 641; [1976] R.T.R. 437, HL 7–008, 7–009, 7–012, 7–015, 7–016, 7–017
Moorhead v. Smith (Thomas) & Sons Ltd [1963] 1 Lloyd's Rep. 164 14–058
Mora Shipping Inc v. Axa Corporate Solutions Assurance SA [2005] EWCA Civ 1069; [2005] 2 Lloyd's Rep. 769; [2005] 2 C.L.C. 349; [2006] I.L.Pr. 10, CA 19–013, 20–030
Moralice (London) Ltd v. Man (E.D. and F.) [1954] 2 Lloyd's Rep. 526 .... 11–018, 23–196
Moran Galloway & Co. v. Uzielli [1905] 2 K.B. 555; 74 L.J.K.B. 494; 54 W.R. 250; 21 T.L.R. 378; 10 Com.Cas. 203 20–039
Moray Park Fruit Co. Ltd v. Crewe and Newcombe [1934] SAS.R 8–056
Mordaunt Bros. v. British Oil and Cake Mills Ltd [1910] 2 K.B. 502 .... 8–013, 15–094, 15–095
Morelli v. Fitch and Gibbons [1928] 2 K.B. 636; [1928] All E.R.Rep. 610; 97 L.J.K.B. 812; 140 L.T. 21; 44 T.L.R. 737; 72 S.J. 503 .... 11–048, 11–056, 17–072
Morgan v. Bain (1874) L.R. 10 C.P. 15 .... 3–048, 8–078, 8–086, 9–010
—— v. Gath (1865) 3 H. & C. 748; 34 L.J.Ex. 165; 13 L.T. 96; 11 Jur. (N.S.) 654; 13 W.R. 756; 159 E.R. 726 .... 8–046, 8–047

Morgan v. Griffith (1871) L.R. 6 Ex. 70; 40 L.J.Ex. 46; 23 L.T. 783; 19 W.R. 957 ... 10–014
—— v. Marquis (1854) 9 Exch. 145 ... 5–125
—— v. Russell & Sons [1909] 1 K.B. 357; 78 L.J.K.B. 187; 100 L.T. 118; 25 T.L.R. 120; 55 S.J. 136 ... 1–097, 1–098
Morgan Guarantee Trust Co. v. Vend Technologies 100 A.D. 2d 782 (1984) ... 25–156
Morison v. Gray (1824) 2 Bing. 260; 9 Moore C.P. 484; 3 L.J. (o.s.) C.P. 261; 130 E.R. 305 ... 15–013, 18–088
—— v. Lockhart (1912) S.C. 1017 ... 1–100, 5–024
—— v. London County and Westminster Bank Ltd [1914] 3 K.B. 356; 83 L.J.K.B. 1202; 111 L.T. 114; 30 T.L.R. 481; 58 S.J. 453; 19 Com.Cas. 273 ... 22–023
Morley v. Attenborough (1849) 3 Exch. 500; 18 L.J.Ex. 148; 12 L.T. (o.s.) 532; 13 J.P. 427; 13 Jur. 282; 154 E.R. 943 ... 4–032
—— v. Maybray Motors Ltd (1971) 25 Hire Trading (No. 3) 15 ... 7–090, 7–107
Morris, *Re* [1922] 1 I.R. 81 ... 22–144
Morris v. Martin (C.W.) & Sons Ltd [1966] 1 Q.B. 716; [1965] 3 W.L.R. 276; 109 S.J. 451; [1965] 2 All E.R. 725; [1965] 2 Lloyd's Rep. 63 ... 5–010, 5–057, 6–026, 6–030, 18–150
—— v. Ritchie [1934] N.Z.L.R. 196 ... 1–083
—— v. Robinson (1824) 3 B. & C. 196 ... 1–072, 1–073, 1–084
Morris Graphics Inc. v. Trans Freight Lines Inc. [1990] A.M.C. 2764 ... 21–085
Morris Motors Ltd v. Lilley [1959] 1 W.L.R. 1184; 103 S.J. 1003; [1959] 3 All E.R. 737 ... 11–019
Morrison, *Re* (1906) 25 N.Z.L.R. 513 ... 7–063, 7–077
Morrison and Mason Ltd v. Clarkson Bros. (1898) 25 R. 427; 35 Sc.L.R. 335; 5 S.L.T. 277 ... 12–055
Morrisson v. Robertson 1908 S.C. 332; 45 S.L.R. 264; 15 S.L.T. 697 ... 5–046, 7–023
Morritt, *Re; ex p.* Official Receiver (1886) 18 Q.B.D. 222, 56 L.J.Q.B. 139; 56 L.T. 42; 35 W.R. 277; 3 T.L.R. 266 ... 7–110
Morrow v. Carty [1957] N.I. 174 ... 9–024
Mortgage Loan Finance Co. of Australia v. Richards (1932) S.R. (N.S.W.) 50 ... 7–032
Mortimer v. Bell (1865) 1 Ch.App. 10; 135 L.J.Ch. 25; 13 L.T. 348; 29 J.P. 803; 11 Jur. (n.s.) 897; 14 W.R. 68 ... 3–009
Mortimer-Rae v. Barthel (1979) 105 D.L.R. 289 ... 7–008, 7–043
Morton v. Lamb (1797) 7 T.R. 125; 101 E.R. 890 ... 8–004
Moschi v. Lep Air Services Ltd [1973] A.C. 331; [1972] 2 W.L.R. 1175; 116 S.J. 372; [1972] 2 All E.R. 393 ... 12–067, 15–110, 19–066
Moss v. Hancock [1899] 2 Q.B. 111; 68 L.J.Q.B. 657; 80 L.T. 693; 63 J.P. 517; 47 W.R. 698; 15 T.L.R. 353; 43 S.J. 749; 19 Cox C.C. 324 ... 1–084
—— v. Old Colony Trust Co. 140 N.E. 803 (1923) ... 23–112, 23–134
—— v. Smith (1850) 9 C.B. 94 ... 18–136
—— v. Sweet (1851) 16 Q.B. 493; 20 L.J.Q.B. 167; 16 L.T. (o.s.) 341; 15 Jur. 536; 117 E.R. 968 ... 5–040, 5–041, 5–050, 5–055
Motis Exports Ltd v. Dampskibsselskapet AF 1912 A/S (No.1); *sub nom.* Dampskibsselskabet AF 1912 v. Motis Export Ltd [2000] 1 All E.R. (Comm) 91; [2000] 1 Lloyd's Rep. 211; [2000] C.L.C. 515; (2000) 97(3) L.S.G. 37; *The Times*, January 26, 2000, CA; affirming [1999] 1 All E.R. (Comm) 571; [1999] 1 Lloyd's Rep. 837; [1999] C.L.C. 914; *The Times*, March 31, 1999, QBD (Comm Ct) ... 18–027, 18–063, 18–075, 18–084
Motor Mart Ltd v. Webb [1958] N.Z.L.R. 773 ... 1–062, 5–147
Motor Oil Hellas (Corinth) Refineries SA v. Shipping Corp. of India (The Kanchenjunga) [1990] 1 Lloyd's Rep. 391 ... 8–030, 12–006, 12–031, 12–034, 12–035, 12–036, 12–037, 12–054, 18–358, 19–150, 19–151
Motor Trade Finance Ltd v. H.E. Motors Ltd, unreported (H.L.), March 26, 1926 ... 1–066
Mott (Frank) & Co. Ltd v. Muller & Co. (London) Ltd (1922) 13 Ll.L.R. 492 ... 17–030, 17–035
Mouat (J.N.) v. Betts Motors Ltd [1959] A.C. 71; [1958] 3 W.L.R. 598; 102 S.J. 810; [1958] 3 All E.R. 402; [1958] 2 Lloyd's Rep. 321 ... 16–069, 17–006
Mount Albert Borough Council v. Australasian etc. Life Assurance Society Ltd [1938] A.C. 224; [1937] 4 All E.R. 206; 107 L.J.P.C. 5; 157 L.T. 522; 54 T.L.R. 5 ... 25–156, 25–161, 25–165, 25–167, 25–174
Mount (D.F.) Ltd v. Jay and Jay (Provisions) Ltd [1960] 1 Q.B. 159; [1959] 3 W.L.R. 537; 103 S.J. 636; [1959] 3 All E.R. 307; [1959] 2 Lloyd's Rep. 269 ... 5–065, 5–097, 5–122, 5–139, 7–062, 7–069, 7–072, 7–077, 7–085, 8–013, 15–095, 15–098, 18–197, 18–205

Mountford v. Scott [1975] Ch. 258 1–050
Mowbray v. Merryweather [1895] 2 Q.B. 640 .... 10–019, 17–060, 17–075
Mowbray Robinson & Co. v. Rosser (1922) 91 L.J.K.B. 524; 126 L.T. 748; 38 T.L.R. 413; 66 S.J. 315 .... 18–268, 21–099
Moyce v. Newington (1878) 4 Q.B.D. 32; 48 L.J.Q.B. 125; 37 L.T. 535; 43 J.P. 191; 27 W.R. 319; 14 Cox C.C. 182 7–024
Mubarak Ali v. Wali Mohamed & Co. (1938) 18 K.L.R. 23 7–082
Mucklow v. Mangles (1808) 1 Taunt. 318; 127 E.R. 856 .... 5–005, 5–080, 5–091
Muhammad Issa el Sheikh Ahmad v. Ali [1947] A.C. 424 .... 16–046, 16–054
Muirhead v. Industrial Tank Specialities Ltd [1986] Q.B. 507; [1985] 3 W.L.R. 993; [1985] 3 All E.R. 705; [1985] E.C.C. 225 .... 5–011, 14–059, 18–149
Muller, Maclean & Co. v. Leslie and Anderson [1921] W.N. 235; (1921) 8 Ll.L.R. 328 .... 9–021, 16–026, 16–028, 19–213, 19–216, 21–012
Mulliner v. Florence (1878) 3 Q.B.D. 484; 47 L.J.Q.B. 700; 38 L.T. 167; 42 J.P. 293; 26 W.R. 385 .... 1–072, 7–002, 7–110, 15–057
Munchener Ruckversicherungs-Gesellschaft AG (t/a Munich Reinsurance Co) v. Commonwealth Insurance Co [2004] EWHC 914; [2004] 2 C.L.C. 665; [2005] Lloyd's Rep. I.R. 99, QBD 25–030
Munro v. Balnagown Estates 1949 S.L.T. 85 5–024
—— v. Liquidator of Balnagown Estates Co. 1949 S.C. 49 1–100
—— v. Willmott [1949] 1 K.B. 295; [1949] L.J.R. 471; 64 T.L.R. 627; 92 S.J. 662; [1948] 2 All E.R. 983 .... 3–006, 7–005, 15–106
Munro & Co. v. Bennet & Son 1911 S.C. 337 12–055
Munro (Robert A.) & Co. Ltd v. Meyer [1930] 2 K.B. 312 .... 8–076, 8–077, 8–080, 11–020, 13–028, 13–033
Murgatroyd v. Wright [1907] 2 K.B. 333; 76 L.J.K.B. 747; 97 L.T. 108; 23 T.L.R. 517; 14 Mans. 201 7–114
Murphy v. Brentwood D.C. [1991] 1 A.C. 398; [1990] 3 W.L.R. 414; [1990] 2 All E.R. 908; (1990) 22 H.L.R. 502; (1990) 134 S.J. 1076; (1990) 21 Con.L.R. 1; (1991) 89 L.G.R. 24; (1990) 6 Const. L.J. 304; (1990) 154 L.G.Rev. 1010 .... 12–124, 12–078, 14–087, 18–149
Murray v. King (1821) 5 B. & A. 165 22–133
Museprime Properties v. Adhill Properties [1990] 36 E.G. 114; (1990) 61 P. & C.R. 111 [1990] 2 E.G.L.R. 196 .... 10–009, 13–055
Muskham Finance Ltd v. Howard [1963] 1 Q.B. 904; [1963] 2 W.L.R. 87; 106 S.J. 1029; [1963] 1 All E.R. 81 7–018
Mussen v. Price (1803) 4 East 147; 102 E.R. 786 9–063
—— v. Van Diemen's Land Co. [1938] Ch. 253 16–038
Mutual Life and Citizens' Assurance Co. Ltd v. Evatt [1971] A.C. 793; [1971] 2 W.L.R. 23; *sub nom.* Mutual Life Citizens' Assurance Co. v. Evatt 114 S.J. 932; [1971] 1 All E.R. 150; [1970] 2 Lloyd's Rep. 441 .... 12–013, 23–185
Myers [G.H.) & Co. v. Brent Cross Service Co. [1934] 1 K.B. 46 .... 1–041, 1–043, 14–046, 14–051
Myton Ltd v. Schwab-Morris [1974] 1 W.L.R. 331; (1973) 118 S.J. 117; [1974] 1 All E.R. 326; (1973) 28 P. & C.R. 1 9–052

N.S.W. Leather Co. Pty Ltd v. Vanguard Insurance Co. Ltd (1991) 25 N.S.W.L.R. 699 .... 19–104, 20–021, 20–106, 21–100
N.V. Arnold Otto Meyer v. Aune [1939] 3 All E.R. 168 .... 19–024, 19–029
N.V. Bunge v. Cie. Noga d'Importation et d'Exportation (The Bow Cedar) [1980] 2 Lloyd's Rep. 601; [1981] Com.L.R. 92 .... 11–016, 11–096, 11–102, 13–033, 13–040
N.V. Devos Gebroeder v. Sunderland Sportswear Ltd 1987 S.L.T. 331 11–073
N.V. Handel Maatschappij J. Smits v. English Exporters (London) Ltd [1955] 2 Lloyd's Rep. 317 .... 25–009, 25–010, 25–011, 25–066, 25–086, 25–089
N.V. Handel My. J. Smits Import-Export v. English Exporters (London) Ltd [1957] 1 Lloyd's Rep. 517 .... 18–247, 20–007, 20–009, 20–044
N.V. Kwik Hoo Tong Handel Maatschappij v. Finlay (James) & Co. [1927] A.C. 604 .... 25–007, 25–012, 25–024
N.V. Stoomv Maats "De Maas" v. Nippon Yusen Kaisha [1980] 2 Lloyd's Rep. 56 2–015
N.Z. Securities Finance Ltd v. Wrightcars Ltd [1976] 1 N.Z.L.R. 77 7–077
Naamlooze Vennootschap, etc., Vredobert v. European Shipping Co. (1924) 20 Ll.L.R. 296 1–082

Nadreph Ltd v. Willmett & Co. (1977) 122 S.J. 744; [1978] 1 All E.R. 746; *sub nom.* Nadreth v. Willmett & Co. [1978] 1 W.L.R. 1537 17–056
Naken v. General Motors of Canada Ltd (1977) 92 D.L.R. (3d) 100 14–103
Nanka-Bruce v. Commonwealth Trust Ltd [1926] A.C. 77; 94 L.J.P.C. 169; 134 L.T. 35 .... 5–016, 5–036, 5–072, 7–021, 7–022
Napier and Ettrick (Lord) v. R. F. Kershaw [1993] A.C. 713; [1993] 2 W.L.R. 42; [1993] 1 All E.R. 385; (1993) 137 S.J.L.B. 44; [1993] 1 Lloyd's Rep. 197; *The Independent*, December 11, 1992; *The Times*, December 16, 1992, HL; reversing, *The Times*, July 17, 1992; *Financial Times*, July 22, 1992, CA 24–012
Napier (F.E.) v. Dexters Ltd (1926) 26 Ll.L.R. 184 5–077, 16–004, 16–024, 18–166, 18–167, 18–168, 18–224, 18–228, 20–043, 20–055, 20–070, 20–074, 20–075, 20–076, 20–077, 20–084, 20–127, 20–128, 20–130, 20–134, 20–141
Napier (N.G.) Ltd v. Corbett, 1962 S.L.T. (Sh. Ct.) 90 9–066
—— v. Patterson 1959 S.C.(J.) 48 9–066
Napoli, The (1898) 15 T.L.R. 56 5–035
Nash v. Barnes [1922] N.Z.L.R. 303 7–043
—— v. Halifax Building Soc. [1979] Ch. 584 3–032
—— v. Inman [1908] 2 K.B. 1; [1908–10] All E.R.Rep. 317; 77 L.J.K.B. 626; 98 L.T. 658; 24 T.L.R. 401; 52 S.J. 335 .... 2–030, 2–031, 2–032
Nathan, *Re, ex p.* Stapleton (1879) 10 Ch.D. 586; 40 L.T. 14; 27 W.R. 327 8–086
Nathan v. Giles (1814) 5 Taunt. 558; 1 Marsh. 226 .... 18–063, 18–216
—— v. Ogdens Ltd (1905) 93 L.T. 553; 21 T.C.R. 775; 49 S.J. 726 22–041
National American Corporation v. Federal Republic of Nigeria 425 F.Supp. 1365 (1977) 23–183
National Bank of Australasia Ltd v. Scottish Union and National Insurance Co. Ltd [1952] A.C. 493; [1952] 2 T.L.R. 254; 96 S.J. 529 .... 25–165, 25–167
National Bank of Egypt v. Hannevig's Bank Ltd (1919) 1 Ll.L.R. 69 .... 19–024, 19–038, 23–127, 23–173
National Bank of Greece and Athens SA v. Metliss [1958] A.C. 509; [1957] 3 W.L.R. 1056; 101 S.J. 972; [1957] 3 All E.R. 608 25–177
National Bank of South Africa v. Banca Italiano De Sconto (1922) 10 Ll.L.R. 531 .. 23–206
National Carriers Ltd v. Panalpina (Northern) Ltd [1981] A.C. 675; [1981] 2 W.L.R. 45; (1980) 125 S.J. 46; [1981] 1 All E.R. 161; (1982) 43 P. & C.R. 72 .. 6–041, 6–054, 6–060
National City Bank of New York v. Partola Manufacturing Co. 181 N.Y.S. 464 (1920) 23–164
National Coal Board v. Gamble [1959] 1 Q.B. 11; [1958] 3 W.L.R. 434; 122 J.P. 453; 102 S.J. 621; [1958] 3 All E.R. 203; 42 Cr.App.R. 240 ... 5–035, 5–061, 5–070, 5–072, 5–082
National Employer's Mutual General Insurance Assn. Ltd v. Jones [1990] 1 A.C. 24; (1989) 8 Tr.L. 43 .... 4–001, 7–066, 7–082
National Importing and Trading Co. Inc. v. E.A. Bear & Co. 155 N.E. 343 (1927) .. 18–267
National Mutual Life Association of Australasia Ltd v. Att-Gen. for New Zealand [1956] A.C. 369; [1956] 2 W.L.R. 532; 100 S.J. 149; [1956] 1 All E.R. 721 ... 25–158, 25–167
National Park Bank of New York v. Berggren & Co. (1914) 110 L.T. 907; [1914–15] All E.R. 548; 30 T.L.R. 387; 19 Com.Cas. 234 22–061
National Permanent Benefit Building Soc., *Re; ex p.* Williamson (1869) 5 Ch.App. 309; 22 L.T. 284; 34 J.P. 341; 18 W.R. 388 2–035
National Savings Bank Association Ltd v. Tranah (1867) L.R. 2 C.P. 556; 36 L.J.C.P. 260; 16 L.T. 592; 15 W.R. 1015 9–030
National Surety Corporation v. Midland Bank and Trust Co., 408 F.Supp. 684 (1976) 23–239
National Telephone Co. v. Constables of St. Peter Port [1900] A.C. 317; 69 L.J.P.C. 74; 82 L.T. 398 2–043
National Westminster Bank v. Halesowen Presswork and Assemblies [1972] A.C. 785; [1972] 2 W.L.R. 455; 116 S.J. 138; [1972] 1 All E.R. 641; [1972] 1 Lloyd's Rep. 101; HL reversing [1971] 1 Q.B. 1; [1970] 3 W.L.R. 625; [1970] 3 All E.R. 473, CA; reversing [1970] 2 W.L.R. 754; 113 S.J. 939; [1970] 1 All E.R. 33 ...... 13–039, 22–139, 22–144
—— v. Morgan [1985] A.C. 686; [1985] 2 W.L.R. 588; (1985) 129 S.J. 205; [1985] 1 All E.R. 821; (1985) 17 H.L.R. 360; 1985 F.L.R. 266; (1985) 135 New L.J. 254; (1985) 82 L.S.Gaz. 1485 .... 14–049, 14–052A

Naughton v. O'Callaghan [1990] 3 All E.R. 191 .... 3–022, 17–054
Naugle Pole & Tie Co. v. Wilson [1929] 3 W.W.R. 730 5–036
Naviera Mogor SA v. Soc. Metallurgique de Normandie (The Nogar Marin) [1988] 1 F.T.L.R. 349; [1988] 1 Lloyd's Rep. 412 .... 18–164, 18–165
Navrom v. Callitsis Management SA [1987] 2 Lloyd's Rep. 276; affirmed [1988] 2 Lloyd's Rep. 416 .... 8–089, 8–091, 8–094, 8–098, 8–100
Navulshaw v. Brownrigg (1852) 2 De G.M. & G. 441 7–047
Naxos, The. *See* Compagnie Commerciale Sucres et Denrées v. C. Czarnikow Ltd
Naylor Benzon Co. Ltd v. Krainische Industrie Gesellschaft [1918] 2 K.B. 486; 87 L.J.K.B. 1066; 118 L.T. 783; 34 T.L.R. 536 6–042
Naylor (Isaac) & Sons Ltd v. New Zealand Co-operative Wool Marketing Association Ltd [1981] 1 N.Z.L.R. 361 25–192
Nea Tyhi, The [1982] 1 Lloyd's Rep. 606; [1982] Com.L.R. 9 .... 5–009, 18–028, 18–029, 18–040, 18–149
Neal v. Viney (1808) 1 Camp. 471; 170 E.R. 1025 5–028
Neale v. Rose (1898) 3 Com.Cas. 236 19–049
Neate v. Ball (1801) 2 East. 117; 102 E.R. 313 5–043
Nederlandsche Banden-Industrie Michelin v. E.G. Commission [1983] E.C.R. 3461 ... 3–042
Nederlandsche Cacaofabrik v. David Challen Ltd (1898) 14 T.L.R. 322 8–068
Neill v. Whitworth (1865) 18 C.B. (N.S.) 435; 34 L.J.P.C. 155; 11 L.T. 677; 11 Jur. (N.S.) 158; 13 W.R. 461 .... 8–005, 20–015, 21–025, 21–027
Nelson v. Chalmers (William) & Co. Ltd 1913 S.C. 441 5–092
Nelson Pine Industries Ltd v. Seatrans New Zealand Ltd (The Pembroke) [1995] 2 Lloyd's Rep. 290, (NZ High Ct) 18–039, 21–091
Neptune Orient Lines Ltd v. J.V.C. (U.K.) Ltd (The Chevalier Rose) [1983] 2 Lloyd's Rep. 438 .... 2–012, 13–017, 13–097, 21–083
Nessa v. Chief Adjudication Officer [1999] 1 W.L.R. 1937; [1999] 4 All E.R. 677; [1999] 2 F.L.R. 1116; [1999] 3 F.C.R. 538; [2000] Fam. Law 28; (1999) 96(42) L.S.G. 42; (1999) 149 N.L.J. 1619; (1999) 143 S.J.L.B. 250; *The Times*, October 27, 1999; *The Independent*, October 27, 1999, HL; affirming [1998] 2 All E.R. 728; [1998] 1 F.L.R. 879; [1998] 2 F.C.R. 461; [1998] Fam. Law 329; (1998) 142 S.J.L.B. 78; *The Times*, February 11, 1998, CA 25–056
Neste Oy v. Lloyd's Bank plc [1983] 2 Lloyd's Rep. 658; [1982] Com.L.R. 185; (1983) 133 New L.J. 597 .... 5–152, 7–045
Netherlands Trading Society v. Wayne and Haylitt Co. (1952) 36 Hong Kong L.R. 109 .... 23–131, 23–205
Neuzen v. Korn (1993) 103 D.L.R. (4th) 473 1–089
Nevill, *Re, ex p.* White (1871) 6 Ch.App. 397; 40 L.J.By. 73; 24 L.T. 45; 19 W.R. 488; affirmed *sub nom.* John Towle & Co. v. White (1873) 29 L.T. 78 ..... 1–049, 5–045, 5–152
New v. Swain (1828) 1 Dans. & L. 193 15–035
New Braunfels National Bank v. Okorne 780 S.W. 2d 313 (Tex. App. 1989) 23–198
New Chinese Antimony Co. Ltd v. Ocean S.S. Co. Ltd [1917] 2 K.B. 664, CA 18–028
New Civilbuild Pte Ltd v. Guobena [1999] 1 S.L.R. 374; affirmed [2000] 2 S.L.R. 378, CA 23–282
New System Private Telephones (London) Ltd v. E. Hughes & Co. [1939] 2 All E.R. 844; 161 L.T. 140; 55 T.L.R. 917; 83 S.J. 588 6–055
New Zealand Forest Ltd v. Pongakawa Sawmill Ltd [1992] 3 N.Z.L.R. 304 5–149
New Zealand Shipping Co. Ltd v. Satterthwaite (A.M.) & Co. Ltd (The Eurymedon) *See* Satterthwaite (A.M.) & Co. Ltd v. New Zealand Shipping Co. Ltd (The Eurymedon)
—— v. Société des Ateliers et Chantiers de France [1919] A.C. 1 8–099
Newborne v. Sensolid (Great Britain) Ltd [1954] 1 Q.B. 45; [1953] 2 W.L.R. 596; 97 S.J. 209; [1953] 1 All E.R. 708 .... 3–012, 18–037
Newman v. Bourne and Hollingsworth (1915) 31 T.L.R. 209 6–011
—— v. Hackney L.B.C. (1982) 80 L.G.R. 611; [1982] R.T.R. 296 14–112
—— v. Lipman [1951] 1 K.B. 333; 114 J.P. 561; 94 S.J. 673; [1950] 2 All E.R. 332; 49 L.G.R. 457 .... 1–027, 1–047
—— v. Oughton [1911] 1 K.B. 792; 80 L.J.K.B. 673; 104 L.T. 211; 22 T.L.R. 254; 55 S.J. 272 .... 7–092, 11–028
Newman Industries Ltd v. Indo-British Industries Ltd [1957] 1 Lloyd's Rep. 211 C.A.; reversing [1956] 2 Lloyd's Rep. 219 .... 15–021, 16–019, 19–214, 23–098

Newsom v. Thornton (1805) 6 East 17; 2 Smith K.B. 207 . . . . 18–006, 18–088
Newton v. Pyke (1908) 25 T.L.R. 127 11–028
Newton Abbot Development Co. Ltd v. Stockman Bros. (1931) 47 T.L.R. 616 13–039
Newtons of Wembley Ltd v. Williams [1965] 1 Q.B. 560; [1964] 3 W.L.R. 888; 108 S.J. 619; [1964] 3 All E.R. 532 . . 7–024, 7–025, 7–030, 7–040, 7–043, 7–070, 7–071, 7–074, 7–076, 7–081, 7–086, 12–003, 15–118, 15–126
Ngo Chew Hong Edible Oils Pte. Ltd v. Scindia Steam Navigation Co. Ltd (The Jalamohan) [1988] 1 Lloyd's Rep. 443 18–039
Niblett v. Confectioners' Materials Ltd [1921] 3 K.B. 387 . . . . . . 4–003, 4–004, 4–025, 4–026, 4–027, 4–030, 4–032, 11–030, 11–044
Nichimen Corp. v. Gatoil Overseas Inc. [1987] 2 Lloyd's Rep. 46 . . . . . 8–030, 9–053, 9–055, 19–087, 19–151, 23–086, 23–096
Nichol v. Godts (1854) 10 Exch. 191; 2 C.L.R. 1468; 23 L.J.Ex. 314; 23 L.T. (o.s.) 162 . . . . 11–004, 11–022, 13–022
Nicholls v. LeFeuvre (1835) 2 Bing. N.C. 81; 1 Hodg. 255; 4 L.J.C.P. 281; 132 E.R. 32; *sub nom.* Slaver v. Le Feuvre, Nicholls v. Le Feuvre, 2 Scott 146 . . . . 15–085, 15–089
—— v. White (1911) 103 L.T. 800 8–009
Nichols v. Marsland (1876) 2 Ex.D. 1 8–097
Nicholson v. Bradfield Union (1866) L.R. 1 Q.B. 620; 7 B. & S. 744; 35 L.J.Q.B. 176; 14 L.T. 830; 30 J.P. 549; 12 Jur. (n.s.) 686; 14 W.R. 731 . . . . 8–065, 8–072
—— v. Deere (1987) 34 D.L.R. (4th) 542; affirmed (1989) 57 D.L.R. (4th) 639 12–124
—— v. Harper [1895] 2 Ch. 415; 64 L.J.Ch. 672; 73 L.T. 19; 59 J.P. 727; 43 W.R. 550; 11 T.L.R. 435; 39 S.J. 524 . . . . 7–035, 7–057, 7–062, 7–073, 7–078, 8–011
Nicholson & Venn v. Smith-Marriott (1947) 177 L.T. 189 . . . . 3–020, 11–019, 12–128, 13–025, 13–029
Nickoll and Knight v. Ashton, Edridge & Co. [1901] 2 K.B. 126 . . . . . 1–128, 6–049, 19–126, 20–098, 21–028
Nickson v. Jepson (1817) 2 Stark. 227; 171 E.R. 629 9–065
Nicol v. Hennessey (1896) 44 W.R. 584; 12 T.L.R. 485; 40 S.J. 601; 1 Com.Cas. 410 1–073
Nicolene Ltd v. Simmonds [1953] 1 Q.B. 543; [1953] 2 W.L.R. 717; 97 S.J. 247; [1953] 1 All E.R. 822; [1953] 1 Lloyd's Rep. 189 . . . . 2–016, 23–092
Nicolls v. Bastard (1835) 2 Cr. M. & R. 659 1–072
Nile Co. for the Export of Agricultural Crops v. H. & J.M. Bennett (Commodities) Ltd [1986] 1 Lloyd's Rep. 555 . . . . 2–017, 6–044, 13–039, 18–301, 18–303, 18–304, 19–064A, 19–126, 20–040, 20–098, 20–102, 25–119
Ningchow, *The* [1916] P. 221; 115 L.T. 554; 31 T.L.R. 470; 13 Asp.M.L.C. 509 7–110
Nippon Yusen Kaisha v. International Import and Export Co. Ltd (The Elbe Maru) [1978] 1 Lloyd's Rep. 206 . . . . 13–017, 21–083
—— v. Ramjiban Serowgee [1938] A.C. 429; [1938] 2 All E.R. 285; 10 L.J.P.C. 89; 159 L.T. 266; 54 T.L.R. 546; 82 S.J. 292; 43 Com.Cas. 223; 19 Asp.M.L.C. 154 . . . . 5–135, 15–029, 15–043, 15–061, 18–084, 18–080, 18–165, 18–166, 18–167, 18–168, 18–210, 18–212, 18–228, 18–234, 20–083, 20–141, 21–010, 21–011
Niru Battery Manufacturing Co v. Milestone Trading Ltd (No.1) [2003] EWCA Civ 1446; [2004] Q.B. 985; [2004] 2 W.L.R. 1415; [2004] 1 All E.R. (Comm) 193; [2004] 1 Lloyd's Rep. 344; [2004] 1 C.L.C. 647; [2004] W.T.L.R. 377; (2003) 100(44) L.S.G. 33; *The Times*, October 30, 2003, CA 18–009, 18–193, 19–076, 23–164
Nisshin Shipping Co Ltd v. Cleaves & Co Ltd [2003] EWHC 2602; [2004] 1 All E.R. (Comm) 481; [2004] 1 Lloyd's Rep. 38; [2003] 2 C.L.C. 1097; (2003) 153 N.L.J. 1705, QBD 18–005, 18–056, 25–202
Nisho Iwai Europe v. Korea First National Bank (2003) 752 N.Y.S. 2d 259 23–067
Nissho Iwai Petroleum Co. Inc. v. Cargill International SA [1993] 1 Lloyd's Rep. 80 2–015, 20–048
Nitrate Corp. of Chile Ltd v. Pansuiza Compania de Navegacion.
Nitrigin Eireann Teoranta v. Inco Alloys [1992] 1 W.L.R. 498 [1982] 1 All E.R. 854; [1992] *Gazette*, January 22, 34; [1991] W.P.C. 17; 135 S.J.L.B. 213; 60 B.L.R. 65; 141 N.L.J. 1518; *The Times*, November 4, 1991; *The Independent*, November 28, 1991 . . . . 12–078, 14–087, 14–092

Njegos, The [1936] P. 90; [1935] All E.R. 863; 105 L.J.P. 49; 155 L.T. 109; 52 T.L.R. 216; 18 Asp.M.L.C. 609 .... 25–010, 25–071, 25–202
Noble Resources Ltd v. Cavalier Shipping Corp. (The Atlas) [1996] 1 Lloyd's Rep. 642 .... 18–027, 18–073, 18–141, 18–188, 18–252, 20–070
Noblett v. Hopkinson [1905] 2 K.B. 214; 74 L.J.K.B. 544; 92 L.T. 462; 69 J.P. 269; 53 W.R. 637; 21 T.L.R. 448; 49 S.J. 459 .... 5–013, 5–080, 5–088
Nockels v. Crosby (1825) 3 B. & C. 814; 5 Dow. & Ry. K.B. 751; 107 E.R. 935 12–067
Nokes v. Doncaster Amalgamated Collieries Ltd [1914] A.C. 1014; [1940] 3 All E.R. 549; 109 L.J.K.B. 865; 163 L.T. 343; 56 T.L.R. 988; 85 S.J. 45 3–044
Noordam, The (No.2) [1920] A.C. 904; 89 L.J.P. 234; 123 L.T. 477; 36 T.L.R. 581; 15 Asp.M.L.C. 27; 3 P.Cas. 599 .... 1–078, 1–080
Norbrook Laboratories Ltd v. Export Credit Guarantees Department (CA of N.I., unreported, October 10, 1992) 24–015
Norden S.S. Co. v. Dempsey (1876) 1 C.P.D. 654; 45 L.J.Q.B. 764; 24 W.R. 984 25–157
Nordisk Oversoisk Handelsselskab A/S v. Eriksen & Christensen (1920) 5 Ll.L.R. 71 20–030 ....
Nordskog v. National Bank (1922) 10 Ll.L.R. 652 23–067
Norfolk, Baltimore & Carolina Line Inc., *Re*, 478 F.Supp. 383 (1979) 21–086
Norfolk Southern Railway Co v. James N. Kirby Pty Ltd (2004) 125 S.Ct 385 .... 18–150, 21–074, 21–076, 21–104
Norgren (C.A.) Co. v. Technomarketing (1983) *The Times*, March 3, 1983 1–027
Norman v. Ackland [1915] SAL.R. 177 8–040
—— v. Bennett [1974] 1 W.L.R. 1229 14–112
—— v. Ricketts (1886) 3 T.L.R. 182 9–041
North, *Re* [1895] 2 Q.B. 264 8–034
North v. Great Northern Railway (1860) 2 Giff. 64; 29 L.J.Ch. 301; 1 L.T. 510; 6 Jur. (N.S.) 244 .... 17–099, 17–103
North American Manufacturers Export Associates Inc. v. Chase National Bank of City of New York 77 F.Supp. 55 (1948) 23–139
North Central Wagon Co. v. Manchester, Sheffield and Lincolnshire Railway (1887) 35 Ch.D. 191 5–167
North Central Wagon Finance Co. Ltd v. Brailsford [1962] 1 W.L.R. 1288; 106 S.J. 878; [1962] 1 All E.R. 502 .... 1–016, 1–066
—— v. Graham, *See* North General Wagon and Finance Co. v. Graham.
—— v. White and Powell [1955] C.L.Y. 1204 3–005
North Eastern Co-op. Soc. v. Newcastle-Upon-Tyne C.C. (1987) 282 E.G. 1409; [1987] 1 E.G.L.R. 142 2–051
North Ocean Shipping Co. Ltd v. Hyundai Construction Co. Ltd (The Atlantic Baron) [1979] Q.B. 705; [1979] 3 W.L.R. 419; (1978) 123 S.J. 352; [1978] 3 All E.R. 1170 .... 3–010, 14–052A
North of England Pure Oil-Cake Co. v. Archangel Maritime Insurance Co. (1875) L.R. 10 Q.B. 249 21–020
North Sea Energy Holdings NV v. Petroleum Authority of Thailand [1999] 1 All E.R. (Comm.) 173; [1999] 1 Lloyd's Rep. 483, CA; affirming [1997] 2 Lloyd's Rep. 418, QBD (Comm Ct) 9–020, 10–024, 16–050, 18–312, 19–161, 20–048
North Staffordshire Loan and Discount Co. v. Wythies (1861) 2 F. & F. 563 22–131
North Sydney Investment and Tramway Co. Ltd v. Higgins [1899] A.C. 263; 68 L.J.P.C. 42; 80 L.T. 303; 47 W.R. 481; 15 T.L.R. 232; 6 Mans. 321 9–041
North Valley Bank v. National Bank of Austin, 437 F.Supp. 70 (1977) 23–203
North Western Bank, *ex p.* (1872) L.R. 15 Eq. 69; 42 L.J. Bey. 6; 27 L.T. 461; 21 W.R. 69 1–063
North Western Bank v. Poynter, Son and Macdonalds [1895] A.C. 56; 64 L.J.P.C. 27; 72 L.T. 93; 11 R. 125 .... 7–031, 15–038, 15–054, 18–207, 25–121, 25–136, 25–140
North Western Rubber Co. Ltd and Huttenbach & Co., *Re* [1908] 2 K.B. 907; 78 L.J.K.B. 51; 99 L.T. 680 .... 11–016, 13–032, 13–033
Northern Grain Co. v. Wiffler (1918) 223 N.Y. 169 15–090
Northern Steel & Hardware Co. Ltd v. John Batt & Co. (London) Ltd (1917) 33 T.L.R. 516 .... 6–021, 18–247
Northgran Finance Ltd v. Ashley [1963] 1 Q.B. 476; [1962] 3 W.L.R. 1360; 106 S.J. 877; [1962] 3 All E.R. 973 3–005
Northland Airlines Ltd v. Dennis Ferranti Meters Ltd. (1970) 114 S.J. 845; *The Times*, February 13, 1970 2–015

Northumberland County Bank v. Eyer 58 Pa.St. 97 (1868) 23–049
Northwest Co. Ltd v. Merland Oil Co. of Canada and Gas and Oil Products Ltd [1936] 4 D.L.R. 248; [1936] 2 W.W.R. 557 .... 4–020, 4–032
Northwest Securities v. Alexander Breckon [1981] R.T.R. 518 .... 5–003, 7–002
Nortier (A.A.) & Co. v. Wm. Maclean Sons & Co. (1921) 9 Ll.L.R. 192 ... 16–022, 16–026, 19–213, 20–070, 20–073, 20–120, 20–121
Norton v. Florence Land and Public Works Co. (1877) 7 Ch.D. 332; 38 L.T. 377; 26 W.R. 123 25–181
Norwich City Council v. Harvey [1989] 1 W.L.R. 828; (1989) 133 S.J. 694; [1989] 1 All E.R. 1180; (1989) 45 Build.L.R. 14; (1989) 139 New L.J. 40 18–149
Norwich Pharmacal Co. v. Customs and Excise Commissioners [1974] A.C. 133; [1973] 3 W.L.R. 164; 117 S.J. 567; *sub nom.* Norwich Pharmacal Co. v. Commissioners of Customs and Excise [1973] 2 All E.R. 943; [1973] F.S.R. 365; [1974] R.P.C. 101 .... 21–073, 21–097
Norwich Union Fire Ins. v. Lykes Bros. S.S. Co. 741 F.Supp. 1051 (1990) 21–086
Nottidge v. Dering [1909] 2 Ch. 647; 79 L.J.Ch. 65; 101 L.T. 491 4–023
Nottingham Building Society v. Eurodynamics Systems [1995] F.S.R. 605, C.A. affirming [1993] F.S.R. 468 8–078
Nottingham Patent Brick and Tile Co. v. Butler (1886) 16 Q.B.D. 778; 55 L.J.Q.B. 280; 54 L.T. 444; 34 W.R. 405; 2 T.L.R. 391 10–009
Nova (Jersey) Knit Ltd v. Kammgam Spinnerei G.m.b.H. [1977] 1 W.L.R. 713; (1977) 121 S.J. 170; [1977] 2 All E.R. 463; [1977] 1 Lloyd's Rep. 463 .... 9–032, 17–049, 22–062, 22–064, 22–069
Nova Petroleum International Establishment v. Tricon Trading Ltd [1989] 1 Lloyd's Rep. 312 .... 19–018, 19–058, 19–074, 19–145, 19–148
Novaknit Hellas SA v. Kumar Bros International Ltd [1998] Lloyd's Rep. Bank. 287; [1998] C.L.C. 971, CA 22–043
Nugent v. Smith (1876) 1 C.P.D. 423; 45 L.J.Q.B. 697; 34 L.T. 827; 41 J.P. 4; 25 W.R. 117; 3 Asp.M.L.C. 198 .... 8–097, 8–099
Nunes (J.) Diamonds Ltd v. Dominion Electric Protection Co. [1972] S.C.R. 769; (1972) 26 D.L.R. 699 12–124
Nutt v. Butler (1804) 5 Esp. 176; 170 E.R. 777 1–095
Nyberg v. Handelaar [1892] 2 Q.B. 202; 61 L.J.Q.B. 709; 67 L.T. 361; 56 J.P. 694; 40 W.R. 545; 8 T.L.R. 549, 36 S.J. 485 .... 1–063, 5–125
Nykredit Mortgage Bank plc v. Edward Erdman Group (No.2) [1997] 1 W.L.R. 1627; [1998] 1 All E.R. 305; [1998] Lloyd's Rep. Bank, 39; [1998] C.L.C. 116; [1998] 1 Costs L.R. 108; [1998] P.N.L.R. 197; [1998] 1 E.G.L.R. 99; [1998] 05 E.G. 150; (1998) 95(1) L.S.G. 24; (1998) 142 S.J.L.B. 29; [1997] N.P.C. 165; (1998) 75 P. & C.R. D28; *The Times*, December 3, 1997, H.L. 19–188, 19–202

O.K. Petroleum A.B. v. Vitol Energy SA (The Chemical Venture and The Jade) [1995] 2 Lloyd's Rep. 160; *The Times*, May 29, 1995, QBD 18–063, 19–088
OT Africa Line Ltd v. Magic Sportswear Corp [2005] EWCA Civ 710; [2006] 1 All E.R. (Comm) 32; [2005] 2 Lloyd's Rep. 170; [2005] 1 C.L.C. 923; 2005 A.M.C. 2179; *The Times*, June 21, 2005, CA 25–089, 25–156
O.T.M. Ltd v. Hydranautics [1981] 2 Lloyd's Rep. 211 2–013
Oakley v. Ultra Vehicle Design Ltd (In Liquidation); *sub nom.* Ultra Motorhomes International Ltd, Re [2005] EWHC 872; [2005] I.L.Pr. 55; [2006] B.P.I.R. 115, Ch D 25–030
Oatway [1903] 2 Ch. 356 7–003
Obagi v. Stanborough Developments (1995) 69 P.&C. R. 573 18–320
Obaseki Bros. v. Reif & Son Ltd [1952] 2 Lloyd's Rep. 364 .... 20–109, 20–118
Obestain Inc. v. National Mineral Development Corp. Ltd (The Sanix Ace) [1997] 1 Lloyd's Rep. 465 .... 5–009, 5–010, 18–114, 18–116, 18–117, 18–119
O'Byrne v. Sanofi Pasteur MSD Ltd (formerly Aventis Pasteur MSD Ltd) (C127/04) *The Times*, February 15, 2006, ECJ 14–081, 14–092
OCCL Bravery, The [2000] 1 Lloyd's Rep. 394 .... 21–082, 21–086, 21–104
Ocean Chemical Transport Inc. v. Exnor Craggs Ltd [2000] 1 All E.R. (Comm) 519; [2000] 1 Lloyd's Rep. 446, CA 4–025, 13–036, 13–092, 18–281, 25–090
Ocean Marine Navigation Ltd v. Koch Carbon Inc (The Dynamic) [2003] EWHC 1936; [2003] 2 Lloyd's Rep. 693, QBD 19–215, 20–126

Ocean Rig ASA v. Safra National Bank of New York 72 F. Supp. 2d 193 23–196
Ocean Tramp Tankers Corporation v. V/O Sovfracht (The Eugenia) [1964] 2 Q.B. 226; [1964] 2 W.L.R. 114; 107 S.J. 931; [1964] 1 All E.R. 161; [1963] 2 Lloyd's Rep. 155; [1963] C.L.Y. 3200 .... 6–034, 6–049
Oceanfocus Shipping Ltd v. Hyundai Merchant Marine Co. Ltd (The Hawk) [1999] 1 Lloyd's Rep. 176, QBD (Comm Ct) 18–028, 18–029, 18–030, 18–164
Oceanic Sun Line Special Shipping Co. Inc. v. Fay (1988) 165 C.L.R. 197, HC (Aus) 25–079
Oceano Grupo Editorial SA v. Rocio Muriano Quintero (Case C–240/98-C–244/98); Salvat Editores SA v. Prades (C241/98); Salvat Editores SA v. Badillo (C242/98) Salvat Editores SA v. Berroane (C243/98); Salvat Editores SA v. Feliu (C244/98) [2000] E.C.R. 1–4941; [2002] 1 C.M.L.R. 43, ECJ ... 25–055, 25–102
Ockenden v. Henly (1858) E.B. & E. 485; 27 L.J.Q.B. 361; 31 L.T. (O.S.) 179; 4 Jur. (N.S.) 999 .... 15–132, 17–090
Ocular Sciences Ltd v. AspectVision Care Ltd (No.2) [1997] R.P.C. 289; (1997) 20(3) L.P.D. 20022, Pat Ct 8–026
Oddy v. Phoenix Assurance Co. [1966] 1 Lloyd's Rep. 134; (1966) 116 New.L.J. 554 8–097
Odenfeld, The. *See* Gator Shipping Corp. v. Trans-Atlantic Occidental Shipping Establishment.
Odessa, The [1916] 1 A.C. 145; 85 L.J.P.C. 49; 114 L.T. 10; 32 T.L.R. 103; 60 S.J. 292; 13 Asp.M.L.C. 215 .... 1–063, 1–126
Oelbermann v. National City Bank of New York 79 F. 2d 534 (1935) 23–066
Office of Fair Trading v. Lloyds TSB Bank Plc [2006] EWCA Civ 268; (2006) 156 N.L.J. 553; *The Times*, April 7, 2006, CA (Civ Div); reversing [2004] EWHC 2600; [2005] 1 All E.R. 843; [2005] 1 All E.R. (Comm) 354; [2005] E.C.C. 27; (2004) 154 N.L.J. 1728, QBD 14–154, 25–055, 25–089
Office of Fair Trading v. MB Designs (Scotland) Ltd, 2005 S.L.T. 691; 2005 S.C.L.R. 894; 2005 G.W.D. 22–393; *The Times*, August 11, 2005, OH 14–041, 14–135
Official Assignee of Madras v. Mercantile Bank of India Ltd [1935] A.C. 53 .... 7–033, 7–036, 8–013, 18–006, 18–167, 18–197, 18–234, 18–236
Official Solicitor of the Supreme Court v. Thomas [1986] 2 E.G.L.R. 1; (1986) 279 E.G. 407 9–030
Offord v. Davies (1862) 12 C.B. (N.S.) 748; 31 L.J.C.P. 319; 6 L.T. 579; 9 Jur. (N.S.) 22; 10 W.R. 758; 142 E.R. 1336 2–010
Offshore International SA v. Banco Central SA [1977] 1 W.L.R. 399; (1977) 121 S.J. 252; [1976] 3 All E.R. 749; *sub nom.* Offshore International SA v. Banco Central SA and Hijos de J. Barreras SA [1976] 2 Lloyd's Rep. 402 .. 23–140, 23–239, 23–241, 23–248, 25–076, 25–161
Ogden v. Benas (1874) L.R. 9 C.P. 513; 43 L.J.C.P. 259; 30 L.T. 683; 38 J.P. 519; 22 W.R. 805 22–028
Ogdens Ltd v. Nelson [1905] A.C. 109 8–079
Ogg v. Shuter (1875) 1 C.P.D. 47; 45 L.J.Q.B. 44; 33 L.T. 492; 24 W.R. 100; 3 Asp.M.L.C. 77 .... 5–003, 5–137, 20–077, 20–084
Ogle v. Atkinson (1814) 5 Taunt. 759; 1 Marsh. 323; 128 E.R. 890 ... 5–097, 18–214, 18–221
—— v. Earl Vane (1868) L.R. 3 Q.B. 272 .... 8–030, 8–069, 8–087, 16–073, 17–010
O'Hanlan v. Great Western Railway (1865) 6 B. & S. 484; 6 New Rep. 147; 34 L.J.Q.B. 154; 12 L.T. 480; 30 J.P. 710; 11 Jur. (N.S.) 797; 13 W.R. 741 ..... 16–069, 16–070, 17–005
Ojjeh v. Waller [1999] C.L.Y. 4405 11–019
Okell v. Smith (1815) 1 Stark. 107; 171 E.R. 416, N.P. 5–049, 6–027, 12–032
Old Colony Trust Co. v. Continental Bank 288 F. 979 (1921) 23–068, 23–071
—— v. Lawyers' Title and Trust Co. 297 F. 152 (1924) 23–141, 23–203, 23–206
Oldershaw v. King (1857) 2 H. & N. 517; 27 L.J.Ex. 120; 3 Jur. (N.S.) 1152; 5 W.R. 753 23–137
Oldfield Asphalts Ltd v. Grovedale Coolstores (1994) Ltd [1998] 3 N.Z.L.R. 479 1–128
Olds Discount Co. Ltd v. Krett [1940] 2 K.B. 117 .... 1–066, 7–057
Olearia Tirrena SpA v. N.V. Algemeene Oliehandel (The Osterbek) [1973] 2 Lloyd's Rep. 86, C.A. affirming [1972] 2 Lloyd's Rep. 341 ... 18–172, 20–031, 20–046, 20–125
Oleificio Zucchi SpA v. Northern Sales Ltd [1965] 2 Lloyd's Rep. 496 ...... 6–019, 11–040, 12–012, 13–040, 18–254, 19–111

Olgeirsson v. Kitching [1986] 1 W.L.R. 304; (1986) 130 S.J. 110; (1985) 150 J.P. 117; [1986] 1 All E.R. 746; [1986] Crim.L.R. 341; [1986] R.T.R. 129; (1985) 83 L.S.Gaz. 617 14–108
Oliver Ashworth (Holdings) Ltd v. Ballard (Kent) Ltd *See* Ballard (Kent) Ltd
Ollett v. Jordan [1918] 2 K.B. 41; 87 L.J.K.B. 934; 119 L.T. 50; 82 J.P. 221; 62 S.J. 636; 16 L.G.R. 487; 26 Cox C.C. 275 .... 5–013, 5–019, 5–073, 6–019, 11–052, 18–255
Olley v. Marlborough Court Ltd [1949] 1 K.B. 532; [1949] L.J.R. 360; 65 T.L.R. 95; 93 S.J. 40; [1949] 1 All E.R. 127 .... 2–012, 13–013, 18–047
Olympia & York Canary Wharf Ltd (No.2), Re; *sub nom.* Bear Stearns International v. Adamson [1993] B.C.C. 159 8–026
Olympia Oil and Cake Co. and Produce Brokers Co. *Re* [1915] 1 K.B. 233; 84 L.J.K.B. 281; 111 L.T. 1107; 12 Asp.M.L.C. 570; 19 Com.Cas. 359 ... 19–083, 19–113
—— v. ——, *See* Produce Brokers Co. v. Olympia Oil and Cake Co.
Omnium D'Enterprises v. Sutherland [1919] 1 K.B. 618 8–079
On Demand Information Plc (In Administrative Receivership) v. Michael Gerson (Finance) Plc [2002] UKHL 13; [2003] 1 A.C. 368; [2002] 2 W.L.R. 919; [2002] 2 All E.R. 949; [2002] 1 All E.R. (Comm) 641; [2002] B.C.C. 673; [2002] C.L.C. 1140; (2002) 99(21) L.S.G. 31; (2002) 146 S.J.L.B. 110; *The Times*, May 2, 2002, HL; reversing [2001] 1 W.L.R. 155; [2000] 4 All E.R. 734; [2000] 2 All E.R. (Comm) 513; [2002] B.C.C. 122; (2000) 150 N.L.J. 1300; *The Times*, September 19, 2000, CA 16–038, 16–039
O'Neil v. Armstrong [1895] 2 Q.B. 418 .... 6–048, 8–079
Oppenheim v. Fraser (1876) 34 L.T. 524; 3 Asp.M.L.C. 146 .... 18–235, 21–039
—— v. Russell (1802) 3 Bos. & P. 42; 127 E.R. 24 15–089
Oppenheimer v. Attenborough [1908] 1 K.B. 221 .... 7–032, 7–037, 7–043
—— v. Cattermole; *sub nom.* Nothman v. Cooper [1976] A.C. 249; [1975] 2 W.L.R. 347; [1975] 1 All E.R. 538; [1975] S.T.C. 91; 50 T.C. 159; [1975] T.R. 13; 119 S.J. 169, HL; affirming [1973] Ch. 264; [1972] 3 W.L.R. 815; [1972] 3 All E.R. 1106; 116 S.J. 802, CA; reversing [1972] Ch. 585; [1972] 2 W.L.R. 1045; [1972] 2 All E.R. 529; [1971] T.R. 507; (1971) 116 S.J. 256, Ch. D 25–043, 25–119
—— v. Frazer and Wyatt [1907] 2 K.B. 50; 76 L.J.K.B. 806; 97 L.T. 3; 23 T.L.R. 410; 51 S.J. 373; 12 Com.Cas. 147 .... 7–037, 7–038, 7–043, 7–045, 7–074
Opthalmic Innovations (U.K.) v. Opthalmic Innovations International Inc. [2004] EWHC 2948 (Ch.); [2005] I.L.Pr. 109 .... 25–019, 25–020, 25–021, 25–060
Orchard v. Simpson (1857) 2 C.B. (N.S.) 299; 140 E.R. 431 16–070
Organ Retention Group Litigation, Re. *See* A v. Leeds Teaching Hospital NHS Trust
Oricon Waren-Handels G.m.b.H. v. Intergraan N.V. [1967] 2 Lloyd's Rep. 82 .... 8–055, 11–087, 23–027
Orient Co. Ltd v. Brekke Howlid [1913] 1 K.B. 531; 82 L.J.K.B. 427; 108 L.T. 507; 18 Com.Cas. 101 19–042
Oriental Pacific (U.S.A.) Inc. v. Toronto Dominion Bank 357 N.Y.S. 2d 957 (1974) 23–027, 23–196, 23–234
Orinoco Navigation Ltd v. Ecotrade SpA (The Ikariada) [1999] 2 All E.R. (Comm) 257; [1999] 2 Lloyd's Rep. 365; [1999] C.L.C. 1713, QBD 25–156
Orion Insurance Co. plc v. Sphere Drake Insurance plc [1992] 1 Lloyd's Rep. 239 ... 2–019
Ornstein v. Alexandra Furnishing Co. (1895) 12 T.L.R. 128 .... 1–056, 5–052, 12–065
—— v. Hickerson 40 F. Supp. 305 23–102
Orteric, The [1920] A.C. 724; 123 L.T. 448; 15 Asp.M.L.C. 10 5–015, 5–138, 5–140, 18–216
Osborn v. Hart (1871) 23 L.T. 851; 19 W.R. 331 .... 10–005, 11–020
Osborn (L.) & Co. Ltd v. Davidson Bros. [1911] V.L.R. 416 8–082
Oscar Chess Ltd v. Williams [1957] 1 W.L.R. 370; 101 S.J. 186; [1957] 1 All E.R. 325 1–009, 3–020, 10–003, 10–006, 10–008, 10–011, 10–017, 10–018, 11–012, 11–019, 13–083, 14–041
O'Sullivan *Re* (1892) 61 L.J.Q.B. 228 15–072
O'Sullivan v. Management Agency and Music Ltd [1985] Q.B. 428; [1984] 3 W.L.R. 448; (1984) 128 S.J. 548; [1985] 3 All E.R. 351; (1984) 81 L.S.Gaz. 2693 16–007
—— v. Williams [1992] 3 All E.R. 385; [1992] R.T.R. 402; (1992) 142 N.L.J. 717; *The Times*, March 13, 1992; *The Independent*, March 20, 1992, CA 5–010, 18–114, 18–149
Ottoman Bank of Nicosia v. Chakarian (No.1) [1930] A.C. 277 25–193
—— v. Chakarian (No.2) [1937] All E.R. 570; [1938] A.C. 260; 107 L.J.P.C. 15; 158 L.T. 1; 54 T.L.R. 122 25–166

Oulu Osakayettio of Oulu, Finland v. Arnold Laver & Co. [1940] 1 K.B. 750; [1940] 2 All E.R. 243; 109 L.J.K.B. 669; 162 L.T. 415; 56 T.L.R. 545; 84 S.J. 453; 45 Com.Cas. 193 19–009
Overbrooke Estates Ltd. v. Glencombe Properties Ltd. [1974] 1 W.L.R. 1335; 118 S.J. 775; [1974] 3 All E.R. 511 .... 13–055, 13–064
Overland Shoes Ltd v. Schenkers Ltd; Overland Shoes Ltd v. Schenkers International Deutschland GmbH [1998] 1 Lloyd's Rep. 498; (1998) 95(11) L.S.G. 36; (1998) 142 S.J.L.B. 84; *The Times*, February 26, 1998, CA 9–026, 13–090, 18–275, 18–280
Overseas Buyers Ltd v. Granadex [1980] 2 Lloyd's Rep. 608 .... 6–047, 8–092, 18–309, 18–320, 18–328
Overseas Medical Supplies Ltd v. Orient Transport Services Ltd [1999] 1 All E.R. (Comm) 981; [1999] 2 Lloyd's Rep. 273; [1999] C.L.C. 1243, CA 13–089, 13–090 13–095, 13–096, 18–280
Overseas Union Bank Ltd v. Chua (1964) 30 M.L.J. 165 .... 23–205, 23–235
Overstone Ltd v. Shipway [1962] 1 W.L.R. 117; 106 SJ. 14; [1962] 1 All E.R. 52 ..... 4–017, 16–005
Owen, *Re* Owen v. I.R.C. [1949] W.N. 201; [1949] L.J.R. 1128; 93 S.J. 287; [1949] 1 All E.R. 901; [1949] T.R. 189 9–030
Owen v. Tate [1976] Q.B. 402; [1975] 3 W.L.R. 369; [1975] 2 All E.R. 129; (1974) 119 S.J. 575, CA 9–044
Owen (Edward) Engineering Ltd v. Barclays Bank International Ltd [1977] 3 W.L.R. 764; (1977) 121 S.J. 617; [1978] 1 All E.R. 976; [1978] 1 Lloyd's Rep. 166; [1977] 6 Build. L.R. 1 .... 23–164, 23–272, 23–276
Owens v. Denton (1835) 1 C.M. & R. 711 9–041
Owenson v. Morse (1796) 7 T.R. 64; 101 E.R. 856 9–030
Owners of Cargo Laden on Board the Albacruz v. Owners of the Albazero; *sub nom.* Concord Petroleum Corp v. Gosford Marine Panama SA [1977] A.C. 774; [1976] 3 W.L.R. 419; [1976] 3 All E.R. 129; [1976] 2 Lloyd's Rep. 467; 120 S.J. 570, HL 18–065, 18–114
Owners of Cargo Lately Laden on Board the David Agmashenebeli v. Owners of the David Agmashenebeli [2002] EWHC 104; [2002] 2 All E.R. (Comm) 806; [2003] 1 Lloyd's Rep. 92; [2003] 1 C.L.C. 714, QBD 18–028, 18–081, 18–082, 18–084, 18–090, 18–093, 18–113, 18–136
Owners of the SS Istros v. FW Dahlstroem & Co [1931] 1 K.B. 247; (1930) 38 Ll. L. Rep. 84, KBD 13–044
Oxendale v. Wetherell (1829) 9 B. & C. 386; 4 Man. & Ry. K.B. 429; 7 L.J. (O.S.) K.B. 264; 109 E.R. 143 .... 8–046, 8–047, 8–072
Oxford v. Moss (1978) 68 Cr. Hpp.R. 183; [1979] Crim.L.R. 119 1–080
—— v. Sangers Ltd [1965] 1 Q.B. 491; [1995] 2 W.L.R. 145; 129 J.P. 98; [1965] 1 All E.R. 96 1–027
Ozalid Group Export Ltd v. African Continental Bank Ltd [1979] 2 Lloyd's Rep. 231 .... 23–169, 25–192

P.J. van der Zijden Wildhander N.V. v. Tucker & Cross Ltd [1975] 2 Lloyd's Rep. 240 .... 18–344, 19–140, 19–141
P.Q. v. Australian Red Cross Society [1992] 1 V.R. 19 1–089
P & O Developments Ltd v. Guy's and St. Thomas' NHS Trust (1998) 62 Con.L.R. 38 17–078
P. & O. Oil Trading Ltd v. Scanoil A.B. (The Orient Prince) [1985] 1 Lloyd's Rep. 389 .... 18–002, 19–074
P. and O. Steam Navigation Co. v. Shand (1865) 3 Moo.P.C. (N.S.) 272; 6 New Rep. 387; 12 L.T. 808; 11 Jur. (N.S.) 771; 13 W.R. 1049; 2 Mar.L.C. 244 25–010
PT Pan Indonesia Bank TBK v. Marconi Communications International Ltd. *See* Marconi Communications International Ltd v. PT Pan Indonesia Bank TBK
PT Putrabali v. Fratelli de Lorenzi SNC, unreported, October 15, 2001 19–022
PT Putrabali Adyamulia v. Societe est Epices; PT Putrabali Adyamulia v. Enrico Webb James SNC [2003] 2 Lloyd's Rep. 700, QBD 19–022, 19–083
Paal Wilson & Co. A/S v. Partenreederei Hannah Blumenthal [1983] 1 A.C. 854; [1982] 3 W.L.R. 1149; [1983] 1 All E.R. 34; (1982) 126 S.J. 835; [1983] Com.L.R. 20; [1983] 1 Lloyd's Rep. 103, H.L. 6–034, 6–041, 8–031

Paccar International Inc. v. Commercial Bank of Kuwait 587 F. 2d 783 (C.D. Cal. 1984) 23–153
Pacific and General Insurance Co. Ltd v. Hazell; Pacific and General Insurance Co. Ltd v. Home and Overseas Insurance Co. Ltd [1997] L.R.L.R. 65; [1997] B.C.C. 400; [1997] 6 Re. L.R. 157, QBD (Comm Ct) 9–044
Pacific Associates Inc. v. Baxter [1900] 1 Q.B. 993; [1989] 3 W.L.R. 1150; (1989) 133 S.J. 123; [1989] 2 All E.R. 159; (1989) 44 Build. L.R. 33, CA 9–044, 18–149
Pacific Molasses Co. and United Molasses Trading Co. v. Entre Rios Compania Naviera SA (The San Nicholas) [1976] 1 Lloyd's Rep. 8, CA 20–070, 25–071
Pacific Motor Auctions Property Limited v. Motor Credits (Hire Finance) Ltd [1965] A.C. 867; [1965] 2 W.L.R. 881; 109 S.J. 210; [1965] 2 All E.R. 105, P.C. 7–038, 7–039, 7–043, 7–055, 7–059, 7–077
Pacific Produce Co. Ltd v. Franklin Co-operative Growers Ltd [1968] N.Z.L.R. 521 11–040
Pacific Trading Co. Ltd v. Wiener (Robert O.) (1923) 14 Ll.L.R. 51 .... 11–013, 11–015
Paclantic Financing Co. Inc. v. Moscow Narodny Bank [1984] 1 W.L.R. 930; (1984) 128 S.J. 349; [1984] 1 Lloyd's Rep. 469; (1984) 81 L.S.Gaz. 899, CA 22–062
Pacol Ltd v. Trade Lines Ltd (The Henrik Sif) [1982] (1982) 126 S.J. 312; [1982] Com.L.R. 92; 1 Lloyd's Rep. 456 .... 7–012, 18–054
Page v. Cowasjee Eduljee (1866) L.R. 1 P.C. 127; 3 Moo.P.C. (N.S.) 361; 16 E.R. 189; *sub nom.* Page v. Eduljee, 14 L.T. 176 .... 4–001, 4–032, 15–117, 17–106
Pagnan and Fratelli v. Tradax Overseas SA [1980] 1 Lloyd's Rep. 665 8–065
Pagnan (R) & Fratelli v. Corbisa Industrial Agropacuaria [1970] 1 W.L.R. 1306; 114 S.J. 568; [1970] 1 All E.R. 165; [1970] 2 Lloyd's Rep. 14, CA 16–056, 16–075, 17–002, 17–007, 17–019, 17–020, 17–026, 17–040, 17–054
—— v. Finagrain (The Adolph Leonhart) [1986] 2 Lloyd's Rep. 395 8–090, 19–088, 20–020
Pagnan (R) & Fratelli v. Lebanese Organisation for International Commerce (The Caloric) [1981] 2 Lloyd's Rep. 675; [1981] Com.L.R. 152 .... 19–088, 19–176, 19–181
—— v. N.G.J. Schouten N.V. (The Philipinas 1) [1973] 1 Lloyd's Rep. 349 20–046
Pagnan SpA v. Feed Products Ltd [1987] 2 Lloyd's Rep. 601, CA 2–011, 2–017, 20–014, 20–031
—— v. Granaria B.V. [1986] 2 Lloyd's Rep. 547, CA 2–011
—— v. Tradax Ocean Transportation SA [1987] 3 All E.R. 565; [1987] 2 Lloyd's Rep. 342 .... 6–047, 8–088, 8–099, 18–314, 18–317, 18–318, 18–325, 20–040
Palacath v. Flanagan [1985] 2 All E.R. 161; [1985] 1 E.G.L.R. 86; (1985) 274 E.G. 143; (1985) 135 New L.J. 364 .... 2–052, 13–039
Palaniappa Chettiar v. Arunasalam Chettiar [1962] A.C. 294; [1962] 2 W.L.R. 548; *sub nom.* Palaniappa Chettiar v. Arunsalam Chettiar, 106 S.J. 110 3–033
Palmco Shipping Inc. v. Continental Ore Corporation [1970] 2 Lloyd's Rep. 21 19–037
Palmer v. Pratt (1824) 2 Bing. 185; 9 Moo.C.P. 358; 3 L.J. (O.S.) C.P. 250 22–043
—— v. Simmonds (1854) 2 Drew 221; 2 W.R. 313; 61 E.R. 704 5–153
—— v. Temple (1839) 9 A. & E. 508; 1 Per. & Dav. 379; 8 L.J.Q.B. 179 16–040
Palmolive Co. (of England) Ltd v. Freedman [1928] Ch. 264; L.J.Ch. 40; 138 L.T. 274; 44 L.T.R. 86; 71 S.J. 927 3–037
Pan-American Bank and Trust Co. v. National City Bank of New York 6F. 2d 762 (1925) 23–174, 23–232
Pan-American World Airways Inc. v. Aetna Casualty and Surety Co., The [1970] 1 Lloyd's Rep. 77, U.S.C.A.; affirming [1974] 1 Lloyd's Rep. 207, U.S.D.C. 8–097
Pan Ocean Shipping Co. v. Creditcorp (The Trident Beauty) [1994] 1 W.L.R. 161; [1994] 1 All E.R. 470; [1994] 1 Lloyd's Rep. 365; (1994) 144 New L.J. 1203; *The Times*, February 1, 1994; *The Independent*, February 1, 1994, HL 18–123, 18–147
Panaghia Tinnou. The [1986] 2 Lloyd's Rep. 586 20–018
Panalpina International Transport Ltd v. Densil Underwear Ltd [1981] 1 Lloyd's Rep. 187 16–046
Panatown v. McAlpine Construction Ltd *See* Alfred McAlpine Construction Ltd v. Panatown (No. 1)
Panchaud Fréres SA v. Etablissements General Grain Co. [1970] 1 Lloyd's Rep. 53, CA 8–101, 12–034, 12–037, 19–144, 19–151, 19–160
Pancommerce SA v. Veecheema B.V. [1983] 2 Lloyd's Rep. 304; [1983] Com.L.R. 230, CA; [1982] 1 Lloyd's Rep. 645 .... 6–052, 6–053, 8–091, 8–092, 8–102, 18–340, 18–352, 18–353

Panoutsos v. Hadley (Raymond) Corporation [1917] 2 K.B. 473 .... 9–028, 12–034, 12–035, 19–207, 23–055, 23–084, 23–095
Panozza (Allan J.) Property Ltd v. Allied Interstate (Queensland) Pty. Ltd [1976] 2 N.S.W.L.R. 192 .... 25–191, 25–204
Pantanassa [1970] P. 187; [1970] 2 W.L.R. 981; *sub nom.* Pantanassa The, (1969) 114 S.J. 372; [1970] 1 Lloyd's Rep. 153 .... 19–051, 19–120
Pao On v. Lau Yiu Long [1980] A.C. 614; [1979] 3 W.L.R. 435; (1979) 123 S.J. 319; [1979] 3 All E.R. 65, PC 14–052A
Paragon Finance plc v. Nash; Paragon Finance plc v. Staunton
Paragon Finance plc. v. Staunton *See* Paragon Finance plc v. Nash [2001] EWCA Civ 1466; [2002] 1 W.L.R. 685; [2002] 2 All E.R. 248; [2001] 2 All E.R. (Comm) 1025; (2001) 98(44) L.S.G. 36; (2001) 145 S.J.L.B. 244; *The Times*, October 25, 2001, CA 14–038, 14–150
Paramount Export Co. v. Asia Trust Bank 238 Col. Rep. 920 (App. 1987) 23–203
Parana Plantations Ltd. *Re* [1946] 2 All E.R. 214; 90 S.J. 430 25–167
Parchim, The [1918] A.C. 157; 87 L.J.P. 18; 117 L.T. 738; 34 T.L.R. 53; 14 Asp.M.L.C. 196 .... 1–126, 5–015, 5–027, 5–084, 5–112, 18–209, 18–214, 18–242, 19–009, 19–099, 20–001, 20–008, 20–070, 20–077, 20–079, 20–080, 20–081, 20–088, 20–093, 25–133
Paris v. Goodwin [1954] N.Z.L.R. 823 7–032
Paris Savings and Loan Association v. Walden, 730 S.W. 2d 355 (Ct App. Tex. 1987) 23–150
Parker, *Re* (1843) 3 Mont. D. & De G. 332; 7 Jur. 910 22–092
Parker v. British Airways Board [1982] Q.B. 1904; [1982] 2 W.L.R. 503; [1982] 1 All E.R. 834; 125 S.J. 119, CA 7–116
Parker v. Gordon (1806) 7 East, 385; 3 Smith K.B. 358; 6 Esp. 41 22–099
—— v. Gossage (1835) 2 C.M. & R. 617; 1 Gale 288; Tyr. & Gro. 105; 5 L.J.Ex. 4 15–024
—— v. Palmer (1821) 4 B. & A. 387; 106 E.R. 978 .... 11–022, 11–074, 12–051
—— v. Patrick (1793) 5 T.R. 715 7–029
—— v. Schuller (1901) 17 T.L.R. 299 .... 19–002, 19–008
—— v. South Eastern Railway (1877) 2 C.P.D. 416 .... 2–012, 13–012, 13–015
Parkinson v. College of Ambulance [1925] 2 K.B. 1; 93 L.J.K.B. 1066; 133 L.T. 135; 40 T.L.R. 886; 69 S.J. 107 3–031
—— v. Lee (1802) East, 314; 102 E.R. 389 11–074
Paros Shipping Corp. v. Nafta (GB) Ltd (The Paros) [1987] 2 Lloyd's Rep. 269, QBD (Comm Ct.) 25–071
Parrish & Heimbecker Ltd v. Gooding Lbr. Ltd (1986) 67 D.L.R. (2d) 495 6–041
Parsons v. Mather & Platt Ltd [1977] 1 W.L.R. 855; (1977) 121 S.J. 204; [1977] 2 All E.R. 715 16–013
—— v. New Zealand Shipping Co. [1901] 1 K.B. 548; 70 L.J.K.B. 404; 84 L.T. 218; 48 W.R. 355; 17 T.L.R. 274; 9 Asp.M.L.C. 170; 6 Com.Cas. 41 .... 11–018, 18–033, 18–037, 18–043, 18–273, 19–146
—— v. Sexton (1874) 4 C.B. 899; 16 L.J.C. 181; 9 L.T. (o.s.) 410; 11 Jur. 849; 136 E.R. 763 5–020
Parsons & Co. v. Electricity Trust (1976) 16 SAS.R. 93 25–167
Parsons Bros. Ltd v. Shea (1965) 53 D.L.R. (2d) 86 .... 6–051, 6–063
Parsons Corp. v. CV Scheepvaartonderneming Happy Ranger (The Happy Ranger) [2002] EWCA Civ 694; [2002] 2 All E.R. (Comm.) 24, CA; reversing [2002] 1 All E.R. (Comm.) 176; [2001] 2 Lloyd's Rep. 530, QBD (Comm Ct) 18–017, 18–039, 18–009, 18–015, 18–018, 18–024, 18–047, 18–048, 18–049, 18–063, 18–067, 18–071, 18–076, 18–084, 20–089, 18–102, 21–106, 25–072
Parsons (H.) (Livestock) Ltd v. Uttley Ingham & Co. Ltd [1978] Q.B. 791 .... 1–043, 11–064, 12–121, 16–043, 16–044, 16–047, 17–047, 17–074
Partabmull Rameshwar v. Sethia (K.C.) (1944); Partabmull Rameshwar v. Sethia (K.C.) (1944); Sethia (1944) v. Partabmull Rameshwar *See* Sethia (K.C.) Ltd. v. Partabmull Rameshwar.
Partenreederei M/S Heidberg v. Grosvenor Grain & Feed Co. Ltd (The Heidberg) [1994] 2 Lloyd's Rep. 287 .... 18–047, 18–048, 25–079, 25–080
Partridge v. Crittenden [1968] 1 W.L.R. 1204 .... 1–027, 2–002

Partridge & Co. (N.Z.) Ltd v. Bignell and Holmes [1924] N.Z.L.R. 769 12–055
Pasley v. Freeman (1789) 3 T.R. 51 10–016
Pastor v. National Republic Bank of Chicago, 56 111.App. 421, 371 N.E. 2d 1127 (1975) 23–068
Patel v. Standard Chartered Bank [2001] All E.R. 66 23–117
Paterson Zochonis & Co Ltd v. Elder Dempster & Co Ltd; *sub nom.* Paterson Zochnois & Co Ltd v. Elder Dampster & Co Ltd; Elder Dempster & Co Ltd v. Paterson Zochonis & Co Ltd; Griffiths Lewis Steam Navigation Co Ltd v. Paterson Zochonis & Co Ltd [1924] A.C. 522; (1924) 18 Ll. L. Rep. 319, HL 18–098, 19–095, 19–097
Paton v. Payne (1897) 35 S.L.R 112 8–025
Paton's Trustees v. Finlayson 1923 S.C. 872 .... 1–100, 15–038, 15–049
Patrick v. Harrison (1792) 3 Bro. C.C. 476; 29 E.R. 653 22–064
—— v. Russo-British Grain Export Co. Ltd. [1927] 2 K.B. 535; 137 L.T. 815; 43 T.L.R. 724 .... 16–046, 17–029, 17–030, 17–035
Patry v. General Motors Acceptance Corp. of Canada Ltd (2000) 187 D.L.R. (4th) 99. 7–046
Patten v. Thomas Motors Property Ltd [1965] N.S.W.R. 1457 .... 4–010, 4–011
—— v. Thompson (1816) 5 M. & S. 350; 105 E.R. 990 8–012
Pattison v. Robinson (1816) 5 M. & S. 105; 105 E.R. 990 8–012
Paul v. Dod (1846) 2 C.B. 800; 15 L.J.C.P. 177; 7 L.T. (o.s.) 44; 10 Jur. 335; 135 E.R. 1158 9–063
—— v. Joel (1858) 27 L.J.Ex. 380, affirmed (1859) 28 L.J. Ex 143 22–124
Paul (H.W.) Ltd v. Pim (W.H.) Junior & Co. Ltd [1922] 2 K.B. 360; 91 L.J.K.B. 556; 38 T.L.R. 95; 66 S.J. 93; 27 Com.Cas. 98 .... 21–032, 21–037, 21–038, 21–039
Paul (R. & W.) Ltd v. National S.S. Co. Ltd (1937) 59 Ll.L.R. 28 .... 18–119, 18–139, 18–215
Paul & Co. v. Glasgow Corp. (1900) 3 F. (Ct. of Sess.) 119 .... 10–020, 11–082
Paul & Frank Ltd v. Discount Bank (Overseas) Ltd [1967] Ch. 348; [1966] 3 W.L.R. 490; [1966] 2 All E.R. 922; 110 S.J. 423, Ch D 24–027, 24–029, 24–030
Pavia & Co. SpA v. Thurmann-Nielsen [1952] 2 Q.B. 84; [1952] 1 All E.R. 492; [1952] 1 T.L.R. 586; [1952] 1 Lloyd's Rep. 153, C.A., affirming [1951] 2 All E.R. 866 .... 9–053, 18–309, 18–313, 23–088, 23–089, 23–090
Payne v. Cave (1789) 3 Term Rep. 148 2–004
—— v. Elsden (1900) 17 T.L.R. 161 4–032
—— v. Minister of Food (1953) 103 L.J. 141, Cty. Ct. 11–019, 17–065,
—— v. Wilson [1895] 2 Q.B. 537; 65 L.J.Q.B. 150; 73 L.T. 12; 43 W.R. 657 7–070
Payne & Routh v. Lillico & Sons (1920) 36 T.L.R. 569 .... 8–049, 8–054, 19–012
Paynter v. James (1867) L.R. 2 C.P. 348; 15 L.T. 600; 15 W.R. 493; 2 Mar.L.C. 450 8–004
Payzu Ltd v. Saunders [1919] 2 K.B. 581 ..... 8–077, 8–080, 9–051, 16–052, 17–026, 17–027
Peachdart Ltd. *Re* [1984] Ch. 131; [1983] 3 W.L.R. 873; (1983) 127 S.J. 839; [1983] 3 All E.R. 204; (1984) 81 L.S.Gaz. 204 ..... 1–060, 5–142, 5–144, 5–145, 5–146, 5–147, 5–149, 5–150, 5–156, 5–160
Peacock v. Pursell (1863) L.J.C.P. 266; 8 L.T. 636; 14 C.B. (N.S) 728; 10 Jur. (N.S.) 175; 11 W.R. 834 .... 22–114, 22–115, 23–097
Peacocke Co. v. Williams (1909) 28 N.Z.L.R. 354 22–041
Pearce v. Brain [1929] 2 K.B. 310; 98 L.J.K.B. 559; 141 L.T. 264; 93 J.P.Jo. 380; 45 T.L.R. 501; 73 S.J. 402 .... 1–036, 2–028, 2–039
—— v. Brooks (1866) L.R. 1 Ex. 213; 4H. & C. 358; 35 L.J.Ex. 134; 14 L.T. 288; 20 J.P. 295; 12 Jur. (N.S.) 342; 14 W.R. 614 3–029
Pearl Mill Co. v. Ivy Tannery Co. Ltd [1919] 1 K.B. 78 .... 8–031, 8–039
Pearne v. Lisle (1749) Amb. 75 17–099
Pearson v. Dawson (1858) E.B. & E. 448; 27 L.J.Q.B. 248; 31 L.T. (o.s.) 1015; 120 E.R. 576 .... 15–060, 15–093, 15–096
—— v. Rose & Young Ltd [1951] 1 K.B. 275; 66 T.L.R. (Pt. 2) 886; 94 S.J. 778; [1950] 2 All E.R. 1027, CA 1–083, 7–036, 7–036, 7–037, 7–038, 7–044, 7–046, 7–074, 7–075
Pearson (S.) & Son Ltd v. Dublin Corporation [1907] A.C. 351 ..... 4–022, 12–016, 13–016
Pease v. Gloahec (The Marie Joseph) (1866) L.R. 1 P.C. 219; Brown & Lush 449; 2 Moo.P.C.C. (N.S.) 556; 35 L.J.P.C. 66; 15 L.T. 6; 12 Jur. (N.S.) 677; 15 W.R. 201; 2 Mar.L.C. 394 .... 7–021, 18–084, 18–086

Peco Arts Inc. v. Hazlitt Gallery Ltd [1983] 1 W.L.R. 1315; (1983) 127 S.J. 806; [1983] 3 All E.R. 193; (1984) 81 L.S.Gaz. 203 10–006
Pcene v. Taylor (1916) 32 T.L.R. 674 8–074
Peer International Corp v. Termidor Music Publishers Ltd (No.1); *sub nom.* Peer International Corp v. Termidor Music Publishers Co Inc [2003] EWCA Civ 1156; [2004] Ch. 212; [2004] 2 W.L.R. 849; [2003] E.M.L.R. 34; [2004] R.P.C. 23; (2003) 26(11) I.P.D. 26070; (2003) 100(37) L.S.G. 31; *The Times*, September 11, 2003, CA 25–121, 25–131
Peeters v. Opie (1671) 2 Wms. Saund. 350 10–026
Peevins v. Downing (1876) 1 C.P.D. 220 8–025
Pegler Ltd v. Wang U.K. Ltd (No. 1) [2000] B.L.R. 218; 70 Con. L.R. 68; [2000] I.T.C.L.R. 617; [2000] Masons C.L.R. 19, QBD (T & CC) 11–070, 13–037, 13–090, 13–095
Peirce v. London Horse and Carriage Repository [1922] W.N. 170 7–031
Pelhams (Materials) Ltd v. Mercantile Commodities Syndicate [1953] 2 Lloyd's Rep. 281 12–047
Pellecat v. Angell (1835) 2 Cr.M. & R. 311 25–119
Penarth Dock Engineering Co. v. Pounds [1963] 1 Lloyd's Rep. 359 .... 9–004, 9–008
Pendred Hairdressing Ltd v. Customs and Excise Commissioners (1973) 1 V.A.T.T.R. 81 1–047
Pennington v. Crossley & Sons (1897) 77 L.T. 43; 13 T.L.R. 513; 41 S.J. 661 9–042
—— v. Reliance Motor Works Ltd [1923] 1 K.B. 127; 92 L.J.K.B. 202; 128 L.T. 384; 38 T.L.R. 670; 66 S.J. 667 15–054
Pennsylvania Shipping Co. v. Cie. Nationale de Navigation [1936] 2 All E.R. 1167; 155 L.T. 294; 80 S.J. 722; 42 Com.Cas. 45; 55 Ll.L.R. 271 .... 1–011, 10–040, 12–119
People's Bank of Halifax v. Estey (1904) 34 S.C.R. 429 .... 7–009, 7–011
Pepper (Inspector of Taxes) v. Hart [1993] A.C. 593; [1992] 3 W.L.R. 1032; [1993] 1 All E.R. 42; [1993] I.C.R. 291; [1992] S.T.C. 898; [1993] I.R.L.R. 33; [1993] R.V.R. 127; [1992] N.P.C. 154; (1993) N.L.J. Rep. 17; *The Times*, November 30, 1992; *The Independent*, November 26, 1992, HL 1–005
Pera Shipping Corp v. Petroship SA (The Pera) [1985] 2 Lloyd's Rep. 103, CA 13–020
Peregrine Systems Ltd v. Steria Ltd [2005] EWCA Civ 239; [2005] All E.R. (D.) 215 (Mar); [2005] Info. T.L.R. 294, CA 8–037
Percival v. Blake (1826) 2 C. & P. 514; 172 E.R. 233 12–065
—— v. Oldacre (1865) 18 C.B. (N.S.) 398 10–003
Percival Ltd v. London C.C. Asylums Committee (1918) 87 L.J.K.B. 677; 82 J.P. 157; 16 L.G.R. 367 .... 2–009, 8–058, 8–059, 8–060
Percy (G.) Trentham Ltd v. Archital Luxfer Ltd [1993] 1 Lloyd's Rep. 24 2–017
Perkins v. Bell [1893] 1 Q.B. 193; 62 L.J.Q.B. 91; 67 L.T. 792; 41 W.R. 195; 9 T.L.R. 147; 37 S.J. 130; 4 R. 212 .. 12–043, 12–047, 12–048, 20–108, 20–109, 20–110, 21–045
Perks v. Clark *See* Clark v. Perks
Perlmutter v. Beth David Hospital (1955) 123 N.E. (2d) 792 .... 1–046, 1–089
Perrett v. Collins [1998] 2 Lloyd's Rep. 255; [1999] P.N.L.R. 77; *The Times*, June 23, 1998, CA 18–149
Perry v. Attwood (1856) 6 E. & B. 691 9–041
—— v. Equitable Life Assurance Society of the United States of America (1929) 45 T.L.R. 468 25–006
Perry (Howard E.) & Co. Ltd v. British Railways Board [1980] I.C.R. 743; [1980] 1 W.L.R. 1375; (1980) 124 S.J. 591; [1980] 2 All E.R. 579 17–098
Perry v. Phillips (Sidney) & Son (A Firm) [1982] 1 W.L.R. 1297; [1982] 3 All E.R. 705; (1982) 126 S.J. 626; 22 Build.L.R. 120; 263 E.G. 888; 79 L.S.Gaz. 1175, CA 16–047
Peruvian Guano Co. v. Dravfus Bros [1892] A.C. 166; 61 L.J.Ch. 749; 66 L.T. 536; 7 Asp.M.L.C. 225; 87 T.L.R. 327 15–116
Pesquieras v. Beer (1949) 82 W.L. Rep. 501 8–097
Petch v. Tutin (1846) 15 M. & W. 110; 15 L.J.Ex. 280; 153 E.R. 782 .... 1–106, 5–095
Petelin v. Cullen (1975) 132 C.L.R. 355 .... 7–018, 13–013
Peter der Grosse, The (1875) 1 P.D. 414 18–028
Peter Symmons & Co. v. Cooke (1981) 131 N.L.J. 758 13–074
Peters v. Fleming (1840) 6 M. & W. 42 .... 2–030, 2–031
Peters & Co. v. Planner (1895) 11 T.L.R. 169 .... 12–012, 13–028, 13–052

Peterson v. Ayre (1853) 13 C.B. 353; 138 E.R. 1235 17–037
Peto v. Blades (1814) 5 Taunt. 657; 128 E.R. 849 .... 4–001, 4–032
Petrofina (Great Britain) Ltd v. Martin [1966] Ch. 146; [1966] 2 W.L.R. 318; 109 S.J. 1009; [1966] 1 All E.R. 126, CA 3–034
Petrofina SA v. Aut Ltd (The Maersk Nimrod) [1991] 1 Lloyd's Rep. 269 19–010
—— v. Compagnia Italiana Transporto Olii Minerali of Genoa (1937) 53 T.L.R. 650 13–040
Petromec Inc v. Petroleo Brasileiro SA Petrobras (No.3) [2004] EWHC 1180; [2005] 1 Lloyd's Rep. 219, QBD 1–043, 5–093
Petrotrade Inc. v. Stinnes Handel G.m.b.H. [1995] 1 Lloyd's Rep. 142; *The Times*, July 27, 1994, ... 8–024, 10–037, 16–067, 16–069, 17–005, 18–232, 20–014, 20–029, 20–105, 20–107
Pettitt v. Mitchell (1842) 4 Man. & G. 819; Car. & M. 424; 5 Scott N.R. 721; 121 L.J.C.P. 9; 6 Jur. 1016; 134 E.R. 337 .... 12–039, 12–042, 13–029
Peyman v. Lanjani [1985] Ch. 457; [1985] 2 W.L.R. 154; (1984) 128 S.J. 853; [1984] 3 All E.R. 703; (1984) 48 P. & C.R. 398; (1985) 82 L.S.Gaz. 43, CA 12–006, 12–037, 14–047, 18–358, 19–150, 19–151
Pfeiffer (John) Pty Ltd v. Rogerson (2002) 172 A.L.R. 625 .... 25–190, 25–191
Pfeiffer Weinkellerei-Weinenkauf GmbH & Co. v. Arbuthnot Factors Ltd [1988] 1 W.L.R. 150; [1988] 132 S.J. 89; [1987] B.C.L.C. 522; (1987) 3 B.C.C. 608..... 5–142, 5–147, 5–151, 5–153, 5–160, 5–161, 25–141
Pfizer Corporation v. Ministry of Health [1965] A.C. 512; [1965] 2 W.L.R. 387; 109 S.J. 149; [1965] 1 All E.R. 450; [1965] R.P.C. 261 1–071
Pharmaccutical Society of Great Britain v. Boots Cash Chemists (Southern) Ltd [1952] 2 Q.B. 795; [1952] 2 T.L.R. 340; 116 J.P. 507; 96 S.J. 513 2–002
—— v. Dickson [1970] A.C. 403; [1968] 3 W.L.R. 286; (1968) 112 S.J. 601; [1968] 2 All E.R. 686, HL 3–039
Phelps v. McQuade (1917) 220 N.Y. 232 3–014
Phelps, Stokes & Co. v. Comber (1885) 29 Ch.D. 813; 54 L.J.Ch. 1017; 52 L.T. 873; 33 W.R. 829; 5 Asp.M.L.C. 428 .... 15–085, 15–090
Phibco Energy Inc. v. Coastal (Bermuda) Ltd (The Aragon) (1987) [1991] 1 Lloyd's Rep. 61 20–029
Phibro Energy A.G. v. Nissho Iwai Corp. (The Homan Jade) [1991] 1 Lloyd's Rep. 38 .... 18–232, 19–063, 19–071, 20–034
Philip Alexander Securities & Futures Ltd v. Bamberger; *sub nom.* Phillip Alexander Securities & Futures Ltd v. Bamberger; Philip Alexander Securities & Futures Ltd v. Gilhaus [1996] C.L.C. 1757; [1997] Eu. L.R. 63; [1997] I.L.Pr. 73; *The Times*, July 22, 1996, CA 25–114
Philip Bros. Inc. v. Oil Country Specialists 709 S.W. 2d 262 C. A. Tex (1986) 23–153
Philips v. Astling (1809) 2 Taunt. 206 22–133
Philips Hong Kong Ltd v. Att.-Gen. of Hong Kong (1993) 61 B.L.R. 41; (1993) 9 Const. L.J. 202; *The Times*, February 15, 1993, P.C. 16–032
Phillimore v. Barry (1808) 1 Camp. 513; 170 E.R. 1040, N.P. 5–018
Phillips v. Britannia Hygienic Laundry Co. Ltd [1923] 1 K.B. 539; 92 L.J.K.B. 389; 128 L.T. 690; 39 T.L.R. 207; 67 S.J. 365; 21 L.G.R. 168; [1923], 2 K.B. 832, C.A. 17–074
—— v. Brooks Ltd [1919] 2 K.B. 243 .... 5–026, 7–021, 7–023, 7–028
—— v. Cycle and General Finance Cpn. [1977] C.L.Y. 364 11–019
—— v. Dalziel [1948] W.N. 429; 64 T.L.R. 628, 112 J.P. 445; [1948] 2 All E.R. 810; 47 L.G.R. 31, D.C. 2–002
—— v. Homfray (1883) 24 Ch. D. 439; 49 L.T. 5; 32 W.R. 6 1–073
—— v. Huth (1860) 6 M. & W. 572 7–039
—— v. Lamdin [1949] 2 K.B. 33; [1949] L.J.R. 1293; 93 S.J. 320; [1949] 1 All E.R. 770 17–099
Phillips Products Ltd v. Hyland Ltd [1987] 1 W.L.R. 659; (1985) 129 S.J. 47; [1987] 2 All E.R. 620; (1988) 4 Const. L.J. 53, CA 13–064, 13–089
Philpott v. Bryant (1827) 3 C. & P. 244 22–110
Phillpotts v. Evans (1839) 5 N. & W. 475; 9 L.J.Ex. 33; 151 E.R. 200 .... 16–082, 17–016
Phoebus D. Kyprianou Coy v. Pim (Wm. H.) Jr. & Co. Ltd [1977] 2 Lloyd's Rep. 570 .... 20–115, 20–135, 21–041
Phoenix Bessemer Steel Co., *Re, ex p.* Carnforth Haematite Iron (1876) 4 Ch.D. 108; 46 L.J.Ch. 115; 35 L.T. 776; 25 W.R. 187 .... 3–048, 8–004, 8–078, 8–083, 15–025, 15–037, 15–108

Phoenix Distributors Ltd v. Clarke (L.B.) (London) Ltd [1966] 2 Lloyd's Rep. 285; 116 New L.J. 1713; [1966] C.L.Y. 10833 .... 11–044, 11–059
Phoenix General Insce. Co. of Greece SA v. Halvanon Insce. Co. Ltd [1988] Q.B. 216; [1987] 2 W.L.R. 512; (1987) 131 S.J. 257; [1987] 2 All E.R. 152; [1987] F.L.R. 48, CA 3–028
Phosphate Mining Co. v. Rankin Gilmore & Co. (1915) 21 Com.Cas. 248 8–094
Photo Production Ltd v. Securicor Transport Ltd [1980] A.C. 827; [1980] 2 W.L.R. 283; (1980) 124 S.J. 147; [1980] 1 All E.R. 556; [1980] 1 Lloyd's Rep. 545, HL .. 4–020, 8–006, 8–080, 10–027, 10–030, 10–033, 12–018, 12–022, 12–067, 12–108, 13–020, 13–034, 13–049, 13–046, 13–047, 13–048, 13–052, 16–032, 16–036, 16–056, 18–059, 18–276, 19–207, 23–131
Phrantzes v. Argenti [1960] 2 Q.B. 19; [1960] 2 W.L.R. 521; [1960] 1 All E.R. 778; 104 S.J. 271, QBD 25–146, 25–190
Picardi (t/a Picardi Architects) v. Cuniberti [2002] EWHC 2923; [2003] B.L.R. 487; 94 Con. L.R. 81; (2003) 19 Const. L.J. 350, QBD 14–035
Pickard v. Sears (1837) 6 A. & E. 469 7–010
Pickin v. Graham (1833) 1 Cr. & M. 725; 3 Tyr. 923; 2 L.J. Ex. 253; 149 E.R. 591 .. 22–131
Pickering v. Busk (1812) 15 East. 38 7–011
Pickersgill (William) & Sons Ltd v. London, etc. Insurance Co. [1912] 3 K.B. 614; [1911–13] All E.R. 861; 82 L.J.K.B. 130; 107 L.T. 305; 28 T.L.R. 591; 57 S.J. 11, 12 Asp.M.L.C. 263; 18 Com.Cas. 1 10–009
Pickford v. Grand Junction Railway (1841) 8 M. & W. 372 8–004
Pignatoro v. Gilroy [1919] 1 K.B. 459; 88 L.J.K.B. 726; 120 L.T. 480; 35 T.L.R. 191; 63 S.J. 265; 24 Com.Cas. 174 .... 5–007, 5–077, 6–002
Pigot v. Cubley (1864) 15 C.B. (N.S.) 701; 3 New Rep. 607; 33 L.J.C.P. 134; 9 L.T. 804; 10 Jur. (N.S.) 318; 12 W.R. 467 7–110
Pilgram v. Rice-Smith [1977] 1 W.L.R. 671; [1977] 2 All E.R. 658; [1977] Cr.App.R. 142; [1977] Crim.L.R. 371, D.C. 2–002, 5–082
Pilkington v. Wood [1953] Ch. 770 16–052
Pini & Co. v. Smith & Co. (1895) 22 R. 699; 32 Sc.L.R. 474; 3 S.L.T. 20 ... 12–043, 12–055
Pinnel's Case (1602) 5 Co.Rep. 117a 9–024
Pinnock Bros. v. Lewis and Peat Ltd [1923] 1 K.B. 680 .... 11–016, 11–020, 13–023, 13–025, 13–041, 13–051, 17–060, 17–076, 17–077, 17–081, 17–083, 17–084
Pinto Leite & Nephews, *ex p.* Visconde des Olivaes, *Re* [1929] 1 Ch. 221; [1928] All E.R. 371; 98 L.J.Ch. 211; 140 L.T. 587; [1928] B & C.R. 188 23–170
Pioneer Container, The, *See* K.H. Enterprise (Cargo Owners) v. Pioneer Container (Owners).
Pioneer Shipping Ltd v. B.T.P. Tioxide Ltd (The Nema) [1982] A.C. 724; [1981] 3 W.L.R. 292; (1981) 125 S.J. 542; [1981] 2 All E.R. 1030; [1981] 2 Lloyd's Rep. 239; [1981] Com.L.R. 197 .... 6–041, 18–300, 19–140
Pirelli General Cable Works Ltd v. Oscar Faber & Partners [1983] 1 A.C. 1; [1983] 2 W.L.R. 6; (1983) 127 S.J. 16; [1983] 1 All E.R. 65; (1983) 265 E.G. 979, H.L. 12–121, 14–086
Pitrie v. Racey (1963) 37 D.L.R. (2d) 495 5–045
Plaimar Ltd v. Waters Trading Co. Ltd (1945) 72 C.L.R. 304 ...... 16–028, 19–006, 19–007, 19–016, 19–029, 19–043, 19–075, 19–214
Plasticmoda Societa per Azioni v. Davidsons (Manchester) Ltd [1952] 1 Lloyd's Rep. 527, C.A. 9–028, 23–092, 23–096
Platform Home Loans Ltd v. Oyston Shipways Ltd [2000] 2 A.C. 190; [1999] 2 W.L.R. 518; [1999] 1 All E.R. 833; [1999] C.L.C. 867; (1999) 1 T.C.L.R. 18; [1999] P.N.L.R. 469; [1999] 1 E.G.L.R. 77; [1999] 13 E.G. 119; [1999] E.G.C.S. 26; (1999) 96(10) L.S.G. 31; (1999) 149 N.L.J. 283; (1999) 143 S.J.L.B. 65; [1999] N.P.C. 21; *The Times*, February 19, 1999; *The Independent*, March 5, 1999, HL; reversing [1998] Ch. 466; [1998] 3 W.L.R. 94; [1998] 4 All E.R. 252; [1998] P.N.L.R. 512; [1998] 1 E.G.L.R. 108; [1998] 13 E.G. 148; [1997] E.G.C.S. 184; (1998) 95(1) L.S.G. 26; (1998) 142 S.J.L.B. 46; [1997] N.P.C. 185; *The Times*, January 15, 1998, CA; reversing in part [1996] 2 E.G.L.R. 110; [1996] 49 E.G. 112; [1996] E.G.C.S. 146, ChD 19–202
Playford v. Mercer (1870) 22 L.T. 41; 3 Mar.L.C. 335 .... 4–023, 8–005
Playing Cards (Malaysian) Sdn. Bhd. v. China Mutual Navigation Co. Ltd [1980] 1 M.L.J. 182 .... 18–034, 18–047

Pletts v. Beattie [1896] 1 Q.B. 519; 65 L.J.M.C. 86; 74 L.T. 148; 60 J.P. 185; 12 T.L.R. 227; 40 S.J. 297; 18 Cox C.C. 264 .... 5–013, 5–078, 5–081, 5–088
Pletts v. Campbell [1985] 2 Q.B. 229 5–088
Plevins v. Downing (1876) 1 C.P.D. 220; 45 L.J.Q.B. 695; 35 L.T. 263; 40 J.P. 791 ... 8–069, 9–006
Plimley v. Westley (1835) 2 Bing.N.C. 249; 1 Hodg. 324; 2 Scott 423; 5 L.J.C.P. 51; 132 E.R. 98 9–030
Plischke (Johann) and Sohne GmbH v. Allison Brothers Ltd [1936] 2 All E.R. 1009 .... 15–074, 15–077
Pocahontas Fuel Co. v. Ambatielos (1922) 27 Com.Cas. 148 13–014
Podair Trading Ltd, *Re* [1949] 2 K.B. 277 8–099
Podar Trading Co., Bombay v. Francois Tagher, Barcelona [1949] 2 K.B. 277; [1949] L.J.R. 1470; [1949] 2 All E.R. 62; 65 T.L.R. 433; 93 S.J. 406; 82 Ll.L.Rep. 705, DC 8–098, 16–037
Polak v. Everett (1876) 1 Q.B.D. 669; 46 L.J.Q.B. 218; 35 L.T. 350; 24 W.R. 689 ... 22–134, 23–097, 23–194
Polar Refrigeration Service Ltd v. Moldenhauer (1967) 61 D.L.R. (2d) 462 12–055
Polenghi Bros. v. Dried Milk Co. (1904) 10 Com.Cas. 42; 92 L.T. 64 .... 6–016, 12–042, 16–026, 16–028, 16–092, 19–069, 19–075, 19–076, 19–083, 19–145, 19–212, 19–213, 20–129
Polhill v. Walter (1832) 3 B. & Ad. 114; 1 L.J.K.B. 92; 110 E.R. 43 .... 12–012, 19–197
Polish SS. Co. v. Atlantic Maritime Co. [1985] Q.B. 41; [1984] 3 W.L.R. 300; (1984) 128 S.J. 469; [1984] 3 All E.R. 59; [1984] 2 Lloyd's Rep. 37, CA 16–008
Pollard v. Bank of England (1871) L.R. 6 Q.B. 623; 40 L.J.Q.B. 233; 24 L.T. 415; 19 W.R. 1168 22–118
Pollock (W.S.) & Co. v. Macrae 1922 S.C. (H.L.) 192 .... 13–036, 13–051
Polly Peck International plc v. Nadir (No.2) [1992] 4 All E.R. 769; [1993] B.C.L.C. 187; (1992) 142 N.L.J. 671; *The Independent*, March 20, 1992, *The Times*, March 24, 1992, CA 22–091
Polsky v. S. & A. Services Ltd [1951] 1 All E.R. 185 1–066
Polyproplene [1988] 4 C.M.L.R. 347 3–041
Pongakawa Sawmills Ltd v. New Zealand Forest Products Ltd [1992] 3 N.Z.L.R. 304 1–060
Pontifex v. Midland Railway (1877) 3 Q.B.D. 23; 47 L.J.Q.B. 28; 37 L.T. 403; 26 W.R. 209 15–08
Pontypridd Union v. Drew [1927] 1 K.B. 214; 95 L.J.K.B. 1030; 136 L.T. 83; 90 J.P. 169; 42 T.L.R. 677; 70 S.J. 795; 24 L.G.R. 405 2–032
Pool Shipping v. London Coal Co. of Gibraltar [1939] 2 All E.R. 432; 44 Com.Cas. 276; 64 W.L.R. 268 8–102
Poole v. Dicas (1835) 1 Bing. (N.C.) 649; 1 Scott 600; 1 Hodg. 162; 7 C. & P. 79; 4 L.J.C.P. 196 22–136
—— v. Smith's Car Sales (Balham) Ltd [1962] 1 W.L.R. 744; 106 S.J. 284; [1962] 2 All E.R. 482, CA 5–041, 5–044, 5–045, 5–050, 5–054, 5–055, 5–056, 5–057
Pordage v. Cole (1669) 1 Wms. Saund. 319 .... 8–004, 10–026, 19–164
Port Jackson Stevedoring Property Ltd v. Salmond and Spraggon (Australia) Property Ltd (The New York Star) *See* Salmond v. Spraggon (Australia) Property Ltd v. Port Jackson Stevedoring Property Ltd (The New York Star)
Port Line Ltd v. Ben Line Steamers Ltd [1985] 2 Q.B. 146; [1958] 2 W.L.R. 581; 102 S.J. 237; [1958] 1 All E.R. 787; [1958] 1 Lloyd's Rep. 290 .... 7–047, 18–005, 21–077
Port Sudan Cotton Co. v. Govindaswamy Chettiar & Sons [1977] 1 Lloyd's Rep. 5, CA 2–011, 2–013, 2–015, 2–017, 20–042
Port Swettenham Authority v. T.W. Wu & Co. (M) Sdn. Bhd. [1979] A.C. 580; [1978] 3 W.L.R. 530; (1978) 122 S.J. 523; [1978] 3 All E.R. 337; [1979] 1 Lloyd's Rep. 11, PC 5–057, 6–026, 6–029, 6–030
Portalis v. Tetley (1867) L.R. 5 Eq. 140; 37 L.J.Ch. 139; 17 L.T. 344; 16 W.R. 503; 3 Mar.L.C. 34 7–052
Portaria Shipping Co. v. Gulf Pacific Navigation Co. Ltd [1981] Com.L.R. 111; [1981] 2 Lloyd's Rep. 180 .... 8–026, 9–052
Porter v. General Guarantee Cpn. Ltd [1982] R.T.R. 384 .... 10–006, 14–041
Portman v. Middleton (1858) 4 C.B. (N.S.) 322; 27 L.J.C.P. 231; 4 Jur. (N.S.) 689; 6 W.R. 598; 140 E.R. 1108; *sub nom.* Portman v. Nichol 31 L.T. (O.S.) 152 .... 17–044, 17–045

Postmaster-General v. W.H. Jones & Co. (London) Ltd [1957] N.Z.L.R. 829 .... 5–098, 15–046
Potter v. Customs & Excise Commissioners [1985] S.T.C. 45; (1984) 81 L.S.Gaz. 3342, CA 1–049, 5–170
Potton Homes Ltd v. Coleman Contractors Ltd (1984) 28 Build.L.R. 19; (1984) 81 L.S.Gaz. 1044, CA 23–272
Potts (Walter) & Co. Ltd v. Brown Macfarlane & Co. Ltd (1934) 30 Com.Cas. 64 .. 12–039, 12–040, 12–041
Poulton v. Lattimore (1829) 9 B. & C. 259; 4 Man. & Ry. K.B. 208; 7 L.J. (o.s.) K.B. 225; 109 E.R. 96 .... 11–003, 17–049
Poulton & Son v. Anglo-American Oil Co. Ltd (1911) 27 T.L.R. 216; (1910) 27 T.L.R. 38 .... 8–012, 15–034, 15–035, 15–040, 15–060, 15–092
Pound (A.V.) & Co. Ltd v. Hardy (M.W.) & Co. Inc. [1956] A.C. 588; [1956] 2 W.L.R. 683; 100 S.J. 208; [1956] 1 All E.R. 639, *sub nom.* Hardy (M.W.) & Co. Inc. v. Pound (A.V.) & Co. Ltd [1956] 1 Lloyd's Rep. 255, H.L. 6–046, 8–040, 18–310, 18–311, 18–314, 18–329, 18–330, 18–331, 18–335, 20–043, 25–009, 25–119, 25–168, 25–177 ....
Poussard v. Spiers (1876) 1 Q.B.D. 410 8–080
Powell v. Horton (1836) 2 Bing.N.C. 668; 2 Hodg. 12; 3 Scott 110; 5 L.J.C.P. 204; 132 E.R. 257 11–021
—— v. Hoyland (1851) 6 Exch. 67 7–021
Power v. Barham (1836) 4 A. & E. 473; 1 Har. & W. 683; 6 Nev. & M.K.B. 62; 5 L.J.K.B. 88; 111 E.R. 865 .... 10–003, 10–006
Power Curber International Ltd v. National Bank of Kuwait SAK [1981] 1 W.L.R. 1233; (1981) 125 S.J. 585; [1981] 3 All E.R. 607; [1981] 2 Lloyd's Rep. 394; [1981] Com.L.R. 224 .... 23–140, 25–161
Prager v. Blatspiel, Stamp and Heacock Ltd [1924] 1 K.B. 566; 93 L.J.K.B. 410; 13; L.T. 672; 40 T.L.R. 287; 68 S.J. 46; 15–106
Preload Co. of Canada Ltd v. Regina (City) (1958) 24 W.W.R. 433, affirmed [1959] S.C.R. 801 1–047
President of India v. La Pintada Compania Navigacion SA [1985] A.C. 104; [1984] 3 W.L.R. 10; [1984] 128 S.J. 414; [1984] 2 All E.R. 773; [1984] 2 Lloyd's Rep. 9, H.L. 16–007, 16–012, 16–030, 16–046, 23–107
—— v. Lips Maritime Corporation [1988] A.C. 395; [1987] 3 W.L.R. 572; (1987) 131 S.J. 1085; [1987] 3 All E.R. 110; [1987] 2 F.T.L.R. 477; [1987] 2 Lloyd's Rep. 311, HL 16–007, 16–035, 25–192
—— v. Metcalfe S.S. Co. Ltd (The Dunelmia) [1970] 1 Q.B. 289; [1969] 3 W.L.R. 1120; 113 S.J. 792; [1969] 3 All E.R. 1549 ... 5–027, 18–051, 18–053, 18–057, 18–111, 18–114, 18–118, 18–119, 18–157, 20–008
Preston v. Albuery [1964] 2 Q.B. 796; [1964] 2 W.L.R. 218; 107 S.J. 891; [1963] 3 All E.R. 897, DC 5–060, 5–061, 5–088
Price v. Groom (1848) 2 Exch. 542 7–009
—— v. Nixon (1814) 5 Taunt. 338; 128 E.R. 720 .... 9–061, 9–062
—— v. Price (1847) 16 M. & W. 232 9–030
Priest v. Last [1903] 2 K.B. 148 .... 11–040, 11–055, 11–057, 11–059, 14–071, 17–072
Primetrade AG v. Ythan Ltd [2005] EWHC 2399; [2006] 1 All E.R. 367; [2006] 1 All E.R. (Comm) 157; [2005] 2 C.L.C. 911, QBD 18–011, 18–016, 18–104, 18–113, 18–125, 18–126, 18–129, 18–136, 18–209, 25–072, 25–082
Prince v. Oriental Bank Corporation (1878) 3 App.Cas. 325; 47 L.J.P. 42; 38 L.T. 41; 26 W.R. 543 .... 22–092, 22–128
Princes Buitoni Ltd v. Hapag-Lloyd A.G. [1991] 2 Lloyd's Rep. 383 .... 21–076, 21–106
Pringle-Associated Mortgage Corp. v. Southern National Bank, 571 F. 2d. 871 (1978) 23–203
Print Concept GmbH v. GEW (EC) Ltd [2001] EWCA Civ 352; [2002] C.L.C. 352; [2001] E.C.C. 36, CA 25–019, 25–060, 25–073
Prinz Adalbert, The [1917] A.C. 586; 86 L.J.P.C. 165; 116 L.T. 802; 33 T.L.R. 490; 61 S.J. 610; 14 Asp.M.L.C. 81 ..... 1–049, 5–015, 5–138, 5–140, 15–046, 18–063, 18–217, 18–221, 18–222, 18–223, 18–232, 18–242
Pritchett Co. v. Currie [1916] 2 Ch. 545; [1916–17] All E.R. 705; 85 L.J.Ch. 753; 115 LT. 325 1–043
Pritchett & Gold and Electric Power Storage Co. Ltd v. Currie [1916] 1 Ch. 515; 85 L.J.Ch. 753; 115 L.T. 325 .... 5–023, 5–032, 5–068, 5–091

ProCD Inc. v. Zeidenberg 86 F. 3d 1447 (7th Cir. 1996) 2–012
Proctor v. Jones (1826) 2 C. & P. 532; 172 E.R. 241 8–010
Proctor & Gamble Philippine Manufacturing Corp. v. Kurt A. Becher [1988] F.T.L.R. 450; [1988] 2 Lloyd's Rep. 21, CA 19–150, 19–151, 19–160, 19–192, 19–197, 19–198, 19–199, 19–200, 19–202
—— v. Peter Cremer GmbH & Co. (The Manila) [1988] 3 All E.R. 843 ... 19–150, 19–151, 19–160
Prodexport State Co. for Foreign Trade v. E.D. & F. Man Ltd [1973] Q.B. 389; [1973] 3 W.L.R. 845; 116 S.J. 1632; [1972] 1 All E.R. 355; [1972] 2 Lloyd's Rep. 375 .... 6–048, 18–341, 25–119
Produce Brokers Co. Ltd v. Olympia Oil and Cake Co. Ltd [1916] 1 A.C. 314 ..... 13–032, 13–033, 18–210
Produce Brokers Co. v. Olympia Oil and Cake Co. *Sub nom.* Olympia Oil & Cake Co. v. Produce Brokers Co. [1917] 1 K.B. 320; 86 L.J.K.B. 421; 116 L.T. 1; 33 T.L.R. 95; [1916–17] All E.R. Rep. 753, CA 19–016, 19–083
Produce Brokers Ltd v. Weiss [1918] 118 L.T. 111; 87 L.J.K.B. 472 .... 18–345, 19–017, 19–057, 19–063, 19–138, 19–140, 19–180
Produce Brokers New Company (1924) Ltd v. Wray, Sanderson & Co. Ltd (1931) 39 Ll.L.R. 257 .... 19–006, 19–119
Producer Meats (North Island) Ltd v. Thomas Borthwick & Sons (Australia) Ltd [1964] N.Z.L.R. 700 13–022
Professional Modular Surface v. Uniroyal 440 N.E. 2d 177 (Ct. App. 111, 1982) 23–139
Promos S.A. v. European Grain & Shipping Ltd [1979] 1 Lloyd's Rep. 375 19–042, 19–048
Proops v. Chaplin (W.H.) & Co. (1920) 37 T.L.R. 112 17–065
Prosper Homes v. Hambro's Bank Executor and Trustee Co. (1979) 39 P. & C.R. 395 18–358
Prosser v. Hooper (1817) 1 Moo.C.P. 106 11–011
Provimi Hellas A.E. v. Warinco A.G. [1978]; 1 Lloyd's Rep. 373, CA 6–047, 8–092, 18–322, 18–345
Provincial Treasurer of Alberta v. Kerr [1933] A.C. 710 25–121
Prudential Assurance Co. Ltd v. Newman Industries Ltd [1981] Ch. 257; [1980] 3 W.L.R. 543; (1986) 124 S.J. 756, [1980] 2 All E.R. 841 14–103
Prudential Mortgage Co. Ltd v. Marylebone B.C. (1910) 8 L.G.R. 901; 74 J.P.Jo. 339 1–066
Prutscher v. Fidelity Internatinal Bank 502 F.Supp. 535 (1980) 23–150
Public Utilities Commission of City of Waterloo v. Burroughs Business Machines Ltd (1974) 6 O.R. (2d) 257; 52 D.L.R. (3d) 481 .... 1–086, 12–055, 12–065
Public Works Commissioner v. Hills [1906] A.C. 368; 75 L.J.P.C. 69; 94 L.T. 833 ... 16–032, 16–038
Publishers' Association v. Rowland (1915) 32 W.L.R. 646 5–077
Puckford v. Maxwell (1794) 6 T.R. 52 9–030
Pugh v. Duke of Leeds (1778) 2 Cowp. 714 8–034
Pullin v. Stokes (1794) 2 H.B1. 312 23–137
Pullman Trailmobile Canada Ltd v. Hamilton Refrigeration Ltd (1979) 96 D.L.R. 322 5–081
Pump Distributors Property Ltd v. Atherton (Queensland) Property Ltd [1969] Qd. R 213 .... 9–015, 9–017
Purcell v. Henderson (1885) 16 L.R.Lr. 213 9–044
Pye v. British Automobile Commercial Syndicate Ltd [1906] 1 K.B. 425; 75 L.J.K.B. 270; 22 T.L.R. 287 16–034
Pye Ltd v. BG Transport Service Ltd [1966] 2 Lloyd's Rep. 300; 116 N.L.J. 1713, QBD 25–112
Pyke (Joseph) & Son (Liverpool) Ltd v. Richard Cornelius & Co. [1955] 2 Lloyd's Rep. 747 .... 8–092, 18–345, 18–349
Pym v. Campbell (1856) 6 E. & B. 370 .... 2–049, 10–024
Pyrene Co. Ltd v. Scindia Navigation Co. Ltd [1954] 2 Q.B. 402; [1954] 2 W.L.R. 1005; 98 S.J. 354; [1954] 2 All E.R. 158; [1954] 1 Lloyd's Rep. 32 .... 6–021, 18–047, 18–122, 18–142, 18–146, 18–164, 18–245, 18–264, 20–001, 20–003, 20–004, 20–007, 20–013, 20–014, 20–018, 20–020, 20–021, 20–028, 20–054, 20–055, 20–059, 20–060, 20–061, 20–062, 20–066, 20–072, 20–073, 20–089, 20–090, 20–094, 20–141, 21–104

Pyrmont Ltd v. Schott [1939] A.C. 145; [1938] 4 All E.R. 713; 108 L.J.P.C. 30; 160 L.T. 118; 55 T.L.R. 178; 83 S.J. 132 25–166

Quantum Corp Inc v. Plane Trucking Ltd; *sub nom*. Quantum Corp Ltd v. Plane Trucking Ltd,
[2002] EWCA Civ 350; [2002] 1 W.L.R. 2678; [2003] 1 All E.R. 873; [2002] 2 All E.R. (Comm) 392; [2002] 2 Lloyd's Rep. 25; [2002] C.L.C. 1002; (2002) 99(20) L.S.G. 31; *Times*, April 18, 2002, CA 21–058, 21–076, 21–077, 21–105
Queensland Electricity Generating Board v. New Hope Collieries [1989] 1 Lloyd's Rep. 205, P.C. 2–017
Quenerduaine v. Cole (1883) 32 W.R. 185 2–015
Quickmaid Rental Services Ltd v. Reece (1970) 114 S.J. 372; *The Times*, April 22, 1970, CA 10–012
Quinn v. Burch Bros. (Builders) Ltd [1966] 2 Q.B. 370; [1966] 2 W.L.R. 1017; 110 S.J. 214; [1966] 2 All E.R. 283; 1 K.I.R. 9 .... 6–028, 16–049, 16–051, 16–058

R. v. Amey; R. v. Meah [1983] 1 W.L.R. 346; (1983) 147 J.P. 124; (1982) 127 S.J. 85; [1983] 1 All E.R. 865; (1983) 76 Cr.App.R. 206 14–106
—— v. Aston (1850) 14 Jur. 1045 8–036
—— v. Avro (1993) 12 Tr.L.R. 83; (1993) 157 J.P. 759; (1993) 157 J.P.N. 490, C.A. 14–107
—— v. Barnet LBC, exp. Nilish Shah [1983] 2 A.C. 309; [1983] 2 W.L.R. 16; [1983] 1 All E.R. 226; 81 L.G.R. 305; (1983) 133 N.L.J. 61; (1983) 127 S.J. 36, HL; reversing [1982] Q.B. 688; [1982] 2 W.L.R. 474; [1982] 1 All E.R. 698; 80 L.G.R. 571; *The Times*, November 12, 1981, CA; affirming [1981] 2 W.L.R. 86; [1980] 3 All E.R. 679; 79 L.G.R. 210; 125 S.J. 64, DC 25–056
—— v. Baxter [1972] 1 Q.B. 1; [1971] 2 W.L.R. 1138; 115 S.J. 246; [1971] 2 All E.R. 359 18–281
—— v. Birmingham City Council, *ex p.* Ferrero [1993] 1 All E.R. 530; 89 L.G.R. 977; (1991) 10 Tr.L.R. 129; (1991) 155 J.P. 721; [1991] C.O.D. 476; (1991) 155 J.P.N. 522; (1991) 155 L.G.Rev. 645; (1991) 3 Admin. L.R. 613; *The Independent*, May 24, 1991; *The Times*, May 30, 1991, CA 14–118
—— v. Birmingham Profiteering Committee (1919) 89 L.J.K.B. 57; 122 L.T. 348; 84 J.P. 13; 36 T.L.R. 92; 18 L.G.R. 40 1–046
—— v. Bull 160 J.P. 24 (1996) 14–112
—— v. Carr-Briant [1943] K.B. 607 14–108
—— v. Chappell (1984) 128 S.J. 629; (1984) 80 Cr.App.R. 31; (1984) 6 Cr.App.R.(S.) 242; [1984] Crim.L.R. 574, CA 14–107
—— v. Charles [1977] A.C. 177; (1976) 68 Cr.App.R. 334, *sub nom.* Metropolitan Police Commissioner v. Charles [1977] Crim.L.R. 615 9–034
—— v. Chorley Justices, *ex p.* Jones, *The Times*, March 24, 1990 14–106
—— v. Church (Peter Leslie) (1970) 53 Cr.App.R. 65 7–006
—— v. Crutchley (Deborah) and Tonks (Trevor Reginald) (1994) 15 Cr.App.R. (S.) 627; [1994] Crim.L.R. 309; *The Times*, January 3, 1994, CA 14–106
—— v. Curr (1980) 2 Cr. App. R. (S.) 153, CA 14–138
—— v. Deller (1952) 36 Cr.App.R. 184, C.C.A. 1–066
—— v. Demers [1900] A.C. 103; 69 L.J.P.C. 5; 81 L.T. 795 .... 2–009, 8–059
—— v. Dickinson [1920] 3 K.B. 552; 90 L.J.K.B. 140; 123 L.T. 716; 85 J.P. 24; 36 T.L.R. 860; 26 Cox C.C. 636; 18 L.G.R. 657 1–084
—— v. Director General of Fair Trading, ex p. FH Taylor & Co [1981] I.C.R. 292, DC 14–128
—— v. Eaton (1966) 110 S.J. 329; (1966) 50 Cr.App.R. 189; 116 New L.J. 754; [1966] Crim.L.R. 333, C.C.A. 5–042, 5–045
—— v. Ferguson [1970] 1 W.L.R. 1246; 114 S.J. 472; [1970] 2 All E.R. 820; 54 Cr.App.R. 410, CA 7–006
—— v. Ford Motor Co. Ltd [1974] 1 W.L.R. 1220; 118 S.J. 596; [1974] 3 All E.R. 489; [1974] R.T.R. 509; 72 L.G.R. 655 .... 11–019, 12–012
—— v. Godfrey (Samuel David) (1994) 15 Cr.App.R. (S.) 536, CA 14–100
—— v. Gomex [1991] 3 All E.R. 394 5–013
—— v. Gomez [1993] A.C. 442; [1992] 3 W.L.R. 1067; [1993] 1 All E.R. 1; (1993) 96 Cr.App.R. 359; (1993) 137 S.J. (L.B.) 36; (1993) 157 J.P. 1; [1993] Crim.L.R. 304; (1993) 157 J.P.N. 15, HL 7–023, 7–037, 7–074

R. v. Goodall (Malcolm Brian) [2002] EWCA Crim 511, CA 14–107
—— v. Grimes (1752) Fost. 79n 1–084
—— v. Gregory 1998 WL 1670525 14–112
—— v. Hammertons Cars Ltd [1976] 1 W.L.R. 1243; 120 S.J. 553; [1976] 3 All E.R. 758; [1976] R.T.R. 516; (1976) 63 Cr.App.R. 234 14–112
—— v. Harris [1984] A.C. 327 7–023
—— v. Herbert (1960) 25 Jo.Cr.L. 163 1–089
—— v. Horsham J.J., *ex p.* Richards [1985] 1 W.L.R. 986; (1985) 149 J.P. 567; (1985) 129 S.J. 467; [1985] 2 All E.R. 1114; (1985) 82 Cr.App.R. 254, DC 14–106
—— v. International Trustee [1937] A.C. 500; [1937] 2 All E.R. 164; 106 L.J.K.B. 236; 156 L.T. 352; 53 T.L.R. 507; 81 S.J. 316; 42 Com.Cas. 246; 57 Ll.L.R. 145 .... 25–006, 25–007, 25–010, 25–089, 25–119
—— v. Inwood (Roland Joseph) (1974) 60 Cr.App.R. 70, CA 14–106
—— v. Johnson [1978] E.C.R. 2247 3–042
—— v. Jones [1898] 1 Q.B. 119; 67 L.J.Q.B. 41; 77 L.T. 503; 46 W.R. 191; 14 T.L.R. 79; 42 S.J. 82; 19 Cox C.C. 87 9–057
—— v. Killian (John); R. v. Lang (Peter John) [2002] EWCA Crim 404; (2002) 166 J.P. 169; (2002) 166 J.P.N. 230, CA 14–113
—— v. Lambert (Steven); R. v. Ali (Mudassir Mohammed); R. v. Jordan (Shirley) [2001] UKHL 37; [2002] 2 A.C. 545; [2001] 3 W.L.R. 206; [2002] 1 All E.R. 2; [2001] 3 All E.R. 577; [2001] 2 Cr. App. R. 28; [2001] H.R.L.R. 55; [2001] U.K.H.R.R. 1074; [2001] Crim. L.R. 806; (2001) 98(33) L.S.G. 29; (2001) 145 S.J.L.B. 174; *The Times*, July 6, 2001; *Independent*, July 19, 2001; *Daily Telegraph*, July 17, 2001, HL 14–108
—— v. Lambie [1982] A.C. 449; [1981] 3 W.L.R. 88; (1981) 125 S.J. 480; [1981] 2 All E.R. 776; [1981] Crim.L.R. 712, H.L. 9–034
—— v. Lawrence [1972] A.C. 626; [1971] 3 W.L.R. 225; 115 S.J. 565; 55 Cr.App. 7, 471; *sub nom.* Lawrence v. Commissioner of Police for the Metropolis [1971] 2 All E.R. 1253, HL 5–046, 7–037, 7–074
—— v. Leigh (1764) 1 Leach 52 1–084
—— v. Liverpool City Council, ex p. Baby Products Association Ltd (2000) 2 L.G.L.R. 689; [2000] B.L.G.R. 171; [2000] C.O.D. 91; *The Times*, December 1, 1999, QBD 14–117
—— v. Long [1960] 1 Q.B. 681; [1959] 3 W.L.R. 953; 124 J.P. 4; 103 S.J. 922; [1959] 3 All E.R. 559 8–035
—— v. Marshall (Roy) (1990) 90 Cr.App.R. 73, CA 14–140
—— v. Miller (1979) 68 Cr.App.R. 56 14–106
—— v. Modupe (1992) Tr.L.R. 59; (1991) 135 S.J. 249; [1991] C.C.L.R. 29; [1991] Crim.L.R. 530; (1992) 156 J.P.N. 300; *The Times*, February 27, 1991; *The Daily Telegraph*, March 14, 1991, CA 7–070, 7–090
—— v. Morris (David); *sub nom.* Anderton v. Burnside [1984] A.C. 320; [1983] 3 W.L.R. 697; (1984) 148 J.P. 1; (1983) 127 S.J. 713; [1983] 3 All E.R. 288; (1984) 77 Cr.App.R. 309 .... 5–013, 5–026, 5–082, 7–037, 7–074
—— v. Oldham Metropolitan B.C. *ex p.* Garlick [1993] 1 All E.R. 447; (1992) 24 H.L.R. 726; [1993] 1 F.L.R. 645; [1993] Fam.Law 219; *The Times*, August 26, 1992, CA 2–029
—— v. Palmer (Peter Leslie) (1994) 15 Cr.App.R.(S.) 550; [1994] Crim.L.R. 228, CA 14–106
—— v. Piper 160 J.P. 116 (1996) 14–113
—— v. Registered Designs Appeal Tribunal, *ex p.* Ford Motor Co. [1995] 1 W.L.R. 18; [1995] R.T.R. 68; (1995) 139 S.J.L.B. 42; (1995) 92 (08) L.S.Gaz. 39; *The Times*, December 16, 1994, HL 1–078
—— v. Rothery [1976] R.T.R. 550 1–089
—— v. Saddlers' Co. (1863) 10 H.L.C. 404; 32 L.J.Q.B. 337; 9 L.T. 60; 28 J.P. 36; 9 Jur. (N.S.) 1081; 11 W.R. 1004 15–024
—— v. Secretary of State, *ex p.* Factortame [1990] 2 A.C. 85; [1989] 2 W.L.R. 997; [1989] 2 All E.R. 692; [1989] 3 C.M.L.R. 1; [1989] C.O.D. 531; (1989) 139 N.L.J. 715, HL 1–005
—— v. Secretary of State for Health, *ex p.* U.S. Tobacco International Inc. [1992] Q.B. 353; [1991] 3 W.L.R. 529; [1992] 1 All E.R. 212; (1992) 11 Tr.L.R. 1; [1991] C.O.D. 268; (1991) 3 Admin.L.R. 735; *The Independent*, January 4, 1991; *The Times*, January 4, 1991; *The Daily Telegraph*, January 21, 1991; *The Guardian*, January 22, 1991, DC 14–0115

R. v. Secretary of State for Trade and Industry, ex p. Consumers' Association (Case C-82/96) 14–040
—— v. Shropshire Justices (1838) 8 A. & E. 173 8–035
—— v. Southwood [1987] 1 W.L.R. 1361; (1987) 131 S.J. 1038; [1987] 3 All E.R. 556; (1987) 85 Cr.App.R. 272; [1987] R.T.R. 273 14–112
—— v. Stevens and Agnew (1804) 5 East. 244 8–033
—— v. Sunair Holidays Ltd [1974] 1 W.L.R. 1105; 117 S.J. 429; [1973] 2 All E.R. 1233; 57 Cr.App.R. 782; [1973] Crim.L.R. 587, CA 14–113
—— v. Thompson [1980] Q.B. 229; [1980] 2 W.L.R. 521; (1978) 124 S.J. 240; [1980] 2 All E.R. 102; [1978] 1 C.M.L.R. 47 1–084
—— v. Thomson Holidays Ltd [1974] Q.B. 592; [1974] 2 W.L.R. 371; [1974] 1 All E.R. 823; (1973) 58 Cr.App.R. 429 14–107
—— v. Tideswell [1905] 2 K.B. 273; 74 L.J.K.B. 725; 93 L.T. 111; 69 J.P. 318; 21 T.L.R. 531; 21 Cox C.C. 10 .... 5–035, 5–037, 5–061, 5–082
—— v. Torbay Justices, *ex p.* Royal British Legion (Paignton) Social Club [1981] C.L.Y. 229 1–121
—— v. Warwickshire County Council, *exp.* Johnson [1993] A.C. 583; [1993] 2 W.L.R. 1; [1993] 1 All E.R. 299; (1993) 137 S.J.L.B. 37; 91 L.G.R. 130; (1993) 12 Tr.L.R. 1; [1993] Crim.L.R. 940; (1993) 143 N.L.J. 126; (1993) 157 J.P.N. 201; *The Times*, December 16, 1992, HL 2–002, 14–108, 14–124
—— v. Welsh [1974] R.T.R. 478, CA 1–089
—— v. Wheeler (1991) 92 Cr.App.R. 279, CA 4–004, 4–022, 4–032, 5–013, 5–017
—— v. White (1853) 22 L.J.M.C. 123 1–087
—— v. Williams [1980] Crim.L.R. 589 .... 5–013, 7–021
—— v. Wood Green Profiteering Committee (1920) 89 L.J.K.B. 55; (1919) 122 L.T. 120; W.N. 291; 84 J.P. 22; 36 T.L.R. 47; 18 L.G.R. 68 .... 1–046, 1–047
R. (on the application of Khatun) v. Newham LBC; *sub nom.* Khatun v. Newham LBC; Newham LBC v. Khatun; R. (on the application of Zeb) v. Newham LBC; R. (on the application of Iqbal) v. Newham LBC [2004] EWCA Civ 55; [2005] Q.B. 37; [2004] 3 W.L.R. 417; [2004] Eu. L.R. 628; [2004] H.L.R. 29; [2004] B.L.G.R. 696; [2004] L. & T.R. 18; (2004) 148 S.J.L.B. 268; [2004] N.P.C. 28; *The Times*, February 27, 2004; *Independent*, March 4, 2004, CA ... 14–931
R. & B. Customs Brokers Co Ltd v. United Dominions Trust Ltd [1988] 1 W.L.R. 321; [1988] 1 All E.R. 847; [1988] R.T.R. 134; (1988) 85(11) L.S.G. 42; (1988) 132 S.J. 300, CA .. 11–027, 11–041, 11–049, 11–057, 11–072, 13–074, 13–075, 13–090, 14–011, 14–029, 14–037, 14–071, 14–112, 18–264, 18–280, 28–282
R Griggs Group Ltd v. Evans (No.2) [2004] EWHC 1088; [2005] Ch. 153; [2005] 2 W.L.R. 513; [2005] E.C.D.R. 12; [2004] F.S.R. 48; (2004) 27(9) I.P.D. 27095; *The Times*, May 27, 2004, Ch D 25–121
Rabe v. Otto (1903) 89 L.T. 562; 20 T.L.R. 27 9–063
Rabey v. Gilbert (1861) 30 L.J.Ex. 170; 6 H. & N. 536 22–131
Radcliffe v. Bartholomew [1892] 1 Q.B. 161 8–034
Radford v. De Froberville [1977] 1 W.L.R. 1262; *sub nom.* Radford v. De Froberville [1978] 1 All E.R. 33; (1977) 121 S.J. 319; (1977) 35 P. & C.R. 316 16–053
Raeburn v. Burness (1895) 11 T.L.R. 399; 1 Com.Cas. 22 2–015
Raffles v. Wichelhaus (1864) 2 H. & C. 906 3–016
Rafsanjan Pistacchio Producers Co-operative v. Bank Leumi (U.K.) plc [1992] 1 Lloyd's Rep. 513 18–054
Rafuse Motors Ltd v. Mardo Construction Ltd (1963) 41 D.L.R. 340 12–055
Raiffeisen Hauptgenossenschaft v. Louis Dreyfus & Co. Ltd [1981] 1 Lloyd's Rep. 345; [1980] Com.L.R. 13 .... 8–091, 8–092, 8–101, 18–345, 18–346, 19–160
Raiffeisen Zentralbank Osterreich AG v. Five Star General Trading LLC (The Mount I) [2001] EWCA Civ 68; [2001] Q.B. 825; [2001] 2 W.L.R. 1344; [2001] 3 All E.R. 257; [2001] 1 All E.R. (Comm) 961; [2001] 1 Lloyd's Rep. 597; [2001] C.L.C. 843; [2001] Lloyd's Rep. I.R. 460; (2001) 98(9) L.S.G. 38; (2001) 145 S.J.L.B. 45; *The Times*, February 21, 2001, CA; reversing in part [2000] 1 All E.R. (Comm) 897; [2000] 2 Lloyd's Rep. 684; [2000] C.L.C. 1359; (2000) 97(25) L.S.G. 38; *The Times*, June 21, 2000, QBD (Comm Ct) 25–001, 25–019, 25–020, 25–030, 25–149, 25–177
Raiffeisen Zentralbank Osterreich AG v. National Bank of Greece SA [1999] 1 Lloyd's Rep. 408; *The Times*, September 25, QBD 25–076

Railway Sleepers Supply Co., *Re* (1885) 29 Ch.D. 204; 54 L.J.Ch. 720; 52 L.T. 731; 33 W.R. 595 .... 8–034, 8–035
Rainbow v. Hawkins [1904] 2 K.B. 322; 73 L.J.K.B. 641; 91 L.T. 149; 53 W.R. 46; 20 T.L.R. 508; 48 S.J. 494 .... 2–005, 18–045
Raineri v. Miles [1981] A.C. 1050 8–026
Rajapakse v. Fernando [1920] A.C. 892 4–011
Ralli v. Denistoun (1851) 6 Exch. 483; 20 L.J.Ex. 278; 17 L.T.O.S. 127; 15 E.R. 633 25–177
—— v. Universal Marine Insurance Co. (1862) 4 De G.F. & J. 1; 31 L.J.Ch. 313; 6 L.T. 34; 8 Jur. (N.S.) 495; 10 W.R. 278; 1 Mar.L.C. 194; 45 E.R. 1082 19–051
Ralli Bros. v. Compania Naviera Sota y Aznar [1920] 2 K.B. 287; 89 L.J.K.B. 999; 123 L.T. 375; 36 T.L.R. 456; 64 S.J. 462; 15 Asp.M.L.C. 33; 25 Com.Cas. 227 .... 18–339, 25–119, 25–120, 25–168
Ramchurn Mullick v. Luchmeechund Radakissen (1854) 9 Moore. P.C. 46 22–098
Ramdas Vithaldas Dubar v. S. Amerchand & Co. (1916) 85 L.J.P.C. 214; 32 T.L.R. 594; L.R. 43 Ind.App. 164, PC 18–139, 21–044, 21–054, 21–068
Ramsay v. Margrett [1894] 2 Q.B. 18; 63 L.J.Q.B. 513; 70 L.T. 788; 10 T.L.R. 355; 1 Mans. 184; 9 R. 407 .... 1–016, 1–017, 8–011
Randall v. Newson (1877) 2 Q.B.D. 102; 46 L.J.Q.B. 259; 36 L.T. 164; 25 W.R. 313 .... 11–003, 11–025, 17–074
—— v. Raper (1858) E.B. & E. 84; 27 L.J.Q.B. 266; 31 L.T. (O.S.) 81; 4 Jur. (N.S.) 662; 6 W.R. 445; 120 E.R. 438 17–066
Randy Knitwear Inc. v. American Cyanamid Co. 11 N.Y. 2d 5 (1962) 14–078
Rankin v. Potter (1873) L.R. 6 H.L. 83; 42 L.J.C.P. 169; 29 L.T. 142; 22 W.R. 1; 2 Asp.M.L.C. 65; *sub nom.* Potter v. Rankin (1870) L.R. 5 C.P. 341, Ex.Ch. 1–069, 5–079
Ranson (T.W.) Ltd v. Manufacture d'Engrais, etc. (1922) 13 Ll.L.R. 205 ... 19–024, 19–043
Rapalli v. K.L. Take Ltd [1958] 2 Lloyd's Rep. 469, CA 2–011, 2–012, 8–050, 11–020, 11–044
Raphael v. Bank of England (1855) 17 C.B. 161 7–047
Rasbora v. JCL Marine; *sub nom.* Atkinson v. JCL Marine [1977] 1 Lloyd's Rep. 645, QBD 11–044, 12–121, 13–030, 13–063, 13–072, 13–089, 18–281
Raven, The. *See* Banco Central SA and Trevelian Navigation Inc. v. Lingoss & Falce and B.F.I. Line.
Rawlings v. General Trading Co. [1921] 1 K.B. 635; 90 L.J.K.B. 404; 124 L.T. 562; 37 T.L.R. 252; 65 S.J. 220; 26 Com.Cas. 171 3–009
Rawlinson v. Mort (1905) 93 L.T. 555 .... 1–060, 5–159
Rawson v. Johnson (1801) 1 East. 203; 102 E.R. 79 8–004
Rawton, *ex p.* (1810) 17 Ves. Jun. 426 22–092
Ray v. Barker (1879) 4 Ex.D. 279; 48 L.J.Q.B. 569; 41 L.J. 265; 27 W.R. 745 5–054
Raymond Lyons & Co. Ltd v. Metropolitan Police Commissioner [1975] Q.B. 321; [1975] 2 W.L.R. 197; (1974) 119 S.J. 82; [1975] 1 All E.R. 335, DC 7–006
Rayn v. McCalley 228 S.W. 2d 61 (1950) 25–132
Rayner v. Davies; *sub nom.* Davies v. Rayner [2002] EWCA Civ 1880; [2003] 1 All E.R. (Comm) 394; [2003] 1 C.L.C. 169; [2003] I.L.Pr. 15, CA 25–048
Rayner (J.H.) & Co. Ltd v. Hambro's Bank Ltd [1943] 1 K.B. 37; [1942] 2 All E.R. 694; 112 L.J.K.B. 27; 167 L.T. 380; 59 T.l.R. 21; 86 S.J. 302; 74 Ll.L.R. 10 ... 23–028, 23–115, 23–174, 23–196, 23–206, 23–213
Raynham Farm Co. Ltd v. Symbol Motor Cpn. (1987) 6 Tr.L.Rep. 143; *The Times*, January 27, 1987 11–019
Read v. Croydon Corporation [1938] 4 All E.R. 631; 108 L.J.K.B. 72; 160 L.T. 176; 103 J.P. 25; 55 T.L.R. 212; 82 S.J. 991; 37 L.G.R. 53 .... 1–071, 14–094
—— v. Hutchinson (1813) 3 Camp. 352; 170 E.R. 1048, N.P. 1–034, 1–035
—— v. Legard (1851) 6 Exch. 636 2–041
Reardon Smith Line Ltd v. Australian Wheat Board [1956] A.C. 266; [1956] 2 W.L.R. 403; [1956] 1 All E.R. 456; [1956] 1 Lloyd's Rep. 1, P.C. 16–049
—— v. Black Sea and Baltic General Insurance Co. Ltd [1939] A.C. 562; [1939] 3 All E.R. 444; 108 L.J.K.B. 692; 161 L.T. 79; 55 T.L.R. 929; 83 S.J. 796 .... 18–059, 19–032
—— v. Hansen Tangen [1976] 1 W.L.R. 989 .... 18–266, 18–273, 19–146
—— v. Ministry of Agriculture, Fisheries & Food [1963] A.C. 691; [1963] 2 W.L.R. 439; 107 S.J. 133; [1963] 1 All E.R. 545; [1963] 1 Lloyd's Rep. 12 ...... 8–036, 8–091

Reardon Smith Line Ltd v. Ministry of Agriculture, Fisheries & Food [1960] 1 Q.B. 439; [1959] 3 W.L.R. 665; [1959] 3 All E.R. 434; [1959] 2 Lloyd's Rep. 229; 103 S.J. 920 8–097
—— v. Yngvar Hansen-Tangen [1976] 1 W.L.R. 989; 120 S.J. 719; *sub nom.* Reardon Smith Line v. Hansen-Tangen; Hansen-Tangen v. Sanko Steamship Co. [1976] 3 All E.R. 570, HL 1–082, 1–114, 10–031, 11–013, 11–014, 11–015, 11–018, 13–029
Reay v. British Nuclear Fuels Plc; Hope v. British Nuclear Fuels Plc [1994] Env. L.R. 320; [1994] P.I.Q.R. P171; [1994] 5 Med. L.R. 1; *Independent*, November 22, 1993 (C.S.); *Guardian*, October 15, 1993, QBD 14–091
Reckett v. Barnett and Slater Ltd [1929] A.C. 176; [1928] All E.R. 1; 98 L.J.K.B. 136; 140 L.T. 208; 45 T.L.R. 36; 34 Com.Cas. 126 7–047
Red Sea Tankers Ltd v. Papachristides (The Hellespont Ardent) [1997] 2 Lloyd's Rep. 547, QBD (Comm Ct) 18–129
Reddall v. Union Castle Mail S.S. Co. Ltd (1914) 84 L.J.K.B. 360; 112 L.T. 910; 13 Asp.M.L.C. 51; 20 Com.Cas. 86 15–075
Rederiaktiebolget Amphitrite v. The King [1921] 3 K.B. 500 6–048
Redfern v. Rosenthal (1902) 18 T.L.R. 718; 86 L.T. 855 22–060
Redgrave v. Hurd (1881) 20 Ch.D. 1; 51 L.J.Ch. 113; 45 L.T. 485; 30 W.R. 251 .... 10–008, 10–009, 12–003
Redhead v. Westwood (1889) 59 L.T. 293; 4 T.L.R. 671 1–066
Redler Grain Silos Ltd v. BICC Ltd [1982] 1 Lloyd's Rep. 435, CA 5–003, 19–098, 19–204
Reed v. Mestaer (1804) Comyn's Law of Contract (h) 2nd ed., p. 181 9–063
Reeman v. Department of Transport [1997] 2 Lloyd's Rep. 648; [1997] P.N.L.R. 618, CA 18–149
Rees Hough Ltd v. Redland Reinforced Plastics Ltd (1984) 1 Constr.L.J. 67 13–090
Reese River Silver Mining Co. v. Smith (1869) L.R. 4 H.L. 64 7–024
Reeves v. Barlow (1884) 12 Q.B.D. 436; 53 L.J.Q.B. 192; 50 L.T. 782; 32 W.R. 672 .... 5–066, 5–093, 5–167
—— v. Capper (1838) 5 Bing.N.C. 136; 1 Arn. 427; 6 Scott 877; 8 L.J.C.P. 44; 2 Jur. 1067 15–038
Reg. Glass Property Ltd v. Rivers Locking Systems Ltd (1968) 120 C.L.R. 516 1–043
Regal (Hastings) Ltd v. Gulliver [1967] 2 A.C. 134n; [1942] 1 All E.R. 378 1–080
Regazzoni v. K.C. Sethia (1944) Ltd [1958] A.C. 301; [1957] 3 W.L.R. 752; [1957] 3 All E.R. 286; [1957] 2 Lloyd's Rep. 289; 101 S.J. 848, HL; affirming [1956] 2 Q.B. 490; [1956] 3 W.L.R. 79; [1956] 2 All E.R. 487; [1956] 1 Lloyd's Rep. 435; 100 S.J. 417, CA; affirming [1956] 2 W.L.R. 204; [1956] 1 All E.R. 229; [1955] 2 Lloyd's Rep. 766; 100 S.J. 55, QBD 25–119
Regent O.H.G. Aisenstadt und Barig v. Francesco of Jermyn Street Ltd [1981] 3 All E.R. 327; [1981] Com.L.R. 78 .... 8–048, 8–077, 8–083, 19–165
Regent Oil Co v. Aldon Motors [1965] 1 W.L.R. 956; [1965] 2 All E.R. 644; 109 S.J. 433, CA 6–045
Regie National des Usines Renault SA v. Maxicar SA (Case C-38/98) [2000] E.C.R. 1–2973; [2000] E.C.D.R. 415; (2000) 23(7) I.P.D. 23050; *The Times*, May 23, 2000, ECJ (5th Chamber); [2000] E.C.R. 1–2973; [2000] E.C.D.R. 138, AGO 25–043
Reid v. Fairbanks (1853) 13 C.B. 692; 1 C.L.R. 787; 1 L.T. (o.s.) 166; 138 E.R. 1371; *sub nom.* Read v. Fairbanks, 22 L.J.C.P. 206; 17 Jur. 918 .... 5–092, 7–005
—— v. Furnival (1833) 1 Cr. & M. 538; 5 C. & P. 499; 2 L.J.Ex. 199 22–060
—— v. Macbeth & Gray [1904] A.C. 223; 73 L.J.P.C. 57; 90 L.T. 422; 20 T.L.R. 316 .... 1–082, 5–093
Reid (Joseph) Property Ltd v. Schultz (1949) 49 S.R. 231 .... 5–022, 5–034
Reid Motors Ltd v. Wood [1978] 1 N.Z.L.R. 319 .... 15–112, 15–134
Rein v. Stein [1892] 1 Q.B. 753; 61 L.J.Q.B. 401; 66 L.T. 469 .... 9–047, 9–048, 19–069, 19–086
Reinhart & Co. v. Joshua Hoyle & Sons Ltd [1961] 1 Lloyd's Rep. 346, CA 19–045, 21–012
Reinhold & Co. and Hansloh, *Re See* Arbitration, An between Reinhold & Co. and Hansloh.
Rekstin v. Severo Sibirsko Gosudarstvenmoe Akcionernoe [1933] 1 K.B. 47; 102 L.J.K.B. 16; 147 L.T. 231; 48 T.L.R. 578; 76 S.J. 494 22–118

Rendell v. Associated Finance Property Ltd [1957] V.R. 604 5–149
—— v. Turnbull & Co. (1908) 27 N.Z.L.R. 1067 . . . . 1–128, 6–035
Rennet v. Mathieson (1903) 40 Sc.L.R. 421; 5 F. (Ct. Sess.) 591; 10 S.L.T. 765 1–065
Renton (G.H.) & Co. v. Palmyra Trading Corporation of Panama [1957] A.C. 149; [1957] 2 W.L.R. 45; 101 S.J. 43; [1956] 3 All E.R. 957; [1956] 2 Lloyd's Rep. 379 . . . . 13–094, 19–037
Republic of India v. India Steamship Co Ltd. *See* India v. India Steamship Co Ltd
Republica de Guatemala v. Nunez [1927] 1 K.B. 669; 96 L.J.K.B. 441; 136 L.T. 743; 43 T.L.R. 187; 71 S.J. 35 25–127
Resolute Maritime Inc. v. Nippon Kaiji Kyokai (The Skopas) [1983] 1 W.L.R. 857; (1983) 127 S.J. 491; [1983] 2 All E.R. 1; [1983] 1 Lloyd's Rep. 431 . . . . 12–014, 18–045
Reunion Europeene v. Spliethoff's Bevrachtingskantoor (Case C-51/97) [1998] E.C.R. 1–6511 25–202
Reuter, Hufeland & Co. v. Sala (1879) 4 C.P.D. 239; 48 L.J.Q.B. 492; 40 L.T. 476; 27 W.R. 631; 4 Asp.M.L.C. 121 . . . . . . 6–021, 8–026, 8–046, 8–047, 8–054, 8–064, 8–065, 8–066, 8–072, 8–073, 8–083, 12–031, 15–121
Rew v. Payne, Douthwaite & Co. (1885) 53 L.T. 932; 5 Asp.M.L.C. 515 . . . . 5–138, 16–089, 18–221, 18–233
Rewe v. Bundesmonopoleverwaltung für Branntwein (case 120/78) [1979] E.C.R. 649 3–042
Rewia, The [1991] 2 Lloyd's Rep. 325 . . . . 18–127, 18–181, 25–063
Reynolds v. Ashby & Son [1904] A.C. 466; 73 L.J.K.B. 946; 91 L.T. 607; 54 W.R. 129; 20 T.L.R. 766 1–095
—— v. Chettle (1811) 2 Camp. 596 22–110
—— v. Coleman (1887) 36 Ch.D. 453; 56 L.J.Ch. 903; 57 L.T. 588; 35 W.R. 813 9–047
—— v. Wrench (1888) 23 L.J.N.C. 27 13–029
Rhode v. Thwaites (1827) 6 B. & C. 388 5–075
Rhode Island Locomotive Works v. South Eastern Railway Co. (1886) 31 L.C.J. 86 . . . . 25–183, 25–184
Rhodes, *Re* (1890) 44 Ch.D. 94; 59 L.J.Ch. 298; 62 L.T. 342; 38 W.R. 385 2–041
Rhymney Railway v. Brecon and Merthy Tydfil Junction Railway (1900) 69 L.J.Ch. 813; 83 L.T. 111; 49 W.R. 116; 16 T.L.R. 517; 44 S.J. 643 12–019
Rice v. Baxendale (1861) 7 H. & N. 96; 30 L.J.Ex. 371 16–070
Richard v. Royal Bank of Canada, 23 F. 2d 430 (1928) 23–205, 23–236
Richards v. Phillips [1969] 1 Ch. 39; [1968] 3 W.L.R. 33; [1968] 112 S.J. 460; [1968] 2 All E.R. 859, C.A. 2–004
—— v. Symons (1845) 8 Q.B. 90; 15 L.J.Q.B. 35; 6 L.T. (o.s.) 124; 10 Jur. 6 15–053
Richardson, *Re* (1885) 30 Ch.D. 396; 55 L.J.Ch. 241; 53 L.J.Ch. 241; 53 L.T. 746; 34 W.R. 286 7–110
—— v. Dunn (1841) 2 Q.B. 218; 1 Gal. & Dav. 417; 10 L.J.Q.B. 282; 6 Jur. 126; 114 E.R. 85 8–046
—— v. L.R.C. Products Ltd [2000] Llloyd's Rep.Med. 280 14–086
—— v. Worrell; Westall v. McDonald (1987) 58 T.C. 642; [1985] S.T.C. 693; (1985) 82 L.S.Gaz. 2501 1–084
Richardson, Spence & Co. v. Rowntree [1894] A.C. 217 . . . . 2–012, 13–013
Richardsons & Samuel, *Re* [1898] 1 Q.B. 261 8–097
Richco International Ltd v. Bunge & Co. A.G. (The New Prosper) [1991] 2 Lloyd's Rep. 93 . . . . 20–043, 20–045
Richmond Gas Co. & Richmond (Surrey) Corporation, *Re* [1893] 1 Q.B. 56, 62 L.J.Q.B. 172; 67 L.T. 554; 56 J.P. 776; 41 W.R. 41; 9 T.L.R. 5; 36 S.J. 866; 5 R. 29 1–071
Richo International v. Alfred C. Toepfer International GmbH; Bonde, The [1991] 1 Lloyd's Rep. 136; *The Times*, June 4, 1990, D.C. 13–035, 20–020, 20–033, 20–046
Rickard v. Moore (1878) 38 L.T. 841 12–045
Rickards (Charles) Ltd v. Oppenhaim [1950] 1 K.B. 616; 66 T.L.R. (Pt. 1) 435; 94 S.J. 161; [1950] 1 All E.R. 420, CA 8–030, 9–006, 9–055, 12–034, 15–123, 20–035
Riddiford v. Warren (1901) 20 N.Z.L.R. 572 . . . . 1–008, 1–011, 3–008, 10–002, 10–008
Ridgway v. Hungerford Market Co. (1853) 3 A. & E. 171 9–016
—— v. Ward (1884) 14 Q.B.D. 110; 54 L.J.M.C. 20; 51 L.T. 704; 49 J.P. 150; 33 W.R. 166; 1 T.L.R. 112; 15 Cox C.C. 603 . . . . 5–013, 5–080, 5–088

Riekermann, *Re* [1968] C.M.L.R. D78 3–041
Rimmer v. Webster [1902] 2 Ch. 163 .... 7–008, 7–009, 7–013, 7–016
Ringstad v. Gollin & Co. Pty Ltd (1924) 35 C.L.R. 303 8–070
Ripley v. M'Clure (1849) 4 Exch. 345; 18 L.J.Ex. 419; 14 L.T. (o.s.) 180 9–017
Risdon Iron and Locomotive Works Ltd v. Furness [1906] 1 K.B. 49, CA; affirming [1905] 1 K.B. 304, KBD 25–085
River Gurara (Cargo-owners) v. Nigerian National Shipping Line Ltd (The River Gurara) [1998] Q.B. 610; [1997] 3 W.L.R. 1128; [1997] 4 All E.R. 498; [1998] 1 Lloyd's Rep. 225; [1997] C.L.C. 1322; (1997) 94(33) L.S.G. 27; (1997) 141 S.J.L.B. 175; *The Times*, July 29, 1997, CA; affirming [1996] 2 Lloyd's Rep. 53; [1996] C.L.C. 927; *The Times*, March 6, 1996, QBD (Adm Ct) 18–034, 21–076, 21–086, 21–087
River Gurara, The *See* River Gurara (Cargo-owners) v. Nigerian National Shipping Line Ltd (The River Gurara)
River Stave Co. v. Sill (1886) 12 O.R. 557 25–127
Rivtow Marine Ltd v. Washington Ironworks (1973) 40 D.L.R. (3d) 530 .... 12–076, 14–084
Riyad Bank v. Ahli United Bank (UK) Plc [2005] EWHC 279; [2005] 2 Lloyd's Rep. 409, QBD 18–116
Roache v. Australian Mercantile Land and Finance Co. Ltd (No. 2) [1966] 1 N.S.W.L.R. 384 .... 7–039, 7–041
Roadworks (1952) Ltd v. Charman [1994] 2 Lloyd's Rep. 99, QBD (Comm Ct) 10–024
Robb v. Gow (1905) 8 F. 90 (Ct. Sess.) 9–042
Robbie (N.W.) & Co. Ltd v. Witney Warehouse Co. Ltd [1963] 1 W.L.R. 1324; 107 S.J. 1038; [1963] 3 All E.R. 613, CA 5–161, 7–028
Robbins of Putney Ltd v. Meek [1971] R.T.R. 345 .... 16–055, 16–077
Roberta, The [1938] P. 1; 107 L.J.P. 40; 158 L.T. 391; 53 T.L.R. 1048; 58 Ll.L.R. 231 25–205
Roberts v. Brett (1865) 11 H.L.C. 337; 20 C.B. (N.S.) 148; 34 L.J.C.P. 241; 12 L.T. 286; 11 Jur. (N.S.) 377; 13 W.R. 587; 2 Mar.L.C. 226; 11 E.R. 1363 8–036
—— v. Gray [1913] 1 K.B. 520; 82 L.J.K.B. 362; 108 L.T. 232; 29 T.L.R. 149; 57 S.J. 143 2–032
Roberts & Co. v. Marsh [1915] 1 K.B. 42; 84 L.J.K.B. 388; 111 L.T. 1060; 30 T.L.R. 609 22–041
Roberts Hair Fashions v. Customs and Excise Commissioners [1973] 1 V.A.T.T.R. 140 1–047
Robertson, *Re, ex p.* Crawcour (1878) 9 Ch.D. 419; 47 L.J.Bcy. 94; 39 L.T. 2; 26 W.R. 733 1–066
Robertson v. Hall's Trustee (1896) 24 R. (Ct. Sess.) 120 1–065
Robertson v. Jackson (1845) 2 C.B. 412; 15 L.J.C.P. 28; 6 L.T.O.S. 256; 10 Jur. 98; 135 E.R. 1006 25–157
Robertson (J.S.) (Aust.) Pty Ltd v. Martin (1956) 94 C.L.R. 30 .... 12–051, 20–108, 23–310
Robey & Co. v. Snaefell Mining Co. Ltd (1887) 20 Q.B.D. 152; 37 L.J.Q.B. 134; 36 W.R. 224 .... 9–047, 9–048, 16–016
Robey & Co.'s Perseverance Ironworks v. Ollier (1872) L.R. 7 Ch.App. 695; 27 L.T. 362; 20 W.R. 956; 1 Asp.M.L.C. 413 18–241
Robin and Rambler Coaches Ltd v. Turner [1947] 2 All E.R. 284 .... 4–006, 4–010, 7–021
Robinson v. Canadian Pacific Railway Co. [1892] A.C. 481; 61 L.J.P.C. 79; 67 L.T. 505; 8 T.L.R. 722 1–002
—— v. Golden Chips (Wholesale) Ltd [1971] N.Z.L.R. 257, CA 3–036
—— v. Graves [1935] 1 K.B. 579 .... 1–041, 1–045, 1–047, 14–046
—— v. Harman (1848) 1 Exch. 850; 18 L.J.Ex. 202; 13 L.T. (o.s.) 141 16–031
—— v. Macdonnell (1816) 5 M. & S. 228 1–106
—— v. Read (1829) 9B & C. 449; 4 Man. & Ry.K.B. 349; 7 L.J. (o.s.) K.B. 236; 109 E.R. 167 9–031
—— v. Reynolds (1841) 2 Q.B. 196; 1 Gal. & Dav. 526 22–062
Robophone Facilities Ltd v. Blank [1966] 1 W.L.R. 1428; 110 S.J. 544; [1966] 3 All E.R. 128, CA 2–007, 16–005, 16–033, 16–046
Robshaw Bros. Ltd v. Mayer [1957] Ch. 125; [1956] 3 W.L.R. 1049; 100 S.J. 916; [1956] 3 All E.R. 833 1–034
Rocco Giuseppe & Figli v. Tradax Export SA [1984] 1 W.L.R. 742; (1984) 128 S.J. 243; [1983] 3 All E.R. 598; [1983] 2 Lloyd's Rep. 434 16–013

Rockwell International v. Citibank 719 F. 2d 583 (1983) 23–146, 23–153
Rodger v. Comptoir D'Escompte de Paris (1869) L.R. 2 P.C. 393; 5 Moo.P.C.C. (N.S.) 538; 38 L.J.P.C. 30; 21 L.T. 33; 17 W.R. 468; 3 Mar.L.C. 271; 16 S.R. 618 ... 15–080, 18–084, 18–088
Rodocanachi, Sons & Co. v. Milburn Bros. (1886) 18 Q.B.D. 67; 56 L.J.Q.B. 202; 56 L.T. 594; 35 W.R. 241; 3 T.L.R. 115; 6 Asp.M.L.C. 100 ..... 17–027, 17–031, 18–051
Rodwell v. Phillips (1842) 9 M. & W. 501 1–093
Roe v. R.A. Naylor Ltd [1917] 1 K.B. 712; 87 L.J.K.B. 958; 119 L.T. 359 13–013
Roebuck v. Mungovin [1994] 2 A.C. 224; [1994] 2 W.L.R. 290; [1994] 1 All E.R. 568; [1994] 1 Lloyd's Rep. 481; [1994] P.I. Q.R. P209; (1994) 138 S.J. (LB) 59; (1994) 144 New.L.J. 197; *The Times*, February 4, 1994; *The Independent*, February 8, 1994, HL 18–174
Roerig v. Valiant Trawlers Ltd [2002] EWCA Civ 21; [2002] 1 W.L.R. 2304; [2002] 1 All E.R. 961; [2002] 1 Lloyd's Rep. 681; [2002] P.I.Q.R. Q8; (2002) 152 N.L.J. 171, CA 25–191
Rogers, *Re* (1874) L.R. 9 Ch.App. 432; 43 L.J.Bcy. 76; 30 L.T. 104; 38 J.P. 533; 22 W.R. 397 .... 4–001, 4–031
Rogers v. Hosegood [1900] 2 Ch. 388; [1990–3] All E.R. 915; 69 L.J.Ch. 652; 83 L.T. 186; 48 W.R. 659; 16 T.L.R. 489; 44 S.J. 607 11–028
—— v. Markel Corp (formerly Markel Holdings Inc) (Contractual Construction) [2004] EWHC 1375, QBD 25–191
—— v. Markel Corp (formerly Market Holdings Inc) (Liability) [2004] EWHC 2046, QBD 25–191, 25–192
—— v. Mississippi and Dominion Steamship Co. (1888) 14 Q.L.R. 99 25–186
—— v. Parish (Scarborough) Ltd [1987] Q.B. 933 .... 1–005, 11–044, 11–038, 11–048, 11–049, 14–010, 14–065
Rohde v. Thwaites (1872) 6 B. & C. 388; 9 Dow. & Ry. K.B. 293; 108 E.R. 495; *sub nom.* Phode v. Thwaites, 5 L.J. (O.S.) K.B. 163 5–068
Rolimpex Centrale Handlu Zagranicznego v. Haji E. Dossa & Sons Ltd [1971] 1 Lloyd's Rep. 380 13–040
Rolls v. Miller (1884) 27 Ch.D. 71; 53 L.J.Ch. 682; 50 L.T. 597; 32 W.R. 806 11–028
Rolls Royce Power Engineering Plc v. Ricardo Consulting Engineers Ltd [2003] EWHC 2871; [2004] 2 All E.R. (Comm) 129; 98 Con. L.R. 169, QBD 13–067, 18–114
Rolph v. Crouch (1867) L.R. 3 Ex. 44; 37 L.J.Ex. 8; 17 L.T. 249; 16 W.R. 252 4–029
Romer and Haslam, *Re* [1893] 2 Q.B. 286; 62 L.J.Q.B. 610; 4 R. 486; 69 L.T. 547; 42 W.R. 51 .... 9–030, 9–031
Ronaasen (E.A.) & Son v. Arcos Ltd *See* Arcos Ltd v. Ronaasen (E.A.) & Son.
Ronson International Ltd v. Patrick; *sub nom.* Patrick v. Royal London Mutual Insurance Society Ltd CA affirming [2005] EWHC 1767; [2005] 2 All E.R. (Comm) 453; [2006] Lloyd's Rep. I.R. 194 QBD 18–357, 19–064
Roots v. Lord Dormer (1832) 4 B. & Ad. 77; Nev. & M.K.B. 667; 100 E.R. 384 2–004
Roper v. Johnson (1873) L.R. 8 C.P. 167 .... 8–067, 8–068, 8–087, 12–021, 16–052, 16–071, 16–081, 17–008, 17–014, 17–015, 20–116
Rorison v. McKey [1952] N.Z.L.R. 398 13–029
Roscorla v. Thomas (1842) 3 Q.B. 234; 2 Gal. & Dav. 508; 11 L.J.Q.B. 214; 6 Jur. 929; 114 E.R. 496 .... 10–012, 14–066
Rose (F.E.) Ltd v. Pim (W.H.) & Co. Ltd [1953] 2 Q.B. 450; [1953] 3 W.L.R. 497; 97 S.J. 556; [1953] 2 All E.R. 739; [1953] 2 Lloyd's Rep. 238 ..... 1–009, 3–020, 12–128
Rose & Frank Co. v. Crompton (J.R.) & Bros. Ltd [1925] A.C. 445; [1924] All E.R. Rep. 245, 94 L.J.K.B. 120; 132 L.T. 641, 30 Com.Cas. 163, HL 1–013, 2–019, 2–047, 13–064
Rosenberg v. International Banking Corporation (1923) 14 Ll.L.R. 344 23–132
Rosenbruch v. American Export Isbrandtsen Lines 357 F. Supp. 982 (1973) [1974] 1 Lloyd's Rep. 119, M.S. District Ct 21–086
Rosenhain v. Commonwealth Bank of Australia (1922) 31 C.L.R. 46 .... 22–042, 22–045
Rosenthal (J.) & Sons Ltd v. Esmail (T/A H.M.H. Esmail & Sons); *sub nom.* Esmail (T/A H.M.H. Esmail & Sons) v. Rosenthal (J.) & Sons [1965] 1 W.L.R. 1117; [1965] 2 All E.R. 860; [1965] 2 Lloyd's Rep. 171; 109 S.J. 553, H.L.; affirming [1964] 2 Lloyd's Rep. 447, 108 S.J. 839, CA 8–047, 8–065, 8–066, 8–073, 8–082, 8–084, 9–015, 9–017, 9–020, 11–021, 12–064, 13–051, 19–170, 19–174

Rosevear China Clay Co., (*Re* Cock), *ex p.* (1879) 11 Ch.D. 560; 48 L.J.Bcy. 100; 40 L.T. 730; 27 W.R. 591; 4 Asp.M.L.C. 144 .. 15–068, 15–069, 15–082, 20–012, 20–070, 20–141
Ross v. Allis-Chalmers Australia Property Ltd (1981) 55 A.L.J.R. 8 10–006
—— v. London County Westminster and Parr's Bank Ltd [1919] 1 K.B. 678; 88 L.J.K.B. 927; 120 L.T. 636 22–019
Rossano v. Manufacturers Life Insurance Co. [1963] 2 Q.B. 352; [1962] 3 W.L.R. 157; 106 S.J. 452; [1962] 2 All E.R. 214; [1962] 1 Lloyd's Rep. 187 .... 25–008, 25–010
Roth & Co. v. Taysen, Townsend & Co., and Grant & Co. (1895) 73 L.T. 628; 12 T.L.R. 100; 8 Asp.M.L.C. 120; 1 Com.Cas. 240 (1896) 12 T.L.R. 211 ...... 12–021, 16–031, 17–015, 20–105, 20–116, 20–140
Roth Schmidt & Co. v. Nagase (D.) & Co. (1920) 2 Ll.L.R. 36 .... 13–031, 16–037, 18–275
Rother Iron Works Ltd v. Canterbury Precision Engineers Ltd [1974] Q.B. 1; [1973] 2 W.L.R. 281; (1972) 117 S.J. 122; [1973] 1 All E.R. 394, CA 7–028
Rotherham M.B.C. v. Frank Haslam Milan & Co. Ltd (1996) 78 B.L.R. 1 .... 11–050, 11–059
Rouquette v. Overmann (1875) L.R. 10 Q.B. 525; 44 L.J.Q.B. 221; 33 L.T. 420 22–049
Rourke v. Short (1856) 5 E. & B. 904; 25 L.J.Q.B. 196; 26 L.T. (o.s.) 235; 2 Jur. (n.s.) 352; 4 W.R. 247; 119 E.R. 717 2–048
Rousillon v. Rousillon (1880) 14 Ch D. 351 25–119
Routledge v. Grant (1828) 4 Bing. 653 2–010
—— v. McKay [1954] 1 W.L.R. 615 .... 3–020, 10–008, 10–011, 10–018, 10–022, 11–012
Rover International Ltd v. Cannon Film Sales Ltd [1989] 1 W.L.R. 912 ..... 4–006, 12–068, 16–040, 19–166
Rowe, *Re, ex p.* Derenburg & Co. [1904] 2 K.B. 483; 73 L.J.K.B. 594; 91 L.T. 220; 52 W.R. 628; 48 S.J. 475; 11 Mans. 130 9–044
Rowe v. Turner Hopkins & Partners [1980] 2 N.Z.L.R. 550 6–028
Rowett, Leakey & Co. v. Scottish Provident Institution [1927] 1 Ch. 55; 95 L.J. Ch. 434; 135 L.T. 558; 42 T.L.R. 504, CA 25–156
Rowland v. Divall [1923] 2 K.B. 500 ..... 4–001, 4–002, 4–006, 4–007, 4–009, 4–010, 4–012, 4–020, 4–032, 12–007, 12–068, 12–097, 14–007, 17–090
Rowton, *ex p.* (1810) 17 Ves.Jun. 426 22–085
Royal & Sun Alliance Insurance Plc v. MK Digital FZE (Cyprus) Ltd [2005] EWHC 1408; [2005] 2 Lloyd's Rep. 679; [2005] 2 C.L.C. 146; [2005] I.L.Pr. 51, QBD 21–073
Royal Baking Powder Co. v. Hessey 76 F. 2d 645 (1935) 25–127
Royal Bank of Canada and Saskatchewan Communications, *Re* (1985) 20 D.L.R. (4th) 415 5–092
Royal Bank of Scotland v. Cassa di Risparmio delle Provincie Lombard [1992] 1 Bank L.R. 251; *Financial Times*, January 21, 1992, CA 23–027, 23–029, 23–131
Royal Bank of Scotland v. Etridge (No.2) [2001] UKHL 44; [2002] 2 A.C. 773, [2001] 3 W.L.R. 1021; [2001] 4 All E.R. 449; [2001] 2 All E.R. (Comm) 1061; [2002] 1 Lloyd's Rep. 343; [2001] 2 F.L.R. 1364; [2001] 3 F.C.R. 481; [2002] H.L.R. 4; [2001] Fam. Law 880; [2001] 43 E.G.C.S. 184; (2001) 151 N.L.J. 1538; [2001] N.P.C. 147; *The Times*, October 17, 2001; *The Daily Telegraph*, October 23, 2001, HL 14–052A
Royal Boskalis Westminster NV v. Mountain [1999] Q.B. 674; [1998] 2 W.L.R. 538; [1997] 2 All E.R. 929; [1997] L.R.L.R. 523, CA 25–119
Royal Design Studio Pte Ltd v. Chang Development Pte Ltd [1991] 2 M.L.J. 229 ... 23–280, 23–282
Royal Trust Co. Ltd v. Campeau Corp. (1981) 118 D.L.R. (3d) 207 25–119
Royal Typewriter Co.; Division Litton Business Systems Inc. v. M.V. Kulmerland and Hamburg-Amerika Linie; Kulmerland, The [1973] 2 Lloyd's Rep. 428, U.S.C.A.; affirming *sub nom.* Royal Typewriter Co.; Division Litton Business Systems Inc. v. M.V. Kulmerland and Hamburg-America Linie; Hapag-Lloyd A.G. (Sued as Hamburg-America Linie) v. Pioneer Terminal Corporation, International Terminal Operating Co. Inc. and Sullivan Security Services Inc. Kulmerland. The [1973] 1 Lloyd's Rep. 318, U.S.D.C 21–086
Royscot Trust Ltd v. Rogerson [1991] 2 Q.B. 297 [1991] 3 W.L.R. 57; [1991] 3 All E.R. 294 .... 4–022, 12–015
Ruben (E. & S.) Ltd v. Faire Bros. & Co. Ltd [1949] 1 K.B. 254; [1949] L.J.R. 800; 93 S.J. 103; [1949] 1 All E.R. 215 .... 2–026, 8–007, 11–096, 12–048

Ruck v. Hatfield (1822) 5 B. & A. 632; 106 E.R. 1321 .... 15–073, 18–167, 20–141
Rubicon Computer Systems Ltd v. United Paints Ltd (2000) 2 T.C.L.R. 453, CA 4–026, 4–029, 4–030, 10–033
Ruby S.S. Corp. v. Commercial Union Assurance Co. Ltd (1933) 46 Ll. L. Rep. 265, CA; affirming (1932) 44 Ll. L. Rep. 263, KBD 25–081
Rudder v. Microsoft Corporation (1999) 2 C.P.R. (4th) 474 2–012
Rudolph A. Oetker v. IFA Internationale Frachtagentor A.G. (The Almak) [1985] 1 Lloyd's Rep. 557 .... 18–038, 18–040, 18–087, 19–190
Rugg v. Minett (1809) 11 East. 210; 103 E.R. 985 .... 5–030, 6–037, 6–039
—— v. Weir (1864) 16 C.B. (N.S.) 471; 143 E.R. 1211 9–062
Rumpai-Zenecon Construction Pte Ltd v. Arab Bank Ltd [1997] 3 S.L.R. 770 (Ct of Appeal, Singapore) 23–029
Rusholme and Bolton and Roberts Hadfield Ltd v. Read (S.G.) & Co. (London) Ltd [1955] 1 W.L.R. 146; 99 S.J. 132; [1955] 1 All E.R. 180 ..... 23–308, 23–309, 23–310
Russell v. Nicolopulo (1860) 8 C.B. (N.S.) 362; 2 L.T. 185; 8 W.R. 415; 141 E.R. 1206 11–091
—— v. Niemann (1864) 17 C.B.N.S. 163 8–097
—— v. Phillips (1850) 14 Q.B. 891; 19 L.J.Q.B. 297; 14 Jur. 806 .... 22–103, 22–104
Rutherford & Son Ltd v. Miln & Co. 1941 S.C. 125 13–029
Rutter v. Palmer [1922] 2 K.B. 87 .... 5–058, 6–031
Ruxley Electronics and Construction Ltd v. Forsyth [1996] 1 A.C. 344 ..... 14–006, 14–025, 16–048, 17–021, 17–023, 17–071, 17–099
Ryall v. Rowles (1749) 9 Bli. (N.S.) 377 1–063
Ryan v. Ridley & Co. (1902) 19 T.L.R. 45; 8 Com.Cas. 105 .... 8–004, 19–085, 19–207
Ryder v. Wombwell (1868) L.R. 4 Ex. 32; 38 L.J.Ex. 8; 19 L.T. 491; 17 W.R. 167 .... 2–030, 2–031, 2–034
Rylands v. Kreitman (1865) 19 C.B. (N.S.) 351; 144 E.R. 823 8–049

S. (A Minor) (Abduction: European Convention), Re [1998] A.C. 750; [1997] 3 W.L.R. 597; [1997] 4 All E.R. 251; [1998] 1 F.L.R. 122; [1997] 3 F.C.R. 293; [1997] Fam. Law 782; (1997) 94(34) L.S.G. 28; (1997) 147 N.L.J. 1310; (1997) 141 S.J.L.B. 205; *The Times*, July 30, 1997, HL; affirming [1997] 1 F.L.R. 958; [1997] 1 F.C.R. 588; [1997] Fam. Law 388; *The Times*, January 8, 1997, CA; reversing [1996] 1 F.L.R. 660; [1996] 3 F.C.R. 115; [1996] Fam. Law 204, Fam Div 25–056
SA Sucre Export v. Northern River Shipping Ltd (The Somovskiy 3068) [1994] 2 Lloyd's Rep. 266 .... 18–053, 18–063
S. & M. Hotels v. Legal and General Assurance Soc. [1972] 1 Lloyd's Rep. 157; 115 S.J. 888 8–097
S.C.C.M.O. (London) Ltd v. Soc. Generale de Compensation [1956] 1 Lloyd's Rep. 290 .... 18–277, 19–207, 20–098,
S.C.F. Finance Co. Ltd v. Masri [1986] 1 Lloyd's Rep. 293; *The Times*, August 12, 1986, CA 25–010, 25–073
S.G.S. (N.Z.) Ltd v. Quirke Export Ltd [1988] 1 N.Z.L.R. 52 13–036
SHV Gas Supply & Trading SAS v. Naftomar Shipping & Trading Co Ltd Inc (The Azur Gaz) [2005] EWHC 2528; [2006] 1 Lloyd's Rep. 163; [2005] 2 C.L.C. 815, QBD 8–037, 8–091, 18–269, 18–357, 19–013, 19–074, 19–159, 20–030
S.I. A.T. Di Del Ferro v. Tradax Overseas Ltd [1980] 1 Lloyd's Rep. 53, CA; affirming; [1978] 2 Lloyd's Rep. 470 .... 10–034, 12–031, 13–014, 18–048, 18–095, 18–169, 18–171, 18–286, 19–005, 19–008, 19–010, 19–031, 19–034, 19–040, 19–041, 19–147, 19–172
S.W.E. Corp. v. T.F.L. Freedom 704 F.Supp. 380 (1989) 21–085, 21–086
Sachs v. Miklos [1948] 2 K.B. 23; [1948] L.J.R. 1012; 64 T.L.R. 181; [1948] 1 All E.R. 67, CA 3–006, 7–002, 15–106
Safadi v. Western Assurance Co. (1933) 46 Ll.L.Rep. 140 8–091
Saffron v. Societe Miniere Cafrika (1858) 32 A.C.J.R. 286; 100 C.L.R. 231 .... 5–086, 16–019, 18–239, 19–067, 19–214, 20–001, 20–003, 20–070, 20–130, 23–097, 23–098, 23–109
Saga of Bond Street Ltd v. Avalon Promotions Ltd [1972] 2 Q.B. 325; [1972] 2 W.L.R. 1250 (Note); [1972] 2 All E.R. 545 (Note), CA 9–032
Sainsbury v. Matthews (1838) 4 M. & W. 343 1–093

Sainsbury (H.R. & S.) Ltd v. Street [1972] 1 W.L.R. 834; (1972) 116 S.J. 507, D.C. .. 1–115, 1–127, 6–038, 6–053, 18–338, 18–354
Saint v. Pilley (1875) L.R. 10 Ex. 137; 44 L.J.Ex. 266; 33 L.T. 93; 23 W.R. 753 1–095
St. Albans City and District Council v. International Computers Ltd [1995] F.S.R. 686; affirmed; [1996] 4 All E.R. 481, CA 1–031, 1–041, 1–086, 11–070, 13–089, 13–090, 13–091, 13–095, 14–082, 16–036
St. John Shipping Corp. v. Joseph Rank Ltd [1957] 1 Q.B. 267; [1956] 3 W.L.R. 870; 100 S.J. 841; [1956] 3 All E.R. 683 .... 3–028, 14–097, 18–333
St. Joseph, The [1933] P. 119, [1933] All E.R. 901; 102 L.J.P. 49; 149 L.T. 352; 49 T.L.R. 367; 18 Asp.M.L.C. 375 25–202
Saint Line Ltd v. Richardsons Westgarth & Co. Ltd [1940] 2 K.B. 99 ...... 13–036, 13–037, 17–041, 17–046
St. Margaret's Trust v. Castle [1964] C.L.Y. 1685 .... 7–032, 7–038
St. Marylebone Property Co. Ltd v. Payne [1994] 2 E.G.L.R. 25 13–057
St. Paul Fire & Marine Ins. Co. v. Sea-Land Service Inc. 735 F.Supp. 129 (1990) 745 F.Supp. 1989 (1990) 21–086
St. Pierre v. South American Stores (Gath and Chaves) Ltd [1936] 1 K.B. 382; [1935] All E.R. 408; 105 L.J.K.B. 436; 154 L.T. 546 25–150
Saipern SpA and Conoco (U.K.) Ltd v. Dredging V02 B.V. and Geosite Surveys Ltd (The Volvox Hollandia) (No. 2) [1993] 2 Lloyd's Rep. 315 18–149
Sainter v. Ferguson (1849) 1 Mac. & G. 286 16–033
Sajan Singh v. Sardara Ali [1960] A.C. 167 3–030
Saks v. Tilley (1915) 32 T.L.R. 148 .... 5–016, 5–026
Sale Continuation Ltd v. Austin Taylor & Co. Ltd [1968] 2 Q.B. 849; [1967] 3 W.L.R. 142; 111 S.J. 472; [1967] 2 All E.R. 1092 ... 18–180, 18–189, 18–210, 23–099, 23–100, 23–126
Salmon v. Watson (1817) 4 Moore C.P. 73 5–028
Salmond and Spraggon (Australia) Property Ltd v. Port Jackson Stevedoring Property Ltd (The New York Star) [1981] W.L.R. 138; (1980) 124 S.J. 756; [1980] 3 All E.R. 257, PC 13–016, 14–065, 18–016, 18–127
Salo v. Anglo-British Columbia Packing Co. [1929] 1 D.L.R. 874 1–041
Salomon & Co. and Naudszus, *Re*, (1899) 81 L.T. 325; 8 Asp.M.L.C. 59 .... 19–040, 19–066
Salot v. Naidoo [1981] 3 SAL.R. 959 22–043
Salsi v. Jet Speed Air Services [1977] 2 Lloyd's Rep. 57 .... 2–012, 21–073
Salter v. Woollams (1841) 2 M. & G. 650; Drinkwater 146; 3 Scott N.R. 59; 10 L.J.C.P. 145; 133 E.R. 906 .... 8–012, 8–013
Salvage Association v. CAP Financial Services [1995] F.S.R. 654 .... 1–086, 11–070, 13–090, 13–095
SAM Business Systems Ltd v. Hedley & Co [2002] EWHC 2733; [2003] 1 All E.R. (Comm) 465; [2003] Masons C.L.R. 11; (2003) 147 S.J.L.B. 57, QBD 1–086, 12–009, 13–056, 13–060
Samcrete Egypt Engineers and Contractors SAE v. Land Rover Exports Ltd [2001] EWCA Civ 2019 [2002] C.L.C. 533, CA 25–001, 25–019, 25–020, 25–030, 25–065, 25–068
Samuel (P.) & Co. Ltd v. Dumas [1924] All E.R. Rep. 66 8–097
Samuels v. Davis [1943] 1 K.B. 526; [1943] 2 All E.R. 3; 112 L.J.K.B. 561; 168 L.T. 296 .... 1–041, 1–047
San Nicholas, The *See* Pacific Molasses Co. and United Molasses Trading Co. v. Entre Rios Compania Naviera SA (The San Nicholas)
Sanchez v. Medicina Asturiana SA (C183/00) [2002] E.C.R. I-3901 14–080
Sanday v. Keighley, Maxted & Co. (1922) 91 L.J.K.B. 624; 127 L.T. 327; 38 T.L.R. 561; 66 S.J. 437; 15 Asp.M.L.C. 596; 27 Com.Cas. 296 ...... 18–270, 20–053, 21–030
Sanday (Samuel) & Co. v. Cox, McEuen & Co. (1921) 10 Ll.L.R. 459 18–345
Sandeman & Sons v. Tyzack and Branfoot Steamships Co. Ltd [1913] A.C. 680; [1911–13] All E.R. 1013; 83 L.J.C.P. 23; 109 L.T. 580; 29 T.L.R. 694; 57 S.J. 752; 12 Asp.M.L.C. 437 5–148
Sandeman Coprimar SA v. Transitos y Transportes Integrales SL [2003] EWCA Civ 113; [2003] Q.B. 1270; [2003] 2 W.L.R. 1496; [2003] 3 All E.R. 108; [2003] 1 All E.R. (Comm) 504; [2003] 2 Lloyd's Rep. 172; [2003] 2 C.L.C. 551; [2003] R.T.R. 31; *The Times*, February 13, 2003, CA 18–150
Sanders v. Jameson (1848) 2 C. & K. 557 .... 12–042, 12–063, 13–038

Sanders v. Vanzeller (1843) 4 Q.B. 260; 3 Gar. & Dav. 580; 12 L.J.Ex. 497 18–098
Sanders Bros v. Maclean & Co (1882–83) L.R. 11 Q.B.D. 327, CA 18–006, 18–063, 18–066, 18–090, 18–092, 18–094, 18–082, 18–179, 18–264, 19–063, 19–066, 19–068, 19–102, 23–132
Sanderson v. Armour, 1921 S.C. 18 8–080
—— v. Berwick-on-Tweed Corp. (1884) 13 Q.B.D. 547 4–026
Sandford v. Dairy Supplies Ltd [1941] N.Z.L.R. 141 16–029
Sands v. Clarke (1849) 19 L.J.C.P. 84; 8 C.B. 751; 14 Jur. 352 22–116
—— v. Norman (1903) 4 S.R.N.S.W. 234; 21 N.S.W.W.N. 89 1–034
Sanitary Packing Co. Ltd v. Nicholson and Bain (1916) 33 W.L.R. 594; 9 W.W.R. 1420 .... 25–009, 25–161
Sanix Ace, The. *See* Obestain Inc v. National Mineral Development Corp Ltd (The Sanix Ace)
Sanko S.S. Co. Ltd v. Kano Trading Ltd [1978] 1 Lloyd's Rep. 156, CA 11–014
Sanschagrin v. Echo Flour Mills Co. (1922) 70 D.L.R. 380 6–041
Santa Carina, The; Vassopulos v. May Shipping [1977] 1 Lloyd's Rep. 478, CA 23–314
Santa Marta Bay Scheepvaart and Handelsmaatschappig N.V. v. Scanbulk A/S (The Rijn) [1981] 2 Lloyd's Rep. 267 21–040
Santor v. A. & M. Karagheusian Inc. 207 A. 2d. 305 (1965) 14–079
Saphena Computing Ltd v. Allied Collection Agencies Ltd [1995] F.S.R. 616, CA 1–086
Sard v. Rhodes (1836) 1 M. & W. 153 9–032
Sargant & Sons v. East Asiatic Co. Ltd (1915) 85 L.J.K.B. 277; 32 T.L.R. 119; 21 Com.Cas. 344 19–030
Sargant (W.J.) & Sons v. Eric Paterson & Co. (1923) 129 L.T. 471; 39 T.L.R. 378 ... 6–043, 6–049, 6–043
Sargent (J.) (Garages) Ltd v. Motor Auctions (West Bromwich) Ltd [1977] R.T.R. 121, CA 7–002, 7–009, 7–015, 7–034, 7–075
Saskatoon Sand & Gravel Ltd v. Steve (1970) 40 D.L.R. (3d) 248 1–098
Sassoon (E.D.) & Co. v. Western Assurance Co. [1912] A.C. 561 8–097
Sassoon (M.A.) & Sons Ltd v. International Banking Corporation [1927] A.C. 711; 96 L.J.P.C. 153; 137 L.T. 501 .... 23–055, 23–061, 23–063, 23–163, 23–187, 23–188, 23–194
Satanita, The *See* Clarke v. Dunraven.
Satef-Huttenes Albertus SpA v. Paloma Tercera Shipping Co. SA (The Pegase) [1981] 1 Lloyd's Rep. 175; [1980] Com.L.R. 9 ...... 16–046, 17–035, 17–040, 20–003
Satisfaction Stores, *Re* [1929] 2 D.L.R. 435; 60 N.S.R. 357 .... 25–133, 25–183, 25–185
Satterthwaite (A.M.) & Co. Ltd v. New Zealand Shipping Co. Ltd (The Eurymedon) [1975] A.C. 154; [1972] 2 Lloyd's Rep. 544, N.Z.C.A 13–017, 14–0465 18–141, 18–142, 18–146
Saudi Crown, The [1986] 1 Lloyd's Rep. 261 ...... 18–028, 18–029, 18–040, 18–147, 18–149, 19–191
Saul v. Jones (1858) 28 L.J.Q.B. 37; 1 E. & B. 59; 5 Jur. (N.S.) 220; 7 W.R. 47 22–110
Saunders v. Anglia Building Soc. [1971] A.C. 1004; [1970] 3 W.L.R. 1078; *sub nom.*
Saunders v. Anglia Building Society, 114 S.J. 885 .... 3–013, 3–024, 7–016, 7–017, 7–018
—— v. ——(No.2) [1971] A.C. 1039; [1971] 2 W.L.R. 349; [1971] 1 All E.R. 243; 22 P. & C.R. 300; 115 S.J. 112, HL 13–013
—— v. Pilcher [1949] 2 All E.R. 1097; 31 T.C. 314, CA; Pilcher v. I.R.C. [1949] T.R. 405, TC 1–093, 1–094, 1–100
Saunders v. Topp (1849) 4 Exch. 390; 18 L.J.Ex. 374; 154 E.R. 1264 12–045
Saunt v. Belcher and Gibbons Ltd (1920) 90 L.J.K.B. 541; 125 L.T. 283; 26 Com.Cas. 115 .... 12–043, 12–048, 20–109
Sauter Automation Ltd v. Goodman Mechanical Services Ltd (1986) 34 Build.L.R. 81 .... 5–093, 5–148
Savage v. First National Bank and Trust Co. 413 F.Supp. 447 (1976) 23–139, 23–239, 23–241
Savage (J.J.) & Sons Property Ltd v. Blakney (1970) 119 C.L.R. 435 .... 10–006, 10–017
Savatin Corporation v. National Bank of Pakistan 447 F. 2d 727 (1971) 23–054
Saxty v. Wilkin (1843) 11 M. & W. 622; 12 L.J.Ex. 381; 7 Jur. 704; 152 E.R. 954; *sub nom.* Saxby v. Wilkins 1 L.T. (O.S.) 233 1–039
Sayer v. Wagstaff (1844) 5 Beav. 415 .... 9–030, 9–031
Sayers v. Harlow U.D.C. [1958] 1 W.L.R. 623; 122 J.P. 351; 102 S. J. 419; [1958] 2 All E.R. 342, CA 6–028

Sayers v. International Drilling Co. N.V. [1971] 1 W.L.R. 1176; 115 S.J. 466; [1971] 3 All E.R. 163; [1971] 2 Lloyd's Rep. 105; 11 K.I.R. 65, CA . . . 25–008, 25–010, 25–066
Scaliaris v. Ofverberg (G.) & Co. (1921) 37 T.L.R. 307 . . . . 11–088, 12–043, 20–038, 20–109
Scammel (G.) & Nephew Ltd v. H.C. & J.G. Ouston [1941] A.C. 251 2–016
Scandinavian Trading Co. A/B v. Zodiac Petroleum SA (The Al Hofuf) [1981] 1 Lloyd's Rep. 81; [1981] 2 Lloyd's Rep. 425; [1981] Com.L.R. 214 . . . . . 8–025, 9–005, 9–016, 10–037, 19–064, 19–167, 20–001, 20–032
Scandinavian Trading Tanker Co. A/B v. Flota Petrolera Ecuatoriana (The Scaptrade) [1983] Q.B. 529; (1982) 126 S.J. 853; (1983) 133 New. L.J. 133, CA 9–024, 9–055, 15–121, 15–134, 16–038, 19–150
Scania Finance Ltd v. Monteum Ltd 00/TLQ/1911, QBD 13–090
Scanlon v. First National Bank of Mexico 162 N.E. 567 (1928) 23–183, 23–188, 23–194
Scarf v. Jardine (1882) 7 App.Cas. 345 . . . . 5–079, 7–024
Scarfe v. Morgan (1838) 4 M. & W. 270 3–030
Scarth, *Re* (1874) 10 Ch.App. 234; 44 L.J.Bcy. 29; 31 L.T. 737 1–072
Schawel v. Reade [1913] 2 I.R. 64 . . . . 10–006, 10–020
Schenkers Ltd v. Overland Shoes Ltd *See* Overland Shoes Ltd v. Schenkers Ltd.
Schering Ltd v. Stockholms Enskilda Bank Aktiebolag [1946] A.C. 219, HL 6–044
Schiffahrt und Kohlen G.m.b.H. v. Chelsea Maritime Ltd (The Irene's Success) [1982] Q.B. 481; [1982] 2 W.L.R. 422; (1982) 126 S.J. 101; [1982] 1 All E.R. 218; [1981] 2 Lloyd's Rep. 635; [1981] Com.L.R. 219 . . . . 5–009, 18–123
Schijveschuurder v. Canon (Export) Ltd [1952] 2 Lloyd's Rep. 196 . . . . 20–038, 23–083
Schmoll Fils & Co. v. Scriven Bros. & Co. (1924) 19 Ll.L.Rep. 118 . . . . 18–264, 19–072, 19–157, 19–166
Schnapper, *Re* [1936] 1 All E.R. 322 25–166
Schneider v. Foster (1857) 2 H. & N. 4; 157 E.R. 2 9–063
—— v. Heath (1813) 3 Comp. 506 12–012
Schofield v. Emerson Brantingham Implement Co. (1918) 43 D.L.R. 509; [1918] 1 W.W.R. 306; 11 Sask.L.R. 11 12–055
Schofield (J.W.) & Sons. v. Rownson, Drew & Clydesdale Ltd (1922) 10 Ll.L.R. 480 . . . . 12–043, 20–010, 20–109
Scholefield Goodman & Sons Ltd v. Zyngier [1986] A.C. 562; [1985] 3 W.L.R. 953; (1985) 129 S.J. 811; [1985] 3 All E.R. 105; [1984] V.R. 445 22–049
Scholey v. Walton (1844) 12 M. & W. 510 9–041
Schorsch Meier G.m.b.H. v. Hennin [1975] Q.B. 416; [1974] 3 W.L.R. 823; 118 S.J. 881; [1975] 1 All E.R. 152; [1975] 1 C.M.L.R. 20; [1975] 1 Lloyd's Rep. 1, CA 25–194
Schotsmans v. Lanes & Yorks Railway (1867) L.R. 2 Ch.App. 332; 36 L.J.Ch. 361; 16 L.T. 189; 15 W.R. 537; 2 Mar.L.C. 485, L.C. & L.J. 15–066, 15–067, 15–073, 15–088, 19–220, 20–141
Schroeder v. Central Bank (1876) 34 L.T. 735; 24 W.R. 710; 2 Char.Pr.Cas. 77 22–047
Schroeder (A.) Music Publishing Co. Ltd v. Macaulay [1974] 1 W.L.R. 1308; 118 S.J. 734; [1974] 3 All E.R. 616, HL 3–035
Schuster v. McKellar (1857) 7 E. & B. 704; 26 L.J.Q.B. 281; 29 L.T. (o.s.) 225; 3 Jur. (N.S.) 1320; 5 W.R. 656; 119 E.R. 1407 . . . . 5–135, 18–065, 18–198, 18–232
Schwarzwaldmilch v. Einfuhr-und-Vorratsstelle fur Fette (Case 4/68) [1968] E.C.R. 377 8–100
Scorell v. Boxall (1827) 1 Y. & J. 396 1–093
Scotson v. Pegg (1861) 6 H. & N. 295; 30 L.J.Ex. 225; 3 L.T. 753; 9 W.R. 280; 158 E.R. 121 18–117
Scott v. Avery (1865) 5 H.L.C. 811; 25 L.J.Ex. 308; 28 L.T. (o.s.) 207; 2 Jur. (N.S.) 815; 4 W.R. 746 . . . . 13–041, 14–100
—— v. Brown Doering McNab & Co. [1892] 2 Q.B. 724 . . . . 3–009, 3–031
—— v. Coulson [1903] 2 Ch. 249; 72 L.J.Ch. 600; 88 L.T. 653; 19 T.L.R. 440 3–020, 3–022, 12–128
Scott v. England (1844) 2 Dow. & L. 520; 14 L.J.Q.B. 43; 4 L.T. (o.s.) 141; 9 Jur. 87 16–021
—— v. Foley, Aikman & Co. (1899) 16 T.L.R. 55; 5 Com.Cas. 53 . . 10–019, 17–060, 17–075
—— v. Hanson (1829) 1 Russ. & M. 128 10–005
—— v. Lifford (1808) 1 Camp. 246 22–060
—— v. McGreath (1899) 1 G.L.R. 268 12–047

Scott v. Pettit (1803) 3 B. & P. 469; 127 E.R. 255 .... 15–068, 15–072
—— v. Pilkington (1862) 2 B. & S. 11 25–081
Scott (Donald H.) v. Barclays Bank Ltd [1923] 2 K.B. 1; 92 L.J.K.B. 772; 129 L.T. 108; 39 T.L.R. 198; 67 S.J. 456; 28 Com.Cas. 253 ... 19–001, 19–044, 19–045, 19–047, 23–054, 23–196, 23–205, 23–219, 23–230, 23–231
Scottish Transit Trust Ltd v. Scottish Land Cultivators Ltd 1955 S.C. 254; 1955 S.L.T. 417 1–065
Scragg (Ernest) & Sons Ltd v. Perseverance Banking and Trust Co. Ltd [1973] 2 Lloyd's Rep. 101, CA 5–138
Scriven Bros. & Co. v. Hindley & Co. [1913] 2 K.B. 564; 83 L.J.K.B. 40; 109 L.T. 526 3–016
Scrivener v. G.N. Railway (1871) 19 W.R. 388 15–059
Scully v. South [1931] N.Z.L.R. 1187 1–093
Scruttons Ltd v. Midland Silicones Ltd [1962] A.C. 446; [1962] 2 W.L.R. 186; 106 S.J. 34; [1962] 1 All E.R. 1; *sub nom.* Midland Silicones v. Scruttons [1961] 2 Lloyd's Rep. 365 .... 13–017, 18–146, 20–013, 20–062
Sea Calm Shipping Co. SA v. Chantiers Nayal de L'Esterels (The Uhenbels) [1986] 2 Lloyd's Rep. 294 .... 18–047, 19–150
Sea Success Maritime Inc v. African Maritime Carriers Ltd [2005] EWHC 1542; [2005] 2 All E.R. (Comm) 445; [2005] 2 Lloyd's Rep. 692; [2005] 2 C.L.C. 167; *The Times*, September 6, 2005, QBD 19–038
Seaconsar Far East v. Bank Marrozi Jomhouri Islami Iran [1994] 1 A.C. 438; [1993] 3 W.L.R. 756; [1993] 4 All E.R. 456; [1994] 1 Lloyd's Rep. 1; (1993) 137 S.J.L.B. 239; (1993) 143 N.L.J. 1479; *The Times*, October 15, 1993, *The Independent*, October 20, 1993, HL reversing [1993] 2 Lloyd's Rep. 236; *The Times*, November 25, 1992, CA 23–183, 23–196
Seaconsar (Far East) Ltd v. Bank Markazi Jomhouri Islami Iran [1999] 1 Lloyd's Rep. 36; [1998] C.L.C. 1543, CA; affirming [1997] 2 Lloyd's Rep. 89; [1997] C.L.C. 611, QBD (Comm Ct) 18–061, 23–157, 23–158, 23–183
Sealace Shipping Co. Ltd v. Oceanvoice Ltd (The Alecos M.) [1991] 1 Lloyd's Rep. 120 .... 17–023, 20–112
Sealand of the Pacific Ltd v. Ocean Cement Ltd (1973) 33 D.L.R. (3d) 625 12–013
Seapremium Shipping Ltd v. Seaconsortium Ltd, April 11, 2001 25–034
Seath v. Moore (1886) 11 App.Cas. 350; 55 L.J.P.C. 54; 54 L.T. 690; 5 Asp.M.L.C. 586 .... 5–017, 5–091, 5–092, 5–093, 6–002, 6–033
Seaver v. Lindsay Light Co. 135 N.E. 329 (1922) 19–008
Second National Bank of Allegheny v. Lash Corporation, 299 F.371 (1924) 23–203
Second National Bank of Hoboken v. Columbia Trust Co. 288 F.17 (1923) 23–134, 23–171, 23–210
Second National Bank of Toledo v. Samuel (M.) & Sons Inc. 12 F. 2d 963 (1926) .. 23–188, 23–195, 23–210
Securities (N.Z.) Finance Ltd v. Wrightcars Ltd [1976] 1 N.Z.L.R. 77 .... 7–063, 7–066
Seddon v. Cruikshank (1846) 16 M. & W. 71 5–028
—— v. North Eastern Salt Co. Ltd [1905] 1 Ch. 326 12–005
Seeberg v. Russian Wood Agency (1934) 50 Ll.L. Rep. 146 8–097
Seely v. White Motor Co. 45 Cal.Rptr. 17 (1965) 14–079
Segap Garages Ltd v. Gulf Oil (Great Britain) Ltd, *The Times*, October 24, 1988, C.A. 8–006, 9–018, 9–019, 19–165
Seguros "Illimani" SA v. M/V. Popi 929 F. 2d 89 (1991) 21–086
Selliger v. Kentucky 213 U.S. 200 (1909) 25–128, 25–129
Sells v. Thomson (1914) 17 D.L.R. 737 5–078
Sere Holdings Ltd v. Volkswagen Group UK Ltd [2004] EWHC 1551, HC 13–057
Servais Bouchard v. Prince's Hall Restaurant Ltd (1904) 20 T.L.R. 574 ...... 3–038, 17–103
Service, Reeve & Co. (London) Ltd v. Central Iron and Metal Co. (1926) 24 Ll.L.R. 340 20–107
Services Europe Atlantique Sud (S.E.A.S.) v. Stockholms Rederiaktebolag S.V.E.A., The Folias [1979] A.C. 685; [1978] 3 W.L.R. 804; (1978) 122 S.J. 758; [1979] 1 All E.R. 421; [1979] 1 Lloyd's Rep. 1, HL 25–193, 25–194, 25–200
Sethia (K.C.) Ltd v. Partabmull Rameshwar [1951] 2 All E.R. 352n; affirming [1950] 1 All E.R. 51; [1951] 2 Lloyd's Rep. 89 .... 6–047, 6–057, 18–311, 18–316, 18–325, 25–119, 25–168

Sethia (S.L.) Liners Ltd v. State Trading Corp. of India [1985] 1 W.L.R. 1398; (1985) 129 S.J. 889; [1986] 2 All E.R. 395; (1986) 83 L.S.Gaz. 200, CA 19–085, 20–018, 20–020
Seven Pioneer, The [2001] 2 Lloyd's Rep. 57, HC (NZ) 5–009, 5–131, 5–135, 18–148, 18–149, 18–214, 20–067, 20–083
Sewell v. Burdick (1884) 10 App.Cas. 74; (1884) 13 Q.B.D. 159 .... 1–063, 5–001, 7–110, 15–053, 18–047, 18–051, 18–052, 18–088, 18–089, 18–100, 18–114, 18–129, 18–139, 18–147, 18–201, 18–216, 18–237, 23–132
Shackleford, The, Surrey Shipping Co. v. Compagnie Continentare SA [1978] 1 W.L.R. 1080; (1978) 122 S.J. 555; [1978] 2 Lloyd's Rep. 154, CA 12–037
Shackleton, *Re, ex p.* Whittaker (1875) L.R. 10 Ch. App. 466; 44 L.J.Bcy. 91; 32 L.T. 443; 23 W.R. 555 7–028
Shaddock (L.) & Associates Property Ltd v. Parramatta City Council (1981) 150 C.L.R. 225, High Ct. Aust 12–013
Shaffer v. Brooklyn Park Garden Apartments, 250 N.W. 2d 172 (Minn. 1977) 23–068
Shaffer (James) Ltd v. Findlay Durham and Brodie [1953] 1 W.L.R. 106; 97 S.J. 26, C.A. 8–078
Shamil Bank of Bahrain EC v. Beximco Pharmaceuticals Ltd (No.1); *sub nom.* Beximco Pharmaceuticals Ltd v. Shamil Bank of Bahrain EC [2004] EWCA Civ 19; [2004] 1 W.L.R. 1784; [2004] 4 All E.R. 1072; [2004] 2 All E.R. (Comm) 312; [2004] 2 Lloyd's Rep. 1; [2004] 1 C.L.C. 216; (2004) 101(8) L.S.G. 29; *The Times*, February 3, 2004, CA 25–028, 25–029, 25–076
Shamsher Jute Mills v. Sethia (London) Ltd [1987] 1 Lloyd's Rep. 388 .... 20–057, 23–110, 23–111
Shand v. Du Buisson (1874) L.R. 18 Eq. 283; 43 L.J.Ch. 508; 22 W.R. 483 22–047
Shanghai Commercial Bank Ltd v. Bank of Boston International 53 A.D. 2d 830; 385 N.Y.S. 2d 548 (1976) 23–026
Shanklin Pier Ltd v. Detel Products Ltd [1951] 2 K.B. 854; 95 S.J. 563; [1951] 2 All E.R. 471; [1951] 2 Lloyd's Rep. 187 .... 10–013, 14–062
Shanning International Ltd v. Lloyds TSB Bank plc; *sub nom.* Lloyds TSB Bank plc v. Rasheed Bank; Shanning International Ltd (In Liquidation) v. Rasheed Bank [2001] UKHL 31; [2001] 1 W.L.R. 1462; [2001] 3 C.M.L.R. 14; (2001) 98(32) L.S.G. 36; *The Times*, July 2, 2001; *The Daily Telegraph*, July 10, 2001, HL; affirming [2000] Lloyd's Rep. Bank, 215; [2000] 3 C.M.L.R. 450; [2000] Eu. L.R. 551, CA; affirming *The Times*, January 19, 2000, QBD (Comm Ct) 23–135
Sharif v. Azad [1967] 1 Q.B. 605; [1966] 3 W.L.R. 1285; [1966] 3 All E.R. 785; 110 S.J. 791; *The Times*, October 6, 1966, CA 25–119, 25–120
Sharneyford Supplies Ltd v. Edge [1986] Ch. 128; [1985] 3 W.L.R. 1; (1985) 129 S.J. 316; [1985] 1 All E.R. 976; (1985) 50 P. & C.R. 343; (1985) 35 New L.J. 288 12–015
Sharp v. Bailey (1829) 9 B. & C. 44; 4 Man. & Ry. K.B. 4 22–132
—— v. Batt (1930) 25 Tas.L.R. 33 .... 6–023, 6–024, 6–027
—— v. Christmas (1892) 8 T.L.R. 687 .... 5–061, 9–005, 15–120, 15–122
—— v. Sphere Drake Insurance (The Moonacre) [1992] 2 Lloyd's Rep. 501 20–039
Sharp (W. & J.) v. Thomson (1915) 20 C.L.R. 127 11–075
Sharpe (C.) & Co. Ltd v. Nosawa [1917] 2 K.B. 814 ...... 16–053, 19–066, 19–069, 19–178, 19–179, 19–080, 19–181, 19–184, 19–169, 20–114
Shaw v. Commissioner of Metropolitan Police [1987] 1 W.L.R. 1332 .. 7–009, 7–012, 7–036, 7–070, 7–075
—— v. Groom [1970] 2 Q.B. 504; [1970] 2 W.L.R. 299; (1969) 114 S.J. 14; [1970] 1 All E.R. 702; P. & C.R. 137, C.A. 3–028
—— v. Shaw [1954] 2 Q.B. 429; [1954] 3 W.L.R. 265; 98 S.J. 509; [1954] 2 All E.R. 638; C.A. 3–029
—— v.——[1965] 1 W.L.R. 537; 109 S.J. 233; [1965] 1 All E.R. 638, C.A. 3–031
Shaw MacFarlane & Co. v. Waddell & Sons (1900) 2 F. (Ct. of Sess.) 1070 20–029
Shearson Lehman Hutton Inc. v. Maclaine Watson & Co. Ltd [1989] 1 All E.R. 1056; [1989] 2 Lloyd's Rep. 570; (1990) 140 New L.J. 247 .... 8–104, 18–054
—— v. (No.2) [1990] 3 All E.R. 723; [1990] 1 Lloyd's Rep. 441; *The Times*, January 9, 1990, QBD (Comm Ct) 16–062, 16–063, 16–066, 16–067, 16–069, 16–074
—— v. TVB Treithandgesellschaft für Vermogensverwaltung and Beteiligungen GmbH (C–89/91) January 19, 1993; *Financial Times*, January 26, 1993, ECJ 16–008, 16–061, 16–064, 16–068, 16–072, 17–004, 17–007, 25–045

Sheffield v. Conran (1987) 22 Con.L.R. 108, C.A. 19–171
Sheffield Corporation v. Sheffield Electric Light Co. [1898] 1 Ch. 203; 67 L.J.Ch. 113; 77 L.T. 616; 62 J.P. 87; 46 W.R. 485 8–034
Sheikh Bros. Ltd v. Ochsner [1957] A.C. 136; [1957] 2 W.L.R. 254; 101 S.J. 128, P.C. 3–022
Sheik Mohammad Habib Ullah v. Bird & Co. (1921) 37 T.L.R. 405 .... 17–011, 17–028
Sheldon v. Cox (1824) 3 B. & C. 420; 5 Dow. & Ry K.B. 277; 107 E.R. 789 1–035
—— v. R.H.M. Outhwaite (Underwriting Agencies) Ltd [1996] A.C. 102; [1995] 2 W.L.R. 570; [1995] 2 All E.R. 558; [1995] 2 Lloyd's Rep. 197; [1995] 4 Re. L.R. 168; (1995) 92(22) L.S.G. 41; (1995) 145 N.L.J. 687; (1995) 139 S.J.L.B. 119; *The Times*, May 5, 1995; *The Independent*, May 9, 1995; Lloyd's List, May 24, 1995 (I.D.), HL; reversing [1994] 3 W.L.R. 999; [1994] 4 All E.R. 481; [1995] 4 Re.L.R. 20; *The Times*, July 1, 1994; *The Independent*, July 8, 1994, CA; reversing [1994] 1 W.L.R. 754; *The Times*, December 8, 1993, QBD 7–116
Sheldrake v. DPP; Attorney General's Reference (No.4 of 2002), Re [2004] UKHL 43; [2005] 1 A.C. 264; [2004] 3 W.L.R. 976; [2005] 1 All E.R. 237; [2005] 1 Cr. App. R. 28; (2004) 168 J.P. 669; [2005] R.T.R. 2; [2004] H.R.L.R. 44; [2005] U.K.H.R.R. 1; 17 B.H.R.C. 339; [2005] Crim. L.R. 215; (2005) 169 J.P.N. 19; (2004) 101(43) L.S.G. 33; (2004) 148 S.J.L.B. 1216; *The Times*, October 15, 2004, HL 14–108
Shell-Mex Ltd v. Elton Cop Dyeing Co. Ltd (1928) 34 Com.Cas. 39 .... 16–026, 16–093, 19–213
Shell Tankers (U.K.) Ltd v. Astro Comino Armadora SA (The Pacific Colocotronis) [1981] 2 Lloyd's Rep. 40, C.A.; [1980] 1 Lloyd's Rep. 366 25–184
Shell Transport and Trading Co. and Consolidated Petroleum Co, *Re* (1904) 20 T.L.R. 517; 48 S.J. 509 8–005
Shell U.K. Ltd v. Lostock Garages Ltd [1977] 1 W.L.R. 1187; [1977] 1 All E.R. 481, CA 3–029, 3–038, 8–061
Shelley v. Paddock [1980] Q.B. 348; [1980] 2 W.L.R. 647; (1979) 123 S.J. 706; [1986] 1 All E.R. 1009, CA 3–029, 3–032
Shelton v. Braithwaite (1841) 8 M. & W. 252; 10 L.J.Ex. 218; 5 Jur. 28 22–130
Shenstone v. Hilton [1894] 2 Q.B. 452; 63 L.J.Q.B. 584; 71 L.T. 339; 10 T.L.R. 557; 10 R. 390 .... 7–058, 7–065, 7–079, 7–084
Shenyin Wangou-Aps Management Pte Ltd v. Commerzbank (South East Asia) Ltd [2001] 4 S.L.R. 275 .... 22–010, 22–014
Shepherd v. Harrison (1871) L.R. 5 H.L. 116; 40 L.J.Q.B. 148; 24 L.T. 857; 20 W.R. 1; 1 Asp.M.L.C. 66 .... 5–138, 13–028, 18–194, 18–212, 18–221
—— v. Johnson (1802) 2 East 211 17–008
—— v. Kain (1821) 5 B. & A. 240; 106 E.R. 1180 13–028
Shepherd (F.C.) & Co. v. Jerrom.b.H. [1987] Q.B. 301; [1986] 3 W.L.R. 801; [1986] I.C.R. 802; (1986) 130 S.J. 665; [1986] 3 All E.R. 589; [1986] I.R.L.R. 358 CA 18–354
Shepley v. Davis (1814) 5 Taunt, 617; 1 Marsh. 252; 128 E.R. 832 .... 5–061, 5–065
Sheridan v. New Quay Co. (1858) 4 C.B. (N.S.) 618; 28 L.J.C.P. 58; 33 L.T. (O.S.) 238; 5 Jur. (N.S.) 248; 140 E.R. 1234 .... 18–214, 18–223, 20–083, 21–020
Shields (Trading as W. Ryder & Co.) v. Honeywill and Stein Ltd [1953] 1 Lloyd's Rep. 357, CA 11–055, 11–057, 12–042
Shillingford (as Business Trustee of A.C. Shillingford & Co.) v. Baron (Trading as A.A. Baron & Co.) [1959] 2 Lloyd's Rep. 453, PC 11–040
Shiloh Spinners Ltd v. Harding [1973] A.C. 691; [1973] 2 W.L.R. 28; (1972) 117 S.J. 34; [1974] 1 All E.R. 90; 25 P. & C.R. 48 .... 5–145, 16–038, 16–039
Shine v. General Guarantee Corp. [1988] 1 All E.R. 911 11–048
Shinhan Bank Ltd v. Sea Containers Ltd [2000] 2 Lloyd's Rep. 406; [2000] Lloyd's Rep. Bank, 365; [2000] C.L.C. 1473, QBD (Comm Ct) 23–144
Shinko Boeki Co. Ltd v. S.S. Pioneer Moon 507 F.2d. 342 (1974) [1975] 1 Lloyd's Rep. 199 21–086
Shipping Co. of India Ltd v. Naviera Letasa SA [1976] 1 Lloyd's Rep. 132 21–040
Shipping Development Corp. SA v. V/O Sojusneftexport (The Delian Spirit) [1972] 1 Q.B. 103; [1971] 2 W.L.R. 1434; 115 S.J. 345; [1971] 2 All E.R. 1067; [1971] 1 Lloyd's Rep. 506 21–040
Shipton v. Casson (1826) 5 B. & C. 378; 8 Dow. & Ry. K.B. 130; 4 L.J. (O.S.) K.B. 199; 108 E.R. 141 .... 8–046, 8–049, 8–072

Shipton, Anderson & Co. Ltd and Harrison Bros. & Co. Ltd, *Re*, an Arbitration [1915] 3 K.B. 676 .... 1–126, 5–026, 5–132, 5–135, 6–041, 6–050, 18–212
Shipton, Anderson & Co. v. Weil Bros. & Co. [1912] 1 K.B. 574; 81 L.J.K.B. 910; 106 L.T. 372; 28 T.L.R. 269; 17 Com.Cas. 153 .... 8–049, 8–050, 19–012
—— v. Weston (John) & Co. (1922) 10 Ll.L.R. 762 ...... 18–061, 18–252, 18–254, 19–010, 19–011, 19–033, 19–050, 19–147, 19–151
Shipton, Anderson & Co. (1927) Ltd v. Micks, Lambert & Co. [1936] 2 All E.R. 1032 .... 15–108, 15–112, 15–130
Shogun Finance Ltd v. Hudson; *sub nom.* Hudson v. Shogun Finance Ltd [2003] UKHL 62; [2004] 1 A.C. 919; [2003] 3 W.L.R. 1371; [2004] 1 All E.R. 215; [2004] 1 All E.R. (Comm) 332; [2004] 1 Lloyd's Rep. 532; [2004] R.T.R. 12; (2003) 100(46) L.S.G. 25; (2003) 153 N.L.J. 1790; (2003) 147 S.J.L.B. 1368; *The Times*, November 20, 2003, HL 1–054, 2–024, 3–005, 3–011, 3–014, 5–046, 7–023, 7–089, 7–090, 7–091, 14–007
Shohfi v. Rice 135 N.E. 141 (1922) 25–170
Short v. Simpson (1866) L.R. 1 C.P. 248; Har. & Ruth. 181; 35 L.J.C.P. 147; 13 L.T. 674; 12 Jur. (N.S.) 258; 14 W.R. 307; 2 Mar.L.C. 307 18–114
Shute v. Robins (1828) 3 C. & P. 80 (do.); Mood. & M. 133 22–098
Shuttleworth v. Clews [1910] 1 Ch. 176; 79 L.J.Ch. 121; 101 L.T. 708 15–132
Sibree v. Tripp (1846) 15 M. & W. 23 .... 9–031, 22–118
Siderius Inc. v. Wallace Co. 583 S.W. 2d 852 (1981) 23–150
Sidhu v. British Airways plc; Abnett (known as Sykes) v. British Airway plc [1997] A.C. 430; [1997] 2 W.L.R. 26; [1997] 1 All E.R. 193; [1997] 2 Lloyd's Rep. 76; 1997 S.C. (H.L.) 26; 1997 S.L.T. 492; 1997 S.C.L.R. 114; (1997) 94(2) L.S.G. 26; (1996) 146 N.L.J. 1851; (1997) 141 S.J.L.B. 26; *The Times*, December 13, 1996; *The Independent*, December 17, 1996, HL; affirming [1995] P.I.Q.R. P427, CA 18–149
Siebe Gorman & Co. Ltd v. Barclays Bank Ltd [1979] 2 Lloyd's Rep. 142 .... 5–142, 5–161, 22–145
Siemon (W.) & Sons Ltd v. Samuel Allen & Sons Ltd [1925] Q.S.R. 269 20–018
Sierra Leone Telecommunications Co. Ltd v. Barclays Bank plc; *sub nom.* Sierratel v. Barclays Bank plc [1998] 2 All E.R. 820; [1998] C.L.C. 501; (1998) 95(17) L.S.G. 32; *The Times*, February 25, 1998, QBD (Comm Ct) 25–076
Siffken v. Wray (1805) 6 East 371; 2 Smith K.B. 480; 102 E.R. 1328 .... 15–014, 15–065
Sikes & Co., *Re* (1829) Mont. & M. 263 22–090
Silbert Sharp and Bishop Ltd v. Geo. Wills & Co. Ltd [1919] SAL.R. 114 .. 11–030, 12–043
Sill v. Worswick (1791) 1 H.B1. 665 25–121
Sillence, *Re* (1877) 7 Ch.D. 238 8–036
Silver v. Ocean S.S. Co. [1930] 1 K.B. 416; [1929] All E.R. Rep. 611; 99 L.J.K.B. 104; 142 L.T. 244; 46 T.L.R. 78; 73 S.J. 849; 18 Asp.M.L.C. 74; 35 Com.Cas. 140; 35 Lloyd's Rep. 49 .... 18–028, 18–029, 18–030
Simaan General Contracting Co. v. Pilkington Glass Ltd (No.2) [1988] Q.B. 758; [1988] 2 W.L.R. 761; (1988) 132 S.J. 463; [1988] 1 All E.R. 791; [1988] F.T.L.R. 469 .... 12–120, 18–149
Sime Darby & Co. Ltd v. Everitt & Co. (1923) 14 Ll.L.R. 120 .... 18–258, 20–017
Simm v. Anglo-American Telegraph Co. (1879) 5 Q.B.D. 188; 49 L.J.Q.B. 392; 42 L.T. 37; 44 J.P. 280; 28 W.R. 290 .... 5–065, 7–014
Simmonds v. Millar & Co. (1898) 15 T.L.R. 100; 4 Com.Cas. 64 17–001
Simmons v. Swift (1826) 5 B. & C. 857; 8 Dow. & Ry. K.B. 693; 5 L.J. (N.S.) K.B. 10; 108 E.R. 319 .... 5–017, 5–035
Simon v. Lloyd (1835) 2 C.M. & R. 80 9–030
—— v. Pawsons and Leafs Ltd (1932) 148 L.T. 154; 38 Com.Cas. 151 ...... 17–033, 17–069
Simonds v. Braddon (1857) 2 C.B. 324 21–024
Simonin v. Mallac (1860) 2 Sw. & Tr. 67 .... 25–084, 25–098
Simpson v. Connolly [1953] 1 W.L.R. 911; 97 S.J. 490; [1953] 2 All E.R. 474 1–034
—— v. Crippin (1872) L.R. 8 Q.B. 14; 42 L.J.Q.B. 28; 27 L.T. 546; 21 W.R. 141 .... 8–080, 8–081, 8–084, 9–010
—— v. Eggington (1855) 10 Exch. 845 9–044
—— v. Fogo (1863) 1 H. & M. 195; 1 New Rep. 422; 8 L.T. 61; 9 Jur. (N.S.) 403; 11 W.R. 418; 1 Mar.L.C. 312; 71 E.R. 85 25–123

Simpson v. Henderson (1829) Moo. & M. 300 8–036
—— v. Nichols (1838) 3 M. & W. 240 3–030
—— v. Thompson (1877) 3 App.Cas. 279; 38 L.T. 1; 3 Asp.M.L.C. 567 5–011
Sims v. Marryat (1851) 17 Q.B. 281 4–001
Sinason-Teicher Inter-American Grain Corp. v. Oilcakes and Oilseeds Trading Co. Ltd [1954] 1 W.L.R. 1394; 98 S.J. 804; [1954] 3 All E.R. 468; [1954] 2 Lloyd's Rep. 327, CA 9–015, 20–117, 23–089, 23–091
Sindall (William) plc v. Cambridgeshire County Council [1994] 1 W.L.R. 1016 12–004
Sinfra AG v. Sinfra Ltd [1939] 2 All E.R. 675 25–081
Singer & Friedlander v. Creditanstalt-Bankverein [1981] Com.L.R. 69 (Com. Ct. of Vienna) 23–069
Singer (U.K.) Ltd v. Tees and Hartlepool Port Authority [1988] F.T.L.R. 442; [1988] 2 Lloyd's Rep. 164 .... 13–082, 13–084, 18–280
Singh v. Ali [1960] A.C. 167; [1960] 2 W.L.R. 180; 104 S.J. 84; [1960] 1 All E.R. 269 15–118
Singh (Dyal) v. Kenyan Insurance [1954] A.C. 287; [1954] 2 W.L.R. 607; 98 S.J. 231; [1954] 1 All E.R. 847 7–111
Sinidino, Ralli & Co. v. Kitchen & Co. (1883) Cab. & El. 217 13–033
Siporex Trade SA v. Banque Indosuez [1986] 2 Lloyd's Rep. 146; (1986) 136 New. L.J. 538 .... 23–273, 23–284, 23–285
Sir James Laing & Sons v. Barclay, Curle & Co. *See* Laing (Sir James) & Sons v. Barclay, Curle & Co.
Skandinaviska Kreditaktiebolaget v. Barclays Bank (1925) 22 Ll.L.R. 523 .. 23–173, 23–203, 23–206
Skarp, The [1935] P. 134; [1935] All E.R. Rep. 560; 104 L.J.P. 63; 154 L.T. 309; 51 T.L.R. 541; 41 Com.Cas. 1; 18 Asp.M.L.C. 576 18–174
Skilbeck v. Garbett (1845) 7 Q.B. 846 22–127
Skips A/S Nordheim v. Syrian Petroleum Co. Ltd (The Varenna) [1984] Q.B. 599; [1984] 2 W.L.R. 156; (1983) 127 S.J. 840; [1983] 3 All E.R. 645; [1983] 2 Lloyd's Rep. 592 .... 18–049, 18–052, 18–054, 18–110
Skipskredittforeningen v. Emperor Navigation [1998] 1 Lloyd's Rep. 66; [1997] 2 B.C.L.C. 398; [1997] C.L.C. 1151, QBD (Comm Ct) 9–026, 13–039, 13–055, 13–060, 13–080, 13–083
Skov AEG and Nilka v. Mikkelsen (January 2006, ECJ) 14–080
Skrine v. Gordon (1875) 9 Ir.R.C.L. 479 2–031
Sky Petroleum Ltd v. V.I.P. Petroleum Ltd [1974] 1 W.L.R. 576; (1973) 118 S.J. 311; [1974] 1 All E.R. 954 .... 17–099, 17–103
Slater v. Finning Ltd [1997] A.C. 473; [1996] 3 W.L.R. 190; [1996] 3 All E.R. 398 .. 11–057, 14–084
—— v. Hoyle and Smith [1920] 2 K.B. 11; 89 L.J.K.B. 401; 122 L.T. 611; 36 T.L.R. 132; 25 Com.Cas. 140 ..... 16–056, 17–039, 17–052, 17–054, 17–057, 17–058, 17–080, 17–082
Slee, *Re, ex p.* North Western Bank (1872) L.R. 15 Eq. 69; 42 L.J.Bcy. 6; 27 L.T. 461; 21 W.R. 69 7–051
Sleigh v. Sleigh (1850) 5 Exch. 574; 19 L.J.Ex. 345 22–132
Slingsby v. District Bank [1931] 2 K.B. 588 .... 22–026, 22–061
—— v. Westminster Bank (No. 1) [1931] 1 K.B. 173; 100 L.J.K.B. 195; 144 L.T. 369; 47 T.L.R. 1; 36 Com.Cas. 54 22–019
Smallman v. Smallman [1972] Fam. 25; [1971] 3 W.L.R. 588; 115 S.J. 527; [1971] 3 All E.R. 717 1–051
Smart v. Hyde (1841) 8 M. & W. 723; 1 Dowl. (N.S.) 60; L.J.Ex. 479 13–038
—— v. Jones (1864) 15 C.B. (N.S.) 717; 3 New Rep. 648; 33 L.J.C.P. 154; 10 L.T. 271; 10 Jur. (N.S.) 678; 12 W.R. 430; 143 E.R. 966 1–097
Smart Brothers Ltd v. Holt [1929] 2 K.B. 303; [1929] All E.R. 322; 98 L.J.K.B. 532; 141 L.T. 268; 45 T.L.R. 504; 35 Com.Cas. 53 5–14
Smeaton, Hanscomb & Co. Ltd v. Sassoon I. Setty, Son & Co. [1953] 1 W.L.R. 1468; 97 S.J. 862; [1953] 2 All E.R. 1471; [1953] 2 Lloyd's Rep. 580 ...... 13–033, 13–038, 13–041, 13–051, 20–038
Smeed v. Foord (1859) 1 E. & E. 602; 28 L.J.Q.B. 178; 32 L.T. (O.S.) 314; 5 Jur. (N.S.) 291; 7 W.R. 266 .... 17–040, 17–046
Smith, *Re, ex p.* Bright (1879) 10 Ch.D. 566; 48 L.J.Bcy. 81; 39 L.T. 649; 27 W.R. 385 .... 1–049, 5–045, 5–153

Smith v. Anderson (1880) 15 Ch.D. 247; 50 L.J.Ch. 39; 43 L.T. 329; 29 W.R. 21 11–028
—— v. Bedouin Steam Navigation Co. [1896] A.C. 70 18–028
—— v. Bridgend CBC; *sub nom.* Cosslett (Contractors) Ltd (In Administration) (No.2), Re [2001] UKHL 58; [2001] 3 W.L.R. 1347; [2002] 1 All E.R. 292; [2001] B.C.C. 740; [2002] 1 B.C.L.C. 77; [2001] N.P.C. 161, HL; reversing [2000] B.C.C. 1155; [2000] 1 B.C.L.C. 775, CA 5–093, 5–143
—— v. Bush (Eric S.); Harris v. Wyre Forest District Council [1990] 1 A.C. 831; [1989] 2 W.L.R. 790; (1989) 133 S.J. 597; (1990) 9 Tr.L.Rep. 1; [1989] 2 All E.R. 514 .... 10–009, 12–013, 13–065, 13–066, 13–089, 13–107, 18–045
—— v. Chance (1819) 2 B. & Ald. 753; 106 E.R. 540 .... 8–007, 8–012, 8–018
—— v. Compton (1832) 3 B. & Ad. 407; 1 L.J.K.B. 146; 110 E.R. 146 4–029
—— v. Cox [1940] 2 K.B. 558; [1940] 3 All E.R. 546; 109 L.J.K.B. 732; 163 L.T. 330; 56 T.L.R. 899; 84 S.J. 598 9–044
—— v. Ferrand (1827) 7 B. & C. 19 9–031
—— v. Gale [1974] 1 W.L.R. 9; 117 S.J. 854; [1974] 1 All E.R. 401 2–051
—— v. Goral [1952] 3 D.L.R. 328 .... 4–023, 4–027, 4–030
—— v. Goss (1808) 1 Camp. 282; 170 E.R. 958, N.P. 15–068
—— v. Green (1875) 1 C.P.D. 92; 45 L.J.Q.B. 28; 33 L.T. 572; 40 J.P. 103; 24 W.R. 142 17–074
—— v. Hughes (1871) L.R. 6 Q.B. 597; 40 L.J.Q.B. 221; 25 L.T. 329; 19 W.R. 1059 .... 3–017, 11–073
—— v. Johnson (1899) 15 T.L.R. 179; Emden's B.C., 4th ed. 668 .... 17–060, 17–062
—— v. Land and House Property Corp. (1884) 28 Ch.D. 7 10–006
—— v. Lazarus, unreported, 1981, CA 14–009
—— v. Marryat (1851) 17 Q.B. 281 4–032
—— v. Mawhood (1845) 14 M. & W. 452 3–028
—— v. Mercer (1867) L.R. 3 Ex. 51; 37 L.J.Ex. 24; 17 L.T. 317 22–134
—— v. Morgan [1971] 1 W.L.R. 803; 115 S.J. 288; [1971] 2 All E.R. 1500; 22 P. & C.R. 618 .... 2–017, 2–046
—— v. Myers (1871) L.R. 7 Q.B. 139; 41 L.J.Q.B. 91; 26 L.T. 103; 20 W.R. 186; 1 Asp.M.L.C. 222 .... 21–026, 21–032
—— v. O'Bryan (1864) 11 L.T. 346; 10 Jur. (N.S.) 1107; 13 W.R. 79 10–019
—— v. Peters (1875) L.R. 20 Eq. 511; 44 L.J.Ch. 613; 23 W.R. 783 .... 2–049, 17–103
Smith v. South Wales Switchgear Ltd [1978] 1 W.L.R. 165; (1977) 122 S.J. 61; [1978] 1 All E.R. 18; (1977) 8 Build.L.R. 5 .... 13–013, 13–020, 13–022
—— v. Spurling Motor Bodies Ltd (1961) 105 S.J. 967 2–027
—— v. Surman (1829) 9 B. & C. 561; 4 Man. & Ry. K.B. 455; 75 L.J. (O.S.) K.B. 296; 109 E.R. 209 .... 1–091, 1–093
—— v. Union Bank of London (1875) L.R. 10 Q.B. 291 .... 22–023, 22–059
—— v. Vertue (1860) 30 L.J.C.P. 56; 9 C.B. (N.S.) 214; 3 L.T. 538; 7 Jur. (N.S.) 395; 9 W.R. 146 22–104
Smith v. Winter (1852) 12 C.B. 487; 21 L.J.C.P. 158; 19 L.T. (O.S.) 111 16–015
Smith (E. & E. Brian) (1928) Ltd v. Wheatsheaf Mills Ltd [1939] 2 K.B. 302; [1939] 2 All E.R. 251; 108 L.J.K.B. 602; 160 L.T. 389; 55 T.L.R. 599; 83 S.J. 456; 44 Com.Cas. 210 12–031
Smith and Ferguson v. Ledyard Goldwaithe & Co., 49 Ala. 279 (1873) 23–063
Smith and Palmer v. Scarffe and Abbott (1741) 7 Mod. 426 22–104
Smith Bros. (Hull) Ltd v. Gosta Jacobsson & Co. [1961] 2 Lloyd's Rep. 522 .... 11–018, 13–033
Smith, Coney & Barrett v. Becker, Gray & Co. [1916] 2 Ch. 86 .... 6–042, 6–046, 18–335
Smith New Court Securities v. Scrimgeour Vickers (Asset Management) Ltd; Smith New Court Securities Ltd v. Citibank NA [1997] A.C. 254; [1996] 3 W.L.R. 1051; [1996] 4 All E.R. 769; [1997] 1 B.C.L.C. 350; (1996) 93(46) L.S.G. 28; (1996) 146 N.L.J. 1722; (1997) 141 S.J.L.B. 5; *The Times*, November 22, 1996; *The Independent*, November 27, 1996, HL 4–022
Smorgon v. Australia and New Zealand Banking Group Ltd (1976) 134 C.L.R. 475 22–142
Smurthwaite v. Hannay [1894] A.C. 495 5–148
—— v. Wilkins (1862) 11 C.B. (N.S.) 842; 31 L.J.C.P. 214; 5 L.T. 842; 7 L.T. 65; 10 W.R. 386; 1 Mar.L.C. 198 18–132

Smyth (Ross T.) & Co. Ltd v. Bailey (T.D.), Sons & Co. [1940] 3 All E.R. 60; 164 L.T. 102; 45 Com.Cas. 292 . . . . 5–059, 5–066, 5–071, 5–131, 5–135, 8–054, 8–075, 8–076, 8–077, 8–078, 8–080, 12–020, 18–209, 18–210, 18–280, 19–008, 19–010, 19–021, 19–023, 19–057, 19–080, 19–099, 19–100, 19–103, 20–080
—— v. Lindsay (W.N.) Ltd [1953] 1 W.L.R. 1280; 97 S.J. 744; [1953] 2 All E.R. 1064; [1953] 2 Lloyd's Rep. 378 . . . . 6–046, 8–092, 18–345, 19–013, 19–129
Snee v. Prescot (1753) 1 Atk. 245; 26 E.R. 157 15–085
Snell v. Heighton (1883) 1 Cab. & Ell. 95 5–061
Snelling v. John G. Snelling Ltd [1973] 1 Q.B. 87; [1972] 2 W.L.R. 588; 116 S.J. 217; [1972] 1 All E.R. 79 . . . . 10–014, 13–017
Snook v. London & West Riding Investments Ltd [1967] 2 Q.B. 768; [1967] 2 W.L.R. 1020; 111 S.J. 71; [1967] 1 All E.R. 518 . . . . 1–066, 3–005, 7–010
Snow (John) & Co. Ltd v. D.G.B. Woodcraft Co. Ltd [1985] B.C.L.C. 54 . . . . . 5–146, 5–148
Soares v. Glyn (1845) 8 Q.B. 24 20–046
Sobell Industries Ltd v. Cory Bros. & Co. [1955] 2 Lloyd's Rep. 82 . . . . 3–004, 23–308, 23–310
Socap International Ltd v. Rich (Mare) & Co. A.G. [1990] 2 Lloyd's Rep. 175 20–115
Social Services Tax Act, *Re* (1970) 74 W.W.R. 246 . . . . 1–085, 1–087
Sociedad Iberica de Molturacion SA v. Tradax Export SA [1978] 2 Lloyd's Rep. 545 . . . . 8–092, 19–140
Società Italiano Vetro v. Commission [1992] 11 E.C.R. 1403 3–041
Société Anonyme L'Industrielle Russo-Belge v. Scholefield & Son (1902) 7 Com.Cas. 114 . . . . 8–054, 8–062
Société Bertrande v. Ott (Paul) K.G. [1978] E.C.R. 1431; [1978] 3 C.M.L.R. 499 25–045
Société Co-operative Suisse des Céréales et Matières Fouragàres v. La Plata Cereal Co. SA (1947) 80 Ll.L.R. 530 6–041, 6–046, 18–339, 18–345, 20–042, 20–046, 25–119
Société D'Avances Commerciales (London) Ltd v. A. Besse & Co. (London) Ltd [1952] 1 T.L.R. 644; [1952] 1 Lloyd's Rep. 242 . . . . 6–057, 18–320, 25–161
Société de Banque Susse v. Société Generale Alsacienne de Banque [1989] J.T. 1342, ... 23–202
Société des Hótels le Touquet Paris-Plage v. Cummings [1922] 1 K.B. 451; [1921] All E.R. 408; 91 L.J.K.B. 288; 126 L.T. 513; 38 T.L.R. 221; 66 S.J. 269 . . . . 25–161, 25–166, 25–194
Société des Industries Metallurgiques SA v. The Bronx Engineering Co. Ltd [1975] 1 Lloyd's Rep. 465 17–099
Société Générale Sucrière v. E.C. Commission; Unione Nazionale Consumators; *Re* [1975] E.C.R. 1663 3–041
Société Italo-Belge pour le Commerce et l'Industrie v. Palm and Vegetable Oils (Malaysia) Sdn. Bhd. (Post Chaser, The) [1982] 1 All E.R. 19; [1981] 2 Lloyd's Rep. 695; [1981] Com.L.R. 249 . . . . 8–022, 8–030, 8–036, 9–024, 10–037, 12–035, 12–036, 18–357, 19–018, 19–064, 19–150, 19–180, 20–033, 21–025
Société Metallurgique D'Aubrives & Villerupt v. British Bank of Foreign Trade (1922) 11 Ll.L.R. 168 . . . . 23–142, 23–234, 23–235
Société Nouvelle des Papeteries de l'PAa v. BV Machinefabriek B.O.A. 1992 N.J. 750 . . . . 25–060, 25–065
Society of Lloyd's v. Canadian Imperial Bank of Commerce [1993] 2 Lloyd's Rep. 579 . . . . 23–145, 23–241
—— v. Fraser [1998] C.L.C. 1630; [1999] Lloyd's Rep. I.R. 156, CA; affirming [1998] C.L.C. 127, QBD (Comm Ct) 25–112
—— v. Leighs; Society of Lloyd's v. Lyon; Society of Lloyd's v. Wilkinson [1997] C.L.C. 1398; [1997] 6 Re. L.R. 289; *The Times*, August 11, 1997, CA; affirming [1997] C.L.C. 759, QBD 13–039
Sohio Supply Co. v. Gatoil (USA) Inc. [1989] 1 Lloyd's Rep. 588 23–087
Sokoloff v. National City Bank (1927) 224 N.Y.S. 102, affirmed 227 N.Y.S. 907, affirmed (1928) 164 N.E. 745 21–015
Solarte v. Palmer (1831) 7 Bing, 530; affirmed (1834) 1 Bing N.C. 194, HL 22–121
Solholt, The *See* Sotiros Shipping Inc. and Aeco Maritime SA v. Sameiet (The Solholt)
Solle v. Butcher [1950] 1 K.B. 671; 66 T.L.R. (Pt. 1) 448; [1949] 2 All E.R. 1107 . . . . 1–130, 3–013, 3–020, 3–025, 12–005, 12–128

Solloway v. McLaughlin [1937] 4 All E.R. 328; [1938] A.C. 247; 107 L.J.P.C. 1; 54 T.L.R. 69 7–002
Solo Industries UK Ltd v. Canara Bank [2001] EWCA Civ 1059; [2001] 1 W.L.R. 1800; [2001] 2 All E.R. (Comm) 217; [2001] 2 Lloyd's Rep. 578; [2001] Lloyd's Rep. Bank, 346; [2001] C.L.C. 1651; (2001) 98(29) L.S.G. 37; (2001) 145 S.J.L.B. 168; *The Times*, July 31, 2001; *The Independent*, July 6, 2001, CA; affirming 1999 Folio 13, QBD (Comm Ct) 23–145, 23–276
Soltykoff, *Re* [1891] 1 Q.B. 413; 60 L.J.Q.B. 339; 39 W.R. 337; 55 J.P. 100; 8 Morr. 27 2–035
Somes v. British Empire Co. (1860) 8 H.L.C. 338; 30 L.J.Q.B. 229; 21 L.T. 547; 6 Jur. (N.S.) 761; 8 W.R. 707 .... 9–009, 15–044, 15–088
Sonat Offshore SA v. Amerada Development Ltd [1987] 2 F.T.L.R. 220; [1988] 1 Lloyd's Rep. 145; (1988) 39 B.L.R. 1 .... 8–089, 8–099
Soneco Ltd v. Barcross Finance Ltd [1978] R.T.R. 444 .... 7–093, 7–100, 7–105
Sonicare International Ltd v. East Anglia Freight Terminal Ltd; Sonicare International Ltd v. Neptune Orient Lines Ltd [1997] 2 Lloyd's Rep. 48, CC (Central London) 18–150, 18–065, 21–073
Soon Hua Seng Co. v. Glencore Grain [1996] 1 Lloyd's Rep. 398 ... 19–002, 19–006, 19–027 19–075
Soproma SpA v. Marine and Animal By-products Corp. [1966] 1 Lloyd's Rep. 367; 116 New L.J. 867 .... 15–021, 18–059, 19–026, 19–027, 19–070, 19–207, 23–028, 23–083, 23–084, 23–096, 23–097, 23–098, 23–196, 23–203, 23–213, 23–214, 23–218, 23–222, 23–223
Sorrentino Fratelli v. Buerger [1915] 1 K.B. 307; 84 L.J.K.B. 1937; 113 L.T. 840; 13 Asp.M.L.C. 164; 21 Com.Cas. 33 3–043
Sotiros Shipping Inc. and Aeco Maritime SA v. Sameiet Solholt (The Solholt) (1983) 127 S.J. 305; [1983] 1 Lloyd's Rep. 605; [1983] Com.L.R. 114 .... 12–118, 16–052, 17–026, 19–184, 20–116, 20–137
Sottomayor v. de Barros (No. 1) (1877–78) L.R. 3 P.D. 1; (1877) 26 W.R. 455, CA; reversing (1876–77) L.R. 2 P.D. 81, PDAD 25–084
Sottomayor v. de Barros (No. 2) (1879–80) L.R. 5 P.D. 94; [1874–80] All E.R. Rep. 97, PDAD 25–084
Soules CAF v. PT Transap (Indonesia) [1999] 1 Lloyd's Rep. 917, QBD (Comm Ct) 19–008, 19–024, 19–031, 19–039, 19–147, 19–159, 19–161
South African Breweries v. King [1900] 1 Ch. 273; 69 L.J.Ch. 171; 82 L.T. 32; 48 W.R. 289; 16 T.L.R. 172; 44 S.J. 228 25–010
South African Republic v. Compagnie Franco-Belge du Chemin de Fer du Nord [1898] 1 Ch. 190; 77 L.T. 555; 46 W.R. 151; 14 T.L.R. 65; 42 S.J. 66 25–191
South African Reserve Bank v. Samuel & Co. (1931) 40 Ll.L.R. 291 .... 23–066, 23–115
South Australian Asset Management Corp. v. York Montague Ltd [1997] A.C. 191; [1996] 3 W.L.R. 87 .... 16–043, 16–046, 19–202
South Australian Insurance Co. v. Randell (1869) L.R. 3 P.C. 101; 6 Moo.P.C.C. (N.S.) 341; 22 L.T. 843; 16 E.R. 755 .... 1–034, 1–038, 1–058, 1–062, 5–152
South Caribbean Trading Ltd v. Trafigura Beheer BV [2004] EWHC 2676; [2005] 1 Lloyd's Rep. 128, QBD 8–030, 12–035, 19–209
South Coast Basalt Property Ltd v. R.W. Miller & Co. Property Ltd [1981] 1 N.S.W.L.R. 356 11–061
South Hetton Coal Co. v. Haswell Shotton & Easington Coal & Coke Co. [1898] 1 Ch. 465; 67 L.J.Ch. 238; 78 L.T. 366; 46 W.R. 355; 14 T.L.R. 277; 42 S.J. 345 2–003
South Staffs Tramways Co. Ltd v. Sickness and Accident Assurance Assn. [1891] 1 Q.B. 402; 60 L.J.Q.B. 260; 64 L.T. 279; 55 J.P. 372; 39 W.R. 292; 7 T.L.R. 267 8–034
South Western General Property Co. Ltd v. Marton (1982) 263 E.G. 1090; (1983) 2 T.L.R. 14 .... 13–057, 13–060
Southern (James) & Co. v. Austin (E.) & Son (1921) 6 Ll.L.R. 24 .... 20–109, 20–119
Southern Water Authority v. Carey [1985] 2 All E.R. 1077 18–149
Sovereign Bank of Canada v. Bellhouse, Dillon & Co. (1911) 23 Que.K.B. 413 ..... 23–114, 23–136
Sovereign Finance Ltd v. Silver Crest Furniture Ltd (1997) 16 Tr. L.R. 370; [1997] C.C.L.R. 76, QBD 13–030, 13–090

Soward v. Palmer (1818) 8 Taunt, 277; 2 Moo.C.P. 274 22–114
Sowler v. Potter [1940] 1 K.B. 271 3–013
Spaeth v. Hare (1842) 1 Dowl, (n.s.) 595 9–063
Spalding v. Ruding (1843) 6 Beav. 376; 12 L.J.Ch. 503; 1 L.T. (o.s.) 384; 7 Jur. 733; 49 E.R. 871 .... 15–099, 18–080
Span Terza (No. 2), The [1984] 1 W.L.R. 27; [1984] 1 Lloyd's Rep. 119; (1984) 81 L.S.G. 283; (1984) 128 S.J. 32, HL 5–014
Sparkes v. Marshall (1836) 2 Bing. 761; 2 Hodg, 44; 3 Scott 172; 5 L.J.C.P. 286 5–076
Spartali v. Benecke (1850) 10 C.B. 212; 19 L.J.C.P. 293; 15 L.T. (o.s.) 183; 138 E.R. 87 .... 5–017, 15–033
Specialist Plant Services Ltd v. Braithwaite Ltd (1987) 3 B.C.C. 119 ... 5–149, 5–150, 5–167
Spectra International plc v. Hayesoak Ltd [1998] 1 Lloyd's Rep. 162, CA; reversing [1997] 1 Lloyd's Rep. 153, CC (Central London) 18–150
Spectrum Plus Ltd (In Liquidation), Re; *sub nom.* National Westminster Bank Plc v. Spectrum Plus Ltd (In Creditors Voluntary Liquidation) [2005] UKHL 41; [2005] 2 A.C. 680; [2005] 3 W.L.R. 58; [2005] 4 All E.R. 209; [2005] 2 Lloyd's Rep. 275; [2005] B.C.C. 694; [2005] 2 B.C.L.C. 269; (2005) 155 N.L.J. 1045; *The Times*, July 1, 2005; *Independent*, July 6, 2005, HL 5–142, 5–152
Speedway Safety Products Property Ltd v. Hazell & Moore Industries Property Ltd [1982] 1 N.S.W.L.R. 255 .... 11–003, 11–007, 11–011
Spence v. Chadwick (1847) 10 Q.B. 5 8–097
—— v. Crawford [1939] 3 All E.R. 271 .... 12–007, 12–068
—— v. Union Marine Insurance Co. (1868) L.R. 3 C.P. 427 5–148
Spencer v. Claude Rye (Vehicles) Ltd, *The Guardian*, December 19, 1972 11–057
—— v. Harding (1870) L.R. 5 C.P. 561; 39 L.J.C.P. 332; 23 L.T. 237; 19 W.R. 48 2–003
Spencer v. North Country Finance Ltd [1963] C.L.Y. 212; *The Guardian*, February 20, 1963 .... 1–066, 3–005, 7–010
Sperry International Trade Inc. v. Government of Israel 532 F.Supp. 901 (1982) ... 23–135, 23–153
Sperry Rand Corp. v. Norddeutscher Lloyd, The Bischolstein [1974] 1 Lloyd's Rep. 122; [1973] A.M.C. 1392 21–086
Spettabile Consorzio Veneziano di Armamento di Navigazione v. Northumberland Shipbuilding Co. Ltd (1919) 121 L.T. 628 .... 8–078, 9–010, 17–104
Spiliada Maritime Corp. v. Cansulex Ltd [1987] A.C. 460; [1986] 3 W.L.R. 972; (1986) 130 S.J. 925; [1986] 3 All E.R. 843; [1987] 1 F.T.L.R. 103; [1987] 1 Lloyd's Rep. 1; [1987] E.C.C. 168; (1986) 130 S.J. 925; (1987) 84 L.S.Gaz. 113; (1986) 136New L.J. 1137, H.L.; reversing [1985] 2 Lloyd's Rep. 116; (1985) 82 L.S.Gaz. 1416, C.A. 18–053
Spillers Ltd v. Mitchell (J.W.) Ltd (1929) 33 W.L.R. 89 19–033
Spinney's (1948), Spinney's Centres SAL. and Doumet (Michell) Doumet (Joseph) and Distributors and Agencies SAL, v. Royal Insurance Co. [1980] 1 Lloyd's Rep. 406 8–097
Spiro v. Glencrown Properties Ltd [1991] Ch. 537; [1991] 2 W.L.R. 931; [1991] 1 All E.R. 600; (1990) 134 S.J. 1479; [1991] 02 E.G. 167; (1990) 62 P. & C.R. 402; (1990) 134 N.L.J. 1754; (1991) 141 N.L.J. 124; *The Independent*, December 5, 1990 .... 1–050, 5–044, 7–070
—— v. Lintern [1973] 1 W.L.R. 1002; 117 S.J. 584; [1973] 3 All E.R. 319 .... 7–008, 7–011, 7–012
Sport International Bussum B. V. v. Inter-Footwear Ltd [1984] 1 W.L.R. 776; (1984) 128 S.J. 383; [1984] 2 All E.R. 321; (1984) 81 L.S.Gaz. 1992 .... 15–134, 16–037, 16–038
Sprague v. Booth [1909] A.C. 576; 78 L.J.P.C. 164; 101 L.T. 211 8–040
Sprange v. Barnard (1789) 2 Bro.C.C. 585 5–153
Spring Motors Distributors v. Ford Motor Co. 489 A. 2d 660 (1985) 14–079
Spurling (J.) Ltd v. Bradshaw [1956] 1 W.L.R. 461 .... 13–013, 13–014, 13–052
Spurrier v. La Cloche [1902] A.C. 446; 71 L.J.P.C. 101; 86 L.T. 631; 18 T.L.R. 606; 51 W.R. 1 .... 25–007, 25–010, 25–089
Square v. Model Farm Dairies (Bournemouth) Ltd [1939] 2 K.B. 365; [1939] 1 All E.R. 259; 108 L.J.K.B. 198; 160 L.T. 165; 55 T.L.R. 384; 83 S.J. 152 .... 14–094, 17–072
Stabilad Ltd v. Stephens & Carter Ltd (No. 2) [1999] 2 All E.R. (Comm) 651, CA ... 2–017

Stach (Ian) Ltd v. Baker Bastey Ltd [1958] 2 Q.B. 130; [1958] 2 W.L.R. 419; 102 S.J. 177; [1958] 1 All E.R. 542 .... 9–053, 20–001, 20–003, 20–014, 20–028, 20–030, 20–041, 20–045, 23–080, 23–088, 23–094, 23–105
Stadium Finance Ltd v. Robbins [1962] 2 Q.B. 664; [1962] 3 W.L.R. 453; 106 S.J. 369; [1962] 2 All E.R. 633 .... 1–083, 7–032, 7–038, 7–043, 7–044, 7–046, 7–075
Staffordshire Area Health Authority v. South Staffordshire Water Authority [1978] 1 W.L.R. 1387; (1978) 122 S.J. 331; [1978] 3 All E.R. 769; (1978) 77 L.G.R. 17 6–054
Staffs, Motor Guarantee Ltd v. British Wagon Co. Ltd [1934] 2 K.B. 305 .... 1–066, 7–032, 7–038, 7–058, 7–070
Stag Line Ltd v. Foscolo, Mango & Co. Ltd [1932] A.C. 328; [1931] All E.R. Rep. 666; 101 L.J.K.B. 165; 146 L.T. 305; 48 T.L.R. 127; 75 S.J. 884; 18 Asp.M.L.C. 266; 37 Com.Cas. 54 .... 18–059, 21–090
—— v. Tyne Shiprepair Group Ltd (The Zinnia) [1984] 2 Lloyd's Rep. 211; (1985) 4 Tr.L. 33 13–090
Stagg, Mantle & Co. v. Brodrick (1895) 12 T.L.R. 12, CA 22–045, 22–051
Staimen Steel Ltd v. Frank Canada Ltd (1985) 23 D.L.R. (4th) 180 12–045
Stamp v. United Dominions Trust Ltd [1967] 1 Q.B. 418; [1967] 2 W.L.R. 541; 131 J.P. 177; 110 S.J. 904; [1967] 1 All E.R. 251; [1966] C.L.Y. 7650 7–006
Standard Bank London Ltd v. Apostolakis [2003] I.L.Pr. 499 25–045
Standard Bank London Ltd v. Apostolakis (No.1) [2002] C.L.C. 933; [2000] I.L.Pr. 766, QBD 25–045, 25–102
Standard Bank London Ltd v. Apostolakis (No.2) [2001] Lloyd's Rep. Bank. 240; [2002] C.L.C. 939, QBD 25–045, 25–048
Standard Bank London Ltd v. Bank of Tokyo Sudwestdeutsche Landesbank Girozentrale v. Bank of Tokyo Ltd [1995] 2 Lloyd's Rep. 169, *The Times*, April, 15, 1995, QBD 2–021, 23–155
Standard Chartered Bank v. Pakistan National Shipping Corp. (No. 1) [1998] 1 Lloyd's Rep. 656, CA; reversing [1995] 2 Lloyd's Rep. 364 (QBD Admin Ct) 18–028, 18–029, 19–196, 19–197
Standard Chartered Bank v. Pakistan National Shipping Corp (No.2); Standard Chartered Bank v. Mehra [2002] UKHL 43; [2003] 1 A.C. 959; [2002] 3 W.L.R. 1547; [2003] 1 All E.R. 173; [2002] 2 All E.R. (Comm) 931; [2003] 1 Lloyd's Rep. 227; [2002] B.C.C. 846; [2003] 1 B.C.L.C. 244; [2002] C.L.C. 1330; (2003) 100(1) L.S.G. 26; (2002) 146 S.J.L.B. 258; *The Times*, November 7, 2002, HL; reversing in part [2000] 1 All E.R. (Comm) 1; [2000] 1 Lloyd's Rep. 218; [2000] Lloyd's Rep. Bank. 40; [2000] C.L.C. 133; *The Times*, March 15, 2000; *Independent*, December 9, 1999, CA (Civ Div); reversing in part [1998] 1 Lloyd's Rep. 684; *The Times*, May 27, 1998, QBD 18–021, 18–022, 18–028, 18–045, 18–046, 18–147, 19–197, 23–142, 23–187
Standard Chartered Bank v. Pakistan National Shipping Corp. (No.3) [2001] EWCA Civ 55; [2001] 1 All E.R. (Comm) 822; [2001] C.L.C. 825CA; affirming [1999] 1 All E.R. (Comm.) 417; [1999] 1 Lloyd's Rep. 747; [1999] C.L.C. 761, QBD (Comm Ct) 18–028, 18–029, 19–176
Standard Chartered Bank v. Pakistan National Shipping Corp. (No. 4) [2001] Q.B. 167; [2000] 3 W.L.R. 1692; [2000] 2 All E.R. (Comm) 929; [2000] 2 Lloyd's Rep. 511; [2000] Lloyd's Rep. Bank, 342; [2000] C.L.C. 1575; *The Times*, October 3, 2000, CA 18–028, 18–029
Standard Electrica SA v. Hamburg Süd-amerikanische Dampfschiffahrts-Gesellschalt 375 F. 2d 943 (1967) [1967] 2 Lloyd's Rep. 193 21–086
Stanmore Wesson & Co. v. Breen (1886) 12 App.Cas. 698 19–196
Stansbie v. Troman [1948] 2 K.B. 48; [1948] L.J.R. 1206; 64 T.L.R. 226; 92 S.J. 167; [1948] 1 All E.R. 599; 46 L.G.R. 349 16–049
Stapleton, *ex p.* (1879) 10 Ch.D. 586 .... 3–048, 15–027, 15–037, 15–108, 16–074
Stapylton Fletcher Ltd (In Administrative Receivership) *Re* [1994] 1 W.L.R. 1181; [1995] 1 All E.R. 192; [1994] B.C.L.C. 681; [1994] B.C.C. 532 .... 1–059, 1–108, 1–119, 5–081, 5–110, 5–113, 5–130, 18–254, 19–204, 21–007
Starkey v. Bank of England [1903] A.C. 114 18–045
Star Public Saw Mill Co. v. Robert Bruce & Co. Ltd (1923) 17 Ll.L.R. 7 19–014
Star Shipping A.G. v. China National Foreign Trade Transportation Corp.; Star Texas, The [1993] 2 Lloyd's Rep. 445, CA 25–031

Star Texas, The *See* Star Shipping A.G. v. China National Foreign Trade Transportation Corp.; Star Texas, The.
Starside Properties Ltd v. Mustapha [1974] 1 W.L.R. 816; 118 S.J. 388; [1974] 2 All E.R. 567; 28 P. & C.R. 95 .... 15–134, 16–038, 16–038
Startup v. Cortazzi (1835) 2 C.M. & R. 165; 5 Tyr. 698; 4 L.J.Ex. 218 17–009
—— v. Macdonald (1843) 6 M. & G. 593; 7 Scott N.R. 269; 12 L.J.Ex. 477; 1 L.T. (o.s.) 172; 134 E.R. 1029, Ex.Ch. 8–033, 8–041, 9–007
State Savings Bank of Victoria v. Patrick Intermarine Acceptances Ltd (In Liquidation) [1981] 1 N.S.W.L.R. 175 (Australia) 22–049
State Trading Corporation v. Mar (Sugar) Ltd [1981] Com.L.R. 235 23–276
State Trading Corp. of India v. Campagnie Francaise d'Importation et de Distribution [1983] 2 Lloyd's Rep. 679 .... 9–055, 19–150
—— v. M. Golodetz Ltd [1989] 2 Lloyd's Rep. 277 ... 9–016, 9–018, 9–053, 10–037, 12–027, 18–276, 18–357, 19–058, 19–063, 19–148, 19–162, 19–166, 19–207
Staunton v. Wood (1851) 16 Q.B. 638; 16 L.T. (o.s.) 486; 15 Jur. 1123; 117 E.R. 1025 .... 8–036, 9–051
Steam Herring Fleet Ltd v. V.S. Richards & Co. Ltd (1901) 17 T.L.R. 731 .... 17–040, 17–041, 17–046
S.S. Den of Airlie Co. Ltd v. Mitsui & Co. (1911–12) 17 Com.Cas. 116 ..... 18–116, 21–020
Steamship "Induna" Co. Ltd v. British Phosphate Commissioners; The Loch Dee [1949] 2 K.B. 430; [1949] L.J.R. 1058; 65 T.L.R. 149; 93 S.J. 237; [1949] 1 All E.R. 522 8–091
S.S. Istros v. F.W. Dahlstroem & Co. [1931] 1 K.B. 247; 100 L.J.K.B. 141; 144 L.T. 124; 18 Asp.M.L.C. 177; 36 Com.Cas. 65
Steedman v. Drinkle [1916] 1 A.C. 275; 85 L.J.P.C. 79; 114 L.T. 248; 32 T.L.R. 231 16–038
Steel Authority of India Ltd v. Hind Metals Inc. [1984] 1 Lloyds Rep. 405; (1984) 134 New, L.J. 204 25–007
Steel Co. of Canada Ltd v. Dominion Radiator Co. Ltd (1919) 48 D.L.R. 350 8–027
Steele v. M'Kinlay (1880) 5 App.Cas. 754; 43 L.T. 358; 29 W.R. 17 .... 22–053, 22–054
Steels & Busks Ltd v. Bleecker Bik & Co. Ltd [1956] 1 Lloyd's Rep. 228 ... 11–022, 11–061, 11–079
Stein v. Hambro's Bank of Northern Commerce (1921) 9 Ll.L.R. 433; (1922) 10 Ll.L.R. 529 .... 23–136, 23–171, 23–210
Stein Forbes & Co. v. County Tailoring Co. Ltd (1916) 86 L.J.K.B. 448; 115 L.T. 215; 13 Asp.M.L.C. 422 .... 5–071, 9–021, 16–023, 16–026, 16–028, 18–209, 19–006, 19–069, 19–075, 19–081, 19–098, 19–099, 19–213, 19–214, 21–015
Steinmeyer v. Warner Consolidated Corporation, 42 Cal. App. 3d 515, 116 Cal.Reptr. 57 (1974) 23–239, 23–248
Stennett v. Hancock and Peters [1939] 2 All E.R. 578; 83 S.J. 379 .... 14–063, 14–076
Stensby, The [1974] 2 All E.R. 786 .... 25–071, 25–202
Stent Foundations Ltd v. M.J. Gleeson Group plc [2001] B.L.R. 134; (2001) 17 Const. L.J. 186, QBD (T&CC) 13–019
Stephens v. Wilkinson (1831) 2 B. & A. 320; 9 L.J. (o.s.) K.B. 231; 109 E.R. 1162 .. 15–117, 17–106
Sterns Ltd v. Vickers Ltd [1923] 1 K.B. 78 ..... 5–061, 5–099, 5–110, 6–004, 6–006, 18–177, 18–193, 18–300, 18–301, 18–302, 18–303, 18–304, 21–008
Steven v. Bromley & Son [1919] 2 K.B. 722, 728 2–008
Stevenson v. Beverley Bentinck Ltd [1976] 1 W.L.R. 483; 120 S.J. 197; [1976] 2 All E.R. 606; [1976] R.T.R. 543 .... 7–092, 11–028
—— v. McLean (1880) 5 Q.B.D. 346; 49 L.J.Q.B. 701; 42 L.T. 897 2–015
—— v. Newnham (1853) 13 C.B. 285; 22 L.J.C.P. 110; 20 L.T. (o.s.) 279; 17 Jur. 600 7–021
—— v. Rogers [1999] Q.B. 1028; [1999] 2 W.L.R. 1064; [1999] 1 All E.R. 613; (1999) 96(2) L.S.G. 29; (1999) 149 N.L.J. 16; (1999) 143 S.J.L.B. 21; *The Times*, December 31, 1998, CA 11–045, 13–075, 14–011, 14–029, 14–112
Stewart v. Chapman [1951] 2 K.B. 792 8–034
—— v. Greenock Marine Insurance Co. (1847) 2 H.L.C. 159 1–069
—— v. Kennedy (1890) 15 App.Cas. 75 17–100
—— v. Kennet (1809) 2 Camp. 177 22–122
—— v. Oriental Fire & Marine Insce. Co. Ltd [1985] Q.B. 988; [1984] 3 W.L.R. 741; (1984) 128 S.J. 645; [1984] 3 All E.R. 777; [1984] 2 Lloyd's Rep. 109 3–028

Stewart v. Reavell's Garage [1952] 2 Q.B. 545; [1952] 1 T.L.R. 1266; 96 S.J. 314; [1952] 1 All E.R. 1191 .... 1–041, 1–043, 14–046
—— v. Rogerson (1871) L.R. 6 C.P. 424 15–088
—— v. Royal Bank of Scotland plc 1994 S.L.T. (Sh Ct) 27, Sh Ct (Glasgow) 25–076
Stewart Gill v. Horatio Myer & Co. [1992] Q.B. 600; [1992] 2 W.L.R. 721; [1992] 2 All E.R. 257; (1991) 11 Tr.L.R. 86; (1992) 142 N.L.J. 241, CA 1–043, 9–026, 13–027, 13–064, 13–087, 13–090, 18–275
Stewart (Robert) & Sons Ltd v. Carapanayoti & Co. Ltd [1962] 1 W.L.R. 34; 106 S.J. 16; [1962] 1 All E.R. 418; [1961] 2 Lloyd's Rep. 387 .... 16–032, 16–037
Stickney v. Keeble [1915] A.C. 386 8–026
Stindt v. Roberts (1848) 17 L.J.Q.B. 166; 5 Dow. & L. 460; 2 Saund, & C. 212; 12 Jur. 518 18–099
Stock v. Inglis, *See* Inglis v. Stock.
Stock v. Urey [1954] N.I. 71 .... 4–012, 4–029
Stockloser v. Johnson [1954] 1 Q.B. 476; [1954] 2 W.L.R. 439; 98 S.J. 178; [1954] 1 All E.R. 630 .... 15–134, 16–038, 16–040
Stockman v. Parr (1843) 11 M. & W. 809; 1 Car. & Kir. 41; 12 L.J.Ex. 415; 7 Jur. 886 22–124
Stocks v. Wilson [1913] 2 K.B. 235; 82 L.J.K.B. 598; 108 L.T. 834; 29 T.L.R. 352; 20 Mans. 129 .... 2–028, 2–031, 2–034, 2–038, 2–040, 15–118, 25–127
Stocznia Gdanska SA v. Latvian Shipping Co. [1996] 2 Lloyd's Rep. 132 .... 1–041, 1–047
Stocznia Gdanska SA v. Latvian Shipping Co. [2001] 1 Lloyd's Rep. 537; [2001] C.L.C. 1290, QBD (Comm Ct) 12–021, 12–037
Stocznia Gdanska SA v. Latvian Shipping Co (Repudiation) [2002] EWCA Civ 889; [2002] 2 All E.R. (Comm) 768; [2002] 2 Lloyd's Rep. 436; [2003] 1 C.L.C. 282, CA 19–209
Stolt Loyalty, The [1995] 1 Lloyd's Rep. 598, CA; affirming [1993] 2 Lloyd's Rep. 281, QBD (Adm Ct) 18–054
Stonard v. Dunkin (1810) 2 Camp. 344; 170 E.R. 1178, N.P. 5–065, 7–014
Stoneleigh Finance Ltd v. Phillips [1965] 2 Q.B. 537; [1965] 2 W.L.R. 508; 109 S.J. 68; [1965] 1 All E.R. 513 .... 1–066, 7–007, 7–011
Stora Enso oyj v. Port of Dundee [2006] CSHO 40 .... 5–029, 18–212, 18–244
Stoveld v. Hughes (1811) 14 East 308; 104 E.R. 619 15–093
Straker v. Graham (1839) 4 M. & W. 721; 8 L.J.Ex. 86; 7 Dowl. 223 22–098
Strand Electric Engineering Co. Ltd v. Brisford Entertainments Ltd [1952] 2 Q.B. 246; [1952] 1 T.L.R. 939; 96 S.J. 260; [1952] 1 All E.R. 796 .... 7–002, 9–009
Strass v. Spillers and Bakers Ltd [1911] 2 K.B. 759; 80 L.J.K.B. 1218; 104 L.T. 284; 11 Asp.M.L.C. 590; 16 Com.Cas. 166 19–051
Strathlorne S.S. Co. Ltd v. Baird (Hugh) & Sons Ltd 1916 S.C. (H.L.) 134 23–027
Street v. Blay (1831) 2 B. & Ad. 456; 109 E.R. 1212 .... 11–003, 12–046, 12–057, 12–063
Strohmenger v. Attenborough (1894) 11 T.L.R. 7 7–083
Ströms Brucks Aktie Bolag v. Hutchison [1905] A.C. 515; 74 L.J.P.C. 130; 93 L.T. 562; 21 T.L.R. 718; 10 Asp.M.L.C. 138; 11 Com.Cas. 13 .... 16–068, 19–157
Strong v. Hart (1827) 6 B. & C. 160 9–031
Strongman (1945) Ltd v. Sincock [1955] 2 Q.B. 525; [1955] 3 W.L.R. 360; 99 S.J. 540; [1955] 3 All E.R. 90 .... 3–029, 10–013
Stroud Architectural Services v. John Laing Construction [1994] B.C.C. 18; [1994] 2 B.C.L.C. 276; 35 Con.L.R. 135; (1993) 9 Const. L.J. 337 .... 5–134, 5–144, 5–158
Strutt v. Smith (1834) 1 Cr. M. & R. 312; 4 Tyr. 1019; 3 L.J.Ex. 357; 149 E.R. 1099 16–016
Stubbs v. Holywell Railway (1867) L.R. 2 Ex. 311; 36 L.J.Ex. 166; 16 L.T. 631; 15 W.R. 869 18–354
Stucley v. Bailey (1862) 1 H. & C. 405; 31 L.J.Ex. 483; 10 W.R. 720; 158 E.R. 943 10–005
Studdy v. Beesty (1889) 60 L.T. 647 22–131
—— v. Sanders (1826) 5 B. & C. 628; 8 Dow. & Ry. K.B. 403; 4 L.J. (o.s.) K.B. 290; 108 E.R. 234 .... 5–097, 16–021, 16–023
Stunzi Sons Ltd v. House of Youth Pty. Ltd (1960) 60 S.R. (N.S.W.) 220 23–315
Subro Valour, The [1995] 1 Lloyd's Rep. 509 .... 18–115, 20–082, 20–088
Sudan Import and Export Co. (Khartoum) Ltd v. Sociètè Generale de Compensation [1958] 1 Lloyd's Rep. 310, CA; affirming [1957] 2 Lloyd's Rep. 528 .... 16–081, 16–082, 20–116, 20–135, 20–140

Sudbrook Trading Estate Ltd v. Eggleton [1983] 1 A.C. 444; [1982] 3 W.L.R. 315; (1982) 126 S.J. 512; [1982] 3 All E.R. 1; (1982) 44 P. & C.R. 153 ...... 2–017, 2–050
Sugar Distributors Ltd v. Monaghan Cash & Carry Ltd [1982] I.L.R.M. 399 5–152
Sugar Properties (Derisley Wood) Ltd (1987) 3 B.C.C. 88; [1988] B.C.L.C. 146 1–081
Suiker Unie v. Commission of the European Communities. *See* Cooperatieve Vereniging Suiker Unie UA v. Commission of the European Communities (40/73)
Suisse Atlantique Sociètè d'Armement Maritime SA v. N.V. Rotterdamsche Kolen Centrale [1967] A.C. 361..... 4–020, 8–081, 12–019, 12–034, 12–066, 13–031, 13–034, 13–036, 13–037, 13–043, 13–046, 13–047, 13–048, 13–051, 13–052, 15–111, 16–032, 16–036, 23–131
Sullivan v. Jacob (1828) 1 Moll. 472 17–100
Sully v. Frean (1854) 10 Exch. 535; 156 E.R. 551 22–062
Sumitomo Bank v. Co-operative Centrale Raiffeisen-Bocerenleenbank BA *See* Co-operative Centrale Raiffeisen-Boerenleenbank BA v. Sumitomo Bank
Summer v. Challenor (1926) 70 S.J. 760 6–011
Summers v. Cook (1880) 28 Grant's Ch.R. 179 (Can.) 1–093
Sumner, Permain & Co. v. Webb & Co. [1922] 1 K.B. 55; 91 L.J.K.B. 228; 126 L.T. 294; 38 T.L.R. 45; 66 S.J.W.R. 17; 27 Com.Cas. 105 .... 11–044, 11–059, 18–239, 20–038
Sumpter v. Hedges [1898] 1 Q.B. 673 6–040
Sunair Holidays Ltd v. Dodd [1970] 1 W.L.R. 1037; 114 S.J. 372; [1970] 2 All E.R. 410; 68 L.G.R. 550 14–113
Sunrise Maritime Inc. v. Uvisco Ltd (The Hector) [1998] 2 Lloyd's Rep. 287; [1998] C.L.C. 902, QBD (Comm Ct)...... 18–029, 18–047, 18–054, 18–084, 18–165 20–008, 20–020
Super Servant Two, The [1990] 1 Lloyd's Rep. 1 .... 8–088, 8–089, 8–097, 8–099
Superior Overseas Development Corporation v. British Gas Corporation [1982] 1 Lloyd's Rep. 262 6–054
Surf City, The [1995] 2 Lloyd's Rep. 242 .... 18–209, 19–099
Surzur Overseas Ltd v. Ocean Reliance Shipping Co. Ltd [1997] C.L.Y. 906 .... 9–026, 13–090, 13–100, 25–092, 25–162
Sutcliffe v. Chief Constable of West Yorkshire (1995) 159 J.P. 770; [1996] R.T.R. 86; *The Times*, June 5, 1995, CA 6–026, 6–029
Sutcliffe v. Thackrah [1974] A.C. 727; [1974] 2 W.L.R. 295; 118 S.J. 148; [1974] 1 All E.R. 859; [1974] 1 Lloyd's Rep. 318 .... 2–052, 13–039
Sutherland v. Allhusen (1866) 14 L.T. 666; 2 Mar.L.C. 349 .... 20–014, 20–016, 20–042
—— v. Nicol [1951] W.N. 110; 95 S.J. 187 1–002
Sutro (L.) & Co. and Heilbut Symons & Co., *Re* [1917] 2 K.B. 348 .. 5–100, 6–049, 18–208, 19–032, 21–082
Sutters v. Briggs [1922] 1 A.C. 1; 91 L.J.K.B. 1; 125 L.T. 737; 38 T.L.R. 30; 66 S.J.W.R. 9 .... 22–075, 22–144
Sutton
—— v. Buck (1810) 2 Taunt. 302; 127 E.R. 1094 5–010
—— v. Page (1846) 3 C.B. 204 9–041
Suzuki & Co. v. Burgett & Newsam (1921) 8 Ll.L.Rep. 495; (1922) 10 Ll.L.R. 223 .. 19–013 19–027, 19–030, 19–145, 19–151
—— v. Companhia Mercantile Internacional (1921) 8 Ll.L.R. 174; 9 Ll.L.R. 171 19–088
Swaddling v. Administration Officer (Case C–90/97) 1999 All E.R. (EC) 217; [1999] E.C.R. 1–1075; [1999] 2 C.M.L.R. 679; [1999] C.E.C. 184; [1999] 2 F.L.R. 184; [1999] Fam. Law 382; *The Times*, March 4, 1999, ECJ (5th Chamber) 25–056
Swain v. Shepherd (1832) 1 Moo. & Rob. 223, N.P. 5–009, 5–040, 5–041, 8–014
Swan v. North British Australasian Co. Ltd (1863) 2 H. & C. 175 .... 7–016, 7–017
Swanwick v. Southern (1839) 9 A. & E. 895; 1 Per. & Dav. 648; 112 E.R. 1453 ..... 5–038, 5–061
Sweet & Maxwell Ltd v. Universal News Services Ltd [1964] 2 Q.B. 699; [1964] 3 W.L.R. 356; 108 S.J. 478; [1964] 3 All E.R. 30 .... 2–017, 8–077
Sweeting v. Turner (1871) L.R. 7 Q.B. 310; 41 L.J.Q.B. 58; 25 L.T. 796; 36 J.P. 597; 20 W.R. 185 .... 5–017, 6–033
Swift v. Winterbotham (1873) L.R. 8 Q.B. 244 12–012
Swift Canadian Co. Ltd v. Banet 224, F. 2d 36 (1955) 20–102

Swinyard v. Bowes (1816) 5 M.& S. 62 22–134
Swire v. Leach (1865) 18 C.B. (N.S.) 492; 5 New Rep. 314; 34 L.J.C.P. 150; 11 L.T. 680; 11 Jur. (N.S.) 179; 13 W.R. 385 1–072
Swiss Bank Corporation v. Brinks Mal Ltd [1986] Q.B. 853; [1986] 3 W.L.R. 12; (1986) 130 S.J. 446; [1986] 2 All E.R. 188; [1986] 2 Lloyd's Rep. 79 .... 13–020, 13–052
—— v. Lloyds Bank Ltd [1982] A.C. 584; [1981] 2 W.L.R. 893; (1981) 125 S.J. 495; [1981] 2 All E.R. 449 .... 5–161, 18–234, 18–236
Sydney City Council v. West (1965) 114 C.L.R. 481; (1965) 39 A.L.J.R. 323 13–049
Sydney Harbour Trust Commissioners v. Wilson (1907) 7 S.R. (N.S.W.) 225 5–076
Syers v. Jonas (1848) 2 Exch. 111; 154 E.R. 426 .... 11–074, 11–076
Sykes, Cloghran Stud Farm Co. v. Trustee *Re* (1932) 101 L.J.Ch. 298; [1931] B. & C.R. 215 25–182
Sykes (F. & G.) (Wessex) Ltd v. Fine Fare Ltd [1967] 1 Lloyd's Rep. 53 .... 2–017, 2–046
Symes v. Hughes (1870) L.R. 9 Eq. 475; 39 L.J.Ch. 304; 22 L.T. 462 .... 1–043, 1–095, 3–033
—— v. Laurie [1985] 2 Qd. R. 547 1–096
Symonds v. Clark Fruit and Produce Co. Ltd [1919] 1 W.W.R. 587 12–051
Symons v. Mulkern (1882) 46 L.T. 763; 30 W.R. 875 22–141
Syndic in Bkpcy of Salim Nasrallah Khoury v. Khayat [1943] 2 All E.R. 406; [1943] A.C. 507 25–160
Syros Shipping Co. SA v. Elaghill Trading Co. (The Proodos C.) [1980] 2 Lloyd's Rep. 390 19–160
Sze Hai Tong Bank Ltd v. Rambler Cycle Co. Ltd [1959] A.C. 576; [1959] 3 W.L.R. 214; 103 S.J. 561; [1959] 3 All E.R. 182; [1959] 2 Lloyd's Rep. 114 .... 13–042, 13–044, 13–052, 18–063
Sztejn v. Schroder (Henry J.) Banking Corporation 31 N.Y.S. 2d 631 (1941) 23–141, 23–150, 23–191
Szymanowski & Co. v. Beck & Co. *See* Beck & Co. v. Szymanowski & Co.

T.C. Industrial Plant Property Ltd v. Robert's Queensland Property Ltd [1964] A.L.R. 1083 17–070
T.N.T. (Melbourne) Property Ltd v. May & Baker (Australia) Property Ltd (1966) 115 C.L.R. 353 13–049
Taddy & Co. v. Sterious & Co. [1904] 1 Ch. 354; 73 L.J.Ch. 191; 89 L.T. 628; 52 W.R. 152; 20 T.L.R. 102; 48 S.J. 117 3–037
Tagart, Beaton & Co. v. James Fisher & Sons [1903] 1 K.B. 391; 72 L.J.K.B. 202; 88 L.T. 451; 51 W.R. 599; 9 Asp.M.L.C. 381; 8 Com.Cas. 133 18–051
Tai Hing Cotton Mill Ltd v. Kamsing Knitting Factory [1979] A.C. 91 [1978] 2 W.L.R. 62; (1977) 121 S.J. 662; [1978] 1 All E.R. 515 .... 12–021, 16–072, 16–074, 16–082, 17–010, 17–014, 17–015, 17–016, 17–018, 19–179, 20–116
—— v. Liu Chong Hing Bank Ltd [1986] A.C. 80; [1985] 3 W.L.R. 317; (1985) 129 S.J. 503; [1985] 2 All E.R. 947 12–073
Tailby v. Official Receiver (1888) 13 App.Cas. 523 .... 1–107, 5–094
Talbot v. Bank of Hendersonville 495 S.W. 2d 548 (1972) 23–027, 23–129, 23–206, 23–234
Tamplin v. James (1880) 15 Ch. D. 215; 43 L.T. 520; 29 W.R. 311 17–100
Tamplin (F. A.) S.S. Co. Ltd v. Anglo-American Petroleum Co. Ltd [1916] 2 A.C. 397; 85 L.J.K.B. 1389; 32 T.L.R. 677; 1 Com.Cas. 299; 115 L.T. 315; 13 Asp.M.L.C. 467 6–050
Tamvaco v. Lucas (No. 1) (1859) 1 E. & E. 581; 28 L.J.Q.B. 150; 1 L.T. 161; 5 Jur. (N.S.) 731; 7 W.R. 568 .... 8–046, 8–049, 19–012, 19–036, 19–054, 19–147
—— v. —— (No. 2) (1862) 2 B. & S. 89; 3 F. & F. 10; 31 L.J.Q.B. 296; 6 L.T. 697; 10 W.R. 733; 1 Mar.L.C. 231; 122 E.R. 34, Ex.Ch. 19–012, 19–051, 19–120
Tancred v. Allgood (1859) 4 H. & N. 438 5–010
Tancred Arrol & Co. v. Steel Co. of Scotland Ltd (1890) 15 App.Cas. 125; 62 L.T. 738 .... 8–056, 8–059, 8–060, 8–062
Tankexpress A/S v. Compagnie Financiere Belge des Petroles SA [1949] A.C. 76; [1949] L.J.R. 170; 93 S.J. 26; [1948] 2 All E.R. 939 .... 9–038, 9–042, 12–035
Tankrederei Ahrenkeil GmbH v. Fruhuil SA; Multitank Holsatia, The [1988] 2 Lloyd's Rep. 486 8–031
Tanner v. Scovell (1845) 14 M. & W. 28; 14 L.J.Ex. 321; 153 E.R. 375 15–084

Tansley v. Turner (1835) 2 Bing. 151; 1 Hodg. 267; 2 Scott 238; 4 L.J.C.P. 272; 132 E.R. 60 .... 5–024, 5–037, 15–039, 15–049
Tapfield v. Hillman (1843) 6 M. & G. 245; 6 Scott N.R. 967; 12 L.J.C.P. 311; 7 Jur. 771; 134 E.R. 883 5–094
Tappenbeck, *Re. ex p.* Banner (1876) 2 Ch.D. 278; 45 L.J.Bcy. 73; 34 L.T. 199; 24 W.R. 476 .... 5–005, 5–138, 18–229, 18–230, 18–231
Tarleton v. Allhusen (1834) 2 A. & E. 32 9–030
Tarling v. Baxter (1827) 6 B. & C. 360; 9 Dow. & Ry. K.B. 272; 5 L.J. (o.s.) K.B. 164; 108 E.R. 484 .... 5–017, 5–018, 5–135
—— v. O'Riordan (1878) 2 L.R.lr. 82 .... 8–046, 8–064, 8–065, 8–072, 8–073, 8–082, 8–084
Tate, *Re, ex p.* Moffatt (1840) 1 Mont. D. & De G. 282; 4 Jur. 659 15–129
Tate & Lyle plc v. Commission of the European Communities (T202/98); British Sugar plc v. Commission of the European Communities (T204/98); Napier Brown plc v. Commission of the European Communities (T207/98) [2001] All E.R. (EC) 839; [2001] 5 C.M.L.R. 22; *The Times*, September 3, 2001, CFI (4th Chamber) 3–041
Tate & Lyle Food and Distribution Ltd v. Greater London Council [1982] 1 W.L.R. 149; (1981) 125 S.J. 865; [1981] 3 All E.R. 716 16–007
Tattersall v. National S.S. Co. Ltd (1884) 12 Q.B.D. 297 13–035
Tatung (U.K.) Ltd Galex Telesure Ltd [1989] 5 B.C.C. 325 .... 5–153, 5–160
Tavoulareas v. Tsavliris; Tavoulareas v. Alexander G Tsavliris & Sons Maritime Co (No.1) [2005] EWHC 2140; [2006] 1 All E.R. (Comm) 109; [2006] I.L.Pr. 14, QBD 25–020
Taylor, *Re* [1985] J.B.L. 390 7–070
Taylor v. Bank of Athens (1922) 27 Com.Cas. 142 .... 19–187, 19–189, 19–190, 19–192, 19–198, 19–202
—— v. Blakelock (1886) 32 Ch.D. 560; 56 L.J.Ch. 390; 55 L.T. 8 5–161
—— v. Bowers (1876) 1 Q.B.D. 291 3–033
—— v. Bullen (1850) 5 Exch. 779; 20 L.J.Ex. 21; 16 L.T. (o.s.) 154; 155 E.R. 341 .. 11–011, 13–028, 13–029
—— v. Caldwell (1863) 3 B. & S. 826 1–115
—— v. Chester (1869) L.R. 4 Q.B. 309 .... 3–030, 3–031
—— v. Combined Buyers Ltd [1924] N.Z.L.R. 627 .... 5–019, 11–008, 11–012, 11–013, 11–040, 12–038, 12–046, 12–048, 12–055, 12–057
—— v. G.E. Railway [1901] 1 K.B. 774; 70 L.J.K.B. 499; 84 L.T. 770; 49 W.R. 431; 17 T.L.R. 394; 45 S.J. 381; 6 Com.Cas. 121 15–078
—— v. Johnson (1983) 57 A.L.J.R. 197; 151 C.L.R. 422; [1983] 45 H.L.R. 265 12–128
—— v. Lewis Ltd (1927) 28 Ll.L. Rep. 329 8–091
—— v. National Union of Mineworkers (Derbyshire Area) (1985) 14 I.R.L.R. 99 2–043
Taylor v. Oakes, Roncoroni & Co. (1922) 38 T.L.R. 349; 127 L.T. 267 .... 8–080, 9–012, 9–015, 9–016, 9–017, 9–018, 9–020, 19–159, 19–167, 19–168, 20–109
—— v. Plumer (1815) 3 M. & S. 562 7–005
—— v. Thompson [1930] W.N. 16 5–021
—— v. Wakefield (1856) 6 E. & B. 765; 27 L.T. (o.s.) 185; 2 Jur. (n.s.) 1086; 119 E.R. 1049 8–011
Taylor (J.W.) & Co. Ltd v. Landauer & Co. [1940] 4 All E.R. 335; 164 L.T. 299; 57 T.L.R. 47; 85 S.J. 119 .... 6–047, 18–311, 18–320, 18–330
Taylor & Sons Ltd v. Bank of Athens (1922) 91 L.J.K.B. 776; 128 L.T. 795;27 Com.Cas. 142 17–038
Taypotat v. Surgeson [1985] 3 W.W.R. 18 1–043
Teal v. Auty (1820) 2 Br. & B. 99 1–093
Tebbitts Brothers v. Smith (1917) 33 T.L.R. 508 8–056
Technicon Investments Ltd. *Re* [1985] B.C.L.C. 434 24–008
Teheran-Europe Co. Ltd v. S.T. Belton (Tractors) Ltd [1968] 2 Q.B. 545; [1968] 3 W.L.R. 205; (1968) 112 S.J. 501; [1968] 2 All E.R. 886; [1968] 2 Lloyd's Rep. 37 .... 11–059, 11–070, 18–204, 18–239, 23–308, 23–314, 25–170
Tekron Resources Ltd v. Guinea Investment Co Ltd [2003] EWHC 2577; [2004] 2 Lloyd's Rep. 26, QBD 25–043, 25–119
Telefunken (A.E.G.) A.G. v. E.C. Commission [1983] E.C.R. 3151 3–041
Telfair Shipping Corp. v. Athos Shipping Corp. SA [1983] 1 Lloyd's Rep. 127, C.A.; [1981] Lloyd's Law Rep. 74; [1981] Com.L.R. 105 .... 8–078, 12–034, 19–150

Telford and Wrekin Council v. Jordan (2001) 165 J.P. 107, QBD 14–112
Tellrite Ltd v. London Confirmers Ltd [1962] 1 Lloyd's Rep. 236 . . . . 23–309, 23–313
Tempest v. Fitzgerald (1820) 3 B. & Ald. 680, 106 E.R. 809 8–009
—— v. Ord. (1815) 1 Mad. 89; 56 E.R. 35 9–030
Temple-Eastex Inc. v. Addison Bank 672 S.W. 2d 793 (1984) 23–245
Tempus Shipping v. Louis Dreyfus [1930] 1 K.B. 699 8–097
Tenax Steamship Co. v. The Brimes (Owners) [1975] Q.B. 929; [1974] 3 W.L.R. 613; 118 S.J. 808 . . . . 2–011, 2–015, 9–030, 9–038, 9–051
Tennant v. Strachan (1829) 4 C. & P. 31; Mood. & M. 377 22–090
Tennants (Lancashire) Ltd v. C.S. Wilson & Co. Ltd [1917] A.C. 495; 86 L.J.K.B. 1191; 116 L.T. 780; 33 T.L.R. 454; 61 S.J. 23 Com.Cas. 41 . . . . . 6–054, 8–092, 8–094, 8–102, 18–344, 18–352, 18–353
Tennant Radiant Heat Ltd v. Warrington Development Corp. [1988] 1 E.G.L.R. 41; [1988] 11 E.G. 71; (1988) 4 Const.L.J. 321 16–051
Tepea B.V. v. E.C. Commission [1978] 3 C.M.L.R. 392; [1979] F.S.R. 11; [1978] E.C.R. 1391 3–041
Terfloth and Kennedy Ltd v. Christy Crops Ltd (1977) 27 N.S.R. (2d) 433 11–077
Terkol Rederierne v. Petroleo Brasileiro SA (The Badagry) [1985] 1 Lloyd's Rep. 395 6–052
Terry v. Moss's Empires Ltd (1915) 32 T.L.R. 92 8–040
—— v. Vancouver Motors U-Drive Ltd [1942] 4 D.L.R. 399 7–021
Tetley v. Shand (1871) 25 L.T. 658; 20 W.R. 206 12–031
Tetra Pak International SA v. Commission of the European Communities (C333/94 P); *sub nom.*Tetra Pak International SA v. Commission of the European Communities (T83/91) [1997] All E.R. (EC) 4; [1996] E.C.R. I-5951; [1997] 4 C.M.L.R. 662, ECJ (5th Chamber); affirming [1994] E.C.R. II-755; [1997] 4 C.M.L.R. 726, CFI 3–042
Tetra Pak Rausing SA. v. Commission (Tetra Pak I) [1990] II E.C.R. 309 3–041
Tetroc Ltd v. Cross-Con (International) Ltd [1983] 1 Lloyd's Rep. 192 21–073
Texaco Ltd v. Eurogulf Shipping Co. Ltd [1987] 2 Lloyd's Rep. 541 . . . . 8–078, 8–079, 19–156, 20–051
—— v. Mulberry Filling Station Ltd [1972] 1 All E.R. 513 3–038
Texaco Melbourne, The. *See* Attorney General of the Republic of Ghana and Ghana National Petroleum Corp. v. Texaco Overseas Tankers; Texaco Melbourne, The.
—— v. Nason (Europe) Ltd [1991] 1 Lloyd's Rep. 146 . . . . . 5–009, 18–097, 18–245, 19–091 20–008, 20–067, 21–060
Texas Instruments Ltd v. Nason (Europe) Ltd [1991] 1 Lloyd's Rep. 146, QBD 18–245
Thair v. Pertainina [1994] 3 Sing. L.R. 257 (Singapore CA) 25–146
Thai-Europe Tapioca Service v. Seine Navigation Co. Inc.; Maritime Winner, The [1989] 2 Lloyd's Rep. 506 8–031
Thain v. Anniesland Trade Centre 1997 S.L.T. (Sh Ct) 102; 1997 S.C.L.R. 991; 1997 G.W.D. 32–1654, Sh. Pr. 11–044, 11–048, 11–057, 11–073
Thairwall v. G.N. Railway [1910] 2 K.B. 509; 79 L.J.K.B. 924; 103 L.T. 186; 26 T.L.R. 555; 54 S.J. 652; 17 Mans. 247 . . . . 9–042, 22–041
Thake v. Maurice [1986] Q.B. 644; [1986] 2 W.L.R. 337; [1986] 1 All E.R. 479; (1986) 136 New L.J. 92; 83 L.S.Gaz. 123, CA 14–051
Thalmann Freres v. Texas Star Flour Mills (1900) 82 L.T. 833; 16 T.L.R. 460; 9 Asp.M.L.C. 87; 5 Com.Cas. 321 18–267
Thames and Mersey Marine Insurance Co. Ltd v. Hamilton Frazer & Co. (1887) 12 App.Cas. 484 8–097
Thames Canning Co. v. Eckhardt (1915) 8 O.W.N. 395; 34 O.L.R. 72; 23 D.L.R. 805 12–043
Thames Ironworks Co. v. Patent Derrick Co. (1860) 1 J. & H. 93 7–110
Thames Sack & Bag Co. v. Knowles (1918) 88 L.J.K.B. 585; 119 L.T. 287 . . . . . 5–060, 9–005, 17–097
Thames Tideway Properties Ltd v. Serfaty [1999] 2 Lloyd's Rep. 110, CC (Central London) 13–015
Thames Valley Power Ltd v. Total Gas & Power Ltd [2005] EWHC 2208 (Comm); [2006] 1 Lloyd's Rep. 441 8–097
Themehelp Ltd v. West [1996] Q.B. 84; [1995] 3 W.L.R. 751; [1995] 4 All E.R. 215, *The Times*, May 2, 1995, *The Independent*, June 26 (C.S.), CA 23–144, 23–280

Theodohos, The [1977] 2 Lloyd's Rep. 428, QBD (Adm Ct.) 25–064
Thermo Engineers Ltd v. Ferrymaster Ltd [1981] 1 W.L.R. 1470; [1981] 1 All E.R. 1142; [1981] 1 Lloyd's Rep. 300; [1981] Com. L.R. 9 21–059
Thew v. Cole; King v. Daltray [2003] EWCA Civ 1828; [2004] R.T.R. 25; *The Times*, January 15, 2004, CA 9–065
Thomas v. Heelas, November 27, 1986 (C.A.T. No. 1065) 7–024, 7–029
—— v. Jennings (1896) 66 L.J.Q.B. 5; 75 L.T. 274; 45 W.R. 93, 12 T.L.R. 637; 40 S.J. 731 1–095
—— v. Robinson [1977] 1 N.Z.L.R. 385 .... 5–149, 7–005, 15–116
—— v. Sorrell (1673) Vaughan 330 8–022
—— v. Times Book Co. Ltd [1966] 1 W.L.R. 911 8–010
Thomas Cook (New Zealand) Ltd v. Inland Revenue Commissioner [2004] UKPC 53; [2005] S.T.C. 297; 77 T.C. 197; [2004] S.T.I. 2378, PC (NZ) 22–019
Thomas (E. & D.) v. H.S. Alper & Sons [1953] C.L.Y. 3277; *The Times*, June 26, 1953 8–023
Thomas (P.) Gonzalez Corp. v. Muller's Mtihle, Muller G.m.b.H. *See* Gonzalez (Thomas P.) Corp. v. Muller's Muhle, Muller GmbH
Thomas (T.W.) & Co. Ltd v. Portsea Shipping Co. Ltd [1912] A.C. 1...... 18–049, 18–055, 18–084
Thompson v. Asda MFI Group Ltd [1988] Ch. 241; [1988] 2 W.L.R. 1093; [1988] 2 All E.R. 722; [1988] I.R.L.R. 340; (1988) 132 S.J. 497, Ch D............... 10–024
Thompson v. Dominy (1845) 14 M. & W. 403; 14 L.J.Ex. 320; 5 L.T. (o.s.) 268 .... 18–063, 18–084, 18–089, 18–097, 18–098
—— v. Giles (1824) 2 B. & C. 422 .... 22–073, 22–090
—— v. L.M. & S. Railway [1930] 1 K.B. 41; 98 L.J.K.B. 615; 141 L.T. 382 .... 2–012, 13–013, 13–016
—— v. Lohan (T.) (Plant) Ltd [1987] 1 W.L.R. 649; [1987] 2 All E.R. 631; (1987) 131 S.J. 358; [1988] T.L.R. 65 .... 13–064, 13–097
—— v. Palmer [1893] 2 Q.B. 80; 62 L.J.Q.B. 502; 69 L.T. 366; 42 W.L.R. 22; 4 R. 422 .... 9–047, 16–015
—— v. Stimpson [1961] 1 Q.B. 195; [1960] 3 W.L.R. 818; 104 S.J. 912; [1960] 3 All E.R. 500 8–035
Thompson and Shackell Ltd. v. Veale (1896) 74 L.T. 130 7–070
Thompson (George) (Australia) Property Ltd. v. Vittadello [1978] V.R. 199 .... 22–050, 22–055, 22–104
Thompson (W.L.) Ltd. v. Robinson (Gunmakers) Ltd [1955] Ch. 177; [1955] 2 W.L.R. 185; 99 S.J. 76; [1955] 1 All E.R. 154 ...... 16–063, 16–064, 16–066, 16–068, 16–079 16–085, 17–007
Thomson v. Christie Manson & Woods Ltd [2005] EWCA Civ 555; [2005] P.N.L.R. 38, CA 3–008, 10–006
Thoni G.m.b.H. v. R.T.P. Equipment Ltd. [1979] 2 Lloyd's Rep. 282 .... 9–032, 22–064
Thor Line A.B. v. Alltrans Group of Canada (The T.F.L. Prosperity) [1984] 1 W.L.R. 48 18–278
Thoresen v. Capital Credit Corporation and Active Bailiff Service (1962) 37 D.L.R. (2d) 317 7–052
Thoresen & Co (Bangkok) Ltd v. Fathom Marine Co Ltd [2004] EWHC 167; [2004] 1 All E.R. (Comm) 935; [2004] 1 Lloyd's Rep. 622, QBD 2–017
Thorley (Joseph) Ltd. v. Orchis S.S. Co. Ltd [1907] 1 K.B. 660; 76 L.J.K.B. 595; 96 L.T. 488; 23 T.L.R. 338; 51 S.J. 289; 10 Asp.M.L.C. 431; 12 Com.Cas. 51 18–059
Thorman v. Dowgate S.S. Co. [1910] 1 K.B. 410; 79 L.J.K.B. 287; 102 L.T. 242; 11 Asp.M.L.C. 481; 15 Com.Cas. 67 8–089
Thorn v. City Rice Mills (1889) 40 Ch. D. 357; 58 L.J. Ch. 297; 60 L.T. 359; 37 W.R. 398; 5 T.L.R. 172 9–048
—— v. Commissioners of Public Works (1863) 32 Beav. 490; 55 E.R. 192 17–099
Thornalley v. Gostelow (1947) 80 Ll.L. Rep. 507 2–036
Thorne v. Smith (1851) 10 C.B. 659; 2 L.M. & P. 43; 20 L.J.C.P. 71; 16 L.T.O.S. 365; 15 Jur. 469; 138 E.R. 261 9–030
Thorne (L.G.) & Co. Property Ltd. v. Borthwick (Thomas) & Son Ltd [1956] S.R. 81 11–076
Thorneley v. Tuckwell (Butchers) Ltd. [1964] Crim.L.R. 127 5–085
Thornett v. Haines (1846) 15 M. & W. 367 3–009

Thornett and Fehr and Yuills Ltd, *Re* [1921] 1 K.B. 219; *sub nom*. Thornett & Fehr v. Yuilis Ltd, 90 L.J.K.B. 361; 124 L.T. 218; 37 T.L.R. 31; 26 Com.Cas. 59 ..... 6–041, 8–054, 17–002, 21–040
Thornett and Fehr v. Beers & Son. [1919] 1 K.B. 486; 88 L.J.K.B. 684; 120 L.T. 570; 24 Com.Cas. 133 .... 11–008, 11–010, 11–042, 13–029
Thornton v. Maynard (1875) L.R. 10 C.P. 695; 44 L.J.C.P. 382; 33 L.T. 433 22–069
—— v. Shoe Lane Parking Ltd [1971] 2 Q.B. 163; [1971] 2 W.L.R. 585; [1970] 115 S.J. 75; [1971] 1 All E.R. 686; [1971] R.T.R. 79; [1971] 1 Lloyd's Rep. 289 ... 2–002, 2–012, 13–013, 13–016
—— v. Simpson (1816) 6 Taunt. 556; Holt N.P. 164; 2 Marsh 267; 128 E.R. 1151, N.P 8–065
Thornton Springer v. NEM Insurance Co Ltd [2000] 2 All E.R. 489; [2000] 1 All E.R. (Comm) 486; [2000] C.L.C. 975; [2000] Lloyd's Rep. I.R. 590; (2000) 97(13) L.S.G. 42; (2000) 144 S.J.L.B. 147, QBD 18–030
Thurnell v. Balbirnie (1837) 2 M. & W. 786; Murp. H. 235; 6 L.J.Ex. 255; 1 Jur. 847; 150 E.R. 975 2–049
Thorpe v. Fasey [1949] Ch. 649; [1949] L.J.R. 1613; 65 T.L.R. 561; 935 S.J. 552; [1949] 2 All E.R. 393 12–068
Three Rivers District Council v. Bank of England (No. 2) [1996] 2 All E.R. 363 1–005
Thrige v. United Shipping Co Ltd (1924) 18 Ll. L. Rep. 6, CA 18–067
Through Transport Mutual Insurance Association (Eurasia) Ltd v. New India Assurance Co Ltd (The Hari Bhum) (No.1) [2004] EWCA Civ 1598; [2005] 1 All E.R. (Comm) 715; [2005] 1 Lloyd's Rep. 67; [2004] 2 C.L.C. 1189; [2005] I.L.Pr. 30; (2004) 148 S.J.L.B. 1435, CA 18–047
Thunderbird Industries LLC v. Simoco Digital UK Ltd; sub nom. Simoco Digital UK Ltd, Re [2004] EWHC 209; [2004] 1 B.C.L.C. 541, Ch D 8–025
Thyssen Stahl AG v. Commission of the European Communities (T141/94) [1999] E.C.R. 11–347; [1999] 4 C.M.L.R. 810, CFI (2nd Chamber) 3–041
Tiernan v. Magen Insurance Co. Ltd [2000] I.L.Pr. 517, QBD (Comm Ct) 25–020, 25–030, 25–031
Tigress, The (1863) Browne & Lush 338; 1 New Rep. 449; 32 L.J. Adm. 97; 8 L.T. 117; 9 Jur. (N.S.) 361; 11 W.R. 538; 1 Mar.L.C. 323; 167 E.R. 286 ... 15–026, 15–085, 15–088, 15–092
Tilley v. Bowman Ltd [1910] 1 K.B. 745; 79 L.J.K.B. 547; 102 L.T. 318; 54 S.J. 342; 17 Mans. 97 7–028
—— v. Thomas (1867) L.R. 3 Ch. App. 61 8–026
Tilly Russ, The [1985] Q.B. 931 25–202
Timothy v. Simpson (1834) 6 Car. & P. 499 2–002
Tingey & Co. v. John Chambers [1967] N.Z.L.R. 785 7–043
Tinsley v. Milligan [1994] 1 A.C. 340; [1993] 3 W.L.R. 126; [1993] 2 All E.R. 65; (1993) 68 P. & C.R. 412; [1993] 2 F.L.R. 963; [1993] W.P.C. 97; [1993] E.G.C.S. 118; *The Times*, June 28, 1993; *The Independent*, July 6, 1993, HL ... 3–030, 3–031
Titanium Metals Corporation of America v. Space Metals Inc., 529 P. 2d 431 (Utah 1974) 23–205, 23–236
Tito v. Waddell (No. 2) [1977] Ch. 106; [1977] 2 W.L.R. 496; [1977] 3 All E.R. 129 3–043
Toby Constructions Products Property Ltd v. Computa Bar (Sales) Property Ltd [1983] 2 N.S.W.L.R. 48 .... 1–086, 11–087
Todd v. Armour (1882) 9 R. 901; 19 S.L.R. 656 .... 25–130, 25–131
Toepfer v. Continental Grain Co. [1973] 117 S.J. 649; [1974] 1 Lloyd's Rep. 11 .... 11–016, 11–079, 11–085, 13–040, 19–187
—— v. Cremer [1975] 2 Lloyd's Rep. 118; (1975) 119 S.J. 506, C.A. affirming [1975] 1 Lloyd's Rep. 406 ...... 8–078, 8–095, 8–099, 12–007, 18–321, 19–181, 19–166, 19–208
—— v. Lenerson Poortman N.V. [1980] 1 Lloyd's Rep. 143 .... 8–025, 8–036, 10–037, 14–006, 18–190, 19–061, 19–063, 19–066, 19–104, 20–033
—— v. Schwarze [1980] 1 Lloyd's Rep. 385 .... 8–091, 8–092, 8–101
—— v. Sosimage SpA [1980] 2 Lloyd's Rep. 397 20–046
—— v. Warinco A.G. [1978] 2 Lloyd's Rep. 569 .... 11–016, 12–035, 20–107
Toepfer (Alfred C.) International GmbH v. Itex Italrani Export SA [1993] 1 Lloyd's Rep. 137 .... 20–043, 20–051

Tolhurst v. Assoc. Portland Cement Manufacturers (1900) Ltd [1903] A.C. 414 ..... 3–043, 3–044, 8–058
Tomkinson v. First Pennsylvania Banking and Trust Co. [1961] A.C. 1007; [1960] 2 W.L.R. 969; 104 S.J. 466; [1960] 2 All E.R. 332 .... 25–007, 25–008, 25–010, 25–014, 25–177, 25–194
Tomlinson (A.) (Hauliers) v. Hepburn [1966] A.C. 451; [1966] 2 W.L.R. 453; 110 S.J. 86; [1966] 1 All E.R. 418; [1966] 1 Lloyd's Rep. 309 5–012
Tommey v. Finextra Ltd (1962) 106 S.J. 1012 1–131
Toms v. Wilson (1862) 4 B. & S. 455; 2 New Rep. 454; 32 L.J.Q.B. 382; 8 L.T. 799; 10 Jur. (N.S.) 201; 11 W.R. 952; 122 E.R. 529, Ex.Ch.; (1867) 17 L.T. 266 .... 8–036, 9–059
Tooke v. Hollingworth. *See* Hollingworth v. Tooke.
Tool Metal Manufacturing Co. Ltd v. Tungsten Electric Co. Ltd [1955] 1 W.L.R. 761; 99 S.J. 470; [1955] 2 All E.R. 657; 72 R.P.C. 209 9–024
Toprak Mahsulleri Ofisi v. Finagrain Cie Commerciale [1979] 2 Lloyd's Rep. 98 ... 18–030, 19–128, 19–166, 19–181, 19–183, 20–099, 21–040, 25–119
Tor Line A.B. v. Alltrans Group of Canada Ltd [1984] 1 W.L.R. 48; (1984) 128 S.J. 18; [1984] 1 All E.R. 103; [1984] 1 Lloyd's Rep. 123 4–020
Torkington v. Magee [1902] 2 K.B. 427 18–147
Torni, The [1932] P. 78; 48 T.L.R. 471; 43 Ll.L.R. 78 25–202
Torquay Hotel Co. Ltd v. Cousins [1969] 2 Ch. 106; [1969] 2 W.L.R. 289; (1968) 113 S.J. 52; [1969] 1 All E.R. 522 8–099
Torvald Klaveness A/S v. Arni Maritime Corp. (The Gregos) [1994] 1 W.L.R. 1465; [1994] 4 All E.R. 998; [1995] 1 Lloyd's Rep. 1; (1994) 144 N.L.J. Rep. 1550; *The Times*, October 28, 1994, *The Times*, 15 November, 1994; *The Independent*, November 15, 1994, HL reversing [1993] 2 Lloyd's Rep. 335; *The Times*, June 4, 1993; *The Independent*, July 5, 1993 (C.S.) CA reversing [1992] 2 Lloyd's Rep. 40; *Financial Times*, February 14, 1992, QBD 18–357, 19–063
Tota Societa Italiana per Azioni v. Liberian Trans-Ocean Navigation Corp. [1971] 2 Lloyd's Rep. 469 25–165
Total Gas Marketing Ltd v. Arco British Ltd [1998] 2 Lloyd's Rep. 209; [1998] C.L.C. 1275; *The Times*, June 8, 1998, HL; affirming (1998) 95(5) L.S.G. 28; (1998) 142 S.J.L.B. 47; *The Times*, December 22, 1997, CA 10–024, 18–318
Total International Ltd v. Addax B.V. [1996] 2 Lloyd's Rep. 333 ... 11–013, 11–016, 12–023
Total Liban SA v. Vitol Energy SA [2001] Q.B. 643; [2000] 3 W.L.R. 1142; [2000] 1 All E.R. 267; [1999] 2 All E.R. (Comm) 65; [1999] 2 Lloyd's Rep. 700; [1999] C.L.C. 1301, QBD (Comm Ct) 17–036, 17–104
Touche, Ross & Co. v. Manufacturers Hanover Trust Co. 434 N.Y.S. 2d 575 (1980) 23–149, 23–241
Towers v. Barrett (1786) 1 T.R. 133 12–067
Towerson v. Aspatric Agricultural Co-operative Society Ltd (1872) 27 L.T. 276 11–079
Towle (John) & Co. v. White. *See* Nevill, *Re, ex p.* White.
Town Investments Ltd v. Dept. of the Environment [1978] A.C. 359 .... 11–028, 13–070
Townley v. Crump (1835) 4 A. & E. 58; 1 Har. & W. 564; 5 Ner. & M.K.B. 606; 5 L.J.K.B. 14; 111 E.R. 709 .... 8–009, 15–040
Tractors (K.L.) Ltd, *Re* (1961) 106 C.L.R. 318 2–028
Tradax Export SA v. André & Cie SA [1976] 1 Lloyd's Rep. 416, [1977] 1 Lloyd's Rep. 484 ... 6–046, 8–091, 8–092, 8–095, 8–098, 8–099, 8–101, 8–102, 18–345, 18–346, 19–013, 19–141
—— v. Carapelli SpA [1977] 2 Lloyd's Rep. 157 .... 8–092, 18–345
—— v. Cook Industries Inc. [1982] 1 Lloyd's Rep. 385; affirming [1981] 1 Lloyd's Rep. 236 .... 8–092, 8–101, 18–349, 18–350
—— v. Dorada Compania Naviera SA of Panama (The Lutetian) [1982] 2 Lloyd's Rep. 140; [1982] Com. L.R. 130, QBD (Comm Ct) 7–012
—— v. European Grain Shipping Ltd [1983] 2 Lloyd's Rep. 100 ... 11–015, 12–032, 18–273, 19–147, 19–157, 19–174
—— v. Italgrani di Francesco Ambrosiano [1986] 2 Lloyd's Rep. 112, CA 8–025, 8–036, 8–039, 8–040, 10–037, 18–321, 19–064, 20–029, 20–030, 20–033, 20–046, 20–049
Tradax Internacional SA v. Bunge SA [1977] 2 Lloyd's Rep. 604 11–016
—— v. Goldschmidt SA [1977] 2 Lloyd's Rep. 60 .... 10–031, 16–026, 18–273, 18–357, 19–066, 19–147, 20–022, 20–027, 20–084, 20–105, 20–106, 20–107, 20–126, 20–129

Trade and Transport Inc. v. Iino Kaiun Kaisha Ltd [1973] 1 W.L.R. 210; (1972) 117 S.J. 123; [1973] 2 All E.R. 144; [1972] 2 Lloyd's Rep. 154 ..... 8–088, 8–091, 13–046
Trade Star Line Corp. v. Mitsui & Co. Ltd (The Arctic Trader); Mitsui & Co. Ltd v. J. Lauritzen A/S [1996] 2 Lloyd's Rep. 449; [1997] C.L.C. 174, CA .. 18–051, 18–052, 18–110, 18–164, 18–165
Traders Finance Corp. v. Dawson Implements Ltd (1959) 15 D.L.R. (2d) 515 25–131
Traders Group Ltd v. Gouthro (1969) 9 D.L.R. 387 7–038
Tradigrain SA v. King Diamond Marine Ltd (The Spiros C); *sub nom*. Tradigrain SA v. King Diamond Shipping SA (The Spiros C) [2000] 2 All E.R. (Comm) 542; [2000] 2 Lloyd's Rep. 319; [2000] C.L.C. 1503, CA; reversing [1999] 1 All E.R. 837; [1999] 2 Lloyd's Rep. 91; [1999] C.L.C. 1136, QBD (Comm Ct) 18–022, 18–048, 18–084
Trading and General Investment Corp. v. Gault, Armstrong & Kemble Ltd [1986] 1 Lloyd's Rep. 195 22–088
Trading Society Kwik-Hoo-Tong v. Royal Commission on Sugar Supply (1923) 16 Ll.L.R. 250; (1924) 19 Ll.L.R. 343 .... 20–029, 20–119
Trafalgar House Construction (Regions) Ltd v. General Surety & Guarantee Co. Ltd [1996] A.C. 199; [1995] 3 W.L.R. 204; [1995] 3 All E.R. 737; 73 B.L.R. 32; 44 Con. L.R. 104; (1995) 92(28) L.S.G. 39; (1995) 145 N.L.J. 1221; (1995) 139 S.J.L.B. 177; *The Times*, July 4, 1995, HL; reversing 66 B.L.R. 42; 38 Con. L.R. 53; (1994) 10 Const. L.J. 240, CA 23–273
Tramp Shipping Corp. v. Greenwich Marine Inc. [1975] I.C.R. 261; [1975] 1 W.L.R. 1042; [1975] 2 All E.R. 989; [1975] 2 Lloyd's Rep. 314; 119 S.J. 300, CA 8–097
Trans Trust S.P.R.L. v. Danubian Trading Co. Ltd [1952] 2 Q.B. 297; [1952] 1 T.L.R. 1066; 96 S.J. 312; [1952] 1 All E.R. 970; [1952] 1 Lloyd's Rep. 348 .. 16–046, 16–092, 16–055, 17–036, 17–104, 19–207, 23–052, 23–081, 23–105
Transcatalana de Commercio SA v. Incrobasa Industriale Commercio Brasileira SA (The Vera) [1995] 1 Lloyd's Rep. 215, Q.B.D. 19–150, 19–151, 20–015
Transcontainer Express Ltd v. Custodian Security Ltd [1988] 1 F.T.L.R. 54; [1988] 1 Lloyd's Rep. 128 .... 5–009, 5–010, 5–011, 18–149
Transmotors Ltd v. Robertson, Buckley & Co. Ltd [1970] 1 Lloyd's Rep. 224 .... 2–012, 5–057, 6–030
Transocean Reederei GmbH v. Euxine Shipping Co. (The Imvros) [1999] 1 All E.R. (Comm) 724; [1999] 1 Lloyd's Rep. 848; [1999] C.L.C. 928, QBD (Comm Ct) 21–089
Transoceanica Francesca, The and Nicos V, The [1987] 2 Lloyd's Rep. 155, QBD (Adm Ct) 25–194
Transpacific Discovery SA v. Cargill International SA (The Elpa) [2001] 1 All E.R. (Comm) 937; [2001] 2 Lloyd's Rep. 596; [2001] C.L.C. 1252, QBD (Comm Ct) 19–035 ....
Transpacific Eternity SA v. Kanematsu Corp. (The Antares 111) [2002] 1 Lloyd's Rep. 233, QBD (Comm Ct) 5–102, 5–136, 5–137, 18–165, 21–011
Transpetrol Ltd v. Transol Olieprodukten Nederland B.V. [1989] 1 Lloyd's Rep. 309 .... 19–018, 23–087, 23–202
Transport and General Credit Corporation Ltd v. Morgan [1939] Ch. 531; [1939] 2 All E.R. 17; 108 L.J.Ch. 179; 160 L.T. 380; 55 T.L.R. 483; 83 S.J. 338 .... 1–010, 15–028
Trasimex Holding SA v. Addax BV (The Red Sea) [1999] 1 Lloyd's Rep. 28, CA; affirming [1997] 1 Lloyd's Rep. 610, QBD (Comm Ct) 11–018, 18–002, 19–008, 19–111, 19–144, 19–145, 19–155, 19–157
Travel Vac SL v. Sanchis (Case C–423/97) [1999] All E.R. (EC) 656; [1999] E.C.R. 1–2195; [1999] 2 C.M.L.R. 1111; (1999) 96(31) L.S.G. 43, EC.1 25–055
Travelers Casualty & Surety Co of Europe Ltd v. Sun Life Assurance Co of Canada (UK) Ltd [2004] EWHC 1704; [2004] I.L.Pr. 50; [2004] Lloyd's Rep. I.R. 846, QBD 25–033, 25–057
Travellers' Indemnity Co. v. Flushing National Bank, 396 N.Y.S. 2d 754 (1977) 23–244
Travers v. Richardson (1920) 20 S.R.N.S.W. 367 8–040
Travers (Joseph) and Sons v. Cooper [1915] 1 K.B. 73 6–029
—— v. Longel Ltd (1948) 64 T.L.R. 150 .... 11–007, 11–011, 11–014, 11–022, 11–077, 11–081
Treacy v. D.P.P. [1971] A.C. 537; [1971] 2 W.L.R. 112; (1970) 115 S.J. 12; [1971] 1 All E.R. 110; (1970) 55 Cr.App.R. 113 18–281

Trebanog Working Men's Club & Institute Ltd v. Macdonald [1940] 1 K.B. 576; [1940] 1 All E.R. 454; 109 L.J.K.B. 288; 162 L.T. 305; 104 J.P. 171; 56 T.L.R. 404; 84 S.J. 357; 38 L.G.R. 160; 31 Cox C.C. 372 1–121
Tredegar Iron and Coal Co. (Ltd) v. Gielgud (1883) 1 Cab & El. 27 16–069
—— v. Hawthorn Bros. & Co. (1902) 18 T.L.R. 716 .... 8–082, 12–021, 16–080, 16–081, 16–082, 17–015, 17–016, 20–116, 20–140
Tregelles v. Sewell (1862) 7 H. & N. 574; 158 E.R. 600 .... 5–098, 19–002, 21–016
Trendtex Trading Corp. v. Central Bank of Nigeria [1978] Q.B. 529; [1977] 2 W.L.R. 356; 121 S.J. 85; [1977] 1 All E.R. 881; [1976] 2 C.M.L.R. 465 23–135
—— v. Credit Suisse [1980] Q.B. 679; [1981] 3 W.L.R. 766; (1981) 125 S.J. 761; [1981] 3 All E.R. 520 25–202
Trent and Humber Co., Bailey & Leetham's Case, *Re* (1869) L.R. 8 Eq. 94; 38 L.J.Ch. 485; 20 L.T. 301; 17 W.R. 1079 .... 17–040, 17–041
Trent Valley Woollen Manufacturing Co. v. Oelrichs (1894) 23 S.C.R. 682 25–157
Treseder-Griffin v. Co-operative Insurance Society Ltd [1956] 2 Q.B. 127; [1956] 2 W.L.R. 866; 100 S.J. 283; [1956] 2 All E.R. 33; [1956] 1 Lloyd's Rep. 377 1–084
Triangle Underwriters Inc. v. Honeywell Inc. 604 F. 2d. 737 (1979) 1–086
Trident Beauty, The. *See* Pan Ocean Shipping Co. v. Creditcorp (The Trident Beauty).
Trifinery v. Banque Paribas 762 F. Supp. 1119 (SD N.Y. 1991) 23–196
Trimbey v. Vignier (1834) 1 Bing.N.C. 151; 4 Moo. & S. 695; 3 L.J.C.P. 246; 131 E.R. 1075 25–086
Trinidad Shipping Co. v. Alston [1920] A.C. 888; 89 L.J.P.C. 185; 123 L.T. 476; 36 T.L.R. 654; 15 Asp.M.L.C. 31 25–119
Tripp v. Armitage (1839) 4 M. & W. 687; 1 Horn & H. 442; 8 L.J.Ex. 107; 3 Jur. 249; 150 E.R. 1597 .... 1–043, 5–093
Tromp, The [1921] P. 337; 90 L.J.P. 379; 125 L.T. 637; 37 T.L.R. 752; 15 Asp. 338 20–008
Troson v. Dent (1853) 8 Moo.P.C. 419;14 E.R. 159 5–009
Tropwood A.G. of Zug v. Jade Enterprises; Tropwood, The [1982] 1 Lloyd's Rep. 232; [1982] Com.L.R. 17, CA 2–017
Trow v. Ind. Coope (West Midlands) Ltd [1967] 2 Q.B. 899; [1967] 3 W.L.R. 633; 111 S.J. 375; [1967] 2 All E.R. 900 8–034
Trucks & Spares Ltd v. Maritime Agencies Ltd [1951] 2 All E.R. 982; [1951] 2 Lloyd's Rep. 345 18–055
Trueman v. Hurst (1875) 1 Term Rep. 40 2–035
Truk (UK) Ltd v. Tokmakidis GmbH [2000] 2 All E.R. (Comm) 594; [2000] 1 Lloyd's Rep. 543, QBD (Merc Ct) 12–041, 12–051, 12–055
Truman v. Attenborough (1910) 103 L.T. 218; 26 T.L.R. 601; 54 S.J. 682 ..... 5–042, 5–046, 7–022
Trust Bank Central Ltd v. Southdown Properties Ltd [1991] 1 N.Z. Conv. c. 190 5–159
Trustee of the Property of F.C. Jones & Sons v. Jones [1996] 3 W.L.R. 703 7–003
Trustees of Henry Smith's Charity v. Willson [1983] Q.B. 316; [1983] 2 W.L.R. 77; (1982) 126 S.J. 673; [1983] 1 All E.R. 73 19–151
Tryg Baltica International (UK) Ltd v. Boston Compania de Seguros SA [2004] EWHC 1186; [2005] Lloyd's Rep. I.R. 40, QBD 25–030, 25–031
Trytel, *Re* [1952] W.N. 355; [1952] 2 T.L.R. 32 18–234
Tsakiroglou & Co. Ltd v. Noblee Thorl GmbH [1962] A.C. 93; [1961] 2 W.L.R. 633; 105 S.J. 346; [1961] 2 All E.R. 179; [1961] 1 Lloyd's Rep. 329 HL; affirming [1960] 2 Q.B. 348; [1960] 2 W.L.R. 869; [1960] 2 All E.R. 160; [1960] 1 Lloyd's Rep. 349; 104 S.J. 426, CA 5–100, 6–041, 6–049, 6–054, 8–092, 8–099, 10–030, 18–268, 19–025, 19–032, 19–127, 19–131, 19–132, 21–082
—— v. Transgrains SA [1958] 1 Lloyd's Rep. 562 .... 19–009, 19–089
Tucker v. Farm & General Investment Trust Ltd [1966] 2 Q.B. 421; [1966] 2 W.L.R. 1241; 110 S.J. 267; [1966] 2 All E.R. 508 .... 1–106, 6–033
—— v. Linger (1883) 8 App.Cas. 508; 52 L.J.Ch. 941; 49 L.T. 373; 48 J.P. 4; 32 W.R. 40 23–027
Tudor Grange Holdings Ltd v. Citibank N.A. [1992] Ch. 53; [1991] 3 W.L.R. 750; [1991] 4 All E.R. 1; (1991) 135 S.J.L.B. 3; [1991] B.C.L.C. 1009; *The Times*, April 30, 1991 13–090
Tudor Marine Ltd v. Tradax Exports; The Virgo [1976] 2 Lloyd's Rep. 135 18–233

Tuet v. Rodriguez 176 So. 2d 550 (1965) 23–175
Tufton Associates Ltd v. Dilman Shipping [1992] 1 Lloyd's Rep. 71 19–171
Tukan Timber Ltd v. Barclays Bank plc [1987] 1 F.T.L.R. 154; [1987] F.L.R. 208 ... 23–145, 23–277
Tungsten Electric Co. Ltd v. Tool Manufacturing Co. Ltd (1950) 69 R.P.C. 108 9–024
Turkiye is Bankasi A.S. v. Bank of China [1993] 1 Lloyd's Rep. 132; [1994] 3 Bank L.R. 34, QBD 23–286
Turley v. Bates (1863) 2 H. & C. 200; 3 New Rep. 478; 10 L.T. 35; 10 Jur. (N.S.) 368; 12 W.R. 438; 159 E.R. 83; *sub nom*. Furley v. Bates 33 L.J.Ex. 43 ..... 5–036, 5–039
Turnbull (Peter) & Co. Proprietary Ltd v. Mundas Trading Co. (Australasia) Ltd [1954] 2 Lloyd's Rep. 198 .... 8–024, 9–019, 20–014, 20–049
Turner v. Anquetil [1953] N.Z.L.R. 952 .... 10–005, 10–017, 10–018, 10–022
—— v. Barclay (1854) 9 Moo.P.C. 264 25–004
—— v. Haji Goolam Mahommed Azam [1904] A.C. 826; 74 L.J.P.C. 17; 91 L.T. 216; 20 T.L.R. 599; 9 Asp.M.L.C. 588 18–054
—— v. Hardcastle (1862) 11 C.B. (N.S.) 683; 31 L.J.C.P. 193; 5 L.T. 748 1–072
—— v. Hayden (1825) 4 B. & C. 1; 6 Dow, & Ry. K.B. 5; Ry. & M. 215; 107 E.R. 959 22–114
—— v. Leech (1821) 4 B. & A. 451 22–122
—— v. Moon [1901] 2 Ch. 825; 70; L.J.Ch. 822; 85 L.T. 90; 50 W.R. 237 ..... 4–023, 4–024
—— v. Mucklow (1862) 6 L.T. 690; 8 Jur. (N.S.) 870; 10 W.R. 668 11–059
—— v. Sampson (1911) 27 T.L.R. 200 .... 7–032, 7–038
—— v. Samson (1876) 2 Q.B.D. 23; 46 L.J.Q.B. 167; 35 L.T. 537; 25 W.R. 240, CA 22–132
—— v. Trisby (1719) 1 Str. 168 2–030
—— v. Trustees of Liverpool Docks (1851) 6 Exch. 543; 20 L.J.Ex. 393; 17 L.T. (O.S.) 212 .... 5–137, 5–140, 18–185, 20–077, 20–084A
Turul, The [1919] A.C. 515; 88 L.J.P.C. 43; 120 L.T. 393; 35 T.L.R. 217; 14 Asp.M.L.C. 423 8–099
Tuthill v. Union Savings Bank 561 N.Y.S. 2d. 286 (App.Dir. 1990) 23–245
Tweddle v. Atkinson (1861) 1 B. & S. 393 18–096
Twentsche Overseas Trading Co. Ltd v. Uganda Sugar Factory Ltd (1944) 113 L.J.P.C. 25; 172 L.T. 163 6–041
Twenty First (21st) Century Logistic Solutions Ltd (In Liquidation) v. Madysen Ltd [2004] EWHC 231; [2004] 2 Lloyd's Rep. 92; [2004] S.T.C. 1535; [2004] B.T.C. 5720; [2004] B.V.C. 779; [2004] S.T.I. 497; (2004) 101(12) L.S.G. 35; *The Times*, February 27, 2004, QBD 3–029
Twogood, *ex p*. (1812) 19 Ves.Jun. 229 22–073
Tye v. Fynmore (1813) 3 Camp. 462; 170 E.R. 1446, N.P. 11–078
Tyers v. Rosedale and Ferryhill Iron Co. (1875) L.R. 10 Ex. 195; 44 L.J.Ex. 130; 33 L.T. 56; 23 W.R. 871, Ex. Ch.; (1873) L.R. 8 Ex. 305 ... 8–031, 8–069, 8–087, 9–006, 16–073, 17–011, 17–012
Tzortzis v. Monark Line A/B [1968] 1 W.L.R. 406; 112 S.J. 108; [1968] 1 All E.R. 949 25–007

U.C.B. Corporate Services Ltd v. Thomason [2005] EWCA Civ 225; [2005] 1 All E.R. (Comm) 601, CA 12–004
U.G.S. Finance Ltd v. National Mortgage Bank of Greece 107 S.J. 552 [1964] 1 Lloyd's Rep. 446 .... 9–019, 13–043, 13–050
U.S v. Lutz (1944) 142 F. 2d. 985 5–131
Ullock v. Reddelein (1828) 5 L.J. K.B. 208; (1628) Dan. & Ll. 6 5–100
Ulster Bank v. Synnott (1871) I.R. 5 Eq. 595 23–128
Ultraframe (UK) Ltd v. Tailored Roofing Systems Ltd [2004] EWCA Civ 585; [2004] 2 All E.R. (Comm) 692; [2004] B.L.R. 341, CA 3–038
Underhill v. Fernandez 92 U.S. 510 (1876) 22–015
Underwood (A.L.) Ltd v. Barclays Bank Ltd [1924] 1 K.B. 775; 93 L.J.K.B. 690; 131 L.T. 271; 40 T.L.R. 302; 68 S.J. 716; 29 Com.Cas. 182 22–073
Underwood Ltd v. Burgh Castle Brick and Cement Syndicate [1922] 1 K.B. 123; 91 L.J.K.B. 355; 126 L.T. 401; 38 T.L.R. 44 .... 5–007, 5–016, 5–023, 5–029, 5–030, 5–031, 5–102, 6–002, 6–017, 16–019, 21–043
Union Bank of Australia Ltd v. McClintock [1922] 1 A.C. 240; 91 L.J.P.C. 108; 126 L.T. 588 22–023

Union Bank of Australia Ltd v. Murray-Aynsley [1898] A.C. 693; 67 L.J.P.C. 123 ... 22–145
Union Bank of Medina v. Shea, 58 N.W. 985 (1894) ... 23–236
Union Credit Bank Ltd v. Mersey Docks and Harbour Board [1899] 2 Q.B 205; 68, L.J.Q.B. 842; 81 L.T. 44; 4 Com.Cas. 227 ... 7–013, 7–017
Union Industrielle et Maritime v. Petrosul International Ltd (The Roseline) [1987] 1 Lloyd's Rep. 18 ... 18–011, 18–045, 20–008, 20–067
Union Transport Finance Ltd v. Ballardie [1937] 1 K.B. 510 ... 7–058
—— v. British Car Auctions Ltd [1978] 2 All E.R. 385; (1977) 246 E.G. 131, February 16, 1977 (C.A. Transcript No. 87 of 1977) ... 7–002
Union Transport plc v. Continental Lines SA; *sub nom.* Cross AM Lines [1992] 1 W.L.R. 15; [1992] 1 All E.R. 161; [1992] 1 Lloyd's Rep. 229; [1992] I.L.Pr. 385; (1992) 89(2) L.S.G. 30; (1992) 136 S.J.L.B. 18; *The Times*, December 16, 1991; *The Independent*, January 10, 1992; *The Financial Times*, December 17, 1991, HL; reversing [1991] 2 Lloyd's Rep. 49, CA ... 19–002, 25–079, 25–080
Unit Construction Co. v. Bullock [1960] A.C. 351; [1959] 3 W.L.R. 1022; [1959] 3 All E.R. 831; 52 R. & I.T. 828; 38 T.C. 712; (1959) 38 A.T.C. 351; [1959] T.R. 345; 103 S.J. 1027, HL; reversing [1959] Ch. 315; [1959] 2 W.L.R. 437; [1959] 1 All E.R. 591; 52 R. & I.T. 294; (1959) 38 A.T.C. 36; [1959] T.R. 37; 103 S.J. 238, CA; reversing [1959] Ch. 147; [1958] 3 W.L.R. 504; [1958] 3 All E.R. 186; 51 R. & I.T. 625; (1958) 37 A.T.C. 292; [1958] T.R. 277; 102 S.J. 654, Ch D ... 25–063
United Australia Ltd v. Barclays Bank Ltd [1941] A.C. 1 ... 1–073, 1–074, 22–114
United Baltic Corporation v. Burgett & Newsam (1921) 8 W.L.R. 190 ... 19–030
United Bank Ltd v. Banque Nationale de Paris [1992] 2 S.L.R. 64 (Singapore Sup. Ct.) ... 23–157, 23–159, 23–190, 23–199
—— v. Cambridge Sporting Goods Corp. 360 N.E. 2d. 943 (N.Y. 1976) ... 23–027, 23–129, 23–141, 23–150
United Brands Co. v. E.C. Commission [1978] C.M.L.R. 429; [1978] 3 C.M.L.R. 83; [1978] E.C.R. 207 ... 3–041
United City Merchants (Investments) Ltd v. Royal Bank of Canada (The American Accord) [1983] 1 A.C. 168; [1982] 2 W.L.R. 1039; [1982] 2 All E.R. 720; [1982] Lloyd's Rep. 1 ... 19–196, 20–021, 21–083, 21–096, 23–054, 23–135, 23–136, 23–142, 23–143, 23–146, 23–204, 23–206, 25–216
United Dominions Trust v. Taylor 1980 S.L.T. (Sh.Ct.) 28 ... 14–141
—— v. Western [1976] Q.B. 513 ... 1–054, 7–011, 7–017, 7–018
United Dominions Trust (Commercial) Ltd v. Parkway Motors Ltd [1955] 1 W.L.R. 719; 99 S.J. 436; [1955] 2 All E.R. 557 ... 7–070
United Forty Pound Loan Club v. Bexton [1891] 1 Q.B. 28n ... 1–066
United Fresh Meat Co. Ltd v. Charterhouse Cold Storage Ltd [1974] 1 Lloyd's Rep. 286 ... 13–046
United Plastics Ltd v. Reliance Electric (N.Z.) Ltd [1977] 2 N.Z.L.R. 125 ... 15–040, 15–053, 15–054
United Railways of the Havana and Regla Warehouses Ltd, *Re* [1961] A.C. 1007; [1960] 2 W.L.R. 969; 104 S.J. 466; [1960] 1 All E.R. 332 ... 25–007, 25–010, 25–014, 25–033, 25–177
United Scientific Holdings Ltd v. Burnley B.C.; Cheapside Land Development Co. v. Messels [1978] A.C. 904; [1977] 2 W.L.R. 806, (1977) 121 S.J. 223; (1977) 33 P. & C.R. 220 ... 8–025, 8–026, 8–080, 9–005, 14–006
United Securities Corp. v. Tomlin 198A. 2d 179 (1964) ... 25–189
United Service Co., *Re* (1870) L.R. 6 Ch.App. 212; 40 L.J.Ch. 286; 24 L.T. 115; 19 W.R. 457 ... 22–140, 22–142
United Shoe Machinery Co. of Canada v. Brunet [1909] A.C. 330; 78 L.J.P.C. 101; 100 L.T. 579; 25 T.L.R. 442; 53 S.J. 396 ... 3–036, 12–003, 12–006
United States of America and Republic of France v. Dollfus Mieg et Cie and Bank of England [1952] A.C. 582; [1952] 1 T.L.R. 541; 96 S.J. 180; [1952] 1 All E.R. 572 ... 1–072, 4–012
United States Steel Products Co. v. G.W Railway [1916] 1 A.C. 189; 85 L.J.Q.B. 1; 113 L.T. 886; 31 T.L.R. 561; 59 S.J. 648; 21 Com.Cas. 105 ... 15–088, 15–089
United States Surgical Corporation v. Hospital Products International Property Ltd [1983] 2 N.S.W.L.R. 157 ... 25–145
United Technologies Corp. v. Citibank N.A. 469 F.Supp. 473 (1979) ... 23–150
United Trading Corporation SA v. Allied Arab Bank Ltd [1985] 2 Lloyd's Rep. 554, C.A. ... 23–142, 23–277

Unitel Film und Fernseh Produktionsgesellschaft mbH & Co, Re [1978] 3 C.M.L.R. 306; [1978] F.S.R. 627, CEC 3–041
Unity Finance Ltd v. Hammond (1965) 109 S.J. 70 7–018
Universal Bulk Carrier Pte Ltd v. Andre & Cie SA; *sub nom.* Andre et Cie SA v. Universal Bulk Carriers Ltd [2001] EWCA Civ 588; [2001] 2 All E.R. (Comm) 510; [2001] 2 Lloyd's Rep. 65, CA; affirming [2000] 1 Lloyd's Rep. 459; [2001] C.L.C. 1179, QBD (Comm Ct) 18–357, 20–032
Universal Cargo Carriers' Corporation v. Citati [1957] 2 Q.B. 401; [1957] 2 W.L.R. 713; 101 S.J. 320; [1957] 2 All E.R. 70; [1957] 1 Lloyd's Rep. 174 ..... 8–078, 8–079, 9–016, 12–020, 19–161
Universal Guarantee Property Ltd v. Metters Ltd [1965] 1 W.L.R. 691; 109 S.J. 331; [1965] 2 All E.R. 98; [1965] 1 Lloyd's Rep. 525; [1966] W.A.R. 74 .... 7–010, 7–032, 7–038
Universal Permanent Building Society v. Cooke [1952] Ch. 95; [1951] 2 T.L.R. 962; [1951] 2 All E.R. 893, CA 4–011
Universe Tankship Inc. of Monrovia v. International Transport Workers' Federation [1983] 1 A.C. 366; [1982] 2 W.L.R. 803; [1982] I.C.R. 262; [1982] 2 All E.R. 67; [1982] 1 Lloyd's Rep. 537 .... 14–052A
Untalan, Hong Kong and Shanghai Banking Corp. v. United Overseas Bank Ltd [1992] 2 S.L.R. 195 22–090
Upman v. Elkan (1871) 7 Ch.App. 130; 41 L.J.Ch. 246; 25 L.T. 813; 36 J.P. 295; 20 W.R. 131 21–097
Urquhart, Lindsay & Co. Ltd v. Eastern Bank Ltd [1922] 1 K.B. 318; 91 L.J.K.B. 274; 126 L.T. 534; 27 Com.Cas. 124 .... 23–054, 23–139, 23–171
Utaniko Ltd v. P&O Nedlloyd BV (N.1); East West Corp v. DKBS 1912; *sub nom.* East West Corp v. Dampskibsselskabet AF 1912 A/S [2003] Q.B. 1509; [2003] 3 W.L.R. 916; [2003] 2 All E.R. 700; [2003] 1 All E.R. (Comm) 524; [2003] 1 Lloyd's Rep. 239; [2003] 1 C.L.C. 797; (2003) 100(12) L.S.G. 31, *The Times*, February 13, 2003, CA (Civ Div); affirming [2002] EWHC 83; [2002] 1 All E.R. (Comm) 676; [2002] 2 Lloyd's Rep. 182, QBD ... 5–009, 5–010, 18–016, 18–018, 18–021, 18–025, 18–034, 18–061, 18–063, 18–065, 18–066, 18–067, 18–080, 18–089, 18–097, 18–098, 18–104, 18–113, 18–114, 18–115, 18–123, 18–149, 18–150, 18–153, 18–216, 18–245, 19–050, 19–099, 19–014, 20–008, 20–082, 25–156

V/O Rasnoimport v. Guthrie & Co. Ltd [1966] 1 Lloyd's Rep. 1 ... 18–030, 18–031, 18–033, 18–045, 18–136
Vacwell Engineering Co. Ltd v. B.D.H. Chemicals Ltd [1971] 1 Q.B. 111; [1976] 3 W.L.R. 67; 114 S.J. 472, C.A.; varying [1971] 1 Q.B. 88; [1969] 3 W.L.R. 927 .... 11–057, 12–121, 14–061, 16–043, 16–049
Vaine v. Rigden (1870) L.R. 5 Ch.App. 663 7–110
Vale v. Bayee (1775) 1 Cowp. 294; 98 E.R. 1094 5–098
Valibhoy (A.A.) & Sons (1907) Pte Ltd v. Bank Nationale de Paris [1994] 2 S.L.R. 772 .... 22–076, 22–083, 22–088
Valpy v. Gibson (1847) 4 C.B. 837; 16 L.J.C.P. 241; 9 L.T. (o.s.) 434; 11 Jur. 826; 136 E.R. 737 .... 2–047, 15–038, 15–054, 15–069, 18–248
—— v. Oakeley (1851) 16 Q.B. 941; 20 L.J.Q.B. 380; 17 L.T. (o.s.) 124; 16 Jur. 38; 117 E.R. 1142 .... 9–030, 15–036, 17–003
Valsabbia v. E.C. Commission [1980] E.C.R. 907 8–100
Van Casteel v. Booker (1848) 2 Exch. 691; 18 L.J.Ex. 9; 12 L.T. (o.s.) 65; 154 E.R. 668 .... 5–131, 15–017, 15–073, 18–048, 18–214
Van Cutsem v. Dunraven [1954] C.L.Y. 2998; *The Times*, January 15, 1954 1–081
Van den Hurk v. Martens (R.) & Co. Ltd [1920] 1 K.B. 850; 89 L.J.Q.B. 545; 123 L.T. 110; 25 Com.Cas. 170 ..... 12–043, 16–053, 17–007, 17–054, 20–109, 20–118, 21–102
Van der Zijden Wildhandel (P.J.) N.V. v. Tucker & Cross Ltd [1975] 2 Lloyd's Rep. 240 .... 8–089, 8–091, 8–092, 8–093, 19–140, 19–125
Van Grutten v. Digby (1862) 31 Beav. 561 25–086
Van (H. & E.) der Sterren v. Cibernetics (Holdings) Property Ltd (1970) 44 A.L.J.R. 157 .... 13–038, 13–049
Vanbergen v. St. Edmunds Properties Ltd [1933] 1 K.B. 345; 102 L.J.Q.B. 174 9–024
Vanden Avenne-Izegem P.V.B.A. v. Finagrain SA [1985] 21 Lloyd's Rep. 99 .... 18–349, 18–350

Vandyke v. Hewitt (1800) 1 East 96 25–119
Vane v. Lord Barnard (1708) Gilb. Rep. 6 4–023
—— v. Vane (1873) 8 Ch.App. 383; 42 L.J.Ch. 299; L.T. 320; 21 W.R. 252 7–046
Vantol (J.H.) Ltd v. Fairclough Dodd & Jones Ltd [1955] 1 W.L.R. 642; 99 S.J. 336; [1955] 2 All E.R. 516; [1955] 1 Lloyd's Rep. 546; revsd. *sub nom.* Fairclough Dodd and Jones Ltd v. J.H. Vantol Ltd [1957] 1 W.L.R. 136; 101 Sol. Jo. 86; [1956] 3 All E.R. 921; [1956] 2 Lloyd's Rep. 437, HL ... 8–088, 8–092, 8–095, 8–099, 17–099, 18–345, 19–011, 19–138, 19–140, 19–141
Varga v. John Labatt Ltd (1956) 6 D.L.R. (2d) 336 13–017
Vargas Pena Apeztieguia y Cia v. Peter Cremer GmbH [1987] 1 Lloyd's Rep. 394 .. 12–032, 18–238, 19–147, 19–154, 19–189, 19–191, 19–192, 20–106, 20–118
Varley v. Whipp [1900] 1 Q.B. 513; 69 L.J.Q.B. 333; 48 W.R. 333; 48 W.R. 363; 44 S.J. 263 .... 5–016, 5–019, 5–020, 5–068, 10–026, 11–006, 11–008, 11–009, 11–013, 11–019, 12–038, 12–045
Varverakis v. Compagnia de Navegacion Artico SA; Merak, The [1976] 2 Lloyd's Rep. 250, CA 1–051
Vaswani v. Italian Motors (Sales and Services) Ltd [1996] 1 W.L.R. 270; [1996] R.T.R. 115; (1996) 93(2) L.S.G. 27; (1996) 140 S.J.L.B. 27; *The Times*, December 15, 1995, PC (HK) 8–078, 9–023
Vaughan v. Moffatt (1868) 38 L.J.Ch. 144 7–037
Vautier v. Fear [1916] G.L.R. 524 1–046
Veba Oil Supply and Trading GmbH v. Petrotrade Inc. (The Robin) [2001] EWCA Civ 1832; [2002] 1 All E.R. 703; [2002] 1 All E.R. (Comm) 306; [2002] 1 Lloyd's Rep. 295; [2002] B.L.R. 54, CA; affirming [2001] 1 All E.R. (Comm) 1051; [2001] 2 Lloyd's Rep. 731, QBD (Comm Ct) 11–079, 13–040
Veedfald v. Arhus Amtskommune (C203/99) [2001] E.C.R. I-3569; [2003] 1 C.M.L.R. 41; (2002) 66 B.M.L.R. 1; *The Times*, June 4, 2001, ECJ 14–081
Veflings (George) Rederi A/S v. President of India [1978] 1 W.L.R. 982; (1978) 122 S.J. 247; [1978] 3 All E.R. 838; [1978] 1 Lloyd's Rep. 467 .... 25–167, 25–194
Veithardt and Hall Ltd v. Rylands Bros. Ltd (1917) 86 L.J.Ch. 604; 116 L.T. 706 6–042
Venizelos SA v. Chase Manhattan Bank, 425 F.2d 461 (1970) 23–196
Venning v. Leckie (1810) 13 East. 7; 104 E.R. 267 1–081
Venus Electric Ltd v. Brevel Products Ltd (1978) 85 D.L.R. (3d) 282 11–060
Verheijdens Veevoeder Commissiehandel B.V. v. I.S. Joseph Co. Inc. [1981] 1 Lloyd's Rep. 102 13–040
Vermaazs (J.) Scheepvaartbedrif NV v. Association Technique de l'Importation Charbonnière [1966] 1 Lloyd's Rep. 582 8–097
Vernede v. Weber (1856) 1 H. & N. 311; 25 L.J.Ex. 326; 27 L.T. (o.s.) 274; 156 E.R. 1222 21–024
Vernitron Ltd v. The Commissioners [1978] V.A.T.T.R. 157 5–170
Verschures Creameries Ltd v. Hull & Netherlands S.S. Co. Ltd [1921] 2 K.B. 608; 91 L.J.Q.B. 39; 125 L.T. 165 1–074
Vervaeke v. Smith [1983] 1 A.C. 145; [1982] 2 W.L.R. 855; [1982] 2 All E.R. 144; 126 S.J. 293, HL 7–019
Vesta, The [1921] 1 A.C. 774; 90 L.J.P. 250; 25 L.T. 261; 37 T.L.R. 505; 15 Asp.M.L.C. 194 .... 1–056, 5–043
Viale v. Michael (1874) 30 L.T. 463 22–125
Vic Mill Ltd, *Re* [1913] 1 Ch. 465; 82 L.J.Ch. 251; 108 L.T. 444; 57 S.J. 404 .... 16–064, 16–067, 16–075, 16–078, 16–079, 16–085
Vickers v. Vickers (1867) L.R. 4 Eq. 527; 36 L.J.Ch. 946 2–049
Victor Chandler International Ltd v. Customs and Excise Commissioners [2000] 1 W.L.R. 1296; [2000] 2 All E.R. 315; (2000) 97(11) L.S.G. 36; (2000) 150 N.L.J. 341; (2000) 144 S.J.L.B. 127; *The Times*, March 8, 2000; *The Independent*, March 10, 2000, CA; reversing [1999] 1 W.L.R. 2160; [2000] 1 All E.R. 160; (1999) 96(31) L.S.G. 42; (1999) 143 S.J.L.B. 219; *The Times*, August 17, 1999; *The Independent*, October 4, 1999, Ch D 18–202
Victor Hydraulics Ltd v. Engineering Dynamics Ltd [1996] 2 N.Z.L.R. 235 .... 13–014, 13–036
Victoria Dairy Co. of Worthing v. West (1895) 11 T.L.R. 233 1–066
Victoria Fur Traders Ltd v. Roadline U.K. Ltd [1981] 1 Lloyds Rep. 571 21–052
Victoria Laundry (Windsor) Ltd v. Newman Industries Ltd [1949] 2 K.B. 528; 65 & L.R. 274; 93 S.J. 371; [1949] 1 All E.R. 997 .... 16–043, 16–044, 16–045, 16–046, 17–031, 17–040, 17–041, 17–042

Victory Carriers Inc. v. United States, 467 F. 2d 1334 (1972) 23–239
Vidgen (Len) Ski & Leisure Ltd v. Timaru Marine Supplies (1982) Ltd [1986] N.Z.L.R. 349 .... 5–146, 5–151, 5–152, 5–153
Viditz v. O'Hagan [1900] 2 Ch. 87, CA; reversing [1899] 2 Ch. 569, Ch D 25–084, 25–086
Vidler & Co. (London) Ltd v. R. Silcock & Sons Ltd [1960] 1 Lloyd's Rep. 509 ..... 6–047, 18–320, 18–345
Vigers v. Pike (1842) 8 Cl. & F. 562 12–007
Vigers Bros. v. Sanderson Brothers [1901] 1 K.B. 608; 70 L.J.Q.B. 383; 84 L.T. 464; 49 W.R. 411; 17 T.L.R. 316; 45 S.J. 328; 6 Com.Cas. 99 ...... 5–020, 5–085, 10–026, 11–018, 12–046, 12–057, 13–033, 18–266, 18–278, 18–244, 20–109, 20–110
Vimig Pty Ltd v. Contract Tooling Pty Ltd (1986) 9 N.S.W.L.R. 731 .... 1–008, 1–011
Vinava Shipping Co. v. Finelvet A.G. (The Chrysalis). *See* Finelvet A.G. v. Vinava Shipping Co.
Vincentelli v. Rowlett (John) & Co. (1911) 105 L.T. 411; 12 Asp.M.L.C. 34; 16 Com.Cas. 310 .... 18–051, 19–045, 19–050, 25–202
Virani Ltd v. Manuel Revert y Cia SA [2003] EWCA Civ 1651; [2004] 2 Lloyd's Rep. 14, CA 25–166, 25–193, 25–194, 25–200
Virgo Steamship Co. SA v. Skaarup Shipping Corp. (The Kapetan Georgis) [1988] F.T.L.R. 180; [1988] 1 Lloyd's Rep. 352 18–149
Viscount Supply Co. Ltd. *Re* (1963) 40 D.L.R. 501 .... 25–011, 25–133, 25–183
Vishipco Line v. Chase Manhatten Bank (1981) 66 F. 2nd 854 .... 22–015, 22–017
Viskase Ltd v. Paul Kiefel GmbH [1999] 1 W.L.R. 1305; [1999] 3 All E.R. 362; [1999] 1 All E.R. (Comm.) 641; [1999] C.L.C. 957; [2000] 1 L.Pr. 29; *The Times*, March 30, 1999, CA 11–049
Vita Food Products Inc. v. Unus Shipping Co. Ltd [1939] A.C. 277; [1939] 1 All E.R. 513; 108 L.J.P.C. 40; 160 L.T. 579; 55 T.L.R. 402; 83 S.J. 295; 44 Com.Cas. 123 .... 25–006, 25–014, 25–028, 25–089, 25–119
Vitkovice Hornia Hutni Tezirstvo v. Korner [1951] A.C. 869, [1951] 2 T.L.R. 188; 95 S.J. 527; [1951] 2 All E.R. 334 .... 9–047, 9–048, 25–154
Vitol SA v. Esso Australia Ltd (The Wise) [1989] 2 Lloyd's Rep. 45; reversing [1989] 1 Lloyd's Rep. 96 .... 6–011, 19–074, 19–150, 19–151
—— v. Norelf Ltd (The Santa Clara) [1996] Q.B. 800, [1996] 3 W.L.R. 105; [1996] 3 All E.R. 193, H.L. 8–006, 12–021, 12–027, 18–209, 18–174, 19–217
—— v. Phibro Energy A.G. (The Mathraki) [1990] 2 Lloyd's Rep. 84 ...... 8–036, 16–086, 19–016, 19–018, 19–218
Vivacqua Irmaos SA v. Hickerson 190 So. 657 (1939) 23–102
Vivian v. Coca-Cola Export Cpn. [1984] 2 N.Z.L.R. 289 14–006
Vladimir Ilich, The [1975] 1 Lloyd's Rep. 322 12–037
Voest-Alpine International Corporation v. Chase Manhattan Bank N.A., 545 F.Supp. 301 (1982) 23–206, 23–210
Voest-Alpine Intertrading GmbH v. Chevron International Oil Co. Ltd [1987] 2 Lloyd's Rep. 546 2–017
Voest-Alpine Trading USA Corp. v. Bank of China, CA H–95–4954, March 13, 2000, Dist Ct 23–158, 23–198
Vogan v. Oulton (1899) 81 L.T. 435; 16 T.L.R. 37 17–075
Volk v. Vervaecke [1969] C.M.L.R. 273 3–041
Vosper Thorneycroft Ltd v. Ministry of Defence [1976] 1 Lloyd's Rep. 58 2–017
Voss, *Re. ex p.* Llansamlet Tin Plate Co. (1873) L.R. 16 Eq. 155 .... 8–086, 17–008, 17–011
Voss v. APL Co Pte Ltd [2002] 2 Lloyd's Rep. 707, CA (Sing) 18–071, 18–073, 18–074, 18–076, 18–078, 18–264
Vowles v. Island Finances Ltd [1940] 4 D.L.R. 357 7–056
Vsesojwzoje Objedinenije "Exportles" v. T.W. Allen & Sons Ltd [1938] 3 All E.R. 375; 82 S.J. 682; 61 Ll.L.Rep. 217 .... 13–033, 13–038

W.L.R. Traders Ltd v. British and Northern Shipping Agency Ltd and Leftley (I.) [1955] 1 Lloyd's Rep. 554 20–039
WRM Group v. Wood [1998] C.L.C. 189, CA 9–026, 13–039, 13–090
Wackerbarth v. Masson (1812) 3 Camp. 270; 170 E.R. 1378 .... 9–004, 20–015
Waddington v. Oliver (1805) 2 B. & P.N.R. 61; 127 E.R. 544 .... 8–045, 8–071

Waddington & Sons v. Neale & Sons (1907) 96 L.T. 786; 23 T.L.R. 464 ..... 7–041, 7–051, 7–079
Wadsworth v. Lydall [1981] 1 W.L.R. 598; (1981) 125 S.J. 309; [1981] 2 All E.R. 401 ..... 16–007, 16–030, 16–046, 16–055, 23–107
Wagg (Helbert) & Co. Ltd, *Re* [1956] Ch. 323; [1956] 2 W.L.R. 183; 100 S.J. 53 ..... 6–038, 25–006, 25–010, 25–028, 25–119, 25–177
Wagon Mound (No. 1), The [1961] A.C. 388; [1961] 2 W.L.R. 126; 105 S.J. 85; [1961] 1 All E.R. 404; [1961] 1 Lloyd's Rep. 1 12–073
——(No.2), The [1967] 1 A.C. 617; [1966] 3 W.L.R. 498; 110 S.J. 447; [1966] 2 All E.R. 709 17–072
Wagstaff v. Shorthorn Dairy Co. (1884) Cab. & El. 324 ..... 17–060, 17–061, 17–066
Wahbe Tamara and Sons Co. v. Bernhard Rothfos [1980] 2 Lloyd's Rep. 553 ..... 25–010, 25–079
Wahbe Tamari & Sons Ltd v. "Colprogeca" Sociedade Geral de Fibras, Cafes & Produtos Colonials Lda [1969] 2 Lloyd's Rep. 18 ..... 23–053, 23–082
Wahda Bank v. Arab Bank plc [1994] 2 Lloyd's Rep. 411; (1993) 90(4) L.S.Gaz. 38; (1993) 137 S.J.L.B. 24; *The Times*, December 23, 1992 QBD 23–281, 25–076
—— v. ——[1996] 1 Lloyd's Rep. 470 25–161
Waight v. Waight and Walker [1952] P. 282; [1952] 2 T.L.R. 177; 96 S.J. 496; [1952] 2 All E.R. 290 5–167
Waimiha Sawmilling Co. Ltd v. Howe [1920] N.Z.L.R. 681 1–093
Wait, *Re* [1926] Ch. 962: on appeal [1927] 1 Ch. 606; 71 S.J. 56; *sub nom.* Wait, *Re*, Trustee v. Humphries & Bobbitt 96 L.J.Ch. 179; 136 L.T. 552; *sub nom.* Wait. *Re*, *ex p.* Collins 43 T.L.R. 150 ..... 1–010, 1–011, 1–107, 1–108, 1–115, 1–118, 1–119, 1–119, 5–005, 5–060, 5–064, 5–066, 5–094, 5–099, 5–110, 6–038, 7–067, 10–008, 16–028, 17–096, 17–097, 17–098, 17–099, 17–100, 18–234, 18–286, 18–287, 18–291, 18–292, 18–299, 19–016, 19–101, 19–204, 19–206, 21–032
Wait v. Baker (1848) 2 Exch. 1; 17 L.J.Ex. 307, 154 E.R. 380 ... 5–003, 5–004, 5–031, 5–069, 5–085, 5–098, 5–131, 5–132, 5–137, 12–046, 12–057, 15–102, 18–210, 19–016, 20–026, 20–070, 20–077, 20–084
Wait and James v. Midland Bank (1926) 31 Com.Cas. 172 ..... 5–062, 5–063, 5–104, 5–107, 21–007
Wakefield v. Alexander & Co. (1901) 17 T.L.R. 217 22–070
Waldwiese Sftung v. Lewis [2004] EWHC 2589 25–060
Walford v. Miles [1992] 2 A.C. 128; [1992] 2 W.L.R. 184; [1992] 1 All E.R. 453; (1992) 64 P. & C.R. 166; [1992] 1 E.G.L.R. 207; (1992) 11 E.G. 115; [1992] N.P.C. 4; *The Times*, January 27, 1992; *The Independent*, January 29, 1992, HL 2–016
Walker v. Boyle; Boyle v. Walker [1982] 1 W.L.R. 495; (1981) 125 S.J. 724; [1981] 1 All E.R. 634; (1982) 44 P & C.R. 20 ..... 12–016, 13–060
—— v. Milner (1866) 4 F. & F. 745 ..... 10–003, 10–005
—— v. Weedair (N.Z.) Ltd [1959] N.Z.L.R. 777 1–087
Walkers, Winser and Hamm and Shaw, Son & Co., *Re*, [1904] 2 K.B. 152 .. 11–021, 11–074, 11–095, 11–096, 13–013, 13–032, 13–033
Walkinshaw v. Diniz [2002] EWCA Civ 180, CA; affirming [2001] 1 Lloyd's Rep. 632, QBD (Comm Ct) 8–031
Wall v. Rederiaktiebolaget Luggude [1915] 3 K.B. 66; 84 L.J.K.B. 1663; 114 L.T. 286; 31 T.L.R. 487; 13 Asp.M.L.C. 271; 21 Com.Cas 132 16–036
Wallace v. Breeds (1811) 13 East. 522; 1 Rose 109; 104 E.R. 473 5–061
—— v. Woodgate (1824) 1 C. & P. 575; Ry. & Moo. 193 ..... 15–038, 15–055
Waller v. Drakeford (1853) 1 E. & B. 749; 22 L.J.Q.B. 274; 17 J.P. 663; 17 Jur. 853 7–010
Wallersteiner v. Moir [1974] 1 W.L.R. 991; 118 S.J. 464; [1974] 3 All E.R. 217 3–032
—— v. ——(No. 2) [1975] Q.B. 373; [1975] 2 W.L.R. 389; 119 S.J. 97; [1975] 1 All E.R. 849 16–007
Walley v. Montgomery (1803) 3 East 584; 102 E.R. 721 ..... 18–216, 18–222, 18–226
Wallis v. Russell [1902] 2 I.R. 585 1–002, 11–008, 11–025, 11–042, 11–055, 11–057, 11–059, 11–062
—— v. Smith (1882) 21 Ch.D. 243; 52 L.J.Ch. 145; 47 L.T. 389; 31 W.R. 214 ..... 16–030, 16–034

Wallis, Son & Wells v. Pratt & Haynes [1910] 2 K.B. 1003; 79 L.J.K.B. 1013; 103 L.T. 118; 26 T.L.R. 572, CA on appeal [1911] A.C. 394; [1911–13] All E.R. Rep. 284; 80 L.J.K.B. 1058; 103 L.T. 146; 27 T.L.R. 431; 55 Sol.Jo. 496, HL 10–026, 11–008, 11–019, 11–022, 12–037, 13–024, 13–043, 15–007, 17–047, 17–066
Walls v. Centaur Co. Ltd (1921) 126 L.T. 242 .... 13–013, 13–017, 14–077
Walter v. Everard [1891] 2 Q.B. 369; 60 L.J.Q.B. 738; 65 L.T. 443; 55 J.P. 693; 39 W.R. 676; 7 T.L.R 469 2–035
—— v. James (1871) L.R. 6 Ex. 124; 40 L.J.Ex. 104; 24 L.T. 188; 19 W.R. 472 9–044
Walters v. Neary (1904) 21 T.L.R. 146 22–055
Waltham Forest L.B.C. v. T.G. Wheatley (Central Garage) Ltd (No. 2) [1978] R.T.R. 333, [1977] Crim.L.R. 761 14–112
Walton v. British Leyland UK Ltd , unreported, 1968 14–061
Walton v. British Leyland (U.K.) Ltd [1980] Product Liability International 156 12–124
—— v. Mascall (1844) 13 M. & W. 452 .... 9–059, 16–016, 22–133
Walton (Grain and Shipping) Ltd v. British Italian Trading Co. Ltd [1959] 1 Lloyd's Rep. 223 ..... 6–045, 6–046, 8–099, 18–316, 18–318, 18–325, 18–331, 18–339, 18–340, 18–342, 18–343, 25–119
Wancke v. Wingren (1889) 58 L.J.Q.B. 519; 5 T.L.R. 696 .... 19–008, 21–016
Ward (R.V.) Ltd v. Bignall [1967] 1 Q.B. 534; [1967] 2 W.L.R. 1050; 111 S.J. 190; [1967] 2 All E.R. 449 ... 5–016, 5–018, 5–026, 5–146, 9–051, 15–001, 15–011, 15–101, 15–102, 15–123, 15–124, 15–127, 15–128, 15–133, 16–014, 16–060, 16–083, 16–087, 19–098, 19–207, 21–004
Ward v. Hobbs (1878) 4 App.Cas. 13; 48 L.J.Q.B. 281; 40 L.T. 73; 43 J.P. 252; 27 W.R. 114; affirming (1877) 3 Q.B.D. 150 .... 12–012, 12–077, 13–028, 13–052
—— v. Oxford Railway Co. (1852) 2 De G.M. & G. 750; 22 L.J.Ch. 905; 1 W.R. 9 22–116
—— v. Royal Exchange Shipping Co. (1887) 58 L.T. 174 5–161
Wardars (Import and Export) Co. Ltd v. Norwood (W.) & Sons Ltd [1968] 2 Q.B. 663; [1968] 2 W.L.R. 1440; [1960] 1 All E.R. 602; [1968] 2 Lloyd's Rep. 1 .... 5–007, 5–076, 5–081, 5–089, 5–097, 6–002, 18–194, 18–253, 21–003, 21–007
Warde (Michael J.) v. Feedex International Inc. [1995] 2 Lloyd's Rep. 289 .... 10–037, 19–074, 19–207, 20–032
Waren Import Gesellschaft Krohn & Co. v. Alfred C. Toepfer (The Vladimir Ilich) [1975] 1 Lloyd's Rep. 322 19–022
—— v. Internationalé Graanhandel Thegra N.V. [1975] 1 Lloyd's Rep. 146 .... 18–170, 18–171, 18–172, 18–174, 18–182, 18–194, 18–291
Warin and Craven v. Forrester (1876) 4 R. (Ct. of Sess.) 190 ...... 20–007, 20–008, 20–016, 20–028, 20–135, 21–011
Warinco A.G. v. Fritz Mauthner [1978] 1 Lloyd's Rep. 151 .... 8–092, 18–141, 18–345, 19–349
—— v. Samor SpA [1979] 1 Lloyd's Rep. 450, CA; reversing [1977] 2 Lloyd's Rep. 582 .... 8–078, 8–081, 9–010, 12–019, 20–118
Waring v. Cox (1808) 1 Camp. 369; 170 E.R. 989, N.P. 18–084, 18–088
Warlow v. Harrison (1858) 1 E. & E. 295 2–005
Warman v. Southern Counties Car Finance Cpn. Ltd (W.J. Ameris Car Sales) [1949] 2 K.B. 576; [1949] L.J.R. 1182; 93 S.J. 319; [1949] 1 All E.R. 711 ...... 4–005, 4–006
Warmings Used Cars Ltd v. Tucker [1956] SAS.R. 249 .... 1–039, 4–032
Warner v. Central Trust Co. 715 F. 2d 1121 (1983) 23–151
Warner Bros & Co. Ltd v. Israel 101 F. 2d 59 (1939) 19–004, 19–006, 19–008
Warner Bros. Records Inc. v. Rollgreen Ltd [1976] Q.B. 430; [1975] 2 W.L.R. 816; (1974) 119 S.J. 253; [1975] 2 All E.R. 105 18–234
Warren v. Forbes [1959] V.R. 14 5–028
—— v. Nut Farms of Australia Pty. Ltd [1981] W.A.R. 134 1–094
Warwick v. Nairn (1855) 10 Exch. 762; 156 E.R. 648 22–062
—— v. Rogers (1843) 5 Man. & G. 340; 6 Scott N.R. 1; 12 L.J.C.P 113 22–118
Warwicke v. Noakes (1797) Peake 98 9–041
Warwickshire County Council, *ex p.* Johnson. *See* R. v. Warwickshire County Council, *ex p.* Johnson.
Washbourn v. Burrows (1847) 1 Exch. 107 1–091
Waterhouse v. Skinner (1801) 2 B. & P. 447 8–004

Waters v. Monarch Fire and Life Assurance Co. (1856) 5 E. & B. 870; 25 L.J.Q.B. 102; 26 L.T.O.S. 217; 2 Jur. (N.S.) 375; 4 W.R. 245; 119 E.R. 705 5–012
—— v. Towers (1853) 8 Exch. 401; 22 L.J.Ex. 186; 155 E.R. 1404 17–046
Water-Tube Boilermakers's Agreement, *Re* [1959] 1 W.L.R. 1118; 103 S.J. 695; [1959] 3 All E.R. 267 1–085
Wales Ltd v. G.L.C. (1983) 25 Build.L.R. 1 6–054
Watford Electronics Ltd v. Sanderson CFL Ltd [2001] EWCA Civ 317; [2001] 1 All E.R. (Comm) 696; [2001] B.L.R. 143; (2001) 3 T.C.L.R. 14; (2001) 98(18) L.S.G. 44; *The Times*, March 9, 2001, CA; reversing [2000] 2 All E.R. (Comm) 984, QBD (T&CC) 11–069, 13–020, 13–030, 13–037, 13–056, 13–089, 13–090
Wathes (Western) Ltd v. Austins (Menswear) Ltd [1976] 1 Lloyd's Rep. 14 .... 13–046, 13–048
Watkins v. Rymill (1883) 10 Q.B.D. 178; 52 L.J.Q.B. 121; 48 L.T. 426; 47 J.P. 357; 31 W.R. 337 13–016
Watson, *ex p., Re* Love (1877) 5 Ch.D. 35; 46 L.J.Bcy. 97; 36 L.T. 75; 25 W.R. 489; 3 Asp.M.L.C. 396 .... 15–069, 15–080, 15–085
Watson, *Re* (1890) 25 Q.B.D 27 1–066
—— v. Buckley, Osborne, Garrett & Co. Ltd [1940] 1 All E.R. 174 .... 1–041, 1–046, 12–074, 14–063
—— v. Coupland [1945] 1 All E.R. 217; 175 L.T. 92; 109 J.P. 90; 43 L.G.R. 60 5–066
—— v. Duff, Morgan & Vermont Holdings Ltd [1974] 1 W.L.R. 450; (1973) 117 S.J. 910; [1974] 1 All E.R. 794 5–161
—— v. Gray (1900) 16 T.L.R. 308 .... 17–040, 17–046
—— v. Russell (1864) 5 B. & S. 968; 34 L.J.Q.B. 93; 11 L.T. 641; 13 W.R. 231 22–064
Watson Bros. v. Hornby [1942] 2 All E.R. 506 2–047
Watt v. Westhoven [1933] V.L.R. 458; 39 Argus L.R. 448 .... 1–008, 1–011, 10–008
Watts v. Christie (1849) 11 Beav. 546; 18 L.J.Ch. 173; L.T. (O.S.) 297; 13 Jur. 244 ... 22–145
—— v. Friend (1830) 10 B. & C. 446; L. & Welsh. 193; 5 Man. & Ry. K.B. 439; 8 L.J. (O.S.) K.B. 181; 109 E.R. 516 1–093
Watts v. Morrow [1991] 1 W.L.R. 1421; [1991] 4 All E.R. 937; [1991] 2 E.G.L.R. 152; [1991] E.G.C.S. 88; [1992] *Gazette*, January 8, 33; 23 H.L.R. 608; 54 B.L.R. 86; 43 E.G. 121; 26 Con.L.R. 98; 8 Const.L.J. 73; 141 N.L.J. 1331; *The Independent*, August 20, 1991; *The Guardian*, September 4, 1991, CA 16–047
—— v. Seymour [1967] 2 Q.B. 647; [1967] 2 W.L.R. 1072; 131 J.P. 309; 111 S.J. 294; [1967] 1 All E.R. 1044 .... 1–027, 3–030, 15–118
Watts & Co. Ltd v. Mitsui & Co. Ltd [1917] A.C. 227; 86 L.J.Q.B. 873; 116 L.T. 353; 33 T.L.R. 262; 61 S.J. 382; 13 Asp.M.L.C. 580; 22 Com.Cas. 242 .... 16–031, 16–036, 18–336
Waugh v. Morris (1873) L.R. 8 Q.B. 202 6–045
Wavin Nederland B.V. v. Excomb Ltd [1983] New L.J. 937 5–148
Waymell v. Reed (1794) 5 T.R. 599 25–119
Wayne's Merthyr Steam Coal and Iron Co. v. Morewood & Co. (1877) 46 L.J.Q.B. 476 .... 9–063, 16–020
Weatherby v. Banham (1832) 5 C. & P. 228; 172 E.R. 950, N.P. 2–014
Webb v. Austin (1844) 7 Han. & G. 701; 8 Scott N.R. 419; 13 L.J.C.P. 203; 3 L.T.O.S. 282 4–011
—— v. Chief Constable of Merseyside Police; Chief Constable of Merseyside v. Porter; *sub nom.* Porter v. Chief Constable of Merseyside [2000] Q.B. 427; [2000] 2 W.L.R. 546; [2000] 1 All E.R. 209; (1999) 96(47) L.S.G. 33; (2000) 144 S.J.L.B. 9; *The Times*, December 1, 1999, CA 7–006
—— v. Fairmaner (1838) 3 M. & W. 473; 6 Dowl, 549; 1 Horn & H. 108; 7 L.J.Ex. 140; 2 Jur. 397; 150 E.R. 1231 8–034
—— v. Ireland and the Attorney General [1988] I.R. 353 7–005
Webber v. Lee (1882) 9 Q.B.D. 315; 51 L.J.Q.B. 485; 47 L.T. 215; 47 J.P. 4; 30 W.R. 866 1–090
Webster v. Bosanquet [1912] A.C. 394; 81 L.J.P.C. 205; 106 L.T. 357; 28 T.L.R. 271, P.C. 16–032
—— v. Higgin 92 S.J. 454; [1948] 2 All E.R. 127 .... 2–027, 10–012, 10–019, 13–015, 13–024, 13–030
Weddel New Zealand Ltd [1996] 5 N.Z.B.L.C. 104, 055 1–060
Weeks v. Goode (1859) 6 C.B. (N.S.) 367; 33 L.T. (O.S.) 93 15–056

Weibking, Re [1902] 1 K.B. 713 5–093
Weiner v. Gill [1906] 2 K.B. 574; affirming [1905] 2 K.B. 172 .... 5–004, 5–042, 5–047, 5–048 7–009, 7–010, 7–013
—— v. Harris [1910] 1 K.B. 285 .... 1–049, 5–045, 7–032, 7–043
Weir (Andrew) & Co. v. Dobell & Co. [1916] 1 K.B. 722; 85 L.J.Q.B. 873; 115 L.T. 387; 13 Asp.M.L.C. 496; 21 Com.Cas. 296 16–052
Weis & Co. v. Produce Brokers (1921) 7 Ll.L.R. 211 .... 18–235, 18–309, 19–030
Weis & Co. Ltd and Credit Colonial et Commercial (Antwerp), *Re* [1916] 1 K.B. 346; *sub nom.* Weiss (C.) & Co. Ltd v. Credit Colonial et Commercial (Antwerp) 85 L.J.Q.B. 533; 114 L.T. 168; 13 Asp.M.L.C. 242; 21 Com.Cas. 186 ... 6–021, 6–043, 19–037, 19–136
Welby v. Drake (1825) 1 C. & P. 557 9–025
Weld-Blundell v. Stephens [1920] A.C. 956; 89 L.J.Q.B. 705; 123 L.T.R. 593; 36 T.L.R. 640; 64 S.J. 529 .... 16–043, 16–049
Weldon v. GRE Linked Life Assurance Ltd [2000] 2 All E.R. (Comm) 914, QBD ... 9–039
Weldtech Equipment Ltd. *Re* [1991] B.C.C. 16 .... 5–144, 5–153, 5–160, 25–144
Welex AG v. Rosa Maritime Ltd (The Epsilon Rosa) (No.2) [2003] EWCA Civ 938; [2003] 2 Lloyd's Rep. 509; [2003] 2 C.L.C. 207, CA affirming [2002] EWHC 2033; [2002] 2 Lloyd's Rep. 701; [2003] I.L.Pr. 18, QBD 19–041, 25–079
Welex AG v. Rosa Maritime Ltd (The Epsilon Rosa) (No.2) [2003] EWCA Civ 938; [2003] 2 Lloyd's Rep. 509; [2003] 2 C.L.C. 207, CA (Civ Div); affirming [2002] EWHC 2033; [2002] 2 Lloyd's Rep. 701; [2003] I.L.Pr. 18, QBD 19–041, 25–079
Wells v. Hopkins (1839) M. & W. 7; 2 Horn & H. 11; 3 Jur. 797; 151 E.R. 3 11–073
Wells Fargo Asia Ltd v. Citibank N.A. (1991) 936 F. 2d. 723 (2nd Cir.) 22–016, 22–017
Wells Fargo Nevada National Bank v. Corn Exchange National Bank, 23 F. 2d 1 (1927) 23–234
Wells (Merstham) Ltd v. Buckland Sand & Silica Co. Ltd [1965] 2 Q.B. 170; [1964] 2 W.L.R. 453; 108 S.J. 177; [1964] 1 All E.R. 41 .... 2–027, 10–012, 12–011, 14–062
Welsh Development Agency v. Export Finance Co. [1992] B.C.L.C. 270; [1992] B.C.L.C. 148; *Financial Times*, November 27, 1991; *The Times*, November 28, 1991, CA 1–066, 22–144
Welsh Irish Ferries Ltd. *Re* [1986] Ch. 471; [1985] 3 W.L.R. 610; 1985 P.C.C. 303; (1985) 129 S.J. 683; [1985] 1 Lloyd's Rep. 372 .... 5–153, 21–106
Wenning v. Robinson (1964) 64 S.R.N.S.W. 157 .... 2–047, 2–049, 2–050
Werner v. A. L. Grootemaat & Sons Inc., 259 N.W. 2d 310 (1977) 23–244
—— v. Humphreys (1841) 2 M. & G. 853; Drink water 206; 3 Scott N.R. 226; 10 L.J.C.P. 214; 133 E.R. 989 .... 3–050, 5–091
Werner Lehara International Inc. v. Harn's Trust and Savings Bank 484 F.Supp. 65 (1980) 23–149
Wertheim v. Chicoutimi Pulp Co. [1911] A.C. 301; 80 L.J.P.C. 91; 104 L.T. 226; 16 Com.Cas. 297 .... 16–031, 16–056, 16–063, 17–039, 17–040, 17–058
West v. Dillicar [1920] N.Z.L.R. 139 7–012
West (H.W.) Ltd v. McBlain [1950] N.I. 144 4–011
West Middlesex Water-Works Co. v. Suwercrop (1829) 4 Car. & P. 87; Mood. & M. 408, N.P. 1–087
Westdeutsche Landesbank Girozentrale v. Islington L.B.C. [1996] A.C. 669; [1996] 3 W.L.R. 802; [1996] 2 All E.R. 961, HL 7–003, 7–047, 16–007, 22–090
West Virginia Housing Development v. Sroka 415 F.Supp. 1107 (1976) 23–027, 23–051, 23–196, 23–250
West Yorks Darracq Agency Ltd v. Coleridge [1911] 2 K.B. 326; 80 L.J.Q.B. 1122; 105 L.T. 215; 18 Mans. 307 9–025
Western Digital Corporation v. British Airways plc [2001] Q.B. 733; [2000] 3 W.L.R. 1855; [2001] 1 All E.R. 109; [2000] 2 All E.R. (Comm) 647; [2000] 2 Lloyd's Rep. 142; [2000] C.L.C. 1276; (2000) 144 S.J.L.B. 273; *The Times*, June 28, 2000, CA; reversing in part [1999] 2 All E.R. (Comm) 270; [1999] 2 Lloyd's Rep. 380; [1999] C.L.C. 1681; *The Times*, July 23, 1999, QBD (Comm Ct) 5–009, 18–149, 20–008, 21–073
Western Tractor Ltd v. Dyck (1969) 7 D.L.R. (3d) 535 13–030
Westfalische Central-Genossenschaft GmbH v. Seabright Chemicals Ltd (1979), unreported 8–102, 8–103
Westminster Bank v. Banca Nazionale Di Credito (1928) Ll.L.R. 306 ..... 23–203, 23–219, 23–221

Westminster Bank v. Zang [1966] A.C. 182; [1966] 2 W.L.R. 110; 109 S.J. 1009; [1966] 1 All E.R. 114; [1966] 1 Lloyd's Rep. 49 22–073
Westminster Building Co Ltd v. Beckingham [2004] EWHC 138; [2004] B.L.R. 163; [2004] B.L.R. 265; [2004] T.C.L.R. 8; 94 Con. L.R. 107, QBD 14–035
Westminster Property Group p.l.c. *Re* [1985] 1 W.L.R. 676; (1985) 129 S.J. 115; [1985] 2 All E.R. 426; 1985 P.C.C. 176; (1985) 82 L.G.Gaz. 1085, CA 1–027, 1–034, 2–044
Weston v. Downes (1778) 1 Doug. 23 12–067
Westpac Banking Corp. v. Commonwealth Steel Co. Ltd 735 (Aust.) 23–054, 23–137
Westpac Banking Corporation and Commonwealth Steel Co. v. South Carolina National Bank [1986] 1 Lloyd's Rep. 311, PC 18–016, 23–054, 23–127, 23–221
Westwood v. Secretary of State for Employment [1985] A.C. 20; [1984] 2 W.L.R. 418; [1985] I.C.R. 209; (1984) 128 & S.J. 221; [1984] 1 All E.R. 874 ..... 16–031, 16–052, 16–056, 16–075
Westzinthus, *Re* (1833) 5 B. & A. 817; 2 Nev. & M.K.B. 644; 3 L.J.K.B. 56; 110 E.R. 992 .... 15–099, 18–080
Wharton v. Mackenzie (1844) 5 Q.B. 606 2–031
—— v. Wright (1844) 1 Car. & K. 585; (1845) 6 L.T. (o.s.) 148 22–125
Wheatley v. Silkstone Co. (1885) 29 Ch.D. 715; 54 L.J.Ch. 778; 52 L.T. 798; 33 W.R. 797 5–161
Wheeler v. Pearson (1857) 2 Saund. & M. 170; 28 L.T. (o.s.) 255; 5 W.R. 227 5–101
—— v. Roberts (unreported) July 11, 1994, CA 22–060
Whenuapair Joinery (1988) Ltd v. Trust Bank Central Ltd [1994] 1 N.Z.L.R. 406 1–060
Whincup v. Hughes (1871) L.R. 6 C.P. 78; 40 L.J.C.P. 104; 24 L.T. 76; 19 W.R. 439 6–040, 12–069
Whistler v. Forster (1863) 14 C.B. (N.S.) 248; 32 L.J.C.P. 161; 8 L.T. 317; 11 W.R. 648 .... 7–001, 22–055, 22–061, 22–063
White v. Garden (1851) 10 C.B. 919; 20 L.J.C.P. 166; 15 Jur. 630; 138 E.R. 364 7–021
—— v. Garnier (1824) 2 Bing. 23; 1 C. & P. 324; 9 Moore C.P. 41; 2 L.J. (o.s.) C.P. 101; 130 E.R. 212 15–056
—— v. Jones [1995] 2 A.C. 207 .... 18–104, 18–122, 18–144, 18–149
—— v. Warwick (J.) & Co. Ltd [1953] 1 W.L.R. 1285; 97 S.J. 740; [1953] 2 All E.R. E.R. 1021 .... 12–073, 13–022
—— v. Wilks (1814) 5 Taunt. 176; 1 Marsh, 2; 128 E.R. 654 5–061
—— v. Williams [1912] A.C. 814; 82 L.J.P.C. 11; 107 L.T. 99; 28 T.L.R. 521; 121 Asp. M.L.C. 208; 17 Com.Cas. 309 .... 8–005, 19–088
White and Carter (Councils) Ltd v. McGregor [1962] A.C. 413; [1962] 2 W.L.R. 17; 105 S.J. 1104; [1961] 3 All E.R. 1178; 1962 S.C.(H.L.) 1 ...... 8–082, 9–021, 15–110, 15–111, 16–003, 16–004, 16–005, 16–022, 16–028, 16–035, 16–059, 16–080, 16–082, 17–016, 18–210, 19–214, 20–126, 20–128, 20–132
White Sea Timber Trust Ltd v. W.W. North Ltd (1932) 148 L.T. 263; 49 T.L.R. 142; 44 Ll.L.R. 390; 77 S.J. 30; 18 Asp.M.L.C. 367 ...... 13–033, 18–272, 18–273, 18–279
Whitehead v. Anderson (1842) 9 M. & W. 518; 11 L.J.Ex. 157; 152 E.R. 219 ...... 15–008, 15–065, 15–070, 15–074, 15–078, 15–079, 15–085, 15–086
Whitehorn Bros. v. Davison [1911] 1 K.B. 463 ... 4–010, 5–042, 5–044, 5–046, 7–022, 7–024, 7–028, 7–029, 7–038, 7–046
Whitehouse v. Frost (1810) 12 East 614; 104 E.R. 239 5–061
—— v. Liverpool New Gas Light and Coke Co. (1848) 5 C.B. 798; 17 L.J.C.P. 237; 136 E.R. 1093 8–058
Whiteley v. Hilt [1918] 2 K.B. 808 .... 4–013, 15–116, 17–098, 17–099
Whittingham v. Bloxham (1831) 4 C. & P. 597 5–010
Whittington v. Seale-Hayne (1900) 82 L.T. 49; 16 T.L.R. 181; 44 S.J. 229 12–003
Wibau Maschinenfabric Hartman SA v. Mackinnon Mackenzie & Co. (The Chanda) [1989] 2 Lloyd's Rep. 494; *The Independent*, April 28, 1989 .. 18–059, 18–278, 21–091, 21–093
Wichita Eagle and Beacon Publishing Co. Inc. v. Pacific National Bank, 343 F.Supp. 332 (1971); 493 F. 2d 1285 (1974) 23–239, 23–241, 23–248, 23–268
Wickham Holdings Ltd v. Brooke House Motors Ltd [1967] 1 W.L.R. 295; [1967] 1 All E.R. 117 .... 4–013, 4–014, 7–002, 7–106, 17–107
Wickman Machine Tool Sales Ltd v. L. Schuler A.G. [1974] A.C. 235; [1973] 2 W.L.R. 683; 117 S.J. 340; [1973] 2 All E.R. 39; [1973] 2 Lloyd's Rep. 53 .... 10–024, 10–037

Widenmeyer v. Burn, Stewart & Co. 1967 S.C. 85 1–036
Wiebe v. Butchart's Motors Ltd [1949] 4 D.L.R. 838 12–007
Wiehe v. Dennis Bros. (1913) 29 T.L.R. 250 .... 6–026, 18–209, 18–244, 18–264, 18–280, 18–282, 19–098, 19–114, 19–172
Wieler v. Schilizzi (1856) 17 C.B. 619; 25 L.J.C.P. 89; 139 E.R. 1219 .... 11–003, 11–004
Wight v. Eckhardt Marine GmbH; sub nom. Wight v. Eckhardt GmbH [2003] UKPC 37; [2004] 1 A.C. 147; [2003] 3 W.L.R. 414; [2003] B.C.C. 702; [2004] 2 B.C.L.C. 539; *The Times*, June 6, 2003, PC 25–177
Wilensko Slaski Towarzystwo Drewno v. Fenwick & Co. (West Hartlepool) Ltd [1938] 3 All E.R. 429; 54 T.L.R. 1019; 44 Com.Cas. 1 .... 8–050, 11–018, 13–033
Wilhelm, The (1866) 14 T.L. 636; 2 Mar.L.C. 343 16–049
Wilkie v. Fleming (1919) 3 W.W.R. 569 5–032
Wilkins v. Bromhead (1844) 6 M. & E. 963; 7 Scott N.R. 921; 13 L.J.C.P. 74;2 L.T. (o.s.) 328; 8 Jur. 83; 134 E.R. 1182 .... 5–075, 5–076, 5–091
—— v. Jadis (1831) 2 B. & Ad. 188; 9 L.J. (o.s.) K.B. 173 22–099
Wilkinson v. Barclay [1946] 1 All E.R. 387; 115 L.J.Q.B. 363; 62 T.L.R. 375 .... 13–033, 13–034, 13–051
Wilkinson v. Johnson (1824) 3 B. & C. 428; 5 Dow. & Ry. K.B. 403; 3 L.J. (o.s.) K.B. 58 22–056
—— v. Lloyd (1845) 7 Q.B. 27; 4 L.T. (o.s.) 432; 9 Jur. 328 .... 8–007, 8–018
—— v. London and County Banking Co. (1884) 1 T.L.R. 63 22–114
William Grant & Sons International Ltd v. Marie Brizard Espana SA, 1998 S.C. 536, OH 25–060
Williams v. Attorney General [1990] 1 N.Z.L.R. 646 5–011
Williams v. Burrell (1845) 1 C.B. 402; 14 L.J.C.P. 98; 4 L.T.O.S. 415; 9 Jur. 282; 135 E.R. 596 4–029
—— v. Cohen (1871) 25 L.T. 300 .... 20–086, 20–089
—— v. Naamlooze (1915) 21 Com.Cas. 253 8–096
—— v. Natural Life Health Foods Ltd [1998] 1 W.L.R. 830; [1998] 2 All E.R. 577; [1998] B.C.C. 428; [1998] 1 B.C.L.C. 689; (1998) 17Tr. L.R. 152; (1998) 95(21) L.S.G. 37; (1998) 148 N.L.J. 657; (1998) 142 S.J.L.B. 166; *The Times*, May 1, 1998, HL 18–045
—— v. Reynolds (1865) 6 B. & S. 495; 6 New Rep. 293; 34 L.J.K.B. 221; 12 L.T. 729; 11 Jur. (N.S.) 973; 13 W.R. 940; 122 E.R. 1278 17–029
—— v. Roffey Bros. & Nicholls (Contractors) Ltd [1991] 1 Q.B. 1 12–035
—— v. Trimm Rock Quarries Ltd (1965) 109 Sol.Jo. 454 14–061
—— v. Wheeler (1860) 8 C.B. (N.S.) 299 25–087
—— v. Williams (1882) 20 Ch.D. 659; 51 L.J.Ch. 385; 46 L.T. 275; 46 J.P. 726; 30 W.R. 438; 15 Cox C.C. 37 1–089
—— v. Williams 1980 S.L.T. 25; (1980) 11 Fam.Law 23 22–061
Williams & Glyn's Bank Ltd v. Belkin Packaging Ltd [1983] W.W.R. 481; [1981] 123 D.L.R. (3d) 612 .... 22–061, 22–062
Williams (J.D.) & Co. v. McCauley Parsons & Jones [1994] C.C.L.R. 78 3–005
Williams Bros. Ltd v. Agius (Ed. T.) Ltd [1914] A.C. 510; 83 L.J.K.B. 715; 110 L.T. 865; 30 T.L.R. 351; 58 S.J. 377; 19 Com.Cas. 200 .... 17–016, 17–027, 17–028, 17–031, 17–033
Williams Ice Cream Co. Inc. v. Chase National Bank, 199 N.Y.S. 314 (1923) 23–218
Williamson v. Rider [1963] 1 Q.B. 89; [1962] 3 W.L.R. 119; 106 S.J. 263; [1962] 2 All E.R. 268 22–043
Willis v. Barrett (1816) 2 Stark. 29 22–046
—— v. F.M.C. Machinery and Chemicals Ltd (1976) 68 D.L.R. (3d) 127 11–057
—— v. Glenwood Cotton Mills 200 F. 301 (1912) 25–173, 25–174
Willis (R.H.) & Son v. British Car Auctions Ltd [1978] 1 W.L.R. 438; (1978) 122 S.J. 62; [1978] 2 All E.R. 392; [1978] R.T.R. 244 7–002
Willmore (Trading as Linsenden Poultry) v. South Eastern Electricity Board [1957] 2 Lloyd's Rep. 375 1–071
Wills (George) & Sons Ltd v. R.S. Cunningham Son & Co. Ltd [1924] 2 K.B. 220; [1923] All E.R. 299; 93 L.J.K.B. 1008; 131 L.T. 400; 40 T.L.R. 108 8–093
—— v. Thomas Brown & Sons (1922) 12 Ll.L.R. 292 .... 6–019, 6–041, 11–067, 18–257, 18–258, 18–274, 20–018, 20–038, 20–114
Wilmshurst v. Bowker (1841) 10 L.J.C.P. 161; (1844) 7 Man. & G. 882; 8 Scott N.R. 571; 12 L.J.Ex. 475 .... 18–102, 18–216, 19–221

Wilson v. Anderton (1830) 1 B. & A. 450; 9 L.J. (o.s.) K.B. 48 15–088
—— v. Barclay 1957 S.L.T. (Sh.Ct.) 40; (1957) 73 Sh.Ct.Rep. 114 4–012
—— v. Church (1879) 13 Ch.D. 1; 41 L.T. 50 12–067
—— v. Dunville (1879) L.R. 4 Ir. 249 .... 11–059, 11–067
—— v. First County Trust Ltd (No.2); *sub nom.* Wilson v. Secretary of State for Trade and Industry [2003] UKHL 40; [2004] 1 A.C. 816; [2003] 3 W.L.R. 568; [2003] 4 All E.R. 97; [2003] 2 All E.R. (Comm) 491; [2003] H.R.L.R. 33; [2003] U.K.H.R.R. 1085; (2003) 100(35) L.S.G. 39; (2003) 147 S.J.L.B. 872; *The Times*, July 11, 2003; *Independent*, November 3, 2003 (C.S), HL 2–023, 14–145
—— v. General Iron Screw Colliery Co. (1877) 47 L.J.Q.B. 239; 37 L.T. 789; 3 Asp.M.L.C. 536 17–041
—— v. Lombank Ltd [1913] 1 W.L.R. 1294 5–010
—— v. Love [1896] 1 Q.B. 626; 65 L.J.Q.B. 474; 74 L.T. 580; 44 W.R. 450, CA 16–032
—— v. Rickett, Cockerell & Co. Ltd [1954] 1 Q.B. 598; [1954] 2 W.L.R. 629; 98 S.J. 233; [1954] 1 All E.R. 868 .... 11–048, 11–065, 12–066, 14–014, 14–025, 17–074
—— v. Robertsons (London) Ltd [2005] EWHC (Ch.); [2005] 3 All ER 873 14–147
—— v. United Counties Bank [1920] A.C. 102; 88 L.J.K.B. 1033 H.L 16–030, 16–058
—— v. Wright [1937] 4 All E.R. 371; 82 S.J. 14; 59 Ll.L.Rep. 86 .... 20–038, 20–042
Wilson (J. Raymond) & Co. Ltd v. Norman Scatchard Ltd (1944) 77 Ll.L.R. 373 ... 20–001, 20–011, 20–086
Wilson and Meeson v. Pickering [1946] K.B. 422; [1947] L.J.R. 18; 175 L.T. 65; [1946] 1 All E.R. 394 .... 7–008, 7–016
Wilson Holgate & Co. Ltd v. Belgian Grain and Produce Co. Ltd [1920] 2 K.B. 1; 89 L.J.Q.B. 300; 122 L.T. 524; 35 T.L.R. 530; 14 Asp.M.L.C. 566; 25 Com.Cas. 1 .... 19–042, 19–047, 19–048, 23–230
Wilson Smithett & Cape (Sugar) Ltd v. Bangladesh Sugar & Food Industries Corp. [1986] 1 Lloyd's Rep. 378 2–019
Wilson, Smithett & Cope Ltd v. Terruzzi [1976] Q.B. 683 .... 1–104, 25–113
Wiltshire Iron Co., *Re* (1868) L.R. 3 Ch.App. 443 5–098
Wimble, Sons & Co. v. Lillico & Son (1922) 38 T.L.R. 296 .... 11–018, 13–023, 13–028
—— v. Rosenberg & Sons [1913] 3 K.B. 743; 82 L.J.K.B. 1251; 109 L.T. 294; 29 T.L.R. 752; 57 S.J. 784; 12 Asp.M.L.C. 373; 18 Com.Cas. 65 ... 1–002, 6–021, 8–015, 18–245, 18–246, 18–247, 18–248, 18–250, 20–001, 20–002, 20–003, 20–007, 20–012, 20–042, 20–043, 21–011, 21–029, 21–101
Wimshurst v. Deeley (1845) 2 C.B. 253; 135 E.R. 942 8–025
Wincanton Ltd v. P. & O. Trans European Ltd [2001] EWCA Civ 227; [2001] C.L.C. 962, CA 1–059
Windschuegl (Charles H.) Ltd v. Alexander Pickering & Co. Ltd (1950) 84 Ll.L.R. 89 .... 6–057, 18–313, 18–318, 18–320, 18–328, 19–013
Wing on Bank Ltd v. American National Bank and Trust Co. 457 F. 2d 328 (1972) 23–158, 23–203
Wingold v. William Looser & Co. [1951] 1 D.L.R. 429 8–039
Wings Ltd v. Ellis [1985] A.C. 272; [1984] 3 W.L.R. 965; (1984) 128 S.J. 766; (1985) 149 J.P. 33; [1984] 3 All E.R. 577; [1985] L.G.R. 193 14–113
Winkfield, The [1902] P. 42; 71 L.J.P. 21; 85 L.T. 668; 50 W.R. 246; 18 T.L.R. 178; 46 S.J. 163; 9 Asp.M.L.C. 259 .... 1–072, 5–010, 18–114
Winks v. Hassall (1829) 9 B. & C. 372; Dan. & Ll. 312; 7 L.J. (o.s.) K.B. 265; 109 E.R. 138 .... 8–012, 15–044
Winkworth v. Christie Manson and Woods Ltd [1980] Ch. 496; [1980] 2 W.L.R. 937; [1980] 1 All E.R. 1121 .... 25–121, 25–122, 25–131, 25–138
Winnipeg Condominium Corp. Np. 36 v. Bird Construction Co. [1995] 1 S.C.R. 85; (1995) 121 D.L.R. (4th) 193 12–126
Winnipeg Fish Co. v. Whitman Fish Co. (1909) 41 S.C.R. (Can.) 453 12–040
Winsley Bros. v. Woodfield Importing Co. [1929] N.Z.L.R. 480 11–032
Winsor (J. Barry) and Associates Ltd v. Belgo-Canadian Manufacturing Co. Ltd (1976) 76 D.L.R. 685 4–004
Winter, Re (1878) 8 Ch. D.225 5–093
Wirth v. Austin (1875) L.R. 10 C.P. 689; 32 L.T. 669 22–116
Wise, *Re* (1842) 3 Mont. D. & De G. 103; 7 Jur. 95; 12 L.J.Bcy. 28 22–090
Wiseman v. Vandeputt (1690) 2 Vern. 203; 23 E.R. 742 15–061

Wiskin v. Terdich Bros. Property Ltd [1928] Arg.L.R. 242 8–018
With v. O'Flanagan [1936] Ch. 575; [1936] 1 All E.R. 727; 105 L.J.Ch. 247; 154 L.T. 634; 80 S.J. 285 10–009
Withers v. General Theatre Corporation Ltd [1933] 2 K.B. 536; 102 L.J.Q.B. 719; 149 L.T. 487 17–002
—— v. Lyss (1815) 4 Camp. 237; Holt N.P. 18; 171 E.R. 76, N.P 5–035
—— v. Reynolds (1831) 2 B. & Ad. 882 .... 8–078, 8–085
Witt & Scott Ltd v. Blumenreich [1949] N.Z.L.R. 806 .... 23–308, 23–314
Witter (Thomas) Ltd v. T.B.P. Industries Ltd [1996] 2 All E.R. 573 .... 12–010, 13–022, 13–023, 13–030, 13–056, 13–087, 19–197
Wolf (W.) & Sons v. Carr, Parker & Co. Ltd (1915) 31 T.L.R. 407 6–042
Wolfenden v. Wilson (1873) 33 U.C.R. 442 1–043
Wood v. Baxter (1883) 49 L.T. 45 .... 4–001, 4–032
—— v. Bell (1856) 5 E. & B. 772 .... 5–017, 5–092, 5–093
—— v. Copper Miners' Co. (1854) 14 C.B. 428; 2 C.L.R. 1735; 23 L.J.C.P. 29; 1 Jur. (N.S.) 65; 139 E.R. 176; (1856) 17 C.B. 594n., Ex.Ch. 8–058
—— v. Donnelley (R.R.) & Sons Co. 888 F. 2d 313 (3rd Cir. 1989) 23–245
—— v. Jackson (1910) 12 G.L.R. 413 (N.Z.) 22–041
—— v. Leadbitter (1845) 13 M. & W. 838 8–022
—— v. Letrik Ltd. *The Times*, January 13, 1932 14–062
—— v. Manley (1839) 11 A. & E. 34; 3 Per. & Dav. 5; 9 L.J.Q.B. 27; 3 Jur. 1028; 113 E.R. 325 8–022
—— v. Roberts (1818) 2 Stark, 417 9–025
—— v. Rowcliffe (1846) 6 Hare 183 7–032
—— v. Smith (1829) 4 C. & P. 45; M. & M. 539; 5 M. & Ry. 124; 8 L.J. (O.S.) K.B. 50 10–019
—— v. Tassell (1844) 6 Q.B. 234; 115 E.R. 90 .... 8–007, 8–012, 8–018
Wood Components of London v. James Webster & Brother Ltd [1959] 2 Lloyd's Rep. 200 11–077
Wood Hall Ltd v. Pipeline Authority (1979) 53 A.L.J.R. 487 .... 23–274, 23–289
Wood Preservation Ltd v. Prior [1969] 1 W.L.R. 1077 1–051
Wood Pulp Cartel, *Re* [1988] 4 C.M.L.R. 901 3–041
Woodar Investment Development Ltd v. Wimpey Construction U.K. Ltd [1980] 1 W.L.R. 277; (1980) S.J. 184; [1980] 1 All E.R. 571 ... 8–078, 12–019, 12–021, 13–017, 13–052, 14–071, 18–114
Woodchester Equipment (Leasing) Ltd v. British Association of Canned, etc. Food Importers Ltd [1995] C.C.L.R. 51 3–005
Woodhouse A.C. Israel Cocoa Ltd SA v. Nigerian Produce Marketing Co. Ltd [1972] A.C. 741; [1972] 2 W.L.R. 1090; 116 S.J. 329; [1972] 2 All E.R. 271; [1972] 1 Lloyd's Rep. 439 .... 8–030, 9–024, 12–035, 25–167
Woodland v. Fuller (1840) 11 A. & E. 859 7–113
Woodley v. Coventry (1863) 2 H. & C. 164; 2 New Rep. 35; 32 L.J.Ex. 185; 8 L.T. 249; 9 Jur. (N.S.) 548; 11 W.R. 599 .... 5–065, 7–015, 15–096
Woodman v. Photo Trade Processing Ltd (1981) 13–089
Woods v. Dean (1862) 32 L.J.Q.B. 1; 3 B. & S. 101; 7 L.T. 561; 1 W.R. 22 22–131
—— v. Russell (1822) 5 B. & Ald. 942; 1 Dow. & Ry. K.B. 587; 106 E.R. 1436 ..... 5–092, 5–093
—— v. Thiedemann (1862) 1 H. & C. 478; 10 W.R. 846 23–128
Woodstead Finance Ltd v. Petrou (1985) 136 New L.J. 188; *The Times*, January 23, 1986 14–150
Woodward, *ex p.* Huggins, *Re* (1886) 54 L.T. 683; 3 Morn, 75 1–057
—— v. Pell (1868) L.R. 4 Q.B. 55; 9 B. & S. 994; 38 L.J.Q.B. 30; 19 L.T. 557; 17 W.R. 117 22–108
Wooldridge v. Sumner [1963] 2 Q.B. 43; [1962] 3 W.L.R. 616; 106 S.J. 489; [1962] 2 All E.R. 978 13–106
Woolf v. Collis Removal Service [1948] 1 K.B. 11; [1947] L.J.R. 1377; 177 L.T. 405; 63 T.L.R. 540; [1947] 2 All E.R. 260 .... 13–041, 13–046
—— v. Horne (1877) 2 Q.B.D. 355; 46 L.J.Q.B. 534; 36 L.T. 705; 41 J.P. 501; 25 W.R. 728 .... 9–005, 18–038, 20–125
Worcester Works Finance Ltd v. Cooden Engineering Co. Ltd [1972] 1 Q.B. 210; [1971] 3 W.L.R. 661; 115 S.J. 605; [1971] 3 All E.R. 708 .... 5–034, 7–042, 7–047, 7–059, 7–060, 7–061, 7–062, 7–064, 7–065, 7–078, 7–079, 7–080, 15–112, 15–117

Worcester Works Finance Ltd v. Medens Ltd (1973) 117 S.J. 143 .... 4–013, 7–009
—— v. Ocean Banking Corp. Ltd March 29, 1972 7–100
Workers Trust and Merchant Bank Ltd v. Dojap Investments Ltd [1993] A.C. 573; [1993] 2 W.L.R.702; [1993] 2 All E.R. 370; [1993] 1 E.G.L.R. 203; [1993] E.G.C.S. 38; [1993] N.P.C. 33; 66 P. & C.R. 15; 137 S.J.L.B. 83; 143 N.L.J. 616, PC 15–132, 15–133, 16–039
Workman, Clark & Co. Ltd v. Lloyd Brazileno [1908] 1 K.B. 968; 77 L.J.Q.B. 953; 99 L.T. 477; 24 T.L.R. 458; 11 Asp.M.L.C. 126 .... 5–092, 8–077, 16–003, 16–005, 16–027, 16–028, 19–212, 19–213, 19–214
World Harmony, The; Konstontinidis v. World Tankers Co. [1967] P. 341 5–011
WorldLink Inc. v. HSBC Bank, No. 604118/1999 (NY Sup. Ct. May 23, 2000) 23–142
Wormell v. R.H.M. Agricultural (East) Ltd [1987] 1 W.L.R. 1091; (1987) 131 S.J. 1085; [1987] 3 All E.R. 75; [1988] T.L.R. 114, CA; reversing [1986] 1 W.L.R. 336; [1986] 1 All E.R. 769; (1985) 129 S.J. 166; 83 L.S.Gaz. 786 .... 11–039, 11–057, 14–010, 14–014, 14–084
Worsley v. Tambrands Ltd [2000] C.P. Rep. 43; (1999) 96(48) L.S.G. 40; *The Times*, February 11, 2000, CA 14–084
Wren v. Holt [1903] 1 K.B. 610; 72 L.J.Q.B. 340; 88 L.T. 282; 67 J.P. 191; 51 W.R. 435; *sub nom.* Holt v. Wren, 19 T.L.R. 292 .... 11–008, 11–053, 11–044, 11–059, 11–065, 14–011, 16–047, 17–072
Wright v. Lawes (1801) 4 Esq. 82; 170 E.R. 649, N.P. 7–021
Wright (Frank H.) (Constructions) Ltd v. Frodoor Ltd [1967] 1 W.L.R. 506 2–051
Wright, Stephenson & Co. v. Adams & Co. (1908) 28 N.Z.L.R. 193 8–067
Wrightson v. McArthur and Hutchinsons (1919) Ltd [1921] 2 K.B. 807; 90 L.J.Q.B. 842; 125 L.T. 383; 37 T.L.R. 575; 65 S.J. 553; [1921] B. & C.R. 136 .... 8–008, 15–038
Wrightup v. Chamberlain (1839) 7 Scott. 598; 2 Arn. 28 17–077
Wroth v. Tyler [1974] Ch. 30; [1973] 2 W.L.R. 405; (1972) 117 S.J. 90; [1973] 1 All E.R. 897; 25 P. & C.R. 138 .... 16–042, 16–045, 16–055, 17–100
Wurtembergische Fire Insurance Co. v. Pan Atlantic Underwriters Ltd 519 N.Y.S. 2d 57 (1987) 23–153
Wycombe Marsh Garages Ltd v. Fowler [1972] 1 W.L.R. 1156; 116 S.J. 467; [1972] 3 All E.R. 248; [1972] R.T.R. 503; [1972] Crim.L.R. 456 14–106
Wylde v. Legge (1901) 84 L.T. 121 7–070
—— v. Radford (1863) 33 L.J.Ch. 51; 9 L.T. 471; 9 Jur. (N.S.) 1169; 12 W.R. 38 22–140
Wylie v. Porah (1907) 23 T.L.R. 687; 12 Com.Cas. 317 21–027

Wylie & Lockhead v. Mitchell (1870) 8 M. 552 5–149

X v. Schering Health Care Ltd; *sub nom.* XYZ v. Schering Health Care Ltd [2002] EWHC 1420; (2003) 70 B.M.L.R. 88; *Daily Telegraph*, August 1, 2002, QBD .. 1–071
XAG v. A Bank [1983] 2 All E.R. 464 25–076
XL Insurance v. Owens Corning [2001] 1 All E.R. (Comm) 530; [2000] 2 Lloyd's Rep. 500; [2001] C.P. Rep. 22; [2001] C.L.C. 914, QBD (Comm Ct) 25–024, 25–033, 25–057
Xantho, The (1886) L.R. 11 P.D. 170 8–097

Yachetti v. John Duff & Sons Ltd [1943] 1 D.L.R. 194; [1942] O.R. 682 (CAN.) ... 11–044, 11–057
Yangtsze Insurance Association v. Lukmanjee [1918] A.C. 585; 87 L.J.P.C. 111; 118 L.T. 736; 34 T.L.R. 320; 14 Asp.M.L.C. 296 5–102, 18–089, 21–014, 21–017, 21–018, 21–020
Yarrow, *Re*, Collins v. Weymouth (1889) 59 L.J.Q.B. 18; 61 L.T. 642; 38 W.R. 175 ... 1–066
Yates v. Pym (1816) 6 Taunt. 446; 128 E.R. 1107; *sub nom.* Yeats v. Pim, 2 Marsh 141 11–021
Yelo v. S.M. Machado [1952] 1 Lloyd's Rep. 183 .. 18–027, 19–029, 20–020, 20–024, 20–028, 20–029, 20–038, 20–105, 20–106, 23–220
Yeoman Credit Ltd v. Apps. [1962] 2 Q.B. 508; [1961] 3 W.L.R. 94; 105 S.J. 567; [1961] 2 All E.R. 281 ...... 3–005, 10–031, 12–023, 12–066, 13–030, 13–042, 13–044, 13–051, 14–047, 17–090

Yeoman Credit Ltd v. Gregory [1963] 1 W.L.R. 343; 107 S.J. 315; [1963] 1 All E.R. 245; [1962] 2 Lloyd's Rep. 302 .... 22–110, 22–126, 22–129
—— v. McLean [1962] 1 W.L.R. 131; 105 S.J. 990 4–017
—— v. Odgers Vospers Motor House (Plymouth) (Third Party) [1962] 1 W.L.R. 215; 106 S.J. 75; [1962] 1 All E.R. 789 .... 1–054, 2–027, 14–044
—— v. Waragowski [1961] 1 W.L.R. 1124; 105 S.J. 588; [1961] 3 All E.R. 145 16–005
Yeramex International v. The Tendo 1977 A.M.C. 1807 21–086
Yin (Chai San) v. Sam (Liew Kwee) [1962] A.C. 304; [1962] 2 W.L.R. 765; 106 S.J. 217 3–028
Yonge v. Toynbee [1910] 1 K.B. 215; 79 L.J.Q.B. 208; 102 L.T. 57; 26 T.L.R. 211 .... 14–042, 18–045
Yorkshire Railway Wagon Co. Ltd v. Maclure (1882) 21 Ch.D. 309 1–066
Youell v. Bland Welch & Co Ltd (No.1) [1992] 2 Lloyd's Rep. 127, CA 13–020
Young v. Glover (1857) 3 Jur. (N.S.) 637 22–103
—— v. Dalgleish (D.S.) & Son (Hawick) 1994 S.C.L.R. 696, Sh.Ct 7–021, 7–024
—— v. Higgon (1840) 6 M. & W. 49 .... 8–034, 8–035
—— v. Kitchin (1878) 3 Ex.D. 127 18–123
—— v. Matthews (1866) L.R. 2 C.P. 127; 36 L.J.C.P. 61; 15 L.T. 182 5–030
—— v. Moeller (1855) 5 E. & B. 755; 4 W.R. 149 18–099
—— v. Sun Alliance Ltd [1977] 1 W.L.R. 104; [1976] 3 All E.R. 561; 120 Sol.Jo. 469; 239 E.G. 805; [1976] 2 Lloyd's Rep. 189, CA 8–097
—— v. Timmins (1831) 1 Cr. & J. 331 3–035
Young and Marten Ltd v. McManus Childs Ltd [1969] 1 A.C. 454; [1968] 3 W.L.R. 630; 112 S.J. 744; [1968] 2 All E.R. 1169 .... 1–041, 1–043, 11–043, 11–050
Young, Hamilton & Co., *Re. ex p.* Carter [1905] 2 K.B. 381 .... 5–167, 18–238
Young (T.) & Sons v. Hobson and Partner (1949) 65 T.L.R. 365 ... 8–015, 18–245, 21–042, 21–043
Youngs v. Youngs [1940] 1 K.B. 760 1–016
Yrazu v. Astral Shipping Co. (1904) 20 T.L.R. 153; 9 Com.Cas. 100 8–099
Yuill v. Scott-Robson [1908] 1 K.B. 270; 77 L.J.Q.B. 259; 98 L.T. 364; 24 T.L.R. 180; 52 S.J. 192; 11 Asp.M.L.C. 40; 13 Com.Cas. 166 19–045
Yungmann v. Briesemann (1892) 67 L.T. 642; 41 W.R. 148; 4 R. 119 .... 15–056, 15–057

Z. Ltd v. A.-Z. and AA.-LL. [1982] 1 Q.B. 558; [1982] 2 W.L.R. 288; (1982) 126 S.J. 100; [1982] 1 All E.R. 556 .... 5–014, 23–137
Zagury v. Furnell (1809) 2 Camp. 240; 170 E.R. 1142, N.P. 5–035
Zahnrad Fabrik Passau G.m.b.H v. Terex Ltd 1986 S.L.T. 84 .... 5–149, 25–141, 25–142, 25–143
Zambia Steel & Building Supplies v. Clark (James) & Eaton [1986] 2 Lloyd's Rep. 225, CA 2–013
Zanzibar v. British Aerospace (Lancaster House) Ltd [2000] 1 W.L.R. 2333; [2000] C.L.C. 735; *The Times*, March 28, 2000, QBD (Comm Ct) 12–010, 13–022, 13–056, 13–060
Zawadski v. Sleigh (1975) 119 S.J. 318; [1975] R.T.R. 113; [1975] Crim.L.R. 180 14–112
Zebrarise Ltd v. De Nieffe [2004] EWHC 1842; [2005] 2 All E.R. (Comm) 816; [2005] 1 Lloyd's Rep. 154, QBD 25–001, 25–024, 25–077, 25–191
Zeevi & Sons Ltd v. Grindlays Bank (Uganda) Ltd 371 N.Y.S. 2d 892 (1975) 23–171
Zemel v. Commercial Warehouses (1945) 40 A. (2d) 642 16–070
Zendman v. Winston (Harry) Inc. Ill N.E. 2d 871 (1953) 25–131
Zigurds, The [1932] P. 113 25–188
Zinc Corporation Ltd v. Hirsch [1916] 1 K.B. 541; 85 L.J.Q.B. 565; 114 L.T. 222; 32 T.L.R. 232; 21 Com.Cas. 273 .... 6–042, 8–099
Zivnostenska Banka v. Frankman [1950] A.C. 57; [1949] 2 All E.R. 671, HL; reversing [1949] 1 K.B. 199; [1948] 2 All E.R. 1025; 92 S.J. 705, CA; reversing [1948] 1 K.B. 730, KBD 25–119
Zoan v. Rouamba [2000] 1 W.L.R. 1509; [2000] 2 All E.R. 620; [2000] C.C.L.R. 18; (2000) 150 N.L.J. 99; *The Times*, March 7, 2000, CA 1–022, 8–034, 9–065
Zockoll Group Ltd v. Mercury Telecommunications Ltd (No.2) [1999] E.M.L.R. 385; [1998] I.T.C.L.R. 104, CA 13–094
Zouch v. Empsey (1821) 4 B. & Ald. 522 8–035
Zuiho Maru, The [1977] 2 Lloyd's Rep. 552 .... 6–053, 8–097, 8–102

Zuker v. Paul (1982) 135 D.L.R. (3d) 481 4–028
Zwinger v. Samuda (1817) 7 Taunt. 265; 1 Moore C.P. 12; Holt N.P. 395; 129 E.R. 106 7–013

TABLE OF STATUTES

1677 Statute of Frauds (29 Car. 2 c.3) 1–041, 1–090, 1–091, 1–092, 8–009, 12–044, 12–045, 15–050, 22–053
s.4 . . . 1–091, 1–093, 1–095, 1–096, 25–087
s.17 . . . 1–078, 1–091, 1–093, 2–022
1689 Distress for Rent Act (2 Will. & Mar. c.5)—
s.1 7–111
1709 Landlord and Tenant Act (8 Ann. c.18) 7–111
1730 Landlord and Tenant Act (4 Geo. 2 c.28)—
s.5 7–111
1737 Distress for Rent Act (11 Geo. 2 c.19)—
s.10 7–111
1820 Insolvent Debtors Act (1 Geo. 4 c.3) 15–024
1823 Factors Act (4 Geo. 4 c.83) . . 1–018, 7–031
s.1 7–053
1825 Factors Act (6 Geo. 4 c.94) . . 1–018, 7–031, 7–047
1828 Statute of Frauds Amendment Act (9 Geo. 4 c.14) 1–091
1833 Public Notaries Act (3 & 4 Will. 4 c.70)—
s.2 22–135
1838 Judgments Act (1 & 2 Vict. c.110)—
s.17 . . . . . . 16–007, 16–013, 25–191
1842 Factors Act (5 & 6 Vict. c.39) 1–018, 7–031, 7–047
1845 Gaming Act (8 & 9 Vict. c.109)
s.18 . . . . 1–104, 6–012
1853 Stamp Act (16 & 17 Vict. c.59) 22–024, 22–025
s.19 . . . . . 22–024, 22–025, 22–027, 22–028
1854 Railway and Canal Traffic Act (17 & 18 Vict. c.31)—
s.7 13–007
Stamp Act (17 & 18 Vict. c.83)—
s.11 22–019
1855 Bills of Lading Act (18 & 19 Vict. c.111) 5–008, 5–110, 15–013, 18–023, 18–034, 18–065, 18–080, 18–096, 18–100, 18–101, 18–108, 18–113, 18–116, 18–129, 18–132, 18–134, 18–138,
1855 Bills of Lading Act—*cont.* 18–139, 18–146, 18–147, 18–149, 18–190, 18–227, 18–292, 19–093
s.1 . . . . . . 18–023, 18–080, 18–100, 18–114, 18–123, 18–129, 18–142, 18–220, 18–237, 19–093, 19–094, 19–102, 22–021
s.3 . . . . . . 18–033, 18–034, 18–037, 18–043
1855 Mercantile Law Amendment Act (19 & 20 Vict. c.97) 11–055
s.2 17–096
s.5 15–014
1858 Chancery Amendment Act (21 & 22 Vict. c.27) 12–114, 17–100, 17–102
Mersey Docks Consolidation Act (21 & 22 Vict. c.xcii)—
s.200 18–198
1861 Admiralty Court Act (24 & 25 Vict. c.10)—
s.6 18–079
Larceny Act (24 & 25 Vict. c.96)—
s.100 1–084
1867 Policies of Assurance Act (30 & 31 Vict. c.144) 18–147
1870 Inland Revenue Repeal Act (33 & 34 Vict. c.99)—
s.2 22–024
1873 Judicature Act (36 & 37 Vict. c.66) 1–008, 18–147
1874 Infants Relief Act (37 & 38 Vict. c.62) 2–029, 2–035, 2–037, 15–118
s.1 . . . . 2–035, 2–037, 25–127
1877 Factors Acts Amendment Act (40 & 41 Vict. c.39) 1–018, 7–031
s.3 7–055
s.4 7–069
1878 Bills of Sale Act (41 & 42 Vict. c.31) 1–012, 1–016, 1–017, 2–024, 5–167, 5–168, 15–009, 15–117, 15–129, 24–030
s.3 5–167
s.4 . . . 1–016, 1–017, 1–079, 5–167, 5–168, 18–238, 24–030

1878 Bills of Sale Act—*cont.*
s.8 .... 1–016, 5–167
s.10 .... 1–016, 5–167
Innkeepers Act (41 & 42 Vict. c.38)—
s.1 7–111
1881 Conveyancing Act (44 & 45 Vict. c.41)—
s.7..................... 4–023
1882 Bills of Sale Act (1878) Amendment Act (45 & 46 Vict. c.43) 1–012, 1–016, 1–017, 1–064, 1–065, 1–066, 1–067, 2–024, 5–167, 5–168
s.4 .... 1–016, 5–167
s.5 1–016
s.7A 1–016
s.8 .... 1–016, 5–167
s.9 .... 1–016, 5–167
s.10 5–167
s.12 1–016
s.17..................... 1–016
Bills of Exchange Act (45 & 46 Vict. c.61) 1–002, 15–007, 22–030, 22–033, 22–034, 22–035, 22–036, 22–040, 22–074, 22–075, 22–085, 22–086, 22–120, 22–121, 25–077
s.2 ...... 22–020, 22–031, 22–036, 22–050, 22–055, 22–057, 22–059
s.3(1) 22–036, 22–038, 22–041, 22–043, 22–045, 22–118
(2) 22–038
(3) 22–041
(b) 22–042
(4) 22–038
s.4 .... 22–025, 22–040, 22–053
s.5(1) 22–046
(2) 22–019
s.7(1) 22–046
(2) 22–046
s.8 9–030
(2) 22–046
(3) 22–046
(4) 22–046
s.9(1) 22–045
(2) 22–045
s.10(1) 22–043
(2) 22–043, 22–103
s.11(1) 22–043
(2) 22–043
s.12 ..... 22–062, 22–103, 22–126
s.14(1) 9–055, 22–044
(2) 22–044
(3) 22–044
(4) 22–044
1882 Bills of Exchange Act—*cont.*
s.15 22–138
s.16(1) ... 22–070, 22–086, 23–163
(2) 22–086, 22–136
s.17(1) 22–047
(2) 22–103
s.18(1) 22–103
(2) 22–103
(3) 22–103
s.19(2) 22–104, 22–107
(a) 22–104
(b) 22–104
(c) 22–104
(d) 22–104
s.20(2) 22–062
s.21(1) 22–058
(2) 22–062
(2) 2–035
s.23 22–050
(1) 22–050
(2) 22–050
s.24 22–107
s.27(1)(a) 22–068
(2) 22–060, 22–064
(3) ... 22–060, 22–067, 22–075
s.28(2) 22–064
s.29 22–061
(1) 22–061, 22–068
(2) ... 22–061, 22–062, 22–063
s.30(1) 22–061
(2) 22–061
s.31(1) 22–055
(2) 22–055
(3) 18–103, 22–055
(4) 22–055
s.32 22–055
s.33 22–055
s.34(1)–(3)..................... 22–056
(4) 22–056
s.36(3) 22–061
s.38(1) 22–062
(2) ... 22–062, 22–063, 22–064
s.39(1) 22–097
(2) 22–097
(3) 22–097
(4) 22–097
s.40(1) 22–098
(2) 22–098
(3) 22–098
s.41 22–116
(1) 22–098, 22–099
(a) 19–069, 22–098, 22–099
(b) 22–099
(c) 22–099
(d) 22–099
(e) 22–099
(2) .. 22–099, 22–102, 22–116
(3) 22–102
s.42 ...... 18–223, 22–100, 22–105

1882 Bills of Exchange Act—*cont.*
s.43(1) 22–105
(a) 22–107
(2) ... 22–097, 22–105, 23–011, 23–163, 23–178
s.44(1) 22–106
(2) 22–106
(3) 22–106
s.45 .... 22–108, 22–114
(1) 22–109
(2) 22–109
(3) 22–108
(4) 22–110
(b)–(d) 22–111
(c) 19–069, 22–111
(5) 22–111
(6) 22–113
(7) 22–113
(8) 22–108
s.46 .... 22–116, 22–132
(1) 22–116, 22–130
(2) 22–116, 22–131
(c) 22–132
s.47 18–223
(1) 22–117
(2) ... 22–117, 23–011, 23–163, 23–178
s.48 22–121
s.49 22–122
(1) 22–122
(2) 22–122
(3) 22–123
(4) 22–123
(5) 22–124
(6) 22–124
(7) 22–124
(8)–(11) 22–125
(8) 22–125
(9) 22–125
(10) 22–125
(11) 22–125
(12) .. 22–126, 22–128, 22–137
(13) 22–128, 22–129
(14) 22–126
(15) 22–127
s.50(1) 22–130
(2)(a) 22–131
(b) 22–131
(c) 22–132
(d) 22–132
s.51 ...... 22–040, 22–135, 22–137
(1) 22–136
(2) 22–136
(3) 22–136
(4) 22–137
(5) 22–136
(6) 22–137
(7) 22–137
s.52(1) 22–114

1882 Bills of Exchange Act—*cont.*
s.52(2) 22–114
(3) ... 22–120, 22–133, 22–136
(4) 22–108
s.53(1) 22–047
(2) 22–047
s.54(1) 22–047
(2) 22–062
s.55(1)(a) 22–048
(b) 22–048
(2) 22–062
(a) 22–049
(b) 22–049
(c) 22–049
s.56 .... 22–050, 22–054
s.57 16–007
(2) 25–194
(3) 22–114
s.58(2) 22–071
(3) 22–071
s.59 22–026
(2)(b) 22–056
s.60 ..... 22–022, 22–024, 22–025, 22–026
s.64 22–062
s.65 .... 22–136, 22–138
s.67 .... 22–136, 22–138
s.69 ...... 22–020, 22–021, 22–022
s.70 .... 22–020, 22–114
s.71 22–066
(3) 22–052
(4) 25–194
s.73 .... 22–019, 22–032
s.74(1) 22–114
s.75A 22–047
s.76 9–030
s.81 9–030
s.81A 9–030
s.89(4) 22–040
s.90 .... 7–046, 7–099, 18–105
s.91 .... 22–050, 22–103
s.92 .... 22–044, 22–126
(b) 22–044
s.93 .... 22–135, 22–137
s.94 22–135
s.97(2) 22–033
1883 Revenue Act (46 & 47 Vict. c.55)—
s.17 22–030
1887 Merchandise Marks Act (50 & 51 Vict. c.28) 14–112
1888 Law of Distress Amendment Act (51 & 52 Vict. c.21) 7–111

1889 Factors Act (52 & 53 Vict. c.45) 1–018, 1–077, 1–082, 3–002, 7–031, 7–032, 7–036, 7–044, 7–046, 7–047, 7–051, 7–052, 7–054, 7–069, 15–009, 18–083, 18–070, 18–197, 25–135, A–030
s.1 7–055
(1) 1–018, 3–004, 7–032, 7–043, 7–055, 7–063, 7–069, 7–078
(2) 5–122, 7–034, 7–035, 7–057, 7–072, 15–038
(3) 1–079, 7–035, 7–055, 7–069
(4) 5–065, 7–034, 7–036, 7–039, 7–042, 7–049, 7–055, 7–069, 7–072, 8–013, 15–097, 18–006, 18–009, 18–010, 18–013, 18–018, 18–078, 18–083, 18–164, 18–167, 18–196, 18–201, 18–205, 18–207, 21–054, 21–061, 21–068, 21–083
(5) 7–049, 7–055, 7–063, 7–069, 7–079, 7–080, 7–083, 15–099
(6) 7–034, 7–055, 7–069
ss.2–4 15–099
s.2 ... 1–018, 3–002, 5–156, 7–013, 7–036, 7–068, 7–070, 7–074, 7–075, 7–077, 7–081, 7–086, 7–108, 12–020, 15–009, 18–006, 18–087, 18–070, 25–131
(1) 1–065, 7–034, 7–038, 7–048, 7–081, 18–237
(2) 7–038, 7–040, 7–071, 7–076
(3) 7–039, 7–074
(4) 7–037, 7–074
ss.3–5 7–063
s.3 ... 7–049, 7–051, 7–069, 7–079, 7–083, 18–197
s.4 ... 7–049, 7–051, 7–069, 7–079, 7–080, 7–083, 18–088
s.5 ... 7–042, 7–049, 7–051, 7–064, 7–080, 7–083
s.5, proviso 7–050
s.6 .... 7–032, 7–041, 7–043
s.7(1) 7–053
(2) 7–053
s.8 ... 1–018, 3–002, 5–004, 5–121, 7–031, 7–036, 7–047, 7–055, 7–063, 7–065, 7–084, 7–108, 15–009, 15–102, 18–006, 18–087, 18–070, 20–084

1882 Bills of Exchange Act—*cont.*
s.9 ... 1–018, 1–052, 3–002, 5–004, 5–122, 5–139, 5–156, 7–031, 7–036, 7–047, 7–065, 7–069, 7–077, 7–079, 7–082, 7–083, 7–084, 7–108, 8–013, 15–009, 15–092, 15–100, 18–006, 18–087, 18–070, 25–147
s.10 .. 1–018, 7–031, 7–036, 7–072, 8–013, 15–009, 15–097, 18–006, 18–086, 18–087
s.11 .. 7–036, 7–042, 7–055, 7–062, 7–069, 7–077, 15–097
s.12 7–031
(1) 7–054
(2) 3–045, 7–050, 7–051, 7–054
(3) 7–048
s.13 7–031
1890 Inland Revenue Regulation Act (53 & 54 Vict. c.21)—
s.40 22–024
Partnership Act (53 & 54 Vict. c.39) 1–002
s.14 13–077
Factors (Scotland) Act (53 & 54 Vict. c.40) 1–018, A–030
Bills of Sale Act (53 & 54 Vict. c.53) 1–016, 1–017
1891 Bills of Sale Act (54 & 55 Vict. c.35) 1–016, 1–017, 18–238
Stamp Act (54 & 55 Vict. c.39) 1–078
s.54 1–027
s.55 1–027
s.59(1) 1–030
Sch. 1–078
1892 Betting and Loans (Infants) Act (55 & 56 Vict. c.4)—
s.5 2–035
1893 Sale of Goods Act (56 & 57 Vict. c.71) 1–001, 1–002, 1–003, 1–004, 1–006, 1–008, 1–009, 1–012, 1–014, 1–027, 1–030, 1–081, 3–045, 4–002, 4–006, 4–032, 5–016, 5–017, 5–030, 5–034, 5–035, 5–040, 5–059, 5–068, 5–094, 5–096, 5–138, 6–029, 7–022, 7–037, 8–018, 8–080, 9–002, 10–008, 10–026, 10–027, 11–003, 11–006, 11–013, 11–024, 11–025, 11–027, 11–029, 11–031, 11–041, 11–055, 11–074, 12–023, 12–081, 13–083, 15–001, 15–007, 15–010,

1893 Sale of Goods Act—*cont.* .. 15–013, 15–014, 15–024, 15–029, 15–036, 15–061, 15–074, 15–077, 15–092, 15–094, 15–128, 16–021, 16–061, 17–051, 17–054, 17–096, 17–099, 18–234, A–031, A–034, A–035, A–036
s.1(1) 1–001
(2) 1–052, 1–080
s.4 .. 1–092, 2–021, 2–022, 12–044, 15–050
(1) 7–077, 8–009
(3) 9–002
s.7 .... A–034
s.11(1)(b) 10–027, 10–031
(c) .. 4–009, 5–019, 10–018, 10–026, 12–039, 12–046, 12–057, A–034
ss.12–15 .... 1–052, A–034
s.12 .... 4–032, A–034
(1) 4–002
(a) 4–002
(2) 4–025
(3) 4–023, 4–028
s.13 .... 13–061, A–034
s.14 ...... 1–082, 11–024, 11–025, 13–061, 17–072, A–034
(1) ... 11–025, 11–031, 11–051, 11–060, 11–070, 17–059
(2) 4–003, 11–006, 11–025, 11–027
(3) 14–024
(5) 11–068
s.15 .... 13–061, A–034
s.19(3) 18–212
s.21 .... A–034
s.22(2) 1–012
s.24 .... A–036
s.25 8–013
(1) 7–055
(2) 7–068, A–034
s.26 .. 1–001, 7–113, A–035, A–036
s.30(1) 9–014
(3) 9–014
s.34(1) 12–050
s.35 .... 12–050, 12–053
s.45(1) 15–068, 21–070
s.47 8–013
s.47 proviso 15–097
s.50(3) 16–065
s.51(3) 16–071
s.52 .... 1–108, 17–096, 17–098
s.55 ...... 11–001, 13–083, 14–142
(3)–(11) 13–057
(4) 13–079
s.57 16–094
s.60 .... 17–096, A–036

1893 Sale of Goods Act—*cont.*
s.61(1) 1–089
(2) ... 10–008, 10–031, 12–023
s.62 .... A–034
(1) 1–078, 1–079, 1–082, 1–090, 1–093, A–034
Sch A–036
1894 Merchant Shipping Act (57 & 58 Vict. c.60)—
s.497 7–111
s.498 7–111
1895 Law of Distress Amendment Act (58 & 59 Vict. c.24) 7–111
1897 Police (Property) Act (60 & 61 Vict. c.30)—
s.1(1) 7–006
s.2 .... 7–006, 7–111
s.2A 7–006, 7–111
1900 Money-lenders Act (63 & 64 Vict. c.51) 7–090, 14–143
s.6 11–028
1904 Trafford Park Act (c.ccxxv)—
ss.33, 34 18–198
1906 Fertilisers and Feeding Stuffs Act (6 Edw. 7 c.27) 14–097
Marine Insurance Act (6 Edw. 7 c.41) 1–002
ss.4–8 6–012
s.5(1) 5–012
s.5(2) 5–012
s.14(2) 5–012
s.20 10–007
s.22 19–047
s.26(3) 5–012
s.31(2) 18–059
s.33(3) 18–059
s.46(1) 18–059
s.50(3) 19–042, 19–047
ss.56–61 .... 6–035, 12–084
Sch.1, r.17 1–079
1908 Statute Law Revision Act (8 Edw. 7 c.49) A–036
Law of Distress Amendment Act (8 Edw. 7 c.53)—
s.1 5–014
s.4 7–111
s.4A 7–111
1914 Bankruptcy Act (4 & 5 Geo. 5 c.59) 1–012, 3–045, 5–166
s.38(c) 3–047, 5–166, 18–236
s.43 5–168
Welsh Church Act (4 & 5 Geo. 5 c.91)—
s.37 22–135
1916 Larceny Act (6 & 7 Geo. 5 c.50)—
s.1(3) 1–079

1917 Bills of Exchange (Time of Noting) Act (7 & 8 Geo. 5 c.48)—
s.1 22–137
1920 Overseas Trade (Credits and Insurance) Act (10 & 11 Geo. 5 c.29) 24–007
1921 Liverpool Mineral and Metal Storage Co. Ltd. (Delivery Warrants) Act (c.iii)—
s.3 18–198
s.4 18–198
1922 Finance Act (12 & 13 Geo.5 c.17)—
s.21(6) 24–008
1924 Carriage of Goods by Sea Act (14 & 15 Geo. 5 c.22) .. 18–059
Sch 21–047
1925 Settled Land Act (15 & 16 Geo. 5 c.18)—
s.38 1–100
s.49(2) 1–100
s.66 1–100
s.90 1–100
Law of Property Act (15 & 16 Geo. 5 c.20) 1–092
s.40 .... 1–092, 2–022
s.41 8–026
s.52 1–097
s.76 4–023
s.136 .... 5–161, 18–147
(1) 18–097, 18–147
(2) 18–147
s.146 16–038
s.205(1)(ix) 1–092
(xxi) 1–027
(xxiv) 1–027
Sch.2, Pt 1 4–023
Administration of Estates Act (15 & 16 Geo. 5 c.23)—
s.39(1) 7–110
1926 Fertilisers and Feeding Stuffs Act (16 & 17 Geo. 5 c.45)—
s.2(2) 14–094, 17–077, 19–001, 25–171
1927 Auctions (Bidding Agreements) Act (17 & 18 Geo. 5 c.12)—
s.1(2) 3–009
Moneylenders Act (17 & 18 Geo. 5 c.21) 14–143
Landlord and Tenant Act (17 & 18 Geo. 5 c.36)—
s.19(1) 23–078
1928 Currency and Bank Notes Act (18 & 19 Geo. 5 c.13) .. 22–019
1932 Carriage by Air Act (22 & 23 Geo. 5 c.36)—
Sch.1, art.5 21–052
1932 Bills of Exchange Act (1882) Amendment Act (22 & 23 Geo. 5 c.44)—
s.1 22–030
1934 Overseas Trade Act (24 & 25 Geo. 5 c.12) 24–007
Law Reform (Miscellaneous Provisions) Act (24 & 25 Geo. 5 c.41)—
s.3 .... 16–007, 23–107, 25–168
(1) 16–007
(c) 16–007
Finance Act (1 Edw. 8 & 1 Geo. 6 c.54)—
Sch.IV 24–008
1937 Export Guarantees Act (1 Edw. 8 & 1 Geo. 6 c.61) 24–007
1938 Hire-Purchase Act (1 & 2 Geo. 6 c.53)—
s.8 13–007
(3) 13–053
1939 Export Guarantees Act (2 & 3 Geo. 6 c.5) 24–007
War Risks Insurance Act (2 & 3 Geo. 6 c.57) A–034
s.15(1)(e) A–034
Import, Export and Customs Powers (Defence) Act (2 & 3 Geo. 6 c.69) 18–308
Trading with the Enemy Act (2 & 3 Geo. 6 c.89)—
s.1(2) 6–042
(3) 6–042
s.2(1) 6–042
s.15(3) 6–042
(5) 6–042
Finance (No.2) Act (2 & 3 Geo. 6 c.109)—
s.13(3) 24–008
(9) 24–008
1940 Finance Act (3 & 4 Geo. 6 c.29)—
s.55 24–008

1943 Law Reform (Frustrated Contracts) Act (6 & 7 Geo. 6 c.40) 6–001, 6–006, 6–039, 6–047, 6–058, 6–059, 6–069, 16–007, 18–136, 18–331, 18–342, 19–142, 19–143, 20–104, 21–018, 25–176, 25–191, A–034
s.1 ... 6–069, 6–070, 6–071, 22–011
(1) 25–176
(2) 6–060, 6–063, 6–066, 6–068, 6–071, 18–292, 19–143, 20–104
s.1(3) 6–061, 6–063, 6–064, 6–066, 6–068, 6–071, 19–143, 20–104
(a) 6–061, 6–063, 6–066
(b) 6–061, 6–063
(4) 6–060, 6–061
(5) 6–060, 6–061, 6–063, 6–070, 19–143, 20–104
(6) 6–061, 6–064
s.2(1) 18–292, 19–143, 21–018
(3) 6–063, 6–065, 6–071, 18–292, 19–142
(4) 6–062, 6–069, 6–071, 19–143, 20–104
(5)(c) 1–030, 1–041, 1–116, 6–058, 19–143, A–034
1945 Law Reform (Contributory Negligence) Act (8 & 9 Geo. 6 c.28) 6–034, 12–121, 14–084, 16–051
s.1(1) 16–051
s.4 6–034
Water Act (8 & 9 Geo 6 c.42)—
s.27 13–098
(2) 13–098
Bretton Woods Agreements Act (9 & 10 Geo. 6 c.19) 25–120
1947 Frustrated Contracts Act (Northern Ireland) (c.2) A–034
s.2(5)(c) A–034
Exchange Control Act (10 & 11 Geo. 6 c.14) 22–001
Transport Act (10 & 11 Geo. 6 c.49)—
s.29 1–070
1948 Companies Act (11 & 12 Geo. 6 c.38)—
s.95 .. 5–149, 5–150, 5–161, 18–238
(1) 5–142, 5–143
(2) 5–142
(c) 5–150
(f) 5–144
s.108(4) 1–085
Export Guarantees Act (11 & 12 Geo. 6 c.54) 24–007
1949 Export Guarantees Act (12, 13 & 14 Geo. 6 c.14) 24–007
1952 Customs and Excise Act (15 & 16 Geo. 6 & 1 Eliz. 2 c.44)—
s.4 1–084
1953 Emergency Laws (Miscellaneous Provisions) Act (1 & 2 Eliz. 2 c.47)—
s.2 6–042
Sch.2
para.2(1) 6–042
(2) 6–042
Sch.3
para.3(a) 6–042
(b) 6–042
Merchandise Marks Act (1 & 2 Eliz. 2 c.48) 14–112
1954 Currency and Bank Notes Act (2 & 3 Eliz. 2 c.12)—
s.1 9–028
(2) 15–022
(6) 15–022
Law Reform (Enforcement of Contracts) Act (2 & 3 Eliz. 2 c.34) 1–092, 12–044
s.1 2–022
Hire-Purchase Act (2 & 3 Eliz. 2 c.51)—
s.54 1–052
1956 Hotel Proprietors Act (4 & 5 Eliz. 2 c.62) 7–111
1957 Cheques Act (5 & 6 Eliz. 2 c.36)—
s.1(1) 22–026
(2)(b) 22–027
s.4(1) 22–028
(b) 22–073
(2)(d) 22–027, 22–028
s.5 22–030
s.6(3) 22–030
1958 Trading Representations (Disabled Persons) Act (6 & 7 Eliz. 2 c.49) 14–141

1959 Restriction of Offensive Weapons Act (c.37)—
s.1 2–002
1960 Corporate Bodies' Contracts Act (8 & 9 Eliz. 2 c.46)—
s.1 2–021
1961 Restriction of Offensive Weapons Act (9 & 10 Eliz. 2 c.22)—
s.1 2–002
Carriage by Air Act (9 & 10 Eliz. 2 c.27) 21–051
s.1 21–047
(1) 21–052
(3) 21–055
(5)(a) 21–047
(b) 21–047
(c) 21–047
(6) 21–051
Sch.1—The Warsaw Convention as amended at the Hague in 1955 and by Protocols No.3 and No.4 signed at Montreal in 1975 (1955 amended Convention) .. 21–047, 21–051, 21–055, 21–077, 21–105
art.1(2) 21–051
art.2(2) 21–051
art.5 21–052
art.6 21–052
(2) 21–053
art.11(1) 21–052
art.12 21–055
(1) 21–052
(3) .. 21–052, 21–054, 21–067
(4) .. 21–052, 21–055, 21–057
art.13 5–009
(1) .. 21–052, 21–055, 21–057
(2) 21–052
art.14 5–009
art.15 21–106
(1) 21–055, 21–062
(2) 21–052
(3) 21–052, 21–061
art.22(5) 25–194
art.24 5–009
art.31 .... 21–051, 21–077, 21–104, 21–106
art.34 21–051
Sch.1A—The Warsaw Convention with the Amendments made in it by The Hague Protocol and Protocol No.4 of Montreal 1975 (MP4 Convention) .. 21–047, 21–051, 21–077, 21–104, 21–105
art.1(2) 21–051
art.12(2) 21–054
Sch.1B—Montreal Convention 1999 ...... 21–047, 21–051, 21–054, 21–104
art.4(1) 21–052
(2) 21–052
art.38 .... 21–051, 21–077, 21–104
Factories Act (9 & 10 Eliz. 2, c.34) 17–075
Consumer Protection Act (9 & 10 Eliz. 2 c.40) 14–114
ss.1, 2 14–114
Mock Auctions Act (9 & 10 Eliz. 2 c.47) 14–141
s.3(1) 2–004
Housing Act (9 & 10 Eliz. 2 c.65)—
s.33 13–007
1962 Carriage by Air (Supplementary Provisions) Act (10 & 11 Eliz. 2 c.43) 21–047
Transport Act (10 & 11 Eliz. 2 c.46) 13–007
1963 Weights & Measures Act (c.31) 14–111
1964 Plant Varieties and Seeds Act (c.14) 14–096, 14–097
s.16 14–096
s.17 14–096
(1) 13–053
(5) 14–097
Continental Shelf Act (c.29)—
s.1 1–097
Hire-Purchase Act (c.53) 1–019, 1–020, 1–052, 1–053, 1–083, 7–046, 7–099, 7–108, A–034
Pt III 1–019, 1–052, 7–087, 7–088, 7–090, 7–091, 7–092, 7–100, 7–105, 7–108, 14–007, 25–131
ss.27–29 .... 1–006, 7–087
s.27 ...... 3–014, 7–106, 11–027, 13–073
(1) 7–088, 7–094, 14–007
(2) 7–094, 7–097, 7–098, 7–105
(3) 4–004, 7–094, 7–095, 7–096, 7–097, 7–098, 7–105, 7–106

1964 Hire-Purchase Act—*cont.*
s.27(4) 7–094, 7–096, 7–097, 7–105
(5) 2–022, 7–108, A–034
(6) 4–004, 7–104, 7–106
s.28 .... 7–099, 7–104
(1) 7–091, 7–100
(2) 7–091, 7–101
(3) 7–102
(4) 7–103
(5) 7–104
s.29 1–020
(1) 1–053, 1–083, 7–087, 7–088, 7–091
(2) 7–092
(3) 7–091, 7–099
(4) 7–087, 7–089
(5) 7–098, 7–107
s.37 1–019
Emergency Laws (Re-enactments and Repeals) Act (c.60) 18–308
Trading Stamps Act (c.71) ... 1–040, 11–050, 13–085
s.4 1–040
1965 Carriage of Goods by Road Act (c.37) 21–047, 21–058, 21–104
s.1(1) 21–058
(2) 21–062
s.2 21–058
s.14(2) 21–058
Sch 21–058
art.1(1) 21–058
(2) 21–105
art.2 21–059
(1) 21–058, 21–059
art.3 21–058
art.4 .... 21–059, 21–060
art.5 21–060
art.9 21–060
art.12 25–187
(1) 21–060, 21–106
(2) .. 21–060, 21–063, 21–064
(3) .. 21–060, 21–062, 21–064
(4) 21–060
(5) 21–060
(a) 21–060
art.13 ..... 5–009, 21–060, 21–106, 25–187, 25–202
art.15(1) 21–060
art.23(3) 21–104
art.27(2) 25–194
art.34 21–058
Protocol of Signature 21–058
Nuclear Installations Act (c.57)—
s.12 14–082
1965 Hire-Purchase Act (c.66) 1–019, 1–021, 1–052, 7–087, 14–143, 14–147, A–034
s.1(1) 1–052, 1–053, 1–055
s.5 .... 2–023, 3–003
s.12(3) 1–054
ss.17–20 1–052
s.20 .... 1–052, A–034
s.29 1–054
(3)(c) 1–052
s.31 1–054
s.54 .... 1–052, A–034
s.58 1–054
(1) A–034
(3) A–033
(5) A–033
s.59(4) 7–087
Sch.5 7–087
Hire-Purchase (Scotland) Act (c.67) A–034
s.20 .... A–034
s.50 .... A–034
s.54(1) A–034
(3) A–033
(5) A–033
1966 Hire-Purchase Act (Northern Ireland) A–034
s.20 .... A–034
s.54 .... A–034
s.62(5) A–034
s.65(1) A–034
(3) A–033
(5) A–033
1967 Misrepresentation Act (c.7) .. 1–009, 1–011, 10–008, 10–009, 10–010, 10–018, 10–026, 10–040, 12–050, 12–052, 12–063, 12–119, 13–056, 13–064, 13–079, 13–087, 13–089, 13–107, 16–090
s.1 10–040
(a) 12–119, 13–058
(b) 12–005, 15–115, 15–118
s.2 13–058
(1) 4–022, 10–010, 10–011, 10–013, 12–002, 12–004, 12–012, 12–013, 12–014, 12–016, 13–059, 14–041, 17–089, 18–045, 19–200, 25–205
(2) 4–022, 12–004, 12–005, 12–010, 12–027, 15–118, 15–125
(3) 12–004
s.3 .... 4–022, 13–008, 13–030, 13–041, 13–053, 13–054, 13–055, 13–060, 13–065, 13–067, 13–069, 13–084, 13–087, 13–090, 13–091,

1967 Misrepresentation Act—*cont.*
s.3 ..... 13–099, 13–100, 13–101, 13–107, 14–041
s.4 .... 1–001, 10–008, 12–046, A–035
(1) 4–009, 5–019, 12–038
(2) 12–050, A–035
s.6(3) A–035
Export Guarantees Act (c.11) 24–007
Uniform Laws on International Sales Act (c.45) 1–079, 25–003, A–034
s.1(3) 18–003, 25–003
(4) A–034
(c) 25–160
Sch.1 ..... 5–002, 18–003, 18–004, 25–003, 25–025, 25–026, 25–099, 25–100, 25–160
art.1 21–023
(1) 1–024
art.3 18–003
art.4 .... A–034
art.5 1–079
art.9(3) 18–003, 18–004
art.71 19–076
art.72(1), (2) 19–076
art.73(3) 18–086
Sch.2 1–024
Industrial and Provident Societies Act 1967 (c.48)—
s.1(1) 1–016
Criminal Law Act (c.58)—
s.10(2) 1–012
Sch.3, Pt I 1–012
Misrepresentation Act (Northern Ireland)—
s.4 .... 1–001, A–035
1968 National Loans Act (c.13)—
s.10(4)(a) 24–007
(5) 24–007
Export Guarantees Act (c.26) 24–007
Trade Descriptions Act (c.29) ... 3–028, 10–001, 11–027, 12–012, 14–097, 14–107 14–109, 14–112, 14–132
s.1 14–112
(1) 11–027
s.2 14–112
s.3 14–112
s.4 14–112
s.5 14–112
s.7 14–112
s.8 14–112
s.9 14–112
s.11 14–124
s.14 14–108
(1) 14–112
1968 Trade Descriptions Act—*cont.*
s.19 14–108
s.20 14–108
s.23 14–108
s.24 14–108
s.28 14–108
s.29 14–108
s.35 .... 10–001, 14–097
Theft Act (c.60) 5–046, 7–006, 7–037, 7–074
s.1 5–046
s.4 1–079
(4) 1–088
s.13 1–085
s.15 5–046
(1) 7–115
s.16 .... 14–052A
s.21 7–115
s.22 .... 1–079, 4–001
s.23 1–079
s.24 .... 1–079, 4–001
s.26 1–079
s.28 .... 1–079, 7–006, 7–115
(3) 7–006
s.34(2)(b) 1–079
Medicines Act (c.67) 14–140
Pt VI 14–140
Port of London Act (c.xxxii)—
s.146(4) 18–198, 25–135
1969 Arbitration Act—
s.49(3) 25–191
Employers Liability (Defective Equipment) Act (c.37) 14–076, 17–075
Family Law Reform Act (c.46) 2–029
s.1 2–029
s.9 2–029
Auctions (Bidding Agreements) Act (c.56)—
s.3(1), (2) 3–009
1970 Export Guarantees and Payments Act (c.15) 24–007
Administration of Justice Act (c.31)—
s.40 .... 14–004, 14–141
s.44 16–013
s.44A 25–191
Agriculture Act (c.40) 14–097
Pt IV 14–094, 14–096, 14–097
s.65(4) 14–097
s.66(1) 14–094
s.68 14–096
(6) 13–053, 14–097
ss.69–71 14–096
s.71(4) 13–053, 14–097
s.72 ..... 14–094, 19–001, 25–171
(1) 14–094
(3) 13–054

1970 Matrimonial Proceedings and Property Act (c.45)—
s.41(1) 2–042, 3–007
1971 Unsolicited Goods and Services Act (c.30) 14–005
s.3A 14–005
Consumer Protection Act (c.15) 14–114
Carriage of Goods by Sea Act (c.19) . . 13–098, 18–013, 18–018, 18–028, 18–035, 18–044, 21–047, 21–106, 25–025, 25–072, 25–195
s.1 18–044
(2) 18–059, 18–149, 21–047, 21–092, 21–106
(3) 21–106
(4) 18–035, 18–044
(6)(a) 18–048, 21–106
(b) 18–018, 18–035, 18–044, 18–074, 21–047, 21–058, 21–059, 21–073, 21–081, 21–105, 21–106
Sch.—Hague Visby Rules . . 18–013, 18–018, 18–034, 18–035, 18–044, 18–067, 18–078, 18–121, 18–148, 18–272, 20–089, 21–058, 21–059, 21–065, 21–081, 21–082, 21–085, 21–087, 21–089, 21–092, 21–093, 21–104, 21–105, 21–106, 25–025, 25–071, 25–072, 25–195
art.I 1–079
(a) 18–034, 18–044
(b) . . 18–009, 18–044, 18–067, 21–047, 21–059, 21–104, 21–106
(c) . . . 18–272, 21–059, 21–089
(e) 20–089
art.II 18–034
art.III
r.1 18–142
r.2 18–142
r.3 . . . . . . 18–034, 18–037, 18–040, 18–167, 21–104
(a)–(c) 18–035
(a) 18–034
(b) 18–028, 18–034
(c) 18–028, 18–034
r.4 . . . . . . 18–028, 18–034, 18–035, 18–037, 18–038, 18–040, 18–042 18–044, 18–045, 18–152, 20–065
r.6 . . . . 18–059 18–116, 21–091, 21–092
r.7 . . . . 18–027, 21–104
r.8 21–106
1971 Sch.—Hague Visby Rules—*cont.*
art.IV
r.2 . . . . 21–090, 21–092, 21–093
r.4 21–093
r.5 . . . . 18–059, 21–091, 21–104
r.5(a) 21–085, 21–091, 21–092
r.5(c) 21–087, 21–092
art.IV*bis*(1) 18–121, 18–149, 18–151
art.V 21–059
art.VI 21–059, 21–106
art.X 18–044
1971 Coinage Act (c.24)—
s.2 . . . . 9–028, 15–022
Unsolicited Goods and Services Act (c.30) 14–004
s.1 . . . . 2–014, 14–004
(1) 14–004
(2) 14–004
s.2 14–004
s.3 14–004
s.6(2) 14–004
Banking and Financial Dealings Act (c.80) 22–044
s.1 22–044
s.2 22–044
s.3 22–044
(1) 22–044
(2) 22–044
1972 Overseas Investment and Export Guarantees Act (c.40) 24–048
s.1 24–007
s.2 24–007
Trading Representations (Disabled Persons) Amendment Act (c.45) 14–141
European Communities Act (c.68)—
s.2 3–041
(2) 6–014, 14–008, 14–045, 14–115, 14–140
s.9(1) 2–043
1973 Supply of Goods (Implied Terms) Act (c.13) 1–005, 1–006, 1–014, 1–020, 1–031, 1–052, 1–109, 11–010, 11–024, 11–025, 11–028, 11–029, 11–030, 11–031, 11–051, 11–052, 11–065, 11–068, 11–070, 11–088, 13–008, 13–047, 13–048, 13–053, 13–061, 13–083, 13–084, 13–079, 13–088, 13–089, 13–103, 13–105, 14–008, 14–142, 14–152, A–034
ss.1–7 . . . . 1–001, A–035

1973 Supply of Goods (Implied Terms) Act—*cont.*
s.1 .... 1–015, 4–002, 4–032
s.3 1–005
s.4 .... 13–084, 14–142
(5) 18–280
ss.8–11 14–152
s.8 .... 1–019, 4–035
s.9 11–023
s.10 .... 11–050, 11–069
(2) 1–020
(3) 1–020, 3–005
(4) 11–088
s.11 .... 1–019, 11–087
s.11A 12–024
s.12(1) 1–019
s.14 .... 1–019, 1–052, 4–009
(1) A–034
s.15 1–019
(1) 4–035, A–034
s.16 1–040
s.18(2) 1–001, A–035
Fair Trading Act (c.41) 3–040, 13–053, 13–063, 13–105, 14–097, 14–125, 14–126, 14–128, 14–131, 14–137, 14–142
Pt III 14–028, 14–040, 14–128, 14–129, 14–130, 14–140
Pt XI 14–141
s.1 14–125
s.2(3) 14–127
s.3 14–127
s.13 14–127
s.16 14–127
s.22 .... 1–006, 14–141
(2) 14–127
(4) 14–127
ss.23–33 14–127
s.24 14–108
s.26 .... 14–094, 14–097
s.29 14–108
s.30 14–108
ss.34–42 .... 14–128, 14–130
s.34 14–128
(1) 14–128
(2) 14–040, 14–128
(3) 14–128
s.37 14–128
s.119 14–141
s.124(3) 13–098
s.129 14–108
s.132 14–108
s.134(2) 1–006
s.137(2) 1–079, 1–085
Sch.5 14–127
Hallmarking Act (c.43) 14–112
Domicile and Matrimonial Proceedings Act (c.45)
s.5(2) 25–056

1973 Powers of Criminal Courts Act (c.62)—
s.35 14–106
1974 Prices Act (c.24)—
s.4 14–111
(1)(a) 14–111
(b) 14–111
Health and Safety at Work, etc., Act (c.37)—
s.6 14–116
s.15 14–115
s.47(2) 14–095
Consumer Credit Act (c.39) .. 1–016, 1–019, 1–020, 1–021, 1–022, 1–052, 1–053, 1–055, 3–003, 3–005, 5–021, 7–070, 7–088, 7–090, 7–111, 9–035, 9–036, 9–065, 9–066, 11–023, 11–028, 11–051, 11–056, 13–057, 14–133, 14–138, 14–140, 14–143, 14–147, 14–152, 15–134, 16–029, 16–038, 16–042, A–013, A–034
Pt IX 14–145
s.8 .... 9–066, 14–001, 14–143
(1) 5–021, 7–070, 9–065
(2) 1–021, 1–022, 1–055, 5–021, 7–070, 7–088, 7–108, 9–065, 14–147
(3) 1–022
s.9 .... 5–021, 9–065, 9–066
(1) 1–022, 14–143
(3) 7–088, 14–147
(4) 14–147
s.10 .... 9–066, 14–150
(1) 1–022
(a) 14–148, 14–149
(b) 14–147, 14–148
(3)(a) 14–148
(b) 14–148
s.11 14–154
(a) 14–147, 14–148, 14–149
(b) 14–149
s.12 1–022
(a) ... 14–147, 14–148, 14–149
(b) 14–149, 14–154
s.13 1–022
s.14 14–149
s.15 14–001
s.16 .... 1–022, 9–066, 14–143
(5) 1–022
(a) 1–055
s.16A 14–144
s.16B 7–088, 14–144
s.17 .... 1–021, 14–149
s.19 14–150
(1)(b) 14–150

1974 Consumer Credit Act—*cont.*
s.20 14–150
(1) 1–022
s.21(1) 14–146
s.23(3) 14–146
s.39(1) 14–146
s.40 14–146
ss.43–47 14–155
s.44 14–150
s.51 14–149
s.52 14–150
s.56 .... 1–054, 3–005, 10–013, 14–044, 14–153, 14–154
(1) 14–153
(b) 14–153
(c) 14–154
(2) 3–005, 14–153, 14–154
(3) 3–005, 13–057, 14–153
(b) 1–054
(4) 14–153
s.57 1–054
(3) 3–005, 13–063
ss.60–64 2–023
ss.60–65 25–088
s.60 ...... 7–090, 13–007, 14–145, 14–150
(3), (4) 2–023
s.61 .... 7–090, 14–145
ss.62–64 14–145
s.63(4) 14–149
s.64(2) 14–149
s.65 .... 2–023, 7–090
(1) 14–145
s.66 14–149
ss.67–73 ... 2–020, 14–045, 14–145
s.69 1–054
(1), (6) 3–005
s.70(5) 14–149
s.74(2) 1–021
s.75 .... 3–005, 9–036, 10–013, 14–154
(1) 14–154, 25–089
(2) 14–154
(3) 14–154
s.76 14–145
s.77 14–145
s.77A 14–145
s.78 14–145
(4) 14–145
s.81 9–046
s.83 9–036
s.84 .... 9–036, 14–149
s.85 14–149
s.87 14–145
ss.86A–86F 14–144
s.88 14–144
ss.90–92 14–145
s.90 .... 1–021, 7–002, 14–147
s.91 1–021
s.93 14–145

1974 Consumer Credit Act—*cont.*
s.94 14–145
s.95 14–145
s.96 14–145
s.97 14–145
s.98 14–145
s.99 .... 1–021, 14–147, 16–035
s.100 ...... 1–021, 14–147, 16–035
(1) 16–042
(3) 16–042
s.102 1–054
(1) 3–005
s.105 14–145
s.107 14–145
s.108 14–145
s.113(2) 2–023
s.120 7–111
s.121 7–111
s.126 14–145
ss.127–144 14–145
s.127 2–023
(3) 2–023, 3–003, 14–144, 14–145
s.129 ..... 14–035, 14–145, 14–147
s.130 1–021
(4) 7–089
s.131 1–021
s.133 .... 1–021, 14–147
s.134 .... 1–021, 14–147
s.136 14–035
ss.137–140 .... 1–021, 14–133, 14–150, 14–156, 15–134, 16–009, 16–042
s.137(2)(a) 1–021
s.138 14–150
(1) 16–042
s.139(2) 16–042
ss.140A–140D 14–150
s.141 14–145
s.145 14–146
(2) ... 3–005, 11–056, 14–146, 14–153
(a)(i) 11–056
(ii) 11–056
(b) 11–056
(c) 11–056
s.147 14–146
s.149 14–146
s.171(4) 14–149
s.173 13–007
(3) 2–023
s.179 14–149
s.187 14–154
s.189(1) 1–021, 1–022, 1–052, 1–053, 1–055, 1–062, 1–079, 3–005, 4–035, 5–005, 5–021, 5–044, 7–070, 7–088, 7–108, 9–065, 14–143, 14–144, 14–146, 14–147, 14–148, 14–153, 14–154, 16–029, A–034

1974 Consumer Credit Act—*cont.*
s.189(2) 14–146
s.192 . . . . 1–052, 1–053, 4–035, 7–070, 7–111
(4) 1–001, 1–052, 11–088, A–036
Sch.2, Pt II, Example 16 . . 14–149
Sch.3 14–143
Sch.4 . . . . 1–016, 7–087, 7–111, 14–007, 25–131, A–034
para.2 . . . . 1–052, 7–070
para.3 . . . . 1–001, A–035
para.4 . . . . 7–070, A–035
para.6(1) 1–019
para.22 . . . . 1–019, 1–053, 7–087
para.35 . . . . 4–035, 11–088
para.36 4–035
Sch.5 7–111
Solicitors Act (c.47)—
s.57 14–105
1975 Unsolicited Goods and Services Act (c.13) 14–005
Export Guarantees Act (c.38) 24–007
Litigants in Person (Costs and Expenses) Act (c.47) . . . 14–102
1976 Congenital Disabilities (Civil Liability) Act (c.28) 14–087
Fatal Accidents Act (c.30) . . . 16–051
Restrictive Practices Court Act (c.33) 3–040
Restrictive Trade Practices Act (c.34) 3–039, 3–040
Resale Prices Act (c.53) 3–037, 3–040
s.1 3–037
s.10 3–037
s.11 3–037
s.26 3–037
International Carriage of Perishable Foodstuffs Act (c.58)—
s.19 21–071
Insolvency Act (c.60) 3–045
Energy Act (c.76) 14–140
s.15(3) 14–140
Weights and Measures etc. Act 1976 (c.77) 14–111
1977 Restrictive Trade Practices Act (c.19) 3–040
Torts (Interference with Goods) Act (c.32) 3–032, 5–010, 14–007, 15–013, 15–088, 17–106
s.1 . . . . 5–003, 5–010
s.2 5–003
(1) 5–010, 7–002, 15–005, 15–116, 17–098
s.3 . . 4–012, 5–003, 15–116, 17–098
1977 Torts (Interference with Goods) Act—*cont.*
s.3(2) 4–012, 19–204
(a) . . 7–002, 15–116, 16–089, 17–098
(b) 7–002, 15–116
(c) 7–002
(3)(b) . . . 7–002, 15–116, 17–098
(4) 15–116, 17–098
(6) 4–013, 15–116, 17–098
(7) 4–007, 7–005
s.4 7–002
s.5 1–072
(1) 1–072, 4–012, 4–013
(b) 1–072
(2) 1–072
(3) 1–072, 4–012, 4–013
(4) 4–012
(5) 4–012
s.6 4–029
(1) 4–007, 7–005, 14–007
(2) 4–007, 7–005
(3) 4–007
(4) 4–007, 7–005
s.7(1) 5–010
(2) 5–010
(3) 5–010
(4) 5–010
s.8 . . . . 1–072, 15–096
(1) 5–010, 15–077
(2) 5–010
s.9 4–014
(3) 4–007
s.10(1) 5–125, 5–129
(b) 5–121
s.11(1) 4–012, 6–034, 7–002
s.12 . . . . 3–006, 7–111, 14–004, 15–106
(1) 4–014, 4–017
(2)(b) 4–012
s.13 . . . . . . 7–111, 14–004, 15–106
s.14(1) 1–079
Price Commission Act (c.33)—
s.16 14–111
Patents Act (c.37) 3–036
s.44 3–036
Administration of Justice Act (c.38)—
s.4 25–194
Unfair Contract Terms Act (c.50) 1–001, 1–006, 1–013, 1–014, 1–031, 1–042, 1–092, 2–004, 4–018, 4–020, 6–014, 6–025, 8–063, 8–088, 9–026, 11–005, 11–011, 11–027, 11–059, 12–016, 12–121, 13–008, 13–010, 13–011, 13–012, 13–016, 13–020,

1977 Unfair Contract Terms Act (c.50)—*cont.* ... 13–021, 13–022, 13–030, 13–041, 13–046, 13–047, 13–053, 13–055, 13–056, 13–059, 13–062, 13–063, 13–064, 13–067, 13–069, 13–070, 13–077, 13–079, 13–083, 13–084, 13–088, 13–089, 13–092, 13–094, 13–099, 13–102, 13–103, 13–105, 13–106, 13–107, 14–028, 14–029, 14–030, 14–031, 14–036, 14–037, 14–038, 14–040, 14–041, 14–042, 14–047, 14–052A, 14–071, 14–083, 14–100, 14–112, 14–132, 14–142, 14–152, 16–011, 16–036, 16–037, 17–049, 18–005, 18–259, 18–264, 18–275, 18–280, 18–281, 18–282, 18–282, 18–283, 18–292, 18–342, 19–048, 20–094, 20–110, 20–113, 22–089, 22–093, 25–042, 25–090, 25–097, 25–099, 25–100, 25–104, 25–114, 25–115, 25–118, 25–160, 25–169, 25–171, A–027
Pt I 8–051, 12–050, 12–073, 13–055, 14–008, 14–010, 14–011, A–030
Pt I ... 4–021, 5–098, 6–013, 6–025
Pt II 13–063
Pt III 13–063
s.1 13–092
(3) 1–006, 1–031, 11–028, 13–063, 13–070, 13–083, 13–085, 13–092, 13–094
ss.2–7 .... 1–013, 25–091, 25–093, 25–118
ss.2–4 1–092
s.2 ...... 13–064, 13–066, 13–087, 13–092, 13–094, 13–097, 13–103, 13–106, 14–029, 14–042, 14–052A, 14–069, 25–090, 25–091
(1) 13–087, 13–092, 13–106, 14–036, 14–069, 14–142
(2) 13–093, 13–096, 13–106, 14–069
(3) 13–096, 13–106
s.3 ... 1–006, 2–033, 6–031, 8–104, 9–026, 12–117, 13–064, 13–087, 13–092, 13–094, 13–097, 13–099, 13–102, 13–103, 14–029, 14–042, 14–052A, 14–069, 18–280, 18–281, 25–091

1977 Unfair Contract Terms Act—*cont.*
s.3(1) 13–094, 19–014
(2)(a) 13–094
(b) 8–104
(i) 13–094, 14–038
(ii) 13–094 19–014
s.4 .... 1–006, 13–087, 13–097, 13–099, 14–029 14–069, 25–091
ss.5–7 .... 13–064, 13–066
s.5 .... 1–006, 13–017, 13–097, 14–042, 14–069, 14–142, 25–091, 25–115
(2)(a) 14–001, 14–069
(b) 14–069
(3) 14–069
s.6 ... 1–006, 1–030, 1–031, 1–041, 4–018, 9–026, 12–117, 13–064, 13–066, 13–083, 13–084, 13–085, 13–087, 13–092, 13–093, 13–094, 13–096, 13–097, 14–029, 14–042, 14–069, 14–142, 18–280, 18–281, 25–091, 25–160, A–034
(1) 1–014, 1–015, 1–041, 13–063, 13–083
(a) 4–018, 4–031, 4–034, 14–029, 25–160, 25–171
(b) 4–035
(2) 1–006, 11–047, 13–030, 13–064, 13–083, 13–084, 13–087, 13–103, 14–019, 14–028, 14–037, 14–083, 18–280
(a) 13–064, 13–083, 14–029, 25–115, 25–171
(b) 13–083
(3) 2–033, 13–083, 13–084, 13–087, 18–280
(4) 1–006, 4–018, 13–063, 13–070, 13–083
s.7 .. 1–030, 1–031, 1–041, 13–085, 13–087, 13–088, 13–092, 13–093, 13–096, 14–042, 14–069, 25–091
(1) 13–085
(2) 13–085, 14–047, 14–142
(3) 13–085
(3A) 4–036, 13–085, 14–047
(4) 1–041, 13–085
s.8 ...... 4–022, 14–052A, 25–093
(1) 13–054
s.9(1) 13–046
s.10 .... 13–097, 14–069
s.11 .... 1–006, 14–029, 22–089
(1) 6–014, 13–020, 13–054, 13–055, 13–060, 13–079, 13–087, 13–096

1977 Unfair Contract Terms Act—*cont.*
s.11(2) ... 13–012, 13–013, 13–020, 13–088
(3) 13–066, 13–107
(4) ... 13–060, 13–089, 13–091, 13–096
(5) ... 13–079, 13–092, 14–037, 25–205
s.12 ...... 4–018, 11–027, 13–010, 13–011, 13–070, 13–071, 14–001 14–002, 14–008, 14–010, 14–011, 14–071, 14–112, 18–259, 25–098
(1) ... 11–028, 13–083, 18–280, 18–282, 25–045, 25–099, 25–111
(a) 14–011, 14–029
(b) 14–029, 14–037
(c) 14–011, 14–029, 14–037, 14–069
(1A) 14–011, 14–029
(2) ... 13–080, 14–029, 14–037, 25–205
(a) 14–011
(3) 13–082
s.13 ...... 4–018, 12–073, 13–057, 13–064, 13–087, 14–142
(1) ... 13–064, 13–065, 13–066, 13–097, 13–107
(b) 9–026, 13–097, 18–275, 18–280, 25–115
(2) ... 13–055, 13–069, 14–100
(3) 25–205
s.14 ...... 1–079, 13–066, 13–075, 14–142, A–034
s.15 14–142
ss.16–17 1–013
ss.16–21 25–091
s.16 13–087
s.17 .... 13–087, 13–095
s.18 13–087
s.20 1–006
s.20(1)(a) 25–171, A–034
(2)(a) 25–171, A–034
s.22 .... 18–281, 25–114
s.25(1) 1–079, 12–024, A–030, A–034
s.26 .. 1–006, 1–014, 4–035, 4–036, 13–099, 18–275, 18–281, 19–014, 25–090, 25–098, 25–104, 25–114, 25–160
(1) 4–018, 18–275
(2) 13–099
(3) 4–018, 25–090, 25–114
(a) 18–281
(b) 18–281
(4) 4–018, 18–281, 25–114
(a) 18–281
(b) 18–281

1977 Unfair Contract Terms Act—*cont.*
s.26(4)(c) 18–281
s.27 ...... 1–013, 4–036, 13–098, 14–028, 25–090, 25–112, 25–113, 25–118
(1) 1–014, 4–018, 4–035, 13–100, 18–281, 25–090, 25–091, 25–092, 25–093, 25–103, 25–104, 25–118, 25–160, 25–162
(2) 4–018, 4–035, 13–101, 25–040, 25–090, **25–094**, 25–096, 25–098, 25–099, 25–100, 25–103, 25–104, 25–113, 25–115, 25–116, 25–117, 25–156, 25–160, 25–163
(a) 25–094, 25–099, 25–097, 25–098, 25–099, 25–116
(b) 25–048, 25–090, 25–094, 25–096, 25–098, 25–099, 25–103, 25–116
(3) 25–090
s.29 13–098
(1) 14–031
(a) 18–292
(b) 18–283
s.31(1) 13–062
(2) 1–001, 13–062
Sch.1 14–031
para.1(a) 14–031, 19–048
(b) 1–092
Sch.2 ..... 1–006, 13–013, 13–088, 13–090, 13–096, 14–029, 14–034, 18–280
para.(a) 2–033, 14–034, 18–280
(c) 18–280
Sch.3 .... 1–001, A–035
para.1(1)(a) 18–292
para.8 18–281
Sch.4 1–001
1978 Export Guarantees and Overseas Investment Act (c.18) 24–007, 24–009
Interpretation Act (c.30)—
s.4(a) 14–008
s.5 .... 7–088, 22–036, 24–008
s.6 11–056
(c) 2–026
s.17 .... A–031
Sch.1 .... 7–088, 22–036, 24–008
Theft Act (c.31)—
s.3 5–013
State Immunity Act (c.33)—
s.3(3)(b) 23–135
Consumer Safety Act (c.38) 14–114, 14–115

1978 Consumer Safety Act—*cont.*
s.1 14–115
s.3 14–117
Civil Liability (Contribution) Act (c.47) 4–014, 14–083
s.1 4–014
(1) 16–049
1979 Carriage by Air and Road Act (c.28) 21–047, 21–058
s.4(1) 25–194
(2) 21–104
Sch.1
art.5(1) 21–052
(2) 21–052
art.6 21–052
(2) 21–052
art.11(1) 21–052
art.12(1) 21–052
(3) 21–052
(4) .. 21–052, 21–055, 21–057
art.13(1) .. 21–052, 21–055, 21–057
(2) 21–052
art.15 21–106
art.31 21–051
Estates Agents Act (c.38) ... 14–138
s.3(1)(d) 14–138
s.4 14–138
Merchant Shipping Act (c.39)—
s.17 18–149
Sch.4 18–149
Weights and Measures Act (c.45) 14–111
Sale of Goods Act (c.54) 1–001, 1–004, 1–005, 1–006, 1–007, 1–009, 1–014, 1–015, 1–017, 1–018, 1–019, 1–021, 1–027, 1–030, 1–031, 1–039, 1–040, 1–041, 1–052, 1–055, 1–056, 1–057, 1–062, 1–064, 1–065, 1–067, 1–071, 1–075, 1–076, 1–078, 1–081, 1–086, 1–088, 1–092, 1–093, 1–095, 1–096, 1–097, 1–101, 1–104, 1–112, 1–114, 1–115, 2–001, 2–019, 2–022, 2–026, 2–044, 2–045, 3–001, 3–045, 3–048, 4–035, 4–036, 5–002, 5–034, 5–060, 5–090, 5–122, 6–014, 7–047, 7–109, 8–018, 8–074, 9–005, 10–029, 10–033, 10–036, 11–028, 11–039, 11–078, 11–089, 12–009, 12–022, 12–023, 12–038,
1979 Sale of Goods Act (c.54)—*cont.* ... 12–057, 12–060, 12–074, 12–078, 12–079, 12–080, 12–119, 12–120, 12–129, 13–025, 13–042, 13–061, 13–062, 13–064, 13–088, 14–005, 14–006, 14–008, 14–013, 14–028, 14–047, 14–050, 14–132, 14–152, 15–001, 15–007, 15–009, 15–038, 15–061, 15–112, 16–016, 16–043, 16–046, 17–088, 17–096, 17–100, 17–102, 18–010, 18–013, 18–018, 18–137, 18–196, 18–197, 18–205, 18–243, 18–244, 18–251, 18–255, 18–259, 18–260, 18–299, 19–008, 19–012, 19–101, 19–108, 19–203, 19–220, 20–094, 20–111, 20–129, 21–054, 21–055, 21–056, 21–057, 21–061, 21–062, 21–063, 21–064, 21–068, 21–069, 21–070, 21–071, 21–083, 25–111, 25–133, 25–180, A–034
Pt 5 ..... 13–077, 13–078, 13–079, 15–013
Pt 5A 6–016, 8–045, 12–071, 12–080, 12–083, 12–085, 12–090, 12–092, 12–093, 12–095, 12–096, 12–097, 12–098, 12–102, 12–103, 12–104, 12–105, 12–106, 12–108, 12–109, 12–111, 12–114, 12–115, 12–116, 12–117, 12–118, 13–011, 13–071, 13–072, 13–081, 13–083, 14–002, 14–005, 14–023, 14–028, 14–049, 14–150, 16–002, 17–003, 17–048, 17–050, 17–059, 17–094, 17–096, 17–101, 17–103, 18–284, 19–012, 19–065, 19–077, 19–111, 19–123, 19–144, 19–194, 19–203, 19–206, 20–029, 20–038, 20–074, 20–105, 20–110, 20–113, 20–120, 20–122, 21–102
s.1 .... 4–023, **A–002**, A–033
(1) 1–001, 1–034
(2) 1–001
(3) 1–001
(4) 1–001, 21–022
(6) 6–037

1979 Sale of Goods Act—*cont.*
s.2 ... 1–019, 1–025, 1–029, 1–030, 1–063, 2–026, 2–051, 13–021, 18–088, **A–003**
(1) 1–025, 1–033, 1–084, 2–044, 4–001, 4–006, 15–017, 15–101, 15–119, 16–014
(2) 1–025, 1–080, 12–079, 12–120
(3) 1–025, 1–051, 1–109, 1–112, 5–019, 5–021
(4) .. 1–025, 1–027, 6–035, 7–02
(5) 1–025, 1–026, 5–021, 6–035, 7–022, 7–070, 15–012
(6) 1–025, 1–027, 6–035
s.3 ... 1–007, 1–076, 2–028, 2–029, 2–031, 2–041, 3–001, 13–021, 18–088, **A–003**
(2) 1–076, 2–030
(3) 2–030
s.4 ... 1–012, 1–067, 2–021, **A–004**
(2) 2–021
s.5 .... 1–103, **A–005**
(1) 1–101, 1–102, 5–021, 5–090, 7–001
(2) 1–111, 1–112, 6–038, 14–049
(3) 1–015, 1–103, 1–105, 5–021, 5–090
s.6 ... 1–011, 1–015, 1–025, 1–116, 3–019, 3–023, 6–035, 6–040, 12–079, 12–080, 12–081, 12–082, 12–083, 12–085, 12–086, 12–088, 12–089, 12–091, 13–021, 15–120, 18–136, 19–008, 19–108, 19–113, **A–005**
(1) 5–090
(2) 1–014
(3) 1–014
s.7 ... 1–015, 1–116, 5–170, 6–002, 6–003, 6–035, 6–036, 6–037, 6–038, 6–039, 6–040, 6–041, 6–051, 6–058, 12–021, 12–079, 12–080, 12–081, 12–082, 12–083, 12–084, 12–085, 12–088, 13–021, 13–071, 15–120, 18–136, 19–108, 19–124, 19–125, 20–096, 20–097, 21–028, **A–005**, A–034
s.8 ...... 15–017, 15–061, 15–119, 16–014, **A–006**
(1) 2–045, 2–047
(2) 1–067, 2–016, 2–046, 2–047
(3) 2–047
s.9 ... 2–045, 2–049, 2–050, 2–051, 15–017, 16–014, **A–006**
(1) 2–049, 2–051, 5–069
(2) 2–049, 17–088, 17–102

1979 Sale of Goods Act—*cont.*
s.10 .... **A–007**
(1) 9–051, 9–052, 14–006, 15–109, 15–122, 15–123, 16–016, 19–207
(b) 5–125
(2) 8–025, 9–005, 14–006
(3) 8–032
ss.11–15 18–255
s.11 ..... 10–027, 10–033, 12–117, 15–109, **A–007**, A–033
(2) 8–028, 8–064, 12–034, 15–109, 19–150, 20–107
(3) 1–007, 4–005, 4–021, 4–029, 5–073, 10–027, 10–028, 10–031, 12–022, 12–023, 12–109, 13–025, 14–021
(4) 1–052, 4–009, 4–011, 5–019, 8–028, 8–047, 8–073, 8–082, 8–084, 9–002, 10–018, 10–026, 12–022, 12–028, 12–029, 12–038, 12–060, 12–063, 13–025, 15–109, 15–118, 19–150, 20–107, A–033, A–034
(6) 3–001, 6–034
(7) 1–001
ss.12–15 .... 1–006, 1–014, 1–031, 1–052, 13–021, 13–066, 14–152, 18–265 25–099, 25–100, 25–196, A–033, A–034
s.12 .. 1–006, 1–014, 1–015, 1–040, 4–018, 4–022, 4–036, 12–081, 14–007, 15–102, 17–047, 17–090, 18–284, 25–160, 25–171, **A–008**, A–033, A–034
(1) 1–110, 4–002, 4–003, 4–004, 4–005, 4–006, 4–009, 4–011, 4–018, 4–019, 4–020, 4–021, 4–023, 4–027, 4–030, 4–031, 4–032, 4–034, 5–170, 7–001, 11–044, 12–025, 12–089, 12–097, 14–021, 15–119, 17–081, 17–090
(2) 4–011, 4–017, 4–030, 4–031, 4–032, 10–033, 19–073
(a) ... 4–023, 4–024, 4–030, 5–170
(b) ... 4–002, 4–024, 4–025, 4–026, 4–029, 4–030, 15–117
(3)–(5) 1–015
(3) 1–112, 4–002, 4–021, 4–023, 4–025, 4–032, 4–036, 7–001
(4) 4–033, 4–034
(5) 4–033, 4–034

1979 Sale of Goods Act—*cont.*
(5A) 4–006, 4–024, 4–029, 4–033
(6) 1–001, 4–002, 4–032
ss.13–15 .... 13–066, 14–013, 14–142, 17–047, 18–267, 18–276, 18–280, 18–284, 19–173, 20–029
s.13 .. 1–011, 1–014, 3–020, 5–019, 5–068, 10–026, 11–001, 11–008, 11–011, 11–014, 11–016, 11–018, 11–021, 11–023, 11–025, 11–029, 11–065, 11–074, 11–079, 12–024, 12–025, 12–074, 12–101, 12–115, 12–117, 12–118, 13–013, 13–023, 13–025, 13–029, 13–030, 13–051, 13–064, 13–067, 13–079, 13–080, 13–081, 13–083, 13–088, 14–009, 14–011, 14–013, 14–023, 14–032, 17–047, 17–074, 18–267, 18–276, 18–284, 19–065, 19–164, 19–194, 25–170, 25–171, **A–009**, A–010, A–033, A–034
(1) ... 10–029, 11–001, 11–002, 11–003, 11–004, 11–005, 13–023, 13–026, 14–009, 14–021
(1A) 11–001, 18–284
(2) 11–022, 11–086
(3) 11–010, 14–009, A–033
(4) 1–001
s.14 .. 1–001, 1–012, 1–014, 1–082, 3–001, 10–019, 11–001, 11–016, 11–017, 11–025, 11–049, 12–024, 12–025, 12–074, 12–101, 12–115, 12–117, 12–118, 13–013, 13–023, 13–025, 13–028, 13–029, 13–030, 13–033, 13–049, 13–064, 13–067, 13–070, 13–075, 13–079, 13–080, 13–083, 13–083, 13–088, 14–002, 14–010, 14–011, 14–023, 14–044, 14–084, 14–112, 17–047, 17–066, 17–072, 17–074, 18–255, 18–284, 19–065, 19–147, 19–194, 25–111, 25–114, 25–115, 25–118, 25–170, 25–171, **A–009**, A–010, A–033, A–034
s.14(1) 1–006, 1–012, 11–024, 11–030, 11–042, 11–070, 11–089, 20–038

1979 Sale of Goods Act—*cont.*
s.14(2) 1–006, 1–040, 6–034, 10–019, 10–029, 11–003, 11–006, 11–007, 11–008, 11–025, 11–026, 11–027, 11–029, 11–030, 11–033, 11–036, 11–041, 11–042, 11–044, 11–045, 11–047, 11–050, 11–051, 11–052, 11–053, 11–054, 11–055, 11–057, 11–058, 11–059, 11–065, 11–066, 11–070, 11–071, 11–072, 11–083, 11–084, 11–085, 12–025, 12–066, 12–071, 13–025, 17–072, 18–255, 18–274, 20–038
(2)–(2F) 1–006, **11–026**
(2A) 11–031, 11–039, 11–081, 14–010, 14–014
(2B) 11–038, 11–039, 11–081, 14–010, 14–014, 17–051
(2B)(a) 14–013
(e) 18–255
(2C) 11–033, 11–041, 11–042, 11–085
(a) 14–014
(b) 14–014, 17–060
(c) 11–036, 11–083
(2D)–42(2F) 14–012, 14–150
(2D) 11–037, 14–010
(2E) .. 11–036, 11–037, 14–010
(2F) 11–037, 14–010
(3) 1–006, 1–021, 1–061, 3–005, 6–034, 11–009, 11–025, 11–026, 11–028, 11–029, 11–031, 11–040, 11–044, 11–046, 11–047, 11–048, 11–049, 11–051, 11–058, 11–059, 11–060, 11–062, 11–065, 11–067, 11–069, 11–070, 11–071, 11–072, 11–086, 12–082, 13–025, 14–010, 14–013, 17–047, 17–059, 17–084, 18–254, 18–255, 18–274, 20–017, 20–038
(b) 1–054
(4) 11–088
(5) 1–006, 11–029, 11–053, 13–080, 14–009, 14–021
(6) 1–005, 11–026, 11–039, 11–051, 14–010, 18–284
(7) 1–001
(8) 1–001, A–036

1979 Sale of Goods Act—*cont.*
s.15 .... 1–014, 1–025, 11–001, 11–024, 11–065, **11–074**, 11–087, 12–024, 12–025, 12–074, 12–101, 12–115, 12–117, 12–118, 13–013, 13–025, 13–064, 13–079, 13–080, 13–083, 13–088, 14–013, 14–027, 17–047, 18–284, 19–065, 19–164, 19–194, 25–170, 25–171, A–009, **A–010**, A–033, A–034
(2) 11–074
(a) 13–028, 13–029
(b) 12–039
(c) 1–006, 11–079, 11–085, 13–023, 13–028, 17–058
(3) 11–074, 18–284, A–033
(4) 1–001
s.15A 1–006, 8–084, 10–038, 11–001, 11–018, 11–026, 11–051, 12–024, 12–025, 14–026, 18–284, 19–012, 19–145, 19–173, 19–194, 19–203, 20–029, 20–032, 20–033, 20–038, 20–105, 20–106, 20–113, 21–025, 21–030, **A–010**
(1) 18–284
(i)(a) 12–024, 18–284, 19–173
(b) 12–024, 18–284
(2) .. 12–024, 18–284, 19–012
(3) 12–024
s.15B **A–010**
ss.16–19 .... 25–133, 25–155
s.16 .. 1–015, 1–108, 5–059, 5–061, 5–110, 5–116, 5–130, 6–004, 12–078, 12–079, 15–012, 15–097, 17–097, 18–194, 18–201, 18–209, 18–287, 18–288, 18–291, 18–292, 18–293, 18–296, 18–299, 19–098, 19–102, 21–007, **A–011**
ss.17–20 1–082
s.17 .. 5–001, 5–018, 5–021, 5–022, 5–023, 5–026, 5–030, 5–031, 5–033, 5–036, 5–039, 5–059, 5–090, 5–094, 5–131, 17–097, 18–201, 18–209, **A–011**
(1) 12–078, 5–016, 5–066, 19–098
(2) 5–016, 5–027, 5–066
s.18 .. 1–056, 1–108, 1–117, 5–016, 5–017, 5–030, 5–035, 5–040, 18–288, **A–011**
r.1–5 5–001
rr.1–3 .... 1–099, 21–005

1979 Sale of Goods Act—*cont.*
r.1 ... 1–027, 1–039, 1–051, 1–114, 5–017, 5–019, 5–020, 5–121, 5–022, 5–023, 5–026, 5–027, 5–029, 5–030, 5–033, 5–036, 5–131, 10–026, 12–038, 12–046, 12–079, 15–048, 18–209, 19–098, 20–070, 21–043, A–011
r.2 ... 5–021, 5–023, 5–024, 5–030, 5–031, 5–037, 6–037, 20–073, 21–005, A–011
r.3 ... 2–045, 5–021, 5–035, 5–072, 6–037, 20–073, A–011
r.4 ... 1–056, 5–040, 5–043, 5–044, 5–046, 5–047, 6–009, 6–037, 7–070, 9–002, 12–057, A–011
(b) 5–050, 5–052
r.5 ... 1–036, 1–099, 5–009, 5–019, 5–035, 5–067, 5–073, 5–090, 5–094, 5–108, 5–116, 8–014, 12–066, 15–010, 15–105, 18–288, 19–093, 20–070, 21–003, 21–052, 21–060, A–011
(1) 5–060, 5–068, 5–085, 5–091, 5–095, 5–103, 5–106, 5–126, 12–046, 12–064, 15–012, 18–210, 18–288, 20–084, 21–003, 21–044
(2) 5–009, 5–096, 5–098, 5–102, 5–103, 5–131, 5–133, 18–211, 18–214, 20–070, 20–071, 21–044, 21–098
(3) 5–103, 5–104, 5–106, 5–107, 5–108, 18–288, 18–289, 21–007
(a) 18–288
(4) 5–107, 5–108, 18–288, 18–289, 21–007
s.19 .... 5–021, 5–101, 6–037, 15–047, 15–063, 21–052, 21–060, **A–011**
(1) 5–026, 5–071, 5–081, 5–131, 5–133, 5–136, 5–138, 5–144, 5–146, 5–148, 18–211, 18–212, 18–213, 21–011
(2) 5–071, 5–136, 5–137, 15–047, 15–073, 18–211, 18–214, 20–071, 20–077, 20–082, 20–083, 21–098
(3) 5–026, 5–071, 5–136, 5–138, 9–030, 18–087, 18–194, 18–211, 18–212, 18–221, 18–222, 18–223, 18–224, 18–225
s.20 ... 1–062, 5–007, 5–170, 6–010, 9–003, 14–007, 14–011, 18–260, 18–263, 19–099, 20–071, 25–154, 25–155, **A–012**

1979 Sale of Goods Act—*cont.*
s.20(1)–(3) 19–123, 20–094
(1) 6–002, 6–033, 6–037, 12–057, 18–244, 18–260, 18–263, 18–264, 19–110, 20–058, 20–071, 21–011, 25–154, 25–160
(2) 6–025, 6–034, 6–035, 8–015, 8–042, 9–003, 9–008, 18–244, 18–260, 19–121, 20–092, 20–096
(3) 1–007, 6–031, 6–032, 9–008, 12–065, 18–244, 19–114, 19–122
(4) 5–098, 6–013, 6–014, 6–025, 6–031, 6–032, 8–014, 11–049, 12–075, 14–010, 18–260, 18–261, 18–262, 18–263, 18–264, 18–281, 18–307, 19–080, 19–110, 19–123, 19–124, 20–071, 20–094, 20–096, 20–097, 20–120, 21–003, 21–006, 21–007, 21–011, 21–013, 21–020, 21–043, 21–100, 25–154
s.20A 1–015, 5–035, 5–059, 5–061, 5–079, 5–094, 5–099, 5–104, 5–109, 5–110, 5–112, 5–120, 5–122, 5–124, 5–125, 5–126, 5–127, 5–128, 5–129, 5–130, 6–006, 6–007, 6–051, 7–014, 7–067, 7–085, 8–002, 8–017, 12–078, 12–079, 18–116, 18–120, 18–193, 18–194, 18–201, 18–209, 18–288, 18–293, 18–294, 18–295, 18–296, 18–297, 18–299, 18–300, 18–306, 19–098, 19–102, 19–204, 20–070, 20–086, 20–096, 21–004, 21–006, 21–007, 25–133, 25–155, A–011, **A–012**, A–030
(1) 5–064, 5–109, 5–110, 5–111, 5–112, 5–116, 5–123, 5–130, 17–097, 18–137, 18–209, 18–294, 18–297, 19–015, 19–204, 20–086, 20–096, 21–038
(a) 18–295, 18–296, 18–297, 18–306, 20–086
(b) 5–111, 5–130, 18–295, 18–296, 18–297, 18–306, 20–086
(2) 5–099, 5–109, 5–129, 5–130, 17–097, 18–137, 18–296, 18–297, 18–298, 18–299, 19–098, 20–086
(3)–(6) 5–117

1979 Sale of Goods Act—*cont.*
s.20A(3) ... 5–111, 5–130, 18–296, 18–297
(4)–(6) 5–129
(4) ... 5–118, 5–121, 18–290, 18–306
(5) 5–120, 8–017
(6) 5–119, 18–297
s.20B 5–124, 5–125, 5–127, 5–129, 8–002, 8–017, 18–193, 18–299, 19–204, **A–012**, A–030
(1) 5–124, 5–125, 5–126, 7–085, 8–017, 19–204, 18–299
(a) 5–124, 5–125
(b) 5–124, 5–125, 18–299
(2) 5–124, 5–125
(3) 5–127
(a) 5–127
(b) 5–127
(c) 5–127, 6–006
ss.21–25 .... 1–075, 1–101
ss.21–26 ... 1–015, 15–102, 25–131
s.21 .. 7–001, 7–108, **A–013**, A–034
(1) 1–075, 5–121, 7–001, 7–008, 7–011, 7–013, 7–015
(2) 7–008
(a) ... 1–012, 1–018, 3–002, 7–031, 7–109
(b) ... 1–012, 7–109, 15–106
s.22 .... 7–001, **A–013**, A–033
(1) 7–020, A–033
(3) 1–001
ss.23–26 7–001
s.23 .. 3–012, 7–001, 7–021, 7–022, 7–023, 7–024, 7–025, 7–027, 7–028, 7–029, 7–030, 7–068, 7–071, 7–077, 15–112, **A–013**
ss.24–26 18–006
s.24 ... 1–018, 3–002, 5–004, 5–121, 5–122, 5–123, 5–126, 5–129, 7–001, 7–036, 7–042, 7–055, 7–056, 7–057, 7–058, 7–059, 7–061, 7–063, 7–064, 7–067, 7–072, 7–077, 7–080, 7–085, 12–020, 15–001, 15–009, 15–011, 15–102, 15–103, 15–104, 18–080, 18–087, 18–094, 18–205, 18–240, 18–290, 18–299, 19–204, 20–084, 21–054, 25–131, 25–135, **A–013**
s.25 ... 1–001, 3–002, 5–065, 7–001, 7–022, 7–027, 7–036, 7–057, 7–062, 7–064, 7–065, 7–066, 15–001, 15–009, 15–060, 15–092, 15–097, 15–098, 15–100, 15–115, 15–125, 15–126, 18–087, 18–223, 18–225, 18–227, 18–240, 21–054, 25–131, 25–135, **A–013**, A–033

1979 Sale of Goods Act—*cont.*
(1) 1–018, 1–052, 1–096, 5–004, 5–122, 5–139, 5–156, 5–157, 7–025, 7–063, 7–069, 7–070, 7–071, 7–072, 7–073, 7–074, 7–075, 7–076, 7–077, 7–081, 7–082, 7–083, 7–085, 7–086, 7–108, 15–055, 18–067, 18–197, 18–205, A–034
(2) 1–021, 1–052, 7–070, 25–147, A–033
(b) 1–021
(3) 1–001
(4) 1–001, 7–070, A–036
s.26 .. 1–018, 3–004, 7–001, 7–031, 7–055, 7–063, 7–069, 7–078, 13–021, **A–013**
s.27 .. 2–026, 8–001, 9–001, 9–002, 9–021, 12–044, 15–017, 15–028, 15–061, 15–119, 16–016, **A–014**
(1) 13–021
s.28 .. 2–026, 5–018, 8–004, 8–085, 9–021, 9–047, 9–057, 12–080, 15–002, 15–017, 15–032, 15–034, 15–061, 15–063, 15–119, 15–120, 15–121, 15–122, 16–016, 16–021, 16–028, 17–009, 18–325, 19–075, 20–055, 20–127, 21–018, 21–042, **A–014**
ss.29–37 1–116
s.29 .... 8–013, 15–041, **A–014**
(1) 8–018
(2) 8–019, 9–047, 18–249, 19–069, 21–002
(3) 8–037, 14–006, 21–007, 21–029
(4) 5–097, 6–013, 8–012, 8–013, 15–052, 18–193, 18–196, 18–307, 21–007
(5) 8–032, 8–033, 8–041, 9–007, 17–008, 25–157
(6) 8–005, 21–002
s.30 .... 2–008, 8–053, 8–054, 11–018, 12–028, 12–029, 12–060, 21–033, **A–014**
(1) 5–086, 6–040, 8–046, 8–047, 8–048, 8–050, 8–051, 8–052, 8–054, 8–063, 8–064, 8–072, 8–073, 8–077, 8–083, 9–002, 9–014, 12–030, 12–069, 12–086, 12–101, 18–338, 18–355, 20–074, 20–127
(2) 5–086, 8–049, 8–050, 8–051, 8–054, 8–063, 9–002, 12–030

1979 Sale of Goods Act—*cont.*
s.30(2A) 1–006, 5–085, 8–051, 8–053, 12–030, 18–284, 19–012, 19–036, 19–145, 19–173, 20–032, 20–033, 20–038, 20–074, 20–105, 20–106, 20–113, 21–036
(2B) 8–051
(3) 5–086, 8–049, 9–002
(4) 5–085, 9–014, 11–018, 12–060, 18–273
(5) 8–052, 8–062, 8–063, 19–012
s.31 ...... 16–027, 20–112, **A–014**
(1) 8–052, 8–064, 9–002, 12–101
(2) 6–069, 8–006, 8–037, 8–039, 8–048, 8–069, 8–070, 8–074, 8–077, 8–083, 8–084, 9–003, 9–010, 12–019, 12–028, 12–031, 12–099, 15–042, 15–107, 15–109
s.32 ...... 5–009, 14–007, 14–011, 15–046, 18–244, **A–014**
(1)–(3) 20–094
(1) 5–050, 5–098, 8–014, 8–015, 12–043, 12–061, 15–046, 16–059, 18–245, 18–250, 18–264, 20–012, 21–042, 21–099, 25–009
(2) 6–033, 8–015, 18–245, 18–248, 18–252, 18–264, 19–025, 19–046, 19–102, 19–123, 20–091, 20–094, 21–042, 21–043
(3) 1–002, 6–031, 6–033, 8–015, 8–016, 18–245, 18–246, 18–247, 18–248, 18–250, 18–252, 18–261, 18–264, 19–046, 19–117, 19–123, 20–039, 20–091, 21–013, 21–029, 21–101
(4) 5–098, 6–021, 6–031, 8–014, 8–015, 11–049, 12–043, 14–010, 18–260, 18–261, 18–262, 18–264, 18–281, 18–307, 19–046, 19–123, 20–012, 20–038, 20–094, 21–011, 21–013, 21–042, 21–099, 21–100
s.33 .... 5–101, 6–033, 18–160, 18–244, 18–249, 18–250, 18–251, 18–252, 19–204, 19–118, 20–091, **A–014**
s.34 .... 2–021, 8–028, 12–039, 13–064, 19–150, 19–153, 19–156, A–015, A–033

1979 Sale of Goods Act—*cont.*
(1) 9–002, 12–039, 12–048, 19–156
(2) 5–078, 11–074, 12–039, 16–016, 17–054, 21–099
s.34A 9–002
s.35 .. 1–041, 2–021, 5–047, 8–028, 8–047, 8–072, 8–073, 9–002, 12–006, 12–009, 12–027, 12–037, 12–038, 12–039, 12–044, 12–048, 12–050, 12–052, 12–055, 12–066, 12–109, 12–118, 13–102, 14–021, 14–027, 14–047, 19–153, 19–154, 19–155, 19–157, 19–142, 19–174, 21–102, **A–015**, A–033
(1) 9–002, 12–044, 12–050, 12–059, 19–153, 20–107, A–033
(a) .. 8–047, 12–044, 14–021
(b) .. 8–047, 12–044, 14–021
(2) 1–001, 8–047, 9–002, 12–044, 12–050, 12–109, 13–064, 13–102, 14–021, 19–150, 19–153, 20–107
(a) 12–050
(b) 12–050
(3) ... 12–045, 12–050, 12–063, 12–109, 13–102, 14–021, 19–154, 20–105
(4) 8–047, 8–072, 9–002, 12–053, 14–021, 14–027, 19–153, 20–107
(5) ... 12–053, 12–055, 14–021, 19–150, 19–153, 20–107
(6) ... 12–031, 12–054, 12–090, 12–109, 12–112, 12–118
(a) 14–021, 14–027
(b) .. 8–047, 8–072, 12–051, 12–052, 19–154, 19–174, 20–111
(7) 8–028, 8–073, 9–002, 12–062, 12–109
s.35A 8–028, 8–073, 12–038, 12–060, 12–100, 19–158, A–007, **A–015**
(1) 5–085, 12–060
(a), (b) 12–060
(2)–(4) 12–060
(2) 8–084
s.36 .... 6–011, 9–002, 12–065, 12–097, 17–093, A–015
s.37 .... 9–003, 9–006, 9–009, 16–017, 16–030, 16–060, 16–088, 19–216, 19–219, 20–139, A–016
(1) 6–015, 6–033, 9–009

1979 Sale of Goods Act—*cont.*
s.37(2) 9–005, 9–009
s.38 .... 8–004, 9–022, 15–028, 15–045, 15–061, 15–101, **A–017**
(1) ... 15–001, 15–006, 15–016, 15–017, 15–018, 15–022, 15–030, 15–033, 15–045, 15–103, 15–109, 15–119, 15–129, 16–017
(a) 15–017, 15–028, 15–042, 15–062, 15–119
(b) 9–030, 15–002, 15–018, 15–019, 15–036, 15–056, 15–062, 16–018
(2) 3–043, 15–008, 15–013, 15–014, 15–015, 15–016, 15–065, 18–229, 25–182
s.39 .... 1–064, 3–045, 9–022, 15–004, 15–005, 15–013, 15–022, 15–023, 15–024, 16–017, **A–017**
(1) 1–012, 7–111, 9–061, 15–001, 15–002, 15–004, 15–009, 15–061, 15–063, 15–065
(a) 15–044, 18–010
(b) 3–048
(c) 15–004, 15–011, 15–119, 19–220
(2) 5–018, 9–022, 9–061, 15–010, 15–011, 15–012, 15–029, 15–063, 15–102, 18–149, 19–220
s.40 .... 1–001, 15–001, **A–017**
ss.41–43 ... 1–064, 15–002, 18–010
ss.41–48 15–001
s.41 .. 3–045, 5–003, 5–005, 8–004, 9–022, 15–010, 15–024, **A–018**
(1) ... 15–002, 15–022, 15–024, 15–028, 15–030, 15–032, 15–033, 15–034, 15–037, 15–038, 15–044, 15–048, 15–049, 15–062
(a) 15–034
(b) 9–061, 15–017, 15–033, 15–035, 15–056
(c) .. 3–048, 9–061, 15–017, 15–033, 15–037, 15–056
(2) ... 15–039, 15–040, 15–049, 15–050
s.42 ...... 9–022, 15–017, 15–028, 15–030, 15–041, 15–051, 15–084, **A–018**
s.43 ...... 15–028, 15–045, **A–018**
(1) ... 15–045, 15–049, 15–050, 15–056
(a) 15–045, 15–046, 15–048, 15–062, 18–010, 18–149, 20–083

1979 Sale of Goods Act—*cont.*
s.43(1)(b) 15–038, 15–045, 15–049, 15–055, 15–074, 15–117
(c) 15–036, 15–040, 15–041, 15–045, 15–056
(2) 5–021, 15–006, 15–017, 15–056, 15–059, 16–016
ss.44–46 .... 9–022, 15–002
s.44 .. 3–045, 5–003, 5–005, 7–060, 15–001, 15–017, 15–019, 15–022, 15–024, 15–026, 15–059, 15–061, 15–062, 15–088, 15–091, 15–100, **A–019**
ss.45–47 15–061
s.45 ..... 15–017, 15–061, 15–064, 15–066, 15–081, 15–082, 18–248, **A–019**
(1) ... 15–049, 15–068, 15–071, 15–074, 15–083, 15–085, 15–117, 21–057, 21–071, 21–103, 25–110
(2) ... 15–049, 15–055, 15–074, 15–076, 15–117, 18–248
(3) ... 15–052, 15–077, 15–080, 15–081, 15–084, 15–117, 21–057, 21–071
(4) ... 15–070, 15–072, 15–081, 15–085, 25–123
(5) ... 15–073, 15–082, 18–248, 20–012, 20–141, 21–103
(6) ... 15–039, 15–055, 15–065, 15–074, 15–078, 15–083, 21–071, 25–123
(7) 15–041, 15–084
s.46 .... **A–019**
(1) 15–085
(2) 15–085, 21–057
(3) 15–085, 15–086
(4) ... 15–005, 15–062, 15–085, 15–088, 15–103, 16–089, 21–057, 21–071
s.47 .. 1–018, 5–004, 5–065, 5–139, 7–001, 7–036, 7–069, 7–072, 15–005, 15–028, 15–092, 15–094, 15–095, 15–100, 18–006, **A–020**
(1) ... 15–060, 15–092, 15–093, 15–096, 18–205
(2) ... 15–009, 15–040, 15–055, 15–060, 15–061, 15–067, 15–092, 15–097, 15–098, 18–086, 18–087, 18–197, 18–225, 18–227, 19–220, 25–181
(b) 15–097, 15–099, 18–086

1979 Sale of Goods Act—*cont.*
s.48 .... 7–001, 7–111, 12–095, 15–028, 15–091, 15–102, 15–127, **A–020**
(1) ... 15–003, 15–043, 15–062, 15–088, 15–091, 15–101, 15–102
(2) 5–004, 5–139, 7–056, 7–060, 7–068, 15–003, 15–004, 15–043, 15–101, 15–102, 15–103, 15–104, 15–119, 15–124
(3) 5–146, 7–060, 8–026, 9–051, 15–001, 15–003, 15–011, 15–017, 15–022, 15–043, 15–062, 15–101, 15–102, 15–104, 15–105, 15–106, 15–109, 15–119, 15–120, 15–122, 15–123, 15–124, 15–125, 15–127, 15–128, 15–129, 15–130, 15–131, 15–132, 16–060, 16–083, 16–087, 19–207
(4) 5–146, 9–051, 15–003, 15–101, 15–105, 15–125, 15–127, 15–128, 15–129, 16–060, 16–083, 16–087, 19–207
ss.48A–48E 12–100
ss.48A–48F 14–002, 14–005, 14–023, 25–196
s.48A 4–021, **12–072**, **A–021**
(1) 19–187
(b) 19–065, 19–077, 19–123, 19–144, 19–203, 19–206, 20–029, 20–038, 20–105, 20–110, 20–113, 20–120, 20–122, 21–102
(2) 12–106, 19–206
(a) 14–024, 18–284, 19–012, 19–071, 19–194, 20–122
(b) 19–077, 19–145
(i) 12–091, 19–144, 19–187, 19–206, 20–105, 20–120, 21–102
(ii) ... 19–065, 19–207, 20–029, 20–105, 20–113
(3) 11–001, 11–026, 11–051, 11–074, 12–075, 12–118, 13–064
(4)(a) 12–075
s.48B 4–021, **12–076**, 12–077, 12–090, 12–104, 12–113, 12–118, 14–024, 18–284, 19–071, 19–150, 19–194, 19–206, 20–074, 20–122, **A–022**
(1) 12–102, 19–012, 19–144, 19–203

1979 Sale of Goods Act—*cont.*
s.48B(2) ... 6–016, 12–083, 12–108
(a) 12–080, 12–088
(3) 12–079, 12–088, 12–102, 12–104, 12–106, 12–108, 12–114, 19–144, 19–203
(a) 19–144, 19–206
(b) 19–206
(4) 12–081, 12–102, 12–104, 12–114
(5) 12–102
s.48C 4–021, 12–077, 12–079, **12–088**, 12–092, 12–097, 12–103, 12–107, 12–113, 12–118, 19–077, 19–150, 19–203, 19–207, 20–105, **A–022**
(1) 12–100, 12–102, 19–144, 19–203, 20–120
(a) 12–093, 19–187, 19–203, 19–206
(b) 19–144, 19–145, 19–203, 19–206, 20–029, 20–105, 20–113, 21–102
(2) 12–106, 12–108, 19–206, 20–029, 20–113, 21–102
(b) 12–089, 12–095, 19–150
(3) 19–203
s.48D 12–090, 12–106, **12–110,** 12–111, 12–112, 18–284, 19–012, 19–071, 19–150, 19–181, 19–194, 20–032, 20–038, 20–074, 20–105, 21–036, **A–022**
(1) 12–078, 12–118
(2)(a) 12–103, 20–029
(b) 12–111
(3) 12–106
s.48E 12–102, 12–104, **12–113**, 12–114, 19–203, 20–113, **A–022**
(2) 12–083, 12–114, 14–005, 14–025, 17–101, 19–206, 20–122
(3) 12–091, 12–097, 12–102, 12–104, 12–114, 19–145, 19–206, 20–122
(a) 12–096
(4) 12–114, 19–145, 19–206, 20–122
(5) 12–097
(6) 12–083, 12–114
s.48F 4–021, 6–016, 11–001, 12–071, 12–074, 12–091, 12–101, 12–115, 19–012, 19–065, 19–077, 19–145, 20–113, **A–022**

1979 Sale of Goods Act—*cont.*
s.49 ...... 5–170, 15–001, 15–006, 15–010, 15–059, 16–001, 16–003, 16–014, 16–028, 16–029, 19–212, 19–215, 20–131, 25–190, **A–027**
(1) 5–006, 9–010, 9–021, 16–001, 16–003, 16–004, 16–016, 16–021, 16–023, 16–026, 16–029, 16–059, 16–092, 19–211, 20–126, 20–128
(2) 1–028, 1–029, 5–006, 9–010, 9–021, 16–001, 16–003, 16–004, 16–016, 16–023, 16–025, 16–026, 16–027, 16–028, 16–029, 16–060, 16–092, 18–292, 18–296, 19–213, 19–214, 20–129
s.50 .. 5–006, 5–146, 6–015, 9–002, 15–001, 15–010, 15–127, 16–061, 16–085, 16–088, **A–027**
(1) 9–010, 12–044, 16–021, 16–023, 16–027, 16–060, 16–061, 19–216, 20–133
(2) ... 16–043, 16–044, 16–049, 16–061, 16–065, 16–077, 17–001, 17–002, 17–021, 20–137
(3) ... 15–109, 16–004, 16–045, 16–052, 16–061, 16–062, 16–064, 16–065, 16–066, 16–071, 16–072, 16–075, 16–077, 16–081, 16–083, 16–085, 17–002, 17–004, 17–005, 17–007, 17–010, 17–014, 17–052, 19–166, 19–176, 19–216, 19–216, 20–133, 20–140, 25–191
s.51 ...... 4–005, 17–001, 17–002, 17–008, 17–047, 17–093, **A–025**
(1) ... 17–001, 17–002, 19–175
(2) ... 16–043, 16–044, 16–049, 16–077, 17–001, 17–002, 17–007, 17–010, 17–021, 17–023, 19–175, 20–119
(3) ... 16–045, 16–052, 16–061, 16–071, 16–072, 17–001, 17–002, 17–004, 17–005, 17–007, 17–008, 17–009, 17–010, 17–014, 17–017, 17–019, 17–020, 17–025, 17–037, 17–038, 17–052, 17–093, 19–175, 19–179, 19–180, 19–181, 19–183, 19–217, 20–114, 20–115, 20–116, 20–119, 20–140, 21–031

1979 Sale of Goods Act—*cont.*
s.52 ... 1–010, 1–082, 1–116, 3–025, 12–071, 12–078, 12–079, 15–116, 16–003, 16–028, 16–089, 16–093, 17–096, 17–097, 17–098, 17–099, 17–100, 18–292, 19–204, 19–206, **A–025**
(1) 17–096
(2) 17–096
(3) 17–096, 17–100
(4) 17–096
s.53 .... 4–024, 4–029, 16–061, 17–007, 17–047, 17–048, 19–203, **A–025**
(1) ... 9–026, 12–092, 12–106, 14–020, 15–109, 16–020, 17–047, 19–187, 20–118
(a) 6–034, 14–018, 16–001, 17–049, 17–050, 17–051
(b) 17–051
(2) ... 16–061, 17–007, 17–038, 17–047, 17–051, 17–058, 17–088, 19–187, 19–188, 19–189, 20–118, 20–119
(3) ... 12–093, 16–061, 17–007, 17–017, 17–028, 17–029, 17–033, 17–047, 17–052, 17–054, 17–056, 17–063, 17–066, 17–067, 17–072, 17–073, 17–082, 19–166, 19–187, 19–188, 19–189, 20–118, 20–120
(4) ... 16–020, 17–047, 17–049, 17–050
(5) 17–047
s.53A A–025
s.54 .. 1–007, 3–001, 4–005, 4–006, 4–029, 9–068, 12–067, 16–007, 16–046, 16–060, 16–086, 16–088, 17–001, 17–037, 17–038, 17–047, 17–088, 17–090, **A–026**
s.55 ..... 11–068, 12–089, 15–001, 15–028, 15–049, 15–053, 15–061, 15–092, 16–003, **A–027**, A–033, A–034
(1) 1–006, 1–013, 1–014, 1–015, 6–014, 6–037, 8–032, 8–062, 8–063, 9–057, 13–005, 13–033, 15–031
(2) 11–068
(3) 1–001, 18–280
s.56 .... 1–001, **A–027**, A–033, A–034
s.57 .. 1–006, 1–015, 2–001, 2–004, **A–028**
(1) 2–004
(2) 2–004, 2–005

1979 Sale of Goods Act—*cont.*
s.57(3) 3–009
(4) 3–009
(5) 3–009
(6) 3–009
s.58 .... **A–029**
s.59 .. 5–040, 5–050, 8–037, 9–009, 12–055, 15–123, **A–029**
s.60 ..... 15–086, 15–088, 16–094, 17–088, 17–102, **A–029**
s.61 ...... 11–038, **A–030**, A–034
(1) 1–018, 1–025, 1–027, 1–029, 1–063, 1–078, 1–080, 1–081, 1–084, 1–090, 1–093, 1–098, 1–100, 1–101, 1–102, 1–113, 4–003, 4–021, 4–029, 5–001, 5–016, 5–022, 5–025, 5–030, 5–035, 5–059, 5–060, 5–097, 5–099, 5–105, 5–112, 5–113, 5–120, 5–122, 6–002, 6–004, 6–006, 6–007, 6–009, 6–013 6–034, 6–035, 6–036, 6–038, 6–050, 6–058, 7–027, 7–055, 7–062, 7–069, 7–077, 7–099, 8–002, 8–003, 8–013, 8–017, 8–019, 10–022, 10–023, 10–028, 11–035, 11–056, 11–078, 12–050, 12–074, 12–079, 12–081, 12–083, 12–085, 13–025, 13–040, 15–001, 15–012, 15–013, 15–045, 15–049, 15–065, 15–068, 15–074, 15–097, 15–101, 16–021, 16–025, 16–094, 17–097, 17–102, 18–006, 18–013, 18–018, 18–137, 18–193, 18–201, 18–255, 18–290, 18–294, 18–295, 19–008, 19–071, 19–102, 19–113, 19–203, 19–204, 21–002, 21–054, 21–083, 25–004, A–033, A–034
(3) 7–029, 7–046, 7–055, 7–068, 7–069, 7–086, 7–099, 15–097, 18–105
(4) 1–001, 3–048, 15–001, 15–002, 15–017, 15–024, 15–037, 15–061, 15–062
(5) 5–023, 5–035, 5–068, 8–005, 21–002
(5A) 4–021, 5–098, 6–013, 6–025, 8–014, 8–051, 12–024, 12–073, 13–102, 14–008, 14–010, 14–011, 18–259, 25–111
(6) 1–001
s.62 .... 1–012, **A–031**
(1) 1–012, 3–045, 15–027, 15–097, A–036

1979 Sale of Goods Act—*cont.*
s.62(2) 1–007, 1–008, 1–010, 1–011, 2–001, 3–001, 3–002, 3–008, 3–010, 3–011, 3–027, 6–034, 6–038, 7–008, 7–031, 10–008, 10–031, 10–033, 12–023, 15–012, 15–088, 15–092, 17–088, 17–102, 18–263, A–036
(3) 1–012, 1–016
(4) 1–012, 1–017, 1–064, 1–065, 5–146
s.63 .. 4–018, 6–058, 7–087, 7–108, **A–031**, A–034, A–036
s.64 .... **A–032**
Sch.1 ..... 1–001, 13–021, A–002, **A–033**
para.1 .... A–033
para.2 .... A–007, A–033
para.3 .... 4–002, 4–023, 4–032, A–008, A–033
para.4 .... A–009, A–033
para.5 .... 1–001, 1–021, A–009, A–033
para.6 .... A–033
para.7 .... A–010, A–033
para.8 .... A–013, A–033
para.9 .... 1–001, 1–021, 7–070, A–013, A–033
para.10 .... A–015, A–033
para.11 1–052, 11–068, 18–280, A–027, A–033, A–034
para.12 .... A–027, A–033
para.13 .... A–027, A–033
para.14 .... A–030, A–033
para.15 .... A–030, A–033
Sch.2 ...... 1–001, 4–018, 13–083, A–031, **A–034**
para.1 .... **A–034**
para.2 .... 6–058, **A–034**
para.3 .... **A–034**
para.4 .... 7–087, 7–108, **A–034**
para.5 .... **A–034**
para.6 .... **A–034**
para.7 .... **A–034**
para.8 .... **A–034**
para.9 .... **A–034**
para.10 .... **A–034**
para.11 .... **A–034**
para.12 .... **A–034**
para.13 .... **A–034**
para.14 .... **A–034**
para.15 .... 25–160, **A–034**
para.16 .... **A–034**
para.17 .... 1–052, **A–034**
para.18 .... **A–034**
para.19 .... **A–034**
para.20 .... **A–034**
para.21 .... **A–034**

1979 Sale of Goods Act—*cont.*
para.22 .... **A–034**
Sch.3 .... A–031, **A–035**
Sch.4 .... A–031, **A–036**
para.1 .... A–036
para.2 .... 7–070, A–036
para.3 .... A–036
para.4 .... A–036
para.5 .... A–036
para.6 .... A–036

1980 Competition Act (c.21) 3–040, 14–125
Magistrates' Court Act (c.43)—
s.127(1) 14–108
Limitation Act (c.58) 7–117
s.2 7–115
s.3(1) 7–115
(2) 7–115, 7–117
s.4(1) 7–115
(2) 7–115
(3) 7–115
(4) 7–115
(5)(b) 7–115
s.5 4–030
s.11(4) 14–092
s.11A 14–092
(3) 14–061, 14–092
(4) 14–092
(5)–(7) 14–092
s.14A(4) 14–092
s.14B 14–092
s.27A 7–117
(1) 7–117
(2) 7–117
(3) 7–117
(4) 7–117
(5) 7–117
(6) 7–117
s.32 .... 4–022, 7–115
(1)(b) 7–116

1981 Statute Law (Repeals) Act (c.19)—
s.1(1) 1–001, A–034
Sch.1 1–001
Pt XI A–034
Finance Act (c.35)—
s.136(2) 22–044
Deep Sea Mining (Temporary Provisions) Act (c.53) 1–097
Supreme Court Act (c.54)—
s.35A 6–067, 16–007, 16–008, 23–107, 25–191
(1) 16–007
(2) 16–007
(3) 16–007
(4) 16–007, 16–009
(5) 16–007
(6) 16–007
(7) 16–007

1981 Supreme Court Act—*cont.*
s.35A(8) 16–007
s.39 23–112
s.50 12–114
s.138 7–113
s.138A 7–111
s.138B 7–111
s.152(4) 1–001
Sch.7 1–001
1982 Civil Jurisdiction and Judgments Act (c.27) 25–063
s.3(3) 25–018
s.42 25–063
Sch.1, art.17 25–072
Sch.3C 25–082
art.17 25–072
Sch.4 25–176
Supply of Goods and Services Act (c.29) 1–031, 1–032, 1–040, 1–041, 1–067, 1–071, 1–086, 2–019, 2–044, 4–036, 11–027, 12–079, 13–085, 14–008, 14–047, 14–051
Pt 1B 14–023, 14–049
Pt 2 1–031
ss.1–5 1–031
s.1 .... 1–031, 14–049
(1) 1–031, 4–036
(2) 1–031, 4–036
(3) 1–031
ss.2–5 .... 1–031, 13–066
s.2 .... 4–036, 14–047
(3) 4–036
s.3 .... 11–023, 14–047, 14–051
(2) 1–041
s.4 .... 3–001, 11–027, 11–050, 11–069, 14–047, 14–051
(4) 3–005
(7) 11–088
s.5 .... 14–051, 11–087
s.5A 12–024
ss.6–10 1–031
s.6 1–031
ss.7–10 13–066
s.7 .... 1–031, 14–047
s.8 .... 11–023, 14–047
s.9 .... 3–001, 11–050, 11–069, 14–047
(7) 11–088
s.10 11–087
s.10A 12–024
s.11 1–031
(1) 1–031
(3) 1–031
ss.11M–11S 14–049
s.11N(3) 14–049
(4) 14–049
s.11S(a) 14–051
(b) 14–051
1982 Supply of Goods and Services Act—*cont.*
s.12–15 14–051
s.12(4) 14–051
s.13 14–051
s.14 .... 14–052A
s.15 .... 2–047, 14–052A
s.16(3)(a) 14–051
s.17(2) 4–036
s.18 1–079
s.20(3) 1–031
(5) 1–031
(6) 1–031
Administration of Justice Act (c.53)—
s.15 16–007
Sch.1 16–007
1983 Currency Act (c.9)—
s.1 9–028
(3) 15–022
Car Tax Act (c.53)—
s.5(2)(c) 5–051
Sch.1, para.12(h) 5–051
1984 Telecommunications Act (c.12)—
s.4 18–202
Foreign Limitation Periods Act (c.16) 25–204
s.1(1) 25–204
s.2(1) 25–204
(2) 25–204
Road Traffic Regulation Act (c.27)—
s.101 7–111
County Courts Act (c.28)—
s.38 7–112
s.64 14–101
s.69 .... 6–067, 16–007, 25–191
(1) 16–007
(2) 16–007
(3) 16–007
(4) 16–007, 16–009
(5) 16–007
(6) 16–007
(7) 16–007
s.69A 23–107
s.74 16–013
(5A) 25–191
s.85 5–014
ss.89–102 7–111
s.89(2) 7–114
s.99 7–114
s.100 7–112
s.102 7–111
s.103(2) 7–114
Food Act (c.30) 14–110
s.2 14–110
s.6 14–110

1984 Food Act—*cont.*
s.11 14–110
Police and Criminal Evidence Act (c.60) 7–007
s.19 7–007
s.22 7–007
1985 Companies Act (c.6) .. 1–016, 2–043
Pt XII 1–065, 25–128
s.35(1) 2–043
(2) 2–043
s.35A(1) 2–043
(2)(b) 2–043
(c) 2–043
s.36 2–021
s.36A 2–021
ss.258–260 24–008
s.349(4) 1–085
s.395 .... 1–016, 5–142, 5–144, 5–149, 5–153, 5–154, 5–166, 18–238, 25–151
(1) 5–143, 25–144
s.396 ...... 5–142, 18–238, 25–151
(1) 5–143, 25–144
(b) 18–238
(c) .. 1–016, 5–143, 5–145, 5–150
(iii) 18–238, 24–029
(e) .. 5–143, 5–160, 18–238
(f) ... 5–143, 5–144, 5–160
(2)(b) 1–079
(c) 18–214
s.409 .... 5–143, 25–144
ss.410–424 5–143
s.612 3–045
s.621 7–111
s.622 7–111
s.736 24–008
Insolvency Act (c.65) 1–012, 3–045, 5–160
s.109(1) 5–143
s.235 .... 7–111, A–030
s.235(3) 1–001, 3–046, 3–047, 3–048, 15–024
s.238 3–049
Sch.6
para.10 5–143
Sch.10 1–001
Pt II 7–111
Pt III 3–046, 3–047, 3–048, 15–024, A–030
Bankruptcy (Scotland) Act (c.66)—
s.75(2) 1–001, A–030
Sch.8 .... 1–001, A–030
Weights and Measures Act (c.72) .. 14–109, 14–111, 14–140
Pt I 14–111
Pt II 14–111
Pt III 14–111
Pt IV 14–111
1985 Weights and Measures Act—*cont.*
s.7 14–111
s.11(2) 14–111
s.21 14–111
s.22(1) 14–111
s.28 14–111
s.29 14–111
s.35(1) 14–108
Law Reform (Miscellaneous Provisions) (Scotland) Act (c.73)—
s.11 22–047
1986 Agricultural Holdings Act (c.5)—
s.10 1–095
Consumer Safety (Amendment) Act (c.29) 14–114
s.3 14–118
s.6 14–118
Latent Damage Act (c.37) ... 12–121
s.1 14–092
s.3 18–149
(1) 5–009
Gas Act (c.44)—
s.10 1–071
Sch.2B 1–071
Insolvency Act (c.45) 3–045, 5–164, 5–166, 15–024
Pt I 5–005, 5–164
Pt IV 3–049
Pt V 3–049
Pt VIII–XI 1–012
s.1A 5–164
s.10 5–005
s.14 7–111
s.15 .... 5–005, 7–111
s.42 7–111
s.43 7–111
ss.72A–72G 5–161
ss.72B–72G 5–165
s.72A 5–165, 7–111
s.86 3–049
s.127 3–049
s.129 3–049
s.134 7–111
s.165 7–111
s.166 7–111
s.167 7–111
s.183(4) 1–079
s.184(6) 1–079
s.233 8–086
s.238 1–016
s.239 1–016
s.244 16–009
s.251 .... 5–005, 5–162
s.267(2) 15–024
s.268 15–024
s.271(1) 15–024

1986 Insolvency Act—*cont.*
s.278(a) 3–046
s.283 18–236
s.285 7–028
s.286 7–111
s.287 7–111
(2)(b) 15–120
s.311(5) 15–027
s.314 15–027
ss.315–321 .... 15–027, 15–037
s.315 3–046
s.323 3–046
ss.339–342 3–047
s.343 16–009
s.344 5–168
(3)(a) 5–168
(b)(i) 5–168
(4) 5–168
s.346 7–111
s.347 7–111
s.372 8–086
s.423 .... 1–016, 3–047
s.436 .... 5–005, 5–162
Sch.1 7–111
Sch.A1 .... 5–005, 5–164
para.2 5–164
para.7 5–164
para.8 5–164
para.12(1)(g) 5–164
para.29 5–164
para.32 5–164
Sch.B1 .... 5–005, 5–162
para.3(1) 5–162
(2) 5–162
(4) 5–162
paras 10–13 5–162
para.13(1)(e) 3–049
paras 14–21 5–162
paras 22–34 5–162
para.43 .... 5–005, 5–162
para.44 5–162
para.59 7–111
(3) 5–163
paras 70–72 7–111
para.72 .... 5–005, 5–163
(1) 5–163
(2) 5–163
(3) 5–163
(4) 5–163
(5) 5–163
para.111(1) 5–162, 5–163
Sch.4, Pt III 7–111
Sch.5 .... 7–111, 15–027
Sch.14 7–111
Financial Services Act (c.60)—
s.132 3–028
1987 Minors' Contracts Act (c.13) 2–029, 2–034, 2–034, 2–037
s.1(1) 2–037
1987 Minors' Contracts Act—*cont.*
s.3 ... 2–028, 2–034, 2–035, 2–038, 2–039
s.4 2–037
Recognition of Trusts Act (c.14) 25–145
art.6 25–145
art.7 25–145
Finance Act (c.16)—
s.68(1) 22–001
Debtors (Scotland) Act (c.18)—
s.108 .... A–017
s.108(3) 1–001
Sch.8 .... 1–001, A–017
Consumer Protection Act (c.43) 1–071, 1–089, 3–028, 11–039, 12–001, 13–017, 13–019, 13–053, 13–104, 14–061, 14–063, 14–079, 14–083, 14–084, 14–087, 14–091, 14–095, 14–097, 14–109, 14–114
Pt I 1–023, 12–127, 14–002, 14–020, 14–031, 14–076, 14–080, 14–081, 14–082, 14–091, 14–092, 14–093, 14–114
Pt II 13–019, 14–076, 14–085, 14–114, 14–122
Pt III 1–084, 1–085, 14–124
s.1(1) 14–051, 14–089
(2) 1–079, 14–082
(3) 14–083
s.2 14–087
(1) 14–083
(2) 14–083, 14–088
(a) 14–083
(b) .. 14–020, 14–063, 14–083
(c) 14–063, 14–083
(3) 14–020, 14–063, 14–083
(c) 14–083
(5) 14–083, 14–089, 14–093
(6) 14–081
s.3 ...... 12–127, 14–013, 14–084, 14–116
(1) 14–084
(2) 14–084, 14–085
(a) 14–084
(b) 14–084
(c) 14–084
s.4 14–088
(1)(a) 14–088
(b) 14–088
(c) 14–088
(ii) 14–088
(d) 14–088
(e) 14–081, 14–089
(f) 14–090

1987 Consumer Protection Act—*cont.*
s.4(2) 14–088, 14–092
(b) 14–088
s.5 14–084
(1) 14–087
(2) 14–087
(3) 14–001, 14–087
(4) 14–061, 14–087
(5)–(8) 14–092
s.6 14–092
(2) 14–083
(3) 14–087
(4) 14–084
(8) 14–082
s.7 . . . . . . 13–019, 13–104, 14–069, 14–083
s.10 . . . . . 14–095, 14–114, 14–116, 14–118, 14–119
(1)(b) 14–116
(3)(a) 14–088
(7) 14–001, 14–116
(a)–(f) 14–116
s.11 . . . . . 14–085, 14–095, 14–114, 14–115, 14–118
(1)(a)–(c) 14–115
(2)(a) 14–115
(f) 14–115
(g) 14–115
(j) 14–115
(5) 14–115
s.12 . . . . 14–095, 14–115
s.13 . . . . . 14–095, 14–117, 14–118, 14–122
(1)(a) 14–117
(b) 14–117
(6) 14–117
(7) 14–117
s.14 . . . . 14–095, 14–118
(1) 14–118
(7) 14–118
s.15 14–118
s.16 14–118
s.19 14–116
s.20 . . . . 2–002, 14–124
(1) 14–124
s.21 14–124
s.22(1)(b) 1–084
(c) 1–085
s.25 14–124
(2) 14–124
s.26 14–124
s.29 14–108
s.32 14–108
s.39 . . . . 14–095, 14–116
(1) 14–108
(2) 14–108
(3) 14–108
s.40(1) 14–108
(2) 14–108

1987 Consumer Protection Act—*cont.*
s.41(1) 14–095, 14–115
(2) 14–095
(3) 14–097
(4) . . . 13–019, 13–104, 14–095
s.45 14–082
(1) 1–079, 14–087, 14–058, 14–118
s.46 . . . . . 14–088, 14–092, 14–115, 14–116
s.48(3) 14–115
s.50(7) 14–081, 14–093
Sch.1 14–092
Sch.2 14–117
Sch.5 14–115

1988 Merchant Shipping Act (c.12)—
Pt I 1–082
Consumer Arbitration Agreements Act (c.21) 13–041, 14–100
Income and Corporation Taxes Act (c.1)—
s.416(2) 24–008
s.840 24–008
Road Traffic Act (c.52)—
s.65 14–097

1989 Electricity Act (c.29)—
ss.16–17 1–071
s.112(4) 1–079, 1–085
Sch.6 1–071
Sch.18 . . . . 1–079, 1–085
Law of Property (Miscellaneous Provisions) Act (c.34) 1–092, 2–022
s.1 2–021
s.2 . . . 1–092, 1–096, 1–097, 1–100, 2–022, 8–022
(6) 1–092
(8) 1–092
s.3 1–100
Companies Act (c.40) 1–016
Pt IV 5–143
ss.92–104 5–143
s.92 1–016
s.93 18–238
s.108 2–043
(1) 2–043
s.207 22–036
Statute Law (Repeals) Act (c.43)—
s.1(2) 7–111
Sch.2 7–111

1990 Food Safety Act (c.16) 14–108, 14–109, 14–110, 14–140
Pt II 14–110
s.2 14–110
s.5 14–108
ss.7–26 14–110

1989 Statute Law (Repeals) Act—*cont.*
s.7 14–110
s.8 14–110
s.9 14–110
s.10 14–110
s.11 14–110
s.12 14–110
s.13 14–110
s.14 14–110
s.15 14–110
s.16 14–110
s.17 14–110
s.18 14–110
s.19 14–110
s.20 14–108
s.21 17–065
(1) 14–108
(2) 14–108
(3) 14–108
(4) 14–108
(5) 14–108
s.32 14–108
s.33 14–108
s.34 14–108
s.36 14–108
Contracts (Applicable Law) Act (c.36) 13–100, 13–101, 25–001, 25–002, 25–015, 25–027, 25–092
s.2(1) 25–015, 25–027
(1A)(a) 25–075
(2) ... 25–027, 25–038, 25–042, 25–054, 25–103, 25–119, 25–176
(3) 25–022, 25–027
s.3 25–018
(2) 25–018
(3) 25–019
(a) 25–019
s.5 .... 4–018, 18–281, 25–027, 25–090, 25–091, 25–092, 25–160
Sch.1 .... 25–001, 25–002, 25–003, 25–004, 25–005, 25–008, 25–011, 25–012, 25–014, 25–015, 25–017, 25–018, 25–019, 25–024, 25–025, 25–026, 25–027, 25–028, 25–043, 25–069, 25–071, 25–074, 25–075, 25–076, 25–077, 25–078, 25–082, 25–083, 25–084, 25–085, 25–087, 25–088, 25–089, 25–090, 25–096, 25–098, 25–119, 25–120, 25–121, 25–145, 25–154, 25–157, 25–158, 25–161, 25–165, 25–167, 25–170, 25–171,

1990 Contracts (Applicable Law) Act—*cont.*
Sch.1—*cont.* 25–173, 25–176, 25–177, 25–179, 25–180, 25–183, 25–190, 25–191, 25–194, 25–203
art.1(1) 25–020, 25–021
(2)(a) 25–024, 25–084
(b) 25–024
(c) 25–024, 25–077
(d) 25–024, 25–089
(e) 25–024, 25–085
(f) 25–024, 25–073, 25–082, 25–085
(g) 25–024, 25–145
(h) 25–024, 25–029, 25–08, 25–194, 25–203
(3) ... 25–024, 25–074, 25–075
(4) 25–024, 25–074
art.2 25–020
art.3 ..... 25–031 25–047, 25–057, 25–067, 25–074, 28–092, 25–163
(1) .. 25–029, 25–030, 25–031, 25–033, 25–034, 25–035, 25–086, 25–092, 25–095, 25–145, 25–162, 25–164
(2) ... 25–035, 25–082, 25–086
(3) ... 4–018, 25–023, 25–037, 25–038, 25–039, 25–040, 25–041, 25–042, 25–054, 25–093, 25–103, 25–118, 25–171
(4) 25–034
art.4 ..... 25–029, 25–031, 25–033, 25–034, 25–035, 25–057, 25–066, 25–067, 25–068, 25–073, 25–074, 25–087, 25–092, 25–096, 25–097, 25–105, 25–162, 25–163, 25–164
(1) .. 25–057, 25–071, 25–086, 25–145
(2)–(4) 25–058
(2) .. 25–058, 25–059, 25–061, 25–062, 25–063, 25–064, 25–065, 25–066, 25–068, 25–069, 25–071, 25–073, 25–074, 25–076, 25–079, 25–092, 25–087, 25–162
(3) 25–058, 25–073
(4) ... 25–058, 25–069, 25–071
(5) .. 25–058, 25–059, 25–062, 25–063, 25–065, 25–066, 25–071, 25–073, 25–074, 25–076

1990 Contracts (Applicable Law) Act—*cont.*
art.5 ...... 4–018, 13–101, 25–036, 25–038, 25–040, 25–044, 25–045, 25–046, 25–047, 25–049, 25–051, 25–053, 25–054, 25–055, 25–056, 25–059, 25–067, 25–074, 25–086, 25–093, 25–099, 25–105, 25–114, 25–116, 25–118, 25–160, 25–171
(1) 25–045
(2) .. 25–047, 25–048, 25–051, 25–053, 25–054, 25–055, 25–067, 25–086, 25–098
(3) 25–067
(4)(a) 25–045
(b) 25–045
(5) 25–045
art.6 25–038
art.7 .... 25–038, 25–055
(1) .. 25–038, 25–042, 25–054, 25–055, 25–103, 25–119
(2) ... 4–018, 25–040, 25–042, 25–055, 25–056, 25–072, 25–088, 25–089, 25–099, 25–114, 25–116, 25–119, 25–160, 25–171, 25–195
art.8(1) .. 25–034, 25–078, 25–079, 25–080, 25–082, 25–083, 25–089, 25–119, 25–120
(2) 25–079, 25–083
art.9 ..... 25–035, 25–086, 25–087, 25–206
(1) 25–086
(2) 25–086
(3) 25–086
(4) ... 25–034, 25–079, 25–086
(5) 25–044, 25–086
(6) 25–086, 25–119
art.10(1) 25–082, 25–154, 25–156, 25–161, 25–168
(a) 25–156, 25–161, 25–165
(b) 25–120, 25–156, 25–161, 25–167, 25–174
(c) 25–146, 25–179, 25–180, 25–190, 25–191, 25–193, 25–195, 25–196, 25–199, 25–201
(d) 25–173, 25–174, 25–175, 25–177, 25–204
(e) 25–176
(2) 25–156, 25–157, 25–167, 25–195, 25–196
art.11 .... 25–024, 25–084
art.12 .... 25–149, 25–182
(1) 25–149, 25–202
(2) 25–149. 25–202
arts 13–15 25–046

1990 Contracts (Applicable Law) Act—*cont.*
art.14 .... 25–029, 25–087, 25–203
(1) 21–198
(2) 25–087, 25–206
art.15 25–026
art.16 ..... 4–018, 25–043, 25–119, 25–120
art.17 .... 25–001, 25–015, 25–027
art.18 25–019
art.19(1) 25–021
(2) 25–022
art.20 25–025
art.21 .... 25–025, 25–026, 25–071, 25–120, 25–145, 25–195
art.22 .... 25–038, 25–119
(1)(a) 25–042
(b) 25–176
art.23 25–025
art.24 25–025
art.25 25–025
Sch.2 25–015
Sch.3 ..... 25–015, 25–01, 25–019
art.2, preamble 25–018
(a) 25–018
(b) 25–018
art.3 25–019
Sch.3A 25–015
Sch.3B 25–015
Sch.4 ..... 4–018, 18–281, 25–027, 25–090, 25–091, 25–092, 25–160
Human Fertilisation and Embryology Act (c.37) ... 1–089
Courts & Legal Services Act (c.41)—
s.15 7–111
s.58 14–105
(1) 14–105
(4)(a) 14–105
(b) 14–105
(c) 14–105
(5) 14–105
s.58A 14–105
Sch.20 7–111
Environmental Protection Act (c.43)—
s.82 14–105
1991 Property Misdescriptions Act (c.29) 14–113
s.1(5)(d) 14–113
Road Traffic Act (c.40)—
s.67 7–10
Age of Legal Capacity (Scotland) Act (c.50) 2–029
s.3 1–001
s.10 .... A–003

1991 Age of Legal Capacity (Scotland) Act—*cont.*
Sch.2 .... 1–001, A–003
Export and Investment Guarantees Act (c.67) 24–004, 24–007
s.1 .... 24–008, 24–009
(1) 24–008
(2) 24–008
(3) 24–008
(4) 24–008
s.2 .... 24–008, 24–048, 24–049
(1) 24–008
(2) 24–008
(3) 24–008
s.3 24–009
(1) 24–009
(2) 24–009
(3) 24–009
(4) 24–009
(6) 24–009
(7) 24–009
s.4(3)(b) 24–008
s.6 24–010
ss.8–12 24–004
s.11(2) 24–008
s.13(1) 24–004, 24–008
s.15(6) 24–007
1992 Timeshare Act (c.35) 14–045, 14–054, 14–133
Carriage of Goods by Sea Act (c.50) 5–008, 5–009, 5–110, 15–009, 15–013, 18–005, 18–011, 18–013, 18–016, 18–018, 18–020, 18–023, 18–025, 18–026, 18–027, 18–040, 18–041, 18–044, 18–056, 18–060, 18–065, 18–067, 18–068, 18–073, 18–074, 18–077, 18–079, 18–080, 18–081, 18–082, 18–083, 18–088, 18–096, 18–097, 18–100, 18–101, 18–103, 18–108, 18–110, 18–111, 18–113, 18–114, 18–115, 18–116, 18–117, 18–118, 18–123, 18–129, 18–132, 18–137, 18–138, 18–139, 18–140, 18–147, 18–149, 18–152, 18–153, 18–157, 18–165, 18–169, 18–174, 18–182, 18–183, 18–184, 18–188, 18–195, 18–202, 18–203, 18–204, 18–207, 18–227, 18–286, 18–292, 18–296, 18–302, 19–008, 19–089, 19–090, 19–092, 19–093, 19–094, 19–096, 19–097, 19–104,
1992 Carriage of Goods by Sea Act (c.50)—*cont.* ... 20–059, 20–060, 20–141, 21–020, 21–050, 21–076, 21–077, 21–083, 21–094, 25–070
s.1(1) 18–101, 18–164, 18–202, 21–094
(d) 18–101
(2)(a) 18–014, 18–018, 18–040, 18–041, 18–044, 18–073, 18–103, 18–155, 21–076
(b) 18–027, 18–079, 18–103, 18–156, 19–030, 20–064, 21–076
(3) 18–013, 18–018, 18–040, 18–044, 18–083, 18–154, 19–092, 21–098
(a) .. 18–154, 18–156 18–177
(b) 18–025, 18–154
(4) 18–149, 18–169, 18–176, 18–177, 18–153, 18–183, 18–195, 18–286, 18–296, 19–092
(a) 18–041, 18–177, 18–179, 18–180 21–076
(b) 18–177, 18–153, 18–182, 18–183, 18–195
(5) 7–036, 18–202, 18–203, 19–092
(a) 18–202
(b) 18–202
(c) 18–202
s.2 ...... 18–027, 18–036, 18–073, 18–150, 19–096
(1) 18–036 18–056, 18–057, 18–102, 18–107, 18–108, 18–109, 18–110, 18–113, 18–114, 18–115, 18–116, 18–117, 18–118, 18–119, 18–120, 18–121, 18–122, 18–124, 18–125, 18–126 18–130, 18–131, 18–132, 18–133, 18–137, 18–139, 18–142, 18–144, 18–146, 18–147, 18–157, 18–160, 18–162, 18–175, 18–183, 18–185, 18–186, 18–189, 18–245, 19–030, 19–094, 20–061, 20–068
(a) 18–023, 18–040, 18–088, 18–102, 18–103, 18–104, 18–105, 18–106, 18–114, 18–115, 18–132, 18–142, 18–151, 18–186, 18–220, 19–091, 19–094, 19–219

1992 Carriage of Goods by Sea Act—*cont.*
s.2(1)(b) 18–025, 18–073, 18–119, 18–153, 18–159, 18–161, 19–091
(c) 18–023, 18–041, 18–073, 18–116, 18–120, 18–175, 18–184, 18–187, 18–195, 18–286, 18–302, 19–091
(2) 18–040, 18–080, 18–081, 18–083, 18–110, 18–113 18–135, 18–136, 18–138, 18–159, 18–220, 19–094
(a) 18–088, 18–113
(b) .. 18–113, 19–104, 19–094
(3) 18–137
(a) 18–073, 18–175, 18–195, 18–206
(b) 18–175, 18–185
(4) 18–110, 18–114, 18–119, 18–119, 18–120, 18–121, 18–122, 18–130, 19–050, 19–094, 19–104
(a) 18–119, 18–120, 18–121, 18–122, 19–050
(b) 18–119, 18–121
(5) 5–009, 18–023, 18–025, 18–114, 18–115, 18–117, 18–118, 18–119, 18–121, 18–132, 18–134, 18–142, 18–160, 18–161, 18–186, 19–050, 19–104, 20–061, 21–098
(a) .. 5–009, 18–115, 18–118, 18–186
(b) 18–118, 18–161, 18–187, 18–195
s.3 ...... 18–027, 18–088, 18–101, 18–110, 18–126, 18–129, 18–134, 18–162, 18–189, 18–190, 18–192, 18–302, 19–030, 21–020
(1) 18–101, 18–124, 18–125, 18–127, 18–132, 18–133, 18–134, 18–137, 18–139, 18–191, 19–219
(a)–(c) 18–101, 18–0140
(a) .. 18–124, 18–126 18–128, 18–129, 18–131, 18–132, 18–147, 18–162, 18–189
(b) 18–124, 18–126, 18–129, 18–131, 18–133, 18–147, 18–162, 18–189
(c) 18–124, 18–126, 18–129, 18–131, 18–162, 18–189

1992 Carriage of Goods by Sea Act—*cont.*
(2) 18–134, 18–137, 18–162, 18–190, 18–191
(3) 18–134, 18–162, 18–171, 19–219
s.4 ...... 18–027, 18–030, 18–031, 18–036, 18–037, 18–038, 18–039, 18–040, 18–041, 18–042, 18–043, 18–044, 18–045, 18–103, 18–107, 18–132, 18–135, 18–136, 18–148, 18–164, 18–191, 19–030, 19–035, 21–035, 20–065
(a) 18–036, 18–038, 19–030
(b) 18–036, 18–037, 18–038
s.5 18–042
(1) 18–048, 18–106, 18–107, 18–114, 18–118 18–142, 18–153, 18–154, 18–175, 18–176, 18–177, 18–179, 18–202
(b) 18–179, 18–184
(2) 18–023, 18–040, 18–042, 18–043, 18–080, 18–104, 18–105, 18–113, 18–125, 18–131, 18–220, 19–219, 20–065
(a) 18–088, 18–118, 18–150, 18–204, 19–094
(b) 18–014, 18–103, 18–104, 18–118, 18–147, 18–186, 19–094
(c) .. 18–081, 18–083, 18–113
(3) 18–025, 18–041, 18–154, 18–155, 18–159, 18–161, 18–176, 18–177, 18–182, 18–183, 18–187, 18–195, 19–092
(4) 18–135, 18–136, 18–137, 18–176, 18–185
(a) 18–135, 18–136
(b) 18–135, 18–180
(5) 18–034, 18–044
s.6(2) 18–033, 18–100
(3) 18–011
Car Tax (Abolition) Act (c.58) 5–051
1993 Charities Act 1993 (c.10)—
s.65 2–043
European Economic Area Act (c.51) 25–074
1994 Coal Industry Act (c.21)—
s.7 1–097
s.8 1–097
Value Added Tax Act (c.23)—
s.6(2)(c) 5–051
s.36(4)(b) 5–170

1994 Value Added Tax Act—*cont.*
Sch.4
para.1(1) 1–081
para.3 .... 1–085, 1–087
para.4 1–084
Sale of Goods (Amendment) Act 1994 (c.32) ... 1–001, 7–020
s.1 .... 1–082, A–013
s.3(2) A–013
Sale and Supply of Goods Act 1994 (c.35) 1–001, 11–025, 11–050, 11–074, 11–085, 12–030, 12–051, 12–053, 12–054, 12–060, 12–062, 13–102, 14–047
s.1 ..... 11–026, 14–010, 17–051, 18–209
(1) 14–013, 18–255
(2) A–010
s.2 ..... 12–039, 12–050, 12–054, 12–062, 12–063, 13–102
(1) 12–044, 12–051, 12–053, 14–021, 20–111, A–015
(2)(a) A–015
(b) A–015
s.3 12–060
(1) A–015
(2) 12–038, A–007
s.4 18–266
(1) 18–045, 12–024
(2) 8–051 A–010, A–014
s.5(1) A–010
(2) A–014
(3) A–025
s.7 ...... 1–031, 11–001, 11–023, 11–050, 11–051, 11–069, 11–074, 11–087, 11–088, 12–024, 12–050, 14–009
(1) 1–031
s.8(2) 11–028
Sch.2 ..... 1–031, 10–027, 11–001, 11–023, 11–050, 11–051, 11–069, 11–074, 11–087, 11–088, 12–024, 12–050
para.4 .... 1–019, 4–035
para.5 14–009
para.5(2) A–007
para.5(3) A–008
para.5(3)(b) A–008
para.5(4)(a) A–009
para.5(4)(b) A–009
para.5(5)(a) A–009
para.5(5)(b) A–009
para.5(6)(a) A–010
para.5(6)(b) A–010
para.5(7) A–025
para.5(8) A–027
para.5(9)(a)(i) A–030
para.5(9)(c) A–030

1994 Sale and Supply of Goods Act—*cont.*
para.6 14–047
para.6(1) 1–031
para.6(2) 1–031
para.10 .... A–007
Sch.3 ..... 5–085, 11–050, 11–069, 11–074, 11–087, A–007, A–010, A–014, A–030
Law of Property (Miscellaneous Provisions) Act (c.36)—
s.3 4–023
1995 Merchant Shipping Act (c.21) 1–082, 2–023
s.1(1) 1–082
(2) 1–082
s.8(5) 1–082
s.313 1–082
(1) 1–081
Sch.I,
para.2(1) 1–082, 2–023
Sale of Goods (Amendment) Act 1995 (c.28) .. 1–001, 1–010, 1–015, 1–081, 1–107, 1–112, 5–110, 11–078, 12–079, 15–096, 15–097, 18–194, 18–287, 18–295
s.1(1) 1–015, 18–194, 19–098, A–011
(2) 5–103, 5–107, 18–288, A–011
(3) 1–20, 5–061, 5–110, 12–079, 17–097, 19–098, A–012
s.2(a) 18–295, A–030
(b) 5–120, 8–017, A–030
(c) 1–078, 1–115, A–030
(d) 1–108, 1–113, 1–116, 5–022, 5–112, 6–007, 6–036, 12–083, 12–085, 17–097, 18–193, A–030
s.3(1) 1–081
(2) 1–081
Civil Evidence Act (c.38)—
s.13 18–202
Private International Law (Miscellaneous Provisions) Act (c.42)— 25–148
Pt III 25–148, 25–190
s.1(1) 25–191
s.2 25–191
s.11(1) 25–148
(2)(c) 25–148
s.12 25–148
(1) 25–148
1996 Treasure Act (c.24) 1–097
Police Act (c.16)—
s.81(3) 18–202

1996 Arbitration Act (c.23) 2–052, 13–041, 14–100
s.9 .... 13–041, 14–100
s.29 13–040
s.48(5)(b) 17–100
s.49 .... 6–067, 16–012, 25–191
(3) 16–012
(4) 16–013
(6) 16–012
s.74 13–040
ss.85–91 13–069
s.86 .... 13–041, 14–100
ss.89–91 13–041
s.89(1), (2) 14–100
s.90 ...... 13–041, 13–103, 14–100
s.91 14–100
(1) 14–100
s.107(2) 14–100
Sch.4 14–100
1997 Police (Property) Act (c.30)—
s.1 7–111
1998 Petroleum Act (c.17)—
s.1 1–087
s.2 .... 1–087, 1–097
Late Payment of Commercial Debts (Interest) Act (c.20) ... 1–023, 16–010, 16–013, 25–153, 25–162, 25–163, 25–164, 25–191
Pt I 25–162
Pt II 16–010, 25–162
s.1(1) 16–010, 25–162
(2) 25–162
(3) 16–010
s.2(1) 16–010, 25–162
(2) 16–010, 25–162
(3) 16–010, 25–162
(4) 16–010
(5) 16–010, 25–162
(7) 16–010, 25–162
s.3(1) 16–010, 25–162
(2) 16–010
(3) 16–010
(4) 16–010
s.4(3) 16–011
(4) 16–011
(5)(a) 16–011
(b) 16–011
(7) 16–011
s.5(1) 16–011
(2) 16–011
(3) 16–011
(4) 16–011
(5) 16–011
s.6 16–010
ss.7–10 .... 16–010, 25–162
s.9 16–010
s.11 16–011
s.11(3) 16–011
s.11(4)–(7) 16–011
1998 Late Payment of Commercial Debts (Interest) Act—*cont.*
s.12 .... 16–010, 25–162
s.12(1) ... 25–091, 25–162, 25–163, 25–164
(b) 25–163
(2) ... 25–094, 25–163, 25–164
(3) ... 25–162, 25–163, 25–164
s.13 16–010
s.14 16–011
s.16 16–010
s.17(5) 25–134
Competition Act (c.41) 3–040, 14–125, 14–138
Pt I 3–040
Chap. I 3–036, 3–037, 3–040
Chap. II 3–040
Chap. III 14–138
s.2(1) 3–040, 14–138
s.3 3–040
(6) 3–040
ss.3–11 14–138
s.4 3–040
s.6 3–040
s.18 3–040
s.19 3–040
ss.25–44 14–138
s.60 3–040
s.70 3–036
s.74(3) 3–037
Sch.1 3–040
Schs 1–4 3–040
Sch.3 3–040
Sch.14 3–037
1999 Access to Justice Act (c.22)—
s.27(1) 14–105
Food Standards Act (c.28) .. 14–110
s.40(1) 14–110
Sch.5 14–110
Contracts (Rights of Third Parties) Act (c.31) ... 2–026, 3–037, 13–018, 14–019, 14–077, 14–080, 17–030, 17–045, 17–072, 17–080, 17–085, 17–096, 18–005, 18–021, 18–024, 18–026, 18–055, 18–056, 18–096, 18–101, 18–112, 18–117, 18–145, 18–188, 18–204, 19–090, 19–092, 19–094, 19–096, 19–097, 20–003, 20–059, 20–060, 20–061, 20–062, 20–064, 20–068, 20–069, 21–050, 21–077, 21–094, 25–082
s.1 ...... 13–018, 18–005, 18–024, 18–055, 18–056, 18–057, 18–096, 18–101, 18–117,

1999 Contracts (Rights of Third Parties) Act—*cont.*
s.1—*cont.* 18–145, 18–188, 19–092, 19–094, 19–097, 20–059, 20–061, 20–062, 20–063, 20–065, 20–066, 20–068, 21–077
(1) 2–026, 13–018, 14–019, 18–057, 20–060, 20–061, 20–068
(a) 18–005
(b) .. 17–072, 18–005, 20–068
(c) 20–068
(2) 2–026, 13–018, 14–019, 17–072, 18–005, 18–024
(3) 2–026, 13–018, 14–019, 18–005, 18–204, 19–094, 19–096
(4) 18–005, 18–024, 18–048, 18–056, 20–060, 20–068
(5) 14–019
(6) 13–018, 18–005
s.2 .... 18–005, 18–024
(1) 18–005, 18–056, 20–060
(3) 18–005
(4) 18–005
(5) 18–005, 19–092
s.3 18–005
(1) 13–018
(2) 13–018, 18–005, 21–077
(a) 19–096
(3) 18–005
(4) 18–005, 21–077
(6) 18–005
s.4 ...... 18–005, 18–117, 19–092, 20–061
s.5 .... 18–005, 18–117
(1) 17–080
s.6 18–005
(2) 18–005
(5) 18–005, 18–024, 18–055, 18–057, 18–058, 18–096, 18–101, 18–117, 18–145, 18–188, 19–090, 19–092, 19–094, 19–096, 19–097, 20–059, 20–060, 20–061, 20–062, 20–063, 20–064, 20–065, 20–066, 20–068, 21–050, 21–077
(a) 19–092, 21–077
(b) .. 18–096, 21–050, 21–077
(f) 18–188
(6) 18–024, 18–026, 18–055, 18–101, 18–117, 18–145, 18–188, 20–060, 20–061, 20–063, 20–064, 20–066, 20–068
(a) 18–096, 18–188, 19–092, 20–059

1999 Contracts (Rights of Third Parties) Act—*cont.*
s.6(6)(b) 18–188, 19–092
(7) 18–024, 18–055, 18–101, 18–117, 18–145, 18–188, 20–060, 20–063, 20–064, 20–066, 20–068
(a) 18–096, 18–188, 19–092, 20–059
(8) 18–096, 21–050, 21–077
(c)(iii) 21–077
s.7 .... 18–145, 21–077
(1) 13–018, 18–005, 20–069
(4) 14–019
2000 Powers of Criminal Courts (Sentencing) Act (c.6) .. 14–106
s.130(1) 14–106
(b) 14–106
(3) 14–107
(4) 14–107
(5) 14–106
(6)–(8) 14–106
(11) 14–106
(12) 14–106
s.131(1) 14–107
s.132 14–106
s.133 14–106
s.134 14–107
s.143 7–111
s.144 7–111
s.148 .... 1–084, 7–006
(2)(a) 7–006
(b) 7–006
(c) 7–006
(8) 7–006
(9) 7–006
s.149 7–006
Electronic Communications Act (c.7) 1–024, 2–021
Pt I 9–036
Pt II 22–036
s.7 2–021
Financial Services and Markets Act (c.8) 14–146, 24–036, 25–074, 25–075
ss.26–28 .... 3–028, 3–032
s.31 14–146
(1)(b) 14–143
s.147(1) 14–146
s.194 14–143
s.203 14–143
s.204 14–143
s.225(4) 14–146
s.412 1–104
Sch.3 14–143
para.15(3) 14–146
Sch.17 14–146

2000 Limited Liability Partnerships Act (c.12)—
s.1(2) 2–043
(3) 2–043
Utilities Act (c.27)—
s.44 1–071
s.51 1–071
s.80 1–071
s.84 1–071
Sch.4 1–071
Insolvency Act (c.39) 5–005
s.1 5–164
2001 Criminal Justice and Police Act (c.16) 7–006
s.50 7–007
s.51 7–007
s.52 7–007
ss.53–57 7–007
s.58 7–007
s.59 7–007
s.60 7–007
s.61 7–007
Sch.1 7–007
2002 Office of Communications Act (c.11)
s.1(1) 14–140
Proceeds of Crime Act (c.29) 7–007
Pt 2 (ss.6–91) 7–007
Pt 5 7–117
ss.40–47 7–007
s.77 7–007
s.78 7–007
s.81 7–007
s.83 7–007
s.241 7–111
s.242 7–111
s.267 7–111
s.281 7–111
s.281(3)(a) 7–111
(b) 7–111
(c) 7–111
s.288 7–111
s.316(1) 7–117
(4) 7–117
(5) 7–117
(6) 7–117
(7) 7–117
s.352 7–007
Sch.7 7–111
Sch.11, para.40 7–007
Sch.12 7–007
Police Reform Act (c.30)
s.59 7–007
s.60 7–007
s.77 .... 7–007, 7–111
s.84 7–007
Sch.4
para.9 7–007
para.19 7–007
para.24 7–007
2002 Enterprise Act (c.40) 1–023, 13–105, 14–125, 14–137, 14–138
Pt 3 3–040
Pt 8 ...... 1–023, 14–028, 14–040, 14–043, 14–050, 14–059, 14–074, 14–103, 14–130, 14–131, 14–134, 14–135, 14–136, 14–140, 14–156
s.2(1) 14–125
(2) 14–125
s.3 14–125
s.4 14–125
s.5 14–125
s.6 .... 14–125, 14–137
s.7 .... 14–125, 14–137
s.8 13–098
s.10 14–127
(2)(a) 14–127
(b) 14–127
s.11 14–127
(2) 14–127
(5) 14–127
ss.210–236 14–130
s.210 14–131
(2) 14–131
(3) 14–131
(4) 14–131
(5) 14–131
(6) 14–131
(7) 14–133
(8) 14–131
s.211 .... 13–105, 14–028, 14–059, 14–140, 14–156
(1) 14–040, 14–131
(2) 14–131
(a)–(g) 14–131
(e) 14–040
(f) 14–040
(g) 14–040
s.212 .... 14–028, 14–059, 14–140, 14–156
(1) 14–133
(5) 14–133
s.213 14–134
(1) 14–134
(2) 14–134
(3) 14–134
(5) 14–134
(6) 14–134
s.214(1)(a) 14–135
(b) 14–135
(3) 14–135
(4)(a) 14–135
(b) 14–135
s.215(2) 14–134
(3) 14–134
(4) 14–134
(5)(a) 14–135

2002 Enterprise Act—*cont.*
s.216 14–135
(6) 14–135
s.217(1) 14–135
(2) 14–135
s.218 14–135
s.219 14–135
s.221 14–134
s.222 14–135
(3) 14–133
(4) 25–008
s.223 14–135
(3) 1–043, 1–079
s.248 .... 5–005, 5–162, 7–111
s.250 .... 5–161, 5–165, 7–111
s.278 14–130
Sch.13 ... 14–028, 14–059, 14–131, 14–133, 14–140
Sch.16 ...... 5–005, 5–162, 7–111
para.44 5–005
para.111(1) 5–005
Sch.26 14–130
2003 Licensing Act (c.17)
s.192 12–079
Railway and Transport Safety Act (c.20)
s.103 21–047
Sch.6 21–047
Courts Act (c.39)
Sch.7
para.7(1) 7–113
(3) 7–113
para.8(1) 7–113
(2) 7–113
(3) 7–113
(4) 7–113
(5) 7–113
para.10 7–111
Sch.8 7–111
2003 Criminal Justice Act (c.44)
Sch.1
para.4 7–007
para.14 7–007
para.19 7–007
2004 Human Tissue Act (c.30) 1–089
s.32 1–089
(8) 1–089
(9) 1–089
2005 Mental Capacity Act (c.9)—
s.7 .... 1–076, 2–030, 2–032, 2–041
Sch.6,
para.24 .... 1–076, 2–030, 2–041
Serious Organised Crime and Police Act (c.15)
s.97 7–007
s.109 7–111
Sch.6,
para.2 7–111
Gambling Act (c.19) 1–104
s.334(1)(c) 1–104
(e) 1–104
2006 Consumer Credit Act (c.14) .. 1–019, 1–021, 1–022, 2–003, 3–005, 5–021, 7–070, 7–108, 9–065, 14–143, 14–145, 14–151
ss.1–3 1–021
s.4 7–088
ss.8–15 14–146

TABLE OF STATUTORY INSTRUMENTS

1946 Bretton Woods Agreements Order in Council (SR&O 1946/36) 23–135, 25–120
art.3 25–120
Sch., Pt I, art.VIII 23–135
1954 Import of Goods (Control) Order (SI 1954/23) 18–308
1964 Hire-Purchase and Credit Sale Agreements (Control) Order 1964 (SI 1964/942) 7–090
1965 Hire-Purchase (Documents) (Legibility and Statutory Statements) Regulations 1965 (SI 1965/1646) 2–023
Rules of the Supreme Court (SI 1965/1776) 17–090
Ord.11
r.1(1) 25–001
(d)(iii) 25–020
(e) 25–012, 25–157, 25–161
Ord.14 23–029
r.1 .... 22–062, 23–135
Ord.15
r.10A 5–010
r.11A 5–010
r.12 14–103
Ord.18
r.7(4) 8–004, 9–017
Ord.29
r.4 15–120
1967 Carriage by Air Acts (Application of Provisions) Order (SI 1967/480)—
Sch.2, Pt B, Sect. A
art.6 21–051
art.6(2) 21–053
art.11(1) 21–052
art.12 21–055
(1) 21–052
(3) 21–054, 21–067
(4) .. 21–052, 21–055, 21–057
art.13(1) .. 21–052, 21–055, 21–057
(2) 21–052
art.15 21–106
(1) .. 21–055, 21–062, 21–069
(3) 21–052
art.31 .... 21–051, 21–104
Strategic Goods (Control) Order (SI 1967/983) 18–308
1979 Mail Order Transactions (Information) Order (SI 1976/1812) 14–126
1976 Consumer Protection (Restrictions on Statements) Order (SI 1976/1813) ... 1–006, 4–018, 11–011, 13–067, 13–084, 13–105, 14–065, 14–069, 14–075, 14–126, 14–142
1977 Business Advertisements (Disclosure) Order (SI 1977/1918) 13–105, 14–126, 14–141
1978 Consumer Transactions (Restrictions on Statements) (Amendment) Order (SI 1978/127) 1–006, 4–018, 13–084, 13–105, 14–126, 14–142
art.5 14–065
Torts (Interference with Goods) Act 1977 (Commencement No.2) Order (SI 1978/627) 4–007, 4–012
Export of Goods (Control) Order (SI 1978/796) 18–308
1979 Price Marking (Food and Drink on Premises) Order (SI 1979/361) 14–111
Price Marking (Bargain Offers) Order (SI 1979/364) 14–124
1980 Consumer Credit (Total Charge for Credit) Regulations (SI 1980/51) 1–022, 14–150
Price Marking (Petrol) Order (SI 1980/1121) 14–111
Trade Descriptions (Sealskin Goods) (Information) Order (SI 1980/1150) ... 14–112
1981 County Court Rules (SI 1981/1687)—
Ord.13,
r.7(f) 15–121
Ord.19 14–101
1982 Supply of Goods and Services Act 1982 (Commencement) Order (SI 1982/1770) 1–031
Supply of Services (Exclusion of Implied Terms) Order (SI 1982/1771) 14–051
1983 Supply of Services (Exclusion of Implied Terms) Order (SI 1983/902) 14–051

1983 Consumer Credit Act 1974 (Commencement No.8) Order (SI 1983/1551) ... 4–035, 7–087, 14–143
art.6(1), (2) 14–143
(3) 14–143
Consumer Credit (Agreements) Regulations (SI 1983/1553) 2–023, 14–145, 14–150
Sch.2, Pt I, para.15 14–149
Consumer Credit (Credit-Token Agreements) Regulations (SI 1983/1555) 14–149
Consumer Credit (Guarantees and Indemnities) Regulations (SI 1983/1556) .. 14–145
Consumer Credit (Cancellation Notices and Copies of Documents) Regulations (SI 1983/1557) 14–145
reg.8 14–149
Consumer Credit (Linked Transactions) (Exemptions) Regulations (SI 1983/1560) 14–150
Consumer Credit (Enforcement, Default and Termination Notices) Regulations (SI 1983/1561) 14–145
Consumer Credit (Settlement Information) Regulations (SI 1983/1564) 14–145
Consumer Credit (Running-Account Credit Information) Regulations (SI 1983/1570) 14–145
Sale of Goods Act 1979 (Appointed Day) Order (SI 1983/1572) ... 7–070, A–009, A–013
Consumer Credit (Increase of Monetary Limits) Order (SI 1983/1878) ... 1–021, 5–021, 9–065, 14–143
1984 Consumer Credit (Cancellation Notices and Copies of Documents) (Amendment) Regulations (SI 1984/1108) 14–145
Consumer Credit (Enforcement, Default and Termination Notices) (Amendment) Regulations (SI 1984/1109) 14–145
1984 Consumer Credit (Agreements) (Amendment) Regulations (SI 1984/1600) ... 2–023, 14–145, 14–150
Gas Catalytic Heaters (Safety) Regulations (SI 1984/1802) 14–115
1985 Supply of Services (Exclusion of Implied Terms) Order (SI 1985/1) 14–051
International Transport Conventions Act 1983 (Certification of Commencement of Convention) Order (SI 1985/612) 21–047
Consumer Credit (Exempt Advertisements) Order (SI 1985/621) 14–155
Consumer Credit (Agreements and Cancellation Notices and Copies of Documents) (Amendment) Regulations (SI 1985/666) 2–023, 14–145, 14–150
Consumer Credit (Exempt Agreements) (No.2) Order (SI 1985/757) 1–022
Consumer Credit (Total Charge for Credit) (Amendment) Regulations (SI 1985/1192) 1–022, 14–150
Asbestos Products (Safety) Regulations (SI 1985/2042) 14–115
Nightwear (Safety) Regulations (SI 1985/2043) 14–115
1986 Removal and Disposal of Vehicles Regulations (SI 1986/183)—
reg.15 7–111
Insolvency Rules (SI 1986/1925)—
r.4.90 25–191
1987 Nightwear (Safety) (Amendment) Regulations (SI 1987/286) 14–115
Bunk Beds (Entrapment Hazards) (Safety) Regulations (SI 1987/1337) 14–115
Consumer Protection Act 1987 (Commencement No.1) Order (SI 1987/1680) ... 14–093
arts.6–9 14–114
art.8 14–114
Asbestos Products (Safety) (Amendment) Regulations (SI 1987/1979) 14–115

1987 Consumer Protection (Cancellation of Contracts Concluded away from Business Premises) Regulations (SI 1987/2117) ... 1–023, 2–020, 14–045, 14–133, 25–055
reg.2(1) ... 14–045
reg.3(1)(a)–(d) ... 14–045
(2) ... 14–045
(3) ... 14–045
reg.4(1), (5) ... 14–045
(6) ... 14–045
reg.4A ... 14–045
reg.5–8 ... 14–045
1988 Control of Misleading Advertisements Regulations (SI 1988/915) ... 4–121, 14–133, 14–140
reg.2(1) ... 14–140
reg.4 ... 14–140
(3) ... 14–140
reg.5 ... 14–040, 14–136, 14–140
reg.6(1) ... 14–140
Consumer Protection (Cancellation of Contracts Concluded away from Business Premises) (Amendment) Regulations (SI 1988/958) ... 14–045, 25–055
Furniture and Furnishings (Fire) (Safety) Regulations (SI 1988/1324) .. 14–115
Ceramic Ware (Safety) Regulations (SI 1988/1647) .. 14–115
Consumer Credit (Agreements and Cancellation Notices and Copies of Documents) (Amendment) Regulations (SI 1988/2047) ... 2–023, 14–145, 14–150
Distress for Rent Rules (SI 1988/2050) ... 7–111
1989 Merchant Shipping Act 1988 (Commencement No.3) Order (SI 1989/353) ... 1–082
Consumer Credit (Cancellation Notices and Copies of Documents) (Amendment) Regulations (SI 1989/591) ... 14–145
Consumer Credit (Total Charge for Credit and Rebate on Early Settlement) (Amendment) Regulations (SI 1989/596) ... 1–022, 14–150
1989 Consumer Credit (Exempt Agreements) Order (SI 1989/869) 1–022, 1–055, 14–143
art.3(1)(a)(i) ... 1–022, 1–055, 9–065, 14–148
(ii) ... 1–022, 9–065, 14–148, 14–149
art.4(1)(a) ... 1–022
(5) ... 1–022
(6) ... 1–022
art.5 ... 1–022
Food Imitations (Safety) Regulations (SI 1989/1291) .. 14–115
Consumer Credit (Exempt Agreements) (Amendment) Order (SI 1989/1841) ... 1–022, 14–143
All-Terrain Motor Vehicles (Safety) Regulations (SI 1989/2288) ... 14–115
Consumer Credit (Exempt Agreements) (Amendment) (No.2) Order (SI 1989/2337) ... 1–022, 14–143
Oral Snuff (Safety) Regulations (SI 1989/2347) .. 14–115
Furniture and Furnishings (Fire) (Safety) (Amendment) Regulations (SI 1989/2358) ... 14–115
1991 Price Indications (Method of Payment) Regulations (SI 1991/199) ... 14–124
Value Added Tax (Refunds for Bad Debts) Regulations (SI 1991/371) ... 5–170
Contracts (Applicable Law) Act 1990 (Commencement No.1) Order (SI 1991/707) ... 25–015
High Court and County Courts Jurisdiction Order (SI 1991/724) ... 14–102
art.5(1) ... 14–102
Estate Agents (Undesirable Practices) (No.2) Order (SI 1991/1032) ... 14–138
Estate Agents (Specified Offences) (No.2) Order (SI 1991/1091) ... 14–138
County Courts (Interest on Judgment Debts) Order (SI 1991/1184) .. 14–035, 16–013
Price Marking Order (SI 1991/1382) ... 14–111
Consumer Credit (Exempt Agreements) (Amendment) Order (SI 1991/1393) ... 14–143

1991 Construction Products Regulations (SI 1991/1620) .. 14–115
Consumer Credit (Exempt Agreements) (Amendment) (No.2) Order (SI 1991/1949) 1–022, 14–143
Export and Investment Guarantees Act 1991 (Commencement) Order (SI 1991/2430) 24–007
Value Added Tax (Buildings and Land) Order (SI 1991/2569)—
art.4(a) 2–043
art.7 2–043
Heating Appliances (Fireguards (Safety) Regulations (SI 1991/2693) .. 14–115
Simple Pressure Vessels (Safety) Regulations (SI 1991/2749) 14–115
Order Consumer Credit (Exempt Agreements) (Amendment) (No.3) (SI 1991/2844) 1–022, 14–143
1992 Price Indications (Bureaux de Change) (No.2) Regulations (SI 1992/737) ... 14–124
Property Misdescriptions (Specified Matters) Order (SI 1992/2834) 14–113
Asbestos (Prohibitions) Regulations (SI 1992/3067) .. 14–115
Supply of Machinery (Safety) Regulations (SI 1992/3073) 14–115
Personal Protective Equipment (EC Directive) Regulations (SI 1992/3139) .. 14–115
Plastic Materials and Articles in Contact with Food Regulations (SI 1992/3145) 14–115
Active Implantable Medical Devices Regulations (SI 1992/3146) 14–115
Banking Coordination (Second Council Directive) Regulations (SI 1992/3218)—
reg.61(1), (3), (4) 14–146
reg.82(1) 14–143
Sch.10,
Pt II
para.54 14–143
Package Travel, Package Holidays and Package Tours Regulations (SI 1992/3288) 14–050, 14–054, 14–133
reg.13(3)(b) 8–100
1992 Package Travel, Package Holidays and Package Tours Regulations—*cont.*
reg.15(2)(c)(i) 8–100
1993 Furniture and Furnishings (Fire) (Safety) (Amendment) Regulations (SI 1993/207) 14–115
Consumer Credit (Exempt Agreements) (Amendment) Order (SI 1993/346) 1–022, 14–143
Judgment Debts (Rate of Interest) Order (SI 1993/564) 16–013
High Court and County Courts Jurisdiction (Amendment) Order (SI 1993/1407) ... 14–102
Consumer Credit (Exempt Agreements) (Amendment) (No.2) Order (SI 1993/2922) 1–022, 14–143
Imitation Dummies (Safety) Regulations (SI 1993/2923) 14–115
Commercial Agents (Council Directive) Regulations (SI 1993/3053) 1–048, 3–004, 25–073
reg.1(2) 3–004
reg.17 25–073
reg.18 25–073
Personal Protective Equipment (EC Directive) (Amendment) Regulations (SI 1993/3074) 14–115
Commercial Agents (Council Directive) (Amendment) Regulations (SI 1993/3173) 3–004, 25–073
1994 Return of Cultural Objects Regulations (SI 1994/501) 25–131
Plugs and Sockets etc. (Safety) Regulations (SI 1994/1768) 14–115
Contracts (Applicable Law) Act 1990 (Amendment) Order (SI 1994/1900) ... 25–015
Supply of Machinery (Safety) (Amendment) Regulations (SI 1994/2063) .. 14–115
Personal Protective Equipment (EC Directive) (Amendment) Regulations (SI 1994/2326) 14–115
General Product Safety Regulations (SI 1994/2328) .. 14–116, 14–119, 14–122
reg.2(1) 14–119

1994 Consumer Credit (Exempt Agreements) (Amendment) Order (SI 1994/2420) 1–022, 14–143
Dangerous Substances and Preparations (Safety) (Consolidation) Regulations (SI 1994/2844) .. 14–115
Medical Devices Regulations (SI 1994/3017) 14–115
Construction Products (Amendment) Regulations (SI 1994/3051) .. 14–115
Simple Pressure Vessels (Safety) (Amendment) Regulations (SI 1994/3098) 14–115
Motor Vehicle Tyres (Safety) Regulations (SI 1994/3117) 14–115
Medicines for Human Use (Marketing Authoris ations Etc.) Regulations (SI 1994/3144) .. 14–116, 14–123
Unfair Terms in Consumer Contracts Regulations (SI 1994/3159) 1–001, 1–014, 1–023, 13–003, 13–009, 13–041, 13–063, 13–067, 13–069, 13–103, 14–030, 14–034, 14–040, 14–100, 14–128, 16–009, 16–041, 25–042, 25–101
reg.2(1) 14–100
reg.3(2) .. 13–067, 14–033, 19–048
(a) 14–033
(b) 14–033
reg.4(4) 14–100, 25–102
reg.5(1) 1–014
reg.8 .... 14–040, 14–128
Sch.3 25–102
para.1(q) 14–100
Price Indications (Resale of Tickets) Regulations (SI 1994/3248) 14–124
Electrical Equipment (Safety) Regulations (SI 1994/3260) 14–115
1995 Public Supply Contracts Regulations (SI 1995/201)—
reg.21 2–003
Toys (Safety) Regulations (SI 1995/204) 14–115
High Court and County Courts Jurisdiction (Amendment) Order (SI 1995/205) 14–102
art.4A 14–102
1995 N-nitrosamines and N-nitrosatable Substances in Elastomer or Rubber Teats and Dummies (Safety) Regulations (SI 1995/1012) 14–115
Consumer Credit (Exempt Agreements) (Amendment) Order 1995 (SI 1995/1250) 1–022, 14–143
Appliances (Safety) Regulations (SI 1995/1629) .. 14–115
Package Travel, Package Holidays and Package Tours (Amendment) Regulations (SI 1995/1648) .. 14–050
Active Implantable Medical Devices (Amendment and Transitional Provisions) Regulations (SI 1955/1671) 14–115
Consumer Credit (Exempt Agreements) (Amendment) (No.2) Order (SI 1995/2914) 1–022, 14–143
Investment Services Regulations (SI 1995/3275) .. 14–143
reg.38(1) 14–146
(3) 14–146
1996 Private International Law (Miscellaneous Provisions) Act 1995 (Commencement) Order (SI 1996/995) 25–148
Consumer Credit (Exempt Agreements) (Amendment) Order (SI 1996/1445) 1–022, 14–143
Dangerous Substances and Preparations (Safety) (Consolidation) (Amendment) Regulations (SI 1996/2635) 14–115
Utilities Contracts Regulations (SI 996/2911)—
reg.21 2–003
Deregulation (Bills of Exchange) Order (SI 1996/2993) 22–108, 22–114
Personal Protective Equipment (EC Directive) (Amendment) Regulations (SI 1996/3039) 14–115
Consumer Credit (Exempt Agreements) (Amendment) (No.2) Order (SI 1996/3081) 1–022, 14–143

1996 1996 High Court and County Courts Jurisdiction (Amendment) Order (SI 1996/3141) 14–102
Arbitration Act 1996 (Commencement No.1) Order (SI 1996/3146)—
art.3 14–100
Motor Vehicle Tyres (Safety) (Amendment) Regulations (SI 1996/3227) .. 14–115
1997 Trading Schemes Regulations (SI 1997/30) 14–141
Trading Schemes (Exclusion) Regulations (SI 1997/31) 14–141
Motor Vehicle Tyres (Safety) (Amendment) Regulations (SI 1997/815) ... 14–115
Lifts Regulations (SI 1997/831) 14–115
Timeshare Regulations (SI 1997/1081) 14–045
Return of Cultural Objects (Amendment) Regulations (SI 1997/1719) .. 25–131
Wheeled Child Conveyances (Safety) Regulations (SI 1997/2866) 14–115
1998 Consumer Credit (Increase of Monetary Limits) (Amendment) Order (SI 1998/996) 1–021, 1–022, 5–021, 7–070, 7–088, 9–068, 14–143
Consumer Credit (Further Increase of Monetary Amounts) Order (SI 1998/997) 14–145, 14–149
Package Travel, Package Holidays and Package Tours (Amendment) Regulations (SI 1998/1208) ... 8–099, 14–050
Plastic Materials and Articles in Contact with Food Regulations (SI 1998/1376) 14–115
County Courts (Interest on Judgment Debts) (Amendment) Order (SI 1998/2400) 16–013
Pencils and Graphic Instruments (Safety) Regulations (SI 1998/2406) .. 14–115
1998 Late Payment of Commercial Debts (Interest) Act 1998 (Commencement No.1) Order (SI 1998/2479)—
art.2(2) 16–010
Late Payment o Commercial Debts (Rate of Interest) Order (SI 1998/2480) ... 16–010
Late Payment of Commercial Debts (Interest) Act 1998 (Transitional Provisions) Regulations (SI 1998/2481) 16–010
Late Payment of Commercial Debts (Rate of Interest) (No.2) Order (SI 1998/2765) 16–010
Commercial Agents (Council Directive) (Amendment) Regulations (SI 1998/2868) 3–004, 25–073
Consumer Protection (Cancellation of Contracts Concluded away from Business Premises) (Amendment) Regulations (SI 1998/3050) ... 1–023, 14–045
reg.2(b) 14–045
(c) 14–045
Civil Procedure Rules (SI 1998/3132) 7–112, 14–102, 14–104, 17–096, 18–185
r.6.20(6) .. 25–012, 25–157, 25–161
r.6.21(2A) 25–020
Pt 12, r.6 16–007
Pt 16, PD, para.9 25–194
r.16.4(1)(a) .. 8–004, 9–009, 9–018
(2) 16–007
Pt 19 III 14–104
r.19(1) 18–185
(2)(a) 18–185
r.19.10 14–104
r.19.11 14–104
(2)(a) 14–104
r.19.12(1)(a) 14–104
r.19.13(b) 14–104
r.20.2 5–014
Pt 24 9–032
r.25.1(i)(c)(v) 7–112, 15–120
r.26.6 14–101
(4) 14–102
r.26.6(5) 14–102
r.26.7 14–102
r.26.8 14–102
Pt 27 14–101
r.27.6 14–101
r.27.8 14–101
r.27.14 14–101
(2)(b) 14–101

1998 Civil Procedure Rules—*cont.*
Pt 28 14–102
Pt 29 14–102
Pt 29, PD, 29.2.2 14–102
Pt 36 16–007
PD, para.9 25–194
r.36.22 16–007
Pt 40, PD 40B, para.10 ... 25–194
r.44.4 4–016
Pt 48 14–104
r.48.6A 14–104
Pt 49, PD 49F, para.8 7–112
r.61.10 7–113
Sch.1 .... 5–014, 7–111
RSC
Ord.17,
r.6 7–112
Ord.45,
r.4(1) 15–116, 17–096
Ord.46 .... 5–014, 7–111
Ord.47 7–111

1999 High Court and County Courts Jurisdiction (Amendment) Order (SI 1999/1014) ... 14–102
art.5 14–102
art.6 14–102
Carriage by Air Acts (Implementation of Protocol No.4 of Montreal 1975) Order (SI 1999/1312) ... 21–047
Cross Border Credit Transfer Regulation (SI 1999/1876) 22–006
Consumer Credit (Exempt Agreements) (Amendment) Order (SI 1999/1956) 1–022, 14–143
Pressure Equipment Regulations (SI 1999/2001) .. 14–115
Unfair Terms in Consumer Contracts Regulations (SI 1999/2083) 1–001, 1–014, 1–023, 1–031, 1–092, 2–033, 4–019, 4–020, 4–031, 4–034, 5–169, 6–014, 6–025, 6–031, 8–063, 8–105, 9–026, 13–053, 13–095, 13–103, 14–002, 14–030, 14–031, 14–037, 14–040, 14–042, 14–047, 14–052A, 14–069, 14–100, 14–102, 14–112, 14–128, 14–136, 15–132, 15–134, 16–009, 16–038, 16–041, 17–049, 18–264, 18–275, 18–282, 18–283, 18–342, 19–048, 20–094, 20–110, 20–113, 25–042, 25–055, 25–101, 25–102,

1999 Unfair Terms in Consumer Contracts Regulations—*cont.*
25–103, 25–104, 25–106, 25–107, 25–109, 25–114, 25–116, 25–154, 25–169
Pt II 14–040
reg.2(a) 14–031
(b) 14–031
reg.3 14–040
(1) ... 4–019, 14–001, 14–031, 14–037, 18–282, 18–283, 25–042, 25–045, 25–101
(2) 25–101
reg.4 .... 13–103, 25–045
(1) .. 14–002, 14–031, 18–282, 25–101
(2)(b) 18–283
(3) 14–034
regs 5–8 25–114
reg.5 ..... 6–014, 14–037, 14–039, 25–045, 25–103
(1) ... 4–019, 13–103, 14–031, 14–034, 14–052A, 25–102
(2) 14–031
regs 5(2)–(4) 14–052A
reg.5(3) 14–031
(4) 14–031
(5) .. 14–100, 25–161, 25–171
reg.6 .... 13–079, 14–051
(1) 14–034
(2) 14–031, 14–033, 14–052A, 19–048
(a) 14–032, 14–033
(b) 14–032, 14–033
reg.7 14–032
reg.8 .... 4–019, 14–047
(1) .. 14–034, 14–047, 14–100, 18–282, 20–113
(2) 14–034
reg.9 .... 13–100, 14–028, 25–042, 25–102, 25–103, 25–104, 25–109, 25–112, 25–115, 25–154, 25–171
regs 10–15 14–128
reg.10(1) 14–040, 25–106
reg.11 25–106
reg.12 .... 14–136, 25–106
(1) 14–040, 25–106
(2) 14–040
(4) 14–040
reg.13 14–040
Sch.1 .... 14–040, 14–136, 25–101, 25–106
Sch.2 .... 1–031, 9–023, 9–026, 13–063, 14–035, 14–036, 25–045
para.1(a) 14–034, 14–036
(b) 4–019, 14–036, 14–039

1999 Unfair Terms in Consumer Contracts Regulations—*cont.*
Sch.2—*cont.*
para.1(c) 14–036, 19–014
(d) 14–036, 14–038
(e) 14–036, 14–038
(f) 8–105, 14–036
(g) 8–105, 14–036, 18–342
(h) 8–105, 14–036
(i) 14–036
(j) 8–105, 14–036, 14–038
(k) 8–105, 14–036, 14–038
(l) 14–036, 14–038, 25–161
(m) 14–036, 25–171
(n) 14–036, 14–039
(o) 14–036, 14–039
(p) 14–036
(q) 14–036, 14–100, 19–048
para.2(a) 14–036
(b) 14–036
(c) 14–036, 14–038
(d) 14–036, 14–038
Dangerous Substances and Preparations (Safety) (Consolidation) (Amendment) Regulations (SI 1999/2084) 14–115
Unfair Arbitration Agreements (Specified Amount) Order (SI 1999/2167) 14–100
Asbestos (Prohibitions) (Amendment) Regulations (SI 1999/2373) .. 14–115
Asbestos (Prohibitions) (Amendment) (No.2) Regulations (SI 1999/2977) 14–115
Road Vehicles (Brake Linings Safety) Regulations (SI 1999/2978) 14–115
Price Marking Order (SI 1999/3042) 1–023, 14–111
art.3 14–111
art.4(1) 14–111
(2) 14–111
art.5 14–111
art.7 14–111
Consumer Credit (Total Charge for Credit, Agreements and Advertisements) (Amendment) Regulations (SI 1999/3177) 2–023, 14–145

1999 Dangerous Substances and Preparations (Safety) (Consolidation) (Amendment) (No.2) Regulations (SI 1999/3193) 14–115
2000 Pressure Systems Safety Regulations (SI 2000/128) ... 14–115
Civil Procedure (Amendment) Rules (SI 2000/221) 14–104
Conditional Fee Agreements Regulations (SI 2000/692) 14–105
Conditional Fee Agreements Order (SI 2000/823)—
art.3 14–105
art.4 14–105
Control of Misleading Advertisements (Amendment) Regulations (SI 2000/914) 14–140
In Vitro Diagnostic Medical Devices Regulations (SI 2000/1315) 14–115
Air Navigation Order (SI 2000/1562) 1–082
Contracts (Applicable Law) Act 1990 (Amendment) Order (SI 2000/1825) ... 25–015
Export and Investment Guarantees (Limit on Foreign Currency Commitments) Order (SI 2000/2087) ... 24–010
Consumer Protection (Distance Selling) Regulations (SI 2000/2334) ... 1–023, 2–001, 2–014, 8–038, 8–106, 9–036, 14–045, 14–054, 14–055, 14–056, 14–057, 14–060, 14–125, 14–126, 14–133, 25–042, 25–045, 25–108, 25–109
reg.2 14–126
reg.3(1) ... 2–014, 14–001, 14–054, 14–057, 14–059, 25–107
reg.4 2–014
reg.5 .... 14–054, 25–107
(1)(a) 14–054
(b) 14–054
(f) 2–004
reg.6 25–107
(1) 14–054
(2) 14–054
(3) 14–054
reg.7 ...... 8–106, 14–055, 25–107
(1)(a)(i)–(vi) 14–055
(vi) 14–055
(vii) 14–055
(viii) 14–055
(ix) 14–055

2000 Consumer Protection (Distance Selling) Regulations —*cont.*
reg.7(1)(b) 8–106, 14–055, 14–056
(c) 14–055, 14–056, 14–058
(2) 8–106
(3) 14–055
(4) 14–055
regs 7–19(1) 14–054
regs 7–20 14–054
reg.8(1) 14–055
(2)(a) 14–055
(b) 14–055
(iii) 14–055
(c) 14–055
(d) 14–055
(e) 14–055
reg.9 14–055
reg.10(2) 14–057
(3) 14–057
(4) 14–057
(5) 14–057
regs 10–13 .... 2–020, 25–107
reg.11(2) 14–057
(3) 14–057
(4) 14–057
reg.12 14–057
reg.13 .... 14–054, 14–055, 14–057
(1)(c) 14–057
(d) 2–012, 14–057
(e) 14–057
reg.14 25–107
(1) 14–057
(3) 14–057
reg.15 14–057
reg.16 14–057
reg.17(2) 14–058
(3) 14–058
(4) 14–058
(10) 14–058
reg.18 14–057
reg.19 .... 8–038, 14–052A
(1), ... 8–038, 8–106, 14–056
(2) 8–038, 8–106
(2)–(4) 14–056
(2)–(8) 14–054
(3), (4) 8–106
(5) 8–106, 14–056
(6) 8–106
(7) 14–055, 14–056
reg.20 .... 14–054, 14–056
reg.21 .... 9–036, 14–057
(3) 14–057
(5) 14–149
reg.22 2–014
reg.24 .... 2–014, 14–004
(2) 14–004
(3) 14–004

2000 Consumer Protection (Distance Selling) Regulations —*cont.*
reg.24(4) 14–004
(5)(a) 14–004
(b) 14–004
(c) 14–004
(7) 14–005
(8) 14–005
reg.25 .... 14–052A
(1) 14–059
(2) 25–112, 25–115
(5) 25–103, 25–107, 25–108, 25–109
reg.26(1) 14–059
reg.27 .... 14–059, 14–136
Sch.1 .... 14–054, 25–107
Sch.2 14–054
Late Payment of Commercial Debts (Interest) Act 1998 (Commencement No.4) Order (SI 2000/2740) ... 16–010
Consumer Protection Act 1987 (Product Liability) (Modification) Order (SI 2000/2771) 14–082
Dangerous Substances and Preparations (Safety) (Consolidation) and Chemicals (Hazard Information and Packaging for Supply) (Amendment) Regulations (SI 2000/2897) 14–115
Banking Consolidation Directive (Consequential Amendments) Regulations (SI 2000/2952) .. 14–143
reg.8 14–143
Collective Conditional Fee Agreements Regulations (SI 2000/2988) 14–105
2001 Biocidal Products Regulations (SI 2001/880) 14–115
Postal Service Act 2000 (Consequential Modifications) No.1 Order (SI 2001/1149) 22–108
Unfair Terms in Consumer Contracts (Amendment) Regulations (SI 2001/1186) 1–023, 4–019, 4–031, 8–105, 14–103, 14–136, 25–055
High Court and County Courts Jurisdiction (Amendment) Order (SI 2001/1387) ... 14–102

2001 Stop Now Orders (EC Directive) Regulations (SI 2001/1422) 14–028, 14–040, 14–045, 14–050, 14–129, 14–133, 14–156, 25–055, 25–106
reg.2(1) .. 14–040, 14–129, 14–140
reg.2(3) 14–129
(a) 14–140
(g) 14–040
reg.3 14–129
reg.4 14–129
Sch.1 14–129
para.1 14–140
para.7 14–040
Sch.2 14–129
para.1 14–129
Sch.3 14–129
Financial Services and Markets Act 2000 (Law Applicable to Contracts of Insurance) Regulations (SI 2001/2635) 25–074, 25–075
reg.2(2) 25–075
High Court and County Courts Jurisdiction (Amendment No.2) Order (SI 2001/2685) 14–102
Financial Services and Markets Act 2000 (law Applicable to Contracts of Insurance) (Amendment) Regulations (SI 2001/3542) .. 25–074, 25–075
Financial Services and Markets Act 2000 (Consequential Amendments and Repeals) Order (SI 2001/3649) 2–023, 14–043, 14–144, 14–150
art.320 25–075
Value Added Tax (Special Provisions) (Amendment) Order (SI 2001/3753) ... 22–036
Civil Jurisdiction and Judgments Order (SI 2001/3929) 25–016
Return of Cultural Objects (Amendment) Regulations (SI 2001/3972) .. 25–131
2002 Electronic Signatures Regulations (SI 2002/318) 1–024
reg.4 9–036
Carriage by Air Acts (Implementation of Montreal Convention 1999) Order (SI 2002/263) 21–047
art.2 ..... 21–047, 21–051
(1) 21–055
(25) 21–051
2002 Late Payment of Commercial Debts Regulations (SI 2002/1674) 1–023, 25–153, 25–163
Late Payment of Commercial Debts (Rate of Interest) (No.3) Order (SI 2002/1675) 1–023
Health Act 1999 (Commencement No. 13) Order (SI 2003/1689) 14–115
Dangerous Substances and Preparations (Safety) (Consolidation) (Amendment)Regulations (SI 2002/1770) 14–115
Electronic Commerce (EC Directive) Regulations (SI 2002/2013) 1–023, 2–021, 14–060, 25–051, 25–053
reg.2(1) 25–037
reg.3 14–060
reg.4 25–036
(4) 25–036, 25–051
reg.6 14–060
reg.7 14–060
reg.8 14–060
reg.9 ..... 2–012, 14–060
(1) 14–060
(4) 14–060
reg.11 14–060
(1) 14–060
(2)(a) 2–016, 25–050
Sch. 25–051
2003 Uncertificated Securities (Amendment) (Eligible Debt Securities) Regulations (SI 2003/1633) .. 22–036
2003 Dangerous Substances and Preparations (Safety) (Consolidation) (Amendment No.3) Regulations (SI 2002/3010) 14–115
Tobacco Products (Manufacture, Presentation and Sale) (Safety) Regulations (SI 2002/3041) 14–115
Sale and Supply of Goods to Consumers Regulations (SI 2002/3045) ... 1–001, 1–023, 1–031, 5–098, 6–014, 11–033, 12–001, 12–055, 12–071, 13–017, 14–008, 14–047, 14–066, 14–133, 18–259, 19–144, 19–203, 20–105, 20–120, 25–042, 25–045, 25–055, 25–111, 25–171
reg.1(1) 14–008

2003 Sale and Supply of Goods to Consumers Regulations—*cont.*
reg.2 ..... 1–079, 13–077, 14–008, 14–070, 14–071, 14–072, 14–074
regs 3–5 25–111
reg.3 .... 14–010, 14–012
reg.4 .... 5–098, 8–014
reg.5 .... 14–005, 14–023
reg.6 .... A–030
reg.7 14–047
reg.9 .... 14–023, 14–051
reg.10 14–047
reg.13 14–150
reg.14 .... 14–011, 18–256
(2) 14–029
(3) 14–029
reg.15 ... 14–008, 14–066, 14–070, 14–073, 14–074, 25–111, 25–114
(1) 14–062, 14–070, 14–072
(2) 14–070, 14–073
(3) 14–070, 14–073
(5) 14–070, 14–073
(6) 14–074
(7) 14–074
2003 Electronic Commerce (EC Directive) (Extension) Regulations (SI 2003/115) ... 14–060
Biocidal Products (Amendment) Regulations (SI 2003/429) 14–115
Conditional Fee Agreements (Miscellaneous Amendments) Regulations (SI 2003/1240) 14–105
Motor Vehicle Tyres (Safety) (Amendment) Regulations (SI 2003/1316) .. 14–115
Enterprise Act 2002 (Super-Complaints to Regulators) Order (SI 2003/1368) 14–127
Enterprise Act 2002 (Part 8 Community Infringements Specified UK Laws) Order (SI 2003/1374) 14–133
art.2 14–133
art.3 ..... 14–028, 14–040, 14–059, 14–074, 14–140, 14–156
Sch. 14–028, 14–040, 14–059, 14–074, 14–140, 14–156
Enterprise Act 2002 (Part 8 Notice to OFT of Intended Prosecution Specified Enactments, Revocation and Transitional Provision) Order (SI 2003/1376) 8–099
2003 Enterprise Act 2002 (Commencement No.3, Transitional and Transitory Provisions and Savings) Order (SI 2003/1397)
art.2 14–130
Sch 14–130
The Enterprise Act 2002 (Part 8 Designated Enforcers: Criteria for Designation, Designation of Public Bodies as Designated Enforcers and Transitional Provisions) Order (SI 2003/1399) 14–134
art.3 14–134
art.4 14–134
art.5 14–134
Sch. 14–134
Enterprise Act 2002 (Part 9 Restrictions on Disclosure of Information) (Amendment and Specification) Order (SI 2003/1400) ... 8–099, 14–043, 14–115
Enterprise Act 2002 (Part 8 Domestic Infringements) Order (SI 2003/1593) ... 14–132
art.2 ..... 14–028, 14–059, 14–140, 14–156
(i) 14–040
Sch. 14–028, 14–140, 14–156
Pt II 14–059
Medical Devices (Amendment) Regulations (SI 2003/1697) 14–115
Secretary of State for Constitutional Affairs Order (SI 2003/1887)—
art.9 14–105
Sch.2 14–105
Asbestos (Prohibitions) (Amendment) Regulations (SI 2003/1889) .. 14–115
Timeshare Act 1992 (Amendment) Regulations (SI 2003/1922) 14–043
Packaging (Essential Requirements) Regulations (SI 2003/1941) 14–115
Conditional Fee Agreement (Miscellaneous Amendments) (No.2) Regulations (SI 2003/2344) 14–105
Electronic Commerce (EC Directive) (Extension) (No.2) Regulations (SI 2003/2500) 14–060

2003 Timeshare (Cancellation Information) Order (SI 2003/2579) 14–043
Motor Vehicle Tyres (Safety) (Amendment) (No.2) Regulations (SI 2003/2762) 14–115
Communications Act 2003 (Consequential Amendments No.2) Order (SI 2003/3182) 14–100, 14–103, 14–136
Control of Misleading Advertisements (Amendment) Regulations (SI 2003/3183) 14–140
reg.3 14–140
reg.4 14–140
Road Vehicles (Brake Linings Safety) (Amendment) Regulations (SI 2003/3314) 14–115
2004 Price Marking Order (SI 2004/102) 14–111
Carriage of Dangerous Goods and Use of Transportable Pressure Equipment Regulations (SI 2004/568) 14–115
Tobacco Advertising and Promotion (Point of Sale) Regulations (SI 2004/765) 14–115
Enterprise Act 2002 (Part 8) (Designation of the Financial Services Authority as a Designated Enforcer) Order (SI 2004/935) 14–134
Electronic Commerce (EC Directive) (Extension) Regulations (SI 2004/1178) .. 14–060
Packaging (Essential Requirements) (Amendment) Regulations (SI 2004/1188) 14–115
Tobacco Advertising and Promotion (Specialist Tobacconists) Regulations (SI 2004/1277) 14–115
Dangerous Substances and Preparations (Safety) (Consolidation) (Amendment) Regulations (SI 2004/1417) 14–115
Recreational Craft Regulations (SI 2004/1464) 14–115
Consumer Credit (Disclosure of Information) Regulations (SI 2004/1481) ... 2–023, 14–144
2004 Consumer Credit (Agreements) (Amendment) Regulations (SI 2004/1482) ... 2–023, 14–144, 14–150
reg.11 14–149
Consumer Credit (Early Settlement) Regulations (SI 2004/1483) 14–145
Consumer Credit (Advertisements) Regulations (SI 2004/1484) 14–150, 14–155
Enterprise Act 2002 (Bodies Designated to make Super-Complaints) Order (SI 2004/1517) 14–127
Tobacco Advertising and Promotion (Brandsharing) Regulations (SI 2004/1824) 14–115
Fireworks Regulations (SI 2004/1836) 14–115
Carriage by Air Acts (Application of Provisions) Order (SI 2004/1899) .. 21–047, 21–051
art.2 21–047
art.5 .... 21–047, 21–051
art.6 21–047
art.9 21–077
Sch.1 21–051
Sch.2
Pt I 21–047
Pt IIA 21–047, 21–051
Pt IIA, Ch.1 21–047
Pt IIB 21–047
art.1(2) 21–051
art.5 21–052
Sch.3 21–047
Pt IIB 21–047
Sch.4 21–077
Financial Services (Distance Marketing) Regulations (SI 2004/2095) ... 8–038, 8–106, 9–036, 14–054, 14–100, 14–103, 14–133, 14–136, 25–055, 25–100, 25–107
reg.14 9–036
(4) 14–149
reg.26 14–133
Cosmetic Products (Safety) Regulations (SI 2004/2152) 14–115
Cosmetic Products (Safety) (Amendment) Regulations (SI 2004/2361) .. 14–115

2004 Consumer Credit (Miscellaneous Amendments) Regulations (SI 2004/2619) 14–144, 14–145, 14–150, 14–155

Cosmetic Products (Safety) (Amendment) (No.2) Regulations (SI 2004/2988) 14–115

Food Safety Act 1990 (Amendment) Regulations (SI 2004/2990) 14–110

Recreational Craft (Amendment) Regulations (SI 2004/3201) 14–115

Consumer Credit Act 1974 (Electronic Communications) Order (SI 2004/3236) 14–144, 14–150

art.4 14–149

Consumer Credit (Enforcement, Default and Termination Notices) (Amendment) Regulations (SI 2004/3237) .. 14–144

Fireworks (Amendment) Regulations (SI 2004/3262) 14–115

General Food Regulations (SI 2004/3279) 14–110

reg.4 14–110

reg.5 14–110

reg.7 14–108

reg.9 14–110

reg.10 14–110

Contracts (Applicable Law) Act 1990 (Commencement No.2) Order (SI 2004/3448) 25–015

2005 Supply of Extended Warranties on Domestic Electrical Goods Order (SI 2005/37) 2–020, 14–043

art.1(2) 14–043

(3) 14–043

art.3(1)(a) 14–043

(b) 14–043

(c) 14–043

(2) 14–043

(3) 14–043

(4) 14–043

art.4 14–043

art.5 14–043

art.6 14–043

art.8(1)(b) 14–043

(4) 14–043

2005 Regulatory Reform (Unsolicited Goods and Services Act 1971) (Directory Entries and Demands for Payment) Order (SI 2005/55) 14–005, 14–054

art.2(6) 14–005

art.4 14–005

Sch., Pt 1 14–005

High Court and County Courts Jurisdiction (Amendment) Order (SI 2005/587) 14–102

Unsolicited Goods and Services Act 1971 (Electronic Commerce) (Amendment) Regulations (SI 2005/148) 14–005

Consumer Protection (Distance Selling) (Amendment) Regulations (SI 2005/689) 1–023, 8–038, 8–106, 14–054, 25–055, 25–100

reg.2 .... 14–055, 14–057

Sch.

para.1(2) 14–055

para.2 14–057

para.3 14–057

Supply of Machinery (Safety) (Amendment) Regulations (SI 2005/831) 14–115

Regulatory Reform (Trading Stamps) Order (SI 2005/871) 1–040

Materials and Articles in Contact with Food (England) Regulations (SI 2005/898) 14–115

Enterprise Act 2002 (Part 8) (Designation of the Consumers' Association) Order (SI 2005/917) 14–134

General Product Safety Regulations (SI 2005/1803) .. 14–116, 14–117, 14–119, 14–122

Pt 4 14–123

reg.1(2) 14–116

reg.2 .... 14–119, 14–120, 14–121, 14–123

reg.3(1) 14–119

(2) 14–119

reg.4 14–119

reg.5(1) 14–120

(2) 14–120

(3) 14–120

(4) 14–120

reg.6 14–120

(1) 14–085

(2) 14–085

(3) 14–085

(4) 14–085

2005 General Product Safety Regulations—*cont.*
reg.7 14–120
reg.8(1) 14–121
(a) 14–121
(b) 14–121
reg.9 .... 14–120, 14–121
(1) 14–123
reg.10 14–122
reg.11 14–122
reg.12 14–122
reg.13 14–122
reg.14 14–122
reg.15 .... 14–119, 14–122
(4) 14–122
(5) 14–122
reg.16(6) 14–122
reg.17 14–122
reg.18 14–122
reg.20(1)–(3) 14–120, 14–121
(4) 14–122
reg.21 14–122
reg.22 14–122
reg.23 14–122
reg.24 14–122
reg.25 14–122
reg.26 14–122
reg.27 14–122
reg.28 14–122
reg.29 .... 14–120, 14–121
reg.30 14–119
reg.33(1) 14–123
(2)–(4) 14–123
(5) 14–123
reg.35 14–123
(4) 14–123
reg.42 14–095
reg.46(2) 14–116
(4) 14–117
Cosmetic Products (Safety) (Amendment) Regulations (SI 2005/1815) .. 14–115
Dangerous Substances and Preparations (Nickel) (Safety) Regulations (SI 2005/2001) 14–115

2005 Railways (Convention on International Carriage by Rail) Regulations (SI 2005/2092) 21–047, 21–065, 25–194
reg.1 21–047
reg.3 21–047
Conditional Fee Agreements (Revocation) Regulations (SI 2005/2305)—
reg.2 14–105
reg.3(1) 14–105
Enterprise Act 2002 (Bodies Designated to make Super-complaints) (Amendment) Order (SI 2005/2340)—
art.2(2) 14–127
Biocidal Products (Amendment) Regulations (SI 2005/2451) 14–115
Enterprise Act 2002 (Part 8 Community Infringements Specified UK Laws) (Amendment) Order (SI 2005/2418) 14–133
Enterprise Act 2002 (Bodies Designated to make Super-complaints) (Amendment) Order (SI 2005/2468) 14–127
Consumer Protection (Code of Practice for Traders on Price Indications) Approval Order (SI 2005/2705) 14–125
Medicines (Marketing Authorisations Etc.) Amendment Regulations (SI 2005/2759)—
reg.4 14–133
Sch., para.19 14–133
Medical Devices (Amendment) Regulations (SI 2005/2909) 14–115
Cosmetic Products (Safety) (Amendment) (No.2) Regulations (SI 2005/3346) 14–115

TABLE OF EUROPEAN COMMUNITIES LEGISLATION

European Community Treaties and Conventions

Accession Convention providing for the accession of Austria, Finland and Sweden, signed November 29, 1996 25–015
Accession Convention providing for the accession of Spain and Portugal to the Rome Convention signed May 18, 1992 25–015
European Economic Agreement (Oporto, May 2, 1992; [1994] O.J. L1/3) ... 25–042, 25–074, 25–101, 25–107
Treaty of Rome (March 25, 1957)—
art.3 3–042
art.12 25–114
art.14 3–041
art.15 3–041
art.16 3–041
art.23 3–042
arts 23–37 .... 3–041, 3–042
art.28 .... 3–042, 25–114
art.29 25–114
arts 30–37 1–084
art.30 3–042
art.49 25–114
art.65 25–017
art.65(b) 25–017
art.81 .... 3–036, 3–037, 3–040, 8–061
art.81(1) 3–041
art.81(2) 3–041
art.81(3) 3–041
art.82 .... 3–040, 3–041, 8–061
art.85 .... 3–038, 3–040
(1) 3–041
art.86 .... 3–038, 3–040
art.153 (ex art.129a) 14–001
art.234 (ex art.177) 25–018
European Convention on Human Rights and Fundamental Freedoms (1950) 2–023, 25–043
art.6 14–144

Decisions

Council Decision 2001/76/EC of December 22, 2000 replacing the Decision of April 4, 1978 on the application of certain guidelines in the field of officially supported export credits [2001] O.J. L32/1 24–054
Council Decision 2001/77/EC of December 22, 2000 on the application of principles of a framework agreement on project finance in the field of officially supported export credits [2001] O.J. L32/55 24–054

Directives

1970 Dir.70/509 Council Directive on the adoption of a common credit insurance policy for medium- and long-term transactions with public buyers [1970] O.J. L254/1 24–054
Dir.70/510 Council Directive on the adoption of a common credit insurance policy for medium- and long-term transactions with private buyers [1970] O.J. L254/26 24–054
1984 Dir.84/450 Council Directive on misleading advertising so as to include comparative advertising [1984] O.J. L250/17 .... 14–001, 14–133, 14–140, 25–055, 25–100
1985 Dir.85/374 Council Directive on the approximation of the laws, regulations and administrative provisions of the Member States concerning liability for defective products [1985] O.J. L210/29 1–023, 14–001, 14–079, 14–080, 14–081
art.7(e) 14–089
art.9(b) 14–087
art.11 14–092
art.15.1(b) 14–089
art.16.1 14–087
Dir.85/577 Council Directive to protect the consumer in respect of contracts negotiated away from business premises [1985] O.J. L372/31 .... 1–023, 14–045, 14–133, 25–055

1986 Dir.86/653 Council Directive on the coordination of the laws of the Member States relating to self-employed commercial agents [1986] O.J. L382/17 ..... 1–048, 3–004, 25–073
art.17 25–073
art.18 25–073

1987 Dir.87/102 Council Directive for the approximation of the laws, regulations and administrative provisions of the Member States concerning consumer credit [1987] O.J. L43/48 14–133

1988 Dir.88/357 Council Directive on the coordination of laws, regulations and administrative provisions relating to direct insurance other than life assurance and laying down provisions to facilitate the effective exercise of freedom to provide services and amending Directive 73/239/EEC (Second Directive on Direct Insurance other than Life Assurance) [1988] O.J. L172/1 25–075
art.7 25–075

1990 Dir.90/314 Council Directive on package travel, package holidays and package tours [1990] O.J. L158/59 ...... 8–097, 14–001, 14–050, 14–133
art.4(6) 8–100

Dir.90/619 Council Directive on the coordination of laws, regulations and administrative provisions relating to direct life assurance, laying down provisions to facilitate the effective exercise of freedom to provide services and amending Directive 79/267/EEC [1990] O.J. L330/50 .... 25–075, 25–107

1992 Dir.92/49 Council Directive on the coordination of laws, regulations and administrative provisions relating to direct insurance other than life assurance and amending Directives 73/239/EEC and 88/357/EEC (third non-life insurance Directive) [1992] O.J. L228/1) 25–075

Dir.92/59 Council Directive on general product safety [1992] O.J. L228/24 .... 14–001, 14–123

1993 Dir.93/13 Council Directive on unfair terms in consumer contracts [1994] O.J. L95/29 ...... 1–014, 1–023, 13–009, 13–099, 14–001, 14–030, 14–036, 14–071, 14–133, 25–042, 25–055, 25–101, 25–102, 25–103, 25–112
Preamble, para.1 25–103
Recital 10 25–101
art.2(b) 14–029, 14–130
art.3(3) 25–102
art.6(2) 25–101, 25–103
art.7(2) 14–040
art.10 .... 14–022, 14–030
Annex 25–102

1994 Dir.94/47 Directove of the European Parliament and of the Council on the protection of purchasers in respect of certain aspects of contracts relating to the purchase of the right to use immovable properties on a timeshare basis [1994] O.J. L280/83 .... 14–045, 14–133

1997 Dir.97/7 Directive of the European Parliament and of the Council on the protection of consumers in respect of distance contracts (Distance Selling Directive) [1997] O.J. L144/19 .... 1–023, 14–001, 14–054, 14–060, 14–133, 25–042, 25–055, 25–100, 25–107, 25–109, 25–112
art.3(2) 14–054
art.10(2) 25–107, 25–109
art.11 14–061
Annex 1 25–107

1997 Dir.97/55 Council Directive of the European Parliament and of the Council amending Directive 84/450/EEC concerning misleading advertising so as to include comparative advertising [1997] O.J. L290/19 14–140

1998 Dir.98/6 Directive of the European Parliament and of the Council on consumer protection in the indication of the prices of products offered to consumers [1998] O.J. L190/86 . . . . 1–023, 14–111

Dir.98/27 Directive of the European Parliament and of the Council on injunctions for the protection of consumers' interests (Injunctions Directive) [1998] O.J. L166/51 . . . . . 1–023, 14–001, 14–045, 14–129, 14–134, 25–055, 25–100, 25–106, 25–107

Dir.98/29 Council Directive on harmonisation of the main provisions concerning export credit insurance for transactions with medium and long-term cover [1998] O.J. L148/22 24–054

1999 Dir.99/34 Directive of the European Parliament and of the Council on the approximation of the laws, regulations and administrative provisions of the Member States concerning liability for defective products [1999] O.J. L141/20 . . . . 1–023, 14–082

Art.4 14–083

Dir.99/44 Directive of the European Parliament and of the Council on certain aspects of the sale of consumer goods and associated guarantees (Consumer Sales Directive) [1999] O.J. L171/12 . . . . . 1–023, 1–079, 1–106, 6–014, 13–077, 14–001, 14–005, 14–008, 14–022, 14–013, 14–016, 14–024, 14–025, 14–026, 14–029, 14–049, 14–050, 14–133, 16–001, 17–048, 17–050, 17–090,

1999 Dir.99/44 Directive of the European Parliament and of the Council on certain aspects of the sale of consumer goods and associated guarantees (Consumer Sales Directive)—*cont.*

. . . . 17–093, 17–100, 18–259, 19–071, 19–204, 25–042, 25–055, 25–111, 25–112

Recital 10 14–026

Recital 12 14–024

art.1 . . . . 1–079, 1–087

art.1.2(a) 14–008, 14–011, 14–029, 14–071

(b) 14–011, 14–070

(c) 14–011

(e) 14–070

(f) 14–024

art.1.3 14–011

art.1.4 14–049

art.2.1 . . . . . 6–014, 14–011, 18–259

art.2.2 14–012

art.2.2(c) 14–013

art.2.2(d) 14–010, 14–014

art.2.4 . . . . 14–010, 14–012, 14–013

art.2.5 . . . . 14–049, 14–051, 14–052

art.3 . . . . . 14–016, 14–024, 19–071

art.3.1 6–014,

art.3.2 . . . . 12–100, 14–026

art.3.3 . . . 12–106, 14–024, 19–071, 19–204

art.3.4 14–024

art.3.5 . . . 12–100, 14–026, 17–093, 19–071

art.3.6 . . . . 12–095, 12–100, 14–026

art.4 14–024

art.5.1 14–016

art.5.2 14–016

art.5.3 14–015

art.6 . . . . . 14–008, 14–066, 14–070

art.6.1 . . . . 14–062, 14–070

art.6.2 . . . 14–065, 14–072, 14–073, 14–075

art.6.3 14–073

art.6.4 14–073

art.6.5 14–074

art.7.1 . . . . 6–014, 12–117, 14–016, 14–028

art.7.2 . . . 14–028, 25–042, 25–112, 25–114, 25–115, 25–116, 25–117, 25–118

art.8.1 14–024

art.8.2 . . . . 12–071, 14–008, 14–013

art.11.1 14–008

1999 Dir.99/93 Directive of the European Parliament and of the Council on a Community framework for electronic signatures [2000] O.J. L13/12 2–021
art.6(1) 9–036
2000 Dir.2000/31 Directive of the European Parliament and of the Council on certain legal aspects of information society services, in particular electronic commerce, in the Internal Market (Directive on Electronic Commerce) [2000] O.J. L178/1 ...... 1–023, 14–060, 25–036, 25–037, 25–051
Recital 19 ...... 25–037, 25–053, 25–064
Recital 23 25–051
Recital 55 25–051
art.1.1 14–060
art.1.4 25–051
art.3.3 ...... 25–036, 25–051
art.5 14–060
art.6 14–060
art.7 14–060
art.9 14–060
art.10 14–060
art.10(3) 14–060
art.11 14–060
art.11.1 ...... 25–050, 25–053
art.11(3) 25–050
Annex 25–051
Dir.2000/35 Directive of the European Parliament and of the Council on combating late payment in commercial transactions [2000] O.J. L200/35 .... 1–023, 16–010, 25–141, 25–153, 25–163
Recital 21 25–153
art.4 ...... 5–141, 25–153
(1) 25–153
(2) 25–153
art.6(1) 25–153
2001 Dir.2001/95 Directive of the European Parliament and of the Council on general product safety [2002] O.J. L11/4 14–119
Recital 25 14–123
Recital 30 14–123
Recital 31 14–123
Recital 32 14–123
art.8(1)(b)–(f) 14–123
(2) 14–122
art.10 14–123
2001 Dir.2001/95 Directive of the European Parliament and of the Council on general product safety—*cont.*
art.11 14–123
art.12 14–123
art.13 14–123
art.13(2) 14–123
art.13(3) 14–123
2002 Dir.2002/65 Directive of the European Parliament and of the Council concerning the distance marketing of consumer financial services and amending Council Directive 90/619/EEC and Directives 97/7/EC and 98/27/EC [2002] O.J. L271/91 ...... 14–133, 25–055, 25–100, 25–107
Dir.2002/83 Directive of the European Parliament and of the Council concerning life assurance [2002] O.J. L345/1 25–075
Recital 1 25–075
art.32 25–075
art.72 25–075
Annex VI 25–075
2005 Dir.2005/29 Council Directive concerning unfair business-to-consumer commercial practices in the internal market and amending Council Directive 84/450/EEC, Directives 97/7/EC, 98/27/EC and 2002/65/EC of the European Parliament and of the Council and Regulation (EC) No 2006/2004 of the European Parliament and of the Council (Unfair Commercial Practices Directive) [2005] O.J. L149/22 1–023, 14–139, 14–140, 25–055, 25–100
art.2 14–139
art.14 14–140

Regulations

1962 Reg.17/62 First Regulation implementing Articles 85 and 86 of the Treaty [1962] O.J. L24 3–041

1971 Reg.1408/71 Council Regulation on the application of social security schemes to employed persons and their families moving within the Community [1971] O.J. L149/366 ... 25–056

1983 Reg.1984/83 Commission Regulation on the application of Art.85(3) of the Treaty to categories of exclusive purchasing agreements [1984] O.J. L173/5 ... 3–038

1989 Reg.556/89 Commission Regulation on the application of Art.85(3) of the Treaty to certain categories of know-how licensing agreements [1989] O.J. L359/46 ... 3–041

1999 Reg.2790/99 Commission Regulation on the application of Art.81(3) of the Treaty to categories of vertical agreements and concerted practices [1999] O.J. L336/21 ... 3–038, 3–041

2000 Reg.1346/2000 Council Regulation on insolvency proceedings [2000] O.J. L160/1 ... 25–141, 25–150
- art.1 ... 25–150
- art.3(1) ... 25–150
  - (2) ... 25–150
  - (3) ... 25–150
  - (4) ... 25–150
- art.4 ... 25–150
- art.4(2)(m) ... 25–152
- art.5 ... 25–150
- art.7 ... 25–150
  - (1) ... 25–151, 25–152
  - (2) ... 25–152
  - (3) ... 25–152
- art.27 ... 25–150

2001 Reg.44/2001 Council Regulation on jurisdiction and the recognition and enforcement of judgments in civil and commercial matters [2001] O.J. L12/1 .. 25–016, 25–017, 25–018, 25–020, 25–063

2001 Reg.44/2001 Council Regulation on jurisdiction and the recognition and enforcement of judgments in civil and commercial matters—*cont.*
- art.15(1)(c) ... 25–048
  - (3) ... 25–051
- arts 15–17 ... 25–045
- art.23 ... 25–072
- art.60(1)(b) ... 25–063
- art.65 ... 25–018
- art.68 ... 25–018

2002 Reg.178/2002 Regulation of the European Parliament and of the Council of 28 January 2002 laying down the general principles and requirements of food law, establishing the European Food Safety Authority and laying down procedures in matters of food safety [2002] O.J. L31/1 ... 14–110
- art.14 ... 14–110
  - (2) ... 14–110
  - (3)–(9) ... 14–110

Reg.1400/2002 Commission Regulation on the application of Art.81(3) of the Treaty to categories of vertical agreements and concerted practices in the motor vehicle sector [2002] O.J. L203/30 ... 3–041

2003 Reg.1/2003 Council Regulation on the implementation of the rules on competition laid down in Articles 81 and 82 of the Treaty [2003] O.J. L1/1 .. 3–040

2004 Reg.2006/2004 Regulation of the European Parliament and of the Council of 27 October2004 on cooperation between national authorities responsible for the enforcement of consumer protection laws (the Regulation on consumer protection cooperation) [2004] O.J. L364/1 ... 14–136, 25–100

TABLE OF INTERNATIONAL CONVENTIONS

Brussels Convention on Jurisdiction and the Enforcement of Judgments in Civil and Commercial Matters 1968 (EC 46 (1978); Cmnd. 7395) 25–016, 25–018, 25–022, 25–043, 25–045, 25–063
art.5(1) 25–176
art.13 25–045
(3) 25–048
Protocol 25–018
art.2(2) 25–018
Brussels Protocol on the interpretation of the Rome Convention by the European Court of Justice, (Brussels, December 19, 1988) (*See Contracts (Applicable Law) Act 1990, Sch.3*) 25–015
CIM Convention (Cmnd. 2187 (1961)) 21–047
Convention concerning International Carriage by Rail ('The COTIF Convention') (Berne, May 9, 1980) Cmnd. 8535 (1982) (*See International Transport Conventions Act 1983*) 21–047, 21–065, 25–187, 25–195, 25–202
art.2(2) 21–065, 21–077
art.3 21–065
(3) 21–065, 21–077
(4) 21–065
art.6(1)(b) 21–047
(2) 21–047
art.10 21–065
art.28 25–202
arts 30, 31 25–187
arts 54, 55 25–202
Convention concerning International Carriage by Rail (as modified by the Vilnius Protocol) 21–065
art.24(1) 21–065
CIM Uniform Rules 21–047, 21–061, 21–065, 21–066, 21–067, 21–068, 21–069, 21–070, 21–071, 21–082, 21–105, 21–106
art.1(1) 21–065
(2) 21–065, 21–077
art.2 21–065
art.8(4) 21–068
art.11(1) 21–066
(3) 21–066
(5) 21–066, 21–068
art.12(1) 21–066
art.13 21–066
CIM Uniform Rules—*cont.*
art.18 21–066
art.28 21–068
(1) 21–066, 21–068
(4) 21–066, 21–067, 21–069
(5) 21–066
art.30 21–106
(1) 21–067
(2) 21–067, 21–068
(3) 21–067, 21–068
(a) 21–068
(4) 21–066, 21–067, 21–068, 21–071
(a) 21–067, 21–068
(b) 21–067
(c) 21–066, 21–067
(d) 21–067, 21–071
art.31 .... 21–071, 21–106
(1) 21–067, 21–069, 21–071
(b) 21–067
(c) 21–067
(d) 21–066
(2) 21–067
(3)(a) 21–067, 21–068
(c) 21–067
(d) 21–067
(4) 21–067
art.32(1) 21–056, 21–067, 21–071
(c) 21–070
art.34(3) 21–067
art.36 21–065
art.48(1) 21–065, 21–077
(a) 21–065
art.54 5–009
CIM Uniform Rules (as modified by the Vilnius Protocol) 21–065, 21–066, 21–067, 21–068, 21–070, 21–071
art.1 21–065
art.6 21–066
(1) 21–068
art.7 21–066
art.8(4) 21–068
art.12 21–066
art.17 21–066
art.18 .... 21–066, 21–067
(1) 21–067
(2) 21–067
(d) 21–070
(3) 21–067
(4) 21–067
art.19 21–067

Convention for the Settlement of Certain Conflicts of Laws in Connection with Bills of Exchange and Promissory Notes, signed at Geneva on June 7, 1930 (League of Nations Treaty Series, Vol. CXLIII, p. 319, No.3314) 22–034
Convention for the Settlement of Certain Conflicts of Laws in Connection with Cheques, signed at Geneva on March 19, 1931 (League of Nations Treaty Series, Vol. CXLIII, p. 409, No.3317) 22–034
Convention on the Contract for the International Carriage of Goods by Road ('The CMR Convention') (Geneva, May 19, 1956) (*See Carriage of Goods by Road Act 1965, s.1, Sch.*) 5–009, 21–047, 21–058, 21–059, 21–060, 21–061, 21–062, 21–063, 21–064, 21–074, 21–076, 21–077, 21–082, 21–104, 21–105, 21–106, 25–195, 25–202
Convention on the Law applicable to Contractual Obligations (Rome, June 19, 1980) ("the Rome Convention") (*See Contracts (Applicable Law) Act 1990, Sch.1 for references to the Rome Convention and articles thereof*)
Convention on the Stamp Laws in Connection with Bills of Exchange and Promissory Notes, signed at Geneva on June 7, 1930 (League of Nations Treaty Series, Vol. CXLIII, p. 339, No.3315) 22–034
Convention on the Stamp Laws in Connection with Cheques, signed at Geneva on March 19, 1931 (League of Nations Treaty Series, Vol. CXLIII, p. 9, No.3301) 22–034
Convention relating to a Uniform Law on the Formation of Contracts for the International Sale of Goods signed at the Hague on July 1, 1964 (*See Uniform Laws on International Sales Act 1967, Sch.2*) 1–024
Convention relating to a Uniform Law on the International Sale of Goods signed at the Hague on July 1, 1964 (*See Uniform Laws on International Sales Act 1967, Sch.1*) 1–023
Council of Europe Convention on Products Liability with regard to Personal Injury and Death 14–080
Funchal Convention signed in Funchal on May 18, 1992 (*See Contracts (Applicable Law) Act 1990, Sch.3A*) 25–015
Guadalajara Convention of 1961 (*See Carriage by Air Acts (Application of Provisions) Order (SI 2004/1899)* 21–047
Hague Convention on the Law Applicable to International Sale of Goods of June 15, 1955 ...... 25–025, 25–060
  art.2(3) 25–034
Hague Convention on the Law Applicable to the International Sale of Goods 1986 25–025
  art.10 25–034
  art.12(d) 25–154
Hague Convention on the Law Applicable to Trusts and their Recognition 1986 25–145
Hague-Visby Rules: *See* Table of Statutes under Carriage of Goods by Sea Act 1971, Sch.
Hamburg Rules (a Convention adopted by the United Nations Conference on Carriage of Goods by Sea at Hamburg on March 30, 1978, not yet in force) 21–047, 21–087
  art.6(2) 21–087
    (a) 21–087
International Monetary Fund Agreement (Washington, December 27, 1945; TS 21 (1946))—
  art.VIII 2(b) 25–120
Lugano Convention on Jurisdiction and the Enforcement of Judgments in Civil and Commercial matters 1988–
  art.5(1) 25–082
Luxembourg Convention on the accession to the Rome Convention by Greece (Luxembourg, April 10, 1984) (*See Contracts (Applicable Law) Act 1990, Sch.2*) 25–015
Montreal Convention 1999 (*see Carriage by Air Act 1961, Sch.1B*)
Rome Convention on the Law Applicable to Contractual Obligations 1980 ("the Rome Convention") *See (Convention on the Law Applicable to Contractual Obligations 1980 above and Contracts (Applicable Law) Act 1990, Sch.1 for references to the Convention and articles thereof*)

UNCTAD/ICC Rules for Multimodal Transport Documents (ICC Publication No.481) 21–082
UNCTAD/ICC Uniform Rules
r.2.6(a) 21–076
Uniform Law for Cheques, signed at Geneva on March 19, 1931 (League of Nations Treaty Series, Vol. CXLIII, p. 357, No.3316) 22–034
Uniform Law on Bills of Exchange and Promissory Notes promulgated by the Geneva Convention signed at Geneva on June 7, 1930 (League of Nations Treaty Series, Vol. CXLIII, p. 259, No.3313) 22–034, 22–035, 22–052
art.9 22–072
art.16 22–059
arts 21–25 22–100
arts 30–32 23–054
art.38 22–108
arts 43–46 22–120
art.43 23–011
Uniform Law on the Formation of Contracts for the International Sale of Goods 1964 (ULFIS) .. 25–003
Uniform Law on the International Sale of Goods (ULIS) *(See Uniform Laws on International Sales Act 1967, Sch.1)*
United Nations Convention on Contracts for the International Sale of Goods 1980 ("the Vienna Convention") ... 1–024, 2–001, 5–002, 12–001, 12–065, 12–099, 12–106, 12–129, 14–012, 16–028, 18–004, 18–006, 18–244, 18–267, 18–269, 18–271, 18–272, 18–283, 19–010, 19–080, 19–083, 19–122, 19–145, 19–204, 19–207, 19–215, 19–216, 19–217, 20–106, 20–107, 20–115, 20–116, 20–118, 20–121, 20–123, 20–126, 20–133, 21–045, 25–019, 25–025, 25–026
arts 1–5 18–004
art.1 18–283
art.2 1–079
(a) 18–283
(d) 19–008
art.3(1) 1–044
(2) 1–047
art.4(b) 18–006, 19–204
art.6 ... 18–004, 18–283, 19–083, 20–030, 20–046, 20–088, 20–105
art.7 19–204
(1) 19–215, 20–126
United Nations Convention on Contracts for the International Sale of Goods 1980 ("the Vienna Convention")—*cont.*
art.8(3) 18–004
art.9 .... 19–128, 20–046, 20–088, 20–105
(1) 18–004
(2) 18–004, 20–030
art.10(a) 25–056
art.12 2–020
art.14 2–002
art.16(2) 2–010
art.18(1) 2–014
(2) 2–015
art.19(2) 2–011, 13–013
art.24 2–015
art.25 .... 8–080, 8–081, 12–129, 18–244, 18–267, 18–270, 19–102, 19–144, 19–146, 19–161, 19–204, 19–207, 20–038, 20–046, 20–105
art.28 .... 12–129, 19–204, 19–215
arts 30–34 19–144
art.30 .... 4–002, 8–001, 12–129, 18–006, 19–002, 19–059, 19–144, 19–147, 21–002
art.31 ...... 8–002, 8–014, 8–018, 8–019, 18–267, 19–069, 21–014
art.31(a)–(c) 21–014
(a) 18–245, 19–059, 19–144, 19–169, 20–012, 20–037, 21–010, 21–042, 21–099
(c) 20–014, 21–002
art.32 6–031
(1) 18–006, 19–002, 19–023, 19–144
(2) 8–015, 18–245, 19–025, 19–102, 21–042
(3) 18–246, 18–247, 19–103, 20–039, 21–101
art.33 ...... 8–004, 8–025, 8–037, 20–105
(a) 18–267
(b) 18–267, 19–013, 20–030
art.34 ... 8–018, 12–031, 12–129, 18–006, 18–267, 19–002, 19–063, 19–071, 19–186
art.35 ... 18–265, 18–267, 20–038, 20–105
(1) 11–001, 18–267, 20–017
(2)(a) 11–026
(b) 11–051, 18–274
(c) 11–074
(d) 11–026, 21–002
art.36(1) 11–050, 18–254, 19–111
(2) 11–040
art.37 .... 12–129, 19–071
art.38 .... 12–129, 20–109
(1) 19–155, 20–109, 21–102
(2) 19–141, 20–109, 21–102
(3) 20–109
art.39 12–129

United Nations Convention on Contracts for the International Sale of Goods 1980 ("the Vienna Convention")—*cont.*
art.39(1) 12–032, 12–033, 19–150, 19–159, 19–160, 20–109
(2) 19–150
art.40 19–159
arts 41–44 4–002
art.41 .... 12–129, 18–265
(1)(b) 19–145
art.42 18–265
art.43 12–129
art.45(1)(b) 19–175
art.46(1) 12–129, 19–204
(2) 12–129, 19–204
(3) 12–129, 19–204
art.47 .... 8–025, 8–030, 12–129, 18–004, 19–144, 20–105
(1) 18–267, 19–150, 20–029
art.48 .... 8–025, 12–031, 12–077, 12–129
art.49 .... 8–025, 12–129
(1) 18–004, 19–147
(a) 18–267, 18–270, 19–063, 19–144, 19–145, 19–149, 20–029, 20–038, 20–105
(b) 18–267, 19–144, 20–029, 20–038, 20–105
(2) 12–129, 19–150, 19–207
(a) 19–150
(b)(i) 19–150, 20–109
(ii) 19–150
art.50 ... 12–129, 19–187, 19–188, 20–120
art.51 .... 8–046, 12–099, 12–129
(2) 12–100, 12–101
art.52 12–129
(1) 8–043
(2) 8–049
art.53 .... 9–001, 9–021, 19–207
art.55 2–047
art.58 8–004
(1) 18–006, 19–076, 20–055
, 1st sentence 19–075
, 2nd sentence 19–075
(2) 18–006
(3) 19–076, 20–055
art.59 8–004
art.60 9–003
(a) 20–042, 20–125
(b) 19–207
arts 61–65 9–009
art.61 9–010
(1)(b) 19–216
art.62 19–215
art.63 9–007
(1) 19–207, 20–046
art.64 20–046
(1) 20–125
(a) 19–207, 19–208
(b) 19–207

United Nations Convention on Contracts for the International Sale of Goods 1980 ("the Vienna Convention")—*cont.*
art.64(2) 19–207
arts 66–70 6–002
art.66 ... 6–001, 19–116, 19–117, 19–121, 20–092
arts 67–69 19–116
art.67 ... 6–031, 18–006, 19–082, 19–084, 19–108
(1) 18–244, 18–254, 19–114, 20–088, 20–090, 21–043, 21–100
, 1st sentence ... 19–110, 19–111
(2) ... 1–113, 6–004, 6–033, 19–083, 19–113
art.68 .. 18–006, 18–244, 19–082, 19–083, 19–084, 19–113, 19–108, 20–088
, 1st sentence 19–082, 19–083, 19–112, 19–113
, 2nd sentence 19–082, 19–083, 19–110, 19–113
, 3rd sentence 19–083, 19–113
art.69(1) 1–113, 18–244, 19–121, 19–122, 20–088, 20–092, 21–003, 21–100
(2) 18–244, 19–121, 20–092, 21–020
art.70 .. 18–244, 19–116, 19–117, 19–121, 20–092
arts 71–73 .... 8–025, 8–078
art.71 .... 12–129, 18–006, 19–179
(1) 19–161, 20–105
(2) 18–086, 19–220, 20–141, 21–057, 21–103
art.72 .... 12–129, 19–179, 20–105
(1) 19–161
(2) 19–161
(3) 19–161
art.73 .... 8–077, 12–099
arts 74–76 19–187
art.74 .. 19–175, 19–187, 19–188, 19–216, 19–218, 20–138
art.75 .. 19–175, 19–186, 19–187, 19–216, 20–137
art.76 ... 19–179, 19–187, 19–216, 20–140
(1) 19–175, 19–177, 19–186, 19–188, 20–133, 21–031
(2) 19–175, 19–186, 19–216, 20–115, 20–134, 20–135, 21–046
art.77 19–215
art.79 ... 11–043, 12–129, 19–124, 20–095
(2) 19–130
arts 81–88 12–129
arts 81–84 12–057
art.81(1) 19–161
art.82 .. 12–059, 12–098, 19–150, 19–174
art.83 19–150
arts 85–88 .... 12–065, 12–129
art.88 .... 19–220, 20–141
art.96 2–020

United Nations Convention on Independent Guarantees and Standby Letters of Credit, adopted by the General Assembly on December 11, 1995 23–301
United Nations Convention on International Bills of Exchange and International Promissory Notes adopted by the United Nations Commission on International Trade Law (UNCITRAL) on August 14, 1987 and by the General Assembly on December 9, 1988 22–035
art.1 22–035
art.2 22–035
United Nations Convention on the International Multimodal Transport of Goods (United Nations Document TD/MT/Conf. 16 adopted on May 24, 1980) 21–082
Vilnius Protocol 1999 ..... 21–047, 21–066, 21–067, 21–068
Warsaw Convention *unamended* (see SI 2004/1899, Sch.2, Pt II)
Warsaw Convention of 1929 *as amended* at the Hague in 1955 and Montreal in 1975 (*See Carriage by Air Act 1961, Sch.1*) ... 5–009, 21–047, 21–051, 21–052, 21–053, 21–055, 21–058, 21–104, 21–105, 21–106
Warsaw Convention *re-amended* (*See Carriage by Air and Road Act 1979*) 21–047, 21–051, 21–052, 21–053, 21–055, 21–056, 21–057, 21–104, 21–105, 21–106

TABLE OF FOREIGN LEGISLATION

AUSTRALIA

Commonwealth

Bills of Exchange Act 1909–73 22–034
Trade Practices Act 1973 13–063
Trade Practices Act 1974—
Pt. V 14–044, 14–139
Trade Practices Act 1974 14–013
Trade Practices Amendment Act 1978 14–001

New South Wales

ontracts Relief Act 1980 13–049
Contracts Review Act 1980 .... 13–003, 13–063
s.7 13–007

South Australia

Bulk Handling of Grain Act 1955 ... 1–057
Door to Door Sales Act 1971 14–045
Door to Door Sales Act 1979 14–045
Sale of Goods Act 1895—
s.14 17–072

Victoria

Consumer Affairs Act 1972 14–102
Consumer Affairs Act 1978 14–102

CANADA

Canada Grain Act R.S.C. 1985, c.G–10 1–057
Consumer Protection Act 1996 (Saskatchewan)—
s.47 14–014

British Columbia

Trade Practice Act 1996 14–102

FRANCE

Civil Code 25–030
s.1138 25–154
s.1147 25–205
s.1583 25–132
s.1648 25–196

GERMANY

AGB-Gesetz (Standard Contract Terms Law) 1976 ..... 13–003, 13–063
s.1 13–095
s.5 13–020
s.10 13–007
s.11 13–007
Civil Code—
s.326 25–196
s.441(3) 19–187
s.446 25–154
s.477 25–199
s.929 25–132

HONG KONG

Law Reform (Frustrated Contracts) Ordinance—
s.3 22–011

INDIA

Contract Act 1872—
s.20 3–022
Sale of Goods Act 1930—
s.2(4) 18–167

ISRAEL

Standard Contracts Law 1964 13–007
Standard Contracts Law 1982 ..... 13–003, 13–095

ITALY

Civil Code—
art.1341 13–007
art.1362 25–032
art.1495 25–196

NEW ZEALAND

Bills of Exchange Act 1908 22–034
Sale of Goods Act 1908 1–087

SWITZERLAND

Code of Obligations—
s.185 25–154
Swiss Private International Law Act 1987—
art.117 25–060
(3)(a) 25–060

UNITED STATES

American Federal Bills of Lading Act 1916 .... 18–074, 18–081
s.3 18–015
s.4 18–069
s.9 18–070
s.11 18–081
s.31 18–074
s.31(b) 18–074
s.32 18–074
Carriage of Goods by Sea Act 1936 21–074, 21–085, 21–086, 21–104
Constitution
art.III, para.2 C1.1 21–076
Harter Act 1893 18–074
Magnuson-Moss Warranty Act 1975 14–065
USC (1994)
s.80103(b)(1)(B) 18–074
s.80105 18–074
s.80109 18–123
s.80110(b) 18–070
s.80111(c) 18–081
Uniform Bills of Lading Act 1909—
s.1 18–079
s.32 18–096
Uniform Commercial Code 1990 ... 1–001, 5–002, 6–053, 12–062, 12–129, 13–007, 14–022
s.1–201(6) 18–012, 18–079, 18–268, 21–082
s.1–201(15) 18–079, 21–082
s.1–206(16) 21–081
art.2 .... 18–268, 19–047, 21–096
s.2–105(6) 12–062
s.2–106 .... 1–026, 1–027
s.2–163 12–082
s.2–207 2–011
s.2–302 .... 13–003, 13–007, 13–063
s.2–304 2–044
(1) 1–034
s.2–306 8–060
s.2–312(2) 4–004, 4–032
(3) 4–027
s.2–313 10–015
s.2–314 11–026
(2)(f) 14–014
s.2–315 11–051
s.2–317 11–068
s.2–318 14–078
s.2–319(1)(c) 20–016
s.2–320 18–268, 19–047, 19–078, 21–096
(2)(c) 19–047
(e) 19–066
s.2–325 23–085
s.2–327 1–056
s.2–503 25–154
Uniform Commercial Code 1990—*cont.*
s.2–508 ... 2–008, 8–052, 12–031, 14–022
s.2–509 .... 19–083, 19–113, 25–154
s.2–510 .... 6–011, 12–059
s.2–513(1) 12–043
s.2–601 2–008
s.2–603 12–065
s.2–604 12–065
s.2–605 12–032
s.2–608 .... 12–038, 14–022
s.2–609 12–129
s.2–614(1) 19–126, 20–015
s.2–615(b) 6–053, 18–353
s.2–615(c) 6–053
s.2–616 6–053
s.2–706 15–131
s.2–709(1) 9–056
s.2–615(b) 16–028
s.2–711(3) 12–065
art.3 .... 22–034, 22–035
s.3–310 23–099
s.3–416 22–052
s.3–419 (Revised Version) 22–052
s.3–507(2) 23–011
art.5 .... 23–026, 23–057
s.5–103(c) 23–026
(1)(f) 23–249
s.5–106 .... 23–054, 23–114
s.5–109 23–139
s.5–109(a) 23–146, 23–150
(b) 23–142
s.5–110 23–191
s.5–111 .... 23–164, 23–171
s.5–114 .... 23–054, 23–061
s.5–114(2) 23–150
s.5–116(2) 23–068
art.7 .... 18–015, 18–204
s.7–102(1)(e) 18–079
s.7–104 18–084
(a) 18–015
(b) 18–015
(2) 18–079
s.7–106 18–204
s.7–207(2) 1–057
s.7–304 18–069
s.7–307 18–123
s.7–502 .... 18–074, 18–084
(d) 18–096
s.7–503 18–084
(1) 18–085
art.8 22–034
Uniform Sales Act 1–001
s.7(2) 12–082
s.9(2) 1–034
Uniform Warehouse Receipts Act—
s.23 1–057

Part One

NATURE AND FORMATION OF THE CONTRACT OF SALE

Chapter 1

THE CONTRACT OF SALE OF GOODS

	PARA.
1. The Sale of Goods Acts	1–001
2. Related statutes	1–016
3. The contract of sale	1–025
(a) Sale and agreement to sell	1–025
(b) Contract of sale distinguished from other transactions	1–030
4. Subject-matter of the contract	1–078
(a) Goods	1–078
(b) Classes of goods	1–101
(c) Part interests in goods	1–121
(d) Non-existent goods	1–122

1. The Sale of Goods Acts

The Sale of Goods Act 1979. The Sale of Goods Act 1979, which **1–001**
received the Royal Assent on December 6, 1979 and came into force on January 1, 1980,[1] consolidates the law relating to the sale of goods. It applies to the whole of the United Kingdom. It replaces the Sale of Goods Act 1893[2] and parts of a number of other enactments,[3] and incorporates changes which had already been made in those Acts by amending legislation.[4] The Act of 1979 is expressed to be retrospective in its effect, so as to apply to all contracts of sale of goods made on or after January 1, 1894 (the date when the Act of 1893 became operative).[5] The wording of the Act of 1979 is not identical with that of the enactments which it consolidates, and in particular the definition of some statutory terms is altered. So far as concerns contracts made after January 1, 1980, there is no need to look beyond the substantive provisions,[6] but as regards contracts made earlier than that date, it is necessary in the case of particular sections to refer to the transitional provisions set out in Schedule 1.[7]

---

[1] Excepting parts of s.14 (implied terms as to quality or fitness) and s.25 (sale by buyer in possession), which were not brought into force until May 19, 1985: see s.14(7), (8) and Sch.1, para.5; s.25(3), (4) and Sch.1, para.9; and SI 1983/1572.
[2] Excluding s.26 (effect of writs of execution), which was not repealed until January 1, 1982: Supreme Court Act 1981, s.152(4) and Sch.7.
[3] Principally the Misrepresentation Act 1967, s.4; Misrepresentation (Northern Ireland) Act 1967, s.4; Supply of Goods (Implied Terms) Act 1973, ss.1–7, 18(2).
[4] Principally the Consumer Credit Act 1974, s.192(4) and Sch.4, para.3; Unfair Contract Terms Act 1977, s.31(2) and Schs 3, 4.
[5] See s.1(1).
[6] See s.1(4).
[7] See ss.1(2), (3) and ss.11(7), 12(6), 13(4), 14(7), 15(4), 22(3), 25(3), 35(2), 55(3), 56, 61(6), and Sch.1.

Since its enactment, the Sale of Goods Act 1979 has been the subject of three amending Acts,[8] as well as a number of minor statutory amendments.[9]

However, changes of much greater significance have been introduced by other legislation,[10] in many cases by statutory instrument, not all of which have involved amendment of the Act itself. In particular, a number of measures dealing with consumer sales,[11] implementing directives applicable throughout the European Union, have made major inroads into the traditional domestic law, to the extent that consumer sales can now fairly be regarded as a distinct branch of the law.[12]

The Sale of Goods Bill, as originally drafted by Sir Mackenzie Chalmers in 1888, was intended to apply only in the common law jurisdictions of England, Wales and Ireland, but in the course of its passage through Parliament it was amended so as to extend its operation to Scotland. The effect of this was that a common legislated code was superimposed on two fundamentally different legal systems. The Act of 1893 did not attempt to sweep away all the basic conceptual and procedural differences between the two systems: there was a generous duplication of terminology; and some provisions were specifically made to apply only in one jurisdiction or the other.[13] The Act of 1979 preserves all these features. This work is concerned primarily with English law.

The Act of 1893 has been adopted with little modification in many jurisdictions of the British Commonwealth. In the United States, the first of the two uniform codes governing sales, the Uniform Sales Act, was substantially modelled upon the English legislation, so that decisions and commentaries relating to it may be relevant and helpful in England.[14] But this legislation has now been replaced in all states except Louisiana by the

---

[8] Sale of Goods (Amendment) Act 1994, Sale and Supply of Goods Act 1994, Sale of Goods (Amendment) Act 1995.

[9] In s.61(4) (definition of "insolvent"), the words from "whether he has committed" onwards were repealed by the Insolvency Act 1985, s.235(3) and Sch.10, and the words "and whether he has become a notour bankrupt or not" by the Bankruptcy (Scotland) Act 1985, s.75(2) and Sch.8; and s.40 (attachment by seller in Scotland) was repealed by the Debtors (Scotland) Act 1987, s.108(3) and Sch.8. One paragraph of Sch.2 to the 1979 Act was repealed by the Statute Law (Repeals) Act 1981, s.1(1) and Sch.1; and (for Scotland only) part of s.3 by Sch.2 to the Age of Legal Capacity (Scotland) Act 1991.

[10] The principal primary legislation is the Unfair Contract Terms Act 1977 (below, para.13–008).

[11] Notably the Unfair Terms in Consumer Contracts Regulations 1999 (SI 1999/2083, replacing SI 1994/3159) and the Sale and Supply of Goods to Consumers Regulations 2002 (SI 2002/3045). See further below, para.1–023. These and other Regulations concerned with consumer protection are discussed in Chs 13 and 14.

[12] Macleod, *Consumer Sales Law* (2002).

[13] See generally Bridge, [1991] L.M.C.L.Q. 52.

[14] The principal draftsman was Williston, who also wrote the leading commentary on it: Williston, *The Law Governing Sales of Goods at Common Law and under the Uniform Sales Act*. The Revised (or 3rd) edition of 1948 was the last to deal with the Uniform Sales Act; more recent editions have been based on the Uniform Commercial Code.

Uniform Commercial Code,[15] which is not derived from the English Act and is in many respects fundamentally different from it.

Construction of codifying statute.[16] The Sale of Goods Act 1893 was, to quote its full title, "An Act for codifying the Law relating to the Sale of Goods." The purpose of a codifying enactment is "to present an orderly and authoritative statement of the leading rules of law on a given subject, whether they are to be found in statute law or common law."[17] The question naturally arises how far it is legitimate to have regard to the earlier law in construing the codifying Act. In general, it may be said that the correct approach is to treat the statute as marking a new departure, and to disregard what it replaces. A code is not necessarily a simple restatement of the earlier rules; it may alter or amend them, and include some wholly new provisions. There is no presumption that any particular proposition was intended to corroborate the existing law rather than to substitute a new rule.[18] In the leading case on the construction of a codifying enactment, *Bank of England v Vagliano Brothers*, Lord Halsbury L.C. said[19]: "I am wholly unable to adopt the view that, where a statute is expressly said to codify the law, you are at liberty to go outside the code so created, because before the existence of that code another law prevailed." In the same case Lord Herschell said[20]: "I think the proper course is in the first instance to examine the language of the statute and to ask what is its natural meaning, uninfluenced by any considerations derived from the previous state of the law, and not to start with inquiring how the law previously stood, and then, assuming that it was probably intended to leave it unaltered, to see if the words of the enactment will bear an interpretation in conformity with this view. 1–002

---

[15] Cited hereafter as U.C.C. References are to the official text of 2001 (as revised). For comparative studies, see Ogilvie, 2 Tasmania Univ.L.Rev. 12, 176, 288 (1964); Sutton, 6 Melbourne Univ.L.Rev. 150 (1967) and 7 Alberta L.Rev. 130 (1969); Adams [2002] J.B.L. 553; Fridman and Thompson in Ziegel and Foster (eds), *Aspects of Comparative Commercial Law* (1969), Chs 2, 3. See also the Ontario Law Reform Commission's *Report on the Sale of Goods* (1979) and Ziegel (ed.), *Papers and Comments Delivered at the 9th Annual Workshop on Commercial and Consumer Law* (1981), pp.1–58.

[16] See generally Halsbury, *Laws of England* (4th ed.), Vol.44(1), paras 1226, 1418; *Craies on Statute Law* (7th ed.), pp.364 *et seq.*

[17] Halsbury, *op. cit.*, para.1226. Other codifying Acts are the Bills of Exchange Act 1882, Partnership Act 1890 and Marine Insurance Act 1906.

[18] *Bank of England v Vagliano Brothers* [1891] A.C. 107 at 145. It has, however, been suggested that a codifying Act should not be presumed to have altered a well-established rule of law without clear words to that effect: see *British and Foreign Marine Insce. Co. Ltd v Samuel Sanday & Co.* [1916] 1 A.C. 650 at 673; *Sutherland v Nicol* [1951] W.N. 110.

[19] Above, at p.120. (The decision concerned the Bills of Exchange Act 1882; but the Sale of Goods Act 1893 is *in pari materia*.)

[20] Above, at pp.144–145. See also *Robinson v Canadian Pacific Ry. Co.* [1892] A.C. 481 at 487; *Abbott & Co. v Wolsey* [1895] 2 Q.B. 97 at 99; *Bristol Tramways Carriage Co. Ltd v Fiat Motors Ltd* [1910] 2 K.B. 831 at 836; *Wimble, Sons & Co. v Rosenberg & Sons* [1913] 3 K.B. 743 at 762; *Laurie & Morewood v Dudin & Sons* [1926] 1 K.B. 223 at 234–235; *Farrell v Alexander* [1977] A.C. 59 at 73, 82, 97 (Rent Acts). Contrast *Wallis v Russell* [1902] 2 I.R. 585 at 590.

"If a statute, intended to embody in a code a particular branch of the law, is to be treated in this fashion, it appears to me that its utility will be almost entirely destroyed, and the very object with which it was enacted will be frustrated. The purpose of such a statute surely was that on any point specifically dealt with by it, the law should be ascertained by interpreting the language used instead of, as before, by roaming over a vast number of authorities in order to discover what the law was, extracting it by a minute critical examination of the prior decisions . . . I am of course far from asserting that resort may never be had to the previous state of the law for the purpose of aiding in the construction of the provisions of the code. If, for example, a provision be of doubtful import, such resort would be perfectly legitimate. Or, again, if in a code words be found which have previously acquired a technical meaning, or been used in a sense other than their ordinary one, . . . the same interpretation might well be put upon them in the code. I give these as examples merely; they, of course, do not exhaust the category. What, however, I am venturing to insist upon is, that the first step taken should be to interpret the language of the statute, and that an appeal to earlier decisions can only be justified on some special ground."

Despite these observations, recourse is often had in practice to cases which were decided before the Act of 1893 not only where the statute is ambiguous or silent, but also where it seems to be generally accepted that a provision in that Act was intended to give effect to a particular decision or to continue the established law. This is borne out both by the large number of pre-1894 cases which are cited in all textbooks (including the present work), and also by an examination of the precedents relied upon in modern cases.[21]

In some instances, the Act is based on a rule of Scots law which had no counterpart in English common law.[22] But these are isolated provisions: the Act of 1893 is in no sense a codification of the law of Scotland as it stood at that time.

1–003 **Application of Code to modern conditions.** The observations of Lord Halsbury L.C., cited in the preceding paragraph, should, however, be read in the light of the comments of Lord Diplock in *Ashington Piggeries Ltd v Christopher Hill Ltd.*[23] He said[24]: "The provisions of the Act are in the main confined to statements of what promises are to be implied on the part of the buyer and the seller in respect of matters upon which the contract is silent, and to statements of the consequences of performance or non-performance of promises, whether expressed or implied, where the contract

[21] See Diamond, 31 M.L.R. 361 (1968). For a striking example of this approach, see *Cehave NV v Bremer Handelsgessellschaft mbH, The Hansa Nord* [1976] Q.B. 44 (below, para.10–003), where the Court of Appeal relied extensively on 19th-century textbooks and decisions in rejecting the twofold classification of terms, as either conditions or warranties, which it was generally accepted that the Sale of Goods Act 1893 had established.
[22] *e.g.* s.32(3): below, para.18–246.
[23] [1972] A.C. 441.
[24] *ibid.* at p.501.

does not state what those consequences are to be. Even a code whose content is so limited must proceed by classifying promises, both those which are expressed and those to be implied; the circumstances which give rise to implied promises, and how they are to be performed and the consequences of performing each class of promise or of failing to perform it. Because of the source of the rules stated in the Sale of Goods Act 1893 the classification adopted is by reference to the promises made in relatively simple types of contracts for the sale of goods which were commonly made in the nineteenth century and had been the subject of judicial decision before 1893. But although the language in which the rules are expressed is appropriate to these simple types of contracts, it has to be applied today to promises made in much more complicated contracts which cannot be readily allotted to any single class of contract which appears to be primarily envisaged by a particular section or subsection of the code. Unless the Sale of Goods Act 1893 is to be allowed to fossilise the law and to restrict the freedom of choice of parties to contracts for the sale of goods to make agreements which take account of advances in technology and changes in the way in which business is carried on today, the provisions set out in the various sections and subsections of the code ought not to be construed so narrowly as to force upon parties to contracts for the sale of goods promises and consequences different from what they must reasonably have intended. They should be treated rather as illustrations of the application to simple types of contract of general principles for ascertaining the common intention of the parties as to their mutual promises and their consequences, which ought to be applied by analogy in cases arising out of contracts which do not appear to have been within the immediate contemplation of the draftsman of the Act in 1893."

Construction of consolidating statute. The object of the Sale of Goods Act 1979, in contrast with that of 1893, was to consolidate the existing statutory law, that is, to present the whole body of such law in complete form, repealing the former statutes.[25] There is a presumption in construing a consolidating Act that no alteration of the previous law was intended, so that it is legitimate to have regard to judicial decisions on the superseded statutes in order to determine the meaning of the consolidating measure. The presumption applies even if the language of the two provisions is not identical; but this view must yield to plain words to the contrary[26]; and where the words of the consolidating Act are clear, the court in construing it should treat it as standing on its own feet, without recourse to its legislative antecedents.[27] 1–004

Construction of subsequent amendments. Differing views have been expressed by the judges on the approach to be taken in construing the more recent amendments to the Act. For example, when in 1973 a new statutory 1–005

[25] *Conservators of the River Thames v Smeed, Dean & Co.* [1897] 2 Q.B. 334 at 346. See generally Halsbury, *Laws of England* (4th ed.), Vol.44(1), paras 1225, 1417; *Craies on Statute Law* (7th ed.), pp.136 *et seq.*

[26] *MacConnell v E. Prill & Co.* [1916] 2 Ch. 57 at 63; *Gilbert v Gilbert and Boucher* [1928] P. 1 at 8; *Grey v Inland Revenue Commrs* [1960] A.C. 1 at 13; *Beswick v Beswick* [1968] A.C. 58.

[27] *Farrell v Alexander* [1977] A.C. 59; *Edwards v Clinch* [1981] Ch. 1 at 5.

provision defining the (now discarded) term "merchantable quality" was introduced,[28] Mustill L.J. said that since the language of the new subsection was clear and free from technicality it should be sufficient in the great majority of cases to enable the judge to arrive at a decision without exploring the intricacies of the prior law.[29] In contrast, in *M/S Aswan Engineering Establishment Co v Lupdine Ltd*,[30] Lloyd L.J. said: "It is not possible to appreciate the change which the definition is said to have brought about without first looking at the law as it stood before 1973"; and then reviewed the earlier law in a passage extending over eight pages of the report of his judgment.

The question also arises whether it is legitimate to refer to Law Commission reports, government white papers and Parliamentary debates in order to interpret or explain amending legislation. In the *Aswan Engineering* case[31] Lloyd L.J. said that he could "see no conceivable reason" why the court should not have been referred to the Law Commission papers which preceded the enactment of the 1973 Act, "and good reasons why we should". More recently, it has been settled that such reports and papers may be looked at, but only for the purpose of ascertaining the mischief which the amending statute is intended to cure, and not in order to ascertain the meaning of the words used by Parliament to effect such a cure.[32] The conditions on which the records of Parliamentary debates in *Hansard* and other Parliamentary material may be referred to as an aid to statutory interpretation have now been settled by the House of Lords.[33]

1–006 **General scope of the Act.** The Sale of Goods Act 1979, like its predecessor of 1893, applies to contracts for the sale of all types of goods. In so far as special rules exist governing particular categories of goods, they are to be found in other enactments.[34]

---

[28] Supply of Goods (Implied Terms) Act 1973, s.3, introducing new s.14(6) to the Sale of Goods Act 1979 (since repealed): see below, para.11–025.

[29] *Rogers v Parish (Scarborough) Ltd* [1987] Q.B. 933 at 942.

[30] [1987] 1 W.L.R. 1 at 6.

[31] *ibid.* at p.14.

[32] *Pepper (Inspector of Taxes) v Hart* [1993] A.C. 593 at 630. In *R. v Secretary of State for Transport Ex p. Factortame Ltd* [1990] 2 A.C. 85, the House of Lords also referred to a Law Commission report in order to draw an inference as to Parliamentary intention from the fact that Parliament had not expressly implemented one of the Law Commission's recommendations.

[33] *Pepper (Inspector of Taxes) v Hart*, above; *Melluish (Inspector of Taxes) v BMI (No.3) Ltd* [1996] 1 A.C. 454. The conditions are: (i) reference may only be made to statements made by a Minister or other promoter of the Bill; (ii) this may be done only where the legislation is ambiguous or obscure, or where a literal or *prima facie* construction would lead to absurdity; and (iii) the statements relied on must be directed to the specific matter in issue. The court's approach may be more flexible if the object of the legislation is to introduce into the law of the United Kingdom the provisions of an E.C. Directive: *Three Rivers DC v Bank of England (No.2)* [1996] 2 All E.R. 363; indeed, the courts of this country are under a duty to construe its domestic legislation in the light of the wording and purpose of any relevant Directive (*Marleasing SA v La Comercial Internacional de Alimentacion SA* [1992] 1 C.M.L.R. 305).

[34] *cf.* the special rules as to the transfer of title to motor vehicles in the Hire-

With one or two exceptions (*e.g.* section 57, dealing with sales by auction), most provisions of the original legislation of 1893 were made to apply generally to every kind of contract, regardless of the circumstances in which it might have been formed and of the standing of the parties. It was a feature (and, perhaps, a fault) of this legislation that virtually no distinctions were made between commercial sales and private sales,[35] between merchants' sales and retail sales, or between sales of new and of second-hand goods.

Important changes, however, were made in this respect by later legislation, the terms of which have been consolidated in the Act of 1979 or are expressly saved by it.[36] The effect of these provisions is that it is no longer possible to regard the Sale of Goods Act as a single code of rules which in principle applies to all contracts of sale. Factors such as that one of the parties is acting in the course of a business[37] or through an agent who is so acting,[38] that a party is dealing as consumer[39] or does not deal as consumer,[40] that the goods are of a type ordinarily supplied for consumer use or consumption,[41] or that the transaction has an international element[42] may bring a wide range of special statutory rules into operation. The circumstances of the parties and the nature or description of the goods may also have a bearing on the question whether a contractual term satisfies the "requirement of reasonableness" imposed by some sections of the Unfair Contract Terms Act 1977[43]; and similar considerations may be relevant to the question whether the goods supplied under a contract of sale are of "satisfactory quality" for the purposes of sections 14(2)–(2C) and 15(2)(C) of the Sale of Goods Act 1979.[44]

Other measures applicable particularly to sales made to a consumer buyer include a number of statutory instruments enacted in order to implement EC directives in this area. These are discussed in Chapter 14.

Purchase Act 1964, ss.27–29 (below, paras 7–087 *et seq.*), and the statutory warranties implied by law in the sale of certain classes of goods (below, paras 14–094 *et seq.*). In addition, the sale of many types of goods is regulated by legislation for which the sanctions are primarily penal: see below, paras 14–108 *et seq.*

[35] The most notable exception was that a term as to fitness for purpose would be implied only where (*inter alia*) the goods were of a description which it was in the course of the seller's business to supply (s.14(1)), and a term as to merchantable quality only where goods were bought by description from a seller who dealt in goods of that description (s.14(2)): see now the wider wording of the corresponding provisions (s.14(3), (2)) of the 1979 Act, below, paras 11–051 *et seq.*, 11–026 *et seq.*

[36] Supply of Goods (Implied Terms) Act 1973; Unfair Contract Terms Act 1977 (see Sale of Goods Act 1979, s.55(1)).

[37] Unfair Contract Terms Act 1977, s.1(3) (but see *ibid.* s.6(4)), below, paras 11–062 *et seq.*; Sale of Goods Act 1979, s.14(2), (3), below, paras 11–027 *et seq.*

[38] Sale of Goods Act 1979, s.14(3), (5), below, para.11–029.

[39] Unfair Contract Terms Act 1977, ss.3, 4, 6(2); for a definition of "dealing as consumer" for this purpose see s.12, below, paras 13–071 *et seq.* The Unfair Terms in Consumer Contracts Regulations 1999 (SI 1999/2083) also apply only to contracts concluded between a seller or supplier and a consumer, but for the purpose of these Regulations there is a different definition of "consumer": see below, para.14–031.

[40] Sale of Goods Act 1979, s.15A, below, paras 12–024 *et seq.*; s.30(2A), below, paras 12–030 *et seq.*

[41] *Unfair Contract Terms Act 1977*, s.5, below, paras 13–081 *et seq.*

[42] *ibid.* s.26, below, paras 13–099 *et seq.*

[43] *ibid.* s.11 and Sch.2, below, paras 13–086 *et seq.*

[44] See below, paras 11–026 *et seq.*

The Sale of Goods Act contains no penal provisions[45] and prescribes no special rules of evidence or procedure. The liability of the parties in tort to each other and to third parties is unaffected, except in so far as the Act deals with questions of the property in and the right to possession of the goods which are the subject of a contract of sale.

1–007 **Saving of common law rules.** The Sale of Goods Act 1979 codifies only the special rules of law which are peculiar to the sale of goods. It is set against the background of the general law of contract and of personal property. Section 62(2) of the Act provides that "the rules of the common law, including the law merchant, except in so far as they are inconsistent with the provisions of this Act, and in particular the rules relating to the law of principal and agent and the effect of fraud, misrepresentation, duress or coercion, mistake, or other invalidating cause, apply to contracts for the sale of goods." This section confirms that the rules of the general law continue in operation to supplement the code. Certain other sections of the Act also make express provision for the application of particular common law rules, for example, those relating to the capacity of parties to contract and to transfer and acquire property[46]; the discharge of certain obligations by reason of impossibility[47]; the liabilities of one contracting party as a bailee of the goods of the other[48]; and the right of a buyer or seller to recover interest, special damages and money paid on a failure of consideration.[49]

1–008 **The Act and equity.** The use of the expression "the rules of the common law" in section 62(2) gives rise to an issue which has never been authoritatively determined in this country, although it has been ignored on so many occasions that it may now be considered settled simply for want of objection. Put shortly, the question is whether or not the phrase is intended to include the rules of equity. The argument that the rules of equity are not preserved draws support from three different sources. First, it would generally be agreed that the most natural and usual sense in which the expression "the rules of the common law" is understood by contract lawyers is the most technical, *viz.* in contradistinction to the rules of equity. It is in this sense that the term is used in the Judicature Act 1873. Secondly, at the time when the Act was passed, it was still unsettled whether certain equitable principles (in particular, those regarding innocent misrepresentation) were generally applicable to all contracts, and specifically to sales of

[45] Note, however, the Consumer Transactions (Restrictions on Statements) Order 1976 (SI 1976/1813, as amended by SI 1978/127), which makes it an offence to purport to include in a consumer sale transaction any term which is declared void by ss.6 or 20 of the Unfair Contract Terms Act 1977. This, in effect, makes it an offence to purport to contract out of liability for certain undertakings as to title, quality, etc., implied in favour of a consumer-buyer under ss.12–15 of the Sale of Goods Act 1979. See below, para.14–142.

[46] s.3; see below, paras 2–028—2–043.

[47] s.11(3); see below, paras 6–034 *et seq.*

[48] s.20(3); see below, paras 6–026 *et seq.*

[49] s.54; see below, paras 9–068, 16–007 (interest); 16–046, 16–086 (special damages); 12–067, 17–090 (money paid).

goods. The use of the words "the rules of the common law" rather than, say, "the existing rules of law" could therefore be taken as a legislative declaration either that these equitable principles had not been extended to sales of goods by the Judicature Act[50] or that, even if this had been the effect of the Judicature Act, it was no longer to be the case after the Act of 1893. Thirdly, the New Zealand Court of Appeal,[51] and the Full Court in the State of Victoria,[52] each held in early decisions that the use of the expression "the common law" did not in the context include the rules of equity. (Subsequently, however, courts of comparable standing in both Australia and New Zealand have either distinguished or declined to follow these rulings.[53])

In opposition to this view, it has been pointed out that "the common law" is a term of variable meaning, capable in suitable contexts of meaning "judge-made" as opposed to statute law, or even "the law hitherto existing" as opposed to that presently being enacted.[54] Either of these constructions would allow for the continuance of the principles of equity under section 62(2). Various writers have argued in favour of this interpretation.[55]

It is submitted that it would now be difficult to argue that the principles of equity are not applicable to sales of goods, in view of the many cases in which they have been tacitly assumed to apply. Thus, a remedy for innocent misrepresentation based on equitable principles was granted in *Goldsmith v Rodger*[56]; and the same principles have been considered in a number of other cases, though relief was refused on the facts.[57] In *F E Rose Ltd v W H Pim & Co. Ltd*,[58] no question was raised as to the jurisdiction of the court to grant rectification in equity of a written contract for the sale of goods. Moreover, as has been pointed out,[59] it has always been accepted that the benefit of a contract of sale of goods may be assigned in equity, and that a breach of such a contract may be restrained by injunction.[60] In the 1–009

---

50 *Riddiford v Warren* (1901) 20 N.Z.L.R. 572 at 576, 582.

51 *ibid.*; distinguished in *Thomas Borthwick & Sons (Australasia) Ltd v South Otago Freezing Co. Ltd* [1978] 1 N.Z.L.R. 538 at 545, but followed in *Cutelli v Brian Cotter Motors Ltd* (1993) 5 T.C.L.R. 500.

52 *Watt v Westhoven* [1933] V.L.R. 458; but see now *Graham v Freer* (1980) 35 S.A.S.R. 424; and *cf. Leason Pty Ltd v Princes Farm Pty Ltd* [1983] 2 N.S.W.L.R. 381; *Vimig Pty Ltd v Contract Tooling Pty Ltd* (1986) 9 N.S.W.L.R. 731.

53 Above, nn.51, 52.

54 See Glanville Williams, 61 L.Q.R. 302 (1945); Fleming, 25 A.L.J. 443 (1951).

55 Glanville Williams, *op cit.*; earlier eds of *Anson's Law of Contract* and Morison, *Rescission of Contracts* (1916), cited by Fleming, *op. cit.*, p.446; Atiyah, *The Sale of Goods* (11th ed.), pp.530–531; Treitel, *The Law of Contract* (11th ed.), pp.374–375; Goode, *Commercial Law* (3rd ed.), p.192.

56 [1962] 2 Lloyd's Rep. 249; *cf. Abram Steamship Co. Ltd v Westville Shipping Co. Ltd* [1923] A.C. 773 (Scotland).

57 *T. & J. Harrison v Knowles and Foster* [1918] 1 K.B. 608; *Leaf v International Galleries* [1950] 2 K.B. 86; *Long v Lloyd* [1958] 1 W.L.R. 753; *cf. Huyton S A v Distribuidora Internacional de Productos Agricolas SA de CV* [2003] EWCA Civ 1104; [2004] All E.R. (Comm) 402.

58 [1953] 2 Q.B. 450.

59 Treitel, *The Law of Contract* (11th ed.), p.374.

60 *Jones & Sons Ltd v Earl of Tankerville* [1909] 2 Ch. 440; *Esso Petroleum Co. Ltd v Harper's Garage (Stourport) Ltd* [1968] A.C. 269; *Thomas Borthwick & Sons (Australasia) Ltd v South Otago Freezing Co. Ltd* [1978] 1 N.Z.L.R. 538 at 545.

particular case of innocent misrepresentation, the enlarged remedies given to a plaintiff by the Misrepresentation Act 1967 appear to be available to contracts generally, without any restriction. The Law Reform Committee in its report[61] on the subject clearly assumed that there was no exception as regards sales of goods, and indeed went out of its way to recommend an amendment of the Sale of Goods Act so that the position under the Act would be consistent with the proposed new remedies for misrepresentation. The Misrepresentation Act gave effect to this recommendation, but did not settle by any express terms the question here debated.

There is, of course, nothing in the Sale of Goods Act to prevent the parties to a contract for the sale of goods from incorporating equitable principles into their bargain by express agreement.[62]

1–010 **Compatibility with particular provisions.** Even if the wording of section 62(2) is not so construed as to make the whole of equity inapplicable to sale of goods, it may be argued that particular provisions in the Act have the effect of displacing the individual rules of equity with which they more or less correspond. It may be presumed, in other words, that the legislature intended that a rule declared by the Act should constitute a complete and definitive statement of the law governing that aspect of the subject. This to some extent appears from section 62(2) itself: the rules of law referred to are to apply "except in so far as they are inconsistent with the provisions of this Act." The argument receives strong support from an *obiter dictum* of Atkin L.J. in *Re Wait*,[63] where it was contended that a buyer, although not entitled to a remedy of specific performance under section 52 of the Act, should be considered an equitable assignee of the goods by virtue of the doctrine in *Holroyd v Marshall*.[64] In rejecting this view Atkin L.J. said[65]: "The Code was passed at a time when the principles of equity and equitable remedies were recognised and given effect to in all our courts, and the particular equitable remedy of specific performance is specially referred to in section 52. The total sum of legal relations (meaning by the word 'legal' existing in equity as well as in common law) arising out of the contract for the sale of goods may well be regarded as defined by the Code. It would have been futile in a Code intended for commercial men to have created an elaborate structure of rules dealing with rights at law, if at the same time it

---

[61] Cmnd. 1782 (1962).

[62] *Cf.*, *e.g. Aluminium Industrie Vaassen BV v Romalpa Aluminium Ltd* [1976] 1 W.L.R. 676 (right to trace), below, paras 5–141 *et seq.*

[63] [1927] 1 Ch. 606.

[64] (1861) 10 H.L.C. 191; see below, paras 1–108, 5–094, 17–096, 19–204 and, for the position following the enactment of the Sale of Goods (Amendment) Act 1995, below, paras 5–109 *et seq.*, 18–287 *et seq.*

[65] [1927] 1 Ch. 606 at 635–636. See also the view expressed in *Transport and General Credit Corp. Ltd v Morgan* [1939] Ch. 531 at 546, that there is no room for the concept of a vendor's equitable lien in a sale of ordinary commercial goods over and above the seller's possessory lien provided for by the Act: below, para.15–028. An equitable lien was held to have been established in favour of an unpaid seller of goods in *Electrical Enterprises Retail Pty Ltd v Rogers* (1988) 15 N.S.W.L.R. 473, and a buyer's equitable lien in *Hewett v Court* (1983) 149 C.L.R. 639 (where, however, the Sale of Goods Act was not in issue because the contract (for the supply of a prefabricated house) was held to be for work and materials).

was intended to leave, subsisting with the legal rights, equitable rights inconsistent with, more extensive, and coming into existence earlier than the rights so carefully set out in the various sections of the Code.

"The rules for transfer of property as between seller and buyer, performance of the contract, rights of the unpaid seller against the goods, unpaid sellers' lien, remedies of the seller, remedies of the buyer, appear to be complete and exclusive statements of the legal relations both in law and equity."

In this case there was a direct conflict between the remedy which the court was asked to grant and the restrictions on the award of specific performance—itself a remedy of equitable origin—which are expressly laid down by the Act; and the conclusion reached by Atkin L.J. could have been justified by the very wording of section 62(2). A problem of greater difficulty arises when it is less obvious whether an equitable principle and a provision in the Act cover the same ground. For example, it may be argued (with some historical support) that there is no place in a code of the law of sale for a doctrine of innocent misrepresentation, since the rules as to conditions and warranties may be regarded as a complete statement of the obligations of the parties (or at least of the seller) in regard to misstatements. There is direct support for this view in some older decisions in other jurisdictions,[66] and it is plain that judges have occasionally felt the force of the general argument that it is incongruous to allow a remedy for misrepresentation more extensive than could be had by suing on the same statement as a warranty or condition.[67] 1–011

So far as concerns innocent misrepresentation, it is probable that the Misrepresentation Act 1967 has made all these arguments obsolete. But the basic issue remains alive, as the facts of *Re Wait*[68] show; and it could conceivably arise again in another context, so that the courts may yet be obliged to consider how far a particular equitable rule is consistent with express provisions of the Act.

Other savings. Provision for the saving of other parts of the law prior to 1894 is made by the remainder of section 62. Section 62(1) enacts that "the rules in bankruptcy relating to contracts of sale apply to those contracts, notwithstanding anything in this Act." The law formerly in force concerning bankruptcy was mainly contained in the Bankruptcy Act 1914; but this Act was repealed by the Insolvency Act 1985, and replaced by the Insolvency 1–012

---

[66] *Riddiford v Warren* (1901) 20 N.Z.L.R. 572 at 582; *Watt v Westhoven* [1933] V.L.R. 458 at 463; but see now *Graham v Freer* (1980) 35 S.A.S.R. 424; *Leason Pty Ltd v Princes Farm Pty Ltd* [1983] 2 N.S.W.L.R. 381; *Vimig Pty Ltd v Contract Tooling Pty Ltd* (1986) 9 N.S.W.L.R. 731.

[67] *Pennsylvania Shipping Co. v Cie. Nationale de Navigation* [1936] 2 All E.R. 1167 (*contra Cie. Française des Chemins de Fer Paris-Orléans v Leeston Shipping Co.* (1919) 1 Ll.L.R. 235 at 237–238); *Leaf v International Galleries* [1950] 2 K.B. 86 at 89–91, 92–93, 95. A similar consideration appears to have induced the court in *Beale v. Taylor* [1967] 1 W.L.R. 1193 (below, para.11–019) very readily to hold that a statement by the seller as to the year of manufacture of a car was part of the "description" of the goods within the terms of s.13, and not merely a representation.

[68] Above.

Act 1986, Parts VIII–XI. The provisions of this legislation which have a bearing on contracts for the sale of goods are discussed in a later section,[69] and noted at other relevant points in the text. Section 62(3) provides that "nothing in this Act or the Sale of Goods Act 1893 affects the enactments relating to bills of sale, or any enactment relating to the sale of goods which is not expressly repealed or amended by this Act or that." The Bills of Sale Acts referred to are those of 1878 and 1882,[70] which are still in force; they are discussed later in the present chapter. Other enactments relating to the sale of goods which are saved by section 62(3) include the Factors Acts,[71] various statutes conferring powers of sale of goods upon persons other than the owner[72]; those providing for statutory warranties in relation to particular classes of goods[73]; and a number of penal statutes.[74] Further statutory provisions in force when the Act of 1893 was passed are saved by virtue of particular sections.[75] Section 62(4) preserves the existing law as regards transactions by way of security in the following terms: "the provisions of this Act about contracts of sale do not apply to a transaction in the form of a contract of sale which is intended to operate by way of mortgage, pledge, charge, or other security." This is mainly of significance in Scotland, since in England such transactions are severely restricted by the Bills of Sale Act (1878) Amendment Act 1882.[76]

1–013 **Freedom of contract.** Section 55(1) provides that "where a right, duty or liability would arise under a contract of sale of goods by implication of law, it may (subject to the Unfair Contract Terms Act 1977) be negatived or varied by express agreement, or by the course of dealing between the parties, or by such usage as binds both parties to the contract." This section maintains in principle the traditional freedom of the parties to a contract to fix the terms of their own bargain, although significant restrictions on this freedom are made by the Unfair Contract Terms Act 1977, to which the section itself makes reference.[77] In addition to this general provision, the right of the parties to vary or negative the effect of particular sections of the Act is frequently affirmed by those sections. It should be observed that the "right, duty or liability" which may be the subject of contrary agreement between the parties is one "arising under a contract of sale." Section 55(1) does not, and could not, authorise the parties to create their own rules as to what should amount to a binding or enforceable contract or to disregard the vitiating effect of such factors as incapacity, misrepresentation or

---

[69] See below, paras 3–045 *et seq*.
[70] See below, paras 1–016 *et seq.*, 1–065 *et seq*.
[71] See below, para.1–018; and *cf.* ss.21(2)(a), 39(1).
[72] See below, paras 7–109 *et seq.*; and *cf.* s.21(2)(b).
[73] See below, paras 14–094 *et seq.*; and *cf.* s.14(1).
[74] See below, paras 14–108 *et seq*.
[75] See, *e.g.* s.4 (formalities), below, paras 2–021 *et seq.*; s.14 (warranties), above, n.73, s.21(2)(a) and s.39(1) (Factors Acts, etc.), above, n.71; s.21(2)(b) (powers of sale), above, n.72. Certain early statutes relating to the sale of horses, formerly preserved by s.22(2) of the 1893 Act, were repealed by the Criminal Law Act 1967, s.10(2), Sch.3, Pt I.
[76] See below, paras 1–065 *et seq*.
[77] See below, para.1–014.

illegality. It is generally permissible, however, to agree that a contract shall be governed by the law of another country[78]; or shall be considered a gentlemen's agreement not binding in law at all.[79]

Statutory restrictions on contracting out. The Unfair Contract Terms Act 1977, which incorporates amendments first made to the Sale of Goods Act 1893 by the Supply of Goods (Implied Terms) Act 1973, qualifies the general operation of section 55(1). This Act severely restricts, and in some instances negatives altogether, the freedom of parties to exclude or vary the terms implied into a contract of sale of goods by sections 12 to 15 of the Sale of Goods Act 1979. Section 6(1) of the Act of 1977 provides that liability for breach of the obligations arising from section 12 of the Sale of Goods Act (which implies undertakings by the seller as to title, etc.) cannot be excluded or restricted by reference to any contract term[80]; while sections 6(2) and 6(3) respectively state that, as against a person dealing as consumer, liability for breach of the obligations arising from sections 13, 14 and 15 of the Sale of Goods Act (which imply undertakings by the seller as to the conformity of the goods with description or sample, and as to their quality and fitness for a particular purpose) are similarly made incapable of exclusion or restriction[81] and, as against a person dealing otherwise than as consumer, the freedom to exclude or restrict these liabilities is subjected to an overriding test of reasonableness.[82] None of these statutory limitations applies, however, to an international supply contract as is described in section 26 of the Unfair Contract Terms Act 1977,[83] nor to a contract governed by section 27(1) of that Act, that is, a contract to which the law of this country applies only by virtue of the provisions of a "choice of law" clause.[84] 1–014

The Unfair Terms in Consumer Contracts Regulations 1999,[85] which implement the provisions of the European Community Directive on Unfair Contract Terms,[86] do not in terms restrict or limit the freedom of parties to include particular provisions in their contract, but achieve much the same result by declaring that an unfair term (as therein defined) in a contract concluded with a consumer by a seller or supplier shall not be binding on the consumer.[87]

Statutory provisions not capable of exclusion or variation. There are some provisions of the Sale of Goods Act 1979 to which it is almost certain that the power of variation conferred on the parties by section 55(1) cannot 1–015

---

[78] See below, paras 25–001 *et seq.* As regards the effect of a choice of law clause on the operation of ss.2–7 and ss.16–17 of the Unfair Contract Terms Act 1977, see s.27 of that Act, discussed below, para.13–101.
[79] *Rose & Frank Co. v J R Crompton & Bros Ltd* [1925] A.C. 445; below, para.2–019.
[80] See below, paras 4–018 *et seq.*
[81] See below, paras 13–062, 13–083 *et seq.*
[82] See below, paras 13–083 *et seq.*
[83] See below, paras 13–099, 25–090.
[84] See below, paras 13–101, 25–091.
[85] SI 1999/2083 (replacing SI 1994/3159).
[86] 93/13/EEC.
[87] Unfair Terms in Consumer Contracts Regulations 1999, reg.8(1); below, para.13–103.

apply, in spite of the unqualified language used. Thus, section 16, which stipulates that (subject to section 20A)[88] no property can pass in goods which are unascertained, and section 5(3), which declares that a purported present sale of future goods operates only as an agreement to sell, do not appear to be capable of variation by agreement.[89] Clearly, too, the parties to a contract of sale cannot by their agreement abrogate or qualify the rights of third persons so as to prevent the latter from gaining a good title under sections 21 to 26[90]; although they may prevent the sections from operating at all by (for instance) making their own bargain one of hire-purchase and not of sale. More controversial are the questions whether sections 6 and 7, which deal with the perishing of goods the subject of a contract of sale, may be negatived by agreement.[91] Former doubts whether a seller might exclude his obligations as to title under section 12 without removing the transaction altogether from the scope of the Act appear to have been resolved by the provisions of section 12(3) to (5).[92] Finally, some at least of the provisions of section 57, regarding the conduct of sales by auction, are probably mandatory.[93]

2. RELATED STATUTES

1–016 **Bills of Sale Acts.** The Bills of Sale Acts, which are left unaffected by the specific terms of section 62(3) of the Act, are those of 1878 and 1882,[94] as modified by the later Acts of 1890 and 1891.[95] These Acts are still in force.[96]

---

[88] Section 20A and the words in brackets were inserted by the Sale of Goods (Amendment) Act 1995, s.1(1): see below, paras 5–109 *et seq.*

[89] See below, paras 5–090, 1–105; and *cf. Karlshamns Olje Fabriker v Eastport Navigation Corp (The Elafi)* [1982] 1 All E.R. 208 at 212; *Jansz v GMB Imports Pty Ltd* [1979] V.R. 581 at 586. Related questions are whether specific performance is available in the case of an agreement to sell unascertained goods (see below, para.17–097), whether there may be an attornment by a bailee in relation to unascertained goods (see below, para.8–012); and whether an unpaid seller's lien may be defeated while the goods are still unascertained (see below, paras 15–012, 15–095); but these problems arise at common law rather than under the Act. *cf.* Nicol, 42 M.L.R. 129 (1979), Goode, *Proprietary Rights and Insolvency in Sales Transactions* (2nd ed.), Ch.1, and the Law Commission's Working Paper No.112, *Rights to Goods in Bulk* (1989) and its Report No.215, *Sale of Goods Forming Part of a Bulk* (1993).

[90] See below, Ch.7.

[91] See below, paras 1–123 *et seq.*

[92] These provisions were first introduced by the Supply of Goods (Implied Terms) Act 1973, s.1: see below, paras 4–032 *et seq.* Liability for breach of the obligations arising from s.12 cannot be excluded: see Unfair Contract Terms Act 1977, s.6(1).

[93] See below, paras 2–004, 3–009.

[94] Bills of Sale Act 1878; Bills of Sale Act (1878) Amendment Act 1882.

[95] Bills of Sale Act 1890; Bills of Sale Act 1891. See also Consumer Credit Act 1974, Sch.4, inserting new s.7A in the Act of 1882.

[96] The *Report of the Committee on Consumer Credit* (the Crowther Report), Cmnd. 4596 (1971), paras 5.3.4, 6.2.60, recommended their repeal, but no provision to this effect was made by the Consumer Credit Act 1974. A similar recommendation is contained in Professor Diamond's Report, *A Review of Security Interests in Property* (HMSO 1989), and is repeated in the Law Commissions consultations report *Company Security Interests* (No.176, 2004), para.1.3.

A bill of sale is, at common law, a written instrument (whether in the form of a deed or otherwise) effecting a transfer of personal property.[97] The expression is still used with this meaning in connection with the transfer of ships.[98] For the purposes of the Acts of 1878 and 1882, however, the term is used in a more restricted sense, to describe documents which effect or record the transfer of the ownership of goods[99] without any corresponding transfer of possession. The definition given by the Act of 1878[1] is a long and very complex piece of legislative drafting; it has been summarised by a learned writer as follows: "a bill of sale is a document, granted by the owner of goods (the grantor) giving some other person (the grantee) a legal or equitable right to the goods, and entitling the grantee to take possession of those goods."[2] The Act of 1878 applies to all bills of sale, whether absolute, *i.e.* effecting an out-and-out transfer of ownership to the grantee, or by way of security only; the Act of 1882 is limited in its application to bills of sale given by way of security.

The object of the Act of 1878 is to prevent a person from giving the appearance of being creditworthy by retaining the possession of goods which he has secretly sold or assigned to someone else. The Act declares that the document effecting or evidencing[3] such a transaction shall be deemed fraudulent and void as against the trustee in bankruptcy or an assignee for the benefit of creditors of the grantor, and against persons levying execution against such goods, unless certain formalities have been complied with[4] and the document has been registered in the office of the High Court within seven days of its execution.[5] Two comments in particular should be made on the effect of this Act. In the first place, it strikes at documents, and not transactions. If an absolute transfer of the ownership of goods is effected orally without any change of possession, the bargain, though perhaps impeachable on other grounds,[6] is not void under the Bills of Sale Act.[7] Secondly, if the document is not in proper form and registered as a bill of sale, the transaction is void only as against the persons named. As between the parties themselves and as regards third parties generally, the bargain is altogether valid and effective.

---

97 Diamond, 23 M.L.R. 399 (1960).

98 See below, para.1–082.

99 The term used by these Acts is "personal chattels," which is defined by s.4 of the Act of 1878.

1 Bills of Sale Act 1878, s.4.

2 Diamond, 23 M.L.R. 399, 402 (1960).

3 It is sometimes a difficult question whether a document is intended to be a memorandum of the bargain passing the property in the goods, and therefore caught by the Act, or a mere receipt for purchase-money forming no part of the bargain: contrast *Ramsay v Margrett* [1894] 2 Q.B. 18 with *Youngs v Youngs* [1940] 1 K.B. 760.

4 The bill must set forth the consideration for which it was given, and it must be attested by a solicitor, whose duty it is to explain the effect of the bill to the grantor before execution.

5 Bills of Sale Act 1878, ss.8, 10.

6 *e.g.* as a transaction at an undervalue which may be set aside under s.238 or s.423 of the Insolvency Act 1986, or as a preference which may be avoided under s.239 of that Act.

7 *Ramsay v Margrett* [1894] 2 Q.B. 18.

MAGDALEN COLLEGE LIBRARY

Bills of sale given by way of security for the payment of money are regulated by the much more stringent requirements of the 1882 Act. In particular the form of the document must be substantially that prescribed by the Act itself and the document must contain a schedule listing and specifically describing the goods comprised in the bill. Again, the document must be properly attested, and registered within seven days. Failure to comply with the provisions of the 1882 Act renders the security[8] void, not merely as against creditors and their representatives as under the 1878 Act, but even as between the parties themselves.[9]

The provisions of the 1882 Act do not apply to debentures issued by any company and secured on the capital stock or goods, chattels and effects of such company.[10] But particulars of a charge created or evidenced by an instrument which, if executed by an individual, would require registration as a bill of sale must be registered under the provisions of the Companies Act 1985, failing which it will be void against the liquidator or administrator and any creditor of the company.[11]

1–017 **Effect of Bills of Sale Acts on sales of goods.** It will be apparent that the only situation in which a sale of goods may be caught by the Act of 1878 is where the sale is made or evidenced by a written document, and possession of the goods is retained by the seller. Though effective as between the parties, such a transaction will be void as against the creditors of the seller in the event of his bankruptcy or of execution being levied against him. However, the scope of the Act of 1878 is very much restricted as regards commercial transactions by section 4, which excepts from the provisions of that legislation "transfers or assignments of any ship or vessel or any share thereof, transfers of goods in the ordinary course of business of any trade or calling, bills of sale of goods in foreign parts or at sea, bills of lading, India warrants, warehouse-keepers' certificates, warrants or orders for the delivery of goods, or any other documents used in the ordinary course of business as proof of the possession or control of goods, or authorising or purporting to authorise, either by indorsement or by delivery, the possessor of such document to transfer or receive goods thereby represented."[12] The

---

[8] Money lent may, however, be recovered in an action for money had and received: *Davies v Rees* (1886) 17 Q.B.D. 408; *North Central Wagon Finance Co. Ltd v Brailsford* [1962] 1 W.L.R. 1288.

[9] Bills of Sale Act (1878) Amendment Act 1882, ss.4, 5, 8 and 9. Note also that by virtue of s.12, every bill of sale made or given in consideration of any sum under £30 is void.

[10] *ibid*. s.17. "Company" has been restrictively interpreted so as to exclude (*e.g.*) a society incorporated under the Industrial and Provident Societies Acts: *Great Northern Railway Co. v Coal Co-operative Soc.* [1896] 1 Ch. 187. For the present position regarding such societies, however, see Industrial and Provident Societies Act 1967, s.1(1).

[11] Companies Act 1985, ss.395, 396(1)(c). (Note that these sections were provisionally repealed and replaced by the Companies Act 1989, ss.92 *et seq.*; but it is now accepted that the new provisions will not be brought into force. The proposed reforms would not have made any change of substance to the requirement of registration described in the text.)

[12] Further exemptions, affecting certain commercial letters of hypothecation, are made by the Bills of Sale Acts of 1890 and 1891.

MAGDALEN COLLEGE LIBRARY

exemption of transfers of goods "in the ordinary course of business of any trade or calling" covers virtually all sales except those where the seller is a private person.[13] Even in the latter case, the Act of 1878 will not apply: (a) where there is no document; (b) where the buyer does not need to rely on the document given by the seller in order to prove his title or right to possession[14]; or (c) where the evidence as regards possession is inconclusive—for instance, when the parties are members of a common household—so that possession may be deemed to have followed the transfer of title.[15]

There is ordinarily no reason why the Bills of Sale Act of 1882 should in any way affect a sale of goods, for there is a clear difference between a sale out-and-out and a transaction intended only to secure a debt until it is paid.[16] But an apparent sale may sometimes mask an intention to effect a security, the true object of the parties being suppressed; or a sale may be but one step in a composite arrangement which amounts overall to a loan on security. In regard to such transactions the Act of 1882 applies, but the Sale of Goods Act is expressly excluded.[17] Cases dealing with the distinction between a genuine sale and concealed security are examined in a later section.[18]

Factors Acts. The Factors Act 1889,[19] which replaces and in part extends a series of earlier Factors Acts,[20] deals with the powers of disposition of a "mercantile agent," that is, one having in the customary course of his business as such agent authority either to sell goods, or to consign goods for the purpose of sale, or to buy goods, or to raise money on the security of goods.[21] Where such an agent is in possession of goods, or of the documents of title to goods, with the consent of the owner, the Factors Act provides that any sale, pledge or other disposition of the goods, made by him while acting in the ordinary course of business of a mercantile agent, shall be as valid as if he were expressly authorised by the owner of the goods to make it, provided that the party with whom he deals acts in good faith.[22] Similar protection is afforded to innocent third parties to whom goods or documents are transferred either by a seller who remains in possession of goods or documents after a sale,[23] or by a buyer who obtains possession of goods or documents with the consent of the seller.[24] 1–018

The Sale of Goods Act 1979 by section 21(2)(a) expressly leaves unaffected the provisions of the Factors Acts,[25] and in sections 61(1) and 26

[13] Diamond, 23 M.L.R. 399, 406 (1960).
[14] *Ramsay v Margrett* [1894] 2 Q.B. 18; see above, para.1–016.
[15] *Cf. French v Gething* [1922] 1 K.B. 236.
[16] See below, para.1–064.
[17] Sale of Goods Act 1979, s.62(4); see below, paras 1–065 *et seq*.
[18] See below, paras 1–065 *et seq*.
[19] See below, para.7–031.
[20] These were the Factors Acts of 1823, 1825, 1842 and 1877.
[21] Factors Act 1889, s.1(1): see below, paras 3–004, 7–032.
[22] *ibid.* s.2: see below, paras 7–031 *et seq*.
[23] *ibid.* s.8: see below, paras 7–055 *et seq*.
[24] *ibid.* s.9: see below, paras 7–069 *et seq*.
[25] The plural refers to the English Act of 1889 and the Factors (Scotland) Act 1890, which extends the application of the English Act to Scotland. *cf.* also Sale of Goods Act 1979, s.61(1).

it adopts certain definitions from those Acts.[26] Moreover, in sections 24, 25(1) and 47 of the Sale of Goods Act 1979 three sections of the Factors Act 1889 (sections 8, 9 and 10 respectively) are substantially reproduced. Unfortunately, there are differences in wording, which are not insignificant, between the earlier and the later enactment in each case, but no provision is made for the repeal of the former[27]; and so it is necessary in some situations to consider the wording of both statutes.[28] The provisions of the Factors Acts are discussed at relevant places in the course of this work.[29]

1–019 **The Hire-Purchase Acts[30] and the Consumer Credit Act Acts.[31]** A hire-purchase agreement properly so called[32] is not a contract of sale, at least until the hirer has exercised his option to buy, and accordingly the Sale of Goods Act has no application to such an agreement. On the other hand, both a conditional sale agreement[33] and a credit-sale agreement[34] are contracts for the sale of goods within the meaning of section 2 of the Sale of Goods Act 1979, and are therefore governed by that Act, except in so far as other statutes provide to the contrary.

Contracts of hire-purchase were governed solely by the rules of the common law until 1938. Since that date, there has been a succession of enactments imposing statutory controls over such agreements. The statutory controls have applied for the most part only to transactions coming within defined financial or other limits. Many of these statutory controls have been extended also to conditional sale agreements, and some to credit-sale agreements as well. The legislation presently in force relating to hire-purchase agreements comprises: (i) the Hire-Purchase Act 1964, Part III and section 37; (ii) sections 8, 11, 12(1), 14 and 15 of the Supply of Goods (Implied Terms) Act 1973[35]; and (iii) the Consumer Credit Act 1974.[36] The Act of 1974 repealed and replaced with its own provisions all the earlier legislation governing hire-purchase agreements, apart from the measures mentioned above[37]; and in particular, it superseded the Hire-Purchase Act 1965 which had previously regulated the subject.

---

[26] The definition of "mercantile agent" in s.26 reproduces the wording of that in the Factors Act 1889, s.1(1), but with different punctuation.
[27] The Law Reform Committee in its Twelfth Report, Cmnd. 2958 (1966), para.19, recommended that, to avoid confusion, ss.8 and 9 of the Factors Act 1889 should be repealed. The opportunity to do so was not taken when the law of sale of goods was consolidated by the Act of 1979.
[28] See below, paras 7–055, 7–069.
[29] See especially below, paras 7–031 *et seq.*; paras 7–055 *et seq.*
[30] See Guest, *The Law of Hire-Purchase* (1966); Goode, *Hire-Purchase Law and Practice* (2nd ed.).
[31] See Guest and Lloyd, *Encyclopedia of Consumer Credit Law* (loose-leaf); Goode, *Consumer Credit Law* (1989); Goode, *Consumer Credit Law and Practice* (loose-leaf), and below, paras 14–143 *et seq.*
[32] Defined below, para.1–053.
[33] Defined below, para.1–052.
[34] Defined below, para.1–055.
[35] As amended by the Sale and Supply of Goods Act 1994, Sch.2, para.4.
[36] The Consumer Credit Act 2006, which has not been brought into force as this edition goes to press, makes extensive changes to parts of the 1974 Act. Where relevant, these are noted at appropriate places in the text which follows.
[37] Pt III of the Hire-Purchase Act 1964 was re-enacted by the Consumer Credit Act 1974, with certain changes of terminology: see Sch.4, para.22.

Neither the Consumer Credit Acts nor the earlier legislation purports to codify the law governing hire-purchase and other instalment credit transactions, and so it is still necessary to have recourse to the common law for many purposes; and, of course, for those transactions which fall outside the limits of the statutory control, it is the common law alone which is applicable.

Scope of the earlier Acts. The Hire-Purchase Act 1964, so far as it remains unrepealed, deals only with motor vehicles which have been let under a hire-purchase agreement or conditional sale agreement, and operates irrespective of the value of the goods affected, the amount of credit provided, or the corporate or non-corporate status of the hirer or buyer.[38] **1–020**

The Supply of Goods (Implied Terms) Act 1973 also applies to all hire-purchase agreements; but certain provisions are confined to the case "where the creditor bails or hires goods under a hire-purchase agreement in the course of a business."[39]

The wording of the Hire-Purchase Act 1964, like that of the Consumer Credit Act 1974,[40] assimilates the position under a conditional sale agreement to that under a hire-purchase agreement.

Scope of the Consumer Credit Acts. The Consumer Credit Act 1974 is designed to establish a comprehensive code of regulation[41] for the supply of "consumer credit"—that is, credit given to individuals[42] to an amount not exceeding £25,000[43] in a particular transaction.[44] The Act also provides for the licensing of those who carry on a business which involves the granting **1–021**

---

[38] Hire-Purchase Act 1964, s.29; see below, para.7–085.

[39] s.10(2), (3); see below, para.11–045. (This wording, replacing the original version "where the owner lets goods . . ." was introduced by the Consumer Credit Act 1974).

[40] See below, para.1–021.

[41] See further below paras 14–143—14–156.

[42] Defined (s.189(1)) as including a partnership or other unincorporated body of persons not consisting entirely of bodies corporate. The term clearly excludes a corporation, but not a sole trader. (Note that this definition is modified by the Consumer Credit Act 2006, s,1 (above, para.1–019) so as to exclude partnerships of more than three members—in other words, such partnerships will be treated in the same way as corporate bodies for the purposes of the 1974 Act.) For other definitions of "consumer", see below, paras 14–001, n.2, 14–011, 14–029, 14–031, 14–045, 14–053, 14–071, 14–100.

[43] This sum was substituted for the former figure of £15,000 by the Consumer Credit (Increase of Monetary Limits) (Amendment) Order 1998 (SI 1998/996), effective May 1, 1998. (Note that the Consumer Credit Act 2006, s.2 (above, para.1–019) proposes to removes this financial limit, so that all consumer credit agreements will be regulated by the 1974 Act unless specifically exempted. A new exemption, however, is to be introduced by statutory instrument where the debtor has a "high net worth" and agrees to forego the protection of the Act: see the 2006 Act, s.3).

[44] s.8(2). Note, however, that certain provisions of the Act (*e.g.* ss.137–140, which deal with extortionate credit bargains) apply to all credit agreements where the debtor is an individual, without regard to the amount of credit given: see s.137(2)(a). (Under the Consumer Credit Act 2006 (above, para.1–019), these provisions will be superseded by new clauses dealing with "unfair relationships").

of credit and regulates the practice of seeking business, advertising and giving quotations in relation thereto. It replaces not only the previous hire-purchase legislation but also that dealing with pawnbrokers and moneylenders, and in addition it extends to transactions which were not previously regulated by statute, such as consumer hire agreements.

It should be noted that the financial limit of the Act of 1974 is fixed by reference to the amount of credit provided (*i.e.* in the case of a contract of hire-purchase or similar transaction, the balance financed), in contrast with the Hire-Purchase Act 1965, where the reference was to the hire-purchase price or the total purchase price, which included the deposit (if any) and credit charges. As with the Hire-Purchase Act, there is an exemption for smaller credit-sale agreements: where the amount of credit provided is under £50,[45] many of the statutory provisions do not apply.[46] (Note again, however, that the reference is to the amount of credit and not to the total price.)

A number of sections of the Consumer Credit Act 1974[47] expressly continue the assimilation of conditional sale agreements to hire-purchase agreements which was a feature of the Hire-Purchase Acts.

It should be noted that the definitions of "hire-purchase", "conditional sale" and "credit-sale" under the Consumer Credit Act 1974 are not identical with those of the earlier legislation.[48] These differences are reflected in certain of the transitional provisions of the Sale of Goods Act 1979.[49]

1–022 **The meaning of "credit".** The term "credit" in the Consumer Credit Act 1974 is defined in wide terms[50] which are capable of embracing all contracts for the supply of goods where payment of the price is deferred so as to be paid either in one amount or in instalments. Any such agreement is a "consumer credit agreement" within the meaning of section 8(2) of the Act if the debtor is an individual and the amount of credit provided does not exceed £25,000[51]; and as such it will, prima facie, be subject to the provisions of the Act. Certain agreements are, however, exempted from the operation of the Act by virtue of section 16[52] and, further, by the same section the Secretary of State is empowered to grant exemption from the regulating provisions of the Act for certain other agreements, including those where the number of payments to be made by the debtor does not exceed a specified number, or where the rate of the total charge for credit does not exceed a specified rate, or where the agreement has a connection

---

[45] Substituted for the original figure of £30 by SI 1983/1878, effective May 20, 1985.
[46] ss.17, 74(2).
[47] ss.90, 91, 99, 100, 130, 131, 133, 134; and *cf.* Sale of Goods Act 1979, s.25(2).
[48] See below, paras 1–052—1–055.
[49] Sale of Goods Act 1979, s.25(2)(b) and Sch.1, para.9; *cf.* also s.14(3) and Sch.1, para.5("credit-broker").
[50] s.9(1): "'credit' includes a cash loan and any other form of financial accommodation."
[51] Substituted for the former figure of £15,000 by SI 1998/996, effective May 1, 1998. Note the abolition of this financial limit by the Consumer Credit Act 2006 (above para.1–019).
[52] Principally mortgages of land in favour of a local authority or building society.

with a country outside the United Kingdom.[53] Orders have been made under this provision[54] exempting (*inter alia*) a debtor-creditor-supplier agreement[55] for fixed-sum credit[56] (other than a hire-purchase agreement or a conditional sale agreement) under which the number of payments to be made by the debtor does not exceed four and those payments are required to be made within a period not exceeding 12 months from the date of the agreement,[57] a debtor-creditor-supplier agreement[58] for running-account credit[59] where the number of payments to be made at the end of each payment period does not exceed one (*e.g.* normal trade credit),[60] a debtor-creditor agreement[61] where the total charge for credit does not exceed 12.7 per cent (where the creditor is a credit union) or, in certain other cases where credit is offered to a particular class or classes of the public, 1 per cent above the highest of the clearing banks' base rates,[62] and credit agreements with a foreign connection.[63] A consumer credit agreement is a "regulated agreement" for the purposes of the Act of 1974 if it is not exempted by or under these provisions.[64]

EC legislation. The law of sale of goods in the United Kingdom has been supplemented, and to some extent modified, by legislation emanating from the European Community. In particular, a number of European Community directives applicable to the sale of goods have been adopted and implemented into the domestic law of this country by statute or regulation. The most important of these are: (i) the Consumer Protection Act 1987, Part I,[65] dealing with "product liability"; (ii) the Unfair Terms in Consumer Contracts Regulations 2004[66] (which, apart from a few specified exceptions, apply to consumer contracts generally and not just to sales of goods), restricting the use of terms which are considered unfair; (iii) the Consumer Protection (Cancellation of Contracts Concluded away from Business Premises) Regulations 1987,[67] giving consumers the right to cancel 1–023

[53] s.16(5).
[54] Consumer Credit (Exempt Agreements) Order 1989 (SI 1989/869), as amended by SIs 1989/1841, 1989/2337, 1991/1949, 1991/2844, 1993/346, 1993/2922, 1994/2420, 1995/1250, 1996/1445, 1996/3081, 1999/1956, replacing Consumer Credit (Exempt Agreements) (No.2) Order 1985 (SI 1985/757), as amended.
[55] Defined in ss.12, 189(1) of the 1974 Act.
[56] Defined in ss.10(1), 189(1) of the 1974 Act.
[57] SI 1989/869, art.3(1)(a)(i). (See *Zoan v Rouamba* [2000] 2 All E.R. 620.)
[58] Defined in ss.12, 189(1) of the 1974 Act.
[59] Defined in ss.10(1), 189(1) of the 1974 Act.
[60] SI 1989/869, art.3(1)(a)(ii).
[61] Defined in ss.13, 189(1) of the 1974 Act.
[62] SI 1989/869, art.4 (as amended by SI 1999/1956); for the meaning of "total charge for credit", see s.20(1) of the Act and SI 1980/51, reg.6, as amended by SIs 1985/1192, 1989/596 and 1999/3177.
[63] SI 1989/869, reg.5.
[64] Consumer Credit Act 1974, s.8(3).
[65] Implementing Directive 1985/374/EEC ([1988] O.J. L307/54), as amended by 1999/34/EC [1999] O.J. L141/20); below, para.14–080.
[66] SI 1999/2088 (as amended by SI 2001/1186) (replacing SI 1994/3159, which implemented Directive 1993/13/EEC ([1993] O.J. L95/29)); below, paras 13–009, 13–103, 14–031. Note also the Enterprise Act 2002, Pt 8, as the enforcement of this legislation.
[67] SI 1987/2117 (implementing Directive 1985/577/EEC ([1985] O.J. L372/31)), as amended by SI 1988/958 and SI 1998/3050; below, para.14–045.

contracts entered into in certain circumstances; (iv) the Consumer Protection (Distance Selling) Regulations 2000,[68] which are designed to give similar protection where a contract is concluded by telephone or other form of distance communication; (v) the Price Marking Order 2004,[69] dealing with the indication of prices of products offered to consumers; (vi) the Enterprise Act 2002[70] empowering the office of Fair Trading and other qualified bodies to obtain injunctions for the protection of consumers' interests; the Sale and Supply of Goods to Consumers Regulations 2002,[71] dealing with particular aspects of the sale of consumer goods and associated guarantees; the Electronic Commerce (EC Directive) Regulations 2002,[72] which are concerned, *inter alia*, with contracts concluded by email or through the internet; and the Late Payment of Commercial Debts Regulations,[73] designed to combat the practice of paying commercial debts late. A directive on unfair business-to-consumer commercial practices was adopted on May 11, 2005 and awaits implementation.[74] In addition there are many European Community measures dealing with the sale of particular categories of goods, *e.g.* medicinal and tobacco products.

1–024 **The Uniform Laws on International Sales, and the Vienna Convention on Contracts for the International Sale of Goods.** In the post-war period, two separate projects have been initiated which have resulted in the conclusion of international conventions governing contracts for the international sale of goods. The first of these took the form of two linked Conventions, signed at The Hague on July 1, 1964: the Uniform Law on the International Sale of Goods (ULIS) and the Uniform Law on the Formation of Contracts for the International Sale of Goods (ULFIS). These Conventions were implemented as part of the domestic law of the United Kingdom by the Uniform Laws on International Sales Act 1967,[75] but with the reservation that the code contained in the Conventions should not apply to any contract of sale unless the parties expressly so provided in their contract. However, international support for the Uniform Laws was disap-

[68] SI 2000/2334 (as amended by SI 2005/689) (implementing Directive 1997/7/EC ([1997] O.J. L144/19)); below, para.14–053.

[69] SI 2004/102 (replacing SI 1999/3042) (which implemented Directive 1998/6/EC ([1998] O.J. L190/86)), below, para.14–111.

[70] Pt 8 (implementing Directive 1998/27/EC ([1998] O.J. L166/51)).

[71] SI 2002/3045 (implementing Directive 99/44/EC ([1999] O.J. L171/12)); below, paras 14–008 *et seq.* 14–065 *et seq.*

[72] SI 2002/2013 (implementing Directive 2000/31/EC ([2000] O.J. L178/1)); below, para.14–060.

[73] SI 2002/1674 (implementing Directive 2000/35/EC ([2000] O.J. L200/35)). Note also the Late Payment of Commercial Debts (Interest) Act 1998 and the Late Payment of Commercial Debts (Rate of Interest) (No.3) Order 2002 (SI 2002/1675), below, para.16–010.

[74] Directive 2005/99/EC ([2005] O.J. L149/22); Collins (ed.), *The Forthcoming EC Directive on Unfair Commercial Practices* (2004).

[75] See Graveson, Cohn and Graveson, *The Uniform Laws on International Sales Act 1967* (1968); Schmitthoff, *Export Trade* (10th ed.), Ch.14; Lagergren [1958] J.B.L. 131; Nadelmann, 112 Univ. of Pennsylvania L.Rev. 697 (1964); Aubrey, 14 I.C.L.Q. 1011 (1965); Szakats, 15 I.C.L.Q. 749 (1966); Lagergren [1966] J.B.L. 22; Simmonds, 111 S.J. 781 (1967); Feltham, 30 M.L.R. 670 (1967).

pointing, with only a handful of ratifications. A second initiative, the United Nations Convention on Contracts for the International Sale of Goods (commonly known as the Vienna Convention)[76] is now clearly destined to supersede them. This Convention was adopted at a United Nations Conference held in Vienna in March and April 1980, and is based on a draft formulated by a working group set up by the United Nations Commission on International Trade Law (UNCITRAL). Although initially contemplated as a revision of the ULIS and ULFIS texts, in its final form the Convention (which includes provisions on formation) departs radically from the earlier models.

The Convention came into force on January 1, 1988, having received the requisite 10 ratifications some 12 months previously; and it has now been ratified or acceded to by some 65 States, including the United States, Australia, China and most members of the EU and EEA—indeed, almost all of the UK's main trading partners.

The United Kingdom was represented on the working group throughout its deliberations, but it was not a signatory to the Convention and has not acceded to it.[77] There is no provision for a reservation such as that under which the United Kingdom ratified the Uniform Laws Conventions, although some other reservations are permitted.

The Convention is expressed to apply to contracts of sale of goods between parties whose places of business are in different States: (a) when those States are Contracting States, and (b) when the rules of private international law lead to the application of the law of a Contracting State.[78] It will therefore govern a contract of sale made by a party who has his place of business in this country only where the other party is based in a Contracting State and condition (b) above applies, or where the parties agree that the contract shall be regulated by the Convention. It is, of course, open to the parties to a contract to which the Convention would ordinarily be applicable to agree that it shall instead be governed by the domestic law of a specified country, subject to the general controls which are placed on the power of the parties to choose the applicable law.[79]

Mention should also be made of another international agreement concluded under the aegis of UNCITRAL, the Model Law on Electronic Commerce (1996), which sets out provisions designed to ensure that

---

[76] There is a growing literature on the Convention. See, *e.g.* Honnold, *Uniform Law for International Sales under the 1980 United Nations Convention* (3rd ed.) and *Documentary History of the Uniform Law for International Sales* (1989); Schlechtriem, *Commentary on the U.N. Convention on the International Sale of Goods 1980* (2nd ed.); Bianca and Bonell (eds), *Commentary on the International Sales Law* (1987); Schmitthoff, *Export Trade* (10th ed.), Ch.14; *Bridge, The International Sale of Goods: Law and Practice* (1999); Nicholas, 105 L.Q.R. 201 (1989); Enderlein and Maskow, *International Sales Law: United Nations Convention on Contracts for the International Sale of Goods* (1992); Galston and Smit (eds), *International Sales: the U.N. Convention on Contracts for the International Sale of Goods* (1984); Ferrari *et al.*, *The Draft UNCITRAL Digest and Beyond* (2003).

[77] For a discussion of the UK position, see the DTI's consultation document, *United Nations Convention on Contract for the International Sale of the Goods. (The Vienna Sales Convention)*, URN 97/875 (1987).

[78] Art.1(1).

[79] See below, paras 25–001 *et seq.*

contracts concluded by electronic means are legally recognised. The Model Law has no force of its own, but depends upon the enactment by individual States of domestic legislation which incorporates its terms. The United Kingdom's Electronic Communications Act 2000 covers some of this ground (*e.g.* in relation to the recognition of electronic signatures[80]), but does not directly address many other contractual issues dealt with by the Model Law.

3. THE CONTRACT OF SALE

(a) *Sale and Agreement to Sell*

1–025 **The contract of sale: statutory definitions.** In any discussion of the law of sale it is important to distinguish between the concepts which in English law are termed "contract of sale", "sale" and "agreement to sell". These expressions are defined by the Sale of Goods Act 1979 in section 2 and again, in part, in section 61(1). These sections read:

> "2.—(1) A contract of sale of goods is a contract by which the seller transfers or agrees to transfer the property in goods to the buyer for a money consideration, called the price.
>
> (2) There may be a contract of sale between one part owner and another.
>
> (3) A contract of sale may be absolute or conditional.
>
> (4) Where under a contract of sale the property in the goods is transferred from the seller to the buyer the contract is called a sale.
>
> (5) Where under a contract of sale the transfer of the property in the goods is to take place at a future time or subject to some condition later to be fulfilled the contract is called an agreement to sell.
>
> (6) An agreement to sell becomes a sale when the time elapses or the conditions are fulfilled subject to which the property in the goods is to be transferred."
>
> "61.—(1) In this Act, unless the context or subject matter otherwise requires,—
>
> 'contract of sale' includes an agreement to sell as well as a sale;
>
> 'sale' includes a bargain and sale as well as a sale and delivery . . ."

The term "contract of sale" is therefore a general expression embracing both "sale" and "agreement to sell". It may be added that a contract of sale must be one or the other: there is no intermediate category.[81] The variant "contract for sale" is sometimes employed in the Act for reasons of euphony[82]; it may be considered as equivalent to "contract of sale" for all purposes.

---

[80] s.7. See also the Electronic Signatures Regulations 2002 (SI 2002/318).

[81] Williston, *Sales* (3rd ed.), para.6, suggested that a present agreement that the property in goods shall pass at some time in the future, without any further act on the part of the seller, might fall into an intermediate category. However, by s.2(5) of the Act, these are declared to be agreements to sell in English law.

[82] *e.g.* s.15; "contract for sale by sample"; *cf.* s.6: "contract for the sale of specific goods". "Contract for sale" is the standard expression in the Uniform Commercial Code: see U.C.C., para.2–106.

Corresponding definitions of "buyer" and "seller" are given by section 61(1) of the Act: "buyer" means a person who buys or agrees to buy goods, and "seller" means a person who sells or agrees to sell goods.

Agreement to sell. A contract of sale is called an agreement to sell where the transfer of the property in the goods is to take place at a future time or subject to some condition later to be fulfilled.[83] Equivalent expressions are "executory contract of sale", "executory sale" and (especially in the United States) "contract to sell". An agreement to sell is simply a contract, and as such cannot give rise to any rights in the buyer which are based on ownership or possession, but only to claims for breach of contract. In the normal case at least, so long as the property in the goods remains in the seller, they are his to deal with as he chooses (except that he may be in breach of his contract with the buyer); they are liable to seizure in distress or execution as his property; and they pass to the trustee of his estate in the event of his bankruptcy. **1–026**

Sale. The Sale of Goods Act 1979 defines a sale in the following passages: first "where under a contract of sale the property in the goods is transferred from the seller to the buyer the contract is called a sale"[84]; and secondly, "an agreement to sell becomes a sale when the time elapses or the conditions are fulfilled subject to which the property in the goods is to be transferred."[85] It is therefore possible for a sale within the statutory meaning to come about in one of two ways: either by a contract which itself operates to transfer the goods from the ownership of the seller to that of the buyer, the property passing when the contract is made[86]; or by a contract which is initially only an agreement to sell, but is later performed or executed by the transfer of the property. In either case it is clear that the sale involves not only a contract, but also a conveyance of the property in the goods, and so it may confer on the buyer the right to bring a claim in tort for wrongful interference with the goods[87] as well as rights in contract. **1–027**

The expression "sale" is sometimes used purely in the sense of "conveyance", so as to refer to that aspect of the transaction which concerns the transfer of the property, divorced from all contractual considerations. Benjamin, writing before the Act of 1893, defined a sale as "a transfer of the absolute or general property in a thing for a price in money",[88] and similarly in the United States the Uniform Commercial Code provides that a "sale" consists in the passing of title from the seller to the buyer for a price.[89] A "sale" in this sense may be accomplished on the making of the

---

[83] s.2(5).
[84] s.2(4).
[85] s.2(6).
[86] s.18, rule 1: below, paras 5–017 *et seq*.
[87] See below, paras 5–009 *et seq*. Such claims may, however, be defeated by the seller's right to a lien on the goods for the price (below, paras 15–028 *et seq*.). As regards specific performance of a contract to sell goods, see below, paras 17–096 *et seq*.
[88] *Sale of Personal Property* (2nd ed., 1873), p.1.
[89] U.C.C., para.2–106; but note that the price need not be in money: below, paras 1–034, 2–044.

contract of sale (in which case it is conveniently termed, as in the United States, a "present sale"),[90] or by the performance of an agreement to sell. The term "sale" is accordingly somewhat ambiguous.

The expressions "executed sale" and "actual sale" are used as equivalent to "sale", mainly to emphasise the distinction between that term and "agreement to sell".

By section 61(1) of the Act, "sale" includes a bargain and sale as well as a sale and delivery. These expressions are explained in a later paragraph.[91]

The interpretation of terms such as "sale", "sell" and "purchase" as used in other statutory provisions is not always consistent with the definitions given by this Act.[92]

1–028 **Sale distinguished from agreement to sell.** It has been stated above that an agreement to sell is purely a contract, while a sale is both a contract and a conveyance, under which the property in the goods is transferred to the buyer. From this distinction a number of differences follow, at least in principle. When a party to an agreement to sell makes default, the remedy of the other party is normally[93] an action for damages; but where there is a sale, the seller may sue for the price, and the buyer may assert the remedies of an owner for wrongful interference with the goods not only against the seller, but in appropriate circumstances also against third parties. Again, the risk of loss or damage to the goods, and the corresponding right to profits and increases accruing, is normally in the owner of the goods, *i.e.* the seller under an agreement to sell, and the buyer under a sale. These and other incidents of the passing of the property are examined more fully in later chapters.[94] It is sufficient to note here that the differences in principle which have been emphasised above may be considerably modified in practice both by the operation of particular rules of law (*e.g.* the seller's right to a lien for the price, and the provisions of the Factors Acts) and also by the general power of the parties to a contract of sale to make their own bargain, varying the principles which would otherwise apply.

---

[90] *ibid*.

[91] See below, para.1–029.

[92] *Cf.* the decisions concerning the sale of liquor in clubs, below, para.1–121. See also the definitions of "purchase" and "sale" in the Law of Property Act 1925, s.205(1)(xxi)(xxiv); and *cf.* "conveyance on sale" in the Stamp Act 1891, ss.54 (since repealed), 55, explained in *Coats v I.R.C.* [1897] 2 Q.B. 423; *IRC v Maple & Co. (Paris) Ltd* [1908] A.C. 22. Other expressions judicially considered have included: "make a sale" (*Milner v Staffs. Congregational Union (Inc.)* [1956] Ch.275); "sale by way of wholesale dealing" (*Oxford v Sangers Ltd* [1965] 1 Q.B. 491); "offer for sale" (*Fisher v Bell* [1961] 1 Q.B. 394; *cf. Newman v Lipman* [1951] 1 K.B. 333; *Partridge v. Crittenden* [1968] 1 W.L.R. 1204); "offer to sell" (*British Car Auctions Ltd v Wright* [1972] 1 W.L.R. 1519; *C.A. Norgren Co. v Technomarketing, The Times*, March 3, 1983); "sell" (*Mischeff v Springett* [1942] 2 K.B. 331; *Watts v Seymour* [1967] 2 Q.B. 647); "agreement . . . for the sale purchase or exchange of any property" (*Doyle v East* [1972] 1 W.L.R. 108); "exposing goods for supply" (*Haringey LBC v Piro Shoes Ltd* [1976] Crim.L.R. 462); "are to be sold" (*Re Westminster Property Group Plc* [1985] 1 W.L.R. 676).

[93] Exceptionally, he may sometimes sue for the price under s.49(2): below, para.16–025.

[94] See below, Chs 5 and 6.

It should be observed that the questions whether the goods have been delivered and whether the price has been paid are in themselves immaterial to the distinction between a sale and an agreement to sell.

Bargain and sale, and sale and delivery. By section 61(1), "sale" includes a bargain and sale as well as a sale and delivery. At common law, an action for the price of goods could be brought only upon one or other of two counts: the *indebitatus* count for goods sold and delivered, which would not lie before delivery, and the *indebitatus* count for goods bargained and sold, which was applicable where the property had passed to the buyer and the contract had been completed in all respects except delivery, and delivery was not part of the consideration for the price or a condition precedent to its payment.[95] The statement in section 61(1) may be intended to mean that the former procedural distinction is not preserved for any substantive purpose by the Act, or that the old principles which determine when an action for the price will lie have been confirmed by the Act—both of which propositions are true.[96] But the statement in section 61(1) adds nothing to the definition of "sale" made by section 2 of the Act. 1–029

(b) *Contract of Sale Distinguished from Other Transactions*

Contract of sale distinguished from other transactions. The provisions of the Sale of Goods Act 1979 are directly applicable only to contracts of sale of goods as defined in section 2. For this reason, and sometimes also for other purposes,[97] it is important to distinguish contracts for the sale of goods from (a) contracts for the sale of property other than "goods", which are governed either by the general law or by their own special legislation; and (b) certain other transactions affecting goods which in some degree resemble sales, but do not fall wholly within the statutory definition. The first of these distinctions is examined fully later in this chapter[98]; we proceed now to discuss the second. 1–030

Benjamin, writing before the Act of 1893, listed as the essential elements of a contract of sale: parties competent to contract; mutual assent; a thing, the absolute or general property in which is transferred from the seller to the buyer; and a price in money paid or promised.[99] The transactions now to be described, although in some respects analogous to contracts of sale, lack one or more of these features: they are not sales at common law, and they are not governed by the Act or by any other statutory provision dealing with sales of goods.[1]

---

[95] *Colley v Overseas Exporters* [1921] 3 K.B. 302 at 309–310; Bullen and Leake, *Precedents of Pleadings* (3rd ed., 1868), p.39.

[96] *ibid.* But note that an action for the price may also lie under s.49(2) by special agreement, although the property has not passed: below, para.16–025.

[97] See, *e.g.* the statutes mentioned in n.1, *infra*.

[98] See below, paras 1–078 *et seq*.

[99] *Sale of Personal Property* (2nd ed., 1873), pp.1–2.

[1] *e.g.* Law Reform (Frustrated Contracts) Act 1943, s.2(5)(c), below, paras 6–058 *et seq.* (provisions of that Act not applicable to contracts for the sale of specific goods); Unfair Contract Terms Act 1977, ss.6, 7 (different provisions as regards exemptions): below, paras 13–083 *et seq.* and *cf.* the exemption from stamp duty formerly granted to contracts for the sale of goods by the Stamp Act 1891, s.59(1): below, para.1–079.

In determining whether a contract is one of sale or some other kind of transaction it is the substance and not merely the form of the bargain which must be considered. Thus, the fact that a person to whom goods are delivered is described as a "sole agent" does not prevent the court from holding that he is a buyer of the goods and not an agent for sale.[2] Conversely, goods may be invoiced as if sold to a consignee for convenience in book-keeping, when the transaction is in law no more than a bailment to an agent or a delivery on "sale or return".[3]

In particular, regard must be had to the true nature of the transaction when the issue is whether a sale is to be upheld as genuine or to be considered a cloak for a loan on security and accordingly void under the Bills of Sale Acts.[4]

1–031 **Common law and statutory rules governing transactions analogous to sales.** At common law, many of the principles of the law of sale were applied, in terms which were either identical or at least very similar, to other transactions which were closely analogous, *e.g.* contracts of barter, contracts for work and materials and contracts of hire.[5] This was particularly the case in regard to the implied terms as to title, description, quality and fitness and sample which were codified as sections 12 to 15 of the Sale of Goods Act. Following recommendations made by the Law Commission in 1979,[6] the legislature enacted the Supply of Goods and Services Act 1982. This Act has replaced these common law implied terms by statutory provisions modelled on those sections of the Sale of Goods Act.[7] The relevant parts of the Act of 1982, which applies in England, Wales and Northern Ireland but not in Scotland,[8] came into operation on January 4, 1983.[9] Sections 1 to 5 deal with "contracts for the transfer of goods," which are defined by section 1 as follows:

"(1) In this Act in its application to England and Wales and Northern Ireland[10] a 'contract for the transfer of goods' means a contract under which one person transfers or agrees to transfer to another the property in goods, other than an excepted contract.

(2) For the purposes of this section an excepted contract means any of the following:—

[2] See below, para.1–049.
[3] See below, para.1–048.
[4] See below, paras 1–065—1–066.
[5] For a general discussion of the common law rules see the Law Commission's *Report on Implied Terms in Contracts for the Supply of Goods* (Law Com. No.95, HMSO, 1979), Pts II and III.
[6] *ibid.* paras 130–131.
[7] Even so, there are some contracts which fall outside both the Sale of Goods Act and the Act of 1982, and which fall to be dealt with by reference to analogous common law implied terms: see; *e.g. St Albans City & District Council v International Computers Ltd* [1996] 4 All E.R. 481 (supply of computer software), below, para.1–086.
[8] s.20(6).
[9] s.20(3): the Act does not operate retrospectively (s.20(5)). Pt II of the Act, which relates to the supply of services, came into force on July 4, 1983: see SI 1982/1770.
[10] The words "in its application to England and Wales and Northern Ireland" were inserted by the Sale and Supply of Goods Act 1994, s.7(1) and Sch.2, para.6(1), (2).

(a) a contract of sale of goods;
(b) a hire-purchase agreement;
(c) a contract under which the property in goods is (or is to be) transferred in exchange for trading stamps[11] on their redemption;
(d) a transfer or agreement to transfer which is made by deed and for which there is no consideration other than the presumed consideration imported by the deed;
(e) a contract intended to operate by way of mortgage, pledge, charge or other security.

(3) For the purposes of this Act in its application to England and Wales and Northern Ireland[12] a contract is a contract for the transfer of goods whether or not services are also provided or to be provided under the contract, and (subject to subsection (2) above) whatever is the nature of the consideration for the transfer or agreement to transfer."

It is clear that the supply of goods under a contract for work and materials will come within this definition, as will a contract of barter or exchange; but gifts are excluded. Sections 2 to 5 set out the statutory implied terms about title, conformity with description, etc. which apply to these contracts.[13]

In sections 6 to 10 of the Act of 1982, similar implied terms are formulated to govern contracts for the hire of goods.[14] Necessarily, there is no implied term as to title, but only a term about the bailor's "right to transfer possession"[15]; otherwise, the model of the Sale of Goods Act is closely followed.

These statutory implied terms in contracts for the transfer or hire of goods may, in general, be negatived or varied by express agreement, or a course of dealing, or usage, in a similar manner to those in a contract of sale[16]; but this provision is without prejudice to the operation of any other enactment or to other rules of law[17]; and, in particular, the power to

---

[11] On the redemption of trading stamps, see below, para.1–040.
[12] The words "in its application to England and Wales and Northern Ireland" were inserted by the Sale and Supply of Goods Act 1994, s.7(1) and Sch.2, para.6(1), (2).
[13] See further below, paras 4–036, 11–023, 11–050, 11–069, 11–087.
[14] Defined by s.6 (as amended) as follows:
"(1) In this Act in its application to England and Wales and Northern Ireland a 'contract for the hire of goods' means a contract under which one person bails or agrees to bail goods to another by way of hire, other than an excepted contract.
(2) For the purposes of this section an excepted contract means any of the following:—
(a) a hire-purchase agreement;
(b) a contract under which goods are (or are to be) bailed in exchange for trading stamps on their redemption.
(3) For the purposes of this Act in its application to England and Wales and Northern Ireland a contract is a contract for the hire of goods whether or not services are also provided or to be provided under the contract, and (subject to subsection (2) above) whatever is the nature of the consideration for the bailment or agreement to bail by way of hire."
[15] s.7.
[16] s.11; *cf.* above, para.1–013.
[17] s.11(3).

exclude them is subject to the restrictions imposed by the Unfair Contract Terms Act 1977.[18]

Apart from these rules relating to implied terms which have now been largely codified, it is a matter for speculation whether and to what extent other common law principles, analogous to those of the law of sale of goods, apply to these transactions. In particular, the presumptive rules as to the passing of property and risk may be different,[19] and possibly also the remedies of the parties for breach of contract.[20]

Recent legislation effecting changes to the law of sale of goods has included equivalent provisions dealing with transactions analogous to sales. Thus, the Sale and Supply of Goods Act 1994, which made a number of amendments to the law governing sales of goods,[21] also made amendments of a corresponding nature to other contracts for the supply of goods, such as contracts of hire and barter, while the Unfair Terms in Consumer Contracts Regulations 1999[22] deal in the same terms with both the sale of goods and the supply of goods (under a contract of any kind) to consumers. The Sale and Supply of Goods to Consumers Regulations 2002[23] make modifications to the Sale of Goods Act 1979, the Supply of Goods and Services Act 1982 and the Supply of Goods (Implied Terms) Act 1973 in closely similar terms, so that no distinction is made between contracts of sale and the analogous contracts governed by the latter two statutes.

1–032 **Sale distinguished from gift.** If no valuable consideration is given for the transfer of property in goods, there is a gift, but not a sale. Nor, since there is no contract, does the transaction come within other legislation governing contracts for the supply of goods, such as the Supply of Goods and Services Act 1982. Delivery (either actual or constructive) is essential to make a gift of a chattel at common law, unless the gift is by deed.[24] A promise to make a gift is ineffective and unenforceable for want of consideration, unless by deed[25]; and so is a purported present gift of future property.[26]

1–033 **"Free offers" under promotional schemes.** Where, under a scheme to promote a product or services, a supplier offers something "free" to those who become his customers (for instance, a free medallion to every motorist

[18] s.11(1); and see Unfair Contract Terms Act 1977, s.7. Note, however, that s.7 of the Act of 1977 applies only to "business liability" (as defined *ibid.* s.1(3)), whereas s.6 (which deals with contracts of sale and hire-purchase) is not so restricted. Furthermore, a term in a consumer contract which purported to exclude the statutory implied terms could well be regarded as "unfair" under the Unfair Terms in Consumer Contracts Regulations 1999 (SI 1999/2083), Sch.2, and accordingly not binding on the consumer-buyer.

[19] See, *e.g. Flynn v Mackin & Mahon* [1974] I.R. 101.

[20] *Hyundai Heavy Industries Ltd v Papadopoulos* [1980] 1 W.L.R. 1129, discussed below, paras 16–027, 16–040.

[21] Sale and Supply of Goods Act 1994, s.7 and Sch.2.

[22] SI 1999/2083.

[23] SI 2002/3045, below, Ch.14.

[24] *Cochrane v Moore* (1890) 25 Q.B.D. 57. For the rules regarding delivery, see Crossley Vaines, *Personal Property* (5th ed.), pp.305 *et seq.*; Bell, *Modern Law of Personal Property* (1989), pp.221–223.

[25] The promise, if by deed, is not specifically enforceable but may found an action for substantial damages; *Cannon v Hartley* [1949] Ch.213.

[26] On assignments of future property, see below, paras 1–107 *et seq*.

who buys four gallons of petrol), there is scope for a difference of opinion whether the thing is itself the subject of a sale or, indeed, of a contract at all. In *Esso Petroleum Co. Ltd v Customs and Excise Commissioners*,[27] a majority of the House of Lords held that there was no "sale", but was divided on the question whether this was because the consideration for the supply was not a money price[28] but rather the customer's entering into the main contract,[29] or whether there was no contract at all, but merely the promise of a gift, for want of any intention to create a legally binding relationship.[30]

Sale distinguished from barter or exchange.[31] To constitute a sale it is necessary that the consideration for the transfer of the property in the goods should be in money.[32] This may be either paid or promised (*i.e.* the sale may be for cash or on credit); but if the consideration is something other than money[33] the contract is not, strictly speaking, one of sale in English law.[34] 1–034

Where goods are supplied or promised in exchange for goods, the transaction is a barter or exchange. Similarly, goods may be given in consideration for work done,[35] for the making of another contract,[36] for

---

[27] [1976] 1 W.L.R. 1; *cf. GUS Merchandise Corp. Ltd v Customs & Excise Commrs* [1981] 1 W.L.R. 1309 (liability to value added tax on "gifts" to mail-order representatives); and *Att.-Gen. v L D Nathan & Co. Ltd* [1990] 1 N.Z.L.R. 129, where the *Esso Petroleum* case was not followed.

[28] Sale of Goods Act 1979, s.2(1), below, para.1–034.

[29] [1976] 1 W.L.R. 1 at 5, 6, 11.

[30] *ibid.* at pp.5, 10.

[31] See the Law Commission's Report, n.1, above, Forte (1983) 28 J. Law Soc. Scotland 108; Jacobs (1986) 15 Anglo-Amer. L.R. 234.

[32] s.1(1); *cf. Re Westminster Property Group Plc* [1985] 1 W.L.R. 676 (shares). A price payable in a foreign currency will normally be regarded as "money" for this purpose: see *Daewoo Australia Pty Ltd v Suncorp-Metway Ltd* (2000) 33 A.C.S.R. 481, and *cf.* below, para.1–084. Where the parties agree to treat fungible goods as money, the transaction is virtually a sale, though *semble* not a sale within the statutory definition. *Cf. Barbe v Parker* (1789) 1 H.Bl. 283 (gold case valued as cash); *South Australian Insurance Co. v Randell* (1869) L.R. 3 P.C. 101 (wheat), discussed below, paras 1–057, 1–062. A bill of exchange or other negotiable instrument will be regarded as money only if it is given and accepted as conditional payment of a money price (see below, paras 9–031 *et seq.*), and not if it is exchanged as such: *Read v Hutchinson* (1813) 3 Camp. 352. A trading "check" or similar voucher may be treated as a consideration in money: see *Davies v Customs and Excise Commissioners* [1975] 1 W.L.R. 204 (value added tax). As regards payment by credit card, see *infra*, n.39 and below, para.9–033.

[33] Foreign currency may, depending on the circumstances, be treated as a medium of exchange (*i.e.* money) or as a commodity (*i.e.* goods): see below, para.1–084, and *Daewoo Australia Pty Ltd v Suncorp-Metway Ltd* (above). A contract to exchange a sum in one foreign currency for a sum in another could well be regarded as a species of barter.

[34] The distinction is not made in the uniform legislation in the United States, where the price may be payable in money or otherwise; if it is payable in whole or in part in goods, each party is a seller of the goods which he is to transfer: U.C.C. para.2–304(1); Uniform Sales Act, s.9(2). A similar provision was proposed by Chalmers in his original draft Bill: see Chalmers, *The Sale of Goods* (1st ed., 1890), p.87.

[35] *Garey v Pyke* (1839) 10 Ad. & El. 512; *cf. Doyle v East* [1972] 1 W.L.R. 1080 (agreement to convey land in return for building work).

[36] *Esso Petroleum Co. Ltd v Customs and Excise Commissioners* [1976] 1 W.L.R. 1 at 5, 7, 11.

rent, or for board and lodging,[37] or in return for the extinction of a right[38] or the abandonment of a claim, or any other valuable consideration.[39] None of these bargains is a true sale. The same is true, it is submitted, where the owner of waste materials or other unwanted goods pays someone to take them away.[40]

1–035 The implications of this distinction have not been fully explored.[41] It is of course clear that the Sale of Goods Act has no direct application to contracts of barter or exchange. There is reasonable agreement among the authorities that it is not open to a disappointed party, who has parted with his own goods without receiving the expected return, to sue for the value of the goods delivered as a price[42]; his remedy is to claim unliquidated damages for non-delivery of the goods promised in exchange, or possibly[43] to sue the other party in tort on the basis that the property in such goods has passed to him. It would seem, on principle, that he should be debarred from claiming a price even when the goods have been valued for the purpose of the bargain, unless the transaction can be construed as two reciprocal sales, or a sale with a subsidiary agreement for payment in kind.[44] He may, however, claim a liquidated sum when this is agreed to be paid as *part* of the exchange,[45] or when, after goods have been exchanged for goods on a running account, a cash balance is agreed to be due.[46]

1–036 The right of a party to assert the remedies of an owner in relation to the goods bartered in exchange depends upon whether the property in such goods is capable of passing by virtue of the contract itself, or whether delivery is essential. This point has never been authoritatively determined. Many of the cases are inconclusive[47]; and such dicta as there are appear to be evenly balanced.[48] Unfortunately, in the most recent case of *Koppel v*

---

[37] *Keys v Harwood* (1846) 2 C.B. 905.

[38] In *Simpson v Connolly* [1953] 2 All E.R. 474, Finnemore J. held that an agreement to extinguish an existing debt if land (or goods) were transferred to the creditor was not a sale. But in *Sands v Norman* (1903) 4 S.R.N.S.W. 234, the opposite conclusion was reached on facts not materially distinguishable. The decision in the former case is, it is submitted, strictly correct. See also *Robshaw Bros Ltd v Mayer* [1957] Ch.125.

[39] *Read v Hutchinson* (1813) 3 Camp. 352 (bill of third party, without recourse); *cf. Robshaw Brothers Ltd v Mayer*, above (assumption of tenant's obligations). But where a seller of goods agrees to accept payment by credit card, without recourse to the buyer in the event of non-payment by the credit-card company, it appears that the transaction is a sale: see below, para.9–033.

[40] Such a transaction has been held to be a "sale" under the wider definition adopted in the United States; see *H. S. Crocker Co. v McFaddin*, 148 Cal.App. 2d 639 (1957).

[41] See the discussion in the Law Commission's Report, n.5, above, paras 48–55.

[42] *Read v Hutchinson*, above; *Harrison v Luke* (1845) 14 M. & W. 139.

[43] See below, para.1–036.

[44] *Cf. Messenger v Greene* [1937] 2 D.L.R. 26.

[45] *Sheldon v Cox* (1824) 3 B. & C. 420; *Bull v Parker* (1842) 12 L.J.Q.B. 93.

[46] *Ingram v Shirley* (1816) 1 Stark. 185; contrast *Garey v Pyke* (1839) 10 Ad. & El. 512; *Harrison v Luke* (1845) 14 M. & W. 139 (no balance struck).

[47] See, *e.g. Pearce v Brain* [1929] 2 K.B. 310.

[48] Contrast the views of Lord Esher M.R. and Fry L.J. in *Cochrane v Moore* (1890) 25 Q.B.D. 57 at 75, 73 respectively. (But it is not certain whether "sale" is used throughout this case in the strict sense of a transaction for a money consideration.)

Koppel,[49] where the view was expressed that the property in such a case passed under the contract itself, it was assumed that the Sale of Goods Act applied. A related question concerns the time when the risk passes to the transferee of bartered goods.[50]

A transaction is a true barter only when the goods (or services or other equivalent) of the one party are specifically traded or promised for the goods of the other. It is possible to distinguish certain other situations where an element of price is discernible, so that they may be treated as sales. There is plainly nothing to prevent parties from expressly agreeing that what might have been a barter shall take the form of reciprocal sales, with a mutual set-off of prices and, if necessary, a cash adjustment. For example, plant or stock-in-trade may be sold to a company for *a price to be satisfied* by the allotment of shares, rather than *in consideration of* the allotment. In *Aldridge v Johnson*,[51] it was agreed that 32 bullocks valued at £192 should be transferred by Aldridge to Knights and that 100 quarters of barley valued at £215 should be transferred by Knights to Aldridge, the difference of £23 to be paid in cash. An agreement such as this is quite capable of being construed as reciprocal sales; and this is what the court appears to have done. But had the deal been that 100 quarters of barley be traded for 32 bullocks, or for 32 bullocks plus a sum of money, without any valuation of the consideration on either side, it could only be regarded as a barter.[52] It would be attributing a wholly false intention to the parties to allow one to sue the other for a reasonable price of what he had delivered, as on a sale: the remedy must be founded upon the non-delivery of the agreed exchange. **1–037**

It is also possible to treat a transaction as a sale where the buyer has the *option* of delivering goods,[53] or the seller the option of taking goods,[54] in lieu of the payment of an agreed money price, and the option is not exercised. The courts seem to have been fairly ready to give the former construction to "trade-in" or "part-exchange" contracts, in order to allow the party "selling" the principal goods an action for their price. **1–038**

---

[49] [1966] 1 W.L.R. 802. *Cf. Aldridge v Johnson* (1875) 7 E. & B. 885 (below, para.1–037), where it appears that principles analogous to those in s.18, rule 5, of the Act (below, paras 5–068 *et seq.*) were applied by the court.

[50] *Cf. Widenmeyer v Burn, Stewart & Co.* 1967 S.C. 85 (Scots common law).

[51] (1857) 7 E. & B. 885; *cf. Davey v Paine Bros (Motors) Ltd* [1954] N.Z.L.R. 1122 (exchange of cars valued at same price).

[52] In *Chappell & Co. Ltd v Nestlé Co. Ltd* [1960] A.C. 87 a gramophone record was offered in return for 1s 6d. and three chocolate wrappers. The question whether the transaction was a sale or a barter was not argued, but Lord Reid expressed doubts that it could be considered a sale (at p.109). On the other hand, the Sale of Goods Act was assumed to be applicable to similar facts in *Buckley v Lever Bros Ltd* [1953] 4 D.L.R. 16. *Cf. Clarke v Reilly & Sons* (1962) 96 I.L.T.R. 96 (where the agreement appears to have been to exchange a new car for a used car plus £192, neither vehicle being valued), and the similar case of *Flynn v Mackin and Mahon* [1974] I.R. 101.

[53] See below, para.1–039; and *cf. Messenger v Greene* [1937] 2 D.L.R. 26 (goods sold for a money price, but understanding that pulpwood would be accepted in payment).

[54] *South Australian Insurance Co. v Randell* (1869) L.R. 3 P.C. 101.

1–039 **Consideration partly in money: trading-in.** It is very common for goods to be "traded-in" or transferred to the seller in part exchange by the buyer, especially in sales of cars and other consumer durables. The exact nature of such a bargain depends on the interpretation of the facts in each case. It is clearly possible to construe it as reciprocal contracts of sale with a set-off of prices.[55] In this event, the Sale of Goods Act 1979 will apply to both parts of the transaction, so that the property and risk in the goods traded-in may pass to the seller of the principal goods by virtue of the agreement, independently of delivery.[56] Alternatively, it is possible to hold that there is only one contract of sale, of the principal goods, coupled with a subsidiary arrangement that if the buyer delivers to the seller the other goods, an agreed allowance will be made. It is then up to the buyer to satisfy this condition and, if he fails to do so, the seller may simply sue for his price. On such a construction, it is plain that no property in the goods traded-in will pass to the principal seller until delivery is made; and the Act will not apply to this part of the transaction, since the consideration for the goods delivered is not a money price, but the partial release of a debt.[57] Most of the cases which have come before the courts have been found capable of this interpretation.[58]

1–040 **Trading stamps.** The exchange of trading stamps or other tokens for goods appears to be a barter and not a sale. This was tacitly recognised by the Trading Stamps Act 1964,[59] which made special provision for the implication into such transactions of warranties as to title, quiet possession, freedom from encumbrance and quality similar to those prescribed by sections 12 and 14(2) of the Sale of Goods Act 1979.

1–041 **Sale distinguished from contract for work and materials.**[60] It is sometimes extremely difficult to decide whether a particular agreement is more properly described as a contract of sale of goods, or a contract for the performance of work or services to which the supply of materials or some

---

[55] *Cf. Davey v Paine Bros (Motors) Ltd* [1954] N.Z.L.R. 1122.

[56] Under s.18, r.1: below, para.5–017.

[57] Above, para.1–034.

[58] *Forsyth v Jervis* (1816) 1 Starke 437; *Keys v Harwood* (1846) 2 C.B. 905; *G. J. Dawson (Clapham) Ltd v H. & G. Dutfield* [1936] 2 All E.R. 232; *Warmings Used Cars Ltd v Tucker* [1956] S.A.S.R. 249. Contrast the old case of *Harris v Fowle* (1787) cited in *Barbe v Parker* (1789) 1 H.Bl. 283. It is in keeping with this view that a buyer suing on a warranty under the old system of pleading was allowed simply to plead the gross price: *Hands v Burton* (1808) 9 East. 349; *Saxty v Wilkin* (1843) 11 M. & W. 622. Contrast *Clarke v Reilly & Sons* (1962) 96 I.L.T.R. 96 and *Flynn v Mackin and Mahon* [1974] I.R. 101, above, para.1–037, n.52.

[59] s.4 (as amended by the Supply of Goods (Implied Terms) Act 1973, s.16). This Act has been repealed by the Regulatory Reform (Trading Stamps) Order 2005 (SI 2005/871). These contracts now fall within the ambit of the Supply of Goods and Services Act 1982.

[60] *Cf.* the Law Commission's Report on *Implied Terms in Contracts for the Supply of Goods* (Law Com. No. 95, HMSO, 1979), paras 56 *et seq.*; Webb [2000] J.B.L. 513.

other goods[61] is incidental[62]: for example, when an order is given to a tailor to make a suit or to an artist to paint a portrait, or when a meal is supplied in a restaurant. Since both the old forms of pleading and the provisions of the Statute of Frauds formerly made a distinction between the two types of contract, the success or failure of an action could frequently turn on the drawing of an artificial line of demarcation. In modern law the distinction is much less important. It is true of course that the Sale of Goods Act cannot apply to a contract for work and materials,[63] but the courts have shown little hesitation in ruling that analogous common law rules are applicable (for instance, in implying warranties as to fitness for purpose),[64] and the Supply of Goods and Services Act 1982 now implies similar terms by statute.[65] It is possible that different rules may govern, say, the passing of property and risk or the consequences of a frustrating event,[66] and perhaps the remedies of the parties in the event of a breach[67] in the two classes of contract; but otherwise the distinction now appears to be of little significance,[68] except in relation to other statutory provisions which apply only to a "sale" or a "contract of sale". Many of the transactions with which we are concerned may, if the parties choose, be expressed either as a contract of sale or a contract for work; their legal relationship will then be different during the performance of the work, but the same ultimate result will be achieved. For instance, we may take the case posed by Roman lawyers of a bystander who agrees with a fisherman to pay an agreed sum for what is yielded by the

---

[61] Where the product supplied falls outside the statutory definition of "goods", the contract may be construed as being neither for the sale of goods nor for the supply of services, but *sui generis*: see *St Albans City & District Council v International Computers Ltd* [1996] 4 All E.R. 481; *Beta Computers (Europe) Ltd v Adobe Systems (Europe) Ltd* 1996 S.L.T. 604 (computer software), below, para.1–086.

[62] In *Hyundai Shipbuilding & Heavy Industries Co. Ltd v Papadopoulos* [1980] 1 W.L.R. 1129,1134, 1148 and *Stoczina Gdanska SA v Latvian Shipping Co.* [1996] 2 Lloyd's Rep. 132, 138 it was held that a contract to build a ship, though a contract of sale of goods, had *also* some of the characteristics of a building contract.

[63] *Cf.*, however, *Jones v Gallagher* [2004] EWCA Civ 10; [2005] 1 Lloyd's Rep. 377, where the court, having held that the contract (to supply and install kitchen fittings) came within the Supply of Goods and Services Act 1982, s.3(2) (and was thus not a contract of sale of goods), nevertheless assumed that s.35 of the Sale of Goods Act 1979 governed the question of the transferees' right to reject. (See Bradgate, 120 L.Q.R. 558 (2004).)

[64] See, *e.g. Harmer v Cornelius* (1858) 5 C.B.(N.S.) 236; *Myers & Co. v Brent Cross Service Co.* [1934] 1 K.B. 46; *Watson v Buckley, Osborne, Garrett & Co. Ltd* [1940] 1 All E.R. 174; *Samuels v Davis* [1943] 1 K.B. 526; *Stewart v Reavell's Garage* [1952] 2 Q.B. 545; *Ingham v Emes* [1955] 2 Q.B. 366; *Young & Marten Ltd v McManus Childs Ltd* [1969] 1 A.C. 454; contrast *Helicopter Sales (Australia) Pty Ltd v Rotor-Work Pty Ltd* (1974) 132 C.L.R. 1 (no warranty when manufacturer's spare part fitted); and *cf. St Albans City and District Council v International Computers Ltd* [1996] 4 All E.R. 481, below, para.1–086 (contract for supply of computer software).

[65] See above, para.1–031.

[66] *Cf.* Law Reform (Frustrated Contracts) Act 1943, s.2(5)(c), below, para.6–058.

[67] *Hyundai Shipbuilding & Heavy Industries Co. Ltd v Papadopoulos*, above, (seller's right to payment of instalments of price following termination of contract): see below, para.16–040.

[68] Note, however, the different provisions regarding exemption clauses contained in ss.6 and 7 of the Unfair Contract Terms Act 1977, both as regards the implied terms as to title (ss.6(1), 7(4)) and in the restriction of the scope of s.7 to "business liability."

next cast of his net.[69] This may be expressed indifferently as an agreement by the fisherman to sell his catch, or to catch fish for reward. Again, chickens may be bailed to a grower for rearing until maturity on behalf of the bailor, whose property they are to remain throughout, or they may be sold to the grower with an agreement to repurchase them when reared. In either case it is possible to make any desired provisions for the remuneration of the grower and for the allocation of cost and risk.

1–042 Where the parties have not settled the question by the form of their contract, the decision whether the bargain is one for the performance of work or the sale of a chattel must be made by the court. It is now well established that the court does so by having regard to "the substance" of the contract[70]—a test which assumes that every contract must be in substance one or the other.[71] This is a legitimate inquiry where the supply of the goods and the performance of the work are, to some extent at least, separate elements in the bargain; but it breaks down in the case where *all* the work goes into the making of the goods to be supplied, so that the two are inseparable. This point has unfortunately not been appreciated. In the former type of contract, the determination of "the substance" is a matter of degree, involving an assessment of the relative importance of the two elements; but in the latter type the designation of the contract as one of work or sale must depend upon either an arbitrary formula or a superficial impression. We examine first some contracts where a logical decision is possible.

1–043 **Chattel to be affixed to land or another chattel.** Where work is to be done on the land of the employer[72] or on a chattel belonging to him, which involves the use or affixing of materials belonging to the person employed, the contract will ordinarily be one for work and materials, the property in the latter passing to the employer by accession[73] and not under any contract of sale.[74] Sometimes, however, there may instead be a sale of an article with an additional and subsidiary agreement to affix it. The property then passes before the article is affixed, by virtue of the contract of sale itself or an appropriation made under it. Obviously, the question whether the intention

[69] Dig. 18.1.8. This was the illustration given of *emptio spei*, or the sale of an expectation dependent upon a chance. Benjamin thought the contract was one of work and labour: *Sale of Personal Property* (2nd ed.), pp.66–67. In *Salo v Anglo-British Columbia Packing Co.* [1929] 1 D.L.R. 874, a contract by fishermen to catch fish for a cannery was held to be a contract of sale, even though the sellers submitted to a measure of control by the buyer.
[70] *Robinson v Graves* [1935] 1 K.B. 579.
[71] But see *Hyundai Shipbuilding & Heavy Industries Ltd v Papadopoulos*, above.
[72] Barber, "Title to Goods, Material and Plant under Construction Contracts," in Palmer and McKendrick (eds.), *Interests in Goods* (2nd ed.), Ch.15. Note also the definition of "supply of goods" in the Enterprise Act 2002, s.232(3), below, para.1–079, n.97; Bennett, "Attachment of Chattels to Land," *ibid.*, Ch.11.
[73] *Tripp v Armitage* (1839) 4 M. & W. 687; *Clark v Bulmer* (1843) 11 M. & W. 243. This reasoning would apply *a fortiori* where a heart pacemaker is implanted by a surgical operation.
[74] See, however, *Taypotat v Surgeson* [1985] 3 W.W.R. 18, where it was held that the property in a prefabricated house being constructed off-site passed to the buyer prior to being affixed to the land.

of the parties is substantially one of improving the land or principal chattel (to which the furnishing of materials is incidental) on the one hand or one of making a sale (to which the agreement to affix is incidental) on the other hand is a matter of degree, which may be difficult to determine in practice; but there is no theoretical difficulty. In decided cases, the following have been held contracts for work and materials: to supply and install machinery in a building[75]; to renew and alter the engines and other machinery in a ship[76]; to erect a building[77]; to construct a built-in cocktail cabinet in a house[78]; to fit new brake-linings to a car.[79] In contrast, a contract to supply black-out curtains and rails and to fit them in premises has been held a sale of goods,[80] and so have a contract to manufacture a bulk food hopper and (for an additional charge) to deliver and erect it,[81] and a contract to design and install a security system in a block of apartments.[82]

Materials supplied wholly or principally by employer.[83] Where an article is to be manufactured, and all the materials are supplied by the person for whom the work is to be done, it is obvious that there can be no sale unless 1–044

[75] *Buxton v Bedall* (1803) 3 East 303; *Clark v Bulmer*, above; *Appleby v Myers* (1867) L.R. 2 C.P. 651; *cf. Stewart Gill Ltd v Horatio Myer & Co. Ltd* [1992] Q.B. 600 at 603; *Petromec Inc. v Petroleo Parasileiro S.A. Petrobas* [2004] EWHC 1180 (Comm.); [2005] 1 Lloyd's Rep. 219. Exceptionally, the parties may agree that the supplier of the goods is to retain title to them, either conditionally (*e.g.*, until the contract price has been paid) or absolutely. As to the effectiveness of such a provision, see below, para.1–060.

[76] *Anglo-Egyptian Navigation Co. v Rennie* (1875) L.R. 10 C.P. 271.

[77] *Tripp v Armitage*, above: *cf. Young & Marten Ltd v McManus Childs Ltd* [1969] 1 A.C. 454 (roofing sub-contract); *Laminated Structures & Holdings Ltd v Eastern Woodworkers Ltd* (1962) 32 D.L.R. (2d) 1 (roof trusses); *Aristoc Industries Pty Ltd v R. A. Wenham (Builders) Pty Ltd* [1965] N.S.W.R. 581 (lecture-theatre seats); *Reg. Glass Pty Ltd v Rivers Locking Systems Ltd* (1968) 120 C.L.R. 516 (burglar-proof door); *Brunswick Glass Co. Ltd v United Contractors Ltd* (1975) 12 N.B.R. (2d) 631 (electric doors); *Hewett v Court* (1983) 57 A.L.J.R. 211 (contract to construct movable house and position it on site). Contrast *Symes v Laurie* [1985] 2 Qd. R. 547 (contract to sever house from land, move it and re-erect it on new site held a sale of goods).

[78] *Brooks Robinson Pty Ltd v Rothfield* [1951] V.L.R. 405; *cf. Jones v Gallagher* [2004] EWCA Civ 10; [2005] 1 Lloyd's Rep. 377 (fitted kitchen).

[79] *Stewart v Reavell's Garage* [1952] 2 Q.B. 545; *cf. G. H. Myers & Co. v Brent Cross Service Co.* [1934] 1 K.B. 46 (connecting rods); *Helicopter Sales Pty Ltd v Rotor-Work Pty Ltd* (1974) 132 C.L.R. 1 (spare parts for helicopter).

[80] *Love v Norman Wright (Builders) Ltd* [1944] K.B. 484. The premises were those of a third party but this was held to be immaterial; see the judgment at p.487. *Cf. Wolfenden v Wilson* (1873) 33 U.C.R. 442 (contract to make and erect tombstone); *Pritchett v Currie* [1916] 2 Ch. 545 (electric storage battery); *Collins Trading Co. Pty Ltd v Maher* [1969] V.R. 20 (supply and installation of oil heater); *Philip Head & Sons Ltd v Showfronts Ltd* [1970] 1 Lloyd's Rep. 140 (contract to sew and lay fitted carpet); *Symes v Laurie* [1985] 2 Qd.R. 547 (house to be severed, moved to a new site and re-erected, held a sale of goods); *James Slater & Hamish Slater (a firm) v Finning Ltd* [1996] C.L.C. 1236 (supply and fitting of camshaft to marine engine).

[81] *H. Parsons (Livestock) Ltd v Uttley Ingham & Co. Ltd* [1978] Q.B. 791 at 805, 809; *contra* Lord Denning at p.800, who thought that the contract was divisible into two parts.

[82] *Management Corp. Strata Title Plan No. 1166 v Chubb Singapore Pte. Ltd* [1999] 3 S.L.R. 540.

[83] *Cf.* Vienna Convention on Contracts for the International Sale of Goods (above, para.1–024), Art. 3(1): contract to be considered a sale unless employer undertakes

there is a specific transfer of the materials followed by a repurchase of the product.[84] Where each party provides some of the materials or components, the task of the court is to determine which of them has supplied the "principal materials"; it then follows that the materials supplied by the other vest by accession in the owner of the principal materials.[85] It has been held that the question which are the principal materials depends on all the circumstances, and that their relative value is not conclusive. In *Dixon v London Small Arms Co.*[86] rifles were made by the defendants for the Crown, the stock in the rough and the steel barrel being supplied by the Crown at an agreed figure which was deducted from the price of each finished rifle. This was held to be an ordinary contract for the sale of goods to be manufactured, and not one of employment of contractors or agents by the Crown at piecework rates.

1–045 The case where a printer is employed to print a book is analogous. The principal property here is the creative work embodied in the author's manuscript; the printer merely does work and supplies materials to give it another form.[87] Yet the courts appear at times to have come very near to the extraordinary view that the printer sells a product comprising only paper and ink.[88] The latter would be the case in the ordinary commercial printing of office stationery, visiting cards and so on.[89]

If the employer supplies the principal materials, the contract must be one for work and labour; but it should be observed that the converse does not hold, for even in the case where *all* the materials are supplied by the worker, the contract is not necessarily a sale.[90]

1–046 **Services independent of creation or furnishing of product.** Where work or skill is involved over and above what goes into the making of the goods delivered, it is possible and often correct to view the contract as "substantially" one for work or services.[91] A doctor or veterinary surgeon who

---

to supply "a substantial part" of materials. See also Webb [2000] J.B.L. 513.

[84] *Cf. Accurate Bailiffs & Collection Agency Ltd. v ITM Industries Ltd* (1993) 78 B.C.L.R. (2d) 1 (materials for construction of boat purchased by builder on buyer's account: held not a sale of goods).

[85] This question may arise in a case where the seller of component materials for use in a manufacturing process purports to reserve title to the materials supplied: see below, paras 1–060, 5–149, 5–150.

[86] (1876) 1 App.Cas. 632. *Cf. Hill & Sons v Edwin Showell & Sons Ltd* (1918) 87 L.J.K.B. 1106 (steel made into cartridge cases).

[87] The leading case is *Clay v Yates* (1856) 1 H. & N. 73, where the contract was held to be one for work and materials. The argument in the text is supported not by the judgments delivered in the case itself but by the subsequent explanation in *Lee v Griffin* (1861) 1 B. & S. 272 at 273–274. It is unlikely that the situation would be different where a separate publisher is involved.

[88] See, *e.g. Lee v Griffin*, above, at p.278.

[89] *Cf. Canada Bank Note Engraving & Printing Co. v Toronto Ry Co.* (1895) 22 A.R. 462 (debentures).

[90] *Robinson v Graves* [1935] 1 K.B. 579 (below, para.1–047).

[91] Another feature which has been considered indicative of a contract of services is that the contract between the supplier and his customer or client is unique in each case: *Barbee v Rogers* 425 S.W. (2d) 342 (1968) (supply of contact lenses).

supplies medicines does so as an incident to a contract for professional services, which include diagnosis and advice over and above any work in the making up of the medicine.[92] In contrast, a chemist who makes up a prescription sells it, since his work and skill goes entirely into the product—it is simply a component reflected in the price of the goods.[93] This, it is submitted, is the reason for excepting from the category of sales the case of a solicitor who draws a document or an architect who draws a plan.[94] The client obtains consultation and advice; he pays for a professional assessment of his situation as well as for the skill needed in the actual drafting.[95]

It has been held that where a meal is supplied to a customer in a restaurant there is a sale of goods,[96] the element of service being subsidiary; but it is submitted that a meal supplied to a lodger or a resident hotel guest is part of a contract for services.[97]

Where goods (*e.g.* machinery) are supplied on terms that the price paid includes maintenance for a given period after delivery, it is plainly correct to regard the services as incidental and to construe the contract as one for the sale of goods.

Work wholly a component of article produced.[98] The most difficult type of contract remains to be discussed. In this case the whole of the work or skill involved goes into the creation of the product which is ultimately delivered in performance of the contract: for example, a contract to make a suit of clothing or to build a ship. The work or skill is here a component—perhaps the most important—of the thing produced, but it is a component and nothing more. It is not logical to ask whether in such a case the parties contracted primarily or substantially for the performance of work *or* for the transfer of a chattel: they contracted for both.[99] In *Clay v Yates*[1] Pollock 1–047

[92] *Dodd v Wilson & McWilliam* [1946] 2 All E.R. 691 (veterinary surgeon). *Cf. Clarke v Mumford* (1811) 3 Camp. 67 (farrier); *Watson v Buckley, Osborne, Garrett & Co. Ltd* [1940] 1 All E.R. 174 (hairdresser); *Perlmutter v Beth David Hospital* (1955) 123 N.E. (2d) 792 (blood transfusion).

[93] *R. v Wood Green Profiteering Committee* (1920) 89 L.J.K.B. 55; *cf. Buchan v Ortho Pharmaceutical (Canada) Ltd* (1984) 8 D.L.R. (4th) 373 (oral contraceptive supplied by pharmacist on doctor's prescription). For the position under the National Health Service, see below, para.1–071.

[94] *Grafton v Armitage* (1845) 2 C.B. 336 (engineer devising and building machine); *cf. ibid.*, at p.339, *per* Erle J. (attorney preparing deed); *Gibbon v Pease* [1905] 1 K.B. 810; *Vautier v Fear* [1916] G.L.R. 524 (architect's plans); *Art Direction Ltd v UPS Needham (N.Z.) Ltd* [1977] 2 N.Z.L.R. 12 (artwork).

[95] For this reason, the case of *Lee v Griffin* (1861) 1 B. & S. 272 (supply of dentures) might well be open to reconsideration. See also below, para.1–086 (bespoke computer software).

[96] *Lockett v A. & M. Charles Ltd* [1938] 4 All E.R. 170; *cf. R. v Birmingham Profiteering Committee* (1919) 89 L.J.K.B. 57.

[97] See, however, *Horgan v Driscoll* (1908) 42 I.L.T. 238.

[98] *Cf.* Vienna Convention on Contracts for the International Sale of Goods (above, para.1–024), Art. 3(2): "This Convention does not apply to contracts in which the preponderant part of the obligations of the party who furnishes the goods consists in the supply of labour or other services."

[99] *Cf. Hyundai Shipbuilding & Heavy Industries Ltd v Papadopoulos* [1980] 1 W.L.R. 1129 at 1134, 1148; *Stoczina Gdanska SA v Latvian Shipping Co.* [1996] 2 Lloyd's Rep. 132 at 138 (contract to build ship held to have characteristics of both types of transaction).

[1] (1856) 1 H. & N. 73.

C.B. suggested that the court should ask whether it was the work or the materials supplied that was of the essence of the contract, a question to be determined by comparing the importance, though not perhaps necessarily the value, of the two items. This in turn was rejected in *Lee v Griffin*,[2] where the court virtually held that any contract capable of being described as a sale should be so classified: "If the contract be such that, when carried out, it would result in the sale of a chattel, the party cannot sue for work and labour; but if the result of the contract is that the party has done work and labour which ends in nothing that can become the subject of a sale, the party cannot sue for goods sold and delivered. The case of an attorney employed to prepare a deed is an illustration of this latter proposition . . . I do not think that the test to apply to these cases is whether the value of the work exceeds that of the materials used in its execution; for, if a sculptor were employed to execute a work of art, greatly as his skill and labour, supposing it to be of the highest description, might exceed the value of the marble on which he worked, the contract would, in my opinion, nevertheless be a contract for the sale of a chattel."[3] Accordingly the court held that a contract by a dentist to make and fit dentures for a patient was for the sale of goods.[4] The rule so established in *Lee v Griffin* has been summarised as follows[5]: if the contract is intended to result in transferring for a price from B to A a chattel in which A had no previous property, it is a contract for the sale of a chattel.[6]

In *Robinson v Graves*,[7] however, the Court of Appeal reintroduced, purportedly as a qualification to this rule, what is in effect the criterion of relative importance as between work and materials which had been rejected in *Lee v Griffin*,[8] although the court professed to be considering what was the substance of the *contract* rather than the more substantial component in the *product* ultimately delivered. In *Robinson v Graves*, Greer L.J. said: "If

---

[2] (1861) 1 B. & S. 272; *cf. R. v Wood Green Profiteering Committee* (1920) 89 L.J.K.B. 55.

[3] (1861) 1 B. & S. 272 at 278.

[4] *Cf. Samuels v Davis* [1943] 1 K.B. 526.

[5] Benjamin, *Sale of Personal Property* (8th ed.), pp.161–162.

[6] Consistent with this view are: *R. v Wood Green Profiteering Committee*, above (chemist's prescription); *Re Blyth Shipbuilding Co. Ltd* [1926] Ch. 494 (construction of ship); *Cammell Laird & Co. Ltd v Manganese Bronze & Brass Co. Ltd* [1934] A.C. 402 (construction of ship's propellers); *Newman v Lipman* [1951] 1 K.B. 333 (photograph taken in street; contrast *Lyle v Ajax Distributing Agency Pty Ltd* (1975) 11 S.A.S.R. 9, where similar contract held to be for work and materials); *J Marcel (Furriers) Ltd v Tapper* [1953] 1 W.L.R. 49 (fur jacket made to order); *Preload Co. of Canada Ltd v Regina (City)* (1958) 24 W.W.R. 433, affirmed [1959] S.C.R. 801 (supply of pre-stressed concrete pipes); *Ashington Piggeries Ltd v Christopher Hill Ltd* [1972] A.C. 441 (animal food compounded to customer's formula); *Deta Nominees Pty Ltd v Viscount Plastic Products Pty Ltd* [1979] V.R. 167 (plastic-moulding dies to customer's specification); all were held or assumed to be sales of goods. See also *Huntwave Ltd v Customs and Excise Commissioners* [1973] V.A.T.T.R. 72; *Pendred Hairdressing Ltd v Customs and Excise Commissioners, ibid.* 81; *Roberts Hair Fashions v Customs and Excise Commissioners*, *ibid.* 140 (shampoos, etc. in hairdresser's stock not "materials held for sale").

[7] [1935] 1 K.B. 579. Contrast *Isaacs v Hardy* (1884) Cab. & El. 287 (contract to execute painting held sale of goods).

[8] Above.

you find . . . that the substance of the contract was the production of something to be sold . . . then that is a sale of goods. But if the substance of the contract, on the other hand, is that skill and labour have to be exercised for the production of the article and that it is only ancillary to that that there will pass from the artist to his client or customer some materials in addition to the skill involved in the production of the portrait, that does not make any difference to the result, because the substance of the contract is the skill and experience of the artist in producing the picture".[9] This statement, with respect, overlooks the fact that what passes to the client is not the materials but the finished picture, of which both the work and the materials are components. *Lee v Griffin* and *Robinson v Graves* cannot be reconciled: the reasoning in each case could have been applied to the facts of the other. It has yet to be appreciated that a decision of this problem can be reached only by adopting one or the other of these equally arbitrary rules.[10]

Sale distinguished from contract of agency. When a supplier agrees to procure goods for another, he may do so as the latter's agent[11] or as a principal party standing towards him in the relationship of a seller. The situation is parallel to that already discussed[12] in which the agreement is to manufacture and supply goods: the manufacturer may produce the goods for himself and sell them when completed, or he may be employed to work on the other party's behalf. A supplier who is a seller ordinarily contracts to supply the goods at an agreed price whatever may be the cost to himself, and he undertakes absolutely to do so[13]; a supplier who is an agent merely binds himself to use due diligence to fulfil the order; but on the other hand, he is bound to get the goods as cheaply as he reasonably can,[14] and his remuneration is normally by way of commission.[15] 1–048

Conversely when goods are delivered to another for sale to a third party, the recipient may be an outright buyer, or he may take the goods "on sale or return"[16]; alternatively, he may be merely the supplier's agent to sell the

---

[9] [1935] 1 K.B. 579 at 587.

[10] In *Deta Nominees Pty Ltd v Viscount Plastic Products Pty Ltd*, above, the Supreme Court of Victoria rejected as "illogical and unsatisfactory" the test laid down in *Robinson v Graves*, and stated that the reasoning in *Lee v Griffin* was to be preferred.

[11] In this case, the relationship between the parties may be governed by the Commercial Agency Regulations 1993 (SI 1993/3053, implementing E.C. Directive 1986/653/EEC ([1986] O.J. L382/17)); Bowstead and Reynolds on Agency (18th ed.), Ch.11.

[12] Above, para.1–044.

[13] See, however, *Monkland v Jack Barclay Ltd* [1951] 2 K.B. 252, where the seller's obligation under a contract of sale was construed as being no more than an undertaking to use his best endeavours to procure delivery of the goods.

[14] *Ireland v Livingston* (1872) L.R. 5 H.L. 395. Note that an agent employed to procure goods on commission may be treated as a quasi-seller for some purposes, *e.g.* as having power to stop the goods in transit: see below, paras 15–013, 15–065.

[15] *Miller v Newman* (1842) 4 Man. & G. 646; contrast *Cobbold v Caston* (1824) 1 Bing. 399.

[16] *i.e.* as a bailee who may elect to buy, and in some cases may be deemed to have elected to buy, the goods bailed to him: see below, para.1–056; paras 5–040 *et seq.* See also *Comet Group plc v British Sky Broadcasting Ltd, The Times*, April 26, 1991 (joint venture).

goods[17] or an agent on a *del credere* commission—that is, an agent who guarantees to his principal that the buyer will duly pay the price.[18] It is possible also for the buyer under a contract of sale to agree that the property in the goods shall remain in the seller until the price has been paid or some other condition has been fulfilled and that, should he before that time resell the goods, he will do so as the seller's agent and be accountable to him for the proceeds of the sub-sale on a fiduciary basis.[19]

1–049 To determine the nature of the transaction in these cases, the whole agreement must be looked to. It is not conclusive that the consignee should be described in the contract as an "agent" or even "sole agent"[20] or conversely that the transaction should be called a "sale".[21] Certain stipulations may be consistent with both sale (and especially "sale or return") and agency, and therefore cannot be taken as indicative of either: for instance, the transfer to the consignee of the property in goods shipped upon his acceptance of drafts[22]; a provision that the property in the goods shall remain in the consignor until disposed of[23]; or the fact that the price of sale to third parties is fixed by the consignor.[24] Exceptionally, an agent *may* be remunerated by allowing him to keep the surplus over and above a specified price which he is to receive on account of his principal,[25] while a buyer *may* be paid a sum described as a "commission".[26] It is, however, evidence towards a sale that the recipient is entitled to sell at whatever price he thinks fit, accounting to the supplier only for a predetermined sum,[27] and this interpretation is given further support if he is to alter or improve the goods.[28] An agent, even a *del credere* agent, acts in accordance with the instructions of his principal, and is normally remunerated by commission.[29] The nature of the consignee's obligation to account to the consignor is perhaps the strongest indication of his position: if he is bound to furnish particulars of his sales and customers, he is probably an agent; if not, he may be deemed to be selling to his own customers. If he has to account periodically for the proceeds of his sales, rather than pay wholesale

---

[17] In particular, he may be the supplier's "mercantile agent" or (in 19th century terminology) his "factor," empowered to sell in his own name. See below, para.3–004.
[18] See below, para.3–004.
[19] *Aluminium Industrie Vaassen BV v Romalpa Aluminium Ltd* [1976] 1 W.L.R. 676: see below, para.5–141.
[20] *The Kronprinzessin Cecilie* (1917) 33 T.L.R. 292; *W T Lamb & Sons v Goring Brick Co. Ltd* [1932] 1 K.B. 710; *Potter v Customs and Excise Commrs*. [1985] S.T.C. 45 ("Tupperware" dealers held buyers, not agents).
[21] *Weiner v Harris* [1910] 1 K.B. 285.
[22] *The Prinz Adalbert* [1917] A.C. 586.
[23] *Weiner v Harris*, above; *Michelin Tyre Co. Ltd v McFarlane (Glasgow) Ltd* (1917) 55 Sc.LR. 35, HL.
[24] *Michelin Tyre Co. Ltd v McFarlane (Glasgow) Ltd*, above. On the fixing of resale prices generally, see below, para.3–037.
[25] *Re Smith, ex p. Bright* (1879) 10 Ch.D. 566 at 570, *per* Jessel M.R.
[26] *Kelly v Enderton* [1913] A.C. 191; *Gannow Engineering Co. Ltd v Richardson* [1930] N.Z.L.R. 361.
[27] *Re Nevill, ex p. White* (1871) 6 Ch.App. 387, affirmed *sub nom. John Towle & Co. v. White* (1873) 29 L.T. 78.
[28] *Re Nevill, ex p. White*, above, at p.400.
[29] *Weiner v Harris*, above: *cf. Miller v Newman* (1842) 4 Man. & G. 646.

prices, he is likely to be considered an agent. But if when he sells (whether for cash or on credit) to a retail purchaser, he at once becomes debtor to the supplier for the listed price, the transaction is quite inconsistent with agency or *del credere* agency, and consistent only with sale or return.[30]

Contract of sale distinguished from option to buy. An option to buy goods granted to a possible purchaser is, in a strict legal sense, an offer to sell which the offeror promises for valuable consideration (or by deed) not to revoke.[31] The owner of the goods may, in popular language, be said to have "agreed to sell" them, but in law there is no such agreement unless the parties are mutually bound.[32] An agreement to sell connotes an agreement to buy,[33] and in the absence of any binding obligation to buy there is no contract of sale.[34] The holder of an option is free to exercise it or not as he may choose, and unless and until he does so, he has neither bought nor agreed to buy. Once an option to buy has been exercised, there is of course a contract of sale of goods within the meaning of the Act. 1–050

Two particular types of transaction which involve an option to buy call for special consideration, and are discussed shortly: hire-purchase agreements[35] and deliveries on "sale or return".[36]

Option distinguished from conditional right or obligation. The Sale of Goods Act recognises that there may be conditional contracts of sale,[37] and it may be inferred that the Act applies to such contracts, at least so far as this is practicable. The terms "condition" and "conditional" raise questions of great difficulty in the law of contract, and in particular in the law of sale, because of the different meanings and shades of meaning which may be given to them.[38] Some of these difficulties are discussed in a later chapter.[39] If by the term "conditional contract" is meant an agreement whose very existence is dependent upon the fulfilment of some condition (in the sense that there are to be no binding obligations until that event has occurred)[40] 1–051

---

[30] *Michelin Tyre Co. Ltd v McFarlane (Glasgow) Ltd* (1917) 55 Sc.L.R. 35, HL; *cf. Macdonald v Westren* (1888) 15 R. (Ct. of Sess.) 988; *Weiner v Harris*, above; *International Harvester Co. of Australia Pty Ltd v Carrigan's Hazeldene Pastoral Co.* (1958) 100 C.L.R. 644. See also the discussion below, para.1–060, of the situation where a manufacturer sells his product as agent for the supplier of the component materials.

[31] *Mountford v Scott* [1975] Ch.258 at 264; Mowbray, 74 L.Q.R. 242 (1958). Contrast the view expressed in *Spiro v Glencrown Properties Ltd* [1991] Ch. 537 (option to purchase land).

[32] *Helby v Matthews* [1895] A.C. 471. (See, however, *Re Asia Oil & Minerals Ltd* (1986) 10 A.C.L.R. 333 at 335 (share option treated as conditional contract); *cf. Laybutt v Amoco Australia Ltd* (1974) 132 C.L.R. 57 at 73–76 and *Spiro v Glencrown Properties Ltd* [1991] Ch.537(nature of option to buy land)).

[33] *Helby v Matthews*, above, at p.477.

[34] *Helby v Matthews*, above; *Wm. Cory & Son Ltd v I.R.C.* [1965] A.C. 1088.

[35] Below, paras 1–053—1–054.

[36] Below, paras 1–056.

[37] s.2(3); and *cf.* s.18, rule 1.

[38] See below, paras 10–024 *et seq.*; Smith, 14 M.L.R. 173 (1951); Stoljar, 69 L.Q.R. 485 (1953).

[39] See below, paras 10–024 *et seq.*

[40] Below, para.10–024 and *cf. Damon Compania Naviera SA v Hapag-Lloyd International SA* [1985] 1 W.L.R. 435 (provision for payment of deposit not a condition precedent to the formation of contract to sell ship).

then each party is free to withdraw from it, and may proceed with it or not as he chooses. The best-known examples of such agreements are transactions "subject to contract" or "subject to confirmation". This use of the term "conditional contract" is probably otiose.[41] A contract may perhaps more properly be said to be conditional[42] if all or some of the obligations of one or both of the parties are conditional upon a stated fact or event. For example, there may be an agreement to buy and sell a car, provided that it passes a mechanical test.[43] In this case the parties are bound respectively to sell and to buy, subject only to the fulfilment of the condition, and neither is free to withdraw, except on the failure of the event. This is so even where the fulfilment of the condition is dependent upon an action of one of the parties[44]—for instance, in the example given, the seller must allow the car to be submitted to the test, and if he refuses to do so, he will be in breach of contract.[45] For this reason, a conditional right or obligation in the sense here described is always distinguishable from an option.

1–052 **Conditional sale agreements.** It may be a term of a contract of sale that the transfer of the property in the goods is subject to some condition to be fulfilled after the making of the contract. In particular, it may be agreed that the property shall not pass to the buyer until the price has been paid in full; and the expression "conditional sale" (and its variant "conditional purchase") is regularly used to describe such a contract,[46] at least in the common case where the price is payable by instalments. Such contracts are now in part governed by the Consumer Credit Act 1974, which employs the following definition[47]: "'conditional sale agreement' means an agreement for the sale of goods or land under which the purchase price or part of it is payable by instalments, and the property in the goods or land is to remain in the seller (notwithstanding that the buyer is to be in possession of the goods or land) until such conditions as to the payment of instalments or otherwise as may be specified in the agreement are fulfilled."

It was held in *Lee v Butler*[48] that a person who was in possession of goods under a conditional sale agreement had "agreed to buy" within the terms of

---

[41] *ibid*.
[42] See, however, *Eastham v Leigh London & Provincial Props. Ltd* [1971] Ch.871, where for the purposes of a revenue statute a contract was held not to be "conditional" merely because it contained some conditional obligations.
[43] *Cf. Mackay v Dick* (1881) 6 App.Cas. 251, discussed below, paras 10–025, 10–039.
[44] *Marten v Whale* [1917] 2 K.B 480 at 486–487; *Varverakis v Cia. de Navegacion Artico SA (The "Merak")* [1976] 2 Lloyd's Rep. 250; *Wood Preservation Ltd v Prior* [1969] 1 W.L.R. 1077 (shares); *Smallman v Smallman* [1972] Fam. 25 (divorce settlement); *IRC v Ufitex Group Ltd* [1977] 3 All E.R. 924 (shares), and see further below, para.10–025.
[45] *ibid*.
[46] See, however, *Re Bond Worth Ltd* [1980] Ch.228 at 245, where Slade J. said that contracts containing a "retention of title" clause (below, paras 1–060, 5–141) were "absolute contracts for the sale of goods within the meaning of section 1(2) of the Sale of Goods Act 1893, though this is not to say that they did not comprise other features in addition."
[47] Consumer Credit Act 1974, s.189(1). The definition in the Hire-Purchase Act 1965, s.1(1), was the same, except that the words "or land" were omitted throughout. (The definitions discussed in this and the paragraphs following are not affected by the Consumer Credit Act 2006.)
[48] [1893] 2 Q.B. 318.

section 9 of the Factors Act 1889, so that he could pass a good title to a third party under that provision.[49] The conditional sale agreement was therefore not fully effective as a security to the seller for the unpaid purchase price[50]; and it was to overcome this difficulty that the hire-purchase agreement was devised.

A conditional sale agreement is a contract of sale both at common law and within the Sale of Goods Act 1979. The provisions of this Act will, therefore, govern such questions as the implication of terms as to title and quality into such agreements.[51] But in a number of statutes concerned with the supply of goods on instalment credit terms, it has been recognised that the buyer in a conditional sale transaction and the hirer under a hire-purchase agreement stand in closely analogous situations; and in these Acts the law of sale of goods has been modified or excluded so as to make the same legal rules applicable to both. Thus, conditional sale agreements relating to motor vehicles are affected by Part III of the Hire-Purchase Act 1964, which makes an exception to the principle *nemo dat quod non habet* in favour of a private purchaser of a motor vehicle.[52] The protection given by the Consumer Credit Act 1974 to those who acquire goods on hire-purchase, within the financial and other limitations which make the transaction a "regulated agreement" as defined by that Act,[53] extends also to buyers under a conditional sale agreement, so that, within those limitations, the two types of transaction are to all intents and purposes equated. In particular, the power of a buyer in possession to pass a good title to a third party (which was the basis of the decision in *Lee v Butler*[54]) is removed as regards all conditional sale agreements coming within the statutory control.[55]

---

[49] On this section, and the similar provision in s.25(1) of the Sale of Goods Act 1979, see below, paras 7–067 *et seq*.

[50] See now, however, s.54 of the Hire-Purchase Act 1964 and s.25(2) of the Sale of Goods Act 1979, discussed *infra* and below, para.7–070.

[51] For the period between the commencement of the Hire-Purchase Act 1965 and the coming into operation of the Supply of Goods (Implied Terms) Act 1973, conditional sale agreements were treated for the purpose of the implication of these statutory terms on the stricter basis which then applied to hire-purchase agreements, and ss.12–15 of the Sale of Goods Act 1893 were declared not to apply: see ss.17–20 and 29(3)(c) of the 1965 Act. The Supply of Goods (Implied Terms) Act 1973 repealed the latter sections and dealt separately, but in similar terms, with contracts of sale of goods and hire-purchase agreements; and accordingly conditional sale agreements were once again treated for this purpose as contracts of sale, as is the case also under the Sale of Goods Act 1979, ss.12–15, which replace the corresponding provisions in the 1973 Act. But s.14 of the 1973 Act, like the repealed s.20 of the 1965 Act, provides that s.11(4) of the Sale of Goods Act 1979 (dealing with loss of the right to reject goods for breach of condition) shall not apply to conditional sale agreements which are "consumer sales" (defined in Sch.2, para.17 and Sch.1, para.11, to the Act of 1979), and makes alternative provision in that case. On implied terms generally, see below, Chs 4, 11.

[52] See below, paras 7–087 *et seq*.

[53] For the scope of these limitations, see above, para.1–021.

[54] Above.

[55] This was, in fact, already the position under s.54 of the Hire-Purchase Act 1965. With the coming into force of the Consumer Credit Act 1974 (see above, para.1–019), s.54 of the 1965 Act has been replaced by equivalent provisions contained in

1–053 **Hire-purchase agreements.**[56] At common law, a hire-purchase agreement may be defined as a contract for the hiring of goods under which there is conferred on the hirer an option to buy the goods.[57] The salient features of such an agreement are: first, that during the currency of the agreement the property in the goods remains in the owner, while the hirer is a mere bailee having no power to dispose of them; and, secondly, that the hirer has an option to buy the goods but not a binding obligation to do so.[58] In practice, hire-purchase is a device used in order to give possession and the use of goods to an intending buyer over a period during which he pays the price, with interest, by instalments while the seller retains the title to the goods as security for the unpaid balance of the price. The success of the hire-purchase form has been due to two decisions in the House of Lords in the year 1895[59]: *McEntire v Crossley Bros*,[60] in which it was held that a hire-purchase transaction was not caught by the Bills of Sale Acts, since there was no assignment or right to seize granted to another by the *owner* of the goods; and *Helby v Matthews*,[61] in which it was held that the hirer, having an option but not an *obligation* to buy the goods, had not "agreed to buy" them, even conditionally; and therefore had no power to confer a good title on a third party and so to defeat the owner's security as had been the case in *Lee v Butler*.[62]

Many aspects of hire-purchase practice are now regulated by legislation, and in particular by the Hire-Purchase Act 1964 and the Consumer Credit Act 1974.[63]

---

s.25(2) of the Sale of Goods Act 1979, and by an amendment to s.9 of the Factors Act 1889 (made by the Consumer Credit Act 1974, s.192(3), (4) and Sch.4, para.2). These amendments provide that, for the purposes of s.25(1) of the Act of 1979 and s.9 of the Act of 1889, the buyer under a conditional sale agreement is to be taken not to be a person who has bought or agreed to buy goods, and that "conditional sale agreement" means an agreement for the sale of goods which is a consumer credit agreement within the meaning of the Consumer Credit Act 1974 under which the purchase price or part of it is payable by instalments, and the property in the goods is to remain in the seller (notwithstanding that the buyer is to be in possession of the goods) until such conditions as to the payment of instalments or otherwise as may be specified in the agreement are fulfilled.

[56] See Guest, *The Law of Hire-Purchase* (1966); Goode, *Hire-Purchase Law and Practice* (2nd ed.).

[57] The consideration for the exercise of the option is commonly a nominal sum. But this fact (and the fact that in practice payment may not be required) will not prevent a contract from being construed as one of hire-purchase: *Close Asset Finance Ltd v Care Graphics Machinery Ltd, The Times*, March 21, 2000.

[58] In *Forthright Finance Ltd v Carlyle Finance Ltd* [1997] 4 All E.R. 90, the agreement provided that the "hirer" (a company) was bound to pay all the instalments due under the contract and that the "hirer" should then become the owner of the goods unless it exercised an option *not* to take title. The Court of Appeal held that, since the "hirer" was contractually bound to pay all the instalments and that it was extremely unlikely that such an option would ever been exercised, the contract was one of conditional sale.

[59] It was also, no doubt, a factor contributing to its popularity that the transaction was not within the control of the Moneylenders Acts: Guest, *op. cit.*, paras 134–135.

[60] [1895] A.C. 457.

[61] [1895] A.C. 471.

[62] [1893] 2 Q.B. 318; see above, para.1–052.

[63] See above, para.1–019.

For the purpose of this legislation, a hire-purchase agreement is defined as follows[64]: "'hire-purchase agreement' means an agreement, other than a conditional sale agreement, under which—(*a*) goods are bailed or (in Scotland) hired in return for periodical payments by the person to whom they are bailed or hired, and (*b*) the property in the goods will pass to that person if the terms of the agreement are complied with and one or more of the following occurs—(i) the exercise of an option to purchase by that person, (ii) the doing of any other specified act by any party to the agreement, (iii) the happening of any other specified event."

Other statutes have special definitions of "hire-purchase" and "hire-purchase agreement" which in many cases include conditional sale agreements and sometimes other transactions as well.[65]

Financing of hire-purchase agreements. In modern practice the credit given to a customer who takes goods on hire-purchase is commonly not carried personally by the dealer or shopkeeper from whose stock the goods were selected, but instead by a specialist finance house which pays or advances cash to the dealer, and may also undertake the collection of the instalments. This is usually done in one of two ways. In the "block discounting" method, the dealer himself lets the goods on hire-purchase to his customer, and then assigns or agrees to assign ("discounts") to the finance company his contractual rights under the hire-purchase agreement. Such a transaction is a sale of book-debts or assignment of a chose in action, but it is not a sale of goods. The dealer may, however, assign not merely his rights under the agreement but also his interest in the goods themselves. The latter transaction is a sale of goods, and may in some cases be caught by the provisions of the Bills of Sale Acts.[66] In other cases, the "direct collection" system is used, under which the dealer first sells the goods to the finance company, and the company then lets the goods on hire-purchase directly to the customer. Here there *is* a sale of goods from the dealer to the finance company, but there is normally no contract at all between the dealer and his customer. Despite the fact that he negotiates the terms of the transaction which is ultimately concluded between the finance company and the customer, he is not in all cases or for all purposes the agent of the former at common law,[67] and he will rarely be the agent of 1–054

---

[64] Consumer Credit Act 1974, s.189(1); Hire-Purchase Act 1964, s.29(1) (as amended by the Consumer Credit Act 1974, s.192 and Sch.4, para.22). The definition of "hire-purchase agreement" for the purposes of the Hire-Purchase Act 1964 prior to May 19, 1985 (the date on which the Act of 1974 became fully operative) was much wider. It read: "'hire-purchase agreement' means an agreement for the bailment of goods under which the bailee may buy the goods, or under which the property in the goods will or may pass to the bailee" (Hire-Purchase Act 1965, s.1(1)).

[65] The different statutory definitions are collected and examined by Guest, *op. cit.*, paras 52–56.

[66] These and other questions arising out of such transactions are fully discussed in Guest, *op. cit.*, Chs 3, 13.

[67] *Mercantile Credit Co. Ltd v Hamblin* [1965] 2 Q.B. 242 at 269; *Branwhite v Worcester Works Finance Ltd* [1969] 1 A.C. 552; *cf. Financings Ltd v Stimson* [1962] 1 W.L.R. 1184; *Carlyle Finance Ltd v Pallas Industrial Finance* [1999] 1 All E.R. (Comm.) 659 (authorisation to deliver vehicle); *Shogun Finance Ltd v Hudson* [2003] U.K.H.L. 62; [2004] 1 A.C. 919 at [51] and see below, para.3–005.

the customer.[68] But the courts have sometimes found that there has been a collateral contract entered into between the dealer and the customer, in order to fix the dealer with liability for representations which he has made as to the quality of the goods[69]; and now by statute the dealer is deemed to be the agent of the finance company for many purposes in connection with agreements falling within the statutory control.[70] This imputed agency cannot be negatived.[71]

1–055 **Credit-sale agreements.** The Consumer Credit Act 1974 makes special provision for "credit-sale agreements" and regulates the formation and formalities of agreements within certain financial and other limits,[72] but for all other purposes these are contracts for the sale of goods within the meaning of the Sale of Goods Act.

The Consumer Credit Act 1974 defines a credit-sale agreement as follows: "'credit-sale agreement' means an agreement for the sale of goods, under which the purchase price or part of it is payable by instalments, but which is not a conditional sale agreement."[73] In practice, however, the statutory control of credit-sale agreements normally extends only to transactions under which the purchase price is payable by five or more instalments, for power is given to the Secretary of State to exclude from the regulating provisions of the Act of 1974 consumer credit agreements[74] where the payments to be made by the debtor do not exceed a specified number[75]; and he has specified a maximum of four, provided that the payments are to be made within 12 months from the date of the agreement.[76]

1–056 **Delivery on "sale or return".** A person to whom goods are delivered on "sale or return" has a true option to buy, in the sense that he is free to buy or not as he chooses. In such a transaction the goods are bailed to a

---

68 But if the customer signs an agreement containing blank spaces, leaving it to be completed by the dealer, he will be bound by what the dealer writes: *United Dominions Trust Ltd v Weston* [1976] 1 Q.B. 513.

69 *Brown v Sheen & Richmond Car Sales Ltd* [1950] 1 All E.R. 1102; [1950] W.N. 316; *Andrews v Hopkinson* [1957] 1 Q.B. 229; *Yeoman Credit Ltd v Odgers* [1962] 1 W.L.R. 215.

70 Consumer Credit Act 1974, ss.56, 57, 69, 102, replacing (from May 19, 1985) Hire-Purchase Act 1965, ss.12(3), 31, 58: see below, para.3–005. For the scope of the statutory control, see above, para.1–021. See further Sale of Goods Act 1979, s.14(3)(b): below, para.11–056.

71 Consumer Credit Act 1974, s.56(3)(b), replacing Hire-Purchase Act 1965, s.29.

72 See above, para.1–021.

73 s.189(1). For the definition of "conditional sale agreement", see *ibid:* and above, para.1–052.

74 For the definition of "consumer credit agreement," see s.8(2) and above, para.1–022.

75 s.16(5)(a).

76 Consumer Credit (Exempt Agreements) Order 1989 (SI 1989/869), art. 3(1)(a)(i). This makes the position the same, in effect, as that under the repealed Hire-Purchase Act of 1965, which (by s.1(1)) defined a credit-sale agreement as "an agreement for the sale of goods under which the purchase price is payable by five or more instalments, not being a conditional sale agreement."

prospective buyer on the understanding that he may buy them at a stated price: he may elect either to buy or to return the goods,[77] and by the terms of the agreement, or in accordance with the presumed intention of the parties set out in section 18, rule 4, of the Sale of Goods Act 1979, will be deemed to have bought them in certain events if he does not give notice of rejection.[78] Since the property remains in the bailor until there is an election to buy, and the bailee is not until such time under any obligation to buy, there is no contract of sale within the meaning of the Act. Nevertheless, the Act does contain certain provisions concerning the passing of the property in these transactions.[79]

It is of course competent for the parties to enter into a quite different bargain, in which it is agreed that the property shall pass on or before delivery, subject to the right of the person taking the goods to return them and revest the property in the seller should they not suit him, either within a fixed time or a reasonable time.[80] In this case there is a sale subject to a condition subsequent, and the transaction comes within the scope of the Sale of Goods Act.

Confusion may be caused by the practice in the United States where the term "sale or return" is used to describe the latter transaction and "sale on approval" the former.[81] In this country there is no recognised name for a sale with condition subsequent,[82] while the expressions "on sale or return," "on approval," "on trial" and "on approbation" are all commonly treated as equivalent. Each transaction must be construed by reference to all the facts and circumstances in order to ascertain the true intention of the parties; but the wording of section 18 makes it plain that, unless a different intention appears, the delivery will be presumed to have been made on the terms set out in rule 4 of that section.

Sale distinguished from bailment. A contract of sale is to be distinguished from a bailment.[83] A bailment is a delivery of a thing by one person to another for a limited purpose upon the terms that the bailee will return the same thing[84] to the bailor, or deliver it to someone in accordance with the bailor's instructions, after the purpose has been fulfilled.[85] Where 1–057

---

[77] Depending upon the terms of the contract, the buyer may be entitled to accept part of the goods and return the remainder: *Atari Corporation (UK) Ltd v Electronics Boutique Stores (UK) Ltd* [1998] Q.B. 539.

[78] See below, paras 5–040 *et seq.* The parties may, alternatively, agree that notice of rejection shall not be sufficient for this purpose, but that the goods must actually be returned: *Ornstein v Alexandra Furnishing Co.* (1895) 12 T.L.R. 128.

[79] *ibid.*

[80] See, *e.g. Head v Tattersall* (1871) L.R. 7 Ex. 7; *The Vesta* [1921] 1 A.C. 774; and *cf.* below, para.5–043.

[81] See U.C.C., s.2–327.

[82] In retail transactions, such a term is commonly referred to as a "satisfaction guarantee".

[83] *Re Woodward, ex p. Huggins* (1886) 54 L.T. 683 (agistment of ewes).

[84] This is the traditional view: on mixed and substituted goods, see below, para.1–059.

[85] See Jones, *Law of Bailments* (1823), p.1: Story, *Bailment* (1843), para.2; Paton, *Bailment in the Common Law* (1952), Ch.1; Palmer, *Bailment* (2nd ed.), pp.131 *et seq.*; *Chitty on Contracts* (29th ed.), Vol. 2, Ch.33.

the terms are that the recipient will pay money or deliver some other valuable commodity or deliver an equivalent amount of the same commodity[86] to the bailor, and not return the identical subject-matter, either in its original form or an altered form, this is a transfer of property for value[87] and not a bailment.[88] In *South Australian Insurance Co. v Randell*,[89] corn was deposited by farmers with a miller, who mixed it with other corn and held the whole on the terms that a farmer could claim at any time a quantity of grain of the same quality equal to that which he had delivered (without reference to any specific bulk from which it was to be taken), or in lieu thereof the market price of an equivalent quantity and quality ruling on the day on which he made his demand. It was held that, there being no obligation to preserve the identity of each consignment of corn delivered and to return it intact upon demand, the transaction was a transfer of property for value, and not a bailment, to the miller, who was in consequence entitled to claim in respect of the grain on an insurance policy which covered his own property. This decision has been followed in a number of cases concerning the bulk handling of commodities for the purpose of storage, processing or marketing,[90] although the position is now regulated by statute in many jurisdictions.[91]

1–058 **Intermixture where ownership retained by contributors.** It is possible, however, for goods to be delivered by their owner to another person to be mixed with similar goods belonging to that person or to other owners on terms that there shall be neither a bailment *stricto sensu* nor a transfer of the property for value. In *Coleman v Harvey*,[92] coins containing an estimated 166 kilogrammes of silver were delivered by the plaintiff to a company which undertook to refine the metal and to hold 166 kilogrammes of the resulting refined silver ingots on the plaintiff's behalf. The coins were supplied (as the court found) on the terms that the property in the silver was to remain in the plaintiff throughout the refining process, notwithstand-

[86] But it would appear to follow from the decision in *Mercer v Craven Grain Storage Ltd* [1994] C.L.C. 328 that there can sometimes be a bailment where it has been agreed that what will be returned to the owner may not (or will not) be the identical goods: see below, para.1–059.

[87] Sometimes loosely called a "sale" (not, however, a sale under the Sale of Goods Act 1979, since there is no money price: see above, para.1–034).

[88] *South Australian Insurance Co. v Randell* (1869) L.R. 3 P.C. 101.

[89] Above.

[90] See, *e.g.* *Lawlor v Nicol* (1898) 12 Man. L.R. 224; *Chapman Bros v Verco Bros & Co. Ltd* (1933) 49 C.L.R. 306; *Farnsworth v Federal Commr. of Taxation* (1949) 78 C.L.R. 504; *Crawford v Kingston* [1952] 4 D.L.R. 37 (cattle).

[91] See, *e.g.* U.C.C., Art. 7–207(2), replacing Uniform Warehouse Receipts Act, s.23; Canada Grain Act, R.S.C. 1985, c. G-10; Bulk Handling of Grain Act 1955 (as amended) (South Australia).

[92] [1989] 1 N.Z.L.R. 723; *cf. Good v Bruce* [1917] N.Z.L.R. 514 (butterfat delivered to producers' co-operative); *Caltex Oil (Australia) Pty Ltd v The Dredge "Willemstad"* (1976) 136 C.L.R. 529 at 561 (crude oil piped to refinery); *Re Coro (Canada) Inc.* (1997) 36 O.R. (3d.) 563 (gold used in electro-plating process); *Glencore International AG v Metro Trading Inc.* [2001] 1 All E.R. (Comm.) 103 (mixing of oil of different grades). See Watts, 106 L.Q.R. 552 (1990); Goode, *Proprietary Rights and Insolvency in Sales Transactions* (2nd ed.), pp.85 *et seq*; Hickey, 66 M.L.R. 368 (2003).

ing the fact that his coins would be mixed with other source-materials containing silver which belonged to the company itself. The Court of Appeal of New Zealand held that this was a contract *sui generis*, a contract of consensual intermixture under which each of the parties should be treated as having a proprietary interest in the mass of refined silver proportionate to his own contribution. The contract was not a bailment (at least as traditionally understood[93]), since there was no obligation to hold or deliver the original coins *in specie*, while *Randell's* case[94] was to be distinguished since in that case the miller's obligation to redeliver corn did not require that he should do so out of the original bulk or, indeed, from any particular source.

Mixed and substituted goods. In the cases discussed above it was held, or at least assumed, that a transaction could not be a bailment unless there was an obligation to redeliver or otherwise deal with the identical goods which the owner had delivered to the bailee. But recent decisions suggest that it may be necessary to qualify this view. In *Mercer v Craven Grain Storage Ltd*[95] growers deposited grain with the defendant (a co-operative society) where it was held in a commingled mass which was continually drawn upon whenever grain was sold and replenished as more grain was added. This was done pursuant to a contract between the society and each grower which provided that the grain deposited should remain the property of the farmer concerned until it was sold on his behalf. The House of Lords held that such an arrangement was not inconsistent with a bailment: title remained in such of the growers as were interested in the mix at any given time in proportion to their respective contributions to the bulk.[96] It thus appears to be recognised that there can be a bailment in which the bailee is authorised to substitute other goods for those bailed.[97] But it is doubtful whether a bailor's proprietary rights in such a situation would survive if at any time the bulk were to be totally depleted, even if other goods were immediately substituted.[98] **1–059**

---

[93] See below, para.1–059.
[94] (1869) L.R. 3 P.C. 101, above, para.1–057.
[95] [1994] C.L.C. 328; *Glencore International AG v Metro Trading Inc.* (above).
[96] Compare the position of the buyers of the wines which were physically segregated from the seller's trading stock (but not allocated to them individually) in *Re Stapylton Fletcher Ltd* [1994] 1 W.L.R. 1181 at 1200 and the "Walker & Hall claimants" in *Re Goldcorp Exchange Ltd* [1995] 1 A.C. 74: see below, para.5–130.
[97] Smith, 111 L.Q.R. 10 (1995). *Cf.* the arrangement known as "gratuitous quasi-bailment" or *mutuum*, where goods are loaned on the understanding that they are not to be returned *in specie* but replaced by equivalent goods. In *Wincanton Ltd v P. & O. Trans European Ltd* [2001] EWCA Civ 227; [2001] C.L.C. 962, it was held that the common law rules governing this concept applied only to consumable goods and not (*e.g.*) to pallets.
[98] In *Re Goldcorp Exchange Ltd* (above) part of the bulk had been wrongly disposed of and there was insufficient remaining to meet the claims of all those concerned. The court held that each claimant should recover only his proportionate part of the "lowest intermediate balance" of the bulk held by the appellant company at any time after his proprietary right arose. It would follow that all claims would be lost when the bulk was reduced to nil. See further Smith, *ibid*.

1–060 **Sale or bailment in manufacturing cases.**[99] A variation of the same question arises where goods are supplied to a manufacturer who uses them, together with goods of his own, to make a product which is then redelivered to the original supplier for a price or charge. Here (in the absence of any express agreement between the parties as to the title to the finished product[1]), if the principal materials are those of the supplier, the subordinate components vest in him by accession as the work progresses, and the contract overall is a *bailment* of the supplier's goods with a view to their improvement by the work and materials of the manufacturer.[2] If, in contrast, the principal materials are held to be those of the manufacturer, the contract is a *sale* of the finished product, the property in the supplier's goods being divested in the course of the work and later revested in him by the sale.[3]

A similar question may arise where it is understood that the finished product is to be sold by the manufacturer to third parties and that the price of the component will be paid, or may be paid, to the supplier only after the product itself has been paid for by its purchaser. The manufacturer in such a case may be a buyer of the component and a seller of the completed goods, and his obligation to the supplier will then be as a debtor for the price of the component (though the debt may be secured by some form of charge on the moneys received). Alternatively, he may agree that the property in the goods to be manufactured will be vested in the supplier throughout, and that he will sell it to the third party as the supplier's agent, and be accountable to him for the price.[4]

Where materials are supplied to a manufacturer for use in the making of a product which it is not intended shall be or become the property of the supplier, the agreement is inconsistent with a contract of bailment (at least once the materials have been so used) and is essentially one of sale and purchase. In these circumstances, a purported reservation of title to the component materials in favour of the supplier will be ineffective, and the supplier's title to it will cease to exist if it loses its identity in the manufacturing process.[5] What constitutes the "identity" of goods in this context is a matter of potential debate, which appears so far to have been determined on a purely impressionistic basis in the cases.[6]

---

[99] Webb [2000] J.B.L. 513.

[1] On the sale of goods with a reservation of title by the seller, see below, paras 5–141 *et seq.*

[2] *Jones v De Marchant* (1916) 28 D.L.R. 561 (furs made into coat).

[3] See *Dixon v London Small Arms Co.* (1876) 1 App.Cas. 632; above, para.1–044.

[4] *Aluminium Industrie Vaassen BV v Romalpa Aluminium Ltd* [1976] 1 W.L.R. 676; see below, paras 5–141 *et seq.* The supplier will not, however, be fully in the position of an undisclosed principal—*e.g.* he may not be liable on a warranty of quality: see [1976] 1 W.L.R. 676 at 690.

[5] *Borden (UK) Ltd v Scottish Timber Products Ltd* [1981] Ch. 25; see below, para.5–149; and *cf. Hendy Lennox (Industrial Engines) Ltd v Grahame Puttick Ltd* [1984] 1 W.L.R. 485 (component engine still identifiable).

[6] "Identity" has been held to have been lost in *Borden (UK) Ltd v Scottish Timber Products Ltd* (above) (resin used in the manufacture of chipboard); *Re Peachdart Ltd* [1984] Ch.131 (leather when cut into pieces ready to be made into handbags (*sed quaere*?)); *Modelboard Ltd v Outer Box Ltd (in liq.)* [1993] B.C.L.C. 623

A similar issue arises where goods are supplied for the purpose of being used in the construction of a building or otherwise being affixed to land, on terms whch purport to reserve title to the seller. Save in the exceptional case where the goods retain their separate identity as goods, notwithstanding that they are so affixed,[7] the supplier's property in the goods will be extinguished once the process of affixing is complete.[8]

Sale or bailment of sacks and other containers. It is a question of construction whether sacks, barrels, pallets, bottles and similar containers in or on which goods are sold are themselves the subject of a sale or are merely bailed to the buyer, remaining at all times the property of the seller or the original manufacturer.[9] It is not decisive of the issue that a charge is made for the non-return of the container, nor will the payment of such a charge necessarily transfer the ownership of the container to the person who pays it.[10] Nevertheless, where mineral water was sold to a buyer in bottles which were merely bailed and not sold, it was held that the bottle had been "supplied under a contract of sale" within the terms of what is now section 14(3) of the Sale of Goods Act 1979. There was therefore an implied condition that the bottle as well as its contents was reasonably fit for the buyer's purpose, entitling the latter to damages when the bottle exploded.[11] **1–061**

Bailment incidental to contract of sale. The decision in *South Australian Insurance Co. Ltd v Randell*[12] shows that where there has been a sale of goods and the property has passed to the buyer, it is not possible to regard **1–062**

(cardboard made into boxes); *Chaigley Farms Ltd v Crawford, Kaye & Grayshire Ltd* [1996] B.C.C. 957 (carcasses of slaughtered animals); *ICI New Zealand Ltd v Agnew* [1998] 2 N.Z.L.R. 129 (plastic pallets made into containers by process in theory reversible). The *Chaigley Farms* case is at odds with *Re Weddel New Zealand Ltd* [1996] 5 N.Z.B.L.C. 104, 055 (reversed on other grounds [1997] 2 N.Z.L.R. 455), where the New Zealand court gave effect to the intention of the parties that the property in animals sent for slaughter should remain with the sellers, not only in the carcasses but even after the meat had been further processed. See also *Pongakawa Sawmill Ltd v New Zealand Forest Products Ltd* [1992] 3 N.Z.L.R. 304 (seller of logs held to have retained property after they had been sawn into timber).

[7] *e.g.*, perhaps, an identifiable machine installed in a factory, or a statue erected in a garden (*Cf. Rawlinson v Mort* (1905) 93 L.T. 555 (organ built into church remained property of donor)). The seller's claim in some such cases might not, however, prevail against a subsequent purchaser or mortgagee of the land who was unaware of the reservation of title.

[8] *Charles Henshaw & Sons Ltd v Antlerport Ltd* [1995] C.L.C. 1312 at 1322 ("incorporation of immovable property into the structure of a building is normally wholly destructive of any reversionary right of the seller of the components"). *Cf. Whenuapai Joinery (1988) Ltd v Trust Bank Central Ltd* [1994] 1 N.Z.L.R. 406 (joinery built into house).

[9] *Cantrell & Cochrane Ltd v Neeson* [1926] N.I. 107; *Barlow & Co. v Hanslip* [1926] N.I. 113n.; *cf. William Leitch & Co. Ltd v Leydon* [1931] A.C. 90; *Beecham Foods Ltd v North Supplies (Edmonton) Ltd* [1959] 1 W.L.R. 643. See also *Manders v Williams* (1849) 4 Exch. 339, where containers were bailed subject to the option of the supplier to treat them as sold to the consignee if not returned.

[10] *Barlow & Co. v Hanslip*, above.

[11] *Geddling v Marsh* [1920] 1 K.B. 668; below, para.11–030.

[12] (1869) L.R. 3 P.C. 101, above, para.1–057.

the transaction as a bailment, even if the buyer is bound at a later date to reconvey similar goods. It does not follow, however, that a bailment is inconsistent with particular stages of a contract of sale: indeed, it is very common for the owner of goods to bail them to another, with a view to his buying them, or for a person who has sold goods to agree to retain them on the buyer's behalf. Where goods are delivered on "sale or return," or let on hire-purchase, there is a bailment of the goods until the option to buy is exercised, when the transaction becomes a sale. Similarly, a person who has agreed to buy goods and has been given possession may be regarded as a bailee of the goods until the property passes to him[13] and this is an important feature of many contracts where the seller reserves title under a "Romalpa" clause.[14] The Sale of Goods Act 1979[15] expressly recognises that either a seller or a buyer may be a bailee of the goods of the other party in the course of a contract of sale.

1–063 **Sale distinguished from pledge.** A pledge[16] is a bailment—that is, a delivery of possession—of goods, or of documents of title to goods, in order to secure a debt. The creation of a charge over goods or documents of title or the proceeds of goods, without any delivery of possession (which is sometimes called a hypothecation[17]) is operative in equity only.

A pledge differs from other bailments and from possessory liens in that the pledgee has a common law right, in the event of default in payment of the debt of the pledgor, to sell the goods without first obtaining the authority of the court. For this reason, the pledgee is sometimes said to have a "special property" in the goods[18]; and a pledge is then defined as a transfer by the owner of this "special property" in the goods, in contrast with a sale, where the "absolute property" is transferred.[19] This use of the term "special property" has been criticised.[20]

By section 2 of the Sale of Goods Act 1979, a sale is defined as a transfer of "the property" in goods—that is, "the general property in goods, and not

---

[13] *Motor Mart Ltd v Webb* [1958] N.Z.L.R. 773; *cf.* Consumer Credit Act 1974, s.189(1), "hire-purchase agreement".
[14] *Aluminium Industrie Vaassen BV v Romalpa Aluminium Ltd* [1976] 1 W.L.R. 676; below, paras 5–141 *et seq*.
[15] s.20.
[16] See *Chitty on Contracts* (29th ed.), Vol. 2, paras 33–118 *et seq.*; Palmer and Hudson in Palmer and McKendrick, (eds) *Interests in Goods* (2nd ed.), Ch.24.
[17] *Ryall v Rowles* (1749) 9 Bli.(N.S.) 377; *Ex p. North Western Bank* (1872) L.R. 15 Eq. 69.
[18] *The Odessa* [1916] 1 A.C. 145 at 158–159; *cf. Harper v Godsell* (1870) L.R. 5 Q.B. 422 at 426. The term "special property" (or "a" property as distinct from "the" property) is also used to refer to the interest of a bailee, or other person having an immediate right to possession, which entitles him to sue for conversion or other wrongful interference with the goods: see *Nyberg v Handelaar* [1892] 2 Q.B. 202. *Cf.* also *Giles v Grover* (1832) 6 Bli. N.S. 277 at 292–293 (sheriff's interest in goods seized).
[19] *Sewell v Burdick* (1884) 10 App.Cas. 74 at 93; *cf.* the view of Bowen L.J. in the court below, (1884) 13 Q.B.D. 159 at 175.
[20] *The Odessa*, above, where the expression "special interest" is suggested as more appropriate.

merely a special property."[21] It follows that neither the pledge itself, nor an assignment of his interest by the pledgee to a third party, can be a sale of goods. The pledgor, however, retains the general property, which he may transfer to a third party subject to the rights of the pledgee. This is not merely the assignment of a chose in action; it may properly be termed a sale of the goods.[22]

Sale distinguished from other transactions by way of security. In a pledge, it is possession of the goods which is given to the creditor as security, coupled with the power to sell them in the event of default. Possession is the security also in a *lien*, where a person who is already a bailee of goods or documents belonging to another is given a right, either by law or pursuant to an agreement between the parties, to retain them until a claim against the owner is satisfied. The right of a lien-holder, in contrast with that of a pledgee, is usually lost if he voluntarily parts with possession, and it is not assignable. Since there is no transfer of the property in the goods, a lien is plainly distinguishable from a sale. 1–064

Sections 39 and 41 to 43 of the Sale of Goods Act 1979 confer on an unpaid seller of goods a lien or a right of withholding delivery until payment or tender of the price.[23]

In a *mortgage* of goods, the legal title to the goods is transferred to a creditor in order to secure the debt. It resembles a sale in that the general property in the goods passes; but whereas in a sale it passes absolutely, so that the buyer becomes the owner and the seller has no further interest in the goods, in a mortgage the mortgagor is entitled to redeem: that is, to have the goods retransferred to him upon payment of the debt. There is a continuing relationship of debtor and creditor throughout the currency of the mortgage, with both parties retaining an interest in the goods until either the debt is paid or the security is realised upon default.[24]

But confusion can arise where a transfer of property which is really intended to operate as a security is expressed unconditionally, so as to appear an outright sale. Again, a sale which is coupled with another transaction, such as an agreement or option to repurchase, or a bailment of the goods (and especially a letting on hire-purchase) back to the seller, may have the same practical consequences as a loan on security. Such transactions may be affected by two statutory provisions: first, the Sale of Goods Act 1979, section 62(4), which expressly excludes from its application "a transaction in the form of a contract of sale which is intended to operate by way of . . . security"; and secondly the Bills of Sale Act of 1882,[25] which

---

[21] s.61(1), "property". For a full discussion of the meaning of this term as is used in the Act, see Battersby and Preston (1972) 35 M.L.R. 268. The use of this term also prevents a contract for the creation or assignment of, *e.g.* a life interest in goods from being a contract of sale: see the article cited, at p.271.

[22] *Franklin v Neate* (1844) 13 M. & W. 481.

[23] Below, paras 15–001 *et seq.*, 15–028 *et seq.*

[24] The differences are explored in such cases as *Beckett v Tower Assets Co. Ltd* [1891] 1 Q.B. 1, on appeal, [1891] 1 Q.B. 638; *Gavin's Trustee v Fraser*, 1920 S.C. 674. See also *Cushing v Dupuy* (1880) 5 App.Cas. 409 (apparent sale really a mortgage, but referred to inaccurately as a pledge).

[25] Above, para.1–016.

requires all documents granting a security over goods, in circumstances where the grantor retains possession, to be in due form and registered, failing which the security is declared void.

1–065 **Apparent sale intended to operate as security.** The provisions of the Sale of Goods Act 1979 relating to contracts of sale do not apply to a transaction in the form of a contract of sale which is intended to operate by way of mortgage, pledge, charge or other security.[26] Since any transaction coming within these terms will almost certainly[27] be caught by the Bills of Sale Act of 1882,[28] it is not surprising that there is no English decision about the meaning or effect of the section.[29] Such a bargain would be void unless it complied with the formal and other requirements of the Act of 1882, in which case it would not be "in the form of a contract of sale". In Scotland, however, the section is of real significance, since it is only under the Sale of Goods Act 1979 that there can be a transfer of the ownership of goods without delivery. It is therefore vital for an assignee of goods who has not been given possession to show that there has been a genuine sale, governed by the Act, and not a transaction caught by section 62(4) which would be ineffective under Scots common law.[30]

1–066 **Sale part of composite arrangement.** A sale, even when coupled with an agreement or option to repurchase the goods sold, is theoretically distinct from a transaction by way of security, for there is no continuing relationship of debtor and creditor. Nevertheless, such a composite arrangement approximates in its effect to the giving of a loan on security and may be used to cloak an intention to create a security. This is particularly true of a sale followed by a letting-back of the goods to the seller, under a contract of hire or a hire-purchase agreement[31] either directly or through a nominee. If such *de facto* security transactions were upheld by the courts, the restrictions of the Bills of Sale Act of 1882 would be evaded: but the courts

---

[26] Sale of Goods Act 1979, s.62(4); *cf. Lloyds & Scottish Finance Ltd v Cyril Lord Carpets Sales Ltd* [1992] B.C.L.C. 609 (book-debts).

[27] There are, however, some transactions to which the Act of 1882 does not apply—*e.g.* those relating to ships—which could conceivably be affected by s.62(4).

[28] Or, in the case of a company, by the provisions of Pt XII of the Companies Act 1985.

[29] Note, however, *Joblin v Watkins & Roseveare (Motors) Ltd* [1949] 1 All E.R. 47 (purported sale with option to repurchase at a higher price held a device to give temporary financial accommodation, and not a "sale" within Factors Act 1889, s.2(1)); and see *Re Curtain Dream plc.* [1990] B.C.L.C. 925 (sale and resale back to seller held a charge).

[30] The principal Scottish cases are: *Robertson v Hall's Trustee* (1896) 24 R. (Ct.Sess.) 120; *Jones & Co.'s Trustee v Allan* (1901) 4 F. (Ct.Sess.) 374; *Rennet v Mathieson* (1903) 5 F. (Ct.Sess.) 591; *Hepburn v Law*, 1914 S.C. 918; *Gavin's Trustee v Fraser*, 1920 S.C. 674; *Newbigging v Ritchie's Trustee*, 1930 S.C. 273; *Scottish Transit Trust Ltd v Scottish Land Cultivators Ltd*, 1955 S.C. 254; *G. & C. Finance Corp. Ltd v Brown*, 1961 S.L.T. 408; *Ladbroke Leasing Ltd v Reekie Plant Ltd* 1983 S.L.T. 155; *Armour v Thyssen Edelstahlwerke AG* [1991] 2 A.C. 339.

[31] See Diamond, 23 M.L.R. 399, 516 (1960); Guest, *The Law of Hire-Purchase* (1966), Ch. 4; Goode, *Law of Hire-Purchase* (2nd ed.), pp.78 *et seq.*; Fitzpatrick, [1969] J.B.L. 211; Spink and Ong [2004] C.L.J. 199.

have always had regard to the reality of the position rather than the form or literal wording of the documents in determining the scope of the Act of 1882, and arrangements of this kind have been held void on many occasions. However, the attitude of the courts has not been invariably fatal to such transactions. Depending on the "true intention" of the parties (to be ascertained not only from the principal document but also from any collateral agreement and also by parol evidence) the bargain may either be struck down as a concealed loan on security or upheld as a genuine composite transaction taking effect according to its tenor.[32] The decisions of the courts have been summarised by Cairns J. in *North Central Wagon Finance Co. v Brailsford*[33] as follows:

> "1. If a person deliberately, and with a clear understanding of what he is doing, and with all appropriate formalities, sells his property to a finance company and then hires it back under a hire-purchase agreement, the agreement is not a bill of sale.[34] 2. If the purpose of the transaction is to enable the hirer to dispose of the property to a customer, the courts will the more readily hold that the agreement is not a bill of sale.[35] 3. If the hire-purchase agreement is a mere device to cloak a loan, the document is a bill of sale.[36] 4. In considering whether the real transaction is one of loan it is necessary to look behind the documents to discover its true nature.[37] 5. If the facts are not truly stated in the documents, this is a circumstance tending to show that the documents are a mere cloak."[38]

The task of determining the "true intention" of the parties is not made easier by the fact that the interpretations between which the court must choose are not mutually exclusive: very often, the parties will have intended *both* to raise money on the security of the goods *and* to do so by the sale and hiring back of the goods. It is scarcely surprising that the actual decisions are difficult to reconcile, and that no universally applicable criteria for distinguishing the two situations have been formulated.[39]

---

[32] *Re Lovegrove* [1935] Ch.464 at 495–496.
[33] [1962] 1 W.L.R. 1288 at 1292.
[34] *Yorkshire Ry Wagon Co. Ltd v Maclure* (1882) 21 Ch.D. 309; *British Ry Traffic & Electric Co. v Kahn* [1921] W.N. 52.
[35] *Staffs. Motor Guarantee Ltd v British Wagon Co. Ltd* [1934] 2 K.B. 305.
[36] *Yorkshire Ry Wagon Co. Ltd v Maclure* (1882) 21 Ch.D. 309 at 317.
[37] *Polsky v S & A Services Ltd* [1951] 1 All E.R. 185, 1062n.
[38] *Polsky v S & A Services Ltd*, above, at p.189; *cf. Re George Inglefield Ltd* [1933] Ch. 1 at 27–28 (book-debts).
[39] See, in addition to the cases mentioned in nn.32 to 38, above: *Re Robertson* (1878) 9 Ch.D. 419; *Crawcour v Salter* (1881) 18 Ch.D. 30; *Re Gelder* [1881] W.N. 37; *Manchester, Sheffield and Lincolnshire Ry v North Central Wagon Co.* (1888) 13 App.Cas. 554; *Redhead v Westwood* (1889) 59 L.T. 293; *Re Yarrow* (1889) 61 L.T. 642; *United Forty Pound Loan Club v Bexton* (1890) [1891] 1 Q.B. 28n.; *Re Watson* (1890) 25 Q.B.D. 27; *Madell v Thomas & Co.* [1891] 1 Q.B. 230; *McEntire v Crossley Bros Ltd* [1895] A.C. 457; *Victoria Dairy Co. of Worthing v West* (1895) 11 T.L.R. 233; *Clapham v Ives* (1904) 91 L.T. 69; *Maas v Pepper* [1905] A.C. 102; *Prudential Mortgage Co. Ltd v Marylebone BC* (1910) 8 L.G.R. 901; *British Ry Traffic and Electric Co. v West (HA) & Co. Ltd* (1921), Jones and Proudfoot, *Notes on Hire-*

It is possible to detect in the reported cases a trend towards upholding these transactions as genuine. This, coupled with the fact that the issue is nowadays less frequently litigated, may suggest that the sale and lease-back has come to be accepted, at least in a commercial context, as a standard form of transaction.

1–067 **Sale distinguished from transactions not fully consensual.** It is not every transaction involving a transfer of property and a payment that constitutes a sale. A sale is always a consensual transaction; even when the word "sale" is used in the narrower sense of a pure conveyance, there is necessarily an antecedent or contemporaneous agreement to sell. There must be mutual assent, in the objective sense in which this expression is always understood in the law of contract, to all the elements which make up a sale.[40] The seller must agree to transfer the property and the buyer to take it, and they must agree to do so in return for money which is paid and received *as the price* of the goods. Where the consent of the parties does not extend so far, or does not exist at all, there is no sale. Such transactions or events are sometimes termed "quasi-contracts of sale" or "implied contracts of sale",[41] but there is no true analogy with a contract of sale properly so called, and the Sale of Goods Act is not applicable to them.[42] Examples are given in the paragraphs which follow.

1–068 **Transfer of property pursuant to award.** An *award* that one party to an arbitration shall deliver goods to the other on being paid a certain sum is not a sale of goods. It is not effective in itself to transfer the property, even though the money is tendered, without the assent of the first party to transfer it,[43] and perhaps not until actual delivery. The party claiming the goods has no proprietary claim in respect of them: his sole remedy is on the award.

Purchase Law (2nd ed.), p.87; *Colchester Motor Hire-Purchase Co. Ltd v Wragge* (1923), Jones and Proudfoot, *op. cit.*, p.90; *Elsey & Co. Ltd v Palmer* (1924), Jones and Proudfoot, *op. cit.*, p.99; *Motor Trade Finance Ltd v H.E. Motors Ltd*, unreported HL, March 26, 1926; *King v Chester & Cole Ltd* (1928), Jones and Proudfoot, *op. cit.*, p.102; *Automobile and General Finance Corp. Ltd v Morris* (1929) 73 S.J. 451; *Modern Light Cars Ltd v Seals* [1934] 1 K.B. 32; *Olds Discount Co. Ltd v Krett* [1940] 2 K.B. 117; *Re Apex Supply Co. Ltd* [1942] Ch. 108; *R. v Deller* (1952) 36 Cr.App.R. 184; *Spencer v North Country Finance Co. Ltd* [1963] C.L.Y. 212; *Stoneleigh Finance Ltd v Phillips* [1965] 2 Q.B. 537; *Bennett v Griffin Finance Ltd* [1967] 2 Q.B. 46; *Kingsley v Sterling Industrial Securities Ltd* [1967] 2 Q.B. 747; *Snook v London & West Riding Investments Ltd* [1967] 2 Q.B. 768; *Re Curtain Dream Plc.* [1990] B.C.L.C. 925; *Dodds v Yorkshire Bank Finance* [1992] C.C.L.R. 92; contrast *Welsh Development Agency v Export Finance Co. Ltd* [1992] B.C.L.C. 148 (goods bought by finance company and then resold by seller acting as its agent: transaction upheld as genuine and not a charge).

[40] Exceptionally, the amount of the price may be left undetermined, in which case s.8(2) of the Act declares that the buyer must pay a reasonable price: see below, para.2–047.

[41] This use of the expression "implied contract of sale" must be distinguished from that where the parties' agreement is inferred from their conduct. Such a transaction is a true sale, as is recognised by s.3 of the Act: see below, para.2–008.

[42] Nor, it would appear, would the Supply of Goods and Services Act 1982 apply to such non-consensual transactions: Atiyah, *The Sale of Goods* (11th ed.), p.9.

[43] *Hunter v Rice* (1812) 15 East 100.

Transfer of property on payment of indemnity. Where, under a contract of indemnity, one person compensates another for the total loss or destruction of a thing, all rights in respect of the thing are ceded by operation of law to the indemnifier by the person compensated.[44] But this transaction does not amount to a sale of the thing or of such rights to the indemnifier: the property passes merely as an incident in the performance of the contract of indemnity, by virtue of the doctrine of subrogation. 1–069

Compulsory acquisition of goods. Where property is compulsorily acquired pursuant to an authority conferred by statute there is no "sale" of the property, even though compensation is payable and its amount may be fixed by negotiation between the parties. The expression "compulsory purchase" commonly used in this connection is misleading.[45] 1–070

Supply of goods under a public duty. The supply of goods pursuant to a statutory obligation or other public duty has been held not to be a sale of such goods, even though the person to whom they are supplied is required to make a payment. It was held by the House of Lords in *Pfizer Corp. v Ministry of Health*[46] that the supply of drugs or appliances to a member of the public under the National Health Service scheme, whether by a hospital or a pharmacist, was not a sale, although a prescription charge was paid in return.[47] Lord Reid said[48]: ". . . in my opinion there is no sale in this case. Sale is a consensual contract requiring agreement, express or implied. In the present case there appears to me to be no need for any agreement. The patient has a statutory right to demand the drug on payment of two shillings. The hospital has a statutory obligation to supply it on such payment. And if the prescription is presented to a chemist he appears to be bound by his contract with the appropriate authority[49] to supply the drug on receipt of such payment. There is no need for any agreement between the patient and either the hospital or the chemist, and there is certainly no room for bargaining." 1–071

---

[44] *Rankin v Potter* (1873) L.R. 6 H.L. 83 at 118; *cf. Stewart v Greenock Marine Insce. Co.* (1847) 2 H.L.C. 159 at 183.
[45] *Kirkness v John Hudson & Co. Ltd* [1955] A.C. 696 (compulsory acquisition of railway wagons under Transport Act 1947, s.29); *cf. Minister of Finance v Kicking Horse Forest Products Ltd* (1975) 57 D.L.R. (3d) 220 (timber).
[46] [1965] A.C. 512.
[47] Since the transaction is not consensual, the Supply of Goods and Services Act 1982 will also not apply. However, if the goods supplied are defective, there may be liability under the Consumer Protection Act 1987: below, para.14–080; *cf. X v Schering Health Care Ltd* [2002] EWHC 1420; (2003] 70 B.M.L.R. 88.
[48] [1965] A.C. 512 at 535–536.
[49] The contract between the pharmacist and the National Health Service executive council has been held to be one for services and not a contract of sale: *Appleby v Sleep* [1968] 1 W.L.R. 948.

On the same reasoning, the supply of electricity,[50] gas[51] or water by a public authority[52] is not a "sale" of such commodities, so that, independently of any question whether the term "goods" is appropriate,[53] the Sale of Goods Act does not apply. There is no *contractual* obligation on which an action may be brought against the authority for failure to make the supply available or to provide a supply fit for the purpose of the consumer.[54] Whether such an action will lie under the statute depends upon its terms.[55] Furthermore, it would be open to the parties to supplement their arrangement by a collateral contract; and it should be noted that in some circumstances (*e.g.* under the Gas Code, para.8[56]) the parties are deemed to have entered into a contract. A remedy may also be available in negligence.[57]

1–072 **Satisfaction of judgment in tort.**[58] An action of trespass, conversion or other wrongful interference with goods may in appropriate circumstances be brought by the owner of goods against a person who has wrongfully dealt with or detained them. Where in such a case judgment is given for damages on the footing that the claimant is being compensated for the whole of his interest in the goods, and the defendant satisfies the judgment, the property or interest of the plaintiff in the goods will pass by operation of law to the defendant.[59] But an *unsatisfied* judgment in such an action

---

[50] For the terms on which a supply of electricity is made to a customer, see the Electricity Act 1989, ss.16–17 and Sch.6 (as substituted by the Utilities Act 2000, ss.44, 51 and Sch.4).

[51] In a similar way, the Gas Act 1986, s.10 and Sch.2B (in part as substituted by the Utilities Act 2000, ss.80, 84) prescribes terms for the supply of gas.

[52] It is not relevant for this purpose whether the supplier is a public body or a corporation (whether publicly or privately owned): see, *e.g.* the cases concerning gas and waterworks companies referred to in n.54, *infra*.

[53] See below, para.1–085. In *East Midlands Electricity Board v Grantham* [1980] C.L.Y. 271 the supply of electricity was regarded as a supply of services.

[54] *Milnes v Huddersfield Corp.* (1886) 11 App.Cas. 511 at 523; *Re Richmond Gas Co. & Richmond (Surrey) Corp.* [1893] 1 Q.B. 56 at 59; *Clegg Parkinson Co. v Earby Gas Co.* [1896] 1 Q.B. 592 at 595; *Read v Croydon Corp.* [1938] 4 All E.R. 631 at 648–649; *Willmore v South Eastern Electricity Board* [1957] 2 Lloyd's Rep. 375 at 380; *cf. Malone v Metropolitan Police Commissioner* [1979] Ch. 344 at 375 (supply of telephone services not contractual).

[55] Compare *Read v Croydon Corp.*, above, with *Atkinson v Newcastle & Gateshead Waterworks Co.* (1877) 2 Ex.D. 441 and *Willmore v South Eastern Electricity Board*, above.

[56] Gas Act 1986, Sch. 2B.

[57] *Read v Croydon Corp.*, above. Alternatively, the buyer may bring an action for breach of statutory duty under the Consumer Protection Act 1987.

[58] In the original Sale of Goods Bill, cl. 2, this type of transaction was to have been treated as a sale of the goods from the plaintiff to the defendant as from the time when the judgment was satisfied: Chalmers, *Sale of Goods* (1st ed., 1890), p.5.

[59] Torts (Interference with Goods) Act 1977, s.5. This section reaffirms and amplifies the rules of common law, although in terms it refers only to the "extinguishment" of the claimant's title and not also to the consequential vesting of that title in the wrongdoer. For the effect of contributory negligence, see s.5(1)(b); and for the position where the damages paid are limited by virtue of an enactment or rule of law to a lesser amount, see s.5(3). Decisions at common law include *Anon.*, in Jenkins, *Eight Centuries of Reports*, 4th cent., case 88 (trespass); *Adams v*

does not pass the property,[60] nor will a satisfied judgment for less than the full value.[61] A settlement of a claim for damages for wrongful interference has the same effect as a satisfied judgment.[62]

In some cases also, a bailee of goods may bring an action against a wrongdoer by virtue of his right of possession, and may recover the full value of the goods.[63] The effect of a payment by the defendant which satisfies such a judgment is to extinguish altogether the *owner's* property in the goods and to vest it in the defendant. The payment of damages to the bailee is in this case a complete defence to the wrongdoer in any subsequent action by the owner, whose only remedy is to recover from the bailee the proceeds of the action as representing the goods, or the surplus over and above the value of the bailee's interest, as the case may be.[64]

If the wrongdoer has disposed of the goods to a third party and is then sued for the tort, the effect of a satisfied judgment in the action between owner and tortfeasor will be to pass the property in the goods to the third party. In none of these situations, however, is there a true sale.

Waiver of tort. Where a person obtains possession of the goods of another and wrongfully sells them to a third party, the owner has alternative remedies in tort and for restitution available against each of the other parties. He may, as has been seen, recover the value of the goods in an action of tort, and in such a case the satisfaction of a judgment by either of the other parties will effect a transfer of the property in the goods by operation of law to the defendant or to any person claiming through him. He may also "waive the tort" and recover judgment for the value of the goods in an action for money had and received brought against either party,[65] or for the proceeds of the wrongful sale in a similar action against 1–073

Broughton (1737) 2 Str. 1078 (trover); *Cooper v Shepherd* (1846) 3 C.B. 266 (trover); *Hiort v London & North Western Ry Co.* (1879) 4 Ex.D. 188 at 199 (conversion); *Eberle's Hotels & Restaurant Co. v Jones* (1887) 18 Q.B.D. 459 at 468 (detinue); *United States of America v Dollfus Mieg et Cie* [1952] A.C. 582 at 622 (conversion). See also the following cases, where the principle was applied when the claim was for the value of the plaintiff's interest in the goods although this was less than their full value: *Brierly v Kendall* (1852) 17 Q.B. 937; *Chinery v Viall* (1860) 5 H. & N. 288; *Mulliner v Florence* (1878) 3 Q.B.D. 484; *Belsize Motor Supply Co. v Cox* [1914] 1 K.B. 244; *Whitely v Hilt* [1918] 2 K.B. 808.

[60] *Marston v Phillips* (1863) 9 L.T. 289 (trover); *Brinsmead v Harrison* (1871) L.R. 6 C.P. 584, affd. (1872) L.R. 7 C.P. 547 (trover); *Ex p. Drake* (1877) 5 Ch.D. 866 (detinue); *Re Scarth* (1874) 10 Ch.App. 234 (detinue); *Ellis v John Stenning & Son* [1932] 2 Ch. 81 (conversion). If, in an action for wrongful interference, the plaintiff recovers the property itself, an alternative judgment for its value becomes inoperative: *Ellis v John Stenning & Son*, above, at p.90.

[61] *Morris v Robinson* (1824) 3 B. & C. 196 at 206–207. See also below, para.4–012.

[62] Torts (Interference with Goods) Act 1977, s.5(1), (2).

[63] *Nicolls v Bastard* (1835) 2 Cr.M. & R. 659 at 660; *The Winkfield* [1902] P. 42 at 60; *Eastern Construction Co. Ltd v National Trust Co. Ltd* [1914] A.C. 197 at 209–211. By virtue of the Torts (Interference with Goods) Act 1977, s.8, however, the bailee would now in most cases be required to identify the owner and his interest, so that the defendant could seek to join him as a third party to the proceedings, and in that event the full value of the goods would not be awarded to the bailee.

[64] *Turner v Hardcastle* (1862) 11 C.B.(N.S.) 683 at 708; *Swire v Leach* (1865) 18 C.B.(N.S.) 492; *The Winkfield*, above.

[65] *Morris v Robinson* (1824) 3 B. & C. 196 (buyer); *Nicol v Hennessey* (1896) 44 W.R. 584 (seller).

the seller.[66] It is plain that the *satisfaction* of a judgment for the full value of the goods would operate to transfer the title as in a tort action; but there are suggestions, especially in some early cases, that the election to waive the tort and to proceed by way of an action for money had and received is in itself an affirmation or adoption of a wrongful or supposed contract of sale, taking effect (it is variously suggested) when the action is brought, or when judgment is obtained or at least consented to by the plaintiff. One apparent consequence of such an election would be that the property would pass by virtue of the sale so adopted, without the need for a satisfied judgment. These opinions must now all be reconsidered in the light of the decision of the House of Lords in *United Australia Ltd v Barclays Bank Ltd*.[67] In this case it was held that a bank was liable in damages for the conversion of a cheque collected by it on behalf of a wrongdoer, notwithstanding that the holder of the cheque had first proceeded without success against the wrongdoer for the amount of the cheque as money had and received to its use. Nothing short of judgment and satisfaction in the first action would amount to a bar to a second action against a different defendant. The so-called waiver of tort was purely fictional, a device which as a matter of pleading allowed a plaintiff in an earlier period to choose the more advantageous restitutionary remedy. It is therefore authoritatively settled that merely to bring an action for restitution is not an adoption or affirmation of a sale in any realistic sense, and cannot have the effect of passing the property to the defendant. Nor will such a consequence follow from *obtaining* a judgment without satisfaction: confusion is caused here by the fact that to obtain a judgment on one ground bars an action on a different ground, but the same facts, against the *same party*, on the principle of *res judicata*.[68] The decision in the *United Australia* case makes it plain that the property remains in the plaintiff until there is a satisfied judgment.

1–074 **Ratification of unauthorised sale distinguished.** The waiver of tort in the *United Australia*[69] case was a pure fiction: there was no act on the part of the wrongdoer which could in reality have been ratified by the claimant as having been performed on his behalf. But the House of Lords distinguished the situation where a true ratification is in fact possible, *e.g.* where the wrongdoer is the agent or bailee of the claimant. In this case the acts of the claimant *may* amount to an election to affirm an unauthorised contract of sale made by or with the defendant, with the effect that he is divested of the property in his goods in favour of the buyer because he has adopted the sale as his own. "If the [claimant] in truth treats the wrongdoer as having acted as his agent, overlooks the wrong, and by consent of both parties is content to receive the proceeds this will be a true waiver. It will arise necessarily where the [claimant] ratifies in the true sense an unauthorised act of an agent: in that case the lack of authority disappears,

[66] *Lamine v Dorrell* (1705) 2 Ld.Raym. 1216; *Phillips v Homfray* (1883) 24 Ch.D. 439 at 462.
[67] [1941] A.C. 1.
[68] *Lamine v Dorrell*, above; *Hitchin v Campbell* (1772) 2 Wm.Bl. 827; *United Australia Ltd v Barclays Bank Ltd*, above, at p.28.
[69] *United Australia Ltd v Barclays Bank Ltd* [1941] A.C. 1.

and the correct view is not that the tort is waived, but by retroaction of the ratification has never existed."[70] What will amount to an act of ratification will depend on the facts.

In *Bradley & Cohn Ltd v Ramsay & Co.*[71] opals were delivered by the claimants on approval to one Braun, the price asked being £750. Braun then purported to sell them to the defendants, who acted in good faith, for £300. The claimants first took proceedings against Braun for £750, or alternatively for the return of the stones or damages, and consented to judgment for £750 which was, in effect, a judgment for the price of the stones. It was held that their act in consenting to judgment in this form amounted to an acknowledgment that the goods had been sold to Braun, so that the claimants had no right to bring a further action in conversion against the defendants. In *Verschures Creameries Ltd v Hull & Netherlands S.S. Co. Ltd*,[72] the defendants, who were carriers, disregarded instructions from the claimants not to deliver certain goods to a customer to whom they had been consigned. The claimants invoiced the goods to the customer and later sued him and recovered judgment for the price of the goods. When they failed to get satisfaction, they endeavoured to hold the defendants responsible in tort for the misdelivery, but they were held to be barred from this course by their election to treat the goods as sold, which implied a ratification of the unauthorised delivery.

The contrast between these cases and the *United Australia* case is plain: the owner of goods is not deemed to adopt a sale made by a fraudulent stranger, or thief, merely because he sues him for the proceeds as money had and received[73]; he must, by claiming a price or otherwise, have ratified a sale that could in reality have been his own.

Transfer of title to goods by non-owner. In a number of situations, 1–075
power is given by law to a person who is not the owner of goods to confer a good title to those goods upon a person who buys them from him. This topic forms the subject of Chapter 7 of this work. For the purposes of the Sale of Goods Act 1979, the transaction between these two parties themselves is a contract of sale of goods.[74] However, as between the former owner, who loses his title to the goods in the process of such a transaction, and the buyer of the goods, who gains it, the absence of any consensual element will prevent the situation from being a sale within the statutory meaning, except in the rare case where by agreement, implication or estoppel the person selling does so, or is deemed to do so, as the former owner's agent.[75]

---

[70] *ibid.* at p.28.
[71] (1912) 106 L.T. 771.
[72] [1921] 2 K.B. 608.
[73] See the opinion of Lord Atkin [1941] A.C. 1 at 28.
[74] This is plain from the language of ss.21–25 of the Act.
[75] *e.g.* where the seller sells as agent of necessity (below, para.3–006), or under a power to sell *as agent* conferred upon the holder of a lien or other security, and probably also in at least some situations "where the owner of the goods is by his conduct precluded from denying the seller's authority to sell" (s.21(1), below, paras 7–008 *et seq.*).

1–076 **Transactions involving persons subject to incapacity.** Where necessaries are sold and delivered to a minor or to a person who by reason of drunkenness is incompetent to contract, the Sale of Goods Act 1979 provides that he must pay a reasonable price for them.[76] A body of opinion at the present time favours the view that the obligation to pay a reasonable price is restitutionary and not contractual in nature.[77] If this view is correct, it could be argued that such transactions (and *a fortiori*, contracts by such persons for non-necessaries) are not "contracts for the sale of goods" within the meaning of the Act, by reason of the lack of full consent. But it is submitted that a minor, though not liable to be *sued* on his contract or to have it enforced against him, has, subject to certain limitations, a capacity to make and to perform it; he *can* effectively buy and sell[78]; and he can therefore rely on such provisions of the Act as are consistent with this. Section 3 itself virtually assumes this by its use of the expression "*sold* and delivered". Certainly there are decided cases in which the Act has been applied to a minor's contract without question.[79]

1–077 **Sale of goods distinguished from licence to use goods subject to intellectual property rights.** A common feature of contracts for the supply of a computer program or intellectual property of a similar kind is that, although such a contract may include a sale of goods (*e.g.* in the form of a hardware system or a computer disk),[80] an essential part of the transaction is a licence to use the program granted by the owner of the copyright (who need not be the seller of the goods) to the buyer. Where the seller is not the owner of the copyright, there will be a separate contract between the owner and the buyer in which the seller acts as the owner's agent. Where he is the owner, the question whether the licence is incidental to the sale or an independent part of a composite transaction will be a matter for construction by the court.

4. SUBJECT-MATTER OF THE CONTRACT

(a) *Goods*

1–078 **Meaning of "goods".** Section 61(1) provides that "'goods' includes all personal chattels other than things in action and money, and in Scotland all corporeal moveables except money; and in particular 'goods' includes

[76] s.3(2); (as amended by the Mental Capacity Act 2005, Sched 6, para.24) see below, paras 2–028 *et seq*. A similar provision is contained in s.7 of the Mental Capacity Act 2005 with respect to a person who lacks capacity to contract.
[77] See *Chitty on Contracts* (29th ed.), Vol. 1, paras 8–011, 30–190 *et seq.*; *Anson's Law of Contract* (28th ed.), pp.222–226; Cheshire, Fifoot and Furmston, *The Law of Contract* (14th ed.), pp.480, 741. Contrast Treitel, *The Law of Contract* (11th ed.), pp.541–543; Goff and Jones, *The Law of Restitution* (6th ed.), para.25–003.
[78] The question is more fully examined below, para.2–032.
[79] See, *e.g. Godley v Perry* [1960] 1 W.L.R. 9.
[80] Alternatively, the contract may be one for the supply of a service to which the delivery of any such goods is incidental. See further below, para.1–085.

emblements, industrial growing crops, and things attached to or forming part of the land which are agreed to be severed before sale or under the contract of sale and includes an undivided share in goods."[81] The definition in section 62(1) of the Act of 1893 was in similar terms. The same word is used (and, in some instances, defined) in a number of other statutes, and it has frequently been the subject of judicial consideration; but caution is clearly necessary in applying these definitions and interpretations to situations governed by the Act. "The word [goods] is of very general and quite indefinite import, and primarily derives its meaning from the context in which it is used."[82] "In a will or in a policy of marine insurance, in the marriage service or in a schedule of railway rates, in the title of a probate action or in an enactment relating to the rights of an execution creditor, the word may sometimes be of the narrowest and sometimes of the widest scope."[83] However, the definition in the Act (from its use of the word "includes") is not intended to be exhaustive, so that other definitions may not be altogether irrelevant. Of more doubtful value are definitions and interpretations of expressions roughly synonymous with "goods", *e.g.* "article",[84] "chattel" or "personal chattels", "commodity", "movable" (corporeal, tangible movable),[85] and "thing".[86] The expanded phrase "goods, wares, and merchandizes" was used in section 17 of the Statute of Frauds (and in a variant form in the Stamp Act 1891 and the Factors Acts).[87] There is much old learning on the meaning of this expression, but in some respects at least its meaning may not be as wide as that of "goods" in the Sale of Goods Act.[88] Finally, in some cases other terms—*e.g.* land or money—have been contrasted with goods, but extreme care is necessary in drawing inferences from these cases as to the meaning of "goods".

Part-interests in goods are now declared to be "goods" for the purposes of the Act.[89]

---

[81] The words "and includes an undivided share in goods" were added to the definition by the Sale of Goods (Amendment) Act 1995, s.2(c).

[82] *The Noordam (No.2)* [1920] A.C. 904 at 908–909. In this case bearer securities were held to be "goods" for the purposes of an Order-in-Council relating to reprisals.

[83] *ibid.* at p.909.

[84] On the meaning of this word, see C. K. Allen, 77 L.Q.R. 237 (1961); 78 L.Q.R. 29 (1962); and *Re Att.-Gen.'s Reference (No.5 of 1980)* [1981] 1 W.L.R. 88 (video cassette); *R. v Registered Designs Appeal Tribunal, ex p. Ford Motor Co. Ltd* [1995] 1 W.L.R. 18 (motor vehicle parts).

[85] The term "movable" is of importance in England only in the conflict of laws: below, para.25–004.

[86] The term "goods" is sometimes used in European Community documents in the wider sense of "assets": see, *e.g.* the EC Regulation on Insolvency Proceedings, 1346/2000/EC ([2000] O.J. L160/1), Art. 2(h).

[87] See below, para.1–079.

[88] It is doubtful whether *fructus industriales* not yet grown to maturity were within s.17 of the Statute of Frauds, but they may clearly now be "goods" the subject of an agreement to sell within the Act: see below, para.1–093.

[89] See above, n.81 and below, para.1–081.

1–079 **"Goods" and similar terms in other statutes.**[90] Some of the more important statutory terms and definitions are as follows:

Bills of Sale Act 1878, s.4: "personal chattels."[91]

Factors Act 1889, s.1(3): "The expression 'goods' shall include wares and merchandise."

Marine Insurance Act 1906, Schedule 1 (Form of Policy), r.17: "The term 'goods' means goods in the nature of merchandise, and does not include personal effects or provisions and stores for use on board. In the absence of any usage to the contrary, deck cargo and living animals must be insured specifically, and not under the general denomination of goods."

Uniform Laws on International Sales Act 1967: the Uniform Law contains no definition of "goods", but declares by Article 5 that its provisions are not to apply to sales: (a) of stocks, shares, investment securities, negotiable instruments or money; (b) of any ship, vessel or aircraft which is or will be subject to registration; (c) of electricity.[92]

In the Consumer Credit Act 1974, s.189(1), the Unfair Contract Terms Act 1977, ss.14 and 25(1), the Supply of Goods and Services Act 1982, s.18 and the Sale of Supply of Goods to Consumers Regulations 2002,[93] reg. 2 the expression "goods" is declared to have the same meaning as in the Sale of Goods Act, or is defined in the same terms.

Theft Act 1968, s.34(2)(b): "'goods,' except in so far as the context otherwise requires, includes money and every other description of property except land, and includes things severed from the land by stealing."[94]

Carriage of Goods by Sea Act 1971, Schedule, Art. 1: "'Goods' includes goods, wares, merchandise, and articles of every kind whatsoever except live

---

[90] *Cf.* Vienna Convention on Contracts for the International Sale of Goods (above, para.1–024), Art. 2:
"This Convention does not apply to sales:
- (a) of goods bought for personal, family or household use, unless the seller, at any time before or at the conclusion of the contract, neither knew nor ought to have known that the goods were bought for any such use;
- (b) by auction;
- (c) on execution or otherwise by authority of law;
- (d) of stocks, shares, investment securities, negotiable instruments or money;
- (e) of ships, vessels, hovercraft or aircraft;
- (f) of electricity."

[91] For the statutory definition, see above, para.1–016.

[92] Above, para.1–024.

[93] SI 2002/3045. Note, however, that EC Directive 1999/44/EC, which these Regulations implement, defines (in Art. 1) "consumer goods" as "any tangible movable item, with the exception of
–goods sold by way of execution or otherwise by authority of law,
–water and gas where they are not put up for sale in a limited volume or set quantity,
–electricity."
Note also the Treaty of Rome, Art.9, discussed below, para.3–042, n.5.

[94] This definition is needed for the offence of handling stolen goods (s.22) and for various other sections which refer to "stolen goods" (ss.23, 24, 26, 28). The definition of "property" capable of being stolen (s.4) is wider, and for many purposes includes land; it replaces the more limited definition of "things" capable of being stolen given by s.1(3) of the Larceny Act 1916. See generally J. C. Smith, *The Law of Theft* (8th ed.), paras 2–90 *et seq.*, 4–50 *et seq.*; A.T.H. Smith, *Property Offences* (1994), paras 3–32 *et seq.*

animals and cargo which by the contract of carriage is stated as being carried on deck and is so carried."

Fair Trading Act 1973, s.137(2): "'goods' includes buildings and other structures, and also includes ships, aircraft and hovercraft."[95]

Torts (Interference with Goods) Act 1977, s.14(1): "'goods' includes all chattels personal other than things in action and money."

Companies Act 1985, s.396(2)(b): "'goods' means any tangible movable property (in Scotland, corporeal moveable property) other than money."

Insolvency Act 1986, ss.183(4), 184(6): "'goods' includes all chattels personal."

Consumer Protection Act 1987, s.45(1): "'goods' includes substances, growing crops and things comprised in land by virtue of being attached to it and any ship, aircraft or vehicle."[96]

Enterprise Act 2002, s.232(2): "Goods include–

(a) buildings and other structures;

(b) ships, aircraft and hovercraft."[97]

Meaning of "personal chattels". By the definition in the Act,[98] "goods" includes all personal chattels other than things in action and money. The term "personal chattels" or "chattels personal"[99] is used in contrast with "chattels real",[1] which refers primarily to leasehold interests in land. "Personal chattels" may be subdivided into choses in possession and choses in action. Only the former come within the statutory definition of "goods." "Choses or things in possession include all things which are at once tangible, movable and visible, and of which possession can be taken, for example animals, household articles, money, jewels, corn, garments, and everything else that can properly be put in motion and transferred from place to place."[2] 1–080

The statutory exclusion of things (or choses) in action means that shares and other securities, debts, bills of exchange and other negotiable instruments, bills of lading, insurance policies, patents, copyrights and trade marks and other incorporeal property are not capable of being "goods" for the purposes of the Act, although they may sometimes have this meaning in other contexts.[3] It follows *a fortiori* that intangibles which are not recog-

---

[95] This provision formerly concluded with the words "but does not include electricity" (repealed by Electricity Act 1989, s.112(4) and Sch.18). As regards electricity, see below, para.1–085.

[96] Pt I of this Act deals with liability for damage caused by a defective "product", a term defined (by s.1(2)) as "any goods or electricity".

[97] Note also s.232(3): "The supply of goods includes – (a) supply by way of sale, lease, hire or hire-purchase; (b) in relation to buildings and other structures, construction of them by one person for another."

[98] s.61(1): above, para.1–078.

[99] "Chattels personal" was the expression used in the definition of "goods" in s.62(1) of the Sale of Goods Act 1893.

[1] For a full discussion of these terms, see Crossley Vaines, *Personal Property* (5th ed.), Ch.1.

[2] Halsbury, *Laws of England* (4th ed.), Vol.35, para.1205, based on 2 Bl.Comm. 387.

[3] *The Noordam* [1920] A.C. 904.

nised by the law as "property" (*e.g.* information,[4] or an opportunity[95]) do not come within the definition. The same would be true of images, music, etc., which, although able to be the subject of copyright or other intellectual property rights and which (like computer software[6]) are capable of being "delivered" on-line, independently of any physical medium, are not capable of being owned as such.

A sale of goods on c.i.f. terms[7] is a sale of goods and not a sale of documents, even though the seller's principal obligation may be performed by the delivery of documents.[8]

1–081 **Undivided interest in goods.** The Sale of Goods Act, both as originally drafted in 1893 and as consolidated in 1979, made only one reference to part interests in goods: in section 2(2) it is stated that "There may be a contract of sale between one part owner and another". It is probable that this subsection was inserted for the removal of doubt, it being taken for granted that the owner of a part interest in goods could sell it to any person other than a co-owner.[9] The Sale of Goods (Amendment) Act 1995,[10] however, now extends the definition of "goods" in section 61(1) by adding the words "and includes an undivided share in goods". It is thus made clear beyond doubt[11] that the sale of an undivided share in goods, such as a one-half or one-third interest in a horse or a boat, whether the seller and buyer[12] hold as joint tenants or as tenants in common, is governed by the Act. This may not be possible for all purposes, but at least it will be the case to the extent to which the context or subject-matter allows.[13] Plainly, certain provisions are not capable of literal application to transactions involving a

[4] Kohler and Palmer, "Information as Property", in Palmer and McKendrick (eds) *Interests in Goods* (2nd ed.), Ch.1; *cf. Oxford v Moss* [1979] Crim.L.R. 119 (information not capable of being stolen); Hammond, 100 L.Q.R. 252 (1984)); *Malone v Metropolitan Police Commissioner* [1980] Q.B. 49 (no property in spoken words); but see *Boardman v Phipps* [1967] 2 A.C. 46 (breach of confidence). As regards computer software, see below, para.1–086.

[5] See, however, *Keech v Sandford* (1726) Sel.Cas.t. King 61; *Regal (Hastings) Ltd v Gulliver* [1967] 2 A.C. 134n. (fiduciary liable to account).

[6] Below, para.1–086.

[7] See below, paras 19–001 *et seq.*

[8] See further below, para.19–008.

[9] The doubt would not have been whether such a transaction was possible, but rather as to whether it should be classed as a sale of goods. See further *Chalmers' Sale of Goods* (18th ed.), pp.78, 116.

[10] In force from September 19, 1995, but not with retrospective effect: s.3(1), (2).

[11] Most decisions prior to the amendment (apart from the special case of the supply of liquor in members' clubs: see below, para.1–121) had held such a transaction to be a sale: see *Venning v Leckie* (1810) 13 East 7; *Marson v Short* (1853) 2 Bing. (N.C.) 118; *Van Cutsem v Dunraven* [1954] C.L.Y. 2998; *Jones v Samios* [1985] A.C.L.D. 381 (Queensland). Note also *Re Sugar Properties (Derisley Wood) Ltd* (below, para.1–081, n.15) (Bills of Sale Acts).

[12] On a literal construction, the subsection does not cover the case where a sole owner or part-owner contracts to transfer part of his interest to another so as to create a tenancy in common between them. Goode, *Commercial Law* (3rd ed.), p.199 takes the view that this would not be a contract of sale within the Act. The two cases first cited in the preceding note held the contrary at common law.

[13] s.61(1), opening words: "In this Act, unless the context or subject matter otherwise requires . . .".

part interest—for instance, the implied warranty as to quiet possession and the rules as to delivery; but the Law Commissions (on whose recommendation the amendment was based) took the view that any problems so raised were not important enough to warrant a complicated set of special statutory provisions: "The Act's provisions based on possession or physical delivery will simply disapply themselves and the intentions of the parties will prevail."[14]

It should be borne in mind that the amendments made in 1995 apply only for the purposes of the Sale of Goods Act 1979 and other statutes which adopt the definition used in the latter Act. In *Re Sugar Properties (Derisley Wood) Ltd*[15] shares representing respectively four and eight one-fortieth interests in two stallions were considered to be choses in action and not "goods" or "personal chattels" for the purposes of the Bills of Sale Acts. There is no reason why this ruling should not be regarded as still authoritative in that context.

A transfer of the whole of the property in goods is a "supply of goods" for the purposes of the Value Added Tax legislation, but a transfer of an undivided share of the property in goods is a "supply of services".[16]

Ships[17] and aircraft. The definition of goods in section 62(1) of the Act is wide enough to include ships and other vessels; but in some respects the transfer and ownership of ships is expressly regulated by the Merchant Shipping Act 1995,[18] or by equivalent laws in other countries, so that the Sale of Goods Act cannot be applied *simpliciter*. In a case dealing with a registered American ship in 1867, Turner L.J. said: "A ship is not like an ordinary personal chattel; it does not pass by delivery, nor does possession of it prove the title to it. There is no market overt[19] for ships; in the case of American ships the laws of the United States provide the means of evidencing the title to them".[20] Prior to April 1, 1989, when the Merchant Shipping Act 1988, Part I, came into force,[21] it was a requirement that all British ships above a prescribed tonnage should, unless specially exempted, be registered, but registration has now been made optional.[22] A registered ship may be transferred only by a bill of sale in the statutory form (unless 1–082

[14] *Sale of Goods forming Part of a Bulk* (L.Com. No. 215, 1993), para.5.5.
[15] (1987) 3 B.C.C. 88 at 92.
[16] Value Added Tax Act 1994, Sch.4, para.1(1).
[17] In regards to houseboats, see, below, para, 1-096, n.37.
[18] A "ship" in these Acts includes every description of vessel used in navigation (s.313(1)). For the scope of this definition, see the commentary to s.313 in *Current Law Statutes Annotated* (1995), Vol. 2, p.21–320, and *cf. Perks v Clark* [2001] EWCA Civ 1228; [2001] 2 Lloyd's Rep. 430 (drilling rigs).
[19] The rule of law relating to sales of goods in market overt has been abolished: Sale of Goods (Amendment) Act 1994, s.1, below, para.7–020.
[20] *Hooper v Gumm* (1867) 2 Ch.App. 282 at 290. These remarks are subject to certain limitations: see *Naamlooze Vennootschap, etc., Vredobert v European Shipping Co.* (1924) 20 Ll.L.R. 296 at 300.
[21] SI 1989/353.
[22] Merchant Shipping Act 1995, s.1(1); *cf.* the definition of "United Kingdom ship" in s.1(2).

the transfer will result in the ship ceasing to have a British connection).[23] But a ship in the course of construction,[24] or a ship not required to be or not capable of being registered, or which has ceased to be registered as a British ship[25] is subject to the general rules as to passing of property laid down in sections 17 to 20 of the Sale of Goods Act; and apart from the rules as to transfer of property, it would seem that even a registered ship[26] may be subject to the Act.[27] Thus, in *Behnke v Bede Shipping Company Ltd*,[28] section 52 was invoked to obtain specific performance of a contract to sell a British ship.

It seems that closely analogous rules would govern the ownership and sale of aircraft, which are subject to similar registration provisions.[29]

1–083 **Motor vehicles.** Motor vehicles are goods for all purposes under the Sale of Goods Act and the Factors Act.[30] They are the subject of a special exception to the principle *nemo dat quod non habet* by virtue of the provisions of the Hire-Purchase Act 1964.[31] The registration document of a motor vehicle (formerly referred to as a "log-book") is not a document of title,[32] but the sale of a motor vehicle without its registration document may not be a sale in the ordinary course of business.[33] It has also been held to be an implied condition in a hire-purchase contract relating to a car that a registration document will be supplied.[34]

---

[23] Merchant Shipping Act 1995, Sch.1, para.2(1). There is now a single register for all British ships; but a separate part of the register deals with fishing vessels, and there is also power for the register to be otherwise divided into parts, *e.g.* for small ships: s.8(5).

[24] *Reid v Macbeth & Gray* [1904] A.C. 223; *cf. McDougall v Aeromarine of Emsworth Ltd* [1958] 1 W.L.R. 1126.

[25] *Cf. Manchester Ship Canal Co. v Horlock* [1914] 2 Ch. 199 (vessel ceasing to be a registered ship when constructive total loss transferable without bill of sale).

[26] Including an oil production platform: *Davy Offshore Ltd v Emerald Field Contracting Ltd* [1992] 2 Lloyd's Rep. 142.

[27] In *Lloyd del Pacifico v Board of Trade* (1929) 35 Ll.L.R. 217, the application of s.14 of the Sale of Goods Act 1893 to a registered ship was considered, but the case failed on the facts. *Cf. Reardon-Smith Line Ltd v Yngvar Hansen-Tangen* [1976] 1 W.L.R. 989 (charterparty of ship not yet built: analogy with contract for sale of future goods by description discussed by House of Lords); and *Hyundai Shipbuilding & Heavy Industries Ltd v Papadopoulos* [1980] 1 W.L.R. 1129 (analogy with building contract).

[28] [1927] 1 K.B. 649.

[29] Air Navigation Order 2000 (SI 2000/1562); *cf. Cadogan Finance Ltd v Lavery* [1982] Com.L.R. 248, below, para.7–015.

[30] It is immaterial for this purpose that the vehicle lacks an ignition key or a registration certificate: *Stadium Finance Ltd v Robbins* [1962] 2 Q.B. 664.

[31] See below, paras 7–087 *et seq.* A motor vehicle is defined for this purpose as "a mechanically-propelled vehicle intended or adapted for use on roads to which the public has access": Hire-Purchase Act 1964, s.29(1).

[32] See below, para.7–036.

[33] Contrast *Pearson v Rose & Young Ltd* [1950] 1 K.B. 275 and *Stadium Finance Ltd v. Robbins* [1962] 2 Q.B. 664 with *Astley Industrial Trust Ltd v Miller* [1968] 2 All E.R. 36: below, para.7–044.

[34] *Bentworth Finance Ltd v Lubert* [1968] 1 Q.B. 680.

Coins and other money as goods. The Act defines goods so as to exclude money.[35] Banknotes and current coin of the realm when exchanged or transferred as such are therefore not "sold" as "goods", whatever the form which the consideration takes. But the term "money" is capable of various meanings,[36] and it is uncertain whether the word as it is used in section 61(1) should be understood in a general or a restricted sense, or indeed whether the same meaning should be given to the word in section 2(1)[37] and in section 61(1). In *Moss v Hancock*,[38] a £5 Jubilee gold piece which was current coin, but also a curiosity having a greater value than its denomination, was stolen from its owner and sold for £5 to a dealer in curiosities. On the conviction of the thief, an order was made for its restitution under the Larceny Act,[39] the court drawing the inference of fact that it had been sold as a curiosity and not passed on as currency. This case indicates that a coin may be bought and sold as a non-negotiable thing if the parties choose to treat it so; but the court nevertheless ordered its restitution as "money".[40] It is a possible but not a necessary inference that the transaction was a sale of "goods" within section 61(1) of the Act—possible only if "money" is there given a restricted meaning.[41] In any event it is plain that such a dealing cannot affect third parties who subsequently handle the money as currency. 1–084

Foreign money is capable of being bought and sold, at least in the sense that the rate of exchange is a matter for negotiation; and it may not be legal tender in the place where it is to be delivered; but these facts alone may be insufficient to deprive it of its character as "money" and to bring it within the definition of "goods" in section 61(1).[42] If the foreign money is not

---

35 s.61(1).

36 Halsbury, *Laws of England* (4th ed.), Vol. 32, para.102; Mann, *The Legal Aspect of Money* (6th ed.), Ch.1.

37 ". . . a money consideration, called the price."

38 [1899] 2 Q.B. 111; *cf. Treseder-Griffin v Co-operative Insurance Soc. Ltd* [1956] 2 Q.B. 127 (gold coin treated as currency); *Jenkins v Horn (Inspector of Taxes)* [1979] 2 All E.R. 1141 (gold sovereigns treated as commodity although also legal tender; *cf. Morris v Ritchie* [1934] N.Z.L.R. 196); *Buckingham (Inspector of Taxes) v Securities Properties Ltd, The Times*, December 7, 1979 (sorting money not "industrial processing of goods"). Contrast *R. v Thompson* [1980] Q.B. 229 (current silver coin not "goods" though traded at price above face value). Krugerrands have been held not to be "goods" within Arts 30–37 (now Arts 28–31) of the Treaty of Rome (free movement of goods), but were deemed "goods" within the Customs and Excise Act 1952, s.4, for the purposes of a forfeiture order: see *R. v Thompson*, above, and *cf. Allgemeine Gold- und Silberscheideananstalt v Customs & Excise Commrs* [1980] Q.B. 390; *Bennett-Cohen v The State* (Zimbabwe S.Ct., February 4, 1985).

39 Larceny Act 1861, s.100; see now Powers of Criminal Courts (Sentencing) Act 2000, s.148.

40 See, however, *R. v Dickinson* [1920] 3 K.B. 552, where gold sovereigns were deemed "goods" for the purposes of a forfeiture order; *cf. Allgemeine Gold- und Silberscheideananstalt v Customs & Excise Commrs*, above (Krugerrands).

41 Note also the opening words of s.61(1): "unless the context or subject-matter otherwise requires, . . ."

42 In *R. v Grimes* (1752) Fost. 79n. and *R. v Leigh* (1764) 1 Leach 52, foreign money was held not to be "goods, wares, or merchandise" for the purpose of a criminal statute. *Cf.*, however, nn.38 and 40, above. The purchase or sale of foreign currency is treated as the supply of a "service or facility" for the purposes of Pt III of the Consumer Protection Act 1987: s.22(1)(b).

delivered or deliverable *in specie* the contract may not, on a strict analysis, be one of sale at all.[43]

The *price* in a contract of sale of goods may be agreed to be paid in a foreign currency.[44]

Cheques, credit cards[45] and similar instruments are in a sense "money"[46] in that they are a means by which payments are made and credit transferred; but whether viewed as money or as choses in action they are clearly excluded from the statutory definition of "goods".

Gaming chips used for the purpose of betting in a casino may in other contexts be "goods", but when exchanged by a patron for money they are not "bought".[47]

1–085 **Electricity and other forms of energy.** There is no doubt that energy, whether in mechanical, electrical[48] or other form, including heat and refrigeration, is capable of being bought and sold. It has been judicially referred to as a "thing" and an "article"[49] and also as a "commodity",[50] and as "tangible personal property"[51] but there has been no decision whether it comes within the term "goods" for the purposes of the Sale of Goods Act.[52] In *Bentley Bros v Metcalfe & Co.*[53] mechanical power from a shaft was supplied by a landlord to his tenant, who also rented the machine which it drove. It was held that since the power was consumed in the process, it was bought and not hired and it was further held that there was an implied contractual obligation to supply power fit for the user's purpose.

---

[43] See Williston, *Sales* (3rd ed.), para.66b and (on contracts for "differences") below, para.1–104.

[44] *Daewoo Australia Pty Ltd v Suncorp-Medway Ltd* (2000) 33 A.C.S.R. 481; below, para.2–044.

[45] On the legal character of credit card sales, see *Richardson v Worrell* [1985] S.T.C. 693, *Re Charge Card Services Ltd* [1989] Ch.497 and below, para.9–033.

[46] "They [credit cards] are frequently referred to as 'plastic money'": *per* Browne-Wilkinson V.-C. in *Re Charge Card Services Ltd* (above), at p.509.

[47] *Lipkin Gorman (a firm) v Karpnale Ltd* [1991] 2 A.C. 548 at 575.

[48] The supply of electricity is treated as the supply of a "service or facility" for the purposes of Pt III of the Consumer Protection Act 1987: s.22(1)(c). The abstraction of electricity is now a special statutory offence: Theft Act 1968, s.13. *Cf. Low v Blease* (1975) 119 Sol.Jo. 695.

[49] *Bentley Bros v Metcalfe & Co.* [1906] 2 K.B. 548 at 552–553.

[50] *British Electric Traction Co. v IRC* [1902] 1 K.B. 441.

[51] *Re Social Services Tax Act* (1970) 74 W.W.R. 246 (steam supplied for heating: held a contract for services and not a "sale").

[52] *Cf. AGL Victoria Pty Ltd v Lockwood* (2004) 22 A.C.L.C. 237 at [69] *et seq.* Electricity was assumed to come within the term "goods, wares, or merchandise" in *County of Durham Electrical Power Co. v I.R.C.* [1909] 2 K.B. 604, but the point was left open. In *East Midlands Electricity Board v Grantham* [1980] C.L.Y. 271, electricity was held not to be "goods" for the purposes of s.108(4) of the Companies Act 1948 (now Companies Act 1985, s.349(4)); but contrast *Hutt Valley Energy Board v Hayman* (1988) 4 N.Z.C.L.C. 64, 244 (gas treated as goods), and *cf. Re Water-Tube Boilermakers' Agreement* [1959] 1 W.L.R. 1118 at 1147 (restrictive practices). The Fair Trading Act 1973, s.137(2) formerly excluded electricity from its definition of the term "goods", but this exception was repealed by the Electricity Act 1989, s.112(4) and Sch.18.See further the other statutory definitions of "goods" above, para.1–079.

[53] Above.

By a special statutory provision,[54] the supply of any form of power, heat, refrigeration or ventilation is declared to be a supply of goods and not of services for the purposes of the law relating to value added tax.

There are clearly difficulties in attributing to energy all the legal qualities of a physical object. For instance, it cannot be possessed *per se*—it is capable of being kept or stored only by changing the physical or chemical state of other property which is itself the subject of possession.

Computer software.[55] The question whether computer software should be classed as "goods" for any purpose has been a matter of debate in the different common law jurisdictions for some decades. However, the issue has been authoritatively dealt with by Sir Iain Glidewell (*obiter*) in the Court of Appeal ruling in *St Albans City & DC v International Computers Ltd*.[56] The question in that case was whether a contract for the supply of software was subject to any implied term as to quality or fitness for purpose. In his Lordship's view a computer disk was clearly within the definition of "goods" for the purpose of the Sale of Goods Act 1979 and the Supply of Goods and Services Act 1982, while equally clearly a program, "being instructions or commands telling the computer hardware what to do", of itself was not.[57] If a disk carrying a program[58] was transferred by way of sale or hire and the program was defective, the seller or hirer of the disk would be in breach of the terms as to quality and fitness implied by these Acts.[59] However, in the *St Albans City* case, as is equally common, the defective program was not sold or hired: it had simply been transferred from a disk on to the claimants' computer without delivery of the disk; the property in the program remained in the supplier and under the contract the claimants were licensed to use it. The program was not 1–086

---

[54] Value Added Tax Act 1994, Sch.4, para.3.

[55] Bainbridge, *Software Licensing* (2nd ed.), Ch. 43 Carr and Arnold, *Computer Software: Legal Protection in the United Kingdom* (2nd ed.), Ch.8; Macdonald, 58 M.L.R. 585 (1995); Napier [1992] C.L.J. 46, 55 *et seq*.

[56] [1996] 4 All E.R. 481.

[57] Chissick and Kelman, *Electronic Commerce Law and Practice* (3rd ed.), paras 3.08–3.09 consider that the distinction made by Sir Iain Glidewell between a program supplied in the form of a disk and one transmitted directly via the internet or over the telecommunications system (the former being regarded as a sale of goods and the latter not) is illogical, because different results could follow where identical digital products were sold, merely because a different medium was used. The learned authors submit that digitised services should be treated as "a dematerialised form of goods", and draw support from the judgment in *Advent Systems Ltd v Unisys Corp.* 925 F. 2d. 670 (1991). (See also the similar criticism in Atiyah, *The Sale of Goods* (11th ed.), pp.78–79.)

[58] Or a whole computer system, including hardware and software: *Toby Constructions Products Pty Ltd v Computa Bar (Sales) Pty Ltd* [1983] 2 N.S.W.L.R. 48 (N.S.W.S.Ct.—a decision regarded by Sir Iain Glidewell as "clearly correct"); *cf. Burroughs B.M.L. v Feed-Rite Mills (1962) Ltd* (1973) 42 D.L.R. (2d) 303; *Public Utilities Commission for the City of Waterloo v Burroughs Business Machines Ltd* (1974) 6 O.R. (2d.) 257 (Ont. C.A.); *Triangle Underwriters Inc. v Honeywell Inc.* 604 F. 2d. 737 (1979). It is immaterial in such a case that it is contemplated that certain services will also be supplied (*ibid.*).

[59] *Brocket v DGS Retail Ltd* [2004] C.L. Jan. 332.

"goods" and so there was no statutory implication of any term as the quality or fitness for purpose. However, his Lordship went on to hold that, in the absence of any express term, such a contract would be subject to an implied term at common law that the program would be reasonably fit for (*i.e.* capable of achieving) its intended purpose.[60]

Even where a disk (or other physical medium) is sold or hired, however, it does not follow that the program which is encoded on it is necessarily also sold or hired. Frequently, the property in the copyright in the program is vested in a third party, such as its author, and the supplier agrees in a composite transaction to make available to his customer both the medium and the right of access to, and use of, the program by procuring a licence for its use. Of such a transaction Lord Penrose in *Beta Computers (Europe) Ltd v Adobe Systems (Europe) Ltd*[61] said: "In my opinion the only acceptable view is that the supply of proprietary software for a price is a contract *sui generis* which may involve elements of nominate contracts such as sale, but would be inadequately understood if expressed wholly in terms of any of the nominate contracts. Further, it is in my opinion unacceptable to analyse the transaction in this case as if it were two separate transactions relating to the same subject matter. There is but one contract. If on a proper analysis it does not fit the basic characteristics of any one nominate contract, the preferable view . . . is that it is innominate but reflects elements also found typically in nominate contract forms."

A contract to write a new program for a customer is, of course, capable of being simply a contract for the supply of services.[62]

1–087 **Water, oil, gases.**[63] It is submitted that water,[64] oil,[65] gas[66] (whatever its source) and even air[67] (*e.g.* in the form of compressed air) are capable of

---

[60] *Cf. Saphena Computing Ltd v Allied Collection Agencies Ltd* [1995] F.S.R. 616 at 643.

[61] 1996 S.L.T. 604, 609; *SAM Business Systems Ltd v Hedley & Co.* [2002] EWHC 2733 (TCC); [2003] 1 All E.R. (Comm) 465.

[62] *The Salvage Association v C.A.P. Financial Services Ltd* [1995] F.S.R. 654.

[63] Note the special definition applying to water and gas in EC Directive 1999/44/EC, art. 1 (above, para.1–079, n.93).

[64] But not flowing water: see generally Halsbury, *Laws of England* (4th ed.), Vol. 49(2), paras 47 *et seq*. Water was held to be "goods" within the Sale of Goods Act 1908 (N.Z.) in *Hamilton v Papakura DC* [2000] 1 N.Z.L.R. 265, and to be included in the term "goods, wares, or merchandise" in *West Middlesex Water-Works Co. v Suwercrop* (1829) 4 Car. & P. 87; and water in pipes to be larcenable in *Ferens v O'Brien* (1883) 11 Q.B.D. 21. It was held an "article" in *Longhurst v Guildford Godalming & District Water Board* [1963] A.C. 265; *cf. Walker v Weedair (NZ) Ltd* [1959] N.Z.L.R. 777. *Cf. Re Social Services Act* (1970) 74 W.W.R. 246 (steam).

[65] Oil in a tanker was held to be a movable in *Anglo-Iranian Oil Co. Ltd v Jaffrate* [1953] 1 W.L.R. 246 at 259–260 (Aden S.Ct). All "petroleum" (including mineral oil and natural gas) in its natural state within Great Britain is vested in the Crown: Petroleum Act 1998, ss.1, 2. See generally Goode, *Proprietary Rights in Insolvency and Sales Transactions* (2nd ed.), Ch.2.

[66] *Marleau v People's Gas Supply Co.* [1940] 4 D.L.R. 433 (acetylene); *Bradshaw v Boothe's Marine Ltd* [1973] 2 O.R. 646 (propane); *Britvic Soft Drinks v Messer UK Ltd* [2002] 1 Lloyd's Rep. 20; *Bacardi-Martin Beverages Ltd v Thomas Hardy Packaging Ltd [2002] EWCA Civ 549,* [2002] 2 Lloyd's Rep 379; (carbon dioxide); *Contigroup Companies Inc. v Glencore A.G.* [2004] EWHC 2750 (Comm); [2005] Lloyd's Rep. 241 (butane). *Cf. Erie County Natural Gas & Fuel Co. v Carroll* [1911]

being bought and sold as goods: if of mineral origin, there must clearly be a severance from the soil, and if originally *res nullius*, a reduction into possession. A right to take water or to extract oil or gas may, however, be given or granted by a landowner as a disposition of an interest in land (a *profit à prendre*) and not merely as a sale of goods, severed or to be severed. This is the case with all minerals.[68]

Animals.[69] Domestic animals are capable of being owned absolutely, and are "goods" for the purposes of the Act. There is, however, no absolute property in wild animals[70] while living, and they are neither "goods" nor "chattels". A qualified property may be obtained in such animals by lawfully taking them and reducing them into possession: they may then be bought and sold and are presumably "goods". But this qualified property is lost if a wild animal regains its natural liberty and has no *animus revertendi*.[71] 1–088

The grant by a landowner of hunting or sporting rights is a disposition of an interest in the land itself or *profit à prendre*, and not a sale of goods.

Wild animals when dead may be the subject of absolute ownership, and may therefore be "goods".

Human remains and parts of the body. The law recognises no right of property in a dead body or any part thereof,[72] and for this reason human remains cannot ordinarily be considered "goods" capable of being bought and sold.[73] But there is probably no universal rule to this effect: in *Dobson v North Tyneside Health Authority*,[74] it appears to have been accepted that, once a person has, by the lawful exercise of work or skill, so dealt with a human body or part of a human body that it has acquired some attributes distinguishing it from a mere corpse awaiting burial (or part thereof), it can be the subject of property in the ordinary way, and of a right to retain possession.[75] Examples given included stuffing or embalming a corpse or preserving an anatomical or pathological specimen for a scientific collection, or preserving a human freak such as a double-headed foetus that has some value for exhibition purposes. It would follow that such items may be "goods" and the subject of a contract of sale. 1–089

A.C. 105, where the point was not decided; *R. v White* (1853) 22 L.J.M.C. 123 (larceny).

[67] But the supply of ventilation or air conditioning would probably be construed as a contract for services (see, however, Value Added Tax Act 1994, Sch.4, para.3, above, para.1–085, n.54).

[68] See below, para.1–098.

[69] See generally Halsbury, *Laws of England* (4th ed.), Vol. 21, paras 502, 508 *et seq.* Wild creatures are specially dealt with in the Theft Act 1968: see s.4(4).

[70] Including bees: *Kearry v Pattinson* [1939] 1 K.B. 471.

[71] *Hamps v Darby* [1948] 2 K.B. 311 at 321.

[72] *Williams v Williams* (1882) 20 Ch.D. 659 at 664–665; *Dobson v North Tyneside Health Authority* [1996] 4 All E.R. 474.

[73] *Cf. Bourne (Inspector of Taxes) v Norwich Crematorium Ltd* [1967] 1 W.L.R. 691 (cremation not "subjection of goods or materials to any process").

[74] Above, applying *dicta* in *Doodeward v Spence* (1908) 6 C.L.R. 406 at 413–414 (H. Ct. Aus.).

[75] See *Re Organ Retention Group Litigation* [2004] EWHC 644 (QB); [2005] Q.B. 506 at [128] (possession of child's body).

The law relating to human tissue and organs (*e.g.* kidneys used for transplants) and bodily products (*e.g.* hair, blood, urine) and genetic materials (*e.g.* ova, sperm[76] and embryos) has developed rapidly in recent years. There is now a growing literature on the subject.[77] Many of these items appear to be capable of being stolen.[78] The provision of a blood transfusion has been held in one well-known American case to be a contract for the supply of services,[79] but there is authority also that blood supplied by a blood bank is a sale of goods.[80] In yet another American case it was held that a patient had no property rights in parts of his body after they had been removed in an operation.[81] Human hair has, of course, been bought and sold for wig-making for centuries.

The sale of human organs and others material for transplantation[82] and other commercial dealing in such organs is forbidden by the Human Tissue Act 2004.[83]

1–090 **Goods and land.**[84] Section 61(1) provides that ". . . 'goods' includes emblements, industrial growing crops, and things attached to or forming part of the land which are agreed to be severed before sale or under the contract of sale."[85]

It is necessary that any definition of goods should draw a line of demarcation between goods and land, as must a definition of land. The problem arises most obviously in relation to: first, crops, trees, and other

---

[76] *Cf. ter Neuzen v Korn* (1993) 103 D.L.R. (4th) 473 (artificial insemination using H.I.V. infected semen: held (by jury on direction of judge) not a sale of goods).

[77] Scott, *The Body as Property* (1981); Meyers, *The Human Body and the Law* (2nd ed.); Kennedy and Grubb, *Medical Law*: (3rd ed.), Ch.15; Magnusson, "Property Rights in Human Tissue", in Palmer and McKendrick (eds), *Interests in Goods* (2nd ed.), Ch.2; Skegg, 44 Anglo-Am.L.R. 412 (1974); Smith [1976] Crim.L.R. 622; Dickens, 27 U. of Tor. L.J. 142 (1977) Harris, 16 O.J.L.S. 55 (1996). See also the Report of the Committee of Inquiry into Human Fertilization and Embryology (Warnock Report), Cmnd. 9314, 1984, and n.83, below.

[78] *R. v Welsh* [1974] R.T.R. 478 (urine); *R. v Rothery* [1976] R.T.R. 550 (blood); *R. v. Herbert* (1960) 25 Jo.Cr.L. 163 (hair). See further Smith, [1976] Crim.L.R. 622.

[79] *Perlmutter v Beth David Hospital* 123 N.E. (2d) 792 (1955); *cf. E. v Australian Red Cross Society* (1991) 105 A.L.R. 53; *PQ v Australian Red Cross Society* [1992] 1 V.R. 19.

[80] *Belle Bonfils Memorial Blood Bank v Hansen* 579 P 2d 1158 (1978); *cf. A. v National Blood Authority* [2001] 3 All E.R. 289 (blood a "product" within Consumer Protection Act 1987).

[81] *Moore v Regents of the University of California*, 51 Cal. 3rd 120 (1990) (spleen and genetic materials).

[82] Defined as any material which – (a) consists of or includes human cells, (b) is, or is intended to be removed, from a human body and (c) is intended to be used for the purpose of transplantation (s.32(8)). Excluded are: gametes, embryos and "material which is the subject of property because of an application of human skill" (s.32(9)).

[83] S.32. The Act also makes provision for the giving of authorisation for the removal of parts of the body for medical purposes. See also the Human Fertilisation and Embryology Act 1990, which regulates the keeping or use of human gametes and human embryos outside a woman's body and scientific research involving these materials. See Price, 68 M.L.R. 798 [2004].

[84] See Hudson, 22 *Conveyancer*, 137 (1958).

[85] The relevant part of the definition of "goods" in s.62(1) of the Sale of Goods Act 1893 was in identical terms.

growth of the soil; secondly, buildings, fixtures and other erections upon land[86]; and thirdly, minerals, water, sand, gravel, clay and the very soil itself. Here the principal question is whether a contract providing for the severance and removal of such commodities is a sale of goods or an agreement to grant an interest in the land in the nature of a *profit à prendre*. (An analogous question arises in the case of things not attached to the land, for instance, a contract granting the right to take game or fish.[87])

Unfortunately, the most important of the statutory definitions of "goods" and "land" have not been formulated with reference to each other, with the result that there are some curious inconsistencies in their interpretation. This was particularly so under the Statute of Frauds, where the definitions left something of a hiatus, but the position is just as confused under the modern definitions which have replaced them, and which appear in some respects to overlap.

Goods and land under the Statute of Frauds. Under the Statute of Frauds 1677, sales of "goods, wares and merchandizes" were governed by section 17, while "any contract of sale of lands, tenements, or hereditaments, or any interest in or concerning them" fell to be considered under section 4. Although the principal requirement of these sections was substantially the same, *viz.* that the agreement or some memorandum or note thereof should be in writing, there were differences which were sometimes important: for instance, under section 17 there was no need for writing when the value[88] was under £10, and it could be dispensed with in any case by proof of part acceptance or part payment or the giving of an earnest. 1–091

It was generally agreed that if something attached to land was to be severed by the seller and then sold, the contract was one for the sale of "goods, wares and merchandizes" within section 17[89]; but if the contract was to give the buyer a right or licence to enter upon the land and take or sever and remove such things from the land, it fell outside that section. In most cases, the contract was then one for the sale of an "interest in or concerning lands" within section 4, but this did not always follow, especially in the case of the class of crops known as *fructus industriales*.[90]

Goods and land under the modern statutes. Section 17 of the Statute of Frauds was replaced by section 4 of the Sale of Goods Act 1893, which has since itself been repealed.[91] There is now no general requirement that a 1–092

---

[86] A contract to *erect* a building or to install something in or upon land in such a manner that it is to become a fixture, and on terms that no property is to pass until it is affixed, is a contract for work and materials and not a sale of goods: *Brooks Robinson Pty Ltd v Rothfield* [1951] V.L.R. 405.

[87] *Webber v Lee* (1882) 9 Q.B.D. 315.

[88] In the original statute, the price. The effect of Lord Tenterden's Act (Statute of Frauds Amendment Act 1828) was to substitute "value" for "price": *Harman v Reeve* (1856) 18 C.B. 587.

[89] *Smith v Surman* (1829) 9 B. & C. 561; *Cf. Washbourn v Burrows* (1847) 1 Exch.107 at 115.

[90] See below, para.1–093. Similar principles governed the right of a tenant to sever and remove certain fixtures: see *Evans v Roberts* (1826) 5 B. & C. 829 at 835, and below, para.1–095.

[91] Law Reform (Enforcement of Contracts) Act 1954.

contract for the sale of goods should be evidenced by a note or memorandum in writing. Section 4 of the Statute of Frauds was also replaced, so far as concerned contracts relating to land, by section 40 of the Law of Property Act 1925, but this section has now in turn been repealed and replaced by section 2 of the Law of Property (Miscellaneous Provisions) Act 1989.[92] The main change in the law effected by this most recent statute is to require that a contract for the sale or other disposition of an interest in land should, with certain exceptions, be *made in writing* and signed by or on behalf of *each party* to the contract, whereas under both the Statute of Frauds and the Act of 1925 such a contract, to be enforceable, had to be *evidenced by* a note or memorandum in writing and signed "by the party to be charged therewith." Although these differences are not relevant for the purposes of the present discussion, it is important to consider the meaning of the phrases "any contract for the sale or other disposition of land or any interest in land" (as used in the Act of 1925) and "any contract for the sale or other disposition of an interest in land" (as in the Act of 1989). Curiously, the term "land" is not defined in the latter statute,[93] but it is a reasonable assumption that the definition prescribed by the 1925 Act should apply by implication.[94] This reads that "land" includes[95]: "land of any tenure, and mines and minerals, whether or not held with the surface, buildings or parts of buildings . . . and other corporeal hereditaments, and an easement, right, privilege or benefit in, over or derived from land." It follows from this definition that an agreement giving a person the right to enter upon another's land and extract minerals or remove a building or shoot and take away game may come within the scope of section 40 of the Law of Property Act 1925 (and, by implication, section 2 of the Act of 1989), even though it may also be a contract for the sale of goods as defined by the Sale of Goods Act 1979.[96] This definition of "goods" is wider than that in the Statute of Frauds, and has in consequence removed many doubts as to the meaning of "goods" for the purpose of its own provisions, but it cannot affect the meaning of "land" or "an interest in land" for the purpose of the other legislation. The result is that both statutes may apply to certain transactions.[97]

1–093 **Crops.** A contract for the sale of crops, timber or other growth of the soil was not in every case regarded as one affecting an interest in land within section 4 of the Statute of Frauds. Here a distinction was drawn

[92] This reform follows the recommendation of the Law Commission in its report, *Formalities for Contracts for Sale, etc. of Land* (Law Com. No. 164 (1987)).
[93] The expression "interest in land" is, however, defined by s.2(6) as meaning "any estate, interest or charge in or over land or in or over the proceeds of sale of land."
[94] s.2(8) declares that s.40 of the 1925 Act "is superseded by this section."
[95] s.205(1)(ix).
[96] Above, para.1–078.
[97] A similar problem may arise under the Unfair Contract Terms Act 1977, which is generally applicable to sales of goods, but exempts from the operation of ss.2–4 "any contract so far as it relates to the creation or transfer of an interest in land, or to the termination of such an interest, whether by extinction, merger, surrender, forfeiture or otherwise": see Sch.1, para.1(b). The Unfair Terms in Consumer Contracts Regulations 1999 contain no definition of "goods" and, indeed, appear to apply to sales of land to a consumer: see *Chitty on Contracts* (29th ed.), Vol. 1, paras 15–014 *et seq.*

between *fructus naturales, i.e.* the natural growth of the soil, such as grass, timber and fruit on trees, which were regarded at common law as part of the soil, and *fructus industriales*, fruits or crops produced "in the year, by the labour of the year"[98] in sowing and reaping, planting and gathering, *e.g.* corn and potatoes.[99] The latter are traditionally "chattels",[1] being considered the "representative"[2] of the labour and expense of the occupier, and a thing independent of the land in which they are growing.[3] Under the Statute of Frauds, growing crops, if *fructus industriales*, were treated as chattels and not as part of the land or an interest in land; accordingly an agreement for the sale of such crops, whether mature or immature, and whether the property in them was purportedly transferred before or after severance, was not governed by section 4.[4] Strangely enough, it was never directly decided whether a contract for unsevered *fructus industriales* was a sale of "goods, wares and merchandizes" within section 17.[5]

Fructus naturales were regarded until severance as part of the soil, and an agreement conferring any right or interest in them upon a buyer before severance was a "contract for sale of an interest in land" governed by section 4.[6] If they were to be severed before sale, section 17 applied. However, in *Marshall v Green*[7] in 1875, a further qualification or refinement was introduced. In this case standing timber was sold, to be cut down *by the buyer* and removed as soon as possible. It would probably have been more in keeping with the earlier authorities to hold that since the seller was not to cut (*i.e.* render the subject-matter "goods") before sale,[8] the contract was in effect a licence or grant to the buyer of an interest in the land, but the court held the transaction to be within section 17 and not section 4, on the ground that since the severance was to be immediate, the buyer would derive no benefit from the trees remaining in the soil. This case has been

---

98 *Saunders v Pilcher* [1949] 2 All E.R. 1097 at 1104.

99 There was some uncertainty regarding crops which either took more than a year to mature, or matured within a year but lasted for two or three seasons only. The former was probably not *fructus industriales* (or emblements) at all, while in the latter case the first crop was capable of being emblements but that of subsequent years was *fructus naturales*. See *Graves v Weld* (1833) 5 B. & Ad. 105 (clover); *Kingsbury v Collins* (1827) 4 Bing. 202 (teasels); *Flanagan v Seaver* (1859) 9 Ir.Ch.R. 230 (clover and rye-grass). A special rule was applied to hops, which grow from permanent roots but demand repeated annual cultivation: each successive crop is *fructus industriales*: *Latham v Atwood* (1635) Cro.Car. 515; *English Hop Growers v. Dering* [1928] 2 K.B. 174.

1 Not necessarily, however, "goods": see below, n.3.

2 *Evans v Roberts* (1826) 5 B. & C. 829 at 836.

3 Accordingly, they passed to the executor and not the heir and were liable to seizure in execution levied against the tenant: *ibid.*, at pp.832, 835–836.

4 *Watts v Friend* (1830) 10 B. & C. 446, where the crop was not sown at the time of the agreement.

5 There are dicta to this effect in *Evans v Roberts*, above, at pp.837, 840; *cf. Emmerson v Heelis* (1809) 2 Taunt. 38; *Sainsbury v Matthews* (1838) 4 M. & W. 343; *Jones v Flint* (1839) 10 Ad. & El. 753. *Contra Blackburn on Sale*, (3rd ed.), pp.12–16.

6 *Crosby v Wadsworth* (1805) 6 East 612; *Teal v Auty* (1820) 2 Br. & B. 99; *Scorell v Boxall* (1827) 1 Y. & J. 396; *Carrington v Roots* (1837) 2 M. & W. 248; *Rodwell v Phillips* (1842) 9 M. & W. 501.

7 (1875) 1 C.P.D. 35, following notes to *Duppa v Mayo* (1669) 1 Wms. Saund. (6th ed.), 277.

8 As in *Smith v Surman* (1829) 9 B. & C. 561.

criticised[9]; but it may still be of some importance, since the point there in issue survives the replacement of section 4 of the Statute of Frauds by the more recent statutes.[10]

The enlarged definition of "goods" in section 61(1) of the Sale of Goods Act 1979[11] renders many of the old distinctions obsolete for the purposes of the Act (although not, of course, for the purposes of other Acts).[12] Crops and other produce, whether *fructus naturales* or *fructus industriales* (except in the case of a sale without severance to a landlord, incoming tenant or purchaser of the land[13]), will always be "goods" for the purpose of a contract of sale, since the agreement between the parties must be that they shall be severed either "before sale" or "under the contract of sale" as provided by section 61(1).[14] Whether or not *fructus industriales* were "goods, wares and merchandizes" under the former law, they are plainly always "goods" within the meaning of the Act. And it is no longer material whether *fructus naturales* are to derive further benefit from the soil before severance.

The Act also declares that the term "goods" includes "emblements" and "industrial growing crops". Technically, the right to *emblements* is a right which the law gives to the tenant of an estate of uncertain duration to take the crop which is growing at the determination of his estate of those vegetables produced by agricultural labour which ordinarily yield a "present annual profit", such as corn and potatoes; and it includes the right of free entry, egress and regress to cut and carry them away.[15] This right also extends to a tenant in fee, on whose death the emblements vest in his executor or administrator and not in his heir.[16] As a subject of *sale*, the term "emblements" as used in the Act appears to be intended to mean simply *fructus industriales*.

The term "industrial growing crops" was added to the definition when the Act was extended to Scotland. It does not, however, seem to be an expression in regular use in Scots law; and its meaning may be wider than *fructus industriales*.[17] But in any event the definition overall is wide enough to include everything that grows.

1–094 **Transfer of land with sale of crops.** Where a purchaser of land or an incoming tenant agrees to take the crops then growing together with the land, it is a question of construction whether the contract is entire, so that

[9] See, *e.g. Lavery v Pursell* (1888) 39 Ch.D. 508 at 515–517; *cf. Summers v Cook* (1880) 28 Grant's Ch.R. 179 (Can.). In *Marshall v Green* itself, it was pointed out that whether a standing tree will derive benefit from the land may depend as much upon the season of the year as the length of time before it is cut down: see (1875) 1 C.P.D. 35 at 39.

[10] See above, para.1–092.

[11] See above, para.1–090. The definition in s.62(1) of the Sale of Goods Act 1893 was in similar terms.

[12] See above, para.1–092.

[13] See below, para.1–094.

[14] See, *e.g. Waimiha Sawmilling Co. Ltd v Howe* [1920] N.Z.L.R. 681 (timber); *Knight & McLennan v National Mortgage & Agency Co.* [1920] N.Z.L.R. 748 (grass seed); *Scully v South* [1931] N.Z.L.R. 1187 (turnips).

[15] Co. Litt. 55a; *Graves v Weld* (1833) 5 B. & Ad. 105.

[16] 2 Bl.Comm. 404.

[17] It is possible that the crops mentioned above, para.1–093, n.99 are intended to be included in "industrial growing crops."

the crops are regarded as part of the land, or severable, in which case the crops are sold as goods. It would appear that this issue can arise only in relation to *fructus industriales*. In *Saunders v Pilcher*,[18] a cherry orchard was sold together with the crop of cherries which was almost ready for picking. The buyer's contention that the sale of the cherries as goods was severable from the conveyance of the land was rejected: cherries being *fructus naturales* were part of the land. In contrast, in *English Hop Growers v Dering*,[19] the land demised carried a crop of hops nearing maturity. The lessor was held to have disposed of the crop as hops (in breach of a covenant to sell only to the claimants) and not merely to have alienated the whole as land, on the simple ground that hops are *fructus industriales* and "not part of the land while growing".[20] It was apparently not considered relevant that no separate price was agreed for the hops. In this respect the case goes further than older cases under the Statute of Frauds, where the issue was whether the price of the crops could have been sued for in a separate action.[21]

Fixtures.[22] In general, the word "fixture" means anything which has become so attached to the land as to form in law part of the land.[23] Whether or not chattels have been affixed to the land in this sense depends partly upon the degree of annexation and partly upon the purpose of annexation.[24] When goods become fixtures (for instance, when materials are used to erect a building) they become the property of the owner of the land, and the title of their previous owner is extinguished,[25] and this is so whether or not the person affixing them has any authority to do so.[26] When fixtures are severed (as when a building is demolished) they again become goods, but do not revert to their former ownership, except in the special case of "tenant's fixtures". Under this exception, a tenant[27] has the right at any time during the term to sever and remove "trade", "ornamental" and "domestic" fixtures[28] (and, in the case of a tenant for years, but not a tenant for life,[29] "agricultural" fixtures[30]) which he has himself affixed, and when so severed they are restored to his ownership.[31] **1–095**

[18] [1949] 2 All E.R. 1097; *Warren v Nut Farms of Australia Pty Ltd* [1981] W.A.R. 134.
[19] [1928] 2 K.B. 174.
[20] *ibid.* at p.179. For a contrary view, see *Saunders v Pilcher*, above, at p.1105.
[21] Contrast *Mayfield v Wadsley* (1824) 3 B. & C. 357 (contract held severable) with *Earl of Falmouth v Thomas* (1832) 1 Cr. & M. 89 (contract held entire).
[22] Bennett, "Attachment of Chattels to Land," in Palmer and McKendrick (eds), *Interests in Goods* (2nd ed.), Ch.11.
[23] Megarry and Wade, *The Law of Real Property* (6th ed.), para.14–311.
[24] *ibid.*
[25] *Bain v Brand* (1876) 1 App.Cas. 762 at 772; *Melluish (Inspector of Taxes) v B.M.I. (No. 3) Ltd* [1996] A.C. 454.
[26] *Reynolds v Ashby & Son* [1904] A.C. 446; *Crossley Bros Ltd v Lee* [1908] 1 K.B. 86; *Re 876267 Alberta Ltd* [2003] 10 W.W.R. 90.
[27] Or, in the case of a tenant for life, his executor after his death: *Leigh v Taylor* [1902] A.C. 157.
[28] For the meaning of these terms, see Megarry and Wade, *op. cit.*, at paras 14–318, 14–319.
[29] Agricultural Holdings Act 1986, s.10.
[30] For the meaning of these terms, see Megarry and Wade, *op. cit.*, para.14–320.
[31] Megarry and Wade, *op. cit.*, at paras 14–316 *et seq.*

Even whilst attached, tenant's fixtures may be treated for some purposes as chattels; for instance, they may be taken in execution under a *fi. fa.* against the tenant as goods and chattels, thus bearing a close resemblance to emblements.[32]

A sale of unsevered tenant's fixtures by a tenant to the landlord or to an incoming tenant or purchaser was regarded at common law as merely a surrender or abandonment of the right to sever them, and was not a sale of goods.[33] It was further established that a sale of unsevered tenant's fixtures to a stranger who did not take the land was by the same reasoning only a transfer of the right to sever and not a sale of goods. But if the *seller* undertook to sever, so that the property was to pass after severance, the contract was an agreement for the sale of goods.[34]

Other fixtures were at common law part of the realty. Unless the agreement was that they should be first severed and then sold as goods, a contract to sell them (whether to a tenant or to a stranger) was a contract concerning an interest in land within section 4 of the Statute of Frauds, but not a sale of goods.[35]

The definition of "goods" in the Sale of Goods Act 1979[36] seems to be sufficiently wide to include all contracts for the sale of fixtures where severance (not necessarily by the seller) is contemplated.

1–096 **Buildings.** Buildings, walls and other erections upon land are part of the land for all purposes whilst they remain affixed to it.[37] But a building may be sold for removal, or for demolition and removal of the materials of which it is made. Prior to the Act, such a contract was one for the sale of an interest in land within section 4 of the Statute of Frauds, if the buyer was to sever.[38] Under the Act, this is an agreement for the sale of goods. But in the nature of things, it is impossible for the property to pass until severance. Further, the extended definition given to the term "goods" by the Act may not prevent the contract from being considered to be a contract relating to land for other purposes.[39] A contract under which the owner of land agrees to sever or demolish a building and sell it when severed is, and has always been, a contract of sale of goods.

A contract to *erect* a building or to install something in or upon land or an existing building in such a manner that it is to become a fixture, and on

---

[32] *Hallen v Runder* (1834) 1 C.M. & R. 266.

[33] *Blackburn on Sale* (1st ed.), p.20; *Hallen v Runder*, above, distinguishing *Lee v Risdon* (1816) 7 Taunt. 188; *Horsfall v Key* (1848) 2 Ex. 778; *Saint v Pilley* (1875) 44 L.J.Ex. 266; *Lee v Gaskell* (1876) 1 Q.B.D. 700; *Thomas v Jennings* (1896) 66 L.J.Q.B. 5 at 8. *Cf. Nutt v Butler* (1804) 5 Esp. 176; *Macintosh v Trotter* (1838) 3 M. & W. 184.

[34] *Blackburn on Sale* (1st ed.), pp.9–11.

[35] *Lee v Risdon*, above.

[36] Above, para.1–090.

[37] *Elitestone Ltd v Morris* [1997] 1 W.L.R. 687. In regard to houseboats, contrast *Chelsea Yacht & Boat Co. Ltd v Pope* [2001] 2 All E.R. 409 (houseboat held to be a chattel) with *Cinderella Rockerfellas Ltd v Rudd* [2003] EWCA Civ 529; [2003] 3 All E.R. 219 (held rateable as land).

[38] *Lavery v Pursell* (1888) 39 Ch.D. 508.

[39] *e.g.* it may need to be made in writing under s.2 of the Law of Property (Miscellaneous Provisions) Act 1989 (above, para.1–092); and see below, para.1–100.

terms that no property is to pass until it is affixed, is a contract for work and materials and not a sale of goods.[40] But some provisions of the Sale of Goods Act may apply to such a contract.[41]

Minerals, gravel and soil. Minerals,[42] sand and gravel, soil and surface and underground water when *in situ* are not merely "attached or affixed" to the land, but part of the land itself.[43] The owner of these commodities may sell them to another, or grant him the right to get them, in a number of ways. He may, where appropriate, sell that part of the land which contains them, since there may be separate owners of the different strata of a piece of land, or ownership of a mine distinct from the ownership of the surface. This is not merely the grant by the owner of an *interest* in his land, but an alienation of a physical part of his estate. Alternatively, the owner may by grant vest the minerals in his land in another, together with the right to enter upon his land and get and remove them. Such a grant is a *profit à prendre* (in the case of minerals sometimes called a mining lease): it is both a "disposition of an interest in land" within section 2 of the Law of Property (Miscellaneous Provisions) Act 1989, and also a transfer of a proprietary interest in the minerals themselves. It can be created only by deed.[44] 1–097

Instead of making a formal grant, the landowner may by simple contract agree that the other party may enter upon his land and take away the minerals or other products. This is a mere contractual licence which confers on the other party no right of ownership in the unsevered minerals, but it is still a "disposition of an interest in land" requiring to be made in writing under section 2 of the Law of Property (Miscellaneous Provisions) Act 1989; and the rights of the licensee may be enforced by injunction.[45]

---

[40] *Brooks Robinson Pty Ltd v Rothfield* [1951] V.L.R. 405 (supply and installation of cocktail cabinet); *Hewett v Court* (1983) 57 A.L.J.R. 211 (construction and erection on site of movable house). Contrast *Symes v Laurie* [1985] 2 Qd. R. 547 (contract to sever house from land, move it and re-erect it on new site held a sale of goods).

[41] *e.g.* s.25(1) ("... the delivery of the goods ... under any sale, pledge *or other disposition thereof* ..."): see below, para.7–079.

[42] See generally Goode, *Proprietary Rights and Insolvency in Sales Transactions* (2nd ed.), Ch.2; *Cheshire and Burn's Modern Law of Real Property* (16th ed.), pp.172 *et seq*. Special rules apply to particular minerals: thus, gold and silver are vested in the Crown by royal prerogative: *Case of Mines* (1567) 1 Plowd. 310; *Att.-Gen. v Morgan* [1891] 1 Ch. 432; coal, in the Coal Authority: Coal Industry Act 1994, ss.7, 8; petroleum in its natural condition in strata, in the Crown: Petroleum Act 1998, s.2. As regards the continental shelf, see Continental Shelf Act 1964, s.1; and the hard mineral resources of the deep sea bed, Deep Sea Mining (Temporary Provisions) Act 1981. On treasure see the Treasure Act 1996.

[43] Chattels deposited on the land in some cases become part of the land itself: *Boileau v Heath* [1898] 2 Ch. 301 (refuse of iron manufacture); *Morgan v Russell & Sons* [1909] 1 K.B. 357 (cinder and slag); *cf. Smart v Jones* (1864) 15 C.B.(N.S.) 717 (cinders) and *Elwes v Brigg Gas Co.* (1886) 33 Ch.D. 562 (prehistoric boat), in which the point was not decided. See also *Mills v Stokman* (1967) 116 C.L.R. 61, where it was held that waste dumped from a slate quarry was part of the land, either on analogy with the cases cited above, or possibly because it had never been effectively severed.

[44] Law of Property Act 1925, s.52.

[45] *James Jones & Sons Ltd v Earl of Tankerville* [1909] 2 Ch. 440 at 443; *cf. Frogley v Earl of Lovelace* (1859) Johns. 333; *McManus v Cooke* (1887) 35 Ch.D. 681.

Finally, the landowner may contract to sell severed minerals simply as goods.[46] There may be a sale of minerals which have already been extracted, or an agreement to sell minerals not yet won, which the landowner is to mine before the property passes. These are, both at common law and under the Act, contracts for the sale of goods. The buyer can have no interest in or right to the goods themselves under such a contract before severance.

1–098 A difficult question is whether a contract for the sale of minerals to be won by the *buyer* can ever be a contract for the sale of "goods" within the extended definition of that word formulated in section 61(1) of the Act. The language used, "emblements, industrial growing crops, and things attached to or *forming part of* the land which are agreed to be severed before sale or under the contract of sale", is clearly wide enough to include the soil itself and mineral products; but there seems to be a reluctance among commentators to extend the analogy of *fructus naturales* so far. It has indeed been suggested[47] that the sale of sand from a quarry is in all cases a sale of an interest in "the land itself", echoing the argument of counsel in *Morgan v Russell & Sons*[48] that the words "things attached to and forming part of the land" mean "things of the same nature as 'emblements and industrial growing crops' and have no application to a contract for the sale of the land itself or part thereof." Williston[49] considered that the sale of a *definite* amount of ore *to be mined promptly* by the buyer should be treated as a contract to sell goods; but the validity of the qualifications introduced by the learned author is doubtful. The requirement of prompt severance, even if it could be said to have survived the Act in the case of trees and other growing things,[50] has never been relevant in the case of minerals, which cannot derive further benefit from remaining unsevered. The stipulation that there can be no sale of goods where the buyer may remove an indefinite quantity has more support. The case of *Kursell v Timber Operators & Contractors Ltd*[51] is an authority to the contrary as regards timber; but in *Morgan v Russell and Sons*[52] the fact that the amount contracted for was indefinite carried weight with at least one member of the court.[53] In this case a contract for the sale of cinders and slag, held to have become part of the soil, which was to be removed by the buyer, was considered not to be a sale of goods under the Act. "The contract appears

---

[46] *Cf. Anglo-Iranian Oil Co. Ltd v Jaffrate* [1953] 1 W.L.R. 246 at 259–260.
[47] Atiyah, *The Sale of Goods* (11th ed.), p.83. (The comment of the learned author is not restricted to sales where the sand is to be severed by the buyer. In this respect, at least, it is surely too wide.)
[48] [1909] 1 K.B. 357.
[49] *Sales* (3rd ed.), para.64.
[50] See below, para.1–099, where it is submitted that this is no longer a valid requirement.
[51] [1927] 1 K.B. 298.
[52] [1909] 1 K.B. 357; *cf. Mills v Stokman* (1967) 116 C.L.R. 61 (contract to enter and remove slate (including waste slate abandoned after severance) held a *profit à prendre*).
[53] Lord Alverstone C.J. [1909] 1 K.B. 357 at 365. Note also *Egmont Box Co. Ltd v Registrar-General of Lands* [1920] N.Z.L.R. 741, in which there was held to be no sale of goods where there was a *right* but not an *obligation* to enter and cut timber.

to me to be exactly analogous to a contract which gives a man a right to enter upon land with liberty to dig from the earth *in situ*, so much gravel or brick earth or coal on payment of a price per ton."[54] But the judgments as a whole give no clear indication of the point at which, or the grounds on which, this analogy is to give way to the wording of the Act.

Time allowed for severance. Williston[55] contended that although the statute does not in terms require prompt severance, "it is reasonable to imply this requirement, since the English Act was intended to state previously existing law, which was expressed in . . . *Marshall v Green*."[56] With respect, there is no greater case for this presumption than for an argument that the Act was intended to sweep away differences and difficulties which existed previously. Looking to the words of the Act itself, it is submitted that whether severance is to be immediate or otherwise is no longer material. 1–099

Passing of property. Things attached to or forming part of the land—buildings, fixtures, crops, minerals and soil—which are agreed to be severed before sale or under the contract of sale, are declared to be "goods" by section 61(1) of the Act. Some of these things were indeed "chattels," if not goods, at common law. The owner of land to which such things are attached may, for the purposes of a contract of sale, treat them as "goods" within the Act[57]; but this conventional characterisation cannot displace the overriding fact that for many purposes they remain land. It is an open question whether, even as a matter *inter partes*, the property in such things can pass before severance[58]: certainly the statutory presumption that goods must be "in a deliverable state" before the property will pass[59] would be difficult to displace. This is borne out by the many cases in which it was thought not open to argument that property passed only on severance.[60] In the graphic phrase used in *Liford's Case*,[61] "timber trees cannot be felled with a goose quill." 1–100

---

[54] [1909] 1 K.B. 357 at 365. *Cf. Saskatoon Sand & Gravel Ltd v Steve* (1970) 40 D.L.R. (3d) 248 and *Atlantic Concrete Ltd v LeVatte Construction Co. Ltd* (1975) 62 D.L.R. (3d) 663, where agreements to remove gravel were held *profits à prendre*; and contrast *Amco Enterprises Pty Ltd v Wade* [1968] Qd.R. 445 (held a sale of goods).

[55] *Sales* (3rd ed.), para.62.

[56] (1875) 1 C.P.D. 35.

[57] It is traditionally said that whether such things are sold as goods or conveyed as an interest in land, in the nature of an easement or profit, depends on whether the property is intended to be transferred to the buyer before or after severance (see, *e.g. Blackburn on Sale* (3rd ed.), pp.5–16). But this supposed test is unworkable, for it overlooks the difficulties discussed in the text, *infra*, and also the rule that an informal contract is insufficient to create an interest in land.

[58] See the discussion in Gow, *The Mercantile and Industrial Law of Scotland* (1964), p.80; and *cf. Saunders v Pilcher* [1949] 2 All E.R. 1097 at 1103.

[59] s.18, rr. 1–3, 5.

[60] *Morison v Lockhart*, 1912 S.C. 1017; *Paton's Trustees v Finlayson*, 1923 S.C. 872; *Kursell v Timber Operators* [1927] 1 K.B. 298; *Munro v Liquidator of Balnagown Estates Co.*, 1949 S.C. 49; *cf. Brantom v Griffits* (1877) 2 C.P.D. 212 (growing crops for similar reasons held not within Bills of Sale Acts). The contracts described in para.1–094, above, might be an exception.

[61] (1614) 11 Co.Rep. 46b at 50a.

In any case the mere agreement of the parties cannot affect the claims of third parties who enjoy paramount rights in the land. In *Morison v Lockhart*,[62] the heir in possession of an entailed estate entered into a contract to sell standing timber, which the buyer was to cut down and remove. Before all the timber had been cut, the seller died, and the right of his successor as heir to the estate to claim the uncut trees was upheld by the court. Although the Act declares that a sale of uncut timber is a contract for the sale of *goods*, it cannot confer upon the seller the power to sell what is not his goods, but someone else's land, by the law of entail.[63] Similarly, despite the fact that a thing is defined to be "goods" by section 61(1) of the Act, it may also be "land" or an "interest in land" within the Law of Property (Miscellaneous Provisions) Act 1989, so that a contract relating to it will need to be made in writing under section 2 of that statute.[64]

(b) *Classes of Goods*

1–101 **Statutory classifications.** Two classifications of "goods" are made by the Sale of Goods Act 1979. The first is the division into *existing goods* and *future goods*,[65] both terms being defined in section 5(1) and the latter again in section 61(1). The second is the distinction made between *specific goods*, defined in section 61(1), and *unascertained goods*,[66] which is not expressly defined but must by inference mean "goods *not* identified and agreed upon at the time a contract of sale is made." It is no doubt intended that each pair of terms should be both mutually exclusive[67] and also complementary so as together to embrace all goods. But existing goods may be either specific or unascertained, and the same is true of future goods; so that the classifications cut across one another.[68]

Mention may also be made of the terms "fungible goods"[69] and "goods having a potential existence"[70] (neither of which is used in the Act), and "ascertained goods"[71] (which is used but not defined).

---

[62] Above.

[63] See Settled Land Act 1925, ss.38, 49(2), 66, 90 for the position where the sale is made under the powers given by that Act.

[64] Prior to the abolition of the rule in *Bain v Fothergill* (1874) L.R. 7 H.L. 158 (by the Law of Property (Miscellaneous Provisions) Act 1989, s.3), a question might have arisen in relation to facts similar to those in *Morison v Lockhart* (above) whether the seller would be liable to the purchaser for damages for loss of his bargain. It will now clearly be open to a court to award such damages, whether the transaction is viewed as a sale of goods or of an interest in land.

[65] See below, para.1–102.

[66] See below, para.1–113.

[67] It is arguable that goods possessed but not owned by the seller are both "existing" and "future" goods within s.5(1), but this depends on the meaning of "acquired". The use in s.5(1) of the wording "either . . . or" suggests the contrary. The words "or possessed" in s.5(1) are probably included in order to meet the special cases dealt with in ss.21–25 (sales by a person not the owner).

[68] See below, para.1–114.

[69] See below, para.1–120.

[70] See below, para.1–106.

[71] See below, para.1–117.

Existing and future goods. Section 5(1) of the Act provides that "the goods which form the subject of a contract of sale may be either existing goods, owned or possessed[72] by the seller, or goods to be manufactured or acquired by him after the making of the contract of sale, in this Act called future goods."[73] It is clear that goods which the seller neither owns nor possesses may be "existing" in an everyday sense and yet "future goods" for the purposes of the Act. For instance, the seller may agree to sell goods which at the time of the contract are in the ownership and possession of a third party, and which he expects or hopes to acquire before performance is due.[74] 1–102

The statutory definition of "future goods" refers simply to goods to be "manufactured or acquired" by the seller. But a more elaborate classification may be made as follows: (a) goods to be manufactured by the seller, whether from materials which are now in existence or not; (b) goods which are to become, or may become, the property[75] of the seller, whether by purchase, gift, succession, occupation[76] or otherwise; (c) goods expected to come into existence as the property of the seller in the ordinary course of nature, *e.g.* the young to be born of his livestock, or the milk to be produced by his cows; (d) things attached to or forming part of land (whether belonging to the seller or another) which are to be severed in the future, *e.g.* minerals to be won, timber to be cut, fixtures to be detached[77]; and (e) crops in the category *fructus industriales* to be grown by the seller in the future.[78]

Contracts for the sale of future goods. Section 5 makes it clear that future goods may be the subject of a contract of sale.[79] Whatever its outward form, such a contract can operate only as an agreement to sell.[80] 1–103

Agreement to pay differences distinguished. An agreement to sell goods in the future, which the seller does not own at the time but intends to go into the market and buy, is a sale of goods within the Act provided that an actual delivery of the goods is contemplated. The fact that the motive of either party is to speculate is immaterial. This may be distinguished from the case where the contract of sale is colourable only, and the parties agree 1–104

---

[72] See n.67, above.
[73] The definition of "future goods" is repeated in s.61(1).
[74] It is clear that such goods may be either "specific" or "unascertained": see below, paras 1–112—1–113.
[75] Or, possibly, to come into his possession: see the wording of s.5(1).
[76] *e.g.* wild creatures: see above, para.1–088.
[77] Goods in classes (c) and (d) may in some cases be said to have a "potential existence": see below, para.1–106.
[78] Such crops, if already growing, and things in class (d) which are agreed to be severed before sale or under the contract of sale are by s.61(1) "goods" and, *semble, existing* goods within the statutory definition: but see above, para.1–100.
[79] In *Ajello v Worsley* [1898] 1 Ch. 274, it was held that a person could lawfully advertise goods for sale which he did not then have, and with which the manufacturers had refused to supply him.
[80] s.5(3); below, para.1–105.

or intend[81] that there shall be merely a settlement based on "differences" or "fluctuations" in the market price of such goods, without delivery. The question whether an actual delivery is contemplated is one of fact.[82] The distinction between the two categories of bargain was formerly important because the latter has traditionally been regarded as a wager on the future price of the commodity and, as such, was void under the Gaming Act 1845, s.18.[83] With the coming into force of the Gambling Act 2005, section 18 has ceased to have effect[84] and the fact that a contract relates to gambling no longer prevents its enforcement. However, the distinction will continue to be relevant in other jurisdictions where gaming contracts are illegal, either at common law or by statute; and in any case it would seem clear that agreements to pay differences are outside the scope of the Sale of Goods Act.

1–105 **Effect of purported sale of future goods.** Both at common law and under section 5(3) of the Act, a purported sale of future goods operates not as a sale but as an agreement to sell. This is so even if the seller executes a deed of bargain and sale. "It is a common learning in the law that a man cannot grant or charge that which he hath not."[85] "The law has long been settled that a person cannot by deed, however solemn, assign that which is not in him—in other words, there cannot be a prophetic conveyance."[86] Such a transaction, when viewed as an agreement to sell, would not appear to have any characteristics differing from an agreement to sell *stricto sensu*. The property will pass subsequently in accordance with what must be presumed to be the intention of the parties. In the special circumstances of such a case, it may be possible to infer a licence to the buyer to seize the goods after they have become the seller's property. And if the goods are sufficiently identified, the property in the goods may pass when they come into the seller's ownership, without any act on the part of either party. This may be especially true of "goods having a potential existence".

1–106 **Goods having a potential existence.** At common law, a distinction was recognised between future goods in which the seller had, and those in which he had not, what was called a potential property. The former class embraced all things which were the natural produce or expected increase of

---

[81] If only one of the parties intends, or is prepared, to make or accept delivery according to the contract, the transaction is a sale, even though the other party may have had no such intention: *Wilson, Smithett & Cope Ltd v Terruzzi* [1976] Q.B. 683 at 710.

[82] On the question of intention, see *Grizewood v Blane* (1851) 11 C.B. 526; *Cooper v Stubbs* [1925] 2 K.B. 753; *Barnett v Sanker* (1925) 41 T.L.R. 660; *Forget v Ostigny* [1895] A.C. 318.

[83] While this Act was in force, a statutory exception was made for hedging and similar contracts entered into by way of business and for certain kinds of investment transaction specified by the Treasury: Financial Services and Markets Act 2000, s.412.

[84] Gambling Act 2005, s.334(l)(c). The Financial Services and Markets Act 2000, s.412 *(above)* is now redundant: *ibid.*, s.334(l)(e).

[85] Perkins' Profitable Book, tit. Grant, s.65.

[86] *Belding v Read* (1865) 3 H. & C. 955 at 961.

something already owned or possessed[87] by the seller: a man might sell the crop of hay to be grown in his field, or the wool of the sheep or the milk from the cows presently owned by him. There is old authority for the proposition that such property could be the subject of an immediate grant or assignment,[88] and not merely of an agreement to sell (as was the case where the subject of the contract was to be acquired later, *e.g.* the wool of any sheep which the seller might buy within a year).[89] It is plain that this view has not survived the Act; although, as a matter of inference, such goods may more readily be deemed to become the buyer's as soon as they are extant (or severed), without any further act of appropriation, since they are capable of prospective identification.

Assignment of future property in equity. In equity, it is not necessary for the transfer of property (that is, of beneficial ownership) that there should be any formal conveyance or delivery of possession: a contract for valuable consideration, by which it is agreed to make a transfer of property, may pass to the intended assignee an immediate beneficial interest in or equitable title to the property.[90] But where such an agreement relates to property not existing or not owned at the time by the intending transferor, it cannot have any present operation. If, however, he later acquires property identifiable as that described in the contract, an equitable interest in favour of the intended transferee will immediately attach to the property. In other words, the transferor will then become a trustee of the property for the transferee, and the right of the latter will prevail against anyone except a bona fide purchaser of the legal title. 1–107

The leading case in which this doctrine was applied to after-acquired personal property is *Holroyd v Marshall*,[91] decided by the House of Lords in 1862. Here a person had mortgaged the chattels in his mill, with a covenant by him that all chattels added to the mortgaged goods or substituted for them should also be bound by the mortgage. It was held that immediately new chattels were placed in the mill an equitable title to them vested in the mortgagee, no further act by either party being necessary.

Under the rule of equity, the mode or form of assignment is immaterial provided that the intention of the parties is clear, value is given, and the property is of such a nature and so described as to be capable of being ascertained and identified.[92] Furthermore, a purported *immediate* assign-

---

[87] Where the ownership and possession are separated, *e.g.* in the case of a letting, the property in the produce or progeny is prima facie in the possessor: *Tucker v Farm & General Investment Trust Ltd* [1966] 2 Q.B. 421.

[88] *Grantham v Hawley* (1615) Hob. 132; *Petch v Tutin* (1846) 15 M. & W. 110. *Cf. Fitzwilliam v Parson of Arcsay* (1443) Y.B. 21 Hen. 6 at 43 (tithes).

[89] *Robinson v Macdonnell* (1816) 5 M. & S. 228 (oil from whales to be caught).

[90] *Holroyd v Marshall* (1862) 10 H.L.Cas. 191; *Collyer v Isaacs* (1881) 19 Ch.D. 342; *Re Clarke* (1887) 36 Ch.D. 348; *Tailby v Official Receiver* (1888) 13 App.Cas. 523; and see generally Ashburner, *Principles of Equity* (2nd ed.), pp.245–247; *Snell's Equity* (31st ed.), paras 3–28 *et seq.*.

[91] Above.

[92] The situation must be such that the goods upon acquisition can be "unequivocally identified with the individual contract relied on" (*per* Lord Mustill in *Re Goldcorp Exchange Ltd* [1995] 1 A.C. 74 at 95–96.

ment for value of future property is regarded as a contract to assign within the rule. In principle, the rule is applicable generally to all kinds of property, real and personal, including goods and choses in action. But a special limitation must be made as regards the sale of future goods, as a result of the decision in *Re Wait*.[93]

1–108 **Equitable principle inapplicable to contracts for sale of future goods.** In *Re Wait*,[94] W agreed to buy 1,000 tons of wheat of a particular description c.i.f. Bristol, expected to be shipped shortly from a port in the United States. On the following day, he resold 500 tons of the same wheat to sub-purchasers. Wheat of the contract description was shipped in bulk, and a bill of lading for 1,000 tons sent to W. Shortly afterwards the sub-purchasers, without having received any documents of title and before there had been any appropriation of the 500 tons, paid the price to W, who then became bankrupt before the ship arrived. The trustee in bankruptcy claimed to be entitled to the whole 1,000 tons. The sub-purchasers brought an action for specific performance, which failed because the 500 tons were not "specific or ascertained goods" within section 52 of the Act of 1893[95]; and in the alternative they alleged that the contract had operated as an equitable assignment giving them a beneficial interest or equitable lien in respect of 500 tons of the wheat in the hands of the trustee. This plea was rejected by a majority of the Court of Appeal. Lord Hanworth M.R.[96] based his opinion simply on the point that the principle of *Holroyd v Marshall*[97] could not apply unless the property in question had been subsequently identified. But Atkin L.J. was prepared to go further, and to hold that the supposed equitable claim would not lie even in this event: to grant such relief would "appear to embarrass to a most serious degree the ordinary operations of buying and selling goods, and the banking operations which attend them."[98] The codification of the law, since the decision in *Holroyd v Marshall*, made the claim of the sub-purchasers even more difficult to sustain: "Without deciding the point, I think that much may be said for the proposition that an agreement for the sale of goods does not import any agreement to transfer property other than in accordance with the terms of the Code, that is, the intention of the parties to be derived from the terms of the contract, the conduct of the parties and the circumstances of the case, and unless a different intention appears, from the rules set out in section 18 . . . A seller or a purchaser may, of course, create any equity he pleases by way of charge, equitable assignment or any other dealing with or

[93] [1927] 1 Ch. 606. (Note that this case would now be decided differently in consequence of the reforms introduced by the Sale of Goods (Amendment) Act 1995 (below, paras 5–109 *et seq.*). However, the effect of this amending legislation is to enable the transfer of the *legal* property in goods which form part of a larger bulk; the equitable principles discussed in *Re Wait* remain unaffected.)
[94] [1927] 1 Ch. 606.
[95] Below, paras 17–097 *et seq.* (The enlarged definition of "specific goods" introduced by s.2(d) of the Sale of Goods (Amendment) Act 1995 would still not extend to such goods: see below, para.1–116.)
[96] [1927] 1 Ch. 606 at 617 *et seq.*
[97] (1861) 10 H.L.Cas. 191; above, para.1–107.
[98] [1927] 1 Ch. 606 at 629–630.

disposition of goods, the subject-matter of sale; and he may, of course, create such an equity as one of the terms expressed in the contract of sale.[99] But the mere sale or agreement to sell or the acts in pursuance of such a contract mentioned in the Code will only produce the legal effects which the Code states."[1]

Re Wait was followed and applied in *Re London Wine Co. (Shippers) Ltd*,[2] where a company had contracted to sell to various customers wine held on its behalf in a number of warehouses. Each purchaser received from the company a document called a "Certificate of Title" in respect of wine for which he had paid, describing him as the "sole and beneficial owner" of the wine in question. But there had been no appropriation from bulk of any wine to answer particular contracts. The company went into receivership, and the court was asked to determine the rights of three categories of buyer: (1) those in which a single purchaser of a particular wine by generic description had purchased the company's whole stock of that wine at the date of purchase, but in which there had been no act of appropriation and (apart from the "Certificate of Title") no acknowledgment by the company or the warehouseman that wine of that description was held to the buyer's order; (2) those which were similar to (1) except that there were a number of purchasers of the particular wine whose purchases together exhausted the whole of the company's stocks of that wine; and (3) those which were similar to (2) except that the purchases did not exhaust the company's stocks and in which cases, although there had been no acts of appropriation, there had been acknowledgements (*e.g.* in the form of warehouse receipts) that the appropriate quantity of wine was held to the customer's order. There were alternative arguments that in all three categories the goods had become subject to a valid and effective trust.

Oliver J. held that no property in the wine had passed to the purchasers in categories (1) and (2): the wine had been sold by description and was not a sale of the specific parcel which by coincidence the company then held; the order could have been fulfilled from any source, and the goods had not become "ascertained" within section 16 of the Act. In regard to category (3), although there was an estoppel against the warehouseman and, on the facts, also against the company, this gave rise to no proprietary right or claim, but would only enable the representee to recover damages. Further, there was no trust of the property in any of the three categories for want of certainty as to the subject-matter of the alleged trust. Accordingly, the receiver was directed to treat all the wine in question as the property of the company.

Absolute and conditional contracts for the sale of future goods. The Act provides, by section 2(3), that a contract of sale may be absolute or conditional. In the case of future goods, the issue naturally arising is 1–109

---

[99] *Cf. Aluminium Industrie Vaassen BV v Romalpa Aluminium Ltd* [1976] 1 W.L.R. 676; below, para.5–141.

[1] [1927] 1 Ch. 606 at 635–636. For a suggested qualification to the remarks of Atkin L.J., see below, para.18–234.

[2] [1986] P.C.C. 121 (in fact decided in 1975). See also *Re Goldcorp Exchange Ltd (In Receivership)* [1995] 1 A.C. 74; *Re Stapylton Fletcher Ltd* [1994] 1 W.L.R. 1181.

whether the obligations of both parties are conditional upon the goods in question coming into existence or being acquired by the seller, or whether the obligation of one party or the other is absolute. It is a question of construction which form the bargain between the parties has taken.

1–110 **Seller's obligation unconditional.** A seller may contract unconditionally to sell goods which he does not then own. Whether he intends to acquire goods to answer the contract or to manufacture or grow them himself is immaterial unless the terms of the bargain indicate that they are to be so acquired or produced.[3] The principle is the same where the goods contracted for are specific. If the seller cannot deliver them on the due date, he is liable for non-delivery[4]; and if he is unable to give a good title, he will be in breach of section 12(1) of the Act.[5]

1–111 **Obligation of both parties conditional.** If the seller's promise is to deliver the goods only if he should acquire them, or only if they should come into existence, and that of the buyer is similarly contingent, no action will lie on these promises if the condition is not fulfilled.[6] It is probably this situation which is contemplated by section 5(2) of the Act.[7] An illustration is to be found in the sale of goods "to arrive": these words are ordinarily construed to mean "if they arrive", and not to import any promise on the part of the seller that the event shall happen. If they fail to arrive, neither party incurs any liability.[8]

1–112 **Buyer's obligation unconditional, or sale of a chance.** The third alternative is that the seller's undertaking is to deliver the goods only if they come into existence or are otherwise acquired by him,[9] while the buyer agrees to pay the price whether this happens or not. Here the buyer takes the risk of the failure of the event, and the seller cannot be liable for non-delivery on that account. The subject-matter of such a contract may also be described not as "goods" but as a chance of obtaining goods; and accordingly it may be contended that the transaction falls outside the scope of the Act; but the contrary view is surely preferable in view of the plain language of sections 2(3) and 5(2).[10] Irrespectively of the question whether the Act is applicable, however, a chance may properly be the subject of a lawful contract.

---

[3] *Cf. Blackburn Bobbin Co. Ltd v T. W. Allen & Sons Ltd* [1918] 2 K.B. 467; below, para.6–035; and *cf. Hayward Bros Ltd v Daniel & Son* (1904) 91 L.T. 319.
[4] Below, para.17–001.
[5] Below, para.4–002.
[6] On contingent obligations, see above, para.1–051.
[7] "There may be a contract for the sale of goods the acquisition of which by the seller depends on a contingency which may or may not happen."
[8] *Lovatt v Hamilton* (1839) 5 M. & W. 639; *Johnson v Macdonald* (1842) 9 M. & W. 600: below, para.21–022.
[9] The event upon which such acquisition depends must necessarily be beyond the seller's own control.
[10] The parties may in a similar way agree that one or other of them shall take the chance that the goods may have ceased to exist (below, para.1–123). A buyer may also take the "chance" that the seller's title is defective: see below, para.4–032, but the fact that provision is made for such contracts by s.12(3) precludes any argument that the Act is inapplicable.

Specific and unascertained goods.[11] The second major classification of goods made by the Act is that into specific goods and unascertained goods. "Specific goods" by section 61(1) means "goods identified and agreed on at the time a contract of sale is made and includes an undivided share, specified as a fraction or percentage, of goods identified and agreed on as aforesaid."[12] "Unascertained goods" is not defined, but by inference must mean goods not identified and agreed on at that time. 1–113

Specific goods. Goods cannot be specific in the statutory sense unless they are so at the time of the contract: they cannot become "specific" (although they may become "ascertained"[13]) at a later stage. Specific goods are by the agreement of the parties designated as the unique goods which can be delivered by the seller in performance of his obligations; their individuality is established, so that there is no room for further selection or substitution. The question whether goods must be in existence[14] at the time of the contract in order to come within the statutory definition of "specific goods" has not been determined. It is clear that goods may be "identified and agreed on", so as to be specific, merely by words of description, *e.g.* the black horse now in my stable (there being only one). It is arguable that goods not yet in existence may be as particularly described, *e.g.* the whole crop of fruit to be produced from my orchard in the coming season.[15] It is sometimes asserted that future goods can never be specific, at least so far as concerns the passing of property,[16] but this is surely only an inexact way of stating that the property in such goods can never pass on the making of the contract under section 18, rule 1 of the Act.[17] There is reason enough for this in the requirement of rule 1 that the goods must be in a deliverable state at the time of the contract, as well as in the fact that a contract to sell future goods as such can never be "unconditional"; but there is nothing which compels us to read into the definition of "specific goods" a condition that they should presently exist. 1–114

The question remains an open one, and is probably of no consequence.[18] Further, it must be borne in mind that goods may "exist" in an everyday sense and yet be "future goods" rather than "existing goods" for the purposes of the Act.[19]

---

[11] *Cf.* Vienna Convention on Contracts for the International Sale of Goods (above, para.1–024), Arts 67(2), 69(1) ("goods identified to the contract").

[12] The words from "and includes" to the end were added by the Sale of Goods (Amendment) Act 1995, s.2(d): see below, para.1–116.

[13] Below, para.1–118.

[14] As regards goods which have never existed or have ceased to exist, see below, paras 1–122 *et seq.*

[15] *Cf. Reardon Smith Line Ltd v Yngvar Hansen-Tangen* [1976] 1 W.L.R. 989 (ship yet to be built "identified" by serial construction number, etc.).

[16] Atiyah, *The Sale of Goods* (11th ed.), p.84; *cf.* Chalmers, *Sale of Goods Act* (18th ed.), p.271.

[17] Below, para.5–017.

[18] In later chapters of this work it is assumed that such goods are "unascertained".

[19] Above, para.1–102.

1–115 **Suggested wider meaning of "specific goods".** In *Howell v Coupland*,[20] which was decided before the Act, a contract to sell 200 tons of potatoes from a particular crop to be grown by the seller was considered to be a sale of "specific" goods, the perishing of which frustrated the contract under the rule in *Taylor v Caldwell*.[21] But it has since been held in *Re Wait*[22] that the plain language of the Act now prevents so wide a meaning being given to "specific goods", so far as concerns the application of the statute: an unascertained or unappropriated portion of a larger designated mass, whether the latter is "existing goods" or "future goods", must be outside the statutory definition.

1–116 **Undivided share as "specific goods".** An amendment to the definition of "specific goods" made by the Sale of Goods (Amendment) Act 1995, s.2(d) adds the words "and includes an undivided share, specified as a fraction or percentage, of goods identified and agreed on as aforesaid." This provision follows an amendment to the definition of "goods" so as to include an undivided share in goods,[23] and is said to have been added for the purposes of clarification.[24] In the view of the Law Commissions, "where there is a sale of an undivided share, specified as a fraction, of specific goods (such as a horse, or greyhound, or item of furniture, or the cargo of a named ship), it would be inconvenient if the share were to be regarded as unascertained goods. This would mean that, in the case of property which could not be divided without losing its identity (such as a living horse), property in the share could never pass."[25] Accordingly, they recommended that it should be made clear in the Act that such a share in specific goods should itself be regarded as specific goods.

The Law Commissions further stated that, since an undivided share in goods cannot be physically possessed or delivered, separately from the whole of the goods, the provisions of the Act based on possession or physical delivery "would simply disapply themselves and the intentions of the parties would prevail".[26] This is, perhaps, more obviously the case where the goods cannot be divided up (*e.g.* a one-quarter share in a boat or a horse). Where the goods are bulk goods which are capable of physical separation, and it is contemplated by the contract that they will be divided up and the portion due to the buyer will be physically delivered, some parts of the Act will be applicable to such delivery.[27]

The Law Commissions in their report did not consider the implications of the extended definition of "specific goods" in contexts other than the passing of property and delivery and acceptance. It is clear that sections 6

---

[20] (1876) 1 Q.B.D. 258; below, para.6–038. *Cf. Lister v Munro* [1924] N.Z.L.R. 1137 (progeny of specific ewes).
[21] (1863) 3 B. & S. 826.
[22] [1927] 1 Ch. 606 at 621, 631: see below, para.6–038, and see also *H R & S Sainsbury Ltd v Street* [1972] 1 W.L.R. 834.
[23] Sale of Goods (Amendment) Act 1995, s.2(c), above, para.1–081.
[24] *Sale of Goods forming Part of a Bulk* (L. Com. No. 215, Scot. L. Com. No. 145, 1993), para.5(4).
[25] *ibid*.
[26] *ibid*., para.5(5).
[27] *e.g.* ss.29–37.

and 7 (perishing of specific goods)[28] and section 52 (specific performance)[29] will now apply to contracts for the sale of part-interests in specific goods, as will the Law Reform (Frustrated Contracts) Act 1943, s. 2(5)(c). Whether the change will be of any practical consequence remains to be seen.

Unascertained goods. Goods which are not "specific" as defined by the Act are unascertained goods. There are three main categories of unascertained goods: (a) generic goods, or goods referred to only as being of a particular kind or description, *e.g.* 100 tons of barley, or a new Ford Fiesta car; (b) goods not yet in existence, which have to be manufactured or produced by the seller or to accrue to him in some other way; and (c) a part[30] as yet unidentified of a specified bulk, *e.g.* 100 tons out of the 1,000 tons (or out of the unmeasured but larger quantity) now stored in the seller's warehouse. 1–117

Ascertained goods. The Act in section 16 speaks of unascertained goods becoming "ascertained", and in sections 17(1) and 52 uses the expression "specific or ascertained goods", but this term is not defined in the Act. It is plain that "ascertained goods" means goods originally unascertained which become identified in accordance with the parties' agreement *after* the contract of sale is made; and this was assumed to be the meaning of the term by Atkin L.J. in *Re Wait*.[31] 1–118

The amendment to the statutory definition of the term "specific goods" so as to include an undivided share in specific goods[32] is not matched by any similar extended definition of "ascertained goods"—no doubt because this latter expression is not defined in the Act. This is of no significance so far as concerns the passing of property, for the new section 20A expressly deals with goods which are identified by subsequent agreement between the parties; but it would appear that specific performance under section 52[33] will not be available to a buyer of an undivided share in goods which become ascertained after the making of the contract of sale.

Application of the distinction. The distinction between specific and unascertained goods is of most importance in relation to the passing of property. Under the Act, the property in specific goods may pass to the buyer when the contract is made,[34] but no property is transferred under a contract for the sale of unascertained goods unless and until the goods are ascertained.[35] Nor can there by a valid trust of unidentified property.[36] It is 1–119

---

[28] Below, paras 6–035 *et seq.*

[29] Below, paras 17–096 *et seq.*

[30] As regards the sale of a part specified as a fraction or percentage of the whole, see below, para.1–121.

[31] [1927] 1 Ch. 606 at 630.

[32] Above, para.1–116.

[33] Nor, presumably, under the general law: *Re Wait* (above).

[34] s.18, r. 1; below, para.5–017.

[35] s.16; below, para.5–069.

[36] *Re Wait* [1927] 1 Ch. 606; *Re London Wine Co. (Shippers) Ltd* [1986] P.C.C. 121; *Re Goldcorp Exchange Ltd (in receivership)* [1995] 1 A.C. 74; *Re Stapylton Fletcher Ltd* [1994] 1 W.L.R. 1181.

probably[37] also the rule at common law that possession cannot be effectively transferred in goods which are not yet ascertained, so that, for instance, there can be no attornment by a bailee of such goods[38]; and on similar reasoning the defeat of a seller's lien, although possible in the case of unascertained goods, is not readily inferred.[39]

Under section 52 of the Act, the court may in its discretion decree specific performance of a contract to deliver specific or ascertained goods, but there is no right either under the Act or on any general equitable principle to specific performance of a contract for the sale of unascertained goods.[40]

Sections 6 and 7 of the Act, which deal with the perishing of the contract goods respectively before and after the formation of a contract of sale, apply only to specific goods. The broad principles of common law which lie behind these statutory rules are, however, of more general application, and extend to the perishing of a specific source from which unascertained goods are to be derived or selected.[41] Even so, as regards at least one class of unascertained goods, *viz.* purely generic goods, it does not appear that a plea of impossibility or frustration based on the "perishing" of such goods or their source is capable of being sustained.[42]

1–120 **Fungible goods.** The expression "fungible goods" is not used in the Act; but it is common in countries of civil law jurisdiction and in the United States. It is used to define goods of which every particle or unit is indistinguishable from, or at least commercially equivalent to, every other particle or unit, *e.g.* grain, flour, or oil. Whether the term can be extended so as to include units capable of separate identification (*e.g.* barrels of flour, or the individual cattle in a herd) depends on whether it was the intention of the parties to regard them as equivalent.[43]

(c) *Part Interests in Goods*[44]

1–121 **Part owners.** Section 2(2) of the Sale of Goods Act 1979 states that there may be a contract of sale between one part owner and another. It is arguable that this provision is wide enough to include the transfer by a

[37] See, however, dicta to the contrary in *Comptoir d'Achat et de Vente du Boerenbond Belge S/A v Luis de Ridder Lda (The Julia)* [1949] A.C. 293 at 312. See generally Nicol, 42 M.L.R. 129 (1979).

[38] *Re London Wine Co. (Shippers) Ltd* [1986] P.C.C. 121 at 166; *Maynegrain Pty Ltd v. Compafina Bank* [1982] 2 N.S.W.L.R. 141 at 146–147 (reversed in part on another point (1984) 58 A.L.J.R. 389, PC). There may, however, be an estoppel as against the bailee himself. See further below, para.8–012.

[39] Below, para.15–095.

[40] *Re Wait* [1927] 1 Ch. 606; below, para.17–097. See also above, para.1–108.

[41] Below, para.6–038.

[42] Below, para.6–041.

[43] On fungible goods generally, see Williston, *Sales* (3rd ed.), para.159.

[44] See further 2 Bl.Comm. 399; Halsbury, *Laws of England* (4th ed.), Vol. 35, para.1243; Goode, *Proprietary Rights and Insolvency in Sales Transactions* (2nd ed.), p.6; Hill and Bowes-Smith, "Joint Ownership of Chattels", in Palmer and McKendrick, *Interests in Goods* (2nd ed.), Ch.10.

tenant in common both of the whole of his interest and also of a portion only of his interest (so that, in consequence, the proportions in which the part owners hold their shares are altered).[45] The subsection does not refer expressly to certain other transactions which appear analogous, for example, the transfer by the owner of a part interest in goods of the whole of that interest to a third party, or the transfer by the owner of goods of one or more part interests in them so as to make the transferee or transferees and himself co-owners.[46] There was some doubt prior to 1995 whether these transactions were all sales of goods within the Act; but since the Sale of Goods (Amendment) Act 1995 has amended the definition of "goods" in section 61(1) by adding the words "and includes an undivided share in goods"[47] it would now seem clear that this is the case.

A person who has agreed to buy goods is in no sense the owner of such goods, and therefore cannot make another a part owner of them. All that he can do is assign in part, or charge, his rights under the contract.

Section 20A of the Act, as inserted by the Sale of Goods (Amendment) Act 1995, s.1(3), provides that where there is a contract for the sale of a specified quantity of unascertained goods forming part of an identified bulk (such as 1,000 tonnes of wheat out of the cargo of wheat aboard a named ship) and the buyer has paid all or part of the price, property in an undivided share in the bulk is transferred to the buyer and the buyer becomes an owner in common of the bulk.[48] The provisions of the Act dealing with part interests in goods (*e.g.* s.2(2), above) would clearly apply to any subsequent dealings with such goods by the buyer. Apart from this special case, there cannot be part ownership in unascertained goods.

The cases on the supply of liquor to members of members' clubs are anomalous. The courts have consistently taken the view that the liquor is in law (or at least beneficially[49]) the joint property of all the members and that the supply of a drink to an individual member, even though it is paid for by him, is a "mere distribution of property" in which the members have a common interest or "the transfer of a special property" in the goods and is

---

[45] Goode, *Commercial Law* (3rd ed.), p.199 expresses the view that there cannot be a contract of sale unless the transferor intends to part with the whole of his interest.

[46] Goode, *ibid.*, considers that the latter of these transactions would be outside the statutory definition of a contract of sale—even, it would appear, after the 1995 amendments. The Law Commissions, however, took a contrary view, stating that the new definition "would . . . make it clear not only that there can be a sale of an undivided share in goods, whether by a sole owner or by someone who is already a part owner, but also that such a sale is a sale of goods for the purposes of the Act" (*Sale of Goods forming Part of a Bulk* (L. Com. No. 215, 1993, para.5.3). If, as is submitted, this latter view is correct, it would follow that a part-owner may also make a sale of a portion only of his interest (since that interest is now defined in the Act as "goods").

[47] See above, para.1–081.

[48] See below, paras 5–109 *et seq.*

[49] In *Trebanog Working Men's Club & Institute Ltd v Macdonald* [1940] 1 K.B. 576, where the club was incorporated, it was held to be a trustee of the liquor for the members collectively.

not a "sale" for the purposes of the licensing and revenue Acts.[50] Some further ingenuity of reasoning may be called for if this line of cases is to survive the changes made by the Sale of Goods (Amendment) Act 1995.[51]

(d) *Non-existent Goods*

1–122 **Non-existent goods.** The parties may reach an agreement about the sale of goods which without their knowledge have ceased to exist, either in whole or in part. Even short of actual destruction, the goods may have been lost or damaged or suffered such deterioration as to make it impossible for the seller to deliver them as "the contract goods". The parties may also agree to sell and purchase goods which have never in fact existed. The effect of such transactions is discussed in the sections which follow.

It is plain that, whatever may be the effect (whether under the Sale of Goods Act or otherwise) of the destruction or non-existence of the goods on the *contractual* relationship between the parties, the absence of a subject-matter makes it impossible for there to be any actual *sale*: there is nothing in respect of which a title can be transferred to the buyer.

1–123 **Effect on contract.** The absence of a real subject-matter does not, however, necessarily have the consequence of depriving a bargain of all effect. The question is essentially one of construction of the contract which the parties have made. If it has been made on the basis of a common assumption that the goods exist, the failure of that assumption will nullify their agreement, so that both parties are excused from all liability, apart from that of making restitution of anything already paid. But this is not the only possibility: "there may be a good contract about a non-existent subject-matter if on the true construction of the contract the risk of non-existence is thrown on one party."[52] On the one hand, the seller may have warranted that the goods in question do exist, in which case he will be liable for his inability to deliver, although the buyer will not have to pay the price.[53] On the other hand, the buyer may by the terms of the contract expressly or

---

[50] *Graff v Evans* (1882) 8 Q.B.D. 373; *Davies v Burnett* [1902] 1 K.B. 666; *Trebanog Working Men's Club & Institute Ltd v Macdonald*, above; *French v Hoggett* [1968] 1 W.L.R. 94; *R. v Torbay Justices, ex p. Royal British Legion (Paignton) Social Club* [1958] C.L.Y. 229; *cf. Carlton Lodge Club v Customs & Excise Commrs* [1975] 1 W.L.R. 66 (such a transaction not a "sale", but nevertheless a "supply" of liquor for the purpose of liability to value added tax). See also the definition of "Supply of alcohol" in the Licensing Act 2003, s. 14.

[51] A possible alternative explanation of these decisions is that a "sale", as contemplated by the Sale of Goods Act 1979, is a bilateral, and not a multilateral, transaction: below, para.2–026. In any case, the term "sale" undoubtedly has a special meaning in the Licensing Acts: see the Licensing Act 2003, s. 192 ("sale by retail"), and *Doak v Bedford* [1964] 2 Q.B. 587. Atiyah, *Sale of Goods* (11th ed.), p.35, suggests that these contracts may come within the Supply of Goods and Services Act 1982. There are plainly difficulties in applying such provisions as the implied terms as to quality to a multilateral transaction of this kind. See further above, para.1–027, n.92.

[52] Treitel, *The Law of Contract* (11th ed.), p.296. *Cf. McRae v Commonwealth Disposals Commission* (1950) 84 C.L.R. 377, below, para.1–132.

[53] This follows from s.28: see below, paras 9–021, 17–090.

implicitly have taken the chance that the goods do not exist: he will then be bound to pay the price whether there are such goods or not, although the seller will be excused from any obligation to deliver in the latter event.

Goods which have perished. The Sale of Goods Act 1979, by section 6, deals only with the first of these three[54] possibilities. This section declares that, "where there is a contract for the sale of specific goods, and the goods without the knowledge of the seller have perished at the time when the contract is made, the contract is void." Among the questions which arise in relation to this section are the meaning in the context of the terms "specific goods" and "perish"; and further, if the language used does not cover all possible categories of goods and types of event, whether the same or an analogous principle will govern the position at common law. Very similar problems are raised by section 7, which provides for the corresponding case where specific goods perish *after* the making of the contract.[55] The decisions which have been given under section 6 may therefore throw light on the interpretation of section 7, and vice versa. **1–124**

Meaning of "specific goods". By section 61(1) of the Act, "specific goods" means "goods identified and agreed on at the time a contract of sale is made and includes an undivided share, specified as a fraction or percentage, of goods identified and agreed on as aforesaid."[56] Although it has been suggested that the term might be given a wider interpretation for the purposes of sections 6 and 7, it is submitted that the only proper meaning must be that assigned by the statute.[57] It follows that a contract for the sale of goods not yet appropriated from a specific larger quantity (*e.g.* 500 tonnes out of the 1,000 tonnes now aboard the *Challenger*)[58] will not be within the section, and the same is true of unascertained goods to be derived from a designated source. It is probable, however, that the common law would reach a similar result even in a case not covered by the section: if the larger quantity in such a contract had itself "perished"[59] at the time **1–125**

[54] There is, at least in theory, a fourth possibility (that both parties shall be bound): Treitel, *loc. cit.* This would be the case if the parties were to enter into a contract for the sale of goods on a "lost or not lost" basis, containing obligations on both sides. The situation where goods sold on c.i.f. terms perish before the tender of documents is due is analogous: see below, para.19–059.

[55] Below, paras 6–035 *et seq.*

[56] Above, para.1–114; the words from "and includes" to the end were added by the Sale of Goods (Amendment) Act 1995, s.2(d): see above, para.1–116.

[57] Above, para.1–115, and below, para.6–038.

[58] As regards contracts for the sale of an undivided share in specific goods, see above, para.1–081 and below, para.1–129.

[59] Where part only of the bulk has perished, the vital question (unless the parties have expressly or impliedly agreed otherwise) will be whether what remains is sufficient to satisfy the contract. A more difficult question arises where there are unrelated contracts to sell (for instance) 500 tonnes out of a specific bulk of 1,000 tonnes to A and a further 500 tonnes to B, and part has perished so as to leave enough to fulfil one contract but not both. Unless one of the contracts is expressly or by implication made subject to the other, it would seem that neither buyer can claim priority, and neither contract is avoided. The seller may elect to perform

when the contract was made, or the source referred to had failed,[60] the parties would be discharged from their obligations either by the common law doctrine of mistake or because of the non-fulfilment of an implied condition precedent.[61]

1–126 **Meaning of "perish".** The Act does not define the term "perish", which is also used in section 7. Goods which have been stolen were held by Wright J. to have perished within the meaning of the section in *Barrow, Lane & Ballard Ltd v Phillip Phillips & Co. Ltd*[62]: this was undoubtedly true on the facts of the case, where 109 bags of a specific parcel of 700 bags of groundnuts had been stolen, so that *the parcel* had ceased to exist in a commercial sense; but it is open to question whether the mere fact of theft in the case of, say, a car means that it has "perished" in a commercial sense, at least before all hope of its recovery has been abandoned.[63] It is possible that goods which have been requisitioned[64] or condemned as prize[65] would be held to have "perished," and the leading case of *Couturier v Hastie*[66] (on which it is generally thought that section 6 was based by the draftsman of the Act[67]) perhaps suggests that this may also be the case where the goods have already been sold by a ship's master acting under a lawful power.[68]

1–127 **Perishing of part.** *Barrow, Lane & Ballard Ltd v Phillip Phillips & Co. Ltd*[69] is also authority for the proposition that, where a contract for the sale of a specific parcel of goods is indivisible, the perishing of part of the goods will render the contract void under section 6. It would seem to follow that where the contract is divisible, the destruction of part will not avoid the contract for the remainder; but this appears to put a gloss on the wording of the section. In any case, the mere fact that the goods, or the price (as distinct from the contract)[70] are divisible will not oblige either party to perform the contract as regards the remainder after part has been

---

whichever contract he pleases, but he must pay damages for breach of the other. See below, para.6–052, and *cf. J. Lauritzen A.S. v Wijsmuller BV (The "Super Servant Two")* [1990] 1 Lloyd's Rep. 1 (hire of transportation unit). The seller may, however, allocate the available goods *pro rata* (or on any other reasonable basis) among the various buyers if he has the protection of a "prohibition of export" or *force majeure* clause: see below, paras 18–353 *et seq.* For the position where either or both of the buyers have paid all or part of the price, see below, paras 5–109 *et seq.*

[60] Above, para.1–115; but there cannot ordinarily be any failure of a source of purely generic goods: below, para.6–041.

[61] Below, para.3–021.

[62] [1929] 1 K.B. 574.

[63] Atiyah, *The Sale of Goods* (11th ed.), p.111.

[64] *Cf. Re Shipton, Anderson & Co. Ltd and Harrison Bros & Co. Ltd* [1915] 3 K.B. 676. But see below, paras 6–035, 6–050.

[65] *Cf. The Odessa* [1916] 1 A.C. 145; *The Parchim* [1918] A.C. 157.

[66] (1856) 5 H.L. Cas. 673; below, para.1–134: but the result of the master's act in this case was that the specific cargo in question ceased to exist *as a cargo*.

[67] See Chalmers, *Sale of Goods Act 1893* (2nd ed., 1894), p.17.

[68] The same might be true of a sheriff's sale. But in most cases the seller would simply be in breach of his obligations under s.12: below, Ch.4.

[69] [1929] 1 K.B. 574; above, para.1–126.

[70] See below, paras 8–074 *et seq.*, 17–089.

destroyed: at best, the void bargain may serve to supply the terms of a new contract for the remainder which the parties may expressly or impliedly agree to make in its place.[71]

It has, however, been suggested that the buyer may always if he wishes waive his right to full and complete delivery and insist on having the remainder if he is willing to pay the full contract price, or perhaps, in a proper case, the appropriate part of a divisible price.[72] It is difficult to see how this can be reconciled with the statutory provision that the contract is void, although an analogous conclusion has been reached in one case[73] where the court was able to rule that the statute was not applicable.

Deterioration and damage. Goods may be held to have perished not only if they have been physically destroyed, but also if they have ceased to exist in a commercial sense as the contract goods—that is, if their merchantable character, as such, has been lost—or if they suffer such a change in their nature as to prevent their use for the purposes contemplated by the transaction.[74] This may be the consequence of damage externally caused or of deterioration from inherent natural causes. Substantially similar questions may arise in determining whether a contract has been frustrated (*e.g.* by the stranding of a ship whose continued "existence" was necessary for performance[75]), whether freight has been earned by the delivery of "the goods" which were shipped,[76] and whether under a policy of insurance there has been a constructive total loss.[77] The cases in which this difficult issue of degree has been determined are not easy to reconcile: thus potatoes which have so far deteriorated as to be unfit for human consumption, though still answering to the description "potatoes", have been held not to have perished,[78] but there is a New Zealand case[79] where the contrary was held on similar facts; and in *Asfar & Co. v Blundell*[80] dates which had begun to ferment after wetting and contamination were held to have ceased to exist in a commercial sense as "dates", even though the 1–128

---

[71] In *Barrow, Lane & Ballard Ltd v Phillip Phillips & Co. Ltd*, above, payment was made and accepted for part of the goods which were in fact delivered, although the contract was for an indivisible parcel. *Cf. H. R. and S. Sainsbury Ltd v Street* [1972] 1 W.L.R. 834, where the goods (part of a crop to be grown) were not specific and it was held that s.7 was not applicable. In these circumstances, Mackenna J. ruled that it was a question of the construction of the contract whether, in the event of the failure of part of the crop, the seller was nevertheless bound to deliver the quantity which had in fact been produced, and on the facts held this to be the case.

[72] Williston, *Sales* (3rd ed.), para.162. These views are reflected in the American Uniform Sales Act, s.7(2) and in U.C.C., para.2–163.

[73] *H R and S Sainsbury Ltd v Street* [1972] 1 W.L.R. 834.

[74] *Oldfield Asphalts Ltd v Grovedale Coolstores (1994) Ltd* [1998] 3 N.Z.L.R. 479 (building sold for removal damaged by fire).

[75] *Nickoll & Knight v Ashton, Edridge & Co.* [1901] 2 K.B. 126 at 133.

[76] *Duthie v Hilton* (1868) L.R. 4 C.P. 138; *Asfar & Co. v Blundell* [1896] 1 Q.B. 123.

[77] *Montreal Light, Heat & Power Co. v Sedgwick* [1910] A.C. 598 (cement ruined by wetting); and see Marine Insurance Act 1906, ss.56–61. But the questions whether goods are merely defective in quality or so defective as to fail to answer the contract description may not be exactly parallel: see below, para.11–020.

[78] *Horn v Minister of Food* [1948] 2 All E.R. 1036; below, para.6–035; (a case on s.7).

[79] *Rendell v Turnbull & Co.* (1908) 27 N.Z.L.R. 1067.

[80] Above.

consignment was still of considerable value. Again, in the old case of *Barr v Gibson*,[81] a ship which had foundered and was seriously damaged beyond practical, but not perhaps theoretical, repair was held not to have lost its character as a ship; but the more modern case of *Nickoll & Knight v Ashton, Edridge & Co.*[82] indicates that this decision would not now be followed.

The question of liability for damage and deterioration which falls short of "perishing" in a commercial sense is determined by the ordinary principles governing the assumption of risk and the related issue of whether the quality of the goods has been warranted.[83]

1–129 **Undivided share.** The definition of "specific goods" in section 61(1) of the Act was extended in 1995 by the addition of the words "and includes an undivided share, specified as a fraction or percentage, of goods identified and agreed on as aforesaid."[84] It follows that section 6 (and also section 7) applies to a contract for the sale of such a share—*e.g.* a one-quarter share in an identified racehorse or boat, or a 50 per cent share in the cargo of oil aboard a named vessel. If the horse, boat or cargo should have "perished" in any of the senses falling within section 6, as discussed above, plainly the contract for the sale of the undivided share will be void. Section 7 will similarly apply to the case where there is an agreement to sell such a share (but only where the risk has not passed to the buyer). However, at least in the case of the cargo of oil, it is possible that the terms of the contract may provide otherwise—*e.g.* that if, when the cargo is apportioned, part has been lost, the buyer shall be entitled to take delivery of a predetermined percentage or quantity out of what remains.

1–130 **Effect of the section.** Section 6 provides that in the circumstances mentioned, "the contract is void". The true position appears to be that, although there is a bargain based upon mutual assent, such assent is nullified either by the common mistake[85] of the parties so that it is "emptied of all content"[86] or by the failure of an implied condition precedent that the goods are in existence.[87] The consequence is on either view that each party is excused from all his obligations under the contract, and any money paid in advance by the buyer can be recovered.[88]

1–131 **Relevance of knowledge and fault.** Section 6 applies only where the goods have perished "without the knowledge of the seller." In *Bell v Lever Bros Ltd*,[89] Lord Atkin said: "I apprehend that if the seller with knowledge

[81] (1838) 3 M. & W. 390.
[82] Above.
[83] Below, Ch.6 and paras 11–040, 11–049, 11–066 *et seq.*
[84] Sale of Goods (Amendment) Act 1995, s.2(d); above, para.1–081.
[85] *Bell v Lever Bros Ltd* [1932] A.C. 161 at 217. On mistake generally, see below, paras 3–011 *et seq.*
[86] Cheshire, Fifoot and Furmston, *The Law of Contract* (14th ed.), p.255.
[87] *Bell v Lever Bros Ltd* above, pp.224 *et seq.*; *Solle v Butcher* [1950] 1 K.B. 671 at 691; *McRae v Commonwealth Disposals Commission* (1950) 84 C.L.R. 377 at 407.
[88] Where the goods have perished in part, and the remainder is tendered, the provisions of s.30(1) do not apply: *Barrow, Lane & Ballard Ltd v Phillip Phillips & Co. Ltd* [1929] 1 K.B. 574 at 585. But there may be a new contract as regards that part: see above, para.1–127.
[89] [1932] A.C. 161 at 217.

that a chattel was destroyed purported to sell it to a purchaser, the latter might sue for damages for non-delivery though the former could not sue for non-acceptance, but I know of no case where a seller has so committed himself." The same may be true of the case where the seller *ought* to have known of the destruction or non-existence of the goods,[90] and possibly also where the goods have perished as a consequence of the seller's own act or fault.[91]

Alternative construction: seller absolutely liable. In the ordinary case of a contract for the sale of specific goods, the parties may naturally be presumed to have made their bargain on the understanding that the goods were then in existence, so that the provisions of section 6 will govern the position. But it is an over-simplification to suppose that this approach is adequate to deal with all contracts for the sale of goods which prove to be non-existent. In the Australian case of *McRae v Commonwealth Disposals Commission*,[92] the seller was held to have warranted that the goods existed, so that he was liable in damages for non-delivery. The defendant Commission had advertised for sale an oil-tanker, which was described as stranded on a named reef off the coast of New Guinea, and subsequently accepted the [claimants'] offer to buy it. In fact there was no tanker at all in the locality, nor indeed any reef, and the cost of the [claimants'] abortive salvage expedition was claimed in an action for non-delivery. The trial judge held that the contract of sale was void; but in the High Court a different view was taken: "The buyers relied upon, and acted upon, the assertion of the seller that there was a tanker in existence. It is not a case in which the parties can be seen to have proceeded on the basis of a common assumption of fact so as to justify the conclusion that the correctness of the assumption was intended by both parties to be a condition precedent to the creation of contractual obligations . . . The only proper construction of the contract is that it included a promise by the Commission that there was a tanker in the position specified."[93] Damages were accordingly awarded. 1–132

Some writers[94] have found difficulty in reconciling the decision in *McRae's* case with the language of section 6; but the section was expressly held inapplicable by the court, in accordance with the reasoning quoted above. It would be possible to distinguish the statutory wording on the literal ground that the tanker had not "perished", for it had never existed; but the High Court itself based its reasoning on principle and not on mere wording. It is submitted that the provisions of section 6 can always be overriden by an express or implied warranty that the goods exist,[95] and this

---

[90] *Cf. McRae v Commonwealth Disposals Commission* (1950) 84 C.L.R. 377, below, para.1–132; Atiyah, *The Sale of Goods* (11th ed.), p.107, suggests that in such a case the seller should be held liable for misrepresentation.

[91] *Cf.* s.7, below, para.6–035; *Lebeaupin v Crispin & Co.* [1920] 2 K.B. 714; *Tommey v Finextra Ltd* (1962) 106 S.J. 1012 (car undeliverable because sold to third party).

[92] (1950) 84 C.L.R. 377. See Slade, 70 L.Q.R. 389 at 396–397 (1954); Shatwell, 33 Can.Bar.Rev.164 (1955).

[93] (1950) 84 C.L.R. 377 at 409–410.

[94] *e.g.* Cheshire, Fifoot and Furmston, *The Law of Contract* (14th ed.), pp.257–258.

[95] Or, conceivably, that they exist and will continue to exist for a stated period.

approach may be supported by an appeal to section 55 of the Act.[96] If this submission is not accepted, but it is felt that justice entitles the buyer to relief, recourse may perhaps be had to the fiction of a collateral contract or to the law of misrepresentation.[97]

It follows that section 6 should be regarded only as a prima facie rule. Where goods have perished without the knowledge of the seller, there is a presumption[98] that the parties have contracted on the implied understanding that they continue to exist; but this presumption will be displaced if the construction of the contract so demands.

1–133 **Warranty that goods have existed.** It is pertinent to ask whether there is a principle of general application that the seller of specific goods impliedly warrants either that the goods have at some time been in existence or that to the best of his knowledge they do exist. There is some support for this view in the decided cases[99]: that *McRae's* case is not only reconcilable with the principle underlying section 6, but is itself an illustration of a general principle which is logically presupposed by that of section 6. A similar argument may be based on section 12(1)[1]; for if a seller impliedly undertakes that he has title, he necessarily also warrants that, at least so far as he knows or ought to know, there is in existence a thing to which the title relates.

1–134 **Alternative construction: buyer absolutely liable.** A third possible construction of the contract is that the buyer has assumed the risk of the existence of the goods, and has promised to pay the price whether or not the seller is able to make delivery. In these circumstances the subject-matter of the contract is perhaps better described as a chance or venture than as goods.[2] The bargain may be that he should get nothing at all if the goods cannot be delivered, or that he should have something else in their place—*e.g.* that he should succeed to the seller's right to claim for their loss under an insurance policy. The latter was unsuccessfully argued to be the true construction of the contract in *Couturier v Hastie*.[3] There, a cargo of corn had been shipped at Salonica in February for delivery in London. In May, the claimants sold the cargo through the agency of the defendants, who were acting under a *del credere* commission and therefore liable as a buyer for the price. In fact the cargo had, unknown to either party, been

---

[96] Above, para.1–013; and *cf.* below, para.1–133. See further Atiyah, 73 L.Q.R. 340 (1957); Atiyah, *The Sale of Goods* (11th ed.), pp.105–107. *Contra* Treitel, *The Law of Contract* (11th ed.), p.297.

[97] Cheshire Fifoot, and Furmston, *op. cit.*, p.258 (where it is pointed out that the consideration for such a collateral contract may be illusory). On collateral contracts, see K. W. Wedderburn [1959] C.L.J. 58 and below, paras 2–027, 10–012; and on misrepresentation, see below, paras 12–002 *et seq.*

[98] Atiyah, *op. cit.*, p.97.

[99] *Bell v Lever Bros Ltd*, above, para.1–130; Atiyah, 73 L.Q.R. 340 at 349 (1957); *cf. Goldsborough, Mort & Co. v Carter* (1914) 19 C.L.R. 429 at 437. But see *Barrow Lane & Ballard Ltd v Phillip Phillips & Co. Ltd* [1929] 1 K.B. 574 at 582.

[1] Below, para.4–002.

[2] Above, para.1–112.

[3] (1856) 5 H.L.Cas. 673, affirming (1853) 9 Exch.102; Atiyah, 73 L.Q.R. 340 (1957).

sold *en route* by the ship's captain before the date of the contract, as it had begun to deteriorate after suffering damage in a storm. The claimants failed in their claim for the price. The case is commonly supposed to have laid down the rule that a contract for the sale of goods which have without the seller's knowledge perished is void; and indeed it was probably on this understanding of the case that section 6 of the Act was drafted.[4] But this proposition was not part of the *ratio decidendi* in any of the judgments which were delivered in the course of the hearing of *Couturier v Hastie*: the issue at all stages was not the validity, but the true construction, of the contract made by the parties. Counsel for the claimants contended that the contract was for the sale and purchase, not of the specific cargo, but of the adventure as represented by the shipping documents—an argument which had some substance in view of the written terms "free on board and including freight and insurance; . . . payment upon handing over shipping documents."[5] The failure of this argument meant necessarily that the action for the price could not succeed, not because of any ruling that the contract was void, but simply because the cargo which was held to be the subject-matter of the contract had not been delivered. In an action for the price of goods which the seller is incapable of delivering, the only issue is whether the liability of the buyer is to be construed as absolute. It is submitted that such a construction is still possible in an appropriate case without infringing the principle declared by section 6.

Goods not known to exist. The requirement of mutual assent naturally 1–135
precludes there being any effective contract for the sale of goods which are not known by either party to exist—for example, jewellery contained in a secret drawer of a cabinet which is itself the subject of a contract of sale.[6] This would be subject to an exception where the terms of the contract or the nature of the subject-matter may be taken to include the possibility of unknown additional goods—*e.g.* "the contents" of a house, or oysters which may contain pearls.

---

[4] See Chalmers, *Sale of Goods Act 1893* (2nd ed., 1894), p.17.

[5] See below, para.19–109. It is arguable even on this interpretation, however, that the decision is out of keeping with modern cases on risk in c.i.f. contracts: see paras 19–110 *et seq.*

[6] *Merry v Green* (1841) 7 M. & W. 623.

CHAPTER 2

FORMATION OF THE CONTRACT[1]

PARA.

1. Agreement 2–001
2. Formalities 2–021
3. Parties 2–026
4. The price 2–044

1. AGREEMENT

Application of general contractual principles. A contract of sale, like any other contract, depends on agreement,[2] which is usually shown by the acceptance of an offer. The question whether agreement has been reached is determined objectively. The rules as regards the making and communication of offer and acceptance and the revocation and termination of offers are common to all contracts, and may be found in general works on the law of contract.[3] The Sale of Goods Act 1979—apart from section 57, which deals with sales by auction[4]—contains no special provisions concerning this aspect of the contract of sale, which is therefore governed by the ordinary principles of the common law.[5] It is only in a few respects that the application of these principles to the sale of goods calls for special mention. **2–001**

Where a contract of sale is concluded by electronic means and the buyer is a consumer, the Consumer Protection (Distance Selling) Regulations 2000[6] will necessarily apply.

---

[1] References to corresponding provisions of the Vienna Convention on Contracts for the International Sale of Goods (above, para.1–024) are given at relevant places in this chapter. On electronic commerce, see Saxby *et al., Encyclopedia of Information Technology Law* (loose-leaf), Ch.3; Gringrass, *The Laws of the Internet* (2nd ed.), Ch.2; Stokes (ed.), *Encyclopedia of ECommerce Law* (2005); Morgan and Stedman, *Computer Contracts* (6th ed.); Smith, *Internet Law and Regulation* (3rd ed.); Murray, in Edwards and Waelde (eds.), *Law & the Internet* (2nd ed.), Ch.2; Chissick and Kelman, *Electronic Commerce, Law and Practice* (3rd ed.), Ch.3; Lloyd, *Information Technology Law* (4th ed.); the Law Commission's Advice, *Electronic Commerce: Formal Requirements in Commercial Transactions* (December 2001); and, for a comparative study, Freedman, "Electronic Contracts under Canadian Law—a Practical Guide" (2001) 28 Manitoba L.J.1.

[2] If there is no agreement, or the transaction is not fully consensual, it is not a sale: above, para.1–067.

[3] *e.g. Chitty on Contracts* (29th ed.), Vol. 1, Ch.2; Treitel, *The Law of Contract* (11th ed.), Ch.2.

[4] Below, para.2–004.

[5] s.62(2); above, para.1–007.

[6] SI 2000/2334, below, para.14–054.

2–002 **Offer distinguished from invitation to treat.**[7] An *offer*, which is intended to be binding on the person making it and capable of acceptance without further negotiation, must be distinguished from an *invitation to treat*, which is a statement or conduct inviting the making of an offer.[8] In the law of sale of goods, it is well settled that the display of goods in a shop or shop-window is ordinarily[9] nothing more than an invitation to treat.[10] The shopkeeper does not make an offer to sell; it is the customer who makes an offer to buy, which the shopkeeper may accept or reject at his pleasure. There is therefore no sale or agreement to sell, even in a self-service shop or supermarket,[11] until the seller assents; and the latter is not bound to sell at the price which has been advertised or displayed.[12] On the other hand, where goods are exhibited for sale on an unattended stall[13] or in an automatic vending machine,[14] the display may itself be construed as an offer capable of acceptance by the act of the customer.[15] A similar construction

---

[7] *Cf.* Vienna Convention on Contracts for the International Sale of Goods (above, para.1–024), Art. 14.

[8] *Chitty on Contracts* (29th ed.), Vol. 1, para.2–004; Treitel, *The Law of Contract* (11th ed.), pp.10–16; Winfield, 55 L.Q.R. 499 at 516 (1939); Ellison Kahn, 72 S.A.L.J. 246 at 250 (1955). In *Michael Gerson (Leasing) Ltd v Wilkinson* [2001] Q.B. 514, the statement "I am willing to make an outright sale for £319,000 plus VAT" was regarded as being probably an invitation to treat rather than an offer.

[9] But circumstances may show that the seller does intend the display to be an offer: *Cf. Warwickshire County Council, Ex p. Johnson* [1993] 1 All E.R. 299 (statement "We will beat any TV HiFi and Video price by £20 on the spot" held to be a "continuing offer" to sell at such a price).

[10] *Timothy v Simpson* (1834) 6 Car. & P. 499 at 500; *Pharmaceutical Society of Great Britain v Boots Cash Chemists (Southern) Ltd* [1952] 2 Q.B. 795; *Fisher v Bell* [1961] 1 Q.B. 394; *Esso Petroleum Co. Ltd v Customs & Excise Commissioners* [1976] 1 W.L.R. 1 at 11 (statement of price of petrol on pumps not an offer to sell; contrast the case of "self–service" pumps, where it appears that the garage makes an open offer to sell at the stated prices: *Re Charge Card Services Ltd* [1989] Ch.497 at 510). In penal statutes the term "offer for sale" has sometimes been construed less strictly, as equivalent to "expose for sale": contrast *Fisher v Bell*, above, *Wiles v Maddison* [1943] 1 All E.R. 315, *Partridge v Crittenden* [1968] 1 W.L.R. 1204 and *British Car Auctions Ltd v Wright* [1972] 1 W.L.R. 1519 ("offer to sell") with *Keating v. Horwood* (1926) 28 Cox C.C. 198 and *Phillips v Dalziel* [1948] 2 All E.R. 810. The Restriction of Offensive Weapons Act 1961, s.1, amending the Restriction of Offensive Weapons Act 1959, s.1, nullifies the decision in *Fisher v Bell*, above, by the use of the wider phrase "offers ... or exposes or has in his possession for the purpose of sale."

[11] *Pharmaceutical Society of Great Britain v Boots Cash Chemists (Southern) Ltd*, above. As regards the passing of property when goods are sold in a self–service shop, see *Martin v Puttick* [1968] 2 Q.B. 82; *Lacis v Cashmarts* [1969] 2 Q.B. 400; *Pilgram v Rice-Smith* [1977] Cr.App.R. 142; *Davies v Leighton* [1978] Crim.L.R. 575; and below, paras 5–026, 5–082.

[12] He may, however, be guilty of an offence if he refuses to sell or demands a higher price: Consumer Protection Act 1987, s.20; *Warwickshire County Council v Johnson*, above.

[13] *Cf. Chapelton v Barry U.D.C.* [1940] 1 K.B. 532 (chairs for hire on self–service basis, receipt given by attendant *after* acceptance).

[14] *Cf. Thornton v Shoe Lane Parking Ltd* [1971] 2 Q.B. 163 (car park).

[15] A similar inference can be drawn in all situations where the customer's act in selecting the goods is, for practical purposes, irreversible—*e.g.* where he fills the petrol tank of his car from a self-service pump (*Re Charge Card Services Ltd*, above), or chooses the items for a meal from a self-service hotplate.

would seem to be appropriate in the case of a contract made parmaat to a web-page advertisement, where the buyer is required to give his consent to purchase by technological means, *e.g.* by clicking on an icon on a computer screen,[16] but in others contracts made online or by email the normal rule is likely to apply.

The same general principle applies in the case of an advertisement,[17] catalogue or price list[18] of goods: each is normally construed as an invitation to treat, for otherwise (it is said) a seller whose stock is necessarily limited might be made liable to an indefinite number of buyers.[19]

An offer is also to be distinguished from a preliminary inquiry which merely seeks information.[20]

Tenders. An advertisement or other invitation calling for tenders for the purchase of goods or for the supply of goods is not normally an offer but an invitation to treat.[21] The offer is made by the person submitting the tender, and in the absence of any undertaking to the contrary there is no obligation on the other party to accept the highest or lowest tender (as the case may be) or, indeed, any tender.[22] Exceptionally, however, the person issuing the invitation may bind himself to accept the best tender, and an agreement will then be concluded automatically with the person who has made the best bid.[23] Alternatively, he may be held to have undertaken at least to consider the tender, so that failure on his part to do so will give rise to liability under a collateral contract.[24] **2–003**

---

[16] The so-called "click-wrap" contracts. On the acceptance of such offers, see below, para.2–022, n.24. On the question whether such a seller might render himself liable to an indefinite number of buyers, see *infra*, n.19. In some cases, contracts of sale may be concluded automatically without human input at the time by either seller or buyer—*e.g.* where a stock control system is programmed to order replacement of items which fall below a set threshold. Questions such as those discussed in the present paragraph are likely to be resolved by the terms of an electronic data interchange (EDI) agreement between the parties.

[17] *Partridge v Crittenden*, above.

[18] *Grainger & Sons v Gough* [1896] A.C. 325.

[19] *ibid.* at p.334; *Esso Petroleum Co. Ltd v Customs & Excise Commissioners* [1976] 1 W.L.R. 1 at 11. See, however, *Chitty on Contracts* (29th ed.), Vol. 1, para.2–014; Treitel, *The Law of Contract* (11th ed.), p.12.

[20] *Interfoto Picture Library Ltd v Stiletto Visual Programmes Ltd* [1989] Q.B. 433 at 436 (bailment); *cf. Harvey v Facey* [1893] A.C. 552 (purchase of land).

[21] *Spencer v Harding* (1870) L.R. 5 C.P. 561.

[22] Exceptionally, legislation implementing EC directives on public procurement contracts requires public authorities and public utilities who invite tenders for the supply of goods either to accept the lowest price tendered or the tender which is the "most economically advantageous" (the latter being determined by reference to pre-announced specified criteria): see the Public Supply Contracts Regulations 1995 (SI 1995/201), reg. 21 and the Utilities Contracts Regulations 1996 (SI 1996/2911), reg. 21.

[23] *Harvela Investments Ltd v Royal Trust Co. of Canada (C.I.) Ltd* [1986] A.C. 207 at 225 (shares); *MJB Enterprises Ltd v Defence Construction (1951) Ltd* (2000) 193 D.L.R. (4th) 1; (1999) 15 Const. L.J. 455 (building contract: see Duncan Wallace 117 L.Q.R. 1 (2001)); *cf. South Hetton Coal Co. v Haswell Shotton & Easington Coal & Coke Co.* [1898] 1 Ch. 465.

[24] *Blackpool & Fylde Aero Club Ltd v Blackpool BC* [1990] 1 W.L.R. 1195.

2–004 **Sales by auction.** An auction sale is a sale by competitive bidding, normally held in public,[25] at which prospective purchasers are invited to make successively increasing bids for the property, which is then usually sold to the highest bidder.[26] An auction sale is to be distinguished from a sale by fixed bidding (*e.g.* where offers are made by "sealed tender"), when each bidder must specify a fixed amount and has no opportunity to adjust his bid by reference to rival bids.[27] Section 57 of the Sale of Goods Act 1979 codifies, in regard to sales of goods, some of the special rules governing auction sales.[28]

Where goods are put up for sale by auction in lots, each lot is prima facie deemed to be the subject of a separate contract of sale.[29]

A sale by auction is complete when the auctioneer announces its completion by the fall of the hammer, or in other customary manner.[30] Until such announcement is made any bidder may retract his bid.[31] It follows that neither the display of a lot nor the auctioneer's request for bids is an offer capable of being accepted even by the highest bidder, but amounts only to an invitation to treat.[32] Each bid is an offer which the auctioneer, as agent for the seller, is free to accept or reject.[33]

In a "Dutch auction", the seller asks prospective purchasers successively decreasing prices until one is accepted. Under this system, it is the seller who makes the offer and the buyer's bid is an acceptance.[34]

---

[25] "Online" or "Web" auctions conducted over the internet are now common. In such auctions there is no act of the auctioneer corresponding to the fall of the hammer: instead, it is usual to set a closing time on the website, by which time all bids must be placed and (unless there is a reserve price which has not been reached) the highest bid is deemed to have been accepted when the auction closes.

[26] *Harvela Investments Ltd v Royal Trust Co. of Canada (C.I.) Ltd*, above; *cf. Frewen v Hays* (1912) 106 L.T. 516 at 518.

[27] The distinction is discussed further in *Harvela Investments Ltd v Royal Trust Co. of Canada (C.I.) Ltd*, above, at pp.230–234.

[28] *Cf.* U.C.C., para.2–328. Auction sales are specifically excluded from the Consumer Protection (Distance Selling) Regulations 2000 (below, para.14–054): see reg. 5(1)(f). On the question whether a buyer at a public auction is to be regarded as dealing as consumer for the purposes of the Unfair Contract Terms Act 1977, see below, para.14–029.

[29] s.57(1), affirming the rule established at common law in *Emmerson v Heelis* (1809) 2 Taunt. 38; *Roots v Lord Dormer* (1832) 4 B. & Ad. 77.

[30] This is so even where the auctioneer has accepted a bid in breach of his advertised conditions of sale, and notwithstanding that another bidder was prepared to pay a higher price: *Hordern House Pty Ltd v Arnold* [1989] V.R. 402.

[31] s.57(2), affirming the rule established at common law in *Payne v Cave* (1789) 3 Term Rep. 148.

[32] *British Car Auctions Ltd v Wright* [1972] 1 W.L.R. 1519.

[33] Where there is a dispute respecting bids, the conditions of sale commonly empower the auctioneer to reopen the bidding, even though a bid has been apparently accepted as the final bid. On the meaning of "dispute respecting a bid" in such a case, see *Richards v Phillips* [1969] 1 Ch. 39. An auctioneer who declines to reopen the bidding in such a case may be liable in contract to a disappointed bidder: *Ulbrick v Laidlaw* [1924] V.L.R. 247.

[34] *Demerara Turf Club Ltd v Wight* [1918] A.C. 605; *cf.* Mock Auctions Act 1961, s.3(1).

Sales without reserve. Where an auction sale is advertised as being "without reserve" the auctioneer, and perhaps also the seller as principal, is regarded as having undertaken to sell the goods to the highest bidder.[35] This does not, however, mean that the putting up of the goods is an offer, capable of being accepted by the making of a bid (or the highest bid). The language of section 57(2) makes it fairly clear that even in a sale "without reserve" each bid is merely an offer. If the goods are withdrawn before the auction is complete,[36] the remedy of the highest bidder is to sue not on the basis of a concluded sale,[37] but for the breach of a collateral contract that the sale will be without reserve,[38] or of a warranty by the auctioneer that he has authority to sell without reserve.[39] But even where a sale is advertised as being without reserve, the seller and the auctioneer will be under no liability if the sale does not take place or the goods in question are not put up for sale; for a statement of intention to hold a sale does not amount to an offer to hold it.[40] **2–005**

Sale subject to reserve price. Where notice has been given that a sale is subject to a reserve price, the act of the auctioneer in knocking down the goods to a bidder is not a conclusive acceptance if the reserve price has not in fact been reached.[41] **2–006**

Conditional offers. If an offer is expressly made "subject to confirmation", or if a document which sets out the terms by which a party is prepared to be bound contains a stipulation that he shall not be so bound until he has signed the document or shown his assent in some other specified way, there is no contract until the signature or other confirmation has been given and the other party informed. But this requirement may be waived by the first party's conduct, and the second party for his part may waive his right to be notified of the confirmation.[42] **2–007**

---

[35] *Warlow v Harrison* (1858) 1 E. & E. 295 at 309; *Barry v Davies* [2000] 1 W.L.R. 1962; *cf. Mainprice v Westley* (1865) 6 B. & S. 420; *Johnston v Boyes* [1899] 2 Ch. 73; *Rainbow v Howkins* [1904] 2 K.B. 322. See the discussion between Slade and Gower in 68 L.Q.R. 238 at 457 (1952) and 69 L.Q.R. 21 (1953).

[36] Or if the seller himself makes a higher bid: *Warlow v Harrison*, above. On the right of the seller to bid, see below, para.3–009.

[37] *Fenwick v Macdonald, Fraser & Co.* (1904) 6 F. (Ct.Sess.) 850.

[38] *Barry v Davies* (above); *Warlow v Harrison*, above; *cf. Harris v Nickerson* (1873) L.R. 8 Q.B. 286 at 288. Consideration would be provided by his bidding for the goods in reliance on the auctioneer's advertisement, which is both a detriment to the bidder, since he runs the risk of being bound, and a benefit to the auctioneer, as the bidding is driven up: see *Chitty on Contracts* (29th ed.), Vol. 1, para.3–172, and *Barry v Davies*, above.

[39] This was the view of the minority in *Warlow v Harrison*, above.

[40] *Harris v Nickerson*, above.

[41] *McManus v Fortescue* [1907] 2 K.B. 1; *Fay v Miller, Wilkins & Co.* [1941] Ch. 360. But the auctioneer may in such circumstances be liable to the purchaser on an implied warranty that the reserve price has, in fact, been reached (*ibid.*).

[42] *E. M. Denny & Co. Ltd v Wholesalers (Australia) Pty Ltd* [1959] 1 Lloyd's Rep. 167; *Financings Ltd v Stimson* [1962] 1 W.L.R. 1184; *Robophone Facilities Ltd v Blank* [1966] 1 W.L.R. 1428.

An offer may be subject to an implied condition—for instance, in the case of an offer to buy goods, that the goods should not be damaged prior to acceptance by the seller. If the goods should then become damaged, the offer can no longer be accepted.[43]

2–008 **Offer inferred from conduct.** An offer may sometimes be inferred from conduct: for instance, where a seller tenders goods different from those which he has agreed to sell, he may be deemed to offer to sell the goods actually tendered.[44]

2–009 **Standing offer.** A party may offer to sell such quantities of goods of a certain description as the other party may from time to time order, usually within stated limits. Similarly, a party may offer to buy such quantities as the other may acquire (or produce) and tender from time to time. The "acceptance" of such an offer does not create any binding obligation; but on each occasion when an order is placed or a consignment tendered, the party who has made the offer is bound to sell or buy the quantity in question.[45] Apart from this, the offer may be withdrawn at any time, unless consideration has been given in return for an undertaking to keep it open.[46] The offeree for his part is not bound to place any order or tender any goods unless he has expressly or impliedly promised to do so.[47]

2–010 **Revocation of offer.** As a general rule, an offer may be revoked at any time prior to acceptance. This is so even though the offeror has promised to keep it open for a certain time, or indefinitely, unless he has given the offeree a binding option supported by consideration or made by deed.[48] To be effective, the revocation must be communicated to the offeror.[49]

---

[43] *Financings Ltd v Stimson*, above.
[44] *Steven v Bromley & Son* [1919] 2 K.B. 722 at 728; *cf. Hart v Mills* (1846) 15 L.J.Ex. 200; *Charterhouse Credit Co. Ltd v Tolly* [1963] 2 Q.B. 683 at 710; and see also s.30, below, paras 8–045 *et seq*. On the tender of unsolicited goods, see below, para.2–014, and on the tender of non-conforming goods generally, see below, paras 12–022 *et seq.*; 17–047 *et seq.* and 17–093 *et seq.*; and *cf.* U.C.C., paras 2–508, 2–601.
[45] *Great Northern Ry v Witham* (1873) L.R. 9 C.P. 16; *Percival v London CC Asylums Committee* (1918) 87 L.J.K.B. 677. See below, paras 8–058 *et seq*.
[46] *Percival v London CC Asylums Committee*, above.
[47] *Churchward v R.* (1865) L.R. 1 Q.B. 173; *R. v Demers* [1900] A.C. 103.
[48] *Routledge v Grant* (1828) 4 Bing. 653; *Offord v Davies* (1862) 12 C.B.(N.S.) 748; *Chitty on Contracts* (29th ed.), Vol. 1, para.2–086. Contrast Vienna Convention on Contracts for the International Sale of Goods (above, para.1–024), Art. 16(2): "an offer cannot be revoked: (*a*) if it indicates, whether by stating a fixed time for acceptance or otherwise, that it is irrevocable, or (*b*) if it was reasonable for the offeree to rely on the offer as being irrevocable and the offeree has acted in reliance on the offer." See further the Law Commission's Working Paper No. 60 (1975), *Firm Offers*.
[49] *Chitty on Contracts* (29th ed.), Vol. 1, para.2–087. There is no exception for revocations sent by post or similar means: *cf.* below, para.2–015.

Acceptance. In order to make a valid contract an offer must be accepted; the acceptance must be unqualified[50]; and, as a general rule, it must be communicated[51] to the offeror.[52] These principles apply to contracts for the sale of goods. In cases where there have been prolonged negotiations or correspondence between the parties, it may be difficult to determine whether (and if so, at what point) agreement has in fact been reached, or whether an agreement once concluded has been effectively varied at a later stage.[53] But acceptance may be inferred from conduct: for example, by sending goods which have been ordered.[54] In these circumstances the normal requirement that acceptance should be communicated may be taken to have been waived by the offeror; but whether the offer can be so construed is a question for the court to determine.[55] 2–011

Incorporation of standard or printed terms.[56] A problem which commonly arises is whether a party is bound by terms embodied in a notice, ticket, receipt or other standard form document drawn up by the other party and introduced, or allegedly introduced, into the contract at some stage of the negotiations. If the document has been signed, the terms contained in it are incorporated in the contract, whether or not the party signing has read or understood it.[57] If the document is not signed, the terms 2–012

---

[50] Contrast Vienna Convention on Contracts for the International Sale of Goods (above, para.1–024), Art. 19(2): "a reply to an offer which purports to be an acceptance but contains additional or different terms which do not materially alter the terms of the offer constitutes an acceptance unless the offeror, without undue delay, objects orally to the discrepancy or dispatches a notice to that effect. If he does not so object, the terms of the contract are the terms of the offer with the modifications contained in the acceptance". *Cf.* U.C.C., para.2–207; and see below, para.2–012.

[51] For the meaning of "communicated", see *Entores Ltd v Miles Far East Corp.* [1955] 2 Q.B. 327 at 332 and *Tenax Steamship Co. Ltd v The Brimnes (Owners) (The Brimnes)* [1975] Q.B. 929, and below, para.2–015.

[52] *Chitty on Contracts* (29th ed.), Vol. 1, paras 2–041 *et seq.*

[53] *Compagnie de Commerce, etc. v Parkinson Stove Co.* [1953] 2 Lloyd's Rep. 487; *Port Sudan Cotton Co. v Govindaswamy Chettiar & Sons* [1977] 1 Lloyd's Rep. 166; *Pagnan SpA v Granaria BV* [1986] 1 Lloyd's Rep. 547; *Pagnan SpA v Feed Products Ltd* [1987] 2 Lloyd's Rep. 601; *Manatee Touring Co. v Oceanbulk Maritime SA* [1999] 2 All E.R. (Comm.) 306.

[54] Chitty, *op. cit.*, para.2–027; *cf. Brogden v Metropolitan Ry* (1877) 2 App.Cas. 666; *Carlyle Finance Ltd v Pallas Industrial Finance* [1999] 1 All E.R. (Comm.) 659 (delivery of car to customer before formal acceptance of offer). On "shrink-wrap" contracts (where a buyer of computer software is deemed to have accepted the terms of a licence to use the software by the act of opening the package in which the disk or other medium is contained), see below, para.2–012.

[55] *Cf. Rapalli v K. L. Take Ltd* [1958] 2 Lloyd's Rep. 469; *Boyers & Co. v D. & R. Duke* [1905] 2 I.R. 617.

[56] See *Chitty on Contracts* (29th ed.), Vol. 1, paras 12–008 *et seq.*; Treitel, *The Law of Contract* (11th ed.), Ch.7; Sales, 16 M.L.R. 318 (1953); Spencer [1973] C.L.J. 104; Samek, 52 C.B.R. 351 (1974); Coote, *Exception Clauses* (1964); Yates, *Exclusion Clauses in Contracts* (2nd ed.); Chin, *Excluding Liability in Contracts* (1985); and see also below, Ch.13.

[57] *The Luna* [1920] P. 22 (towage); *L'Estrange v F. Graucob Ltd* [1934] 2 K.B. 394; *P.S. Chellaram & Co. Ltd v China Ocean Shipping Co. (The "Zhi Jiang Kou")* [1991] 1 Lloyd's Rep. 493 (S.Ct. N.S.W.; carriage of goods; very small print). There is an exception in the case of misrepresentation: *Curtis v Chemical Cleaning & Dyeing Co.* [1951] 1 K.B. 805 (cleaning contract).

will not be incorporated unless they were brought to the party's notice before or at the time of the making of the contract. This will be held to be the case if the other party has taken such steps as were reasonably sufficient to draw his attention to the existence of the conditions.[58] Where the clauses contained in a document include a particularly onerous or unusual condition, the party seeking to rely on it must show that it was brought fairly and reasonably to the attention of the other party[59]: "the more unusual a clause is, the greater the notice which must be given of it."[60] A party may also be held bound by the other's standard terms if these have habitually been used or referred to in a course of dealing between the parties,[61] but for this purpose consistent dealing to a substantial extent rather than a number of scattered transactions must be shown.[62] Where a contract is made in a commercial setting, it appears that the court will more readily infer that the parties intended to deal on standard terms, particularly where these are well known, or customary in the trade.[63] The express inclusion of some terms only out of a set of standard terms may lead to the inference that the remainder of the set were not intended to apply.[64]

---

[58] *Parker v South Eastern Ry* (1877) 2 C.P.D. 416 at 421, 423; *Richardson, Spence & Co. v Rowntree* [1894] A.C. 217; *Hood v Anchor Line (Henderson Bros) Ltd* [1918] A.C. 837 at 844; *Thompson v L. M. & S. Ry* [1930] 1 K.B. 41 (cases on carriage of passengers); *Burnett v Westminster Bank Ltd* [1966] 1 Q.B. 742 (banking).

[59] *Interfoto Picture Library Ltd v Stiletto Visual Programmes Ltd* [1989] Q.B. 433 (bailment); *cf. Parker v South Eastern Ry Co.* (1877) 2 C.P.D. 416 at 428 (carriage of passenger); *J. Spurling Ltd v Bradshaw* [1956] 1 W.L.R. 461 at 466 (bailment); *Thornton v Shoe Lane Parking Ltd* [1971] 2 Q.B. 163 at 170, 172–173 (parking); *Hollingworth v Southern Ferries Ltd* [1977] 2 Lloyd's Rep. 70 at 78–79 (carriage of passenger).

[60] *J. Spurling Ltd v Bradshaw* (above), at p.466.

[61] *Rapalli v K. L. Take Ltd* [1958] 2 Lloyd's Rep. 469 at 484; *Henry Kendall & Sons v. William Lillico & Sons Ltd* [1969] 2 A.C. 31; *S.I.A.T. Di Del Ferro v Tradax Overseas Ltd* [1978] 2 Lloyd's Rep. 470; *McCrone v Boots Farm Sales Ltd* 1981 S.L.T. 103; *George Mitchell (Chesterhall) Ltd v Finney Lock Seeds Ltd* [1983] Q.B. 284 at 295 (affirmed [1983] 2 A.C. 803); *Johnson Matthey Bankers Ltd v State Trading Corp. of India Ltd* [1984] 1 Lloyd's Rep. 427; *cf. J. Spurling Ltd v Bradshaw* (above); *Cockerton v Naviera Aznar SA* [1960] 2 Lloyd's Rep. 450 (carriage of passenger); *Transmotors Ltd v Robertson Buckley & Co. Ltd* [1970] 1 Lloyd's Rep. 224; *Eastman Chemical International AG v N.M.T. Trading Ltd* [1972] 2 Lloyd's Rep. 25; *Gillespie Bros & Co. Ltd v Roy Bowles Transport Ltd* [1973] Q.B. 400 (cases on carriage of goods); *Lamport & Holt Lines Ltd v Coubro & Scrutton (M. & I.) Ltd* [1981] 2 Lloyd's Rep. 659 (affirmed [1982] 2 Lloyd's Rep. 42) (contract for services); *Circle Freight International Ltd v Medeast Gulf Exports Ltd* [1988] 2 Lloyd's Rep. 427 (carriage of goods); *Banque Paribas v Cargill International SA* [1992] 1 Lloyd's Rep. 96 at 98; Hoggett, 33 M.L.R. 518 (1970).

[62] *Chevron International Oil Co. Ltd v A/S Sea Team* [1983] 2 Lloyd's Rep. 356; *cf. McCutcheon v David McBrayne Ltd* [1964] 1 W.L.R. 125 (carriage of goods); *Hollier v. Rambler Motors Ltd* [1972] 2 Q.B. 71 (repairs to car); *British Crane Hire Corp. Ltd v. Ipswich Plant Hire Ltd* [1975] Q.B. 303 (hire of machine); *Salsi v Jet Air Services Ltd* [1977] 2 Lloyd's Rep. 57 (carriage by air); *Lamport & Holt Lines Ltd v Coubro & Scrutton (M. & I.) Ltd* (above); *Neptune Orient Lines Ltd v J.V.C. (U.K.) Ltd* [1983] 2 Lloyd's Rep. 438 (carriage of goods).

[63] *Chevron International Oil Co. Ltd v A/S Sea Team* [1983] 2 Lloyd's Rep. 356; *cf. British Crane Hire Corp. Ltd v Ipswich Plant Hire Ltd* [1975] Q.B. 303 (hire of machine).

[64] *Johnson Matthey Bankers Ltd v State Trading Corp of India Ltd* [1984] 1 Lloyd's Rep. 427.

A standard form document is not as a rule effective to vary the terms of a contract already made[65]; but this may be possible where the contract is of a continuing nature,[66] or where agreement has been reached only on an informal or provisional basis and the written terms are delivered to confirm and supplement what has been agreed.[67] Again, it must be shown that adequate notice has been given of the existence of the new terms, and that the party receiving them has by his conduct accepted them.

Goods are commonly offered for sale on the internet on the basis that a person may become the buyer by clicking in a box or on an icon on his computer screen (sometimes referred to as a "click-wrap" contract). In such a case the seller would be regarded as having made an offer, rather than an invitation to treat, and the act of the buyer as an acceptance.[68] If the seller wished to make his offer subject to a set of conditions,[69] care would need to be taken to ensure that the conditions were brought to the attention of the buyer before he was invited to record his acceptance: it might not be thought sufficient to refer him to conditions set out lower down on the screen, or elsewhere on the seller's website.[70]

Problems of a special kind may arise in the case of so-called "shrink-wrap" contracts. Here, a supplier of computer software (usually in the form of a disk) tenders it in a package which contains a warning that, by tearing the wrapping from the package, the buyer agrees to be bound by the terms of the "end-user licence"—that is, a licence granted to the buyer by the owner of the copyright in the program to make use of the copyright material for specifically limited purposes. The terms of the licence may be written on the outside of the package or visible through the wrapper. In that case, a court in this country would no doubt apply the principles set out above and, provided that sufficient notice of the terms had been given, hold that a contract had been created between the copyright owner and the buyer. However, in a leading ruling by the United States Court of Appeals, Seventh Circuit, *ProCD Inc. v Zeidenberg*,[71] it was held that such licences could be enforceable even if the terms were not accessible before the

---

[65] *Jayaar Impex Ltd v Toaken Group Ltd* [1996] 2 Lloyd's Rep. 437; *cf. Chapelton v Barry U.D.C.* [1940] 1 K.B. 532 (hire of deck chair); *Olley v Marlborough Court Ltd* [1949] 1 K.B. 532 (hotel); *Thornton v Shoe Lane Parking Ltd* [1971] 2 Q.B. 163 (parking); *Hollingworth v Southern Ferries Ltd (The "Eagle")* [1977] 2 Lloyd's Rep. 70; *Daly v General Steam Navigation Co. Ltd (The "Dragon")* [1979] 1 Lloyd's Rep. 257 (cases on carriage of passengers).

[66] *Burnett v Westminster Bank Ltd*, above.

[67] *Henry Kendall & Sons v William Lillico & Sons Ltd*, above; Hoggett, 33 M.L.R. 518 (1970).

[68] "Click–wrap" contracts have been held enforceable in the United States (*Hotmail Corp. v Van Money Pie Inc.* C98–20064 (N.D. Cal., April 20, 1998)) and in Canada (*Rudder v Microsoft Corp.* (1999) 2 C.P.R. (4th) 474).

[69] Saxby *et al.*, *Encyclopedia of Information Technology Law* (loose-leaf), paras 3.317 *et seq.* contains a useful discussion of terms suitable for use in contracts concluded electronically, and at paras 3.328 *et seq.* a discussion of terms appropriate for inclusion in electronic data interchange agreements.

[70] On the duty of a service provider to provide information on the technical steps to be followed to conclude the contract, etc. (otherwise than by email) see the Electronic Commerce (EC Directive) Regulations 2002 (SI 2002/2013), reg. 9.

[71] 86 F. 3d 1447 (7th Cir. 1996).

wrapper was removed—*e.g.* if a document setting out the terms was enclosed inside the package, or if the terms appeared on the computer screen before the program was run. All that was necessary was that the buyer should be aware that the software was sold with a restricted licence, that the terms were not objectionable on the grounds of illegality or unconscionability, and that the buyer should have an opportunity to reject and return the goods if, before *using* the program, he found the terms of the licence unsatisfactory.

This issue has not yet come before our own courts, but in *Beta Computers (Europe) Ltd v Adobe Systems (Europe) Ltd*,[72] Lord Penrose was required to determine a related question. A company had ordered from a supplier a standard computer software package which carried a notice that opening the package indicated the buyer's acceptance of end-user licence conditions, the terms of which could be read through the wrapping. The company claimed that it was entitled to return the package unopened. The issue was thus between the supplier and the buyer of the package and not (as in the *ProCD* case) between the copyright owner and the buyer. The supplier contended that its contract with the buyer was a simple contract of sale of goods and that it was not concerned with the position as between the copyright owners and the buyer; but it was held that it was an essential feature of the transaction that the supplier had agreed to make available to the buyer both the goods and the right to use the software so that, until the buyer had had an opportunity to decide whether the conditions were acceptable, it was not bound and could reject the goods.[73]

2–013 **The "battle of forms".**[74] Sometimes each of the parties to the negotiations for a contract may purport to introduce his own set of standard terms; and it then becomes a difficult question for the court to determine which set of terms is to prevail. On principle, if an offer is made on certain terms and the offeree stipulates for different terms, there is a counter-offer, and no contract results unless the new terms are accepted. But if, as is common, the parties have acted on the assumption that they have made a contract, and perhaps rendered substantial performance, it may be difficult for the court to conclude that there is no contract. The question is then commonly resolved by determining whether as each set of terms was introduced, sufficient steps were taken to draw the attention of the other party to them: if so, it may be inferred that that party has acquiesced in them unless his own terms can be said to have displaced them by a similar process of notification and implied acceptance.[75] A party may attempt to avoid this

---

[72] 1996 S.L.T. 604.

[73] Note that under the Consumer Protection (Distance Selling) Regulations 2000 (SI 2000/2334), reg. 13(d), a consumer forfeits the right to cancel a contract (see below, para.14–057) for the supply of audio or video recordings or computer software if he unseals them.

[74] See *Chitty on Contracts* (29th ed.), Vol. 1, paras 2–032—2–036; Adams [1983] J.B.L. 297.

[75] *A. Davies & Co. (Shopfitters) Ltd v William Old Ltd* (1969) 67 L.G.R. 395; *cf. British Road Services v A V Crutchley Ltd* [1968] 1 All E.R. 811 at 817 (affirming [1967] 2 All E.R. 785); *Port Sudan Cotton Co. v Govindaswamy Chettiar & Sons*

inference by an express stipulation that his own set of terms shall be paramount, but even in these circumstances he will not succeed in imposing his own terms if his conduct is not consistent with such a result.[76] If, however, the court concludes that no binding contract exists, a remedy on the basis of *quantum meruit* may be available if the goods have been delivered and accepted and cannot be returned.[77]

Unsolicited goods. At common law a person to whom goods are sent with an express or implied offer to sell them may be deemed to have accepted such an offer and become the buyer by (for instance) using the goods, and perhaps by any conduct which makes it impossible to restore them *in integrum* to the seller.[78] Acceptance cannot, however, be inferred from mere silence or inactivity, even if the offeror so stipulates.[79] These rules were modified by the Unsolicited Goods and Services Act 1971, which provided by section 1 that in specified circumstances a person who received unsolicited goods could treat the transaction as an unconditional gift of the goods. This provision has now been repealed,[80] and replaced (where the recipient of the goods is a consumer[81]) by the Consumer Protection (Distance Selling) Regulations 2000, reg. 24,[82] which is similar terms. The regulation applies where unsolicited goods are sent to a person with a view to his acquiring them, and he has no reasonable cause to believe that they were sent with a view to their being acquired for the purposes of a business, and he has neither agreed to acquire nor agreed to return them. In these circumstances the recipient may, as between himself and the sender, use, 2–014

[1977] 2 Lloyd's Rep. 5; *Butler Machine Tool Co. Ltd v Ex-Cell-O Corp. (England) Ltd* [1979] 1 W.L.R. 401; *OTM Ltd v Hydranautics* [1981] 2 Lloyd's Rep. 211; *Zambia Steel & Building Supplies Ltd v James Clark & Eaton Ltd* [1986] 2 Lloyd's Rep. 225; *Chichester Joinery Ltd v John Mowlem & Co. Plc* (1987) 42 Build.L.R. 100. In the *Butler Machine Tool* case, Lord Denning M.R. favoured the broader approach of construing all the documents together.

[76] *Butler Machine Tool Co. Ltd v Ex-Cell-O Corp. (England) Ltd* (above).

[77] *Cf. Peter Lind & Co. Ltd v Mersey Docks & Harbour Board* [1972] 2 Lloyd's Rep. 234 (construction contract).

[78] *Chitty on Contracts* (29th ed.), Vol. 1, para.2–028; *Weatherby v Banham* (1832) 5 C. & P. 228.

[79] *Felthouse v Bindley* (1862) 11 C.B.(N.S.) 869; *cf.* Vienna Convention on the International Sale of Goods (above, para.1–024), Art. 18(1). Exceptionally, it is possible that silence may bind an offeree in some circumstances, *e.g.* where there has been a course of dealing between the parties in which offers to buy goods have always been accepted as a matter of course by the despatch of the relevant goods; or where the situation gives rise to an estoppel against the offeree; or where the offer is made on a form provided by the offeree which stipulates that silence shall amount to acceptance: see further *Chitty on Contracts* (29th ed.), Vol. 1, paras 2–068—2–072. The question whether an agreement to abandon an arbitration can be inferred from the inactivity of one or both of the parties has been considered in a number of cases: see *Chitty*, *op. cit.*, paras 2–003, 2–074.

[80] See reg. 22 (which, however, uses the word "omit", rather than words of repeal). It is possible that s.1 is intended to remain in force in regard to contracts other than "distance contracts" (as defined in reg. 3(1)), since the Regulations as a whole apply only to such "distance contracts": see reg. 4.

[81] Defined (reg. 3(1)) as "any natural person who, in contracts to which these Regulations apply, is acting for purposes outside his business".

[82] SI 2000/2334, effective October 31, 2000. See further below, paras 14–054 *et seq.*

deal with or dispose of the goods as if they were an unconditional gift to him, and the rights of the sender to the goods are extinguished. In contrast with section 1 of the 1971 Act, the deemed gift takes effect immediately and is not dependent on the expiration of any period of time or the sending by the recipient of any notice to the supplier. The regulation is also backed by criminal sanctions.

2–015 **Time and place of contract.** The rules which determine the time when, and the place where, a contract of sale is deemed to be completed are the same as in the general law of contract. In the case of contracts made by telephone, teleprinter, facsimile (fax), and other forms of virtually instantaneous communication, an acceptance is, generally speaking, complete only when it has been received by the offeror.[83] But in the case of acceptances sent by post or (in countries where this service is still available) by telegram or cable the effective time is normally that when the letter of acceptance is posted or the telegram handed in.[84] For these and all other rules regarding offer and acceptance reference should be made to standard works on the law of contract.[85]

The position in regard to contracts concluded over the internet is not clear. Since the communication between the parties is virtually instantaneous, it would seem to follow that the analogy with contracts concluded by telex and similar means would be applied. However, in the

[83] *Entores Ltd v Miles Far East Corp.* [1955] 2 Q.B. 327; *WA Dewhurst & Co. Pty Ltd v Cawrse* [1960] V.R. 278 (acceptance by telephone); *cf. The Brimnes, Tenax Steamship Co. Ltd v The Brimnes (Owners)* [1975] Q.B. 929 (notice of withdrawal of vessel under charterparty); *Diamond v Bank of London & Montreal Ltd* [1979] Q.B. 333 (misrepresentation); *NV Stoomt Maats "De Maas" v Nippon Yusen Kaisha* [1980] 2 Lloyd's Rep. 56 (reference to arbitration: telex message received out of office hours); *Gill & Duffus Landauer Ltd v London Export Corp. GmbH* [1982] 2 Lloyd's Rep. 627; *Brinkibon Ltd v Stahag Stahl und Stahlwarenhandelsgesellschaft mbH* [1983] 2 A.C. 34; *JSC Zestafoni Nikoladze Ferroalloy Plant v Ronly Holdings Ltd* [2004] EWHC 245 (Comm.), [2004] 2 Lloyd's Rep. 335 at [75]. In regard to the meaning of "received" in this context, Lord Wilberforce has said: "No universal rule can cover all such cases; they must be resolved by reference to the intentions of the parties, by sound business practice and in some cases by a judgment where the risks should lie." ([1983] 2 A.C. 34 at 42). *cf. Nissho Iwai Petroleum Co. Inc. v Cargill International SA* [1993] 1 Lloyd's Rep. 80 (delay in answering telephone).

[84] *Chitty on Contracts* (29th ed.), Vol. 1, para.2–046; *Adams v Lindsell* (1818) 1 B. & Ald. 681; *Byrne v van Tienhoven* (1880) 5 C.P.D. 344; *Henthorn v Fraser* [1892] 2 Ch.27; *cf. Alexander v Steinhardt, Walker & Co.* [1903] 2 K.B. 208; *Port Sudan Cotton Co. v Govindaswamy Chettiar & Sons* [1977] 1 Lloyd's Rep. 5; contrast *Holwell Securities Ltd v Hughes* [1974] 1 W.L.R. 155 (exercise of option not effective until received). On contracts made by telegram or cable see *Stevenson v McLean* (1880) 5 Q.B.D. 346; *Quenerduaine v Cole* (1883) 32 W.R. 185; *Cowan v O'Connor* (1888) 20 Q.B.D. 640; *Raeburn v Burness* (1895) 1 Com.Cas. 22; *Bruner v Moore* [1904] 1 Ch. 305. As regards the risk of errors in transmission, see *Henkel v Pape* (1870) L.R. 6 Ex. 7 and *Northland Airlines Ltd v Dennis Ferranti Meters Ltd, The Times*, February 13, 1970 (reversed on other grounds (1970) 114 S.J. 845). Contrast Vienna Convention on Contracts for the International Sale of Goods (above, para.1–024), Arts 18(2), 24, under which the acceptance becomes effective only when it "reaches" the offeror: in the case of an acceptance sent by post, by delivery to his address.

[85] *e.g. Chitty, op. cit.*, Ch.2.

case of a "click-wrap" contract, where the offer is made on a website and the other party accepts by clicking on a box or icon on his computer screen,[86] it would appear to be the case that the contract is completed then and there, and that the offeror has waived the right to have the acceptance communicated.[87] In regard to contracts formed by e-mail correspondence, the communications are, once again, instantaneous or nearly so, and so it is likely again that the courts would look to the telex cases for precedents; but it has been argued, on the other hand, that the parallel here is closer to contracts concluded through the post, so that the acceptance should take effect at the time when and the place where the offeree's e-mail is sent.[88]

Certainty of terms. It is basic to the law of contract that the parties must make their own bargain and settle its terms. If they leave a vital part of it undetermined, or subject to further negotiation, the court cannot add what it considers reasonable or usual terms: it can only declare that there is no binding contract.[89] Still less will it infer that the parties have entered into a contract based on their conduct, where the alleged terms are too imprecise **2–016**

---

[86] See n.68, above.

[87] This analysis is, however, not in accord with the EC Directive on Electronic Commerce (above, para.1–023 and below, para.14–060) which provides (Art. 11(1)) that:

> "Member States shall ensure, except when otherwise agreed by parties who are not consumers, that in cases where the recipient of the service places his order through technological means, the following principles apply:
> — the service provider has to acknowledge the receipt of the recipient's order without undue delay and by electronic means,
> — the order and the acknowledgement of receipt are deemed to be received when the parties to whom they are addressed are able to access them."

The latter of these requirements is repeated in virtually identical language in reg. 11(2)(a) of the Electronic Commerce (EC Directive) Regulations 2002 (below, para.14–060). This could, it is submitted, lead to difficulties if it were held to follow that a message constituting an acceptance of an offer is deemed to be received *at the place where* the offeror is able to access it, for the service provider could well be situated in a jurisdiction where neither of the parties is based. See further *Chitty on Contracts* (29th ed.), Vol. 1, para.2–049; Atiyah, *Sale of Goods* (11th ed.), p.70.

[88] Chissick and Kelman, *Electronic Commerce: Law and Practice* (3rd ed.), paras 3.43 *et seq.*, who point out that (i) the sender of an e-mail message does not normally receive any immediate or continuous feedback concerning the delivery of the message; (ii) the e-mail is sent off into the internet and routed through various computers until it reaches its destination; (iii) the same issues of uncertainty for sending messages through the post apply to e-mail as well. See also the discussion in Saxby *et al., Encyclopedia of Information Technology Law* (loose-leaf), paras 3.305 *et seq.* (Note that the first indent of Art. 11(1) of the E.C. Directive on electronic commerce and reg. 11(2)(a) of the 2002 Regulations (above) does not apply to contracts concluded exclusively by e-mail).

[89] Chitty, *op. cit.*, Vol. 1, paras 2–10 *et seq.*; *Courtney & Fairbairn Ltd v Tolaini Bros (Hotels) Ltd* [1975] 1 W.L.R. 297 (building contract). However, if before a contract is formally concluded one party delivers goods which are accepted by the other, the court may be prepared to hold that this has been done pursuant to a preliminary or informal contract containing terms (*e.g.* as to the quality of the goods) which are not the subject of the continuing negotiations: *Britvic Soft Drinks Ltd v Messer UK Ltd* [2001] 1 Lloyd's Rep. 20, at [70]; affirmed on other grounds [2002] EWCA Civ 548; [2002] 2 Lloyd's Rep. 368.

to be capable of enforcement.[90] Equally, if no certain meaning can be attributed to the language used by the parties to a supposed bargain and the ambiguity cannot be resolved by recourse to parol evidence, there is no enforceable contract.[91] Apart from a special rule which allows the seller to claim a reasonable price where no price has been agreed,[92] this principle applies to contracts for the sale of goods.

So, in *G. Scammel & Nephew Ltd v H C & J G Ouston*,[93] an order was given for the supply of a van "on hire-purchase terms over a period of two years." The expression "on hire-purchase terms" was held not to be sufficiently certain for the contract to be enforceable. Lord Wright said[94]: "The law has not defined and cannot of itself define what are the normal and reasonable terms of a hire-purchase agreement. Though the general character of such an agreement is familiar, it is necessary for the parties in each case to agree upon the particular terms." Other expressions which have been construed in decided cases as too vague to be enforceable include "subject to war clause"[95] and "subject to *force majeure* conditions."[96] In *Walford v Miles*[97] a "lock-out" agreement (*i.e.* an agreement by the intending vendors of a business not to negotiate with any third party) was held void for uncertainty because its duration was not specified.

2–017 The courts strive, however, to uphold rather than to destroy bargains which the parties believe themselves to have concluded, and this is especially true in commercial dealings in a trade with which both parties are familiar.[98] "Business men often record the most important agreements in crude and summary fashion; modes of expression sufficient and clear to them in the course of their business may appear to those unfamiliar with the business far from complete or precise. It is accordingly the duty of the court to construe such documents fairly and broadly, without being too astute or subtle in finding defects; but, on the contrary, the court should seek to apply the old maxim of English law, *verba ita sunt intelligenda ut res magis valeat quam pereat*."[99] In accordance with this approach, the court may import terms from trade custom, or from a previous course of dealing

[90] *Baird Textiles Holdings Ltd v Marks & Spencer Plc* [2001] EWCA Civ 274; [2002] 1 All E.R. (Comm.) 737.

[91] *Chitty*, *op. cit.*, para.2–136; but note that a meaningless term may be disregarded: *Nicolene Ltd v Simmonds* [1953] 1 Q.B. 543. *Cf. ERJ Lovelock Ltd v Exportles* [1968] 1 Lloyd's Rep. 163; *Hobbs Padgett & Co. (Reinsurance) Ltd v JC Kirkland Ltd* (1969) 113 S.J. 832.

[92] Sale of Goods Act 1979, s.8(2); below, para.2–047.

[93] [1941] A.C. 251.

[94] *ibid.* at p.273.

[95] *Bishop & Baxter Ltd v Anglo-Eastern Trading Co. Ltd* [1944] K.B. 12.

[96] *British Electrical & Associated Industries (Cardiff) Ltd v Patley Pressings Ltd* [1953] 1 W.L.R.280; *cf. Astra Trust Ltd v Adams & Williams* [1969] 1 Lloyd's Rep. 81 (purchase of yacht "subject to satisfactory survey").

[97] [1992] A.C. 128.

[98] *G Scammell & Nephew Ltd v HC & JG Ouston* [1941] A.C. 251 at 255; and see Fridman, 76 L.Q.R. 521 (1960).

[99] *Hillas & Co. Ltd v Arcos Ltd* (1932) 147 L.T. 503 at 514; *Mamidoil-Jetoil Greek Petroleum Co. SA v Okta Crude Oil Refinery A.D.* [2001] EWCA Civ 406; [2001] 2 Lloyd's Rep. 76 (oil refining); *cf.* U.C.C., para.2–204.

between the parties; and it will endeavour to define what is "usual" or what is "reasonable" where the parties have stipulated for "usual" or "reasonable" terms. In *Hillas & Co. Ltd v Arcos Ltd*,[1] the House of Lords decided that an option was enforceable, although expressed in vague terms, because the uncertainty could be resolved by reference to the principal contract of which the option was a part, the parties' previous dealings, and the practice in their trade.

It has been held,[2] too, that in a commercial agreement the further the parties have gone on with their contract (and *a fortiori* when it has been fully executed on the part of the plaintiff[3]), the more ready the courts will be to give effect to their intentions by resolving uncertainties rather than holding that there was no binding agreement. Accordingly, an agreement to buy such quantities "as may be agreed between the parties hereto" (during the second year of a contract intended to last for at least five years) has been construed as an agreement to take a reasonable quantity.[4] In *Foley v Classique Coaches Ltd*,[5] a contract which had been in other respects performed provided that the defendants would buy all their requirements of petrol "at a price to be agreed by the parties in writing and from time to time": the Court of Appeal held that the contract was sufficiently certain to be binding and that in default of further agreement the obligation was to pay a reasonable price. On the other hand, in *May & Butcher Ltd v The King*,[6] the price and other details were left to be agreed and the contract was held void for uncertainty. It is perhaps significant that the transaction was wholly executory; and that the contract was not merely silent on the points in question, but expressly stated that further agreement was required. In contrast, it was no doubt an important factor in the cases earlier referred to that the contract contained some machinery or formula (*e.g.* an arbitration clause) which, if liberally construed, was wide enough to provide a method alternative to agreement by which the uncertainty could be resolved. In these circumstances, the apparent lack of certainty can be cured in the first instance by recourse to this machinery; and if the agreed procedure has for some reason broken down, the court is less inhibited in imposing its own criteria to resolve the issue.[7]

---

[1] Above.

[2] *F. & G. Sykes (Wessex) Ltd v Fine Fare Ltd* [1967] 1 Lloyd's Rep. 53 at 57; *Port Sudan Cotton Co. v Govindaswamy Chettiar & Sons* [1977] 1 Lloyd's Rep. 5 at 13.

[3] *British Bank for Foreign Trade Ltd v Novinex Ltd* [1949] 1 K.B. 623; *cf. G. Percy Trentham Ltd v Archital Luxfer Ltd* [1993] 1 Lloyd's Rep. 25 (construction sub-contract).

[4] *F. & G. Sykes (Wessex) Ltd v Fine Fare Ltd*, above.

[5] [1934] 2 K.B. 1.

[6] [1934] 2 K.B. 17n., HL.

[7] See further *R & J Dempster Ltd v Motherwell Bridge & Engineering Co. Ltd*, 1964 S.L.T. 353 (agreement to sub-contract manufacturing work; prices by custom settled after delivery to customers); *Sweet & Maxwell Ltd v Universal News Services Ltd* [1964] 2 Q.B. 699 (renewal of lease, to include such covenants "as shall reasonably be required" by landlord); *King's Motors (Oxford) Ltd v Lax* [1970] 1 W.L.R. 426 (renewal of lease, rental "as may be agreed upon"); *Smith v Morgan* [1971] 1 W.L.R. 803 (right of pre-emption of land "at a figure to be agreed upon": vendor bound to act bona fide in naming price); *Brown v Gould* [1972] Ch. 53 (renewal of lease;

2–018 **Goods supplied without contract.** Where it is not shown that a contract has been established, but goods have been supplied and accepted in the belief that such a contract existed or in anticipation that terms would be agreed, the supplier may claim their reasonable value, at least where the goods cannot be restored to the supplier.[8]

---

formula to determine rent); *Courtney & Fairbairn Ltd v Tolaini Bros (Hotels) Ltd* [1975] 1 W.L.R. 297 (building contract; agreement to negotiate price); *Vosper Thorneycroft Ltd v Ministry of Defence* [1976] 1 Lloyd's Rep. 58 (shipbuilding: entitlement to additional payment); *Att.-Gen. v Barker* [1976] 2 N.Z.L.R. 495 (renewal of lease); *Beer v Bowden* [1981] 1 W.L.R. 522 (rent revision "as shall be agreed"); *Thomas Bates & Son Ltd v Wyndham's (Lingerie) Ltd* [1981] 1 W.L.R. 505 (rent review clause in lease rectified so as to include provision for arbitration); *Tropwood AG of Zug v Jade Enterprises Ltd (The "Tropwood")* [1982] 1 Lloyd's Rep. 232 (charterparty; payment "for such length of time as owners and charterers may agree upon"); *Sudbrook Trading Estate Ltd v Eggleton* [1983] 1 A.C. 444 (option to purchase "at such price as may be agreed upon" by parties' valuers: fair value payable); *Cedar Trading Co. Ltd v Transworld Oil Ltd (The "Gudermes")* [1985] 2 Lloyd's Rep. 623 (agreement to settle dispute "at a price acceptable to the defendants" not enforceable); *Nile Co. for the Export of Agricultural Crops v H & JM Bennett (Commodities) Ltd* [1986] 1 Lloyd's Rep. 555 (contract to reach a settlement of dispute by agreement held unenforceable); *Pagnan SpA v Granaria BV* [1986] 1 Lloyd's Rep. 547 (prices and other terms never finally agreed: contract void); *Pagnan SpA v Feed Products Ltd* [1987] 2 Lloyd's Rep. 601 (contract binding although certain subsidiary and inessential terms left to be settled later); *Grace Shipping Inc. v C.F. Sharpe (Malaysia) Pte. Ltd* [1987] 1 Lloyd's Rep. 207 (contract of affreightment: contract binding notwithstanding failure to stipulate place of arbitration); *Voest Alpine Intertrading GmbH v Chevron International Oil Co. Ltd* [1987] 2 Lloyd's Rep. 546 ("book-out" procedure in circular string contract; base price "to be agreed": upheld); *Didymi Corp. v Atlantic Lines & Navigation Co. Inc.* [1988] 2 Lloyd's Rep. 108 (charterparty: agreement to pay increased hire; rate capable of ascertainment by inference from other provisions of contract); *Queensland Electricity Generating Board v New Hope Collieries Pty Ltd* [1989] 1 Lloyd's Rep. 205 (agreement to extend coal supply contract beyond initial period; arbitration clause held sufficiently comprehensive to enable fair and reasonable revised price structure to be achieved); *CPC Consolidated Pool Carriers GmbH v CTM Cia. Transmediterranea SA (The "CPC Gallia")* [1994] 1 Lloyd's Rep. 68 ("subject to details/ logical amendments"—no binding contract); *Metal Scrap Trade Corp. v Kate Shipping Co. Ltd (The "Gladys") (No. 2)* [1994] 2 Lloyd's Rep. 402 (contract for sale of ship not binding: blank spaces in standard form still to be completed); *Little v Courage* (1994) 70 P. & C.R. 469 at 476 (lease: "best endeavours to agree", not binding); contrast *Lambert v HTV Cymru (Wales) Ltd* [1998] E.M.L.R. 629 (copyright: undertaking "to use all reasonable endeavours to obtain first rights of negotiation" held enforceable); *Stabilad Ltd v Stephens & Carter Ltd (No. 2)* [1999] 2 All E.R. (Comm.) 651 (royalties: discretion of one party to decide whether precondition satisfied: void for uncertainty); *Gillatt v Sky Television Ltd* [2000] 1 All E.R. (Comm.) 461 (shares: dispute resolution provided for by contract: court not free to substitute own opinion); *Baird Textile Holdings Ltd v Marks and Spencer Plc* [2001] EWCA Civ 274, [2002] 1 All E.R. (Comm.) 737 (terms too vague to enforce). *Ignazio Messina & Co. v Polskie Linie Oceaniczne* [1995] 2 Lloyd's Rep. 566 (no legally binding agreement until amendments to standard form contract agreed); *Thoresen Co. (Bangkok) Ltd v Fathom Marine Co Ltd.* [2004] EWHC 167 (Comm.); [2004] 1 All E.R. (Comm.) 935 (sale of ship "subject to details": no binding contract). See generally Fridman, 76 L.Q.R. 521 (1960); Samek, 47 Can. Bar Rev. 203 (1970).

[8] *British Steel Corp. v Cleveland Bridge & Engineering Co. Ltd* [1984] 1 All E.R. 504; *Cf. Peter Lind & Co. Ltd v Mersey Docks & Harbour Board* [1977] 2 Lloyd's Rep. 234 (construction contract). See further Jones, 18 U.W. Ont.L.Rev. 44 (1980).

2–019 **Intention to establish contractual relationship.**[9] An agreement will sometimes be held not to be binding as a contract on the ground that the parties did not intend to create a legal relationship,[10] but in the case of a contract made in a commercial context such an intention will be presumed.[11] The parties to an apparent contract of sale of goods may expressly negative such an intention, in which case the courts will treat their undertakings as not binding in law.[12] But they will enforce an obligation *dehors* the agreement to pay a reasonable price for goods actually supplied under it.[13]

A transaction may be a valid contract as to part and an honorary engagement as to the remainder.[14] But if the contract as a whole is not legally binding, it is not possible to sever part and treat it as enforceable.[15]

There are also situations (for example, when goods are supplied pursuant to a statutory obligation) where the relationship between the parties gives rise to legal, but not contractual, obligations.[16] Neither the Sale of Goods Act 1979 nor the Supply of Goods and Services Act 1982 applies in these circumstances.

2–020 **Right of cancellation.** A number of legislative measures in the field of consumer protection give a party to a contract (*e.g.* a buyer under a contract of sale of goods) who is a "consumer" (as defined for the purposes of the legislation in question) the right to cancel the contract within a specified period (commonly referred to as a "cooling-off period"), by giving notice of cancellation to the other party.[17] The consequence is, as a general rule, that the contract is "treated as if it had not been made". These provisions are discussed in detail in a later chapter.[18]

---

[9] As regards "letters of intent," see *Wilson Smithett & Cape (Sugar) Ltd v Bangladesh Sugar & Food Industries Corp.* [1986] 1 Lloyd's Rep. 378 and, generally, *Chitty on Contracts* (29th ed.),Vol. 1, para.2–123; and Ball, 99 L.Q.R. 572 (1983).

[10] Chitty, *op. cit.*, paras 2–153 *et seq*; *Baird Textile Holdings Ltd v Marks & Spencer Plc* [2001] EWCA Civ 274; [2002] 1 All E.R. (Comm.) 737.

[11] *ibid*. See, however, *Kleinwort Benson Ltd v Malaysia Mining Corp. Bhd.* [1989] 1 W.L.R. 379, where a "letter of comfort" written by a holding company with reference to its subsidiary's indebtedness was construed as containing no promise as to its future conduct and as merely an undertaking of moral, and not legal, responsibility.

[12] *Rose & Frank Co. v J. R. Crompton & Bros Ltd* [1925] A.C. 445.

[13] *ibid*.

[14] *Guthing v Lynn* (1831) 2 B. & Ad. 232 (buyer of horse to pay more if it proved "lucky").

[15] *Orion Insurance Co. Plc v Sphere Drake Insurance Plc* [1992] 1 Lloyd's Rep. 239.

[16] Above, para.1–071.

[17] See, *e.g.* Consumer Credit Act 1974, ss.67–73; Consumer Protection (Cancellation of Contracts Concluded away from Business Premises) Regulations 1987 (SI 1987/2117) and Consumer Protection (Distance Selling) Regulations 2000 (SI 2000/2334), regs 10–13; Supply of Extended Warranties on Domestic Electrical Goods Order 2005 (SI 2005/37); and see Hellwege [2004] C.L.J. 712.

[18] Below, paras 14–054, 14–057.

2. FORMALITIES[19]

2–021 **Statutory provision.** At common law, a contract for the sale of goods required no formality. This is reflected in section 4 of the Sale of Goods Act 1979, which provides that, subject to that Act[20] and any other Act,[21] a contract of sale may be made in writing (either with or without seal[22]), or by word of mouth, or partly in writing and partly by word of mouth, or may be implied from the conduct of the parties. Section 4(2) provides that nothing in the section shall affect the law relating to corporations.[23]

2–022 **Repeal of section 4 of the 1893 Act.** The Statute of Frauds 1677, s.17, imposed important limitations on the enforceability of contracts for the sale of goods where the goods were of the value of £10 or more: no action could be brought on such a contract unless the buyer had accepted[24] part of the goods or given something in earnest or in part payment, or unless some note or memorandum in writing of the contract had been made and signed by the party to be charged or his agent. This provision was later incorporated into the Sale of Goods Act 1893 as section 4; but in 1954, following the recommendations of the Law Revision Committee, section 4 was repealed,[25] so that the common law rule was restored. There is therefore now no general formal requirement affecting contracts of sale.

Cases decided under the repealed legislation may still be of some relevance, especially those which were concerned with the distinction

---

[19] *Cf.* Vienna Convention on Contracts for the International Sale of Goods (above, para.1–024), Arts 12, 96. On electronic signatures, see the Electronic Communications Act 2000, s.7, and *Standard Bank London Ltd v Bank of Tokyo Ltd* [1995] 2 Lloyd's Rep. 169; and on formal requirements generally in e-commerce transactions, the Law Commission's *Electronic Commerce: Formal Requirements in Commercial Transactions* (2001), *Chitty on Contracts* (29th ed.), Vol. 1, paras 4–05 *et seq.*; Saxby *et al., Encyclopedia of Information Technology Law* (loose-leaf), paras 3.312 *et seq.*; Mason, *Electronic Signatures in Law* (2003). On the EC Directive on Electronic Signatures, the Electronic Communications Act 2000 and the Electronic Commerce (EC Directive) Regulations 2002 (SI 2002/2013), see Saxby *et al., op. cit.,* paras 3.239 *et seq.*

[20] This reference is otiose: it replaces a similar provision in the Act of 1893 referring to s.4 of that Act, which was repealed in 1954: see below, para.2–022.

[21] Below, para.2–023.

[22] Sealing is no longer necessary for the execution of any document by an individual (Law of Property (Miscellaneous Provisions) Act 1989, s.1), or by a company (Companies Act 1985,s.36A). As regards other forms of corporation, see Corporate Bodies' Contracts Act 1960, s.1.

[23] All corporate bodies may now make contracts in exactly the same way as natural persons: see Companies Act 1985, s.36 and Corporate Bodies' Contracts Act 1960, s.1. This provision is accordingly no longer of any significance.

[24] This term had a meaning different from that used in ss.34–35; see below, para.9–002.

[25] Law Reform (Enforcement of Contracts) Act 1954, s.1. The later repeal of s.40 of the Law of Property Act 1925 by the Law of Property (Miscellaneous Provisions) Act 1989 (see above, para.1–092) has no relevance in this context.

between contracts of sale of goods and other types of contract,[26] for the Sale of Goods Act 1979 will apply only to contracts in the former category.

Formal requirements under other statutes. Under the Merchant Shipping Act 1995, a registered ship or share therein must be transferred by a bill of sale satisfying the prescribed requirements, and registered.[27] 2–023

The formalities required for the making of hire-purchase, credit-sale and conditional sale agreements[28] are strictly prescribed by the Consumer Credit Act 1974, ss.60–64,[29] and regulations made thereunder,[30] so far as concerns "regulated agreements" as defined by that Act.[31] A regulated agreement which is not properly executed is enforceable against a debtor or hirer on an order of the court only,[32] except with his consent given at the time[33]; and any security given is similarly not enforceable without an order of the court.[34]

These statutes (and others, such as the Bills of Sale Acts[35]) require the use of a written document and a signature, and possibly also that the signature be witnessed. The application of such provisions to contracts concluded by electronic means is uncertain.[36] The question of electronic bills of lading and other documents of title is discussed in a later chapter.[37]

---

[26] Above, paras 1–078 *et seq*. Because of the overlap between the different statutory definitions of "goods" and "land", it is possible that some contracts (*e.g.* for the sale of minerals) may still require writing under s.2 of the Law of Property (Miscellaneous Provisions) Act 1989: see above, para.1–092, and Hudson, 22 Conv.(N.S.) 137 (1958).

[27] Merchant Shipping Act 1995, Sch.1, para.2(1); above, para.1–082. This rule does not apply where the transfer will result in the ship ceasing to have a British connection (*ibid.*).

[28] Defined above, paras 1–052—1–055.

[29] For the previous law, see Hire-Purchase Act 1965, s.5, and Hire-Purchase (Documents) (Legibility and Statutory Statements) Regulations 1965 (SI 1965/1646).

[30] See Consumer Credit (Agreements) Regulations 1983 (SI 1433/1553, as amended by SIs 1984/1600, 1985/666, 1988/2047 1999/3177, 2001/3649, 2004/1881, 2004/1482).

[31] For the meaning of "regulated agreement", see above, para.1–022.

[32] Consumer Credit Act 1974, s.65. Section 127(3), which precludes the court from making an enforcement order if *no* document containing the prescribed terms (whether or not in the prescribed form and complying with the regulations) has been signed by the debtor, has been declared incompatible with the Human Rights Convention: *Wilson v First County Trust Ltd (No.2)* [2001] EWCA Civ 633; [2002] Q.B. 74.

[33] *ibid.* s.173(3).

[34] *ibid.* s.113(2). For the powers of the court, see s.127; and for the power of the Office of Fair Trading to waive or modify the statutory requirements in a particular case, see s.60(3), (4).

[35] Above, para.1–016.

[36] See the authorities referred to at para.2–021, n.19, above, where it is noted that the term "signature" is capable of various meanings and that the legislative definitions vary. It should be noted also that the legislation on electronic signatures referred to in that note is primarily concerned with systems for the authentication of such signatures, rather than the factual question whether a person has "signed" a document.

[37] Below, para.18–202.

2–024 **Written contracts of sale.** Although it is not necessary to make a contract of sale in writing, if the parties choose to do so their contract will be governed by the ordinary rules of evidence which affect written contracts. In particular, under the "parol evidence rule", where a document is intended by the parties to express the entire agreement between them, extrinsic evidence generally cannot be used to add to, vary, subtract from or contradict the terms of the written instrument.[37a] But this rule is subject to many exceptions.[38]

2–025 **Sales and assignments by deed.**[39] A contract for the sale of goods may be made by deed, although there will rarely be any commercial reason why this form should be adopted. Goods may also be assigned by deed, *e.g.* for the benefit of creditors, or by way of gift. In this case, the property will be effectively transferred to the assignee without delivery of the goods[40]; but if the assignor in fact remains in possession, the transaction may infringe the Bills of Sale Acts.[41]

3. PARTIES

2–026 **Number of parties.** The Sale of Goods Act 1979 plainly assumes throughout that a contract of sale of goods will be a bilateral contract between a "seller" and a "buyer". There is no difficulty in extending the scope of the Act to include the case where several persons sell or buy the same property jointly.[42] But a multipartite transaction in which three or more persons agree on the fusion or partition or reallocation of their interests in property may not be a contract of sale within the meaning of the Act, even though money is paid in return.[43] This may be true also of certain other transactions by or between part-owners.[44]

The 1979 Act does not deal specifically with the type of contract under which A agrees to pay B for goods to be supplied to C, and prima facie it would appear that such a contract falls outside the scope of the Act in view of the language of sections 2, 27 and 28.[45] If, however, the transaction can

---

37a Extrinsic evidence intended to show that the party named in a written contract was not the true contracting party was rejected in *Shogun Finance Ltd v Hudson* [2003] UKHL 62; [2004] 1 A.C. 919. See on this issue McLauchlan, 121 L.Q.R. 9 (2005).

38 For a full discussion, see *Phipson on Evidence* (16th ed.), Ch.42; *Cross and Tapper on Evidence* (10th ed.), pp.718 *et seq.*; *Chitty on Contracts* (29th ed.), Vol. 1, paras 12–095 *et seq*. See also the Law Commission's Report, *The Parol Evidence Rule* (L.Com. No. 154, Cmnd. 9700, 1986), where the view is expressed that the supposed rule is not as far-reaching as has previously been thought.

39 A seal is no longer required for the execution of a deed by an individual or a company: see para.2–021, n.22, above.

40 *French v Gething* [1922] 1 K.B. 236.

41 Above, paras 1–016—1–017.

42 Interpretation Act 1978, s.6(c).

43 See *Graff v Evans* (1882) 8 Q.B.D. 373 and the other cases cited above, para.1–121.

44 *ibid*.

45 It is possible that no property would pass to C without delivery to him: *cf.* *Cochrane v Moore* (1890) 25 Q.B.D. 57 at 72–73. But the principles of the Act might be applied by analogy: see above, para.1–036.

be construed as one in which the property in the goods passes to A as a step towards its transfer to C (either by way of sub-sale or gift), there is plainly a sale to A.[46] And there may be situations where the facts are so uncertain or the position so ambiguous that a court could well infer that there was a contract of sale between B and C: for example, where a customer (A) orders meals in a restaurant[47] owned by B for himself and his friend (C). On one view (and more particularly where it is not settled at the time when the contract is made whether A is to pay for both meals or each is to pay for his own), A can be taken to have acted as C's agent, so that there is a contract of sale between C and B as well as one between A and B. Alternatively, if the circumstances are such that it is held that the only contract is one made between A and B, C may be able to avail himself of the remedies now accorded to third parties under the Contracts (Rights of Third Parties) Act 1999. By virtue of this Act, a person who is not a party to a contract may in his own right enforce a term of the contract (a) if the contract expressly provides that he may, or (b) if the term purports to confer a benefit on him (unless on a proper construction of the contract it appears that the parties did not intend the term to be enforceable by him).[48] The third party must be expressly identified in the contract by name, as a member of a class or as answering to a particular description but need not be in existence when the contract is entered into.[49] In a suitable case this could enable a person who was not a party to a contract for the sale of goods to avail himself of the remedies accorded to a seller or a buyer by the Sale of Goods Act 1979. But the Act of 1999 is concerned only with *benefits* conferred by the contract: there is no corresponding provision making the third party liable to perform any of the obligations which it may contain.

Collateral contract. A person who is not a party to a contract of sale of goods or contract of hire-purchase may be liable to one of the parties on a collateral contract, the consideration for such collateral contract usually[50] being the making by the other party of the contract of sale. So, in *Wells (Merstham) Ltd v Buckland Sand & Silica Co. Ltd*,[51] the plaintiffs bought 2–027

---

[46] *E. & S. Ruben Ltd v Faire Bros & Co. Ltd* [1949] 1 K.B. 254; *Four Point Garage Ltd v Carter* [1985] 3 All E.R. 12; *cf.* the unsuccessful argument for the prosecution in *Appleby v Sleep* [1968] 1 W.L.R. 948, above, para.1–071.

[47] Such a contract was held to be a contract for the sale of goods in *Lockett v A & M Charles Ltd* [1938] 4 All E.R. 170: see above, para.1–046.

[48] s.1(1), (2).

[49] s.1(3).

[50] But the collateral contract may have its own independent consideration: *cf.* the common credit-card arrangement in which the seller, buyer and credit-card company enter into three separate bilateral contracts: *Re Charge Card Services Ltd* [1989] Ch. 497.

[51] [1965] 2 Q.B. 170. *Cf. Couchman v Hill* [1947] K.B. 554; *Webster v Higgin* [1948] 2 All E.R. 127; *Brown v Sheen & Richmond Car Sales Ltd* [1950] 1 All E.R. 1102; *Harling v Eddy* [1951] 2 K.B. 739; *Andrews v Hopkinson* [1957] 1 Q.B. 229; *Smith v Spurling Motor Bodies Ltd* (1961) 105 S.J. 967; *Yeoman Credit Ltd v Odgers* [1962] 1 W.L.R. 215. *Cf. J. Evans & Son (Portsmouth) Ltd v Andrea Merzario Ltd* [1976] 1 W.L.R. 1078 (sea carriage of goods); *Esso Petroleum Co. Ltd v Mardon* [1978] Q.B. 801 (lease of petrol station); and see below, paras 10–012 *et seq.*; 12–011, 13–016, 14–042, 14–044, 14–062; Wedderburn [1959] C.L.J. 58.

sand from a firm of merchants in reliance upon an assurance given by the defendants (who produced the sand) that its analysis made it suitable for propagating chrysanthemums. When the assurance proved to be untrue, the defendants were held liable to the buyers on a collateral contract.[52]

2–028 **Capacity of parties.** Section 3 of the Act declares that "capacity to buy and sell is regulated by the general law concerning capacity to contract and to transfer and acquire property." The capacity of different categories of persons to contract is dealt with in the paragraphs which follow. There are in general no limitations on the capacity of any person to *acquire* goods in English law.[53] The capacity of a person to *dispose* of goods is not necessarily co-extensive with his capacity to contract to do so[54]: in the context of the law of sale, a question not based on contractual capacity will arise where a person under a disability who has purportedly sold goods brings an action to have the transfer avoided and the property revested in him. There is authority for the view that even in those cases where the contract is said to be *void*, property once transferred is irrecoverable,[55] or at least not recoverable unless there has been a total failure of consideration.[56] The particular category of incapacity may make a difference.[57] In any event, a claim for the return of goods sold under a contract of sale which is *voidable* on the grounds of incapacity[58] is liable to be defeated by the rights of third parties or other equitable bars to such claims.[59]

2–029 **Contractual capacity of minors.**[60] A natural person under full age is known as a minor or infant. By the Family Law Reform Act 1969, the age of majority was reduced from 21 to 18[61]; but this Act did not alter the

---

[52] See below, paras 10–012 *et seq*; 14–042 *et seq*. An alternative remedy in such cases might also now lie on the principle of *Hedley Byrne & Co. Ltd v Heller & Partners Ltd* [1964] A.C. 465 (negligent misstatement); *cf. Esso Petroleum Co. Ltd v Mardon*, above, and see below, para.12–013.

[53] Halsbury, *Laws of England* (4th ed.), Vol. 35, para.1231.

[54] *Chitty on Contracts* (29th ed.), Vol. 1, paras 8–065—8–067; *Chaplin v Leslie Frewin (Publishers) Ltd* [1966] Ch. 71 (copyright).

[55] *Stocks v Wilson* [1913] 2 K.B. 235 at 246; *Chaplin v Leslie Frewin (Publishers) Ltd*, above (cases concerning minors). But see now, as regards restitution of such property by the minor, Minors' Contracts Act 1987, s.3, below, para.2–038.

[56] *Pearce v Brain* [1929] 2 K.B. 310 (barter). The proper question should perhaps be whether *restitutio in integrum* can be made: see Treitel, 73 L.Q.R. 194 at 202–205 (1957); Goff and Jones, *The Law of Restitution* (5th ed.), para.25–006.

[57] *Bell Houses Ltd v City Wall Properties Ltd* [1966] 1 Q.B. 207 at 221 (reversed on other grounds [1966] 2 Q.B. 656); *Cabaret Holdings Ltd v Meeanee Sports & Rodeo Club Inc.* [1982] 1 N.Z.L.R. 673 (*ultra vires* contracts of company held unenforceable); contrast *Re K.L. Tractors Ltd (in liq.)* (1961) 106 C.L.R. 318 (action allowed for price of goods sold *ultra vires*); and *cf. Hazell v Hammersmith & Fulham LBC* [1992] 2 A.C. 1 at 36: "The consequences of any *ultra vires* transaction may depend on the facts of each case."

[58] *e.g.* on the grounds of mental incapacity or drunkenness: below, para.2–041.

[59] See below, paras 12–005 *et seq*.

[60] See *Chitty on Contracts* (29th ed.), Vol. 1, paras 8–002 *et seq.*; Treitel, *The Law of Contract* (11th ed.), pp.539–557.

[61] s.1. The Act came into force on January 1, 1970, and all persons then aged 18 or over, but under 21, attained their majority on that date. A person attains the age of 18 at the commencement of the 18th anniversary of his birth: s.9.

substantive legal rules governing minors' contracts.[62] Such contracts continued to be governed by the common law as altered by the Infants Relief Act 1874 and as codified in part by section 3 of the Sale of Goods Act 1979. However, by the Minors' Contracts Act 1987,[63] the Act of 1874 ceased to apply to any contract made by a minor after June 9, 1987, so that the common law position has been restored.[64] The general rule at common law[65] is that a contract made by a minor is voidable at his option[66]; but contracts for "necessaries"[67] and beneficial contracts of service are binding on him.[68] So far as concerns the sale of goods, a minor's contracts fall into three categories: (a) contracts for the purchase of necessaries, (b) contracts for the purchase of non-necessaries and (c) contracts to sell.[69]

Necessaries.[70] Section 3(2) of the Sale of Goods Act 1979[71] reads as follows: "Where necessaries are sold and delivered to a minor or to a person who by reason of drunkenness is incompetent to contract, he must pay a reasonable price for them."[72] "Necessaries" in this subsection means goods suitable to the condition in life of the minor or other person concerned and to his actual requirements at the time of the sale and delivery.[73] Whether goods in any case are necessaries is a question of mixed law and fact. It is a matter of law whether on the evidence given the article is capable of being found a necessary, and a matter of fact whether, having regard to the actual requirements of the buyer, it is a necessary in the particular circumstances of the case.[74] The onus of proving that goods are necessaries lies on the seller, who must show both that the goods are suitable to the condition in life of the buyer and that they were suitable to 2–030

---

[62] Recommendations for reform of these rules were made by the Latey Committee on the Age of Majority (Cmnd. 3342, 1967), whose report led to the passing of the Act of 1969, but these recommendations have not so far been implemented. See also the Law Commission's Report on Minors' Contracts (L.Com. No. 134, 1984), which led to the passing of the Minors' Contracts Act 1987 (below).
[63] This Act applies only in England and Wales. For the position in Scotland, see the Age of Legal Capacity (Scotland) Act 1991.
[64] In some respects, however, the common law has been modified by the Act of 1987, *e.g.* as regards restitution of property: see below, para.2–037.
[65] A very young child may lack the capacity to make a contract at all—or at least a contract of any but the most simple kind: *R. v Oldham Metropolitan BC, ex p. Garlick* [1993] 1 F.L.R. 645 (five-year-old held incapable of contracting for the occupation of residential premises).
[66] The term "voidable" is used in more than one sense, meaning at times "not binding unless ratified" and at other times "binding unless repudiated": see Chitty, *op. cit.*, para.8–005.
[67] Below, para.2–030.
[68] See *Chitty on Contracts* (29th ed.), Vol. 1, paras 8–005 *et seq*.
[69] Various statutes provide that the sale of particular categories of goods (*e.g.* liquor, fireworks) to minors, or to minors under a specified age, is unlawful.
[70] The term "necessaries" may include services as well as goods, *e.g.* lodging and legal advice: see *Chitty on Contracts* (29th ed.), Vol. 1, paras 8–011, 8–013; but only the cases concerned with goods are discussed here.
[71] As amended by the Mental Capacity Act 2005, Sch.6, para 24.
[72] See also (mental incapacity) Mental Capacity Act 2005, s.7, discussed below, para.2–041.
[73] s.3(3).
[74] *Ryder v Wombwell* (1868) L.R. 4 Ex. 32.

his actual requirements at the time of the sale and delivery.[75] It is immaterial that the seller was unaware of the buyer's situation: the mere fact that he was already adequately provided with goods of the type in question will defeat the seller's claim.[76]

The term "necessaries" is not confined to the bare necessities of life: food, clothing and medicine are clearly necessaries, but these are not the only things embraced by the expression. It includes also goods purchased for real use, so long as they are not merely ornamental.[77] "Articles of mere luxury are always excluded, though luxurious articles of utility are in some cases allowed."[78] Further, although it is settled that only those contracts are enforceable against a minor which "relate to his person",[79] the principle of liability extends to necessaries for his wife and children.[80]

2–031 **Examples of necessaries.** It should be borne in mind that the question whether goods are necessaries is always a relative one and depends both on the situation of the particular person and on the social needs and customs of the day. Subject to this caveat, the following may be cited as examples of goods held or found to be necessaries: military uniform,[81] horses and harness,[82] a greatcoat,[83] a watch-chain and rings,[84] a racing bicycle[85] and rings and gifts for a fiancée.[86] In contrast, the following have been held not to be necessaries in the circumstances of the particular cases: a chronometer for a naval officer,[87] expensive dinner-parties,[88] cigars and tobacco in large quantities,[89] jewellery intended for presents,[90] clothing which included 11 fancy waistcoats,[91] and curios and collector's items.[92] Articles bought for the purposes of trade cannot be necessaries.[93]

2–032 **Executory contracts for necessaries.** Section 3 of the Act refers only to the case where goods are sold *and delivered*.[94] It is uncertain whether this

---

[75] *Nash v Inman* [1908] 2 K.B. 1.
[76] *Barnes & Co. v Toye* (1884) 13 Q.B.D. 410; *Johnstone v Marks* (1887) 19 Q.B.D. 509; *Nash v Inman*, above.
[77] *Peters v Fleming* (1840) 6 M. & W. 42.
[78] *Chapple v Cooper* (1844) 13 M. & W. 252 at 258.
[79] *Cowern v Nield* [1912] 2 K.B. 419 at 422.
[80] *Turner v Trisby* (1719) 1 Str. 168; *Chapple v Cooper*, above.
[81] *Coates v Wilson* (1804) 5 Esp. 152.
[82] *Hart v Prater* (1837) 1 Jur. 623; *Hill v Arbon* (1876) 34 L.T. 125; *cf. Skrine v Gordon* (1875) 9 Ir.R.C.L. 479; *Re Mead* [1916] 2 I.R. 285.
[83] *Brayshaw v Eaton* (1839) 5 Bing. N.C. 231.
[84] *Peters v Fleming* (1840) 6 M. & W. 42.
[85] *Clyde Cycle Co. v Hargreaves* (1898) 78 L.T. 296.
[86] *Elkington v Amery* [1936] 2 All E.R. 86; contrast *Hewlings v Graham* (1901) 70 L.J.Ch.568.
[87] *Berroles v Ramsay* (1815) Holt N.P. 77.
[88] *Wharton v Mackenzie* (1844) 5 Q.B. 606.
[89] *Bryant v Richardson* (1866) 14 L.T. 24.
[90] *Ryder v Wombwell* (1869) L.R. 4 Ex. 32; but see n.86, above.
[91] *Nash v Inman* [1908] 2 K.B. 1.
[92] *Stocks v Wilson* [1913] 2 K.B. 235.
[93] *Cowern v Nield* [1912] 2 K.B. 419; *Mercantile Union Guarantee Corp. v Ball* [1937] 2 K.B. 498; see further *Chitty on Contracts* (29th ed.), Vol. 1, para.8–017.
[94] *Cf.* Mental Capacity Act 2005, s.7 ("supplied"), see below, para.2–041.

amounts to a statutory declaration that the only circumstances in which a minor is liable to pay for necessaries are those where there has been actual delivery, or whether there may possibly be a residual liability under an executory contract for the sale of necessaries on common law principles. There are various difficulties here. In the first place, it is uncertain whether any such liability exists at common law, although in the broadly analogous case of beneficial contracts of service an executory contract is enforceable against a minor.[95] Secondly, there is some support for the view that the obligation to pay for necessaries supplied is not contractual but quasi-contractual[96]—a view which is encouraged by the statutory liability to pay not the agreed contract price, but a reasonable price. Finally, both at common law and under the statute the question whether goods are necessary to a minor is determined at least in part by reference to the time of delivery,[97] so that there may be considerable uncertainty in deciding whether an executory contract is or is not one for necessaries.[98]

On the other hand, it appears from the language used in section 3 of the Act (and, in particular, the use of the word "sold") that the transaction is at least in part consensual; and this view is fortified both by the analogous case of beneficial contracts of service[99] and by the fact that in other respects the contract is apparently enforceable.[1] It has accordingly been argued that liability is basically contractual,[2] except that an excessive price will be disallowed.

Requirement of overall benefit. It is generally true that a minor is not liable even on a contract for necessaries unless the agreement is, taken as a whole, for his benefit.[3] There is no known case in which this point has been taken in a contract of sale of goods (as distinct from a contract of hire or hire-purchase[4]), but it is conceivable that objection might be made to a contract of sale containing wide exemption clauses or other onerous terms.[5] **2–033**

Mixed goods. Prior to the reforms enacted by the Minors' Contracts Act 1987, it was held that in the case of an entire contract[6] for a quantity of goods of which some only were necessaries, a buyer who was a minor was **2–034**

---

95 *Roberts v Gray* [1913] 1 K.B. 520.

96 See *Nash v Inman* [1908] 2 K.B. 1 at 8–9; *Pontypridd Union v Drew* [1927] 1 K.B. 214 at 220; Cheshire, Fifoot and Furmston, *Law of Contract* (14th ed.), pp.480, 741; Miles, 43 L.Q.R. 389 (1927).

97 Winfield, 58 L.Q.R. 82 (1942).

98 *Chitty on Contracts* (29th ed.), Vol. 1, paras 8–011—8–011.

99 *Roberts v Gray*, above.

1 Below, para.2–036.

2 Treitel, *The Law of Contract* (11th ed.), pp.541–543; Goff and Jones, *The Law of Restitution* (6th ed.), para.25–003 ("A minor's contract to buy necessary goods for less than a reasonable price is surely valid"); *cf. Nash v Inman*, above, at p.12. And see above, para.1–076.

3 *Fawcett v Smethurst* (1914) 84 L.J.K.B. 473.

4 *ibid.*; *Mercantile Union Guarantee Corp. v Ball* [1937] 2 K.B. 498; and *cf. Chaplin v Frewin (Publishers) Ltd* [1966] Ch. 71 (assignment of copyright).

5 *Cf. Flower v London & North Western Ry Co.* [1894] 2 Q.B. 65 (contract of carriage). *Quaere* whether the contract as a whole would be declared invalid, or only the relevant terms? An alternative course would be for the court to strike down the clauses under the Unfair Contract Terms Act 1977, ss.3, 6(3) and Sch.2, para.(a) or the Unfair Terms in Consumer Contracts Regulations 1999 (SI. 1999/2083).

6 Below, para.8–072.

not liable to pay anything at all.[7] But there seems to be no reason in such a case why a reasonable price should not be paid for such of the things delivered to him as are held to be necessaries; and the court would now also be able to make an order for the restitution under section 3 of the 1987 Act of the other goods, provided that they had not been consumed.[8]

2–035 **Loans for the purchase of necessaries.** A minor is not liable to repay money lent to him[9] even where the advance was made to enable him to buy necessaries. If, however, such a loan is in fact used for the purchase of necessaries, the lender may to that extent recover his loan under the equitable principle of subrogation.[10]

A bill of exchange or other security given for the price of necessaries is not binding on the infant at common law,[11] and the same is true of an account stated even though the account refers to necessaries supplied.[12] But the creditor can always ignore the security or account stated and claim a reasonable price under section 3.[13]

2–036 **Liability of seller.** Where necessaries have been sold and delivered, the seller is liable for breaches of the conditions and warranties expressly or impliedly falling to be fulfilled by him under the contract of sale,[14] and for misrepresentations. He is also liable on an executory contract for damages for non-delivery, since a plea of minority operates only in the minor's favour.[15]

2–037 **Goods other than necessaries.** A contract by a minor for the purchase of goods other than necessaries is enforceable by the minor but is not binding on him unless he ratifies it on coming of full age. Ratification may be by words or conduct, and if ratified the contract will be binding on him without the need for consideration for the new promise.[16]

A minor is not liable on a warranty of goods sold by him, even where the warranty has been given fraudulently.[17]

---

[7] *Stocks v Wilson* [1913] 2 K.B. 235 at 241–242.

[8] This has in effect been the decision in many cases, *e.g. Ryder v Wombwell* (1868) L.R. 4 Ex. 32; *Elkington v Amery* [1936] 2 All E.R. 86.

[9] The contract would now be voidable. Prior to the Minors' Contracts Act 1987, it would have been "absolutely void": Infants Relief Act 1874, s.1; Betting and Loans (Infants) Act 1892, s.5.

[10] *Marlow v Pitfeild* (1719) 1 P.Wms. 558; *Re National Permanent Benefit Building Soc.* (1869) 5 Ch.App. 309 at 313; *Martin v Gale* (1876) 4 Ch.D. 428.

[11] Under the Infants Relief Act 1874, it would have been void: *Re Soltykoff* [1891] 1 Q.B. 413. The liability of other parties to the bill is unaffected: Bills of Exchange Act 1882, s.22(2).

[12] *Trueman v Hurst* (1875) 1 Term Rep. 40.

[13] *Re Soltykoff*, above, at p.415. A covenant by deed to pay the price of necessaries may be disregarded in the same way: *Walter v Everard* [1891] 2 Q.B. 369.

[14] *Godley v Perry* [1960] 1 W.L.R. 9; *Cf. Thornalley v Gostelow* (1947) 80 Ll.L.R. 507 (where a minor and an adult were co-plaintiffs, but infancy was not pleaded).

[15] *Farnham v Atkins* (1670) 1 Sid. 446; *Bruce v Warwick* (1815) 6 Taunt. 118; below, para.2–039.

[16] Such a ratification was declared to be void by the Infants Relief Act 1874, but the common law position, as stated in the text, has now been restored by the Minors' Contracts Act 1987, ss.1(1), 4.

[17] *Howlett v Haswell* (1814) 4 Camp. 118; *Green v Greenbank* (1816) 2 Marsh. 485.

Trading contracts to which a minor was a party were "absolutely void" under section 1 of the Infants Relief Act 1874; but this provision was repealed by the Minors' Contracts Act 1987,[18] with the result that trading contracts are now governed by the same rules as other contracts.

Liability of minor to make restitution.[19] At common law, restitution of 2–038
money or property obtained by a minor under a void or unenforceable contract would not be ordered, but an obligation to make restitution in equity lay in certain limited circumstances where he had fraudulently misrepresented his age.[20] Section 3 of the Minors' Contracts Act, however, now gives the court a discretionary power to order restitution: it may, if it is just and equitable to do so, require the minor to transfer to the other contracting party any property acquired by the minor under the contract, or any property represented by it. These last words clearly allow the court to make a form of tracing order. The jurisdiction of the court does not depend on proof of fraud. But if property has been delivered to the minor and consumed or lost, there will be no remedy.

Contracts to sell. A contract by a minor to sell goods to an adult is 2–039
enforceable by the minor against the other party, but he is not liable to be sued upon it.[21] Such a contract can, however, be effective to pass the property to the buyer.[22] The minor, for his part, cannot claim restitution unless there has been a total failure of consideration.[23] The right of the other party to recover his price where the goods had not been delivered or had been rejected for breach of condition depended at common law on his ability to prove fraud on the part of the minor.[24] However, this rule has now been superseded by the discretionary power to order a minor to make restitution which has been conferred on the court by section 3 of the Minors' Contracts Act 1987.[25]

Liability of minor in tort. A minor who is a party to a contract cannot be 2–040
sued in tort where this would be an indirect way of enforcing the contract, but he may be liable for a tort which falls wholly outside the scope of the contract.[26] No action in deceit may be brought in respect of a misrepresentation that he is of full age which has induced the other party to contract with him.[27] But it appears that a minor may be liable for other types of fraud and misrepresentation,[28] *e.g.* (perhaps) a fraudulent representation by an under-age seller regarding the mileage of a used car.

---

[18] ss.1(1), 4.

[19] *Chitty on Contracts* (29th ed.), Vol. 1, paras 8–048 *et seq.*

[20] *Stocks v Wilson* [1913] 2 K.B. 235; *R Leslie Ltd v Sheill* [1914] 3 K.B. 607.

[21] *Cowern v Nield* [1912] 2 K.B. 419.

[22] *Pearce v Brain* [1929] 2 K.B. 310 (exchange of goods). *Cf. Chaplin v Frewin (Publishers) Ltd* [1966] Ch. 71 at 90 (assignment of copyright).

[23] *Pearce v Brain*, above.

[24] *Cowern v Nield*, above.

[26] para.2–038, above.

[26] *Chitty on Contracts* (29th ed.), Vol. 1, paras 8–046 *et seq.*

[27] *Stocks v Wilson* [1913] 2 K.B. 235.

[28] *Cowern v Nield* [1912] 2 K.B. 419.

2–041 **Drunkenness and mental incapacity.** By virtue of section 3(2) of the Sale of Goods Act 1979,[29] a person who by reason of drunkenness is incompetent to contract is liable to pay a reasonable price for necessaries sold and delivered to him[30] in the same way as a minor.[31] Section 7 of the Mental Capacity Act 2005, which deals with mental incapacity, is expressed in similar terms, except that it refers to services as well as goods and uses the word "supplied" instead of "sold and delivered". In all other respects, the capacity of such persons is governed by the general law concerning capacity to contract, for which reference should be made to standard works.[32] The basic rule is that such a person is bound by his contract unless he did not understand what he was doing, and the other party was aware of his incapacity. If the incapable person can show this, the contract is voidable at his option.[33]

2–042 **Married women.** There are no limitations on the capacity of a married woman to make a contract for the sale of goods.[34] A married woman has an implied authority to pledge her husband's credit for necessaries, which normally arises from the fact of cohabitation.[35]

2–043 **Corporate bodies.** A corporate body incorporated by special statute or which derives its powers from statute[36] may act only within the powers expressly or impliedly conferred by that legislation. The capacity of certain other incorporated bodies[37] is restricted in law to activities which are expressly or by implication within the scope of the objects clause contained in their memorandum of association, rules or other equivalent document, *e.g.* industrial and provident societies, building societies and credit unions. A contract of sale of goods which is not within the powers of any such body corporate is at common law *ultra vires* and void[38]; though it is possible that such a contract, if executed, is effective to transfer property rights.[39]

Companies incorporated under the Companies Act 1985 and its predecessors were formerly also subject to the *ultra vires* doctrine, but since February 4, 1991,[40] the law has been changed, so that the validity of an act done by a company (except a company which is a charity) may not be called

---

[29] As amended by the Mental Capacity Act 2005, Sch.6, para.24.
[30] Or to his dependants: *Read v Legard* (1851) 6 Exch. 636.
[31] *Re Rhodes* (1890) 44 Ch.D. 94.
[32] *Chitty on Contracts* (29th ed.), Vol. 1, paras 8–070 *et seq.*
[33] *Hart v O'Connor* [1985] A.C. 1000.
[34] Chitty, *op. cit.*, para.8–068.
[35] Chitty, *op. cit.*, Vol. 2, para.31–049. But the former power of a deserted wife to pledge her husband's credit as agent of necessity was abrogated by the Matrimonial Proceedings and Property Act 1970, s.41(1): below, para.3–007.
[36] *e.g.* a local authority: *Hazell v Hammersmith & Fulham LBC* [1992] 2 A.C. 1.
[37] This *ultra vires* rule also applies, anomalously, to trade unions, which are not incorporated (*Taylor v National Union of Mineworkers (Derbyshire Area)* (1985) 14 I.R.L.R. 99).
[38] *Chitty on Contracts* (29th ed.), Vol. 1, paras 9–020 *et seq.*; Gower and Davies, *Modern Company Law* (7th ed.), Ch.7.
[39] *Ayers v S. Australian Banking Co.* (1871) L.R. 3 P.C. 548; *National Telephone Co. v. Constables of St Peter Port* [1900] A.C. 317.
[40] See SI 1990/2569, arts. 4(a), 7.

into question on the ground of lack of capacity by reason of anything in the company's memorandum.[41] Charitable companies remain subject to the doctrine, but there is statutory protection in favour of a person who does not know at the time the act is done that the company is a charity, or who gives full consideration in money or money's worth in relation to the act in question and does not know that the act is not permitted by the company's memorandum.[42]

Notwithstanding the abolition of the *ultra vires* doctrine, a contract made with a company may be open to challenge on the ground that the directors (or other person or persons representing the company) have no authority to bind the company in a matter that is outside the scope of its objects clause or which infringes some other constitutional provision. The Companies Act 1985 provides, however, that in favour of a person dealing with a company in good faith, the power of the board of directors to bind the company, or to authorise others to do so, shall be deemed to be free of any limitation under the company's constitution.[43] A person is not regarded as acting in bad faith by reason only of his knowing that an act is beyond the powers of the directors under the company's constitution,[44] and good faith is presumed unless the contrary is proved.[45] These statutory provisions will not, however, protect a person who receives property from a company in circumstances which make him accountable for it as a constructive trustee.[46]

4. THE PRICE

Price must be in money. The consideration in a contract of sale of goods must in English law be a price in money[47] either paid or promised. Where the consideration for the transfer of property in goods takes some other form, the contract is one of exchange or barter and the Sale of Goods Act 2–044

---

[41] Companies Act 1985, s.35(1) (as inserted by Companies Act 1989, s.108(1)). Between January 1, 1973, and the coming into effect of this provision, limited protection was given to third parties dealing with a company in good faith by the European Communities Act 1972, s.9(1), which was later consolidated as s.35(1), (2) of the Companies Act 1985 (now repealed). The Company Law Reform Bill currently before Parliament re-enacts the provisions discussed in the present paragraphs in similar language. Limited liability partnerships, which are bodies corporate, have unlimited capacity: Limited Liability Partnerships Act 2000, s.1(2), (3).

[42] Charities Act 1993, s.65.

[43] Companies Act 1985, s.35A(1) (as inserted by Companies Act 1989, s.108). The meaning of the expression "good faith" is discussed in *Barclays Bank Ltd v TOSG. Trust Fund Ltd* [1984] B.C.L.C. 1 at 17.

[44] *ibid.*, s.35A(2)(b).

[45] *ibid.*, s.35A(2)(c).

[46] *Cf. International Sales and Agencies Ltd v Marcus* [1982] 3 All E.R. 551 (a case on the former statute).

[47] Sale of Goods Act 1979, s.2(1); *Re Westminster Property Group Plc* [1985] 1 W.L.R. 676 (shares): contrast U.C.C., para.2–304 (above, para.1–034). A contract under which payment is to be by credit card is within the Act: *Re Charge Card Services Ltd* [1987] Ch. 150 at 164 (a point not considered on appeal [1989] Ch. 497).

1979 will not apply to it, although it may in some respects be governed by analogous principles, either at common law or under the Supply of Goods and Services Act 1982. Where it is agreed that the consideration may consist partly in money and partly in some other form, as where goods are traded-in in part exchange, the contract may sometimes be construed as one of sale, or even as two contracts of sale with a set-off of prices and such adjustment as is necessary.[48] It is open to the parties to agree that the price shall be payable in any currency.[49]

2–045 **Fixing of price.** Section 8(1) of the Sale of Goods Act 1979 provides that the price in a contract of sale may be fixed by the contract,[50] or may be left to be fixed in a manner agreed by the contract, or may be determined by the course of dealing between the parties. Where the parties expressly state a price, no problem usually arises. They may, however, agree on a price stated, not as a lump sum, but at a certain rate, to be calculated by reference to the number, weight, measurement or appraisal of the goods. Under such a contract, the property or the risk may sometimes pass to the buyer before the price has been calculated[51]; and if in such a case the calculation becomes impossible—for instance, by the destruction of the goods—the court must decree payment of an estimated price based on such evidence as is available.[52]

The price may also be left to be fixed by other means. Where it is to be assessed by a third party, the Act makes special provision in section 9.[53] It may be agreed that some outside circumstance shall determine the price—*e.g.* the manufacturer's recommended price,[54] or the market price ruling at a particular time and place. Even an agreement that one of the parties shall have power to fix the price himself is valid, and his determination is binding, provided that he has acted *bona fide*.[55]

2–046 **Price to be agreed.** If the price is left to be agreed upon subsequently between the parties, there will ordinarily be no binding contract, on the grounds of uncertainty,[56] unless and until they later reach agreement on a price. Moreover, an agreement to leave the price open to further negotiation will normally exclude any inference that the price should be a reasonable price in accordance with the provisions of section 8(2).[57] But, in

---

[48] Above, para.1–039.

[49] *Miliangos v George Frank (Textiles) Ltd* [1976] A.C. 443; *Daewoo Australia Pty Ltd v. Suncorp-Metway Ltd* (2000) 33 A.C.S.R. 481: below, para.25–187.

[50] The contract may lawfully provide that the price is to be fixed by one or other of the parties: *May & Butcher v The King* [1934] 2 K.B. 17n at 21; *Lombard Tricity Finance Ltd v Paton* [1989] 1 All E.R. 918 at 923 (rate of interest).

[51] Where the *seller* is to weigh or measure, the property will normally not pass until this is done: s.18, r. 3: below, para.5–035.

[52] *Martineau v Kitching* (1872) L.R. 7 Q.B. 436; *Castle v Playford* (1872) L.R. 7 Ex. 98.

[53] Below, para.2–049.

[54] As regards resale price maintenance, see below, para.3–037.

[55] Williston, *Sales* (3rd ed.), para.167; *May & Butcher v R.* [1934] 2 K.B. 17n. at 21; *cf. Esso Petroleum Co. Ltd v Harper's Garage (Stourport) Ltd* [1966] 2 Q.B. 514 at 541, 563, 573, reversed in part on another point [1968] A.C. 269.

[56] Above, paras 2–016—2–017.

[57] Below, para.2–047.

accordance with the principle that the courts will endeavour to uphold bargains which the parties believe themselves to have concluded,[58] especially in the case of executed or partially executed contracts, it may sometimes be possible either to infer an intention that at any rate a reasonable price should be paid if no price is later settled,[59] or to have regard to other circumstances, such as the course of dealing between the parties.[60] Where an approximate price has already been agreed, the inference that the sale shall be at a reasonable price near the sum or within the range mentioned may readily be drawn.[61]

Reasonable price where none fixed. Section 8(2) of the Act states that where the price is not determined as mentioned in section 8(1)[62] the buyer must pay a reasonable price; and what is a reasonable price is a question of fact dependent on the circumstances of each particular case.[63] This was also the rule at common law, where it was ultimately settled that the principle applied to executory agreements as well as to executed sales.[64] 2–047

The reasonable price of goods for the purpose of this subsection is usually ascertained by reference to the current market price at the time and place of delivery, even although some other figure (*e.g.* the cost of production) may also be in a sense "reasonable".[65] But the market price may not be the sole or conclusive test. This was made clear in the leading case of *Acebal v Levy*,[66] where it was said that a reasonable price "may, or may not, agree with the current price of the commodity at the port of shipment, at the precise time when such shipment is made. The current price of the day may be highly unreasonable from accidental circumstances, as on account of the commodity having been purposely kept back by the vendor himself, or with reference to the price at other ports in the immediate vicinity, or from various other causes."[67]

The basis of claim in such cases is contractual. But a reasonable price or *quantum valebant* may also be awarded in other circumstances where the obligation is quasi-contractual, that is, where no agreement to pay such a

---

58 Above, para.2–017.

59 *Foley v Classique Coaches Ltd* [1934] 2 K.B. 1; *cf. Jewry v Bush* (1814) 5 Taunt. 302; *Bryant v Flight* (1839) 5 M. & W. 114; *British Bank for Foreign Trade Ltd v Novinex Ltd* [1949] 1 K.B. 623; *F & G Sykes (Wessex) Ltd v Fine Fare Ltd* [1967] 1 Lloyd's Rep. 53; *Smith v Morgan* [1971] 1 W.L.R. 803.

60 *Cf. Hillas & Co. Ltd v Arcos Ltd* (1932) 147 L.T. 503 (above, para.2–017).

61 *Laing v Fidgeon* (1815) 6 Taunt. 108.

62 Above, para.2–045. As regards a contract to sell "at valuation," see *Wenning v Robinson*, below, para.2–049, n.75.

63 s.8(3); *Hoadly v McLaine* (1834) 10 Bing. 482.

64 *Acebal v Levy* (1834) 10 Bing. 376; *Valpy v Gibson* (1847) 4 C.B. 837 (but see the doubts repressed in *Hall v Busst* (1960) 104 C.L.R. 206 at 234). An analogous rule applies in the case of a contract to supply a service: Supply of Goods and Services Act 1982, s.15. *Cf.* Vienna Convention on Contracts for the International Sale of Goods (above, para.1–024), Art. 55, which provides that where the contract does not expressly or implicitly fix or make provision for determining the price, the parties are prima facie considered to have impliedly made reference to the current trade price.

65 *Cf. Watson Bros v Hornby* [1942] 2 All E.R. 506.

66 Above.

67 (1834) 10 Bing. 376 at 383.

sum can be attributed to the parties.[68] This may occur when goods have been delivered under a contract which is discharged by breach after part performance[69] or which is for some reason void[70] or not legally enforceable.[71]

2–048 **Varying or alternative prices.** Where the parties agree that the price shall be larger or smaller, depending upon the happening of some future or uncertain event or the truth of some unknown fact, the transaction may be void as a wager.[72] For example, a racehorse may be sold for a price which it is agreed shall be increased if he should win his next two races.[73] In these circumstances the transaction will be valid if the event is one which can affect the value of the property so as to justify the difference in price. This would normally be true of the example of the racehorse just given; but in *Brogden v Marriott*,[74] where the terms of sale of a horse were that the price should be £200 if within a month it trotted 18 miles in an hour, but one shilling if it failed to do so, the difference in price was held to be so far out of proportion to any possible difference in the value of the horse that the transaction was held to be a wager.

2–049 **Agreement to sell at valuation of third party.**[75] The parties to a contract of sale may agree that the price shall be fixed by one or more independent persons appointed by them. In such circumstances the parties are bound by their bargain, and the price when so determined is as much part of the contract as if they had originally fixed it themselves. In the case of an *agreement to sell* goods, section 9 of the Sale of Goods Act 1979 makes special provision as follows: "(1) Where there is an agreement to sell goods on the terms that the price is to be fixed by the valuation of a third party, and he cannot or does not make the valuation, the agreement is avoided; but if the goods or any part of them have been delivered to and appropriated by the buyer he must pay a reasonable price for them. (2) Where the third party is prevented from making the valuation by the fault of the seller or buyer, the party not at fault may maintain an action for damages against the party at fault."

The assessment of the price by the valuer is in such circumstances a condition precedent to the operation of the parties' obligations respectively to buy and to sell; and it is in accordance with general contractual principles both that the failure of the condition should nullify the agreement[76] and

---

[68] *Chitty on Contracts* (29th ed.), Vol. 1, paras 29–067 *et seq*.
[69] Below, paras 12–017 *et seq*.
[70] *e.g.* for uncertainty (above, para.2–017), mistake (below, para.3–011) or illegality (below, para.3–027).
[71] *Rose & Frank Co. v Crompton & Bros Ltd* [1925] A.C. 445, above, para.2–019.
[72] As regards contracts to pay "differences", see above, para.1–104.
[73] *Crofton v Colgan* (1859) 10 Ir.R.C.L. 133.
[74] (1836) 5 L.J.C.P. 302; and see *Rourke v Short* (1856) 5 E. & B. 904 (price of rags dependent upon whether seller or buyer was correct in a dispute).
[75] In the Australian case *Wenning v Robinson* (1964) 64 S.R.N.S.W. 157, it was held that a contract to sell stock-in-trade "at valuation", without mention of any particular valuer, should be construed as a contract to sell at a fair valuation (or value), and that it was open to the court to fix such a value.
[76] See *Chitty on Contracts* (29th ed.), Vol. 1, para.12–028; and *cf. Pym v Campbell* (1856) 6 E. & B.370, where it was understood that there was to be *no* agreement unless and until approval was given by a third person.

that a party who by his own act or default has prevented the fulfilment of the condition should be liable for breach of an implied undertaking that he would not do so.[77] The terms of section 9 confirm decisions under the common law prior to the Act.[78]

Failure to appoint valuer. The wording of section 9 of the Act, which is discussed in the preceding paragraphs, is appropriate to the case where a specific person is identified as the intended valuer by the terms of the contract. In *Sudbrook Trading Estate Ltd v Eggleton*[79] (a case dealing with an option to purchase land), the House of Lords drew a distinction between such a contract and one where the price is to be fixed by a valuer or valuers to be chosen by the parties at a later date. Such a contract can be construed as an agreement to sell at a fair and reasonable price by the application of objective standards; and if the intended machinery for ascertaining the price breaks down for any reason (*e.g.* the failure of one party to appoint a valuer), the court will substitute its own machinery to ascertain a fair and reasonable price, and enforce the contract accordingly. Nothing in section 9 of the Act of 1979 appears to prevent the application of this reasoning to a contract for the sale of goods. **2–050**

Failure of valuation. It follows from section 9(1) that if the valuer declines to act, or is unable to do so, or if he dies,[80] neither party has any remedy against the other, except for the restitution of his money or property. The court has normally no power to substitute for the parties' own agreement a contract to pay a reasonable price.[81] The valuer for his part cannot be compelled by either or both parties to act,[82] although he may be liable in damages if he has *contracted* to do so. **2–051**

The parties are normally bound by the valuation, if it has been made pursuant to their agreement, even if it is excessive or inadequate. The remedy of the party who pays too high a price, or receives too little, is against the valuer.[83] Exceptionally, however, a valuation may be impeached

---

[77] Chitty, *op. cit.*, para.13–011.

[78] *Thurnell v Balbirnie* (1837) 2 M. & W. 786; *Vickers v Vickers* (1867) L.R. 4 Eq. 527; *Cooper v Shuttleworth* (1856) 25 L.J.ExCh.114; *Clarke v Westrope* (1856) 18 C.B. 765; *Cf. Smith v Peters* (1875) L.R. 20 Eq. 511 (party ordered by mandatory injunction not to prevent valuation).

[79] [1983] 1 A.C. 444; *cf. Wenning v Robinson* (n.75, above; contract to sell goods "at valuation"), but contrast *Gillatt v Sky Television Ltd* [2000] 1 All E.R. (Comm.) 461, where it was held that an agreement to refer the valuation to "an independent chartered accountant" was an essential term of the contract, and that the court was not entitled to substitute its own opinion.

[80] *Firth v Midland Ry* (1875) L.R. 20 Eq. 100.

[81] Above, para.2–046.

[82] *Cooper v Shuttleworth* (1856) 25 L.J.Exch.114.

[83] *Campbell v Edwards* [1976] 1 W.L.R. 403; *Arenson v Arenson* [1973] Ch. 346 at 363, *per* Lord Denning M.R. (dissenting: decision reversed on appeal, *sub. nom. Arenson v Casson Beckman Rutley & Co.* [1977] A.C. 405, without reference to this point).

on the ground of fraud or collusion, and also where it can be shown that the valuer has proceeded upon some fundamentally erroneous principle.[84]

Section 9 is by its terms confined to an agreement to sell. If the passing of the property in the goods has not been made conditional upon the making of the valuation, expressly or by implication, and it has in fact passed to the buyer, he must in default of a valuation pay a reasonable price on common law principles.[85] If it is so conditional, then the transaction will be an agreement to sell within the terms of section 2 of the Act, and section 9 will apply.

2–052 **Position of valuer.** An agreement to refer a price to a valuer is not an arbitration, unless there is already a dispute between the parties.[86] The provisions of the Arbitration Act 1996 will therefore not apply.[87]

Where the valuer has been fraudulent or negligent, he may be personally liable to a party who suffers loss as a result.[88] The appointment of a valuer, being made by agreement between the parties, is irrevocable except by their joint consent.[89]

---

[84] *Collier v Mason* (1858) 25 Beav. 200; *Finnegan v Allen* [1943] K.B. 425; *Dean v Prince* [1954] Ch. 409; *Frank H. Wright (Constructions) Ltd v Frodoor Ltd* [1967] 1 W.L.R. 506; *Smith v Gale* [1974] 1 W.L.R. 9. In the absence of reasons or calculations, it may not be possible to show such an error: *Campbell v Edwards* [1976] 1 W.L.R. 403; *Baber v Kenwood Manufacturing Co. Ltd* [1978] 1 Lloyd's Rep. 174; *Burgess v Purchase & Sons (Farms) Ltd* [1983] Ch. 216 (shares); *Jones v Sherwood Computer Services Plc.* [1992] 2 All E.R. 170 (calculation of turnover). See also *Chitty* on *Contracts* (29th ed.), para.32–166, n.674.

[85] Above, paras 2–046, 2–047. It is also possible that a contract might be so construed as to allow either party to avoid the sale on failure of the valuation, by the operation of an implied condition subsequent: Benjamin, *Sale of Personal Property* (8th ed.), p.150.

[86] *Re Carus-Wilson and Greene* (1886) 18 Q.B.D. 7; *Re Hammond and Waterton* (1890) 62 L.T. 808; *Palacath v Flanagan* [1985] 2 All E.R. 161; *North-Eastern Co-op Soc v Newcastle-upon-Tyne CC* (1987) 282 E.G. 1409; see further *Russell on Arbitration* (21st ed.), para.2–014.

[87] Nevertheless, the court has an inherent power to stay proceedings brought before it in breach of an agreement to decide disputes by some alternative method: *Channel Tunnel Group Ltd v Balfour Beatty Construction Ltd* [1993] A.C. 334.

[88] *Sutcliffe v Thackrah* [1974] A.C. 727; *Arenson v Casson Beckman Rutley & Co.* [1977] A.C. 405.

[89] *Mills v Bayley* (1863) 2 H. & C. 36.

CHAPTER 3

APPLICATION OF GENERAL CONTRACTUAL PRINCIPLES

	PARA.
1. Agency	3–002
2. Fraud and misrepresentation	3–008
3. Duress and undue influence	3–010
4. Mistake	3–011
5. Illegality	3–027
6. Assignment	3–043
7. Bankruptcy, insolvency and death	3–045

Introductory. A contract of sale of goods is a species of contract—indeed, it may be regarded as the paradigm contract—so that the law of sale as codified in the Sale of Goods Act 1979 and elaborated in this work is essentially no more than the application of the principles of the general law of contract to the special case of the selling and buying of goods, and the effect of these principles upon the property rights which are the subject of the transaction. In a number of sections, the Act expressly stipulates that a particular aspect of a contract of sale shall be regulated by the general rules of the law of contract[1]; and other sections are declaratory of common law principles which are of wider application than the sale of goods.[2] More generally, section 62(2) declares that "The rules of the common law, including the law merchant, except in so far as they are inconsistent with the provisions of this Act, and in particular the rules relating to the law of principal and agent and the effect of fraud, misrepresentation, duress or coercion, mistake, or other invalidating cause, apply to contracts for the sale of goods." In this chapter are discussed both the topics mentioned in section 62(2) and also a number of other rules of the general law which are by the wide terms of the section made applicable to sales of goods. **3–001**

1. AGENCY[3]

General principles of agency applicable. Section 62(2) preserves the common law rules relating to the law of principal and agent and declares them applicable to contracts for the sale of goods. Particular rules as to **3–002**

---

[1] *e.g.* ss.3, 11(6), 54.
[2] *e.g.* implied terms as to quality (s.14) applied also at common law in contracts for the supply of goods generally, and have now been similarly codified, as regards such contracts, by the Supply of Goods and Services Act 1982, ss.4, 9: see above, para.1–031. For a general discussion, see the report of the Law Commission on *Implied Terms in Contracts for the Supply of Goods* (Law Com. No.95, HMSO, 1979).
[3] See generally *Chitty on Contracts* (29th ed.), Vol. 2, Ch.31; *Bowstead and Reynolds on Agency* (18th ed.).

"mercantile agents" are contained in the Factors Act 1889, and these also are expressly declared by section 21(2)(a) of the Sale of Goods Act 1979 to be unaffected. The most important of these latter provisions are those which empower a mercantile agent in certain circumstances to transfer a good title to a bona fide purchaser or pledgee of the goods or documents of title to goods.[4]

3–003 Generally speaking, whatever a party may do in matters of contract he may do by means of an agent. A party to a contract of sale of goods is therefore bound by the act of his agent, provided that it is within the scope of his actual or apparent authority. But a contract of hire-purchase, conditional sale or credit-sale which is a "regulated agreement" under the Consumer Credit Act 1974 must be signed by the debtor personally, or the agreement (and any contract of guarantee) cannot be enforced.[5]

3–004 **Particular types of agent.** A *mercantile agent* is one[6] having in the customary course of his business as such agent authority either to sell goods, or to consign goods for the purpose of sale, or to buy goods, or to raise money on the security of goods.[7] A *factor*, as traditionally defined, is a species of mercantile agent who is normally entrusted by a seller of goods with the possession either of the goods or of the documents of title representing them: he may contract in his own name, and receive payment of moneys due from the buyer.[8] A *broker*, in contrast, usually acts as an agent for a buyer or seller without having such possession; and his authority does not extend to contracting in his own name or to making or receiving payment.[9] (This distinction between "factors" and "brokers" was, however, more important in nineteenth-century commerce than it is today, and the term "factor" in this sense is now little used.) An *auctioneer* sells at an open sale, either with or without having possession of the goods, to the bidder who offers the best price. He has no implied authority to give warranties as to the goods.[10] A *del credere* agent is one who, usually for an extra commission, undertakes to indemnify the seller for whom he acts against the non-payment by the buyer of the price or other sums for which he may be liable under the contract.[11]

---

[4] Factors Act 1889, s.2; below, paras 7–032 *et seq.*; and see also ss.8, 9 (substantially re-enacted as ss.24 and 25 of the Sale of Goods Act 1979), below, paras 7–055, 7–069.

[5] Consumer Credit Act 1974, s.127(3). (This provision is to be repealed by the Consumer Credit Act 2006.) See further below, para.2.023. For the position under the previous law, see Hire-Purchase Act 1965, s.5.

[6] The statutory definitions in fact here repeat the term "mercantile agent", confirming decisions given under earlier, repealed, Factors Acts that the employment should come within some known category of commercial agency: Chalmers, *Sale of Goods Act 1979* (18th ed.), p.291.

[7] Factors Act 1889, s.1(1); Sale of Goods Act 1979, s.26. For the special provisions of the Factors Act as regards dispositions of goods and documents of title by mercantile agents, see below, paras 7–032 *et seq*.

[8] *Chitty on Contracts* (29th ed.), Vol. 2, para.31–012.

[9] *ibid*.

[10] *Chitty*, *op. cit.*, para.31–014. For the provisions of the Act governing sales by auction, see above, para.2–004 and below, para.3–009. See also *Chelmsford Auctions Ltd v Poole* [1973] Q.B. 542 (action for price by auctioneer in own name).

[11] *Chitty*, *op. cit.*, para.31–013.

A person may act as a principal in some respects and as agent in others: thus, a confirming house (or "commission agent"), which provides agency services for an overseas buyer, may stand as principal (*i.e.* as the buyer of the goods) in relation to the seller, and at the same time be in the position of an agent *vis-à-vis* that overseas buyer.[12]

Civil law systems recognise a special category of *commercial agent*. Although such a distinct category of agency relationships has not traditionally been the subject of separate treatment by the common law, it has now become necessary to identify them because they are governed by an EC directive[13] which has been implemented in this country by domestic legislation.[14] A commercial agent is defined as "a self-employed intermediary who has continuing authority to negotiate the sale or purchase of goods on behalf of another person (the 'principal'), or to negotiate and conclude the sale and purchase of goods on behalf of and in the name of that principal".[15] The legislation provides, *inter alia*, for the payment of compensation by the principal on termination of the agency relationship.[16]

Dealers as agents in instalment credit transactions.[17] Where a customer enters into a hire-purchase, conditional sale or credit-sale agreement directly with a finance company through the medium of a dealer who has displayed the goods, the dealer is to be taken as the agent of the finance company only to a limited extent at common law.[18] An agency may be inferred despite a denial in the agreement itself.[19] The dealer is not as a rule the hirer's or buyer's agent for any purpose.[20] 3–005

---

[12] *Ireland v Livingston* (1872) L.R. 5 H.L. 395 at 409; *Sobell Industries Ltd v Cory Bros & Co.* [1955] 2 Lloyd's Rep. 82 at 90–91; *Anglo-African Shipping Co. of New York Inc. v J. Mortner Ltd* [1962] 1 Lloyd's Rep. 610 at 616–617. *Cf. Aluminium Industrie Vaassen BV v Romalpa Aluminium Ltd* [1976] 1 W.L.R. 676, below, para.5–141.

[13] EC Directive 1986/653/EEC ([1986] O.J. L382/17).

[14] SI 1993/3053, as amended by SI 1993/3173 and SI 1998/2868.

[15] *ibid.*, reg. 1(2).

[16] For a more detailed account, see *Chitty on Contracts* (29th ed.), Vol. 2, para.31–005; *Bowstead and Reynolds on Agency* (18th ed.), Ch.11.

[17] Chitty, *op. cit.*, para.31–019.

[18] Guest, *The Law of Hire–Purchase* (1966), paras 365–367; *North Central Wagon & Finance Co. Ltd v White and Powell* [1955] C.L.Y 1204; *Campbell Discount Co. Ltd v Gall* [1961] 1 Q.B. 431; *Bentworth Finance Ltd v White* (1962) 112 L.J. 140; *Financings Ltd v Stimson* [1962] 1 W.L.R. 1184 at 1188; *Yeoman Credit Ltd v Apps* [1962] 2 Q.B. 508; *Northgran Finance Ltd v Ashley* [1963] 1 Q.B. 476; *Car & Universal Finance Co. Ltd v Caldwell* [1965] 1 Q.B. 525; *Mercantile Credit Co. Ltd v Hamblin* [1965] 2 Q.B. 242 at 269; *Kingsley v Sterling Industrial Securities Ltd* [1967] 2 Q.B. 747; *Snook v London & West Riding Investments Ltd* [1967] 2 Q.B. 786; *Branwhite v Worcester Works Finance Ltd* [1969] 1 A.C. 552; *J.D. Williams & Co. v McCauley Parsons & Jones* [1994] C.C.L.R. 78; *Woodchester Equipment (Leasing) Ltd v British Association of Canned, etc. Food Importers Ltd* [1995] C.C.L.R. 51; *Shogun Finance Ltd v Hudson* [2003] UKHL 62; [2004] 1 A.C. 919 at [51]; Guest, 79 L.Q.R. 33 (1963); Hughes, 27 M.L.R. 395 (1964); and see above, para.1–054.

[19] *Financings Ltd v Stimson*, above; contrast *Bentworth Finance Ltd v White*, above.

[20] Guest, *op. cit.*, paras 371–372; *Branwhite v Worcester Works Finance Ltd*, above. *Cf. British Ry Traffic & Electric Co. Ltd v Roper* (1939) 162 L.T. 217; *Spencer v North Country Finance Co. Ltd* [1963] C.L.Y. 212; *United Dominions Trust Ltd v Western* [1976] 1 Q.B. 513.

Where such a transaction is a "regulated agreement"[21] under the Consumer Credit Act 1974, however, the dealer will normally come within the statutory definition of "credit-broker"[22] and, as such will, if he conducts negotiations with the debtor ("antecedent negotiations"[23]) in relation to the goods, be deemed to be the agent[24] of the finance company in respect of any representations[25] made by him to the debtor and any other dealings between them.[26] Further, he may render the finance company liable under the implied condition as to fitness for purpose if the particular purpose for which the goods are sold or supplied is made known to him, expressly or by implication, by the debtor.[27] He will also be the "agent" of the finance company for the purpose of receiving a notice of cancellation, notice of withdrawal and a notice rescinding the agreement.[28]

But the Act goes even further, and has the effect of imputing an agency in certain situations which at common law would be regarded as comprising two distinct and unrelated transactions. Where the dealer is himself the seller or supplier of goods and finance is provided by way of loan or other credit by a finance house in pursuance of arrangements with the dealer (*e.g.* in the case of check trading, or where a credit card is used), "antecedent negotiations" in relation to the transaction financed are deemed to be conducted by the dealer as agent for the creditor as well as in his own capacity, so that the creditor will be liable for any misrepresentations and contractual statements made by the dealer.[29]

3–006 **Agency of necessity.**[30] In certain circumstances of emergency a power is conferred by law upon one person to act on behalf of another, either where no contract of agency exists, or where the authority already given to an agent is inadequate to meet the situation. Under this principle the master of a ship may sell a cargo in order to protect the ship or cargo, as may any carrier of perishable goods; and a carrier or bailee of animals may incur expense in maintaining them. The doctrine of agency of necessity will apply only where there is a real emergency (as distinct from mere inconvenience[31]),

---

[21] For the meaning of "regulated agreement", see above, para.1–022. (The provisions discussed in this paragraph are not affected by the Consumer Credit Act 2006.)
[22] For definition, see Consumer Credit Act 1974, ss.145(2), 189(1).
[23] For definition, see Consumer Credit Act 1974, s.56.
[24] Such agency cannot be excluded: see Consumer Credit Act 1974, s.56(3).
[25] Defined in s.189(1) to include any condition or warranty, and any other statement or undertaking, whether oral or in writing.
[26] Consumer Credit Act 1974, s.56.
[27] Sale of Goods Act 1979, s.14(3); Supply of Goods (Implied Terms) Act 1973, s.10(3); Supply of Goods and Services Act 1982, s.4(4).
[28] Consumer Credit Act 1974, ss.57(3), 69(1), (6), 102(1).
[29] s.56(2). See also the substantive provisions of s.75, making the creditor jointly and severally liable with the dealer in respect of such claims. The sections are discussed below, paras 14–153 *et seq*.
[30] *Chitty on Contracts* (29th ed.), Vol. 2, paras 31–033 *et seq.*; *Bowstead and Reynolds on Agency* (18th ed.), Ch.4; Goff and Jones, *The Law of Restitution* (6th ed.), paras.17–002 *et seq.*; and see *China Pacific SA v Food Corp. of India* [1982] A.C. 939.
[31] *Cf. Sachs v Miklos* [1948] 2 K.B. 23; *Munro v Willmott* [1949] 1 K.B. 295 (sale of goods by bailee when owner untraceable: liable in conversion; but see now Torts (Interference with Goods) Act 1977, s.12).

where communication with the principal is impossible, and where the act is honestly done on his behalf.

Agency of a married woman. There is a rebuttable presumption that a wife has authority to purchase necessaries, and to pledge her husband's credit for the purpose, during cohabitation. This presumption ceases if the parties are separated, but the wife may then still have her husband's express or implied authority to contract on his behalf.[32] 3–007

2. FRAUD AND MISREPRESENTATION

Application of common law principles. Section 62(2) of the Sale of Goods Act 1979 preserves the application of the rules of the common law[33] relating to fraud and misrepresentation to contracts for the sale of goods, save in so far as they are inconsistent with the provisions of the Act itself. The important issues which are likely to arise in this context are those concerning statements made by the seller as to the description or quality of the goods sold.[34] These questions are discussed in a later chapter.[35] In other respects, the topics of fraud and misrepresentation do not call for special consideration in relation to contracts for the sale of goods; and reference should be made to standard works on the law of contract.[36] 3–008

Fraud at auction sales. In relation to goods sold by auction, section 57(4) of the Sale of Goods Act 1979 provides that "where a sale by auction is not notified to be subject to a right to bid by or on behalf of the seller, it is not lawful for the seller to bid himself or to employ any person to bid at the sale, or for the auctioneer knowingly to take any bid from the seller or any such person." Any sale contravening this rule may be treated as fraudulent by the buyer.[37] 3–009

The Act further provides by section 57(3) that "a sale by auction may be notified to be subject to a reserve or upset price, and a right to bid may also be reserved expressly by or on behalf of the seller"; and subsection (6) continues: "where, in respect of a sale by auction, a right to bid is expressly

---

[32] *Chitty on Contracts* (29th ed.), Vol. 2, para.31–04; *Bowstead and Reynolds on Agency* (18th ed.), paras 3–040 *et seq.* Note that a wife's former power to bind her husband as his agent of necessity has been abolished: Matrimonial Proceedings and Property Act 1970, s.41(1).

[33] For a discussion of the meaning of this context of the expression "the common law", see above, para.1–008.

[34] But see *Riddiford v Warren* (1901) 20 N.Z.L.R. 572 and *Goldsmith v Rodger* [1962] 2 Lloyd's Rep. 249, where the misrepresentation was made by the buyer.

[35] Below, Ch.10, and paras 12–121 *et seq.*

[36] *e.g. Chitty on Contracts* (29th ed.), Vol. 1, Ch.6; Treitel, *The Law of Contract*, (11th ed.), Ch.9. A claim against an auctioneer alleging that goods had been misdescribed in the sale catalogue failed in *Thomson v Christie Manson & Woods Ltd* [2005] EWCA Civ 555; [2005] P.N.L.R 38.

[37] s.57(5). The common law rule appears to have been the same: *Bexwell v Christie* (1776) 1 Cowp. 395 at 396; *Thornett v Haines* (1846) 15 M. & W. 367; *Green v Baverstock* (1863) 14 C.B.(N.S.) 204.

reserved (but not otherwise) the seller or any one person on his behalf may bid at the auction." It would appear to follow from these provisions that where more than one person bids on behalf of the seller at an auction, the transaction is voidable on the grounds of fraud, and perhaps also void for illegality.[38]

An agreement between bidders to form a "ring" or "knockout"—that is, to refrain from bidding in competition with each other in order to depress the price—is not illegal at common law[39]; but where one of the parties to such an agreement is a dealer[40] it is now provided by statute that the contract of sale is voidable at the seller's option[41]; and further that, if the buyer has obtained possession of the goods and restitution is not made to the seller, the parties to the agreement are to be jointly and severally liable to make good any loss sustained by him by reason of the operation of the agreement.[42]

3. DURESS AND UNDUE INFLUENCE

3–010 **Duress and undue influence.** The common law principles of duress (including economic duress[43]), and the wider equitable doctrine of undue influence, appear to apply without any special qualification to contracts for the sale of goods.[44]

4. MISTAKE[45]

3–011 **Application of common law[46] rules.** Section 62(2) expressly preserves the rules of the common law relating to the effect of mistake on contracts for the sale of goods, except in so far as they are inconsistent with the

---

[38] *Mortimer v Bell* (1865) 1 Ch.App. 10 (fraud); *cf. Scott v Brown Doering McNab & Co.* [1892] 2 Q.B. 724 (conspiracy to inflate share prices held illegal).

[39] *Rawlings v General Trading Co.* [1921] 1 K.B. 635; *Cohen v Roche* [1927] 1 K.B. 169.

[40] A dealer is defined for the purposes of the section (by reference to s.1(2) of the Auctions (Bidding Agreements) Act 1927) as follows: "a person who in the normal course of his business attends sales by auction for the purpose of purchasing goods with a view to reselling them".

[41] Auctions (Bidding Agreements) Act 1969, s.3(1).

[42] *ibid.* s.3(2).

[43] *North Ocean Shipping Co. Ltd v Hyundai Construction Co. Ltd (The "Atlantic Baron")* [1979] Q.B. 705; *Atlas Express Ltd v Kafco (Importers & Distributors) Ltd* [1989] Q.B. 833; *CTN Cash & Carry Ltd v Gallagher Ltd* [1994] 4 All E.R. 714.

[44] Sale of Goods Act 1979, s.62(2). For these topics, see *Chitty on Contracts* (29th ed.), Vol. 1, Ch.7; Treitel, *The Law of Contract* (11th ed.), Ch.10.

[45] See generally *Chitty on Contracts* (29th ed.), Vol. 1, Ch.5; Treitel, *The Law of Contract*, (11th ed.), Ch.8; Lawson, 52 L.Q.R. 79 (1936); Cheshire, 60 L.Q.R. 175 (1944); Tylor, 11 M.L.R. 257 (1948); Slade, 70 L.Q.R. 385 (1954); Bamford, 32 S.A.L.J. 166 (1955); Shatwell, 33 Can.Bar Rev. 164 (1955); Atiyah, 73 L.Q.R. 340 (1957); Atiyah and Bennion, 24 M.L.R. 421 (1961); McTurnan, 41 Can.Bar Rev. 1 (1963); Stoljar, 28 M.L.R. 265 (1965); Atiyah, 2 Ottawa L.Rev. 337 (1968). As regards mistake of identity, see also the articles cited *infra*, n.48.

[46] On the (now limited) scope of equitable principles and remedies in relation to mistake, see below, paras 3–025—3–026.

provisions of the Act. The concept of mistake traditionally embraces a number of disparate principles many of which are capable of explanation on other grounds[47]: there can be little doubt, however, that all of such principles are, in theory, applicable to sales of goods—even if, as will appear, their practical operation has been markedly restricted by trends in the law in recent years. These separate aspects of the subject of "mistake" at common law may be enumerated as follows.

First, a mistake as to the identity of a party or as to the terms being offered may operate so as to negative consent, that is, to show that there has been no certain agreement to which one party can hold the other bound, and the supposed transaction is accordingly void.

Secondly, although the parties have reached agreement in the same terms on the same subject-matter, if their agreement is based on a fundamental assumption of fact which turns out to have been mistaken, the courts may treat such a mistake as avoiding the bargain which had apparently been made.

Thirdly, a document mistakenly signed by a party may sometimes be held void under the special plea known as *non est factum*.

In each of the above cases the effect of the mistake, if operative, is to render the transaction void at common law.

In equity, mistake may be a ground for refusing an order for specific performance. It is also the basis of the special remedy of rectification of a written contract. And it may justify a decree of rescission.

The application of these different topics to contracts of sale will be examined in turn.

Mistake of identity.[48] It is only in special circumstances that the identity of the person with whom a contract is made is material. Where the identity of a party is not material, or is not regarded by the other party as material, a mistake will not of itself affect the validity of the contract.[49] In most cash sale transactions, one customer is as good as another[50]; and the same is true at a public auction.[51] But where identity is material, a person cannot force a contractual relationship on to another by purporting to accept an offer which he knows or ought to know was not intended to be made to him.[52] Where an offer meant for A is purportedly accepted by B, the apparent contract is void, and can confer no rights on anyone. 3–012

---

[47] See, *e.g.* the articles by Slade and Atiyah cited in n.45, above; and *cf.* below, para.3–021.

[48] See *Chitty on Contracts* (29th ed.), Vol. 1, paras 5–076 *et seq.*; Treitel, *The Law of Contract* (11th ed.), pp.298 *et seq.*; Goodhart, 57 L.Q.R. 228 (1941); Cheshire, 60 L.Q.R. 175 at 183 (1944); Glanville Williams, 23 Can.Bar Rev. 271 (1945); Tylor, 11 M.L.R. 257 at 259 (1948); Slade 70 L.Q.R. 385 at 390 (1954); Wilson, 17 M.L.R. 515 (1954); Unger, 18 M.L.R. 259 (1955); Shatwell, 33 Can.Bar Rev. 164 at 189 (1965); Hall [1961] C.L.J. 86; Stoljar, 28 M.L.R. 265 at 280 (1965).

[49] *Lewis v Averay* [1972] 1 Q.B. 198 at 209, citing Cheshire and Fifoot, *The Law of Contract*, (7th ed.), pp.213–214; *cf. Newborne v Sensolid (Great Britain) Ltd* [1954] 1 Q.B. 45 at 47, 51–52; *Fawcett v Star Car Sales Ltd* [1960] N.Z.L.R. 406; *Midland Bank Plc v Brown Shipley & Co. Ltd* [1991] 1 Lloyd's Rep. 576 (mistake as to identity of messenger).

[50] *Ingram v Little* [1961] 1 Q.B. 31 at 57.

[51] Chitty, *op. cit.*, para.5–077; *Dennant v Skinner and Collom* [1948] 2 K.B. 164.

[52] *Boulton v Jones* (1857) 2 H. & N. 564; 6 W.R. 107.

The most likely circumstances in which this question will be of importance in the context of the sale of goods are where a fraudulent buyer first induces the owner of goods to sell them to him by misrepresenting his identity, and then purportedly resells them to an innocent third person. The first transaction is, of course, voidable at the option of the original seller on the grounds of fraud; but if he has not taken steps effectively to avoid it before the resale, the third person may have obtained a good title to the goods under the provisions of section 23 of the Sale of Goods Act 1979.[53] It is only where the original owner can go further and establish that the first transaction was void and inoperative because of the mistake of identity that he will be able to claim the goods as never having ceased to be his property.[54]

3–013 **Identity distinguished from attributes.** It is usually said[55] that the mistake made by a contracting party must, to be operative, be as to the identity of the other party and not merely as to some attribute of his, *e.g.* solvency. It may be inferred from this that there must, as a general rule, be an identified third person with whom the contract was in fact believed to have been made.[56] In *Cundy v Lindsay*,[57] a letter was written by a fraudulent person named Blenkarn ordering a quantity of handkerchiefs from the respondents; he signed his name in a way which allowed it to be confused with an established firm named Blenkiron & Co. who carried on business in the same street. The goods were sent to Blenkiron & Co. at the address given by Blenkarn, who received them and sold them to the appellants. It was held that there was no contract between Blenkarn and the respondents, for their intention had been to deal only with Blenkiron & Co.; and so the property in the handkerchiefs had remained throughout with the respondents. In contrast, in *King's Norton Metal Co. Ltd v Edridge, Merrett & Co. Ltd*[58] one Wallis sent an order for wire to the claimants and used for the purpose the name of "Hallam & Co.", which was represented on the notepaper as a firm of considerable substance, whereas in reality it existed only in name. Again, the goods were sent on credit and disposed of by resale to the innocent defendants; but this time there was held to have been no operative mistake: the claimants had intended to contract with the writer of the letter whoever he was, and had been mistaken not as to his identity but as to his creditworthiness. The transaction was in consequence only voidable for fraud, and not void, and Wallis was accordingly able to confer a good title on the defendants.

---

[53] Below, para.7–024.
[54] The Law Reform Committee in 1966 recommended that contracts which under the present law are void because of mistake of identity should be treated as voidable so far as third parties are concerned (Cmnd. 2958 (1966), para.15). No legislation to this effect has been introduced.
[55] But see below, para.3–015.
[56] See, however, Treitel, *The Law of Contract* (11th ed.), p.303.
[57] (1878) 3 App.Cas. 459; *cf. Hardman v Booth* (1863) 1 H. & C. 803.
[58] (1897) 14 T.L.R. 98. The case of *Sowler v Potter* [1940] 1 K.B. 271 is difficult to reconcile with this decision and must be regarded as no longer good law. It was criticised in *Solle v Butcher* [1950] 1 K.B. 671 at 691; *Gallie v Lee* [1969] 2 Ch. 17 at 33, 41, 45 affirmed *sub nom. Saunders v Anglia Building Soc.* [1971] A.C. 1004); and *Lewis v Averay* [1972] 1 Q.B. 198 at 206.

Mistake *inter praesentes*.[59] The same distinction must be made where parties negotiate face to face; but here there is a strong presumption[60] that the party intended to contract with the physical person actually present and not with the other individual whom he mistakenly believed that person to be. So, in *Lewis v Averay*[61] a person calling himself Green and claiming to be a well-known actor of that name called at Lewis's home in response to an advertisement and induced the latter to sell him a car and to allow him to take it away in exchange for a cheque which proved worthless. By the time the fraud was discovered, the car had been purchased in good faith by Averay. The Court of Appeal was unanimously of the opinion that the first transaction was not void for mistake, so that the principle of *King's Norton Metal Co. Ltd v Edridge, Merrett & Co. Ltd*[62] was applied and that of *Cundy v Lindsay*[63] not followed. A similar decision had been reached many years earlier in *Phillips v Brooks Ltd*[64]; but in the more recent case of *Ingram v Little*[65] the Court of Appeal had, by a majority, held the contrary on facts which it is difficult to distinguish from *Lewis v Averay*. In *Ingram v Little* the owners of a car had first refused to allow a would-be buyer calling himself Hutchinson to take it away against an uncleared cheque, but later agreed to do so after he had given them the initials and address of a real Mr. Hutchinson whose existence they were able to verify by consulting a telephone directory. The majority of the Court of Appeal held that, "in the very special and unusual facts of the case",[66] the presumption of an intention to deal with the person physically present was rebutted. Such special facts, if they are to be found in *Ingram v Little*,[67] must have been constituted by the initial refusal to deal further with the *soi-disant* Hutchinson until the genuineness of the name and address given by him had been established: this made his identity as that person a matter of vital importance to the contract which was thereafter concluded.[68] It is submitted that it will only be in very rare cases that such special facts will be found. 3–014

In *Shogun Finance Ltd v Hudson*[69] a rogue, giving the name and address of a real person named Patel and producing a driving licence in the name of Patel as identification, induced a motor dealer to arrange for him to acquire a Shogun vehicle on hire-purchase from the claimant finance company. The company authorised the dealer to complete the transaction after satisfying itself as to the creditworthiness of the real Patel.

---

[59] In *Shogun Finance Ltd v Hudson* [2003] UKHL 62; [2004] 1 A.C. 919 the House of Lords rejected an argument that the cases discussed in this paragraph were relevant to the case of a written contract.

[60] *Ingram v Little* [1961] 1 Q.B. 31 at 61, 66 (citing Benjamin, *Sale of Personal Property* (8th ed.), p.102); *Edmunds v Merchants Despatch Co.* (1883) 135 Mass. 283; *Phelps v McQuade* (1917) 220 N.Y. 232; *Lewis v Averay* (above).

[61] Above.

[62] (1897) 14 T.L.R. 98; above, para.3–013.

[63] (1878) 3 App.Cas. 459; above, para.3–013.

[64] [1919] 2 K.B. 243; contrast *Lake v Simmons* [1927] A.C. 487.

[65] Above.

[66] *Lewis v Averay*, above, at p.208.

[67] Lord Denning M.R. in *Lewis v Averay* (above) was of opinion that *Ingram v Little* could not in fact be distinguished: see his judgment at p.206.

[68] *Lewis v Averay*, above, at p.209.

[69] [2003] UKHL 262; [2004] 1 A.C. 919.

The rogue signed a hire-purchase agreement[70] in the name of Patel, drove the vehicle away, and shortly afterwards sold the vehicle to the defendant and disappeared. The House of Lords, by a majority of three to two, held that, as a matter of the construction of the written document, the real Mr Patel, as an identified person, was the party whose offer the finance company had intended to accept, and that no-one other than he could be the hirer under that document. On principle, extrinsic evidence was not admissible to contradict the document on that point. In addition, there was no *consensus ad idem* leading to a contract between the finance company and the rogue. The principle of *Cundy v Lindsay* was to be followed. In consequence, where a contract is in writing, the identity of the parties is to be established by the names recorded in that contract.[71]

It was strongly argued for the defendant that the law should make a break from the past by abolishing the distinction between contracts made in writing and contracts concluded by parties dealing on a face-to-face basis, and that the presumption established in *Lewis v Averay* should apply in all cases (as had been advocated initially by Lord Denning in the latter case). *Cundy v Lindsay* should no longer be followed. This view was accepted by Sedley L.J. in the Court of Appeal and by Lords Nicholls of Birkenhead and Millett (dissenting) in the House of Lords. In the result, however, *Cundy v Lindsay* remains authoritative.

Since most contracts entered into on the internet are made between parties who are unknown to each other, the potential for one of them to enter into a contract under a mistake as to the identity of the other is high. It remains to be seen whether the precedents set by the existing cases are sufficient to meet the situations which may arise.

3–015 **Validity of distinction.** The distinction so made between the identity of a person and his attributes has been criticised both on the ground that it is essentially lacking in validity[72] and also because what is important is not so much the nature of the mistake made as whether it is material. A mistake as to identity may, as has been observed,[73] be immaterial and therefore of no effect, while in exceptional circumstances a mistake as to a particular attribute may have such a material bearing on a transaction as to invalidate an apparent consent.[74]

3–016 **Mistake as to terms offered.** The terms offered by a party (including his description of the subject-matter) may contain a latent ambiguity, so that they may reasonably be understood by the offeree in a sense other than that

[70] The claim of the defendant depended on his being able to establish an exception to the principle *nemo dat quod non habet* under the statutory rule in the Hire-Purchase Act 1964, s.27: see below, para.7–087.
[71] *Cf. Hector v Lyons* (1988) 58 P. & C.R. 156.
[72] *Lewis v Averay* (above), at p.206; Contrast Treitel, *The Law of Contract* (11th ed.), pp.301–302; Cheshire, Fifoot and Furmston, *The Law of Contract* (13th ed.), p.279; Glanville Williams, 23 Can.Bar Rev. 271 (1945).
[73] Above, para.3–012.
[74] Treitel, *op. cit.*, p.302; *cf. Lake v Simmons* [1927] A.C. 487 (mistake that customer was wife and agent of known person). *Quaere* whether creditworthiness can ever be a material attribute for this purpose?

which was quite as reasonably intended by the offeror. If the parties are genuinely at cross-purposes in this way, the contract is void for want of certainty.[75] In the leading case of *Raffles v Wichelhaus*,[76] there was a contract for the sale of cotton "to arrive ex *Peerless* from Bombay". There were in fact two ships called *Peerless* sailing from Bombay, one in October and the other in December: the buyer had contemplated delivery by the earlier vessel and the seller by the later one. In the absence of evidence to resolve the ambiguity it was held that there was no binding contract.

Even where by the normal standard of objective interpretation there is no uncertainty as to the proposed terms, a party will not be allowed to hold another to the contract if he knew that that party intended to contract on different terms or if he has intentionally or negligently allowed him to believe that different terms were being offered. In *Hartog v Colin & Shields*,[77] the parties had negotiated for the sale of some Argentine hare skins at certain prices per *piece* (which was the usual basis of assessment in the trade), but the defendants in their offer mistakenly quoted prices at so much per *pound*. It was held that the buyers must be taken to have known that the defendants did not intend to contract on these terms, and that the alleged contract resulting from their purported acceptance of the offer was not binding. A case where a party's negligence was found to have caused a mistake and so prevented him from holding the other party to an alleged contract is *Scriven Bros & Co. v Hindley & Co.*,[78] where the goods sold at auction on behalf of the claimants included both hemp and tow, packed in bales bearing identical markings; but care had not been taken by the auctioneers, in compiling their catalogue and in showing the defendants samples, to distinguish between the two commodities. The defendants bid an extravagant price for a lot of tow in the belief that it was hemp, but it was ruled that the supposed sale could not be enforced against them.

Mistake as to quality distinguished.[79] The principle described in the preceding paragraph is confined in its application to a mistake in the *terms* being offered by the other party. A mistaken belief that what the other party is offering has some particular quality or attribute will not avoid a contract, although a mistaken assumption that the other has *warranted* the goods to have such a quality or attribute will do so, in the circumstances described above. This is brought out by the case of *Smith v Hughes*.[80] There a farmer sold certain oats to a horse-trainer, exhibiting a sample; but the latter rejected them on the ground that they were new oats when he had intended to buy old oats. It was not clear from the evidence whether the seller had described the subject-matter of the sale as "old oats", or merely as "oats" (the buyer himself in the latter case erroneously, and perhaps to the knowledge of the seller, having assumed that they were old). In the view 3–017

[75] There may, of course, be an estoppel against one party.
[76] (1864) 2 H. & C. 906.
[77] [1939] 3 All E.R. 566.
[78] [1913] 3 K.B. 564.
[79] For the position where *both* parties are mistaken as to a question of quality, see below, para.3–020.
[80] (1871) L.R. 6 Q.B. 597.

of the Court of Queen's Bench this was the crucial question, and because the issue had not been so put to the jury, a new trial was ordered: "In order to relieve the defendant it was necessary that the jury should find not merely that the [claimant] believed the defendant to believe that he was buying old oats, but that he believed the defendant to believe that he, the [claimant], was contracting to sell old oats."[81] Where such a mistake as to quality is made by the buyer, the seller's "passive acquiescence in the self-deception of the buyer"[82] has no effect on the validity of the contract.

3–018 **Common mistake nullifying assent.** Where the parties have reached agreement, but both[83] have contracted on the basis of a particular assumption of fact which is fundamental to their bargain, and the assumption proves to be mistaken, the contract is void: the mistake nullifies their apparent consent. However, if the parties to such a contract have acted on the assumption that it is valid to the detriment of either or both of them, they may be estopped by convention from denying its validity.[84] This proposition, although apparently well supported by the cases, must now be regarded as confined within fairly narrow limits as a result of the decision of the House of Lords in *Bell v Lever Bros Ltd*,[85] where an agreement for the termination of a service contract in return for a substantial payment was held binding although, unknown to the parties, the employee could at the time have been summarily dismissed.

The difficulty in interpreting this decision lies in giving meaning to the notion of a "fundamental" mistake when the assumption erroneously made by the parties in the case itself was as to the very validity of the contract which was the subject of their bargain. Some guidance may, however, be obtained from the speeches of the majority in the case and in particular from that of Lord Atkin.

3–019 ***Res extincta and res sua***. It has long been recognised that a common mistake as to the *existence* of the subject-matter of a contract will normally render the contract void. Lord Atkin in *Bell v Lever Bros Ltd* said: "the agreement of A and B to purchase a specific article is void if in fact the article had perished before the date of sale. In this case, though the parties in fact were agreed about the subject-matter, yet a consent to transfer or take delivery of something not existent is deemed useless, the consent is nullified."[86] Lord Atkin then referred to section 6 of the Sale of Goods Act, where this principle is in part codified.[87] He went on to describe the situation, usually considered to be analogous, which is commonly known as

---

[81] *ibid.* at p.611.
[82] *ibid.* at p.603.
[83] It is arguable that the fact that the mistake is shared by both parties is irrelevant: Atiyah and Bennion, 24 M.L.R. 421 at 422 (1961).
[84] *Furness Withy (Australia) Pty Ltd v Metal Distributors (UK) Ltd (The "Amazonia")* [1990] 1 Lloyd's Rep. 236.
[85] [1932] A.C. 161; discussed and followed in *Great Peace Shipping Ltd v Tsavliris Salvage (International) Ltd* [2002] EWCA Civ 1907; [2003] Q.B. 679.
[86] [1932] A.C. 161 at 217.
[87] See above, paras 1–124 *et seq.*

res sua: "Corresponding to mistake as to the existence of the subject-matter is mistake as to title in cases where, unknown to the parties, the buyer is already the owner of that which the seller purports to sell to him. The parties intended to effectuate a transfer of ownership: such a transfer is impossible: the stipulation is *naturali ratione inutilis*."[88]

Common mistake as to quality. Greater difficulty arises from the passage in the speech of Lord Atkin dealing with mistake as to quality of the thing contracted for. "In such a case," he said,[89] "a mistake will not affect assent unless it is the mistake of both parties, and is as to the existence of some quality which makes the thing without the quality essentially different from the thing as it was believed to be." This statement, although clearly appearing to recognise that a contract may be avoided on the ground of mistake as to quality, can hardly be taken at its face value in view of the illustrations given in *Bell v Lever Bros Ltd* itself, and of the decisions in that and subsequent cases. None of the following can on this authority be considered "fundamental" mistakes: a mistake as to the soundness of a horse sold[90]; or as to the genuineness of a picture believed to be an old master[91]; or as to the year of first registration of a car[92]; the erroneous belief that "horsebeans" and "feveroles" were the same commodity[93]; or that "Calcutta kapok, Sree brand" was a type of pure kapok.[94] On the other hand, there are dicta to the effect that a contract for a horse believed to be a racehorse would be void if it proved to be a carthorse,[95] and that table linen "with the crest of Charles I and the authentic property of that monarch" is so essentially different from Georgian linen that if it turns out to be the latter, a contract to buy it is void.[96] More recently, in *Associated Japanese Bank (International) Ltd v Crédit du Nord SA*,[97] a guarantee of the lessor's obligations under a contract for the lease of certain machines was held to be void when it turned out that the machines were fictitious. 3–020

88 [1932] A.C. 161 at 218. *Cf.* the opinion of Lord Thankerton, at pp.235–236; and see also *Cooper v Phibbs* (1867) L.R. 2 H.L. 149 (lease of fishery) and *Bligh v Martin* [1968] 1 W.L.R.804 (conveyance of land).

89 [1932] A.C. 161 at 218.

90 *ibid.* at p.224.

91 *ibid.*; *cf. Leaf v International Galleries* [1950] 2 K.B. 86 (criticised by Treitel, *The Law of Contract* (10th ed.), pp.268–269, and *Harlingdon & Leinster Enterprises Ltd v Christopher Hull Fine Art Ltd* [1991] 1 Q.B. 564 (where mistake was not pleaded).

92 *Routledge v McKay* [1954] 1 W.L.R. 615; *Oscar Chess Ltd v Williams* [1957] 1 W.L.R. 370; but if the date is part of the description under which the goods are sold, the seller will be liable under s.13: *Beale v Taylor* [1967] 1 W.L.R. 1193.

93 *F. E. Rose (London) Ltd v Wm. H. Pim Jnr. & Co. Ltd* [1953] 2 Q.B. 450 at 460.

94 *Harrison & Jones Ltd v Bunten & Lancaster Ltd* [1953] 1 Q.B. 646.

95 *Lever Bros Ltd v Bell* [1931] 1 K.B. 557 at 597 (reversed on appeal *sub nom. Bell v Lever Bros Ltd*, above).

96 *Nicholson & Venn v Smith-Marriott* (1947) 177 L.T. 189; disapproved in *Solle v Butcher* [1950] 1 K.B. 671 at 692.

97 [1989] 1 W.L.R. 255; *cf. Scott v Coulson* [1903] 2 Ch. 249 (sale of life policy believed to be current, assured in fact dead).

3–021 Different opinions have been expressed about the present state of the law in the light of these decisions. It has been said that common mistake is now restricted in its effect to the case of *res extincta*[98]; that only a mistake as to quality which goes to the *identity* of the thing contracted for will invalidate a contract[99]; that the question is one of the true construction of the "total" contract, so that the contract will be void only if a term can be implied that the failure of the particular underlying assumption is to have such a consequence[1]; and that the question is primarily one of the allocation of risk, which, particularly in the context of sales of goods, leaves little scope for any operative doctrine of mistake as to quality which would override the basic principle that the buyer must normally accept all risks as to the state and condition of the goods except those for which the seller has accepted responsibility by giving warranties, express or implied.[2] Each of these views was considered by Steyn J. in his judgment in *Associated Japanese Bank (International) Ltd v Creédit du Nord SA*,[3] where the defendants were sued as guarantors of the liability of a lessee under agreements for the lease of four industrial machines. In fact, the machines did not exist, and both the claimants and the defendants had been induced to enter into the guarantee agreement by the fraud of the supposed lessee. Steyn J. ruled that the guarantee was subject to an express condition precedent that there was a lease in respect of four existing machines, with the consequence that the guarantee was void for failure of this condition; but he held in the alternative (1) that if there was no express condition, an implied condition to the same effect was to be read into the contract; (2) that the guarantee was void at common law on the ground of essential mistake as to subject-matter; and (3) that even if it were not void at common law the contract should be set aside on equitable principles. This final ground must now be regarded as unsound because of the rejection of any separate doctrine of "mistake in equity" by the Court of Appeal in *Great Peace Shipping Ltd v Tsavrilis Salvage (International) Ltd*.[4] In *Great Peace* itself, the defendants contracted to hire the *Great Peace* to provide salvage services to a ship which had suffered structural damage. Both parties acted in the mistaken belief that it was the nearest ship to the stricken vessel: in fact, it was more than 10 times further away than they thought, and another ship was better placed to provide assistance. The defendants cancelled the hiring and declined to make any payment for it, arguing that the purported contract was void by reason of a fundamental mistake. The Court of Appeal, after an exhaustive examination of the cases, rejected this contention and held that the contract was binding.[5] Lord Phillips of Worth Matravers M.R., giving the judgment of the court, said that the following elements must be

---

[98] Cheshire, Fifoot and Furmston, *The Law of Contract* (11th ed.), p.208 (but see now the current (14th) edition at p.263).
[99] Treitel, *The Law of Contract* (11th ed.), p.292.
[1] Atiyah & Bennion, 24 M.L.R. 421 (1961) (but see the *Great Peace* case (above) at [73]).
[2] McTurnan, 41 Can.Bar Rev. 1 (1963).
[3] [1989] 1 W.L.R. 255.
[4] [2002] EWCA Civ 1407; [2003] Q.B. 679, below, para.3–025.
[5] An alternative argument that the contract was voidable on equitable grounds also failed: see below, para.3–025.

present if a common mistake is to avoid a contract:[6] (i) there must be a common assumption as to the existence of a state of affairs; (ii) there must be no warranty by either party that the state of affairs exists; (iii) the non-existence of the state of affairs must not be attributable to the fault of either party; (iv) the non-existence of the state of affairs must render performance of the contract impossible; and (v) the state of affairs may be the existence, or a vital attribute, of the consideration to be provided or circumstances which must subsist if performance of the contractual adventure is to be possible. It followed that, while not disagreeing with the judge's ruling in the *Associated Japanese Bank* case that the "narrow test" laid down by Lord Atkin had been satisfied in that case, the court considered that the mistake in *Great Peace* was not such as to make performance of the contract impossible.

Other fundamental assumptions. In *Bell v Lever Bros Ltd*[7] it was accepted as a general proposition that "whenever it is to be inferred from the terms of a contract or its surrounding circumstances that the consensus has been reached on the basis of a particular contractual assumption, and that assumption is not true, the contract is avoided"—provided that the assumption was "fundamental to the continued validity of the contract", or "a foundation essential to its existence". Although it is not easy to reconcile the acceptance of this proposition with the decision in *Bell v Lever Bros Ltd* itself or with subsequent cases,[8] it is apparent that, if the principle so stated is correct, a contract for the sale of goods could be avoided on the grounds of a false and fundamental assumption as to something other than the existence or quality of the goods.[9] The proposition was applied in *Sheikh Bros Ltd v Ochsner*,[10] where a contract granting the respondent a licence to enter and cut sisal on the appellant's land contained a provision that the respondent would deliver to the appellant a minimum of 50 tons of processed sisal per month. In fact the land was, unknown to either party, incapable of producing this amount of sisal; and the Privy Council held that the contract was void. 3–022

---

[6] At [76], adapting a passage from the judgment of Lord Alverstone C.J. in *Blakeley v Muller & Co.* (1903) TLR 186 (a frustration case).

[7] [1932] A.C. 161 at 225–226, 235–236.

[8] Above, paras 3–018, 3–020.

[9] The discussion of common mistake in *Associated Japanese Bank (International) Ltd v Crédit du Nord SA* [1989] 1 W.L.R. 255 (above, para.3–021) is confined to mistake as to the "subject-matter" of the contract. Mistake was not pleaded in *Naughton v O'Callaghan* [1990] 3 All E.R. 191 (misrepresentation as to true pedigree of racehorse).

[10] [1957] A.C. 136; the decision was based primarily on the wording of the Indian Contract Act 1872, s.20, but the English cases on the law of mistake were also relied on. *Cf. Clifford v Watts* (1870) L.R. 5 C.P. 577 (licence to dig clay). See also *Scott v Coulson* [1903] 2 Ch. 249 (life policy not known to have matured); *Griffith v Brymer* (1903) 19 T.L.R. 434 (room to view procession which had been cancelled); *Galloway v Galloway* (1914) 30 T.L.R. 531 (deed of separation between parties in fact unmarried); *Magee v Pennine Insurance Co. Ltd* [1969] 2 Q.B. 507 at 517, *per* Fenton Atkinson L.J. (insurance policy wrongly believed valid); *Associated Japanese Bank (International) Ltd v Crédit du Nord SA* [1989] 1 W.L.R. 255 (guarantee of lease of fictitious machines); and contrast *Amalgamated Investment & Property Co. Ltd v John Walker & Sons Ltd* [1977] 1 W.L.R. 164 (purchase of building believed available for redevelopment).

3–023 **Mistake as to quantity.** There are no modern cases[11] directly concerned with the issue of mistake as to quantity. In so far as a quantity of goods is sold as a specific parcel, a mistake as to the actual number or measurement of the goods comprised in it would seem to be directly analogous to a mistake as to quality or value. Moreover, it has been held that the loss or destruction of part of such goods may amount to the "perishing" of the specific parcel within the terms of section 6 of the Sale of Goods Act 1979.[12] If, on the other hand, goods are sold by reference to their quantity, it is a matter of the construction of the contract whether the parties are either permitted or bound respectively to tender and to accept a different quantity of goods from that contracted for.[13]

3–024 **Documents mistakenly signed, and rectification of written contracts.** Where a person has been induced to sign a document contrary to his true intention, he may be able to plead the legal defence of *non est factum*. And where a document intended to record the agreement reached by parties does not truly state the agreed terms, there is equitable jurisdiction to rectify the written document. Neither of these topics raises any question peculiar to the law of sale of goods; and so reference may be made to general works on the law of contract.[14]

3–025 **Mistake in equity.** The courts of equity may refuse to order specific performance of a contract against a party who has entered into the contract under a mistake of fact.[15] This jurisdiction has been superseded in the law of sale of goods by the special provisions of section 52 of the Sale of Goods Act 1979, which gives the court a discretionary power in the case of a contract for specific or ascertained goods to direct that the contract shall be performed specifically, either unconditionally or upon such terms and conditions as to damages, payment of the price and otherwise as may seem just. The language here is plainly wide enough to enable a court to make allowance for a party's mistake. In exercising this jurisdiction the court's concern is not as to the validity or otherwise of the contract, but as to the suitability of a particular remedy.

3–026 **Rescission for mistake.** It is open to a party who alleges a common mistake to make application to a court of equity to have the contract set aside rather than to treat it as void, or have it declared void, at law.[16] There is little reason to invoke this jurisdiction in most contracts for the sale of

---

[11] For an old case, see *Cox v Prentice* (1815) 3 M. & S. 344, discussed by Treitel, *The Law of Contract* (11th ed.), p.294.
[12] *Barrow, Lane & Ballard Ltd v Phillip Phillips & Co. Ltd* [1929] 1 K.B. 574; above, paras 1–125—1–126.
[13] Below, Chs 8, 9.
[14] See, *e.g.* as regards *non est factum*, *Chitty on Contracts* (29th ed.), Vol. 1, paras 5–086 *et seq.*; Treitel, *The Law of Contract* (11th ed.), pp.326–329; *Saunders v Anglia Building Society* [1971] A.C. 1004 and Stone, 88 L.Q.R. 190 (1972); and as regards rectification, Chitty, *op. cit.*, paras 5–092 *et seq.*; Treitel, *op. cit.*, pp.321–326.
[15] As regards specific performance of contracts for the sale of goods, see below, paras 17–096, 19–204, 20–121.
[16] *Chitty on Contracts* (29th ed.), Vol. 1, paras 5–048 *et seq.*

goods since the special features which make it attractive apply mainly in conveyancing and other more complex transactions.

In such a case, equity goes no further than to provide an alternative remedy to those which would be available at law. The notion that there was a separate doctrine of "mistake in equity", associated with the case of *Solle v Butcher*,[17] must now be considered discredited, following the ruling in the *Great Peace* case.[18]

5. ILLEGALITY[19]

General contractual principles applicable. A contract may be unenforceable on the ground of illegality or because it is contrary to public policy. It is, indeed, commonly said to be "void" on these grounds; but since illegal contracts may not be totally without effect and may sometimes be enforced by an innocent, or even a relatively innocent, party, the word "void" must be understood in a special sense in this context, and is perhaps better not used at all. The Sale of Goods Act 1979, s.62(2), may be taken to declare that the general principles governing illegality shall apply to contracts for the sale of goods because of the use of the phrase "other invalidating cause". 3–027

Illegal contracts generally. A contract is illegal if it involves the commission of a legal wrong or if it is contrary to public policy. The illegal element may be in the terms of the contract itself, or in the purpose for which the contract is made, or in the manner of its performance.[20] The nature of the illegality may vary from the commission of a crime at one extreme to a covenant in unreasonable restraint of trade at the other; and its formal source may be found in statute[21] or in the common law (including the rules 3–028

---

[17] [1950] 1 K.B. 671.

[18] *Great Peace Shipping Ltd v Tsavliris Salvage (International) Ltd* [2002] EWCA Civ 1407; [2003] Q.B. 679, above, para.3–021. See Reynolds, 119 L.Q.R. 177 (2003); Midwinter, 119 L.Q.R. 180 (2003); and contrast Yeo, 121 L.Q.R. 393 (2005).

[19] See generally *Chitty on Contracts* (29th ed.), Vol. 1, Ch.16; Treitel, *The Law of Contract* (11th ed.), Ch.11; Hamson, 10 C.L.J. 249 (1949); Grodecki, 71 L.Q.R. 254 (1955); Higgins, 25 M.L.R. 149 (1962); Furmston, 16 Univ. of Toronto L.J. 267 (1966); Coote, 35 M.L.R. 38 (1972); Shand [1972A] C.L.J. 144.

[20] See, however, *Euro-Diam Ltd v Bathurst* [1990] Q.B. 1 (offence under foreign law committed only incidentally in course of performance held irrelevant to claim).

[21] A contract may be invalid at common law by reason of illegality which has its formal source in a statute on the same principles as apply in the case of other types of illegality; but in addition, one or both of the parties may be deprived of their remedies under a contract because of a prohibition expressed or implied in the statute itself. For this purpose a statute may (a) prohibit the making or enforcement of a contract absolutely: *Re Mahmoud and Ispahani* [1921] 2 K.B. 716 (*cf. Yin v Sam* [1962] A.C. 304); *Bedford Insce. Co. Ltd v Instituto de Resseguros do Brasil* [1985] Q.B. 966; *Stewart v Oriental Fire & Marine Insce. Co. Ltd* [1985] Q.B. 988; *Phoenix General Insce. Co. of Greece SA v Halvanon Insce. Co. Ltd* [1988] Q.B. 216; *Re Cavalier Insce. Co. Ltd* [1989] 2 Lloyd's Rep. 430 (insurance; but see now Financial Services and Markets Act 2000, ss.26–28); *Mohamed v Alaga & Co.* [1998] 2 All E.R.

of public policy). It is not necessary in a work on the sale of goods to discuss the subject at length; but certain topics call for some special mention. These are, first, the effect of illegality (as described above) on the contract itself and related transactions; secondly, its effect on the passing of property in the goods which are the subject of a contract of sale; thirdly, its effect as regards restitutionary remedies; and, finally, the application of the doctrine of restraint of trade and the allied questions (now regulated by statute) of monopolies, restrictive practices and resale price maintenance. These matters will be dealt with in the present chapter. The Consumer Protection Act 1987, the Trade Descriptions Act 1968, and other statutes which prohibit or regulate certain specific types of sale are discussed in Chapter 14, below.

3–029 **Effect of illegality on contract.** A contract which is affected by illegality cannot be enforced by a party who was aware of or privy to the illegality.[22] If both parties are in this position, it cannot be enforced by either of them.[23] But a party who is innocent of the illegality is not deprived of a remedy: he may not, of course, compel performance of the illegal promise, and he is entitled[24] (and, indeed, bound) himself to desist from further performance; but he may sue for a price,[25] or claim on a quantum meruit in respect of such performance as he has himself rendered[26]; and he may sue for

---

720 (introduction fee) or (b) prohibit the performance of a contract in a particular way: *Anderson Ltd v Daniel* [1924] 1 K.B. 138; *Marles v Philip Trant & Sons Ltd* [1954] 1 Q.B. 29) or (c) prohibit certain acts in the course of the performance of a contract without affecting the enforceability of the contract itself: *Smith v Mawhood* (1845) 14 M. & W. 452; *cf. St. John Shipping Corp. v Joseph Rank Ltd* [1957] 1 Q.B.267; *Archbolds (Freightage) Ltd v S. Spanglett Ltd* [1961] 1 Q.B. 374 (carriage); *Shaw v Groom* [1970] 2 Q.B. 504 (tenancy); *Crédit Lyonnais v P. T. Barnard & Associates Ltd* [1976] 1 Lloyd's Rep. 557 and *S. A. Ancien Maison Marcel Bauche v Woodhouse Drake & Carey (Sugar) Ltd* [1982] 2 Lloyd's Rep. 516 (cases on exchange control). For the special rules and problems involved in the construction of statutes for this purpose, see *Chitty on Contracts* (29th ed.), Vol.1, paras 16–141 *et seq.*; Treitel, *The Law of Contract* (11th ed.), pp.429–439, 513–514; Buckley, 38 M.L.R. 535 (1975).

[22] *Langton v Hughes* (1813) 1 M. & S. 593; *Anderson Ltd v Daniel* [1924] 1 K.B. 138; *Marles v Philip Trant & Sons Ltd* [1954] 1 Q.B. 29; *cf. Bostel Bros Ltd v Hurlock* [1949] 1 K.B. 74 (building contract); *Ashmore, Benson, Pease & Co. Ltd v A V Dawson Ltd* [1973] 1 W.L.R. 828 (carriage). *Cf. 21st Century Logistic Solutions Ltd v Madysen Ltd* [2004] EWHC 231 (Q.B.); [2004] 2 Lloyd's Rep. 92 (intention to defraud too remote to affect contract).

[23] *Pearce v Brooks* (1866) L.R. 1 Ex. 213; *J. M. Allan (Merchandising) Ltd v Cloke* [1963] 2 Q.B. 340 (contracts of hire). The court will refuse to enforce a contract tainted by illegality even where it has not been pleaded by either party: *Birkett v Acorn Business Machines Ltd* [1999] 2 All E.R. (Comm.) 429. Exceptionally, and only in certain cases (*e.g.* a promise in restraint of trade), the illegal part of a contract may be severed and the balance enforced: for this topic, see *Chitty on Contracts* (29th ed.), Vol. 1, paras 16–186 *et seq*.

[24] *Curragh Investments Ltd v Cook* [1974] 1 W.L.R. 1559.

[25] *Cf. Pearce v Brooks* (1866) L.R. 1 Ex. 213 at 219, 221; *Mason v Clarke* [1955] A.C. 778 at 793, 805 (*profit à prendre*).

[26] *Cf. Clay v Yates* (1856) 1 H. & N. 73 (contract to print book).

damages for breach of the contract.[27] For this purpose, a party is an innocent party if he was unaware of the facts making the contract illegal or of the illegal purpose which the other party had in mind, and also if the other party intended to perform (or has in fact performed) the contract in an illegal manner without his knowledge.[28] An innocent party may also, at least in some cases,[29] sue for breach of a collateral warranty or collateral contract—for instance, an assurance given by the other party that the licence necessary for the lawful performance of the principal contract had been or would be obtained.[30]

Effect of illegality on passing of property.[31] Although a contract which is tainted with illegality cannot be enforced, at least by a party who is privy to the illegality, it is well settled that property can pass under an illegal contract of sale: where goods have been delivered in pursuance of such a contract they cannot be recovered back by the seller, and the buyer may assert his proprietary rights both against the seller and against a stranger. Thus, in *Sajan Singh v Sardara Ali*,[32] a lorry was sold by the appellant to the respondent in a transaction which was illegal because it involved a fraud on the transport licensing authorities. The appellant retook possession of the lorry without the respondent's consent, and claimed to be entitled to retain it. The Privy Council held that, notwithstanding the illegality of the contract, the fact that it had been fully executed and carried out meant that the property in the lorry had passed to the buyer: "the transferee, having obtained the property, can assert his title to it against all the world, not because he has any merit of his own, but because there is no one who can assert a better title to it."[33] This principle has been held to apply even where the transferee has not taken possession of the property, so long as the title to it was intended under the contract to pass to him, and had so passed.[34] It would appear, however, that if the transfer of property was itself 3–030

[27] *Bloxsome v Williams* (1824) 3 B. & C. 232; *Marles v Philip Trant & Sons Ltd*, above; *cf. Shaw v Shaw* [1954] 2 Q.B. 429 (contract to marry). If an innocent party suffers loss through the performance of an illegal contract which he has been compelled to observe, there is some support for the view that this *per se* would entitle him to damages: *Shell U.K. Ltd v Lostock Garages Ltd* [1977] 1 W.L.R. 1187 at 1200.

[28] See the cases cited in nn.24–27, above.

[29] This may not be the case where a contract is absolutely prohibited by statute (*Re Mahmoud and Ispahani* [1921] 2 K.B. 716): *Cf.* Treitel, *The Law of Contract* (11th ed.), pp.486–487.

[30] *Cf. Strongman (1945) Ltd v Sincock* [1955] 2 Q.B. 525 (building contract). Alternatively, a remedy may lie in deceit: *Burrows v Rhodes* [1899] 1 Q.B. 816; *Shelley v Paddock* [1980] Q.B. 348.

[31] See Hamson, 10 C.L.J. 249 (1949); Higgins, 25 M.L.R. 149 (1962); Coote, 35 M.L.R. 38 (1972).

[32] [1960] A.C. 167; *cf. Taylor v Chester* (1869) L.R. 4 Q.B. 309 (pledge); *Belvoir Finance Co. Ltd v Stapleton* [1971] 1 Q.B. 210; *Tinsley v Milligan* [1994] A.C. 340 (equitable interest).

[33] [1960] A.C. 167 at 176–177.

[34] *Belvoir Finance Co. Ltd v Stapleton*, above; *Kingsley v Sterling Industrial Securities Ltd* [1967] 2 Q.B. 747 at 783; *cf. Watts v Seymour* [1967] 2 Q.B. 647. These cases appear to mark a departure from the earlier authorities, which all stress the fact of delivery: see *Simpson v Nichols* (1838) 3 M. & W. 240 at 244; *Scarfe v Morgan* (1838) 4 M. & W. 270 at 281; *Elder v Kelly* [1919] 2 K.B. 179.

absolutely forbidden by statute, there would be no room for its application.[35]

3–031 **Restitution in illegal contracts.** The general consequence of illegality affecting a contract is that neither party can sue to recover money paid or property transferred pursuant to it.[36] To this rule there are, however, certain exceptions. The first is that an owner of property may bring an action based on his proprietary rights, provided that he is not obliged to rely on the illegal transaction in support of his claim, but sues independently of it.[37] Thus, the owner of goods who has let them on hire-purchase may sue the hirer for wrongful interference with the goods if the latter has acted in denial of his rights as owner (*e.g.* by selling the goods), even though the hire-purchase transaction was itself illegal.[38] But he should not be able to enforce the return of the goods where his claim to be entitled to do so is based purely on the terms of the illegal contract itself—for instance, on the exercise of a right to determine the hiring for non-payment of rent.[39] In such circumstances, the special property[40] of the hirer as a bailee which is conferred by virtue of the principle stated in the previous paragraph prevails over the owner's general proprietary rights, at least for the expected term of the hiring.[41]

3–032 **Parties not *in pari delicto*.** The rule against recovery of money or property applies only where the parties are *in pari delicto*, that is, where the law regards them as equally implicated in the illegality. A second exception is made where this is not so. A party will be allowed to sue to recover his property where, for instance, he is ignorant of the facts which render the transaction unlawful, or where he is unaware of the defendant's intention to perform the contract in an illegal manner.[42] A plaintiff will not be *in pari delicto* if he has been the victim of fraud or oppression,[43] or if the law which

[35] *Cf. Re Mahmoud and Ispahani* [1921] 2 K.B. 716; *Amar Singh v Kulubya* [1964] A.C. 142 (lease).

[36] *Chitty on Contracts* (29th ed.), Vol. 1, para.16–171; Treitel, *The Law of Contract* (11th ed.), pp.490–492; Goff and Jones, *The Law of Restitution* (6th ed.), Ch. 24; *Scott v Brown, Doering, McNab & Co.* [1892] 2 Q.B. 724 (shares); *Parkinson v College of Ambulance* [1925] 2 K.B. 1 (procurement of honour); *Bigos v Bousted* [1951] 1 All E.R. 92 (foreign currency). The contrary dictum in *Shaw v Shaw* [1965] 1 W.L.R. 537 at 539 (tenancy) does not appear to be supportable.

[37] *Bowmakers Ltd v Barnet Instruments Ltd* [1945] K.B. 65; *Belvoir Finance Co. Ltd v Stapleton* [1971] 1 K.B. 210; *Tinsley v Milligan* [1994] A.C. 340.

[38] *Bowmakers Ltd v Barnet Instruments Ltd*, above; *cf. Belvoir Finance Co. Ltd v Stapleton*, above (action in conversion against salesman): see now Torts (Interference with Goods) Act 1977.

[39] The contrary was in fact decided in *Bowmakers Ltd v Barnet Instruments Ltd*, above; but see the criticism of Hamson, 10 C.L.J. 249 (1949); *Chitty on Contracts* (29th ed.), Vol. 1, para.16–175. For another view, see Coote, 35 M.L.R. 38 (1972).

[40] For the meaning of this term, see above, para.1–063.

[41] *Taylor v Chester* (1869) L.R. 4 Q.B. 309 (pledge); *cf. Feret v Hill* (1854) 15 C.B. 207 (lease).

[42] *Mason v Clarke* [1955] A.C. 778 (*profit à prendre*).

[43] *Kettlewell v Refuge Assce. Co.* [1908] 1 K.B. 545, affirmed [1909] A.C. 243 (insurance); *Shelley v Paddock* [1980] Q.B. 348 (exchange control); contrast *Harse v Pearl Life Assce. Co.* [1904] 1 K.B. 558 (innocent misrepresentation): *sed quaere*? See also *Atkinson v Denby* (1861) 6 H. & N. 778, affirmed (1862) 7 H. & N. 934 (composition with creditors).

makes the transaction illegal is designed for the protection of persons in the plaintiff's position.[44] In all these circumstances, property transferred or money paid may be recovered in normal restitution proceedings, even after the contract has been executed.

Repudiation of executory contract. Under a third exception to the general rule, a party may recover money paid or property transferred under an illegal contract if he repudiates the illegal purpose before it has been fully or substantially carried out.[45] It is essential that the repentance be voluntary and bona fide, and not merely a belated change of attitude assumed when the illegal object becomes unattainable.[46] In *Taylor v Bowers*,[47] the plaintiff assigned goods to A in fraud of his creditors, and A further assigned them to B, who was privy to the fraudulent scheme. Before any creditor had in fact been defrauded, the plaintiff changed his mind and sought to repudiate the transaction and recover the goods. It was held that since the illegal object of the assignment had not been carried out, he was entitled to succeed. 3–033

Restraint of trade.[48] Covenants and contracts in restraint of trade (although not in themselves unlawful[49]) are prima facie unenforceable[50] at common law; but they may be upheld if they are shown to be reasonable in the interests both of the parties themselves and of the public. Although the concept of restraint of trade is not capable of exhaustive definition,[51] it has been described as follows[52]: "A contract in restraint of trade is one in which a party (the covenantor) agrees with any other party (the covenantee) to restrict his liberty in the future to carry on trade with other persons not parties to the contract in such manner as he chooses." The question of the 3–034

---

[44] *Marles v Phillip Trant & Sons Ltd* [1953] 1 All E.R. 645 (reversed on another ground, but approved on this point, [1954] 1 Q.B. 29 at 36). *Cf. Browning v Morris* (1778) 2 Cowp. 790 at 792; *Kiriri Cotton Co. Ltd v Dewani* [1960] A.C. 192 (tenant); *Wallersteiner v Moir* [1974] 1 W.L.R. 991 (company); *Belmont Finance Corp. Ltd v Williams Furniture Ltd* [1979] Ch. 250 (company); *Nash v Halifax Building Soc.* [1979] Ch. 584 (building society); *Re Cavalier Insce. Co. Ltd* [1989] 2 Lloyd's Rep. 430 (insurance: and see now Financial Services and Markets Act 2000, ss.26–28.).

[45] *Taylor v Bowers* (1876) 1 Q.B.D. 291; *cf. Bone v Ekless* (1860) 29 L.J.Ex. 438; *Symes v Hughes* (1870) L.R. 9 Eq. 475; *Bigos v Bousted* [1951] 1 All E.R. 92; *Palaniappa Chettiar v Arunasalam Chettiar* [1962] A.C. 294. As to what amounts to "substantial" performance of the illegal object, see *Kearley v Thomson* (1890) 24 Q.B.D. 742.

[46] *Bigos v Bousted*, above.

[47] (1876) 1 Q.B.D. 291.

[48] See *Chitty on Contracts* (29th ed.) Vol. 1, paras 16–075 *et seq.*; Heydon, *The Restraint of Trade Doctrine* (1971).

[49] *Boddington v Lawton* [1994] I.C.R. 478.

[50] It is sometimes possible to sever the unreasonable part of the covenant and to enforce the remainder, or to enforce the contract without the covenant where the latter is not substantially the whole consideration: see Chitty, *op. cit.*, paras 16–191 *et seq.*

[51] *Esso Petroleum Co. Ltd v Harper's Garage (Stourport) Ltd* [1968] A.C. 269 at 298–299, 332.

[52] *Petrofina (Great Britain) Ltd v Martin* [1966] Ch.146 at 180; accepted as "helpful" in the *Esso* case, above, at pp.307, 317.

validity of such covenants falls to be considered most often in connection with the sale of the goodwill of a business and with contracts of employment and partnership; but it is not confined to these situations. In the context of sales of goods, it may arise in several ways. First, a contract of sale may itself purport to impose restrictions on the use or subsequent disposal of the goods by the buyer. Secondly, two traders may seek by an agreement to regulate their future dealings *inter se* and, in particular, one of them may undertake to deal exclusively with the other. Thirdly, an arrangement may be made between two or more parties to establish a common policy under which each of them will deal with the world at large—for instance, by price-fixing, control of production or distribution, or adoption of standard terms of trading. These agreements may all be affected by the common law doctrine of restraint of trade; but it is necessary also to consider the relevant provisions of the competition legislation, both the domestic law of the United Kingdom and that of the European Community.[53]

3–035 **Exception in cases of general commercial acceptance.** Although no class of contract may be said to have gained absolute exemption from the operation of the doctrine of restraint of trade,[54] it has been accepted that contracts of a kind which have gained general commercial acceptance and have not been traditionally subject to the doctrine will not be subjected to it, so as to impose upon a plaintiff the burden of justifying their terms as reasonable.[55] Special or unusual features in particular contracts may, however, bring such contracts within the ambit of the doctrine,[56] and this may be particularly so where a contract has been made between parties of unequal bargaining power.[57] For instance, a normal co-operative selling scheme established by the growers or producers of a particular commodity may not call for justification,[58] but it will do so if it appears to impose an excessive and unusual fetter on a member's liberty.[59] Almost all of the contracts relating to sales of goods in which questions of restraint of trade arise seem to fall into well-known categories which have become so recognised and accepted as no longer to call for justification, except where the circumstances are unusual.

3–036 **Restraints affecting goods sold.** It is not altogether certain that the common law rules apply to the case of restrictions imposed by a contract of sale on the liberty of the buyer to use and dispose of the goods sold to him

---

[53] paras 3–040 *et seq.*
[54] *Esso Petroleum Co. Ltd v Harper's Garage (Stourport) Ltd* [1968] A.C. 269 at 333.
[55] *ibid.* at pp.306, 319–320, 323, 328, 333.
[56] *ibid.* at pp.294, 328–329, 333; *cf. Young v Timmins* (1831) 1 Cr. & J. 331 (employment); *Att.-Gen. for Australia v Adelaide S.S. Co. Ltd* [1913] A.C. 781; *McEllistrim v Ballymacelligott Co-op. Soc. Ltd* [1919] A.C. 548.
[57] *A Schroeder Music Publishing Co. Ltd v Macaulay* [1974] 1 W.L.R. 1308; *Clifford Davis Ltd v WEA Records Ltd* [1975] 1 W.L.R. 61.
[58] *English Hop Growers Ltd v Dering* [1928] 2 K.B. 174.
[59] *McEllistrim v Ballymacelligott Co-op. Soc. Ltd*, above.

under that contract.[60] An alternative view is that a buyer in such circumstances is not subjected to any restraint in the exercise of a right already enjoyed by him, but has merely obtained a new, limited, right which he was free to acquire or not as he might choose.[61] This reasoning was used in *United Shoe Machinery Co. of Canada v Brunet*,[62] where the lessee of certain shoemaking machinery covenanted with the lessor not to use it in conjunction with machinery hired from anyone else. It was held that the agreement was not in restraint of trade. In so far as a contract of sale of goods purports to impose restrictions on the buyer's liberty to deal with goods *other* than those sold, it is thought that the doctrine of restraint of trade will in principle apply.[63] As regards patented articles, the Patents Act 1977[64] formerly prohibited the use of a patent for the purpose of extending a monopoly beyond the terms of the patent itself—for instance, by attaching a condition requiring a purchaser of the patented goods to acquire or use other goods supplied by the patent-holder. However, this provision has now been repealed, and it is left to the broad ambit of the Chapter I prohibition in the Competition Act 1998, together with Article 81 of the E.C. Treaty, to deal with such questions.[65]

Resale price maintenance. Where a manufacturer or other supplier of goods seeks to impose upon his purchaser a condition that the goods shall not be resold for less than a specified price, the arrangement is known as "resale price maintenance." Such a condition is binding *inter partes* at common law[66]; but the rules of privity of contract made it virtually impossible at common law[67] to ensure that a similar obligation was adhered to by subsequent distributors of the goods,[68] and in practice (before the advent of modern legislation) traders had recourse to non-legal sanctions such as the withholding of further supplies and the circulation of stop-lists. 3–037

The enforcement of resale price maintenance provisions is now greatly restricted by statute. The relevant legislation was, until March 1, 2000, the Resale Prices Act 1976 but, with effect from that date, this Act was repealed,[69] and the issue of resale price maintenance is now dealt with

[60] See *Chitty on Contracts* (29th ed.), Vol. 1, paras 16–120 *et seq.; Esso Petroleum Co. Ltd v Harper's Garage (Stourport) Ltd* [1968] A.C. 269 at 298, 309, 325; *Cleveland Petroleum Co. Ltd v Dartstone* [1969] 1 W.L.R. 116; *Robinson v Golden Chips (Wholesale) Ltd* [1971] N.Z.L.R. 257; *Amoco Australia Pty Ltd v Rocca Bros Motor Engineering Pty Ltd* [1975] A.C. 561.

[61] See, however the criticism in Heydon, *The Restraint of Trade Doctrine* (1971), pp.55–59.

[62] [1909] A.C. 330; criticised (but not on this ground) in the *Esso* case, above at p.297. See also *British United Shoe Machinery Co. Ltd v Somervell Bros* (1906) 95 L.T. 711.

[63] *Chitty on Contracts* (29th ed.), Vol. 1, para.16–129.

[64] s.44 (repealed by the Competition Act 1998, s.70); Chitty, *op. cit.*, para.16–130.

[65] See below, paras 3–040, 3–041 *et seq.*

[66] *Elliman Sons & Co. v Carrington & Son Ltd* [1901] 2 Ch. 275; *Palmolive Co. (of England) Ltd v Freedman* [1928] Ch.264; *English Hop Growers Ltd v Dering* [1928] 2 K.B. 174 at 181; *Imperial Tobacco Co. Ltd v Parslay* [1936] 2 All E.R. 515.

[67] *i.e.* prior to the enactment of the Contracts (Rights of Third Parties) Act 1999.

[68] *Taddy & Co. v Sterious & Co.* [1904] 1 Ch. 354; *McGruther v Pitcher* [1904] 2 Ch. 306; *Dunlop Pneumatic Tyre Co. Ltd v Selfridge & Co. Ltd* [1915] A.C. 847.

[69] Competition Act 1998, s.74(3) and Sch.14.

under the more general provisions of the Chapter I prohibition in the Competition Act 1998 and Article 81 of the EC Treaty.[70]

3–038 **Exclusive dealing agreements.** An agreement under which a person agrees to take the whole of his requirements of a particular class of goods from one supplier, or to stock exclusively goods of a particular brand, may be affected by the doctrine of restraint of trade, but only in cases where the restraint is unusual.[71] Examples of such contracts are those relating to "tied" public-houses,[72] and "solus" agreements between petrol retailers and the suppliers of fuel and oil.[73] If the limitations on the buyer's freedom of action are declared unreasonable or contrary to the public interest, the restraint is void.[74] The same principle governs the converse case where it is agreed that a producer of goods will sell the whole of his output to a single buyer; but again if the agreement is of a normal commercial character it will not require justification.[75]

3–039 **Restrictive trading agreements.** The rules of restraint of trade apply also to agreements under which a number of traders seek to regulate the conditions under which they will deal with outside parties. Common illustrations include co-operative and other marketing associations[76] and professional and trading societies. In *Pharmaceutical Society of Great Britain*

---

[70] See below paras 3–040, 3–041 *et seq.*

[71] Above, para.3–035. *Cf. Ultraframe (UK) Ltd v Tailored Roofing Systems Ltd* [2004] EWCA Civ 585; [2004] 2 All E.R. (Comm.) 692 (construction of exclusive purchase agreement).

[72] *Catt v Tourle* (1869) 4 Ch.App. 654; *Clegg v Hands* (1890) 44 Ch.D. 503; and see *Chitty on Contracts* (29th ed.), Vol. 1, para.16–124 and *Servais Bouchard v Prince's Hall Restaurant Ltd* (1904) 20 T.L.R. 574 (supply of burgundy to restaurant). In *Esso Petroleum Co. Ltd v Harper's Garage (Stourport) Ltd* [1968] A.C. 269 at 298, 311, 315, 319–320, 328, 333 the view was expressed that the tied public–house cases had become so generally accepted as no longer to require justification in normal cases; while Lord Pearce (at p.325) thought that the doctrine did not apply at all—as had Collins M.R. in the *Servais Bouchard* case, above.

[73] *Esso* case, above, and earlier cases there discussed; *Cleveland Petroleum Co. Ltd v Dartstone Ltd* [1969] 1 W.L.R. 116; *Texaco Ltd v Mulberry Filling Station Ltd* [1972] 1 All E.R. 513; *Amoco Australia Pty Ltd v Rocca Bros Motor Engineering Co. Pty Ltd* [1975] A.C. 561; *Shell U.K. Ltd v Lostock Garage Ltd* [1977] 1 W.L.R. 1187; *Alec Lobb (Garages) Ltd v Total Oil (G.B.) Ltd* [1985] 1 W.L.R. 173; [1985] 1 W.L.R. 598, *Esso Petrolum Ltd v Niad Ltd* [2001] All E.R. (D) 324. Exclusive dealing agreements may also be affected by Arts 81 and 82 of the Treaty of Rome (below, para.3–041), and those relating to beer and petrol were specifically regulated by EEC Reg. 1984/83; but now come under the "Verticals" Regulation (Reg. 1999/2790, (O.J. 1999 L 336/21)).

[74] Above, para.3–034; but the remainder of the contract may be enforceable (n.50, above). "Sole agency" cases have also now passed into general commercial acceptance (see the *Esso* case, above, at pp.311, 320, 328; and *cf. Lamb v Goring* [1932] 1 K.B. 710; *Foley v Classique Coaches Ltd* [1934] 2 K.B. 1), except where the restraint is unusually severe (*Att.-Gen. for Australia v Adelaide S.S. Co. Ltd* [1913] A.C. 781).

[75] *English Hop Growers Ltd v Dering* [1928] 2 K.B. 174; *Esso* case, above, at p.296.

[76] *McEllistrim v Ballymacelligott Co-op. Soc. Ltd* [1919] A.C. 548. *Cf. Att.-Gen. for Australia v Adelaide S.S. Co. Ltd* [1913] A.C. 781; *English Hop Growers Ltd v Dering* [1928] 2 K.B. 174.

v Dickson[77] the defendant society sought to amend its rules so as to prevent its members from extending the classes of goods in which they might deal beyond those traditionally sold by chemists; but the amendment was held not reasonable either in the interests of the members or in the public interest. In most cases, however, such agreements now fall within the scope of the competition legislation.

Legislative control of restrictive trading agreements.[78] Until March 1, 2000, the domestic competition law of the United Kingdom was governed by a number of statutes, principally the Restrictive Trade Practices Acts of 1976 and 1977, the Restrictive Practices Court Act 1976, the Resale Prices Act 1976 and the Competition Act 1980, together with parts of the Fair Trading Act 1973. For all purposes relevant to the present work,[79] this legislation has been repealed from the date above and replaced by a single Act, the Competition Act 1998. In place of the earlier law, the Act of 1998 has introduced a new system of regulation, based closely upon Articles 81 and 82 of the Treaty of Rome.[80] The former Monopolies and Mergers Commission has been succeeded by a new body, the Competition Commission, and wide powers of investigation and enforcement are conferred on the Office (formerly the Director General) of Fair Trading ("DFT") and certain sectoral regulators. **3–040**

Part I of the 1998 Act introduced provisions, modelled respectively on Articles 81 and 82, which are referred to in the Act as the "Chapter I" and "Chapter II" prohibitions. Under the Chapter I prohibition, agreements between undertakings, decisions by associations of undertakings or concerted practices which may affect trade within the United Kingdom and which have as their object or effect the prevention, restriction or distortion of competition within the United Kingdom are prohibited, unless exempted in accordance with the provisions of the Act.[81] An agreement which is so prohibited is void.

The Chapter II prohibition proscribes any conduct on the part of one or more undertakings which amounts to the abuse of a dominant position in a market, if it may affect trade within the United Kingdom.[82] Again, there is provision for excluded cases.[83]

The very close similarity between the wording of these provisions of the 1998 Act and Articles 81 and 82 of the Treaty will mean that the domestic competition law of the United Kingdom and that of the European

---

77 [1970] A.C. 403.
78 *Chitty on Contracts* (29th ed.), Vol. 2, para.42–077 *et seq.*; Whish, *Competition Law* (5th ed.), Chs 9, 10.
79 The parts of the Fair Trading Act 1973 dealing with mergers were not affected by the Competition Act 1998, but have since been repealed and replaced by the Enterprise Act 2002, Pt 3.
80 Formerly Arts 85 and 86 respectively. See below, paras 3–041 *et seq.*
81 Competition Act 1998, s.2(1). For the statutory exemptions, see s.3 and Schs 1–4. The Secretary of State also has power to exclude agreements in certain circumstances (s.3(6)), as may the OFT (s.4). Sections 6 *et seq.* make provision for block exemptions.
82 s.18.
83 s.19 and Schs 1, 3.

Community are likely to develop in parallel. Indeed, section 60 of the Act specifically directs that questions arising in relation to competition within the United Kingdom are to be dealt with in a manner which is consistent with the treatment of corresponding questions arising in Community law.

Both the European Court[84] and the Commission[85] have stressed the importance of avoiding conflict in situations where both the domestic courts and the Commission have jurisdiction in competition cases.[86]

3–041 **E.C. competition law.**[87] Agreements between undertakings, decisions by associations of undertakings and concerted practices[88] which may affect trade between Member States and which have as their object or effect the prevention, restriction or distortion of competition within the common market are prohibited by Article 81(1) (formerly Article 85(1)) of the Treaty of Rome.[89] Such agreements or decisions are declared by Article 81(2) to be "automatically void." The provisions of the Treaty are part of the law of the United Kingdom and are directly applicable, to the exclusion of any contrary rule of the national law.[90] In addition to the sanction of nullity, infringements may be dealt with under the administrative powers of the Commission of the European Communities, which may impose fines, may also order the termination of an agreement or practice, and may grant exemptions[91] from the operation of Article 81(1).[92]

---

84 *Delimitis* [1991] I E.C.R. 2303; *Masterfoods v H.B. Ice Cream* [2001] 4 C.M.L.R. 449.

85 Note, however, that by Council Regulation 1/2003 ([2003] O.J. L1/1) (the "Modernisation Regulation") the relationship between the Commission and the courts and authorities in Member States has been significantly redefined, with a greater share of the jurisdiction being given to the latter.

86 See *Chitty on Contracts* (29th ed.), Vol. 2, para.42–067; Bellamy and Child, *European Community Law of Competition* (5th ed.), paras 10–019—10–028.

87 See *Chitty on Contracts* (29th ed.), Vol. 2, paras 42–004 *et seq.*; Albers-Lorens, *EC Competition Law and Policy* (2002); Bellamy and Child, *European Community Law of Competition* (5th ed.); Goyder, *E.C. Competition Law* (4th ed.); Jones and Sufrin *EC Competition Law* (2nd ed.); (2002); Kerse and Khan, *E.C. Antitrust Procedure* (5th ed.); Korah (ed.), *Competition Law of the European Community* (2nd ed.), and *An Introductory Guide to E.C. Competition Law and Practice* (8th ed.); Megret, Waelbroeck *et al.*, *Droit de la CEE* (1972), Vol. 4; Mathijsen, *A Guide to European Community Law* (8th ed.); Van Bael and Bellis, *Competition Law of the EEC* (4th ed.); Whish, *Competition Law* (5th ed.); Wyatt and Dashwood, *European Union Law* (4th ed.). On the application of Competition Law in the European Economic Area, see Chitty, *op cit.*, para.42–010.

88 For the meaning of this term, see *A. C. F. Chemiefarma v E.C. Commission* (the "*Quinine*" case) [1970] E.C.R. 661; *I.C.I. Ltd v E.C. Commission* (the "*Dyestuffs*" case) [1972] C.M.L.R. 557 at 622; *Belgische Radio en Televisie v S.V.S.A.B.A.M.* [1974] I E.C.R. 51; *Société Générale Sucrière v E.C. Commission* (the "*Sugar*" case) [1975] E.C.R. 1663; *S. A. Musique Diffusion Française v E.C. Commission* (the "*Pioneer*" case) [1983] E.C.R. 1825; *A.E.G. Telefunken A.G. v E.C. Commission* [1983] E.C.R. 3151; *Polypropylene* [1988] 4 C.M.L.R. 347; *Hercules v Commission* [1991] II E.C.R. 1711; *Società Italiano Vetro v Commission* [1992] II E.C.R. 1403; *Thyssen Stahl AG v E.C. Commission* [1999] 4 C.M.L.R. 810; *Tate & Lyle p.l.c. v E.C. Commission* [2001] 5 C.M.L.R. 22; *Ferry Operators* [1997] 4 C.M.L.R. 789.

89 See also Arts 14, 15, 23–37, 82 and 86.

90 European Communities Act 1972, s.2; *Bosch v de Geus* [1962] C.M.L.R. 1.

91 Art. 81(3).

92 Reg. 17 of 1962.

The term "undertaking" includes individuals (but not employees), partnerships, companies, trade associations and public bodies[93]; but agreements between associated companies within the same group are normally outside the scope of the Article.[94]

The Article has been interpreted so as to include not only agreements which prevent, restrict or distort competition as between the *parties* to the agreement, but also those that affect the competitive position of one of the parties *vis-à-vis* others (*e.g.* an exclusive distributorship agreement between G, a German manufacturer and C, a French distributor, which restricted the ability of other firms to distribute G's products in France in competition with C[95]).

The Article is not contravened where the effect of the agreement on the market as a whole is insignificant.[96]

Article 81(1) does not apply to pure agency agreements[97] or to agreements which operate exclusively outside the E.U.[98] But an agreement between undertakings outside the Community may fall within Article 85(1) if it affects competition within the E.U.[99]

Block exemptions under Article 81(3) were originally granted separately for exclusive distribution agreements and exclusive purchasing agreements, and also for particular categories of goods and services (e.g. technology transfer and franchising agreements, insurance, and liner shipping consortia); but these have now largely been replaced by a single block exemption covering most vertical agreements.[1] This new block exemption covers agreements between parties who are not in competition with each other, provided that the market share of the supplier (or, in some cases, the buyer) does not exceed 30 per cent of the relevant market. A separate block exemption, however, continues to deal with the distribution of motor vehicles.[2]

Article 82 of the Treaty of Rome prohibits "any abuse by one or more undertakings of a dominant position within the common market in so far as

---

93 But not Member States or governmental authorities: *Diego Cali & Fgili v Servicio Ecologici Porto di Genova* [1997] E.C.R. I–1547.

94 *Hydrotherm v Compact* [1984] E.C.R. 2999; *Polypropylene* [1988] 4 C.M.L.R. 347; *Höfner & Elser v Macroton* [1991] E.C.R. I–1979; *Enichem v Commission* [1991] E.C.R. II–1623; *Commission v Italy* [1998] 5 C.M.L.R. 889; *Suicker Unie v EC Commission* [1975] E.C.R. 1663; *Re UNITEL* [1978] 3 C.M.L.R. 306; *FENIN v EC Commission* [2003] 5 C.M.L.R. 34.

95 *Consten SA and Grundig-Verkaufs GmbH v EC Commission* [1966] C.M.L.R. 418.

96 *Volk v Vervaecke* [1969] C.M.L.R. 273; *Metro-SB-Grossmaärkte GmbH & KG v EC Commission* [1978] 2 C.M.L.R. 1; *Miller International Schallplatten GmbH v EC Commission* [1978] E.C.R. 131; *Delimitis v Henniger Bräu* [1991] I E.C.R. 935; and see the Commission's *Notice on Agreements of Minor Importance* of December 21, 2001, [2001] O.J. C368/13.

97 See the Commission's *Guidelines*, [2000] O.J. C291/1, Section II, paras 12–20, *Société Générale Sucrière v EC Commission* [1975] E.C.R. 1663.

98 *Re Grosspillex* [1964] 2 C.M.L.R. 237; *Re Riekermann* [1968] C.M.L.R. D78; *cf. Tepea BV v EC Commission* [1978] 3 C.M.L.R. 392 (agreement affecting trade only within one Member State and between that Member State and the outside world).

99 *Re Wood Pulp Cartel* [1988] 4 C.M.L.R. 901.

1 Reg. 2790/99, [1999] O.J. L336/21 (the "Verticals" Regulation); see *Chitty on Contracts* (29th ed.), Vol. 2, para.42–046).

2 Reg. 1400/02, [2002] O.J. L203/30.

it may affect trade between Member States." Such abuse may, in particular, consist in imposing unfair purchase or selling prices or other unfair trading conditions, such as refusal of supplies, special rebates and turnover-related discounts.[3]

3–042 **Free movement of goods.**[4] Article 3 of the Treaty of Rome includes among the declared activities of Community law "the prohibition, as between Member States, of customs duties and quantitative restrictions on the import and export of goods,[5] and of all other measures having equivalent effect." This objective is amplified by substantive rules of Community law set out in subsequent Articles of the Treaty.[6] In particular, Article 23 (formerly Article 9) states that the Community shall be based on a customs union, to cover all trade in goods, involving the prohibition of customs duties and comparable charges between one Member State and another, and the adoption of a common customs tariff in relation to non-member countries. Article 28 (formerly Article 30) abolishes quantitative restrictions—that is, quotas— and all measures having equivalent effect as between Member States, subject to certain exceptions (the so-called "escape clauses")[7] justified on the grounds of public morality, public policy or security, health, the protection of national artistic, etc., treasures and the protection of industrial or commercial policy. The abolition of customs barriers and quotas between Member States has been largely achieved; but progress towards the ultimate goal of entirely unrestricted movement of goods within the Community has been less rapid: in particular, there are considerable delays at frontiers caused by the lack of a co-ordinated policy on Value Added Tax, and many technical or "non-tariff" trade barriers continue to hinder the free passage of goods. Nevertheless, there has been much concern to see the position improved, and the European Court has

---

[3] On the meaning of "dominant position" for the purposes of this Article, see *Europemballage and Continental Can Co. Inc. v EC Commission* [1973] C.M.L.R. 199; *United Brands Co. v EC Commission* [1978] C.M.L.R. 429; and see generally *Hoffman-La Roche v EC Commission* [1979] C.M.L.R. 211; *NV Nederlandsche Banden-Industrie Michelin v EC Commission* [1983] E.C.R. 3461; *Garden Cottage Foods Ltd v Milk Marketing Board* [1984] A.C. 130; *Tetra Pak Rausing SA v Commission* (*Tetra Pak I*) [1990] E.C.R. II–309; *Hilti AG v Commission* [1994] 1 C.E.C. 590; *Tetra Pak International DC SA v EC Commission (No.2)* [1997] 4 C.M.L.R. 662 (*Tetra Pak II*).

[4] Burrows, *Free Movement in European Community Law* (1987); Gormley, *Prohibiting Restrictions on Trade within the EEC* (1985); Oliver, *Free Movement of Goods in the European Community* (4th ed.); Bellamy and Child, *European Union Law of Competition* (5th ed.), paras 1–032 *et seq.*; Mathijsen, *Guide to European Community Law* (8th ed.), pp.173 *et seq.*; Whish, *Competition Law* (5th ed.), pp.211 *et seq.*, Woods, *Free Movement of Goods and Services within the EC* (2004); Wyatt and Dashwood; *European Union Law* (4th ed.), pp.364 *et seq.*

[5] "Goods," within Art. 9, is a term "wider than ordinary merchandise": it means "products which can be valued in money and which are capable, as such, of forming the subject of commercial transactions": *EC Commission v Italy (Case 7/68)* [1968] E.C.R. 423. Coins may constitute "goods" if they are not a means of payment within the EU: *R. v Johnson* [1978] E.C.R. 2247.

[6] Arts 23–37.

[7] Art. 30 (formerly Art. 36).

consistently pursued a policy of strict interpretation of the "escape clauses".[8]

6. ASSIGNMENT

Assignment of rights under contract of sale. The rights of either party under a contract of sale may in general[9] be assigned in accordance with the normal rules governing the assignment of choses in action.[10] Thus a claim for the price of goods sold may be assigned by the seller to a third party, and the right to receive a price which is not due, though not immediately assignable, may be the subject of an agreement to assign. In the same way, a buyer's right to have delivery of the goods may be transferred to another party, provided that no additional obligation is sought to be imposed on the seller (*e.g.* to make delivery in a different way). As a general rule,[11] obligations of a party to a contract cannot be assigned, except by a novation with the consent of all parties.[12] It therefore follows that where the right of a party is conditional upon the performance by him of his own obligations, that right cannot be assigned (except with the consent of the other party) in any way which discharges him from his own duty of performance. He may, of course, arrange with the intended assignee that the latter will perform the contract on his behalf, and in many cases the other party will be bound to accept that performance[13]; but the other party will be entitled to hold him liable for any breach that may be committed, and is not bound to look for satisfaction to the substituted party.[14] 3–043

Rights of a personal nature. Where the skill, judgment or other qualities of a party are an essential feature of a contract, it is well settled that the rights which depend on this feature are incapable of assignment. Rights under a contract of service are invariably of this nature, but it is only rarely 3–044

---

[8] Notably in the leading case commonly known as *Cassis de Dijon*: *Rewe v Bundesmonopole-verwaltung für Branntwein (Case 120/78)* [1979] E.C.R. 649.

[9] On the effectiveness of a stipulation in the contract that a right shall be incapable of assignment, see *Linden Gardens Trust Ltd v Lenesta Sludge Disposals Ltd* [1994] 1 A.C. 85, and *Chitty on Contracts* (29th ed.), Vol. 1, para.19–043.

[10] For a full discussion see *Chitty on Contracts* (29th ed.), Vol. 1, Ch.19. An assignment by a buyer of his rights under a contract for the sale of goods must be distinguished from a sub-sale, and in particular a sub–sale effected or performed by a transfer of the documents of title to goods: as to this, see below, paras 7–067 *et seq.*, 15–092 *et seq.* The statutory power of an agent or consignee to exercise the seller's rights against the goods when he has himself paid the price, or is directly responsible for it (Sale of Goods Act 1979, s.38(2), below, para.15–013 *et seq.*) may be regarded as a form of assignment.

[11] Exceptionally, the circumstances may be such as to show that the assignee, in accepting the benefits of the contract, agreed also to accept the associated burdens: see *Tito v Waddell (No. 2)* [1977] Ch. 106 at 290–307; and Chitty, *op. cit.*, paras 19–077—19–078.

[12] Chitty, *op. cit.*, paras 20–076 *et seq.*, 19–084.

[13] *Cf. British Waggon Co. v Lea* (1880) 5 Q.B.D. 149.

[14] *Tolhurst v Assoc. Portland Cement Manufacturers (1900) Ltd* [1903] A.C. 414; *cf. Sorrentino Fratelli v Buerger* [1915] 1 K.B. 307 at 312–313.

that the rights under a contract of sale of goods are construed as essentially personal. In *Cooper v Micklefield Coal & Lime Co.*,[15] however, it was held that the buyer's rights under a contract to deliver coal by instalments on credit were not assignable, the giving of credit being in the circumstances personal to the particular buyer. And in *Kemp v Baerselman*,[16] where a supplier agreed to provide a cake manufacturer with all the eggs that he should require for manufacturing purposes for one year, it was held that the rights of the buyer, being measured by his personal requirements, were not capable of being assigned to a company formed to take over his business. This decision may be contrasted with the earlier case of *Tolhurst v Associated Portland Cement Manufacturers (1900) Ltd*,[17] where the appellant agreed to supply a company for 50 years with all the chalk which it might require at certain works, and the company assigned the benefit of the contract to the respondents. The House of Lords held that the respondents could enforce the contract, since the quantities were to be assessed by reference to the needs of the works in question, and not the requirements of the contracting party as a person.

7. BANKRUPTCY, INSOLVENCY AND DEATH

3–045 **Application of bankruptcy rules.** Section 62(1) of the Sale of Goods Act provides that "the rules in bankruptcy[18] relating to contracts of sale apply to those contracts notwithstanding anything in this Act."[19] The principal statute governing this subject in England is now the Insolvency Act 1986, consolidating the Insolvency Act 1985, which repealed the earlier law (including the Bankruptcy Act 1914 and much of the Insolvency Act 1976). The effect of the bankruptcy of a party to a contract of sale is, in the main, the same as that in regard to contracts generally[20]; but the consequences so far as concerns the rights of the parties in respect of the goods affected may be of particular importance. In addition, the insolvency of a buyer short of or prior to actual bankruptcy is the subject of special provision in certain sections of the Sale of Goods Act 1979.[21]

---

15 (1912) 107 L.T. 457.
16 [1906] 2 K.B. 604. *cf. Nokes v Doncaster Amalgamated Collieries Ltd* [1914] A.C. 1014 at 1024 (amalgamation of companies).
17 [1903] A.C. 414.
18 At the time when the Sale of Goods Acts of 1893 and 1979 were enacted, many of the rules of bankruptcy law were incorporated into company law by statute, so as to apply in the winding up of insolvent companies: see, for the list of these provisions, Companies Act 1985, s.612 (now repealed). The reference in s.62(1) to the "rules of bankruptcy law" would therefore naturally have been taken to extend to the law governing insolvent companies. However, the Insolvency Act 1986 now deals with bankruptcy and corporate insolvency in separate parts (albeit in similar terms), and there is no provision corresponding to the former s.612. But it is submitted that "the rules of bankruptcy law" should not be construed narrowly, in the light of this change, so as to refer only to the bankruptcy of individuals: rather, they should be read broadly as "the rules of insolvency law".
19 Certain bankruptcy rules are also expressly saved by the Factors Act 1889, s.12(2).
20 See on this topic *Chitty on Contracts* (29th ed.), Vol. 1, paras 20–015 *et seq.*
21 ss.39, 41, 44: below, Ch.15.

Effect of bankruptcy and insolvency on contract of sale. Neither the bankruptcy nor the insolvency of a person affects his capacity to contract, or operates of itself to terminate a contract already made by him. But when a bankruptcy order is made, all the property belonging to or vested in the bankrupt at the commencement of the bankruptcy[22] or accruing to him thereafter—including debts due to him and his rights under any contract[23]—passes by law to the trustee of his estate. Prima facie, therefore, it may be crucial to establish whether the property in goods the subject of a contract of sale has passed to the buyer[24] prior to the commencement of the bankruptcy of one party or the other, since a claim to the goods themselves is likely to be of greater value than a demand for payment or the return of a sum of money. 3–046

When a bankruptcy order is made against a bankrupt, the normal legal remedies cease to be available against him, and are replaced by a right to prove in the bankruptcy. But since the trustee in bankruptcy takes "subject to equities", any set-off, cross-claim or defence which might have been pleaded against the bankrupt is available against the trustee.[25]

The trustee in bankruptcy may disclaim onerous property, subject to the right of any person injured by the disclaimer to prove for his loss.[26]

Transactions at an undervalue and preferences. Where a person is adjudged bankrupt and he has, within certain periods before the presentation of the bankruptcy petition, entered into a transaction at an undervalue or given a preference to any person, the court may make an order nullifying the transaction and restoring the parties to their previous position; but such an order cannot be made if it would prejudice a third party who has acted in good faith and without notice of the relevant circumstances.[27] 3–047

Insolvency of buyer. The Sale of Goods Act 1979 makes special provision for certain situations involving an insolvent buyer. For this purpose, a person is deemed to be insolvent who either has ceased to pay his debts in the ordinary course of business, or cannot pay his debts as they become due.[28] Thus, an unpaid seller is entitled to stop the goods in transit, after he 3–048

---

[22] The bankruptcy commences with the day on which the bankruptcy order is made: see Insolvency Act 1986, s.278(a). (Note that the "doctrine" of relation back, and the associated concept of "act of bankruptcy," which gave retrospective operation to some rules of bankruptcy under the former law, were repealed by the Insolvency Act 1985: see s.235(3) and Sch.10, Part III.)

[23] Excluding rights of a personal nature: Chitty, *op. cit.*, para.20–026.

[24] Below, Ch.5 and in particular, in relation to undivided shares in goods forming part of a bulk, paras 5–109 *et seq.*

[25] Insolvency Act 1986, s.323; and *cf.* Chitty, *op. cit.*, paras 20–039 *et seq.*

[26] *ibid.*, s.315; and *cf.* Chitty, *op. cit.*, paras 20–035 *et seq.*

[27] Insolvency Act 1986, ss.339–342, 423. (Note that the "reputed ownership" provision of the former law (Bankruptcy Act 1914, s.38(c)), under which the trustee in bankruptcy could in certain circumstances claim property which did not belong to the bankrupt but was in his possession at the commencement of the bankruptcy, was repealed by the Insolvency Act 1985: see s.235(3) and Sch.10, Part III.)

[28] s.61(4); the words "whether he has committed an act of bankruptcy or not" were deleted from this subsection by the Insolvency Act 1985, s.235(3) and Sch.10, Part III.

has parted with the possession of them, in the case of the insolvency of the buyer,[29] and he may also refuse delivery except against payment of the price in cash, notwithstanding the fact that he has agreed to give credit, and that the property may have passed.[30] Further, although insolvency does not *per se* put an end to a contract, a *notice* of his insolvency given by the buyer which amounts to a declaration of his inability or unwillingness to pay for the goods may in a proper case be treated by the seller as a repudiation of the contract.[31]

3–049 **Companies.**[32] The winding up, or liquidation, of a company, and in particular an insolvent company, bears some similarity to the bankruptcy of a natural person. The legislation governing winding up is now contained in Parts IV and V of the Insolvency Act 1986. The winding up of a company is deemed to commence, in the case of a voluntary liquidation, at the time of the passing of the resolution for winding up[33]; but where the company is wound up compulsorily—*i.e.* by court order—the liquidation is deemed to commence not at the date when the order is made but at the time when the petition for winding up was presented.[34] A disposition of the company's property made after the commencement of a winding up is, unless the court otherwise orders, void[35]; and so it is possible for a contract of sale to be invalidated with retrospective effect. There are legislative provisions for the avoidance of transactions at an undervalue, preferences, etc., in the liquidation of a company similar to those which apply in the bankruptcy of an individual.[36]

3–050 **Death of party.**[37] The death of a party ordinarily has no effect on a contract of sale of goods: the rights and obligations created thereby enure for the benefit of, or against, the estate of the party.[38] An exceptional case is where the personality of a party is essential to the contract, so that his death discharges the obligations by virtue of the doctrine of frustration.[39] But few contracts for the sale of goods will be capable of this interpretation.[40]

---

29 s.39(1)(b); below, paras 15–061 *et seq.*

30 s.41(1)(c); below, paras 15–028 *et seq.*

31 *Re Phoenix Bessemer Steel Co.* (1876) 4 Ch.D. 108; *Morgan v Bain* (1874) L.R. 10 C.P. 15 at 25–26; *ex p. Stapleton* (1879) 10 Ch.D. 586; *Mess v Duffus* (1901) 6 Com.Cas. 165. See below, para.15–108.

32 See above, para.3–045, n.18.

33 Insolvency Act 1986, s.86.

34 Insolvency Act 1986, s.129; but if before the presentation of the petition a resolution for voluntary winding up has been passed, the winding up is deemed to have commenced at the time of the passing of the resolution. Exceptionally, when a winding-up order (instead of an administration order) is made on an application for administration, the winding up is deemed to commence on the making of the order (*ibid.*, Sch.B1, para.13(1)(e)).

35 Insolvency Act 1986, s.127.

36 Insolvency Act 1986, ss.238 *et seq.*; *cf.* para.3–047, above.

37 See generally *Chitty on Contracts* (29th ed.), Vol. 1, paras 20–001 *et seq.*

38 *Werner v Humphreys* (1841) 2 M. & G. 853.

39 *Chitty, op. cit.*, paras 20–006, 23–036.

40 Above, para.3–044.

Part Two

PROPERTY AND RISK

CHAPTER 4

THE TITLE OF THE SELLER

	PARA.
1. The seller's right to sell the goods	4–002
2. Freedom from encumbrances and quiet possession	4–023
3. Sale of a limited title	4–032
4. Analogous provisions	4–035

In general. Section 2(1) of the Sale of Goods Act 1979 defines a contract of sale of goods as "a contract by which the seller transfers or agrees to transfer the property in goods to the buyer for a money consideration, called the price."[1] It is, however, submitted that there can be a valid contract of sale even though, for example, because the goods have been stolen from their true owner, the seller will never be able to transfer the property in the goods to the buyer. An agreement for the sale of the property of another, as opposed to an actual sale, is not null and void.[2] If the seller agrees to divest himself of the general or absolute property in the goods in favour of the buyer, there is a contract of sale notwithstanding that he is not the owner of the goods and has no right to sell them.[3] Moreover, at common law, it did not necessarily follow from the very act of selling the goods that the seller warranted his title or right to sell.[4] There was an implied undertaking on his part that he did not *know* that he had no right to sell; but otherwise, in the absence of such fraud or knowledge, the seller of specific goods was not liable in damages for bad title unless there was an express warranty, or the equivalent to it, by declaration or conduct.[5] Usage of trade might be sufficient to raise such a warranty; and in ordinary sales, *e.g.* from an open shop or warehouse, the seller was considered to warrant that the buyer would have a good title to keep the goods purchased.[6] **4–001**

---

[1] See above, para.1–025.

[2] *National Employers' Mutual General Insurance Assn Ltd v Jones* [1990] 1 A.C. 24 at 50; *cf.*, *ibid.* pp.39–40, 42 (CA) (this point did not arise on appeal to the House of Lords). *cf.* also *Rowland v Divall* [1923] 2 K.B. 500 at 506; *Customs and Excise Commissioners v Oliver* [1980] 1 All E.R. 353 at 355. The concept of property is discussed by Kiralfy, 12 M.L.R. 424 (1949), and by Battersby and Preston, 35 M.L.R. 268 at 272–275 (1972) who suggested that "property" in the Act meant "a title to the absolute legal interest in the goods solds": below, para.5–001, n.1. *cf.* Battersby [2001] J.B.L. 1.

[3] But if both the seller and buyer know the goods have been stolen or otherwise unlawfully acquired the contract may be unenforceable on the ground of illegality: see Theft Act 1968, ss.22, 24. *cf.* below, para.4–032, n.5.

[4] *Noy's Maxims* (c.42).

[5] *Furnis v Leicester* (1619) Cro. Jac. 474; *Crosse v Gardner* (1688) Carth. 90; *Medina v Stoughton* (1699) 1 Salk. 210; *Peto v Blades* (1814) 5 Taunt. 657; *Early v Garrett* (1829) 9 B. & C. 928 at 932; *Morley v Attenborough* (1849) 3 Exch. 500 at 513; *Sims v Marryat* (1851) 17 Q.B. 281. "Warranty" is used here in the sense of guarantee.

[6] *Morley v Attenborough*, above, at p.512; *Eichholz v Bannister* (1864) 17 C.B.(N.S.) 708.

However, the circumstances surrounding the transaction might create no such inference, and the sale would then be subject to the principle of *caveat emptor* .[7]

1. THE SELLER'S RIGHT TO SELL THE GOODS

4–002 **Right to sell the goods.** Section 12(1) of the Sale of Goods Act 1979[8] provides that in a contract of sale, other than one to which subsection (3) of section 12 applies,[9] there is an implied term on the part of the seller that in the case of a sale he has a right to sell the goods, and in the case of an agreement to sell he will have such a right at the time when the property is to pass.[10] The liability thus imposed is a strict liability, and does not depend upon the fault or knowledge of the seller. Nor does it depend upon any disturbance of the buyer's possession of the goods by the true owner.[11] It has been stated that the corresponding provision in the 1893 Act re-enacted the rule of common law,[12] but it seems that it both clarified the rule and extended the protection afforded to the buyer.[13]

4–003 A seller will clearly have no "right to sell the goods" where he has no title to the goods and can pass none to the buyer. There will likewise be a breach of this term if he has only a special property or right to possession of the goods, *e.g.* as bailee, so that the buyer does not acquire the general property in them.[14] But in *Niblett v Confectioners' Materials Co. Ltd*[15] it was held that the words "a right to sell the goods" embraced more than an ability to pass a good title. In that case, the claimants bought from the defendants a quantity of tinned milk to be shipped from New York to London, payment against documents. Some of the milk arrived bearing the labels "Nissly" brand. These infringed the trade mark of third parties, at whose instance the milk was seized by the customs. The claimants obtained the release of the goods by removing and destroying the labels, and then sold them unlabelled for the best price obtainable. The Court of Appeal held that they were entitled to damages for breach of section 12(1)[16] since

[7] See, *e.g. Peto v Blades*, above; *Morley v Attenborough*, above; *Chapman v Speller* (1850) 14 Q.B. 621; *Page v Cowasjee Eduljee* (1866) L.R. 1 P.C. 127 at 144; *Bagueley v Hawley* (1867) L.R. 2 C.P. 625; *Re Rogers* (1874) L.R. 9 Ch.App. 432 at 437; *Wood v Baxter* (1883) 49 L.T. 45; and below, para.4–032. By 1893, the exceptions could be stated to have become the rule: *Rowland v Divall* [1923] 2 K.B. 500 at 505.

[8] By s.1 of the Supply of Goods (Implied Terms) Act 1973 this provision became s.12(1)(a) instead of s.12(1) of the 1893 Act, but again became s.12(1) in the 1979 Act. See s.12(6) and Sch.1, para.3, of the 1979 Act.

[9] See below, para.4–032.

[10] Compare the corresponding provisions in the Vienna Convention on Contracts for the International Sale of Goods, Arts 30, 41–44 (see above, para.1–024).

[11] As in the case of s.12(2)(b); below, para.4–025.

[12] *Rowland v Divall* [1923] 2 K.B. 500 at 505 ("but as a condition, not a warranty").

[13] *Niblett v Confectioners' Materials Ltd* [1921] 3 K.B. 387 at 402; see above, para.4–001.

[14] Sale of Goods Act 1979, s.61(1): "Property". See also *McDonald v Provan (of Scotland Street) Ltd*, 1960 S.L.T. 231 ("cannibalised" vehicle sold).

[15] [1921] 3 K.B. 387, disapproving *Montforts v Marsden* (1895) 12 R.P.C. 266 at 269.

[16] The court also considered whether there had been a breach of the condition as to merchantable quality contained in s.14(2) of the (unamended) 1893 Act; see below, para.11–025.

the defendants did not have a right to sell the goods at the time when the property was to pass. Scrutton L.J. said[17]: "The defendants impliedly warranted that they had then a right to sell them. In fact they could have been restrained by injunction from selling them, because they were infringing the rights of third persons. If a vendor can be stopped by process of law from selling he has not the right to sell." Atkin L.J. considered that, although the defendants could have passed the property in the goods but for the intervention of the third party, they had nevertheless no right to sell the goods owing to "the existence of a title superior to that of the vendor, so that the possession of the vendee may be disturbed."[18] The claimants could have been restrained at the suit of the third parties in the same way as the defendants.

It is submitted that this case does not lay down any general principle to the effect that there is a breach of section 12(1) whenever the seller could be restrained by process of law from selling the goods, even if the possession of the buyer could in no way be disturbed. The words "a right to sell the goods" mean, it is submitted, that the seller has the power to vest full and complete rights over the goods in the buyer. The seller makes no promise about his own proprietary rights; only that he will be able to create the appropriate rights in the buyer.[19] Thus if a seller without title sells goods in circumstances in which the buyer acquires a good title to the goods, there would be no breach of section 12(1) of the Act.[20] Still less would the buyer be entitled to claim that the seller had no "right to sell the goods" merely because the sale exposed the seller to a penalty imposed on him personally by the criminal law. The *ratio decidendi* of *Niblett's* case does not, it is submitted, extend beyond the situation where the property rights which the seller purports to create in the buyer are encumbered by a right vested in a third party such as a copyright, design, patent, or trade mark, or right of prohibition or seizure, which affects the goods in the hands of the buyer.[21] 4–004

Time at which the right to sell must exist. Where the contract of sale purports to effect a present transfer of the property in the goods from the seller to the buyer, the seller must have a right to sell the goods at the time 4–005

---

[17] At p.398.

[18] At p.402.

[19] *Karlshamns Oljefabriker v Eastport Navigation Corp. (The Elafi)* [1981] 2 Lloyd's Rep. 679 at 685.

[20] *Niblett v Confectioners' Materials Co. Ltd* [1921] 3 K.B. 387 at 401; *Anderson v Ryan* [1967] I.R. 34; *R. v Wheeler* (1991) 92 Cr.App.R. 279 at 283. However, in *Barber v NWS Bank Plc* [1996] 1 W.L.R. 641, where a conditional sale agreement contained an express term that the seller was the owner of the goods, it was held that the buyer could rescind the contract and recover the instalments paid notwithstanding that he might have acquired a good title under s.27(3) of the Hire-Purchase Act 1964 (see below, para.7–087) because s.27(6) of the 1964 Act preserved the liability of the seller. *cf.*, U.S. Uniform Commercial Code, para.2–312(1).

[21] See also *Egekvist Bakeries v Tizel & Blinick* [1950] 1 D.L.R. 585 (affirmed [1950] 2 D.L.R. 592); *Lloyds & Scottish Finance Ltd v Modern Cars & Cars & Caravans (Kingston) Ltd* [1966] 1 Q.B. 764 (below, paras 4–026, 4–030, 7–113); *J. Barry Winsor and Associates Ltd v Belgo-Canadian Manufacturing Co. Ltd* (1976) 76 D.L.R. (3d) 685 (law prohibiting resale). Contrast Atiyah, *The Sale of Goods* (11th ed.), p.113; Palmer and McKendrick, *Interests in Goods* (2nd ed., 1998), Ch.12, p.308.

of the contract. But where the contract of sale is merely an agreement to sell,[22] it is sufficient if the seller has a right to sell the goods at the time when the property is to pass. So, for example, in the case of a conditional sale agreement under which the purchase price is payable by instalments and the property in the goods is not to pass to the buyer until all the instalments are paid notwithstanding that the buyer is to have possession of the goods in the meantime, section 12(1) does not require that the seller has a right to sell the goods when the agreement is made but only at the time when the property is to pass. If, therefore, before that time it emerges that the seller has no title to the goods agreed to be sold, the buyer will be unable to treat the contract as repudiated and recover the instalments paid unless he proves that it will be impossible for the seller to pass a good title when the payments are completed[23] or that the situation is such as to lead a reasonable person to conclude that the seller does not intend, or will not then be able, to do so.[24] However, it may be an express term of such an agreement that the seller is the owner of the goods at the time the agreement is entered into,[25] or it may be a necessary inference from the terms of the agreement and the surrounding circumstances that the seller must be the owner of the goods at the time of their delivery to the buyer and remain their owner until the time when the property is to pass.[26]

4–006 **Remedies of the buyer.** As regards England and Wales and Northern Ireland, the term implied by section 12(1) is a condition.[27] Breach of this condition may give rise to a right on the part of the buyer to treat the contract as repudiated[28] and to claim damages for any loss suffered by reason of the breach.[29] Further, where the breach consists of a failure by the seller to pass a good title to the goods sold, the buyer is prima facie entitled to recover the whole of the purchase price paid as on a total failure of consideration.[30] This principle was established by the Court of Appeal in *Rowland v Divall* .[31] In that case, the defendant bought a motor-car in good

---

[22] See above, para.1–026.
[23] *Chitty on Contracts* (29th ed.), Vol.1, para.24–028.
[24] *ibid.*, para.24–018.
[25] *Barber v NWS Bank Plc* [1996] 1 W.L.R. 641; below, para.4–021.
[26] See *Karflex Ltd v Poole* [1933] 2 K.B. 251, as interpreted in *Mercantile Union Guarantee Corp. Ltd v Wheatley* [1938] 1 K.B. 490, and *Warman v Southern Counties Car Finance Corp. Ltd* [1949] 2 K.B. 576 (hire-purchase).
[27] Sale of Goods Act 1979, s.12(5A).
[28] *ibid.*, s.11(3).
[29] *ibid.* s.51.
[30] *ibid.* s.54. See, before the 1893 Act, *Eichholz v Bannister* (1864) 17 C.B. (N.S) 708.
[31] [1923] 2 K.B. 500, followed in *Butterworth v Kingsway Motors Ltd* [1954] 1 W.L.R. 1286; *Margolin v Wright Pty Ltd* [1959] Arg.L.R. 988; *McNeill v Assoc. Car Markets Ltd* (1962) 35 D.L.R. (2d) 581; *Barber v NWS Bank Plc* [1996] 1 W.L.R. 641. See also *Karflex Ltd v Poole* [1933] 1 K.B. 251; *Mercantile Union Guarantee Corp. Ltd v Wheatley* [1938] 1 K.B. 490; *Warman v Southern Counties Car Finance Corp. Ltd* [1949] 2 K.B. 576; *Malaney v Union Transport Finance Ltd*, 1959 S.L.T. 37; *Rover International Ltd v Cannon Film Sales Ltd* [1989] 1 W.L.R. 912 at 925, 938; *David Securities Pty Ltd v Commonwealth Bank of Australia* (1992) 175 C.L.R. 353 at 382; *Baltic Shipping Co. v Dillon* (1993) 176 C.L.R. 344 at 351. If the "price" paid by the buyer consists wholly or in part of chattels, the buyer cannot recover the chattels given in part exchange from a person who buys them from the seller in good faith and for value: *Robin and Rambler Coaches Ltd v Turner* [1947] 2 All E.R. 284.

faith from a thief and resold it to the claimant, a car dealer, for £334. The claimant repainted the car and exposed it for sale in his showroom for two months until he sold it to a third party for £400. Two months later, the police took possession of the car on behalf of the true owner. The claimant refunded to the third party the money which he had been paid and brought an action to recover from the defendant the £334.[32] The Court of Appeal held that his action should succeed. Even though the claimant and his sub-purchaser had had the use of the car for four months and could not restore the car to the defendant, nevertheless the consideration for the payment had totally failed: "the buyer has not received any part of that which he contracted to receive—namely, the property and right to possession—and, that being so, there has been a total failure of consideration."[33] It was not unreasonable in this case that the claimant should recover the whole of the purchase price since he had paid out an amount in excess of this sum to the third party. But the principle laid down has been criticised[34] on the ground that its application may result in the buyer recovering more than the loss which he has actually suffered. Where the buyer has had the use and benefit of the goods for a considerable time before the seller's lack of title is discovered, he is not compelled to bring this into account. It is also to be noted that the application of this principle does not appear to depend upon any claim being made against the buyer either by the true owner or by a sub-purchaser. Although there would no doubt be difficulty in calculating the financial value of the benefit derived by the buyer from his possession of the goods,[35] especially where the goods have passed through a chain of buyers, it is submitted that the rule in *Rowland v Divall* deserves reconsideration, and that any claim by the buyer should be limited to the recovery of the actual loss which he has sustained by reason of the defect of title.[36] In any event, there must be considerable doubt whether the principle thus laid down can properly be applied where the buyer's inability to return the goods is solely due to the fact that he has consumed or resold them, at any rate if no claim has been made against him. In *Rowland v Divall*, the car had been seized by the police, and it was said[37]: "the reason of [the

---

32 The original owner's insurers sold the car to the claimant for £260, and the defendant contended that his liability was limited to that amount: see the report in (1923) 129 L.T. 757.

33 At p. 507. See also ss.2(1), 54 of the Act.

34 Law Reform Committee, Twelfth Report (*Transfer of Title to Chattels*), 1966, Cmnd. 2958, para.36. See also Treitel, 30 M.L.R. 139 at 145–149 (1967); Law Commission Report (1969), Law Com. No.24, paras 11–19; Law Commission Working Paper No. 65 (1975); Law Commission Report (1983), Law Com. No.121, paras 1.9–1.12; Law Commission Working Paper No.85 (1983), paras 6.1–6.21. See the discussion of this point in Palmer and McKendrick, *Interests in Goods* (2nd ed., 1998), Ch.12, p.318; Goff and Jones, *Law of Restitution* (6th ed.), pp.20–14, 20–017; Burrows, *Law of Restitution* (2nd ed.), pp.340–341.

35 This consideration was one which led the Law Commission in its Final Report on Sale and Supply of Goods (1987), Law Com. No.160, paras 6.1–6.5, to recommend no change in the law; but the Commission also appeared to approve the substance of the rule.

36 But if a claim has been made against him by the true owner for the full value of the goods, then his minimum loss should be the amount of the true owner's claim.

37 [1923] 2 K.B. 500 at 505.

claimant's] inability to return the car—namely, the fact that the defendant had no title to it—is the very thing of which he is complaining, and . . . it does not lie in the defendant's mouth to set up as a defence to the action his own breach of the implied condition that he had a right to sell." But this reasoning would not apply where *restitutio in integrum* was precluded by an act on the part of the buyer, and his inability to return the goods was in no way due to the seller's defect of title.[38]

4–007 **Improvements.**[39] A statutory qualification to the principle in *Rowland v Divall* exists by virtue of section 6(3) of the Torts (Interference with Goods) Act 1977.[40] If proceedings are brought by the buyer against the seller for recovery of the purchase price because of failure of consideration, then, if the seller acted in good faith, an allowance is to be made, where appropriate,[41] for any improvement to the goods effected by the seller[42] or by any person from whom the seller derived (whether immediately or not) his supposed "title" to the goods.[43] The improver must have improved the goods in the mistaken but honest belief that he had a good title to them.[44] Thus if a stolen car is purchased by A, who installs a new engine in the honest belief that he is the owner of the vehicle, and the car is then sold by A to B, in any proceedings by B against A to recover the purchase price on the ground of failure of consideration, the amount recoverable may be reduced to the extent to which the value of the goods is attributable to the improvement.[45] Likewise, in the above example, if there were a further sale of the car by B to C, and C claimed to recover the purchase price from B, the same allowance might fall to be made even though A, and not B, was the improver of the vehicle.[46] The reason for this provision is that, by subsections (1) and (2) of section 6 of the 1977 Act, the damages for wrongful interference recoverable by the true owner from A, B or C are to be reduced to the extent of the improved value.[47]

4–008 **Change of position.** If the buyer claims to recover the purchase price on the ground of failure of consideration, this is a claim in restitution. In principle, therefore, it would be open to the seller to raise the defence of change of position, which was recognised by the House of Lords in *Lipkin Gorman v Karpnale Ltd* [48] as a general defence to a restitutionary claim. The defence was there stated to be "available to a person whose position has so changed that it would be inequitable in all the circumstances to require him to make restitution or alternatively to make restitution in

---

[38] *Cf. Linz v Electric Wire Co. of Palestine Ltd* [1948] A.C. 371.
[39] See Palmer and McKendrick, *Interests in Goods* (2nd ed., 1998), Ch.36.
[40] Operative June 1, 1978: SI 1978/627 (c.15).
[41] Such an allowance might not be appropriate if the true owner has, in fact, repossessed the goods from the buyer in that action: see below, para.7–005.
[42] s.6(1).
[43] ss.6(2), (4).
[44] s.6(1).
[45] ss.6(2), (3).
[46] s.6(2).
[47] See also ss.3(7), 9(3); and below, para.7–005.
[48] [1991] 2 A.C. 548 at 558, 562, 567–568, 577.

full".[49] In *Barber v NWS Bank Plc*[50] the seller was in breach of an express term as to title and the buyer sued to recover the purchase price. The seller raised the defence of change of position. The Court of Appeal considered the defence very briefly and found it not to have been made out on the facts of the case.[51] The seller was therefore required to refund the purchase price in full. The court did not, however, specifically reject the defence. Nevertheless, it is submitted that the defence should not be available to a seller who, even innocently, has in breach of an express or implied term of the contract failed to convey a good title to the goods which he purported to sell. In *Lipkin Gorman v Karpnale Ltd*[52] Lord Goff said that "it is commonly accepted that the defence should not be open to a wrongdoer" and it is submitted that "wrongdoing" can include a breach of contract by the payee from whom recovery is sought where it is that breach of contract which provides the basis for the restitutionary claim. It is therefore not inequitable to disregard any change of position by the seller as a result of the payment and to require him to make full restitution of the money which he has obtained in return for an undertaking which he has, in breach of contract, failed to fulfil.

Acceptance of the goods. By section 11(4) of the Sale of Goods Act 1979[53] the acceptance of the goods by the buyer will normally take away his right to treat the contract as repudiated for breach of condition, and he will be compelled to sue for damages for breach of warranty only.[54] In *Rowland v Divall*[55] it was argued for the seller that the case fell within this provision, but Atkin L.J. held[56] that this subsection had no application to the breach of section 12(1) of the Act in that case.[57] 4–009

Feeding title. There is authority[58] for the view that the principle in *Rowland v Divall* will not be applicable if, before the buyer elects to treat the contract of sale as repudiated, his title has been "fed" by the 4–010

---

49 At p.580. See Goff and Jones, *Law of Restitution* (6th ed.), Ch.40.
50 [1996] 1 W.L.R. 641.
51 At p. 648.
52 [1991] 2 A.C. 548 at 579.
53 Previously s.11(1)(c) of the 1893 Act, as amended by s.4(1) of the Misrepresentation Act 1967. *cf.* s.14 of the Supply of Goods (Implied Terms) Act 1973 (conditional sales).
54 See below, para.12–038.
55 [1923] 2 K.B. 500.
56 At pp.506–507.
57 *Cf.* Ellinger, 5 Victoria Univ. of Wellington L.R. 168 (1969). It is arguable that s.11(4) should apply to the claim to reject under s.12(1), even if it does not apply to the claim to recover the purchase price for total failure of consideration. *Quaere* whether s.11(4) would apply if the buyer knows of the seller's lack of title. (See Atiyah, *The Sale of Goods* (11th ed.), p.119, n.34).
58 *Lucas v Smith* [1926] V.L.R. 400 at 403–404; *Butterworth v Kingsway Motors Ltd* [1954] 1 W.L.R. 1286; *Patten v Thomas Motors Pty Ltd* [1965] N.S.W.R. 1457. See also *Whitehorn Bros v Davison* [1911] 1 K.B. 463 at 475; *Blundell-Leigh v Attenborough* [1921] 3 K.B. 235 at 240, 242; *Robin and Rambler Coaches Ltd v Turner* [1947] 2 All E.R. 284. In *Bennett v Griffin Finance* [1967] 2 Q.B. 46 at 50, Winn L.J. expressly reserved his opinion on this point.

subsequent acquisition by the seller of a good title to the goods sold. In *Butterworth v Kingsway Motors Ltd*[59] the hirer of a motor-car under a hire-purchase agreement wrongfully sold the car to A during the currency of the agreement. A resold the car to B, who in his turn sold it to the defendants. The claimant bought the car from the defendants and used it for several months before he was informed that the car was the property of the finance company which had let it on hire to the hirer. The claimant immediately wrote to the defendants rescinding the contract of sale and demanding the return of the purchase price. Eight days later the hirer paid to the finance company the balance outstanding under the hire-purchase agreement and exercised the option to purchase contained therein. Pearson J. held that the claimant was entitled to recover from the defendants the price paid by him as money paid upon a consideration which had totally failed, since, at the time he rescinded the contract, the hirer had not yet purchased the car.[60] But the acquisition of a good title by the hirer went to feed the title of the intermediate purchasers.[61] No decision was reached on the point whether there would have been a total failure of consideration if the hirer had purchased the goods *before* the claimant purported to rescind the contract of sale. But Pearson J. considered that it would be an extraordinary position if the claimant should then seek to say: "There has been a total failure of consideration by purchase of this car, although here is the car in my possession and I am entitled to retain it against the world."[62] If this view is correct, then a buyer whose title has been fed cannot subsequently elect to rescind the contract of sale and recover the purchase price.

4–011 In *West (H.W.) Ltd v McBlain*,[63] however, Sheil J. rejected the proposition that the subsequent acquisition by the seller of a good title to the goods can affect the remedies of the buyer, since "you can never revivify that which never had life." A literal application of the wording of section 12(1) would support this view. Where there is merely an agreement for a sale, there will be no breach of section 12(1) if the seller acquires a good title before the time at which the property is to pass. But where a seller without title purports to effect a present sale of the goods, or where he fails to pass the property to the buyer at the time when it is agreed that it shall pass, the wording of section 12(1) might be said to rule out any argument that the buyer's right to treat the contract as repudiated could be affected by the subsequent acquisition by the seller of a good title to the goods, whether or not the buyer had previously elected to exercise that right. It is also difficult to justify the principle of "feeding title" analytically.[64] The opinion has been expressed[65] that it is analogous to that of "feeding the

---

59 [1954] 1 W.L.R. 1286.

60 See also *Lucas v Smith*, above; *McNeill v Assoc. Car Markets Ltd* (1962) 35 D.L.R. (2d) 581.

61 The defendants, whose title had been fed, were nevertheless entitled to recover from their immediate vendor the amount which they had been compelled to refund to the claimant, less the value of the car at the time their title was fed.

62 At p.1295.

63 [1950] N.I. 144.

64 See Ellinger, 5 Victoria Univ. of Wellington L.R. 168 (1969).

65 *Lucas v Smith* [1926] V.L.R. 400 at 403–404; *Patten v Thomas Motors Pty Ltd* [1965] N.S.W.R. 1457.

estoppel" which is applied between the grantor and grantee of an interest in land.[66] But the analogy is not exact since the buyer of goods (unlike the grantee of an interest in land), even if precluded from rescinding the contract of sale, can nevertheless sue for damages on the ground that the seller had originally no right to sell the goods.[67] It would also seem difficult to account for this situation by reference to section 11(4) of the Act[68] as in *Rowland v Divall* this provision was said to be inapplicable to sales without title.[69] Nevertheless, it is submitted that, for the reasons stated by Pearson J. in *Butterworth v Kingsway Motors Ltd*,[70] a subsequent acquisition of title by the seller should go to feed the title of the buyer and that, if the buyer has not then elected to treat the contract as repudiated, he should not be entitled to do so, nor should he be able to recover the purchase price.

Settlement with true owner. By section 5(1) of the Torts (Interference with Goods) Act 1977,[71] where damages for wrongful interference are, or would fall to be, assessed on the footing that the claimant is being compensated—(a) for the whole of his interest in the goods, or (b) for the whole of his interest in the goods subject to a reduction for contributory negligence,[72] payment of the assessed damages (under all heads),[73] or as the case may be settlement of a claim for damages for the wrong (under all heads),[74] extinguishes the claimant's title to that interest. Thus if the true owner claims damages for wrongful detention of goods,[75] or for their conversion, from a buyer who has bought goods from a seller without title, full payment by the buyer of a money judgment or settlement of the true owner's claim will extinguish the true owner's title to the goods. Although the subsection might appear to be merely negative in effect, it is submitted that such payment or settlement operates (as it does in the case of a satisfied judgment at common law)[76] to vest in the buyer the true owner's title to the goods. In such an event, there is some doubt whether the buyer could treat the contract of sale as repudiated and recover the purchase price once his title has thus been "fed".[77] He would, however, be able to 4–012

[66] *Webb v Austin* (1844) 7 Man. & G. 701; *Rajapakse v Fernando* [1920] A.C. 892 at 897; *Universal Permanent Building Society v Cooke* [1952] Ch. 95; *First National Bank Plc v Thompson* [1996] Ch. 231.

[67] *Butterworth v Kingsway Motors Ltd* [1954] 1 W.L.R. 1286; see above, para.4–010, n.61.

[68] *Cf.* Ellinger, 5 Victoria Univ. of Wellington L.R. 168 (1969).

[69] [1923] 2 K.B. 500 at 506–507. But the buyer might be said to be suing under s.12(2) of the Act: below, para.4–023.

[70] Above, para.4–010.

[71] See also s.5(4). *Cf.* s.5(3), (5); and above,

[72] *Cf.* s.11(1).

[73] See s.3 of the 1977 Act.

[74] *ibid.*

[75] Under s.3(2) of the Act, a judgment for damages may be given in lieu of, or as an alternative to, an order for specific delivery of the goods.

[76] *U.S.A. v Dollfus Mieg* [1952] A.C. 582 at 622. *Cf. Ellis v John Stenning & Son* [1932] 2 Ch.81 (unsatisfied judgment). See above, para.1–072.

[77] *Ed Learn Ford Sales Ltd v Giavannone* (1990) 74 D.L.R. (4th) 761. But see *Rowland v Divall* [1923] 2 K.B. 500 (above, para.4–006, n.32) where the claimant had in fact purchased the car from the true owner's insurers.

recover from the seller damages consisting of the amount which he had paid to the true owner (including costs), together with his own costs reasonably incurred in defending any action against him.[78] The amount of those damages might well exceed the purchase price of the goods. In a Scottish case, *Wilson v Barclay*,[79] the buyer of goods "paid off" the true owner and then sought to recover the sum thus paid from the seller, but it was held that he could recover the purchase price of the goods and no more. It is difficult, however, to see why this should be so, if the settlement with the true owner is reasonable, and it is submitted that the buyer's claim should not be limited in this way.[80]

4–013 Section 5(3) of the Torts (Interference with Goods) Act 1977 expressly declares that section 5(1) is not to apply "where damages are assessed on the footing that the claimant is being compensated for the whole of his interest in the goods, but the damages paid are limited to some lesser amount by virtue of any enactment or rule of law." Where goods let on hire-purchase have been wrongfully sold by the hirer, the measure of damages recoverable by the owner of the goods from the buyer is the balance outstanding under the hire-purchase agreement if less than the value of the goods.[81] If section 5(3) were held to apply to this situation, it would mean that payment or settlement by the buyer of the outstanding balance would not extinguish the true owner's title or vest that title in the buyer. It is, however, submitted that damages in such a case are assessed on the footing that the owner is being compensated in full for the whole of his interest in the goods: his interest is only a limited interest since the hirer acquires, by virtue of the hire-purchase agreement, a proprietary interest in the goods beyond that of a simple bailee for hire.[82] On this assumption, if the buyer pays or settles the outstanding balance, the title of the owner will vest in him.[83] Moreover, it would be expected that this acquisition of title by the buyer would "feed" the title of subsequent purchasers of the goods.[84] However, in *Worcester Works Finance Ltd v Medens Ltd*,[85] where goods let

---

[78] See below, para.4–016.
[79] (1957) 73 Sh.Ct.Rep. 114.
[80] *Little v Kingsbury Motors Ltd* (1961) 112 L.J. 60 (Cty.Ct.); *Bowmaker (Commercial) Ltd v.Day* [1965] 1 W.L.R. 1396. See also *Stock v Urey* [1954] N.I. 71 and below, para.4–029 (s.12(2)(b) of the Act).
[81] *Wickham Holdings Ltd v Brooke House Motors Ltd* [1967] 1 W.L.R. 295; *Belvoir Finance Co. Ltd v Stapleton* [1971] 1 Q.B. 210; *Chubb Cash Ltd v John Crilley & Son* [1983] 1 W.L.R. 599. *Cf. Astley Industrial Trust Ltd v Miller* [1968] 2 All E.R. 36. See also s.3(6) of the Torts (Interference with Goods) Act 1977, and below, para.7–002, n.12.
[82] *Whitely v Hilt* [1918] 2 K.B. 808; *Karflex Ltd v Poole* [1933] 1 K.B. 251 at 264, 265; *Wickham Holdings Ltd v Brooke House Motors Ltd*, above, at p.300; *Belvoir Finance Co. Ltd v Stapleton*, above, at p.220. *Cf. Helby v Matthews* [1895] A.C. 471 at 481. See also above, para.1–072.
[83] He would be entitled to recover from the hirer damages consisting of the outstanding balance and any costs which he had paid to the owner, together with his own costs reasonably incurred in defending any action against him; see above, para.4–011; below, para.4–017.
[84] See above, para.4–010.
[85] (1973) 117 S.J. 143.

on hire-purchase were wrongfully disposed of by the hirer to B, the Court of Appeal held that the fact that the owner had negotiated a cash settlement with B in respect of B's liability in conversion did not preclude the owner from claiming damages in conversion against the defendants, who subsequently purchased the goods.

Chain transactions.[86] Goods may be sold many times over in breach of section 12(1) before they are ultimately traced by the true owner. A thief, for example, may sell the goods which he has stolen to A, who sells to B, who sells to C. Each party in this chain transaction will be liable for conversion of the goods, for each sale and delivery of the goods, albeit innocent, constitutes an act inconsistent with the true owner's title to the goods. In practice, however, the true owner will seek to recover possession of the goods or their value[87] from the buyer who is actually in possession of them, *i.e.* from C, and it is against C that an action for wrongful interference will be brought. C will then claim against B as a Part 20 defendant, and, in turn, B will claim against A as a Part 20 defendant (2nd claim). Since the thief will normally be insolvent or will have disappeared when the day of reckoning arrives, the person who will have to bear the loss is A, the first innocent purchaser in the chain. But if any buyer in the centre of the chain is insolvent, the person who purchased the goods from him will have to bear the loss. Such a purchaser cannot sue the previous sellers in the chain for between him and them there is no privity of contract, and sales of goods do not, in English law, effect an assignment by the seller to the buyer of the seller's rights under a previous contract of sale. Nor, it is submitted, can any buyer who is sued in conversion claim contribution from previous sellers under the Civil Liability (Contribution) Act 1978.[88] They are not liable "in respect of the same damage"[89] since each successive sale is a separate and distinct conversion of the goods. 4–014

Where A sells goods without title to B, who resells them to C from whom they are repossessed by the true owner, the measure of the damages recoverable by B from A will depend on whether or not it was in the reasonable contemplation of A and B at the time of the contract of sale that B would, or would probably, resell the goods. If a probable resale of the goods was in the contemplation of the parties at that time, then B will be entitled to recover from A the amount of any sums which he has paid, or has become liable to pay, to his sub-purchaser, C, or the amount of the purchase price paid by B to A,[90] whichever is the greater. If, however, such a resale was not contemplated, then the measure of the damages recover- 4–015

[86] See also below, paras 17–081 *et seq*.
[87] *Cf. Wickham Holdings Ltd v Brooke House Motors Ltd* [1967] 1 W.L.R. 295; above, para.4–013, n.82.
[88] But see s.9 of the Torts (Interference with Goods) Act 1977.
[89] Civil Liability (Contribution) Act 1978, s.1.
[90] Unless B's title has been fed: see above, para.4–010, n.61. Also if B pays out the true owner in order to give title to C, B can recover only the sum paid out and not the whole of the purchase price: *Ed Learn Ford Sales Ltd v Giavannone* (1990) 74 D.L.R. (4th) 761.

able was stated by Pearson J. in *Butterworth v Kingsway Motors Ltd* [91] to be the lesser of the two following amounts, *viz* . (a) the purchase price paid by B to A, and (b) the amount of any sums which B has paid, or has become liable to pay, to his sub-purchaser, C, less the profit (if any) made by B on the resale.

4–016 In assessing the liability of each seller in the chain to his immediate buyer, the costs reasonably incurred by the buyer must be taken into account, and if there is a chain of forward sales the costs of all parties are passed on cumulatively up the chain to the first solvent seller.[92] Although it could be argued that, in the example given above, A should not be bound to compensate B for any costs incurred by B in relation to his sub-purchaser, C, where no resale of the goods was contemplated, it may be that knowledge of an intended resale is this time immaterial.[93] A will, of course, be liable for B's costs in the proceedings which A has unsuccessfully defended against B. But in assessing the amount of the sums which B has paid, or become liable to pay, to C,[94] this amount will include the costs payable by B to C, and B's own costs incurred in resisting the claim by C, provided that it was reasonable in the circumstances to resist C's claim.[95] If C in his turn has reasonably resisted a claim against him by the true owner, then the costs of these proceedings will also have to be taken into account. Thus in *Bowmaker (Commercial) Ltd v Day*,[96] a hirer of a motor-car wrongfully sold it to A, who sold it to B, who sold it to C, who sold it to the claimant. The car was then seized by the true owner. The claimant brought an action against C claiming damages for breach of warranty of title, and against the owner claiming damages for conversion. C joined B as third-party, and B joined A as fourth party. MacKenna J. held that the car was throughout the property of the true owner and that: (i) since the claimant had acted reasonably in joining the true owner as a party to the action, his costs as between solicitor and client[97] of suing the true owner were recoverable from C, and judgment should be entered against C for these costs, with costs as between party and party; (ii) in the third-party proceedings, C was entitled to be indemnified by B in respect of the damages and costs which he, C, was liable to pay to the claimant, and to be reimbursed for his own costs as between solicitor and client of defending the claimant's claim, and that C was also entitled to the costs of the third party proceedings; (iii) A was likewise liable to indemnify B against the sums payable by B to C for damages and costs and against B's own costs, as between solicitor and client, of defending C's claim.

4–017 **Buyer lets goods on hire-purchase.** Where a seller of goods without title sells the goods to a buyer and it is in the reasonable contemplation of the parties at the time of the sale that the buyer will, or will probably, let the

---

[91] [1954] 1 W.L.R. 1286 at 1297, 1299, 1300.
[92] *Kasler and Cohen v Slavouski* [1928] 1 K.B. 78.
[93] *Butterworth v Kingsway Motors Ltd* [1954] 1 W.L.R. 1286; *Bowmaker (Commercial) Ltd v Day* [1965] 1 W.L.R. 1396. But the point was not argued in these two cases. *Cf.* below, para.17–083.
[94] See above, para.4–015.
[95] *Butterworth v Kingsway Motors Ltd*, above.
[96] [1965] 1 W.L.R. 1396.
[97] Assessment is now on a "standard basis"; CPR, r.44.4.

goods on hire-purchase to a third party, the measure of damages recoverable by the buyer appears to be as follows: (i) any sum which the buyer is liable to pay to the hirer to compensate him for the loss which he suffers by reason of the repossession of the goods by the true owner; (ii) any sums unpaid by the hirer under the hire-purchase agreement with the buyer, including the amount of the buyer's finance charges,[98] and (iii) any costs payable to the hirer,[99] and the buyer's own costs of resisting an action by the hirer if it should have been reasonable to do so.

Exemption clauses. [1] The ability of the seller to exclude by contract the application of section 12(1) is limited by statute in two respects. First, by section 6(1)(a) of the Unfair Contract Terms Act 1977,[2] liability for breach of the obligations arising from section 12 of the Sale of Goods Act 1979 cannot be excluded or restricted[3] by reference to any contract term. This prohibition is not limited to a "business liability",[4] or to cases where the buyer deals as consumer.[5] Prima facie, therefore, the term implied by section 12(1) will be implied notwithstanding any contractual provision to the contrary. This will be so notwithstanding any contract term which applies or purports to apply the law of some country outside the United Kingdom (a "choice of law" clause), where (either or both)—(a) the term appears to the court or arbitrator to have been imposed wholly or mainly for the purpose of enabling the party imposing it to evade the operation of the 1977 Act, or (b) in the making of the contract one of the parties dealt as consumer,[6] and he was then habitually resident in the United Kingdom, and the essential steps necessary for the making of the contract were taken there, whether by him or by others on his behalf.[7] However, where the law applicable to the contract is the law of any part of the United Kingdom only by choice of the parties (and apart from that choice would be the law of some country outside the United Kingdom) section 6 of the 1977 Act does not operate as part of the law applicable to the contract.[8] Further, the prohibition against exclusion or restriction of liability imposed by section 6 4–018

98 *Bowmaker (Commercial) Ltd v Day* [1965] 1 W.L.R. 1396 at 1397. But it is submitted that, in appropriate cases, an allowance should be made for the accelerated return to the owner of his capital outlay: *Overstone Ltd v Shipway* [1962] 1 W.L.R. 117; *Yeoman Credit Ltd v McLean* [1962] 1 W.L.R. 131; *Goulston Discount Co. Ltd v Sims* (1967) 111 S.J. 682, CA. See also *Lloyds & Scottish Finance Ltd v Modern Cars and Caravans (Kingston) Ltd* [1966] 1 Q.B. 764 (s.12(2)).

99 *Cf. Bankamerica Finance Ltd v Nock* [1988] 1 A.C. 1002.

1 See Palmer and McKendrick, *Interests in Goods* (2nd ed., 1998), Ch.12, p.314.

2 As amended by s.63 of and Sch.2. to the 1979 Act. See also the Consumer Transactions (Restriction on Statements) Order 1976, SI. 1976/1813, as amended by SI 1978/127 (criminal offence), and below, para.14–142.

3 See s.13 of the 1977 Act.

4 s.6(4) of the 1977 Act.

5 See s.12 of the 1977 Act and below, para.13–071.

6 *ibid.*

7 s.27(2) of the 1977 Act. See also the Contracts (Applicable Law) Act 1990, Sch.1, arts 3(3), 5, 7(2), 16 and below, paras 13–101, 25–037, 25–042, 25–054, 25–094, 25–160.

8 s.27(1) of the 1977 Act, as amended by s.5 of and Sch.4 to the Contracts (Applicable Law) Act 1990. See below, paras 13–100, 25–091.

of the 1977 Act does not apply to liability arising under an international supply contract[9] (which includes a contract for the international sale of goods).[10]

4–019 Secondly, where the seller, in making the contract, is acting for purposes relating to his business[11] and the buyer is a consumer, *i.e.* a natural person who, in making the contract, is acting for purposes outside his business,[12] a contract term which purports to exclude the term implied by section 12(1) of the 1979 Act or to exclude or restrict the liability of the seller for breach of that implied term may not be binding on the consumer by virtue of the Unfair Terms in Consumer Contracts Regulations 1999.[13] It is submitted that, in a contract of sale, any attempt to exclude or limit the rights of a consumer to reject the goods and recover the price paid or to recover damages in the event that the seller has no right to sell the goods would prima facie be regarded as improper[14] and "unfair" within the meaning of those Regulations,[15] and hence not binding on the consumer.[16]

4–020 If, however, the contract of sale falls within one of the exceptions provided for in the 1977 Act and falls outside the 1999 Regulations, for example, because the buyer is not a consumer, then it is open to the seller by means of an appropriately drafted exemption clause to exclude or restrict his liability for breach of the obligations arising from section 12(1), or to exclude or restrict any right or remedy of the buyer in respect of that liability.[17] Whether or not any particular exemption clause is sufficient to relieve the seller of liability depends upon whether the clause, construed in the light of its wording and the commercial or other purpose of the contract, was intended by the parties to cover the liability which it sought to exclude or restrict.[18] But it has been said that an exemption clause should not be construed so as to lead to an incongruity or absurdity, or so as to deprive the contract of all contractual effect.[19] It would therefore seem that

[9] Defined in s.26(3), (4) of the 1977 Act; see below, paras 13–099, 18–281.
[10] s.26(1) of the 1977 Act.
[11] Reg.3(1) "seller"; below, para.14–031.
[12] Reg.3(1); below, para.14–031.
[13] SI 1999/2083 as amended by SI 2001/1186. These Regulations revoked and replaced the Unfair Terms in Consumer Contracts Regulations 1994, SI 1994/3159. See below, para.14–030.
[14] Sch.2, para.1(b).
[15] Reg.5(1).
[16] Reg.8.
[17] See the discussion on this point in Hudson, 20 M.L.R. 236 (1957); Samek, 33 Aust.L.J. 392 (1960); Guest, 77 L.Q.R. 98 at 100 (1961); Hudson, 24 M.L.R. 690 (1961); Reynolds, 79 L.Q.R. 534 at 541 (1963); Battersby and Preston, 35 M.L.R. 268 at 274 (1972). Twelfth Report of the Law Reform Committee (1966), Cmnd. 2958, para.38.
[18] *Suisse Atlantique Société d'Armement Maritime SA v NV Rotterdamsche Kolen Centrale* [1967] 1 A.C. 361; *Photo Production Ltd v Securicor Transport Ltd* [1980] A.C. 827; see below, paras 13–043, 13–049.
[19] *Suisse Atlantique Société d'Armement Maritime SA v NV Rotterdamsche Kolen Centrale*, above, at pp.398, 412, 432. See also *Tor Line AB v Alltrans Group of Canada Ltd* [1984] 1 W.L.R. 48 at 58–59.

a court would be reluctant to conclude that an exemption clause, framed in general terms, was intended by the parties to relieve the seller of his obligation to pass the property in the goods to the buyer. The court would have to be satisfied that the parties truly intended merely the sale and purchase of a chance (*emptio spei*)[20] that the seller might or might not have a good title to the goods,[21] for "the whole object of a sale is to transfer property from one person to another."[22] A clause which merely restricted his liability or restricted any right or remedy available to the buyer might, however, be upheld.

Express undertaking as to title. The seller may in the contract of sale 4–021
expressly warrant that he is the owner of the goods or that he has a good title to them or that they are his sole and unencumbered property. Such an express undertaking would probably be construed as a condition[23] and might at first sight appear to add little to the term implied by section 12(1). However, it is submitted that the presence of an express undertaking could enlarge the remedies of the buyer. First, in the case of an agreement to sell, the seller would warrant that he is the owner of the goods at the time the agreement is entered into and not merely that he will be the owner of the goods at the time when the property is to pass.[24] Secondly, in those situations where the seller himself has no title to the goods but nevertheless passes a good title to the buyer,[25] it is arguable that the buyer has the right to reject the goods and treat the contract as repudiated for breach of condition[26] even though the sale has created in him rights which are good against the true owner of the goods and the rest of the world. The contrary argument is that the buyer's title has been "fed" by operation of law and that he cannot rely on the breach of condition when he is in the same position as he would have been had the undertaking been duly fulfilled.

An express undertaking as to title would also negate any inference of an intention that the seller should transfer only such title as he or a third person might have.[27]

However, if the buyer "deals as consumer",[28] it is unlikely that a breach of the express term[29] will entitle him to the special consumer remedies

[20] See below, para.4–032. See also *Northwest Co. Ltd v Merland Oil Co. of Canada and Gas and Oil Products Ltd* [1936] 4 D.L.R. 248.
[21] *Suisse Atlantique Société d'Armement Maritime SA v NV Rotterdamsche Kolen Centrale*, above, at pp. 392, 399, 427, 432.
[22] *Rowland v Divall* [1923] 2 K.B. 500 at 507.
[23] *Barber v NWS Bank Plc* [1996] 1 W.L.R. 641.
[24] *ibid*.
[25] See above, para.4–004.
[26] s.11(3).
[27] s.12(3); below, para.4–032.
[28] By s.61 (5A) references to this expression are to be construed in accordance with Pt I of the Unfair Contracts terms Act 1977; See below para.13–071
[29] s.48 F; below para.12–074.

conferred by Pt 5A of the Act[30] as these appear to be limited to breaches of terms that relate to the physical characteristics[31] of the goods.[32]

4–022 **Fraud or misrepresentation by seller.** The liability of the seller will prima facie not be affected by the fact that he knows he has no right to sell the goods. Such knowledge, however, if coupled with a misrepresentation, may render him liable in damages for deceit. The measure of such damages will be assessed in accordance with tortious principles,[33] which may give the buyer the right to recover an amount more or less than that which would be recoverable in an action for breach of contract.[34] Otherwise, in the absence of misrepresentation, the deliberate concealment by the seller of his lack of a right to sell the goods, *e.g.* a defective title, would not appear to enlarge the buyer's remedies. However, the deliberate commission of a breach of section 12 of the Act by the seller in circumstances in which it is unlikely to be discovered for some time will postpone the running of the limitation period against the buyer[35] and it may also prevent the seller from relying upon an otherwise valid exemption clause inserted in a contract, for no exemption clause can protect a person against liability for personal fraud.[36]

An innocent misrepresentation by the seller as to his right to sell the goods[37] will also render him liable in damages unless he proves that he had reasonable ground to believe and did believe up to the time the contract was made that the facts represented were true.[38] Again, the damages will be assessed according to the rules for damages in tort.[39] In any event, whether the representation is fraudulent or innocent, the buyer is entitled[40] to rescind the contract of sale.[41]

---

[30] s.48A; below para.12–072.

[31] *Cf.* See also "repair as defined in s.61(1) "bring the goods into conformity with the contract".

[32] See art. 2 of Directive 1999/44/EC and below para.14–012.

[33] *Doyle v Olby (Ironmongers) Ltd* [1969] 2 Q.B. 158; *Smith New Court Securities Ltd v Scrimgeour Vickers (Asset Management) Ltd* [1997] A.C. 254 at 263, 267.

[34] Liability is based on the "out of pocket rule", although consequential damages can be recovered (even if unforeseeable, provided these are not too remote), but not damages for "loss of the bargain". However, "lost opportunity" damages may be recoverable: *East v Maurer* [1991] 1 W.L.R. 461; *Clef Aquitaine SARL v Laporte Materials (Barrow) Ltd* [2001] 1 Q.B. 488; see below, para.12–012.

[35] Limitation Act 1980, s.32. But see below, para.4–030.

[36] *Pearson (S.) & Son Ltd v Dublin Corp.* [1907] A.C. 351; *Boyd & Forrest v Glasgow & SW Ry*, 1915 S.C.(H.L.) 21 at 36. See also Misrepresentation Act 1967, s.3 (as amended by s.8 of the Unfair Contract Terms Act 1977). But this principle does not necessarily apply to cases of mere non-disclosure, as opposed to a positive representation.

[37] Being a statement of private rights, as distinct from the general law, it is treated as a misrepresentation of fact: see *Chitty on Contracts* (29th ed.), Vol.1, para.6–011.

[38] Misrepresentation Act 1967, s.2(1); see below, para.12–014.

[39] *Royscot Trust Ltd v Rogerson* [1991] 2 Q.B. 297 (measure of damages for fraud applied); see below, para.12–015.

[40] Unless the right to rescind has been lost or rescission is refused: see below, paras 12–005—12–009. See also above, para.1–009.

[41] Where a seller without title nevertheless passes a good title to the buyer (see above, para.4–004), it is possible that the court would exercise its discretion to refuse rescission under s.2(2) of the Misrepresentation Act 1967; below, para.12–004. See *R. v Wheeler* (1991) 92 Cr.App.R. 279.

2. FREEDOM FROM ENCUMBRANCES AND QUIET POSSESSION

Freedom from encumbrances. By section 12(2)(a) of the Sale of Goods Act 1979,[42] in a contract of sale, other than one to which subsection (3) of section 12 applies,[43] there is also "an implied term that the goods are free, and will remain free until the time when the property is to pass, from any charge or encumbrance not disclosed or known to the buyer before the contract is made."[44] It seems probable that this implied term was originally derived from the law of land.[45] But, unlike the similar covenant encountered in relation to conveyances of land,[46] the term set out in section 12(2)(a) will be broken by the mere existence of a charge or encumbrance over the goods; breach does not, as in the case of land,[47] depend upon an actual assertion of the charge or encumbrance by claim or demand on the part of a third party.[48] The words "charge or encumbrance" denote some proprietary right, whether legal or equitable, over or affecting the goods,[49] or a possessory right such as a lien.[50] It is to be observed that the wording of section 12(2)(a) differs from that of section 12(1), where the operative time at which the seller must have a right to sell the goods is the time of the passing of property. If the contract of sale is not a sale but an agreement to sell,[51] the goods must be free from any charge or encumbrance at the time of the agreement to sell and must remain free until the time when the property is to pass. It is, however, only possible to apply the section 12(2)(a) wording literally to the case of an agreement to sell specific goods in the ownership of the seller, since the goods may be unascertained or in the ownership of some third party or even not in existence at the time of an agreement to sell. 4–023

---

[42] s.12(3) of the (unamended) 1893 Act. See s.1 of and Sch.1, para.3, to the 1979 Act. See also U.S. Uniform Commercial Code, para.2–312(1)(b).
[43] See below, para.4–032.
[44] *McDonald v Provan (of Scotland Street) Ltd*, 1960 S.L.T. 231 ("cannibalised" vehicle sold).
[45] It has, on the other hand, been said that this term derives from a passage in Benjamin, *Sale of Personal Property*, (2nd ed.), p.574, which pointed out that the transfer of documents of title would not be a sufficient delivery by the seller if the goods represented by the documents were subject to liens or charges in favour of the bailee of the goods; but such a situation would relate to the seller's duty to deliver the goods (see *Playford v Mercer* (1870) 22 L.T. 41).
[46] See Conveyancing Act 1881, s.7; Law of Property Act 1925, s.76 and Sch.2, Pt I; (now repealed); Law of Property (Miscellaneous Provisions) Act 1994, s.3; Megarry and Wade, *Law of Real Property* (6th ed.), para.5–058.
[47] *Vane v Lord Barnard* (1708) Gilb.Rep. 6 at 8; *Nottidge v Dering* [1909] 2 Ch. 647 at 656 (affirmed [1910] 1 Ch. 297). *Cf. Turner v Moon* [1901] 2 Ch. 825. See also *Collinge v Underwood* (1839) 9 A. & E. 633 (limitation); *Hughes–Hallett v Indian Mammoth Gold Mines Ltd* (1883) 22 Ch.D. 561.
[48] The original warranty contained in the unamended Act of 1893 (s.12(3)) was expressed *in futuro*, and probably similarly required an assertion of the charge or encumbrance for breach.
[49] *Athens Cape Naviera SA v Deutsche Dampfschiffahrtgesellschaft "Hansa" Aktiengesellschaft* [1985] 1 Lloyd's Rep. 528 at 532 ("encumbrances"). See also *Jones v Barnett* [1899] 1 Ch.611 at 620; *Smith v Goral* [1932] 3 D.L.R. 328.
[50] *ibid.*
[51] See above, para.1–026.

4–024 As regards England and Wales and Northern Ireland the term implied by section 12(2)(a) is a warranty.[52] The measure of the damages recoverable for breach of this warranty is uncertain. Where a claim is made by the owner or other person entitled to the benefit of the charge or encumbrance, there will be a breach of the term as to quiet possession implied by section 12(2)(b) and the damages will be assessed accordingly.[53] But if no such claim is asserted, it is arguable that the damages will be nominal only, since the buyer will not have sustained any loss as a result of the breach. In such a case, however, it is submitted that the buyer is entitled to damages representing any diminution in the value of the goods,[54] having regard to the likelihood that such a claim will in future be made, or to recover any expenses reasonably incurred by him to discharge or remove the charge or encumbrance and acquire an unencumbered title to the goods.

4–025 **Quiet possession.** By section 12(2)(b) of the Sale of Goods Act 1979, in a contract of sale, other than one to which subsection (3) of section 12 applies, there is also "an implied term that the buyer will enjoy quiet possession of the goods except so far as it may be disturbed by the owner or other person entitled to the benefit of any charge or encumbrance so disclosed or known."[55] Breach of this term is not confined to physical interference with the buyer's possession of the goods. In *Niblett v Confectioners' Materials Co. Ltd*,[56] Atkin L.J. considered that the term[57] had been broken on the facts of that case,[58] since the buyers had to strip off the labels before they could assume possession of the goods, and in *Microbeads AG v Vinhurst Road Markings Ltd*,[59] the Court of Appeal held that a breach occurred upon a claim being made by the patentee of a patent affecting the goods. The use of the word "possession" suggests that the term takes effect upon delivery of the goods to the buyer, whether or not the property in the goods has then passed,[60] and that it would cease to have effect if the buyer has consumed the goods[61] or parted with possession of them, for example, by their sale and delivery to a sub-purchaser.

4–026 The extent of the implied term is nevertheless not entirely clear.[62] It can scarcely be intended to impose upon a seller the obligation of guaranteeing the buyer's possession against every disturbance that may occur.[63] The term

[52] s.12(5A).
[53] See below, para.4–029.
[54] s.53. See *Turner v Moon* [1901] 2 Ch. 825 (land). Alternatively, the buyer might claim a declaration and indemnity against future claims: see below, para.17–104.
[55] Derived from s.12(2) of the unamended Act of 1893: "shall have and enjoy quiet possession of the goods."
[56] [1921] 3 K.B. 387 at 407. The other members of the Court of Appeal did not consider this point.
[57] *i.e.* the warranty contained in s.12(2) of the unamended 1893 Act.
[58] See above, para.4–003.
[59] [1975] 1 W.L.R. 218; see below, para.4–027.
[60] But interference with the buyer's right to possession would probably suffice.
[61] *Ocean Chemical Transport Inc. v Exnor Craggs Ltd* [2000] 1 Lloyd's Rep. 446 at [13].
[62] See Palmer and McKendrick, *Interests in Goods* (2nd ed., 1998), Ch.12, p.310.
[63] *Empresa Exportadora de Azucar v Industria Azucarera Nacional SA (The Playa Larga)* [1983] 2 Lloyd's Rep. 171 at 178; *Gatoil International Inc. v Tradax Petroleum Ltd* [1985] 1 Lloyd's Rep. 350 at 361.

will certainly protect the buyer against disturbance of his possession by a breach of the contract of sale or tortious act on the part of the seller.[64] It should also protect him against disturbance by the lawful acts of third persons,[65] unless such disturbance is due to some act or omission on the part of the buyer or of a person deriving title from or connected with the buyer. But in *Niblett's* case,[66] Atkin L.J. suggested that the term resembled the covenant for quiet enjoyment of real property by a vendor who conveyed as beneficial owner in being subject to certain limitations. If this analogy were followed, the term would extend only to disturbance by the lawful acts of third persons claiming under the seller and not of those claiming by title paramount.[67] In *Mason v Burningham*,[68] however, Lord Greene M.R. was not prepared to introduce any such gloss, and the Court of Appeal held that the term had been broken when the buyer was compelled to return the goods bought to their true owner. Lord Greene's interpretation has subsequently been adopted by the Court of Appeal[69] and is clearly the correct one on the present wording of section 12(2)(b).[70] On the other hand, the term will not normally protect the buyer against disturbance of his possession by the wrongful acts of third parties.[71] If, however, such wrongful acts occur with the concurrence or connivance of the seller and are sufficiently connected with the contract of sale,[72] the seller will incur liability. In *Empresa Exportadora de Azucar v Industria Azucarera Nacional SA (The Playa Larga)*[73] the seller under a c. & f. contract was involved in and party to a decision by the seller's government to withdraw at the port of discharge a ship loaded with the goods appro-

---

[64] *Niblett v Confectioners' Materials Co. Ltd* [1921] 3 K.B. 387 at 403; *Healing (Sales) Pty Ltd v English Electrix Pty Ltd* (1968) 121 C.L.R. 584; *Gatoil International Inc. v Tradax Petroleum Ltd*, above, at pp. 360, 361; *Rubicon Computer Systems Ltd v United Paints Ltd* (2000) 2 T.C.L.R. 454.

[65] *Niblett v Confectioners' Materials Co. Ltd*, above, at p. 403; *Microbeads AG v Vinhurst Road Markings Ltd* [1975] 1 W.L.R. 218; *Louis Dreyfus Trading Ltd v Reliance Trading Ltd.* [2004] EWHC 525 (Comm.), [2004] 2 Lloyd's Rep. 243. *cf. Gatoil International Inc. v Tradax Petroleum Ltd*, above, at p. 361, where Bingham J. referred to an "interference with possession or quiet enjoyment persisted in as a result of any act or omission of [the sellers] by any third party with whom they were in contractual relations."

[66] [1921] 3 K.B. 387 at 398, 403.

[67] *Jones v Lavington* [1903] 1 K.B. 253; *Markham v Paget* [1908] 1 Ch. 697; Megarry and Wade, *The Law of Real Property* (6th ed.), paras 5–051, 14–197.

[68] [1949] 2 K.B. 545 at 563.

[69] *Microbeads v Vinhurst Road Markings Ltd* [1975] 1 W.L.R. 218 at 223, 227. See also *Egekvist Bakeries v Tizel & Blinick* [1950] 2 D.L.R. 585.

[70] The words "the owner" in s.12(2)(b) refer, not to the owner of the goods, but to the owner of "any charge or encumbrance so disclosed or known."

[71] Even if claiming through the seller: *Chantflower v Priestley* (1603) Cro.Eliz. 914; *Sanderson v Berwick-on-Tweed Corp* (1884) 13 Q.B.D. 547; *Malzy v Eichholz* [1916] 2 K.B. 308; *Bergfeldt v Markell* [1921] 1 W.W.R. 453; *Matania v National Provincial Bank Ltd* [1936] 2 All E.R. 633; *Niblett v Confectioners' Materials Ltd*, above, at p. 403.

[72] In *The Playa Larga*, *infra* (at p.180) the relationship of buyer and seller was held still to exist as the buyer acquired conditional property only in the goods on acceptance of the shipping documents, retaining his right to reject the goods on arrival.

[73] [1983] 2 Lloyd's Rep. 171.

priated to the contract. It was held that the seller had committed a breach of the implied term as to quiet possession.

4–027 The term is not confined to a disturbance of quiet possession arising from a defect of title existing at the time of the sale. In *Microbeads AG v Vinhurst Road Markings Ltd*[74] the goods sold were, at the time the property in them was to pass to the buyer, not the subject of any patent. Subsequently a patent specification was published, letters patent granted and a claim for infringement made against the buyer. The Court of Appeal held that, although there was no breach of the term implied by section 12(1) of the Act, the seller was in breach of the term as to quiet possession.[75]

4–028 **Disclosed or known encumbrances.** The term as to freedom from encumbrances will not be implied in relation to any charge or encumbrance disclosed[76] or known[77] to the buyer before[78] the contract is made, and there is no implied term that the buyer will enjoy quiet possession of the goods in so far as it may be disturbed by the owner or other person entitled to the benefit of any charge or encumbrance so disclosed or known.

4–029 **Remedies of the buyer.** As regards England and Wales and Northern Ireland the term implied by section 12(2)(b) is a warranty.[79] The buyer is not without more[80] entitled to treat the contract as repudiated by reason of a breach of the term, and can claim damages for breach of warranty only.[81] The measure of damages is to be ascertained by reference to subsections 53 (2) and (3) and section 54 of the 1979 Act.[82] Where, as a result of the breach, the buyer is evicted from possession of the goods, the normal measure of damages appears to be the value of the goods at the time of eviction.[83] So if the buyer has repaired or improved the goods while they

---

[74] [1975] 1 W.L.R. 218, followed in *Gencab of Canada Ltd v Murray-Jensen Manufacturing Co. Ltd* (1980) 114 D.L.R. (3d) 92.

[75] See also *Smith v Goral* [1952] 3 D.L.R. 328; *Healing (Sales) Pty Ltd v English Electrix Pty Ltd* (1968) 121 C.L.R. 584; *The Playa Larga*, above. *cf.* U.S. Uniform Commercial Code, para.2–312(3). Contrast *Montforts v Marsden* (1895) 12 R.P.C. 266 (disapproved in *Niblett v Confectioners' Materials Co. Ltd*, above).

[76] The unamended 1893 Act (s.12(3)) contained the word "declared" and not "disclosed."

[77] *Cf. Zuker v Paul* (1982) 135 D.L.R. (3d) 481 (registration in statutory register insufficient).

[78] The unamended 1893 Act (above) referred to "before or at the time when the contract is made."

[79] Sale of Goods Act 1979, s.12(5A).

[80] But see *Rubicon Computer Systems Ltd v United Paints Ltd* (2000) 2 T.C.L.R. 454 (where the installation and activation by the seller of a time lock device in a computer system was held by the Court of Appeal to be a repudiatory breach).

[81] Sale of Goods Act 1979, ss.11(3), 61(1): "Warranty".

[82] *Louis Dreyfus Trading Ltd v Reliance Trading Ltd* [2004] EWHC 525 (Comm.), [2004] 2 Lloyds Rep. 243. See below, para.17–047. See also s.54; below, para.16–045.

[83] *Healing (Sales) Pty Ltd v English Electrix Pty Ltd*, above. See also *Jenkins v Jones* (1882) 9 Q.B.D. 128 (land). *cf. Lloyds & Scottish Finance Ltd v Modern Cars and Caravans (Kingston) Ltd* [1966] 1 Q.B. 764 and *Rubicon Computer Systems Ltd v United Paints Ltd*, above (recovery of price paid); *The Playa Larga* [1983] 2 Lloyd's Rep. 171 (market value of substitute goods on earliest date after eviction on which buyer should have covered himself in the market by buying in).

were in his possession, the damages recoverable from the seller on eviction can include the amount expended on the goods, provided that it was in the ordinary course of events to effect such repairs and improvements, even though the seller had no foreknowledge that this damage was likely to result.[84] Where the buyer is not evicted from possession, the measure of damages is prima facie the difference between the value of the goods at the time of delivery to the buyer and the value they would have had if free from the adverse claim.[85] If the buyer reasonably incurs expenditure to avoid or discharge the adverse claim, that sum can be recovered as damages from the seller.[86] The buyer may also recover any legal costs reasonably incurred by him in attempting to resist the adverse claim[87] and any damages which he may be forced to pay to the claimant.[88] Consequential losses, if not too remote, are recoverable. Thus, in appropriate cases,[89] the buyer may recover damages for loss of profits[90] or for deterioration of the goods[91] caused by the breach.

Overlap with section 12(1). It is clear that liability under section 12(2) may often coincide with that under section 12(1). Nevertheless there is a significant difference in the wording of the two provisions.[92] First, in England and Wales and Northern Ireland the term implied by section 12(1) is a condition, whereas the terms implied by section 12(2) are warranties. Secondly, section 12(1) is related to defect of title at the time of sale,[93] whereas section 12(2)(b) covers a situation where the buyer's right to quiet possession is disturbed before or after the time when property passes. It is possible for the seller to transfer to the buyer a good title to the goods, but the buyer's possession may yet be subsequently disturbed, *e.g.* by the 4–030

---

[84] *Mason v Burningham* [1949] 2 K.B. 545. See also *Bunny v Hopkinson* (1859) 27 Beav. 565; *Rolph v Crouch* (1867) L.R. 3 Ex. 44 (land). S.6 of the Torts (Interference with Goods) Act 1977 (above, para.4–007) does not appear to apply to such a claim.

[85] *Louis Dreyfus Trading Ltd v Reliance Trading Ltd* [2004] EWHC 525 (Comm), [2004] 2 Lloyd's Rep. 243. But this presumption may be rebutted; *ibid*.

[86] *Niblett v Confectioners' Materials Co. Ltd*, [1921] 3 K.B. 387. *Stock v Urey* [1954] N.I. 71; *Ed Learn Ford Sales Ltd v Giavannone* (1990) 74 D.L.R. (4th) 761. See also *Smith v Compton* (1832) 3 B. & Ad.407; *Lock v Furze* (1866) L.R. 1 C.P. 441; *G.W. Ry v Fisher* [1905] 1 Ch. 316 (land).

[87] *Lloyds & Scottish Finance Ltd v Modern Cars and Caravans (Kingston) Ltd*, above; *Bowmaker (Commercial) Ltd v Day* [1965] 1 W.L.R. 1396. See also *Smith v Compton*, above; *Williams v Burrell* (1845) 1 C.B. 402; *Rolph v Crouch*, above; *Sutton v Baillie*, (1891) 65 L.T. 528 (land).

[88] *Williams v Burrell*, above; *Rolph v Crouch*, above (land).

[89] See below, para.17–066.

[90] *Lloyds & Scottish Finance Ltd v Modern Cars and Caravans (Kingston) Ltd*, above. See also *Rolph v Crouch*, above; *Grosvenor Hotel Co. v Hamilton* [1894] 2 Q.B. 836 (land).

[91] *Gatoil International Inc. v Tradax Petroleum Ltd* [1985] 1 Lloyd's Rep. 350 at 361.

[92] *Microbeads AG v Vinhurst Road Markings Ltd* [1975] 1 W.L.R. 218.

[93] *ibid*. *cf.* s.12(2)(a).

seller,[94] or by the lawful action of a third party,[95] or by a claim for infringement of a patent granted after the time when the property passes.[96] Thirdly, the term as to quiet possession is only broken when the buyer's possession is actually disturbed,[97] and the limitation period will begin to run against him from this time,[98] whereas the term implied by section 12(1) is breached at the latest at the time when the property is to pass.

4–031 **Exemption clauses.** The prohibition imposed by section 6(1)(a) of the Unfair Contract Terms Act 1977[99] against exclusion or restriction of liability applies equally to liability arising under section 12(2) as it does to liability arising under section 12(1) and is subject to the same exceptions. If the buyer is a consumer an exemption clause may also not be binding on him under the Unfair Terms in Consumer Contracts Regulations 1999.[1]

3. SALE OF A LIMITED TITLE[2]

4–032 **Limited title.** Subsections (1) and (2) of section 12 are excluded,[3] and different terms are implied, in a contract to which section 12(3) of the 1979 Act applies,[4] *viz.* "a contract of sale in the case of which there appears from the contract or is to be inferred from its circumstances an intention that the seller should transfer only such title as he or a third person may have." It is therefore quite clear that the seller may, by an express term of the contract, indicate his intention to transfer only such a title. The true consideration would then seem to be the assignment of the right, whatever it is, that the seller or the third party has at the time of the sale.[5] There is, however, more

---

[94] *Healing (Sales) Pty Ltd v English Electrix Pty Ltd* (1968) 121 C.L.R. 584; *Rubicon Computer Systems Ltd v United Paints Ltd* (2000) 2 T.C.L.R. 454. See also *The Playa Larga* [1983] 2 Lloyd's Rep. 171; above, para.4–026.

[95] *Lloyds & Scottish Finance Ltd v Modern Cars and Caravans (Kingston) Ltd*, above (but it is submitted that, in this case, there was also a breach of s.12(1); see above, para.4–004). See also *Smith v Goral* [1952] 3 D.L.R. 328; *Louis Dreyfus Trading Ltd v Reliance Trading Ltd* [2004] EWHC 525 (Comm), [2004] 2 Lloyd's Rep. 243.

[96] *Microbeads AG v Vinhurst Road Markings Ltd*, above.

[97] *Howell v Richards* (1809) 11 East 633 at 642; *Baynes & Co. v Lloyd & Sons* [1895] 1 Q.B. 820 at 824; *Niblett v Confectioners' Materials Co. Ltd* [1921] 3 K.B. 387 at 403; *Microbeads AG v Vinhurst Road Markings Ltd*, above.

[98] Limitation Act 1980, s.5. As a result, the seller could remain potentially liable for a very long period of time. *Cf. The Playa Larga*, above, at p.178.

[99] See above, para.4–018.

[1] SI 1999/2083, as amended by SI 2001/1186; above, para.4–019, below, para.14–030.

[2] See Palmer and McKendrick, *Interests in Goods* (2nd ed., 1998), Ch.12, p.314.

[3] See the opening words of s.12(1)(2); above, paras 4–002, 4–023, 4–024.

[4] Introduced by s.1 of the Supply of Goods (Implied Terms) Act 1973: see s.12(6) of and Sch.1, para.3 to the 1979 Act.

[5] *Chapman v Speller* (1850) 14 Q.B. 621 at 624. It would seem that this might be the proper construction of the contract if the buyer knew of the seller's defective title: *Clark v England* (1916) 29 D.L.R. 374 at 376; *Northwest Co. Ltd v Merland Oil Co. of Canada and Gas and Oil Products Ltd* [1936] 4 D.L.R. 248 (but see above, para.4–001, n.3). See also the Law Commission's First Report on *Exemption Clauses in Contracts (Amendments to the Sale of Goods Act 1893)* (1969), Law Com. No.24; U.S. Uniform Commercial Code, s.2–312(2).

difficulty as to when such an intention is properly to be inferred from the circumstances of the contract. In a number of nineteenth-century cases which were decided before the passing of the Sale of Goods Act 1893, no warranty of title was implied, for instance, where goods were sold, or known to have been sold, by a sheriff[6] or auctioneer,[7] where an unredeemed pledge was sold, or known to have been sold, by a pawnbroker[8] and where the hull of a stranded vessel was sold at a public auction by the master of a ship.[9] It is doubtful, however, to what extent these cases are now to be regarded as authoritative.[10] They were decided at a time when the general rule was still that of *caveat emptor*, even if by that time it could be said to have been "eaten up by exceptions".[11] The original text of section 12 of the 1893 Act stated that the condition and warranties to be implied by that section were to be implied "unless the circumstances of the contract are such as to show a different intention"; and in *Payne v Elsden*[12] no condition as to title was implied on the part of an auctioneer who sold goods distrained upon by a bailiff. In *Niblett v Confectioners' Materials Co. Ltd*[13] Atkin L.J. thought that the qualification contained in the 1893 Act had been inserted to exclude sales by a sheriff under an execution[14] and also "other cases where by implication or by express terms there is no warranty of title."[15] Again, in the Australian case of *Warmings Used Cars v Tucker*[16] it was held that there was no intention to guarantee title in circumstances where the seller was virtually in the position of a commission agent purchasing goods from a third party for sale to the buyer. These latter cases may well give some guidance as to when an intention to transfer only such title as the seller or the third person may have will be inferred.[17]

Implied terms. Where the seller purports to transfer only such title as he or a third person may have, he does not thereby exclude in their entirety the terms as to freedom from encumbrances[18] and quiet possession.[19] By section 12(4) of the 1979 Act there is an implied term that all charges or 4–033

---

[6] *Peto v Blades* (1814) 5 Taunt. 657; *Chapman v Speller* (1850) 14 Q.B. 621; *Bagueley v Hawley* (1867) L.R. 2 C.P. 625; *Re Rogers* (1874) L.R. 9 Ch.App. 432 at 437.
[7] *Bagueley v Hawley*, above; *Wood v Baxter* (1883) 49 L.T. 45.
[8] *Morley v Attenborough* (1849) 3 Exch. 500.
[9] *Page v Cowasjee Eduljee* (1866) L.R. 1 C.P. 127.
[10] See above, para.4–001.
[11] *Smith v Marryat* (1851) 17 Q.B. 281 at 291; *Rowland v Divall* [1923] 2 K.B. 500 at 505.
[12] (1900) 17 T.L.R. 161, relying on *Wood v Baxter*, above.
[13] [1921] 3 K.B. 387; above, para.4–003.
[14] At p.401. See also *Rowland v Divall*, above, at p.505, and below, para.7–111.
[15] [1921] 3 K.B. 387 at 401. *cf.* p. 395. In this case the question was left open whether the sellers would have been held to have warranted their right to sell had the contract been specifically for milk "Nissly brand" (at p.398).
[16] [1956] S.A.S.R. 249.
[17] In *R. v Wheeler* (1991) 92 Cr.App.R. 279 it was suggested that s.12(3) might apply if the sale took place in market overt (now abolished) since, even if the seller had no title, the purchaser in good faith acquired title.
[18] See above, para.4–023.
[19] See above, para.4–025. See also the Law Commission's First Report on *Exemption Clauses in Contracts (Amendments to the Sale of Goods Act 1893)* (1969), Law Com. No.24, paras 16–18.

encumbrances known to the seller and not known to the buyer have been disclosed to the buyer before the contract is made. Further, by section 12(5) of the 1979 Act there is also an implied term that none of the following will disturb the buyer's quiet possession of the goods, namely—(a) the seller; (b) in a case where the parties to the contract intend that the seller should transfer only such title as a third person may have, that person; (c) anyone claiming through or under the seller or that third person otherwise than under a charge or encumbrance disclosed or known to the buyer before the contract is made. In England and Wales and Northern Ireland, these implied terms are warranties.[20]

4–034 **Exemption clauses.** The prohibition imposed by section 6(1)(a) of the Unfair Contract Terms Act 1977[21] against exclusion or restriction of liability applies equally to liability arising under subsections (4) and (5) of section 12 as it does to liability arising under subsection (1) and is subject to the same exceptions. If the buyer is a consumer an exemption clause may also not be binding on him under the Unfair Terms in Consumer Contracts Regulations 1999.[22]

4. ANALOGOUS PROVISIONS

4–035 **Instalment credit contracts.** In the case of a hire-purchase agreement,[23] the implied terms as to title will be those contained in section 8 of the Supply of Goods (Implied Terms) Act 1973,[24] which cannot be excluded by agreement of the parties.[25] But credit sale agreements[26] and conditional sale agreements[27] are subject to the provisions of the Sale of Goods Act 1979.

4–036 **Contracts for the transfer of property in goods.** In a contract under which one person transfers or agrees to transfer to another the property in goods,[28] other than a contract of sale of goods, hire-purchase and certain other excepted contracts,[29] the terms about title will be those implied by section 2 of the Supply of Goods and Services Act 1982. Those terms are very similar to the terms implied by the Sale of Goods Act 1979,[30] and

---

[20] s.12(5A).
[21] See above, para.4–018.
[22] SI 1999/2083, as amended by SI 2001/1186; above, para.4–019, below, para.14–030.
[23] As defined in s.15(1) of the Supply of Goods (Implied Terms) Act 1973, as amended by s.192 to and Sch.4, para.36, of the Consumer Credit Act 1974 (operative May 19, 1985, by SI 1983/1551).
[24] As substituted by s.192 of and Sch.4, para.35 to the Consumer Credit Act 1974 (operative May 19, 1985, by SI 1983/1551) and amended by Sch.2, para.4 of the Sale and Supply of Goods Act 1994.
[25] Unfair Contract Terms Act 1977, s.6(1)(b). But see ss.26, 27(1) of the 1977 Act, and also s.27(2).
[26] See s.189(1) of the Consumer Credit Act 1974.
[27] Defined in s.189(1) of the Consumer Credit Act 1974.
[28] Supply of Goods and Services Act 1982, s.1(1).
[29] *ibid.*, s.1(2).
[30] s.12.

again cannot be excluded by agreement of the parties.[31] Thus, in a contract for work and materials,[32] a condition will be implied on the part of the contractor as to his right to transfer the property in the materials and warranties will be implied as to freedom from encumbrances and quiet possession of the materials.

---

[31] Unfair Contract Terms Act 1977, s.7(3A) (inserted by the Supply of Goods and Services Act 1982, s.17(2)). But see ss.26, 27 of the 1977 Act.
[32] Other than a contract to which s.2(3) of the 1982 Act applies (which corresponds to s.12(3) of the 1979 Act).

CHAPTER 5

PASSING OF PROPERTY

	PARA.
1. Effects of the passing of property	5–003
2. Specific goods	5–016
(a) Specific goods in a deliverable state	5–016
(b) Specific goods to be put into a deliverable state	5–030
(c) Specific goods to be weighed, measured or tested	5–035
3. Goods delivered on approval or on sale or return	5–040
4. Unascertained goods	5–059
(a) Appropriation with the assent of the other party	5–068
(b) Appropriation of future goods	5–090
(c) Appropriation by delivery	5–096
(d) Appropriation of goods forming part of an identified bulk	5–103
5. Undivided shares in goods forming part of a bulk	5–109
6. Reservation of the right of disposal	5–131

In general. A contract of sale of goods contemplates transfer of the general property[1] in the goods sold from the seller to the buyer. The question whether and at what time the property passes to the buyer is dependent upon the intention of the parties.[2] But since the parties may have had no intention, or expressed no intention, in this respect, a number of presumptions were evolved by the common law which were to be applied unless a different intention appeared. These presumptions are now contained in section 18, rules 1 to 5, of the Sale of Goods Act 1979, and for convenience are dealt with in this chapter according to whether the subject-matter of the contract is specific goods,[3] goods delivered on approval or on sale or return,[4] or unascertained goods.[5] The passing of property in undivided shares in goods forming part of a bulk,[6] and the reservation by the seller of the right of disposal of goods, as permitted by section 19 of the Act,[7] are also considered here. **5–001**

Property, possession and risk.[8] The property in the goods is to be distinguished from the possession of them. The property in the goods may be transferred to the buyer before or after the goods have been delivered to **5–002**

[1] See the definition of "property" in s.61(1) of the Sale of Goods Act 1979, and *Sewell v Burdick* (1884) 10 App.Cas. 74 at 92–93. *Cf.* Battersby and Preston, 35 M.L.R. 268 (1972); Ho [1997] C.L.J. 571; Battersby [2001] J.B.L. 1. See also Atiyah, *The Sale of Goods* (11th ed.), p.315; Smith, *Property Problems in Sale* (Tagore Law Lectures, 1978); Palmer and McKendrick, *Interests in Goods* (2nd ed., 1998), Ch.3.
[2] Sale of Goods Act 1979, s.17; see below, paras 5–016, 5–066.
[3] See below, para.5–016.
[4] See below, para.5–040.
[5] See below, para.5–059.
[6] See below, para.5–109.
[7] See below, para.5–130.
[8] See Goode, *Proprietary Rights and Insolvency in Sales Transactions* (2nd ed.).

him or to his agent, or it may be transferred at the time of delivery. Property plays a "pivotal" role in the Sale of Goods Act,[9] although, in commercial practice, the location of the ownership of the goods may frequently be of less importance than the location of the risk[10] and the transfer of ownership of less significance than the delivery of the goods or of the documents of title to the goods. The approach of the modern commercial codes[11] has been to divorce questions of risk from the passing of property, and in c.i.f. and f.o.b. contracts property and risk are often separated.[12] But the passing of property is of considerable importance in English law, even though some of its effects may be negatived where there has been no delivery of possession.[13]

1. EFFECTS OF THE PASSING OF PROPERTY

5–003 **Title of the buyer.** When the property in the goods passes to the buyer, there will be transferred to him a title to an absolute legal interest in the goods sold.[14] Prima facie he will be entitled to obtain damages or an order for delivery up of the goods if the seller thereafter wrongfully interferes with the goods.[15] But in an action for wrongful interference the claimant must prove possession or an immediate right to possession of the goods at the time of the interference. An unpaid seller of goods who is in possession of them is entitled to a lien over the goods until payment or tender of the price.[16] Thus, unless the goods have been sold on credit, and the term of credit has not expired,[17] a buyer who has not paid or tendered the price will not be entitled to delivery of the goods. He will therefore have no immediate right to possession upon which a claim for wrongful interference can be founded.[18]

---

[9] See *ibid.*, p.12.
[10] See below, para.6–002. But see below, para.18–208.
[11] *e.g.* the American Uniform Commercial Code (UCC), the Uniform Law on International Sales (ULIS) and the Vienna Convention on Contracts for the International Sale of Goods(above, para.1–024). See also *Incoterms 2000* (ICC Publication 560).
[12] See below, paras 19–098, 20–070.
[13] See Lawson, 65 L.Q.R. 352 (1949).
[14] For failure by the seller to confer a good title, see above, para.4–002; for transfer of title by non-owners, see below, Ch.7.
[15] Torts (Interference with Goods) Act 1977, ss.1, 2, 3. See also *Langton v Higgins* (1859) 4 H. & N. 402; *Chinery v Viall* (1860) 5 H. & N. 288; *Mirabita v Imperial Ottoman Bank* (1878) 3 Ex.D. 164; *Denny v Skelton* (1916) 115 L.T. 305; *Healing (Sales) Pty Ltd v Inglis Electrix Ltd* (1968) 121 C.L.R. 584; see also *Redler Grain Silos Ltd v BICC Ltd* [1982] 1 Lloyd's Rep. 435 (injunction) and below, para.7–002 (measure of damages). Contrast (where no property passed): *Wait v Baker* (1848) 2 Exch. 1; *Ogg v Shuter* (1875) 1 C.P.D. 47; *Laurie & Morewood v Dudin & Sons* [1926] 1 K.B. 223; *Gale v New* [1937] 4 All E.R. 645. *Cf. Joseph v Ralph Wood & Co.* [1951] W.N. 224; *Jarvis v Williams* [1955] 1 W.L.R. 71; *Northwest Securities v Alexander Breckon* [1981] R.T.R. 518. See below, para.17–105.
[16] Sale of Goods Act 1979, s.41 (below, para.15–028). See also stoppage in transit under s.44 (below, para.15–061).
[17] If the buyer is not insolvent: see below, paras 15–024, 15–037.
[18] *Lord v Price* (1874) L.R. 9 Ex. 54.

Title of third parties. Before the property has passed to the buyer, the seller can dispose of the goods and pass title to a third party, even though this disposition is in breach of the contract of sale.[19] Conversely, after the property in the goods has passed to the buyer, the buyer can dispose of the goods and pass title to a third party.[20] In such cases, the third party acquires his title by virtue of the fact that title to the goods was vested in the seller or buyer, as the case may be. But even if the property in the goods has passed to the buyer, a seller who continues or is in possession of the goods, or of the documents of title to the goods, can pass a good title to a third party who receives them in good faith[21] and an unpaid seller in possession of the goods can pass a good title by a resale consequent upon the exercise of his lien or stoppage in transit.[22] Similarly, even if the property in the goods is still in the seller, a buyer who obtains with his consent possession of the goods or of the documents of title to the goods can in certain circumstances pass a good title to a third party who receives them in good faith.[23] 5–004

Insolvency. Passing of property is a relevant issue where one of the parties to a contract of sale becomes bankrupt or goes into receivership or liquidation. If the property has passed to the buyer, and the seller becomes insolvent, a pre-paying buyer will be able to claim the goods to the exclusion of the other creditors of the seller[24]; if it has not yet passed to him, though he has paid the whole or part of the price, he has only a personal claim as a creditor in respect of the breach of contract.[25] In the case of the buyer's insolvency, the seller can claim the goods if the property has not passed,[26] but if it has and the goods have delivered to the buyer, he will normally be able to claim only as a creditor for the price.[27] Nevertheless, where the seller is unpaid, but is in possession of the goods, he will be able to assert his lien[28] and, if the goods are in transit, his right of stoppage in transit.[29] 5–005

Where an application has been made for an administration order in respect of the buyer company, if the seller has retained the property in the goods under a hire-purchase or conditional sale agreement,[30] a chattel

---

[19] *Wait v Baker* (1848) 2 Exch. 1.
[20] See, *e.g. Kirkham v Attenborough* [1897] 1 Q.B. 201; *London Jewellers v Attenborough* [1934]2 K.B. 206; *Dennant v Skinner* [1948] 2 K.B. 164. Contrast (property in seller): *Weiner v Gill* [1906] 2 K.B. 574.
[21] Sale of Goods Act 1979, s.24; Factors Act 1889, s.8; see below, para.7–055.
[22] Sale of Goods Act 1979, s.48(2); below, para.15–102.
[23] Sale of Goods Act 1979, s.25(1); Factors Act 1889, s.9; see below, para.7–069. See also s.47 of the 1979 Act: below, para.15–092.
[24] See, *e.g. Aldridge v Johnson* (1857) 7 E. & B. 885; *Re Blyth Shipbuilding and Dry Docks Co. Ltd* [1926] Ch. 494.
[25] See, *e.g. Mucklow v Mangles* (1803) 1 Taunt. 318; *Atkinson v Bell* (1828) 8 B. & C. 277; *Hayman & Son v M'Lintock*, 1907 S.C. 936; *Re Wait* [1927] 1 Ch. 606; *Carlos Federspiel & Co. SA v Charles Twigg & Co. Ltd* [1957] 1 Lloyd's Rep. 240.
[26] *Re Ferrier* [1944] Ch. 295; *Aluminium Industrie Vaassen BV v Romalpa Aluminium Ltd* [1976]1 W.L.R. 676; below, para.5–141.
[27] *Re Tappenbeck* (1876) 2 Ch.D. 278.
[28] Sale of Goods Act 1979, s.41; below, para.5–028.
[29] *ibid.* s.44; below, para.5–061.
[30] Defined in s.436 of the Insolvency Act 1986 by reference to s.189(1) of the Consumer Credit Act 1974.

leasing agreement or a retention of title agreement,[31] no step may be taken to repossess goods in the company's possession under the agreement except with permission of the court.[32] A similar moratorium is imposed where an administration order has been made,[33] and the administrator may be authorised by the court to dispose of the goods and thus overreach the seller's proprietary rights in the goods.[34] A moratorium, restricted to "eligible" companies,[35] is also imposed where the directors of the buyer company propose a voluntary arrangement under Part I of the Insolvency Act 1986.[36]

5–006 **Remedies of seller.** The remedies of the seller depend on whether or not the property has passed. As a normal rule, if the property has passed, the seller is entitled to sue for the price,[37] but, if it has not, only for damages for non-acceptance.[38]

5–007 **Risk.** The prima facie rule (except in consumer transactions)[39] is that risk passes with property.[40] The question whether or not the property has passed may therefore be of relevance where the goods are lost, damaged, destroyed or deteriorate[41] and also where the buyer claims to have an insurable interest in the goods at the time these events occur.[42] But there are a number of important exceptions to this prima facie rule and the risk may sometimes pass to the buyer before the property passes or remain with the seller notwithstanding the passing of property.[43]

5–008 **Bills of lading.** One of the most important incidents of the passing of property in the case of contracts for the sale of goods to be carried by sea no longer applies. Previously the acquisition by a buyer of contractual rights and liabilities under the contract of carriage contained in a bill of lading was, under the Bills of Lading Act 1855, linked to the passing of property in the goods mentioned in the bill.[44] This is no longer the case. The 1855 Act

---

[31] Defined in s.251 of the Insolvency Act 1986.

[32] Insolvency Act 1986, Sch.B1, paras 44, 111(1), inserted by s.248 of and Sch. 16 to the Enterprise Act 2002; below, para.5–162.

[33] Insolvency Act 1986, Sch.B1, para.43 (but in this case the administrator may consent to repossession as well as the court); para. 5–162.

[34] Insolvency Act 1986, Sch.B1, para.72; below 5–163.

[35] *i.e.* small companies, excluding companies such as banks, insurance companies, companies involved in the performance of market contracts.

[36] Insolvency Act 1986, Sch.A1, inserted by the Insolvency Act 2000; below, para.5–164.

[37] Sale of Goods Act 1979, s.49(1); below, para.16–001.

[38] *ibid.* s.50; below, para.16–060. But see s.49(2) and below, para.16–028 for exceptions.

[39] See below para.6–013.

[40] Sale of Goods Act 1979, s.20; see below, para.6–002.

[41] See, *e.g. Elphick v Barnes* (1880) 5 C.P.D. 321; *Healey v Howlett & Sons* [1971] 1 K.B. 337; *Pignataro v Gilroy* [1919] 1 K.B. 459; *Underwood Ltd v Burgh Castle Brick & Cement Syndicate* [1922] 1 K.B. 343; *Wardar's (Import & Export) Co. Ltd v W. Norwood & Sons Ltd* [1968] 2 Q.B. 663.

[42] See below, para.6–012.

[43] See below, para.6–003.

[44] See below, para.18–100.

was repealed by the Carriage of Goods by Sea Act 1992, which broke the link between the acquisition of such contractual rights and liabilities and the passing of property. The 1992 Act transfers to and vests contractual rights of suit in the lawful holder of a bill of lading or the person named as consignee in a sea waybill or ship's delivery order.[45] Contractual liabilities to the carrier are imposed upon the person in whom such rights are vested if he takes or demands delivery from the carrier of any of the goods or makes a claim under the contract of carriage against the carrier in respect of any of the goods.[46]

Title to sue. Where goods are consigned by the seller to a carrier for carriage to the buyer, and are lost or damaged in transit or delivered by the carrier to the wrong person, an action may lie against the carrier in contract or in tort.[47] The passing of property may sometimes be relevant to the claimant's title to sue. 5–009

If the claim is one for damages for breach of the contract of carriage, the proper claimant will normally be the buyer if the property and risk in the goods have passed to him upon their delivery to the carrier.[48] In *Dunlop v Lambert*,[49] however, the House of Lords held that a seller of goods could recover substantial damages against the carrier if there was privity of contract[50] between himself and the carrier for the carriage of the goods, notwithstanding that during the transit the property (and risk) was not in him. The seller is then accountable to the buyer for the damages recovered as money had and received.[51] Despite the anomalous nature of this rule, which permits a person to recover damages for loss sustained, not by himself, but by a third party,[52] the principle in *Dunlop v Lambert* is prima

[45] See below, para.18–103.
[46] See below, para.18–123.
[47] *Hayn, Roman & Co. v Culliford* (1879) 4 C.P.D. 182; *Lee Cooper Ltd v CH Jeakins & Sons Ltd* [1967] 2 Q.B, 1; *Margarine Union GmbH v Cambay Prince Steamship Co. Ltd (The Wear Breeze)* [1969] 1 Q.B. 219; *Chabra Cpn. Pte. Ltd v Jag Shakti (Owners)* [1986] A.C. 337; *Obestain Inc. v National Mineral Development Corp. Ltd (The Sanix Ace)* [1987] 1 Lloyd's Rep. 465; *Hispanica de Petroleos SA v Vencedora Oceanica Navegacion SA (The Kapetan Markos No.2)* [1987] 2 Lloyd's Rep. 321; *Gatewhite Ltd v Iberia Lineas Aereas de Espana Sociedad* [1990] 1 Q.B. 326; *Anonima Petroli Italiana SpA v Marlucidez Armadora SA (The Filiatra Legacy)* [1991] 2 Lloyd's Rep. 337 at 341; Reynolds [1986] L.M.C.L.Q. 97.
[48] Sale of Goods Act 1979, s.18, r.5, 5(2); below, para.5–096. Privity of contract may be established by deeming the consignor to have entered into the contract of carriage as agent for the consignee: *Dawes v Peck* (1799) 8 Term R. 330; *Brown v Hodgson* (1809) 2 Camp. 36; *Fragano v Long* (1825) 4 B. & C. 219; *Tronson v Dent* (1853) 8 Moo.P.C. 419; *Cork Distilleries Co. v G.S. & W. Ry* (1874) L.R. 7 H.L. 269 at 277, 281; *Texas Instruments Ltd v Nason (Europe) Ltd* [1991] 1 Lloyd's Rep. 146 at 148; Sale of Goods Act 1979, s.32. Contrast (consignor's action): *Swain v Shepherd* (1832) 1 Moo. & Rob. 223; *Coats v Chaplin* (1842) 3 Q.B. 483 at 489, 491. But see (overseas sales) below, paras 18–096, 19–090, 20–059.
[49] (1839) 6 Cl. & F. 600. See also *Dan's and Jordan v James* (1776) 5 Burr 2680; *Joseph v Knox* (1813) 3 Camp. 320; *Mead v S.E. Ry Co.* (1870) 18 W.R. 735; *Hayn, Roman & Co. v Culliford* (above), at pp.185–186; *Obestain Inc. v National Mineral Development Corp. Ltd* (*The Sanix Ace*), above.
[50] A "special contract", *i.e.* otherwise than as common carrier.
[51] *Albacruz (Cargo Owners) v Albazero (Owners) (The Albazero)* [1977] A.C. 774 at 844, 845.
[52] *ibid.* at pp.844–846.

facie still good law.[53] However, different considerations apply where goods are carried by sea.[54] The Carriage of Goods by Sea Act 1992 provides that, where rights of suit under the contract of carriage are transferred to the lawful holder of a bill of lading, this extinguishes any entitlement to those rights which derives from a person's having been an original party to the contract of carriage.[55]

With respect to claims against the carrier in tort, the claimant must show that, at the time of the loss, damage or misdelivery, he was either the legal owner of the goods or had a possessory title to the goods.[56] In *Leigh & Sillavan Ltd v Aliakmon Shipping Co. Ltd (The Aliakmon)*[57] the House of Lords held that a shipowner owed no duty of care to a buyer under a c. & f. contract in respect of negligent damage to the goods carried in his ship when, at the material time, the buyer had no property in or possessory title to the goods, even though as between the buyer and the seller the goods were at the buyer's risk. Their Lordships rejected the contention that an action in tort for negligence would lie at the suit of a c.i.f. or c. & f. buyer to whom the risk but not yet the property had passed.[58] The rule that the claimant must show a proprietary or possessory title to the goods at the relevant time also applies to claims in tort against a carrier of goods by land.[59]

However, in the case of goods carried internationally by rail,[60] road[61] and air,[62] the relevant international convention normally[63] states who is entitled

---

[53] *ibid.* at p.847; *Linden Gardens Trust Ltd v Lenesta Sludge Disposals Ltd* [1994] 1 A.C. 85.

[54] *The Albazero*, above, at pp.847, 848; below, para.18–114.

[55] s.2(5)(a), *cf.* s.2(5) (tailpiece) (sea waybills and ships delivery orders).

[56] *Margarine Union GmbH v Cambay Prince Steamship Ltd* (*The Wear Breeze*), above, at pp.233, 250. See also *Freeman v Birch* (1833) 3 Q.B. 492n. (bailee); *Bristol and West of England Bank v Midland Ry* [1891] 2 Q.B. 653; *Chabbra Cpn. Pte. Ltd v Jag Shakti (Owners)* [1986] A.C. 337 (pledgee); *East West Corp. v DKBS 1912* [2002] EWHC 83 (Comm), [2003] Q.B.1509 at [18] (shipper). See also the cases cited in n.49, above. On the meaning of "a possessory title", see *Transcontainer Express Ltd v Custodian Security Ltd* [1988] 1 Lloyd's Rep. 128 at 138; Palmer and McKendrick, *Interests in Goods* (2nd ed., 1998), Ch.3; below, para.18–148. But see s.3(1) of the Latent Damage Act 1986 (claim for damage to goods caused before acquisition of title).

[57] [1986] A.C. 785. The decision to the contrary in *Schiffahrt und Kohlen GmbH v Chelsea Maritime Ltd* (*The Irene's Success*) [1981] 2 Lloyd's Rep. 635 and observations of Sheen J. in *The Nea Tyhi* [1982] 1 Lloyd's Rep. 606 were disapproved. See also *Mitsui & Co. Ltd v Flota Mercante Grancolombiana (The Ciudad de Pasto)* [1988] 2 Lloyd's Rep. 208 (f.o.b.); *Conoco U.K. Ltd v Limni Maritime Co. Ltd (The Sirina)* [1988] 2 Lloyd's Rep. 613 (f.o.b.); *The Seven Pioneer* [2001] 2 Lloyd's Rep. 57 (f.o.b.). But see now the Carriage of Goods by Sea Act 1992 and below, para.18–148.

[58] At pp.807, 811, 821.

[59] At p.816.

[60] COTIF Convention (as amended): CIM Rules, Art. 54, see below, paras 21–065—21–071.

[61] CMR Convention, Art.13. See below, paras 21–058—21–064, and *Chitty on Contracts* (29th ed.), Vol.2, paras 36–120 *et seq.*

[62] Warsaw Convention (as amended), Arts 13, 14, 24. See below, paras 21–051—21–057, and Chitty, *op. cit.*, para.35–069 But see *Western Digital Corp. v British Airways Plc* [2001] Q.B. 733 (owner can sue though not named as consignor or consignee).

[63] The CMR Convention is not comprehensive on this point, see Chitty, *op.cit.*, para.36–136.

to claim against the carrier, and the rights of action conferred by the convention do not ordinarily depend upon ownership of the goods.

More generally, apart from actions against a carrier of the goods, the passing of property between seller and buyer is normally of less relevance to their title to sue than the acquisition or retention of possession of the goods. At common law, where goods which are the subject-matter of a contract of sale are destroyed or damaged by the negligence of a third party, an action in tort may be maintained against the wrongdoer by any person who, at the material time, had possession of the goods or an immediate right to possess the goods.[64] The same principle applies where the goods are wrongfully converted by a third party.[65] An owner of goods who, at the material time, did not have possession or an immediate right to possession of the goods may also be entitled to maintain an action, but as a general rule only in respect of injury done to his reversionary interest in the goods.[66] These common law rules remain largely unaffected by the Torts (Interference with Goods) Act 1977.[67] At common law, however, a wrongdoer could not raise against a claimant in actual possession of the goods a plea of *jus tertii* —that the true owner of the goods was a person other than the claimant.[68] Also, at common law, the general rule was that a claimant in actual possession of goods (such as a bailee) could recover from the wrongdoer the full value of the goods, even if not accountable to his bailor.[69] But the Act now enables the defendant in an action for wrongful interference to raise the defence of *jus tertii*[70] and further requires the claimant to identify any person who, to his knowledge, has or claims any interest in the goods.[71] In order to avoid double liability where more than one person has a claim, the Act apportions damages between the claimants,[72] or, where one claimant sues for and recovers damages for the full value of the goods, requires him to account to any other person having a 5–010

---

[64] *Croft v Alison* (1821) 4 B. & Ald. 590; *Whittingham v Bloxham* (1831) 4 C. & P. 597; *The Winkfield* [1902] P. 42; *Chabbra Corp. Pte. Ltd v Jag Shakti (Owners)* [1986] A.C. 337; *Trans-container Express Ltd v Custodian Security Ltd* [1988] 1 Lloyd's Rep. 128 at 138; Palmer and McKendrick, *Interests in Goods* (2nd ed., 1998), Ch.3, p.66.

[65] See below, para.7–002.

[66] *Tancred v Allgood* (1859) 4 H. & N. 438 at 448; *Mears v L. & S.W. Ry* (1862) 11 C.B.(N.S.) 850; *Meux v G.E. Ry* [1895] 2 Q.B. 387; *France v Parkinson* [1954] 1 W.L.R. 581; *Morris v CW Martin & Sons Ltd* [1966] 1 Q.B. 716, 729; *The Sanix Ace* [1987] 1 Lloyd's Rep. 465, 468; *East West Corp v DKBSAF 1912* [2003] Q.B. 1509, 1532; *HSBC Rail (UK) Ltd v Network Rail Infrastructure Ltd* [2005] EWHC 403 (Comm); [2006] 1 W.L.R. 643; at [27].

[67] The Act introduced the collective term "wrongful interference with goods" to cover conversion, trespass, negligence and any other tort so far as it results in damage to goods or an interest in goods (s.1); but, except that detinue was abolished (s.2(1)), did not affect the basis for liability.

[68] *Armory v Delamirie* (1722) 1 Sta. 505; *Sutton v Buck* (1810) 5 E. & B. 802; *Jeffries v G.W. Ry* (1856) 5 E. & B. 802 at 805; *Glenwood Lumber Co. v Phillips* [1904] A.C. 405; *Wilson v Lombank Ltd* [1913] 1 W.L.R. 1294.

[69] *The Winkfield* [1902] P. 42; *Glenwood Lumber Co. v Phillips*, above. *Cf. Chabbra Corp. Pte. Ltd v Jag Shakti (Owners)* [1986] A.C. 337.

[70] s.8(1).

[71] s.8(2).

[72] s.7(1)(2).

right to claim.[73] And where, as a result of enforcement of double liability, any claimant is unjustly enriched to any extent, he is liable to reimburse the wrongdoer to that extent.[74]

5–011 The decision of the House of Lords in *Leigh & Sillavan Ltd v Aliakmon Shipping Co. Ltd (The Aliakmon)*[75] reinforces a number of previous decisions[76] which effectively preclude a buyer to whom the property in the goods has not passed, and who has no possessory title to the goods (but only a contractual right as between himself and the seller in relation to the goods), from any right of action in tort against a third party who negligently destroys or damages the goods in respect of economic loss thereby inflicted upon him.

5–012 **Insurance.**[77] The passing of property is rarely of relevance to insurance. A person can insure goods to their full value against any loss, on behalf of anyone who may be entitled to an interest in the goods at the time the loss occurs, provided that it appears from the terms of the policy that it was intended to cover their interest.[78] Also, a buyer will have an insurable interest in goods if they are at his risk, whether or not the property has passed to him.[79]

5–013 **Criminal offences.** A number of criminal statutes refer to a "sale" of goods, and it is a matter of construction whether that term embraces agreements to sell as well as sales of goods[80] or refers only to an actual sale completed by the passing of property.[81] In the latter case, the question whether, or when, or in what place, the property has passed to the buyer may be a relevant consideration in deciding whether or not an offence has been committed.[82]

---

[73] s.7(3). See *O'Sullivan v Williams* [1992] 3 All E.R. 385.
[74] s.7(4).
[75] [1986] A.C. 785 at 809, 816. See also *Transcontainer Express Ltd v Custodian Security Ltd* [1988] 1 Lloyd's Rep. 128 at 131. *Cf. Williams v Attorney General* [1990] 1 N.Z.L.R. 646.
[76] *Cattle v Stockton Waterworks Co.* (1875) L.R. 10 Q.B. 453; *Simpson v Thompson* (1877) 3 App.Cas. 279 at 289–290; *The Charlotte* [1908] P. 206; *Chargeurs Reéunis Compagnie Française de Navigation à Vapeur v English & American Shipping Co.* (1921) 9 Ll.L.R. 464; *Elliott Steam Tug Co. Ltd v The Shipping Controller* [1922] 1 K.B. 127 at 139; *The World Harmony* [1967] P. 341; *Candlewood Navigation Corp. Ltd v Mitsui O.S.K. Lines Ltd* [1986] A.C. 1; *Muirhead v Industrial Tank Specialities Ltd* [1986] Q.B. 507.
[77] See *Chitty on Contracts* (29th ed.), Vol. 2, paras 41–003-41–015, Palmer and McKendrick, *Interests in Goods* (2nd ed., 1998), Ch.4.
[78] *Waters v Monarch Fire and Life Assurance Co.* (1856) 5 E. & B. 870; *Tomlinson v Hepburn* [1966] A.C. 451 at 467; Marine Insurance Act 1906, ss.14(2), 26(3).
[79] *Anderson v Morice* (1876) 1 App.Cas. 713 at 724; Marine Insurance Act 1906, s.5(1), (2).
[80] See above, para.1–026.
[81] See above, para.1–027.
[82] See, *e.g. Ridgway v Ward* (1884) 14 Q.B.D. 110; *Pletts v Beattie* [1896] 1 Q.B. 519; *Noblett v Hopkinson* [1905] 2 K.B. 214; *Ollett v Jordan* [1918] 2 K.B. 41; *Mischeff v Springett* [1942] 2 K.B. 331. See also *Badische Anilin und Soda Fabrik v Basle*

Legal process. Passing of property may be relevant where a third party asserts a lien over the goods,[83] or the goods are the subject of some legal process such as execution[84] or distress,[85] an order for their arrest[86] or seizure, or a freezing injunction,[87] on account of a debt due or claimed from the person who is alleged to be the owner of the goods. 5–014

Prize. Goods may be condemned as prize if they are the property of an alien enemy in time of war. Whether and at what moment the property passed to the buyer is sometimes relevant to their status as prize,[88] although it will not always be the determining factor. 5–015

2. SPECIFIC GOODS

(a) *Specific Goods in a Deliverable State*

Intention of the parties. Section 17(1) of the 1979 Act provides that, where there is a contract for the sale of specific goods[89] the property in them is transferred to the buyer at such time as the parties to the contract intend it to be transferred. By section 17(2), for the purpose of ascertaining the intention of the parties regard is to be had to the terms of the contract,[90] the conduct of the parties and the circumstances of the case.[91] In 5–016

Chemical Works [1898] A.C. 200; *Badische Anilin Fabrik v Hickson* [1906] A.C. 419 (infringement of a patent); *Furby v Hoey* [1947] 1 All E.R. 236; *Lacis v Cashmarts* [1969] 2 Q.B. 400; *Elsner v Mirams* [1975] Crim.L.R. 519; *Edwards v Ddin* [1976] 1 W.L.R. 942; *Davies v Leighton* [1978] Crim.L.R. 575; *R. v Williams* [1980] Crim.L.R. 589; *Eddy v Niman* (1981) 73 Cr.App.R. 237 (theft, but see *R. v Morris* [1984] A.C. 320 and s.3 of the Theft Act 1978); *Dobson v General Accident Fire and Life Assurance Corp. Plc* [1990] 1 Q.B. 274; *R. v Wheeler* (1991) 92 Cr.App.R. 279; *R. v Gomez* [1991] 3 All E.R. 394. Contrast *Henry Kendall & Sons v William Lillico & Sons Ltd* [1969] 2 A.C. 31.

[83] A particular lien such as, for example, an artificer's lien for repairs.

[84] CPR, 20.2, RSC, Ord. 46; County Courts Act 1984, s.85.

[85] Law of Distress Amendment Act 1908, s.1.

[86] See *The Span Terza* [1984] 1 Lloyd's Rep. 119; *The Gosforth* (Commercial Court of Rotterdam, February 20, 1985) discussed in [1986] L.M.C.L.Q. 4.

[87] *Cf. Z Ltd v A-Z and AA-LL* [1982] 1 Q.B. 538 at 590–591.

[88] *e.g. The Parchim* [1918] A.C. 157; *The Prinz Adalbert* [1917] A.C. 586; *The Annie Johnson*[1918] P. 154; *The Dirigo* [1919] P. 204; *The Orteric* [1920] A.C. 724; *The Kronprinsessan Margareta* [1921] 1 A.C. 486; *The Glenroy* [1946] A.C. 124. See below, para.18–242.

[89] Defined in s.61(1); above, para.1–113. This subsection also refers to "ascertained goods"; see below, para.5–066.

[90] See, *e.g. Saks v Tilley* (1915) 32 T.L.R. 148 (goods sent with bill drawn on buyer and invoice marked "settled by acceptance"); *Underwood Ltd v Burgh Castle Brick and Cement Syndicate* [1922] 1 K.B. 343 (f.o.r.); *Re Anchor Line (Henderson Bros) Ltd* [1937] Ch. 1 (see below, para.5–027); *Gale v New* [1937] 4 All E.R. 645 (sale of metal on artillery range "where collected by contractor").

[91] See, *e.g. Nanka-Bruce v Commonwealth Trust Ltd* [1926] A.C. 77 (see below, para.5–036); *Kursell v Timber Operators and Contractors Ltd* [1927] 1 K.B. 298 (see below, para.5–022); *Lord Eldon v Hedley Bros* [1935] 2 K.B. 1 (custom); *Re Capon* [1940] 2 All E.R. 135 (auctioned pigs passed to buyer despite agreement that they were to be property of auctioneer who provided price); *Jarvis v Williams* [1955] 1 W.L.R. 71 (agreement to cancel sale); *Lambert v G & C Finance Corp.* (1963) 107 S.J. 666 (retention of car log-book); *Ward (R.V.) Ltd v Bignall* [1967] 1 Q.B. 534 (payment deferred).

Varley v Whipp[92] Channell J. commented: "It is impossible to imagine a clause more vague than this, but I think it correctly represents the state of the authorities when the [1893] Act was passed." In order, however, to assist in ascertaining the intention of the parties, the Act of 1979 lays down three rules in section 18[93] which govern the time at which property passes in specific goods unless a different intention appears.[94] But these rules are only presumptions: "the law permits [the parties] to settle the point for themselves by any intelligible expression of their intention."[95]

5–017 **Section 18, rule 1.** The first rule set out in section 18 of the 1979 Act relates to "an unconditional contract for the sale of specific goods in a deliverable state." In this case, unless a different intention appears, the property in the goods passes to the buyer when the contract is made,[96] and it is immaterial whether the time of payment or the time of delivery, or both, be postponed. This rule codifies the common law at the date of the passing of the 1893 Act.[97]

5–018 **Postponement of delivery or payment.** Under English law, as distinct from the civil law, the property in a specific chattel may pass under a contract of sale without delivery.[98] This principle seems to have been formulated in the common law as early as the fifteenth century.[99] Further, by 1893 it was well established that the passing of property was not conditional on payment or tender of the price.[1] Under section 28 of the 1979 Act, unless otherwise agreed, delivery of the goods and payment of the price are concurrent conditions[2]; and under section 39(2) a seller who still retains the property in the goods has a right to withhold delivery and to retain possession of the goods until payment similar to and co-extensive with an unpaid seller's lien.[3] But, in principle, the Act treats the passing of property as a matter distinct and separate from the right of the buyer to delivery of the goods and the right of the seller to receive payment for

---

[92] [1900] 1 Q.B. 513 at 517.
[93] See below, paras 5–017—5–039.
[94] See below, paras 5–026, 5–032, 5–039.
[95] *McEntire v Crossley Bros Ltd* [1895] A.C. 457 at 467.
[96] *Dennant v Skinner and Collom* [1948] 2 K.B. 164; *Clarke v Reilly & Sons* (1962) 96 I.L.T.R. 96; *Koppel v Koppel* [1966] 1 W.L.R. 802; *R. v Wheeler* (1991) 92 Cr.App.R. 279.
[97] Shep.Tou Ch.224–225; *Simmons v Swift* (1826) 5 B. & C. 857 at 862; *Tarling v Baxter* (1827) 6 B. & C. 360 at 364; *Dixon v Yates* (1833) 5 B. & Ad. 313 at 340; *Spartali v Benecke* (1850) 10 C.B. 212 at 223; *Wood v Bell* (1856) 5 E. & B. 772 at 791–792; *Gilmour v Supple* (1858) 11 Moore P.C. 551 at 566; *Sweeting v Turner* (1871) L.R. 7 Q.B. 310 at 313; *Seath v Moore* (1886) 11 App.Cas. 350 at 370.
[98] *Badische Anilin und Soda Fabrik v Hickson* [1906] A.C. 419 at 424. See also *Hinde v White house* (1806) 7 East 558; *Phillimore v Barry* (1808) 1 Camp. 513. For an unconvincing explanation of this principle, see *Dixon v Yates* (1833) 5 B. & Ad. 313 at 340; *Badische Anilin und Soda Fabrik v Hickson*, above, at p.424.
[99] See Fifoot, *History and Sources of the Common Law: Tort and Contract* (1949), p.228; Ibbetson (1991) 107 L.Q.R. 480 at 490. Contrast *Cochrane v Moore* (1890) 25 Q.B.D. 57 at 71 ("comparatively modern").
[1] *Tarling v Baxter* (1827) 6 B. & C. 360. *Cf. Noy's Maxims*, 87–89.
[2] See below, para.8–004.
[3] See below, para.15–028.

them.[4] Thus "if postponement of the purchase price and the delivery of the goods can properly be described as a postponement of the completion of the purchase, the property will pass on the entering into the contract, although in that sense the completion of the purchase is deferred."[5] Of course, the parties may agree that the passing of property is conditional on payment or delivery, or both, and such an agreement may be implied as well as expressed[6]; and it has been said that "in modern times very little is needed to give rise to the inference that the property in specific goods is to pass only on delivery or payment."[7]

Unconditional contract. Considerable difficulty attaches to the meaning of the words "unconditional contract" contained in rule 1 of section 18.[8] The more natural interpretation is that "unconditional" means not subject to any condition upon the fulfilment of which the transfer of property depends.[9] It is submitted that this interpretation is the correct one. An alternative interpretation, however, is that the words connote a contract which contains no condition unfulfilled by the seller, in the sense of an essential stipulation the breach of which may give rise to a right to treat the contract as repudiated.[10] In *Varley v Whipp*[11] an action was brought by the seller for the price of a particular reaping machine which he had described to the buyer as "new the previous year, and only used to cut fifty or sixty acres." The machine was old, and there was thus a breach of the condition implied by section 13 of the Act.[12] The buyer rejected the machine when delivered to him and it was held that he was not liable for the price. Channell J. said that section 18, rule 1, of the Act did not apply since "this was not an unconditional contract for the sale of specific goods",[13] although there was no suspensive condition in the contract of sale. This case might appear to support the alternative interpretation given above and to establish that, where an essential stipulation is broken by the seller, the property in specific goods passes to the buyer only if and when he accepts the goods.[14] 5–019

---

[4] *Dennant v Skinner and Collom* [1948] 2 K.B. 164 at 172.

[5] *Re Anchor Line (Henderson Bros) Ltd* [1937] 1 Ch. 1 at 9.

[6] s.17; see above, para.5–016.

[7] *Ward (RV) Ltd v Bignall* [1967] 1 Q.B. 534 at 545. See also *Minister of Supply and Development v Servicemen's Co-op. Joinery Manufacturers' Ltd* (1951) 82 C.L.R. 621 at 635, 640; *Dobson v General Accident Fire and Life Assurance Corp. Plc* [1990] 1 Q.B. 274; and below, para.16–028.

[8] See Gower, 13 M.L.R. 362 at 364 (1950); Smith, 14 M.L.R. 173 (1951); Stoljar, 16 M.L.R. 174 (1953); Atiyah, *The Sale of Goods* (11th ed.), p.322; Bridge, *The Sale of Goods* (1997), p.65. Most of the difficulty has arisen out of the fact that, before 1967, a literal application of s.11(1)(c) of the 1893 Act (amended by s.4(1) of the Misrepresentation Act 1967 and re-enacted by s.11(4) of the 1979 Act) would take away the buyer's right to reject for breach of condition once the property in the goods had passed: see below, para.12–038.

[9] Sale of Goods Act 1979, s.2(3); above, para.1–025; below, para.5–071.

[10] See *Taylor v Combined Buyers Ltd* [1924] N.Z.L.R. 627; *Armaghdown Motors Ltd v Gray Motors Ltd* [1963] N.Z.L.R. 5 at 8.

[11] [1900] 1 Q.B. 513. See also *Ollett v Jordan* [1918] 2 K.B. 41 at 45 (on s.18, r.5); below, para.5–073.

[12] See below, para.11–001.

[13] At p.517.

[14] See *Leaf v International Galleries* [1950] 2 K.B. 86 at 89–90.

5–020 It is to be noted, however, that *Varley v Whipp* concerned a sale of goods by description. Channell J. appears to have regarded the description as an identification of the goods contracted to be sold, for he says[15]: "If a man says he will sell the black horse in the last stall in his stable, and the stall is empty, or there is no horse in it, but only a cow, no property could pass. Again, if he says he will sell a four-year-old horse in the last stall, and there is a horse in the stall, but it is not a four-year-old, the property would not pass. But if he says he will sell a four-year-old horse, and there is a four-year-old horse in the stall, and he says the horse is sound, this last statement would only be a collateral warranty." It is therefore not unreasonable to suppose that he intended to lay down a different proposition, *viz.* that where goods are sold by description, and the description identifies the goods,[16] no property will pass in any goods other than those which correspond with the description.[17] If such is the case, the inapplicability of section 18, rule 1, did not result merely from the fact that the contract contained a condition unfulfilled by the seller. It was inapplicable because the goods which the seller delivered in pretended fulfilment of the contract were not those identified by the terms of the contract of sale.

5–021 **Conditional contract.** Where a contract for the sale of specific goods is made subject to a condition upon the fulfilment of which the transfer of property depends, the property will not pass to the buyer when the contract is made, but only when the condition is fulfilled.[18] Until this time, the contract takes effect as an agreement to sell, and not as a sale of the goods.[19] Notwithstanding the presumption contained in section 18, rule 1, the contract may be held to be conditional by virtue of the intention of the parties ascertained in accordance with section 17[20] or as the result of the reservation by the seller of the right of disposal of the goods.[21] Circumstances in which a conditional contract for the sale of specific goods will be presumed to have been intended by the parties are further contained in section 18, rules 2 and 3, of the Act, which are discussed below.[22] If the passing of property is conditional on payment of the price,[23] it is submitted that property in the goods does not pass by virtue of the seller claiming or

[15] [1900] 1 Q.B. 513 at 517.
[16] *cf. Parsons v Sexton* (1874) 4 C.B. 899.
[17] See *Vigers Brothers v Sanderson Brothers* [1901] 1 Q.B. 608 (below, para.5–086). The difficulty lies in reconciling the concepts of "specific goods" and a "sale of goods by description" (see Stoljar, 16 M.L.R. 174 (1953)).
[18] Sale of Goods Act 1979, s.2(3), (5); see above, paras.1–025, 1–026, 1–109.
[19] *ibid.*, s.2(5); see above, para.1–026.
[20] See above, para.5–016; below, paras 5–026—5–029. See also s.5(1), (3) of the 1979 Act: above, para.1–102.
[21] Sale of Goods Act 1979, s.19; see below, para.5–131.
[22] Below, paras 5–030, 5–035.
[23] Payment by a negotiable instrument which is subsequently dishonoured does not ordinarily pass property: *M'Laren's Trustee v Argylls Ltd*, 1915 S.L.T. 241; see below, para.9–030. But a tender of the price wrongfully refused by the seller would appear to do so: see below, para.18–226; *Cf. City Motors (1933) Pty Ltd v Southern Aerial Super Service Pty Ltd* (1961) 106 C.L.R. 477 (where differing views were expressed on whether tender after wrongful repudiation by the seller not accepted by the buyer will pass the property).

suing for or even recovering judgment for the price.[24] But if by the terms of the contract the seller has, on default by the buyer in paying the price, the option to terminate the contract and recover the goods or to recover the price, and elects to sue for the price, his election, unless otherwise agreed, passes the property in the goods to the buyer.[25] If he elects to recover the goods, then, unless otherwise agreed, he abandons his claim to the price or the unpaid part of the price, and is relegated to a claim for damages for breach of contract.[26]

A conditional contract of sale under which the purchase price or part of it is payable by instalments may be regulated by the Consumer Credit Act 1974 if the buyer is an "individual" (which includes a partnership, but only if it consists of two or three persons not all of whom are bodies corporate).[27]

Specific goods. Section 18, rule 1, will not apply unless the goods are "specific goods" as defined in section 61(1) of the Act.[28] In *Kursell v Timber Operators and Contractors Ltd*[29] a contract was entered into for the sale and purchase of all timber of a certain height in a designated Latvian forest, the buyer being given 15 years to cut the timber. Shortly afterwards the forest was expropriated by the Latvian State. It was held that the property in the timber had not passed to the buyer under the rule. Sargant and Scrutton L.JJ. were of the opinion that the timber was not specific goods.[30] The contract was ambiguous. The more probable construction was that the buyer was entitled to cut such timber as would have attained the requisite height when it came to be felled within the 15-year period. If this was so, the goods were not specific as the timber to be sold depended on the trees' rate of growth. But even if the contract was construed to mean timber which had attained that height at the time the contract was made, Sargant L.J. considered that it was not specific goods since, though identifiable, it was not "identified" at that time.[31] 5–022

By virtue of the extended definition in section 61(1) of the Act,[32] "specific goods" includes an undivided share, specified as a fraction or percentage, of goods identified and agreed on at the time a contract of sale is made.

---

[24] See also s.43(2); below, paras 15–006, 15–059.
[25] *McEntire v Crossley Brothers* [1895] A.C. 457 at 464, 465. See also *Kin Tye Loong v Seth* (1920) 89 L.J. (P.C.) 113 (proof in bankruptcy for price).
[26] *Hewison v Ricketts* (1894) 63 L.J.Q.B. 711; *Att.-Gen. v Pritchard* (1928) 97 L.J.K.B. 561; *Taylor v Thompson* [1930] W.N. 16. See below, para.15–114.
[27] ss.5, 8(1), 189(1) (as amended by the Consumer Credit Act 2006). The financial limit in the 1974 Act was raised from £5,000 to £15,000 as from May 20, 1985, by SI 1983/1878 and to £25,000 from May 1, 1998, by SI 1998/996. The 2006 Act removes the financial limit but exempts agreements exceeding £25,000 where the agreement is entered into by the debtor wholly or predominantly for the purposes of a business carried on, or to be carried on, by him. The £25,000 is calculated by reference to the balance financed (s.9 of the 1974 Act), see below, para.14–143.
[28] See above, para.1–113.
[29] [1927] 1 K.B. 298. Contrast *Joseph Reid Pty Ltd v Schultz* (1949) 49 S.R.(N.S.W.) 231.
[30] Lord Hanworth M.R. based his judgment on s.17 of the Act.
[31] At p.314. Contrast *Lord Eldon v Hedley Bros* [1935] 2 K.B. 1.
[32] Inserted by s.2(d) of the Sale of Goods (Amendment) Act 1995; see above, para.1–116. But see below, para.5–025.

5–023 **Deliverable state.** The goods must also be in a deliverable state at the time the contract is made. "Goods are in a deliverable state when they are in such a state that the buyer would under the contract be bound to take delivery of them."[33] It could be contended that goods are not in a deliverable state whenever an express or implied condition relating to the state of the goods has been broken by the seller, since the buyer would not then under the contract be bound to take delivery of them.[34] But in practice, this requirement has received a more restrictive interpretation. In *Underwood Ltd v Burgh Castle Brick and Cement Syndicate*[35] a contract was made for the sale of a heavy condensing engine to be delivered free on rail in London. At the time of the contract the engine was affixed to the seller's trade premises in Millwall and had to be separated from its concrete bed and dismantled before it could be delivered on rail. While the main body of the engine was being loaded on a railway truck, part of it was accidentally broken. The Court of Appeal held that the property had not passed at the time of the accident and that the engine was still at the seller's risk.[36] Section 18, rule 1, did not apply, because the engine was not at the time of the contract in a deliverable state, inasmuch as it was affixed to the freehold and could not be put in a state in which the buyer was bound to accept it until it was detached and taken to pieces. Bankes L.J. said[37]: "A 'deliverable state' does not depend upon the mere completeness of the subject matter in all its parts. It depends on the actual state of the goods at the date of the contract and the state in which they are to be delivered by the terms of the contract." The goods must therefore be in a physical condition in which the buyer can take delivery and in which it has been agreed that he shall take delivery under the contract.[38]

5–024 In the above case, the seller was bound to do something to the engine for the purpose of putting it into a deliverable state-a situation expressly provided for in section 18, rule 2.[39] But although nothing remains to be done on the part of the seller before the goods are delivered, if the buyer must put the goods into a deliverable state before taking delivery, the property will not pass (unless so intended by the parties) at the time of the contract of sale. Thus, in the case of a contract for the sale of specific timber growing on the seller's land, on the terms that such timber is to be cut and carried away by the buyer, the property will not pass at the time of the contract, but only on severance.[40]

---

33 Sale of Goods Act 1979, s.61(5). See also below, paras 5–031, 5–035.

34 Atiyah, 19 M.L.R. 315 (1956). This view was subsequently abandoned by the author.

35 [1922] 1 K.B. 343. See also *Acraman v Morrice* (1849) 8 C.B. 449.

36 Relying on ss.17 and 18, r.2, of the Act.

37 At p.345. See also Rowlatt J. at first instance: [1922] 1 K.B. 123 at 124.

38 See also *Pritchett & Gold and Electric Power Storage Co. Ltd v Currie* [1916] 1 Ch. 515; *Philip Head & Sons Ltd v Showfronts Ltd* [1970] 1 Lloyd's Rep. 140; *Hendy Lennox (Industrial Engines) Ltd v Grahame Puttick Ltd* [1984] 1 W.L.R. 485 at 495; below, para.5–068.

39 See below, para.5–030.

40 *Jones v Earl of Tankerville* [1909] 2 Ch. 440 at 442; *Morison v Lockhart*, 1912 S.C. 1017; *Kursell v Timber Operators and Contractors Ltd* [1927] 1 K.B. 298; *Munro v Balnagown Estates*, 1949 S.L.T. 85. *Cf. Tansley v Turner* (1835) 2 Bing.(N.C.) 151. See above, para.1–100.

5–025 A contract for the sale of an undivided share, specified as a fraction or percentage, of a specific bulk[41] does not fall within section 18, rule 1, if it is the parties' intention that the undivided share is subsequently to be separated from the bulk and delivered to the buyer, since the goods[42] will not be in a deliverable state at the time the contract is made. But if the parties intend that the undivided share is to remain permanently undivided, for example, where a half share in a racehorse is sold to each of A and B, the rule could apply.

5–026 **Different intention.** The presumption contained in section 18, rule 1, will not apply where a different intention appears.[43] The most common situation is where the parties intend that the property in the goods shall not pass to the buyer until the price is paid[44] or a bill of exchange has been accepted.[45] Once the property has passed under section 18, rule 1, the parties could no doubt agree that it is to be divested from the buyer and revested in the seller; but convincing evidence is required that the parties so intended by a mere subsequent agreement that the goods are to remain the property of the seller until the price has been paid.[46] It is also necessary to consider whether any arrangement as to payment of the price is intended to suspend the passing of property or relates only to the circumstances in which the seller is prepared to deliver the goods to the buyer.[47] Thus, where specific goods are sold across the counter in a shop, property in the goods may pass under the rule when the contract is made, notwithstanding that the goods have not been paid for or that the method of payment, *e.g.* cash, or credit, or acceptance of a cheque, has still to be agreed.[48] But it may also be the intention of the parties that property is to pass only on delivery or payment.[49] In a supermarket, property in the goods taken from the shelf will pass to the customer only upon payment of the proper amount at the checkpoint.[50]

---

[41] *i.e.* "specific goods" within the extended definition in s.61(1): see above, paras 1–116, 5–022.

[42] By s.61(1), "goods" include an undivided share in goods.

[43] This refers back to s.17.

[44] *McEntire v Crossley Bros Ltd* [1895] A.C. 457; *Re an Arbitration between Shipton, Anderson & Co. and Harrison Bros & Co.* [1915] 3 K.B. 676; *Mooney v Lipka* [1926] 4 D.L.R. 647; *Re Anchor Line (Henderson Bros) Ltd* [1937] Ch. 1; *Ward (R.V.) Ltd v Bignall* [1967] 1 Q.B. 534. See also s.19(1); below, para.5–131.

[45] *Saks v Tilley* (1915) 32 T.L.R. 148. But see *Leigh & Sillavan Ltd v Aliakmon Shipping Co. Ltd* (*The Aliakmon*) [1986] A.C. 785. See also s.19(3); below, para.5–138.

[46] *Dennant v Skinner and Collom* [1948] 2 K.B. 164 at 172.

[47] *ibid.* at p.172. See also *Phillips v Brooks* [1919] 2 K.B. 243, as subsequently interpreted in *Lake v Simmons* [1927] A.C. 487 at 501.

[48] This point may be of importance where the contract is entered into under a mistake as to the person; see *Phillips v Brooks*, above; *Lake v Simmons*, above. *Cf. Ingram v Little* [1961] 1 Q.B. 31 at 49; above, para.3–012. But cases on mistake should not be carried over into the criminal law: *R. v Morris* [1984] A.C. 320.

[49] *Mooney v Lipka*, above; see also *Lambert v G. & C. Finance Corp.* (1963) 107 S.J. 666 (retention of car log-book); *Cheetham & Co. v Thornham Spinning Co.* [1964] 2 Lloyd's Rep. 17 (retention of shipping document).

[50] *Lacis v Cashmarts* [1969] 2 Q.B. 400 at 407; *Davies v Leighton* [1978] Crim.L.R. 575; *R. v Morris* [1984] A.C. 320.

5–027 A provision in the contract relating to risk[51] or to liability to insure[52] has been taken to indicate where the property lay, for risk normally follows property in a commercial transaction.[53] But in *Re Anchor Line (Henderson Brothers) Ltd*[54] where specific goods were purchased on terms that payment was to be deferred, the allocation to the buyer of the entire responsibility for the goods was considered by the Court of Appeal to be one of the factors which showed that property had not passed under section 18, rule 1, since such a clause would be unnecessary if the rule was intended to apply. It is clear that in each instance regard must be had to the terms of the contract, the conduct of the parties and the circumstances of the case.[55]

5–028 **Sale of goods and interest in land.** Where a contract for the sale of specific goods is part of an entire contract for the sale or assignment of an interest in land and goods connected therewith, *e.g.* furniture or crops, the passing of property in the goods is prima facie conditional on the passing of the interest in land,[56] and this is so even if a separate price is stated for the goods.[57]

5–029 **Sales on special terms.** Where specific goods are sold on f.o.r. terms, the property in the goods usually does not pass before delivery to the carrier[58] as is also the case under an f.o.b. contract.[59] Section 18, rule 1, will also not normally apply to "ex ship",[60] f.c.a.,[61] f.a.s.,[62] c.i.f.,[63] c.i.p.[64] and c. & f. contracts[65] as a different intention generally appears in these circumstances.[66]

---

[51] *Martineau v Kitching* (1872) L.R. 7 Q.B. 436 at 454; *The Parchim* [1918] A.C. 157 at 168, 171; *McPherson, Thom, Kettle & Co. v Dench Bros* [1921] V.L.R. 437 at 442; *Carlos Federspiel & Co. SA v Charles Twigg & Co. Ltd* [1957] 1 Lloyd's Rep. 240 at 255; *President of India v Metcalfe Shipping Co. Ltd* [1970] 1 Q.B. 289. Contrast *Mitsui & Co. Ltd v Flota Mercante Grancolombiana SA* (*The Ciudad de Pasto*) [1988] 2 Lloyd's Rep. 208 at 214, 217.
[52] *Allison v Bristol Marine Insurance Co. Ltd* (1876) 1 App.Cas. 209 at 229. See also Atiyah, *Sale of Goods*, (11th ed.), p.326.
[53] See below, para.6–002.
[54] [1937] Ch. 1. See also *Martineau v Kitching*, above, at p.451; and below, para.5–084.
[55] s.17(2); see above, para.5–016.
[56] *Neal v Viney* (1808) 1 Camp. 471; *Lanyon v Toogood* (1844) 13 M. & W. 27. *Cf. Warren v Forbes* [1959] V.R. 14 at 24. See also *Cordew v Drakeford* (1811) 3 Taunt. 382; *Salmon v Watson* (1819) 4 Moore C.P. 73; *Seddon v Cruikshank* (1846) 16 M. & W. 71; *Commissioner of Stamps v Queensland Meat Export Co. Ltd* [1917] A.C. 624.
[57] *Neal v Viney*, above; *Salmon v Watson*, above.
[58] *Underwood v Burgh Castle Brick and Cement Syndicate* [1922] 1 K.B. 343; see above, para.5–023; below, para.21–043.
[59] See below, paras 18–208, 20–070.
[60] (Or "DES" contract.) See below, paras 18–208, 21–020.
[61] See *Incoterms 2000*, "FCA".
[62] See below, paras 18–208, 21–011.
[63] See below, para.19–298.
[64] See *Incoterms 2000*, "CIP"; *Stora Enso DYJ v Port of Dundee* 2006 CSOH 40 (Court of Session).
[65] (Or "CFR".) See below, para.21–013.
[66] For "ex works", see below, paras 5–089, 21–003; containers, below, para.21–098.

(b) *Specific Goods to be put into a Deliverable State*

Section 18, rule 2. The second rule set out in section 18 of the 1979 Act provides that, "where there is a contract for the sale of specific goods[67] and the seller is bound to do something to the goods, for the purpose of putting them into a deliverable state, the property does not pass until the thing be done, and the buyer has notice that it has been done." It is to be noted that this rule, unlike rule 1, is negative in form; but it is likewise only a presumption and is subject to the intention of the parties.[68] It is based on the common law prevailing before the 1893 Act[69] and was applied by the Court of Appeal in *Underwood Ltd v Burgh Castle Brick and Cement Syndicate*.[70] 5–030

Deliverable state. The meaning of "deliverable state" has already been discussed.[71] Where specific goods are sold f.o.r. or f.o.b., it is possible to contend that they are not in a deliverable state until they have been delivered to the carrier[72]; but it is preferable to regard such contracts as instances where the property passes to the buyer in accordance with the intention of the parties under section 17.[73] The fact that a seller has to pay wharfage or warehousing rent[74] or customs dues[75] before the goods are released to the buyer is not something to be done by him for the purpose of putting them into a deliverable state. The rule will, however, be applicable to a contract for the sale of a particular chattel to be completed by the seller. Although a contract for goods to be manufactured by the seller is normally one for the sale of unascertained or future goods,[76] yet if a designated chattel is purchased in the course of manufacture, the parties may have so far agreed upon it as to create "what the civilians called *obligatio certi corporis*."[77] Property will not pass until the chattel is completed by the seller[78] and the buyer has notice that this has been done, unless it is clear that the parties intended that property in the chattel should pass in its incomplete state.[79] 5–031

---

67 s.61(1); see above, para.1–113.

68 See the opening words of s.18 (which refers back to s.17) and *Young v Matthews* (1866) L.R. 2 C.P. 127.

69 *Rugg v Minett* (1809) 11 East 210; *Acraman v Morrice* (1849) 8 C.B. 449; Blackburn, *Contract of Sale* (1st ed.), p.151 (cited in *Gilmour v Supple* (1858) 11 Moo.P.C. 551). But see below, para.5–034.

70 [1922] 1 K.B. 343; above, para.5–023.

71 See above, para.5–023.

72 *Anderson v Morice* (1875) L.R. 10 C.P. 609 at 618 (affirmed (1876) 1 App. Cas. 713).

73 See above, para.5–023. In *Underwood v Burgh Castle Brick and Cement Syndicate*, above, both ss.18, r. 2, and 17 were relied on. See also *Anderson v Morice* (1876) 1 App.Cas. 713 at 749 and below, paras 5–102, 20–070.

74 *Hammond v Anderson* (1803) 1 B. & P.N.R. 69; *Greaves v Hepke* (1818) 2 B. & Ald. 131.

75 *Hinde v Whitehouse* (1806) 7 East 558.

76 See below, paras 5–060, 5–090.

77 *Laidler v Burlinson* (1837) 2 M. & W. 602 at 610. See also *Wait v Baker* (1848) 2 Exch. 1 at 8–9.

78 *Laidler v Burlinson*, above.

79 See below, para.5–092, 5–093.

5–032 **Obligation of the seller.** For the rule to operate so as to suspend the passing of the property to the buyer, it seems that it must be a term of the contract of sale that the seller is bound to do something to the goods for the purpose of putting them into a deliverable state. But if, for example, the seller of a second-hand car agrees to carry out certain repairs to the vehicle before it is delivered to the buyer, or the supplier of component parts of machinery agrees to assemble and install them, it is a matter of construction whether the passing of property in the goods to the buyer is conditional on this being done[80] or whether the seller's obligation is a supplemental obligation which does not condition the passing of property to the buyer.[81]

5–033 **Acts done by the buyer.** The rule only applies when the obligation to put the goods in a deliverable state is placed on the seller.[82] But where such an obligation is placed on the buyer, or the nature of the subject-matter of the contract requires that this be done by him, the result may in certain circumstances be the same: section 18, rule 1, will not apply[83] and the situation will be governed by the intention of the parties under section 17 of the Act.[84]

5–034 **Notice to the buyer.** The requirement that "the buyer has notice that it has been done" did not form part of the common law, but was introduced by the 1893 Act.[85] As the 1979 Act does not provide that the seller shall give notice, but that the buyer shall have notice, it is submitted that "notice" means "knowledge." In accordance with the principle that there is in general no constructive notice in commercial transactions,[86] constructive notice would be insufficient.

---

80 *Wilkie v Fleming* (1919) 3 W.W.R. 569; *McDill v Hilson* (1920) 53 D.L.R. 228; *Jerome v Clements Motor Sales Ltd* (1958) 15 D.L.R. (2d.) 689; *Hartley v Saunders* (1962) 33 D.L.R. (2d.) 638; *Anderson v Ryan* [1967] I.R. 34 at 37.

81 *Pritchett & Gold and Electrical Power Storage Co. Ltd v Currie* [1916] 2 Ch. 515; *Marca v Bertholet* [1928] 2 D.L.R. 691. Since the thing to be done by the seller under the Act is to put the goods into a "deliverable" state, it is argued in Benjamin's *Sale of Personal Property* (8th ed.), p.311, that prima facie the property in goods will pass, even though something remains to be done by the seller in relation to the goods sold, *after* their delivery to the buyer.

82 In *Acraman v Morrice* (1849) 8 C.B. 449, it was held that the buyer could not make the property pass by performing the acts which it was the seller's duty to do.

83 See above, para.5–016.

84 *Kursell v Timber Operators and Contractors Ltd* [1927] 1 K.B. 298; above, para.5–022.

85 "The buyer has notice thereof." *Quaere* whether this requirement could be dispensed with if the parties impliedly intended the property to pass without such notice: see *Joseph Reid Pty Ltd v Schultz* (1949) 49 S.R. (N.S.W.) 231.

86 *Joseph v Lyons* (1884) 15 Q.B.D. 280 at 287; *Manchester Trust v Furness* [1895] 2 Q.B. 539 at 545; *Greer v Downs Supply Co.* [1927] 2 K.B. 28 at 36, 37; *Worcester Works Finance Ltd v Cooden Engineering Co. Ltd* [1972] 1 Q.B. 210 at 218.

(c) *Specific Goods to be Weighed, Measured or Tested*

Section 18, rule 3. The third rule set out in section 18 of the 1979 Act provides that, unless a different intention appears, "where there is a contract for the sale of specific goods[87] in a deliverable state[88] but the seller is bound to weigh, measure, test or do some other act or thing with reference to the goods for the purpose of ascertaining the price, the property does not pass until the act or thing be done, and the buyer has notice that it has been done." It is construed to cover the situation where specific goods are bought on terms that the price depends on their extent or quality (which is unknown), and the price cannot be computed until the extent or quality of the goods is ascertained.[89] The rule codifies the common law before the passing of the 1893 Act[90] but with the additional requirement that the buyer should have notice.[91] 5–035

Obligation of the seller. The duty to weigh, measure, test, etc., must be one which is to be performed by the seller[92] and not by the buyer or a third party. If this obligation is placed by the contract on the buyer, or if it is agreed that the price shall be ascertained by measurement by a third party, it will be necessary to have regard to the intention of the parties[93] in order to discover whether the passing of property was conditional on such an event. A mere right on the part of the buyer or a third party to weigh the goods will not have this effect. In *Nanka-Bruce v Commonwealth Trust Ltd*[94] a seller sold cocoa to a buyer at an agreed price per load of 60 lbs. It was recognised that the buyer would resell the cocoa to other merchants and that when these other merchants took delivery of the cocoa it would be weighed at their premises and the weight tested there. The Privy Council held that the weighing by the merchants was not a condition which suspended the passing of the property to the buyer. Lord Shaw said[95]: "To effect such suspension or impose such a condition would require a clear contract between vendor and vendee to that effect. In this case there was no contract whatsoever to carry into effect the weighing, which was simply a means to satisfy the purchaser that he had what he had bargained for and that the full price claimed per the contract was therefore due." 5–036

---

87 s.61(1); see above, para.1–113.
88 s.61(5); see above, paras.5–023, 5–031.
89 *The Napoli* (1898) 15 T.L.R. 56; *National Coal Board v Gamble* [1959] 1 Q.B. 11 at 21. Contrast *R. v Tideswell* [1905] 2 K.B. 273 at 277. If the acts done by the seller are necessary to ascertain, not the extent, but the identity of the goods to be sold (*e.g.* where the seller has to measure out 500 gallons of oil from a bulk of 1,000 gallons), the goods will not be specific goods, and the situation will be governed by ss.18, r.5 and 20A of the Act.
90 *Hanson v Meyer* (1805) 6 East 614; *Zagury v Furnell* (1809) 2 Camp. 240; *Withers v Lyss* (1815) 4 Camp. 237; *Simmons v Swift* (1826) 5 B. & C. 857; *Logan v Le Mesurier* (1847) 6 Moo.P.C. 116; Blackburn, *Contract of Sale* (1st ed.), p.151.
91 See above, para.5–034.
92 *Turley v Bates* (1863) 2 H. & C. 200.
93 Ascertained in accordance with ss.17 and 18, r.1. See *Naugle Pole & Tie Co. v Wilson* [1929] 3 W.W.R. 730.
94 [1926] A.C. 77. This case, however, appears to have been concerned with a sale of unascertained goods.
95 At p.79.

5–037 The rule applies where the seller is bound to weigh, measure or test the goods, and also where he is bound to do "some other act or thing" with reference to the goods[96] for the purpose of ascertaining the price. The mere adding up of separate items previously measured is not sufficient to suspend the passing of the property for "it is too trifiing an incident to say that the measure is not complete".[97] But presumably counting the quantity of the goods could be a sufficient act, provided the extent of the goods was unknown and counting was not merely a mental act to calculate the price of the goods the extent of which was already ascertained.[98]

5–038 **Ascertaining the price.** The act to be done by the seller must be necessary for the purpose of ascertaining the price. The rule will obviously not apply where goods are sold for a lump sum, since there will then be no necessity to ascertain the price.[99] Nor will it apply where the goods have been measured before the contract of sale, and all that remains is to ascertain the price by the measure previously made.[1] Also, if the price per unit of specific goods is agreed and their weight or measurement given, it is immaterial that the contract provides that they are to be weighed or measured by the seller, for this act is merely for the satisfaction of the buyer.[2]

5–039 **Different intention.** It is difficult to see why this rule should have found a place in English law which has never placed so much weight as Roman law on certainty of price.[3] But in any event it is subject to the general rule relating to the intention of the parties contained in section 17.[4] In particular, where goods have been delivered to the buyer[5] or where it has been acknowledged that they are held to the buyer's order,[6] the property may be held to have passed notwithstanding that they are still to be measured by the seller. Moreover, in *Martineau v Kitching*[7] it was said that, if the parties provisionally fix a price for the goods, although this is afterwards to be more accurately calculated by weighing by the seller, the inference is that they did not intend to suspend the passing of property. It

[96] The words "with reference to the goods" suggest that the act to which the seller is obliged need not physically concern the actual goods sold. Contrast the wording of s.18, r.2.

[97] *Tansley v Turner* (1835) 2 Bing. (N.C.) 151.

[98] *R. v Tideswell* [1905] 2 K.B. 273 at 277.

[99] *Hanson v Meyer* (1805) 6 East 614 at 627; *Alexander v Gardner* (1835) 1 Bing. (N.C.) 671.

[1] *Hinde v Whitehouse* (1806) 7 East 558; *Gilmour v Supple* (1858) 11 Moo.P.C. 551.

[2] *Swanwick v Southern* (1839) 9 A. & E. 895.

[3] Dig. 18. 1. 35 5–7. See also Blackburn, *Contract of Sale* (1st ed.), p.153, who thought it was a rule somewhat hastily adopted from the civil law.

[4] *Turley v Bates* (1863) 2 H. & C. 200; *Martineau v Kitching* (1872) L.R. 7 Q.B. 436 at 449; *Kennedy's Trustee v Hamilton and Manson* (1897) 25 R. 252; *Lord Eldon v Hedley Bros* [1935] 2 K.B. 1.

[5] *Kershaw v Ogden* (1865) 3 H. & C. 717.

[6] *Howes v Watson* (1824) 2 B. & C. 243.

[7] (1872) L.R. 7 Q.B. 436 at 451. See also *Anderson v Morice* (1874) L.R. 10 C.P. 58 at 73 (affirmed (1876) 1 App.Cas. 713). *Cf. Logan v Le Mesurier* (1847) 6 Moo.P.C. 116.

would seem that the presumption contained in the rule can be rebutted without great difficulty.

3. GOODS DELIVERED ON APPROVAL OR ON SALE OR RETURN

Section 18, rule 4. The fourth rule set out in section 18 of the Sale of Goods Act 1979 provides that, unless a different intention appears,[8] "when goods are delivered to the buyer on approval or on sale or return or other similar terms the property in the goods passes to the buyer: (a) when he signifies his approval or acceptance to the seller or does any other act adopting the transaction; (b) if he does not signify his approval or acceptance to the seller but retains the goods without giving notice of rejection, then, if a time has been fixed for the return of the goods, on the expiration of that time, and, if no time has been fixed, on the expiration of a reasonable time."[9] This rule codifies in substance[10] the common law before the 1893 Act.[11] 5–040

Approval or on sale or return.[12] The rule requires that the goods must have been delivered to the buyer "on approval or on sale or return or other similar terms." Goods will be considered to have been delivered on approval where it is agreed by the parties[13] that they shall be retained and purchased by the buyer at the notified price if he approves them, but not if they are disapproved.[14] The meaning of a contract "on sale or return" is that the goods are to be taken as sold at the option of the buyer,[15] if not previously rejected,[16] unless returned to the seller within the time fixed by the contract or within a reasonable time.[17] A contract can be one on sale or 5–041

---

[8] See the opening words of s.18.

[9] What is a reasonable time is a question of fact: s.59.

[10] *Cf. Moss v Sweet* (1851) 16 Q.B. 493 at 495, where it was said that goods sold on sale or return must be returned to cancel the transaction; but, under the Act, the buyer may prevent the passing of property by giving notice of rejection (see below, para.5–052) without returning the goods.

[11] *Burch v Scory* (1699) 12 Mod. 309; *Bailey v Gouldsmith* (1791) Peake 78; *Humphries v Carvalho* (1812) 16 East 45; *Gibson v Bray* (1817) 8 Taunt. 76; *Swain v Shepherd* (1832) 1 M. & Rob. 223; *Beverley v Lincoln Gas Light & Coke Co.* (1837) 6 A. & E. 829; *Johnson v Kirkaldy* (1840) 4 Jur.Rep. 988; *Moss v Sweet* (1851) 16 Q.B. 493; *Elphick v Barnes* (1880) 5 C.P.D. 321; *Blanckensee v Blaiberg* (1885) 2 T.L.R. 36.

[12] See above, para.1–056.

[13] *Cf. Alexander v Glenbroome Ltd* [1957] 1 Lloyd's Rep. 157 (buyer merely thinks he has the chance of returning the goods if he does not like them).

[14] *Gibson v Bray* (1817) 8 Taunt. 76; *Swain v Shepherd* (1832) 1 M. & Rob. 223; *Elphick v Barnes* (1880) 5 C.P.D. 321; *Marsh v Hughes-Hallett* (1900) 16 T.L.R. 376; *London Jewellers Ltd v Attenborough* [1934] 2 K.B. 206.

[15] But not if at the option of the seller: *Manders v Williams* (1849) 4 Exch. 339.

[16] See below, para.5–052.

[17] *Harrison v Allen* (1824) 2 Bing. 4; *Johnson v Kirkaldy* (1840) 4 Jur.Rep. 988; *Moss v Sweet* (1851) 16 Q.B. 493 at 495; *Kirkham v Attenborough* [1897] 1 Q.B. 201; *Bryce v Ehrmann* (1904) 7 F. 5, 13; *Bradley & Cohn Ltd v Ramsey & Co.* (1912) 107 L.T. 771; *Genn v Winkel* (1912) 107 L.T. 434; *Poole v Smith's Car Sales (Balham) Ltd* [1962] 1 W.L.R. 744. Depending on the terms of the contract, the buyer may be entitled to purchase part of the goods and return the remainder: *Atari Corp. (U.K.) Ltd v Electronics Boutiques Stores (U.K.) Ltd* [1998] Q.B. 539.

return whether or not the recipient of the goods under the contract intends to buy them himself or to sell them to third parties.[18] Goods are delivered on "other similar terms" where, for example, they are sent on trial[19] or on approbation.[20] But, in order to bring a transaction within this rule, the circumstances must show that the buyer has an option to purchase on the statutory terms, that is to say, if and when the specific acts or conduct on his part set out in the rule have occurred. For this reason, it is necessary to distinguish certain closely related forms of transaction where a different intention appears.

5–042 **Special condition precedent.** Although the contract may otherwise be one on approval or on sale or return, the rule will not apply if the terms of the contract specify any other event as essential to the passing of the property. In *Weiner v Gill*[21] goods were delivered to the buyer on the terms of a document which stated: "On approbation. On sale for cash only or return. Goods had on approbation or on sale or return remain the property of [the seller] until such goods are paid for or charged." The Court of Appeal held that a pledge of the goods by the buyer, which would otherwise have constituted an act adopting the transaction,[22] did not pass the property under the rule. The property was intended to pass only when the buyer had paid for the goods or was debited with the price by the seller, who had retained the property in the goods until these conditions were fulfilled. It is a question of construction in each case whether or not the particular words used, *e.g.* "until invoiced"[23] or "terms net cash",[24] are a condition precedent to the passing of property. The existence of such a condition will be of considerable importance where a third party claims to have acquired a good title to the goods from the buyer.[25]

5–043 **Condition subsequent.** It may be the intention of the parties that the property in the goods shall pass immediately to the buyer or on delivery of the goods to him with a provision that, if the goods are not approved, they are to be returned and the property is to revest in the seller.[26] The sale is then said to be subject to a condition subsequent.[27] Thus, if garments are

---

[18] *Poole v Smith's Car Sales (Balham) Ltd*, above, at p.748.
[19] *Ellis v Mortimer* (1805) 1 B. & P.N.R. 257; *Humphries v Carvalho* (1812) 16 East 45; *Beverley v Lincoln Gas Light & Coke Co.* (1837) 6 A. & E. 829.
[20] *Blanckensee v Blaiberg* (1885) 2 T.L.R. 36. See also *Bevington v Dale* (1902) 7 Com.Cas. 112 ("on memorandum").
[21] [1906] 2 K.B. 574. See also *Edwards v Vaughan* (1910) 26 T.L.R. 545 (cash); *Kempler v Bravingtons* (1925) 133 L.T. 680 (until charged); *R. v Eaton* (1966) 50 Cr.App.R. 189 (until paid for).
[22] See below, para.5–047.
[23] *Bryce v Ehrmann* (1904) 7 F. 5; *Truman v Attenborough* (1910) 26 T.L.R. 601; *R. v Eaton*, above.
[24] *Whitehorn Brothers v Davison* [1911] 1 K.B. 463.
[25] See below, paras 5–047, 7–021—7–070.
[26] *Neale v Ball* (1801) 2 East 117; *Head v Tattersall* (1871) L.R. 7 Ex. 7; *Chapman v Withers* (1888) 20 Q.B.D. 824; *The Vesta* [1921] 1 A.C. 774. See also *Cranston v Mallow and Lien*, 1912 S.C. 112. *Cf. Maine v Lyons* (1913) 15 C.L.R. 671 (condition not fulfilled).
[27] See above, para.1–056.

purchased from a shop on the understanding that they can be exchanged if they are not of the right size, the natural inference is that the property passes immediately, subject to the right of the buyer to exchange the goods for others by returning them to the seller. Even if the right to return the goods is absolute, section 18, rule 4, will not apply in this situation. The distinction is of importance not merely with reference to the passing of property but also with reference to the risk.[28]

Bailment. The position of a person who has received goods on approval or on sale or return is that he has the option of becoming the purchaser of them, being free to do so or not as he chooses.[29] One analysis of the transaction is that the seller makes to the buyer an irrevocable offer to sell, which the buyer may accept by signifying his acceptance to the seller or in one of the other ways set out in the rule.[30] Alternatively, the seller may be regarded as having granted to the buyer an option to purchase. The granting of the option imposes no obligation on the buyer and an obligation on the seller which is contingent on the exercise of the option.[31] Whichever analysis is adopted, pending acceptance of the offer or the exercise of the option, the buyer is in lawful possession of the goods[32] and holds them as bailee.[33] In certain situations, it may therefore be difficult to distinguish a contract on sale or return from a bailment for hire[34] or from a simple bailment with an option to purchase,[35] or from a bailment on terms that the bailee is to have the power to sell or dispose of the goods to third parties.[36] If such is the true nature of the transaction, property will not pass to the bailee under section 18, rule 4, *e.g.* simply by the expiration of a reasonable time. 5–044

Agency. It is also necessary to distinguish between a sale or return transaction and one of agency.[37] This may be no easy matter. It may well be that goods are delivered to a person on the assumption that he is to find a buyer for them, if he can, otherwise he is to return them. The question then arises whether the transaction is one of sale or return or one in which he is 5–045

---

[28] See below, para.6–010.

[29] See above, para.5–041.

[30] *Kirkham v Attenborough* [1897] 1 Q.B. 201 at 203; *Atari Corp. (UK) Ltd v Electronics Boutiques Stores (UK) Ltd* [1998] Q.B. 539.

[31] *Spiro v Glencrown Properties Ltd* [1991] Ch. 537 (land).

[32] *Colwill v Reeves* (1811) 2 Camp. 575.

[33] *Atari Corp. (UK) Ltd v Electronics Boutiques Stores (UK) Ltd*, above. See below, para.5–057.

[34] *General Motors Acceptance Corp. (UK) Ltd v I.R.C.* (1986) 59 T.C. 651.

[35] In some respects, this type of transaction is not dissimilar from a hire-purchase agreement, where the hirer has an option to purchase the goods or return them to the owner, and the owner is bound contingently to sell: *Helby v Matthews* [1895] A.C. 471. But a hire-purchase agreement is distinguishable by the presence of a bailment for hire. *Cf.* Consumer Credit Act 1974, s.189(1): "hire-purchase agreement". See above, paras 1–021, 1–053.

[36] *Whitehorn Brothers v Davison* [1911] 1 K.B. 463 at 480. See also *Poole v Smith's Car Sales (Balham) Ltd* [1962] 1 W.L.R. 744.

[37] See *Bowstead and Reynolds on Agency* (17th ed.), para.1–032 and above, para.1–048.

an agent selling the goods on behalf of his principal. In determining this question the court is not bound by the terminology used by the parties: the whole agreement must be looked at to determine the reality of the transaction.[38] In *Weiner v Harris*[39] jewellery was delivered to a retail dealer "on sale for cash only or return". The contract further provided that the jewellery was not to be kept as his own stock, that it was to be entered at cost price in a special book kept by him, and that his remuneration for selling it was to be one-half the profit. Immediately he sold the jewellery he was to remit to the seller the cost price and half the profit. The Court of Appeal held that, on these facts, the relationship between the parties was one of principal and agent. On the other hand, in *Re Nevill*,[40] cotton goods were delivered to one Nevill with a price list, it being understood that he was not to pay for them unless he sold them. He rendered monthly accounts of the sales actually made, debiting himself with the price according to the price list, but giving no particulars of the persons with whom he dealt. After a lapse of another month, he was expected to pay in cash according to these accounts. He sometimes dyed or treated the cotton goods before selling them. It was held that the transaction was one of sale or return, and that he was not a *del credere* agent. No exception can be taken to this decision but Mellish L.J. said[41]: "If the consignee is at liberty . . . to sell at any price he likes, and receive payment at any time he likes, but is to be bound, if he sells the goods, to pay the consignor for them at a fixed price and a fixed time-in my opinion, whatever the parties may think, the relation is not that of principal and agent." This might suggest that, where a person is allowed to retain all the profit made by him over and above the agreed price, his duty being to pay the agreed price or to return the goods if unsold, the transaction must inevitably be one of sale or return. But such an agreement may be consistent with the relationship of principal and agent.[42] All the circumstances of the contract should be looked at. The essence of sale or return is that the person to whom the goods have been delivered has the right for a period to retain them[43] and is given the option during that period either himself to purchase the goods or to sell or dispose of them to another on his own account. The distinction between the two types of transaction may be relevant not only to the passing of property between seller and buyer, but also to the acquisition of title by third parties[44] and the extent of the seller's claim against the buyer.[45]

---

[38] *Re Nevill* (1870) L.R. 6 Ch.App. 397 at 399, 403; *Weiner v Harris* [1910] 1 K.B. 285 at 290, 292, 294. See also *Livingstone v Ross* [1901] A.C. 327; *Lamb & Sons v Goring Brick Co. Ltd* [1932] 1 K.B. 710 (sale or agency).

[39] [1910] 1 K.B. 285. See also *Bell, Rannie & Co. v White's Trustee* (1885) 22 Sc.L.R. 597; *Janesich v Attenborough* (1910) 102 L.T. 605.

[40] (1870) L.R. 6 Ch.App. 397, affirmed *sub. nom. Towle & Co. v White* (1873) 29 L.T. 78, HL. See also *Michelin Tyre Co. Ltd v Macfarlane (Glasgow) Ltd* (1917), 55 Sc.L.R. 35, HL; *Kempler v Bravingtons* (1925) 133 L.T. 680; *Poole v Smith's Car Sales (Balham) Ltd* [1962] 1 W.L.R. 744 (noted 25 M.L.R. 726 (1962)); *Pitrie v Racey* (1963) 37 D.L.R. (2d) 495; *R. v Eaton* (1966) 50 Cr.App.Rep. 189.

[41] At p.403.

[42] *ibid*,, at p.405. See also *Re Smith* (1879) 10 Ch.D. 566 at 570.

[43] *Janesich v Attenborough*, above.

[44] See below, paras 5–047, 7–031.

[45] *Re Nevill*, above; *Michelin Tyre Co. Ltd v Macfarlane (Glasgow) Ltd*, above.

Fraud by buyer. Where the seller has been induced to deliver goods to the buyer on approval or on sale or return by a fraudulent representation by the buyer that he has a customer to whom he can sell the goods, the transaction is voidable but not void.[46] It was at one time argued that such a situation constituted the former offence of larceny by a trick; that the buyer was not in possession of the goods with the seller's consent; and that section 18, rule 4, did not therefore apply. But in *London Jewellers Ltd v Attenborough*[47] the court rejected this argument and held that the offence committed was one of obtaining by false pretences and not larceny by a trick.[48] There is no doubt that the position remains unaltered as a result of the passing of the Theft Act 1968.[49] If, however, the transaction has been entered into as the result of a false representation which gives rise to an operative mistake on the part of the seller as to the buyer's identity, it will be void *ab initio*[50] and the rule will not apply. 5–046

Approval or acceptance. The first situation stipulated in rule 4 for the passing of property is when the buyer "signifies his approval or acceptance to the seller or does any other act adopting the transaction." There is no real problem concerning approval or acceptance,[51] but the words "or does any other act adopting the transaction" have occasioned some difficulty. They have been said to be "unfortunately chosen",[52] "difficult to construe"[53] and "not very happy".[54] It is, however, now settled law that, if a buyer who has received goods on sale or return sells[55] or pledges[56] the goods to a third party, he thereby adopts the transaction and property passes to him. In *Kirkham v Attenborough*[57] a buyer of goods on sale or return pledged them with a pawnbroker in order to secure an advance. The Court of Appeal held that the property in the goods passed to the buyer by this act so that the pawnbroker acquired a good title to the goods. Lord Esher M.R. said[58]: "There must be some act which shows that he adopts the transaction; but any act which is consistent only with his being the purchaser is sufficient." 5–047

---

[46] *Truman v Attenborough* (1910) 26 T.L.R. 601; *Whitehorn Brothers v Davison* [1911] 1 K.B. 463.

[47] [1934] 2 K.B. 206. See also *Whitehorn Brothers v Davison*, above.

[48] Even if it were larceny by a trick, the distinction would probably be irrelevant: see below, paras 7–037, 7–074.

[49] s.1 (theft) and s.15 (obtaining property by deception): *R. v Lawrence* [1972] A.C. 626. See also *Dobson v General Accident Fire and Life Assurance Corp. Plc* [1990] 1 Q.B. 274.

[50] *Hardman v Booth* (1863) 1 H. & C. 803; *Cundy v Lindsay* (1878) 3 App.Cas. 459; *Morrisson v Robertson*, 1908 S.C. 332; *Lake v Simmons* [1927] A.C. 487 at 500; *London Jewellers Ltd v Attenborough*, above, at pp.217, 223; *Ingram v Little* [1961] 1 Q.B. 31. See also *Shogun Finance Ltd v Hudson* [2003] UKHL 62, [2004] 1 A.C. 919 and above, para.3–012.

[51] But the definition in s.35 of the Sale of Goods Act 1979 is not really appropriate to this situation. See below, para.12–044.

[52] *Kirkham v Attenborough* [1897] 1 Q.B. 201 at 203.

[53] *ibid.*, at p.204.

[54] *London Jewellers Ltd v Attenborough* [1934] 2 K.B. 206 at 214.

[55] *Re Florence* (1879) 10 Ch.D. 591 at 593; *Genn v Winkel* (1912) 107 L.T. 434.

[56] *Kirkham v Attenborough* [1897] 1 Q.B. 201; *Weiner v Gill* [1906] 2 K.B. 574 at 578.

[57] [1897] 1 Q.B. 201.

[58] At p.203.

The peculiarity of this situation lies in the fact that a person who is intended to purchase or sell the goods and who pledges them contrary to his "mandate" should be treated as a buyer.[59] But it was said in this case that a pledge constitutes an act adopting the transaction either because "he ought not to have done this unless he meant to treat himself as purchaser, and by doing it he makes himself a purchaser",[60] or because "if he pledges [the goods] he no longer has the free control over them so as to be in a position to return them".[61] The same principle applies to sales on approval.[62]

5–048 It seems that the delivery of possession of the goods to a third party for a special purpose consistent with the terms of the contract is not an act adopting the transaction.[63] Also, if a buyer on sale or return[64] offers to sell the goods, or delivers them on sale or return to another, this will not in itself pass the property to him. Such was the opinion of Fletcher Moulton and Buckley L.JJ. in *Genn v Winkel*.[65] But in the same case it was held that, if A delivers goods on sale or return to B, who delivers them on the same terms to C, any act on the part of C which constitutes an adoption of the transaction between himself and B or which passes the property to him from B will constitute an adoption of the first transaction by B.

5–049 Where goods are delivered to a buyer on trial, there appears to be no authority whether a use of the goods which is more than necessary for a fair test or trial amounts to an adoption of the transaction by him. It is, however, submitted that an excessive use of the goods is an act from which the court would be entitled to infer an adoption.[66] And where a motor-car was delivered to a buyer on sale or return, it was held that the receipt of a vehicle log-book issued to him by the local authority on his application was an act adopting the transaction.[67]

5–050 **Expiration of time.** If the buyer does not signify his approval or acceptance to the seller, and does not do any act adopting the transaction,[68] then, if a time has been fixed for the return of the goods, property will pass to him on the expiration of that time[69] and, if no time has been fixed, on the

---

[59] *London Jewellers Ltd v Attenborough*, above, at p.214.
[60] At p.203. See also *London Jewellers Ltd v Attenborough*, above, at p.215.
[61] At p.204.
[62] *London Jewellers Ltd v Attenborough*, above. See also *Blanckensee v Blaiberg* (1885) 2 T.L.R.36 (on approbation).
[63] *Weiner v Gill* [1906] 2 K.B. 574 at 578; *Genn v Winkel* (1912) 107 L.T. 434; *Ellis v Steinberg's Trustee* [1925] 4 D.L.R. 733.
[64] *Quaere* whether this also applies to sales on trial, or even on approval, where it is not intended that the buyer should sell the goods.
[65] (1912) 107 L.T. 434.
[66] See, *e.g. Okell v Smith* (1815) 1 Stark. 107. *Cf. Elliott v Thomas* (1838) 3 M. & W. 170.
[67] *Astley Industrial Trust Ltd v Miller* [1968] 2 All E.R. 36.
[68] This is presumably the case, although not expressly provided for in the rule. An act which adopts the transaction will also preclude the buyer from returning the goods within the allowed time: see *Kirkham v Attenborough* [1897] 1 Q.B. 201; *Genn v Winkel* (1912) 107 L.T. 434.
[69] *Harrison v Allen* (1824) 2 Bing. 4; *Johnson v Kirkaldy* (1840) 4 Jur.Rep. 988; *Marsh v Hughes-Hallett* (1900) 16 T.L.R. 376.

expiration of a reasonable time.[70] What is a reasonable time is a question of fact,[71] and the conduct of the seller may be relevant in determining what in all the circumstances is a reasonable time.[72] Time begins to run from the date on which the goods are actually delivered to the buyer.[73] If A delivers goods on sale or return to B for 14 days, and after seven days B delivers them on sale or return to C, then B should stipulate for a time limit of seven days in his contract with C. For if C retains the goods beyond the date fixed in the contract between A and B, B will (unless he has given notice of rejection) be held to have purchased the goods, since the time fixed for the return of the goods has expired.[74]

Stock financing schemes. For the purpose of value added tax, there is no tax point if goods sent or taken on approval or sale or return or similar terms are removed before it is known whether a supply will take place. The basic tax point occurs at the time when it becomes certain that the supply has taken place, but not later than 12 months after the removal.[75] Thus goods become chargeable to value added tax when the buyer adopts the transaction, or at the end of any time limit of less than 12 months which may be fixed by the seller for the return of the goods. If there is no time limit fixed, or a time limit longer than 12 months, the basic tax point occurs at the end of 12 months from the date on which the goods were dispatched by the seller, unless adoption has already taken place. Because of this ability to postpone the date on which value added tax becomes chargeable, stock financing schemes have been devised under which goods are sold, or delivered on sale or return, by the manufacturer to a finance company, and then delivered on sale or return by the finance company to distributors, and/or under which goods are delivered on sale or return by distributors to dealers. Such schemes were for the most part developed in relation to motor vehicles, since chargeability to car tax (now abolished)[76] could similarly be postponed where a vehicle was delivered under an agreement providing for its sale or return.[77] The buyer may be required to pay to the seller a charge (variously described as a "display charge" or "handling charge") in respect of the period during which the goods are in his possession prior to adoption or expiration of the time limit fixed or 5–051

---

[70] Sale of Goods Act 1979, s.18, r. 4(b); *Burch v Scory* (1699) 12 Mod. 309; *Bailey v Gouldsmith* (1791) Peake 78; *Gibson v Bray* (1817) 8 Taunt. 76; *Beverley v Lincoln Gas Light & Coke Co.* (1837) 6 A. & E. 829; *Moss v Sweet* (1851) 16 Q.B. 493; *Poole v Smith's Car Sales (Balham) Ltd* [1962] 1 W.L.R. 744; *Cf.* below, para.5–052 (rejection).

[71] Sale of Goods Act 1979, s.59.

[72] *Heilbutt v Hickson* (1872) L.R. 7 C.P. 438 at 472; *Poole v Smith's Car Sales (Balham) Ltd*, above.

[73] *Jacobs v Harbach* (1886) 2 T.L.R. 419 (delivery to a carrier does not, as in s.32(1) of the Act, constitute delivery to the buyer for the purpose of computing the time fixed for the return of the goods).

[74] *Genn v Winkel* (1912) 107 L.T. 434.

[75] Value Added Tax Act 1994, s.6(2)(c).

[76] Car Tax (Abolition) Act 1992.

[77] Car Tax Act 1983, s.5(2)(c), Sch.1, para.12(*h*). See also *Fraser v London Sports Car Centre* [1985] S.T.C. 75 (stock relief).

specified.[78] Adoption by the buyer occurs, for example, when he purchases the goods or appropriates them for his stock or for use by himself or another, or makes them the subject of a taxable supply to another person, whether by sale, hire, hire-purchase or credit sale agreement.

5–052 **Notice of rejection.** Property will not pass to the buyer by the expiration of time[79] where he has notified the seller of his rejection of the goods within the appropriate time.[80] If goods are sold on approval, then, in the absence of provision to the contrary, the buyer can reject the goods for reasons other than that the goods are defective or unsatisfactory.[81] The form of the notice depends upon the terms, express or implied, of the particular contract. But any intimation to the seller which clearly demonstrates that the buyer does not wish to exercise his option to purchase will ordinarily suffice,[82] although it is open to the parties to agree that the buyer shall be entitled to reject only by returning the goods or in some other specified manner.[83] In *Atari Corp. (U.K.) Ltd v Electronics Boutiques Stores (U.K.) Ltd*[84] the Court of Appeal held that, in the absence of a contrary intention, the notice did not have to be in writing or identify precisely the goods to which it related: it sufficed to identify the goods generically (*e.g.* "unsold stock") or in such other way as to enable individual identification later by some objective means. The Court of Appeal further held that the goods did not have to be physically capable of collection at the time the notice was issued.

5–053 **Effect of notice.** The effect of a notice of rejection is to determine the contract and to cause an immediate right to possession of the goods to vest in the seller, who normally will be entitled to sue the buyer for wrongful interference if he neglects or refuses to deliver up the goods.[85] But whether the buyer must make the goods available to the seller immediately or whether he is allowed a reasonable time to enable this to be done will depend upon the terms of the contract, express or implied, having regard in particular to the position of the parties and the commercial circumstances.[86] Where the buyer does deliver up the goods to the seller after rejecting

---

[78] *General Motors Acceptance Corp. (U.K.) Ltd v I.R.C.* (1986) 59 T.C. 651 (not "letting on hire"). Some schemes provide for the payment by the buyer to the seller initially of the net trade price of the goods: see *Fraser v London Sports Car Centre*, (above).

[79] Notice of rejection must also be given before the property in the goods has passed by acceptance, adoption or approval: above, para.5–047.

[80] Sale of Goods Act 1979, s.18, r. 4(b).

[81] *Berry v Star Brush Co.* (1915) 31 T.L.R. 603.

[82] *Atari Corp. (U.K.) Ltd v Electronics Boutiques Stores (U.K.) Ltd* [1998] Q.B. 539. See also *Bradley & Cohn Ltd v Ramsey & Co.* (1911) 28 T.L.R. 13; (1912) 106 L.T. 771 where it was held at first instance that a refusal to pay the seller's price was a rejection of the goods. Contrast *Ellis v Mortimer* (1805) 1 B. & P.N.R. 257.

[83] *Ornstein v Alexandra Furnishing Co.* (1895) 12 T.L.R. 128.

[84] [1998] Q.B. 539.

[85] *Ellis v Mortimer* (1805) 1 B. & P.N.R. 257 at 259; *Atari Corp. (U.K.) Ltd v Electronics Boutiques Stores (U.K.) Ltd* [1998] Q.B. 539. See also *Mitchell v Ealing B.C.* [1979] Q.B. 1 (bailee insurer of goods after neglect or refusal to deliver up).

[86] *Atari Corp. (U.K.) Ltd v Electronics Boutiques Stores (U.K.) Ltd*, above.

them, he is prima facie entitled to recover any deposit paid by him under the contract.[87]

Inability to return. In *Re Ferrier*,[88] where goods delivered on sale or return were seized by the sheriff in an execution against the buyer's property so that they could not be returned within the time fixed by the contract, it was held that the goods were not "retained by the buyer" and that the seller was entitled to recover the goods. On the other hand, if the buyer himself delivers the goods on sale or return to a third party, and the goods are misappropriated or lost, then the property will be considered to have passed if he cannot return the goods within the stipulated or a reasonable time.[89] It would therefore seem that, if the buyer voluntarily parts with the goods to a third party, he will be held to have purchased the goods if he is unable to return them; but if while they are in his possession they are detained by a third party for whose acts the buyer is not responsible,[90] the property will not pass. 5–054

Loss or destruction of the goods. Inability to return the goods due to their loss or destruction without default on the part of the buyer does not render him liable for the price so long as the loss or destruction occurs before the stipulated time or (if no time is fixed) before a reasonable time has elapsed. In *Elphick v Barnes*,[91] a horse was delivered to the buyer on condition that it was to be tried by him for eight days, and returned at the end of this period if he did not think it suitable. The horse died on the third day without any fault on the part of the buyer. It was held that it was at the seller's risk[92] and that he could not maintain an action for the price.[93] On the other hand, where the goods are lost or destroyed by some act or default on the part of the buyer or on the part of those for whom he is responsible,[94] it would seem that his inability to return the goods will render him liable for the price.[95] 5–055

Goods returned in a damaged condition. If the buyer returns the goods within the time allowed by the contract, but in a damaged condition, it is submitted that, on the principle in *Elphick v Barnes*,[96] the seller would be 5–056

---

[87] *Hurst v Orbell* (1838) 8 A. & E. 107.
[88] [1944] Ch. 295.
[89] *Ray v Barker* (1879) 4 Ex.D. 279; *Genn v Winkel* (1912) 107 L.T. 434.
[90] *Aliter*, if they are detained by an employee of the buyer in the course of his employment, even if acting for his own benefit: *Poole v Smith's Cars (Balham) Ltd* [1962] 1 W.L.R. 744.
[91] (1880) 5 C.P.D. 321.
[92] See below, para.6–009.
[93] Denman J. (at p.325) interpreted the earlier dicta in *Moss v Sweet* (1851) 16 Q.B. 493 at 495, as relating to destruction of or injury to the goods being the act of the buyer, and not as occurring by inevitable accident. See also *Poole v Smith's Cars (Balham) Ltd* [1962] 1 W.L.R. 744 at 753.
[94] See *Poole v Smith's Cars (Balham) Ltd*, above, at p.753; and below, para.5–057, n.2.
[95] *Elphick v Barnes*, above, at p.325; *Poole v Smith's Cars (Balham) Ltd*, above, at p.753.
[96] (1880) 5 C.P.D. 321.

bound to take back the goods, provided the damage occurred by no fault on the part of the buyer or of those for whom he is responsible.[97] But if the goods are damaged by such fault, then it is possible that the seller could refuse to take back the goods in their damaged condition and the buyer would be liable for the price.[98] It can, however, be argued that the buyer should be permitted to return the goods, but be liable in damages for the loss sustained by the seller, though not for the price. This argument might well succeed if the damage to the goods was not extensive.

5–057 **Burden of proof.** Since the buyer is to be regarded as a bailee of the goods while they are in his possession,[99] he will bear the burden of proving that the loss of or damage to the goods occurred without his fault.[1] Also, where he has entrusted the care or custody of the goods to a servant or agent, he may be responsible for any misuse or theft of the goods by such person, even though the servant or agent acted fraudulently for his own benefit.[2]

5–058 **Risk on buyer.** It is open to the parties expressly or impliedly to provide in their agreement that the goods shall be at the absolute risk of the buyer while in his possession[3] or that the buyer is to be liable for the price if the goods are damaged.[4]

4. UNASCERTAINED GOODS

5–059 **Goods must be ascertained.** Section 16 of the Sale of Goods Act 1979 provides that "subject to section 20A below, where there is a contract for the sale of unascertained goods no property[5] in the goods is transferred to the buyer unless and until the goods are ascertained". It is to be noted that

---

97 See below, para.5–057, n.2.

98 In *Elphick v Barnes*, above, at p.325, Denman J. also refers to "injury to the goods" being the act of the buyer. See also *Poole v Smith's Cars (Balham) Ltd*, above, at p.753.

99 See above, para.5–044; below, para.6–027.

1 *Houghland v R. R. Low (Luxury) Coaches Ltd* [1962] 1 Q.B. 694; *James Buchanan Ltd v Hay's Transport Services Ltd* [1972] 2 Lloyd's Rep. 535 at 542; *Port Swettenham Authority v T. W. Wu & Co. (M) Sdn. Bhd.* [1979] A.C. 580; *Mitchell v Ealing London B.C.* [1979] Q.B. 1; and see, below, para.6–027.

2 *Morris v C. W. Martin & Sons Ltd*, above, disapproving, *e.g. Cheshire v Bailey* [1905] 1 K.B. 237; *Mintz v Silverton* (1920) 36 T.L.R. 399. See also *Coupeé Co. v Maddick* [1891] 2 Q.B. 413; *Aitchison v Page Motors Ltd* (1935) 154 L.T. 128; *Houghland v R. R. Low (Luxury Coaches) Ltd*, above; *Transmotors Ltd v Robertson Buckley & Co. Ltd* [1970] 1 Lloyd's Rep. 224; *Port Swettenham Authority v T. W. Wu & Co. (M) Sdn. Bhd.*, above; and below, para.6–027. *Cf. Poole v Smith's Cars (Balham) Ltd* [1962] 1 W.L.R. 744 at 753.

3 *Bianchi v Nash* (1836) 1 M. & W. 545 (express stipulation); *Bevington v Dale* (1902) 7 Com.Cas. 112 (custom of trade). It would also, presumably, be open to the buyer to provide that he should be under no liability: *Rutter v Palmer* [1922] 2 K.B. 87.

4 *Bianchi v Nash* (above).

5 Defined in s.61(1); for risk, see below, para.6–004.

this section does not state that property will pass if and when the goods are ascertained. Property in ascertained goods passes when the parties intend it to pass.[6] But the section lays down in clear terms that, except where s.20A applies,[7] whatever the intentions of the parties, no property can pass in unascertained goods.[8]

Unascertained goods.[9] A contract for the sale of unascertained goods is not a sale, but an agreement to sell.[10] The Act does not define "unascertained goods", but it would appear that three categories of goods are included. The first is that of generic goods, that is to say, of a certain quantity of goods in general, without any specific identification of them, such as "50 hogsheads of sugar".[11] The second type is certain types of future goods.[12] The third is that of an unascertained part of a larger quantity of ascertained goods, such as "500 tons of wheat out of a cargo of 1,000 tons" on board a certain ship.[13] The common characteristic seems to be that the goods cannot presently be identified and can be referred to by description only.[14] 5–060

Separation from bulk. Section 16 is, however, subject to section 20A of the 1979 Act,[15] which was inserted by section 1(3) of the Sale of Goods (Amendment) Act 1995. Previously if a seller agreed to sell to a buyer a specified quantity of unascertained goods forming part of an identified bulk, then, as a general rule, no property in the goods agreed to be sold would pass to the buyer unless and until the goods had become ascertained 5–061

---

[6] *Ross T. Smyth & Co. Ltd v T. D. Bailey Sons & Co.* (1940) 67 Ll.L.R. 147 at 155; *Ginzberg v Barrow Haematite Steel Co. Ltd* [1966] 1 Lloyd's Rep. 343; *Karlshamns Oljefabriker v East Port Navigation Corp.* (*The Elafi*) [1981] 2 Lloyd's Rep. 679 at 683 (despite the fact that s.17 of the Act refers only to a "contract for the sale of specific or ascertained goods").

[7] See below, para.5–109.

[8] *Karlshamns Oljefabriker v East Port Navigation Corp.* (*The Elafi*) above, at p.683. See also (before the 1893 Act) *Heilbutt v Hickson* (1872) L.R. 7 C.P. 438 at 449; and above, para.1–015.

[9] See above, para.1–117.

[10] *Badische Anilin Fabrik v Hickson* [1906] A.C. 419 at 421; *Mischeff v Springett* [1942] 2 K.B. 331; *Preston v Albuery* [1964] 2 Q.B. 796 at 804; see above, para.1–026.

[11] *Austen v Craven* (1812) 4 Taunt. 644. See also *Re London Wine Co. (Shippers) Ltd* [1986] P.C.C. 121: "36 dozen and 11 bottles of Vosne Romanée les Genévrières 1969, lying in bond."

[12] Defined in s.61(1): see above, para.1–102, below, para.5–090. All future goods are not necessarily unascertained, *e.g.* a specific chattel which is to be acquired by the seller after the making of the contract of sale. Also future goods are referred to separately from unascertained goods in s.18, r.5(1) (below, para.5–068) and, in this section of this book, the subject of appropriation of future goods is dealt with separately at para.5–090, below. See on this point para.1–102, above.

[13] *Re Wait* [1927] 1 Ch. 606. See also the cases cited in para.5–061, n.17. In the case of a contract for the sale of generic goods, the seller may subsequently identify the source from which the contract goods are to come, *e.g.* a particular ship, warehouse or consignment: see *Thames Sack & Bag Co. v Knowles* (1919) 88 L.J.K.B. 585; *The Aramis* [1989] 1 Lloyd's Rep. 213; and below, paras 18–210, 19–015 (notice of appropriation). But the goods may remain still unascertained.

[14] See s.18, r.5(1); below, paras 5–068, 5–085.

[15] See below, para.5–109.

by being separated from the bulk.[16] Thus, where the ascertainment of the goods depended upon their being severed, weighed, measured, delivered or in some way separated by the seller from bulk, no property would pass until this was done.[17] Nor would any property pass where the power of separation was in a third party[18] or in the buyer, unless and until the power had been exercised. But section 20A now provides that, subject to certain conditions, property in an undivided share in the bulk is transferred to the buyer and he becomes an owner in common of the bulk. This matter is dealt with in greater detail in Section 5 of this Chapter. Nevertheless the general rule that goods must be separated from bulk before they can become ascertained is still of importance to the passing of property in two respects. First, if the conditions specified in section 20A for the transfer of an undivided share in the bulk are not satisfied, for example, because the buyer has not paid the price for any of the goods which are the subject of the contract and which form part of the bulk,[19] or, if the buyer has paid the price for only some of the goods, as regards those goods for which no payment has been made,[20] then separation of the goods from the bulk is required before any property can pass. Secondly, where the property in an undivided share in the bulk has passed to the buyer under section 20A, the goods comprised in that undivided share still remain unascertained and they must first become ascertained by being separated from the bulk before sole ownership of the goods themselves (as opposed to co-ownership of the bulk) can pass to the buyer.[21]

5–062 A specified quantity of unascertained goods forming part of an identified bulk may nevertheless become ascertained by process of exhaustion. In *Wait and James v Midland Bank*[22] buyers purchased from sellers under three separate contracts respectively 250, 750 and 250 quarters of wheat "ex store Avonmouth ex Thistleros". The buyers themselves took delivery of 400 quarters and, as a result of deliveries to other purchasers, there came a time when there remained in the warehouse only 850 quarters of the whole cargo (all of which was originally owned by the sellers). Roche J. held that

---

[16] *Gillett v Hill* (1834) 2 C. & M. 530 at 535.

[17] *Wallace v Breeds* (1811) 13 East 522; *Busk v Davis* (1814) 2 M. & S. 397; *White v Wilks* (1814) 5 Taunt. 176; *Shepley v Davis* (1814) 5 Taunt. 617; *Swanwick v Southern* (1839) 9 A. & E. 895 at 900; *Jenkyns v Usborne* (1844) 7 M. & G. 678; *Boswell v Kilborn* (1862) 15 Moo.P.C. 309; *Campbell v Mersey Docks and Harbour Board* (1863) 14 C.B. (N.S.) 412 at 415; *Snell v Heighton* (1883) 1 Cab. & Ell. 95; *Sharp v Christmas* (1892) 8 T.L.R. 687; *R. v Tideswell* [1905] 2 K.B. 273; *Hayman & Son v M'Lintock*, 1907 S.C. 936; *Healy v Howlett & Sons* [1917] 1 K.B. 337; *Laurie & Morewood v Dudin & Sons* [1926] 1 K.B. 223 (overruling *Whitehouse v Frost* (1810) 12 East 614); *National Coal Board v Gamble* [1959] 1 Q.B. 11; *Preston v Albuery* [1964] 2 Q.B. 796.

[18] *Healy v Howlett & Sons*, above; *Sterns Ltd v Vickers* [1923] 1 K.B. 78 at 84. *Karlshamns Oljefabriker v East Port Navigation Corp.* (*The Elafi*) [1981] 2 Lloyd's Rep. 679 at 673; *Re London Wine Co. (Shippers) Ltd* [1986] P.C.C. 121; *The Aramis*, above.

[19] See below, para.5–115.

[20] See below, para.5–118.

[21] See below, para.5–116.

[22] (1926) 31 Com.Cas. 172.

what remained in the warehouse had been ascertained to be the quantity of goods agreed to be sold by the sellers to the buyers, and that the property had passed.[23] On the other hand, where the goods sold are generic goods, not part of any identified bulk, the fact that the seller originally had or that there now remains only a quantity of goods sufficient to satisfy his contract with the buyer will not cause the goods to be ascertained. He may fulfil the contract from any other source.[24]

As *Wait and James v Midland Bank* shows, goods will not be prevented from becoming ascertained by exhaustion by the fact that they were agreed to be sold by the seller to the buyer under two or more separate contracts, even though they have not been allocated distinctly to each of those contracts. Likewise they will still be ascertained where those separate contracts were with different sellers or different buyers, but have become vested in a single buyer. *A fortiori* if the whole of an identified bulk is sold under separate contracts to a single buyer, or those separate contracts become vested in a single buyer, the goods become ascertained.[25] This is sometimes referred to as ascertainment by "consolidation". In such situations the property may then pass.[26] **5–063**

Equitable interests. A buyer of unascertained goods to whom the property in the goods has not yet passed but who has nevertheless pre-paid the whole or part of the purchase price does not thereby acquire any equitable interest in the goods.[27] He does not in consequence have any equitable proprietary claim to the goods in the event of the seller's insolvency. Attempts to establish an equitable interest by way of trust,[28] lien,[29] assignment[30] or the equitable remedy of specific performance[31] have met with no success. If the goods agreed to be sold form part of an identified bulk, property in an undivided share in the bulk will pass to him if the conditions specified in section 20A(1) of the Act[32] are satisfied; but otherwise the fact that the goods form part of an identified bulk does not confer upon him any equitable rights over the bulk. **5–064**

As a normal rule, a buyer who has pre-paid the price has no claim in equity to trace the money paid.[33] If the seller becomes insolvent, any claim by him for the return of the purchase price is a personal claim and not a proprietary claim which ranks prior to other unsecured creditors of the

---

[23] See also *Karlhamns Oljefabriker v Eastport Navigation Corp. (The Elafi)* [1981] 2 Lloyd's Rep. 679, and below, para.5–105 and para.5–107 (appropriation).
[24] *Re London Wine Co. (Shippers) Ltd*, above.
[25] *Karlshamns Oljefabriker v Eastport Navigation Corp. (The Elafi)*, above.
[26] But see (on appropriation of the goods to the contract), below, para.5–107.
[27] *Re Wait* [1927] 1 Ch. 606 at 636; *Leigh and Sillavan Ltd v Aliakmon Shipping Co. Ltd* [1986] A.C. 785 at 812–813, *Re Goldcorp Exchange Ltd* [1995] 1 A.C. 74.
[28] *Re London Wine Co. (Shippers) Ltd* [1986] P.C.C. 121; *Re Goldcorp Exchange Ltd*, above.
[29] *Re Wait*, above.
[30] *Re Wait*, above, at pp.623, 634, 636; *Re London Wine Co. (Shippers) Ltd*, above.
[31] *ibid*.
[32] See below, para.5–109.
[33] *Re Goldcorp Exchange Ltd*, above.

seller. He will have pre-paid the price in order to perform his side of the bargain under which he would in due course have been entitled to claim delivery, and the money would have become, and been intended to become, part of the seller's general assets. It is not impressed with a trust,[34] nor, as a general rule, can any fiduciary relationship between buyer and seller be extracted from the contract of sale. In *Re Goldcorp Exchange Ltd*[35] the Judicial Committee of the Privy Council rejected the plea that it should create a residual restitutionary right to allow the buyer to assert a proprietary interest over the purchase price paid.

5–065 **Estoppel.** Where the goods agreed to be sold are in the possession of a third person such as a warehouseman, the acceptance by the warehouseman of a delivery order given by the seller to the buyer, and even the transfer of the goods to be sold into the name of the buyer in his books, will not pass the property in the goods to the buyer while they are still unascertained.[36] But if the goods are in the possession of the seller or of a warehouseman and the seller gives a delivery order to the buyer, or the buyer gives a delivery order to his sub-purchaser,[37] then a confirmation of the delivery order by the seller or the warehouseman may estop them from denying that the recipient is entitled to delivery of the quantity of goods comprised in the order.[38] However, for such an estoppel to arise, there must, first, be an existing bulk from which it is agreed the goods are to come.[39] Secondly, there must be a representation by words or conduct that the buyer or sub-purchaser is entitled to delivery of the goods[40]: the mere receipt of a delivery order[41] without any acknowledgment will not suffice.[42] Thirdly, it must be shown that the buyer or sub-purchaser has relied on the representation and thereby been prejudiced.[43] Estoppel does not in itself pass the

---

[34] *cf. Re Kayford Ltd* [1975] 1 W.L.R. 279.
[35] [1995] 1 A.C. 74.
[36] *Buck v Davis* (1814) 2 M. & S. 397; *Shepley v Davis* (1814) 5 Taunt. 617; *Hayman & Son v M'Lintock* 1907 S.C. 936; *Laurie & Morewood v Dudin & Sons* [1926] 1 K.B. 223.
[37] If the buyer obtains a document of title to the goods (within the meaning of s.1(4) of the Factors Act 1889) and transfers that document or another document of title to his sub-purchaser, the sub-purchaser may be entitled to the goods or at least to maintain an action in conversion against the seller: *Capital and Counties Bank Ltd v Warriner* (1896) 12 T.L.R. 216; *Ant. Jurgens Margarinefabrieken v Louis Dreyfus & Co.* [1914] 3 K.B. 40; *Mount Ltd v Jay and Jay Provisions Ltd* [1960] 1 Q.B. 159. See ss.25, 47 of the 1979 Act (below, paras 7–072, 15–097). See Nicol, 42 M.L.R. 129 (1979).
[38] *Stonard v Dunkin* (1810) 2 Camp. 344; *Haws v Watson* (1824) 2 B. & C. 540; *Gosling v Birnie* (1831) 7 Bing. 339; *Gillett v Hill* (1834) 2 C. & M. 530; *Woodley v Coventry* (1863) 2 H. & C. 164; *Knights v Wiffen* (1870) L.R. 5 Q.B. 660; *Simm v Anglo-American Telegraph Co.* (1879) 5 Q.B.D. 188 at 215; *Capital and Counties Bank Ltd v Warriner*, above; *Maynegrain Pty Ltd v Compafina Bank* [1982] 2 N.S.W.L.R. 141 (revsd. on different grounds by the Privy Council (1984) A.L.J.R. 389); and see below, para.7–014.
[39] *Re Goldcorp Exchange Ltd* [1995] 1 A.C. 74.
[40] In *Colley v Overseas Exporters* [1921] 3 K.B. 302 at 312, it was stated that the rule laid down in *Carr v L. & N.W. Ry* (1875) L.R. 10 C.P. 307 at 317, must be satisfied.
[41] Contrast the position in relation to documents of title: below, para.8–013.
[42] *Laurie & Morewood v Dudin & Sons*, above. *Cf. Gillett v Hill*, above.
[43] *Knights v Wiffen*, above, at p.665.

property in the goods, but the buyer or sub-purchaser is entitled to maintain an action for wrongful interference if the goods are not delivered to him; the seller is also precluded from setting up an unpaid seller's lien. A representation made by a warehouseman can operate against the seller if the seller authorised the representation or consented to it being made.[44] But the estoppel only creates a cause of action between the person in whose favour the estoppel arises and the person estopped[45]: a purchaser for value or chargee of the goods without notice will not be bound by the estoppel.[46] Since the estoppel confers no property in the goods *in specie*, it does not preclude him from claiming as his goods which were actually sold or charged to him and to which he has the real title.[47]

A representation to the agent of a disclosed principal acting as such will enure to the benefit of the principal, and the same is probably true where the principal is undisclosed.[48]

Intention of the parties. Once the goods have become ascertained, that is to say, once they have become "identified in accordance with the agreement after the time [the] contract of sale is made",[49] the property will pass when the parties intend that it shall pass[50] and, for the purpose of ascertaining the intention of the parties, regard must be had to the terms of the contract, the conduct of the parties, and the circumstances of the case.[51] It is open to them to agree, for example, that the property shall pass *ipso facto* immediately the goods become ascertained[52] or even that it shall pass at some time after the goods have been delivered to the buyer.[53] 5–066

Appropriation. Although the passing of property is dependent upon the intention of the parties, unless a different intention appears, the law imputes to them an intention that property is not to pass unless and until the goods have been appropriated to the contract. Such appropriation is dealt with in section 18, rule 5, of the Sale of Goods Act 1979. The first paragraph of this rule sets out the general requirements for the passing of property in unascertained or future[54] goods by appropriation, and further 5–067

---

44 *Knights v Wiffen*, above.
45 *Simm v Anglo-American Telegraph Co.* (1879) 5 Q.B.D. 188 at 206–207.
46 *Re London Wine Co. (Shippers) Ltd* [1986] P.C.C. 121; *Re Goldcorp Exchange Ltd* [1995] 1 A.C. 74. *Cf. Eastern Distributors Ltd v Goldring* [1957] 2 Q.B. 600; below, para.7–011.
47 *Re London Wine Co. (Shippers) Ltd*, above (floating charge); *Re Goldcorp Exchange Ltd*, above (*ibid.*).
48 *Maynegrain Pty Ltd v Compafina Bank*, above. See *Bowstead and Reynolds on Agency* (17th ed.), para.8–169.
49 *Re Wait* [1927] 1 Ch. 606 at 630.
50 Sale of Goods Act 1979, s.17(1); see above, para.5–016.
51 s.17(2); *Ross T. Smyth & Co. Ltd v T. D. Bailey Son & Co.* (1940) 67 Ll.L.R. 147 at 155.
52 *Reeves v Barlow* (1884) 12 Q.B.D. 436; *Karlshamns Oljefabriker v East Port Navigation Corp. (The Elafi)* [1981] 2 Lloyd's Rep. 679 at 686. See also below, para.5–078.
53 *Bellamy v Davey* [1891] 3 Ch. 540; *Armitage v John Haigh & Sons* (1893) 9 T.L.R. 287; *Sir James Laing & Sons v Barclay, Curle & Co.* [1908] A.C. 35; *Watson v Coupland* [1945] 1 All E.R. 217.
54 See below, para.5–068.

provides that appropriation by one party shall not be effective to pass the property without the assent of the other.[55] The second paragraph of the rule provides for appropriation by delivery.[56] The third and fourth paragraphs of the rule provide for appropriation in situations where goods forming part of an identified bulk have become ascertained by process of exhaustion and consolidation.[57]

(a) *Appropriation with the Assent of the Other Party*

5–068 **Section 18, rule 5(1).** By section 18, rule 5(1): "Where there is a contract for the sale of unascertained[58] or future[59] goods by description,[60] and goods of that description[61] and in a deliverable state[62] are unconditionally appropriated to the contract, either by the seller with the assent of the buyer or by the buyer with the assent of the seller, the property in the goods then passes to the buyer; and the assent may be express or implied, and may be given either before or after the appropriation is made."

This paragraph codifies the common law before the Sale of Goods Act 1893.[63]

5–069 **Meaning of appropriation.** The word "appropriated" has been said to be "a term of legal art [which] has a certain definite meaning".[64] It is, however, extremely difficult to discover the true meaning of appropriation since the word does not appear to have been used with any consistency in the cases. In *Wait v Baker*[65] Parke B. pointed out that appropriation may be understood in different senses: "It may mean a selection on the part of the vendor, where he has the right to choose the article which he has to supply in performance of his contract. Or the word may mean, that both parties have agreed that a certain article shall be delivered in pursuance of the contract, and yet the property may not pass in either case . . . 'Appropriation' may also be used in another sense, *viz.* where both parties agree upon the specific article in which the property is to pass, and nothing remains to

---

[55] See below, para.5–074.
[56] See below, para.5–096.
[57] See below, para.5–103.
[58] See above, para.5–060.
[59] See above, para.5–060 n.12; below, para.5–090.
[60] See s.13 of the Act (below, para.11–001). A sale by description is not necessarily a sale of unascertained or future goods: see *Varley v Whipp* [1900] 1 Q.B. 513 (above, para.5–019), but a sale of unascertained goods appears to be always a sale of goods by description.
[61] See below, para.5–085.
[62] Defined in s.61(5) of the Act. See *Pritchett & Gold and Electrical Power Storage Co. Ltd v Currie* [1916] 2 Ch. 515; *Philip Head & Sons Ltd v Showfronts Ltd* [1970] 1 Lloyd's Rep. 140; *Hendy Lennox (Industrial Engines) Ltd v Grahame Puttick Ltd* [1984] 1 W.L.R. 485 at 495; above, paras 5–023, 5–031, 5–105; below, para.5–034.
[63] *Rohde v Thwaites* (1872) 6 B. & C. 388 at 392; *Aldridge v Johnson* (1857) 7 E. & B. 885 at 898; *Campbell v Mersey Docks and Harbour Board* (1863) 14 C.B. (N.S.) 412 at 414, 415.
[64] *Re Blyth Shipbuilding and Dry Docks Co.* [1926] Ch. 494 at 518.
[65] (1848) 2 Exch. 1 at 8. See also the different sense in s.9(1) of the 1979 Act: above, para.2–049.

be done in order to pass it." For property to pass under a contract for the sale of unascertained or future goods, it is undoubtedly necessary that appropriation in the last sense should have occurred. In essence, however, "appropriation is to be understood as an overt act manifesting an intent to identify specific goods as those to which the bargain of the parties shall apply"[66]: it is the act of one party only, and its purpose is to identify the goods to be sold. But since its relevance in this context is in relation to the transfer of ownership by mutual agreement of the parties, it will only have effect where, by reason of prior or subsequent assent of the other party, it is agreed that such act shall pass the property to the buyer. The act of appropriation must therefore so far identify the goods that the passing of property thereby becomes possible.

Appropriation in this sense will only be held to have occurred where the contract has become irrevocably attached to the goods in question.[67] This may be illustrated by taking as an example a contract entered into for the sale of a quantity of unascertained goods, *e.g.* 100 tons of coal. It will be the duty of one or other of the parties to appropriate, *i.e.* identify, the particular goods to be sold. This duty may be placed upon the buyer, as where the contract provides that he is to separate the goods from bulk and carry them away.[68] More usually it will be placed on the seller. The duty to appropriate carries with it the power to select the goods which are to be delivered in fulfilment of the contract. But it is clear that the act of the party appropriating in simply selecting the goods which he intends to be delivered cannot pass the property in them by appropriation[69]; something more is required. Either the selection will have subsequently to be approved by the other party, so that both parties are agreed that those are the goods to be sold, or one party, *e.g.* the seller, must have been previously authorised to do an act which passes the property to the buyer by appropriation. In the latter case, the act must be one which irrevocably determines the appropriating party's election to specify the goods, and not one by which he may still be at liberty to select other goods. It is here that most difficulty arises, since it may not be easy in any individual case to decide whether the selection made by the seller is a mere revocable manifestation of his intention, or the final determination of a selection conclusively binding on him.[70] Property, however, will only pass where the identity of the goods has been finally and irrevocably established by the mutual assent of both parties. This is a question of law.[71] **5–070**

Unconditional appropriation. The appropriation must be unconditional, that is to say, the party appropriating must intend that the property shall pass by the appropriation, if assented to by the other party, and not upon **5–071**

---

[66] Williston, *Sales*, s.273(a). See also below, para.18–210.
[67] See below, para.5–080.
[68] See, *e.g. National Coal Board v Gamble* [1959] 1 Q.B. 11.
[69] *Carlos Federspiel & Co. SA v Charles Twigg & Co. Ltd* [1957] 1 Lloyd's Rep. 240 at 255; see below, para.5–080.
[70] See below, paras 5–078—5–081, 5–082.
[71] Blackburn, *Contract of Sale* (3rd ed.), p.137.

the occurrence of some further event, *e.g.* payment or tender of the price.[72] By section 19(1) of the Act, the seller may, by the terms of the contract or appropriation, reserve the right of disposal of the goods until certain conditions are fulfilled[73]; he may be deemed to have done so in the circumstances set out in section 19(2) and (3).[74] So, for example, in the case of the usual c.i.f. contract, the seller reserves the right of disposal by retaining the documents against payment or securing of the price by the buyer, and "the notice of appropriation under an ordinary c.i.f. contract is not intended to pass, and does not pass, the property".[75]

5–072 A conditional appropriation may be inferred from the circumstances of the contract. Even though the goods may have been so far appropriated that the parties are agreed that those goods alone are to be delivered, yet the appropriation may be conditional on some final act being done by the seller before the property is to pass. In *Carlos Federspiel & Co. SA v Charles Twigg & Co. Ltd*,[76] Pearson J. said: "Usually, but not necessarily, the appropriating act is the last act to be performed by the seller. For instance, if delivery is to be taken at the seller's premises and the seller has appropriated the goods when he has made the goods ready and identified them and placed them in position to be taken by the buyer and has so informed the buyer, and if the buyer agrees to come and take them, that is the assent to the appropriation. But if there is a further act, an important and decisive act, to be done by the seller, then there is prima facie evidence that probably the property does not pass until the final act is done." It is difficult to find examples of such a situation.[77] But reference has already been made[78] to section 18, rule 3, of the Sale of Goods Act 1979 which deals with contracts for the sale of specific goods where the seller is bound to weigh, measure or test the goods for the purpose of ascertaining the price. There is little doubt that, where the goods were previously unascertained, but have been appropriated to the contract, the passing of property would likewise be conditional on the performance of such an obligation by the seller.[79]

5–073 The normal meaning of the word "unconditional" in this context is that the appropriation is not subject to any condition, express or implied, upon the fulfilment of which the passing of property depends.[80] But in *Ollett v*

---

[72] *Godts v Rose* (1854) 17 C.B. 229; *Stein Forbes & Co. Ltd v County Tailoring Co. Ltd* (1916) 86 L.J.K.B 448 at 449. See also *Cheetham & Co. Ltd v Thornham Spinning Co. Ltd* [1964] 2 Lloyd's Rep. 17 (retention of shipping documents by seller).

[73] See below, para.5–151.

[74] See below, paras 5–137, 5–140.

[75] *Ross T. Smyth & Co. Ltd v T. D. Bailey, Son & Co.* [1940] 3 All E.R. 60 at 66; see below, para.19–100.

[76] [1957] 1 Lloyd's Rep. 240 at 255.

[77] But Pearson J. gave as an example an f.o.b. contract (at p.256) and see also contracts for the sale of goods to be manufactured by the seller: below, para.5–090.

[78] Above, para.5–035.

[79] *Langton v Higgins* (1859) 4 H. & N. 402 at 408, 410; *Jenner v Smith* (1869) L.R. 4 C.P. 270 at 276; *National Coal Board v Gamble* [1959] 1 Q.B. 11 at 21. *Cf. Nanka-Bruce v Commonwealth Trust Ltd* [1926] A.C. 77 (above, para.5–036).

[80] See above, para.5–019.

Jordan,[81] a criminal case, Darling J. appears to have held that there was no unconditional appropriation of certain herrings despatched by rail because the seller was in breach of an implied condition that they should be fit for food on arrival at their destination. If it was intended to suggest that any failure by a seller to fulfil a stipulation in a contract of sale, the breach of which may give rise to a right on the part of the buyer to treat the contract as repudiated,[82] will prevent the passing of property under section 18, rule 5, it is submitted that such interpretation is erroneous. The facts of the case are, however, open to the alternative explanation that the parties intended the passing of property to be suspended until the goods had been received, inspected and approved by the buyer.

Assent of the other party. Since it is by agreement of the parties that an appropriation involving a change of ownership is made, where an election to appropriate rests with one party, the appropriation must be made with the assent, express or implied, of the other. Such assent may be given either before or after the appropriation is made. Williston has said[83]: "The act of appropriation has no legal consequences unless previously or subsequently assented to by the other party. If the buyer assents in advance to an appropriation by the seller, he is in effect an offeror, and such an appropriation as the buyer has authorised is an acceptance. If the buyer's assent is subsequent to the appropriation, the seller is the offeror and the buyer the acceptor of an agreement for the specification of the goods." This analogy should not, however, be taken too far. There is no need to find any formal offer and acceptance. It is sufficient that one party has assented, expressly or impliedly, to the appropriation by the other. 5–074

Subsequent assent of the buyer. Where the seller selects certain goods in such a manner as to identify them as those which he intends to deliver in pursuance of the contract of sale and informs the buyer that these goods have been appropriated to the contract, if the buyer subsequently approves the appropriation by words or conduct, he will be considered to have assented to the appropriation and the property will then pass without delivery. In *Rhode v Thwaites*[84] the buyer bought 20 hogsheads of sugar out of a quantity of sugar in bulk belonging to the seller. Four hogsheads were filled up and delivered. Sixteen hogsheads were then filled up and appropriated by the seller, who gave notice to the buyer to take them away, which he promised to do. It was held that the property had passed. The same principle applies where the buyer approves goods manufactured for him by the seller, if the seller has completed the goods and notified the buyer thereof.[85] 5–075

---

[81] [1918] 2 K.B. 41.
[82] Sale of Goods Act 1979, s.11(3).
[83] Williston, *Sales*, s.273(a).
[84] (1827) 6 B. & C. 388. See also *Donaghy's Rope and Twine Co. Ltd v Wright Stephenson & Co. Ltd* (1906) 25 N.Z.L.R. 641.
[85] *Wilkins v Bromhead* (1844) 6 M. & G. 963. See also *Elliott v Pybus* (1828) 10 Bing. 512, and below, para.5–091.

5–076 Assent may be implied from conduct, as where a buyer is informed that the goods appropriated to the contract are those on board a particular ship, and he receives and retains the invoice and bill of lading[86] or gives instructions for an insurance policy to be effected on the goods.[87] Payment of the price after notification that the goods are ready for delivery may also amount to assent,[88] provided it is specifically made in respect of those goods.[89] Further, where goods have been separated from bulk and are in a deliverable state, the tender of a delivery order by the buyer and its acceptance by a warehouseman constitutes an appropriation of the goods by the seller with the assent of the buyer.[90]

5–077 If the seller notifies the buyer that certain goods have been appropriated to the contract, but the buyer refuses to accept the goods[91] or to pay the price,[92] the property will not pass unless there is some other act on the part of the buyer which indicates his assent to the appropriation.[93] Assent may, however, in some circumstances be inferred from silence, as in *Pignataro v Gilroy*,[94] where a contract was entered into for the sale of 140 bags of rice to be delivered within 14 days. The buyer sent the seller a cheque for the rice and asked for a delivery order. The seller sent him a delivery order for 125 bags lying at the wharf of a third party and informed him that the remaining 15 bags were ready for delivery at the seller's place of business. The buyer neglected to take delivery of these 15 bags for one month, and in the meantime they were stolen. It was held that assent could be inferred from a month's silence without objection.

5–078 **Previous assent of buyer.** Property will pass by appropriation of the goods to the contract where the buyer has by express words previously assented to such appropriation by the seller,[95] or where he has done so by implication. The assent of the buyer is in fact an *authority* conferred by him on the seller to pass the property in the goods by appropriation.[96] In each case, therefore, it will be necessary to enquire whether or not such authority has been given. For example, where goods are sold by sample, the seller may not be taken to have any authority to pass the property by appropriation, for the parties may have intended that the buyer should have the right

---

[86] *Alexander v Gardner* (1835) 1 Bing. (N.C.) 671.
[87] *Sparkes v Marshall* (1836) 2 Bing. (N.C.) 761.
[88] *Wilkins v Bromhead* (1844) 6 M. & G. 963. See also *Elliott v Pybus* (1828) 10 Bing. 512 (where the buyer requested additional time to pay the balance of the price); *Sydney Harbour Trust Commissioners v Wilson* (1907) 7 S.R.(N.S.W.) 225.
[89] *Bishop v Crawshay* (1824) 3 B. & C. 415.
[90] *Wardar's (Import & Export) Co. Ltd v W. Norwood & Sons Ltd* [1968] 2 Q.B. 663.
[91] *Jenner v Smith* (1869) L.R. 4 C.P. 270; *Publishers' Assn v Rowland* (1915) 32 W.L.R. 646 (Sask.)
[92] *Godts v Rose* (1855) 17 C.B. 229.
[93] *Elliott v Pybus* (1828) 10 Bing. 512. But see *F. C. Napier v Dexters Ltd* (1926) 26 Ll.L.R. 62.
[94] [1919] 1 K.B. 459. But contrast *Atkinson v Bell* (1828) 8 B. & C. 277 (two months' silence before seller's bankruptcy).
[95] *Pletts v Beattie* [1896] 1 Q.B. 519.
[96] *Jenner v Smith* (1869) L.R. 4 C.P. 270 at 277, 278. It can therefore be revoked: *Ginner v King* (1890) 7 T.L.R. 140; *Sells v Thomson* (1914) 17 D.L.R. 737.

to compare the goods with the sample[97] before a change of ownership occurs.[98] Secondly, it will be necessary to enquire what are the terms of that authority and whether the appropriation has been carried out in accordance with those terms. Thus the terms of the contract may expressly or impliedly provide that appropriation by the seller can only be effected in a certain manner, *e.g.* by delivery to a carrier, as in the case of a normal f.o.b. or f.o.r. contract, so that the property will not pass before this time.[99] Only such an appropriation as the buyer has authorised will pass the property.[1]

The most difficult problems on this point for the most part arise where it is alleged that the buyer has impliedly authorised the seller to appropriate the goods to the contract by selecting the particular goods to be sold and that the seller has done some act which sufficiently indicates such an appropriation. In his treatise on the Law of Sale, Lord Blackburn wrote[2]: "Where from the terms of an executory agreement to sell unspecified goods, the vendor is to despatch the goods, or to do anything to them that cannot be done till the goods are appropriated, he has the right to choose what the goods shall be; and the property is transferred the moment the dispatch or other act has commenced, for then an appropriation is made, finally and conclusively, by the authority conferred in the agreement, and in Lord Coke's language 'the certainty and thereby the property begins by election'."[3] In *Aldridge v Johnson*,[4] where this statement was approved, the claimant agreed to buy 100 quarters of barley out of 200 which he had seen in bulk and agreed to. It was arranged that he should send 200 sacks for the barley, which the seller would fill and despatch to the claimant by railway. The seller filled 155 sacks, leaving 45 unfilled. On the eve of his bankruptcy, the seller emptied the barley out of the filled sacks into bulk. It was held that the property had passed in the barley in the 155 sacks. Lord Campbell C.J. said[5]: "I consider that here was *a priori* an assent by the [claimant]. He has inspected and approved of the barley in bulk. He sent his sacks to be filled out of that bulk" and "looking to all that was done, when the bankrupt put the barley into the sacks *eo instanti* the property in each sack-full vested in the [claimant]." Similarly in *Langton v Higgins*[6] the claimants contracted to buy from a farmer all the oil of peppermint to be distilled from the crop of peppermint which might be grown on his farm in a certain year. The farmer requested the claimants to send bottles for the oil and, when these were received, he filled them with oil, labelled them with the weight, and made out invoices for the oil. Before the oil was delivered to the carrier for conveyance to the claimants, the farmer sold some of the 5–079

---

[97] Sale of Goods Act 1979, s.34; see below, para.12–039.
[98] *Jenner v Smith*, above.
[99] For special trade terms, see below, paras 20–070, 21–010, 21–043.
[1] See also below, para.5–085.
[2] *A Treatise on the Effect of the Contract of Sale on the Legal Rights of Property and Possession in Goods, Wares and Merchandize* (3rd ed.), p.138.
[3] *Heyward's Case* (1595) 2 Co.Rep. 35a at 37a. See also *Rankin v Potter* (1873) L.R. 6 H.L. 83 at 119; *Scarf v Jardine* (1882) 7 App.Cas. 345 at 360.
[4] (1857) 7 E. & B. 885. But see now s.20A of the 1979 Act; below, para.5–109.
[5] At p.899.
[6] (1859) 4 H. & N. 402.

filled bottles to the defendant. It was held that the property in the oil in the bottles had passed to the claimants, who could maintain an action for conversion of the oil against the defendant. Bramwell B. said[7]: "The seller puts the article into the buyer's bottles, then is there any rule to say that the property does not pass? The buyer in effect says, 'I will trust you to deliver into my bottles, and by that means to appropriate to me, the article which I have bought off you'. . . In all reason, when a vendee sends his ship, or cart, or cask, or bottle to the vendor, and he puts the article sold into it, that is a delivery to the vendee." Both of these cases were approved by Lord O'Hagan in the House of Lords case of *Anderson v Morice*.[8]

5–080 However, in his treatise Lord Blackburn went on to say[9]: "But however clearly the vendor may have expressed an intention to choose particular goods, and however extensive may have been his preparations for performing the agreement with those particular goods, yet until the act has actually commenced the appropriation is not final, for it is not made by the authority of the other party, nor binding on him." Thus in *Mucklow v Mangles*[10] a buyer ordered a barge to be made for him, and advanced money on account as the work proceeded. The buyer's name was painted on the stern, but before completion the builder committed an act of bankruptcy and two days after completion the barge was seized in an execution against him. It was held that no property passed until the barge was completed and delivered, Heath J. saying[11]: "A tradesman often finishes goods, which he is making in pursuance of an order given by one person, and sells them to another." In *Noblett v Hopkinson*[12] an order was placed for half a gallon of beer to be delivered the next day, a Sunday, and paid for in advance. The beer was drawn off, put into a bottle belonging to the seller, and put on one side overnight. It was held that there was no appropriation assented to by the buyer on the Saturday, so that the seller committed an offence by selling the beer on the Sunday when the buyer took delivery of it. Also in *Carlos Federspiel & Co. SA v Charles Twigg & Co. Ltd*[13] sellers agreed to sell to overseas buyers a quantity of bicycles, the price being quoted f.o.b. The bicycles were packed at the seller's premises and marked with the buyers' name. The sellers further informed the buyers of the shipping marks of the consignment and told them that the goods had been registered for shipment. While the goods were awaiting shipment, the sellers became insolvent. It was held that, quite apart from the f.o.b. terms of the contract,[14] the property had not passed by appropriation. Pearson J. said[15]: "A mere setting apart or selection by the seller of the goods which

---

[7] At p.409.
[8] (1876) 1 App.Cas. 713 at 740.
[9] At p.138.
[10] (1808) 1 Taunt. 318. See also *Atkinson v Bell* (1828) 8 B. & C. 277.
[11] At p.320.
[12] [1905] 2 K.B. 214. See also *Ridgway v Ward* (1884) 14 Q.B.D. 110 at 116–117; *Addy v Blake* (1887) 19 Q.B.D. 478; *Cocker v McMullen* (1900) 81 L.T. 784. *Cf. Furby v Hoey* [1947] 1 All E.R. 236.
[13] [1957] 1 Lloyd's Rep. 240.
[14] It was not, in fact, strictly an f.o.b. contract.
[15] At p.255.

he expects to use in performance of the contract is not enough. If that is all, he can change his mind and use those goods in performance of some other contract and use some other goods in performance of this contract. To constitute an appropriation of the goods to the contract the parties must have had, or be reasonably supposed to have had, an intention to attach the contract irrevocably to those goods, so that those goods and no others are the subject of the sale and become the property of the buyer."

It is apparent that there can be acts on the part of the seller other than actual delivery to the buyer or to a carrier which will determine his election to specify the particular goods to be sold and thereby attach the contract irrevocably to those goods. But Chalmers observes[16]: "If the decisions be carefully examined, it will be found in every case where the property has been held to pass, there has been an actual or constructive delivery of the goods to the buyer." This statement was approved by Pearson J. in the *Carlos Federspiel* case, *supra*. "I think" he said[17] "that is right, subject only to this possible qualification, that there may be after such constructive delivery an actual delivery still to be made by the seller under the contract. Of course, that is quite possible, because delivery is the transfer of possession, whereas appropriation transfers ownership. So there may be first an appropriation, constructive delivery, whereby the seller becomes bailee for the buyer, and then a subsequent actual delivery involving actual possession, and when I say that I have in mind in particular the cases cited, namely, *Aldridge v Johnson* and *Langton v Higgins*." If these statements represent the law, then it will be difficult to establish that property has passed by appropriation by the seller, unless there has been at least a constructive delivery of the goods to the buyer[18] or unless the buyer has assented *after* the appropriation has been made. Indeed, it seems clear that, although the goods have been set apart and identified by the seller, such acts as packing the goods, labelling them with the buyer's name, and even informing the buyer that they are ready for delivery, will not in themselves, unless so agreed,[19] determine irrevocably the election of the seller so as to pass the property by appropriation if the buyer has not subsequently assented thereto.[20] Nevertheless, it may be that, if the seller sends to the buyer an invoice or delivery order which precisely and unambiguously identifies the particular goods selected, the property could pass upon receipt of the document, provided the goods are then in a deliverable state.[21] 5–081

[16] (18th ed.), p.151.
[17] [1957] 1 Lloyd's Rep. 240 at 255.
[18] *Wardar's (Import and Export) Co. Ltd v W Norwood & Sons Ltd* [1968] 2 Q.B. 663.
[19] *Pletts v Beattie* [1896] 1 Q.B. 519; *Furby v Hoey* [1947] 1 All E.R. 236.
[20] *Hendy Lennox (Industrial Engines) Ltd v Grahame Puttick Ltd* [1984] 1 W.L.R. 485 at 495. Contrast *Hayes Bros Buick Opel Jeep Inc. v Can. Permanent Trust Co.* (1976) 15 N.B.R. (2d) 166; *Re Stapylton Fletcher Ltd* [1994] 1 W.L.R. 1181.
[21] *Hendy Lennox (Industrial Engines) Ltd v Grahame Puttick Ltd*, above, at p.495. See also *Pullman Trailmobile Canada Ltd v Hamilton Refrigeration Ltd* (1979) 96 D.L.R. (3d) 322. The prior assent of the buyer to the appropriation would be easier to establish if the price has already been paid. *Cf.* s.19(1), below, para.5–131.

5–082 **Assent of the seller.** Less difficulty is caused where the appropriation is made by the buyer with the assent of the seller, as, for example, where the buyer is to separate the goods from bulk and carry them away, for there will normally be an appropriation by actual delivery.[22] It will, however, be necessary to ascertain whether the parties intended that property should pass on appropriation by virtue of a previous assent of the seller[23] or whether they intended that the seller should subsequently assent to the appropriation by approving the buyer's choice.[24]

5–083 **Assent of agent.** The assent to the appropriation need not be given by the buyer or seller himself; it can be given by a servant, or "by an agent of the party, by the warehouseman or wharfinger, for instance."[25]

5–084 **Relevance of risk.** In cases of doubt or ambiguity, it may be relevant to inquire what were the parties' intentions with regard to risk. Ownership and risk are prima facie associated in commercial transactions.[26] Therefore, if it appears that there is reason for thinking, on the construction of the relevant documents, that the goods were, at all material times, still at the seller's risk, that may be some indication that the property has not passed to the buyer.[27]

5–085 **Conformity with contract.** Section 18, rule 5(1), requires that the appropriation be of goods "of that description", *i.e.* the description by which the goods are sold. Prima facie, therefore, no property will pass if the goods which are the subject-matter of the appropriation are other than those described in the contract of sale.[28] Similarly, where the seller appropriates to the contract the goods which he contracted to sell mixed with goods of a different description not included in the contract, it has been held that no property will pass by the appropriation in any of the

[22] But the appropriation may be conditional on some further act on the part of the seller, *e.g.* weighing the goods in order to ascertain the price: *R. v Tideswell* [1905] 2 K.B. 273 at 277; *National Coal Board v Gamble* [1959] 1 Q.B. 11 at 21; see above, para.5–072.

[23] *Congreve v Evetts* (1854) 10 Exch. 298; *Hope v Hayley* (1856) 5 E. & B. 830; *Carr v Acraman* (1856) 11 Exch. 566 at 568; *Chidell v Galsworthy* (1859) 6 C.B. (N.S.) 471.

[24] But in the case of the selection of goods by a customer from the shelves of a self-service shop property does not pass until the price is paid: *Pilgram v Rice-Smith* [1977] 2 All E.R. 658; *Davies v Leighton* [1978] Crim.L.R. 575; *R. v Morris* [1984] A.C. 320.

[25] *Campbell v Mersey Docks and Harbour Board* (1863) 14 C.B. (N.S.) 412 at 416.

[26] See below, para.6–002.

[27] *Carlos Federspiel & Co. SA v Charles Twigg & Co. Ltd* [1957] 1 Lloyd's Rep. 240 at 255. See also *Martineau v Kitching* (1872) L.R. 7 Q.B. 436 at 454; *Allison v Bristol Marine Insurance Co. Ltd* (1876) 1 App.Cas. 209 at 229; *The Parchim* [1918] A.C. 157 at 168, 171. *Cf. Martineau v Kitching*, above, at p.451; *Mitsui & Co. Ltd v Flota Mercante Grancolombiana (The Ciudad de Pasto)* [1988] 2 Lloyd's Rep. 208 at 214, 217. See above, para.5–027.

[28] *Wait v Baker* (1848) 2 Exch. 1 at 7; *Vigers v Sanderson* [1901] 1 K.B. 608; *Hammer & Barrow v Coca-Cola* [1962] N.Z.L.R. 723; *Thorneley v Tuckwell (Butchers) Ltd* [1964] Crim.L.R. 127.

goods.[29] If the goods appropriated by the seller are fundamentally different from those described in the contract of sale, it is no doubt reasonable to assume that the parties did not intend that the seller could, by such an appropriation, pass the property in the non-conforming goods to the buyer.[30] But if the goods appropriated fail to conform with the description in the contract in some less fundamental respect, it may be that the parties intended that property in the goods should nevertheless pass to the buyer, although the buyer could (if he chose to do so) reject them and re-transfer the property to the seller. In *Kwei Tek Chao v British Traders and Shippers Ltd*[31] Devlin J. stated that, under a c.i.f. contract, what the buyer obtains, when the title under the documents is given to him, is the property in the goods, subject to the condition that they revest if upon examination he finds them to be not in accordance with the contract. On this basis an appropriation of non-conforming goods would in some circumstances likewise pass a conditional property to the buyer, subject to his right to reject.[32]

Where the seller delivers to the buyer a quantity of goods larger than he contracted to sell,[33] it has been held that no property in any of the goods will pass on the ground that no particular goods have been appropriated to the contract.[34] But again it may be the intention of the parties that property in the goods shall pass to the buyer, subject to a re-transfer in whole or in part if the buyer elects to reject the goods or the excess.[35] On the other hand where the seller appropriates a quantity of goods less than he contracted to sell, the property in those goods will pass, although the buyer's right of property so acquired is defeasible at his option if the seller fails to deliver the total quantity contracted to be sold.[36] Thus, where goods are contracted for simply as being a certain quantity of goods, but are appropriated by instalments, the ordinary rules of appropriation will apply, and the property in the portion from time to time appropriated will prima facie pass to the buyer.[37] This principle does not, however, apply where a quantity of goods is contracted for as an undivided whole, as, for instance, **5–086**

---

[29] *Levy v Green* (1859) 1 E. & E. 969. But it is submitted that this case deserves reconsideration, especially in the light of the repeal of s.30(4) of the 1979 Act by Sch.3 of the Sale and Supply of Goods Act 1994. The buyer may now accept the conforming goods and reject those which do not conform: see s.35A(1) of the 1979 Act.

[30] See also above, para.5–020.

[31] [1954] 2 Q.B. 459; see below, para.19–174.

[32] *Pullman Trailmobile Canada Ltd v Hamilton Refrigeration Ltd* (1979) 96 D.L.R. (3d) 322. See also *McDougall v Aeromarine of Emsworth Ltd* [1958] 1 W.L.R. 1126 (future goods); below, para.5–092, n.57.

[33] See s.30(2) of the Act: below, para.8–049. But see s.30(2A).

[34] *Cunliffe v Harrison* (1851) 6 Exch. 903 (action for goods sold and delivered).

[35] *Karlshamns Oljefabriker v Eastport Navigation Corp. (The Elafi)* [1981] 2 Lloyd's Rep. 679 at 683; Sale of Goods Act 1979, s.30(2), (3).

[36] *Colonial Insurance Co. of New Zealand v Adelaide Marine Insurance Co.* (1886) 12 App.Cas. 128. *Cf. Saffron v Société Minière Cafrika* (1958) 100 C.L.R. 231.

[37] *Aldridge v Johnson* (1857) 7 E. & B. 885; *Langton v Higgins* (1859) 4 H. & N. 402. *Colonial Insurance Co. of New Zealand v Adelaide Marine Insurance Co.*, above. But see s.30(1) of the Act, below, para.8–046.

the entire load of a vessel. The property in the goods constituting the load will not ordinarily pass until the whole load is made up and appropriated on completion.[38]

5–087 **Appropriation by mistake.** Where goods other than those which conform with the contract description are mistakenly appropriated to the contract, it may be that no property will pass.[39] But, in such a case it is submitted that the seller will be permitted to appropriate other goods of the correct description, provided he does so within the time allowed by the contract.[40] On the other hand, if the goods conform with the contract, a mistake by the party appropriating or his agent as to the particular parcel of goods appropriated may be immaterial. In *Denny v Skelton*,[41] where authority to appropriate a certain quantity of goods had previously been conferred by the buyer on the seller's agent, but the agent mistakenly appropriated the parcel of goods intended for another to the buyer (though in accordance with his authority), it was held that the property in the goods thus appropriated had passed to the buyer. However, no property will pass if the goods are appropriated to a person other than the person to whom the seller's agent is authorised by the buyer to deliver them.[42]

5–088 **Place of sale.** Where goods are appropriated to the contract by one party with the assent of the other, the place where the sale is concluded by conveyance of the property is the place where the goods are at the time of the appropriation,[43] and not where the assent is given or the goods are delivered.[44]

5–089 **"Ex works", etc. contracts.** Where goods are sold "ex works", "ex factory", "ex warehouse", "ex store" or on other similar terms, there is some uncertainty when the property passes, for the exact terms of such contracts are somewhat indefinite.[45] In some situations the property may pass when the goods have been appropriated by the seller and placed at the disposal[46] of the buyer at the designated works, factory, etc., provided the buyer has been given reasonable notice as to when the goods will be at his

---

[38] *Anderson v Morice* (1876) 1 App.Cas. 713. See also *Bryans v Nix* (1839) 4 M. & W. 775 (but *cf.* p.793); *Borrowman v Drayton* (1876) 2 Ex.D. 15.
[39] See above, para.5–085.
[40] *Cf. Borrowman, Phillips & Co. v Free and Hollis* (1878) 4 Q.B.D. 500 (contractual appropriation under c.i.f. contract); below, para.19–021.
[41] (1916) 115 L.T. 305. Contrast *Campbell v Mersey Docks and Harbour Board* (1863) 14 C.B. (N.S.) 412 (but goods in this case were not ascertained).
[42] *Hoare v G.W. Ry* (1877) 37 L.T. 186.
[43] *Daniel v Whitfield* (1885) 15 Q.B.D. 408; *Pletts v Beattie* [1896] 1 Q.B. 519; *Badische Anilin Fabrik v Hickson* [1906] A.C. 419. But see below, paras 25–128—25–140 (conflict of laws).
[44] Where the appropriation is by delivery to the buyer or to a carrier, the place of sale is the place of delivery: *Ridgway v Ward* (1884) 14 Q.B.D. 110; *Pletts v Campbell* [1895] 2 Q.B. 229; *Badische Anilin und Soda Fabrik v Basle Chemical Works* [1898] A.C. 200; *Cocker v McMullen* (1900) 81 L.T. 784; *Noblett v Hopkinson* [1905] 2 K.B. 214. *Cf. Preston v Albuery* [1964] 2 Q.B. 796 at 805.
[45] *Fisher Reeves & Co. v Armour & Co.* [1920] 3 K.B. 614 at 620, 622–623, 624.
[46] See below, para.8–007.

disposal. In others it may be necessary that the buyer should have subsequently assented to the appropriation, or that the goods should have been delivered to him or to a carrier, before the property will pass.[47]

(b) *Appropriation of Future Goods*

Future goods. Future goods are defined in the Sale of Goods Act 1979 as "goods to be manufactured or acquired by the seller after the making of the contract of sale".[48] These may form the subject of a contract of sale[49]; but, where by a contract of sale the seller purports to effect a present sale of future goods, the contract operates as an agreement to sell the goods.[50] Property passes when the parties intend it to pass,[51] but, in the absence of a different intention, the passing of property in future goods is governed by section 18, rule 5, of the Act. 5–090

Goods to be manufactured and sold. Where there is a contract for the sale of goods to be manufactured by the seller, the property in the goods will usually pass to the buyer when the goods have been completed and appropriated to the contract by the seller with the assent of the buyer.[52] Such a contract is prima facie a contract for the sale of the goods when finished.[53] Normally, therefore, no appropriation will be held to have been made until the goods are completed and ready for delivery; and the buyer must then assent to the appropriation before the property can pass.[54] Even if the goods have been appropriated by mutual agreement before completion, the appropriation is usually conditional upon their being completed and in a deliverable state.[55] The property will not be held to have passed before this time. 5–091

Passing of property before completion. This presumption must, however, yield to a different intention of the parties. The terms of the contract may provide that property in goods to be manufactured and sold shall pass to 5–092

---

[47] *Wardar's (Import and Export) Co. Ltd v W. Norwood & Sons Ltd* [1968] 2 Q.B. 663. See also below, paras 5–097, 5–098, 21–003.
[48] s.6(1). See also s.5(1), and above, para.1–102.
[49] s.5(1).
[50] s.5(3); see above, para.1–105.
[51] s.17; *Davy Offshore Ltd v Emerald Field Contracting Ltd* [1992] 2 Lloyd's Rep. 142.
[52] Sale of Goods Act 1979, s.18, r.5(1); *Elliott v Pybus* (1828) 10 Bing. 512; *Wilkins v Bromhead* (1844) 6 M. & G. 963; *B. & H. Constructions Pty Ltd v Campbell* [1963] N.S.W.R. 333. For cases in which the property passed, by virtue of a different intention, later than this time, see *Bellamy v Davey* [1891] 3 Ch. 540; *Armitage v John Haigh & Sons* (1893) 9 T.L.R. 287; *Sir James Laing & Sons v Barclay, Curle & Co.* [1908] A.C. 35.
[53] *Clarke v Spence* (1836) 4 A. & E. 448 at 466; *Laidler v Burlinson* (1837) 2 M. & W. 602; *Seath v Moore* (1886) 11 App.Cas. 350 at 370.
[54] *Mucklow v Mangles* (1808) 1 Taunt. 318 (above, para.5–080); *Bishop v Crawshay* (1824) 3 B. & C. 415; *Atkinson v Bell* (1828) 8 B. & C. 277.
[55] *Laidler v Burlinson*, above; *Werner v Humphreys* (1841) 2 M. & G. 853. Contrast *Carruthers v Payne* (1828) 5 Bing. 270; *Girardot v Fitzpatrick* (1869) 21 L.T. 470; *Pritchett & Gold and Electrical Power Storage Co. Ltd v Currie* [1916] 1 Ch. 515. The seller may also, expressly or impliedly, have reserved the right of disposal: see below, para.5–131.

the buyer while they are in the course of manufacture and before they are completed. Such an agreement is one which is sometimes found in contracts for the construction of ships, where it is the practice to provide for the property in the uncompleted ship to pass to the buyer as and when an instalment of the price is paid corresponding to a certain stage in the progress of construction. There is no doubt that a contract can be so framed as to pass the property at any stage[56] before completion.[57] But it is a question of the construction of the contract in each case, at what stage the property shall pass; and a question of fact in each case, whether that stage has been reached.[58] In *Seath v Moore*[59] Lord Watson said: "Where it appears to be the intention, or in other words the agreement, of the parties to a contract that at a particular stage of its construction, the vessel, so far as then finished, shall be appropriated to the contract of sale, the property of the vessel as soon as it has reached that stage of completion will pass to the purchaser, and subsequent additions made to the chattel thus vested in the purchaser will, *accessione*, become his property." Difficulty can, however, arise where the court is asked to infer such an intention. In the same case Lord Watson continued[60]: "Such an intention or agreement ought (in the absence of any circumstances pointing to a different conclusion) to be inferred from a provision in the contract to the effect that an instalment of the price shall be paid at a particular stage, coupled with the fact that the instalment has been duly paid[61] and that until the vessel reached that stage the execution of the work was regularly inspected by the purchaser, or some one on his behalf." Payment by instalments and inspection have been said to raise "a strong prima facie presumption" that the property is intended to pass[62]; but it would seem that, although they may be marks pointing to still remains as to what the contract really means.[63] Although these principles were enunciated with special reference

---

[56] *Cf. McDougall v Aeromarine of Emsworth Ltd* [1958] 1 W.L.R. 1126 at 1129, where it was said that a clause providing for the passing of property on payment of the first instalment (when nothing was specifically in existence) would be ineffective. *Cf. Nelson v William Chalmers & Co. Ltd*, 1913 S.C. 441.

[57] *Seath v Moore* (1886) 11 App.Cas. 350 at 370; *Sir James Laing & Sons v Barclay, Curle & Co.* [1908] A.C. 35 at 43; *Re Blyth Shipbuilding and Dry Docks Co. Ltd* [1926] Ch. 494. But property passes defeasibly, subject to the ship being in a deliverable state when complete: *Nelson v William Chalmers & Co. Ltd* 1913 S.C. 441 at 452; *McDougall v Aeromarine of Emsworth Ltd*, above.

[58] *Seath v Moore*, above, at p.370.

[59] (1886) 11 App.Cas. 350 at 380, relying on *Woods v Russell* (1822) 5 B. & Ald. 942; *Clarke v Spence* (1836) 4 A. & E. 448; *Wood v Bell* (1856) 5 E. & B. 722; 6 E. & B. 355. See also *Reid v Fairbanks* (1853) 13 C.B. 692; *Clarke v Millwall Dock Co.* (1886) 17 Q.B.D. 494; *Howden Bros Ltd v Ulster Bank Ltd* [1924] I.R. 117.

[60] At p.380.

[61] But Lord Watson also says (*ibid.*): "I do not think it is indispensable to order to sustain [the] inference, that there shall be a stipulation for payment of an instalment in the original contract, or that the stipulated instalment shall have been actually paid." See also (action for amount of instalment) *Workman Clark & Co. Ltd v Lloyd Brazilenño* [1908] 1 K.B. 968.

[62] *Clarke v Spence*, above; *Seath v Moore*, above, at p.370.

[63] *Sir James Laing & Sons v Barclay, Curle & Co.*, above, at p.43 (provision that delivery not to be considered completed until trials held prevented passing of

to ships, there is no reason to suppose that they will not equally apply to a contract for the manufacture and sale of any other chattel.[64]

Materials for construction.[65] Where an article to be manufactured and sold becomes, in an uncompleted state, the property of the buyer, materials provided by the seller and portions of the fabric intended to be used in the execution of the contract may become by accession the buyer's property, but only if and when they have been affixed to or in a reasonable sense made part of the article.[66] This principle can nevertheless be varied by contrary agreement, so that property may pass in such materials (provided they are ascertained) at some earlier stage.[67] Contracts for work and materials, such as building contracts, may provide, for example, that any materials brought on site are to vest in the employer.[68] However, in *Reid v Macbeth*[69] where a contract for the construction of a ship provided that "the vessel, as she is constructed . . . and all materials from time to time intended for her [wherever situated] shall immediately as the same proceeds become the property of the purchasers," the House of Lords held as a matter of construction that various iron and steel plates lying in railway stations, which had been passed by the Lloyd's surveyor and which had been marked with their proposed position in the ship, were still the property of the seller as they had not yet become part of the ship's structure. 5–093

property). See also *Laidler v Burlinson* (1837) 2 M. & W. 602 (payment by instalments but not at particular stages); *Re Royal Bank of Canada and Saskatchewan Communications* (1985) 20 D.L.R. (4th) 415. It is to be noted that there were additional factors in the cases relied upon by Lord Watson (see n.61, above): *Woods v Russell* (registration and charter of ship by buyer with assent of seller); *Clarke v Spence* (approval by buyer's agent); *Wood v Bell* (buyer's name stamped on vessel and acknowledgment by seller that buyer's property).

[64] *Seath v Moore*, above, at pp.370, 380, 385. See also *Beale v Mouls* (1847) 10 Q.B. 976.

[65] See Palmer and McKendrick, *Interests in Goods* (2nd ed., 1998), Ch. 15.

[66] *Seath v Moore* (1886) 11 App.Cas. 350 at 381. See also *Wood v Bell* (1856) 5 E. & B. 772; 6 E. & B. 355 (which overruled the earlier cases of *Woods v Russell* (1822) 5 B. & Ald. 942 and *Goss v Quinton* (1842) 3 M. & G. 825 on this point); *Tripp v Armitage* (1839) 4 M. & W. 687; *Clark v Bulmer* (1843) 11 M. & W. 243; *Petromec Inc. v Petroleo Brasileiro SA Petrobas* [2004] EWHC 1180 (Comm), [2005] 1 Lloyd's Rep. 219 at [36].

[67] *Anglo-Egyptian Navigation Co. v Rennie* (1875) L.R. 10 CP. 271; *Reeves v Barlow* (1884) 12 Q.B.D. 436; *Petromec Inc. v Petroleo Brasileiro SA Petrobas* [2004] EWHC 1180 (Comm), [2005] Lloyd's Rep. 219 at [35–36]; see above, para.5–031. *Cf. McDougall v Aeromarine of Emsworth Ltd* [1958] 1 W.L.R. 1126 at 1129. See also *Banbury and Cheltenham Direct Ry v Daniel* (1884) 54 L.J.Ch. 265.

[68] *Reeves v Barlow* (1884) 12 Q.B.D. 436 (not bill of sale); *Re Weibking* [1902] 1 K.B. 713; *Hart v Porthgain Harbour Co. Ltd* [1903] 1 Ch. 690; *Bennett & White (Calgary) Ltd v Municipal District of Sugar City No. 5* [1951] A.C. 786; *Sauter Automation Ltd v Goodman Mechanical Services Ltd* (1986) 34 Build.L.R. 81. *Cf.*, *Re Winter* (1878) 8 Ch.D. 225; *Re Keen & Keen* [1902] 1 K.B. 555; *Re Cosslett (Contractors) Ltd* [1998] Ch. 495; *Smith v Bridgend C.B.C.* [2002] 1 A.C. 336 (charge).

[69] [1904] A.C. 223. *cf. Baker v Gray* (1856) 17 C.B. 462 (property to pass on user); *Anglo-Egyptian Navigation Co. v Rennie* (1875) L.R. 10 C.P. 271; *Banbury and Cheltenham Ry v Daniel* (1884) 54 L.J Ch 265 (on certificate); *Re Blyth Shipbuilding and Dry Docks Co.* [1926] Ch.494 (on appropriation).

5–094 **Sales of goods to be acquired.** There is a divergence between the rules of common law relating to contracts for the sale of goods to be acquired by the seller after the making of the contract of sale and those of equity relating to assignments of property to be acquired in the future. At common law, such a contract did not before 1893[70] and does not now transfer ownership to the buyer immediately the seller acquires the goods. But equity adopts a different attitude to assignments of or agreements to assign after-acquired property for valuable consideration. As soon as the assignor acquires the property, provided it is identifiable as that comprised in the assignment, a beneficial interest passes to the assignee, and the property is held in trust for him by the assignor.[71] In *Re Wait*[72] it was sought to apply this principle in an action for specific performance of a c.i.f. contract for the sale of an unascertained part of an ascertained bulk—500 tons of wheat, part of a quantity of 1,000 tons shipped on a designated vessel for carriage to England from the United States. The Court of Appeal rejected its application to this situation.[73] In his judgment, however, Atkin L.J.[74] stated that the equitable principle had been abrogated by the provisions of the Sale of Goods Act 1893 so far as after-acquired goods were concerned; it was never intended to leave subsisting equitable rights inconsistent with, and more extensive than, those set out in the Act. The facts of *Re Wait* itself would no longer raise this issue, since an undivided share in the bulk of 1,000 tons would now be transferred to the buyer under section 20A of the 1979 Act[75] and he would become an owner in common of the bulk. But, apart from the special case of the sale of goods forming part of a bulk,[76] if the statement of Atkin L.J. is correct, the passing of property in goods to be acquired by the seller after the making of the contract of sale is governed exclusively by section 17 and by the rules contained in section 18, rule 5, of the Act. Assuming that the goods have become ascertained, it is not inconceivable (especially where the buyer has pre-paid the price) that the parties intended by their contract that property should pass to the buyer as soon as the goods were acquired by the seller.[77] But, in the absence of such an intention, property will only pass when the goods have been appropriated to the contract by one party with the assent

[70] *Lunn v Thornton* (1843) 1 C.B. 379; *Tapfield v Hillman* (1843) 6 M. & G. 245.
[71] *Holroyd v Marshall* (1862) 10 H.L.C. 191 at 209; *Collyer v Isaacs* (1881) 19 Ch.D. 342; *Re Clarke* (1887) 36 Ch.D. 348; *Tailby v Official Receiver* (1888) 13 App.Cas. 523; *Re Gillott's Settlement* [1934] Ch.97. See also above, para.1–107.
[72] [1927] 1 Ch. 606. See also *Re London Wine Co. (Shippers) Ltd* [1986] P.C.C. 121; *Leigh and Sillavan Ltd v Aliakmon Shipping Co. Ltd (The Aliakmon)* [1986] A.C. 785 at 812; *Re Goldcorp Exchange Ltd* [1995] 1 A.C. 74; and above, paras 1–108, 5–064; below, paras 18–253, 19–204.
[73] Sargant L.J. dissenting. Both Lord Hanworth M.R. and Atkin L.J. were agreed that no specific appropriation of the goods in question had occurred to attract the operation of the equitable principle, a point reiterated in *Re Goldcorp Exchange Ltd*.
[74] At p.636. See also *Leigh and Sillavan Ltd v Aliakmon Shipping Co. Ltd (The Aliakmon)* above, at pp.812, 813.
[75] See below, para.5–109.
[76] See below, paras 5–103, 5–109—5–110.
[77] Under s.17.

of the other[78] or by delivery. In the interim period no equitable or beneficial interest will pass to the buyer. It is submitted that the view of Atkin L.J. should be adopted, since, as he pointed out,[79] to permit the creation of beneficial interests in goods would fundamentally affect the whole course of business transactions.

Potential property. Sales of crops to be grown by the seller and the produce thereof may be governed by section 18, rule 5(1) of the 1979 Act.[80] But, at common law, a contract for the sale of future goods in which the seller had a potential property operated as an immediate grant of the goods and not merely as an agreement to sell. In such a case the property passed immediately the goods came into existence, and not on appropriation of the goods with the assent of the other party.[81] There is little doubt, however, that this principle has not survived, although the parties are at liberty to agree that property in the goods shall pass as soon as they have come into existence[82] or when they have been severed from the realty.[83] **5–095**

(c) *Appropriation by Delivery*

Section 18, rule 5(2). Appropriation by delivery is dealt with specifically by section 18, rule 5(2) of the 1979 Act. This paragraph provides: "Where, in pursuance of the contract,[84] the seller delivers the goods to the buyer or to a carrier or other bailee or custodier[85] (whether named by the buyer or not) for the purpose of transmission to the buyer, and does not reserve the right of disposal,[86] he is to be taken to have unconditionally appropriated the goods to the contract." This is in accordance with the common law before the Sale of Goods Act 1893.[87] **5–096**

Delivery to the buyer. The property in ascertained goods[88] will, in the absence of a contrary intention, pass by delivery[89] to the buyer or his agent.[90] Where the goods at the time of sale are in the possession of a third **5–097**

---

[78] *Lunn v Thornton*, above, at p.387. In most of the cases before the 1893 Act, property passed by virtue of the buyer taking possession of the goods in pursuance of an authority previously conferred by the seller: *Congreve v Evetts* (1854) 10 Exch. 298; *Hope v Hayley* (1856) 5 E. & B. 830; *Carr v Acraman* (1856) 11 Exch. 566 at 568; *Chidell v Galsworthy* (1859) 6 C.B. (N.S.) 471.
[79] At pp.639–641.
[80] See, *e.g.* *Langton v Higgins* (1859) 4 H. & N. 402. It is arguable, however, that there can be a present sale of *fructus industriales*.
[81] *Grantham v Hawley* (1615) Hob. 132; *Petch v Tutin* (1846) 15 M. & W. 110. See also *Howell v Coupland* (1874) L.R. 9 Q.B. 462, and generally above, para.1–106.
[82] As in the case, *e.g.* of milk from cows owned by the seller: see above, para.1–106.
[83] See above, para.1–106.
[84] See below, para.5–100.
[85] The Scottish equivalent of bailee.
[86] See below, para.5–131.
[87] See the cases cited in para.5–098, n.97, below.
[88] See above, para.5–059, below, para.5–099.
[89] Defined in s.61(1) of the Act as "voluntary transfer of possession from one person to another," see below, para.8–002.
[90] *Ogle v Atkinson* (1814) 5 Taunt. 759; *Studdy v Sanders* (1826) 5 B. & C. 628; *Colonial Insurance Co. of New Zealand v Adelaide Marine Insurance Co.* (1886) 12 App.Cas. 128; *Denny v Skelton* (1916) 115 L.T. 305. At a filling station, property in the fuel will pass when it is put into the vehicle's fuel tank: *Edwards v Ddin* [1976] 1 W.L.R. 942; *Re Charge Card Services Ltd* [1989] Ch. 497.

person, *e.g.* a warehouseman or wharfinger, delivery will take place when the third person attorns to the buyer, that is to say, acknowledges to the buyer that he holds the goods on his behalf,[91] but not before.[92] If a delivery order[93] is merely received without acknowledgment by the warehouseman or wharfinger, no delivery, and therefore no transfer of ownership, will occur.[94] Yet if the goods are unascertained, no property will pass unless they become ascertained by reason of the attornment.[95]

5–098 **Delivery to carrier or other bailee.** If, in pursuance of a contract of sale, the seller is authorised or required to send the goods to the buyer, section 32(1) of the Act[96] provides that delivery of goods to a carrier (whether named by the buyer or not) for the purpose of transmission to the buyer is prima facie deemed to be a delivery of goods to the buyer. Rule 5(2) is consistent with this presumption in that delivery of goods to a carrier is treated as delivery of goods to the buyer for the purposes of passing of property. By such delivery the seller is to be taken to have unconditionally appropriated the goods to the contract so that the property will then pass.[97] The rationale of the rule was thus stated by Parke B. in *Wait v Baker*[98]: "The moment the goods, which have been selected in pursuance of the contract, are delivered to the carrier, the carrier becomes the agent of the vendee; and if there is a binding contract between the vendor and the vendee . . . then there is no doubt that the property passes by such delivery to the carrier". The carrier is prima facie constituted the buyer's agent for the purpose of taking delivery, although, if the terms of the contract or appropriation show that the carrier is the agent of the seller, the property will not normally pass until the goods are actually delivered to the buyer or his agent.[99] However, section 32(4) of the Act provides that, in a case where the buyer deals as consumer,[1] section 32(l) must be "ignored" and "delivery

[91] *Wardar's (Import and Export) Co. Ltd v Norwood & Sons Ltd* [1968] 2 Q.B. 663.
[92] Sale of Goods Act 1979, s.29(4); see below, para.8–012.
[93] But contrast the position where a document of title is issued or transferred: below, para.8–013.
[94] *Laurie & Morewood v Dudin & Sons* [1926] 1 K.B. 223; *Mount (D.F.) Ltd v Jay and Jay(Provisions) Co. Ltd* [1960] 1 Q.B. 159.
[95] *Re London Wine Co. (Shippers) Ltd* [1986] P.C.C. 121; above, para.5–065.
[96] See; below, para.8–014.
[97] *Vale v Bayee* (1775) 1 Cowp. 294; *Dutton v Solomonson* (1803) 3 B. & P. 582; *King v Meredith* (1811) 2 Camp. 639; *Fragano v Long* (1825) 4 B. & C. 219 at 223; *Bryans v Nix* (1839) 4 M. & W.775 at 791; *Dunlop v Lambert* (1839) 6 Cl. & F. 600 at 620; *Evans v Nichol* (1841) 3 M. & G. 614; *Tregalles v Sewell* (1862) 7 H. & N. 574 at 584; *Re Wiltshire Iron Co.* (1868) L.R. 3 Ch.App. 443; *Mirabita v Ottoman Imperial Bank* (1878) 3 Ex.D. 164 at 172. See also *Cork Distilleries Co. v GS Ry* (1874) L.R. 7 H.L. 269 at 277 ("carriage forward"). When a buyer orders unascertained goods to be delivered to him by post, the despatch of the goods to him by post will (*semble*) pass the property in them: *Badische Anilin und Soda Fabrik v Basle Chemical Works* [1898] A.C. 200. *Cf. Postmaster-General v W H Jones & Co. (London) Ltd* [1957] N.Z.L.R. 829 (no right of stoppage in transit).
[98] (1849) 2 Exch.1 at 7. See also *James v The Commonwealth* (1939) 62 C.L.R. 339 at 377.
[99] *Badische Anilin und Soda Fabrik v Basle Chemical Works*, above, at p.207; *Harrison v Lia* [1951] V.L.R. 470 at 475. See also below, para.8–014.
[1] Defined in s.61(5A) by reference to Pt I or the Unfair Contract Terms Act 1977; below, para.13–070.

of the goods to the carrier is not delivery to the buyer".[2] The effect of this provision in relation to rule 5(2) is not entirely clear. It was introduced by Regulation 4 of the Sale and Supply of Goods to Consumers Regulations 2002[3] which is headed "Amendment to rules on passing of risk and acceptance of goods in consumer cases". This heading would suggest that the amendment was not intended to affect the passing of property but only the passing of risk. Taken together with section 20(4) of the Act[4] it was designed to ensure that risk of loss or damage to the goods remained with the seller during transit and did not pass until the goods were delivered to the consumer. No corresponding amendment was made to rule 5(2) concerning the passing of property. Moreover, rule 5(2) is not limited to delivery to a carrier but extends to delivery to any other bailee for transmission to the buyer. It is therefore submitted that rule 5(2) continues to apply even though the buyer deals as consumer and that delivery to a carrier is, in the absence of a contrary intention, still to be taken as an unconditional appropriation of the goods to the contract, passing the property to the buyer.

Appropriation must identify goods. Unless the goods have become ascertained before or by virtue of the delivery, they will not be deemed to have been unconditionally appropriated to the contract.[5] Mere delivery of a quantity of unascertained goods, *e.g.* to a carrier, will not pass the property. Thus in *Healy v Howlett & Sons*[6] the defendant, a Billingsgate fish merchant, instructed the claimant, a fish exporter in Ireland, carrying on business in Valentia Co. Kerry, to send him 20 boxes of mackerel. The claimant consigned to an Irish railway company at Valentia 190 boxes of mackerel and telegraphed the railway officials at Holyhead to deliver 20 boxes to the defendant, and the remaining 170 boxes to two other consignees. The Irish train from Valentia to Dublin was delayed, and the fish deteriorated before they were earmarked at Holyhead. It was held that the property had not passed to the defendant before the boxes were earmarked, and that the fish was still at the seller's risk when it deteriorated. Ridley J. said[7]: "The essence of the authorities which decide that appropriation of goods to the contract by delivery to the carrier at the beginning of the transit may be sufficient to pass the property is that it should be known to whom the goods are appropriated, and not that the question as to who is to bear any loss that may happen should be open to any discussion or be determined by accident."[8] In order that delivery to the carrier in Ireland should have passed the property, each box ought at least to have been marked with the name of its consignee. 5–099

---

[2] See below para.8–014.
[3] SI 2002/3045. See below para.12–071.
[4] See below, para.6–013.
[5] *Re Wait* [1927] 1 Ch. 606. Contrast *Inglis v Stock* (1885) 10 App.Cas. 263 at 267–268; *Sterns Ltd v Vickers* [1923] 1 K.B. 78 (but both these cases concerned risk).
[6] [1917] 1 K.B. 337.
[7] At p.345.
[8] It is, however, arguable that the risk (though not the property) should have been held to have passed to the buyer in this case.

On the other hand, if the contract is for a specified quantity of goods forming part of an identified bulk[9] such as the load of a particular vehicle, and the buyer has paid the price for some or all of the contract goods, then, under section 20A of the Act,[10] property in an undivided share in the bulk is transferred to the buyer and he becomes an owner in common of the bulk.[11] In a commercial transaction, it is probable that the risk in respect of the undivided share will pass to the buyer at the same time as the property in that share even though no part of the bulk has been allocated to any individual contract.[12]

5–100 **Authority to appropriate.** The premiss underlying the rule that delivery to a carrier constitutes an unconditional appropriation of the goods is that the buyer is deemed to have authorised the seller to pass the property by such delivery. It therefore follows that the delivery to the carrier must be made "in pursuance of the contract", that is to say, the goods must be despatched by the authorised mode of transmission[13] and by the authorised carrier, if named.[14] They must also be despatched within the time fixed by the contract[15] and may also (it appears) have to conform with the contract description.[16]

5–101 **Different intention.** Property will not pass by delivery to the buyer or his agent, or to a carrier, if the seller, by the terms of the contract or appropriation, reserves the right of disposal of the goods until certain conditions are fulfilled.[17] The circumstances of the sale may also raise the implication that property is not intended to pass until the price is paid.[18] Further, where goods are delivered to a carrier, it may be the intention of the parties that such delivery shall not pass the property even conditionally.[19] In particular, where the seller agrees, not merely to send the goods to the buyer, but to deliver them at a prescribed place, and no intention appears from the contract that the property shall pass before delivery, no change of ownership will occur unless and until the goods are actually delivered at that place.[20]

---

[9] Defined in s.61(1) of the Act.
[10] See below, para.5–109.
[11] s.20A(2).
[12] See below, para.6–006.
[13] *Ullock v Reddelein* (1828) 5 L.J. (O.S.) K.B. 208. See also *Re Sutro (L) & Co. and Heilbut Symons & Co.* [1917] 2 K.B. 348. *Cf. Tsakiroglou & Co. Ltd v Noblee Thorl GmbH* [1962] A.C. 93 at 113.
[14] *Cooke v Ludlow* (1806) 2 B. & P.N.R. 119.
[15] *Aron & Co. v Comptoir Wegimont* [1921] 3 K.B. 435.
[16] See above, para.5–085.
[17] See s.19 of the Act; below, para.5–131.
[18] *Davies v Leighton* [1978] Crim.L.R. 575 (goods in supermarket).
[19] See c.i.f. contracts (below, para.19–098) and f.o.b. contracts (below, para.20–070).
[20] *Dunlop v Lambert* (1839) 6 Cl. & F. 600 at 621, 622; *Wheeler v Pearson* (1857) 5 W.R. 227; *Calcutta & Burmah Steam Navigation Co. v De Mattos* (1863) 32 L.J.Q.B. 322 at 328; *Comptoir d'Achat et de Vente du Boerenbond Belge S/A v Luis de Ridder Limitada* [1949] A.C. 293. The question of the true construction of the contract may be one of considerable difficulty: *Badische Anilin und Soda Fabrik v Basle Chemical Works* [1898] A.C. 200 at 207. For risk of deterioration, see s.33 of the Act (below, para.18–249), and below, para.6–022.

Special terms. An example of the principle contained in section 18, rule 5(2), can be found in f.o.r. contracts, where the property will not pass until delivery to the railway,[21] and in f.o.b. contracts, where the property prima facie will not pass before the goods cross the ship's rail at the named port of shipment,[22] although in the latter case at least the seller will more usually be found to have reserved the right of disposal against payment or securing of the price.[23] Where goods are sold "carriage paid" or on other similar terms[24] to an agreed point at a named destination, the property will normally pass when the goods are delivered to the first carrier for transmission to the buyer. But, in the case of c.i.f. and c. & f. contracts, the inference that property passes on shipment is usually rebutted; the ordinary intention of the parties is that property in the goods shall pass on unconditional transfer of the bill of lading against payment or securing of the price by the buyer.[25] Reservation of the right of disposal is also presumed in the case of an f.a.s. contract[26] so that property will not normally pass when the goods are delivered alongside the vessel at the port of shipment.[27] In "ex ship" contracts, property does not ordinarily pass until the goods have crossed the ship's rail at the port of delivery.[28] 5–102

(d) *Appropriation of Goods forming part of an Identified Bulk*

Section 18, rule 5(3). By section 18, rule 5(3): "Where there is a contract for the sale of a specified quantity of unascertained goods in a deliverable state forming part of a bulk which is identified either in the contract or by subsequent agreement between the parties and the bulk is reduced to (or to less than) that quantity, then, if the buyer under that contract is the only buyer to whom goods are then due out of the bulk— 5–103

(a) the remaining goods are to be taken as appropriated to that contract at the time when the bulk is so reduced; and

(b) the property in those goods then passes to that buyer".

This paragraph was introduced by section 1(2) of the Sale of Goods (Amendment) Act 1995. It should be noted, however, that this paragraph and paragraph (4) below are not intended to be an exhaustive statement of the circumstances in which unascertained goods forming part of an identified bulk may be appropriated to the contract. Appropriation of such goods may occur under section 18, rule 5(1) or (2),[29] provided that the goods have then become, or thereby become, ascertained.

---

[21] *Underwood Ltd v Burgh Castle Brick and Cement Syndicate* [1922] 1 K.B. 343; see also below, para.21–043.

[22] See below, para.20–071.

[23] See below, paras 5–131, 20–075.

[24] *e.g.* "carriage forward" or "freight paid". See above, para.5–098, n.97.

[25] See below, para.19–098 (c.i.f.), para.20–071 (f.o.b.) and para.20–013 (c. & f.).

[26] *Transpacific Eternity SA v Kanematsu Corp. (The Antares III)* [2002] 1 Lloyd's Rep. 233.

[27] See below, para.20–011.

[28] *Yangtsze Insurance Association v Lukmanjee* [1918] A.C. 585 at 589; see below, para.21–020.

[29] See above, paras 5–068, 5–096.

5–104 **Illustration.** A buyer contracts to purchase, and pays for, a specified quantity (say 100 tonnes) of unascertained goods forming part of an identified bulk (say 1,000 tonnes of wheat in a particular warehouse). Under section 20A of the Act,[30] property in an undivided share in the bulk is transferred to the buyer and the buyer becomes an owner in common of the bulk. If, because of deliveries to other buyers or other removal of wheat from the warehouse, there comes a time when the quantity of wheat in the warehouse is reduced to 100 tonnes or less and the buyer is then the only buyer to whom wheat is due out of the 1,000 tonnes, the quantity of wheat remaining becomes ascertained goods by process of "exhaustion"[31] Further, under rule 5(3), if that quantity of wheat is in a deliverable state, it is taken as appropriated to the buyer's contract and the property in the wheat itself (as opposed to an undivided share in the bulk) passes to the buyer.[32]

Likewise, in this illustration, if the buyer has not paid any part of the price so that property in an undivided share in the bulk has not passed to him under section 20A,[33] the 100 tonnes is taken as appropriated to his contract and the property in these goods passes to him from the seller (in the absence of a contrary intention that property is to pass only on payment of the price).[34]

5–105 **"Bulk".** Section 61(1) of the Act defines "bulk" to mean "a mass or collection of goods of the same kind which—(a) is contained in a defined space or area, and (b) is such that any goods in the bulk are interchangeable with any other goods therein of the same number or quantity". This definition is considered in paragraph 5–113 in Section 5 of this Chapter. The bulk may be identified in the contract or by subsequent agreement of the parties.[35]

5–106 **Deliverable state.** The meaning of the words "in a deliverable state" has already been discussed earlier in this Chapter.[36] Despite the position of these words in rule 5(3), it is submitted that the goods need not be in a deliverable state at the time the contract is made, or at the time the bulk is or becomes identified, but that it was the intention of the draftsman—consistently with the passing of property in contracts for the sale of unascertained goods under rule 5(1)—that the goods must be in a deliverable state at the time of the deemed appropriation, that is to say, at or after the time when the identified bulk is reduced to (or to less than) the contract quantity.

5–107 **Section 18, rule 5(4).** By section 18, rule 5(4): "Paragraph (3) above applies also (with the necessary modifications) where a bulk is reduced to or (to less than) the aggregate of the quantities due to a single buyer under

---

[30] Below, para.5–109.
[31] See above, para.5–107; below, para.18–288.
[32] See below, para.5–116.
[33] See below, para.5–115.
[34] *Wait and James v Midland Bank* (1926) 31 Com. Cas. 172; *Karlshamns Oljefabriker v Eastport Navigation Corp.* (*The Elafi*) [1981] 2 Lloyd's Rep. 679. But see below, paras 5–108, 18–288 (contrary intention).
[35] See, on this requirement, below, para.5–116.
[36] Above, para.5–024.

separate contracts relating to that bulk and he is the only buyer to whom goods are then due out of that bulk". This paragraph, too, was inserted by section 1(2) of the Sale of Goods (Amendment) Act 1995. Thus, in the illustration given above, if the seller has agreed to sell the 100 tonnes to the buyer under two or more separate contracts, the remaining wheat becomes ascertained by "consolidation"[37] and the property in it passes under rule 5(4) even though no portion of it has been appropriated to any particular contract. The same result ensures even if the contracts have been made with different sellers, or with different buyers, but have become vested in a single buyer.[38]

Different intention. Section 18, rule 5, as a whole applies only "unless a different intention appears". In relation to paragraph (4), there may be situations where the circumstances are such as to show that the parties intend that the remaining goods are to be divided up and each portion appropriated to a particular contract before the property in the goods is to pass. And in relation to both paragraphs (3) and (4) the parties may intend that property is to pass only on delivery, or on transfer of the shipping documents against payment or securing of the price.[39] The seller may also have reserved the right of disposal,[40] in which case property will not pass under these paragraphs until the conditions imposed by the seller (usually payment in full of the price) have been fulfilled. **5–108**

5. UNDIVIDED SHARES IN GOODS FORMING PART OF A BULK[41]

Section 20A. Subsections (1) and (2) of section 20A provide: **5–109**

"(1) This section applies to a contract for the sale of a specified quantity of unascertained goods if the following conditions are met—

(a) the goods or some of them form part of a bulk which is identified either in the contract or by subsequent agreement between the parties; and

(b) the buyer has paid the price for some or all of the goods which are the subject of the contract and which form part of the bulk.

(2) Where this section applies, then (unless the parties agree otherwise), as soon as the conditions specified in paragraphs (a) and (b) of subsection (1) above are met or at such later time as the parties may agree—

---

[37] See above, para.5–063; below, para.18–288; *Wait and James v Midland Bank*, above.
[38] *Karlshamns Oljefabriker v Eastport Navigation Corp.* (*The Elafi*), above.
[39] See below, para.18–288.
[40] Below, para.5–131.
[41] See Burns 59 M.L.R. 260 (1996); Ulph [1996] L.M.C.L.Q. 93; Palmer and McKendrick, *Interests in Goods* (2nd ed., 1998), Ch. 16; and below, para.18–289.

(a) property in an undivided share in the bulk is transferred to the buyer, and
(b) the buyer becomes an owner in common of the bulk."

5–110 **Background to the section.** Section 20A was inserted into the 1979 Act by section 1(3) of the Sale of Goods (Amendment) Act 1995. It qualifies section 16 of the 1979 Act which provides that property cannot pass in the case of a contract for the sale of unascertained goods unless and until the goods are ascertained. Previously if A agreed to sell to B a specified quantity of unascertained goods forming part of an identified bulk, for example, 100 tonnes of wheat out of 1,000 tonnes lying in a particular warehouse, no property in the 100 tonnes could pass to B unless and until that quantity had become ascertained,[42] either by being separated from the bulk[43] or by process of "exhaustion"[44] or "consolidation".[45] Even if A sold 500 tonnes to B and 500 tonnes to C, thereby divesting himself of all interest in the bulk, no property in any of the wheat could pass to B or C until their respective quantities had likewise become ascertained.[46] If the seller became insolvent while the goods were still in bulk,[47] or if the bulk was arrested by a creditor of the seller,[48] the buyer or buyers would have no claim to the goods even though they had pre-paid the whole or part of the price. No equitable interest in the goods was acquired by a pre-paying buyer: he would have a claim for damages for breach of contract, or for return of the price, but in either case only as an unsecured creditor.[49]

This problem was of particular concern to traders in commodities who frequently purchase goods while still in bulk, whether on land or in the course of transit by sea. It was further compounded by the fact that the right to sue the carrier of goods by sea on the contract contained in a bill of lading was, under the Bills of Lading Act 1855, linked to the transfer of the property in the goods covered by the bill.[50] As a result, the purchaser of part of a bulk normally had no right to sue the carrier in contract if the goods were lost or damaged in transit. Nor could he sue the carrier in tort, even though the risk had passed to him.[51] The English and Scottish Law Commissions recommended the reform of the Bills of Lading Act 1855 and

---

[42] See above, para.5–061.
[43] *ibid*.
[44] See above, para.5–062.
[45] See above, para.5–063.
[46] *Healy v Howlett & Sons* [1917] 1 K.B. 337 at 344; *Sterns Ltd v Vickers Ltd* [1923] 1 K.B. 78 at 84; *Laurie & Morewood v Dudin & Sons* [1925] 2 K.B. 383 at 387 (affirmed [1926] 1 K.B. 233); *Karlshamns Oljefabriker v Eastport Navigation Corp. (The Elafi)* [1981] 2 Lloyd's Rep. 679 at 683; *Re London Wine Co. (Shippers) Ltd* [1986] P.C.C. 121. *Cf. Inglis v Stock* (1885) 10 App.Cas. 263 at 267–268, 274.
[47] *Laurie & Morewood v Dudin & Sons*, above; *Re Wait* [1927] 1 Ch. 606; *Re London Wine Co. (Shippers) Ltd*, above. See above, para.5–005.
[48] See *The Gosforth* (Commercial Court of Rotterdam, February 20, 1985) discussed in [1986] L.M.C.L.Q. 4.
[49] See above, paras 5–005, 5–064.
[50] See below, para.18–100.
[51] *Leigh & Sillavan Ltd v Aliakmon Shipping Co. Ltd* [1986] A.C. 785; above, para.5–009.

of section 16 of the 1979 Act.[52] The former reform was implemented by the Carriage of Goods by Sea Act 1992 and the latter by the Sale of Goods (Amendment) Act 1995. Subject to the conditions set out in subsection (1) of section 20A, property in an undivided share of the bulk is now transferred to the buyer and he becomes an owner in common of the bulk. While it was previously not impossible, in certain circumstances, for this to occur,[53] section 16 no longer stands in the way of the buyer acquiring a proprietary interest in the bulk. That interest protects him in the event of the insolvency of the seller; it enables him to assert a claim in tort against a carrier or other person if the goods are negligently destroyed or damaged while still in bulk; and the whole or part of that interest can be sold or traded on to another co-owner or to a third party so as to transfer a similar interest to the purchaser.

Sale of a specified quantity of unascertained goods. The first requirement of subsection (1) is that there should be "a contract for the sale of a specified quantity of unascertained goods". The quantity may be specified by number, measurement, weight, or in any other way, but cannot be wholly indefinite. The question therefore arises whether a contract for the sale of "80 to 100 tonnes" or "100 tonnes, 5 per cent more or less" at seller's option is a contract for the sale of a specified quantity. Such contracts are by no means exceptional in commodity transactions and it would defeat the purpose of the section if they were excluded from its ambit. But the problem then is to determine what is the precise share of the buyer in the bulk. Since, however, that share depends upon the quantity of goods *paid for* and due to the buyer out of the bulk,[54] in most cases the margin afforded to the seller will not affect the determination of the buyer's share. 5–111

The goods must also be unascertained. If a buyer purchases "50 cases of Chateau Palmer 1997 from your Park Street cellar" and there are presently in that cellar more than 50 cases of that wine, there is a contract for the sale of unascertained goods.[55] But if at the time of the contract there are only 50 cases, and it is agreed that those cases alone are to be the subject of the contract of sale, the contract is a contract for the sale of specific goods, since the goods will be "identified and agreed on at the time a contract of sale is made".[56] Also if a buyer purchases an undivided share, specified as a fraction ("one-half") or percentage ("50 per cent"), of a bulk which is identified and agreed on at the time the contract of sale is made, then, by virtue of the extended definition of "specific goods" in section 61(1) of the Act[57] the contract is one for the sale of specific, and not unascertained, goods.[58] Section 20A does not apply. More difficulty, however, surrounds a 5–112

---

[52] Rights of Suit in Respect of Carriage of Goods by Sea, Law Com. No. 196, Scot. Law Com. No. 130 (1991); Sale of Goods forming Part of a Bulk, Law Com. No. 215, Scot. Law Com. No. 145 (1993).
[53] *Re Stapylton Fletcher Ltd* [1994] 1 W.L.R. 1181; and see below, para.5–130.
[54] s.20A(1)(b), (3).
[55] See above, para.5–060.
[56] See above, para.5–113.
[57] Inserted by s.2(d) of the Sale of Goods (Amendment) Act 1995.
[58] See above, para.5–116.

contract for the sale of an undivided share, specified as a fraction or percentage, of a bulk which is not in existence at the time the contract of sale is made, *e.g.* "one-half of the cargo to be shipped on the *Parchim* next November" or "50 per cent of the potatoes to be grown on Blackacre". Since it would appear that a contract for the sale of the entire bulk is not a contract for the sale of specific goods,[59] the contract is not a contract for the sale of specific, but unascertained, goods. It is a moot point whether, in such a situation, the specified fraction or percentage is a "specified quantity" for the purposes of subsection (1). If the quantity of goods in the bulk is itself specified ("one-half of the cargo of 800 tonnes to be shipped on the *Parchim* next November"), or even possibly estimated ("50 per cent of the potatoes to be grown on Blackacre, expected to yield 20 tonnes"), there are strong grounds for saying that a specified fraction or percentage of that bulk is a "specified quantity" as the quantity in question can be determined by a simple arithmetical calculation. But if the extent of the bulk is unspecified, then it is very doubtful whether a specified fraction or percentage of that bulk can be considered to be a "specified quantity".[60]

The same difficulty arises in the case of a contract for the sale of an undivided share, specified as a fraction or percentage, of a bulk which is not identified and agreed on at the time the contract of sale is made, but which is only identified by subsequent agreement between the parties.

5–113 **Bulk.** The second requirement is that the goods or some of them form part of a bulk.[61] "Bulk" is defined in section 61(1) of the 1979 Act to mean "a mass or collection of goods of the same kind which—(a) is contained in a defined space or area; and (b) is such that any goods in the bulk are interchangeable with any other goods therein of the same number or quantity." In addition to the obvious examples of a warehouse, store, compound, silo, hopper, hold or tank, the words "a defined space or area" will include a ship, vehicle or aircraft, and even a discrete stack, heap or pile, but not merely a particular geographical source, *e.g.* Bordeaux,[62] or a company's general trading stock.[63] The word "contained" should be given the larger meaning of being kept within limits rather than being enclosed or kept within a container. It seems probable that a mass which itself has a defined space or area, *e.g.* a roll of carpet, is within the definition.

The goods in the bulk must be of the same kind and interchangeable with any other goods therein of the same number or quantity. In other jurisdictions such goods are known as "fungible" goods.[64] It is submitted that this does not require that each unit or particle of the goods must be identical. Whether they are of the same kind and interchangeable depends upon whether, under the terms of the contract or by trade practice, they are to be regarded as such. Thus the bulk may consist of a quantity of items of

---

[59] See above, para.1–115.
[60] See also below, para.18–294.
[61] See also below, para.18–295.
[62] *Re Stapylton Fletcher Ltd* [1994] 1 W.L.R. 1181.
[63] *Re London Wine Co. (Shippers) Ltd* [1986] P.C.C. 121; *Re Goldcorp Exchange Ltd* [1995] 1 A.C. 74.
[64] See above, para.1–120.

varying colours or sizes, but it may be the intention of the parties to regard them as equivalent to one another despite their differences, and this criterion will then be satisfied.

It is immaterial that the entire quantity of goods in the bulk is unknown (although this will be relevant to determining the extent of the undivided share of the buyer in the bulk), or that the bulk is not in existence at the time of the contract of sale. It would also appear to be immaterial that the goods comprised in the bulk are constantly changing, for example, by oil being withdrawn from a tank and the tank being replenished by fresh oil,[65] or that they are mixed with goods of a different description, provided that they are easily separable.[66]

Since the goods agreed to be sold or some of them must form part of a bulk, it is clear that there must be an attribution of those goods to the bulk. Thus if there is a contract for the sale of a specified number of cases of a designated wine, but the bulk out of which this numerical quantity is to take effect is not agreed, the section does not apply, even though the seller intended to satisfy the contract from stock lying in a particular warehouse and even though the combined purchases of that wine by various purchasers would exhaust the whole of his stock.[67] The words "or some of them" have been inserted to cover the situation where only some of the contract goods are attributed to the bulk in question, the remainder being attributed to another bulk or not being attributed to any bulk at all.

Identified bulk. The third requirement is that the bulk must be identified, either in the contract or by subsequent agreement between the parties. It must be certain from which bulk the goods are to come. However, this must be established by agreement between the parties. A unilateral identification of the bulk by either seller or buyer will not suffice, even if communicated to the other party, unless the other party can be taken to have agreed or assented to that identification. Particular problems arise in relation to this requirement in the case of c.i.f. contracts, where the seller gives to the buyer a notice of appropriation, declaration of shipment or notice of nomination identifying the cargo on a named ship, part of which cargo is appropriated (in the contractual sense) to the buyer's contract.[68] **5–114**

Payment of price. The fourth requirement is that the buyer must have paid the price for some or all of the goods which are the subject of the contract and which form part of the bulk. Payment need not necessarily be in cash, and it is submitted that any other recognised form of payment, for example, a bill of exchange[69] or letter of credit,[70] will suffice. A performance **5–115**

---

[65] Quaere whether this is also the case where the entire quantity of oil in the bulk is withdrawn and the tank is then subsequently replenished: see *Mercer v Craven Grain Storage Ltd.* [1994] C.L.C. 328, HL; Smith, 111 L.Q.R. 10 (1995); and above, para.1–059.

[66] *e.g.* 100 sheep from an identified cargo of sheep and goats.

[67] *Re London Wine Co. (Shippers) Ltd*, above.

[68] See below, para.18–295.

[69] See below, para.9–030. But if the bill is dishonoured, then it would seem that the buyers undivided share would revert to the seller. *Cf.*, below, para.18–295.

[70] See below, paras 18–295, 23–097, 23–112.

bond or payment guarantee will not, it seems, constitute payment. Payment can be made by the buyer himself or by another person, *e.g.* a bank, on his behalf.

5–116 **Undivided share.** The buyer acquires an undivided share in the bulk and becomes an owner in common of the bulk as soon as the conditions specified in section 20A(1) are satisfied. The parties may nevertheless agree otherwise, and presumably may do so either expressly or by implication. Thus the parties may agree that property in the goods agreed to be sold is to pass to the buyer on delivery and (by implication) that the buyer is to acquire no property in an undivided share in the bulk in the meantime. The parties may also agree that property in an undivided share and ownership in common of the bulk is to be transferred to the buyer at a time later than that at which the conditions specified in section 20A(1) are satisfied. The seller may, for example, be found to have reserved the right of disposal (even in respect of an undivided share in the bulk) until payment in full of the price of the goods. And in the case of a c.i.f. or c. & f. contract it may be that property in an undivided share will not be transferred to the buyer except upon transfer of the shipping documents against payment in full of the price.[71]

By becoming an owner in common of the bulk, the buyer does not thereby become the sole owner of the actual contract goods themselves. The contract goods, while in bulk, remain unascertained, and section 16 still governs the transfer of the property in those goods to the buyer. Those goods must therefore be ascertained, normally by being physically separated from the bulk,[72] before the buyer can become the sole owner of them. Once the contract goods have become ascertained, the property in them is transferred to the buyer at such time as the parties intend it to be transferred, having regard in appropriate cases to the rules for ascertaining that intention contained in section 18, rule 5.

5–117 **Extent of the undivided share.** Subsections (3) to (6) of section 20A provide—

"(3) Subject to subsection (4) below, for the purposes of this section, the undivided share of a buyer in a bulk at any time shall be such share as the quantity of goods paid for and due to the buyer out of the bulk bears to the quantity of goods in the bulk at that time.

(4) Where the aggregate of the undivided shares of buyers in a bulk determined under subsection (3) above would at any time exceed the whole of the bulk at that time, the undivided share in the bulk of each buyer shall be reduced proportionately so that the aggregate of the undivided shares is equal to the whole bulk.

(5) Where a buyer has paid the price for only some of the goods due to him out of a bulk, any delivery to the buyer out of that bulk shall, for

---

[71] See below, para.18–297.

[72] See above, para.5–061. But see above, paras 5–062, 5–063 (exhaustion and consolidation).

the purposes of this section, be ascribed in the first place to the goods in respect of which payment has been made.

(6) For the purposes of this section payment of part of the price for any goods shall be treated as payment for a corresponding part of the goods."

Proportionate share. Since the buyer becomes an owner in common of the bulk, he will be the owner (together with others) of the entire bulk, although—as between the co-owners of the bulk—only a proportionate share of the bulk in its undivided state is attributed to him. If a seller agrees to sell to each of 10 buyers 100 tonnes of wheat from a quantity of 1,000 tonnes lying in a particular store, then each buyer who has paid for some or all of the wheat contracted to be sold to him becomes, together with the other buyers, co-owner of the entire 1,000 tonnes, but the undivided share of each buyer in the bulk is such share as the quantity of wheat paid for and due to that buyer bears to the bulk of 1,000 tonnes. 5–118

Assuming that each buyer has pre-paid the whole of the price for his 100 tonnes, there is transferred to him the property in an undivided share of one-tenth of the 1,000 tonnes. Should one of the buyers not have paid any part of the price for his 100 tonnes, or should the seller have sold only 900 tonnes, then each buyer who has paid becomes, together with the seller and the other co-owners who have paid, co-owner of the entire 1,000 tonnes, and again there is transferred to him the property in an undivided share of one-tenth of the 1,000 tonnes. If deliveries or withdrawals are made from the bulk from time to time, the undivided share of each paid-up buyer in the residue is such share as the amount due to him bears to the quantity of goods in the bulk at any given time. Thus if 400 tonnes of the 1,000 tonnes are removed by other buyers, leaving 600 tonnes still in bulk, the undivided share of a buyer who is entitled to 100 tonnes is one-sixth of the 600 tonnes remaining. And if a buyer has already taken delivery of part of his contract quantity, say 40 tonnes, leaving 60 still due to him, his undivided share is one-tenth of that 600 tonnes.

Subsection (4) attempts to solve the problem of what happens if the aggregate of the undivided shares of buyers in a bulk at any time exceeds the whole of the bulk at that time, *e.g.* in the first example mentioned above, where the store containing 1,000 tonnes is reduced by loss, destruction, theft or wastage to 800 tonnes, or where the seller or another person wrongfully removes 200 tonnes. In such a case, the undivided share in the remaining 800 tonnes of each of the ten buyers is reduced proportionately, that is to one-tenth of the 800 tonnes.[72a] Reduction also occurs where a co-owning buyer has taken delivery of the goods due to him under his contract but in excess of his undivided share.[73] It is doubtful, however, whether the subsection applies to a case where the seller purports to sell more than the quantity of goods in the bulk, for example, where he sells 100 tonnes to each of 12 purchasers from a bulk which consists of only 1,000 tonnes. This matter is discussed in paragraph 5–121 below.

[72a] If part only of a bulk is destroyed, but an amount to which the buyers are entitled still survives, there will be no abatement under subs.(4).

[73] See s.20B(1)(a); below, para.5–124.

The section does not deal with the converse case where the aggregate of the undivided shares of buyers in a bulk is less than the whole of the bulk at that time, *e.g.* where the store is assumed to contain 1,000 tonnes, but in fact contains 1,100 tonnes, or where 100 tonnes are added by the seller to the store. In such a case, each buyer becomes co-owner (together with the seller and the other buyers) of the 1,100 tonnes and there is transferred to him property in an undivided share of one-eleventh of the bulk of 1,100 tonnes.

Since the bulk may consist of a quantity that is constantly changing by withdrawals and additions, the proportionate share of the buyer in the bulk may alter from time to time and may therefore be very different at one time, for example, the date of the seller's liquidation, from another time.

5–119 The section does not venture any solution in the event that the quantity of goods in the bulk is unknown, but it may be unnecessary to do so. The extent of the buyer's undivided share will only be of relevance at a specific time, and it should be possible to determine the quantity of goods in the bulk at that time or to calculate the proportionate share on the basis of an estimate.

5–120 Subsection (5) deals with the situation where a buyer has paid for only some of the goods due to him out of a bulk and provides that any delivery to him out of the bulk is to be ascribed in the first place to the goods in respect of which payment has been made. Thus if his contract is for 100 tonnes, but he has paid for only 40 tonnes, a delivery to him of 25 tonnes is ascribed to the 40 tonnes paid for, and reduces his undivided share in the bulk accordingly. Since "delivery" in relation to sections 20A and 20B includes such appropriation of goods to the contract as results in property in the goods being transferred to the buyer,[74] the separation from bulk of a quantity of goods and their appropriation to the buyer's contract in such a way that property in those goods themselves (as opposed to property in an undivided share in the bulk) passes to the buyer is treated in the same way as a physical delivery.

Part payments are, however, very frequently not related to any specific quantity of the contract goods and in such a case subsection (6) provides that such a payment is to be treated as payment for a corresponding part of the goods.

5–121 **Overselling.** It is by no means clear what are the consequences if a seller of goods in bulk, either deliberately or inadvertently, sells more than the quantity of goods in the bulk, for example, where he sells 200 tonnes of wheat to each of two pre-paying buyers from a bulk which consists of 400 tonnes but then proceeds to sell a further 200 tonnes from the same bulk to a third, later buyer. The first two buyers in point of time ("the original buyers") will initially each acquire an undivided share of one-half of the bulk of 400 tonnes. But the question arises as to the effect (if any) of the

[74] s.61(1) "delivery", as amended by s.2(b) of the Sale of Goods (Amendment) Act 1995.

later sale on the property rights so acquired. On one view, each buyer (including the later buyer) would share equally and proportionately in the 400 tonnes and, under section 20A(4),[75] the shares of each of the three buyers would abate rateably to one-third of the 400 tonnes. But this solution, though a convenient one, is open to the objection that it does not take into account the title conflict provisions of the Act. These do not contemplate an apportionment of the loss caused in such a situation. The better view, it is submitted, is that the original buyers would retain their undivided shares of the 400 tonnes in full and the later buyer would get nothing. Ownership of the bulk would have passed entirely from the seller to the two original buyers as owners in common. The seller would therefore have nothing left to sell and the later buyer can acquire no better title than the seller had: *nemo dat quod non habet*. This solution would be consistent with section 21(1) of the 1979 Act[76] and could be said to have the merit of preferring the earlier buyers over the later on a "first come, first served" basis. Account may, however, then have to be taken of the provisions of section 24 of the Act[77] under which, in certain circumstances, a seller who sells goods to one buyer but continues in possession of the goods or of the documents of title to the goods, and who subsequently sells the same goods to a second buyer, can pass a good title to the goods to the second buyer and the title thus acquired overrides that of the first. If section 24 applies in the situation of overselling referred to above, the claim of the later buyer would prevail over and (it seems) eat into the undivided shares of the original buyers, the owners in common of the goods. This is because, under section 24, the sale to the later buyer is stated to have "the same effect as if the [seller] were expressly authorised by the owner of the goods to make the same". Each of the two original buyers, as co-owners of the goods, would therefore be deemed to have authorised the seller to sell 200 tonnes of the bulk co-owned by them to the later buyer. The later buyer would become an owner in common with them of the bulk, but would be entitled to his 200 tonnes in full, the share of each of the two original buyers reducing to one-half of the remaining 200 tonnes, that is to 100 tonnes each.

In other contexts where section 24 is invoked the later buyer usually 5–122
claims title to *identified* goods as against a previous buyer to whom the seller had sold those goods.[78] The question therefore arises whether the section is apt to cover successive sales of unascertained goods while still in bulk. There is nothing in the section which specifically limits its application to proprietary claims to identified goods. But, for the section to apply, certain requirements must be satisfied. Of the requirements that are relevant in this context, the first is that the seller must have "sold" goods, *i.e.* to the original buyers.[79] This would ordinarily require the transfer to them of the general property in the goods. It could be argued that there has

[75] See above, para.5–118.
[76] Below, para.7–001.
[77] Or s.8 of the Factors Act 1889; see below, para.7–055.
[78] Below, paras 7–055—7–068.
[79] See below, para.7–056.

been no sale in this sense because there has been transferred to each of the original buyers only an undivided share in the bulk and not the general property in any of the goods. But section 61(1) of the Act now provides that, unless the context or subject-matter otherwise requires, "goods" include an undivided share in goods. This at least suggests that there can be a sale of an undivided share.[80] Moreover the seller will in fact have transferred the general property in the whole of the bulk to the two original buyers as owners in common.[81] It is therefore submitted that the seller has "sold" goods for the purposes of section 24 and accordingly the first requirement is satisfied. Secondly, the seller must continue or be in possession of the goods sold or of the documents of title to the goods.[82] Whether this requirement is satisfied is a question of fact in each individual case. But in many cases the seller of goods in bulk will continue in possession of the bulk or be deemed to do so where the bulk is held by a third party such as a warehouseman subject to his control or for him or on his behalf.[83] Or the seller may continue in possession of a bill of lading or other document of title covering the goods in the bulk. Thirdly, there must be a delivery or transfer of the goods or documents of title to the goods by the seller to the later buyer.[84] This requirement will obviously be satisfied where (say) 200 tonnes are separated from the bulk and are physically delivered to the later buyer.[85] It will also probably be satisfied by the transfer of a document of title, *e.g.* a delivery order, for 200 tonnes from the seller to the later buyer even though the goods remain part of the bulk.[86] But there is much more doubt whether there can be a "delivery" of the goods to the later buyer while still in bulk if, for example, a person in possession of the goods simply attorns to the later buyer, that is to say, acknowledges to the later buyer that 200 tonnes of the goods in the bulk are now held on the later buyer's behalf. It may well be that there is no transfer of possession, actual or constructive, of any of the goods by the seller to the later buyer as they are still unascertained.[87] However, it has been pointed out above that "goods" includes an undivided share in goods and it is in consequence arguable that there can be delivery of an undivided share from seller to buyer by a transfer of constructive possession of that undivided share by attornment. The fourth requirement is that the delivery or transfer must be under a sale or other disposition of the goods by the seller to the later buyer[88] and again it is submitted that this requirement is satisfied by the sale of an undivided share in goods.[89] Fifthly, the later buyer must be without notice and in good faith.[90] This is a question of fact.

---

[80] See above, para.1–121. *Cf.* Goode, *Commercial Law* (3rd ed.), p.199.
[81] s.20A(2).
[82] See below, para.7–057.
[83] Factors Act 1889, s.1(2).
[84] See below, para.7–062.
[85] See also s.61(1) n.80, above.
[86] *Capital and Counties Bank Ltd v Warriner* (1896) 12 T.L.R. 216; *Ant. Jurgens Margarine-fabrieken v Louis Dreyfus & Co.* [1914] 3 K.B. 40; *Mount Ltd v Jay and Jay Provisions Ltd*[1960] 1 Q.B. 159 (s.25(1) of the 1979 Act and s.9 of the Factors Act 1889; below, para.7–077).
[87] See above, para.1–119; below, para.8–012, n.51.
[88] See below, para.7–064.
[89] See above, para.1–121 *Cf.* Goode, *Commercial Law* (3rd ed.), p.199.
[90] See below, para.7–068.

5–123 Section 24 of the Act may therefore play a significant role in determining upon whom the loss should fall in a situation of the overselling of goods in bulk. But then further problems arise: for example, where a seller sells to A 100 tonnes from a bulk consisting of 200 tonnes and then proceeds to sell a further 130 tonnes to B (each buyer paying his full price at the time of sale). If the overselling of 30 tonnes to B attracts the application of section 24, does this result in B being entitled to that 30 tonnes in full, leaving the balance of 170 tonnes in the bulk to abate rateably between A and B. In that case B will get 115 tonnes and A 85 tonnes of the bulk of 200 tonnes. Or does the overselling of 30 tonnes to B eat into the title of A alone, so that B will be entitled to 130 tonnes and A to 70? The former solution is, it is submitted, the correct one. Since the oversale of 30 tonnes is deemed to have been authorised by both the owners in common, A and B, it will override and eat into that joint title. Alternatively, if section 24 is in fact inapplicable in this situation, then A and B will become owners in common of the 200 tonnes in equal shares and B alone must bear the risk of the oversale to him of 30 tonnes since the seller could not sell to him what he had not got. These uncertainties could well be exacerbated by the possibility of a series of oversales of goods in the same bulk, each eating into the current undivided shares, and possibly accompanied by the removal from time to time of parcels of goods from the bulk.[91] It is unfortunate that a measure designed to improve the position of pre-paying buyers may in the event require complex calculations to determine each buyer's share at any given time.

5–124 **Deemed consent by co-owner to dealings in bulk goods.** By subsections (1) and (2) of section 20B:

"(1) A person who has become an owner in common of a bulk by virtue of section 20A above shall be deemed to have consented to—

(a) any delivery of goods out of the bulk to any other owner in common of the bulk, being goods which are due to him under his contract;

(b) any dealing with or removal, delivery or disposal of goods in the bulk by any other person who is an owner in common of the bulk in so far as the goods fall within that co-owner's undivided share in the bulk at the time of the dealing, removal, delivery or disposal.

(2) No cause of action shall accrue to anyone against a person by reason of that person having acted in accordance with paragraph (a) or (b) of subsection (1) above in reliance on any consent deemed to have been given under that subsection".

5–125 **Co-ownership of goods.**[92] If two or more persons own goods in common, then each is a co-owner of the goods and not merely the owner of a share of them. At common law it was "well established that one tenant in

---

[91] See below, para.5–126.

[92] See Palmer and McKendrick, *Interests in Goods* (2nd ed., 1998), Ch.10.

common cannot maintain an action against his companion unless there has been a destruction of the particular chattel or something equivalent to it".[93] But if one co-owner completely ousted another from the use, enjoyment or benefit of co-owned goods or, without the consent of the other, disposed of the co-owned goods in a way which gave good title to the entire property in the goods to the disponee, this was "equivalent to a destruction" of the other's interest in the goods and an action in conversion would lie.[94] This common law rule is restated in section 10(1) of the Torts (Interference with Goods) Act 1977, which extended its scope to cases where an unauthorised disposition by a co-owner, had it been authorised, would have given a good title to the entire property in the goods to the disponee.[95] It follows that, were it not for section 20B, a buyer to whom property in an undivided share in a bulk had been transferred under section 20A and who had become, together with others, co-owner of the bulk could not lawfully appropriate or take delivery of any goods in the bulk in excess of his undivided share (the exact extent of which from time to time might be uncertain and might be less than his contractual entitlement). The solution adopted in subsection (1) of section 20B is, first, to provide that each co-owner of the bulk is deemed to have consented to deliveries to any other co-owner of the quantity due to the latter under his contract. Secondly, each co-owner is deemed to have consented to any dealing with or removal, delivery or disposal of goods in the bulk by another co-owner (including the seller) falling within the latter's undivided share at the time. "Delivery" in this context has the extended meaning referred to in paragraph 5–120 above. It is to be noted, however, that a co-owner who sells to a third party the quantity of goods due to him under his contract, but in excess of his undivided share, is still liable in conversion as regards the excess.

Third parties who purchase goods from buyers in the circumstances set out in subsection (1)(b) are protected by subsection (2) from actions by other co-owners of the bulk. Subsection (2) also protects warehousemen, carriers, liquidators and receivers who release goods to co-owning buyers in reliance on the deemed consent in subsection (1)(a). There is no requirement that such persons act in good faith or without notice.

5–126 The deemed consent to removals from the bulk applies only where "a person has become an owner in common of the bulk by virtue of section 20A". It has been pointed out in paragraphs 5–121—5–123 above that, in an "overselling" situation where the seller has sold more goods than there are in the bulk, a later buyer might establish a good title to an undivided share of the goods in the bulk (and would thus become an owner in common of the bulk) under section 24 of the 1979 Act. The question then arises whether the undivided share so acquired would be vulnerable to depletion under section 20B(1). For instance, in the example given in paragraph 5–121 above, if the original buyers remove from the bulk the

93 *Morgan v Marquis* (1854) 9 Exch. 145 at 148.
94 See *Clerk and Lindsell on Torts* (19th ed.), paras 14–73—14–75; Derham, 68 L.Q.R. 507 (1952).*Cf.* pledges, but see *Nyberg v Handelaar* [1892] 2 Q.B. 202 and below, para.18–299.
95 s.10(1)(b).

whole or part of their contractual entitlement, leaving less than 200 tonnes in the bulk for the later buyer, could they claim that they were protected against an action in conversion by the later buyer on the ground that he would be deemed to have consented to the removal under section 20B(1)? It has been contended[96] that they could not do so, on the ground that the later buyer would not have become an owner in common of the bulk by virtue of section 20A but by virtue of section 24. On the other hand the effect of section 24 is merely that the sale to the later buyer is treated as having been authorised by the original buyers (the then owners of the goods). It does not explain why this sale results in the later buyer becoming an owner in common of the bulk. This consequence, it is submitted, must come about by virtue of section 20A[97] or at least by virtue both of section 20A and section 24. In the result the later buyer, like any co-owner of the bulk, should be taken to have consented to removals from the bulk in the circumstances set out in section 20B(1).

Other savings. Subsection (3) of section 20B states: 5–127

"(3) Nothing in this section or section 20A above shall—

(a) impose an obligation on a buyer of goods out of a bulk to compensate any other buyer of goods out of that bulk for any shortfall in the goods received by that other buyer;
(b) affect any contractual arrangement between buyers of goods out of a bulk for adjustments between themselves; or
(c) affect the rights of any buyer under his contract."

Paragraphs (a) and (b) are self-explanatory, but the effect of paragraph (c) is less certain. Clearly sections 20A and 20B do not affect the right of a buyer to claim damages against the seller for non-delivery should he receive less than the quantity of goods due to him under his contract (although such a claim would be as an unsecured creditor in the event of the seller's insolvency). What is less clear is whether paragraph (c) requires that sections 20A and 20B must be left out of account in deciding when the risk of loss, damage, destruction or deterioration of the goods in the bulk is transferred to the buyer, with the result that such risk would (in a commercial transaction) normally pass to him only upon the transfer to him of the sole property in the contract goods themselves. This matter is discussed in Chapter 6 of this book.[98]

Trading the undivided share. A buyer who has contracted to buy a specified quantity of unascertained goods forming part of an identified bulk, and to whom the property in an undivided share in the bulk has been transferred under section 20A, may agree to re-sell to a sub-purchaser the whole or part of the contract quantity. The provisions of section 20A 5–128

---

[96] Bridge, *The Sale of Goods* (1997), p.463.
[97] Assuming that the later buyer has pre-paid.
[98] Below, para.6–006.

likewise apply to the sub-sale and, if the conditions set out in subsection (1) of that section are satisfied, property in an undivided share in the bulk is transferred to the sub-purchaser and the sub-purchaser becomes an owner in common of the bulk. The effect of the sub-sale is therefore to pass the whole or part of the buyer's interest in the bulk at the time of the sale from the buyer to the sub-purchaser.[99] Undivided shares in a bulk can thus be traded, or fragmented and traded, while the goods still remain in bulk.[1]

5–129 **Situations outside section 20A: specific goods.** It has already been noted that a contract for the sale of specific goods does not fall within section 20A and that a contract for the sale of an undivided share, specified as a fraction or percentage, of a bulk which is identified and agreed on at the time the contract is made is contract for the sale of specific goods.[2] The question therefore arises as to what interest (if any) is transferred to the buyer of such an undivided share while the goods still form part of the bulk. The answer would appear to be, at common law, an interest identical with that set out in section 20A(2), namely, property in the undivided share in the bulk and ownership in common of the bulk. This proprietary interest will pass when the parties intend it to pass, which may be before, or at the time, or after the price is paid. The rules set out in subsections (4) to (6) of section 20A are, however, an innovation and do not in their terms apply. In cases of overselling,[3] if a seller purports to sell 25 per cent of the bulk to five separate buyers, it would seem that a proprietary interest passes to the four whose contracts were first in time, but none to fifth, rather than each buyer suffering an abatement of his share.[4] Section 20B also does not apply, so that the position is governed by section 10(1) of the Torts (Interference with Goods) Act 1977.[5]

5–130 **Other situations.** Where one or more of the other conditions set out in subsection (1) of section 20A are not met, for example, where the buyer has not paid the price for any of the goods which are the subject of the contract and which form part of the bulk,[6] or where the buyer has paid the price for only some of the goods, as regards those goods for which no payment has been made,[7] or where section 20A is excluded by agreement of the parties,[8] section 16 of the Act precludes any property in the goods being transferred

---

[99] See also below, para.7–085 (s.25(1)).
[1] See above, para.1–121. Contrast Goode, *Commercial Law* (3rd ed.), p.199.
[2] See above, paras 1–116, 5–112.
[3] *cf. ante*, paras 5–121—5–123.
[4] But where the seller is in possession of the goods or documents of title, he may be able to pass a good title to the fifth buyer under s.24 of the Sale of Goods Act 1979 (below, para.7–055). In such a case, it would seem that the title of the fifth buyer overrides and "eats unto" the title of the other four, so that his proprietary interest will be 25 per cent of the bulk, the remaining 75 per cent being apportioned between the other four. See also above, para.5–121—5–123.
[5] Above, para.5–125.
[6] s.20A(1)(b).
[7] s.20A(3).
[8] s.20A(2).

to the buyer unless and until the goods are ascertained. No undivided share in the bulk is transferred to the buyer and the seller remains the sole owner of the goods while they are still in bulk. If the seller becomes insolvent, no claim can be made by the buyer to the goods,[9] even in equity,[10] and his status is that of an unsecured creditor.

It is, however, open to the parties to a contract to provide expressly that the buyer of unascertained goods forming part of an identified bulk is to become a co-owner of the bulk.[11] There can also be exceptional situations where, apart from section 20A, a bulk is or becomes ascertained and, by intention of the parties, property in the bulk passes to the buyers as owners in common while it is still undivided. In *Re Stapylton Fletcher Ltd*[12] a company sold to various buyers specified quantities of particular wines and agreed to store them for the buyers until required. The buyers paid the purchase price in full. Records were maintained showing what wines were held in store for each buyer. Wine so purchased was taken out of the trading stock of the company and placed in a separate unit for storage. In that unit wine of a particular type and vintage was stored in a separate stack, but no case or bottle was marked with the name of or allocated to any individual buyer. The company went into administrative receivership and the administrative receivers sought directions from the court as to whether the buyers had any interest in the wines. It was held that the wines had become ascertained for the purposes of section 16 when they were segregated from the company's trading stock for storage and that property in the wines had then, by common intention, passed to the buyers of the wine as tenants in common.

A buyer of such goods may also be entitled to assert a claim to the goods by virtue of an estoppel.[13]

6. RESERVATION OF THE RIGHT OF DISPOSAL

Right of disposal. It has already been shown that the property in specific goods will not pass to the buyer under section 18, rule 1, of the Act unless the contract of sale is unconditional,[14] and that property in unascertained goods will not pass under section 18, rule 5(1), (2), unless the goods have become ascertained and have been unconditionally appropriated to the contract.[15] Section 19(1) of the 1979 Act makes express provision for a conditional contract or appropriation enabling the seller to retain a *jus disponendi* over the goods: "Where there is a contract for the sale of 5–131

[9] See above, para.5–019.
[10] See above, para.5–071.
[11] This has been provided for expressly in certain commodity association standard terms.
[12] [1994] 1 W.L.R. 1181. Contrast *Re London Wine Co. (Shippers) Ltd* [1986] P.C.C. 121; *Re Goldcorp Exchange Ltd* [1995] 1 A.C. 74; *Customs and Excise Commissioners v Everwine Ltd* [2003] EWCA Civ. 953.
[13] See above, para.5–065.
[14] See above, para.5–019.
[15] See above, para.5–071.

specific goods[16] or where goods are subsequently appropriated to the contract,[17] the seller may, by the terms of the contract or appropriation, reserve the right of disposal of the goods until certain conditions are fulfilled." The condition most frequently encountered in such a reservation is the payment or tender of the price,[18] but the seller is at liberty to reserve the right of disposal on whatever conditions he himself wishes to impose.[19] The reservation may be express or implied; and the question whether or not the seller intended to retain the property in the goods, and on what terms, is a question of inference from what the parties said or did at the time.[20] It would appear that, having regard to section 17 of the Act, the effect of section 19(1) could be displaced by proof of an intention contrary to that expressed in the subsection.[21]

5–132 The reservation of the right of disposal may be inserted by the seller as a stipulation in the terms of the contract of sale, that is to say, by agreement of the parties.[22] Such reservation may be express or implied.[23] If the contract is one for the sale of specific goods, the seller must, by the terms of the contract, reserve the right of disposal, since appropriation is not necessary to pass property in specific goods. If the contract is one for the sale of unascertained goods, the parties may agree, either by the terms of the contract[24] or appropriation, that the right of disposal be reserved. But the seller may also, when appropriating unascertained goods to the contract[25] unilaterally reserve the right of disposal of the goods and impose conditions to be fulfilled before the property will pass.[26] A conditional appropriation of this nature will effectively prevent the property from passing, even though by reserving the right of disposal the seller is in breach of the terms of the contract of sale.[27]

---

[16] See above, paras 1–113, 5–022.
[17] See above, para.5–067.
[18] Terms "C.O.D." would appear to have this effect: *US v Lutz* (1944) 142 F.2d 985.
[19] *Wait v Baker* (1848) 2 Exch. 1 at 7–9. See also below, para.5–146.
[20] *Van Casteel v Booker* (1848) 2 Exch.691; *Browne v Hare* (1859) 4 H. & N. 822; *Falk v Fletcher* (1865) 18 C.B. (N.S.) 403; *Ross T Smyth & Co. Ltd v T D Bailey Son & Co.* (1940) 67 Ll.L.R. 147 at 155; *Leigh & Sillavan Ltd v Aliakmon Shipping Co. Ltd (The Aliakmon)* [1985] Q.B. 350 (affirmed [1986] A.C. 785); *Enichem Anic SpA v Ampelos Shipping Co. Ltd (The Delfini)* [1990] 1 Lloyd's Rep. 252 at 269; *The Seven Pioneer* [2001] 2 Lloyd's Rep. 57 at 62.
[21] *The Aliakmon* [1985] Q.B. 350 at 388. But contrast *ibid.* p.364 (CA) (decision affirmed *sub. nom. Leigh and Sillavan Ltd v Aliakmon Shipping Co. Ltd* [1986] A.C. 785).
[22] See, *e.g. Re Shipton Anderson & Co. and Harrison Bros & Co.'s Arbitration* [1915] 3 K.B. 676.
[23] See below, para.18–211.
[24] It is submitted that reservation by the terms of the contract is not confined to specific goods; alternatively, by the terms of the contract, the parties may determine the terms of appropriation, *i.e.* whether it is conditional or unconditional.
[25] See above, para.5–074.
[26] See, *e.g. Godts v Rose* (1855) 17 C.B. 229; Bradgate [1988] J.B.L. 477.
[27] *Ellershaw v Magniac* (1843) 6 Exch. 570n.; *Wait v Baker* (1848) 2 Exch. 1; *Gabarron v Kreeft* (1875) L.R. 10 Ex. 274. See also below, para.18–211. But see *City Motors v Southern Aerial Super Services* (1961) 106 C.L.R. 477.

5–133 The principle is of general application. But section 19(1) further provides: ". . . and in such case, notwithstanding the delivery of the goods to the buyer, or to a carrier or other bailee or custodier[28] for the purpose of transmission to the buyer, the property in the goods does not pass to the buyer until the conditions imposed by the seller are fulfilled." The seller can thus, by the terms of a contract or appropriation, derogate from the presumption contained in section 18, rule 5(2) of the Act[29] that such delivery is deemed to be an unconditional appropriation of the goods to the contract.[30] The most obvious instance of such derogation is provided by c.i.f. contracts, where the property in the goods sold does not normally pass upon shipment,[31] nor even upon notice of appropriation,[32] but the seller reserves the right of disposal until the shipping documents are transferred against payment or securing of the price.[33]

5–134 Where the seller reserves the right of disposal, he prima facie retains both the legal and the equitable title to the goods. It is submitted that, notwithstanding that the goods are ascertained and have been appropriated to the contract, no equitable interest passes to the buyer, and the seller retains both the legal and beneficial ownership of the goods agreed to be sold.[34] However, it is open to the parties to agree that the seller is to retain the beneficial ownership only[35] or that the seller, though he retains the legal ownership of the goods, is to hold them on trust for the buyer.[36]

5–135 **Delivery in exchange for payment.** If the terms of the contract or appropriation expressly provide that delivery of the goods, or of a document giving control of the goods, is to be made or given against payment of the price or the provision of security for the price,[37] the seller may be held to have reserved the right of disposal and retained ownership of the goods until payment has been made or a security provided.[38] But

---

[28] The Scottish equivalent of a bailee.
[29] See above, para.5–096.
[30] See below, para.18–211.
[31] See below, para.19–099.
[32] See above, para.5–071, below, paras 18–210, 19–100.
[33] See above, paras 5–029, 5–071; below, para.19–102 See also (f.o.b. contracts), below, para.20–075.
[34] *Leigh and Sillavan Ltd v Aliakmon Shipping Co. Ltd (The Aliakmon)* [1986] A.C. 785 at 812–813.
[35] But a reservation of beneficial ownership might operate only by way of grant of legal and beneficial ownership, followed by a re-grant of beneficial ownership to the seller: *Re Bond Worth Ltd* [1980] Ch. 228; *Abbey National Building Society v Cann* [1991] 1 A.C. 56; *Stroud Architectural Systems Ltd v John Laing Construction Ltd* [1994] 2 B.C.L.C. 276; below, para.5–144 (registration as charge). *Cf. Re Connolly Bros Ltd (No. 2)* [1912] 2 Ch. 25.
[36] *cf. Re London Wine Co. (Shippers) Ltd* [1986] P.C.C. 121.
[37] See below, para.19–102.
[38] *Loeschman v Williams* (1815) 4 Camp. 181; *Bishop v Shillito* (1819) 2 B. & Ald. 329n.; *Godts v Rose* (1855) 17 C.B. 229; *Schuster v McKellar* (1857) 7 E. & B. 704; *Moakes v Nicolson* (1865) 19 C.B. (N.S.) 290; *Cohen v Foster* (1892) 61 L.J.Q.B. 643; *Re Shipton Anderson & Co. and Harrison Bros & Co.'s Arbitration* [1915] 3 K.B. 676; *Ross T Smyth & Co. Ltd v T D Bailey Sons & Co.* [1940] 3 All E.R. 60; *Ginzberg v Barrow Haematite Steel Co. Ltd* [1966] 1 Lloyd's Rep. 343; *The Seven Pioneer* [2001] 2 Lloyd's Rep. 57. *Cf. Castle v Playford* (1872) L.R. 7 Ex. 98; *Armstrong v Allen Bros* (1892) 67 L.T. 738. See below, para.19–102.

such an inference is not inevitable, and it is a question of fact in each case whether the passing of property is conditional upon such an event.[39]

5–136 **Carriage of goods by sea.** The cases which illustrate the reservation of the right of disposal by unilateral action of the seller when appropriating the goods have mostly arisen in connection with the sale of goods to be carried by sea, where the seller wishes to secure himself against insolvency or default of the buyer. The need for such security is nowadays often met by the use of bankers' commercial credits,[40] but property rights as between buyer and seller may still be important.[41] Traditionally there are a number of ways by which the seller can obtain security by reserving the right of disposal of the goods. Partial provision is made for these in subsections (2) and (3) of section 19,[42] but for the rest they depend for their effectiveness upon the implication of a retention of the *jus disponendi* under section 19(1).

5–137 **Bill of lading to seller's order.** One method of obtaining security is for the seller to take a bill of lading making the goods deliverable to his own order or that of his agent,[43] thereby evincing an intention that the property is not to pass to the buyer until certain conditions (to be ascertained from the terms of the contract and what the parties said or did at the time) are fulfilled. Such a device was recognised by the common law as effective to prevent the passing of property to the buyer[44] and is given statutory recognition in section 19(2) of the Sale of Goods Act 1979, which provides as follows: "Where goods are shipped, and by the bill of lading the goods are deliverable to the order of the seller or his agent, the seller is prima facie to be taken to reserve the right of disposal." This subsection lays down a prima facie rule,[45] but the presumption contained in it may be rebutted by proof of a contrary intention from the contract or the circumstances of the

---

39 *Tarling v Baxter* (1827) 6 B. & C. 360; *Browne v Hare* (1859) 4 H. & N. 822; *Re Middleton* (1864) 3 De G.J. & Sm. 201; *Nippon Yusen Kaisha v Ramjiban Serowgee* [1938] A.C. 429; *Enichem Anic SpA v Ampelos Shipping Co. Ltd (The Delfini)* [1990] 1 Lloyd's Rep. 252. See also above, paras 5–026, 5–071.

40 See below, Ch.23.

41 See, *e.g. Leigh & Sillavan Ltd v Aliakmon Shipping Co. Ltd (The Aliakmon)* [1986] A.C. 785; *Mitsui & Co. Ltd v Flota Mercante Grancolombiana (The Ciudad de Pasto)* [1988] 2 Lloyd's Rep. 208; *Transpacific Eternity SA v Kanematsu Corp. (The Antares III)* [2002] 1 Lloyd's Rep.233 and see above, paras 5–003—5–115.

42 See below, paras 5–137—5–138.

43 For the effect of an agent disobeying his mandate: see *The Argentina* (1867) L.R. 1 A. & E. 370.

44 *Ellershaw v Magniac* (1843) 6 Exch. 570n.; *Wait v Baker* (1848) 2 Exch.1; *Jenkyns v Brown* (1849) 14 Q.B. 496; *Turner v Trustees of Liverpool Docks* (1851) 6 Exch. 543; *Ogg v Shuter*(1875) 1 C.P.D. 47; *Mirabita v Imperial Ottoman Bank* (1878) 3 Ex.D. 164 at 172.

45 *Mitsui & Co. Ltd v Flota Mercante Grancolombiana (The Ciudad de Pasto)*, above; *Enichem Anic SpA v Ampelos Shipping Co. Ltd (The Delfini)*, above, at p.269; *Anonima Petroli Italiana SpA v Marlucidez Armadora SA (The Filiatra Legacy)* [1990] 1 Lloyd's Rep. 354 at 357, [1991] 2 Lloyd's Rep. 337 at 343; *Transpacific Eternity SA v Kanematsu Corp. (The Antares III)*, above, at p.236.

case. The operation of section 19(2) is discussed in detail later in this work.[46]

Documentary bills. A documentary bill is a bill of exchange which is accompanied by the documents of title to the goods.[47] Where goods are shipped, the bill of exchange will be accompanied by the shipping documents, and it must be accepted or paid before the property in the goods will pass to the buyer. Partial provision[48] is made for this by section 19(3) of the Sale of Goods Act 1979, which is enacted in the following terms: "Where the seller of goods draws on the buyer for the price, and transmits the bill of exchange and the bill of lading to the buyer together to secure[49] acceptance or payment of the bill of exchange, the buyer is bound to return the bill of lading if he does not honour the bill of exchange, and if he wrongfully retains the bill of lading the property in the goods does not pass to him." It is generally acknowledged that this subsection was intended to embody the decision of the House of Lords in the case of *Shepherd v Harrison*,[50] decided before the passing of the 1893 Act. The buyer and any other person who wrongfully deals with the bill of lading in these circumstances will be liable to the seller in damages for conversion.[51] 5–138

The subject of documentary bills is discussed in a later chapter in this work,[52] but it should be noted that, by reason of section 9 of the Factors Act 1889,[53] the transmission directly to the buyer of the bill of lading together with the bill of exchange affords little protection *vis-à-vis* third parties against wrongful dispositions by the buyer.[54] 5–139

Discount of documentary bills. The seller may draw a bill of exchange on the buyer for the price and then discount the bill with a banker, depositing an indorsed bill of lading with the banker to secure the advance 5–140

[46] See below, para.18–214. See also below, para.20–077 (application to f.o.b. contracts). On electronic bills of lading, see Law Commission Advice (2001), *Electronic Commerce: Formal Requirements in Commercial Transactions*, para.5.3 and below, paras 18–202—18–207.

[47] See Chalmers and Guest, *Bills of Exchange* (16th ed.), para.6–043; and below, para.18–221.

[48] s.19(3) applies only in its terms where the bill of exchange is accompanied by a bill of lading, and where the seller draws upon the buyer for the price. But presumably, by virtue of s.19(1), the same principle would apply in the case of other documents, and where the seller draws upon a banker for the price (*Brandt v Bowlby* (1831) 2 B. & Ad. 932).

[49] *i.e.* in order to secure.

[50] (1871) L.R. 5 H.L. 116. See also *Mirabita v Imperial Ottoman Bank* (1878) 3 Ex.D. 164 at 172; *Rew v Payne, Douthwaite & Co.* (1885) 53 L.T. 932; *Cahn v Pockett's Bristol Channel Steam Packet Co.* [1899] 1 Q.B. 643; *The Prinz Adalbert* [1917] A.C. 586; *The Orteric* [1920] A.C. 724; *The Glenroy* [1946] A.C. 124. Contrast *Re Tappenbeck* (1876) 2 Ch.D. 278; *Koönig v Brandt* (1901) 84 L.T. 748.

[51] *Ernest Scragg & Sons Ltd v Perseverance Banking and Trust Co. Ltd* [1973] 2 Lloyd's Rep. 101.

[52] See below, para.18–221. On electronic bills of lading, see the Law Commission Advice, above, n.46, para.5.3 and below, paras 18–202—18–207.

[53] And s.25(1) of the Sale of Goods Act 1979; see below, para.7–089. See also ss.47, 48(2) of the 1979 Act: below, paras 15–092, 15–101.

[54] *Cahn v Pockett's Bristol Channel Steam Packet Co.*, above. *Cf. Mount (D.F.) Ltd v Jay & Jay (Provisions) Ltd* [1960] 1 Q.B. 159.

and leaving the banker to present[55] the bill of exchange for payment or acceptance by the buyer in return for the bill of lading.[56] In such a case, the general property in the goods does not pass to the banker, who holds the bill of lading as pledgee.[57] The property will not pass to the buyer until he has accepted the bill of exchange or paid or tendered the price.[58]

5–141 **"Romalpa" clauses.**[59] Reservation of the right of disposal of the goods greatly increased in importance as the result of the decision of the Court of Appeal in *Aluminium Industrie Vaassen BV v Romalpa Aluminium Ltd.*[60] In that case, the claimants, a Dutch company, sold to the defendants, an English company, aluminium foil, some of which was then sold by the defendants to sub-purchasers and the sub-purchasers paid the defendants therefor. The claimants' standard conditions of sale provided (*inter alia*) that (i) the ownership of the foil was to be transferred to the defendants only when they had met all that was owing to the claimants; (ii) until the date of payment the defendants were, if the claimants so desired, to store the foil in such a way that it was clearly the property of the claimants; (iii)

---

55 The banker does not, by presenting the bill of exchange for acceptance, warrant that the bill of lading is genuine: *Leather v Simpson* (1871) L.R. 11 Eq. 398; *Baxter v Chapman* (1873) 29 L.T. 642; *Guaranty Trust Co. of New York v Hannay* [1918] 2 K.B. 623.

56 See *Turner v Trustees of Liverpool Docks* (1851) 6 Exch. 543; *Mirabita v Imperial Ottoman Bank* (1878) 3 Ex.D. 164; *The Miramichi* [1915] P.71; *The Prinz Adalbert* [1917] A.C. 586 at 589; *The Orteric* [1920] A.C. 724 at 733; *Comptoir Commercial Anversois v Power, Son & Co.* [1920] 1 K.B. 868 at 877, 893.

57 *Banner v Johnston* (1871) L.R. 5 H.L. 157; *Re Howe* (1871) L.R. 6 Ch.App. 838; *Lutscher v Comptoir d'Escompte de Paris* (1876) 1 Q.B.D. 709; *Bristol & West of England Bank v Midland Ry* [1891] 2 Q.B. 653; *The Orteric*, above; *Brandt v Liverpool Brazil and River Plate Steam Navigation Co. Ltd* [1924] 1 K.B. 575. See below, para.18–216.

58 *Mirabita v Imperial Ottoman Bank*, above; *The Charlotte* [1908] P.206; *The Prinz Adalbert*, above; *Midland Bank Ltd v Eastcheap Dried Fruit Co.* [1962] 1 Lloyd's Rep. 359.

59 See Parris, *Effective Retention of Title Clauses* (1986); Dickson, *Retention of Title Clauses* (1987); McCormack, *Reservation of Title* (2nd ed., 1995); Davies, *Effective Retention of Title* (1991); Wheeler, *Retention of Title Clauses: Impact and Implications* (1991); Goode, *Proprietary Rights and Insolvency in Sales Transactions* (2nd ed.), Ch.V; Worthington, *Proprietary Interests in Commercial Transactions* (1996); Palmer and McKendrick, *Interests in Goods* (2nd ed., 1998), Ch.28. The periodical literature on this subject is so voluminous that little would be achieved by attempting to list all the articles. On the conflicts of laws problems involved, see below, para.25–141. On reform of the law, see the Law Commission's Consultation Paper No. 164 (2002); Consultative Report on Company Security Interests (Consultation Paper No. 176 (2004)); Company Security Interests Developing a Final Scheme (April 2005); Law Commission Final Report on Company Security Interests, Law Com. No. 296 (2005). Under Art. 4 of Directive 2000/35/EC on combating late payment in commercial transactions ([2000] O.J. L200/35) the United Kingdom is required to provide, in conformity with the applicable national provisions designated by private international law, that the seller retains title to goods until they are fully paid for if a retention of title clause has been expressly agreed between the buyer and the seller before delivery of the goods. See below, para.25–153. See also Council Regulation 1346/2000/EC of May 29, 2000 on insolvency proceedings ([2000] O.J. L160/1), below, para.25–150.

60 [1976] 1 W.L.R. 676.

articles manufactured from the foil supplied were to become the property of the claimants as surety for the full payment of the sums owed by the defendants to the claimants; (iv) until such payment, the defendants were to keep the articles for the claimants in their capacity of fiduciary owners and, if required, were to store them in such a way that they could be recognised as such; (v) the defendants were to be entitled to sell the articles to third parties in the ordinary course of business on condition that, if the claimants so required, the defendants would "hand over" to the claimants the claims they might have against those third parties. The defendants' bankers appointed a receiver under powers contained in a debenture. On the date of his appointment the defendants were indebted to the claimants for over £122,000. After his appointment, the receiver certified that he held foil delivered by the claimants to the defendants to the value of some £50,000 and that an amount of £35,000 was held by him in a separate account representing the proceeds of foil supplied and then resold by the defendants to third parties. The claimants claimed an order for delivery up of the foil so held and a declaration that they were entitled to a charge on the money in the account of the receiver. They claimed to be entitled to trace the proceeds of the sub-sales of their property in that account. The defendants conceded that they were bailees of the foil supplied, but contended that, once they had resold the foil, the relationship between them and the claimants was simply that of debtor and creditor so that the claimants had no right to trace. The Court of Appeal held that, by virtue of the relationship of bailor and bailee, and as expressly contemplated in the claimants' conditions, a fiduciary relationship arose and the claimants were entitled to trace and claim the proceeds of the sub-sales in priority to the general body of the defendants' creditors and in priority to the defendant's bankers under their debenture. As a result of this decision, it has become extremely common for sellers to insert in their standard conditions of sale a "Romalpa" clause which, as a minimum, stipulates that the seller is to retain ownership of the goods until payment of the price, but which may contain more extensive provisions.

The existence of "Romalpa" clauses in contracts of sale is of serious 5–142
concern to creditors of manufacturing and trading companies and in particular to banks who might otherwise be secured by a floating charge on the assets of the buyer company or by a fixed charge[61] on its book debts and other receivables. It is also of concern to factoring companies to whom the buyer company may have sold or discounted its receivables.[62] Attacks on the effectiveness of "Romalpa" clauses have been made mainly on two grounds. The first is that the clause gives rise to a charge created by the buyer company within section 396 of the Companies Act 1985[63] and so requires to be registered under section 395 of that Act.[64] The second is that

---

[61] But see *Re Spectrum Plus Ltd* [2005] UKHL 41, [2005] 2 A.C.680.

[62] *Pfeiffer Weinkellerei-Weinenkauf GmbH & Co. v Arbuthnot Factors Ltd* [1988] 1 W.L.R. 150; *Compaq Computer Ltd v Abercorn Group Ltd* [1991] B.C.C. 484; below, para.5–161.

[63] Formerly s.95(2) of the Companies Act 1948.

[64] Formerly s.95(1) of the Companies Act 1948.

the particular clause, in its terms or upon its true construction, does not confer such extended rights as are claimed by the seller in reliance on its provisions. Since "Romalpa" clauses may take many forms, and since the case-law on their validity and interpretation has become progressively complex and refined, this area of the law is, in the words of Staughton J.,[65] "presently a maze if not a minefield". It will therefore be necessary to consider separately the various provisions that may be inserted in such clauses.

5–143 **Company charges.** Section 395(1) of the Companies Act 1985, provides that a charge created by a company registered in England and Wales[66] and being a charge of a description referred to in section 396(1)[67] is (so far as any security on the company's property or undertaking is conferred by the charge) void against the liquidator[68] and any creditor of the company, unless the prescribed particulars of the charge are delivered to the registrar of companies for registration within 21 days after the date of its creation. In a number of cases, which are discussed in the paragraphs which follow, the courts have held that the effect of certain forms of "Romalpa" clause was to create a charge on the property of the buyer company and that the clause was to that extent void for non-registration against a liquidator or creditor of the buyer company under section 395(1) of the 1985 Act or its predecessor, section 95(1) of the Companies Act 1948.[69]

The buyer company, while it is a going concern, cannot itself assert the invalidity of the charge.[70]

5–144 **Retention of title.** It is an essential feature of any "Romalpa" clause that ownership of the goods is retained by the seller until at least[71] the purchase price of the goods is paid. But in *Re Bond Worth Ltd*[72] the clause in

[65] *Hendy Lennox (Industrial Engines) Ltd v Grahame Puttick Ltd* [1984] 1 W.L.R. 485 at 493.

[66] Registration in Scotland of charges created by companies is dealt with in ss.410–424 of the Act, and charges on property in England and Wales created by an oversea company by s.409.

[67] These include: s.396(1)(c) "a charge created or evidenced by an instrument which, if executed by an individual, would require registration as a bill of sale"; s.396(1)(e) "a charge on book debts of the company"; and s.396(1)(f) "a floating charge on the company's undertaking or property."

[68] Or, by an amendment made by the Insolvency Act 1985, s.109(1) and Sch.6, para.10, against an administrator.

[69] New provisions relating to the registration of company charges were inserted by Pt.4 of the Companies Act 1989 (ss.92–104) but these were never brought into force and are proposed to be repealed by the Companies Reform Bill (2006). The Bill may, however, eventually contain provisions modifying the provisions of the 1985 Act relating to company charges. See Law Commission, Consultative Report on *Company Security Interests,* Law Com. No.176 (2004); Law Commission Final Report on *Company Security Interests,* Law Com. No.296 (2005).

[70] *Re Monolithic Building Co. Ltd* [1915] 1 Ch. 643; *Independent Automatic Sales Ltd v Knowles and Foster* [1962] 1 W.L.R. 974; *Smith v Bridgend C.B.C.* [2002] 1 A.C. 336 at 348.

[71] See below, para.5–146.

[72] [1980] Ch. 228, followed in *Stroud Architectural Systems Ltd v John Laing*

question provided that "equitable and beneficial ownership shall remain with us [the seller] until full payment has been received." This, together with other features of the clause,[73] was held by Slade J. to give rise to a floating charge created by the buyer company on its property[74] and to require registration. There can, however, be no valid objection to a clause by which the seller retains legal, and not merely beneficial or equitable, ownership of the goods agreed to be sold until such time as the conditions stipulated in the clause, *e.g.* payment of the price, are fulfilled, since this is expressly provided for in section 19(1) of the Sale of Goods Act 1979.[75] Moreover, no question of any charge by the buyer company requiring registration under section 395 of the Companies Act 1985 can arise, because a company can create a charge only on its own property, and if the company never has acquired property in the goods the subject of an agreement for sale it cannot charge them.[76] Nevertheless, where goods are sold to a manufacturing or trading company, and particularly where a period of credit is allowed, it can scarcely be supposed that the buyer company is meanwhile to have no right to consume the goods in manufacture or to resell the goods in the ordinary course of its business. Accordingly a term may be implied to that effect in order to give business efficacy to the contract.[77] An implied, or even express,[78] provision of this nature will not, however, invalidate the seller's retention of ownership of the goods until such time as they are so consumed or sold.[79]

Construction Ltd [1994] B.C.L.C. 276. See also *Emerald Stainless Steel Ltd v South Side Distribution Ltd*, 1983 S.L.T. 162 (where the clause in question inconsistently provided that the goods "shall be and remain the property of the [seller] and shall be held by the customer as trustee for the [seller]."). Contrast Gregory, 106 L.Q.R. 550 (1990); Hicks [1992] J.B.L. 398.

[73] See below, para.5–150.

[74] Companies Act 1948, s.95(2)(f). See now Companies Act 1985, s.396(1)(f).

[75] *Aluminium Industrie Vaassen BV v Romalpa Aluminium Ltd* [1976] 1 W.L.R. 676 at 687, 691, 693; *Frigoscandia (Contracting) Ltd v Continental Irish Meat Ltd* [1982] I.L.R.M. 396; *Re Peach dart Ltd* [1984] Ch. 131 at 141; *Hendy Lennox (Industrial Engines) Ltd v Grahame Puttick Ltd* [1984] 1 W.L.R. 485 at 491–3; *Re Andrabell Ltd* [1984] 3 All E.R. 407 at 410; *Clough Mill Ltd v Martin* [1985] 1 W.L.R. 111 at 116, 121–2, 125; *Re Weldtech Equipment Ltd* [1991] B.C.C. 16.

[76] *Clough Mill Ltd v Martin* (above), at pp.116, 122, 125. See also *Hendy Lennox (Industrial Engines) Ltd v Grahame Puttick Ltd*, above, at p.492. However, a sale of goods to a finance company and a repurchase of the goods from the finance company subject to a retention of title clause in favour of the finance company may create a registrable charge: *Re Curtain Dream Plc* [1990] B.C.L.C. 925. See above, para.1–066.

[77] *Aluminium Industrie Vaassen BV v Romalpa Aluminium Ltd* (above), at pp.680, 687, 689, 692, 694; *Re Bond Worth Ltd* [1980] Ch. 228 at 246; *Borden (UK) Ltd v Scottish Timber Products Ltd* [1981] Ch. 25 at 34, 44, 46; *Hendy Lennox (Industrial Engines) Ltd v Grahame Puttick Ltd*, above, at p.491; *Re Andrabell Ltd* (above), at p.411; *Four Point Garages Ltd v Carter* [1985] 3 All E.R. 12. See also below, para.5–156, n.65.

[78] *Aluminium Industrie Vaassen BV v Romalpa Aluminium Ltd*, above, at p.688; *Re Peachdart Ltd*, above; *Clough Mill Ltd v Martin*, above.

[79] *Aluminium Industrie Vaassen BV v Romalpa Aluminium Ltd*, above; *Re Peachdart Ltd*, above;*Hendy Lennox (Industrial Engines) Ltd v Grahame Puttick Ltd*, above; *Cf. Borden (UK) Ltd v Scottish Timber Products Ltd*, above; *Re Bond Worth Ltd*, above.

5–145 Retention of title clauses often contain in addition provisions whereby the seller is to be entitled to retake possession of the goods agreed to be sold and in which the seller retains title, and to keep or re-sell them, in the event that payment is not made on its due date or in the event, for example, of any petition being presented or resolution passed for the winding-up of the buyer company, or of the insolvency of the buyer.[80] Such a provision would again not give rise to a charge created by the buyer company[81]: the seller retains property in the goods and his right to recover possession is a right against his own goods.[82] Nor would the addition of a "right of entry and seizure" clause affect the position.[83] It has, however, been stated that, where material in its raw state is delivered to a manufacturing company, it would be impossible to suppose that the parties intended the seller to have the right, until the material had been fully paid for, to retake any partly or completely manufactured article derived from it.[84] But if the goods agreed to be sold sufficiently retain their identity, even though incorporated by process of manufacture in a finished product, the right of repossession and resale may still be available.[85]

5–146 Although certain "Romalpa" clauses retain ownership only in such goods as have not been paid for by the buyer, others go further and retain ownership of goods until all goods comprised in the same invoice[86] or in the same contract[87] have been paid for in full, or even until "all accounts" owing by the buyer to the seller have been settled.[88] Under section 19(1) of the Sale of Goods Act 1979, there is no reason why the seller should not specify what ever conditions he thinks fit to be fulfilled before property passes,[89] even if, in the case of an "all accounts" clause, this might mean in

---

[80] *Aluminium Industrie Vaassen BV v Romalpa Aluminium Ltd*, above; *Re Peachdart Ltd*, above; *Hendy Lennox (Industrial Engines) Ltd v Grahame Puttick Ltd*, above; *Clough Mill Ltd v Martin*, above.

[81] Companies Act 1985, s.396(1)(c).

[82] *McEntire v Crossley Brothers Ltd* [1895] A.C. 457; *Smart Brothers Ltd v Holt* [1929] 2 K.B. 303 at 308.

[83] *Shiloh Spinners Ltd v Harding* [1973] A.C. 691.

[84] *Re Peachdart Ltd*, above, at p.142. See below, para.5–149.

[85] *Hendy Lennox (Industrial Engines) Ltd v Grahame Puttick Ltd*, above. See below, para.5–149.

[86] *Re Peachdart Ltd* [1984] Ch. 131.

[87] *Re Bond Worth Ltd* [1980] Ch. 228; *Clough Mill Ltd v Martin* [1985] 1 W.L.R. 111.

[88] *Aluminium Industrie Vaassen BV v Romalpa Aluminium Ltd* [1976] 1 W.L.R. 676; *Borden (UK) Ltd v Scottish Timber Products Ltd* [1981] Ch. 25; *John Snow & Co. Ltd v D. G. B. Woodcraft Co. Ltd* [1985] B.C.L.C. 54; *Len Vidgen Ski & Leisure Ltd v Timaru Marine Supplies (1982) Ltd* [1986] N.Z.L.R. 349; *Armour v Thyssen Edelstahlwerke AG* [1991] 2 A.C. 339.

[89] *Aluminium Industrie Vaassen BV v Romalpa Aluminium Ltd*, above; *Re Peachdart Ltd*, above; *Clough Mill Ltd v Martin*, above; *John Snow & Co. Ltd v DGB Woodcraft & Co. Ltd*, above; *Len Vidgen Ski & Leisure Ltd v Timaru Marine Supplies (1982) Ltd*, above; *Armour v Thyssen Edelstahlwerke AG*, above, at p.353. Contrast Goodhart and Jones, 43 M.L.R. 480 at 508 (1980); Goodhart, 49 M.L.R. 96 (1986); Bradgate [1987] Conv. 434. In Scotland, "all accounts" clauses were at one time struck down as attempts to obtain security without possession, and by virtue of s.62(4), to fall outside the Sale of Goods Act 1979: *Emerald Stainless Steel Ltd v South Side Distribution Ltd* 1983 S.L.T. 162; *Deutz Engines Ltd v Terex Ltd*, 1984 S.L.T. 273; but they have since been upheld by the House of Lords in *Armour v Thyssen Edelstahlwerke AG*, above.

practice that the property would never pass as between seller and buyer. As a result, however, because other debts are still outstanding, the seller may still retain ownership of goods which have been delivered to and paid for by the buyer. In *Clough Mill Ltd v Martin*,[90] the Court of Appeal considered whether, in such a case: (1) account must be taken of the part payment already received in deciding how much the seller should be entitled to repossess and sell, and (2) if he does resell, he is accountable to the buyer in respect of any profit made on resale by reason of a rise in the market value of the goods. Robert Goff L.J. took the hypothetical example of a condition by which title to the goods was retained until payment in full for all the goods delivered under the contract had been received by the seller. In his opinion,[91] a distinction should be drawn between a situation where the contract of sale was still subsisting and one where the contract had been determined by the seller's acceptance of the buyer's repudiation.[92] In the former case, it would be possible to conclude, on the basis of an implied term in the contract, that the seller could resell only so much of the goods as was necessary to pay the outstanding balance of the purchase price; that the rest of the goods would remain available to the buyer for the purposes of the contract; and that if he resold more, then he would be accountable to the buyer for the surplus. In the latter case, however, such an implied term could not be given effect to, unless it survived the determination. So the seller could exercise his rights as owner uninhibited by any contractual restrictions. He could sell the goods on his own account: though he would be bound to repay any part of the purchase price already paid by the buyer which had to be appropriated to the goods sold, because such sum would be recoverable by the buyer on the ground of failure of consideration. Donaldson M.R., however, in his judgment[93] did not draw any such distinction. In his view, the word "until" in such a condition as "reserves the right to dispose of the [goods] until payment in full for all the [goods] has been received" connoted not only a temporal, but also a quantitative limitation. The seller could go on selling the goods until they were paid for in full, but if thereafter he continued to sell, he would be accountable to the buyer for having sold goods which, upon full payment having been achieved, were the buyer's goods. In *Armour v Thyssen Edelstahlwerke AG*[94] (where an "all accounts" clause was upheld) the House of Lords did not find it necessary to form a concluded view as to the solution of these problems. But it is submitted that, until the conditions on which the passing of property depends have been satisfied in relation to any particular parcel of goods, the seller is prima facie entitled to recover possession of them, and, if he does so, this rescinds the contract of sale.[95] In any event the

[90] [1985] 1 W.L.R. 111.

[91] At pp.117–118, with whom Oliver L.J. (at p.124) agreed.

[92] See also *Borden (UK) Ltd v Scottish Timber Products Ltd*, above, at p.44.

[93] At pp.125–126.

[94] [1991] 2 A.C. 339 at 353 (an appeal from Scotland).

[95] *Hewison v Ricketts* (1894) 63 L.J.Q.B. 711; *Att.-Gen. v Pritchard* (1928) 97 L.J.K.B. 561; see below, para.15–114. For more extended discussion of the whole problem, see Goodhart and Jones, 43 M.L.R. 480 (1980); Goodhart, 49 M.L.R. 96 (1986); McCormack [1989] Conv. 92; Bradgate, 54 M.L.R. 726 (1991).

contract of sale will be rescinded if the seller resells the goods, whether he does so in the exercise of a right of resale expressly reserved in the contract[96] or of his statutory right conferred by section 48(3) of the Sale of Goods Act 1979.[97] As a result: (i) he abandons any claim to recover the balance of the price of the goods comprised in the contract,[98] (ii) he must repay to the buyer the price attributable to the goods repossessed (subject to any counterclaim which he may have for damages[99] for breach of the contract), and (iii) he is not obliged to account to the buyer for any part of the resale value of the goods.[1]

5–147 In the *Romalpa* case itself the clause in question provided that, until the date of payment, the buyer company, if the seller so desired, was to store the goods in such a way that they were clearly the property of the seller, and it was conceded that the buyer was a bailee of the goods.[2] In *Borden (U.K.) Ltd v Scottish Timber Products Ltd*,[3] however, Bridge L.J. stated[4] that if goods were delivered for use in the manufacturing process at a time before they could have been paid for, in circumstances in which the seller had no right to call for their return or object to their use in the manufacture, and it was never intended that the product of manufacture should be recovered, either in its original or in its altered form or at all, it seemed quite impossible for him to say that there was a contract of bailment. In subsequent cases, the courts have found it unnecessary to decide whether the relationship of seller and buyer in relation to the goods is one of bailor and bailee.[5] Also in the *Romalpa* case, where the buyer company was expressly entitled (subject to certain conditions) to sell the goods to a third party, Roskill L.J. stated[6] that, as between buyer and seller, the buyer resold the goods as agent for the seller. However, the efficacy of a retention of title provision does not appear to depend on whether or not the goods are delivered to the buyer as bailee or whether or not, if the goods are sold, they are sold by the buyer as principal or agent. These

[96] s.48(4); see below, para.15–128.
[97] *Ward (RV) Ltd v Bignall* [1967] 1 Q.B. 534; see below, para.15–127.
[98] *Hewison v Ricketts*, above; *Att.-Gen. v Pritchard*, above.
[99] Under s.50 of the 1979 Act: *Ward (RV) Ltd v Bignall*, above.
[1] *Armour v Thyssen Edelstahlwerke AG*, above, at p.353; see also below, paras 15–127, , 15–128.
[2] *Aluminium Industrie Vaassen BV v Romalpa Aluminium Ltd* [1976] 1 W.L.R. 676 at 680. See also *Re Bond Worth Ltd* [1980] Ch. 228 at 263; *Borden (UK) Ltd v Scottish Timber Products Ltd* [1981] Ch. 25 at 38; *Re Peachdart Ltd* [1984] Ch. 131 at 141; *Hendy Lennox (Industrial Engines) Ltd v Grahame Puttick Ltd* [1984] 1 W.L.R. 485 at 497, 498; *Re Andrabell Ltd* [1984] 3 All E.R. 407 at 415.
[3] [1981] Ch. 25.
[4] At p.35. Buckley L.J. (at p.45) left open the question whether the buyer was properly to be regarded as a bailee in that case. See also *Pfeiffer Weinkellerei-Weineinkauf GmbH & Co. v Arbuthnot Factors Ltd* [1988] 1 W.L.R. 150 at 159. *Cf. Motor Mart Ltd v Webb* [1958] N.Z.L.R. 772.
[5] *Re Peachdart Ltd*, above, at pp.141, 142; *Hendy Lennox (Industrial Engines) Ltd v Grahame Puttick Ltd*, above, at pp.499–500; *Re Andrabell Ltd*, above, at p.414. But see *Clough Mill Ltd v Martin* [1985] 1 W.L.R. 111 at 116.
[6] [1976] 1 W.L.R. 676 at 690. See also Goff and Megaw L.JJ., *ibid.* at pp.693, 694. *Cf. Michelin Tyre Co. Ltd v Macfarlane (Glasgow) Ltd* (1917) 55 Sc.L.R. 35, HL.

matters are of relevance (if at all) only to the question of accountability of the buyer for the proceeds of sale.[7]

5–148 In conclusion it may be said that a reservation of title provision, if properly drafted, will normally be effective and will enable the seller to retain ownership of the goods agreed to be sold until those events which are expressly or impliedly set out in the provision occur. Nevertheless, in practice, considerable difficulties may arise in attempting to enforce the provision.[8] The seller may be unable to prove that the "Romalpa" clause was effectively incorporated into the contract of sale[9]; he may be unable to distinguish his goods from those supplied by other suppliers or those that have been paid for from those that have not[10]; and in many cases the goods will have been sold or converted into other products when he seeks to exercise his rights.

5–149 **Products.** Goods agreed to be sold subject to a reservation of title provision may be incorporated into other goods owned by the buyer or be subjected to the buyer's manufacturing processes to make other products. The effect of such acts on the title of the seller has been considered in a number of cases. In *Borden (UK) Ltd v Scottish Timber Products Ltd*,[11] a seller supplied resin for the manufacture of chipboard by the buyer company, reserving ownership of the resin until all goods supplied by him to the buyer company had been paid for in full. The Court of Appeal held that, once the resin was used in the manufacturing process, it ceased to exist, and with it the seller's title thereto; that, once the resin had lost its identity in the chipboard, it could no longer be traced into the chipboard or the proceeds of its sale; and that no term could properly be implied in the contract that the seller should have any interest in or charge over the

---

[7] See below, para.5–151.

[8] See Wheeler, *Retention of Title Clauses: Impact and Implications* (1991); Spencer [1989] J.B.L. 220.

[9] See, on this point, *Wavin Nederland BV v Excomb Ltd* [1983] New L.J. 937; *John Snow & Co. Ltd v DGB Woodcraft & Co. Ltd* [1985] B.C.L.C. 54; *Sauter Automation Ltd v Goodman (HC) (Mechanical Services) Ltd* (1986) 34 Build.L.R. 81. *Cf., Re Bond Worth Ltd*, above; *Kruppstahl AG v Quitmann Products Ltd* [1982] I. L.R.M. 551. But under s.19(1) of the Sale of Goods Act 1979, the seller may, by the terms of the contract *or appropriation*, reserve the right of disposal of the goods: see above, para.5–132, and Bradgate [1988] J.B.L. 477.

[10] But see on intermixture of chattels: *Indian Oil Corp. v Greenstone Shipping SA (Panama)* [1988] Q.B. 345; *Glencore International AG v Metro Trading International Inc.* [2001] 1 Lloyd's Rep. 283 at 320; Palmer and McKendrick, *Interests in Chattels* (2nd ed., 1998), Chs 10, 36. See also *Lupton v White* (1808) 15 Ves.Jun. 432 at 439–441; *Spence v Union Marine Insurance Co.* (1868) L.R. 3 C.P. 427; *Smurthwaite v Hannay* [1894] A.C. 495; *Sandeman & Sons v Tyzack and Branfoot Steamships Co. Ltd* [1913] A.C. 680 at 695; *Gill & Duffus (Liverpool) Ltd v Scruttons Ltd* [1953] 2 All E.R. 977; *Borden (UK) Ltd v Scottish Timber Products Ltd* [1981] Ch. 25 at 41; *Re Andrabell Ltd* [1984] 3 All E.R. 407; *Clough Mill v Martin* [1985] 1 W.L.R. 111 at 124; *Mercer v Craven Grain Storage Ltd* [1994] C.L.C. 328, HL; *Forsythe International (U.K.) Ltd v Silver Shipping Co. Ltd* [1994] 1 W.L.R. 1334; and the cases cited above, paras 1–058, 1–059; below, para.7–004, n.30.

[11] [1981] Ch. 25.

chipboard. In *Re Peachdart Ltd*,[12] quantities of leather supplied by the seller under a retention of title clause[13] had, at the time a receiver was appointed of the assets of the buyer company, been worked upon by the buyer to manufacture handbags. Some of these were wholly, but others only partly, completed. Vinelott J. held that the parties must have intended that at least after a piece of leather had been appropriated to be manufactured into a handbag and work had started on it, the leather would cease to be the exclusive property of the seller and that the seller would thereafter have a charge on the handbags in the course of manufacture and on the end products. That charge required registration under section 95 of the Companies Act 1948.[14] And in *Clough Mill Ltd v Martin*,[15] Robert Goff L.J. stated[16] that "where A's material is lawfully used by B to create new goods, whether or not B incorporates other material of his own, the property in the new goods will generally vest in B, at least where the goods are not reducible to the original materials." On the other hand, in *Hendy Lennox (Industrial Engines) Ltd v Grahame Puttick Ltd*,[17] diesel engines were sold to the buyer company subject to a retention of title clause and were incorporated into diesel generating sets. The process of incorporation did not in any way alter or destroy the substance of an engine, and it could be removed from the set, if necessary, within several hours. Staughton J. held that the proprietary rights of the seller were not affected by the incorporation: the engines remained engines, albeit connected to other things. These cases move into very difficult and uncertain[18] areas of law relating to the creation of a new product from materials owned by another[19] or the

---

[12] [1984] Ch. 131. See also *Modelboard Ltd v Outer Box Ltd* [1993] B.C.L.C. 623 (cardboard made into boxes); *Ian Chisholm Textiles v Griffiths* [1994] B.C.C. 96 (cloth cut and worked on); *Chaigley Farms Ltd v Crawford, Kaye & Grayshire Ltd* [1996] B.C.C. 957 (slaughtered cattle); *ICI New Zealand v Agnew* [1998] 2 N.Z.L.R. 129 (plastic pellets made into containers). Contrast *Armour v Thyssen Edelstahlwerke AG* [1991] 2 A.C. 339 (cut steel); *New Zealand Forest Products Ltd v Pongakawa Sawmill Ltd* [1992] 3 N.Z.L.R. 304 (sawn timber); *Coleman v Harvey* [1989] 1 N.Z.L.R. 723 (refined silver).

[13] The clause, in fact, contained an express provision relating to products: see below, para.5–150.

[14] See now s.395 of the Companies Act 1985.

[15] [1985] 1 W.L.R. 111.

[16] At p.119. See also Donaldson M.R. at p.125.

[17] [1984] 1 W.L.R. 485. Contrast *Specialist Plant Services Ltd v Braithwaite Ltd* (1987) 3 B.C.C.119 (materials for repair).

[18] See *Clough Mill Ltd v Martin* [1985] 1 W.L.R. 111 at 124.

[19] The principle of *specificatio* (Bracton, Lib. II, cap. ii and iii; 2 Bl.Comm. 405). The ownership of the new product normally vests in the maker (if bona fide), subject to his liability in damages to the owner of the materials converted. See Matthews, 10 Anglo-American L.R. 121 (1981); Whittaker 100 L.Q.R. 35 (1984); Palmer and McKendrick *Interests in Goods* (2nd ed., 1998), Ch.10, p.228, Ch.36, p.934; and, in Scotland, Stair II, 1, 41; Erskine II, 1, 16; Bell, Prin. para.1298; *International Banking Corp. v Ferguson Shaw & Sons* 1910 S.C. 182; *Wylie & Lockhead v Mitchell* (1870) 8 M. 552; *McDonald v Provan of Scotland Street Ltd* 1960 S.L.T. 231; *ZahnradFabrik Passau GmbH v Terex Ltd* 1986 S.L.T. 84; Gretton and Reid 1985 S.L.T. 329 at 333. *Cf. Jones v De Marchant* (1916) 28 D.L.R. 561; *Glencore International AG v Metro Trading International Inc.* [2001] 1 Lloyd's Rep. 283 at 320; and the cases cited in para.5–148, n.10.

attachment of one person's chattel to that of another.[20] They appear to establish that, in the absence of an express provision to the contrary,[21] the seller's property in the goods will be lost and vest in the buyer if the identity of the goods is destroyed in the manufacturing process or if they are transformed by manufacture into different goods, but may be retained if the goods are in their original state and can easily be removed from the finished product. But other intermediate possibilities exist. The question whether or not goods which are still identifiable, but have to a greater or less extent been worked on by the buyer or incorporated in other articles, remain the property of the seller would seem to depend upon what intention is to be imputed to the parties, having regard to such factors as the nature of the goods, the product, the degree and purpose of incorporation, and the manufacturing or other process applied.[22]

"Romalpa" clauses not infrequently contain a specific provision whereby ownership of products manufactured with the goods agreed to be sold is to vest in the seller or the seller is to acquire ownership of any articles in which such goods are incorporated. In *Borden (UK) Ltd v Scottish Timber Products Ltd*,[23] the opinion was expressed[24] that if the seller had any interest or share in the chipboard or proceeds of sale of the chipboard, or property representing proceeds of sale of the chipboard, any such interest or share must have been agreed to be granted and must have been created as security for the payment of the debts incurred and to be incurred by the buyer company to the seller in respect of the supply of resin, and so require registration as a charge under section 95 of the Companies Act 1948.[25] In that case, however, the seller's goods had been combined with the buyer's materials to create a new product, and the same reasoning would not necessarily apply where they could be proved to have been manufactured solely from the seller's goods. But in *Re Bond Worth Ltd*,[26] where the seller supplied raw acrilan to be spun, dyed and woven into carpets, a provision that the seller was to have "equitable and beneficial ownership of the products" was held void against a receiver of the assets of the buyer **5–150**

[20] The principle of accession (2 Bl.Comm. 404; 2 Kent's Comm. (10th ed.) 300). See *Akron Tyre Co. Pty Ltd v Kittson* (1951) 82 C.L.R. 477; *Rendell v Associated Finance Pty Ltd* [1957] V.R. 604; *Thomas v Robinson* [1977] 1 N.Z.L.R. 385; *McKeown v Cavalier Yachts* (1988) 13 N.S.W.L.R. 303; *Crossley Vaines on Personal Property* (5th ed.), p.430; Sawer 9 Aust. L.J. 50 (1935); Slater, 37 Can. Bar Rev. 597 (1959); Guest, 27 M.L.R. 505 (1964); Matthews [1981] *Current Legal Problems* 159; Matthews [1981] C.L.J. 340; Palmer and McKendrick, *op. cit.*, Ch.10, p.227, Ch.36, p.931; and, in Scotland, Bell, *Prin.* para.1297–1298; *Wylie & Lochhead v Mitchell* (above), at p.557; *Zahnrad Fabrik Passau GmbH v Terex Ltd*, above; Gretton and Reid 1985 S.L.T. 329 at 333.

[21] Such a term will not be implied: *Borden (UK) Ltd v Scottish Timber Products Ltd* [1981] Ch. 25 at 42, 44, 46.

[22] See the cases cited in nn.12, 20, above.

[23] [1981] Ch. 25. See also *Kruppstahl v Quitmann Products Ltd* [1982] I. L.R.M. 551 (joint ownership provision).

[24] *Per* Templeman L.J. at pp.44, 45. See also Buckley L.J. at pp.46, 47.

[25] As a charge under s.95(2)(c) of the 1948 Act (see now s.396(1)(c) of the Companies Act 1985).

[26] [1980] Ch. 228.

company on the ground that it created a charge over carpets in the process of manufacture and finished carpets in stock. Also in *Re Peachdart Ltd*,[27] where leather was supplied to be made into handbags, a provision that "the relationship of the buyer to the seller shall be fiduciary in respect of . . . other goods in which [the contract goods] are incorporated or used" was likewise held to create a charge over completed and uncompleted handbags manufactured from the leather supplied. All of these cases assume that the application of the manufacturing process to the goods agreed to be sold vested ownership of the products in the buyer company, so that the buyer company was creating a charge over its property as security for payment of a debt. On the other hand, in *Clough Mill Ltd v Martin*,[28] where yarn was supplied to be manufactured into fabric, neither Robert Goff L.J.[29] nor Oliver L.J.[30] saw any objection in principle to an agreement of the parties that property in any new product created by manufacture should vest in the seller: the buyer would not *confer* upon the seller any interest in property defeasible on payment of a debt, since, when the new product came into existence, the property in it would *ipso facto* vest in the seller. Nevertheless, both they and Donaldson M.R. were of the opinion[31] that the specific provision in that case whereby "if any of the material is incorporated in or used as material for other goods before . . . payment the property in the whole of such goods shall be and remain with the seller until such payment has been made" would give rise to a charge on the new product in favour of the seller. The provision could not be read literally to produce the result of a windfall to the seller of the full value of the new product, deriving as it might from the labour of the buyer and also from materials that were the buyer's, and having regard to the fact that the new product might incorporate also materials supplied by other sellers on similar terms. It would not, therefore, vest in the seller legal title to the new product on its creation, but rather vest title in the buyer subject to the creation of a charge. It therefore seems likely that, save in the most exceptional circumstances, any "products" provision would be held to create a registrable charge. Similarly a provision whereby the ownership of any article in which the goods supplied are incorporated is to pass to the seller would also create such a charge.[32]

5–151 **Proceeds of sale.** It is submitted that a mere retention of title provision will not, of itself, impose upon the buyer an obligation to account to the seller for the proceeds of sale of the goods in which property is retained.[33]

---

27 [1984] Ch. 131.

28 [1985] 1 W.L.R. 111.

29 At p.119.

30 At p.124. But see Donaldson M.R. at p.125 and *Borden (UK) Ltd v Scottish Timber Products* [1981] Ch. 25 at 46.

31 At pp.120, 124, 125. See also *Modelboard Ltd v Outer Box Ltd* [1993] B.C.L.C. 623; *ICI New Zealand v Agnew* [1998] 2 N.Z.L.R. 129.

32 *Specialist Plant Services Ltd v Braithwaite Ltd* (1987) 3 B.C.C. 119.

33 *Michelin Tyre Co. Ltd v Macfarlane (Glasgow) Ltd* (1917) 55 Sc.L.R. 35, HL; *Hendy Lennox (Industrial Engines) Ltd v Grahame Puttick Ltd* [1984] 1 W.L.R. 485; *Re Andrabell Ltd* [1984] 3 All E.R. 407; *Pfeiffer Weinkellerei-Weineinkauf GmbH & Co. v Arbuthnot Factors Ltd* [1988] 1 W.L.R. 150.

It is not necessary to imply any term to that effect to give business efficacy to the transaction.[34] If the buyer company is permitted to and does resell the goods, it will normally do so for its own account.[35] Even if it holds the goods until payment as bailee for the seller or sells the goods as agent on behalf of the seller,[36] it does not necessarily do so in a fiduciary capacity,[37] since not all bailees or agents are fiduciaries for their bailors or principals.[38]

In order to render the buyer accountable to the seller, and in such a way as to confer upon the seller a proprietary interest in the proceeds of sale to the exclusion of other creditors of the buyer, many "Romalpa" clauses expressly provide that the buyer shall hold the proceeds on trust or in a fiduciary capacity for the seller. The legal title to the proceeds then vests in the buyer, but they are in the beneficial ownership of the seller, who therefore has the right to trace them in accordance with the principles in *Re Hallett's Estate*.[39] In the *Romalpa* case itself,[40] it was held that the intention of the clause in question was to create a fiduciary relationship between the buyer company and the seller, so that the buyer company was accountable to the seller for the proceeds of sale in accordance with those principles. *Re Bond Worth Ltd*,[41] however, emphasises the fact that the buyer company should not expressly or impliedly be empowered to use the proceeds of sale as its own money. If the buyer company is not bound to keep the proceeds separate, but is entitled to mix them with its own money and deal with them as it pleases, and when called upon to hand over an equivalent sum of money, then it is not a trustee of the proceeds, but merely a debtor.[42] In that case, the clause provided that "our beneficial entitlement shall attach to the proceeds of resale or to the claim for such proceeds", but permitted (so it was held) the buyer company to use the goods, products and moneys derived from resale as it pleased and for its own purposes during the subsistence of the retention of title provision; this was incompatible with **5–152**

---

[34] *Cf. Aluminium Industrie Vaassen BV v Romalpa Aluminium Ltd* [1976] 1 W.L.R. 676 at 690, 692, 694. In *Len Vidgen Ski & Leisure Ltd v Timaru Marine Supplies (1982) Ltd* [1986] N.Z.L.R. 349, such an obligation was implied.

[35] *Pfeiffer Weinkellerei-Weineinkauf GmbH & Co. v Arbuthnot Factors Ltd*, above, at p.159.

[36] See above, para.5–147.

[37] *Cf. Re Hallett's Estate* (1880) 13 Ch.D. 696 at 708–711; *Aluminium Industrie Vaassen BV v Romalpa Aluminium Ltd* (above), at p.690.

[38] *Kirkham v Peel* (1880) 43 L.T. 171; *Re Coomber* [1911] 1 Ch. 723 at 728; *Henry v Hammond* [1913] 2 K.B. 515; *Boardman v Phipps* [1967] 2 A.C. 46 at 126; *Hendy Lennox (Industrial Engines) Ltd v Grahame Puttick Ltd*, above, at pp.497–499; *Re Andrabell Ltd*, above, at pp.411–416; *Compaq Computer Ltd v Abercorn Group Ltd* [1991] B.C.C. 484 at 496.

[39] (1880) 13 Ch.D. 696.

[40] [1976] 1 W.L.R. 676. See also *Sugar Distributors Ltd v Monaghan Cash & Carry Ltd* [1982] I.L.R.M. 399 at 402; *Foundaries du Lion v International Factors Ltd* [1985] I.L.R.M. 66; *Len Vidgen Ski & Leisure Ltd v Timaru Marine Supplies (1982) Ltd* [1986] N.Z.L.R. 349.

[41] [1980] Ch. 228.

[42] *Henry v Hammond*, above, at p.521; *Neste Oy v Lloyd's Bank Plc* [1983] 2 Lloyd's Rep. 658 at 665.

the relationship of trustee and beneficiary.[43] The *Romalpa* decision was distinguished[44] on a number of grounds, and in particular because the receiver had kept the relevant proceeds of sale in a separate account and they had never been mixed with other moneys. A "Romalpa" clause should therefore state expressly that the proceeds of resale should be placed in a separate account so as to be identifiable as being in the beneficial ownership of the seller. In the absence of any such express provision, it is unlikely that it would be implied.[45] In particular, where a period of credit is allowed, the normal inference must be that, in respect of resales made during that period, the buyer company is to be free to use the proceeds of sale as it thinks fit.[46]

5–153 It is clear, however, that, for reasons of cash flow alone, no buyer would willingly accept that the seller was absolutely entitled to claim the entire proceeds of resale. The parties may in consequence be held to have intended that the seller's interest in the proceeds is to be defeasible upon payment of the sums owing from the buyer company to the seller, and is, in consequence, an interest by way of security rather than an absolute interest. If such is the true construction of the provision,[47] then it is submitted that a charge is created over the proceeds of sale.[48] If created by the buyer company,[49] it will require registration under section 395 of the Companies

---

[43] [1980] Ch. 228 at 261, following *Re Nevill* (1870) L.R. 6 Ch.App. 397 (affirmed sub. nom. *Towle & Co. v White* (1873) 29 L.T. 78, HL); *Foley v Hill* (1848) 2 H.L.C. 28; *South Australian Insurance Co. v Randall* (1869) L.R. 3 P.C. 101. See also the invalidation of the trust device on different grounds in *Clark Taylor & Co. Ltd v Quality Site Development (Edinburgh) Ltd* 1981 S.L.T. 308 (commented upon by Wilson, 1983 S.L.T. 106 at 108; Gretton [1983] J.B.L. 334; Halliday 1984 S.L.T. 153) and the distinction between fixed and floating charges drawn in *Re Spectrum Plus Ltd* [2005] UKHL 41; [2005] 2 A.C. 680.

[44] At pp.263–264. See also *Hendy Lennox (Industrial Engines) Ltd v Grahame Puttick Ltd*, above, at pp.497–499; *Re Andrabell Ltd*, above, at pp.414, 415.

[45] But in *Len Vidgen Ski & Leisure Ltd v Timaru Marine Supplies (1982) Ltd* [1986] N.Z.L.R. 349, such a provision was implied from the words "the proceeds of sale . . . shall be the property of" the seller.

[46] *Hendy Lennox (Industrial Engines) Ltd v Grahame Puttick Ltd*, above, at p.499; *Re Andrabell Ltd*, above, at p.416. Contrast *Aluminium Industrie Vaassen BV v Romalpa Aluminium Ltd*, above, at pp.689, 692; *Len Vidgen Ski & Leisure Ltd v Timaru Marine Supplies (1982) Ltd*, above.

[47] *Re Kent & Sussex Sawmills Ltd* [1947] Ch. 177 at 181; *Re Welsh Irish Ferries Ltd* [1986] Ch. 471. *Cf. Re Smith* (1879) 10 Ch.D. 566.

[48] *Borden (UK) Ltd v Scottish Timber Products Ltd* [1981] Ch. 25 at 45, *Re Bond Worth Ltd* [1980] Ch. 228 at 248, 259; *Tatung (UK) Ltd v Galex Telesure Ltd* [1989] 5 B.C.C. 325; *Re Weldtech Equipment Ltd* [1991] B.C.C. 16; *Compaq Computer Ltd v Abercorn Group Ltd* [1991] B.C.C. 484. Contrast (trust receipts) *Re David Allester Ltd* [1922] 2 Ch. 211. But in the case of trust receipts, the bank's rights as pledgee arise under the original pledge. *Cf., Ladenburg v Goodwin Ferreira & Co. Ltd* [1912] 3 K.B. 275. See the discussion, below, para.18–238.

[49] *Tatung (UK) Ltd v Galex Telesure Ltd*, above; *Compaq Computer Ltd v Abercorn Group Ltd*, above; (*i.e.* by contract, and not by virtue of the relationship of fiduciary bailee and bailor). Contrast *Aluminium Industrie Vaassen BV v Romalpa Aluminium Ltd* [1976] 1 W.L.R. 676 at 682–683, where Mocatta J. (at first instance) considered that the fact that the proceeds of sale belonged in equity to the seller resulted from the property in the goods never having passed to the buyer, and not (presumably) from the creation of a charge by the buyer.

Act 1985. It is perhaps for this reason, and possibly because such a provision might appear more acceptable to the buyer, that "Romalpa" clauses sometimes contain a provision that the buyer is to hold as trustee on behalf of the seller, not the entire proceeds of resale of the goods, but only such part of those proceeds as represent or are equivalent to the price at which the goods resold were invoiced by the seller to the buyer.[50] Although a declaration of trust of an unquantified part of a specific fund would fail for uncertainty,[51] there is no reason to suppose that a trust of a quantified amount forming part of a fund would likewise fail.[52] Moreover, in *Associated Alloys Pty Ltd v CAN 001 452 106 Pty Ltd (in liquidation)*,[53] the High Court of Australia, by a majority,[54] upheld a clause which required the buyer company to hold on trust for the seller such part of the proceeds of sale as were equal to the amount owing by the buyer at the time of the receipt of the proceeds.[55] The High Court approached the matter in an innovative manner. It held that there was an implied term in the contract of sale that, upon receipt of the relevant proceeds, the obligation in debt of the buyer to the seller was discharged. The clause did not therefore create any "charge" over the proceeds to secure a debt: it was simply an agreement to constitute a trust of after-acquired property. It may be that such a provision would likewise be upheld in England,[56] provided that the parties thereby intended that the seller should have an absolute and indefeasible interest in the trust money and provided that the buyer company was not free to use that money as it pleased.[57]

A "proceeds of sale" provision may be stated to extend, not only to the proceeds of sale of the goods supplied by the seller under the contract of sale, but also to the proceeds of sale of products manufactured with or incorporating those goods. The same difficulties as are mentioned above apply equally to any such provision. But where a claim to the proceeds of sale of products is made, an additional difficulty may arise that the products will incorporate the labour of the buyer and may incorporate materials of the buyer or even of third parties.[58] In such a case, it is submitted that it is strongly arguable that the parties true intention was that the proceeds should vest in the buyer company subject to the grant of a charge, which charge (being created by the buyer company) would require registration under section 395 of the Companies Act 1985.[59] **5–154**

[50] In *Len Vidgen Ski & Leisure Ltd v Timaru Marine Supplies (1982) Ltd* [1986] N.Z.L.R. 349, this point was left open by Barker J. (no express provision).
[51] *Sprange v Barnard* (1789) 2 Bro.C.C. 585; *Palmer v Simmonds* (1854) 2 Drew 221.
[52] *Hunter v Moss* [1994] 1 W.L.R. 452.
[53] (2000) 202 C.L.R. 558.
[54] Kirby J. dissenting.
[55] However, the seller's claim failed because it was unable to identify whether any payments made by a sub-purchaser to the buyer were related, within the meaning of the clause, to the goods supplied by the seller under any particular contract.
[56] *cf. Pfeiffer Weinkellerei-Weineinkauf GmbH & Co. v Arbuthnot Factors Ltd* [1988] 1 W.L.R. 150 at 160.
[57] These limitations are not, however, found in the Australian decision.
[58] See above, para.5–149.
[59] *Borden (UK) Ltd v Scottish Timber Products Ltd* [1981] Ch. 25 at 44–45.

5–155 If the buyer company is in fact accountable to the seller for the whole or part of the proceeds of resale of the goods, considerable practical problems nevertheless arise for a seller who seeks to enforce his rights.[60] First, he must identify the proceeds of sale as those of his goods.[61] If his goods have been invoiced to sub-purchasers together with other goods, this may be no easy matter. Secondly, in many cases, there will be no monies available to satisfy his claim, but at most debts payable by sub-purchasers to the buyer company which remain to be got in. Thirdly, even if such monies are available, the buyer company will most probably not have placed the proceeds of sale into a separate account but mixed them with its own monies. The difficulties of tracing into a mixed fund in the hands of a liquidator (especially where there are claims by other suppliers under "Romalpa" clauses) may in the final stage prove insurmountable.

5–156 **Title of sub-purchasers.** The title of sub-purchasers from the buyer of goods supplied subject to a reservation of title provision in a "Romalpa" clause will ordinarily not be affected by the fact that the buyer is not the owner of the goods.[62] They will acquire a good title under section 25(1) of the Sale of Goods Act 1979[63] or under section 2 of the Factors Act 1889,[64] or because the buyer has the express or implied authority of the seller to sell the goods in the ordinary course of business and confer a good title on sub-purchasers.[65] However, the buyer may in turn agree to sell the goods to a sub-purchaser subject to a retention of title provision, and deliver the goods to the sub-purchaser. In such a case unless and until the sub-purchaser has paid the price of the goods or satisfied such other conditions as may have been stipulated by the buyer for the passing of property to the sub-purchaser, the seller is entitled to claim the goods as his property in the hands of the sub-purchaser.[66]

5–157 **Building and construction contracts.**[67] Goods may be supplied by a sub-contractor to the main contractor under a contract of sale subject to a stipulation that property in the goods agreed to be sold is not to pass to the

[60] See Wheeler, *Retention of Title Clauses: Impact and Implications* (1991).
[61] See n.55, above.
[62] *Hendy Lennox (Industrial Engines) Ltd v Grahame Puttick Ltd* [1984] 1 W.L.R. 485 at 495.
[63] See below, para.7–069; *Aluminium Industrie Vaassen BV v Romalpa Aluminium Ltd* [1976] 1 W.L.R. 676 at 681; *Re Peachdart Ltd* [1984] Ch. 131 at 141; *Archivent Sales and Developments Ltd v Strathclyde R.C.* (1984) 27 Build.L.R. 98; *Four Point Garage Ltd v Carter* [1985] 3 All E.R. 12. Contrast *Re Interview Ltd* [1975] I.R. 382 and *W. Hanson (Harrow) Ltd v Rapid Civil Engineering Ltd* (1987) 38 Build.L.R. 106 (knowledge by sub-purchaser that goods subject to a "Romalpa" clause); *Feuer Leather Corp. v Frank Johnstone & Sons* [1981] Com.L.R. 251; [1983] Com.L.R. 12 (bad faith); *Forsythe International (UK) Ltd v Silver Shipping Co. Ltd* [1993] 2 Lloyd's Rep. 268 (no delivery).
[64] See below, para.7–031.
[65] *Re Bond Worth Ltd* [1980] Ch. 228 at 246; *Four Point Garage Ltd v Carter*, above. See also *above*, para.5–144, n.77.
[66] *Hanson (W) (Harrow) Ltd v Rapid Civil Engineering Ltd* (1987) 38 Build.L.R. 106; *Re Highway Foods International Ltd* [1995] 1 B.C.L.C. 209. In the latter case it was held that the sub-purchaser could not rely on the words "or under any agreement for sale, . . . or other disposition" in s.9 of the Factors Act 1889; below, para.7–084.
[67] See Palmer and McKendrick (eds), *Interests in Goods* (2nd ed., 1998), Ch.15.

main contractor until paid for in full. The goods are then delivered to the site but, before they are affixed to the building,[68] the main contractor becomes insolvent and the sub-contractor seeks to recover the unfixed goods from the employer.[69] The sub-contractor's claim may well fail on the ground that the main contractor was a buyer in possession and could in consequence pass a good title to the employer under section 25(1) of the Sale of Goods Act 1979.[70] But there could be a number of obstacles to the successful assertion by the employer of a good title to goods supplied by a sub-contractor subject to a "Romalpa" clause. First, the contract between the sub-contractor and the main contractor may not be a contract of sale but a contract for work and materials,[71] so that section 25(1) of the 1979 Act will not apply as the main contractor will not have "bought or agreed to buy" the goods.[72] Secondly, there may have been no sale, pledge or other disposition of the goods by the main contractor to the employer sufficient to enable the employer to assert that he has acquired a good title by virtue of section 25(1).[73] Thirdly, the employer may not be without notice of the right of the sub-contractor with respect to the goods as required by section 25(1).[74] This may be because the sub-contractor has been nominated by the employer and the employer is in consequence aware of the terms of the sub-contract, including the retention of title provision. Or it may be because the relevant disposition to the employer took place only after he became aware of the provision.[75]

In *Stroud Architectural Systems Ltd v John Laing Construction Ltd*[76] the claimants claimed from the main contractor the return of goods which they had supplied to a sub-contractor company. The goods had been supplied subject to a term by which they had retained equitable (but not legal) ownership of the goods until the price was paid. The price had not been paid when the sub-contractor company went into receivership. It was held that the legal title to the goods had passed to the sub-contractor company subject to a floating charge in favour of the claimants.[77] Since that charge had not been registered it was void against the receiver; but it was not void against the main contractor as the main contractor was not a creditor of the **5–158**

---

[68] *cf. Aircool Installations v British Telecommunications* [1995] C.L.Y. 821 (Cty. Ct.) (goods affixed).

[69] Certain standard forms of building contract provide that unfixed materials delivered to the site are not to be removed without the consent of the architect or supervising officer. But such a provision in the main contract would not be binding on a sub-contractor who was not a party to the main contract: *Dawber Williamson Roofing Ltd v Humberside CC* (1979) 14 Build. L.R. 70.

[70] *Archivent Sales and Developments Ltd v Strathclyde RC* (1984) 27 Build.L.R. 98.

[71] See above, para.1–041.

[72] *Dawber Williamson Roofing Ltd v Humberside CC* (1979) 14 Build.L.R. 70 (concession); see below, para.7–070.

[73] *Hanson (W) (Harrow) Ltd v Rapid Civil Engineering Ltd* (1987) 38 Build.L.R. 106; see below, para.7–079.

[74] See below, para.7–086.

[75] *Hanson (W) (Harrow) Ltd v Rapid Civil Engineering Ltd*, above.

[76] [1994] B.C.L.C. 276.

[77] Following *Re Bond Worth Ltd* [1980] Ch. 228 and *Abbey National Building Society v Cann* [1991] 1 A.C. 56.

sub-contractor company. Nevertheless the goods were not recoverable from the main contractor because, unless the charge had ceased to float and become fixed, the claimants had no right to possession of the goods.

5–159 **Fixtures.**[78] Goods supplied subject to a "Romalpa" clause may be attached to land or premises so as to become fixtures. The seller normally has no claim to goods which have become fixtures as against a mortgagee[79] or landlord of the buyer. However, if the clause reserves to the seller the right to enter premises and retake the goods agreed to be sold, the seller may in certain circumstances,[80] as against a mortgagee of the buyer's land, sever and remove the goods where the mortgage is a legal mortgage created before the goods were affixed and the fixtures are trade fixtures.[81] Also the seller has the right, as against a landlord of the buyer, to sever and remove tenant's fixtures if and so long as the buyer as tenant is entitled to do so.[82] Otherwise the goods, having become part of the realty, are irrecoverable by the seller.[83]

5–160 **Claims against sub-purchasers.** "Romalpa" clauses sometimes provide that, where the goods supplied are resold by the buyer to sub-purchasers before payment has been received by the seller, any claim against sub-purchasers for the purchase price of the goods under the sub-contracts is to vest in or to be transferred to the seller. Such provisions may take a number of forms. Their intention is to enable the seller to intercept the proceeds of resale in the event of the insolvency of the buyer and to maintain a direct action against sub-purchasers for the sub-sale price of the goods. This result might possibly be achieved by a provision to the effect that, if the buyer resells any of the goods which are the seller's property, any claim against sub-purchasers is to vest immediately in the seller.[84] If literally construed, such a provision would mean that, as soon as any claim came into existence, it would become the property of the seller. But it seems unlikely that the parties would be held to have thereby intended to exclude absolutely and unconditionally any claim by the buyer against the sub-purchaser for the sub-sale price of the goods. In the *Romalpa* case,[85] a provision that the buyer company was, if the seller so required, to "hand over" to the seller

---

[78] See generally: Goode, *Hire-Purchase Law and Practice* (2nd ed.), Ch.32; Guest, *The Law of Hire-Purchase* (1966), Ch.18; Guest and Lever 27 Conv. N.S. 30 (1966); Bennett and Davis, 110 L.Q.R. 448 (1994); Palmer and McKendrick, *Interests in Goods* (2nd ed., 1998), Chs 11, 15, and above, para.1–095.
[79] *Trust Bank Central Ltd v Southdown Properties Ltd* [1991] 1 N.Z. Conv. c.190.
[80] Provided that the mortgage does not expressly prohibit the removal of fixtures and provided that the mortgagee has not taken possession of the mortgaged land.
[81] *Gough v Wood & Co.* [1894] 1 Q.B. 713 at 720; *Huddersfield Banking Co. Ltd v Henry Lister & Son Ltd* [1895] 2 Ch. 273; *Ellis v Glover & Hobson Ltd* [1908] 1 K.B. 388 at 396.
[82] *Crossley Bros Ltd v Lee* [1908] 1 K.B. 86; *Becker v Riebold* (1913) 30 T.L.R. 142. See Goode, *op. cit.*, p.376; Guest, *op cit.*, p.960; and above, para.1–095.
[83] *Aircool Installations v British Telecommunications* [1995] C.L.Y. 821 (Cty. Ct.); *Charles Henshaw & Sons Ltd v Antlerport Ltd* [1995] C.L.C. 1312 at 1322. *Cf. Rawlinson v Mort* (1905) 93 L.T. 555.
[84] See Goode [1964] J.B.L. 523 at 525.
[85] [1976] 1 W.L.R. 676 at 688, 692.

the claims it had against sub-purchasers emanating from the transaction was held not to be a present equitable assignment of those claims. But if the provision falls to be considered as such an equitable assignment,[86] it would again seem unlikely to be construed as an absolute assignment, vesting the buyer's claim to the price unconditionally in the seller.[87] More probably it would be considered to be an assignment to secure the indebtedness of the buyer and so be registrable as a charge created by the buyer company on its book debts under section 396(1)(e) of the Companies Act 1985.[88] If the provision takes the form of a declaration of trust, but is yet considered to be by way of security for the payment of a debt, it might still be regarded as a charge created by the buyer company on its book debts or as a floating charge on its property.[89]

Priorities. In the event that the "Romalpa" clause is held to give rise to an absolute assignment to the seller of debts owed to the buyer by sub-purchasers of the goods agreed to be sold, problems of priority may arise as between the seller and other assignees, *e.g.* where the buyer has factored the debts. In *Pfeiffer Weinkellerei-Weinenkauf GmbH & Co. v Arbuthnot Factors Ltd*,[90] a retention of title clause purported to create in favour of the seller an equitable assignment of the future debts owed by sub-purchasers of the goods from the buyer company. Phillips J. held that, if the assignment had been valid,[91] the claim of the seller to the debts would have been postponed to that of a subsequent assignee to whom the buyer had assigned the debts absolutely under a factoring agreement and who had given notice of the assignment to the sub-purchasers. Priority as between the two assignments was determined by the rule in *Dearle v Hall*,[92] that is to say, that the assignee who first gives notice to debtors of his assignment has the prior right, unless he knows of the previous assignment when he takes his assignment. The factoring company had been the first to give notice of its assignment to the sub-purchasers. Phillips J. further held that the fact that one of the assignments (in this case the assignment to the factoring company) satisfied the requirements of a statutory assignment under section 136 of the Law of Property Act 1925 did not enable the assignee to claim a legal title to the debts and so obtain priority as a bona fide 5–161

---

[86] *Compaq Computer Ltd v Abercorn Group Ltd* [1991] B.C.C. 484 at 500.
[87] *cf. Hughes v Pump House Hotel Co.* [1902] 2 K.B. 190.
[88] See *Independent Automatic Sales Ltd v Knowles and Foster* [1962] 1 W.L.R. 974; *Re Interview Ltd*, [1975] I.R. 182; *Pfeiffer Weinkellerei-Weineinkauf GmbH & Co. v Arbuthnot Factors Ltd* [1988] 1 W.L.R. 150; *Re Weldtech Equipment Ltd* [1991] B.C.C. 16; *Compaq Computer Ltd v Abercorn Group Ltd*, above. In *Re Peachdart Ltd* [1984] Ch. 131, Vinelott J. (at p.143) held that the charge was also void as regards the book debts against the bank, which under its debenture had a prior fixed charge.
[89] Companies Act 1985, s.396(1)(e), (f). See *Re Bond Worth Ltd*, above, at p.50; *Tatung (UK) Ltd v Galex Telesure Ltd* [1989] 5 B.C.C. 325.
[90] [1988] 1 W.L.R. 150. See also *Compaq Computer Ltd v Abercorn Group Ltd* [1991] B.C.C. 484.
[91] The assignment was held to have created a registrable charge on the book debts of the buyer company (see above, para.5–160) and to be void against the factor for want of registration under s.95 of the Companies Act 1948.
[92] (1828) 3 Russ. I. See *Chitty on Contracts* (29th ed.), Vol. 1, para.19–067.

purchaser for value without notice.[93] Priorities still fell to be determined as if the statutory assignment had been effected in equity, not in law.

In the case of competing assignments, the rule in *Dearle v Hall* displaces the general principle that equitable interests rank in priority in the order of their creation. However, it is arguable that, if the clause takes the form of a declaration by the buyer company that it will hold on trust for the seller any claim against sub-purchasers for the sub-sale price of the goods and the proceeds of their resale, then the title of the seller as *cestui que trust* does not need to be perfected by notice and will rank prior to that of a subsequent assignee who has given notice to the sub-purchasers.[94] But this argument assumes that the clause does in fact create a trust in favour of the seller. If the clause on its true construction constitutes an agreement between the buyer and the seller that the debts owing by the buyer to the seller are to be paid out of a specific fund coming to the buyer, namely the proceeds of the sub-sales, then it would appear that this gives rise to an equitable assignment,[95] and priority between this assignment and other competing assignments will be determined by the rule in *Dearle v Hall*.

The appointment of a receiver by a debenture holder converts the incomplete assignment constituted by a floating charge into a completed equitable assignment of the assets charged by it.[96] But if a floating charge[97] has been created on the property of the buyer company, and before the charge crystallises the seller has, by a "Romalpa" clause, reserved title to the goods in such a way as to have an equitable interest in the proceeds of resale which does not require registration as a charge, then such interest will prevail over that of the receiver, who cannot obtain priority by being the first to give notice to sub-purchasers of the goods resold.[98] The power of

---

[93] This view was followed by Mummery J. in *Compaq Computer Ltd v Abercorn Group Ltd*, above. But Phillips J. left open the question whether, if a statutory assignee has actually been paid the debts, it can claim precedence as a bona fide purchaser for value of the legal title in the payments received: *Taylor v Blakelock* (1886) 32 Ch.D. 560. This was conceded in the *Compaq* case, above, at p.500. *Cf.*, Oditah, 9 O.J.L.S. 513 (1989).

[94] *Hill v Peters* [1918] 2 Ch. 273, considered in *BS Lyle Ltd v Rosher* [1959] 1 W.L.R. 8 at 15, 17, 22–23, 24. See Goode, 92 L.Q.R. 528 at 556 (1976); Donaldson, 93 L.Q.R. 324 (1977); Goode, 93 L.Q.R. 487 (1977); McLaughlan, 96 L.Q.R. 90 (1980); Goode, *Legal Problems of Credit and Security* (3rd ed), para.5–36; Oditah, *Legal Aspects of Receivables Financing* (1991), p.259.

[95] *Compaq Computer Ltd v Abercorn Group Ltd* [1991] B.C.C. 484 at 500, citing *Swiss Bank Corp. v Lloyds Bank Ltd* [1982] A.C. 584 at 613.

[96] *NW Robbie & Co. Ltd v Witney Warehouse Ltd* [1963] 1 W.L.R. 1324; *George Barker (Transport) Ltd v Eynon* [1974] 1 W.L.R. 462 at 467; *Watson v Duff, Morgan & Vermont Holdings Ltd* [1974] 1 W.L.R. 450 at 456.

[97] For the position with respect to a prior fixed charge, see *Siebe Gorman & Co. Ltd v Barclays Bank Ltd* [1979] 2 Lloyd's Rep. 142.

[98] *Wheatley v Silkstone Co.* (1885) 25 Ch.D. 715; *Ward v Royal Exchange Shipping Co.* (1887) 58 L.T. 174; *Re Ind Coope & Co.* [1911] 2 Ch. 223. *Cf. English and Scottish Mercantile Investment Co. Ltd v Brunton* [1892] 2 Q.B. 700. The position is more complicated where the debenture contains a "negative pledge" clause which prohibits the company from creating any charge or assignment of its assets ranking in priority to or *pari passu* with the floating charge: see Farrar, 38 Conv. 315 (1974); Ferran [1988] C.L.J. 213; *Ian Chisholm Textiles Ltd v Griffiths* [1994] 2 B.C.L.C. 291. See also *Re Connolly Bros Ltd (No. 2)* [1912] 2 Ch. 25; *Abbey National Building Society v Cann* [1991] 1 A.C. 56.

a floating charge holder to appoint an administrative receiver has, however, been severely curtailed by ss.72A–72G of the Insolvency Act 1986.[99]

Administration orders.[1] Schedule B1 to the Insolvency Act 1986[2] enables an administrator of a company to be appointed, in certain circumstances, by the court,[3] by the holder of a floating charge[4] or by the company or its directors.[5] The administrator is required[6] to perform his functions with the objective of (a) rescuing the company as a going concern, (b) achieving a better result for the company's creditors as a whole than would be likely if the company were wound up (without first being in administration), or (c) realising property in order to make a distribution to one or more secured or preferential creditors. He must perform his functions as quickly and efficiently as is reasonably practicable[7] and, subject to this, he must perform them in the interests of the company's creditors as a whole.[8] The ability of the seller to enforce a "Romalpa" clause will be affected where the company is in, or is about to go into, administration. Once an administration order has been made, no step may be taken to repossess goods in the company's possession under a retention of title agreement[9] (or under a hire-purchase, conditional sale or chattel leasing agreement)[10] except with the consent of the administrator or with the permission of the court.[11] An interim moratorium is also imposed where an administration application has been made and either the application has not yet been granted or dismissed or the application has been granted but the administration order has not yet taken place. In that case, the goods may not be repossessed except with the permission of the court.[12] 5–162

Paragraph 72 of Schedule Bl to the 1986 Act further empowers the court to make an order enabling an administrator to dispose of goods which are in the possession of the company under a retention of title agreement as if all the rights of the owner were vested in the company.[13] Such an order may be made only on the application of the administrator and where the court thinks that the disposal of the goods would be likely to promote the purpose of the administration in respect of the company.[14] Protection is, however, afforded to the owner of the goods in that the order must provide for the net proceeds of disposal of the goods, and any additional moneys 5–163

---

[99] Inserted by s.250 of the Enterprise Act 2002.
[1] See Charlesworth and Morse, *Company Law* (17th ed., 2005).
[2] Inserted by s.248 of and Sch.16 to the Enterprise Act 2002.
[3] Sch B1, paras 10–13.
[4] Sch.B1, paras 14–21.
[5] Sch.B1, paras 22–34.
[6] Sch.B1, para.3(1).
[7] Sch.B1, para.3(4).
[8] Sch.B1, para.3(2).
[9] Defined in s.251 of the 1986 Act.
[10] See Sch.B1, para.111(1) and s.436 of the 1986 Act.
[11] Sch.B1, para.43.
[12] Sch.B1, para.44.
[13] Sch.B1, para.72(1), 111(1).
[14] Sch.B1, para.72(2).

required to be added to the net proceeds so as to produce the amount to be determined by the court as the net amount which would be realised on a sale of the goods at market, to be applied to discharging the sums payable under the agreement.[15] The administrator may thus, with the authority of the court, overreach the rights of the seller of goods that are subject to a "Romalpa" clause. An administrator who makes a successful application for such an order must send a copy of the order to the registrar of companies within 14 days of the date of the order,[16] in default, he may be guilty of a criminal offence.[17] However, a person who deals with the administrator of a company in good faith and for value need not inquire whether the administrator is acting within his powers.[18]

5–164 **Voluntary arrangements.** Amendments made to the Insolvency Act 1986 by the Insolvency Act 2000 enable the directors of a buyer company to obtain a similar moratorium for the company where they propose a voluntary arrangement under Part I of the 1986 Act.[19] This facility is, however, restricted to "eligible companies", that is to say, small companies, but excluding companies such as banks, insurance companies and companies involved with the performance of market contracts.[20] The moratorium is a temporary one only, commencing at the time certain documents are filed or lodged with the court[21] and ending at the end of the day on which the meetings of the company and its creditors are first held,[22] unless it is extended.[23] The effect of the moratorium is to preclude the seller under a retention of title agreement from taking any steps to repossess the goods in the buyer company's possession without permission of the court.[24]

5–165 **Receivership.** Save in exceptional cases,[25] the power of a floating charge holder to appoint an administrative receiver has now been taken away by s.72A of the Insolvency Act 1986.[26] However, it has been held that, where goods are supplied on credit to a company subject to a retention of title clause, and the company goes into receivership, the court will not grant an injunction to restrain the receivers from dealing with the goods if they give an undertaking to pay for such of the goods as are used or sold.[27]

5–166 **Non-corporate buyer.** Where the buyer is not a company, but is an individual, sole trader, partnership or unincorporated body of persons, a "Romalpa" clause cannot be attacked on the ground that it gives rise to a

---

15 Sch.B1, para.72(3).
16 Sch.B1, para.72(4).
17 Sch.B1, para.72(5).
18 Sch.B1, para.59(3).
19 Insolvency Act 1986, s.1A and Sch.A1 inserted by the Insolvency Act 2000, s.1.
20 Sch.A1, para.2.
21 Sch.A1, paras 7, 8.
22 Sch.A1, paras 8, 29.
23 Sch.A1, para.32.
24 Sch.A1, para.12(1)(g).
25 Insolvency Act 1986, ss.72B-72G, inserted by s.250 of the Enterprise Act 2002.
26 Inserted by s.250 of the Enterprise Act 2002.
27 *Lipe Ltd v Leyland Daf Ltd* [1993] B.C.C. 385.

charge which requires registration under section 395 of the Companies Act 1985, since that provision applies only to companies. But the seller must still show that the clause, in its express terms or on its true construction, creates the rights for which he contends. Many of the problems of scope and interpretation which have been discussed above in relation to sales to companies will therefore equally arise where the buyer is not a company. Certain statutory provisions[28] must, however, also be taken into account where the buyer is unincorporated.

A "Romalpa" clause may be affected by the Bills of Sale Acts 1878 and 1882.[29] A clause by which the seller reserves to himself title in the goods to be sold will not be caught by these Acts. The buyer does not give or confer any assurance of or right to seize goods which are his property.[30] But the situation may be different where the application of a manufacturing process to the goods vests title to the manufactured product in the buyer.[31] If the buyer, by a "Romalpa" clause contained in a document,[32] then grants to the seller the legal title, or some equitable right, to the product and the seller has power, either with or without notice, and either immediately or at any future time, to seize or take possession of the product, the document will constitute a bill of sale.[33] The same applies to any article in which the goods supplied are incorporated.[34] An absolute bill of sale, that is, one which transfers the chattels comprised in it absolutely to the seller, will be void against the buyer's creditors unless registered.[35] If it is a security bill, then it will be void even as between the parties to it unless made in the statutory form.[36] **5–167**

The Bills of Sale Acts do not apply to choses in action.[37] But section 344 of the Insolvency Act 1986[38] provides that, where a person engaged in any business makes a general assignment to another person of his existing or **5–168**

---

[28] The most serious threat to the seller's retention of title was at one time the "reputed ownership" provision in s.38(c) of the Bankruptcy Act 1914. But the 1914 Act was entirely repealed by the Insolvency Act 1985. The Insolvency Act 1986 (which replaced the 1985 Act) contains no such provision.

[29] Bills of Sale Act 1878; Bills of Sale Act 1878 (Amendment) Act 1882.

[30] *McEntire v Crossley Brothers Ltd* [1895] A.C. 457 at 462. However, a sale of goods to a finance company and a repurchase of the goods from the finance company subject to retention of title clause in favour of the finance company may give rise to a bill of sale: *Re Curtain Dream Plc* [1990] B.C.L.C. 925; see above, para.1–066.

[31] See above, para.5–149.

[32] *North Central Wagon Co. v Manchester, Sheffield and Lincolnshire Ry* (1887) 35 Ch.D. 191 at 207; *Beckett v Tower Assets Co.* [1891] 1 Q.B. 638 at 647; *Waight v Waight and Walker* [1952] 2 All E.R. 290 at 292.

[33] Bills of Sale Act 1878, s.3. But Tettenborn [1981] J.B.L. 173 suggests that it falls within the exception created by s.4 of the 1878 Act. See also *Reeves v Barlow* (1884) 12 Q.B.D. 436; All cock, 131 N.L.J. 842 (1981); and (trust receipts) *Re Young, Hamilton & Co.* [1905] 2 K.B. 381 (affirmed *ibid.*, p.772); below, para.18–238.

[34] *Specialist Plant Services Ltd v Braithwaite Ltd* (1987) 3 B.C.C. 119; above, para.5–150, n.32. *Cf. Akron Tyre Co. Pty Ltd v Kittson* (1951) 82 C.L.R. 477.

[35] Bills of Sale Act 1878, ss.8, 10.

[36] Bills of Sale Act 1878 (Amendment) Act 1882, ss.4, 8, 9, 10.

[37] Bills of Sale Act 1878, s.4.

[38] Re-enacting, in more modern words, s.43 of the Bankruptcy Act 1914. For the purpose of the subsection, "assignment" includes an assignment by way of security or charge: s.344(3)(a).

future book debts, or any class of them, and is subsequently adjudged bankrupt, the assignment is void against the trustee of the bankrupt's estate as regards book debts which were not paid before the presentation of the bankruptcy petition unless the assignment has been registered[39] under the Bills of Sale Act 1878. An assignment under a "Romalpa" clause by the buyer to the seller of existing or future debts due to the buyer from sub-purchasers of the goods would be caught by this provision.[40] In practice it would be impossible for the debtors or contracts to be specified with sufficient particularity to remove them[41] from the operation of this subsection.

5–169 **Unfair clauses.** Where the buyer is a consumer, that is, where he is acting for purposes outside his business, trade or profession, certain types of extended "Romalpa" clause might be held to be unfair and so not binding on him under the Unfair Terms in Consumer Contracts Regulations 1999.[42]

5–170 **Disadvantages of a "Romalpa" clause.** It is submitted that, *vis-à-vis* sub-purchasers, the buyer prima facie sells as principal and not as agent for the seller,[43] so that the seller would not be liable to a sub-purchaser in respect of defects in the goods or for a breach of an express undertaking given by the buyer concerning the goods. Nevertheless, certain disadvantages may flow from the inclusion of a "Romalpa" clause in a contract of sale. If the seller retains title to the goods, then prima facie the risk remains with him.[44] Also, under section 49 of the Sale of Goods Act 1979, a seller may maintain an action for the price of the goods (as opposed to an action for damages for non-acceptance) only where the property in the goods has passed to the buyer, unless the price is payable on a certain day irrespective of delivery.[45] It is therefore important to provide that risk shall pass to the buyer and that the seller may maintain an action for the price notwithstanding that he retains ownership of the goods.[46] If the risk remains with the seller and the contract is one for the sale of specific goods, the loss or destruction of the goods may avoid the contract.[47] Further, if any adverse right over the goods is created before the time when the property is to pass, the seller may be in breach of the undertakings as to title implied by section 12(1) and section 12(2)(a) of the 1979 Act.[48] Yet another practical disadvantage is that, under section 36(4)(b) of the Value Added Tax Act 1994 the availability of Value Added Tax relief on bad debts is limited, *inter*

[39] See s.344(4).
[40] *Cf.* McCormack, *Reservation of Title* (2nd ed.), p.140.
[41] See s.344(3)(b)(i) of the 1986 Act.
[42] See below, para.14–030.
[43] *Aluminium Industrie Vaassen BV v Romalpa Aluminium Ltd* [1976] 1 W.L.R. 676 at 690; *Re Bond Worth Ltd* [1980] Ch. 228 at 262–263; McCormack 11 B.L.R. 109 (1990).
[44] Sale of Goods Act 1979, s.20; see below, para.6–002.
[45] See below, paras 16–021, 16–025.
[46] See below, para.6–003, 16–028.
[47] Sale of Goods Act 1979, s.7; below, para.6–035.
[48] See above, para.4–002.

alia, to situations where "in the case of a supply of goods, the property in the goods has passed to the person to whom they were supplied or to a person deriving title from, through or under that person", although Customs and Excise conceded entitlement to bad debt relief if title had passed to the insolvent debtor by the time the relief was claimed, *e.g.* if title had been formally transferred to the liquidator as agent for the debtor company before the claim was made.[49]

[49] CCAB. TR 388 (May 7, 1980); VAT Leaflet 700/18/86 (April 1, 1986). See also (on VAT) Value Added Tax (Refunds for Bad Debts) Regulations 1991, SI 1991/371; *Vernitron Ltd v The Commissioners* [1978] V.A.T.T.R. 157; *Potter v Customs and Excise Commissioners* [1985] S.T.C. 45.

Chapter 6

RISK AND FRUSTRATION

	PARA.
1. Risk	6–002
(a) Property and risk	6–002
(b) Consumer sales	6–013
(c) Carriage of goods to the buyer	6–017
(d) Delay in delivery of the goods	6–023
(e) Liability as bailee	6–026
(f) Benefits	6–033
2. Frustration	6–034
(a) Specific goods which have perished	6–035
(b) Other instances of frustration	6–041
(c) Express clauses	6–056
(d) Consequences of frustration	6–058

In general. It is important to distinguish between risk and frustration in relation to contracts of sale of goods, although it is sometimes difficult to delimit exactly the scope of each of these principles.[1] A question of risk will arise when the goods which have been agreed to be sold[2] are lost or destroyed, damaged or deteriorate, and it is necessary to decide whether the seller or the buyer shall bear the loss. If the risk lies on the seller and the goods are lost or damaged, so that he is no longer able to deliver goods in accordance with the contract or at all, he will not be entitled to recover the price from the buyer and must refund any part of the price paid in advance. But the contract is not discharged. If he cannot replace the goods with other goods which comply with the contract, he may be liable in damages for non-delivery since he will not be released from his obligation to deliver. Conversely, if the goods are lost when they are at the buyer's risk, the buyer must nevertheless pay the price.[3] The seller will be released from his obligation to deliver,[4] but not necessarily from his other obligations, *e.g.* to transfer shipping documents. If the goods are damaged, the buyer will not be entitled to refuse to accept them when tendered if they are otherwise conforming goods. **6–001**

Frustration, on the other hand, discharges the contract of sale. Where the contract is frustrated, both parties will forthwith and automatically be released from all obligations falling due after the frustrating event occurs[5]

[1] See Sealy [1972B] C.L.J. 225 at 245, and below, paras 6–037—6–038.
[2] In some instances, the question of risk will also be relevant where the goods have been sold and the property has passed: see below, para.6–023.
[3] *Castle v Playford* (1872) L.R. 7 Ex. 98; *Martineau v Kitching* (1872) L.R. 7 Q.B. 436. An estimate may be required of what would be payable had the loss not occurred: *ibid*.
[4] *McPherson, Thom, Kettle & Co. v Dench Bros* [1921] V.L.R. 437 at 445. *Cf.* Vienna Convention on Contracts for the International Sale of Goods, Art. 66 (above, para.1–024).
[5] Subject to the provisions of the Law Reform (Frustrated Contracts) Act 1943; below, para.6–058.

and the contract will be discharged as from that time. Loss of or damage to the goods is ordinarily dealt with as a question of risk, although instances can arise where such loss or damage avoids or frustrates the contract.[6] Normally, however, a frustrating event, (*e.g.* supervening illegality) does not involve loss of or damage to the goods, but inhibits performance of the contract of sale.

1. RISK[7]

(a) *Property and Risk*

6–002 **Risk follows property.** "As a general rule," said Blackburn J. in *Martineau v Kitching*,[8] "*res perit domino*, the old civil law maxim,[9] is a maxim of our law; and when you can show that the property passed, the risk of the loss prima facie is in the person in whom the property is." This principle is embodied in section 20(1) of the Sale of Goods Act 1979, which enacts: "Unless otherwise agreed, the goods remain at the seller's risk until the property in them is transferred to the buyer,[10] but when the property in them is transferred to the buyer the goods are at the buyer's risk whether delivery[11] has been made or not."[12] The presumption therefore is that risk and property pass together. But property and risk may be separated by agreement[13] or by usage[14] and, where the buyer deals as consumer, risk passes only on delivery of the goods.[15]

6–003 **Contrary agreement.** The parties may, by agreement, evince an intention that the passing of risk is to be separated from the passing of property; and an agreement that one or other shall bear the risk may be inferred from their course of dealing, or by usage binding on both.[16] The parties may

---

[6] See below, paras 6–035, 6–051.
[7] See Sealy [1972B] C.L.J. 225.
[8] (1872) L.R. 7 Q.B. 436 at 454. See also *Hansen v Craig and Rose* (1859) 21 D. 432 at 438.
[9] The rule of Roman law was, in fact, that risk passes when the sale is *perfecta*, and not when the property passes: Just.Inst., above *III.23.3.* A more accurate statement of the civil law is given by Lord Normand in *Comptoir D'Achat et de Vente du Boerenbond Belge SA v Luis de Ridder Limitada* (*The Julia*) [1949] A.C. 293 at 319. See also *Seath v Moore* (1886) 11 App.Cas. 350 at 371, 378.
[10] See above, Ch.5. But see s.7 of the Act: below, para.6–035.
[11] Defined in s.61(1) of the Act: see below, para.8–002.
[12] See *e.g. Healy v Howlett & Sons* [1917] 1 K.B. 337; *Pignataro v Gilroy* [1919] 1 K.B. 459; *Underwood Ltd v Burgh Castle Brick and Cement Syndicate* [1922] 1 K.B. 343; *Wardars (Import and Export) Co. Ltd v W Norwood & Sons Ltd* [1968] 2 Q.B. 663. *Cf.* Vienna Convention on Contracts for the International Sale of Goods, Arts 66–70 (above, para.1–024).
[13] See below, para.6–003.
[14] *Bevington v Dale* (1902) 7 Com.Cas. 112.
[15] See below, para.6–013.
[16] *Martineau v Kitching* (1872) L.R. 7 Q.B. 436; *Castle v Playford* (1872) L.R. 7 Ex. 98; *Anderson v Morice* (1875) L.R. 10 C.P. 609 at 616 (affirmed (1876) 1 App.Cas. 713); *Bevington v Dale* (1902) 7 Com.Cas. 112; *Horn v Minister of Food* [1948] 2 All E.R. 1036; and see below, paras 6–004, 6–010, 6–020.

agree that the risk shall pass only on delivery of the goods. Risk can clearly pass before property where the goods are specific or ascertained, although an intention that the buyer shall assume the risk before the property has vested in him must either be expressed or clearly inferred from the circumstances.[17] In cases where specific goods perish before the property and risk in them passes to the buyer, regard must be had to the provisions of section 7 of the Act.[18]

Identification of the goods. Where the parties agree that the risk is to pass to the buyer before the property, it is clear that the goods must be sufficiently identifiable as those to which the risk relates.[19] It might therefore be thought that the contract must have been one for the sale of specific goods,[20] or, if it was one for the sale of unascertained goods, that the goods should have become ascertained[21] before the risk could pass. But this is not necessarily the case. In certain situations, the risk in goods not yet separated from bulk[22] may be transferred to the buyer notwithstanding that the property in the goods is still vested in the seller. In the case of f.o.b. contracts, for example, the risk in relation to an unascertained part of an ascertained cargo may pass to the buyer on shipment.[23] Also, in *Sterns Ltd v Vickers Ltd*[24] the defendants sold to the claimants 120,000 gallons of white spirit, part of a larger quantity of 200,000 gallons lying in a tank belonging to a storage company, and handed to the claimants a delivery warrant by which the storage company undertook to deliver that quantity of spirit to the claimants' order. The claimants indorsed the warrant to a sub-purchaser, but as he did not desire to take delivery at that time he made his own arrangements for further storage with the company and paid them rent. After some months, but before the quantity purchased had been separated from bulk, the spirit in the tank deteriorated in quality. The Court of Appeal held that, whether or not the property had passed,[25] upon acceptance of the delivery warrant, the risk passed to the claimants and the loss fell on them. Scrutton L.J. said[26]: "The transfer of the undivided interest carries with it the risk of loss from something happening to the goods, such as a deterioration in their quality, at all events after the vendor has given the purchaser a delivery order upon the party in possession of them, and that party has assented to it . . . The vendors had done all that 6–004

---

[17] *Comptoir D'Achat et de Vente du Boerenbond Belge SA v Luis de Ridder Limitada*, above, at p.319. But see c.i.f. and f.o.b. contracts, below, paras 6–018, 19–110, 20–087.
[18] See below, para.6–035.
[19] See also below, para.6–017 and Vienna Convention on Contracts for the International Sale of Goods, Art. 67(2) (above, para.1–024).
[20] Defined in s.61(1): see above, para.1–113.
[21] See s.16 of the Act; above, para.5–059.
[22] See above, para.5–061.
[23] *Stock v Inglis* (1884) 12 Q.B.D. 564, affirmed *sub nom. Inglis v Stock* (1885) 10 App.Cas. 263 (below, para.6–018). See also Incoterms (2000) (F.o.b.), B.5 and below, para.18–300.
[24] [1923] 1 K.B. 78.
[25] See above, para.5–059.
[26] At pp.84–85.

they undertook to do. The purchasers had the right to go to the storage company and demand delivery, and if they had done so at the time they would have got all that the defendants had undertaken to sell them. What the purchasers here are trying to do is to put the risk after acceptance of the warrant upon persons who had then no control over the goods, for it seems plain that after acceptance of that warrant the vendors would have had no right to go to the storage company and request them to refuse delivery to the purchaser."

6–005 This case, however, depends upon its special facts.[27] In *Comptoir d'Achat et de Vente du Boerenbond Belge SA v Luis de Ridder Limitada* (*The Julia*)[28] Lord Normand said[29]: "In those cases in which it has been held that the risk without the property has passed to the buyer it has been because the buyer rather than the seller was seen to have an immediate and practical interest in the goods, as for instance when he has an immediate right under the storekeeper's delivery warrant to the delivery of an undivided bulk in store or an immediate right under several contracts with different persons to the whole of the bulk not yet appropriated to the several contracts." In that case, the risk was held not to have passed to the buyers under an ex facie c.i.f. contract (which was performed as an "ex ship" or "on arrival" contract)[30] for the purchase of 500 tons of rye shipped as part of a larger parcel covered by a single bill of lading which was retained by the sellers or their agents, even though the buyers had received and accepted a delivery order for the rye addressed to the seller's agents at the port of discharge against payment of the price. It is submitted that, at common law, in a domestic sale,[31] the tender to and acceptance by the buyer of a delivery order will normally not pass the risk in part of an undivided bulk stored by a third party, unless and until the third party has (at least) agreed with or acknowledged to the buyer that he will hold the goods on his behalf.

6–006 Section 20A of the 1979 Act,[32] however, now provides that, where there is a contract for the sale of a specified quantity of unascertained goods forming part of an identified bulk, then, as soon as the conditions mentioned in that section are met, property in an undivided share in the bulk is transferred to the buyer and he becomes an owner in common of the bulk. It might be supposed that, unless otherwise agreed, the risk in respect of that undivided share would pass to the buyer at the same time. But section 20B(3)(c)[33] states that nothing in section 20A is to "affect the rights of any buyer under his contract". On one view this saving provision leads to the conclusion that, in deciding whether or not the risk has passed

---

[27] See below, para.18–300. By the terms of the warrant, the storage company may have attorned to the buyer. *Cf.* below, para.18–300, n.20.
[28] [1949] A.C. 293. See also *Cunningham Ltd v R. A. Munro & Co. Ltd* (1922) 28 Com.Cas. 42 (goods prepared for execution of fob contract).
[29] At p.319. See also Lord Porter at p.312.
[30] See above, para.5–102; below, paras 19–003, 20–016.
[31] *cf.* below, para.18–300 (overseas sales).
[32] See above, para.5–109.
[33] See above, para.5–126.

to the buyer in goods not yet separated from bulk, the passing of property under section 20A is to be wholly disregarded and that the allocation of risk is to be determined without reference to the effects of that section. On another view, however, the purpose of the saving provision is simply to make it clear that the rights of the buyer, *e.g.* to sue for damages for non-delivery of the contract goods, are preserved and not to provide that section 20A should be left out of account in determining risk. The latter view is, it is submitted, the better one.[34]

Nevertheless it is suggested that the allocation of risk in cases governed by section 20A cannot satisfactorily be answered merely by referring to the principle that "risk passes with property". The "property" that is transferred to the buyer under section 20A is property in an undivided share and not, until the goods are separated from bulk and appropriated to the contract, the sole property in the goods themselves. It is arguable that, as a general rule, the goods are at the buyer's risk only when the sole property is transferred to him and not from the time of the transfer to him of an undivided share (though the definition of "goods" in section 61(1) includes an undivided share in goods). Yet it would seem remarkable that a seller who has, for example, sold to two buyers each 50,000 gallons of spirit out of a particular tank containing 100,000 gallons should continue to bear the risk (other than in appropriate circumstances as bailee) of damage to or deterioration of the goods rendering them unfit for the purpose for which the buyer requires them, even though the seller, having been paid in full for the entire quantity sold, is no longer the owner of the goods and has divested himself of all interest in them. If the entire bulk from which the goods are to come is not merely damaged or deteriorates but is lost or destroyed, the choice is between placing this risk on the buyer or holding that the contract is frustrated,[35] in which case some apportionment of the loss may arise under the Law Reform (Frustrated Contracts) Act 1943.[36] The matter is not susceptible of an easy solution, but it may be that a court would adopt the opinion of Scrutton L.J. in *Sterns Ltd v Vickers Ltd*[37] that "the transfer of the undivided interest carries with it the risk from something happening to the goods", even in the absence of the additional features referred to by him in that case. Fortunately many situations where section 20A is likely to apply concern the sale and carriage of goods by sea where the rules establishing risk will normally not be affected by its provisions.[38]

A similar problem arises where the bulk from which the goods are to come is identified and agreed on at the time the contract of sale is made and the seller agrees to sell an undivided share, specified as a fraction or percentage, of that bulk, for example, where the seller agrees to sell one-fifth of the white spirit currently lying in a particular tank. Under the **6–007**

---

[34] Especially since risk primarily affects the liabilities, rather than the rights, of the buyer under his contract.

[35] See below, para.6–051.

[36] See below, para.6–058.

[37] [1923] 1 K.B. 78 at 84 (with whom Eve J. agreed).

[38] See below, paras 18–300, 19–110, 20–087.

extended definition of "specific goods" in section 61(1) of the Act[39] the undivided share is, as well as the bulk, specific goods for the purposes of the Act. To this situation section 20A has no application, since that section applies only to a contract for the sale of a specified quantity of *unascertained* goods forming part of an identified bulk. But the effect of such a contract is nevertheless the same at common law: to transfer to the buyer property in an undivided share in the bulk and the buyer becomes an owner in common of the bulk.[40] In this case the property in the undivided share will be transferred at such time as the parties intend it to be transferred. The same result ensues in the case of a sale of an undivided share, specified as a fraction or percentage, of specific goods where the parties envisage that the undivided share will remain permanently undivided and never be separated from the "bulk" of which it forms part, *e.g.* a contract for the sale of a quarter share in a named racehorse.[41] In either case, it is probable that, unless otherwise agreed, the risk in relation to the undivided share will be transferred to the buyer at the same time as the property in the undivided share, so that if the bulk of which the undivided share forms part is lost, destroyed, damaged or deteriorates, the risk will lie on the buyer and he will remain liable to pay the contract price.

6–008 Assuming that the risk in relation to an undivided share may pass to the buyer in any of the situations referred to above, the question arises as to the consequences of the loss, destruction, damage or deterioration of part only of the bulk. If the seller has sold shares amounting to the whole of the bulk to a number of buyers, then as between them the most likely result appears to be that each buyer will bear the risk *pro rata* to the extent of his share in the bulk.[42] But more difficulty surrounds the situation where the seller has agreed to sell only some of the bulk. Where he has, for example, agreed to sell to a buyer an undivided share, specified as a fraction or percentage, say one-fifth, of the white spirit currently lying in a particular tank, and one-half of the spirit in the tank is destroyed, it would seem that the buyer remains liable to pay the contract price but is entitled to delivery of only one-fifth of the spirit that remains, bearing the risk in respect of the destroyed portion *pro rata* with the seller. On the other hand, if, for example, the bulk consists of 100,000 gallons and the seller has agreed to sell to a buyer (and has been paid for) 20,000 gallons out of that quantity, the loss of 50,000 gallons of the bulk will still enable the seller to fulfil his contract with the buyer out of the spirit that remains. It is arguable that the seller must still deliver 20,000 gallons and that the buyer would only commence to bear the risk if less than that quantity remained.[43] But if the risk in relation to the undivided share of 20,000 gallons purchased by the buyer is held to have passed to him together with the property in that undivided share, then he should bear a *pro rata* share of the loss. He will be

---

[39] As amended by s.2(d) of the Sale of Goods (Amendment) Act 1995; see above, paras 5–112, 5–128.
[40] See above, para.5–129.
[41] See above, para.1–116.
[42] See below, para.18–306.
[43] Burns, 59 M.L.R. 260 at 269 (1996); Goode, *Commercial Law*, (3rd ed.), 227, 257.

entitled to delivery of only 10,000 of the 50,000 gallons which remain and cannot recover that part of the purchase price paid which relates to the undelivered quantity.

Goods delivered on approval or on sale or return. Where goods are delivered to a buyer on approval or "on sale or return" or other similar terms, then, in the absence of a contrary agreement,[44] the risk lies on the seller unless and until the property has passed to the buyer,[45] provided that any loss of or damage to the goods occurs without the buyer's fault.[46] 6–009

Condition subsequent. The parties may, however, intend that the property in the goods should pass to the buyer immediately, but subject to a condition subsequent[47] which will revest the property in the seller should the buyer disapprove the goods.[48] Since section 20 provides that risk prima facie passes with property, it would be expected that the buyer would bear the risk of any loss of or damage to the goods which occurred before he disapproved them. But in the pre-Act case of *Head v Tattersall*[49] the claimant bought from the defendant, an auctioneer, a horse which was described in the auction catalogue as having been hunted with the Bicester hounds. The contract of sale contained a condition that "horses not answering the description must be returned before 5 o'clock on Wednesday evening next; otherwise the purchaser shall be obliged to keep the lot with all faults." The horse had not, in fact, been hunted with the Bicester hounds, and the claimant returned it before the stated time. In the meantime, however, it had been injured by no fault of the claimant while in his possession. In an action by the claimant for the recovery of the price, the defendant pleaded an implied term that the horse, if returned, should be returned in the same state as that in which it was delivered, and without having been injured. The Court of Exchequer held that the injury did not cause the claimant to lose his right to return the horse. This case would appear to establish no more than that the buyer's right to reject goods for failure to correspond with their contractual description is not taken away by the fact that they have in the meantime been damaged without his fault.[50] But in his judgment Cleasby B. said[51]: "As a general rule, damage from the depreciation of a chattel ought to fall on the person who is the owner of it. Now here the effect of the contract was to vest the property in the buyer subject to a right of rescission in a particular event when it would revest in 6–010

---

44 *Bianchi v Nash* (1836) 1 M. & W. 545; *Bevington v Dale* (1902) 7 Com.Cas. 112.
45 Sale of Goods Act 1979, s.18, r.4; above, para.5–040.
46 See above, para.5–055. The buyer is, however, not technically a buyer within the definition in s.61(1) since he has not "bought or agreed to buy" the goods: see *Edwards v Vaughan* (1910) 26 T.L.R. 545, and above, para.5–044. But s.18, r.4, refers to "buyer" and "seller".
47 See above, para.5–043.
48 See above, para.5–043.
49 (1871) L.R. 7 Ex. 7. See Sealy [1972B] C.L.J. 225.
50 Bramwell B. (at p.13) also considered that the contract could have been rescinded even if the horse had died without the buyer's default. See also *Chapman v Withers* (1888) 20 Q.B.D. 824.
51 At pp.13, 14.

the seller. I think in such a case that the person who is eventually entitled to the property in the chattel ought to bear any loss arising from any depreciation in its value caused by an accident for which nobody is in fault. Here the defendant is the person in whom the property is revested, and he must therefore bear the loss." It is submitted, however, that this statement should not be taken to extend to a situation where the buyer is permitted, without any breach on the part of the seller, to return the goods sold to him, *e.g.* where clothing purchased is not of the appropriate size. It would then be the intention of the parties that the contract should be subject to a condition of the type pleaded by the defendant in *Head v Tattersall*, so that the goods would effectively be at the buyer's risk until they are returned to the seller.

6–011 **Risk in relation to rejected goods.** The case of *Head v Tattersall*[52] raises the more general issue of the incidence of risk in respect of rejected goods.[53] If, after the property in the goods has passed to the buyer, he justifiably rejects the goods, the question arises whether and, if so, in what circumstances the risk of any loss of or damage to or deterioration of the goods in the intervening period revests in[54] or is deemed to have remained with the seller.[55] This matter is discussed in Chapter 12 of this work.[56] If goods are rightfully rejected, but the seller neglects or refuses to collect them,[57] the buyer would appear thereafter to be an involuntary bailee,[58] being liable only for deliberate injury to the goods or for gross negligence, but not for ordinary negligence.[59]

6–012 **Insurable interest.** The question of the allocation of risk is often of importance where a claim is made on an insurance policy, since the insured must have an insurable interest in the goods at the time of the loss.[60] It will be sufficient that the goods are at his risk even though he has no property in them.[61] The topic of insurance is, however, outside the scope of this work and reference should be made to specialist treatises on insurance law.

---

52 (1871) L.R. 7 Ex.7.

53 See Law Comm. Working Paper No. 85 (1983), paras 2.60, 4.76–4.80; Law Comm. Report, *Sale and Supply of Goods* (1987), Cmnd. 137, para.5.40; Uniform Commercial Code, para.2–510(1).

54 See *Head v Tattersall*, above, at pp.13, 14; *Vitol SA v Esso Australia Ltd* [1989] 1 Lloyd's Rep. 96.

55 See (in Scots law) *Kinnear v J & D Brodie* (1902) 3 F. 540 at 544, 545; *Boyd & Forrest v Glasgow & SW Ry Co.* 1915 S.C. (HL) 21 at 29.

56 Below, para.12–057.

57 See s.36 of the Act; below, para.12–065.

58 *Heugh v L & NW Ry Co.* (1870) L.R. 5 Ex. 51 (carrier).

59 *Hiort v Bott* (1874) L.R. 9 Ex. 86 at 90; *Howard v Harris* (1884) Cab. & El. 253. But contrast *Newman v Bourne and Hollingsworth* (1915) 31 T.L.R. 209; *Summer v Challenor* (1926) 70 S.J. 760; *Elvin and Powell Ltd v Plummer Roddis Ltd* (1933) 50 T.L.R. 158; *Houghland v RR Low (Luxury Coaches) Ltd* [1962] 1 Q.B. 694 at 698; *Chitty on Contracts* (29th ed.), Vol. 2, para.33–036.

60 See *Anderson v Morice* (1876) 1 App.Cas. 713; Marine Insurance Act 1906, ss.4–8, and generally *Chitty on Contracts* (29th ed.), Vol. 2, paras 41–003—41–016. But see also Marine Insurance Act 1906, s.4; and above, para.5–012.

61 See, *e.g. Inglis v Stock* (1885) 10 App.Cas. 263; *Colonial Insurance Co. of New Zealand v Adelaide Marine Insurance Co.* (1886) 12 App.Cas. 128.

(b) *Consumer Sales*

Buyer dealing as consumer. The presumption that risk passes with property does not apply where the buyer "deals as consumer"—a technical expression which is to be construed in accordance with Part I of the Unfair Contract Terms Act, 1977.[62] In such a case, section 20(4) of the 1979 Act provides that subsection (1) of section 20 "must be ignored" and that "the goods remain at the seller's risk until they are delivered to the consumer".[63] Thus, even though the property in the goods has passed to the buyer, the risk will pass to him only on delivery. This may better accord with the expectations of the parties in a consumer transaction: that the risk is to pass to the buyer only when he comes into possession of the goods and not before. However, it must be appreciated that delivery does not inevitably entail the transfer of actual physical possession of the goods by the seller to the buyer. Delivery may be actual or constructive.[64] There may be a delivery of goods to the buyer even though they never leave the physical custody of the seller[65] or of a third party (such as a warehouseman) who is holding the goods.[66] Transfer of physical possession is also unnecessary in cases of symbolic delivery[67] and the transfer of the goods to a third party nominated by the buyer, and not to the buyer himself, can constitute delivery.[68] Nevertheless, subject to these qualifications, in most business-to-consumer sales it will be the physical transfer of the goods by the seller to the buyer that will pass the risk. 6–013

Contrary agreement. Section 20(4) was inserted into the 1979 Act by the Sale and Supply of Goods to Consumers Regulations 2002[69] which were made under section 2(2) of the European Communities Act 1972 with a view to implementing Directive 1999/44/EC on certain aspects of the sale of consumer goods and associated guarantees.[70] Article 7.1 of the Directive[71] invalidates (though by reference to national law) the waiver or restriction of the rights of the consumer resulting from the Directive. However, although the Directive requires the seller to deliver to the consumer goods which are in conformity with the contract of sale[72] and provides that the seller is to be liable to the consumer for any lack of conformity which exists at the time the goods were delivered[73] the preamble to the Directive expressly states that "the references to the time of delivery do not imply that Member States have to change their rules on the passing of the risk".[74] It is therefore 6–014

---

[62] s.61(5A); see below, para.13–071.
[63] See the *Special Supplement to Benjamin's Sale of Goods* (6th ed), para.1–078.
[64] s.61(1) and below, para.8–002.
[65] See below, para.8–009.
[66] s.29(4) and below, para.8–012.
[67] See below, para.8–008.
[68] See below, para.8–007.
[69] SI 2002/3045; see below, para.12–071.
[70] See below, para.14–008.
[71] See below, para.14–028.
[72] Art.2.1.
[73] Art.3.1.
[74] para.(14).

submitted that the changes in the law relating to risk effected by the Regulations were not required by the Directive and that the consumer's rights deriving therefrom are not "rights resulting from the Directive"[75] There is consequently nothing in the Directive to prevent the parties in a consumer transaction from agreeing that the risk shall pass to the buyer at some time before delivery of the goods. Nor is there anything in the 1979 Act to prevent such an agreement.[76] Nevertheless, a term in the contract of sale to that effect may in some circumstances be subject to the test of reasonableness imposed by the Unfair Contract Terms Act 1977[77] or to the test of fairness imposed by the Unfair Terms in Consumer Contracts Regulations 1999.[78] Under the 1977 Act, the term is required to be "a fair and reasonable one to be included having regard to the circumstances which were or ought reasonably to have been known to or in the contemplation of the parties when the contract was made",[79] the burden of proof resting upon the seller.[80] Under the 1999 Regulations a term which has not been individually negotiated is to be regarded as unfair (and so void against the consumer) if, contrary to the requirement of good faith, it causes a significant imbalance in the parties' rights and obligations arising under the contract to the detriment of the consumer.[81] It is probable that, in a consumer transaction, a term in a standard form contract by which it was agreed that the risk should pass to the buyer before delivery would now be regarded as unreasonable or unfair unless there were special circumstances (for example, the perishable nature of the goods[82] or the fact that the buyer was, or the seller was not, in control of them) which would justify such a term.

6–015 **Refusal to take delivery.** If the buyer wrongfully refuses to take delivery when tendered, it is possible that the seller could treat the delivery as having been duly made and the risk would then pass. More probably, however, the seller would be put to an election either to treat the contract as repudiated, accept the repudiation and sue for damages for non-acceptance[83] or to treat the contract as still continuing and to sue for damages under section 37(1) of the Act.[84] That subsection provides that if the buyer does not, within a reasonable time of being requested to do so, take delivery of the goods, he is liable "for any loss occasioned by his neglect or refusal to take delivery". Such loss could, it is submitted, in appropriate circumstances include loss arising from damage to or destruction or deterioration of the goods occurring after a reasonable time had elapsed while the goods were still at the seller's risk.

---

[75] See the *Special Supplement to Benjamin's Sale of Goods* (6th ed.), paras 1–077, 1–093.
[76] s.55(1).
[77] See below, para.13–086.
[78] See below, para.14–030.
[79] s.11(1) of the 1977 Act.
[80] s.61(5A) of the 1979 Act.
[81] Reg.5.
[82] See below, para.6–025.
[83] s.50; see below, para.16–060—16–081.
[84] See below, para.9–009.

Repair and replacement. If the buyer deals as consumer[85] and the goods do not conform to the contract of sale[86] at the time of delivery, Part 5A of the Act gives to the buyer a right to require the seller to repair or replace the goods.[87] The Act is silent as to the incidence of risk during the period of repair or replacement. But since it is provided that the costs incurred in repair or replacement must be borne by the seller,[88] it seems probable that the risk of loss of or damage to the goods during that period would be placed on the seller so that he will bear the risk, for example, of loss or damage in transit from the time the goods leave the possession of the buyer until the repaired or replaced goods are re-delivered to the buyer. The question, however, arises whether the buyer can require the seller to repair or replace goods which did not conform to the contract of sale at the time of delivery but which have been lost or damaged after delivery without any fault on the part of the buyer. It is submitted that, having regard to the fact that the risk ordinarily passes to the buyer on delivery, he must in principle bear the risk of such loss or damage and could not require the seller to repair or replace the lost or damaged goods unless the loss or damage was attributable to the non-conformity. It is nevertheless arguable that the risk should re-vest in the seller immediately the buyer notified him that he required the goods to be repaired or replaced,[89] or even that it might do so as soon as the non-conforming goods were delivered since it is then that the buyer's right to require repair or replacement in fact accrues. 6–016

(c) *Carriage of Goods to the Buyer*

Delivery to carrier. In those instances where the property in the goods passes to the buyer on delivery to a carrier,[90] the risk prima facie passes with the property.[91] It has, however, been previously pointed out that, if the contract is one for the sale of unascertained goods, the property will normally not pass to the buyer by delivery to the carrier unless and until the goods become ascertained,[92] and it seems that the risk will not in principle pass until that time.[93] Also, where the buyer deals as consumer, delivery of the goods to a carrier is not delivery of the goods to the buyer[94] and the risk will pass only on their delivery to the buyer.[95] Otherwise, in a commercial transaction, the risk in principle passes on delivery to the carrier. 6–017

---

[85] See above, para.6–013; below, para.13–070.
[86] S.48F; see below, para.12–074.
[87] See below, para.12–076.
[88] s.48B(2).
[89] See also below, para.12–085.
[90] See above, para.5–096.
[91] *Underwood Ltd v Burgh Castle Brick and Cement Syndicate* [1922] 1 K.B. 343 (above, para.5–023). *Cf.* Vienna Convention on Contracts for the International Sale of Goods, Art. 67 (above, para.1–024).
[92] *Healy v Howlett & Sons* [1917] 1 K.B. 337 (above, para.5–099).
[93] *ibid.*
[94] s.32(4).
[95] s.20(4); above, para.6–013.

6–018 Special rules have nevertheless been developed in relation to overseas sales. The case of *Stock v Inglis*[96] shows that risk in relation to the unascertained part of a larger bulk may pass under an f.o.b. contract on shipment, even though the goods remain unascertained. Further, where goods are sold on c.i.f. terms, the property will usually pass to the buyer only on unconditional delivery of the bill of lading.[97] But the risk is prima facie transferred on shipment or as from shipment, and the seller is often entitled to tender the shipping documents to the buyer and claim the price where the goods have been lost in transit.[98] These and other special rules[99] are dealt with later in this book.

6–019 **Seller's responsibilities at point of delivery.** The prima facie rule that risk passes on delivery to the carrier in a commercial transaction is, however, subject to a number of qualifications. In particular, it is to be qualified by the principle enunciated in *Beer v Walker*[1] and also by Diplock J. in *Mash and Murrell Ltd v Joseph I Emanuel Ltd*[2] that, when goods are sold under a contract which involves transit before use, there is an implied term in the contract of sale that the goods should be despatched in such a condition that they can endure the normal journey and upon arrival at their destination[3] be suitable for the ordinary purpose for which such goods are intended to be used and be of satisfactory quality. This does not mean that the seller guarantees the state of the goods on arrival at their destination; his undertaking relates to their state at the place of delivery to the carrier and to their capacity to survive normal transit. The effect therefore is that "an extraordinary deterioration of the goods due to abnormal conditions experienced during the transit [is one] for which the buyer takes the risk. A necessary and inevitable deterioration during transit which will render them unmerchantable on arrival is normally one for which the seller is liable."[4]

---

[96] (1884) 12 Q.B.D. 564, affirmed (1885) 10 App.Cas. 263. See below, paras 18–301, 20–086. *Cf.* Vienna Convention on Contracts for the International Sale of Goods, Art. 67(2) (above, para.1–024); Incoterms (2000) (F.o.b.), B.5.

[97] See above, para.5–102; below, para.19–102.

[98] See below, paras 19–080, 19–082. See also Incoterms (2000), (C.i.f.), B.5.

[99] C.& f. contracts (below, para.21–013); f.a.s. contracts (below, para.21–011); "ex ship" contracts (below, para.21–020); containers (below, para.21–100).

[1] (1877) 46 L.J.Q.B. 677. See also *Burrows v Smith* (1894) 10 T.L.R. 246.

[2] [1961] 1 W.L.R. 862, reversed on other grounds: [1962] 1 W.L.R. 16 (c. & f. contract). See also *Ollett v Jordan* [1918] 2 K.B. 41 at 48; *Evanghelinos v Leslie and Anderson* (1920) 4 Ll.L.R. 17 at 18; *Broome v Pardess Co-operative Society* [1939] 3 All E.R. 978 (reversed on other grounds: [1940] 1 All E.R. 603); *AB Kemp Ltd v Tolland* [1956] 2 Lloyd's Rep. 681 at 685; *H Glynn (Covent Garden) Ltd v Wittleder* [1959] 2 Lloyd's Rep. 409; *Gardano and Giampieri v Greek Petroleum George Mamidakis & Co.* [1962] 1 W.L.R. 40 at 53; *Georgetown Seafoods Ltd v Usen Fisheries Ltd* (1977) 78 D.L.R. (3d) 542; *Gatoil International Inc. v Tradax Petroleum Ltd* [1985] 1 Lloyd's Rep. 350 at 358. *Cf. Bowden Bros & Co. Ltd v Little* (1907) 4 C.L.R. 1364; *George Wills & Son Ltd v Thomas Brown & Sons* (1922) 12 Ll.L.R 292; *Kelly, Douglas & Co. Ltd v Pollock* (1958) 14 D.L.R. (2d) 526; *Oleificio Zucchi SpA. v Northern Sales Ltd* [1965] 2 Lloyd's Rep. 496; *Cordova Land Co. Ltd v Victor Bros Inc.* [1966] 1 W.L.R. 793. See also below, paras 11–049, 11–067, 18–255.

[3] And for a reasonable time thereafter to allow for disposal or use: see *Mash and Murrell Ltd v Joseph I Emanuel Ltd*, above.

[4] *Mash and Murrell Ltd v Joseph I Emanuel Ltd*, above, at p.871. But see Sassoon, 28 M.L.R. 189 (1965) and below, para.6–022.

6–020 **Payment on arrival.** The risk will not necessarily be placed upon the seller during transit merely because the price is payable on delivery of the shipping documents[5] or at a time calculated with reference to the arrival of the goods at their destination,[6] or is to be ascertained by some act to be done to them after their arrival.[7] Such provisions may be intended only to regulate the time of payment, or the amount of the price, if the goods are not lost. But where the contract expressly or by implication provides that the whole or part of the price of the goods is to be payable only if the goods arrive at their destination, or are actually delivered to the buyer, the risk of loss during transit will remain with the seller in so far as he cannot claim the price of the goods or the unpaid part of it until the goods actually arrive, even though the property may have passed to the buyer.[8]

6–021 **Notification of shipment.** Section 32(3) of the Act of 1979[9] provides: "Unless otherwise agreed, where goods are sent by the seller to the buyer by a route involving sea transit, under circumstances in which it is usual to insure, the seller must give such notice to the buyer as may enable him to insure them during their sea transit; and if the seller fails to do so, the goods are at his risk during such sea transit." The rule embodied in this subsection is taken from Scots law, and possibly has been extended.[10] It will apply to an f.o.b. contract under which the contract of carriage is made by the seller[11] and also to a c. & f. contract.[12] A buyer under a c.i.f. contract is not entitled to receive timely notice of shipment by virtue of this provision unless there are risks not covered by the seller against which it is usual for the buyer to insure,[13] because in such contracts it is the seller's duty to insure.[14] "Ex ship" contracts are likewise excluded from the operation of

---

[5] *Anderson v Morice* (1876) 1 App.Cas. 713.
[6] *Fragano v Long* (1825) 4 B. & C. 219.
[7] *Castle v Playford* (1872) L.R. 7 C.P. 436.
[8] *Calcutta & Burmah Steam Navigation Co. v De Mattos* (1863) 32 L.J.Q.B. 322 at 328; 33 L.J.Q.B. 214. See also *Dupont v British South Africa Co.* (1901) 18 T.L.R. 24; *Polenghi v Dried Milk Co.* (1904) 10 Com.Cas. 42 (purported "c.i.f." contracts, below, para.21–015) and below, para.21–020 ("ex ship" contracts). The question whether the seller is, in addition, liable for damages for non-delivery will depend on the construction of the contract: see *Calcutta & Burmah Steam Navigation Co. v De Mattos*, above.
[9] This sub section does not apply (and is indeed otiose) where the buyer deals as consumer: s.32(4).
[10] *Fleet v Morrison* (1854) 16 D. 1122 at 1124; *Hastie v Campbell* (1857) 19 D. 557 at 567; *Wimble Sons & Co. v Rosenberg & Sons* [1913] 3 K.B. 743 at 762. *Cf.* Vienna Convention on the International Sale of Goods, Art. 32 (above, para.1–024).
[11] *Wimble Sons & Co. v Rosenberg & Sons*, above, followed in *Northern Steel and Hardware Co. Ltd v John Batt & Co. (London) Ltd* (1917) 33 T.L.R. 516. See also *Pyrene Co. Ltd v Scindia Navigation Co. Ltd* [1954] 2 Q.B. 402 at 424 and below, paras 18–246, 20–039, 20–091.
[12] See below, para.21–013.
[13] *Law and Bonar Ltd v British American Tobacco Co. Ltd* [1916] 2 K.B. 605. See also *Re Weis & Co. Ltd and Credit Colonial et Commercial (Antwerp)* [1916] 1 K.B. 346, and below, paras 18–246, 19–117.
[14] In many c.i.f. contracts, however, an express term is inserted requiring a declaration of shipment, and the breach of such a stipulation entitles the buyer to treat the contract as discharged: see *Reuter v Sala* (1879) 4 C.P.D. 239 and below, para.19–017. *Cf. Aure v Van Cauwenberghe & Fils* [1938] 2 All E.R. 300.

the rule.[15] It is probable that this subsection could be extended by analogy to cases where goods are carried otherwise than by sea transit, *e.g.* by land or air, or by combined land and sea transit.[16] It is a moot point whether, under the subsection, the entire risk during transit is to be borne by the seller or only such risks as would have been covered by insurance had timely notice been given. The former is more likely from the wording of the subsection.

6–022 **Goods sent at seller's risk.** Section 33 of the 1979 Act provides that, where the seller of goods agrees to deliver them at his own risk at a place other than that where they are when sold, the buyer must nevertheless (unless otherwise agreed)[17] take any risk of deterioration in the goods necessarily incident in the course of transit.[18] It will be observed that the terms of this section only apply to cases where the seller has agreed to assume the risk during transit, either by express agreement or by implication as in the case of "ex ship"[19] or arrival contracts; but it is probable that the same principle applies in situations where, under the normal rules as to the passing of risk,[20] the goods would be at his risk during transit.[21] If such is the case, the section will apply even where the buyer deals as consumer[22] and in consequence the goods are then still at the seller's risk.[23] The effect of this section is that "[the vendor] must indeed stand the risk of any extraordinary or unusual deterioration; but the vendee is bound to accept the article if only deteriorated to the extent that it is necessarily subject to in the course of transit from one place to the other."[24] The question arises, however, whether and, if so, to what extent this section must be qualified by the principle in *Beer v Walker*[25] and *Mash and Murrell Ltd v Joseph I. Emanuel Ltd*[26] previously referred to.[27] It is to be noted that this latter principle was enunciated with reference to cases where, under the terms of the contract, the seller's duty was merely to despatch the goods, so that the risk passed to the buyer on delivery to the carrier. It was not stated to extend to the situation envisaged in section 33 of the Act.[28–29] Nevertheless, it would seem that the words "necessarily incident to the course of transit" should not be taken to extend to cases where the particular goods are despatched by the seller in such a state as to be unable to withstand normal transit, but only to cover deterioration which all goods of the kind called for by the contract would necessarily suffer during transit.

---

[15] See below, para.21–014.
[16] See below, para.18–246 and para.21–101 (containers).
[17] The seller may expressly or impliedly agree to assume the risk of even necessary deterioration.
[18] For a discussion of "transit," see below, para.18–250.
[19] See below, para.21–014.
[20] *i.e.* under s.20(1). It is doubtful whether the same principle would apply in the cases envisaged by s.32(2), (3) of the Act: see below, para.18–252.
[21] *Bull v Robison* (1854) 10 Exch. 342.
[22] See above, paras 6–013, 6–017
[23] See above, para.6–013.
[24] (1854) 10 Exch. at p.346. See also below, para.18–251.
[25] (1877) 46 L.J.Q.B. 677.
[26] [1961] 1 W.L.R. 862, reversed on other grounds [1962] 1 W.L.R. 16.
[27] See above, para.6–019.
[28–29] Sassoon, 28 M.L.R. 189 (1965).

(d) *Delay in Delivery of the Goods*

6–023 **Effect of delay.** Section 20(2) of the Sale of Goods Act 1979 states: "But where delivery[30] has been delayed through the fault[31] of either buyer or seller the goods[32] are at the risk of the party at fault as regards any loss which might not have occurred but for such fault."[33] It should be observed that this subsection relates to delay in delivery, and not to delay in the passing of property.[34] It contemplates a situation where the risk would otherwise lie with one party, but because of delay in delivery through the fault of the other party, the latter must bear the risk of any loss which might not have occurred but for such fault.[35]

6–024 **Entire risk not transferred.** The subsection does not, however, throw the entire risk upon the party at fault, but only the risk of such loss as is causally attributable to his fault.[36] It is nevertheless arguable that the use of the word "might"[37] places on the party in fault the onus of showing positively that this loss would have occurred independently of his fault. But this was not the view taken by Sellers J. in *Demby Hamilton & Co. Ltd v Barden*[38] where the subsection was applied. In that case, the sellers had agreed to sell 30 tons of apple juice which the buyer had ordered "as per sample" for delivery to third parties. The sellers crushed the apples and put the juice into casks pending delivery. The buyer took delivery of part of the juice, but was late in taking delivery of the remainder as he could get no instructions from the third parties. Because of the delay, the remaining part of the juice became putrid and had to be destroyed. Although the property had not passed to the buyer, it was held that he bore the risk of deterioration. Sellers J. said[39]: "I am not going so far in this case as to say that I place the onus on the buyer to show that the loss did not occur or might not have occurred. I think that all the facts and circumstances have to be looked at in very much the same way as a jury would look at them in order to see whether the loss can properly be attributed to the failure of the

---

30 Defined in s.61(1); see below, para.8–002.
31 Defined in s.61(1) as meaning "wrongful act or default".
32 The "goods" in this context mean the contractual goods assembled by the seller for the purpose of fulfilling the contract and making delivery: *Demby Hamilton & Co. Ltd v Barden* [1949] 1 All E.R. 435 at 437.
33 *Martineau v Kitching* (1872) L.R. 7 Q.B. 436 at 456; *J & J Cunningham Ltd v Robert A. Munro Ltd* (1922) 28 Com.Cas. 42 at 46; *Sharp v Batt* (1930) 25 Tas.L.R. 33; *Horn v Minister of Food* [1948] 2 All E.R. 1036; *Demby Hamilton & Co. Ltd v Barden*, above; *Gatoil International Inc. v Tradax Petroleum Ltd* [1985] 1 Lloyd's Rep. 350 at 362. See also below, para.19–121 (c.i.f.) and below, para.20–092 (f.o.b.).
34 *cf.* Blackburn J. in *Martineau v Kitching*, above, at p.456, but his statement of the civil law is scarcely accurate. The principle in this subsection, however, does appear to represent the Roman law: De Zulueta, *Roman Law of Sale* (1945), pp.31, 32.
35 It would seem that the subsection can be applied to the situation where the property has passed to the buyer, but the goods are still at the seller's risk, as well as to the situation where the property and risk are still both in the seller.
36 *Demby Hamilton & Co. Ltd v Barden* [1949] 1 All E.R. 435 at 437.
37 The word "might" was substituted for "would" at the instance of Lord Watson during the passage of the Bill (the 1893 Act) through the House of Lords.
38 [1949] 1 All E.R. 435. See also *Sharp v Batt* (1930) 25 Tas.L.R. 33.
39 At p.437.

buyer to take delivery of the goods at the proper time." He also stated that it was the duty of the sellers to act reasonably, and, if possible, to avoid any loss, *e.g.* in certain circumstances to dispose of the goods elsewhere and acquire other goods for the postponed time of delivery.[40]

6–025 **Consumer sales.** Section 20(2) does not apply where the buyer deals as consumer.[41] Section 20(4) of the Act states that, in such a case, the subsection "must be ignored". It is difficult to see why this should be so. Under section 20(4) the goods remain at the seller's risk until they are delivered to the consumer.[42] But there is no reason why the seller should continue to bear the risk until delivery where delivery has been delayed through the fault of the buyer. If (as in *Demby Hamilton & Co Ltd v Barden*[43]) the goods deteriorate because the buyer fails to take delivery, the risk of deterioration should be borne by the buyer even if he deals as consumer. Nevertheless the Act provides that the risk still remains with the seller. It is however, open to the parties to insert in their agreement a term equivalent to the rule set out in section 20(2) and it seems probable that such a term would be upheld as being reasonable and fair under the Unfair Contract Terms Act 1977[44] and the Unfair Terms in Consumer Contracts Regulations 1999,[45] at least in situations where the goods are perishable and likely to deteriorate in the event of delay.

(e) *Liability as Bailee*

6–026 **Seller or buyer as bailee.** Section 20(3) of the Act states: "Nothing in this section affects the duties or liabilities of either seller or buyer as a bailee or custodier[46] of the goods of the other party."[47] If the property has passed to the buyer under the contract of sale, but the seller remains in possession of the goods, he does so as bailee[48] until the time for delivery has arrived. Notwithstanding that the goods are at the buyer's risk, the seller must take reasonable care of the goods according to the circumstances of the particular case.[49] Conversely, where the property in the goods

---

[40] At p.438. *Cf. Sharp v Batt*, above. See also below, para.12–031.
[41] Defined in s.61(5A) by reference to Pt I or the Unfair Contract Terms Act 1977; see below, para.13–071.
[42] See above, para.6–013.
[43] [1949] 1 All E.R.435; above, para.6–024.
[44] See below, para.13–086.
[45] See below, para.14–030.
[46] The Scottish equivalent of bailee.
[47] See *Wiehe v Dennis Bros* (1913) 29 T.L.R. 250; see also below, para.18–244.
[48] *Wiehe v Dennis Bros*, above (where it was said that he was a gratuitous bailee).
[49] *Houghland v RR Low (Luxury Coaches) Ltd* [1962] 1 Q.B. 694 at 698; *Morris v C. W. Martin & Sons Ltd* [1966] 1 Q.B. 716 at 726, 731. See also *Coggs v Bernard* (1703) 2 Ld.Raym. 909 at 916; *Bullen v Swan Electric Engraving Co.* (1907) 23 T.L.R. 258; *Blount v War Office* [1953] 1 W.L.R 736 at 739; *James Buchanan & Co. Ltd v Hay's Transport Services Ltd* [1972] 2 Lloyd's Rep. 535 at 543; *Port Swettenham Authority v TW Wu & Co. (M) Sdn. Bhd* [1979] A.C. 580 at 589; *Mitchell v Ealing London BC* [1979] Q.B. 1; *China Pacific SA v Food Corp. of India* [1982] A.C. 939 at 960; *Sutcliffe v Chief Constable of West Yorkshire* [1998] R.T.R. 86; *Chitty on Contracts* (29th ed.), Vol. 2, paras 33–032, 33–036.

remains in the seller and they are at his risk, but possession of them is delivered to the buyer, the buyer must nevertheless take reasonable care of the goods.[50]

After the time for delivery has arrived, the duties of the seller as bailee of the goods are somewhat uncertain. Where the delay in delivery is due to the fault of the buyer, the seller might be held to be a gratuitous, or even an involuntary bailee. It is submitted, however, that he is under a duty to take reasonable care of the goods.[51] It is further submitted that this is so even if section 37(1) of the Act applies,[52] in which case the seller will be entitled to claim a reasonable charge for the care and custody of the goods.[53] The position would then be as follows: (i) if the risk has passed to the buyer, and delay in delivery is due to the fault of the buyer, the seller is still under a duty to take reasonable care of the goods; and (ii) if the risk remains with the seller, but delay in delivery is due to the fault of the buyer, the buyer must assume the risk of any loss which might not have occurred but for such fault,[54] yet the seller must still take reasonable care of the goods. Further, if the risk has passed to the buyer, but delivery is delayed due to the seller's fault, the seller must assume the risk of any loss which might not have occurred but for such fault,[55] and in addition must take reasonable care of the goods. **6–027**

Remedies. Some of the situations mentioned above envisage that the destruction or deterioration of the goods may be due partly to the buyer's fault in neglecting to take delivery of the goods at the appropriate time and partly to the failure by the seller to take sufficient care of them while in his possession. It has not yet been settled, however, whether this is an appropriate case for the apportionment of the loss under the provisions of the Law Reform (Contributory Negligence) Act 1945.[56] Moreover, there would appear to be no reliable authority on the consequence of the failure by a bailee to take sufficient care of the goods. But where the seller claims against the buyer damages for failure to accept the goods, or payment of **6–028**

---

[50] See above, paras 5–044, 5–055 (goods on sale or return).

[51] *Demby Hamilton & Co. Ltd v Barden* [1949] 1 All E.R. 435 at 438. Contrast the note in 3 Salk. 61; *Okell v Smith* (1815) 1 Stark. 107; *Sharp v Batt* (1930) 25 Tas.L.R. 33 at 56; Dig. 18.6.17 (*dolus* or *culpa lata* only).

[52] See below, para.9–009.

[53] The right to charge appears to be correlative to the duty to take reasonable care: *China Pacific SA v Food Corp. of India*, above. But even where there is no right to charge, *e.g.* because the seller asserts an unpaid sellers lien (see below, para.15–028) it is submitted that the duty to take reasonable care continues.

[54] See above, para.6–023.

[55] *ibid.*

[56] See the definition of "fault" in s.4 of the 1945 Act, and *Sayers v Harlow UDC* [1958] 1 W.L.R. 623; *Quinn v Burch Bros (Builders) Ltd* [1966] 2 Q.B. 370 at 381; *de Meza v Apple* [1974] 1 Lloyd's Rep. 508; [1975] 1 Lloyd's Rep. 498; *Rowe v Turner Hopkins & Partners* [1980] 2 N.Z.L.R. 550; *Basildon DC v JE Lesser Ltd* [1985] Q.B. 839; *AB Marintrans v Comet Shipping Co. Ltd* [1985] 1 Lloyd's Rep. 568; *Forsikringsaktieselskabet Vesta v Butcher* [1989] A.C. 852, CA; *Chitty on Contracts* (29th ed.), Vol. 1, para.26–042. See also the Torts (Interference with Goods) Act 1977, s.11(1).

the price, it is submitted that in appropriate cases an allegation made by the buyer that the seller is in breach of his duty as bailee could be raised by way of defence, and not merely as a counterclaim for damages, in the action.[57]

6–029 **Burden of proof.** The burden of proving that the loss was not caused by failure to take reasonable care would appear to rest upon the bailee.[58]

6–030 **Vicarious liability.** Where the bailee has entrusted the goods to his servant or agent, he may be vicariously liable for the theft of or damage negligently caused to the goods by that servant or agent, notwithstanding that the servant or agent was acting for his own benefit.[59]

6–031 **Extension or exclusion of liability.** The liability of the bailee for the safe custody of the goods may be extended[60] or excluded or restricted[61] by the express or implied agreement of the parties.

6–032 **Consumer sales.** Where the buyer deals as consumer[61a] s.20(4) of the Act[61b] provides that s.20(3) is to be ignored and the goods remain at the seller's risk until they are delivered to the consumer. Ignoring ss.(3) would appear to have no discernible effect as the seller or buyer (as the case may be) who is in possession of the goods as the bailee will continue to be under a duty at common law to take reasonable care of the goods.

(f) *Benefits*

6–033 **Benefits to goods.** It is a moot point whether any fruits of or accessions[62] or other benefits to the goods accrue (i) to the person who bears the risk, or (ii) to the person in whom the property is vested, or (iii) to the person in

---

[57] See, *e.g.* ss.14(2), (3), 53(1)(a) of the 1979 Act, and *Horn v Minister of Food* [1948] 2 All E.R. 1036.

[58] *Coggs v Bernard* (1703) 2 Ld.Raym. 909 at 914, 915; *Bullen v Swan Electric Engraving Co.* (1907) 23 T.L.R. 258; *Travers & Sons v Cooper* [1915] 1 K.B. 73 at 90; *Brook's Wharf and Bull Wharf v Goodman Bros* [1937] 1 K.B. 534 at 538; *Houghland v RR Low (Luxury Coaches) Ltd* [1962] 1 Q.B. 694; *James Buchanan Ltd v Hay's Transport Services Ltd* [1972] 2 Lloyd's Rep. 535 at 543; *Port Swettenham Authority v TW Wu & Co. (M) Sdn. Bhd.* [1979] A.C. 580; *Mitchell v Ealing London BC* [1979] Q.B. 1; *Sutcliffe v Chief Constable of West Yorkshire* [1996] R.T.R. 86.

[59] *Coupé Co. v Maddick* [1891] 2 Q.B. 413; *Aitchison v Page Motors Ltd* (1935) 154 L.T. 128; *Houghland v RR Low (Luxury Coaches) Ltd*, above, at p.698; *Morris v C W Martin & Sons Ltd* [1966] 1 Q.B. 716 at 728, 740; *Transmotors Ltd v Robertson, Buckley & Co. Ltd* [1970] 1 Lloyd's Rep. 224; *Port Swettenham Authority v T W Wu & Co. (M) Sdn. Bhd.*, above. Contrast *Morris v CW Martin & Sons Ltd*, above, at pp.725, 737.

[60] *Bianchi v Nash* (1836) 1 M. & W. 545; *Bevington v Dale* (1902) 7 Com.Cas. 112; *Horn v Minister of Food* [1948] 2 All E.R. 1036.

[61] See *Rutter v Palmer* [1922] 2 K.B. 87 (but not a case of sale). But see s.3 of the Unfair Contract Terms Act 1977 and the Unfair Terms in Consumer Contracts Regulations 1999, SI 1999/2803; below, paras 13–094, 14–030, which may be applicable.

[61a] Defined in s. 61 (5A) by reference to Part I of the Unfair Contract Terms Act 1977; see belows, para.13–071.

[61b] See above, para.6–013.

[62] See Guest, 27 M.L.R. 505 (1964); Matthews [1981] *Current Legal Problems* 159.

possession of the goods. The Roman law principle was that benefits accrued to the person who bore the risk: *nam et commodum eius debet, cuius periculum est*.[63] And in *Sweeting v Turner*[64] Blackburn J. said: "Any calamity befalling the goods after the sale is completed must be borne by the purchaser and, by a parity of reasoning, any benefit to them is his benefit, and not that of the vendor"[65]; but this presupposes a situation where the risk passes with the property. In *Tucker v Farm and General Investment Trust Ltd*[66] the Court of Appeal held that, in the absence of a contrary stipulation, where livestock are let on hire-purchase and produce young, the young belong to the hirer (the bailee in possession) and not to the owner of the dams. It is difficult, therefore, to lay down even a prima facie rule. But it is submitted that benefits should normally be regarded as belonging to the owner of the goods,[67] rather than to the person who is in possession of them or who bears the risk. However, where the goods are sufficiently identified as those which are the subject-matter of the contract of sale, the parties may be taken to have intended that the buyer should be entitled to any benefits to the goods upon acquiring the property in them.

2. FRUSTRATION[68]

Generally. A contract of sale may be frustrated where, after the contract has been entered into,[69] but before the property in the goods has passed to the buyer,[70] without default of either party,[71] the contract has become impossible of legal performance, or incapable of being performed because the circumstances in which performance is called for render it a thing radically different from that which was undertaken by the contract.[72] The principle of frustration is, of course, not confined to contracts of sale of 6–034

[63] *Justinian, Inst.*, above III.23.3; Cod. 4.48.1.
[64] (1871) L.R. 7 Q.B. 310 (not a case of benefit).
[65] At p.313.
[66] [1966] 2 Q.B. 421. *Cf. Juelle v Trudeau* (1968) 7 D.L.R. (3d) 82.
[67] *Mirabita v Imperial Ottoman Bank* (1878) 3 Ex.D. 164 at 169; *Seath v Moore* (1886) 11 App.Cas. 350 at 380; see above, paras 1–043, 1–105, 5–092.
[68] See Treitel, *Frustration and Force Majeure* (2nd ed., 2004); McKendrick (ed.), *Force Majeure and Frustration of Contract* (2nd ed.).
[69] As contrasted with initial impossibility (above, para.1–122) or initial illegality (above, para.3–027).
[70] In most cases, the passing of property will preclude the operation of frustration, but in some circumstances the relevant time will be the passing of the risk, or even the delivery of goods to the buyer where, *e.g.* he is an alien enemy (see below, para.6–042). In the case of instalment sales, the property in some of the goods may have passed, but the contract still be frustrated as to the remainder.
[71] See *Bank Line Ltd v Arthur Capel & Co.* [1919] A.C. 435 at 452; *Maritime National Fish Ltd v Ocean Trawlers Ltd* [1935] A.C. 524 at 530; *Joseph Constantine S.S. Line Ltd v Imperial Smelting Corp. Ltd* [1942] A.C. 154 at 170–171; *Ocean Tramp Tankers Corp. v V/O Sovfracht (The Eugenia)* [1964] 2 Q.B. 226; *Denmark Productions Ltd v Boscobel Productions Ltd* [1969] 1 Q.B. 699; *Paal Wilson & Co. A/S v Partenreederi Hannah Blumenthal* [1983] 1 A.C. 854 at 882, 909; *J Lauritzen A/S v Wijsmuller BV (The Super Servant Two)* [1990] 1 Lloyd's Rep. 1 at 8–10; Treitel, *op. cit.*, Ch.14; *Chitty on Contracts* (29th ed.), Vol. 1, para.23–059 (self-induced frustration).
[72] See below, para.6–041.

goods,[73] but the rules of common law relating thereto are applicable to contracts of sale by virtue of section 62(2) of the Sale of Goods Act 1979.[74]

(a) *Specific Goods which have Perished*

6–035 **Section 7.** Provision is made for one particular instance of frustration by section 7 of the Sale of Goods Act 1979, which enacts: "Where there is an agreement to sell specific goods and subsequently the goods, without any fault on the part of the seller or buyer, perish before the risk passes to the buyer, the agreement is avoided." Before this section will apply, a number of requirements must be satisfied. First, the goods to which the agreement relates must be specific goods.[75] Secondly, there must be an agreement to sell, and not a sale of, the goods. The section contemplates a situation where the goods perish after an agreement to sell[76] has been entered into, but before the property in the goods is transferred to the buyer.[77] Thirdly, the goods must have "perished". Although an opinion to the contrary has been expressed,[78] it would seem that the goods need not have been totally destroyed, provided that they have been so altered in nature by damage or deterioration that they have become for business purposes something other than that which is described in the contract of sale.[79] Fourthly, the risk must not yet have passed to the buyer. If, therefore, notwithstanding that the property in the goods remains in the seller, the goods are at the buyer's risk,[80] this section will not apply.[81] It would also seem that, where delay in delivery is due to the fault of the buyer, so that the goods are at his risk as regards any loss which might not have occurred but for his fault,[82] the section is likewise inapplicable. This interpretation is to some extent confirmed by the fifth requirement that the goods must perish without any fault[83] on the part of the seller or buyer. This last requirement would appear to include situations where the seller or buyer is at fault by virtue of the breach of his obligations as bailee of the goods.[84]

---

[73] See generally *Chitty on Contracts* (29th ed.), Vol. 1, Ch.23.
[74] See also s.11(6).
[75] Defined in s.61(1) of the Act; see above, para.1–113.
[76] Sale of Goods Act 1979, s.2(5): see above, para.1–026.
[77] s.2(4), (6): see above, para.1–025.
[78] *Horn v Minister of Food* [1948] 2 All E.R. 1036 (rotten potatoes held not to have perished). *Cf. Rendel v Turnbull & Co.* (1908) 27 N.Z.L.R. 1067.
[79] See *Duthie v Hilton* (1868) L.R. 4 C.P. 138 (freight); *Asfar v Blundell* [1896] 1 Q.B. 123 (insurance); *Montreal Light, Heat and Power Co. v Sedgwick* [1910] A.C. 598 (insurance); Marine Insurance Act 1906, ss.56–61. See also *Barr v Gibson* (1838) 3 M. & W. 390 at 400. A partial destruction or loss, *e.g.* by theft, may also be covered where the contract is entire and not severable: *Lovatt v Hamilton* (1839) 5 M. & W. 639; *Barrow, Lane & Ballard Ltd v Phillip Phillips & Co. Ltd* [1929] 1 K.B. 574 (on s.6 of the Act), but not (*semble*) the requisitioning of the goods: see below, para.6–050. Decisions on s.6 (above, para.1–124) may be a useful guide to the meaning of terms in s.7.
[80] See above, para.6–003. For this reason, s.7 will not apply to c.i.f. contracts for the sale of specific goods after shipment: see below, para.19–124. But see *Fibrosa Spolka Akcyjna v Fairbairn Lawson Combe Barbour Ltd* [1943] A.C. 32 at 83. For f.o.b. contracts, see below, para.20–014; and "ex ship," see below, para.21–028.
[81] *Horn v Minister of Food*, above.
[82] s.20(2); see above, para.6–023.
[83] Defined in s.61(1) of the Act as meaning "wrongful act or default".
[84] See above, para.6–026.

6–036 Specific goods are defined in section 61(1) of the Act to mean "goods identified and agreed on at the time a contract of sale is made" and are stated to include "an undivided share, specified as a fraction or percentage, of goods identified and agreed on as aforesaid".[85] A contract for the sale of a quarter share in a named racehorse is therefore an agreement for the sale of specific goods. But even if the parties intend that the specified fraction or percentage is subsequently to be separated from the bulk of which it forms part, a contract for the sale of such an undivided share can still be an agreement for the sale of specific goods. Thus if a contract for the sale of the whole of the wine in a particular stack or bin (whether described as such or as a numerical quantity) would be an agreement to sell specific goods, an agreement to sell an undivided share, specified as a fraction ("one-half") or percentage ("50 per cent"), of that wine is likewise an agreement to sell specific goods. The effect of such an agreement is to transfer to the buyer, at such time as the parties to the contract intend it to be transferred, property in an undivided share in the bulk, and the buyer becomes an owner in common of the bulk.[86] Once such a transfer occurs it is submitted that section 7 ceases to apply. Section 61(1) defines "goods" to include an undivided share in goods and it would appear that, since the property in "goods" is transferred from the seller to the buyer, there is an actual sale of the undivided share and not merely an agreement to sell such a share. Since section 7 applies only where there is an agreement to sell, and not where a sale has taken place, the contract will not be avoided if the bulk of which the fraction or percentage forms part perishes after the property in the undivided share has passed but before that share has been separated from the bulk. Even if this argument is not accepted, section 7 would still be inapplicable if (as has previously been contended[87] will be the case in the absence of an agreement to the contrary) the risk has passed to the buyer together with the property in the undivided share before the perishing of the goods.

It is important to note that if, in the above example, the seller agrees to sell a specified quantity, say 200 bottles, of wine from the same specific stack or bin, this is not an agreement to sell specific, but unascertained, goods. Should the bulk perish, the agreement will not be avoided under section 7.[88]

6–037 **Scope of section 7.** In its terms, section 7 of the Act will apply to all agreements for the sale of specific goods where the transfer of the property in the goods is to take place at a future time or subject to some condition[89] thereafter to be fulfilled,[90] unless the risk has passed to the buyer. Prima facie, it will be applicable to the circumstances envisaged in section 18, rules 2 and 3, of the Act,[91] and also to cases where the seller has reserved

---

[85] As amended by s.2(d) of the Sale of Goods (Amendment) Act 1995; see above, paras 1–116, 5–129.
[86] See above, para.5–129.
[87] Above, para.6–007.
[88] But see below, para.6–051 (frustration).
[89] See above, para.5–021.
[90] Sale of Goods Act 1979, s.2(5); above, para.1–025.
[91] See above, paras 5–030, 5–035; *Rugg v Minett* (1809) 11 East 210. But it is questionable whether it would apply to s.18, r. 4: *Edwards v Vaughan* (1910) 26 T.L.R. 545.

the right of disposal of specific goods in accordance with section 19.[92] It is, however, submitted that section 7 does not lay down an absolute rule, but may be negatived or varied by express agreement, or by the course of dealing between the parties, or by such usage as binds both parties to the contract.[93] A court may thus be at liberty to find that the contract has not been avoided, that the goods were intended to be at the seller's risk until the property therein was transferred to the buyer, and that the seller is liable in damages for failure to deliver the goods.[94]

6–038 **Howell v Coupland.** It is generally thought that section 7 of the Act was formulated in reliance on the decision of the Court of Appeal in *Howell v Coupland*,[95] where the defendant agreed to sell to the claimant 200 tons of potatoes to be grown on a particular field. The crop failed, so that the defendant was able to deliver only 80 tons. It was held that he was relieved of liability to deliver the other 120 tons by reason of impossibility of performance.[96] Sir Mackenzie Chalmers was of the opinion that section 7 applied to specifically described goods, whether in existence at the time the contract was made or not.[97] But this interpretation does not accord with the definition of "specific goods" in section 61(1) of the Act.[98] It seems better[99] to regard the situation in *Howell v Coupland* either as an instance of a sale upon a contingency covered by section 5(2) or as a sale subject to a condition implied at common law as preserved by section 62(2) of the Act. It was not decided in *Howell v Coupland* whether the seller might have refused delivery of the 80 tons which he in fact delivered. This will depend on the presumed intention of the parties. A condition may be implied that, in such circumstances, the contract is wholly discharged. Alternatively, a condition may be implied that the buyer shall have the option of accepting part delivery.[1] In this type of case, therefore, one or both parties may be relieved, in whole or in part, from further performance of his obligations under the contract. But the contract is not avoided by section 7 of the Act; nor is it otherwise discharged automatically by frustration.

6–039 **Consequences of section 7.** The effect of the operation of section 7 is that the agreement is avoided. Both parties are released from all obligations which have not yet accrued at the time at which the goods perish. Prima facie, however, any obligation which has accrued before this time must be performed,[2] and any obligation which has accrued and been

---

[92] See above, para.5–131.
[93] Sale of Goods Act 1979, s.55(1). However, s.7 is not prefaced by the words "unless otherwise agreed" as is (for example) s.20(1), and it is arguable that s.55(1) in its terms does not apply to such a provision.
[94] See, *e.g. Logan v Le Mesurier* (1847) 6 Moo.P.C. 116.
[95] (1876) 1 Q.B.D. 258.
[96] *ibid.* at p.262. See also the decision at first instance (1874) L.R. 9 Q.B. 462.
[97] Chalmers, *Sale of Goods Act 1893* (18th ed.), p.100.
[98] See Treitel, *Frustration and Force Majeure* (2nd ed., 2004), para.4–049, and above, paras 1–113, 5–022.
[99] *Re Wait* [1927] 1 Ch. 606 at 630–631; *Sainsbury Ltd v Street* [1972] 1 W.L.R. 834.
[1] *Sainsbury Ltd v Street*, above. *Cf. Lovatt v Hamilton* (1839) 5 M. & W. 639; *Lipton Ltd v Ford* [1917] 2 K.B. 647.
[2] *Chandler v Webster* [1904] 1 K.B. 493 is still good law in this respect.

performed remains undisturbed. Nevertheless, if the price, or any part of it, has already been paid by the buyer, it is recoverable from the seller, provided there has been a total failure of consideration.[3] But no provision is made under section 7 for apportionment of the loss; nor can the seller retain or recover any sum in respect of expenses incurred by him before the time of discharge in, or for the purpose of, the performance of the agreement.[4] The rights and obligations of the parties are in principle determined as at the time the goods perish.

It has, however, been suggested[5] that, if part of the specific goods agreed to be sold has been delivered to the buyer, but the remainder subsequently perishes before the risk passes to the buyer, the buyer can recover that part of the price due and paid which is attributable to the goods not yet received, even though the consideration has only partially failed.[6] This is no doubt so where part of the price can be attributed to a corresponding part of the goods, *e.g.* where there is a unit price for the goods.[7] But it is argued that the same principle applies even where the payment cannot easily be apportioned, on the ground that the risk in respect of the non-delivered goods is on the seller when they perish. The suggestion has also been made that, where part of the goods has been delivered to the buyer, even though the contract of sale is not severable and the price only payable on delivery of the whole of the goods,[8] the buyer cannot claim to retain the goods without paying for the part retained. Provided that the buyer has an option to retain or return those goods,[9] it is argued that he should be held liable *quantum meruit* upon a new implied contract which arises from his acceptance of the benefit, and his refusal to disgorge it.[10] The validity of the first suggestion may depend on whether the incidence of risk is relevant to the operation of section 7. The validity of the second suggestion depends on the questionable assumption that the buyer is in fact under a duty to return the goods received. But a solution by which the buyer would recover payment made for any part of the goods not delivered, yet be bound to pay 6–040

[3] *Fibrosa Spolka Akcyjna v Fairbairn Lawson Combe Barbour Ltd* [1943] A.C. 32. See also *Rugg v Minett* (1809) 11 East 210; *Logan v Le Mesurier* (1847) 6 Moo.P.C. 116; *McDill v Hilson* (1920) 53 D.L.R. 228.

[4] See below, para.6–058, on the non-applicability of the Law Reform (Frustrated Contracts) Act 1943. Contrast *Cantiare San Rocco SA v Clyde Shipbuilding and Engineering Co. Ltd* [1924] A.C. 226 (Scots law).

[5] Atiyah, *The Sale of Goods*, (11th ed.), p.367.

[6] By the same token, if the price is due but unpaid, the buyer would be relieved from payment in respect of the goods destroyed.

[7] See (in a different context) *Deveaux v Connolly* (1849) 8 C.B. 640; *Biggerstaff v Rowatts' Wharf Ltd* [1896] 2 Ch. 93; *Behrend & Co. Ltd v Produce Brokers Ltd* [1920] 3 K.B. 530; *Ebrahim Dawood Ltd v Heath Ltd* [1961] 2 Lloyd's Rep. 512; *David Securities Pty Ltd v Commonwealth Bank of Australia* (1992) 66 A.L.J.R. 768 at 779.

[8] *Cf. Cutter v Powell* (1795) 6 T.R. 320; *Appleby v Myers* (1867) L.R. 2 C.P. 651; *Whincup v Hughes* (1871) L.R. 6 C.P. 78.

[9] *Cf. Sumpter v Hedges* [1898] 1 Q.B. 673; *Forman & Co. Pty Ltd v The Ship "Liddesdale"* [1900] A.C. 190. *Quaere* whether such an option exists if the buyer has resold the goods: see Atiyah, *op. cit.*, p.364.

[10] *Cf.* s.30(1) of the 1979 Act, and the result in *Barrow, Lane and Ballard v Phillip Phillips & Co.* [1929] 1 K.B. 574 (s.6).

a reasonable sum for any part delivered and retained, would arguably produce a more just allocation of the loss between the buyer and seller than would otherwise occur by the strict application of common law principles.

(b) *Other Instances of Frustration*

6–041 **Unascertained goods.** Section 7 of the 1979 Act deals only with the particular case of specific goods which have perished, and it is of course possible for a contract for the sale of specific goods to be frustrated by other events, *e.g.* by the requisitioning of the goods.[11] Where, however, the contract is one for the sale of unascertained generic goods, it is obvious from the very nature of the contract that the circumstances necessary for frustration will only rarely arise. The seller is normally free to obtain supplies from any source he chooses, and *genus numquam perit*. Thus it has been said "a bare and unqualified contract for the sale of unascertained goods will not (unless most special facts compel an opposite implication) be dissolved by the operation of the principle [of frustration], even though there has been so grave and unforeseen a change of circumstances as to render it impossible for the vendor to fulfil his bargain."[12] In most cases, therefore, it is no defence for the seller to plead that goods of the description mentioned in the contract are no longer available from the source from which he intended to obtain them: the contract is not frustrated.[13] Only if the parties have contracted expressly or impliedly on the basis of a *common* assumption that the goods are to come from that particular source and no other will frustration occur.[14] Even if the source contemplated is the sole source from which the goods can be obtained, a mere interruption or reduction of supplies due to commonplace difficulties such as breakdown of machinery or inadequacies of transport will not frustrate the contract: they are "the warp and woof of industrial and commercial aggravation".[15] Nevertheless it must not be supposed that an

---

[11] *Re Shipton, Anderson & Co. and Harrison Bros & Co.* [1915] 3 K.B. 676; see below, para.6–050.

[12] *Blackburn Bobbin Co. Ltd v TW Allen & Sons Ltd* [1918] 1 K.B. 540 at 550 (affirmed [1918] 2 K.B. 467). See below, para.19–128.

[13] *King v Parker* (1876) 34 L.T. 886; *Jacobs v Crèdit Lyonnais* (1884) 12 Q.B.D. 589; *Gelling v Crispin* (1917) 23 C.L.R. 443; *Blackburn Bobbin Co. Ltd v T W Allen & Sons Ltd*, above; *Lebeaupin v Crispin & Co.* [1920] 2 K.B. 714; *Re Thornett and Fehr and Yuills Ltd* [1921] 1 K.B. 219; *George Wills & Sons Ltd v RS Cunningham, Son & Co. Ltd* [1924] 2 K.B. 220; *Twentsche Overseas Trading Co. Ltd v Uganda Sugar Factory Ltd* (1944) 113 L.J.P.C. 25; *Monkland v Jack Barclay Ltd* [1951] 2 K.B. 252 at 258; *Beves & Co. Ltd v Farkas* [1953] 1 Lloyd's Rep. 103; *Hong Guan & Co. Ltd v R. Jumabhoy & Sons Ltd* [1960] A.C. 684; *Parrish & Heimbecker Ltd v Gooding Lbr. Ltd* (1968) 67 D.L.R. (2d) 495. *Cf. Lipton v Ford* [1917] 2 K.B. 647; *Brooke Tool Manufacturing Co. Ltd v Hydraulic Gears Co. Ltd* (1920) 89 L.J.K.B. 263.

[14] *Re Badische Co. Ltd* [1921] 2 Ch. 331; *Société Co-operative Suisse des Ceéreales et Matières Fouragères v La Plata Cereal Co. SA* (1947) 80 Ll.L.R. 530; *Sanschagrin v Echo Flour Mills Co.* (1922) 70 D.L.R. 380. See also *Howell v Coupland* (1876) 1 Q.B.D. 258; above, para.6–038.

[15] *Intertradex SA v Lesieur Tourteaux SARL* [1977] 2 Lloyd's Rep. 146 at 154 (affirmed [1978] 2 Lloyd's Rep. 509). See also *George Eddy Co. Ltd v Corey* [1951] 4 D.L.R. 90.

unqualified contract for the sale of unascertained goods can never be frustrated.[16] Frustration can occur if the contract becomes physically or legally impossible of performance or if "without default of either party the contractual obligation has become incapable of being performed because the circumstances in which performance is called for would render it a thing radically different from that undertaken by the contract."[17]

Outbreak of war. By section 1(2) of the Trading with the Enemy Act 1939[18] it is a criminal offence to supply any goods to or for the benefit of an enemy[19] or to obtain any goods from an enemy in time of war. Indeed, both at common law and under this statute, all commercial intercourse between a British subject[20] and an enemy becomes illegal upon the outbreak of war.[21] As a result, any existing contract of sale which involves such intercourse by reason of the performance or further performance of the contract is frustrated by the outbreak of war, or upon one of the parties acquiring the status of an enemy.[22] Even if the contract contains a clause which suspends its entire operation during the period of war, it nevertheless becomes illegal and is discharged.[23] It is otherwise, however, if the parties expressly provide that, in the event of war, an illegal method of performance is to be cancelled and a legal method substituted therefor.[24] 6–042

---

16 *Re Badische Co. Ltd*, above, at pp.381–383. See also *E Hulton Co. Ltd v Chadwick and Taylor Ltd* (1918) 34 T.L.R. 230 (all-round embargo on goods in question) and below, paras 18–298 *et seq.*

17 *Davis Contractors Ltd v Fareham U.D.C.* [1956] A.C. 696 at 729. See also *Acetylene Co. of GB v Canada Carbide Co.* (1922) 8 Ll.L.R. 456; *Tsakiroglou & Co. Ltd v Noblee Thorl GmbH* [1962] A.C. 93; *National Carriers Ltd v Panalpina (Northern) Ltd* [1981] A.C. 675 at 688, 700, 717; *Pioneer Shipping Ltd v BTP Tioxide Ltd* [1982] A.C. 724 at 744, 745, 751; *Paal Wilson & Co. A/S v Partenreederei Hannah Blumenthal* [1983] 1 A.C. 854; *Exportadora de Azucar v Industria Azucarera Nacional SA* [1983] 2 Lloyd's Rep. 171; *Atisa SA v Aztec AG* [1983] 2 Lloyd's Rep. 579.

18 s.1(2), (3), as amended by Emergency Laws (Miscellaneous Provisions) Act 1953, s.2 and Sch.2, para.2(1), (2).

19 Defined in ss.2(1), 15(3), (5) of the Act, as amended by Emergency Laws (Miscellaneous Provisions) Act 1953, s.2 and Sch.3, para.3(a), (b).

20 Or a person owing temporary allegiance to the Crown. See also *Kuenigl v Donnersmarck* [1955] 1 Q.B. 515 at 539.

21 See generally McNair and Watts, *The Legal Effects of War* (4th ed.); Rogers, *Effect of War on Contracts* (1940); Trotter, *Law of Contract during and after* War (4th ed.); Webber, *Effect of War on Contracts* (2nd ed.); Howard, *Trading with the Enemy* (1943) and Suppt (1945); Treitel, *Frustration and Force Majeure* (2nd ed., 2004), para.8–004.

22 *W Wolf & Sons v Carr, Parker & Co. Ltd* (1915) 31 T.L.R. 407; *Zinc Corp. Ltd v Hirsch* [1916] 1 K.B. 541; *Distington Hematite Iron Co. v Possehl* [1916] 1 K.B. 811; *Veithardt and Hall Ltd v Rylands Bros Ltd* (1917) 116 L.T. 706; *Ertel Bieber & Co. v Rio Tinto Co.* [1918] A.C. 260; *Naylor Benzon Co. Ltd v Krainische Industrie Gesellschaft* [1918] 2 K.B. 486; *Re Continho Caro & Co.* [1918] 2 Ch. 384; *Re Badische Co. Ltd* [1921] 2 Ch. 331; *Cantiare San Rocco SA v Clyde Shipbuilding and Engineering Co. Ltd* [1924] A.C. 226; *Fibrosa Spolka Akcyjna v Fairbairn Lawson Combe Barbour Ltd* [1943] A.C. 32.

23 *Distington Hematite Iron Co. v Possehl*, above; *Veithardt and Hall Ltd v Rylands Bros Ltd*, above; *Ertel Bieber & Co. v Rio Tinto Co.*, above; *Naylor Benzon & Co. Ltd v Krainische Industrie Gesellschaft*, above; *Re Badische Co. Ltd*, above; *Fibrosa Spolka Akcyjna v Fairbairn Lawson Combe Barbour Ltd*, above, at p.41.

24 *Smith Coney and Barrett v Becker Gray & Co.* [1916] 2 Ch. 86 at 92.

6–043 A contract of sale of goods which contemplates the carriage of the goods by sea will be frustrated if the named port of shipment becomes an enemy port.[25] In the case of a c.i.f. contract, frustration may also occur if the port of destination becomes an enemy port or falls under enemy occupation or control,[26] or if the goods are in transit and have been shipped upon enemy vessels.[27] A buyer under c.i.f. contract is therefore entitled to refuse the tender of documents consisting of an enemy bill of lading, or even an enemy insurance policy.[28] But if the contract provides for shipment to one of several ports of destination, the buyer being empowered to declare to which port the goods shall be carried, the declaration of an enemy port in time of war is a complete nullity and the buyer may subsequently declare a lawful port: the contract is not frustrated.[29]

6–044 It is important to make clear that the principle of frustration does not involve the destruction of the contract so far as already performed. That which is abrogated is the further performance of the contract, as from the outbreak of war.[30] Rights which have already accrued under the contract of sale (*e.g.* a claim for the price) are not destroyed, though the right of suing in respect thereof is suspended for the duration of the war where the claimant is an enemy.[31]

6–045 **Other supervening illegality.** A contract of sale of goods may be discharged by frustration if legislation is passed making further performance of it illegal. The illegality, however, must render the contract impossible of legal performance in accordance with its terms,[32] or be of such a character and duration that it vitally and fundamentally affects the nature of the performance contemplated by the parties to the contract when it was made.[33] If the illegality is merely temporary, the contract will not necessarily be frustrated.[34] It will also remain valid and binding if the

[25] *Esposito v Bowden* (1857) 7 E. & B. 763. *Cf. WJ Sargant & Sons v Eric Paterson & Co.* (1923) 129 L.T. 471. See below, paras 19–136, 20–098 (c.i.f. and f.o.b.).

[26] *Fibrosa Spolka Akcyjna v Fairbairn Lawson Combe Barbour Ltd* [1943] A.C. 32; see below, para.19–136.

[27] *Duncan, Fox & Co. v Schrempft and Bonke* [1915] 3 K.B. 355; *Arnhold Karberg & Co. v Blythe Green Jourdain & Co.* [1916] 1 K.B. 495. *Cf. Re Weis & Co. and Crèdit Colonial et Commercial (Antwerp)* [1916] 1 K.B. 346 (capture of ship). See below, para.19–136.

[28] *Arnhold Karberg & Co. v Blythe Green Jourdain & Co.*, above.

[29] *Hindley & Co. Ltd v General Fibre Co. Ltd* [1940] 2 K.B. 517; see below, para.19–129.

[30] *Schering Ltd v Stockholms Enskilda Bank Aktiebolag* [1946] A.C. 219 at 241, 248.

[31] *ibid.*; *Arab Bank Ltd v Barclays Bank* [1954] A.C. 495; *Re a Claim by Helbert Wagg & Co. Ltd* [1956] Ch. 323 at 354.

[32] *Denny, Mott and Dickson Ltd v James B Fraser & Co. Ltd* [1944] A.C. 265; *Nile Co. for the Export of Agricultural Crops v H & JM Bennett (Commodities) Ltd* [1986] 1 Lloyd's Rep. 555. See also below, paras 6–046, 18–334 (export and import prohibitions).

[33] *Metropolitan Water Board v Dick, Kerr & Co. Ltd* [1918] A.C. 119 at 126; *Denny, Mott and Dickson Ltd v James B. Fraser & Co. Ltd*, above, at p.273.

[34] *Andrew Millar & Co. Ltd v Taylor & Co. Ltd* [1916] 1 K.B. 402. *Cf. Bank Line Ltd v Capel (A.) Ltd* [1919] A.C. 435 at 454; *Court Line Ltd v Dant and Russell Inc.* [1939] 3 All E.R. 314; *Atlantic Maritime Co. Inc. v Gibbon* [1954] 1 Q.B. 88; *Walton (Grain and Shipping) Ltd v British Italian Trading Co. Ltd* [1959] 1 Lloyd's Rep. 223. See also below, para.18–336.

illegality relates only to some subsidiary provision[35] or to one of the methods by which it may be performed.[36]

Where performance is to take place in England, and such performance is rendered illegal under English law, even a contract valid under its governing law will not be enforced.[37] A contract of sale may also be frustrated by reason of supervening illegality under a foreign law which governs the contract. This topic is discussed in the chapter on Conflict of Laws later in this work.[38]

Export and import prohibitions.[39] A contract of sale of goods which provides[40] that the goods will be exported from one country to another may be frustrated if, after the contract is made, legislation prohibits its performance by placing an embargo on the export or import of the goods.[41] However, it is necessary in each case to consider the effect of the embargo on the performance required by the contract. The contract must be one which can only be performed by export from or import to the country to which the embargo applies.[42] Also, if the embargo is not an absolute one, but subject to exceptions or "loopholes," the contract will not be frustrated if they could have been made use of to effect performance.[43] Regard must also be had to those terms which govern the time of performance. Each party will be well advised to wait for a reasonable time before declaring to the other his inability to perform: he should wait and see whether the embargo will be final in the sense of extending throughout the period allowed for performance. A premature decision by one party that the contract has been frustrated may constitute a breach by him if the embargo is merely temporary.[44] Further, if the embargo does not come into operation immediately, there may still be sufficient time within which performance can and must take place.[45] 6–046

---

35 *Regent Oil Co. Ltd v Aldon Motors Ltd* [1965] 1 W.L.R. 956; *Congimex etc. SARL v Tradax Export SA* [1983] 1 Lloyd's Rep. 250.

36 *Waugh v Morris* (1873) L.R. 8 Q.B. 202; *Hindley & Co. Ltd v General Fibre Co. Ltd* [1940] 2 K.B. 517; *Cornelius v Banque Franco-Serbe* [1942] 1 K.B. 29.

37 See below, para.25–119.

38 *ibid.*

39 See below, para.18–334, for a fuller discussion of this question.

40 See *McMaster & Co. v Cox, McEwen & Co.* 1921 S.C. (HL) 24, as interpreted in *A. v Pound & Co. Ltd v M. W. Hardy & Co. Inc.* [1956] A.C. 588 at 604, 611 (f.o.b. contract). See also *Smith, Coney & Barrett v Becker, Gray & Co.* [1916] 2 Ch. 86; *Beves & Co. v Farkas* [1953] 1 Lloyd's Rep. 103.

41 See *e.g. Société Cooperative Suisse des Céréales et Matières Fouragères v La Plata Cereal Co. SA* (1947) 80 Ll.L.R. 530 at 543.

42 *Congimex etc. SARL v Tradax Export SA* [1983] 1 Lloyd's Rep. 250.

43 See below, paras 8–092, 18–349 (*force majeure*).

44 *Andrew Millar & Co. Ltd v Taylor & Co. Ltd* [1916] 1 K.B. 402. *Cf. Embiricos v Sydney Reid & Co.* [1914] 3 K.B. 45; *Atlantic Maritime Co. Inc. v Gibbon* [1954] 1 Q.B. 88; *Walton (Grain and Shipping) Ltd v British Italian Trading Co. Ltd* [1959] 1 Lloyd's Rep. 223. See below, para.18–336.

45 *Ross T Smyth & Co. Ltd v W. N. Lindsay Ltd* [1953] 1 W.L.R. 1280; *Tradax Export SA v Andreé & Cie SA* [1976] 1 Lloyd's Rep. 416.

6–047 If the embargo prohibits the export or import of goods except under licence, one of the parties may thereby be placed under an implied duty to use reasonable endeavours to obtain a licence.[46] Failure to fulfil that duty will preclude the party in default from relying on frustration as a ground of discharge, unless he proves that any steps he could have taken to obtain a licence would have been useless.[47] A similar, but distinct,[48] problem arises where legislation in force at the time the contract is made imposes a similar prohibition. If one party has expressly[49] or impliedly undertaken to use reasonable endeavours to obtain a licence,[50] but with due diligence has been unable to do so, he will normally be released from liability.[51] There is some doubt, however, whether such inability to obtain a licence under an existing licensing system is properly to be regarded as frustration.[52]

6–048 A foreign government which is a party to a contract of sale may be precluded from relying on an export or import prohibition which it has itself imposed, since the frustration is then "self induced"[53]; but a State trading organisation, independent of government, will be discharged from its contractual liabilities if the prohibition is beyond its control.[54]

6–049 **Sale and carriage of goods.** A contract of sale of goods which provides or contemplates that the goods will be carried to the buyer by a carrier will seldom be frustrated by the fact that one of the parties is subsequently

---

[46] *JW Taylor & Co. Ltd v Landauer & Co.* [1940] 4 All E.R. 335; *Dalmia Dairy Industries Ltd v National Bank of Pakistan* [1978] 2 Lloyd's Rep. 223 at 253 (affirmed *ibid*). See below, paras. 18–309, 18–313.

[47] *JW Taylor & Co. Ltd v Landauer & Co.*, above; *Brauer & Co. (Great Britain) Ltd v James Clark (British Materials) Ltd* [1952] 2 All E.R. 497 at 501; *Beves & Co. Ltd v Farkas* [1953] 1 Lloyd's Rep. 103 at 112; *Vidler & Co. (London) Ltd v R Silcock & Sons Ltd* [1960] 1 Lloyd's Rep. 509 at 514; *Malik & Co. v Central European Trading Agency Ltd* [1974] 2 Lloyd's Rep. 279 at 282; *Provimi Hellas AE v Warinco AG* [1978] 1 Lloyd's Rep. 373; *Overseas Buyers Ltd v Granadex* [1980] 2 Lloyd's Rep. 608 at 612. See below, para.18–320.

[48] See below, para.18–323.

[49] See the effect of the words "subject to licence" below, paras.6–057, 18–318.

[50] For cases in which a party has been held under an absolute obligation to perform, *e.g. Partabmull Rameshwar v KC Sethia (1944) Ltd* [1950] 1 All E.R. 352; affirmed [1951] 2 All E.R. 352n; *Peter Cassidy Seed Co. Ltd v Osuustukkukauppa I.L.* [1957] 1 W.L.R. 273; *Czarnikow (C) Ltd v Centrala Handlu Zagranicznego Rolimpex* [1979] A.C. 351; *Pagnan SpA v Tradax Ocean Transportation SA* [1987] 3 All E.R. 565 (subject to *force majeure* clause); see below, para.18–317.

[51] See, *e.g. Re Anglo-Russian Merchant Traders Ltd and John Batt & Co. (London) Ltd* [1917] 2 K.B. 679; and below, para.18–317.

[52] This will be of particular importance if the provisions of the Law Reform (Frustrated Contracts) Act 1943 are invoked. See below, paras 6–058, 18–334.

[53] *O'Neil v Armstrong* [1895] 2 Q.B. 418; *Prodexport State Co. for Foreign Trade v E. D. & F. Man Ltd* [1973] Q.B. 389. But see *Rederiaktiebolaget Amphitrite v The King* [1921] 3 K.B. 500; *Commissioner of Crown Lands v Page* [1960] 2 Q.B. 274 at 291, *Chitty on Contracts* (29th ed.), paras 10–006–10–007; and see below, para.18–342.

[54] *Czarnikow (C) Ltd v Central Handlu Zagranicznego Rolimpex* [1979] A.C. 351; *Empresa Exportadora de Azucar v Industria Azucarera Nacional SA* [1983] 2 Lloyd's Rep. 171 at 191–2.

unable to obtain the necessary transport.[55] For example, a c.i.f. contract for the sale of unascertained goods[56] will not normally[57] be frustrated by the inability of the seller to ship the goods, *e.g.* due to outbreak of hostilities,[58] shortage of shipping space[59] or other extraneous cause[60] preventing shipment at the place and during the time stipulated by the contract.[61] And the same is true of an f.o.b. contract.[62] It is possible that the closure of a route expressly designated in a c.i.f. contract will effect a discharge[63]; but, in the absence of special circumstances,[64] a c.i.f. contract is not frustrated if the route envisaged at the time the contract is made subsequently becomes unavailable, provided that an alternative route exists which is not such as fundamentally to alter the nature of the contract.[65] The closure of a route envisaged by one party to the contract of sale will clearly not frustrate the contract.[66]

Requisitioning. Where the goods which are the subject-matter of the contract of sale are specific goods[67] or have become ascertained, the requisitioning (or expropriation) of the goods may bring about a frustration of the contract.[68] If, however, the goods have not yet become ascertained, it is submitted that a requisitioning of the goods which the seller intended to use in fulfilment of the contract will not normally effect a discharge, unless it was made on the common assumption of both parties that the goods requisitioned should be, in whole or in part, the contract goods.[69] In any event, the requisitioning must be of such a character or duration as to 6–050

[55] *Lewis Emanuel & Son Ltd v Sammut* [1959] 2 Lloyd's Rep. 629 (below, para.19–132). *Cf. Nickoll and Knight v Ashton Edridge & Co.* [1901] 2 K.B. 126 (below, para.19–126)—named ship not available to load during shipment period.
[56] But see *Gaon & Co. v Société Interprofessionelle des Oléagineaux Fluides Alimentaires* [1959] 2 Lloyd's Rep. 30 at 41; *Carapanayoti & Co. Ltd v ET Green Ltd* [1959] 1 Q.B. 131 at 147; *Lewis Emanuel & Son Ltd v Sammut* [1959] 2 Lloyd's Rep. 629 at 640; *Tsakiroglou & Co. Ltd v Noblee Thorl GmbH* [1962] A.C. 93.
[57] Contrast *Acetylene Co. of GB v Canada Carbide Co.* (1922) 8 Ll.L.R. 456 (below, para.19–128).
[58] *Ashmore & Son v CS Cox & Co.* [1899] 1 Q.B. 436; *WJ Sargant & Sons v Eric Paterson & Co.* (1923) 129 L.T. 471. But see above, para.6–042 (outbreak of war).
[59] *Lewis Emanuel & Son Ltd v Sammut*, above. *Cf. Acetylene Co. of GB v Canada Carbide Co*, above.
[60] *Kearon v Pearson* (1861) 7 H. & N. 386 (frost).
[61] See below, para.19–130.
[62] See below, para.20–100.
[63] But see the comments on *Re L Sutro & Co. and Heilbut Symons & Co.* [1917] 2 K.B. 348 in *Tsakiroglou & Co. Ltd v Noblee Thorl GmbH*, above, at p.113.
[64] See *Tsakiroglou & Co. Ltd v Noblee Thorl GmbH*, above; *Ocean Tramp Tankers Corporation v V/O Sovfracht ("The Eugenia")* [1964] 2 Q.B. 226 at 240, 243.
[65] *Tsakiroglou & Co. Ltd v Noblee Thorl GmbH*, above; below, para.19–127.
[66] See above, para.6–041; below, para.20–095 (f.o.b. contracts).
[67] Defined in s.61(1) of the 1979 Act; see above, para.1–113.
[68] *Re Shipton, Anderson & Co. and Harrison Bros & Co.* [1915] 3 K.B. 676 (but *Cf.* p.682); *Dale SS Co. Ltd v Northern SS Co. Ltd* (1918) 34 T.L.R. 271; *Kursell v Timber Operators and Contractors Ltd* [1927] 1 K.B. 298 at 312.
[69] See above, para.6–041. *Cf. Lipton v Ford* [1917] 2 K.B. 647.

render performance of the contract impossible or fundamentally different from that contemplated by the parties.[70]

6–051 **Goods destroyed.** Except in the case of specific goods which have perished,[71] the loss or destruction of the goods, or damage to them, is normally dealt with as a question of risk.[72] In *Appleby v Myers*,[73] however, the claimants contracted to supply and erect on the defendant's premises certain machinery, the price to be paid on completion of the work. Before completion, the premises and all the machinery and materials thereon were destroyed by fire. It was held that the contract was frustrated by the destruction of the premises. In this case, the contract was one for work and materials and was to be performed exclusively in relation to the particular premises. If the fire had left the premises untouched, and only injured part of the work which the claimants had already done, the court was of the opinion that they would have had to do that work over again and the contract would not have been discharged.[74] In most cases, therefore, where the contract is for the sale of unascertained goods, the loss or destruction of the goods manufactured, assembled or installed by the seller before the risk passes to the buyer will not discharge the contract of sale.[75]

Exceptionally, however, where the goods, though unascertained, are intended by both parties to be taken from an ascertained bulk, and that bulk is lost or destroyed, the contract may be held to have been frustrated.[76] Where property in an undivided share in the bulk has been transferred to the buyer under section 20A of the Act[77] or at common law[78] it is probable that, unless otherwise agreed, the risk in relation to that undivided share passes to the buyer at the same time[79] so that the contract will not be frustrated by the subsequent loss or destruction of the bulk. But there will be cases where the property in an undivided share is not transferred to the buyer while the goods still form part of the bulk[80] and in those cases the loss or destruction of the bulk could frustrate the contract.

6–052 **Insufficiency of goods.** A seller may, because of a prohibition of export or other extraneous supervening event, have insufficient goods of the contractual description available to fulfil all of his existing contracts for

---

[70] See *FA Tamplin SS Co. Ltd v Anglo-American Petroleum Co. Ltd* [1916] 2 A.C. 397 (ship under charterparty); *Metropolitan Water Board v Dick, Kerr & Co. Ltd* [1918] A.C. 119 (building contract); *Bank Line Ltd v Arthur Capel & Co.* [1919] A.C. 435 (ship under charterparty).

[71] Sale of Goods Act 1979, s.7; above, para.6–035.

[72] See above, para.6–001. This may even include a situation where unascertained goods become ascertained, *e.g.* by a contractual notice of appropriation, and are subsequently lost or destroyed before the risk passes to the buyer. *Cf.* Treitel, *Frustration and Force Majeure* (2nd ed., 2004), para.3–022.

[73] (1867) L.R. 2 C.P. 651. See also *Parsons Bros Ltd v Shea* (1965) 53 D.L.R. (2d) 86.

[74] At p.660.

[75] *Cf. Fibrosa Spolka Akcyjna v Fairbairn, Lawson, Combe Barbour Ltd* [1943] A.C. 32 at 83.

[76] See above, para.6–038, *Howell v Coupland* (1874) L.R. 9 Q.B. 462 at 466; (1876) 1 Q.B.D. 258 at 262, 263. But see above, paras 6–036, 6–041.

[77] See above, para.5–109.

[78] See above, para.5–129.

[79] See above, para.6–006.

[80] See, for example, above, para.5–130.

those goods, but nevertheless have sufficient goods to satisfy one or some of them. Suppose that a seller has contracts with A and B for the supply from a defined source of unascertained goods of the same contractual description. He has sufficient goods available to fulfil his contract with A, but the occurrence of such an event renders it impossible for him to perform his contracts with both A and B. It is clear that he cannot claim that both contracts are frustrated on the ground that he cannot perform both contracts in full. But, on one view, he should be entitled reasonably to appropriate what goods he has to A's contract, and will then be discharged by frustration from performance of his contract with B. The contrary view is that he could not excuse non-performance of his contract with B by reference to his commitments to A, nor could he give priority to A's contract over that of B.[81] He can therefore perform his contract with A for which he has sufficient goods, but will then be liable for the breach of his contract with B which is unfulfilled, since it is by his own act or election ("self-induced frustration") that he has chosen to perform his contract with A in preference to that of B.[82] This issue was considered incidentally in *J. Lauritzen A/S v Wijsmuller BV (The Super Servant Two)*.[83] In that case the defendants agreed to transport a large drilling rig by sea on terms that the transportation unit to be used for the carriage was to be *Super Servant One* or *Super Servant Two* at the defendants' option. The defendants intended to use *Super Servant Two* for the contract, but before the time for performance that unit sank. They had in the meantime entered into contracts with other persons which they could only perform by using *Super Servant One*. They therefore declined to use that unit to carry out the contract and claimed that the contract was frustrated. The Court of Appeal held that the contract was not frustrated by the loss of the *Super Servant Two*: the contract could still have been performed by using *Super Servant One*, but the defendants themselves elected not to do so. This case did not, of course, concern the sale of goods, and it is distinguishable in that the contract reserved to the defendants the express option to use either of the named units for its performance.[84] Nevertheless, in his judgment, Dillon L.J. rejected the proposition[85] that a party who, because of a supervening event, is deprived of the means of satisfying all his existing contracts may elect to use such means as are available to him to perform some of the contracts and claim that the others are discharged by frustration.[86] If the view of Dillon L.J. is correct,[87] then, in the absence of any appropriately drafted *force majeure*

---

[81] *Hong Guan & Co. Ltd v R Jumabhoy & Sons Ltd* [1960] A.C. 684 at 701–702 ("subject to *force majeure* and shipment" clause).
[82] *Maritime National Fish Ltd v Ocean Trawlers Ltd* [1935] A.C. 524; *Pancommerce SA v Veecheema BV* [1982] 1 Lloyd's Rep. 645 at 651 (on appeal [1983] 2 Lloyd's Rep. 304 at 307). See also *J. Lauritzen AS v Wijsmuller BV (The Super Servant Two)* [1989] 1 Lloyd's Rep. 148 at 152–159 (affirmed [1990] 1 Lloyd's Rep. 1).
[83] [1990] 1 Lloyd's Rep. 1. *Cf. Terkol Rederierne v Petroleo Brasileiro SA (The Badagry)* [1985] 1 Lloyd's Rep. 395.
[84] [1990] 1 Lloyd's Rep. 1 at 4. See also *Barkworth v Young* (1856) 26 L.J.Ch. 153 at 163.
[85] Advanced by Treitel, *Law of Contract* (7th ed.), p.675.
[86] [1990] 1 Lloyd's Rep. 1 at 13–14. See also *ibid.* at pp.9–10 (Bingham L.J.).
[87] See the criticism advanced by Treitel, *Frustration and Force Majeure* (2nd ed., 2004), para.14–024 and below, para.18–354.

clause in the contract of sale,[88] even a reasonable allocation by the seller of available goods to A will not relieve him of liability for breach of his contract with B, notwithstanding that an extraneous event for which he is not responsible has rendered it impossible for him to perform both contracts in full.

6–053 **Prorating.** The American Uniform Commercial Code[89] makes provision for an event which thus affects only part of a seller's capacity to perform by adoption of the principle of "prorating".[90] The seller must allocate production and deliveries among his customers and may so allocate in any manner which is fair and reasonable. He must notify the buyer seasonably that there will be delay or non-delivery and of the estimated quota made available to the buyer. The buyer may then either modify the contract by agreeing to take his available quota in substitution or terminate and thereby discharge the unexecuted portion of the contract.[91] In making the allocation the seller may, at his option, include regular customers not then under contract as well as his own requirements for further manufacture.[92] In English law, however, it has been held that where a seller has a legal commitment to A, and a non-legal moral commitment to B, and he can honour his obligations to A, or B, but not to both, he is not justified in law in partially honouring both obligations.[93] Still less (it may be presumed) would any account be taken of the seller's own manufacturing requirements. The possibility of *pro rata* apportionment in appropriate circumstances among existing contracts has been recognised where the seller relies on a *force majeure* clause in the contract of sale, even when the clause refers to the seller being "prevented" from performing the contract by the stipulated event.[94] But, in the absence of such a clause, there is no obligation on the seller to effect such an apportionment or on the buyer to accept the lesser quantity tendered, nor, if the seller does apportion, does it appear that he will be relieved by reason of frustration from liability for non-delivery of the undelivered balance.[95]

6–054 **Contract becomes unprofitable for seller.** The fact that a contract of sale has become, because of a rise in prices or costs or by the occurrence of an extraneous event, unprofitable for the seller is insufficient to frustrate the

[88] For the position where there is such a clause, see below, paras 8–102, 18–353.
[89] s.2–615(b), (c).
[90] See Hudson, 31 M.L.R. 535 (1968), 123 S.J. 137 (1978).
[91] s.2–616.
[92] s.2–615(b).
[93] *Pancommerce SA v Veecheema BV* [1983] 2 Lloyd's Rep. 304 at 307.
[94] See below, paras 8–102, 18–353.
[95] It is, however, arguable that, if an export prohibition is only partial, and restricts export to a stated percentage of the quantity of goods contracted to be sold, the seller would be bound to deliver the permitted quantity if required by the buyer, being discharged of liability in respect of the remainder: see *Sainsbury (HR & S) Ltd v Street* [1972] 1 W.L.R. 834, and below, paras 18–338, 18–354. Contrast *Kawasaki Steel Corp. v Sardoil SpA* [1977] 2 Lloyd's Rep. 552 at 555 (express clause required).

contract.[96] Although it has been suggested[97] that it would be possible for a court to find that "a serious and sudden depreciation of monetary value could disrupt the intended equivalence of performances on either side" and bring about a radical change in the obligation sufficient to frustrate a contract, the better view is that a devaluation of the currency in which the price is expressed[98] or the effect of inflation on the profitability of a fixed-price contract (even if of long duration)[99] are risks which must be borne by the seller.[1]

Change in circumstances of buyer. A contract of sale of goods will not be frustrated by the fact that, after the contract has been made, events subsequently occur which render the goods of no practical use to the buyer[2] or which prevent him from using the goods for a purpose intended by him,[3] unless it can be shown that the continuing existence of such purpose was the basis on which both parties entered into the contract.[4] 6–055

(c) *Express Clauses*

Provisions of contract. The parties may in their contract make express provision for the effects of an event which would otherwise frustrate the contract, for example, that one party is to bear the risk of such an event,[5] or that the contract is to be performed in an alternative manner,[6] or that it is 6–056

---

96 *Instone (S) & Co. Ltd v Speeding Marshall & Co. Ltd* (1915) 32 T.L.R. 202; *Bolckow Vaughan & Co. v Compania Minera de Sierra Minera* (1916) 33 T.L.R. 111; *Tennants (Lancashire) Ltd v C. S. Wilson & Co. Ltd* [1917] A.C. 495; *Blackburn Bobbin Co. Ltd v TW Allen & Sons Ltd* [1918] 2 K.B. 467; *E Hulton & Co. Ltd v Chadwick & Taylor Co. Ltd* (1918) 34 T.L.R. 230; *Beves & Co. Ltd v Farkas* [1953] 1 Lloyd's Rep. 103; *Davis Contractors Ltd v Fareham UDC* [1956] A.C. 696 at 729; *Tsakiroglou & Co. Ltd v Noblee Thorl GmbH* [1962] A.C. 93; *Exportelisa SA v Rocco Giuseppe & Figli Soc Coll* [1978] 1 Lloyd's Rep. 433; *National Carriers Ltd v Panalpina (Northern) Ltd* [1981] A.C. 675 at 700. *Cf. Brauer & Co. (GB) Ltd v James Clark (Brush Materials) Ltd* [1952] 2 All E.R. 497 at 500, 501.

97 Mann, *Legal Aspects of Money* (6th ed.), 9.47.

98 See Downes, 101 L.Q.R. 98 (1985), and below, para.25–166.

99 *British Movietonews v London and District Cinemas Ltd* [1952] A.C. 166 at 185; *Wates Ltd v GLC* (1983) 25 Build.L.R. 1 at 34; *Cf. Staffordshire Area Health Authority v South Staffordshire Water Authority* [1978] 1 W.L.R. 1387 at 1397–8.

1 The seller may protect himself by express provisions in the contract of sale whereby the price is to be adjusted, *e.g.* in the event of a rise in raw material, labour or transport costs, or (in longterm contracts) by a "hardship" clause: see *Superior Overseas Development Corp. v British Gas Corp.* [1982] 1 Lloyd's Rep. 262; *Wates Ltd v GLC*, above.

2 *New System Private Telephones (London) Ltd v E. Hughes & Co.* [1939] 2 All E.R. 844 (hire).

3 *McMaster & Co. v Cox McEuen & Co.* 1921 S.C. (HL) 24 (export); *Congimex etc. SARL v Tradax Export SA* [1983] 1 Lloyd's Rep. 250 (import). See also *Herne Bay Steamboat Co. v Hutton* [1903] 2 K.B. 683 (charter of ship).

4 As in the case of prohibitions against export (above, para.6–046) and *Krell v Henry* [1903] 2 K.B. 740 (hire of rooms). See also *Appleby v Myers* (1867) L.R. 2 C.P. 651 (above, para.6–051). Contrast *Atlantic Paper Stock Ltd v St Anne-Nackawic Pulp & Paper Co.* (1976) 56 D.L.R. (3d) 409.

5 *Cf. Kodros Shipping Corp. v Empresa Cubana de Fletes* [1981] 2 Lloyd's Rep. 612.

6 *Kuwait Supply Co. v Oyster Marine Management Inc.* [1994] 1 Lloyd's Rep. 637.

to continue or to be merely suspended,[7] or that one party is to have the option to continue with or cancel the contract,[8] or that certain notices must be given before one party is relieved of his liability to perform.[9] Where the contract makes provision (that is full and complete provision so intended) for a specified contingency, this will normally preclude the court from holding that the contract is frustrated.[10] But if, on its true construction, the clause in question is found not to be intended to make full and complete provision for the situation created by the frustrating event, then it is still open to the court to find that the contract has been frustrated.[11]

6–057 Conversely, in many contracts of sale, clauses are inserted which provide for the cancellation, variation, suspension or extension of the contract, or of particular obligations arising thereunder, upon the happening of certain events, even though such events may be insufficient in law to bring about frustration.[12] And, in overseas sales,[13] the contract of sale may contain the term "subject to licence" or "subject to licence being granted" or "subject to quota"[14] or some such similar provision. There is then introduced into the contract a condition that the licence must be obtained and that neither party will be liable[15] to perform the duties under the contract unless the licence is obtained.[16]

---

[7] Contrast *Ertel Bieber & Co. v Rio Tinto Co. Ltd* [1918] A.C. 260 (outbreak of war rendering contract illegal).
[8] *Bank Line Ltd v Capel (A) & Co.* [1919] A.C. 435; *Empresa Exportadora de Azucar v Industria Azucarera Nacional SA* [1983] 2 Lloyd's Rep. 171.
[9] *Empresa Exportadora de Azucar v Industria Azucarera Nacional SA*, above.
[10] *Bank Line Ltd v Capel (A) & Co.*, above, at pp.455, 456; *Joseph Constantine Steamship Line Ltd v Imperial Smelting Corp. Ltd* [1942] A.C. 154 at 163; *Empresa Exportadora de Azucar v Industria Azucarera Nacional SA*, above, at pp.188–189; *Kuwait Supply Co. v Oyster Marine Management Inc.*, above.
[11] *Metropolitan Water Board v Dick, Kerr & Co. Ltd* [1918] A.C. 119; *Bank Line Ltd v Capel (A) & Co.*, above; *Fibrosa Spolka Akcyjna v Fairbairn, Lawson, Combe Barbour Ltd* [1943] A.C. 32 at 40; *Kodros Shipping Corp. v Empresa Cubana de Fletes*, above; *Empresa Exportadora de Azucar v Industria Azucarera Nacional SA*, above.
[12] See below, para.8–088.
[13] See below, para.18–318.
[14] *Cf. Partabmull Rameshwar v KC Sethia (1944) Ltd* [1951] 1 All E.R. 352n.
[15] But "subject to licence" will itself be subject to the duty on the part of one party to use reasonable endeavours to obtain a licence: *Charles H Windschuegl Ltd v Alexander Pickering & Co. Ltd* (1950) 84 Ll.L.R. 89 at 92. See above, para.6–047; below, para.18–314. See also *Kyprianou v Cyprus Textiles Ltd* [1958] 2 Lloyd's Rep. 60 (duty to co-operate).
[16] *Charles H Windschuegl Ltd v Alexander Pickering & Co. Ltd*, above, at p.92; *Société D'Avances Commerciales (London) Ltd v A Besse & Co. (London) Ltd* [1952] 1 T.L.R. 644 at 646; *Brauer & Co. (GB) Ltd v James Clark (Brush Materials) Ltd* [1952] 2 All E.R. 497 at 501; *Aaronson Bros Ltd v Maderera del Tropico SA* [1967] 2 Lloyd's Rep. 159 at 160; *Czarnikow (C) Ltd v Central Handlu Zagranicznego Rolimpex* [1979] A.C. 351. *Cf. Peter Cassidy Seed Co. Ltd v Osuustukkukauppa I.L.* [1957] 1 W.L.R. 273 ("as soon as export licence granted".) See below, paras 18–328, 18–329.

(d) *Consequences of Frustration*

Consequences. The consequences of frustration of a contract of sale of goods governed by English law are in principle governed by the common law as modified by the provisions of the Law Reform (Frustrated Contracts) Act 1943.[17] But this Act exempts from its operation "any contract to which section 7 of the Sale of Goods Act 1979 . . . applies, or . . . any other contract for the sale, or for the sale and delivery, of specific goods, where the contract is frustrated by reason of the fact that the goods have perished."[18] The reference to section 7 of the 1979 Act is clear,[19] but the remainder of this provision is enigmatic. Cases where specific goods perish would, apart from section 7, normally not give rise to frustration, but be determined as questions of risk. It is possible that this provision was merely inserted *ex abundanti cautela* to avoid any misunderstanding that the 1943 Act was intended to apply to cases where the risk lay on the buyer or seller.[20] 6–058

The Act of 1943 will, however, apply to cases where a contract for the sale of unascertained goods is frustrated, and where a contract for the sale of specific goods is frustrated otherwise than by the fact that the goods have perished.[21] The provisions of the 1943 Act give rise to a number of difficulties of interpretation which were considered in *BP Exploration Co. (Libya) Ltd v Hunt (No.2)*.[22] 6–059

Sums paid or payable before time of discharge. Section 1(2) of the 1943 Act provides: "All sums paid or payable to any party in pursuance of the contract before the time when the parties were so discharged (in this Act referred to as 'the time of discharge') shall, in the case of sums so paid, be recoverable as money received by him for the use of the party by whom the sums were paid, and, in the case of sums so payable, cease to be so payable." Thus if the buyer has paid to the seller the whole or part of the purchase price of the goods or other sums in pursuance of the contract before[23] the frustrating event occurs, the buyer is entitled as of right to the 6–060

---

[17] See *Chitty on Contracts* (29th ed.), Vol. 1, para.23–068.

[18] s.2(5)(c), as amended by s.63 and Sch.2, para.2 of the Sale of Goods Act 1979.

[19] See above, paras 6–035, 6–039.

[20] See Atiyah, *Sale of Goods* (11th ed.), p.365; Treitel, *Frustration and Force Majeure* (2nd ed., 2004), para.15–094; Goff and Jones, *The Law of Restitution* (6th ed.), 20–079—20–081. *Cf.* Macleod, *Sale and Hire Purchase* (1971), p.258. However, where the contract is for the sale of a specified fraction or percentage of a specific bulk, then by virtue of the extended definition of "specific goods" in s.61(1) of the1979 Act the contract is one for the sale of specific goods. In such a case, the loss or destruction of the bulk before the risk has passed to the buyer might (arguably) frustrate the contract. See above, paras 6–036, 6–051.

[21] It seems that a contract frustrated by supervening illegality will attract the provisions of the Act: see McNair, 60 L.Q.R. 160 at 162–163 (1944). For the application of the Act to c.i.f. and f.o.b. contracts, see below, paras 19–143, 20–104.

[22] [1979] 1 W.L.R. 783. (Robert Goff J.); [1981] 1 W.L.R. 232, CA; [1983] 2 A.C. 352, HL.

[23] The subsection does not provide for the recovery of money paid *after* the time of discharge, even if, for example, it has been paid in ignorance of the facts which frustrated the contract, or in ignorance that known facts have operated to frustrate the contract. But sums so paid might, in certain circumstances, be recoverable as money paid under a mistake.

repayment of those sums in full[24]; and if the purchase price or other sums payable in pursuance of the contract have not been paid, but are payable before[25] the frustrating event occurs, they cease to be payable by him. However, a proviso to this subsection states that "if the party to whom the sums were so paid or payable incurred expenses before the time of discharge in, or for the purpose of, the performance of the contract, the court may, if it considers it just to do so having regard to all the circumstances of the case, allow him to retain or, as the case may be, recover the whole or any part of the sums so paid or payable, not being an amount in excess of the expenses so incurred."[26]

Thus, for example, expenses incurred by the seller in acquiring the goods, or in manufacturing goods to be manufactured by him, or in packing the goods, before the frustrating event occurs may, to the extent that the court considers it just to do so, be set off against the sums paid or payable by the buyer before that event.[27] It would seem that "expenses" here means net expenses, exclusive of any profit element. But they will include such sum as appears to be reasonable in respect of overhead expenses and in respect of any work or services performed personally by the seller.[28] The view has been expressed that "the allowance for expenses is probably best rationalised as a statutory recognition of the defence of change of position."[29] If this be so, expenses incurred prior to, and in anticipation of, the making of the contract might be unfairly excluded.[30] The discretion conferred by the proviso is a broad one and does not require an equal division of the loss.[31] In exercising its discretion the court would no doubt take into consideration whether the expenses incurred by the seller had been wholly wasted or whether, for example, goods of a realisable value (in respect of which the expenses had been incurred) still remained in the hands of the seller. Further, in an individual case it may be just to allow the seller to retain or recover only a proportionate part of his expenses instead

---

[24] See *BP Exploration Co. (Libya) Ltd v Hunt (No.2)* [1981] 1 W.L.R. 232 at 240, CA; [1983] 2 A.C. 352 (recovery of the "farm-in" payment).

[25] Sums payable *after* the time of discharge cease to be payable at common law.

[26] See also s.1(5).

[27] Expenses can only be set off against "the sums so paid or payable," *i.e.* those paid or due before the time of discharge. Expenses in excess of such sums are irrecoverable under s.1(2). Also if no advance payment is provided for, or if the consideration is something other than the payment of money, no expenses can be recovered under ss.(2).

[28] s.1(4). *Quaere* whether debts incurred by the seller in respect of work or services performed by a third party, *e.g.* a carrier are included. In principle, there would seem to be no reason why these should not be included.

[29] *BP Exploration Co. (Libya) Ltd v Hunt (No.2)* [1979] 1 W.L.R. 783 at 800 (this point was not mentioned on appeal).

[30] See Treitel, *Frustration and Force Majeure* (2nd ed., 2004), para.15–071, and *Lloyd v Stanbury* [1971] 1 W.L.R. 535; *Anglia Television Ltd v Reed* [1972] 1 Q.B. 60; below, paras 16–086, 17–064 (damages). See also *Brewer Street Investments Ltd v Barclays Woollen Co. Ltd* [1954] 1 Q.B. 428; *William Lacey (Hounslow) Ltd v Davis* [1957] 1 W.L.R. 932 (restitution). *Cf. Dextra Bank & Trust Co. Ltd v Bank of Jamaica* [2002] 1 All E.R. (Comm.) 193.

[31] *Gamerco SA v ICM/Fair Warning (Agency) Ltd* [1995] 1 W.L.R. 1226.

of transferring, in effect, the whole of this loss to the buyer,[32] or even to deny any set-off of expenses at all.[33]

No provision is made in the subsection for any increase in the sum recoverable by the buyer, or in the amount of expenses to be allowed to the seller, to allow for the time value of money.[34]

Payment for valuable benefit obtained. Subsection (3) of section 1 of the 1943 Act further provides: "Where any party to the contract has, by reason of anything done by any other party thereto in, or for the purpose of, the performance of the contract obtained a valuable benefit[35] (other than a payment of money to which the last foregoing subsection applies) before the time of discharge, there shall be recoverable by him from the said other party such sum (if any) not exceeding the value of the said benefit to the party obtaining it, as the court considers just, having regard to all the circumstances of the case and, in particular—(a) the amount of any expenses[36] incurred before the time of discharge by the benefited party in, or for the purpose of, the performance of the contract, including any sums paid or payable by him to any other party in pursuance of the contract and retained or recoverable by that party under the last foregoing subsection, and (b) the effect, in relation to the said benefit, of the circumstances giving rise to the frustration of the contract." Robert Goff J. stated in *BP Exploration Co. (Libya) Ltd v Hunt (No.2)*[37] that this subsection must be applied in two distinct stages. First, the benefit has to be identified and valued, and such value forms the upper limit of the award. Secondly, the court may award a sum (the "just sum"), not greater than the value of such benefit, as it considers just having regard to all the circumstances of the case, including in particular the matters specified in section 1(3)(a) and (b). 6–061

The benefit. In *BP Exploration Co. (Libya) Ltd v Hunt (No.2)*[38] Robert Goff J. held that the benefit should be identified, not as the performance rendered by the party conferring the benefit, but as the product of that performance. If, therefore, before the frustrating event occurred, the seller has delivered to the buyer part of the goods contracted for, the benefit consists of the goods delivered[39] which may be worth more or less than the expenses incurred by the seller in their manufacture, supply, delivery, etc. The value of the benefit to the party receiving it has then to be assessed. The benefit was, in his opinion, to be valued as at the date of frustration, but no allowance was to be made for the time value of money, that is to say, 6–062

[32] Contrast Lord Simon in *National Carriers Ltd v Panalpina (Northern) Ltd* [1981] A.C. 675 at 707 (no apportionment).

[33] *Gamerco SA v ICM/Fair Warning (Agency) Ltd*, above.

[34] *BP Exploration Co. (Libya) Ltd v Hunt (No.2)* [1981] 1 W.L.R. 232 at 244, CA (this point was not dealt with by the House of Lords). But see below, para.6–067 (interest).

[35] See also s.1(5), (6).

[36] See also s.1(4).

[37] [1979] 1 W.L.R. 783 at 810 (this approach appears to have been impliedly accepted by the Court of Appeal [1981] 1 W.L.R. 232 at 237).

[38] [1979] 1 W.L.R. 783 at 801–802.

[39] *Cf.* s.2(4); below, para.6–069.

for the fact that that party had had the use of money obtained by the disposal of the goods (or, presumably, the use of the goods themselves) prior to the date of frustration.[40] If the benefit was obtained partly by reason of performance of the contract by the seller and partly by reason of work done by the buyer, the court had to do its best to apportion the benefit, and to decide what proportion was attributable to the seller's performance.[41] These points were not considered by the Court of Appeal[42] or by the House of Lords.[43]

6–063 Robert Goff J. further took the view that the circumstances referred to in section 1(3)(a) and (b) should be taken into account in valuing the benefit.[44] For example, under section 1(3)(a), the relevant expenses of the buyer and the amount (if any) retained or recoverable by the seller under section 1(2) in respect of the seller's expenses would fall to be deducted from the value of the benefit.[45] And section 1(3)(b) had also to be applied. This provision, in his opinion, made it clear that the party conferring the benefit was to take the risk of depreciation or destruction by the frustrating event.[46] So, for instance, if part of the contract goods were delivered to the buyer, but that part was destroyed by the frustrating event[47] or was rendered by the frustrating event of no value without delivery of the remainder, then the value of the benefit at the date of frustration[48] would be nil.[49] Again, however, these views were not considered by the Court of Appeal or by the House of Lords and it is arguable[50] that, on an alternative interpretation of section 1(3), the circumstances referred to in (a) and (b) are to be taken into account, not in valuing the benefit, but in the assessment of the just sum. In that event those circumstances would not go to reduce the value of the benefit (which forms the upper limit of the award), but be circumstances, *inter alia*, relevant to fixing a sum which the court considers it just to award to the seller.

6–064 Section 1(6) further provides that, where any person has assumed obligations under the contract in consideration of the conferring of a benefit by any other party to the contract upon any other person, whether a party to the contract or not, the court may, if in all the circumstances it is just to do so, treat for the purpose of section 1(3) any benefit so conferred

---

40 [1979] 1 W.L.R. 783 at 801–802.
41 *ibid.* at p.802.
42 [1981] 1 W.L.R. 232.
43 [1983] 2 A.C. 352.
44 [1979] 1 W.L.R. 783 at 801, 803, 804.
45 Contrast *Chitty on Contracts* (29th ed.), Vol. 1, para.23–087 (just sum).
46 [1979] 1 W.L.R. 783 at 803. See also s.2(3); below, para.6–071.
47 See, *e.g. Appleby v Myers* (1867) L.R. 2 C.P. 651 (above, para.6–051); *Parsons Bros Ltd v O'Shea* (1965) 53 D.L.R. (2d) 86.
48 *Cf.* Glanville Williams, *Law Reform (Frustrated Contracts) Act 1943* (2nd ed., 2004), pp.48–50; Treitel, *Frustration and Force Majeure* (1994), para.15–064, who argues that s.1(3) requires the court to look at the facts as they were before and not after the frustrating event.
49 Assuming no obligation to insure: s.1(5), below, para.6–070.
50 Treitel, *op. cit.*, para.15–064. See also *BP Exploration Co. (Libya) Ltd v Hunt (No.2)* [1981] 1 W.L.R. 232 at 237–238, CA.

as a benefit obtained by the person who has assumed the obligations as aforesaid.

The "just sum". The Act gives no indication of the way in which the just sum is to be assessed[51] and in *BP Exploration Co. (Libya) Ltd v Hunt (No.2)* the Court of Appeal recognised that it might be assessed in a number of different ways.[52] At first instance, Robert Goff J. had, in the circumstances of that case, assessed the just sum on the basis of reimbursing the claimants the expenditure which they had incurred under the contract before the frustrating event.[53] The Court of Appeal refused to upset this assessment and stated that it would not be justified in setting aside the judge's method of assessment merely because it thought there were better ways: the method of assessment would have to be shown to be "palpably wrong."[54] Although the assessment will depend upon the particular circumstances of each case, the method adopted by Robert Goff J. could be applied to contracts of sale of goods. On a reimbursement basis, the just sum would then be such amount as would fairly compensate the seller for the expenditure incurred by him in performance of the contract. This could, in appropriate cases, include development costs and machine and tool costs, as well as expenses of manufacture. However, any award would have to be limited to the value of the benefit obtained by the buyer by reason of the seller's performance.[55] The terms of the contract between the parties and the circumstances surrounding the making of it might also be relevant to the assessment of the just sum, in particular with respect to their intentions regarding the allocation of risks.[56] It has further been suggested[57] that, in a contract of sale of goods, since the buyer will only have been prepared to contract for the goods on the basis that he paid no more than the contract price, it might be unjust to compel him, by an award under the Act, to pay more than that price, or a rateable part of it, in respect of the goods he has received. 6–065

Cross-claims. Claims or cross-claims, or both, may be made by either party under both subsections (2) and (3) of section 1 of the Act.[58] 6–066

---

[51] In *BP Exploration Co. (Libya) Ltd v Hunt (No.2)*, Robert Goff J. at [1979] 1 W.L.R. 783 at 799, explained the principle underlying the Act to be "the prevention of unjust enrichment of either party to the contract at the other's expense", but the Court of Appeal at [1981] 1 W.L.R. 232 at 243, stated "We get no help from the use of words which are not in the statute."

[52] [1981] 1 W.L.R. 232 at 242–244. The method of assessment was not considered by the House of Lords.

[53] Less the value of the benefits in kind which the claimants had received before that time.

[54] [1981] 1 W.L.R. 232 at 243.

[55] See above, para.6–062.

[56] This appears to have been impliedly accepted by the House of Lords in *BP Exploration Co. (Libya) Ltd v Hunt (No.2)* [1983] 2 A.C. 352, although held to be inapplicable on the facts of the case. See also s.2(3).

[57] By Robert Goff J. in *BP Exploration Co. (Libya) Ltd v Hunt (No.2)* [1979] 1 W.L.R. 783 at 805–806.

[58] *ibid.* at pp.807–8. But see s.1(3)(a).

6–067 **Interest.** The court may award interest under section 35A of the Supreme Court Act 1981[59] on any sum adjudged to be payable under the Act from the date on which the cause of action arose.[60] The cause of action arises on the occurrence of the frustrating event.[61]

6–068 **Effect of prior breach.** A breach of the relevant contract prior to frustration does not affect the right of a party to repayment under subsection (2) of section 1, nor the award of a just sum under subsection (3). The innocent party should raise his accrued right to damages as a set-off or counterclaim in the proceedings in which the claim is made.[62]

6–069 **Severability.** Where it appears to the court that a part of any contract to which the 1943 Act applies can properly be severed[63] from the remainder of the contract, being a part wholly performed before the time of discharge, or so performed except for the payment in respect of that part of the contract of sums which are or can be ascertained under the contract, the court is to treat that part of the contract as if it were a separate contract and had not been frustrated and is to treat section 1 of the Act as only applicable to the remainder of the contract.[64] So if, for example, there is a contract for the sale of goods to be delivered by four stated instalments, which are to be separately paid for,[65] and the contract is frustrated after delivery of the second instalment, but before the third instalment has been completely delivered or delivered at all, the court may treat the first two instalments as a separate contract and not frustrated, applying section 1 only to the third and fourth instalments and the payments therefor.

6–070 **Insurance monies.** Section 1(5) of the 1943 Act provides that moneys payable under a contract of insurance by reason of the frustrating event are not to be taken into account in assessing the sum which ought to be recovered or retained under section 1, unless there was an obligation to insure imposed by an express term of the frustrated contract or by or under any enactment.

6–071 **Contractual provision to the contrary.** By section 2(3) of the 1943 Act, where any contract to which the Act applies contains any provision which, upon the true construction of the contract, is intended to have effect in circumstances arising which operate, or would but for the provision operate, to frustrate the contract, or is intended to have effect whether such circumstances arise or not, the court is to give effect to the provision and is only to give effect to section 1 of the Act to such extent, if any, as appears to the court to be consistent with the provision. The parties can thus, by an

---

[59] See also County Courts Act 1984, s.69; Arbitration Act 1996, s.49; and below, paras 16–007, 16–012.
[60] *BP Exploration Co. (Libya) Ltd v Hunt (No.2)* [1983] 2 A.C. 352.
[61] *ibid*.
[62] [1979] 1 W.L.R. 783 at 808.
[63] See below, para.8–074.
[64] Law Reform (Frustrated Contracts) Act 1943, s.2(4).
[65] See Sale of Goods Act 1979, s.31(2) (below, para.8–077).

express provision in the contract, regulate the consequences of frustration, and effect must then be given to their intention. In *BP Exploration Co. (Libya) Ltd v Hunt (No.2)*,[66] the House of Lords held that there was nothing in the terms of the contract in that case, or in the circumstances surrounding the making of it, to indicate, either expressly or by necessary implication, that the parties had in contemplation the risks of the type of event which operated to frustrate the contract; or that, having had such risks in contemplation, they included in the contract any provision which, expressly or by necessary implication, was to take effect in the event of such risks materialising. This would indicate that the subsection can apply so as to oust section 1 of the Act, not only where the parties have expressly so provided, but also where, in accordance with ordinary principles of construction, their intentions in that respect can be ascertained by "necessary implication".[67] A contract of sale of goods may, on its true construction, provide that no payment is to be made unless and until full performance has been achieved. Such a situation will arise where the contract is "entire"[68] and not a severable[69] contract. It would appear, however, that such a provision would not, by necessary implication, automatically preclude an award under section 1(3) of the Act.[70] Only if, upon a true construction of the contract, the seller has contracted on terms that he is to receive no payment in the event which has occurred, will the fact that the contract is entire have the effect of precluding an award under the Act.[71] Also the fact that the buyer has made an advance payment or a payment on account, which in normal circumstances would be irrecoverable, will not automatically preclude the operation of section 1(2),[72] but only if the buyer has made an "out-and-out" payment which, on the true construction of the contract, was intended to be irrecoverable in the event that has occurred.[73]

---

[66] [1983] 2 A.C. 352.
[67] See also Robert Goff J. [1979] 1 W.L.R. 783 at 806.
[68] See below, para.8–072.
[69] See s.2(4) of the Act, and below, para.8–074.
[70] *BP Exploration Co. (Libya) Ltd v Hunt (No.2)* [1979] 1 W.L.R. 783 at 807.
[71] *ibid.* at pp.806, 807.
[72] *ibid.* at p.807.
[73] *ibid.* See also *Fibrosa Spolka Akcyjna v Fairbairn, Lawson, Combe, Barbour Ltd* [1943] A.C. at 43, 77.

CHAPTER 7

TRANSFER OF TITLE BY NON-OWNERS

		PARA.
1.	In general	7–001
2.	Estoppel	7–008
3.	Sale in market overt	7–020
4.	Sale under a voidable title	7–021
5.	Mercantile agents	7–031
6.	Seller in possession	7–055
7.	Buyer in possession	7–069
8.	Motor vehicles subject to a hire-purchase or conditional sale agreement	7–087
9.	Miscellaneous provisions	7–109
10.	Limitation	7–115

1. IN GENERAL

Nemo dat quod non habet. The general rule in English law[1] is that no one can transfer a better title to goods than he himself possesses.[2] This rule is often expressed in terms of the Latin maxim *nemo dat quod non habet*.[3] It is partially set out in section 21(1) of the Sale of Goods Act 1979, which provides "Subject to this Act,[4] where goods are sold by a person who is not their owner,[5] and who does not sell them under the authority or with the consent of the owner, the buyer acquires no better title to the goods than the seller had." At one time, the only effective exception to this rule was that of a sale in market overt.[6] But, in response to commercial[7] and social demands, further exceptions to the rule have been progressively introduced both by the common law and by statute. As Denning L.J. has remarked[8]: "In the development of our law, two principles have striven for mastery. The first is for the protection of property: no one can give a better title than he himself possesses. The second is for the protection of commercial transactions: the person who takes in good faith and for value without **7–001**

---

[1] The same rule applies in Scots law: *Morrisson v Robertson* 1908 S.C. 332. The Roman law at the time of Justinian was thus stated (Dig. 50. 17. 54): "Nemo plus juris ad alium transferre potest quam ipse haberet." See the Twelfth Report of the Law Reform Committee (1966), Cmnd. 2958.

[2] *Whistler v Forster* (1863) 14 C.B.(N.S.) 248 at 257.

[3] But a person may make a valid agreement to sell a thing not yet his: Sale of Goods Act 1979, ss.5(1), 12(1), (3) (above, para.4–001).

[4] ss.21, 23–26, 47, 48.

[5] For sales by part owners, see above, paras 1–081, 1–121, 5–128.

[6] See below, para.7–020 (now abolished).

[7] Chorley, 48 L.Q.R. 51 at 64 (1932).

[8] *Bishopsgate Motor Finance Corp. Ltd v Transport Brakes Ltd* [1949] 1 K.B. 322 at 336–337.

notice should get a good title. The first principle has held sway for a long time, but it has been modified by the common law itself and by statute so as to meet the needs of our own times." The second principle is fairly precisely delineated by a finite number of exceptions to the *nemo dat* rule. These are discussed in the sections which follow.

7–002 **Remedies of the owner.** An owner[9] who has an immediate right to possession of goods is entitled to recover possession of them from a person who is wrongfully in possession of the goods. He may either retake them without action[10] or bring an action for delivery up of the goods[11] or for damages for wrongful interference.[12] Further, any person who has wrongfully converted the goods either to his own use or to the use of another will be liable to an action for damages for wrongful interference at the suit of the owner[13] provided that, at the time of the conversion, the owner had an immediate right to possession of the goods.[14] Thus, even though the owner has been deprived of his title by the operation of one of the exceptions to the *nemo dat* rule, he will nevertheless be entitled to institute proceedings

---

[9] See *infra*, n.13.

[10] On recaption of chattels, see *Clerk and Lindsell on Torts* (19th ed.), para.31–12; Eighteenth Report of the Law Reform Committee (1971), Cmnd. 4774, paras 116–126. Contrast s.90 of the Consumer Credit Act 1974 (no recovery of "protected" goods otherwise than by action).

[11] Torts (Interference with Goods) Act 1977, s.3(2)(a), (b). The remedy of specific delivery of goods is, however, discretionary: see s.3(3)(b) of the 1977 Act. See also s.4 and CPR 25.1(1)(e) (interim remedy) and below, para.15–116.

[12] Torts (Interference with Goods) Act 1977, s.3(2)(c). Normally the measure of damages will be the value of the goods at the date of conversion if the goods have not been returned, detinue having been abolished by s.2(1): *Solloway v McLaughlin* [1938] A.C. 247 at 257; *BBMB Finance (HK) Ltd v Eda Holdings Ltd* [1990] 1 W.L.R. 409. *Cf. IBL Ltd v Coussens* [1991] 2 All E.R. 133. But consequential damages are recoverable if not too remote: see *Clerk and Lindsell on Torts* (19th ed.), paras 13–99—13–117. *Sachs v Miklos* [1948] 2 K.B. 22; *Strand Electric Engineering Co. Ltd v Brisford Entertainments Ltd* [1952] 2 Q.B. 246; *J. Sargent (Garages) Ltd v Motor Auctions (West Bromwich) Ltd* [1977] R.T.R. 121; *Hillesden Securities Ltd v Ryjack Ltd* [1983] 1 W.L.R. 959; *Kuwait Airways Corp. v Iraq Airways Co.* (*Nos 4 and 5*) [2002] UKHL 19, [2002] 2 A.C. 883; Palmer and McKendrick, *Interests in Chattels* (2nd ed., 1998), Chs 32–34. For cases where both claimant and defendant have an interest in the goods, see *Gillard v Brittan* (1841) 8 M. & W. 575; *Brierly v Kendall* (1852) 17 Q.B. 937; *Chinery v Viall* (1860) 5 H. & N. 288; *Massey v Sladen* (1868) L.R. 4 Ex. 13; *Mulliner v Florence* (1878) 3 Q.B.D. 484; *Moore v Shelley* (1883) 8 App.Cas. 285; and (goods let under hire-purchase agreement) *Wickham Holdings Ltd v Brook House Motors Ltd* [1967] 1 W.L.R. 295; *Belvoir Finance Co. Ltd v Stapleton* [1971] 1 Q.B. 210; *Chubb Cash Ltd v John Crilley & Son* [1983] 1 W.L.R. 599; below, para.7–105. *Cf. Astley Industrial Trust Ltd v Miller* [1968] 2 All E.R. 36.

[13] *cf. North West Securities v Alexander Breckon* [1981] R.T.R. 518 (action by non-owner who had entered into binding contract to purchase the goods). An equitable owner has no right to sue in conversion unless he had possession or an immediate right to possession of the converted goods: *MCC Proceeds Inc. v Lehman Brothers International (Europe)* [1998] 4 All E.R. 675, not following *International Factors Ltd v Rodriguez* [1979] Q.B. 351.

[14] *Union Transport Finance Ltd v British Car Auctions Ltd*, February 16, 1977 (CA Transcript No. 87 of 1977); *R. H. Willis & Son v British Car Auctions Ltd* [1978] 1 W.L.R. 438 (auctioneers).

in tort for wrongful interference against any person who converted the goods before his title was extinguished.[15] Contributory negligence on the part of the owner is no defence in proceedings founded on conversion.[16]

Alternatively the owner may "waive the tort"[17] and pursue a restitutionary claim to recover any sum received as a result of the sale or use of the goods by the wrongdoer in an action in restitution for money had and received.[18] Further the proprietary right of the owner is recognised, both at common law and in equity, by allowing him to "trace" or "follow" his property into the proceeds of its sale, so long as these have not been dissipated,[19] or into other identifiable assets which have been purchased with those proceeds.[20] This will be particularly important where the defendant is insolvent and the owner seeks to establish a claim in priority to the defendant's general creditors. At common law, tracing is a limited remedy. It is available only where the proceeds of sale have not been mixed with other moneys, *e.g.* in a bank account,[21] or (if a claim is made to other assets) where these have been purchased exclusively with the unmixed proceeds.[22] But equity will trace into a mixed fund or into assets purchased with the mixed fund[23] and will follow the moneys into the hands of anyone other than a bona fide purchaser for value without notice,[24] giving the owner a charge over the fund or assets in question.[25] However, tracing in equity requires the owner to establish that the defendant or a third party[26] is in a fiduciary relationship to him,[27] and that he has an equitable proprietary interest in the property claimed.[28] **7–003**

[15] See below, paras 7–105, 7–115.
[16] Torts (Interference with Goods) Act 1977, s.11(1). *Cf.*, Tettenborn [1993] C.L.J. 128.
[17] See *Chitty on Contracts* (29th ed.), Vol. 1, para.29–141; Goff and Jones, *The Law of Restitution* (6th ed.), Ch.36; Burrows, *The Law of Restitution* (2nd ed., 2002), Ch.14; and above, para.1–073.
[18] See Palmer and McKendrick, *Interests in Goods* (2nd ed., 1998), Chs 32, 35.
[19] *Re Diplock* [1948] Ch.465 at 521, 546.
[20] *Chitty on Contracts*, *op. cit.*, Vol. 1, para.29–158; Goff and Jones, *op. cit.*, Ch.2. See *Foskett v McKeown* [2001] 1 A.C. 182.
[21] *Taylor v Plumer* (1815) 3 M. & S. 562; *Banque Belge pour l'Etranger v Hambrouck* [1921] 1 K.B. 321 at 329; *Re Diplock*, above, at p.518; *Agip (Africa) Ltd v Jackson* [1991] 1 Ch. 447; *Lipkin Gorman v Karpnale Ltd* [1991] 2 A.C. 548.
[22] *Re Diplock*, above, at p.519; *Re J. Leslie Engineering Co. Ltd* [1976] 1 W.L.R. 292 at 297; *Lipkin Gorman v Karpnale Ltd*, above, at p.573; *Trustee of the Property of FC Jones & Sons v Jones* [1997] Ch.159.
[23] *Re Diplock*, above, at p.520.
[24] *ibid.*, at pp.521, 546.; *Foskett v McKeown* [2001] 1 A.C. 102, 129.
[25] See, *e.g. Re Hallett's Estate* (1880) 13 Ch.D. 696; *Re Oatway* [1903] 2 Ch. 356. See also *Clayton's Case* (1816) Mer. 572 (withdrawals from mixed fund) and *Chitty on Contracts*, *op. cit.*, Vol. 1, para.29–164.
[26] *i.e.*, a third party through whose hands the owner's property has passed.
[27] *Re Diplock*, above, at p.532. But if goods or money are stolen or obtained by fraud, equity imposes a constructive trust on the fraudulent recipient: *Westdeutsche Landesbank Girozentrale v Islington London BC* [1996] A.C. 669 at 716.
[28] *Re Diplock*, above, at pp.520, 529; *Westdeutsche Landesbank Girozentrale v Islington London B.C.*, above.

7–004 Where goods of the owner are wrongfully mixed by the defendant with goods of his own, which are substantially of the same nature and quality,[29] and they cannot in practice be separated, the mixture is held in common and the owner is entitled to receive out of it a quantity equal to that of his goods which went into the mixture, any doubt about that quantity being resolved in favour of the owner.[30] He is also entitled to claim damages from the defendant in respect of any loss he may have suffered, in respect of quality or otherwise, by reason of the admixture.[31]

7–005 **Improvements.**[32] By section 6(1) of the Torts (Interference with Goods) Act 1977, if in proceedings for wrongful interference against a person (the "improver") who has improved the goods, it is shown that the improver acted in the mistaken but honest belief that he had a good title to them, an allowance is to be made for the extent to which, at the time as at which the goods fall to be valued in assessing damages, the value of the goods is attributable to the improvement. This subsection in substance restates the common law.[33] However, subsection (2) of section 6 goes further and extends the availability of such an allowance, not merely to the case where the defendant is the improver, but where he is a purchaser,[34] acting in good faith, who derives (whether immediately or not) his supposed "title" to the goods from the improver.[35] In addition, section 3(7) of the 1977 Act provides that, if the court makes an order for delivery up of the goods (with or without the alternative of paying damages by reference to their value) it may assess the allowance to be made in respect of the improvement, and by the order require, as a condition for delivery of the goods, that allowance to be made by the claimant.[36] It is questionable, however, whether a person from whom the goods are seized by the owner has a similar claim.[37] The Act is silent on this point, but a New Zealand case[38] has held that the owner is liable for the conversion of the components constituting the improvements, unless these have by accession[39] become merged in the goods, and

---

[29] See above, para.1–120 (fungible goods). *Cf. Borden (U.K.) Ltd v Scottish Timber Products Ltd* [1981] Ch.25 (new product), above, para.5–149 *cf.Glencore International AG v Metro Trading International Inc.* [2001] 1 Lloyd's Rep. 283 (commingling).

[30] *Indian Oil Corp. Ltd v Greenstone Shipping SA (Panama)* [1988] Q.B. 345 at 370–371. See also *Glencore International AG v Metro Trading International Inc.*, above, and the cases cited above, para.5–148, n.10 and the discussion in Palmer and McKendrick, *Interests in Goods* (2nd ed., 1998), Ch.10, p.227, Ch.36, p.935.

[31] *Indian Oil Corp. Ltd v Greenstone Shipping SA (Panama)*, above., at p.371.

[32] See Palmer and McKendrick, *Interests in Goods* (2nd ed., 1998), Chs 33, 35, 36.

[33] *Reid v Fairbanks* (1853) 13 C.B. 692 at 797. But see *Munro v Willmott* [1949] 1 K.B. 295 (improvement with knowledge of lack of title). See also Gordon (1955) 71 L.Q.R. 346; Guest (1964) 27 M.L.R. 505 at 516; Matthews [1981] C.L.J. 340; Matthews [1981] *Current Legal Problems* 159.

[34] See also s.6(4) (other dispositions)—an ambiguous provision: see Palmer and McKendrick, *op. cit.*, Ch.36, p.926.

[35] See also above, para.4–007.

[36] *Greenwood v Bennett* [1973] 1 Q.B. 195. *Cf. Webb v Ireland and the Attorney General* [1988] I.R. 353 at 373.

[37] Matthews [1981] C.L.J. 340 at 346.

[38] *Thomas v Robinson* [1977] 1 N.Z.L.R. 385.

[39] See Guest (1964) 27 M.L.R. 505; Matthews [1981] *Current Legal Problems* 159 at 171; Palmer and McKendrick, *op. cit*, Chs 10, 36 and above, para.5–149 n.20.

that the improver could further be compensated for the added value he had given to the goods.[40]

7–006 **Restitution and seizure orders.** Where goods have been stolen, and a person is convicted of any offence with reference to the theft (whether or not the stealing is the gist of his offence),[41] section 148 of the Powers of the Criminal Courts (Sentencing) Act 2000[42] gives to the court by or before which the offender is convicted the power to order anyone having possession or control of the goods to restore the stolen goods to any person entitled to recover them from him.[43] This power also extends to cases where goods have been obtained by blackmail[44] or by deception.[45] The power is discretionary, but a restitution order can be made even where the person convicted has sold the goods to a person acting in good faith, or has borrowed money on them from a person so acting.[46] Although a restitution order can be made in favour of a person "entitled to recover" the goods, and that person may or may not be their owner, it is submitted that the court could not, by such an order, deprive a bona fide disponee of a good title which he had obtained under one of the exceptions to the *nemo dat* rule.[47] Moreover it has been stated that the court should exercise this power only in "the plainest cases"[48] and that it should not be exercised when difficult questions of law affecting title to goods arise, since such matters are more suitable for the civil courts.[49]

A similar procedure exists under the Police (Property) Act 1897,[50] which applies to property which has come into the possession of the police in connection with their investigation of any suspected offence. This power is again discretionary, but does not depend upon the apprehension or conviction of the offender. The court may make an order for the delivery of the property "to the person appearing . . . to be the owner thereof."[51] However, it has been stated that this procedure should not be used in cases involving "tricky questions of title".[52]

---

[40] See also *Greenwood v Bennett*, above (interpleader action) at pp.202, 203 and [1973] C.L.J. 23; 36 M.L.R. 89 (1973); [1973] J.B.L. 64; Palmer and McKendrick, *op. cit.*, Chs 33, p.854, 35, p.898, 36, p.929.

[41] Or where a person is convicted of any other offence, but an offence with reference to theft is taken into consideration in determining his sentence.

[42] Re-enacting s.28 of the Theft Act 1968.

[43] s.148(2)(a). For the other types of order that may be made, see s.148(2)(b), (c), and s.149.

[44] s.148(8), (9); Theft Act 1968, s.24(4).

[45] s.148(8), (9); Theft Act 1968, ss.15(1), 24(4).

[46] s.148(4).

[47] *Cf.* Kentisbeer [1977] Crim.L.R. 696.

[48] *R. v Ferguson* [1970] 1 W.L.R. 1246 at 1249.

[49] *Stamp v United Dominions Trust Ltd* [1967] 1 Q.B. 418; *R. v Church* (1970) 53 Cr.App.R. 65.

[50] s.1(1), as amended by the Criminal Justice Act 1972, s.58 and the Powers of the Criminal Courts (Sentencing) Act 2000, s.144. See also s.2 and s.2A (inserted by s.77 of the Police Reform Act 2002).

[51] See *Raymond Lyons & Co. Ltd v Metropolitan Police Commissioner* [1975] Q.B. 321.

[52] *Raymond Lyons & Co. Ltd v Metropolitan Police Commissioner*, above, at p.326. *Cf.*, *Irving v National Provincial Bank Ltd* [1962] 2 Q.B. 73 (burden of proof).

7–007 Power to seize and retain property is also given to the police by the Police and Criminal Evidence Act 1984.[53] But the exercise of this power transfers to the police no title to the property and the person from whom the property is seized can normally rely on his previous possession of the property as conferring sufficient title to recover the property from the police.[54]

Numerous other statutes confer a power of seizure.[55] Where there is an obligation to return the property seized,[56] it is to be returned to the person from whom it was seized unless some other person has a "better right" to the property than the person from whom it was seized.[57] Very broad powers are, however, conferred by the Proceeds of Crime Act 2002[58] upon the Crown Court[59] to make confiscation orders[60] in respect of property[61] where it decides that a defendant has benefited from his criminal conduct. In particular the court may make an order in respect of property held by the recipient of a "tainted gift" [62] from the defendant (which includes a transfer at a significant undervalue).[63] It is immaterial that the recipient of a tainted gift received it in good faith.

2. ESTOPPEL

7–008 **Title by estoppel.** Section 21(1) of the Sale of Goods Act 1979 provides that the rule *nemo dat quod non habet* is not to apply where "the owner of the goods is by his conduct precluded from denying the seller's authority to sell." It might be supposed that this exception embodies the broad principle enunciated by Ashhurst J. in *Lickbarrow v Mason*[64] that "wherever one of two innocent persons must suffer by the acts of a third, he who has enabled such third person to occasion the loss must sustain it." But it is clear that this dictum, if too literally construed, is much too wide: it has often been

---

[53] ss.19, 22, supplemented by the Police Reform Act 2002, Sch.4, para.19 and the Criminal Justice Act 2003, Sch.1, para.4.
[54] *Webb v Chief Constable of Merseyside Police* [2000] Q.B. 427; *Costello v Chief Constable of Derbyshire Constabulary* [2001] EWCA Civ. 381; [2001] 1 W.L.R. 1437.
[55] Criminal Justice and Police Act 2001, ss.50, 51, 52, and Sch.1 amended by the Police Reform Act 2002, s.59 and Sch.4, paras 9, 24; Proceeds of Crime Act 2002, s.352, Sch.11, para.40, Criminal Justice Act 2003, Sch.1, para.19.
[56] Criminal Justice and Police Act 2001, ss.53–57 amended by the Police Reform Act 2002, s.60 and Sch.4, para.2; Proceeds of Crime Act 2002, Sch.11, para.40 Sch.12, Criminal Justice Act 2003, Sch.1, paras.14, 19.
[57] *ibid.*, s.58. See also s.59 (application to the appropriate judicial authority) and ss.60, 61 (duty to secure), amended by the Police Reform Act 2002, s.60; Proceeds of Crime Act 2002, Sch.11, par.40, Sch.12.
[58] Part 2 (s. 6–91).
[59] The power may be extended to magistrates' courts by an order made under s.97 of the Serious Organised Crime and Police Act 2005.
[60] Restraint orders may also be made (ss.40–47).
[61] Defined in s.84.
[62] Defined in s.77.
[63] ss.78, 81, 83.
[64] (1787) 2 T.R. 63 at 70, reversed *sub nom. Mason v Lickbarrow* (1790) 1 Hy.Bl. 357.

criticised[65] and seldom applied.[66] At the other end of the scale, it might be thought that the language of the exception ("authority to sell") confined its operation to cases of agency by estoppel[67] or apparent (or ostensible) authority.[68] But section 62(2) of the Act expressly preserves the rules of the common law relating to the law of principal and agent,[69] so that there is little doubt that the exception relates to situations other than those in which the seller is the agent of the true owner of the goods or in which the owner holds out the seller to be his agent. The cases in which this provision has been canvassed indicate that it was intended to give statutory effect to a particular principle of estoppel in English law,[70] and that the terminology used may have been intended to render this principle intelligible in Scots law where the specific term "estoppel" is unknown. The true owner of goods can be estopped from denying the apparent ownership of the seller, so that the buyer acquires a good title to the goods by estoppel. Such an estoppel may arise either (i) by reason of a representation made by the true owner that the seller is the owner of the goods, or (ii) by negligence on the part of the true owner which enables the seller to create an appearance of ownership. For reasons of commercial convenience, however, the effect of its application is to transfer to the buyer a real title and not a metaphorical title by estoppel.[71] The estoppel is thus an unusual one in that it not only binds the true owner personally and those claiming under him, but confers a good title against all the world.

Estoppel by representation. Where the true owner of goods, by words or conduct,[72] voluntarily[73] represents or permits it to be represented that another person is the owner of the goods, any sale[74] of the goods by that 7–009

---

[65] *Farquharson Bros & Co. v King & Co.* [1902] A.C. 325 at 335, 342; *Rimmer v Webster* [1902] 2 Ch. 163 at 169; *London Joint Stock Bank v Macmillan* [1918] A.C. 777 at 836; *Jones Ltd v Waring and Gillow Ltd* [1926] A.C. 670 at 693; *Mercantile Bank of India Ltd v Central Bank of India Ltd* [1938] A.C. 287 at 298–299; *Wilson and Meeson v Pickering* [1946] K.B. 422 at 425; *Jerome v Bentley & Co.* [1952] 2 All E.R. 114 at 118; *Central Newbury Car Auctions Ltd v Unity Finance Ltd* [1957] 1 Q.B. 371 at 389, 396.

[66] *Cf. Commonwealth Trust v Akotey* [1926] A.C. 72, which was disapproved in *Mercantile Bank of India Ltd v Central Bank of India Ltd*, above; *Central Newbury Car Auctions Ltd v Unity Finance Ltd*, above, at p.383.

[67] See *Bowstead and Reynolds on Agency* (17th ed.), paras 2–099, 8–029.

[68] *ibid.* para.8–013.

[69] See also s.21(1), (2) of the Act.

[70] *Cf. Eastern Distributors Ltd v Goldring* [1957] 2 Q.B. 600 at 607. See also *Halsbury's Laws of England* (4th ed.), Vol. 16, para.1060; *Bowstead and Reynolds on Agency* (17th ed.), paras 8–126, 8–129; *Spiro v Lintern* [1973] 1 W.L.R. 1002 at 1010.

[71] *Eastern Distributors Ltd v Goldring*, above; *Mercantile Credit Co. Ltd v Hamblin* [1965] 2 Q.B. 242 at 275; *Stoneleigh Finance Ltd v Phillips* [1965] 2 Q.B. 537 at 578; *Moorgate Mercantile Co. Ltd v Twitchings* [1977] A.C. 890 at 918.

[72] See Pickering, 55 L.Q.R. 400 (1939).

[73] *Debs v Sibec Developments Ltd* [1990] R.T.R. 91.

[74] In *Shaw v Commissioner of Metropolitan Police* [1987] 1 W.L.R. 1332, the Court of Appeal held that estoppel did not operate in favour of one who had merely agreed to buy, and had not bought, the goods. But, in principle, there is no reason why estoppel should not apply to cases where the goods are pledged or otherwise disposed of for value to a third party: see *ibid.* at p.1337.

person is as valid against the true owner as if the seller were actually the owner thereof, with respect to anyone buying the goods in reliance on the representation.[75] Although the representation may be by words or conduct, it must be clear and unequivocal.[76] It is therefore well established that the mere parting with possession of goods is not conduct which estops the true owner from setting up his title.[77] Parting with possession alone is not a representation of ownership, even if the person receiving the goods has the authority of the true owner to deliver them to third parties.[78] If the rule were otherwise, any bailor would be estopped from denying his bailee's right to sell the goods, and there would be no necessity at all for the Factors Acts.[79] There must be something more. The true owner must have so acted as to mislead the buyer into the belief that the seller was entitled to sell the goods.[80] Delivery of possession of the goods is therefore neither a necessary nor a sufficient condition to raise such an estoppel. In the case of a motor vehicle, delivery to another of possession of the vehicle together with a vehicle registration document does not constitute a representation that the bailee has authority to sell the vehicle.[81] Nor does the fact that the true owner has negotiated a cash settlement with a person who has wrongfully dealt with the goods in respect of that person's liability in conversion estop him from claiming damages for conversion against a subsequent purchaser of the goods.[82]

7–010 The representation that the seller has a right to sell the goods must be made by the true owner or his agent.[83] The true owner will not be estopped by a representation of ownership made by the seller himself,[84] unless he

---

[75] *Cole v North Western Bank* (1875) L.R. 10 C.P. 354 at 363; *Colonial Bank v Cady* (1890) 15 App.Cas. 267 at 285; *Farquharson Bros & Co. v King & Co.* [1902] A.C. 325 at 330; *Rimmer v Webster* [1902] 2 Ch. 163 at 173; *People's Bank of Halifax v Estey* (1904) 34 S.C.R. 429. See also *Bowstead and Reynolds on Agency* (17th ed.), para.8–129. An estoppel could also arise if the true owner represents or permits it to be represented that he has no interest in the goods: *Shaw v Commissioner of Metropolitan Police*, above, at pp.1335, 1338. *Cf. Moorgate Mercantile Co. Ltd v Twitchings* [1977] A.C. 890.

[76] *Moorgate Mercantile Co. Ltd v Twitchings*, above.

[77] *Price v Groom* (1848) 2 ExCh.542; *Hollins v Fowler* (1875) L.R. 7 H.L. 757 at 764; *Johnson v Crédit Lyonnais Co.* (1877) 3 C.P.D. 32 at 36; *Meggy v Imperial Discount Co.* (1878) 3 Q.B.D. 711 at 717, 719; *Farquharson Bros & Co. v King & Co.*, above, at p.330; *Weiner v Gill* [1905] 2 K.B. 172 at 182, affirmed [1906] 2 K.B. 574; *Jerome v Bentley & Co.* [1952] 2 All E.R. 114 at 118; *Central Newbury Car Auctions Ltd v Unity Finance Ltd* [1957] 1 Q.B. 371 at 394, 396; *McVicar v Herman* (1958) 13 D.L.R. (2d) 419; *Mortimer-Rae v Barthel* (1979) 105 D.L.R. (3d) 289. See also *Beverley Acceptances Ltd v Oakley* [1982] R.T.R. 417.

[78] *Farquharson Bros & Co. v King & Co.*, above, at pp.332–333, 340.

[79] *Johnson v Crédit Lyonnais Co.*, above, at p.40; *Farquharson Bros & Co. v King & Co.*, above, at p.343; *Weiner v Gill*, above, at p.182. See below, para.7–031.

[80] *People's Bank of Halifax v Estey* (1904) 34 S.C.R. 429.

[81] *Central Newbury Car Auctions Ltd v Unity Finance Ltd*, above. See also *Beverley Acceptances Ltd v Oakley*, above; *Mcmanus v Eastern Ford Sales Ltd* (1981) 28 D.L.R. (3d) 346. *Cf. Canaplan Leasing Inc. v Dominion of Canada General Insurance Co.* (1990) 69 D.L.R. (4th) 531.

[82] *Worcester Works Finance Ltd v Medens Ltd* (1973) 117 S.J. 143; but see above, para.4–013.

[83] *Central Newbury Car Auctions Ltd v Unity Finance Ltd*, above; *J. Sargent (Garages) Ltd v Motor Auctions (West Bromwich) Ltd* [1977] R.T.R. 121.

[84] *Farquharson Bros & Co. v King & Co.*, above; *Weiner v Gill*, above.

authorised the representation or consented to its being made.[85] The representation must also be addressed to the particular buyer who alleges that he relied on it, or it must be made under such circumstances of publicity as to justify the inference that the buyer knew of it and relied on it.[86] It therefore follows that a buyer who is unaware of the representation cannot establish such reliance, nor, if he knows of the seller's defect of title, can he claim to have been misled. Whether or not the sale is in the ordinary course of business is relevant only in so far as it throws light on the bona fides of the buyer.[87]

There are very few cases of actions for conversion in which a plea of estoppel by representation has succeeded.[88] But in *Henderson v Williams*[89] an estoppel arose where the true owner instructed that goods in the possession of a warehouseman be transferred to the order of another, who sold them as owner.[90] Further, in *Eastern Distributors Ltd v Goldring*,[91] M was the owner of a van and wished to raise money on it. He agreed with a car dealer that the dealer should represent to the claimant finance company that he (M) wished to take the van on hire-purchase. He signed blank forms of hire-purchase agreement and a delivery note stating that he had taken delivery of the van. The effect of this was to arm the dealer with documents which enabled him to represent to the company that he (the dealer) was the owner of the van and had the right to sell it. Since M had consented and was privy to this representation, it was held by the Court of Appeal that he was estopped from denying the dealer's apparent ownership of the van. The company therefore acquired a good title under section 21(1) of the Act when they purchased the van from the dealer in reliance on the representation. **7–011**

Even though the true owner of goods has made no initial representation, he might nevertheless by his subsequent conduct be precluded from denying the seller's authority to sell. Thus if the true owner knows that the **7–012**

---

[85] *Pickard v Sears* (1837) 6 A. & E. 469; *Gregg v Wells* (1839) 10 A. & E. 90; *Waller v Drakeford* (1853) 1 E. & B. 749. See also *Eastern Distributors Ltd v Goldring* [1957] 2 Q.B. 600, and the cases cited in para.7–011, n.91. *Cf. Freeman v Cooke* (1848) 2 ExCh.654; *First Energy (U.K.) Ltd v Hungarian International Bank Ltd* [1993] 2 Lloyd's Rep. 194.

[86] *Dickinson v Valpy* (1829) 10 B. & C. 128 at 140; *Farquharson Bros & Co. v King & Co.*, above, at p.341; *Universal Guarantee Pty Ltd v Metters Ltd* [1966] W.A.R. 74. *Cf. Carr v L. & N.W. Ry.* (1875) L.R. 10 C.P. 307.

[87] *Lloyds & Scottish Finance Ltd v Williamson* [1965] 1 W.L.R. 404.

[88] *Mercantile Bank of India Ltd v Central Bank of India Ltd* [1938] A.C. 287 at 302.

[89] [1895] 1 Q.B. 521. See also *Pickering v Busk* (1812) 15 East 38 (agency); *Canadian Laboratory Supplies Ltd v Engelhard Industries Ltd* [1980] 2 S.C.R. 450.

[90] In this case, the warehouseman also acknowledged to the buyer that he held the goods to the seller's order subsequent to the contract of sale; see below, para.8–012.

[91] [1957] 2 Q.B. 600, noted 73 L.Q.R. 455 (1957); 20 M.L.R. 650 (1957). See also *People's Bank of Halifax v Estey* (1904) 34 S.C.R. 429; *Motor Finance and Trading Co. Ltd v Brown* [1928] S.A.S.R. 153; *Spencer v North Country Finance Co. Ltd* [1963] C.L.Y. 212, CA; *Stoneleigh Finance Ltd v Phillips* [1965] 2 Q.B. 537; *Snook v London and West Riding Investments Ltd* [1967] 2 Q.B. 786. Contrast *Campbell Discount Co. Ltd v Gall* [1961] 1 Q.B. 431 (disapproved in *United Dominions Trust Ltd v Western* [1976] Q.B. 513); *Dent-Brocklehurst v Lombank, The Guardian*, March 14, 1962; *Mercantile Credit Co. Ltd v Hamblin* [1965] 2 Q.B. 242. *Cf. Spiro v Lintern* [1973] 1 W.L.R. 1002 (land).

seller has contracted to sell his goods to a buyer who mistakenly believes them to be the property of the seller, it is submitted that the true owner may be under a duty to disclose to the buyer the fact that the contract was entered into without his authority. Such a duty will arise where a reasonable man would expect the true owner, acting honestly and responsibly, to make known to the buyer that he claimed title to the goods. Should he fail in this duty, and the buyer is thereby induced to believe in the validity of the contract and to buy the goods in reliance on that belief, the true owner ought then to be estopped from asserting his title against the buyer.[92] Also if, without any representation, the true owner and the buyer act upon[93] an agreed assumption that the seller is entitled to sell the goods, each may be estopped by convention against the other from denying that the seller was so entitled.[94]

7–013 **Documents of title.** The mere delivery by the true owner to another person of the possession of documents of title to goods does not, at common law,[95] estop him from asserting his title against one who has purchased[96] the goods from that person.[97] Even though, in one sense, he could be said to have enabled the seller to represent that he was the owner of the goods by investing him with the indicia of title,[98] it is clear that the delivery of possession of documents of title in itself has no greater effect than the delivery of possession of the goods themselves.[99] There must be some further act on the part of the true owner which amounts to a representation by him of the seller's right to sell, as for example, where he executes a document in which he acknowledges that he has been paid in full for the goods by the seller.[1] Most cases in which the true owner has been precluded from recovering the goods from the buyer prove, on examination, to be cases where the true owner's relationship with the seller was that of principal and agent. The true owner may deliver the document of title to

---

[92] *Spiro v Lintern* above (land); *Moorgate Mercantile Co. Ltd v Twitchings* [1977] A.C. 890 at 903; *Pacol Ltd v Trade Lines Ltd* (*The Henrik Sif*) [1982] 1 Lloyd's Rep. 456 at 465; *Tradax Export SA v Dorada Compania Naviera SA* (*The Lutetian*) [1982] 2 Lloyd's Rep. 140 at 157. See also *Mangles v Dixon* (1852) 3 H.L.C. 702 at 734; *West v Dillicar* [1920] N.Z.L.R. 139; [1921] N.Z.L.R. 617. Contrast *Shaw v Commissioner of Metropolitan Police* [1987] 1 W.L.R. 1332; *The Good Luck* [1989] 2 Lloyd's Rep. 238.

[93] *Astilleros Canaries SA v Cape Hatteras Shipping Co. SA* [1982] 1 Lloyd's Rep. 518.

[94] *Amalgamated Investments & Property Co. Ltd v Texas Commerce International Bank Ltd* [1982] Q.B. 84. See *Chitty on Contracts* (29th ed.), Vol. 1, para.3–107.

[95] But see Factors Act 1889, s.2; below, para.7–031.

[96] Or receives the goods, *e.g.* as pledgee.

[97] *Boyson v Coles* (1817) 6 M. & S. 14; *Kingsford v Merry* (1856) 1 H. & N. 502; *Lamb v Attenborough* (1862) 1 B. & S. 830; *Cole v North Western Bank* (1875) L.R. 10 C.P. 354 at 363; *Johnson v Crédit Lyonnais* (1877) 3 C.P.D. 32; *Mercantile Bank of India Ltd v Central Bank of India Ltd* [1938] A.C. 287. *Cf. Union Credit Bank Ltd v Mersey Docks and Harbour Board* [1899] 2 Q.B. 205.

[98] *Commonwealth Trust v Akotey* [1926] A.C. 72; *Central Newbury Car Auctions Ltd v Unity Finance Ltd* [1957] 1 Q.B. 371 at 382–386. A car registration document is not a document of title: *Beverley Acceptances Ltd v Oakley* [1982] R.T.R. 417, and see below, para.7–036, n.45.

[99] *Mercantile Bank of India Ltd v Central Bank of India Ltd*, above, at p.303.

[1] *Rimmer v Webster* [1902] 2 Ch. 163 at 173; *Abigail v Lapin* [1934] A.C. 491.

the seller and at the same time authorise him to sell or otherwise deal with the goods.[2] Or he may indorse the document of title in blank and transfer it to a broker who, by the nature of his employment, may be taken prima facie to have the right to sell the goods.[3] In such an event, the true owner may be "estopped" from asserting his title to the goods if the agent disregards the terms of his mandate and wrongfully sells the goods to a third party. It has been argued[4] that these cases are anomalous within the law of agency inasmuch as there is no actual or apparent[5] authority. But they would appear to depend on the existence of some initial authority given to the agent rather than on estoppel by a representation of apparent ownership under the provisions of section 21(1) of the Act.

Goods in bulk. The principle of estoppel referred to above must be distinguished from a closely related[6] principle of estoppel by which, at common law,[7] the seller of an unascertained part of an identified bulk may be precluded from asserting as against the buyer or his sub-purchaser that the latter is not entitled to delivery of the goods.[8] It was thus described by Cotton L.J. in *Simm v Anglo-American Telegraph Co.*[9]: "If an action is brought upon the ground that the property in goods has passed to the vendor of the [claimant sub-purchaser], and if that question depends upon whether a particular parcel of goods has been set apart and appropriated to the contract between the vendor of the [claimant] and his defendant, an admission by the defendant, the owner of the goods, that there has been a setting apart of the goods, would be effectual as against him to pass the property[10] in the goods to the [claimant's] vendor; as against the [claimant] who has paid for the goods, the defendant is estopped from denying that the goods have been set apart, and the [claimant] is entitled to rely upon the admission of the defendant which if true would have given the [claimant] a good title to the goods."[11] 7–014

---

[2] *Weiner v Gill* [1906] 2 K.B. 574 at 582; *Fry v Smellie* [1912] 3 K.B. 282. See also *Bowstead and Reynolds on Agency* (17th ed.), para.8–134. *Cf. Lloyds Bank Ltd v Bank of America National Trust and Savings Association* [1938] 2 K.B. 147.

[3] *Colonial Bank v Cady* (1890) 15 App.Cas. 267 at 278, 283; *Fuller v Glyn, Mills, Currie & Co.* [1914] 2 K.B. 168, as interpreted in *Mercantile Bank of India Ltd v Central Bank of India Ltd*, above, at p.302. *Cf. Zwinger v Samuda* (1817) 7 Taunt. 265.

[4] *Bowstead and Reynolds on Agency* (17th ed.), para.8–135.

[5] The existence of the principal may not be known to the buyer.

[6] See *Henderson v Williams* [1895] 1 Q.B. 521.

[7] But see now s.20A of the Act: above, para.5–109.

[8] See above, para.5–065.

[9] (1879) 5 Q.B.D. 188 at 215.

[10] In fact, the estoppel does not pass the property, but prevents the seller from denying that the purchaser is entitled to delivery: see above, para.5–065.

[11] *Stonard v Dunkin* (1810) 2 Camp. 344; *Hawes v Watson* (1824) 2 B. & C. 540; *Gosling v Birnie* (1831) 7 Bing. 339; *Gillett v Hill* (1834) 2 C. & M. 530; *Woodley v Coventry* (1863) 2 H. & C. 164; *Knights v Wiffen* (1870) L.R. 5 Q.B. 660; *Capital and Counties Bank Ltd v Warriner* (1896) 12 T.L.R. 216. Contrast *Gillman Spencer & Co. v Carbutt & Co.* (1889) 61 L.T. 281; *Laurie & Morewood v Dudin & Sons* [1926] 1 K.B. 223; *Re London Wine Co. (Shippers) Ltd* [1986] P.C.C. 121; *Re Goldcorp Exchange Ltd* [1995] 1 A.C. 74.

7–015 **Estoppel by negligence.** The true owner of goods may by his conduct[12] be "precluded from denying the seller's authority to sell" within section 21(1) of the Act where he has been negligent in allowing the seller to create an appearance of ownership of the goods. But the circumstances in which negligence on the part of the true owner can raise such an estoppel are narrowly circumscribed. It is necessary for the buyer to show, first, that the true owner owed him a duty to be careful; secondly, that in breach of that duty the true owner was negligent; and, thirdly, that this negligence was the proximate or real cause of the buyer being induced to buy the goods and part with the purchase price to the seller.[13]

7–016 The requirement of a duty of care is essential to this type of estoppel.[14] In the absence of such a duty, the true owner will not be prejudiced or affected by his carelessness in relation to the goods, however gross this may have been. Thus a failure on his part to take normal precautions to prevent his goods being stolen by a thief[15] or to report the theft to the police,[16] a careless loss of the goods,[17] a culpable credulity in entrusting possession of goods, or of the documents of title to goods, to another,[18] or a careless failure to register in a central register his interest in a vehicle let by him on hire-purchase,[19] will not of itself preclude him from recovering the goods from a person who has bought them from a seller without title, even though it could be said that it was the carelessness of the true owner which enabled the seller to pass the goods off as his own. The mere neglect of what would

---

[12] See Pickering, 55 L.Q.R. 400 (1939).

[13] *Mercantile Credit Co. Ltd v Hamblin* [1965] 2 Q.B. 242 at 271; *Moorgate Mercantile Co. Ltd v Twitchings* [1977] A.C. 890 at 903, 906, 912, 919, 920, 921, 924, 927, 928. *Gator Shipping Corp. v Trans-Asiatic Oil Ltd* [1978] 2 Lloyd's Rep. 357 at 377–378; *Cadogan Finance Ltd v Lavery and Fox* [1982] Com.L.R. 248.

[14] *Johnson v Crédit Lyonnais Co.* (1877) 3 C.P.D. 32 at 42; *Farquharson Bros & Co. v King & Co.* [1902] A.C. 325 at 335–336; *Rimmer v Webster* [1902] 2 Ch. 163 at 172; *Heap v Motorists' Advisory Agency* [1923] 1 K.B. 577 at 587; *Mercantile Bank of India Ltd v Central Bank of India Ltd* [1938] A.C. 287 at 299; *Wilson and Meeson v Pickering* [1946] K.B. 422; *Central Newbury Car Auctions Ltd v Unity Finance Ltd* [1957] 1 Q.B. 371 at 381, 389, 395; *Mercantile Credit Co. Ltd v Hamblin*, above, at pp.265, 271–273, 275, 278; *Moorgate Mercantile Co. Ltd v Twitchings*, above, at pp.903, 912, 919, 924, 930; *J. Sargent (Garages) Ltd v Motor Auctions (West Bromwich) Ltd* [1977] R.T.R. 121; *McManus v Eastern Ford Sales Ltd* (1981) 128 D.L.R. (3d) 246; *Beverley Acceptances Ltd v Oakley* [1982] R.T.R. 417 at 439. See also *Bank of Ireland v Evans' Trustees* (1855) 5 H.L.C. 389 at 410; *Swan v North British Australasian Co. Ltd* (1863) 2 H. & C. 175 at 181; *R. E. Jones Ltd v Waring & Gillow Ltd* [1926] A.C. 670. Contrast *Commonwealth Trust v Akotey* [1926] A.C. 72.

[15] *Farquharson Bros & Co. v King & Co.*, above, at p.335; *Jerome v Bentley & Co.* [1952] 2 All E.R. 114 at 118; *Central Newbury Car Auctions Ltd v Unity Finance Ltd*, above, at pp.381, 394.

[16] *Debs v Sibec Developments Ltd* [1990] R.T.R. 91.

[17] *Farquharson Bros & Co. v King & Co.*, above, at pp.335–336; *Central Newbury Car Auctions Ltd v Unity Finance Ltd*, above, at p.381.

[18] *Johnson v Crédit Lyonnais Co.*, above; *Farquharson Bros & Co. v King & Co.*, above; *Mercantile Bank of India Ltd v Central Bank of India Ltd*, above; *Central Newbury Car Auctions Ltd v Unity Finance Ltd*, above; *McManus v Eastern Ford Sales Ltd*, above; *Beverley Acceptances Ltd v Oakley*, above.

[19] *Moorgate Mercantile Co. Ltd v Twitchings* [1977] A.C. 890. See also *Cadogan Finance Ltd v Lavery and Fox* [1982] Com.L.R. 248 (aircraft).

be prudent conduct in respect of the true owner himself is insufficient.[20] It has, however, been cogently said[21] that "the principal task is to find what situations or relationships may give rise to the duty to be careful," and on this point decided cases provide no reliable affirmative guidance.[22] The mere fact that the true owner could reasonably foresee that his carelessness would lead the buyer to believe that the seller was the owner of the goods, or that the true owner had no interest in the goods, does not in itself impose such a duty[23]; the circumstances must be such that a legal duty of care is owed to the buyer.[24] In *Mercantile Credit Co. Ltd v Hamblin*[25] the defendant signed in blank hire-purchase documents addressed to the claimant finance company without reading them and handed these documents to a dealer intending that the dealer should use them to obtain for her a loan on the security of her car. She thus enabled the dealer to offer to sell the car as his own to the finance company, which offer was accepted by the company. The Court of Appeal held that there was a sufficient relationship of proximity between the defendant and the finance company to give rise to a duty of care.[26] In this case, however, the documents were addressed to a specific recipient and the defendant (had she read them) ought to have known that the finance company would rely on them for the very purpose for which the company required them.[27]

Assuming that the existence of a duty of care can be established, it is necessary for the buyer to show a breach of that duty by the failure of the true owner to take reasonable care.[28] The buyer must further show that this breach of duty was the effective cause of his loss, that is to say, that the negligence of the true owner was the proximate and real cause of his being induced to buy the goods and part with the purchase price to the seller.[29] From time to time the courts have exhibited a tendency to hold that, where the seller has been guilty of fraud, the effective cause of the buyer's loss is the fraud of the seller, and not the negligence of the true owner.[30] But it is 7–017

[20] *Swan v North British Australasian Co. Ltd*, above, at p.181.
[21] *Mercantile Credit Co. Ltd v Hamblin* [1965] 2 Q.B. 242 at 271.
[22] In *Wilson v Meeson and Pickering* [1946] K.B. 422 at 427, it was suggested that the principle was confined to negotiable instruments. But see the cases discussed in *Mercantile Credit Co. Ltd v Hamblin*, above; *Saunders v Anglia Building Society* [1971] A.C. 1004.
[23] *Moorgate Mercantile Co. Ltd v Twitchings*, above.
[24] See *Mercantile Credit Co. Ltd v Hamblin*, above; and below, para.7–017.
[25] [1965] 2 Q.B. 242. But this was a case of documents signed in blank: see below, para.7–018, nn.39 and 40. See also *Coventry v GE Ry* (1883) 11 Q.B.D. 776.
[26] But the claimant failed to establish any breach of the duty or that the defendants' negligence was the effective cause of its loss (see *infra*).
[27] *cf. Caparo Industries Plc v Dickman* [1990] 2 A.C. 605.
[28] *Johnson v Crédit Lyonnais Co.* (1877) 3 C.P.D. 32; *Mercantile Credit Co. Ltd v Hamblin*, above; *Moorgate Mercantile Co. Ltd v Twitchings*, above.
[29] *Swan v North British Australasian Co. Ltd* (1863) 2 H. & C. 175 at 182; *Carr v L. & NW Ry* (1875) L.R. 10 C.P. 307 at 318; *Coventry v G. E. Ry* (1883) 11 Q.B.D. 776; *Union Credit Bank Ltd v Mersey Docks and Harbour Board* [1899] 2 Q.B. 205; *Mercantile Credit Co. Ltd v Hamblin*, above, at pp.266, 275; *Moorgate Mercantile Co. Ltd v Twitchings*, above, at pp.919, 921, 928.
[30] *Mercantile Credit Co. Ltd v Hamblin*, above. See also *Carlisle and Cumberland Banking Co. v Bragg* [1911] 1 K.B. 489 (overruled in *Saunders v Anglia Building Society* [1971] A.C. 1004); *Campbell Discount Co. Ltd v Gall* [1961] 1 Q.B. 431 (disapproved in *United Dominions Trust Ltd v Western* [1976] Q.B. 513).

submitted that, in most cases, the seller's fraud, although the immediate cause of the buyer's loss, is the very kind of thing that due care on the part of the true owner would have prevented, so that the negligence of the true owner should be regarded as an effective cause, albeit concurrent with the fraud of the seller.[31]

7–018 **Non est factum.** Where the true owner of goods has signed a document which transfers title to the goods to another, he will not be permitted to disown his signature simply by asserting that he did not understand that which he signed.[32] But where, for example, by reason of the fraud of the seller, he is induced to sign a document which purports to effect a transaction essentially different in substance or in kind from the transaction intended,[33] he may be entitled to rely on the principle of *non est factum*, not only as against the seller, but also against an innocent purchaser of the goods from the seller.[34] However, this plea is one which, as against an innocent purchaser,[35] is defeated by the presence of negligence: he will not be entitled to recover the goods from such a purchaser unless he proves[36] that he exercised reasonable care in signing the document. What is reasonable care will depend on the circumstances of the case and the nature of the document being signed. As a normal rule, if a person of full understanding and capacity forbears, or carelessly omits, to read what he signs, the plea of *non est factum* will not be available[37]; he takes the risk of a fraudulent substitution. But there may be rare occasions where, by reason of his illiteracy or senility, the nature of the fraud perpetrated by the seller or other circumstances, he could discharge the burden of proof.[38] The same principles apply where the true owner signs documents in blank, entrusting these to the seller to be completed in accordance with an agreement between them.[39] If the seller, in breach of the agreement, completes the blanks and is thereby enabled to represent that he is the owner of the goods to the buyer who purchases them in reliance on that representation, the true owner will be bound, unless the transaction contemplated by the agreement was essentially different in substance or in kind and he proves that he exercised reasonable care.[40]

---

[31] *United Dominions Trust Ltd v Western*, above; *Moorgate Mercantile Co. Ltd v Twitchings*, above, at pp.912, 928. *Cf. ibid.* at p.921; *Gator Shipping Corp. v Trans-Asiatic Oil Ltd* [1978] 2 Lloyd's Rep. 357 at 378; *Cadogan Finance Ltd v Lavery and Fox* [1982] Com.L.R. 248.
[32] *Blay v Pollard & Morris* [1930] 1 K.B. 628; *Muskham Finance Ltd v Howard* [1963] 1 Q.B. 904 at 914.
[33] *Saunders v Anglia Building Society* [1971] A.C. 1004 at 1017, 1022, 1026.
[34] *Muskham Finance Ltd v Howard*, above. See also *Mercantile Credit Co. Ltd v Hamblin* [1965] 2 Q.B. 242. *Cf. Saunders v Anglia Building Society*, above.
[35] But not as against a seller who is aware of the facts: *Petelin v Cullen* (1975) 132 C.L.R. 355.
[36] *Saunders v Anglia Building Society*, above, at pp.1016, 1019, 1027, 1028.
[37] *ibid.*, at pp.1026, 1027, 1036.
[38] *ibid.*, at p.1025. See also *Mercantile Credit Co. Ltd v Hamblin*, above.
[39] *United Dominions Trust Ltd v Western* [1976] Q.B. 513 (disapproving *Campbell Discount Ltd v Gall* [1961] 1 Q.B. 431). See also *British Railway Traffic and Electric Co. Ltd v Roper* (1939) 162 L.T. 217, *General and Finance Facilities Ltd v Hughes* (1966) 110 S.J. 147. *Cf. Unity Finance Ltd v Hammond* (1965) 109 S.J. 70.
[40] *Mercantile Credit Co. Ltd v Hamblin*, above.

Estoppel by judgment. Estoppel by judgment, or estoppel *per rem judicatam*, is a rule of evidence[41] whereby a party is debarred from relitigating a cause of action which has been conclusively determined by a judgment of a court of competent jurisdiction in previous proceedings between the same parties or their privies, or an issue raised in such proceedings which it was necessary to determine for the purposes of those proceedings.[42] So far as title to goods is concerned, where ownership of the goods has thus been determined in legal proceedings, the estoppel will operate for, or against, the parties to those proceedings and also their privies, that is to say, persons who claim title through or under a party. However, a person claiming title is "privy" to the interests of those through whom he claims that title for the purposes of the operation of the doctrine of estoppel *per rem judicatam* only if the title he claims was acquired after the date of the judgment.[43] If the title claimed was acquired before the date of the judgment, he will not be estopped.[44] 7–019

3. Sale in Market Overt

Market overt. Section 22(1) of the Sale of Goods Act 1979 provided: "Where goods are sold in market overt, according to the usage of the market, the buyer acquires a good title to the goods, provided he buys them in good faith and without notice of any defect or want of title on the part of the seller." This ancient rule applied to sales from shops in the City of London and, outside the City of London, to sales from any open, public and legally constituted market, including fairs. It did not apply in Scotland or in Wales, or to ships, or to goods belonging to the Crown. The rule was highly technical in its application and replete with artificiality.[45] It was abolished by the Sale of Goods (Amendment) Act 1994, which came into force on January 3, 1995, and applies to any contract for sale of goods made after that date. 7–020

4. Sale Under a Voidable Title

Seller with a voidable title. By section 23 of the Sale of Goods Act 1979: "When the seller of goods has a voidable title to them, but his title has not been avoided at the time of the sale, the buyer acquires a good title to the goods, provided he buys them in good faith and without notice of the seller's defect of title." The paradigm case of the operation of this section is 7–021

---

[41] *Vervaeke v Smith* [1983] 1 A.C. 145; *Republic of India v India Steamship Co Ltd* [1993] A.C. 410, 422.
[42] *Chitty on Contracts* (29th ed.), Vol. 1, 25–001; *Halsbury's Laws of England* (4th ed., 2003), Vol. 16(2), para.974.
[43] *Doe d. Foster v Earl of Derby* (1834) 1 A. & E. 783, 790; *Hodson v Walker* (1872) I.R. 7 Ex. 55.
[44] *Powell v Wiltshire* [2005] Q.B. 117.
[45] See the 4th edition of this book, paras 7–016—7–022.

where A, the true owner of the goods, is induced by the fraud of B (the seller) to sell goods to B which B then resells to C, an innocent buyer. The effect of the fraud is not absolutely to avoid the contract of sale between A and B, but to render it voidable at the option of A. Property in the goods passes to B, although B's title is subject to A's right to avoid it. Provided that A has not effectively exercised this right at the time of the sale of the goods by B to C, then C will acquire an indefeasible title to the goods notwithstanding the fact that B had only a voidable title to them.[46]

7–022 **Voidable title.** The transaction between the true owner and the seller must be such as to transfer to the seller a voidable title to the goods sold. It is therefore necessary to distinguish between the situation where the true owner intends to pass the property in the goods to the seller, *e.g.* a sale of the goods,[47] and the situation where the true owner intends to transfer to the seller nothing more than possession of the goods. In the former case, the seller acquires a title to the goods, albeit a voidable title; in the latter, he merely acquires possession of the goods, but no title to them. Thus if the contract between the true owner and the seller is only an agreement to sell,[48] or if the transaction is one of hire-purchase or conditional sale,[49] or if the seller is in possession of the goods on "sale or return," approval, or similar terms,[50] and at the time of the sale to the innocent buyer the property has not yet passed to the seller, section 23 of the Act has no application. It would seem, however, that where the true owner transfers to the seller possession of the goods, and intends to confer a power to pass the property in them to a third party, the section may apply.[51] And even if the transaction which passes the voidable title to the seller is subsequent in time to the sale to the innocent buyer, it may well be that the section could still apply, for the innocent buyer's title might be considered to have been "fed".[52] On the other hand, in a case before the 1893 Act, *Kingsford v Merry*,[53] the Court of Exchequer Chamber held that, where a person induced the true owner to deliver goods to him by falsely representing that

---

[46] *Wright v Lawes* (1801) 4 Esq. 82; *Load v Green* (1846) 15 M. & W. 216 at 219; *White v Garden* (1851) 10 C.B. 919; *Powell v Hoyland* (1851) 6 ExCh.67 at 72; *Stevenson v Newnham* (1853) 13 C.B. 285 at 302; *Pease v Gloahec* (1866) L.R. 1 P.C. 219; *Cundy v Lindsay* (1878) 3 App.Cas. 459 at 463–464, 466; *King's Norton Metal Co. v Edridge, Merrett & Co.* (1897) 14 T.L.R. 98; *Phillips v Brooks Ltd* [1919] 2 K.B. 243; *Nanka Bruce v Commonwealth Trust* [1926] A.C. 77; *Terry v Vancouver Motors U-Drive Ltd* [1942] 4 D.L.R. 399; *Dennant v Skinner and Collom* [1948] 2 K.B. 164; *Robin and Rambler Coaches Ltd v Turner* [1947] 2 All E.R. 284; *Hendrickson v Mid-City Motors Ltd* [1951] 3 D.L.R. 276; *Macleod v Kerr* 1965 S.C. 253; *Lewis v Averay* [1972] 1 Q.B. 198; *Young v D. S. Dalgleish & Son (Hawick)* 1994 S.C.L.R. 696 (Sh. Ct.).

[47] Sale of Goods Act 1979, s.2(4); see above, para.1–027.

[48] s.2(5). But see s.25 of the Act; below, para.7–069. *Cf. Nanka Bruce v Commonwealth Trust* [1926] A.C. 77.

[49] But see below, para.7–087.

[50] *Truman v Attenborough* (1910) 26 T.L.R. 601. But see above, para.5–040.

[51] *Whitehorn Brothers v Davison* [1911] 1 K.B. 463, discussed in *Folkes v King* [1923] 1 K.B. 282.

[52] *Whitehorn Brothers v Davison*, above.

[53] (1856) 1 H. & N. 503. *Cf. Babcock v Lawson* (1880) 5 Q.B.D. 284.

he had purchased them from one who had agreed to buy the goods from the true owner, he could pass no title to a third party. Even though the true owner intended to pass to him both the property and possession of the goods, the relationship between the true owner and himself was not "the relation of vendor and vendee of the goods, and there was no contract between them which the [true owner] might either affirm or disaffirm."[54]

Voidable and void. An innocent buyer will only acquire a good title to goods under section 23 if the title of the seller is voidable, but not if the seller has no title at all. The title of the seller may be voidable at the option of the true owner, for example, on the ground of fraud at common law[55] or in equity,[56] misrepresentation,[57] non-disclosure,[58] duress[59] or undue influence.[60] In these instances, the true owner is normally entitled to rescind the contract between himself and the seller, but the contract is not void *ab initio*. If, however, it is completely void, for example, on the ground of mistake as to identity[61] or because of a lack of coincidence between the terms of the offer and of the acceptance,[62] then no property in the goods will pass to the seller, and the buyer will not acquire a good title under this section even if he purchases the goods in good faith and without notice of the seller's defect of title.[63] For the same reason, the buyer will not acquire a good title under this section as against the true owner of the goods from whom they have been stolen,[64] whether by the seller or some other person. 7–023

Avoidance. A voidable title "is a good title until a person entitled to avoid elects to avoid it, and does avoid it, in which case that which was a title, though a voidable title, becomes an avoided title."[65] The true owner may therefore defeat the operation of section 23 by avoiding the seller's title *before* the seller re-sells the goods to the buyer. It is not necessary that there should be a judgment of a court to effect such an avoidance. The true 7–024

---

54 At p.516.

55 See *Chitty on Contracts* (29th ed.), Vol. 1, paras 6–042, 6–100.

56 *ibid.* para.6–100.

57 *ibid.* Ch.6.

58 *ibid.* paras 6–139 *et seq.*

59 *ibid.* paras 7–001 *et seq.*

60 *ibid.* paras 7–047 *et seq.*

61 *Hardman v Booth* (1862) 32 L.J.Ex. 105; *Cundy v Lindsay* (1878) 3 App.Cas. 459; *Morrisson v Robertson* 1908 S.C. 332; *Ingram v Little* [1961] 1 Q.B. 31; *Shogun Finance Ltd v Hudson* [2003] UKHL 62, [2004] 1 A.C.69. Contrast *King's Norton Metal Co. v Edridge, Merrett & Co.* (1897) 14 T.L.R. 98; *Phillips v Brooks Ltd* [1919] 2 K.B. 243; *Hendrickson v Mid-City Motors Ltd* [1951] 3 D.L.R. 276; *Lewis v Averay* [1972] 1 Q.B. 198. See *Chitty on Contracts* (29th ed.), Vol. 1, paras 5–076—5–085; above, para.3–012.

62 *Morrison v Robertson*, 1908 S.C. 332. *Cf. R. v Williams* [1980] Crim.L.R. 589. See also *Chitty on Contracts* (29th ed.), Vol. 1, paras 5–055—5–075.

63 *cf.* Twelfth Report of the Law Reform Committee (1966) Cmnd. 2958, para.15.

64 *i.e.* without the true owner's consent. But the mere fact that the wrongdoer is guilty of the crime of theft is in itself insufficient: see *R. v Lawrence* [1972] A.C. 626; *Dobson v General Accident and Life Assurance Corp. Plc* [1990] 1 Q.B. 274. *Cf. R. v Harris* [1984] A.C. 327. *R. v Gomez* [1993] A.C. 442.

65 *Whitehorn Brothers v Davison* [1911] 1 K.B. 463 at 481. See also *Eisinger v General Accident Fire and Life Assurance Corp. Ltd* [1955] 1 W.L.R. 869.

owner may achieve this result by rescinding the contract between himself and the seller. As a general rule, he must communicate to the seller his intention to rescind, and the seller's title will not be avoided until this has been done.[66] An uncommunicated intention, for example, by speaking to a third party or making a private note, will be ineffective. This rule, however, is not an absolute one. It would seem that the true owner may rescind the contract merely by retaking possession of the goods[67]; and a further exception or qualification was recognised by the Court of Appeal in *Car and Universal Finance Co. Ltd v Caldwell*.[68] In that case, the defendant was fraudulently induced to sell a motor car to N in return for a cheque. When the cheque was dishonoured, the defendant immediately informed the police and the Automobile Association of the fraud, but neither he nor they were able to communicate with N. Subsequently N sold the car, which came into the hands of the claimants, who bought it in good faith and without notice of any defect of title. At first instance, Lord Denning M.R. decided that the defendant had effectively rescinded the contract between himself and N, so that the claimants acquired no title to the car. "I hold," he said,[69] "that where a seller of goods has a right to avoid a contract for fraud, he sufficiently exercises his election if he at once, on discovering the fraud, takes all possible steps to regain the goods even though he cannot find the rogue or communicate with him." This decision was upheld by the Court of Appeal, but on the narrower ground that, in this case, N intended quite deliberately to disappear and render it impossible for the defendant to communicate with him or to recover the car. The court left open the question whether or not the general principle would apply in a case where one party to a contract makes an innocent misrepresentation which entitles the other to elect to rescind and then innocently so acts that the other cannot find him to communicate his election to him.[70]

7–025 This decision has been criticised[71] and its effect appears to have been considerably curtailed by the subsequent decision of the Court of Appeal in *Newtons of Wembley Ltd v Williams*.[72] From this latter case it would seem that, if a rogue obtains possession of goods from the true owner under a contract of sale induced by his fraud, he can pass a good title to an innocent buyer under section 25(1) of Sale of Goods Act 1979[73] notwithstanding the

[66] *Reese River Silver Mining Co. v Smith* (1869) L.R. 4 H.L. 64 at 74; *Scarf v Jardine* (1882) 7 App.Cas. 345 at 361; *Car and Universal Finance Co. Ltd v Caldwell* [1965] 1 Q.B. 525 at 550, 554, 558.

[67] *Re Eastgate* [1905] 1 K.B. 465; *Car and Universal Finance Co. Ltd v Caldwell*, above, at pp.554, 558.

[68] [1965] 1 Q.B. 525. See also *Newtons of Wembley Ltd v Williams* [1965] 1 Q.B. 560; *Thomas v Heelas*, November 27, 1986 (C.A.T. No. 1065). Contrast *Moyce v Newington* (1878) 4 Q.B.D. 32 at 35; *Macleod v Kerr* 1965 S.C. 253; *Young v D. S. Dalgleish & Son (Hawick)* 1994 S.C.L.R. 696 (Sh. Ct.).

[69] At p.532.

[70] [1965] 1 Q.B. 525 at 555, 559.

[71] Twelfth Report of the Law Reform Committee (1966), Cmnd. 2958, paras 16, 40(4).

[72] [1965] 1 Q.B. 560; see below, para.7–076.

[73] See below, para.7–071.

fact that the true owner has avoided the rogue's voidable title before the innocent buyer purchased the goods. Although, in this case, the contract between the true owner and the rogue appears to have been an agreement to sell, and not a sale of, the goods, the wording of section 25(1) extends to cases where the rogue has "bought" the goods as well as to cases where he has "agreed to buy" them.[74] Provided, therefore, that the other requirements of that subsection are fulfilled,[75] it is submitted that rescission of the contract of sale by the true owner will not prevent an innocent buyer from acquiring a good title under section 25(1) even if he cannot do so under section 23.

In any event, in order to avoid the seller's voidable title, the true owner must be in a position to rescind the contract made between himself and the seller, that is to say, the remedy of rescission must not for any reason have become barred.[76] In particular, the true owner must not have elected to affirm the contract and so lost his right to rescind.[77] **7–026**

Sale to buyer. Section 23 applies in its terms only to the situation where the person with a voidable title is a "seller" and the person seeking to establish a good title as against the true owner is a "buyer" of the goods. It is submitted that, in this context,[78] there must be an actual sale of the goods, and that an agreement for a sale which did not purport to transfer the property in the goods immediately and unconditionally to the buyer would be insufficient. It is to be noted that no requirement is imposed by this section that the seller should have obtained possession of the goods[79] or that the sale by him to the buyer should have been made "in the ordinary course of business"[80] or that the goods should have been delivered to the buyer; but these facts may well be relevant if the bona fides of the buyer is impugned. **7–027**

At common law, however, a similar rule to that set out in section 23 applies to a person with a voidable title who pledges the goods with an innocent pledgee[81] or who creates an equitable right by an incomplete pledge.[82] But a trustee in bankruptcy does not stand in the position of an **7–028**

---

[74] It could, however, be argued that, if the rogue's voidable title is avoided, he has not "bought" the goods. *Cf.* Twelfth Report of the Law Reform Committee (1966), Cmnd. 2958, para.24.
[75] See below, paras 7–069—7–086. S.25(1) imposes requirements not found in s.23.
[76] See below, paras 12–005—12–009, and *Chitty on Contracts* (29th ed.), Vol. 1, paras 6–120—6–130.
[77] See below, para.12–006, and *Chitty on Contracts* (29th ed.), Vol. 1, para.6–121. See also below, para.12–009 (lapse of time, but this does not extend to cases of fraud).
[78] See s.61(1) of the 1979 Act (opening words).
[79] *cf.* s.25 of the Act; below, para.7–072.
[80] See below, para.7–081.
[81] *Parker v Patrick* (1793) 5 T.R. 715; *Babcock v Lawson* (1880) 5 Q.B.D. 284; *Whitehorn Brothers v Davison* [1911] 1 K.B. 463; *Phillips v Brooks* [1919] 2 K.B. 243.
[82] *Attenborough v London & St Katherine's Docks* (1878) 3 C.P.D. 450.

innocent buyer, for he takes "subject to equities".[83] Thus, where the true owner of goods is fraudulently induced to sell them to another, who subsequently becomes bankrupt, he can rescind the contract of sale and recover the goods.[84]

7–029 **Good faith and notice.** The buyer will acquire a good title to the goods, provided he buys them in good faith[85] and without notice[86] of the seller's defect of title. In *Whitehorn Brothers v Davison*,[87] the Court of Appeal held that the true owner bears the burden of proving that the requirements of section 23 have not been complied with and, in particular that the buyer bought with notice or otherwise than in good faith. This ruling reverses the burden of proof which is applied in the case of other similar provisions[88] and it is submitted that it deserves reconsideration.[89] However, in *Thomas v Heelas*,[90] the Court of Appeal considered itself bound by that decision. But Sir George Waller held that the buyer nevertheless bore the burden of proving that a sale of the goods took place before the first buyer's title was avoided, and Woolf L.J. held that the burden of proof lay on the buyer to establish that there was in fact a sale to which section 23 could apply. O'Connor L.J. agreed with both judgments.

7–030 There is no reason to suppose that only the first buyer from a seller with a voidable title can rely upon section 23. If A, the true owner, is fraudulently induced to sell goods to B, and B resells them to C, who resells them to D, then D will acquire a good title if he buys in good faith and without notice, even though C had notice of B's defect of title.[91] Also, if D is not an innocent buyer, but C bought in good faith and without notice, D's title is indefeasible,[92] for he purchased the goods from C who had a good title to them.

---

[83] *Load v Green* (1846) 1 M. & W. 216. See also *Graham v Johnson* (1869) L.R. 8 Eq. 36 (assignee); *Robbie & Co. Ltd v Witney Warehouse Co. Ltd* [1963] 1 W.L.R. 1324; *Rother Iron Works Ltd v Canterbury Precision Engineers Ltd* [1974] Q.B. 1 (receivers); *Mersey Steel and Iron Co. v Naylor Benzon & Co.* (1882) 9 Q.B.D. 648 (affirmed (1884) 9 App.Cas. 434) (winding-up).

[84] *Re Eastgate* [1905] 1 K.B. 465; *Tilley v Bowman Ltd* [1910] 1 K.B. 745. *Cf. Re Shackleton* (1875) L.R. 10 Ch.App. 466. But see s.285 of the Insolvency Act 1986.

[85] By s.61(3) of the 1979 Act, a thing is deemed to be done "in good faith" when it is in fact done honestly, whether it is done negligently or not. See below, para.7–046.

[86] For the meaning of "notice", see below, para.7–047.

[87] [1911] 1 K.B. 463.

[88] See below, paras 7–045, 7–068, 7–086.

[89] See the Twelfth Report of the Law Reform Committee (1966), Cmnd. 2958, para.25. The buyer is in a better position to prove the circumstances of his acquisition of the goods than the true owner.

[90] November 27, 1986 (C.A.T. No. 1065).

[91] *Cf. Newtons of Wembley Ltd v Williams* [1964] 1 W.L.R. 1028 (affirmed [1965] 1 Q.B. 560); below, para.7–086.

[92] *Peirce v London Horse and Carriage Repository* [1922] W.N. 170, CA (unless, possibly, D is party to the fraud).

5. Mercantile Agents

Agency. The rules of common law relating to the law of principal and agent are expressly stated to be applicable to contracts of sale of goods by section 62(2) of the Sale of Goods Act 1979.[93] An agent of the true owner may therefore pass a good title by selling or disposing of the goods to another if such an act is within the scope of his actual authority, whether express or implied.[94] A sale or disposition made by an agent acting within his apparent or usual authority will likewise be effective to pass a good title.[95] At common law, however, the mere fact that an agent is entrusted by his principal with the possession of goods or the documents of title to goods does not of itself enable him to make a disposition which is binding on his principal,[96] nor does an authority to sell the goods include a power to pledge.[97] Merchants may nevertheless be misled in commercial transactions by the appearance of authority thus created. In response to pressure from the mercantile community,[98] the legislature progressively intervened during the course of the nineteenth century by means of the Factors Acts[99] to protect persons dealing in good faith with mercantile agents or with certain apparent owners of goods.[1] The Factors Act 1889 embodied and extended the protection afforded by previous Acts. 7–031

Mercantile agents. The provisions of the Act of 1889 relating to the question of agency apply to dispositions by mercantile agents. For the purposes of this Act, the expression "mercantile agent" is defined in section 1(1) to mean "a mercantile agent having in the customary course of his business as such agent authority either to sell goods, or to consign goods for the purpose of sale, or to buy goods, or to raise money on the security of goods."[2] The mere fact that a person is an agent is therefore insufficient to enable him to pass a good title by disposing of the goods.[3] The authority given to him by the owner or with which he is customarily endowed must be such that, if carried to its normal result, it would end in his selling the goods, or consigning them for sale, buying goods or raising money on the 7–032

---

[93] See also Factors Act 1889, ss.12, 13.
[94] Such a disposition need not be made "in the ordinary course of business" of the agent (*cf.* para.7–043, below).
[95] See *Bowstead and Reynolds on Agency* (17th ed.), paras 3–006, 8–013.
[96] See above, para.7–013.
[97] *Fuentes v Montis* (1868) L.R. 4 C.P. 93.
[98] Chorley, 48 L.Q.R. 51 at 68 (1932).
[99] Factors Act 1823, 1825, 1842, 1877.
[1] See also ss.8, 9, 10 of the Factors Act 1889; below, paras 7–055, 7–069, 15–097; and s.21(2)(a) of the 1979 Act.
[2] This definition is repeated in s.26 of the Sale of Goods Act 1979.
[3] *Hellings v Russell* (1875) 33 L.T. 380 (forwarding agent); *Brown & Co. v Bedford Pantechnicon Co. Ltd* (1884) 5 T.L.R. 449 (agent to obtain orders); *Kendrick v Sotheby & Co.* (1967) 111 S.J. 470 (agent to obtain photograph of goods).

security of goods.[4] Thus a mere clerk or servant,[5] carrier,[6] warehouseman[7] or other bailee[8] will not be a mercantile agent. But the words "in the customary course of his business as such agent" do not require that he should be a person whose occupation corresponds to that of some known kind of commercial agent, such as a factor.[9] He can be a mercantile agent even though his general occupation is that of an independent dealer in the goods in question[10] or if he is authorised to act as a mercantile agent on a single occasion[11] or by only one principal.[12] The substance of his relationship with his principal must also be looked at. So a person to whom goods are consigned "on sale or return" may be found in reality to be a mercantile agent[13] and likewise one to whom goods are supplied for the purposes of display under a "stocking plan".[14] Once it is established that he is a mercantile agent, it is immaterial that he intends to act fraudulently and for his own benefit[15] or that his authority is limited either expressly[16] or by virtue of trade custom.[17] However, a person who simply sells his own goods is not a mercantile agent.[18]

---

[4] *City Bank v Barrow* (1880) 5 App.Cas. 664 at 678; *Turner v Sampson* (1911) 27 T.L.R. 200 at 202; *Moody v Pall Mall Deposit and Forwarding Co. Ltd* (1917) 33 T.L.R. 306. But see *Stadium Finance Ltd v Robbins* [1962] 2 Q.B. 664 at 674, and below, para.7–044.

[5] *Lamb v Attenborough* (1862) 1 B. & S. 831; *Heyman v Flewker* (1863) 13 C.B.(N.S.) 519 at 527; *International Sponge Importers v Watt* 1909 S.L.T. 24 (affirmed [1911] A.C. 279). But see s.6 of Factors Act 1889 (clerk of mercantile agent).

[6] *Heyman v Flewker*, above, at p.527; *Oppenheimer v Attenborough & Son* [1908] 1 K.B. 221 at 226; *Lowther v Harris* [1927] 1 K.B. 393 at 398.

[7] *Cole v North Western Bank* (1875) L.R. 10 C.P. 354.

[8] *Wood v Rowcliffe* (1846) 6 Hare 183 (tenant); *Heyman v Flewker*, above, at p.527 (custodian); *Johnson v Crédit Lyonnais* (1877) 3 C.P.D. 32 (seller in possession); *Heap v Motorists' Advisory Agency Ltd* [1923] 1 K.B. 577 at 588 (gratuitous bailee); *Staffs Motor Guarantee Ltd v British Wagon Co. Ltd* [1934] 2 K.B. 305 at 313 (hirer under hire-purchase agreement); *Kendrick v Sotheby & Co.* (1967) 111 S.J. 470 (bailee). See also below, para.7–038.

[9] *Lowther v Harris* [1927] 1 K.B. 393; *Mortgage Loan & Finance Co. of Australia v Richards* (1932) S.R.(N.S.W.) 50. *Cf. Heyman v Flewker*, above, at p.527.

[10] *Weiner v Harris* [1910] 1 K.B. 285 (overruling *Hastings v Pearson* [1893] 1 Q.B. 62).

[11] *Lowther v Harris*, above; *Mortgage Loan & Finance Co. of Australia v Richards*, above. *Cf. Budberg v Jerwood and Ward* (1934) 51 T.L.R. 99; *Heap v Motorists' Advisory Agency Ltd*, above, at p.589.

[12] *Lowther v Harris*, above; *Budberg v Jerwood and Ward*, above, at p.100.

[13] *Weiner v Harris*, above. See also *Janesich v Attenborough* (1910) 102 L.T. 605, and above, para.5–045.

[14] *St Margaret's Trust v Castle* [1964] C.L.Y. 1685; *Pacific Motor Auctions Pty Ltd v Motor Credits (Hire Finance) Ltd* [1965] A.C. 867 at 889. *Cf. Brown & Co. v Bedford Pantechnicon Co. Ltd* (1884) 5 T.L.R. 449; *Universal Guarantee Pty Ltd v Metters Ltd* [1966] W.A.R. 74.

[15] See the cases cited in para.7–037, n.51, below.

[16] *Turner v Sampson* (1911) 27 T.L.R. 200; *Paris v Goodwin* [1954] N.Z.L.R. 823.

[17] *Oppenheimer v Attenborough & Son* [1908] 1 K.B. 221.

[18] *Belvoir Finance Co. Ltd v Harold G. Cole & Co. Ltd* [1969] 1 W.L.R. 1877. See also *Mehta v Sutton* (1913) 109 L.T. 529 (joint venture); *Evans v Ritchie* (1964) 44 D.L.R.(2d) 675. *Cf. Lloyd's Bank Ltd v Bank of America National Trust and Savings Association* [1938] 2 K.B. 147 at 162.

Trust receipts.[19] Where a bill of lading is pledged with a bank as security for an advance, and the bank releases the bill of lading to the pledgor in return for a trust receipt in order to enable him to sell the goods, the trust receipt is construed as an authority stating the terms on which the pledgor is to realise the goods on the bank's behalf[20] so that the pledgor becomes a mercantile agent of the bank.[21] 7–033

Disposition by mercantile agent.[22] Section 2(1) of the Factors Act 1889 provides: "Where a mercantile agent is with the consent[23] of the owner,[24] in possession of goods[25] or of the documents of title[26] to goods, any sale,[27] pledge,[28] or other disposition[29] of the goods, made by him when acting in the ordinary course of business of a mercantile agent,[30] shall, subject to the provisions of this Act, be as valid as if he were expressly authorised by the owner of the goods to make the same[31]; provided that the person[32] taking under the disposition acts in good faith,[33] and has not at the time of the disposition notice[34] that the person making the disposition has not authority to make the same." 7–034

Possession of the agent. At the time of the disposition[35] the mercantile agent must be in possession of the goods[36] or of the documents of title to goods. By section 1(2) of the Act, a person is deemed to be in possession of goods or of the documents of title to goods, where the goods or documents are in his actual custody or are held by any other person subject to his control or for him or on his behalf.[37] 7–035

---

[19] See below, paras 18–235, 23–133.
[20] *Re David Allester Ltd* [1922] 2 Ch. 211.
[21] *Lloyds Bank Ltd v Bank of America National Trust and Savings Association* [1938] 2 K.B. 147. For the meaning of "the owner" in this connection, see below, para.7–035, n.48. *Cf. North Western Bank Ltd v Paynter* [1895] A.C. 56; *Official Assignee of Madras v Mercantile Bank of India Ltd* [1935] A.C. 53.
[22] See also *Bowstead and Reynolds on Agency* (17th ed.), para.8–143.
[23] See below, para.7–037.
[24] See below, para.7–037, n.48, para.7–048, n.17.
[25] See s.1(2) of the Act, and below, para.7–035.
[26] See s.1(4) of the Act, and below, para.7–036.
[27] See below, para.7–048.
[28] See below, para.7–049.
[29] See below, para.7–041.
[30] See below, para.7–043.
[31] See below, para.7–048.
[32] See s.1(6) of the Act.
[33] See below, para.7–046.
[34] See below, para.7–047.
[35] *Beverley Acceptances Ltd v Oakley* [1982] R.T.R. 417.
[36] Defined in s.1(3) of the 1889 Act; but the term does not include certificates of stock: *Freeman v Appleyard* (1862) 32 L.J.Ex. 175. For an extended meaning of the word "goods" to include a motor vehicle together with its registration book, see *Pearson v Rose and Young Ltd* [1951] 1 K.B. 275 at 291 (below, para.7–044).
[37] *Capital and Counties Bank v Warriner* (1896) 12 T.L.R. 216 (below, para.7–072); *City Fur Manufacturing Co. v Fureenbond* [1937] 1 All E.R. 799 (below, para.7–057). *Cf. Nicholson v Harper* [1895] 2 Ch. 415.

7–036 **Documents of title.** The expression "document of title" is stated by section 1(4) of the Act to include any bill of lading,[38] dock warrant,[39] warehousekeeper's certificate,[40] and warrant or order for the delivery of goods, and any other document used in the ordinary course of business as proof of the possession or control of goods, or authorising or purporting to authorise, either by endorsement or by delivery, the possessor of the document to transfer or receive goods thereby represented.[41] Apart from the provisions of the Factors Act 1889, the transfer of document such as a delivery order would not have effect as a transfer of the constructive possession of goods without attornment.[42] But for the purposes of section 2 of the Act[43] it would seem that a mercantile agent can, by the transfer of such a document, confer title upon the transferee without the need for any attornment.[44]

A motor vehicle registration document is not, in the United Kingdom, a document of title within this definition,[45] nor is an invoice, even with proof that it has been paid.[46] It has yet to be established whether an electronic bill of lading or other electronic document could be considered to be a document of title for the purposes of this subsection.[47]

7–037 **Consent of the owner.** The possession by the mercantile agent must be with the consent of the owner,[48] and, for the purposes of the Act, the consent of the owner is presumed in the absence of evidence to the

---

[38] See below, para.18–062.
[39] See below, para.18–198.
[40] *cf. Gunn v Bolckow Vaughan & Co.* (1875) L.R. 10 Ch.App. 491.
[41] For delivery orders, see below, paras 18–193—18–197; mate's receipts, below, para.18–167; sea waybills, below, para.18–152; air waybills, cargo receipts and consignment notes, issued on international carriage of goods by air, road and rail, below, paras 21–053, 21–061, 21–068.
[42] See below, paras 8–013, 18–193.
[43] And for the purposes of ss.24, 25 of the Sale of Goods Act 1979 (reproducing ss.8, 9 of the Factors Act 1889) see below, paras 7–055, 7–069. For the position in relation to s.10 of the Factors Act 1889 and s.47 of the Sale of Goods Act 1979, see below, paras 15–092, 15–097.
[44] *Official Assignee of Madras v Mercantile Bank of India* [1935] A.C. 53 at 60. See also *Ant. Jurgens Margarinefabrieken v Louis Dreyfus & Co.* [1914] 3 K.B. 40. Contrast *Laurie and Morewood v Dudin & Sons* [1925] 2 K.B. 383; [1926] 1 K.B. 223; *Joblin v Watkins & Roseveare (Motors) Ltd* [1949] 1 All E.R. 47. See also s.11 of the 1889 Act and below, para.18–196.
[45] *Joblin v Watkins and Roseveare (Motors) Ltd*, above; *Pearson v Rose and Young Ltd* [1951] 1 K.B. 275; *Central Newbury Car Auctions Ltd v Unity Finance Ltd* [1957] 1 Q.B. 371; *J. Sargent (Garages) Ltd v Motor Auctions (West Bromwich) Ltd* [1977] R.T.R. 121; *Beverley Acceptances Ltd v Oakley* [1982] R.T.R. 417; *Shaw v Commissioner of Metropolitan Police* [1987] 1 W.L.R. 1322 at 1335–1336.
[46] *Anglo-Irish Asset Finance v D.S.G. Financial Services* [1995] C.L.Y. 4491.
[47] *cf.*, Carriage of Goods by Sea Act 1992, s.1(5); Faber [1996] L.M.C.L.Q. 232 at 240. Law Commission Advice (2001) *Electronic Commerce: Formal Requirements in Commercial Transactions*, para.5; Law Commission Consultative Report (2004) on *Company Security Interests*, Law Com No. 176, para 3.20; Law Commission Final Report (2005) on *Company Security Interests*, Law Com. No. 296. See also "Legal Aspects of a Bolero Bill of Lading" at www.bolero.net, and below, para.18–205.
[48] The "owner" is the person who could have given express authority with regard to dealing with the goods or documents of title, and a mercantile agent can be in possession with the consent of the owner even if he (the agent) has an interest in the

contrary.[49] If, however, the owner can prove that the mercantile agent was in possession without his consent, no title will pass under the Act.[50] The fact that the mercantile agent has obtained possession of the goods by means of fraud will not of itself negative consent.[51] Nevertheless, it was at one time believed that, if he obtained possession in circumstances amounting to larceny by a trick—as opposed to obtaining by false pretences—there would be no true consent.[52] This view was later discarded.[53] In any event the distinction between these two criminal offences has been rendered obsolete by the passing of the Theft Act 1968.[54] In the result, the *de facto* consent of the owner will suffice, even though the mercantile agent may be guilty of theft. It would seem, however, that consent could be negatived by an operative mistake as to identity on the part of the owner[55] and it has even been suggested that it could be negatived by illegality.[56]

Section 2(1) of the Act has further been interpreted in such a way as to require the owner to have consented to the agent being in possession of the goods or documents of title as mercantile agent. "This means that the owner must consent to the agent having them for a purpose which is in some way or other connected with his business as a mercantile agent. It may not actually be for sale. It may be for display or to get offers, or merely to put in his showroom: but there must be a consent to something of that kind before the owner can be deprived of his goods."[57] If, therefore, the owner merely consents to the mercantile agent being in possession of the **7–038**

property shared with the owner: *Lloyds Bank Ltd v Bank of America National Trust and Savings Association* [1938] 2 K.B. 147 at 161–162. See also *Beverley Acceptances Ltd v Oakley* [1982] R.T.R. 417 (pledgee without whose consent goods cannot be sold by the true owner). *Cf. Cook v Rodgers* (1946) 46 S.R.(N.S.W.) 229 (hirer is not the owner).

[49] Factors Act 1889, s.2(4).

[50] *Cf. Vaughan v Moffatt* (1868) 38 L.J.Ch.144 (a case before the 1893 Act).

[51] *Cole v North Western Bank* (1875) L.R. 10 C.P. 354 at 373; *Folkes v King* [1923] 1 K.B. 282; *Lowther v Harris* [1927] 1 K.B. 393.

[52] *Oppenheimer v Frazer and Wyatt* [1907] 2 K.B. 50; *Oppenheimer v Attenborough & Son* [1908] 1 K.B. 221 at 232; *Mehta v Sutton* (1913) 109 L.T. 529; *Heap v Motorists' Advisory Agency Ltd* [1923] 1 K.B. 577; *Lake v Simmons* [1926] 2 K.B. 51 at 71; [1927] A.C. 487 at 509–510.

[53] *Folkes v King*, above, at pp.296, 305; *Buller & Co. Ltd v T. J. Brooks Ltd* (1930) 142 L.T. 576 at 578; *Pearson v Rose and Young Ltd* [1951] 1 K.B. 275; *Ingram v Little* [1961] 1 Q.B. 31 at 70. See also *Whitehorn Bros v Davison* [1911] 1 K.B. 463; *Du Jardin v Beadman Bros* [1952] 2 Q.B. 712; and below, para.7–074.

[54] The offences are now (i) theft, and (ii) obtaining property by deception. Neither refers to consent of the owner: *R. v Lawrence* [1972] A.C. 626. See also *Dobson v General Accident Fire and Life Assurance Corp. Plc* [1990] 1 Q.B. 274. *Cf. R. v Morris* [1984] A.C. 320; *R. v Gomez* [1993] A.C. 442.

[55] *Du Jardin v Beadman Bros*, above, at p.718. See *Chitty on Contracts* (29th ed.), Vol. 1 para.5–076; and above, para.3–012.

[56] *Belvoir Finance Co. Ltd v Harold G. Cole & Co. Ltd* [1969] 1 W.L.R. 1877 at 1881. *Sed quaere?*

[57] *Pearson v Rose and Young Ltd* [1951] 1 K.B. 275 at 288. See also *Turner v Sampson* (1911) 27 T.L.R. 200; *Moody v Pall Mall Deposit and Forwarding Co. Ltd* (1917) 33 T.L.R. 306. *Cf. Universal Guarantee Pty Ltd v Metters Ltd* [1966] W.A.R. 74 ("display or return").

goods for the purpose of holding them as bailee for other purposes,[58] *e.g.* for repair, the subsection will be inapplicable. Similarly, if the agent is first entrusted with the goods as mercantile agent, but later becomes a bailee of the goods in some other capacity it may be that he cannot pass a good title as bailee, even though there may have been no break in the continuity of his physical possession of the goods.[59]

7–039 Where a mercantile agent has obtained possession of any documents of title[60] to goods by reason of his being or having been, with the consent of the owner, in possession of the goods represented thereby, or of any other documents of title to the goods, his possession of the first-mentioned documents is deemed to be with the consent of the owner.[61]

7–040 **Withdrawal of consent.** By section 2(2) of the Act, where a mercantile agent has, with the consent of the owner, been in possession of goods or the documents of title to goods, any sale, pledge, or other disposition, which would have been valid if the consent had continued, is valid notwithstanding the determination of the consent: provided that the person taking under the disposition has not at the time thereof notice that the consent has been determined.[62]

7–041 **Disposition.** Protection is afforded by section 2(1) of the Act to "any sale, pledge, or other disposition of the goods" made by the mercantile agent, or by a clerk or other person authorised in the ordinary course of business[63] to make contracts of sale or pledge on his behalf.[64] Where a mercantile agent deposited with an auctioneer goods entrusted to him for

---

[58] *Cole v North Western Bank* (1875) L.R. 10 C.P. 354 at 369; *Oppenheimer v Frazer and Wyatt* [1907] 1 K.B. 519 at 529 (above); *Folkes v King* [1923] 1 K.B. 282 at 295; *Heap v Motorists' Advisory Agency Ltd* [1923] 1 K.B. 577 at 588; *Staffs Motor Guarantee Ltd v British Wagon Co. Ltd* [1934] 2 K.B. 305; *Pearson v Rose and Young Ltd*, above, at p.288; *Stadium Finance Ltd v Robbins* [1962] 2 Q.B. 664 at 674; *Roache v Australian Mercantile Land and Finance Co. Ltd (No. 2)* [1966] 1 N.S.W.L.R. 384 at 388; *Kendrick v Sotheby & Co.* (1967) 111 S.J. 470; *Astley Industrial Trust Ltd v Miller* [1968] 2 All E.R. 36 at 40; *Belvoir Finance Co. Ltd v Harold G. Cole & Co. Ltd* [1969] 1 W.L.R. 1877 at 1881; *Traders Group Ltd v Gouthro* (1969) 9 D.L.R. (3d) 387; *McManus v Eastern Ford Sales Ltd* (1981) 128 D.L.R. (3d) 246; *Henderson v Prosser* [1982] C.L.Y. 21. *Cf. St Margaret's Trust v Castle* [1964] C.L.Y. 1685; *Pacific Motor Auctions Pty Ltd v Motor Credits (Hire Finance) Ltd* [1965] A.C. 867 at 889.

[59] *Staffs Motor Guarantee Ltd v British Wagon Co. Ltd*, above; *Astley Industrial Trust Ltd v Miller*, above, at pp.41–42. The principle in *Pacific Motor Auctions Pty Ltd v Motor Credits (Hire Finance) Ltd*, above, which is referred to in para.7–059, below, may not apply to s.2(1) of the Factors Act 1889. But see s.2(2) of the Act, below, para.7–040.

[60] Defined in s.1(4) of the Act: see above, para.7–036.

[61] s.2(3). This subsection overruled the decisions in *Hatfield v Phillips* (1845) M. & W. 665 and *Phillips v Huth* (1860) 6 M. & W. 572.

[62] *Moody v Pall Mall Deposit and Forwarding Co. Ltd* (1917) 33 T.L.R. 306; *Newtons of Wembley Ltd v Williams* [1965] 1 Q.B. 560 (see below, para.7–080). This subsection overruled *Fuentes v Montis* (1868) L.R. 4 C.P. 93.

[63] See below, para.7–043.

[64] Factors Act 1889, s.6.

sale, and subsequently obtained an advance from the auctioneer on the proceeds of sale, this was held not to be a pledge or other disposition of the goods.[65] Similarly where a mercantile agent delivered to the purchaser of a car the registration document and a post-dated cheque, it being agreed that the agent could repurchase the car within a limited period of time, it was held on the facts that there was no "sale, pledge or other disposition" of the car, but only a device to enable the agent to obtain temporary financial accommodation.[66]

In the case of a sale or pledge, consideration is provided by the buyer or pledgee.[67] It would also seem that consideration must likewise be given for any other disposition,[68] so that a gift by the mercantile agent of the goods entrusted to him would not bind the owner. By section 5 of the Act, the consideration necessary for the validity of a sale, pledge, or other disposition, of goods may be either a payment in cash, or the delivery or transfer of other goods, or of a document of title to goods,[69] or of a negotiable security, or any other valuable consideration. 7–042

Ordinary course of business. The disposition by the mercantile agent[70] must be made by him "when acting in the ordinary course of business of a mercantile agent." It was pointed out by Buckley L.J. in *Oppenheimer v Attenborough & Son*[71] that this expression differs in language and intent from the phrase "in the customary course of his business" contained in section 1(1) of the Act, which is part of the definition of a mercantile agent and deals with the circumstances under which the agent gets his authority. Even if he has such authority and is thus a mercantile agent within the meaning of section 1(1), he must still dispose of the goods while "acting in such a way as a mercantile agent would act; that is to say, within business hours, at a proper place of business, and in other respects in the ordinary way in which a mercantile agent would act, so that there is nothing to lead [the disponee] to suppose that anything wrong is being done, or to give him notice that the disposition is one which the mercantile agent had no authority to make."[72] But once this test is satisfied, it has been said to be immaterial that the disposition is one which is not customary in his 7–043

---

[65] *Waddington & Sons v Neale & Sons* (1907) 96 L.T. 786; *Roache v Australian Mercantile Land and Finance Co. Ltd* (*No. 2*) [1966] 1 N.S.W.L.R. 384 at 386.
[66] *Joblin v Watkins and Roseveare (Motors) Ltd* [1949] 1 All E.R. 47.
[67] For pledges in respect of an antecedent debt or liability, see below, para.7–051.
[68] See *Bank of Scotland v Gardiner* (1907) 15 S.L.T. 229 ("value" in Scotland). *Cf. Worcester Works Finance Ltd v Cooden Engineering Co. Ltd* [1972] 1 Q.B. 210 (on s.24 of the Sale of Goods Act 1979); below, para.7–064, n.95. In any event, a gratuitous disposition by a mercantile agent would not be made by him "when acting in the ordinary course of business of a mercantile agent."
[69] See ss.1(4), 11, of the 1889 Act (above, para.7–036).
[70] Or by a clerk or other person duly authorised by him; see Factors Act 1889, s.6.
[71] [1908] 1 K.B. 221 at 230.
[72] *ibid.*, at pp.230–231. *Cf. ibid.*, at pp.226, 227, 231, and *Newtons of Wembley Ltd v Williams* [1965] 1 Q.B. 560 at 580. See also *Weiner v Harris* [1910] 1 K.B. 285.

particular trade or business[73] or one which is made on unusual terms.[74] A sale from dealer to dealer can be in the ordinary course of business,[75] and likewise a sale by a dealer to a finance company,[76] provided the other circumstances are in order. On the other hand, a sale by a mercantile agent under which the price was to be paid direct to the agent's creditor,[77] a sale of stock under pressure in which the purchase price was to be set-off against a debt owed by the agent to the purchaser,[78] a sale by the agent of his entire stock-in-trade,[79] and a pledge by a mercantile agent through the medium of a friend[80] have been held not to be in the ordinary course of business. It is a question of fact in each case whether this requirement has been satisfied.

7–044 A sale of a second-hand vehicle without its registration document will normally not be a sale in the ordinary course of business.[81] But in *Pearson v Rose and Young Ltd*[82] a mercantile agent obtained possession of a second-hand motor car with the consent of the owner and subsequently obtained possession of its registration document (the "log-book" then in use) without the consent of the owner. The agent then sold the car *with* the registration document to a third party. The Court of Appeal held that the Factors Act 1889 did not confer a good title in these circumstances. Denning L.J. and Vaisey J. so held[83] on the ground that the "goods" in this case meant the car together with the registration document, and the agent was not in possession of both of these with the owner's consent.[84] Somervell L.J., however, was of the opinion[85] that, since the owner had withheld his consent to the possession of the registration document, the sale was not in

---

[73] *Oppenheimer v Attenborough & Son* [1908] 1 K.B. 221 (unless the custom of the trade is so notorious that the disponee must consequently have had notice of the agent's want of authority: *ibid.*, at pp.230, 231). *Cf. Mehta v Sutton* (1913) 109 L.T. 529 (Paris pearl trade); *Mortimer-Rae v Barthel* (1979) 105 D.L.R. (3d) 289 (sale of entire stock-in-trade).
[74] *Janesich v Attenborough & Son* (1910) 102 L.T. 605. *Cf. Tingey & Co. v John Chambers* [1967] N.Z.L.R. 785 (price not in cash).
[75] *Lowther v Harris* [1927] 1 K.B. 293 at 297; *Davey v Paine Bros (Motors) Ltd* [1954] N.Z.L.R. 1122 at 1129.
[76] *Stadium Finance Ltd v Robbins* [1962] 2 Q.B. 664 at 671.
[77] *Biggs v Evans* [1894] 1 Q.B. 88. *Cf. Lloyds and Scottish Finance Ltd v Williamson* [1965] 1 W.L.R. 404 at 408 (authority to sell as apparent principal).
[78] *Pacific Motor Auctions Pty Ltd v Motor Credits (Hire Finance) Ltd* (1963) 109 C.L.R. 87; [1965] A.C. 867 at 881 (but in this case the sale was also outside business hours). See also *Nash v Barnes* [1922] N.Z.L.R. 303. Contrast *Ceres Orchard Partnership v Fiatagari Australia Pty Ltd* [1995] 1 N.Z.L.R. 112 (set-off but no forced sale).
[79] *Mortimer-Rae v Barthel* (1979) 105 D.L.R. (3d) 289.
[80] *De Gorter v Attenborough & Son* (1904) 21 T.L.R. 19. But see s.6 of the Act.
[81] *Pearson v Rose and Young Ltd* [1951] 1 K.B. 275; *Stadium Finance Ltd v Robbins* [1962] 2 Q.B. 664; *Lambert v G. & C. Finance Corp.* (1963) 107 S.J. 666; *Durham v Asser* (1968) 67 D.L.R. (2d) 574; *Henderson v Prosser* [1982] C.L.Y. 21. Contrast *Astley Industrial Trust Ltd v Miller* [1968] 2 All E.R. 36 (new car). See also para.7–075, n.75.
[82] [1951] 1 K.B. 275.
[83] At pp.290, 291.
[84] See also *George v Revis* (1966) 111 S.J. 51; below, para.7–075.
[85] At p.283.

the ordinary course of business of a mercantile agent. Neither of these reasons is wholly satisfactory,[86] and in *Stadium Finance Ltd v Robbins*[87] the Court of Appeal considered them in relation to a case involving similar facts.[88] The court unanimously rejected the first reason in *Pearson's* case, but Willmer L.J. nevertheless approved the second reason, *i.e.* that such a sale would not be in the ordinary course of business. It is difficult to see, however, why the sale of a car with its registration document should not be in the ordinary course of business merely because the document has been obtained without the owner's consent.[89] It is submitted that the only convincing ground on which it might be argued that *Pearson's* case was rightly decided is that, without the registration document, the owner did not consent to the agent being in possession of the car in his capacity of mercantile agent, but only as bailee.[90]

Good faith and notice.[91] The person dealing with the mercantile agent must act in good faith and must not have notice of the agent's want of authority to dispose of the goods at the time the disposition is made to him. The burden of proving these facts rests on him.[92] If two or more persons together deal with the agent, bad faith or notice on the part of any one of them will deprive all of the protection of the Act.[93] 7–045

The expression "in good faith" is not defined in the Act of 1889[94] but would appear to mean "honestly", that is to say, not fraudulently or dishonestly.[95] It is submitted that negligence or carelessness is not in itself sufficient evidence of bad faith and the fact that the person dealing with the agent did not behave with the prudence to be expected of a reasonable man does not mean that he acted in bad faith.[96] On the other hand, negligence or carelessness, when considered in connection with the surrounding circumstances, may be evidence of bad faith.[97] But the facts and circum- 7–046

---

[86] See Goodhart, 67 L.Q.R. 3 (1951); Powell, *Law of Agency* (2nd ed.), p.228; *Bowstead and Reynolds on Agency* (17th ed.), para.8–153.

[87] [1962] 2 Q.B. 664.

[88] But in this case the car was sold *without* its registration document.

[89] *Astley Industrial Trust Ltd v Miller*, above, at p.42.

[90] *Stadium Finance Ltd v Robbins*, above, at p.674. But see *Pearson v Rose and Young Ltd*, above, at p.288 (above, para.7–038).

[91] See Palmer and McKendrick, *Interests in Goods* (2nd ed., 1998), Ch.17.

[92] *Oppenheimer v Frazer and Wyatt* [1907] 2 K.B. 50 at 62; *Heap v Motorists' Advisory Agency Ltd* [1923] 1 K.B. 557 at 590.

[93] *Oppenheimer v Frazer and Wyatt*, above.

[94] But see s.61(3) of the Sale of Goods Act 1979 and s.90 of the Bills of Exchange Act 1882. These provisions codified the common law: see J. W. Jones, *Position and Rights of a Bona Fide Purchaser for Value of Goods Improperly Obtained* (Cambridge, 1921).

[95] *Mogridge v Clapp* [1892] 3 Ch. D. 383 at 392. See also *Barclays Bank Plc v T.O.S.G. Trust Fund* [1984] B.C.L.C. 18 ("genuinely and honestly in the circumstances of the case"); *Dodds v Yorkshire Bank Finance* [1992] C.C.L.R. 92, CA; *GE Capital Bank Ltd v Rushton* [2005] EWCA Civ 1556, [2006] 1 W.L.R. 899 (Hire-Purchase Act 1964).

[96] *Re Gomersall* (1875) 1 Ch.D. 137 at 146. See also *Vane v Vane* (1873) 8 Ch.App. 383 at 399; *Jones v Gordon* (1877) 2 App.Cas. 616; *Moody v Pall Mall Deposit and Forwarding Co. Ltd* (1917) 33 T.L.R. 306; Bills of Exchange Act 1882, s.90; Sale of Goods Act 1979, s.61(3).

[97] *Re Gomersall*, above, at p.146.

stances should then be such as to lead to the inference that the disponee must have had a suspicion that there was something wrong, and that he refrained from asking questions because he thought that further enquiry would reveal an irregularity.[98] Proof that the goods were purchased at a much lower price than the ordinary trade price is not absolute proof of bad faith, but it may be evidence of fraudulent knowledge on his part.[99] Also an unusually high rate of interest charged on a pledge may be evidence of bad faith on the part of a pledgee.[1] Although it has been said that the courts view with suspicion any dealing with a secondhand motor vehicle without the registration document,[2] a failure on the part of the buyer to ask for the registration document of a second-hand vehicle does not necessarily show bad faith[3] and may be of little evidentiary value in the case of the sale of a new vehicle.[4]

7–047 It is submitted that, in the context of the Factors Act 1889 and of the Sale of Goods Act 1979,[5] "notice" of a fact prima facie means actual knowledge of that fact. But, as was pointed out by Lord Tenterden in *Evans v Trueman*[6]: "A person may have knowledge of a fact either by direct communication, or by being aware of the circumstances which must lead a reasonable man applying his mind to them, and judging from them, to the conclusion that the fact is so. Knowledge acquired in either of these ways is enough, I think, to exclude a party from the benefit of the provisions of this statute[7]: a slight suspicion, I think, will not." In *Navulshaw v Brownrigg*[8] Lord St. Leonards L.C. approved this statement but added that the final words of the statement appeared to be laid down a little too much at large: mere suspicion should not amount to notice. It is, however, established that suspicion in the mind of a person, and the means of knowledge in his power wilfully disregarded, would amount to notice.[9] But the main problem is the

---

[98] *Jones v Gordon*, above, at p.629; *Whitehorn Brothers v Davison* [1911] 1 K.B. 463 at 478; *Patry v General Motors Acceptance Corp. of Canada Ltd* (2000) 187 D.L.R. (4th) 99 at 105; *Cf. Mercantile Credit Co. Ltd v Waugh* (1978) 32 *Hire Trading* (No. 2), p.16.

[99] *Re Gomersall*, above, at p.150; *Heap v Motorists' Advisory Agency Ltd* [1923] 1 K.B. 577 at 590; *Davey v Paine Bros (Motors) Ltd* [1954] N.Z.L.R. 1122 at 1130. *Cf. GE Capital Bank Ltd v Rushton* [2005] EWCA Civ 1556, [2006] 1 W.L.R. 899 at [43].

[1] *Janesich v Attenborough & Son* (1910) 102 L.T. 605 at 607.

[2] *Pearson v Rose and Young Ltd* [1951] 1 K.B. 275 at 289. See also *Heap v Motorists' Advisory Agency Ltd*, above, at p.591; *Bishopsgate Motor Finance Corp. Ltd v Transport Brakes Ltd* [1949] 1 K.B. 322 at 338. *Cf.* Goodhart, 67 L.Q.R. 3 (1951). But a private purchaser from a vehicle dealer would not ordinarily expect to see the registration document.

[3] *Stadium Finance Ltd v Robbins* [1962] 2 Q.B. 664 at 672, 675.

[4] *Astley Industrial Trust Ltd v Miller* [1968] 2 All E.R. 36.

[5] See above, para.7–029, below, paras 7–068, 7–086.

[6] (1830) 1 Moody & R. 10 at 12. See also *Gobind Chunder Sein v Ryan* (1861) 15 Moo.P.C. 231 at 254.

[7] Factors Act 1825.

[8] (1852) 2 De G.M. & G. 441 at 451 (commenting on the Factors Act 1842).

[9] *Heap v Motorists' Advisory Agency Ltd* [1923] 1 K.B. 577 at 591; *Worcester Works Finance Ltd v Cooden Engineering Co. Ltd* [1972] 1 Q.B. 210 at 218 ("deliberately turning a blind eye"); *Feuer Leather Corp. v Frank Johnstone & Sons Ltd* [1981] Com.L.R. 251 at 253. See also *May v Chapman* (1847) 16 M. & W. 355 at 361; *Raphael v Bank of England* (1855) 17 C.B. 161 at 174 (bills of exchange cases).

extent to which the courts will adopt an objective approach to the question of notice, *e.g.* Lord Tenterden's reference to a "reasonable man". The doctrine of constructive notice does not normally apply to commercial transactions[10] and there is no general duty on the buyer of goods in an ordinary commercial transaction to make inquiries as to the right of the seller to dispose of the goods.[11] Nevertheless, in most cases, the court will not be able to decide, for example, whether a person who has bought goods from a mercantile agent had notice of the agent's want of authority except by drawing an inference from the circumstances surrounding the transaction. It is certainly appropriate that the court should apply an objective test to those circumstances, that is to say, to determine from those circumstances whether the buyer as a reasonable man must have known of the agent's want of authority or must have suspected that authority and wilfully shut his eyes to the means of knowledge available to him.[12] In a somewhat different context,[13] however, Neill J. went further and expressed the opinion[14] that "if by an objective test clear notice was given, liability cannot be avoided by proof merely of absence of actual knowledge." If this view is correct, then, in the absence of actual notice, the question becomes "looking objectively at the circumstances which are alleged to constitute notice, do those circumstances constitute notice? This must be a matter of fact and degree to be determined in the particular circumstances of the case."[15]

Effect of sale. The effect of a sale of the goods by a mercantile agent will normally be to transfer a good title to the goods to the buyer.[16] It is to be noted, however, that section 2(1) of the Factors Act 1889 states that any 7–048

[10] *Manchester Trust v Furness* [1895] 2 Q.B. 539; *Greer v Downs Supply Co.* [1927] 2 K.B. 28; *Port Line Ltd v Ben Line Steamers Ltd* [1958] 2 Q.B. 146 at 167; *Worcester Works Finance Ltd v Cooden Engineering Co. Ltd*, above, at p.218; *Feuer Leather Corp. v Frank Johnstone & Sons Ltd*, above, at p.253; *Neste Oy v Lloyds Bank Plc* [1983] 2 Lloyd's Rep. 658 at 665; *Westdeutsche Landesbank Girozentrale v Islington L.B.C.* [1996] A.C. 669 at 704.

[11] *Hambro v Burnand* [1904] 2 K.B. 10 at 20; *Dobell, Beckett & Co. v Neilson* (1904) 7 F. 281 at 288; *Curtice v London City and Midland Bank* [1908] 1 K.B. 293 at 298; *Reckett v Barnett and Slater Ltd* [1928] 2 K.B. 244 at 258, 266 (revd. [1929] A.C. 176); *Feuer Leather Corp. v Frank Johnstone & Sons Ltd*, above, at p.253. *Cf. Lord Sheffield v London Joint Stock Bank* (1888) 13 App.Cas. 333 at 341, 346, 348 (which was criticised in *London Joint Stock Bank v Simmons* [1892] A.C. 201 at 210, 221); *Heap v Motorists' Advisory Agency Ltd* [1923] 1 K.B. 577 at 591.

[12] *Ceres Orchard Partnership v Fiatagari Australia Pty Ltd* [1995] 1 N.Z.L.R. 112 at 117.

[13] The purchase of goods subject to a trust or fiduciary duty.

[14] *Feuer Leather Corp. v Frank Johnstone & Sons Ltd*, above, at p.253.

[15] *ibid.* See also *Forsythe International (U.K.) Ltd v Silver Shipping Co. Ltd* [1993] 2 Lloyd's Rep. 268 at 279.

[16] It is submitted that no title would pass by a mere agreement for a sale. Unlike ss.8, 9 of the Factors Act 1889 (see below, paras 7–055, 7–069), the words "agreement for sale" are not included in s.2(1) of the Act; but an agreement for a sale might be held to be a "disposition" of the goods; *Shenstone v Hilton* [1894] 2 Q.B. 452 (s.9). Nevertheless, no property in the goods would be transferred by such a disposition; *Re Highway Foods International Ltd* [1995] B.C.L.C. 209 (s.9), below para.7–084.

sale, pledge or other disposition of the goods "shall ... be as valid as if [the agent] were expressly authorised by the owner of the goods to make the same." This means that the buyer will not acquire an absolute title to the goods, but only such title as was, at the time of the sale to him, vested in the owner of the goods.[17] But even if the owner of the goods is bound by the sale, he may nevertheless recover from the buyer the price agreed to be paid for the goods, or any part of that price, subject to any right of set-off on the part of the buyer against the agent.[18]

7–049 **Effect of pledge.** A pledge of the documents of title[19] to goods is, under section 3 of the 1889 Act, deemed to be a pledge of the goods.[20] The expression "pledge" is defined[21] to include any contract pledging, or giving a lien or security on, goods, whether in consideration of an original advance or of any further or continuing advance or of any pecuniary liability.[22] This definition is very wide, and, it seems, could include a mortgage, charge, or bill of sale, and possibly even a letter of hypothecation[23] without the transfer of possession. But it does not include an arrangement by which the agent is merely granted temporary financial accommodation stopping short of an actual pledge.[24]

7–050 Where goods are pledged without authority by a mercantile agent in consideration of an advance in cash, the owner has the right to redeem the goods at any time before the sale thereof on satisfying the claim for which the goods were pledged.[25] If the pledgee sells the goods, the owner can recover from him the balance of money remaining in his hands as the proceeds of the sale of the goods.[26] But where the goods are pledged by a mercantile agent in consideration of the delivery or transfer of other goods, or of a document of title to goods, or of a negotiable security, the pledgee acquires no right or interest in the goods so pledged in excess of the value of the goods, documents or security when so delivered or transferred in exchange.[27]

---

[17] *i.e.*, in the agents 'principal'. In any event, the expression "the owner" would appear to mean a person who could have lawfully authorised the agent to deal with the goods, and not, *e.g.* a hirer from the true owner: *Cook v Rodgers* (1946) 46 S.R. (N.S.W.) 229.
[18] Factors Act 1889, s.12(3). For the right of set-off, see *Bowstead and Reynolds on Agency* (17th ed.), para.8–108. See also *ibid.*, para.8–113 (Illustration 9).
[19] See above, para.7–036.
[20] See also Factors Act 1889, s.1(4).
[21] *ibid.*, s.1(5).
[22] The words "pecuniary liability" must be read in conjunction with ss.4, 5 of the Act: above, para.7–042; below, para.7–051.
[23] *Re Slee* (1872) L.R. 15 Eq. 69.
[24] *Waddington & Sons v Neale & Sons* (1907) 96 L.T. 786; *Joblin v Watkins and Roseveare (Motors) Ltd* [1949] 1 All E.R. 47; see above, para.7–041.
[25] See Factors Act 1889, s.12(2). The owner is also bound to pay the agent, if by him required, any money in respect of which the agent would by law be entitled to retain the goods or the documents of title thereto, or any of them, by way of lien as against the owner: *ibid*.
[26] *Kaltenbach v Lewis* (1885) 10 App.Cas. 617. But see s.12(2) of the 1889 Act (deduction of amount of lien).
[27] Factors Act 1889, s.5, proviso.

A pledge created as security for an antecedent debt or liability is effective against the owner,[28] although it is specifically provided[29] that, in such a case, the pledgee is to acquire no further right to the goods than could have been enforced by the pledgor at the time of the pledge. If, therefore, a mercantile agent without the owner's authority pledges goods[30] entrusted to him with a bank as security for an existing overdraft, the owner is only bound by the pledge to the extent of any money in respect of which the agent would by law be entitled to retain the goods by way of lien as against the owner,[31] and he can redeem the goods from the pledgee upon payment of that amount. 7–051

Where a mercantile agent pledges goods with A in order to secure an advance which does not exhaust their value, and, subsequently, with the consent of A, makes a further pledge in favour of B for the balance of their value, the owner will be bound by the latter pledge as well as by the former one, because the former pledge does not prevent the goods being held subject to the agent's control.[32] It is a moot point, however, whether the Factors Act 1889 will apply if the goods entrusted to a mercantile agent are pledged by him without authority together with other goods in order to secure an advance based on the total value of all the goods so pledged.[33] It would scarcely be equitable if the owner could only redeem his goods upon payment to the pledgee of the whole sum.[34] On the other hand, it would be equally inequitable if the pledgee was not entitled to the benefit of the Act merely because the advance covered other goods. It is submitted that, in these circumstances, the unauthorised pledge should bind the owner, but that he should be entitled to redeem the goods upon payment to the pledgee of a reasonable or *pro rata* share of the advance. 7–052

Lien of consignee. Where the owner of goods has given possession of the goods to another person for the purpose of consignment or sale, or has shipped the goods in the name of another person, and the consignee of the goods has not had notice[35] that such person is not the owner of the goods, the consignee, in respect of advances made to or for the use of such person, has the same lien on the goods as if such person were the owner of the goods, and may transfer any such lien to another person.[36] This, however, 7–053

---

[28] *Cf. Macnee v Gorst* (1867) L.R. 4 Eq. 315 (before the 1889 Act). But see s.5 of the 1889 Act.
[29] Factors Act 1889, s.4.
[30] Or documents of title: *ibid.*, s.3.
[31] See also *ibid.*, s.12(2) and above, para.7–050, n.25.
[32] *Portalis v Tetley* (1867) L.R. 5 Eq. 140. *Cf. Beverley Acceptances v Oakley* [1982] R.T.R. 417 (first pledgee obtains possession: subsequent unauthorised pledge of goods not valid as against first pledgee).
[33] See *Kaltenbach v Lewis* (1883) 24 Ch.D. 54 at 78; (1885) 10 App.Cas. 617 at 635; *Re the Farmer's and Settler's Co-op. Society Ltd* (1909) 9 S.R. (N.S.W.) 41, 54; *Thoresen v Capital Credit Corporation and Active Bailiff Service* (1962) 37 D.L.R. (2d) 317; (1964) 43 D.L.R. (2d) 94.
[34] *Cf.* s.12(2) of the 1889 Act.
[35] See above, para.7–047.
[36] Factors Act 1889, s.7(1). See *Mildred, Goyeneche & Co. v Maspons* (1883) 8 App. Cas. 874 (on s.1 of the Factors Act 1823).

does not limit or affect the validity of any sale, pledge or disposition by a mercantile agent.[37]

7–054 **Rights of owner preserved.** The provisions of the Factors Act 1889 do not authorise an agent to exceed or depart from his authority as between himself and his principal, nor do they exempt him from any liability, civil or criminal, for so doing.[38] They also do not prevent the owner from recovering the goods from the agent or his trustee in bankruptcy[39] at any time before the sale or pledge of the goods.[40]

6. SELLER IN POSSESSION

7–055 **Seller in possession.** A further exception to the rule *nemo dat quod non habet* is provided by section 24 of the Sale of Goods Act 1979,[41] which enacts: "Where a person[42] having sold[43] goods[44] continues or is in possession[45] of the goods, or of the documents of title[46] to the goods, the delivery or transfer[47] by that person, or by a mercantile agent[48] acting for him, of the goods or documents of title under any sale, pledge,[49] or other disposition[50] thereof, to any person[51] receiving the same in good faith[52] and without notice[53] of the previous sale, has the same effect as if the person making the delivery or transfer were expressly authorised by the owner of the goods to make the same." This section re-enacts in substance[54] section 8 of the Factors Act 1889, to part of which Act reference may be made for the interpretation of its wording.[55] It is derived from section 3 of the Factors Act 1877, which was passed to remedy the situation revealed by *Johnson v Crédit Lyonnais Co.*[56] and "with the object of mitigating the asperity of the

---

[37] *ibid.*, s.7(2).
[38] *ibid.*, s.12(1).
[39] See *Bowstead and Reynolds on Agency* (17th ed.), paras 8–160, 8–164.
[40] Factors Act 1889, s.12(2).
[41] Formerly s.25(1) of the Sale of Goods Act 1893.
[42] Defined in s.1(6) of the Factors Act 1889 to include any body of persons corporate or incorporate.
[43] See below, para.7–056.
[44] Different definitions of goods are contained in s.1(3) of the Factors Act 1889 and s.61(1) of the Sale of Goods Act 1979.
[45] See below, para.7–057.
[46] Defined by s.61(1) of the Sale of Goods Act 1979 to have the same meaning as in s.1(4) of the Factors Act 1889. See above, para.7–036.
[47] See below, para.7–062, and s.11 of the Factors Act 1889.
[48] Defined in s.26 of the 1979 Act and s.1(1) of the Factors Act 1889.
[49] See s.1(5) of the Factors Act 1889; but see below, para.7–063, n.83.
[50] See below, para.7–064.
[51] See above, n.42.
[52] Defined in s.61(3) of Sale of Goods Act 1979; see above, para.7–046.
[53] See above, para.7–047.
[54] But omitting after the words "sale, pledge, or other disposition thereof" the further words "or under any agreement for sale, pledge, or other disposition thereof."
[55] ss.1, 11 only: see *Inglis v Robertson* [1898] A.C. 616 at 629–630.
[56] (1877) 3 C.P.D. 32 at 40.

common law towards an innocent party purchasing goods from a person who has all the trappings of ownership but in truth has no proper title to the goods."[57] A seller who has parted with the property in the goods, but nevertheless is in possession of them, or of the documents of title to the goods, can pass a good title to a third party.

Buyer and seller. For the purposes of this section, the relationship of buyer and seller must exist between the parties to the original sale. But the need to invoke section 24 only arises when the property in the goods has passed to the buyer under the contract of sale, for if the property has not passed the seller can pass a good title by virtue of his ownership of the goods.[58] The section therefore applies in those cases where the seller has actually sold the goods, and is not needed where there has been merely an agreement to sell.[59] 7–056

Possession of seller. The seller must also be in possession of the goods sold, or of the documents of title[60] to the goods. By section 1(2) of the Factors Act 1889, this is deemed to be the case where the goods or documents are in the seller's actual custody or control or are held by any other person subject to his control or for him or on his behalf. The same interpretation is to be applied to the word "possession" in section 24.[61] Thus, if a seller sells goods which are stored for him by a warehouseman, but subsequently pledges the goods and causes them to be delivered by the warehouseman to an innocent third party in return for an advance, the buyer cannot recover the goods from the third party without paying off the advance.[62] Goods which are currently let by the seller to hirers under hire-purchase agreements are not within this provision.[63] 7–057

It used to be thought that the seller must, for the purposes of section 24, be in possession or continue in possession as seller, and that the section would not apply if he continued in possession by virtue of a separate agreement in some other capacity, *e.g.* as bailee under that agreement. This was the view taken by MacKinnon J. in *Staffs Motor Guarantee Ltd v British Wagon Co. Ltd*[64] where a motor dealer sold a lorry to the defendants, a finance company, who then let it on hire to him under a hire-purchase 7–058

---

[57] *Pacific Motor Auctions Pty Ltd v Motor Credits (Hire Finance) Ltd* [1965] A.C. 867 at 882.

[58] See above, para.5–004. If the property has passed, where the seller is an unpaid seller, he can also pass a good title under s.48(2) of the 1979 Act on the exercise of his power of re-sale: this subsection may overlap with s.24. See below, para.15–102.

[59] *Vowles v Island Finances Ltd* [1940] 4 D.L.R. 357. See above, para.1–026.

[60] See above, para.7–036.

[61] See also (s.25) *Archivent Sales and Developments Ltd v Strathclyde R.C.* (1984) 27 Build. L.R. 98; *Forsythe International (U.K.) Ltd v Silver Shipping Co. Ltd* [1993] 2 Lloyd's Rep. 268 at 275. But see *Michael Gerson (Leasing) Ltd v Wilkinson* [2001] Q.B. 514 at 527.

[62] *City Fur Manufacturing Co. v Fureenbond* [1937] 1 All E.R. 799. *Cf. Nicholson v Harper* [1895] 2 Ch. 415.

[63] *Anglo-Irish Asset Finance v D.S.G. Financial Services* [1995] C.L.Y. 4491.

[64] [1934] 2 K.B. 305.

agreement, the lorry remaining at all times in his possession. The dealer subsequently sold and delivered the lorry to the claimants, another finance company, who were unaware of the previous transaction. MacKinnon J. held that the dealer was not in possession of the lorry as a person who "having sold goods continues or is in possession of the goods" within the meaning of section 24, but as bailee of the goods under the hire-purchase agreement. He could therefore pass no title to the claimants under this section. This reasoning was adopted by the Court of Appeal in a number of subsequent cases,[65] although it was not applied where the agreement under which the seller purported to have become a bailee of the goods was in fact a sham.[66]

7–059 These decisions were, however, not followed by the Judicial Committee of the Privy Council in *Pacific Motor Auctions Pty Ltd v Motor Credits (Hire Finance) Ltd.*[67] The Board there held that the words "continues ... in possession" indicated that section 24 did not contemplate as relevant a change in the legal title under which the seller was in possession of the goods, for this legal title could not continue. Before the sale he would be in possession as an owner, whereas after the sale he would be in possession as bailee holding the goods for the new owner.[68] In order to defeat the operation of section 24, there would have to be a break in the *physical* possession of the seller, *i.e.* by delivering the goods to the buyer[69] or to some third person.[70] The section did not cease to apply where the seller simply attorned to the buyer as bailee.[71] Although this decision is strictly only of persuasive authority in England, it has been followed by the Court of Appeal in *Worcester Works Finance Ltd v Cooden Engineering Co. Ltd*,[72] where it was said: "It does not matter what private arrangement may be made by the seller with the purchaser—such as whether the seller remains bailee or trespasser or whether he is lawfully in possession or not. It is sufficient if he remains continuously in possession of the goods that he has sold to the purchaser."[73]

7–060 The section applies, not only where the seller "continues in possession", but also where he "is in possession" of the goods. It has been stated that these latter words "refer only to a case where the person who sold the

---

[65] *Dore v Dore, The Times*, March 18, 1953; *Eastern Distributors Ltd v Goldring* [1957] 2 Q.B. 600; *Halfway Garage (Nottingham) v Lepley, The Guardian*, February 8, 1964. See also *Ahrens Ltd v Cohen, Sons & Co. Ltd* (1934) 50 T.L.R. 411 at 412.
[66] *Union Transport Finance Ltd v Ballardie* [1937] 1 K.B. 510.
[67] [1965] A.C. 867.
[68] See *Dore v Dore*, above.
[69] *Mitchell v Jones* (1905) 24 N.Z.L.R. 932; *Worcester Works Finance Ltd v Cooden Engineering Co. Ltd* [1972] 1 Q.B. 210 at 217–218. In the latter case Lord Denning M.R. suggested (*ibid.*) that the break ought to be "substantial".
[70] *Olds Discount Co. Ltd v Krett* [1940] 2 K.B. 117.
[71] But in the *Pacific Motor Auctions* case, the Board stated (at p.889) that the seller had not attorned.
[72] [1972] 1 Q.B. 210. See also *Astley Industrial Trust Ltd v Miller* [1968] 2 All E.R. 36; *Mercantile Credit Ltd v F. C. Upton & Sons Pty Ltd* (1974) 47 A.L.J.R. 301.
[73] [1972] 1 Q.B. 210 at 217.

goods had not got the goods when he sold them, but they came into his possession afterwards."[74] It is possible, however, that the words in question would also cover a situation where the seller, having lost or parted with possession of the goods, regained possession of them, provided he did so as seller and not in some other capacity.[75]

7–061 Section 24 does not require that the seller should continue or be in possession of the goods or documents of title with the consent of the buyer.[76]

7–062 **Delivery or transfer.** The act which passes title is "the delivery or transfer . . . of the goods or documents of title."[77] It is submitted that the words "delivery or transfer" must be read distributively, and that there must be either a delivery of the goods or transfer of documents of title.[78] It would be insufficient merely to transfer the goods without delivery[79] or to deliver documents of title, unless the document is by custom or by its express terms transferable by delivery, or makes the goods deliverable to the bearer.[80] The voluntary surrender of the goods by the seller to the disponee is a delivery of the goods to the disponee.[81]

7–063 The delivery or transfer must be made by the seller, or by a mercantile agent[82] acting for him. It must also take place "under any sale, pledge[83] or other disposition thereof" or (by virtue of section 8 of the Factors Act

---

[74] *Worcester Works Finance Ltd v Cooden Engineering Co. Ltd* [1972] 1 Q.B. 210 at 217, citing *Mitchell v Jones* (1905) 24 N.Z.L.R. 932.
[75] For example, if the seller lawfully exercised his right of stoppage in transit and thus resumed possession of the goods (see Sale of Goods Act 1979, s.44) and resold them (quite apart from s.48(2) or (3) of the Act). But see Palmer and McKendrick, *Interests in Goods* (2nd ed., 1998), Ch.13, p.334.
[76] *Worcester Works Finance Ltd v Cooden Engineering Co. Ltd* [1972] 1 Q.B. 210 at 220. But it is submitted that an unlawful repossession of the goods sold by the seller would not enable him to pass a good title, as he would not then be in possession as seller.
[77] "Delivery" is defined in s.61(1) of the Sale of Goods Act 1979, and "transfer" in s.11 of the Factors Act 1889. For "documents of title", see above, para.7–036.
[78] *Nicholson v Harper* [1895] 2 Ch. 415 at 418. But see s.11 of the 1889 Act (delivery of documents). The documents of title transferred need not be the same documents as those in the possession of the seller by virtue of the contract of sale: see *Mount Ltd v Jay and Jay (Provisions) Ltd* [1960] 1 Q.B. 159 at 168–169 and below, para.7–077 (s.25). Assuming that an electronic bill of lading or other electronic document can be a document of title (see above, para.7–036), the question arises whether the electronic transmission of such a document amounts to "transfer" (see below, para.18–205).
[79] *Nicholson v Harper*, above; *Ahrens Ltd v Cohen, Sons & Co. Ltd* (1934) 50 T.L.R. 411 at 412. *Cf. Worcester Works Finance Ltd v Cooden Engineering Co. Ltd* [1972] 1 Q.B. 210. But see below, para.7–063.
[80] Factors Act 1889, s.11. See below, para.18–016 (bill of lading indorsed in blank).
[81] *Worcester Works Finance Ltd v Cooden Engineering Co. Ltd*, above. Contrast *Forsythe International (U.K.) Ltd v Silver Shipping Co. Ltd* [1993] 2 Lloyd's Rep. 268 at 277–279 (mere inaction insufficient).
[82] Defined in s.26 of the 1979 Act and s.1(1) of the Factors Act 1889.
[83] By s.1(5) of the Factors Act 1889, "pledge" includes a lien, or security, on goods. But ss.3–5 of the Factors Act, being contained in the group of sections headed "Dispositions by Mercantile Agents", do not appear to apply to s.8 of that Act: *Inglis v Robertson* [1898] A.C. 616 at 629–630.

1889) "under any agreement for sale, pledge, or other disposition thereof." This wording contemplates that the delivery or transfer should be effected in consequence of the disposition or agreement. Thus in *Nicholson v Harper*[84] where one G sold to the claimant wine already stored in the cellars of a warehouseman and afterwards pledged it with the same warehouseman to secure an advance, it was held that section 24 was inapplicable, since there had been no delivery or transfer to the warehouseman after the sale. This case also suggested that an actual delivery of the goods is required and that a constructive delivery,[85] *i.e.* by the warehouseman ceasing to hold the goods as bailee for the seller and holding them instead as pledgee on his own account, would not suffice.[86] The reference in the section to a person "receiving" the goods might further be said to support the view that there must be a change in the physical possession of the goods.[87] However, in *Gamer's Motor Centre (Newcastle) Pty Ltd v Natwest Wholesale Australia Pty Ltd*,[88] the High Court of Australia held (in the context of section 25(1) of the Act) that there can be a delivery of the goods, even though they never leave the physical possession of the person disposing of them, if the character of his possession changes by his becoming a bailee of the goods for the disponee.[89] In *Forsythe International (U.K.) Ltd v Silver Shipping Co. Ltd*[90] (again in the context of section 25(1)) Clarke J. was of the opinion that delivery could be constructive and the same proposition was accepted by the Court of Appeal in *Michael Gerson (Leasing) Ltd v Wilkinson*[91] in relation to section 24. In the latter case equipment was sold to and leased back from a finance company and then sold to and leased back from a second finance company. The equipment remained throughout in the physical possession of the seller. It was held that there was a constructive delivery of the equipment by the seller to the second finance company when the seller acknowledged to that company that he held the equipment sold on its behalf.[92] The character of his possession then changed from possession on his own account to possession for the company. This was immediately followed by redelivery to the seller as bailee. There is therefore little doubt that a constructive delivery is now sufficient.

7–064 **Disposition.** "Disposition" involves some transfer of an interest in property,[93] and it has been said that it extends "to all acts by which a new interest (legal or equitable) in the property is effectually created."[94] The

---

[84] [1895] 2 Ch. 415.
[85] See below, paras 8–008, 8–009.
[86] See also *Hull Rope Works Co. Ltd v Adams* (1895) 73 L.T. 446 at 448; *Ahrens Ltd v Cohen, Sons & Co. Ltd*, above, at p.412; *Bank of New South Wales v Palmer* [1970] 2 N.S.W.R. 532; *NZ Securities Finance Ltd v Wrightcars Ltd* [1976] 1 N.Z.L.R. 77.
[87] *Bank of New South Wales v Palmer*, above, at p.536; *NZ Securities Finance Ltd v Wrightcars Ltd*, above.
[88] (1987) 163 C.L.R. 236; below, para.7–077. See also *Re Morrison* (1906) 25 N.Z.L.R. 513.
[89] See below, para.8–009.
[90] [1993] 2 Lloyd's Rep. 268; below, para.7–077.
[91] [2001] Q.B. 514 (approved concession).
[92] See below, para.8–009.
[93] *Worcester Works Finance Ltd v Cooden Engineering Co. Ltd* [1972] 1 Q.B. 210 at 218, 219, 220.
[94] *ibid.*, at p.218, citing *Carter v Carter* [1896] 1 Ch. 62 at 67.

reference to an equitable interest is, however, problematical; and it further seems unlikely that a purely gratuitous disposition, *e.g.* a gift, would suffice.[95] In its context, the word "disposition" must also mean something more than a mere transfer of possession.[96] It is a moot point, however, whether a bailment by the seller which creates some sort of proprietary interest in the bailee analogous to the specific instance mentioned of a pledge, would constitute a "disposition" within the meaning of section 24. For example, if a seller in possession wrongfully lets the goods to a hirer under a hire-purchase agreement, there must be some doubt whether the buyer is bound by this hire-purchase agreement,[97] since it can be argued that this only transfers possession of the goods to the hirer[98] and the seller does not sell or dispose of the property in the goods, or agree so to do.[99] If, however, the hirer were subsequently to exercise his option to purchase the goods under the agreement, he might acquire a good title, provided that a constructive delivery of the goods can be spelt out in consequence of this disposition.[1]

An assignment or mortgage by the seller of "his property" will not extend to goods which are the property of the buyer, even though the seller is in possession of the goods after the sale.[2]

Effect of delivery or transfer. The delivery or transfer is stated to have "the same effect as if the person making the delivery or transfer were expressly authorised by the owner of the goods to make the same." If, therefore, it takes place under a sale of goods, the purchaser from the original seller will acquire a good title to the goods.[3] If it takes place by virtue of a pledge, the pledgee will acquire an interest as pledgee which will be enforceable against the original buyer. Similarly, if it takes place under some other disposition of the goods, the disponee's interest will be binding on the original buyer.[4] But where the delivery or transfer takes place under an *agreement*[5] for sale, pledge, or other disposition of the goods, the situation is more problematic.[6] It would at least appear to protect the disponee from an action for conversion by the original buyer,[7] and it is possible that the contractual right acquired by the disponee under the agreement would be enforceable against the original buyer,[8] although this is 7–065

---

[95] *Cf. Kitto v Bilbie, Hobson & Co.* (1895) 72 L.T. 266 at 267; *Worcester Works Finance Ltd v Cooden Engineering Co. Ltd*, above, at p.219. See Preston, 88 L.Q.R. 239 (1972). The provisions of section 5 of the Factors Act 1889 are not applicable: see above, para.7–055, n.55.

[96] *Worcester Works Finance Ltd v Cooden Engineering Co. Ltd*, above, at pp.219, 220.

[97] *cf.* Goode, *Hire-Purchase Law and Practice* (2nd ed.), pp.606, 607.

[98] *cf. Karflex Ltd v Poole* [1933] 2 K.B. 251 at 264–265.

[99] *Helby v Matthews* [1895] A.C. 471 at 477.

[1] See above, para.7–063. But, by that time, the hirer might no longer be without notice.

[2] *Kitto v Bilbie, Hobson & Co.* (1895) 72 L.T. 266 (s.25); *Ahrens Ltd v Cohen, Sons & Co. Ltd* (1934) 50 T.L.R. 411.

[3] For a different view, see Rutherford and Todd [1979] C.L.J. 346.

[4] *Worcester Works Finance Ltd v Cooden Engineering Co. Ltd* [1972] 1 Q.B. 210.

[5] Factors Act 1889, s.8.

[6] The same problems arise under s.9 of the 1889 Act, below, para.7–084.

[7] *Shenstone & Co. v Hilton* [1894] 2 Q.B. 452 (s.9); below, paras 7–079, 7–084.

[8] Contrast *Hanson (W.) (Harrow) Ltd v Rapid Civil Engineering Ltd* (1987) 38 Build.L.R. 106 (s.25).

by no means explicit in the wording of the statute. But the disponee will acquire no title to the goods which he has agreed to purchase.[9]

7–066 The fact that the delivery or transfer is to have the same effect as if the person making the delivery or transfer were expressly authorised by the *owner* of the goods might at first sight appear to indicate that a purchaser from a seller in possession would acquire an absolute title, and not merely such title as, immediately before the delivery or transfer, was vested in the original buyer. But this is not the case. If goods have been stolen from A by B, who sells them to C, B cannot pass a good title as seller in possession on a subsequent sale to D. D's title will only be effective as against C, the original buyer, and not as against A, the true owner of the goods.[10] On the other hand, if X sells goods to Y, who re-sells them to Z, it is possible that X could pass a good title as seller in possession on a subsequent sale to P. It is arguable that the delivery or transfer of the goods or documents of title under the sale by X to P should have the same effect as if it were authorised by Z, the owner of the goods.[11] In this case, P's title might be effective not only against Y, the original buyer, but also against Z, the sub-purchaser from Y.

7–067 **Goods in bulk.** Under section 20A of the 1979 Act, where there is a contract for the sale of a specified quantity of unascertained goods forming part of an identified bulk, a pre-paying buyer will have transferred to him property in an undivided share in the bulk and he will become an owner in common of the bulk.[12] The effect of section 24 in a situation where the seller of goods sells to successive buyers more than the quantity of goods in the bulk has been discussed in Chapter 5, paragraph 5–122 above. Section 24 may also be invoked where, for example, a buyer purchases and pays for a specified quantity of goods from a larger quantity of goods forming the cargo of a named vessel, but the seller continues or is in possession of a bill of lading covering the whole of the cargo and pledges the bill with a bank to secure an advance.[13] In such a case, provided the bank is in good faith and without notice of the sale, it can rely on section 24 to assert the priority of its pledge over the property interest of the buyer. It would appear to be immaterial that the goods which are the subject-matter of the pledge are then unascertained.[14]

7–068 **Good faith and notice.** The person receiving[15] the goods or documents of title must receive them in good faith[16] and without notice[17] of the previous sale.[18] It would appear that, if he is mala fide or has notice, then a

---

[9] *Re Highway Foods International Ltd* [1995] B.C.L.C. 209 (s.9).
[10] See below, para.7–082 (s.25).
[11] But see *National Employers' Mutual General Insurance Ltd v Jones* [1990] 1 A.C. 24.
[12] See above, para.5–109.
[13] As in *Re Wait* [1927] 1 Ch. 606 (decided before s.20A was inserted into the Act).
[14] *Capital and Countries Bank v Warriner* (1896) 12 T.L.R. 216 (on s.25(1): below, para.7–085). But see above, para.5–122; below, para.8–012, n.51 (attornment).
[15] See Rutherford and Todd [1979] C.L.J. 346.
[16] Defined in s.61(3) of the Sale of Goods Act 1979; see above, para.7–046.
[17] See above, para.7–047.
[18] *cf.* s.48(2) of the 1979 Act; below, para.15–102.

subsequent purchaser of the goods from him could not claim the protection of section 24.[19] The burden of proving good faith and absence of notice appears to rest upon him.[20]

7. BUYER IN POSSESSION

Buyer in possession. By section 25(1) of the Sale of Goods Act 1979[21] "Where a person[22] having bought or agreed to buy[23] goods[24] obtains, with the consent of the seller,[25] possession[26] of the goods or the documents of title[27] to the goods, the delivery or transfer[28] by that person, or by a mercantile agent[29] acting for him, of the goods or documents of title,[30] under any sale, pledge,[31] or other disposition[32] thereof, to any person[33] receiving the same in good faith[34] and without notice[35] of any lien or other right of the original seller in respect of the goods, has the same effect as if the person making the delivery or transfer were a mercantile agent in possession of the goods or documents of title with the consent of the owner."[36] This subsection re-enacts in substance[37] section 9 of the Factors Act 1889, to which Act reference may be made for the interpretation of its wording. At common law, a disposition by a buyer in possession was subject to the ordinary rule that *nemo dat quod non habet*.[38] A limited exception was established by section 4 of the Factors Act 1877[39] and this was extended and reformulated in the Act of 1889. **7–069**

---

[19] See below, para.7–086. *Cf.* s.23 of the Act, above, para.7–030.
[20] *Heap v Motorists Advisory Agency Ltd* [1923] 1 K.B. 577 (Factors Act 1889, s.2); above, para.7–045.
[21] Formerly in s.25(2) of the Sale of Goods Act 1893.
[22] Defined in s.1(6) of the Factors Act 1889 to include any body of persons corporate or incorporate.
[23] See below, para.7–070.
[24] Different definitions of goods are contained in s.1(3) of the Factors Act 1889 and s.61(1) of the Sale of Goods Act 1979.
[25] See below, para.7–074.
[26] See below, para.7–072.
[27] Defined in s.61(1) of the Sale of Goods Act 1979 in the same terms as in s.1(4) of the Factors Act 1889. See above, para.7–036.
[28] See below, para.7–077 and s.11 of the Factors Act 1889.
[29] Defined in s.26 of the 1979 Act and s.1(1) of the Factors Act 1889.
[30] It seems that these need not be the same documents as those of which the buyer has obtained possession: *Mount Ltd v Jay & Jay (Provisions) Co. Ltd* [1960] 1 Q.B. 159 at 168. *Cf.* Sale of Goods Act 1979, s.47; below, para.15–098.
[31] See Factors Act 1889, ss.1(5), 3, 4; below, para.7–083.
[32] See below, para.7–079.
[33] See above, n.22.
[34] Defined in s.61(3) of the Sale of Goods Act 1979. See above, para.7–046.
[35] See above, para.7–047.
[36] See below, para.7–081.
[37] But omitting after the words "sale, pledge, or other disposition thereof" the further words "or under any agreement for sale, pledge, or other disposition thereof." See below, paras 7–079, 7–084.
[38] *Jenkyns v Usborne* (1844) 7 M. & G. 678 at 700; *McEwan v Smith* (1849) 2 H.L.C. 309; *Cole v North Western Bank* (1875) L.R. 10 C.P. 354 at 373.
[39] This only applied to a buyer in possession of documents of title, but did not require delivery or transfer by him.

7–070 **"Bought or agreed to buy."** In order to claim the protection of this subsection, the person to whom the buyer has delivered or transferred the goods or the documents of title must show that the buyer has "bought or agreed to buy" the goods. In most cases, the subsection will be invoked where there has been merely an agreement to sell,[40] that is to say, where there is a contract of sale, but the transfer of the property in the goods to the buyer is to take place at a future time or subject to some condition later to be fulfilled.[41] The buyer must, however, be contractually bound to purchase the goods under a contract of sale.[42] If a person has acquired possession of the goods under a contract for work and materials,[43] or if he has merely an option to purchase the goods, but is not bound to do so, as for example under a hire-purchase agreement[44] or under an agreement on sale or return,[45] he will not be able to pass a good title by virtue of section 25(1) since he has not "agreed to buy" the goods. It has been held to be immaterial that the agreement is unenforceable for failure to comply with

---

[40] *Lee v Butler* [1893] 2 Q.B. 318; *Hull Rope Works Co. v Adams* (1895) 73 L.T. 446; *Thompson and Shackell Ltd v Veale* (1896) 74 L.T. 130; *Horton v Gibbins* (1897) 13 T.L.R. 408; *Wylde v Legge* (1901) 84 L.T. 121; *Marten v Whale* [1917] 2 K.B. 480. But a buyer is deemed not to be a person who has bought or agreed to buy goods if he is a buyer under a conditional sale agreement which is a consumer credit agreement, *i.e.* an agreement for the sale of goods which is a consumer credit agreement within the meaning of the Consumer Credit Act 1974 (as amended) under which the purchase price or part of it is payable by instalments, and the property in the goods is to remain in the seller (notwithstanding that the buyer is to be in possession of the goods) until such conditions as to payment of instalments or otherwise as may be specified in the agreement are fulfilled: see Sale of Goods Act 1979, s.25(2), (4), Sch.1, para.9 and Sch.4, para.2; Consumer Credit Act 1974 s.192 and Sch.4, paras 2, 4; Sale of Goods Act 1979 (Appointed Day) Order 1983 (SI 1983/1572). A conditional sale agreement will be a consumer credit agreement if the buyer is an "individual" (which includes a partnership consisting of two or three persons not all of whom are bodies corporate). Under the 1974 Act an agreement was a consumer credit agreement only if the amount of credit did not exceed £25,000. But the Consumer Credit Act 2006 removed the limit. It is still a consumer credit agreement even though it falls within the exemption for agreements exceeding £25,000 where the agreement is entered into by the debtor wholly or predominantly for the purposes of a business carried on, or to be carried on, by him: see Consumer Credit Act 1974, ss.8(1), (3), 16B, 189(1); and below para.14–143.

[41] Sale of Goods Act 1979, s.2(5); above, para.1–025. The condition may not, in fact, be fulfilled: *Marten v Whale*, above.

[42] *Shaw v Commissioner of Metropolitan Police* [1987] 1 W.L.R. 1332 at 1334–1335.

[43] *Dawber Williamson Roofing Ltd v Humberside C.C.* (1979) 14 Build.L.R. 70; above, para.1–041.

[44] *Helby v Matthews* [1895] A.C. 471; *Payne v Wilson* [1895] 2 Q.B. 537; *Belsize Motor Supply Co. v Cox* [1914] 1 K.B. 244; *Lewis v Thomas* [1919] 1 K.B. 319; *Modern Light Cars Ltd v Seals* [1934] 1 K.B. 32; *Staffs Motor Guarantee Ltd v British Wagon Co. Ltd* [1934] 2 K.B. 305; *United Dominions Trust (Commercial) Ltd v Parkway Motors Ltd* [1955] 1 W.L.R. 719; *Astley Industrial Trust Ltd v Miller* [1968] 2 All E.R. 36; *Spiro v Glencrown Properties Ltd* [1991] Ch.537; *Close Asset Finance Ltd v Care Graphics Machinery Ltd* [2000] C.C.L.R. 43. But, if the hirer is contractually bound to pay all the instalments and is then deemed to have purchased the goods unless he elects otherwise (*i.e.* a negative option), he will be treated as having "agreed to buy" the goods: *Forthright Finance Ltd v Carlyle Finance Ltd* [1997] 4 All E.R. 90.

[45] *Edwards v Vaughan* (1910) 26 T.L.R. 545. But see *London Jewellers Ltd v Attenborough* [1934] 2 K.B. 206, and s.18, r. 4 of the Sale of Goods Act 1979 (above, para.5–040); Taylor [1985] J.B.L. 390.

an evidentiary requirement as to form[46] or that it is voidable at the election of the seller on the ground of fraud.[47] But if the agreement is absolutely void, *e.g.* for mistake as to the person[48] or even possibly for illegality,[49] there will have been no agreement to buy the goods.

At first sight it seems curious that a disposition by a person who has *bought* the goods should also have been included, since, as a normal rule, a buyer to whom the property in goods has passed under a contract of sale will be able to confer a good title by virtue of his property in them.[50] In such a case no question will arise as to the good faith of the person receiving them, nor will the other limitations[51] imposed by this subsection be of any relevance. But there may be some situations where the property in the goods sold will have passed to the buyer, and he will have obtained possession of them, but subject to some right or interest still vested in the seller. For example, it seems that an unpaid seller might still retain his lien over the goods notwithstanding that they are in the buyer's possession if such possession has been given to the buyer temporarily and for a limited purpose[52]; or special rights may have been reserved by agreement to the seller under which he retains an interest in the goods.[53] In these situations, a disponee of the goods from the buyer might not obtain a good title except by relying on section 25(1) of the Act.[54] However, the most important application of the word "bought" in this subsection is where the buyer has obtained both property in and possession of the goods under the contract of sale, but his title has subsequently been avoided by the seller.[55] In this case, it would seem that, having obtained possession of the goods with the consent of the seller,[56] the buyer may be able to pass a good title to a disponee.[57] **7–071**

---

[46] *Hugill v Masker* (1889) 22 Q.B.D. 364 (Statute of Frauds provision, now repealed). See also *R. v Modupe* [1991] Crim. L.R. 531 (non-compliance with the requirements of the Consumer Credit Act 1974).

[47] *Newtons of Wembley Ltd v Williams* [1965] 1 Q.B. 560. See also below, para.7–076.

[48] *Du Jardin v Beadman Brothers Ltd* [1952] 2 Q.B. 712 at 718. See above, para.3–012.

[49] *Belvoir Finance Co. Ltd v Harold G. Cole & Co. Ltd* [1969] 1 W.L.R. 1877 at 1881 (s.2, of the 1889 Act "consent").

[50] *Inglis v Robertson* [1898] A.C. 616 at 630.

[51] See below, paras 7–072—7–086.

[52] See below, para.15–049, s.25(1) refers to notice of "any lien". See also *Jeffcott v Andrew Motors Ltd* [1960] N.Z.L.R. 721.

[53] *Dodsley v Varley* (1840) 12 A. & E. 632 (below, para.15–053). S.25(1) refers to notice of "any . . . other right of the original seller in respect of the goods."

[54] See also Smith, 7 *Journal of the Society of Public Teachers of Law* 225 (1963); Battersby and Preston, 35 M.L.R. 268 at 281–282 (1972).

[55] Sale of Goods Act 1979, s.23; above, para.7–024.

[56] See Factors Act 1889, s.2(2); above, para.7–040; below, para.7–076.

[57] *Newtons of Wembley Ltd v Williams* [1965] 1 Q.B. 560; above, para.7–025; below, para.7–076.

7–072 **Possession of buyer.** The buyer must have obtained possession of the goods or the documents of title[58] to the goods. Possession may be actual or, in some situations, constructive. In *Four Point Garage Ltd v Carter*[59] the buyer of a motor car requested the seller to deliver the vehicle direct to a sub-purchaser from the buyer, and the seller did so. It was held that the buyer had obtained possession of the vehicle constructively for the purposes of section 25(1) of the Act. Further, by section 1(2) of the Factors Act 1889, a buyer will be deemed to be in possession of goods or of the documents of title to goods, where the goods or documents of title are in his actual custody or are held by any other person subject to his control or for him or on his behalf. The same interpretation is to be applied to the word "possession" in section 25(1).[60] In *Capital and Counties Bank Ltd v Warriner*,[61] the seller issued transfer notes to goods in favour of the buyer and sent them to a warehouseman. The warehouseman acknowledged receipt of the notes to the buyer, and subsequently issued delivery orders for the goods to the buyer, who pledged the delivery orders with an innocent pledgee. It was held that the pledgee was entitled to the goods. If the buyer obtains documents of title, it would seem to be immaterial that the goods which they represent are still unascertained.[62]

7–073 The wording of section 25(1), however, contemplates that the buyer must obtain possession of the goods or the documents of title *after* he has agreed to buy the goods. If, therefore, he first obtains possession of goods, *e.g.* as bailee, and subsequently agrees to purchase them, the subsection will not apply. The question also arises whether the buyer must obtain possession pursuant to the prior agreement to sell or whether it is sufficient, while the relationship of buyer and seller continues, that he obtains possession under some collateral arrangement, for example, on hire or on loan from the seller. It is submitted that the latter view is to be preferred.[63]

---

[58] Defined in s.61(1) of the Sale of Goods Act to have the same meaning as in s.1(4) of the Factors Act 1889. See *Ant. Jurgens Margarinefabrieken v Louis Dreyfus & Co.* [1914] 3 K.B. 40. Contrast *Laurie and Morewood v Dudin & Sons* [1926] 1 K.B. 223. A vehicle registration book (or registration document) is not a document of title: see below, para.7–075. See also s.47 of the Sale of Goods Act 1979; below, para.15–092.

[59] [1985] 3 All E.R. 12.

[60] See *Archivent Sales and Developments Ltd v Strathclyde R.C.* (1984) 27 Build.L.R. 98; *Forsythe International (U.K.) Ltd v Silver Shipping Co. Ltd* [1993] 2 Lloyd's Rep. 268 at 275. See also (s.24) *City Fur Manufacturing Co. v Fureenbond* [1937] 1 All E.R. 799 at 802. But see *Michael Gerson (Leasing) Ltd v Wilkinson* [2001] Q.B. 514 at 521.

[61] (1896) 12 T.L.R. 216 (the seller was also held to be estopped).

[62] *ibid.*; *Ant. Jurgens Margarinefabrieken v Louis Dreyfus & Co.*, above (Factors Act 1889, s.10); *Mount Ltd v Jay & Jay Provisions Ltd* [1960] 1 Q.B. 159. But see Nicol, 42 M.L.R. 129 (1979); Goode, *Proprietary Rights and Insolvency in Sales Transactions* (2nd ed.), pp.64–68.

[63] *Marten v Whale* [1917] 2 K.B. 480. *Cf. Edwards v Vaughan* (1910) 26 T.L.R. 545; *Buller & Co. Ltd v T. J. Brooks Ltd* (1930) 142 L.T. 476. Differing views were expressed on this point in *Langmead v Thyer Rubber Co. Ltd* (1947) S.R.(S.A.) 29 at 34, 41.

7–074 **Consent of seller.** A seller of goods cannot be deprived of his title to the goods under the provisions of section 25(1) of the Act unless the goods or documents of title were in the possession of the buyer with his consent.[64] The consent of the seller is to be presumed in the absence of evidence to the contrary[65] so that the burden is on him to prove the lack of consent. The meaning of "consent" in this context has, however, given rise to considerable difficulty, but it is at least clear that, if there is consent in fact, it is immaterial that the buyer obtained possession of the goods by means of fraud.[66] Previously there was some doubt whether the buyer could be said to have obtained possession with the consent of the seller if possession had been obtained in circumstances amounting to larceny by a trick, as opposed to obtaining by false pretences. It was argued that the crime of larceny required that the thief should have taken possession without the consent of the owner, so that any buyer who was guilty of this crime could not have obtained possession with the consent of the seller within the meaning of the subsection.[67] Later cases, however, established that the question of larceny or no larceny was irrelevant for the purposes of section 2 of the Factors Act 1889,[68] and this view was followed in relation to the requirement of consent in section 25(1) of the 1979 Act.[69] The crime of larceny was abolished by the Theft Act 1968.[70] It would therefore now seem to be settled law that, unless the contract of sale between the buyer and seller can be shown to be void, *e.g.* for mistake as to identity,[71] the *de facto* consent of the seller will suffice, even though the buyer may be guilty of theft. Nor is it material for this purpose that the seller's consent was given subject to the fulfilment of a condition subsequent on the part of the buyer, which condition has not been fulfilled.[72]

7–075 A vehicle registration document is not, in the United Kingdom, a document of title.[73] If, however, a vehicle is sold and possession of it delivered to the buyer, the seller may retain possession of the registration

---

[64] *Michael Gerson (Leasing) Ltd v Wilkinson* [2001] Q.B. 514.

[65] Factors Act 1889, s.2(4). See also s.2(3).

[66] *Du Jardin v Beadman Brothers Ltd* [1952] 2 Q.B. 712; *Newtons of Wembley Ltd v Williams* [1965] 1 Q.B. 560. See also *London Jewellers Ltd v Attenborough* [1934] 2 K.B. 206.

[67] *Oppenheimer v Frazer and Wyatt* [1907] 2 K.B. 50; *Heap v Motorists' Advisory Agency Ltd* [1923] 1 K.B. 577 (both on s.2 of the Factors Act 1889; see above, para.7–037).

[68] *Folkes v King* [1923] 1 K.B. 282 at 296, 305; *Pearson v Rose and Young Ltd* [1951] 1 K.B. 275; see above, para.7–037.

[69] *Du Jardin v Beadman Brothers Ltd* [1952] 2 Q.B. 712.

[70] The two relevant offences are now (i) theft, and (ii) obtaining property by deception. Neither refers to the consent of the owner: *R. v Lawrence* [1972] A.C. 626. See also *Dobson v General Accident Fire and Life Assurance Corp. Plc* [1990] 1 Q.B. 274. *Cf. R. v Morris* [1984] A.C. 320; *R. v Gomez* [1993] A.C. 442.

[71] *Du Jardin v Beadman Brothers Ltd*, above, at p.718. See also *Belvoir Finance Co. Ltd v Harold G. Cole and Co. Ltd* [1969] 1 W.L.R. 1877 at 1881 (illegality): *sed quaere?*

[72] *Cahn v Pockett's Bristol Channel Steam Packet Co. Ltd* [1899] 1 Q.B. 643. See also *Marten v Whale* [1917] 2 K.B. 480 (condition precedent). See below, para.18–225.

[73] *Joblin v Watkins and Roseveare (Motors) Ltd* [1949] 1 All E.R. 47; *Pearson v Rose and Young Ltd* [1951] 1 Q.B. 275; *Central Newbury Car Auctions Ltd v Unity Finance*

document until the price is paid or some other condition is fulfilled.[74] Where the vehicle is second-hand, there is authority for the view that the buyer would not be acting in the ordinary course of business if he disposed of the vehicle without its registration document and the disponee would not in consequence acquire a good title to the vehicle.[75] Further, in *George v Revis*,[76] where the buyer stole the registration document which had been retained by the seller, it was held that he could pass no title to the vehicle under section 25(1).

7–076 It has already been noted[77] that section 2(2) of the Factors Act 1889 in effect provides that consent to possession of goods or documents of title given by the owner to a mercantile agent is deemed to continue notwithstanding that it has been determined, unless the disponee knows that the consent has been determined. It has been held that section 25(1) of the Sale of Goods Act 1979 should be read in conjunction with this subsection,[78] so that the consent of the seller to the buyer's possession of the goods or documents of title is likewise deemed to continue.[79] In *Newtons of Wembley Ltd v Williams*,[80] the claimant agreed to sell a car to A on terms that the property should not pass to A until the whole purchase price had been paid or a cheque honoured. Possession of the car was given to A, but his cheque was dishonoured and the claimant in consequence forthwith rescinded the contract of sale.[81] Subsequently A sold the car to B in Warren Street car market,[82] and B resold the car to the defendant. The Court of Appeal held that the defendant had a good title to the car. A had obtained possession of it with the claimant's consent and, although the claimant had determined this consent by rescinding the contract of sale, the consent was nevertheless deemed to continue. B had purchased the car in good faith and without notice either of A's defect in title or of the fact that the consent of the claimant had been determined, and so had acquired a good title under section 25(1) of the Act. Accordingly B could in turn pass a good title to the defendant.

7–077 **Delivery or transfer.** As in the case of section 24 of the Act,[83] it is submitted that the words "delivery or transfer" must be read distributively, so that there must be either a delivery of the goods or transfer of

Ltd [1957] 1 Q.B. 371; *J. Sargent (Garages) Ltd v Motor Auctions (West Bromwich) Ltd* [1977] R.T.R. 121; *Beverley Acceptances Ltd v Oakley* [1982] R.T.R. 417; *Shaw v Commissioner of Metropolitan Police* [1987] 1 W.L.R. 1322 at 1335–1336.
[74] Thus indicating a reservation of the right of disposal of see above, para.5–130.
[75] *Lambert v G. & C. Finance Corp.* (1963) 107 S.J. 666. See above, para.7–044; below, para.7–081, n.21.
[76] (1966) 111 S.J. 51. But see (on s.2 of the Factors Act 1889) *Pearson v Rose and Young Ltd* [1951] 1 K.B. 275; *Stadium Finance Ltd v Robbins* [1962] 2 Q.B. 664 (above, para.7–044) and below, para.7–081, n.21. The criticisms of these decisions apply equally in this case.
[77] See above, para.7–040.
[78] See below, para.7–081.
[79] *Cahn v Pockett's Bristol Channel Steam Packet Co. Ltd* [1899] 1 Q.B. 643 at 658.
[80] [1965] 1 Q.B. 560.
[81] See *Car and Universal Finance Co. Ltd v Caldwell* [1965] 1 Q.B. 525.
[82] See below, para.7–081, n.20.
[83] See above, para.7–062.

documents of title[84] in order to substantiate a title under section 25(1).[85] If goods which have been agreed to be sold are attached by the buyer to property mortgaged by him to a third party, and by such attachment become an accession[86] thereto, there is a sufficient "delivery" to the mortgagee, at any rate if followed by the mortgagee taking possession of the mortgaged property.[87] The question, however, arises whether an actual delivery of the goods is required,[88] or whether a constructive delivery will suffice.[89] The reference in the subsection to a person "receiving" the goods might suggest that there must be a change in the physical possession of the goods for the subsection to apply.[90] But in *Gamer's Motor Centre (Newcastle) Pty Ltd v Natwest Wholesale Australia Pty Ltd*[91] the defendant sellers delivered to car dealers possession of certain vehicles under an agreement for a sale by which they reserved the property in the vehicles until the price was paid.[92] The dealers immediately sold the vehicles to the claimants, retaining possession of them for the purposes of display but granting to the claimants the right to take possession of the vehicles at any time without notice.[93] The High Court of Australia, by a bare majority,[94] held that the claimants had acquired a good title to the vehicles under the equivalent provision to section 25(1). Transfer of the physical possession of the vehicles by the dealers to the claimants was not required; there was a sufficient delivery when the character of the dealers' possession changed and they became bailees of the vehicles for the claimants on the terms of the agreement.[95] This decision may be supported on the ground that a seller who has consented to a person obtaining possession of goods under an agreement for a sale should bear the risk if the goods are then wrongfully disposed of by that person to a bona fide disponee, whether or not the disponee has obtained physical possession of the goods. However, it is

---

84 *Ant. Jurgens Margarinefabrieken v Louis Dreyfus & Co.* [1914] 3 K.B. 40. *Cf. Laurie and Morewood v Dudin & Sons* [1925] 2 K.B. 383; [1926] 1 K.B. 223. The documents of title transferred need not be the same documents as those issued under the original contract of sale: see *Mount Ltd v Jay and Jay (Provisions) Ltd* [1960] 1 Q.B. 159 at 168–169. See also above, para.7–036, and Factors Act 1889, s.11. Assuming that an electronic bill of lading or other electronic document can be a document of title (see above. para.7–036), the question arises whether the electronic transmission of the document constitutes a "transfer" (see below, para.18–205).

85 *Nicholson v Harper* [1895] 2 Ch. 415 at 418 (on s.24).

86 See Guest, 27 M.L.R. 505 (1964); Matthews [1981] *Current Legal Problems* 159.

87 *Hull Rope Works Co. Ltd v Adams* (1895) 73 L.T. 446 at 448.

88 See *Nicholson v Harper* [1895] 2 Ch. 415 (above, para.7–063); *Ahrens Ltd v Cohen, Sons & Co. Ltd* (1934) 50 T.L.R. 411 at 412; *Bank of New South Wales v Palmer* [1970] 2 N.S.W.R. 532; *NZ Securities Finance Ltd v Wrightcars Ltd* [1976] 1 N.Z.L.R. 77.

89 "Delivery" is defined in s.61(1) of the Act: see below, para.8–002.

90 *Bank of New South Wales v Palmer*, above, at p.536; *NZ Securities Finance Ltd v Wrightcars Ltd*, above. But see below, para.8–009, n.48 ("actually receive" in s.4(1) of the Sale of Goods Act 1893, now repealed).

91 (1987) 163 C.L.R. 236. See also *Re Morrison* (1906) 25 N.Z.L.R. 513.

92 See above, para.5–141.

93 (1987) 163 C.L.R. 236 at 257, 263; *Michael Gerson (Leasing) Ltd v Wilkinson* [2001] Q.B. 514.

94 Mason, Brennan, Dawson JJ. (Tookey and Gaudron JJ. dissenting).

95 See above, para.7–059.

arguable that this virtually eliminates the requirement—which is absent from section 2 of the Factors Act[96] —that there should be a "delivery" in addition to a "sale, pledge or other disposition" of the goods,[97] since, on a sale by the buyer to a third party, the character of the buyer's possession necessarily changes to that of a bailee for the purchaser.[98] *Nicholson v Harper*[99] (on section 24) suggested that there must be a delivery of physical possession of the goods to the disponee, but in *Forsythe International (U.K.) Ltd v Silver Shipping Co. Ltd*[1] Clarke J. approved the reasoning in *Gamer's* case and expressed the opinion that delivery could be constructive. The same view was accepted (in relation to section 24) by the Court of Appeal in *Michael Gerson (Leasing) Ltd v Wilkinson*[2] and it must now be taken to represent English law.

7–078 The delivery or transfer must be by the person who has bought or agreed to buy the goods, or by a mercantile agent[3] acting for him. In *Four Point Garage Ltd v Carter*,[4] it was held that, where the seller at the request of the buyer delivered the goods directly to a sub-purchaser, such delivery was effected by him as agent for the buyer, so that there was a delivery by the person who had bought or agreed to buy the goods.

The voluntary surrender of the goods to the disponee is a delivery of the goods to the disponee[5] but not mere acquiescence or inaction.[6]

7–079 **Sale, pledge or other disposition.** The delivery or transfer must also take place "under any sale, pledge,[7] or other disposition thereof" or (by virtue of section 9 of the Factors Act 1889) "under any agreement for sale, pledge, or other disposition thereof." In *Shenstone & Co. v Hilton*[8] goods let to a hirer under a hire-purchase agreement were delivered by the hirer to auctioneers to be sold by auction. Bruce J., treating the hirer as a buyer,[9] held that the auctioneers were protected by section 9 of the Factors Act 1889 on the ground that the delivery of goods on the terms that they should

---

[96] See above, para.7–034. It is also absent from s.23 of the Sale of Goods Act 1979.
[97] Or, under s.9 of the Factors Act 1889, any agreement for sale, etc.
[98] A point emphasised in *Pacific Motor Auctions Pty Ltd v Motor Credits (Hire Finance) Ltd* [1965] A.C. 867; above, para.7–059.
[99] [1895] Ch.415 (above, para.7–063); but that was a case where the disponee was already in possession of the goods, to which different considerations might apply. *Cf. Archivent Sales and Developments Ltd v Strathclyde R.C.* (1984) 27 Build.L.R. 98.
[1] [1993] 2 Lloyd's Rep. 268.
[2] [2001] Q.B. 514; above, para.7–063.
[3] Defined in s.26 of the 1979 Act and s.1(1) of the Factors Act 1889.
[4] [1985] 3 All E.R. 12.
[5] *Worcester Works Finance Ltd v Cooden Engineering Co. Ltd* [1972] 1 Q.B. 210.
[6] *Forsythe International (UK) Ltd v Silver Shipping Co. Ltd* [1993] 2 Lloyd's Rep. 268 at 277–279.
[7] See ss.1(5), 3 and 4 of the Factors Act 1889 and below, para.7–083. Contrast *Waddington & Sons v Neale & Sons* (1907) 96 L.T. 786 (deposit of goods with auctioneer with instructions to sell held not a pledge, even though advance obtained on goods in contemplation of sale).
[8] [1894] 2 Q.B. 452. *Cf. Hanson (W.) Harrow Ltd v Rapid Civil Engineering Ltd*, above.
[9] This case was wrongly decided in that it treated a hirer under a hire-purchase agreement as a buyer: *Helby v Matthews* [1895] A.C. 471.

be sold by the person to whom they were delivered, for the benefit of the person delivering them, was "an agreement for the disposition" of the goods within the meaning of that section.[10] An assignment or mortgage of "his property" by a person who has agreed to buy goods, the ownership of which remains in the seller, is not a disposition of the goods by that person.[11]

The meaning of "disposition" has already been discussed in relation to section 24.[12] It would seem that a purely gratuitous disposition is excluded,[13] although the consideration necessary for the validity of a sale, pledge,[14] or other disposition of the goods in this context may be "either a payment in cash, or the delivery or transfer of other goods, or of a document of title to goods, or of a negotiable security, or any other valuable consideration."[15] 7–080

Effect of delivery or transfer. The delivery or transfer is stated to have "the same effect as if the person making the delivery or transfer were a mercantile agent in possession of the goods or documents of title with the consent of the owner." This provision gives rise to considerable difficulty[16] for it is only intelligible if reference is made to section 2(1) of the Factors Act 1889 to see what the position is in the case of an actual mercantile agent.[17] Under that subsection, a sale, pledge, or other disposition of the goods will only be validated if it is made by him when acting in the ordinary course of business of a mercantile agent. The problem then arises: if the buyer in possession is not in fact a mercantile agent, how can he be acting in the ordinary course of business as a mercantile agent? In *Newtons of Wembley Ltd v Williams*,[18] Pearson L.J. said: "I suppose it follows that when one is applying the hypothesis in section 2 one assumes that he is a mercantile agent: if he has a business it is assumed to be the business of a mercantile agent; or the other way of putting it is that the transaction will be validated if this buyer is doing something that would constitute acting in 7–081

---

[10] Bruce J. also held that a "disposition" of the goods need not be restricted to a disposition in the nature of a sale. See also *Worcester Works Finance Ltd v Cooden Engineering Co. Ltd*, above (voluntary surrender of goods).

[11] *Kitto v Bilbie Hobson & Co.* (1895) 72 L.T. 266 at 267; *Ahrens Ltd v Cohen, Sons & Co. Ltd* (1934) 50 T.L.R. 411 at 412. See also *Dawber Williamson Roofing Ltd v Humberside C.C.* (1979) 14 Build.L.R. 70 (building contract).

[12] See above, para.7–065, and *Hull Rope Works Co. Ltd v Adams*, above; *Thomas Graham & Sons Ltd v Glenrothes Development Corp.*, 1968 S.L.T. 2; *Worcester Works Finance Ltd v Cooden Engineering Co. Ltd* [1972] 1 Q.B. 210 at 218, 219, 220; *Hanson (W.) (Harrow) Ltd v Rapid Civil Engineering Ltd* (1987) 38 Build.L.R. 106; Preston, 88 L.Q.R. 239 (1972).

[13] *Thomas Graham & Sons Ltd v Glenrothes Development Corp.*, 1968 S.L.T. 2. *Cf. Worcester Works Finance Ltd v Cooden Engineering Co. Ltd* [1972] 1 Q.B. 210. See also above, para.7–064.

[14] But see ss.1(5), 4 of the Factors Act 1889; below, para.7–083.

[15] Factors Act 1889, s.5; *Thomas Graham & Sons Ltd v Glenrothes Development Corp.*, above.

[16] *Newtons of Wembley Ltd v Williams* [1965] 1 Q.B. 560 at 579 ("an obscure provision"). See also the Twelfth Report of the Law Reform Committee, 1966 (Cmnd. 2958), para.22, and the cases cited in n.23, *infra*.

[17] See above, para.7–032.

[18] [1965] 1 Q.B. 560 at 579.

the ordinary course of business if he were a mercantile agent." As the law now stands,[19] it would in consequence seem that the transaction between the buyer and the disponee must take place within business hours, at a proper place of business[20] and in other respects in the ordinary way in which a mercantile agent would act,[21] so that a transaction, *e.g.* from a private house, might be excluded.[22] But it is submitted that this test cannot possibly be applied satisfactorily where the buyer has no business. It would be better if this requirement were discarded as inapposite to section 25(1); the question of the way in which the goods were disposed of would then be relevant to the bona fides of the person receiving them, but not otherwise.[23]

7–082 Provided that the requirements of section 25(1) are fulfilled, a purchaser from the buyer in possession will normally acquire a good title to the goods purchased.[24] A problem, however, arises by virtue of the fact that the subsection states that the delivery or transfer shall have the same effect as if the buyer were a mercantile agent in possession of the goods or documents of title with the consent of the *owner*. This might appear to indicate that, if a thief who had stolen goods from their true owner sold or agreed to sell the goods and delivered possession of them to a buyer (whether bona fide or not), the buyer could pass a good title under section 25(1) to a person purchasing the goods from him, because the consent of the thief would be treated as equivalent to the consent of the true owner. However, in *National Employers' Mutual General Insurance Ltd v Jones*[25] the House of Lords examined the history of the Factors Acts and concluded that section 9 of the Factors Act 1889 (and section 25(1) of the 1979 Act) was intended only to divest the title of the seller, and that it did not divest the title of the person from whom the goods had been stolen.

7–083 Where the disposition by the buyer in possession consists of a pledge of the goods[26] otherwise than for an antecedent debt or liability due from the buyer to the pledgee,[27] the pledgee will acquire an interest in the goods

---

[19] See also *Lambert v G & C Finance Corp.* (1963) 107 S.J. 666; *Martin v Duffy* [1985] Northern Ireland Judgment Bulletin 80, 84.

[20] *e.g.* in Warren Street car market for the sale of a car: *Newtons of Wembley Ltd v Williams*, above. See also *Archivent Sales and Developments Ltd v Strathclyde RC* (1984) 27 Build.L.R. 98 (building site for contractor's materials).

[21] A sale of a second-hand vehicle without a registration document is not in the ordinary course of business: *Lambert v G & C Finance Corp.*, above. See also the cases cited in para.7–044, above, n.81.

[22] *Cf. Lee v Butler* [1893] 2 Q.B. 318.

[23] See *Langmead v Thyer Rubber Co. Ltd* [1947] S.A.S.R. 29 at 39; *Jeffcott v Andrew Motors Ltd* [1960] N.Z.L.R. 721 at 729. See also *Gamer's Motor Centre (Newcastle) Pty Ltd v Natwest Wholesale Australia Pty Ltd* (1987) 163 C.L.R. 236 at 243, 252, 259; *Forsythe International (UK) Ltd v Silver Shipping Co. Ltd* [1993] 2 Lloyd's Rep. 268 at 280.

[24] See the cases cited above, para.7–070, n.40.

[25] [1990] 1 A.C. 24. See also *Mubarak Ali v Wali Mohamed & Co.* (1938) 18 K.L.R. 23 (Kenya Sup.Ct.), *Elwin v O'Regan and Maxwell* [1971] N.Z.L.R. 1124 at 1130; *Avco Corp. v Borgal and Brandon v Leckie* (1972) 29 D.L.R. (3d) 633.

[26] Defined in s.1(5) of the Factors Act 1889. See also s.3 of this Act (pledge of documents of title).

[27] But see s.4 of the 1889 Act; it would seem that s.9 of this Act and s.25(1) of the 1979 Act should be read subject to this provision. *Cf. Inglis v Robertson* [1898] A.C. 616 at 629–630; and above, para.7–051.

which can be asserted against their true owner.[28] But where goods are pledged in consideration of the delivery or transfer of other goods, or of a document of title to goods, or of a negotiable security, the pledgee acquires no right or interest in the goods so pledged in excess of the value of the goods, documents, or security when so delivered or transferred in exchange.[29]

The effect of a transfer or delivery by the buyer under an *agreement*[30] for the sale, pledge, or disposition of the goods is by no means certain,[31] but in *Shenstone & Co. v Hilton*[32] it was held that auctioneers were protected by the words "delivery under any agreement for sale" from an action in conversion at the suit of the original seller. No title will, however, pass under an agreement for a sale.[33] 7–084

Sub-sales of goods forming part of a bulk. Section 20A of the 1979 Act provides that, in certain circumstances, a pre-paying buyer of a specified quantity of goods forming part of an identified bulk can acquire a proprietary interest in the goods while still in bulk.[34] The buyer becomes the owner (together with others) of the bulk and is entitled to an undivided share of the goods in the bulk. The buyer can sell on his undivided share to a sub-purchaser who will normally have no need to rely on section 25(1) of the Act as he simply acquires the buyer's share.[35] But if, at the time of the sub-sale, the original seller still retains certain rights over the undivided share, the sub-purchaser may need to rely on the subsection to defeat the seller's claim. In such a case, there is authority for the view that the delivery of a document of title (*e.g.* a delivery order) by the original seller to the buyer and the subsequent transfer of a document of title by the buyer to the sub-purchaser will entitle the sub-purchaser to invoke section 25(1) against the seller even though the goods are still in bulk and so are unascertained.[36] But, where there are no documents of title, it is much less certain whether the buyer can be said to have obtained, for the purposes of the subsection, "possession" of an undivided share of the co-owned goods in the bulk, for example, by an acknowledgement by the person in possession of the goods that he holds a specified quantity of the goods on the buyer's behalf.[37] Section 25(1) also requires that there should be a delivery of the goods by the buyer to the sub-purchaser under the sub-sale. A physical delivery of 7–085

---

[28] *Strohmenger v Attenborough* (1894) 11 T.L.R. 7.
[29] Factors Act 1889, s.5.
[30] Factors Act 1889, s.9.
[31] See above, para.7–065 (s.8 of the 1889 Act.)
[32] [1894] 2 Q.B. 452 (above, para.7–079). *Cf. Hanson (W) (Harrow) Ltd v Rapid Civil Engineering Ltd* (1987) 38 Build. L.R. 106.
[33] *Re Highway Foods International Ltd* [1995] B.C.L.C. 209.
[34] See above, para.5–109.
[35] See above, para.5–128.
[36] *Capital and Counties Bank Ltd v Warriner* (1896) 12 T.L.R. 216; *Ant. Jurgens Margarinefabrieken v Louis Dreyfus & Co.* [1914] 3 K.B. 40; *Mount Ltd v Jay and Jay Provisions Ltd* [1960] 1 Q.B. 159.
[37] See above, para.1–119, and *Maynegrain Property Ltd v Compafina Bank* [1982] 2 N.S.W.L.R. 141 at 146 (revd. on different grounds by the Privy Council (1984) A.L.J.R. 389).

the goods will obviously satisfy this requirement.[38] But again it is doubtful whether there can be a constructive delivery of an undivided share of goods while still in bulk.[39]

A sub-purchaser of a quantity of goods in bulk may also wish to rely on section 25(1) if, at the time of the sub-sale, the buyer's undivided share has reduced, *e.g.* because of wastage or the removal of goods from the bulk, to an amount less than the quantity to which the buyer is entitled under his contract with the original seller. If the buyer then sells on the contractual quantity to a sub-purchaser, the sub-purchaser will, in principle, acquire no title to the excess over the buyer's then undivided share, since *nemo dat quod non habet*. Section 25(1) will not, of course, entitle the sub-purchaser to obtain a larger share at the expense of any co-owning buyer of the bulk.[40] But if, at the time of the sub-sale, the original seller retains an undivided share of the bulk, and provided the requirements of the subsection are satisfied, the sub-sale would override and eat into that undivided share to the extent of the excess.

7–086 **Good faith and notice.** The person receiving[41] the goods or documents of title must receive them in good faith[42] and without notice[43] of any lien[44] or other right of the original seller in respect of the goods.[45] It would seem that, if the first purchaser from the buyer is mala fide or has notice, then a subsequent purchaser of the goods from him will not be entitled to claim the protection of section 25(1).[46] The burden of proving good faith and absence of notice appears to rest upon the person receiving the goods.[47]

8. MOTOR VEHICLES SUBJECT TO A HIRE-PURCHASE OR CONDITIONAL SALE AGREEMENT[48]

7–087 **Disposition of motor vehicles.** An important exception to the rule *nemo dat quod non habet* is provided for in Part III (sections 27 to 29) of the Hire-Purchase Act 1964[49] (re-enacted with terminological changes in

[38] See also s.61(1) "delivery".
[39] See above, para.5–122 (s.24), below, para.8–012, n.51.
[40] But see s.20B(1) (removals); above, para.5–124.
[41] See Rutherford and Todd [1979] C.L.J. 346 (on s.24).
[42] Defined in s.61(3) of the Sale of Goods Act 1979; see above, para.7–046.
[43] See above, para.7–047.
[44] *Jeffcott v Andrew Motors Ltd* [1960] N.Z.L.R. 721.
[45] *Barrow v Cole* (1811) 3 Camp. 92; *Cahn v Pockett's Bristol Channel Steam Packet Co. Ltd* [1899] 1 Q.B. 643; *Re Interview Ltd* [1981] I.R. 382; *Hanson (W) (Harrow) Ltd v Rapid Civil Engineering Ltd*, above. In *Forsythe International (UK) Ltd v Silver Shipping Co. Ltd* [1993] 2 Lloyd's Rep. 268 at 280, Clarke J. construed "other right" as meaning some right in relation to the goods themselves, such as a right of ownership or possession.
[46] *Newtons of Wembley Ltd v Williams* [1964] 1 W.L.R. 1028 (affirmed on different grounds [1965] 1 Q.B. 560). Contrast Cornish, 27 M.L.R. 472 (1964).
[47] *Heap v Motorists' Advisory Agency Ltd* [1923] 1 K.B. 577 (Factors Act 1889, s.2); *Lambert v G & C Finance Corp.* (1963) 107 S.J. 666; *Forsythe International (UK) Ltd v Silver Shipping Co. Ltd*, above, at p.279.
[48] See Davies [1995] J.B.L. 36.
[49] Pt III of the 1964 Act was not repealed by the Hire-Purchase Act 1965, but it was amended by s.59(4) of and Sch.5 to the 1965 Act. It was further amended by s.63 of and Sch.2, para.4 to the Sale of Goods Act 1979.

Schedule 4 to the Consumer Credit Act 1974).[50] Part III of the 1964 Act enables the hire-purchaser or conditional buyer of a motor vehicle to pass a good title in certain circumstances to a third party. The person letting the vehicle on hire-purchase or, as the case may be, the seller is referred to as the "creditor",[51] and the person to whom the vehicle is let on hire or, as the case may be, the buyer is referred to as the "debtor".[52]

Scope of provisions. Part III of the 1964 Act is of *prima facie* application "where a motor vehicle[53] has been bailed under a hire-purchase agreement, or has been agreed to be sold under a conditional sale agreement, and, at a time before the property in the vehicle has become vested in the debtor, he disposes of the vehicle to another person."[54] The terms "hire-purchase agreement" and "conditional sale agreement" embrace all such agreements within the meaning given in section 189(1) of the Consumer Credit Act 1974[55] even if they fall outside the financial limits of the exemption relating to businesses[56] and even if the debtor is not an "individual".[57] Credit sale agreements[58] and simple hire or leasing agreements are not included. 7–088

The debtor. The debtor is stated in section 29(4) to be the person who at the material time either is the person to whom the vehicle is bailed under a hire-purchase agreement or is, in relation to a conditional sale agreement, the buyer.[59] This subsection, however, provides that such a person is the debtor "whether the agreement has before that time been terminated or not." This qualification was clearly introduced to cover the situation where the terms of the agreement provide that, if the debtor disposes of, or attempts to dispose of, the vehicle, the agreement is *ipso facto* determined. But this concept of "once a debtor always a debtor" raises certain difficulties. It could in theory apply, for example, where the creditor under a hire-purchase agreement had already retaken possession of the vehicle, since there is no requirement that the debtor should be in possession of the vehicle at the time at which he disposes of it to the third party. But it is 7–089

---

[50] Para.22 (as amended by s.63 of and Sch.2, para.4 to the Sale of Goods Act 1979). This re-enactment became operative on May 19, 1985: see SI 1983/1551 (c. 44).

[51] s.29(1). This includes the person to whom the creditor's rights and duties have passed by assignment or operation of law.

[52] s.29(4). See below, para.7–089.

[53] Defined in s.29(1). This definition would not necessarily cover agricultural or building vehicles.

[54] s.27(1). "Person" includes a body corporate, see Interpretation Act 1978, s.5 and Sch.1.

[55] Hire-Purchase Act 1964, s.29(1).

[56] Consumer Credit Act 1974, s.16B (inserted by s.4 of the Consumer Credit Act 2006). The 2006 Act removes the general financial limit in s.8(2) of the 1974 Act; see below, para.14–143.

[57] See 189(1) of the Consumer Credit Act 1974, as amended by the Consumer Credit Act 2006.

[58] The property in goods sold under a credit sale agreement will have passed to the buyer.

[59] This includes the "statutory bailee", *i.e.* the person who at that time is, by virtue of s.130(4) of the Consumer Credit Act 1974, treated as a bailee of the vehicle after the making of a time order even though the agreement has been terminated.

scarcely feasible to construe the provision as conferring upon the debtor a capacity to confer a good title which capacity will last for ever, and it is submitted that the "notional" debtor situation should not be extended to cases where the creditor has recovered possession of the vehicle.[60]

7–090 A second problem arises where the hire-purchase or conditional sale agreement is void or voidable. If the agreement is completely void, *e.g.* for mistake as to the person,[61] then the person in possession of the vehicle is not a "debtor" and the operation of Part III of the 1964 Act will be excluded. It is, however, submitted that Part III of the Act will apply if the agreement is illegal[62] —notwithstanding that it might be said to be "void" for illegality,[63] or if the agreement is unenforceable against the debtor by reason of the fact that it failed to satisfy the formal and other requirements of the Consumer Credit Act 1974.[64] But more difficulty arises where the agreement is voidable, *e.g.* for fraud or misrepresentation on the part of the debtor, and has subsequently been avoided. It is arguable that, if the creditor avoids the agreement before the disposition occurs, such avoidance rescinds the agreement *ab initio* and does not merely "terminate" it. The debtor therefore ceases to be the person who at the material time is the person to whom the vehicle is bailed under that agreement or who is the buyer in relation to that agreement, and so cannot pass a good title. It is, however, submitted that the words "whether the agreement has before that time been terminated or not" can be construed to cover this situation and that the provisions of Part III of the Act will apply.[65]

7–091 **Disposition.** A "disposition" of a vehicle by the debtor to a purchaser[66] here means "any sale or contract of sale (including a conditional sale agreement), any bailment under a hire-purchase agreement and any transfer of the property in goods in pursuance of a provision in that behalf contained in a hire-purchase agreement, and includes any transaction purporting to be a disposition (as so defined)."[67] This definition clearly embraces a sale of a vehicle by the debtor, but not a gift, mortgage, lien, exchange[68] or assignment on death or bankruptcy. Part III of the Act is also

---

[60] In any event, in most cases, the absence of the vehicle will lead to the inference that the disponee must have had a suspicion that there was something wrong and so preclude him from establishing that he was in good faith: see above, para.7–046; below, para.7–099.

[61] See above, para.3–012; *Shogun Finance Ltd v Hudson* [2003] UKHL 62, [2004] 1 A.C. 919; *Moorgate Mercantile Co. Ltd v Bowman* (1974) 28 *Hire Trading* (No.2), p.15 (Cty.Ct.).

[62] *cf. Belvoir Finance Co. Ltd v Harold G Cole & Co. Ltd* [1969] 1 W.L.R. 1877 (non-compliance with Hire-Purchase and Credit Sale Regulations (now revoked)).

[63] But see *Morley v Maybray Motors Ltd* (1971) 25 *Hire Trading* (No.3), p.15 (Cty.Ct.).

[64] *e.g.*, ss.60, 61, 65. See *R. v Modupe* [1991] Crim. L.R. 530.

[65] *Chartered Trust Plc v Conlay* [1998] C.L.Y. 2516 (Cty. Ct.). Contrast *Morley v Maybray Motors Ltd*, above; Goode, *Hire-Purchase Law and Practice* (2nd ed.), p.620.

[66] See s.29(3).

[67] s.29(1); *Dodds v Yorkshire Bank Finance* [1992] C.C.L.R. 92.

[68] For the distinction between exchange and sale, see above, para.1–034.

inapplicable if the disposition is made by a person other than the debtor,[69] for example, by a bailee of the debtor or by a thief.

Private purchaser. Assuming that the debtor has disposed of the vehicle to a third party, a distinction is drawn between a "trade or finance purchaser" (who does not acquire a good title) and a "private purchaser" (who acquires a good title if bonafide). A "trade or finance purchaser" is a purchaser who, at the time of the disposition made to him, carries on a business[70] which consists, wholly or partly, (a) of purchasing motor vehicles for the purpose of offering or exposing them for sale, or (b) of providing finance by purchasing motor vehicles for the purpose of bailing them under hire-purchase agreements or agreeing to sell them under conditional sale agreements.[71] The fact that he purchases the goods for his own use does not alter his status as a trade or finance purchaser.[72] A "private purchaser" means a purchaser who, at the time of the disposition made to him, does not carry on any such business.[73] It is to be noted that, although Part III of the Act is primarily designed to protect the private individual, it will also protect, for example, a company which purchases vehicles for the purpose of utilising them in its business or even of letting them out on hire. 7–092

Trade or finance purchaser. Obvious examples of trade or finance purchasers are motor dealers, and finance companies.[74] No title passes to a trade or finance purchaser, and he can only take advantage indirectly of the Act's provisions, *i.e.* where he derives title from a bona fide private purchaser.[75] 7–093

Situations covered. The Act specifies three sets of circumstances where the third party will acquire a good title. These are set out in subsections (2), (3) and (4) of section 27, to which reference should be made for their precise wording. 7–094

First, under section 27(2), where the disposition[76] is to a private purchaser, and he is a purchaser of the motor vehicle in good faith and without notice of the hire-purchase agreement or conditional sale agreement, that disposition has effect as if the creditor's title to the vehicle had

---

[69] Unless the person disposing of the vehicle is the actual or ostensible agent of the debtor: *Ford Motor Credit Co. Ltd v Harmack* [1972] C.L.Y. 1649, CA (company director); *Majid v TMV Finance Ltd* [1999] C.L.Y. 2448 (agent). See also *Keeble v Combined Lease Finance Plc* [1996] C.C.L.R. 63, CA (partners and joint debtors). and s.28(1), (2); below, para.7–100.

[70] This directs attention to the activities of the purchaser prior to and at the time of the disposition and to the purpose for which the vehicle was bought: *GE Capital Bank Ltd v Rushton* [2005] EWCA Civ 1556, [2006] 1 W.L.R. 899 at [39–40].

[71] s.29(2). The financing of hiring or leasing contracts, or trading by means of block discounting, would not be sufficient, but the financing of credit sales would probably mean that the financier was a trade purchaser.

[72] *Stevenson v Beverley Bentinck Ltd* [1976] 1 W.L.R. 483. But see *GE Capital Bank Ltd v Rushton*, above, at [39].

[73] s.29(2).

[74] But see above, n.71.

[75] *Cf. Soneco Ltd v Barcross Finance Ltd* [1978] R.T.R. 444.

[76] *i.e.* the disposition referred to in s.27(1); above, para.7–088.

been vested in the debtor immediately before that disposition. Thus, for example, if a motor vehicle owned by A is let under a hire-purchase agreement to B, who wrongfully sells it to C, an innocent private purchaser, C will acquire a good title to the vehicle.

7–095 Secondly, under section 27(3), where the person to whom the disposition[77] is made (referred to as "the original purchaser") is a trade or finance purchaser, then if the person who is the first private purchaser of the motor vehicle after that disposition (referred to as "the first private purchaser") is a purchaser of the vehicle in good faith and without notice of the hire-purchase agreement or conditional sale agreement, the disposition of the vehicle to the first private purchaser has effect as if the title of the creditor to the vehicle had been vested in the debtor immediately before he disposed of it to the original purchaser. Thus if a motor vehicle owned by A is let under a hire-purchase agreement to B, who wrongfully sells it to C, a trade or finance purchaser, who then sells it to D, an innocent private purchaser, D will acquire a good title to the vehicle. Even if the vehicle has passed through the hands of a number of trade or finance purchasers, section 27(3) will protect the first private purchaser, provided that he is *bona fide* and has no notice of the hire-purchase agreement.[78]

7–096 Thirdly, under section 27(4), where, in a case falling within section 27(3), the disposition whereby the first private purchaser becomes a purchaser of the vehicle in good faith and without notice of the hire-purchase agreement or conditional sale agreement is itself a bailment under a hire-purchase agreement, and the person who is the creditor in relation to that agreement disposes of the vehicle to the first private purchaser, or a person claiming under him,[79] by way of transferring to him the property in the vehicle in pursuance of a provision in the agreement in that behalf, the latter disposition (whether or not the person to whom it is made is then a purchaser in good faith and without notice of the original hire-purchase agreement or conditional sale agreement) will, as well as the former disposition, have effect as mentioned in section 27(3). Suppose, therefore, that a motor vehicle owned by A is let under a hire-purchase agreement to B. B wrongfully sells the vehicle to a finance company, which lets it under a hire-purchase agreement to C. Provided that C was, at the time of the letting, the first private purchaser of the vehicle in good faith and without notice of the original hire-purchase agreement, the letting under his hire-purchase agreement is a valid letting; and if, in pursuance of this agreement, the finance company transfers the property in the vehicle to C, he acquires a good title even though at the time the property is transferred he has been informed of the original hire-purchase agreement and so has notice thereof.

---

[77] *ibid*.
[78] If the first private purchaser is mala fide or has notice, then subsequent private purchasers will not be protected even if in good faith and without notice. See below, para.7–097.
[79] Presumably this refers to a lawful assignee, whether the assignment is voluntary or by operation of law, but not to a wrongful disponee.

Anomalies. Certain anomalies are created by this structure of protection. It will be noted that, under section 27(2), a good title is conferred upon *any* private purchaser (provided he is in good faith and without notice) to whom the debtor has himself disposed of the vehicle. But under section 27(3) and (4) only the *first* private purchaser after the disposition by the debtor to a trade or finance purchaser is protected, and then only if he is in good faith and without notice. Thus, for example, if a debtor under a hire-purchase agreement himself wrongfully lets the vehicle on hire-purchase to A, but subsequently repossesses it and sells it to B, B will acquire a good title. Yet if he sells the vehicle to a finance company which lets the vehicle on hire-purchase to A, but subsequently repossesses it and sells it to B, B will not acquire a good title as he is not the *first* private purchaser. Further, the protection afforded in the circumstances mentioned in section 27(4) (notice acquired of the original agreement between the time of letting and the time the property is transferred to him) will only apply where the vehicle is let to the debtor by a trade or finance purchaser, and not where the vehicle is let to him by the original debtor. 7–097

A problem also arises in the following situation: a motor vehicle owned by A is let under a hire-purchase agreement to B, who wrongfully sells it to C, a trade or finance purchaser. C lets the vehicle to D (a private purchaser) under a hire-purchase agreement. Before the property is transferred to him in pursuance of this second agreement, D wrongfully sells the vehicle to a private purchaser, E. Assuming that D was at the time of the letting to him in good faith and without notice of the original hire-purchase agreement, and that E is likewise innocent, will E acquire a good title? It is submitted that he will not do so.[80] He cannot acquire a good title merely by virtue of section 27(3), since he is not the first private purchaser. However, the letting (disposition) to D has, under section 27(3), effect "as if the title of the creditor ... to the vehicle has been vested in the debtor ... immediately before he disposed of it to the original purchaser." It could therefore be argued that the title of the trade or finance purchaser, C, was notionally "fed", so that E could rely upon section 27(2) and acquire that title. But it is submitted that the title of C is only notionally "fed" for the purpose of establishing the validity of the letting to D. C, in fact, has no title; he was the "creditor" in relation to the second hire-purchase agreement; and E can only acquire such title of C[81] as is deemed to be vested in D immediately before the sale of the vehicle by D to E, *i.e.* none. 7–098

Good faith and notice. The expression "in good faith" is not defined in the 1964 Act, but presumably a purchaser is deemed to be in good faith when he acts honestly, whether he acts negligently or not.[82] Section 29(3) of the Act further provides that "a person shall be taken to be a purchaser of a 7–099

---

[80] *cf.* Goode, *Hire-Purchase Law and Practice* (2nd ed.), p.627. But see above, para.7–095.

[81] See s.29(5); below, para.7–107.

[82] See Bills of Exchange Act, 1882, s.90; Sale of Goods Act 1979, s.61(3); *Dodds v Yorkshire Bank Finance* [1992] C.C.L.R. 92, CA; *GE Capital Bank Ltd v Rushton* [2005] EWCA Civ 1556, [2006] 1 W.L.R. 899; and above, para.7–046.

motor vehicle without notice of a hire-purchase agreement or conditional sale agreement if, at the time of the disposition made to him, he has no actual notice that the vehicle is or was the subject of any such agreement." Constructive notice is therefore insufficient. Despite the use of the words "a" and "any" in section 29(3), it has been held by the Court of Appeal in *Barker v Bell*[83] that there must be actual notice of the relevant, and not of any, hire-purchase agreement or conditional sale agreement. In the same case, Lord Denning M.R. and Fenton Atkinson L.J. expressed the opinion that the words "or was" did not embrace a hire-purchase or conditional sale agreement which had been supposedly paid off. Thus, if the purchaser is informed that the vehicle has been the subject of a hire-purchase agreement, but (untruthfully) that the debtor has paid off the amount outstanding under the agreement and so acquired a title to the vehicle, the purchaser will still be protected. The burden of proving good faith and absence of notice appears to rest upon the purchaser.[84]

7–100 **Presumptions.** Once it is proved in any proceedings (whether civil or criminal) relating to a motor vehicle (i) that the vehicle was bailed under a hire-purchase agreement, or was agreed to be sold under a conditional sale agreement, and (ii) that a person[85] (whether a party to the proceedings or not) became a private purchaser of the vehicle in good faith and without notice of the hire-purchase or conditional sale agreement (the "relevant agreement"), certain *rebuttable* presumptions arise in favour of a claimant who seeks to rely on the protection conferred by Part III of the 1964 Act.[86] These presumptions may enable him to overcome the difficulty of proving the precise chain of dealings between himself and the debtor, or the state of mind of the parties to those transactions; but they do not apply where all the transactions are fully known.[87]

7–101 First, it is presumed that the disposition to the private purchaser mentioned above (known as "the relevant purchaser") was made by the debtor.[88]

7–102 Secondly, if it is proved that the disposition was not made by the debtor, then it is presumed (a) that the debtor disposed of the vehicle to a private purchaser who was a purchaser of the vehicle in good faith and without notice of the relevant agreement, and (b) that the relevant purchaser is or was a person claiming under the person to whom the debtor so disposed of the vehicle.[89]

---

[83] [1971] 1 W.L.R. 983.
[84] *Mercantile Credit Co. Ltd v Waugh* (1978) 32 *Hire Trading* (No. 2), p.16. But see s.28, *infra*.
[85] Such a purchaser must be one in the "chain" between the debtor and the person claiming that he has title under Pt III of the Act, and not a purchaser from or subsequent to the claimant: *Worcester Works Finance Ltd v Ocean Banking Corp. Ltd*, March 29, 1972 (Uttoxeter Cty. Ct.).
[86] s.28(1).
[87] *Soneco Ltd v Barcross Finance Ltd* [1978] R.T.R. 444.
[88] s.28(2). See *Ford Motor Credit Co. Ltd v Harmack* [1972] C.L.Y. 1649, CA.
[89] s.28(3).

Thirdly, if it is proved that the disposition of the vehicle to the relevant purchaser was not made by the debtor, and that the person to whom the debtor disposed of the vehicle[90] was a trade or finance purchaser, then it is presumed (a) that the person who, after the disposition of the vehicle to the trade or finance purchaser, first became a private purchaser of the vehicle was a purchaser in good faith and without notice of the relevant agreement, and (b) that the relevant purchaser is or was a person claiming under the trade or finance purchaser.[91] **7–103**

Admissions. Section 28(5) of the 1964 Act also provides: "without prejudice to any other mode of proof, where in any proceedings[92] a party thereto admits a fact, that fact shall, for the purposes of this section,[93] be taken as against him to be proved in relation to those proceedings." If applied literally, this subsection would render any admission, however informal, made at any stage in proceedings irrevocably binding upon the party who made it.[94] **7–104**

Extent of protection. It is important to note that the only persons who can claim protection under Part III of the 1964 Act are those who are, or who claim under, either a private purchaser (in the case of section 27(2)) or the first private purchaser (in the case of section 27(3) and (4)) who must in both cases be in good faith and without notice of the hire-purchase or conditional sale agreement. An intermediate trade or finance purchaser is not protected, and will be liable in conversion to the original owner of the vehicle.[95] In the case of section 27(3) and (4), if the first private purchaser is mala fide, or has notice, no subsequent private purchaser will acquire a good title. And, in any event, no person who is or claims under a purchaser who is mala fide or has notice will be entitled to protection.[96] As one commentator has remarked: ". . . if the first private purchaser is not in good faith, then it does not matter how much good faith is mustered by any number of subsequent purchasers, for they are all damned."[97] **7–105**

Section 27(6) of the 1964 Act provides that nothing in section 27 is to exonerate the debtor from any liability (whether criminal or civil) to which he would be subject apart from that section; and, in a case where the debtor disposes of a motor vehicle to a trade or finance purchaser, nothing in that section is to exonerate (a) that trade or finance purchaser, or (b) any other **7–106**

---

[90] The "original purchaser": see above, para.7–095.
[91] s.28(4).
[92] *Quaere* whether the subsection can be applied equitably in criminal proceedings.
[93] s.28 (presumptions).
[94] See the discussion of the subsection in Goode, *Hire-Purchase Law and Practice* (2nd ed.), p.630.
[95] s.27(6), *infra*. The measure of damages in conversion is the balance outstanding under the hire-purchase agreement, if this is less than the value of the goods: *Wickham Holdings Ltd v Brooke House Motors Ltd* [1967] 1 W.L.R. 295; *Belvoir Finance Co. Ltd v Stapleton* [1971] 1 Q.B. 210. *Cf. Astley Industrial Trust Ltd v Miller* [1968] 2 All E.R. 36; *Chubb Cash Ltd v John Crilley & Son* [1983] 1 W.L.R. 599.
[96] *Soneco Ltd v Barcross Finance Ltd* [1978] R.T.R. 444.
[97] M. G. Bridge, *Sale of Goods* (1988), p.663.

trade or finance purchaser who becomes a purchaser of the vehicle and is not a person claiming under the first private purchaser, from any liability (whether criminal or civil) to which he would be subject apart from that section. In *Barber v NWS Bank plc*[98] a hirer of a motor car under a hire-purchase agreement wrongfully disposed of the vehicle which came into the hands of the defendant finance company (a trade or finance purchaser). The defendant then agreed to sell the vehicle under a conditional sale agreement to the claimant, a bona fide private purchaser without notice of the existing hire-purchase agreement. The conditional sale agreement contained a term by which the defendant was found to have expressly warranted that it was the owner of the vehicle. After paying a number of instalments under the conditional sale agreement the claimant discovered that the motor car did not belong to the defendant. He rescinded the agreement and claimed back the instalments which he had paid. The Court of Appeal held that he was entitled to do so. Even though, on completion of the instalments, he would have acquired a good title to the vehicle under section 27(3), section 27(6) preserved the liability of the defendant for breach of the express term in the conditional sale agreement.

7–107 **Nature of title acquired.** The third party does not acquire a guaranteed title to the vehicle, but only such title (if any) as, immediately before the disposition by the debtor, was vested in the person who then was the creditor in relation to the hire-purchase agreement, or the conditional sale agreement.[99]

7–108 **Relation to other statutes.** The provisions of Part III of the 1964 Act override the *nemo dat quod non habet* rule contained in section 21 of the Sale of Goods Act 1979, but operate without prejudice to the provisions of the Factors Act[1] or of any other enactment[2] enabling the apparent owner of goods to dispose of them as if he were the true owner.[3] In particular, a conditional sale agreement which is not made by an "individual" (which expression includes a partnership consisting of two or three persons not all of whom are bodies corporate)[4] as the buyer of the vehicle to which the agreement relates may attract the provisions of both the 1964 Act and of section 25(1) of the Sale of Goods Act 1979.[5]

9. MISCELLANEOUS PROVISIONS

7–109 **Common law and statutory powers.** Nothing in the Sale of Goods Act 1979 affects (a) the provisions of the Factors Acts or any enactment enabling the apparent owner of goods to dispose of them as if he were their

---

[98] [1996] 1 W.L.R. 641.
[99] s.29(5). See *Morley v Maybray Motors Ltd* (1971) 25 *Hire Trading (No. 3)*, p.15 (Cty.Ct.).
[1] Factors Act 1889, ss.2, 8, 9; see above, paras 7–031, 7–055, 7–069.
[2] See above, para.7–007; below, para.7–111.
[3] s.27(5) (amended by s.63 of and Sch.2, para.4 to the Sale of Goods Act 1979).
[4] Consumer Credit Act 1974, s.189(1) (amended by the Consumer Credit Act 2006).
[5] See above, para.7–070, n.40.

true owner[6]; (b) the validity of any contract of sale under any special common law or statutory power of sale or under the order of a court of competent jurisdiction.[7]

Common law powers include those of a pledgee of goods or documents of title to goods,[8] an agent of necessity,[9] and an executor or administrator.[10] 7–110

Statutory powers include those of an unpaid seller of goods,[11] an enforcement officer,[12] the trustee for civil recovery,[13] a registrar or other officer of a county court,[14] an administrator,[15] administrative receiver[16] and liquidator[17] of a company, a trustee in bankruptcy[18] and a receiver or manager of a bankrupt's estate,[19] a landlord who has distrained upon goods in the possession of a tenant,[20] a criminal court,[21] the police,[22] a local 7–111

---

[6] Sale of Goods Act 1979, s.21(2)(a); see above, para.7–008, below, para.7–013.
[7] Sale of Goods Act 1979, s.21(2)(b).
[8] *Martin v Reid* (1862) 11 C.B.(N.S.) 730; *Pigot v Cubley* (1864) 15 C.B. (N.S.) 701; *Halliday v Holgate* (1868) L.R. 3 Ex. 299; *Burdick v Sewell* (1884) 13 Q.B.D. 159 at 174; *Re Richardson* (1885) 30 Ch.D. 396 at 403; *Re Morritt* (1886) 18 Q.B.D. 222 at 232, 235; *The Ningchow* [1916] P.221. *Cf. Johnson v Stear* (1863) 15 C.B.(N.S.) 330 (premature sale). But a lien confers no power of sale at common law: *Thames Ironworks Co. v Patent Derrick Co.* (1860) 1 J. & H. 93; *Mulliner v Florence* (1878) 3 Q.B.D. 484, except (*semble*) in the case of a bank: Ellinger, Lomnicka and Hooley *Modern Banking Law* (4th ed.), p.803.
[9] See *Bowstead and Reynolds on Agency* (17th ed.), para.4–001.
[10] *Vaine v Rigden* (1870) L.R. 5 Ch.App. 663 at 668; *Attenborough v Solomon* [1913] A.C. 76 at 82; Administration of Estates Act 1925, s.39(1). But this is not really an exception, since the executor or administrator has the full ownership of the goods.
[11] Sale of Goods Act 1979, ss.39(1), 48; below, para.15–101.
[12] Companies Act 1985, ss.621, 622 (as amended by s.235 and Sch.10, Pt. II, of the Insolvency Act 1985); Insolvency Act 1986, s.346; (as amended by the Courts Act 2003, Sch.8); the Courts Act 2003, Sch.7, para.10; CPR Sch.1, RSC, Ord. 46, 47. See *Curtis v Maloney* [1951] 1 K.B. 736; *Dyal Singh v Kenyan Insurance Ltd* [1954] A.C. 287. *Cf. Jones Brothers (Holloway) Ltd v Woodhouse* [1923] 2 K.B. 117.
[13] Proceeds of Crime Act, 2002, s.267 and Sch.7.
[14] County Courts Act 1984, ss.89–102 (as amended by Sch.14 of the Insolvency Act 1986 and s.15 and Sch.20 of the Courts and Legal Services Act 1990).
[15] Insolvency Act 1986, Sch.B1, paras. 59, 70–72, inserted by s.248 and Sch.16 of the Enterprise Act 2002.
[16] *ibid.* ss.42, 43, Sch.1. But administrative receivership has been abolished (subject to certain exceptions) by s.72A of the 1986 Act, inserted by s.250 of the Enterprise Act 2002.
[17] *ibid.* ss.165, 166, 167, Sch.4, Pt III.
[18] *ibid.* s.134, Sch.5.
[19] *ibid.* ss.286, 287.
[20] Distress for Rent Act 1689, s.1; Landlord and Tenant Act 1709; Landlord and Tenant Act 1730, s.5; Distress for Rent Act 1737, s.10; Law of Distress Amendment Act 1888; Law of Distress Amendment Act 1895; Law of Distress Amendment Act 1908, ss.4 (amended by s.192 and Sch.5 of the Consumer Credit Act 1974), 4A (inserted by s.192 and Sch.4 of the Consumer Credit Act 1974); County Courts Act 1984, s.102 (as amended by Sch.14 of the Insolvency Act 1986); Insolvency Act 1986, s.347; Distress for Rent Rules 1988 SI 1988/2050.
[21] Powers of the Criminal Courts (Sentencing) Act 2000, s.143.
[22] Police (Property) Act 1897, s.2, as amended by the Police (Property) Act 1997, s.1, and applied by the Powers of the Criminal Courts (Sentencing) Act 2000, s.144. See also s.2 and s.2A (inserted by s.77 of the Police Reform Act 2002).

authority which has taken possession of an abandoned vehicle,[23] a pawnee under the Consumer Credit Act 1974,[24] a bailee of uncollected goods, an innkeeper,[25] and certain warehousemen.[26]

7–112 The Civil Procedure Rules provide for the sale of relevant property which is of a perishable nature or which for any other good reason it is desirable to sell quickly.[27] They also provide for the sale of a ship in Admiralty proceedings.[28]

7–113 **Sale of goods bound by writ or warrant of execution.** By para.8(1) of Sch.7 to the Courts Act 2003,[29] a writ of execution against goods issued from the High Court binds the property[30] in the goods of the execution debtor from the time the writ is received by the person who is under a duty to endorse it.[31] But sub paras (2) and (3) of para.8 go on to provide that the writ does not prejudice the title to any goods of the execution debtor acquired by a person in good faith and for valuable consideration,[32] unless the person acquiring the goods of the execution debtor had notice,[33] at the time of the acquisition that, the writ or any other writ by which the goods of the execution debtor might be seized or attached had been received by the person under a duty to endorse it but had not been executed.[34] A writ of execution does not prevent the property in the goods passing upon a sale of them by the execution debtor, although the buyer, if he has notice or is not in good faith, takes the goods subject to the rights of the execution creditor.[35] The effect of subparas (2) and (3) is, therefore, to enable the execution debtor to pass to a bona fide purchaser a title to the goods unencumbered by the charge created by the writ of execution. Once,

---

23 Road Traffic Regulation Act 1984, s.101 (as amended by s.67 of the Road Traffic Act 1991); Removal and Disposal of Vehicles Regulations 1986, SI 1986/183, reg. 15; *Bulbruin Ltd v Romanyszyn* [1994] R.T.R. 273.
24 ss.120, 121 (operative May 19, 1985).
25 Innkeepers Act 1878, s.1. See also the Hotel Proprietors Act 1956.
26 Merchant Shipping Act 1894, ss.497, 498.
27 CPR 25.1(1)(c)(v); County Courts Act 1984, s.38.
28 CPR 61.10, 2D-61.
29 This Schedule replaced s.138 of the Supreme Court Act 181 (as amended), which replaced s.26 of the Sale of Goods 1893.
30 Defined in para.8(5).
31 *e.g.* by an enforcement officer (para.7 (1)). A person endorses a writ by endorsing on the back of it the date and time when he receives it. (para.7 (3)).
32 See *Beebee & Co. v Turner's Successors* (1931) 48 T.L.R. 61 (trustee under a deed of arrangement). *Cf. Re Cooper* [1958] Ch.922 at 928 (trustee in bankruptcy). See also *Ellis & Co. v Cross* [1915] 2 K.B. 654 (revocable deed of arrangement).
33 See above para.7–047 and *Ehlers v Kauffman* (1883) 49 L.T. 806 (position of trustees under deed of assignment).
34 Or notice that an application for a warrant of execution had been made to a county court and that the warrant issued on the application remained unexecuted in the hands of the district judge: para.8(4).
35 *Giles v Grover* (1832) 1 Cl. & Fin. 72; *Woodland v Fuller* (1840) 11 A. & E. 859 at 867; *McPherson v Temiskaming Lumber Co. Ltd* [1913] A.C. 145 at 156; *Lloyds and Scottish Finance Ltd v Modern Cars and Caravans (Kingston) Ltd* [1965] 1 W.L.R. 404. For the remedies of the buyer under s.12(2)(b) of the Sale of Goods Act 1979, see above, para.4–029.

however, the writ has been executed by seizure of the goods, then, even though the execution debtor is still in possession of the goods, he cannot pass an unencumbered title to a buyer, notwithstanding that the buyer purchases the goods in good faith and without notice of the receipt of the writ of execution.[36]

Similar provision is made by section 99 of the County Courts Act 1984[37] in respect of the sale of goods which are subject to a warrant of execution issued by a county court. 7–114

10. LIMITATION

Limitation.[38] Where goods have been converted, the owner of the goods has six years thereafter[39] in which to bring an action in respect of that and all subsequent acts of conversion whether or not committed by the same person.[40] After the expiration of that period, unless he has previously recovered possession, section 3 (2) of the Limitation Act 1980 provides that his title to the goods is extinguished.[41] However, these rules are qualified where the goods have been stolen.[42] As against a purchaser in good faith of stolen goods or a person who has converted the goods following such a purchase, the owner's title is extinguished, and his right to claim damages barred, after six years from the date of purchase.[43] But otherwise the right of a person from whom goods are stolen to bring an action in respect of the theft or of any conversion following the theft is not barred by limitation, nor is his title to the goods extinguished.[44] And the same applies to cases where the goods are obtained by deception[45] or blackmail.[46] Theft and these allied offences are therefore "imprescriptible" as against the person from whom the goods are stolen, and no subsequent converter (other than a bona fide purchaser or person claiming through such a purchaser) can claim the benefit of limitation.[47] 7–115

---

36 *Lloyds and Scottish Finance Ltd v Modern Cars and Caravans (Kingston) Ltd*, above.

37 See also ss.89(2), 103(2) of the 1984 Act and *Murgatroyd v Wright* [1907] 2 K.B. 333.

38 See Palmer and McKendrick, *Interests in Goods* (2nd ed., 1998), Ch.37.

39 Unless he has recovered possession in the meantime.

40 Limitation Act 1980, ss.2, 3(1).

41 But see below, para.7–117.

42 See the Twenty-first Report of the Law Reform Committee 1977 (Cmnd. 6923), paras 3.1 *et seq.*

43 Limitation Act 1980, s.4(1)(2).

44 Limitation Act 1980, s.4(1), (2), (3), (4). See also Powers of the Criminal Courts (Sentencing) Act 2000, s.148 (restitution order), above, para.7–006.

45 Limitation Act 1980, s.4(5)(b); Theft Act 1968, s.15(1).

46 Limitation Act 1980, s.4(5)(b); Theft Act 1968, s.21.

47 By s.4(4) of the 1980 Act, the claimant bears the burden of proving that the goods were stolen from him or anyone through whom he claims, but the defendant bears the burden of proving that he is or claims through a bona fide purchaser. See *Kuwait Airways Corp. v Iraqi Airways Co. (Nos 4 and 5)* [2002] UKHL 19, [2002] 2 A.C. 883 at [103].

7–116 Although, in respect of stolen goods, the requirement of good faith relates to the time of purchase, it may be that a purchaser who subsequently discovers, within the limitation period, that the goods bought by him have been stolen is under a duty to take reasonable steps to acquaint the true owner with his possession and the whereabouts of the goods.[48] If such is the case, it is arguable that a conscious failure to take such steps amounts to a deliberate concealment of a fact relevant to the true owner's right of action, which would start time running again.[49]

7–117 **Property obtained through unlawful conduct.** Part 5 of the Proceeds of Crime Act 2002 enables the enforcement authority (in England and Wales, the Director of the Asset Recovery Agency)[50] to recover, in civil proceedings before the High Court, property[51] which is, or represents, property obtained through "unlawful conduct".[52] Section 27A of the Limitation Act 1980[53] provides that none of the time limits given in the preceding provisions of the 1980 Act is to apply to such proceeding's.[54] The Director is allowed 12 years in which to bring proceedings for a recovery order.[55] The 12 year period runs from the date on which the Director's cause of action accrues—(broadly) when the property obtained by unlawful conduct is so obtained.[56] Moreover, a third party may intervene in the proceedings and apply for a declaration that the property sought to be recovered belongs to him.[57] On such an application he must establish that he was deprived of the property he claims, or of property which it represents, by unlawful conduct, *i.e.* that he was the victim of a crime,[58] and that the property belongs to him.[59] In such a case, if he would (but for the preceding provisions of the 1980 Act) have had a cause of action in respect of the conversion of a chattel, section 3(2) of the 1980 Act does not prevent his asserting on the application that the property belongs to him.[60] If the court makes a declaration in his favour, his title to the chattel is to be treated as not having been extinguished by section 3(2).[61]

---

[48] *Parker v British Airways Board* [1982] Q.B. 1004 at 1007 (finder).
[49] Limitation Act 1980, s.32(1)(b), (2); *Sheldon v R.M. Outhwaite (Underwriting Agencies) Ltd* [1996] A.C. 102.
[50] s.316(1).
[51] s.316(4), (5), (6), (7).
[52] ss.241, 242, 316(1).
[53] Inserted by s.288 of the 2002 Act.
[54] s.27A(1).
[55] s.27A(2), (3) as amended by s.109 of and Sch.6, para.2, to the Serious Organised Crime and Police Act 2005.
[56] s.27A(4).
[57] s.281 of the 2002 Act.
[58] s.281(3)(a), (b).
[59] s.281(3)(c).
[60] s.27A(5) of the 1980 Act.
[61] s.27A(6).

Part Three

PERFORMANCE OF THE CONTRACT

Chapter 8

DELIVERY

	PARA.
1. In general	8–001
2. Methods of delivery	8–007
3. Place of delivery	8–018
4. Time of delivery	8–025
5. Quantity of goods delivered	8–045
6. Delivery by instalments	8–064
7. Clauses excusing delivery	8–088

1. In General

Seller's duty to deliver. It is the duty of the seller to deliver the goods to the buyer in accordance with the terms of the contract of sale.[1] The delivery of the goods must be distinguished from the passing of property in them, since the property may pass either before or contemporaneously with or after delivery.[2] Although the buyer may already have become the owner of the goods, a further act is required on the part of the seller or his bailee[3] whereby the buyer is placed in a position to be able to obtain custody of or control over the goods. **8–001**

Meaning of delivery. Section 61(1) of the Sale of Goods Act 1979 defines delivery as "voluntary transfer of possession from one person to another."[4] The words "delivery" and "deliver" are not, however, used in a single consistent sense in the Act. For example, with respect to the seller's duty to deliver the goods, it is normally sufficient for the seller to place the goods specified by the contract at the disposition of the buyer in a deliverable state without any reciprocal act on the part of the buyer.[5] The use of the word "possession" in the subsection is also a source of uncertainty, since this concept is notoriously resistant to definition.[6] It might well be thought to signify the actual physical custody of the goods. But delivery may take place even though there is no transfer of the actual **8–002**

---

[1] Sale of Goods Act 1979, s.27; *Buddle v Green* (1857) 27 L.J.Ex. 33 at 34. See also Vienna Convention on Contracts for the International Sale of Goods, Art. 30 (above, para.1–024). For damages for non-delivery, see below, para.17–001.

[2] See above, para.5–002.

[3] See below, para.8–012.

[4] *cf.* Vienna Convention on Contracts for the International Sale of Goods, Art. 31 (above, para.1–024). The additional words of this definition relate only to ss.20A and 20B of the Act: see above, paras 5–120, 5–125, below, para.8–017.

[5] See below, para.8–007.

[6] See Harris, *Oxford Essays in Jurisprudence* (1961), p.69; Pollock and Wright, *Possession in the Common Law* (1888).

physical custody of the goods from one person to another. For example, where a bailee of the goods on behalf of the seller acknowledges that he holds them on behalf of the buyer, there is a delivery of the goods to the buyer even though there is no change in their actual physical custody.[7] Further, in certain circumstances, the physical transfer of the goods themselves is not required, and delivery may be effected by the transfer of documents of title to the goods.[8] It is therefore suggested that the meaning of delivery is best ascertained from the various acts which have been recognised by the law as constituting an effective delivery of the goods to the buyer in a given situation.[9] It is also necessary to have regard to the purpose for which delivery is relevant. For instance, in a commercial transaction, an authorised delivery of the goods to a carrier for transmission to the buyer is normally a sufficient fulfilment of the seller's duty to deliver the goods to the buyer.[10] But such a delivery does not defeat an unpaid seller's right of stoppage in transit,[11] although actual delivery of the goods to the consignee will defeat this right. Delivery for the purpose of one rule need not necessarily be delivery for the purpose of another separate rule.[12]

8–003 **Goods to be delivered.** If the contract is one for the sale of specific goods[13] or if the property in the goods has passed to the buyer,[14] the seller must deliver the particular goods contracted for, and cannot deliver other similar goods. But if the contract is one for the sale of unascertained goods,[15] the seller is at liberty to deliver any goods which answer the contract description, unless or until the particular goods to be sold have been sufficiently and irrevocably identified, *e.g.* by a notice of appropriation.[16] Such a contractual appropriation binds the seller to deliver the particular goods even though the property may not have passed.

8–004 **Delivery and payment.** The parties are free to make whatever arrangements they choose as to the relative times at which delivery and payment are to be made.[17] But by section 28 of the 1979 Act: "Unless otherwise agreed, delivery of the goods and payment of the price are concurrent conditions, that is to say, the seller must be ready and willing to give possession of the goods to the buyer in exchange for the price[18] and the

---

7 See below, para.8–012. See also below, para.8–009 (seller becomes bailee).
8 See below, paras 8–013, 18–007.
9 See below, paras 8–007 *et seq*.
10 See below, para.8–014.
11 See below, para.15–061.
12 *cf.* Benjamin, *Sale of Personal Property* (8th ed.), p.686. See also the difference of opinion in the High Court of Australia in *Gamer's Motor Centre (Newcastle) Pty Ltd v Natwest Wholesale Australia Pty Ltd* (1987) 163 C.L.R. 236; above, para.7–077.
13 Defined in s.61(1) of the Act: see above, para.1–113.
14 See above, Ch.5.
15 See above, para.1–117.
16 A notice of appropriation, *e.g.* under a c.i.f. contract (see below, para.19–100) may sufficiently and irrevocably identify the goods to be sold even though the property in the goods does not pass by such notice.
17 *Amos and Wood Ltd v Kaprow* (1948) 64 T.L.R. 110. See also below, paras 8–025, 9–051.
18 See below, para.9–021.

buyer must be ready and willing to pay the price in exchange for[19] possession of the goods."[20] It has been said that this implies that delivery and payment are to be made at the same time.[21] But it is to be noted that section 28 does not prescribe that actual payment or tender of the price is a condition precedent to the seller's obligation to deliver the goods,[22] although it may be made so by agreement of the parties. All that is necessary is that the buyer should be "ready and willing" to pay the price.[23] However, an unpaid seller[24] of goods who is in possession of them is entitled to retain possession of them until payment or tender of the price where the goods have been sold without any stipulation as to credit,[25] or where the goods have been sold on credit but the term of credit has expired, or where the buyer becomes insolvent.[26]

Expenses of delivery. Unless otherwise agreed, the expenses of and incidental to putting the goods into a deliverable state[27] are required by section 29(6) of the Act to be borne by the seller. But the Act does not set out any rule as to the expenses of delivery itself. At common law, however, the rule is that the expenses of and incidental to making delivery fall on the seller; those of preparing to receive, or receiving, delivery on the buyer.[28] This rule may be varied by agreement between the parties, and special rules have been elaborated where the sale is on c.i.f.,[29] f.o.b.,[30] "ex ship"[31] or other similar terms.[32] **8–005**

---

[19] See *Ryan v Ridley & Co.* (1902) 8 Com.Cas. 105 (exchange in commercial sense).
[20] *cf.* Vienna Convention on Contracts for the International Sale of Goods, Arts 33, 58, 59 (above, para.1–024).
[21] *Forrestt & Son Ltd v Aramayo* (1900) 83 L.T. 335 at 338.
[22] *cf. Bloxam v Sanders* (1825) 4 B. & C. 941 at 948–949.
[23] *Pordage v Cole* (1669) 1 Wms.Saund. 319; *Morton v Lamb* (1797) 7 T.R. 125; *Rawson v Johnson* (1801) 1 East 203 at 212; *Waterhouse v Skinner* (1801) 2 B. & P. 447. See also *Lawrence v Knowles* (1839) 5 Bing.N.C. 399; *Pickford v Grand Junction Ry* (1841) 8 M. & W. 372 at 378; *De Medina v Norman* (1842) 9 M. & W. 820 at 827; *Bankart v Bowers* (1866) L.R. 1 C.P. 484; *Paynter v James* (1867) L.R. 2 C.P. 348; *Re Phoenix Bessemer Steel Co.* (1876) 4 Ch.D. 108. Previously it was necessary for the buyer expressly to aver that he was ready and willing to pay the price, but this was dispensed with by RSC, Ord. 18, r. 7(4). But see now CPR 16.4(1)(a). See also below, para.8–064 (instalment deliveries).
[24] See Sale of Goods Act 1979, s.38 (below, para.15–016).
[25] For the position where goods have been sold on credit, see below, paras 15–017, 15–033.
[26] Sale of Goods Act 1979, s.41 (below, para.15–024).
[27] Defined in s.61(5) of the Act as being "in such a state that the buyer would under the contract be bound to take delivery of them": see above, para.5–023.
[28] *Cf. Neill v Whitworth* (1865) 18 C.B.(N.S.) 435, affirmed (1866) L.R. 1 C.P. 684 ("to be taken from the quay"); *Playford v Mercer* (1870) 22 L.T. 41 ("from the deck"); *Acme Wood Flooring Co. v Sutherland Innes Co.* (1904) 9 Com.Cas. 170 ("c.i.f. to buyer's wharf"); *Re Shell Transport and Trading Co. and Consolidated Petroleum Co.* (1904) 20 T.L.R. 517 (cost of preparing place of delivery); *White v Williams* [1912] A.C. 814 ("cost of stevedoring"); *Jager v Tolme and Runge* [1916] 1 K.B. 939 ("free of customs formalities"); *Fisher, Reeves & Co. v Armour & Co.* [1920] 3 K.B. 614 ("ex store, Rotterdam").
[29] See below, paras 19–009, 19–011.
[30] See below, paras 20–008, 20–012.
[31] See below, para.21–014.
[32] See "ex works", below, para.21–002.

8–006 **Breach by seller.** A breach by the seller of an obligation on his part relating to delivery will not necessarily amount to a repudiation by him of the contract of sale.[33] But it will do so if the breach is a breach of condition.[34] The seller will also be held to have repudiated the contract[35] if (i) he makes it plain to the buyer by words or conduct that he is unable or unwilling to carry out such an obligation, or (ii) he is in fact finally and completely disabled from performing the obligation, or (iii) he fails to perform the obligation, provided that, in each case, the resulting or actual breach would or does amount to a fundamental breach of the contract.[36] Acceptance by the buyer of the repudiation brings to an end all primary obligations of the parties which have not yet fallen due for performance, but does not prejudice the buyer's right to claim damages for non-delivery.[37] Acceptance may be by words or conduct, provided that it clearly and unequivocally conveys to the seller that the buyer is treating the contract as at an end.[38] The buyer may alternatively elect to treat the contract as still continuing. In such a case the contract is kept alive for the benefit of both parties, and the seller may normally[39] take advantage of any supervening circumstances which would justify him in declining to complete it.[40]

2. METHODS OF DELIVERY

8–007 **How delivery effected.** Delivery of the goods to the buyer may be made by any method which the parties agree shall constitute delivery. For example, it may be agreed that the goods shall be delivered, not to the buyer himself, but to a third party nominated by the buyer.[41] In the absence of any such agreement, express or implied, the seller sufficiently performs his duty to deliver by making the goods available to the buyer in a deliverable state at the place[42] and time[43] designated in the contract of

[33] In particular, in the case of instalment deliveries, by s.31(2) of the Act: see below, para.8–077.
[34] See, for example, below, para.8–025 (time of delivery), 8–046 (insufficient delivery), para.8–049 (excessive delivery). But, in the case of instalment deliveries, a breach in relation to an instalment will not necessarily amount to a repudiation: s.31(2), below, para.8–077.
[35] See *Chitty on Contracts* (29th ed.), Vol. 1, Ch.24, and below, paras 8–025, 8–078, 8–080.
[36] *Afovos Shipping Co. SA v R. Pagnan & F.lli* [1984] 1 W.L.R. 195 at 203.
[37] *Photo Production Ltd v Securicor Transport Ltd* [1980] A.C. 827 at 849; *Gill & Duffus SA v Berger & Co. Inc.* [1984] A.C. 382 at 390. For the measure of damages, see below, para.17–001.
[38] *Vitol SA v Norelf Ltd* [1996] A.C. 800.
[39] But see the exceptions referred to in para.9–019, below .
[40] *Avery v Bowden* (1855) 5 E. & B. 714; (1856) 6 E. & B. 953; *Johnstone v Milling* (1886) 16 Q.B.D. 460 at 470; *Fercometal S.A.R.L. v Mediterranean Shipping Co. SA* [1989] A.C. 788; *Segap Garages Ltd v Gulf Oil (Great Britain) Ltd, The Times*, October 24, 1988, CA. See below, para.9–018.
[41] *Bull v Sibbs* (1799) 8 T.R. 327 at 328; *E. & S. Ruben Ltd v Faire Bros & Co. Ltd* [1949] 1 K.B. 254; *Four Point Garage Ltd v Carter* [1985] 3 All E.R. 12.
[42] See below, para.8–018.
[43] See below, para.8–025.

sale so as to enable the buyer to obtain custody of or control over the goods.[44]

Symbolic delivery. Delivery may be effected by handing to the buyer the key of a warehouse or other place where the goods are stored, provided that a licence to enter and take the goods can be implied therefrom.[45] Also delivery of a bill of lading has been said to be a symbolic or constructive delivery of the goods.[46] But it is doubtful whether a token delivery such as, for example, might support a *donatio mortis causa* or a gift *inter vivos*[47] could be considered a delivery for the purpose of a sale of goods. 8–008

Seller becomes bailee. Although the goods may remain in the physical custody of the seller after the sale, if it is agreed between the buyer and the seller that the seller shall thenceforth retain possession of the goods, not as seller, but as bailee for the buyer, there will be a sufficient delivery of the goods to the buyer.[48] 8–009

Licence to remove goods. The removal of the goods by the buyer in pursuance of a licence to remove them conferred upon him by the seller constitutes a delivery of the goods.[49] 8–010

Goods in possession of buyer. Where the goods at the time of the sale are already in the possession of the buyer, it would seem that completion of 8–011

---

[44] *Smith v Chance* (1819) 2 B. & Ald. 753 at 755; *Wood v Tassell* (1844) 6 Q.B. 234; *Wilkinson v Lloyd* (1845) 7 Q.B. 27 at 44. See also *European Grain & Shipping Ltd v David Geddes (Proteins) Ltd* [1977] 2 Lloyd's Rep. 591 ("available for delivery").

[45] *Ellis v Hunt* (1789) 3 T.R. 464 at 468; *Chaplin v Rogers* (1800) 1 East 192 at 195; *Elmore v Stone* (1809) 1 Taunt. 458 at 460; *Gough v Everard* (1864) 2 H. & C. 1 at 10; *Ancona v Rogers* (1876) 1 Ex.D. 285 at 290; *Hilton v Tucker* (1888) 39 Ch.D. 669 at 676; *Lloyds Bank Ltd v Swiss Bankverein* (1913) 108 L.T. 143 at 146; *Dublin City Distillery Ltd v Doherty* [1914] A.C. 823 at 843; *Wrightson v McArthur and Hutchinsons (1919) Ltd* [1921] 2 K.B. 807 at 816. *Cf. Milgate v Kebble* (1841) 3 M. & G. 100. See also Pollock and Wright, *Possession in the Common Law* (1888), pp.60–70.

[46] See below, para.18–062.

[47] See Crossley Vaines, *Personal Property* (5th ed.), pp.305–310.

[48] *Hurry v Mangles* (1808) 1 Camp. 452; *Elmore v Stone* (1809) 1 Taunt. 458; *Marvin v Wallace* (1856) 25 L.J.Q.B. 369; *Castle v Sworder* (1860) 6 H. & N. 828; *Cusack v Robinson* (1861) 30 L.J.Q.B. 264; *Nicholls v White* (1911) 103 L.T. 800; *Dublin City Distillery Ltd v Doherty* [1914] A.C. 823 at 843, 852. *Cf. Goodall v Skelton* (1794) 2 H.Bl. 316; *Tempest v Fitzgerald* (1820) 3 B. & Ald. 680; *Carter v Toussaint* (1822) 5 B. & Ald. 855; *Proctor v Jones* (1826) 2 C. & P. 532; *Holderness v Shackels* (1828) 8 B. & C. 612; *Townley v Crump* (1835) 4 A. & E. 58. These cases were, however, for the most part decided on the meaning of the words "actually receive" in s.4(1) of the 1893 Act (formerly part of the Statute of Frauds 1677), now repealed. But see *Gamer's Motor Centre (Newcastle) Pty Ltd v Natwest Wholesale Australia Pty Ltd* (1987) 163 C.L.R. 236; *Michael Gerson (Leasing) Ltd v Wilkinson* [2001] Q.B. 514; and below, para.15–028 (unpaid seller's lien).

[49] *Congreve v Evetts* (1854) 10 ExCh.298 at 308. Contrast *Thomas v Times Book Co Ltd* [1966] 1 W.L.R. 911 (gift).

the sale by the passing of property prima facie operates also as a delivery of the goods.[50]

8–012 **Goods in possession of third person.** By section 29(4) of the 1979 Act: "Where the goods at the time of sale[51] are in the possession of a third person, there is no delivery by seller to buyer unless and until the third person acknowledges to the buyer that he holds the goods on his behalf." This subsection is declaratory of the common law, and means that a bailee or other third person[52] in possession of the goods must attorn to the buyer before delivery will be held to have taken place.[53] One effect of such an acknowledgment is that the third person thenceforth ceases to hold the goods on behalf of and to the order of the seller and instead holds them on behalf of and to the order of the buyer.[54] The acknowledgment by the third person must be given with the consent of both the buyer and the seller,[55] and each party to the contract of sale must do all that is necessary, so far as it depends upon him, to obtain it.[56] If the buyer, having fulfilled his part, cannot obtain the acknowledgment, he may be able to treat the contract as discharged.[57] Conversely, if the failure to obtain the acknowledgment is due to the buyer's fault alone, it may be that the seller can treat the delivery as duly made.[58]

---

[50] *Manton v Moore* (1796) 7 T.R. 67; *Eden v Dudfield* (1841) 1 Q.B. 302; *Lillywhite v Devereux* (1846) 15 M. & W. 285. *Cf. Taylor v Wakefield* (1856) 6 E. & B. 765. See also Pollock and Wright, *Possession in the Common Law* (1888), p.72; *Chalmers Sale of Goods* (18th ed.), p.264; *Ramsay v Margrett* [1894] 2 Q.B. 18; *French v Gething* [1922] 1 K.B. 236 (joint possession). *Cf. Nicholson v Harper* [1895] 2 Ch. 415 (above, para.7–063); *Minister of Supply and Development v Servicemen's Co-operative Joinery Manufacturers* (1951) 82 C.L.R. 621.

[51] "The time of sale" appears to mean the time when property passes. Where the goods are unascertained, and there is an acknowledgment by a third person, it is arguable that this is ineffectual, except by way of estoppel (see above, para.5–065): *Busk v Davis* (1814) 2 M. & S. 397. But see above, para.5–122.

[52] Other than a servant of the seller.

[53] *Farina v Home* (1846) 16 M. & W. 119; *Smith v Chance* (1819) 2 B. & Ald. 753; *Bentall v Burn* (1824) 3 B. & C. 423; *Lackington v Atherton* (1844) 7 M. & G. 360 at 365; *M'Ewan & Sons v Smith* (1849) 2 H.L.Cas. 309; *Buddle v Green* (1857) 27 L.J.Ex. 33; *Gunn v Bolckow, Vaughan & Co.* (1875) L.R. 10 Ch.App. 491; *Dublin City Distillery Ltd v Doherty* [1914] A.C. 823 at 847–848, 864–865; *Peter Dumenil & Co. Ltd v James Ruddin Ltd* [1953] 1 W.L.R. 815; *Wardar's (Import and Export) Co Ltd v Norwood & Sons Ltd* [1968] 2 Q.B. 663. See also *Hammond v Anderson* (1803) 1 B. & P.N.R. 69 (acknowledgment and part delivery); *Salter v Woollams* (1841) 2 M. & G. 650 (acknowledgment before sale later withdrawn); *Wood v Tassell* (1844) 6 Q.B. 234 (part delivery). *Cf. Harman v Anderson* (1809) 2 Camp. 243; *Marshall v Green* (1875) 1 C.P.D. 35; *Poulton & Son v Anglo-American Oil Co. Ltd* (1911) 27 T.L.R. 216. See also below, paras 18–163, 18–193, 18–194, 21–053, 21–061, 21–068 (overseas sales).

[54] See below, para.18–174 on the other effects of acknowledgment.

[55] *Godts v Rose* (1855) 17 C.B. 229; *Poulton & Son v Anglo-American Oil Co. Ltd*, above.

[56] *Smith v Chance*, above; *Winks v Hassall* (1829) 9 B. & C. 372; *Bartlett v Holmes* (1835) 13 C.B. 630; *Buddle v Green*, above.

[57] *Pattison v Robinson* (1816) 5 M. & S. 105 at 110. *Cf. Peter Dumenil & Co. Ltd v James Ruddin Ltd*, above. See also *Alicia Hosiery Ltd v Brown, Shipley & Co. Ltd* [1970] 1 Q.B. 195, and below, para.18–173.

[58] *Bartlett v Holmes*, above.

Issue or transfer of document of title. Subsection (4) of section 29 states that nothing in section 29 affects the operation of the issue or transfer of any document of title to goods. The issue or transfer of a document of title may therefore dispense with the need for any acknowledgment by the third person in possession of the goods. A bill of lading is a document of title[59] and the transfer[60] of a bill of lading by the seller to the buyer transfers constructive possession of the goods without any need for an attornment by the carrier.[61] In section 61(1) of the Sale of Goods Act 1979, a "document of title" is defined to have the same meaning as it has in the Factors Act.[62] It might therefore be supposed that the issue or transfer of any "document of title" within the extended definition of those words contained in section 1(4) of the Factors Act 1889[63] would likewise confer constructive possession of the goods without attornment. But the wording of the qualification in section 29(4) is merely negative in nature, and, as between *seller and buyer*,[64] no "document of title" other than a bill of lading will (except under statute or by trade custom) have this effect.[65] Other documents such as delivery orders,[66] warrants,[67] wharfinger's or warehouseman's certificates[68] or similar documents[69] will not normally dispense with the need for attornment by the bailee.[70] 8–013

Delivery to carrier. By section 32(1) of the 1979 Act: "Where, in pursuance of a contract of sale,[71] the seller is authorised or required to 8–014

---

59 See below, para.18–062.
60 By endorsement (where necessary) and delivery: see below, para.18–016.
61 See below, para.18–062.
62 See above, para.7–036; below, para.18–006.
63 See above, para.7–036.
64 *Cf.* in relation to ss.9, 10 of the Factors Act 1889 and ss.25, 47 of the Sale of Goods Act 1893: *Ant. Jurgens Margarinefabriken v Louis Dreyfus & Co.* [1914] 3 K.B. 40; *Official Assignee of Madras v Mercantile Bank of India Ltd* [1935] A.C. 53 at 60; *Mount (D.F.) Ltd v Jay and Jay (Provisions) Co. Ltd* [1960] 1 Q.B. 159. *Cf. Inglis v Roberston* [1898] A.C. 616. See above, para.7–072, below, para.15–097.
65 *Bentall v Burn* (1824) 3 B. & C. 423; *Lackington v Atherton* (1844) 7 M. & G. 360; *Farina v Home* (1846) 16 M. & W. 119; *M'Ewan & Sons v Smith* (1849) 2 H.L.C. 309; *Coventry v Gladstone* (1868) L.R. 6 Eq. 44; *Mordaunt Bros v British Oil and Cake Mills Ltd* [1910] 2 K.B. 502; *Dublin City Distillery Co. v Doherty* [1914] A.C. 823; *Laurie and Morewood v Dudin & Sons* [1925] 2 K.B. 383, affirmed [1926] 1 K.B. 223; *Peter Dumenil & Co. Ltd v James Ruddin Ltd* [1953] 1 W.L.R. 815. *Cf. Merchant Banking Co. of London v Phoenix Bessemer Steel Co.* (1877) 5 Ch.D. 205 (custom); para.18–198, below (statute). See also *Gunn v Bolckow Vaughan & Co.* (1875) L.R. 10 Ch.App. 491; *Comptoir d'Achat et de Vente du Boerenbond Belge SA v Luis de Ridder Limitada* [1949] A.C. 293; *Margarine Union GmbH v Cambay Prince Steamship Co. Ltd* [1969] 1 Q.B. 219.
66 See below, paras 18–169, 18–193.
67 See below, para.18–169, 18–198
68 See *Gunn v Bolckow Vaughan & Co.*, above.
69 See below, para.18–163 (mate's receipts), para.21–053 (air waybills), paras 21–061, 21–068 (road and rail consignment notes).
70 The issue of a warrant by, *e.g.* a warehouseman may, however, constitute an acknowledgement: see below, para.18–174. *Cf.* also *Salter v Woollams* (1841) 2 M. & G. 650 (buyer agrees to treat issue or transfer of document as delivery to himself).
71 The subsection would appear not to apply to the sale of goods on approval, or on sale or return, or other similar terms: *Swain v Shepherd* (1832) 1 Mood. & Rob. 223; *Jacobs v Harbach* (1886) 2 T.L.R. 419; see above para.5–044.

send[72] the goods to the buyer, delivery of the goods to a carrier (whether named by the buyer or not) for the purpose of transmission to the buyer is prima facie deemed to be a delivery of the goods to the buyer."[73] This subsection embodies a rule which was well-established at common law, and is also relevant, when read in conjunction with section 18, rule 5, of the Act, to the passing of property in unascertained goods by delivery,[74] and to risk.[75] On the other hand, if the carrier is the servant or agent of the seller himself, the subsection will not apply.[76] It must also be noted that, while the goods are in transit, the seller may be able to exercise a right of stoppage in transit.[77] By s.32(4), however, where the buyer deals as consumer,[78] s.32(1) is to be "ignored" and "if in pursuance of a contract of sale the seller is authorised or required to send the goods to the buyer, delivery of the goods to the carrier is not delivery of the goods to the buyer." The effect of this amendment[79] is to place the risk of loss or damage to goods during transit on the seller[80] since, in a consumer sale, the goods remain at the seller's risk until they are delivered to the consumer.[81]

8–015 **Contract of carriage.** By section 32(2) of the 1979 Act: "Unless otherwise authorised by the buyer, the seller must make such contract with the carrier on behalf of the buyer as may be reasonable having regard to the nature of the goods and the other circumstances of the case; and if the seller omits to do so, and the goods are lost or damaged in course of transit, the buyer may decline to treat the delivery to the carrier as a delivery to himself[82] or may hold the seller responsible in damages."[83] In *Young (T.) & Sons v Hobson and Partner*,[84] this subsection was successfully relied upon by the buyer in an action against him for the price of electrical engines dispatched under an f.o.r. contract.[85] The contract of carriage

[72] See below, para.18–245.
[73] *cf.* Vienna Convention on Contracts for the International Sale of Goods, Art. 31 (above, para.1–024). See also below, para.19–011 (c.i.f. contracts); para.20–002 (f.o.b. contracts); para.21–072 (containers).
[74] See above, para.5–098.
[75] See above, para.6–017.
[76] *Dunlop v Lambert* (1839) 6 Cl. & F. 600 at 620; *Badische Anilin und Soda Fabrik v Basle Chemical Works* [1898] A.C. 200 at 207; *Galbraith and Grant Ltd v Block* [1922] 2 K.B. 155 at 156.
[77] See below, para.15–061.
[78] Defined in s. 61 (5A); below, para.13–071.
[79] Introduced by Reg. 4 of the Sale and Supply of Goods to Consumers Regulations 2002, SI 2002/3045, above para.6–014.
[80] See above, para.6–017.
[81] s.20 (4); above para.6–013.
[82] In effect, the risk of such loss or damage is thus thrown on the seller.
[83] *Clarke v Hutchins* (1811) 14 East 475; *Cothay v Tute* (1811) 3 Camp. 129; *Buckman v Levi* (1813) 3 Camp. 414. See also Vienna Convention on Contracts for the International Sale of Goods, Art. 32(2) (above, para.1–024) and below, para.18–245. On the relationship between subsections (1), (2) and (3) of s.32, see *Wimble, Sons & Co. Ltd v Rosenberg & Sons* [1913] 3 K.B. 743. By s.32(4), s.32(2) must be ignored where the buyer deals as consumer, the risk of loss or damage remaining with the seller in any event during transit: see above, paras 6–013, 6–017.
[84] (1949) 65 T.L.R. 365.
[85] See below, para.21–042.

arranged by the seller provided that the engines were to be carried at owner's risk when they could have been sent at the same cost, subject to an inspection by the railway, at carrier's risk. The engines arrived damaged, and the Court of Appeal held that the contract was not a reasonable one in the circumstances. The duty of the seller under this subsection[86] is, however, merely to make a reasonable contract on ordinary terms: it is not to ensure that the buyer will in any event have a remedy against the carrier.[87] The seller is entitled to assume that the duration of the transit will not be prolonged beyond that which is usual, taking into account ordinary vicissitudes[88]; and, although he is bound to possess reasonable knowledge of the characteristics of the goods he is selling and must ensure that the contract of carriage provides for the taking of any necessary precautions to preserve them during the transit in question, he need not stipulate for exceptional measures to be taken.[89]

From the wording of the subsection it would seem that, if the seller is in breach of this duty, the buyer would be entitled to decline to treat the delivery to the carrier as a delivery to himself notwithstanding that the loss or damage might have occurred even without such breach.[90]

Insurance. The duty to make a reasonable contract of carriage does not carry with it a duty to insure the goods during transit unless so agreed or unless it is customary for the seller to assume such a duty. But, where the goods are sent by the seller to the buyer by a route involving sea transit,[91] the seller may be required by section 32(3) of the Act to give such notice to the buyer as may enable the buyer to insure them during their sea transit.[92] 8–016

Delivery of goods forming part of a bulk. The definition of "delivery" in section 61(1) of the 1979 Act is qualified[93] in relation to sections 20A and 20B to include "such appropriation of goods to the contract as results in property in the goods being transferred to the buyer". Section 20A deals with undivided shares in goods forming part of a bulk[94] and section 20B with the deemed consent by a co-owner to dealings in bulk goods.[95] For the limited purpose of interpreting the word "delivery" in section 20A(5)[96] and 20B(1),[97] an appropriation which passes the property in the goods to a buyer is equated with physical delivery. But in all other respects the fact 8–017

---

86 *Cf. Clarke v Hutchins*, above, at p.476.

87 *Wimble, Sons & Co. Ltd v Rosenberg & Sons*, above, at p.757.

88 *Gatoil International Inc. v Tradax Petroleum Ltd* (*The Rio Sun*) [1985] 1 Lloyd's Rep. 350 at 359–360.

89 *ibid. Cf. B.C. Fruit Market Ltd v National Fruit Co.* (1921) 59 D.L.R. 87 (express term in contract of sale).

90 Contrast s.20(2) of the Act (above, para.6–024).

91 *Quaere* whether s.32(3) also applies by analogy to cases not involving sea transit: see above, para.6–021.

92 See above, para.6–021; below, paras 18–246, 19–117, 20–039, 20–091, 21–013.

93 A qualification inserted by s.2(b) of the Sale of Goods (Amendment) Act 1995.

94 See above, para.5–109.

95 See above, para.5–124.

96 above, para.5–120.

97 above, para.5–124.

that the contract is one for the sale of goods out of a bulk does not dispense with the need for the goods to be delivered to the buyer.

3. PLACE OF DELIVERY

8–018 **General rule.** Whether it is for the buyer to take possession of the goods or for the seller to send them to the buyer is a question depending in each case on the contract, express or implied.[98] Before the 1893 Act, it appears to have been the rule of the common law that the seller was prima facie not bound to send or carry the goods to the buyer. His duty was to afford the buyer the opportunity of taking possession of the goods at the agreed place of delivery.[99] It is submitted that there is nothing in the 1979 Act to displace this common law presumption.[1]

8–019 **Place of delivery**. Where the parties to a contract of sale have expressly or impliedly agreed upon the method by which delivery shall be effected, this agreement may well determine the place of delivery.[2] In the absence of any agreement, express or implied, as to the place of delivery, section 29(2) of the 1979 Act provides that the place of delivery is the seller's place of business, if he has one, and if not, his residence.[3] This subsection unfortunately does not provide for the contingency that the seller may have more than one place of business, nor does it establish whether the place of business or residence is that at the time of the conclusion of the contract or at the time when delivery is to be made. But in most cases the appropriate place of delivery can no doubt be established from the circumstances surrounding the contract of sale and the respective positions of the parties.

Section 29(2) nevertheless states that, if the contract is for the sale of specific goods,[4] which, to the knowledge of the parties when the contract is made are in some other place, then that place is the place of delivery.[5] It is possible that this presumption might also be applied where the goods are unascertained goods which, to the knowledge of the parties at that time, are to be taken from an identified bulk or are to be manufactured or produced at a particular place.[6]

8–020 **Option as to place of delivery.** Where the place of delivery is not specified in the contract of sale, but one of the parties is given an option as to the place of delivery, it is a condition precedent to the other party's

---

[98] Sale of Goods Act 1979, s.29(1). *Cf.* Vienna Convention on Contracts for the International Sale of Goods, Arts 31, 34 (above, para.1–024).

[99] *Smith v Chance* (1819) 2 B. & Ald. 753 at 755; *Wood v Tassell* (1844) 6 Q.B. 234; *Wilkinson v Lloyd* (1845) 7 Q.B. 27 at 44.

[1] Contrast *Wiskin v Terdich Bros Pty Ltd* [1928] Arg.L.R. 242 ("please supply us").

[2] See above, para.8–017.

[3] *Cf.* Vienna Convention on Contracts for the International Sale of Goods, Art. 31 (above, para.1–024).

[4] Defined in s.61(1) of the Act; see above, para.1–113.

[5] See also Vienna Convention on Contracts for the International Sale of Goods, Art. 31.

[6] *ibid*.

liability to accept or deliver the goods that he should receive prior notice of the place of delivery.[7]

Tender of documents. The place of tender of documents in overseas transactions is considered later in this work.[8] 8–021

Licence to enter and remove goods. If the terms of the contract of sale provide that the goods sold or to be sold are to be taken away from the land or premises of the seller, a licence is impliedly granted to the buyer to enter and remove the goods.[9] No special formalities are normally required for the grant of such a licence, but a licence to enter and remove growing crops,[10] minerals,[11] etc., may require to be made by signed writing as a "contract for the disposition of an interest in land" within section 2 of the Law of Property (Miscellaneous Provisions) Act 1989.[12] A licence to enter and remove goods, whether express or implied, is irrevocable by the seller, at any rate if the property in the goods has passed to the buyer.[13] But, as a normal rule, such a licence will not be binding on third parties, *e.g.* upon purchasers or assignees of the land.[14] 8–022

Delivery at buyer's premises. Where the seller is required by the terms of the contract of sale to deliver the goods at the premises of the buyer, he discharges his obligation if he delivers them there without negligence to a person apparently having authority to receive them.[15] 8–023

Delivery at wrong place. Where the seller delivers or tenders delivery of the goods at a place other than that stipulated, the remedies of the buyer depend on whether the stipulation is a condition, the breach of which entitles the buyer to refuse delivery at that place and to treat the contract as repudiated, or is merely an intermediate term.[16] In the case of a c.i.f.[17] or 8–024

---

[7] *Davies v McLean* (1873) 21 W.R. 264. See also the buyer's duty under an f.o.b. contract to nominate the vessel and port of shipment below, paras 20–014, 20–041. *Cf. Bulk Trading Corp. Ltd v Zenziper Grains and Feedstuffs* [2001] 1 Lloyd's Rep. 356 (f.o.t. contract).

[8] See below, paras 19–069, 20–022.

[9] *Liford's Case* (1614) 11 Co.Rep. 46b at 52a; *Jones (James) & Sons Ltd v Earl of Tankerville* [1909] 2 Ch. 440 at 442; *Mohanlal Hargovind of Jubbulpore v Commissioner of Income Tax* [1949] A.C. 521. For the remedy of injunction in these circumstances, see below, para.17–101.

[10] See above, para.1–093.

[11] See above, para.1–097.

[12] See above, paras 1–092, 1–097.

[13] *Thomas v Sorrell* (1673) Vaughan 330 at 351; *Wood v Manley* (1839) 11 A. & E. 34; *Wood v Leadbitter* (1845) 13 M. & W. 838 at 845; *Marshall v Green* (1875) 1 C.P.D. 35; *Jones (James) & Sons Ltd v Earl of Tankerville*, above, at p.443.

[14] *Ashburn Anstalt v Arnold* [1989] Ch. 1. *Cf.* Megarry and Wade, *The Law of Real Property* (6th ed.), paras 17–014—17–020.

[15] *Galbraith and Grant Ltd v Block* [1922] 2 K.B. 155; *Computer 2000 Distribution Ltd v ICM Computer Solutions Plc.* [2004] EWCA Civ 1634, [2005] Info. I.L.R 147. *Cf. E & D Thomas v H.S. Alper & Sons* [1953] C.L.Y. 3277, CA. Contrast *Linden Tricotagefabrik v White and Meacham* [1975] 1 Lloyd's Rep. 384.

[16] See below, para.10–033.

[17] *Bowes v Shand* (1877) 2 App. Cas. 455 at 467, 480; *Aruna Mills Ltd v Dhanrajmal Gobindram* [1968] 1 Q.B. 655 at 665.

f.o.b.[18] contract the port of shipment is a condition. But in other cases the place of delivery might well be considered to be an intermediate term, breach of which would entitle the buyer to treat the contract as repudiated only if delivery at the wrong place deprived him substantially of the whole benefit of the contract. If the buyer chooses or is compelled to accept the delivery, he may recover the costs and expenses incurred in forwarding the goods to the agreed place of delivery.[19] However, he may be held to have waived or to be estopped from insisting on strict compliance with the terms of the contract as to the place of delivery by taking or agreeing to take delivery at some other place.[20]

4. TIME OF DELIVERY

8–025 **Express stipulations.** According to section 10(2) of the Sale of Goods Act 1979, whether a stipulation as to time (other than as to time of payment) is or is not of the essence of the contract depends on the terms of the contract. The parties are therefore at liberty to stipulate in the contract that time is to be of the essence in relation to the seller's obligation to deliver within an agreed time. If no such stipulation is inserted, but the parties have nevertheless fixed a time for the delivery of the goods, section 10(2) would still require that the nature of this term be determined by reference to the terms of the contract. It was, however, pointed out by McCardie J. in *Hartley v Hymans*[21] that the common law and law merchant did not make the question whether time was of the essence depend upon the terms of the contract, unless those terms were express on the point. It looked rather to the nature of the contract and the character of the goods dealt with. There is no presumption or rule of law that stipulations as to time of delivery are of the essence of a contract of sale of goods.[22] But, in commercial contracts, they are frequently so construed, even though this is not expressly stated in the words of the contract.[23] If, in such a case, the

[18] *Petrotrade Inc. v Stinnes Handel GmbH* [1995] 1 Lloyd's Rep. 142.
[19] *Peter Cremer v Brinkers' Groudstoffen BV* [1980] 2 Lloyd's Rep. 605.
[20] *Peter Turnbull & Co. Pty Ltd v Mundas Trading Co. (Australasia) Ltd* [1954] 2 Lloyd's Rep. 198.
[21] [1920] 3 K.B. 475 at 483.
[22] *Compagnie Commerciale Sucres et Denrees v C. Czarnikow Ltd* [1990] 1 W.L.R. 1337 at 1347; *Thunderbird Industries LLC v Simoco Digital UK Ltd* [2004] EWHC 209 (Ch), [2004] 1 B.C.L.C. 541 at [14].
[23] *Wimshurst v Deeley* (1845) 2 C.B. 253; *Bowes v Shand* (1877) 2 App.Cas. 455 at 463; *Reuter v Sala* (1879) 4 C.P.D. 239 at 246, 249; *Harrington v Brown* (1917) 23 C.L.R. 297: *Hartley v Hymans* [1920] 3 K.B. 475 at 484, *Brooke Tool Manufacturing Co. Ltd v Hydraulic Gears Co. Ltd* (1920) 89 L.J.K.B. 263; *Finagrain SA Geneva v P. Kruse Hamburg* [1976] 2 Lloyd's Rep. 508; *United Scientific Holdings Ltd v Burnley B.C.* [1978] A.C. 904 at 924, 937, 944, 950, 958; *Toepfer v Lenersan-Poortman NV* [1980] 1 Lloyd's Rep. 143; *Cerealmangimi SpA v Toepfer* [1981] 1 Lloyd's Rep. 337; *Bunge Corp. v Tradax Export SA* [1981] 1 W.L.R. 711 at 716, 719, 729; *Société Italo-Belge pour le Commerce et l'Industrie v Palm and Vegetable Oils (Malaysia) Sdn. Bhd.* [1981] 2 Lloyd's Rep. 695 at 699; *Compagnie Commerciale Sucres et Denrees v C. Czarnikow Ltd*, above, at p.1347. *Cf. McDougall v Aeromarine of Emsworth Ltd*

seller fails to deliver the goods within the time limited for delivery, there is a breach of condition and the buyer is entitled to reject the goods and treat the contract as repudiated.[24] However, a stipulation as to time of delivery may on its true construction[25] be merely an "innominate" or "intermediate" term,[26] the breach of which entitles the buyer to treat the contract as repudiated only if the delay in delivery is so prolonged as to deprive him of substantially the whole benefit which it was intended he should receive from the contract.[27]

Notice making time of the essence. At common law, stipulations as to the time of completion were in general regarded as being of "the essence" of a contract of sale of land. But this was not so in equity, which was accustomed to afford relief either by granting specific performance to the party who was out of time or by restraining the other party from enforcing his consequential rights at law.[28] Today the equitable rule prevails.[29] But, even in equity, the innocent party could bring to an end equity's interference with the legal rights of the parties by giving to the party in default a notice requiring him to perform his obligation within a reasonable time.[30] It is, however, submitted that these equitable rules have only a very limited application to contracts of sale of goods,[31] since equity would not ordinarily 8–026

[1958] 1 W.L.R. 1126. Contrast *Paton v Payne* (1897) 35 S.L.R. 112, HL. See also below, para.19–063 (tender of documents).

[24] *Plevins v Downing* (1876) 1 C.P.D. 220 at 226; *Coddington v Paleologo* (1867) L.R. 2 Ex. 193 at 196–197. See also the later cases in n.23 (above). *Cf.* Vienna Convention on Contracts for the International Sale of Goods, Arts 33, 47, 48, 49, 71–73 (above, para.1–024). For delivery by instalments, see below, para.8–077.

[25] Applying the principle stated by Bowen L.J. in *Bentsen v Taylor, Sons & Co.* [1893] A.C. 274 at 281 (approved in *Bunge Corp. v Tradax Export SA* [1981] 1 W.L.R. 711 at 719, 725). See also *Compagnie Commerciale Sucres et Denrees v C Czarnikow Ltd*, above, at p.1347.

[26] See below, para.10–033.

[27] *Scandinavian Trading Co. A/B v Zodiac Petroleum SA* [1981] 1 Lloyd's Rep. 81 (time for provision of cargo and loading of chartered ships); *Tradax Export SA v Italgrani di Francesco Ambrosio* [1986] 1 Lloyd's Rep. 112 (time for delivery "at buyers' call"). But contrast *Compagnie Commerciale Sucres et Denrees v C. Czarnikow Ltd*, above.

[28] *Tilley v Thomas* (1867) L.R. 3 Ch.App. 61 at 67; *Stickney v Keeble* [1915] A.C. 386 at 415; *Jamshed Khodaram Irani v Burjorji Dhonjibhai* (1915) 32 T.L.R. 156 at 157; *Lock v Bell* [1931] 1 Ch. 35 at 43; *United Scientific Holdings Ltd v Burnley Borough Council* [1978] A.C. 904 at 924, 940; *Raineri v Miles* [1981] A.C. 1050; *British and Commonwealth Holdings Plc. v Quadrex Holdings Inc.* [1989] Q.B. 842 at 857; *Behzadi v Shaftesbury Hotels Ltd* [1992] Ch. 1.

[29] Law of Property Act 1925, s.41.

[30] *Stickney v Keeble*, above; *Ajit v Sammy* [1967] 1 A.C. 255; *United Scientific Holdings Ltd v Burnley Borough Council*, above, at pp.934, 946; *British and Commonwealth Holdings plc v Quadrex Holdings Inc.*, above, at p.857; *Behzadi v Shaftesbury Hotels Ltd*, above.

[31] Contrast Stannard, 120 L.Q.R. 137 (2004). But (1) where one party waives timely performance of an obligation by the other party and no period of postponement is fixed, he may give notice that he requires performance within a reasonable time and that time then becomes of the essence (see below, paras 8–030, 9–006), and (2) under s.48(3) of the 1979 Act, an unpaid seller may give notice of his intention to re-sell and then re-sell the goods if the buyer does not pay or tender the price within

intervene to relieve a party from the consequences at common law of a breach of a time stipulation in such a contract.[32] Although the extent of equitable intervention outside contracts of sale of land is possibly unclear,[33] there is likely to be little scope for notices making time of the essence in the case of a delay in the delivery of goods.[34] If one party is guilty of the breach of a stipulation as to the time of delivery and the stipulation is a condition, the other party is entitled without more to treat the contract as repudiated and there is no need for him to serve a notice giving a further opportunity to deliver within a reasonable time. If the stipulation is not a condition but an intermediate term, then a notice purporting to make time of the essence will not automatically make a failure of performance a repudiatory breach, for one party cannot unilaterally vary the terms of a contract by turning what was previously a non-essential term of the contract into an essential term.[35] Should such a notice be served, the failure to deliver within the time fixed by the notice will not, in itself, constitute a repudiation irrespective of the consequences of the breach.

8–027 **Express provision giving right to terminate.** Where there is an express provision in the contract entitling the buyer to terminate the contract in the event that delivery is not made within a certain period after the agreed date for delivery, it is unlikely that that agreed date will be regarded as of the essence of the contract.[36]

8–028 **Affirmation and acceptance.** Even though time is of the essence, the buyer is not bound to reject the goods for late delivery and may elect either to waive the breach or to treat it as a breach of warranty only.[37] Further, where the contract of sale is not severable[38] and the buyer has accepted[39] the goods or part of them[40], a late delivery can in any event only be treated as a breach of warranty, and not as a ground for rejecting the goods and treating the contract as repudiated, unless there is an express or implied term of the contract to that effect.[41]

---

a reasonable time (see below, para.15–119). See also below, para.8–039 (delivery on request).

[32] *Reuter v Sala* (1879) 4 C.P.D. 239 at 249; *Stickney v Keeble*, above. But see below, para.15–130 (relief against forfeiture).

[33] *United Scientific Holdings Ltd v Burnley Borough Council*, above, at pp.924, 940, 957.

[34] *cf.*, *Portaria Shipping Co. v Gulf Pacific Navigation Co. Ltd* [1981] 2 Lloyd's Rep. 180 at 185 (payment); Vienna Convention on Contracts for the International Sale of Goods (above, §1–024), Arts 47, 48, 63, 64.

[35] *Behzadi v Shaftesbury Hotels Ltd*, above, at pp.12, 24; *Re Olympia & York Canary Wharf Ltd (No. 2)* [1993] B.C.C. 159 at 171; *Ocular Sciences Ltd v Aspect Vision Care Ltd* [1997] R.P.C. 289, 432; *Dalkia Utilities Services Plc v Celtech International Ltd* [2006] EWHC 63 (Comm), [2006] 1 Lloyd's Rep. 599 at [131]. See also *Green v Sevin* (1879) 13 Ch.D. 589 at 599.

[36] *Steel Co. of Canada Ltd v Dominion Radiator Co. Ltd* (1919) 48 D.L.R. 350, PC.

[37] See s.11(2) of the 1979 Act; below, para.12–034. For damages, see below, para.17–038.

[38] See below, para.8–074.

[39] See ss.34, 35 of the 1979 Act; below, para.12–044.

[40] But see ss.35(7), 35A of the 1979 Act; below, paras 12–060, 12–062.

[41] See s.11(4) of the 1979 Act; below, para.12–038.

Variation of time of delivery. The buyer and seller may agree to vary the time of delivery stipulated in the contract. But such an agreement will only be binding if it is supported by some consideration moving from the promisee,[42] for example, the exchange of mutual promises to make and accept delivery at a later date.[43] 8–029

Waiver. Where the buyer voluntarily accedes to a request by the seller that delivery of the goods be postponed, he may be held to have waived his right to insist that the goods be delivered within the time fixed by the contract of sale.[44] Such a waiver may be by words or conduct and no consideration for the waiver need be proved to have moved from the seller. The buyer may likewise be estopped from asserting his right if, by words or conduct, he has led the seller to believe that he will accept delivery at a later time than that stipulated in the contract.[45] But the seller must prove a clear and unequivocal representation to that effect, and also that he has altered his position in reliance on the representation, or at least acted or omitted to act in reliance on it so that it would be inequitable in all the circumstances for the buyer to go back on the representation.[46] If it would not be inequitable for the buyer to do so, he will not be estopped.[47] The mere reservation by the buyer of "his rights" under the contract will not preclude a waiver or estoppel where the remaining circumstances justify a finding to that effect.[48] If the seller establishes such a waiver or estoppel, then the buyer will not thereafter be entitled to reject the goods on the ground that they were not delivered within the contract time.[49] 8–030

---

[42] *South Caribbean Trading Ltd v Trafigura Beheer BV* [2004] EWHC 2676 (Comm.), [2005] 1 Lloyd's Rep. 128.

[43] *Ibid*. at [105].

[44] *Ogle v Earl Vane* (1868) L.R. 3 Q.B. 272; *Hartley v Hymans* [1920] 3 K.B. 475; *Besseler Waechter Glover & Co. v South Derwent Coal Co.* [1938] 1 Q.B. 408; *Rickards (Charles) Ltd v Oppenhaim* [1950] 1 K.B. 616; *Chitty on Contracts* (29th ed.), Vol. 1, paras 22–040—22–046, *cf*. Vienna Convention on Contracts for the International Sale of Goods, Art. 47 (above, para.1–024).

[45] *Hartley v Hymans*, above; *Rickards (Charles) Ltd v Oppenhaim*, above; *Toprak Mahsulleri Ofisi v Finagrain Compagnie Commerciale Agricole et Financiere SA* [1979] 2 Lloyd's Rep. 98, 109, 115; *Fleming & Wedeln GmbH & Co. v Sanofi SA/AG* [2003] EWHC 561 (Comm.), [2003] 2 Lloyd's Rep. 472 at [62].

[46] *Finagrain SA Geneva v P. Kruse Hamburg* [1976] 2 Lloyd's Rep. 508. See also *Woodhouse v Nigerian Produce Marketing Co. Ltd* [1972] A.C. 741 at 755; *Bremer Handelsgesellschaft mbH v Vanden Avennue-Izegem PVBA* [1978] 2 Lloyd's Rep. 109 at 116, 120, 126, 130, 131; *Bunge GmbH v C.C.V. Landbouwbelang G.A.* [1980] 1 Lloyd's Rep. 458; *Cerealmangimi SpA v Toepfer* [1981] 1 Lloyd's Rep. 337; *Cook Industries v Meunerie Liegeois* [1981] 1 Lloyd's Rep. 359; *Cremer v Granaria BV* [1981] 2 Lloyd's Rep. 583; *Société Italo-Belge pour le Commerce et l'Industrie v Palm and Vegetable Oils (Malaysia) Sdn. Bhd.* [1982] 1 All E.R. 19; *Bremer Handelsgesellschaft mbH v Raiffeissen* [1982] 1 Lloyd's Rep. 599; *Bremer Handelsgesellschaft mbH v Deutsche Conti-Handelsgesellschaft mbH* [1983] 2 Lloyd's Rep. 45; *Motor Oil Hellas (Corinth) Refineries SA v Shipping Corp. of India* [1990] 1 Lloyd's Rep. 391 at 399, but see *WJ Alan & Co. v El Nasr Export & Import Co. Ltd* [1972] 2 Q.B. 189 at 213; *Bremer Handelsgesellschaft mbH v C. Mackprang* [1979] 1 Lloyd's Rep. 221 at 225–226, 228, 230.

[47] *South Caribbean Trading Ltd v Trafigura Beheer BV* [2004] EWHC 2676 (Comm), [2005] 1 Lloyd's Rep. 128 at [112].

[48] *Bremer Handelsgesellschaft mbH v C Mackprang*, above, at pp.225, 230; *Nichimen Corp. v Gatoil Overseas Inc.* [1987] 2 Lloyd's Rep. 46 at 51.

[49] *Hartley v Hymans*, above.

Where the period of postponement is not specified, the buyer can give reasonable notice to the seller requiring that the goods be delivered within a certain time[50] and, if he so specifies a new time-limit, delivery at the time thus specified becomes of the essence of the contract.[51] Where the period of postponement is specified, the new delivery date applies; but the buyer does not thereby waive his right to continue to treat the time of delivery as of the essence if it was originally so.[52]

Since the waiver is for the benefit of the seller, he too is precluded from relying on the time originally specified in the contract.[53] If the market price of the goods rises or falls during the period of postponement, and the seller ultimately fails to deliver the goods, the measure of damages will be assessed by reference to the time of his ultimate default, and not by reference to the time originally specified.[54]

8–031 **Abandonment.** A failure by the seller to tender delivery and of the buyer to require delivery over an extended period of time will not necessarily give rise to the inference that the parties have impliedly agreed to abandon the contract.[55] The party seeking to establish abandonment must show that the other party so conducted himself as to lead him to assume, and that he did assume, that the contract was agreed to be abandoned *sub silentio*.[56]

8–032 **Computation of time.** Where one party to a contract of sale is allowed a certain period of time within which to fulfil his obligations under the contract, *e.g.* to deliver the goods or to pay for them, and this period of time is expressed in terms of years or months, the word "year" is prima

---

[50] *ibid. Cf. Etablissements Chainbaux S.A.R.L. v Harbormaster Ltd* [1955] 1 Lloyd's Rep. 303; *Fleming & Wedeln GmbH & Co. v Sanofi SA/AG* [2003] EWHC 561 (Comm), [2003] 2 Lloyd's Rep. 472 (notice not required).

[51] *Rickards (Charles) Ltd v Oppenhaim* [1950] 1 K.B. 616; *Jacobson van den Berg & Co. (UK) Ltd v Biba Ltd* (1977) 121 S.J. 333.

[52] *Buckland v Farmar & Moody* [1979] 1 W.L.R. 221; *Nichimen Corp. v Gatoil Overseas Inc.*, above.

[53] *Besseler Waechter Glover & Co. v South Derwent Coal Co.*, above.

[54] *Ogle v Earl Vane*, above; *Johnson v Agnew* [1980] A.C. 367 at 400–401; *Johnson Matthey Bankers Ltd v State Trading Corp. of India Ltd* [1984] 1 Lloyd's Rep. 427; *Fleming & Wedeln GmbH & Co. v Sanofi SA/AG*, above; see also below, paras 16–073, 17–011, 17–012.

[55] *Allied Marine Transport Ltd v Vale do Rio Doce Navegacao SA* [1985] 1 W.L.R. 925 (interpreting *Pearl Mill Co. v Ivy Tannery Co. Ltd* [1919] 1 K.B. 78). *Cf. André et Cie SA v Marine Transocean Ltd* [1981] Q.B. 694 at 700, 713. See also *Tyers v Rosedale and Ferryhill Iron Co.* (1875) L.R. 10 Ex. 195 and *Chitty on Contracts* (29th ed.), Vol. 1, para.22–027.

[56] *Paal Wilson & Co. A/S v Partenreederei Hannah Blumenthal* [1983] 1 A.C. 854 at 924. See also *Allied Marine Transport Ltd v Vale do Rio Doce Navegacao SA*, above; *Collin v Duke of Westminster* [1985] Q.B. 581; *MSC Mediterranean Shipping Co. SA v BRE Metro Ltd* [1985] 2 Lloyd's Rep. 239; *Cie Française d'Importation et Distribution v Deutsche Continental Handelsgesellschaft* [1985] 2 Lloyd's Rep. 592; *Gebr. van Weelde Scheepvartkantor BV v Compania Naviera Sea Orient SA* [1987] 2 Lloyd's Rep. 223; *Food Corp. of India v Antclizo Shipping Corp.* [1988] 1 W.L.R. 603 (where the test to be applied is discussed); *Tankrederei Ahrenkeil GmbH v Frahuil SA* [1988] 2 Lloyd's Rep. 486; *Thai-Europe Tapioca Service Ltd v Seine Navigation Co. Inc.* [1989] 2 Lloyd's Rep. 506; *Walkinshaw v Diniz* [2002] EWCA Civ. 180; [2001] 1 Lloyd's Rep. 632 at 652.

facie to be construed as meaning a period of 12 consecutive months[57] and "month" as meaning a calendar month.[58] As a normal rule, a "week" is a period of seven consecutive days; and "day" is a period from midnight to midnight[59] and not a consecutive period of 24 hours.[60] No attention is paid to fractions of a day, so that a number of "days" means a number of complete days, and includes Sundays and holidays.[61] These presumptions may, however, be displaced by a contrary intention appearing from the contract, or by trade custom.[62]

If one party is allowed "until" a certain day to perform a particular act, or if the act is to be performed "by" a certain day, this may be construed to include or exclude that day according to the context of the words in the contract[63]; but normally he will have the whole of that day[64] in order to complete his performance.[65] **8–033**

If the period of time is to be computed "from" or "after" a date, act or event, or if something is to be done "in" or "within" a certain period of time "from" or "of" a date, act or event, there is no hard and fast rule as to whether the day of the date, act or event is to be excluded or included.[66] Attempts have been made from time to time to formulate subsidiary rules of construction.[67] It has, for example, been said that, where time is to be computed from the performance of an act, and the act is one to which the party against whom time is to run is privy, there is less hardship in holding that the day of the act should be included, because that party has had the benefit of some part of the day.[68] It has also been stated that, where the computation is to be for the benefit of the person affected as much time should be given as the language admits of, and where it is for his detriment the language should be construed as strictly as possible.[69] However, **8–034**

---

[57] *Bracegirdle v Heald* (1818) 1 B. & Ald. 722.

[58] Sale of Goods Act 1979, s.10(3). See also *Dodds v Walker* [1981] 1 W.L.R. 1027; *Chitty, op. cit.*, para.21–026.

[59] *The Katy* [1895] P. 56; *Cartwright v MacCormack* [1963] 1 W.L.R. 18.

[60] *Chitty, op. cit.*, para.21–022. *Cf. Cornfoot v Royal Exchange Assurance Corp.* [1904] 1 K.B. 40.

[61] But see s.29(5) of the Sale of Goods Act 1979; below, para.8–041.

[62] *ibid.*, s.55(1).

[63] *R. v Stevens and Agnew* (1804) 5 East 244 at 255–257; *Kerr v Jeston* (1842) 1 Dowl.(N.S.) 538 at 539; *Bellhouse v Mellor, Proudman and Mellor* (1859) 4 H. & N. 116 at 123.

[64] But see s.29(5) of the 1979 Act: below, para.8–041.

[65] *Startup v Macdonald* (1843) 6 M. & G. 593. See also *Isaacs v Royal Insurance Co. Ltd* (1870) L.R. 5 Ex. 296 at 299, 301; *Afovos Shipping Co. SA v Pagnan & Filli* [1983] 1 W.L.R. 195.

[66] *Lester v Garland* (1808) 15 Ves.Jun. 248 at 258; *Re North* [1895] 2 Q.B. 264 at 269; *Sheffield Corp. v Sheffield Electric Light Co.* [1898] 1 Ch. 203 at 209.

[67] See the test of "shortening the period to one day": *Webb v Fairmaner* (1838) 3 M. & W. 473 at 477; *Young v Higgon* (1840) 6 M. & W. 49; *Re Railway Sleepers Supply Co.* (1885) 29 Ch.D. 204 at 207; *Carapanayoti v Comptoir Commercial André et Cie SA* [1972] 1 Lloyd's Rep. 139 at 143, 144, 145.

[68] *Lester v Garland*, above, at p.256.

[69] *Re North*, above, at p.270; *Carapanayoti v Comptoir Commercial André et Cie SA*, above, at pp.143, 144, 146.

decisions as to the computation of time with reference to statutes, deeds and contracts reveal no consistent principle[70] and "the rational mode of computation is to have regard in each case to the purpose for which the computation is to be made"[71] and to the precise words used.[72] Nevertheless, in contracts of sale of goods, it is submitted that the computation of the time of performance from a particular date, act or event is prima facie exclusive of the day of the date, act or event[73] and inclusive of the day of performance,[74] although this presumption may be displaced by a contrary intention appearing from the wording of the contract and the circumstances surrounding it.[75]

8–035 Where one party is given "at least" or "not less than" a certain period of time from (or before) a date, act or event, then that period of time must completely elapse before his performance becomes due.[76]

8–036 **Words and phrases.** The following words and phrases relating to time have been considered by the courts[77]: "as soon as possible",[78]

---

[70] For examples of exclusive computation, see *Lester v Garland*, above ("within"); *Blunt v Heslop* (1838) 8 A. & E. 577 ("after"); *South Staffs Tramways Co. Ltd v Sickness and Accident Assurance Assn* [1891] 1 Q.B. 402 ("from"); *Radcliffe v Bartholomew* [1892] 1 Q.B. 161 ("within"); *Re North*, above ("for"); *Goldsmith's Company v West Metropolitan Ry* [1904] 1 K.B. 1 ("from"); *Stewart v Chapman* [1951] 2 K.B. 792 ("within"); *Cartwright v MacCormack* [1963] 1 W.L.R. 18 ("from"); *Re Figgis* [1969] Ch. 123 ("from"); *Re Lympe Investments Ltd* [1972] 1 W.L.R. 523 ("thereafter"); *Dodds v Walker* [1981] 1 W.L.R. 1027 ("after"); *Zoan v Rouamba* [2000] 1 W.L.R. 1509 ("after"). For examples of inclusive computation, see *Pugh v Duke of Leeds* (1778) 2 Cowp. 714 ("from"); *English v Cliff* [1914] 2 Ch. 376 at 383 ("from"); *Hare v Gocher* [1962] 2 Q.B. 641 ("beginning with"); *Trow v Ind Coope (West Midlands) Ltd* [1967] 2 Q.B. 899 ("beginning with"); *Zoan v Rouamba*, above ("beginning with").

[71] *Re North* [1895] 2 Q.B. 264 at 269.

[72] *Carapanayoti v Comptoir Commercial André et Cie* [1972] 1 Lloyd's Rep. 139 at 144.

[73] *Webb v Fairmaner* (1838) 3 M. & W. 473 (payment for goods). See also *Goldsmith's Company v West Metropolitan Ry* [1904] 1 K.B. 1; *Carapanayoti v Comptoir Commercial André et Cie*, above, at p.142.

[74] But see below, para.8–041.

[75] See *Chitty on Contracts* (29th ed.), Vol. 1, paras 12–093, 21–024.

[76] The "clear day" principle: see *Zouch v Empsey* (1821) 4 B. & Ald. 522 ("at least"); *R. v Shropshire Justices* (1838) 8 A. & E. 173 ("at least"); *Young v Higgon* (1840) 6 M. & W. 49 ("at least"); *Chambers v Smith* (1843) 12 W. & W. 2 ("not less than"); *Re Railway Sleepers Supply Co.* (1885) 29 Ch.D. 204 ("not less than"); *Re Hector Whaling Ltd* [1936] Ch.208 ("not less than"); *R. v Long* [1960] 1 Q.B. 681 ("before"); *Thompson v Stimpson* [1961] 1 Q.B. 195 ("not less than"); *Carapanayoti v Comptoir Commercial André et Cie* [1972] 1 Lloyd's Rep. 139 ("not later than . . . before").

[77] See also *Chitty on Contracts* (29th ed.), Vol. 1, para.21–021; Odgers, *Construction of Deeds and Statutes* (5th ed.), pp.126–140.

[78] *Attwood v Emery* (1856) 1 C.B.(N.S.) 110 at 115; *Hydraulic Engineering Co. v McHaffie* (1878) 4 Q.B.D. 670; *Société Italo-Belge pour le Commerce et l'Industrie v Palm and Vegetable Oils (Malaysia) Sdn. Bhd.* [1981] 2 Lloyd's Rep. 695 at 700.

"directly",[79] "forthwith",[80] "immediately",[81] "prompt",[82] "three working days",[83] "delivery on April 17th, complete 8th May",[84] "not later than",[85] "at latest"[86] and "during [February] at buyer's call".[87]

No time fixed. Section 29(3) of the 1979 Act provides: "Where under the contract of sale the seller is bound to send the goods to the buyer, but no time for sending them is fixed, the seller is bound to send them within a reasonable time." This, however, is but one instance of a more general rule that, if the contract is silent as to the time of delivery, the goods must be delivered within a reasonable time.[88] What is a reasonable time is a question of fact.[89] When deciding whether or not a reasonable time for delivery has elapsed, it would seem that a court is not limited to what the parties contemplated or ought to have foreseen at the time of entry into the contract but can take account of a broad range of factors involved in the transaction.[90] A failure to deliver the goods within a reasonable time may 8–037

---

79 *Duncan v Topham* (1849) 8 C.B. 225; *Ministry of Agriculture v Kelly* [1953] N.I. 151.
80 *Simpson v Henderson* (1829) Moo. & M. 300; *Doe* d. *Pittman v Sutton* (1849) 9 C. & P. 706; *Roberts v Brett* (1865) 11 H.L.C. 337 at 335; *Hudson v Hill* (1874) 43 L.J.C.P. 273; *Re Sillence* (1877) 7 Ch.D. 238; *Re Southam* (1881) 19 Ch.D. 179 at 183; *Keith Prowse & Co. v National Telephone Co.* [1894] 2 Ch. 147 at 155; *Hillingdon London B.C. v Cutler* [1968] 1 Q.B. 124. See also *Staunton v Wood* (1851) 16 Q.B. 638 (delivery of goods forthwith and payment within 14 days).
81 *R. v Aston* (1850) 14 Jur. 1045; *Alexiadi v Robinson* (1861) 2 F. & F. 679; *Toms v Wilson* (1862) 4 B. & S. 455; *Massey v Sladen* (1868) L.R. 4 Ex. 13; *Re Burghardt* (1875) 1 Ch.D. 297; *Moore v Shelley* (1883) 8 App.Cas. 285; *Bradley & Sons v Colonial Continental Trading Ltd* [1964] 2 Lloyd's Rep. 52.
82 *European Grain & Shipping Ltd v David Geddes (Proteins) Ltd* [1977] 2 Lloyd's Rep. 591 (GAFTA form 109).
83 *Vitol SA v Phibro Energy A.C.* [1990] 2 Lloyd's Rep. 84 (citing *Reardon Smith Line Ltd v Ministry of Agriculture Fisheries and Food* [1963] A.C. 691).
84 *Coddington v Paleologo* (1867) L.R. 2 Ex. 193.
85 *Toepfer v Lenersan-Poortman NV* [1980] 1 Lloyd's Rep. 143.
86 *Gill & Duffus SA v Société pour l'Exportation des Sucres SA* [1986] 1 Lloyd's Rep. 322.
87 *Tradax Export SA v Italgrani di Francesco Ambrosio* [1986] 1 Lloyd's Rep. 112. See also *Compagnie Commerciale Sucres et Denrees v C. Czarnikow Ltd* [1990] 1 W.L.R. 1337 ("buyer . . . shall be entitled to call for delivery").
88 *Ellis v Thompson* (1838) 3 M. & W. 445 at 456; *Jones v Gibbons* (1853) 8 ExCh.920 at 922; *Hick v Raymond and Reid* [1893] A.C. 22; *British Motor Body Co. Ltd v Thomas Shaw (Dundee) Ltd*, 1914 S.C. 922; *SHV Gas Supply & Trading SAS v Naftomar Shipping and Trading Co. Ltd. Inc.* [2005] EWHC 2528 (Comm), [2006] 1 Lloyd's Rep. 163. See also *Hartwells of Oxford Ltd v British Motor Trade Association* [1951] Ch.50; *Monkland v Jack Barclay Ltd* [1951] 2 K.B. 252 at 260. See also Vienna Convention on Contracts for the International Sale of Goods, Art. 33 (above, para.1–024).
89 Sale of Goods Act 1979, s.59. What is a reasonable time may be affected by usage: *Bradley & Sons v Colonial Continental Trading Co.* (1964) 108 S.J. 599. If circumstances hamper performance without the fault of the seller, this may extend a "reasonable time" beyond its normal span: *Hick v Raymond and Reid*, above, at p.33; *Re Carver & Co. and Sassoon & Co.* (1911) 17 Com.Cas. 59; *Hartwells of Oxford Ltd v British Motor Trade Association* above; *SHV Gas Supply & Trading SAS v. Naftomar Shipping and Trading Co. Ltd. Inc.*, above.
90 *Peregrine Systems Ltd v Steria Ltd* [2005] EWCA Civ 239, [2005] All E.R. Info. T.L.R. 294 at [15].

amount to a breach which entitles the buyer to treat himself as discharged from further liability under the contract of sale.[91]

8–038 **Distance selling.** Regulation 19 of the Consumer Protection (Distance Selling) Regulations 2000[92] provides that, in the case of a contract concerning goods which is concluded between a supplier and a consumer by means of distance communication,[93] unless the parties agree otherwise, the supplier must perform the contract within a maximum of 30 days beginning with the day after the consumer sent his order to the supplier.[94] If the supplier is unable to perform the contract because the goods are not available, within the period for performance, he is required to inform the consumer and reimburse any sum paid by or on behalf of the consumer.[95] The reimbursement must be made as soon as possible and in any event not later than 30 days commencing with the day after the day on which the period for performance expired.[96] The effect of non-performance within the allotted period is to avoid the contract.[97] But this does not prevent the consumer from claiming damages for non delivery.[98]

8–039 **Delivery on request.** If the seller is under an obligation[99] to deliver the goods to the buyer "on request" or "as required" or on similar terms, he is not bound to deliver the goods unless and until the buyer has requested him to do so.[1] Once the buyer has made his request, he is then under a duty to deliver the goods as soon as the buyer is ready to receive them.[2] Where the time for the buyer's request is not limited or fixed, the general rule is that the seller is not discharged by the fact that the buyer has not made any request within a reasonable time after the contract.[3] But the seller may, after the expiration of a reasonable time, give the buyer notice that he should make known his requirements; and, if the buyer does not then

---

[91] *Thomas Borthwick (Glasgow) Ltd v Bunge & Co. Ltd* [1969] 1 Lloyd's Rep. 17 at 28. But see s.31(2) of the Act (delivery by instalments); below, para.8–077. For the measure of damages where no time is fixed for delivery, see below, para.17–010.
[92] SI 2000/2334 as amended by SI 2004/2095, SI 2005/689; see below, para.14–054.
[93] For the scope of the Regulations, see below, para.14–054.
[94] Reg. 19(1).
[95] Reg. 19(2)(3).
[96] Reg. 19(4).
[97] Reg. 19(5).
[98] *ibid*.
[99] See below, para.8–058.
[1] *Birks v Trippet* (1666) 1 Wms.Saund. 32; *Bowdell v Parsons* (1808) 10 East 359; *GN Ry v Harrison* (1852) 12 C.B. 576; *Jones v Gibbons* (1853) 8 ExCh.920 at 922. But even if no request is received, the seller may be in breach of contract if he disposes of the goods or if he declares his unwillingness to deliver: *Bowdell v Parsons*, above; *Leeson v North British Oil and Candle Co*. (1874) Ir.R. 8 C.L. 309; *Wingold v William Looser & Co*. [1951] 1 D.L.R. 429.
[2] *European Grain & Shipping Ltd v David Geddes (Proteins) Ltd* [1977] 2 Lloyd's Rep. 591; *Tradax Export SA v Italgrani di Francesco Ambrosio* [1986] 1 Lloyd's Rep. 112; *Compagnie Commerciale Sucres et Denrées v C. Czarnikow Ltd* [1990] 1 W.L.R. 1337; *Becher (Kurt A.) GmbH v Roplak Enterprises* [1991] 1 Lloyd's Rep. 277 at 283.
[3] *Jones v Gibbons*, above; *Pearl Mill Ltd v Ivy Tannery Co. Ltd* [1919] 1 K.B. 78 at 81–83.

request delivery of the goods within a reasonable time, after notice, the seller may treat himself as discharged from further liability.[4]

Delivery conditional on buyer's act. If delivery by the seller is to take place upon the performance of some act by the buyer, *e.g.* giving delivery instructions,[5] supplying containers, or providing a means of carriage,[6] the seller is not in default for non-delivery until the stipulated act has been performed.[7] Where each party is bound[8] to co-operate with the other[9] to secure delivery of the goods to the buyer, the implication is that each will use due diligence in performing his part.[10] 8–040

Hour of delivery. By section 29(5) of the 1979 Act, demand or tender of delivery may be treated as ineffectual unless made at a reasonable hour. What is a reasonable hour is a question of fact.[11] 8–041

Delayed delivery. The buyer is entitled to claim damages for late delivery of the goods.[12] Further, where delivery has been delayed through the fault of either buyer or seller, the goods are at the risk of the party at fault as regards any loss which might not have occurred but for such fault.[13] 8–042

Early delivery. If a time has been fixed for delivery, it would appear that delivery before that date could be refused by the buyer.[14] If, however, the buyer accepted the early delivery, he would probably be held to have waived his right to object that the delivery had been made before the due date.[15] 8–043

---

4 *Jones v Gibbons*, above; *Pearl Mill Ltd v Ivy Tannery Co. Ltd*, above, at p.81. *Cf. Allied Marine Transport Ltd v Vale do Rio Doce Navegacao SA* [1985] 1 W.L.R. 925 at 938–939. But see s.31(2) of the Act (delivery by instalments): below, para.8–077.
5 See *Horn v Ministry of Food* [1948] 2 All E.R. 1036. See also *Miguel Mico (London) Ltd v H. Widdop & Co.* [1955] 1 Lloyd's Rep. 491.
6 See below, para.20–042 (f.o.b. contracts).
7 *Travers v Richardson* (1920) 20 S.R.N.S.W. 367; *Norman v Ackland* [1915] S.A.L.R. 177; *Tradax Export SA v Italgrani di Francesco Ambrosio*, above; *Compagnie Commerciale Sucres et Denrees v C. Czarnikow Ltd*, above. See also below, para.20–046.
8 See Bateson [1960] J.B.L. 187; Burrows, 31 M.L.R. 390 (1968).
9 On the duty to co-operate, see *Mackay v Dick* (1881) 6 App.Cas. 251 at 263; *Sprague v Booth* [1909] A.C. 576 at 580; *Kleinert v Abosso Gold Mining Co.* (1913) 58 S.J.(P.C.) 45; *Terry v Moss's Empires Ltd* (1915) 32 T.L.R. 92; *Colley v Overseas Exporters Ltd* [1921] 3 K.B. 302 at 309; *Pound (AV) & Co. Ltd v Hardy (MW) & Co. Inc.* [1956] A.C. 588 at 608, 611; *Kyprianou v Cyprus Textiles Ltd* [1958] 2 Lloyd's Rep. 60. *Cf. Mona Oil Equipment and Supply Co. Ltd v Rhodesia Ry* [1949] 2 All E.R. 1014; *Hargreaves Transport Ltd v Lynch* [1969] 1 W.L.R. 215; *Becher (Kurt A.) GmbH v Roplak Enterprises*, above, at pp.282–284. See also *Chitty on Contracts* (29th ed.), Vol. 1, para.13–013 (export and import licences).
10 *Ford v Cotesworth* (1868) L.R. 4 Q.B. 127; (1870) L.R. 5 Q.B. 544.
11 This replaces the technical rules of law laid down in *Startup v Macdonald* (1843) 6 M. & G. 593.
12 See below, para.17–038.
13 Sale of Goods Act 1979, s.20(2); above, para.6–023.
14 But it is doubtful whether he could treat the contract as repudiated. *Cf. Bowes v Shand* (1877) 2 App.Cas. 455 (c.i.f. contract); Vienna Convention on Contracts for the International Sale of Goods, Art. 52(1) (above, para.1–024).
15 See above, para.8–030.

8–044 **Time in overseas sales.** The nature and effect of stipulations as to the time of shipment in c.i.f.[16] and f.o.b.[17] contracts, and the time allowed for tender of documents,[18] are discussed later in this book.

5. QUANTITY OF GOODS DELIVERED

8–045 **Delivery of the correct quantity.**[19] It is the duty of the seller to deliver to the buyer the exact quantity of goods stipulated in the contract of sale. This duty is a strict one, and any failure in this respect normally entitles the buyer to reject the incorrect quantity of goods delivered.[20]

8–046 **Insufficient delivery.** By section 30(1) of the Sale of Goods Act 1979: "Where the seller delivers to the buyer a quantity of goods less than he contracted to sell, the buyer may reject them, but if the buyer accepts the goods so delivered he must pay for them at the contract rate."[21] Two alternatives are open to the buyer under this subsection. First, he can reject the insufficient quantity delivered and sue for any loss occasioned by the seller's breach[22]; and, if the price has already been paid, it can be recovered as paid upon a consideration which has totally failed. Secondly, he can—if he so chooses— retain the quantity delivered, paying for this at the contract rate,[23] and recover such part of the price as has been paid for the undelivered balance.[24] He can also claim damages for breach[25]: by accepting the quantity delivered, the buyer does not give up his right to recover damages for non-delivery of the balance.[26] He cannot, however, without the

[16] See below, para.19–013.
[17] See below, para.20–029.
[18] See below, para.19–060.
[19] See the Final Report of the Law Commission on the Sale and Supply of Goods (1987) Cmnd. 137, paras 6.17–6.23.
[20] But see below, paras 8–050, 8–051. It is submitted that the special remedies provided by part 5A of the 1979 Act are not available for breach of a quantity stipulation.
[21] This subsection embodies the common law rule stated in *Shipton v Casson* (1826) 5 B. & C. 378 at 382–383; *Oxendale v Wetherell* (1829) 9 B. & C. 386 at 387–388; *Colonial Insurance Co. v Adelaide Insurance Co.* (1886) 12 App.Cas. 128 at 138–140. *Cf.* Vienna Convention on Contracts for the International Sale of Goods, Art. 51 (above, para.1–024).
[22] *Tamvaco v Lucas* (1859) 1 E. & E. 581 and 591; *Borrowman v Drayton* (1876) 2 Ex.D. 15; *Reuter v Sala* (1879) 4 C.P.D. 239; *Harland and Wolff Ltd v Burstall & Co.* (1901) 6 Com.Cas. 113; *Cobec Brazilian Trading and Warehousing Corp. v Toepfer* [1983] 2 Lloyd's Rep. 386 at 391. See also *Gorrissen v Perrin* (1857) 2 C.B.(N.S.) 681, and below, para.8–064 (instalments). If the whole quantity is not made up, the seller cannot sue for the price: *Waddington v Oliver* (1805) 2 B. & P.N.R. 61. *Cf. Morgan v Gath* (1865) 3 H. & C. 748. See also below, para.8–077.
[23] *cf. Shipton v Casson*, above, at p.383 ("value" of goods).
[24] *Oxendale v Wetherell*, above; *Richardson v Dunn* (1841) 2 Q.B. 218; *Biggerstaff v Rowatt's Wharf Ltd* [1896] 2 Ch. 93; *Behrend & Co. v Produce Brokers Co. Ltd* [1920] 3 K.B. 530. *Cf. Morgan v Gath*, above.
[25] *Household Machines Ltd v Cosmos Exporters Ltd* [1947] K.B. 217. *Cf. Morgan v Gath*, above.
[26] *European Grain & Shipping Ltd v Peter Cremer* [1983] 2 Lloyd's Rep. 211.

consent of the seller, divide his acceptance by retaining a portion of the goods delivered and rejecting the rest: he must accept the whole of the insufficient delivery, or reject the whole of it.[27]

The words "accepts the goods" in section 30(1) must presumably be construed in accordance with section 35 of the Act.[28] If, therefore, having examined or having had a reasonable opportunity of examining the goods,[29] the buyer intimates to the seller that he has accepted the quantity of goods delivered[30] or does any act in relation to those goods which is inconsistent with the ownership of the seller,[31] he will not subsequently be entitled to reject them on the ground of the shortfall. Difficulties may, however, arise if, after the lapse of a reasonable time, he retains the quantity of goods delivered without intimating to the seller that he has rejected them,[32] because he believes the whole quantity of goods will subsequently be made up. If this belief proves false, is he then precluded from rejecting the goods and bound to pay for the insufficient quantity delivered? An affirmative answer might have to be given to this question on a literal application of section 35 of the Act[33]; although it is arguable that the buyer's belief is a factor which should be taken into account in determining whether a reasonable time has elapsed. Subsection (1) of section 30, however, appears to envisage a situation where the buyer knows that the seller will not deliver the contract quantity, and it is submitted that (in the absence of estoppel) the buyer never "accepts" the insufficient quantity of goods delivered merely by retaining them in the expectation that the seller will subsequently deliver the balance.[34] 8–047

Section 30(1) is subject to section 31(2)[35] of the 1979 Act. Thus, where the goods are to be delivered by instalments, the buyer cannot reject the whole of the goods on the ground that there has been short delivery of one or more instalments unless such short delivery is a repudiation of the whole contract.[36] 8–048

Excessive delivery. By section 30(2) of the 1979 Act: "Where the seller delivers to the buyer a quantity of goods larger than he contracted to sell, the buyer may accept the goods included in the contract and reject the rest, 8–049

---

27 *Champion v Short* (1807) 1 Camp. 53, as explained in *Tarling v O'Riordan* (1878) 2 L.R.Ir. 82. *Cf.* Hudson, 92 L.Q.R. 506 (1976).

28 See below, para.12–044. See also s.11(4) of the Act (below, para.12–038) and *Rosenthal & Sons Ltd v Esmail* [1965] 1 W.L.R. 1117.

29 s.35(2).

30 s.35(1)(a).

31 s.35(1)(b). But see s.35(6)(b) (buyer not deemed to have accepted the goods merely because the goods are delivered to another under a sub-sale or other disposition).

32 s.35(4).

33 See also *Morgan v Gath* (1865) 3 H. & C. 748.

34 *Reuter v Sala* (1879) 4 C.P.D. 239; *Finagrain v Kruse* [1976] 2 Lloyd's Rep. 508; *Gill & Duffus SA v Berger & Co. Inc.* [1983] 1 Lloyd's Rep. 622 at 627, 629 (reversed on other grounds [1984] A.C. 382). *Cf. Oxendale v Wetherell* (1829) 9 B. & C. 386.

35 See below, para.8–077.

36 *Regent OHG Aisenstadt und Barig v Francesco of Jermyn Street Ltd* [1981] 3 All E.R. 327.

or he may reject the whole." And by section 30(3): "Where the seller delivers to the buyer a quantity of goods larger than he contracted to sell and the buyer accepts the whole of the goods so delivered he must pay for them at the contract rate."[37] The buyer is therefore entitled to refuse the whole of the goods tendered if they exceed the quantity agreed, and the seller has no right to insist upon the buyer's selecting the correct amount out of the larger quantity delivered.[38] The buyer may, however, select the correct quantity[39] and reject the rest. Or he may treat the excessive delivery as a proposal for a new contract[40] and accept the whole, paying for the excess at the contract rate,[41] in which case it appears that he will be precluded from claiming damages for delivery of the wrong quantity of goods.[42]

8–050 **Restrictions on buyer's right to reject.** Two restrictions are imposed on the right to reject the goods conferred by subsections (1) and (2) of section 30. First, at common law, a shortfall or excess in quantity which is "microscopic"[43] and which is not capable of influencing the mind of the buyer[44] will not entitle him to reject the goods, for *de minimis non curat lex*.[45] Some slight elasticity in carrying out a commercial contract for the supply of goods in bulk is unavoidable, and the courts will not allow the buyer to take advantage of a merely trivial difference in quantity if the delivery is substantially of the quantity named.[46] Thus, in *Shipton Anderson*

[37] *Hart v Mills* (1846) 15 M. & W. 85; *Cunliffe v Harrison* (1851) 6 ExCh.903; *Tamvaco v Lucas* (1859) 1 E. & E. 581; *Rylands v Kreitman* (1865) 19 C.B.(N.S.) 351; *Kreuger v Blanck* (1870) L.R. 5 Ex. 179; *Frangopulo v Lomas & Co.* (1902) 18 T.L.R. 461; *Payne and Routh v Lillico & Sons* (1920) 36 T.L.R. 569. *Cf. Dixon v Fletcher* (1837) 3 M. & W. 146. See also Vienna Convention on Contracts for the International Sale of Goods, Art. 52(2) (above, para.1–024).

[38] *Cunliffe v Harrison*, above, at p.906. It is by no means certain, however, that the buyer could reject the whole of the goods tendered if the seller did not seek to recover from him a sum in excess of that agreed to be paid or to make him separate out the correct quantity, and if the delivery of the excess quantity was not otherwise a burden to the buyer: see *Levy v Green* (1857) 8 E. & B. 575 at 587; (1859) 1 E. & E. 969 at 975; *Rylands v Kreitman*, above, at p.358; *Shipton, Anderson & Co. v Weil Bros & Co.* [1912] 1 K.B. 574 at 577.

[39] But (*semble*) not part of the correct quantity: *Champion v Short* (1807) 1 Camp. 53 (above, para.8–46, n.27), nor part of the excess. But see *Hart v Mills*, above, at p.86; Hudson (1976) 92 L.Q.R. 506.

[40] *Hart v Mills*, above, at p.87; *Cunliffe v Harrison*, above, at p.906; *Gabriel Wade and English v Arcos Ltd* (1929) 34 Ll.L.R. 306 at 309. *Quaere* whether the buyer could do this when, for example, the buyer orders one article, perhaps of a special nature, and two are mistakenly delivered. The seller may have no more available and thus be in contractual difficulties with another customer. See the Final Report of the Law Commission on the Sale and Supply of Goods (1987) Cmnd. 137, para.6.23.

[41] *cf. Shipton v Casson* (1826) 5 B. & C. 378 at 383; above, para.8–046, n.23.

[42] *Gabriel Wade and English v Arcos Ltd*, above. *Sed quaere*? In this case separation of the correct quantity was not commercially possible and the buyer suffered loss as a result of the delivery of the excess. But see *ibid.* p.307 (offer by seller to take excess).

[43] *Arcos Ltd v E. A. Ronaasen & Son* [1933] A.C. 470 at 480.

[44] *Shipton Anderson & Co. v Weil Brothers & Co.* [1912] 1 K.B. 574 at 577.

[45] See also below, para.19–012.

[46] *Harland and Wolff Ltd v Burstall & Co.* (1901) 6 Com.Cas. 113 at 116.

and Co. v Weil Brothers & Co.[47] an excess of 55 lbs. of wheat over and above an agreed limit of 4,950 tons was held to fall within the rule. It seems, however, that the seller cannot invoke the rule except as a defence to an allegation that he has not substantially performed his obligation under the contract of sale[48] and the burden of proving that the deficiency or excess falls within the rule rests upon him.[49] The *de minimis* rule does not apply to documentary credits.[50]

The second restriction is statutory. Subsection (2A) of section 30[51] provides: "A buyer who does not deal as consumer may not—(a) where the seller delivers a quantity of goods less than he contracted to sell, reject the goods under subsection (1) above, or (b) where the seller delivers a quantity of goods larger than he contracted to sell, reject the whole under subsection (2) above, if the shortfall or, as the case may be, excess is so slight that it would be unreasonable for him to do so". It should be noted that this restriction applies only where the buyer does not "deal as consumer", a phrase which is to be construed in accordance with Part I of the Unfair Contract Terms Act 1977.[52] Subsection (2A) is not merely a re-statement in statutory terms of the *de minimis* rule, despite the reference to the shortfall or excess being "slight". A shortfall or excess which is more than *de minimis* can therefore fall within its scope. It would no doubt be unreasonable for a buyer to reject the goods delivered on the ground of a slight shortfall in the contract quantity if it was not essential to him to receive the whole of that quantity and if he could be adequately compensated in damages for non-delivery of the undelivered balance. With respect to an excessive delivery, it might be unreasonable for a buyer to reject the whole of the goods delivered on the ground of a slight excess over the contract quantity if, for example, it was commercially practical for him to separate out the correct quantity and reject the excess or if he was not required by the seller to pay for the excess. The burden of proving that the buyer does not "deal as consumer"[53] and that a shortfall or excess falls within subsection (2A)[54] lies on the seller. 8–051

Cure by seller of insufficient or excessive delivery. Where the seller tenders or delivers an insufficient or excessive quantity of goods and the goods are in consequence rejected by the buyer, it is submitted that, in 8–052

---

[47] [1912] 1 K.B. 574. See also *Easterbrook v Gibb* (1887) 3 T.L.R. 401. *Cf. Harland and Wolff Ltd v Burstall & Co.*, above; *Jackson v Rotax Motor and Cycle Co.* [1910] 2 K.B. 937 at 949; *Wilensko Slaski Towarzystwo Drewno v Fenwick & Co. (West Hartlepool) Ltd* [1938] 3 All E.R. 429; *Rapalli v K L Take Ltd* [1958] 2 Lloyd's Rep. 469.

[48] *Margaronis Navigation Agency Ltd v Henry W Peabody & Co. of London Ltd* [1965] 1 Q.B. 300.

[49] *E A Ronaasen & Son v Arcos Ltd* (1932) 48 T.L.R. 356, affirmed *sub nom. Arcos Ltd v E A Ronaasen & Son*, above.

[50] See below, para.23–196. But see U.C.P., Art. 39.

[51] Inserted by s.4(2) of the Sale and Supply of Goods Act 1994.

[52] See below, para.13–071.

[53] s.61(5A) of the 1979 Act.

[54] s.30(2B).

principle, the seller could subsequently make delivery of the correct quantity, which the buyer would then be bound to accept unless the time for delivery had by then expired.[55] But the seller could not cure an insufficient or excessive delivery by delivering the correct quantity outside the contract period. Nor could he, in any event, cure an insufficient delivery by delivering or promising to deliver the balance at a later time, since, unless the buyer has agreed to accept delivery by instalments,[56] the buyer is entitled to delivery of the whole of the goods at one and the same time.[57]

8–053 **Derogation from section 30.** All the provisions of section 30 of the Act (including subsection (2A))[58] are subject to any usage of trade, special agreement, or course of dealing between the parties.[59]

8–054 **Words of approximation.** The most common way for the parties to derogate from the provisions of section 30 by special agreement is to state the quantity of goods to be delivered as an approximate quantity, leaving a margin for excess in or deficiency of the specified quantity by using such words as "about" or "more or less".[60] By such a stipulation, the seller gains a certain moderate and reasonable latitude as to the quantity of goods which he is contractually bound to deliver[61]; but the buyer will nevertheless be entitled to invoke the provisions of subsections (1) and (2) of section 30 if that reasonable latitude is exceeded.[62] It would also seem that such a stipulation will only protect the seller where the deficiency or excess arises in an honest attempt to perform the contract, and cannot be relied upon by him to reduce his liability where he refuses to perform.[63] The parties may also stipulate certain limits within which the seller is entitled to deliver more or less than a specified quantity, *e.g.* "200 tons, 5 per cent more or less"[64] or determine the quantity to be delivered by reference to a maximum or minimum quantity, *e.g.* "not less than 100 packs"[65]; but he must then not deliver a quantity outside those limits.

---

[55] See below, paras 12–029, 12–031. See also US Uniform Commercial Code, para.2–508.
[56] See below, para.8–065.
[57] Sale of Goods Act 1979, s.31(1); below, para.8–064.
[58] See below, paras 19–012, 19–173 (overseas sales).
[59] Sale of Goods Act 1979, s.30(5).
[60] In the case of instalment contracts (see below, para.8–064), it is a question of construction whether such words qualify the whole quantity of goods or the amount of an instalment: *Société Anonyme l'Industrielle Russo-Belge v Scholefield & Son* (1902) 7 Com.Cas. 114. See also *Ross T Smyth & Co. Ltd v T D Bailey Son & Co.* [1940] 3 All E.R. 60.
[61] See also U.C.P., Art. 39a; below, para.23–211.
[62] *Cross v Eglin* (1831) 2 B. & Ad. 106; *Bourne v Seymour* (1855) 16 C.B. 337; *Reuter v Sala* (1879) 4 C.P.D. 239; *Harland and Wolff Ltd v Burstall & Co.* (1901) 6 Com.Cas. 113; *Carson v Union SS Co.* [1922] N.Z.L.R. 778 at 782. But see below, para.8–056 (words of estimate).
[63] *Hassell v Bagot Shakes and Lewis Ltd* (1911) 13 C.L.R. 374 at 380. But see below, para.17–002.
[64] *Re Thornett and Fehr and Yuills* [1921] 1 K.B. 219. See also *Doe v Bowater Ltd* [1916] W.N. 155; *Payne and Routh v Lillico & Sons* (1920) 36 T.L.R. 569 (2 per cent more or less); and below, para.17–002.
[65] *Leeming v Snaith* (1851) 16 Q.B. 275. See also *Graham v Jackson* (1811) 14 East 498; *Bekh v Page* (1859) 5 C.B.(N.S.) 708; *Arbuthnot v Streckheisen* (1866) 35 L.J.C.P. 305 (maximum quantities). *Cf. Hayward v Scougall* (1809) 2 Camp. 56.

Words of adjustment. The parties may also agree, for example, that payment shall be made against bill of lading weights but that a final adjustment will be made on discharged weights. If the buyer seeks such an adjustment, he must proceed in accordance with the procedure stipulated in the contract and will not have any claim for an adjustment or for short delivery if the required procedure is not fulfilled.[66] 8–055

Words of estimate. The goods to be delivered may be specified by reference to a particular parcel of goods, or to other circumstances, with the addition of words indicating the quantity which it is expected may be delivered, *e.g.* "all naphtha made by the seller, say from 1,000 to 1,200 gallons a month."[67] In such a case, these words may be construed as words of estimate only, and not as a warranty as to the quantity to be delivered, so that the buyer will have no right of action if the quantity delivered differs materially from the estimated amount,[68] provided that the seller has acted in good faith. 8–056

Sale of a cargo. The word "cargo" is a word of varied meaning,[69] but, in a contract of sale of goods, it normally means the whole or entire cargo of a vessel.[70] If there is then added to the word "cargo" a statement of a particular quantity of goods, *e.g.* "about 450 tons", this statement is usually construed as one of expectation and estimate only, and not as a guarantee by the seller that he will deliver the specified quantity.[71] 8–057

Goods "as required." Difficult questions of construction may arise where the quantity of goods to be delivered is stated in terms of the buyer's "requirements" or defined by the use of the words "as required" or "as may be required" or some similar expression. 8–058

In the first place, the extent of the seller's liability must be ascertained. The agreement between the parties may be found to be no more than a standing offer on the part of the seller to supply such goods as the buyer may from time to time order.[72] In such a case, so long as this offer has not

---

66 *Krohn & Co. v Mitsui and Co. Europe GmbH* [1978] 2 Lloyd's Rep. 419. *Cf. Oricon Waren- Handels GmbH v Intergraan NV* [1967] 2 Lloyd's Rep. 82.

67 *Gwillim v Daniell* (1835) 2 C.M. & R. 61.

68 *McConnel v Murphy* (1873) L.R. 5 P.C. 203 (all spars manufactured, say about 600 spars); *McLay & Co. v Perry & Co.* (1881) 44 L.T. 152 (specific heap of iron, understood about 150 tons); *Tancred Arrol & Co. v Steel Co. of Scotland Ltd* (1890) 15 App.Cas. 125 (whole steel required for Forth Bridge, understood to be 30,000 tons more or less); *Goldsborough Mort & Co. Ltd v Carter* (1914) 19 C.L.R. 429 (about 4,500 sheep); *Tebbitts v Smith* (1917) 33 T.L.R. 508 (quantity salved, estimated 8–10 tons); *Re Harrison and Micks, Lambert & Co.* [1917] 1 K.B. 755 (remainder of cargo, 5,400 quarters more or less); *Moray Park Fruit Co. Ltd v Crewe and Newcombe* [1934] S.A.S.R. (season's pack of raisins, between 90 and 100 tons, according to what is treated). The parties may also mutually take the risk of the quantity of goods delivered being more or less than that quantity on which the price was calculated: *Covas v Bingham* (1853) 2 E. & B. 836.

69 *Colonial Insurance Co. of New Zealand v Adelaide Marine Insurance Co.* (1886) 12 App.Cas. 128 at 129.

70 See below, para.21–034.

71 See below, para.21–033.

72 *Great Northern Ry v Witham* (1873) L.R. 9 C.P. 16.

been withdrawn, the seller will be bound to execute any order placed by the buyer[73] subject to any limit imposed by the terms of the offer. But he will be free to withdraw his offer before any order or any particular order is placed.[74] On the other hand, the agreement may be construed to mean "I hereby bind myself to execute any order which you may place",[75] in which case the seller will not be entitled to withdraw if this promise is supported by some consideration.[76] Or the seller may bind himself to supply, for example, all the goods required by the buyer for use in the buyer's business over a particular period, and in this case also the seller will be under an obligation to satisfy those requirements when requested to do so.[77]

8–059 Secondly, the terms of the agreement must be examined in order to determine the extent of the buyer's liability. The word "required", or any similar word, may be equivalent to "ordered" or "demanded", so that the buyer will only be liable if he actually places an order for goods, but will not be bound to purchase any goods at all.[78] Where there is a standing offer by the seller, for example, the buyer will not normally incur any liability by "accepting" such an offer, his acceptance being merely a recognition that the offer has been made; in the absence of an express stipulation, he will be under no obligation to give any order.[79] On the other hand, the true construction of the agreement may be that the buyer binds himself to purchase such goods as he may "require" in the sense that he undertakes to procure all that he may need from the seller and from no other source.[80] In such a case, he is under a contractual obligation to purchase his requirements from the seller.

8–060 Where there is a bilateral contract to supply and purchase the "requirements" of the buyer, the seller cannot force upon the buyer the estimated quantity[81] of his requirements where the goods are bona fide not required, as, for instance, where the buyer has discontinued the business for which

---

73 *ibid.*; *Percival Ltd v LCC Asylums, etc. Committee* (1918) 87 L.J.K.B. 677 at 679.

74 *Great Northern Ry v Witham*, above.

75 *Percival Ltd v LCC Asylums, etc. Committee*, above, at p.679.

76 But see Adams, 94 L.Q.R. 73 (1978).

77 *Whitehouse v Liverpool New Gas Light & Coke Co.* (1848) 5 C.B. 798; *Wood v Copper Miners' Co.* (1854) 14 C.B. 428 at 468; *Eastern Counties Ry v Philipson* (1855) 16 C.B. 2; *Percival Ltd v LCC Asylums, etc. Committee*, above, at p.679; *Kier (J.L.) & Co. v Whitehead Iron & Steel Co. Ltd* [1938] 1 All E.R. 591. See also *Tolhurst v Associated Portland Cement Manufacturers (1900) Ltd* [1903] A.C. 414 (assignee). *Cf. Hamlyn & Co. v Wood* [1891] 2 Q.B. 488.

78 *Burton v GN Ry* (1854) 9 Exch.507; *Churchward v R.* (1865) L.R. 1 Q.B. 173; *R. v Demers* [1900] A.C. 103; *Att.-Gen. v Stewards Ltd* (1901) 18 T.L.R. 131; *Moon v Mayor of Camberwell* (1904) 89 L.T. 595; *Percival Ltd v LCC Asylums, etc. Committee* (1918) 87 L.J.K.B. 677; *Cory Bros & Co. Ltd v Universe Petroleum Co. Ltd* (1933) 46 Ll.L.R. 308.

79 *Percival Ltd v LCC Asylums, etc. Committee*, above.

80 *Tancred Arrol & Co. v Steel Co. of Scotland Ltd* (1890) 15 App.Cas. 125; *Percival Ltd v LCC Asylums, etc. Committee*, above, at p.679.

81 Specified quantities will normally be regarded as words of estimate only; see *Tancred Arrol & Co. v Steel Co. of Scotland Ltd* (1890) 15 App.Cas. 125; *Percival Ltd v LCC Asylums, etc. Committee* (1918) 87 L.J.K.B. 677; *Cory Bros & Co. Ltd v Universe Petroleum Co. Ltd* (1933) 46 Ll.L.R. 308; and above, para.8–056.

the goods are required.[82] Conversely, the buyer cannot enforce delivery of a greater quantity of goods than are bona fide required.[83] If the buyer brings an action for damages against the seller for failure to satisfy his requirements, it is essential for him to prove that there was a need on his part for the goods of which delivery was required.[84]

An "exclusive dealing" agreement under which the buyer promises to purchase the whole of his requirements of goods from a single source and to buy from no other may nevertheless be void and unenforceable as being in unreasonable restraint of trade[85] or be affected by the Competition Act 1998 or by Article 81 or 82 of the Treaty of Rome.[86] 8–061

Usage. The obligation of the seller to deliver the exact quantity of goods stipulated in the contract, and the meaning of terms as to quantity, may be subject to a usage prevailing in a particular trade.[87] 8–062

Exemption clauses. The right to reject the goods conferred by subsections (1) and (2) of section 30 of the Act may be taken away by special agreement of the parties.[88] But since any clause purporting to deprive the buyer of this right is in the nature of an exemption clause, the actual wording of the clause must be closely scrutinised to see whether, on its true construction, it was intended to protect the seller in the event of the breach which has actually taken place.[89] In particular, it has been held that such words as "the buyers shall not reject the goods herein specified, but shall accept and pay for them in terms of contract against shipping documents" do not prevent the buyer from rejecting the goods delivered if they are not of the correct quantity.[90] Such a clause may also be unenforceable in certain circumstances, except in so far as it satisfies the requirement of reasonableness, by virtue of the Unfair Contract Terms Act 1977,[91] or, in a consumer contract, it may not be binding on the consumer by virtue of the Unfair Terms in Consumer Contracts Regulations 1999.[92] 8–063

---

[82] *Berk v International Explosives Co.* (1901) 7 Com.Cas. 20.
[83] *Kier (JL) & Co. v Whitehead Iron and Steel Co. Ltd* [1938] 1 All E.R. 591. *Cf.* U.S. Uniform Commercial Code, para.2–306.
[84] *ibid*.
[85] *Esso Petroleum Ltd v Harper's Garage (Stourport) Ltd* [1968] A.C. 269; *Amoco Australia Pty Ltd v Rocca Bros Motor Engineering Co. Pty Ltd* [1975] A.C. 561; *Shell U.K. Ltd v Lostock Garage Ltd* [1977] 1 W.L.R. 1187. *Cf. Cleveland Petroleum Ltd v Dartstone Ltd* [1969] 1 W.L.R. 116; *Alec Lobb (Garages) Ltd v Total Oil (Great Britain) Ltd* [1985] 1 W.L.R. 173. See *Chitty on Contracts* (29th ed.), Vol. 1, paras 16–120 *et seq.*, and above, para.3–038.
[86] See *Chitty on Contracts* (29th ed.), Vol. 2, Ch.42, and above, paras 3–040, 3–041.
[87] Sale of Goods Act 1979, ss.30(5), 55(1); *Devaux v Conolly* (1849) 8 C.B. 640; *Moore v Campbell* (1854) 10 Exch.323; *Lister and Biggs v Barry & Co.* (1886) 3 T.L.R. 99; *Lomas & Co. v Barff Ltd* (1901) 17 T.L.R. 437 (revsd. on other grounds, 18 T.L.R. 461); *Société Anonyme l'Industrielle Russo-Belge v Scholefield* (1902) 7 Com.Cas. 114. Contrast *Cross v Elgin* (1831) 2 B. & Ad. 106; *Tancred Arrol & Co. v Steel Co. of Scotland Ltd* (1890) 15 App.Cas. 125 at 136. See also *Chitty on Contracts* (29th ed.), Vol. 1, paras 12–127—12–133, 13–018.
[88] Sale of Goods Act 1979, ss.30(5), 55(1).
[89] See below . para.13–020 and *Chitty on Contracts, op. cit.*, paras 14–005, 14–027.
[90] *Green v Arcos Ltd* (1931) 47 T.L.R. 336. See also below, para.13–033.
[91] See below, para.13–086.
[92] See below, para.14–030.

6. DELIVERY BY INSTALMENTS

8–064 **Instalment deliveries.** Unless otherwise agreed, the buyer of goods is not bound to accept delivery of them by instalments,[93] nor is he entitled to call for delivery by instalments.[94] He may, however, waive the requirement that all the goods must be delivered at one and the same time, and the acceptance by him of an instalment without objection may constitute such a waiver.[95]

8–065 **Agreement to deliver by instalments.** It is open to the parties expressly to provide for delivery by instalments, and such a provision may also be inferred from the language used in the contract of sale[96] or from the circumstances of the case.[97] Where there is a contract for a quantity of goods, some of which are existing, while others are to be manufactured, and no particular time is specified for delivery, the inference is that the goods are to be delivered by instalments.[98]

8–066 **Election by the seller of a single or instalment delivery.** Where the seller has an option to deliver either by a single delivery or by instalments, and is required by the contract to declare which method of delivery he will adopt, he must make his election within the time stipulated in the contract[99] and deliver the goods accordingly. If no such declaration is required, he exercises his option by making a single or instalment delivery as the case may be.[1] In *Reuter v Sala*[2] the sellers, having the option to ship by vessel or

---

[93] Sale of Goods Act 1979, s.31(1); *Champion v Short* (1807) 1 Camp. 53 at 54; *Reuter v Sala* (1879) 4 C.P.D. 239; *Honck v Muller* (1881) 7 Q.B.D. 92 at 99; *Behrend & Co. v Produce Brokers Co.* [1920] 3 K.B. 530 at 534–535; *Cobec Brazilian Trading and Warehousing Corp. v Toepfer* [1983] 2 Lloyd's Rep. 386. See also above, para.8–046, on the rights of the buyer in such a case (s.30(1) of the Act).

[94] *Kingdom v Cox* (1848) 5 C.B. 522 at 526; *Reuter v Sala*, above, at p.247; *Honck v Muller*, above, at p.99.

[95] *Champion v Short*, above; *Leidemann v Gray* (1857) 26 L.J. Ex. 162; *Tarling v O'Riordan* (1878) 2 L.R. Ir. 82 at 86. The waiver may be a waiver of the breach, or merely of the right to reject under s.30(1) of the Act: see s.11(2) (below, para.12–034); *Bentsen v Taylor, Sons & Co.* [1893] 2 Q.B. 274. *Cf. Cobec Brazilian Trading and Warehousing Corp. v Toepfer*, above (no waiver).

[96] *Brandt v Lawrence* (1876) 1 Q.B.D. 344 ("shipment by steamer or steamers"); *Jackson v Rotax Motor and Cycle Co.* [1910] 2 K.B. 937 ("delivery as required"); *Ballantine & Co. v Cramp* (1923) 129 L.T. 502 ("each month's or steamer's contract to be considered a separate contract"); *Howells v Evans* (1926) 42 T.L.R. 310 (engravings "to be sent to me as published"); *Esmail v J. Rosenthal & Sons Ltd* [1965] 1 W.L.R. 1117 ("shipments: Feb. 1961. each shipment under this contract shall be deemed as a separate contract"); *Pagnan and Fratelli v Tradax Overseas SA* [1980] 1 Lloyd's Rep. 665 (GAFTA 100). *Cf. Reuter v Sala*, above; *Cobec Brazilian Trading and Warehousing Corp.*, above.

[97] *Thornton v Simpson* (1816) 6 Taunt. 556; *Nicholson v Bradfield Union* (1866) L.R. 1 Q.B. 620; *Colonial Insurance Co. of New Zealand v Adelaide Marine Insurance Co.* (1886) 12 App.Cas. 128 at 138; *Pagnan and Fratelli v Tradax Overseas SA*, above, at p.672.

[98] *Tarling v O'Riordan*, above, at p.86.

[99] *Reuter v Sala* (1879) 4 C.P.D. 239. If no time is fixed, then within a reasonable time. See above, para.8–037.

[1] *Rosenthal & Sons Ltd v Esmail* [1965] 1 W.L.R. 1117.

[2] (1879) 4 C.P.D. 239.

vessels, declared and tendered as one entire whole the contract quantity shipped on board a single vessel under three bills of lading. The buyers discovered that one of the bills of lading covered goods shipped outside the shipment period. They therefore refused to accept the declaration, as it was not for the full quantity. After the time limited for declaring had expired, the sellers substituted a new declaration of goods on the same vessel which had been shipped within the shipment period. It was held that they were not entitled to do so and the buyers could reject the goods.[3] It may be, however, that the seller could subsequently revoke his election, and re-tender to the buyer the insufficient quantity as an instalment, provided that his new declaration was still in time and he was able to deliver the remainder of the goods in accordance with the contract.[4]

Amount of instalments not specified. Where the amount of the instalments is not specified, the prima facie inference would seem to be that the instalments should be rateably distributed over the period appointed for the delivery of the goods.[5] But the terms of the contract or the surrounding circumstances, *e.g.* problems of supply, manufacture or transport, may indicate that rateable deliveries were not intended.[6] In such a case, it is then a question of fact whether or not the quantity delivered or tendered was a reasonable one.[7] What is reasonable will depend upon the time and amount of delivery having regard to the total quantity contracted for and the length of the period within which delivery is to be completed.[8] 8–067

Average instalments. Where the goods are to be delivered by "average" or "about equal" instalments for each specified unit of the period within which the whole delivery is to take place, or on similar terms, a moderate deficiency or excess at the end of one unit of time may be compensated for subsequently, provided that, at the expiration of any particular time, it cannot be said (as a question of fact) that a fair average has not been achieved in relation to the sum of the instalments delivered.[9] In the latter event, the seller will have committed a breach of the contract[10] and will not, 8–068

---

[3] At pp.245–248. But see the different reasoning of Cotton L.J. at pp.249–250. Brett L.J. dissented. *Cf. Brandt v Lawrence* (1876) 1 Q.B.D. 344.

[4] *Reuter v Sala*, above, at p.248; *Borrowman v Free* (1878) 4 Q.B.D. 500; *Ashmore & Son v Cox & Co.* [1899] 1 Q.B. 436 at 440; *Getreide Import Gesellschaft mbH v Itoh & Co. (America) Inc.* [1979] 1 Lloyd's Rep. 592. See above, para.8–049; below, para.12–031.

[5] *Roper v Johnson* (1873) L.R. 8 C.P. 167; *Bergheim v Blaenavon Iron Co.* (1875) L.R. 10 Q.B. 319 at 328; *Wright, Stephenson & Co. v Adams & Co.* (1908) 28 N.Z.L.R. 193.

[6] *Bergheim v Blaenavon Iron Co.*, above, at pp.326, 328; *Calaminus v Dowlais Iron Co.* (1878) 47 L.J.Q.B. 575.

[7] *Bergheim v Blaenavon Iron Co.*, above, at p.326; *Brandt v Lawrence* (1876) 1 Q.B.D. 344; *Calaminus v Dowlais Iron Co.*, above, at p.578.

[8] *Coddington v Paleologo* (1867) L.R. 2 Ex. 193 at 197.

[9] *Barningham v Smith* (1874) 31 L.T. 540 at 542, 543; *Nederlandsche Cacaofabrik v David Challen Ltd* (1898) 14 T.L.R. 322. *Cf. Ireland v Merryton Coal Co.* (1894) 21 R. 989.

[10] *Ballantine v Cramp* (1923) 129 L.T. 502. For the measure of damages, see *Barningham v Smith*, above. *Cf. Bergheim v Blaenavon Iron Co.* (1875) L.R. 10 Q.B. 319. See also *Roper v Johnson* (1873) L.R. 8 C.P. 167.

for example, be entitled to make up the deficiency by thrusting on the buyer the residue not delivered.[11] The buyer may, however, be held to have waived an excessive delivery by accepting it.[12] Circumstances may likewise exist where he could be held to have waived an insufficient delivery.[13] It is also possible that the delivery and acceptance of smaller instalments than those contracted for could indicate an extension of the time for complete performance by mutual agreement of the parties,[14] or even an agreement to abandon the undelivered balance of the instalments.[15]

8–069 **Postponement of delivery by instalments.** If, at the request (express or implied) of the buyer[16] or the seller[17] delivery of goods by instalments is postponed, the party granting the concession is not entitled to treat the contract as repudiated[18] on the ground that the goods have not been delivered or accepted within the time fixed by the contract of sale, since he will be held to have waived[19] his right to insist that the goods be delivered or accepted within the contract period. If no period of postponement is stipulated, he can give notice to the other party[20] fixing a reasonable time thereafter within which the goods are to be delivered or accepted.[21] It would seem that the party seeking the concession cannot be compelled to deliver or accept at one time the whole quantity of goods which, but for the postponement, should have been delivered in the period of postponement, but only by such instalments and at such intervals as were originally provided for.[22]

8–070 Where the parties have agreed that the delivery of goods by instalments is to be postponed while a particular state of affairs continues, the seller is bound to deliver and the buyer to accept the undelivered instalments within a reasonable period from the time when the specified state of affairs ceases to exist.[23] What is a reasonable period is a question of fact to be determined in the light of the contemplated duration of the contract, the means which

---

[11] *Barningham v Smith*, above, at p.543. See also *Nederlandsche Cacaofabrik v David Challen Ltd*, above (acceptance).
[12] In which case, the excess should be taken into account in assessing the "average" for future instalments.
[13] *Barningham v Smith*, above.
[14] *A. B. Donald Ltd v Corry* [1916] N.Z.L.R. 228.
[15] *Lockie v Walter Reid & Co. Ltd* [1916] Q.S.R. 10. But see above, para.8–031.
[16] *Hickman v Haynes* (1875) L.R. 10 C.P. 598; *Tyers v Rosedale and Ferryhill Iron Co. Ltd* (1875) L.R. 10 Ex. 195; *Levey & Co. v Goldberg* [1922] 1 K.B. 688.
[17] *Ogle v Earl Vane* (1868) L.R. 3 Q.B. 272; *Hartley v Hymans* [1920] 3 K.B. 475; *Besseler Waechter Glover & Co. v South Derwent Coal Co.* [1938] 1 K.B. 408. *Cf. Plevins v Downing* (1876) 1 C.P.D. 220.
[18] But see s.31(2) of the Act: below para.8–077.
[19] See above, para.8–030.
[20] *Cf. Tyers v Rosedale and Ferryhill Iron Co. Ltd*, above.
[21] *Hartley v Hymans*, above. See also above, para.8–030, and below, paras 16–073, 17–011, 17–012 (measure of damages).
[22] This point was left open in *Tyers v Rosedale and Ferryhill Iron Co. Ltd*, above, at p.199.
[23] *De Oleaga v West Cumberland Iron and Steel Co.* (1879) 4 Q.B.D. 472. *Cf. Ringstad v Gollin & Co. Pty Ltd* (1924) 35 C.L.R. 303 (original delivery schedule projected forward).

the seller has to make up the arrears,[24] and possibly other circumstances.[25] If, however, circumstances have so changed during the period of postponement that to treat the contract as still subsisting would be to force on the parties a radically different obligation, the contract may be discharged by frustration.[26]

Right of discharge. Whether or not one party is entitled to treat himself as discharged from further performance by reason of a default by the other party under a contract for the delivery of goods by instalments depends, in the first instance, upon whether the contract is entire or severable, *i.e.* divisible.[27] A contract is an entire contract where the liability of one party to perform is dependent upon complete performance of his obligations by the other. A contract is severable if liability under it accrues from time to time as performance of a part or parts of the contract takes place. 8–071

Entire contracts. Even though the contract is one for the delivery of goods by instalments, it may, on its true construction, be an entire and indivisible contract for the delivery of the quantity of goods stated therein.[28] Full and complete delivery of the total quantity of the goods is then prima facie a condition precedent to the liability of the buyer to pay any part of the price.[29] The mere receipt by the buyer of one or more instalments does not preclude him from rejecting those instalments if the total quantity of goods is not made up.[30] But the buyer must pay for any instalments which he has in the meantime sold and delivered to a third party[31] and for any of the goods which he retains after the lapse of a reasonable time from the end of the period stipulated for complete delivery.[32] 8–072

Each party is bound to deliver or accept the instalments when required or delivered in accordance with the terms of the contract.[33] Provided that there is nothing at the time of the tender of an instalment to show that the seller is not prepared to fulfil the contract in its entirety, the buyer is not entitled, before accepting an instalment, to wait and see whether the seller 8–073

---

[24] Or the means which the buyer has at his disposal to take delivery.

[25] *De Oleaga v West Cumberland Iron and Steel Co.*, above, at pp.475, 476.

[26] *Geipel v Smith* (1872) L.R. 7 Q.B. 404; *De Oleaga v West Cumberland Iron and Steel Co.*, above, at p.476; *Metropolitan Water Board v Dick, Kerr & Co.* [1918] A.C. 119. See also above, para.6–034; but *cf.* para.19–128.

[27] See *Chitty on Contracts* (29th ed.), Vol. 1, paras 21–027, 24–043, 24–044; Glanville Williams, 57 L.Q.R. 373–375 (1941).

[28] *Reuter v Sala* (1879) 4 C.P.D. 239. See also *Leidemann v Gray* (1857) 26 L.J. Ex. 162; *Tarling v O'Riordan* (1878) 2 L.R.Ir. 82 at 86, 87, 89.

[29] *Hungerford v Halliford* (1626) 3 Bulst. 323 at 325; *Waddington v Oliver* (1805) 2 B. & P.N.R. 61; *Shipton v Casson* (1826) 5 B. & C. 378 at 382; *Oxendale v Wetherell* (1829) 9 B. & C. 386 at 387–388.

[30] *Reuter v Sala* (1879) 4 C.P.D. 239. See also s.30(1) of the Act (above, para.8–046). *Cf. Brandt v Lawrence* (1876) 1 Q.B.D. 344.

[31] s.35 (but see s.35(6)(b)). *Cf. Nicholson v Bradfield Union* (1866) L.R. 1 Q.B. 620 at 655.

[32] s.35(4); *Oxendale v Wetherell*, above. See also s.30(1) of the Act (above, paras 8–046, 8–047).

[33] *Brandt v Lawrence* (1876) 1 Q.B.D. 344; *Tarling v O'Riordan* (1878) 2 L.R. Ir. 82.

will fulfil his obligations in respect of the delivery of further instalments.[34] In the case of an entire contract, a partial breach by the seller is treated as a total breach, and the buyer is prima facie entitled to reject the whole of the goods for any breach of condition.[35] However, if part of the goods has been accepted,[36] the right to reject the whole will be lost by virtue of section 11(4) of the 1979 Act.[37] It is only where the breach consists in an eventual short delivery that the buyer may, it seems, reject the goods, even though an instalment has been retained by him after delivery.[38]

8–074 **Severable contracts.** Contracts for the delivery of goods by instalments will more often be construed as severable (or divisible) contracts than as entire. Performance by each party of his obligations under an instalment contract may be severable[39] in the sense that a breach relating to one or more instalments must be considered in the light of its effect on the contract as a whole, so that the innocent party will not necessarily be entitled to treat the whole contract as repudiated by such a breach.[40] The 1979 Act does not define such contracts, although section 31(2) refers to "a contract for the sale of goods to be delivered by stated instalments, which are to be separately paid for" as attracting the consequences of a severable contract.[41] This definition is not, however, exhaustive,[42] and it seems clear that severability can be implied from the terms of the contract or from the circumstances.[43] In *Jackson v Rotax Motor and Cycle Co.*[44] there was a contract for the sale of 600 motor horns of slightly varying descriptions and prices on terms "Delivery as required, usual terms 2½ per cent, franco franco London." The goods were delivered in 19 cases over two months. It was held by the Court of Appeal that the words "delivery as required" showed that the parties contemplated delivery by instalments and not delivery of all the goods at one and the same time.[45] It was further held that, although there was no specific provision for separate payment of instalments, this was the intention of the parties and the contract was severable. "I find it impossible to suppose" said Farwell L.J.[46] "that the parties were intending this to be an entire contract with all the consequences that would follow." It would seem that the inference that the contract is severable will, in many cases, lead to a substantially more just result than an inference that the contract is entire.[47] However, it is

---

[34] *Brandt v Lawrence*, above, as interpreted in *Reuter v Sala* (1879) 4 C.P.D. 239.
[35] *Longbottom & Co. Ltd v Bass Walker & Co. Ltd* [1922] W.N. 245.
[36] See s.35 of the Act: below, para.12–044. But see ss.35(7), 35A (right of partial rejection).
[37] *Rosenthal & Sons Ltd v Esmail* [1965] 1 W.L.R. 1117. See below, para.12–038.
[38] See the discussion, above, para.8–047 (on s.30(1) of the Act).
[39] See *Chitty on Contracts* (29th ed.), Vol. 1, paras 21–027, 24–044.
[40] See s.31(2) of the Act: below, para.8–077.
[41] See below, para.8–077.
[42] *ibid.* See also *Longbottom & Co. Ltd v Bass Walker & Co. Ltd* [1922] W.N. 245.
[43] *Brandt v Lawrence* (1876) 1 Q.B.D. 344. See also *Peene v Taylor* (1916) 32 T.L.R. 674 (trade usage).
[44] [1910] 2 K.B. 937.
[45] See above, para.8–065.
[46] At p.947.
[47] In *Ballantine & Co. v Cramp and Bosman* (1923) 129 L.T. 502 at 504, McCardie J. said that "one must look at the practical working of this matter".

submitted that the acceptance by the buyer without objection of delivery by instalments of goods which ought under the terms of the contract to have been delivered to him by a single delivery[48] should not, without more, raise an inference that the contract should be severable.

Not the same as separate contracts. A severable contract for the delivery of goods by instalments is not the same as a series of separate contracts. "A contract for the sale of goods by instalments is a single contract, not a complex of as many contracts as there are instalments under it."[49] To a series of separate contracts quite different principles would apply. For example, a breach as to one of the contracts would never entitle the innocent party to treat the remainder as repudiated, unless there were exceptional circumstances showing the contracts to be interdependent. It has been said[50] that the test to determine whether there is one severable contract or several single contracts is "Did the parties assent to all the promises as a single whole, so that there would have been no bargain whatever if any promise or set of promises were struck out?" **8–075**

"Each delivery a separate contract." Even if the contract expressly provides that each delivery is to be treated as a separate contract, this does not create a number of separate contracts: "such clauses are subsidiary clauses, which generally have effect upon questions of performance. There is still only one contract and one contract quantity, though, for certain purposes, particular instalments or shipments and parcels may be treated in separation from the others."[51] Such a contract is normally a severable contract[52] although a breach in respect of one instalment may (though not necessarily) entitle the innocent party to treat the whole contract as discharged.[53] However, on questions of performance, such a clause may negative the possibility[54] of making up a deficiency on one instalment on the delivery of a subsequent instalment[55] or require that each instalment exactly corresponds to the contract description.[56] **8–076**

Discharge by breach. By section 31(2) of the 1979 Act: "Where there is a contract for the sale of goods to be delivered by stated instalments, which are to be separately paid for, and the seller makes defective deliveries in respect of one or more instalments, or the buyer neglects or refuses to take **8–077**

---

[48] See above, para.8–047.

[49] *Maple Flock Co. Ltd v Universal Furniture Products Co. Ltd* [1934] 1 K.B. 148 at 154; *Ross T Smyth & Co. Ltd v T D Bailey Son & Co.* [1940] 3 All E.R. 60 at 73. See also *Mersey Steel and Iron Co. v Naylor, Benzon & Co.* (1884) 9 App.Cas. 434 at 439.

[50] Williston, *Sales* (rev. ed.), para.466b.

[51] *Ross T Smyth & Co. Ltd v T D Bailey Son & Co.*, above, at p.73.

[52] *ibid.*; *Ballantine & Co. v Cramp and Bosman* (1923) 129 L.T. 502. But see *Berk & Co. v Day and White* (1897) 13 T.L.R. 475; *Goddard v Raake O/Y Osakeyhtio* (1935) 53 Ll.L.R. 208; *Cobec Brazilian Trading and Warehousing Corp. v Toepfer* [1983] 2 Lloyd's Rep. 386.

[53] *Robert A Munro & Co. Ltd v Meyer* [1930] 2 K.B. 312.

[54] See above, para.8–068.

[55] *Higgin v Pumpherston Oil Co. Ltd* (1893) 20 R. 532.

[56] *Ballantine & Co. v Cramp and Bosman*, above, at p.504.

delivery of or pay for one or more instalments, it is a question in each case depending on the terms of the contract[57] and the circumstances of the case whether the breach of contract is a repudiation of the whole contract or whether it is a severable breach giving rise to a claim for compensation[58] but not to a right to treat the whole contract as repudiated."[59] This subsection prevails over section 30(1).[60] It is, however, only a partial statement of the law applicable on this particular point to severable instalment contracts. The breach by the seller is described as "defective deliveries" and the breach by the buyer as a neglect or refusal to take delivery or pay. If strictly construed, the subsection would not embrace cases where the seller fails to make any delivery at all, or fails to make a particular delivery, or where the contract is not one for the delivery of goods by *stated* instalments, or where the instalments are not to be separately paid for. But the common law, upon which this subsection is based, applies the same principles to severable contracts in these situations.[61]

8–078 **Repudiation by renunciation.** One party will be entitled to treat an instalment contract as repudiated if the other party renounces his obligations under it, *i.e.* if by words or by conduct he makes quite plain his intention not to perform, or his inability to perform, those obligations,[62] provided that the non-performance would amount to a fundamental breach of the contract.[63] In cases of renunciation, it has been said that "the real

[57] *Cf. Ebbw Vale Steel Co. v Blaina Iron Co.* (1901) 6 Com.Cas. 33 (payment on dates stipulated made condition precedent to future deliveries).

[58] The word "compensation" covers a claim by the seller for an unpaid instalment or instalments, as well as a claim for damages: *Workman Clark & Co. Ltd v Brazileno* [1908] 1 K.B. 968 at 978. *Sed quaere* whether the breach gives rise to such a claim.

[59] *cf.* Vienna Convention on Contracts for the International Sale of Goods, Art. 73 (above, para.1–024).

[60] *Regent OHG Aisenstadt und Barig v Francesco of Jermyn Street Ltd* [1981] 3 All E.R. 327; above, para.8–048.

[61] See *Clarke v Burn* (1866) 14 L.T. 439; *Coddington v Paleologo* (1867) L.R. 2 Ex. 193; *Leeson v North British Oil and Candle Co. Ltd* (1874) Ir.R. 8 C.L. 309; *Jackson v Rotax Motor and Cycle Co.* [1910] 2 K.B. 937; *Edilson v Joyce* [1917] N.Z.L.R. 648 at 651; *Payzu Ltd v Saunders* [1919] 2 K.B. 581; *Continental Contractors Ltd v Medway Oil and Storage Co. Ltd* (1925) 27 Ll.L.R. 124 at 127, 131, 134; *Robert A. Munro Ltd v Meyer* [1930] 2 K.B. 312; *Ross T Smyth & Co. Ltd v T D Bailey, Son & Co.* [1940] 3 All E.R. 60.

[62] *Spettabile Consorzio Veneziano di Armamento di Navigazione v Northumberland Shipbuilding Co. Ltd* (1919) 121 L.T. 628 at 634–635; *Maple Flock Co. v Universal Furniture Products (Wembley) Ltd* [1934] 1 K.B. 148 at 157; *Universal Cargo Carriers' Corporation v Citati* [1957] 2 Q.B. 401 at 436 (affirmed in part and reversed in part on different grounds [1957] 1 W.L.R. 979; [1958] 2 Q.B. 254); *The Mihalis Angelos* [1971] 1 Q.B. 164 at 196; *Woodar Investment Development Ltd v Wimpey Construction UK Ltd* [1980] 1 W.L.R. 277 at 287; *Anchor Line Ltd v Keith Rowell Ltd* [1980] 2 Lloyd's Rep. 351 at 353; *Chilean Nitrate Sale Corp. v Marine Transportation Co. Ltd* [1982] 1 Lloyd's Rep. 570 at 580; *Texaco Ltd v Eurogulf Shipping Co. Ltd* [1987] 2 Lloyd's Rep. 541 at 544; *Aktion Maritime Corp. of Liberia v S. Kasmas Brothers Ltd* [1987] 1 Lloyd's Rep. 283 at 286; *Nottingham Building Soc. v Eurodynamics Systems* [1995] F.S.R. 605. See also *Forslind v Becheley Crundall*, 1922 S.C.(HL) 173 at 179.

[63] *Federal Commerce & Navigation Co. Ltd v Molena Alpha Inc.* [1979] A.C. 757; *Afovos Shipping Co. SA v R. Pagnan & Filli* [1983] 1 W.L.R. 195 at 203. On fundamental breach, see the cases cited in para.8–080, nn.77, 78.

matter for consideration is whether the acts or conduct of the [party in default] do or do not amount to an intimation of an intention to abandon and altogether to refuse performance of the contract."[64] This test is equally applicable to a default in delivery on the part of the seller and to a default in acceptance or payment on the part of the buyer.[65] In *Withers v Reynolds*[66] the buyer impliedly agreed to pay for each instalment on delivery, but fell into arrear in paying for several instalments and eventually insisted on the seller allowing him credit for the goods delivered. It was held that the seller was entitled to treat this conduct as a repudiation of the contract and to refuse to deliver further instalments. On the other hand, in *Freeth v Burr*,[67] where the buyer refused to pay for one instalment of several deliveries of iron under the erroneous impression that he was entitled to withhold payment as a set-off against damages for late delivery of an earlier instalment by the seller, but still urged the delivery of further instalments, it was held that the seller was not discharged. Also in the leading case of *Mersey Steel and Iron Co. v Naylor Benzon & Co.*[68] where the buyer refused, pending the hearing of a bankruptcy petition against the seller, to pay for two instalments already delivered as he had been erroneously advised not to do so without leave of the court, but still expressed his willingness to accept delivery and make the payments if possible, the House of Lords

---

[64] *Freeth v Burr* (1874) L.R. 9 C.P. 208 at 213. See also *Mersey Steel and Iron Co. v Naylor Benzon & Co.* (1884) 9 App.Cas. 434 at 438–439; *Anchor Line Ltd v Rowell Ltd* [1980] 2 Lloyd's Rep. 351; *Chilean Nitrate Sales Corp. v Marine Transportation Co. Ltd* [1980] 1 Lloyd's Rep. 638; *Aktion Maritime Corp. of Liberia v S. Kasmas & Brothers Ltd* [1987] 1 Lloyd's Rep. 283 at 286.

[65] See the cases cited in nn.66, 68 (*infra*).

[66] (1831) 2 B. & Ad. 882. See also *Morgan v Bain* (1874) L.R. 10 C.P. 15 (buyer informs seller that he is insolvent); *Leeson v North British Oil and Candle Co. Ltd* (1874) Ir. R. 8 C.L. 309 (seller informs buyer he cannot deliver balance of instalments); *Bloomer v Bernstein* (1874) L.R. 9 C.P. 588 (failure to take up bill of lading for second instalment and insolvency of buyer); *Booth v Bowron* (1892) 8 T.L.R. 641 (cash on delivery, but buyer insists on credit); *Berk & Co. Ltd v Day and White* (1897) 13 T.L.R. 475 (buyer ships goods to non-contract destination); *Braithwaite v Foreign Hardwood Co.* [1905] 2 K.B. 543 (buyer refuses to accept first instalment); *Warinco AG v Samor SpA* [1979] 1 Lloyd's Rep. 450 (buyer refuses to accept first instalment and any future instalment of same quality); *Metro Meat Ltd v Fares Rural Co. Pty Ltd* [1985] 2 Lloyd's Rep. 13 (refusal by seller to discuss shipment of last two of five instalments). *Cf.* Vienna Convention on Contracts for the International Sale of Goods, Arts 71–73 (above, para.1–024).

[67] (1874) L.R. 9 C.P. 208.

[68] (1884) 9 App.Cas. 434. See also *Kent v Godts* (1855) 26 L.T.(O.S.) 88 (buyer refuses to accept instalment in erroneous belief that it is of inferior quality): *Corcoran v Proser* (1873) 22 W.L.R. 222 (buyer refuses to pay price without deduction for short weight); *Re Phoenix Bessemer Steel Co.* (1876) 4 Ch.D. 108 (request for credit by buyer after meeting of his creditors); *Dominion Coal Co. Ltd v Dominion Iron and Steel Co. Ltd* [1909] A.C. 293 (rightful rejection of one instalment by buyer and notice to seller that future deliveries would not be accepted); *Household Machines v Cosmos Exports* [1947] K.B. 217 (buyer refuses to pay until seller makes future deliveries); *Bunge GmbH v CCV Landbouwbelang G.A.* [1980] 1 Lloyd's Rep. 458 (buyer imposes time-limit not provided for in contract); *Dalkia Utilities Services Plc v Celtech International Ltd* [2006] EWHC 63 (Comm), [2006] 1 Lloyd's Rep. 599 at [134] (mixed message). Contrast *Continental Contractors Ltd v Medway Oil and Storage Co. Ltd* (1925) 23 Ll.L.R. 124 at 131 (party willing to perform but will never be able to do so).

refused to ascribe to the buyer's conduct, under these circumstances, the character of a renunciation of the contract. The courts are inclined to hold that a genuine mistake of fact[69] or of law[70] or as to the construction of the contract[71] does not amount to a repudiation of it; and even the commencement of an action by one party claiming rescission of the contract does not necessarily entitle the other to treat the contract as repudiated, as the action may be brought simply to determine the respective rights of the parties.[72]

8–079 **Repudiation by inability to perform.** Where one party has, by his own act or default, finally and completely disabled himself from performing his obligations under an instalment contract, the other party will be entitled to treat the contract as repudiated,[73] provided that the resulting non-performance would amount to a fundamental breach.[74] Inability to perform is, however, less easy to establish than renunciation. It is not sufficient for the innocent party to show that he had reasonable grounds to believe that the other party would be unable to perform. He will only be justified in treating the contract as repudiated if the other party is in fact unable to perform.[75]

8–080 **Repudiation by failure of performance.** Failure of performance by one party, even in the absence of an express or implied renunciation of the contract,[76] will entitle the other party to treat an instalment contract as

---

[69] *Kent v Godts*, above; *Peter Dumenil & Co. Ltd v James Ruddin Ltd* [1953] 1 W.L.R. 815; *Alfred C Toepfer v Peter Cremer* [1975] 2 Lloyd's Rep. 118.
[70] *Freeth v Burr*, above; *Mersey Steel and Iron Co. v Naylor Benzon & Co.*, above; *Ross T. Smyth v T D Bailey, Son & Co.* [1940] 3 All E.R. 60.
[71] *James Shaffer Ltd v Findlay Durham and Brodie* [1953] 1 W.L.R. 106; *Sweet and Maxwell Ltd v Universal News Services Ltd* [1964] 2 Q.B. 699; *Woodar Investment Development Ltd v Wimpey Construction U.K. Ltd* [1980] 1 W.L.R. 277; *Telfair Shipping Corp. v Athos Shipping Corp. SA* [1983] 1 Lloyd's Rep. 127; *The Design Company v Elizabeth King*, unreported, July 7, 1992, CA; *Vaswani v Italian Motors (Sales and Services) Ltd* [1996] 1 W.L.R. 270. Contrast *Federal Commerce & Navigation Co. Ltd v Molena Alpha Inc.* [1979] A.C. 757.
[72] *Spettabile Consorzio Veneziano di Armamento di Navigazione v Northumberland Shipbuilding Co. Ltd* (1919) 121 L.T. 628; *Woodar Investment Development Ltd v Wimpey Construction U.K. Ltd*, above.
[73] *Keys v Harwood* (1846) 2 C.B. 905; *Lovelock v Franklyn* (1846) 8 Q.B. 371; *O'Neil v Armstrong* [1895] 2 Q.B. 418; *Ogdens Ltd v Nelson* [1905] A.C. 109; *Measures Bros Ltd v Measures* [1910] 2 Ch. 248; *Omnium D'Enterprises v Sutherland* [1919] 1 K.B. 618; *British & Beningtons Ltd v NW Cachar Tea Co.* [1923] A.C. 48 at 72; *Universal Cargo Carriers Corporation v Citati* [1957] 2 Q.B. 401 (affirmed in part [1957] 1 W.L.R. 979 and reversed in part [1958] 2 Q.B. 254); *Texaco Ltd v Eurogulf Shipping Co. Ltd* [1987] 2 Lloyd's Rep. 541 at 544; *Smith's Leading Cases* (13th ed.), Vol. 2, p.40. *Cf. Hamlyn & Co. v Wood* [1891] 2 Q.B. 488.
[74] *Afovos Shipping Co. SA v R. Pagnan & F.lli* [1983] 1 W.L.R. 195 at 203. For fundamental breach, see para.8–080, nn.77, 78.
[75] *Universal Cargo Carriers Corporation v Citati* [1957] 2 Q.B. 401 at 449–450; *Continental Contractors Ltd v Medway Oil and Storage Co. Ltd* (1925) 23 Ll.L.Rep. 124 at 128.
[76] *Ross T Smyth & Co. Ltd v T D Bailey, Son & Co.* [1940] 3 All E.R. 60 at 72. The same set of facts may give rise to a repudiation on the ground of failure of performance and an implied renunciation: see *Mersey Steel and Iron Co. v Naylor Benzon & Co.* (1884) 9 App.Cas. 434 at 441, 444.

repudiated, provided that the breach is fundamental, that is to say, provided that it goes "to the root or essence of the contract"[77] or deprives the innocent party of substantially the whole benefit which it was intended that he should receive from the contract.[78] In *Simpson v Crippin*,[79] the buyer took delivery of less than one-third of the goods comprised in the first instalment and the seller purported to treat this as a repudiation of the contract. It was held that he was not entitled to do so. On the other hand, in *Robert A. Munro Ltd v Meyer*,[80] after nearly half the total quantity of goods had been delivered by instalments, they were found to be seriously defective. The buyer was held to be entitled to treat himself as discharged by reason of the serious and persistent nature of the breach. Whether or not the contract has been repudiated by failure of performance is a question of fact in each case.

The most relevant factors in determining whether the breach is or is not of sufficient gravity have been said to be: "First, the ratio quantitatively which the breach bears to the whole, and secondly the degree of probability **8–081**

---

[77] *Poussard v Spiers* (1876) 1 Q.B.D. 410 at 414; *Honck v Muller* (1881) 7 Q.B.D. 92 at 100. *Mersey Steel and Iron Co. v Naylor Benzon & Co.* (above), at pp.443–444; *Robert A. Munro Ltd v Meyer* [1930] 2 K.B. 312; *Heyman v Darwins Ltd* [1942] A.C. 356 at 397; *Suisse Atlantique Société d'Armement Maritime SA v NV Kolen Centrale* [1967] 1 A.C. 361 at 442; *Decro-Wall International SA v Practitioners in Marketing Ltd* [1971] 1 W.L.R. 361 at 374; *Cehave NV v Bremer Handelsgesellschaft mbH* [1976] Q.B. 44 at 60, 73; *Federal Commerce & Navigation Co. Ltd v Molena Alpha Inc.* [1979] A.C. 757 at 779. See also *Chitty on Contracts* (29th ed.), Vol. 1, para.24–040. *Cf.* Vienna Convention on Contracts for the International Sale of Goods, Art. 25 (above, para.1–024).

[78] *Hongkong Fir Shipping Co. Ltd v Kawasaki Kisen Kaisha Ltd* [1962] 2 Q.B. 26 at 66; *Cehave NV v Bremer Handelsgesellschaft mbH*, above, at p.82; *United Scientific Holdings Ltd v Burnley B.C.* [1978] A.C. 904 at 928, 945; *Federal Commerce & Navigation Co. Ltd v Molena Alpha Inc.*, above, at p.783; *Photo Production Ltd v Securicor Transport Ltd* [1980] A.C. 827 at 849; *Nitrate Corp. of Chile Ltd v Pansuiza Compania de Navegacion* [1980] 1 Lloyd's Rep. 638 (affirmed [1982] 1 Lloyd's Rep. 570).

[79] (1872) L.R. 8 Q.B. 14 (*Cf. infra*, n.80). See also *Jonassohn v Young* (1863) 4 B. & S. 296 (shipment of inferior goods and detention of buyer's ship); *Clarke v Burn* (1866) 14 L.T. 439 (late delivery); *Dickinson v Fanshaw* (1892) 8 T.L.R. 271 (failure to take full delivery); *Payzu Ltd v Saunders* [1919] 2 K.B. 581 (failure to pay punctually); *Sanderson v Armour*, 1921 S.C. 18 (one instalment defective); *Taylor v Oakes, Roncoroni & Co.* (1922) 127 L.T. 267 (*ibid.*); *Maple Flock Co. Ltd v Universal Furniture Products (Wembley) Ltd* [1934] 1 K.B. 148 (*ibid.*); *Ross T Smyth & Co. Ltd v T D Bailey, Son & Co.*, above (tender by seller of amended invoice); *Amos & Wood Ltd v Kaprow* (1948) 64 T.L.R. 110 (late payment).

[80] [1930] 2 K.B. 312. See also *Hoare v Rennie* (1859) 5 H. & N. 19 (short delivery of first instalment); *Honck v Muller* (1881) 7 Q.B.D. 92 (failure by buyer to take delivery of first instalment). There has been much discussion as to the extent to which these two cases can be reconciled with *Simpson v Crippin*, above, but, since the Sale of Goods Act 1893, they must all be regarded as decisions on their own facts: see *Mersey Steel & Iron Co. v Naylor Benzon & Co.*, above, at pp.444–445, 446–447. See further *Coddington v Paleologo* (1867) L.R. 2 Ex. 193 (late delivery manifest at commencement of the delivery period); *Millar's Karri and Jarrah Co. v Weddel Turner & Co.* (1908) 100 L.T. 128 (two shipments, one not in accordance with contract).

or improbability that such a breach will be repeated."[81] The importance of the second factor was emphasised by Bigham J. in *Millar's Karri and Jarrah Co. v Weddel, Turner & Co.*,[82] where he said: "If the breach is of such a kind, or takes place in such circumstances as reasonably to lead to the inference that similar breaches will be committed in relation to subsequent deliveries, the whole contract may there and then be regarded as repudiated and may be rescinded. If, for instance, a buyer fails to pay for one delivery in such circumstances as to lead to the inference that he will not be able to pay for subsequent deliveries[83] ; or if a seller delivers goods differing from the requirements of the contract, and does so in such circumstances as to lead to the inference that he cannot, or will not, deliver any other kind of goods in the future, the other contracting party will be under no obligation to wait and see what may happen; he can at once cancel the contract and rid himself of the difficulty." It has also been said that, the further the parties have proceeded with the performance of the contract, the less likely it is that one party will be entitled to claim that it has been discharged by a single breach,[84] and that the degree to which delivery of one instalment is linked to another is a relevant factor.[85]

8–082 **Effect of repudiation.** Even though the contract provides that each instalment is to be separately paid for, or that each delivery is to be treated as a separate contract,[86] in the event of a repudiation by one party accepted by the other,[87] the innocent party is entitled to refuse all further performance if tendered and to treat himself as discharged from further liability.[88] Notwithstanding that the buyer has received and accepted an earlier instalment, he is entitled to reject further goods delivered and to treat the whole contract as repudiated.[89] Moreover, it may well be that, if the

[81] *Maple Flock Co. Ltd v Universal Furniture Products (Wembley) Ltd* [1934] 1 K.B. 148 at 157. *Cf.* Vienna Convention on Contracts for the International Sale of Goods, Art. 25 (above, para.1–024).

[82] (1908) 100 L.T. 128 at 129.

[83] See below, para.8–086.

[84] *Cornwall v Henson* [1900] 2 Ch. 298 at 304. But see *Hoare v Rennie* (1859) 4 H. & N. 19; *Simpson v Crippin* (1872) L.R. 8 Q.B. 14; *Honck v Muller* (1881) 7 Q.B.D. 92; above, para.8–079, n.71.

[85] *Warinco AG v Samor SpA* [1977] 2 Lloyd's Rep. 582 at 588 (revd. [1979] 1 Lloyd's Rep. 450).

[86] See above, para.8–076.

[87] The innocent party is not bound to accept the repudiation, but may treat the contract as continuing. The seller may, in certain circumstances, complete performance of the contract and sue for the price: *White and Carter (Councils) Ltd v McGregor* [1962] A.C. 413; *Tredegar Iron and Coal Co. Ltd v Hawthorn Bros & Co.* (1902) 18 T.L.R. 716; *Anglo-African Shipping Co. of New York Inc. v J. Mortner Ltd* [1962] 1 Lloyd's Rep. 81 at 610; *Decro-Wall International SA v Practitioners in Marketing Ltd* [1971] 1 W.L.R. 361; *Gator Shipping Corp. v Trans-Asiatic Oil Ltd SA* [1978] 2 Lloyd's Rep. 357. But see the qualifications to this principle referred to in paras 16–023, 20–126, below, and in *Chitty on Contracts* (29th ed.), Vol. 1, para.24–011.

[88] See the cases cited in nn.77, 78, above.

[89] *Tarling v O'Riordan* (1878) 2 L.R.Ir. 82; *Molling & Co. v Dean & Sons Ltd* (1901) 18 T.L.R. 217; *Jackson v Rotax Motor and Cycle Co. Ltd* [1910] 2 K.B. 937; *Rosenthal & Sons Ltd v Esmail* [1965] 1 W.L.R. 1117 at 1132. The provisions of s.11(4) of the 1979 Act (below, para.12–038) do not apply where the contract is severable.

instalments already delivered can be regarded as parts of an indivisible whole, *e.g.* individual volumes of a set of books, parts of a machine, or a suit of clothes,[90] then the buyer will be entitled to rescind the contract *ab initio* by returning the instalments already delivered and recovering the whole, or any part, of the price paid.[91]

Effect of non-repudiatory breach. The effect of a non-repudiatory breach was thus described by Brett J. in his dissenting judgment[92] in *Reuter v Sala*[93] : "Where in a mercantile contract of purchase and sale of goods to be delivered and accepted the terms of the contract allow the delivery to be by successive deliveries, the failure of the seller or buyer to fulfil his part in any one or more of those deliveries does not absolve the other party from tendering or accepting in the case of other subsequent deliveries, although the contract was for the purchase and sale of a specified quantity of goods, and although the failure of the party suing as to one or more deliveries was incurable in the sense that he never could fulfil his undertaking to accept or deliver the whole of the specified quantity. The reasons . . . are that such a breach by the party suing is a breach of only a part of the consideration moving from him; that such a breach can be compensated in damages without any necessity for annulling the whole contract, that the true construction of such contracts is that it is not a condition precedent to the obligation to tender or accept a part, that the other party should have been or should always be ready, and willing, and able to accept or tender the whole." Unless the breach is such as to entitle him to treat the contract as repudiated, a buyer is not entitled to refuse to accept and pay for an instalment because of a defect in or short delivery of an earlier instalment[94]; nor can he insist on waiting to see whether proper delivery of subsequent instalments will take place before he accepts and pays for an instalment.[95] 8–083

The contract is also severable in the sense that a breach of condition in respect of any particular instalment normally[96] entitles the buyer to reject that instalment, and he can exercise this right of rejection despite having accepted an earlier instalment.[97] Where default has been made in the delivery or acceptance of a particular instalment, it has been suggested that 8–084

---

[90] *Honck v Muller* (1881) 7 Q.B.D. 92 at 99 (assuming each part is to be separately paid for).
[91] It could, however, be argued that, by making the contract severable, the buyer could rescind only as to future instalments.
[92] Cited with approval by Farwell L.J. in *Jackson v Rotax Motor and Cycle Co.* [1910] 2 K.B. 937 at 947.
[93] (1879) 4 C.P.D. 239 at 256.
[94] *Brandt v Lawrence* (1876) 1 Q.B.D. 344; *L. Osborn & Co. Ltd v Davidson Bros* [1911] V.L.R. 416. In this respect, s.30(1) of the 1979 Act must be read subject to s.31(2): see *Regent OHG Aisenstadt und Barig v Francesco of Jermyn Street Ltd* [1981] 3 All E.R. 327.
[95] *Howell v Evans* (1926) 134 L.T. 570.
[96] But see s.15A of the 1979 Act: below, para.12–024.
[97] *Tarling v O'Riordan* (1878) 2 L.R.Ir. 82; *Molling & Co. v Dean & Sons Ltd* (1901) 18 T.L.R. 217; *Jackson v Rotax Motor and Cycle Co. Ltd* [1910] 2 K.B. 937; *Rosenthal & Sons Ltd v Esmail* [1965] 1 W.L.R. 1117 at 1132. The provisions of s.11(4) of the 1979 Act do not apply where the contract is severable. See also s.35A(2).

the effect of such a default (assuming that it does not amount to a repudiation of the whole contract) is to strike that instalment out of the contract, which is *pro tanto* discharged.[98] If such be the case, the seller cannot afterwards claim to deliver or the buyer claim to have the instalment in respect of which default has been made, the sole remedy of the innocent party lying in damages.[99] However, it is submitted that the seller is entitled to cure the default by delivering a substitute instalment in conformity with the contract, provided that he does so within the time limited for delivery of that instalment.[1] Moreover, if it is the case that the effect of the default is to strike the instalment out of the contract, which is *pro tanto* discharged, it does not follow that, in applying section 31(2),[2] the default is to be ignored for the purpose of deciding whether or not there has been a repudiation of the whole contract. The fact that the innocent party has received no part of the performance promised to him in respect of that instalment should, it is submitted, be taken into account in appropriate cases[3] to determine the proportion of the contract as a whole which the party in default has failed to perform.

8–085 **Default in payment.** Where there is a contract for the sale and delivery of goods by instalments which are to be separately paid for, then, unless otherwise agreed,[4] delivery of an instalment and payment of its price are concurrent conditions.[5] But payment for instalments previously delivered is not normally[6] a condition precedent or concurrent condition to the liability of the seller to deliver subsequent instalments,[7] although an unqualified refusal to pay may amount to a repudiation of the contract by the buyer.[8] However, if the contract of sale is not severable, the seller may usually exercise his right of lien or his right to withhold delivery of future instalments until he is paid for instalments already delivered.[9]

8–086 **Insolvency of buyer.** The insolvency of the buyer does not in itself amount to a repudiation of the contract[10] ; but "when one contracting party gives notice to the other that he is insolvent, and does nothing more, the

---

[98] *Simpson v Crippin* (1872) 42 L.J.Q.B. 28 at 33 (*cf.* L.R. 8 Q.B. 14 at 17); *Barningham v Smith* (1874) 31 L.T. 540 at 543; *De Oleaga v West Cumberland Iron and Steel Co*. (1879) 4 Q.B.D. 472 at 475. *Sed quaere* whether this is always the case.
[99] *De Oleaga v West Cumberland Iron and Steel Co.*, above, at p.475.
[1] See above, para.8–052; below, para.12–031.
[2] See above, para.8–077.
[3] See above, para.8–080.
[4] Terms of credit may be specially agreed: see below, para.9–061.
[5] It is submitted that s.28 of the 1979 Act applies in this situation.
[6] *Cf. Ebbw Vale Steel Co. v Blaina Iron Co.* (1901) 6 Com.Cas. 33 (express provision).
[7] *Clarke v Burn* (1866) 14 L.T. 239; *Re Edwards* (1873) L.R. 8 Ch.App. 289 at 293; *Mersey Steel and Iron Co. v Naylor Benzon & Co*. (1884) 9 App.Cas. 434; *Longbottom & Co. Ltd v Bass, Walker & Co.* [1922] W.N. 245 at 246. See below, para.15–042.
[8] *Withers v Reynolds* (1831) 2 B. & Ad. 882; *Booth v Bowron* (1892) 8 T.L.R. 641.
[9] *Re Edwards*, above; *Longbottom & Co. v Bass Walker & Co.*, above; *Re Grainex Canada Ltd* (1987) 34 D.L.R. (4th) 646; see below, paras 15–028, 15–042.
[10] *Re Edwards* (1873) L.R. 8 Ch.App. 289 at 294; *Morgan v Bain* (1874) L.R. 10 C.P. 15 at 26.

other party has a right to assume that he intends to abandon the contract"[11] and the seller may accept this as discharging him from further liability under the contract. The insolvency of the buyer will, however, in any event entitle the seller, notwithstanding he may have agreed to allow credit for the goods, to refuse to deliver any more goods under the contract until the price of the goods not yet delivered is tendered to him; and, if a debt is due to him for goods already delivered, he is entitled to refuse to deliver any more till he is paid the debt due for those already delivered, as well as the price of those still to be delivered.[12] But these rules only apply where there is an admitted insolvency: the summoning of an informal meeting of the principal creditors of the buyer, with a view to making some arrangement with regard to his financial difficulties, has been held not to amount to a declaration of insolvency and entitle the seller to refuse further deliveries except upon immediate cash payments.[13]

Measure of damages. The severable nature of the contract is also reflected in the way that damages are to be calculated.[14] In the case of instalment contracts, damages are prima facie to be calculated by reference to the time at which each successive instalment ought to have been delivered or accepted.[15] This principle is, however, subject to the duty of the party not in default to mitigate his loss.[16] 8–087

7. Clauses Excusing Delivery

***Force majeure* clauses.**[17] By a clause in the contract of sale, the seller[18] may be entitled[19] to suspend delivery, or extend the time for delivery or even cancel the whole or part of the contract upon the happening of a 8–088

---

[11] *Morgan v Bain*, above, at p.26. See also *Re Edwards*, above, at p.294; *Re Nathan* (1879) 10 Ch.D. 586 at 590.

[12] *Re Edwards*, above, at p.293. But *cf. Merchant Banking Co. Ltd v Phoenix Bessemer Steel Co.* (1877) 5 Ch.D. 205 at 220 (instalment already paid for) and Insolvency Act 1986, ss. 233, 372 (supplies of gas, water, electricity, etc.). See also below, paras 15–028, 15–042 (lien).

[13] *Re Phoenix Bessemer Steel Co.* (1876) 4 Ch.D. 108. See also *Mess v Duffus & Co.* (1901) 6 Com.Cas. 165 and below, para.15–025.

[14] See below, paras 16–071, 17–008.

[15] *Brown v Muller* (1872) L.R. 7 Ex. 319; *Roper v Johnson* (1873) L.R. 8 C.P. 167; *Re Voss* (1873) L.R. 16 Eq. 155; *Barningham v Smith* (1874) 31 L.T. 540. Contrast *Ogle v Earl Vane* (1868) L.R. Q.B. 272; *Tyers v Rosedale and Ferryhill Iron Co.* (1873) L.R. 8 Ex. 305, (1875) L.R. 10 Ex. 195; *Hickman v Haynes* (1875) L.R. 10 C.P. 598. See below, paras 16–071, 17–008.

[16] See below, paras 16–052, 16–081, 17–014.

[17] See Treitel, *Frustration and Force Majeure* (2nd ed., 2004); McKendrick (ed.) *Force Majeure and Frustration of Contract* (2nd ed., 1995).

[18] A *force majeure* clause may also be expressed to operate in favour of the buyer, or of both parties.

[19] The contract may even be cancelled automatically: *Continental Grain Export Corp. v STM Grain Ltd* [1979] 2 Lloyd's Rep. 460; *Bremer Handelsgesellschaft mbH v Finagrain SA* [1981] 2 Lloyd's Rep. 259; *Pagnan SpA v Tradax Ocean Transportation SA* [1987] 2 Lloyd's Rep. 342.

specified event or events beyond his control. Clauses of this type are often referred to as "*force majeure*" clauses, and they are frequently found in commercial contracts. Such clauses may assume a variety of forms, and a term "the usual force majeure clauses to apply" has been held void for uncertainty.[20] *Force majeure* clauses have been said not to be exemption clauses,[21] although it is difficult to draw any clear line of demarcation between the two types of clause,[22] since the effect of each may be to relieve a contracting party of an obligation or liability to which he would otherwise be subject, and *force majeure* clauses may nevertheless be affected by the Unfair Contract Terms Act 1977.[23]

8–089 Frequently a number of events are specified and then followed by the words "or any other causes beyond our control". Such general words in a commercial document are prima facie to be construed as having their natural and larger meaning and are not limited to events *ejusdem generis* with those previously enumerated.[24] Moreover, the words "beyond our control" will normally be construed to refer, not only to the unspecified cases, but also to the specific events.[25] Clauses which excuse performance in general terms may be construed as *force majeure* clauses. Thus a clause which provides that the date of delivery is approximate only, and that the seller is not to be responsible for any delay or non-delivery, does not confer upon him an absolute discretion whether to deliver or not and so render the contract nugatory, but only to excuse him if non-delivery is due to a cause outside his control.[26] In the absence of a clear indication to the contrary,[27] a *force majeure* clause will not be construed to cover events brought about by a party's negligence or wilful default, even though a specified event would in other contexts not be limited to an event occurring without negligence.[28]

---

[20] *British Electrical and Associated Industries (Cardiff) Ltd v Patley Pressings Ltd* [1953] 1 W.L.R. 280. But such a term could refer to clauses used in a particular trade.

[21] *Fairclough, Dodd & Jones Ltd v J.H. Vantol Ltd* [1957] 1 W.L.R. 136 at 143. See also *Trade and Transport Inc. v Iino Kaiun Kaisha Ltd* [1973] 1 W.L.R. 210 at 230–231; *The Super Servant Two* [1990] 1 Lloyd's Rep. 1 at 7, 12. *Cf. Cero Navigation Corp. v Jean Lion & Cie* [2000] 1 Lloyd's Rep. 292 at 299.

[22] See Treitel, *op. cit.*, para.12–018; McKendrick (ed.), *op. cit*.

[23] See below, para.8–104.

[24] *Chandris v Isbrandtsen-Moller Co. Inc.* [1951] 1 K.B. 240 at 245–246; *PJ Van der Zijden Wildhandel NV v Tucker & Cross Ltd* [1975] 2 Lloyd's Rep. 240; *Navrom v Callitsis Ship Management SA* [1987] 2 Lloyd's Rep. 276 at 281 (affirmed [1988] 2 Lloyd's Rep. 416). See also *Anderson v Anderson* [1895] 1 Q.B. 749 at 753; *Larsen v Sylvester* [1908] A.C. 295. Contrast *Thorman v Dowgate S.S. Co.* [1910] 1 K.B. 410; *Jenkins v Watford* (1918) 87 L.J.K.B. 136; *Sonat Offshore SA v Amerada Hess Development Ltd* [1988] 1 Lloyd's Rep. 145 at 149, 158, 163.

[25] *Frontier International Shipping Corp. v Swissmarine Corp. Inc.* [2004] EWHC 8 (Comm), [2005] 1 Lloyd's Rep. 390 at [11].

[26] *Barnett v Ira L and AC Berk Pty Ltd* (1952) 52 S.R. (N.S.W.) 268. See also *Hartwells of Oxford Ltd v B.M.T.A.* [1951] Ch.50; *Monkland v Jack Barclay Ltd* [1951] 2 K.B. 252.

[27] *Gyllenhammar & Partners International Ltd v Sour Brodogradevna Industrija* [1989] 2 Lloyd's Rep. 403 at 406.

[28] *Sonat Offshore SA v Amerada Hess Development Ltd* [1988] 1 Lloyd's Rep. 145; *The Super Servant Two* [1990] 1 Lloyd's Rep. 1.

A *force majeure* clause which is prefaced by such words as "while every effort will be made to carry out this contract" will be rendered nugatory unless the seller has in fact made reasonable efforts to ensure that the contract is performed.[29] 8–090

Burden of proof. The burden of proof is on the seller to prove the facts bringing the case within the clause.[30] He must therefore prove the occurrence of one of the events referred to in the clause and that he has been prevented, hindered or delayed (as the case may be)[31] from performing the contract by reason of that event.[32] He must further prove; (i) that his non-performance was due to circumstances beyond his control; and (ii) that there were no reasonable steps that he could have taken to avoid or mitigate the event or its consequences.[33] However, in *Trade and Transport Inc. v Iino Kaiun Kaisha Ltd*[34] where the clause in question referred to "unavoidable hindrances", Kerr J. stated that a party would be debarred from relying upon such a clause if the existence of facts which show that the clause was bound to operate should reasonably have been known to that party prior to the conclusion of the contract, and would have been expected by the other party to be so known. But subsequently in *Channel Island Ferries Ltd v Sealink United Kingdom Ltd*,[35] Parker L.J. expressed doubts[36] whether, because of pre-contract improvidence, a party would be disabled from relying on a *force majeure* clause, even if such clause would otherwise have applied; there was no principle of law that a party who entered into a contract could not rely on its terms because he was improvident in entering into it. It may, nevertheless, be argued that the parties to a contract cannot 8–091

---

[29] *B & S Contracts and Design Ltd v Victor Green Publications Ltd* [1984] I.C.R. 419.

[30] *Channel Island Ferries Ltd v Sealink UK Ltd* [1988] 1 Lloyd's Rep. 323 at 327.

[31] See below, paras 8–092, 8–093, 8–094.

[32] *PJ Van der Zijden Wildhandel NV v Tucker & Cross Ltd* [1975] 2 Lloyd's Rep. 240 at 242; *Tradax Export SA v André et Cie* [1976] 1 Lloyd's Rep. 416 at 423, 425; *Bremer Handelsgesellschaft mbH v Vanden Avenne-Izegem PVBA* [1978] 2 Lloyd's Rep. 109 at 114; *Avimex SA v Dewulf & Cie* [1979] 2 Lloyd's Rep. 57; *André & Cie SA v Etablissements Michel Blanc et Fils* [1979] 2 Lloyd's Rep. 427; *Continental Grain Export Corp. v STM Grain Ltd* [1979] 2 Lloyd's Rep. 460; *Toepfer v Schwarze* [1980] 1 Lloyd's Rep. 385; *Thomas P. Gonzalez Corp. v Millers Mühle, Müller GmbH* [1980] 1 Lloyd's Rep. 445; *Raiffeisen Hauptgenossenschaft v Louis Dreyfus & Co. Ltd* [1981] 1 Lloyd's Rep. 345; *Pancommerce SA v Veecheema BV* [1983] 2 Lloyd's Rep. 304; *Hoecheong Products Co. Ltd v Cargill Hong Kong Ltd* [1995] 1 W.L.R. 404 at 409; *Agrokor AG v Tradigrain SA* [2000] 1 Lloyd's Rep. 497 at 500.

[33] *B & S Contracts and Designs Ltd v Victor Green Publications Ltd* [1984] I.C.R. 419; *Channel Island Ferries Ltd v Sealink (UK) Ltd* [1988] 1 Lloyd's Rep. 323 at 327, 328; *Hoecheong Products Co. Ltd v Cargill Hong Kong Ltd*, above, at p.409; *Mamidoil-Jetoil Greek Petroleum Co SA v Okta Crude Oil Refunery AD (No.3)* [2003] 2 Lloyd's Rep. 635 at [32].

[34] [1973] 1 W.L.R. 210 at 224–227. See also *Ciampa v British India Steam Navigation Co. Ltd* [1915] 2 K.B. 774 at 779; *Taylor v Lewis Ltd* (1927) 28 Ll.L.Rep. 329 at 332; *Safadi v Western Assurance Co.* (1933) 46 Ll.L.Rep. 140 at 143. *Cf. Steamship "Induna" Co. Ltd v British Phosphate Commissioners* [1949] 2 K.B. 430 at 436.

[35] [1988] 1 Lloyd's Rep. 323.

[36] At p.328, with whose judgment Caulfield L.J. agreed. But see the more qualified statements (at pp.328–329) of Ralph Gibson L.J. See also *Reardon Smith Line Ltd v Ministry of Agriculture* [1960] 1 Q.B. 493–495, [1962] 1 Q.B. 42 at 83, 107, 128 (this point did not arise in the House of Lords [1963] A.C. 691).

reasonably have intended that one party should be entitled to rely on a *force majeure* clause which, as the result of facts known to him at the time of entering into the contract, he could reasonably foresee would inevitably come into operation and so affect the performance expected of him by the other party.[37] However, it has been held that there is no justification for limiting the ordinary meaning of words in a *force majeure* clause to events or states of fact not in existence at the date of the contract or to those which are unpredictable at the time it was made.[38]

8–092 **"Prevented" clauses.** Where the seller seeks to invoke the protection of a clause which states that he is to be relieved of liability if he is "prevented" from carrying out his obligations under the contract or is "unable" to do so, he must show that performance has become physically or legally impossible, and not merely more difficult or unprofitable.[39] It is not sufficient, for example, for him to show that his intended supplier is unable to supply the goods if he can obtain goods of the contract description from another supplier.[40] But the word "prevented" has always to be interpreted in the context of the particular contract. Thus, where the method of performance arranged by the seller is prohibited by government embargo, but he is nevertheless able to perform in an alternative manner, it is a question of construction of the clause, and of fact, whether his performance has been effectively "prevented" by the embargo.[41] In particular, c.i.f. sellers in a

---

[37] See also the Force Majeure (Exemption) Clause of the I.C.C.; below, para.8–098. But see *Hoecheong Products Co. Ltd v Cargill Hong Kong Ltd* [1995] 1 W.L.R. 404 at 408 (where it was pointed out that this proposition is untested).

[38] *Navrom v Callitsis Ship Management SA* [1988] 2 Lloyd's Rep. 416 at 420. See also *R Pagnan & Fratelli v Finagrain Compagnie Commerciale Agricole et Financière SA* [1986] 2 Lloyd's Rep. 395 at 401; *SHV Gas Supply Trading SAS v Naftomar & Trading Co. Ltd. Inc.* [2005] EWHC 2528 (Comm), [2006] 1 Lloyd's Rep. 163 at [29].

[39] *Blythe & Co. v Richards Turpin & Co.* (1916) 114 L.T. 753; *Tennants (Lancashire) Ltd v CS Wilson & Co. Ltd* [1917] A.C. 495; *Re Comptoir Commercial Anversois and Power Son & Co.* [1920] 1 K.B. 168; *Brauer & Co. (G.B.) Ltd v James Clark (Brush Materials) Ltd* [1952] 2 All E.R. 497; *Ross T. Smyth & Co. (Liverpool) Ltd v WN Lindsay Ltd* [1953] 2 Lloyd's Rep. 378; *Fairclough, Dodd & Jones Ltd v JH Vantol Ltd* [1957] 1 W.L.R. 136 at 143, 144; *Tsakiroglou & Co. v Noblee Thorl GmbH* [1962] A.C. 93; *Warinco AG v Fritz Mauthner* [1978] 1 Lloyd's Rep. 151; *Exportelisa SA v Giuseppe & Figli Soc. Coll.* [1978] 1 Lloyd's Rep. 433; *Huilerie l'Abeille v Société des Huileries du Niger* [1978] 2 Lloyd's Rep. 203; *Channel Island Ferries Ltd v Sealink U.K. Ltd* [1988] 1 Lloyd's Rep. 323 at 327; *Thames Valley Power Ltd v Total Gas Ltd* [2005] EWHC 2208 (Comm), [2006] 1 Lloyd's Rep. 441 at [50].

[40] *Joseph Pyke & Son (Liverpool) Ltd v Richard Cornelius & Co.* [1955] 2 Lloyd's Rep. 747; *Fairclough, Dodd & Jones Ltd v J H Vantol Ltd*, above, at p.146; *Koninklijke Bunge v Cie. Commerciale d'Importation* [1973] 2 Lloyd's Rep. 44; *P J Van der Zijden Wildhandel NV v Tucker & Cross Ltd* [1975] 2 Lloyd's Rep. 240; *Exportelisa SA v Giuseppe & Figli Soc. Coll.*, above; *Hoecheong Products Co. Ltd v Cargill Hong Kong Ltd*, above.

[41] *Tradax Export SA v André et Cie* [1976] 1 Lloyd's Rep. 416; *Warinco AG v Fritz Mauthner* [1978] 1 Lloyd's Rep. 151; *Bremer Handelsgesellschaft mbH v C. Mackprang* [1979] 1 Lloyd's Rep. 221; *Avimex SA v Dewulf & Cie* [1979] 2 Lloyd's Rep. 57; *André et Cie SA v Etablissements Michel Blanc et Fils* [1979] 2 Lloyd's Rep. 427; *Bunge SA v Deutsche Conti Handelsgesellschaft mbH* [1979] 2 Lloyd's Rep. 455;

"circle" or "string" have in some cases been held entitled to rely on a clause of this nature when they or some shipper higher up the "string" were prevented by government embargo from shipping the goods, even though they could have attempted to purchase substitute goods afloat, on the ground that such an attempt would in the circumstances have been impractical and commercially unreasonable.[42] Once the seller has discharged the burden of proving that performance has been prevented by the relevant event, he need not normally prove that he could have performed but for the occurrence of the event.[43] An independent state trading organisation may be able to establish that it has been prevented from delivering by "government intervention beyond its control" if an export embargo is imposed by its own government.[44] But, where it is alleged that performance has been prevented by refusal of a licence, the party required to obtain the licence may be obliged to show that he has made reasonable efforts to obtain the licence or that a licence would inevitably have been refused[45]; and, if an embargo is not absolute, but subject to certain

---

Continental Grain Export Corp. v STM Grain [1979] 2 Lloyd's Rep. 460; *Toepfer v Schwarze* [1980] 1 Lloyd's Rep. 385; *Bremer Handelsgesellschaft mbH v Westzucker GmbH* [1981] 1 Lloyd's Rep. 207; *Raiffeisen Hauptgenossenschaft v Louis Dreyfus & Co. Ltd* [1981] 1 Lloyd's Rep. 345; *Bremer Handelsgesellschaft mbH v C. Mackprang Jnr.* [1981] 1 Lloyd's Rep. 292; *Cook Industries Inc. v Meunerie Liegeois SA* [1981] 1 Lloyd's Rep. 359; *Tradax Export SA v Cook Industries Inc.* [1982] 1 Lloyd's Rep. 385; *Bremer Handelsgesellschaft mbH v Raiffeisen Hauptgenossenschaft* [1982] 1 Lloyd's Rep. 599; *Bremer Handelsgesellschaft mbH v Continental Grain Co.* [1983] 1 Lloyd's Rep. 269; *Bremer Handelsgesellschaft mbH v Bunge Corp.* [1983] 1 Lloyd's Rep. 476; *Pancommerce SA v Veecheema BV* [1983] 2 Lloyd's Rep. 304; *Deutsche Conti-Handelsgesellschaft mbH v Bremer Handelsgesellschaft mbH* [1984] 1 Lloyd's Rep. 447; *Cook Industries v Tradax Export SA* [1985] 2 Lloyd's Rep. 454; *Bremer Handelsgesellschaft v Westzucker GmbH* [1989] 1 Lloyd's Rep. 582. *Cf. Koninklijke Bunge v Compagnie Continentale d'Importation* [1973] 2 Lloyd's Rep. 44; *Tradax Export SA v Carapelli SpA* [1977] 2 Lloyd's Rep. 157; *Bremer Handelsgesellschaft mbH v Vanden Avenne- Izegem PVBA* [1978] 2 Lloyd's Rep. 109; *Sociedad Iberica de Molturacion SA v Tradax Export SA* [1978] 2 Lloyd's Rep. 545; *Bunge SA v Kruse* [1979] 1 Lloyd's Rep. 279 (affirmed [1980] 2 Lloyd's Rep. 142); *André et Cie SA v Tradax Export SA* [1983] 1 Lloyd's Rep. 254. See McKendrick (ed.), *Force Majeure and Frustration of Contract* (2nd ed.), Ch.12, Treitel, *Frustration and Force Majeure* (2nd ed., 2004), paras 12–037—12–038.

[42] *Tradax Export SA v André et Cie*, above, at p.423; *Bremer Handelsgesellschaft mbH v Vanden Avenne-Izegem PVBA*, above, at p.115; *Continental Grain Export Corp. v STM Grain*, above, at p.473; *Cook Industries Inc. v Tradax Export SA* [1983] 1 Lloyd's Rep. 327 (affirmed [1985] 2 Lloyd's Rep. 454). See below, para.18–350.

[43] *Bremer Handelsgesellschaft mbH v Vanden Avenne-Izegem PVBA*, above, at pp.114, 121; *Bremer Handelsgesellschaft mbH v C Mackprang Jnr* [1980] 1 Lloyd's Rep. 210 (affirmed [1981] 1 Lloyd's Rep. 292); *Continental Grain Export Corp. v S.T.M. Grain*, above. *Cf. Tradax Export SA v André et Cie*, above; *Toepfer v Schwarze* [1977] 2 Lloyd's Rep. 330 (affirmed [1980] 1 Lloyd's Rep. 385); *André et Cie SA v Etablissements Michel Blanc et Fils* [1979] 2 Lloyd's Rep. 427.

[44] *C Czarnikow Ltd v Centrala Handlu Zagranicznego Rolimplex* [1979] A.C. 351. *Cf. Empresa Exportadora de Azucar v Industria Azucarera Nacional SA* [1983] 2 Lloyd's Rep. 171. *Cf. Mamidoil-Jetoil Greek Petroleum SA v Okta Crude Oil Refinery AD* [2003] EWCA Civ 1031, [2003] 1 Lloyds' Rep. 1, [2003] 2 Lloyds' Rep. 635.

[45] *Re Anglo-Russian Merchant Traders and John Batt & Co. (London) Ltd* [1917] 2 K.B. 679; *Brauer & Co. (G.B.) Ltd v James Clarke (Brush Materials) Ltd* [1952] 2 All E.R. 497; *Malik Co. v Central European Trading Agency Ltd* [1974] 2 Lloyd's Rep. 279; *Provimi Hellas AE v Warinco AG* [1978] 1 Lloyd's Rep. 373; *Overseas Buyers Ltd v Granadex* [1980] 2 Lloyd's Rep. 608.

exceptions, a seller may be obliged to show that he has no goods of the contract description available to him within the "loopholes" to which the embargo is subject.[46]

8–093 Even though the word "prevented" is not used in the clause, it may be so construed.[47] If the clause provides that the seller is to be "excused" or "not to be responsible" upon the occurrence of certain events or any other causes beyond his control, he must show that he has been prevented from fulfilling the contract by one of the specified events or some other cause beyond his control.[48] It has been held that a clause in the form "unforeseen contingencies excepted" will only be effective if performance has become impossible.[49]

8–094 **"Hindered."** A wider scope is, however, given to the word "hindered"[50] and Lord Loreburn said[51]: "to place a merchant in the position of being unable to deliver unless he dislocates his business and breaks his contracts in order to fulfil one surely hinders delivery." Where, due to executive restrictions following a strike, charterers could not load unless they dislocated their businesses and broke other contracts, loading was "hindered".[52] A contract of sale of goods which contemplates the carriage of goods by sea may be hindered by the shortage of ships due to enemy action and an increased risk with resultant rise in freight rates.[53] Normally, however, a mere rise in price rendering the contract more expensive to perform will not constitute "hindrance".[54] The words "impeded", "impaired" and "interfered with" may, in context, be construed as equivalent to "hindered".

8–095 **"Delayed."** If provision is made for an extension of time for delivery if "performance" is "delayed" by circumstances beyond a party's control, the word "delayed" is not necessarily to be treated as equivalent to

---

[46] *Tradax Export SA v André et Cie*, above; *Bremer Handelsgesellschaft mbH v C Mackprang* [1979] 1 Lloyd's Rep. 221; *André et Cie SA v Etablissements Michel Blanc et Fils*, above; *Avimex SA v Dewulf & Cie.*, above; *Bunge SA v Deutsche Conti Handelsgesellschaft mbH*, above; *Overseas Buyers Ltd v Granadex*, above; *Raiffeisen Hauptgenossenschaft v Louis Dreyfus & Co. Ltd*, above; *Bremer Handelsgesellschaft mbH v Westzucker GmbH (No. 2)* [1981] 2 Lloyd's Rep. 130; *Cook Industries Ltd v Tradax Export SA* [1985] 2 Lloyd's Rep. 454. *Cf. Bremer Handelsgesellschaft mbH v Vanden Avenne-Izegem PVBA*, above.

[47] *Channel Island Ferries Ltd v Sealink UK Ltd* [1988] 1 Lloyd's Rep. 323 at 327.

[48] *PJ Van der Zijden Wildhandel NV v Tucker & Cross Ltd* [1975] 2 Lloyd's Rep. 240. See also *Hong Guan & Co. Ltd v R. Jumabhoy & Sons Ltd* [1960] A.C. 684 ("subject to").

[49] *George Wills & Sons Ltd v RS Cunningham Son & Co. Ltd* [1924] 2 K.B. 220. *Cf. Ashmore & Son v CS Cox & Co.* [1899] 1 Q.B. 436.

[50] *Crawford & Rowat v Wilson Sons & Co.* (1896) 12 T.L.R. 170; *Instone & Co. Ltd v Speedy Marshall & Co.* (1915) 114 L.T. 370; *Phosphate Mining Co. v Rankin Gilmour & Co.* (1915) 21 Com.Cas. 248. See also *Navrom v Callitsis Ship Management SA* [1988] 2 Lloyd's Rep. 416 ("hindrances").

[51] *Tennants (Lancashire) Ltd v CS Wilson & Co. Ltd* [1917] A.C. 495 at 510.

[52] *Reardon Smith Line Ltd v Ministry of Agriculture* [1962] 1 Q.B. 42 (revd. in part [1963] A.C. 691).

[53] *Peter Dixon & Sons Ltd v Henderson Craig & Co.* [1919] 2 K.B. 778.

[54] *Tennants (Lancashire) Ltd v CS Wilson & Co. Ltd*, above, at pp.509, 510, 522, 526.

"prevented"[55] and circumstances which merely hinder delivery may fall within the provision.[56]

Other expressions. Other, wider expressions may, however, be used, *e.g.* "rendered uneconomic". 8–096

Specified events. The following words and phrases have been the subject of consideration by the courts: Act of God,[57] storm tempest or flood,[58] fire,[59] perils and dangers or accidents of the sea,[60] war,[61] war-like operations,[62] civil war,[63] riot,[64] civil commotion,[65] strikes,[66] acts of the Queen's enemies,[67] 8–097

---

[55] *Fairclough Dodd & Sons Ltd v JH Vantol Ltd* [1957] 1 W.L.R. 136.

[56] *Re Lockie and Craggs* (1901) 86 L.T. 388. But see also *Matsoukis v Priestman & Co.* [1915] 1 K.B. 681; *Alfred C. Toepfer v Peter Cremer* [1975] 2 Lloyd's Rep. 578; *Tradax Export SA v André et Cie* [1976] 1 Lloyd's Rep. 416; *Bremer Handelsgesellschaft mbH v Vanden Avenne- Izegem PVBA* [1978] 2 Lloyd's Rep. 109; *Bremer Handelsgesellschaft mbH v J. Mackprang* [1979] 1 Lloyd's Rep. 221; *Avimex SA v Dewulf & Cie* [1979] 2 Lloyd's Rep. 57; McKendrick (ed.), *Force Majeure and Frustration of Contract* (2nd ed.), Ch.12.

[57] *Nugent v Smith* (1876) 1 C.P.D. 423 at 437, 438, 441, 444; *Nichols v Marsland* (1876) 2 Ex.D. 1; *Greenock Corpn v Caledonian Ry* [1917] A.C. 556.

[58] *Oddy v Phoenix Assurance Co. Ltd* [1966] 1 Lloyd's Rep. 134; *S & M Hotels Ltd v Legal & General Assurance Socy Ltd* [1972] 1 Lloyd's Rep. 157; *Young v Sun Alliance Ltd* [1977] 1 W.L.R. 104.

[59] *Thames and Mersey Marine Insurance Co. Ltd v Hamilton Fraser & Co.* (1887) 12 App. Cas. 484; *The Diamond* [1906] P. 282; *Tempus Shipping v Louis Dreyfus* [1930] 1 K.B. 699.

[60] *Thames and Mersey Marine Insurance Co. Ltd v Hamilton Fraser & Co.*, above; *The Xantho, ibid.* at p.503; *Hamilton Fraser & Co. v Pandorf & Co.* (1887) 12 App. Cas. 518; *The Glendarroch* [1894] P. 226; *ED Sassoon & Co. v Western Assurance Co.* [1912] A.C. 561; *Grant Smith & Co. and McDonnell Ltd v Seattle Construction and Dry Dock Co.* [1920] A.C. 162; *P Samuel & Co. Ltd v Dumas* [1924] All E.R. 66; *Canada Rice Mills Ltd v Union Marine and General Insurance Co. Ltd* [1940] 4 All E.R. 169; *Goodfellow Lumber Sales v Verreault* [1971] 1 Lloyd's Rep. 185; *The Super Servant Two* [1990] 1 Lloyd's Rep. 1; *Great China Metal Industries Co. Ltd v Malaysian International Shipping Corp. Bhd.* [1999] 1 Lloyd's Rep. 512.

[61] *Curtis v Mathews* [1919] 1 K.B. 425; *Pesquieras v Beer* (1949) 82 Ll.L. Rep. 501 at 514; *Kawasaki Kisen Kabushiki Kaisha v Banham SS Co. Ltd (No. 2)* [1939] 2 K.B. 544. See McKendrick (ed.), *Frustration and Force Majeure* (2nd ed.), Ch.8.

[62] *Clan Line Steamers Ltd v Liverpool and London War Risks Insurance Assn Ltd* [1943] K.B. 209 at 221. *Cf. Pan American World Airways Inc. v Aetna Casualty and Surety Co.* [1974] 1 Lloyd's Rep. 207 (affirmed [1975] 1 Lloyd's Rep. 77). See McKendrick (ed.), *op. cit*. Ch.8.

[63] *Spinney's (1948) Ltd v Royal Insurance Co. Ltd* [1980] 1 Lloyd's Rep. 406.

[64] *London and Lancashire Fire Insurance Ltd v Bolands Ltd* [1924] A.C. 836.

[65] *Levy v Assicurazione Generali* (1940) 67 Ll.L.R. 174 at 179.

[66] *Re Richardsons & Samuel* [1898] 1 Q.B. 261 at 267, 268; *Williams v Naamlooze* (1915) 21 Com.Cas. 253 at 257; *Seeberg v Russian Wood Agency* (1934) 50 Ll.L.Rep. 146; *Reardon Smith Line Ltd v Ministry of Agriculture* [1960] 1 Q.B. 439 (affirmed [1962] 1 Q.B. 42. This point did not arise in the House of Lords [1963] A.C. 691); *J. Vermaazs Scheepvaartbedrif NV v Association Technique de l'Importation Charbonnière* [1966] 1 Lloyd's Rep. 582; *Tramp Shipping Corp. v Greenwich Marine Inc.* [1975] 1 W.L.R. 1042; *B. & S. Contracts and Design Ltd v Victor Green Publications Ltd* [1984] I.C.R. 419; *Channel Island Ferries Ltd v Sealink (UK) Ltd* [1987] 1 Lloyd's Rep. 559, [1988] 1 Lloyd's Rep. 323. See McKendrick (ed.), *op. cit.*, Ch.6.

[67] *Russell v Niemann* (1864) 17 C.B.N.S. 163. *Cf. Spence v Chadwick* (1847) 10 Q.B. 5.

and prohibition of export.[68] However, expressions used in the context of another type of contract, for example, a policy of insurance or a charter-party, may not necessarily be appropriate to a contract of sale of goods. Moreover, even if the circumstances do not fall precisely within the meaning of a particular specified event, they may still be operative by virtue of the addition of more general words in the clause.

8–098 ***"Force majeure."*** Sometimes the actual expression "*force majeure*" is employed. *Force majeure* is not a term of art in English law,[69] although it is well known in continental legal systems, for example that of France.[70] The meaning of *force majeure* may nevertheless be ascertained by reference. Thus the incorporation into a contract of sale of the Force Majeure (Exemption) Clause of the International Chamber of Commerce[71] will mean that a party is not liable for failure to perform any of his obligations in so far as he proves: (1) that the failure was due to an impediment beyond his control; and (2) that he could not reasonably be expected to have taken the impediment and its effects upon his ability to perform the contract into account at the time of the conclusion of the contract; and (3) that he could not reasonably have avoided or overcome it or at least its effects.

8–099 It has rightly been observed that the concept of *force majeure* in English law is wider than that of "Act of God" or *vis major*,[72] as these latter expressions appear to denote events due to natural causes, without any human intervention.[73] In *Lebeaupin v Crispin & Co.*[74] McCardie J. reviewed the previous authorities on *force majeure*, and it now seems that war,[75] strikes,[76] legislative or administrative interference, for example, an embargo,[77] the refusal of a licence,[78] or seizure,[79] abnormal storm or

[68] The number of cases is voluminous. See below, paras 18–342 *et seq*; McKendrick (ed.), *op cit.*, Ch. 12; Treitel, *op. cit.*, para.12–033.

[69] *Hackney BC v Doré* [1922] 1 K.B. 431 at 437; *Re Podar Trading Co. Ltd and Tagher* [1949] 2 K.B. 277 at 286; *Thomas Borthwick (Glasgow) Ltd v Faure Fairclough Ltd* [1968] 1 Lloyd's Rep. 16 at 28; *Navrom v Callitsis Ship Management SA* [1987] 2 Lloyd's Rep. 276 at 281, 282 (affirmed [1988] 2 Lloyd's Rep. 416).

[70] Cod. Civ., para.1148; Carbonnier, *Droit Civil* (19th ed., 1995), IV, No. 1620; Marty and Raynaud, *Droit Civil* (1988), II, Vol. I, para.552; Mazeaud and Chabas, *Leçons de Droit Civil* (8th ed.), II, para.573. But see *Jacobs v Crédit Lyonnais* (1884) 12 Q.B.D. 589; *Navrom v Callitsis Ship Management SA*, above, at pp.281, 282, for supposed differences between French and English law.

[71] I.C.C. Publication No. 421.

[72] *Matsoukis v Priestman & Co.* [1915] 1 K.B. 681 at 686; *Lebeaupin v Crispin & Co.* [1920] 2 K.B. 714 at 719.

[73] *Nugent v Smith* (1876) 1 C.P.D. 423 at 427, 431, 444.

[74] [1920] 2 K.B. 714.

[75] *Zinc Corporation v Hirsch* [1916] 1 K.B. 541 at 544. *Cf.* p.549.

[76] *Matsoukis v Priestman & Co.*, above; *Torquay Hotel Co. Ltd v Cousins* [1969] 2 Ch. 106. *Cf. Hackney BC v Doré* [1922] 1 K.B. 431; *B & S Contracts and Design Ltd v Victor Green Publications Ltd* [1984] I.C.R. 419.

[77] *Lebeaupin v Crispin & Co.*, above, at p.270; *Tradax Export SA v André et Cie* [1976] 1 Lloyd's Rep. 109. *Cf. Re Podar Trading Co. Ltd and Tagher* [1949] 2 K.B. 277.

[78] *Walton (Grain) Ltd v British Italian Trading Co.* [1959] 1 Lloyd's Rep. 223; *Coloniale Import- Export v Loumidis Sons* [1978] 2 Lloyd's Rep. 560. But see *Brauer & Co. (GB) Ltd v James Clark (Brush Materials) Ltd* [1952] 2 All E.R. 497 at 501; *Pagnan SpA v Tradax Ocean Transportation SA* [1987] 3 All E.R. 565.

[79] *Yrazu v Astral Shipping Co.* (1904) 20 T.L.R. 153 at 154–155; *The Turul* [1919] A.C. 515.

tempest,[80] flooding which inhibits shipment from river ports,[81] interruption of the supply by rail of raw material,[82] and even the accidental breakdown of machinery[83] can amount to *force majeure*,[84] but not "bad weather, football matches or a funeral,"[85] a failure of performance due to the provision of insufficient financial resources[86] or to a miscalculation,[87] a rise in cost or expense,[88] the failure by a third party to fulfil his contract,[89] or any act, negligence, omission or default on the part of the party seeking to be excused.[90] The words "*force majeure*" are, however, rarely unqualified. The type of circumstance envisaged by the parties will often be set out, so that those circumstances may apply to limit, extend or explain the meaning of "*force majeure*".[91] Further the clause may refer to performance being "prevented", "hindered" or "delayed" by *force majeure*.[92] The expression must therefore be construed with regard to the words which precede and follow it and also with regard to the nature and general terms of the contract.[93]

---

[80] *Lebeaupin v Crispin & Co.*, above, at p.720.
[81] *Alfred C Toepfer v Peter Cremer* [1975] 2 Lloyd's Rep. 118; *Tradax Export SA v André et Cie*, above; *Bunge GmbH v Alfred C Toepfer* [1978] 1 Lloyd's Rep. 506; *Avimex SA v Dewulf & Cie* [1979] 2 Lloyd's Rep. 57.
[82] *cf. Intertradax SA v Lesieur-Tourteaux SARL* [1978] 2 Lloyd's Rep. 509.
[83] *Matsoukis v Priestman & Co.*, above; *Thomas Borthwick (Glasgow) Ltd v Faure Fairclough Ltd* [1968] 1 Lloyd's Rep. 16 at 28. *Sed quaere? Cf. Sonat Offshore SA v Amerada Hess Development Ltd* [1988] 1 Lloyd's Rep. 145 at 158.
[84] See also *Yrazu v Astral Shipping Co.*, above, at pp.154–155 (casualty to ship or cargo).
[85] *Matsoukis v Priestman & Co.*, above, at p.687.
[86] *The Concadoro* [1916] 2 A.C. 199.
[87] *Yrazu v Astral Shipping Co.*, above. See also *Atlantic Paper Stock Ltd v St Anne Nackawic Pulp and Paper Co. Ltd* (1975) 56 D.L.R. (3d) 409 (lack of business sense).
[88] *Brauer & Co. (GB) Ltd v James Clark (Brush Materials) Ltd* [1952] 2 All E.R. 497.
[89] *Lebeaupin v Crispin*, above. See also *Thomas Borthwick (Glasgow) Ltd v Faure Fairclough Ltd*, above (failure of Conference to provide vessel). *Cf. John Batt & Co. (London) Ltd v Brooker, Dore & Co. Ltd* (1942) 72 Ll.L.Rep. 149; *Coastal (Bermuda) Petroleum Co. Ltd v VTT Vulcan Petroleum SA (No. 2)* [1996] 2 Lloyd's Rep. 383.
[90] *New Zealand Shipping Co. v Société des Ateliers et Chantiers de France* [1919] A.C. 1 at 6; *Hong Guan & Co. Ltd v R. Jumabhoy & Sons Ltd* [1960] A.C. 684 at 700; *Sonat Offshore SA v Amerada Hess Development Ltd* above; *The Super Servant Two* [1990] 1 Lloyd's Rep. 1 at 5–8, 11–13.
[91] *Sonat Offshore SA v Amerada Hess Development Ltd*, above, at p.158.
[92] See above, paras 8–092, 8–094, 8–095.
[93] *Lebeaupin v Crispin & Co.*, above, at p.702; *Re Podar Trading Co. Ltd and Tagher*, above, at p.286; see also *Matsoukis v Priestman & Co.* [1915] 1 K.B. 681 (excepted only the cause of *force majeure* and/or strikes); *Dixon & Sons v Henderson Craig & Co.* [1919] 2 K.B. 778 (hindered or prevented by *force majeure*); *Brauer & Co. (GB) Ltd v James Clark (Brush Materials) Ltd* [1952] 2 All E.R. 497 (prevented by *force majeure*); *Fairclough Dodd & Jones Ltd v JH Vantol Ltd* [1957] 1 W.L.R. 136 (prohibition of export or any other cause comprehended by *force majeure*); *Hong Guan & Co. Ltd v R Jumabhoy & Sons Ltd* [1960] A.C. 684 (subject to *force majeure* and shipment); *Tsakiroglou & Co. Ltd v Noblee Thorl GmbH* [1962] A.C. 93 (*force majeure* preventing shipment); *Alfred C Toepfer v Peter Cremer* [1975] 2 Lloyd's Rep. 118 (delay in shipment occasioned by any cause comprehended in the term "*force majeure*); *Tradax Export SA v André et Cie* [1976] 1 Lloyd's Rep. 416 (*ibid.*); *Bunge*

8–100 If the reference to *force majeure* is indeed unqualified, *e.g.* "subject to *force majeure*" or "*force majeure* excepted", then it is submitted that, in English law, performance of the relevant obligation must have been prevented by an event of *force majeure* and not merely hindered or rendered more onerous.[94] However, there does not appear to be any requirement that the circumstances alleged to constitute *force majeure* should be unforeseeable,[95] although the seller still bears the burden of proving that his non-performance was due to circumstances beyond his control and that there were no reasonable steps that he could have taken to avoid or mitigate the event or its consequences.[96]

8–101 **Conditions precedent.** A clause excusing delivery, or permitting the seller to postpone or suspend delivery, may provide that certain procedures are to be followed or notices given to the buyer within a stipulated period of time before he is entitled to rely on the clause. Such measures may be a condition precedent on which the availability of the protection provided by the clause depends,[97] or merely an intermediate

---

GmbH v Alfred C. Toepfer [1978] 1 Lloyd's Rep. 506 (*ibid.*); *Bremer Handelsgesellschaft mbH v Vanden Avenne-Izegem PVBA* [1978] 2 Lloyd's Rep. 109 (*ibid.*); *Avimex SA v Dewulf & Cie* [1979] 2 Lloyd's Rep. 57 (*ibid.*); *Marifortuna Naviera SA v Govt. of Ceylon* [1970] 1 Lloyd's Rep. 247 ("*force majeure* excepted"); *Huilerie l'Abeille v Société des Huileries du Niger* [1978] 2 Lloyd's Rep. 203 ("strikes . . . or any other cause comprehended by the term *force majeure*"); *The Super Servant Two* [1990] 1 Lloyd's Rep. 1 ("*force majeure,* . . . perils or danger and accidents of the sea").

[94] But, in the context of EC Regulations, the European Court has sometimes held that the expression *force majeure* is not limited to cases where performance is impossible, but extends to unusual circumstances, outside the control of the person concerned, the consequences of which, in spite of the exercise of all due care, could not have been avoided except at the cost of excessive sacrifice: see *Internationale Handelsgesellschaft v Einfuhr-und-Vorratsstelle* [1970] E.C.R. 1125; *De Jong Verenigde v VIB* [1985] E.C.R. 2061. Contrast *Schwarzwaldmilch v Einfuhr-und- Vorratsstelle fur Fette* (Case 4/68) [1968] E.C.R. 377; *Valsabbia v EC Commission* [1980] E.C.R. 907. These cases are discussed in McKendrick (ed.), *Force Majeure and Frustration of Contract* (2nd ed.), Ch.13.

[95] *Navrom v Callitsis Ship Management SA* [1987] 2 Lloyd's Rep. 276 at 281, 282, and see para.8–091, above . Contrast Council Directive 90/314/EEC on package travel, package holidays and package tours ([1993] O.J. L158/59), Art. 4(6), which defines *force majeure* as "unusual and *unforeseeable* circumstances beyond the control of the party by whom it is pleaded, the consequences of which could not have been avoided even if all due care had been exercised": see the Package Travel, Package Holidays and Package Tours Regulations 1992 (SI 1992/3288 as amended by SI 1998/1208, SI 2003/1376, SI 2003/1400), regs 13(3)(b), 15(2)(c)(i); *Charlson v Warner* [2000] C.L.Y. 4043 (Cty. Ct.).

[96] See above, para.8–091.

[97] *Tradax Export SA v André et Cie* [1976] 1 Lloyd's Rep. 416; *Finagrain SA Geneva v P Kruse Hamburg* [1976] 2 Lloyd's Rep. 508; *Berg & Son Ltd v Vanden Avenne-Izegem PVBA* [1977] 1 Lloyd's Rep. 499; *Toepfer v Schwarze* [1977] 2 Lloyd's Rep. 380 (affirmed [1980] 1 Lloyd's Rep. 385); *Bunge GmbH v CCV Landbouwbelang G.A.* [1978] 1 Lloyd's Rep. 217; *Bremer Handelsgesellschaft mbH v Vanden Avenne-Izegem PVBA* [1978] 2 Lloyd's Rep. 109; *Intertradax SA v Lesieur Tourteaux SARL* [1978] 2 Lloyd's Rep. 509; *Bremer Handelsgesellschaft mbH v C. Mackprang* [1979] 1 Lloyd's Rep. 221; *Bunge GmbH v Alfred C. Toepfer* [1979] 1 Lloyd's Rep. 554; *Johnson Matthey Bankers Ltd v State Trading Corp. of India* [1984] 1 Lloyd's Rep. 427; *Bremer Handelsgesellschaft mbH v Westzucker GmbH (No. 3)* [1989] 1 Lloyd's

term,[98] the non-fulfilment of which does not necessarily deprive him of his right to rely on the clause.[99] The buyer may also be held to have waived, or to be estopped from asserting, non-compliance with the measures set out in the clause.[1]

Insufficiency of goods. A seller may as a result of an event of *force majeure* have insufficient goods of the contract description to meet all his existing contracts, but nevertheless have at his disposal enough goods to satisfy one or more of those contracts. In such a case he may be entitled to rely upon an appropriately worded *force majeure* clause as an excuse for non-performance of those contracts which are unfulfilled, even though the clause refers to his being "prevented" from delivering the goods and not merely to his being "hindered" from doing so.[2] If he has a number of existing contracts to fulfil, but cannot fulfil all of them, he can rely upon *force majeure* as to the others.[3] He may allocate the available goods in any 8–102

Rep. 582.; *Mamidoil-Jetoil Greek Petroleum Co. SA v Okta Crude Oil Refinery AD* [2003] 1 Lloyd's Rep. 1; [2003] EWCA Civ 1031; [2003] 2 Lloyd's Rep. 635 at [34]. *Cf., Hoecheong Products Co. Ltd v Cargill Hong Kong Ltd* [1995] 1 W.L.R. 404 (certificate required to attest only to occurrence of *force majeure* event). See also below, para.18–357.

[98] See below, para.10–033.

[99] *Bremer Handelsgesellschaft mbH v Vanden Avenne-Izegem PVBA*, above, at p.113. See also *Bunge SA v Kruse* [1979] 1 Lloyd's Rep. 279 (affirmed [1980] 2 Lloyd's Rep. 142); *SHV Gas Supply & Trading SAS v Naftomar Shipping & Trading Co. Ltd. Inc.* [2005] EWHC 2528 (Comm), [2006] 1 Lloyd's Rep. 163 at [39]. *Cf. Tradax Export SA v André et Cie*, above. See below, para.18–357.

[1] *Bremer Handelsgesellschaft mbH v Vanden Avenne-Izegem PVBA*, above; *Bremer Handelsgesellschaft mbH v C. Mackprang Jnr* [1979] 1 Lloyd's Rep. 221 (waiver or estoppel). Contrast *Finagrain SA Geneva v P. Kruse Hamburg*, above; *Berg & Son Ltd v Vanden Avenne-Izegem PVBA*, above; *Toepfer v Schwarze* [1977] 2 Lloyd's Rep. 380 (affirmed [1980] 1 Lloyd's Rep. 385); *Avimex SA v Dewulf & Cie* [1979] 2 Lloyd's Rep. 57; *Bunge SA v Kruse* [1979] 1 Lloyd's Rep. 279; *Bremer Handelsgesellschaft mbH v C. Mackprang Jnr* [1981] 1 Lloyd's Rep. 292; *Raiffeisen Hauptgenossenschaft v Louis Dreyfus & Co. Ltd* [1981] 1 Lloyd's Rep. 345; *Tradax Export SA v Cook Industries Inc.* [1981] 1 Lloyd's Rep. 236 (affirmed [1982] 1 Lloyd's Rep. 385); *Bremer Handelsgesellschaft mbH v Finagrain SA* [1981] 2 Lloyd's Rep. 259; *Bunge SA v Compagnie Européenne des Cereales* [1982] 1 Lloyd's Rep. 306; *Bremer Handelsgesellschaft mbH v Raiffeisen Hauptgenossenschaft E.G.* [1982] 1 Lloyd's Rep. 599; *Bremer Handelsgesellschaft mbH v Bunge Corp.* [1983] 1 Lloyd's Rep. 476; *Bremer Handelsgesellschaft mbH v Deutsche- Conti Handelsgesellschaft mbH* [1983] 1 Lloyd's Rep. 689 (no waiver or estoppel). See also *Panchaud Frères SA v Etablissements General Grain Co.* [1970] 1 Lloyd's Rep. 53, 57; *Bunge SA v Kruse* [1980] 2 Lloyd's Rep. 142; *André et Cie v Cook Industries Inc.* [1987] 2 Lloyd's Rep. 463. See below, paras 18–322, 18–358 and Treitel, *Frustration and Force Majeure* (2nd ed., 2004), para.12–045.

[2] *Bremer Handelsgesellschaft mbH v Continental Grain Co.* [1983] 1 Lloyd's Rep. 269 at 280–281, 291–294. See also *Westfalische Central-Genossenschaft GmbH v Seabright Chemicals Ltd* (1979), unreported (Robert Goff J.), cited *ibid.*

[3] *Tennants (Lancashire) Ltd v CS Wilson & Co. Ltd* [1917] A.C. 495 at 511–512; *Pool Shipping v London Coal Co. of Gibraltar* [1939] 2 All E.R. 432; *Tradax Export SA v André et Cie. SA* [1976] 1 Lloyd's Rep. 416 at 423; *Kawasaki Steel Corp. v Sardol SpA* [1977] 2 Lloyd's Rep. 552 at 555; *Bremer Handelsgesellschaft mbH v Vanden Avenne-Izegem PVBA* [1978] 2 Lloyd's Rep. 109 at 115; *Intertradex SA v Lesieur Tourteaux SARL* [1978] 2 Lloyd's Rep. 509; *Bremer Handelsgesellschaft v Continental Grain Co.*, above.

way which the trade would consider proper and reasonable, whether this is *pro rata*, or in chronological order, or on some other basis.[4] But he cannot make any allocation to those of his customers to whom he has a non-legal moral commitment[5]; nor would it be reasonable to allocate supplies to new contracts in order to take advantage of a resultant rise in price.[6]

8–103 The principle of "pro-rating" has already been referred to.[7] Whether a seller is ever under a duty to distribute available goods *pro rata* among existing contracts has yet to be decided.[8] However, it is unlikely that, in the absence of any special circumstances or recognised trade custom to that effect, there would be implied on the part of the seller any obligation as such to apportion *pro rata*.[9] But some sharing out may be regarded as reasonable in the trade in question, although it would not invariably be required—for example, "if the quantity available is too small[10] to be sensibly apportioned among the relevant purchasers; or his storage problems or a perishable product require one purchaser to be preferred to another; or (perhaps) if a ship already chartered and tendered were reasonably to be loaded; and there may be other cases."[11] Nevertheless the liability of the seller for breach of a particular contract will not be reduced by reference to a notional distribution which he did not in fact make.[12]

8–104 **Unfair Contract Terms Act 1977.** *Force majeure* clauses may attract the test of reasonableness imposed by section 3 of the Unfair Contract Terms Act 1977.[13] It seems unlikely that a clause which merely permits the seller to suspend, postpone or cancel delivery upon the happening of events beyond his control would, in a commercial contract, be held to be unreasonable,[14] although there are possibly circumstances where such a clause would be so held, for example, in an exclusive dealing agreement, if the seller was entitled to suspend delivery in such events, but the buyer was nevertheless not entitled, during the suspension, to purchase supplies from elsewhere.

---

[4] *Intertradex SA v Leiseur Tourteaux SARL*, above, at p.512; *Bremer Handelsgesellschaft mbH v C. Mackprang*, above, at p.224; *Westfalische Central-Genossenschaft GmbH v Seabright Chemicals Ltd*, above, at pp.291–294. See also below, para.18–353.

[5] *Pancommerce SA v Veecheema BV* [1983] 2 Lloyd's Rep. 304 at 307.

[6] *Westfalische Central-Genossenschaft GmbH v Seabright Chemicals Ltd*, above.

[7] See above, para.6–053. See also below, para.18–353.

[8] *Continental Grain Export Corp. v STM Grain Ltd* [1979] 2 Lloyd's Rep. 460 at 473.

[9] *Westfalische Central-Genossenschaft GmbH v Seabright Chemicals Ltd*, above; *Bremer Handelsgesellschaft mbH v Continental Grain Co.*, above, at pp.280–281, 293. *Cf. Bremer Handelsgesellschaft mbH v C. Mackprang*, above, at p.224.

[10] *Bremer Handelsgesellschaft mbH v Vanden Avenne-Izegem PVBA* [1978] 2 Lloyd's Rep. 109 at 115.

[11] *Westfalische Central-Genossenschaft GmbH v Seabright Chemicals Ltd*, above; *Bremer Handelsgesellschaft mbH v Continental Grain Co.*, above, p.293.

[12] *Bremer Handelsgesellschaft mbH v Bunge Corp.* [1982] 1 Lloyd's Rep. 108 at 114; *Bremer Handelsgesellschaft mbH v Continental Grain Co.*, above, at pp.280–281, 292–293.

[13] s.3(2)(b). See *Chitty on Contracts* (29th ed.), Vol. 1, para.14–152. Contrast Treitel, *Frustration and Force Majeure* (2nd ed., 2004), para.12–018.

[14] See *Shearson Lehman Hutton Inc. v Maclaine Watson & Co. Ltd* [1989] 2 Lloyd's Rep. 570 at 612.

Unfair Terms in Consumer Contracts Regulations 1999. These Regulations[15] are discussed in Chapter 14.[16] A *force majeure* clause in a consumer contract may not be binding on the consumer if, contrary to the requirement of good faith,[17] it causes a significant imbalance in the parties' rights and obligations arising under the contract, to the detriment of the consumer[18] or if it is not drafted in plain, intelligible language.[19] Examples of unfair terms might be *force majeure* clauses which require the consumer to accept a suspension of delivery or delayed delivery or the delivery of substitute goods without giving him the opportunity to cancel the contract, or which deny him a full refund in the event of cancellation of the contract by the seller upon the occurrence of an event of *force majeure*.[20] 8–105

Distance Selling Regulations 2000. Regulation 19(7) of the Consumer Protection (Distance Selling) Regulations 2000[21] provides that, in the case of a contract concerning goods which is concluded between a supplier and a consumer by means of distance communication,[22] where the supplier is unable to supply the goods ordered by the consumer within the time limited by the contract or the Regulations,[23] he may provide substitute goods of equivalent quality and price. But this possibility must have been provided for in the contract and the supplier must, prior to the conclusion of the contract, have given the consumer the information required by Regulation 7[24] and in the manner there laid down.[25] Substitution is, however, only permitted if the supplier is *unable* to supply the goods and this inability must arise because the goods are "unavailable".[26] 8–106

---

15 SI 1999/2083, as amended by SI 2001/1186.
16 See below, para.14–030.
17 See below, para.14–034.
18 See below, para.14–035.
19 See below, para.14–032, n.93.
20 See, in particular, Sch.2, para.1 (f), (g), (h), (j), (k), of the Regulations, and below, para.14–036. *Cf.* Treitel, *op. cit.* para.12–018.
21 SI 2000/2334, as amended by SI 2004/2095, SI 2005/689; see below, para.14–054.
22 For the scope of the Regulations, see below, para.14–054.
23 Reg. 19(1); see above, para.14–056.
24 Reg. 7(1)(b) and (c); below, para.14–055.
25 Reg. 7(2); below, para.14–055, n.37.
26 Regs. 7(i)(f), 19(2).

CHAPTER 9

ACCEPTANCE AND PAYMENT

	PARA.
1. Acceptance	9–002
2. Payment	9–021
(a) Methods of payment	9–028
(b) Place of payment	9–047
(c) Time of payment	9–051

Buyer's duty to accept and pay. Section 27 of the Sale of Goods Act 1979 prescribes that it is the duty of the buyer to accept and pay for the goods in accordance with the terms of the contract of sale.[1] **9–001**

1. ACCEPTANCE

Meaning of acceptance. The words "accept" and "acceptance" have been used in a number of different senses in the 1979 Act,[2] and in its predecessor, the Sale of Goods Act 1893.[3] For example, section 11(4) of the 1979 Act provides that, where the buyer has accepted the goods or part of them,[4] the breach of any condition to be fulfilled by the seller can in certain circumstances only be treated as a breach of warranty, and not as a ground for rejecting the goods and treating the contract as repudiated.[5] In this context, the relevant definition of the word "accept" is to be found in section 35 of the 1979 Act.[6] Subject to his having had a reasonable opportunity to examine the goods,[7] section 35(1) states: "The buyer is deemed to have accepted the goods (a) when he intimates to the seller that he has accepted them, or (b) when the goods have been delivered to him and he does any act in relation to them which is inconsistent with the ownership of the seller". The buyer is also deemed to have accepted the goods when after the lapse of a reasonable time he retains the goods without intimating to the seller that he has rejected them.[8] However, this definition does not seem entirely appropriate to the duty of the buyer to accept the goods: it is somewhat difficult to say that there is a positive *duty* on the buyer to accept the goods in the sense of section 35. Breach of the **9–002**

---

[1] *cf.* Vienna Convention on Contracts for the International Sale of Goods, Art. 53 (above, para.1–024).
[2] See ss.11(4), 18 r. 4, 27, 30(1), (2), (3), 31(1), 34(1), 35(1), 36, 50.
[3] See s.4(3) of the 1893 Act.
[4] But see s.34A (right of partial rejection). *Cf.*, s.35(7).
[5] See below, para.12–038.
[6] See below, para.12–044.
[7] s.35(2).
[8] s.35(4).

"duty to accept" in section 27 of the Act normally consists in the buyer expressly or impliedly rejecting the goods, and, in practice, the duty is conceived in a more negative form, *i.e.* a duty not unjustifiably to reject the goods.

9–003 **Acceptance and taking delivery.** The Act appears to draw a distinction between acceptance of the goods and taking delivery of them.[9] This distinction is not very precisely delineated, but undoubtedly exists in fact. For example, the buyer may fail to take delivery of the goods for some time,[10] but nevertheless subsequently accept the goods.[11] Or he may accept the goods (in the sense of signifying his approval of them after examination), but subsequently fail to take delivery of them.[12] The Act does not in its terms impose on the buyer any independent duty to take delivery, although it prescribes certain sanctions in the event of a neglect or refusal to take delivery or of a delay in taking delivery.[13] But taking delivery is one of the most important aspects of the duty to accept since a neglect or refusal to take delivery will very often constitute a rejection (express or implied) of the goods by the buyer,[14] and in consequence amount to a non-acceptance of them.

9–004 **Place of taking delivery.** Where a place of delivery is stipulated in the contract, the buyer is not entitled to require the seller to permit him to take delivery at any other place.[15]

9–005 **Time of taking delivery.** The time at which the buyer must take delivery of the goods will normally be the time at which the goods are to be delivered by the seller. Although there is no express provision to this effect in the Sale of Goods Act 1979, it is submitted that, in the absence of a contrary intention,[16] delivery by the seller and the taking of delivery by the buyer are concurrent obligations, that is to say, each party must be ready and willing to give or take possession of the goods at the time appointed for delivery. If the contract expressly or impliedly fixes a time at or within which the buyer is to take delivery of the goods, such a stipulation may or may not be of the essence of the contract.[17] A stipulation of this nature has been held to make time of the essence where the goods were perishable[18] and where the contract was subject to "spot" conditions, *i.e.* the goods being available and ready for immediate delivery and removal on a certain date from a certain place.[19] In mercantile contracts, provisions as to time

---

[9] See above, para.9–002, n.2, and ss.20, 37. *Cf.* Vienna Convention on Contracts for the International Sale of Goods, Art. 60 (above, para.1–024).
[10] ss.20(2), 37.
[11] See below, para.20–139 (f.o.b. contracts).
[12] See below, para.19–219 (c.i.f. contracts).
[13] ss.20(2), 37; below, paras 9–008, 9–009.
[14] See, *e.g.* s.31(2); below, para.9–010.
[15] *Wackerbath v Masson* (1812) 3 Camp. 270; *Maine Spinning Co. v Sutcliffe & Co.* (1917) 87 L.J.K.B. 382.
[16] See, for example, c.i.f. contracts: below, Ch.19.
[17] See s.10(2) of the Act; above, para.8–025.
[18] *Sharp v Christmas* (1892) 8 T.L.R. 687.
[19] *Thames Sack and Bag Co. Ltd v Knowles & Co. Ltd* (1919) 88 L.J.K.B. 585.

are frequently, but not always, regarded as being of the essence of the contract.[20] And in *Bunge Corporation v Tradax Export SA*,[21] the House of Lords stated that, in a mercantile contract, when a term has to be performed by one party as a condition precedent to the ability of the other party to perform another term, especially an essential term, the term as to time for the performance of the former obligation will in general fall to be treated as a condition. In that case, a term in an f.o.b. contract that the buyer was to give "at least 15 consecutive days' notice of readiness of vessel(s) and of the approximate quantity to be loaded" was held to be a condition since, until such notice was given, the seller could not nominate a loading port so as to ensure that the contract goods would be available for loading on the ship's arrival at that port before the end of the shipment period. Similarly, where time is of the essence in respect of the seller's obligation to deliver and the buyer does not, for example in the case of an f.o.b. contract, nominate an effective ship[22] or give notice of expected time of arrival of the vessel[23] within the time stipulated for that purpose to enable the seller to ship the goods in time, the seller will be entitled to treat the contract as repudiated and claim damages for non-acceptance. But, in cases where the property in the goods has passed to the buyer, if the contract merely states that the goods bought are to be carried away by the buyer within a certain period of time, a default in this respect will not necessarily entitle the seller to treat the contract as repudiated and resell the goods.[24] In such a case, a stipulation as to the time of taking delivery might be construed as an "intermediate" or "innominate" term,[25] the breach of which will not discharge the seller unless the delay is so prolonged as to frustrate the commercial purpose of the contract.

Waiver. Where the seller expressly or impliedly accedes to a request by the buyer that the time of delivery be postponed, he will be held to have waived his right to insist that the buyer take delivery at the time appointed for delivery under the contract of sale.[26] In such an event, he will not be entitled to rely on that right in order to claim damages for non-acceptance of the goods, or (*semble*) to assert any other remedy,[27] on the ground that 9–006

[20] *United Scientific Holdings Ltd v Burnley B.C.* [1978] A.C. 904 at 924, 937, 944, 950, 958. See also *Bunge Corp. v Tradax Export SA* [1981] 1 W.L.R. 711 at 716, 719, 729; *Compagnie Commerciale Sucres et Denrees v C. Czarnikow Ltd* [1990] 1 W.L.R. 1337 at 1346–1349.

[21] [1981] 1 W.L.R. 711 at 729 (see also *ibid.*, at pp.714, 716, 717, 718).

[22] See below, para.20–046.

[23] *Scandinavian Trading Co. A/B v Zodiac Petroleum SA* [1981] 1 Lloyd's Rep. 81. See also below, para.20–043 (effective shipping instructions).

[24] *Greaves v Ashlin* (1813) 3 Camp. 426; *Woolfe v Horn* (1877) 2 Q.B.D. 355. *Cf. Penarth Dock Engineering Co. v Pounds* [1963] 1 Lloyd's Rep. 359 at 361 and s.37(2) of the Act (below, para.9–009).

[25] See below, para.10–033.

[26] *Hickman v Haynes* (1875) L.R. 10 C.P. 598; *Levey & Co. v Goldberg* [1922] 1 K.B. 688; *Besseler Waechter Glover & Co. v South Derwent Coal Co.* [1938] 1 K.B. 408. *Cf. Plevins v Downing* (1876) 1 C.P.D. 220. See also below, paras 16–073, 17–011, 17–012 (damages).

[27] See s.37 of the 1979 Act, below, para.9–009. The seller could, however, reserve his right to claim damages for loss or expense occasioned by the delay.

the buyer has failed to take delivery at the appointed time. Conversely, since the concession is made for the benefit of the buyer, he too is precluded from relying on the terms of the contract as to the time of delivery.[28] If no period of postponement is fixed, the seller may give notice to the buyer that he requires the buyer to take delivery of the goods within a reasonable time, and the buyer must then take delivery within that time.[29]

9–007 **Hour of taking delivery.** A demand or tender of delivery may be treated as ineffectual unless made at a reasonable hour. What is a reasonable hour is a question of fact.[30]

9–008 **Risk after delay.** Where delivery has been delayed through the fault of the buyer the goods are at his risk as regards any loss which might not have occurred but for such delay,[31] subject to the duties or liabilities of the seller as a bailee of the goods of the buyer.[32]

9–009 **Failure to take delivery after request.** By section 37(1) of the 1979 Act: "When the seller is ready and willing to deliver the goods, and requests the buyer to take delivery, and the buyer does not within a reasonable time[33] after such request take delivery of the goods, he is liable[34] to the seller for any loss[35] occasioned by his neglect or refusal to take delivery, and also for a reasonable charge for the care and custody of the goods."[36] It could be contended that the reference to a charge for the "care and custody" of the goods suggests that this subsection is only applicable where the property in the goods has passed to the buyer; but it is submitted that this would be too narrow an interpretation. However, the seller can claim under section 37(1) only if he can show that he was ready and willing to deliver the goods in accordance with his contractual obligation.[37] Moreover, if he asserts an

---

[28] *Hickman v Haynes*, above; *Levey & Co. v Goldberg*, above.
[29] *cf. Charles Rickards Ltd v Oppenhaim* [1950] 1 K.B. 616. See also *Tyers v Rosedale & Ferryhill Iron Co.* (1875) L.R. 10 Ex. 195 (duty of seller to deliver within reasonable time if so requested by the buyer). *Cf.* Vienna Convention on Contracts for the International Sale of Goods, Art. 63 (above, para.1–024).
[30] Sale of Goods Act 1979, s.29(5). See also *Startup v Macdonald* (1843) 6 M. & G. 593, and above, para.8–041.
[31] Sale of Goods Act 1979, s.20(2); see above, para.6–023.
[32] s.20(3); see above, para.6–026.
[33] This is a question of fact: see s.59 of the Act.
[34] In *Penarth Dock Engineering Co. v Pounds* [1963] 1 Lloyd's Rep. 359, an action was successfully maintained in trespass for leaving the goods bought on the seller's premises. *Sed quaere*?
[35] In *Penarth Dock Engineering Co. v Pounds*, above, at p.361, the measure of damages awarded was not the loss suffered by the seller, but the unauthorised benefit obtained by the buyer in having free storage. *Cf. Strand Electric and Engineering Co. Ltd v Brisford Entertainments Ltd* [1952] 2 Q.B. 246 at 253–254. See also *Greaves v Ashlin* (1813) 3 Camp. 426 at 427; *Somes v British Empire Co.* (1860) 8 H.L.C. 338 at 344 (reasonable sum for storage). On the merger of such loss in damages for non-acceptance, see below, para.16–088.
[36] This section is based on common law principles before the Act: *Greaves v Ashlin*, above; *Bloxam v Sanders* (1825) 4 B. & C. 941 at 950; *Somes v British Empire Co.*, above.
[37] CPR 16.4(1)(a).

unpaid seller's lien[38] over the goods, he can make no claim for a reasonable charge under this subsection since he keeps the goods for his own benefit and not for the benefit of the buyer.[39] But he is not precluded from claiming storage charges from the buyer merely because he has agreed in a contract with a person from whom he himself bought the goods that he would be liable to pay storage charges to that person only to the extent that he could recover such charges from the buyer.[40]

Subsection (2) of section 37 states that nothing in section 37 affects the rights of the seller where the neglect or refusal of the buyer to take delivery amounts to a repudiation of the contract.[41]

Repudiation of the contract. A wrongful neglect or refusal by the buyer 9–010 to take delivery of the goods may constitute a repudiation by him of the contract of sale. But it will not necessarily do so. In particular, "where there is a contract for the sale of goods to be delivered by stated instalments, which are to be separately paid for, and the buyer neglects or refuses to take delivery of one or more instalments, it is a question in each case depending on the terms of the contract and the circumstances of the case whether the breach of contract is a repudiation of the whole contract or whether it is a severable breach giving rise to a claim for compensation but not to a right to treat the whole contract as repudiated."[42] Such neglect or refusal will not amount to a repudiation unless (i) the buyer makes it plain by words or conduct that he is unable or unwilling to accept the goods, or (ii) he has, by his own act or default, finally and completely disabled himself from accepting them, or (iii) he fails to perform his obligation to accept the goods, provided that in each case the buyer's act or default would be or is a breach which goes to the root of the contract of sale.[43] A neglect or refusal to take delivery may, however, be a breach of condition, as, for example, where a buyer under an f.o.b. contract neglects or refuses to nominate an effective ship timeously or at all[44] or where a buyer under a c.i.f. contract refuses to accept the tender of shipping documents which on their face are

---

[38] See below, para.15–028.

[39] *Somes v British Empire Co.*, above.

[40] *Harlow and Jones Ltd v Panex International Ltd* [1967] 2 Lloyd's Rep. 509 at 531: "It seems to me an eminently sensible commercial arrangement."

[41] See above, para.8–077; below, para.9–010. *Cf.* Vienna Convention on Contracts for the International Sale of Goods, Arts 61–65 (above, para.1–024).

[42] Sale of Goods Act 1979, s.31(2). See (no repudiation): *Kent v Godts* (1855) 26 L.T. (O.S.) 88; *Simpson v Crippin* (1872) L.R. 8 Q.B. 14; *Dickinson v Fanshaw* (1892) 8 T.L.R. 271; *Dominion Coal Co. Ltd v Dominion Iron and Steel Co. Ltd* [1909] A.C. 293; *Spettabile Consorzio Veneziano di Armamento e Navigazione v Northumberland Shipbuilding Co. Ltd* (1919) 121 L.T. 628; *Warinco AG v Samor SpA* [1979] 1 Lloyd's Rep. 450. *Cf.* (repudiation) *Morgan v Bain* (1874) L.R. 10 C.P. 15; *Bloomer v Bernstein* (1874) L.R. 9 C.P. 588; *Honck v Muller* (1881) 7 Q.B.D. 92; *Braithwaite v Foreign Hardwood Co. Ltd* [1905] 2 K.B. 543. See above, paras 8–077 *et seq*.

[43] *Warinco AG v Samor SpA* [1977] 2 Lloyd's Rep. 582 at 588 (reversed on its facts [1979] 1 Lloyd's Rep. 450); *Anchor Line Ltd v Keith Rowell Ltd* [1980] 2 Lloyd's Rep. 351 at 354, 359; *Afovos Shipping Co. SA v R Pagnan and Filli* [1983] 1 W.L.R. 195 at 203. See also the cases cited in n.42, above, and above, paras 8–078, 8–079, 8–080.

[44] See below, para.20–046.

in conformity with the contract.[45] A repudiation or breach of condition[46] by the buyer entitles the seller, if he so chooses, to treat himself as discharged from his further obligations under the contract.[47] Even though the time for delivery has not yet arrived, if the buyer makes it plain that he is unable or unwilling to accept the goods, or it is clear that through his own default he will be unable to accept them, the seller may treat this as an anticipatory[48] repudiation of the contract and at once bring an action for damages for the breach.[49]

9–011 **Relevance of seller's inability to perform.**[50] If the seller brings an action against the buyer for damages for non-acceptance of the goods, there is some doubt as to whether and in what circumstances the buyer may raise as a defence to liability, or in reduction of the damages payable, the fact that the seller was or would have been incapable of performing the contract in accordance with its terms. This problem has been considered in a number of cases, but four cases in particular deserve special mention.

9–012 The first of these is the decision of the Court of Appeal in *Braithwaite v Foreign Hardwood Co. Ltd*,[51] where there was a c.i.f.[52] contract for the delivery of rosewood by instalments, cash being payable against bill of lading. While the first instalment was still upon the seas, the buyers unjustifiably repudiated the contract by refusing to accept any wood under it. The seller's agents subsequently informed the buyers that they were ready to hand over the bill of lading for cash as provided by the contract.[53] But the buyers adhered to their repudiation and the seller resold. The bill of lading for the second instalment was likewise refused and again the seller resold. The buyers subsequently discovered that a portion of the first instalment did not answer to the quality of the rosewood in the contract. In an action for non-acceptance brought by the seller, they contended that the seller had elected to treat the contract as still subsisting and had thus kept the contract open for the benefit of both parties[54]; accordingly he had to show that he was ready and willing to deliver the goods in accordance with the contract, which he could not do with regard to the first instalment, so

---

[45] *Gill & Duffus SA v Berger & Co. Inc.* [1984] A.C. 382; below, para.9–014.
[46] But in an instalment contract, the breach of a condition will not necessarily give rise to this right: see s.31(2), n.42, above.
[47] See also (for remedies) s.50(1) of the Act (below, para.16–060) and s.49(1), (2) (below, paras 16–021, 16–025). *Cf.* Vienna Convention on Contracts for the International Sale of Goods, Art.61 (above, para.1–024).
[48] On the nature of "anticipatory breach", see *The Mihalis Angelos* [1971] 1 Q.B. 64 and *Chitty on Contracts* (29th ed.), Vol. 1, paras 24–021, 24–026, 24–030.
[49] See below, para.9–017.
[50] See Lloyd, 37 M.L.R. 121 (1974); Dawson, 96 L.Q.R. 239 (1980).
[51] [1905] 2 K.B. 543. See also below, para.19–167.
[52] This appears from the other reports of this case, see below, para.19–168, n.43.
[53] [1905] 2 K.B. 543 at 549 (*Cf.* pp.544, 553). See the interpretation put upon these facts in *Taylor v Oakes Roncoroni & Co.* (1922) 38 T.L.R. 349 at 351 (affirmed *ibid.*, at p.517); *Brett v Schneideman Bros Ltd* [1923] N.Z.L.R. 938 at 972; *Esmail v J. Rosenthal & Sons Ltd* [1964] 2 Lloyd's Rep. 447 at 466; *Fercometal SARL v Mediterranean Shipping Co. SA* [1989] A.C. 788, and see below, paras 9–015, 19–168.
[54] But see below, para.9–015.

that he was not entitled to any damages in respect of that instalment. This contention was rejected by the Court of Appeal which held that the buyers, by their repudiation of the whole contract, had waived the performance by the seller of the conditions precedent which would otherwise have been necessary to the enforcement by him of the contract. Collins M.R. assumed that the seller had elected to keep the contract alive as against the buyers notwithstanding their repudiation,[55] but stated[56]: "It is not competent for the [buyers] now to hark back and say that the [seller] was not ready and willing to perform the conditions precedent devolving upon him, and that if they had known the facts they might have rejected the instalment when tendered to them . . . The [buyers] are not in a position now, by reason of their after-acquired knowledge, to set up a defence which they previously elected not to make."

The second case is the decision of the House of Lords in *British and Beningtons Ltd v North Western Cachar Tea Co. Ltd*.[57] In that case, the buyers had agreed to purchase certain tea to be delivered in London at a bonded warehouse or ex ship. By order of the Shipping Controller, the ships carrying the tea had been diverted to various ports in England and Scotland. The buyers repudiated the contract on the ground that reasonable time for delivery had expired. The arbitrator found that a reasonable time had not expired. He awarded damages against the buyers on the ground that they were guilty of an anticipatory breach of contract by their refusal to accept the tea. On appeal, the buyers argued that, in order to maintain an action for damages for breach, it was incumbent on the sellers to prove that they were ready and willing to perform the contract and it was further alleged that the sellers never were ready and willing to deliver the tea in London. The House of Lords upheld the decision of the arbitrator. The reason given by Lord Atkinson[58] for so holding was that, the buyers having wrongfully repudiated the contract, the sellers were not bound to prove that they were ready and willing at the date of the repudiation to deliver the tea in London. He relied, in particular, upon the decision of the Court of Appeal in *Braithwaite v Foreign Hardwood Co. Ltd*. Lord Sumner,[59] however, in his speech stated that *Braithwaite's* case was "not quite easy to understand".[60] In his opinion, that case, as reported, did not lay it down that a buyer, who had repudiated a contract for a wrong reason, had, therefore, no other opportunity of defence either as to the whole or as to part, but must fail utterly.[61] "I do not see," he said,[62] "how the fact, that the 9–013

[55] At p.551, contrary to the finding of Kennedy J. at first instance.
[56] [1905] 2 K.B. 543 at 552.
[57] [1923] A.C. 48. See also below, para.19–161.
[58] At p.66.
[59] With whom all the other members of the House of Lords (except Lord Atkinson) agreed.
[60] [1923] A.C. 48 at 70. Lord Sumner had appeared as counsel for the unsuccessful party in *Braithwaite's* case, a fact which is commented upon by Scrutton L.J. in *Continental Contractors Ltd v Medway Oil and Storage Co. Ltd* (1925) 23 Ll.L.R. 55 at 124.
[61] [1923] A.C. 48 at 71. See also the cases cited in below, para.9–016, n.76.
[62] *ibid.*, at p.72.

buyers have wrongly said 'we treat this contract as being at an end, owing to your unreasonable delay in the performance of it' obliges them, when that reason fails, to pay in full, if, at the very time of this repudiation, the sellers had become wholly and finally disabled from performing essential terms of the contract altogether. *Braithwaite's* case says nothing, which affects the regular consequences, when it appears at the time of the breach the plaintiff is already completely disabled from doing his part at all." Nevertheless, Lord Sumner was not satisfied that the sellers could not have forwarded the tea to London, or that the tea, when so forwarded, would not have been still such as the contract provided for. Accordingly he agreed that the award of the arbitrator was correct.

9–014 The third case is that of *Gill & Duffus SA v Berger & Co. Inc.*[63] In that case, sellers sold to buyers by sample 500 tonnes of Argentine "bolita" beans c.i.f. Le Havre. The contract provided for payment against shipping documents on first presentation and that a certificate of quality at port of discharge given by General Superintendance Co. Ltd should be final. On arrival at Le Havre the ship discharged only 445 tonnes of the consignment and over-carried the balance of 55 tonnes to Rotterdam, where it was transhipped and brought back to Le Havre and was discharged there some 12 days later. In the meantime the sellers tendered to the buyers the shipping documents covering the whole contract quantity of 500 tonnes. These were rejected by the buyers on the (invalid) ground that they did not include a certificate of quality. The sellers did not treat this rejection as a repudiation of the contract. They procured a certificate of quality with respect to the 445 tonnes and re-tendered the shipping documents to the buyers together with this certificate. This tender was again refused. The sellers treated this refusal as a wrongful repudiation and elected to rescind the contract. In arbitration proceedings, the arbitration appeal board found that the 445 tonnes contained a commercially significant number (1.8 per cent) of coloured beans, whereas "bolita" beans were white, and that the goods did not correspond with the contract description. At first instance, Lloyd J. held[64] that the finality of the certificate extended to the admixture of coloured beans. He upheld the seller's claim in respect of the 445 tonnes, but upheld the buyers' claim in respect of the 55 tonnes which were not covered by the certificate and which had been found by the board not to be in accordance with the contract description. On appeal,[65] the Court of Appeal found in favour of the buyers. Since the 55 tonnes did not conform to the contract, the buyers were entitled to reject the whole 500 tonnes under section 30(1) and (3) of the Sale of Goods Act 1893[66] notwithstanding the finality of the certificate in respect of the 445 tonnes. The House of Lords, however, defined the legal issues involved in an entirely different manner. Their Lordships pointed out that it had never been contended that the shipping documents tendered and re-tendered by the sellers did not

[63] [1984] A.C. 382; see Treitel [1984] L.M.C.L.Q. 565 and below, para.19–163.
[64] [1982] 1 Lloyd's Rep. 101.
[65] [1983] 1 Lloyd's Rep. 622.
[66] s.30(1) and (4) of the 1979 Act.

upon the face of them conform to the terms of the contract. Accordingly, the refusal of the buyers to accept the re-tendered documents and to pay the contract price amounted to a breach of condition or fundamental breach of the contract of sale. It was not open to a buyer under a c.i.f. contract to justify the rejection of conforming documents if it should subsequently turn out that the goods shipped under the documents did not in fact conform with the contract.[67] Since the sellers had elected to treat the contract as repudiated by reason of the buyer's rejection, they were forthwith released from further performance of their obligations under the contract. Admittedly a c.i.f. buyer who had accepted the shipping documents retained the right to reject the goods if, on delivery, they were found not to be in conformity with the contract.[68] But this was because the c.i.f. contract remained on foot. It followed, therefore, that the buyers could not raise as a defence to liability for the wrongful rejection of the documents any contention that the sellers would not have been able to deliver goods under the documents which conformed with the contract of sale. This question went to quantum of damages alone. On this point the House of Lords held that the buyers lacked any finding of fact that, on the balance of probabilities, a similar certificate would not have been issued in respect of the 55 tonnes. The buyers were therefore liable to the sellers for non-acceptance of the whole of the 500 tonnes.

The fourth case, *Fercometal SARL v Mediterranean Shipping Co. SA (The Simona)*[69] did not concern the sale of goods. A voyage charterparty contained a term which gave to the charterers the option of cancelling the charter should the vessel not be willing to load on or before a certain date. Prior to that date the charterers prematurely purported to exercise their right of cancellation. This constituted an anticipatory breach and repudiation of the contract. This repudiation was not accepted by the shipowners. Nevertheless the vessel was not ready to load by the stipulated date and the charterers then sent a second notice cancelling the charter. The shipowners argued, on the authority of the *Braithwaite* case, that they were absolved from tendering further performance under the contract while the charterers maintained their repudiatory attitude so that the charterers could not rely on the vessel's non-readiness to load to entitle them to cancel the charterparty. The House of Lords, however, held that the shipowners, by affirming the contract, had kept it alive for the benefit of both parties. The charterers were, therefore, notwithstanding their repudiation, entitled by their second notice to cancel the charter upon the shipowner's failure to have the vessel ready to load in accordance with its terms. In his speech,[70] Lord Ackner examined the *Braithwaite* decision and concluded that the buyer's repudiation had in fact been accepted by the seller. He endorsed the view previously expressed on the point by Salmon L.J. in *Esmail v J.* 9–015

[67] Disapproving the opinions to the contrary in *Henry Dean & Sons (Sydney) Ltd v O'Day Pty Ltd* (1927) 39 C.L.R. 330.
[68] *Kwei Tek Chao v British Traders & Shippers Ltd* [1954] 2 Q.B. 459 at 487–488.
[69] [1989] A.C. 788.
[70] With whom all the members of the House of Lords agreed.

Rosenthal & Sons Ltd[71] and the further statement of Salmon L.J. in that case[72] that "The key to *Braithwaite's* case lies in the fact (at first sight artificial) that in that case the documents were never tendered by the seller; there was merely an offer to tender. It was at this stage that the seller accepted the buyers' wrongful repudiation and the contract was rescinded. Accordingly the contract came to an end before the seller had committed any breach. There was no question of the buyers bringing the contract to an end after a fundamental breach by the seller. What might or might not have happened had there been no total breach by the buyers accepted by the seller could not affect the issue of liability but it might be most material on the question of damages. It seems to me that that interpretation is the only one which can bring it into line with the well-established principle referred to and restated in *Heyman and Another v Darwins Ltd*[73] to the effect that a wrongful repudiation by one party has no legal effect until accepted by the other."[74] The decision in *Braithwaite* was therefore not an authority for the proposition advanced by the shipowners, alternatively, if it was, it was wrong.[75]

9–016 As a result of these cases, the following questions arise for consideration:

(1) whether it is a principle of law that a buyer cannot justify his anticipatory refusal to accept goods under a contract on the ground that, if he had not refused, the goods when delivered would not have been in accordance with the contract or that the seller would have been otherwise unable to perform the contract in accordance with its terms;

(2) if such is the principle, how it can be reconciled with the well-known rule of law[76] that a party who refuses to perform a contract may yet justify

[71] [1964] 2 Lloyd's Rep. 447 (this point was not discussed on appeal to the House of Lords in *J. Rosenthal & Sons Ltd v Esmail* [1965] 1 W.L.R. 1117). The analysis of Greer J. in *Taylor v Oakes Roncoroni and Co.* (1922) 38 T.L.R. 349 at 351 (affirmed *ibid.*, at p.517) was adopted. But there is some doubt whether this explanation is entirely consistent with the facts of *Braithwaite's* case: see below, paras 19–167—19–171.

[72] At p.466.

[73] [1942] A.C. 356.

[74] [1989] A.C. at p.805.

[75] Other cases or statements which may now be regarded as suspect are: *Brett v Schneideman Bros Ltd* [1923] N.Z.L.R. 938; *Sinason Teicher Inter-American Grain Corp. v Oilcakes and Oilseeds Trading Co. Ltd* [1954] 1 W.L.R. 935 at 944 (affirmed *ibid.*, at p.1394); *Pump Distributors Pty Ltd v Atherton (Queensland) Pty Ltd* [1969] Qd.R. 213; *Bunge Corp. v Vegetable Vitamin Foods (Private) Ltd* [1985] 1 Lloyd's Rep. 613; *Bulk Oil (Zug) AG v Sun International Ltd* [1984] 1 Lloyd's Rep. 531, 546. But see below, para.9–019 (estoppel).

[76] *British and Beningtons Ltd v N.W. Cachar Tea Co. Ltd* [1923] A.C. 48 at 71–72; *Ridgway v Hungerford Market Co.* (1853) 3 A. & E. 171 at 177, 178, 180; *Boston Deep Sea Fishing and Ice Co. v Ansell* (1888) 39 Ch.D. 339 at 352, 364; *Taylor v Oakes Roncoroni & Co.* (1922) 127 L.T. 267 at 269; *Etablissements Chainbaux SARL v Harbormaster Ltd* [1955] 1 Lloyd's Rep. 303 at 314; *Universal Cargo Carriers Corp. v Citati* [1957] 2 Q.B. 401 at 443–445 (affirmed in part [1957] 1 W.L.R. 979, and reversed in part [1958] 2 Q.B. 259); *Denmark Productions Ltd v Boscobel Productions Ltd* [1969] 1 Q.B. 699 at 722, 732; *The Mihalis Angelos* [1971] 1 Q.B. 164 at 195, 200, 204; *Cyril Leonard & Co. v Simo Securities Trust* [1972] 1 W.L.R. 80 at 85, 87, 89; *Scandinavian Trading Co. A/B v Zodiac Petroleum SA* [1981] 1 Lloyd's Rep. 81 at 90; *State Trading Corp. of India Ltd v M Golodetz Ltd* [1988] 2 Lloyd's Rep. 182, [1989] 2 Lloyd's Rep. 277.

his refusal if there were at the time facts in existence which would have provided a good reason, even though he did not know of them at the time of his refusal;

(3) whether the principle applies both to situations where the seller elects to treat the refusal as a repudiation of the contract and to situations where he elects not to accept the repudiation but continues to press the buyer to accept delivery or even tenders the goods;

(4) whether, on the assumption that the future inability of the seller to perform is immaterial to the buyer's liability, proof of such inability to perform would nevertheless be material to the quantum of damages.

For the purposes of exegesis, it is necessary to distinguish between situations where the seller accepts the repudiation and brings the contract to an end and those where he does not accept the repudiation and treats the contract as still continuing.

Repudiation accepted by seller.[77] Where the repudiation by the buyer is accepted by the seller, it is clear that the seller is thereafter absolved from delivering or tendering the goods to the buyer, since such an act would in the circumstances be nugatory.[78] Further, if and in so far as an averment by the seller of his readiness and willingness to perform the contract is necessary to establish his cause of action,[79] the buyer's repudiation exonerates the seller from proving that he was ready and willing to perform any conditions precedent to the buyer's performance (or concurrent conditions).[80] If the seller brings an action against the buyer for the price of the goods or for damages for non-acceptance, the buyer cannot escape liability by showing that, if he had not repudiated, there would have been no performance by the seller at the time fixed for performance or that the performance would have been defective.[81] The future inability of the seller 9–017

---

[77] See also below, para.19–166.

[78] *Jones v Barkley* (1781) 2 Doug. 684 at 694; *Ripley v M'Clure* (1849) 4 ExCh.345; *Cort. v Ambergate Ry* (1851) 17 Q.B. 127; *Bank of China, Japan and the Straits v American Trading Co.* [1894] A.C. 266 at 274; *Braithwaite v Foreign Hardwood Co. Ltd* [1905] 2 K.B. 543 at 552; *Cohen & Co. v Ockerby & Co. Ltd* (1917) 24 C.L.R. 288; *Cooper Ewing & Co. v Hamel and Horley Ltd* (1922) 13 Ll.L.R. 446 at 590, 592; *British and Beningtons Ltd v North Western Cachar Tea Co. Ltd* [1923] A.C. 48 at 63–66; *YP Barley Producers Ltd v EC Robertson Pty Ltd* [1927] V.L.R. 194 at 209; *Gill & Duffus SA v Berger & Co. Inc.* [1984] A.C. 382 at 395–396.

[79] By RSC Ord. 18, r. 7(4) compliance with conditions precedent was implied. But see now CPR 16.4(1)(a). *Cf. Jefferson v Paskell* [1916] 1 K.B. 57.

[80] *Braithwaite v Foreign Hardwood Co. Ltd*, above, at pp.551, 554; *Cooper, Ewing & Co. Ltd v Hamel & Horley Ltd*, above, at p.593; *Taylor v Oakes Roncoroni & Co.* (1922) 38 T.L.R. 349 at 517; *British and Beningtons Ltd v North Western Cachar Tea Co. Ltd*, above, at p.66 (*Cf. ibid.*, at p.70); *Brett v Schneideman Bros Ltd* [1923] N.Z.L.R. 938; *Continental Contractors Ltd v Medway Oil and Storage Co. Ltd* (1925) 23 Ll.L.R. 55 at 124, 128, 132; *YP Barley Producers Ltd v E C Robertson Pty Ltd*, above, at p.309. *Cf. Cohen & Co. v Ockerby & Co. Ltd* (1917) 24 C.L.R. 288. Contrast Dawson, 96 L.Q.R. 239 (1980).

[81] *Cooper, Ewing & Co. Ltd v Hamel and Horley Ltd*, above, at p.593; *Taylor v Oakes Roncoroni & Co.* above, at p.351; *British and Beningtons Ltd v North Western Cachar Tea Co. Ltd*, above, at p.72; *Brett v Schneideman Bros Ltd*, above; *Pump Distributors Pty Ltd v Atherton (Queensland) Pty Ltd* [1969] Qd.R. 213; *Gill & Duffus SA v Berger & Co. Inc.*, above.

to perform the contract in accordance with its terms is irrelevant since his election to treat the contract as repudiated brings to an end all primary obligations of the parties which have not yet fallen due for performance at the time of acceptance of the repudiation.[82] However, if, at the time of the repudiation, the seller has (unknown to the buyer) already committed a breach which would have justified the repudiation[83] or (*semble*) if it is clear that the seller was at that time finally and completely disabled from performing,[84] the buyer can successfully resist an action for non-acceptance of the goods. Although he repudiated the contract for the wrong reason or for no reason at all, he may yet justify his action if there were at the time facts in existence which would have provided a good reason.[85]

9–018 **Repudiation not accepted by seller.** Where the repudiation is not accepted by the seller, the contract is then kept alive for the benefit of both parties: the seller remains subject to all the obligations and liabilities under it and takes the risk that he will, when the time for performance arrives, be unable to perform the contract in accordance with its terms or at all, or that some other event will occur which releases the buyer from liability.[86] Since the seller continues to be bound to deliver the goods in accordance with the contract, it is a good defence to liability for the buyer to show that, notwithstanding his refusal to accept the goods, the seller has failed or is unable to perform his obligations under the contract in some fundamental respect at the time appointed for their performance.[87] Even if the buyer persists in his refusal to accept, he does not thereby waive performance by the seller of the conditions precedent devolving on him.[88] In *The Simona*[89] Lord Ackner said: "When A wrongfully repudiates his contractual obliga-

---

[82] *Gill & Duffus SA v Berger & Co. Inc.*, above.

[83] This was not the case in *Braithwaite v Foreign Hardwood Co. Ltd*, above; see *Taylor v Oakes Roncoroni & Co.* (1922) 38 T.L.R. 349 at 351 (affirmed *ibid.*, at p.517); *Esmail v Rosenthal & Sons Ltd* [1964] 2 Lloyd's Rep. 447 at 466; and see above, para.9–015. Also, in the case of a c.i.f. contract, the fact that the buyer has shipped non-conforming goods does not justify a subsequent wrongful rejection of conforming documents: *Gill & Duffus SA v Berger & Co.* [1984] A.C. 382; above, para.9–014; below, para.19–163.

[84] *Cooper, Ewing & Co. Ltd v Hamel & Horley Ltd*, above; *British and Beningtons Ltd v North Western Cachar Tea Co. Ltd*, above, at p.72. See also *Chitty on Contracts* (29th ed.), Vol. 1, para.24–028. But *cf.*, *Gill & Duffus SA v Berger & Co. Inc.*, above.

[85] See the cases cited in para.9–016, n.76.

[86] *Avery v Bowden* (1855) 5 E. & B. 714; (1856) 6 E. & B. 953; *Frost v Knight* (1872) L.R. 7 Ex. 111 at 112; *Johnstone v Milling* (1886) 16 Q.B.D. 460 at 470; *Michael v Hart & Co.* [1902] 1 K.B. 482; *Heyman v Darwins Ltd* [1942] A.C. 356 at 361; *Segap Garages Ltd v Gulf Oil (Great Britain) Ltd, The Times*, October 24, 1988; *Fercometal SARL v Mediterranean Shipping Co. SA (The Simona)* [1989] A.C. 788 (above para.9–015). *Cf.* "Anticipatory Breach," by Mustill L.J., *Butterworth's Lectures 1989–1990* (1990).

[87] *Cohen & Co. v Ockerby & Co. Ltd* (1917) 24 C.L.R. 288; *Taylor v Oakes Roncoroni & Co.* (1922) 38 T.L.R. 349 at 351 (affirmed *ibid.*, at p.517); *Bowes v Chaleyer* (1923) 32 C.L.R. 159 at 169, 192, 197–199; *State Trading Corp. of India v M Golodetz Ltd* [1989] 2 Lloyd's Rep. 277. See further Treitel, 106 L.Q.R. 185 at 188 (1990).

[88] Contrast the cases decided before the *Simona* case (above), cited in para.9–015, n.75. But see *Foran v Wight* (1989) 168 C.L.R. 385; below, para.9–019.

[89] *Fercometal SARL v Mediterranean Shipping Co. SA (The Simona)* [1989] A.C. 788 at 805 (above, para.9–015).

tions in anticipation of the time for their performance, he presents the innocent party B with two choices. He may either affirm the contract by treating it as still in force or he may treat it as finally and conclusively discharged. There is no third choice, as a sort of via media, to affirm the contract and yet to be absolved from tendering further performance unless and until A gives reasonable notice that he is once again able and willing to perform. Such a choice would negate the contract being kept alive for the benefit of *both* parties and deny to the party who unsuccessfully sought to rescind, the right to take advantage of any supervening circumstance which would justify him in declining to complete."

Nevertheless, even where the seller has not accepted the buyer's repudiation, there may be circumstances where a refusal to accept, persisted in by the buyer, may release the seller from performance of one or more of his obligations under the contract. The first is where the buyer has, by words or conduct, represented to the seller that he will no longer require performance of that obligation, and the seller acts upon that representation. In *The Simona*,[90] Lord Ackner said: "Of course, it is always open to A, who has refused to accept B's repudiation of the contract, and thereby kept the contract alive, to contend that in relation to a particular right or obligation under the contract, B is estopped from contending that he, B, is entitled to exercise that right or that he, A, has remained bound by that obligation. If B represents to A that he no longer intends to exercise that right or requires the obligation to be fulfilled by A and A acts upon that representation, then clearly B cannot be heard thereafter to say that he is entitled to exercise that right or that A is in breach of contract by not fulfilling that obligation." But their Lordships held that no estoppel had been established on the facts in that case. The need to prove the necessary clear and unequivocal representation and reliance to found an estoppel would, in English law, keep this exception within fairly narrow bounds. However, a different view from that of Lord Ackner was expressed by Brennan J. in the High Court of Australia in *Foran v Wight*,[91] where he said[92]: "I would hold .. that an intimation of non-performance of an essential term of a contract amounts to a repudiation and dispenses a party who acts upon it from performance of his dependent obligation though he does not rescind the contract. Therefore I am unable with respect to agree with Lord Ackner's rejection of what his Lordship described as a third choice . . . The proposition that, if a repudiation by anticipatory breach is not accepted, the contract subsists is undoubted; but it does not follow that an intimation by one party that tender of performance by the other will be nugatory cannot, if acted on, dispense the other from his obligation of performance under the contract by raising an equitable estoppel. It may be that Lord Ackner acknowledges some role for estoppel in this context . . . 9–019

[90] [1989] A.C. 788 at 805. See also *UGS Finance Ltd v National Mortgage Bank of Greece* [1964] 1 Lloyd's Rep. 446 at 452; *Cerealmangimi SpA v Toepfer* [1981] 1 Lloyd's Rep. 337; and below, para.19–160.
[91] (1989) 168 C.L.R. 385 (Mason J. dissenting). See also *Mahoney v Lindsay* (1980) 55 A.L.J.R. 118.
[92] At pp.421–422.

In my view an equity by estoppel arising from an intimation by A that he does not intend to perform which conveys to B that performance by him would be nugatory absolves B 'from tendering further performance unless and until A gives reasonable notice that he is once again able and willing to perform.'" It is arguable that the difference of opinion between the House of Lords and Brennan J. lies only in the ease with which the requirements of representation and reliance may be satisfied in order to give rise to an estoppel. But the approach adopted by Brennan J. suggests that an anticipatory repudiation by the buyer—though not accepted by the seller as discharging the contract—would in itself amount to a representation that it was pointless for the seller to complete the contract and, if acted upon, would relieve the seller from complying with the dependent conditions which he would otherwise be bound to perform, unless the buyer communicated to him a change of stance before the time for performance arrived. Such an approach, it is submitted, is inconsistent with the decision of the House of Lords in *The Simona*.

Secondly, where the non-performance by the seller of his obligations is prevented by the buyer's breach of contract or by an event due to the fault of the buyer, the buyer cannot set up that non-performance as a defence to liability.[93]

Thirdly, where the buyer repudiates the contract by insisting that it be performed in a manner not required by its terms,[94] and the seller attempts to arrange a substitute performance acceptable to the buyer, the buyer may not be entitled to rely upon a failure by the seller to perform an obligation if that failure results from the seller's efforts to comply with his demand.[95]

9–020 **Effect on quantum.** The further question which arises is whether the fact that the seller would, at the time appointed for performance, have been unable to perform, or that his performance would have been defective, while affording no defence to the buyer against liability, might nevertheless be material in assessing the quantum of damages. The termination of the primary obligations of the parties under the contract by reason of the seller's acceptance of the buyer's repudiation does not prejudice the seller's right to claim damages from the buyer for any loss sustained in consequence of the non-performance by the buyer of his primary obligations under the contract, future as well as past.[96] In *Gill & Duffus SA v Berger & Co. Inc.*,[97] however, Lord Diplock said[98] that the prima facie measure of damages (in that case, the difference between the contract price and the

---

[93] *Heyman v Darwins Ltd* [1942] A.C. 356 at 361; *Fercometal SARL v MSC Mediterranean Shipping Co. SA (The Simona)* [1987] 2 Lloyd's Rep. 236 at 240, CA; *Segap Garages Ltd v Gulf Oil (Great Britain) Ltd, The Times*, October 24, 1988. See also *Bulk Oil (Zug) AG v Sun International Ltd* [1984] 1 Lloyd's Rep. 531, 546.

[94] See *e.g. BV Oliehandel Jonglarid v Coastal International Ltd* [1983] 2 Lloyd's Rep. 463.

[95] *Peter Turnbull & Co. Ltd v Mundas Trading Co. (Australasia) Pty Ltd* [1954] 2 Lloyd's Rep. 198, as explained in *Fercometal SARL v MSC Mediterranean Shipping Co. SA (The Simona)* [1987] 2 Lloyd's Rep. 236 at 242–243, CA.

[96] *Gill & Duffus SA v Berger & Co. Inc.* [1984] A.C. 382.

[97] [1984] A.C. 382; above, para.9–014.

[98] At p.392.

price obtainable on the market for the documents representing the goods at the date of the acceptance of the repudiation) might "fall to be reduced by any sum which the buyers could establish they would have been entitled to set up in diminution of the contract price by reason of a breach of warranty as to description or quality of the goods represented by the shipping documents that had actually been shipped by the sellers if those goods had in fact been delivered to them." And again he stated[99]: "As already mentioned, if the seller sued the buyer for damages for his failure to pay the price against tender of conforming shipping documents, the buyer, if he could prove that the seller would not have been able to deliver goods under those shipping documents that conformed with the contract of sale, would be able to displace the prima facie measure of damages by an amount by which the value of the goods was reduced below the contract price by that disconformity." These remarks were made in the context of the buyer's repudiation of a c.i.f. contract[1] and would appear to be limited to the situation where, prior to that repudiation, the seller had already committed a breach of the contract (in that case, the alleged failure to ship conforming goods). The question is therefore left open whether the buyer would likewise be entitled to plead, in diminution of the damages payable to the seller, that, in the absence of his anticipatory repudiation of the contract, the seller would have been unable on the due date for performance to have performed the contract in accordance with its terms or at all. On this question authority is divided.[2] But it is submitted that the court should be entitled to take into account all contingencies which would have extinguished or reduced the seller's loss.[3] Otherwise the seller would be entitled to windfall damages in respect of a loss which, in fact, he would never have sustained. This will necessarily involve the court in an assessment of what would have happened if the contract had not been repudiated[4] and of the seriousness of the seller's potential breach.[5] In cases of total inability to perform, the damages might in consequence be nominal only. In other cases, where the seller's inability to perform was induced by the buyer's refusal to accept, it might be inappropriate for any reduction to

---

[99] At p.396.

[1] See below, para.19–166.

[2] See *Braithwaite v Foreign Hardwood Co. Ltd* (1905) 92 L.T. 637 (*Cf.*, *ibid.*, [1905] 2 K.B. 543); *British and Beningtons Ltd v North Western Cachar Tea Co. Ltd* [1923] A.C. 48 at 71, 72; *YP Barley Producers Ltd v EC Robertson Pty Ltd* [1927] V.L.R. 194; *Esmail v Rosenthal & Sons Ltd* [1964] 2 Lloyd's Rep. 447 at 466. Contrast *Taylor v Oakes, Roncoroni & Co.* (1922) 38 T.L.R. 349 at 517; *Continental Contractors Ltd v Medway Oil and Storage Co. Ltd* (1925) 23 Ll.L.R. 55 at 124, 132; *Brett v Schneideman Bros Ltd* [1923] N.Z.L.R. 938 at 968–978.

[3] See *The Mihalis Angelos* [1971] 1 Q.B. 164 (damages reduced by inevitable exercise of right to terminate contract), followed in *Kurt A Becher GmbH & Co. KG v Roplak Enterprises KG (The World Navigator)* [1991] 2 Lloyd's Rep. 23; *North Sea Energy Holdings NV v Petroleum Authority of Thailand* [1999] 1 Lloyd's Rep. 483; *BS & N Ltd (BVI) v Micado Shipping Ltd (Malta) (The Seaflower)* [2000] 2 Lloyd's Rep. 37, *Golden Strait Corp. v Nippon Yusen Kubishika Kaisha (The Golden Victory)* [2005] EWCA Civ 1190, [2005] 2 Lloyd's Rep. 47. See *Chitty on Contracts* (29th ed.), Vol. 1, para.26–041.

[4] *Gill & Duffus SA v Berger & Co. Inc.*, above, at p.397.

[5] *Bunge Corp. v Vegetable Vitamin Foods (Private) Ltd* [1985] 1 Lloyd's Rep. 613.

be made. The burden of proving the seller's inability to perform the contract in accordance with its terms would appear to rest on the buyer, at least in so far as he seeks to displace the prima facie measure of damages by an amount by which the value of the goods was reduced below the contract price by disconformity.[6] But this would not absolve a seller who claims in respect of some special or consequential loss from his ordinary obligation to prove the circumstances which gave rise to that loss.[7]

2. PAYMENT

9–021 **In general.** It is the duty of the buyer to pay for the goods in accordance with the terms of the contract of sale.[8] The method,[9] place[10] and time[11] of payment are, therefore, in the first instance, to be determined by reference to the terms of the contract of sale, although, by section 28 of the Sale of Goods Act 1979, unless otherwise agreed, delivery of the goods and payment of the price are concurrent conditions, that is to say, the seller must be ready and willing to give possession of the goods to the buyer in exchange for the price and the buyer must be ready and willing to pay the price in exchange for possession of the goods.[12] An obligation on the part of the buyer to pay the price does not necessarily connote a right on the part of the seller to sue for the price.[13] As a normal rule, an action will lie at the suit of the seller for the price only where, under the contract of sale, the property in the goods has passed to the buyer, and the buyer wrongfully neglects or refuses to pay for the goods according to the terms of the contract.[14] This rule suffers an exception where, under the contract, the price is payable on a day certain irrespective of delivery[15] and there may be further exceptions.[16] Otherwise the seller's action is one for damages for non-acceptance.[17]

9–022 **Unpaid seller's lien.** An unpaid seller[18] may nevertheless be entitled to a lien or right of retention[19] over the goods where the price is due but unpaid, or where the buyer is insolvent.[20] An unpaid seller may also, in certain

---

[6] *Gill & Duffus SA v Berger & Co. Inc.*, above, at p.396. Contrast *Fercometal SARL v MSC Mediterranean Shipping Co. SA (The Simona)* [1986] 1 Lloyd's Rep. 171 (Leggatt J.).
[7] *Bremer v Rayner* [1979] 2 Lloyd's Rep. 216 at 224, 228.
[8] Sale of Goods Act 1979, s.27. *Cf.* Vienna Convention on Contracts for the International Sale of Goods, Art. 53 (above, para.1–024).
[9] See below, para.9–028.
[10] See below, para.9–047.
[11] See below, para.9–051.
[12] See above, para.8–004; below, para.9–057.
[13] *Stein Forbes & Co. v County Tailoring Co.* (1916) 86 L.J.K.B. 448; *Muller, Maclean & Co. v Leslie and Anderson* (1921) 8 Ll.L.R. 328; *White and Carter (Councils) Ltd v McGregor* [1962] A.C. 413 at 437.
[14] Sale of Goods Act 1979, s.49(1); below, para.16–021.
[15] *ibid.*, s.49(2); below, para.16–025.
[16] See below, para.16–028.
[17] See below, para.16–060.
[18] As defined in s.38 of the 1979 Act; see below, para.15–016.
[19] Sale of Goods Act 1979, s.39(2); below, para.15–028.
[20] *ibid.*, ss.39, 41, 42; below, paras 15–024—15–027.

circumstances, have a right of stoppage in transit where the buyer is insolvent.[21]

Amount of payment. The buyer is bound to pay to the seller the full contract price of the goods unless by their contract the parties have agreed that a discount shall be allowed. If a discount is allowed to the buyer for payment within a stated period, the full price is payable at the end of that period should the reduced price not then have been paid.[22] The parties may agree that the price ultimately payable by the buyer is to be adjusted by reference to the seller's prices prevailing at the time of delivery, or that the stipulated price shall be increased by index-linking[23] or some other factor.[24] 9–023

As a general rule, the payment by the buyer to the seller of a lesser sum than the full contract price (if indisputably due) will not, even if the seller agrees to accept it in full settlement, discharge his obligation to pay the balance, since there will be no consideration for the seller's promise to forgo the residue of the debt.[25] But payment of a lesser sum at a different place or at an earlier time or by a different method[26] will, if made for the benefit of the seller,[27] operate as a valid discharge.[28] Further, the seller may be estopped[29] from going back on his promise to forgo the residue of the debt if it would be inequitable for him to do so.[30] In such a case, the promise to forgo the balance must be clear and unequivocal[31] and it may 9–024

---

[21] *ibid.*, ss.39, 44–46; below, paras 15–061—15–091.

[22] *Amos and Wood Ltd v Kaprow* (1948) 64 T.L.R. 110. *Aliter* if the discount is a "trade discount" or one not expressed to have been allowed only for payment within a stated period.

[23] See *Chitty on Contracts* (29th ed.), Vol. 1, para.21–072.

[24] *cf.*, *Vaswani v Italian Motors (Sales and Services) Ltd* [1997] 1 W.L.R. 270, PC (increase must be in accordance with terms of the contract). Also, where the buyer is a consumer, a term in the contract to this effect may be held to be unfair and not binding on him under the Unfair Terms in Consumer Contracts Regulations 1999, SI 1999/2083, Sch.2, para.1(l), para.2(d); below, para.14–030.

[25] *Pinnel's Case* (1602) 5 Co.Rep. 117a; *Foakes v Beer* (1884) 9 App.Cas. 605; *D. & C. Builders Ltd v Rees* [1966] 2 Q.B. 617; *James Cook Hotel Ltd v Canx Corporate Services Ltd* [1989] 3 N.Z.L.R. 213. See *Chitty on Contracts* (29th ed.), Vol. 1, paras 3–115 *et seq.*

[26] The acceptance of a negotiable instrument issued by the debtor for a smaller amount would at one time suffice (*Goddard v O'Brien* (1882) 9 Q.B.D. 37), but this is no longer so *D & C Builders Ltd v Rees*, above. For the effect of the acceptance of a cheque for part of a debt which is tendered in settlement, see the cases and discussion in McLaughlan 12 N.Z.U.L.R. 259 and *James Cook Hotel Ltd v Canx Corporate Services Ltd*, above; *Haines House Haulage Co. Ltd v Gamble* [1989] 3 N.Z.L.R. 221.

[27] *Vanbergen v St Edmunds Properties Ltd* [1933] 2 K.B. 223.

[28] *Pinnel's Case*, above. *Cf. Couldery v Bartrum* (1881) 19 Ch.D. 394 at 399.

[29] The principle of equitable forbearance or "promissory" estoppel: see *Chitty on Contracts* (29th ed.), Vol. 1, paras 3–128 *et seq.*

[30] *Central London Property Trust Ltd v High Trees House Ltd* [1947] K.B. 130; *Tungsten Electric Co. Ltd v Tool Manufacturing Co. Ltd* (1950) 69 R.P.C. 108; *Tool Metal Manufacturing Co. Ltd v Tungsten Electric Co. Ltd* [1955] 1 W.L.R. 761; *Cf. Ajayi v R. T. Briscoe (Nigeria) Ltd* [1964] 1 W.L.R. 1326; *D. & C. Builders v Rees* [1966] 2 Q.B. 617. See *Chitty on Contracts* (29th ed.), Vol. 1, paras 3–085, 3–128.

[31] *Woodhouse AC Israel Cocoa Ltd SA v Nigerian Produce Marketing Co. Ltd* [1972] A.C. 741; see *Chitty on Contracts* (29th ed.), Vol. 1, para.3–090.

well be that the buyer must also have altered his position[32] in reliance on the promise made to him before the seller will be held to be estopped.[33]

9–025 Part payment of the price by a third party,[34] or by the buyer himself as part of a composition with his creditors,[35] will also discharge his obligation to pay the balance if such part payment is accepted by the seller in satisfaction of the whole debt.

9–026 **"No set-off" clauses.** A contract term which requires the buyer to pay the price in full without any set-off or deduction in respect of any claim which he may have against the seller[36] may be held to be unreasonable and unenforceable under the Unfair Contract Terms Act 1977[37] or, where the buyer is a consumer, may be held to be unfair and not binding on him under the Unfair Terms in Consumer Contracts Regulations 1999.[38]

9–027 **Default in payment.** Default by the buyer in payment may entitle the seller to treat the contract as repudiated. Such a right will arise if the time of payment is of the essence or a fundamental term of the contract of sale.[39] Otherwise the seller must show that the failure to pay is a breach which goes to the root of the contract[40] or that the buyer has made it plain by words or conduct that he is unable or unwilling to pay for the goods.[41]

---

32 *Société Italo-Belge pour le Commerce et l'Industrie v Palm & Vegetable Oils (Malaysia) Sdn. Bhd. (The Post Chaser)* [1981] 2 Lloyd's Rep. 695 at 700–702. See also *Tungsten Electric Co. Ltd v Tool Metal Manufacturing Co. Ltd*, above, at pp.112, 115–116; *Combe v Combe* [1951] 2 K.B. 215 at 220, 225; *Tool Metal Manufacturing Co. Ltd v Tungsten Electric Co. Ltd*, above, at pp.764, 784, 799; *Morrow v Carty* [1957] N.I. 174; *Beesly v Hallwood Estates Ltd* [1960] 1 W.L.R. 549 at 560 (affirmed on other grounds [1961] Ch.105); *Ajayi v R T Briscoe (Nigeria) Ltd*, above, at p.1330; *Woodhouse AC Israel Cocoa Ltd SA v Nigerian Produce Marketing Co. Ltd*, above; *Scandinavian Trading Tanker Co. AB v Flota Petrolera Ecuatoriana (The Scaptrade)* [1983] Q.B. 549 (affirmed [1983] 2 A.C. 694). See also *Chitty on Contracts* (29th ed.), Vol. 1, paras 3–094, 3–135.

33 See also the question of the "suspensive" nature of the doctrine as a necessary limitation to its application: *Chitty on Contracts* (29th ed.), Vol. 1, para.3–096, 3–129; Wilson, 67 L.Q.R. 330 (1951); [1965] C.L.J. 93.

34 *Welby v Drake* (1825) 1 C. & P. 557; *Hirachand Punamchand v Temple* [1911] 2 K.B. 330.

35 *Wood v Roberts* (1818) 2 Stark. 417; *Good v Cheesman* (1831) 2 B. & Ad. 328; *Cook v Lister* (1863) 13 C.B. (N.S.) 543; *West Yorks Darracq Agency Ltd v Coleridge* [1911] 2 K.B. 326.

36 *e.g.*, under Sale of Goods Act 1979, s.53(1); below, para.17–047.

37 ss.3, 6, 13(1)(b); below, para.13–086. See *Stewart Gill Ltd v Horatio Myer & Co. Ltd* [1992] Q.B. 600; *Fastframe Ltd v Lochinski*, unreported, CA, March 3, 1993 (noted in 57 M.L.R. 960 (1994)); *Esso Petroleum Co. Ltd v Milton* [1997] 1 W.L.R. 938; *Surzur Overseas Ltd v Ocean Reliance Shipping Co. Ltd* [1997] C.L.Y. 906; *Skipskredittforeningen v Emperor Navigation* [1998] 1 Lloyd's Rep. 66; *Schenkers Ltd v Overland Shoes Ltd* [1998] 1 Lloyd's Rep. 498; *WRM Group v Wood* [1998] C.L.C. 189.

38 SI 1999/2083, Sch.2, para.1(b)(o); below, para.14–030.

39 See below, para.9–051.

40 See above, paras 8–006, 8–071, 8–077—8–080, 8–086.

41 See above, paras 8–006, 8–078, 8–085.

(a) *Methods of Payment*

Cash. Unless otherwise agreed, the buyer must pay or tender[42] the price of the goods to the seller in cash at the time and place indicated by the contract of sale, and the seller need not accept payment or tender otherwise than in lawful money.[43] The parties may, however, expressly or impliedly agree that payment may be made in some other manner, and, in the absence of any express stipulation, the method of payment may be determined by the course of dealing between the parties or by trade custom.[44] Notwithstanding that the method of payment has been agreed in the contract of sale, the seller may waive strict compliance with the contractual terms.[45] 9–028

Method to be arranged. Where the method of payment is to be arranged subsequent to the contract, and the buyer wrongfully refuses or neglects to make an arrangement within a reasonable time, it has been held that he is bound to pay the price of the goods sold in cash if then due.[46] 9–029

Payment by negotiable instrument. Payment may, by agreement, be made by means of a negotiable instrument such as a bill of exchange,[47] cheque or promissory note. It is a well-established rule that payment by means of a negotiable instrument[48] is prima facie conditional on the instrument being honoured at maturity.[49] The seller's remedy to sue for the 9–030

---

[42] For the general principles of law relating to tender, see *Chitty on Contracts* (29th ed.), Vol. 1, paras 21–083 *et seq*.

[43] See, *e.g. Gordon v Strange* (1847) 1 ExCh.477. For legal tender, see the Currency and Bank Notes Act 1954, s.1; Coinage Act 1971, s.2; Currency Act 1983, s.1.

[44] It is submitted that, in modern conditions, when an account is sent to the buyer, trade custom will permit payment by cheque and by post: see below, para.9–042. See also payment in overseas sales, below, paras 19–075, 20–055, 22–006, 22–018, 22–031.

[45] *Panoutsos v Raymond Hadley Corp. of New York* [1917] 2 K.B. 473; *Plasticmoda Societa per Azioni v Davidsons (Manchester) Ltd* [1952] 1 Lloyd's Rep. 527; *Enrico Furst & Co. v WE Fischer* [1960] 2 Lloyd's Rep. 340; *WJ Alan & Co. Ltd v El Nasr Export and Import Co.* [1972] 2 Q.B. 189; and see below, para.9–055.

[46] *Hall v Conder* (1857) 2 C.B. (N.S.) 22 (affirmed *ibid.*, at p.53).

[47] For the use of bills as a means of payment in overseas transactions, see below, para.22–031. See also s.19(3) of the Sale of Goods Act 1979; above, para.5–138.

[48] It has been said that the rule does not apply to non-negotiable instruments: *James v Williams* (1845) 13 M. & W. 828, but it is probable that a cheque crossed non-negotiable or "account payee" is still within the rule: Bills of Exchange Act 1882, ss.8, 76, 81, 81A. *Cf. Plimley v Westley* (1835) 2 Bing.N.C. 249.

[49] *Owenson v Morse* (1796) 7 T.R. 64 at 66; *Sayer v Wagstaff* (1844) 5 Beav. 415 at 423; *Griffiths v Owen* (1844) 13 M. & W. 58 at 64; *James v Williams*, above, at p.833; *Baker v Walker* (1845) 14 M. & W. 465 at 468; *Belshaw v Bush* (1851) 11 C.B. 191 at 205; *Crowe v Clay* (1854) 9 ExCh.604 at 608; *Griffiths v Perry* (1859) 1 E. & E. 680 at 688; *Currie v Misa* (1875) L.R. 10 Ex. 153 at 163 (affirmed (1876) 1 App.Cas. 554); *Cohen v Hale* (1878) 3 Q.B.D. 371 at 373; *Re, Romer and Haslam* [1893] 2 Q.B. 286 at 296, 300, 303. In *Gunn v Bolckow, Vaughan & Co.* (1875) L.R. 10 Ch.App. 491 at 501, and in *Bolt and Nut Co. (Tipton) Ltd v Rowlands Nicholls & Co. Ltd* [1964] 2 Q.B. 10 at 18, 21, the presumption was said to be even more strong between traders. The rule also applies if the instrument is given to the seller by a third party: *Belshaw v Bush*, above; *Allen v Royal Bank of Canada* (1925) 95 L.J.P.C. 17, and where the instrument is, at the seller's request, payable to a third party: *Price v Price* (1847) 16 M. & W. 232 at 241; *National Savings Bank Association Ltd v Tranah* (1867) L.R. 2 C.P. 556.

price[50] is suspended during the currency of the instrument.[51] If the instrument is honoured at maturity, the amount expressed therein is effectively paid[52]; if it is dishonoured, the seller's remedy revives.[53] By section 38(1)(b) of the Sale of Goods Act 1979,[54] the seller of goods is deemed to be an "unpaid seller" within the meaning of that Act when a bill of exchange or other negotiable instrument has been received as conditional payment, and the condition on which it has been received has not been fulfilled by reason of the dishonour of the instrument or otherwise.

9–031 A negotiable instrument may nevertheless, by agreement, be taken as an absolute payment, in which case the buyer cannot be sued for the price of the goods, the seller's only remedy being to sue on the instrument.[55] It is a question of fact whether the instrument has been accepted as a conditional or absolute payment[56]; but the intention to take an instrument in absolute payment for the goods sold must be clearly shown, and not deduced from ambiguous expressions such as that the instrument was taken "in payment"

---

[50] If the instrument is given for only part of the price, judgment cannot be signed in default for the whole price unless the instrument has been dishonoured: *Nut & Bolt Co. (Tipton) Ltd v Rowlands Nicholls & Co. Ltd*, above.

[51] *Simon v Lloyd* (1835) 2 C.M. & R. 80; *Sayer v Wagstaff*, above, at p.423; *Baker v Walker*, above; *Burliner v Royle* (1880) 5 C.P.D. 354 at 357; *Re Matthew* (1884) 12 Q.B.D. 506; *Elwell v Jackson* (1885) 1 T.L.R. 458; *Re Romer and Haslam*, above, at p.296; *Hadley & Co. Ltd v Hadley* [1898] 2 Ch. 680; *Allen v Royal Bank of Canada*, above.

[52] *Sayer v Wagstaff*, above, at p.423; *Thorne v Smith* (1851) 10 C.B. 659; *Cohen v Hale*, above, at p.373. On the time when payment by cheque is effective, see *Hadley & Co. Ltd v Hadley*, above; *Marreco v Richardson* [1908] 2 K.B. 584; *The Brimnes* [1975] Q.B. 929 at 948, 969; *Cf. Re Owen decd.* [1949] 1 All E.R. 901; *Re Hone* [1951] Ch.85; *Official Solicitor of the Supreme Court v Thomas, The Times*, March 3, 1986. See also *Bottomley v Nuttall* (1858) 5 C.B.(N.S.) 122 (*pro tanto* discharge).

[53] *Puckford v Maxwell* (1794) 6 T.R. 52; *Owenson v Morse* (1796) 7 T.R. 64; *Tempest v Ord* (1815) 1 Mad. 89; *Sayer v Wagstaff* (1844) 5 Beav. 415 at 423; *Valpy v Oakeley* (1851) 16 Q.B. 941: *Crowe v Clay* (1854) 9 ExCh.604 at 608; *Griffiths v Perry* (1859) 1 E. & E. 680; *Currie v Misa* (1875) L.R. 10 Ex. 153 at 163; *Cohen v Hale* (1878) 3 Q.B.D. 371; *Burliner v Royle* (1880) 5 C.P.D. 354 at 357; *Re Romer and Haslam* [1893] 2 Q.B. 286 at 296, 300; *Hadley & Co. Ltd v Hadley* [1898] 2 Ch. 680 at 683; *M'Laren's Trustee v Argylls Ltd*, 1915 2 S.L.T. 241. But where the instrument has been negotiated and is still outstanding in the hands of third parties, the creditor's remedy is still suspended: *Price v Price* (1847) 16 M. & W. 232; *Belshaw v Bush* (1851) 11 C.B. 191; *Davis v Reilly* [1898] 1 Q.B. 1; *Re a Debtor* [1908] 1 K.B. 344 (overruling *Burden v Halton* (1828) 4 Bing. 454). *Cf. Tarleton v Allhusen* (1834) 2 A. & E. 32; *Hadwen v Mendisabel* (1825) 10 Moore C.P. 477; *National Savings Bank Association Ltd v Tranah* (1867) L.R. 2 C.P. 556. Nevertheless, the dishonour of an instrument outstanding in the hands of a third party may revive the unpaid seller's lien: *Valpy v Oakeley*, above; *Gunn v Bolckow, Vaughan & Co.* (1875) L.R. 10 Ch.App. 491. *Cf. Bunney v Poyntz* (1833) 2 L.J.K.B. 55. See below, para.15–036. For the retrospective effect of revival, see *Griffiths v Perry*, above; *Cohen v Hale*, above; *Hadley & Co. Ltd v Hadley*, above.

[54] See below, para.15–018.

[55] *Sard v Rhodes* (1836) 1 M. & W. 153; *Sayer v Wagstaff* (1844) 5 Beav. 415; *Sibree v Tripp* (1846) 15 M. & W. 23. It does not seem necessary in this situation for the instrument to be negotiable: *Lewis v Lyster* (1835) 2 C.M. & R. 704 at 706.

[56] *Gunn v Bolckow, Vaughan & Co.* (1875) L.R. 10 Ch.App. 491 at 501.

for the goods,[57] or "in discharge"[58] or "in settlement"[59] of the price. However, if the seller has the opportunity of receiving cash from the buyer's agent, and voluntarily elects for his own convenience to take the agent's (or a third party's) bill or note[60] in preference to cash, the liability of the buyer to pay the price will be discharged.[61]

Negotiable instrument equivalent to cash. Where an application is made by the seller under CPR Part 24 for summary judgment on a claim on a bill of exchange, cheque or promissory note given as payment for goods supplied, the general rule is that summary judgment will be given on the claim save in exceptional circumstances. "We have repeatedly said in this court that a bill of exchange or promissory note is to be treated as cash. It is to be honoured unless there is a good reason to the contrary."[62] It is well established that a claim by the buyer for unliquidated damages for breach of the underlying contract of sale is not such a reason, nor is it available as a set-off or counterclaim.[63] The court may, however, dismiss the application if there has been a total failure of consideration[64] and, in the exercise of its discretion, may dismiss it as to part only of the claim if there has been a partial failure of consideration in a liquidated amount[65] or even if there is a liquidated counterclaim arising out of the same transaction which can be raised by way of legal set-off.[66] But, in such a case, the court may make a conditional order requiring the buyer to pay into court the amount in dispute.[67] 9–032

---

57 *Maillard v Duke of Argyle* (1843) 6 M. & G. 40.
58 *Kemp v Watt* (1846) 15 M. & W. 672.
59 *Re Romer and Haslam* [1893] 2 Q.B. 286.
60 But not a cheque: *Everett v Collins* (1810) 2 Camp. 515; *Smith v Ferrand* (1827) 7 B. & C. 19 at 24, 25; *Anderson v Hillies* (1852) 12 C.B. 499 at 504, 505.
61 *Marsh v Pedder* (1815) 4 Camp. 257 at 263; *Strong v Hart* (1827) 6 B. & C. 160; *Smith v Ferrand*, above; *Robinson v Read* (1829) 9 B. & C. 449 at 455; *Anderson v Hillies*, above; *The Huntsman* [1894] P. 214 at 219. Contrast *Robinson v Read*, above; *Davison v Donaldson* (1882) 9 Q.B.D. 623. But see generally Reynolds, 86 L.Q.R. 318 at 326–327, 334 (1970).
62 *Fielding & Platt Ltd v Najjar* [1969] 1 W.L.R. 356 at 361, *per* Lord Denning M.R. See also *Brown Shipley & Co. Ltd v Alicia Hosiery Ltd* [1966] 1 Lloyd's Rep. 668 at 669; *Cebora SNC v SIP Industrial Products Ltd* [1976] 1 W.L.R. 271 at 274, 278, 279; *Montecchi v Simco (UK) Ltd* [1979] 1 Lloyd's Rep. 509 at 511; and below, paras 22–062—22–064.
63 *Nova (Jersey) Knit Ltd v Kammgarn Spinnerei GmbH* [1977] 1 W.L.R. 713 at 732. See also the cases cited in n.62, above.
64 *Montebianco Industrie Tessili SpA v Carlyle Mills (London) Ltd* [1981] 1 Lloyd's Rep. 509 at 511. See also *Fielding & Platt Ltd v Najjar*, above; *All Trades Distributors v Agencies Kaufman* (1969) 113 S.J. 995; *Nova (Jersey) Knit Ltd v Kammgarn Spinnerei GmbH*, above, at pp.726, 732.
65 *Saga of Bond Street Ltd v Avalon Promotions Ltd* [1972] 2 Q.B. 325; *Thoni GmbH v RTP Equipment Ltd* [1979] 2 Lloyd's Rep. 282.
66 *Barclays Bank Ltd v Aschaffenberger Zellstoffwerke AG* [1967] 1 Lloyd's Rep. 387.
67 *All Trades Distributors v Agencies Kaufman*, above; *Saga of Bond Street Ltd v Avalon Promotions Ltd*, above; *Thoni GmbH v RTP Equipment Ltd*, above.

9–033 **Payment by credit or charge card.**[68] Credit card (or charge card) transactions may involve two parties or three parties. In a two-party transaction, the issuer of the card himself supplies goods to the cardholder and the cardholder undertakes to pay for the goods supplied in accordance with the terms of the credit agreement made between them. It is clear that, in a two-party situation, the cardholder remains always liable to pay the card issuer/supplier for the goods purchased by use of the card. In a three-party transaction, the card-issuing company is an entity distinct from the supplier of the goods. Three separate contracts exist: (i) the contract of sale between the supplier and the cardholder; (ii) the contract between the card-issuing company and the supplier by which the card-issuing company undertakes to reimburse[69] the supplier the purchase price of the goods as recorded in the sales voucher, less an agreed discount or commission due to the company; and (iii) the contract between the card-issuing company and the cardholder by which the cardholder agrees to reimburse the company in respect of purchases made by use of the card on the terms agreed between them. In *Re Charge Card Services Ltd*,[70] the Court of Appeal held that, unlike payment by negotiable instrument[71] or letter of credit,[72] there was no presumption that the use of the card constituted conditional payment only by the cardholder. Whether the card was accepted by the supplier as conditional or absolute payment depended on the terms of the contract between the supplier and the cardholder, and those terms would have to be inferred from the parties' conduct and the circumstances known to them at the time of the sale. On the facts of the case, which involved a charge card scheme under which participating garages accepted cards of the card-issuing company in payment for fuel supplied to cardholders and charged the price of the fuel so supplied to the card-issuing company, it was held that payment by means of the card was an absolute discharge of the cardholders' liability to the garages. It was not conditional upon the card-issuing company making payment to the garage which supplied the fuel or upon the cardholder making payment to the card-issuing company. Accordingly, where (as in this case) the card-issuing company had sold its receivables to a factor under an invoice discounting agreement and then became insolvent, leaving the garages unpaid, the debts due from cardholders were payable to the factor, and the garages could not call upon cardholders to pay them direct. Although a contrary conclusion could possibly be reached on different facts in a particular case, it is submitted

68 See Stephenson, *Credit, Debit and Cheque Cards; Law and Practice* (1993); Brindle and Cox, *Law of Bank Payments* (3rd ed.), 4–001, 5–020; Ellinger, Lomnicka and Hooley, *Modern Banking Law* (4th ed.), p.581. below, para.14–149.
69 In some three-party transactions, the documentation may be so formulated as to give rise to assignment by the supplier to the card-issuing company of the debt of the cardholder to the supplier constituted by the purchase of the goods. But see *Commissioners of Customs and Excise v Diners Club Ltd* [1989] 1 W.L.R. 1196.
70 [1989] Ch.497.
71 See above, para.9–030.
72 See below, paras 9–040, 23–098.

that payment by credit or charge card (or by debit card)[73] will normally be taken to discharge the cardholder absolutely from his liability to pay the price of the goods to the supplier. The cardholder's liability will lie only to the card-issuing company.

Payment by cheque accompanied by cheque card. Different considerations, however, apply to the situation where a buyer purchases goods by means of a cheque accompanied by production of a "cheque card" (or "cheque guarantee card"). A bank which issues such a card to its customer undertakes to any person who accepts a cheque drawn payable to him by the customer in payment for goods supplied that the cheque will be paid on presentment, provided the conditions printed or referred to on the card are satisfied. The bank's undertaking was described by Lord Diplock in *Metropolitan Police Commissioner v Charles*[74] as one that "gives the payee a direct contractual right against the bank itself to payment on presentment, provided that the use of the card by the drawer to bind the bank to pay the cheque was within the actual or ostensible authority conferred upon him by the bank." However, unlike the case of credit card, charge card or debit card transactions, there is no written "master" or "merchant" agreement between the issuer of the card and the supplier. Reliance has to be placed by the supplier on the bank's undertaking conveyed to him by the cardholder's representation of his authority from the bank to make a contract on the bank's behalf.[75] Further, the bank does not undertake to pay for the goods supplied, but undertakes not to dishonour the cardholder's cheque on presentation for want of funds in the cardholder's account, so that it is obliged if necessary to advance money to its customer (the cardholder) to meet it. When the bank pays the cheque, it honours its own undertaking as principal to the supplier, and, as agent of its customer, makes payment out of the customer's own moneys, whether or not these have been advanced to him for that purpose. In *Re Charge Card Services Ltd*[76] Millett J., at first instance, stated that the presumption that the giving of a cheque operated as conditional payment only would not be displaced merely by the fact that the cheque was accompanied by a cheque card. On appeal, this point was expressly left open.[77] But it is submitted that Millett J.'s statement is correct. Payment by this means would not raise the inference that the cardholder was absolutely discharged from liability to pay for the goods supplied. 9–034

[73] In the case of a debit card, purchases made by use of the card are not debited to a distinct card account, but are debited directly to a current account maintained by the cardholder with the card issuer (usually a bank or building society). Although payment by these means resembles, in some respects, payment by cheque, it is submitted that the intention is that the cardholder's liability to the supplier is absolutely discharged.

[74] [1977] A.C. 177 at 182.

[75] *ibid. Cf. R. v Lambie* [1982] A.C. 449. But see *First Sport Ltd v Barclays Bank Plc* [1993] 3 All E.R. 789 (forged signature of drawer).

[76] [1987] Ch.150 at 166.

[77] [1989] Ch.497 at 517.

9–035 **Payment by stored value card.**[78] Stored value cards, sometimes referred to as "digital cash cards" or "electronic purses", are cards on which "value" is stored electronically. This card can be used by the cardholder to pay for goods or services supplied, units of value being transferred electronically from buyer to seller. Some cards depend on a magnetic strip, but others carry more complex information stored in a microchip. Some cards are reloadable and can be charged with additional value, while others lack this facility and are considered disposable once the entire value has been spent. In some cases a stored value card can be used by the cardholder to purchase goods or services only from the card issuer or the card issuer's organisation. In other cases, however, as in three-party credit transactions, the card may be used to effect purchases from any supplier who has agreed to accept payment in this form and the supplier will be reimbursed in accordance with the terms of his agreement in respect of purchases made by use of the card. Since stored value cards are a relatively recent phenomenon, the exact relationship between the participants (the scheme originator, participating banks, supplier and cardholder), and the risks to be borne by each party, have yet to be established.[79] But the strong analogy between stored value and cash suggests that payment by stored value card would be regarded as absolute, and not conditional, payment.[80]

9–036 **Internet payments.**[81] Internet transactions may involve conflict of law[82] and jurisdictional issues. But, apart from these, payments made on line over the internet may give rise to certain special problems. The first and most obvious one is that, since payment is usually in advance of delivery, the buyer is at risk that the goods when delivered may not be in conformity with the contract or may never be delivered at all, and that it will most probably be impractical for him to attempt to recover the payment by legal action, particularly when the seller is in a foreign country. Most business-to-business transactions are paid for in the ordinary way through the banking system. But business-to-consumer transactions will more often be paid for by credit, debit or charge card, the card details being communicated electronically over the internet. Where this method of payment is adopted, then, in the event of non-performance or defective performance of the

---

[78] See Edwards and Waelde, *Law and the Internet* (2nd ed.), Ch.4, p.63; O'Mahony, Peirce and Tewari, *Electronic Payment Systems for E-Commerce* (1997); Ellinger, Lomnicka & Hooley, *Modern Banking Law* (4th ed.), Ch.14(7); Brindle and Cox, *Law of Bank Payments* (3rd ed.), para.5–035.

[79] In particular, since the "value" on the card is pre-purchased by the cardholder, the protection afforded by the Consumer Credit Act 1974 does not apply, as there is no provision of "credit" for purchases. But *cf.* s.14(1)(b). The Banking Code (March 2005) excludes from protection "electronic purses". See also Reed and Davies, *Digital Cash—the Legal Implications* (1995); Finlayson-Brown, (1997) 12 J.I.B.L. 362; Effros (ed.), *Current Legal Issues Affecting Central Banks* (1998), Ch.6; Hooley in (Rider ed.), *The Realm of Company Law—Essays in Honour of Professor Leonard Sealy* (1998), 245; Brindle and Cox, *op. cit.*, para.5–043.

[80] Edwards and Waelde, *op. cit.*, Ch.4; p.71; Brindle and Cox, *Law of Bank Payments* (3rd ed.), para.5–041 *Encyclopedia of Banking Law*, i, DI 315.

[81] See Edwards and Waelde, *Law and the Internet* (2nd ed.), Ch.4; Brindle and Cox, *Law of Bank Payments* (3rd ed.), Ch.5.

[82] See below, para.25–049.

contract of sale, the consumer may in some cases have a claim against the issuer of the card under section 75 of the Consumer Credit Act 1974.[83] Nevertheless this method of payment gives rise to the further risk that the seller or some third party who has acquired knowledge of the consumer's card details may misuse the information obtained to cause unauthorised transactions to be debited to the card account. Again, however, a buyer who is a consumer may (subject to certain conditions) be relieved, in whole or in part, from liability to the card issuer on the card account under the Consumer Credit Act 1974,[84] the Consumer Protection (Distance Selling) Regulations 2000,[85] the Financial Services (Distance Marketing) Regulations 2004[86] or the provisions of the Banking Code.[87] But the coverage of the protection afforded by these measures is nevertheless not comprehensive and in any event the nuisance value of the claims generated by misuse of the card is not inconsiderable. In order to increase consumer confidence in on-line transactions, the card information may be encrypted. Encryption involves the application to electronic data of a mathematical algorithm, the encryption "key", in order to render the data indecipherable by anyone not having access to the appropriate decryption key.[88] It may be supported or enhanced by a site verification service provided by a Trusted Third Party (TTP) which confirms the identity of the payee and which may also certify that the payee applies acceptable standards of security in protecting payment details.[89] Part I of the Electronic Communications Act 2000[90] provides for a voluntary approvals regime to cover providers of cryptography support systems.[91] But it is by no means certain whether any liability would arise for financial loss caused to the consumer by failure of encryption and, if so, who would be liable and in what circumstances.[92]

Risks may also arise for the seller or person receiving payment under an internet transaction in that the payment message may not originate from, or bind, the person who purports to have sent it or may have been altered in transmission. Again the risks may be reduced by encryption and by the use of TTPs to ensure that the message comes from an authentic source and has not been tampered with.[93] 9–037

---

[83] See below, para.14–154. But charge card and debit card transactions do not qualify for this protection.
[84] ss. 83, 84.
[85] SI 2000/2334 (as amended), reg, 21. See below, para.14–057.
[86] SI 2004/7406 reg. 14, See 14–054, n.25.
[87] March 2005, 12.12.
[88] Edwards and Waelde, *op. cit.*, Ch.3, p.39; Brindle and Cox, *op. cit.*, para.5–008.
[89] Brindle and Cox, *op. cit.*, paras 5–012, 5–016.
[90] To be brought into force by statutory instrument.
[91] Edwards and Waelde, *op. cit.*, Ch.3, p.47.
[92] Edwards and Waelde, *op. cit.*, Ch.3, p.48; Brindle and Cox, *op. cit.*, para.5–018. But see the duty of care imposed in certain circumstances by the Electronic Signatures Regulations 2002, SI 2002/318, reg.4(1).
[93] See Brindle and Cox, *op. cit.*, paras 5–007—5–019.

9–038 **Use of banking system.** Payment may be made by use of the banking system, for example, by a banker's draft drawn by one bank on another or drawn by one branch on another branch of the same bank,[94] by cheque[95] or credit transfer, or by an order instructing the buyer's bank to transfer some of the balance of the buyer's account to the credit of the seller at another bank or at another branch of the same bank.[96]

9–039 **Direct debits.** Direct debits may be used to effect payments for goods supplied, in particular where there are recurring payments at regular or irregular intervals of variable amounts. The seller obtains the advantage of prompt payment of the amounts due to him by presenting, through the banking system, direct debit forms to the buyer's bank. The seller is, however, required to furnish an indemnity to all banks participating in the direct debit scheme and, under current banking arrangements, any credit entry obtained by direct debiting may in effect be reversed if disputed by the buyer. In *Esso Petroleum Co. Ltd v Milton*[97] the Court of Appeal held that modern commercial practice was to treat payments by direct debit in the same way as payments by cheque, that is to say, as the equivalent of cash,[98] and that, in general, a payment for goods or services by direct debit should preclude a defence of equitable set-off. It is probable that a seller is under an implied obligation to use his best endeavours to implement payment of any direct debit mandate with which he has been provided.[99]

9–040 **Banker's commercial credits.** The purpose and function of, and the law relating to, payment by means of a banker's commercial credit or a bill of exchange drawn thereunder are dealt with in Chapter 23 of this work.

9–041 **Payment by set-off in account stated.** An account stated with the seller in which the seller has, by mutual agreement, been credited with the whole or part of the price of the goods as a set-off against sums admitted to be

---

94 A draft drawn by one branch on another branch of the same bank is not a cheque or bill: *London City and Midland Bank v Gordon* [1903] A.C. 240. For payment by banker's draft in overseas sales, see below, para.22–018.

95 See above, paras 9–030, 9–034.

96 On bank transfers, see *Tankexpress A/S v Compagnie Financie're Belge des Petroles SA* [1949] A.C. 76; *Tenax Steamship Co. Ltd v The Brimnes (Owners) (The Brimnes)* [1975] Q.B. 929; *Delbrueck & Co. v Barclays Bank International Ltd* [1976] 2 Lloyd's Rep. 341; *Mardorf Peach & Co. Ltd v Attica Sea Carriers Corporation of Liberia* [1977] A.C. 850; *Momm v Barclays Bank International Ltd* [1977] 1 Q.B. 790; *A/S Awilco of Oslo v Fulvia SpA di Navigazione of Cagliari (The Chikuma)* [1981] 1 W.L.R. 314; *Afovos Shipping Co. SA v Romano Pagnan and Pietro Pagnan* [1983] 1 W.L.R. 195. See Goode, *Payment Obligations in Commercial and Financial Transactions* (1983), p.90; *Chitty on Contracts* (29th ed.), Vol. 1, para.21–045, Vol. 2, paras 34–367 *et seq*; Brindle and Cox, *Law of Bank Payments* (3rd ed.), Ch.1.

97 [1997] 1 W.L.R. 938.

98 See para.9–032, above.

99 *Weldon v GRE Linked Life Assurance Ltd* [2000] 2 All E.R. (Comm.) 914 at 919 (an insurance case).

due from him to the buyer, is equivalent to an actual cash payment by the buyer of the amount of the credit.[1]

Payment by post. If money is sent by the buyer to the seller, the buyer must normally bear the risk of his payment going astray, *e.g.* being lost in the post.[2] But a particular mode of payment may be expressly or impliedly authorised by the contract, in which case (in the absence of an express stipulation to the contrary) the buyer's obligation is discharged if he complies with that authorised mode.[3] Thus if the contract expressly or impliedly[4] authorises the buyer to remit payment in cash or by cheque through the post, then, unless otherwise agreed, the risk of loss or delay[5] falls on the seller,[6] provided that the letter is properly addressed and sufficiently stamped[7] and payment is made in a form appropriate to its transmission by post.[8] 9–042

Payment to agent. Discussion of the circumstances in which a principal will be bound by payment to and set-offs against his agent lie outside the scope of this book and reference should be made to works of authority on this subject.[9] 9–043

Payment by agent or third party. Payment of the price by a third party who is not liable to the seller for the price[10] does not normally discharge the buyer's obligation to pay, unless the payment is made by the third party for and on account of the buyer and with his prior authority or subsequent 9–044

---

[1] Co.Litt. 213a; *Owens v Denton* (1835) 1 C.M. & R. 711; *Ashby v James* (1843) 11 M. & W. 542; *Scholey v Walton* (1844) 12 M. & W. 510; *Sutton v Page* (1846) 3 C.B. 204; *Callendar v Howard* (1850) 10 C.B. 290; *Re Harmony Tin and Copper Mining Co.* (1873) L.R. 8 Ch.App. 407 at 414; *Larocque v Beauchemin* [1897] A.C. 358 at 365–366; *North Sydney Investment and Tramway Co. Ltd v Higgins* [1899] A.C. 263 at 273; *Harrison v Tew* [1989] Q.B. 307, [1990] 2 A.C. 523. See also *Livingstone v Whiting* (1850) 15 Q.B. 722. Contrast *Cottam v Partridge* (1842) 4 M. & G. 271 (no agreement to set off items); *Perry v Attwood* (1856) 6 E. & B. 691 (items on one side only).

[2] *Luttges v Sherwood* (1895) 11 T.L.R. 233; *Pennington v Crossley & Sons* (1897) 77 L.T. 43; *Baker v Lipton Ltd* (1899) 15 T.L.R. 435.

[3] *Comber v Leyland* [1898] A.C. 524; *Edmundson v Longton Corp.* (1902) 19 T.L.R. 15.

[4] *Cf. Pennington v Crossley & Son*, above (no necessary inference from course of dealing).

[5] *Cf. Tankexpress A/S v Compagnie Financie're Belge des Petroles SA* [1949] A.C. 76. For lost instruments, see *Chitty on Contracts* (29th ed.), Vol. 2, para.34–147.

[6] *Warwicke v Noakes* (1797) Peake 98; *Norman v Ricketts* (1886) 3 T.L.R. 182; *Thairlwall v GN Ry* [1910] 2 K.B. 509. *Cf. Hawkins v Rutt* (1793) Peake 248.

[7] *cf. Getreide-Import-Gesellschaft v Contimár SA Compania Comercial y Maritima* [1953] 1 W.L.R. 793.

[8] *Mitchell-Henry v Norwich Union Life Insurance Socy* [1918] 1 K.B. 123 (£48 in cash in registered packet). See also *Robb v Gow* (1905) 8 F. 90 (Ct.Sess.) (bearer cheque).

[9] See, *e.g. Bowstead and Reynolds on Agency* (17th ed.), paras 3–021, 8–108.

[10] For payment by one of a number of joint (or joint and several) debtors, see *Chitty on Contracts* (29th ed.), Vol. 1, para.17–001.

ratification.[11] If payment is made without the buyer's prior authority, then, unless and until the payment is ratified by the buyer,[12] the payment may be withdrawn by agreement between the third party and the seller.[13]

9–045 **Currency of payment.** The principles of law applicable to the currency of account and the currency of payment are dealt with in Chapter 25 of this book (Conflict of Laws).[14]

9–046 **Appropriation of payments.** Unless otherwise agreed where the buyer owes more than one debt to the seller, he is entitled, when making a payment, to appropriate the sum paid to whichever debt or debts he pleases, and, if the seller receives the payment so made,[15] he must apply it in the manner directed by the buyer.[16] Should the buyer not exercise his right of appropriation, the seller may appropriate the payment to any lawful debt[17] due to him from the buyer,[18] even if such debt is or has become statute-barred.[19] Special rules apply to appropriation of payments where trading is on the basis of a current account,[20] in the case of guaranteed debts[21] and for certain consumer credit agreements.[22]

(b) *Place of Payment*

9–047 **Place of payment.** Where a certain place is appointed by the contract for payment, payment must be made at that place[23]; and a buyer who has not in fact paid will not be in default if the seller fails to attend at that place to

---

[11] Co.Litt. 206b; *Grymes v Blofield* (1594) Cro.Eliz. 541; *Edgcombe v Rodd* (1804) 5 East 294; *James v Isaacs* (1852) 12 C.B. 791; *Kemp v Balls* (1854) 10 Exch.607; *Simpson v Eggington* (1855) 10 Exch.845 at 847–848; *Lucas v Wilkinson* (1856) 1 H. & N. 420; *Walter v James* (1871) L.R. 6 Ex. 124 at 127, *Purcell v Henderson* (1885) 16 L.R.Ir. 213 at 223–224 (affirmed *ibid.*, at p.466); *Re Rowe* [1904] 2 K.B. 483; *Smith v Cox* [1940] 2 K.B. 558; *Owen v Tate* [1976] 1 Q.B. 402; *Pacific Associates Inc. v Baxter* [1990] 1 Q.B. 993 at 1033; *Pacific and General Insurance Co. Ltd v Hazell* [1997] L.R.L.R. 65; *Crantrave Ltd v Lloyds Bank Plc* [2000] Q.B. 917; Birks and Beatson, 92 L.Q.R. 188 (1976); Goff and Jones, *Law of Restitution* (6th ed.), para.1–018. Contrast *Cook v Lister* (1863) 13 C.B. (N.S.) 543 at 594–595; Burrows, *The Law of Restitution* (2nd ed.), p.293; Friedman, 99 L.Q.R. 534 (1983).

[12] The buyer may ratify such payment by pleading payment: *Belshaw v Bush* (1851) 11 C.B. 191; *Simpson v Eggington*, above.

[13] *Walter v James*, above; *Pacific and General Reinsurance Co. Ltd v Hazell*, above.

[14] Below, paras.25–165, 26–167.

[15] If the seller is unwilling to apply it to the debt for which it is tendered, he must refuse it and stand upon his rights (whatever they may be) or make a counter-proposal for the appropriation.

[16] See *Chitty on Contracts* (29th ed.), Vol. 1, paras 21–059, 21–060.

[17] See *ibid.*, para.21–062.

[18] See *ibid.*, para.21–061. For appropriation between principal and interest, see *ibid.*, para.21–067.

[19] See *ibid.*, para.21–063.

[20] See *ibid.*, para.21–066.

[21] See *ibid.*, para.21–064.

[22] Consumer Credit Act 1974, s.81.

[23] If two places are named, there will be no default until the creditor has fixed the place where he will be paid: *Thorn v City Rice Mills* (1889) 40 Ch.D. 357 at 360.

receive the money.[24] But where no place of payment is specified, the place of payment depends upon the intention of the parties to be gathered from the terms of the contract and the position of the parties and circumstances prevailing at the time it was entered into.[25] In many cases the mode of payment prescribed[26] will therefore determine where payment is to be made.[27] If no place of payment can thus be implied, it has been said to be a general rule that "the debtor must follow his creditor and must pay wherever his creditor is."[28] In commercial transactions, however, the general rule would seem to be that payment is to be made at the place where the creditor resided or carried on business at the time of the contract,[29] and it is submitted that, in contracts of sale, this means the seller's place of business, if he has one, or if not, his residence.[30] If, after the conclusion of the contract, the seller changes his place of business or his residence, the question whether or not the place of payment is thereby changed should, it is submitted, depend upon a reasonable inference to be drawn from all the circumstances surrounding the formation and performance of the contract of sale.[31]

Overseas sales. If a seller whose place of business is in England contracts 9–048 to deliver goods to a buyer abroad, the courts will, in the absence of indications to the contrary, readily infer that payment is to be made in England[32]; and the same inference will be made where the seller sends goods to an agent abroad to be sold by him on commission.[33] So far as the currency of payment is concerned, the fact that payment is to be made in English currency may, though not necessarily,[34] indicate payment in England[35]; but the fact that payment is to be made in a foreign currency

---

[24] *Thorn v City Rice Mills*, above; *Re Escalera Silver Lead Mining Co.* (1908) 25 T.L.R. 87.
[25] *Bell & Co. v Antwerp, London and Brazil Line* [1891] 1 Q.B. 103; *Fry & Co. v Raggio* (1891) 40 W.R. 120; *Rein v Stein* [1892] 1 Q.B. 753 at 758; *Thompson v Palmer* [1893] 2 Q.B. 80 at 84. *Duval & Co. Ltd v Gans* [1904] 2 K.B. 685.
[26] See above, paras 9–020—9–046.
[27] See below, para.19–086 (c.i.f. contracts).
[28] *The Eider* [1893] P. 119 at 131, 136. See also Shepp. Touchstone, p.136; *Drexel v Drexel* [1916] 1 Ch. 251 at 259; *Fowler v Midland Electric Corporation for Power Distribution Ltd* [1917] 1 Ch. 656; *Korner v Witkowitzer* [1950] 2 K.B. 128 at 159 (affirmed *sub nom. Vitkovice Horni a Hutni Tezirstvo v Korner* [1951] A.C. 869). *Cf. Fessard v Mugnier* (1865) 18 C.B. (N.S.) 286; *Malik v Narodni Banka Ceskoslovenska* [1946] 2 All E.R. 663.
[29] *Robey & Co. v Snaefell Mining Co. Ltd* (1887) 20 Q.B.D. 152 at 154; *Reynolds v Coleman* (1887) 36 Ch.D. 453 at 464; *Rein v Stein* [1892] 1 Q.B. 753 at 758; *Thompson v Palmer* [1893] 2 Q.B. 80 at 84; *Duval & Co. Ltd v Gans* [1904] 2 K.B. 685 at 692; *Bremer Oeltransport GmbH v Drewry* [1933] 1 K.B. 753 at 766.
[30] See also ss.28, 29(2) of the 1979 Act.
[31] *Cf. Malik v Narodni Banka Ceskoslovenska*, above.
[32] *Robey & Co. v Snaefell Mining Co. Ltd* (1887) 20 Q.B.D. 152; *Hassall v Lawrence* (1887) 4 T.L.R. 23; *Fry & Co. v Raggio* (1891) 40 W.R. 120.
[33] *Rein v Stein* [1892] 1 Q.B. 753 (approved in *Johnson v Taylor Bros* [1920] A.C. 144 at 155); *Duval & Co. v Gans* [1904] 2 K.B. 685. *Cf. Comber v Leyland* [1898] A.C. 524.
[34] *Bremer Oeltransport GmbH v Drewry* [1933] 1 K.B. 753 at 766.
[35] *Fry & Co. v Raggio*, above.

does not necessarily mean that England is not the place where payment is to be made.[36] The provisions of a foreign law applicable to the contract of sale may nevertheless determine the place of payment.[37]

9–049 The rules relating to the place of payment in c.i.f., f.o.b., ex ship, etc., sales are discussed elsewhere in this work.[38]

9–050 **Waiver.** The obligation of the buyer to make the payment at the place expressed or implied in the contract may be held to have been waived by the seller requesting or accepting payment at some other place.[39]

(c) *Time of Payment*

9–051 **Time of payment specified.** The parties to a contract of sale are at liberty to specify in their contract the time at which payment is to be made by the buyer. This time need not necessarily bear any relationship to the time of the transfer of the property in the goods to the buyer, or to the time of delivery.[40] But by section 10(1) of the Sale of Goods Act 1979, unless a different intention appears from the terms of the contract,[41] stipulations as to time of payment are not of the essence of a contract of sale. Thus, if time is not of the essence, a default by the buyer in making payment at the time specified in the contract will not entitle the seller to treat himself as discharged from further liability and to resell the goods[42] unless the buyer's neglect or refusal to pay the price makes it plain that he is unwilling or unable to perform the contract.[43] However, where there has been undue delay in payment, the seller may give notice requiring payment to be made within a reasonable time.[44] The seller may also in the contract of sale expressly reserve the right of resale in case the buyer should make default,[45] and, by section 48(3) of the Act,[46] an unpaid seller has a statutory right of

---

36 *Rein v Stein*, above; *Drexel v Drexel* [1916] 1 Ch. 251; *Vitkovice Horni a Hutni Tezirstvo v Korner* [1951] A.C. 869.
37 See below, para.25–161.
38 See below, para.19–085 (c.i.f.); para.20–056 (f.o.b.); para.21–017 (ex ship).
39 *Gyles v Hall* (1726) 2 P.Wms. 378; *Caine v Coulton* (1863) 1 H. & C. 764. *Cf. Gordon v Strange* (1847) 1 ExCh.477.
40 *Cf. Staunton v Wood* (1851) 16 Q.B. 638 ("delivery forthwith, cash in fourteen days from making of contract"); *Godts v Rose* (1855) 17 C.B. 229 ("free delivered and paid for in fourteen days in cash"); *Minister for Supply and Development v Servicemen's Co-op. Joinery Manufacturers Ltd* (1951) 82 C.L.R 621 ("net cash before delivery").
41 *Maclaine v Gatty* [1921] 1 A.C. 376 at 389 ("punctual payment"). *Cf. Tenax Steamship Co. Ltd v Reinante Transoceanica Navegacion SA Brimnes, The* [1973] 1 W.L.R. 386 at 409. But see below, paras 19–085, 22–067.
42 *Martindale v Smith* (1841) 1 Q.B. 389; *Mersey Steel and Iron Co. v Naylor* (1884) 9 App.Cas. 434 at 444; *Payzu Ltd v Saunders* [1919] 2 K.B. 581.
43 *Anchor Line Ltd v Keith Rowell Ltd* [1980] 2 Lloyd's Rep. 351. See also above, para.8–078 (instalment contracts); below, para.9–065. For a discussion of damages for late payment, see below, para.16–030.
44 See *Chitty on Contracts* (29th ed.), Vol. 1, 21–014. But see above, para. 8–026.
45 Sale of Goods Act 1979, s.48(4); below, para.15–128.
46 See below, para.15–119.

resale where the goods are of a perishable nature, or where he gives notice to the buyer of his intention to resell, and the buyer does not within a reasonable time pay or tender the price. A resale by the seller in these circumstances effectively rescinds the contract of sale.[47]

Time for payment of deposit. It is doubtful whether the reference to "stipulations as to time of payment" in section 10(1) of the Act includes a deposit, but in any event the question whether the time for payment of a deposit is of the essence depends upon the intention of the parties to be ascertained by construing the contract.[48] If the deposit is payable on signature of the contract, a short leeway may in practice be allowed.[49] Provision for payment of a deposit is not usually a condition precedent to the formation of the contract,[50] but may be construed as a fundamental term of the contract entitling the seller to treat the contract as repudiated if it is not duly paid.[51] **9–052**

Time for opening letter of credit. The time within which a letter of credit must be opened is considered later in this work.[52] As a normal rule, stipulations as to the time within which a letter of credit must be provided are of the essence of a contract of sale.[53] **9–053**

Terms relating to time. The meaning of terms relating to the time of performance, and the calculation of the time at which performance is due, have been dealt with in a previous chapter.[54] If payment is due on or by a certain date, the buyer has the whole of that day in which to effect payment.[55] No extension is available if the date of payment is a non-business day.[56] **9–054**

Waiver. Although the time of payment is specified in the contract, the seller may be held to have waived (or be estopped from asserting) his right to insist that payment be made at that time where he has expressly or **9–055**

---

[47] Sale of Goods Act 1979, s.48(4); *Ward v Bignall* [1967] 1 Q.B. 534; below, para.14–127.
[48] *Portaria Shipping Co. v Gulf Pacific Navigation Co. Ltd* [1981] 2 Lloyd's Rep. 180.
[49] *ibid.*, at p.185; *Damon Compania Naviera SA v Hapag-Lloyd International SA* [1985] 1 W.L.R. 435 at 453.
[50] *Damon Compania Naviera SA v Hapag-Lloyd International SA* above. See also *Millichamp v Jones* [1982] 1 W.L.R. 1422. *Cf. Myton Ltd v Schwab-Morris* [1974] 1 W.L.R. 331.
[51] *Myton Ltd v Schwab-Morris*, above, at p.337; *Millichamp v Jones*, above, at p.1430; *Portaria Shipping Co. v Gulf Pacific Navigation Co. Ltd*, above; *Damon Compania Naviera SA v Hapag-Lloyd International SA*, above. See also *Haugland Tankers As v RMK Marine Gemi Yapim Sanayii As* [2005] EWHC 321 (Comm), [2005], 1 Lloyd's Rep. 573 (option fee).
[52] See below, para.23–086.
[53] *Pavia & Co. SpA v Thurmann Nielsen* [1952] 1 Lloyd's Rep. 153; *Ian Stach Ltd v Baker Bastey Ltd* [1958] 2 Q.B. 130; *Nichimen Corp. v Gatoil Overseas Inc.* [1987] 2 Lloyd's Rep. 46. Contrast *State Trading Corp. of India Ltd v M. Golodetz Ltd* [1989] 2 Lloyd's Rep. 277 (counter-trade guarantee).
[54] See above, paras 8–032—8–039.
[55] *Afovos Shipping Co. SA v R. Pagnan & F.lli* [1983] 1 W.L.R. 195.
[56] *Mardorf Peach & Co. Ltd v Attica Sea Carriers Corp. of Liberia* [1977] A.C. 850. But see s.14(1) of the Bills of Exchange Act 1882 (as amended) (due date for bills of exchange).

impliedly led the buyer to believe that he will accept payment at a later time.[57] If no new time for payment has been fixed, the seller is entitled, upon giving reasonable notice, to fix such a time, which may then become of the essence of the contract of sale.[58] The granting by the seller of a fixed extension of time does not constitute a waiver by him of any requirement that the time of payment is of the essence.[59]

9–056 **Payment for goods at buyer's risk.** Where the goods are lost or destroyed when they are at the buyer's risk, the buyer is still liable to pay the price[60] and, if the contract fixes no other time, is under a duty to pay within a reasonable time after the loss or destruction of the goods.[61]

9–057 **No time of payment specified.** If no time of payment is specified in the contract, the time at which payment is to be made may be established in appropriate cases by the previous course of dealing between the parties[62] or by usage.[63] Where no time of payment can thus be implied, payment would appear prima facie to be due when the seller informs the buyer that he is ready and willing to deliver the goods, since by virtue of section 28 of the 1979 Act delivery of the goods and payment of the price are, unless otherwise agreed, concurrent conditions.[64]

9–058 **Overseas sales.** The rules applicable to the time of payment in c.i.f., f.o.b., ex ship, etc., contracts are discussed elsewhere in this work.[65]

9–059 **Payment on demand or notice.** No request or demand for payment is normally necessary.[66] But if the contract expressly provides that a demand is required or that notice must be given by the seller to the buyer, it may be a condition precedent to the buyer's liability that the demand has been made or that notice has been given,[67] and even then a reasonable time must be allowed to the buyer to tender the amount due.[68]

---

[57] *cf. Scandinavian Trader Tanker Co. AB v Flota Petrolera Ecuatoriana* [1983] 2 Q.B. 549, affirmed [1983] 2 A.C. 694 (acceptance of late payments on previous occasions creates no estoppel). See also *Chitty on Contracts* (29th ed.), Vol. 1, paras 3–081—3–114.

[58] *Charles Rickards Ltd v Oppenhaim* [1950] 1 K.B. 616; *State Trading Corp. of India Ltd v Compagnie Française d'Importation et de Distribution* [1983] 2 Lloyd's Rep. 679.

[59] *Buckland v Farmar & Moody* [1979] 1 W.L.R. 221; *Nichimen Corp. v Gatoil Overseas Inc.*, above.

[60] See above, para.6–001.

[61] *Fragano v Long* (1825) 4 B. & C. 219 at 223. See also *Alexander v Gardner* (1835) 1 Bing.N.C. 671. *Cf.* American Uniform Commercial Code, para.2–709(1).

[62] *King v Reedman* (1883) 49 L.T. 473. But see *Ford v Yates* (1841) 2 M. & G. 549. *Cf. Lockett v Nicklin* (1848) 2 Exch.93.

[63] Sale of Goods Act 1979, s.55(1); *R. v Jones* [1898] 1 Q.B. 119.

[64] See above, para.8–004.

[65] See below, para.19–075 (c.i.f.); para.20–056 (f.o.b.); para.21–018 (ex ship).

[66] *Walton v Mascall* (1844) 13 M. & W. 452 at 458; *Bell & Co. v Antwerp, London and Brazil Line* [1891] 1 Q.B. 103 at 107.

[67] *Bell & Co. v Antwerp, London and Brazil Line*, above, at p.107 (place).

[68] *Brighty v Norton* (1862) 3 B. & S. 305; *Toms v Wilson* (1862) 4 B. & S. 455. See also *Massey v Sladen* (1868) L.R. 4 Ex. 13; *Moore v Shelley* (1883) 8 App.Cas. 285; *Cripps (RA) & Son Ltd v Wickenden* [1973] 1 W.L.R. 944.

9–060 Where the amount of the price is to be regulated by some fact within the special cognisance of the seller, *e.g.* the amount paid by third parties to the seller for goods of a similar nature, the price is not payable by the buyer until he receives notice of the amount ascertained.[69]

9–061 **Credit.** The parties to a contract of sale may expressly or impliedly agree that the buyer is to take possession of goods before payment is made, that is to say, a period of credit is to be allowed. Where goods are sold on credit, payment is not due until the period of credit has expired.[70] Before that time, the unpaid seller of goods who is in possession of them is not entitled to refuse delivery of them until payment or tender of the price,[71] unless the buyer becomes insolvent.[72] But the contract may provide that, in certain events falling short of insolvency, no further credit is to be allowed or that the seller is to be entitled to refuse to deliver the goods unless they are paid for in advance.[73]

9–062 **Periods of credit.** If a longer and shorter period of credit is stated by way of estimate in the contract, *e.g.* "to be paid for in from six to eight weeks", it is a question of fact whether or not at any particular date between the two periods the credit has, in a commercial sense, expired.[74] On the other hand, if the buyer has the option of a longer or shorter period of credit, *e.g.* "six *or* nine months" and does not pay the price at the expiration of the shorter period, he may be deemed to have elected for the longer period.[75]

9–063 **Credit where bill or note to be given.** If the terms of the contract stipulate that the goods are to be paid for by a bill or note payable at a future date, *e.g.* "bill at two months", and the bill or note is not given, then, unless credit was made conditional on the giving of the instrument,[76] the buyer is nevertheless entitled to credit until the time when the bill or note, if given, would have matured[77]; but the seller may bring an action for damages for breach of the agreement to give the bill or note.[78] In this

---

[69] *Holmes v Twist* (1614) Hob. 51; *Henning's Case* (1617) Cro.Jac. 432.
[70] *Price v Nixon* (1814) 5 Taunt. 338. But see below, para.15–016.
[71] Sale of Goods Act 1979, ss.39(1), (2), 41(1)(b); see below, para.15–033.
[72] *ibid.* s.41(1)(c); see below, para.15–037.
[73] *Cf. BV Oliehandel Jongland v Coastal International Ltd* [1983] 2 Lloyd's Rep. 463 ("in the case of [the buyer's] financial responsibility being impaired" requires proof of actual impairment equivalent to insolvency).
[74] *Ashforth v Redford* (1873) L.R. 9 C.P. 20.
[75] *Price v Nixon* (1814) 5 Taunt. 338.
[76] *Nickson v Jepson* (1817) 2 Stark. 227; *Rugg v Weir* (1864) 16 C.B. (N.S.) 471. See also *Lee v Risdon* (1816) 7 Taunt. 188.
[77] *Mussen v Price* (1803) 4 East 147; *Dutton v Solomonson* (1830) 3 B. & P. 582; *Day v Picton* (1829) 10 B. & C. 120; *Helps v Winterbottom* (1831) 2 B. & Ad. 431; *Paul v Dod* (1846) 2 C.B. 800; *Rabe v Otto* (1903) 89 L.T. 562. See also *Brooke v White* (1805) 1 B. & P.N.R. 330; *Wayne's Merthyr Steam Coal and Iron Co. v Morewood & Co.* (1877) 46 L.J.Q.B. 476.
[78] The measure of damages is not the price of the goods, but the loss (if any) sustained by not having the instrument: *Mussen v Price*, above, at p.151; *Helps v Winterbottom*, above, at pp.434, 435; *Rabe v Otto*, above. It seems that the duty lies on the seller to tender the bill for acceptance: *Reed v Mestaer* (1804) Comyn's *Law of Contract* (2nd ed.), p.181; *Spaeth v Hare* (1842) 1 Dowl. (N.S.) 595. *Cf. Foster v Eades* (1860) 2 F. & F. 103 at 104.

connection, credit is conditional on the giving of the instrument where the price is payable in cash at a fixed date with an option to the buyer to substitute a bill or note payable at a future date; it is not conditional where the price is payable by such a bill or note with an option to the buyer to substitute cash.[79] But if the buyer, having the option to pay cash or to give a bill or note payable *in futuro*, makes a part payment in cash, he is deemed irrevocably to have elected to pay cash, and cannot claim credit for the payment of the residue until the time when the bill or note would have matured.[80]

9–064 **Trading account.** If so agreed between the parties, payment may be made by remittance on a trading account. The goods will be delivered to the buyer, and his account will be debited by the seller to the amount of the price. At some agreed period of time, *e.g.* at the end of each month, it is expected that the buyer will send a remittance to the seller to settle the balance outstanding on the account. It would seem that the ordinary inference from such an arrangement is that credit is extended to the buyer until such a time as payment is required to be made, or, if no time is fixed, within a reasonable time from a demand for payment made by the seller.

9–065 **Payment by instalments.** The terms of the contract of sale may provide that the entire quantity of goods is to be delivered to the buyer, but that the buyer shall pay the price of the goods by instalments.[81] In such a case credit is granted to the buyer *pro tanto* until each instalment falls due.[82] An agreement for the sale of goods, under which the purchase price or part of it is payable by instalments, but which is not a conditional sale agreement,[83] will also constitute a "credit-sale agreement" within the meaning of that term in the Consumer Credit Act 1974, and may be a regulated consumer credit agreement if the buyer is an "individual" (which expression includes a partnership consisting of two or three persons not all of whom are bodies corporate),[84] and the number of instalments exceeds four.[85]

---

[79] *Anderson v Carlisle Horse Clothing Co.* (1870) 21 L.T. 760. See also *Mussen v Price*, above; *Rugg v Weir*, above; *Rabe v Otto*, above.
[80] *Schneider v Foster* (1857) 2 H. & N. 4; *Rugg v Weir*, above.
[81] For payment *and* delivery by instalments, see above, paras 8–064.
[82] Some agreements contain "acceleration clauses", under which, if any instalment is for a certain period of time in arrear, the whole balance for the time being owing thereupon becomes due and payable.
[83] A conditional sale agreement for the purposes of the Consumer Credit Act 1974 is defined in s.189(1) of that Act. See above, para.1–021.
[84] Consumer Credit Act 1974, ss.8(1), 189(1) as amended by the Consumer Credit Act 2006. The financial limit in the 1974 Act was raised from £5,000 to £15,000 from May 20, 1985, by SI 1983/1878, and to £25,000 from May 1, 1998, by SI 1998/996. The 2006 Act removes the financial limit, but provides an exemption for agreements exceeding £25,000 where the agreement is entered into by the debtor wholly or predominantly for the purposes of a business carried on, or intended to be carried on, by him (ss.8(3), 16B of the 1974 Act). The £25,000 exemption is calculated by reference to the balance financed (s.9 of the 1974 Act).
[85] Credit sale agreements of four instalments or less are not regulated agreements, provided the payments are to be made within a period not exceeding 12 months beginning with the date of the agreement: Consumer Credit (Exempt Agreements) Order 1989, SI 1989/869, art. 3(1)(a)(i). See *Zoan v Rouamba* [2000] 1 W.L.R. 1509; *Ketley v Gilbert* [2001] 1 W.L.R. 986; *Thew v Cole*, [2003] EWCA Civ 1828.

Revolving credit. Many large stores operate "budget credit" or "option" accounts for their customers, under which a customer is permitted to incur a debit balance which must not exceed a certain limit at any one time. In return, the customer undertakes to make to the store a monthly payment of a fixed or minimum sum. Such an agreement may be considered to be a contract for the sale of goods under which the purchase price is payable by instalments.[86] It is also a consumer credit agreement for running-account credit within the Consumer Credit Act 1974.[87] 9–066

Terms negativing credit. The terms of payment contained in the contract of sale may be such as to negative any implication of credit, *e.g.* the term "net cash" means that no credit is to be allowed, and no deductions made by way of discount or rebate or otherwise.[88] 9–067

Interest. The right of the seller to recover interest in any case where by law interest may be recoverable is expressly preserved by section 54 of the Sale of Goods Act 1979. This is discussed in Chapter 16 of this work.[89] 9–068

---

[86] *NG Napier Ltd v Patterson*, 1959 S.C.(J.) 48; *NG Napier Ltd v Corbett*, 1962 S.L.T.(Sh.Ct.) 90.

[87] Consumer Credit Act 1974, ss.8, 9, 10. See also s.16 and the statutory instrument cited in n.85, above, art. 3(1)(a)(ii) (charge cards).

[88] *Biddell Bros v E. Clemens Horst Co.* [1911] 1 K.B. 934 at 939–940 (affirmed *sub nom. E Clemens Horst Co. v Biddell Bros* [1912] A.C. 18).

[89] See below, paras 16–007—16–013.

Part Four
DEFECTIVE GOODS

CHAPTER 10

CLASSIFICATION OF STATEMENTS AS TO GOODS

PARA.

1. Introduction 10–001
2. Puffs and statements of opinion or intention.................. 10–005
3. Misrepresentations inducing the contract...................... 10–008
4. Collateral contracts 10–012
5. Warranties.. 10–015
6. Conditions.. 10–024
7. Intermediate terms.. 10–033
8. Other classifications.. 10–039

1. Introduction

Types of statement. Express statements as to goods, made in connection with a contract of sale, may be divided initially into two groups. **10–001**

(i) *Statements involving no legal liability.* In this category come mere puffs and certain statements of opinion or intention.[1]

(ii) *Statements involving legal liability.* In this category are misrepresentations inducing the contract (whether fraudulent, negligent or entirely innocent)[2]; contractual promises separate from the main contract (collateral contracts)[3]; and contractual promises which are terms of the main contract.[4] Within this last category it was formerly usual to subdivide further into warranties (less important promises within the main contract)[5] and conditions (more important promises within the main contract)[6]; but, as will be later explained,[7] subsequent developments have either added a third category of intermediate or innominate terms (promises which cannot be designated as conditions or warranties because the consequences of their breach may substantially vary in importance) or possibly even called the whole division into question. It is finally possible for misrepresentations inducing the contract to be incorporated into it when it is made, and so to attract also the rules applicable to contractual promises.[8]

By whom made. Statements giving rise to dispute in a contract of sale are normally made by a seller and relate to the goods involved. But they may sometimes be made by a buyer,[9] or even by a third party such as a **10–002**

---

[1] Below, paras 10–005 *et seq.* Some statements which might come into this category as regards the civil law might attract criminal liability under the Trade Descriptions Act 1968; but contravention of the Act does not render a contract void or unenforceable (s.35). See below, paras 14–112 *et seq.*
[2] Below, paras 10–008 *et seq.*
[3] Below, paras 10–012 *et seq.*
[4] Below, paras 10–015 *et seq.*
[5] Below, para.10–023.
[6] Below, paras 10–026 *et seq.*
[7] Below, paras 10–029 *et seq.*
[8] Below, para.10–040.
[9] *e.g. Goldsmith v Rodger* [1962] 2 Lloyd's Rep. 249 (condition of boat).

manufacturer or a dealer "selling" on hire-purchase.[10] Indeed they do not always refer directly to the goods. Thus in *Riddiford v Warren*[11] it was represented by a buyer that he had already been quoted a lower price for the goods by the seller's agent. Discussion in this chapter is concentrated on statements made by sellers relating to goods actually or prospectively the subject of sale: but the same or analogous principles may apply to statements made by buyers and sometimes to those made by third parties.[12]

10–003 **Classification of statements—fact or law?** The proper classification of statements is a matter of interpretation and therefore one of law.[13] But when disputes arise as to exactly what was said and done, these are questions of fact; and when such cases were tried by jury the whole question frequently had to be left to the jury.[14]

10–004 **Development of the law.** It is important to make plain at the outset of this analysis that the law in this area has been the subject of considerable change. Old cases show reluctance to impose liability for statements unless there was deceit, a tort which from 1889 onwards was narrowly defined,[15] or contractual liability was clearly undertaken. Other categories of liability have, however, developed subsequently. Thus an equitable jurisdiction to rescind contracts for non-fraudulent misrepresentation has evolved; separate or collateral contracts have been detected; and liability for negligent statements has been established both in the common law of tort and by statute. Further, the categories in which statements attract liability have been more broadly interpreted (though with some variation between law and equity) and objective standards as to reliance on statements applied. All cases which are not comparatively recent should be read with these developments in mind. Finally, the meanings to be attributed to the terms "warranty" and "condition", much found in the old cases and in the Sale of Goods Act, have changed considerably over the years. All this is explained below.

---

[10] *e.g. Andrews v Hopkinson* [1957] 1 Q.B. 229, below, para.10–005.

[11] (1901) 20 N.Z.L.R. 572 (where rescission was in fact refused on the ground that the jurisdiction was not applicable to sale of goods: see below, para.10–008). See also *Easterbrook v Hopkins* [1918] N.Z.L.R. 428 (estate agent said he had purchaser for representee's business at a certain price, inducing representee to buy another business through him: liability in deceit).

[12] As to collateral contracts and tort liability, see below, paras 10–012 *et seq*. See also below, paras 11–033 *et seq*.

[13] *Behn v Burness* (1863) 3 B. & S. 751 at 754; *Oscar Chess Ltd v Williams* [1957] 1 W.L.R. 370 at 375.

[14] *Bentsen v Taylor, Sons & Co.* [1893] 2 Q.B. 274 at 280. See, *e.g. De Sewhanberg v Buchanan* (1832) 5 C. & P. 343; *Power v Barham* (1836) 4 A. & E. 473; *Percival v Oldacre* (1865) 18 C.B.(N.S.) 398; *Walker v Milner* (1866) 4 F. & F. 745. *Cf. Heilbut, Symons & Co v Buckleton* [1913] A.C. 30 at 51, where it was held that the question should not have been left to the jury.

[15] *Derry v Peek* (1889) 14 App. Cas 337; see below, para.12–012.

2. PUFFS AND STATEMENTS OF OPINION OR INTENTION

Mere puffs. A mere puff is, as the name implies, a statement favourably describing or extolling goods which by virtue of its vagueness or extravagance[16] would not normally be regarded as something to be taken seriously or as grounding any form of liability. *Simplex commendatio non obligat.* Thus in *Walker v Milner*[17] a safe was described as "strong, holdfast, thiefproof" and a burglar gave evidence of breaking into it within half an hour with ordinary implements, despite the fact that police looked through the window every 10 minutes: it was held that there was no liability on such a statement. But the same view might not be taken today of this case, nor of others of similar nature[18]: and in any case the line between puff and statement giving rise to liability is easily crossed. In *Osborn v Hart*[19] the words "superior old port" were held to involve a warranty, *i.e.* a contractual promise, that the port was superior, and much later in *Andrews v Hopkinson*[20] a statement by a car dealer "It's a good little bus; I would stake my life on it; you will have no trouble with it" was likewise held a contractual warranty.[21] The extent to which a statement may be so categorised depends on the degree or obviousness of its untruth, the circumstances of its making, and in particular on the expertise and knowledge attributable to the person to whom it is made. "A statement made may be so preposterous in its nature that nobody could believe that anyone was misled by it. Subject to this observation the question in every case is whether or not one person has been induced to act by the misrepresentation of another."[22] Thus in the sale of second-hand cars, a 10–005

---

16 "Extravagant phrasing which would naturally be discounted by sensible persons": *Turner v Anquetil* [1953] N.Z.L.R. 952 at 957, *per* F. B. Adams J.

17 (1866) 4 F. & F. 745. See also *Lambert v Lewis* [1982] A.C. 225 at 262, CA—"foolproof": no warranty (point not decided in HL).

18 *e.g. Scott v Hanson* (1829) 1 Russ. & M. 128 ("uncommonly rich water meadow"); *Stucley v Bailey* (1862) 1 H. & C. 405 (condition of boat); *Dimmock v Hallett* (1866) L.R. 2 Ch.App. 21 (land "fertile and improvable"); *Chalmers v Harding* (1868) 17 L.T. 571 ("very good secondhand reaper"); *Johnston v McRae* (1907) 26 N.Z.L.R. 299 ("well grown lambs, fit for rape"). See McLauchlan, 8 Victoria U. of Wellington L.Rev. 101 (1975). This is even more so of old cases where the existence of a warranty was held to imply that other statements had no legal force, *e.g. Budd v Fairmaner* (1831) 8 Bing. 48 ("grey four year old colt, warranted sound"—no warranty as to age); *Anthony v Halstead* (1877) 37 L.T. 433 ("black horse, rising five years, quiet to ride and drive, and warranted sound up to this date"—warranty of soundness only). Many such statements would now rank as part of the description of the goods: below, paras 11–012 *et seq.*

19 (1871) 23 L.T. 851 ("almost undrinkable").

20 [1957] 1 Q.B. 229; see also *Carlill v Carbolic Smoke Ball Co.* [1893] 1 Q.B. 256 (statements as to preventive properties of medicine); *Fordy v Harwood*, CA, March 30, 1999 ("Absolutely mint. All the right bits . . . and does it go. Probably cost a fortune to build"). But *cf. Garbett v Rufford Motor Co. Ltd, The Guardian*, March 12, 1962 ("as far as I know this vehicle is mechanically sound"—no warranty); *Hummingbird Motors Ltd v Hobbs* [1986] R.T.R. 276 (odometer reading correct "to the best of my knowledge and belief"—no warranty).

21 Though the warranty here was not given by the seller but by a third party: below, para.10–013.

22 *Easterbrook v Hopkins* [1918] N.Z.L.R. 428 at 442, *per* Sim J. (business a "little gold-mine"—promissory).

statement "good runner" might have no consequences in the case of an indifferent car, but lead to liability if the car was reasonably bought by a private buyer without testing and proved incapable of self-propulsion. A statement as to "good condition"[23] might again have no consequences in the case of a car that was merely indifferent, but equally might give rise to liability if the first passenger in the back seat fell through the floor. Such statements might also have greater legal significance when made to a person who had no opportunity to inspect the goods than when made to one who has.

10–006 **Statements of opinion.** Likewise, genuine statements of opinion and belief may not ground liability. They may be treated like puffs; or the matter may be one upon which the buyer is expected to form his own opinion.[24] Much will depend on the general commercial understanding in the particular type of trade or activity at the time and place where the facts occur. Old examples occur in connection with the sale of pictures. In *Jendwine v Slade*[25] Lord Kenyon held that the listing of pictures in a catalogue as being by Loraine and Teniers amounted to no more than an expression of opinion. On the other hand, in *Power v Barham*,[26] where a seller supplied a bill referring to "Four pictures, views in Venice, Canaletto", *Jendwine v Slade* was distinguished on the grounds that the pictures in the instant case were not so old,[27] and it was held that the matter had been rightly left to the jury, who found a warranty, though Littledale J. thought that "all the auctioneers in London would be alarmed if they thought that such words as these were to be understood as a warranty."[28] Statements of value may sometimes be treated as statements of opinion; but where the value stated purports to be based on the sum paid for the object or offered for it by someone else, the statement should be regarded as being one of fact, and as such may give rise to liability. The same is true in other cases where an opinion carries the implication that there are facts

---

[23] See *Turner v Anquetil* [1953] N.Z.L.R. 952 (advertisement of piano in "good order"—promissory).

[24] See *Ecay v Godfrey* (1947) 80 Ll.L.R. 286 (seller of boat told buyer that it was sound but advised him to have it surveyed); *Oscar Chess Ltd v Williams* [1957] 1 W.L.R. 370 at 375, 378 (car traded in to dealer).

[25] (1797) 2 Esp. 572; see also *Gee v Lucas* (1867) 16 L.T. 357; *Thomson v Christie Manson and Woods Ltd* [2005] EWCA Civ 555; [2005] P.N.L.R 38.

[26] (1836) 4 A. & E. 473. See also as to pictures *Lomi v Tucker* (1829) 4 C. & P. 15; *De Sewhanberg v Buchanan* (1832) 5 C. & P. 343; *Hyslop v Shirlaw* (1905) 7 F. (Ct. of Sess.) 875; *Leaf v International Galleries* [1950] 2 K.B. 86, esp. at pp.89, 94.

[27] Although Lord Kenyon referred to "the work of artists some centuries back", Loraine and Teniers died rather more than 100 years before *Jendwine v Slade*. Canaletto died about 70 years before *Power v Barham*.

[28] At p.476. In *Harlingdon and Leinster Enterprises Ltd v Christopher Hull Fine Art Ltd* [1991] 1 Q.B. 564, it was held that on the facts the sale of a picture described in negotiations and the invoice as being by Gabriele Münter was not a sale by description, on the basis that art dealers do not rely on descriptions by sellers. See below, para.11–011. See also *Peco Arts Inc. v Hazlitt Gallery Ltd* [1983] 1 W.L.R. 1315.

to support it.[29] The nineteenth-century reports contain various examples of assertions that horses were sound.[30] Although such statements used sometimes to be treated as being of opinion, it is again not likely that these and similar assertions (*e.g.* in connection with the sale of cars) would be so readily interpreted in this way today,[31] especially where the person making the statement is possessed of special expertise or means of knowledge.[32] It has been said that "the word 'representation' is an extremely wide term; I cannot see why one should not be making a representation when giving information or when stating one's opinion or belief."[33] Where the representor knew the article to be unsatisfactory, or can otherwise be proved not to have held the opinion which he claimed to hold, he may even be liable in deceit.[34]

Statements of intention. In principle a representation must be of fact[35]; 10–007
hence a statement of intention is not directly actionable unless it constitutes a contractual promise, whether collateral or part of the main contract. But such statements are frequently used in negotiation, and they may constitute representations that facts exist upon which such intentions could reasonably be based. And if it can be established that the intention was not held, the statement that it was will, in addition to the remedies for misrepresentation, give rise to liability in deceit.[36]

---

[29] See *Smith v Land and House Property Corp.* (1884) 28 Ch.D. 7 ("most desirable tenant"); *Armstrong v Strain* [1952] 1 K.B. 232 (value of property); *Brown v Raphael* [1958] Ch. 636 ("believed to have no aggregable estate"); *Esso Petroleum Co. Ltd v Mardon* [1976] Q.B. 801 (likely throughput of petrol station); *Easterbrook v Hopkins* [1918] N.Z.L.R. 428 ("a little goldmine"); *Porter v General Guarantee Corp. Ltd* [1982] R.T.R. 384 (car alleged suitable for use as minicab). But in other cases statements have been held not promissory: *cf. Bisset v Wilkinson* [1927] A.C. 177 (sheep-carrying capacity of land); *J. J. Savage & Sons Pty Ltd v Blakney* (1970) 119 C.L.R. 435 ("estimated speed" of boat); *Ross v Allis-Chalmers Australia Pty Ltd* (1981) 55 A.L.J.R. 8 ("My own experience with our machine is that you should budget on 90 acres per day").

[30] *cf. Hopkins v Tanqueray* (1854) 15 C.B. 130 with *Schawel v Reade* [1913] 2 I.R. 64, HL. Both concerned such statements; that in the first case was not held promissory, that in the second was. The best explanation of the difference is probably that given in *Schawel v Reade*, namely that in the first case the sale took place subsequently at Tattersall's, where sales were known to be without warranty unless the contrary was stated in the catalogue. But see also *Harling v Eddy* [1951] 2 K.B. 739 at 745, 748; Greig, 87 L.Q.R. 179 at 183–184 (1971).

[31] See *Holmes v Burgess* [1975] 2 N.Z.L.R. 311 ("Bloody rot! There is nothing wrong with the horse at all, it is as sound as a bell"—promissory). *Cf.* however *Lucas Laureys v Graham Earl*, QBD (Graham Foskett Q.C.), November 3, 2005 (broker in classic car market was simply passing on information given to him by others).

[32] See *Oscar Chess Ltd v Williams* [1957] 1 W.L.R. 370 at 375 (car traded in to dealer).

[33] *Cremdean Properties Ltd v Nash* (1977) 244 E.G. 547 at 551, *per* Bridge L.J. (lettable office space). See also *Box v Midland Bank Ltd* [1979] 2 Lloyd's Rep. 391 at 399 (statement as to policy of bank).

[34] See below, paras 10–009, 12–012; *Brown v Raphael* [1958] Ch. 636 at 643.

[35] See, *e.g. Bisset v Wilkinson* [1927] A.C. 177 at 182.

[36] *Edgington v Fitzmaurice* (1885) 29 Ch.D. 459; below, para.12–012; *cf.* Marine Insurance Act 1906, s.20.

3. MISREPRESENTATIONS INDUCING THE CONTRACT

10–008 **Misrepresentations inducing the contract.** An untrue statement of fact made by a party to a sale and relating to the goods may not be a contractual promise, but may be classifiable as a misrepresentation which, while not part of the contract, nevertheless constituted or formed part of the inducement to contract. Such misrepresentations are sometimes called "mere representations". In the absence of tort liability for deceit, which was strictly defined,[37] there was formerly no remedy on them at common law. From the early nineteenth-century courts of equity, however, provided relief in contractual situations of this sort in various ways, and after the Judicature Acts it became accepted that there was an equitable jurisdiction to rescind contracts induced by such misrepresentations even though innocent, which thus established them as a category of statement attracting legal consequences. This can be justified on the basis that while the representor may have done no wrong, it is in the circumstances inequitable for him to rely on his strict rights and hold the other party to the transaction. The case from which this development is usually dated[38] did not in fact concern sale of goods, and equally the cases from which the jurisdiction was (rather mysteriously) derived were not sale of goods cases.[39] Relief in respect of such misrepresentations is most obviously appropriate to situations such as that of the sale of land (or, in former days, stocks and shares), where the distinction between representation and contractual promise is easy to make because a considerable interval may separate negotiation and contract, and the contract, when entered into, may be in a standard form making no reference to earlier negotiations, evidence of which may indeed be excluded because the parties are regarded as having reduced the contract to writing.[40] With the enactment of the Sale of Goods Act 1893, it could also be said that the Act purported to be a Code for the sale of goods[41] and made no mention of such a category of statement, nor of such a right to rescind. Doubts were also expressed as to whether or to what extent section 61(2) of the Act,[42] which expressly preserved "the rules of the common law", included or excluded the rules of equity.[43] However,

---

37 See below, para.12–012.
38 *Redgrave v Hurd* (1881) 20 Ch.D. 1.
39 See *Riddiford v Warren* (1901) 20 N.Z.L.R. 572, where the matter is discussed.
40 See *Chitty on Contracts* (29th ed.), Vol.1. paras 12–096 *et seq*.; Treitel, *Law of Contract* (11th ed.), pp.192 *et seq*; McLauchlan, *The Parol Evidence Rule* (Wellington, N.Z., 1976); Law Com. No. 154, Cmnd. 9700 (1986).
41 *Re Wait* [1927] 1 Ch. 606 at 635.
42 s.62(2) of the 1979 Act. The section preserves "in particular the rules relating to . . . the effect of fraud, misrepresentation, duress or coercion, mistake, or other invalidating cause." It has been pointed out that only in equity is non-fraudulent misrepresentation an invalidating cause: Treitel, *Law of Contract* (11th ed.), pp.374–375.
43 See *Riddiford v Warren*, above (identical statute); followed in *Watt v Westhoven* [1933] V.L.R. 458; not followed in *Graham v Freer* (1980) 35 S.A.S.R. 424. This question is discussed *in extenso*, above, paras 1–008 *et seq*. See also Bridge, 20 U.B.C.L.Rev. 53 (1986); *Electrical Enterprises Pty Ltd v Rogers* (1988) 15 N.S.W.L.R. 473.

books on contract have for some decades stated the jurisdiction to rescind for misrepresentation inducing the contract as a general one; in three leading sale of goods cases of the twentieth century the availability of rescission was accepted, though rescission was not, in the event, possible[44]; and rescission for misrepresentation has been held available to a *seller*.[45] Furthermore, the Misrepresentation Act 1967 added considerably to the remedies available in the case of such misrepresentations. There is nothing in the Act excluding its application to sale of goods, and such exclusion would be most surprising; indeed, section 4 made amendments to part of the Sale of Goods Act. It seems clear, therefore, that the remedy of rescission for misrepresentations inducing the contract applies to sale of goods as to other contracts, and that the further remedies provided by the Misrepresentation Act 1967 can be invoked in sale of goods cases.[46]

Right to rescind. A full account of the rules as to when the equitable remedy of rescission for misrepresentation arises should be sought in general works on the law of contract.[47] What rescinding actually entails, and the further remedies provided by the Misrepresentation Act 1967, are discussed elsewhere in this book.[48] A brief indication as to when the right arises is, however, appropriate here. The misrepresentation must be of fact as opposed to opinion[49] or intention.[50] It was formerly regarded as obvious that it must be of fact not law,[51] though the two could be difficult to distinguish.[52] However the House of Lords has recently held that money paid under a mistake of law is as recoverable as money paid under a mistake of fact,[53] and this decision is likely to prompt reconsideration of the distinction elsewhere. In the present context there is a strong case for abandoning it as regards rescission at least. It must be relied on by the 10–009

---

[44] *Leaf v International Galleries* [1950] 2 K.B. 86; *Oscar Chess Ltd v Williams* [1957] 1 W.L.R. 370; *Long v Lloyd* [1958] 1 W.L.R. 753. See also *Routledge v McKay* [1954] 1 W.L.R. 615; *André & Cie v Ets. Michel Blanc & Fils* [1979] 2 Lloyd's Rep. 427.

[45] *Goldsmith v Rodger* [1962] 2 Lloyd's Rep. 249.

[46] See also above, para.1–008. As to the position in Australia see *Hewett v Court* (1983) 149 C.L.R. 639 at 646, 654, 662; *Electrical Enterprises Retail Pty Ltd v Rogers* (1988) 15 N.S.W.L.R. 473; *Graham v Freer* (1980) 35 S.A.S.R. 424; in New Zealand *Thos. Borthwick & Sons (Australasia) Ltd v South Otago Freezing Co. Ltd* [1978] 1 N.Z.L.R. 538 at 545.

[47] See, *e.g. Chitty on Contracts* (29th ed.), Vol.1, Ch.6; Treitel, *Law of Contract* (11th ed.), Ch.9. The cases usually cited are not sale of goods cases, and indeed many of them do not even concern innocent misrepresentation but the tort of deceit.

[48] Below, paras 12–003, 12–014 *et seq*.

[49] Above, para.10–006.

[50] Above, para.10–007.

[51] See *Mackenzie v Royal Bank of Canada* [1934] A.C. 468; *Eaglesfield v Marquis of Londonderry* (1876) 4 Ch.D. 693 at 709. But a misrepresentation of foreign law is a misrepresentation of fact: *André & Cie. v Ets. Michel Blanc & Fils* [1979] 2 Lloyd's Rep. 427.

[52] *cf., e.g. Beattie v Ebury* (1872) L.R. 7 Ch.App. 777, affirmed L.R. 7 H.L. 102; *Cherry and McDougall v Colonial Bank of Australasia* (1869) L.R. 3 P.C. 24.

[53] *Kleinwort Benson Ltd v Lincoln CC* [1999] 2 A.C. 349.

person to whom it was made[54]: he cannot rescind if he did not believe it,[55] or tested its accuracy.[56] But if he does rely on it, it is immaterial that there were also other inducements to contract.[57] It is also possible that it must be material in the objective sense.[58] There must be a positive misrepresentation: silence cannot in general constitute misrepresentation[59] unless a representation arises from conduct,[60] is literally true but misleading,[61] or is falsified by a later event occurring before the contract is entered into.[62] A duty to disclose may, however, arise in contracts *uberrimae fidei* (contracts of insurance and certain family arrangements[63]), or where there is a fiduciary relationship[64] or a contractual duty of disclosure.[65]

10–010 **Damages.** In the case of such misrepresentations the common law, as has already been stated, gave no damages except where they were wilfully or recklessly made, in which case there was an action on the tort of deceit.[66] Since *Hedley Byrne & Co. Ltd v Heller & Partners Ltd*[67] there can sometimes be liability in the tort of negligence in such situations; and since the Misrepresentation Act 1967 there can often be liability in damages under section 2(1) of that Act.[68] Both of these actions may yield damages different from those which would be awarded for breach of a contractual term,[69] the first because it is an action in tort and the second because the wording of section 2(1) seems to require the action thereby created to be treated as a tort, and in some respects as a deceit action.[70]

---

[54] *Jennings v Broughton* (1854) 5 De G.M. & G. 126; *JEB Fasteners Ltd v Marks Bloom & Co.* [1983] 1 All E.R. 583.
[55] Or in some cases if the truth was known to his agent: *Bawden v London, etc., Assurance Co.* [1892] 2 Q.B. 534. See *Bowstead and Reynolds on Agency* (18th ed.), para.8–216.
[56] Even though he did not find out the truth: *Redgrave v Hurd* (1881) 20 Ch.D. 1. *Aliter* if he did not test its accuracy, though he had the opportunity to do so: *ibid*; but *cf. Smith v Eric S Bush* [1990] 1 A.C. 831; Treitel, *Law of Contract* (11th ed.), pp.339–340. Testing accuracy in one respect may indicate reliance in other respects.
[57] *Edgington v Fitzmaurice* (1885) 29 Ch.D. 459.
[58] See Treitel, *Law of Contract* (11th ed.), pp.336–338; Chitty, *Contracts* (29th ed.), Vol.1, paras 6–036, 6–037; *Lonrho Plc v Fayed (No. 2)* [1992] 1 W.L.R. 1 at 5–6; *cf.* Goff and Jones, *Law of Restitution* (6th ed.), para.9–022; *Museprime Properties Ltd v Adhill Properties Ltd* [1990] 2 E.G.L.R. 196.
[59] *Bell v Lever Bros* [1932] A.C. 161 at 227.
[60] *Bodger v Nicholls* (1873) 28 L.T. 441 at 445.
[61] *Nottingham Patent Brick and Tile Co. v Butler* (1886) 16 Q.B.D. 778.
[62] *With v O'Flanagan* [1936] Ch. 575; *Awaroa Holdings Ltd v Commercial Securities and Finance Ltd* [1976] 1 N.Z.L.R. 19. If the representation has become false by the time it is acted on, it does not seem that the representor need know this: see the *Awaroa* case at p.31. As to the application of this principle to change of intention see Hudson [1984] N.I.L.Q. 1800.
[63] See Treitel, *Law of Contract* (11th ed.), pp.394 *et seq.; Chitty on Contracts* (29th ed.) Vol.1, paras 6–139 *et seq.*
[64] *e.g.* parent and child, solicitor and client, agent and principal. See Treitel, *op. cit*, p.399.
[65] See *William Pickersgill & Sons Ltd v London, etc., Insurance Co.* [1912] 3 K.B. 614 at 621. There are few indications as to when such a duty will be implied.
[66] *Derry v Peek* (1889) 14 App.Cas. 337: below, para.12–012.
[67] [1964] A.C. 465: below, para.12–013.
[68] Below, paras 12–014 *et seq.*
[69] As to which see below, paras 12–017 *et seq.*
[70] Below, para.12–015.

Significance of category. The difficulty of separating such statements, in the context of many sales, from the main contract means that the category of misrepresentation inducing the contract will in fact not frequently be invoked in sale situations. The situation will require to be one where the representation is clearly separate from the contract, whether chronologically or because the contract is reduced to writing, or where full contractual liability on it is inappropriate under the criteria for the identification of a contractual promise.[71] There are however cases where this interpretation has been put upon the facts.[72] 10–011

4. COLLATERAL CONTRACTS

Contractual promises separate from the main contract (collateral contracts). Sometimes it may seem appropriate to treat a statement as containing a promise; but there may still be difficulty in regarding it as part of the main contract, whether because it is clearly prior[73] or otherwise external to the contract, or contrary to the terms of the contract, or because the contract is reduced to writing.[74] In such situations it may sometimes be possible to interpret the promise as part of a *separate* or *collateral* contract, often called a "collateral warranty". Where the main contract is not yet concluded when the collateral promise is made, consideration will be provided by entering into the main contract,[75] though when the main contract is already binding there may be more difficulty in finding consideration.[76] *Couchman v Hill*[77] can be explained as involving such a contract. A heifer was auctioned, and the printed conditions of sale excluded warranties. The plaintiff asked whether the heifer was "unserved", saying that he would not bid if she was not. He was held entitled to sue for breach of collateral warranty (the consideration being his bidding) when it proved, 10–012

---

[71] Below, para.10–016.

[72] *e.g. Routledge v McKay* [1954] 1 W.L.R. 615; *Oscar Chess Ltd v Williams* [1957] 1 W.L.R. 370; *Long v Lloyd* [1958] 1 W.L.R. 753; *Davis & Co. (Wines) Ltd v Afa-Minerva (EMI) Ltd* [1974] 2 Lloyd's Rep. 27 (apparently a contract of hire); *Howard Marine and Dredging Co. Ltd v A. Ogden & Sons (Excavations) Ltd* [1978] Q.B. 574 (hire of barge). The possibility of relying on s.2(1) of the Misrepresentation Act 1967 (below, paras 12–014 *et seq.*) can sometimes increase the attractiveness of the argument that a statement is not a term.

[73] See *Miller v Cannon Hill Estates Ltd* [1931] 2 K.B. 113; *Coffey v Dickson* [1960] N.Z.L.R. 1135; *Wells (Merstham) Ltd v Buckland Sand & Silica Ltd* [1965] 2 Q.B. 170 (where no specific contract was in view).

[74] As to which see material cited above, para.10–008, n.40.

[75] See *Heilbut, Symons & Co. v Buckleton* [1913] A.C. 30 at 47.

[76] See *Roscorla v Thomas* (1842) 3 Q.B. 234 (warranty given after sale unenforceable).

[77] [1947] K.B. 554. See also *Harling v Eddy* [1951] 2 K.B. 739 (but see below, para.10–039, for another explanation of these cases); *Webster v Higgin* [1948] 2 All E.R. 127; *City and Westminster Properties (1934) Ltd v Mudd* [1959] Ch. 129; *Mendelssohn v Normand Ltd* [1970] 1 Q.B. 177. But *cf. Lough v Moran Motors Pty Ltd* [1962] Q.S.R. 466 (car: prior warranty inconsistent with later 30-day warranty); *Donovan v Northlea Farms Ltd* [1976] 1 N.Z.L.R. 180. See McLauchlan, *The Parol Evidence Rule* (Wellington, N.Z. 1976), Ch.6, esp. at pp.70 *et seq.*

contrary to the assertion made, that she was in calf: the exclusion of warranties, being part of the main contract, was inapplicable. In the leading case of *Heilbut, Symons & Co. v Buckleton* it was said that "such collateral contracts, the sole effect of which is to vary or add to the terms of the principal contract, are therefore viewed with suspicion by the law. They must be proved strictly."[78] However, Lord Denning M.R. subsequently suggested that "much of what was said in that case is entirely out of date"[79]; and it is certainly true that contractual, as well as tortious liability on statements has of recent years been much more readily accepted. This manifests itself in two principal ways. First, promises are more readily inferred from statements, as in *Esso Petroleum Co. Ltd v Mardon*,[80] where a pre-contractual statement as to the likely throughput of a petrol station was held to involve, as an alternative to liability in tort, a promise that the forecast had been made with reasonable care and skill (though not a promise that such an amount of petrol would actually be sold). In construing such contracts, careful attention must be paid to the exact content of the promise. This is shown by the case itself where the obligation was held not to be strict.[81] Secondly, the apparent inconsistency of such a contract with a written main contract may be regarded as less significant than might have been the case previously. Sometimes this is achieved without adopting the device of the collateral contract, by simply saying that the main contract is not reduced to writing but partly written and partly oral.[82]

10–013 **Uses of such contracts.** Where such a contract is duly established, the main remedy in respect of it is normally an action for damages. As *Couchman v Hill*[83] shows, it may override exemption clauses framed in

---

[78] [1913] A.C. 30 at 47, *per* Lord Moulton. See in general Wedderburn [1959] C.L.J. 58.

[79] *J. Evans & Son (Portsmouth) Ltd v Andrea Merzario Ltd* [1976] 1 W.L.R. 1078 at 1081. See also *Esso Petroleum Co. Ltd v Mardon* [1978] Q.B. 801 at 817–818, 823–827; *Howard Marine and Dredging Co. Ltd v A Ogden & Sons (Excavations) Ltd* [1978] Q.B. 574 at 590. The judgment of Lord Moulton is plainly influenced by his view that it was important that the "House should maintain in its full integrity the principle that a person is not liable in damages for an innocent misrepresentation, no matter in what way or under what form the attack is made": see p.51. Such a principle is no longer valid. Dicta from the case were however cited with approval by Lord Dilhorne in *Independent Broadcasting Authority v EMI Electronics Ltd* (1980) 14 Build.L.R. 1; and it is certainly explicable on the basis of lack of contractual intent.

[80] Above, but *cf.* the *Howard Marine* case, above, where no warranty was found; also *Lambert v Lewis* [1982] A.C. 225 (affirmed on other grounds *ibid.* 271) (no warranty in promotional literature).

[81] *cf. Wells (Merstham) Ltd v Buckland Sand and Silica Ltd* [1965] 2 Q.B. 170 (warranty of analysis of sand absolute).

[82] As in *J Evans & Sons (Portsmouth) Ltd v Andrea Merzario Ltd*, above, *per* Roskill L.J.; *Quickmaid Rental Services Ltd v Reece* (1970) 114 S.J. 372; *A M Bisley & Co. Ltd v Thompson* [1982] 2 N.Z.L.R. 696. See also *Esso Petroleum Co. Ltd v Mardon*, above. See McLauchlan, 3 Dalhousie L.Rev. 136 (1976); *The Parol Evidence Rule* (Wellington, N.Z., 1976), Ch.8; Law Com. No. 154 (Cmnd. 9700) (1986).

[83] Above, para.10–012; *cf.* below, para.13–016. See also *Gallaher Ltd v British Road Services Ltd* [1974] 2 Lloyd's Rep. 440.

general terms. It will also be actionable though the main contract was made between persons other than the representor and representee, *e.g.* where the warranty is given by a dealer in connection with a hire-purchase transaction (in which case the main contract will often not be with the dealer but with a finance company[84]) or by a manufacturer who has not sold the goods directly to the buyer.[85] It may also be actionable though the main contract is unenforceable because of illegality.[86] In many cases it is not clear whether such a promise or warranty as to goods should be regarded as part of a genuinely separate or collateral contract or as part of the main contract, for there is a tendency to refer to all warranties as collateral.[87] Frequently an action in tort, or under section 2(1) of the Misrepresentation Act 1967, will be available in respect of the same representation.[88] It might then be thought that these latter liabilities, both fairly recent in origin, might make it less necessary to rely upon the older device of the collateral contract, the main advantage of which was that it gave a claim in damages despite the fact that the representation was not a term of the contract.[89] But the existence of a duty of care and negligent breach of it may not always be easy to establish,[90] whereas the liability on a collateral contract may in appropriate cases be strict; the requirements of section 2(1) of the Misrepresentation Act may not always be met; and conversely the measure of damages for breach of a collateral contract may often yield a result similar to that in a tort action, depending on the nature of the promise inferred.[91] Further, as shown above, there are other advantages in the contractual action. The action upon a collateral contract is therefore far from dead: it has even been suggested that the contractual action leaves little necessity for the tort action in this area.[92]

Although the basic remedy for breach of such a contract lies in damages, it seems also that breach of such a contract may in appropriate cases entitle the promisee to treat the main contract as discharged, or at least provide him with a defence to an action for non-performance. It might amount to a 10–014

[84] *e.g. Andrews v Hopkinson* [1975] 1 Q.B. 229, above para.10–005; see below, para.14–062. The actual seller may sometimes be liable under Consumer Credit Act 1974, ss.56, 75.

[85] *e.g. Shanklin Pier Ltd v Detel Products Ltd* [1951] 2 K.B. 854; (paint); *Hallmark Pool Corp. v Storey* (1983) 144 D.L.R. (3d) 56 (swimming pool); but *cf. Lambert v Lewis* [1982] A.C. 225 (affirmed on other grounds *ibid.* 271). See below, para.14–062.

[86] *e.g. Strongman (1945) Ltd v Sincock* [1955] 2 Q.B. 525. If the contract was void there might be more difficulty in finding consideration.

[87] Below, para.10–022. See, *e.g. J Evans & Son (Portsmouth) Ltd v Andrea Merzario Ltd* [1976] 1 W.L.R. 1078.

[88] Below, paras 12–012 *et seq.*

[89] It is also an established exception to the parol evidence rule: see above, para.10–008 n.40.

[90] See *Howard Marine and Dredging Co. Ltd v A Ogden & Sons (Excavations) Ltd* [1978] Q.B. 574; and in general *Caparo Industries Plc v Dickman* [1990] 2 A.C. 605; *Henderson v Merrett Syndicates Ltd* [1995] 2 A.C. 145; below, para.12–013.

[91] See *Esso Petroleum Co. Ltd v Mardon*, above, para.10–012.

[92] McLauchlan, 4 Otago L.Rev. 23 (1977). But *cf.* the *Howard Marine* case, above, where in the context of hire a statement was held a misrepresentation but not promissory.

variation of the main contract[93]; or by virtue of its status as a misrepresentation, to grounds for rescission[94]; or perhaps to a ground for barring the vendor's action.[95]

5. WARRANTIES

10–015 **Contractual promises which are terms of the main contract (warranties).** Statements relating to goods sold may finally, of course, amount to contractual promises and as such will be terms of the main contract. Such promises are usually referred to as warranties in the old cases and this term is often still used in considering whether a statement is such that the maker is to be regarded as undertaking contractual liability on it. This usage arose because before the development of *assumpsit* the statement gave rise to an action separate from those upon the main transaction.[96] Thus the development of the law as to contractual promises in sale is for a considerable period represented by the history of the law as to warranties. The evolution of the law of warranty is complex.[97] The warranty was apparently originally conceived of as sounding in tort. It retained this connotation for some time after the evolution of *assumpsit* (itself of tortious origin) and was thought of in connection with the action of deceit. This led to difficulties in applying the idea of warranty to statements as to the future performance of goods as opposed to those concerning their existing properties.[98] Once these difficulties were overcome, however, there seems to have been a contrary tendency towards requiring a promise for all warranties, and thus not regarding a statement of fact as a warranty at all. But as Chalmers said,[99] a representation may amount to a warranty, *i.e.* there may be a statement of fact which is promised to be true, and this was in due course accepted. The course of development of the law of warranty was different in the United States,[1] for there the tortious background of warranty retained its prominence, and this led to more ready inference of warranties from statements

---

93 *cf. Brikom Investments Ltd v Carr* [1979] Q.B. 467.
94 See *Morgan v Griffith* (1870) L.R. 6 Ex. 70 at 73.
95 *cf.* the procedure suggested in *Gore v Van der Lann* [1967] 2 Q.B. 31; see also *Snelling v John G Snelling Ltd* [1973] 1 Q.B. 87.
96 Simpson, *History of the Common Law of Contract* (1975), pp.240 *et seq.*
97 See Greig, 87 L.Q.R. 179 (1971); Stoljar, 15 M.L.R. 425 (1952); 16 M.L.R. 174 (1953); Williston, *Sales* (rev. ed., 1948), paras 195–196; Ames, 2 Harv.L.Rev. 1 (1888).
98 Blackstone, 3 Comm. 165, says that "the warranty can only reach the things in being at the time of the warranty made."
99 *Sale of Goods* (2nd ed., 1894), p.22. The criticism of the English approach made by Williston, *Sales* (rev. ed., 1948), paras 181, 194, and in 27 Harv.L.Rev. 1 (1913), followed by Stoljar, 15 M.L.R. 425 at 426–427 (1962), seems to be based on excessively definite meanings attached to the words "representation" and "agreement." The same point arose in Roman law: see Honoré, *Studies in the Roman Law of Sale in Memory of de Zulueta* (Daube ed., 1959), pp.132, 136: "only a sophisticated generation feels uncomfortable about a stipulatory promise that so-and-so is the case." See D. 21.2.31.
1 See Williston, *Sales* (rev. ed., 1948), para.201; *cf.* Uniform Commercial Code, s.2–313.

of fact inducing the contract. In England however the idea of warranty has long been closely associated with that of contract, and it is clear that liability is only to be imposed where the person giving the warranty can fairly be regarded as having made a contractual promise.[2]

When is a statement a warranty? The oldest cases were reluctant to hold statements to be warranties unless responsibility had been expressly undertaken. In conformity with the tendency of developing law to rely on fixed ritualistic terms it seems that at one time the word "warrant" had to be used. Thus in *Chandelor v Lopus*[3] it was held that a declaration that a goldsmith had affirmed a stone to be a bezar was not sufficient to found a verdict for breach of warranty, for "the bare affirmation that it was a bezar stone without warranting it to be so, is no cause of action." Later cases took a somewhat broader view: in 1789 Buller J. said "it was rightly held by Holt C.J.[4] . . . and has been uniformly adopted ever since, that an affirmation at the time of a sale is a warranty, provided it appear on evidence to have been so intended."[5] This statement is often cited and still provides the starting point of the modern English law. As already stated, a wider interpretation of the idea of warranty, placing less reliance on intention and more on the simple fact of inducement to contract, was adopted in the United States; and some of the older English cases were also susceptible of such an interpretation.[6] Thus Benjamin wrote: "In determining whether it was so intended, a decisive test is whether the vendor assumes to assert a fact of which a buyer is ignorant or merely states an opinion or judgment upon a matter of which the vendor has no special knowledge, and on which the buyer may be expected also to have an opinion and to exercise his judgment."[7] This passage was indeed adopted by the Court of Appeal in 1901.[8] But it was disapproved by the House of Lords in 1913 in *Heilbut, Symons & Co. v Buckleton*.[9] "It may well be" said Lord Moulton[10] "that the features thus referred to . . . may be criteria of value. . . but they cannot be said to furnish decisive tests, because it cannot be said as a matter of law that the presence or absence of those features is conclusive of the intention of the parties." 10–016

Basis of the modern law. The modern English law therefore still starts from the dictum of Holt C.J. that "an affirmation at the time of a sale is a warranty provided it appear on evidence to have been so intended",[11] and this is regularly cited. But the general tendency over the whole law of 10–017

---

[2] *Heilbut, Symons & Co. v Buckleton* [1913] A.C. 30.
[3] (1603) Cro.Jac. 4.
[4] In *Crosse v Gardner* (1688) Carth. 90 and *Medina v Stoughton* (1700) 1 Salk. 210.
[5] *Pasley v Freeman* (1789) 3 T.R. 51 at 57. This was in fact an "improvement" on what Holt C.J. had said: see Stoljar, 15 M.L.R. 425 at 428 (1952).
[6] See, *e.g. Cave v Coleman* (1828) 3 Man. & Ry. 2; *Gee v Lucas* (1867) 16 L.T. 357; *Cowdy v Thomas* (1876) 36 L.T. 22; *De Lassalle v Guildford* [1901] 2 K.B. 215 at 221.
[7] *Sale of Personal Property* (3rd ed.), p.607.
[8] *De Lassalle v Guildford*, above, at p.221.
[9] [1913] A.C. 30. The passage was therefore amended in subsequent editions.
[10] At p.50.
[11] Above, para.10–016.

contract in the twentieth century to treat statements and acts objectively and to place emphasis on the impression they reasonably create[12] has over the last 50 or so years produced a clear movement which, while retaining the overall justification of implementing the intention of the parties, has moved towards the readier imposition of liability. The dicta in *Heilbut, Symons & Co. v Buckle-ton*,[13] which were influenced by the importance of the principle that there was then no liability in damages for innocent misrepresentation, have been called in question.[14] A well-known example of this trend is *Dick Bentley Productions Ltd v Harold Smith (Motors) Ltd*,[15] where Lord Denning M.R. said: "The question whether a warranty was intended depends on the conduct of the parties, on their words and behaviour, rather than on their thoughts. If a representation is made in the course of dealings for a contract for the very purpose of inducing the other party to act upon it, and actually inducing him to act on it, by entering into the contract, that is prima facie ground for inferring that it was intended as a warranty. It is not necessary to speak of it as being collateral. Suffice it to say that it was intended to be acted upon and was in fact acted on."[16] In so far as it makes inducement the *sole* test of whether a statement is a contractual promise, however, this passage probably goes too far. Salmon L.J. in the same case posed the more traditional test: "Was what [the defendant] said intended and understood as a legally binding promise?" The High Court of Australia has also reaffirmed the distinction between promissory and representational statements,[17] and Lord Denning himself subsequently relied on the dictum of Holt C.J. in holding significant statements not to be warranties.[18] It seems therefore that whether a statement is to be regarded as a warranty must be ascertained objectively by asking whether the other party assumed, and a reasonable person in his position would have assumed, that the representor was to be regarded as undertaking legal liability for his assertions.[19] Factors relevant to the ascertainment of this are the importance of the statement, the relative knowledge and means of knowledge of the parties, and the possibility of verification. There must also be a tendency to look to the consequences of

---

12 As to which see, *e.g. Ashington Piggeries Ltd v Christopher Hill Ltd* [1972] A.C. 441 at 502.

13 See above, paras 10–012, 10–016.

14 See above, para.10–012.

15 [1965] 1 W.L.R. 623 at 627. See also *Oscar Chess Ltd v Williams* [1957] 1 W.L.R. 370 at 375. But see Greig, 87 L.Q.R. 179 at 182 (1971).

16 The remainder of this passage should however be treated with caution, inasmuch as it imports the idea that a statement may not be a warranty merely because the maker was not negligent.

17 *J. J. Savage & Sons Pty Ltd v Blakney* (1970) 119 C.L.R. 435 (statement as to estimated speed of boat not a warranty).

18 *Howard Marine and Dredging Co. Ltd v A Ogden & Sons (Excavations) Ltd* [1978] Q.B. 574 at 590–591 (where *collateral* warranty was argued). See also *Independent Broadcasting Authority v EMI Electronics Ltd* (1980) 14 Build.L.R. 1 at 23, *per* Viscount Dilhorne.

19 "The defendant swore that he did not intend to give a warranty. But his subjective intentions are irrelevant, and cannot affect the construction to be put on the advertisement or the inferences to be drawn from his conduct": *Turner v Anquetil* [1953] N.Z.L.R. 952 at 957, *per* F. B. Adams J.

treating a statement as a warranty. These are prima facie that the liability which the representor undertakes is strict and that he answers in damages on the basis that he must put the other party in the same position as that in which he would have been if the statement had been true—*viz.*, for the expectation loss.[20]

10–018 **Examples.** In the *Dick Bentley*[21] case, a statement by a dealer as to the mileage of a second—hand car was held a warranty: on the other hand, in *Oscar Chess Ltd v Williams*[22] an innocent statement made by a private seller to a dealer that a car was a 1948 model (when in fact it was a 1939 model) was held not to be a warranty. In cases such as these, which were prior to the Misrepresentation Act 1967, the result may sometimes have been influenced by the tactics of the parties, in that buyers who wished to reject, but feared that they had lost the right to do so for breach of condition by virtue of section 11(1)(c) of the Sale of Goods Act 1893 as it then stood (it was amended by the 1967 Act and is now section 11(4) of the 1979 Act), might seek to rescind as upon a misrepresentation rather than sue for damages for breach of warranty.[23] But there can be no doubt that the relative standing of the parties is relevant to the question whether there is a warranty: private individuals, for example, may less frequently be regarded as undertaking the strict liability of a warranty.[24] Thus the above two cases can be explained on the basis that statements may be warranties when made by dealers, though they would not be warranties if made by private sellers; for the dealer may be in possession of special knowledge, expertise and means of information not available to ordinary persons.

10–019 **Obvious defects.** As a matter of interpretation it seems reasonable that an express warranty should not normally be regarded as covering obvious defects which the buyer must have noticed.[25] The same would be true of a defect that would be obvious on examination even to a person possessed of no technical knowledge, provided that such examination was actually carried out.[26] But where a warranty is found, in general the maker undertakes strict liability for what he asserts. Therefore it does not seem

---

[20] Both these consequences can be mitigated by a limited view of what is promised: see *e.g. Esso Petroleum Co. Ltd v Mardon* [1976] Q.B. 801, above, para.10–012 (collateral warranty).

[21] Above, para.10–017.

[22] [1957] 1 W.L.R. 370.

[23] *e.g. Long v Lloyd* [1958] 1 W.L.R. 753. See below, para.12–038.

[24] See also *Routledge v McKay* [1954] 1 W.L.R. 615 (no warranty by private seller). But *cf. Beale v Taylor* [1967] 1 W.L.R. 1193 (Koh [1968] C.L.J. 11); and *Turner v Anquetil* [1953] N.Z.L.R. 952, in both of which there was contractual liability on statements contained in advertisements of goods offered by private sellers.

[25] *Baily v Merrell* (1615) 3 Bulst. 94 ("if he sells purple to one and saith to him that it is scarlet, this warrant is to no purpose"); *Margetson v Wright* (1831) 7 Bing. 603 (example given of horse blind in both eyes). See also *Lambert v Lewis* [1982] A.C. 225; below, paras 17–059 *et seq*. A warranty may also be expressly qualified: see *Jones v Cowley* (1825) 4 B. & C. 445; *Wood v Smith* (1829) 5 M. & Ry. 124. S.14 of the Sale of Goods Act 1979 produces the same effect: see below, Ch.11.

[26] See *Holliday v Morgan* (1858) 1 E. & E. 1 (short-sighted horse); *Cowdy v Thomas* (1876) 36 L.T. 22.

right normally to imply any diminution of a warranty made where there is an examination, and the defect is one which would only be discoverable on careful or expert examination[27]; still less is it right to imply such diminution on the basis that though an examination could have been carried out, but was not. Further, it seems on principle that a warranty may sometimes be so phrased as to cover even obvious defects.[28] All matters such as these may, however, be relevant where a statement is sought to be construed as a misrepresentation inducing the contract or as founding liability upon a collateral contract or in tort.

10–020 **Time of warranty.** There is no difficulty in principle about liability for a warranty made before the sale.[29] "If, upon a treaty, about the buying of certain goods. . . the seller should warrant them, and then the buyer should demand the price, and the seller should set the price, and then the buyer should take time to consider for two or three days and then should come and give the seller his price; though the warranty here was before the sale, yet this will be well, because the warranty is the ground of the treaty."[30] But of course the fact that a statement was made before the sale may well be relevant to the question whether it is deemed to be incorporated in it. Thus in *Camac v Warriner*[31] there was a sale of a material called oropholithe. The seller's agent had described this to the buyer eight months earlier as being suitable for roofing, though the buyer had previously bought it for flooring. It was held that the sale had not been "shown to have been made with any reference" to the representation and that there was therefore no liability in respect of it. Nowadays, however, the further questions would arise as to whether the representation induced the contract,[32] or could be treated as a collateral warranty.[33]

10–021 **Warranty of future events.** As previously explained,[34] the old idea of warranty was associated with that of deceit, and the implication was that warranties were affirmations of fact only. Since the amalgamation of

---

[27] This will be clearest where the warranty can be interpreted as genuinely collateral. See *Webster v Higgin* [1948] 2 All E.R. 127 ("the hirer is deemed to have examined (or caused to be examined) the vehicle prior to this agreement and satisfied himself as to its condition", etc.: seller liable on overriding collateral warranty guaranteeing that car in good condition). See also *Mowbray v Merryweather* [1895] 2 Q.B. 640; *Scott v Foley, Aikman & Co.* (1899) 16 T.L.R. 55. *Cf.* Sale of Goods Act 1979, s.14(2).

[28] *Liddard v Kain* (1824) 2 Bing. 183 (warranty that sick horses would be all right within a fortnight); *Butterfield v Burroughs* (1706) 1 Salk. 211 (horse with one eye—warranty absolute on facts); *Smith v O'Bryan* (1864) 13 W.R. 79.

[29] See, *e.g. Cowdy v Thomas* (1876) 36 L.T. 22; *Schawel v Reade* [1913] 2 I.R. 64, HL.

[30] *Lysney v Selby* (1705) 2 Ld.Raym. 1118 at 1120, *per* Holt C.J.

[31] (1845) 1 C.B. 356. See also *Hopkins v Tanqueray* (1854) 15 C.B. 130, as explained in *Harling v Eddy* [1951] 2 K.B. 739; *cf. Schawel v Reade*, above, and *Malcolm v Cross* (1898) 35 Sc.L.R. 794; *Howard Marine and Dredging Co. Ltd v A Ogden & Sons (Excavations) Ltd* [1978] Q.B. 574 at 590–591; *Lambert v Lewis* [1982] A.C. 225; *Paul & Co. v Glasgow Corp.* (1900) 3 F. (Ct. of Sess.) 119; *Baker Perkins Ltd v Thompson* [1960] N.S.W.R. 488.

[32] Above, paras 10–008 *et seq.*

[33] Above, para.10–012. See, *e.g. Coffey v Dickson* [1960] N.Z.L.R. 1135 ("The plant is in good working order").

[34] Above, para.10–015.

warranty into the general law of contract, however, there is no difficulty as to warranties for the future: goods are frequently warranted for a year or some other period, and this is in effect a promise to be answerable for any defect that may manifest itself within that period.[35] Such a warranty would, however, normally have to be clearly proved, and would not easily be implied from a mere assertion of present condition. And sometimes warranties in this form are to be interpreted as warranties of soundness at the time of buying only, liability for which is extinguished if no complaint is made within the specified period.[36]

Warranty as collateral. Many cases treat warranties as collateral, and indeed section 61(1) of the Sale of Goods Act 1979 defines a warranty as "an agreement with reference to goods which are the subject of a contract of sale, but collateral to the main purpose of such contract." This, however, is directly derived from the earlier notion that the warranty was separate from the sale,[37] and is a misleading usage at the present day, for it makes the warranty which is a term of the contract easy to confuse with the warranty which is part, or the subject, of a genuine collateral contract separate from the main contract, breach of which may not lead to the same consequences as breach of the main contract.[38] Rather than use this confusing terminology in respect of terms of the contract,[39] it would be better to concentrate on distinguishing between contractual promises which are terms of the main contract on the one hand, and representations and contractual promises which are not, on the other. 10–022

Warranty as less important promise. It is explained in the following paragraphs that in the nineteenth century a special use of the word "condition" grew up, which treated the word as meaning a promise (or warranty) any breach of which would, in accordance with the parties' supposed intentions, entitle the innocent party to treat the contract as discharged.[40] This led to a further and specialised use of the word "warranty", which became attributed to and reserved for the remaining, less important terms of a contract, breach of which did not give rise to such a right: *viz.*, the promises (or warranties) that were not conditions.[41] Thus 10–023

---

[35] *Chapman v Gwyther* (1866) L.R. 1 Q.B. 463 ("warranted sound for one month"); *J Barre Johnston & Co. v Oldham* (1895) 11 T.L.R. 401. See also *Lambert v Lewis* [1982] A.C. 225: below, paras 17–059 *et seq*; and as to durability of goods below, paras 11–040.

[36] *Chapman v Gwyther*, above. For another type of (collateral) warranty see *Esso Petroleum Co. Ltd v Mardon* [1976] Q.B. 801, above, para.10–012.

[37] Above, para.10–015.

[38] Above, paras 10–012 *et seq*.

[39] For examples of the confusion generated see the leading case on warranties itself, *Heilbut, Symons & Co. v Buckleton* [1913] A.C. 30; also *Couchman v Hill* [1947] K.B. 554; *Harling v Eddy* [1951] 2 K.B. 739; *Routledge v McKay* [1954] 1 W.L.R. 615; *Howard Marine and Dredging Co. Ltd v A Ogden & Sons (Excavations) Ltd* [1978] Q.B. 574; *Turner v Anquetil* [1953] N.Z.L.R. 952 at 954; *Coffey v Dickson* [1960] N.Z.L.R. 1135.

[40] Below, paras 10–026 *et seq*.

[41] Strictly speaking, the warranties which are not also conditions. See *Behn v Burness* (1863) 3 B. & S. 751 at 755 ("a warranty, that is to say a condition").

section 61(1) of the Sale of Goods Act continues by indicating that a breach of warranty "gives rise to a claim for damages, but not to a right to reject the goods and treat the contract as repudiated." This associates a further confusion with the word. However, as will be explained,[42] the law has developed towards a position in which the significance of this dichotomy is much reduced; and it is possible that this special usage of the word may eventually disappear.

6. CONDITIONS

10–024 **Conditions: difficulty of term.** The term "condition" is one that causes great difficulty in law. Among many uses and meanings, the way of defining a condition most relevant to the law of contract is perhaps as an event upon which an obligation or obligations of one or the other party, or of both parties, depend.[43] It is sometimes suggested that the term should also be used to refer to something upon which the existence of the *contract* depends, but if the position really is that there are no binding obligations until the condition occurs, *i.e.* either party can withdraw *pendente condicione*, there is no legal relationship at all until the condition occurs and little significance for the concept.[44] This latter usage comes from the Roman Law, where the position was slightly different and the term consequently more appropriate.[45] It may be suggested therefore that the better use of the word "condition" is to refer to an event qualifying the operation of a promise of the seller or of the buyer or of each. An example occurs where a seller agrees to supply goods subject to availability, which latter he may not necessarily promise.[46] As regards the buyer, there may be a condition (as with a sale on approval) that the goods meet certain requirements, which is not necessarily promised by the seller.[47] The

---

[42] Below, paras 10–029 *et seq.*

[43] *cf. Restatement, Second, Contracts*, paras 224 *et seq.*; Williston, *Sales* (rev. ed., 1948), paras 178 *et seq.*; Williston, *Contracts* (rev. ed., 1936), paras 663 *et seq.*; Stoljar, 69 L.Q.R. 485 (1953) and material there cited; Reynolds, 79 L.Q.R. 534–538 (1963). See also *Wm. Cory & Son Ltd v IRC* [1965] A.C. 1088 at 1108. The term is discussed in *Wickman Machine Tool Sales Ltd v L Schuler AG* [1974] A.C. 235.

[44] Stoljar, *op. cit.*, at pp.489–492. *Cf. Pym v Campbell* (1856) 6 E. & B. 370 (sale of patent subject to approval of invention by third party: "there never was any agreement at all"). This notion is sometimes called an "external condition". The term can also be used in connection with the passing of property, but this is not here relevant. In this area the terms "condition precedent" and "condition subsequent" are also found, but they are of little if any utility in contract: Stoljar, *op. cit.*, at pp.506–511.

[45] *cf.* Stoljar, *op. cit.*, at p.501, n.84; Daube, *Tijdschrift voor Rechtsgeschiedenis*, 1960, pp.261 *et seq.*

[46] *e.g.* sale of goods "to arrive": see *Hollis Bros & Co. Ltd v White Sea Timber Trust Ltd* [1936] 3 All E.R. 895; below, paras 21–014 *et seq.* See also *Total Gas Marketing Ltd v Arco British Ltd* [1998] 2 Lloyd's Rep. 209, HL (approvals and consents). In another context (insurance) see *Roadworks (1952) Ltd v JR Charman* [1994] 2 Lloyd's Rep. 99 at 103.

[47] See *Mackay v Dick* (1881) 6 App.Cas. 251, below, para.10–038; *Millars Machinery Co. Ltd v David Way & Son* (1935) 40 Com.Cas. 204. Cases on agreements "subject to licence being obtained" and the like provide good examples: *e.g. Hargreaves Transport Ltd v Lynch* [1969] 1 W.L.R. 215; see Treitel, *Law of Contract* (11th ed.), pp.62–66; below, paras 18–318, 19–014, 21–022 *et seq.*

obligation of both parties is qualified where, for example, the goods must be valued or tested by a third party.

Promises with regard to conditions. Where promises are qualified in this way, the parties may make, or be regarded as making, various further promises about the performance or fulfilment of any condition. A party may make no promise except not actually to prevent fulfilment of the condition.[48] Again, he may promise to take certain steps towards providing facilities for the fulfilment of the condition, *e.g.* make applications, test machinery to see if it meets requirements.[49] Finally, he may promise that the condition will occur. The idea of a promise is thus different from that of condition and the two should be kept separate: as Williston said[50] "the difference between conditions and promises is so radical in its consequences that there is no excuse for a nomenclature which fails to recognise the distinction." 10–025

Special meaning of "condition" in English law. There became prominent, however, in the nineteenth century a special use of the term "condition" in the law of contract, as meaning a *promise* (or warranty) regarded as so vital to the contract that its complete performance by the party making it is a condition of the liability of the other party to perform his part. If such a promise is not performed, the other party can therefore treat the contract as discharged. For example, in a sale by description, the tendering by the seller of goods complying with the description is normally a condition of the duty of the buyer to accept the goods and pay the price.[51] It may well be desirable to have a name for such promises, to distinguish them from promises the breach of which may be less important and may sound in damages only, but this particular term is a confusing one for the purpose.[52] In the old law, the problem was solved by asking whether the covenant (promise) was dependent (on performance by the other party) or 10–026

---

[48] Even this may not always be implied: see *Thompson v Asda-MFI Group Plc* [1988] Ch. 241 at 266; *North Sea Energy Holdings Ltd v Petroleum Authority of Thailand* [1999] 1 Lloyd's Rep. 483.

[49] See *Mackay v Dick*, above; Treitel, *op. cit.* above.

[50] *Contracts* (rev. ed., 1936), para.665. *Cf. Restatement, Second, Contracts*, para.225(3): "Nonoccurrence of a condition is not a breach by a party unless he is under a duty that the condition occur." See also Montrose, 15 Can.Bar Rev. 325 (1937): "It would appear nonsensical to say a promise is a condition if its performance is a condition."

[51] Sale of Goods Act 1979, s.13; below, paras 11–001 *et seq.*

[52] See *Wallis, Son & Wells v Pratt & Haynes* [1910] 2 K.B. 1003 at 1012, *per* Fletcher Moulton L.J. (whose dissenting judgment was subsequently approved by the House of Lords [1911] A.C. 394): "I do not think that the choice of terms is happy, especially so far as regards the word 'condition', for it is a word which is used in many other connections and has a considerable variety of meaning." A striking example of the confusion caused is to be found in *Varley v Whipp* [1900] 1 Q.B. 513, where the judge, wishing to find that property in specific goods had not passed, was led to attempt to show that the contract was not "unconditional" because it contained conditions in the sense of vital promises. But every contract does. See also *Vigers Bros v Sanderson Bros* [1901] 1 K.B. 608; *Boys v Rice* (1908) 27 N.Z.L.R. 1038. For a different example of confusion arising from this term see *Bentworth Finance Ltd v Lubert* [1968] 1 Q.B. 680; Carnegie, 31 M.L.R. 78 (1968).

independent.[53] But a usage grew up, or at any rate came to be regarded as having grown up, which attributed the word "condition" to a dependent covenant, and this certainly was the use Chalmers intended in the final version of the Sale of Goods Act 1893.[54] Thus in an appended note on the term "condition"[55] he stated that "the term seems to have been imported into the law of contract from the law of conveyancing. In conveyancing a distinction was drawn between 'conditions' and 'covenants' which, in contracts, has now become obliterated . . . in the older cases promissory[56] conditions were referred to as 'dependent covenants or promises' and were contrasted with independent covenants or promises, namely, stipulations the breach of which gives rise to a claim for damages, but not to a right to treat the contract as repudiated. Now the term 'dependent promise' appears to be merged in the wider term 'condition precedent.'"[57] This may be attacked on both historical[58] and practical grounds: Williston wrote that this use of the word condition was "astonishing"; "it cannot be too strongly deprecated."[59] Even Chalmers was forced to admit that[60] "the Act throughout, so far as it relates to England, draws a distinction between the terms 'condition' and 'warranty'. This distinction has often been insisted on, but seldom observed by judges and text writers."[61]

10–027 **Conditions in the modern law.** However this be, the usage was confirmed in the Act, and though there has, as will be explained below,[62] been a more recent movement towards solving problems of discharge by breach

[53] The old learning was to some extent systematised in the notes to *Pordage v Cole* (1669) 1 Wms.Saund. 319. See also notes to *Peeters v Opie* (1671) 2 Wms.Saund. 350 and *Cutter v Powell* (1795) 2 Sm.L.C. 1. In *Boone v Eyre* (1777) 1 H.Bl. 273n Lord Mansfield said: "where mutual covenants go to the whole of the consideration on both sides they are mutual conditions, the one precedent to the other. But where they only go to a part, where a breach may be paid for in damages, there the defendant has a remedy on his covenant and shall not plead it as a condition precedent." See in general *Hong Kong Fir Shipping Co. Ltd v Kawasaki Kisen Kaisha* [1962] 2 Q.B. 26 at 65–73; *Cehave NV v Bremer Handelsgesellschaft mbH (The Hansa Nord)* [1976] Q.B. 44 at 57–60, 72–73; Shea, 42 M.L.R. 623 (1979); Bridge, 28 McGill L.J. 867 (1983); Carter, *Breach of Contract* (2nd ed.), Chs 4–6.

[54] The Bill on which the 1st ed. of his *Sale of Goods* (1890) is a commentary did not reflect this usage entirely: see esp. p.65 where a right to reject for breach of warranty is given. The note on Conditions in the 2nd ed. (1894) says (p.169) that the meaning of warranty in the Act was adopted "after much consideration". It seems that the original draft thought of the term "condition" as being principally relevant to the passing of property: this explains the controversial term "unconditional" in s.18, r. 1, which caused difficulties in connection with s.11(1)(c) (now s.11(4)) leading to the eventual amendment of that provision by the Misrepresentation Act 1967. See above, paras 5–019 *et seq*.; below, para.12–038.

[55] *Sale of Goods* (2nd ed., 1894), pp.164–165.

[56] A term often used to distinguish the special English use of the term from the more general one given, above, para.10–024.

[57] "Precedent" is added to make a distinction with "subsequent". This dichotomy is of little value in this context: see above, para.10–024, n.44.

[58] Stoljar, 15 M.L.R. 425 at 436–441 (1952); 16 M.L.R. 174 at 183–190 (1953).

[59] *Contracts* (rev. ed., 1936), para.665.

[60] *Sale of Goods* (2nd ed., 1894), p.24.

[61] For 19th century cases containing examples of failure to observe it, see the leading case of *Chanter v Hopkins* (1838) 4 M. & W. 399 at 404; *Bannerman v White* (1861) 10 C.B.(N.S.) 844 at 860.

[62] Below, paras 10–029 *et seq*.

by another and broader principle, the notion of breach of condition is still alive here and elsewhere in commercial law.[63] In *Photo Production Ltd v Securicor Transport Ltd*[64] Lord Diplock described this type of discharge by breach as occurring "where the contracting parties have agreed, whether by express words or by implication of law, that *any* failure by one party to perform a particular obligation ('condition' in the nomenclature of the Sale of Goods Act 1893), irrespective of the gravity of the event that has in fact resulted from the breach, shall entitle the other party to elect to put an end to all primary obligations of both parties remaining unperformed." Whether a term is a condition in this sense or not is a matter of construction and is based, in the absence of statutory guidance, on the court's view as to the apparent intentions of the parties. Section 11(3) (formerly 11(1)(b)) reads: "Whether a stipulation in a contract of sale is a condition, the breach of which may give rise to a right to treat the contract as repudiated, or a warranty, the breach of which may give rise to a claim for damages but not to a right to reject the goods and treat the contract as repudiated, depends in each case on the construction of the contract; and a stipulation may be a condition, though called a warranty in the contract."[65] A controlling dictum is that of Bowen L.J. in *Bentsen v Taylor, Sons & Co.*[66]: "There is no way of deciding that question except by looking at the contract in the light of the surrounding circumstances, and then making up one's mind whether the intention of the parties, as gathered from the instrument itself, will best be carried out by treating the promise as a warranty sounding only in damages, or as a condition precedent by the failure to perform which the other party is relieved of his liability."[67]

It should be noted that the wording of section 11(3) of the Sale of Goods Act reproduced above does not state that a breach of condition automatically gives rise to the right to treat the contract as repudiated, but rather that it *may* do so. In this respect it is inconsistent with the dictum of Lord Diplock quoted in the previous paragraph. One view is that no significance should be attached to this particular wording: the word "may" is also used in the same subsection to refer to the warranty, breach of which always gives to a right to damages, and in respect of which another provision, section 61(1), actually states in a definition of the word that **10–028**

---

[63] Below, para.10–034.
[64] [1980] A.C. 827 at 849. This formulation, which bases discharge on the intention of the parties, seems preferable to his earlier reference in *Hong Kong Fir Shipping Co. Ltd v Kawasaki Kisen Kaisha Ltd* [1962] 2 Q.B. 26 at 69 to terms "of which it can be predicated that every breach of such an undertaking must give rise to an event which will deprive the party not in default of substantially the whole benefit which it was intended that he should obtain from the contract." The difficulties caused by the latter wording were discussed by Megaw L.J. in *Bunge Corp. v Tradax Export SA* [1980] 1 Lloyd's Rep. 294; see also [1981] 1 W.L.R. 711 at 727, HL.
[65] s.11 does not apply to Scotland, where the use of the term "condition" in this sense has been abolished: Sale and Supply of Goods Act 1994, Sch.2.
[66] [1893] 2 Q.B. 274 at 281; cited again with approval in *Bunge Corp. v Tradax Export SA*, above, at p.725. See also *Decro-Wall International SA v Practitioners in Marketing Ltd* [1971] 1 W.L.R. 361 at 368, 374, 380.
[67] The release is not, of course, automatic: the innocent party has an option. See below, paras 12–034 *et seq*.

breach "gives rise" to such a right. Another view, however, is that the word "may" indicates that not every breach of condition gives rise to the right to treat the contract as repudiated, in recognition of the fact that in some cases it is possible for the seller to correct the misperformance, as by making a fresh tender of conforming goods if this can be done within any relevant time-limit.[68] In other situations he may not be able to do so, as where he is out of time or by his defective delivery has destroyed the confidence of the buyer in such a way as to amount to a repudiation. On this view, it is possible to say that it is the seller's overall conduct rather than by the breach of the condition itself which entitles the buyer to treat the contract as discharged. This is however not consistent with most judicial dicta, and a complex theory to base (effectively) on the presence of the word "may".

10–029 **Dichotomy of condition and warranty not exhaustive.** This sharp dichotomy between condition, breach of which permits rejection, and warranty, breach of which does not, so clearly articulated by the Sale of Goods Act, tended for some decades to be treated as the principal key to the effects of breach of contract in general, despite the existence of areas where other techniques were used.[69] Its advantage is that it enables parties affected by breach of contract to know their rights, and in particular, in the context of sale, it permits the quick rejection of goods (or, where appropriate, documents). It requires, however, that any term breach of which *might* in some circumstances justify rejection should be classified as a condition so as to permit of this result always.[70] This has facilitated rejection in commercial contracts on purely technical grounds, motivated by movements in the market. Where the definition of the term broken itself contains an element of flexibility (*e.g.* "satisfactory quality"[71]) the problem is less serious: a court disposed not to allow rejection can hold the deficiency not serious enough to constitute a breach.[72] Where however the term is or may be strictly applied (as with the description of goods in commercial contracts[73]) rejection may arguably become too easy.

10–030 A significant manifestation of this problem arose in the case of the stipulation as to seaworthiness in a charterparty, which can be broken in many ways from the slightest to the most grave. In *Hong Kong Fir Shipping Co. Ltd v Kawasaki Kisen Kaisha Ltd*[74] it was argued that this term was a condition. But the Court of Appeal held that it was neither a condition nor a warranty, and that whether or not its breach entitled the innocent party to treat the contract as discharged depended on the nature and effect of the

---

[68] Below, paras 12–028, 12–031.
[69] *e.g.* in relation to instalment contracts: above, para.8–077 *et seq*; and construction contracts, *e.g. Hoenig v Isaacs* [1952] 2 All E.R. 176.
[70] See *Cehave NV v Bremer Handelsgesellschaft mbH (The Hansa Nord)* [1976] Q.B. 44 at 83.
[71] Sale of Goods Act 1979, s.14(2); below, paras 11–024 *et seq*.
[72] See *The Hansa Nord*, above; below, paras 10–031, 11–031, 12–023.
[73] s.13(1): below, para.11–018. See also below, paras 18–266 *et seq*.
[74] [1962] 2 Q.B. 26.

breach. A stringent test for this was laid down by Diplock L.J.: "Does the occurrence of the event deprive the party who has further undertakings still to perform of substantially the whole benefit which it was the intention of the parties as expressed in the contract that he should obtain as the consideration for performing those undertakings?"[75] This test, derived in the main from cases on delay in performance of contracts for carriage of goods by sea[76] is the same as that for frustration, which had at about the same time been said to be a "last ditch".[77] It is plainly more hostile to rejection as a remedy.

This latter approach was subsequently, in *Cehave NV v Bremer Handelsgesellschaft mbH (The Hansa Nord)*,[78] applied to a contract of sale of goods. In that case goods shipped in performance of a c.i.f. contract were on shipment partly in defective condition but not sufficiently so to make the consignment unmerchantable. There was however also a stipulation "shipment to be made in good condition." It was argued that the wording of section 11(3) of the Sale of Goods Act[79] required that all stipulations be classified as conditions or warranties and that this term was a condition, breach of which of itself entitled the buyer to reject the goods. It was held however that the preservation of the common law rules by section 62(2) of the Act[80] prevented the condition/warranty dichotomy from being exclusive; the term was not a condition, and the breach was in the circumstances not sufficiently serious to justify rejection. Preference was subsequently expressed in the House of Lords for this "more modern doctrine".[81] 10–031

Role of conditions. After *The Hansa Nord*[82] there was some tendency to think that the more general approach manifested in that case and in the *Hong Kong Fir*[83] case provided the primary approach to problems of discharge of contract by breach. However, the pendulum swung back somewhat in *Bunge Corp. v Tradax Export SA*.[84] This concerned breach of a stipulation in an f.o.b. sale contract, "Buyer shall give at least 15 days notice 10–032

---

[75] At p.66. See also *Photo Production Ltd v Securicor Transport Ltd* [1980] A.C. 827 at 849, where Lord Diplock used similar wording.

[76] *e.g. Freeman v Taylor* (1831) 8 Bing. 124; *Jackson v Union Marine Insurance Co. Ltd* (1874) L.R. 10 C.P. 125.

[77] *Tsakiroglou & Co. Ltd v Noblee Thörl GmbH* [1960] 2 Q.B. 348 at 370, *per* Harman L.J. (affirmed [1962] A.C. 93); see also Lord Radcliffe in *Davis Contractors Ltd v Fareham UDC* [1956] A.C. 696 at 727 ("not to be lightly invoked").

[78] [1976] Q.B. 44: see notes by Weir [1976] C.L.J. 33, and Reynolds, 92 L.Q.R. 17 (1976). See also *Yeoman Credit Ltd v Apps* [1962] 2 Q.B. 508; *Holmes v Burgess* [1975] 2 N.Z.L.R. 311, a precursor of *The Hansa Nord; Tradax Internacional SA v Goldschmidt SA* [1977] 2 Lloyd's Rep. 604.

[79] Formerly s.11(1)(b): above, para.10–027.

[80] Formerly s.61(2).

[81] *Reardon Smith Line Ltd v Yngvar Hansen-Tangen* [1976] 1 W.L.R. 989 at 998, *per* Lord Wilberforce; see also *Bunge Corp. v Tradax Export SA* [1981] 1 W.L.R. 711 at 715–716.

[82] [1976] Q.B. 44; above.

[83] [1962] 2 Q.B. 26; above.

[84] [1981] 1 W.L.R. 711. See Carter [1981] C.L.J. 219; Reynolds, 97 L.Q.R. 541 (1981).

of readiness of vessels." It was accepted that under the broader test the seller was unable to establish that the nature and consequences of the breach were such as to entitle him to treat the contract as discharged under the *Hong Kong Fir* wording.[85] The House of Lords, however, held that the term was a condition, in the sense that any breach of it entitled the innocent party to treat the contract as discharged; and reaffirmed the role of conditions as providing certainty for the innocent party's remedies in commercial contracts.

7. INTERMEDIATE TERMS

10–033 **Intermediate term?** The question then arose as to how the law on repudiatory breach should be formulated. One possibility was that the *Hong Kong Fir* case and *The Hansa Nord*[86] establish the existence of a third category of "intermediate" or "innominate" terms, breach of which may or may not entitle the innocent party to treat the contract as discharged, in accordance with the nature and consequences of the breach. This has undoubtedly been the prevailing formulation. On this basis the first question the court must ask in such a case is whether the term broken is a condition or a warranty. Any term not so classified will be an intermediate or innominate term, and the rights arising on its breach will depend on the nature and consequences of that breach. But this formulation, it is submitted, lacks flexibility in regard to the category of warranty, a category which in any case is of dubious value and productive of confusion.[87] There may well be circumstances where a deliberate breach of a minor term, or an aggregation of breaches of a minor term or terms, should be treated as repudiatory. To permit this, the prevailing formulation requires a new readiness on the part of the court to classify terms as intermediate rather than as warranties. There is therefore much to be said for a second viewpoint, for which there is also judicial authority,[88] that if a term is not classified as a condition in accordance with the appropriate[89] criteria, the right of the innocent party should simply turn on the nature and consequences of the breach. It would then be for consideration whether the remaining term should be called a "warranty" or not. This analysis is certainly simpler, though it is admittedly difficult to reconcile with the definition in the Sale of Goods Act 1979, where a warranty is defined as a term breach of which only gives rise to a right in damages.[90] It is

[85] Above, para.10–030.
[86] Above, para.10–031.
[87] Above, paras 10–015, 10–016, 10–023, 10–024.
[88] See *The Hansa Nord* [1976] Q.B. 44 at 60F (Lord Denning M.R.), 82–84 (Ormrod L.J.); the speech of Lord Diplock in *Photo Production Ltd v Securicor Transport Ltd* [1980] A.C. 827 at 849–850; and *Cie. General Maritime v Diakan Spirit SA (The Ymnos)* [1982] 2 Lloyd's Rep. 574 at 583, *per* Robert Goff L.J.
[89] See above, para.10–027; below, para.10–037.
[90] See s.11, above, para.10–023. See also *The Ymnos*, above. But it is possible to argue that the general rules as to repudiatory breach are preserved by the general savings in s.62(2) of the Sale of Goods Act 1979: see *The Hansa Nord*, above, at pp.60, 83.

noteworthy however that whereas cases continue to discuss whether terms are conditions, no recent case appears to consider whether a term is such that no breach of it can *ever* give rise to the right to reject; and it may therefore be questioned whether the notion of such a term is a necessary one. The term is twice attributed to contract duties in the Sale of Goods Act 1979, but it has been held that a breach of warranty with serious consequences may be repudiatory.[91]

Differences of approach: commercial disputes. The cases just discussed are all commercial cases, and show a tension between two general approaches to the problem of discharge by breach in such cases. One, achieved by the use of conditions, is, while recognising that commercial people supposedly dislike rejection,[92] to pursue a policy of holding the parties strictly to the terms of the contract, and thus making it fairly easy for the innocent party to treat the contract as discharged. An example of this approach, for which the English courts must be well known in certain trades, is a dictum of Lord Atkin in 1933: "If the seller wants a margin he must and in my experience does stipulate for it . . . . In a falling market I find that buyers are often as eager to insist on their legal rights as courts of law are ready to maintain them."[93] It is frequently justified by reference to the necessity for certainty in commercial transactions,[94] and works best when the term is sharply defined so that either it is clearly broken or it is not—as in time stipulations, of which *Bunge Corp. v Tradax Export SA* is itself an example. Its application is also often justified on the basis that the breach *may* have been specially prejudicial to the other party, and that the court is not entitled to speculate. The other approach, much more hostile to rejection, is justified in a passage from the judgment of Roskill L.J. in *The Hansa Nord*[95]: "In principle contracts are made to be performed and not to be avoided according to the whims of market fluctuation and where there is a free choice between two possible constructions I think the court should tend to prefer that construction which will ensure performance and not encourage avoidance of contractual obligations." 10–034

The tension between these two approaches was acknowledged by Lord Wilberforce in *Bunge Corp. v Tradax Export SA*, where, commenting with approval on the dictum of Roskill L.J. quoted above, he said that the courts "should not be too ready to interpret contractual clauses as conditions"[96] 10–035

[91] *Rubicon Computer Systems Ltd v United Paints Ltd* (2000) 2 T.C.L.R. 453 (Sale of Goods Act 1979, s.12(2)).
[92] *e.g. EA Ronaasen & Son v Arcos Ltd* (1932) 43 Ll.L.R. 1 at 4–6 (affirmed [1933] A.C. 470); *The Hansa Nord*, above, at pp.62–63. And see below, para.13–032, as to non-rejection clauses, which seem common, at any rate as regards quality as opposed to description.
[93] *Arcos Ltd v EA Ronaasen & Son* [1933] A.C. 470 at 479–480. This is a Russian timber case, and there is considerable background to the development of the present law in such cases: see below, para.11–018, n.98.
[94] *e.g. The Mihalis Angelos* [1971] 1 Q.B. 164, *per* Megaw L.J.; *SIAT di del Ferro v Tradax Overseas SA* [1980] 1 Lloyd's Rep. 53 at 62; *Bunge Corp. v Tradax Export SA* [1981] 1 W.L.R. 711.
[95] [1976] Q.B. 44 at 71: above, para.10–031.
[96] [1981] 1 W.L.R. 711 at 715.

but went on to say that he did not doubt "that in suitable cases the courts should not be reluctant, if the intentions of the parties as shown by the contract so indicate, to hold that an obligation has the force of a condition."[97] Which approach is more appropriate and when is a question on which the views of the commercial community would be of interest; but it is certainly not clear that rejection is always economically the most efficient remedy in such cases.[98] There must inevitably be some sort of compromise between the two techniques. Perhaps it is best to regard the second (seriousness of breach) approach as the rule and the first (condition) as the exception, though one highly relevant in the commercial context.[99]

10–036 **Consumer transactions.** The tension described is clearly seen in commercial disputes. For the consumer, rejection is usually the most efficacious, perhaps the only efficacious remedy.[1] In consumer cases the *Hong Kong Fir* test[2] may make rejection too difficult. The stipulations on which consumers are most likely to rely (those as to satisfactory quality and fitness for purpose[3]) are however designated by the Sale of Goods Act as conditions. But they are conditions formulated in a broad way,[4] such as "satisfactory quality", and a court, especially if following commercial precedents, may be reluctant to hold them broken by the presence of small defects which do not appear to justify rejection.[5] The difficulty then is that if the court holds the implied terms not broken, there may be no remedy at all. This would not necessarily be the case in a commercial contract, where there might be express terms also in respect of which damages could be awarded. Such was the case in *The Hansa Nord*.[6]

10–037 **Examples of conditions.** It may be asked what sort of term is likely to be treated as a condition. First, most of the statutory implied terms as to the seller's duties in sale of goods (as to title, conformity with description and quality[7]) are designated as conditions: this is not, however, so of the buyer's duties laid down in the Act. Secondly, the parties may themselves designate terms as conditions, though the court will not be bound by the expressions they use and may hold that notwithstanding the use of the word "condition" its full legal consequences were not intended.[8] Thirdly, the term in

---

[97] *ibid.*, at p.716.

[98] Honnold, 97 U.Pa.L.Rev. 457 (1949), gives a sophisticated analysis of the problem. See also Priest, 91 Harvard L.Rev. 960 (1978); Treitel, *Law of Contract* (11th ed.), pp.760–761.

[99] *e.g. Federal Commerce and Navigation Co. Ltd v Molena Alpha Inc. (The Nanfri)* [1979] A.C. 757 at 785. For further discussion see Treitel, *op. cit.*, at pp.788 *et seq.*

[1] See Llewellyn, 36 Col.L.Rev. 699 at 731 (1936); Law Com.W.P. No. 85, Sc.Law Com.C.M. No. 58 (1983), pp.68 *et seq.*

[2] Above, para.10–030.

[3] Below, paras 11–001 *et seq.*

[4] *cf.* above, para.10–034.

[5] *e.g. Millar's of Falkirk Ltd v Turpie*, 1966 S.L.T. (Notes) 66 (car with defective oil seal merchantable). See further below, para.11–031.

[6] Above, para.10–031.

[7] Above, para.4–002; below, 11–001, 11–024, 11–051, 11–073.

[8] See *Wickman Machine Tool Sales Ltd v L Schuler AG* [1974] A.C. 235 (distributorship contract).

question or a similar term may have been held to be a condition in another case: this will be a strong but not conclusive indication that the term is a condition in the instant case.[9] Fourthly, in *Bunge Corp. v Tradax Export SA*[10] Lord Roskill refers to a situation "in a mercantile contract, when a term has to be performed by one party as a condition precedent to the ability of the other party to perform another term."[11] Fifthly, in the same case Lord Wilberforce said in the passage quoted above[12] that the courts should usually interpret "time clauses in mercantile contracts" as conditions[13]; and Lord Lowry justified this as "a practical expedient founded on and dictated by the experience of businessmen."[14] Sixthly, there must also be a residual category of cases where the implementation of the supposed intentions of the parties requires a term to be treated as one any breach of which gives rise to the right to treat the contract as discharged[15]; equally, the overall interpretation of the contract may lead to the conclusion that a term which on isolated criteria might be a condition was not intended as such.[16] Most of these will occur in connection with large-scale commercial contracts; in this connection it has been said that the court will accord special respect to the findings of commercial arbitrators[17] and reliance placed on the importance of certainty.[18] But the reasoning can be used elsewhere. Thus in *Harling v Eddy*[19] a statement by the seller of a heifer that there was nothing

---

[9] *e.g. Maredelanto Cia. Naviera SA v Bergbau-Handel GmbH (The Mihalis Angelos)* [1971] 1 Q.B. 164 ("expected ready to load" in a charterparty: following *Finnish Government v H Ford & Co. Ltd* (1921) 6 Ll.L.R. 188 (same term in f.o.b. sale)).

[10] [1981] 1 W.L.R. 711 at 729.

[11] *e.g. Toepfer v Lenersan-Poortman NV* [1980] 1 Lloyd's Rep. 143 (c.i.f. sale: time of tender of documents); *Gill & Duffus SA v Société pour l'Exportation des Sucres SA* [1986] 1 Lloyd's Rep. 322 (f.o.b. sale: nomination of loading port); and see *Greenwich Marine Inc. v Federal Commerce and Navigation Co. Ltd (The Mavro Vetranic)* [1985] 1 Lloyd's Rep. 580 at 583.

[12] [1981] 1 W.L.R. 711 at 715, quoted above, para.10–035.

[13] At p.716; *e.g. Cie. Commerciale Sucres et Denrées v C Czarnikow Ltd (The Naxos)* [1990] 1 W.L.R. 1337, HL (readiness of sugar for delivery) (see Treitel [1991] L.M.C.L.Q. 147); *Scandinavian Trading Co. A/B v Zodiac Petroleum SA (The Al Hofuf)* [1981] 1 Lloyd's Rep. 81 (f.o.b. sale: notice of time of arrival of vessel); *Société Italo-Belge v Palm and Vegetable Oils (Malaysia) Sdn. Bhd. (The Post Chaser)* [1982] 1 All E.R. 19 (c.i.f. sale: declaration of ship "as soon as possible"); *cf. Tradax Export SA v Italgrani* [1986] 1 Lloyd's Rep. 112 (f.o.b. sale: time of delivery to vessel not a condition); *Bremer Handelsgesellschaft v Vanden Avenne-Izegem PVBA* [1978] 2 Lloyd's Rep. 109 (duty to advise "without delay" not a condition); *State Trading Corp. of India v M Golodetz Ltd* [1989] 2 Lloyd's Rep. 277 (provision for countertrade not a condition) (see Treitel, 106 L.Q.R. 185 (1990)); *Petrotrade Inc. v Stinnes Handel GmbH* [1995] 1 Lloyd's Rep. 142 (f.o.b. sale: port of shipment a condition). The precision of the stipulation is obviously relevant, though not conclusive, in determining whether it is a condition.

[14] At p.719.

[15] *e.g. Bergerco v Vegoil Ltd* [1984] 1 Lloyd's Rep. 440 (c. & f. sale: "direct ship"); *Warde v Feedex International Inc.* [1985] 2 Lloyd's Rep. 289 (opening of credit).

[16] This was perhaps the basis for the dissenting opinion of Lord Brandon in *The Naxos*, above, n.9: see Treitel [1991] L.M.C.L.Q. 147 at 152–153.

[17] *State Trading Corp. of India v M Golodetz Ltd*, above, at p.284; *The Naxos*, above.

[18] *BS & N Ltd (BVI) v Micado Shipping Ltd (Malta) (The Seaflower)* [2001] 1 Lloyd's Rep. 341 ("majors approval clause" in time charter).

[19] [1951] 2 K.B. 739; see also *Couchman v Hill* [1947] K.B. 554. On this basis these cases would involve contracts partly written and partly oral. But they may also be explained as cases of collateral contract: see above, para.10–012.

wrong with the animal sold and that he would take it back if it turned out not to be as he said was held to import a condition because of the undertaking to take back. Where on the other hand a term can be broken in a number of ways involving results of different degrees of gravity, as in the *Hong Kong Fir* case itself,[20] that is some indication that it should not be classified as a condition.[21]

10–038 **Statutory modification of right to reject for breach of condition in commercial sales.** It must finally be noted that the right to reject for breach of the *statutory implied* conditions has for commercial contracts been modified by statute, which reduces slightly their significance as such. This is dealt with elsewhere.[22]

8. OTHER CLASSIFICATIONS

10–039 **Non-promissory conditions qualifying the liability of one of the parties.** Sometimes a statement as to goods is made, but no promise is made as to its truth. A contract comes into operation, from which neither party can with draw, but if it turns out that the statement is not true, though the representor is not liable, the other party need not proceed. This is an example of what is earlier submitted as being the better use of the term "condition".[23] An example is *Mackay v Dick*[24] where there was a contract for the sale of a digging machine if it fulfilled certain conditions: the understanding was that if it did not, the buyer need not have it, but the seller would not be liable in damages. Where a contract contains such conditions, there may also be related promises. Promises by buyer and seller not to prevent the fulfilment of the condition will normally be implied. Sometimes there are further duties: thus in *Mackay v Dick* the buyer did not give the machine a proper trial and was held liable for the price.[25]

10–040 **Misrepresentations inducing the contract and subsequently incorporated into it.** Until the Misrepresentation Act 1967 it was not clear what happened when a misrepresentation was made prior to the time of contracting in such circumstances that it would clearly rank as a misrepresentation external to the contract and not as a contractual promise, and was subsequently repeated at the time of contracting so as to become part of the contract.[26] Did it lose its earlier classification as a misrepresentation,

---

[20] Above, para.10–030.
[21] See *Toepfer v Lenersan-Poortman NV* [1980] 1 Lloyd's Rep. 143; *Aktion Maritime Corp. v S Kasmas Bros Ltd (The Aktion)* [1987] 1 Lloyd's Rep. 283.
[22] Sale of Goods Act 1979, s.15A, inserted by Sale and Supply of Goods Act 1994, s.4(1): see below, paras 12–024 *et seq.*
[23] Above, para.10–024.
[24] (1881) 6 App.Cas. 251. *Cf. Colley v Overseas Exporters* [1921] 3 K.B. 302.
[25] See above, para.10–025.
[26] *cf. Cie. Française des Chemins de Fer Paris-Orléans v Leeston Shipping Co. Ltd* (1919) 1 Ll.L.R. 235; *Leaf v International Galleries* [1950] 2 K.B. 86; and *Academy of Health and Fitness Pty Ltd v Power* [1973] V.R. 254; with *Pennsylvania Shipping Co. v Cie. Nationale de Navigation* (1936) 155 L.T. 294.

and hence the remedies available for such, and become solely a term in the contract and therefore subject to the rules as to breach of contract? The better view was probably that it did, for the misrepresentation rules were only ancillary and came into existence to fill a lacuna in the law: indeed, their very application to sale of goods was not beyond doubt.[27] However, section 1 of the Misrepresentation Act 1967 provides that "where a person has entered into a contract after a misrepresentation has been made to him, and . . . the misrepresentation has become a term of the contract . . . then, if otherwise he would be entitled to rescind the contract without alleging fraud, he shall be so entitled." The misrepresentation thus retains its status as such as well as forming the basis of a contract term. The problems as to remedies created by this provision are described elsewhere.[28]

---

[27] Above, para.10–008.
[28] Below, paras 12–119 *et seq*.

Chapter 11

TERMS AS TO DESCRIPTION AND QUALITY IMPLIED BY THE SALE OF GOODS ACT

	PARA.
1. Correspondence with description	11–001
2. Quality and fitness for purpose	11–024
(a) Nature of the Act's provisions	11–024
(b) Satisfactory quality	11–026
(c) Fitness for purpose	11–051
3. Sale by sample	11–073
4. Other implied terms	11–088

1. Correspondence with Description

Sale of Goods Act 1979, s.13(1). Sections 13, 14 and 15 of the Sale of Goods Act lay down implied terms as to the description and quality of goods supplied under a contract of sale. They were all in principle excludable by appropriate provisions[1]—*ius dispositivum* rather than *ius cogens*; but this position was subsequently corrected by statute.[2] The first implied term concerns the conformity of the goods with description. Section 13(1) of the Act reads: "Where there is a contract for the sale of goods by description, there is an implied term that the goods will correspond with the description."[3] Section 13(1A)[4] adds that "As regards England and Wales and Northern Ireland, the term implied by subsection (1) is a condition."[5] It should be noted that the subsection applies to all **11–001**

---

[1] s.55 of the 1893 Act.

[2] Below, Ch.13.

[3] See also below, para.18–266 as to international sales. *Cf.* Vienna Convention (above, para.1–024), Art.35(1).

[4] The designation of the term as a condition was originally contained in s.13(1) itself. The present formulation, with the use there of "term" and the addition of s.13(1A), dates from the Sale and Supply of Goods Act 1994 (s.7 and Sch.2) and was adopted to effect the abolition of the term "condition" in the English law sense for Scots law.

[5] In general, breach of a condition entitles rejection: see above, paras 10–024 *et seq.*, below, paras 12–022 *et seq.* In non-consumer cases, a slight breach may, however, not do so (see s.15A of the Act, below, paras 12–024 *et seq.*, 18–284). A buyer who deals as consumer is entitled under the Act to the benefit of a (rebuttable) presumption that the goods were non-compliant at the relevant time if they are non-compliant at any time during six months from delivery (s.48A(3), below, para.12–075). The relevant provision includes non-compliance with description (s.48F). This is part of the new provisions providing special remedies for those who deal as consumers (below, paras 12–071 *et seq.*, 14–008 *et seq*). The point is more likely to be relevant in respect of quality defects and is returned to in that context (see below, paras 11–026, 11–051), as well as in the context of the consumer buyer's remedies (below, paras 12–097 *et seq.*, 12–118 *et seq*). The significance of "delivery" in this context is considered below, para.11–049.

sales and is not restricted to sales in the course of a business. The case law mixes commercial and consumer transactions with the former heavily predominating. It does not seem that any particular conclusions can be drawn from differentiating between types of case, though the strictest applications of the subsection are usually to be found in commercial cases.

11–002 **Historical background of this provision.** Conceptually this is one of the most troublesome provisions of the Act.[6] As is explained later, the phrase "sale by description" has been interpreted to cover almost all sales.[7] Section 13(1) seems therefore to do more than state, for the vast majority of sales, as an implied term something central to the whole contract, the duty to deliver the contract goods. This is really an express term, or the spelling out of an express term,[8] and to call it an *implied* term is an inappropriate diminution of its status which can cause difficulty, for example where a clause provides for exclusion of implied terms. It has therefore been suggested that "those responsible for the statute . . . merely meant to say that the description is not a mere term or a mere warranty but is a condition of the contract by implication of law."[9]

11–003 It seems, however, that the object of the draftsman of the 1893 Act was not simply to state such a duty. The cases from which he sought to derive this rule were cases making an antithesis between sales of specific goods and sales by description.[10] In the case of specific goods the rules as eventually settled were adverse to the buyer: there was no implied term as to quality,[11] and further, when property had passed, which would in the absence of a contrary intention be on the making of the contract, there was no right to reject even for breach of an express term as to quality, only a right to damages.[12] But where the sale was by description the rules were more favourable to the buyer: the seller was regarded as promising that the goods supplied conformed with their description[13] and also that they were merchantable[14] (though these two requirements, which now appear in the

[6] See a valuable discussion in Goode, *Commercial Law* (3rd ed.), pp.290 *et seq*.
[7] Below, para.11–008.
[8] See Williston, *Sales* (rev. ed., 1948), para.223.
[9] *Andrews Bros Ltd v Singer & Co. Ltd* [1934] 1 K.B. 17 at 25, *per* Greer L.J.
[10] For an account of the evolution of the rules in this area, see Stoljar, 15 M.L.R. 425 (1952); 16 M.L.R. 174 (1953). The starting points for further investigations are the 1st ed. of Chalmers, *Sale of Goods* (1890), a commentary on the Sale of Goods Bill as it stood at the time, which contains remarkable differences from the Act as eventually adopted, and the 2nd ed. (1894), a commentary on the Act as passed; Benjamin, *Sale of Personal Property* (2nd ed., 1873), the last edited by Benjamin himself, and the 5th ed. (1906), the first after the Act; also *Blackburn on Sale* (3rd ed., 1885). As to specific goods see above, paras 1–113 *et seq*.
[11] *Barr v Gibson* (1838) 3 M. & W. 390 (wrecked ship still a ship).
[12] *Street v Blay* (1831) 2 B. & Ad. 456; *Mondel v Steel* (1841) 8 M. & W. 858. Unless the goods were totally worthless: *Poulton v Lattimore* (1829) 9 B. & C. 259.
[13] See *Chanter v Hopkins* (1838) 4 M. & W. 399; *Randall v Newson* (1877) 2 Q.B.D. 102.
[14] *Jones v Just* (1868) L.R. 3 Q.B. 197, citing *Laing v Fidgeon* (1815) 4 Camp. 169.

Act,[15] were sometimes run together[16]). Further, in such cases the buyer might be entitled to reject defective goods even though property had passed, unless they had been accepted.[17] It was the first of these latter rules for sales by description that the draftsman sought to express here. But in fact the antithesis between the two types of sale has been largely forgotten, and the notion of sale by description extended—at least in part in order to increase the scope of the former provision as to merchantable quality.[18] The result has been that section 13(1) is now taken as a proposition of almost general application. It has even been suggested that, inasmuch as it simply states the duty central to most sales, it is superfluous.[19]

Situations covered by section 13(1). Taken as it stands, however, without reference to the confused evolution of doctrine which produced it, section 13(1) has been interpreted to cover two types of breach which on their face appear to be of different magnitude. The first is failure to secure exact conformity to the full contractual description of the goods where there is one—a duty which is best specified as a condition if it is to exist, for otherwise there might be a tendency to apply some sort of doctrine of substantial performance, as in other parts of the law.[20] An example of this would be the supply of goods which are in substance the goods stipulated for but which are not packaged in accordance with the contractual requirements.[21] The second is total failure to perform the contract, *e.g.* supplying a second-hand car instead of the new one ordered,[22] where the duty broken, that to supply the contract goods, is so fundamental as hardly to need stating at all and may seem of a quite different order from the earlier duty. The putting of the two together is, however, analytically correct, for the reason why there can be rejection in the first case is that it is assimilated to the second. A buyer can refuse to receive something which is not what he promised to buy. The description of goods may be strictly interpreted with the result that a slight discrepancy may be treated as 11–004

[15] ss.13(1), 14(2): though the term "merchantable" has been replaced by "satisfactory"; below, para.11–026.

[16] By the idea of merchantability under the same description. See, *e.g. Wieler v Schilizzi* (1856) 17 C.B. 619; *Randall v Newson*, above; *Mody v Gregson* (1868) L.R. 4 Ex. 49; *Jones v Just*, above; *Drummond v Van Ingen* (1887) 12 App.Cas. 284 at 291. For a modern example of this reasoning see *Speedway Safety Products Pty Ltd v Hazell & Moore Industries Pty Ltd* [1982] 1 N.S.W.L.R. 255 at 262.

[17] See *Heilbutt v Hickson* (1872) L.R. 7 C.P. 438 at 451: as opposed to specific goods, below, para.12–038. Chalmers (2nd ed.), p.27, quotes from the Digest, 18.1.14, *Si aes pro auro veneat, non valet*. The quotation is misleading, as it refers to a contract void for *error*. The citations of this and other passages by Blackburn J. in *Kennedy v Panama, etc., Mail Co. Ltd* (1867) L.R. 2 Q.B. 580 at 587–588 are also inappropriate, at least by modern standards.

[18] Now "satisfactory quality". See below, paras 11–026, 11–031.

[19] Coote, *Exception Clauses* (1964), p.51; Melville, 19 M.L.R. 26 at 29 (1956); and see Goode, *Commercial Law* (3rd ed.), pp.281–282, 290, 298.

[20] See, *e.g. Graves v Legg* (1854) 9 Exch. 709. For examples of the doctrine of substantial performance see, *e.g. Dakin v Lee* [1916] 1 K.B. 566; *Hoenig v Isaacs* [1952] 2 All E.R. 176 (cases on building contracts).

[21] *e.g. Re Moore & Co. and Landauer & Co.* [1921] 2 K.B. 519; below, para.11–018.

[22] *e.g. Andrews Bros (Bournemouth) Ltd v Singer & Co. Ltd* [1934] 1 K.B. 17, below, para.13–031.

making the goods not what was stipulated for. Where goods are not what was stipulated for, they can be rejected.[23]

11–005 **Exemption clauses.** In connection with the common law rules regarding exemption clauses more serious difficulties arise, the solutions to which are still not generally agreed. The problem is that whereas it is not difficult (though the courts have frequently been reluctant[24]) to interpret exemption clauses in a contract of sale so as to cut down the duty of absolute compliance, the first aspect of section 13(1) referred to above, there is an understandable unwillingness to allow such a clause to cut down the second duty, that of performing the main contractual obligation, unless of course the whole contract is cast in terms only entitling the buyer to something within an extremely vague category. The matter is primarily considered elsewhere, and it is now clear that it has lost much of its importance in England since the enactment of the Unfair Contract Terms Act 1977, which deals more directly with the problem.[25] It has, however, been suggested that the influence of the exemption clause cases, in establishing minimal descriptions, liability for non-compliance with which cannot be excluded, has led to cases suggesting an inappropriate reduction of the duty as to conformity with description in general.[26]

11–006 **"Sale of goods by description".** The nineteenth-century cases were vague as to the exact meaning of the term "sale by description", though some at least gave the phrase a wide operation, probably with the unexpressed desire of avoiding the strict rules applicable to sales of specific goods.[27] There are indications of a tightening up towards the end of the century.[28] But the cases after the Sale of Goods Act 1893 certainly took a wide view: thus in the fifth edition of Benjamin's *Sale of Personal Property* (1906) it was suggested[29] that "a less rigid interpretation may perhaps be put upon the term 'description' as applicable to specific goods under the Code than

---

[23] See the cases on which the section is founded: *Nichol v Godts* (1854) 10 Exch. 191 ("foreign refined rape oil, warranted only equal to samples"—samples and goods delivered both contained hemp oil—held oil supplied did not answer description of goods sold); *Josling v Kingsford* (1863) 13 C.B. (N.S.) 447 ("oxalic acid"—contained 10 per cent sulphate of magnesium); *Azémar v Casella* (1867) L.R. 2 C.P. 677 ("long stable Salem cotton"—Western Madras cotton tendered); *Mody v Gregson* (1868) L.R. 4 Ex. 49 (grey shirtings, each piece to weigh 7 lb.—shirting contained china clay); *Borrowman v Drayton* (1876) 2 Ex.D. 15 (sale of cargo: seller put other goods on board as well—buyer entitled to refuse delivery); *Wieler v Schilizzi* (1856) 17 C.B. 619 ("Calcutta linseed tale quale"—not Calcutta linseed at all).

[24] *e.g. Montague L Meyer Ltd v Kivisto* (1929) 35 Ll.L.R. 265 (timber); below, para.11–015.

[25] As to the common law rules, see below, paras 13–050, 13–051; as to the Unfair Contract Terms Act 1977 see below, paras 13–062 *et seq.*, esp. para.13–067.

[26] See Coote, 50 A.L.J. 17 (1976), criticising *Ashington Piggeries Ltd v Christopher Hill Ltd* [1972] A.C. 441, below, para.11–060, on this account.

[27] Above, para.11–003; and see *Jones v Just* (1868) L.R. 3 Q.B. 197.

[28] See *Heyworth v Hutchinson* (1867) L.R. 2 Q.B. 447; criticised by Benjamin, *Sale of Personal Property* (2nd ed.), pp.742–746; *Kennedy v Panama, etc., Mail Co. Ltd* (1867) L.R. 2 Q.B. 580 at 587–588.

[29] At p.611, discussing *Varley v Whipp* [1900] 1 Q.B. 513, dicta from which are cited below, para.11–008.

would have been placed on it at common law." No doubt this was influenced by two factors. First, when the sale was not by description, a descriptive statement, if held to be contractual at all, might well be found to be a warranty and so merely sound in damages. Secondly, prior to 1973 the condition as to merchantable quality (the general quality requirement applicable till 1995[30]) only applied when goods were bought by description.[31] Indeed, the majority of cases on the notion of "sale by description" actually relate to the applicability of section 14(2), the merchantable quality provision.[32]

The modern law.[33] In *Joseph Travers & Son Ltd v Longel Ltd*[34] Sellers J accepted the following passage from Benjamin's *Sale of Personal Property*.[35]: "Sales by description may . . . be divided into sales (1) of unascertained or future goods, as being of a certain kind or class, or to which otherwise a 'description' in the contract is applied; (2) of specific goods, bought by the buyer in reliance, at least in part, upon the description given, or to be tacitly inferred from the circumstances, and which identifies the goods." 11–007

It is clear, first, that all contracts for the sale of unascertained goods are sales by description.[36] Most sales of future goods will likewise be sales by description, though the sale of a specific article seen and requested by the buyer, which is owned by a third party and would require to be obtained by the seller, will not normally be.[37] But the term is not restricted to unascertained and future goods and has been extended (probably contrary to the intentions of the draftsman) to sales of specific goods[38] which have not been seen at the time of contract: it "must apply to all cases where the purchaser has not seen the goods, but is relying on the description alone."[39] Thus in *Varley v Whipp*[40] it was held that there was a sale by description where the seller met the buyer at Huddersfield and sold him something described as a "second-hand self-binder reaping machine", which was at 11–008

---

[30] See below, para.11–032: the requirement now is one of "satisfactory quality".
[31] See Sale of Goods Act 1893, s.14(2), as it originally stood: below, para.11–027.
[32] See below, n.41. A more recent example is *Lockhart v Osman* [1981] V.R. 57, where a sale by auction was held to be by description because of the advertisement of the auction as a "cattle breeders' sale".
[33] See Feltham [1969] J.B.L. 16.
[34] (1948) 64 T.L.R. 150. A general discussion appears in *Speedway Safety Products Pty Ltd v Hazell & Moore Industries Pty Ltd* [1982] 1 N.S.W.L.R. 255. It is again however in the context of the provision as to merchantable quality, the first version of the wording of s.14(2) being then operative in New South Wales.
[35] 7th ed., p.641, inaccurately reproduced in the 8th ed., p.615.
[36] *Kidman v Fisken Bunning & Co.* [1907] S.A.L.R. 101 at 107. See, *e.g. Wallis, Son and Wells v Pratt and Haynes* [1911] A.C. 394 (seeds). As to unascertained goods, see above, paras 1–117 *et seq*. But in some cases the description may be provided by a sample; below, paras 11–022, 11–074.
[37] As to future goods, see above, para.1–102.
[38] As to specific goods, see above, paras 1–113 *et seq*.
[39] *Varley v Whipp* [1900] 1 Q.B. 513 at 516. See also *Boys v Rice* (1908) 27 N.Z.L.R. 1038 at 1048.
[40] Above.

that time at another place. The term has however been extended even further: "it may also be pointed out that there is a sale by description even though the buyer is buying something displayed before him on the counter: a thing is sold by description, though it is specific, so long as it is sold not merely as the specific thing but as a thing corresponding to a description, *e.g.* woollen undergarments, a hot-water bottle, a second-hand reaping machine, to select a few obvious illustrations."[41]

11–009 **Reliance.** It will be noted that both in *Varley v Whipp*[42] and the passage of Sellers J. quoted above[43] there is reference to reliance by the buyer. A sale is not by description merely because descriptive words are used during the negotiations: for it to be by description in respect of any of these words, the buyer must rely on them in making the contract. This proposition can be criticised on the basis that reliance on a contractual promise is not necessary for it to be actionable.[44] That is so, but the notion of reliance has another, and earlier, significance. In order for a statement or promise to be contractual, it must be such that the other party on *entering into the contract* was relying on its being made good.[45] It is further reliance after that time that is not necessary in order to create a right of action in contract (though it would be necessary if a statement was not a contractual promise but a misrepresentation inducing the contract, and it was sought to claim relief in respect of it). This reliance at the time of formation is similar to the reliance on the seller's skill and judgment that the goods are fit for purpose under section 14(3).

11–010 **Sale of Goods Act 1979, s.13(3): goods selected by buyer.** Although the original Act was not specific on the point, it was long thought that a sale might rank as being by description though the buyer had examined or tried the goods,[46] or himself selected them from stock without anything being

---

[41] *Grant v Australian Knitting Mills Ltd* [1936] A.C. 85 at 100, *per* Lord Wright; see also *Taylor v Combined Buyers Ltd* [1924] N.Z.L.R. 626 at 633 *et seq.; Morelli v Fitch and Gibbons* [1928] 2 K.B. 636; *Australian Knitting Mills Ltd v Grant* (1933) 50 C.L.R. 387 at 417–418; *David Jones Ltd v Willis* (1934) 52 C.L.R. 110 at 118; *Godley v Perry* [1960] 1 W.L.R. 9 at 14; despite doubts expressed in *Wren v Holt* [1903] 1 K.B. 610 and *Wallis v Russell* [1902] 2 I.R. 585 at 631. These cases, and most of those in the following footnotes, are actually cases on s.14(2), below, paras 11–026 *et seq.*, which imposes a condition as to (what was until recently called) merchantable quality, and prior to 1973 was restricted to cases of goods "*bought* by description". It is however submitted that there is no difference between the meaning of that phrase and the meaning of "contract for the sale of goods by description" in s.13: see *Grant v Australian Knitting Mills Ltd*, above, at p.100; *Godley v Perry*, above, at p.14; *Morelli v Fitch and Gibbons*, above, at p.641. Dicta from *Varley v Whipp*, above, a case on s.13, are cited in *Thornett and Fehr v Beers & Son* [1919] 1 K.B. 486, a case on s.14(2).

[42] Above, para.11–008.

[43] Above, para.11–007.

[44] *Centrovincial Estates Plc v Merchant Investors' Assurance Co. Ltd* [1983] Com.L.Rep. 158.

[45] *Harlingdon and Leinster Enterprises Ltd v Christopher Hull Fine Art Ltd* [1991] 1 Q.B. 564: below, para.11–011.

[46] *Beale v Taylor* [1967] 1 W.L.R. 1193 (car); *David Jones Ltd v Willis* (1934) 52 C.L.R. 110 (shoes); *Thornett and Fehr v Beers & Son* [1919] 1 K.B. 486 at 488–489 (vegetable glue).

said.[47] Thus it was probable that even a sale of goods in a self-service shop was a sale by description, provided the goods were described in some way on the shelf, outside packing or by a notice or label.[48] This was, however, put beyond all doubt by section 13(3) of the Sale of Goods Act, which was inserted by the Supply of Goods (Implied Terms) Act 1973 and provides: "A sale of goods is not prevented from being a sale by description by reason only that, being exposed for sale or hire, they are selected by the buyer." Disputes could still occur as to whether the sale of an easily identifiable but undescribed article (*e.g.* a melon out of a pile in a greengrocer's shop, in relation to which there is nothing but a notice stating the price) is a sale by description, but in view of the fact that the condition as to merchantable (now "satisfactory") quality is no longer confined to sales by description, it is difficult to see that there would be much practical significance in the question in England.

Sale not by description. It is clear therefore that sales other than by description are comparatively rare. The passage from Benjamin quoted above continues: "It follows that the only sales not by description are sales of specific goods *as such*. Specific goods may be sold as such when they are sold without any description, express or implied; or where any statement made about them is not essential to their identity; or where, though the goods are described, the description is not relied upon,[49] as where the buyer buys the goods such as they are."[50] In one case a sale (by the receiver of a motor-cycle distributor's business) of "the stock situated at the premises 74–78 Wentworth Avenue, Sydney" was held not to be a sale by description.[51] And in another, sale of a picture between dealers was held to be not 11–011

[47] *H Beecham & Co. Pty Ltd v Francis Howard & Co. Pty Ltd* [1921] V.L.R. 428 (selected timber proved to be affected by dry rot).
[48] See the dicta quoted above, para.11–007.
[49] See *Taylor v Bullen* (1850) 5 Exch. 779 ("the fine teak-built barque 'Intrepid,' A1": held no breach of warranty when barque proved neither teak-built nor A1, because sale based on inventory); *Joseph Travers & Sons Ltd v Longel Ltd* (1948) 64 T.L.R. 150 (war surplus boots referred to as "waders" for convenience); *Leggett v Taylor* (1965) 50 D.L.R. (2d) 516 (car: "not a sale by description but one by inspection"); *Marks v Hunt Bros (Sydney) Pty Ltd* [1958] S.R. (N.S.W.) 380 (notice on car windscreen not part of description where contract written); *cf. Beale v Taylor* [1967] 1 W.L.R. 1193 (advertisement constituted description though car examined, but see Koh [1968] C.L.J. 11); *M'Ivor v Michie* 1953 S.L.T. (Sh. Ct.) 53 (statement as to horsepower part of description when car inspected in dark with torch).
[50] Williston, *Sales* (rev. ed., 1948), para.224, suggested that the term sales by description should "be confined to cases where the identification of the goods which are the subject-matter of the bargain depends upon the description," but thought that "it seems not improbable . . . that the English courts may extend the definition of sale by description to every case where the buyer relies on descriptive words." The English interpretation went far, however, to counteract the narrow view taken in the earlier cases of when a statement was a warranty: see above, para.10–016. Conversely, liberal views in that respect could now enable a stricter view to be taken of s.13.
[51] *Speedway Safety Products Pty Ltd v Hazell & Moore Industries Pty Ltd* [1982] 1 N.S.W.L.R. 255. The result was that the merchantable quality provision did not apply. See also *Prosser v Hooper* (1817) 1 Moo.C.P. 106. In *Hughes v Hall* [1981] R.T.R. 430 a Divisional Court held, in the context of the Consumer Transactions

by description where it was clear that the buyer relied on his own judgment and that the seller disclaimed knowledge as to the supposed painter, despite the fact that there were attributions in early negotiations, in an old auction catalogue referred to, and in an invoice issued after the sale.[52]

11–012 **What is a "description"? Words of description and misrepresentations.** Even where the sale is by description, however, not all descriptive words will necessarily constitute conditions. Such words may, in principle, fall into any of the categories outlined in the previous chapter. It is perhaps unlikely that words which are genuinely descriptive, as opposed to qualitative, will often be treated as mere puffs or the like, so as to ground no liability at all.[53] But it is clear in principle that statements descriptive of goods may amount only to pre-contractual misrepresentations inducing the contract, or as non-promissory conditions precedent.[54] Thus in *Harrison v Knowles and Foster*[55] statements as to the deadweight capacity of two ships were held mere representations; as were statements made by a private seller to a dealer concerning the age of a car in *Oscar Chess Ltd v Williams*.[56]

11–013 **Words of description and warranties.** When words of description are held to be incorporated into the contract, it may be asked whether they can be held to be warranties, *i.e.* terms the breach of which may give rise to no more than the right to damages,[57] or whether they are always by virtue of such incorporation part of the description so as to bring the right to reject for breach of condition into operation. Here again the possibility of a warranty as to description was accepted in older cases on the Sale of Goods Act. In *Harrison v Knowles and Foster*, already referred to,[58] Bailhache J. at

---

(Restriction on Statements) Order 1976 as amended, which makes criminal the use of certain clauses which are void under the Unfair Contract Terms Act 1977 (below, paras 13–105, 14–142) that a clause in the sale of a car, "sold as seen and inspected", would prima facie negative a sale by description; and (though this is more questionable) constituted an attempt to exclude s.13. But another Divisional Court in *Cavendish-Woodhouse Ltd v Manley* (1982) 82 L.G.R. 376, dealing with a sale of furniture "bought as seen", found this a "puzzling decision" and held that the latter words simply indicated that the buyer had seen the goods, which might be relevant if a dispute arose as to their condition at the time of sale. See also below, para.13–066.

[52] *Harlingdon and Leinster Enterprises Ltd v Christopher Hull Fine Art Ltd* [1991] 1 Q.B. 564. Evidence was given that art dealers do not rely on descriptions by sellers. See Brown, 106 L.Q.R. 561 (1990); Bridge [1990] L.M.C.L.Q. 455.

[53] Above, paras 10–005, 10–006. But *cf. Budd v Fairmaner* (1831) 8 Bing. 48 and *Anthony v Halstead* (1877) 37 L.T. 433, above, para.10–005, n.19; *Marks v Hunt Bros (Sydney) Pty Ltd*, above, n.49. And see below, para.11–014.

[54] Above, paras 10–008 *et seq.*, 10–039.

[55] [1918] 1 K.B. 608; see also *Howard Marine and Dredging Co. Ltd v A Ogden & Sons (Excavations) Ltd* [1978] Q.B. 574 (similar statements in hire of barges).

[56] [1957] 1 W.L.R. 370, above, para.10–018. See also *Routledge v McKay* [1954] 1 W.L.R. 615; *Johnston v McRae* (1907) 26 N.Z.L.R. 299; *Boys v Rice* (1908) 27 N.Z.L.R. 1038; *Taylor v Combined Buyers Ltd* [1924] N.Z.L.R. 627 at 638. But *cf. Beale v Taylor* [1967] 1 W.L.R. 1193.

[57] See above, paras 10–023; *cf.* para.10–015.

[58] Above, para.10–011.

first instance[59] suggested a rule that "where the subject matter of a contract of sale is a specific existing chattel a statement as to some quality possessed by or attaching to such chattel is a warranty, and not a condition, unless the absence of such quality or the possession of it to a smaller extent makes the thing sold different in kind from the thing as described in the contract." On this basis he held that a statement as to the deadweight capacity of two ships was a warranty only and so covered by an exemption clause. This is a strict rule. But one of the cases cited[60] is prior to the 1893 Act, and the second, of 1900, actually seems to be contrary[61]: the analysis can also be criticised as unsound historically.[62] The Court of Appeal[63] indicated that if it had not affirmed the decision on other grounds, it would have heard further argument on this point. It seems therefore that a more recent dictum gives a better guide: "as a matter of law . . . every item in a description which constitutes a substantial ingredient in the 'identity' of the thing sold is a condition."[64] On this basis, statements truly relating to contractual description will rarely be warranties, though again the possibility remains open.[65] There may, however, clearly be warranties as to quality[66]; and problems of the time at which a statement was made or the fact that the contract was reduced to writing[67] may sometimes make it appropriate to regard descriptive statements as collateral warranties.[68]

Identification. The way in which descriptive words are to be understood is a matter of interpretation of contract and subject to the normal objective principles governing that topic.[69] The following dictum of Lord Diplock relates to sales of unascertained goods only, but seems relevant to all sales where this problem arises. "The 'description' by which unascertained goods are sold is, in my view, confined to those words in the contract which were intended by the parties to identify the kind of goods which were to be 11–014

---

[59] [1917] 2 K.B. 606 at 610: followed on this point in *Taylor v Combined Buyers Ltd* [1924] N.Z.L.R. 627.
[60] *Barr v Gibson* (1838) 5 M. & W. 390.
[61] *Varley v Whipp* [1900] 1 Q.B. 513; see Stoljar, 16 M.L.R. 174 at 185–186 (1953). In *Taylor v Combined Buyers Ltd*, above, the case was doubted: see pp.643–644.
[62] Stoljar, *op. cit.* above.
[63] [1918] 1 K.B. 608; above, para.10–012.
[64] *Couchman v Hill* [1947] K.B. 554 at 559, *per* Scott L.J., where the test was used to *extend* what was a condition. It was however approved by Lord Wilberforce in *Reardon Smith Line Ltd v Yngvar Hansen-Tangen* [1976] 1 W.L.R. 989 at 998 (below, para.11–014) as *restricting* what was a condition.
[65] See *Taylor v Combined Buyers Ltd*, above, at pp.638 *et seq.*
[66] *e.g. Ashington Piggeries Ltd v Christopher Hill Ltd* [1972] A.C. 441 at 511; *Pacific Trading Co. Ltd v Robert O Wiener* (1923) 14 Ll.L.R. 51; *Total International Ltd v Addax BV* [1996] 2 Lloyd's Rep. 333 ("usual Dakar refinery quality" not part of description but innominate term), below, para.11–016.
[67] See, *e.g. Howard Marine and Dredging Co. Ltd v A Ogden & Sons (Excavations) Ltd* [1978] Q.B. 574.
[68] Above, paras 10–012 *et seq.* In *Couchman v Hill*, above, a heifer was said to be "unserved": this was held to be part of the description, or alternatively a collateral warranty (above, para.10–012). See also *Hodgson v Morella Pastoral Co.* (1975) 13 S.A.S.R. 51 ("due to calf Nov./Feb." part of description).
[69] *Ashington Piggeries Ltd v Christopher Hill Ltd* [1972] A.C. 441 at 502. See also below, para.18–273.

supplied . . . Ultimately the test is whether the buyer could fairly and reasonably refuse to accept the physical goods proffered to him on the ground that their failure to correspond with that part of what was said about them in the contract makes them goods of a different kind from those he had agreed to buy. The key to section 13 is identification."[70] Descriptive words may identify the goods with varying degrees of preciseness. Thus in *Reardon Smith Line Ltd v Yngvar Hansen-Tangen*[71] there was a charter and sub-charter of a ship not yet built, which was described in the sub-charter as "Japanese flag . . . New-building motor tank vessel called Yard No. 354 at Osaka Zosen . . . described as per clause 24 hereof." The vessel built had been subcontracted to an associated yard, Oshima, in whose books it was No. 004. The House of Lords held on the facts that the sub-charterers must take the vessel, Lord Wilberforce drawing a distinction between words which identify in that "their purpose is to state (identify) an essential part of the description of the goods", and words which merely "provide one party with a specific indication (identification) of the goods so that he can find them and if he wishes sub-dispose of them."[72] Words identifying the goods in the second sense can be more liberally construed, so that not every element in them need be given contractual force. Although this case was not one of sale of goods (and indeed Lord Wilberforce expressly doubted the applicability of at least certain types of sale of goods cases to contracts such as that under dispute[73]) it would seem that this distinction too is general.[74]

11–015 **Form of contract.** The form of any written contract is relevant, but not conclusive, to the establishment of the identity of the contract goods. Thus where a clause referred to the contract goods as "Goods in bulk U.S.A. solvent extracted toasted soyabean meal—maximum 7.5 per cent fibre" and was followed by clauses headed "Quantity" and "Quality", it was held that "7.5 per cent fibre" was part of the description.[75] And in one case the fact that words appeared outside a formal specification was held relevant to establish that they did not form part of the description.[76] But in another case an indication that goods must be of "fair average quality" was held not

[70] *ibid.*, at pp.503–504.
[71] [1976] 1 W.L.R. 989; followed in *Sanko SS Co. Ltd v Kano Trading Ltd* [1978] 1 Lloyd's Rep. 156. See Coote, 51 A.L.J. 44 (1977).
[72] At p.999.
[73] See p.998.
[74] *cf. Hopkins v Hitchcock* (1863) 14 C.B.(N.S.) 65 (marks on iron immaterial); *Joseph Travers & Sons Ltd v Longel Ltd* (1948) 64 T.L.R. 150 ("waders"); *cf. Clarke v McMahon* [1939] S.A.S.R. 64 ("Kelvinator" word of description).
[75] *Tradax Export SA v European Grain & Shipping Ltd* [1983] 2 Lloyd's Rep. 100. See below, para.18–273.
[76] See *Montague L. Meyer Ltd v Kivisto* (1929) 35 Ll.L.R. 265 (timber: "to be properly seasoned" not part of description); *cf. Reardon Smith Line Ltd v Yngvar Hansen-Tangen* [1976] 1 W.L.R. 989, above, para.10–014, where there was a separate clause as to description. See below, para.18–273.

part of the description of goods sold despite the fact that it appeared in a clause headed "Quantity and Description".[77]

11–016 **Statements relating to quality.** In principle, identity and quality are separate notions, and statements as to quality are not to be regarded as part of the description of goods. Although the same set of facts can give rise to breaches both of section 13 and of the provisions as to quality contained in section 14 of the Sale of Goods Act 1979,[78] the two sections are to some extent exclusive. Thus stipulations may be said not to form part of the description of goods because they relate to quality[79]; and conversely may be said, especially in the context of an exemption or non-rejection clause as to defects in quality,[80] to relate not to quality but rather to description. In *Arcos Ltd v E E Ronaasen & Son*, discussed below,[81] it was held that goods did not correspond with their description though they were of merchantable quality and entirely fit for the purpose intended. But the line between the two is not easily drawn: where a defect is as to composition or analysis it will frequently be regarded as relevant to the description of the goods, and it is possible for goods to be of such poor quality that they cannot come within the contractual description at all.[82] And it is certainly possible for words relating to quality to form part of the description of goods.[83] Thus in *Toepfer v Continental Grain Co.*[84] the Court of Appeal upheld the decision of commercial arbitrators that in a contract for "Hard Amber Durum Wheat" the word "hard" related to quality (for the purpose of the finality of a certificate as to quality) but had no doubt that it could also be a word of description.[85] In the circumstances the certification was final for these purposes also.[86] And in *Toepfer v Warinco AG*[87] it was held that in a sale of

[77] *Ashington Piggeries Ltd v Christopher Hill Ltd* [1972] A.C. 441 above (claim against third parties) (where however there were other indications in the form of the contract); see also *Pacific Trading Co. Ltd v Robert O Wiener* (1923) 14 Ll.L.R. 51; below, para.18–273. As to the terms "f.a.q." and the like, see below, para.11–079, n.5.

[78] *Pinnock Bros v Lewis and Peat Ltd* [1923] 1 K.B. 690.

[79] *e.g. Ashington Piggeries Ltd v Christopher Hill Ltd* [1972] A.C. 441 at 470, 475, below, para.11–020. See also *Britain SS Co. Ltd v Lithgows Ltd*, 1975 S.L.T. (Notes) 20 (performance capacity of ship's engine); *Total International Ltd v Addax BV* [1996] 2 Lloyd's Rep. 333 ("usual Dakar refinery quality").

[80] *e.g. Pinnock Bros v Lewis and Peat Ltd*, above.

[81] Below, para.11–018.

[82] See the cases cited below, para.11–020 and *Marimpex Mineralöl Handelsgesellschaft mbH v Louis Dreyfus & Cie. Mineralöl GmbH* [1995] 1 Lloyd's Rep. 167 at 178 ("normal Russian gasoil"). But a clause beginning "expected to analyse" may only refer to quality: *Ashington Piggeries Ltd v Christopher Hill Ltd*, above.

[83] *Ashington Piggeries Ltd v Christopher Hill Ltd*, above, at p.470.

[84] [1974] 1 Lloyd's Rep. 11. See also *Re North Western Rubber Co. Ltd and Hüttenbach & Co.* [1908] 2 K.B. 907 (fair quality rubber).

[85] See pp.13, 14, 15.

[86] See *Gill & Duffus SA v Berger & Co. Inc.* [1983] 1 Lloyd's Rep. 622 at 626, 628–630, 632–634; [1984] A.C. 382 at 393–394. *Cf. NV Bunge v Cie. Noga d'Importation et d'Exportation (The Bow Cedar)* [1980] 2 Lloyd's Rep. 601, where it was held that certificates were final as to analysis but not as to the description of the goods as "Brazilian crude groundnut oil"; *Daudruy v Tropical Products SA* [1986] 1 Lloyd's Rep. 535 (palm fatty acid distillate).

[87] [1978] 2 Lloyd's Rep. 569. *Cf. Tradax Internacional SA v Bunge SA* [1977] 2 Lloyd's Rep. 604 at 612 (barley: provision as to impurities not part of description).

soya bean meal the word "fine-ground" was a word of description, with the result that coarse-ground meal could be rejected.

11–017 **Indications of purpose.** Again, a stipulation that goods are suitable for a specific purpose will usually be held not to be part of the description, for otherwise there would be no need for section 14(3) of the Sale of Goods Act.[88] But the general purpose for which goods are to be used may sometimes be an element in their description; thus it has been suggested that goods described as oysters which were not fit for human consumption might not conform with their description,[89] and it is submitted that goods described by such terms as "baby food", "cough mixture", "cold cure" would not conform with description if they proved totally unsuitable to the purposes indicated by those words.[90]

11–018 **Failure of goods to "correspond with description": first type of case.** As previously stated,[91] goods have been held not to correspond with their description in two types of case. The first type comprises cases where although the goods are substantially what is required, there is some small discrepancy from the contract particulars. Most of the decisions involve commercial disputes relating to unascertained or future goods, and the discrepancy may appear quite small in such cases. Thus in *Arcos Ltd v E A Ronaasen & Son*[92] there was a contract for staves of 1/2 inch thick. Only about 15 per cent conformed with this requirement, but the rest were nearly all less than 9/16 inch thick. Despite a finding that the goods were commercially within, and merchantable under, the contract specification, and that they were reasonably fit for their purpose (which was the making of cement barrels), the buyers were held entitled to reject, Lord Atkin saying that "if the seller wants a margin he must, and in my experience does, stipulate for it."[93] The packing of goods may also form part of their

---

88 *Ashington Piggeries Ltd v Christopher Hill Ltd* [1969] 3 All E.R. 1496 at 1512 (affirmed on this point [1972] A.C. 441).
89 *ibid*.
90 See also the cases on "breeding cattle," below, para.11–019, n.9.
91 Above, para.11–004.
92 [1933] A.C. 470. See also *Vigers Bros v Sanderson Bros* [1901] 1 K.B. 608 (timber); *Wilensko Slaski Towarzystwo Drewno v Fenwick & Co. (West Hartlepool) Ltd* [1938] 3 All E.R. 429 (timber); *Wimble, Sons & Co. v Lillico & Son* (1922) 38 T.L.R. 296 (cotton cake: specified percentage of oil and protein content not met); *Ballantine & Co. v Cramp and Bosman* (1923) 129 L.T. 502 (carcases of meat: "average not to exceed 60 lb."); *Rapalli v K L Take Ltd* [1958] 2 Lloyd's Rep. 469 ("medium onions": 6–7 per cent undersized). Contrast *Montague L Meyer Ltd v Vigers Bros Ltd* (1939) 63 Ll.L.R. 10, below, para.11–021 (timber); *Trasimex Holding SA v Addax BV (The Red Sea)* [1999] 1 Lloyd's Rep. 28 (aviation fuel specification). See also below, paras 18–266, 18–273 *et seq.* as to international sales.
93 As to the word "about" as qualifying the duty, see *Vigers Bros v Sanderson Bros*, above; *Joseph Green v Arcos Ltd* (1931) 39 Ll.L.R. 229 at 231; see also *Canada Law Book Co. v Boston Book Co.* (1922) 64 S.C.R. (Can.) 182 ("150 vols. more or less"); above, para.8–054; below, para.11–021.

description. Thus in *Re Moore & Co. and Landauer & Co.*[94] there was a contract for 3,000 tins of Australian canned fruit packed in cases of 30 tins. The seller supplied a substantial number in cases containing only 24 tins, though the total number of tins was correct. It was held that the buyer could reject the whole consignment. An exception is only made in cases of "microscopic deviation".[95] Overseas sales where there are special stipulations as to mode and date of shipment, etc., can be treated under this head also, on the grounds that the extra requirements are part of the description.[96] In *Reardon Smith Line Ltd v Yngvar Hansen-Tangen*[97] Lord Wilberforce thought some of the older cases "excessively technical and due for fresh examination in [the House of Lords]", and at best was prepared to accept them as relating to "unascertained future goods (*e.g.* commodities) as to which each detail of the description must be assumed to be vital."[98] The famous decision in *Bowes v Shand*,[99] that goods can be rejected because shipment was not completed within the specified period, has however been reaffirmed by the House of Lords in the leading case of *Bunge Corp. v Tradax Export SA*[1] and is still clearly valid.[2] It is presumably to be brought within the exception to which Lord Wilberforce referred. It should be noted that remedies for defects in *quantity* are more specific and separately dealt with in section 30 of the Act. They do not normally,

---

[94] [1921] 2 K.B. 519, a case on s.30(4) of the Sale of Goods Act (below, para.12–029). See also *Manbré Saccharin Co. v Corn Products Co.* [1919] 1 K.B. 198 at 207 (size of bags); *Makin v London Rice Mills Co. Ltd* (1869) 20 L.T. 705 (rice in double bags); *Smith Bros (Hull) Ltd v Gosta Jacobsson & Co.* [1961] 2 Lloyd's Rep. 522 (marks on timber part of description); *cf. Parsons v New Zealand Shipping Co.* [1901] 1 K.B. 548 (marks on lamb carcasses irrelevant).

[95] *Arcos Ltd v E A Ronaasen & Son* [1933] A.C. 470 at 479; as to which see *Easterbrook v Gibb* (1887) 3 T.L.R. 401 (vices); *Wilensko Slaski Towarzystwo Drewno v Fenwick & Co. (West Hartlepool) Ltd*, above; *Rapalli v K L Take Ltd*, above; *Margaronis Navigation Agency Ltd v Henry W Peabody & Co.* [1965] 1 Q.B. 300 at 319–320 (loading of cargo); *cf. Moralice (London) Ltd v E. D. and F. Man* [1954] 2 Lloyd's Rep. 526 (where sale financed by bankers' credit, documents and hence goods must correspond exactly: on contract for 5,000 bags buyer can refuse bill of lading for 4,997); below, paras.23–196 *et seq.*

[96] See cases cited below, paras 18–266 *et seq.*, 20–029, 20–038. *Cf.* however *J Aron & Co. (Inc.) v Comptoir Wegimont* [1921] 3 K.B. 435, where such a term was treated as independent of description, so that an exemption clause relating to errors of description did not apply to it.

[97] [1976] 1 W.L.R. 989; above, para.11–014.

[98] At p.998. See also pp.1000–1001 and *Ashington Piggeries Ltd v Christopher Hill Ltd* [1972] A.C. 441 at 489. The rule of strict compliance seems to have been introduced in the teeth of findings by commercial arbitrators, especially in the timber trade: see *Re Moore & Co. and Landauer & Co.* [1921] 2 K.B. 519 at 524; *Montague L Meyer Ltd v Osakeyhtio Carelia Timber Co. Ltd* (1930) 35 Com.Cas. 17 at 19; *Hillas & Co. Ltd v Arcos Ltd* (1931) 40 Ll.L.R. 307 (decision revsd. (1932) 43 Ll.L.R. 359); *E A Ronaasen & Son v Arcos Ltd* (1932) 43 Ll.L.R. 1 at 4–6 (affirmed [1933] A.C. 470); *Joseph Green v Arcos Ltd* (1931) 39 Ll.L.R. 229 at 231. But some of these cases might now be affected by s.15A of the Sale of Goods Act: below, paras 12–024, 12–025, 18–284.

[99] (1877) 2 App.Cas. 455.

[1] [1981] 1 W.L.R. 711 at 724–725.

[2] It probably survives the introduction of 15A of the Sale of Goods Act: below, paras 12–024, 12–025, 18–284.

therefore, involve the application of section 13 unless only damages are claimed.[3]

11–019 **Second type of case.** The second type comprises cases where in the absence of detailed commercial description the goods supplied are to be regarded as not being the goods ordered in a much more general sense. Here the cases have stressed, and hence required, a more considerable discrepancy; though it should be noted that their context is often that of holding an exemption clause inapplicable where the goods supplied are of a different kind.[4] Thus a contract for common English sainfoin seed was not performed by delivery of giant sainfoin[5]; a contract for a new Singer car was not satisfied by delivery of a second-hand model[6]; a contract for a second-hand reaping machine new the previous year, and only used to cut 50 acres, was not performed by delivery of a very old one which had been mended.[7] Consumer cases are more likely to figure in this group than in the first. Thus it has been held that a contract for a "Herald, convertible, white, 1961, twin carbs." was not performed by delivery of a vehicle consisting of parts of two cars, one part manufactured earlier than 1961, welded together.[8] In a New Zealand case, it was held that a contract to sell a pure bred polled Angus bull could be treated as discharged for breach when the bull (which had been inspected and bought at an auction) proved to be "a bull in name only and useful as such for no purpose, though its carcase may be of value."[9]

---

[3] Above, paras 8–045 *et seq.*; below, paras.12–029, 12–030 *et seq.* See however *Canada Law Book Co. v Boston Book Co.* (1922) 64 S.C.R. 182 (English Reports: "150 volumes more or less" held a description: damages claim).

[4] See above, para.11–005; below, para.14–009.

[5] *Wallis, Son & Wells v Pratt & Haynes* [1911] A.C. 394. See also *Payne v Minister of Food* (1953) 103 L.J. 141.

[6] *Andrews Bros Ltd v Singer & Co. Ltd* [1934] 1 K.B. 17; see also *Armaghdown Motors Ltd v Gray Motors Ltd* [1963] N.Z.L.R. 5 (statement that car had not been used as taxi part of description). As to the meaning of "new car" see *Morris Motors Ltd v Lilley* [1959] 3 All E.R. 737; *Phillips v Cycle and General Finance Corp.* [1977] C.L.Y. 364; *R. v Ford Motor Co. Ltd* [1974] 3 All E.R. 489; *Raynham Farm Co. Ltd v Symbol Motor Corp.* (1987) 6 Tr.L.Rep. 143. See also *Anderson v Scrutton* [1934] S.A.S.R. 10 ("new engine"); and in a different context, *Annand & Thompson Pty Ltd v Trade Practices Commission* (1979) 25 A.L.R. 91.

[7] *Varley v Whipp* [1900] 1 Q.B. 513; *cf. Chalmers v Harding* (1868) 17 L.T. 571.

[8] *Beale v Taylor* [1967] 1 W.L.R. 1193 (private buyer and seller); as to cars see also *M'Ivor v Michie* 1953 S.L.T. (Sh. Ct.) 53; but see Koh [1968] C.L.J. 11 and compare *Leggett v Taylor* (1965) 50 D.L.R. (2d) 516; *Marks v Hunt Bros (Sydney) Pty Ltd* [1958] S.R. (N.S.W.) 380 and *Oscar Chess Ltd v Williams* [1957] 1 W.L.R. 370. See also *Ojjeh v Waller* [1999] C.L.Y. 4405 (purple Lalique glass car mascots not genuine).

[9] *Cotter v Luckie* [1918] N.Z.L.R. 811; but *cf. Dell v Quilty* [1924] N.Z.L.R. 1270. See also as to cattle *Handbury v Nolan* (1977) 13 A.L.R. 339 (cow in calf); *Elder Smith Goldsbrough Mort Ltd v McBride* [1976] 2 N.S.W.L.R. 631 (bull sold as breeding bull); *Lockhart v Osman* [1981] V.R. 57 (cattle infected with brucellosis sold at auction advertised as "cattle breeders' sale" did not comply with description). See further *Gorton v Macintosh & Co.* (1883) W.N. 103 (india rubber thread useless); *American Can Co. v Stewart* (1915) 50 I.L.T. 132 (American adding machine did not work for British currency without slight mental operation on part of user); *Nicholson and Venn v Smith Marriott* (1947) 177 L.T. 189 (table linen "the property of Charles I" actually Georgian).

Variations of composition. As regards substances which contain admixtures of other substances, lack ingredients, or have undergone deterioration, the question is normally whether the admixture, lack or deterioration is sufficiently significant to make the basic substance lose its identity from a commercial point of view.[10] Goods may be subject to a defect which is commercially significant in the sense that it reduces their value in the market without suffering a change of description.[11] Often the test employed is quantitative.[12] But where the admixture makes the resultant substance toxic, quite a small amount of foreign matter may prevent the goods from conforming with description.[13] Toxicity is however to some extent a relative notion, for substances may be poisonous to certain creatures and not to others, or in certain quantities and not in others. The extent to which a product should be regarded as toxic may therefore depend on the description under which it is sold, its normal use and so forth. In *Ashington Piggeries Ltd v Christopher Hill Ltd*,[14] herring meal was by a majority held to comply with its description as such though it had become contaminated by a chemical reaction caused by a preservative added to it, in such a way as to make it toxic to mink and in some degree to all animals. Had it been instantly poisonous to all creatures the result would surely have been otherwise. It can however be argued that some of these cases, because of their context, have set too limited a standard for compliance with description.[15] 11–020

Trade custom. Proof of trade custom and normal commercial understanding is admitted to explain or qualify the meaning of descriptions. Thus in *Grenfell v E B Meyrowitz Ltd*[16] an aviator who purchased in 1932 flying 11–021

---

[10] *British Oil and Cake Co. Ltd v J Burstall & Co. Ltd* (1923) 15 Ll.L.R. 46; *Pinnock Bros v Lewis and Peat Ltd* [1923] 1 K.B. 690 (copra cake containing castor seed held not to be copra cake); *Robert A Munro & Co. Ltd v Meyer* [1930] 2 K.B. 312 (cocoa husks in bone meal); *Bostock & Co. Ltd v Nicholson & Sons Ltd* [1904] 1 K.B. 725 ("sulphuric acid commercially free from arsenic"—contained arsenic); see also *Bakker v Bowness Auto Parts Co. Ltd* (1977) 68 D.L.R. (3d) 173 (ethanol-ethylene glycol anti-freeze: contained very little ethylene glycol, but kerosene, methanol and water); and in a different context (entitlement to freight) *Montedison SpA v Icroma SpA (The Caspian Sea)* [1980] 1 W.L.R. 48 (impurities in oil). For an old example of bad quality leading to difference of identity, see *Osborne v Hart* (1871) 23 L.T. 851 ("Can it be said that a contract for the supply of superior old port wine is fulfilled by supplying wine which is described by witnesses as almost undrinkable?").

[11] *Gill & Duffus SA v Berger & Co. Inc.* [1981] 2 Lloyd's Rep. 233 at 236 (beans) (for subsequent proceedings see [1984] A.C. 382).

[12] *Rapalli v K L Take Ltd* [1958] 2 Lloyd's Rep. 469 (5–6 per cent of onions defective in quality); *Glass's Fruit Markets Ltd v Southwell & Son Ltd* [1969] 2 Lloyd's Rep. 398 (potatoes not "sound" if more than negligible amount of blight).

[13] See cases cited above, n.10.

[14] [1972] A.C. 441 (claim against defendants).

[15] See criticism by Coote, 50 A.L.J. 17 (1976) on the basis that such reasoning (i) pays insufficient attention to the distinction between sales of unascertained or future goods and sales of specific goods, and (ii) was unduly influenced by cases on the doctrine of fundamental breach (as then understood) in relation to exemption clauses (to which some of the cases cited above relate).

[16] [1936] 2 All E.R. 1313. (But *cf. Kat v Diment* [1951] 1 Q.B. 34 as to application of false trade description under the old Merchandise Marks Acts.) See also *Powell v*

goggles described in a catalogue as fitted with "safety-glass lenses" was held unable to recover for breach of section 13 where his eye was injured by a splinter from one of the goggles in a flying accident, because the goggles were made from laminated glass and therefore complied with the meaning of the term "safety-glass" as understood at the time. And in *Steels & Busks Ltd v Bleecker Bik & Co. Ltd*[17] the commercial or market standard as to the meaning of "pale crepe rubber; quality as previously delivered" was applied, the court accepting the finding of the arbitrator that the kind of chemical used in its preservation was not relevant to the contract description. This applies also to trade usage as to numbers and quantities: for example, evidence could be adduced as to the meaning of a "baker's dozen". Thus in one case evidence of usage as to permissible excess dimensions of sawn timber was accepted.[18]

11–022 **Sale of Goods Act 1979, s.13(2): sale by sample as well as by description.** This reads: "If the sale is by sample as well as by description it is not sufficient that the bulk of the goods corresponds with the sample if the goods do not also correspond with the description."[19] This provision raises problems as to the extent to which the sample itself provides elements of the description. They are discussed in connection with sales by sample.[20] There may also be cases where the sample is given under circumstances which make it the *only* description of the thing to be supplied: in such cases of course the buyer stipulates for no more than goods of the same description as the sample.[21] And even where descriptive words are used they may form no more than a label for convenience of reference to the subject-matter.[22]

Horton (1836) 2 Bing. N.C. 668 ("mess pork of Scott & Co."); *Lucas v Bristow* (1858) E.B. & E. 907 (best palm oil). But the express terms of a contract cannot be contradicted by usage or custom: *Yates v Pym* (1816) 6 Taunt. 446. See also *Re Walkers, Winser and Hamm and Shaw, Son & Co.* [1904] 2 K.B. 152.

[17] [1956] 1 Lloyd's Rep. 228. See also *Peter Darlington and Partners Ltd v Gosho Co. Ltd* [1964] 1 Lloyd's Rep. 149 ("canary seed on pure basis"); *Glass's Fruit Markets Ltd v Southwell & Son Ltd* [1969] 2 Lloyd's Rep. 398 (potatoes: contract "for sound bags only").

[18] *Montague L. Meyer Ltd v Vigers Bros Ltd* (1939) 63 Ll.L.R. 10. See also *Rosenthal & Sons Ltd v Esmail* [1965] 1 W.L.R. 1117 (cotton poplin).

[19] See *Nichol v Godts* (1854) 10 Exch. 191 ("foreign refined rape oil, warranted only equal to samples"), one of the cases on which s.13(2) was based; *Parker v Palmer* (1821) 4 B. & A. 387 (rice); *Azèmar v Casella* (1867) L.R. 2 C.P. 677 (cotton); *Wallis, Son and Wells v Pratt and Haynes* [1911] A.C. 394 (seed); *Steels and Busks Ltd v Bleecker Bik & Co. Ltd* [1956] 1 Lloyd's Rep. 228 (rubber); *John Bowron & Son Ltd v Rodema Canned Foods Ltd* [1967] 1 Lloyd's Rep. 183 (apricot pulp).

[20] Below, para.11–086.

[21] *Boshali v Allied Commercial Exporters Ltd* (1961) 105 S.J. 987; *Mody v Gregson* (1868) L.R. 4 Ex. 49 at 53; *Carter v Crick* (1859) 4 H. & N. 412 (seed); *RW Cameron & Co. v L Slutzkin Pty Ltd* (1923) 32 C.L.R. 81 (description had no recognised meaning in trade).

[22] *Joseph Travers & Sons Ltd v Longel Ltd* (1948) 64 T.L.R. 150 ("waders"); *Houndsditch Warehouse Co. Ltd v Waltex Ltd* [1944] 2 All E.R. 518 ("braces").

Related contracts. Provisions similar to section 13 are implied into other contracts for the transfer of property in goods[23] (*e.g.* contracts of exchange and for work and materials[24]); hire-purchase agreements[25]; and contracts of hire.[26] 11–023

2. QUALITY AND FITNESS FOR PURPOSE

(a) *Nature of the Act's Provisions*

Basic rule: caveat emptor. The starting point as regards quality in sale of goods is *caveat emptor*[27]: except in so far as there are express contractual stipulations[28] or the goods do not conform with their description[29] or sample,[30] the buyer buys goods as they are. Section 14(1) of the Sale of Goods Act 1979 reads: "Except as provided by this section and section 15 below[31] and subject to any other enactment,[32] there is no implied condition or warranty about the quality or fitness for any particular purpose of goods supplied under a contract of sale." This subsection reproduces with minor amendments wording which in the Act of 1893 originally appeared as a preamble to section 14 and not as a subsection.[33] The provisions which follow impose a condition that the goods must be of satisfactory quality[34] and a more specific condition over and above, that they must in many circumstances be reasonably fit for their purpose.[35] They leave little of the maxim *caveat emptor*. 11–024

History of section 14. The original Sale of Goods Act of 1893 set out these provisions in the reverse order: the condition as to fitness for purpose appeared, as subsection (1), before that as to quality, the standard for which was "merchantable", and followed in subsection (2). Further, the latter provision was confined to cases where goods were bought by description. The reason was historical. As with section 13, the case law which the draftsman sought to embody was to an effect different both from the purpose which a superficial scrutiny might attribute to the section, and also from the effect which subsequent interpretation has given it. In the case of sales by description, not only was there prior to the Act of 1893 a condition that the goods should correspond with the description, but there 11–025

---

23 Supply of Goods and Services Act 1982, s.3.
24 Above, paras 1–034 *et seq*.
25 Supply of Goods (Implied Terms) Act 1973, s.9 as substituted by Consumer Credit Act 1974 and amended by Sale and Supply of Goods Act 1994.
26 Supply of Goods and Services Act 1982, s.8.
27 See *Jones v Just* (1868) L.R. 3 Q.B. 197.
28 Above, paras 10–015 *et seq*.
29 Above, paras 11–001 *et seq*.
30 Below, paras 11–073 *et seq*.
31 Below, para.11–073.
32 As to other statutes, see Ch.14, below.
33 The present words date from the Supply of Goods (Implied Terms) Act 1973.
34 Below, paras 11–026 *et seq*.
35 Below, paras 11–051 *et seq*.

was also a warranty as to merchantability, the two being frequently run together.[36] In the case of specific goods neither of these rules applied. But there was another rule, apparently more general in its scope and therefore possibly applicable to such goods as well as to sales by description, that where the buyer made known to the seller the purpose for which goods were required so as to show that he relied on the seller's skill or judgment, there was a warranty that they were reasonably fit for that purpose.[37] This rule, being more general, was placed first: the merchantable quality rule, being confined to sales by description, was placed second. It was this dichotomy, not (as might appear) one between special and general reliance, which the 1893 Act originally sought to state; though it may have gone further than the cases, and Chalmers observed[38] that the section "probably narrows somewhat the already restricted rule of *caveat emptor*." The section was however interpreted in a surprising way. Early doubts as to whether goods were bought by description,[39] and as to the standards imported by the word "merchantable",[40] led to buyers invoking the subsection as to fitness for purpose more frequently than that as to merchantable quality. As a result, the former subsection became very widely interpreted so as to apply to almost all sales.[41] To modern eyes the whole provision appeared unscientifically drafted and not entirely satisfactory in operation. It was therefore amended by the Supply of Goods (Implied Terms) Act 1973, which reversed the order of the two provisions. What had been subsection (1) became subsection (3), and the former preamble was inserted as subsection (1). By this means the merchantable quality provision remained as subsection (2). The Act also replaced the requirement of sale by description in the original section 14(2) by one that the seller sells in the course of a business, and inserted this also into the reliance section, section 14(3). The other principal change was that it gave a definition of "merchantable quality"; this proved unsatisfactory and was replaced in the Sale and Supply of Goods Act 1994 by a completely new provision, as is explained below.[42] The overall result is, contrary to the original arrangement of the Act, to provide first in section 14(2) a general standard which goods are required to reach, and secondly in section 14(3) "to impose a particular obligation tailored to the particular circumstances of the case".[43]

[36] Above, para.11–003.

[37] See *Jones v Bright* (1829) 5 Bing. 533; *Jones v Just* (1868) L.R. 3 Q.B. 197; *Randall v Newson* (1877) 2 Q.B.D. 102; *Drummond v Van Ingen* (1887) 12 App.Cas. 284 at 290. See also *Wallis v Russell* [1902] 2 I.R. 585 at 615 ("*caveat emptor* does not mean—in law or Latin—that the buyer must 'take *chance*,' it means that he must take '*care*'").

[38] *Sale of Goods* (2nd ed., 1894), p.30.

[39] As to which see above, paras 11–006 *et seq.*

[40] Below, paras 11–031 *et seq.*

[41] See Hughes, 22 M.L.R. 484 (1959); Davies, 85 L.Q.R. 75 (1969); Franzi, 51 A.L.J. 298 (1977); *Mash & Murrell Ltd v Joseph I Emanuel Ltd* [1961] 1 W.L.R. 862 at 865. In *Ashington Piggeries v Christopher Hill Ltd* [1972] A.C. 441 at 496, Lord Wilberforce said that this tendency "reflects a reversion to the more general approach to questions of the seller's liability under implied warranty adopted by the common law, as contrasted with the compartmentalisation into separate but inevitably overlapping provisions adopted by the Sale of Goods Act."

[42] Para.11–031.

[43] *Jewson v Boyhan* [2003] EWCA Civ 1030; [2004] 1 Lloyd's Rep. 505 at [46] and [47] *per* Clarke L.J.

(b) *Satisfactory Quality*

Sale of Goods Act 1979, s.14(2). This subsection is the product of several changes. It is appropriate to start by setting out in full the version of the section now operative. The commentary below follows, in general, the order of the words and provisions of the subsection. As amended by section 1 of the Sale and Supply of Goods Act 1994, it reads: 11–026

"(2) Where the seller sells goods in the course of a business, there is an implied term that the goods supplied under the contract are of satisfactory quality.

(2A) For the purposes of this Act, goods are of satisfactory quality if they meet the standard that a reasonable person would regard as satisfactory, taking account of any description of the goods, the price (if relevant) and all the other relevant circumstances.

(2B) For the purposes of this Act, the quality of goods includes their state and condition and the following (among others) are in appropriate cases aspects of the quality of goods—

(a) fitness for all the purposes for which goods of the kind in question are commonly supplied,
(b) appearance and finish,
(c) freedom from minor defects,
(d) safety, and
(e) durability.

(2C) The term implied by subsection (2) above does not extend to any matter making the quality of goods unsatisfactory—

(a) which is specifically drawn to the buyer's attention before the contract is made,
(b) where the buyer examines the goods before the contract is made, which that examination ought to reveal, or
(c) in the case of a contract for sale by sample, which would have been apparent on a reasonable examination of the sample."[44]

For cases where the buyer deals as consumer, the following provisions also apply:

"(2D) If the buyer deals as consumer or, in Scotland, if a contract of sale is a consumer contract, the relevant circumstances mentioned in subsection (2A) above include any public statements on the specific

[44] *cf.* Vienna Convention (above, 1–024), Art.35(2)(a) (d); Uniform Commercial Code, s.2–314. The 1994 Act was the eventual result of work done earlier by the Law Commission: see Law Com. W.P. No. 85, Scot. Law Com. C.M. No. 58 (1983); Law Com. No. 161, Scot. Law Com. No. 104, Cm. 137 (1987) There is a valuable commentary on the 1994 Act by W. H. Thomas and W. C. H. Ervine in *Current Law Statutes Annotated*. Parliamentary proceedings appear in *Hansard*, H.C. Vol.237, col.233; Vol.243, col.1054; Vol.245, col.526; H.L. Vol.557, cols.472, 960; Vol.558, col.686. A full account of the development was given in the 6th edition of this book.

characteristics of the goods made about them by the seller, the producer or his representative, particularly in advertising or on labelling.

(2E) A public statement is not by virtue of subsection (2D) above a relevant circumstance for the purposes of subsection (2A) above in the case of a contract of sale, if the seller shows that—

(a) at the time the contract was made, he was not, and could not reasonably have been, aware of the statement,
(b) before the contract was made, the statement had been withdrawn in public or, to the extent that it contained anything which was incorrect or misleading, it had been corrected in public, or
(c) the decision to buy the goods could not have been influenced by the statement.

(2F) Subsections (2D) and (2E) above do not prevent any public statement from being a relevant circumstance for the purposes of subsection (2A) above (whether or not the buyer deals as consumer or, in Scotland, whether or not the contract of sale is a consumer contract) if the statement would have been such a circumstance apart from those subsections.

[. . .]

(6) As regards England and Wales and Northern Ireland,[45] the terms implied by subsections (2) and (3) [46] above are conditions." [47]

11–027 **"Sells goods in the course of a business".** These words, which appeared first in the changes of 1973, superseded original reference to a buyer who "deals in goods of that description". They are very similar to the words "in the course of a trade or business—(a) applies a false trade description . . . or (b) supplies or offers to supply any goods . . ." in section 1(1) of the Trade Descriptions Act 1968,[48] and to "makes the contract in the course of a business" in section 12 of the Unfair Contract Terms Act 1977.[49] It seems clear that they cover sales which are an integral part of the business carried on, and sales which are incidental to that business but carried on with a degree of regularity[50]; and in this context a first-time seller must be

[45] The designation of the term as a condition was originally contained in s.14 itself. The present formulation, with the use there of "term" and the addition of s.14(6), dates from the Sale and Supply of Goods Act 1994 (s.7 and Sch.2) and was adopted to facilitate the abolition of the term "condition" in the English sense for Scots law.
[46] As to subs. (3) see below, para. 11–051.
[47] In general, breach of a condition entitles rejection: see above, paras 10–024 *et seq.*, below, paras 12–022 *et seq.* In non-consumer cases, a slight breach of an implied term may, however, not do so (see s.15A of the Act, below, paras 12–024 *et seq.*, 18–284. A buyer who deals as consumer is entitled under the Act to the benefit of a (rebuttable) presumption that the goods were non-compliant at the relevant time if they are non-compliant at any time during six months from delivery (s.48A(3); below, para. 12–075). This is part of new provisions providing special remedies for those who deal as consumers (below, paras 12–071, 14–008 *et seq.* The significance of "delivery" in this context is considered below, para.11–049.
[48] Below, para.14–112.
[49] Below, para.13–062.
[50] *Stevenson v Rogers* [1999] Q.B. 1028 at 1033, citing *R & B Customs Brokers Co. Ltd v United Dominions Trust Ltd* [1988] 1 W.L.R. 321.

covered.[51] They also cover sales in a one-off venture in the nature of trade carried through with a view to profit.[52] It has been held in Scotland that the words cover a person who sells off the whole of his business (a farm), including the items concerned (cattle).[53] Beyond this, difficulty has arisen in respect of the situation where a person in a business not involving sales of this type, or not involving sales at all, makes a sale connected with that business, as where a farmer sells off a surplus tractor, or a medical practitioner or local government department[54] disposing of surplus equipment sells a used word processor. Authority in connection with the other two statutory provisions referred to above requires some degree of regularity in sales of the type concerned for them to rank as being in the course of a business.[55] The first provision however involves criminal liability, and the words form a limit on it; and the second increases protection of buyers by preventing their too easily being regarded as not consumers and so not protected by rules protecting consumers. The two other provisions thus have different purposes. The present provision protects buyers by imposing duties on sellers, and a strict interpretation of it might reduce those duties too easily. It has therefore been held, with the aid of reference to Parliamentary proceedings, that the present provision is not to be affected by the interpretation put on the others, and that the legislative purpose was to exclude only purely private sales outside the confines of a business. Consequent on this, in *Stevenson v Rogers*[56] a fisherman who sold his only boat to procure a new one was held to be selling in the course of a business, though he was not in the business of selling boats and had only done so once before.

Business. An interlocking problem concerns the meaning of the word "business" in connection with this and related provisions.[57] No definition is given except that, as stated above, "business" includes "a profession and 11–028

---

[51] Though the authority stems from dicta concerning the words "deals in goods of that description": see *Ashington Piggerres Ltd v Christopher Hill Ltd* [1972] A.C. 441.

[52] *Davies v Sumner* [1984] 1 W.L.R. 1301 at 1305; see also *Corfield v Sevenways Garage Ltd* [1985] R.T.R. 109.

[53] *Buchanan-Jardine v Hamilink* 1983 S.L.T. 149.

[54] "Business" includes a profession and the activities of any government department or local or public authority": below, para.11–028.

[55] See a line of cases on the Trade Descriptions Act: *Havering LBC v Stevenson* [1970] 1 W.L.R. 1375 (sale of cars by car-hire firm: course of business); *Corfield v Sevenways Garage Ltd* [1985] R.T.R. 109 (sale by repairers, MOT testers: course of business); *Davies v Sumner*, above (sale of car by self-employed courier: not course of business); *Devlin v Hall* [1990] R.T.R. 320 (sale of car by taxi operator: not course of business); and on the Unfair Contract Terms Act: *R & B Customs Brokers Co. Ltd v United Dominions Trust Ltd* [1988] 1 W.L.R. 321. On the problem as it presents itself under that Act see below, para.13–062. As to "private" and "trade" purchasers under s.27 of the Hire Purchase Act 1964 (which deals with transfer of title) see above, para.7–092. See in general Kidner (1987) 38 N.I.L.Q. 46; Pearce [1989] L.M.C.L.Q. 371; Brown [1988] J.B.L. 386; Price, 52 M.L.R. 245 (1989); Jones and Harland, 2 J. Contract Law 266 (1990).

[56] [1999] Q.B. 1028: see Brown, 115 L.Q.R. 384 (1999), suggesting that this may require limiting by attention to the meaning of the word "business", discussed below.

[57] s.14(3), below, para.11–051: and ss.1(3) and 12(1) of the Unfair Contract Terms Act 1977, below, paras 13–061, 13–062.

the activities of any government department or local or public authority", which perhaps indicates that the activity need not be conducted for profit.[58] It has been said that "the word 'business' is an etymological chameleon; it suits its meaning to the context in which it is found. It is not a term of legal art."[59] No doubt the activities of a trading corporation or partnership will normally be regarded as a business. But in the case of non-trading corporations, partnerships and private persons there will obviously be borderline situations where it is not clear whether or not the activity concerned has assumed the status of a business. There are also organisations of a non-profit-making nature such as universities, colleges, schools, nursing homes and so forth which make sales: although the whole activity may perhaps not be appropriately designated as a business, certain portions of it (*e.g.* a university bookshop or hospital restaurant) may be. Such cases must be solved with the aim of the legislation in mind; this seems to be the protection of consumers against those who sell with some degree of professionalism and regularity. The answer will turn on the circumstances of each case, and it is doubtful whether any specific principles can be laid down. At present such authority as there is on the meaning of the word "business" arises in other contexts, such as restrictive covenants,[60] landlord and tenant,[61] trade descriptions,[62] moneylending,[63] bankruptcy,[64] taxation.[65] Such authority is only of indirect relevance.[66] It does seem, however, that there is no need to view the activities of the person or body as a whole: some particular activities may rank as business, some not.[67]

11–029 **Sale through an agent.** The Supply of Goods (Implied Terms) Act 1973 introduced a provision which had no counterpart at all in the original Sale of Goods Act. This now appears as section 14(5) of the Sale of Goods Act 1979 and reads: "The preceding provisions of this section apply to a sale by

---

[58] This is certainly true in the landlord and tenant cases, *infra*, n.61.

[59] *Town Investments Ltd v Dept. of the Environment* [1978] A.C. 359 at 383, *per* Lord Diplock, who goes on to quote a dictum that "anything which is an occupation or duty which requires attention is a business": *Rolls v Miller* (1884) 27 Ch.D. 71 at 88. See also *Smith v Anderson* (1880) 15 Ch.D. 247 at 258–259.

[60] *e.g. Rogers v Hosegood* [1900] 2 Ch. 388 at 390.

[61] *Bramwell v Lacy* (1879) 10 Ch.D. 691 (hospital a business); *Rolls v Miller*, above (home for working girls); *Town Investments* case, above.

[62] *e.g. Blakemore v Bellamy* [1983] R.T.R. 303 (hobby of reconditioning and reselling cars not a business).

[63] As to s.6 of the Moneylenders Act 1900 (repealed by the Consumer Credit Act 1974), see Meston, *The Law Relating to Moneylenders* (5th ed.), pp.1–3, 11 *et seq.*, 39 *et seq*. A leading case was *Litchfield v Dreyfus* [1906] 1 K.B. 584. See also *Newton v Pyke* (1908) 25 T.L.R. 127 (miscellaneous loans to friends or relations at interest did not involve sufficient system and continuity to constitute moneylending business); *Newman v Oughton* [1911] 1 K.B. 792 (isolated transaction does not constitute carrying on of business).

[64] *e.g. Re a Debtor (No. 3 of 1926)* [1927] 1 Ch. 97.

[65] *Inland Revenue Commrs. v Marine Steam Turbine Co. Ltd* [1920] 1 K.B 193; *Lord Advocate v Glasgow Corp.* 1958 S.L.T. 2.

[66] See *Stroud's Judicial Dictionary* (6th ed.), Vol.1, "Business"; Blair, *Sale of Goods Act 1979* (1980), p.100; Harvey, 127 S.J. 163 at 179 (1983). Decisions on the Factors Acts could also be relevant.

[67] *cf. Stevenson v Beverley Bentinck Ltd* [1976] 1 W.L.R. 483.

a person who in the course of a business is acting as agent for another as they apply to a sale by a principal in the course of a business, except where that other is not selling in the course of a business and either the buyer knows that fact or reasonable steps are taken to bring it to the notice of the buyer before the contract is made." The result of this provision is that the implied terms of both subsections (2) and (3) will operate whenever a sale is effected through an agent who sells in the course of a business, unless the buyer has notice, or is taken as having notice, that the seller is selling privately. This was not the case before the amendment of the 1893 Act: the sale was effected by the principal, and the question was whether on the terminology then applicable he dealt in goods of that description or not. It was thought that this could be prejudicial to third parties who bought from professional agents (such as auctioneers) on whom they relied, and had no knowledge of the principal's position in this respect, but should be entitled to assume in the absence of indication to the contrary that the sale was a business sale. The law was thus changed to make the principal prima facie liable in such a case. It should be noted that there are two ways of fixing the buyer with knowledge. If reasonable steps are taken (whether by the principal, the agent or anyone else) to bring the fact to the buyer's attention, this is sufficient even though the buyer never in fact understands that the seller is selling privately. The seller may not however rely on an allegation that the buyer ought reasonably to have discovered the fact from other sources: if he relies on information from such sources, he must prove actual knowledge in the buyer. It may be noted that since the question whether a sale is in the course of a business will not always be an easy one, the "fact" referred to will often not be easy to establish. It has been held that this provision applies even when the principal is completely undisclosed, so that the third party could not possibly know of him.[68] The agent in such a case is also liable as a party to the contract.[69] The decision applies to section 14(3) (on reasonable fitness for purpose[70]) as well as to section 14(2).

"Goods supplied under the contract". This wording did not appear in the original Act, which only referred to "the goods". The present wording was first introduced in 1973 to take into account case law under the old section which read the words "the goods" together with the words in the preamble to the section, which stated that except as specified there was no implied condition or warranty as to quality or fitness of "goods supplied under a contract of sale". The cases, confirmed by the amended wording of the subsection, held that the duty to supply merchantable (now, satisfactory) goods extended beyond the goods sold. Thus it was held under the original wording that the duty may extend to the container in which the goods are supplied, *e.g.* a bottle,[71] and in *Geddling v Marsh*,[72] section 14(3) 11–030

[68] *Boyter v Thomson* [1995] 2 A.C. 629; see Brown, 112 L.Q.R. 225 (1966).
[69] *Bowstead and Reynolds on Agency* (18th ed.), Art.76. But he would not be personally liable where the existence of a principal was disclosed except under the collateral undertakings entered into by auctioneers: see *ibid.*, para.9–021.
[70] Below, para.11–051.
[71] *Morelli v Fitch and Gibbons* [1928] 2 K.B. 636; *Niblett Ltd v Confectioners' Materials Co. Ltd* [1921] 3 K.B. 387.
[72] [1920] 1 K.B. 668. See also *Bradshaw v Boothe's Marine Ltd* (1973) 35 D.L.R. (3d) 43 (propane gas cylinder).

(at that time section 14(1))[73] was held to apply to a defective bottle supplied on the sale of mineral waters even though the bottle was for return when empty, remained the property of the seller and so was not the subject of any sale. But there may be cases where packaging is something totally separate from the thing sold, so that the quality of the goods is not affected by a defect in it: thus in an old case it was held on the sale of a cargo of oil that the subject-matter of that particular sale was merchantable though the oil was in fact delivered in unseasoned casks.[74] In *Wilson v Rickett, Cockerell & Co. Ltd*,[75] a slightly different point arose: on a sale of Coalite, a consignment, satisfactory in other respects, was delivered in which a piece of explosive had become accidentally mixed, probably while the goods were in transit. There was an explosion while some of the Coalite was being burned, and the seller was sued under section 14(2). The Court of Appeal refused to accept the argument that the Coalite was suitable for burning and that the explosive was not part of the goods. Denning L.J. saying "In my opinion [goods] means the goods delivered in purported pursuance of the contract."[76]

11–031 **Satisfactory quality.** The formulation of the general quality requirement set out in section 14(2A) of the Sale of Goods Act 1979 is in substitution for the original requirement of "merchantable" quality of the 1893 Act. This word was particularly appropriate to commercial sales, and led to decisions that goods might be merchantable if, although they were unsuited to the purpose for which they had been bought, they could be used or sold for some other purpose,[77] or if they were only unsuitable in a minor way,[78] or if only a small proportion of a bulk was unmerchantable.[79] Merchants may be assumed to be able to deal with this, but a consumer would be likely to have only one use for goods bought, and for consumer (and other not purely commercial) sales the notion of merchantable quality was inappropriate. A definition inserted in 1973[80] stressed the notion of fitness for purpose (despite this appearing also in section 14(3)), but could have been taken to require fitness for *all* purposes. It also, by using the words "as it is reasonable to expect", gave some scope for argument that, *inter alia*, manufactured products were often somewhat defective. The intention

---

[73] Below, paras 11–051 *et seq*.
[74] *Gower v Von Dedalzen* (1837) 3 Bing.N.C. 717. Contrast *Silbert Sharp and Bishop Ltd v Geo. Wills & Co. Ltd* [1919] S.A.L.R. 114 (sale of cases of pears—goods unmerchantable when cases in bad condition).
[75] [1954] 1 Q.B. 598; see also *Chaproniere v Mason* (1905) 21 T.L.R. 633 (stone in bath bun); *Frost v Aylesbury Dairy Co.* [1905] 1 K.B. 608 (typhoid germs in milk); *Albright & Wilson UK Ltd v Biachem Ltd* [2001] EWCA Civ 301; [2001] 2 All E.R. (Comm.) 537 (two consignments mixed by delivery firm).
[76] At p.607. *Cf. Flippo v Mode O'Day Frock Shops of Hollywood*, 449 S.W. 2d 692 (1970) (bite by spider concealed in slacks: slacks merchantable, as spider not part of goods).
[77] *Henry Kendall & Sons v William Lillico & Sons Ltd* (the *Hardwick Game Farm* case) [1969] 2 A.C. 31 (groundnut extraction).
[78] *Millar's of Falkirk Ltd v Turpie* 1979 S.L.T. (Notes) 66 (car).
[79] *Cehave NV v Bremer Handelsgesellschaft mbH (The Hansa Nord)* [1976] Q.B. 44 (bulk commodity shipment).
[80] By the Supply of Goods (Implied Terms) Act 1973.

behind the present formulation was to eschew fitness for purpose as a controlling notion, and also other general criteria that had been suggested such as acceptability, and to supplement a very general definition with guidelines (including fitness for purpose). The formulation eventually adopted was therefore somewhat anodyne, and also circular: "goods are of satisfactory quality if they meet the standard that a reasonable person would regard as satisfactory".[81] It requires the support of the guidelines which follow, which identify matters which had caused difficulty in disputes. The reasonable person must be one who is in the position of the buyer, with his knowledge; it would not be appropriate for the test to be based on a reasonable third party observer not acquainted with the transaction and its background.[82]

Matters to be taken into account. Two specific matters are here mentioned prior to the guidelines: any description of the goods and the price if relevant. To take an extreme example of description, it is obvious that if goods are sold as scrap, they need not have the quality which might have been expected when they were in working order; and the price may be an indication of the standard to be expected of second-hand goods.[83] It seems likely that the word can cover other descriptive statements than those which would be relevant under section 13.[84] Equally, the price may be an indicator of expected quality. But it cannot be conclusive: the buyer might have agreed too pay too high a price. What he is entitled to is something reasonably in line with what he had paid: "if not to the value of his money, at least to a grade not entirely and hopelessly out of line with what he has paid".[85] On the other hand, goods may be of unsatisfactory quality though the difference between their price and their actual sale value is slight.[86] 11–032

Further matter for consumer sales. The amendments to the Sale of Goods Act introduced for consumer sales by the Sale and Supply of Goods to Consumers Regulations 2002[87] add a further matter of which account is 11–033

[81] Dealing with the problem in a negative way by seeking to define the defects from which the goods must not suffer (a civil law approach deriving from Roman law) was never thought appropriate.

[82] See *Bramhill v Edwards* [2004] EWCA Civ 403; [2004] 2 Lloyd's Rep. 653, *per* Auld L.J. at [39]; also holding that if the judge finds that reasonable persons could disagree, the matter is to be settled by the burden of proof on the person alleging defective quality.

[83] See *Thain v Anniesland Trade Centre* 1997 S.C.L.R. 991 (Sh.Ct.)(a case on the present definition), where a 5/6-year-old Renault car with 80,000 miles on the odometer was sold for £2,995. The gearbox began to fail within two weeks. It was held that the car was as good as could be expected in the circumstances of the sale.

[84] See *Harlingdon and Leinster Enterprises Ltd v Christopher Hull Fine Arts Ltd* [1991] 1 Q.B. 564 at 565, 583: *cf.* 586.

[85] *BS Brown Ltd v Craiks Ltd* [1970] 1 W.L.R. 750 at 760, HL, *per* Viscount Dilhorne (cloth bought for resale as dress material: unsuitable for this but suitable for industrial use: merchantable).

[86] *Jackson v Rotax Motor and Cycle Co. Ltd* [1910] 2 K.B. 937 (dented and scratched motor horns); *IBM Co. Ltd v Shcherban* [1925] 1 D.L.R. 864 (glass covering dial of scale); *Winsley Bros v Woodfield Importing Co.* [1929] N.Z.L.R. 480 (broken shield and set-screw on thicknessing machine).

[87] See above para. 11–026; below, paras 12–071, 14–008 *et seq.*, esp. 14–010.

to be taken: public statements regarding the goods. It applies where the buyer "deals as consumer".[88] The Regulations, while they achieve significant changes regarding consumer remedies, have no other effect in the area of quality requirements, because although the EC Directive which they implement contains provisions on conformity and quality of consumer goods, these are, except as follows, broadly consistent with the general rule of English law and were deemed not to require restating in different words.[89] The new matters to be taken into account are stated in three new subsections added after section 14(2C) and appear above in the full statement of section 14(2).[90]

11–034 **"Public statements, particularly in advertising or labelling".** Such statements when made by the seller might be contractual promises, or misrepresentations inducing the contract. When made by a manufacturer or distributor they might be relevant to the description of the goods even when sold by others (*e.g.* a substance labelled as a "cough mixture" which would have no effect on coughs and hence would not be cough mixture at all). They might also indicate the description of the goods to which the quality provisions are then to be applied, for instance where goods are described as "cleaning fluid" but actually, though the fluid certainly cleans, it is unsafe because of excess acidity, so is not of satisfactory quality, or car polish is polish but does not provide the rust protection claimed. For commercial sales this is still so. However, there was no clear guidance as to when such statements were to be taken into account in the application of the normal rules and criteria in this way, and this was especially so when claims were made in general advertising. This provision gives a specific warrant for taking such matters into account in consumer sales. Its meaning is fairly self-explanatory, but argument may no doubt arise as to what is a "public statement" (though some guidance is given by the reference to advertising or labelling; the former no doubt includes television and radio advertising and posters); and "specific characteristics".

11–035 **By whom made.** The statements must be made by "the seller, the producer or his representative". "Producer" is defined in Regulation 6, amending section 61(1) of the 1979 Act, as meaning "the manufacturer of goods, the importer of goods into the European Economic Area[91] or any person purporting to be a producer by placing his name, trade mark or other distinctive sign on the goods." The words "or his representative" are puzzling: whose representative? The normal grammatical construction would be that only the producer's representative is referred to. This seems to omit cases where the statements are made by a representative of the

---

[88] This phrase, which applies to most of the changes made by the Regulations, is taken from the Unfair Contract Terms Act 1977, and is discussed under that head: see below, paras. 13–070 *et seq.*.

[89] For a detailed comparison between the directive and its implementation in the United Kingdom in this context see *Blackstone's Guide to Consumer Sales and Associated Guarantees* (2003), pp.71 *et seq.*

[90] Para. 11–026.

[91] The EU countries with the addition of Norway, Iceland and Liechtenstein.

seller: but perhaps these will be dealt with under the general law of agency as statements of the seller himself. It is then not clear why the same reasoning could not be used of the producer's representative, unless it be thought that agency reasoning is confined to contract situations. The word "representative" is imprecise even if no other word would obviously be better, and it may give rise to argument.

Withdrawal of statements. The criteria in subsection (2E) seem fairly obvious, and the idea of public correction would refer primarily to a withdrawal in the same medium, or the same level of publicity as that used for the statement in the first place. Situations could certainly arise, however, where a withdrawal of a statement would require more publicity than the original statement itself. It should be noted that it is the seller who has to show these features, since it is his liability under section 14(2) that is in issue; and that subsection (2C)(c) requires that the decision to buy *could not* have been influenced by the statement. This prevents arguments about whether it *was* so influenced, and makes the burden of proof on the seller a heavy one. **11–036**

Preservation of existing laws. Subsection (2F) simply preserves the possibilities of such statements being relevant to the seller's duties under the existing rules, as adumbrated above, and indicates that the substance of section 14(2D) and (2E) may, on appropriate facts, be applicable where the buyer does not deal as consumer. **11–037**

The guidelines: fitness for purpose, appearance and finish, minor defects. Section 14(2B)[92] seeks to solve other problems perceived as arising under the 1973 definition, by specifying non-exhaustive guidelines. "Quality" is first stated to include the state and condition of the goods. This involves no more than a transfer to this place in the Act of words which previously appeared in the interpretation section.[93] Of the following guidelines, fitness for purpose, which was prominent in the 1973 definition, is placed first: it is obviously the most relevant factor and the only objection had been to it appearing to override other factors. It should be noted however that the fitness required is for "*all* the purposes for which goods of the kind in question are commonly supplied." This would seem to require the goods to be fit for all normal purposes, but not for abnormal ones. As such it appears to go somewhat further than the previous law, and it was intended to do so. However, the reference to the purpose for which such goods are *commonly* supplied may preserve some flexibility for the courts.[94] There follows a new element: a specific reference to appearance and finish, directed principally towards consumer goods and intended to deal with such defects as scratches on cars which could be said not to affect their fitness for their purpose. The following reference to freedom from minor defects (some of which would not affect fitness for purpose or safety) has the same **11–038**

---

[92] Above, para.11–026.
[93] s.61.
[94] See Law Com. No. 160, Scot. Law Com. No. 104 (1987), paras 3.31 *et seq.*

objective. It may be that they are unnecessary: dicta on the 1973 definition of Mustill L.J. in *Rogers v Parish (Scarborough) Ltd*[95] had sought to give guidance on this very point. But the Court of Appeal is not always invoked in disputes over the quality of goods supplied. The guidelines should make it clearer to all tribunals at every level, especially in consumer cases, that such defects may render goods of unsatisfactory quality, without the need for guidance from appellate courts.

11–039 **Safety.** Although safety is usually an important aspect of fitness for purpose, it was thought appropriate to add a specific reference to this feature.[96] In commercial contracts it can of course be the case that a buyer buys goods known to be unsafe; and this may occur even in consumer contracts, as in the case of cigarettes. Such variations are picked up by the general wording of sections (2A) and (2B). It had been said before the reforms of 1994 (though in a speech dissenting on the general point in connection with which the words were uttered) that a potentially dangerous article might be unmerchantable if not accompanied by appropriate instructions as to use.[97] It may also be so if misdescribed on its wrapper or in an accompanying document.[98] This seems correct, and indeed there can presumably be goods, not dangerous, which are unusable, or not efficiently usable, without adequate instructions or warnings (for example, as to compatibility with other equipment), and so not up to the present requirement of satisfactory quality, unless such instructions are supplied or available.[99] The specific reference to safety in the new formulation makes this clear. Problems may nevertheless arise when the lack of safety is not known to the buyer or seller. The duty to warn may also be based on a separate implied term,[1] or on tort.[2] The supply of unsafe goods may also be an offence, and give rise to civil liability, under the Consumer Protection Act 1987.[3]

11–040 **Durability.** In principle durability is an aspect of quality on delivery: goods are not of satisfactory quality at that time unless they are capable of enduring for a period reasonable in the circumstances, and the fact that

---

95 [1987] Q.B. 933: "not merely the buyer's purpose of driving the car from one place to another, but of doing so with an appropriate degree of comfort, ease of handling and reliability, and, one may add, of pride in the vehicle's outward and interior appearance".

96 See Law Com. No. 160, Scot. Law Com. No. 104 (1987), paras 3–44, 3–46.

97 *Henry Kendall & Sons v William Lillico & Sons Ltd* [1969] 2 A.C. 31 at 119, *per* Lord Pearce.

98 See *Wormell v RHM Agricultural (East) Ltd* [1986] 1 W.L.R. 36 (revsd. on other grounds [1987] 1 W.L.R. 1091). But *cf. Milne Construction Ltd v Expandite Ltd* [1984] 2 N.Z.L.R. 163 at 185–186 (epoxy resin for bonding concrete); *Buchan v Ortho Pharmaceutical (Canada) Ltd* (1984) 8 D.L.R. (4th) 373 (oral contraceptive) (affirmed on other grounds (1986) 25 D.L.R. (4th) 658). See as to the significance of instructions in consumer sales in general, McLeod, 97 L.Q.R. 550 (1981); Brown [1988] L.M.C.L.Q. 502; Hedley [2001] J.B.L. 114.

99 See *Albright & Wilson UK Ltd v Biachem Ltd* [2001] EWCA Civ 301; [2002] 2 All E.R. (Comm) 537, where misdescription of chemicals caused an explosion.

1 Below, para.11–089.

2 Below, paras 12–121 *et seq.*, 13–099, 13–100.

3 Below, paras 14–080 *et seq.*, 14–095.

they seriously deteriorate or (for example) break down during such a period is evidence that they were not of satisfactory quality. In sales involving extended transport of the goods, it has been said that there is a special continuing duty, that the goods will not only be of the appropriate quality at the time of shipment but will remain so during transit and for a reasonable time thereafter.[4] Even assuming that this exists as a special implied term, for most sales, the fact that the goods do not last the period which might be expected is no more than a symptom of their inappropriate quality, state or condition at the time referred to in paragraph 11–049.[5] The extent of inherent durability to be expected will therefore depend on the circumstances of the sale, such as the description applied to them, the price,[6] whether or not transport of them is contemplated,[7] and so forth. It is however true that the lack of specific reference to enduring quality could encourage tribunals to proceed on the basis that if the qualities required are present at the requisite moment that is enough. This can be an important point in many consumer disputes,[8] and hence a specific reference to durability was included in the guidelines.[9] Even so, there will in many

---

[4] See *Lambert v Lewis* [1982] A.C. 225 at 276, *per* Lord Diplock (domestic sale); see also *Mash & Murrell Ltd v Joseph I Emanuel Ltd* [1961] 1 W.L.R. 862 at 870 (but *cf.* p.872) *per* Diplock J., following dicta in *Beer v Walker* (1877) 46 L.J.Q.B. 677 and *Ollett v Jordan* [1918] 2 K.B. 41 at 47. The decision in *Mash & Murrell* was revsd. on other grounds [1961] 2 Lloyd's Rep. 326 (c. & f. sale: potatoes). In *Cordova Land Co. Ltd v Victor Bros Inc.* [1966] 1 W.L.R. 793, the Court of Appeal did not accept that for the purposes of jurisdiction a breach of a c.i.f. contract occurred at the place where the goods arrived deteriorated, at any rate where the goods were not perishable. It is submitted that no such breach would normally occur even where the goods are perishable. It would in any case be odd to imply a higher duty for perishables than for non-perishables. See also below, paras 18–255 *et seq.*

[5] See *M P Evanghelinos v Leslie & Anderson* (1920) 4 Ll.L.R. 17 (tinned Japanese salmon); *A B Kemp Ltd v Tolland* [1956] 2 Lloyd's Rep. 681 (Italian peaches); *Shillingford v Baron* [1959] 2 Lloyd's Rep. 453 (sugar syrup); *Gardano and Giamperi v Greek Petroleum George Mamidakis & Co.* [1962] 1 W.L.R. 40 at 53 (kerosene); *Oleificio Zucchi SpA v Northern Sales Ltd* [1965] 2 Lloyd's Rep. 496 at 517 (rape seed screenings); *Crowther v Shannon Motor Co.* [1975] 1 W.L.R. 30 (second-hand car: see Hudson, 94 L.Q.R. 566 (1978) suggesting that the dicta give too limited a scope to the need for durability); *Lee v York Coach and Marine* [1977] R.T.R. 35 (second-hand car). In *Preist v Last* [1903] 2 K.B. 148, a hot-water bottle burst after five days' use and there was liability under s.14(3). See also *Knutsen v Mauritzen* 1918 1 S.L.T. 85 (salted mutton for ship's stores); *Godley v Perry* [1960] 1 W.L.R. 9 (catapult: two days); *Pacific Produce Co. Ltd v Franklin Co-operative Growers Ltd* [1968] N.Z.L.R. 521 at 523–524 (onions); *Guarantee Trust of Jersey Ltd v Gardner* (1973) 117 S.J. 564 (hot drink machine: one week); *Georgetown Seafoods Ltd v Usen Fisheries Ltd* (1977) 78 D.L.R. (3d) 542 (fish). See also Vienna Convention (above, para.1–024), Art. 36(2).

[6] See *Thain v Anniesland Trade Centre* 1997 S.C.L.R. 991 (Sh.Ct.), above, para.11–032, n.83.

[7] Thus where all goods of the type involved would suffer a risk of deterioration in transit, such deterioration will not indicate a breach of the seller's obligations. See *Broome v Pardess Cooperative Society of Orange Growers* [1940] 1 All E.R. 603; *cf.* *Bull v Robison* (1854) 10 Exch. 342 (rust on iron). As to deterioration where the seller agrees to deliver at his own risk see above, para.6–022, below, paras 18–249 *et seq.*

[8] See "Faulty Goods" (National Consumer Council, 1981); Ervine, 1984 Jur. Rev. 147.

[9] See Law Com. No. 160, Scot. Law Com. No. 104 (1987), paras 3.47 *et seq.*

cases be difficulty in proving that the lack of durability resulted from a defect in the goods themselves rather than from the way in which they have been treated, used and maintained. And a specific provision as to durability such as this would ideally require an implied promise that the goods would last, and a right to reject which persists for a longer time than the law normally allows, for in the case of goods which may be expected to last for a long period, any lack of durability could take some time to manifest itself. Such an extended right to reject was indeed urged in the consumer interest,[10] but was not taken up in the modifications to the Act.[11]

11–041 **First exception: defects specifically drawn to the buyer's attention.** By subsection (2C) "The term implied by subsection (2) above does not extend to any matters making the quality of the goods unsatisfactory—(a) which is specifically drawn to the buyer's attention before the contract is made." This exception did not appear in the 1893 Act: the present version is a reformulation of wording of 1973, but the change does not appear significant in substance. Under the 1893 Act, the fact that defects had been pointed out might of course affect the description under which the goods were sold and thus the standard of merchantable quality required, and this is now even more likely in view of the statutory definition of satisfactory quality, which actually refers to the description applied to the goods. But the fact that defects are pointed out is now stated as a specific factor relevant to the ascertainment of satisfactory quality. Presumably, the burden is on a seller who seeks to rely on this exception to allege and prove facts bringing himself within it. There is however no requirement that it must have been the seller who drew the buyer's attention to the defect.

11–042 **Second exception: examination of goods.** Section 14(2C) contains a second exception which was, in a different form, the only exception in section 14(2) as it previously stood.[12] By subsection (2C) "The term implied by section 14(2) above does not extent to any matter making the quality of the goods unsatisfactory—(b) where the buyer examines the goods before the contract is made, which that examination ought to reveal." There are only minor differences in drafting between the present and earlier versions: the main change is that the present version (as did that of 1973) specifically requires the examination to have taken place before the contract was

[10] *e.g.* Ontario Law Commission, *Report on Sale of Goods* (1979), Vol.1, pp.215–216; Law Com. No. 95 (1979), pp.32–36; Law Com. W.P. No. 85, Sc. Law Com. C.M. No. 58 (1983), pp.63–64 (dismissing however at pp.85–89 the notion of a long-term right to reject); Goode, *Commercial Law* (3rd ed.), pp.308–309. The EC Directive on the Sale of Consumer Goods and Associated Guarantees (see below, paras 14–008 *et seq.*) provides for a presumption that lack of conformity becoming manifest within six months of delivery shall be presumed to have existed at the time of delivery unless such a presumption is incompatible with the notion of the goods or the nature of the lack of conformity; Art. 5. For implementation see below, para.12–075.

[11] See Law Com. No. 160, Scot. Law Com. No. 104 (1987), paras 5.6–5.13.

[12] If the buyer takes possession of the goods before the contract is actually made, and acquires notice of a defect, it may be that he loses his right under s.14(2) if he fails to return the goods or negotiate for rectification of the defect; see *R & B Customs Brokers Co. Ltd v United Dominions Trust Ltd* [1988] 1 W.L.R. 321.

made.[13] Thus cases on the original provision may be relevant. Examples of defects which examination would not have revealed are arsenic in beer[14] and defective manufacture of a plastic catapult.[15] But it was held under the 1893 provision that if there had been an examination, the buyer would not be able to sue though it was so hastily or inefficiently conducted that the defect was not detected: in *Thornett and Fehr v Beers & Son*[16] the proviso was applied where the buyer had examined barrels of glue only from the outside because of shortage of time, though he had been offered further facilities. This surprising decision seems to have been based on the fact that a full examination had been intended, and every facility for it provided by the seller.[17] The 1893 provision referred to "defects which *such* examination ought to have revealed", and the present wording appears to have been intended to make clear that the examination referred to is that actually carried out. It is in any case clear that for the proviso to operate there must have been some examination, however incomplete: its wording does not cover the situation where the buyer could have examined but did not, however unreasonable this may have been[18]; though under the law as it stood prior to 1893 the warranty of merchantable quality would not have applied in such circumstances.[19] But it is possible that in some cases a buyer may be estopped from saying that he has not examined the goods.[20] Again, the burden is presumably on the seller to allege and prove facts bringing himself within the exception.

Extent of duty. The duty to supply satisfactory goods is and has always been strict; it is no defence that all possible care was taken, nor that the seller had not seen the goods,[21] nor that they were available from one supplier only,[22] nor that the seller relied on an undertaking given by his own supplier.[23] 11–043

---

[13] See *Taylor v Combined Buyers Ltd* [1924] N.Z.L.R. 627 at 635.
[14] *Wren v Holt* [1903] 1 K.B. 610; *Canada-Atlantic Grain Export Co. Inc. v Eilers* (1929) 35 Ll. L. Rep. 206 (barley affected by defect only apperent on bacteriological examination).
[15] *Godley v Perry* [1960] 1 W.L.R. 9 at 15.
[16] [1919] 1 K.B. 486.
[17] Contrast *Frank v Grosvenor Motor Auctions Ltd* [1960] V.R. 607 at 609, where it is suggested that where the purchaser of a car sits in it and looks at it the proviso only applies to such defects as that limited examination could be expected to reveal.
[18] This point appears to have been overlooked in *Bramhill v Edwards*, n.27 below, at [49]–[54].
[19] *Jones v Just* (1868) L.R. 3 Q.B. 197 at 202; *Wallis v Russell* [1902] 2 I.R. 585 at 593–594, 596–597; and see the original draft of this section in Chalmers, *Sale of Goods* (1st ed., 1890), p.20.
[20] This question was left open in *Thornett and Fehr v Beers & Son*, above; see also n.12 above;*Lowe v Lombank Ltd* [1960] 1 W.L.R. 196, below, para.13–030.
[21] *Grant v Australian Knitting Mills Ltd* [1936] A.C. 85 at 100.
[22] *Young & Marten Ltd v McManus Childs Ltd* [1969] 1 A.C. 454.
[23] But *cf.* Vienna Convention (above, para.1–024), Art.79.

11–044 **Examples.** There are few reported cases, and fewer cases of significance, on the interpretation of the phrase "satisfactory quality" since it came into operation in 1995. Perhaps this indicates that the definition has been successful, and that the problems were caused by the specific nature of the previous term "merchantable" and the failure of attempts, whether in judgments or statute, to define it. Attention may be drawn to three cases.[24] In the first it was held that CO_2 contaminated with benzene, a known carcinogen, though in a quantity not injurious to health, was not of satisfactory quality.[25] In the second, electric boilers which depended on peak-rate electricity making them expensive to run, and thus diminishing the home energy rating (dependent on several factors, including, for example, insulation) were held of satisfactory quality.[26] In the third a mobile home that was two inches wider than was permitted under statutory instrument was held of satisfactory quality when evidence had been given that the chances of enforcement of the regulation were small and that this feature was not relevant as regards insurance.[27] Beyond these rather specialised applications of section 14(2), well-established illustrations may be looked to and are certainly still cited, though the difference between the former notion of merchantable quality and the present formulation must always be borne in mind. Examples, other than those already discussed, in which the term as to merchantable quality was held to have been broken include beer contaminated with arsenic,[28] dented and scratched motor horns,[29] buses of weak construction,[30] a power boat which caught fire and became a total loss within 27 hours of delivery,[31] a new car containing defects requiring the provision of a new crankshaft, exhaust, radiator and clutch assembly,[32] underpants containing excess sulphite which irritated the skin,[33] a bottle which broke when the cork was drawn,[34] and tins of preserved milk carrying labels which infringed an English trade mark in such a way that their sale could have been restrained by injunction.[35] The last case was distinguished in a case where tonic water was sold for resale in Argentina, but owing to its containing salicylic acid was in fact unsaleable

---

[24] *Thain v Anniesland Trade Centre*, above, n.6, is also a case on the new definition.

[25] *Britvic Soft Drinks Ltd v Messer UK Ltd* [2002] 1 Lloyd's Rep. 20; partly modified without reference to this point [2003] EWCA Civ 548; [2002] 2 Lloyd's Rep 368.

[26] *Jewson Ltd v Boyhan* [2003] EWCA Civ 1030; [2004] 1 Lloyd's Rep. 505. Sedley L.J. said that s.14(2) is directed primarily at "substandard goods": at [77].

[27] *Bramhill v Edwards* [2004] EWCA Civ 403; [2004] 2 Lloyd's Rep. 653. See Twigg-Flesner (2005) 121 L.Q.R. 205.

[28] *Wren v Holt* [1903] 1 K.B. 610.

[29] *Jackson v Rotax Motor and Cycle Co.* [1910] 2 K.B. 937.

[30] *Bristol Tramways, etc., Carriage Co. Ltd v Fiat Motors Ltd* [1910] 2 K.B. 831.

[31] *Rasbora Ltd v J C L Marine Ltd* [1977] 1 Lloyd's Rep. 645 (under statutory definition).

[32] *Jackson v Chrysler Acceptances Ltd* [1978] R.T.R. 474; see also *Bernstein v Pamson Motors (Golders Green) Ltd* [1987] 2 All E.R. 220; *Rogers v Parish (Scarborough) Ltd* [1987] Q.B. 933. *Cf. Leaves v Wadham Stringer (Cliftons) Ltd* [1980] R.T.R. 308 (car merchantable despite many irritating defects). Claims in respect of new cars were formerly more successful under s.14(3): see below, para.11–057, and as to cars in general, Whincup, 38 M.L.R. 660 (1975).

[33] *Grant v Australian Knitting Mills Ltd* [1936] A.C. 85.

[34] *Morelli v Fitch and Gibbons* [1928] 2 K.B. 636.

[35] *Niblett v Confectioners Materials Co. Ltd* [1921] 3 K.B. 387: but see below.

there by law; it could have been sold anywhere else and so was merchantable, whereas a person buying the tins of milk anywhere in the world might be buying a lawsuit.[36] It was held that goods were not unmerchantable merely because they might prove unsatisfactory if improperly treated or used: thus a pork chop which proved poisonous when undercooked was not unmerchantable, because it would have caused no ill effects had it been properly cooked.[37] On the other hand, goods were held unmerchantable though they could be made merchantable for a trifling cost[38]; and a consignment of a commodity has been held unmerchantable where the proportion of the contents which was unsatisfactory exceeded an amount which would fall under the *de minimis* rule.[39] It may be assumed that many of these cases win (with caution) serve as examples of the present notion of "satisfactory quality".

Doubtful questions: effect of subsequently acquired knowledge. The time at which goods must be of satisfactory quality seems prima facie to be the time of sale.[40] In order to ascertain whether they were then of such quality, however, it is necessary to assume knowledge of the defect which had not then manifested itself and ask whether (on the present wording) a reasonable person would regard the goods with that defect as satisfactory. But in *Henry Kendall & Sons v William Lillico & Sons Ltd*[41] a further problem arose. At the time of sale groundnuts would have been regarded, had the defect been known, as poisonous and therefore would probably have been unsaleable at least at a comparable price. Subsequently however it was discovered that they could be safely fed to some animals at a limited rate of inclusion. In assessing whether they were merchantable at the time 11–045

---

[36] *Summer, Permain & Co. v Webb & Co.* [1922] 1 K.B. 55, where the court had difficulty in distinguishing *Niblett's* case, above, which might therefore be better explained on the basis of breach of s.12(1). See also *Phoenix Distributors Ltd v L B Clarke (London) Ltd* [1966] 2 Lloyd's Rep. 285, affirmed [1967] 1 Lloyd's Rep. 518 (potatoes for export to Poland did not satisfy Polish import requirements but saleable elsewhere); *Buchanan-Jardine v Hamilink* 1983 S.L.T. 149 (temporary embargo on movement of herd at farm did not make cattle not of merchantable quality); *Harlingdon and Leinster Enterprises Ltd v Christopher Hull Fine Art Ltd* [1991] 1 Q.B. 564 (picture not by artist supposed: merchantable).

[37] *Heil v Hedges* [1951] 1 T.L.R. 512 (doubted for modern conditions by Atiyah, *Sale of Goods* (11th ed.), p.179, n.171); *Yachetti v John Duff & Sons Ltd* [1942] O.R. 682 (pork sausages).

[38] *Jackson v Rotax Motor and Cycle Co.* [1910] 2 K.B. 937 (dented and scratched motor horns); *Bernstein v Pamson Motors (Golders Green) Ltd* [1987] 2 All E.R. 220; above, para.11–037.

[39] *Jackson v Rotax Motor and Cycle Co.*, above; *Rapalli v K L Take Ltd* [1958] 2 Lloyd's Rep. 469 (onions 5–6 per cent undersized and 6–7 per cent sprouting). But *cf. FC Bradley & Sons Ltd v Colonial and Continental Trading Ltd* [1964] 2 Lloyd's Rep. 52 (potatoes 2 per cent infected by moth but later fumigated: merchantable); *Cehave NV v Bremer Handelsgesellschaft mbH (The Hansa Nord)* [1976] Q.B. 44, referred to above, para.11–031; *Marimpex Mineralöl Handelsgesellschaft mbH v Louis Dreyfus & Cie Mineralöl GmbH* [1995] 1 Lloyd's Rep. 167 (gasoil: 10 per cent contaminated and not fit for any purpose). Quite slight admixtures can, of course, lead to goods ceasing to comply with description: see above, paras 11–016, 11–020.

[40] Below, para.11–049.

[41] [1969] 2 A.C. 31.

of sale, was the subsequent knowledge of the contamination to be read in the light of the later knowledge of the effect of such contamination available at the time of the trial? Lord Reid thought so on the grounds that "it would be very artificial to bring in some part of the later knowledge and exclude other parts",[42] and Lord Guest agreed on the grounds that to do otherwise would be "to approach the true situation with blinkers".[43] It was therefore held that there had been no breach of section 14(2).

11–046 But, though the general decision as to quality may be accepted, the actual decision as to subsequently acquired knowledge is, it is submitted, more dubious.[44] There is much to be said for the dissenting view of Lord Pearce,[45] with which Lord Wilberforce agreed, that "As it is a hypothetical exercise, one must create a hypothetical market. Nevertheless the hypothetical market should be one that could have existed, not one which could *not* have existed at the date of delivery. Suppose goods contained a hidden deadly poison to which there was discovered by scientists two years after delivery a simple, easy, inexpensive antidote which could render the goods harmless. They would be unmarketable at the date of delivery." It is submitted that this view is preferable, and that the same approach should be applied to the reverse situation, where goods thought safe at the time of sale were subsequently discovered to be unsafe.[46]

11–047 **Goods made up for buyer.** Where the seller makes up or compounds goods in exact accordance with instructions given by the buyer, it seems reasonable that he should answer for the quality of the material or ingredients which he supplies, but not for the quality of the finished product. It seems clear that he is liable to this extent, but it is not clear exactly how this result is to be reached in connection with section 14(2), as opposed to section 14(3).[47] One answer is to say that the condition as to quality of the actual goods is excluded by implication, but that equally by implication it attaches to the materials or ingredients.[48] In the case of a consumer sale, however, this explanation might cause difficulties in view of section 6(2) of the Unfair Contract Terms Act 1977.[49] Here it may be necessary to use another explanation, that the "goods supplied under the contract" are in such a case the ingredients. The use of the word "satisfactory" instead of "merchantable" may assist in reaching appropriate

---

[42] At p.75.
[43] At pp.108–109.
[44] Though such reasoning could certainly in some cases be relevant to a claim for damages. See below, paras 17–057 *et seq.*
[45] At p.119.
[46] See Goode, *Commercial Law* (3rd ed.), pp.313–314. It is arguable that the requirement in section 14(3) (below, paras 11–064 *et seq.*) of reasonable fitness for purpose is more abstract and can be proved to have been satisfied, or not to have been satisfied, in the light of later acquired knowledge. To accept this view would be to place a heavy burden on the seller.
[47] Below, paras 11–051 *et seq.*
[48] See *Ashington Piggeries Ltd v Christopher Hill Ltd* [1972] A.C. 441 at 494; *Bowen v R B Young Products Pty Ltd* [1967] W.A.R. 97 at 105 (poultry feed).
[49] Below, para.13–083.

solutions, if one assumes that the "reasonable person" is in the position of the buyer.[50]

Second-hand goods. There is little authority as to second-hand goods. It was clear before the enactment of the present, and indeed the earlier, statutory definition that a lesser standard is to be exacted than that applicable to new goods: thus a car sold with a reservation as to the condition of the clutch was held merchantable though the actual state of the clutch proved to have been much worse than believed with the result that complete replacement was required at substantial cost.[51] In the same case it was suggested that a second-hand car was merchantable if it was "in a roadworthy condition, fit to be driven along the road in safety"[52]: but while an unroadworthy car would certainly not be merchantable, at least if sold as a car[53] the test was too limited.[54] So in another case a car was held not to be reasonably fit for its purpose under section 14(3)[55] because the engine was "clapped out", though it did not fail completely for a further 2,300 miles.[56] More recently a Fiat sports car bought as an enthusiast's car was held unmerchantable because it had, unknown to the buyer, been submerged in water for 24 hours and written off by an insurance company: though there had been only minor mechanical problems after the buyer took delivery.[57] The new statutory definition[58] gives some guidance. The fact that goods are second-hand affects the description applied to them, their price and may give rise to "other relevant circumstances": and the exception as to examination will be more relevant in second-hand sales. It may also affect their appearance and finish, freedom from minor defects and durability.[59] 11–048

[50] See *Britvic Soft Drinks Ltd v Messer UK Ltd* [2001] 1 Lloyd's Rep. 20 (CO_2 contaminated with benzene: contract required compliance with BS4105 but such compliance did not exclude duty to furnish goods of satisfactory quality). Part of this decision was modified on appeal without reference to this point, [2002] EWCA Civ 548; [2002] 2 Lloyd's Rep. 368.

[51] *Bartlett v Sidney Marcus Ltd* [1965] 1 W.L.R. 1013: see also *Business Applications Specialists Ltd v Nationwide Credit Corp. Ltd* [1988] R.T.R. 332 (car merchantable though broke down after 800 miles); *Lee v York Coach and Marine* [1977] R.T.R. 35 (corrosion in brake piping: unmerchantable).

[52] At p.1017.

[53] *Bernstein v Pamson Motors (Golders Green) Ltd* [1987] 2 All E.R. 220 at 226.

[54] *Business Applications Specialists Ltd v Nationwide Credit Corp. Ltd*, above, following dicta in *Rogers v Parish (Scarborough) Ltd*, [1987] Q.B. 933, above, para.11–038, n.95. See also *Thain v Anniesland Trade Centre* 1997 S.L.T. (Sh. Ct.) 102, above, para.11–032, n.83.

[55] Below, paras 11–051 *et seq*.

[56] *Crowther v Shannnon Motor Co.* [1975] 1 W.L.R. 30 (see Hudson, 94 L.Q.R. 566 (1978)); see also a similar discussion on a second-hand Rolls-Royce, *Keeley v Guy McDonald Ltd* (1984) 134 N.L.J. 706. See further as to cars Whincup, 38 M.L.R. 660 (1975).

[57] *Shine v General Guarantee Corp.* [1988] 1 All E.R. 911.

[58] Above. para.11–026.

[59] As to durability see above, para.11–040.

11–049 **Time element.** It is not clear exactly at what time the goods must be of satisfactory quality. The same problem arises, subject to one slight difference,[60] in connection with section 14(3)[61] and what follows applies in general to both provisions. Some authority (necessarily on the "merchantable" standard) refers to the time of sale,[62] which should on the general principles of the Sale of Goods Act be the time at which the property passes[63], at which time the risk prima facie passes in a commercial transaction.[64] On the other hand it is clear that in commercial c.i.f., c.& f. and f.o.b. contracts, where property and risk are commonly separated, the duty normally relates to the time of shipment, which is normally when the risk passes in such contracts.[65] Although the law might be expected to be better worked out in that area, many sales involve transportation of the goods and there seems no reason for a difference in principle. There are also statements, doubtless correct on the facts of the cases involved, that the duty relates to the time of delivery.[66] In view of the connections between the duties under section 14 and the passing of risk, it seems reasonable to say that the goods must be of the quality requisite under section 14 at the time of the passing of property, or, where property and risk are separated, at the time of the passing of risk,[67] either of which may be at the time of delivery, unless there are other indications.[68] But it would surely be wrong to suggest that where a commercial seller holds specific goods for a buyer, property and risk having passed, and they are damaged before delivery without the seller's fault, the buyer can require compliance with section 14 at the time of delivery; or that where risk has passed but not property (*e.g.* because the seller has reserved it until payment) the duty under the section has not yet attached. On the other hand, in consumer transactions,[69] where risk now passes only on delivery of the goods whether or not the property has passed, it must follow that the duty relates to the tune of delivery.[70]

---

[60] The question of special reliance: below, para.11–067.
[61] Below, paras 11–051 *et seq.*
[62] *A B Kemp Ltd v Tolland* [1956] 2 Lloyd's Rep. 681 at 685, 691; *Crowther v Shannon Motor Co.* [1975] 1 W.L.R. 30 at 33; *R & B Customs Brokers Ltd v United Dominions Trust Ltd* [1988] 1 W.L.R. 321 at 326.
[63] Above, para.1–025.
[64] Above, para.6–002.
[65] Below, paras 19–110, 20–088.
[66] *Henry Kendall & Sons v William Lillico & Sons Ltd* [1969] 2 A.C. 31 at 118; *Lambert v Lewis* [1982] A.C. 225 at 276; *Jackson v Rotax Motor and Cycle Co.* [1910] 2 K.B. 937 at 945; *Lee v York Coach and Marine* [1977] R.T.R. 35 at 43; *Rogers v Parish (Scarborough) Ltd* [1987] Q.B. 933 at 944; *Viskase Ltd v Paul Kiefel GmbH* [1999] 1 W.L.R. 1305 at 1323.
[67] Williston, *Sales* (rev. ed., 1948), para.245. See also Vienna Convention (above, para.1–024), Art. 36(1).
[68] As in *Burnley Engineering Products Ltd v Cambridge Vacuum Engineering Ltd* (1994) 50 Con.L.R. 10, where a period of commissioning was appropriate, this deferring the date for full compliance with the quality obligation, but the risk in other respects may well have been on the purchaser.
[69] *i.e.*, where the buyer "deals as consumer": see above, para.11–033, below, paras 12–073, 13–071, *et seq.*, 14–008.
[70] See ss. 20(4), 32(4); above, paras 6–013 *et seq.* It seems that agreement to the contrary should be valid unless caught by unfair contract terms legislation: *ibid.* See further below, paras 18–256, 18–259 *et seq.*, 21–099.

Related contracts. Provisions similar to section 14(2) are implied into other contracts for the transfer of property in goods (*e.g.* contracts of exchange and for work and materials[71]); hire purchase agreements[72]; and contracts of hire.[73] The changes effected by the Sale and Supply of Goods Act 1994 as to the word "condition" and "satisfactory quality"[74] were written into these also.[75] Questions relating to computer software are more likely to arise in connection with section 14(3).[76] 11–050

(c) *Fitness for Purpose*

Sale of Goods Act 1979, s.14(3). Section 14(3) of the Sale of Goods Act 1979, which was substituted for the former section 14(1) by the Supply of Goods (Implied Terms) Act 1973 and further amended by the Consumer Credit Act 1974, reads: 11–051

> "Where the seller sells goods in the course of a business and the buyer, expressly or by implication, makes known—
>
> (a) to the seller, or
> (b) where the purchase price or part of it is payable by instalments and the goods were previously sold by a credit-broker to the seller, to that credit-broker,[77]
>
> any particular purpose for which the goods are being bought, there is an implied term that the goods supplied under the contract are reasonably fit for that purpose, whether or not that is a purpose for which such goods are commonly supplied, except where the circumstances show that the buyer does not rely, or that it is unreasonable for him to rely, on the skill or judgment of the seller or credit-broker."[78]

Section 14(6)[79] adds that "As regards England and Wales and Northern Ireland, the terms implied by subsections (2) and (3) above are condi-

---

71 Supply of Goods and Services Act 1982, s.4.
72 Supply of Goods (Implied Terms) Act 1973, s.10.
73 Supply of Goods and Services Act 1982, s.9.
74 Above, para.11–031.
75 Sale and Supply of Goods Act 1994, s.7 and Schs 2, 3. A similar result was achieved before the Act by applying the Sale of Goods Act by analogy. See *Young & Marten Ltd v McManus Childs Ltd* [1969] 1 A.C. 454; *Rotherham MBC v Frank Haslam Milan & Co. Ltd* (1996) 78 B.L.R. 1.
76 See below, para.11–069.
77 The references to the credit-broker were operative from 1985.
78 See also below, paras.18–274 *et seq.* as to international sales. *Cf.* Vienna Convention (above, para.1–024), Art. 35(2)(b); Uniform Commercial Code, s.2–315.
79 The designation of the term as a condition was originally contained in s.14(3) itself. The present formulation, with the use there of "term" and the addition of s.14(6), dates from the Sale and Supply of Goods Act 1994 (s.7 and Sch.2) and was adopted to facilitate the abolition of the term "condition" in the English law sense for Scots law.

tions."[80] When cases on fitness for purpose decided before the Act of 1973 are read, the fact that the relevant provision under the original Act of 1893 was designated section 14(1) should be borne in mind.

11–052 **"Sells goods in the course of a business".** These words, first inserted by the Act of 1973, are the same as those in the present section 14(2) and are discussed under that head.[81]

11–053 **Sale through an agent.** Where the seller sells through an agent, the position is now regulated by section 14(5) of the Sale of Goods Act 1979, first inserted in 1973. This provision applies equally to section 14(2) of the Act and is discussed in that connection.[82]

11–054 **"Goods supplied under the contract".** This phrase, also first introduced in 1973, appears also in section 14(2) and is discussed in that connection.[83]

11–055 **"Expressly or by implication makes known . . . to the seller . . . any particular purpose for which the goods are being bought".** These words follow the wording of the 1893 provision with only minor amendments. Cases on the 1893 provision are therefore certainly relevant. The obvious case to which the subsection is applicable is that where a buyer wishes to be supplied with something suitable for a special purpose. In such a case the request may but need not be found within the express contractual agreement: there may be notice of it from extrinsic communications,[84] from the purpose of the contract, *e.g.* where a propeller is ordered for a specific ship under construction,[85] or from the nature of the parties' business, *e.g.* where a dealer whose business is resale buys from another who is well aware of

---

[80] In general, breach of a condition entitles rejection (see above, paras 10–024 *et seq.*, below, paras 12–022 *et seq*). In non-consumer cases, a slight breach of an implied term may, however, not do so (see s.15A of the Act, below, paras 12–024 *et seq.*, 18–284). A buyer who deals as consumer is entitled under the Act to the benefit of a (rebuttable) presumption that the goods were non-compliant at the relevant time if they are non-compliant at any time during six months from delivery (s.48(2)(3); below, para. 12–075). This is part of new provisions providing special remedies for those who deal as consumers (below, paras 12–071, 14–008 *et seq*). The significance of "delivery" in this context is considered above, para.11–049.

[81] Above, paras 11–045, 11–046.

[82] Above, para.11–047.

[83] Above, para.11–048.

[84] *Bristol Tramways, etc., Carriage Co. Ltd v Fiat Motors Ltd* [1910] 2 K.B. 831, below, para.11–073; *Gillespie Bros & Co. v Cheney, Eggar & Co.* [1896] 2 Q.B. 59 (coal), in both of which there was a written contract not referring to the purpose for which the goods were required; *Jacobs v Scott & Co.* (1899) 2 F.(HL) 70 (hay); *Shields v Honeywill and Stein Ltd* [1953] 1 Lloyd's Rep. 357 (isopropyl alcohol).

[85] *Cammell Laird & Co. Ltd v Manganese Bronze and Brass Co. Ltd* [1934] A.C. 402; see also *Manchester Liners Ltd v Rea Ltd* [1922] 2 A.C. 74 (coal); *Hunter Engineering Co. Inc. v Syncrude Canada Ltd* [1989] 1 S.C.R. 426 (gearboxes); *Gibbett v Forwood Products Ltd* [2001] FCA (shavings for packing live crayfish); *cf. Hamilton v Papakura DC* [2002] UKPC 9; [2003] 3 N.Z.L.R. 308 (water supply damaged growing tomatoes: no indication of special purpose had been given, though it was known there were growers in the area).

this.[86] But, partly because of doubts prevalent at one time as to the scope of section 14(2),[87] the former provision was interpreted to cover more situations than this. It was held, first that "the particular purpose" did not only mean a special purpose[88]: if no purpose was indicated, it would be taken that goods were ordered for their normal purpose.[89] Where the description of the goods pointed to one purpose only, therefore, no further indication was required. Thus in *Preist v Last*[90] a person who went into a shop and asked for "a hot-water bottle" was held to rely on the seller's skill or judgment, and to be able to sue under the subsection when the hot-water bottle, by bursting, proved unfit for its purpose. The effect of these decisions, which improved the usefulness of the subsection in consumer situations,[91] was expressly confirmed by the wording of the current provision, which includes the words "whether or not that is a purpose for which such goods are commonly supplied." Where the goods are capable of use for a number or range of purposes, it seems that the seller's liability depends upon whether a special purpose within the range was indicated. If so, the suitability must be for that purpose[92]; otherwise, it must apparently (despite the words "that purpose" in the provision) be for any purpose reasonably foreseeable. Thus in *Ashington Piggeries Ltd v Christopher Hill Ltd*[93] Norwegian suppliers sold herring meal for compounding into feeding stuffs, and it was held that they could reasonably have foreseen that it might be fed to mink.[94]

---

[86] *Henry Kendall & Sons v William Lillico & Sons Ltd* [1969] 2 A.C. 31 (claim against Kendall: goods sold for resale for compounding into cattle and poultry food; claim against Grimsdale: goods sold for compounding into poultry food); *Harlingdon and Leinster Enterprises Ltd v Christopher Hull Fine Art Ltd* [1991] 1 Q.B. 564 (art dealers).

[87] Above, para. 11–025.

[88] The Mercantile Law Amendment Act 1856 used the words "expressly sold for a specified and particular purpose", which is narrower, and there was some authority that the Sale of Goods Act 1893 was to be interpreted on these narrow lines in Scotland: see *Flynn v Scott* 1949 S.C. 442 and *M'Callum v Mason* 1956 S.C. 50. But these were disapproved in *Henry Kendall & Sons v William Lillico & Sons Ltd*, above, at p.83: see also p.123.

[89] *Preist v Last* [1903] 2 K.B. 148 at 153.

[90] Above. See also *Frost v Aylesbury Dairy Co. Ltd* [1905] 1 K.B. 608; *Wallis v Russell* [1902] 2 I.R. 585 at 634: "It savours of absurdity that where an article, such as a razor, is to the knowledge of both buyer and seller only bought for one purpose, an implied warranty should depend in any degree upon the buyer making known to the seller something which not only the latter knows already, but which also forms part of the common knowledge of mankind."

[91] But in less obvious cases it has proved difficult to establish unfitness: see cases on new cars, below, para.11–057, n.3.

[92] *Preist v Last*, above, at p.153.

[93] [1972] A.C. 441.

[94] At p.477, applying the test of remoteness laid down in *Koufos v C Czarnikow Ltd (The Heron II)* [1969] 1 A.C. 350; see also *Henry Kendall & Sons v William Lillico & Sons Ltd* [1969] 2 A.C. 31 at 91 (claim against Grimsdale: foreseeable that poultry food might be fed to pheasants), 114 (claim against Kendall: meal sold for compounding into cattle and poultry feed must be suitable for either). But *cf. Cominco Ltd v Westinghouse Canada Ltd* (1981) 129 D.L.R. (3d) 544 (electric cable not suitable for laying in proximity to other cable: held purpose not sufficiently indicated by buyer) (further proceedings (1983) 147 D.L.R. (3d) 279); *M/S Aswan*

11–056 **Credit-broker.** The references to the credit-broker were introduced by the Consumer Credit Act 1974 and came into force in 1985. The previous wording referred only to the seller. The term "credit-broker" is defined in section 61(1) of the Sale of Goods Act 1979[95] as "a person acting in the course of a business of credit brokerage carried on by him, that is a business of effecting introductions of individuals desiring to obtain credit—(a) to persons carrying on any business so far as it relates to the provision of credit, or (b) to other persons engaged in credit brokerage." The references cover the situation where a dealer sells goods to a finance house which then sells them to the dealer's customer on credit. The seller is liable as to fitness for purpose notwithstanding that the indication of reliance was given to the dealer (credit-broker).[96]

11–057 **"Reasonably fit for that purpose".** Where the subsection applies, the seller's duty is to supply goods reasonably fit for the purpose. The 1893 provision used the same phrase, except that it referred to "such purpose" rather than "that purpose"; cases on it are obviously therefore still valid. A well-known example of its application is *Bristol Tramways, etc., Carriage Co. Ltd v Fiat Motors Ltd*[97] where buses ordered were known to be wanted for heavy passenger work in Bristol, a city containing steep hills, and proved unsuitable: the seller was held liable. In Scotland, it has been said that material bought for manufacturing golf rainwear would be unfit for purpose if, though capable of being made up satisfactorily, it broke down in subsequent use.[98] In the consumer field, examples are provided by a hot-water bottle which burst,[99] a plastic catapult which broke injuring the user's eye,[1] milk containing typhoid germs,[2] a new car which boiled every hundred miles or so,[3] underpants containing excess sulphite which irritated the

---

Engineering Establishment Co. v Lupdine Ltd [1987] 1 W.L.R. 1 (plastic pails for export collapsed when left piled in sun at Kuwait: held purpose indicated was general only, for which goods suitable).

95 This definition differs from that in s.145(2) of the Consumer Credit Act 1974.

96 An argument is possible that a dealer who introduces his customers to one source of finance only does not introduce them to "persons" and so is not a credit-broker. The same argument can arise under the Consumer Credit Act 1974, which sometimes uses the singular and sometimes the plural: *cf.* s.145(2)(a)(i), (ii), (2)(b), (2)(c). But see Interpretation Act 1978, s.6 (plural includes singular). Equally, if he usually sells direct and only occasionally places financed agreements, is he carrying on a "business of credit brokerage"? The definition might also not cover a corporate buyer ("individuals").

97 [1910] 2 K.B. 831; see also *Ashford Shire Council v Dependable Motors Pty Ltd* [1961] A.C. 336 (tractors not fit for road construction work).

98 *NV Devos Gebroeder v Sunderland Sportswear Ltd* 1987 S.L.T. 331 (but the point was not decided).

99 *Preist v Last* [1903] 2 K.B. 148.

1 *Godley v Perry* [1960] 1 W.L.R. 9.

2 *Frost v Aylesbury Dairy Co. Ltd* [1905] 1 K.B. 608. See also *Wallis v Russell* [1902] 2 I.R. 585 (crab).

3 *Spencer v Claude Rye (Vehicles) Ltd, The Guardian*, December 19, 1972; *Jackson v Chrysler Acceptances Ltd* [1978] R.T.R. 474 (both of which concerned cars to be used for holidays); *Finch Motors Ltd v Quin (No. 2)* [1980] 2 N.Z.L.R. 519 (car for towing boat); *R & B Customs Brokers Ltd v United Dominions Trust Ltd* [1988] 1

skin[4] and CO_2 contaminated with benzene, a known carcinogen, though in a quantity not harmful to health.[5] Many of these involve a concurrent breach of section 14(2).[6] But the seller does not promise that the goods are absolutely suitable: a second-hand car may be reasonably fit for its purpose though it is known to require repairs when bought.[7] Nor does he guarantee against the results of misuse.[8] Still less does he promise suitability where because of an unstated peculiarity in the buyer's position, only goods of a special type are in fact suitable for his purpose. Thus in *Griffiths v Peter Conway Ltd*,[9] the buyer of a Harris tweed coat contracted dermatitis from it because, unknown to her, she had an unusually sensitive skin. It was held that, as the coat would not have harmed a normal person, the seller was not liable. More recently, in *Slater v Finning Ltd*[10] a camshaft which was unsuited to the engine of a ship because of features peculiar to that vessel unknown to either party at the time, but which later worked satisfactorily in another ship, was held suitable for its purpose. The duty has sometimes been stated in very wide terms as regards food for human consumption, but it is clear that the sale of food, whether for human consumption or for animals, is no more than an ordinary application of the principle stated in the section.[11] Where potentially dangerous substances are supplied, they may not be fit for their purpose unless accompanied by appropriate instructions, descriptions or warnings[12]; and it seems correct in principle to

---

W.L.R. 321 (leaking car not fit for use on English roads in English weather). *Cf. Leaves v Wadham Stringer (Cliftons) Ltd* [1980] R.T.R. 308 (many irritating faults: fit for purpose). But see *Farnworth Finance Facilities Ltd v Attryde* [1970] 1 W.L.R. 1053 (motor cycle).

[4] *Grant v Australian Knitting Mills Ltd* [1936] A.C. 85.

[5] *Britvic Soft Drinks Ltd v Messer UK Ltd* [2002] 1 Lloyd's Rep. 20; modified without reference to this point [2002] EWCA Civ 548; [2002] 2 Lloyd's Rep. 368; see also *Thain v Anniesland Trade Centre*, above, para.11–032, n.83 (second-hand car).

[6] Above, paras 11–026 *et seq.*; below, paras 11–070 *et seq.*

[7] See below, para.11–058.

[8] *Heil v Hedges* [1951] 1 T.L.R. 512 (pork chop unfit for human consumption when insufficiently cooked: doubted for modern conditions by Atiyah, *Sale of Goods* (11th ed.), p.179, n.171; *Yachetti v John Duff & Sons Ltd* [1942] O.R. 682 (pork sausages); *Decca Radar Co. Ltd v Caserite Ltd* [1961] 2 Lloyd's Rep. 301 (packing cases damaged by stevedores); *cf. Shields v Honeywill & Stein Ltd* [1953] 1 Lloyd's Rep. 357 (isopropyl alcohol known to be required for syrups of delicate flavour); *Lambert v Lewis* [1982] A.C. 225 (trailer coupling, known to be defective and so dangerous but still in use, broke): below, paras 17–059 *et seq.*

[9] [1939] 1 All E.R. 685. See also *Ingham v Emes* [1955] 2 Q.B. 366 (hair dye: plaintiff knew she was specially sensitive but did not say so).

[10] [1997] A.C. 473; see Brown [1997] L.M.C.L.Q. 193. A contrast is possible with *Manchester Liners Ltd v Rea Ltd* [1922] 2 A.C. 74 (coal for ship) and *Cammell Laird & Co. Ltd v Manganese Bronze and Brass Co. Ltd* [1943] A.C. 402 (propellers for ship), in each of which there is some assumption that the seller should have taken steps to find out what was appropriate to the vessel concerned. But in *Slater v Finning* the part ordered was a normal and not a special one, and the ship suffered from a "particular abnormality or idiosyncracy": see Lord Keith of Kinkel at pp.480–483.

[11] *Wallis v Russell* [1902] 2 I.R. 585 at 611–612.

[12] *Vacwell Engineering Co. Ltd v B.D.H. Chemicals Ltd* [1971] 1 Q.B. 88; *Willis v FMC Machinery and Chemicals Ltd* (1976) 68 D.L.R. (3d) 127 (herbicide). But *cf. Lem v Barotto Sports Ltd* (1976) 69 D.L.R. (3d) 276 at 290, where the connection of

say that the absence of such instructions, warnings (for instance as to compatibility with other equipment) or even descriptions, may also make other goods, not potentially dangerous, not reasonably fit for their purpose.[13] The duty to warn may also, however, be based on a separate implied term[14] or on tort.[15]

11–058 **Second-hand goods.** Section 14(3) can apply though the goods are second hand.[16] Where the buyer asks for second-hand goods or knows that such goods are to be supplied, the same standard will obviously not be exacted as in a case where the goods should have been new.[17] But where the buyer merely relies on the seller in general to supply something suitable for his purpose, the supply of second-hand goods may of itself involve a breach of the subsection. The few English cases concerning second-hand cars mostly involve pleas both of section 14(2) and of section 14(3) and are discussed under the former provision.[18]

11–059 **Reliance need not be shown but may be rebutted.** Section 14(3) assumes that where the buyer makes known any particular purpose for which the goods are being bought (these words being widely interpreted as above indicated) there is reliance on the seller. An exception is, however, made where the seller can establish indications to the contrary: "where the circumstances show that the buyer does not rely, or that it is unreasonable for him to rely, on the seller's skill or judgment." It seems that it is not, therefore, necessary for the buyer to allege reliance in his particulars of claim: it is for the seller to allege in defence and prove that there was no reliance, or that reliance was unreasonable.[19] Thus if it can be shown that the seller made it clear to the buyer that he (the seller) did not purport to

---

a duty to warn with s.14 is doubted. The electric cable in *Cominco Ltd v Westinghouse Canada Ltd*, above, n.94, though it had a tendency to cause fire, was presumably not dangerous enough to bring this principle into operation. As to descriptions see *Albright & Wilson UK Ltd v Biachem Ltd* [2001] EWCA 301; [2001] 2 All E.R. (Comm) 537, where wrongly described chemicals caused an explosion on delivery. See also *Buchan v Ortho Pharmaceutical (Canada) Ltd* (1984) 8 D.L.R. (4th) 373 (oral contraceptive) (affirmed on other grounds (1986) 25 D.L.R. (4th) 658).

[13] See *Fillmore's Valley Nurseries Ltd v North American Cyanamid Ltd* (1958) 14 D.L.R. (2d) 297; *Milne Construction Ltd v Expandite Ltd* [1984] 2 N.Z.L.R. 163; *Wormell v RHM Agricultural (East) Ltd* [1986] 1 W.L.R. 336; revsd. on other grounds [1987] 1 W.L.R. 1091. See as to the significance of instructions in consumer sales in general McLeod, 97 L.Q.R. 550 (1981); Brown [1988] L.M.C.L.Q. 502; Hedley [2001] J.B.L. 114.

[14] Below, para.11–088.

[15] Below, paras 12–121 *et seq.*, 13–106, 13–107.

[16] *Bartlett v Sidney Marcus Ltd* [1965] 1 W.L.R. 1013.

[17] *ibid.* (car reasonably fit though requiring repairs); see also *Henry Kendall & Sons v William Lillico & Sons Ltd* [1969] 2 A.C. 31 at 115.

[18] Above, para.11–061. As to ships see *Lloyd del Pacifico v Board of Trade* (1929) 35 Ll.L.R. 217.

[19] *Central Regional Council v Uponor Ltd* 1996 S.L.T. 645.

exercise skill or judgment, the subsection will normally be excluded.[20] The reverse was the case under the original Act of 1893.[21] Other examples where the facts would negative reliance can be found in cases on the former wording. In *Teheran-Europe Co. Ltd v S T Belton (Tractors) Ltd*,[22] air compressors were sold in circumstances which gave the seller notice that they were for resale in Iran. It was held that the buyers relied on their own skill and judgment as to the suitability of these compressors for such resale in Iran.[23] The same may be true where the buyer selects goods from stock for himself,[24] states no purpose at all or a very general purpose for goods that might have several uses,[25] or where, because the buyer knows that the seller has only one commodity to supply, he must be regarded as taking what he buys as it is.[26] It is also possible that where the buyer specifies the level of quality required that may indicate non-reliance on the seller.[27] But

---

[20] A striking illustration is *Corbett Construction Co. Ltd v Simplot Chemical Co. Ltd* [1971] 2 W.W.R. 332 (fertiliser pellets: buyer stated that he required them for use (impregnated with diesel oil) as explosive for blasting operations: seller said it did not manufacture explosive fertiliser). But some indications to this effect could be caught by the Unfair Contract Terms Act 1977, or the rules applied to exemption clauses generally: see Ch.13.

[21] *Grant v Australian Knitting Mills Ltd* [1936] A.C. 85 at 99 *per* Lord Wright; see also *Medway Oil and Storage Co.Ltd v Silica Gel Corp*. (1928) 33 Com.Cas. 195.

[22] [1968] 2 Q.B. 545. See also *M/S Aswan Engineering Establishment Co. v Lupdine Ltd* [1987] 1 W.L.R. 1 (pails for export to Arabian Gulf). *Cf. Sumner, Permain & Co. v Webb & Co.* (1921) 27 Com.Cas. 105 (not reported on this point in [1922] 1 K.B. 55) (tonic water for resale in Argentina); *Phoenix Distributors Ltd v L. B. Clarke (London) Ltd* [1966] 2 Lloyd's Rep. 285, affirmed [1967] 1 Lloyd's Rep. 518 (potatoes for export to Poland). And see below, paras 18–274, 20–038 as to international sales.

[23] It is not clear in what respect the machines were alleged to be unfit for resale in Iran: see p.559. See also *Jewson Ltd v Boyhan* [2003] EWCA Civ 1030; [2004] 1 Lloyd's Rep. 505 (suitability of boilers for flats under development).

[24] *H Beecham & Co. Pty Ltd v Francis Howard & Co. Pty Ltd* [1921] V.L.R. 428 (timber). But *cf. Wilson v Dunville* (1879) L.R. 4 Ir. 249 (distillery grains); *Wallis v Russell* [1902] 2 I.R. 585 (retail sale of boiled crabs), in each of which the buyer exercised some choice. Selection of branded goods off a supermarket shelf would normally involve reliance.

[25] *e.g. Jones v Padgett* (1890) 24 Q.B.D. 650 (cloth ordered by woollen merchant who was also a tailor; required for servants' liveries, for which it was not strong enough, but seller not told this—seller not liable); see also *Henry Kendall & Sons v William Lillico & Sons Ltd* [1969] 2 A.C. 31 at 79–80; *Preist v Last* [1903] 2 K.B. 148 at 153. But *cf.* above, para.11–057.

[26] See *Turner v Mucklow* (1862) 6 L.T. 690 (refuse from dye manufacture); *Ipswich Gaslight Co. v W B King & Co.* (1886) 3 T.L.R. 100 (sale of refuse); *Wren v Holt* [1903] 1 K.B. 610 (public house only stocked Holden's beers: action failed under (what is now) s.14(3) but succeeded under s.14(2)); *Manchester Liners Ltd v Rea Ltd* [1922] 2 A.C. 74 at 90 (coal).

[27] See *Central Regional Council v Uponor Ltd* 1996 S.L.T. 646 (seller specified "British standard": matter remitted for further proof); followed in *British Soft Drinks Ltd v Messer UK Ltd* [2002] 1 Lloyd's Rep. 20 (conformity with BS 4105 not enough); modified on appeal [2002] EWCA Civ 548; [2002] 2 Lloyd's Rep. 368. In *Jewson Ltd v Boyhan*, n.23,above at first instance, the apparent breadth of a dictum of Tomlinson J. in the *Britvic* case, above, that reliance may be on the skill and judgment of "his immediate seller or any person from whom that seller has acquired the goods" (at p.41) was doubted (see at [88]), it is submitted correctly; but *cf.* Sealy [2003] C.L.J. 260–261. See also *Rotherham MBC v Frank Haslam Milan & Co. Ltd* (1996) 78 B.L.R. 1 (reference to BS 1377).

exact knowledge of the purpose is not necessary. In *Henry Kendall & Sons v William Lillico & Sons Ltd*,[28] it was held that, where an importer seeking to introduce a commodity from a new source (Brazilian groundnut extraction) knew that it was being bought by a wholesaler for resale in smaller quantities to be compounded into food for cattle and poultry, this was sufficient knowledge to bring the subsection into operation. The importer was accordingly liable when the extract proved poisonous to poultry, though it could safely be compounded into cattle food.

11–060 **Partial reliance: goods made up for buyer.** Sometimes the circumstances show that there is no reliance as to particular matters, but reliance as to the rest of the contract. This situation is commonly referred to as one of partial reliance, but the phrase is misleading: there is reliance in one area or respect but not in another. Thus a buyer may specify the materials or ingredients for a product and leave the seller to prepare it. In such a case there is no reliance as to the suitability of the end product, but the seller must use materials or ingredients reasonably fit for their purpose. In *Ashington Piggeries Ltd v Christopher Hill Ltd*,[29] an expert in mink farming asked established compounders of animal feeding stuffs to manufacture mink food to an agreed formula. It was held that there was reliance on the compounders to use ingredients reasonably fit for feeding to animals, though not as regards the suitability of the compound specified for mink in particular. Since one of the ingredients supplied was toxic in varying degrees to a number of species of animals, they were held liable under section 14(3) (then section 14(1)). Again, in *Cammell Laird & Co. Ltd v Manganese Bronze and Brass Ltd*,[30] a buyer ordered ship propellers and gave certain specifications. The propellers proved unsatisfactory because of matters outside the specification which had been left to the sellers: the buyer succeeded against the sellers under the subsection. So in a recent case[31] a developer who ordered boilers for converted flats, but did not indicate any specific requirements as to their heating capacity, was held to rely on the supplier only to supply boilers of satisfactory quality. But the reliance must nevertheless "be such as to constitute a substantial and effective inducement which leads the buyer to agree to purchase the commodity."[32]

---

[28] [1969] 2 A.C. 31. See also below, para.18–243.
[29] [1972] A.C. 441.
[30] [1934] A.C. 402. See also *Bowen v R. B. Young Products Pty Ltd* [1967] W.A.R. 97 (poultry mash); *Dixon Kerly Ltd v Robinson* [1965] 2 Lloyd's Rep. 404 (boat); *Venus Electric Ltd v Brevel Products Ltd* (1978) 85 D.L.R. (3d) 282 (hair-dryer motor); *Hunter Engineering Co. Inc. v Syncrude Canada Ltd* [1989] 1 S.C.R. 426; (1989) 57 D.L.R. (4th) 321 (mining gearboxes). *Cf. Edmund Murray Ltd v BSP International Foundations Ltd* (1992) 33 Con.L.R. 1, CA (drilling rig: compliance with detailed requirements undertaken by seller).
[31] *Jewson Ltd v Boyhan* [2003] EWCA Civ 1030; [2004] 1 Lloyd's Rep. 505.
[32] *Medway Oil and Storage Ltd v Silica Gel Corp.* (1928) 33 Com.Cas. 195 at 196.

Dealers. Where dealers buy from each other, particularly in an established market, it may be held that they rely on their own judgment even though it is known that they buy for resale.[33] But this is not always the case.[34] In *Henry Kendall & Sons v William Lillico & Sons Ltd*,[35] a leading case on the law as it stood before 1973, the trial judge thought that in a commercial sale of imported groundnuts reliance was excluded by the fact that the buyer and seller both belonged to the London Cattle Foods Trade Association; in this he followed dicta in a previous case concerning members of the same Association, suggesting that they did not rely on each other's skill or judgment.[36] But the majority of the House of Lords, with the majority of the Court of Appeal,[37] held that though this was relevant it did not in the circumstances show that there was no reliance. To say otherwise would be "to convert a decision on fact into a rule of law and to ignore the fact that not all sales, even on a given market, not to mention sales on different markets, bear the same character or involve the same incidents."[38] 11–061

Opportunity of examination. It seems that at common law, if the buyer has an opportunity of examining the goods there would have been no implied warranty.[39] But in view of the words of the Act, the fact that there was such an opportunity which was not taken would now only be relevant to show lack of reliance; and there may be reliance though the goods will or may be tested or analysed by the buyer on delivery.[40] 11–062

Reliance by an agent. Where the reliance is alleged to be by an agent, difficult questions of fact may arise as to whether the buyer, through his agent, relies on the seller's skill or judgment, or whether he relies on the agent's report to him and not on the seller at all.[41] 11–063

---

[33] See *Henry Kendall & Sons v William Lillico & Sons Ltd* [1969] 2 A.C. 31 at 84, 95, 107, 124, 125; *Steels and Busks Ltd v Bleecker Bik & Co. Ltd* [1956] 1 Lloyd's Rep. 228 (London Rubber Trade Assocation); *Feast Contractors Ltd v Ray Vincent Ltd* [1974] 1 N.Z.L.R. 212 (cartage contractor buying engine). See further above, para.11–011, below, para.18–274.

[34] In *Cointat v Myham & Son* [1913] 2 K.B. 220 the provision was applied to purchases by a butcher from a meat wholesaler. The case was reversed (1914) 110 L.T. 749, on the ground that evidence as to usage of trade had not been received. But there was a decision to similar effect in *B & P Wholesale Distributors v Marko Ltd, The Times*, February 20, 1953.

[35] Above; at first instance, [1964] 2 Lloyd's Rep. 227.

[36] *C E B Draper & Son Ltd v Edward Turner & Son Ltd* [1965] 1 Q.B. 424 at 433, 434.

[37] [1966] 1 W.L.R. 287.

[38] [1969] 2 A.C. at 124, *per* Lord Wilberforce: see also Lord Morris at p.95, but *cf.* Lord Guest at p.107. Lord Reid at p.84 placed emphasis on the fact that the importers were "pushing" the product. See also *South Coast Basalt Pty Ltd v R W Miller & Co. Pty Ltd* [1981] 1 N.S.W.L.R. 356, PC—reliance though buyer and seller associated companies.

[39] *Wallis v Russell* [1902] 2 I.R. 585 at 594, 595, 597, 615. See also *Jones v Just* (1868) L.R. 3 Q.B. 197 at 202–203. The original draft of (what is now) s.14(3) was confined to cases where the buyer "had no opportunity of examining the goods." See Chalmers, *Sale of Goods* (2nd ed., 1894), p.30.

[40] *Henry Kendall & Sons v William Lillico & Sons Ltd* [1969] 2 A.C. 31 at 95.

[41] See *Ashford Shire Council v Dependable Motors Pty Ltd* [1961] A.C. 336 (tractor).

11–064 **Extent of duty.** The duty of the seller is again strict: it is no defence that the seller could not examine the goods (as where they are in sealed tins[42]), nor that all possible care was taken.[43]

11–065 **Orders by patent or other trade name.** Under the 1893 provision, the duty did not apply where there was a contract for the sale of a specified article under its trade name, though, of course, the provisions of sections 13, 14(2) and 15 might apply. It was said that this proviso was intended to meet the case, not of raw commodities or materials, but of manufactured articles.[44] Thus an order for "Cyfartha Merthyr coal" would not be an order of an article under its trade name,[45] though it was said that to order Coalite was to order under a trade name.[46] The cases, however, restricted the proviso to the point where it only applied if an article was ordered by its trade name alone.[47] In *Baldry v Marshall*[48] Bankes L.J. suggested[49] the following test for the operation of the proviso: "Did the buyer specify it under its trade name in such a way as to indicate that he is satisfied, rightly or wrongly, that it will answer his purpose, and that he is not relying on the skill or judgment of the seller, however great that skill or judgment may be?" This test seemed to make the proviso almost superfluous, and it no longer appears. The fact that the buyer orders a specified article under its trade name may, however, indicate more generally that he did not rely, or that it was unreasonable for him to rely, on the seller's skill or judgment.

11–066 **Time element and durability.** The problems here are in general the same as those arising in connection with section 14(2) and are discussed under that provision.[50]

11–067 **Deterioration in transit.** There is, however, one question specific to section 14(3). Where it is contemplated that the goods will be transported, and some goods of the type referred to by the contract would bear

---

[42] *Bigge v Parkinson* (1862) 7 H. & N. 955 at 959. See also *Jackson v Watson & Sons* [1909] 2 K.B. 193.

[43] *Frost v Aylesbury Dairy Co. Ltd* [1905] 1 K.B. 608 (purity of milk); *Henry Kendall & Sons v William Lillico & Sons Ltd* [1969] 2 A.C. 31 at 84; *H. Parsons (Livestock) Ltd v Uttley Ingham & Co. Ltd* [1978] Q.B. 791 at 800. See also above, para.11–043.

[44] *Gillespie Bros & Co. v Cheney Eggar & Co.* [1896] 2 Q.B. 59 at 64.

[45] *ibid*.

[46] *Wilson v Rickett, Cockerell & Co. Ltd* [1954] 1 Q.B. 598 at 610. This is presumably the explanation of *Daniels v White & Sons* [1938] 4 All E.R. 258, where the plaintiff asked for a bottle of R. White's lemonade, and it was held that there was no reliance under (the present) s.14(3); *cf.* however *Wren v Holt* [1903] 1 K.B. 610 (to order beer in a public house known to sell only Holden's beer is to buy by that description). In *Grant v Australian Knitting Mills Ltd* [1936] A.C. 85 at 99, Lord Wright said that the proviso did not apply to the sale there of "Golden Fleece" underpants because this was neither a patent nor a trade name. This seems unlikely; the true explanation is probably that the goods were not bought under this name.

[47] *Chanter v Hopkins* (1838) 4 M. & W. 399 (the case on which the provision was probably based); see also *Paul & Co. v Glasgow Corp.* (1900) 3 F. (Ct. of Sess.) 119 (smoke prevention device).

[48] [1925] 1 K.B. 260 (buyer sought comfortable car for touring purposes: supplied with 8-cylinder Bugatti).

[49] At p.267.

[50] Above, paras 11–049, 11–040.

transportation, and some, though fit for their purpose at the time of sale, would not, it may be held that the buyer relies on the seller's skill and judgment to select goods that will bear transportation.[51] On the other hand, where all goods of the type referred to would necessarily deteriorate in transit or suffer a high risk of doing so, the risk of such deterioriation, unless there are other indications, will be on the buyer.[52]

Express warranties or conditions. By section 55(2) (formerly section 14(5)),[53] "An express condition or warranty does not negative a condition or warranty implied by this Act unless inconsistent with it." In an old case,[54] a contractor agreed to supply troop stores "guaranteed to pass survey of the East India Company's officers." It was held that this did not exclude the implied warranty of fitness. Difficult problems of construction can arise in this connection, as to which no guidance is given.[55] It seems, however, that express conditions or warranties will normally be construed as additional to the implied terms.[56] **11–068**

Related contracts. Provisions similar to section 14(3) are implied into other contracts for the transfer of property in goods[57] (*e.g.* contracts of exchange or work and materials)[58]; hire-purchase agreements[59]; and contracts of hire.[60] Problems relating to computer software not suited to its purpose also raise the question of whether analogous terms apply. The initial approach is to ask whether software counts as "goods".[61] Hardware alone clearly does. It has been held in Australia[62] that a sale of a complete **11–069**

---

[51] *Mash and Murrell Ltd v Joseph I Emanuel Ltd* [1961] 1 W.L.R. 862 at 867–868 (revsd. on other grounds [1961] 2 Lloyd's Rep. 326) (potatoes); *A B Kemp Ltd v Tolland* [1956] 2 Lloyd's Rep. 681; see also *Beer v Walker* (1877) 46 L.J.Q.B. 677 (rabbits); *Burrows v Smith* (1894) 10 T.L.R. 246 (grouse); *Bowden Bros & Co. Ltd v Little* (1907) 4 C.L.R. 1364; *George Wills & Sons Ltd v Thomas Brown & Sons* (1922) 12 Ll.L.R. 292 (herrings in brine for Australia); *Wilson v Dunville* (1879) L.R. 4 Ir. 249 at 257; *cf. Dickson v Zizinia* (1851) 10 C.B. 602. See also above, paras 6–019, 11–060; below, paras 18–274, 20–038 *et seq.*

[52] See *Broome v Pardess Co-operative Society of Orange Growers Ltd* [1940] 1 All E.R. 603; *Bull v Robison* (1854) 10 Exch. 342 (iron). As to deterioration when the seller agrees to deliver at his own risk, see above, para.6–022; below, paras 18–249 *et seq.*

[53] The provision was put into s.55 by the Supply of Goods (Implied Terms) Act 1973.

[54] *Bigge v Parkinson* (1862) 7 H. & N. 955. See also above, para.10–019.

[55] *cf.* Uniform Commercial Code s.2–317, giving guidelines.

[56] *cf. Cammell Laird & Co. Ltd v Manganese Bronze and Brass Co. Ltd* [1934] A.C. 402; above, para.11–060.

[57] Supply of Goods and Services Act 1982, s.4 as amended by Sale and Supply of Goods Act 1994, s.7 and Schs 2, 3.

[58] In the case of contracts for work and materials, the supplier's main business may well be constituted by the services which he offers, and the circumstances in which reliance on him is not reasonable may be more common than in cases of pure sale.

[59] Supply of Goods (Implied Terms) Act 1973, s.10, as amended by Sale and Supply of Goods Act 1994, s.7 and Sch.2.

[60] Supply of Goods and Services Act 1982, s.9 as amended by Sale and Supply of Goods Act 1994, s.7 and Schs 2, 3.

[61] See above, para.1–086.

[62] *Toby Constructions Products Pty Ltd v Computa Bar (Sales) Pty Ltd* [1983] 2 N.S.W.L.R. 48.

system of hardware and software was a sale of goods, and has recently been said in the English Court of Appeal that the same could be true of a program on a disk.[63] Very often however (as in that case) there is no transfer of "property" or even a hiring, but merely a licence, and in the Scottish case of *Beta Computers (Europe) Ltd v Adobe Systems (Europe) Ltd*[64] it was said that such a contract was *sui generis* with elements of sale and licence. Disputes have tended to concern design and supply of systems for tasks for which they have proved inadequate, but the straight issue as to whether they were "goods" has not arisen, by reason of express terms of particular contracts of this type, the implied terms of the Supply of Goods and Services Act 1982, and the implication of analogous terms at common law. The tendency has been (subject to specific contract terms) to imply terms similar to those of the Sale of Goods Act to what might be called the "product" which the contractor is to produce, and duties of reasonable care to the service element.[65] But it can be argued that the strict liability of a seller is inappropriate in computer software contracts in any case and that any analogy with production and circulation of goods is not compelling.[66]

11–070 **Relation between sections 14(2) and 14(3).** There was considerable overlap between sections 14(1) and 14(2), the precursors of the present subsections, and there were many cases in which both were pleaded.[67] The amendments introduced by the Supply of Goods (Implied Terms) Act 1973 and appearing in the 1979 Act actually increased this overlap by removing some of the minor points of difference and introducing other points of similarity. Thus the restriction to sales "in the course of a business" applies to both subsections, replacing wording that differed between them; and the definition of "satisfactory quality", principally relevant to section 14(2), refers, though since the changes of 1994 only in a guideline, to fitness for purpose, the standard specifically set by (the present) section 14(3). The limitation of section 14(2) to sales by description, and the trade name proviso of the former section 14(1) (now section 14(3)) were both eliminated. Two major practical differences between subsections (2) and (3) remain.

11–071 First, section 14(2) requires only that the goods be of satisfactory quality, whereas section 14(3) requires that they be reasonably fit for the purpose expressly or by implication made known. Although in many sales these standards will coincide, because the purpose will be that for which such goods are commonly supplied, a higher standard can be exacted by a buyer

[63] *St Albans City and District Council v International Computers Ltd* [1996] 4 All E.R. 481: see pp.492–494 *per* Sir Iain Glidewell; but see above, para.1–086.
[64] 1996 S.L.T. 605.
[65] See *Salvage Association v CAP Financial Services Ltd* [1995] F.S.R. 654; the *St Albans* case, above; *Jonathan Wren & Co. Ltd v Microdec Plc* (1999) 65 Con.L.R. 157; *Pegler Ltd v Wang UK Ltd* [2000] B.L.R. 218 (where liability was admitted); *Watford Electronics Ltd v Sanderson CFL Ltd* [2001] EWCA Civ 317; [2001] 1 All E.R. (Comm) 696.
[66] See Atiyah, *Sale of Goods* (11th ed.), pp.77–83.
[67] See *Teheran-Europe Co. Ltd v S T Belton (Tractors) Ltd* [1968] 2 Q.B. 545 at 562–563.

who makes his special purpose known, for the seller is then liable if the goods are not reasonably suitable for it, though in general of satisfactory quality. Conversely, the general requirement of satisfactory quality under section 14(2) can be enforced even though section 14(3) is inapplicable because there was no reliance, or reliance was unreasonable.

Secondly, section 14(3) is excluded where the circumstances show that the buyer does not rely, or that it is unreasonable for him to rely, on the seller's skill or judgment: section 14(2) is not so limited, though it does not apply as regards defects drawn to the buyer's attention, nor, where the buyer examines the goods, as regards defects which that examination ought to reveal. These differences of formulation may occasionally lead to differences in result. Thus where a buyer examines the goods, though he shows to some extent that he is not relying on the seller's skill or judgment, it is clear that he may examine goods and still rely in part on it for the purposes of section 14(3); but a claim under section 14(2) might in some cases be excluded by the wording of the proviso as to examination.[68] Conversely under section 14(2) examination only excludes liability for defects which that examination ought to reveal; but in appropriate cases it may show that there was no reliance at all for the purposes of section 14(3). Where a defect is specifically drawn to the buyer's attention, not only is section 14(2) excluded, but that fact will normally indicate that it is unreasonable for the buyer to rely on the seller for the purposes of section 14(3); there could, however, be cases where the buyer relies on the seller as to the fact that the goods, even with such a defect, will be suitable for their purpose. 11–072

3. Sale by Sample

Sale of Goods Act 1979, s.15. This section, which, like section 13, but unlike section 14, is not restricted to business sellers, reads: 11–073

"(1) A contract of sale is a contract for sale by sample where there is an express or implied term to that effect in the contract.
(2) In the case of a contract for sale by sample there is an implied term[69]—

(a) that the bulk will correspond with the sample in quality;
[(b) : repealed][70];

[68] See *R & B Customs Brokers Ltd v United Dominion Trust Ltd* [1988] 1 W.L.R. 321, where the buyer had had possession of the car before the time at which, in the view of the Court of Appeal, the duty under s.14(2) attached, and thus might be regarded as knowing of the defect when it did.

[69] The designation of the term as a condition was originally contained in s.15(2) itself. The present formulation, with the use here of "term" and the addition of s.15(3), dates from the Sale and Supply of Goods Act 1994 (s.7 and Sch.2); and was adopted to effect the abolition of the term "condition" in the English sense in Scots law.

[70] By the Sale and Supply of Goods Act 1994, s.7 and Sch.3. The effect of the repealed wording is reintroduced into s.34(2): below, para.12–039. For the purpose of this change, which is largely for logical consistency, see Law Com. No. 160, Scot. Law Com. No. 104 (1987), para.6.28.

(c) that the goods will be free from any defect, making their quality unsatisfactory, which would not be apparent on reasonable examination of the sample."[71]

(3)[72] As regards England and Wales and Northern Ireland, the term implied by subsection (2) above is a condition."[73]

It is in effect declaratory of the common law.[74]

11–074 **"Sale by sample".** The Act's definition of a sale by sample is not at all helpful. It seems that a sale by sample is a sale whereby the seller expressly or impliedly promises "that the goods sold should answer the description of a small parcel exhibited at the time of the sale."[75] "In truth, a sample is simply a way of describing the subject-matter of the bargain, and the principles which are applicable to contracts to sell and sales by description are applicable here."[76] In many cases a provision as to sample will be express, *e.g.* "as per sample"[77]; in others the showing of a sample may (but will not necessarily) make the sale a sale by sample,[78] and sometimes evidence that sales of the type involved are customarily by sample may be introduced.[79] On general principles the test must be objective: it cannot be that actual intention to sell by sample is required.

---

[71] Until the Sale and Supply of Goods Act 1994 the wording was "rendering them unmerchantable". The change here was to effectuate the policy of substituting "satisfactory quality" for "merchantable quality": see above, para.11–031. The remainder is a "modernised" version of the original wording of the 1893 Act, introduced by the Act of 1979. See Murdoch, 44 M.L.R. 388 (1981), suggesting that the section is superfluous, questions of sale by sample now being adequately covered by ss.13 and 14. The Law Commissions (Law Com.W.P. No. 85, Sc.Law Com.C.M. No. 58) (1983) and Law Com. No. 160, Sc. Law Com. No. 104 (1987) feared that whether this is so or not, repeal might have unexpected and undesirable results and recommended that it be not done unless it was clear that no adverse consequences would follow: see para.6.27 of the 1987 Report.

[72] As to subs.(3) see above, para.11–001, n.4.

[73] In general, breach of a condition entitles rejection: see above, paras 10–024 *et seq.*, below, paras 12–022 *et seq.* In non-consumer cases, a slight breach of an implied term may however not do so (see s.15A of the Act, below, paras 12–024 *et seq.*, 18–284). A buyer who deals as consumer is entitled under the Act to the benefit of a (rebuttable) presumption that the goods were non-compliant at the relevant time if they are non-compliant at any time during six months from delivery (s.48A(3), below, para. 12–075). This is part of new provisions providing special remedies for those who deal as consumers (below, paras 12–071, 14–008 *et seq*). The significance of "delivery" in this context is considered above, para.11–049.

[74] See, *e.g. Hibbert v Shee* (1807) 1 Camp. 113; *Wells v Hopkins* (1839) 5 M. & W. 7; *Smith v Hughes* (1871) L.R. 6 Q.B. 597. *Cf.* Vienna Convention (above, para.1–024), Art. 35(2)(c).

[75] *Parker v Palmer* (1821) 4 B. & A. 387 at 391. See also *Parkinson v Lee* (1802) 2 East 314 at 323.

[76] Williston, *Sales* (rev. ed., 1948), para.250.

[77] *e.g. Re Walkers, Winser and Hamm and Shaw Son & Co.* [1904] 2 K.B. 152 (barley); *Ceramic Brickworks (S) Pte Ltd v Asia-Tech Construction & Engineering Pte Ltd* [1996] 1 Singapore L.R. 200 (bricks). See also *Russell v Nicolopulo* (1860) 8 C.B. (N.S.) 362; and cases on "quality equal to London standard" and "quality as previously delivered" cited below, para.11–079, n.5.

[78] Below, paras 11–075 *et seq.*

[79] *e.g. Syers v Jonas* (1848) 2 Exch. 111 (tobacco).

11–075 **Exhibition of sample does not necessarily make sale one by sample.** The mere fact, however, that a sample is exhibited during negotiation for a sale does not necessarily mean that the sale is by sample: it is only such if the contract made is for goods in agreement with the sample.[80] Frequently samples are displayed to give no more than some indication of the nature of the goods offered. "Whether a seller who exhibits a sample does represent that the bulk is like the sample, or merely that the sample was honestly and properly taken, and that the buyer must take his own risk as to the bulk, is a question of fact in each case."[81] In determining the function of the sample, it should be borne in mind that if the sale is by sample the rules as to satisfactory quality are different from those in sales not by sample: the condition is that the goods shall be free from defects which would not be apparent on reasonable examination of the sample, whether or not such examination was made.[82] The fact that this rule is inappropriate (because an examination was not to be anticipated) would be strong indication that a sale is not to be regarded as one by sample.[83] Purchases by consumers are less likely to be held sales by sample for this reason. Thus a private person buying wine after a tasting might not be buying by sample where a professional buyer might. Where a consumer buys goods at a shop by inspecting a specimen and then ordering something which is supplied in a sealed package from a warehouse or other store, it seems very doubtful whether any examination made was for the purpose of detecting defects, and hence the sale should probably not be regarded as being by sample.[84] Clearer cases can arise when the sale is not by sample because the seller declines to sell by sample but requires the buyer to examine; or where the buyer refuses to buy by sample but requires an express warranty.

11–076 **Written contract.** A number of old cases indicated that where the contract is reduced to writing, and the writing makes no mention of sample, extrinsic evidence might not be introduced to show that a sale by sample was intended.[85] Such evidence could, however, in such cases be introduced to identify the goods by reference to a sample,[86] or to prove a collateral contract that the goods are warranted to be equal to sample,[87] or to indicate trade usage that such sales are by sample.[88] But this was an application of

---

[80] See, *e.g. Gardiner v Gray* (1815) 4 Camp. 144; *Ginner v King* (1890) 7 T.L.R. 140; *Re Faulkners Ltd* (1917) 38 D.L.R. 84 (distinguishing sale by sample from sale from samples); *W & J Sharp v Thomson* (1915) 20 C.L.R. 127 ("Wedgwood Seconds"); *East Asiatic Co. Inc. v Canada Rice Mills Ltd* [1939] 3 D.L.R. 695 ("guaranteed up to type and grade as shown by sample from last year's crop"); *Engineering Plastics Ltd v J Mercer & Sons Ltd* [1985] 2 N.Z.L.R. 72 (where it was argued that the goods supplied were non-conforming because *superior* to sample).

[81] Williston, *Sales* (rev. ed., 1948), para.253.

[82] Below, para.11–080.

[83] It cannot be excluded in a true consumer sale by sample: below, para.13–083.

[84] *cf.* below, para.11–082.

[85] *Tye v Fynmore* (1813) 3 Camp. 462; *Meyer v Everth* (1814) 4 Camp. 22; *Gardiner v Gray* (1815) 4 Camp. 144.

[86] *R W Cameron & Co. v L Slutzkin Pty Ltd* (1923) 32 C.L.R. 81 (descriptive term without fixed commercial meaning).

[87] See *L G Thorne & Co. Pty Ltd v Thomas Borthwick & Son Ltd* [1956] S.R.(N.S.W.) 81 (neatsfoot oil).

[88] *Syers v Jonas* (1848) 2 Exch. 111 (tobacco).

the parol evidence rule, which is now of much less importance than it was formerly.[89]

11–077 **Contract made before sample tendered.** Sometimes the contract is made before the tender of a sample, and itself provides for such tender. This is not the paradigm sale by sample which the Act seeks to regulate and various problems of interpretation may arise. There may first be a question of whether the seller is bound to tender a sample at all, or whether he has an absolute choice as to whether he proceeds with the contract or not.[90] Secondly, there may be a question as to whether the sample must comply with descriptive words contained in the contract,[91] or whether such wording gives a general indication only[92] and, as in the paradigm sale by sample, the description of the goods is in whole or in part to be inferred from the sample.[93] Thirdly, there may be a question as to whether the buyer has an unfettered right to reject the sample[94] or whether he can only do so for good reason such as non-compliance with description.[95] These and similar matters[96] are questions of interpretation.

11–078 **"Bulk".** It is clear that a sale can be a sale by sample, not only where the goods are unascertained,[97] but also where they are specific.[98] In such cases "bulk" may sometimes even mean the goods delivered less the sample. But there can also be a sale by sample though the goods are to be manufactured after contract[99]: in such a case "bulk" means no more than "the contract goods". So also there can presumably be a sale by sample where the contract is simply to supply an article or a few articles identical with the sample: in such a case again the word "bulk" is really inappropriate. Difficulty is caused by the definition of "bulk" given in section 61(1), the interpretation section, of the Sale of Goods Act 1979. This definition was inserted by the Sale of Goods (Amendment) Act 1995, which provides that where there is a sale of a specified quantity of unascertained goods which are part of an identified bulk, a buyer who has paid the price may obtain property in an undivided share of that bulk.[1] The definition is that "'bulk'

---

[89] See Law Com. No. 154, Cmnd. 9700 (1980); Treitel, *Law of Contract* (11th ed.), pp.192 *et seq*.
[90] *cf*. below, para.19–014 ("subject to shipment").
[91] See *John Bowron & Son Ltd v Rodema Canned Foods Ltd* [1967] 1 Lloyd's Rep. 183 (apricot pulp).
[92] As was argued in the above case.
[93] *cf. Joseph Travers & Sons Ltd v Longel Ltd* (1948) 64 T.L.R. 150; *R W Cameron & Co. v L. Slutzkin Pty Ltd* (1923) 32 C.L.R. 81.
[94] As in *Wood Components of London v James Webster & Brother Ltd* [1959] 2 Lloyd's Rep. 200 (wood).
[95] See *John Bowron & Son Ltd v Rodema Canned Foods Ltd*, above, at p.189.
[96] See also *Terfloth and Kennedy Ltd v Christy Crops Ltd* (1977) 27 N.S.R. (2d) 433 (blueberries).
[97] *e.g. Re Walkers, Winser and Hamm and Shaw Son & Co.* [1904] 2 K.B. 152 (barley).
[98] *e.g. Azemar v Casella* (1867) L.R. 2 C.P. 677 (cotton bales).
[99] *e.g. Heilbutt v Hickson* (1872) L.R. 7 C.P. 438 (shoes); *Drummond v Van Ingen* (1887) 12 App.Cas. 284; *Jones v Padgett* (1890) 24 Q.B.D. 650 (cloth).
[1] s.2. See above, paras 5–109 *et seq*.

means a mass or collection of goods of the same type which—(a) is confined in a defined space or area; and (b) is such that any goods in the bulk are interchangeable with any other goods therein of the same number or quantity."[2] It is plain that this definition is directed towards the purposes of the 1995 Act as above described. Despite the apparent generality arising from its position in section 61(1) it is submitted that the definition has no relevance to the notion of "bulk" in connection with the requirement that in sales by sample the bulk correspond with the sample. Although the reference to interchangeability is not irrelevant to (though of little value for) the notion of bulk in connection with sales by sample, it is quite inappropriate to the rules for such sales that the bulk with which the sample must correspond must be contained in a defined space or area.

"The bulk will correspond with the sample in quality". The correspondence required extends beyond description to cover the quality of the goods. The condition is not complied with where the goods do not correspond with sample but could be made to do so at trifling cost and trouble.[3] But correspondence with sample is a notion requiring careful attention. "The extent to which a sample may be held to 'speak' must depend on the contract and what is contemplated by the parties in regard to it."[4] Thus in some cases mere visual comparison is intended: if therefore in such a case the bulk corresponds with the sample on such comparison, there is no breach under this subsection even though there are other differences of a quite substantial nature.[5] There may in other circumstances be a test by touching, or by chemical analysis, or by microscopic examination. But "it is not open to a buyer to submit a sample to an analysis unusual in the trade so as to reveal in it certain attributes or qualities hitherto unsuspected, and then to require, by virtue of the sample clause alone, that the bulk should contain the same qualities."[6] And evidence of trade usage and custom may be admitted as to what constitutes correspondence.[7] There may also be clauses specifying the time in which testing is to 11–079

---

[2] See this definition discussed above, paras 5–113, 5–114; below, para.18–295.

[3] *E and S Ruben Ltd v Faire Bros & Co. Ltd* [1949] 1 K.B. 254 (rubber material); *Aitken, Campbell & Co. Ltd v Boullen and Gatenby*, 1908 S.C. 490 (twill). But if the deficiency is such as to come under the *de minimis* principle it does not justify rejection: *Joe Lowe Food Products Co. Ltd v J A and P Holland Ltd* [1954] 2 Lloyd's Rep. 70 (lumps in dessert powder). Section 15A of the Sale of Goods Act may however be applicable: below, paras 12–024 *et seq.*, 18–284.

[4] *Steels and Busks Ltd v Bleecker Bik & Co. Ltd* [1956] 1 Lloyd's Rep. 228 at 239 (rubber).

[5] *F E Hookway & Co. Ltd v Alfred Isaacs & Son* [1954] 1 Lloyd's Rep. 491 (shellac); *Steels and Busks Ltd v Bleecker Bik & Co. Ltd*, above. But there may in such a case be liability under s.15(2)(c) or for breach of s.13. The two cases cited are not actually cases of sale by sample but relate to the terms "quality equal to London standard" and "quality as previously delivered". But the same principles are applied to those terms, and also to "fair average quality": see *Ashington Piggeries Ltd v Christopher Hill Ltd* [1972] A.C. 441 at 470–471.

[6] *F E Hookway & Co. Ltd v Alfred Isaacs & Co. Ltd*, above, at p.512, *per* Devlin J.

[7] This is probably the best explanation of *Re Walkers, Winser and Hamm and Shaw Son & Co.* [1904] 2 K.B. 152, where evidence was admitted of a custom not to allow rejection of barley where the variation in quality was slight. The contract provided for delivery of goods "about as per sample".

be done or making certain types of certification or testing conclusive: these may in whole or in part be exemption clauses and come under the rules for such clauses.[8] On the other hand there may be cases where, by the express terms of the contract, the goods must correspond with sample and also with analysis: in such cases an extra liability is placed on the seller.[9]

11–080 **"Free from any defect, making their quality unsatisfactory, which would not be apparent on reasonable examination of the sample".** At common law, on a sale by sample, no condition as to any particular quality was ordinarily implied, for "the use of a sample, which to a person of ordinary diligence and experience would disclose the want of that quality, negatives the implication, because it expresses to the buyer a different intention on the part of the seller."[10] There was, however, an implied condition that the goods be free from *latent* defects making them unmerchantable, and it is this that the Act restates, now amended to use the new terminology of "satisfactory quality".[11] The examination referred to need only be a reasonable one in the circumstances, taking into account the practice of the trade and so forth. "The office of a sample is to present to the eye the real meaning and intention of the parties with regard to the subject-matter of the contract, which, owing to the imperfection of language, it may be difficult or impossible to express in words. The sample speaks for itself. But it cannot be treated as saying more than such a sample would tell a merchant of the class to which the buyer belongs, using due care and diligence, and appealing to it in the ordinary way and with the knowledge possessed by merchants of that class at the time. No doubt the sample might be made to say a great deal more. Pulled to pieces and examined by unusual tests which curiosity or suspicion might suggest, it would doubtless reveal every secret of its construction. But that is not the way in which business is done in this country."[12]

11–081 Thus, in one case, a retailer buying plastic catapults tested a sample by pulling back the elastic, with satisfactory results. This was held reasonable examination and the seller was liable when one of the catapults nevertheless proved unmerchantable (under the former term).[13] "The Act speaks,

[8] *"Agroexport" v NV Goorden Import Cy. SA* [1956] 1 Lloyd's Rep. 319; *The Milton B. Medary* [1962] 2 Lloyd's Rep. 192; *W N Lindsay & Co. Ltd v European Grain and Shipping Agency Ltd* [1963] 1 Lloyd's Rep. 437; *C. E. B. Draper & Son Ltd v Edward Turner & Son Ltd* [1964] 1 Lloyd's Rep. 165; revsd. [1965] 1 Q.B. 424; *Toepfer v Continental Grain Co.* [1974] 1 Lloyd's Rep. 11; *NV Bunge v Cie. Noga d'Importation et d'Exportation (The Bow Cedar)* [1980] 2 Lloyd's Rep. 601; *Gill & Duffus SA v Berger & Co. Inc.* [1984] A.C. 382; *Galaxy Energy International Ltd v Eurobunker SpA* [2001] 2 Lloyd's Rep. 725; *Veba Oil Supply and Trading GmbH v Petrotrade Inc.* [2001] EWCA Civ 1832; [2002] 1 Lloyd's Rep. 295. See below, paras 13–031, 13–040, 18–275 *et seq.*

[9] *Towerson v Aspatria Agricultural Co-operative Society Ltd* (1872) 27 L.T. 276.

[10] *Mody v Gregson* (1868) L.R. 4 Ex. 49 at 53, *per* Willes J. (shirting).

[11] See above, para.11–026.

[12] *Drummond v Van Ingen* (1887) 12 App.Cas. 284 at 297, *per* Lord Macnaghten (cloth).

[13] *Godley v Perry* [1960] 1 W.L.R. 9. See also *Joseph Travers & Sons Ltd v Longel Ltd* (1948) 64 T.L.R. 150 (war surplus boots).

not of a 'practicable' but of a 'reasonable' examination."[14] There may also be cases where the sample is too small for the defect to be detected: the term as to quality will then equally apply.[15] The term "satisfactory quality" must be interpreted in accordance with the statutory definition given in section 14(2A) and (2B).[16]

Not confined to business sellers. It is perhaps surprising that at least this part of the section is not confined to business sellers, though it may well be that few transactions which could be described as sales by sample are conducted other than by business sellers.[17] The lack of explanation of the notion of "sale by sample" and the dicta regarding the criteria and methods of comparison certainly seem to envisage merchants.[18] None of the cases here cited on sales by sample appear to be consumer cases. 11–082

"Reasonable examination". But in one respect the liability of the seller is less stringent than that under section 14(2): although the condition of satisfactory quality is excluded if the defect would be apparent on reasonable examination of the sample,[19] there is no requirement that such an examination has actually been made. This is presumably because a sale by sample imports the assumption that examination of the sample will be made, and that the sample is relied on to the extent that it reasonably furnishes information. It is only beyond this that the provision as to satisfactory quality applies. 11–083

Time element. This is discussed in connection with section 14(2).[20] 11–084

Relation with section 14(2). Section 14(2) of the Act, which makes provision as to the duty to supply goods of satisfactory quality,[21] formerly only applied to sales by description. There was then a difference between the effect of that provision, which does not require examination of the goods but provides that where an examination is conducted there is no liability as to defects which that examination ought to reveal, and section 15(2)(c), which excludes liability in respect of matters which would be apparent on reasonable examination of the sample whether such examination took place or not. Since the removal of the restriction of section 14(2) to sales by description, the claimant in a sale by sample who did not examine the sample could perhaps have put himself in a slightly more favourable position by suing under section 14(2). The matter is settled in section 14(2C) of the Sale of Goods Act, inserted by the Sale and Supply of Goods Act 1994 s.1(1) under which it is provided that "The term implied by 11–085

---

[14] *Godley v Perry*, above, at p.15.
[15] See *Jurgensen v F E Hookway & Co. Ltd* [1951] 2 Lloyd's Rep. 129 at 147.
[16] Above, paras 11–026 *et seq.*
[17] *cf.* above, para.11–075.
[18] So also the original Act did not define "merchantable quality": above, para.11–031.
[19] This is reinforced by the same terminology in positive form in s.14(2C)(c).
[20] See above, para.11–049.
[21] Above, paras 11–026 *et seq.*

subsection (2) above does not extend to any matter making the quality of the goods unsatisfactory . . . (c) in the case of a contract for sale by sample, which would have been apparent on a reasonable examination of the sample."[22]

11–086 **Sale by sample and description.** Where a sale is by sample alone, the duty is thus comparatively limited. It is certainly possible for the sample to amount to the sole description of the goods; or for any further description given to be no more than a label for designation of the subject-matter.[23] But where a sale is by description as well as sample, as it often, perhaps usually, will be, section 13(2) must also be complied with: "it is not sufficient that the bulk of the goods corresponds with the sample if the goods do not also correspond with the description."[24] They must also, of course, be of satisfactory quality unless examination of the sample would have revealed the defect[25] and in some cases there may be a sale by sample and a reliance on the seller under section 14(3) over and above this.[26] In view of the fact that the sample itself in some respects indicates the description of the goods, a sale by sample and description may raise problems of reconciliation between these two elements. "The definition of the respective spheres of operation of the description and the sample is a question of construction of the relevant contract, in the light of the relevant surrounding circumstances."[27] In particular, where matters of quality go to description,[28] the exhibition of a sample from which quality can be assessed may impliedly vary the description in this respect; and a certification as to quality may therefore in appropriate cases be conclusive as to compliance with sample and hence with description.[29]

11–087 **Related contracts.** Provisions similar to section 15 are implied into other contracts for the transfer of property in goods[30] (*e.g.* contracts of exchange and for work and materials[31]); hire-purchase agreements[32]; and contracts of hire.[33]

---

[22] See Murdoch 44 M.L.R. 388 at 396–397 (1981); Law Com. No. 160, Scot. Law Com. No. 104 (1987), paras 6, 24–6.27.
[23] Above, para.11–022.
[24] *ibid.*
[25] Above, para.11–080.
[26] Above, paras 11–051 *et seq.*
[27] *Gill & Duffus SA v Berger & Co. Inc.* [1983] 1 Lloyd's Rep. 622 at 632, *per* Robert Goff L.J.
[28] *e.g. Toepfer v Continental Grain Co.* [1974] 1 Lloyd's Rep. 11, above, para.11–016.
[29] *Toepfer v Continental Grain Co.*, above; *Gill & Duffus SA v Berger & Co. Inc.* [1983] 1 Lloyd's Rep. 622 at 626, 628–630, 632–634; [1984] A.C. 382, 393–394. But *cf. NV Bunge v Cie. Noga d'Importation et d'Exportation SA (The Bow Cedar)* [1980] 2 Lloyd's Rep. 601, where the certificate was final as to analysis, but not as to the description of the goods as "Brazilian crude groundnut oil"; *Daudruy v Tropical Products Sales SA* [1986] 1 Lloyd's Rep. 535 (palm fatty acid distillate).
[30] Supply of Goods and Services Act 1982, s.5, as amended by Sale and Supply of Goods Act 1994, s.7 and Schs 2, 3.
[31] Above, paras 1–034 *et seq.*
[32] Supply of Goods (Implied Terms) Act 1973, s.11, as amended by Sale and Supply of Goods Act 1994, s.7 and Sch.2.
[33] Supply of Goods and Services Act 1982, s.10, as amended by Sale and Supply of Goods Act 1994, s.7 and Schs 2, 3.

4. OTHER IMPLIED TERMS

Terms implied by usage. By section 14(4) of the Sale of Goods Act 1979, "An implied term about quality or fitness for a particular purpose may be annexed to a contract of sale by usage."[34] An old example is *Jones v Bowden*,[35] where evidence was admitted that at sales of pimento, where the catalogue did not state that the goods were sea-water damaged, they were warranted free of such damage. The general rules apply, that the usage or custom must be reasonable, universally accepted by the particular trade or profession or at the particular place, certain, not unlawful and not inconsistent with the express or implied terms of the contract.[36] 11–088

Other implied terms. Other terms may when appropriate be implied into a contract of sale, though this is comparatively rare in that the Sale of Goods Act 1979 itself implies most of the terms that are relevant. But it has been held that where goods were ordered from a manufacturer who made such goods, and was not in any other way a dealer in them, there was, in the absence of agreement or contrary usage, an implied term that the goods should be of the manufacturer's own make.[37] Where goods are sold as being of a particular brand, it has been held that there was an undertaking that they would bear the normal label for that brand.[38] It has also been held that the order of an article by its trade name is normally to be taken as meaning an article as it was manufactured at the date of the order, whatever its composition at an earlier date.[39] But it is unwise to treat these isolated decisions on their facts as laying down rules of law. The principles applicable for the implication of terms are the same as those which operate in the law of contract generally.[40] 11–089

---

34 This form of the wording was introduced by the Supply of Goods (Implied Terms) Act 1973. The use of the word "term" rather than "condition or warranty" dates from the Sale or Supply of Goods Act 1994, s.7 and Sch.2, and was adopted to effect the abolition of the term "condition" in Scots law. Similar provisions appear in ss.4(7) and 9(7) of the Supply of Goods and Services Act 1982; and in s.10(4) of the Supply of Goods (Implied Terms) Act 1973, as amended by Consumer Credit Act 1974, s.192(4) and Sch.4, para.35.

35 (1813) 4 Taunt. 847.

36 These four requirements, which are well known and to be found in many authoritative works, were accepted by Roskill J. in *Oricon Waren-Handels GmbH v Intergraan NV* [1967] 2 Lloyd's Rep. 82 at 96.

37 *Johnson v Raylton* (1881) 7 Q.B.D. 438. A provision to this effect was in the 1889 draft of the Sale of Goods Bill, cl.17(4). If this is a term as to quality, its implication is now excluded by s.14(1); but it does not seem to be a term as to quality. It would in any case frequently be inappropriate, *e.g.* where an article normally contains components manufactured by another concern.

38 *Scaliaris v E Ofverberg & Co.* (1921) 37 T.L.R. 307.

39 *Harris & Sons v Plymouth Varnish & Colour Co. Ltd* (1933) 49 T.L.R. 521.

40 See *Chitty on Contracts* (29th ed.), Vol.1, Ch.13; Treitel, *Law of Contract* (11th ed.), pp.201 *et seq*. As to overseas sales, see below, Chaps 18–21. On implied terms in general see *Liverpool City Council v Irwin* [1977] A.C. 239.

CHAPTER 12

REMEDIES IN RESPECT OF DEFECTS

	PARA.
1. Misrepresentation	12–002
2. Breach of contractual term	12–017
3. Additional rights of buyer in consumer cases	12–071
4. Misrepresentations subsequently incorporated into the contract	12–119
5. Tort liability in respect of goods	12–121
6. Mistake as to subject-matter of contract	12–128
7. Vienna Convention	12–129

Introductory. The remedies of a buyer against a seller[1] in respect of defective goods vary in accordance with whether his complaint is (i) as to the falsity of a representation inducing the contract and not subsequently incorporated into it as a term; (ii) as to the breach of a term in the contract; or (iii) as to a misrepresentation inducing the contract and subsequently incorporated into it. The criteria for distinguishing these concepts are discussed in Chapter 10: their consequences, which stem from common law with some statutory modification, are dealt with here. The Sale and Supply of Goods to Consumers Regulations 2002, which implement an EC Directive, have, however, introduced a new set of remedies or breach of certain contract terms which apply to consumers only and are entirely statutory. These are dealt with after the common law remedies, which in fact survive and co-exist with them, raising complications. An action in tort based on negligence in relation to the goods, or under the Consumer Protection Act 1987, may sometimes also be brought against a seller; and it may occasionally be possible to treat a contract as void or inoperative because of mistake made by one or both parties. These last topics are taken in briefly at the end of the present chapter, where there is also brief reference to certain pitfalls connected with the Vienna Convention on International Sales. 12–001

1. MISREPRESENTATION

No rights in contract at common law. Where a misrepresentation is made by a seller which is not incorporated into the contract as a term, no action for damages for breach of the main contract can arise on it. Equally, there can be no right to treat the contract as discharged, except in the case of fraud, where the common law allowed rescission. This jurisdiction has 12–002

[1] As to his remedies against the manufacturer or distributor see below, paras 12–122, 14–061 *et seq.* See also below, para.14–045 on rights to cancel consumer contracts.

effectively been swallowed up by the equitable jurisdiction to rescind, which applies whether a misrepresentation is innocent or fraudulent, though the original rules as to fraud may provide an explanation for various differences which still exist. An action for damages upon a collateral contract, or in tort, or under section 2(1) of the Misrepresentation Act 1967 may also lie in respect of such a misrepresentation: these are discussed later.[2]

12–003 **Representee may rescind in equity.** A jurisdiction to rescind contracts induced by misrepresentation was established in equity in the latter part of the nineteenth century,[3] and it seems that in England at any rate this jurisdiction applies to contracts for the sale of goods despite the fact that it is not mentioned in the Sale of Goods Act. The matter is discussed elsewhere,[4] as are the criteria for identifying such a misrepresentation.[5] A buyer whose purchase is induced by misrepresentation, whether fraudulent, negligent or entirely innocent, may rescind the contract. As a matter of general equity he may not, however, claim damages in such a case, though the court will sometimes order the payment of an indemnity, a money adjustment to assist the effecting of rescission.[6] In order to rescind he must normally either notify the other party[7] or take legal proceedings[8]: though it seems that a rescinding *seller* may retake the chattel without communication.[9] A rescission must normally, at least in this context, be of the whole contract: it is not possible to rescind in part.[10] In this context the right to rescind means that should the buyer in such a case not have paid the price, he can refuse to take delivery of the goods, place them at the seller's disposal[11] or return them, and plead the misrepresentation as a defence to an action for damages or for the price. Should he have paid the price, he can only recover this with the aid of the court.

12–004 **Powers of court under Misrepresentation Act 1967, s.2(2).** Once the matter comes before a court or arbitrator, however, the court or arbitrator may by virtue of section 2(2) of the Misrepresentation Act 1967 in the case

---

[2] Below, paras 12–011 *et seq*.
[3] *Redgrave v Hurd* (1881) 20 Ch.D. 1.
[4] Above, para.10–008.
[5] Above, para.10–009.
[6] See in general *Chitty on Contracts* (29th ed.), Vol.1, paras 6–118, 6–119; *Whittington v Seale- Hayne* (1900) 82 L.T. 49.
[7] But in *Car and Universal Finance Co. Ltd v Caldwell* [1965] 1 Q.B. 525, a person who had by fraud been induced to sell a car in return for a valueless cheque was held entitled to rescind by informing the police and the Automobile Association, it being impossible to trace the buyer. This rule may be confined to cases of fraud and is in any case open to criticism: see 12th Report of Law Reform Committee, Cmnd. 2958 (1966), para.16. See also *Newtons of Wembley Ltd v Williams* [1965] 1 Q.B. 560; *Empresa Cubana de Fletes v Lagonisi Shipping Co. Ltd* [1971] 1 Q.B. 488 at 504; *cf. Macleod v Kerr* 1965 S.L.T. 358; above, paras 7–024, 7–025.
[8] As to whether defence of legal proceedings can constitute rescission, see *Academy of Health and Fitness Pty Ltd v Power* [1973] V.R. 254.
[9] *Re Eastgate* [1905] 1 K.B. 465; *Car and Universal Finance Co. Ltd v Caldwell*, above, at pp.554, 558; above, para.7–024.
[10] *United Shoe Machinery Co. of Canada v Brunet* [1909] A.C. 330. See, however, in a different context *Far Eastern Shipping Co. Public Ltd v Scales Trading Ltd* [2001] 1 All E.R. (Comm.) 319 at 326; *cf. De Molestina v Ponton* [2002] 1 Lloyd's Rep. 271 at 286–287.
[11] *cf.* the rule for breach, below, para.12–065.

of non-fraudulent misrepresentation declare the contract subsisting and award damages in lieu of rescission, even where the original rescission did not require the aid of the court.[12] This subsection reads:

> "Where a person has entered into a contract after a misrepresentation has been made to him otherwise than fraudulently, and he would be entitled, by reason of the misrepresentation, to rescind the contract, then, if it is claimed, in any proceedings arising out of the contract, that the contract ought to be or has been rescinded, the court or arbitrator may declare the contract subsisting and award damages in lieu of rescission, if of opinion that it would be equitable to do so, having regard to the nature of the misrepresentation and the loss that would be caused by it if the contract were upheld, as well as to the loss that rescission would cause to the other party."

Subsection (3) provides that such damages may be awarded notwithstanding the fact that there is also a liability in damages under section 2(1),[13] but that an award under subsection (2) shall be taken into account in assessing damages under subsection (1). It is not stated whether the contractual, or the tortious, or some other measure of damages is intended by subsection (2). If the choice is between the first two, it seems that the tortious measure would be preferable, *i.e.* that the plaintiff should be put in the position in which he would have been had the misrepresentation not been made: to hold him liable for the full expectation on the contract would seem unfair where there is *ex hypothesi* no breach of contract involved. But it is more appropriate that special rules as to damages should be developed in connection with this subsection, perhaps excluding consequential loss and compensating only for the fact that the contract is not rescinded.[14]

Loss of the right to rescind. In accordance with general principles of equity, the right to rescind is lost where the contract has been affirmed, where *restitutio in integrum* is impossible, where the subject-matter of the contract has passed into the hands of a third party, and, except where the misrepresentation is fraudulent, probably by lapse of time.[15] It was formerly probably the law that a contract of sale of a chattel might not be rescinded for innocent misrepresentation where it had been executed,[16] but this rule 12–005

---

[12] See *Atlantic Lines and Navigation Co. Inc. v Hallam Ltd (The Lucy)* [1983] 1 Lloyd's Rep. 188, where Mustill J. suggests that the court may annul retrospectively a rescission which has taken place in the past: see p.202.

[13] Below, para.12–014.

[14] See Treitel, *Law of Contract* (11th ed.), pp.357–358; *Chitty on Contracts* (29th ed.), Vol.1, paras 6–095 *et seq; William Sindall Plc v Cambridgeshire CC* [1994] 1 W.L.R. 1216; Beale, 111 L.Q.R. 60 (1995); *UCB Corporate Services Ltd v Thomason* [2005] EWCA Civ. 225; [2005] 1 All E.R. (Comm) 601 (no loss proved).

[15] See *Chitty on Contracts* (29th ed.), Vol.1, paras 6–112 *et seq.* The significance of these bars on the right to rescind, particularly that relating to third parties, would be much reduced if the decision in *Car and Universal Finance Co. Ltd v Caldwell*, above, para.12–003, n.7, were accepted.

[16] *Seddon v North Eastern Salt Co. Ltd* [1905] 1 Ch. 326; *Angel v Jay* [1911] 1 K.B. 666.

was much criticised[17] and was in England abolished by section 1(b) of the Misrepresentation Act 1967, which provides that a contract may be rescinded notwithstanding that it has been performed.[18] The court may, however, under section 2(2) of the Act[19] award damages in lieu of rescission in such a case if this seems more appropriate.

12–006 **Affirmation.** An affirmation requires in principle a clear indication that the transaction is affirmed, made by a person who has knowledge or obvious means of knowledge of the facts and (probably) of his right to rescind.[20] Express affirmation apart, a contract of sale may be held to be affirmed where the buyer, having discovered a defect, uses the purchased article more than is necessary for the purpose of ascertaining the gravity of the defect. Thus in *Long v Lloyd*,[21] the buyer of a lorry drove it from Hampton Court (where he had taken delivery of it) to Sevenoaks, and then from Sevenoaks to Rochester and back. He found that it was defective, but nevertheless, while making a complaint to the seller, sent it on a long trip to Middlesbrough, on which trip it broke down. He was held by the second trip to have affirmed the contract. There are dicta in this case,[22] based on dicta of Denning L.J. in *Leaf v International Galleries*,[23] indicating that affirmation is the same as acceptance as defined in section 35 of the Sale of Goods Act. It is, however, clear from the wording of section 35 that goods may be accepted though a defect has not been discovered.[24] This does not seem correct as regards affirmation in equity,[25] and it is submitted that, in so far as they lay down a general proposition, both sets of dicta are incorrect.[26]

12–007 **Restitutio in integrum impossible.**[27] *Restitutio in integrum* will be impossible where, for example, the buyer of a car has substantially modified it after purchase,[28] or it has been seriously damaged in an accident,[29] whether or not by his fault, or sold to someone who is not willing to return

---

[17] Hammelmann, 55 L.Q.R. 90 (1939); *Solle v Butcher* [1950] 1 K.B. 671 at 695–696.
[18] *Chitty on Contracts* (29th ed.), Vol.1, para.6–130.
[19] Above, para.12–004.
[20] See *Clough v London & North Western Ry Co.* (1871) L.R. 7 Ex. 26; *Coastal Estates Pty Ltd v Melevende* [1965] V.R. 433; *Peyman v Lanjani* [1985] Ch. 457; *Motor Oil Hellas (Corinth) Refineries SA v Shipping Corp. of India (The Kanchenjunga)* [1990] 1 Lloyd's Rep. 391 at 397–399, HL; and *cf.* below, paras 12–035, 12–037. There may, however, be an estoppel against saying there has been no affirmation: see *Peyman v Lanjani*, above, and below, para.12–037.
[21] [1958] 1 W.L.R. 753. See also *United Shoe Machinery Co. of Canada v Brunet* [1909] A.C. 330.
[22] At p.760.
[23] [1950] 2 K.B. 86 at 91.
[24] Below, paras 12–038 *et seq.*
[25] See *Aaron's Reefs v Twiss* [1896] A.C. 273 at 287, 296. See also below, para.12–037.
[26] See *Leason Pty Ltd v Princes Farm Pty Ltd* [1983] 2 N.S.W.L.R. 381 at 387–388.
[27] *Chitty on Contracts* (29th ed.), Vol. 1, paras 6–112 *et seq.* For further discussion see Treitel, *Law of Contract* (11th ed.), pp.380–381.
[28] *cf. Clarke v Dickson* (1858) E.B. & E. 148.
[29] *cf. Vigers v Pike* (1842) 8 Cl. & F. 562.

it. But on principle testing of the goods, even if it partly consumes them or otherwise affects their condition, should not bar rejection.[30] And the mere fact that goods have deteriorated in market value will not bar rescission if they can be returned.[31] The court has wide powers as to the terms on which it will order rescission, and sometimes does so subject to the payment of compensation for deterioration[32]; it is probable that such an order could be made in a case of sale of goods, though this would doubtless be rare.[33] It seems that the powers are more readily exercised in the case of fraud.[34] In contracts relating to land, a purchaser who rescinds may be allowed to do so only on the terms of paying an occupation rent[35]: there seems however no reason to apply this special rule to sale of goods.[36] Where the representee has improved the property, this does not bar rescission, but may entitle him to a claim in any award of damages.[37]

Third party rights.[38] A disposition of goods in favour of a third party who gives value and acts *bona fide* will also bar rescission, but in the case of rescission of a contract of sale by a buyer this situation is covered by the rule that *restitutio in integrum* is impossible, for the buyer will usually be unable to return the goods. If he can, however, by virtue of the cooperation of the third party, he can rescind, for the rule as to third parties exists to protect the third party, not the party at fault. 12–008

Lapse of time.[39] It seems likely, finally, that in the case of innocent or negligent misrepresentation the right to rescind is lost by mere lapse of time. This is not true in the case of fraud: a party may rescind at any time after learning of the fraud, and lapse of time is only relevant to show affirmation.[40] But in *Leaf v International Galleries*,[41] a case of innocent misrepresentation, the buyer of a picture was held not to be able to rescind five years after the sale, on the grounds that he had had "ample opportunity 12–009

---

[30] *cf.* below, para.12–040.
[31] *Armstrong v Jackson* [1917] 2 K.B. 822 (value of shares). *Cf.* below, para.12–051.
[32] See, *e.g. Erlanger v New Sombrero Phosphate Co.* (1878) 3 App. Cas. 1212 at 1278–1279.
[33] See *Wiebe v Butchart's Motors Ltd* [1949] 4 D.L.R. 838 (rescission of contract for sale of car with compensation for deterioration); *Atlantic Lines and Navigation Co. Inc. v Hallam Ltd (The Lucy)* [1983] 1 Lloyd's Rep. 188 at 202.
[34] *Spence v Crawford* [1939] 3 All E.R. 271 at 288. See *Kellogg Brown & Root Services Corp. v Aerotech Herman Nelson Inc.* (2004) 238 D.L.R. (4th) 595 (heaters falsely represented as new "virtually worthless from the beginning").
[35] See *Hulton v Hulton* [1917] 1 K.B. 813 at 826; Kerr, *Fraud and Mistake* (7th ed.), p.520.
[36] *cf. Rowland v Divall* [1923] 2 K.B. 500; above, para.4–006, below, paras 12–068, 17–090. But see also *Gibbons v Trap Motors* (1970) 9 D.L.R. (3d) 742.
[37] Treitel, *Law of Contract* (11th ed.), pp.381–382.
[38] *Chitty on Contracts* (29th ed.), Vol. 1, para.6–126. Contrast the position as to assignment of choses in action, where an assignee takes subject to equities. See also below, para.12–051.
[39] *Chitty, op. cit.*, para.6–124.
[40] *Clough v L. & N.W.Ry* (1871) L.R. 7 Ex. 26 at 34; *Aaron's Reefs Ltd v Twiss* [1896] A.C. 273 at 294; *Allen v Robles* [1969] 1 W.L.R. 1193; *Fenton v Kenny* [1969] N.Z.L.R. 552.
[41] [1950] 2 K.B. 86.

for examination",[42] and despite a finding of fact that there had been no laches.[43] This particular decision seems based on the idea, which is doubted above,[44] that acceptance under the Sale of Goods Act and affirmation barring rescission for misrepresentation are the same. But the actual result appears reasonable and to be explained on the basis of a rule as to lapse of time. As previously suggested, it does not follow that the right would be lost where one of the acts constituting acceptance under section 35 of the Sale of Goods Act was performed by a buyer who had no knowledge of the defect. The general reasoning of all the judges in the case is based on the idea that there must be an end to a transaction,[45] and it is submitted that this is the best principle for explaining the case. If the goods are used for a substantial period, there may also be an element of unjust enrichment.[46]

12–010 **Damages where right to rescind lost.** Where the right to rescind has been lost it might be expected that the power of the court to declare the contract subsisting and award damages in lieu of rescission under section 2(2) of the Misrepresentation Act 1967 would be especially useful. It does not seem, however, that the power can be exercised at such a time, for it only applies where a person "would be entitled, by reason of the misrepresentation, to rescind the contract", and if it is too late to rescind it would seem that the person who could otherwise do so is not so entitled. It may be that the bars on the right to rescind should be relevant to that drastic right only, and that the court's powers under section 2(2) should remain: this result could be achieved if the section were interpreted to cover cases where a person is *in principle* entitled to rescind. But it is difficult to arrive at this result on the wording of the section, which, by referring to claims "that the contract ought to be or has been rescinded" and to the power of the court to declare the contract subsisting, seems to exclude situations where it is too late to rescind. Although it has recently been said, though by way of *obiter dicta*, that rescission is possible in such a situation,[47] there are now decisions that it is not.[48]

12–011 **Actions for damages: collateral contract.** Where the representation can be treated as part of a collateral contract, an action for damages will lie upon it.[49] Often the promise is treated as absolute.[50] But the court may interpret the promise in a more limited way. Thus in *Esso Petroleum Co.*

---

42 *ibid.*, at p.91.
43 *ibid.*, at p.92.
44 Above, para.12–006.
45 See Denning L.J. at p.91; Jenkins L.J. at p.92; Evershed M.R. at pp.94–95.
46 See *SAM Business Systems Ltd v Hedley & Co.* [2002] EWHC 2733 (TCC); [2003] 1 All E.R. (Comm) 465, where however the basis of a claim to reject is not clear.
47 *Thomas Witter Ltd v TBP Industries Ltd* [1996] 2 All E.R. 573, *per* Jacob J.: but see Beale, 111 L.Q.R. 385 (1995).
48 *Floods of Queensferry Ltd v Shand Construction Ltd* [2000] B.L.R. 81; *Government of Zanzibar v British Aerospace (Lancaster House) Ltd* [2000] 1 W.L.R. 2333; but see Malet, 117 L.Q.R. 524 (2001).
49 Above, para.10–012.
50 *e.g. Wells (Merstham) Ltd v Buckland Sand and Silica Ltd* [1965] 2 Q.B. 170 (warranty as to analysis of sand).

Ltd v Mardon,[51] the defendant was induced to take a lease of a petrol station on certain terms by statements made to him by a very experienced manager of the plaintiffs as to the likely throughput of the station. It was held that there was a promise that the forecast was made with reasonable care and skill but no more.

Liability in tort: deceit. The seller may sometimes be liable under the tort of deceit or fraud. This is committed where a statement is made with knowledge of its falsity, or without belief in its truth, or recklessly, careless whether it be true or false; it must be intended to be acted on and in fact acted on by the person to whom it was made, to his prejudice.[52] The statement need not be made directly to the person who relies on it: it is sufficient if it is made to a third person to be communicated to the plaintiff, or to a class of persons of whom the plaintiff is one, or to the public generally, with a view to its being acted on.[53] If these criteria are fulfilled, it is irrelevant that there was no wrongful motive and no intention to cause loss.[54] The tort requires the making of a statement, but the active concealment of a defect may perhaps sometimes amount to an implied statement.[55] The mere offer to sell defective goods with knowledge that they are defective is not, however, fraud.[56] Where fraud is established, an action for damages in tort against a seller will lie; and it seems clear that the principles of remoteness of damage applicable in cases of intentional tort will apply. These are not limited by notions of foreseeability, but only by the principles of causation: they may therefore lead to a larger award of damages than would be given in an action on the contract, if one was available. It appears that the same principles are applicable to an action under section 2(1) of the Misrepresentation Act 1967, discussed below.[57] In *Doyle v Olby (Ironmongers) Ltd*,[58] an ironmongery business was bought on the inducement of fraudulent representations as to its turnover. The damages awardable were held not to be simply such as to cover the difference in value between the price paid and the benefits actually derived from the business, but to cover also consequential loss suffered by the claimant, who had attempted to run it without being able to afford to do so in such a way as to minimise his losses. There will, however, also be cases 12–012

---

[51] [1976] Q.B. 801. But *cf. Howard Marine and Dredging Co. Ltd v A. Ogden & Sons (Excavations) Ltd* [1978] Q.B. 574 (no warranty as to capacity of barges).
[52] *Derry v Peek* (1889) 14 App.Cas. 337. See in general *Clerk and Lindsell on Torts* (19th ed.), Ch.18.
[53] *Swift v Winterbotham* (1873) L.R. 8 Q.B. 244 at 252–253.
[54] *Polhill v Walter* (1832) 3 B. & Ad. 114; *Brown Jenkinson & Co. Ltd v Percy Dalton (London) Ltd* [1957] 2 Q.B. 621.
[55] See *Schneider v Heath* (1813) 3 Camp. 506; *cf. Horsfall v Thomas* (1862) 1 H. & C. 90; *Ward v Hobbs* (1877) 3 Q.B.D. 150, affirmed (1878) 4 App.Cas. 13; *Peters & Co. v Planner* (1895) 11 T.L.R. 169. See also *Cottee v Douglas Seaton (Used Cars) Ltd* [1972] 1 W.L.R. 1408; *R. v Ford Motor Co. Ltd* [1974] 1 W.L.R. 1220 (Trade Descriptions Act).
[56] *Ward v Hobbs*, above. But see *Hurley v Dyke* [1979] R.T.R. 265 at 280–281, 291, 295 (CA) 302, 303 (HL); and below, paras 12–075, 13–106.
[57] Below, para.12–014.
[58] [1969] 2 Q.B. 158; Treitel, 32 M.L.R. 526 (1969). See also *Archer v Brown* [1985] Q.B. 401.

where an action in tort would yield less damages than one for breach of contract, for contract damages will cover the expectation interest (*i.e.* loss of bargain) which it is assumed, in England at least, cannot be recovered in deceit.[59] The contract may also be rescinded in equity in cases of fraud,[60] if it is not too late to do so,[61] and it should be noted that some of the limits on the right to rescind are more leniently applied in cases of fraud, and in particular that lapse of time does not of itself bar rescission in such a case, but is simply evidence of affirmation.[62]

12–013 **Negligent misrepresentation.** It may also be possible for the buyer to sue the seller in tort for negligent misrepresentation under the principle of *Hedley Byrne & Co. Ltd v Heller & Partners Ltd*.[63] Two main difficulties for some time stood in the way of such an action. The first was the argument that the action is not available between prospective buyer and seller, nor between other persons negotiating for a contractual relationship which later comes into operation.[64] This view is now long rejected,[65] though of course the commercial relationship between the parties (*e.g.* where both are dealers) may indicate that the buyer does not rely, or is not reasonable in relying, on the seller's assertions.[66] The second was the view that a duty of care as regards statements is only owed by someone who carries on a business or profession involving the giving of information or advice; or lets it be known that he claims to exercise skill and competence and is prepared to exercise the necessary diligence to give reliable advice; or (perhaps) has a financial interest in the situation in which he gives advice. This restrictive view was adopted by the majority of the Privy Council in *Mutual Life and Citizens' Assurance Co. Ltd v Evatt*[67]; but the tide subsequently set in favour of an approach similar to the minority opinion,[68] that a duty of care exists where "an inquirer consults a business man in the course of his business and makes it plain to him that he is seeking considered advice and intends to act on it in a particular way."[69] Such a formulation would catch more sellers, who in any case would normally have a financial interest in the

---

[59] But see *Clef Aquitaine SARL v Laporte Materials (Barrow) Ltd* [2001] Q.B. 488.
[60] Above, para.12–003.
[61] Above, paras 12–005 *et seq*.
[62] Above, paras 12–002, 12–009.
[63] [1964] A.C. 465.
[64] See *Hedley Byrne & Co. Ltd v Heller & Partners Ltd*, above, at p.483; *Oleificio Zucchi SpA v Northern Sales Ltd* [1965] 2 Lloyd's Rep. 496 at 519.
[65] *Esso Petroleum Co. Ltd v Mardon* [1976] Q.B. 801; *Capital Motors Ltd v Beecham* [1975] 1 N.Z.L.R. 576; *Sealand of the Pacific Ltd v Ocean Cement Ltd* (1973) 33 D.L.R. (3d) 625 (affirmed (1975) 51 D.L.R. (3d) 702)).
[66] See also *Lambert v Lewis* [1982] A.C. 225 (no duty in respect of promotional literature).
[67] [1971] A.C. 793: see pp.805, 806, 809.
[68] See *Esso Petroleum Co. Ltd v Mardon*, above, at pp.827, 832; *Howard Marine and Dredging Co. Ltd v A. Ogden & Sons (Excavations) Ltd* [1978] Q.B. 574 at 591–592, 600. See also *McInerny v Lloyds Bank Ltd* [1974] 1 Lloyd's Rep. 246 at 253. But in *Caparo Industries Plc v Dickman* [1990] 2 A.C. 605 at 637, Lord Oliver thought it "unnecessary to attempt to resolve the difference of opinion arising from the *Mutual Life* case."
[69] *Mutual Life and Citizens' Assurance Co. Ltd v Evatt* [1971] A.C. 793 at 812, *per* Lord Reid.

transaction within what was (more tentatively) suggested by the majority.[70] The subsequent extensive developments in this part of the law of negligence are beyond the scope of this chapter.[71] But it is obvious that, depending on the nature of what they say, sellers will not in all circumstances be impressed with a duty of care. The action in tort requires the establishment of both duty of care and negligence: it therefore may often offer less prospects of success than those under section 2(1) of the Misrepresentation Act 1967, where no duty need be established and the onus of proof is reversed,[72] or that upon a collateral contract.[73] It used also to be thought that where the complaint was as to negligent advice rather than as to a statement, the tort action would be the only one available; but *Esso Petroleum Co. Ltd v Mardon*,[74] where liability in respect of a negligent prediction was based both in tort and upon a collateral contract, shows that this is not the case. However, where the statement is made by a person not party to the subsequent contract,[75] or where no contract results, the statutory action will not lie[76] and it will be necessary to fall back on a tort action, or an action upon a collateral contract, if either of these is available.

Liability under Misrepresentation Act 1967, s.2(1). Where a buyer is induced to make a contract by a misrepresentation of the seller, he has also a statutory action under section 2(1) of the Misrepresentation Act 1967. The provision reads as follows: "Where a person has entered into a contract after a misrepresentation has been made to him by another party thereto and as a result thereof he has suffered loss, then, if the person making the misrepresentation would be liable to damages in respect thereof had the misrepresentation been made fraudulently, that person shall be so liable notwithstanding that the misrepresentation was not made fraudulently, unless he proves that he had reasonable ground to believe and did believe up to the time the contract was made that the facts represented were true." Under this action the buyer need not prove the essentials of fraud, nor a duty of care, nor that the seller was negligent; instead, the seller must prove that he had reasonable grounds for believing the truth of his representation. Thus in *Howard Marine and Dredging Co. Ltd v A. Ogden & Sons (Excavations) Ltd*,[77] the owner of barges offered for hire mis- 12–014

[70] See pp.805, 809.

[71] See *Clerk and Lindsell on Torts* (19th ed.), paras 8–83 *et seq.*; for useful recent restatements see *James McNaughton Paper Group Ltd v Hicks Anderson & Co.* [1991] 2 Q.B. 113 at 125, *per* Neill L.J.; *Bank of Credit and Commerce International (Overseas) Ltd v Price Waterhouse Ltd* [1998] P.N.L.R. 564 at 583–587, *per* Sir Brian Neill.

[72] See the *Howard Marine* case, above, n.68 where the action under s.2(1) succeeded, but actions in tort and upon a collateral contract failed.

[73] Above, para.10–012.

[74] [1976] Q.B. 801; see above, para.10–012.

[75] As to statements made where it could be foreseen that they would be passed on, see *McInerny v Lloyds Bank Ltd* [1974] 2 Lloyd's Rep. 246 at 253; *Smith v Eric S. Bush* [1990] 1 A.C. 831. As to liability of a broker passing on information from an intending vendor, see *Lucas Laureys v Earl*, QBD (David Foskett Q.C.), November 3, 2005 (no liability).

[76] Below, para.12–014.

[77] [1978] Q.B. 574: criticised, 96 L.Q.R. 15 (1980).

stated their deadweight capacity. It was held that in the circumstances he could not prove reasonable grounds for believing the truth of his representation (in that he had relied on Lloyd's Register, which in this case was incorrect, whereas other documents in his possession gave different indications): though the majority of the Court of Appeal was of the view that the claimant could not have proved him to have been negligent. The subsection is however limited in that it only applies to representations made by one of the parties to the contract. It does not apply to make the agent of one party liable, though the agent's representation might make his principal liable under this provision.[78] It also applies only where a contract actually resulted.

12–015 **Damages recoverable.** It has for some time been clear from the reference to fraud that the action created is of a tortious nature and that damages should be calculated according to the rules for damages in tort.[79] Thus a claimant may recover the loss he had suffered by entering into the contract, including consequential loss,[80] but not the profit he hoped to make on it, nor the value of the thing bought as it was represented to be.[81] But the Court of Appeal has decided that the reference to fraud carries the further consequence that the rules as to damages for deceit, which are not limited by notions of foreseeability,[82] apply.

12–016 **"Fiction of fraud."** The reference to fraud causes, however, further difficulties as to other special rules applicable to the tort of deceit which do not seem necessarily appropriate to what is in effect a statutory action for negligence. Thus it could be argued that the rules that prevent fraud from being established by a combination of the knowledge of the principal and the statement of the agent[83] should apply to actions under this subsection: but the matter has (not surprisingly) been decided in a contrary sense.[84] Where a representation is made by a person who knows it to be false but expressly states that it should be verified and not relied on, although there may be liability for fraud[85] there could be no rescission in the absence of fraud: but it could be argued that the action under section 2(1) might lie in such a case.[86] Again it is said that the limitation period for an action under this subsection might be extended where the cause of action was not known

---

[78] *Resolute Maritime Inc. v Nippon Kaiji Kyokai (The Skopas)* [1983] 1 W.L.R. 857.
[79] *e.g. Sharneyford Supplies Ltd v Edge* [1986] Ch. 128 at 149 ("a new statutory tort") (actual decision revsd [1987] Ch. 305).
[80] *Davis & Co. (Wines) Ltd v Afa-Minerva (E.M.I.) Ltd* [1974] 2 Lloyd's Rep. 27. But this case is puzzling: see Taylor, 45 M.L.R. 139 (1982).
[81] As to which below, paras 17–051 *et seq.*
[82] *Royscot Trust Ltd v Rogerson* [1991] 2 Q.B. 297; but see *Avon Insurance Plc v Swire Fraser Ltd* [2000] 1 All E.R. (Comm.) 573; Treitel, *Law of Contract* (11th ed.), pp.362–364. As to the rules applicable in deceit, see *Doyle v Olby (Ironmongers) Ltd* [1969] 2 Q.B. 158; above, para.12–012.
[83] See *Clerk and Lindsell on Torts* (19th ed.), paras 18–25, 18–26.
[84] *Gosling v Anderson* (1972) 233 E.G. 1743.
[85] *S. Pearson Ltd v Dublin Corp.* [1907] A.C. 351.
[86] Sometimes such a statement might be caught by the Unfair Contract Terms Act 1977: see *Cremdean Properties Ltd v Nash* (1977) 244 E.G. 547; *Walker v Boyle* [1982] 1 W.L.R. 495; below, para.13–054.

to the buyer at the time of the sale, on the ground that it has been concealed by the constructive fraud of the seller, though he was in fact no more than negligent. A final point is that whereas the right to rescind for misrepresentation probably does not apply where the representation, though inducing the contract in fact, was not material in the objective sense, such a representation could, if deliberately false, lead to liability for fraud.[87] An action might arguably lie under section 2(1) on such a representation, though it was no more than negligent. But it is submitted that these suggestions involve reading too much into the wording of the subsection, awkward though it is. Its origin lies in the fact that at the time of drafting there was no other liability for statements on which to draw by way of analogy.

2. BREACH OF CONTRACTUAL TERM

Action for damages. All breaches of contract give rise, in the absence of special provisions, to actions for damages, whether the contract subsists or is discharged.[88] The buyer's claim to damages for breach of contract is dealt with in Chapter 17. **12–017**

Right to treat contract as discharged. Where the breach is serious enough the buyer may also be entitled to treat the contract as discharged, *viz.* refuse to perform his own obligations and refuse to accept further performance. A leading dictum explains the position as follows.[89] "The three sets of circumstances giving rise to a discharge of contract are tabulated by Anson as: (i) renunciation by a party of his liabilities under it; (ii) impossibility created by his own act; and (iii) total or partial failure of performance. In the case of the first two, the renunciation may occur or impossibility be created either before or at the time for performance. In the case of the third it can occur only at the time or during the course of performance. Moreover, if the third be partial, the failure must occur in a matter which goes to the root of the contract. All these acts may be compendiously described as repudiation, though that expression is more particularly used of renunciation before the time of performance has arrived."[90] **12–018**

Renunciation by seller. Where the seller at the time fixed for performance expressly refuses to perform or declares his inability to perform in the way required by the contract, the buyer may obviously treat the contract as discharged. But he may also do so where the seller by his conduct evinces **12–019**

---

[87] See Treitel, *Law of Contract* (11th ed.), p.336, n.67. As to pleading see *Garden Neptune Shipping Ltd v Occidental Worldwide Investment Corp.* [1990] 1 Lloyd's Rep. 330.

[88] See *Johnson v Agnew* [1980] A.C. 367.

[89] See also *Photo Production Ltd v Securicor Transport Ltd* [1980] A.C. 827, where Lord Diplock gives an authoritative analysis of the situation created by a repudiatory breach.

[90] *Heyman v Darwins Ltd* [1942] A.C. 356 at 397, *per* Lord Porter.

an intention (objectively ascertained) not to perform. The term renunciation, and also the term repudiation, are frequently used in connection with problems of breach of instalment contracts, to designate the conduct by one party in respect of a particular instalment or instalments which will amount to a refusal to perform and thus release the other party from his obligations. These problems, and the effects of the buyer's insisting on keeping the contract alive, are discussed elsewhere.[91] In many cases there is an express refusal to perform by one party because he is treating some act of the other party as a renunciation which discharges him; the problem then is as to whether his view is correct, or whether it is incorrect so that he himself must be treated as the party repudiating.[92] To constitute a renunciation, the act or acts concerned must normally indicate a refusal to perform the whole contract. Thus a refusal, actual or implied from conduct, to perform a condition would be renunciatory: but it is now clear that refusal to perform other terms might equally be so,[93] whether because of the likely consequences of the breach or because of its nature, *e.g.* (in some cases) where it is deliberate.[94] But "repudiation of a contract is a serious matter not to be lightly found or inferred."[95] Thus a minor breach, though deliberate and persisted in, will by no means necessarily amount to a repudiation[96]: the party in breach may, for example, honestly be doing the best he can to perform his obligations, or believe himself entitled to act as he does.[97]

12–020 **Impossibility of performance.** Although this type of breach does not usually concern defective goods, for the sake of completeness it should be said that where the seller at the time fixed for performance is unable to perform, the buyer may likewise treat the contract as discharged; and he may do this even though he did not know of the impossibility and

---

[91] See Sale of Goods Act 1979, s.31(2), above, paras 8–077 *et seq.* As regards goods defective in quality, the best test as to when the right to treat the contract as discharged arises is that laid down in *Maple Flock Co. Ltd v Universal Furniture Products (Wembley) Ltd* [1934] 1 K.B. 148 at 157, considered above, para.8–081.

[92] *e.g. Dominion Coal Co. Ltd v Dominion Iron and Steel Co. Ltd and National Trust Co. Ltd* [1909] A.C. 293; *Warinco AG v Samor SpA* [1977] 2 Lloyd's Rep. 582; *Federal Commerce and Navigation Co. Ltd v Molena Alpha Inc. (The Nanfri)* [1979] A.C. 757; *cf. Woodar Investment Development Ltd v Wimpey Construction U.K. Ltd* [1980] 1 W.L.R. 277, HL.

[93] *Cehave NV v Bremer Handelsgesellschaft mbH (The Hansa Nord)* [1976] Q.B. 44; above, paras 10–031 *et seq.*

[94] See *Suisse Atlantique Société d'Armement Maritime SA v NV Rotterdamsche Kolen Centrale* [1967] 1 A.C. 361 at 429, 435; *Mantovani v Carapelli SpA* [1978] 2 Lloyd's Rep. 63 at 72. *Cf.* below, para.13–051.

[95] *Ross T. Smyth & Co. Ltd v T. D. Bailey Son & Co.* [1940] 3 All E.R. 60 at 71, *per* Lord Wright. See also *Woodar Investment Development Ltd v Wimpey Construction U.K. Ltd* [1980] 1 W.L.R. 277 at 283, HL.

[96] See *Rhymney Ry v Brecon and Merthyr Tydfil Junction Ry* (1900) 69 L.J. Ch.813 at 819; *Decro-Wall International SA v Practitioners in Marketing Ltd* [1971] 1 W.L.R. 361 at 374, 379.

[97] This does not, however, of itself prevent the breach from being repudiatory: see *Federal Commerce and Navigation Co. Ltd v Molena Alpha Inc. (The Nanfri)* [1979] A.C. 757; *cf. Woodar Investment Development Ltd v Wimpey Construction U.K. Ltd*, above.

purported to do so for some insufficient, or without giving, any reason.[98] This could occur, for example, where the seller alters, consumes or destroys specific goods before delivery, or where he sells and delivers them to someone other than the buyer.[99]

Anticipatory breach. As the dictum quoted above[1] states, the above two forms of breach entitling the buyer to treat the contract as discharged can also occur before the time for performance is due. In such cases they are referred to as "anticipatory" breaches, and on principle the buyer is entitled to "accept" such a breach and treat the contract as discharged immediately.[2] This normally requires some sort of communication; but in some cases "failure to perform may signify to a repudiating party an election by the aggrieved party to treat the contract as at an end".[3] However, in a decision on the withdrawal clause in a time charterparty, it was categorically stated by Lord Diplock that anticipatory breach depends on repudiation only.[4] This involves the consequence that impossibility of performing a condition, commencing prior to the time for performance, cannot amount to anticipatory breach of contract unless a repudiation can also be found on the facts. It will often be possible to find such a repudiation, but not always. It is difficult to see the justification for this proposition: it was not necessary to the decision, which turned on the interpretation of a particular contractual stipulation.[5] But until dissented from, it must have some force. Where there is an anticipatory breach the buyer can also claim damages immediately, and these are in principle to be assessed with reference to the time at which the contract ought to have been performed,[6] subject to the buyer's duty to mitigate damages.[7] Alternatively he can refuse to accept the 12–021

---

[98] See *Universal Cargo Carriers Corp. v Citati* [1957] 2 Q.B. 401; above, paras 9–010 *et seq.*; below, paras 19–159 *et seq.*

[99] As in *Bowdell v Parsons* (1808) 10 East 359 and *Lovelock v Franklyn* (1846) 8 Q.B. 371. If the property has passed, the buyer may, subject to s.2 of the Factors Act 1889 and s.24 of the Sale of Goods Act 1979 (above, paras 7–034, 7–055), have proprietary remedies; but the breach would still be repudiatory.

[1] Above, para.12–018.

[2] See *Chitty on Contracts* (29th ed.), Vol.1, paras 24–021 *et seq.*; Treitel, *Law of Contract* (11th ed.), pp.857 *et seq.* The refusal or impossibility must still be such as to affect the whole contract: an anticipatory repudiation in a minor respect would not necessarily amount to a renunciation of the whole contract: *Federal Commerce and Navigation Ltd v Molena Alpha Inc. (The Nanfri)* [1979] A.C. 757 at 770, 783; *Woodar Investment Development Ltd v Wimpey Construction U.K. Ltd* [1980] 1 W.L.R. 277 at 298.

[3] *Vitol SA v Norelf Ltd* [1996] A.C. 800 at 811, *per* Lord Steyn (where the acceptance of breach was by the *seller*, who did not tender the documents and sold the goods elsewhere).

[4] *Afovos Shipping Co. SA v Pagnan & Lli (F.) (The Afovos)* [1983] 1 W.L.R. 195; see [1984] L.M.C.L.Q. 189. But *cf. Financings Ltd v Baldock* [1963] 2 Q.B. 104.

[5] *Cf. The Madeleine* [1967] 2 Lloyd's Rep. 224 (a case on early exercise of the right to cancel a time charter).

[6] *Roper v Johnson* (1873) L.R. 8 C.P. 167; *Tai Hing Cotton Mill Ltd v Kamsing Knitting Factory* [1979] A.C. 91.

[7] *Garnac Grain Co. Inc. v H.M.F. Faure and Fairclough Ltd* [1968] A.C. 1130 at 1140; *Roth & Co. v Taysen, Townsend & Co. and Grant & Co.* (1895) 1 Com.Cas. 240. See below, paras 16–051 *et seq.*, 17–015 *et seq.*

repudiation and wait until the time for performance arrives; though if the breach is continuing he may have further opportunities of accepting it.[8] If he does not do so, the seller may repent and tender performance,[9] or may acquire an excuse for non-performance, or may even be discharged by frustration[10] or by the operation of section 7 of the Sale of Goods Act.[11] But, if the breach is not accepted, no duty to mitigate damages will arise.[12]

12–022 **Failure of performance: breach of condition.** The dictum quoted above[13] states that total or partial failure of performance, if accepted, discharges the contract; but goes on to the effect that where the failure is partial it must be such as to go to the root of the contract. Another way of putting it is to say that a total failure of performance discharges the innocent party by implication of the common law; a partial failure does so where upon the court's, or upon a statutory, construction of the contract the parties' intentions are deemed to have regarded a term as so important to the transaction that any breach of it is to be regarded as having the same effect, *viz.* as a condition.[14] Under this second rubric the Sale of Goods Act specifies the terms any breach of which, however slight, may release the innocent party, by designating them as conditions.[15] Thus for the purposes of this chapter "failure of performance" will cover the supply of goods not conforming with description,[16] not of satisfactory quality,[17] not reasonably fit for their purpose,[18] or not conforming with sample in quality.[19] It will also cover breaches of other, express, conditions[20]: whether or not a stipulation is a condition depends in each case on the construction of the contract.[21] It should however be borne in mind that section 11(4) of the Act does not state in so many words that breach of condition entitles the innocent party to treat the contract as repudiated: it only says that it "may" do so. Thus it seems that in some cases at least the innocent party may, if he comes in time, retender conforming goods.[22]

---

[8] *Stocznia Gdanska SA v Latvian Shipping Co.* [2001] 1 Lloyd's Rep. 537 at 564–566, reasoning applicable also to actual breach.
[9] *Sinason-Teicher Inter-American Grain Corp. v Oilcakes and Oilseeds Trading Co. Ltd* [1954] 1 W.L.R. 935 at 944 (affirmed *ibid.*, 1394); *Fercometal SARL v Mediterranean Shipping Co. (The Simona)* [1989] 1 A.C. 788.
[10] *Avery v Bowden* (1855) 5 E. & B. 714; (1856) 6 E. & B. 953.
[11] Above, paras 6–034 *et seq.*
[12] *Tredegar Iron and Coal Co. Ltd v Hawthorn Bros & Co.* (1902) 18 T.L.R. 716; below, para.17–016.
[13] Above, para.12–018.
[14] See *Photo Production Ltd v Securicor Transport Ltd* [1980] A.C. 827 at 849, *per* Lord Diplock; *cf. Bunge Corp. v Tradax Export SA* [1981] 1 W.L.R. 711 at 725; and see Shea, 42 M.L.R. 623 (1979); above, para.10–027.
[15] As to this term see above, para.10–026.
[16] Above, paras 11–001 *et seq.* This condition really concerns total failure of performance: see above, para.11–020.
[17] Above, paras 11–026 *et seq.*
[18] Above, paras 11–051 *et seq.*
[19] Above, paras 11–073 *et seq.*
[20] Above, para.10–026.
[21] Above, paras 10–027 *et seq*; Sale of Goods Act 1979, s.11(3).
[22] Above, para.10–028; below, para.12–031.

12–023 **Failure of performance: other situations.** For a considerable time after the original Sale of Goods Act of 1893, there was ground for thinking that where a stipulation in a contract of sale was not a condition, it must by virtue of the wording of section 11(3) of the Sale of Goods Act,[23] necessarily be a warranty, *viz.*, a term *no* breach of which would entitle the innocent party to treat the contract as discharged. But in *Hong Kong Fir Shipping Co. Ltd v Kawasaki Kisen Kaisha Ltd*,[24] it was held that the term as to seaworthiness in a charterparty could not be designated as either a condition or a warranty, because the events resulting from its breach might be serious or trivial; it was the seriousness of these events which determined whether the charterer could treat the contract as discharged. In *Cehave NV v Bremer Handelsgesellschaft mbH (The Hansa Nord)*,[25] this reasoning was extended to sale of goods: the Court of Appeal held that the wording of the Sale of Goods Act did not exclude terms the breach of which might or might not entitle the innocent party to treat the contract as discharged, depending on the nature and consequences of the breach.[26] The question whether this created a third category of "intermediate" or "innominate" terms, or whether it effectively eliminated the category of warranty as a term no breach of which will entitle discharge, is discussed elsewhere.[27] It is, however, clear that, in sale as in other contracts, breaches of terms which cannot be classified as conditions,[28] and breaches which cannot be related to any single identifiable term may still, if serious enough, be repudiatory. But, as has already been pointed out,[29] the *Hong Kong Fir* case requires a very serious breach and is hostile to rejection as a remedy: this is borne out by its facts, and the facts of *The Hansa Nord* also, where rejection was held not justified.[30]

12–024 **Statutory restriction on right to treat contract as discharged for breach of condition.** Section 4(1) of the Sale and Supply of Goods Act 1994 introduced a new section 15A into the Sale of Goods Act 1979, which is intended to limit the right to reject goods for breach of condition in non-consumer cases where the breach is slight and/or technical.[31] Similar restrictions are also applicable in respect of related contracts.[32] It reads as follows:

---

[23] Above, para.10–027.

[24] [1962] 2 Q.B. 26. See also *Yeoman Credit Ltd v Apps* [1962] 2 Q.B. 508.

[25] [1976] Q.B. 44; above, para.10–012. See also *Holmes v Burgess* [1975] 2 N.Z.L.R. 311.

[26] Relying on the preservation of common law rules by s.62(2) (formerly s.61(2)).

[27] Above, para.10–033.

[28] *e.g. Total International Ltd v Addax BV* [1996] 2 Lloyd's Rep. 333 ("usual Dakar refinery quality").

[29] Above, paras 10–030, 10–034.

[30] *ibid.* (though the word "rejection" is not really appropriate to the *Hong Kong Fir* situation).

[31] The changes were based on Law Com. No. 160, Scot. Law Com. No.104, Cm 137 (1987), esp. in this context paras 4.1 *et seq.*; see also Law Com. W.P. No.85, Scot. Law Com. C.M. No.58 (1983). Parliamentary proceedings appear in *Hansard*, H.C. Vol.237, col.633; vol.243, col.1054; vol.245, col. 526; H.L. vol.557, cols. 472, 960; vol.558, col.686. See also as to this provision below, paras 18–284, 19–173.

[32] Supply of Goods (Implied Terms) Act 1973, s.11A (hire purchase); Supply of Goods and Services Act 1982, s.5A (exchange, contracts for work and materials), s.10A (hire); all inserted by Sale and Supply of Goods Act 1994, s.7 and Sch.2.

"15A (1) Where in the case of a contract of sale—

(a) the buyer would, apart from this subsection, have the right to reject goods by reason of a breach on the part of the seller of a term implied by section 13, 14 or 15 above, but

(b) the breach is so slight that it would be unreasonable for him to reject them,

then, if the buyer deals as consumer,[33] the breach is not to be treated as a breach of condition but may be treated as a breach of warranty.

(2) This section applies unless a contrary intention appears in, or is to be implied from, the contract.

(3) It is for the seller to show that a breach fell within subsection (1)(b) above."

12–025 The drafting of the provision mixes the right to *reject* with that to *treat the contract as discharged*—not always the same.[34] Nevertheless, the second is covered by the reference to "condition", and the first by inference. Secondly, the new section only applies to breaches of the *implied* terms as to description, quality, fitness for purpose and conformity with sample laid down in sections 13, 14 and 15 of the Act. It does not apply to *express* terms, *e.g.* as to time; and it is furthermore excluded by express or implied contrary intention. Thirdly, it does not apply to other terms such as that as to title implied by section 12(1); nor to duties of the buyer[35]; nor when the buyer deals as consumer.[36] Where a term is not a condition or a warranty but an intermediate or innominate term[37] the test for treating the contract as discharged will remain the "nature and consequences" test,[38] which may bar doing so though the breach is more than "slight". Its main application is likely to be in connection with section 13, under which conformity with description is an implied condition, thus triggering off section 15A, and where cases lay down a strict duty regarding such conformity.[39] It will at any rate initially create uncertainties in the law, though the provision that the burden of proof is on the seller to establish that the exception applies will help in resolving these. It may now become more relevant to consider the extent to which descriptive provisions of a contract are part of the description of the goods referred to by the Act. An obvious example is the commercial rule that the date of shipment of goods is likely to rank as part of their description.[40] The Law Commission Report[41] stated that this rule was not intended to be affected by the new provision; though whether this is because the date does not come within the implied term of section 13 as

---

[33] A new s.61(5A) (see Sch.2 of the 1994 Act) provides that this phrase is "to be construed in accordance with Part I of the Unfair Contract Terms Act 1977" (see below, para.13–062); and that the onus of proving that the buyer does not deal as consumer lies on the seller.

[34] Above, para.10–028; below, paras 12–028, 12–031.

[35] *e.g. Bunge Corp. v Tradax Export SA* [1981] 1 W.L.R. 711, above, para.10–032.

[36] Above, n.33

[37] Above, para.10–033.

[38] Above, paras 10–030, 12–023.

[39] Above, para.11–018; below, para.18–284.

[40] *Bowes v Shand* (1877) 2 App. Cas. 455: above, para.11–018; below, para.18–267.

[41] Law Com. No.160, above, para.4.24.

not being part of the description but a separate term, or because it is an express not an implied term, or because section 15A is excluded expressly or by implication, is not clear.[42] Similar problems may arise elsewhere: for example, if the rules as to the condition required of goods on shipment in international sales[43] are now subsumed into the new provision on durability in section 14(2) of the Act,[44] they are now subject to section 15A. If they constitute a separate implied term (as they probably do) they are not.

The Law Commission Report which led to the enactment of the provision sought to prevent what are completely technical rejections in commercial contracts, which may be motivated by caprice or (more likely) adverse movements in the market which lead a buyer to seek escape from a contract. It was, however, stated to be "not intended as a major alteration in the law."[45] It is also stated that the buyer's motives for rejection are not intended to be regarded as relevant, as "subjectivity" is referred to as undesirable.[46] It appears therefore that the test of reasonableness is intended to be an objective one, though it still ought to be geared to a person in the buyer's position rather than an external observer.[47] It would appear that the new section is of severely limited effect and may in the end make little difference in practice. There have been no reported decisions on it since its enactment in 1994. In the meanwhile, however, uncertainties as to its potential application, in particular as to when it is impliedly excluded, may create problems. 12–026

Rights of buyer where contract discharged by breach. Where the buyer is entitled to treat the contract as discharged in accordance with the above criteria, on principle the contract only comes to an end if he accepts the breach. This in general requires a positive act: it has been said that "mere silence or inactivity" may not suffice.[48] Recent authority in the area of *anticipatory* breach by the *buyer*,[49] however, suggests that making another contract, or simply failing to perform further may sometimes constitute acceptance of the breach by conduct.[50] The buyer will usually, nevertheless, reject, and the rejection will constitute a positive act.[51] Thus there will not usually be problems in this connection unless it is sought to prevent a further tender on the basis that the false tender is repudiatory.[52] Thus if the buyer already has the goods, he may notify the seller that he refuses to 12–027

---

[42] See the question discussed more fully in connection with overseas sales, below, paras 18–284 *et seq*.
[43] Above, paras 6–019, 11–040; below, para.18–255.
[44] Above, para.11–040.
[45] Law Com. No.60, paras 4.21, 4.24.
[46] Paras 4.19, 4.21, n.33.
[47] *cf.* above, para.11–031.
[48] *State Trading Corp. of India v M. Golodetz Ltd* [1989] 2 Lloyd's Rep. 277 at 286.
[49] *Vitol SA v Norelf Ltd* [1996] A.C. 800, above, para.12–021. The judgments are however in general terms.
[50] See Treitel, *Law of Contract* (11th ed.), pp.858–859.
[51] Below, para.12–032.
[52] Below, para.12–031.

accept them, unless he is to be regarded as having waived the breach or affirmed the contract at common law,[53] or unless he has impliedly affirmed the contract by accepting them in one of the ways provided by section 35 of the Sale of Goods Act.[54] Rejection for an invalid reason may subsequently be justified by the presence of a valid reason, if it was operative at the time of rejection.[55]

12–028 **Relation between treating contract as discharged and rejection.** It is often assumed that the right to reject for breach of condition carries also with it the right to treat the contract as discharged. Indeed, Devlin J. said that "A right to reject is, after all, only a particular form of the right to rescind the contract."[56] Although this is often so, it does not necessarily follow. First, in severable instalment contracts,[57] the right to reject applies to each instalment,[58] but the right to treat the whole contract as discharged by reason of defects in instalments is a separate question dealt with by section 31(2) of the Sale of Goods Act.[59] Secondly, where the breach by the seller involves a tender of a wrong quantity of the correct goods, the buyer's rights to reject are dealt with by a separate provision of the Act[60] which does not use the terminology of condition at all but simply confers rights of rejection. The right to treat the contract as discharged in such cases must depend on general principle. Finally, even where the term broken is a condition, it has to be noted that in section 11(3), which comes nearest to defining a condition for the purposes of the Act,[61] it is not stated that breach of a condition necessarily confers the right to treat the contract as discharged: it merely says that it "may" do so. Hence there may in some cases be a right to retender conforming goods. Consideration of the last two features follows.

12–029 **Delivery of more or less than contract quantity.** Although it might seem that the quantity of the contract goods is part of their description, section 30 of the Sale of Goods Act, following older cases, lays down special rules

[53] Below, paras 12–034 *et seq*.
[54] Below, paras 12–034 *et seq*. As to situations where the goods cannot be returned, or can only be returned damaged, see below, paras 12–038 *et seq*. As to the possibility that where the term broken was originally a misrepresentation inducing the contract, the court may award damages in lieu of rescission under s.2(2) of the Misrepresentation Act 1967, see below, paras 12–119 *et seq*.
[55] This complex topic is considered above at paras 9–011 *et seq*; and in connection with international sales below at paras 19–159 *et seq*.
[56] *Kwei Tek Chao v British Traders & Shippers Ltd* [1954] 2 Q.B. 459 at 480; but *cf.* Lord Devlin [1966] C.L.J. 192 at 194 ("A tender of . . . goods under a contract for the sale of goods . . . in a condition that does not comply with the terms of the contract is not a breach of contract"— perhaps too far the other way). As to the rights to reject in documentary sales, see below, paras 19–144 *et seq.*, 19–163 *et seq.*, 20–105 *et seq*.
[57] See above, paras 8–074—8–075.
[58] Above, para.8–080. As to acceptance, see below, para.12–060; as to recovery of money, below, para.12–070.
[59] See above, paras 8–080 *et seq*.
[60] s.30: above, paras 8–045 *et seq.*, below, para.12–029.
[61] Above, para.10–022.

for situations where the seller delivers more or less than the contract quantity. They are based on the propositions that the obligation as to quantity is prima facie entire, so that short delivery ranks as no delivery; and that in the case of delivery of too much the seller cannot place upon the buyer the task of sorting out the correct quantity. They produce much the same effect as that of breach of condition, with one exception. The definition of "condition" in section 11(3) indicates that the breach of such a term *may* entitle the buyer to treat the contract as repudiated: there is a possibility that in some cases he cannot, and that the seller can correct by a further conforming tender if he comes in time.[62] In the case of wrong quantity, however, the *only* remedy indicated is that the buyer may reject the tender: there is no indication at all as to whether he can treat the contract as repudiated, which must turn on general principles only. The possibility of further tenders seems therefore slightly greater, subject to the rule that the buyer cannot be compelled to accept delivery by instalments.[63] The main discussion of section 30 is to be found under the heading of Delivery, which is where it appears in the Act.[64]

Exception for slight breaches in respect of quantity. By section 30(2A) of the Sale of Goods Act, a buyer who does not deal as consumer may not reject under subsections (1) or (2) of section 30 where "the shortfall, or, as may be, excess is so slight that it would be unreasonable for him to do so." This implements the policy introduced by the Sale and Supply of Goods Act 1994, which seeks to restrain rejection for slight defects in commercial cases, to breaches in respect of quantity.[65] Since rejection for a shortfall or excess which comes under the principle *de minimis* is already permitted, this provision must allow variations beyond that level, and there is now therefore a further level of "slight" non-compliance where rejection would be unreasonable. As with the main provision, it is for the seller to show that a breach comes within the subsection and so does not justify rejection, and again this will help in the resolution of doubtful cases. It should be noted that the restriction is on the right to reject the *whole*: where there is excess delivery, the right to reject the *excess* persists, however slight the excess. 12–030

Seller's right to retender.[66] There is a certain amount of authority relating to commercial contracts containing specific time limits, and most of it concerned with tender of documents, that a seller who has made a false tender can withdraw it and substitute a conforming tender before the relevant date, subject to paying any special expenditure or loss incurred by the buyer in connection with examining and rejecting the first tender.[67] On 12–031

[62] Above, para.10–027; below, para.12–031.
[63] Above, para.8–064.
[64] Above, paras 8–045 *et seq.*
[65] Above, para.12–024.
[66] See Ahdar [1990] L.M.C.L.Q. 364; Apps [1994] L.M.C.L.Q. 525.
[67] See *Motor Oil Hellas (Corinth) Refineries SA v Shipping Corp. of India Ltd* (*The Kanchenjunga*) [1990] 1 Lloyd's Rep. 391 at 399, *per* Lord Goff of Chieveley. See also Lord Devlin, *op. cit.* above, n.56.

this basis it can be said that the common law gives in a sense some measure of a right to cure defects,[68] a right which has sometimes elsewhere been introduced by statute or equivalent.[69] Thus in *Borrowman, Phillips & Co. v Free and Hollis*,[70] the seller of a cargo of maize tendered a cargo of the vessel *C*, which the buyer refused to accept on the ground that the shipping documents were not tendered with it. The seller insisted on his tender, but the arbitrator decided against him. He therefore tendered the cargo of the *M* within the time fixed for tender, and it was held that the buyer was bound to take it. Presumably, however, there could be situations where a false tender could on general principles be regarded as destroying the confidence of the buyer, and would entitle him to treat the contract as repudiated immediately.[71] And in situations where no time limit was fixed, the scope for the application of this reasoning is more limited. Just as a buyer cannot normally be compelled to accept delivery in instalments unless the contract contemplated this,[72] so also he cannot normally be expected to put up with several attempted deliveries of one consignment. The argument as to loss of confidence would be more often relevant outside the particular contexts referred to above, and particularly in consumer transactions. It would seem therefore that the right at common law to "cure" defects by retender is limited.[73]

---

[68] See Goode, *Commercial Law* (3rd ed.), pp.342–345.

[69] *e.g.* Uniform Commercial Code, s.2–508; Vienna Convention (above, para.1–024), Arts 34, 48. The Law Commissions (Law Com. No.160, Scot. Law Com. No.104) rejected the introduction of a right to cure, largely because of the number of further issues it would raise for resolution: see paras 4.9 *et seq.* esp. para.4.13. The buyer may sometimes be able to hold the seller estopped from making a further tender: *cf.* below, para.20–051. But if the buyer asks for or agrees to repair, the implication from s.35(6) (below, para.12–054) would seem to be that he must accept a second conforming tender: see *J & H Ritchie Ltd v Lloyd Ltd* 2005 S.C. 155 (but note the vigorous dissent of Lord Marnoch); and see Mak [2006] L.M.C.L.Q. 163. As to damages, *cf.* below, para.12–086.

[70] (1878) 4 Q.B.D. 500; *E. & E. Brian Smith (1928) Ltd v Wheatsheaf Mills Ltd* [1939] 2 K.B. 302 at 314 (substitution of documents); *McDougall v Aeromarine of Emsworth Ltd* [1958] 1 W.L.R. 1126 at 1132 (trials of new boat, with specific time limit); *Agricultores Federados Argentinos Soc. Coperativa Lda. v Ampro SA Commerciale Industrielle et Financière* [1965] 2 Lloyd's Rep. 757 at 767 (nomination of vessel under f.o.b. contract); *Gertreide Import Gesellschaft mbH v Itoh & Co.* [1979] 1 Lloyd's Rep. 592 (substitution of declaration of shipment); *S.I.A.T. di del Ferro v Tradax Overseas SA* [1980] 1 Lloyd's Rep. 53 (retender of bill of lading); *Chuan Hiap Seng (1979) Pte. Ltd v Progress Manufacturing Pte. Ltd* [1995] 2 Singapore L.R. 641 (steel pipes). See also *Reuter v Sala* (1879) 4 C.P.D. 239; *Ashmore & Son v C. S. Cox & Co.* [1899] 1 Q.B. 436 at 440; *Tetley v Shand* (1871) 25 L.T. 658; *Millars of Falkirk Ltd v Turpie* 1976 S.L.T. (Notes) 66; below, para.19–071.

[71] *cf. Maple Flock Co. Ltd v Universal Furniture Products (Wembley) Ltd* [1934] 1 K.B. 148 at 157, quoted above, para.8–064.

[72] Sale of Goods Act 1979, s.31(1); above, para.8–064.

[73] But see *McDougall v Aeromarine of Emsworth Ltd*, above, where it was held that there was a condition of the contract that the subject-matter (a boat) be delivered in a reasonable time. There were however specific provisions for trials of the boat before acceptance. As to instalments see above, para.8–084.

12–032 **What constitutes rejection.** For there to be a valid rejection there must be "a clear notice that the goods are not accepted and at the risk of the vendor."[74] An unequivocal rejection prevents a subsequent acceptance of the goods[75] (other than by the agreement of the seller). However, "an unequivocal rejection does not necessarily depend upon the terms of one communication alone. It is necessary to consider the whole of the relevant communications and the buyer's conduct generally."[76] Thus where the buyer acts equivocally, as by proposing to resell, stating that he is reselling them for the account of any interested party, or otherwise dealing with them after a purported rejection, it may be held that he has not in truth rejected.[77] Alternatively, however, this may be evidence of a new agreement between buyer and seller; or simply a conversion by a buyer who has rejected and thus has no power to deal with the goods. It may, however, be that if the seller refuses to accept a clear rejection, a subsequent dealing with the goods by the buyer would not be regarded as a conversion: though it might then be an affirmation.[78] Conduct not known to the seller cannot easily be regarded as an affirmation by the buyer[79]; but it might of course amount to conduct inconsistent with the seller's ownership, which constitutes acceptance regardless of the seller's knowedge.[80]

12–033 **Rejection on wrong grounds.** A rejection on insufficient grounds may sometimes subsequently be justified on other grounds which would have been sufficient at the time. The matter is discussed elsewhere in this book.[81]

12–034 **Waiver, election, estoppel and affirmation.** The buyer may of course, in accordance with the general principle that a person may waive a stipulation in a contract inserted for his benefit, waive his rights in respect of the defects. It is important to note that he may do this in two separate ways, with very different consequences, to each of which the term waiver is not

---

[74] *Grimoldby v Wells* (1875) L.R. 10 C.P. 391; see also *Okell v Smith* (1815) 1 Stark. 107. In *Graanhandel T. Vink BV v European Grain & Shipping Ltd* [1989] 2 Lloyd's Rep. 531 at 533, Evans J. said that "if he does decide to reject the goods he must do so unequivocally and be prepared to take a stand." The Uniform Commercial Code, s.2–605 imposes in certain cases a duty to state grounds for rejection; see also Vienna Convention (above, para.1–024), Art.39(1).

[75] *Graanhandel T. Vink BV v European Grain & Shipping Ltd* [1989] 2 Lloyd's Rep. 531 at 533.

[76] *ibid., per* Evans J.

[77] *ibid.* ("It is clear that a buyer cannot hedge his bets by saying that he rejects the goods if in fact he chooses to resell them for his own protection"). See also *Chapman v Morton* (1843) 11 M. & W. 534; *Tradax Export SA v European Grain & Shipping Ltd* [1983] 2 Lloyd's Rep. 100 esp. at 107; *Vargas Pena Apezteguia y Cia. v Peter Cremer GmbH* [1987] 1 Lloyd's Rep. 394. See also below, para.12–055.

[78] *ibid.*

[79] See *Laurelgates Ltd v Lombard North Central Ltd* (1983) 133 N.L.J. 720.

[80] *Graanhandel T. Vink BV v European Grain & Shipping Ltd*, above, at p.533; see below, paras 12–046 *et seq.*

[81] Above, paras 9–011 *et seq.*; below, paras 19–159 *et seq.* This may not always be so clear under the Vienna Convention (above, para.1–024): see Art.39(1).

infrequently applied.[82] The first sense amounts to a complete excusing of the breach: the buyer says he has no objection to the goods as they are and will not even seek damages. This will be comparatively rare in the case of defective goods.[83] The second sense is a waiver of the right to reject: the buyer says that he does not seek to reject and will be content with damages.[84] This is often called election, or affirmation of the contract.[85] The Sale of Goods Act 1979 distinguishes between these two senses in section 11(2), which provides: "Where a contract of sale is subject to a condition to be fulfilled by the seller, the buyer may waive the condition, or may elect to treat the breach of the condition as a breach of warranty and not as a ground for treating the contract as repudiated."

12–035 **Waiver.** The distinction made in the previous paragraph is very relevant when the buyer seeks to retract a waiver. A waiver in the sense of an indication by the buyer that he is satisfied with the defective performance can be regarded as a promise not to sue; or, if promissory terminology is not thought appropriate, it is at best an informal release.[86] As such it does not, upon orthodox doctrine, bind for the future unless supported by consideration,[87] and if not so supported can be retracted at any time with reasonable notice; though of course it is effective in the sense that the revocation cannot be retrospective, and it is not possible to treat as broken a duty in respect of which rights have been waived and not resumed.[88] It has even been said that "the only way of establishing [such a waiver] would be to show a separate agreement, binding on the buyer, by which he had agreed to surrender the right to damages which automatically vested in him at the time of the breach."[89] This dictum seems however too emphatic, for

[82] See in general on this distinction *Motor Oil Hellas (Corinth) Refineries SA v Shipping Corp. of India (The Kanchenjunga)* [1990] 1 Lloyd's Rep. 391 at 397–399, HL See also *Telfair Shipping Corp. v Athos Shipping Co. SA (The Athos)* [1981] 2 Lloyd's Rep. 74 at 87–88, approved by CA [1983] 1 Lloyd's Rep. 127 at 134; and below, paras 19–150 *et seq*.

[83] Though a waiver as to late delivery may more easily occur: see *Panoutsos v Raymond Hadley Corp. of New York* [1917] 2 K.B. 473; *Hartley v Hymans* [1920] 3 K.B. 475; *Charles Rickards Ltd v Oppenhaim* [1950] 1 K.B. 616.

[84] See *Hain S.S. Co. Ltd v Tate & Lyle Ltd* [1936] 2 All E.R. 597 at 608; *Bentsen v Taylor, Sons & Co.* [1893] 2 Q.B. 274.

[85] See *Suisse Atlantique Société d'Armement Maritime SA v NV Rotterdamsche Kolen Centrale* [1967] 1 A.C. 361 at 398; *The Kanchenjunga*, above, at p.398. This was said to be the true sense of the word "waiver" in *Panchaud Frères SA v Et. General Grain Co.* [1970] 1 Lloyd's Rep. 53 at 57.

[86] See Campbell, 1 N.Z.U.L.R. 232 (1963).

[87] Or under seal. The merits of the situation were fully discussed in the famous case of *Foakes v Beer* (1884) 9 App. Cas. 605. A new view of what constitutes consideration for the modification of a contract, considerably more lenient than had hitherto been assumed to be appropriate, was however taken by the Court of Appeal in *Williams v Roffey Bros & Nicholls (Contractors) Ltd* [1991] 1 Q.B. 1; as to which see Treitel, *Law of Contract* (11th ed.), pp.95–97, and *South Caribbean Trading Ltd v Trafigura Beheer BV* [2004] EWHC 2676 (Comm); [2005] 1 Lloyd's Rep. 128 at [108] *per* Colman J.

[88] See, *e.g.* *Panoutsos v Raymond Hadley Corp. of New York* [1917] 2 K.B. 473; *Tankexpress A/S v Cie. Financière Belge des Petroles SA* [1949] A.C. 76.

[89] *Kwei Tek Chao v British Traders and Shippers Ltd* [1954] 2 Q.B. 459 at 477, *per* Devlin J. *cf. The Democritos* [1975] 1 Lloyd's Rep. 386 at 398 (affirmed [1976] 2 Lloyd's Rep. 149).

under the principle of *Hughes v Metropolitan Railway Co.*[90] the buyer cannot retract where it would be inequitable to do so. This will often mean no more than that he must give notice to enable the seller to resume his former position. Cases may arise where it is inequitable for the buyer ever to retract his waiver, because the seller is not able to resume that position.[91] A clear example in a contract of sale could occur where the seller, in reliance on the buyer's assurances that there was no objection to the goods supplied, has so conducted himself as to prevent himself from making a further, conforming tender, which he could originally have done[92]; or where he for that reason loses an opportunity to tender the goods elsewhere.[93] The exact circumstances in which the principle applies are not yet, however, fully formulated.[94] The prevailing view seems to be that there must be a clear and unequivocal representation that strict legal rights will not be relied on,[95] and "some conduct induced by the representations, differing in some material manner from the way in which the sellers would have conducted themselves if the supposed representation had not been made."[96] It has been said that "No question arises of any particular knowledge on the part of the representor"[97]; and the doctrine has regularly been stated without any such requirement.[98] But if the representor is not aware, or at least has no obvious means of knowledge, of the facts giving rise to his right to treat the contract as discharged, it may be difficult to establish that the representation was unequivocal.[99]

These requirements are not in any case free from doubt, and are sometimes articulated in weaker terms: these may or may not include references to estoppel, though it seems that little turns on the use of this word.[1] Thus as to reliance, it seems clear that failure to act could be sufficient to make the waiver binding.[2] Other cases also suggest that it is not 12–036

---

[90] (1877) 2 App.Cas. 439; see *Chitty on Contracts* (29th ed.), Vol. 1, paras 3–115 *et seq*.
[91] *cf. Birmingham and District Land Co. v L. & N.W. Ry* (1888) 40 Ch.D. 268.
[92] An example accepted in *Toepfer v Warinco AG* [1978] 2 Lloyd's Rep. 569 at 576.
[93] An example given in *Société Italo-Belge pour le Commerce et l'Industrie SA v Palm and Vegetable Oils (Malaysia) Sdn. Bhd. (The Post Chaser)* [1982] 1 All E.R. 19 at 26.
[94] See *Woodhouse A.C. Israel Cocoa Ltd SA v Nigerian Produce Marketing Co. Ltd* [1972] A.C. 741 at 758, *per* Lord Hailsham L.C.
[95] See the *Woodhouse A.C. Cocoa* case, above, at pp.756, 761, 768, 771. See also *Bremer Handelsgesellschaft mbH v C. Mackprang Jr.* [1979] 1 Lloyd's Rep. 221 at 228; *Avimex SA v Dewulf & Cie.* [1979] 2 Lloyd's Rep. 57 at 67. A misrepresentation may, however, be unequivocal without saying "we hereby waive": *Bremer Handelsgesellschaft mbH v Vanden Avenne-Izegem PVBA* [1978] 2 Lloyd's Rep. 109 at 126, HL.
[96] *Finagrain SA v Kruse* [1976] 2 Lloyd's Rep. 508 at 535, *per* Megaw L.J.
[97] *Motor Oil Hellas (Corinth) Refineries SA v Shipping Corp. of India (The Kanchenjunga)* [1990] 1 Lloyd's Rep. 391 at 399, *per* Lord Goff of Chieveley.
[98] See *W. J. Alan & Co. Ltd v El Nasr Export and Import Co.* [1972] 2 Q.B. 189 at 212–214; *Bremer Handelsgesellschaft mbH v C. Mackprang Jr.*, above, at pp.226, 230, explaining dicta in *Bremer Handelsgesellschaft mbH v Vanden Avenne-Izegem PVBA*, above; *Bremer Handelsgesellschaft mbH v Finagrain, etc. SA* [1981] 2 Lloyd's Rep. 259 at 263.
[99] *Bremer Handelsgesellscheft mbH v C. Mackprang Jr.*, above, at p.229; *Avimex SA v Dewulf & Cie.* [1979] 2 Lloyd's Rep. 57 at 67.
[1] *ibid.*, at p.545.
[2] See *Avimex SA v Dewulf & Cie.*, above, at p.67.

necessary for the sellers's action or inaction to be to his detriment, so long as relevant conduct is established.[3] This seems correct, for the detriment is really to be found in the inequitable consequences that would be suffered if the buyer was able to retract his waiver[4]; and later formulations indeed speak only of it being "inequitable", or "unfair or unjust" to allow the representor to go back on his waiver.[5] As an exception to the requirement of consideration this seems about as far as the principle should go. Thus in the leading case of *The Post Chaser*,[6] it was held that where a buyer in a string of contracts accepted documents and later, when they were rejected by the person who bought from him, sought himself to reject them, he was able to do so when the first seller was not able to establish anything beyond an assumption that the buyer was accepting the documents. The alternative would be to adopt a new approach whereby such waivers are effective without consideration, but other rules (*e.g.* as to intention and duress) are developed to distinguish a true and intended waiver from a mere temporary concession. Such an approach was repeatedly urged by Lord Denning M.R.,[7] but is still contrary to the stream of authority. The burden of proof is upon the person seeking to prevent retraction[8]; and the question whether there has been an effective waiver is one of mixed law and fact.[9]

12–037 **Affirmation (election).** A waiver in the sense of an expression of an intention not to reject but to be content with damages, *i.e.* an affirmation of the contract, is however an act of election and cannot be retracted without

[3] See *Finagrain SA v Kruse* [1976] 2 Lloyd's Rep. 508 at 535; *Bremer Handelsgesellschaft mbH v Vanden Avenne-Izegem PVBA* [1978] 2 Lloyd's Rep. 109 at 127 (detriment in "spending time and money in appropriations"); *Bunge SA v Schleswig-Holsteinische, etc. GmbH* [1978] 1 Lloyd's Rep. 480; *Société Italo-Belge, etc. v Palm and Vegetable Oils (Malaysia) Sdn. Bhd. (The Post Chaser)* [1982] 1 All E.R. 19; *The Kanchenjunga*, above, at p.399. Older cases took a stricter view, in requiring change of position: *C.I.R. v Morris* [1958] N.Z.L.R. 1126; *Ajayi v R. T. Briscoe (Nigeria) Ltd* [1964] 1 W.L.R. 1326, PC.

[4] *Grundt v Great Boulder Pty Gold Mines Ltd* (1937) 59 C.L.R. 641 at 674, *per* Dixon J. ("the real detriment or harm from which the law [*sc.*, of estoppel] seeks to give protection is that which would flow from the change of position if the assumption were deserted that led to it").

[5] *Bremer Handelsgesellschaft mbH v C. Mackprang Jr.* [1979] 1 Lloyd's Rep. 221 at 226; *Avimex SA v Dewulf & Cie.* [1979] 2 Lloyd's Rep. 57 at 67; *The Kanchenjunga*, above, at p.399.

[6] *Société Italo-Belge pour le Commerce et l'Industrie v Palm and Vegetable Oils (Malaysia) Sdn. Bhd. (The Post Chaser)* [1982] 1 All E.R. 19. See also *Bremer Handelsgesellschaft mbH v Westzucker GmbH* [1981] 1 Lloyd's Rep. 207 at 212–213; *Cook Industries Inc. v Meunerie Liegois SA* [1981] 1 Lloyd's Rep. 359; *Peter Cremer v Granaria BV* [1981] 2 Lloyd's Rep. 583 at 587; *Bunge SA v Cie Européenne de Céreales* [1982] 1 Lloyd's Rep. 306 at 308; *André et Cie v Cook Industries Inc.* [1986] 2 Lloyd's Rep. 200.

[7] Using the phrase "true accord" to refer to a genuine waiver. See, *e.g. D. & C. (Builders) Ltd v Rees* [1966] 2 Q.B. 617 at 624–625; 15 M.L.R. (1952). A case containing relevant, but sometimes puzzling dicta is *Brikom Investments Ltd v Carr* [1979] Q.B. 467; but it seems doubtful whether general principles are to be extracted from these unreserved judgments. See explanations of the case in Treitel, *Law of Contract* (11th ed.), p.102. The more lenient approach to consideration adopted in *Williams v Roffey Bros & Nicholls (Contractors) Ltd* [1991] 1 Q.B. 1 could, if correct, sometimes enable a similar result to be achieved; but see above, n.87.

[8] See *Finagrain SA v Kruse* [1976] 2 Lloyd's Rep. 508 at 535.

[9] *ibid.*, at pp.532, 540.

the consent of the other party. This seems to be based on the rule that a person must elect or choose between inconsistent rights[10]; though if the seller's breach can be regarded as continuing, as in an instalment contract, the buyer may be able to treat this as a fresh act or acts of repudiation, unless there is some reliance on the affirmation making it inequitable to do so.[11] Similarly, a buyer who rejects cannot thereafter insist on delivery. Such a waiver may be express or implied[12]; but it requires in principle knowledge of the breach waived. It probably also requires that the buyer knows of the right to reject to which the breach gives rise.[13] But by statute acts or omissions may constitute "acceptance", which will, as explained below,[14] bar rejection regardless of the knowledge of the buyer. Thus where a buyer unequivocally states that goods are accepted this is, regardless of his knowledge of defects, an "election statutably implied from acts"[15] and he can no longer reject: the same result flows from the lapse of a reasonable time. And in *Panchaud Frères SA v Etablissements General Grain Co.*,[16] the Court of Appeal held that buyers who rejected goods shipped under a c.i.f. contract on an inadmissible ground could not subsequently justify this on admissible grounds which they could have detected, but did not detect, at the time, and which he only discovered three years later. This decision, which has proved not easy to understand, was justified as based on estoppel by conduct,[17] or on "an inchoate doctrine stemming from the manifest convenience of consistency in pragmatic affairs, negativing any liberty to blow hot and cold in commercial conduct."[18] It has been explained on the basis of an extension of the reasoning behind the notion of acceptance[19] and on the necessity for finality in commercial transactions.[20] As such it does not appear to require that the representor had knowledge of the circumstances or of his rights.[21] One way of expressing it is as based on an

---

[10] See *The Mihalios Xilas* [1979] 1 W.L.R. 1018 at 1034–1035, HL; *Motor Oil Hellas (Corinth) Refineries SA v Shipping Corp. of India (The Kanchenjunga)* [1990] 1 Lloyd's Rep. 391 at 398, HL.

[11] *Stocznia Gdanska SA v Latvian Shipping Co.* [2001] 1 Lloyd's Rep. 537 at 564–566 and authority there cited; Treitel, 114 L.Q.R. 22 (1998).

[12] See *S.N. Kurkjian (Commodity Brokers) Ltd v Marketing Exchange for Africa Ltd* [1986] 2 Lloyd's Rep. 614, where acceptance of arbitration on a dispute as to conformity with description was held an implied abandonment of an objection as to quality.

[13] See *Peyman v Lanjani* [1985] Ch. 457, where there is a full discussion. In the context of rescission for misrepresentation the question was left open in *The Kanchenjunga*, above, at p.398.

[14] Sale of Goods Act 1979, s.35; below, paras 12–038 *et seq*.

[15] *Wallis, Son and Wells v Pratt and Haynes* [1910] 2 K.B. 1003 at 1015 (decision revsd. [1911] A.C. 394).

[16] [1970] 1 Lloyd's Rep. 53. See also *Cerealmangimi SpA v Toepfer (The Eurometal)* [1981] 3 All E.R. 533; below, paras 19–151 *et seq.*, 19–160; Eno, 44 Yale L.J. 782 (1935).

[17] At p.57, *per* Lord Denning M.R.

[18] At p.59, *per* Winn L.J.

[19] Below, paras 12–038 *et seq*.

[20] *B.P. Exploration Co. (Libya) Ltd v Hunt (No.2)* [1979] 1 W.L.R. 783 at 810–812; accepted in *Glencore Grain Rotterdam BV v Lebanese Organisation for International Commerce* [1997] 2 Lloyd's Rep. 386 at 396–397. But for a more limited suggestion see *Bunge SA v Schleswig- Holsteinische, etc. GmbH* [1978] 1 Lloyd's Rep. 480 at 492.

[21] See pp.57, 59.

estoppel as to whether an election has been made.[22] If this is correct, some form of reliance by the representee would be required; on any formulation it only applies where it is inequitable for the representee to change his mind.[23] The doctrine relates to waiver in the second sense of the above meanings, *viz.*, waiver of the right to reject, which was all that was strictly in issue.[24] Similar reasoning has, however, sometimes been invoked in cases on waiver in the first sense,[25] and indeed in other contexts where objection might be taken to various steps in commercial transactions and is not,[26] or where it might more generally be said that a party to litigation is seeking to blow both hot and cold.[27]

12–038 **Statute: acceptance.** The Sale of Goods Act 1979 provides that certain circumstances shall in effect constitute an implied affirmation, in the sense that the buyer is deemed to have affirmed the contract and is thus restricted to a claim for damages, whether or not he has discovered the defect.[28] These circumstances are comprised under the heading of acceptance; they operate in addition to the more general rules discussed above. Section 11(4) provides "Subject to section 35A below,[29] where a contract of sale is not severable, and the buyer has accepted the goods or part of them, the breach of a condition to be fulfilled by the seller can only be treated as a breach of warranty, and not as a ground for rejecting the goods and treating the contract as repudiated, unless there is an express or implied term of the contract to that effect." Before 1967 the right was also lost in the case of

---

22 See *Peyman v Lanjani* [1985] Ch. 457.
23 In the *Glencore Grain* case, above, it was also said (at pp.397–398) that the representation must be unequivocal; but this is not true of the all acceptance rules under s.35 of the Sale of Goods Act (below, paras 12–053 *et seq.*), which are also referred to as relevant.
24 Although the arbitrators found that the buyers were entitled neither to reject nor to damages (see p.56), the only issue was whether the buyers were entitled to reject. See *Edm. J. M. Mertens & Co. PVBA v Veevoeder Import Export Vimex BV* [1979] 2 Lloyd's Rep. 372 at 384–385.
25 *e.g. Bremer Handelsgesellschaft mbH v C. Mackprang Jr.* [1979] 1 Lloyd's Rep. 221 at 226; above, para.12–035.
26 *e.g. The Astraea* [1971] 2 Lloyd's Rep. 494 at 502 (time-bar); *The Shackleford* [1978] 1 W.L.R. 1080 (notice of readiness to unload); *Bunge GmbH v Alfred C. Toepfer* [1978] 1 Lloyd's Rep. 506; [1979] 1 Lloyd's Rep. 554 (notice extending shipment period); *Avimex SA v Dewulf & Cie.* [1979] 2 Lloyd's Rep. 57 (*force majeure* notice).
27 *e.g. The Vladimir Ilich* [1975] 1 Lloyd's Rep. 322 (appropriation alleged contractual subsequently alleged uncontractual); *Alfred C. Toepfer v Peter Cremer* [1975] 2 Lloyd's Rep. 118; *Bunge AG v Fuga AG* [1980] 2 Lloyd's Rep. 513 (similar argument as to notice extending shipment period); *cf. V. Berg & Son Ltd v Vanden Avenne-Izegem PVBA* [1977] 1 Lloyd's Rep. 499; *Avimex SA v Dewulf & Cie.*, above (*force majeure* notice: no inconsistency).
28 See *Bostock & Co. Ltd v Nicholson & Sons Ltd* [1904] 1 K.B. 725 at 734. The Uniform Commercial Code, s.2–608, allows revocation of acceptance in certain circumstances. This goes further than English law: but similar results can often be achieved (especially in consumer disputes) by saying that permitting trials, attempts at repair, etc., do not constitute acceptance; below, para.12–056.
29 These words were inserted by s.3(2) of the Sale and Supply of Goods Act 1994. They refer to the right of partial rejection introduced by that Act: below, para.12–060.

specific goods by the passing of property, and this caused difficulties in that, since in many cases the property would pass on agreement by virtue of section 18, rule 1,[30] there would often in effect be no right to reject. Efforts were made to suggest evasion of this result on the lines that, where the seller had committed a breach such as to entitle rejection, the contract was not unconditional,[31] or the goods not in a deliverable state,[32] or that property would not pass in non-conforming goods.[33] This part of the subsection (then section 11(1)(c)) was, however, removed by section 4(1) of the Misrepresentation Act 1967, though it and the problems generated by it may remain in some other common law jurisdictions. As a result, the loss of the right to reject, where there has been no express affirmation, depends on whether the goods have been accepted in accordance with the terms of section 35.

Buyer's right to examine goods. By section 34 of the Sale of Goods Act 1979, 12–039

> "Unless otherwise agreed, when the seller tenders delivery of goods to the buyer, he is bound on request to afford the buyer a reasonable opportunity of examining the goods for the purpose of ascertaining whether they are in conformity with the contract and, in the case of a contract for sale by sample, of comparing the bulk with the sample."[34]

It should be noted that the right only arises on request, and may be excluded by contrary agreement, express or implied. The right doubtless imposes an obligation on the seller for breach of which the buyer, if he could prove loss different from that consequent upon general failure to perform the contract, could claim damages. But it seems that the main significance of the right of examination is to impose as a prima facie rule a condition precedent on the buyer's duty to accept the goods.[35] Thus, if the seller refuses the buyer the opportunity to examine, the buyer is prima facie not in breach if he refuses to take delivery.[36] Beyond this, the main

[30] Above, paras 5–016 *et seq*.
[31] *Varley v Whipp* [1900] 1 Q.B. 513; above, paras 5–019, 5–020.
[32] Atiyah, 19 M.L.R. 315 (1956).
[33] *Taylor v Combined Buyers Ltd* [1924] N.Z.L.R. 627 at 649; *Armaghdown Motors Ltd v Gray Motors Ltd* [1963] N.Z.L.R. 5.
[34] This provision was originally s.34(2). S.34(1), providing that the buyer was not deemed to have accepted without a reasonable opportunity of examination, now appears in s.35 itself: below, para.12–050. The reference to sample is removed from its former position as s.15(2)(b) (above, para.11–073) and placed here. These changes were made by the Sale and Supply of Goods Act 1994, s.2. See also below, para.19–156 as to documentary sales.
[35] But if the buyer refuses to examine, it may affect the seller's duty to deliver the goods: see *Walter Potts & Co. Ltd v Brown Macfarlane & Co. Ltd* (1934) 30 Com.Cas. 64.
[36] *Lorymer v Smith* (1822) 1 B. & C. 1; *Pettitt v Mitchell* (1842) 4 Man. & G. 819; *Isherwood v Whitmore* (1843) 11 M. & W. 347 (tender of hats in closed casks: buyer need not accept if inspection refused). Conversely if the buyer refuses to examine, the seller may not be in breach if he does not deliver: *Walter Potts & Co. Ltd v Brown Macfarlane & Co. Ltd*, above.

significance of the provision is to reinforce the notion that the right to reject should not normally be lost before the goods have been examined.

12–040 **Testing and fitting.** Where the nature and quality of goods cannot otherwise properly be determined, the right to examine must include the right to test. Tests must be reasonable and normal ones. They may involve the use of the goods for a short time, or the using up of a small portion of the goods.[37] But where a buyer goes beyond what is necessary he may find that he has accepted the goods,[38] unless the seller has acquiesced in further trials.[39] Any cost incurred in fulfilment of the duty to afford the buyer a reasonable opportunity of examination and testing should be the responsibility of the seller. But the cost of the examination and tests themselves should be borne by the buyer,[40] though doubtless he could recover this in damages for breach of contract should the goods prove unsatisfactory. These propositions must yield to the intention of the parties as expressed or implied. Similar reasoning should be applied when the goods require to be fitted, even when this involves what would otherwise be damage to them (as in the case of fitting carpets).

12–041 **Time for examination and testing.** Examination, testing and the like must be carried out within a reasonable time having regard to the nature of the goods and all the circumstances of the case.[41] Failure to examine or test may be evidence of a waiver of the right to do so, and of acceptance of the goods, for it could amount to retaining the goods for a reasonable time without intimation of rejection.[42] Where the goods have not been delivered, it could amount to a waiver of the time for delivery.[43]

12–042 **Contrary agreement.** An agreement that property shall vest in the buyer or payment be made without opportunity to examine or test may be express or implied. The most obvious example occurs in c.i.f. sales, where it is of the nature of the transaction that the buyer must pay against documents without any right to examine the goods; if the goods, when they arrive,

---

[37] *Lucy v Mouflet* (1860) 5 H. & N. 229; *Walter Potts & Co. Ltd v Brown Macfarlane & Co. Ltd* (1934) 30 Com. Cas. 64 at 73. In *Heilbutt v Hickson* (1872) L.R. 7 C.P. 438, shoes intended for the army were tested by the breaking open of the soles of a small number, and later, as suspicion increased, of a larger number. There is no indication as to whether these shoes would have had to be paid for had the consignment been accepted. See also *Winnipeg Fish Co. v Whitman Fish Co.* (1909) 41 S.C.R. 453; *Burroughs Business Machines Ltd v Feed-Rite Mills (1962) Ltd* (1973) 42 D.L.R. (3d) 303, affirmed (1976) 64 D.L.R. (3d) 767 (computer system).
[38] Below, paras 12–044 *et seq.* See *Harnor v Groves* (1855) 15 C.B. 667 (flour); *Heilbutt v Hickson*, above, at p.451. *cf. Finch Motors Ltd v Quin (No.2)* [1980] 2 N.Z.L.R. 519.
[39] *Lucy v Mouflet*, above (cider), where acquiescence was inferred from the seller's silence; *Heilbutt v Hickson*, above, at p.452.
[40] Presumably this would have been the case in *Walter Potts & Co. Ltd v Brown Macfarlane & Co. Ltd*, above, n.34 (inspection of iron by expert).
[41] Williston, *Sales* (rev. ed., 1948), para.476; see also *Heilbutt v Hickson*, above, at p.451; *Truk (U.K.) Ltd v Takmakidis GmbH* [2000] 1 Lloyd's Rep. 543.
[42] See below, para.12–053.
[43] *Walter Potts & Co. Ltd v Brown Macfarlane & Co. Ltd*, above.

prove to be unsatisfactory, he may then, if he acts in time, reject them and recover the price paid.[44] So also in auction sales, examination is normally permitted before sale, but not after,[45] except for the purpose of ascertaining whether the goods received are those bought.[46] Clauses[47] and customs[48] as to time for rejection and as to non-rejection may also be relied on.

Place of examination. In many domestic sales, examination occurs at the seller's place of business when the goods are sold, even though delivery occurs later. But where the seller is authorised or required to send the goods to the buyer, the prima facie rule is that the place of delivery is the place at which the goods are delivered to a carrier,[49] and this would normally be the place for examination. A leading case is *Perkins v Bell*,[50] where barley was sold by sample to be delivered at a railway station near the seller's farm, and the station was held to be the place of examination. However, where the buyer deals as consumer, it is now enacted that delivery to the carrier is not delivery to the buyer[51]; hence the place for examination would normally be the place where the goods are actually presented to the buyer. Even in commercial sales not affected by this provision, it has always been the case that there may be indications to the contrary which show that the parties contemplated another place, though the fact that the buyer alone contemplated examination elsewhere is not without more relevant.[52] Thus where the seller delivers to a carrier, in circumstances making this a delivery to the buyer, but examination at the point of delivery is not reasonable or convenient, the place of examination contemplated may be the buyer's place of business.[53] Yet if the examination could conveniently be conducted at the delivery point, this will normally be the place for it, especially if it was within the reasonable contemplation of the parties that the buyer might wish from there to distribute the goods 12–043

---

[44] *E. Clements Horst & Co. v Biddell Bros* [1912] A.C. 18; see also *Polenghi Bros v Dried Milk Co. Ltd* (1904) 92 L.T. 64; *Gill & Duffus SA v Berger & Co. Inc.* [1984] A.C. 382; below, paras 12–067, 19–145, 19–163.

[45] *Pettitt v Mitchell* (1842) 4 Man. & G. 819.

[46] *Isherwood v Whitmore* (1843) 11 M. & W. 347 (hats in closed casks); *Chalmers v Paterson* (1897) 24 R. 1020 (Ct. of Sess.). The fact that the buyer does not test is not relevant to a claim for damages for breach of s.14: *Shields v Honeywill and Stein Ltd* [1953] 1 Lloyd's Rep. 357.

[47] Below, paras 13–031 *et seq.*, 18–240 *et seq.*

[48] *e.g. Sanders v Jameson* (1848) 2 C. & K. 557 (horses).

[49] Sale of Goods Act 1979, s.32(1), above, para.8–014. As to international sales see below, paras 18–259 *et seq.*

[50] [1893] 1 Q.B. 193. The Uniform Commercial Code, s.2–513(1), allows inspection at any reasonable place and time.

[51] Sale of Goods Act 1979, s.32(4) above, para.8–014. As to international sales see below, paras 18–259 *et seq.*

[52] *Perkins v Bell*, above, at p.197.

[53] *Grimoldby v Wells* (1875) L.R. 10 C.P. 391 (goods transferred from seller's wagon to buyer's wagon part way between premises); *Canterbury Seed Co. Ltd v J. G. Ward Farmers Association* (1895) 13 N.Z.L.R. 96. See also *Thames Canning Co. v Eckardt* (1915) 23 D.L.R. 805; *Silbert Sharp and Bishop Ltd v Geo Wills & Co. Ltd* [1919] S.A.L.R. 114.

direct to sub-buyers, as was the case in *Perkins v Bell*.[54] Where, however, in such a case, examination is not practicable by reason of the nature or packaging of the goods, it may be that the place of examination contemplated is the place of business of the sub-buyer.[55] The normal place of examination may also be varied by agreement between the parties or by the nature of the transaction. In *Heilbutt v Hickson*,[56] there was a sale to London merchants of a large quantity of shoes known to be intended for the French army. Some consignments were examined and accepted by the merchants, but at a later stage certain doubts arose as to the quality of the shoes which led to the seller's agreeing to take them back if they were justifiably rejected by the French army. It was held that this amounted to a variation of the place of examination by agreement between the parties, and that the shoes could be thrown on the seller's hands at Lille when later rejected by the French army at that place on the ground that the soles of many (which had been broken open for examination) contained paper. Brett J. alone went further and was of the opinion[57] that, since the first examination could not, by virtue of the nature of the defect, be a real examination, the place of examination was France in any case. The best discussion as to place of examination is often to be found in cases of overseas sales; but these are subject to special considerations and are treated separately.[58]

12–044 **Acceptance: meaning.**[59] Under section 35(1) of the Sale of Goods Act (as amended by the Sale and Supply of Goods Act 1994[60])

"The buyer is deemed to have accepted the goods subject to subsection (2) below—[61]

(a) when he intimates to the seller that he has accepted them, or

(b) when the goods have been delivered to him and he does any act in relation to them which is inconsistent with the ownership of the seller."[62]

---

[54] Above; see also *Saunt v Belcher and Gibbons Ltd* (1920) 90 L.J.K.B. 541; *Commercial Fibres (Ireland) Ltd v Zabaida* [1975] 1 Lloyd's Rep. 27; *Pini & Co. v Smith & Co.* (1895) 22 R. 699.

[55] *Van der Hurk v R. Martens & Co. Ltd* [1920] 1 K.B. 850 (sodium sulphate packed in drums); *Molling & Co. v Dean & Son Ltd* (1901) 18 T.L.R. 217 (books packed by seller for export). See also *J. W. Schofield & Sons v Rownson, Drew & Clydesdale Ltd* (1922) 10 Ll.L.R. 480; *Bragg v Villanova* (1923) 40 T.L.R. 154; *A. J. Frank & Sons Ltd v Northern Peat Co. Ltd* (1963) 39 D.L.R. (2d) 721.

[56] (1872) L.R. 7 C.P. 438. See also *Scaliaris v E. Ofverberg & Co.* (1921) 37 T.L.R. 307 (ship diverted by Admiralty orders: place of inspection varied).

[57] At p.456; reiterated in *Grimoldby v Wells* (1875) L.R. 10 C.P. 391 at 395–396.

[58] Below, paras 19–156, 20–108 *et seq.*, 21–102.

[59] Stoljar, 1 Melbourne U.L.R. 483 (1957). See also above, para.9–002 *et seq*; below, paras 19–155 *et seq.* as to documentary sales, which raise special problems.

[60] s.2(1).

[61] As to which see below, para.12–050.

[62] Under s.4 of the original Sale of Goods Act 1893 (repealed by the Law Reform (Enforcement of Contracts) Act 1954), which reproduced the provisions of the Statute of Frauds relevant to sales, the defence of lack of written evidence was inapplicable where the buyer had accepted part of the goods sold. There are cases on this provision, but the interpretation of this section was different from that under s.35 and cases on it are of little relevance to the present day. The word "accept" also appears in ss.27 and 50(1) of the Act, where its sense may not be the same as in s.35.

Intimation of acceptance. It might seem at first glance that the draftsman intended the words "intimates to the seller that he has accepted them" to apply to express affirmation of the contract, the reference to an "act inconsistent with the ownership of the seller" to cover implied affirmation by conduct, and the "reasonable time" rule[63] to apply to implied affirmation by inactivity. This is not however so. Although the case originally cited for the "intimation" rule[64] gives no indication as to what was intended, there is nothing to confine the verb "intimate" to express indications of affirmation; and it will be seen below that the "inconsistent act" rule is not explicable on the basis of affirmation by conduct.[65] But an intimation of acceptance, if it need not be express, must certainly be clear. Thus in *Varley v Whipp*[66] the buyer of an unsatisfactory reaping machine wrote a grumbling letter ending "it will be no use to me . . . but I shall be at Huddersfield this week . . . where I shall be pleased to see you." It was assumed that this was not an acceptance, though there was no express statement of intention to reject. There may clearly be express acceptance, as by signing of a delivery note, despite the fact that there has been no reasonable opportunity of examination[67]; or by indicating acceptance of the contract quantity while rejecting excess delivery.[68] In such cases an indication of acceptance amounts to a waiver of the right of examination. However, a person dealing as consumer cannot now lose his right to reject by such a note or by an oral agreement unless he has had an opportunity of examination.[69] 12–045

Act inconsistent with ownership of seller. The first problem arising in connection with this phrase is as to its meaning in cases where the property in the goods has already passed to the buyer, so that the seller has in fact no ownership with which the buyer may act inconsistently. There may clearly be cases where the property has so passed, but where the buyer may nevertheless reject the goods and revest the property in the seller unless he has done something constituting acceptance: it might be argued that this mode of acceptance is inapplicable in such cases. There are indeed old dicta that the notion of acceptance is irrelevant in situations where the property has passed, but these are clearly obsolete.[70] It is also true that the notion that the property does not pass at all when the goods are non-conforming was formerly more frequently resorted to. Thus it was said that under section 18, rule 5(1),[71] which deals with unascertained goods, the 12–046

---

[63] Below, para.12–053.

[64] *Saunders v Topp* (1849) 4 Exch. 390. The buyer of sheep, two days after they had been delivered to him at one place, sent his employee to bring them to another place, where he counted them and said "It is all right." But the case concerns the Statute of Frauds, above, and the communication was apparently not made to the seller.

[65] Below, para.12–046.

[66] [1900] 1 Q.B. 513. See also *Hammer and Barrow v Coca-Cola* [1962] N.Z.L.R. 723; *Rickard v Moor* (1878) 38 L.T. 841; above, para.12–032.

[67] *Hardy & Co. v Hillerns and Fowler* [1923] 2 K.B. 490 at 498. See also *Mechans Ltd v Highland Marine Charters Ltd*, 1964 S.C. 48 (Ct. of Sess.).

[68] *Staiman Steel Ltd v Franki Canada Ltd* (1985) 23 D.L.R. (4th) 180.

[69] Sale of Goods Act 1979, s.35(3), below, paras 12–063, 13–102.

[70] See *Bog Lead Mining Co. v Montague* (1861) 10 C.B.(N.S.) 481.

[71] Above, para.5–068.

seller is not authorised to appropriate non-conforming goods.[72] And although the property in specific goods normally passes on agreement,[73] the right to reject was formerly lost on the passing of property.[74] Thus the problem was first articulately addressed in connection with documentary sales, where property often passes on transfer of the documents, but the buyer undoubtedly retains a right to reject the goods on examination unless he has waived it in some way.[75] The explanation of the phrase adopted in this context is that since by rejecting the goods he has the power of revesting the property in the seller, the property passed in the first place only conditionally.[76] Thus there is ownership left in the seller by way of reversionary interest, and "it is that reversionary interest with which the buyer must not, save with the penalty of accepting the goods, commit an inconsistent act."[77] The old view as to appropriation of non-conforming goods is no longer so readily accepted, and the rule as to loss of the right to reject specific goods has been removed by statute.[78] Hence this explanation must be adopted for all those cases, perhaps the majority, where the property passes to the buyer before he has had an opportunity of examination.

12–047 **Policy behind words.** As has been stated above, it might be thought that the words "does any act . . . inconsistent with the ownership of the seller" were directed towards an implied election to affirm. On general principle an election would require a clear manifestation of intention to affirm, made by a person who knew that he had the right to reject, and known to the seller.[79] In the context of statutory affirmation one might perhaps expect some form of estoppel reasoning: an indication that the buyer was affirming might bar him from rejection against a seller who knew of and relied on it, even though the buyer was unaware that he had a right to reject.[80] But in fact neither the words themselves nor the case-law require that the seller knew of the buyer's act at all, though of course in some situations he may do so. The cases involve two separate types of situation. The first type

---

[72] Above, para.5–085. See Williston, *Sales* (rev. ed., 1948), paras 278a, 473; *Wait v Baker* (1848) 2 Exch. 1; *Vigers Bros v Sanderson Bros* [1901] 1 K.B. 608; *Taylor v Combined Buyers Ltd* [1924] N.Z.L.R. 627 at 648. The argument is, because of the wording of the rule, much stronger where the goods purportedly appropriated were not of the contract description.

[73] Sale of Goods Act 1979, s.18, rule 1; above, para.5–017.

[74] Sale of Goods Act 1893, s.11(1)(c); *Street v Blay* (1831) 2 B. & Ald. 456; above, para.12–038.

[75] Below, paras 19–145 *et seq.*

[76] *Kwei Tek Chao v British Traders and Shippers Ltd* [1954] 2 Q.B. 459 at 487, *per* Devlin J.; approved in *Gill & Duffus SA v Berger & Co. Inc.* [1984] A.C. 382 at 395. See also *Hardy & Co. v Hillerns and Fowler* [1923] 2 K.B. 490 at 496. But for a different view see Goode, *Commercial Law* (3rd ed.), p.350. Acts inconsistent with the seller's ownership performed *subsequently* to a purported rejection may, if known to the seller, indicate that there was no rejection: above, para.12–032.

[77] *ibid.*

[78] s.11(1)(c) of the Sale of Goods Act 1893 was amended by s.4 of the Misrepresentation Act 1967: above, para.12–038.

[79] See above, para.12–037.

[80] *ibid.*

consists of cases where the buyer cannot in practice return the goods because he has consumed them in whole or in part,[81] or used more of them than was necessary for the purpose of fitting or testing,[82] or incorporated them into a structure from which they cannot readily be extricated.[83] Such cases could be explained on a different ground, that of impossibility of *restitutio in integrum*. The second type comprises cases where the buyer has more generally acted, whether or not the seller knew of this, in a way inconsistent with any continuing or reversionary interest of the seller: the words carry some implication that the act would otherwise be a conversion, and are more apposite to situations where no property has passed at all.[84] The only situation of this sort where the loss of the right to reject was clear and articulately justified is the resale and forwarding of the goods to a sub-buyer.[85] The justification given here was that "to hold otherwise would be to expose the vendor to unknown risks, impossible of calculation when the contract was entered into."[86] The assumption seems to have been that if the right to reject were not lost, the goods would remain the seller's property and at his risk and could be sent to and rejected at some place or places (if there were several sub-sales) uncontemplated by the seller. Presumably a pledge with delivery of possession would have the same effect.

Opportunity of examination. From the buyer's point of view the loss of the right to reject in such circumstances might seem unfair if when he forwarded the goods on he had not had an opportunity to examine them. Older cases suggested that there was no acceptance unless inspection was reasonably possible before such further delivery.[87] In *Hardy & Co. v Hillerns and Fowler*,[88] however, it was held by the Court of Appeal that the wording 12–048

---

[81] *Harnor v Groves* (1855) 15 C.B. 667.

[82] Above, para.12–040.

[83] *Mechan & Sons Ltd v Bow, M'Lachlan & Co. Ltd*, 1910 S.C. 758 (ship); *Footersville Pty Ltd v Miles* (1988) 48 S.A.S.R. 525 (house); *Scott v McGreath* (1899) 1 G.L.R. (N.Z.) 268.

[84] Above, para.12–046.

[85] *Chapman v Morton* (1843) 11 M. & W. 534; *Harnor v Groves*, above; *Hunt v Barry* 1905 13 S.L.T. 34; *Hardy & Co. v Hillerns and Fowler* [1923] 2 K.B. 490; *Jordeson & Co. v Stora Kapparbergs Bergslags Aktiebolag* (1931) 41 Ll.L.R. 201; *Pelhams (Materials) Ltd v Mercantile Commodities Syndicate* [1953] 2 Lloyd's Rep. 281; *Kwei Tek Chao v British Traders and Shippers Ltd* [1954] 2 Q.B. 459. In *Chapman v Morton* there had previously been a purported express rejection; but the court held that it was accompanied by conduct making it not unequivocal. See further above, para.12–032.

[86] *Perkins v Bell* [1893] 1 Q.B. 193 at 197; quoted by Greer J. at first instance in *Hardy & Co. v Hillerns and Fowler* [1923] 1 K.B. 658 at 663; both of which were quoted by Branson J. in *Jordeson & Co. v Stora, etc.*, above, who discussed also the slightly different dicta in the Court of Appeal in *Hardy & Co. v Hillerns and Fowler*, above.

[87] See *Molling & Co. v Dean & Son Ltd* (1901) 18 T.L.R. 217 (but the basis of the decision is far from clear and doubt was cast on it in *Hardy & Co. v Hillerns and Fowler*, below); *Heilbutt v Hickson* (1872) L.R. 7 C.P. 438 at 451; *Perkins v Bell* [1893] 1 Q.B. 193; *Saunt v Belcher and Gibbons Ltd* (1920) 90 L.J.K.B. 541; *Taylor v Combined Buyers Ltd* [1924] N.Z.L.R. 627 at 650.

[88] [1923] 2 K.B. 490. *Cf. Breckwoldt v Hanna* (1963) 5 W.I.R. 356 (specific rejection, but part of goods inadvertently sold subsequently—no acceptance).

of the Sale of Goods Act prevented this interpretation: the requirement of acceptance was not (at that time) stated by section 35 to be subject to a reasonable opportunity to examine under the then section 34(1)[89] and indeed could not be, because the part of section 35 dealing with acceptance by intimation that the goods are accepted clearly need not be subject to such a requirement. Thus goods were held to have been accepted where they had in part been forwarded direct from the ship to a sub-buyer, though it was in fact not possible to ascertain their overall quality till a larger amount had been unloaded, and the buyer rejected as soon as he became aware of the breach. This decision was followed in *E. and S. Ruben Ltd v Faire Bros & Co. Ltd*,[90] where goods were ordered by the buyer to be delivered direct to the sub-buyer: it was held that the buyer had taken constructive delivery at the seller's premises and by procuring redelivery thereafter had acted inconsistently with the seller's ownership. It seems however that in that case the shipment by the seller to the sub-buyer was undertaken as a matter of courtesy only,[91] and that it was this fact that may have led to the conclusion that it was at the seller's premises that delivery took place.

12–049 It was also possible to argue that the rule did not apply where the place of examination contemplated was the sub-buyer's premises. The right of the seller is simply to have rejected goods made available to him at the place of examination.[92] Thus an act could be said not to amount to an acceptance unless it actually prevented return of the goods at that place. This view could be reconciled with *Hardy & Co. v Hillerns and Fowler*[93] on the grounds that, in that case, the place of examination was clearly the place where the goods were received from the ship: the only relevant finding was that, at the time of dispatch to the sub-buyer, there had not been time for examination of the whole cargo.[94] A decision to this effect was reached in New Zealand.[95]

12–050 **Clarification of the statute.** The Sale of Goods Act was changed to deal with this problem. By the Misrepresentation Act 1967[96] section 35 was amended to make clear that loss of the right to reject by act inconsistent with the seller's ownership was subject to a reasonable opportunity of the examination which section 34(1) then required.[97] By virtue of section 2 of the Sale and Supply of Goods Act 1994 this now appears, more logically, within section 35 itself,[98] as subsection (2), to which subsection (1) is made subject.[99] It reads:

---

[89] See above, para.12–039.
[90] [1949] 1 K.B. 254; Gower, 12 M.L.R. 368 (1949).
[91] See [1949] 1 All E.R. 215 at 217; *Hammer and Barrow v Coca-Cola* [1962] N.Z.L.R. 723 at 728.
[92] *Kwei Tek Chao v British Traders and Shippers Ltd* [1954] 2 Q.B. 459 at 488. See also *A.J. Frank & Sons v Northern Peat Co.* (1963) 39 D.L.R. (2d) 721.
[93] [1923] 2 K.B. 490.
[94] *Hardy & Co. v Hillerns and Fowler*, above, at p.495.
[95] *Hammer and Barrow v Coca-Cola* [1962] N.Z.L.R. 723.
[96] s.4(2).
[97] Above, para.12–039.
[98] As such, s.34(1) is repealed.
[99] Above, para.12–044.

"(2) Where goods are delivered to a buyer, and he has not previously examined them, he is not deemed to have accepted them under subsection (1) above until he has had a reasonable opportunity of examining them for the purpose—
(a) of ascertaining whether they are in conformity with the contract, and
(b) in the case of a sale by sample, of comparing the bulk with the sample."

Because purchasers are frequently asked to sign notes that goods have been received in good order and the like, it is further provided in a new section 35(3) that this provision cannot be excluded where the buyer deals as consumer.[1]

Ability to return goods to seller. It might then be argued that the real reason why delivery of goods to a sub-buyer may be an act inconsistent with the ownership of the seller is that after this has been done the goods often cannot be returned to the seller at the place of examination, which is where rejection should be effected. Therefore if the goods have not been moved from that place, or if the buyer can recover them intact from his sub-buyer (or pledgee) before he purports to reject, and transport them to the place of examination, a rejection should be effective. Although this might seem reasonable as a matter of policy, the case-law did not support it and suggested that delivery from the place of inspection, at least, barred rejection of itself.[2] The law was therefore altered, or at least clarified, by section 35(6)(b) of the Act (inserted by the Sale and Supply of Goods Act 1994),[3] which provides that "the buyer is not . . . deemed to have accepted the goods merely because—(b) the goods are delivered to another under a sub-sale or other disposition." However, without much discussion of the principles involved, a group of older cases had held lesser acts to be inconsistent with the seller's ownership. If correct, they indicate a looser, less specifically reasoned bar on the right to reject, which could be justified on the basis of estoppel if the seller knew of the acts in question, but which did not in fact require such knowledge. Examples are the execution of a chattel mortgage over the goods,[4] attempting to sell them,[5] putting them up for auction and, when a satisfactory bid was not received, buying them in,[6] or simply putting them up for auction,[7] and registration of change of 12–051

[1] This phrase has the same meaning as in Part I of Unfair Contract Terms Act 1977: Sale of Goods Act 1979, s.61(1) (as amended by Sale and Supply of Goods Act 1994, s.7 and Sch.2). See below, paras 13–071 *et seq*. The onus of proof is on the seller to show that the buyer does not deal as consumer. See above, para.12–024; below, paras 12–056, 13–102.
[2] See *Hardy & Co. v Hillerns and Fowler* [1923] 2 K.B. 490, as explained in *Jordeson & Co. v Stora Kopparbergs Bergslags Aktiebolag* (1931) 41 Ll. L.R. 201.
[3] s.2(1). But suggestions that the provision should be deleted, at least for consumer sales, were not adopted: see Law Com. No. 160, Scot. Law Com. No. 104 (1987), paras 5.32—5.38.
[4] *Metals Ltd v Diamond* [1930] 3 D.L.R. 886.
[5] *Symonds v Clark Fruit and Produce Co. Ltd* [1919] 1 W.W.R. 587.
[6] *Parker v Palmer* (1821) 4 B. & A. 387.
[7] *Hitchcock v Cameron* [1977] 1 N.Z.L.R. 85. See also *Benaim & Co. v L. S. Debono* [1924] A.C. 514, where however the facts are not clear.

ownership of a car.[8] Acts which have not qualified have been unloading goods and stacking them on a wharf,[9] re-bagging rejected corn,[10] repairing goods, sending an invoice for a part of them supplied by the buyer to the seller, and attempting to resell the goods[11] and claiming on the insurance in respect of the consignment.[12] The correctness of some of these cases must be open to question.

12–052 **Dealings with documents.** Special difficulties have occurred in documentary sales where the buyer has made dispositions of documents representing goods, whether by way of pledge or sale, before their arrival. Before the Misrepresentation Act 1967 it was already clear that the buyer in an overseas sale did not accept goods merely by making enquiries about their resale,[13] nor by making a contract for their resale, before goods or documents had arrived,[14] for even if such acts could constitute acceptance, section 35 refers to a situation "when the goods have been delivered to him". Where, however, in an overseas sale there had been a dealing with the actual bills of lading by way of pledge or sale before the arrival of the goods, which frequently occurs, there were difficulties in saying that the goods had not been delivered, for the documents representing the goods had, and this would often amount to delivery of the goods: further, the goods might be regarded as having been delivered by being entrusted to a carrier.[15] But in c.i.f.[16] and some f.o.b.[17] sales the buyer retains the right to reject the goods after examination on arrival. It is now clear that in such sales any disposition of the documents is only a disposition of the conditional property which the buyer has received, and that a pledge or a sale of the documents, does not amount to an act inconsistent with the ownership of the seller within section 35.[18]

12–053 **Reasonable time: opportunity for examination.** Section 35 of the Act originally simply mentioned the "lapse of a reasonable time" without intimation of rejection, as a third factor which would bar rejection. This formulation was perceived as causing a slight difficulty in that the reasonable time was not expressly made subject to the buyer's right to examine, as the "inconsistent act" provision had specifically been.[19] This was not serious, since the possibility of examination could obviously be taken into

---

8 *Armaghdown Motors Ltd v Gray Motors Ltd* [1963] N.Z.L.R. 5.
9 *Libau Wood Co. v H. Smith & Sons Ltd* (1930) 37 Ll. L.R. 296.
10 *Dower & Co. v Corrie, Maccoll & Son* (1925) 23 Ll. L.R. 100.
11 *Truk (U.K.) Ltd v Takmakidis GmbH* [2000] 1 Lloyd's Rep. 543 (a beneficial decision).
12 *J. S. Robertson & Son (Aust.) Pty Ltd v Martin* (1956) 94 C.L.R. 30.
13 *Fisher, Reeves & Co. Ltd v Armour & Co. Ltd* [1920] 3 K.B. 614.
14 *J. & J. Cunningham Ltd v Robert A. Munro & Co. Ltd* (1922) 28 Com.Cas. 42.
15 *Kwei Tek Chao v British Traders and Shippers Ltd* [1954] 2 Q.B. 459 at 486; approved in *Gill & Duffus SA v Berger & Co. Inc.* [1984] A.C. 395. There was a contrary argument by Gower, 12 M.L.R. 368 at 370 (1949).
16 Below, paras 19–145 *et seq*.
17 Below, paras 20–107 *et seq*.
18 *Kwei Tek Chao v British Traders and Shippers Ltd*, above, at p.488. See below, paras 19–154, 19–155.
19 Above, para.12–050.

account in the assessment of the reasonableness of the time. However, it was thought appropriate to clarify this by the amendments to the Sale of Goods Act introduced by the Sale and Supply of Goods Act 1994.[20] Now section 35(4) separately provides that "The buyer is also deemed to have accepted the goods when after the lapse of a reasonable time he retains the goods without intimating to the seller that he has rejected them." Section 35(5) then specifically states that the question whether the buyer has had a reasonable opportunity for examination is relevant, *inter alia*, to the determination whether a reasonable time has elapsed.

Delays caused by attempts to cure defects. There was a fear, particularly among consumer interests, that where buyers permitted sellers to attempt to rectify defects over a period, as is not uncommon with cars and, perhaps less often, electrical goods, they might lose the right to reject, whether because this was an implied indication of acceptance, or an act inconsistent with the seller's ownership, or because the attempts caused a reasonable time to elapse. Although a timely appellate decision could provide useful guidance on this question, it was feared that lower tribunals, perhaps taking the words of the Act strictly, might bar rejection where the equities of the situation made this unfair. As with the guidelines in respect of satisfactory quality, therefore, it was thought best to make specific provision against the difficulty.[21] Section 35(6) of the Act, inserted by the Sale and Supply of Goods Act 1994,[22] therefore now provides that "The buyer is not . . . deemed to have accepted the goods merely because— (a) he asks for or agrees to their repair by or under an agreement with the seller." The word "merely" should be noted: these matters do not *of themselves* trigger off a bar to rejection, but may nevertheless be relevant in considering whether a bar operates. It is submitted that this subsection implies that if the seller repairs the goods to the standard at which they ought to have been within any contract period for delivery (or if there is none, within a reasonable time) the buyer will then accept the goods.[23] 12–054

What is a reasonable time. What is a reasonable time is a question of fact.[24] Section 35 clearly bars rejection in some cases where the buyer did not know of and even could not have ascertained the defect, for example where the defect is one that would only manifest itself after a period of time. It seems also that the policy behind the section is one of finality of transactions,[25] which, while it does not prevent some weight being given to 12–055

[20] s.2(1).
[21] See Law Com. No.160, Scot. Law Com. No.101 (1987), paras 5.61—5.31.
[22] s.2.
[23] See *J.&H. Ritchie Ltd v Lloyd Ltd* 2005 S.C. 155 (but note the vigorous dissent of Lord Marnoch); Mak [2006] L.M.C.L.Q. 163. There could be liability in damages for loss caused by the delay: *cf.* below, para.12–086.
[24] Sale of Goods Act 1979, s.59.
[25] See *Bernstein v Pamson Motors (Golders Green) Ltd* [1978] 2 All E.R. 220 at 230 ("from the point of view of the seller the desirability of being able to close his ledger reasonably soon after the transaction is complete"—even apparently in a consumer case); see also *Motor Oil Hellas (Cornish) Refineries SA v Shipping Corp. of India (The Kanchenjunga)* [1990] 1 Lloyd's Rep. 391 at 398, HL ("the law takes the decision out of his hands").

the discoverability of the defect, prescribes that the right to reject be lost fairly quickly despite this factor. It is certainly clear that the notion of reasonable time prevents the existence of any long-term right to reject in the case of items, such as washing machines, which have defects of durability which by definition will not manifest themselves for a considerable period: and proposals to alter the law to create such a long-term right have been rejected.[26] However, within the fairly short period which this policy seems to require, there is certainly scope for the discoverability of the defect to be taken into account in the ascertainment of reasonable time, as section 35(5) of the Act now requires. Subsections (2)[27] and (6)[28] now make clear that a reasonable opportunity of examining the goods is relevant to the ascertainment of what is a reasonable time and that the buyer's asking or agreeing to repair does not of itself create acceptance.

Before these reforms, a case in which the right to reject a car was held lost in four weeks achieved much prominence in consumer circles.[29] But since the reforms it has been held in the Court of Appeal that the right to reject a yacht was not lost over a period of seven months while inquiries and negotiations about rectification of defects with Swedish suppliers were in progress.[30] This is of course rather a specialised type of consumer purchase. On the other hand, in a subsequent Court of Appeal case regarding kitchen equipment delivered in May it was held that the right to reject had been lost by September, despite the judge of first instance having found that at that time there were at least twenty unremedied breaches of contract.[31] The decision turns largely on the assessment that the judge of first instance was justified in his overall decision that there had on the facts been acceptance. But the practical message emerging from it is that buyers who think they may need to reject (whether or not they know that they may have the right to do so) must be vigilant to assert or preserve their rights.[32]

---

[26] See Law Com. No.160, Sc. Law Com. No.104 (1987), paras 5.6—5.19; above, para.11–040.

[27] Above, para.12–050.

[28] Above, para.12–054.

[29] *Bernstein v Pamson Motors (Golders Green) Ltd*, above (Rougier J.), a case settled before appeal which was much criticised, at any rate by consumer interests, at the time, *e.g.* Cranston and Dehn [1990] J.B.L. 346; Hwang [1992] L.M.C.L.Q. 334. There was an unreported decision pointing the other way, *M. & T. Hurst (Consultants) Ltd v Grange Motors (Brentwood) Ltd* (Russell J., Manchester, October 1981): see Reynolds, 104 L.Q.R.16 (1988).

[30] *Clegg v Olle Anderson* [2003] 2 Lloyd's Rep. 32; [2003] EWCA Civ. 320; see Reynolds (2003) 119 L.Q.R. 544.

[31] *Jones v Gallagher* [2004] EWCA Civ. 10; [2005] 1 Lloyd's Rep. 377. The initial complaint was that the unit was the wrong colour, which the buyers were told would correct itself in time. It is however not clear that the contract was one of sale at all: see Bradgate, 120 L.Q.R. 558 (2004).

[32] Among features taken into account at first instance were that the buyers had used the refrigerator (after it had broken down and been repaired) and the sink, and had put things on the shelves. The buyers might have done better under the Sale and Supply of Goods to Consumers Regulations now operative (below, paras 12–071 *et seq.*), where there are other controls on rescission, but at least no concept of acceptance.

Examples. It has been said in a commercial context that "When one party to a contract becomes aware of a breach of a condition precedent by the other, he is entitled to a reasonable time to consider what he will do, and failure to reject at once does not prejudice his right to reject if he exercises it within a reasonable time . . . He is also entitled during that reasonable time to make enquiries as to the commercial possibilities in order to decide what to do on learning for the first time of the breach of condition which would entitle him to reject."[33] As is to be expected, the resolution of the cases has varied with their facts.[34] Thus the retention of an instalment for 25 days, during which time correspondence took place between the parties, has been held not to be acceptance,[35] but in another case retention for three weeks was held to be acceptance.[36] It has been regarded as relevant that the goods were deteriorating,[37] or that expert opinion could have been obtained earlier,[38] or that the buyer acts as if he is relying on his right to damages, as by negotiating for a reduction in price[39] or calling for adjustments to the goods,[40] or that undue delay may be unfair to the seller.[41] Custom and usage as to rejection in the particular trade will also obviously be relevant. On the other hand the buyer is entitled to test the goods[42] or await their testing by others such as experts or sub-buyers[43]; 12–056

[33] *Fisher, Reeves & Co. Ltd v Armour & Co. Ltd* [1920] 3 K.B. 614 at 624, *per* Scrutton L.J.; followed in *Truk (U.K.) Ltd v Takmakidis GmbH* [2000] 1 Lloyd's Rep. 543, below. See also *Bremer Handelsgesellschaft mbH v Deutsche Conti-Handelsgesellschaft mbH* [1981] 1 Lloyd's Rep. 112 at 116; affirmed [1983] 2 Lloyd's Rep. 45.

[34] See *Couston, Thomson & Co. v Chapman* (1872) L.R. 2 Sc. & Div. 250 (wine: three months too long); *Milner v Tucker* (1823) 1 C. & P. 15 (chandelier: six months); *Percival v Blake* (1826) 2 C. & P. 514 (vat: two months); *Cash v Giles* (1828) 3 C. & P. 407 (threshing machine: some years though only used twice); *Flynn v Scott* 1949 S.C. 442 (car: five weeks); *Eastern Supply Co. v Keir* [1974] 1 M.L.J. 10 (car: two weeks); *Laurelgates Ltd v Lombard North Central Ltd* (1983) 133 N.L.J. 720 (car: several weeks); *Bernstein v Pamson Motors (Golders Green) Ltd* [1987] 2 All E.R. 220, see above, para.12–054 (car: three weeks); *Truk (U.K.) Ltd v Takmakidis GmbH*, above (underlift for recovery vehicle: nine months).

[35] *Hammer and Barrow v Coca-Cola* [1962] N.Z.L.R. 723 (yo-yos). See also *Partridge & Co. (N.Z.) Ltd v Bignell and Holmes* [1924] N.Z.L.R. 769; *A.C. Daniels & Co. Ltd v Jungwoo Logic*, Q.B.D., Judge Hicks Q.C., April 14, 2000 (injection mould: one month).

[36] *Re a Debtor* [1939] Ch. 225. See also *Pini & Co. v Smith & Co.* (1895) 22 R. 699.

[37] *Morrison and Mason Ltd v Clarkson Bros* (1898) 25 R. 427 (pump: 11 months: subjected to rough usage).

[38] *Hyslop v Sherlaw* (1905) 7 F. (Ct. of Sess.) 875 (picture: 18 months); *cf. Burrell v Harding's Executrix* 1931 S.L.T. 76 (picture); *Taylor v Combined Buyers Ltd* [1924] N.Z.L.R. 627 at 652 (car: four months); *Diamond v British Columbia Thoroughbred Breeders' Society Ltd* (1966) 52 D.L.R. (2d) 146 (racehorse: five months).

[39] *Canterbury Seed Co. Ltd v J. G. Ward Farmers' Association Ltd* (1895) 13 N.Z.L.R. 96; see also *Diamond v British Columbia Thoroughbred Breeders' Society Ltd*, above; *Polar Refrigeration Service Ltd v Moldenhauer* (1967) 61 D.L.R. (2d) 462. See also above, para.12–032.

[40] *Morrison and Mason Ltd v Clarkson Bros*, above. See also *Cerealmangimi SpA v Toepfer (The Eurometal)* [1981] 3 All E.R. 533.

[41] See *Maniffature Tessile Laniera Wooltex v J. B. Ashley Ltd* [1979] 2 Lloyd's Rep. 28 (where the delay of four months was reasonable); Patient, 43 M.L.R. 463 (1980).

[42] *Taylor v Combined Buyers Ltd* [1924] N.Z.L.R. 627 at 651; *Finch Motors Ltd v Quin (No.2)* [1980] N.Z.L.R. 519.

[43] *Truk (U.K.) Ltd v Takmakidis GmbH* [2000] 1 Lloyd's Rep. 543.

and the seller may acquiesce in or cause the delay, as when he assures the buyer that the goods, in the hands of a sub-buyer, will be all right after adjustment,[44] or attempts to cure defects[45]: in such cases his act may be held to delay acceptance. The buyer may also need, in some cases, to keep the rejected goods until he can obtain replacements.[46]

12–057 **Rejection of damaged or destroyed goods.** There is a surprising lack of authority as to whether a buyer can reject goods which have been accidentally damaged after delivery, or, in the case of their destruction, proceed as upon a rejection (assuming in the case of damage that this was not caused by reasonable and contemplated tests or modification, as in the case of fitting carpets).[47] One way of dealing with the question is to utilise the requirement of *resitutio in integrum* which applies to rescission for matters external to the contract such as misrepresentation.[48] On this basis the buyer could not reject in such circumstances, at least unless the damage or destruction arose from the seller's breach of contract. It seems more likely, however, that the draftsman of the Sale of Goods Act envisaged the question as turning on the incidence of property. Risk prima facie follows property in commercial transactions.[49] Thus where the property in goods has not passed, they are still prima facie at the seller's risk, subject to the buyer's duties as bailee. This principle will certainly often appropriately apply to sales on approval, where the passing of property is normally subject to a suspensive condition,[50] and where the buyer can be regarded as a mere bailee until he has approved the goods. It would also, however, apply to other cases, where the seller reserves property for other purposes. Furthermore, it seems that the inference that property did not pass in non-conforming goods was formerly more readily adopted: in a sale of unascertained goods it was sometimes said that the buyer did not assent to

---

[44] *Munro & Co. v Bennet & Son*, 1911 S.C. 337 (pump: rejection after two months); *Cork v Greavette Boats Ltd* [1940] 4 D.L.R. 202 (boat: five weeks); *Rafuse Motors Ltd v Mardo Construction Ltd* (1963) 41 D.L.R. (2d) 340 (tractor: 3–4 months); *Schofield v Emerson Brantingham Implement Co.* (1918) 57 S.C.R. 203; (1918) 43 D.L.R. 509 (other proceedings [1920] A.C. 415, PC).

[45] *Burroughs Business Machines Ltd v Feed-Rite Mills (1962) Ltd* (1973) 42 D.L.R. (3d) 303, affirmed (1976) 64 D.L.R. (3d) 767 (computer system: rejection after 11 months); *Barber v Inland Truck Sales Ltd* (1970) 11 D.L.R. (3d) 469 (truck: six months); *Finlay v Metro Toyota Ltd* (1977) 82 D.L.R. (3d) 440 (car: six months).

[46] *Public Utilities Commission of City of Waterloo v Burroughs Business Machines Ltd* (1974) 52 D.L.R. (3d) 481 (computer system: 14 months). Canadian courts have on the whole taken a lenient view towards buyers in respect of the right to reject: see Bridge, *Sale of Goods* (1997), pp.169–170, 177.

[47] The Law Commission (Law Com. No. 160, Scot. Law Com. No.104 (1987)) considered but made no recommendation on this problem: see paras 5.39, 5.40. For an instructive survey as to the positions taken by different legal systems on this topic see Treitel, *Remedies for Breach of Contract* (1988), pp.385 *et seq*.

[48] Above, para.12–007.

[49] Sale of Goods Act, 1979, s.20(1).

[50] Sale of Goods Act 1979, s.18, r.4, above, paras 5–040 *et seq*. See *Elphick v Barnes* (1880) 5 C.P.D. 321.

the appropriation of non-conforming goods.[51] The effect of such reasoning would therefore be in many cases to place the risk on the seller, subject to the buyer's duties as bailee of the goods.

Modern law would more frequently assume that the property had passed to the buyer before the time for rejection.[52] In such situations the same principle would put the risk on the buyer unless the damage or destruction arose from the seller's breach of contract. The position is not however clear. The leading (and almost the only) case is *Head v Tattersall*,[53] where a horse was sold at auction, warranted to have hunted with the Bicester hounds. If it did not answer its description it was to be returned before a certain time, "otherwise the purchaser shall be obliged to keep the lot with all faults." The horse did not comply with the description given, and the purchaser returned it within the specified time, by which time it had been injured without his fault. It was held that he was entitled to do so. It seems that property had passed to him. Some dicta in the case suggest that the contract gave an express liberty to return the horse, and indeed distinguish the situation where a buyer rejects under the general law.[54] On the other hand it can be said that there was not so much an express right of rejection as a time limit on the exercise of the right to reject, which was therefore exercised under the general law[55]: some of the propositions in the judgments as to risk are also general in form.[56] The decision was criticised by Williston on the grounds that risk should follow property.[57] 12–058

It does not seem appropriate at the present day that the matter should turn on the incidence of property: a seller may reserve property for various reasons, the most obvious of which is to retain security in the goods, quite unconnected with considerations as to risk. The matter must therefore be looked at in principle. It might seem initially reasonable to say that it is the seller who has supplied defective goods, and he must therefore bear the risk of damage or destruction prior to rejection unless this has occurred through the fault of the buyer. But the difficulty with this formulation is that if the buyer is the owner of the goods, as will be true in the majority of cases, it is difficult to see in what way he can be at fault in looking after them, however he chooses to treat them. It seems better therefore to lay down a rule that in the absence of other indications the buyer can only reject if he can return the goods in good order, damage caused by fair wear and tear, reasonable testing, fitting and the like in the short period within which rejection is possible being excluded. The risk of accidental damage or destruction 12–059

[51] See Williston, *Sales* (rev. ed., 1948), paras 278a, 473; *Wait v Baker* (1848) 2 Exch.1; *Vigers Bros v Sanderson Bros* [1901] 1 K.B. 608; *Taylor v Combined Buyers Ltd* [1924] N.Z.L.R. 627 at 648 *et seq.* And specific goods could not be rejected when property had passed: Sale of Goods Act 1893, s.11(1)(c); *Street v Blay* (1831) 2 B. & Ad. 456; above, para.12–038.
[52] Above, paras 5–085, 5–086.
[53] (1871) L.R. 7 Ex. 7. See also *Chapman v Withers* (1888) 20 Q.B.D. 824.
[54] See pp.10, 12, 13.
[55] This is true of *Chapman v Withers*, above.
[56] See pp.12–13, 14.
[57] *Sales* (rev. ed., 1948), para.273.

before rejection is therefore on the buyer.[58] Where, however, the goods are not damaged or destroyed but have merely diminished in value because of market movements, they may still be rejected.[59] This view can be supported by the argument that in many cases it is the buyer who is in the best position to insure.[60] It seems likely that one reason why the law on this topic is not yet clearly worked out is that in many cases a buyer who cannot return the goods as they were is, or may (rightly or wrongly) be regarded as barred from rejection by the "inconsistent act" provision of section 35(1).[61]

12–060 **Acceptance of part.** It seems clear that in the case of an instalment contract, *i.e.* one involving severable deliveries, the acceptance rules apply to each instalment separately.[62] Beyond this, however, until the changes made to the Sale of Goods Act by the Sale and Supply of Goods Act 1994 acceptance of part of the goods barred rejection of the remainder by virtue of section 11(4) of the Act as it then stood.[63] There was one exception. Under section 30(4) where goods were delivered mixed with goods of a different description, the buyer might accept the whole, or accept the conforming goods and reject the rest. This provision really represented a different policy as to part rejection and sat very uneasily with the rest of section 30. The policy of the 1994 reforms[64] was to permit part rejection, which is allowed in other sale of goods codes. The Act now therefore[65] makes section 11(4) subject to a new section 35A, subsection (1) of which provides—

"If the buyer—

(a) has the right to reject the goods by reason of a breach on the part of the seller that affects some or all of them, but

---

[58] But for a different view see Sealy [1927B] C.L.J. 225 at 240–244; see also Uniform Commercial Code, s.2–510. The Vienna Convention (Art. 82) is far from clear ("not due to [the buyer's] act or omission"). See further *Kinnear v J. & D. Brodie* (1902) 3 F. 540; *Boyd & Forrest v Glasgow and South-Western Ry Co.*, 1915 S.C. (HL) 21 at 29. The rule preferred in the text seems to be assumed by the Court of Appeal of New Zealand in *Canterbury Seed Co. v J. G. Ward Farmers Assoc. Ltd* (1895) 13 N.Z.L.R. 96.

[59] *cf. Armstrong v Jackson* [1917] 2 K.B. 822, above, para.12–007. It seems indeed that such diminution in value is often a primary motive for exercising a right to reject.

[60] In a c.i.f. sale the buyer receives a transferable insurance policy in respect of transit risks. Where the goods are damaged or destroyed in transit, he may nevertheless reject, or proceed as on a rejection, if they were not shipped in conformity with the contract: he will return the policy to the seller. See below, paras 19–145, 19–158 *et seq.*

[61] Above, paras 12–046 *et seq.* Other disputes may have been solved by assumptions, which might not now seem correct, that the property had not passed.

[62] s.11(4) only provides that acceptance of part of the goods bars rejection where the contract of sale is not severable: above, para.8–028. See the actual result in *Jackson v Rotax Motor and Cycle Co. Ltd* [1910] 2 K.B. 937 at 950; above, para.8–083.

[63] See above, para.12–038.

[64] See Law Com. No.160, Scot. Law Com. No.104 (1987), paras 6.6 *et seq.*

[65] By s.3.

(b) accepts some of the goods, including, where there are any goods unaffected by the breach, all such goods,

he does not by accepting them lose the right to reject the rest."

The provision as to goods mixed with goods of a different description was repealed as superfluous. A full account of it was given in earlier editions of this book.[66]

It is provided that goods are "affected by a breach" for the purposes of this section if by reason of the breach they are not in conformity with the contract.[67] Where the sale is by instalments, the provision applies to each instalment.[68] The section applies unless a contrary intention appears in or is to be implied from the contract.[69]

It should be noted that the buyer is permitted to choose how much of the *non*-conforming goods he rejects: he can reject some and keep some. If, however, he accepts any *conforming* goods he must accept them all; though he can of course reject the whole delivery. If the buyer rejects some of the goods, it might appear that in appropriate cases the seller might make a retender, if he comes in time[70]; but he may encounter a difficulty here in that the buyer may perhaps reject the retender on the ground that he is not bound to accept delivery by instalments.[71] **12–061**

Insofar as the buyer rejects goods and has paid, he must on principle be able to recover back the price of the rejected goods.[72] If he has not paid, he must presumably pay for goods accepted.

The relationship between the right to reject part and the right to treat the contract as discharged may create other problems. Under the previous law, the buyer could only treat the contract as discharged if he rejected the whole delivery.[73] Now that he is entitled to reject part he may presumably still treat the contract as discharged as a result of that rejection. One may next ask whether, when the breach is serious enough, it is the whole contract that he treats as discharged, or only the part of it to which the rejection applies. The answer given to the question may have a practical result, for if he sues for loss of the profit to be made on the contract, the calculation may be different depending on whether the loss is related only to the rejected goods, or to all the goods which should have been supplied under the contract. It may be, for example, that the goods accepted are of no use for a subcontract for which the main contract was to provide the source of supply, but can be used in some other way. It seems likely that the discharge should be regarded as relating to the rejected goods only, for the

---

66 See 4th ed. (1992), paras 12–027 *et seq*.
67 s.35A(3).
68 s.35A(2). As to delivery by instalments see above, paras 8–064 *et seq*.
69 s.35A(4).
70 See above, para.12–031.
71 s.31(1); above, para.8–064.
72 *cf. Devaux v Connolly* (1849) 8 C.B. 640; *Biggerstaff v Rowlatt's Wharf Ltd* [1896] 2 Ch 93; *Behrend & Co. v Produce Brokers Co.* [1920] 3 K.B. 530; *Ebrahim Dawood Ltd v Heath Ltd* [1961] 2 Lloyd's Rep. 512; see below, para.12–069.
73 See above, para.12–038.

buyer could if he wished have rejected the whole consignment. Similar problems may arise if the seller seeks to retender.[74]

12–062 **Commercial units.** It is, however, obvious that there must be some limit on the right to reject part: the mere fact that something is physically separate does not mean that it is necessarily appropriate to reject it separately. For example, if of a pair of shoes one is defective it would not be appropriate to permit rejection of one shoe: the pair should be rejected or none, at least unless the shoes are of an absolutely standard manufacture without differences between pairs or single shoes. The same might be true where a buyer seeks to reject one volume of an encyclopedia comprising several volumes.[75] The Sale and Supply of Goods Act 1994[76] therefore introduced the notion of "commercial unit", which comes from the American Uniform Commercial Code.[77] This feature of the change is (confusingly) introduced in section 35(7), which provides that:

"Where the contract is for the sale of goods making one or more commercial units, a buyer accepting any goods included in a unit is deemed to have accepted all the goods making the unit;"

It results from this formulation that the right to reject part only applies to "commercial units." These are defined in the same section 35(7), which runs on to say:

"and in this subsection 'commercial unit' means a unit division of which would materially impair the value of the goods or the character of the unit".

Examples of the sort of situations intended to be dealt with have already been mentioned above.

12–063 **Provision in contract as to rejection.** The contract may itself provide what constitutes or does not constitute acceptance,[78] and in particular may provide that there must be rejection, if at all, within a specified period.[79] There may be customs to the same effect.[80] By virtue of section 35(3) of the Sale of Goods Act 1979,[81] however, the buyer who deals as consumer cannot lose his right to rely on the rule that he is not deemed to have intimated acceptance without a reasonable opportunity of examination[82] by agreement, waiver or otherwise. Many commercial contracts contain non-rejection clauses which prohibit rejection altogether. All these clauses are

---

[74] See above, para.12–031.
[75] See Law Com. No.160, Scot. Law Com. No.104 (1987), paras 6.12, 6.13.
[76] s.2.
[77] s.2–105(6).
[78] *e.g. "Agroexport" v NV Goorden Import Cy. SA* [1956] 1 Lloyd's Rep. 319, below, para.13–032; *W. N. Lindsay & Co. Ltd v European Grain & Shipping Agency Ltd* [1963] 1 Lloyd's Rep. 437; *W. E. Marshall & Co. v Lewis and Peat (Rubber) Ltd* [1963] 1 Lloyd's Rep. 562.
[79] *e.g. Mellor v Street* (1866) 15 L.T. 223; *R. W. Green Ltd v Cade Bros Farms* [1978] 1 Lloyd's Rep. 602 (provision held unreasonable). Such a term might perhaps indicate that no act within a certain period was to constitute acceptance.
[80] *e.g. Sanders v Jameson* (1848) 2 C. & K. 557 (horses); see also below, para.13–031.
[81] Added by s.2 of the Sale and Supply of Goods Act 1994; see below, para.13–095.
[82] Above, para.12–050.

likely to be classified as exemption clauses and their effect is discussed elsewhere.[83] Section 11(4) of the Sale of Goods Act 1979[84] states that its provisions as to loss of the right to reject do not apply where "there is an express or implied term of the contract to that effect." It is however difficult to envisage a provision that the right to reject is not to be lost on acceptance: an express acceptance would (subject to section 35(3), above) be a waiver of any such provision, a retention within any time allowed would be reasonable and so not an acceptance at all, and no act permitted by the contract would be inconsistent with the seller's ownership.[85] The proviso seems to have been inserted to deal with situations such as that in *Head v Tattersall*,[86] where the contract provided for rejection of a horse within seven days though the property had (probably) passed. In view of the deletion, by the Misrepresentation Act 1967, of that part of section 11(4) which deprived the buyer of the right to reject after the passing of property,[87] the proviso is of little importance: save, perhaps, that it precludes argument that there has been acceptance when there is a time-limit on rejection, and it is sought to reject the goods within this limit but after what would normally be a reasonable time.

Effect of rejection on property. Where the goods have been delivered to the buyer, the property may or may not have passed to him. For example, appropriation of goods not conforming with description would not pass property,[88] but the appropriation of goods not of satisfactory quality might. Again, the seller may reserve property even after delivery.[89] If property has not passed, when the buyer exercises his right to reject he is simply indicating that he does not accept the goods and hence that it will never pass to him. Where, however, the property has passed to the buyer, by rejecting the buyer revests it in the seller. It is then said that the property only passed conditionally in the first place.[90] As has already been explained,[91] this reasoning is convenient in explaining why, for example, a 12–064

83 Below, paras 13–032, 13–033, 18–275, *et seq.*, 19–172.
84 Above, para.12–038.
85 A similar analysis can probably be applied to "no waiver" clauses.
86 (1871) L.R. 7 Ex. 7, above, para.12–058; see also *McDougall v Aeromarine of Emsworth Ltd* [1958] 1 W.L.R. 1126. But it may be that the draftsman really had *Bannerman v White* (1861) 10 C.B.(N.S.) 844 in mind. In that case a buyer was permitted to reject hops about which he had received an assurance that no sulphur had been used in their treatment, though property had passed. The ground given seems to have been that the contract was subject to a non-promissory condition precedent (above, para.10–038) but this is very dubious. To modern eyes this is a case of rejection for breach of condition, but such rejection was probably not possible at the time unless the goods did not correspond with their description, because of *Street v Blay* (1841) 2 B. & Ad. 456. See Stoljar, 16 M.L.R. 154 at 194–195 (1953).
87 Above, para.12–038.
88 Sale of Goods Act 1979, s.18, r. 5(1): above, para.5–085. *Cf.* above, paras 12–057, 12–058.
89 See above, paras 5–131 *et seq.*
90 *Kwei Tek Chao v British Traders and Shippers Ltd* [1954] 2 Q.B. 459 at 487, approved in *Gill & Duffus SA v Berger & Co. Inc.* [1984] A.C. 382 at 395; *McDougall v Aeromarine of Emsworth Ltd* [1958] 1 W.L.R. 1126; *Rosenthal & Sons Ltd v Esmail* [1965] 1 W.L.R. 1117 at 1131. See above, para.12–057, below, para.19–174.
91 Above, para.12–048.

pledge of the documents does not bar rejection of the goods: it is a pledge of the conditional interest only. A *wrongful* rejection would have no effect on the property in the goods unless the seller accepted the repudiation.

12–065 **Rights and duties of buyer and seller as to rejected goods.** By section 36 of the Sale of Goods Act 1979: "Unless otherwise agreed, where goods are delivered to the buyer, and he refuses to accept them, having the right to do so, he is not bound to return them to the seller, but it is sufficient if he intimates to the seller that he refuses to accept them." Where the buyer rightly rejects, therefore he may throw the goods on the seller's hands at the place of examination,[92] a rule which may cause hardship to the seller. The goods therefore continue or become the property,[93] and as such become at the risk[94] and expense, of the seller. The buyer cannot exercise any lien over them in respect of repayment of the price.[95] He is in principle no longer entitled to deal with them except by the express or implied authority of the seller,[96] and in the rare cases where the doctrine of agency of necessity operates, if that is different.[97] He is, however, an involuntary, or at least a gratuitous bailee, and as such owes a duty of care in relation to the goods; and this may entitle him to reimbursement for expenses incurred.[98] Beyond this, however, the goods seem to be at the seller's risk. But the contract may provide that the buyer shall return rejected goods.[99]

12–066 **Tender of totally non-conforming goods.** It has sometimes been suggested that where *totally* non-conforming goods are tendered under the contract, they cannot be treated as the contract goods at all, so that an acceptance of such goods under section 35 cannot occur.[1] It seems,

[92] See *Heilbutt v Hickson* (1872) L.R. 7 C.P. 438 at 456–457. For the situation where the buyer agrees to take goods back on certain terms, and a dispute arises as to whether he has accepted the goods as returned, see *Allard & Co. (Rubber) Ltd v R. J. Hawkins & Co. (Dudley) Ltd* [1958] 1 Lloyd's Rep. 184.
[93] Above, para.12–064.
[94] *Grimoldby v Wells* (1875) L.R. 10 C.P. 391 at 395.
[95] *J. L. Lyons & Co. Ltd v May and Baker Ltd* [1923] 1 K.B. 685. But the buyer is given such a lien by Uniform Commercial Code, s.2–711(3). See also Vienna Convention (above, para.1–024), Arts 85–88.
[96] In *Laurelgates Ltd v Lombard North Central Ltd* (1983) 133 N.L.J. 720, a buyer after rejecting a car continued to use it and also allowed the manufacturer to attempt repairs to it. It was held that these were with the implied authority of the seller and did not invalidate the rejection. See also *Public Utilities Commission of City of Waterloo v Burroughs Business Machines Ltd* (1974) 52 D.L.R. (3d) 481 (computer system).
[97] See above, para.3–006; *Bowstead and Reynolds on Agency* (18th ed.), Art. 33.
[98] *Cf.* Sale of Goods Act 1979, s.20(3), above, para.6–026. See *China Pacific SA v Food Corp. of India (The Winson)* [1982] A.C. 939 (cost of storage after salvage services). The buyer would often be able to found such a claim in breach of contract: see *Kolfor Plant Ltd v Tilbury Plant Ltd* (1977) 121 S.J. 390 (cost of storage on rejection). See also *Chesterman v Lamb* (1834) 2 A. & E. 129. The Uniform Commercial Code, ss.2–603 and 2–604, provides specifically for the buyer's position in such situations, as does the Vienna Convention (above, para.1–024), Arts 84–88, imposing quite stringent duties of preservation.
[99] See *Mellor v Street* (1866) 15 L.T. 223; *Ornstein v Alexandra Furnishing Co.* (1895) 12 T.L.R. 128.
[1] Montrose, 15 Can.Bar.Rev. 760 (1937); Gower, 12 M.L.R. 368 (1949).

however, that a tender of totally non-conforming goods, if made under the contract, is subject to the rules for acceptance, just as is a tender of defective goods[2]; though no doubt there could be circumstances where such a tender could not be related to the contract at all, but would at best be an offer of a separate contract.[3]

Restitution: recovery of money paid. A buyer who justifiably rejects goods may sue for damages[4]: any award will take into account, and may include,[5] any part of the price paid. He may alternatively recover any money he has paid in restitution as upon total failure of consideration.[6] This right is expressly preserved by section 54 of the Sale of Goods Act 1979. Such a claim may be simpler than a claim for damages in that he has no need to prove loss nor to mitigate: it may indeed yield more than a claim for damages would, especially on a falling market,[7] though where other loss can be proved a claim for damages may be preferable. In order to exercise it, the buyer must terminate the contract, *i.e.* treat it as discharged.[8] "If goods have been properly rejected, and the price has already been paid in advance, the proper way of recovering the money back is by action for money paid for a consideration which has totally failed, *i.e.* money had and received; but that form of action is governed by exactly the same rules with regard to affirming or avoiding the transaction as in any other case."[9] Should the buyer affirm the transaction by accepting the goods,[10] it is too late to sue upon a total failure of consideration. Thus in *Yeoman Credit Ltd v Apps*[11] the defendant entered into an agreement for the hire-purchase of a second-hand car. The car proved seriously defective to an extent which the 12–067

---

[2] *Cf. Wilson v Rickett, Cockerell & Co. Ltd* [1954] 1 Q.B. 598, where explosive delivered with Coalite was held to be part of the contractual goods for the purposes of a breach of s.14(2) of the Sale of Goods Act: Denning L.J. referred to the goods "delivered in purported pursuance of the contract".

[3] See *Suisse Atlantique Société d'Armement Maritime v NV Rotterdamsche Kolen Centrale* [1967] 1 A.C. 361 at 404. And where s.18, r. 5, of the Sale of Goods Act 1979 is relevant, the appropriation of non-conforming goods will not be assented to by the buyer, so that property will not pass.

[4] *Millar's Machinery Co. Ltd v David Way & Son* (1935) 40 Com.Cas. 204; *Johnson v Agnew* [1980] A.C. 367.

[5] *e.g. Harling v Eddy* [1951] 2 K.B. 739. See also *Mason v Burningham* [1949] 2 K.B. 545.

[6] *Giles v Edwards* (1797) 7 T.R. 181; *Bragg v Villanova* (1923) 40 T.L.R. 154. See also *Gompertz v Bartlett* (1853) 2 E. & B. 849; *Towers v Barrett* (1786) 1 T.R. 133; *Greville v da Costa* (1797) Peake 113; *Nockels v Crosby* (1825) 3 B. & C. 814; *Wilson v Church* (1879) 13 Ch.D. 1. As to pleading such a debt as a set-off see *Biggerstaff v Rowlatt's Wharf Ltd* [1896] 2 Ch. 93. See in general Goff and Jones, *Law of Restitution* (6th ed.), paras 20–007 *et seq.*; Stoljar, 75 L.Q.R. 53 (1959); below, paras 17–090 *et seq.*

[7] *e.g. Ebrahim Dawood Ltd v Heath Ltd* [1961] 2 Lloyd's Rep. 512.

[8] *Weston v Downes* (1778) 1 Doug. 23. *Cf. Moschi v Lep Air Services Ltd* [1973] A.C. 331 at 345–346, 350–351; *Photo Production Ltd v Securicor Transport Ltd* [1980] A.C. 827.

[9] *Kwei Tek Chao v British Traders and Shippers Ltd* [1954] 2 Q.B. 459 at 475, *per* Devlin J.

[10] Above, paras 12–044 *et seq.*

[11] [1962] 2 Q.B. 508. See also *Heilbutt v Hickson* (1872) L.R. 7 C.P. 438 at 451; *cf. Charterhouse Credit Co. Ltd v Tolly* [1963] 2 Q.B. 683.

court held would have entitled him to reject it, notwithstanding the presence of an exemption clause in the contract. However, the defendant, while complaining as to its state, paid three monthly instalments and kept the car until it was repossessed by the owner after six months. It was held that he could not recover the instalments, but was confined to a claim for damages.

12–068 **Failure of consideration must be total.** On current general principles the buyer cannot sue upon a total failure of consideration unless he can return the goods as they were, except where his inability to do so is because of loss or damage which is at the seller's risk,[12] or is caused by the very breach of which the buyer complains.[13] Old cases, mainly concerning land, took an even stricter view of the requirement that the failure of consideration must be total, and there were decisions that, when the buyer had had any enjoyment of the subject-matter of the contract at all, he could not recover.[14] These cases were connected with the notion that before a party could sue upon a total failure of consideration he must not merely bring the contract to an end but rather wipe it out or avoid it *ab initio*; this was not possible unless true *restitutio in integrum* could be made. This view of the requirements of the restitutionary claim was, however, expressly discountenanced by the House of Lords in the *Fibrosa* case,[15] and these cases should probably nowadays be taken as examples, albeit rather extreme examples, of cases where the contract was affirmed.[16] The mere fact that the buyer has had some enjoyment of the subject-matter should not of itself bar a claim upon a total failure of consideration.[17] Such a view is, however, only maintainable so long as the right to reject must (as at present) be fairly quickly exercised. Strong views have been expressed that the requirement of total failure, on which there are notable difficult cases,[18] should be abandoned, and restitution granted subject to allowances for benefits received[19]; but only statute or the House of Lords can achieve this.

[12] Above, paras 12–057 *et seq.*
[13] A possible explanation of *Rowland v Divall* [1923] 2 K.B. 500. See also *Harling v Eddy* [1951] 2 K.B. 739; Treitel, *Law of Contract* (11th ed.), p.1052. See also *Bostock & Co. Ltd v Nicholson & Sons Ltd* [1904] 1 K.B. 725 at 741 (goods totally worthless).
[14] The most famous case is *Hunt v Silk* (1804) 5 East 449. See also *Beed v Blandford* (1828) 2 Y. & J. 278; *Blackburn v Smith* (1848) 2 Exch.783; *Freeman v Jeffries* (1869) L.R. 4 Ex. 189; *Thorpe v Fasey* [1949] Ch. 649.
[15] *Fibrosa Spolka Akcyjna v Fairbairn Lawsom Combe Barbour Ltd* [1943] A.C. 32, esp. at 52, 70; see also *Bines v Sankey* [1958] N.Z.L.R. 886 at 893.
[16] Goff and Jones, *Law of Restitution* (6th ed.), para.20–013; *Heilbutt v Hickson* (1872) L.R. 7 C.P. 438 at 451. Or even on the basis that the failure of consideration was in the particular circumstances not total: see *Spence v Crawford* [1939] 3 All E.R. 271 at 290.
[17] *Cf. Rowland v Divall* [1923] 2 K.B. 500; Treitel, *Law of Contract* (11th ed.), pp.1049 *et seq.*
[18] Especially *Rowland v Divall* [1923] 2 K.B. 500, concerning the condition as to right to sell: above, para.4–006; Goff and Jones, *Law of Restitution* (6th ed.), paras 20–014 *et seq.* See also *Rover International Ltd v Cannon Film Sales Ltd* [1989] 1 W.L.R. 912; *D.O. Ferguson & Associates Ltd v Sohl* (1992) 62 B.L.R. 95.
[19] See *Goff and Jones, op.cit.* above, Ch.19 and paras 20–012 *et seq.*; Virgo, *Principles of the Law of Restitution* (1999), pp.338–342. See also above, para.12–008.

Recovery of money paid in cases of short delivery. Where the seller delivers less than the contractual amount, the buyer may of course reject the whole tender. But he is allowed alternatively to accept the goods delivered.[20] If he does so he must pay for them at the contract rate: this can usually be justified on the basis that he is voluntarily accepting the offer made. He can also sue for damages: but he can, instead, recover in restitution any excess of price paid over and above what is due for the goods delivered,[21] for the original contract has been discharged by breach, and consideration in respect of which there is failure can be apportioned.[22] It would seem that the same must apply when the buyer rejects part of the goods, as is now permitted.[23] 12–069

Recovery in cases of instalment contracts. Likewise, where the buyer justifiably treats a severable instalment contract[24] as discharged, he can recover any money paid in respect of goods which he is entitled to return or which he is now under no obligation to accept. Even if the contract subsists, he can recover the price of instalments justifiably rejected.[25] But in general it seems that he can neither return instalments previously accepted nor recover payment made in respect of them.[26] 12–070

3. ADDITIONAL RIGHTS OF BUYER IN CONSUMER CASES

Special consumer remedies. A new and alternative range of remedies for consumers is provided by Part 5A of the Sale of Goods Act 1979, inserted by the Sale and Supply of Goods to Consumers Regulations 2002 pursuant to the EC Directive on Consumer Goods and Associated Guarantees of 1999. The purpose of the Directive was to secure similar regimes for (what may loosely be called) consumer sales throughout the EC.[27] The heading to Part 5A refers, as does the Directive, to *rights* of buyers: but in effect these are specialised remedies and will be referred to as such. Although the remedies in question can be regarded as part of specifically consumer law, the requirement of a complete exposition in this chapter of the remedies available for defective goods means that they must be dealt with here, particularly as the existing remedies for defective goods are almost entirely unaffected and are also simultaneously available for use by consumers. The 12–071

---

[20] Sale of Goods Act 1979, s.30(1), above, para.8–045.
[21] *Devaux v Connolly* (1849) 8 C.B. 640; *Biggerstaff v Rowlatt's Wharf Ltd* [1896] 2 Ch. 93; *Behrend & Co. v Produce Brokers Co.* [1920] 3 K.B. 530; *Ebrahim Dawood Ltd v Heath Ltd* [1961] 2 Lloyd's Rep. 512; *cf. Whincup v Hughes* (1871) L.R. 6 C.P. 78 at 81.
[22] See *Goss v Chilcott* [1996] A.C. 788; *David Securities Pty Ltd v Commonwealth Bank of Australia* (1992) 175 C.L.R. 353 at 383; below, para.17–091; Chitty, *Contracts* (29th ed.), Vol. 1, para.29–063; Virgo, *Principles of the Law of Restitution* (1999), pp.338–341.
[23] See above, para.12–061.
[24] Above, paras 8–073 *et seq.*
[25] See above, para.8–082.
[26] But see above, para.8–083. The result seems clear if not the reasons.
[27] As to the Directive, see in general below, paras 14–008 *et seq.*

reader should, however, bear in mind the need to link these remedies with the other elements of consumer law dealt with in Chapter 14.

In addressing these remedies, three major points should be borne in mind. The first is that though the Directive started by laying down basic requirements for conformity of the goods with the contract, in respect of which remedies were then prescribed, beyond a brief mention these do not appear in the United Kingdom Regulations.[28] This was because the U.K. law was regarded as already achieving the same results by its existing implied terms as to description and quality,[29] and consequently it was thought that a new set of provisions regarding this matter was unnecessary. Only in one area was a change to the law regarded as appropriate: the Directive made public statements regarding the goods relevant to the ascertainment of their conformity. This was not necessarily true under the Sale of Goods Act 1979, and a change was effected by amending section 14(2) of the Act.[30] The policy of not restating the conformity requirements may or may not have been justified: the matter is discussed elsewhere.[31] But it is for this reason that the effect of the Regulations that implement the Directive is mostly in respect of consumer *remedies*.

The second is a point that has already been made above: that the regime prescribed does not exclude the existing common law remedies of rejection and damages. Their retention is permitted by the Directive if they are, as seems to have been assumed, "more stringent provisions" than those required by the Directive.[32] Hence Part 5A of the Act is headed "*Additional* rights of the Buyer in Consumer Sales". It will appear in the discussion of Part 5A, however, that the interaction of the existing regime with the new is likely to cause difficulties for consumers and their advisers.

The third point is that the new remedies apply only where goods are supplied but prove defective. Claims in respect of lack of title, and claims for pure non-delivery (obviously less frequently relevant in the consumer context) are left to the general law.[33] As regards non-delivery, this is perhaps more significant to the resolution of disputes than might appear. This is because the remedy of specific performance is exceptional in common law countries, while in other countries for which the uniformity was also intended it may be more easily available. It is conceivable that the new availability of specific performance for repair or (especially) replacement of goods, discussed below[34], may encourage its more frequent use in respect of non-delivery; but there is in fact nothing to alter the normal law on specific performance contained in the relevant provision (section 52 of the Sale of Goods Act[35]).

Reference is sometimes made below to the Vienna Convention on the International Sale of Goods, which is widely operative in Europe and

---

[28] s.48F, below, para.12–074.
[29] Above, Ch.11.
[30] Above, paras 11–033 *et seq.*
[31] Below, paras 14–011 *et seq.*
[32] As to which see Art. 8.2; below, para.14–008.
[33] The difference stems from a Roman law distinction between the general contractual action and separate (aedilician) liability for latent defects, which has never been known to the common law.
[34] See below, paras 12–082, 12–114.
[35] See below, paras 17–096 *et seq.*

elsewhere, though it has not yet been adopted in the United Kingdom. This Convention makes available some of the same remedies as the Directive requires. Although it concerns non-consumer sales, comparison with it is sometimes instructive.

Section 48A: introductory. A general plan of the designated remedies is first provided by section 48A, as follows: 12–072

"(1) This section applies if—

(a) the buyer deals as consumer or, in Scotland, there is a consumer contract in which the buyer is a consumer, and
(b) the goods do not conform to the contract of sale at the time of delivery.

(2) If this section applies, the buyer has the right—

(a) under and in accordance with section 48B below, to require the seller to repair or replace the goods, or
(b) under and in accordance with section 48C below—

(i) to require the seller to reduce the purchase price of the goods to the buyer by an appropriate amount, or
(ii) to rescind the contract with regard to the goods in question.

(3) For the purposes of subsection (1)(b) above goods which do not confirm to the contract of sale at any time within the period of six months starting with the date on which the goods were delivered to the buyer must be taken not to have so conformed at that date.
(4) Subsection (3) above does not apply if—

(a) it is established that the goods did so conform at that date;
(b) its application is incompatible with the nature of the goods or the nature of the luck of conformity."

Application: "deals as consumer". This section provides an introductory statement of remedies unfamiliar to common lawyers. They apply when the buyer "deals as consumer". This phrase was already used in the Sale of Goods Act 1979 before the enactment of the new provisions, and it is there provided by section 61(5A) that "References in this Act to dealing as consumer are to be construed in accordance with Part I of the Unfair Contract Terms Act 1977, and, for the purposes of this Act, it is for a seller claiming that the buyer does not deal as consumer to show that he does not" (the last words in fact repeating the relevant part of the 1977 Act). The remedies therefore require consideration of the criteria stated in section 12 of the Unfair Contract Terms Act 1977, which is dealt with elsewhere in this book.[36] This use of the phrase "deals as consumer" does not link entirely satisfactorily with what appears to have been the intention of the Directive. 12–073

[36] See below, paras 13–070 *et seq*.

12–074 **"The goods do not conform."** The definition of "goods" is that already in the Sale of Goods Act 1979.[37] As stated above,[38] the Directive itself contains detailed provisions on conformity. But for English law this is briefly dealt with in section 48F: "For the purposes of this Part, goods do not conform to a contract of sale if there is, in relation to the goods, a breach of an express term of the contract or a term implied by section 13, 14 or 15 above."[39] This includes not only matters of quality but also the strict requirements as to compliance with description laid down in section 13,[40] and compliance with other, express terms concerning the goods.

12–075 **Presumption of disconformity.** The rule stated in section 48A(3) above, which when taken with subsection (4)(a) can be called a six-month presumption of disconformity,[41] is of definite value where it applies. The right of a buyer to a remedy depends on the goods having been defective at the time of delivery. But it is often difficult for a claimant to establish the existence or inherence at the time of delivery of some defect which would have led to a subsequent deterioration. The seller may plausibly suggest that any deterioration which has occurred results from natural wear and tear, misuse, lack of sufficient care, failure to maintain or service, or some other matter occurring after delivery, and this may be difficult for the buyer to disprove. To do this it may be necessary, for example, to call expert evidence that a particular item was always of poor quality or design (taking its price into account); or of the likely durability of the item in question.[42] The presumption makes such arguments more difficult for the seller to deploy, because if deterioration occurs within the stated period it is he who must prove that the goods conformed on delivery; it is not for the buyer to disprove it. It should be noted that the presumption runs from the date of delivery. This is consistent with the new presumption that where the buyer deals as consumer, that risk passes at that time.[43]

There has been some tendency to represent this provision as creating a compulsory guarantee of quality for six months after delivery. This is not so: the question is simply one of proof of conformity on delivery, bearing in

---

[37] s.61(1); above, paras 1–078 *et seq*; see also above, para.11–069 as to computer goods. The definition of "consumer goods" in the Directive is almost as wide (below, para.14–011).

[38] Above, para.12–027. The word "consumer" itself if only operative in respect of guarantees: below, para.14–071 (though see s.20(4)). As to other definitions see below, paras 14–001, n.2, 14–131.

[39] See above, Ch.11. The implied terms are conditions in English law, but there is no requirement that the express term be a condition. As already stated, the Directive made necessary a small change to the definition of satisfactory quality when the buyer deals as consumer (see above, para.11–071).

[40] See above, paras 11–001 *et seq*.

[41] Subs.4(b) makes an obvious exception for short-lived goods (*e.g.* flowers, some foodstuffs, some cheap artefacts) for which such a presumption would be inappropriate.

[42] Durability may be a factor in the ascertainment of satisfactory quality (see above, para.11–040).

[43] See s.20(4): above, paras 6–013 *et seq*. But it seems that the parties may agree otherwise: *ibid*. As to problems of documentary and other overseas consumer sales see below, paras 18–260 *et seq*. 19–203, 20–113.

mind that disputes tend to arise later. The presumption assists the buyer in establishing that the goods did not conform at the relevant time. In cases where the seller alleges natural wear and tear, misuse, lack of care, failure to maintain or accidental damage after delivery, the burden is now on him to prove this rather than the reverse. The presumption is only drafted to apply for the purposes of the statutory remedies. Whether anything similar could be applied when common law remedies are sought is doubtful.[44]

Repair or replacement of the goods. Section 48B provides: 12–076

"(1) If section 48A above applies, the buyer may require the seller—

(a) to repair the goods, or
(b) to replace the goods.

(2) If the buyer requires the seller to repair or replace the goods, the seller must—

(a) repair or, as the case may be, replace the goods within a reasonable time but without causing significant inconvenience to the buyer;
(b) bear any necessary costs incurred in doing so (including in particular the cost of any labour, materials or postage).

(3) The buyer must not require the seller to repair or, as the case may be, replace the goods if that remedy is—

(a) impossible, or
(b) disproportionate in comparison to the other of those remedies, or
(c) disproportionate in comparison to an appropriate reduction in the purchase price under paragraph (a), or rescission under paragraph (b), of section 48C(1) below.

(4) One remedy is disproportionate in comparison to the other if the one imposes costs on the seller which, in comparison to those imposed on him by the other, are unreasonable, taking into account—

(a) the value which the goods would have if they conformed to the contract of sale,
(b) the significance of the lack of conformity, and
(c) whether the other remedy could be effected without significant inconvenience to the buyer.

(5) Any question as to what is reasonable time or significant inconvenience is to be determined by reference to—

(a) the nature of the goods, and
(b) the purpose for which the goods were acquired."

Power to require repair or replacement. Although such repair or replacement must often occur in practice, the existing common law and the Sale of Goods Act 1979 do not confer a specific power to require it.[45] The 12–077

---

[44] But for a slightly different view see below, para.14–015.
[45] See above, para.12–031.

idea that where possible a contract should by such means be preserved rather than discharged is also found in the Vienna Convention. In sale of goods at least it is not in tune with the common law, which is more disposed to rely on the power to escape from the contract. Article 48 of the Vienna Convention[46] gives the *seller* a power to remedy failure in performance, even after delivery, and in some circumstances to know in advance whether the buyer will accept such a procedure. This is a notoriously controversial provision as its interaction with the buyer's right to "declare the contract avoided" for "fundamental breach" under that Convention is not clear. In the Directive, and hence in these provisions, however, the right is that of the *buyer*. Section 48B simply says that the buyer "may" require the seller to do either of these things. If, however, the buyer does not do so when he could have done, it seems that the next remedies of reduction of the price and rescission in section 48C will not be open to him, since, as will appear, these are conditioned on the exercise of the earlier right. This power in the buyer may therefore yield a similar result to that where the seller has a right to demand to do these things. The seller can point out to the buyer that the other statutory remedies will not be available unless he first demands repair or replacement, and unless the seller is given an opportunity to effect this.

12–078 **Rejection at common law.** But if the remedy of rejection at common law is on general grounds applicable, the buyer can reject on that basis without any such prelude—though if he first requires repair or replacement under the provisions of this section (but not otherwise) it is now provided that he cannot exercise the right until he has given a reasonable time for this to be done.[47]

12–079 **Exercise of the power.** The exercise of the power is hedged around with restrictions which will make its exercise, and hence the exercise of other remedies depending on its non-availability, not easy to establish if the matter is disputed. It is stated in section 48B(3) that the buyer "must" (rather than "may" in the previous subsection) not require repair or replacement in certain circumstances. The first doubt is as to the word "must". On normal principles of statutory construction this would seem to create a duty not to exercise a power which the buyer may normally exercise. The breach of such a duty would then be remediable in damages, though the power would be validly exercised. No doubt this was not intended, and one can only assume that the intention is that attempts to exercise the power are invalid in the circumstances indicated.

The circumstances in which the power "must" not be exercised are then stated as occurring where the remedy is first, impossible (subsection (3)(a)) or second and third, disproportionate in particular respects (subsections (3)(b) and (c)). These criteria apply first to the choice between repair and replacement. One or the other of these may be impossible under (3)(a); or

---

[46] Above, para.1–024; below, para.12–129. As to application in overseas sales see below, para.19–203.
[47] See s.48D(1), below para.12–110.

the exercise of one may be disproportionate to that of the other under (3)(b): for example, that of repair disproportionate to that of replacement, or that of replacement disproportionate to that of repair. The latter sort of case is obvious: often a repair might cost little, whereas a replacement could involve significant expenditure. But equally there may be cases of, for example, cheap electronic devices where replacement is easy but repair would be extremely expensive if not impossible.

Second, it is provided by subsections (3)(a) and (c) that the power may not be exercised where the whole remedy would be impossible or disproportionate to the other remedies of reduction of price or rescission laid down in the following section, section 48C. If the exercise of the remedy is impossible, it is again excluded. As to disproportion, the remedies of reduction of price and rescission are themselves expressed to depend on the non-availability of the remedies of repair or replacement (or failure to carry them out), with the result that there is an element of circularity in the mechanism, which also relies on rather vague terminology.

In many ways all this is a statement of common sense procedures followed by many buyers and sellers. But the balancing of these remedies is likely to lead to unpredictable results where there is a dispute as to what ought to or legitimately could have been done, especially where a dispute leads to the intervention of a court.

"Disproportionate". Subsection (4) makes clear that whether the remedy is to be regarded as "disproportionate" is governed by its cost to the seller in comparison to that of whichever other Part 5A remedy is relevant, as well as the significance of the lack of conformity and the inconvenience likely to be caused to the buyer. That comparative cost is relevant is indeed assumed in the examples given above. There is no suggestion of a cost-benefit analysis between the cost to the seller and the *benefit* to the buyer. It is conceivable that this might be relevant to the question of "significant inconvenience" under section 48B(2)(a). 12–080

Repair—meaning. The duty to repair involves bringing the goods into conformity with the contract requirements[48] within a reasonable time and without causing significant inconvenience to the buyer.[49] A simple example occurs where the buyer requires the seller to put right a defective speedometer in a car. The remedy is obviously more suitable to large and/or complex artefacts such as cars and other machinery, and also for installed items which would be impracticable to return, such as a boiler. It is submitted that the fact that the repair may be expensive to the seller does not *necessarily* make a demand for repair disproportionate within section 48B(4). In the consumer context, the buyer should within reason be entitled to goods which satisfy him, and it would seem that there must be cases where such an entitlement does not have to yield to the argument that a replacement will be more cost-effective to the seller. 12–081

[48] See the definition in s.61(1) of the Sale of Goods Act. Presumably the standard referred to includes full compliance with the requirements of satisfactory quality, including appearance and finish above: above, paras 11–038 *et seq*.
[49] As to the meaning of this see s.48(B)5.

12–082 **Replacement—meaning.** An obvious case for replacement is a cheap item of electronic goods which does not work and cannot easily be repaired. The buyer may demand its replacement. But there may be more difficult situations. If the goods are specific, for example a picture, and cannot be repaired, or repair is simply inappropriate, they clearly cannot be replaced with something else, albeit of a similar nature, which the buyer has not agreed to receive. Equally, if the reason why the goods do not conform with the contract is because they are not suitable for their purpose under section 14(3) of the Sale of Goods Act, and it can be established that *no* goods of the type purchased or ordered would be so, replacement with the same sort of goods would clearly be an inappropriate remedy. Difficulties may arise where the goods are secondhand, or used when replacement is sought, or otherwise inferior to the norm. It would appear that replacement may, if this can be done, sometimes be effected by supplying a similar article. Official documentation issued in connection with the Regulations suggests that a five-year old piano with an inherent fault can be replaced with another of the same or similar specification. Since pianos and musical instruments, like second-hand cars, are usually tested and selected by the buyer and sold as specific goods, this particular example seems doubtful.

12–083 **Cooperation by buyer.** It is submitted that it is implicit in section 48B(2) that if the buyer does require the seller to repair or replace non-conforming goods he is under an obligation to facilitate the fulfilment of the seller's required action, *e.g.* to forward them to the seller where this is appropriate, allow the seller to have reasonable access to the goods, if the repair is to be made on the buyer's premises, or to allow the seller to take possession of the goods if they are to be repaired elsewhere, or if they are to be replaced. There is no express provision in Part 5A for the buyer to be compensated for his loss of the use of the goods during the period while they are being repaired or replaced, but since the common law right to damages is unaffected it seems that a common law claim for damages for this and other consequential loss would be available in addition to the repair or replacement remedy.[50] They would, however, not be available for mere annoyance, disappointment or even distress.[51] If an order for specific performance is made by the court under section 48E(2) the court might possibly be able to impose a "condition" as to "damages" under section 48E(6).[52]

12–084 **Enforcement.** The obligation to repair or replace is secured by conferring on the court the power to make an order for specific performance of it. This is effected by section 48E which confers wide powers, different in nature from those of section 52, and is discussed below.[53] It is doubtful whether any such power existed before. It should be noted that the court is not bound to make such an order, but under section 48E has the power to award another remedy under the Act if it thinks it appropriate.

---

[50] See below, paras 12–086, 12–104.
[51] See *ibid*.
[52] Below, paras 12–113 *et seq*.
[53] See *ibid*.

Risk during repair or replacement. Where the goods are replaced they must presumably be at the seller's risk until the second delivery, that of the replacement goods: otherwise he cannot effect a replacement. But the question of risk while goods are in transit for repair, being repaired or in transit back from the repair operation is not mentioned. The general tenor of Part 5A, with its intention to protect consumers, suggests that all these are for the seller's account because they are caused by the initial nonconformity. If this is correct it would seem that if the goods for repair are entrusted to a normal method of carriage to the seller or someone designated by him, during which they are damaged or lost, the seller must still either repair them or replace them: and the same applies if loss or damage occurs while the seller is repairing them or sending replacement or repaired goods back to the buyer by a similar method of carriage. 12–085

It would also appear that when the buyer demands repair or replacement, the transfer back of risk should occur at the moment at which he does so. Whether or not these rules apply where the goods have meanwhile been destroyed or damaged without the buyer's fault should presumably be settled by the general rule applicable to risk on rejected goods. This is, as stated elsewhere in this book,[54] uncertain: but if the tentative view there expressed is correct, the risk of such loss or damage is on the buyer except as regards matters stemming from the disconformity.

Damages for loss of use during repair or replacement. When the seller fails to deliver a profit-earning chattel on the date fixed for delivery, but the buyer accepts delivery at a later date, the buyer may recover damages for loss of profits during the delay.[55] By analogy, the consumer may in theory have a claim for damages if he can prove "loss" arising from his not having the use of the item while it is being repaired or replaced. But the consumer faces difficulties in proving any such "loss". If he actually incurs extra expense, such as hiring a car during the period of non-use, he will be entitled to damages (subject to the usual rules of causation, remoteness and mitigation) on the ground of the breach of contract leading to the non-conformity.[56] But if his only loss is annoyance, disappointment or frustration, the courts are most unlikely to award damages.[57] Similarly, any short-lived "loss of amenity" suffered by the consumer is unlikely to entitle him to damages.[58] 12–086

Restarting of conformity duties and non-conformity presumption. It seems consistent with the thrust of the Regulations that when the repaired or replaced goods are delivered, the duty of conformity,[59] and hence the right to the buyer's remedies, should arise again at that moment. Equally, the six-month presumption of disconformity[60] should start afresh at that 12–087

54 Above, para.12–056.
55 Below, paras 17–040 *et seq*.
56 Below, para.17–046.
57 Below, paras 16–046, 17–071.
58 *cf.* below, para.17–071.
59 Above, para.12–074. And *cf.* above, para.12–031, n.69; 12–054, n.23.
60 See *ibid*.

time. But difficult problems could occur if the goods are repaired, say, five months after delivery; or if different defects manifest themselves at different times.

12–088 **Reduction of purchase price or rescission of contract.** Section 48C provides:

(1) If section 48A above applies, the buyer may—
  (a) require the seller to reduce the purchase price of the goods in question to the buyer by an appropriate amount, or
  (b) rescind the contract with regard to those goods, if the condition in subsection (2) below is satisfied.

(2) The condition is that—
  (a) by virtue of section 48B(3) above the buyer may require neither repair nor replacement of the goods: or
  (b) the buyer has required the seller to repair or replace the goods, but the seller is in breach of the requirement of section 48B(2)(a) above to do so within a reasonable time and without significant inconvenience to the buyer.

(3) For the purposes of this Part, if the buyer rescinds the contract, any reimbursement to the buyer may be reduced to take account of the use he has had of the goods since they were delivered to him.

12–089 **Reduction of price or rescission of contract: when available.** These two remedies, which are new to the common law, derive from the Roman *actio quanti minoris* and *actio redhibitoria*, though rejection of the goods and termination of the contract for breach, which in many respects is the same as what is here called "rescission" and indeed referred to under this title in some textbooks, is of course a well known common law procedure. Subsection (2) makes clear that these statutory remedies can be exercised only in cases where the buyer does not have the power to require repair or replacement, or the buyer has required repair or replacement but the seller has not effected it within a reasonable time and without significant inconvenience to the buyer. The latter notion of inconvenience to the buyer appears to envisage not only situations where the seller cannot repair or replace without causing such inconvenience, but also situations where he does repair or replace, but significant inconvenience is nevertheless caused. Presumably what is meant is that the repair or replacement, even if tendered, can be rejected by the buyer on the ground of such inconvenience. It should be noted from the wording of section 48C(2)(b) that there is no need for the buyer to have recourse to a court order before invoking the present remedies.

12–090 **Switch to common law remedies.** The above rules concern the exercise of the right to reduce the price or rescind under Part 5A of the Act. If the buyer decides at this point to fall back instead on the common law right to reject and sue for damages, this is subject to the only control of common law rights contained in Part 5A, that of section 48D.[61] This requires that the

[61] Below, para.12–110.

buyer give the seller a reasonable time to cure or replace before the buyer rejects. It would seem, however, that it does not apply if the buyer, rather than purportedly proceeding under section 48B, had informally agreed to attempts to rectify or the like. In such a case he may also be protected from being found to have accepted the goods by section 35(6) of the Act.[62]

Reduction of price. Subsection (l)(a) provides that the buyer may require the seller to reduce the purchase price of the goods in question to the buyer by "an appropriate amount".[63] On general principles it can be exercised even after the price has been paid. These words of subsection l(a) are almost identical to the reference to this remedy in section 48A(2)(b)(i) above, save that that formulation omits the words "in question". The reason for this difference is not clear, but seems unlikely to be of significance. 12–091

The remedy of price reduction is new in English law but is widely available in European legal systems[64] and as stated above derives from the Roman *actio quanti minoris*. The remedy assumes that the buyer accepts the seller's tender of performance even though the goods do not conform to the contract, so that performance is only partial. "The principle underlying price reduction is that the buyer may keep non-conforming goods delivered by the seller, in which case the contract is adjusted to the new situation: the price is reduced, just as if the subject-matter of the contract had from the outset been the non-conforming, less valuable goods actually delivered. Price reduction is thus neither damages nor partial avoidance of the contract, but rather, adjustment of the contract."[65]

The lack of conformity may relate to an express term, description, quantity, quality, time of delivery (where this is an express term of the contract) or otherwise: see section 48F. However, it is submitted that the remedy of price reduction will not be "appropriate" as is required by section 48E(3)[66] if the goods are unable to perform the main function or purpose for which the buyer acquired them. In the case of defective quality, a price reduction is likely to be appropriate when the defect in the quality of the goods relates to an aspect of the goods which does not impede their use as intended by the buyer. For more serious defects in quality, the remedy of replacement or of termination (rescission) will be more appropriate.

Analogies from the previous law. Before Part 5A was enacted, the Sale of Goods Act contained several provisions similar in effect to section 48C. An alternative to claiming damages for breach of warranty is the entitlement of the buyer under section 53(1)[67] to set up (by way of defence) the 12–092

---

[62] Above, para.12–054.

[63] The French version states that the buyer "peut exiger une réduction adequate du prix".

[64] See Lando and Beale eds, *Principles of European Contract Law* (2000). pp.430 *et seq*.

[65] Schlechtriem, *Commentary on the UN Convention on the International Sale of Goods* (2nd (English) ed., 2005), pp.596–597.

[66] Below, para.12–113.

[67] Below, para.17–047.

breach "in diminution or extinction of the price". The measure of damages for breach of warranty of quality is *prima facie* the difference between (a) the value of the defective goods at the time and place of delivery and (b) the value the goods would have had if they had fulfilled the warranty.[68] The concept of a "price allowance" has been used by the courts in applying this subsection.[69]

The new remedy may thus be an alternative to a claim for damages, but it might also lie where the seller is excused from liability in damages.[70] If the price has not been paid, the new remedy of price reduction will operate as a set-off analogous to section 53(1) above. It is implicit in section 48C that the buyer who has already paid the price (or part of it) may recover from the seller any excess of the amount paid which exceeds the reduced price due after it has been reduced by the "appropriate" amount.[71]

12–093 **The amount of the reduction.** By section 48C(l)(a), the amount of the price reduction is to be "appropriate". No guidance is given in Part 5A about the interpretation of this word. But the rules for the assessment of damages can provide an analogy lor assessing the reduction. By section 53(3), the *prima facie* measure of damages for breach of a warranty of quality is the difference between the (lower) value of the defective goods at the time and place of delivery and the (higher) value the goods would then have had if they had fulfilled the warranty (or conformed to the contract). The price is fixed as at the time of contracting but this measure is assessed as at the time of delivery, by which time the market price may have changed. But the comparison between the two values at the time of delivery could alternatively be used to fix the proportion of the price reduction, as is provided by Article 50 of the Vienna Convention ". . . the buyer may reduce the price in the same proportion as the value that the goods actually delivered had at the time of the delivery bears to the value that conforming goods would have had at that time." This provision finds the proportion by using the relative values at the time of delivery, but then applies that proportion to the original price. The price is the ceiling from which the reduction is to be made, which means that the amount of the reduction could be less than the amount awarded as damages for breach (bearing in mind that damages can be awarded for consequential loss, which probably could not be used to assess an "appropriate price reduction").

Section 53(3) does not refer to the price, but to "the value [the goods] would have had if they had fulfilled the warranty". If the value of the goods has risen between the date of the contract and the date of delivery to the buyer, damages under section 53(3) will give the buyer a higher amount of compensation than price reduction, which takes "the price" as the ceiling. But if the value of the goods has fallen since the date of the contract, the price reduction remedy may produce a better result for the claimant than damages. Section 53(3) puts on the buyer the risk of a decline in value after the contract, but on the seller the risk of a post-contract rise in value.[72]

---

68 Below, para.17–051.
69 Below, para.17–053.
70 Other statutory rules apply to frustration: above, paras 6–034 *et seq*.
71 *cf.* Lando and Beale, *op. cit.* above, n.64, Art. 9: 401(2).
72 Some simple examples are given by Nicholas in 105 L.Q.R. at 225–226 (1989) in connection with the Vienna Convention.

In some cases, the amount of the reduction could be easily calculated. *e.g.* if the quantity of items delivered to the buyer was short the reduction could be directly related to the proportion of the shortage in relation to the contractual quantity.[73]

Common law damages. It must be remembered that damages continue to be available in respect of the breach of contract. In view of this, it seems unlikely that the remedy of price reduction will be of much value under English law unless either, as above stated, the ruling price for the goods bought has dropped between sale and delivery, which is obviously more likely to occur in a commercial context: or if the buyer has difficulty in proving damages, for example where he has bought the goods for a gift. It is however true that, at least in theory, the remedy does not require the intervention of a court. 12–094

Statutory recission: meaning. The word "to rescind" in section 48C(l)(b) is not explained in Part 5A. In the French version of the Directive the word is "résolution". In common law "rescind" is most usually taken as undoing the contract *ab initio,* usually in equity.[74] Hence there are "bars on the right to rescission": for example, it can be too late to rescind. It seems unlikely that this sense can be intended here, though the French word "résolution" (as opposed to "résiliation") suggests that it is. It is normally assumed that the word "rescinded" in section 48 of the Sale of Goods Act means no more than "terminated for breach".[75] What seems to be meant in our present context is rejection of defective goods, termination of the contract for breach and recovery of the price if paid.[76] 12–095

Rejection at common law. If the buyer is exercising his common law rights he may reject independently of this provision, and also usually terminate the contract.[77] To some extent the two systems run in parallel, save that the availability of rescission is very carefully prescribed in Part 5A, whereas in English law, if the breach is of condition or otherwise repudiatory there can be rejection provided that the buyer has not accepted the goods.[78] 12–096

Statutory rescission: requirements. Under section 36 of the Act a rejecting buyer has no need to return the goods: "it is sufficient if he intimates to the seller that he refuses to accept them". No guidance is given 12–097

---

[73] *cf.* s.30(1), above, para.8–040.
[74] See *Johnson v Agnew* [1980] A.C. 367.
[75] See above, para.15–101.
[76] The Directive provides that the consumer is not entitled to rescission if the defect is minor (Art. 3.6). This is imprecise and arguably contrary to the policy of the Sale of Goods Act 1979. There is therefore no such provision in Part 5A. See also below, para.14–026.
[77] Above, paras 12–022 *et seq.*, 12–028.
[78] Above, paras 12–044 *et seq.* If a buyer who was found to have accepted the goods sought to transfer back to the statutory regime, he would almost certainly find that he had not complied with the preconditions for its operation. As to statutory rescission on an international consumer sale, see below, para.19–065.

in Part 5A as to how rescission is to be initiated, but it may be assumed that the rule in section 36 is applicable here also. This may in general create complications where buyers are not properly advised as to the procedures they may follow. The only guidance is given in section 48C(2)(b): that to exercise a right under section 48C the buyer must first have required the seller to repair or replace the goods (and presumably only if this is appropriate in the circumstances). Doing so would have given the buyer the benefit of the six-month presumption of disconformity, which is likely to be of value but only applies "for the purposes of this part". An informal acquiescence in attempts to rectify, however, would not seem to rank as a "requiring" under the subsection (nor trigger off the presumption),[79] and hence preserve the operation of the common law rules. It would seem therefore that an essential part of the preservation of the two alternative lines of remedy is that a buyer would need to give some indication that his rescission is intended to operate under section 48C, or be accompanied by a claim to rely on the six-month presumption. Otherwise it might be taken as a simple rejection at common law. But caution is required of a buyer who does give such an indication: this would trigger off the powers in the court under section 48E to rule that some other remedy is more appropriate, or to make deductions for use. To make section 48E(3), superimposed as it is on a different regime, effective, it is difficult to avoid the idea of a specific "requiring" of one the Act's remedies, even if it need not be taken so far as demanding that the applicable section number of the Act be given.[80]

Where the buyer seeks to recover the price paid for goods rejected whether in a single performance contract or an instalment contract, it may be argued that the whole price, or instalment price, could be recovered on the basis that the buyer has had nothing of what he contracted for even if he has in fact had some or considerable use of the goods. This argument has been accepted at common law in relation to breach of the condition as to title contained in section 12(1) of the Sale of Goods Act.[81] It is more doubtful in respect of defective quality, but the problem seems not to have arisen in this context, probably because of the comparatively short limits on the right to rescind put by the rules for acceptance laid down in section 35.[82]

But whether or not such reasoning could have been deployed at common law in the present situation, section 48C(3) provides specifically that in a statutory rescission the reimbursement to the buyer maybe reduced to take account of the use he has had of the goods since they were delivered to him. Short of a court order (which is envisaged by section 48E(5)), which is in virtually identical terms), the amount to be deducted can obviously be contentious between the parties: and the whole idea was rejected by the Law Commissions in 1987[83] as taking away much of the force of the consumer buyer's bargaining position. However, such deduction is only to

[79] See above, para.12–090; below, para.12–118.
[80] It is unknown why s.27E(3)(a) speaks of a seller who "has claims to rescind" as opposed to "claims to rescind".
[81] *Rowland v Divall* [1923] 2 K.B. 500: see above, paras 4–006 *et seq*.
[82] Above, paras 12–044 *et seq*.
[83] See Law Com. No.160, Scot. Law Com. No.104, para.5.7.

be made if the Part 5A rescission remedy is exercised. This rule only applies "for the purposes of this Part" and does not alter the position of a buyer who rejects the goods acting under his common law rights.

Rejection of damaged goods. The notion of rescission implies the return of the goods against a refund of the price (in English law at least), plus an award of damages where appropriate. What is nowhere made clear is whether rescission under section 48C is possible when the goods cannot be returned at all, or cannot be restored in the condition in which they were on delivery. If this is due to a defect in the goods, that is of course something of which the seller cannot complain. This will also be true if part of the goods has been used up by normal testing (for example, tasting of wine) or normal installation (as where a roll of carpet is fitted). On the other hand, if it is due to misuse or mistreatment by the buyer, that he has lost the right to reject is obviously something of which he cannot complain. 12–098

There is, however, a third possibility. If the loss or damage was caused by something for which the buyer was not responsible, for example, purely accidental damage, can the buyer use this as an excuse for non-return, or return the goods damaged? Nothing in Part 5A gives guidance. The general English law is not clear either.[84] It is in that context suggested that the most likely view is that there can be no rejection (though an action for damages would lie); and if that is correct in general it should probably also apply here.[85]

Instalment sales. The Sale of Goods Act approach to instalment sales is, where the contract is severable, to regard each consignment as a separate delivery to which the normal rules for rejection apply. When the question arises as to whether delivery of defective instalments entitles the buyer to treat the whole contract as repudiated, this is governed by section 31(2) of the Act, which embodies a principle of the general law.[86] The provisions of Part 5A do not address the problem, but there is nothing in them which suggests anything other than the same result as regards particular instalments: and it seems appropriate to treat the overall right to treat the whole contract as repudiated as governed by an application by analogy of the statement of the general law in section 31(2). The Vienna Convention here, as elsewhere, has the principle of "fundamental breach" on which to fall back.[87] 12–099

Partial rejection. The reforms of 1994 introduced into the Sale of Goods Act by section 35A a right of partial rejection.[88] The previous law had been that acceptance of any part of the goods barred rejection of the whole (subject to the instalment rules mentioned above). Now where some of the 12–100

---

[84] See above, paras 12–057—12–059.

[85] The Vienna Convention makes specific provision for this problem in Art. 82; but the wording of this is not easy to apply and hence not satisfactory as a guide, and even less so in consumer cases.

[86] See above, paras 8–064 *et seq.*

[87] See Arts 51, 73.

[88] See above, para.12–060.

goods conform, the buyer may if he wishes reject the whole consignment if the non-conformity is a breach of contract, but he may instead reject the defective parts of it (provided that what he rejects are "commercial units"; and provided that he accepts all the conforming goods) and keep the rest. So a consumer buying a box ("case") of a dozen bottles of wine, and buying by the case rather than the bottle, who is able to ascertain without opening any that the contents of three bottles (or the bottles themselves) are defective may reject the case, or may reject the three bottles and retain the rest. Although this is not stated in section 35A, he must presumably pay *pro rata* for the bottles he keeps; or if he has paid, he can recover back part of the price on a *pro rata* basis.[89] There are complications regarding commercial contracts which are not likely to apply in consumer situations.

It is difficult to ascertain what the position is in such a situation under the new remedies of sections 48A–48E. If "the goods" refers, as it does in section 35A referred to above, to the goods tendered under the contract of sale, the buyer can presumably require replacement of the defective bottles. If this cannot be done (for example, because of the scarcity of the type of wine) or is not done, it would appear that the buyer can require the seller to reduce the purchase price of the goods in accordance with section 48C(1): in this context "the goods" presumably means the case delivered. Alternatively, however, he can "rescind the contract *with regard to those goods*." The last five words or their equivalent are not used elsewhere in Part 5A, and it is not clear whether they simply allow partial rejection. The Directive, in the summary of remedies given by Article 3.2. also uses the words "rescinded with regard to those goods", which suggests partial rescission and hence rejection; but Articles 3.5 and 3.6 simply refer to having the contract rescinded[90] which might be taken to suggest that the whole consignment must be returned.

Under the Vienna Convention it is clear that the remedies only apply in respect of the defective part, but this is reinforced in Article 51.2 by a right to terminate the contract (declare it "avoided") where there is a fundamental breach, a general reasoning technique not found in the new sections of the Sale of Goods Act. The result under the Convention is said to be that the buyer may claim replacement of the defective goods, or rescind the contract in respect of them and reduce the overall purchase price: or keep the entire delivery and claim a price reduction, subject always to the doctrine of fundamental breach.[91] This would be a convenient result here also.

12–101 **Quantitative shortages.** Similar problems arise in connection with quantitative shortages. The Sale of Goods Act spells out the consequences of these specifically in section 30: and the right to terminate the contract overall is left to the general law on repudiatory breach. Under the new section 48F (see below) goods "do not conform to a contract of sale if there is, in relation to the goods, a breach of an express term of the contract or a

[89] See above, para.12–061.
[90] (In the French version "la résolution du contrat")
[91] See Schlechtriem, *op. cit.* above, n.65, pp.609–610.

term implied by sections 13, 14 or 15 above." The existence of the special rules in section 30 has meant that quantitative defects are not considered under section 13. However, a stipulation as to quantity, even if not to be regarded as going to description, would probably in any case be an express term of the contract for the purposes of section 48F: section 13 of the Sale of Goods Act is indeed often criticised as stating what is actually an express term as an implied term. Similar considerations as those above seem likely to apply: the buyer may call for the making up of the quantity, assuming that this can be brought within the word "replacement": but if this procedure comes to nothing for the reasons given above, and reduction of the price is not sought or is inappropriate, the question whether the quantity supplied can be kept, or must be returned if the buyer rescinds, does not have a clear answer.

The position under the Vienna Convention is similar to that in respect of delivery of partly defective goods. The buyer may demand the missing goods: or may rescind the contract in respect of that part, with consequent reduction of price.[92] Again, there is the operation of "fundamental breach" in the background. There is a difference under that Convention, however, as the buyer is not entitled to reject part deliveries (Article 51.2) whereas under the Sale of Goods Act a buyer is (unless it is otherwise agreed) not under any obligation to receive delivery in instalments: section 31(1).

In the above two cases of partial rejection and quantitative shortages (and elsewhere) it may well be that the buyer in the United Kingdom would be better advised to rely on the existing and known general law without attempting to apply Part 5A.

Restrictions on the buyer's choice of a Part 5A remedy. The wording of sections 48B(1) and 48C(1) ("... the buyer may ...") appears to give the buyer complete freedom to choose which remedy to "require" or exercise. But there are some explicit restrictions on his choice. For example, by section 48B(3), discussed above, repair or replacement must not be chosen if it is "impossible" or "disproportionate in comparison to" another of the four remedies.[93] 12–102

The court has also, however, an overriding power under section 48E (below) to decide that "another remedy" than the one chosen by the buyer is "appropriate". This means that the buyer's initial choice of remedy must be made in the light of this power, which may substitute that other remedy for the one chosen by the buyer. The concept of one remedy being "disproportionate" under section 48B(4) and (5) is obviously one aspect of the decision whether a remedy is "appropriate", but the absence of any definition of "appropriate" gives the court a very wide power to take into account any other consideration which it deems to be relevant (but probably excluding a cost-benefit analysis, that is, of the cost to the seller in relation to the benefit to the buyer). But it must be noted that the comparison for "appropriateness" is only between the four Part 5A remedies (section 48E(3) and (4)) and not between the chosen remedy and

---

[92] See Schlechtriem, *op. cit.* above, pp.609–610.

[93] "Disproportionate" is defined by s.48B(4) and (5): see above, para.12–080.

the common law remedies of rejection or damages. It appears from section 48E that the court has no power to substitute common law rejection or damages as the "appropriate" remedy which the buyer must accept. Even if the court believes that rejection or damages is an adequate remedy for the buyer, he is entitled to his chosen Part 5A remedy unless one of the other three Part 5A remedies is more "appropriate".

12–103 **Inconsistent remedies.** One aspect of the relationship between the Part 5A remedies is expressly stated: section 48C (discussed above) allows reduction of price or rescission only if the buyer was not able to require repair or replacement (or, if he has done so, the seller has not provided the remedy within a reasonable time and without significant inconvenience to the buyer). It is clearly envisaged from within Part 5A *(e.g.* section 48D(2)(a)) that the buyer retains the right to any remedy previously available to him before Part 5A was enacted. But any remedy sought by the buyer must not be incompatible with any remedy he has previously obtained in respect of the same lack of conformity: for example if he has obtained damages, this may preclude his attempt to require a Part 5A remedy, provided the damages were intended to cover the same aspect of non-conformity and the same "loss" as that for which the Part 5A remedy was designed. Again, termination of the contract, or rescission of the contract under section 48C will preclude a subsequent claim to specific performance or to enforcement of the requirement to repair or replace. Similarly, a requirement to repair or replace, if performed by the seller, will preclude a later rejection or rescission, but not a claim for damages for consequential loss.

12–104 **Relationship of damages to the new remedies.** Apart from the restriction in section 48D on rejection and termination,[94] Part 5A leaves it to the courts to integrate the new with the traditional remedies. In particular, nothing in Part 5A explicitly deals with the buyer's claim to damages. The issue whether repair or replacement is "disproportionate" (section 48B(3) and (4)) or "appropriate" (section 48E(3)) must be decided without reference to the availability of damages. In the result the buyer may choose a Part 5A remedy even where common law would regard damages as "adequate" (a factor that common law would regard as relevant if asked to grant an order of specific performance). The relevance of the words "disproportionate" and "appropriate" is defined by sections 48B and 48E in such a way that the only relevant comparison is with the other Part 5A remedies, and the notion of mitigation (as to which see below) is irrelevant. So, for example, even if the Part 5A remedy chosen by the buyer is disproportionate in the costs which it imposes on the seller in comparison with the damages which would be awarded to the buyer, he is free to choose that remedy. Similarly, when the court is faced with the buyer's choice of requiring the seller to repair, it may not consider awarding damages for the cost of repair by a third party[95]; and when the buyer

[94] See above, para.12–090, below; para.12–110.
[95] Below, para.17–056.

requests replacement the court may not consider awarding damages for the cost of substitute goods.[96]

If the buyer has actually obtained a Part 5A remedy, on general principles of the law of damages any later award of damages to him must take into account the value of that remedy to him. For instance, if the buyer obtained a reduction in price under section 48C he could not later claim damages in respect of the reduction in the value of the performance he received compared with the value of the promised performance: the latter claim would have been met by the reduction in price. There may, however, be other different aspects of the buyer's loss for which damages could be recovered.[97]

Relevance of mitigation rules. Conversely, under the rules of mitigation[98] 12–105
the buyer's damages at common law must be assessed on the basis that he took reasonable steps to avoid or minimise his loss caused by the sellers breach of contract. With the availability of the new remedies under Part 5A, the buyer who sues for damages for defective quality may face the question whether he should have chosen a Part 5A remedy, such as repair or replacement, because the rules of mitigation are wide enough to cover the availability of these new remedies.[99] If the buyer chooses to sue for damages instead of requiring the seller himself to repair or replace defective goods, he might be faced with the seller's allegation that he has failed to mitigate because the seller could have repaired or replaced at lower cost to himself.

Priority among the Part 5A remedies. The question arises as to whether 12–106
(apart from "disproportionate" or "inappropriate" discussed above) there is any implicit order of priority among the Part 5A remedies. They are listed in the order given in section 48A(2)—repair, replacement, price reduction, rescission— but this does not necessarily imply an order of either choice or timing. However, the Directive on which Part 5A was based provided by Article 3.3 that "in the first place, the consumer may require the seller to repair the goods or he may require the seller to replace them, in either case free of charge, unless this is impossible or disproportionate". Although the words "in the first place"[1] are not found in Part 5A, "cure" must be considered by the buyer before the more drastic remedies of replacement or rescission. This is confirmed by the order in which the remedies are set out, which is similar to that of the relevant provisions in the Vienna Convention. This ordering is also inherent in section 48C(2), under which, if the buyer is entitled to choose repair or replacement, he may not choose price reduction or rescission unless, having been required

---

96 Below, para.17–056.
97 See below, paras 17–062 *et seq.* for losses other than diminution in value.
98 Below, paras 16–052 *et seq*.
99 He is unlikely to face a claim that he should have mitigated by choosing a reduction in the price, because even at common law the buyer's claim for damages could take account of a "price allowance" in respect of any defect in the quality of the goods: below, paras 17–047 *et seq*.
1 "dans un premier temps".

to do so, the seller has failed to repair or replace within a reasonable time and without significant inconvenience to the buyer. However, section 48C(2) does not place any restriction on the buyer's choice of a traditional remedy, even though rejection, or diminution or extinction of the price under section 53(1), are very similar to rescission and price reduction under Part 5A. Some ordering is found in section 48D[2] which gives the seller a reasonable time to provide a "cure"—if the buyer first requires repair, he is debarred during a "reasonable time " thereafter from rejecting the goods or requiring their replacement. Similarly, if he first requires replacement, he is debarred until a reasonable time has elapsed from either rejecting the goods or requiring their repair. But apart from section 48B(3) ("impossible" or "disproportionate") and section 48D(3) ("appropriate"), the buyer is free to choose between repair and replacement and (if the conditions in section 48C(2) are met) between price reduction and rescission.

12–107 **No time limits in English law.** The *action redhibitoria* of Roman law (for rescission) and the *action quanti minoris* (for reduction in price) were only available within six and 12 months respectively. Perhaps for this reason civil law systems are accustomed to fixed time limits in respect of rejection of goods. The Directive plainly envisages such limits: it is provided that Member States must give effect to its provisions where the lack of conformity appears within two years of delivery. It also permits Member States to require that notice of a defect is given within two months of its discovery of the defect. Such fixed limits (other than the normal rules for limitation of actions) are unknown to English law, which has relied on the looser notion of acceptance as barring rejection, and as regards damages, on the normal limitation period of six years. A suggestion to introduce fixed periods was rejected by the Law Commission in 1987,[3] largely on the ground that a single time limit is inappropriate to the many types of goods that may be the subject of a contract of sale. The Regulations which implemented the Directive regarded the English rule as more favourable to the consumer and therefore made no change to it.[4] There is therefore in theory no time limit on the right to rescind, whether under section 48C or common law, unless the intervention of a court is required, in which case an action would be barred after the normal limitation period of six years. Equally, the right to reduction of price would only be barred after six years. The result is that exercise of various rights is barred less soon than it would be in a country operating a two-year time limit or something similar. However, this effect is counterbalanced, albeit in an imprecise way, by the increasing difficulty of proving, as time goes on, the inherence of defects at the time of delivery, and as regards rejection, by the rules as to acceptance.

12–108 **Waiver.** The question arises as to whether any principles of waiver or estoppel may prevent a buyer who has sought to exercise one Part 5A remedy from subsequently seeking to exercise another. This needs considering separately with respect to each remedy provided in Part 5A.

---

[2] See below, para.12–110.
[3] See Law Com. No.160, Scot. Law Com. No.104, paras 5.6–5.9, 5.15–5.19.
[4] They also did not avail themselves of the opportunity to set a shorter time limit in respect of second-hand goods.

(i) If the buyer seeks repair, but then changes his mind and seeks replacement of the goods, he may not be entitled to do so if repair is the appropriate remedy, as section 48B(2) and (3) provide criteria for determining which of the two is appropriate. The same would be true if he sought replacement and subsequently changed his demand to one for repair. Part 5A appears to be drafted on the assumption that one or the other is usually appropriate. If. however, there can be a situation where either is appropriate, it is submitted that the buyer's right to change his mind must depend on whether the seller has acted in reliance on the first statement.

(ii) If the buyer seeks repair or replacement but then changes his mind and seeks reduction of the price or rescission, his right to do so is controlled by the provisions of section 48C(2) above, under which the latter two remedies are exercisable only if he had no right to require repair or replacement at all. or if he had such a right and exercised it, but the seller has not complied timeously.

(iii) If the buyer seeks reduction of the price but then before a price reduction is agreed changes his mind and seeks rescission, it would seem that he could do so unless the seller had acted in reliance on his indication that he was seeking a price reduction. Once the price reduction has been agreed, however, it seems that the buyer should not be able to change his mind (unless the seller consents).

(iv) If, however, the buyer indicates that he rescinds, this seems to be an election which changes the rights of the parties, since on general principles the seller must now be released from any duty to perform further.[5] The buyer could therefore change his mind and claim price reduction only with the consent of the seller.

Inactivity of buyer. More difficulties arise where the buyer simply does not indicate an intention to rescind or indeed does no more than simply retain the goods for a period. At common law he may lose the right to reject by acceptance under section 35 of the Sale of Goods Act 1979. This was considerably modified in 1994 to make the rules fairer to consumer buyers.[6] Section 35 does not apply to the new provisions, since by virtue of section 11(3) of the Act it only applies to treating the contract as discharged for breach of condition (though it would doubtless apply to other forms of repudiatory breach). Those responsible for the Directive may be presumed to have considered that the right would be lost, first, under the terms for its availability, secondly by the exercise of the powers of the court, thirdly, by failure to give timely notice of a defect, or finally, by the expiry of a fixed time limit as described above. The third and fourth of these devices were not adopted in the UK regulations, with the result that the right to rescind under Part 5A may, in theory, last for some time. There is here no applicable "reasonable time" provision as under section 35(3). It 12–109

[5] *Photo Production Ltd v Securicor Transport Ltd* [1980] A.C. 827 at 849.
[6] See ss.35(2), (6) and (7) above, paras 12–044 *et seq*.

may, however, be suggested that notwithstanding the apparently complete nature of the rules surrounding the right to rescind under Part 5A, the rules of estoppel[7] could prevent reliance on it.

12–110 **Relation to other remedies.** Section 48D reads:

(1) If the buyer requires the seller to repair or replace the goods the buyer must not act under subsection (2) until he has given the seller a reasonable time in which to repair or replace (as the case may be) the goods.

(2) The buyer acts under this subsection if—

(a) in England and Wales or Northern Ireland he rejects the goods and terminates the contracl for breach of condition;

(b) in Scotland he rejects any goods delivered under the contract and treats it as repudiated;

(c) he requires the goods to be replaced or repaired (as the case may be).

A small difficulty arises in that what the buyer is prevented from doing by section 48D2(a) is rejecting the goods and terminating the contract for *breach of condition.* If the breach is what might be called a *"Hong Kong Fir"* or "fundamental breach"[8], or if there is other repudiatory conduct, he can apparently still do so without allowing the reasonable time. It may well be, however, that allowing a change of course in such circumstances would be a fair result: though equally it may have been an oversight by the draftsman not to cover other grounds for rejecting goods.[9]

12–111 **Limits on common law right to reject.** The above provision, the substance of which is not required by the Directive (which permits but does not take account of existing remedies) imposes the only limit contained in Part 5A on the common law right to reject outside of the new remedies. It requires in effect that a buyer who starts by requiring repair or replacement under Part 5A may not turn to a common law remedy until he has given the seller a reasonable time to repair or replace. (The same effect is created for the statutory remedies of reduction of price and rescission by section 48C(2)(b)). The section is worded only to apply to a buyer who *requires* the seller to repair or replace under the scheme of Part 5A. In so far as the situations can be distinguished, it does not apply to a buyer who makes an informal *request* for repair or replacement which is not complied with, and subsequently proceeds to reject at common law, though of course such a buyer might be caught by the acceptance rules.[10]

12–112 **Acceptance.** Under the common law rules, a buyer who accepts loses the right to reject. Section 48D not only makes clear that that the buyer does not lose the right to reject merely by allowing time for repair: he is actually

[7] See above, paras 12–035 *et seq*.
[8] See above, para.12–023.
[9] It may be pointed out also that the drafting of subsection (1), in so far as it refers to subs.(2)(c), appears circular, but this does not seem to be of practical significance.
[10] Above, para.12–044. See also a above, paras 12–080, 12–097.

compelled, once he chooses such a remedy, to do so. The law as to acceptance was amended in 1994 by the insertion of section 35(6), under which "the buyer is not by virtue of this section deemed to have accepted the goods merely because—(a) he asks for, or agrees to, their repair by or under an arrangement with the seller".[11] If therefore the buyer does not purport to demand the Part 5A remedy of repair or replacement, the result of section 35(6) is that he does not necessarily lose the right to reject by allowing attempts to repair.

Powers of the court. Section 48E reads: 12–113

(1) In any proceedings in which a remedy is sought by virtue of this Part the court, in addition to any other power it has, may act under this section.

(2) On the application of the buyer the court may make an order requiring specific performance or, in Scotland, specific implement by the seller of any obligation imposed on him by virtue of section 48B above.

(3) Subsection (4) applies if—

(a) the buyer requires the seller to give effect to a remedy under section 48B or 48C above or has claims to rescind under section 48C, but
(b) the court decides that another remedy under section 48B or 48C is appropriate.

(4) The court may proceed—

(a) as if the buyer had required the seller to give effect to the other remedy, or if the other remedy is rescission under section 48C
(b) as if the buyer had claimed to rescind the contract under that section.

(5) If the buyer has claimed to rescind the contract the court may order that any reimbursement to the buyer is reduced to take account of the use he has had of the goods since they were delivered to him.

(6) The court may make an order under this section unconditionally or on such terms and conditions as to damages, payment of the price and otherwise as it thinks just.

Enforcement by the court. The most conspicuous provision of section 48E to a common lawyer is that which confers powers on the court to order repair or replacement: powers which, as stated above, a common law court might well not have, or if it had them, would very rarely exercise. This provision gives express sanction to such orders, though the court has a discretion, as is indicated by the word "may" and also by the fact that 12–114

[11] See above, para.12–054.

common law courts in any case treat the exercise of such a power as discretionary. However, subsection (1) gives the court powers to order other remedies in any proceedings in which a remedy is sought by virtue of Part 5A, the Part at present under discussion. Not only can the court determine that repair is inappropriate and order replacement, or *vice versa*, it can also determine that reduction of the price or rescission is more appropriate than either; where the buyer claims to reduce the price, that an order for repair or replacement should be made: and correspondingly if the buyer claims rescission, that one of the other remedies should be ordered.

An order of specific performance to replace the non-conforming goods is in line with the traditional use of such an order to compel one party to a contract to perform exactly the obligation he undertook in the contract. By an order to replace, the seller is ordered to perform his original contractual obligation under the contract of sale as if his previous attempt to do so had not been made. The contract defines exactly what he must do to comply with the order. But it is an unusual use of specific performance to compel the seller to *repair, i.e.* to bring the goods already delivered to the buyer into conformity with the contractual description. Presumably the order to repair must be more specific than this and should inform the seller precisely what he must do to obey the order—and precisely which aspect of non-conformity must be corrected. This has always been a crucial feature of the discretionary decision to make an order of specific performance, because unlike other remedies such as damages or rejection, the sanction behind the order is quasi-criminal, in that breach of the order amounts to contempt of court. It would be strange if Part 5A was intended to give the consumer/buyer wide access to a remedy backed up by the threat of imprisonment or fine. (Even if the draftsman had used a mandatory injunction for the order to repair, this objection would still hold.)[12]

Specific performance as a remedy in contract has always been limited by the principle that it will not be granted where damages are an adequate remedy. Under section 48E(2) and (6) an order for specific performance appears to be discretionary, but the discretion is limited by "possibility" (section 48B(3)), or by a comparison between it and the other three Part 5A remedies ("disproportionate" under section 48B(3) and (4), or "appropriate" under section 48E(3) and (4)). The discretion is therefore unable to compare the availability of damages assessed under the traditional rules as an alternative remedy to specific performance.

Two further points deserve attention. First, it may be asked whether the court may award damages in lieu of specific performance under the discretion conferred on the court by the general law found in Lord Cairns Act 1858 (now section 50 of the Supreme Court Act 1981).[13] It would be surprising if this route was used to circumvent the explicit provisions in Part 5A, which are to the effect that the comparison is to be made with the other Part 5A remedies.

Secondly, under section 48E(6) the order under that section may be made "unconditionally or on such terms and conditions as for damages,

---

[12] See Harris, 119 L.Q.R. 541 (2003).

[13] See below, para.17–100, n.7.

payment of the price and otherwise as it thinks just". The reference is not to damages awarded in lieu of an order—a free-standing award of damages—but to damages being ordered as a condition attached to an order. The corresponding power to impose conditions to an order of specific performance made under the (general) power of section 52[14] has not been used to impose conditions on the seller, but rather on the buyer, *e.g.* to pay the price into court, or to pay a share of freight charges, or to pay interest on the price retained by the buyer pending the order.[15] It would be a novel extension of the power which refers to "damages" in section 48E(6) to interpret it to permit the court to require *the seller* to pay damages to the buyer in addition to complying with the order of specific performance, *e.g.* for some loss not remediable by compliance with the order.

It is difficult to see that a consumer buyer will often wish to have recourse to obtaining a court order. It might be appropriate for a large and/ or valuable item. It seems likely that the mere *entitlement* to these remedies may be enough to persuade the seller to replace or repair. Many sellers would do this anyway, regardless of legal requirements. It also seems that the buyer may, instead of obtaining such an order, proceed to the remedies of section 48C: see above. The obtaining of such an order would therefore be a last resort where the buyer really wanted the goods repaired or (perhaps) replaced.

Conformity with the contract. Section 48F reads: "For the purposes of this Part, goods do not conform to a contract of sale if there is, in relation to the goods, a breach of an express term of the contract or a term implied by section 13,14 or 15 above." This is the only reference in Part 5A or elsewhere to the standard of conformity required of the goods, because while the Directive contains detailed provisions as to this, they were not thought necessary in the UK.[16] As such, section 48F links to the availability of the remedies. It should be noted that the conformity required is not only with the implied terms as to description and quality, but also with express terms relating to the goods. These will often be part of the description of the goods, but not always. 12–115

Defective installation. One related point needs to be noted here. It seems to be the intention of the Directive that defective installation of goods by a seller ranks as part of the sale contract and so is subject to the Part 5A remedies. The U.K. Regulations, however, treat such installation as a contract for services. The new remedies are extended to such contracts, but the underlying obligation is not (as it is in the contract of sale) a strict one, which may not have been an appropriate implementation of the Directive. The Directive also appears to assume that the same remedies should apply where the buyer makes the installation himself but suffers loss because the instructions are defective: but this is not provided for at all, and 12–116

---

[14] See below, paras 17–096 *et seq.*
[15] See below, para.17–100.
[16] See above, para.12–074.

the duties of the seller attach to the time of delivery. The correct solution here appears to be that the lack of appropriate instructions goes to the satisfactory quality of the goods. The matter is considered elsewhere in this book.[17]

12–117 **Contracting out of Part 5A.** This is in general not possible. The Consumer Sales Directive[18] provides that its provisions should not be excludable "directly or indirectly". In the context of Part 5A this is achieved in England by a combination of section 6 of the Unfair Contract Terms Act 1977[19] (which renders ineffective exclusions of sections 13, 14 and 15 of the Sale of Goods Act 1979 where the buyer deals as consumer) and section 13 of the same Act[20] (which defines exclusions to cover exclusion of remedies and is also in words apt to cover exclusion of the six-month presumption of disconformity). However, this prevents only exclusion of the option of exercising such remedies. As has been made clear, the buyer is entitled to pursue the common law remedies if he wishes. Also, an exclusion or restriction of liability for breach of an express term in relation to the goods (such terms being included in the requirement of conformity) would only be subject to section 3 of the 1977 Act.[21]

12–118 **Interaction of new remedies with the existing law.** If one now considers how a dissatisfied consumer who can establish a breach of the conformity requirements of sections 13,14 or 15 of the Sale of Goods Act or of an express term relating to conformity can proceed on the basis of both these sets of remedies the answer appears to be as follows.

If he can establish that the goods were non-conforming on delivery (the rules for which are fairly strict in his favour, though not as strict as they are in commercial cases where there are contract specifications) he can reject them at common law if he comes in time. Recent case law suggests that the previous assumption that this must be done quickly may have been overstressed.[21a] If he has allowed (as opposed to required under section 48B) attempts to repair, this does not necessarily mean that he has accepted the goods. He can also sue for damages. He must however establish the nonconformity himself: he is not entitled to the benefit of the six-month presumption of section 48A(3). since this only relates to the "new" remedies created by Part 5A. It only applies "for the purposes of subsection (1)(b) above" and subsection (1)(b) is part of the designation of when the "new" remedies apply. Subject to this point the common law remedies so far seem superior.

The consumer buyer can instead proceed under the new provisions by requiring repair or replacement while initially retaining his common law rights, if the circumstances under which this can be required, stated in section 48B, apply. Many buyers must in effect do this already, and sellers

[17] Above, para.11–039.
[18] Art.7(1).
[19] See below, para.13–083.
[20] See below, para.13–064.
[21] See below, para.13–094.
[21a] See above, para.12–055.

cooperate without the need for a legal right. If he does not secure this, he could if he wished take proceedings under it to enforce the right, though the result of these might be unpredictable. But the inference from section 48D(1) is that he can, if he has allowed a reasonable time for repair or replacement, instead revert to his common law rights, reject the goods and terminate the contract. It must be assumed that the running of the "reasonable time" for the purposes of the common law notion of acceptance (section 35 of the Sale of Goods Act) is suspended pending the statutory rights being exercised. Section 35(6) provides that the buyer does not accept the goods merely because he asks for or agrees to their *repair*, but it must surely now be inferred that the same applies if he seeks replacement.

The *seller* has no right to demand to repair or replace, though as stated above, he may in practice point out to the buyer that if he does not permit repair or replacement he may lose the prospect of exercising his other rights under Part 5A to price reduction or rescission. If the buyer sues for damages only, he may sometimes find that the court holds that he ought to have mitigated his loss by accepting an offer to cure.[22]

The buyer may, instead of proceeding under the common law rules, proceed under Part 5A. The new provisions give him the benefit of the six-month presumption where this is applicable. However, where repair or replacement are possible and not disproportionate to each other, or to the remedies of reduction of the price and rescission, he must have demanded such repair or replacement (if it was appropriate) to retain the possibility of eventual rescission (rejection) or reduction of the price. If repair or replacement is offered he has no such right unless the offer is not made good.

If the buyer gives an opportunity for repair or replacement and this does not occur, he may, as stated above, revert to the common law position and reject the goods unless he is caught by one of the provisions of section 35. particularly the "reasonable time" provision. But otherwise, he may continue with the Part 5A regime by seeking reduction of the price or rescission (termination) at his choice, and, as explained above,[23] the right to rescind may here persist for a considerable period. If, however, he needs the assistance of the court there is again a danger that a court may then find some other Part 5A remedy more appropriate (which would not be true at common law). The most "dangerous" of these to a person versed in the common law approach is reduction of the price, which may, at least in theory, be imposed on a buyer whose only desire is to get rid of the goods and buy again. Furthermore, if he seeks to rescind and get his money back he may be compelled to make an allowance for the use which he has had of the goods in the interim, which is not true at common law. However, it would appear that the right to damages at common law persists in respect of special or consequential losses.

All the above will prove difficult to apply in practice, especially because (except in the case of an unusually well-advised buyer) these possible

---

[22] See *The Solholt* [1983] 1 Lloyd's Rep. 605; below, paras 16–052 *et seq*.
[23] See para.12–107.

courses of action will often be used only to form the basis for an *ex post facto* explanation of much of the buyer's conduct. In general the Part 5A remedies, which may seem more diverse and to offer more choice, are heavily regulated by matters of proportionality, reasonableness and the like, which in the case of dispute may require determination, usually retrospectively, by a court.

Overall, the common law right to reject requires no preliminaries and hence is more effective if exercised quickly. It need not be lost even if repair or replacement is demanded, but if that is not forthcoming it may be lost quite soon under the acceptance rules. The Part 5A remedy of rescission has the advantage of the six-month presumption, and can go on for longer than the common law right, but is hedged around with statutory controls as to what is appropriate, which may prove difficult to apply. Hence a buyer who can prove that the goods do not conform on delivery may reject immediately or fairly soon thereafter, and may first request repair or replacement without losing this advantage. He *must*, however, consider repair or replacement if he wishes to be able to have a legal right to reduce the price, or to have the benefit of a longer-lasting right to rescind accompanied by the six-month presumption.

It is suggested above that if the sale is by instalments, and the buyer seeks to reject in part, or if the defect is quantitative, the United Kingdom buyer would do better to rely on the existing law, because of the uncertainty of the position under the "rescission" remedy of section 48C. The general law as to repudiatory breach is likely to be needed in the background because the Regulations, and hence Part 5A, do not. as the Directive did not. provide for the coexistence of rules as to "fundamental breach" found in the Vienna Convention.

The overall result shows the problems of superimposing on a system with particular presuppositions and techniques another system with different presuppositions and techniques, and assuming that they can run in tandem.

4. MISREPRESENTATIONS SUBSEQUENTLY INCORPORATED INTO THE CONTRACT

12–119 **Both common law and equity applicable.** Where a misrepresentation such as would normally justify rescission is made prior to a contract, and then is incorporated into the contract as a term, it was not clear before the Misrepresentation Act 1967 whether it was still possible to rely on the right to rescind in equity, regardless of the rules as to breaches of terms in the contract.[24] There might be advantages in doing so. For example, if the representation was incorporated into the contract, but not as a condition, it would often be advantageous to rely on the right to rescind: the same might be the case if the goods had been accepted under the terms of the Sale of

[24] See *Cie. Française de Chemin-de-Fer Paris-Orleans v Leeston Shipping Co. Ltd* (1919) 1 Ll.L.R. 235; *Pennsylvania Shipping Co. v Cie. Nationale de Navigation* (1936) 155 L.T. 294. The problem may still exist in other jurisdictions: see *Academy of Health and Fitness Pty Ltd v Power* [1973] V.R. 254; Bridge, 20 U.B.C.L.Rev. 53 (1986).

Goods Act 1979, but the buyer had no knowledge of defects so that the contract could not be said to have been affirmed in equity.[25] This point was settled by section 1(a) of the Misrepresentation Act 1967, which provides that a contract may be rescinded for misrepresentation notwithstanding that the misrepresentation has become a term of the contract. If it induced the contract, therefore, the misrepresentation may be relied on for the purposes of rescission whether, as incorporated in the contract, its breach justifies discharge or not. Any action in tort equally survives.[26]

Practical difficulties.[27] Certain practical difficulties, however, should be noted. First, if the representee seeks to rescind in court and the representation as incorporated into the contract would give rise to the right to damages only, the court might exercise its discretion under section 2(2) of the Act to declare the contract subsisting and award damages in lieu of rescission. Since the damages awarded under section 2(2) may be less than those given for breach of a contractual promise,[28] the representee should therefore allege breach of contract in the alternative. Secondly, if he seeks to exercise his right of rescission out of court, it is possible that he will debar himself from later suing for damages in contract (any right to sue in tort would remain), for it would seem that rescission destroys the contract. Thus a purported rescission out of court could be dangerous if it later transpired that only contractual damages could provide adequate compensation. It seems that in such a case, however, the court could conceivably exercise its power to declare the contract subsisting under section 2(2)[29] (though it is doubtful whether it would in fact do so); the damages awarded when the court acts under the subsection are of course different from those available for breach of contract,[30] but it has been further suggested[31] that one effect of declaring the contract subsisting might be to revive the right to claim contractual damages for breach of it. Finally, it is arguable that, where a misrepresentation is incorporated into the contract as a condition, and the buyer then seeks to reject for breach of it, the court's jurisdiction to declare the contract subsisting and award damages in lieu of rescission under section 2(2) might still apply, even though under the Sale of Goods Act 1979 the buyer had an absolute right to reject. This, however, seems dubious. The subsection applies only where a party claims "that the contract ought to be or has been rescinded", and it seems on general rounds that the claim in this case is one to reject for breach of a contractual term, not to rescind; the latter term is primarily applicable to the equitable jurisdiction.[32] Further, the section is primarily directed to the situation 12–120

---

[25] Above, para.12–006.
[26] Above, paras 12–012 *et seq*.
[27] See in general Atiyah and Treitel, 30 M.L.R. 369 at 371–372 (1967).
[28] Above, para.12–004.
[29] See *Atlantic Lines and Navigation Co. Inc. v Hallam Ltd (The Lucy)* [1983] 1 Lloyd's Rep. 188 at 202.
[30] *ibid*.
[31] Treitel, *Law of Contract* (11th ed.), p.376.
[32] But see *Kwei Tek Chao v British Traders & Shippers Ltd* [1954] 2 Q.B. 459 at 480: "A right to reject is, after all, only a particular form of a right to rescind the contract."

where a person "would be entitled, by reason of the misrepresentation, to rescind the contract." A person who seeks to reject goods for breach of contract does not really come within these words. Lastly, the reference to the court's power to "declare the contract subsisting" suggests that a rescission destroys the contract: though this may be true of rescission for external misrepresentation, it is a phrase not properly applicable to the situation where a person treats a contract as discharged for breach of a term in it.[33]

5. TORT LIABILITY IN RESPECT OF GOODS

12–121 **Tort action against seller.**[34] Where goods supplied cause personal injury or the destruction of or damage to other property, it is also possible for a dissatisfied buyer to sue the seller in tort,[35] though by so doing he takes on the burden of proving negligence. An action in tort may in some circumstances yield more damages[36] (*e.g.* if expectation of profit cannot be proved,[37] or if the loss claimed is consequential[38]); and the limitation period may run from a different time, *viz.* in the case of negligence actions the suffering of damage[39] rather than that of the supply of the defective goods.[40] The Law Reform (Contributory Negligence) Act 1945, which permits apportionment, applies to tort claims, but its application to contract claims is not yet certain.[41] Circumstances may arise where an exemption clause covers liability in contract but not in tort.[42] There are also differences in respect of jurisdiction, both local and international, and in other respects

---

[33] *Johnson v Agnew* [1980] A.C. 367; Shea, 42 M.L.R. 623 (1979).

[34] See also below, paras 14–080, 14–095 as to consumers.

[35] See *Herschtal v Stewart and Ardern Ltd* [1940] 1 K.B. 155; *Andrews v Hopkinson* [1957] 1 Q.B. 229; *Vacwell Engineering Ltd v B.D.H. Chemicals Ltd* [1971] 1 Q.B. 88 at 108; *Rasbora Ltd v J.C.L. Marine Ltd* [1977] 1 Lloyd's Rep. 645.

[36] As to damages in contract, see below, Ch.17.

[37] *e.g. C.C.C. Films (London) Ltd v Impact Quadrant Films Ltd* [1985] Q.B. 16, though here the damages were recovered in contract.

[38] Under the principles of *The Wagon Mound (No.1)* [1961] A.C. 388; *Clerk and Lindsell on Torts* (19th ed.), paras 2–118 *et seq.* But see *H. Parsons (Livestock) Ltd v Uttley Ingham & Co. Ltd* [1978] Q.B. 791, where consequential loss was recovered in contract: the principle of the case is not clear. As to damages in deceit, see above, para.12–012.

[39] Which in the case of defective buildings is when the damage came into existence: *Pirelli General Cable Works Ltd v Oscar Faber & Partners* [1983] 1 A.C. 1; but *cf. Invercargill CC v Hamlin* [1996] A.C. 624. But the law on this point was modified in part by the Latent Damage Act 1986. See *Clerk and Lindsell on Torts* (19th ed.), Ch.33.

[40] *Battley v Faulkner* (1820) 3 B. & A. 288; *Lynn v Bamber* [1930] 2 K.B. 72 at 74.

[41] *Forsikringsaktieselskapet Vesta v Butcher* [1986] 2 All E.R. 488, affirmed [1989] A.C. 852, CA; for further proceedings see *ibid.*, 880, HL. If it is not applicable the issue turns on causation: see *Lambert v Lewis* [1982] A.C. 225. See *Chitty on Contracts* (29th ed.), Vol. 1, para.26–042; Treitel, *Law of Contract* (11th ed.), pp.982 *et seq.*

[42] *e.g. White v J. Warwick & Co. Ltd* [1953] 1 W.L.R. 1285; but the significance of such decisions is much reduced by the Unfair Contract Terms Act 1977, below, Ch.13.

such as the conflict of laws, which are beyond the scope of this book. It has been said that there is not "anything to the advantage of the law's development in searching for a liability in tort where the parties are in a contractual relationship."[43] Hence the differences between contract and tort as regards the standard of care required of a seller are unlikely to be of substance. But a tort action may of course lie where there is no privity of contract: indeed this is its main utility in this context. Hence such an action may lie against a manufacturer or distributor: and also in favour of a non-buyer, *e.g.* a person to whom the buyer gave the goods in question as a gift.

Manufacturer or distributor. Thus an action in tort may also lie and indeed primarily lies against a manufacturer or distributor who puts into circulation goods which cause physical injury or the destruction of or damage to property.[44] 12–122

Care required. In respect of physical damage, where the manufacturer, distributor or seller knew or ought to have known that the goods were likely to be used without further examination, he owes a duty to take reasonable care in respect of preparation, assembly, installation, packaging, labelling, warning, etc. in so far as these are applicable to him on the facts of the case, or as to any other function he performs or should perform in relation to them.[45] It seems that sale "as seen with all its faults and without warranty" may provide sufficient warning to discharge the duty, even to a third party[46]; but it has been suggested that where the article is actually known to be dangerous more warning may be needed than this,[47] and there is much to be said for such a view. 12–123

Duty to warn as to defects subsequently discovered. Where a seller becomes aware after the sale of a defect in the goods, he may come under a duty to warn the buyer of it.[48] Problems again arise as to whether or not the 12–124

---

[43] *Tai Hing Cotton Mill Ltd v Liu Chong Hing Bank Ltd* [1986] A.C. 80 at 107, *per* Lord Scarman. See also *Aiken v Stewart Wrightson Members Agency Ltd* [1995] 2 Lloyd'd Rep. 618 at 634 *et seq*. But *cf. Henderson v Merrett Syndicates Ltd* [1995] 2 A.C. 145.

[44] *Donoghue v Stevenson* [1932] A.C. 562; below, paras 14–061 *et seq*; as to distributors see *Watson v Buckley, Osborne Garrett & Co. Ltd* [1940] 1 All E.R. 174. There may be argument as to whether the loss is economic: see *Barcardi-Martini Beverages Ltd v Messer U.K. Ltd* [2002] 1 Lloyd's Rep. 62, affirmed [2002] EWCA Civ. 549, [2002] 2 Lloyd's Rep. 379. As to the Contract (Rights of Third Parties) Act 1999 see *Chitty on Contracts* (29th ed.), Vol.1, paras 18–084 *et seq*.

[45] See *Clerk and Lindsell on Torts* (19th ed.), Ch.11.

[46] *Hurley v Dyke* [1979] R.T.R. 265; see below, para.13–106.

[47] See *Hurley v Dyke*, above, at pp.280–281, 303. *Cf.* pp.291, 295, 302.

[48] *e.g. Rivtow Marine Ltd v Washington Ironworks* [1974] S.C.R. 1189; (1973) 40 D.L.R. (3d) 530; *cf. J. Nunes Diamonds Ltd v Dominion Electric Protection Co.* [1972] S.C.R. 769; (1972) 26 D.L.R. (3d) 699; *Nicholson v John Deere* (1987) 34 D.L.R. (4th) 542, affirmed (1989) 57 D.L.R. (4th) 639; *E. Hobbs (Farms) Ltd v Baxenden Chemicals Co. Ltd* [1992] 1 Lloyd's Rep. 54.

loss caused or likely to be caused is physical or purely economic.[49] A manufacturer may be similarly liable.[50]

12–125 **Misrepresentation.** The possibility of an action in tort in respect of misrepresentation has already been dealt with in the discussion of misrepresentations inducing the contract,[51] and is not further considered here. There is, however, some overlap in that an action in respect of defective goods can sometimes be regarded as based on an implied representation as to them.[52]

12–126 **Economic loss: goods which threaten damage or are otherwise unsatisfactory.** There was for a period authority suggesting that a *builder* was liable if he negligently erected a building containing latent defects which merely *threatened* physical damage, not only to persons or other property but also, according to some authority, to the structure itself.[53] Such reasoning could have led to applications in the sale of goods. Though explained by some as involving physical damage, this last liability was in effect a liability in respect of pure economic loss,[54] and raised the possibility of a transmissible warranty against negligence causing economic loss given by a manufacturer and possibly a distributor or seller.[55] These cases have now been overruled or disapproved in England,[56] and liability for such defects is confined to contract[57]; though authority in other jurisdictions is more liberal.[58] It is, however, possible that in some circumstances the manufacturer of a separate part of a structure or article may be liable if it proves defective in such a way as to damage another part of the structure or article,[59] though the question has not really been considered in connection

---

49 See the dissenting judgment of Laskin J. in the *Rivtow Marine* case, above, esp. at pp.1217–1219, 549–550; disapproved in *Murphy v Brentwood DC* [1991] 1 A.C. 398 at 470, 477, 488; *Hamble Fisheries Ltd v L. Gardner & Sons Ltd* [1999] 2 Lloyd's Rep. 1.

50 *Walton v British Leyland (U.K.) Ltd* [1980] *Product Liability International* 156.

51 Above, paras 12–013 *et seq.*

52 See *Langridge v Levy* (1837) 2 M. & W. 519; *Horsfall v Thomas* (1862) 1 H. & C. 90 at 99; *Bodger v Nicholls* (1873) 28 L.T. 441. Not where the sale is "with all faults": *Ward v Hobbs* (1878) 4 App.Cas. 13.

53 *Dutton v Bognor Regis UDC* [1972] 1 Q.B. 373; *Bowen v Paramount Builders (Hamilton) Ltd* [1977] 1 N.Z.L.R. 394; *Anns v Merton LBC* [1978] A.C. 728; *Batty v Metropolitan Property Realisations Ltd* [1978] Q.B. 554.

54 *Murphy v Brentwood DC* [1991] 1 A.C. 398 at 466, *per* Lord Keith of Kinkel; *Nitrigin Eireann Teoranta v Inco Alloys Ltd* [1992] 1 W.L.R. 498.

55 *ibid.*, at p.469, *per* Lord Keith of Kinkel.

56 *Murphy v Brentwood DC*, above; see also *D. & F. Estates Ltd v Church Commissioners for England* [1989] A.C. 177; *Department of the Environment v Thomas Bates & Son Ltd* [1991] 1 A.C. 499; *Clerk and Lindsell on Torts* (19th ed.), paras 8–111 *et seq.*

57 See *Simaan General Contracting Co. v Pilkington Glass Ltd (No.2)* [1988] Q.B. 758.

58 See *Winnipeg Condominium Corp. No.36 v Bird Construction Co.* [1995] 1 S.C.R. 85, (1995) 121 D.L.R. (4th) 193; *Bryan v Maloney* (1995) 182 C.L.R. 609; *Invercargill CC v Hamlin* [1996] A.C. 624, PC (N.Z.).

59 See *Murphy v Brentwood DC*, above, at pp.470, *per* Lord Keith, 478, *per* Lord Bridge of Harwich, 497, *per* Lord Jauncey of Tullichettle. See also Wallace, 107 L.Q.R. 228 at 235 (1991); *Clerk and Lindsell on Torts* (19th ed.), paras 8–113 *et seq.*

with goods as opposed to buildings. And there could be special circumstances where a relationship of proximity, which seems in such situations to mean reliance, could arise between a manufacturer, distributor or seller and a buyer, so as to give rise to a duty of care in respect of economic loss.[60]

Consumer Protection Act. Manufacturers or producers, and in some cases distributors or sellers, may be liable strictly (subject to defences) under Part I of the Consumer Protection Act 1987. This imposes strict liability where physical damage is caused by a defective product. The central feature of the notion of a defective product is that "the safety of the product is not such as persons are entitled to expect".[61] The damage must in general be physical. When an action on this statute is available, it may be more advantageous than an action at common law, in particular because proof of negligence is not required. Where it is not available, however, the tort action may still be used. Regulations may also be made under the Act, breach of which may be actionable as a breach of statutory duty. The Act is discussed elsewhere in this book.[62] 12–127

6. Mistake as to Subject-Matter of Contract

Mistake. It may occasionally be possible to treat a contract as void or inoperative on the ground of a fundamental mistake as to the nature of the subject-matter negativing or nullifying consent, or (perhaps) to seek to have it set aside in equity on the grounds of mistake. This raises the vexed and controversial problem of mistake in the general law of contract, which is dealt with elsewhere.[63] Reference should also be made to general works on the law of contract.[64] It seems that only very rarely, if at all, could these doctrines be invoked between buyer and seller.[65] 12–128

---

[60] In England, such an action might be based on the notion of assumption of responsibility enunciated in *Henderson v Merrett Syndicates Ltd* [1995] 2 A.C. 145. See *Clerk and Lindsell on Torts* (19th ed.), paras 8–87 *et seq.*; *Hamble Fisheries Ltd v L. Gardner & Sons Ltd* [1999] 2 Lloyd's Rep. 1 at 8.

[61] s.3.

[62] Below, paras 14–080 *et seq.*, 14–095.

[63] Above, paras 3–011 *et seq.*

[64] See *Chitty on Contracts*, (29th ed.), Vol.1, Ch.5; Treitel, *Law of Contract* (11th ed.), pp.286 *et seq.*

[65] See *Leaf v International Galleries* [1950] 2 K.B. 86; *Harrison and Jones v Bunten and Lancaster Ltd* [1953] 1 Q.B. 646; *Frederick E. Rose (London) Ltd v William H. Pim Jnr. & Co. Ltd* [1953] 2 Q.B. 450; *Dixon, Kerly Ltd v Robinson* [1965] 2 Lloyd's Rep. 404; *cf. Scott v Coulson* [1903] 2 Ch. 249; *Nicholson and Venn v Smith-Marriott* (1947) 177 L.T. 189; *Associated Japanese Bank (International) Ltd v Credit du Nord SA* [1989] 1 W.L.R. 255. As to the equitable jurisdiction see *Solle v Butcher* [1950] 1 K.B. 671; *Grist v Bailey* [1967] Ch. 532; *Taylor v Johnson* (1983) 151 C.L.R. 422; *Commission for New Towns v Cooper Ltd* [1995] Ch. 259. This jurisdiction is in England more doubtful since *Great Peace Shipping Ltd v Tsavliris Salvage (International) Ltd* [2002] EWCA Civ. 1907; [2003] Q.B. 679: see above, para.3–026.

7. THE VIENNA CONVENTION ON CONTRACTS FOR THE INTERNATIONAL SALE OF GOODS

12–129 **The Vienna Convention.** The nature and scope of the United Nations Convention on Contracts for the International Sale of Goods of 1980, often referred to as the Vienna Convention, has been indicated earlier in this book.[66] The difference between the buyer's remedies under this Convention and under the common law together with the Sale of Goods Act are considerable: indeed it is in the area of remedies that the differences are most striking. The primary remedy is regarded as that of requiring performance of the contract, though there is a proviso that a court is not bound to enter judgment for specific performance unless it would do so under its own law in respect of similar contracts of sale not governed by the Convention.[67] This may seem to avoid different consequences before a common law court; but in fact the initial starting point leads the Convention further to prescribe remedies of requiring repair or in some cases the delivery of substitute goods.[68] The general criteria for (in effect) treating a contract as discharged by breach, called "avoiding the contract", though the right can occur in other cases,[69] refer to a breach which results in "such detriment to the other party as substantially to deprive him of what he is entitled to expect under the contract"[70] and are not dissimilar from, but not the same as, the test laid down in the *Hong Kong Fir* case,[71] which refers to deprivation of "substantially the whole benefit". (There is nothing corresponding to the notion of condition as used in the Sale of Goods Act.) On the other hand the seller may have excuses for non-performance which would not be effective at common law[72]; and has a right to cure defective performance,[73] the relation between which and the right to avoid is not clear. There is also a remedy, partially similar to the *nachfrist* of German law, for fixing an additional time of reasonable length for performance by the other party: if it is not complied with there is a right to avoid the contract even though the breach was insufficient to justify this on general criteria.[74] This remedy is said to be confined to cases of non-delivery, but it is not clear that this is so nor what "non-delivery" is. There is further a special remedy of reduction of the price,[75] deriving from the Roman *actio quanti minoris*, which may lead to a monetary award different from what an award of damages would produce. The right to reject the goods is lost if notice is not given to the seller within a reasonable time after the non-conformity was discovered, or in any case after two years[76]—a fixed period

---

[66] Above, para.1–024. For a detailed comparison with common law see Nicholas, 105 L.Q.R. 201, esp. at 224–234 (1989).
[67] Arts 28, 30, 46(1).
[68] Art.46(2), (3).
[69] See Art.79 (excused failure of performance).
[70] Art.25.
[71] [1962] 2 Q.B. 26 at 66; above, para.12–023.
[72] See Art.79.
[73] Art.48. See also Arts 34, 37.
[74] Arts 47, 49: see also Arts 63, 64.
[75] Art.50.
[76] Art.39.

of a sort not known to common law; and the Convention is replete with requirements for the service of notice and prompt action (especially as to inspection),[77] on which in cases interpreting the Convention many buyers appear to have foundered, by English law standards, unexpectedly. There are complex and detailed provisions regarding short and excessive delivery,[78] and a carefully prescribed right, unknown to English law but similar to a provision of the Uniform Commercial Code,[79] to suspend performance in situations where it is uncertain whether the other party can perform.[80] Bars on the right to avoid, the consequences of its exercise, and problems of preserving goods on rejection are elaborately regulated in a way that differs from the common law.[81] In particular, the buyer is under a duty to care for rejected goods.[82]

Enough has been said to indicate that the Convention, which represents a compromise between common law and civil law techniques, and many parts of which will be understood differently, at any rate at first, by common lawyers and civil lawyers, is a regime on its own requiring careful study and the use of specialised works. It is more complex than the common law, and from the point of view of a buyer gives less robust remedies, being directed instead to a more balanced adjustment of the positions of the parties. The Sale of Goods Act and the extensive common law overlay on that statute provide little or no guide to its application; much will require to be solved in litigation which will interpret in many different countries a completely new regime. Those who may find the regime unsatisfactory should exclude the operation of the Convention in international transactions to which it would otherwise apply.[83]

---

[77] *e.g.* Arts 38, 43, 49(2).
[78] Arts 51, 52.
[79] s.2–609.
[80] Art.71; the consequences of the seller not giving the buyer "adequate assurance of performance" are not clear. See also Art.72 as to anticipatory breach.
[81] See Arts 81–88.
[82] Arts 85–88.
[83] As to international sales see below, Chs 18–21.

CHAPTER 13

EXEMPTION CLAUSES

	PARA.
1. Introduction	13–001
2. Basic principles of formation of contract applied to exemption clauses	13–012
3. Interpretation of exemption clauses	13–020
4. Doctrine of fundamental breach	13–042
5. Control of exemption clauses by statute	13–053

1. INTRODUCTION

Exemption clauses. Parties to contracts often insert into them clauses variously termed "exemption", "exclusion" or "exception" clauses, or "disclaimers", which purport to exclude, qualify, restrict or limit the legal rights, duties, liabilities and remedies which might otherwise arise. In the case of defective goods[1] these sometimes take the form of the specific exclusion of conditions, warranties and other undertakings; sometimes they employ more vague phraseology, such as "with all faults" or "with all faults and errors of description"; sometimes they purport to be acknowledgments or agreements that facts constituting a breach of contract have not occurred (*e.g.* an acknowledgment that goods were satisfactory on delivery); sometimes they purport to exclude or restrict the right to reject, to limit the amount of damages that may be claimed, to restrict set-off, or to impose a time limit on rejection or on claims. Another type of clause, less common in contracts of sale, is a clause requiring one party to indemnify the other against liability in certain circumstances. Such clauses are not exemption clauses but may have a similar effect.[2] **13–001**

Exemption clauses are often open to serious objection, for they may, in reducing the liability of one party, effect a distribution of risks different from that which it may be assumed that contracting parties would reasonably have intended. Such a distribution of risks often results from simple ignorance: one party may have had no reasonable opportunity to become aware of the terms, and if he was aware of them he may not have been able to understand them or to appreciate their full potential implications. Even if these factors are not present, the contract may be made in circumstances where there is inequality of bargaining power: one party has no effective power to negotiate the clauses, nor perhaps even to refuse to contract if he **13–002**

---

[1] As to clauses excusing delivery, see above, paras 8–088 *et seq.*; as to defect in title, above, paras 4–018, 4–032 *et seq.*

[2] See below, para.13–097.

finds the terms unacceptable. Finally, even where there is agreement, particular clauses may on general grounds appear unreasonable. All these problems present themselves most acutely in the case of consumer transactions: but they may also sometimes apply to sales between business concerns, especially where a small business deals with a larger one.

13–003 It should be noted that exemption clauses are part of a much broader problem of unfair contract terms, and that there are different ways of identifying the transactions or clauses to which such objections may be taken. The problem may be regarded as one stemming from the use of sets of standard contract terms, which can be said to amount to a form of private legislation; or as one of economic duress exercised by one party over the other; or as one regarding the use of unconscionable terms in contracts; or as one related to the protection of consumers. Each of these criteria can be found utilised by some legal system.[3] English law has, however, tended to identify the problem almost entirely as one of exemption clauses[4]: besides being rather narrow, this approach presents, as will be shown,[5] problems of definition.

13–004 But it must also be remembered that such clauses can serve perfectly valid purposes of delimiting the risks undertaken by one party; and standard contract terms, especially when drawn up in consultation between interests representing the two sides to a standard commercial transaction, likewise serve a perfectly legitimate purpose in saving time, avoiding disputes, filling gaps, achieving an appropriate balance of risks and so forth.[6] From this point of view, a study of the techniques used by the courts to limit the effect of such clauses is relevant principally in connection with the drafting of such clauses in such a form as to achieve their desired result.

13–005 Statute apart, exemption clauses in contracts of sale are in principle valid under section 55(1) of the Sale of Goods Act 1979.[7] But they have long been subjected to close scrutiny by the courts, and various techniques have been employed to limit their effects.

13–006 **Common law rules affecting such clauses.** Three main techniques have been used at common law to control such clauses. First, by the operation of the basic principles of contract such clauses may be held not incorporated

---

[3] For example, the German *AGB-Gesetz* of 1976, now paras 308, 309 *BGB*, is directed at standard contract terms. The Uniform Commercial Code, s.2–302, is directed at unconscionable clauses in contracts: see White and Summers, *Uniform Commercial Code* (5th ed.), Ch.4. There was pathfinding consumer protection legislation in Sweden: see Bernitz, 20 *Scandinavian Studies in Law* 11 (1976). The Contracts Review Act 1980 (N.S.W.) gives the court power to grant "relief in respect of unjust contracts" but is largely confined to consumer transactions. Finally, the Unfair Terms in Consumer Contracts Regulations 1999 (below, paras 13–103, 14–030 *et seq.*) are directed to consumer contracts.

[4] This in part stems from the Report of the (Molony) Committee on Consumer Protection of 1962 (Cmnd. 1781).

[5] Below, paras 13–044, 13–064—13–065.

[6] See Llewellyn, 52 Harv.L.Rev. 700 (1939); *Macaulay v A. Schroeder Music Publishing Co. Ltd* [1974] 1 W.L.R. 1308, *per* Lord Diplock.

[7] Above, para.1–013.

into the contract; or, though incorporated, nevertheless inoperative because their effect has been misrepresented or they are overridden by a collateral contract; or by virtue of the rules of privity of contract they may be inapplicable in a particular situation.[8] Secondly, such clauses have sometimes (and especially in case of ambiguity) been subjected to interpretation *contra proferentem*, which has often been rigorous.[9] Thirdly, a line of cases dating from about 1950 suggested the existence of a doctrine known as that of fundamental breach of contract, under which exemption clauses might be inoperative in the case of such a breach. Although this doctrine was associated with interpretation, it in two periods appeared to assume the status of a substantive rule of law, regardless of the wording of the clause in question. It is now, however, established, at least in England, that in so far as such reasoning is still relevant it should be assimilated into the rules as to interpretation already mentioned.[10]

Statutory intervention. The common law techniques of control are somewhat unpredictable, as they operate indirectly. In English common law at least, a decision can rarely be based on the articulate proposition that a clause which was agreed to and is applicable on its terms is nevertheless too objectionable in result to be given effect. From time to time, therefore, the legislature has intervened to control such clauses in other fields, though until fairly recently that of sale of goods was little affected.[11] Various techniques have been employed. One is to provide that certain terms are only valid if drawn to the attention of the party adversely affected in certain ways.[12] Another is to provide that a particular type of clause can only be incorporated into the contract under the supervision of the court or of some other body.[13] A third is to prohibit certain types of clause altogether.[14] A fourth is to confer on the courts jurisdiction to control unreasonable clauses. This technique was applied in England more than 100 years ago in connection with contracts for carriage by rail,[15] but became more prominent in the common law world in general when in the United States a general provision of such a nature was inserted into the Uniform Commercial Code.[16] 13–007

The Unfair Contract Terms Act 1977 and earlier legislation. The first major legislative intervention of recent years to affect exemption clauses in general (as opposed to in particular types of transaction) was section 3 of 13–008

[8] See below, paras 13–011 *et seq*.
[9] See below, paras 13–020 *et seq*.
[10] See below, paras 13–042 *et seq*.
[11] The first major legislative intervention in the area was s.8 of the Hire Purchase Act 1938.
[12] *e.g.* Consumer Credit Act 1974, s.60 (empowering regulations as to form and content of agreements). See also Italian Civil Code, art.1341 (requirement of signature for certain types of term).
[13] *e.g.* Housing Act 1961, s.33 (now repealed). The Israeli Standard Contracts Law of 1964 provided a scheme for prior validation of restrictive terms by the Board of Restrictive Trade Practices. It seems at first to have been little used and was replaced by a new version in 1982: see Deutch, 30 McGill L.J. 458 (1985).
[14] *e.g.* Consumer Credit Act 1974, s.173.
[15] See Railway and Canal Traffic Act 1854, s.7 (repealed by Transport Act 1962).
[16] s.2–302 (using the criterion of unconscionability). See also Contracts Review Act 1980 (N.S.W.), s.7.

the Misrepresentation Act 1967, which subjected clauses excluding liability for misrepresentation to a test of reasonableness. The provision is of general application, but though such clauses do appear in contracts for the sale of goods it is probable that its main thrust is to be found in other areas. The Supply of Goods (Implied Terms) Act 1973, however, which applied to sale of goods and hire-purchase, utilised both the third and the fourth of the techniques above mentioned, and also differentiated between consumer and non-consumer transactions. It provided that any purported exclusion of the principal implied obligations of the seller in a sale of goods was void in a consumer sale, and enforceable only subject to a test of reasonableness in other sales. Similar provisions were applied to contracts of hire-purchase. Subsequently the Unfair Contract Terms Act 1977 (which despite its broad title is effectively restricted to exemption clauses, widely defined) repealed and (in substance) re-enacted these provisions, but accompanied them by further provisions of more general scope which render ineffective certain types of clause (principally those exempting from liability for personal injuries caused by negligence) and subject a further range of clauses (principally those exempting from liability for negligence, or contained in standard terms or in consumer transactions) to a requirement of reasonableness. It also amended section 3 of the Misrepresentation Act 1967.

13–009 **The Unfair Terms in Consumer Contracts Regulations 1999.** More recently a further form of legislative control was brought into force by the medium of statutory instrument. The Regulations supersede earlier regulations of 1994 implementing the EC Directive on Unfair Terms in Consumer Contracts, and seek to control not only exemption clauses but also other unfair contract terms: hence their effect extends beyond the scope of this chapter, though they certainly apply to exemption clauses. They are referred to again briefly at the end of this chapter for the sake of completeness,[17] but since they are confined to consumer contracts they are dealt with principally in the chapter on Consumer Protection.[18]

13–010 The provisions of the Misrepresentation Act 1967 and the Unfair Contract Terms Act 1977 are dealt with in a later part of this chapter.[19] The common law rules described above remain in principle applicable; indeed, those as to incorporation in the contract are expressly preserved by the 1977 Act.[20] In fact, those as to incorporation, misrepresentation, collateral contracts and privity of contract are likely to remain of practical importance. There may, however, be a tendency to short-circuit the rules as to interpretation where legislation prohibits certain clauses altogether (as in consumer sales), and also to some extent where the requirement of reasonableness is applied. But it is suggested below[21] that it seems likely that there will still be cases where these rules are invoked. In any case they

---

17 Below, para.13–103.
18 See below, paras 14–001 *et seq.*
19 Below, paras 13–053 *et seq*. As to exclusion of s.12, see above, paras 4–018, 4–032 *et seq*.
20 See below, para.13–012.
21 Below, paras 13–020, 13–086.

may be relevant where the 1977 Act does not apply,[22] for example in many international sales, and in jurisdictions where there is no similar legislation.

Proposals for reform. It has for some time been clear that the interaction of the control of exemption clauses under the Unfair Contracts Terms Act 1977 and that under the Unfair Terms in Consumer Contracts Regulations was unsatisfactory.[23] The former is confined to exemption clauses, but has applications to both consumer and business transactions. The latter is not confined to exemption clauses, but only applies to consumer transactions, and uses definitions and rules that do not entirely coincide with those of the former. The Law Commissions have recently made valuable proposals for assimilating the two, using clearer terminology than that at present operative, and also for introducing an intermediate category of small businesses who in some respects would receive the sort of protection accorded to consumers.[24] It remains to be seen whether they will be implemented: if they are, much of this chapter will require change. The new provisions regarding consumer remedies contained in Part 5A of the Sale of Goods Act 1979[25] are at present dependent on the wording of section 12 of the Unfair Contract Terms Act[26], and hence raise a different and more extensive possibility, that of a Consumer Sales Act.[27] 13–011

2. Basic Principles of Formation of Contract Applied to Exemption Clauses

All basic principles of formation applicable in sale. All the basic principles of formation of contract which can be utilised to control exemption clauses apply in the law of sale of goods; and their operation is expressly preserved in the Unfair Contract Terms Act 1977.[28] Details of these should be sought in general textbooks on contract,[29] but they are briefly indicated here in outline. They provide a technique for the control of exemption clauses, but a rather unpredictable one. 13–012

Incorporation in contract. The clause must be incorporated as a part of the contract. Where it is contained in a document signed by the person sought to be held bound by it, no problem arises in this respect, for a person is bound by what he signs whether he has read it or not,[30] unless its 13–013

---

22 Below, paras 13–021, 13–099 *et seq*.

23 See Reynolds, 110 L.Q.R. 1 (1994)

24 See Law Com. No.292, Sc. Law Com. No.199 (2005).

25 See above, paras 12–071 et seq.

26 See below, paras 13–071 et seq.

27 A possibility put forward by Bridge, 119 L.Q.R. 173 (2003).

28 s.11(2): below, para.9–013. See also Sch.2, below, para.13–088.

29 See *Chitty on Contracts* (29th ed.), Vol.1, Ch.14; Treitel, *Law of Contract* (11th ed.), Ch.7; Coote, *Exception Clauses* (1964); Atiyah, *Sale of Goods* (11th ed.), Ch.14; Yates, *Exclusion Clauses in Contracts* (2nd ed.), Chs 2, 4, 5; Chin, *Excluding Liability in Contracts* (Singapore, 1985); Yates and Hawkins, *Standard Business Contracts* (1986); Macdonald, *Exemption Clauses and Unfair Terms* (1999); Lewison, *The Interpretation of Contracts* (3rd ed.), Ch.12.

30 *L'Estrange v F. Graucob Ltd* [1934] 2 K.B. 394. But *cf*. Spencer [1973] C.L.J. 104.

effect has been misrepresented[31] or *non est factum* can be pleaded.[32] In other cases, however, the question will be whether reasonable notice of the clause has been given to the party affected by it[33] before or at the time of contracting,[34] so as to make it part of the contract. Unusual or unexpected clauses may require more notice.[35] Such notice will not be regarded as having been given if the clause appears on a document that would not be expected to have contractual force, *e.g.* some types of receipt,[36] or a catalogue.[37] An exemption clause may, however, be incorporated by trade usage.[38] By section 11(2) of and Schedule 2 to the Unfair Contract Terms Act 1977[39] the question whether the customer knew or ought to have known of the existence and extent of the term is made relevant to the reasonableness of clauses purporting to exclude the fundamental obligations of the seller under sections 13, 14 and 15 of the Sale of Goods Act

---

[31] Below, para.13–016.

[32] See *Saunders v Anglia Building Society (No.2)* [1971] A.C. 1039. But it will rarely be necessary to rely on this doctrine *inter partes: cf. Petelin v Cullen* (1975) 132 C.L.R. 355.

[33] *Parker v S.E. Ry* (1877) 2 C.P.D. 416; *Richardson, Spence & Co. v Rowntree* [1894] A.C. 217; *Thompson v L.M. and S. Ry* [1930] 1 K.B. 41; *Cockerton v Naviera Aznar SA* [1960] 2 Lloyd's Rep. 450. In *Interfoto Picture Library Ltd v Stiletto Visual Programmes Ltd* [1989] Q.B. 433, Bingham L.J. attributed these rules to the result of an inquiry whether it would be fair or reasonable to hold a party bound: see pp.439, 445. As to sale of goods, see *J. Gordon Alison & Co. Ltd v Wallsend Slipway and Engineering Co. Ltd* (1927) 43 T.L.R. 323 (letterhead stating "all offers are subject to our usual strike and guarabovee clauses, accidents, &c.": not clear enough to incorporate clause exempting from liability for delay or consequential damages). There may be difficulties where two contracting parties use their own printed forms, in deciding which terms apply: see, *e.g. Butler Machine Tool Co. Ltd v Ex-Cell-O Corp. (England) Ltd* [1979] 1 W.L.R. 401; *cf.* Vienna Convention (above, para.1–024), Art. 19.2. And where standard terms change, there may be problems in deciding which set is incorporated: see *Smith v South Wales Switchgear Ltd* [1978] 1 W.L.R. 165, HL. See in general above, paras 2–012, 2–013.

[34] *Olley v Marlborough Court Ltd* [1949] 1 K.B. 532; *Thornton v Shoe Lane Parking Ltd* [1971] 2 Q.B. 163; and see *Chapelton v Barry U.D.C.* [1940] 1 K.B. 532; *Mendelssohn v Normand Ltd* [1970] 1 Q.B. 177. In *Beta Computers (Europe) Ltd v Adobe Systems (Europe) Ltd* 1996 S.L.T. 604, computer software was supplied in a package showing that the software was subject to strict end-user conditions in favour of the author. These terms could be read through the wrapping. It was held that the contract was *sui generis*; and that the person supplied was entitled to return the package unopened to the supplier.

[35] *J. Spurling Ltd v Bradshaw* [1956] 1 W.L.R. 461 at 466; *Thornton v Shoe Lane Parking Ltd*, above; D. & M. Trailers (Halifax) Ltd v Stirling [1978] R.T.R. 468; *Interfoto Picture Library Ltd v Stiletto Visual Programmes Ltd, above; AEG (U.K.) Ltd v Logic Resource Ltd* [1996] C.L.C. 265; Males [1996] L.M.C.L.Q. 335.

[36] *Chapelton v Barry UDC*, above (receipt for hiring deck-chair); *Fillmore's Valley Nurseries Ltd v North America Cyanamid Ltd* (1958) 14 D.L.R. (2d) 297 (invoice); but *cf. Alexander v Railway Executive* [1951] 2 K.B. 882 (railway cloakroom ticket); *Harvey v Ascot Dry Cleaning Co. Ltd* [1953] N.Z.L.R. 549 (dry cleaning ticket); *Roe v R. A. Naylor Ltd* [1917] 1 K.B. 712 (sold note).

[37] *Walls v Centaur Co. Ltd* (1921) 126 L.T. 242.

[38] As to custom and usage of trade, see above, para.11–088; *Cointat v Myham & Son* (1914) 110 L.T. 749 (warranty excluded in meat trade); *Re Walkers, Winser and Hamm and Shaw, Son & Co.* [1904] 2 K.B. 152 (custom as to non-rejection). See also *British Crane Hire Corp. Ltd v Ipswich Plant Hire Ltd* [1975] Q.B. 303, below, para.13–015.

[39] See also below, para.13–088.

1979.[40] But section 11(2) expressly provides that this "does not prevent the court or arbitrator from holding, in accordance with any rule of law, that a term which purports to exclude or restrict any relevant liability is not a term of the contract."

Course of dealing. Disputes frequently arise in commercial cases when the parties have for some time dealt on certain terms, and at some point notice of these ceases or is omitted to be given: to what extent are they to be regarded as continuing to deal on the same terms? It may also happen that a contracting party puts forward terms in a way or at a time which would be inadequate or too late in respect of a single contract, but the parties continue to deal over a period, arguably by tacit reference to them. In *McCutcheon v David McBrayne Ltd*,[41] Lord Devlin said "Previous dealings are relevant only if they prove knowledge of the terms, actual and not constructive, and assent to them." But the House of Lords, in *Henry Kendall & Sons v William Lillico & Sons*,[42] disapproved this view, and placed emphasis on the notion of a consistent course of dealing (which there was not in *McCutcheon's* case): if there is such a course of dealing, the parties must be taken to have assented to the incorporation of the normal terms into the subsequent contract. Here buyers had regularly received more than a hundred contract notes from sellers over a period of three years: they knew of the existence of conditions on the back of the contract note and never raised any query or objection. "The court's task is to decide what each party to an alleged contract would reasonably conclude from the utterances, writings or conduct of the other. The question, therefore, is not what [the buyers] themselves thought or knew about the matter, but what they should be taken as representing to [the sellers] about it or leading [the sellers] to believe. The only reasonable inference from the regular course of dealing over so long a period is that [the buyers] were evincing an acceptance of, and a readiness to be bound by, the printed conditions of whose existence they were well aware although they had not troubled to read them."[43] 13–014

A separate but related principle may apply even where no course of dealing can be shown. Where each party is involved, or used to dealing, in a particular trade and deals in circumstances in which standard terms are normally applicable, it may be held that they deal on the basis of a common 13–015

---

[40] Above, Ch.11.

[41] [1964] 1 W.L.R. 125 at 134. See also *Mendelssohn v Normand Ltd* [1970] 1 Q.B. 177 at 183.

[42] [1969] 2 A.C. 31 at 90, 104–105, 113, 130.

[43] [1969] 2 A.C. 31 at 113, *per* Lord Pearce. See also *Pocahontas Fuel Co. v Ambatielos* (1922) 27 Com.Cas. 148 at 152; *J. Spurling Ltd v Bradshaw* [1956] 1 W.L.R. 461; *Britain and Overseas Trading (Bristles) Ltd v Brooks Wharf and Bull Wharf Ltd* [1967] 2 Lloyd's Rep. 51; *S.I.A.T. di dal Ferro v Tradax Overseas SA* [1980] 1 Lloyd's Rep. 53; *cf. Hollier v Rambler Motors (A.M.C.) Ltd* [1972] 2 Q.B. 71 (consumer situation: no course of dealing); *McCrone v Boots Farm Sales Ltd* 1981 S.C. 68; *Circle Freight Intl. Ltd v Medeast Gulf Exports Ltd* [1988] 2 Lloyd's Rep. 427; *Victor Hydraulics Ltd v Engineering Dynamics Ltd* [1996] 2 N.Z.L.R. 235; above, para.2–012.

understanding that the appropriate terms are to govern, whatever they are, even though not referred to at the time of contracting.[44] This principle could presumably apply even to first-time dealings between traders: it is, if not the same, closely related to the idea of incorporation of terms by custom or usage.

13–016 **Clause incorporated in contract but nevertheless inoperative at common law.** Even though a clause is duly incorporated in the contract and clear in its meaning, it may nevertheless not operate, or be restricted in its operation, if its effect has been misrepresented.[45] The same may be true if a genuine collateral contract not containing the clause and separate from the main contract is found to have been made and broken[46]; an action for breach of the collateral contract may be maintained regardless of the exemption in the main contract. Such a collateral contract is sometimes detected with striking results. Thus in *Couchman v Hill*,[47] there was an auction sale under terms providing that lots were sold "with all faults, imperfections and errors of description." The plaintiff asked the defendant and the auctioneer at the time of sale if a heifer was "unserved", and received an affirmative answer. This was held to be an overriding collateral warranty as to a specific matter, unaffected by the general exemption clause, and an action for damages lay for breach of it.[48] An exemption clause would not be effective to exclude liability for the fraud of a party inducing (as opposed to performing[49]) a contract,[50] or for breach of fiduciary duty[51]; and there are dicta (which, however, have never been

---

[44] *British Crane Hire Corp. Ltd v Ipswich Plant Hire Ltd* [1975] Q.B. 303; *Lacey's Footwear (Wholesale) Ltd v Bowler International Freight Ltd* [1997] 2 Lloyd's Rep. 369; *Thames Tideway Properties Ltd v Serfaty & Partners* [1999] 2 Lloyd's Rep. 110. Contrast *Hollingworth v Southern Ferries Ltd (The Eagle)* [1977] 2 Lloyd's Rep. 70 (consumer case).

[45] *Curtis v Chemical Cleaning and Dyeing Co.* [1951] 1 K.B. 805 (though inasmuch as misrepresentation usually gives rise to rescission of the whole contract the basis of the decision is not clear: in particular it is not clear whether the whole clause cannot be relied on, or merely the part the effect of which was misrepresented). See also *Mendelssohn v Normand Ltd* [1970] 1 Q.B. 177.

[46] Above, para.10–012; see also below, para.13–023.

[47] [1947] K.B. 554. See also *Harling v Eddy* [1951] 2 K.B. 739 (similar facts: but for another explanation of this case see above, para.10–037); *Webster v Higgin* [1948] 2 All E.R. 127 (sale of car): *Mendelssohn v Normand Ltd*, above.

[48] Though the term is puzzlingly referred to as a "condition".

[49] See *Frans Maas (UK) Ltd v Samsung Electronics (UK) Ltd* [2004] EWHC 1502 (Comm); [2004] 2 Lloyd's Rep 251 *per* Gross J. at [134] *et seq.*, quoting Lord Hobhouse in the *HIH* case, below, at [95]. But the context is not of fraud, but rather, of wilful default.

[50] *HIH Casualty & General Insurance Ltd v Chase Manhattan Bank* [2003] UKHL 6; [2003] All E.R. (Comm) 349 at [16], [76]; *S. Pearson & Son v Dublin Corp.* [1907] A.C. 351 at 353–354, 362. But an exemption for gross negligence might be valid: *Armitage v Nurse* [1998] Ch. 241 (trustee); and clear words can probably exclude liability for fraud of an agent: see the *HIH* case, above, at [16], [76]–[81]; but see Handley (2003) 119 LQR. 537. As to sale of forgeries and fakes by auction see Harvey (1997) 16 Tr.Law 96.

[51] See *Gluckstein v Barnes* [1900] A.C. 240. Such a clause could however prevent such a duty from arising.

applied, at least in England[52]) that grossly unreasonable clauses in a contract might not have effect at common law.[53]

Third parties. In accordance with the normal doctrine of privity of contract, a person who is not a party to a contract can at common law neither take the benefit of, nor be bound by, an exemption clause contained in it.[54] This may be very relevant when an action in negligence is brought by or against a third party to the contract of sale.[55] The common law has developed two principal methods of circumventing this rule in the case of exemption clauses.[56] The first involves detecting a separate contract with the third party, incorporating (or even containing no more than) the exemptions of the main contract, made through the agency of one of the parties to the main contract (or more directly if the facts permit of such an inference).[57] If the exemptions are drafted with a view to such interpretation, and if the party to be additionally protected is known from the outset, the separate contract will be easier to infer. The second method involves a promise by one contracting party to the other not to sue the third party; in such a situation an action against the third party would be a breach of contract, and could be stayed[58] or even perhaps made the subject of a claim for damages.[59] Although such a promise could perhaps in some circum- 13–017

[52] But see *Clarke v West Ham Corp.* [1909] 2 K.B. 858.

[53] *Watkins v Rymill* (1883) 10 Q.B.D. 178 at 189; *Thompson v L.M. and S. Ry.* [1930] 1 K.B. 41 at 46; *Parker v S.E. Ry.* (1877) 2 C.P.D. 416 at 428; *John Lee & Sons (Grantham) Ltd v Railway Executive* [1949] 2 All E.R. 581 at 584; *Thornton v Shoe Lane Parking Ltd* [1971] 2 Q.B. 163 at 170; *Gillespie Bros & Co. Ltd v Roy Bowles Transport Ltd* [1973] Q.B. 400 at 416; *Levison v Patent Steam Carpet Cleaning Co. Ltd* [1978] Q.B. 69 at 79. But *cf. Grand Trunk Ry of Canada v Robinson* [1915] A.C. 740 at 747; *Ludditt v Ginger Coote Airways Ltd* [1947] A.C. 233 at 242. Whatever their standing, these dicta are of less significance since the Unfair Contract Terms Act 1977.

[54] See *Chitty on Contracts* (29th ed.), Vol.1, paras 14–039 *et seq.*; Treitel, *Law of Contract* (11th ed.), pp.626 *et seq; Dunlop Pneumatic Tyre Co. Ltd v Selfridge & Co. Ltd* [1915] A.C. 847; *Scruttons Ltd v Midland Silicones Ltd* [1962] A.C. 446.

[55] See above, paras 12–073 *et seq*; below, paras 14–061 *et seq.*; paras 14–076 *et seq.*; but see below, paras 13–019, 14–080 *et seq.*, 14–095 as to the effect of the Consumer Protection Act 1987.

[56] There is a third, that of bailment on terms, which will not usually be relevant in a sale of goods context. See *Chitty on Contracts* (29th ed.), Vol.1, paras 14–054, 14–055.

[57] See *New Zealand Shipping Co. Ltd v A. M. Satterthwaite & Co. Ltd (The Eurymedon)* [1975] A.C. 154; *Port Jackson Stevedoring Pty Ltd v Salmond and Spraggon (Australia) Pty Ltd (The New York Star)* [1981] 1 W.L.R. 138, HL; *Celthene Pty Ltd v W.K.J. Hauliers Pty Ltd* [1981] 1 N.S.W.L.R. 606.

[58] See *Nippon Yusen Kaisha v International Import and Export Co. Ltd (The Elbe Maru)* [1978] 1 Lloyd's Rep. 206; *Broken Hill Pty Co. Ltd v Hapag-Lloyd Aktiengesellschaft* [1980] 2 N.S.W.L.R. 572; *cf. Gore v Van der Lann* [1967] 2 Q.B. 31; *Gillespie Bros & Co. Ltd v Roy Bowles Transport Ltd* [1973] Q.B. 400; *Neptune Orient Lines Ltd v J.V.C. (U.K.) Ltd (The Chevalier Roze)* [1983] 2 Lloyd's Rep. 438; *Deepak Fertilisers and Petrochemicals Corp. v ICI Chemicals and Polymers Ltd* [1998] 2 Lloyd's Rep. 139; [1999] 1 Lloyd's Rep. 387 at 401. For a more radical suggestion, that the defendant can himself plead such a promise in defence, see Birks, 1 Poly.L.Rev. 39 (1975); Birks and Beatson, 92 L.Q.R. 188 at 193 *et seq*. (1976).

[59] *cf. Woodar Investment Development Ltd v Wimpey Construction U.K. Ltd* [1980] 1 W.L.R. 277 at 300–301, HL.

stances be inferred,[60] a clearly formulated promise or set of promises ("circular indemnity clauses") are obviously more likely to be effective. Sale of goods situations involve the application of these principles in two different contexts. The first is that of an action against the seller by a person who did not buy the goods, but, for example, for whom they were bought or to whom they were given. Here the claimant will not be affected by exemptions in the contract of sale unless a contract between him and the seller can be detected[61] or there is a contract between the claimant and the actual buyer containing a promise not to sue. The second is that of a claim by the buyer against a person other than the seller, usually the manufacturer.[62] A clause in a contract of sale entered into by a retailer which purports to protect the manufacturer of the goods will again not be effective as such to do so unless it embodies a separate contract with the manufacturer, or a promise to the retailer not to sue the manufacturer. A contract with the manufacturer is sometimes, however, constituted by a separate guarantee. A person buying goods from a retailer is often given with them a document from the manufacturer which may guarantee them in certain respects, but which often also purports to exclude the manufacturer's liability in tort at common law, and sometimes the retailer's liability (which would be contractual) as well. Since the buyer normally has no privity of contract with the manufacturer and deals with the retailer alone, the manufacturer cannot rely on exemption clauses in the contract of sale when sued in tort, and can only rely on the exemption clause in the "guarantee" if a genuine collateral contract can be inferred between him and the buyer. If such a contract can be found, however, it may in principle protect him; though here conversely the exemption cannot operate in favour of the retailer, even if it purports to do so, unless it can be regarded as incorporated also into the main contract of sale, or again if it embodies a promise not to sue the retailer. The problems arising out of such guarantees are discussed together elsewhere.[63]

13–018 **Contracts (Rights of Third Parties) Act 1999.**[64] Such devices and arguments will become of far less significance in England and Wales by reason of the Contracts (Rights of Third Parties) Act, which confers right

---

[60] See *Snelling v John G. Snelling Ltd* [1973] 1 Q.B. 87 at 98.

[61] For examples of this problem, see *Lockett v A. and M. Charles Ltd* [1938] 4 All E.R. 170 (restaurant); *Walls v Centaur Co. Ltd* (1921) 126 L.T. 242 (purchase from manufacturer by employee of dealer for employee's personal use); *Cockerton v Naviera Aznar SA* [1960] 2 Lloyd's Rep. 450; *Hollingworth v Southern Ferries Ltd (The Eagle)* [1977] 2 Lloyd's Rep. 70 (boat tickets); *Cooke v Midland Ry Co.* (1892) 9 T.L.R. 147; *Hobbs v L. & S.W. Ry Co.* (1875) L.R. 10 Q.B. 111 (railway ticket); *MacRobertson Miller Airline Services v Commissioner of State Taxation (W.A.)* (1975) 133 C.L.R. 125 at 146–147 (airline ticket); *Varga v John Labatt Ltd* (1956) 6 D.L.R. (2d) 336. See also *Daly v General Steam Navigation Co. Ltd (The Dragon)* [1980] 2 Lloyd's Rep. 415; below, para.14–076.

[62] Below, paras 14–061 *et seq*.

[63] See below, paras 14–065 *et seq*. Guarantees of consumer goods are affected by s.5 of the Unfair Contract Terms Act 1977: below, para.13–097; and see below, paras 13–019, 14–080 *et seq.*, 14–008 *et seq.* as to the Consumer Protection Act 1987 and the Sale and Supply and Goods to Consumers Regulations 2002 (SI 2002/3045).

[64] See *Chitty on Contracts* (29th ed.), Vol.1, paras 14–039 *et seq.*, 18–084 *et seq.*; Treital, *Law of Contract* (11th ed.), pp.626 *et seq*.

to sue on third parties to contracts in certain circumstances.[65] This right also entitles such persons to avail themselves of exclusions or limitations of liability.[66] The term must expressly provide that the third party may take the benefit of the clause, or purport to confer such a benefit on him[67]; and the third party must be expressly identified in the contract by name, as a member of a class or as answering a particular description.[68] This may be relevant principally in the second of the two situations discussed above, where a contract of sale between a retailer and an end buyer contains a clause purporting to protect the manufacturer.[69] There will, however, be cases where the existing techniques are still relevant.[70]

Consumer Protection Act 1987. It should be noted that in both the situations referred to above, an action by a buyer against a manufacturer or (sometimes) an action by a third party against a seller, the defendant may also, where the defect causes personal injury or loss of or damage to property, be liable under the Consumer Protection Act 1987, by section 7 of which liability under the Act cannot be limited or excluded by any contract term, notice or other provision.[71] 13–019

3. Interpretation of Exemption Clauses

Strict interpretation. Exemption clauses are, where (as is common) there is room for argument as to their meaning and coverage, strictly construed *contra proferentem*. The first justification for this is that a party seeking to rely on such a clause must prove that he comes within it.[72] It can also be said that a person who puts forward a provision that is for his own benefit should only be allowed to rely on it if its meaning is clear, particularly if he participated in its insertion in the contract.[73] It can also be said that there is "an inherent improbability that the other party to such a contract including such a clause intended to release the *proferens* from a liability that would otherwise fall on him."[74] This assumes that there are 13–020

---

[65] s.1(1)(2).
[66] s.1(6).
[67] s.1(1).
[68] s.1(3).
[69] In the first situation, a donee from a buyer cannot have the burden of the contract between buyer and seller imposed on him, and the Act does not alter this. However, if the contract of sale is for the benefit of the prospective donee within the wording of the Act, and his action was to be regarded as based on the Act ("in reliance on section 1": s.3(1)), he would only be able to enforce it subject to its terms: s.3(2). It appears however that if he sues on his existing common law right, the existing common law applies: s.7(1). See *Chitty on Contracts* (29th ed.), Vol.1, paras 14–044, 14–045, 18–102.
[70] See *Chitty*, above.
[71] See below, paras 14–080 *et seq.*, 14–095 *et seq.*
[72] See *Chitty on Contracts* (29th ed.), Vol.1, para.14–08.
[73] See Staughton L.J. in *Youell v Bland, Welch & Co. Ltd* [1992] 2 Lloyd's Rep 127 at 134; see also *Pera Shipping Corp. v Petroship SA* [1984] 2 Lloyd's Rep. 363 at 365 *per* Staughton J.
[74] *Ailsa Craig Shipping Co. Ltd v Malvern Fishing Co. Ltd* [1983] 1 W.L.R. 964 at 970, *per* Lord Fraser of Tullybelton.

rules whereby such a liability would arise independently of the contract, which is sometimes (*e.g.* where a bailment is involved or where there is a potential liability in tort) but by no means always true; and it moves towards the now abandoned doctrine of fundamental breach, which is discussed below.[75] Whatever the basis of this strict interpretation, it is also applied to indemnity clauses[76]; though, as later explained,[77] there is authority for applying less strict criteria to clauses which merely limit the amount recoverable. Such a technique for controlling the effect of exemption clauses is found in many legal systems. There are numerous examples in the area of sale of goods. Since the Unfair Contract Terms Act came into operation, there has been less need for stringency, at least in the cases where the Act applies (which include domestic sales of goods). There are indeed clear indications that the English courts will take a more relaxed approach than was sometimes taken before the Act,[78] will not strain to detect ambiguities,[79] will not ascribe "tortured meanings" to exemption clauses[80] and will in general simply interpret such clauses in the context of the contract as a whole.[81] But although the Act contains nothing preserving the rules of interpretation, as compared with the rules for formation of contract, which are expressly confirmed,[82] it seems clear that the rules of interpretation must still operate[83]; and it has been said that the true interpretation of a clause must be ascertained before its reasonableness is assessed.[84] And the fact that the Act looks only to the reasonableness of including a particular clause in the contract rather than reasonableness of reliance on the clause in the case in question[85] means that they may be particularly useful when the question is not as to whether a clause is reasonable in itself but as to whether it is appropriate that it should be invoked in a specific set of circumstances.[86] It is, however, clear that all decisions prior to the Act of 1977 should be read in the light of the fact that the court has now in many cases the statutory power to declare exemption clauses ineffective on the facts.

---

[75] Below, paras 13–042 *et seq.*

[76] *Canada Steamship Lines Ltd v R.* [1952] A.C. 192; *Smith v South Wales Switchgear Co. Ltd* [1978] 1 W.L.R. 165; *EE Caledonia Ltd v Orbit Valve Co. Europe* [1994] 1 W.L.R. 221 and 1515; and see *Stent Foundations Ltd v M.J. Gleeson Group Plc* [2001] B.L.R. 134.

[77] Below, para.13–038.

[78] *Howard Marine and Dredging Co. Ltd v A. Ogden & Sons (Excavations) Ltd* [1978] Q.B. 574 at 594; *cf.* 599; *Photo Production Ltd v Securicor Transport Ltd* [1980] A.C. 827 at 843, 851; *George Mitchell (Chesterhall) Ltd v Finney Lock Seeds Ltd* [1983] 2 A.C. 803 at 814.

[79] *Ailsa Craig Shipping Co. Ltd v Malvern Fishing Co. Ltd* [1983] 1 W.L.R. 964 at 966; and see *Livingstone v Roskilly* [1992] 3 N.Z.L.R. 230.

[80] *George Mitchell* case, above, at p.810.

[81] See *Swiss Bank Corp. v Brinks Mat Ltd* [1986] 2 Lloyd's Rep. 79 at 92–93; see also *Darlington Futures Ltd v Delco Australia Pty Ltd* (1986) 161 C.L.R. 500.

[82] See s.11(2); above, para.13–012, below, para.13–021.

[83] See *Green v Cade Bros Farms* [1978] 1 Lloyd's Rep. 602; *George Mitchell* case, above.

[84] *Watford Electronics Ltd v Sanderson CFL Ltd* [2001] EWCA Civ 317; [2001] 1 All E.R. (Comm) 696 at [31] *et seq.*

[85] s.11(1).

[86] *cf.* below, para.13–086.

Cases where Unfair Contract Terms Act inapplicable. The Unfair Contract Terms Act 1977 regulates clauses purporting to exempt from liability for negligence in situations of business liability, clauses in consumer contracts and in standard terms, and attempts to exclude or restrict the implied obligations of the seller under sections 12 to 15 of the Sale of Goods Act.[87] It does not therefore apply to individually negotiated, non-consumer contracts which either do not involve business liability or else do not contain terms seeking to exempt from liability for negligence or for breach of the seller's obligations under sections 12 to 15 of the Act. Nor, more importantly, does it apply to international supply contracts, nor to contracts where English law is the proper law only by choice of the parties.[88] In such situations the cases on strict interpretation are not in principle affected by the presence of powers conferred on the courts by the Act.[89] But it should be noted that all these situations are more likely to have involved free negotiation between parties of equal bargaining power, so that a rigorous approach may well be less appropriate, whether or not this can be justified as a matter of law. "After this Act, in commercial matters generally, when the parties are not of unequal bargaining power, and when risks are normally borne by insurance, not only is the case for judicial intervention undemonstrated, but there is everything to be said, and this seems to have been Parliament's intention, for leaving the parties free to apportion the risks as they think fit and for respecting their decisions."[90] 13–021

Negligence. Clear words are needed to exempt from liability for negligence, for it is "inherently improbable that one party to the contract should intend to absolve the other party from the consequences of the latter's own negligence."[91] This is especially so where (as is usual) the negligence liability stems from a different legal category, the law of tort.[92] Thus it has been held that a term in a contract for the hire of a bicycle, purporting to exempt the owner from liability for personal injuries, only extended to his strict liability in contract and did not cover liability in negligence. A term 13–022

---

[87] By ss.2, 3 and 6: below, paras 13–093, 13–094, 13–083. S.6 also applies to hire purchase; and transactions related to sale are covered by s.7: below, para.13–085.

[88] By ss.26, 27(1): below, paras 13–099 *et seq*. There are also exclusions of specific contracts, not relevant to sale of goods: see SCh.1.

[89] Nor by those under the Unfair Terms in Consumer Contracts Regulations: below, para.13–103.

[90] *Photo Production Ltd v Securicor Transport Ltd* [1980] A.C. 827 at 843, *per* Lord Wilberforce. See also *Darlington Futures Ltd v Delco Australia Pty Ltd* (1986) 161 C.L.R. 500; *Hunter Engineering Co. v Syncrude Canada Ltd* [1989] 1 S.C.R. 426 at 464; (1989) 57 D.L.R. (4th) 321 at 343.

[91] *Gillespie Bros & Co. Ltd v Roy Bowles Transport Ltd* [1973] Q.B. 400 at 419, *per* Buckley L.J.; see, *e.g. A. M. Bisley & Co. Ltd v Thompson* [1982] 2 N.Z.L.R. 696. But *cf. George Mitchell (Chesterhall) Ltd v Finney Lock Seeds Ltd* [1983] 2 A.C. 803 at 814 (a case of a limitation clause: below, para.13–080). Since liability for fraud cannot be excluded (above, para.13–016) a clause may be interpreted as not covering fraud. This may become relevant when reasonableness is in issue: see *Government of Zanzibar v British Aerospace (Lancaster House) Ltd* [2000] 1 W.L.R. 2333 at 2346–2347, not following on this point *Thomas Witter Ltd v TBP Industries Ltd* [1996] 2 All E.R. 573. But compare the position as to set-off, below, para.13–039.

[92] See Howarth, 36 N.I.L.Q. 101 (1985).

specifically referring to negligence, or at least widely expressed (*e.g.* referring to loss "howsoever caused") is necessary.[93] The leading cases on this point do not relate to sale of goods,[94] and clauses exempting from liability for negligence are in any case controlled by the Unfair Contract Terms Act 1977.[95] But a seller may be liable in tort as well as in contract[96]; and where the Act does not apply this line of cases may well be relevant.

13–023 **Exclusion of particular duties.** Sometimes an exemption clause in a contract of sale relates only to certain specific implied duties: in such cases all other implied duties remain. Thus where there is an express disclaimer referring to quality alone, the duty as to compliance with description in a sale by description certainly remains,[97] and in one case where the words "no guarantee of quality or analysis is given" were immediately followed by a requirement that the goods should be in sound merchantable condition at the time of shipment, it was held that the disclaimer did not even extend to merchantability, let alone to non-conformity with description.[98] Again, a general clause such as "Seller not accountable for weight, measure or quality . . . the buyer . . . takes the responsibility of any latent defects" may be held too vague to exclude section 14 of the Sale of Goods Act 1979[99] and in general to refer only to such defects as do not prevent compliance with the statutory conditions. At the other end of the scale, where a sale by sample is of goods "guaranteed equal to sample only", though this phrase might exclude the provision of section 15(2)(c) of the Sale of Goods Act 1979 that the goods be of satisfactory quality,[1] it might not, if the sale is also by description, exclude the requirement of section 13(1) that they correspond with description.[2] Finally, it has been held that a clause purporting to exclude liability for misrepresentation does not exclude liability for a misrepresentation that has become also a warranty within the

---

[93] *White v John Warwick & Co. Ltd* [1953] 1 W.L.R. 1285 at 1294.
[94] See *Alderslade v Hendon Laundry Ltd* [1945] K.B. 189; *Canada Steamship Lines Ltd v R.* [1952] A.C. 192; *Hollier v Rambler Motors (A.M.C.) Ltd* [1972] 2 Q.B. 71; *Smith v South Wales Switchgear Ltd* [1978] 1 W.L.R. 165, HL. See also *Producer Meats (North Island) Ltd v Thomas Borthwick & Sons (Australia) Ltd* [1964] N.Z.L.R. 700; *Hawkes Bay and East Coast Aero Club Inc. v McLeod* [1972] N.Z.L.R. 289; *Chitty on Contracts* (29th ed.), Vol.1, paras 14–010—14–013; Treitel, *Law of Contract* (11th ed.), pp.222–225.
[95] Below, paras 13–092, 13–093.
[96] Above, para.12–121; *cf.* below, para.13–106.
[97] *Josling v Kingsford* (1863) 13 C.B. (N.S.) 447 ("quality approved"); *Azemar v Casella* (1867) L.R. 2 C.P. 677 ("should the quality prove inferior to the guarantee, a fair allowance to be made"); *Pinnock Bros v Lewis and Peat Ltd* [1923] 1 K.B. 690 ("the goods are not warranted free from defect rendering the same unmerchantable, which would not be apparent on reasonable examination": s.13 unaffected. But see further as to this clause below, para.13–025).
[98] *Wimble, Sons & Co. v Lillico & Son* (1922) 38 T.L.R. 296.
[99] Above, paras 11–024 *et seq.*; *Henry Kendall & Sons v William Lillico & Sons* [1969] 2 A.C. 31 at 90–91, 104–105, 114, 130.
[1] Above, para.11–080; *Champanhac & Co. Ltd v Waller Ltd* [1948] 2 All E.R. 724.
[2] Above, paras 11–001 *et seq.* See *Nichol v Godts* (1854) 10 Exch.191. The wording in this case was "warranted only equal to samples." If these words were used nowadays, the question might arise as to whether they exclude even s.15(2)(c), which lays down a *condition* of satisfactory quality.

contract[3]; and that to exclude liability even for misrepresentation alone, the clause would have to be very clearly expressed.[4]

"No warranty is given." Sometimes the terms of a contract contain a provision to the effect that "no warranty is given with goods sold", or a similar clause. It seems that this may simply operate to indicate that statements made at or about the time of contracting are not to be interpreted as express promises or warranties, and does not affect implied terms that are as a matter of law made part of the contract, unless circumstances indicate the contrary.[5] Sometimes it merely gives notice that an agent has no authority to warrant, and so negatives the possibility of apparent authority.[6] But even where it is more generally effective to exclude liability, there may be cases where such a clause is overridden by a prior collateral contract. Thus in *Webster v Higgin*,[7] the words "no warranty is given or implied" were held not clear enough to exclude liability for a promise made prior to the formation of the contract, that a car was in good order. 13–024

Exclusion of warranties. In many contracts, however, no collateral contract can be established, or the clause excluding warranties is drafted in more comprehensive terms. In such a case the word "warranty" will usually be regarded as bearing the same specialised meaning which it bears in the Sale of Goods Act 1979, *i.e.* a term breach of which only gives rise to a right in damages.[8] Thus if only the word "warranty" is used the seller will normally be held not to have contracted out of liability for breach of conditions, *e.g.* those implied by sections 13,[9] 14[10] and 15[11] of the Act. It should be noted that this construction is to some extent peculiar to sale of goods and related transactions such as hire-purchase, for in other contracts 13–025

---

[3] *Thomas Witter Ltd v TBP Industries Ltd* [1996] 2 All E.R. 573.

[4] "He must bring it home that he is limiting his liability for falsehoods he may have told": *ibid.* at p.596 *per* Jacob J.

[5] See *Clarke v Army and Navy Co-operative Society Ltd* [1903] 1 K.B. 155.

[6] See *Clarke v Army & Navy Co-operative Society Ltd*, above, at p.167; but *cf. Mendelssohn v Normand Ltd* [1970] 1 Q.B. 177.

[7] [1948] 2 All E.R. 127; see also *Couchman v Hill* [1947] K.B. 554 ("giving no warranty whatever"); *Harling v Eddy* [1951] 2 K.B. 739 (nothing "is sold with a warranty unless specially mentioned at the time of offering"); *Mendelssohn v Normand Ltd*, above ("no variation of these conditions will bind the [defendants] unless made in writing signed by their duly authorised manager").

[8] Sale of Goods Act 1979, ss.11(3), 61(1); above, paras 10–023.

[9] Above, para.11–001; *Wallis, Son and Wells v Pratt and Haynes* [1911] A.C. 394, discussed *infra*; *W. Barker (Jr) & Co. Ltd v Edward T Agius Ltd* (1927) 33 Com.Cas. 120 ("no warranty is expressed or implied and sellers accept no responsibility in regard to the description, size, quality, condition or fitness"); *Nicholson and Venn v Smith Marriott* (1947) 177 L.T. 189 (auction: "no warranty is given or to be implied by the description in the catalogue"); *Elder Smith Goldsbrough Mort Ltd v McBride* [1976] 2 N.S.W.L.R. 631 (auction).

[10] Above, paras 11–024 *et seq.*; *Baldry v Marshall* [1925] 1 K.B. 260 (exclusion of "guarantee or warranty"); *Cammell Laird & Co. v Manganese Bronze and Brass Co. Ltd* [1934] A.C. 402 at 431 ("to be guaranteed against defective material and workmanship"); *Harling v Eddy*, above.

[11] Above, paras 11–073 *et seq.*

the term "warranty" may be far less precisely used and indeed often refers simply to contractual promises.[12] This interpretation will, however, be applied even where the goods have been accepted so that the breach of condition must be treated as a warranty by virtue of section 11(4),[13] for the term broken is still in its nature a condition. The leading case on this point, *Wallis, Son and Wells v Pratt and Haynes*,[14] involved a very strict interpretation of a widely drafted clause in a sale of seed, running "Sellers give no warranty express or implied as to growth, description, or any other matters, and they shall not be held to guarantee or warrant the fitness for any particular purpose of any grain, seed, flour, cake or any other article sold by them or its freedom from injurious quality or from latent defect." The sellers had purportedly sold by sample common English sainfoin seed. The seed supplied was identical with sample, but was giant sainfoin, a seed of inferior quality which was indistinguishable as seed. The House of Lords, reversing the Court of Appeal,[15] held that the clause did not cover the breach of condition (presumably that in section 13[16]) which had been committed, despite the fact that most descriptive statements are by the Act made conditions,[17] so that the exclusion of warranties as to description was made almost meaningless. So also in *Henry Kendall & Sons v. William Lillico & Sons*,[18] it was held that a clause reading "The goods are not warranted free from defect, rendering same unmerchantable, which would not be apparent on reasonable examination, any statute or rule of law to the contrary notwithstanding" did not cover breaches of the condition as to merchantable (now, satisfactory) quality contained in section 14(2).[19]

13–026 **Exclusion of implied conditions and/or warranties.** Sometimes the terminology has been wider and covered implied warranties and also implied conditions. In such cases it may still be held that *express* warranties and conditions are not affected. Thus in *Andrews Bros (Bournemouth) Ltd v Singer & Co. Ltd*,[20] a clause in a contract for the sale of cars read "All conditions, warranties and liabilities implied by statute, common law or otherwise are excluded." The contract was for "new Singer cars" but a car supplied was not a "new car" within the meaning of the contract. It was held that the clause did not cover the failure to deliver a new Singer car. Despite the fact that section 13(1) of the Sale of Goods Act 1979, which

[12] Above, para.10–015.
[13] Above, paras 12–038 *et seq*.
[14] [1911] A.C. 394.
[15] [1910] 2 K.B. 1003. The Court of Appeal had held that since the right to reject had been lost the condition had become a warranty *ex below facto* and so was covered by the clause.
[16] See [1911] A.C. at 398; as to s.13, above, paras 11–001 *et seq*.
[17] See above, paras 11–013 *et seq*.
[18] [1969] 2 A.C. 31 at 84, 95–96, 107, 109, 114, 126.
[19] Nor would it cover a breach of s.14(3): *ibid.*; nor of s.13: *Pinnock Bros v Lewis and Peat Ltd* [1923] 1 K.B. 690. But *cf. W. N. Lindsay & Co. Ltd v European Grain and Shipping Agency Ltd* [1963] 1 Lloyd's Rep. 437 at 443–444, where a different view is taken of the significance of the word "warranted". See also as to this clause *Canada Atlantic Grain Export Co. v Eilers* (1929) 35 Ll.L.R. 206.
[20] [1934] 1 K.B. 17.

lays down a condition that goods correspond with description,[21] refers to an "implied condition", the court held that the term broken was not implied but express, and so not covered. The same reasoning would apply to an exclusion of implied warranties alone: express warranties would not be excluded.

Intermediate terms. The clauses to which the above two paragraphs relate were drafted at a time when it may have been assumed that, at least in the contract of sale of goods, all terms could be classified as conditions or warranties; or, if they were not drafted at that time, were based on that assumption. It has been explained that the last 25 years have shown that these categories are not exhaustive, and that one of the ways of formulating the law as it now stands is to say that there is a third type of term, the innominate or intermediate term.[22] This may therefore give the courts, where the words "condition" and "warranty" are not accompanied by any other word such as "term", "statement" or "liability", a further opportunity of interpreting such clauses strictly: it may be said that the wording is not apt to cover innominate or intermediate terms. It is, however, possible to interpret the word "warranty" as intended to cover all terms which are not conditions. Indeed, as has been pointed out, this is an alternative way of formulating the law of breach of contract as it stands at present.[23] The problem can from the draftsman's point of view be avoided by the use of a word such as "undertakings". 13–027

"With all faults." In a number of cases this and similar phrases such as "with all faults and imperfections" have been interpreted as referring to matters of quality, merchantability, etc. only, and therefore not affecting the duty in a sale by description to deliver goods conforming to the description.[24] Thus in an old case there was a sale of a "copper-fastened vessel" "with all faults, without allowance for any defect whatsoever", it was held that the clause did not protect the seller where the vessel was not copper-fastened at all, for "with all faults" must mean "with all faults which it may have consistently with its being the thing described."[25] It has also been held that the phrase does not affect the duty in a sale by sample under section 15(2)(a) to supply goods that correspond with sample.[26] Such a phrase 13–028

---

[21] As to which see above, paras 11–001 *et seq.*

[22] Above, paras 10–029 *et seq.*, 12–023.

[23] Above, para.10–033.

[24] Above, paras 11–001 *et seq.*: see *Peters & Co. v Planner* (1895) 11 T.L.R. 169 (Galician eggs); *Robert A. Munro & Co. Ltd v Meyer* [1930] 2 K.B. 312 (meat and bone meal).

[25] *Shepherd v Kain* (1821) 5 B. & A. 240 at 241. See also *Fletcher v Bowsher* (1819) 2 Stark. 561. But *cf. Taylor v Bullen* (1850) 5 Exch. 779. But as to "*as seen* with all its faults and without warranty", see below, para.13–067.

[26] Above, para.11–079; *Champanhac & Co. Ltd v Waller & Co. Ltd* [1948] 2 All E.R. 724 ("as sample taken away . . . with all faults and imperfections").

would, however, negative the duties under section 14[27] or in a sale by sample that under section 15(2)(c),[28] unless there are indications to the contrary.[29]

13–029 **Provisions exempting for errors of description.** Frequently, a clause has required the buyer to take goods "with all faults imperfections and errors of description" or made the seller "not accountable for errors of description" or the like. There is some authority that such a clause would exclude not only the provisions of section 14[30] but also section 13[31] (though presumably not the duty as to conformity with sample in section 15(2)(a)[32] when this is applicable). Equally, however, there are cases where it is suggested that such terminology should be confined to minor errors of description and cannot affect the main duty of the contract.[33] The chief difficulty here is that it seems that most descriptive statements are part of the condition as to description for the purposes of section 13 and will therefore rarely be lesser terms.[34] It is submitted that it is unwise to try to solve the problem by laying down rules: too much turns on the context in which a clause is found. Where the general nature of the article to be sold is clear, a superimposed exemption clause referring to errors of description or the like may be interpreted to operate consistently with the main purpose of the contract. Thus it may be confined to minor errors of description, or treated as showing that words used are not intended to be part of the description but

---

27 Above, paras 11–024 *et seq.*; see, *e.g. Champanhac & Co. Ltd v Waller & Co. Ltd*, above, at p.726; *Lloyd del Pacifico v Board of Trade* (1930) 35 Ll.L.R. 217; *Ward v Hobbs* (1877) 3 Q.B.D. 150, affirmed (1878) 4 App.Cas. 13; *Baglehole v Walters* (1811) 3 Camp. 154. But see *D. & M. Trailers (Halifax) Ltd v Stirling* [1978] R.T.R. 468, where the Court of Appeal expressed doubts as to whether such a clause would exclude s.14. And positive concealment of a defect might give rise to an action in deceit: *Ward v Hobbs, above; Peters & Co. v Planner*, above; above, para.12–012.

28 Above, paras 11–097 *et seq.*; *Champanhac & Co. Ltd v Waller & Co. Ltd*, above.

29 See *Wimble, Sons & Co. v Lillico & Son* (1922) 38 T.L.R. 296, where an express term as to merchantability followed the "with all faults" clause; *Elder Smith Goldsbrough Mort Ltd v McBride* [1976] 2 N.S.W.L.R. 631, where the clause was preceded by a reference to the goods being available for inspection and was held only to cover defects discernible by inspection.

30 Above, paras 11–024 *et seq.*

31 Above, paras 11–001 *et seq.* See *Freeman v Baker* (1833) 5 B. & Ad. 797; *Pettitt v Mitchell* (1842) 4 Man. & G. 819; *Taylor v Bullen* (1850) 5 Exch.779; *Lloyd del Pacifico v Board of Trade* (1930) 35 Ll.L.R. 217 at 223 (but there was no misdescription); *Couchman v Hill* [1947] K.B. 554 at 557. "Faults" and "errors of description" must be read disjunctively: *Lloyd del Pacifico v Board of Trade*, above.

32 Above, para.11–079.

33 See *Lloyd del Pacifico v Board of Trade*, above, at p.224 ("the steamer . . . shall be taken with all faults and errors of description without any allowance or abatement"); *Harrison v Knowles and Foster* [1917] 2 K.B. 606 at 610 (affirmed on other grounds [1918] 1 K.B. 608) ("not accountable for errors in description"); *Cotter v Luckie* [1918] N.Z.L.R. 811 at 816 (auction: clause referred to "error or misdescription as to age, number, sex or condition of any stock offered for sale"); *Nicholson & Venn v Smith Marriott* (1947) 177 L.T. 189 at 191 (auction: "the genuineness or authenticity of any lot is not guaranteed . . . No allowance whatsoever will be made for errors in description, quantity, weight or measurement, but the lots are to be cleared as shown at the sale").

34 Above, paras 11–001 *et seq.*

are merely puffs or names used for convenience of reference to the subject-matter.[35] It may perhaps also be held not to cover a deliberate misdescription.[36] A clause allowing for 10 per cent variation in "quantity, quality, design, finish, colour, ways, weight, combination, construction" has been held ineffective to protect against complete non-conformity with sample.[37] On the other hand, such an exemption clause may sometimes reasonably be interpreted as altering the main purpose of the contract by reducing the definitional content of the subject-matter. It may well be that this latter method of interpretation has received insufficient attention, and that the tendency to determine the purpose of the contract without reference to the exemption clauses contained in it has been too indiscriminately employed.[38] Thus it is certainly possible (statute apart) to sell seeds on the terms that the seller makes no guarantee that they really are the seeds described, and some cases have upheld the validity of such an arrangement.[39] And a monetary limitation of liability in case of supply of the wrong seed has been held effective at common law.[40] Some of the cases cited above may therefore be open to reconsideration in the light of more recent case law.[41]

Clauses in the form of acknowledgments and non-reliance clauses. 13–030
Sometimes clauses which should really be classified as exemption clauses are couched in the form of acknowledgments of fact. Thus in *Lowe v Lombank Ltd*,[42] a hire-purchase case, the hirer entered into a contract containing the clause "The hirer acknowledges that he has examined the goods prior to the signing of this agreement and that there are no defects in the goods which such examination ought to have revealed and that the goods are of merchantable quality. The hirer further acknowledges and agrees that he has not made known to the owners expressly or by implication the particular purpose for which the goods are required, and that the goods are reasonably fit for the purpose for which they are in fact required." In some cases such clauses have simply been treated as exclusions of section 14 of the Sale of Goods Act 1979,[43] and either held

---

[35] *cf. Reardon Smith Line Ltd v Yngvar Hansen-Tangen* [1976] 1 W.L.R. 989 (hull number of newbuilding ship).
[36] Below, para.13–052.
[37] *Mohsin Abdullah Alesayi v Brooly Exim Pte. Ltd* [1993] 3 Singapore L.R. 433 (denim jeans).
[38] *cf.* below, para.13–044.
[39] *Reynolds v Wrench* (1888) 23 L.J.N.C. 27; *Howcroft and Watkins v Perkins* (1900) 16 T.L.R. 217 (sellers "give no warranty express or implied as to description, quality, productiveness, or any other matter . . . and will not be in any way responsible for the crop"); *cf. Howcroft v Laycock* (1898) 14 T.L.R. 460. See also *Carter v Crick* (1859) 4 H. & N. 412; *Rutherford & Son v Miln & Co.*, 1941 S.C. 125.
[40] *George Mitchell (Chesterhall) Ltd v Finney Lock Seeds Ltd* [1983] 2 A.C. 803. But the clause was then held ineffective under statute: below, para.13–089.
[41] *cf.* above, para.13–020.
[42] [1960] 1 W.L.R. 196. See also *Mohar Investment Co. v Wilkins* (1957) 108 L.J. 140; *Thomas Witter Ltd v TBP Industries Ltd* [1996] 2 All E.R. 573 at 597.
[43] Above, paras 11–024 *et seq.*; see *Webster v Higgin* [1948] 2 All E.R. 127; *Yeoman Credit Ltd v Apps* [1962] 2 Q.B. 508; *Harper v South Island Holdings Ltd* [1959] N.Z.L.R. 629; *Cornwall Properties Ltd v King* [1966] N.Z.L.R. 239; *Francis v Trans-Canada Trailer Sales Ltd* (1969) 6 D.L.R. (3d) 705; *Western Tractor Ltd v Dyck* (1969) 7 D.L.R. (3d) 535; *Hall v Queensland Truck Centre Pty Ltd* [1970] Qd.R. 231.

effective, held inapplicable under the doctrine of fundamental breach as then understood,[44] or under the Unfair Contract Terms Act 1977[45] or because of a collateral warranty.[46] It has also been held that clauses excluding evidence ordinarily admissible are to be strictly construed.[47] But such clauses do not purport to exclude terms from the contract, rather to establish facts that render terms inapplicable, and they are certainly not promissory in form.[48] Therefore they should be treated as statements only, which may in appropriate cases tend to prove the truth of what they assert,[49] and may sometimes raise an estoppel. But where the facts acknowledged are not true, the seller will not normally be able to rely on an estoppel, for to do so he must establish that the statement was intended to be acted upon and that he believed it to be true and acted in reliance on it. This will rarely be the case: it certainly was not in *Lowe v Lombank Ltd*.[50] They may also be interpreted strictly.[51] It seems therefore that such clauses will not be conclusive unless they can be regarded as genuinely representing the intention of the parties; save that a clause like that quoted might estop the buyer from establishing that he had not examined the goods, even if he had not, provided the seller reasonably thought he had.[52] A clause saying that goods are sold "as seen tested and approved" can be subjected to the same sort of analysis, save that it might in some cases reduce the description of the contract goods.[53] Similar problems occur in relation to "entire agreement" clauses, which are dealt with elsewhere.[54] They may themselves contain no exclusions of liability (though sometimes they do); but they usually contain or are accompanied by an acknowledgment of non-reliance on representations not incorporated into the contract. To such acknowledgments similar principles apply: they can raise what has been called an "evidential estoppel",[55] but not in favour of a person who did not

---

[44] Below, paras 13–042 *et seq*.

[45] Below, paras 13–062 *et seq.*; *Lutton v Saville Tractors (Belfast) Ltd* [1986] 12 N.I.L.R.B. 1 at 19 ("transparent attempts to escape the operation of s.6(2)(a) of the 1977 Act", *per* Carswell J.); *Sovereign Finance Ltd v Silver Crest Furniture Ltd* [1997] C.C.L.R. 76 (hire-purchase: tripartite transaction).

[46] Above, paras 10–012 *et seq.*, 13–016.

[47] *W. N. Lindsay & Co. Ltd v European Grain & Shipping Agency Ltd* [1963] 1 Lloyd's Rep. 437 at 445; *Nile Co., etc. v H. & J.M. Bennett (Commodities) Ltd* [1986] 1 Lloyd's Rep. 555 at 588.

[48] See *Lowe v Lombank Ltd*, above, at p.204.

[49] See *Criss v Alexander* (1928) 28 S.R. (N.S.W.) 297 (evidence of reliance held wrongly rejected).

[50] Above. See also *Mohsin Abdullah Alesayi v Brooks Exim Pte Ltd* [1993] 3 Singapore L.R. 433 (clause stating (wrongly) that sellers were merely "shippers in transit").

[51] *Rorison v McKey* [1952] N.Z.L.R. 398; *Kemp v Dalziel* [1956] N.Z.L.R. 1030 (inapplicable to matters not ascertainable on inspection).

[52] The question of such an estoppel was left undecided in *Thornett and Fehr v Beers & Son* [1919] 1 K.B. 486.

[53] See *Beale v Taylor* [1967] 1 W.L.R. 1193 at 1196. In *Hughes v Hall* [1981] R.T.R. 430, a criminal case, the words "sold as seen and inspected" were held to imply an exclusion of s.13 of the Sale of Goods Act; but the case was doubted in *Cavendish-Woodhouse Ltd v Manley* [1982] L.G.R. 376. See below, para.13–067.

[54] See below, para.13–056.

[55] *E. Grimstead & Son Ltd v McGarrigan* (CA unreported), October 27, 1999, *per* Chadwick L.J.

rely on the statement as to non-reliance by the other party.[56] In this respect they may not always be effective in practice.

13–031 **Exclusion of conditions, warranties and liabilities express and implied.** It will be recalled that in *Andrews Bros (Bournemouth) Ltd v Singer & Co. Ltd*,[57] a clause excluding all conditions, warranties and liabilities implied by statute, common law or otherwise was held not to apply to express terms. Difficulty was, however, caused by the dictum in that case of Scrutton L.J. "If a vendor desires to protect himself from liability in such a case he must do so by much clearer language than this"[58]; and it is sometimes said that such complete protection was achieved in *L'Estrange v F. Graucob Ltd*.[59] In this case, on the sale of a cigarette vending machine which proved unsatisfactory by reason of becoming easily jammed, the seller was held protected by a clause: "This agreement contains all the terms and conditions under which I agree to purchase the machine specified above, and any *express or* implied condition, statement, or warranty, statutory or otherwise, not stated herein is hereby excluded."[60] It is sometimes suggested that this case is authority for the possibility of excluding all express and implied conditions. But it is difficult to see that a contract which did this would have any content: there must be some basic contractual duty, though no doubt a widely drafted clause could reduce this to something very limited.[61] In fact this particular clause seems (apart from the ever-present problems of unequal bargaining power) unobjectionable: it simply restricts the contractual terms to those stated on the paper. The contract was clearly stated elsewhere in the document as being for "One Six Column Junior Ilam Automatic Machine" and there can be little doubt that as a matter of interpretation the exemption clause did not give the seller the privilege of delivering anything except an article corresponding with that description.

13–032 **Clauses excluding the right to reject.** Clauses frequently appear in commercial transactions excluding the right to reject. It is clear, first, that such clauses do not of themselves exclude the right to sue for damages,[62]

---

[56] *Watford Electronics Ltd v Sanderson CFL Ltd* [2001] EWCA Civ. 317; [2001] 1 All E.R. (Comm) 696; *E. Grimstead & Son Ltd v McGarrigan*, above, questioning dicta in *Thomas Witter Ltd v TBP Industries Ltd* [1996] 2 All E.R. 573. As to the position under s.3 of the Misrepresentation Act 1967 see below, paras 13–055, 13–056.

[57] [1934] 1 K.B. 17; above, para.13–026.

[58] At p.23.

[59] [1934] 2 K.B. 394. Though, contrary to what is sometimes suggested, the clause in the second case cannot have been drafted with these words in mind, as the agreement in the second case was signed eight months before the hearing of the first. See also *Mechanical Horse (Australasia) Pty Ltd v Broken Hill Council* (1941) 41 S.R. (N.S.W.) 135.

[60] Emphasis added.

[61] *cf. Suisse Atlantique Société d'Armement Maritime v NV Rotterdamsche Kolen Centrale* [1967] 1 A.C. 361 at 432; below, para.13–045.

[62] *Szymonowski & Co. v Beck & Co.* [1923] 1 K.B. 457, affirmed on other grounds but approved on this point [1924] A.C. 43 at 52, below, para.13–038; *Ashington Piggeries Ltd v Christopher Hill Ltd* [1972] A.C. 441 at 471 ("the goods shall be taken with all faults and defects, damaged or inferior, if any, at valuation to be arranged mutually or by arbitration"). But if "the goods" are not supplied even the right to reject persists: below, para.15–033. And see further as to this clause below, n.69. Nor does a clause specifying how damages are to be assessed bar rejection: *Roth, Schmidt & Co. v D. Nagase & Co. Ltd* (1920) 2 Ll. L.R. 36.

which might, where the goods are worthless, amount to the whole price paid; though they may be and often are accompanied by a clause which does bar that right.[63] The question next arises how such clauses are to be analysed: whether they are contractual promises to waive the right to reject for breach of condition, or whether they indicate that the terms to which they apply are not conditions but warranties, and thus modify the normal contractual terms. The second interpretation seems preferable, in view of the fact that the cases treat them like other exemption clauses and hold that they do not, unless clearly drafted so as to achieve that effect, apply to complete failure to supply the contract goods,[64] a breach of contract for which there seems no reason why the right to reject should not be waived.[65] This view also has judicial support: an alleged usage to the same effect as such a clause has been said to prevent an implied condition arising, and to turn it from a condition into a mere warranty.[66]

13–033 **Inapplicable to goods not of contract description.** A line of cases relating to sales of timber has established that a clause such as "Buyer shall not reject the goods herein specified but shall accept and pay for them in terms of contract against shipping documents" only prevents rejection where the "goods herein specified" have in fact been supplied and does not apply where the goods supplied do not conform with their description.[67] Reasoning similar to that found in these cases applies also to other similar phraseology[68] and to contracts relating to other commodities.[69] The description of goods has in these cases been widely interpreted to cover not only the measurement and composition of the goods, but also stipulations as to when they

[63] As to such clauses, see below, para.13–034. See also below, paras 18–275 *et seq.*
[64] See below, para.13–033.
[65] Coote, *Exception Clauses* (1964), pp.150–152.
[66] See *Re Walkers, Winser and Hamm and Shaw, Son & Co.* [1904] 2 K.B. 152 at 158; *Re North Western Rubber Co. Ltd and Hüttenbach & Co.* [1908] 2 K.B. 907 at 912 (actual decision overruled by *Produce Brokers Co. Ltd v Olympia Oil and Cake Co. Ltd* [1916] 1 A.C. 314).
[67] *Montague L. Meyer Ltd v Kivisto* (1929) 35 Ll.L.R. 265; *Montague L. Meyer Ltd v Osakeyhtio Carelia Timber Co. Ltd* (1930) 36 Com.Cas. 17; *Montague L. Meyer Ltd v Travaru* (1930) 37 Ll.L.R. 204; *Joseph Green v Arcos Ltd* (1931) 39 Ll.L.R. 229; *White Sea Timber Trust Ltd v W. W. North Ltd* (1932) 44 Ll.L.R. 390; *Vsesojwzoje Objedinenije "Exportles" v T. W. Allen & Sons Ltd* [1938] 3 All E.R. 375.
[68] *Vigers Bros v Sanderson Bros* [1901] 1 K.B. 608 ("buyers shall not reject any of the goods": the clause "does not operate so as to force the buyer to take goods which are neither within nor about the specification nor commercially within its meaning": p.611); *Wilensko, etc. v Fenwick & Co. Ltd* [1938] 3 All E.R. 429 ("the goods herein named"); *Smeaton, Hanscomb & Co. Ltd v Sassoon I. Setty, Son & Co.* [1953] 1 W.L.R. 1468 ("the buyer shall . . . accept the goods as shipped"); *C. Leary & Co. v Francis Briggs & Co.* (1904) 6 F. (Ct. of Sess.) 857. See further as to such clauses, below, paras 18–275 *et seq.*
[69] *Robert A. Munro & Co. Ltd v Meyer* [1930] 2 K.B. 312 (meat and bone meal: "the goods to be taken with all faults and defects, damaged or inferior, if any, at a valuation to be arranged mutually or by arbitration"). But it is not clear that this clause is in any case clear enough to disallow rejection at all: see *Modiano Bros & Son v H. T. Pearson & Co. Ltd* (1929) 34 Ll.L.R. 52; *Ashington Piggeries Ltd v Christopher Hill Ltd* [1969] 3 All E.R. 1496 at 1522–1523; [1972] A.C. 441 at 471.

are to be ready for shipment,[70] as to their marks[71] and their stowage, *e.g.* "under deck".[72] In one case when wider phraseology was used, "whatever the difference of the shipment may be in value from the grade, type or description specified, it is understood that any such question shall not . . . entitle the buyer to reject the delivery or any part thereof" the court, however, fell back on a narrower definition of "description", and held that terms as to shipment were independent and not part of the description so that rejection was still allowed.[73] In *"Agroexport" v NV Goorden Import Cy. SA*,[74] Sellers J. rejected the suggestion that such clauses could not exclude the duty to deliver goods conforming with the contract description and said that the clause in that case clearly did so and was valid.[75] It is submitted, however, that a clause will not easily be held to exclude this duty once the contract description has been determined, but that it may be relevant to the determination of what the contract description is; this seems the proper explanation of the clauses in that case, which formed a comprehensive code for rejection[76] and forbade rejection for some deficiencies while permitting it in others. Similarly in *Wilkinson v Barclay*,[77] another case of sale of timber, a clause: "The lots are offered where and as they are, . . . and the sum offered will be subject to no allowance for any faults, defects, errors of description, measurement, quantity or for any cause and without any warranty whatever" was held to go to description and show that "the amount was not a firm contractual amount." This view is consistent with the analysis of the nature of such clauses offered in the preceding paragraph. Doubts are expressed in some cases as to what such clauses do cover if they do not apply to failure to supply the contract goods[78]: the answer to this depends on the drafting of the clause, but in the "goods herein specified" clause considered above the exclusion seems to be of section 14 of the Sale of Goods Act 1979,[79] and such clauses, by reference to "quality", frequently

---

[70] *Montague L. Meyer Ltd v Osakeyhtio Carelia Timber Co. Ltd*, above. *Cf. Montague L. Meyer Ltd v Kivisto*, above ("to be properly seasoned" not part of description).
[71] *Vsesojwzoje Objedinenije "Exportles" v T. W. Allen & Sons Ltd*, above.
[72] *Montague L. Meyer Ltd v Travaru*, above; *White Sea Timber Trust Ltd v W. W. North Ltd*, above.
[73] *J. Aron & Co. v Comptoir Wegimont* [1921] 3 K.B. 435.
[74] [1956] 1 Lloyd's Rep. 319; see also *Duncombe v Porter* (1953) 90 C.L.R. 295; *W. E. Marshall & Co. v Lewis and Peat (Rubber) Ltd* [1963] 1 Lloyd's Rep. 562 (time limit on rejection); *Gill & Duffus SA v Berger Co. Inc.* [1983] 1 Lloyd's Rep. 622 at 626, 628–630, 632–633; [1984] A.C. 382 at 393–394. *Cf. W. N. Lindsay & Co. Ltd v European Grain and Shipping Agency Ltd, ibid.*, 437 (prescribed procedure not exclusive); *NV Bunge v Cie. Noga d'Importation et d'Exportation (The Bow Cedar)* [1980] 2 Lloyd's Rep. 601; *Daudruy v Tropical Products Sales SA* [1986] Lloyd's Rep. 535 (certificate of analysis not conclusive as to description).
[75] See p.325.
[76] For an example of this in a shipbuilding contract see *China Shipbuilding Corp. v Nippon Yusen Kabukishi Kaisha (The Seta Masu)* [2000] 1 Lloyd's Rep. 367.
[77] [1946] 1 All E.R. 387; actual decision revsd. [1946] 2 All E.R. 337, below, para.13–034.
[78] See *Montague L. Meyer Ltd v Kivisto* (1929) 35 Ll.L.R. 265 at 268; *Montague L. Meyer Ltd v Osakeyhtio Carelia Timber Co. Ltd* (1930) 36 Com.Cas. 17 at 27.
[79] Above, paras 11–024 *et seq.*

make this clear.[80] Terms to similar effect may be imported by custom or usage[81]: they can be regarded either as exclusion clauses incorporated by usage under section 55(1) of the Sale of Goods Act 1979,[82] or as customs as to the meaning of the description of the particular goods in the trade.[83]

13–034 **Clauses excluding any right to damages.** A clause may appear to exclude any right to damages. It seems that such a clause would be interpreted if possible so as only to cover minor matters, or only to exclude rejection[84]; or to confine a buyer to claiming the return of the price and to exclude further liability.[85] But if it clearly applies to an apparent contractual duty and makes no further provision, the effect must be to extinguish that duty[86]; it would then be a matter of construction whether the stipulation concerned would stand as a non-promissory condition precedent[87] or have no effect at all. In *Wilkinson v Barclay*[88] (the relevant wording of the contract in which is given above[89]), it was held at first instance that the effect of the clause used was to bar not only the right of rejection but also the right to claim damages for short delivery. On the other hand, the price paid had been based on the estimated measurements of the timber, and it was held at first instance that this was only payable in respect of timber delivered: the clause did not deprive the buyer of his right to recover back money paid for timber specified but not delivered.[90] The Court of Appeal, however, held that there was an out-and-out sale at a price per cubic foot on the estimated quantity of timber and that it was not intended that there should be an allowance on either side if the estimate proved wrong.[91]

13–035 **Cancelling clauses.** Cancelling clauses can take many forms. Sometimes they simply make the stipulation, on non-performance or non-occurrence of which cancellation can occur, a condition. Sometimes they can permit

---

[80] See, *e.g. Central Meat Products Co. Ltd v J. v McDaniel Ltd* [1952] 1 Lloyd's Rep. 562 ("should any dispute refer to quality or condition, the buyer shall accept the goods . . ."); *Smith Brothers (Hull) Ltd v Gosta Jacobsson & Co.* [1961] 2 Lloyd's Rep. 522 ("Buyer's right of rejection shall not be exercised where the claim is limited to questions of . . . quality unless the shipment . . . as a whole . . . is not in respect of such heads of claim a fair delivery under the Contract from a commercial standpoint"); *Oleificio Zucchi SpA v Northern Sales Ltd* [1965] 2 Lloyd's Rep. 496; *Modiano Bros & Son v H. T. Pearson & Co. Ltd* (1929) 34 Ll.L.R. 52.

[81] See *Re Walkers, Winser and Hamm and Shaw, Son & Co.* [1904] 2 K.B. 152 at 158; *Re North Western Rubber Co. Ltd and Hüttenbach & Co.* [1908] 2 K.B. 907 (actual decision overruled by *Produce Brokers Co. Ltd v Olympia Oil and Cake Co. Ltd* [1916] 1 A.C. 314); but such a custom may be unreasonable: see *Sinidino, Ralli & Co. v Kitchen & Co.* (1883) Cab. & El. 217 at 220. As to custom and usage in general, see above, para.11–088.

[82] Above, para.1–013.

[83] Above, para.11–088.

[84] See cases cited above, para.13–032; *cf. Szymonowski & Co. v Beck & Co.* [1923] 1 K.B. 457 (affirmed [1924] A.C. 43 *sub nom. Szymanowski*), below, para.13–038.

[85] *e.g. R. W. Green Ltd v Cade Bros Farms* [1978] 1 Lloyd's Rep. 602.

[86] See Coote, *Exception Clauses* (1964), pp.152–153; *Photo Production Ltd v Securicor Transport Ltd* [1980] A.C. 827 at 850.

[87] Above, para.10–039.

[88] [1946] 1 All E.R. 387; [1946] 2 All E.R. 337.

[89] Above, para.13–033.

[90] [1946] 1 All E.R. 387. *Cf. Covas v Bingham* (1853) 2 E. & B. 836.

[91] [1946] 2 All E.R. 337.

cancellation whether or not the non-performance or non-occurrence is serious enough to discharge the contract; and the event need not arise from a breach. Sometimes they provide facilities by which a party can effectively buy himself out of the contract. But in other cases they simply entitle one party to escape his obligations on payment of limited damages, or refund of expenses incurred, or even without redress to the other party. Clauses of the last type would no doubt be interpreted strictly[92] unless they make the transaction into a delivery on approval.[93]

Clauses limiting the damages recoverable. Sometimes clauses limit the amount of damages recoverable. Where these are liquidated damages clauses they form a compromise between the parties and are enforceable whether the loss is greater or less than the sum agreed, and thus they may benefit either party.[94] They are therefore not exemption clauses and do not come within the principles here discussed.[95] They will, however, be interpreted only to cover the loss in respect of which they may be regarded as settling the damages. Thus demurrage clauses in contracts for carriage of goods by sea normally fix damages for delay but not for other matters,[96] and on principle it seems that liquidated damages clauses do not bar the remedy of rejection nor the right to recover the price on doing so. Where, however, clauses simply fix a limit[97] or exclude a particular head of damages, *e.g.* "consequential loss",[98] they are exemption clauses and where ambiguous[99] interpreted *contra proferentem*.[1] It has been stated, however, that the principles of strict interpretation "are not applicable in their full rigour when considering the effect of clauses merely limiting [*sc.*, the monetary extent of] liability."[2] The reason given for this difference is that "they must be related to other contractual terms, in particular to the risks to which the 13–036

---

[92] See *N. F. Lanitis & Co. Ltd v Kyoda Shoji (U.K.) Ltd* [1956] 2 Lloyd's Rep. 176 (right of seller to cancel c.i.f. contract "should despatch shipment or delivery of the goods . . . be delayed prevented or prohibited for any cause whatsoever"); *Docker v Hyams* [1969] 1 W.L.R. 1060 (right to cancel sale of yacht for "defects": test of whether defects existed objective).

[93] Above, paras 5–040 *et seq.*

[94] See below, paras 16–029 *et seq.; Chitty on Contracts* (29th ed.), Vol.1, paras 26–109 *et seq.*; Treitel, *Law of Contract* (11th ed.), pp.999 *et seq.*

[95] See the *Suisse Atlantique* case, below, at pp.420–421.

[96] See *A/S Reidar v Arcos Ltd* [1927] 1 K.B. 352; *Suisse Atlantique Société d'Armement Maritime v NV Rotterdamsche Kolen Centrale* [1967] 1 A.C. 361; *The Bonde* [1991] 1 Lloyd's Rep. 136. But a demurrage clause may sometimes be a limitation of damages clause: see the *Suisse Atlantique* case, above, at p.395.

[97] See *Cellulose Acetate Silk Co. Ltd v Widnes Foundry (1925) Ltd* [1933] A.C. 20.

[98] See below, para.13–037.

[99] *S.G.S. (N.Z.) Ltd v Quirke Export Ltd* [1988] 1 N.Z.L.R. 52; *Victor Hydraulics Ltd v Engineering Dynamics Ltd* [1996] 2 N.Z.L.R. 235.

[1] *e.g. W. S. Pollock & Co. v Macrae*, 1922 S.C. (HL) 192, below, para.13–051; *cf. R. W. Green Ltd v Cade Bros Farms* [1978] 1 Lloyd's Rep. 602. See further *Tattersall v National S.S. Co. Ltd* (1884) 12 Q.B.D. 297; *Atlantic Shipping and Trading Co. Ltd v Louis Dreyfus & Co.* [1922] 2 A.C. 250, below, para.13–038; *Leuw v Dudgeon* (1867) L.R. 3 C.P. 17n.; *R. G. MacLean Ltd v Canada Vickers Ltd* (1971) 15 D.L.R. (3d) 15.

[2] *Ailsa Craig Fishing Co. Ltd v Malvern Fishing Co. Ltd* [1983] 1 W.L.R. 964 at 970, *per* Lord Fraser of Tullybelton (and see Lord Wilberforce at p.966); followed in *George Mitchell (Chesterhall) Ltd v Finney Lock Seeds Ltd* [1983] 2 A.C. 803.

defending party may be exposed, the remuneration which he received, and possibly also the opportunity of the other party to insure."[3] It is, however, not easy to justify such a distinction as a tool of legal reasoning, and it has been rejected by the High Court of Australia[4]; and it has been said more recently that it is unlikely that there was any intention to introduce any "mechanistic rule . . . to mitigate the rigour of another."[5] For a start, provisions relating to limitation may be intertwined with exemptions.[6] Secondly, where the sum to which liability is limited is very low, the clause may amount in effect to an exclusion of liability. Thus in a leading case in which this principle was followed[7] the relevant clause limited liability in the event to 0.33 per cent of the loss actually sustained. Nor, thirdly, is it clear which interpretative technique should be applied to clauses imposing time limits on claims. There seems no reason, if special principles are to apply to limitation clauses, why they should not sometimes apply here also.[8] A special variant of clauses limiting the right to damages is the "invoicing back" clause, which is discussed elsewhere.[9]

13–037 **Exclusion of indirect or consequential loss.** Commercial contracts frequently include clauses purporting to exclude liability for consequential loss, or indirect loss (which is interpreted as having the same meaning[10]) or both. The purpose of such clauses would appear to be to exclude liability beyond the difference in value between that of the goods supplied and the value which they ought to have had, together with direct physical damage caused by the goods; in particular, it may be thought that those who use them seek to exclude liability for loss of profits. English courts have however, interpreted such clauses strictly, regarding a straight claim for loss of profits as being direct rather than indirect or consequential. The current authority is that such clauses only exclude losses covered by the second part of the rule in *Hadley v Baxendale*,[11] that is to say, unusual losses for which the defendant would not be liable unless aware of the danger of them. It seems that this is now so well established that only the House of Lords can

---

[3] *ibid.*, at p.966, *per* Lord Wilberforce.
[4] *Darlington Futures Ltd v Delco Australia Pty Ltd* (1986) 161 C.L.R. 500.
[5] *HIH Casualty and General Insurance Ltd v Chase Manhattan Bank* [2003] UKHL 6; [2003] 1 All E.R. (Comm) 349 at [63] *per* Lord Hoffmann, cited by Gross J. in *Frans Maas (UK) Ltd v Samsung Electronics (UK) Ltd* [2004] EWHC 1502 (Comm); [2004] 2 Lloyd's Rep 251 at [131]. See also *Ocean Chemical Transport Inc v Exnor Craggs Ltd* [2000] 1 Lloyd's Rep. 446 at [38] *per* Evans L.J.
[6] As in *W. S. Pollock & Co. v Macrae*, above, n.91.
[7] *George Mitchell (Chesterhall) Ltd v Finney Lock Seeds Ltd*, above. In the Court of Appeal Lord Denning M.R. had criticised this very distinction: [1983] Q.B. 284 at 301.
[8] Below, para.13–038.
[9] Below, para.16–036.
[10] *Saint Line Ltd v Richardsons, Westgarth & Co.* [1940] 2 K.B. 99.
[11] (1854) 9 Exch. 341: see *Chitty on Contracts* (29th ed.), Vol.1, para.26–045; Treitel, *Law of Contract* (11th ed.), pp.965 *et seq.*

reconsider the matter.[12] Quite often such clauses reinforce what might be thought to be their purpose by a specific reference to loss of profits.[13] In such cases a problem of interpretation arises as to whether the loss of profits referred to must be regarded as only covering those arising under the second part of *Hadley v Baxendale*, or whether the reference to profits must be given effect and the exclusion of consequential loss confined to matters outside the express words. There are also problems as to exactly what the second part of the rule in *Hadley v Baxendale* means in practice outside the straightforward examples normally given, in particular as to the requirement of special knowledge.[14]

Clauses imposing time limits. Frequently commercial contracts contain provisions to the effect that legal proceedings, or arbitration,[15] must be commenced, or that defects must be notified, within a certain period, otherwise any claim will be deemed to be waived. Other clauses may be held to impose such a limit impliedly: thus in cases on the sale of horses it has been held that the phrase "warranted sound for one month" did not imply any warranty that the horse would remain sound for one month but rather imposed a bar on claims as to its condition on sale made after the expiry of one month.[16] There may also be customs to similar effect.[17] It has 13–038

[12] *Millar's Machinery Co. Ltd v David Way & Son* (1935) 40 Com.Cas. 204; *Saint Line Ltd v Richardsons, Westgarth & Co.*, above; *Wraight Ltd v PH & T (Holdings) Ltd* (1968) 13 B.L.R. 29; *Croudace Construction Ltd v Cawoods Concrete Products Ltd* [1978] 2 Lloyd's Rep. 55, CA (usually taken as the leading case); *British Sugar Plc v NEI Power Products Ltd* (1998) 87 B.L.R. 42; *Deepak Fertilisers and Petrochemicals Corp. v ICI Chemicals and Polymers Ltd* [1998] 2 Lloyd's Rep. 139; [1999] 1 Lloyd's Rep. 387; *BHP Petroleum Ltd v British Steel Plc* [1999] 1 Lloyd's Rep. 583 (Rix J.), decision varied [2000] 2 Lloyd's Rep. 277; *Hotel Services Ltd v Hilton International Hotels (U.K.) Ltd* [2000] B.L.R. 235; *Pegler Ltd v Wang (U.K.) Ltd* [2000] B.L.R. 218 ("even if Wang shall have been advised of the possibility of such potential loss"); *Watford Electronics Ltd v Sanderson CFL Ltd* [2001] EWCA Civ 317; [2001] 1 All E.R. (Comm) 696.

[13] See *BHP Petroleum Ltd v British Steel Plc*, above, at p.600. See also the clauses in *Britvic Soft Drinks Ltd v Messer U.K. Ltd* [2002] 1 Lloyd's Rep. 20 ("losses, costs or expenses of a purely financial or economic nature (including, but not limited to, loss of profits, loss of use or other consequential loss")) and *Bacardi-Martini Beverages Ltd v Thomas Hardy Packaging Ltd, ibid.*, 62; affirmed [2002] EWCA Civ. 549; [2002] 2 Lloyd's Rep. 379.

[14] See the *BHP* case, above, at first instance at pp.588 *et seq. per* Rix J. In *Caledonia North Sea Ltd v Norton (No. 2) Ltd* [2002] UKHL 4; [2002] All E.R. (Comm) 321 at [100], Lord Hoffmann reserved the question of the correctness of this construction.

[15] But the limit here may only be as to the time within which a party can demand the benefits of arbitration, and not restrict the claim at law. See *Smeaton, Hanscomb & Co. Ltd v Sassoon I. Setty, Son & Co.* [1953] 1 W.L.R. 1468; *Ayscough v Sheed, Thomson & Co. Ltd* (1924) 19 Ll.L.R. 104; below, para.13–041.

[16] *Chapman v Gwyther* (1866) L.R. 1 Q.B. 463. See also *Buchanan v Parnshaw* (1788) 2 T.R. 745; *Mesnard v Aldridge* (1801) 3 Esp. 271; *Bywater v Richardson* (1834) 1 A. & E. 508; *Smart v Hyde* (1841) 8 M. & W. 723; *Head v Tattersall* (1871) L.R. 7 Ex. 7; *Hinchcliffe v Barwick* (1880) 5 Ex.D. 177. But these are examples of interpretation according to usage: in appropriate cases goods can certainly be warranted to remain sound for a fixed period. See above, para.10–021.

[17] *e.g. Sanders v Jameson* (1848) 2 C. & K. 557. As to custom in general, see above, paras 11–088, 11–089.

been said that such clauses are releases rather than waivers,[18] but it is difficult to see how a claim can be released or waived before it accrues and it is probably better to classify them as contractual promises to release or waive. Such clauses have again been interpreted strictly, for they take away normal rights. Thus, in *Ernest Beck & Co. v K. Szymanowski & Co.*, a contract for the sale gross of "200 yard reels" of sewing cotton contained the provision: "The goods delivered shall be deemed to be in all respects in accordance with the contract and the buyers shall be bound to accept and pay for the same accordingly unless the sellers shall within fourteen days after arrival of the goods at their destination receive from the buyers notice of any matter or thing by reason whereof they may allege that the goods are not in accordance with the contract." The cotton on the reels proved on average seriously short in measurement and the buyers claimed damages outside the period. The Court of Appeal[19] held simply that the clause did not affect a claim for damages, but only purported to forbid rejection: the House of Lords[20] went further and held that it only applied to matters of quality and could not be used "so as to convert goods undelivered into goods delivered."[21] So also in *Atlantic Shipping and Trading Co. Ltd v Louis Dreyfus & Co.*,[22] a clause in a charterparty requiring the making of any claim and the appointment of an arbitrator to occur within three months of final discharge was held to apply only to breaches of specific terms in the contract, and not to the warranty of seaworthiness, which was not mentioned in the contract and took effect by implication of law only. But where the breach is less serious, such clauses will of course apply[23]: and there seems no reason why they should not be drafted so as to apply to even the most serious breaches,[24] for it can be said that they do not exclude liability,

---

[18] *Atlantic Shipping and Trading Co. Ltd v Louis Dreyfus & Co.* [1922] 2 A.C. 250 at 262.

[19] [1923] 1 K.B. 457 (*sub nom. Szymonowski).*

[20] [1924] A.C. 43. Atiyah, *Sale of Goods* (11th ed.), p.230 suggests that this is the sort of strained interpretation which might require reconsideration today; *cf.* above, para.13–020.

[21] At pp.51, 52. See also *Gorton v Macintosh & Co.* [1883] W.N. 103; *Minister of Materials v Steel Bros & Co. Ltd* [1952] 1 All E.R. 522 (similar provision relating to claims for defects in quality held not to apply to claims in respect of damage caused by defective packing); *Vsesojwzoje Objedinenije "Exportles" v T. W. Allen & Sons Ltd* [1938] 3 All E.R. 375 ("quality and condition" does not apply to faulty manufacture); *Bunge SA v Deutsche Conti-Handelsgesellschaft mbH (No.2)* [1980] 1 Lloyd's Rep. 352 (limitation on quality claims did not cover technical claims); *Mohsin Abdullah Alesayi v Brooks Exim Pte Ltd* [1993] 3 Singapore L.R. 433 (clause requiring notification of complaints within 24 hours without stating consequences of non-compliance held a guideline only); *cf. H. & E. Van der Sterren v Cibernetics (Holdings) Pty Ltd* (1970) 44 A.L.J.R. 157 (good commercial reason for short time limit).

[22] [1922] 2 A.C. 250.

[23] *Smeaton, Hanscomb & Co. Ltd v Sassoon I. Setty, Son & Co.* [1953] 1 W.L.R. 1468; *Vsesojwzoje Objedinenije "Exportles" v T. W. Allen & Sons Ltd*, above; *W. E. Marshall & Co. v Lewis and Peat Ltd* [1963] 1 Lloyd's Rep. 562; *H. & E. Van der Sterren v Cibernetics (Holdings) Pty Ltd*, above.

[24] See *Bank of Australasia v Clan Line Steamers Ltd* [1916] 1 K.B. 39. The suggestion in *Smeaton, Hanscomb & Co. Ltd v Sassoon I. Setty, Son & Co.*, above, that the time limit clause would not have operated had the seller sent pine logs instead of

but simply require that buyers take vigilant steps to finalise transactions. On the other hand a very short time limit can amount to a bar on rejection or complaint altogether.

Clauses excluding the right of set-off. The right of set-off can be excluded,[25] but the exclusion should be clear[26] as it may be presumed that "neither party intends to abandon any remedies for its breach arising by operation of law."[27] Since however it is only a remedy that is excluded, a clause excluding set-off may extend to preventing set-off even for fraud.[28] 13–039

Certification and testing clauses. Provision is often made for certification and testing by various methods.[29] Such clauses may be treated as exemption clauses and where appropriate subjected to strict interpretation.[30] Sometimes the contractual duty is itself simply to supply goods that satisfy the certifier,[31] or fulfil certain contractual standards and also satisfy the certifier.[32] Unless the contract so provides expressly or by necessary implication, however, approval of the certifier is not conclusive that the contractual terms have been duly performed.[33] But the contract may so 13–040

---

mahogany logs seems misconceived. Why should a buyer have a longer time to complain of a totally false shipment than of a slightly defective one? See the *Suisse Atlantique* case [1967] 1 A.C. 361 at 400–401. On the other hand there could be circumstances where the tender could not be related to the contract at all: above, para.12–066.

[25] *Halesowen Presswork and Assemblies Ltd v National Westiminster Bank Ltd* [1972] A.C. 785; *Gilbert-Ash (Northern) Ltd v Modern Engineering (Bristol) Ltd* [1974] A.C. 689; *Hong Kong and Shanghai Banking Corp. v Kloeckner & Co. AG* [1990] 2 Q.B. 514; *John Dee Group Ltd v WMH (21) Ltd* [1997] B.C.C. 518.

[26] For a case where it was not see *BOC Group Plc v Centeon LLC* [1999] 1 All E.R. (Comm.) 53; *cf. Continental Illinois National Bank & Trust Co. v Papanicolaou* [1986] 2 Lloyd's Rep. 441. Such a clause is not effective in a direct debit situation: *Esso Petroleum Co. Ltd v Milton* [1997] 1 W.L.R. 938.

[27] *Gilbert-Ash (Northern) Ltd v Modern Engineering Co. (Bristol) Ltd*, above, at p.717, *per* Lord Diplock; see also *Nile Co. for Export of Agricultural Crops v H. & J.M. Bennett (Commodities) Ltd* [1986] 1 Lloyd's Rep. 555; *John Dee Group Ltd v WMH (21) Ltd*, above.

[28] *Society of Lloyd's v Leighs* [1997] C.L.C. 1398; *Skipskreditforeningen v Emperor Navigation* [1998] 1 Lloyd's Rep. 66; *WRM Group Ltd v Wood* [1998] C.L.C. 189. As to the position under the Unfair Contract Terms Act 1977 see below, para.13–090.

[29] There are various practical differences between certification and arbitration. There is no general rule of law prohibiting the influencing of certifiers: *Minster Trust Ltd v Traps Tractors Ltd* [1954] 1 W.L.R. 963. Certifiers less frequently perform judicial functions than arbitrators; and it seems that arbitrators acting judicially are not easily liable in negligence. See *Sutcliffe v Thackrah* [1974] A.C. 727; *Arenson v Casson Beckman Rutley & Co.* [1977] A.C. 405; *Palacath Ltd v Flanagan* [1985] 2 All E.R. 161; Arbitration Act 1996, ss.29, 74; and generally *Chitty on Contracts* (29th ed.), Vol.2, para.32–166; Mustill and Boyd, *Commercial Arbitration* (2nd ed.), pp.224–232; Russell, *Arbitration* (22nd ed.), para.4–203.

[30] See *W. N. Lindsay & Co. Ltd v European Grain and Shipping Agency Ltd* [1963] 1 Lloyd's Rep. 437.

[31] See *Minster Trust Ltd v Traps Tractors Ltd*, above.

[32] *Cammell Laird & Co. v Manganese Bronze and Brass Co. Ltd* [1934] A.C. 402.

[33] *Newton Abbot Development Co. Ltd v Stockman Bros* (1931) 47 T.L.R. 616; *Petrofina SA v Compagnia Italiana Trasporto Olii Minerali of Genoa* (1937) 53 T.L.R. 650; *Rolimpex Centrale Handlu Zagranicznego v Haji E. Dobra & Sons Ltd* [1971] 1 Lloyd's Rep. 380; and see *Bird v Smith* (1848) 12 Q.B. 786.

provide: provisions for conclusive certifications as to quality are common.[34] Sometimes much more complex terms are laid down which require specific analysis. Thus in *"Agroexport" v NV Goorden Import Cy. SA*[35] there was what Sellers J. called "a comprehensive code for rejection or acceptance or allowance based on the evidence derived from the certificate of control and the certificates of the analysts as prescribed." The contract, for linseed expellers, provided *inter alia* for no rejection, but acceptance with allowance in the case of deficiency of oil and albuminoids and content of castor seed husk up to a certain percentage, but allowed for rejection beyond this percentage and also if the goods contained more than a certain percentage of sand and/or silica. To this extent it is submitted that it established, not modified,[36] the description of the goods sold. It then provided for sampling and analysis by certain procedures: these operated like time limits and, since they were not followed, the buyer was held to have no valid claim as to the quality and nature of the goods delivered.[37] Although certification will normally be interpreted as relevant to quality only,[38] it can also cover matters of quality which are part of the description of the goods,[39] and there seems no reason why it should not be extended by clear words to cover the nature of the goods, especially where by reason of admixtures it becomes difficult to determine at what point a deficiency in quality affects the nature of the goods.[40] Similarly, it is submitted that an agreed procedure for conclusively ascertaining the amount of the cotton could have barred a claim in *Ernest Beck & Co. v K. Szymanowski & Co.*, discussed above.

---

[34] See *e.g. H. Glynn (Covent Garden) v Wittleder* [1959] 2 Lloyd's Rep. 409; *Oleificio Zucchi SpA v Northern Sales Ltd* [1965] 2 Lloyd's Rep. 496; *Alfred C. Toepfer v Continental Grain Co.* [1974] 1 Lloyd's Rep. 11 (effective though certifier later admitted he had been mistaken); *Gill & Duffus SA v Berger & Co. Inc.* [1984] A.C. 382; *Jones v Sherwood Computer Services Plc* [1992] 1 W.L.R. 277; *Apioil Ltd v Kuwait Petroleum Italia SpA* [1995] 1 Lloyd's Rep. 124; *Galaxy Energy International Ltd v Eurobunker SpA* [2001] 2 Lloyd's Rep. 725 (conclusive save for fraud and manifest error); *Veba Oil Supply and Trading GmbH v Petrotrade Inc.* [2001] EWCA Civ. 1832; [2002] 1 Lloyd's Rep. 295 (where there was such an error). But a certifier may not without authority delegate his function, and if he does the certification may be ineffective: *Kollerich & Cie. SA v State Trading Corp. of India* [1980] 2 Lloyd's Rep. 32. As to communication of certification by telex see *Coastal (Bermuda) Ltd v Esso Petroleum Co. Ltd* [1984] 1 Lloyd's Rep. 11. "Quality" may not cover external condition on loading: *Cremer v General Carriers SA* [1974] 1 W.L.R. 341; nor other matters relating to loading: *Kollerich & Cie SA v State Trading Corp. of India*, above; but *cf.* Sale of Goods Act 1979, s.61(1).

[35] [1956] 1 Lloyd's Rep. 319. *Cf. W. N. Lindsay & Co. Ltd v European Grain and Shipping Agency Ltd*, above, where the procedure was held not to be exclusive.

[36] As Sellers J. seems to suggest at p.325.

[37] Such a procedure was not followed, with the result that a sample taken was inadmissible, in *Verheijdens Veevoeder Commissiehandel BV v I. S. Joseph Co. Inc.* [1981] 1 Lloyd's Rep. 102.

[38] See *NV Bunge v Cie. Noga, etc., SA (The Bow Cedar)* [1980] 2 Lloyd's Rep. 601 (not final as to nature of oil supplied).

[39] *Toepfer v Continental Grain Co.* [1974] 1 Lloyd's Rep. 11; *Gill & Duffus SA v Berger Co. Inc.* [1984] A.C. 382.

[40] *W. N. Lindsay & Co. Ltd v European Grain & Shipping Agency Ltd*, above, at pp.445–446; *cf. Kollerich & Cie. SA v State Trading Corp. of India* [1980] 2 Lloyd's Rep. 32 (clause not so held); *Gill & Duffus SA v Berger Co. Inc.*, above, at p.394.

Arbitration clauses.[41] Arbitration clauses are mere procedural provisions,[42] and can normally be ignored by a party who wishes to sue in court instead,[43] subject to the court's power (and usually duty) to grant a stay.[44] Such clauses are not exemption clauses and thus not subject to the special rules for the interpretation of exemption clauses.[45] This is true even of *Scott v Avery* clauses, *i.e.* clauses making an arbitral award a condition precedent to any right of action, which cannot normally be ignored except by consent of both parties.[46] But where a time limit is involved, this aspect of the clause counts as an exemption,[47] unless the time limit only relates to the appointment of the arbitrator and does not bar the right of action.[48] And since they may be prejudicial to consumers, consumer arbitration agreements are controlled by statute.[49] **13–041**

4. DOCTRINE OF FUNDAMENTAL BREACH

Doctrine of fundamental breach. The 30 years from about 1950 saw a new and apparently independent doctrine regulating the effect of exemption clauses, that of fundamental breach of contract. It was applied in all branches of the law of contract.[50] Its effect was that a party who had committed a fundamental breach of contract was sometimes not able to rely on an exemption clause in his favour contained in the contract. Thus in a number of well-known cases, several of which relate to sale or hire-purchase, a person who had committed a serious breach of contract was not permitted to rely on an exemption clause drafted in very wide terms.[51] Most **13–042**

---

[41] *Chitty on Contracts* (29th ed.), Vol.2, para.32–165; Mustill and Boyd, *Commercial Arbitration* (2nd ed.); Russell, *Arbitration* (22nd ed.). Arbitration is now controlled by the Arbitration Act 1996.

[42] See *Atlantic Shipping and Trading Co. Ltd v Louis Dreyfus* [1922] 2 A.C. 250 at 259; *Heyman v Darwins Ltd* [1942] A.C. 356 at 373–374, 400.

[43] *Doleman & Sons v Ossett Corp.* [1912] 3 K.B. 257 at 267; *Pinnock Bros v Lewis & Peat Ltd* [1923] 1 K.B. 690.

[44] Arbitration Act 1996, ss.9, 86.

[45] *Woolf v Collis Removal Service* [1948] 1 K.B. 11 at 15–17. They are probably caught by s.3 of the Misrepresentation Act 1967: below, para.13–055; specifically excluded from the scope of the Unfair Contract Terms Act 1977: below, para.13–069; but caught by the Unfair Terms in Consumer Contracts Regulations 1994 (below, paras 13–103, 14–030 *et seq.*), as to which see also Arbitration Act 1996, s.90.

[46] *ibid.*

[47] *Atlantic Shipping and Trading Co. Ltd v Louis Dreyfus & Co.* [1922] 2 A.C. 250; Mustill and Boyd, *op. cit.* above, at p.209.

[48] *Smeaton, Hanscomb & Co. Ltd v Sassoon I. Setty, Son & Co.* [1953] 1 W.L.R. 1468; *Ayscough v Sheed, Thomson & Co. Ltd* (1924) 19 Ll. L.R. 104; above.

[49] Arbitration Act 1996, ss.89–91 (formerly Consumer Arbitration Agreements Act 1988); below, para.14–100.

[50] See *Chitty on Contracts* (29th ed.), Vol.1, paras 14–020 *et seq.*; Treitel, *Law of Contract* (11th ed.), pp.225 *et seq.*; Coote, *Exception Clauses* (1964); Yates, *Exclusion Clauses in Contracts* (2nd ed.), Ch.6. See also Guest, 77 L.Q.R. 98 (1961); Reynolds, 79 L.Q.R. 534 (1963); Lord Devlin [1966] C.L.J. 192.

[51] *e.g. Alexander v Railway Executive* [1951] 2 K.B. 882; *Karsales (Harrow) Ltd v Wallis* [1956] 1 W.L.R. 936; *Sze Hai Tong Bank Ltd v Rambler Cycle Co. Ltd* [1959] A.C. 576 at 587, 588; *Yeoman Credit Ltd v Apps* [1962] 2 Q.B. 508 at 520; *Charterhouse Credit Co. Ltd v Tolly* [1963] 2 Q.B. 683.

of the examples in sale of goods and hire-purchase concern what may be regarded as a total failure to supply the contract goods.[52]

13–043 **Doubts as to basis of doctrine: interpretation.** The rationale and scope of this doctrine were the subject of considerable doubt. On one view the relevant cases were no more than a (rather controversial) generalisation on the principles as to the restrictive interpretation of exemption clauses set out, as regards sale of goods, in the previous section of this chapter. Thus in 1964 Pearson L.J. said "As to the question of 'fundamental breach', I think there is a rule of construction that normally an exception or exclusion clause or similar provision in a contract should be construed as not applying to a situation created by a fundamental breach of the contract. This is not an independent rule of law imposed by the Court on the parties willy-nilly in disregard of their contractual intention. On the contrary it is a rule of construction based on the presumed intention of the contracting parties . . . This rule of construction is not new in principle but it has become prominent in recent years in consequence of the tendency to have standard forms of contract containing exceptions clauses drawn in extravagantly wide terms, which would produce absurd results if applied literally."[53]

13–044 **Doctrine as a rule of law.** There were, however, stronger statements in the cases which could be regarded as suggesting that there was actually a rule of law preventing the operation of exemption clauses in situations of fundamental breach.[54] Such a doctrine, apart from not being easily regarded as arising from existing case law, suffered from severe theoretical difficulties.[55] It assumed that what was a fundamental breach of a contract can be determined without reference to the exemption clauses in it (an argument that can even be extended to limitation of liability clauses).[56] It was only easily operable therefore in stylised contracts the normal terms of which are well established as *jus dispositivum* – of which sale of goods and hire purchase are in fact examples. In so far as the doctrine was based on interpretation, the same difficulty can be seen there, though less conspicuously.

13–045 ***Suisse Atlantique* case.** The House of Lords first had an opportunity of considering the doctrine in *Suisse Atlantique Société d'Armement Maritime v NV Rotterdamsche Kolen Centrale*,[57] where a full-scale argument that the

---

[52] See below, paras 13–050, 13–051.
[53] *U.G.S. Finance Ltd v National Mortgage Bank of Greece and National Bank of Greece* [1964] 1 Lloyd's Rep. 446 at 453.
[54] *e.g.* "the law will not allow a clause of exclusion to be pleaded in answer to such a claim": *Charterhouse Credit Co. Ltd v Tolly* [1963] 2 Q.B. 683 at 710. See also *ibid.*, at pp.703–704; *Karsales (Harrow) Ltd v Wallis* [1956] 1 W.L.R. 936 at 940, 943; *Sze Hai Tong Bank Ltd v Rambler Cycle Co. Ltd* [1959] A.C. 576 at 587, 588, 589; *Yeoman Credit Ltd v Apps* [1962] 2 Q.B. 508 at 520; *Astley Industrial Trust Ltd v Grimley* [1963] 1 W.L.R. 584 at 598.
[55] See Coote, *Exception Clauses* (1964), *passim* and esp. at pp.4–7; 40 M.L.R. 31 at 34–41 (1977). This is certainly a valuable insight; but some writers give it considerably less emphasis: see Treitel, 8 J.S.P.T.L. 121 (1964); *Law of Contract* (11th ed.), pp.237–238.
[56] See Wright J. in *SS Istros v F.W. Dahlstroem & Co.* [1931] 1 K.B. 247 at 252–253.
[57] [1967] 1 A.C. 361.

doctrine constituted a rule of law was put forward in the context of the demurrage clause in a voyage charter (not in fact an exemption clause). The House held however that the doctrine was one of interpretation only, and that the clause was in any case not an exemption clause.

Rule of law effectively survived in different form. The *Suisse Atlantique* case did not, however, finally settle the status of the doctrine, largely because of two passages in which Lord Reid and Lord Upjohn appeared to suggest that had the innocent party treated the contract as repudiated by breach, it would have come to an end: then "the whole contract has ceased to exist including the exclusion clause."[58] The point was taken up in *Harbutt's Plasticine Ltd v Wayne Tank and Pump Co. Ltd*,[59] where contractors in breach of contract caused a factory in which they had negligently installed piping to be burned down: the Court of Appeal held that a clause limiting their liability to an amount equivalent to the contract price was applicable as a matter of interpretation, but that it was displaced by the repudiatory breach, which had brought the contract to an end. This reasoning seems to have at least in part been an extension of cases on deviation in the contract of carriage of goods by sea, under which the shipowner loses the benefit of clauses protecting him when he deviates from the normal contractual route,[60] a result said to be based on the notion that his repudiatory breach brought the contract to an end.[61] But in none of these decisions, which in any case have their own difficulties,[62] was it ever suggested that a deviation could displace a clause relating to the contract route which had already been held to be applicable and to justify what would otherwise be a deviation.[63] It is also now clear that although the innocent party is in the case of repudiatory breach at his option discharged from the obligation of further performance, it is misleading to speak of the contract being brought to an end.[64] The case was therefore very difficult to justify analytically. The Unfair Contract Terms Act 1977 even contains a provision to prevent this reasoning being used to displace terms which the court would under the Act regard as reasonable.[65] Nevertheless, in a number of cases between 1970 and 1980, results very similar to those 13–046

[58] Lord Reid at p.398; Lord Upjohn at pp.419, 425.
[59] [1970] 1 Q.B. 447.
[60] See Scrutton, *Charterparties* (20th ed.), pp.256 *et seq*. Similar reasoning has been applied to warehousemen who store goods in places other than those contemplated by the contract: *Lilley v. Doubleday* (1881) 7 Q.B.D. 510; *Davis v Collins* [1945] 1 All E.R. 247; *Woolf v Collis Removal Services* [1948] 1 K.B. 11 at 15; *Garnham, Harris and Elton Ltd v Alfred W. Ellis (Transport) Ltd* [1967] 1 W.L.R. 940.
[61] *Hain S.S. Co. Ltd v Tate and Lyle Ltd* [1936] 2 All E.R. 597 at 601–608, 614, HL; *Chandris v Isbrandtsen-Moller Co. Inc.* [1951] 1 K.B. 240 at 248 (revsd. on other grounds [1950] 2 All E.R. 618).
[62] Coote, *Exception Clauses* (1964), Ch.6; Goff and Jones, *Law of Restitution* (6th ed.), paras 20–053, 20–054; Reynolds, *The Butterworth Lectures* 1990–91 (1992), at 29 *et seq*.
[63] Coote [1970] C.L.J. 221 at 236.
[64] *Heyman v Darwins Ltd* [1942] A.C. 356 at 399; *Photo Production Ltd v Securicor Transport Ltd* [1980] A.C. 827 at 842–845, 849–850, 853. Still less is it appropriate to speak of "rescission *ab initio*": *Johnson v Agnew* [1980] A.C. 367.
[65] s.9(1).

obtaining before the *Suisse Atlantique* case were reached or at least contemplated. Some of these could be explained on the familiar basis of interpretation even though they contained more sweeping dicta[66]; but some involved reasoning that was very difficult to justify, whether in following *Harbutt's* case or in seeking to distinguish it.[67]

13–047 ***Securicor* case: doctrine reaffirmed as one of interpretation.** The fact that a substantive fundamental breach doctrine in some respects survived the *Suisse Atlantique*[68] case can perhaps be regarded as a manifestation of continuing disquiet at the unfair nature of some exemption clauses, though, as Lord Reid had pointed out in it, the protection given by the doctrine was of a rather crude and undiscriminating nature.[69] But the Supply of Goods (Implied Terms) Act 1973, which provided more discriminating control of exemption clauses in contracts of sale and hire-purchase, did something to alleviate the problem, and the Unfair Contract Terms Act 1977,[70] which has a much wider scope, and makes further discriminations, vastly reduced the need for such a doctrine. In *Photo Production Ltd v Securicor Transport Ltd*,[71] an opportunity arose for the House of Lords to give further consideration to the matter. Under a contract for the provision of night patrol services to industrial premises the question was whether a very widely drafted exemption clause covered loss caused by a fire which an employee of the provider had deliberately lit on the premises. The House of Lords again held, reversing the Court of Appeal, and giving a quietus to the reasoning of the *Harbutt's Plasticine* case,[72] that the doctrine of fundamental breach was one of interpretation only; and that on this basis the clause, contained in a contract made between business concerns of equal bargaining power, each well able to insure, involving no more than brief night surveillance visits at a very modest charge, covered what had happened.

13–048 ***George Mitchell Ltd v Finney Lock Seeds Ltd*: doctrine no longer exists as separate entity.** Immediately after the decision in the *Securicor* case it was arguable that the doctrine of fundamental breach was still in existence, but as one of interpretation, holding that exemption clauses will not be

---

[66] *Anglo-Continental Holidays Ltd v Typaldos Lines (London) Ltd* [1967] 2 Lloyd's Rep. 61; *Farnworth Finance Facilities Ltd v Attryde* [1970] 1 W.L.R. 1053; *Mendelssohn v Normand Ltd* [1970] 1 Q.B. 177.

[67] *Kenyon, Son and Craven Ltd v Baxter Hoare & Co. Ltd* [1971] 1 W.L.R. 519; *United Fresh Meat Co. Ltd v Charterhouse Cold Storage Ltd* [1974] 1 Lloyd's Rep. 286; *Wathes (Western) Ltd v Austins (Menswear) Ltd* [1976] 1 Lloyd's Rep. 14; *Levison v Patent Steam Carpet Cleaning Co. Ltd* [1978] Q.B. 69; the judgments in the Court of Appeal in *Photo Production Ltd v Securicor Transport Ltd* [1978] 1 W.L.R. 856 (revsd., [1980] A.C. 827), below, para.13–047. But in *Trade and Transport Inc. v Iino Kaiun Kaisha (The Angelic)* [1973] 1 W.L.R. 210 the reasoning was virtually ignored.

[68] Above, para.13–045.

[69] [1967] 1 A.C. 361 at 406.

[70] Below, paras 13–062 *et seq.*

[71] [1980] A.C. 827. See also *Ailsa Craig Fishing Co. Ltd v Malvern Fishing Co. Ltd* [1983] 1 W.L.R. 964 (sometimes referred to as *Securicor 2*).

[72] Above, 13–046: see Lord Wilberforce at 842–845.

interpreted so as to cover a fundamental breach of contract. None of the relevant authorities were overruled in the *Securicor* case save for three notoriously intractable cases,[73] and there was no actual disavowal of the troublesome dicta in the *Suisse Atlantique* case. References were made to the change in attitude created by the new statutory power to hold exemption clauses ineffective,[74] but they were far from being crucial to the reasoning. On the other hand there was no recognition of the continued existence of the doctrine either, and indeed Lord Diplock, in a seminal explanation of the consequences of breach of contract in the *Securicor* case, ascribed the phrase "fundamental breach" to an ordinary breach of contract other than a breach of condition, sufficiently serious to entitle the innocent party to treat the contract as discharged.[75] The question was resolved in a subsequent leading case, *George Mitchell (Chesterhall) Ltd v Finney Lock Seeds Ltd*,[76] which relates to sale of goods. In that case a buyer ordered 30 lb of "Finney's Late Dutch Special" cabbage seed, but what was delivered proved after sowing to be not late cabbage seed at all; it germinated and grew but the product proved completely valueless and had to be ploughed in. The seller sought to rely on a clause limiting his liability to replacement of the seed or refund of the price paid, and excluding any express or implied conditions or warranties, statutory or otherwise. In the Court of Appeal[77] Oliver L.J. held that the clause only covered delivery of seeds which were correctly described as "Finney's Late Dutch Special". But in the House of Lords Lord Bridge of Harwich said that this came "dangerously near to reintroducing by the back door the doctrine of 'fundamental breach'" which the House in the *Securicor* case "had so forcibly evicted by the front."[78] The subject-matter of the contract was seeds and to them the clause applied. (It was, however, held unreasonable under the Supply of Goods (Implied Terms) Act 1973.[79])

From this it would seem that at any rate in England and Wales the former doctrine of fundamental breach is no longer in existence, even in situations where statutory control is inapplicable; and that the phrase should be reserved for a breach of contract entitling the innocent party to treat the contract as discharged, in accordance with the dicta of Lord Diplock in the *Securicor* case.[80] The applicable principles are those of interpretation already expounded, perhaps with the modification, which was relied on in this case, that actual exemptions from liability are more strictly interpreted than clauses (as in the instant case) which merely limit damages 13–049

---

[73] *Charterhouse Credit Co. Ltd v Tolly* [1963] 2 Q.B. 683; *Wathes (Western) Ltd v Austins (Menswear) Ltd* [1976] 2 Lloyd's Rep. 14; and of course the *Harbutt's Plasticine* case (above, para.13–046) itself.
[74] See [1980] A.C. 827 at 843, 851, 853.
[75] At p.849.
[76] [1983] 2 A.C. 803; Nicol and Rawlings, 43 M.L.R. 567 (1980). *Cf.* another cabbage case, *Kordas v Stokes Seeds Ltd* (1992) 96 D.L.R. (4th) 129.
[77] [1983] Q.B. 284.
[78] [1983] 2 A.C. 803 at 813. See also *Edmund Murray Ltd v B.S.P. International Foundations Ltd* (1992) 33 Con. L.R. 1 at 16, CA.
[79] Below, para.13–089.
[80] See [1980] A.C. at 849.

recoverable.[81] Different views may, however, be taken in other jurisdictions.[82]

13–050 **Supply of wrong thing.** Cases on supply by a seller of the wrong thing used regularly to be discussed as examples of fundamental breach in contracts of sale. It may be inferred from the *George Mitchell* case[83] that at least some are still relevant as examples of strict interpretation, for Lord Bridge said "In my opinion, this is not a 'peas and beans' case at all."[84] The reference is to an ancient example frequently cited as indicating that on a sale of peas, no exemption can normally justify the supply of beans.[85] The inference is that had the case truly been a "peas and beans" case (for example, had daffodil bulbs been supplied, or even perhaps cauliflower seed) an exemption clause might have been ineffective; and also even a limitation of damages clause, since the case concerns such a clause, though elsewhere in the same judgment it is indicated that such clauses are to be less rigorously interpreted.[86]

13–051 The problem has usually arisen in connection with breach of the condition as to description laid down in section 13 of the Sale of Goods Act. It is explained elsewhere[87] that this section was originally not seeking to deal comprehensively with the basic obligation to deliver the contract goods, but that it probably must now be regarded as so doing. Where there is a clear description or specification as to the goods sold, even slight discrepancies may be treated as breaches of condition,[88] and exemption clauses may be interpreted so as not to modify that description or specification.[89] A properly drafted clause may certainly be interpreted as cutting down the duty of absolute compliance with specification.[90] It would

---

[81] But as to this distinction see above, para.13–036.

[82] It seems that the doctrine was never adopted in Australia at all: see *Sydney City Council v West* (1965) 114 C.L.R. 481; *T.N.T. (Melbourne) Pty Ltd v May & Baker (Australia) Pty Ltd* (1966) 115 C.L.R. 353; *Van der Sterren v Cibernetic (Holdings) Pty Ltd* (1970) 44 A.L.J.R. 157; *Darlington Futures Ltd v Delco Australia Ltd* (1986) 161 C.L.R. 500. In general, wide-ranging Trade Practices legislation now provides other opportunities for relief; and in New South Wales there is also a measure of statutory control under the Contracts Relief Act 1980. In Canada, however, it seems that some form of the doctrine had been regarded as valid, but much doubt was cast on it in *Hunter Engineering Co. Inc. v Syncrude Canada Ltd* [1989] 1 S.C.R. 426; 57 D.L.R. (4th) 321.

[83] Above.

[84] [1983] 2 A.C. 803 at 813.

[85] An example taken from the judgment of Lord Abinger C.B. in *Chanter v Hopkins* (1838) 4 M. & W. 399. The context in which he used it, however, was an explanation of the sale of goods by description. See also *U.G.S. Finance Ltd v National Mortgage Bank of Greece* [1964] 1 Lloyd's Rep. 446 at 453 (chalk and cheese).

[86] At p.814; above, para.13–036.

[87] Above, paras 11–002 *et seq*.

[88] Above, para.11–018.

[89] *e.g. Pinnock Bros v Lewis and Peat Ltd* [1923] 1 K.B. 690; *cf. Smeaton Hanscomb & Co. Ltd v Sassoon I. Setty, Son & Co.* [1953] 1 W.L.R. 1468. See above, para.13–033.

[90] See, *e.g. Wilkinson v Barclay* [1946] 1 All E.R. 387; [1946] 2 All E.R. 337, above, paras 13–032, 13–033; *Rosenthal & Sons Ltd v Esmail* [1965] 1 W.L.R. 1117 ("difference of slight nature in quality, designs, shades, dimensions, etc., is allowed").

not, however, easily be regarded as eliminating the duty to supply what appear to be the agreed contract goods.[91] In this connection serious qualitative defects have sometimes been treated as affecting the identity of those goods. Thus in *W. S. Pollock & Co. v Macrae*,[92] a Scottish case, there was a contract for the building and installation of motor marine engines, which included a 12-month guarantee for defective parts caused by bad materials or workmanship followed by the clause "Apart from the above guarantee the works sell their engines under the condition that they are free from any claims arising through the breakdown of any parts or stoppages of the engines, or from any consequential damages arising from same, direct or indirect." The engine delivered was held to have "such a congeries of defects as to destroy the workable character of the machine." It was held by the House of Lords that the words "although they excuse from damage flowing from the insufficiency of a part or parts of the machinery . . . have no application to damage arising when there has been total breach of contract by failing to supply the article truly contracted for."[93] The case is, however, one on interpretation only; it lays down no rule of law that such a clause is inapplicable in the case of a "total breach".[94] It was followed in *Yeoman Credit Ltd v Apps*,[95] where a car was sold which proved to have a congeries of defects rendering it only able to go three or four miles in one-and-a-half hours; an exemption clause reading "No warranty whatsoever is given by the owner as to the age, state or quality of the goods or as to fitness for any purpose and any implied warranties and conditions are hereby expressly excluded" was held inapplicable. Such a clause could, however, be effective in so far as it indicated that the contract goods were to be widely defined. Even the famous "peas and beans" example can be approached in this way. As Lord Devlin put it, "If an anxious hostess is late in the preparation of a meal, she can perfectly well say: 'Send me peas or if you haven't got peas, send beans; but for heaven's sake send something.' That would be a contract for peas, beans or anything else *ejusdem generis* and it is a perfectly sensible contract to make."[96]

Deliberate breach. There was also some authority that as a matter of interpretation exemption clauses might be construed so as not to cover certain situations of deliberate breach. Some fundamental breach cases 13–052

---

[91] *cf. Andrews Bros (Bournemouth) Ltd v Singer & Co. Ltd* [1934] 1 K.B. 17: *Mohsin Abdullah Alesayi v Brooks Exim Pte Ltd* [1993] 2 Singapore L.R. 433 (widely drafted "variation" clause does not permit tender of goods not in conformity with sample at all); above, para.13–026.

[92] 1922 S.C. (HL) 192. See also *Karsales (Harrow) Ltd v Wallis* [1956] 1 W.L.R. 936, (hirepurchase); *R. G. MacLean Ltd v Canada Vickers Ltd* (1971) 15 D.L.R. (3d) 15.

[93] At pp.199, 200.

[94] See *Ailsa Craig Fishing Co. Ltd v Malvern Shipping Co. Ltd*, 1981 S.L.T. 130 (Ct. of Sess.), esp. *per* Lord Emslie at p.138, doubting dicta in *Mechans Ltd v Highland Marine Charters Ltd*, 1964 S.C. 48. The same view was taken in the House of Lords, [1983] 1 W.L.R. 964 at 967, 970.

[95] [1962] 2 Q.B. 508. See the case explained in the *Suisse Atlantique* case [1967] 1 A.C. 361 at 433. *Farnworth Finance Facilities Ltd v Attryde* [1970] 1 W.L.R. 1053, on a new motor-cycle which was unroadworthy and dangerous to the user, can be explained on the same basis. Both these cases actually relate to hire-purchase transactions. *Cf. Astley Industrial Trust Ltd v Grimley* [1963] 1 W.L.R. 584.

[96] [1966] C.L.J. at 212.

indeed seemed to suggest that a deliberate breach was of itself fundamental and so liability in respect of it unexcludable.[97] This is on any basis too wide: for example, a person who deliberately supplies goods not conforming with description, or defective goods, may honestly be doing his best in the circumstances.[98] But "this is not to say that 'deliberateness' may not be a relevant factor: depending on what the party in breach 'deliberately' intended to do, it may be possible to say that the parties never contemplated that such a breach would be excused or limited: and a deliberate breach may give rise to a right for the innocent party to refuse further performance because it indicates the other party's attitude towards future performance."[99] Thus it has been held in Australia that, where a seller supplied goods of a particular description and knowingly inserted into the contract a different description for the purpose of misleading the other party, a very widely drafted exemption clause did not apply.[1] Where there is active concealment as to the nature of, or defects in, goods supplied, another principle may come into play, for this may be deceit.[2]

5. CONTROL OF EXEMPTION CLAUSES BY STATUTE

13–053 **Introduction.** Until fairly recently control of exemption clauses by statute in the field of sale of goods has been rare, though in the field of hire-purchase it has existed longer.[3] A few statutes contain provisions affecting sales of particular types of goods.[4] But a fairly large change was effected by

---

97 *Alexander v Railway Executive* [1951] 2 K.B. 882 at 887–888; *Sze Hai Tong Bank Ltd v Rambler Cycle Co. Ltd* [1959] A.C. 576 at 588, 589; *J. Spurling Ltd v Bradshaw* [1956] 1 W.L.R. 461 at 466 (all cases on bailment). See also *The Cap Palos* [1921] P. 458; *China Shipbuilding Corp. v Nippon Yusen Kabukishi Kaisha (The Seta Maru)* [2000] 1 Lloyd's Rep. 367 at 377.

98 Though this will not *necessarily* prevent the breach from being repudiatory: see *Federal Commerce and Navigation Co. Ltd v Molena Alpha Inc. (The Nanfri)* [1979] A.C. 757; *cf. Woodar Investment Development Ltd v Wimpey Construction U.K. Ltd* [1980] 1 W.L.R. 277, HL.

99 *Suisse Atlantique* case [1967] 1 A.C. 361 at 435, *per* Lord Wilberforce.

1 *Hall v Queensland Truck Centre Pty Ltd* [1970] Qd.R. 231. See also *N. F. Lanitis & Co. Ltd v Kyodo Shoji (U.K.) Ltd* [1956] 2 Lloyd's Rep. 176 (right to cancel contract "should despatch shipment or delivery of the goods . . . be delayed, prevented or prohibited for any cause whatsoever" held only applicable after sellers had put themselves in a position to acquire goods). But *cf. W. E. Marshall & Co. v Lewis & Peat (Rubber) Ltd* [1963] 1 Lloyd's Rep. 562, where a non-rejection clause was held applicable though goods sent were held not to have been a bona fide shipment under the contract; *Photo Production Ltd v Securicor Transport Ltd* [1980] A.C. 827, above, para.13–047, where the exemption clause was held to apply when the employee deliberately lit a fire in the premises which he was patrolling; *Swiss Bank Corp. v Brink's-Mat Ltd* [1986] 2 Lloyd's Rep. 79 at 95; *Frans Maas (UK) Ltd v Samsung Electronics (UK) Ltd* [2004] EWHC 1502 (Comm); [2004] 2 Lloyd's Rep. 251 at [137] *et seq.* (clause covered wilful neglect or default). See also below, para.13–090, n.57.

2 *Ward v Hobbs* (1878) 4 App.Cas. 13; *Peters & Co. v Planner* (1895) 11 T.L.R. 169; above, para.12–012.

3 See, *e.g.* Hire-Purchase Act 1938, s.8(3).

4 *e.g.* Agriculture Act 1970, ss.68(6), 71(4), 72(3) (sale of fertilisers and feeding stuffs); Plant Varieties and Seeds Act 1964, s.17(1).

section 3 of the Misrepresentation Act 1967; the Supply of Goods (Implied Terms) Act 1973 radically changed the law as to exemption clauses in contracts of sale of goods; and the Unfair Contract Terms Act 1977 re-enacted these provisions, albeit in a slightly different form, together with other more general controls on exemption clauses. The Unfair Terms in Consumer Contracts Regulations 1999 impose further controls. The Consumer Protection Act 1987 and the Fair Trading Act 1973 also contain provisions which may affect the validity of exemption clauses.

Misrepresentation Act 1967, s.3. This (as amended by s.8(1) of the Unfair Contract Terms Act 1977[5]) provides: 13–054

> "If a contract contains a term which would exclude or restrict—(a) any liability to which a party to a contract may be subject by reason of any misrepresentation made by him before the contract was made; or (b) any remedy available to another party to the contract by reason of such a misrepresentation, that term shall be of no effect except in so far as it satisfies the requirement of reasonableness as stated in section 11(1) of the Unfair Contract Terms Act 1977; and it is for those claiming that the term satisfies that requirement to show that it does."[6]

Types of clause covered. It seems clear that the section covers all exemption clauses in the normal sense of the term—clauses excluding or restricting liability in particular respects; clauses limiting the time for suit or the amount of damages that may be recovered; clauses seeking to prevent set-off[7] or rejection; and probably even arbitration clauses.[8] Although the wording is not very apt, the section can presumably be invoked by a representee who is simply pleading the misrepresentation as a defence to an action by the misrepresentor. It is, however, probable that it would not apply to a liquidated damages clause, for such clauses do not exclude or restrict liability: they furnish a pre-arranged compromise as to damages payable, which may just as well favour either party.[9] And it has been held that it does not apply to a clause denying authority to an auctioneer to 13–055

---

[5] Below, para.13–086.

[6] For an exhaustive contemporary discussion of (the original version of) this section, see Atiyah and Treitel, 30 M.L.R. 369 at 379–385 (1967).

[7] *e.g. Skipskreditforeningen v Emperor Navigation* [1998] 1 Lloyd's Rep. 66 (but reasonable: below, para.13–087).

[8] Such clauses are in general exempt from the scope of the Unfair Contract Terms Act 1977: below, para.13–062. But the provision achieving this result (s.13(2)) specifically provides that such a clause "is not to be treated *under this Part of this Act* as excluding or restricting any liability." Although s.3 of the Misrepresentation Act 1967 is amended in the relevant Part of the 1977 Act (Pt. I), the wording of s.11(1) of the 1977 Act makes it clear that the amended section is not to be regarded as within Pt. I; the wording of s.13(2) quoted above suggests that for other purposes an arbitration clause *should* be treated as excluding or restricting liability.

[9] Above, para.13–036.

make representations[10]; nor to a disclaimer which is not contained in the contract but put forward externally to it.[11]

13–056 **Entire agreement clauses.** An "entire agreement" clause, providing (in substance) that the terms set out represent the entire agreement between the parties, can be treated as defining the contract terms rather than excluding liability for pre contractual misrepresentation and therefore not caught by the Act,[12] though arguments of this sort are not usually accepted in connection with the Act or the Unfair Contract Terms Act.[13] On this basis such a clause has been held to exclude collateral warranties, whether because there is specific wording which can be given this effect[14] or even where there is not.[15] Even if the argument that such clauses only define the contract terms is accepted in this context, such a clause would not affect rescission and other liability under the 1967 Act or in tort in respect of pre-contractual representations that had not become terms of the contract.[16] But such clauses frequently contain or are accompanied by specific words indicating non-reliance on representations,[17] and these may make them subject to the Act,[18] though variations in wording make generalisation difficult. It does not follow that they are unreasonable,[19] and this may be the better way of dealing with the problem.

13–057 **Limitation of duty.** The main way of attempting to exclude the section appears to be to insert a clause purporting to make it clear that statements made are of opinion only, or otherwise not to be relied upon. But in

---

[10] *Overbrooke Estates Ltd v Glencombe Properties Ltd* [1974] 1 W.L.R. 1335 (a case on the original wording); see Coote [1975] C.L.J. 17; followed in *Museprime Properties Ltd v Adhill Properties Ltd* [1990] 2 E.G.L.R. 196 at 200. *Sed quaere*; see below, para.13–057.
[11] *Collins v Howell-Jones* (1980) 259 E.G. 331 (criticised, 97 L.Q.R. 522 (1981)); *Cremdean Properties Ltd v Nash*, below, para.13–057.
[12] *Inntrepreneur Pub Co. (GL) v East Crown Ltd* [2000] 2 Lloyd's Rep. 611; 696 *Watford Electronics Ltd v Sanderson CFL Ltd* [2001] EWCA Civ 317; [2001] 1 All E.R. (Comm) at [41], where the idea that such a clause is caught is described by Chadwick L.J. as "bizarre". In *McGrath v Shah* (1987) 57 P. & C.R. 452 and *E. Grimstead & Son Ltd v McGarrigan*, CA, October 27, 1999 applicability of the Act had been assumed but not decided.
[13] See below, paras 13–057, 13–065, 13–066.
[14] *Deepak Fertilisers and Petrochemicals Corp. v ICI Chemicals and Polymers Ltd* [1998] 2 Lloyd's Rep. 139; [1999] 1 Lloyd's Rep. 387. See also *The Helene Knutsen* [2003] EWHC 1964 (Comm); [2003] 2 Lloyd's Rep 686, where the clause excluded implied terms based on usage or custom.
[15] *Inntrepreneur Pub Co. (GL) v East Crown Ltd*, above; *Sere Holdings Ltd v Volkswagen Group UK Ltd* [2004] EWHC 1551 (Ch); *cf. Cheverney Consulting Ltd v Whitehead Mann Ltd* [2005] EWHC 2431.
[16] *Deepak Fertilisers and Petrochemicals Corp. v ICI Chemicals and Polymers Ltd* [1999] 1 Lloyd's Rep. 387 at 395; *Inntrepreneur Pub Co (GL) v East Crown Ltd*, above, at p.614; *Government of Zanzibar v British Aerospace (Lancaster House) Ltd* [2001] 1 W.L.R. 2333 at 2344; see also *Thomas Witter & Co. Ltd v TBP Industries Ltd* [1996] 2 All E.R. 573 (must be clear).
[17] As to how such clauses have effect, see above, para.13–030.
[18] See *Inntrepreneur Pub Co. (GL) v East Crown Ltd*, above at p.614; *Inntrepreneur Estates (CPC) Ltd v Worth* [1996] 1 E.G.L.R. 84; *Government of Zanzibar v British Aerospace (Lancaster House) Ltd*, above; *SAM Business Systems Ltd v Hedley & Co* [2002] EWHC 2733 (TCC); [2003] 1 All E.R. (Comm) 465.
[19] See below, para.13–060. This was so in the *SAM Business Systems* case, above.

Cremdean Properties Ltd v Nash,[20] estate agents used a clause reading: "(a) These particulars are prepared for the convenience of an intending purchaser or tenant and although they are believed to be correct their accuracy is not guaranteed and any error, omission or misdescription shall not annul the sale or be grounds on which compensation may be claimed and neither do they constitute any part of an offer of a contract. (b) Any intending purchaser or tenant must satisfy himself by inspection or otherwise as to the correctness of each of the statements contained in these particulars." The Court of Appeal rejected arguments that the effect of these words was to bring about a situation as if no representation had been made; and Bridge L.J. said that he did not think the courts would be ready "to allow such ingenuity in forms of language to defeat the plain purpose at which section 3 is aimed."[21] It is difficult to see why such reasoning should not equally invalidate "authority" clauses, at least where the agent concerned is extremely likely to make representations, which is true of many agents for sale such as auctioneers and estate agents. Where such a clause is used by a company, which can *only* act through agents, it is most doubtful whether it should be taken at its face value. Perhaps in the end it will be possible to distinguish the existing cases and apply the Act to other clauses having an evasive effect.[22]

Not applicable as regards pure contractual terms. The words "by reason of any misrepresentation made by him before the contract was made" seem to confine the section to provisions relating to misrepresentations inducing contracts, and to the exercise of remedies for misrepresentation where such a misrepresentation has been incorporated into the contract but the right to rescind is preserved by section 1(a) of the 1967 Act and the remedies under section 2 of that Act are still applicable.[23] The section does not, therefore, apply to clauses limiting or excluding liability for breach of contractual terms solely; nor perhaps can it be invoked where no more than damages are sought, in contract only, for breach of a term which had first been communicated as an independent misrepresentation. Often, however, exemption clauses are vaguely worded and might apply both to misrepresentations inducing the contract and to contractual terms, whether statements or promises, *e.g.* "with all faults". In such cases it seems that the section can be invoked, for it provides that where a provision would exclude any liability for misrepresentation "that term shall be of no effect except in so far as it satisfies the requirement of reasonableness", *i.e.* it subjects the whole provision to the test. 13–058

[20] (1977) 244 E.G. 547 (also on the unamended wording); see also *South Western General Property Co. Ltd v Marton* (1982) 263 E.G. 1090 (new wording) (see below, para.13–086); *St Marylebone Property Co. Ltd v Payne* [1994] 2 E.G.L.R. 25.

[21] At p.551. Section 13 of the Unfair Contract Terms Act 1977 (below, para.13–064) does not appear to apply, for the reasons given above, n.8. As to this reasoning in general, see below, paras 13–065 *et seq*.

[22] Above, nn. 10, 11. Where the Consumer Credit Act 1974 is applicable, such clauses may be void under s.56(3).

[23] Above, paras 12–064, 12–069. See *Thomas Witter Ltd v T.B.P. Industries Ltd* [1996] 2 All E.R. 573 at 595–597.

13–059 **Only covers liability of party to contract.** The wording of the section makes it clear that it only applies to exemptions from liability in respect of pre-contractual representations made by a person who subsequently becomes a party to a contract—not to those made in circumstances where no contract results, nor to those made by third parties. This is true also of liability under section 2(1) of the same Act.[24] Nor does it apply to disclaimers incorporated into the representation but not subsequently becoming part of the contract[25]: though these might be caught by the Unfair Contract Terms Act 1977.[26]

13–060 **Reasonableness.** The test of reasonableness stated in section 11(1) of the Unfair Contract Terms Act 1977 is that "the term shall have been a fair and reasonable one to be included having regard to the circumstances which were, or ought reasonably to have been, known to or in the contemplation of the parties when the contract was made."[27] The guidelines relevant to sale and related transactions[28] are not applicable to such clauses, though the court may find them relevant[29]; but the guidelines in section 11(4) as to restrictions of liability to a specified sum of money[30] apply where the question of reasonableness arises "under this or any other Act" and so must be taken into account. The main purpose of the amendment of section 3 in this way was to change the time at which the clause must be reasonable to the time of contracting: the original wording provided that the provision was to be "of no effect except to the extent (if any) that . . . the court or arbitrator may allow reliance on it as being fair and reasonable in the circumstances of the case." Under this provision "entire agreement" clauses have been held, if caught by the Act at all, reasonable[31] (though accompanying wording as to non-reliance might not be[32]); as have no-set-off clauses.[33]

13–061 **The Supply of Goods (Implied Terms) Act 1973.** Further control was imposed on exemption clauses by the Supply of Goods (Implied Terms) Act 1973, which implemented the English and Scottish Law Commissions'

---

[24] Above, para.12–014.
[25] In *Cremdean Properties Ltd v Nash*, above, para.13–057, the clause had been held to do so: see p.551 and 241 E.G. 837 (1977).
[26] Below, paras 13–062 *et seq.*
[27] See below, paras 13–086 *et seq.*
[28] Below, para.13–088.
[29] See below, paras 13–088, 13–090.
[30] Below, para.13–091.
[31] *McGrath v Shah* (1987) 57 P. & C.R. 452; *E. Grimstead & Son Ltd v McGarrigan*, CA, October 27, 1999 (in both of which the applicability of the Act was doubted but assumed); *SAM Business Systems Ltd v Headley & Co.* [2002] EWHC 2733 (TCC); [2003] 1 All E.R. (Comm) 465; above, para.13–056.
[32] *Inntrepreneur Estates (CPC) Ltd v Worth* [1996] 1 E.G.L.R. 84; *Government of Zanzibar v British Aerospace (Lancaster House) Ltd* [2001] 1 W.L.R. 2333.
[33] *Skippskreditforeningen v Emperor Navigation* [1998] 1 Lloyd's Rep. 66. See also above, para.13–039 and more generally *Walker v Boyle* [1982] 1 W.L.R. 495; *South Western General Property Co. v Marton* (1982) 263 E.G. 1090; and below, para.13–062 as to the Unfair Contract Terms Act 1977, and para.13–091 as to limits on amount.

First Report on Exemption Clauses.[34] This amended the wording of sections 13, 14 and 15 of the Sale of Goods Act 1893 (changes now assimilated into the Sale of Goods Act 1979)[35] and placed restrictions on contracting out of the obligations imposed by those sections by inserting new provisions into that Act.[36] It also provided in a corresponding way for hire-purchase contracts.

Unfair Contract Terms Act 1977. The Law Commissions' Second Report on Exemption Clauses[37] recommended extending statutory control further, and these proposals were implemented (though not in the precise way recommended) by the Unfair Contract Terms Act 1977. The latter Act removed the provisions controlling exemption clauses from the Sale of Goods Act and reenacted them, in a different form but with substantially the same effect, together with other restrictions on exemption clauses having a more general application in the field of contract (and tort) law.[38] 13–062

Methods used by the 1977 Act.[39] The 1977 Act uses a mixture of the techniques available to control contractual clauses. It contains several different provisions, which overlap considerably: a particular contract term may be potentially affected by more than one of them. Some of its provisions apply to all contracts: some to consumer contracts; and some to standard contract terms (a category which has been identified for control in other countries[40] but had not hitherto in the United Kingdom). Sometimes the Act applies to claims in tort. Sometimes clauses are ineffective: sometimes they are only effective if reasonable. Most of the Act is confined to situations of "business liability": but some of it is applicable to private transactions.[41] The Act took its place at the time with other regulation of unfair contract terms which had been brought into operation in Europe,[42] the United States[43] and Australia.[44] It should, however, be noted that it is in two principal respects more limited than control which is operative elsewhere. First, it is limited to exemption clauses (albeit widely defined): it has no application to other forms of unfair contract term (such as price escalation clauses, clauses providing for forfeiture and clauses providing 13–063

---

[34] Law Com.No.24, Scot. Law Com.No.12 (1969).
[35] Above, Ch.11.
[36] s.55(3)–(11). Its effect was discussed in the first edition of this work (1974).
[37] Law Com. No.69; Sc. Law Com. No.39 (1975).
[38] s.31(1), (2). A useful account of the history of this legislation is given in P. K. J. Thompson, *The Unfair Contract Terms Act 1977* (1978), Ch.1.
[39] See in general *Chitty on Contracts* (29th ed.), Vol. 1, paras 14–059 *et seq.*; Treitel, *Law of Contract* (11th ed.), pp.246 *et seq.*; Yates, *Exclusion Clauses in Contracts* (2nd ed.), Ch.3; Coote, 41 M.L.R. 312 (1978). Part II of the Act applies to Scotland; and Part III to the whole United Kingdom. Discussion here is confined to the law applicable in England, Wales and Northern Ireland. As to international sales, see below, paras 18–280 *et seq.*
[40] *e.g.* the German *AGB-Gesetz* of 1976, now paras 308, 309 *BGB*.
[41] s.1(3); 6(1), (4).
[42] As to which see Hondius, 26 Am.J.Comp.L. 525 (1978).
[43] Uniform Commercial Code, s.2–302.
[44] Trade Practices Act 1973 (Cth.) as amended; Contracts Review Act 1980 (N.S.W.).

that the agent of the party acts as agent of the other in certain respects[45]) which may be regulated in other countries[46]. In this respect the title is misleading.[47] And secondly, its effect is confined to the particular dispute in which a clause is sought to be invoked. Legislation in other countries provides for abstract litigation resulting in declarations and orders that certain terms may not be used.[48] As a measure of control of unfair contract terms the Act should be viewed together with the Enterprise Act 2002, which gives powers to the Office of Fair Trading to procure that certain trade practices, including the use of unfair contract terms, be made illegal by statutory instrument and restrained.[49] But the total result gives less direct control than can be found in some other countries. It should also be said that the Act is complex in its drafting: although time has brought familiarity with the wording, it was unfortunate that such an important measure of relief against unequal bargaining, very considerably directed towards consumers, should have been formulated in such a way.

13–064 **Types of clause covered.** The Unfair Contract Terms Act is directed at exemption clauses only, and most of its provisions refer to clauses "excluding or restricting" liability. Section 13(1) seeks to put a wide interpretation on these words by providing as follows:

> "To the extent that this Part of this Act prevents the exclusion or restriction of any liability it also prevents—(a) making the liability or its enforcement subject to restrictive or onerous conditions; (b) excluding or restricting any right or remedy in respect of the liability, or subjecting a person to any prejudice in consequence of his pursuing any such right or remedy; (c) excluding or restricting rules of evidence or procedure; and (to that extent) sections 2 and 5 to 7 also prevent excluding or restricting liability by reference to terms and notices which exclude or restrict the relevant obligation or duty."[50]

An example of (a) would be a time-limit on claims[51]; of (b), a non-rejection clause[52]; and of (c), a clause framed as an acknowledgment that goods were

---

[45] But see Consumer Credit Act 1974, s.57(3).
[46] The Unfair Terms in Consumer Contracts Regulations (below, paras 13–103, 14–030 *et seq.*) are not so limited. See in particular the types of term listed in Sch.2.
[47] The Bill as first introduced was called the Avoidance of Liability (England and Wales) Bill. As to difficulties caused by this restriction, see above, para.13–044; below, paras 13–064 *et seq.*, 13–094, 13–106.
[48] See Hondius, *op. cit.*, above, n.42. Again, the Unfair Terms in Consumer Contracts Regulations, above, were intended to have a wider effect, and in the United Kingdom to some extent do so: below, paras 14–030 *et seq.*
[49] Below, paras 14–125.
[50] See two cases considering whether provisions in contracts for the hire of excavators together with drivers are caught by the Act: *Thompson v T. Lohan (Plant) Ltd* [1987] 1 W.L.R. 649; *Phillips Products Ltd v Hyland Ltd, ibid.*, at p.659n.
[51] See *BHP Petroleum Ltd v British Steel Plc* [1999] 2 Lloyd's Rep. 583 at 592 (affirmed without reference to this point [2000] 2 Lloyd's Rep. 277).
[52] It does not seem that a clause seeking to prevent the buyer from suing the seller's agents or independent contractors by requiring the proceeds to be paid to the seller

on delivery satisfactory, or providing that receipt by the buyer is "conclusive evidence" to that effect. It is not clear whether (b) covers liquidated damages clauses or not; it is arguable that as they do not always restrict liability, they are not within the wording.[53] A clause excluding rights of set-off has been held caught by the Act.[54] A clause denying authority to an agent to make promises or vary terms has been held in the context of the Misrepresentation Act 1967,[55] however, to prevent accrual of liability rather than exclude or restrict it[56]; and a clause seeking to prevent what might otherwise be a contract from having legal effect may not be a contract term[57] and therefore appears to be caught only by the provisions regarding notices, which relate to tort liability.[58] A purported exclusion or limitation of the new remedies provided for consumers by Part 5A of the Sale of Goods Act 1979[59] would be caught by (b), as a term excluding or limiting any right or remedy in respect of the liability concerned. An exclusion of the six-month presumption of disconformity in that Part[60] would, at any rate in so far as it is applicable to the Part 5A remedies, also be caught by (b) (and perhaps (c), as excluding rules of evidence). As such, in so far as they applied to the statutory implied terms under sections 13, 14 and 15 of the Sale of Goods Act 1979, such provisions would be void under section 6(2) of the Unfair Contract Terms Act 1979.[61]

The final words of section 13(1) raise general problems of definition. It has 13–065 been pointed out in connection with the doctrine of fundamental breach[62] that exemption clauses are an unsatisfactory object of control, **13–065**

---

is caught, since the right pursued is not that in respect of the *seller's* liability: but such a clause might be held to stipulate for a penalty. *Quaere* whether (b) covers attempts to restrict the rights of examination provided by s.34 of the Sale of Goods Act (above, para.12–039). It is submitted that it does, with the result that such attempts are ineffective in consumer sales. The right to compare bulk with sample was formerly in s.15 of the Sale of Goods Act itself and so directly controlled by s.6 of the Unfair Contract Terms Act. Clauses affecting the right to examine may be caught by s.35(3) of the Sale of Goods Act as amended: below, para.13–102. But this only goes to rejection, and in damages claims s.13 of the 1977 Act might prove useful.

[53] The Law Commissions thought that they *should* be subject to scrutiny: Law Com. No.69, Sc.Law Com. No.39, para.166 (1975).

[54] *Stewart Gill Ltd v Horatio Myer & Co. Ltd* [1992] Q.B. 600; and unreasonable, below, para.13–087.

[55] See *Lutton v Saville Tractors (Belfast) Ltd* (1986) 12 N.I.L.R.B. 1 at 19 ("transparent attempts to escape the operation of s.6(2)(a) of the Act" *per* Carswell J.).

[56] *cf. Overbrooke Estates Ltd v Glencombe Properties Ltd* [1974] 1 W.L.R. 1335.

[57] *e.g. Rose & Frank v Crompton Bros Ltd* [1925] A.C. 445 (honour clause); *MacRobertson Miller Airline Services v Commissioner of State Taxation (W.A.)* (1975) 133 C.L.R. 125 (airline ticket); or the common stipulation "subject to contract". This point is particularly relevant to s.3.

[58] Below, para.13–106.

[59] See above, paras 12–071 *et seq*.

[60] s. 48A(3): above, para.12–075. See also para.12–117.

[61] Below, para.13–083. But a term excluding liability for a breach of an express contract term other than one going to description of the goods (to which the Part 5A remedies also apply: see above, para.12–074) would not be caught by s.6 and would only be subject to the requirement of reasonableness under s.3 of the 1977 Act (below, para.13–094).

[62] Above, para.13–044.

because it is difficult to define what they are: a similar result can sometimes be obtained by the different technique of formulating the object of the contract in a limited way. These words seem to be intended to deal with that problem: they extend the notion of an exemption clause to "terms and notices which exclude or restrict the relevant obligation or duty". On their face they are, however, still open to the same objection: what is the "relevant obligation or duty"? A clause can be so drafted as to define rather than exclude or restrict it. However, in *Smith v Eric S. Bush*[63] the House of Lords, in connection with the effect of a surveyor's disclaimer against a third party suing in tort, rejected the idea that a term or notice could define the duty of care owed in tort in respect of negligent statements. Lord Griffiths said that he read the relevant provision of the Act "as introducing a 'but for' test in relation to the notice excluding liability. They indicate that the existence of the common law duty to take reasonable care . . . is to be judged by considering whether it would exist 'but for' the notice excluding liability."[64] This result, while not easy to justify on principle, is in accord with case law on section 3 of the Misrepresentation Act 1967 as amended, which likewise cannot be evaded by simply indicating that representations should not be relied on: and here the result was reached without the benefit of a special provision such as section 13(1) of the 1977 Act.[65]

13–066 *Smith v Eric S. Bush* was a tort case, and the reference to "but for" derives from a provision of the Act relating to tort only, section 11(3). This defines the requirement of reasonableness for a notice not having contractual effect as that "it should be fair and reasonable to allow reliance on it having regard to all the circumstances obtaining when the liability arose or (but for the notice) would have arisen."[66] In tort, the duty of care can be said to be imposed by law—a point indeed made in the case.[67] In contract, however, the only duty is (in general) that undertaken, so that the reasoning of *Smith v Eric S. Bush* could be regarded as inapplicable. Nevertheless it seems likely that in order to prevent evasion of the purposes of the Act the same reasoning would be applied whenever the contract contains implied terms which would operate but for the exemption clause. In sales such terms are implied by sections 12 to 15 of the Sale of Goods Act, and similar terms are implied into related transactions by sections 2 to 5 and 7 to 10 of the Supply of Goods and Services Act 1982. It is probable that this is why the final words of section 13(1) are directed to sections 2 and 5 to 7, which deal with liability in tort and under implied terms. Hence in the context of section 6 of the Act, which deals with exclusion of implied terms in sale of goods and is one of those in respect of which section 13(1) is applicable, it would seem that a clause seeking to delimit the contractual

---

63 [1990] 1 A.C. 831; Allen, 105 L.Q.R. 511 (1989).
64 At p.857; followed in *McCullagh v Lane Fox & Partners Ltd* [1996] 1 E.G.L.R. 35, CA. See also *Johnstone v Bloomsbury H.A.* [1992] Q.B. 333 at 346.
65 *Cremdean Properties Ltd v Nash* (1977) 244 E.G. 547; above, para.13–057.
66 Below, para.13–086.
67 But *cf. Henderson v Merrett Syndicates Ltd* [1995] 2 A.C. 145, where the notion of "assumption of responsibility," is used (the connection with economic loss).

obligation so as to exclude the operation of any of sections 13 to 15 of the Sale of Goods Act[68] would usually be caught by the Act.

Modification of contractual description. The type of clause used in sale of goods contracts most difficult of analysis in this connection is one which seeks to establish that a sale is not by description, or that the description is much reduced or modified from what it would otherwise be, for the purposes of section 13 of the 1979 Act[69]—as by the words "sold as seen and inspected". The Consumer Protection (Restriction on Statements) Order 1976[70] makes it an offence to purport to apply contract terms or notices which are void by virtue of the Unfair Contract Terms Act 1977. In *Hughes v Hall*,[71] a case concerning a prosecution for breach of the Order, the Divisional Court of the Queen's Bench Division held that a clause "sold as seen and inspected" in the sale of a car was a clause purporting to exclude liability for breach of section 13 of the Sale of Goods Act. This may have been in substance correct on the facts, but such a clause certainly ought in appropriate cases to be able to modify the contractual description. However, in *Cavendish-Woodhouse Ltd v Manley*,[72] another Divisional Court in a similar case on the Order, dealing with furniture specified as "bought as seen", found the first case a "puzzling decision" and held that the words did not purport to exclude liability at all but merely indicated that the purchaser had seen the goods which he had bought. The exclusion alleged was of section 14 as to merchantable quality (the term then in use), but on this interpretation *a fortiori* the words did not go to description either. Hence no offence was committed by the use of the clause. The situation as to reduction of description therefore remains uncertain. It is one of the results of selecting exemption clauses as the target for control; and also of the designation of compliance with description as an *implied* term.[73] The only certainty is that the courts are unwilling to tolerate what may appear to be evasions of the Unfair Contract Terms Act (or of section 3 of the Misrepresentation Act).[74] Subject to this rather vague reservation, however, it must surely be possible to establish the contract description as something more limited than normal, *e.g.* that a car is sold as scrap metal or that a substance is sold without indication of its properties. Similar reasoning may also be applied to other clauses, for example clauses making the duty to deliver subject to shipment or availability.[75] Equally, the contract may stipulate a standard of performance which has the effect of eliminating possible defences, such as contributory negligence.[76] 13–067

---

68 Above, paras 11–001 *et seq*.

69 Above, para.11–001.

70 SI 1976/1813, as amended; below, paras 13–105, 14–142.

71 [1981] R.T.R. 430.

72 (1984) 82 L.G.R. 376.

73 See above, para.11–103.

74 Compare the approach to this problem in the Unfair Terms in Consumer Contracts Regulations (below, paras 13–103, 14–030 *et seq*., Reg. 6.

75 *cf.* below, para.19–014.

76 *Rolls Royce Power Engineering Plc v Ricardo Consulting Engineers Ltd* [2003] EWHC 2871 (TCC); [2004] 2 All E.R.(Comm) 129 at [75], [76]. See also *Barclays Bank Plc v Fairclough Building Ltd* [1995] Q.B. 214.

13–068 **Warnings.** The notion of warning is also different from that of exemption, and it seems also that some clauses may be effective as warnings. They may by warning against certain sorts of use indicate the characteristics of the goods supplied and so contribute towards determining their contractual description. Equally, they may make the goods of satisfactory quality, indicating how they should be used and how to avoid misuse.[77] Again, they may provide a defence to liability in tort. Thus use of the phrase "as seen with all its faults and without warranty" was in *Hurley v Dyke*[78] held to discharge a duty of care in tort.[79]

13–069 **Arbitration clauses.** By section 13(2) "an agreement in writing to submit present or future differences to arbitration is not to be treated under this part of this Act as excluding or restricting any liability."[80] It could otherwise be thought that compulsory arbitration might well in many circumstances be prejudicial, at least to consumers.[81] It should be noted that the exclusion only relates to arbitration agreements in writing. But a time limit which bars the right of action would probably be caught by the Act.

13–070 **Basic notions: business liability.** The Act requires the appreciation of two basic notions which are several times utilised. The first is that of "business liability", to which the Act's operation is largely but not entirely confined.[82] This is defined by section 1(3) as "liability for breach of obligations or duties arising—(a) from things done or to be done by a person in the course of a business (whether his own business or another's); or (b) from the occupation of premises used for business purposes of the occupier." Only (a) will of course normally be relevant in matters involving sale of goods. No definition of "business" is given beyond a statement in section 14 that "'business' includes a profession and the activities of any government department or local or public authority," which suggests that a "business" need not be conducted for profit. It has been said that "the word 'business' is an etymological chameleon; it suits its meaning to the context in which it is found. It is not a term of legal art."[83] The whole notion is, in the context of sale of goods, related to the wording "sells goods in the course of a business" in section 14 of the Sale of Goods Act 1979, which deals with the seller's obligations,[84] and to "makes the contract in the course of a business" in section 12 of the Unfair Contract Terms Act itself,

---

[77] See above, para.11–039.
[78] [1979] R.T.R. 265, HL.
[79] See below, para.13–106.
[80] The Unfair Terms in Consumer Contracts Regulations (below, paras 13–103, 14–030 *et seq.*) are not so limited. See also Arbitration Act 1996, ss.85–91 and SI 1999/2167 as to consumer arbitrations. Arbitration clauses may be caught by s.3 of the Misrepresentation Act 1967: above, para.13–041. Arbitration clauses should be distinguished from valuation, certification and testing clauses: above, para.13–040.
[81] See Mustill and Boyd, *Commercial Arbitration* (2nd ed.), p.175; above, para.13–041.
[82] See ss.1(3), 6(4).
[83] *Town Investments Ltd v Dept of the Environment* [1978] A.C. 359 at 383, *per* Lord Diplock.
[84] Above, paras 11–027, 11–052.

which defines the notion of "dealing as consumer".[85] General discussion will be found in connection with these provisions: of the second of them in the following paragraph. The object of the unfair contract terms legislation is in this context presumably to exclude from control only terms put forward by a person acting in a purely private capacity. Much more difficulty may, however, arise in connection with the application of the phrase to tort liability.[86] The reference to "his own business or another's" is presumably inserted to cover situations of agency.

Dealing as consumer. Complexity has been caused by the use of this phrase as denoting also the situations in which a buyer is entitled to the special remedies provided by the new Part 5A of the Sale of Goods Act 1979.[87] Making use of it in this way has necessitated changes to the original text of the 1977 Act. The text of section 12 of the Unfair Contract Terms Act as amended now reads as follows: 13–071

> "(1) A party to a contract 'deals as consumer' in relation to another party if—
>
> (a) he neither makes the contract in the course of a business nor holds himself out as doing so; and
> (b) the other party does make the contract in the course of a business; and
> (c) in the case of a contract governed by the law of sale of goods or hire-purchase, or by section 7 of this Act,[88] the goods passing under or in pursuance of the contract are of a type ordinarily supplied for private use or consumption.
>
> (1A) But if the first party mentioned in subsection (1) is an individual paragraph (c) of that subsection must be ignored.
>
> (2) But the buyer is not in any circumstances to be regarded as dealing as consumer—
>
> (a) if he is an individual and the goods are second hand goods sold at a public auction at which individuals have the opportunity of attending the sale in person;
> (b) if he is not an individual and the goods are sold by auction or by competitive tender.
>
> (3) Subject to this, it is those claiming that a party does not deal as consumer to show that he does not."

Use in the Unfair Contract Terms Act. The original definition of "deals as a consumer", which contained only 1(a), (b) and (c) above, had and has the following features. First, if there is a series of contracts each must be 13–072

---

[85] Below, para.13–071.
[86] P. K. J. Thompson, *The Unfair Contract Terms Act 1977* (1978), pp.15–17.
[87] See above, paras 12–071 *et seq.*
[88] As to which, see below, para.13–085.

considered separately. Secondly, the definition is not confined to consumer buyers: a person may sell as consumer (though as regards the new Part 5A, its only application is to consumer buyers). Thirdly, there is no requirement that the consumer be a natural person: a corporation or a business may be a consumer,[89] and this is still true (by reason of this provision) as regards the new Part 5A. But an overall difficulty has always been that the two prescriptions, those for the buyer and those for the seller, are reciprocally identical and framed to operate in accordance with whether the sale is, on each side, in the course of a business or not. This can lead to unsatisfactory results.

13–073 The focus of difficulty has from the start been the situation of someone who is in business (for the purposes of the wording of the Act) but buys or sells something which it is not part of his business, or not a central part of his business, to buy or sell. An example of the first could be a medical practitioner who needs six chairs for his surgery waiting-room, and buys them on normal terms (does not, for instance, ask for a trade discount) at a furniture retailer. A reciprocal example of the second could be the same practitioner who sells off superseded computer equipment, or a car used in the practice. In neither case does he have in the course of his occupation or business specialised knowledge concerning the goods such as a person who deals in them would have. Therefore, it might be thought that he should rank as a consumer buyer in the first situation and as a private (*i.e.* not a trade) seller in the second. It may well be that many transactions proceed on this basis.

13–074 The case law probably accepts this as regards the first situation (of buying chairs): he does not deal in chairs, about which he knows no more than any consumer, and so deals as consumer. This conclusion favours protection of the consumer and has been reached in connection with the purchase by a firm of surveyors of a Rolls-Royce car "to be used on high days and holidays"[90]; in the leading Court of Appeal case of *R&B Customs Brokers Co. Ltd v United Dominions Trust Ltd*[91] by a freight forwarding company of a car for the use of its managing director; and most recently of the purchase of a Lamborghini car for the managing director of a finance company (the purchase being "seen as a reward"[92]). On this side of the equation, therefore, the purchaser will deal as consumer (and even if a company) unless the purchase is an integral part of his business or involves at least some degree of regularity; and this favours consumer protection.

---

[89] An early case was *Rasbora v J.C.L. Marine Ltd* [1977] 1 Lloyd's Rep. 645, where the buyer of a boat substituted for himself a company formed, for tax reasons, to buy the boat. But the car cases below involve the same situation.
[90] *Peter Symmons & Co. v Cooke* (1981) 131 N.L.J. 758.
[91] [1988] 1 W.L.R. 321. See Kidner (1987) 38 N.I.L.Q. 46; Pearce [1988] L.M.C.L.Q. 371; Brown [1989] J.B.L. 386; Price (1989) 52 M.L.R. 545; Jones and Harland (1990) 2 J. Contract Law 266. As to "private purchasers" and "trade purchasers" under s.27 of the Hire Purchase Act 1964 (which concerns transfer of title) see above, paras 7–092, 7–093.
[92] *Feldaroll Foundry Plc v Hermes Leasing Plc* [2004] EWHC Civ 747.

On the other hand, to apply the same criterion of acting in the course of a business to the seller from whom the consumer purchases, and say that there is no sale in the course of a business unless there is some degree of regularity in performing such sales, would reduce the consumer's protection. Thus in *Stevenson v Rogers*,[93] it was held that the sale by a fisherman of his boat was a sale in the course of business although he was not in the business of selling boats and had only done so once before. This case, which distinguished a line of cases under the Trade Descriptions Act (a criminal statute)[94] was, however, in the context of the duty under section 14 of the Sale of Goods Act 1979 of a person who sells in the course of a business to supply goods of satisfactory quality and fit for their purpose, where a narrow interpretation would reduce the buyer's protection[95]; and the Court made clear that for the purposes of the Unfair Contract Terms Act 1977 the reasoning of the *R&B* case, also a Court of Appeal case, stood, despite the fact that the same terminology is under that Act used both for buyer and for seller. The use of the same wording in section 12 of the 1977 Act creates an inappropriate imbalance which, if legislation does not intervene,[96] may require solution. The objective of protecting consumers suggests that subsection (a) be given a narrow interpretation and subsection (b) a wide one. If *Stevenson v Rogers* can be applied to the Unfair Contract Terms Act 1977, this is the present situation on the case law. However, it is not clear that this can be done, nor how it can be justified as a matter of consistency. 13–075

Buyer holding himself out as buying in the course of a business. This wording is rather unsatisfactory: the idea of holding out usually applies to one person holding *another* out as his *agent*.[97] Apart from the buyer, for whatever reason, posing as a business buyer, it may be that asking for trade terms, discounts and the like could sometimes (not always) come within this wording. 13–076

Use in Part 5A of the Sale of Goods Act 1979. Regardless of this, and despite the somewhat different definition of "consumer" in Regulation 2 of the Sale and Supply of Goods to Consumers Regulations 2002 (which refers to "acting *for purposes* which are outside his trade, business or profession" and so introduces a useful reference to the purpose of a particular transaction), the phrase "deals as consumer" as defined in the 1977 Act remains the trigger for the new remedies of Part 5A of the Sale of Goods Act 1979 introduced in 2002 (though operative in 2003). These implement the Consumer Sales Directive of 1999. The definition of "consumer", taken from the Directive, is (surprisingly) left to a limited role in connection with consumer guarantees. This means that there must be an assessment, not only of the position of the buyer but also that of the seller; and leaves for solution, but in a different context, the question whether the two sides of 13–077

---

[93] [1999] Q.B. 1028.
[94] Especially *Davies v Sumner* [1984] 1 W.L.R. 1301, HL.
[95] See above, para.11–027.
[96] See above, para.13–011.
[97] *cf.* Partnership Act 1890, s.14.

the test should or should not balance out. It also leaves for decision whether the car cases referred to above are correct for the new legislation, though the actual results in them are affected somewhat by the fact that the Directive which the Regulations implement did not envisage corporations and businesses as consumers at all.

13–078 **Changes to accommodate Part 5A of the Sale of Goods Act 1979: subsections (1A) and (2).** The provision in subsection (1)(c), confining the consumer's protection to cases where the sale was of consumer goods, was contrary to the requirements of the Directive, where "consumer goods" were very widely defined. On the other hand, the Directive only sought to protect consumers who were natural persons, and there is no objection to a national law retaining similar protection for companies and businesses. Hence in subsection (1A) what may be called the "consumer goods" requirement was abolished for "individuals" (undefined, presumably "natural persons" as in the Directive) but could be and was retained for those who were consumers but *not* individuals. Next, the original provisions of the Act did not apply to sales by auction or competitive tender, where consumers were presumably expected to look after themselves if they participated in such functions, and it is difficult for the person conducting such a sale to know if a bidder is a consumer or not.[98] But this did not conform with the requirements of the Directive and hence again had to be restricted to consumers who are not individuals, by a modification in subsection (2)(b). On the other hand, the Directive contained a lesser exception denying protection in respect of second-hand goods[99] sold at a public auction which a consumer who is an individual has the opportunity[1] to attend in person; and this is by subsection (2)(a) introduced for individuals, leaving the wider exclusion for companies and businesses above.

13–079 **Repercussions.** These changes, introduced for a different purpose, naturally operate for the 1977 Act itself as well as for the purposes of Part 5A of the Sale of Goods Act 1979 and thus, by altering the meaning of the phrase "deal as consumer" that applies elsewhere, slightly change the effect of the Act. For example, the rules as to reasonableness of consumer contracts (section 3), and the total prohibition on exclusions of sections 13, 14 and 15 of the Act where the buyer deals as consumer, now apply even where the goods are not consumer goods, if the purchaser is an individual. Conversely, individuals are by reason of the amendments now better protected

---

[98] There can also be problems with forced sales. But a subsequent sale by an auctioneer outside the auction would not be protected: *D.&M. Trailers (Halifax) Ltd v Stirling* [1978] R.T.R. 468.

[99] There may be an argument as to what this means. It may be suggested that to qualify, goods must have been used by, or at least in the possession of, someone who might be expected to consume or use them. This would exclude, for example, wholesalers, and persons or business who store, for example, wine for eventual use by its purchasers.

[1] Which he does not need to have exercised; for example he may have sent in a telephone bid.

by the 1977 Act against unfair contract terms if they attend auctions; and their protection in that respect is no longer confined to consumer goods.

Agency problems. A difficulty may arise where a private seller sells through a commercial or professional agent other than an auctioneer (as to whom there is special provision[2]). If he sells to the agent, who then resells in the course of his business, the sale is obviously made by the "agent" (who would in fact not be acting as such), and is made in the course of a business. The same is the case if the principal remains undisclosed, for here again the sale is made by the agent.[3] In other cases of agency, however, in accordance with the normal rules, it is the principal who is the seller, and if he does not act in the course of a business the other party cannot deal as consumer. As against this it may be argued that the terms implied by section 14 of the Sale of Goods Act 1979 are, by subsection (5), expressly rendered applicable when a private seller sells through an agent acting in the course of a business, even as an undisclosed principal, unless the buyer knows, or steps have been taken to inform him, that the seller is a private seller.[4] But for this provision, on a sale by a private seller through a business agent there would be no implied undertakings as to quality at all, so that any purported exclusion would be unobjectionable. Since it is this provision which imposes liability on the seller in such a case, it is arguable that it should be regarded as determining also whether a sale through an agent is in the course of a business for the purpose of defining a consumer sale. In view, however, of the facts that section 14(5) is expressly related only to "the preceding provisions of this section", and that sections 13 and 15 are not affected by this reasoning (because not confined to professional sellers), the former view is perhaps preferable, but it cannot be said that the matter is clear. Difficulties may again occur where a private purchaser buys through a commercial agent. If the agent is authorised to buy on his own account and resell, the sale is to the agent and is obviously in the course of business (though again such a person would not be acting as agent in such a transaction). The same is true if the principal remains undisclosed, for here again the contract is made with the agent. But in other cases of agency it is the principal who is, under general rules, the buyer; and it may be arguable that he deals as consumer. However, where the agent allows it to appear that he is buying for a business customer, *e.g.* by seeking to purchase on trade terms, the principal may sometimes be held to have knowingly suffered himself to be represented as buying in the course of a business, or if the word "knowingly" seems inappropriate, as having represented himself by words or conduct as so doing.[5] Whether he held himself out as so doing in such a case will, in fact, turn on the normal principles of actual and apparent authority.[6] 13–080

Goods "of a type ordinarily supplied for private use or consumption". The requirement that the goods be of such a type formerly conditioned the definition of "deals as consumer" in section 12. As explained 13–081

---

[2] s.12(2): above, para.13–078.
[3] *Bowstead and Reynolds on Agency* (18th ed.), Art. 76.
[4] Above, para.11–029.
[5] Above, para.13–071.
[6] *Bowstead and Reynolds*, *op. cit.* above, Arts 22 *et seq.*, 72.

above, the restriction as to the goods dealt in was removed as regards individuals by the amendment of section 12 consequent on the introduction of new consumer remedies in Part 5A of the Sale of Goods Act 1979. In the result this restriction, rather quaintly, now only applies to contracts made by companies or businesses which deal as consumer in a particular transaction. In this context it can be said still to perform a role in assisting in determining, by reference to the nature of the goods, when there is a dealing as consumer despite the fact that a company or business is involved. Cases where a company has been held to deal as consumer in buying a car have already been referred to.[7] More surprisingly, a company director buying a power boat has been held to deal as consumer.[8]

13–082 **Burden of proof as to dealing as consumer.** As already stated, section 12(3) provides "Subject to this, it is for those claiming that a party does not deal as consumer to show that he does not." This provision may well resolve some of the doubts expressed in the foregoing paragraphs.

13–083 **Provisions applicable specifically to sale of goods: exclusion of sections 13, 14 and 15 of the Sale of Goods Act.** The principal provision of the Unfair Contract Terms Act as to contracts of sale of goods is section 6.[9] By section 6(2)[10]: "As against a person dealing as consumer, liability for breach of the obligations arising from—(a) sections 13, 14 or 15 of the 1979 Act (seller's implied undertakings as to conformity of goods with description or sample, or as to their quality or fitness for a particular purpose)[11] . . . cannot be excluded or restricted by reference to any contract term." There is a corresponding provision for hire-purchase.[12] By section 6(3), "As against a person dealing otherwise than as consumer, the liability specified in subsection (2) above can be excluded by reference to a contract term, but only in so far as the term satisfies the requirement of reasonableness." The applicability of these provisions does not exclude the application of other provisions of the Act also: but these provisions are in some situations stronger than other provisions of the Act in that they prevent certain results from being achieved at all. They also are specifically not limited to business liability.[13] As regards the stronger provision contained in section 6(2)(a), however, the effect is as if it was so limited: for liability under section 14 of the 1979 Act only attaches where the seller sells goods in the course of business, and in any case, for the buyer to deal as consumer, the seller must be contracting in the course of a business.[14] This provision applies therefore only to sales by business suppliers to consumers. Although the new

[7] Above, para.13-074.
[8] *Rasbora Ltd v J. C. L. Marine Ltd* [1977] 1 Lloyd's Rep. 645 (on Supply of Goods (Implied Terms) Act 1973).
[9] s.6 replaced similar provisions inserted into the Sale of Goods Act 1893 by the Supply of Goods (Implied Terms) Act 1973. S.6(1) deals with exclusion of liability as to title: above, paras 4–018 *et seq*.
[10] As amended by Sale of Goods Act 1979, Sch.2.
[11] Above, Ch.11.
[12] s.6(2)(b).
[13] ss.1(3), 6(4).
[14] s.12(1): above, paras 11–027, 11–052, 13–070 *et seq*.

remedies for those dealing as consumers provided by Part 5A of the Sale of Goods Act 1979[15] did not exist when the Unfair Contract Terms Act 1979 was passed, it seems clear that exclusion of them (or, when relevant, of the extended provisions as to the significance of public statements as to quality inserted into section 14 as part of the same changes[16]) should be void.[17] Exclusion of sections 13, 14 and 15 of the Sale of Goods Act in sales by consumer to business concern[18] or by consumer to consumer[19] (where section 14 would be inoperative but sections 13 and 15 would apply) are, as in sales between business concerns, subject to the requirement of reasonableness.

Clause not rendered void. It should be noted that the effect of section 6(2) is not to prohibit or render void clauses which would otherwise have the specified effect (though this had been the technique used by the relevant provisions of the Supply of Goods (Implied Terms) Act 1973).[20] It simply says that the liability may not be excluded or restricted by reference to such clauses. Therefore, a clause drafted in general terms which would incidentally have the specified effect will be ineffective in that respect; but it would seem to remain valid as regards duties to which section 6(2) does not relate. The same wording is used in section 6(3) as regards terms subject to the requirement of reasonableness. The specified liabilities cannot be excluded or restricted except in so far as the clause was a reasonable one to insert in the contract.[21] But such a clause might be valid in respect of contractual duties not affected by the Unfair Contract Terms Act at all. This result is therefore not the same as the result of a clause too widely drafted and assessed under the "reasonableness" provisions.[22] 13–084

Related transactions. Section 7 of the Unfair Contract Terms Act 1977 makes similar but not identical provision for contracts "where the possession or ownership of goods passes[23] under or in pursuance of a contract not governed by the law of sale of goods or hire-purchase." This section applies to contracts of barter, for work and materials, of pledge and of pure hire. Unlike section 6, it is restricted to situations of business liability.[24] Here again there are controls on contract terms "excluding or restricting liability 13–085

---

[15] See above, paras 12–071 *et seq*.
[16] See above, paras 11–033 *et seq*.
[17] See above, para.13–064; including, in so far as it applies to such remedies, the six-month presumption of disconformity: above, para.12–075.
[18] As in *Oscar Chess Ltd v Williams* [1957] 1 W.L.R. 370. As to the application of s.6 to non-rejection clauses see below, para.18–280.
[19] As in *Beale v Taylor* [1967] 1 W.L.R. 1193.
[20] See s.4, amending s.55 of the Sale of Goods Act 1893. But the amendment in 1977 of s.3 of the Misrepresentation Act 1967 left the words "shall be of no effect": above, para.13–054. And the 1978 amendment of the Consumer Protection (Restriction on Statements) Order 1976 (below, paras 13–105, 14–142) still refers to a "term which is void by virtue of section 6 . . . of the Unfair Contract Terms Act 1977": SI 1978/127.
[21] See below, para.13–086.
[22] See below, para.13–087.
[23] It is arguable that this word excludes executory contracts.
[24] s.1(3).

for breach of obligation arising by implication of law from the nature of the contract."[25] Such terms were subsequently laid down by the Supply of Goods and Services Act 1982. Section 7(2) of the 1977 Act provides that "As against a person dealing as consumer, liability in respect of the goods' correspondence with description or sample, or their quality or fitness for any particular purpose, cannot be excluded or restricted by reference to any such term." Because the whole section is restricted to business liability, this provision only applies in transactions involving transfer by a business supplier to a consumer. For those contracts in this category which involve the transfer of title (*e.g.* exchange, or a contract for work and materials) the 1982 Act added a subsection to the Unfair Contracts Act, section 7(3A), under which liability as to title cannot be excluded at all even against a non-consumer: but this again is confined to business liability and so to sale by a commercial seller. Therefore, a private seller is not affected by the Act and can exclude his liability in both respects. Non-consumer transactions are dealt with by section 7(3), which provides that against a person dealing otherwise than as consumer, the liability as to quality or fitness "can be excluded or restricted by reference to such a term, but only in so far as the term satisfies the requirement of reasonableness", and section 7(4) (which was made expressly subject to the new section 7(3A)) imposes the same rule on exclusion of obligations as to title in contracts not involving its transfer (*e.g.* hire, pledge). These subsections again are restricted to business liability,[26] and do not affect private sellers.[27]

13–086 **Reasonableness: onus of proof and meaning.** The general rule, laid down in section 11(5) of the Act, is that "It is for those claiming that a contract term or notice satisfies the requirement of reasonableness to show that it does." This effectively reverses the rule introduced by the Supply of Goods (Implied Terms) Act 1973.[28] The general test as to reasonableness is likewise laid down by section 11(1), which reads "In relation to a contract term, the requirement of reasonableness . . . is that the term shall have been a fair and reasonable one to be included having regard to the circumstances which were, or ought reasonably to have been, known to or in the contemplation of the parties[29] when the contract was made." This makes it clear that reasonableness of contract terms is to be judged at the time of making the contract, not at the time of reliance on the clause: it therefore again effectively reverses the position formerly obtaining under the Misrepresentation Act 1967 and the Supply of Goods (Implied Terms)

---

[25] s.7(1).
[26] s.1(3).
[27] The section excluded redemption of trading stamps, which was dealt with specifically by the Trading Stamps Act 1964, now repealed.
[28] Sale of Goods Act 1893, s.55(4), now repealed. The change was contrary to the recommendations of the two Law Commissions.
[29] The parties referred to are the parties to the particular contract; and the circumstances those known to or in contemplation of *both: Edmund Murray Ltd v B.S.P. International Foundations Ltd* (1992) 33 Con. L.R. 1, CA.

Act 1973.[30] It may be suggested that it is an unsatisfactory rule,[31] for clauses may appear perfectly reasonable at the time of inclusion in the contract, and yet circumstances may arise in which reliance on them may seem unfair and unreasonable even though the actual wording appears to cover what occurred. For this reason it has already been suggested that the rules of interpretation remain of considerable significance.[32]

Clause partly reasonable, partly unreasonable. A related problem is caused by the fact that the relevant sections provide that liability cannot be excluded or restricted by reference to any contract term except in so far as,[33] or can be excluded or restricted only in so far as,[34] the term satisfies the requirement of reasonableness. If it is assumed that the words "except in so far as" are deliberately employed instead of "unless", the inference would seem to be that a clause may be reasonable to the extent that it is designated to apply to one situation and unreasonable to the extent that it is designated for another.[35] Where the clause is so drafted that part of it can be held operative and part inoperative, this approach could[36] be adopted. But in *Stewart Gill Ltd v Horatio Myer Ltd*,[37] the Court of Appeal (perhaps too casually) brushed these difficulties aside and held that a clause preventing withholding of payment in very wide terms[38] which could have unreasonable applications was ineffective. Lord Donaldson of Lymington 13–087

---

[30] The change was favoured by the Scottish, but not by the English, Law Commission.

[31] Though the same time is selected for the operation of the somewhat different criteria under the Unfair Terms in Consumer Contracts Regulations (below, paras 13–103, 14–030 *et seq.*); see Reg.6.

[32] Above, para.13–020.

[33] ss.2, 3, 4.

[34] ss.6, 7.

[35] The full test to be applied in the case, for example, of a contract term potentially affected by s.6(3), obtained by combining that provision with s.11(1), is that "the liability specified . . . can be excluded or restricted by reference to a contract term, but only in so far as the term shall have been a fair and reasonable one to be included having regard to the circumstances which were or ought reasonably to have been known to or in the contemplation of the parties when the contract was made." It is not easy to see exactly what this means. See Coote, 41 M.L.R. 312 at 322 (1978); Treitel, *Law of Contract* (11th ed.), pp.257–258. The part of the Act applicable to Scotland uses the words "if it was not fair and reasonable to incorporate the term in the contract": ss.16, 17, 18. This is clear, and represents the policy of the Scottish Law Commission, (above, n.30). It is tempting to suppose that the English wording was originally prepared to refer to unreasonableness at the time of reliance, to which it was appropriate, and when the policy was changed the wording was not sufficiently altered. This is a problem of the "reasonableness" clauses; the absolute prohibitions of ss.2(1) and 6(2) do not appear to affect the validity of a clause drafted in general terms, but simply prevent it from having certain effects. The difficuties were noted by Mance J. in *Skippskreditforeningen v Emperor Navigation* [1998] 1 Lloyd's Rep. 66 at 75 (in connection with s.3 of the Misrepresentation Act 1967).

[36] Above, para.13–084. This is not however true of the Misrepresentation Act 1967, which uses the words "the term shall be of no effect": above, para.13–054.

[37] [1992] Q.B. 600; followed in *Esso Petroleum Ltd v Milton* [1997] 1 W.L.R. 938. But see Peel, 56 M.L.R. 98 (1993).

[38] The section relied on was s.7, above, para.13–085, together with the wide definition of "exclusion or restriction" in s.13, above, para.13–064.

M.R. said that "The issue is whether 'the term [the whole term and nothing but the term] shall have been a fair and reasonable one to be included.'"[39] Stuart-Smith L.J. added "Nor does it appear to me to be consistent with the policy and purpose of the Act to permit a contractor to impose a contractual term which taken as a whole is completely unreasonable to put a blue pencil through the most offensive parts and say that what is left is reasonable and sufficient to exclude or restrict his liability in a manner relied upon."[40] Similar reasoning has more recently been adopted[41] in the case of a clause purporting to exclude liability for misrepresentation and so caught by section 3 of the Misrepresentation Act 1967 as amended.[42] "The term is not severable. It is either reasonable as a whole or it is not. So one must consider its every potential effect."[43] It must be true, however, that where a provision contains several sentences there may be problems in identifying the "term".

13–088 **Guidelines.** The Supply of Goods (Implied Terms) Act 1973, which dealt with sale and hire-purchase, incorporated into the Sale of Goods Act certain guidelines for the ascertainment of the reasonableness of exemptions from liability for breach of the obligations imposed by sections 13, 14 and 15 of the Sale of Goods Act. These were removed from the Sale of Goods Act and re-enacted with slight changes in the Unfair Contract Terms Act 1977 and extended also to the related transactions dealt with in section 7; but not further. This was unfortunate, as all are applicable to other exemptions, and indeed all but the last are perfectly applicable to contracts other than those mentioned.[44] It is now plain however that they can nevertheless be taken into account in other cases also.[45] It should be noted that, consonant with the policy of the 1977 Act, they all take effect at the time of contracting. The guidelines are as follows[46]:

"(a) the strength of the bargaining positions of the parties relative to each other, taking into account (among other things) alternative means by which the customer's requirements could have been met[47];

(b) whether the customer received an inducement to agree to the term, or in accepting it had an opportunity of entering into a

---

[39] At p.607.

[40] At p.609; *cf. Skippskreditforeningen v Emperor Navigation*, above, where a no-set-off clause was held reasonable under s.3 of the Misrepresentation Act 1967, above, para.13–060.

[41] *Thomas Witter Ltd v T.B.P. Industries Ltd* [1996] 2 All E.R. 573.

[42] Above, paras 13–054 *et seq*. Note para.13–056 as to "entire agreement" clauses.

[43] At p.598 *per* Jacob J.; *cf. Skippskreditforeningen v Emperor Navigation*, above.

[44] And the criteria do not purport to be exclusive: s.11(2) only directs that regard be had to them "in particular".

[45] See below, para.13–090.

[46] Sch.2. Decisions are allocated to these guidelines in *Chitty on Contracts* (29th ed.), Vol. 1, para.14–085.

[47] This provision is briefly discussed in *Denholm Fishselling Ltd v Anderson* 1991 S.L.T. (Sh. Ct.) 24, where it was held that there was no relevant imbalance between fish traders where all dealers sold on the same restrictive conditions but the buyer had a choice of sellers with whom to deal.

similar contract with other persons, but without having to accept a similar term;

(c) whether the customer knew or ought reasonably to have known of the existence and extent of the term (having regard, among other things, to any custom of the trade and any previous course of dealing between the parties)[48];

(d) where the term excludes or restricts any relevant liability if some condition is not complied with, whether it was reasonable at the time of the contract to expect that compliance with that condition would be practicable;

(e) whether the goods were manufactured, processed or adapted to the special order of the customer."

Application of test: old wording. Authority as to the application of these guidelines took some time to appear. In *Rasbora Ltd v J. C. L. Marine Ltd*,[49] it was held that a clause excluding all liability of a boatbuilder could not be relied on where the boat had electrical defects causing its total loss within 27 hours of delivery. Little reasoning was given, but the decision was one under the 1973 Act, under which an exemption "shall not be enforceable to the extent that it is shown that it would not be fair or reasonable to allow reliance on it." The 1977 Act, however, refers, as above explained, to reasonableness of inclusion of the clause at the time of contracting; though the same decision would probably have been reached on the 1977 wording. In *R. W. Green Ltd v Cade Bros Farms*,[50] a short time limit on claims on a bulk sale of seed potatoes was held unreasonable as to latent defects; but a clause limiting liability to repayment of the price was held reasonable both as to patent and latent defects, the parties being merchants of equal bargaining power. This is again a case on the 1973 Act, and again the court was considering the reasonableness of reliance rather than of inclusion. In *Howard Marine and Dredging Co. Ltd v A. Ogden & Sons (Excavations) Ltd*,[51] the Court of Appeal held by a majority that reliance on a clause in a hire of barges specifying that acceptance was conclusive evidence of fitness for use was unreasonable when the complaint was of negligent misrepresentation: but this was a case on the Misrepresentation Act 1967, which at that time also looked to the time of reliance. In the leading case of *George Mitchell (Chesterhall) Ltd v Finney Lock Seeds Ltd*,[52] a clause limiting liability on the sale of seed to refund of the purchase price or replacement 13–089

[48] This guideline appears simply to repeat the normal requirements for incorporation into the contract. But in *AEG (International) Ltd v Logic Resources Ltd* [1996] C.L.C. 265 at 279, Hobhouse L.J. said that this could not be so and that it must apply post-contractually, or it would not be necessary. On this basis he said that the court must look to the "actuality or reality of the consent", which had not been proved. This new approach was not taken by the other members of the court.

[49] [1977] 1 Lloyd's Rep. 645.

[50] [1978] 1 Lloyd's Rep. 602. The guidelines as to limits on damages laid down in s.11(4) would now also be relevant to such a case: below, para.13–091.

[51] [1978] Q.B. 574.

[52] [1983] 2 A.C. 803; above, para.13–048. See Sealy [1984] C.L.J. 29. See also a discussion in connection with a surveyor's contract in *Smith v Eric S. Bush* [1990] 1 A.C. 831 at 858–859.

of the seed was held unreasonable, also under the older wording. The reasons given were that although the matter was not one of discretion, an appellate court should be slow to upset the decision of the judge of first instance unless it was plainly based on wrong principles[53]; the clause was not contained in a well-established contract the text of which had been negotiated between interested parties or trade associations; insurance against liability for supply of the wrong seed was said to be easily obtainable and would not add materially to the cost of the seed; and the evidence showed that the proponent did not in fact usually rely on the terms of the clause but sought to negotiate a settlement against its background.[54] Another factor which has been thought relevant is whether better terms are available at a higher charge.[55] Assessment of the reasonableness of the *inclusion* of the clause may, however, sometimes lead to different results.

13–090 **Present wording.** After a slow start cases on reasonableness are now appearing frequently. The reported cases are mostly in the commercial context, though there may be many unreported decisions involving consumers in lower courts. Useful general criteria in the context of carriage, but plainly relevant elsewhere, have been set out by Potter L.J. in *Overseas Medical Supplies Ltd v Orient Transport Services Ltd*[56] as follows:

(1) the way in which the relevant conditions came into being and are used generally;

(2) the five guidelines as to reasonableness set out in Schedule 2;

(3) in relation to the question of equality of bargaining position the court will have regard not only to the question of whether the customer was obliged to use the services of the supplier, but also to the question of how far it would have been practicable and convenient to go elsewhere;

(4) the question of reasonableness must be assessed having regard to the relevant clause viewed as a whole: it is not right to take any particular part of the clause in isolation, although it must also be viewed against a breach of contract which is the subject of the case;

(5) the reality of the consent of the customer to the supplier's clause will be a significant consideration;

(6) in cases of limitation rather than exclusion of liability, the size of the limit compared with other limits in widely used standard terms may also be relevant;

---

[53] For examples see *Phillips Products Ltd v Hyland* [1987] 1 W.L.R. 659; *St Albans City and DC v International Computers Ltd* [1996] 4 All E.R. 481. See further *Overseas Medical Supplies Ltd v Orient Transport Services Ltd* [1999] 2 Lloyd's Rep. 273 at 276; *Watford Electronics Ltd v Sanderson CFL Ltd* [2001] EWCA Civ 317; [2001] 1 All E.R. (Comm) 696 at [64].

[54] The second and third criteria are also referred to in *Singer Co. (U.K.) Ltd v Tees and Hartlepool Port Authority* [1988] 2 Lloyd's Rep. 164 at 169–170. See also discussion (in connection with a surveyor's disclaimers) in *Smith v Eric S. Bush* [1990] 1 A.C. 831 at 849–854, 857–860.

[55] This factor was taken into account in a County Court consumer decision, *Woodman v Photo Trade Processing Ltd* (1981), discussed in 131 N.L.J. 935 (1981).

[56] [1999] 2 Lloyd's Rep. 273 at 276.

(7) while the availability of insurance to the supplier is relevant, it is by no means a decisive factor;

(8) the presence of a term allowing for an option to contract without the limitation clause but with a price increase in lieu is important; however, if the condition works in such a way as to leave little time to put such option into effect, this may effectively eliminate the option as a factor indicating reasonableness.

Clauses held unreasonable in the context of sale and related contracts include clauses having very wide application in view of the facts of the case,[57] limiting liability to repair or replacement, or containing a specific warranty with onerous terms,[58] time bars,[59] limits on amount recoverable,[60] exclusion of liability for consequential loss[61] and clauses excluding or

---

[57] *Edmund Murray Ltd v BSP International Financiers Ltd* (1992) 33 Con.L.R.1 (drill rig); *Lease Management Services Ltd v Purnell Secretarial Services Ltd* (1993) 13 Tr L.R. 337 (photocopier); *Pegler Ltd v Wang (U.K.) Ltd* [2000] B.L.R. 218 (computer hardware and software); *Britvic Soft Drinks Ltd v Messer U.K. Ltd* [2002] 1 Lloyd's Rep. 20; affirmed on this point [2002] EWCA Civ. 548; [2002] 2 Lloyd's Rep. 368; *Bacardi-Martini Beverages Ltd v Thomas Hardy Packaging Ltd, ibid.*, 62; affirmed [2002] EWCA 549; [2002] 2 Lloyd's Rep. 379 (both on bulk carbon dioxide).

[58] *Charlotte Thirty Ltd v Croker Ltd* (1990) 24 Con.L.R. 46 (industrial plant); *Edmund Murray Ltd v BSP International Financiers Ltd*, above; *AEG (U.K.) Ltd v Logic Resources Ltd* [1996] C.L.C. 265; but *cf. British Fermentation Products Ltd v Compair Reavell Ltd* (1999) 66 Con.L.R.1 (centrifugal air compressor), where such a clause was held reasonable. See also *Stag Line Ltd v Tyne Shiprepair Group (The Zinnia)* [1984] 2 Lloyd's Rep. 211 (ship repair contract: clause requiring return of vessel to yard in case of unsatisfactory work unreasonable).

[59] *Rees-Hough Ltd v Redland Reinforced Plastics Ltd* (1984) 27 B.L.R. 136 (piping: 3 months); *Knight Machinery (Holdings) Ltd v Rennie* 1995 S.L.T. 166 (printing machine: 7 days); *Pegler Ltd v Wang (UK) Ltd* [2000] B.L.R. 218 (computer hardware and software: 2 years); *Bacardi-Martin Beverages Ltd v Thomas Hardy Packaging Ltd*, above (bulk carbon dioxide: 5 days); *cf. Expo Fabrics (UK) Ltd v Martin* [2003] EWCA Civ. 1165 (textiles: 20 days reasonable).

[60] *Salvage Association v CAP Financial Servicees Ltd* [1995] F.S.R. 654 (computer software: £25,000: insurance taken into account); *St Albans City and District Council v International Computers Ltd* [1995] F.S.R. 686; affirmed on this point [1996] 4 All E.R. 481 (computer software: £100,000); but *cf.* holdings of reasonableness in *Watford Electronics Ltd v Sanderson CFL Ltd* [2001] EWCA Civ. 317; [2001] 1 All E.R.) (Comm) 696 (computer software: sum paid); *Britvic Soft Drinks Ltd v Messer UK Ltd* above, n.57; *Bacardi-Martin Beverages Ltd v Thomas Hardy Packaging Ltd*, above, n.57 (both on bulk carbon dioxide (£2m., £500,000).

[61] *Charlotte Thirty Ltd v Croker Ltd* (1990) 24 Con.L.R. 46 (industrial plant); *Edmund Murray Ltd v BSP International Financiers Ltd* (1992) 33 Con.L.R.1 (drill rig); *Pegler Ltd v Wang (UK) Ltd* [2000] B.L.R. 218 (computer hardware and software); *Bacardi-Martini Beverages Ltd v Thomas Hardy Packaging Ltd*, above; but *cf. British Fermentation Products Ltd v Compair Reavell Ltd* (1999) 66 Con.L.R.1 (centrifugal air compressor) and *Watford Electronics Ltd v Sanderson CFL Ltd*, above, where such clauses were held reasonable. The last case contains strong dicta by Chadwick L.J. (at p.158) that "unless satisfied that one party has, in effect, taken advantage of the other—or that a term is so unreasonable that it cannot properly be understood or considered—the court should not interfere." These dicta seem to bring unreasonableness close to unconscionability, a view not taken elsewhere. But *cf.* Peel, 117 L.Q.R. 545 (2001).

significantly restricting rights of set-off.[62] It has been held that availability of insurance, which is specifically made relevant in the case of limits on amount[63] is in general relevant to reasonableness also; but this refers to general availability rather than the actual position between the parties concerned, at least unless the question of insurance was taken into account by the parties at the time the contract was made.[64] It has been held also that clauses in tripartite situations excluding or reducing the financier's liability as seller may still be unreasonable though the financier has not seen the goods.[65]

13–091 **Limits on amount.** Special criteria, applicable to all types of claim, are laid down for clauses restricting liability to specified sums of money (which phrase is probably not confined to clauses limiting liability to a fixed sum in pounds, but must extend to clauses providing methods of calculation, as by a limitation to the contract price or a multiple thereof). Section 11(4) reads:

> "Where by reference to a contract term or notice a person seeks to restrictliability to a specified sum of money and the question arises (under this or any other Act[66]) whether the term or notice satisfies the requirement of reasonableness, regard shall be had in particular . . . to—(a) the resources which he could expect to be available to him for the purpose of meeting the liability should it arise; and (b) how far it was open to him to cover himself by insurance."[67]

It may be asked what view should be taken where the resources could only be provided by selling the business or realising the savings of the person concerned, or the insurance obtained only at prohibitive rates. It seems that the resources are "available" and the insurance "open": but the section only requires these possibilities to be taken into account, it does not make them conclusive of the issue. In respect of insurance, it seems again that the reference is normally to the availability of insurance rather than the actual insurance position of the party concerned at least unless the matter was

[62] *Stewart Gill Ltd v Horatio Myer & Co. Ltd* [1992] Q.B. 600 (overhead conveyor system); but *cf. Schenkers Ltd v Overland Shoes Ltd* [1998] 1 Lloyd's Rep. 498 (freight forwarding); *Surzur Overseas Ltd v Ocean Reliance Shipping Co. Ltd* [1997] C.L.Y. 906; *Skipskredittforeningen v Emperor Navigation* [1998] 1 Lloyd's Rep. 66; (Misrepresentation Act 1967, above, para.13–054); *WRM Group Ltd v Wood* [1998] C.L.C. 189 (reasonable in loan and financial agreements).
[63] Below, para.13–091.
[64] *Flamar Interocean Ltd v Denmac Ltd (The Flamar Pride)* [1990] 1 Lloyd's Rep. 434 at 440.
[65] *Lease Management Services Ltd v Purnell Secretarial Services Ltd* (1993) 14 Tr.L.Rep. 337, followed in *Sovereign Finance Ltd v Silver Crest Furniture Ltd* [1997] C.C.L.R. 76 and *Scania Finance Ltd v Monteum Ltd*, QBD, January 30, 2001; and not following dicta in *R. & B. Customs Brokers Ltd v United Dominions Trust Ltd* [1988] 1 W.L.R. 321 at 332. See further cases on s.3 of the Misrepresentation Act 1967, above, para.13–060.
[66] This provision thus applies to the restrictions imposed by s.3 of the Misrepresentation Act 1967: above, paras 13–054 *et seq*.
[67] This provision was applied in *St Albans City and DC v International Computers Ltd* [1995] F.S.R. 686; affirmed on this point [1996] 4 All E.R. 481.

taken into account at the making of the contract, in which case the general criteria might take this into account.[68] But these factors, while relevant, are in any case not conclusive.[69]

Provisions applicable to all contracts: clauses as to death or personal injury. The next major provision of the Act to be taken into account is section 2. By section 2(1), "A person cannot by reference to any contract term or to a notice given to persons generally or to particular persons exclude or restrict his liability for death or personal injury resulting from negligence."[70] As with the consumer provisions of sections 6 and 7 there is no test of reasonableness: such an effect cannot be achieved at all. An obvious example is a clause in a contract for the sale of electrical or mechanical equipment purporting to absolve the seller from liability for death or personal injuries caused by the equipment. Section 2(1) only applies, however, to business liability[71] and to exclusion of negligence liability[72]: any *strict* contractual liability of a seller can be excluded for death or personal injury unless the clause is also caught by sections 3 or 6.[73] 13–092

Negligence clauses. By section 2(2) "In the case of other loss or damage, a person cannot so exclude or restrict his liability for negligence except in so far as the term or notice satisfies the requirement of reasonableness." An example in the context of sale might be a clause in which the seller disclaimed liability for loss of or damage to the goods prior to delivery, whether by his negligence or not; or one in which he disclaimed liability for loss of or damage caused by the goods to the buyer's property. This provision could therefore be relevant where sections 6 and 7 have no application. 13–093

Clauses in consumer contracts or standard terms. The final major provision of the 1977 Act which must be borne in mind as potentially applicable is section 3, which is directed towards contracts generally, and provides as follows: 13–094

> "(1) This section applies between contracting parties where one of them deals as consumer or on the other's written standard terms of business.
> (2) As against that party, the other cannot by reference to any contract term—

---

[68] *Flamar Interocean Ltd v Denmac Ltd (The Flamar Pride)* [1990] 1 Lloyd's Rep. 434 at 439–440. See above, para.13–090.

[69] A clause limiting a port authority's liability for loading to a sum calculated by reference to the weight of the goods was held reasonable, despite availability of resources and insurance, in *Singer Co. (U.K.) Ltd v Tees and Hartlepool Port Authority* [1988] 2 Lloyd's Rep. 164.

[70] The provision does not make such clauses ineffective, except for this purpose. This is also true of s.6: above, paras 13–084, 13–087.

[71] s.1(3): above, para.13–070.

[72] Defined in s.1 to include breach "(a) of any obligation, arising from the express or implied terms of a contract, to take reasonable care or exercise reasonable skill in the performance of the contract, (b) of any common law duty to take reasonable care and exercise reasonable skill (but not any stricter duty)".

[73] Below, para.13–094; above, para.13–083.

(a) when himself in breach of contract, exclude or restrict any liability of his in respect of the breach; or (b) claim to be entitled—(i) to render a contractual performance substantially different from that which was reasonably expected of him, or (ii) in respect of the whole or any part of his contractual obligation, to render no performance at all, except insofar as . . . the contract term satisfies the requirement of reasonableness."

The section is by virtue of section 1(3) restricted to business liability; but its terms in any case so require. The notion of dealing as consumer has already been discussed[74]: that of standard terms is discussed in the next paragraph. As examples of clauses within section 3(2)(a) may be taken clauses seeking to exempt from liability for breach of contractual undertakings. This provision, however, clearly assumes that there has first been a liability established, the effects of which the clause seeks to exclude or restrict. It can therefore be avoided in appropriate situations by a clause drafted so as to delineate in limited form the contractual duty,[75] unless it appears to be an attempt to evade the Act's provisions.[76] The same is arguably true as to section 3(2)(b) (ii), which again (though less clearly) assumes the prior existence of a contractual obligation. A clause drafted so as to limit that obligation to one of performance in certain events, *e.g.* "subject to availability", would not properly be described as entitling non-performance of the obligation. On this basis section 3(2)(b)(ii) would seem to have little, if any, scope; for a clause which actually permitted non-performance of the contractual obligation would rid the contract of content.[77] It seems likely, however, that in practice this provision will be applied to clauses excusing performance in the event of *force majeure* and the like, which are discussed elsewhere.[78] But section 3(2) (b)(i) is in any case much wider, in that a clause which specifies the contract duty in a way contrary to the reasonable expectations of the other party may not be efficacious if adjudged unreasonable. It will therefore be much more difficult for a contracting party to "draft himself out" of this provision.[79] In the context of sale an example is a clause entitling the seller in certain contingencies to deliver goods other than those specified. The difference permitted would, however, require to be fairly extreme before the performance could rank as "substantially different from that which was reasonably expected".[80]

---

[74] Above, para.13–071 *et seq.*

[75] Subject of course to the absolute prohibitions of ss.2 and 6. *Cf. G. H. Renton & Co. v Palmyra Trading Corp.* [1957] A.C. 149, where a strike clause was held to modify the contract voyage rather than to be inconsistent with it.

[76] See above, paras 13–065 *et seq.*; below, para.13–106.

[77] *cf.* above, para.13–044.

[78] Above, paras 8–088 *et seq.*; paras 18–320 *et seq*; 19–131 *et seq*. Such clauses would normally be reasonable in a commercial contract.

[79] The clauses most regularly cited as examples occur in contracts with tour operators. The provision was held not to apply in *Zockoll Group Ltd v Mercury Telecommunications Ltd* [1999] E.M.L.R. 385 (telecommunications supply contract).

[80] And by the same token such a clause would normally not satisfy the requirement of reasonableness—unless perhaps it allowed the substitution of *more valuable* goods.

Standard terms. The notion of standard terms is undefined, and is unfamiliar to English law, though it has been used in other countries to identify terms requiring control.[81] There is no provision as to burden of proof. Various problems may arise in connection with the notion. It would seem, first, that the terms, though they must be written, need not be printed; and that they may be incorporated into the contract orally,[82] by a notice or by course of dealing.[83] If the terms otherwise qualify as standard terms they must rank as such even when used for the first time. Where standard terms are used with extra clauses added, whether by hand or in typescript, and even if they are added for the particular transaction in question only, unless the addition is the result of individual negotiation it is submitted that all the terms should rank as standard terms: there is no need to seek reasons for restricting the category, for the terms can always be held reasonable. If the additions are negotiated but the dispute concerns the main part of the contract, the parties may be regarded as dealing on standard terms.[84] Questions may arise as to whether the terms must be intended for use in a large or indefinite number of transactions: although this will usually be so, it is submitted that sometimes terms prepared for quite a small group of transactions may justifiably be classed as standard. The terms obviously need not be prepared by or on behalf of one of the parties to the contract. The proponent may use a set of terms prepared by an organisation representing both sides to a transaction (*e.g.* suppliers and buyers); or by an independent organisation representing neither (*e.g.* the International Chamber of Commerce, which prepared INCOTERMS); or by his agent or his agent's trade or professional organisation. In all these cases it may be that adoption of the terms by one party will constitute them his written standard terms of business.[85] In Scotland it has been said that 13–095

[81] See Law Com. No.69 (1975), paras 153–157. A useful definition is to be found in s.1 of the German *AGB-Gesetz* (Standard Contract Terms Law) of 1976 (now contained in s.305(1) *BGB*): "(1) Standard contract terms are all such conditions of contract as are formulated in advance for a large number of contracts, which one contracting party (the proponent) presents to the other at the conclusion of the contract. It is immaterial whether the conditions form a physically separate part of the contract or are set out in the contractual document itself, what scope they have, in what type of writing they are set out, or what form the contract takes. (2) Standard contract terms are not present insofar as the conditions of contract are individually negotiated between the contracting parties." The Israeli Standard Contracts Law of 1982 provides that standard contract "means the text of a contract, all or part of the terms of which have been determined in advance by one party in order to serve as conditions of many contracts between him and persons unidentified as to number or identity": see Deutch, 30 McGill L.J. 458 (1985). Compare the Unfair Terms in Consumer Contracts Regulations (below, paras 13–103, 14–030 *et seq.*), referring to terms which have not "been individually negotiated".

[82] *M'Crone v Boots Farms Sales Ltd* 1981 S.C. 68.

[83] *M'Crone v Boots Farms Sales Ltd*, above.

[84] *Salvage Association v CAP Financial Services Ltd* [1995] F.S.R. 654; *St Albans City and DC v International Computers Ltd* [1995] F.S.R. 686, affirmed on this point [1996] 4 All E.R. 481; *Pegler Ltd v Wang (U.K.) Ltd* [2000] B.L.R. 218; *cf. Flamar Interocean Ltd v Denmac Ltd (The Flamar Pride)* [1990] 1 Lloyd's Rep. 434.

[85] *Chester Grosvenor Hotel Co. Ltd v Alfred McAlpine Management Ltd* (1991) 56 B.L.R. 115; *British Fermentation Products Ltd v Compair Reavell Ltd* (1999) 66 Con.

the phrase "standard form contract" in section 17 of the Scottish part of the Act "is . . . wide enough to include any contract, whether wholly written or partly oral, which includes a set of fixed terms or conditions which the proponer applies, without material variation to contracts of the kind in question."[86] (*Sed quaere* as to "without material variation".) The object of the notion of standard terms must in fact be to identify contracts which are not individually negotiated.[87] Nevertheless, a person may deal on standard terms even where there has been negotiation.[88] The notion provides protection for small businesses dealing with larger business, but it may also operate between large concerns—though here there may be difficulties, where both use standard terms, in determining which deals on the other's terms[89]: for standard terms may obviously be used by buyers as well as by sellers.

13–096 **Requirement of reasonableness under ss.2(2) and (3).** As stated above, the guidelines laid down as to reasonableness in Schedule 2 of the 1977 Act apply only to the exclusion of the seller's statutory obligations regulated by section 6 and to the exclusion of obligations in the related transactions governed by section 7.[90] Other clauses and contracts are governed by the general indications given in section 11(1), and by the guidelines applicable to restrictions to a specified sum of money contained in section 11(4), both of which have already been discussed.[91] It seems clear, however, that the guidelines in section 11(4), and probably also those in Schedule 2, will often be taken into account also, even though there is no requirement to apply them.[92] The burden of proving reasonableness is in all cases on the party alleging it.[93]

13–097 **Supporting provisions: indemnities and manufacturer's guarantees.** Section 4 subjects to the requirement of reasonableness clauses whereby a business supplier does not seek to exclude or restrict his liability, but rather

---

L.R.1 (requiring "proof that the model form is invariably or at least usually used by the party in question. It must be shown that either by practice or by express statement a contracting party has adopted a model form as his standard terms of business"). This may be putting the matter too narrowly: *cf. Overseas Medical Supplies Ltd v Orient Transport Services Ltd* [1999] 2 Lloyd's Rep. 273, above, para.13–090 where applicability of the BIFA Standard Terms and Conditions appears to have been assumed to bring the section into operation.

[86] *McCrone v Boots Farm Sales Ltd*, 1981 S.C. 68 at 74 *per* Lord Dunpark. See *Chester Grosvenor Hotel Co. Ltd v Alfred McAlpine Management Ltd*, above; *Pegler Ltd v Wang (U.K.) Ltd* [2000] B.L.R. 218.

[87] See *Salvage Assn v CAP Financial Services Ltd* [1995] F.S.R. 654.

[88] *St Albans City and DC v International Computers Ltd* [1996] 4 All E.R. 481, affirming on this point [1995] F.S.R. 686; *Salvage Assn v Cap Financial Services Ltd* [1995] F.S.R. 654; but *cf. Flamar Interocean Ltd v Denmac Ltd (The Flamar Pride)* [1990] 1 Lloyd's Rep. 434.

[89] See *Butler Machine Tool Co. v Ex-Cell-O Corp. (England) Ltd* [1979] 1 W.L.R. 401; *Edmund Murray Ltd v BSP International Financiers Ltd* (1992) 33 Con.L.R. 1.

[90] Above, paras 13–085 *et seq.*

[91] Above, paras 13–086 *et seq.*, 13–091.

[92] See, *e.g. Overseas Medical Supplies Ltd v Orient Transport Services Ltd* [1999] 2 Lloyd's Rep. 273 at 276, quoted above, para.13–090; *Flamar Interocean Ltd v Denmac Ltd (The Flamar Pride)* [1990] 1 Lloyd's Rep. 434 at 439 (s.11(4), on the relevance of insurance, taken into account).

[93] s.11(5).

seeks to require a consumer to indemnify him in respect of liability incurred by him to third parties (*e.g.* in tort) or even to the consumer himself (though such an evasion might also be caught by section 13(1)(b)[94] as "subjecting a person to . . . prejudice in consequence of his pursuing any . . . right or remedy"). It does not apply to contracts between business concerns[95] or between private individuals, nor where it is the business concern which must indemnify the consumer. Section 5 subjects to the requirement of reasonableness terms in manufacturer's guarantees excluding or restricting manufacturer's negligence liability in respect of goods ordinarily supplied for private use or consumption[96] which prove defective while in consumer use. It does not apply as between the parties to the contract of sale and is therefore dealt with later, together with requirements for guarantees laid down by the Sale and Supply of Goods to Consumers Regulations 2002.[97] Section 10 seeks to prevent evasion of the Act's provisions by means of a secondary contract purporting to affect the exercise of rights under the main contract—*e.g.* a term in a manufacturer's guarantee, itself valid as a contract, seeking to prevent exercise of rights against the retailer under the main contract. The intention of the section is clear but its wording causes problems: in particular it refers to contract terms "prejudicing or taking away" rights rather than "excluding or restricting" them, and only deals with secondary contracts relating to situations where the Act prevents exclusion or restriction of *liability* rather than obligation or duty. The interconnection with section 13(1)[98] is thus far from clear. On the face of it it might seem to apply to compromises of certain types of valid claim. It is, however, difficult to believe this was intended, and it has been held that it does not do so.[99]

Terms authorised by statute, international agreement or competent authority. Section 29 removes from the scope of the Act terms authorised by statute, or by international agreement to which the United Kingdom is a party. The principal examples of these occur in the area of contracts of carriage.[1] It also exempts from control terms "incorporated or approved by, or incorporated pursuant to a decision or ruling of, a competent authority acting in the exercise of any statutory jurisdiction or function . . ." which are not terms in contracts to which the authority itself is a party. An 13–098

---

[94] Above, para.13–064.
[95] *Thompson v T. Lohen (Plant Hire) Ltd* [1987] 1 W.L.R. 649. Nor, when such a term appears in a commercial contract, does it appear to be caught by anything in the wording of ss.2 or 3. But a clause purporting to exclude the seller's liability to the buyer in respect of claims made on the buyer by third parties might, on some formulations, be caught by ss.2, 3 or 6.
[96] As to which phrase, see above, para.13–081.
[97] Below, paras 14–065 *et seq*. See also paras 14–041, 14–042.
[98] Above, para.13–064. And see para.13–087.
[99] *Tudor Grange Holdings Ltd v Citibank N.A.* [1992] Ch.53; Brown, 108 LQR 223 (1992); Hooley [1991] 3 L.M.C.L.Q. 449. Its application in a situation of carriage sub-contracts was rejected in *Neptune Orient Lines Ltd v J.V.C. (U.K.) Ltd (The Chevalier Roze)* [1983] 2 Lloyd's Rep. 438. See further Treitel, *Law of Contract* (11th ed.), pp.262–263.
[1] *e.g.* the Carriage of Goods by Sea Act 1971 gave effect to the Hague-Visby Rules, which contain many exemptions in favour of the shipowner.

example suggested[2] was section 27(2) of the Water Act 1945 (now repealed), which empowered the relevant Minister to determine questions as to the reasonableness of terms in contracts for supply of water for non-domestic purposes. Under section 8 of the Enterprise Act 2002 the Office of Fair Trading is empowered to approve consumer codes and to provide for the use of an official symbol indicating such approval. Such approval does not bring the terms of an approved code within section 29; but legislation approving contract terms in advance is a device that has been used in other countries.[3]

13–099 **Contracts to which the Act does not apply: international supply contracts.** By section 26 the limits imposed by the Act[4] on excluding or restricting liability by reference to a contract term[5] are inapplicable to international supply contracts. The purpose of this exclusion appears to have been to avoid subjecting English exporters to restrictions not applicable elsewhere: though it seems strange to find an express statement that terms of such contracts "are not subject to any requirement of reasonableness".[6] This provision excludes most international sales from the scope of the Act.[7] It is discussed elsewhere in this book.[8]

13–100 **Contracts where English law applicable by choice of parties only.** The relevant provisions of the Act[9] are also by section 27(1) as amended by the Contracts (Applicable Law) Act 1990 made inapplicable where "the law applicable to a contract is the law of any part of the United Kingdom only by choice of the parties (and apart from that choice would be the law of some country outside the United Kingdom)". As a provision related to the conflict of laws, it is discussed in detail elsewhere in this book.[10]

13–101 **Evasion of Act by choice of foreign law.** By section 27(2) the Act "has effect notwithstanding any contract term which applies or purports to apply the law of some country outside the United Kingdom, where (either or both)—(a) the term appears to the court or arbitrator . . . to have been imposed wholly or mainly for the purpose of enabling the party imposing it to evade the operation of this Act; or (b) in the making of the contract one

---

[2] P. K. J. Thompson, *The Unfair Contract Terms Act 1977* (1978), p.12.
[3] See Hondius, 26 Am.J.Comp.L. 525 at 529 *et seq.* (1978); Berg, 28 I.C.L.Q. 560 (1979); Deutch, *op. cit.* above, n.81.
[4] Including ss.3 and 4; but not those imposed by s.3 of the Misrepresentation Act 1967: above, paras 13–054 *et seq.*
[5] But not those as to notices, which may make a difference where an action is brought in tort. Below, paras 13–106, 13–107.
[6] s.26(2).
[7] *i.e.* the sales discussed in Chs 18–21 below.
[8] Below, paras 18–281, 25–090. For recent cases on the definition, see *Ocean Chemical Transport Inc v Exnor Craggs Ltd* [2000] 1 Lloyd's Rep. 446; *Amirt Flight Authority v BAE Systems Plc* [2003] EWCA Civ. 1447; [2004] 1 All E.R (Comm) 385.
[9] But not s.3 of the Misrepresentation Act 1967: above, paras 13–054 *et seq.*
[10] Below, paras 25–091 *et seq.* For an example see *Surzur Overseas Ltd v Ocean Reliance Shipping Co. Ltd* [1997] C.L.Y. 906. *cf.* Unfair Terms in Consumer Contracts Regulations (below, paras 13–103, 14–030 *et seq.*), Reg. 9.

of the parties dealt as consumer, and he was then habitually resident in the United Kingdom, and the essential steps necessary for the making of the contract were taken there, whether by him or by others on his behalf."[11] The purpose of this provision is obvious, but its wording is not free from difficulties. Its significance lies in the conflict of laws and it also is accordingly discussed elsewhere in this book.[12]

Sale of Goods Act 1979, s.35(3). This subsection, inserted by section 2 of the Sale and Supply of Goods Act 1994,[13] provides that: **13–102**

> "Where the buyer deals as consumer . . . the buyer cannot lose his right to rely on subsection (2) above by agreement, waiver or otherwise."

Subsection (2) is that which provides that where goods are delivered to a buyer which he has not previously examined, he is not deemed to have accepted them until he has had a reasonable opportunity of examining them for the purpose of ascertaining their conformity, and, where relevant, of comparing bulk with sample.[14] The purpose of this provision is therefore to control, in situations of consumer contracts,[15] provisions by virtue of which the consumer may agree that he has inspected the goods and found them satisfactory and thus lost the right to reject them under section 35 of the Sale of Goods Act, or under more general rules as to estoppel, election or waiver, when he has not in fact made such an inspection at all. The result is that the consumer who has not had the opportunity of examination retains the right to reject the goods notwithstanding signature of such a note, or some oral acceptance. Such arrangements usually take the form of "acceptance notes", which a buyer may be required to sign as a condition of receiving the goods (though often these seek to exonerate not sellers but carriers): not all buyers may be warned, or be prudent enough, so insist on accompanying their signatures by some reservation such as "unexamined". The provision only goes, however, to acceptance, and hence to the right to *reject*. In so far as the consumer claims damages he would need to allege that the clause was unreasonable under section 3 of the Unfair Contract Terms Act, if it was a contract term,[16] or on the more general common law reasoning that a supplier who knew that the statement was not true was not justified in relying on it.[17] Although it may seem curious, it appears that this is correct as regards damages, not only where the buyer does not reject, but

---

[11] The subsection does not preserve the effect of s.3 of the Misrepresentation Act 1967: above, paras 13–059 *et seq*.

[12] Below, paras 25–094 *et seq*. Similar protection is conferred by Art. 5 of the Rome Convention on the Law Applicable to Contractual Obligations, effective under the Contracts (Applicable Law) Act 1990.

[13] For references as to the purposes of these statutory amendments see above, para.11–026, n.44.

[14] See above, para.12–039.

[15] The meaning of the term "deals as consumer" is the same as in the 1977 Act: Sale of Goods Act 1979, s.61(5A), inserted by the 1994 Act.

[16] *i.e.*, imposed in advance. Section 6 of the 1977 Act might also be relevant: above, para.13–064, n.52. As to s.3 see above, para.13–094.

[17] Above, para.13–030.

also when he does, unless it could be said that the right to reject carries with it its own right to damages. In non-consumer sales reliance on section 3 would be subject to the further requirement that the clause, if a contract term at all, appears in standard terms, though the common law reasoning would equally apply.

13–103 **The Unfair Terms in Consumer Contracts Regulations 1999.**[18] A further set of provisions controlling unfair contract terms came into effect by statutory instrument, in 1995.[19] They were replaced by the present regulations in 1999. They implement an E.C. Council Directive on unfair terms in consumer contracts. They apply to contracts concluded between a seller or supplier[20 21]); and within this to "a contractual term which has not been individually negotiated"[22]; an idea similar to but not identical with the reference in section 3 of the 1977 Act to dealing on standard terms of business.[23] They interlock with the Unfair Contract Terms Act protection in consumer contracts, to which type of contract some provisions of that Act are confined,[24] and to which the others also apply.[25] No attempt was made however to construct a rational integration of the two sets of provisions, with the result that in a consumer dispute it will be necessary to examine both, as they may apply differently and give different results. Since the Regulations are confined to consumer contracts, they are in general of narrower application than the 1977 Act and are therefore principally discussed in the chapter on Consumer Protection.[26]

13–104 **Other statutes: Consumer Protection Act 1987.** As indicated elsewhere in this book,[27] the Consumer Protection Act 1987 imposes liabilities on manufacturers, producers, and in some cases distributors, which by virtue of sections 7 and 41(4) of the Act cannot be excluded or modified by any contract term, provision or notice.

13–105 **Public enforcement.** The Unfair Contract Terms Act 1977 relied largely on its provisions being raised in private law proceedings. This meant that if the matter was not raised in such proceedings traders could use terms the validity of which were doubtful, or which were even void. The Fair Trading Act 1973 had made a contribution to the problem (which first arose under the precursor of the 1977 Act, the Supply of Goods (Implied Terms) Act 1973) by giving powers to the Director-General of Fair Trading[28] to procure the outlawing of such terms (and other "consumer trade practices") by

---

[18] SI 1999/2083 (effective October 1, 1999), as amended by SI 2001/1186.
[19] Unfair Terms in Consumer Contracts Regulations 1994, SI 1994/3159.
[20] Reg.4.
[21] Defined as a natural or legal person acting for purposes relating to his trade, business or profession.
[22] Reg.5(1).
[23] Above, para.13–095.
[24] *e.g.* s.6(2), above, para.13–083.
[25] *e.g.* s.2, above, paras 13–094, 13–095.
[26] Ch.14; see below, para.14–030 *et seq*. See also below, para.18–282.
[27] Above, paras 12–127, 13–019; below paras 14–080 *et seq.*, 14–095, 14–114.
[28] An office now abolished.

statutory instrument and to restrain their use. Only one statutory instrument effective in the area of sale of goods was ever made.[29] The 1973 Act has now been superseded by the Enterprise Act 2002, which imposes a broad duty on the Office of Fair Trading of "promoting good practice in the carrying out of activities which may affect the economic interests of consumers",[30] and confers considerably greater powers: for example, to prevent infringements by the use of exemption clauses that are invalidated by the Unfair Contract Terms Act 1977.[31] These are dealt with elsewhere in this book.[32]

Liability in tort. The Unfair Contract Terms Act applies also to attempts **13–106**
to exclude liability in tort, whether by contract term or notice: by section 2 these also cannot exclude or restrict liability for death or personal injury resulting from negligence, and in so far as they seek to exempt from liability for negligence leading to other loss or damage, they are subject to the requirement of reasonableness.[33] Where there is strict liability in contract as well as negligence liability in tort, as a matter of construction it may in any case be held that an exemption clause does not cover negligence.[34] But where it does, whether it takes effect by virtue of contract or by way of a notice (*e.g.* affixed to goods sold) it is subject to the Act, which also contains a special provision applicable to tort claims, section 2(3): "Where a contract term or notice purports to exclude or restrict liability for negligence a person's agreement to or awareness of it is not of itself to be taken as indicating his voluntary acceptance of any risk." The purpose of this provision is presumably to reiterate the limits of the doctrine *Volenti non fit injuria*: though it may have some tendency towards narrowing the doctrine, since agreement to a term might be thought to indicate acceptance of a risk.[35] Here, however, a more general difficulty again arises from the selection of exemption clauses as a target for control.[36] Although some terms and notices may clearly be classifiable as intended to exclude or restrict a potential liability, others may seek only to discharge a duty of care by means of a warning or to procure that any injury to another party is in fact attributable to him. Thus in *Hurley v Dyke*[37] on the sale of a seriously defective car for £40 at an auction on the terms "To be sold as seen and with all its faults and without warranty", it was held in the House of Lords (on facts occurring before the Unfair Contract Terms Act was operative)

---

[29] The Consumer Transactions (Restrictions on Statements) Order 1976 (SI 1976/1813) as amended SI, referred to above, paras 13–067, 13–084 and below, para.14–142. See also Business Advertisements (Disclosure) Order 1977 (1977/1918), below, para.14–141.
[30] s.8.
[31] s.211 of the 2002 Act.
[32] See below, paras 14–130 *et seq.*
[33] s.2(1), (2), above, paras 13–092, 13–093.
[34] Above, para.13–022.
[35] Though it is arguable that the defence of *Volenti* has no application to negligence *simpliciter*: *Wooldridge v Sumner* [1963] 2 Q.B. 43 at 69–70; *Clerk and Lindsell on Torts* (19th ed.), paras 3–72 *et seq.*
[36] *cf.* above, paras 13–044, 13–065 *et seq.*
[37] [1979] R.T.R. 265.

that the seller had discharged his duty of care by such a warning, at any rate if he did not know of the car's dangerous condition. Hence he was not liable in respect of injuries suffered by a passenger of the sub-buyer when the car subsequently crashed. The Court of Appeal had also held that, even if the seller was negligent, his negligence was not the cause of the accident.[38] The case concerned liability to a third party: *a fortiori* the notice discharged the seller's liability to the first buyer. The problem arises also in the case of pre-contractual misrepresentations accompanied by a disclaimer or warning.[39] In so far as a disclaimer is involved, the Act doubtless applies[40]; but the warning element is separate.

13–107 It can further be questioned to what extent the wording of section 13(1), which in some cases extends control to "terms and notices which exclude or restrict the relevant obligation or duty"[41] covers disclaimers which seek rather to establish or define the duty of care undertaken. But in *Cremdean Properties Ltd v Nash*[42] the Court of Appeal held that section 3 of the Misrepresentation Act 1967 applied to a clause which purported to indicate that no duty was undertaken in respect of particulars of property supplied by estate agents. And in *Smith v Eric S. Bush*,[43] which has already been discussed,[44] the House of Lords, relying partly on the wording in section 11(3) (a provision not applicable to the Misrepresentation Act), which in connection with notices speaks of "the circumstances obtaining when the liability arose or (but for the notice) would have arisen", held that the 1977 Act plainly covered a notice seeking to limit the duty undertaken by surveyors to third parties who might rely on the results of the survey. Lord Templeman said[45] that "the Act of 1977 requires that all exclusion notices which would in common law provide a defence to an action for negligence must satisfy the requirement of reasonableness." It seems therefore that such arguments will be unsympathetically received. Nevertheless, as has been stated, there can be little doubt that some types of warning may not rank as exemption clauses,[46] but may rather discharge a person's duty of care, so that any loss is not caused by that person's negligence. And although the duty of care in respect of damage to person or property does not arise from assumption of responsibility, and one of the bases on which *Smith v Eric S. Bush* was decided was that liability for economic loss, when it exists, is not usually to be explained on this general basis either,[47] there may still be some cases of such liability which are to be attributed to such

---

[38] At pp.291, 296.
[39] Above, paras 11–041 *et seq.*, 13–055, 13–068.
[40] In *Hurley v Dyke*, Lord Denning M.R. in the Court of Appeal indicated that had the Act been in force when the facts of the case occurred the clause would have been caught by it: see pp.281–282.
[41] See above, para.13–065.
[42] (1977) 244 E.G. 547; above, para.13–057.
[43] [1990] 1 A.C. 831.
[44] Above, paras 13–065, 13–066.
[45] At p.849.
[46] *cf.* above, para.13–068.
[47] See [1990] 1 A.C. 831 at 846, 862, 864. See also *McCullagh v Lane Fox & Partners Ltd* [1996] 1 E.G.L.R. 35.

reasoning.[48] Therefore, the possibility of a clause which only indicates the duty undertaken is one which cannot be totally excluded. It should be noted finally that in the case of notices, the requirement of reasonableness relates to the time when the liability arose (or would have arisen). This is not the same as the rule for contract terms, which are tested at the time of the making of the contract.[49]

---

[48] See *Henderson v Merrett Syndicates Ltd* [1995] 2 A.C. 145.
[49] s.11(3), above, para.13–086.

Part Five
CONSUMER PROTECTION

CHAPTER 14

CONSUMER PROTECTION

	PARA.
1. Introduction	14–001
2. Rights under the civil law	14–004
(a) Rights of buyer against seller	14–004
(b) Exemption clauses and unfair contract terms	14–029
(c) Miscellaneous matters	14–041
(d) Rights under other contracts to supply goods	14–046
(e) Rights under contracts to supply services	14–050
(f) Distance selling	14–053
(g) Rights of buyer against manufacturer and intermediate distributor and others	14–061
(h) Manufacturers' guarantees	14–065
(i) Rights of a user who did not buy the product	14–076
(j) Liability under Part I of the Consumer Protection Act 1987	14–080
(k) Civil liability for breach of statutory duty	14–094
3. The consumer's remedies	14–098
4. Criminal law	14–108
5. Administrative protection	14–125
6. Indirect protection	14–140
7. Consumer credit transactions	14–143

1. INTRODUCTION

Introduction. The contract of sale to which most of this book refers is one in which buyer and seller are assumed to be in a position of general equality, so that the main function of the law is to work out the appropriate consequences of what may be assumed to be the common intention of the parties. It is obvious, however, that in a very large number of sales this is by itself an unsuitable technique. The buyer may by virtue of haste, ignorance, gullibility, inferior bargaining position or simple imprudence enter into a transaction in which the goods supplied, or the terms of the contract, or both, are unsatisfactory to him: and in many circumstances it may be felt that he is deserving of protection. The protection required may be specific, *i.e.* there may be a need for a private remedy in a particular situation; or general, *i.e.* it may be desirable to control unacceptable practices of a particular type. A seller may also, though less often, appear to require such protection against the buyer. The civil law has on the whole, save in the case of conscious deception, taken little account of these problems: its outlook is indeed sometimes expressed by the maxim *caveat emptor*. Even where there is a remedy, its exercise may be troublesome or risky for the consumer. But the general problem has in fact been the subject of attention for many centuries. Attempts to regulate the price of staple commodities (*e.g.* bread), and to control measurements and measuring equipment (*e.g.* in the sale of beer and coal) date back to the Middle Ages.[1] More recently, **14–001**

[1] See Harvey and Parry, *Law of Consumer Protection and Fair Trading* (6th ed.), Ch.1.

however, the movement towards the protection of the consumer, who may in this context be roughly defined as a private buyer from a commercial seller,[2] and who is the person thought most in need of such protection, has increased greatly in strength and prominence. Statutes and regulations have sought to protect consumers; officials have been appointed who have consumer protection as their function or among their functions; organisations of consumers seek to promote their interests; studies are conducted into the problems of consumer protection; and the various organs of the European Union and its predecessors have since 1975 taken a vigorous interest in consumer affairs.[3] Indeed, the European Community is committed to seeking to ensure "a high level of consumer protection" and to contributing "to protecting the health, safety and economic interests of consumers, as well as promoting their right to information, education and to organise themselves in order to safeguard their interests."[4]

14–002 A book on sale of goods which included no reference to consumer protection would give an inaccurate picture, in that the law which it expounded would be misleading, or at best incomplete, for a large number

---

[2] There is no general definition of "consumer": but see; Consumer Credit Act 1974, s.8 ("consumer credit agreement"), s.15 ("consumer hire agreement"); Unfair Contract Terms Act 1977, s.5(2)(a) ("consumer use"), s.12 ("deals as consumer"); Consumer Protection Act 1987, s.5(3) ("damage giving rise to liability"), s.10(7) ("consumer goods"); Unfair Terms in Consumer Contracts Regulations 1999 (SI 1999/2083), reg. 3(1) ("consumer"); Consumer Protection (Distance Selling) Regulations 2000 (SI 2000/2334), reg. 3(1) ("consumer"); Enterprise Act 2002, s.210(2)(6)("consumer").

[3] This stems from a Council Resolution of April 14, 1975: [1975] O.J. C92/1: see Close, 8 Eur.L.Rev. 221 (1983). Examples of EEC activity appear at various points in the text and notes. They include Council Directive No. 1984/450/EEC on misleading advertising, below, para.14–140; Council Directive No. 1985/374/EEC on liability for defective products, below, para.14–080; Council Directive No. 1990/314/EEC on package travel, package holidays and package tours, below, para.14–050; Directive No. 2001/95/EC of the European Parliament and of the Council on general product safety, below, para.14–119; Council Directive No. 1993/13/EEC on unfair terms in consumer contracts, below, para.14–030; Directive 1997/7/EC of the European Parliament and of the Council on the protection of consumers in relation to distance contracts, below, para.14–054; Directive 1998/27/EC of the European Parliament and of the Council on injunctions for the protection of consumers' interests, below, para.14–129; Directive 1999/44/EC of the European Parliament and of the Council on certain aspects of the sale of consumer goods and associated guarantees, below, paras 14–008 *et seq*. For a discussion of some recent issues, see the European Commission's Green Paper, *European Union Consumer Protection*, (COM (2001) 531 final); also the Council Resolution of December 2, 2002 on Community consumer policy strategy 2002–2006 (2003/C 11/01) and for a wide-ranging proposal from the Commission for a programme of Community action in the field of health and consumer protection, see COM (2005) 115 final of April 6, 2005. See, generally, Reich, 14 Sydney L.R. 23 (1992); Lonbay (ed.), *Enhancing The Legal Position of the European Consumer* (1996); Weatherill, *EU Consumer Law and Policy* (2005); Howells and Wilhelmsson, *EC Consumer* Law (1997); Parry, "The Impact of the European Community on the UK Consumer" in Meisel and Cook (eds.), *Property and Protection* (2000), Ch.10. But as to the efficacy of this activity see Borrie, *The Development of Consumer Law and Policy—Bold Spirits and Timorous Souls* (1984), Ch.5. The Council of Europe has also been active in this field.

[4] Art. 153 (ex Art. 129a) of the EC Treaty.

of daily sale transactions. At the same time to give a full account of the law and of the administrative and other measures protecting consumers requires an entirely separate approach, especially if the full economic and regulatory aspects of the subject are to be considered. The area of consumer protection is therefore rightly made the subject of specialised works, to which the reader is directed.[5] At present, the principal rights of a consumer buyer under a contract for the sale of goods or some similar transaction are located in the same enactments as his commercial counterpart, albeit with some important modifications.[6] In future, it may well be that they will be hived off into separate legislation covering consumer sales and perhaps services.[7] In that event more detailed treatment may be required, albeit that it will overlap to a considerable extent with that accorded to commercial sales. Meanwhile, the main purpose of this present part of the book is to draw attention to the particular problems raised by the application of the normal principles of contract and tort to cases involving consumers (many of which are also referred to at the appropriate places elsewhere), and to statutes, statutory instruments and other regulatory techniques which are relevant in the context of a consumer sale. A relatively short account of the provisions of Part I of the Consumer Protection Act 1987 has also been included. The general assumption of the chapter is that it is the buyer who is the consumer: but, as already has been said, it should not be forgotten that similar problems can arise where a private person sells to a commercial concern, *e.g.* in part exchange.

This chapter therefore begins by considering in outline the consumer's rights under the civil law; it briefly draws attention to the ways in which these rights can be enforced; it goes on to the protection conferred by the criminal law; it then considers the administrative functions of the Office of Fair Trading; and finally refers to certain indirect forms of protection, such as control of advertising, and to consumer credit legislation, which is a **14–003**

---

[5] There are two main looseleaf encyclopaedias: *Butterworths Trading and Consumer Law*, and *Encyclopaedia of Consumer Law* (published by Sweet & Maxwell). See also such further general works as Harvey and Parry, *op.cit.*, above; Cranston's *Consumers and the Law* (Scott and Black eds.) (2000); Lowe and Woodroffe, *Consumer Law and Practice* (6th ed.); Oughton and Lowry, *Textbook on Consumer Law* (2nd ed.); Miller, Harvey and Parry, *Consumer and Trading Law: Text, Cases and Materials* (1998); Howells and Weatherill, *Consumer Protection Law* (2005); Ramsay, *Consumer Law and Policy: Text and Materials on Regulating Consumer Markets* (2005). For earlier material, see *The Final Report of the (Molony) Committee on Consumer Protection* (1982), Cmnd. 1781; Cranston, *Regulating Business: Law and Consumer Agencies* (1979). Product liability and consumer credit are separate subjects with a literature of their own: see below, paras 14–061, 14–076 *et seq.* and 14–143 *et seq.*, respectively.

[6] The modifications or variations include those contained in the Sale of Goods Act 1979, s.14, as amended (above, para.11–033, below, para.14–010) and the new Part 5A (ss.48A–48F) remedies (above, paras 12–071—12–118, below, paras 14–023—14–027), together with those contained in the Unfair Contract Terms Act 1977, s.12 (above, paras 13–071—13–082, below, para.14–029). Also, the Unfair Terms in Consumer Contracts Regulations 1999 (SI 1999/2083, as amended) apply only to "contracts concluded between a seller or supplier and a consumer" (reg. 4(1); see below, paras 14–030—14–040.

[7] See Bridge, 119 L.Q.R. 173 (2003).

separate subject in itself. It will be seen that the overall picture is one of considerable complexity.

2. RIGHTS UNDER THE CIVIL LAW

(a) *Rights of Buyer Against Seller*

14–004 **Unordered goods.** It has not been uncommon for sellers to send to consumers goods which had not been ordered, with accompanying literature perhaps indicating that the goods will be taken as having been purchased unless the receiver notifies the sender within a certain time. This technique is sometimes known as "inertia selling". Such goods may be treated under general principles as the offer of a contract, which the receiver is entitled to accept without notifying the seller. He may therefore examine them, and try them out, if this is appropriate in the circumstances, to a limited extent: if he goes further than this, he may accept the offer by conduct and must pay any price stipulated. He is under no obligation to return them.[8] If he decides not to keep the goods, he becomes an involuntary bailee, and (probably) owes no duty to the sender beyond one not to act wilfully or recklessly with regard to them.[9] However, the practice of "inertia selling" has long since been controlled by provisions now contained in the Consumer Protection (Distance Selling) Regulations 2000.[10] Regulation 24 applies where unsolicited goods are sent to a person with a view to his acquiring them and he has no reasonable cause to believe that they were sent with a view to their being acquired for the purposes of a business. In any such case if the recipient has neither agreed to acquire nor agreed to return the goods he may, as between himself and the sender, use, deal with or dispose of them as if they were an unconditional gift to him.[11] The rights of the sender are extinguished.[12] There are associated offences, which include demanding or asserting a right to payment in respect of such unsolicited goods (or services) or threatening to bring legal proceedings in respect of them.[13]

---

[8] See *Capital Finance Co. Ltd v Bray* [1964] 1 W.L.R. 323 at 328–329.

[9] But the position is not entirely clear. See Paton, *Bailment in the Common Law* (1952), Ch.5; Palmer, *Bailment* (2nd ed.), Ch.12.

[10] SI 2000/2334. Previously the relevant provisions were contained in the Unsolicited Goods and Services Act 1971, s.1 (rights of recipients of unsolicited goods).

[11] reg. 24(2).

[12] reg. 24(3).

[13] reg. 24(4) and (5)(a). Also, it is an offence to place or threaten to place a name on a list of defaulters or debtors or to invoke or threaten to invoke any other collection procedure: (reg. 24(5)(b) and (c)). See also Administration of Justice Act 1970, s.40, below, para.14–141. As to unsolicited directory entries, see the Unsolicited Goods and Services Act 1971, s.3, as amended most recently by the Regulatory Reform (Unsolicited Goods and Services Act 1971) (Directory Entries and Demands for Payment) Order 2005 (SI 2005/55) and the Unsolicited Goods and Services Act 1971 (Electronic Commerce) (Amendment) Regulations 2005 (SI 2005/148). Section 3A of the 197l Act (inserted by the Unsolicited Goods and

Non-delivery. At least historically, the remedy for complete non-delivery of goods has almost always been an action for damages[14]: specific performance has been the exception rather than the rule, although it is available in the case of objects of unique character.[15] It is possible that, as a result of the new Part 5A remedies introduced into the Sale of Goods Act 1979[16] in order to give effect to Directive 1999/44/EC,[17] specific performance may be more readily available in future where, in the case of a sale to a consumer, the goods do not conform to the contract at the time of delivery. The matter is considered further elsewhere.[18] These remedies do not apply where the complaint is of non-delivery, as opposed to a non-conforming delivery, but a greater willingness to order the repair or replacement of non-conforming goods might conceivably be reflected in a less restrictive approach to specific performance where the complaint is of simple non-delivery. 14–005

Late delivery. Where the seller is to deliver, the delivery of ordered goods at a time later than that stipulated, or, if no time is stipulated, at a time which is later than might reasonably have been anticipated, is a breach of contract.[19] The Sale of Goods Act provides that whether time is of the essence in a contract of sale depends on the terms of the contract,[20] except in the case of stipulations as to time of payment, which are not of the essence unless a different intention appears from the terms of the contract.[21] In commercial contracts schedules of timing for performance are often laid down, and compliance with each provision may be held a condition, any breach of which entitles the buyer to treat the contract as discharged[22]: such a schedule may also be held to require punctual 14–006

Services Act 1975) gave the Secretary of State power to make regulations as to the contents and form of notes of agreement, invoices and similar documents. However, this has been repealed by SI 2005/55, Art. 2(6) and the relevant particulars are now set out in Part 1 of the Schedule to that Order. Non-compliance with such requirements is to be regarded as asserting a right to payment: Consumer Protection (Distance Selling) Regulations 2000 (SI 2000/2334), reg. 24(7) (as amended by SI 2005/55, Art. 4) and reg. 24(8).

[14] Unless property has passed to the buyer, in which case an action in conversion may be appropriate.

[15] Sale of Goods Act 1979, s.52: below, paras 17–096 *et seq*.

[16] See the Sale and Supply of Goods to Consumers Regulations 2002 (SI 2002/3045), reg. 5, inserting Part 5A (ss.48A–48F). The new s.48E(2) is particularly relevant.

[17] [1999] O.J. L171/12.

[18] See above, para.12–114 and below, para.14–025; also the commentary in *Benjamin's Sale of Goods: Special Supplement to the 6th edition* (2003), pp.66–69.

[19] Sale of Goods Act 1979, s.29(3); above, paras 8–037 *et seq*. For an example in the case of services (car repairs) see *Charnock v Liverpool Corp.* [1968] 1 W.L.R. 1498.

[20] s.10(2): above, para.8–025. See in general *United Scientific Holdings Ltd v Burnley B.C.* [1978] A.C. 904.

[21] s.10(1); above, para.9–051. A different intention may appear in commercial contracts: *e.g. Toepfer v Lenersan-Poortman NV* [1980] 1 Lloyd's Rep. 143. It is less likely to do so in consumer contracts.

[22] *e.g. Bunge Corp. v Tradax Export SA* [1981] 1 W.L.R. 711; *Cie. Commerciale Sucres et Denrées v C. Czarnikow Ltd (The Naxos)* [1990] 1 W.L.R. 1337, above, paras 10–032, 10–034 *et seq*.

performance in related matters as to which no time is specifically stipulated.[23] Consumer contracts are less likely to contain time schedules, and it is doubtful whether they would be subjected to the same overall strict interpretation, even though the consumer may be as reluctant to wait for his goods as the business man. In many consumer contracts, therefore, late delivery will not be a breach serious enough to entitle the buyer to reject unless the delay is long enough to frustrate the object of the contract.[24] The consumer may well be confined to a remedy in damages: and since his loss is likely to consist primarily of inconvenience or disappointment (or both) he may not always find it easy to recover in respect of this.[25]

14–007 **Title.** If the goods supplied under a contract of sale do not belong to the seller, the buyer will acquire no title unless one of the exceptions to the rule *nemo dat quod non habet* applies.[26] The rules as to the passing of property and title are exactly the same for consumers as for commercial buyers except in one respect.[27] By virtue of Part III of the Hire Purchase Act 1964 as amended[28] the "private purchaser" of a motor vehicle from a seller ("debtor") who held on hire-purchase or conditional sale may acquire title if he has acted in good faith; and when such a seller sells to a trade purchaser and the goods are subsequently sold on, the first private purchaser may similarly acquire title. However, such protection is less than complete and the House of Lords has held that the private purchaser is not protected when he buys the vehicle from a rogue who has impersonated a creditworthy individual and thereby gained possession of the vehicle from a dealer. Such a rogue is not a "debtor" within the meaning of section 27(1) of the Act.[29] When the buyer does not acquire title the seller is of course in

---

[23] *e.g. Toepfer v Lenersan-Poortman NV*, above (tender of documents).
[24] Above, paras 8–037, 10–033.
[25] See below, Ch.17. The buyer may derive help from the loss of holiday cases, *e.g. Jarvis v Swans Tours Ltd* [1973] Q.B. 233; *Jackson v Horizon Holidays Ltd* [1975] 1 W.L.R. 1468; *Ichard v Frangoulis* [1977] 1 W.L.R. 556; *Leitner v TUI Deutschland GmbH & Co. KG*, Case C–168/00, [2002] E.C.R. I-2631 (ECJ) (in the context of package holidays); from *Chaplin v Hicks* [1911] 2 K.B. 786 (loss of opportunity to enter beauty contest); from such cases as *Bernstein v Pamson Motors (Golders Green) Ltd* [1987] 2 All E.R. 220 (new car breaking down); *Ruxley Electronics and Construction Ltd v Forsyth* [1996] A.C. 344 (swimming pool not of stipulated depth); *Farley v Skinner* [2002] 2 A.C. 732 (aircraft noise: lack of accurate information by surveyor); and from dicta as to distress and inconvenience such as those in *McCall v Abelesz* [1976] Q.B. 585, 594; *Heywood v Wellers* [1976] Q.B. 446, 458, 461; and *Cox v Philips Industries Ltd* [1976] 1 W.L.R. 638. As to the contrasting position in a commercial context, see *Hayes v James & Charles Dodd (a firm)* [1990] 2 All E.R. 815 (motor repair business and solicitor). See also Treitel, *Law of Contract* (11th ed.), pp.987–991; Phang [2003] J.B.L. 341. See also below, para.14–020, n.8.
[26] Above, Ch.7.
[27] For differences in the rules as to the passing of risk and acceptance of goods in consumer cases (ss.20 and 32 of the Act), see above, paras 6–013—6–014, 6–025, 8–014, and in the context of overseas sales, below, paras 18–259—18–264, 18–307, 19–123 and 20–094. However, these do not affect the passing of property.
[28] Above, paras 7–087 *et seq*. New wording was substituted by Sch.4 to the Consumer Credit Act 1974.
[29] See *Shogun Finance Ltd v Hudson* [2004] 1 A.C. 919, above, para.7–090; also, Elliott, [2004] J.B.L. 381. Nor is a person within the exception if he purchases motor vehicles as a business venture intending to sell them on at a profit: see *GE Capital Bank Ltd v Rushton*, [2006] 1 W.L.R. 899.

breach of a condition of the contract by virtue of section 12 of the Sale of Goods Act[30]: and the wording of this provision is applicable to all sales whether commercial, consumer or purely private. The buyer may therefore reject the goods unless he is too late to do so: and if he does so may recover the price.[31] In any case he may claim damages.[32] It seems that the right to reject and to reclaim the full price is less easily lost in the case of this stipulation.[33] Difficulties may arise where a consumer has improved the item bought and seeks to recover the cost of the improvements from the true owner who claims it. In such a case the improver may, if sued in conversion, be entitled to an allowance under the Torts (Interference with Goods) Act 1977[34]: but if the chattel is simply retaken he may have to rely on the common law.[35]

Implied obligations as to quality, etc.: background and the EC Directive on consumer sales. Historically, English law has not distinguished, at least at a formal level, between implied obligations as to quality, etc. in consumer, as opposed to commercial or "business to business", sales.[36] The same terms have been implied, although the ability to exclude or modify them has long since been much more extensively controlled where sales to consumers are concerned.[37] However, the implementation of Directive 1999/44/EC on certain aspects of the sale of consumer goods and associated guarantees[38] will require such distinctions to be drawn in future and in all probability introduce areas of uncertainty into the law. The implementation has been carried out by the Sale and Supply of Goods to Consumers 14–008

[30] Above, paras 4–002 *et seq*.
[31] Above, paras 4–006 *et seq*.
[32] Above, paras 4–006 *et seq*. For the position with respect to exemption clauses and unfair contract terms, see above, paras 4–018 *et seq*. below, paras 14–029 *et seq*.
[33] *Rowland v Divall* [1923] 2 K.B. 500; above, paras 4–006 *et seq*.
[34] s.6(1); above, paras 4–007 and 7–005.
[35] See *Greenwood v Bennett* [1973] Q.B. 195; Goff and Jones, *Law of Restitution* (6th ed.), pp.236–240.
[36] See above, paras 11–001—11–072. See, however, the modifications to the right to reject in the Sale of Goods Act 1979, s.15A, which apply only in non-consumer cases.
[37] Notably by the Unfair Contract Terms Act 1977, s.6(2) and the Unfair Terms in Consumer Contracts Regulations 1999 (SI 1999/2083), above, paras 13–062 *et seq*. and below, paras 14–029—14–040.
[38] [1999] O.J. L171/12. For discussion of the Directive and its implementation, see *Benjamin's Sale of Goods: Special Supplement to the 6th edition* (2003); *Blackstone's Guide to Consumer Sales and Associated Guarabovees* (2003); Bianca and Grundmann (eds), *EU Sales Directive* (2002); Whittaker, *Liability for Products* (2005), Ch.19; Willett, Morgan-Taylor and Naidoo, [2004] J.B.L. 94, and DTI Consultation Papers on the Sale of Goods Directive of January 4, 2001 and February 26, 2002; as to the Directive, see also Watterson, (2001) 9 Euro. Rev. of Private Law 197; Twigg-Flesner and Bradgate, [2000] Web J. C.L.1; Twigg-Flesner, [1999] Consum. L.J. 177. The Directive had its origins in a much more ambitious Green Paper on *Guarantees for Consumer Goods and After-Sales Services* (COM (93) 509 final). For comments on an earlier draft, see the *Report of the House of Lords Select Committee on the European Communities, Consumer Guarantees* (1996–97 H.L. 57); Bradgate, [1995] Consum. L.J. 94; Beale and Howells, 12 J.C.L. 21 (1997); Shears, Zollers and Hurd, [2000] J.B.L. 262.

Regulations 2002[39] made under section 2(2) of the European Communities Act 1972 and it is mainly in the form of amendments to the Sale of Goods Act 1979.[40] Hence, since there is no separate body of legislation covering consumer sales as such, it is convenient that the principal discussion of the implied obligations and associated remedies for their breach should be reserved for other chapters of this book.[41] The present chapter seeks to do no more than state the position in broad outline and draw some comparisons between the provisions of the 1979 Act and those of the Directive. Two preliminary points should, however, be made. The first is that whereas the Directive refers to the beneficiary of its provisions as "the consumer",[42] the process of implementation in English law has generally been linked to a person who "deals as consumer",[43] an expression which is defined by section 61(5A) of the 1979 Act by reference to its meaning in Part I (section 12) of the Unfair Contract Terms Act 1977.[44] The second preliminary point is that it is important to note that the Directive sets out minimum requirements only and expressly allows Member States to "adopt or maintain in force more stringent provisions, compatible with the Treaty, to ensure a higher level of consumer protection."[45] In other words, assuming compatibility with the Treaty, English law would not be open to challenge if it provides a higher level of protection to consumers or extends such protection to a wider category of persons than those who would be within the scope of the Directive. Problems would arise only if the minimum requirements are not met.

---

[39] SI 2002/3045. Implementation was required (but not achieved) by January 1, 2002 (Art. 11.1), whereas the Regulations came into force only on March 31, 2003 (reg. 1(1)) and accordingly apply only to contracts concluded on or after that date (see Interpretation Act 1978, s.4(a)). The failure to transpose the Directive by the prescribed date gives rise to a possibility of a claim in tort for damages against the UK Government at the suit of a claimant who has incurred loss as a result of the delayed implementation: (see, generally, Joined Cases C6 and 9/90 *Francovich and Bonifaci v Italy* [1991] E.C.R. I-5357, ECJ, Case C-178/94; *Dillenkofer v Germany* [1997] Q.B. 259, [1996] E.C.R. I-4845, ECJ).

[40] However, there are also parallel amendments to the Supply of Goods and Services Act 1982 and, in the case of the implied terms as to quality, to the Supply of Goods (Implied Terms) Act 1973 and further amendments to the Unfair Contract Terms Act 1977, s.12 (see above, paras 13–071 *et seq* and below, para.14–029). A free-standing provision in reg. 15 covers consumer guarantees (see below, paras 14–070, *et seq*).

[41] See, especially, above, paras 11–001—11–072 and 12–038—12–118; and below, paras 17–047—17–080.

[42] As to which, see Art. 1.2(a), and below, para.14–011.

[43] The exception is that the implementation of Art. 6 (Guarantees) by the Sale and Supply of Goods to Consumers Regulations 2002 (SI 2002/3045), reg. 15, refers to the beneficiary as "a consumer", a term which is defined by reg. 2 in a way which is similar (although not identical) to Art. 1(2)(a) of the Directive. See further, below, paras 14–070—14–075.

[44] As to which, see above, paras 13–071—13–082 and below, para.14–029.

[45] Art. 8.2.

Correspondence with description. The condition as to correspondence with description of section 13 of the Sale of Goods Act[46] is potentially applicable in many consumer contracts, for example when goods are acquired by mail order or in response to an advertisement in a catalogue or elsewhere.[47] The condition is implied in all contracts for the sale of goods by description, including private sales.[48] However, the obligation is a limited one and goods may correspond with the contract description and yet be of very poor quality and indeed unsafe.[49] Historically, the strictest application of the rules has been in commercial sales and indeed in consumer transactions it is arguable that the standard of conformity has sometimes been set too low.[50] 14–009

Satisfactory quality and fitness for purpose. The implied conditions as to satisfactory quality and fitness for purpose contained in section 14 of the Act apply only where goods are sold "in the course of a business".[51] They are of considerable importance for the protection of consumers no less than for commercial buyers. Before the amendments introduced by section 1 of the Sale and Supply of Goods Act 1994 the relevant standard of "merchantable quality" was linked to a test of fitness for purpose. Goods were of "merchantable quality" if they were as fit for the purpose or purposes for which goods of that kind are commonly bought as it was reasonable to expect.[52] The functional overtones of this test were seen by many as being less than apt to cover cases where consumer goods worked adequately and yet were poorly finished or generally shoddy in appearance.[53] Under the new test of "satisfactory quality" fitness for purpose is relegated to being an aspect of the quality of goods and the standard is defined by reference to what "a reasonable person would regard as satisfactory, taking account of any description of the goods, the price (if relevant) and all the other relevant circumstances."[54] A more recent amendment introduced to comply 14–010

[46] Above, paras 11–001—11–022. Section 13 was amended by the Sale and Supply of Goods Act 1994, s.7, Sch.2, para.5. The implied term is designated a "condition" only as regards England and Wales and Northern Ireland: s.13(1). For such contracts the controls of the Consumer Protection (Distance Selling) Regulations 2000 (SI 2000/2334) will also be relevant; see below, paras 14–054 *et seq.*
[47] However, s.13 may similarly apply where goods are exposed for sale and selected by the buyer, as in a typical sale in a supermarket: see s.13(3).
[48] See, *e.g. Beale v Taylor* [1967] 1 W.L.R. 1193 (private sale of Herald convertible car).
[49] As in *Smith v Lazarus* (1981), CA unreported, but extracted in Miller, Harvey and Parry, *Consumer and Trading Law: Text, Cases and Materials* (1998), pp.93–94 (motor car). But consumers are less likely to be affected by the limitations on the scope of s.13 associated with the decision in *Harlingdon & Leinster Enterprises Ltd v Christopher Hull Fine Art Ltd.* [1991] 1 Q.B. 564, CA.
[50] Above, paras 11–005, 11–020.
[51] See above, paras 11–027—11–028. The implied terms are designated "conditions" only as regards England and Wales and Northern Ireland: see s.14(5).
[52] s.14(6) of the 1979 Act.
[53] But see *Rogers v Parish (Scarborough) Ltd* [1987] Q.B. 933 at 944, *per* Mustill L.J. and above, para.11–038.
[54] s.14(2A). For a decision applying this provision in a consumer context, see *Bramhill v Edwards* [2004] EWCA Civ 403, [2004] 2 Lloyd's Rep. 505 (mobile home

with the Directive on consumer sales[55] provides that, where the buyer "deals as consumer",[56] the circumstances which are relevant when determining whether the goods meet the statutory standard of satisfactory quality generally include "any public statements on the specific characteristics of the goods made about them by the seller, the producer or his representative, particularly on advertising or on labelling".[57] In addition to fitness for purpose, other specified aspects of the quality of goods include, in appropriate cases, the goods' appearance and finish, freedom from minor defects, safety and durability[58] and no doubt accompanying instructions to the extent that these are reasonably to be expected.[59] This should make it easier for a consumer to establish a breach of section 14, although the mere fact that goods wear out more rapidly than might have been expected will not necessarily imply that they were not of satisfactory quality when sold. Subsequent damage or deterioration (unless it shows that they were not fit at the material time) is governed by the rules as to risk which in such situations would be of general application.[60] The related obligation of reasonable fitness for any particular purpose[61] which has been made known to the seller in circumstances which indicate a reasonable reliance on his skill or judgment will also apply to consumer as well as to commercial sales. However, it may be assumed that businesses will typically indicate such specific requirements more readily than will consumers.[62] Also, it may be doubted whether, in an age of national brand-name advertising, consumers rely on the skill or judgment of the *seller*, rather than that of the manufacturer.[63] This may be so in the case of (say) the specialist hardware shop, but the claim is less plausible where the advice solicited is that of a young assistant in a busy "Do-it-Yourself" type superstore.

---

of satisfactory quality even though strictly speaking it was not by virtue of its width lawful to use it on the road); noted by Twigg-Flesner, 121 L.Q.R. 205 (2005). See also *Jewson Ltd v Boyhan* [2003] EWCA Civ 1030, [2004] 1 Lloyd's Rep. 505 and generally, above, paras 11–031—11–050.

55 See the Sale and Supply of Goods to Consumers Regulations 2002 (SI 2002/3045), reg. 3.

56 As noted above, the words "deals as consumer" are defined by s.61(5A) of the Act by reference to their meaning in Part I (s.12) of the Unfair Contract Terms Act 1977 (see, generally, above, paras 13–071—13–082 and 14–008; and below, para.14–029).

57 See s.14(2D). This is subject to qualifications (s.14(2E) and (2F)). The corresponding provisions in the Directive are contained in Arts 2.2(d) and 2.4. For further discussion, see above, paras 11–033—11–037.

58 s.14(2B). For helpful and detailed discussion, see the Report of the Law Commission and the Scottish Law Commission, *Sale and Supply of Goods* (Law Com. No. 160; Scot. Law Com. No. 104) (Cmnd. 137, 1987), pp.22–35.

59 See *Wormell* v *R.H.M. Agriculture (East) Ltd* [1986] 1 W.L.R. 36 (Piers Ashworth, Q.C.); [1987] 1 W.L.R. 1091, CA.

60 Above, paras 6–002 *et seq*. The risk prima facie passes with the property: In other situations involving sales to consumers, the rules as to the passing of risk may be affected by the new s.20(4) of the Act (above, paras 6–013—6–014 and 6–025); see also the new s.32(4) (delivery of goods to carrier not delivery to buyer), above, para.8–014. As to risk when goods are rejected, see above, para.6–011.

61 See s.14(3) above, paras 11–051 *et seq*.

62 The buyer's particular requirements arising from an unusually sensitive skin were not indicated in *Griffiths v Peter Conway Ltd* [1939] 1 All E.R. 685.

63 But see *Junior Books Co. Ltd v Veitchi Co. Ltd* [1983] 1 A.C. 520 at 547, *per* Lord Roskill.

Compliance with the Directive: definitions. The implied terms as to correspondence with description and satisfactory quality of sections 13 and 14 of the Sale of Goods Act 1979 have as their counterpart Article 2.1 of the Directive which states that: "The seller must deliver goods to the consumer which are in conformity with the contract of sale."[64] "Consumer" is defined as "any natural person who, in the contracts covered by this Directive, is acting for purposes which are not related to his trade, business or profession" and a "seller" as "any natural or legal person who, under a contract, sells consumer goods in the course of his trade, business or profession".[65] So, it is only a "natural" person or an individual (which term would include sole traders but not corporations)[66] who is capable of being a consumer for the purposes of the Directive and then only when he acquires consumer goods for purposes which are not "related to" his trade, etc. A professional author buying replacement cartridges for a printer and an owner of an art gallery who entertains regular clients with a buffet lunch supplied by caterers would not be within the scope of the Directive, although both would of course benefit from the general terms as to quality etc. of the Sale of Goods Act 1979. In the case of sellers, there will be the familiar difficulties of determining whether an activity is a "business", etc. as opposed to a hobby or pastime,[67] but no doubt the words "in the course of" will be construed broadly in the interest of maximising consumer protection.[68] So far as compliance with the minimum harmonisation provisions of the Directive is concerned, the main point to note is that the definition of "consumer goods" is defined very broadly to mean "any tangible movable item, with the exception of: goods sold by way of execution or otherwise by authority of law, water and gas where they are not put up for sale in a limited volume or set quantity, electricity."[69] This has necessitated modifications to the definition of "deals as consumer" within the meaning of section 61(5A) of the 1979 Act (and hence section 12 of the Unfair Contract Terms Act 1977) so that where the buyer is an "individual" the requirement that the goods must be "of a type ordinarily supplied for private use or consumption" is disapplied. The main effect of 14–011

[64] Recital 14 of the Preamble states that "references to the time of delivery do not imply that Member States have to change their rules on the passing of the risk". However, changes to the general rules of ss.20 and 32 of the 1979 Act have, in the result, been made: see above, paras 6–013, 6–014, 6–025 and 8–014.
[65] See, respectively, Art. 1.2(a) and (c).
[66] See by way of analogy Joined Cases C-541/99 and 542/99 *Cape SNC v Idealservice Srl, Idealservice MN RE SAS v OMAI Srl* [2001] E.C.R. I-9049 (corporate buyers not "natural persons" for the purposes of Directive 93/13/EEC on unfair terms in consumer contracts). *Cf.* the expression "deals as consumer" as interpreted for the purposes of the Unfair Contract Terms Act 1977, s.12(1)(a) in *R. & B. Customs Brokers Co. Ltd v United Dominions Trust Ltd* [1988] 1 W.L.R. 321.
[67] See, *e.g. Blakemore v Bellamy* [1983] R.T.R. 303.
[68] As in *Stevenson v Rogers* [1999] Q.B. 1028: see Sealy, [1999] C.L.J. 278; Brown, 115 L.Q.R. 384 (1999). Possibly a distinction might be taken between the words *a* business in s.14 and *his* business in Art. 1.2(c), but this does not seem convincing.
[69] Art. 1.2(b). This would include (say) the purchase of a double-decker bus acquired for driving weekend guests around a country estate.

this is to be seen in the ability of the seller to exclude or restrict liability and in the remedies available to the buyer on breach of the implied terms.[70]

14–012 **Presumption of conformity.**[71] Article 2.2 provides that: "Consumer goods are presumed to be in conformity with the contract if they: (a) comply with the description given by the seller and possess the qualities of the goods which the seller has held out to the consumer as a sample or model; (b) are fit for any particular purpose for which the consumer requires them and which he made known to the seller at the time of conclusion of the contract and which the seller has accepted; (c) are fit for the purposes for which goods of the same type are normally used; (d) show the quality and performance which are normal in goods of the same type and which the consumer can reasonably expect, given the nature of the goods and taking into account any public statements on the specific characteristics of the goods made about them by the seller, the producer or his representative, particularly in advertising or on labelling." The final head (d) is qualified by Article 2.4 which states that: "The seller shall not be bound by public statements, as referred to in paragraph 2(d) if he:—shows that he was not, and could not reasonably have been, aware of the statement in question,—shows that by the time of conclusion of the contract the statement had been corrected, or—shows that the decision to buy the consumer goods could not have been influenced by the statement."[72]

14–013 The above presumptions generally cover much the same ground as sections 13 to 15 of the Sale of Goods Act 1979, albeit that they do so in a less convenient form. Paragraph 2(a) is broadly equivalent to sections 13 and 15,[73] although, as is noted below,[74] when combined with paragraph 2(d) it may go somewhat further than their combined scope. The presumption of conformity linked to paragraph 2(b) is broadly equivalent to section 14(3) of the 1979 Act,[75] although there are differences in terminology which

[70] As was noted above (paras 13–071—13–082 and 14–008), the expression "deals as consumer" is defined in s.61(5A) by reference to Part I (s.12) of the Unfair Contract Terms Act 1977. Section 12 has been amended by the Sale and Supply of Goods to Consumers Regulations 2002 (SI 2002/3045), reg. 14. By s.12(1A) the requirement of s.12(1)(c) that the goods must be "of a type ordinarily supplied for private use or consumption" must be ignored where the buyer is an "individual". Member States may provide (see Art. 1.3) that "consumer goods" do not include second-hand goods sold at public auction where consumers have the opportunity of attending the sale in person. The amended version of s.12 (2)(a) of the 1977 Act contains a provision to this effect: see further, above, para.13–078; also, below, para.14–029. For discussion of the additional remedies which are available where the buyer "deals as consumer", see above, paras 12–071—12–118; also, below, paras 14–023—14–027.

[71] The terminology is that of the Vienna Convention on the International Sale of Goods.

[72] For discussion of Art. 2.5 which is concerned with lack of conformity resulting from incorrect installation of consumer goods, see below, para.14–052.

[73] See above, paras 11–001—11–023; 11–073—11–087 and 14–009. There is, of course, the difference that, whereas the Directive applies only to persons who sell in the course of a trade, business or profession, ss.13 and 15 of the Act apply also to those who sell in a private capacity.

[74] See below, para.14–014.

[75] See above, paras 11–051—11–072; also para.14–010.

might prove to be important. For example, the 1979 Act requires that the goods be *reasonably* fit for the designated purpose whereas the Directive simply uses the word "fit". By way of contrast, the Directive presupposes that the seller has "accepted" the relevant particular purpose whereas the Act requires that the buyer, having made his purpose known whether expressly or impliedly, has reasonably relied on the seller's skill or judgment. It is unclear that such acceptance will be implied from silence whenever the purpose has been made known and reasonable reliance established. However, since any such discrepancy between the 1979 Act and the Directive would appear to operate in favour of the consumer buyer, it would be consistent with the Directive's minimum harmonisation provisions.[76] Paragraph 2(c) adopts an approach which is broadly equivalent to the old test of merchantable quality which applied before the Sale of Goods Act was amended[77] so as to make "fitness for all the purposes for which goods of the kind in question are commonly supplied" an aspect of the quality of goods and, as such, relevant when determining whether they are of satisfactory quality.[78] The Directive omits the word "all", so raising doubts as to the position where the goods are fit for some, but not all, such purposes. However, any such doubts would again suggest that English law may be more favourable to the consumer buyer in this respect and as such would be consistent with the Directive. By way of contrast, the reference in the Directive to the purposes for which goods are "normally used", as opposed to the purposes for which they are "commonly supplied", may possibly be significant in cases where a consumer has used goods for an inappropriate, though "normal", purpose, thereby damaging them or injuring himself. On such facts it might be submitted, although rarely persuasively, that the goods have not met the presumption of conformity of Article 2.2(c).[79]

The presumption of conformity linked to Article 2.2(d) of the Directive partly covers matters which are seen as being relevant to the test of "satisfactory quality" of section 14(2) of the 1979 Act. The Act is generally much more informative and detailed in this regard.[80] However, the Directive is helpful in recognising that the quality and performance which a consumer can reasonably expect may be affected by public statements as to the characteristics of the goods, whether emanating from the seller or producer. It is this provision which has led to the amendment of the 1979 Act[81] to include the new section 14(2D)–(2F).[82] Hitherto, there has been a **14–014**

[76] See Art. 8.2, above, para.14–008

[77] See above, para.11–025; also 14–010. The amendment was introduced by the Sale and Supply of Goods Act 1994, s.1(1).

[78] s.14(2B)(a). See, generally, above, paras 11–026—11–050; also 14–010.

[79] Examples often cited are the use of a screwdriver to open a tin of paint or a chair to stand on. Similar issues arise when considering whether a product is "defective" for the purposes of the Consumer Protection Act 1987, s.3 (see below, paras 14–084—14–086) and submissions based on causation may also be relevant.

[80] See, in particular, the matters listed in s.14(2A) and (2B). No doubt, such matters are often relevant in determining what the consumer buyer can reasonably expect.

[81] By the Sale and Supply of Goods to Consumers Regulations 2002 (SI 2002/3045), reg. 3.

[82] See above, paras 11–033—11–037 and 14–010.

lack of English authority in this area. It seems clear that retailers impliedly adopt statements made by manufacturers which are descriptive of the goods and placed on labels or packaging. It is also probable that express warranties, for example, as to the suitability or characteristics of the goods, will be adopted (unless, of course the retailer indicates otherwise) when they are similarly placed.[83] However, the position is at best doubtful when the claims are made in general advertising. Certainly, it could not have been confidently asserted that implied adoption would occur unless the circumstances of Article 2.4 were present.[84] In all such cases outlined above the obligations of the seller under the Directive are qualified by Article 2.3 which provides in part that: "There shall be deemed not to be a lack of conformity for the purposes of this Article if, at the time the contract was concluded, the consumer was aware, or could not reasonably be unaware of, the lack of conformity." This covers situations in which the matter was drawn to the buyer's attention before the contract was concluded,[85] but may also apply if an examination of the goods was reasonably to be expected, but was not carried out.[86]

14–015 **The six-month presumption of discomformity.** Article 5.3 of the Directive contains a presumption which may assist claimants in borderline cases. It provides that any lack of conformity which becomes apparent within six months of delivery of the goods shall be presumed to have existed at the time of delivery. The presumption is, of course, rebuttable and it will not in any event apply if it is incompatible with the nature of the goods (as when they are perishable) or the nature of the lack of conformity. Nonetheless, it may be of value, for example, in cases where electronic equipment begins to exhibit faults within the six-month period. In implementing the Directive this presumption must be incorporated in so far as it affects the remedial scheme associated with it and this has been effected through an amendment to the 1979 Act in the form of a new section 48A(3) and (4). However, the statutory presumption is located within the remedial scheme of the Part 5A (sections 48A–48F) provisions[87] where the

---

[83] For a case involving allegedly misleading instructions emanating from the manufacturer of a herbicide, see *Wormell v RHM Agriculture (East) Ltd* [1986] 1 W.L.R. 337.

[84] As to which, see above, para.14–012. For other jurisdictions, see, *e.g.* Ontario Law Reform Commission, *Report on Consumer Warranties and Guarantees in the Sale of Goods* (1972), p.35; Australian Trade Practices Act 1974, s.74G; Saskatchewan Consumer Protection Act 1996, s.47; *Green v Jo-Ann Accessory Shop Ltd* (1983) 21 Man.R. (2d.) 261; Uniform Commercial Code, para.2–314(2)(f); *Cochran v McDonald*, 161 P. (2d.) 305 (1945) (Sup. Ct. of Washington). Occasionally, the manufacturer may incur a civil liability, as in *Carlill v Carbolic Smoke Ball Co.* [1893] 1 Q.B. 256; see below, para.14–062.

[85] As in s.14(2C)(a) of the Sale of Goods Act 1979, above, para.11–041.

[86] *cf.* s.14(2C)(b) of the 1979 Act which applies only where an examination was carried out: see above, para.11–042. Since this is on the face of it more advantageous to the consumer buyer it would be permissible under the Directive's minimum harmonisation provisions. Note, however, that s.14(2C)(b) may have been applied incorrectly (albeit *obiter*) in *Bramhill v Edwards* [2004] EWCA Civ 403, [2004] 2 Lloyd's Rep. 653, noted by Twigg-Flesner, 121 L.Q.R. 205 (2005).

[87] As to which, see above, paras 12–071—12–118; also below, paras 14–023—14–027.

emphasis is on repair or replacement of non-conforming goods and it does not apply where a consumer is relying on the traditional common law remedy of rejection. If this distinction proves to be difficult to operate in practice, its effects might be reduced by a court being willing to infer on appropriate facts that goods which were found to be defective within a short period of delivery were probably also similarly defective and non-conforming at the time of delivery. Any such inference would not, of course, be based on the statutory six-month presumption as such.

The two-year time limit. A time limit is contained in Article 5.1 of the Directive which states that: "The seller shall be held liable under Article 3 where the lack of conformity becomes apparent within two years as from delivery of the goods."[88] At one stage this was assumed by some to impose a two-year durability requirement, but it is clear that any such requirement would have been absurd and that this was never intended. It seems that the provision is intended, rather, to supplement the rights of consumers in certain Member States which impose a short statutory warranty period[89] and Article 5.1 goes on to provide that any such "limitation period. . . shall not expire within a period of two years from the time of delivery." The effect of this is potentially reduced in that a further time limit may (but need not) be adopted so as to require a consumer to inform the seller of the lack of conformity within a period of two months from the date on which he detected it.[90] So far as English law is concerned, there is a standard limitation period of six years from the breach of contract and the optional two-month notification requirement has not been adopted. 14–016

Strict contractual liability. One important feature associated with a breach of the implied terms as to correspondence with description, satisfactory quality and fitness for purpose is that liability is strict. In other words, the seller may be liable even though he has exercised all possible care. This is particularly important when personal injury or property damage has been caused by the breach. Although such strict liability clearly attaches to consumer sales, the leading authorities are to be found in commercial cases. Thus in *Henry Kendall & Sons v William Lillico & Sons Ltd*, a case involving animal feeding stuff contaminated by one of its ingredients, Lord Reid said that the implied condition of fitness for a particular purpose covers "defects which are latent in the sense that even the utmost skill and judgment on the part of the seller would not have detected them."[91] Similarly liability was imposed in *Ashington Piggeries Ltd v Christopher Hill Ltd*, another case involving a toxic animal feeding stuff, even though, in the words of Lord Diplock, "in the then state of knowledge, scientific and commercial, no deliberate exercise of human skill or 14–017

[88] There is a qualification for second-hand goods (see Art. 7.1) whereby Member States may allow sellers and consumers to agree contractual terms which reduce this period to one which must not be less than one year.
[89] The example of Germany is given in the House of Lords Select Committee Report, para.94; and see also Beale and Howells, 12 J.C.L. 21 at 32 (1997).
[90] Art. 5.2.
[91] [1969] 2 A.C. 31 at 84.

judgment could have prevented the meal from having its toxic effect upon mink. It was sheer bad luck."[92]

14–018 **Privity of contract.** It is important to emphasise that in English law it is generally only the buyer, or the equivalent contracting party in the case of a contract for the provision of services, who may sue on the contract. A third party cannot sue. Thus in *Daniels and Daniels v R White & Sons Ltd and Tarbard*[93] the plaintiff husband succeeded in his claim against the publican who had sold him lemonade contaminated by carbolic acid, but his wife, who had drunk from the same bottle and suffered similar injury, did not have a contractual claim.[94] Another effect of the privity of contract doctrine is that the purchaser of defective goods may claim under the contract of sale only against the immediate vendor of the goods who will normally be a retailer. If the retailer is insolvent no further contractual action is possible.[95]

14–019 The above position has been modified by the Contracts (Rights of Third Parties) Act 1999. This allows a third party to enforce a contractual term if (a) the contract expressly so provides or (b) the term purports to confer a benefit on him, unless in the latter case it appears from the contract that the parties did not intend the term to be enforceable by the third party.[96] In either case section 1(3) provides that the third party "must be expressly identified in the contract by name, as a member of a class or as answering a particular description but need not be in existence when the contract is entered into." The Act is based on the recommendations of the Law Commission[97] and, as the Commission's hypothetical examples indicate,[98] it will have only a limited effect in typical consumer transactions. For example, it might benefit the recipient of a wedding gift bought from a designated shop which held an "approved" wedding list, but it would not benefit donees more generally. For understandable reasons the Law Commission did not propose a special test of enforceability for consumers in what was intended to operate as a limited general reform.[99]

---

[92] [1972] A.C. 441 at 498: see also, *e.g. Wren v Holt* [1903] 1 K.B. 610 (publican liable for supplying beer contaminated by arsenic); *Frost v Aylesbury Dairy Co. Ltd* [1905] 1 K.B. 608 (milk containing typhoid germs).

[93] [1938] 4 All E.R. 258.

[94] Somewhat surprisingly, her claim in tort against the manufacturer also failed: see below, para.14–061, n.90. Sometimes the difficulty may be avoided by finding that each individual is a contracting party in his or her own right (see, *e.g. Lockett v A. & M. Charles Ltd* [1938] 4 All E.R. 170 and the cases cited below, para.14–077, n.61).

[95] Other things being equal, the retailer who is held liable may be able to pass the loss on up the distribution chain. See below, para.14–064.

[96] s.1(1) and (2).

[97] *Privity of Contract: Contracts for the Benefit of Third Parties* (Law Com No. 242) (1996). See, generally, Adams, Beyleveld and Brownsword, 60 M.L.R. 238 (1997); Smith, 17 O.J.L.S. 643 (1997); Andrews [2001] C.L.J. 353; Stevens, 120 L.Q.R. 292 (2004).

[98] See the Law Commission Report, above, n.97, paras 7.39 *et seq*.

[99] *op.cit.*, paras 7.54 to 7.56. Where the Act applies the third party would not, it seems, benefit from s.6(2) of the Unfair Contract Terms Act 1977 (above para.13–083 and below, para.14–029) since s.1(5) of the 1999 Act is subject to s.7(4). As to the damages which might be awarded to the buyer (*e.g.* of the wedding gift), see by way of analogy *Alfred McAlpine Construction Ltd v Panatown Ltd* [2001] A.C. 518, HL.

Remedies for defective goods: rejection and damages. Until relatively recently, the remedies in respect of defective goods supplied in breach of contract in consumer sales have mirrored those available in commercial sales, namely rejection of the goods and/or a claim for damages.[1] As is noted elsewhere,[2] these remedies have been supplemented (but not replaced) in cases where the buyer "deals as consumer".[3] In some circumstances an action for damages will also lie in tort,[4] including one which arises under Part I of the Consumer Protection Act 1987.[5] The remedy in damages for breach of contract may well be unsuited to the consumer. He may be reluctant to take the risks involved in the institution of legal proceedings[6]; he may feel inadequately compensated by the commercial way in which damages are often assessed on the basis of difference in values[7]; and, as previously mentioned, where (as will normally be the case) he eventually procures substitute goods without difficulty at a similar price, he may not always find it easy to establish inconvenience or disappointment (or both) as acceptable heads of loss within the seller's contemplation.[8] If he can show a quantifiable loss, as where he suffers personal injuries,[9] or property damage[10] or is liable in damages to a third party injured in an accident caused by defects in the goods,[11] he will necessarily have to sue for damages. And if he has not yet paid, he may be able to negotiate by setting off his claim against the price,[12] or at least by withholding part of the price as a tactical move. 14–020

In many cases a consumer will often prefer to reject the goods completely and recover his money if he has paid. In principle, this remedy may be thought to be readily available since the implied obligations as to title, correspondence with description, satisfactory quality and fitness for purpose are all classified as conditions,[13] thus leading to a right to reject on breach.[14] 14–021

---

[1] On appropriate facts a buyer may also seek specific performance of the contract. See paras. 12–071 *et seq.*, below, paras 17–096 *et seq.*

[2] See below, paras 14–023—14–027.

[3] For the meaning of this expression, see above, paras 13–071—13–082, below, para.14–029.

[4] Above, paras 12–121 *et seq.*

[5] See s.2(2)(b) and (3) especially. The Act is discussed below, paras 14–080 *et seq.*

[6] Below, paras 14–098 *et seq.*

[7] Below, paras 17–047 *et seq.* But see *Jackson v Chrysler Acceptances Ltd* [1978] R.T.R. 474.

[8] Above, para.14–006, below, para.17–071. But such damages were recovered by a buyer in *Gascoigne v British Credit Trust* [1978] C.L.Y. para.711; and (though extinguished by items set off) in *Laurelgates Ltd v Lombard North Central Ltd* (1983) 133 N.L.J. 720; also in *Bernstein v Pamson's Motors (Golders Green) Ltd* [1987] 2 All E.R. 220 (totally spoilt day and inconvenience of being without car).

[9] *e.g. Godley v Perry* [1960] 1 W.L.R. 9.

[10] *e.g. Wilson v Rickett, Cockerell & Co. Ltd* [1954] 1 Q.B. 598.

[11] *e.g. Lambert v Lewis* [1982] A.C. 225. The cost of obtaining a temporary substitute (*e.g.* a car) may also be within the seller's contemplation in appropriate cases.

[12] Sale of Goods Act 1979, s.53(1)(a); below, para.17–049.

[13] As to title, see s.12(1) and above, para.4–006; as to correspondence with description, see s.13(1) and above, para.11–001; as to satisfactory quality and fitness for purpose, see s.14(6) and above, para.11–026. In all cases the obligations are designated "conditions" only as regards England and Wales and Northern Ireland.

[14] See s.11(3) of the Act.

Rejection must, however, be firm and not hedged around with qualifications.[15] Moreover, the right will be lost once the buyer has accepted the goods. Briefly, the buyer is deemed to have accepted the goods under section 35 of the Act[16] when he intimates to the seller that he has accepted them or, the goods having been delivered to him, he acts in a way which is inconsistent with the ownership of the seller.[17] In either case, he must generally have had a reasonable opportunity of examining the goods and the buyer who "deals as consumer" cannot lose this right by agreement, waiver or otherwise.[18] Similarly, it is now clear that the buyer is not deemed to have accepted the goods merely because he asks for or agrees to their repair whether by the seller or, more typically, the manufacturer.[19] In practice, it seems likely that the right to reject will usually be lost simply because the buyer has retained the goods for longer than a reasonable time without intimating to the seller that he has rejected them.[20] It may be assumed that acceptance through inertia is by no means uncommon in consumer transactions and some of the cases point to a less than generous approach to what constitutes a reasonable time.[21] A more recent decision of the Court of Appeal involving the sale and purchase of a yacht[22] points to a somewhat more sympathetic approach, although the case was not one involving inertia. Rather, the buyer had been actively seeking and awaiting information from the seller with a view to seeking a compromise through negotiation. Against this background, Hale L.J. commented: "if a buyer is seeking information which the seller has agreed to supply which will enable the buyer to make a properly informed choice between acceptance, rejection or cure, and if cure in what way, he cannot have lost the right to reject."[23] However, the Court of Appeal has subsequently indicated that there is no overriding rule to the effect that the right to reject is not lost whenever information is being sought. What is a reasonable time in which to reject goods is ultimately a question of fact.[24]

---

[15] As in *Lee v York Coach and Marine* [1977] R.T.R. 35.
[16] As amended by the Sale and Supply of Goods Act 1994, s.2(1); see above, para.12–044 *et seq*.
[17] s.35(1)(a) and (b).
[18] s.35(2) and (3).
[19] s.35(6)(a). Previously, an argument to the contrary might have relied on such cases as *Long v Lloyd* [1958] 1 W.L.R. 753.
[20] s.35(4) and (5).
[21] *e.g. Millars of Falkirk Ltd v Turpie*, 1976 S.L.T. (Notes) 66; *Bernstein v Pamson Motors (Golders Green) Ltd* [1987] 2 All E.R. 220; above, para.12–055; but *cf. Farnworth Finance Facilities Ltd v Attryde* [1970] 1 W.L.R. 1053 (hire-purchase); *Laurelgates Ltd v Lombard North Central Ltd* (1983) 133 N.L.J. 720.
[22] *Clegg v Olle Andersson* [2003] EWCA Civ. 320, [2003] 2 Lloyd's Rep. 32, noted by Reynolds, 119 L.Q.R. 544 (2003).
[23] [2003] 2 Lloyd's Rep. 32 at [75].
[24] See *Jones v Gallagher* [2004] EWCA Civ. 10, [2005] 1 Lloyd's Rep. 377 noted by Bradgate, 120 L.Q.R. 558 (2004). Since the case involved the supply and fitting of a kitchen it is not clear why the rules governing sale (as opposed to contracts for work and materials) were considered to be in point.

14–022 An alternative approach is to be seen in the United States where the Uniform Commercial Code softens the rules governing acceptance by permitting revocation of acceptance by the buyer in certain circumstances,[25] though it equally gives the seller the right to cure a defective tender in others.[26] Overall it may be argued that consumers might well, if rejection is inevitably to be difficult, prefer a right to require that defects be remedied within a specified period, and to treat the contract as discharged if this is not done: in return, consumers might have to accept a right in the vendor to cure some cases of defective tender.[27] A right to make a further tender does in fact exist at common law where this can be done within the time specified by the contract[28]; but the possibility has not been much developed and its applicability to the sort of situation created by a consumer sale is doubtful.[29] Nevertheless, the principles of mitigation of damages[30] might sometimes require that such an offer by the vendor be accepted. Despite information to the contrary sometimes given in consumer advice columns and the like, there is, however, at common law no right to *require* cure of defects, whether by repair or replacement. The terms of the contract under which goods are sold may give some such right (or at least entitle the vendor to an opportunity to remedy defects), but a general legal right to this effect would require to be created by statute. This has now been done as part of the process of implementing Directive 1999/44/EC on consumer sales.[31]

14–023 **Remedies required by the Directive.** If the variations between the provisions of the Directive and those of the equivalent implied obligations of sections 13 and 14 of the Sale of Goods Act 1979 are relatively modest, the same cannot be said of the scheme of remedies which is available on breach. The relatively straightforward scheme of the Act with rejection being the primary (albeit short-lived) remedy,[32] and damages being available either in addition or as an alternative, is to be contrasted with the more elaborate scheme of the Directive with its emphasis on repair, replacement or "cure". As noted above,[33] such remedies are not available at common law and hence an amendment to the Sale of Goods Act in the

---

[25] s.2–608 (where goods accepted on reasonable assumption that defects would be cured; and where difficult to discover defects).
[26] s.2–508 (distinguishing between situations where time for performance has and has not expired).
[27] See, *e.g.* Ontario Law Reform Commission Report on Sale of Goods (1979), Vol. II, pp.459 *et seq*. See also the proposals of the Law Commissions: Law Com.W.P. No. 85, Scot. Law Com.C.M. No. 58 (1983). In the result the Law Commissions decided against recommending a "cure" scheme for consumer transactions: see Law Com. No. 160, Scot., Law Com. No. 104 (Cmnd. 137, 1987).
[28] *Borrowman, Phillips & Co. v Free and Hollis* (1878) 4 Q.B.D. 500: above, para.12–031.
[29] *ibid*.
[30] Below, paras 16–052 *et seq*.
[31] Directive 1999/44/EC ([1999] O.J. L171/12).
[32] See above, paras 12–018 *et seq*., 14–020—14–021; below, para.17–093.
[33] See para.14–022.

form of a new Part 5A (sections 48A–48F) was required.[34] The details of the new remedial scheme and its complex relationship to the traditional remedies of rejection and damages are explored elsewhere.[35] This chapter contains no more than a brief outline of the relevant provisions of the Directive.

14–024 Assuming that it can be established that the goods were defective at the time of delivery, the Directive recognises that it is open to the consumer to accept or decline any offer of settlement made by the seller.[36] In the absence of such agreement, Article 3 makes provision for four remedies, namely repair, replacement, an appropriate price reduction and what it terms rescission. General issues as to damages, for example, in respect of personal injury, property damage, and, to the limited extent that it may be available, compensation for disappointment, are left to the national laws of Member States.[37] The wording of the Directive appears to indicate a hierarchy of remedies[38] so that by Article 3.3: "In the first place, the consumer may require the seller to repair[39] the goods or he may require the seller to replace them, in either case free of charge,[40] unless this is impossible or disproportionate." This primary remedy will have to be accorded as a statutory or contractual right and this has been done through amendments to the 1979 Act,[41] but its full implications are uncertain. Whether such a remedy is disproportionate is to be judged objectively and on the basis of the costs imposed on the seller in comparison with an alternative remedy. Account must be taken of "the value the goods would have if there were no lack of conformity, the significance of the lack of conformity, and whether the alternative remedy could be completed without significant inconvenience to the consumer."[42] The first of these elements is important when non-conformity becomes apparent only after a lengthy period of use. A remedy of replacement, etc. might then be adjudged disproportionate, at least without an allowance for the use and depreciation of the goods. The Directive further provides that any repair or

---

[34] The amendment was introduced by the Sale and Supply of Goods to Consumers Regulations 2002 (SI 2002/3045), reg. 5. Corresponding amendments to the Supply of Goods and Services Act 1982 in the form of a new Part 1B (ss.11M–11S) were introduced by reg. 9.

[35] See above, paras 12–071—12–118; also in relation to overseas sales, below, paras 19–065, 19–144, 19–203, 19–206, 20–113, 20–120 and 20–122.

[36] See Recital 12.

[37] Art. 8.1. See, *e.g.* such cases as *Daniels and Daniels v R. White & Sons Ltd and Tarbard* [1938] 4 All E.R. 258 (personal injury); *Wilson v Rickett, Cockerell & Co. Ltd* [1954] 1 Q.B. 598 (property damage); *Bernstein v Pamson's Motors (Golders Green) Ltd* [1987] 2 All E.R. 220 (disappointment and inconvenience). The Directive similarly does not affect the rights of redress available to the seller seeking to pass on loss, as by suing the wholesaler, etc.: see Art. 4.

[38] As to this issue, see also Whittaker, *Liability for Products* (2005), pp.606–610.

[39] "Repair" means "bringing goods into conformity with the contract of sale": Art. 1.2(f).

[40] "Free of charge" refers to "the necessary costs incurred to bring the goods into conformity, particularly the cost of postage, labour and materials.": Art. 3.4.

[41] See ss.48A(2)(a) and 48B.

[42] See Art. 3.3.

replacement must be completed within a reasonable time and without significant inconvenience to the consumer, taking account of the nature of the goods and the purpose for which he required them.[43]

Where the primary remedies of repair or replacement are neither impossible nor disproportionate the consumer is said to be "entitled" to them. In as much as the philosophy underlying the Directive appears to be that the choice is that of the consumer, rather than the seller,[44] it seems that he may elect for one or the other. The question then arises as to what remedy he will have if the seller refuses to accede to the demand, perhaps because he disputes the lack of conformity alleged. In this context the European Commission has disavowed any suggestion that the Directive will require national courts to order specific performance when it would not otherwise be granted. The House of Lords Select Committee regarded the point as very important and such that there should be no room for doubt,[45] but it has not been further clarified. In implementing the Directive a power to order specific performance of the obligation to repair or replace non-conforming goods is recognised by the new section 48E(2) of the 1979 Act, but it would be surprising if an English court were to grant this remedy in relation to the entitlement to repair, except, perhaps, in the most exceptional cases.[46] In the absence of such a remedy, the buyer would then, in effect, have to fall back on alternative remedies which might include damages to meet the costs of having the goods repaired elsewhere.[47] Assuming always that replacement is neither impossible nor disproportionate the objections against granting such a remedy are weaker where this is the outcome being sought. **14–025**

There is, it seems, less room for doubt as to when, in the language of the Directive, rescission is available. For present purposes this is not to be equated with the equitable remedy as traditionally understood in English law, but rather with the entitlement to reject non-conforming goods and to treat the contract as terminated. The structure of the Directive, including the recitals, indicates that rescission is available only if the consumer is entitled to neither repair nor replacement, or if the seller has not completed the remedy within a reasonable time and without significant inconvenience to the consumer.[48] Moreover, in a provision which is not reflected in the implementing provisions of English law the consumer is not entitled to have the contract rescinded if the lack of conformity is minor.[49] **14–026**

---

43 Art. 3.3.

44 See H.L. Select Committee Report (above, para.14–008, n.38), para.98; Beale and Howells, 12 J.C.L. 21 at 34–35 (1997) (commenting on the draft Directive).

45 *ibid.*, para.97.

46 See further above, para.12–114; also Harris, 119 L.Q.R. 541 (2003).

47 No doubt this would be subject to the principles established in *Ruxley Electronics and Construction Ltd v Forsyth* [1996] A.C. 344; see generally Phang [1996] J.B.L. 362; Coote [1997] C.L.J. 537.

48 See Art. 3.2 and 3.5.

49 Art. 3.6. English law has a limited *de minimis* principle, but s.15A of the 1979 Act (which excludes the right to reject for "slight" breaches) does not apply to consumer sales. For s.15A of the Act, see above, para.12–024.

This does not sit easily alongside a claim that the choice of remedies is for the consumer. Indeed, it seems that under the Directive a seller may, in effect, refuse rescission if he is willing and able to repair or replace within a reasonable time and to do so without the consumer being significantly inconvenienced.[50] This is tantamount to a limited right to attempt to "cure" the non-conformity. Assuming rescission to be prima facie available (as when the seller has not repaired or replaced timeously), there are no further bars to its operation. However it is permissible for any reimbursement to the consumer to be reduced to take account of the use he has had of the goods since they were delivered to him.[51] This seems to be equivalent to a price reduction or an award of damages.

14–027 In relation to the above, it is important again to stress that the Directive is one of minimum harmonisation so that Member States may allow existing remedies to operate alongside its provisions (or indeed create new ones), provided that the minimum requirements are not infringed. In the context of English law, no doubt in many cases consumer buyers will be content to accept repair or replacement, but in others they will prefer to reject the goods and recover or withhold the contract price. At least where it is no longer possible to make a substitute tender within the time specified by the contract[52] this remedy will remain. The right to reject will be lost once the buyer has accepted the goods,[53] but he will not be deemed to have accepted them merely by agreeing to an attempted repair[54] (*e.g.* under the remedial scheme associated with the Directive), although care will have to be taken not to retain the goods beyond a reasonable period of time.[55]

14–028 **Binding nature.** As would be expected, the Directive curtails attempts to bind consumers to terms or agreements which waive or restrict the rights it confers. Article 7.1 states that, as provided for in national law, these shall not be binding on the consumer. Section 6(2) of the Unfair Contract Terms Act 1977 is apt to meet this requirement.[56] The Directive also requires Member States to take measures to ensure that consumers are not deprived of protection by choice of law clauses.[57] No steps have been taken to

[50] Note that the entitlement to rescind of Art. 3.2 is in accordance with paragraphs 5 and 6 which contain the above limitations. See also recital 10. Underlying principles of "good faith" would no doubt prevent a consumer from pleading significant inconvenience or undue delay in repair when he had refused to allow the goods to be repaired or replaced.

[51] See recital 15.

[52] *Borrowman, Phillips & Co. v Free and Hollis* (1878) 4 Q.B.D. 500; above, paras 12–031; 14–022.

[53] Under s.35 of the 1979 Act; see generally above paras 12–044—12–065 and 14–021.

[54] s.35(6)(a); above, para.12–054.

[55] s.35(4); above, paras 12–055—12–056.

[56] See, generally, above, paras 13–083—13–084; below, para.14–029. Note also s.13 of the 1977 Act which makes it clear that s.6(2) would also apply to measures purporting to restrict any right or remedy, including, no doubt, the new Part 5A remedies.

[57] Art. 7.2.

implement this provision since the view was apparently taken[58] that English law already covered the point.[59] The question whether it in fact does so is explored elsewhere.[60] Finally, it should be noted that infringements of the Directive may amount both to a "domestic infringement" and to a "Community infringement" for the purposes of the Part 8 provisions of the Enterprise Act 2002 and hence will be subject to the injunctive procedures which they provide.[61]

(b) *Exemption Clauses and Unfair Contract Terms*

Exemption clauses in consumer sales. In consumer, as in commercial, sales the seller who seeks to exclude or limit liability must initially ensure that the relevant clause is effectively incorporated into the contract and apt as a matter of construction to achieve the desired effect.[62] Assuming that this has been done, the Unfair Contract Terms Act 1977 will, in any event, severely limit the seller's ability to rely on such clauses in a consumer sale. In particular, section 6 provides that liability for breach of the implied conditions as to title, correspondence with description, quality and fitness for a particular purpose[63] cannot be excluded or restricted as against a person dealing as consumer.[64] For this purpose a person "deals as consumer" if he neither makes the contract in the course of a business (nor holds himself out as doing so) and the other party does make the contract in the course of a business.[65] Originally, in order to obtain the full protection of section 6, the goods had to be "of a type ordinarily supplied 14–029

---

[58] See the DTI Transposition Note, *Directive 1999/44/EC of the European Parliament and of the Council of May 25, 1999 on certain aspects of the sale of consumer goods and associated guarantees*.

[59] Notably, through the provisions of the Unfair Contract Terms Act 1977, s.27; and see also the Unfair Terms in Consumer Contracts Regulations 1999 (SI 1999/2083), reg. 9.

[60] See below, paras 25–111—25–118; also *Benjamin's Sale of Goods: Special Supplement to the 6th edition* (2003), paras 1–035—1–049.

[61] See s.211 of the Act ("domestic infringements") and the Enterprise Act 2002 (Part 8 Domestic Infringements) Order 2003 (SI 2003/1593), art. 2 and Sch. (the requirements of the Directive having been met by amendments to the Sale of Goods Act 1979 and related legislation); also s.212 and Sch.13 ("Community infringements"), taken together with the Enterprise Act 2002 (Part 8 Community Infringements Specified UK Laws) Order 2003 (SI 2003/1374), art. 3 and Sch. The provisions covering "domestic infringements" supersede those contained in Part III of the Fair Trading Act 1973 and those covering "Community infringements" supersede those contained in the Stop Now Orders (EC Directive) Regulations 2001 (SI 2001/1422). See generally, below, paras 14–130—14–136.

[62] Above, paras 13–012 *et seq*.

[63] As to which see, respectively, above, para.4–018 (title); paras 11–005, 13–083 (correspondence with description); para.13–083 (quality and fitness for purpose).

[64] s.6(1)(a), (2)(a).

[65] s.12(1)(a) and (b). This limitation has been so interpreted that a purchase will be made "in the course of a business" only if it forms part of the regular course of dealings of that business or is an integral part of it: *R & B Customs Brokers Ltd v United Dominions Trust Ltd* [1988] 1 W.L.R. 321. The decision was followed in *Feldarol Foundry Plc v Hermes Leasing (London) Ltd.* [2004] EWCA 747, noted by Twigg-Flesner, 121 L.Q.R. 41 (2005). See above, paras 13–072—13–075. *Cf. Stevenson v Rogers* [1999] Q.B. 1028 and *Davies v Sumner* [1984] 1 W.L.R. 1301.

for private use or consumption".[66] However, this limitation no longer applies[67] if the relevant party is an "individual", which for this purpose may be taken to mean a natural person.[68] Also, by section 12(2) of the Act the buyer is not in any circumstances to be regarded as dealing as consumer: "(a) if he is an individual and the goods are second hand goods sold at public auction at which individuals have the opportunity of attending the sale in person; (b) if he is not an individual and the goods are sold by auction or by competitive tender."[69] These changes have been introduced in order to comply with the requirements of Directive 99/44/EC on certain aspects of the sale of consumer goods and associated guarantees.[70] Where the buyer does not "deal as consumer" an exemption or limitation clause may be effective for the purposes of the Act if it satisfies the requirement of reasonableness.[71] The further and more general protection contained in section 3 of the 1977 Act, which subjects certain other types of exemption clause to the requirement of reasonableness, applies to contracts where one party deals as consumer, or (a situation not confined to consumers) on the other's written standard terms of business.[72] Similarly, a person who deals as consumer is protected against unreasonable indemnity clauses by section 4 of the Act. The restrictions on clauses excluding liability for negligence contained in section 2[73] are, however, general, except that they do not apply where there is no business liability.[74]

14–030 **Unfair Terms in Consumer Contracts Regulations 1999.**[75] More recently, the protection accorded by the 1977 Act has been extended by Regulations which give effect to an EC Council Directive on unfair terms in consumer contracts.[76] The original Regulations date from

---

[66] See s.12(1)(c).

[67] See s.12(1A), which was added by the Sale and Supply of Goods to Consumers Regulations 2002 (SI 2002/3045), reg. 14 (2).

[68] See Joined Cases C-54/99 and C-542/99, *Cape SNC v Idealservice Srl; Idealservice MN RE SAS v OMAI Srl* [2001] E.C.R. I-9049 (ECJ), holding that a company is not a "natural person" for the purposes of Council Directive (EEC) 93/13 on unfair terms in consumer contracts ([1993] O.J. L95/29), Art. 2(b)). Directive 99/44/EC, Art.1(2)(a), similarly defines a "consumer" as a "natural person who, in the contracts covered by this Directive, is acting for purposes which are not related to his trade, business or profession": see above, para.14–011.

[69] s.12(2), as amended by SI 2002/3045, reg. 14(3). See further, above, paras 13–072 *et seq.*

[70] [1999] O.J. L171/12.

[71] As to which, see s.11 and Sch.2.

[72] Above, paras 13–094—13–095.

[73] Above, paras 13–092, 13–093.

[74] Above, para.13–070.

[75] For discussion of the Regulations including comparisons with the 1977 Act, see *Chitty on Contracts* (29th ed.), Ch.15; Treitel, *Law of Contract* (11th ed.), pp.267–283; Beale in Beatson and Friedmann (eds) *Good Faith and Fault in Contract Law* (1995), Ch.9; also Dean, 56 M.L.R. 581 (1993); Collins, 14 O.J.L.S. 229 (1994); Macdonald [1999] C.L.J. 413; Bright, 20 L.S. 331 (2000); Whittaker, 116 L.Q.R. 9 (2000); Beale, 27 J. Con. Pol. 289 (2004).

[76] 1993/13/EEC ([1993] O.J. L95/29). See *Implementation of the EC Directive on Unfair Terms in Consumer Contracts (1993/13/EEC): A Consultation Document* (DTI, 1993) and *Implementation of the EC Directive on Unfair Terms in Consumer*

1994,[77] but they have been replaced in a modified form and renumbered by Regulations made in 1999.[78] Initially, no attempt was made to integrate the two provisions which overlap and yet differ in important respects,[79] although the Law Commission has now undertaken this task.[80] Generally, the Regulations may prove to have only a limited effect on consumer contracts for the sale of goods, but they have a more general importance in the wider context of consumer protection.

Scope of the Regulations. The Regulations apply "in relation to unfair terms in contracts concluded between a seller or a supplier and a consumer."[81] For this purpose the words "seller or supplier" are defined to mean "any natural or legal person who, in contracts covered by these Regulations, is acting for purposes relating to his trade, business or profession, whether publicly owned or privately owned."[82] A "consumer" is in turn defined as "any natural person who, in contracts covered by these Regulations, is acting for purposes which are outside his trade, business or profession."[83] In broad terms, therefore, protection is accorded to private individuals who are dealing with business suppliers of goods or services. The generality of this protection is, however, limited in a number of respects. The most important is that the test of fairness is to be applied only to terms which have not been individually negotiated.[84] This is amplified by regulation 5(2) which states: "A term shall always be regarded as not having been individually negotiated where it has been drafted in advance and the consumer has therefore not been able to influence the substance of the term."[85] If a specific term has been individually negotiated (*e.g.* a delivery date or a modification to a standard package) the Regulations may still apply to the rest of the contract "if an overall assessment of it indicates that it is a pre-formulated standard contract."[86] As in the case of the Unfair Contract Terms Act 1977,[87] some contractual terms are excluded from the scope of the Regulations, namely terms which reflect mandatory statutory or regulatory provisions or the provisions or principles of international 14–031

Contracts (1993/13/EEC): A Further Consultation Document (DTI, 1994). For an assessment of the Directive, see Report from the Commission on the Implementation of Council Directive 1993/13/EC of April 5, 1993 on Unfair Terms in Consumer Contracts (COM(2000)0248 final). See also in relation to overseas sales, below, paras 18–282—18–283 and to conflict of laws issues, below, paras 25–101—25–106.

[77] SI 1994/3159.

[78] SI 1999/2083.

[79] See Reynolds, 110 L.Q.R. 1 (1994).

[80] See *Unfair Terms in Contracts* (Law Com. No. 292, Scot. Law Com. No. 199, Cm. 6464) (2005).

[81] Reg. 4(1).

[82] Reg. 3(1). For a decision of the Court of Appeal holding that the Regulations apply to the terms on which a local authority let accommodation to homeless persons, see *R (Khatun) v Newham London Borough Council* [2005] 1 Q.B. 37.

[83] *ibid*.

[84] Reg. 5(1) does not so state expressly, but it has this effect.

[85] In cases of doubt the onus of proof is on the seller or supplier to establish that the term was individually negotiated: reg. 5(4).

[86] Reg. 5(3).

[87] See Sch.1 to the Act.

conventions.[88] However, the excluded contracts are not identical and, in particular, whereas contracts of insurance are excluded from the scope of the 1977 Act[89] they are not so excluded from the Regulations.[90]

14–032 **Definition of the subject-matter and adequacy of consideration.** Further important limitations are contained in regulation 6(2) which provides that: "In so far as it is in plain intelligible language, the assessment of fairness of a term shall not relate—(a) to the definition of the main subject-matter of the contract, or (b) to the adequacy of the price or remuneration, as against the goods or services supplied in exchange." The limitation in terms of the subject-matter of the contract requires one to ascertain precisely what is being sold and this may be defined more or less broadly. Similar issues arise under section 13 of the Sale of Goods Act[91] with its implied condition that the goods should correspond with the contract description. This cannot be excluded, but the description may be defined sufficiently broadly that no breach occurs. In a different context it is also likely that regulation 6(2)(a) will assist the insurance industry when it argues that an allegedly unfair contract term is no more than a statement of the risk covered.[92] The limitation under head (b) reflects the general rule that courts will not seek to judge whether the consideration for the contract is adequate or if the consumer has made a good or bad bargain. If "plain, intelligible language" has not been used the relevant term will be susceptible to being judged as to its possible unfairness, although there is no implication that it will be found to be unfair.[93]

14–033 The House of Lords has had the occasion to consider what is now regulation 6(2) in an important decision[94] arising out of a standard-form regulated credit agreement requiring a defaulting borrower to pay interest after judgment at the contractual rate. It concluded that such a default provision was not a term which was exempted from assessment as to its fairness, Lord Steyn saying that, "reg. 3(2) [now 6(2)] must be given a restrictive interpretation". His Lordship added: "Unless that is done reg. 3(2)(a) [6(2)(a)] will enable the main purpose of the scheme to be

---

[88] Reg. 2(a) and (b). As to this, see *Chitty on Contracts* (29th ed.), Ch.15, pp.897–899; also Unfair Contract Terms Act 1977, s.29(1). As to choice of law clauses, see reg. 9 and below, paras 25–101 *et seq.*, also Unfair Contract Terms Act 1977, s.27, and below, paras 25–091 *et seq.*

[89] See Sch.1, para.1(a).

[90] Albeit that they are affected by reg. 6(2); *cf.* below, para.14–032.

[91] Above, paras 11–001 *et seq.*

[92] See, *e.g. Bankers Insurance Co. Ltd v South* [2003] EWHC 380, [2004] Lloyd's Rep. I.R. 1 (holiday insurance contract which did not cover accidents arising from claimant's use of jet ski).

[93] See also reg. 7 which provides in part that: "(1) A seller or supplier shall ensure that any written term of a contract is expressed in plain, intelligible language; (2) If there is any doubt about the meaning of a written term, the interpretation which is most favourable to the consumer shall prevail . . ." The latter part of this provision contains the familiar *contra proferentem* principle. There is no direct sanction for non-compliance with the former part, although the use of plain, intelligible language may indicate procedural fairness and suggest that the seller has acted in good faith.

[94] *Director-General of Fair Trading v First National Bank Plc* [2002] 1 A.C. 481.

frustrated by endless formalistic arguments as to whether a provision is a definitional or an exclusionary provision. Similarly, reg. 3(2)(b) [6(2)(b)] dealing with 'the adequacy of the price or remuneration' must be given a restrictive interpretation. After all, in a broad sense all terms of the contract are in some way related to the price or remuneration. That is not what is intended."[95]

The test and effect of unfairness. The central test of "unfairness" is, perhaps inevitably, very open-textured so that a term is to be adjudged unfair if "contrary to the requirement of good faith, it causes a significant imbalance in the parties' rights and obligations arising under the contract, to the detriment of the consumer."[96] Clearly, there is an overlap between the elements of "good faith" and a lack of "significant imbalance", although the former may typically be concerned with procedural fairness and the latter with substantive fairness.[97] In adjudicating on issues of "fairness" and "unfairness" courts must, of course, have regard to relevant decisions of the European Court of Justice. However, these may have only limited value as the European Court will not usually rule on the fairness of a particular term but will limit itself, rather, to interpreting general criteria as used by the Community legislature.[98] Under the 1999 Regulations, assessment of alleged unfairness of the term must take into account the nature of the goods or services for which the contract was concluded, the circumstances attending the conclusion of the contract, and the other terms of the contract or of another contract (*e.g.* a "master contract") on which it is dependent.[99] The earlier 1994 Regulations specified other matters to be taken into account which overlapped considerably with the guidelines for the application of the "reasonableness test" in Schedule 2 to the 1977 Act.[1] For example, the relative strength of the bargaining position of the parties featured in both Schedules.[2] Although this was not carried through into the current Regulations, such matters will remain relevant. As to the consequences of unfairness, regulation 8(1) provides that: "An unfair term in a 14–034

---

[95] *ibid.*, para.[34]. See also *Bairstow Eves London Central Ltd v Smith* [2004] EWHC QB 263 (default provision imposing higher rate of commission if time limit for payment not met not within reg. 6).

[96] Reg. 5(1). See, generally, *Chitty on Contracts* (29th ed.), pp.899–915; Beale in Beatson and Friedmann (eds.), *Good Faith and Fault in Contract Law* (1995), Ch.9, pp.242–245; Willett (ed.), *Aspects of Fairness in Contract* (1996); Whittaker and Zimmermann, *Good Faith in European Contract Law* (2000); Collins, 14 O.J.L.S. 229 (1994); Bright, 20 L.S. 331 at 342–351. A wealth of informative material is to be found in a regular series of bulletins issued by the Office of Fair Trading (OFT): see, especially, *Unfair Contract Terms Guidance* (OFT 311) (2001).

[97] See (*e.g.*) Collins, 14 O.J.L.S. 229 at 249; below, para.14–035.

[98] See Case C-237/02 *Freiburger Kommunalbauten G.M.B.H. Baugesellschaft & Co. K.G. v Hafstetter* [2004] 2 C.M.L.R. 13, noted by MacDonald in 121 L.Q.R. 38 (2005). *Cf.* Joined Cases C-240–244/98 *Oceano Grupo Editorial S.A. v Murciano Qunitero* [2000] E.C.R. I-4941 where the term was, it seems, seen as being unfair in all circumstances.

[99] Reg. 6(1).

[1] See reg. 4(3) and Sch.2 which was headed "Assessment of Good Faith"; also above, para.13–088.

[2] *cf.* Sch.2, para.(a) to the Act and Sch.2, para.(a) to the Regulations.

contract concluded with a consumer by a seller or supplier shall not be binding on the consumer." However, by regulation 8(2) the contract will continue to bind the parties if it is capable of continuing in existence without the unfair term. Whether it is so capable must depend on such matters as the importance of the term within the contract as a whole.

14–035 In the decision of the House of Lords to which reference was made above[3] the House also had to consider whether the default provision satisfied the requirement of fairness. The Director-General of Fair Trading contended that it was "unfair", mainly because typical borrowers would, it was suggested, assume that payment of instalments fixed by the court would discharge their entire obligations and not leave additional contractual obligations outstanding.[4] The House of Lords, disagreeing with the Court of Appeal,[5] was not satisfied that the unfairness of the term had been established. Lord Bingham of Cornhill dealt with the issue of "unfairness" at some length, saying that the "requirement of significance imbalance is met if a term is so weighted in favour of the supplier as to tilt the parties' rights and obligations under the contract significantly in his favour."[6] Such substantive unfairness is complemented by a requirement of good faith as evidenced by fair and open dealing. As to this, Lord Bingham said: "Openness requires that the terms should be expressed fully, clearly and legibly, containing no concealed pitfalls or traps. Appropriate prominence should be given to terms which might operate disadvantageously to the consumer. Fair dealing requires that a supplier should not, whether deliberately or unconsciously, take advantage of the consumer's necessity, indigence, lack of experience, unfamiliarity with the subject matter of the contract, weak bargaining position or any other factor listed in or analogous to those listed in Schedule 2 to the Regulations."[7] In the result the application for an injunction to restrain the use of the default condition was not granted.[8]

14–036 **The indicative or "grey" list.** In order to give further substance to the notion of an unfair contract term, Schedule 2 to the Regulations contains an indicative and non-exhaustive list of terms which may be regarded as

---

[3] *Director-General of Fair Trading v First National Bank Plc* [2002] 1 A.C. 481; above, para.14–033.

[4] This was supported by a submission that typical borrowers would be unaware of safeguards in the Consumer Credit Act 1974, ss.129 and 136 (time orders and powers to amend regulated agreements). Also, the term avoided the effect of the County Courts (Interest on Judgment Debts) Order 1991 (SI 1991/1184).

[5] [2000] Q.B. 672. The Court had itself disagreed with the decision of Evans-Lombe J. ([2000] 1 W.L.R. 98).

[6] [2002] 1 A.C. 481, para.[17]; See also *Picardi v Cuniberti* [2003] B.L.R. 487 (holding *obiter* that an adjudication clause weighted in favour of RIBA members and which an architect could invoke at any time was an unfair contract term). *Cf. Bryen & Langley Ltd v Martin Rodney Boston* [2005] B.L.R. 28 and *Westminster Building Co. Ltd v Andrew Beckingham* [2004] B.L R. 163 (adjudication clause in J.C.T. contract).

[7] *ibid.* As noted above (para.14–034), although Sch.2 is not reproduced in the current version of the Regulations the factors there listed remain important. See also Lord Bingham's judgment in *Interfoto Picture Library Ltd v Stiletto Visual Programmes Ltd* [1989] Q.B. 433, applying similar principles at the earlier stage of incorporation.

[8] See also below, para.14–040.

unfair. This so-called "grey" list, which builds on the indicative list contained in the Annex to Directive 93/13/EEC on unfair terms in consumer contracts,[9] contrasts with some of the provisions in the Unfair Contract Terms Act under which terms are simply ineffective in all circumstances. Where a term falls into this category (as in the case of one which purports to exclude or limit the liability of a business for death or personal injury caused by negligence)[10] there will be no need to consider the issue of unfairness. The claimant will simply rely on the Act. However, the examples of unfairness go well beyond the Act and include, according to paragraph 1, terms which have the object or effect of "(a) excluding or limiting the legal liability of a seller or supplier in the event of the death of a consumer or personal injury to the latter resulting from an act or omission of that seller or supplier; (b) inappropriately excluding or limiting the legal rights of the consumer *vis-à-vis* the seller or supplier or another party in the event of total or partial non-performance or inadequate performance by the seller or supplier of any of the contractual obligations, including the option of offsetting a debt owed to the seller or supplier against any claim which the consumer may have against him; (c) making an agreement binding on the consumer whereas provision of services by the seller or supplier is subject to a condition whose realisation depends on his own will alone; (d) permitting the seller or supplier to retain sums paid by the consumer where the latter decides not to conclude or perform the contract, without providing for the consumer to receive compensation of an equivalent amount from the seller or supplier where the latter is the party cancelling the contract; (e) requiring any consumer who fails to fulfil his obligation to pay a disproportionately high sum in compensation; (f) authorising the seller or supplier to dissolve the contract on a discretionary basis where the same facility is not granted to the consumer, or permitting the seller or supplier to retain the sums paid for services not yet supplied by him where it is the seller or supplier himself who dissolves the contract; (g) enabling the seller or supplier to terminate a contract of indeterminate duration without reasonable notice except where there are serious grounds for doing so; (h) automatically extending a contract of fixed duration where the consumer does not indicate otherwise, when the deadline fixed for the consumer to express this desire not to extend the contract is unreasonably early; (i) irrevocably binding the consumer to terms with which he had no real opportunity of becoming acquainted before the conclusion of the contract; (j) enabling the seller or supplier to alter the terms of the contract unilaterally without a valid reason which is specified in the contract; (k) enabling the seller or supplier to alter unilaterally without a valid reason any characteristics of the product or service to be provided; (l) providing for the price of goods to be determined at the time of delivery or allowing a seller of goods or supplier of services to increase their price without in both cases giving the consumer the corresponding right to cancel the contract if the final price is too high in relation to the price agreed when the contract

---

[9] In relation to this list, see the decision of the ECJ in Case C-478/99 *Commission v Sweden* [2002] E.C.R. I-0414.
[10] *cf.* s.2(1) of the 1977 Act.

was concluded; (m) giving the seller or supplier the right to determine whether the goods or services supplied are in conformity with the contract, or giving him the exclusive right to interpret any term of the contract; (n) limiting the seller's or supplier's obligations to respect commitments undertaken by his agents or making his commitments subject to compliance with a particular formality; (o) obliging the consumer to fulfil all his obligations where the seller or supplier does not perform his; (p) giving the seller or supplier the possibility of transferring his rights and obligations under the contract, where this may serve to reduce the guarantees for the consumer, without the latter's agreement; (q) excluding or hindering the consumer's right to take legal action or exercise any other legal remedy, particularly by requiring the consumer to take disputes exclusively to arbitration not covered by legal provisions, unduly restricting the evidence available to him or imposing on him a burden of proof which, according to the applicable law, should lie with another party to the contract." Paragraphs (1)(g), (j) and (l) are subject to limitations imposed by paragraph 2, covering such areas as financial services, contracts of indeterminate duration, securities, foreign currency and price indexation clauses.[11]

14–037 **Unfair terms in consumer sales.** In the case of the implied conditions as to quality, etc., in contracts for the sale of goods[12] the Regulations will not usually add to the protection accorded by the Unfair Contract Terms Act 1977. However, there are instances where they may do so, as when second-hand goods which are not of satisfactory quality are bought by a private individual at a public auction which individuals had the opportunity of

---

[11] Paragraph 2 provides: "Scope of paragraphs 1(g), (j) and (l)—

(a) Paragraph 1(g) is without hindrance to terms by which a supplier of financial services reserves the right to terminate unilaterally a contract of indeterminate duration without notice where there is a valid reason, provided that the supplier is required to inform the other contracting party or parties thereof immediately.

(b) Paragraph 1(j) is without hindrance to terms under which a supplier of financial services reserves the right to alter the rate of interest payable by the consumer or due to the latter, or the amount of other charges for financial services without notice where there is a valid reason, provided that the supplier is required to inform the other contracting party or parties thereof at the earliest opportunity and that the latter are free to dissolve the contract immediately. Paragraph 1(j) is also without hindrance to terms under which a seller or supplier reserves the right to alter unilaterally the conditions of a contract of indeterminate duration, provided that he is required to inform the consumer with reasonable notice and that the consumer is free to dissolve the contract.

(c) Paragraphs 1(g), (j) and (l) do not apply to:

—transactions in transferable securities, financial instruments and other products or services where the price is linked to fluctuations in a stock exchange quotation or index or a financial market rate that the seller or supplier does not control;

—contracts for the purchase or sale of foreign currency, traveller's cheques or international money orders denominated in foreign currency.

(d) Paragraph 1(l) is without hindrance to price indexation clauses, where lawful, provided that the method by which prices vary is explicitly described.

[12] Above, paras 11–024 *et seq.*, 14–010.

attending in person. As has been noted, the buyer will not "deal as consumer" for the purposes of the Act[13] and yet he will be a "consumer" for the purposes of the Regulations. In such a case it is possible, if unlikely, that an exemption or limitation clause would satisfy the requirement of reasonableness of the Act and yet be unfair within the Regulations.[14] In that event, it would not be binding on the consumer. Conversely, it has been held that a business may "deal as consumer" and hence benefit from the absolute protection of section 6(2) of the 1977 Act[15] and yet, not being a "natural person", would not be within the Regulations.[16]

Potentially unfair contractual terms in consumer sales are by no means limited to those which seek to deny liability for breach of the implied conditions as to quality and related matters. They may take many other forms. Some will, in all probability, fall within the controls both of the 1977 Act and the Regulations. This would be true of a term which purported to enable a seller unilaterally to alter the terms of the contract or the characteristics of the product to be supplied.[17] A standard example is a clause which refers to a right to change specifications without prior notice pursuant to some vaguely worded policy of constant improvement. Other terms may be regarded as unfair within the Regulations and also be subject to control on some alternative basis. Thus a term which requires a consumer "to pay a disproportionately high sum in compensation" for breach of contract or to forfeit a deposit may be "unfair"[18] and also be liable to be struck down as a penalty.[19] Yet other terms are prima facie unfair within the Regulations and in all probability not subject to any alternative controls. This seems to be true of some price variation clauses allowing a seller to increase the price in the event of increased labour or material costs or to fix it at the time of delivery.[20] 14–038

Clearly, the overall effect of the Regulations on consumer contracts for the sale of goods must depend on the precise wording of the term used. The following additional examples are potentially subject to control as unfair terms. First, "entire agreement" clauses frequently seek to confine 14–039

---

[13] See s.12(2)(a) and above, paras 13–078, 14–029.

[14] A further reason why this is unlikely is that whereas by s.11(5) of the 1977 Act the onus of proof is on the party claiming that a clause is reasonable (the seller), the onus is, it seems, on the party claiming that a term is "unfair" within reg. 5 (the consumer) to establish that this is so.

[15] See *R. & B. Customs Brokers Ltd v United Dominions Trust Ltd* [1988] 1 W.L.R. 321; para.14–029, n.65, above; also above, para.13–074. However, a business would not "deal as consumer" if the circumstances fall within s.12(1)(c) (goods not of a type ordinarily supplied for private use or consumption) or s. 12(2)(b) (sales by auction or competitive tender).

[16] Reg. 3(1).

[17] *cf.* s.3(2)(b)(i) of the 1977 Act and Sch.2, paras 1(j) and (k) to the Regulations.

[18] *cf.* Sch.2, paras 1(e) and (d).

[19] See Treitel, *Law of Contract* (11th ed.), pp.1006–1007, where the relationship between the sources of control is discussed in more detail; also below, para.16–041.

[20] *cf.* Sch.2, para.1(l), but note paras 2(c) and (d). See also *Lombard Tricity Finance Ltd v Paton* [1989] 1 All E.R. 918; *Paragon Finance Plc v Staunton* [2001] EWCA Civ 1466; [2001] 2 All E.R. (Comm.) 1025.

the contract to its written terms and conditions (*e.g.* those contained on an order form), so purporting to deny any effect to oral representations or promises made by agents. Alternatively, any variation may require the written consent of a director. Such clauses are potentially unfair and hence potentially unenforceable.[21] Secondly, sellers of goods (*e.g.* furniture or carpets) may seek to protect themselves by stipulating that a delivery date is not binding and that a failure to meet it is not to be treated as a breach of contract nor give rise to any claim for consequential loss. Again, such clauses are potentially unfair,[22] although not invariably so if they are limited to non-delivery which is attributable to genuinely unforeseen circumstances and provision is made for agreeing an alternative date. Thirdly, a term will also be prima facie unfair if it obliges the consumer to perform all his obligations under the contract (*e.g.* to pay in full) even though the seller has failed to perform all his obligations (*e.g.* to install the goods).[23] Finally, it must be stressed that these are only examples and that the "grey list" is, in any event, only illustrative. Terms may be challenged on the ground that they are "unfair" within regulation 5 even though they do not fall within one of the heads of the list.

14–040 **Enforcement provisions.** Although the technique had already been used in the context of consumer protection,[24] the Unfair Terms in Consumer Contracts Regulations were notable for their enforcement provisions enabling injunctions to be sought to prevent the continued use of unfair contract terms. This was particularly important since the general provisions of Part III of the Fair Trading Act 1973 did not extend to such cases.[25] In the 1994 Regulations it was only the Director-General of Fair Trading who had the power to proceed.[26] However, the current 1999 Regulations extend the power to other "qualifying bodies",[27] including regulators, weights and measures authorities and, significantly, the Consumers' Association.[28] The Office of Fair Trading (replacing the Director-General) retains the primary role and is under a duty to consider any complaint made to it that any contract term drawn up for general use is unfair.[29] If it considers the complaint well grounded it may apply for an injunction against any person

[21] *cf.* Sch.2, para.1(n).
[22] *cf.* Sch.2, para.1(b).
[23] *cf.* Sch.2, para.1(o).
[24] See (*e.g.*) the Control of Misleading Advertisements Regulations 1988 (SI 1988/915), reg. 5; also Part III of the Fair Trading Act 1973.
[25] s.34(2) confined the notion of conduct which is "unfair to consumers" to breaches of the criminal and civil law; also below para.14–128.
[26] SI 1994/3159, reg. 8.
[27] SI 1999/2083, reg. 3 and Sch.1 (as substituted by SI 2001/1186, reg. 2(b) and further amended by SI 2003/3182, art. 2 and in SI 2006/253, art. 2) contains a list of such bodies. For an assessment of the Regulations, including the enforcement provisions, see Bright, 2000 L.S. 331.
[28] *ibid.*, Pt Two. The original omission to extend the power to such a body may not have been compatible with Council Directive 1993/13/EC ([1993] O.J. L95/29), Art. 7(2). See Case C–82/96 *R. v Secretary of State for Trade and Industry, ex p.Consumers' Association* (96/C145/05).
[29] Reg. 10(1). The duty does not extend to complaints which appear frivolous or vexatious or which a qualifying body has agreed to consider.

using or recommending the use of the term.[30] A similar power is accorded to qualifying bodies which must, however, notify the Office of Fair Trading of their intention to proceed.[31] If an injunction is granted it "may relate not only to use of a particular contract term drawn up for general use but to any similar term, or a term having like effect, used or recommended for use by any person."[32] There are also extensive powers to obtain documents and information.[33] On a more positive note, it is clear that the unfair contract terms unit of the Office of Fair Trading has played a major role in promoting fairer contract terms and much useful information has been published in a regular series of bulletins.[34] As is noted later,[35] the use of such unfair contract terms may also constitute a "Community infringement" for the purposes of the new Part 8 procedures of the Enterprise Act 2002[36] (replacing the Stop Now Orders (EC Directive) Regulations 2001[37]), thus enabling injunctions to be sought under this alternative source of control.[38] The Law Commission report on Unfair Terms in Contracts is satisfied that the Regulations should retain their own enforcement provisions.[39]

(c) *Miscellaneous Matters*

Representations. Representations as to the goods or other matters made by sellers may constitute contractual promises.[40] If they are external to the contract they may give rise to the right to rescind the contract in equity if it is not too late to do so.[41] There will also be a right to damages in tort if the representation is fraudulent.[42] If it is not, an action may lie under section 2(1) of the Misrepresentation Act 1967, under which the representor must prove that he had reasonable grounds for his belief.[43] There may also be liability in negligence.[44] The latter may often be more difficult to establish 14–041

[30] Reg. 12(1).
[31] Reg. 12(2).
[32] Reg. 12(4).
[33] Reg. 13.
[34] The bulletins, which began in May 1996, are available from the OFT.
[35] See para.14–133.
[36] See s.212 and Sch.13; also the Enterprise Act 2002 (Part 8 Community Infringements Specified UK Laws) Order 2003 (SI 2003/1374), art. 3 and Sch. At least in the case of terms which are subject to control under the Unfair Contract Terms Act 1977, a "domestic infringement" may also be present: see s.211(1) and (2)(e)(f) and (g) of the 2002 Act and the Enterprise Act 2002 (Part 8 Domestic Infringements) Order 2003 (SI 2003/1593), art.2(i) and Sch.
[37] SI 2001/1422. See, in particular, reg. 2(1) and (3)(g); Sch.1, para.7.
[38] A recent example is to be found in *Office of Fair Trading v MB Designs (Scotland) Ltd* 2005 S.L.T. 681 (Outer House: Lord Drummond Young) (interim enforcement order made in relation to clause in standard form contract which sought to deny effect to representations made by salesmen unless they were put into writing and signed). See also, below, paras 14–130—14–136.
[39] See *Unfair Terms in Contracts* (Law Com. No. 292, Scot. Law Com. No. 199, Cm. 6464) (2005), para.3.147.
[40] *e.g. Porter v General Guarantee Corp. Ltd* [1982] R.T.R. 384.
[41] Above, paras 10–008 *et seq.*
[42] Above, para.12–012.
[43] Above, paras 12–014, 12–016.
[44] Above, para.12–013.

than liability under section 2(1), since the onus of proof will be on the claimant throughout[45]; on the other hand, section 2(1) is limited in its operation, and where it is on its wording inapplicable it may be necessary to fall back on the tort action.[46] These rules are general and have no special applicability to consumers, though a consumer may perhaps more readily be held to have relied on a representation than a commercial man, and conversely a statement made by a commercial man to a consumer is more likely to be held a contractual promise than the reverse.[47] Equally the protection against clauses excluding or restricting liability for misrepresentation given by section 3 of the Misrepresentation Act 1967[48] does not distinguish between consumer and other transactions, though the requirement of reasonableness which the section applies to such clauses may enable the court or arbitrator to do so in practice.

14–042 **Collateral contracts, sellers' guarantees and extanded warranties.** Sometimes a statement by a seller as to goods sold can be construed as an offer of a unilateral collateral contract, the consideration for which is provided by entering into the main contract.[49] In such a case it will create liability notwithstanding the fact that the contract is reduced to writing and that the adducing of evidence to add to or vary its terms might otherwise be problematic under principles associated with the parol evidence rule[50]; it may also override an exemption clause.[51] The statement will also normally attract the strict liability associated with contractual liability.[52] Again, a contract of sale may contain some sort of guarantee of the goods sold, or a promise to repair them or to replace defective parts. Such guarantees normally cause dispute only because they involve other exemptions which the seller wishes to invoke. However, if a guarantee can be regarded as part of the main contract, or as a collateral contract duly offered and accepted (again normally by entering into the main contract) it will (subject to the Unfair Contract Terms Act 1977[53] and to the Unfair Terms in Consumer Contracts Regulations[54]) be enforceable by the buyer according to its terms. In many cases consumers are not well advised to accept offers of separate "extended warranty" contracts which are frequently very expensive and do not add significantly (if at all) to the inalienable right to receive goods which are of satisfactory quality under the contract of sale.[55] The general position with respect to manufacturers' guarantees is considered below.[56]

---

[45] *e.g. Howard Marine and Dredging Co. Ltd v A Ogden & Sons (Excavations) Ltd* [1978] Q.B. 574; above, para.12–014. *Cf.* below, para.14–061.
[46] Above, para.12–014. Or on a collateral contract: above, para.10–012; below, paras 14–042, 14–044.
[47] *cf. Dick Bentley Productions Ltd v Harold Smith (Motors) Ltd* [1965] 1 W.L.R. 623 with *Oscar Chess Ltd v Williams* [1957] 1 Q.B. 370: above, paras 10–017 *et seq.*
[48] As substituted by the Unfair Contract Terms Act 1977: above, para.13–054.
[49] See above, para.10–012.
[50] *cf. City and Westminster Properties Ltd v Mudd* [1959] Ch. 129.
[51] *e.g. Couchman v Hill* [1947] K.B. 554; above, para.10–013.
[52] *e.g. Yonge v Toynbee* [1910] 1 K.B. 215; but *cf. Esso Petroleum Co. Ltd v Mardon* [1976] Q.B. 801, above, para.10–012.
[53] ss.2, 3, 6, 7: above, paras 13–062 *et seq.* s.5, which specifically deals with guarantees, does not apply between buyer and seller: below, para.14–069.
[54] SI 1999/2083; above, paras 14–030 *et seq.*
[55] As to which, see above, paras 11–026 *et seq.*, 14–010.
[56] See below, paras 14–065 *et seq.*

14–043 The problems associated with "extended warranties" have over many years been particularly acute in the case of the supply of domestic electrical goods.[57] In December 2003 the Competition Commission issued a critical report which identified practices which restricted or distorted competition and operated against the public interest.[58] This led to the making of the Supply of Extended Warranties on Domestic Electrical Goods Order 2005,[59] which imposes an obligation on suppliers of domestic electrical goods,[60] who also supply or offer to supply extended warranties for those goods,[61] to provide certain information to consumers before the sale of an extended warranty and gives consumers cancellation and termination rights in relation to such warranties. In broad outline, in-store suppliers of such goods must display the price and duration of the warranty whenever the price of the corresponding goods is displayed in store and do so in a clear and legible manner and make it clear that the purchase of such a warranty is optional.[62] In addition, there are obligations to display leaflets containing relevant information[63] and to provide written quotations for extended warranties which must, inter alia, make it clear that such warranties may be available from other persons and that they do not have to be purchased at the same time as the domestic electrical goods to which they relate.[64] The Order also makes provision for cases where the price of domestic electrical goods is advertised in newspapers, etc. or catalogues or on websites.[65] The general principle in relation to cancellation and termination rights is that where an extended warranty has an initial duration of more than one year the consumer has a right to cancel the warranty within a period of 45 days and (where no claim has been made under the warranty) obtain a full refund.[66] Thereafter, he may terminate the warranty by notice (regardless of whether a claim has been made) and receive a pro rata refund of the price paid.[67]

---

[57] See *Extended Warranties on Electrical Goods* (OFT, 1994).

[58] See *A report on the supply of extended warranties on domestic electrical goods within the UK* (Cm. 6089) (2003).

[59] SI 2005/37, which came into force on April 6, 2005 (see art. 1(2)).

[60] Defined to mean " a product designed to be connected to an electricity supply or powered by batteries and used for domestic purposes, but does not include watches, jewellery or fixed installations (other than integrated appliances)" (art. 1(3)). The most obvious examples include television sets, video recorders, hi-fi systems, washing machines, dishwashers and fridges.

[61] The offer to supply may be either direct or on behalf of a third party and either at the same time as the supply of the good to which it relates or immediately subsequent to it (see art. 1 (3)).

[62] Art. 3(1)(a). This does not apply where the price of the goods is displayed on a device for ascertaining whether it is in stock or on an automated self-service machine used for purchasing such goods (art. 3(2)).

[63] Art. 3(1)(b).

[64] Art. 3(1)(c) and (4). This does not apply where the price of the extended warranty is £20 (inclusive of tax) or less (art. 3 (3)). But, subject to this, the written quotation must be kept open for at least 30 days (art. 7).

[65] See, respectively, arts 4, 5 and 6.

[66] Art. 8(1)(a).

[67] Art. 8(1)(b). The pro rata refund is to be calculated by reference to the remaining period of full unexpired months of cover provided by the extended warranty (Art. 8(4)).

14–044 **Hire-purchase transactions.** In certain situations a collateral contract may be made with someone who is neither seller nor manufacturer. Thus in a typical hire-purchase transaction the dealer may not sell the product to the buyer: he may sell it to a finance company who will itself then let it on hire purchase to the buyer. The dealer may nevertheless be liable on his representations on the ground that they constitute part of a collateral contract.[68]

14–045 **Doorstep sales.** There are provisions whereby a sale involving a regulated consumer credit agreement may be cancelled if the agreement is signed by the debtor off trade premises.[69] Where credit is not involved, there was over many years no provision for any such "cooling-off period", although legislation providing for similar rights in respect of what may be called "doorstep sales" existed elsewhere.[70] However, in 1985 the Council of the EEC adopted a Directive on contracts concluded away from business premises,[71] which was implemented in English law in 1987 by regulations made under section 2(2) of the European Communities Act 1972.[72] Broadly speaking, the Regulations apply to contracts for the supply of goods or services to a "consumer"[73] during an unsolicited visit by a trader to the consumer's home (or to that of another person) or to the consumer's place of work.[74] In any such case the consumer has a right to cancel the contract

---

[68] See *Brown v Sheen and Richmond Car Sales Ltd* [1950] 1 All E.R. 1102; *Andrews v Hopkinson* [1957] 1 Q.B. 229; *Yeoman Credit Ltd v Odgers* [1962] 1 W.L.R. 215; *cf. Drury v Victor Buckland Ltd* [1941] 1 All E.R. 269. In *Andrews v Hopkinson* it is suggested at p.237 that the stipulations implied by s.14 of the Sale of Goods Act might apply to such a contract; *sed quaere*. The actual seller, the finance house, may also be liable for such representations: see Consumer Credit Act 1974, s.56.

[69] Consumer Credit Act 1974, ss.67–73: see below, para.14–145.

[70] *e.g.* Door to Door Sales Act 1971–1979 (South Aust.).

[71] Council Directive 1985/577/EEC ([1985] O.J. L372/31). For an important decision concerning this Directive, see Case C–91/92 *Dori v Recreb Srl* [1994] E.C.R. I–3325, ECJ.

[72] Consumer Protection (Cancellation of Contracts Concluded away from Business Premises) Regulations 1987 (SI 1987/2117, as amended by SI 1988/958, SI 1998/3050) SI 2001/3649 and SI 2003/1400. In the case of timeshares, both cash and credit purchasers are covered by the Timeshare Act 1992, as amended most notably by the Timeshare Regulations 1997 (SI 1997/1081) (implementing Directive 1994/47/EC ([1994] O.J. L280/83)) and the Timeshare Act 1992 (Amendment) Regulations 2003 (SI 2003/1922) (provisions for ensuring that purchasers of timeshares are given information about their rights to cancel, as well as the application of the Act to cross-border timeshare purchases). See also the Timeshare (Cancellation Information) Order 2003 (SI 2003/2579, prescribing, inter alia, the form of information on the right to cancel. Both "doorstep selling" and timeshares are within the scope of the injunction procedures of Part 8 of the Enterprise Act and previously the Stop Now Orders (EC Directive) Regulations 2001 (SI 2001/1422), implementing Directive 1998/27/EC ([1998] O.J. L166/51) (the injunctions Directive); see below, paras 14–130—14–136.

[73] That is, a person, other than a body corporate, who is acting for purposes which can be regarded as outside his business: see reg. 2(1).

[74] Reg. 3(1)(a). For the definition of "unsolicited visit", see reg. 3(3), as substituted by SI 1998/3050, reg. 2(b). There is also a limited application to requested visits, but only in respect of goods or services falling outside the scope of the request and then only if the consumer neither knew, nor could reasonably have known, that the

within seven days by serving a notice of cancellation on the trader,[75] the effect of which is generally that the contract is then treated as though it had never been entered into by the consumer.[76] If he does not receive a written notice informing him of this right the contract will not be enforceable against him[77] and such a failure to supply a notice is now a criminal offence.[78] There are exceptions[79] covering inter alia contracts for the construction, sale and rental of immovable property (but contracts for the supply of goods and for their incorporation in immovable property and contracts for the repair of immovable property are covered); contracts for the sale of foodstuffs or beverages or other goods intended for current consumption in the household and supplied by regular roundsmen; certain contracts for the supply of goods or services concluded on the basis of a trade catalogue where the catalogue and the contract clearly inform the consumer of his right to return goods or otherwise cancel the contract within a period of not less than seven days of receipt of the goods; and contracts which do not require the consumer to make total payments exceeding £35 or ones under which credit is provided not exceeding £35. Finally, the Regulations provide for such consequences of cancellation as the repayment of payments and of credit provided and the return of goods received.[80] In a more recent development discussed in a later section broadly equivalent protection has been extended to the modern phenomenon of "distance selling".[81]

(d) *Rights under other Contracts to Supply Goods*

Types of contract involved. The distinction between contracts for the sale of goods and other contracts to supply goods has been considered in detail in an earlier chapter.[82] Some such contracts are of particular importance to consumers. For example, such goods as television sets, chain saws and garden rotavators are often hired and not bought and many costly contracts are for work and materials, rather than sale. This is usually the case in the important area of home improvements (*e.g.* fitted kitchens and bathrooms and the like) and with repairs incorporating replacement parts 14–046

---

supply of such goods or services formed part of the trader's business activities (reg. 3(1)(b)). The regulations also apply to contracts in respect of which an offer was made by the consumer under conditions similar to those described above (reg. 3(1)(c)), and to contracts concluded during an excursion organised by a trader away from premises on which he is carrying on a business (reg. 3(1)(d)).

[75] See reg. 4(5).

[76] See reg. 4(6).

[77] Reg. 4(1).

[78] Reg. 4A, which was added by SI 1998/3050, reg. 2(c).

[79] Reg. 3(2). For a decision concerning the scope of the exclusion for contracts for the sale of immovable property, see Case C-350/03 *Shulte v Deutsche Bausparkasse Badenia AG* [2006] All E.R. (EC) 420 (ECJ).

[80] Regs. 5 (recovery of money paid by consumer); 6 (as amended by SI 1988/958) (repayment of credit); 7 (return of goods by consumer after cancellation); and see also reg. 8 (goods given in part exchange).

[81] See the Consumer Protection (Distance Selling) Regulations 2000 (SI 2000/2334); below, paras 14–053—14–060.

[82] Ch.1, paras 1–030 *et seq*.

in cars and in such goods as washing machines and central heating systems.[83] Less frequently, goods will be acquired by way of barter or exchange,[84] and of course many will be supplied under hire purchase or consumer credit agreements. The latter type of transaction is considered further below.[85]

14–047 **Implied conditions as to quality, etc.** For many years it was important to determine whether a contract to supply goods was one of sale since contracts to hire out goods or for work and materials did not attract the statutory implied terms as to quality and related matters associated with the Sale of Goods Act. The consumer had to fall back on the common law where there was room for argument over whether equivalent terms should be implied. The position was changed by the Supply of Goods and Services Act 1982 which enacts implied terms as to title, correspondence with description, quality and fitness for purpose which (as amended by the Sale and Supply of Goods Act 1994 and the Sale and Supply of Goods to Consumers Regulations 2002[86]) are identical in all essential respects to those implied in contracts of sale.[87] It will be recalled that the seller (and hence the supplier) is strictly liable for breach of such terms and for such consequential personal injury or property damage as is within the standard tests applicable on breach of contract.[88] Attempts to exclude, limit or qualify liability are similarly controlled by the Unfair Contract Terms Act 1977[89] and the Unfair Terms in Consumer Contracts Regulations 1999, which apply both to sellers and suppliers of goods.[90] Thus to this extent the precise mode of supply is less important than was once the case, although

---

[83] The distinction between sale and work and materials is often difficult to draw. See, *e.g. Stewart v Reavell's Garage* [1952] 2 Q.B. 545 (supplying and fitting brake linings to a car: work and materials); *G H Myers & Co. v Brent Cross Services Co.* [1934] 1 K.B. 46 (supplying and fitting connecting rods: work and materials); *Robinson v Graves* [1935] 1 K.B. 579 (painting a portrait: work and materials); *cf. Lee v Griffin* (1861) 1 B. & S. 272 (dentist making and fitting dentures: sale); *Philip Head & Sons Ltd v Showfronts Ltd* [1970] 1 Lloyd's Rep. 140 (supplying, sewing and laying fitted carpet: sale); above, paras 1–041—1–042.

[84] Above, paras 1–034 *et seq*. This appears to include acquisition by using tokens or vouchers.

[85] Below, paras 14–143 *et seq*.

[86] SI 2002/3045.

[87] As to contracts for the transfer of property in goods (including work and materials), see the Supply of Goods and Services Act 1982, ss.2 (title), 3 (correspondence with description) and 4 (quality and fitness, etc.); as to contracts for the hire of goods, see ss.7 (right to transfer possession), 8 (correspondence with description) and 9 (quality and fitness, etc.) The amendments are contained in the Sale and Supply of Goods Act 1994, s.7, Sch.2, para.6 and the Sale and Supply of Goods to Consumers Regulations 2002 (SI 2002/3045), reg. 7 (contracts where there is a transfer of property in goods) and reg. 10 (contracts where goods are hired to consumers). For hire purchase and consumer credit agreements, see below, para.14–152.

[88] See above, para.14–017; below, paras 17–072 *et seq*.

[89] Notably, s.7(2) and (3A); see above, para.13–085.

[90] SI 1999/2083. Thus the central provision in reg. 8(1) states that "An unfair term in a contract concluded with a consumer by a seller or supplier shall not be binding on the consumer." See above, para.14–034.

the goods must still have been supplied under a contract and not as a genuine free promotional gift.[91]

14–048 Notwithstanding the assimilation of the content of the implied terms as to quality, etc. in the various contracts under which goods may be supplied to consumers, the position is altogether more complex when one turns to consider the remedies which are available following a breach of the relevant term. The principal distinction is that the loss of the right to reject through acceptance of the goods under section 35 of the Sale of Goods Act has no direct counterpart in other contracts of supply. In principle, the right to reject goods would then be lost only on affirmation of the contract and this has been said to require that the consumer "knows of the defects and by his conduct elects to go on with the contract despite them."[92] However, authority in this area is sparse and the limit difficult to apply to contracts for work and materials where goods will often have been incorporated into other property.

14–049 A further complication is that the new Part 5A remedies of the Sale of Goods Act 1979 have a corresponding provision in a new Part 1B (sections 11M–11S) of the Supply of Goods and Services Act 1982. This was thought to be necessary in order to comply with Directive 1999/44/E.C. on the sale of consumer goods and associated guarantees.[93] The remedies, which run alongside the traditional remedies, confer additional rights on transferees who deal as consumers in contracts falling within section 1 of the 1982 Act, that is, contracts for work and materials, etc. but not contracts of hire-purchase or of hire.[94] The nature of contracts for work and materials is, however, frequently such that a remedy of replacement of non-conforming goods may be seen as disproportionate.[95]

---

[91] The distinction is not always easy to draw; see *Esso Petroleum Co. Ltd v Customs and Excise Commissioners* [1976] 1 W.L.R. 1; above, para.1–033.

[92] *Farnworth Finance Facilities Ltd v Attryde* [1970] 1 W.L.R. 1053, at 1059, *per* Lord Denning, M.R. (a case of hire purchase). See also *Yeoman Credit Ltd v Apps* [1962] 2 Q.B. 508, *Guarantee Trust of Jersey Ltd v Gardner* (1973) 117 Sol.Jo. 564; *Allen v Robles* [1969] 1 W.L.R. 1193, *Peyman v Lanjani* [1985] Ch.457, *Moore Large & Co. Ltd v Hermes Credit and Guarantee Plc* [2003] 1 Lloyd's Rep. 163, 179–80; Law Com. W.P. No. 85, Scot. Law Com.C.M. No. 58 (1983), paras 261–263.

[93] [1999] O.J. L171/12. See, generally, above, para.14–008. The application of the Directive to such contracts is not clear-cut. It depends in part on the meaning to be attributed to Art. 1.4, which provides that: "Contracts for the supply of consumer goods to be manufactured or produced shall also be deemed contracts of sale for the purpose of this Directive." This might be seen as no more than a reference to contracts for the sale of future goods (as in s.5(1) of the Sale of Goods Act 1979) or to contracts for the supply of custom-made or bespoke items (such as clothing, fitted furniture or expensive yachts). But see also Art. 2.5, below, para.14–052.

[94] For discussion of the Part 5A remedies, see above, paras 12–071—12–118, 14–023—14–027.

[95] For the unavailability of the remedy where it is "disproportionate", see s.11N(3) and (4) of the 1982 Act and, more generally, above, paras 12–080, 14–024.

(e) *Rights under Contracts to Supply Services*

14–050 **Examples of such contracts.** Contracts for the supply of services provide further examples of areas where there is a potential source of consumer dissatisfaction. Many different types of services are involved, including repairs and servicing, bailment (as in the case of home removals and storage, laundry and dry cleaning), film processing, car washes, and the provision of holidays, whether package or tailor-made. Package holidays are now subject to detailed control under the Package Travel, Package Holidays and Package Tours Regulations 1992[96] which implement a Council Directive which was agreed in 1990.[97] Professional services are also relevant, including surveying, insurance and medical, legal and banking services. Many of these areas have their own specialist literature.[98] In this work it is convenient to include a brief reference to some common provisions.

14–051 **Express and implied terms.** Suppliers of services will often make statements about their characteristics or the results which they may be expected to achieve. As in the case of goods, such statements may range from mere advertising puffs to misrepresentations of fact or firm contractual promises.[99] Obviously, much will depend on the precise words used and the context in which they are spoken or otherwise published.[1] The Supply of Goods and Services Act 1982 contains a number of terms which will be implied when the supplier of a service is acting in the course of a business.[2] By section 13 of the Act there is an implied term that he will carry out the service with reasonable care and skill. Subject to an issue which is raised below, the qualified nature of this obligation is to be contrasted with the strict liability attaching to the quality of any goods supplied when performing the service.[3] This may mean that it is important to identify the precise

---

[96] SI 1992/3288, as amended by SI 1995/1648 and SI 1998/1208. Breach of these Regulations may constitute a "Community infringement", so allowing for action under Part 8 of the Enterprise Act 2002 (replacing the Stop Now Orders (EC Directive) Regulations 2001 (SI 2001/1422), below, paras 14–130 *et seq*.

[97] Council Directive 1990/314/EEC ([1990] O.J. L158/59).

[98] See generally Dugdale and Stanton, *Professional Negligence* (4th ed.); Harvey and Parry, *Law of Consumer Protection and Fair Trading* (6th ed.), Ch.7; as to bailment, see Palmer, *Bailment* (2nd ed.).

[99] Above, Ch.10.

[1] For example, it is inherently unlikely that a surgeon will impliedly guarantee that an operation will be a complete success: see *Thake v Maurice* [1986] Q.B. 644; *Eyre v Measday* [1986] 1 All E.R. 488. *cf.* the position of engineers and designers in *Greaves & Co. (Contractors) Ltd v Baynham Meikle & Partners* [1975] 1 W.L.R. 1095 at 1100, *per* Lord Denning, M.R.; *IBA v EMI (Electronics) Ltd* (1980) 14 Build.L.R. 1.

[2] For recommendations leading to the 1982 Act, see the report of the National Consumer Council, "Service Please: Services and the Law" (1991); also Woodroffe, *Goods and Services—The New Law* (1982); Palmer (1983) 46 M.L.R. 619. By s.12(4) the Secretary of State may by Order exclude the application of ss.12–15 to types of services specified in the Order: see The Supply of Services (Exclusion of Implied Terms) Order 1982 (SI 1982/1771); also SI 1983/902 and SI 1985/1. For discussion of these implied terms and of possible further changes, see *Implied Terms in Contracts for the Supply of Services*, Law Com. No. 156 (1986).

[3] See Supply of Goods and Services Act 1982, s.4; above, para.14–047; *G H Myers & Co. v Brent Cross Service Co.* [1934] 1 K.B. 46.

source of the problem. For example, a careful repairer may be liable for supplying and fitting a faulty replacement part correctly and yet not be liable for making an incorrect adjustment to an existing part.[4] Similarly, in the absence of an express warranty or some other unusual circumstance, the repairer would not hitherto have been liable where, although acting with all due care, he had supplied and incorrectly installed goods which were themselves of satisfactory quality and in conformity with the contract.

In the situation envisaged above there is an element of doubt as to the effect of Directive 1999/44/EC on certain aspects of the sale of consumer goods and associated guarantees.[5] The essential obligation of the seller to deliver goods which are in conformity with the contract of sale is supplemented by a provision in Article 2.5 which states in part that: "Any lack of conformity resulting from incorrect installation of the consumer goods shall be deemed to be equivalent to lack of conformity of the goods if installation forms part of the contract of sale of the goods and the goods were installed by the seller or under his responsibility."[6] For the purposes of compliance with the minimum harmonisation provisions of the Directive it can hardly matter that English law would usually describe such a contract as one of work and materials, rather than of sale. The difficulty arises because the corresponding provision which was introduced into the Supply of Goods and Services Act 1982[7] states that goods do not conform to a contract for the supply or transfer of goods if, inter alia, "(b) installation of the goods forms part of the contract for the transfer of goods, and the goods were installed by the transferor, or under his responsibility, in breach of the term implied by section 13. . ."[8] Under section 13 of the 1982 Act the relevant obligation is, as has been noted, one of exercising reasonable care only, whereas it may be assumed (although this is not stated expressly) that the Directive requires that in order to avoid a lack of conformity the installation should in fact *be* carried out correctly. On that basis the exercise of reasonable care would be insufficient. The result is, of course, that there may not be full compliance with the Directive in this respect. 14–052

Another frequent complaint is that there have been unreasonably long delays in carrying out a service. Where the time has not been fixed by the contract or otherwise agreed between the parties section 14 of the 1982 Act 14–052A

---

[4] Although the possibility of a more onerous and stricter obligation is saved by s.16(3)(a) of the 1982 Act.

[5] See above, paras 14–008 *et seq*.

[6] Art. 2.5 further provides that: "This shall apply equally if the product, intended to be installed by the consumer, is installed by the consumer and the incorrect installation is due to a shortcoming in the installation instructions." In principle, this situation is covered by the implied terms as to satisfactory quality of s.14 of the 1979 Act: see above, paras 11–026 *et seq*, 14–010.

[7] By the Sale and Supply of Goods to Consumers Regulations 2002 (SI 2002/3045), reg. 9.

[8] Section 11S(b). By s.11S(a) there will also be a non-conformity if "there is, in relation to the goods, a breach of an express term of the contract or a term implied by section 3, 4 or 5 . . ." Sections 3, 4 and 5 cover, respectively, the terms as to correspondence with description, satisfactory quality, etc. and correspondence with sample. See also above, para.12–116.

provides for an implied term that the supplier will carry out the service within a reasonable time.[9] In the case of distance contracts concluded without the simultaneous physical presence of the supplier and the consumer, alternative provisions apply both as to the time for performance and more generally.[10] A further provision in section 15 of the 1982 Act will apply where the consideration is not fixed or otherwise agreed by or under the contract, the customer then being required to pay "a reasonable charge". Although, other than in the case of distance contracts,[11] it is open to the parties to depart from the above terms, this is subject to the control of the Unfair Contract Terms Act 1977[12] and the Unfair Terms in Consumer Contracts Regulations 1999.[13] Section 15 of the 1982 Act does not assist where a consumer has contracted to pay an extortionate charge for a service. The 1977 Act is similarly inapplicable. Assistance may, however, be derived from the 1999 Regulations, provided always that the term has not been individually negotiated.[14] Regulation 6(2) provides that no assessment shall be made of the fairness of any term which concerns the adequacy of the price against the services supplied. However, this standard provision against inquiring into the adequacy of consideration applies only where the term is in "plain, intelligible language". It remains to be seen how this will be applied to the proverbial "cowboy plumber" called out to unblock a drain or mend a burst pipe.[15]

(f) *Distance Selling*

14–053 **Background.** The paradigm case in the context of the sale of goods to consumers has been one in which buyer and seller were in the physical presence of each other. However, relatively recently there has been a

[9] See *Charnock v Liverpool Corp.* [1968] 1 W.L.R. 1498—an equivalent decision at common law.

[10] See the Consumer Protection (Distant Selling) Regulations 2000 (SI 2000/2334), reg. 19, below, paras 14–053 *et seq.*

[11] *ibid.* reg. 25.

[12] Particularly ss.2 (negligence liability), 3 (liability arising in contract) and 8 (misrepresentation); above, paras 13–062 *et seq.*; 14–029. For a case involving an estate agent where the controls of the Act were satisfied, see *McCullagh v Lane Fox and Partners Ltd* [1996] 1 E.G.L.R. 35.

[13] SI 1999/2083.

[14] Reg. 5(1); see also reg. 5(2) to (4).

[15] Here, as elsewhere, it is possible that some limited form of consumer protection may develop out of the notion of "economic duress": see *North Ocean Shipping Co. Ltd v Hyundai Construction Co. Ltd (The Atlantic Baron)* [1979] Q.B. 705; *Pao On v Lau Yui Long* [1980] A.C. 614; *Universe Tankship Inc. v International Transport Workers' Federation* [1983] 1 A.C. 366; *C.T.N. Cash and Carry Ltd v Gallagher Ltd* [1994] 4 All E.R. 714; Treitel, *Law of Contract* (11th ed.), pp.405–408; Stewart, 14 Melbourne U.L.Rev. 410 (1984). Equitable doctrines, such as that of undue influence and the provision of relief against unconscionable bargains may on occasion be relevant: see *Alec Lobb (Garages) Ltd v Total Oil (Great Britain) Ltd* [1983] 1 W.L.R. 87; [1985] 1 W.L.R. 173; *National Westminster Bank Plc v Morgan* [1985] A.C. 686; *Barclays Bank Plc v O'Brien* [1994] 1 A.C. 180. *Royal Bank of Scotland v Etridge* (*No. 2*) [2002] 2 A.C. 773; Mason, 116 L.Q.R. 66 (2000); Enonchong, *Duress, Undue Influence and Unconscionable Dealing* (2005); Treitel, *op. cit.*, pp.408–427. Also such criminal offences as obtaining a pecuniary advantage by deception under the Theft Act 1968, s.16, may be more effective in practice than civil litigation.

marked shift towards distance selling, whether through methods which have long been familiar (mail order catalogues, Press advertising with accompanying order forms, and the like) or such modern counterparts as telephone sales, the fax, television shopping, email and the internet or online selling. Such transactions create difficulties in applying the traditional rules as to contract formation, for example, to the so-called "click-wrap" contracts formed through clicking in a box or on an icon on the computer screen. These have been considered in an earlier chapter.[16] There are also significant problems of consumer protection in that the buyer will not have seen the specific goods and, depending on the type of transaction, may be susceptible to pressure (as with "cold calling" on the telephone) or prone to buy on impulse (as with internet shopping). The temptation of the double-glazing salesman offering "interest-free" terms, or the convenience of clicking on an icon, may not be easy to resist.

The Distance Selling Regulations. After a protracted period of debate the Distance Selling Directive was agreed in 1997[17] and implemented in the United Kingdom by the Consumer Protection (Distance Selling) Regulations 2000.[18] For this purpose a "distance contract" is defined[19] as "any contract concerning goods or services concluded between a supplier and a consumer[20] under an organised distance sales or service provision scheme run by the supplier who, for the purpose of the contract, makes exclusive use of one or more means of distance communication up to and including the moment at which the contract is concluded."[21] A means of distance communication is one which does not involve the simultaneous physical presence of the supplier and consumer.[22] An indicative list is provided.[23] Hence the Regulations would not apply to private sales from one consumer to another, nor to business-to-business transactions. The requirement that the distance selling be via an "organised scheme" is also apt to exclude a business which does not operate an interactive website, but which responds to an isolated request from a consumer. Similarly, any pre-contractual 14–054

[16] See paras 2–002, 2–012, 2–015. See also in relation to conflict of laws issues, below, paras 25–044—25–056, 25–107—25–110.

[17] Directive 1997/7/EC ([1997] O.J. L144/19). See *Distant Selling: Implementation of EU Directive 97/7 on the Protection of Consumers in Respect of Distant Contracts* (DTI, 1998); *A Guide For Business to the Consumer Protection (Distance Selling) Regulations 2000* (DTI, 2000); *Cremona* [1998] J.B.L. 613; *Brownsword and Howells*, 19 L.S. 287 at 299–307 esp. (1999); Hellwege, [2004] C.L.J. 712.

[18] SI 2000/2334, as amended by SI 2004/2095, SI 2005/55 and SI 2005/689.

[19] Reg. 3(1).

[20] Defined, respectively to mean "any person who, in contracts to which these Regulations apply, is acting in his commercial or professional capacity" and "any natural person who, in contracts to which these Regulations apply, is acting for purposes which are outside his business.": reg. 3(1).

[21] Reg. 3(1).

[22] *ibid*.

[23] See Sch.1, which lists unaddressed printed matter, addressed printed matter, letter, press advertising with order form, catalogue, telephone with human intervention, telephone without human intervention (automatic calling machine, audiotext), radio, videophone (telephone with screen), videotext (microcomputer and television screen) with keyboard or touch screen, electronic mail, facsimile machine (fax) and television (teleshopping).

meeting between a consumer and the supplier or one of his employees would take the contract outwith the scope of the Regulations. Certain contracts are wholly outside the Regulations[24] (including ones which relate to financial services[25] and contracts concluded by means of an automated vending machine, a public pay-phone or at an auction, including an internet auction)[26] and others are excluded from the information and cancellation provisions to which reference is made below.[27] These include contracts for groceries supplied at agreed intervals by "regular roundsmen" (which term would include the fast-disappearing morning milk round, but not periodical home deliveries ordered via the internet from supermarkets) and contracts for the provision of accommodation, transport, catering or leisure services where they are to be provided for a specified date or within a specified period (for example, air travel, concert performances and sporting events).[28]

14–055 **Information to be provided.** One of the central concerns of the Regulations is to require that information be given in good time prior to the conclusion of the contract and in a clear and comprehensible manner appropriate to the means of distance communication used.[29] Such information includes[30] the identity of the supplier, and where payment in advance is required his address, a description of the main characteristics of the goods or services and their price, including all taxes, delivery costs where applicable, arrangements for payment, delivery or performance, the existence of a right of cancellation where one exists,[31] the period for which the offer or the price remains valid[32] and, where appropriate, the minimum duration of the contract.[33] The latter point is particularly important in the case of mobile 'phones, cable or satellite television, book clubs and the like.

---

[24] See reg. 5.

[25] As to which, see the Financial Services (Distance Marketing) Regulations 2004 (SI 2004/2095).

[26] Further exclusions cover contracts for the sale or other disposition of an interest in land (except for a rental agreement) and for the construction of a building where this forms part of such contracts: reg. 5(1)(a) and (b).

[27] See below, paras 14–055, 14–057. One of the more significant exclusions is for "contracts for the provision of accommodation, transport, catering or leisure services, where the supplier undertakes, when the contract is concluded, to provide these services on a specific date or within a specific period": (s.6(2)(b)). The European Court of Justice has held, construing the equivalent provision in Art. 3(2) of the Directive, that "contracts for the provision of . . . transport" includes car rental agreements: see Case C-336/03 *easyCar (UK) Ltd v Office of Fair Trading* [2005] All E.R. (EC) 834.

[28] See reg. 6(2) (excluding regs 7 to 19(1)). Timeshare agreements are excepted from regs 7 to 20 (see reg. 6(1)) and package travel from regs 19(2)–(8) and 20 (see reg. 6(3))—being subject, respectively, to the Timeshare Act 1992 and the Package Travel, Package Holidays and Package Tours Regulations 1992 (SI 1992/3288). Yet other contracts are excluded from cancellation rights, unless the parties have agreed otherwise: see reg. 13, below, para.14–057.

[29] Obviously this would vary from giving information in an advertisement or catalogue to giving it on a website or over the 'phone.

[30] See reg. 7.

[31] Reg. 7(1)(a)(vi). A right of cancellation does not exist in the cases referred to in reg. 13 (below, para.14–057).

[32] Reg. 7(1)(a)(viii).

[33] Reg. 7(1)(a)(ix).

Also, where a premium rate telephone is to be used the cost to the consumer must be specified.[34] In providing such information the commercial purpose must be made clear[35] and, in order to counteract the problems of "cold-calling", in the case of telephone communications this must be done at the beginning of the conversation when the identity of the supplier must also be stated.[36] These pre-contractual requirements are matched by an obligation to provide confirmation in writing, or "in another durable medium which is available and accessible to the consumer,"[37] of information already given,[38] together with certain additional information. This must be done either (a) prior to the conclusion of the contract, or (b) thereafter, in good time and in any event—(i) during the performance of the contract in the case of services; and (ii) at the latest at the time of delivery where goods not for delivery to third parties are concerned.[39] The additional information includes the conditions and procedures for exercising cancellation rights and the responsibility for the return (or recovery) of the goods and associated costs.[40] The supplier's business address must also be provided, as must information about any after-sales services and guarantees.[41] In the case of a contract for services, the consumer must be informed as to how the right to cancel may be affected by his agreeing to performance of the services beginning less than seven working days after the contract was concluded[42]; and where the contract is of unspecified duration or a duration exceeding one year the conditions for exercising any cancellation rights must be specified.[43]

Period for performance. The Regulations seek to combat problems associated with delayed performance by stipulating that, in the absence of agreement to the contrary, the supplier must perform the contract within a 14–056

[34] Reg. 7(1)(a)(vii). The consumer must also be informed of any intention to provide substitute goods or services (if those ordered are unavailable) and that the cost of returning any such goods is to be met by the supplier: reg. 7(1)(b) and (c). See also reg. 19(7).

[35] Reg. 7(3).

[36] Reg. 7(4).

[37] There is room for doubt as to when this requirement would be met. Professors Brownsword and Howells have noted (see 19 L.S. 287 at 303) that the DTI Consultation Paper considers (at para.2.5) that confirmation by electronic mail would suffice where the order has been made by these means and the consumer is the owner of the facilities from which the order is generated. The requirement means, in effect, that the medium must be capable of lasting (even though the confirmation may, in the result, be deleted) and be accessible, although not necessarily, it may be assumed, immediately so. Confirmation provided in response to orders placed via mobile 'phones which allow access to the internet (WAP or GPRS) or similarly by personal digital assistants (PDAs) should also qualify where the recipient has the capacity to store and display information and at least in modern versions to transfer it and print it off. A fortiori confirmation sent by fax where the order has been placed by fax should plainly be sufficient.

[38] Reg. 8(1) and (2)(a). The relevant information is that specified in reg. 7(1)(a)(i) to (vi).

[39] Reg. 8(1).

[40] Reg. 8(2)(b).

[41] Reg. 8(2)(c) and (d).

[42] Reg. 8(2)(b)(iii), which was inserted by SI 2005/689, reg. 2 and Sch., para.1(2). As to services, see also reg. 9.

[43] Reg. 8(2)(e).

maximum of 30 days.[44] Failing this, the consumer must be informed and within a maximum period of 30 days be reimbursed any sum paid by him or on his behalf.[45] The contract is then treated as if it had not been made, except that the consumer retains any rights or remedies under it as a result of the non-performance.[46] Where the supplier is unable to supply the goods or services ordered, an alternative may be substituted, but only where this was provided for in the contract and the necessary information was given before the contract was concluded.[47]

14–057 **Cancellation rights.** Another major feature of the Regulations is that they provide the consumer with cancellation rights during a "cooling off" period. Where notice of cancellation is properly given (and this must be in writing or in another durable medium available and accessible to the supplier)[48] the effect is that the contract is generally treated as if it had not been made.[49] The standard period is one of seven working days beginning with the day after the day on which the consumer receives the goods.[50] Alternative provisions apply where the supplier has failed to comply with the requirements as to giving information or has done so late[51] and separate provision is also made in the case of contracts for the supply of services.[52] Unless the parties have agreed otherwise, certain types of contracts are excluded from the right to cancel. These include contracts for the supply of goods made to the consumer's specifications, or which by reason of their nature cannot be returned or are liable to deteriorate or expire rapidly.[53] Also excluded are contracts for the supply of audio or video recordings or of computer software, if they are unsealed by the consumer.[54] Where cancellation rights exist and are exercised the supplier must reimburse the consumer within a maximum period of 30 days[55] and any related credit agreement is automatically cancelled.[56] There is a further entitlement to cancel a payment where fraudulent use has been made of a payment card in connection with a distant contract.[57]

---

[44] Reg. 19(1). This runs from the day after the order was sent to the supplier.
[45] Reg. 19(2) to (4). The period runs from the day after the day on which the period for performance expired. As to the effect of non-performance on a related credit agreement, see reg. 20.
[46] Reg. 19(5).
[47] Reg. 19(7). As to the information required, see reg. 7(1)(b) and (c).
[48] See reg. 10(3). For a reference to "durable" and "accessible" medium, see above, n.37; as to the detailed requirements for giving notice, see reg. 10(4) and (5).
[49] Reg. 10(2).
[50] Reg. 11(2). For the definition of "working days", see reg. 3(1).
[51] The period is then extended to three months and seven working days, if no information is given and received (reg. 11(4)), or if the information is given late but, within three months, seven working days from the day on which the information was received (reg. 11(3)).
[52] See reg. 12, as extensively amended (along with reg. 13) by SI 2005/689. reg. 2, Sch., paras 2 and 3.
[53] Reg. 13(1)(c).
[54] Reg. 13(1)(d). So too in the case of newspapers, periodicals or magazines—all of which may have a limited shelf life: reg. 13(1)(e).
[55] Reg. 14(1) and (3).
[56] Reg. 15. See also regs 16 (repayment of credit and interest following cancellation of a related credit agreement) and 18 (goods given in part exchange).
[57] Reg. 21. If the consumer maintains that use of the card was not authorised by him the card issuer must prove the contrary: reg. 21(3).

Restoration of goods. Following cancellation the consumer must take reasonable care of the goods and restore them to the supplier if he collects them.[58] In principle, he is not under a duty to return the goods,[59] but the contract may provide otherwise, although any such requirement and the associated obligation as to cost must have been notified.[60] It would not, in any event, apply if the consumer is entitled to reject the goods (for example, because they are not of satisfactory quality). Also, where the contract provides for the possibility of substitute goods the consumer must have been informed that the costs of returning any such goods in the event of cancellation would be met by the supplier.[61] A failure by a consumer to comply with a relevant duty as to restoration, etc. is actionable as a breach of statutory duty.[62] 14–058

Enforcement measures. Although the Regulations specifically provide that a contract term is void if and to the extent that it is inconsistent with their consumer protection measures,[63] this may be insufficient to ensure that they work well in practice. Accordingly, the Office of Fair Trading (formerly the Director-General of Fair Trading) and other designated enforcement authorities[64] are obliged to consider complaints about breaches of the Regulations (unless they appear frivolous or vexatious).[65] They may also apply for injunctions to restrain such breaches, which may be granted on such terms as the court thinks fit to secure compliance.[66] Since such breaches may also constitute a "Community infringement" for the purposes of Part 8 of the Enterprise Act 2002[67] (which has superseded the Stop Now Orders (EC Directive) Regulations 2001)[68] this alternative procedure is also available. 14–059

The Directive on electronic commerce.[69] This Directive which was implemented by the Electronic Commerce (EC Directive) Regulations 2002[70] is expressed as complementing information requirements established in a 14–060

---

58 Reg. 17(3). See also reg. 17(2) (duty to take care of goods prior to cancellation).
59 See reg. 17(4).
60 Reg. 8(2)(b).
61 Reg. 7(1)(c).
62 Reg. 17(10).
63 Reg. 25(1).
64 Defined by reg. 3(1) to include every weights and measures authority.
65 Reg. 26(1).
66 Reg. 27.
67 See s.212 and Sch.13, taken together with the Enterprise Act 2002 (Part 8 Community Infringements Specified UK Laws) Order 2003 (SI 2003/1374), art. 3 and Sch. Depending on the facts, a "domestic infringement" may also be present: see s.211 of the 2002 Act and the Enterprise Act 2002 (Part 8 Domestic Infringements) Order 2003 (SI 2003/1593), art.2(1), Sch., Part II, and, in general, below, para.14–130—14–136.
68 SI 2001/1422.
69 Directive 2000/31/EC ([2000] O.J. L178/1).
70 SI 2002/2013, as amended by, inter alia, SI 2003/115, SI 2003/2500 and SI 2004/1178. The scope of the Regulations is subject to a range of exclusions, for example in relation to taxation and data protection (reg. 3) and there are alternative sources of control in the broad area of financial services and markets.

range of consumer protection measures, particularly the Distance Selling Directive.[71] The overall objective is to contribute to the proper functioning of the internal market by ensuring the free movement of information society services between the Member States.[72] Since these include selling goods on-line they are relevant in the present context. The Directive covers such matters as basic general information which must be provided (name and address of the service provider including his electronic mail address, etc.),[73] information to be provided in commercial communications (including promotional offers and competitions),[74] and unsolicited commercial communications (which must be clearly identified as such).[75] Further provisions apply to contracts concluded by electronic means. These include obligations of ensuring that the conclusion of such contracts is not deprived of legal effectiveness,[76] information to be provided prior to the order being placed (*e.g.* the technical steps to follow to conclude the contract and to correct input errors)[77] and principles which are applicable where orders are placed by technological means. This includes such matters as acknowledging the receipt of the order and the ability to identify and correct input errors before the order is placed.[78] Such protection in relation to the placing of orders is obligatory in its application to consumers, as opposed to businesses.[79]

(g) *Rights of Buyer Against Manufacturer, Intermediate Distributor and Others*

14–061 **Manufacturer's tort liability at common law.** The person principally liable at common law in respect of a sale of defective goods is the seller. Sometimes, as in some mail order transactions, the manufacturer will sell directly to the consumer and thereby incur contractual liability. Usually, however, he will sell via an intermediary, for example a retailer. Although the latter may describe himself as an "agent" or "sole agent" for the manufacturer, he is not normally authorised to create a contract between manufacturer and consumer but simply buys from the manufacturer and sells to the consumer.[80] This statement seems obvious enough in a legal textbook, but in practice efforts are often made (*e.g.* in connection with the

[71] Directive 1997/7/EC ([1997] O.J. L144/19), implemented by the Consumer Protection (Distance Selling) Regulations 2000 (SI 2000/2334), above, paras 14–054 *et seq.*
[72] Directive 2000/31/EC, Art. 1.1.
[73] Art. 5 and the corresponding provision in reg. 6.
[74] Art. 6 and reg. 7.
[75] Art. 7 and reg. 8.
[76] Art 9.
[77] Art. 10 and reg. 9. This does not apply to contracts concluded exclusively by exchange of electronic mail or by equivalent individual communications (reg. 9(4)).
[78] Art. 11 and reg. 11. The same exception for electronic mail (see n.77, above) is applicable.
[79] See reg. 9(1) (information to be provided) and reg. 11(1) (placing of the order) which enable parties who are not consumers to "agree otherwise".
[80] *International Harvester Co. of Australia Pty Ltd v Carrigan's Hazeldene Pastoral Co.* (1958) 100 C.L.R. 644. For discussion of the question when such a person is a genuine agent, see above, paras 1–048 *et seq.*

sale of motor vehicles and electrical equipment) to suggest that a consumer's recourse is principally or solely against the manufacturer. It is true that manufacturers frequently in such cases assume or are willing to assume responsibility for replacement of defective goods or parts, servicing and the like (though the assumption of these duties is frequently contained in some form of guarantee and at least historically has been combined with attempts to exclude other duties); it is also true that manufacturers may have special complaints departments and may be willing to settle claims for the sake of their reputations where retailers might not. But the seller is the person primarily liable. Although it may be relatively unusual for a manufacturer to be directly liable to a consumer in contract, liability may be incurred more frequently in tort. Hitherto such an action would normally lie only in the tort of negligence, under the manufacturers' liability first established in *Donoghue v Stevenson*.[81] This head of liability has been largely superseded by the strict liability provisions of Part I of the Consumer Protection Act 1987. These are discussed below.[82] However, some claims will fall outside the scope of the Act, for example where the sole claim is in respect of property damage not exceeding £275[83] or where claims under the Act are barred by the 10-year cut-off point.[84] The tort of negligence will remain important in any such case. Generally, because of the need to prove negligence, such an action will be less advantageous than an action in contract or under the 1987 Act. Typically, the negligence will lie in the manufacturing process, but there may also be instances of negligence in design[85] or in failing to give an adequate warning of danger or instructions for safe use.[86] It seems that the claimant must show that on the balance of probabilities the defect arose in the course of manufacture,[87] and the maxim *res ipsa loquitur* will not normally be applicable.[88] This may cause serious problems in some cases where the alleged defect is in the production process. On the other hand the claimant need not specify exactly what the negligence was, and the very fact that goods are defective is of itself evidence of negligent manufacture, which may sometimes be difficult to rebut.[89] Although in one case evidence of a "foolproof" method

---

81 [1932] A.C. 562. See in general, in addition to the standard works on tort, Miller and Goldberg, *Product Liability* (2004), Chs. 14–17; Hird in Howells (ed.), *The Law of Product Liability* (2000), Ch.3; Miller, *Product Liability and Safety Encyclopaedia* (1979–2006), Div. III.

82 Below, para.14–080 *et seq.*

83 Consumer Protection Act 1987, s.5(4).

84 See the Limitation Act 1980, s.11A(3), implementing Art. 11 of the Directive; also, below, paras 14–092.

85 *e.g. Williams v Trimm Rock Quarries Ltd* (1965) 109 Sol.Jo. 454; *Walton v British Leyland UK Ltd* (unreported, 1968) Willis J.

86 *e.g. Vacwell Engineering Co. Ltd v BDH Chemicals Ltd* [1971] 1 Q.B. 111, varying [1971] 1 Q.B. 88; *Anglo-Celtic Shipping Co. Ltd v Elliott and Jeffery* (1926) 42 T.L.R. 297.

87 *Evans v Triplex Safety Glass Co. Ltd* [1936] 1 All E.R. 283; *Moorhead v Thomas Smith & Sons Ltd* [1963] 1 Lloyd's Rep. 164. See Miller and Goldberg, *Product Liability* (2004), paras 14.134–14.136; Winfield and Jolowicz, *Tort* (16th ed.), para.5.63; Markesinis and Deakin's *Tort Law* (5th ed.), pp.606–607, 629.

88 See *Donoghue v Stevenson*, above, at p.622; *Mason v Williams and Williams Ltd* [1955] 1 W.L.R. 549 and for a review, Witting, 117 L.Q.R. 392 (2001).

89 See *Grant v Australian Knitting Mills* [1936] A.C. 85 at 101; *Mason v Williams and Williams Ltd*, above.

of manufacture was accepted as disproving negligence,[90] it is thought that the case is exceptional.[91] Where the defective manufacture leads to both physical damage to person or property and to consequential pecuniary loss both will normally be recoverable. If, however, only pecuniary loss is caused, or if the complaint is solely as to a defect in the goods themselves, liability will be incurred only in exceptional cases.[92]

14–062 **Representations and collateral contracts.** In principle a false representation by a manufacturer may lead to liability in tort: but statements (*e.g.* in advertisements) are often too vague to ground liability, and there may also be difficulty in establishing the relevant duty of care.[93] Thus in *Lambert v Lewis*[94] it was held that a manufacturer was not liable to a *retailer* in respect of statements in promotional literature. Sometimes, however, a specific promise or statement is made by or on behalf of a manufacturer which can be regarded as an offer of an independent collateral contract[95] made between manufacturer and eventual buyer. Examples are provided by manufacturers' guarantees, which are discussed below.[96] But there can be other cases. Thus in *Shanklin Pier Ltd v Detel Products Ltd*[97] paint manufacturers represented to the owners of a pier that a paint which they manufactured was suitable for repainting the pier. In reliance on this the pier owners specified to the contractor that this paint should be used. The manufacturers were held to have warranted the suitability of the paint. In such cases therefore a manufacturer may have placed on him the strict liability normally associated with the law of contract. And in the famous case of *Carlill v Carbolic Smoke Ball Co.*[98] manufacturers of a patent medical preparation were held liable on a promise, contained in an advertisement, to pay £1,000 to anyone who used the medicine as prescribed and nevertheless caught influenza. Such contracts will normally be unilateral, *i.e.* the offer will be accepted by (in these cases) doing an act such as specifying the particular paint to be used, or buying or using the

[90] *Daniels and Daniels v R White & Sons Ltd* [1938] 4 All E.R. 258 (criticised, 55 L.Q.R. 6, 352 (1939)).

[91] It was not followed in *Hill v James Crowe (Cases) Ltd* [1978] 1 All E.R. 812. See also *Martin v Thorn Ltd* [1978] W.A.R. 10; *Carroll v Fearon* [1998] P.I.Q.R. P416, *The Times*, January 26, 1998.

[92] See above, para.12–126.

[93] Above, para.12–013.

[94] [1982] A.C. 225; reversed on other grounds: *ibid.*, 271. See also *Muirhead v Industrial Tank Specialities Ltd* [1986] Q.B. 507 at 528–529. But *cf.* Borrie, *The Development of Consumer Law and Practice—Bold Spirits and Timorous Souls* (1984), pp.30–32, suggesting that consumers may rely heavily on promotional literature.

[95] Above, para.10–012.

[96] Below, paras 14–065 *et seq.* Note, in particular, Directive 1999/44/EC, Art. 6.1 which provides that: "A guarantee shall be legally binding on the offerer under the conditions laid down in the guarantee statement *and the associated advertising*." (emphasis supplied). This provision is implemented by the Sale and Supply of Goods to Consumers Regulations 2002 (SI 2002/3045), reg. 15(1).

[97] [1951] 2 K.B. 854; see also *Wells (Merstham) Ltd v Buckland Sand and Silica Ltd* [1965] 2 Q.B. 170 (where there was no particular sale in view when the warranty was given).

[98] [1893] 1 Q.B. 256.

smoke ball. Careful attention must be paid to the question whether the doing of the act can really be regarded as consideration for the promise: in this respect *Carlill's* case can be regarded as very near the borderline.[99] And the promise must be clear. No such contract was derived from the promotional literature in *Lambert v Lewis*.[1]

Intermediate distributors and others. An intermediate distributor may sometimes be subject to strict liability under the Consumer Protection Act 1987. The scope of any such liability is discussed below.[2] In principle, he may also be liable in negligence. But it may be difficult to point to any negligent act, for such a person usually does no more than pass on goods received from the manufacturer. Cases could arise, however, where he might be liable, *e.g.* where he knows or has reason to know that goods are or may be dangerous or dangerously packaged,[3] where he has the responsibility of labelling or packaging products and does so negligently, where it is his duty to release perishable products for resale within a certain period and he negligently releases them after that period, or where it is he who puts goods into circulation, as where they are in his "own brand" packages, imported,[4] or secondhand.[5] Cases may also arise where he is liable for representations, whether in tort or upon a collateral contract. Under similar general principles such other persons as assemblers, repairers and those who hire out products may also incur liability in negligence.[6] 14–063

Part 20 proceedings. Another way of involving the manufacturer or intermediate distributor is by Part 20 (previously known as third- and fourth-party) proceedings. If the buyer sues the seller in contract, the seller may be entitled to an indemnity from the intermediate distributor (if any) and the intermediate distributor from the manufacturer: each may bring the 14–064

---

[99] For a case even nearer the borderline, see *Wood v Letrik Ltd, The Times*, January 13, 1932 (electric comb).

[1] Above. See, however, *Bowerman v Association of British Travel Agents Ltd, The Times*, November 24, 1995, applying the decision in *Carlill's* case to create a contractual relationship between the customer of a failed ABTA tour operator and ABTA itself. In another much publicised incident in 1992–93 the Hoover "free flights" campaign is said to have led to many successful claims: see (*e.g.*) [1995] C.L.Y. para.1570.

[2] See below, paras 14–080 *et seq*. Liability may be incurred, *e.g.* if the distributor is an "own-brander" (s.2(2)(b)), an importer from a non-EC country (s.2(2)(c)), or even a "mere" supplier (s.2(3)).

[3] *Watson v Buckley, Osborne, Garrett & Co. Ltd* [1940] 1 All E.R. 174; and see *Fisher v Harrods Ltd* [1966] 1 Lloyd's Rep. 500 (where the manufacturer had an issued capital of £500, had never made a trading profit and was not insured against liability)

[4] See *Goodchild v Vaclight* [1965] C.L.Y. para.2669.

[5] See *Herschtal v Stewart and Ardern Ltd* [1904] 1 K.B. 155; *Andrews v Hopkinson* [1957] 1 Q.B. 229. See also *Malfroot v Noxal Ltd* (1935) 51 T.L.R. 551.

[6] See, *e.g. Malfroot v Noxal Ltd* (1935) 51 T.L.R. 551 (assembler); *Haseldine v CA Daw & Son Ltd* [1941] 2 K.B. 343 (repairer); *Stennett v Hancock and Peters* [1939] 2 All E.R. 578 (repairer); *Griffiths v Arch Engineering Co. Ltd* [1968] 3 All E.R. 217 (hirer-out).

party from whom he bought the article in as Part 20 defendants.[7] Where this is effected the manufacturer, who is most likely to be in a position to meet the claim, can be brought into the proceedings. It will be seen, however, that this expedient is cumbrous and may be expensive; it is not within the control of the first claimant that this should occur; and should the intermediate distributor be insolvent or have gone out of business the manufacturer could be brought in as liable, if at all, in tort or upon a collateral contract.[8]

(h) *Manufacturers' Guarantees*[9]

14–065 **Introduction.** Manufacturers, especially in the case of commodities in respect of which they undertake servicing, such as electrical equipment, frequently purport to "guarantee" or "warrant" their goods in certain respects. Indeed, it might be argued that such guarantees covering spare parts and service facilities should be obligatory, at least in the case of a limited number of consumer goods. However, any such obligation would not sit easily alongside the reluctance of English law to impose liability for what are essentially economic losses.[10] Where such guarantees are provided they may be contained in the main contract with the retailer or may be set out on a separate document, sometimes attached to the goods. This will then operate in addition to the buyer's rights (*e.g.* to receive goods which are of satisfactory quality under the contract of sale) and not in diminution of them.[11] Indeed, it is an offence for a manufacturer to supply goods which become the subject of a consumer transaction, or to furnish a document in relation to them, without making it clear in an accompanying statement

---

[7] See *Kasler and Cohen v Slavouski* [1928] 1 K.B. 78; *Kubach v Hollands* [1937] 3 All E.R. 907; *Dodd and Dodd v Wilson and McWilliam* [1946] 2 All E.R. 691; *Godley v Perry* [1960] 1 W.L.R. 9.

[8] *e.g. Lambert v Lewis* [1982] A.C. 255 (where it could not be established who the intermediate distributor was).

[9] Trebilcock, 18 McGill L.J. 1 (1972); Miller and Goldberg, *Product Liability* (2004), paras.3.54–3.60; *Final Report of the Committee on Consumer Protection* (the Molony Committee) (Cmnd. 1781, 1962), Ch.12; *Consumer Guarantees: a report by the Director General of Fair Trading* (OFT, 1986); *The Consumer Guarantee* (National Consumer Council, 1989); European Commission, *Green Paper on Guarantees for Consumer Goods and After-Sales Services*, COM (93) 509 final, 1993; *Consumer Guarantees*, a Consultation Document issued by the DTI, February 1992; Report of the House of Lords Select Committee on the European Communities, Consumer Guarantees (1996–97 HL 57); Weatherill, 110 L.Q.R. 545 (1994); Clark [1993] J.B.L. 383; Twigg-Flesner [1999] J.B.L. 568. For North American examples, see the Ontario Law Reform Commission, Report on Consumer Warranties and Guarantees in the Sale of Goods (1972), Pt III; Priest, 90 Yale L.J. 1297 (1981); Whitford, 91 Yale L.J. 1371 (1982). Such guarantees can be made the subject of general statutory control. A famous example is the U.S. Magnuson-Moss Warranty Act of 1975 (15 U.S.C. paras 2301–2312): as to which see, *e.g.* Lee, 51 Indiana L.J. 397 (1976); Vickers [1979] J.B.L. 406.

[10] See the Law Commission report, *Implied Terms in Contracts for the Supply of Goods*, Law Com. No. 95 (1979), paras 115–128 and the report on Sale and Supply of Goods, Law Com. No. 104 (1987), para.3.66.

[11] *cf. Rogers v Parish (Scarborough) Ltd* [1987] Q.B. 933 at 945, *per* Mustill L.J.; also Directive 1999/44/EC, Art. 6.2.

that the guarantee or undertaking does not affect the consumers' statutory rights.[12]

14–066 At common law there has always been an element of doubt as to the circumstances in which manufacturers' guarantees become contractually binding. In large measure these doubts will have been removed following the implementation of Article 6 of Directive 1999/44/EC on certain aspects of the sale of consumer goods and associated guarantees[13] by the Sale and Supply of Goods to Consumers Regulations 2002.[14] However, to the extent that it is necessary to fall back on the common law,[15] then, at least on a traditional analysis, the guarantee will be contractually binding only where offer, acceptance and consideration can be found in accordance with standard principles. An offer of a guarantee may operate as one of a unilateral contract accepted by the purchase of the goods from a retailer.[16] The buyer can then sue the manufacturer provided, at least, that he knew of the guarantee before buying the goods[17] and possibly also if they are of such a general type (*e.g.* a television set or a video recorder) as would almost invariably be covered by a manufacturers' guarantee. Even where a guarantee is not expressed as being limited to the first owner of the goods, it is much less easy to build up a contract between the manufacturer and a subsequent purchaser or donee. It might be possible to argue that the mere act of signing and sending in an acceptance slip to register the guarantee would suffice, the act being characterised both as an acceptance and as the furnishing of consideration.[18] In support of this argument, it is widely accepted that the registration of guarantees provides significant benefit to manufacturers (both in terms of quality control and marketing) whilst the completion and posting of an acceptance slip is not without cost in terms of time and perhaps money.

14–067 **Content and interpretation.** The content of manufacturers' guarantees is, in the nature of things, so variable that generalisations have little value. Typically, there will be a promise to replace defective parts free of any additional charge. This may extend to the cost of labour and/or carriage, but, of course, need not do so. There will also be variations between manufacturers and products in the duration, transferability and territorial

---

[12] Consumer Transactions (Restrictions on Statements) Order 1976 (SI 1976/1813) as amended by SI 1978/127, art. 5. See also below, para.14–142.

[13] [1999] O.J. L171/12.

[14] SI 2002/3045, reg. 15. See further below, paras 14–070—14–075.

[15] The most obvious case in which the necessity may arise is where the person seeking to enforce the guarantee is not a "consumer" for the purposes of Art. 6 and reg. 15; see below, para.14–071

[16] *Carlill v Carbolic Smoke Ball Co.* [1893] 1 Q.B. 256 provides the classic example of such a contract, albeit that acceptance and consideration lay in using, rather than buying, the notorious smoke ball.

[17] *cf. Roscorla v Thomas* (1842) 3 Q.B. 234 (warranty of horse given after sale not enforceable).

[18] See, in a different context, *Chappell & Co. Ltd v Nestlé Co. Ltd* [1960] A.C. 87 (wrappers on chocolate bars part of consideration, although thrown away on receipt).

scope of guarantees. Claims under guarantees may be treated more or less generously, but in the context of litigation (which appears to be conspicuously absent) they will succeed only if the terms of the specific guarantee cover the situation which has arisen. So, in an analogous context it has been held that a clause purporting to "guarantee the efficacy" of dry-rot treatment, which went on to promise to treat timbers reinfested within 10 years free of charge, was to be read as a whole, as constituting no more than a promise to treat timber reinfested within the period, and did not involve a promise to answer for other loss caused by reinfestation.[19]

14–068 **Exemption of manufacturer.** Historically, a major aim of manufacturers' "guarantees" was not the provision of benefits to consumers, but rather the removal of rights. Indeed, the Molony Committee report on Consumer Protection saw the main criticism of the law of sale of goods as being "the ease and frequency with which vendors and manufacturers of goods exclude the operation of the statutory conditions and warranties by provisions in guarantee cards or other contractual documents."[20] In effect, buyers were given limited benefits under the guarantee going beyond those which would otherwise have been available against the manufacturer (*e.g.* the replacement of defective parts) in return for which they agreed to forego any other claims against the manufacturer or even the retailer. The extension of exemption to the latter was unlikely to be effective by virtue of the rules of privity of contract, unless the exemption was also incorporated into the main contract of sale.[21]

14–069 **Unfair Contract Terms Act.** The earlier problems associated with so called manufacturers' guarantees which operated as a disguised form of exemption clauses are now subject to effective statutory control. First, they are subject to section 2(1) of the Unfair Contract Terms Act 1977, which renders ineffective purported exclusions of liability for death or personal injury caused by negligence.[22] An equivalent provision is contained in section 7 of the Consumer Protection Act 1987.[23] In principle they are also subject to sections 2(2) and 3 of the 1977 Act[24]: but these impose only a requirement of reasonableness, and far stronger protection for the

[19] *Adams v Richardson and Starling Ltd* [1969] 1 W.L.R. 1645. It seems, however, that the common law duty of care (an action on which was barred by limitation) was not excluded. For a successful claim under a specialist company's 20-year guarantee against reinfestation by dry rot, see *Ackerman v Protim Services* [1988] 2 E.G.L.R. 259, CA.

[20] Cmnd. 1781 (1962), para.426, Chapter 12 of this Report contains detailed coverage of the then contemporary problems associated with exemption clauses.

[21] For this reason the complexities of *A M Satterthwaite & Co. Ltd v New Zealand Shipping Co. Ltd (The Eurymedon)* [1975] A.C. 154; *Salmond and Spraggon (Australia) Pty Ltd v Port Jackson Stevedoring Pty Ltd (The New York Star)* [1981] 1 W.L.R. 138, and *The Mahkutai* [1996] A.C. 650 would not normally have been relevant.

[22] Above, para.13–092.

[23] Below, para.14–083.

[24] Above, paras 13–093 *et seq*. And in the case of contractual liability to the Unfair Terms in Consumer Contracts Regulations 1999, (SI 1999/2083), since manufacturers are both sellers and suppliers of goods.

consumer is afforded by section 5. This provides: "In the case of goods of a type ordinarily supplied for private use or consumption, where loss or damage—(a) arises from the goods proving defective while in consumer use: and (b) results from the negligence of a person concerned in the manufacture or distribution of the goods, liability for the loss or damage cannot be excluded or restricted by reference to any contract term or notice contained in or operating by reference to a guarantee of the goods." The manufacturer's freedom to exclude his negligence (though not any other) liability by means of a guarantee[25] is therefore eliminated in many situations, and it is submitted that this covers all his negligence liability, including such limited liability as may exist in respect of economic loss.[26] A consequence of this is that if the surrender of rights against the manufacturer is the only consideration for a promise to repair or replace, the latter promise could be unenforceable for want of consideration. Other consideration would not normally, however, be hard to find. The category of "goods ordinarily supplied for private use or consumption" appears elsewhere in the Act.[27] It should be noted that "consumer use" is defined as involving use or possession for use otherwise than *exclusively* for the purposes of a business, which is a wide definition[28]; and that the subsection applies only between manufacturer or distributor and consumer.[29] The position between consumer and retailer is not affected by it, but is regulated by the central provisions of the Act applicable to contracts generally, and by those applicable to contracts of sale in particular.[30] If a term of a manufacturer's guarantee were to seek to prevent a consumer from suing a retailer under the contract of sale it would be an attempted evasion of the retailer's statutory liability by means of a secondary contract. As such it would be rendered ineffective by section 10 of the Unfair Contract Terms Act 1977.[31]

Implementing Directive 1999/44/EC. In recent years important modifications have been introduced into English law as a result of implementing Article 6 of Directive 1999/44/EC on certain aspects of the sale of consumer goods and associated guarantees.[32] The relevant implementing provisions are contained in regulation 15 of the Sale and Supply of Goods to Consumers Regulations 2002[33] which should be read in conjunction with Article 6 of the Directive. The first point to note is that the new provisions do not require that any guarantee be given in relation to goods of whatever kind, nor even that a document described as a "guarantee" should 14–070

[25] Widely defined in s.5(2)(b).
[26] Above, para.12–126.
[27] See s.12(1)(c), above, para.13–081.
[28] s.5(2)(a); *e.g.* it would cover defects in a "company car" in private use at the weekends.
[29] s.5(3).
[30] ss.2, 3, 4, 6, 7: above, paras 13–062 *et seq*.
[31] Above, para.13–097. Such an attempted exclusion might also constitute an offence under the Consumer Transactions (Restrictions on Statements) Order 1976 (SI 1976/1813), as amended; see below, para.14–142.
[32] [1999] O.J. L172/12.
[33] SI 2002/3045.

incorporate basic minimum conditions which give consumers additional rights.[34] The central provision in regulation 15(1) provides, rather, that: "Where goods are sold or otherwise supplied to a consumer which are offered with a consumer guarantee, the consumer guarantee takes effect at the time the goods are delivered as a contractual obligation owed by the guarantor under the conditions set out in the guarantee statement and the associated advertising."[35] In short, in any such case the traditional common law requirements for establishing a contractual obligation are dispensed with and the guarantee will be accorded a statutory contractual status and take effect according to its terms. For the purposes of the Regulations a "consumer guarantee" is defined broadly[36] to mean: "[A]ny undertaking to a consumer by a person acting in the course of his business, given without extra charge,[37] to reimburse the price paid or to replace, repair or handle consumer goods[38] in any way if they do not meet the specifications set out in the guarantee statement or in the relevant advertising."

14–071 In order to benefit from these provisions the person to whom the goods which are linked to the consumer guarantee are sold or otherwise supplied[39] must be a "consumer", which term is defined to mean "any natural person who, in the contracts covered by these Regulations, is acting for purposes which are outside his trade, business or profession."[40] The first element of the definition excludes claimants who are not "natural persons" or, as it might otherwise have been expressed, "individuals".[41] So, a corporate body would not qualify even if it could be regarded as "dealing as consumer" for the purposes of the Unfair Contract Terms Act 1977.[42] The

---

[34] However, there are various provisions (in reg. 15(2), (3) and (5)) which seek to ensure transparency: see further, below, para.14–073.

[35] The somewhat more succinct version in Art. 6.1 of the Directive states that: "A guarantee shall be legally binding on the offerer under the conditions laid down in the guarantee statement and the associated advertising."

[36] See reg. 2. Art.1.2(e) of the Directive is in similar terms.

[37] Accordingly, where an "extra charge" is made the Regulations will not apply, although, depending on the type of goods involved, the situation may fall within alternative controls over extended warranties (see above, para.14–043). Obviously, the cost of any guarantee is reflected in the price of the goods being sold, but the sense of reg. 2 is that a charge will be "extra" only when it is stated separately and not simply built into the price payable.

[38] The expression "consumer goods" is not defined. However, the relevant definition in Art. 1.2(b) of the Directive is very broad and excludes only "goods sold by way of execution or otherwise by authority of law, water and gas where they are not put up for sale in a limited volume or set quantity, electricity."

[39] "Supply" includes supply by way of sale, lease, hire or hire purchase" (see reg. 2). It is submitted that in this context the word "includes" should not be understood as being synonymous with "means". Otherwise, supply under such transactions as contracts for work and materials would not be covered. See also as to the position of donees, etc., below, para.14–072.

[40] See reg. 2.

[41] See Joined Cases C-541/99 and C-542/99 *Cape SNC v Idealservice Srl.*; *Idealservice MN RE SAS v OMAI Srl* [2001] E.C.R. 1–9049. The context was the meaning of the expression "natural person" in Directive 93/13/EEC on unfair terms in consumer contracts, but the principle is the same.

[42] In particular, s.12 as interpreted in such cases as *R & B Customs Brokers Ltd v United Dominions Trust Ltd* [1988] 1 W.L.R. 321; see above, paras 13–074 and 14–029.

second element is apt to exclude such individuals as sole traders or professionals, unless they are acting for purposes which are "outside" or, in the words of the Directive,[43] "not related to" their trade, etc. Such a requirement would not be satisfied if (say) a trader or professional acquired a water cooler or an electric kettle for use on business premises; nor indeed would it be satisfied where the acquisition is both for personal and business use (as perhaps with a laptop computer or a digital camera). In any such case the recipient of the guarantee would have to fall back on the common law.[44]

Subject to the above, there are further elements of doubt as to who is entitled to benefit from the above provisions. As has been noted,[45] regulation 15(1) envisages that the goods be "sold or otherwise supplied to a consumer" but it does not in terms state that the contractual obligation attributed to the corresponding guarantee is owed only to the consumer to whom the goods were originally sold or supplied. A number of scenarios might be envisaged. For example, the guarantee may be clearly expressed as being non-transferable. In that event, it seems clear that it should benefit the original transferee only. At the other extreme, it may state that it is "fully transferable" or the like. In such a case it is submitted that donees and sub-purchasers should be contractually entitled to claim under the guarantee, provided, at least, that both they and the original transferee are "consumers" within the meaning of the Regulations.[46] The intermediate case is one where the guarantee makes no reference to the issue of transferability. It is submitted that in such cases it should be assumed, in the absence of clear implications to the contrary, that it is in principle transferable, subject again to the proviso that all relevant parties are individuals who acquire the goods as "consumers". Otherwise, the reform would be distinctly piecemeal and frequently depend for its efficacy on the original contracting party being willing to step in and enforce its terms. **14–072**

There are a number of provisions in the Directive which seek to promote clarity and transparency. These are reflected in regulation 15. Thus regulation 15(2) requires the guarantor to ensure that the guarantee sets out "in plain intelligible language" the contents of the guarantee, the essential particulars necessary for making claims under it, notably its duration and territorial scope, and the name and address of the guarantor.[47] Further, when the guarantee relates to consumer goods which are offered within the territory of the United Kingdom the guarantor must ensure that the consumer guarantee is written in English.[48] Also, on request by a **14–073**

---

[43] Art. 1.2(a).
[44] As to which, see above, para.14–066.
[45] See above, para.14–070.
[46] A possible implication to the contrary may be suggested by Art. 6.2, which refers (see below, para.14–075) to a consumer's legal rights under sales legislation and at least for the purposes of English law a donee, etc. usually has no such rights. Also, in the case of a donee, a problem would arise if the definition of the word "supply" in reg. 2 is read (contrary to the view advanced in n.39, above) as being exhaustive, rather than as stating that the listed transactions are included within the definition.
[47] See also Art. 6.2 (second indent) of the Directive.
[48] See reg. 15(5); also Art. 6.4.

consumer to the guarantor, or to any other person who offers[49] to consumers the goods which are the subject of the guarantee for sale or supply, the guarantee must within a reasonable time be made available in writing or in another durable medium which is available and accessible to him.[50]

14–074 It is clear from the Directive, although not stated expressly in regulation 15, that a failure to respect the above requirements does not affect the validity of the guarantee or the consumer's entitlement to rely on it.[51] A failure on the part of the guarantor to honour its terms is actionable as a breach of contract and, in principle, the same is true where loss is incurred as a result of non-compliance with other requirements such as that of making the guarantee available to the consumer in writing, etc.[52] However, an action for damages for breach of contract is by no means the sole remedy. An enforcement authority[53] may also apply for an injunction to secure compliance with the requirements of the Regulations as outlined above.[54] Alternatively, since the Directive is a "listed Directive" for the purposes of the Community infringement provisions of Part 8 of the Enterprise Act 2002, injunctions may be sought by virtue of that source of control.[55]

14–075 Finally, the Directive also requires that the guarantee shall "state that the consumer has legal rights under applicable national legislation governing the sale of consumer goods and make clear that those rights are not affected by the guarantee."[56] The latter element is already covered in English law,[57] but the relevant provision does not in terms demand that consumers be informed that they *have* rights under sales legislation. The familiar statement, "This does not affect your statutory rights" would not necessarily be understood to carry the more positive implication.

---

[49] The word "offer" is clearly being used in a colloquial sense which discounts the fact that in English law it is usually the consumer buyer who would make the offer (see (*e.g.*) *Fisher v Bell* [1961] 1 Q.B. 394).

[50] See reg. 15(3); also Art. 6.3. For a reference to the expression "another durable medium which is available and accessible to him", see above, para.14–055, n.37.

[51] Art. 6.5.

[52] It is doubtful whether this applies also to a person who is not a guarantor and who (as a retailer) simply supplies goods which are covered by a guarantee provided by another. It is the "guarantor" (that is, the person who offers a consumer guarantee to a consumer: see reg. 2) who is subject to the contractual obligation envisaged by reg. 15(1).

[53] As defined by reg. 2.

[54] See reg. 15(6) and (7).

[55] See, generally, below, paras 14–130—14–136. Regulation 15 is listed as a corresponding specified UK law giving effect to part of Directive 1999/44/EC (see the Enterprise Act 2002 (Part 8 Community Infringements Specified UK Laws) Order 2003 (SI 2003/1374), art. 3 and Sch).

[56] Art. 6.2 (first indent).

[57] By the Consumer Transactions (Restrictions on Statements) Order 1976 (SI 1976/813), as amended (see above, para.14–069, n.31; below, para.14–142).

(i) *Rights of a User Who Did Not Buy the Product*

Remedies in tort. In England a user who did not buy, but who is injured by, a defective product (*e.g.* a person to whom the buyer gives it or a bystander) may have an action in the tort of negligence against the manufacturer, intermediate distributor or seller or an assembler, repairer or hirer-out, under the principle laid down in *Donoghue v Stevenson*.[58] In an appropriate case he may also have an action under the strict liability provisions of Part I of the Consumer Protection Act 1987 which are discussed below.[59] An action in the tort of negligence is of course subject to the limitations already mentioned.[60] In particular, the claimant must prove negligence and he may also encounter very considerable difficulty if his only loss is pecuniary and not consequential upon damage to person or property. 14–076

Contract. Occasionally such a person may be held to have an action on a separate contract, whether made through the agency of the actual buyer or directly. Thus in *Lockett v A and M Charles Ltd*[61] a husband and wife ate a meal at an hotel as a result of which the wife suffered food poisoning. There was no evidence as to the contractual position except that a man and a woman sat at a table and ordered food, for which the man paid. It was held that there was a contract between the wife and the hotel as well as one between the husband and the hotel and that the wife could sue. But this is simply a decision on the facts: there must be many situations where it is clear that meals are purchased by one person for others to consume.[62] In such a case the buyer can recover in respect of damage suffered by a third party if he himself suffers loss arising out of that damage, *e.g.* by paying medical expenses.[63] Also, in a limited number of cases it may be possible to 14–077

---

[58] [1932] A.C. 562. See, generally, Miller and Goldberg, *Product Liability* (2004), esp. Chs.14–17. An employee injured by defective equipment may be able to sue his employer under the Employer's Liability (Defective Equipment) Act 1969. There is the further, and more general, possibility of an action arising by virtue of the provisions imposing criminal liability in Part II of the Consumer Protection Act 1987: see below, paras 14–115 *et seq*.

[59] Below, paras 14–080 *et seq*.

[60] Above, para.14–061. As to exclusion clauses in manufacturers' guarantees see above, paras 14–068—14–069. For examples of a successful action, see *Kubach v Hollands* [1937] 3 All E.R. 907; *Stennett v Hancock and Peters* [1939] 2 All E.R. 578. *Hill v James Crowe (Cases) Ltd* [1978] 1 All E.R. 812; *Carroll v Fearon*, [1998] P.I.Q.R. P416, *The Times*, January 26, 1998. *Cf. Abouzaid v Mothercare (UK) Ltd* [2000] All E.R. (D) 2436, *The Times*, February 20, 2001 where the claim failed in negligence but succeeded under the 1987 Act.

[61] [1938] 4 All E.R. 170. See also *Cockerton v Naviera Aznar SA* [1960] 2 Lloyd's Rep. 450; *Hollingworth v Southern Ferries Ltd (The Eagle)* [1977] 2 Lloyd's Rep. 70; *Daly v General Steam Navigation Co. Ltd (The Dragon)* [1980] 2 Lloyd's Rep. 415 (boat tickets); *McRobertson Miller Airline Services v Commr. of State Taxation (W.A.)* (1975) 133 C.L.R. 125 at 147 (airline tickets); *Hobbs v L & SW Ry Co.* (1875) L.R. 10 Q.B. 111; *Cooke v Midland Ry Co.* (1892) 9 T.L.R. 147 (railway tickets); *Walls v Centaur Co. Ltd* (1921) 126 L.T. 242 (purchase from manufacturer by employee of dealer, at discount, for employee's personal use).

[62] See *Buckley v La Reserve* [1959] C.L.Y. para.1330.

[63] As in *Preist v Last* [1903] 2 K.B. 148, where a claimant whose wife was scalded by water escaping from a defective hot water bottle which he had purchased recovered for medical expenses. See also *Jackson v Watson & Sons* [1909] 2 K.B. 193.

claim under the Contracts (Rights of Third Parties) Act 1999[64] or on some other basis.[65] However, such situations are unusual and in English law there are no general provisions for an extended liability where damage or loss is caused by defective products.

14–078 **Products liability: United States.** Further developments have occurred in this area in the United States of America. First, section 2–318 of the Uniform Commercial Code extended the benefits of a seller's warranty to personal injuries suffered by any person who is in the family or household of the buyer or who is a guest in his home. This is a narrow formulation and has not been adopted in all states: the authorities responsible for the Code subsequently produced two variants,[66] the first extending liability towards "any natural person who may be expected to use, consume or be affected by the goods and who is injured in person," and a further variant omitting the requirement that the injury be personal. In a related development it has been held that when a manufacturer gives an express warranty, he may be held liable on it, effectively in tort, to a consumer, notwithstanding the absence of a contract with the consumer. Thus in *Baxter v Ford Motor Co.*[67] the manufacturer of a motor car was held liable to a person who had bought from a retailer, on a statement in advertisements that the car was equipped with a "shatterproof" windscreen. Historically this can be justified more easily than might appear, for the idea of warranty was not always so closely connected with contract as modern English law requires.[68] Further, he may in some jurisdictions be liable in contract to a third party on an *implied* statutory warranty of merchantability or the like, again despite the absence of privity. Thus in the famous case of *Henningsen v Bloomfield Motors Inc.*[69] the wife of the buyer of a car, to whom the buyer had given the car, was permitted to sue the dealer and the manufacturer for breach of statutory implied warranty. Finally, any commercial seller of a product, which can include manufacturer, producer, assembler, distributor or retailer, may simply be held strictly liable in tort to any person within the area of risk, regardless of the particular restrictions of any express or statutory warranty. Thus in *Greenman v Yuba Power Products Inc.*[70] the

---

[64] See above, para.14–019.

[65] See (*e.g.*) *Woodar Investment Development Ltd v Wimpey Construction U.K. Ltd* [1980] 1 W.L.R. 277 at 297, *per* Lord Keith of Kinkel, discussing *Jackson v Horizon Holidays Ltd* [1975] 1 W.L.R. 1468 (holiday for family); see also pp.283 (where Lord Wilberforce suggests that the ordering of a meal in a restaurant may be part of a group of situations calling for special treatment), 293, 300–301; Treitel, *The Law of Contract* (11th ed.), pp.593 *et seq*.

[66] Alternatives B and C. For discussion of these provisions, including amendments introduced to the Uniform Commercial Code in 2003, see Miller and Goldberg, *Product Liability* (2004), paras 2.17–2.20.

[67] 12 P. 2d 409; 15 P. 2d 1118; 35 P. 2d 1090 (1934). See also *Randy Knitwear Inc. v American Cyanamid Co.* 11 N.Y. 2d 5, 181 N.E. 2d (1962) where the claim was for economic loss.

[68] Ames, 2 Harv.L.R. 1 (1888); Stoljar, 15 M.L.R. 425 at 427 (1952) and material there cited; Greig, 87 L.Q.R. 179 (1971); above, para.10–015.

[69] 161 A. 2d 69 (1960).

[70] 377 P. 2d 897 (1962). See also *Escola v Coca-Cola Bottling Co.* 150 P. 2d 436 (1944).

husband of the buyer of a power tool, to whom the buyer had given it as a present, was permitted to sue the manufacturer in tort though the statutory implied warranty was for technical reasons not available.

In the highly influential American Law Institute's *Restatement, Second, Torts* (1965), para.402A, liability was expressed as being in respect of products sold in a "defective condition unreasonably dangerous to the user or consumer or to his property".[71] It might be incurred even though the seller had exercised all possible care in the preparation and sale of the product and irrespective of any contractual relation with the user or consumer.[72] The developing case law indicated that persons who were neither users nor consumers (*e.g.* bystanders) could similarly recover and occasionally liability was extended to instances of economic loss.[73] There is an enormous literature on this part of the law[74] and considerable differences in its development from one jurisdiction to another. More recently in 1997 a significant revision was undertaken in the *Restatement (Third) of Torts: Products Liability*.[75] This provides that a person who is "engaged in the business of selling or distributing products who sells or distributes a defective product is subject to liability for harm caused by the defect."[76] However, the crucial words "defective" and "defect" are then defined differently according to the type of defect involved. For manufacturing or production defects liability is strict and will be incurred "even though all 14–079

[71] Not all decisions insisted on the "unreasonably dangerous" requirement: see (*e.g.*) *Cronin v JBE Olson Corp.*, 104 Cal.Rptr. 433 (1972) (Cal.Sup.Ct.).
[72] para.402A (2).
[73] See, *e.g.*, *Santor v A and M Karagheusian Inc.* 207 A.2d 305 (1965), but *cf. Seely v White Motor Co.* 45 Cal.Rptr. 17 (1965); *Spring Motors Distributors v Ford Motor Co.* 489 A.2d 660 (1985); *East River Steamship Corp. v Transamerica Delavel Inc.* 476 U.S. 858 (1986). However, the modern trend is against allowing recovery under a strict liability theory for pure economic loss.
[74] Four earlier and leading English articles are Legh-Jones [1969] C.L.J. 54; Pasley, 32 M.L.R. 241 (1969); Jolowicz, 32 M.L.R. 1 (1969); and Waddams, 37 M.L.R. 154 (1974); and see also Miller & Lovell, *Product Liability* (1977). There are two famous American articles by Prosser, 69 Yale L.J. 1099 (1960) and 50 Minn.L.R. 791 (1966) and others by Keeton, 41 Tex. L.R. 855 (1963) and Traynor, 32 Tenn. L.R. 363 (1965). For a recent authoritative survey, see Owen, *Products Liability Law* (2005); also, Shapo, *The Law of Products Liability* (4th ed., 2002); Madden and Owen, *Products Liability Law* (3rd ed., 2000). For a general and accessible survey, see Owen and Phillips, *Products Liability in a Nutshell* (7th ed., 2005); a selection of the leading cases is contained in Owen, Montgomery and Davis, *Cases and Materials on Products Liability and Safety*. See also the Australian Trade Practices Act 1974 (Cth.) (as amended), Part V, Division 2A; Ontario Law Reform Commission Report on Products Liability (1979); Australian Law Reform Commission Report on Product Liability (1989). For comparisons between English or EEC and American law, see Griffiths, De Val and Dormer, 62 Tulane L.R. 353 (1988); Whitehead and Scott, 2 Eur.Bus. L.R. 171 (1991); Howells and Mildred, 65 Tenn. L.Rev. 9 (1998).
[75] For comment, see (*e.g.*) 62 Tenn. L.R. (Summer, 1994); Owen, Univ of Illinois L.R. 743 (1996); 54 Vanderbilt L.R. (April 2001) (Symposium: John W. Wade Conference on the *Third Restatement of Torts*); Henderson and Twerski, 34 Texas Int. L.J. 1 (1999); Stapleton, 39 Washburn L.J. 363 (2000) and 53 S.Carolina L. Rev. 1225 (2002); Conk, 109 Yale L.J. 1087 (2000).
[76] Ch.1, para.1.

possible care was exercised in the preparation and marketing of the product."[77] By way of contrast, liability for design defects contains elements of fault in that it is related to "foreseeable risks of harm posed by the product" which could have been reduced or avoided by adopting a reasonable alternative design, the lack of which renders the product not reasonably safe.[78] Generally, the ground covered by the *Restatement* is much more extensive than is to be found in the equivalent EC Directive or the Consumer Protection Act 1987 which are discussed below.[79]

(j) *Liability under Part I of the Consumer Protection Act 1987*

14–080 **Background.** Since the early 1970s there has been widespread recognition that English law as outlined above was not apt to produce satisfactory results. In particular, many believed that the need to prove negligence constituted an unacceptable barrier to recovery and that it sat uneasily alongside the strict liability associated with breach of the implied terms as to quality of the Sale of Goods Act. It will be recalled that, subject to very limited exceptions,[80] this liability benefits only a contracting party and not others who may be affected by defective goods.[81] The movement towards reform was motivated in part by the legal difficulties arising from the thalidomide tragedy and it benefited from the experience of the United States.[82] Both the desirability and the details of reform were discussed by the English and Scottish Law Commissions[83] and in the Report of the (Pearson) Royal Commission on Civil Liability and Compensation for Personal Injury.[84] At the more general European level there was also the Council of Europe Convention on Products Liability with regard to Personal Injury and Death.[85] However, reform was eventually associated with an EEC Directive on the approximation of the laws, regulations and administrative provisions of the Member States concerning liability for defective products.[86] The final form of this Directive was eventually agreed

[77] *ibid.*, para.2(a).
[78] *ibid.*, para.2(b). A similar requirement is imposed in respect of allegedly inadequate warnings or instructions: para.2(c).
[79] For example, the *Restatement* has separate provisions covering such matters as prescription drugs and medical devices (para.6), food products (para.7), used products (para.8), post-sale failure to warn or recall (paras 15 and 16). As to the Directive (1985/374/EEC [1985] O.J. L210/29) and the Consumer Protection Act 1987, see below, paras 14–080 *et seq.*
[80] As to the limited exceptions, see (*e.g.*) the Contracts (Rights of Third Parties) Act 1999, above, para.14–019.
[81] See, *e.g. Daniels and Daniels v R White & Sons Ltd and Tarbard* [1938] 4 All E.R. 258, above, para.14–018.
[82] Above, paras 14–078, 14–079.
[83] "Liability for Defective Products", Cmnd. 6831 (1977).
[84] Cmnd. 7054 (1978).
[85] Reproduced in the Law Commission Report and the Pearson Report, above; see also Miller, *Product Liability and Safety Encyclopaedia* (1979–2006), Div. V.
[86] 1985/374/EEC set out in Miller, *op. cit.* above., Div. V. See also Miller and Goldberg, *Product Liability* (2004), Ch.7; Whittaker, *Liability for Products* (2005), Chs 16–18; Fairgrieve (ed.), *Product Liability in Comparative Perspective* (2005);

only in July 1985 and then only with the expedient of a number of optional provisions covering, for example, the position of agricultural produce and the controversial "development risks" or "state of the art" defence. The broad effect of the Directive is to make producers strictly liable for damage caused by defects in their products. Proof of negligence is not required. For this purpose "damage" includes death, personal injury, and damage to or destruction of property (other than the defective product itself) which is of a type ordinarily intended for private use or consumption and used by the injured person mainly for such a purpose. The Directive does not cover damage to commercial property nor indeed cases of pure financial or economic loss.

Introduction. Part I of the Consumer Protection Act 1987 was introduced with a view to implementing the EEC Directive.[87] The link is made explicit in section 1(1) which provides that: "This Part shall have effect for the purpose of making such provision as is necessary in order to comply with the product liability Directive and shall be construed accordingly." Also, the case law of the European Court of Justice confirms that national courts must interpret domestic legislation "as far as possible in the light of the wording and the purpose of relevant provisions of Community law."[88] In the current context this will not be an easy task since the Directive leaves key words undefined and their meaning uncertain.[89] The following paragraphs contain a brief reference to some of the principal issues raised by the Act, namely (i) the products covered; (ii) the persons subject to potential liability; (iii) the definition of a defect; (iv) the types of damage or loss covered; (v) the defences available; and (vi) problems of causation and 14–081

Miller (ed.), *Comparative Product Liability* (1986); Stapleton, *Product Liability* (1994), pp.236–42; Whittaker, 5 Y.B. Eur.L. 233 (1985); Stapleton, 6 O.J.L.S. 392 (1986), Taschner, 34 Texas Int. L.J. 21 (1999). The Directive, unlike Directive 1999/44/EC on certain aspects of the sale of consumer goods and associated guarantees (above, paras 14–008, *et seq.*) does not permit Member States to accord a higher level of protection to consumers in those areas which fall within its scope: see Case C-52/00 *Commission of the European Communities v French Republic* [2002] E.C.R. I-3827; Case C–154/00 *Commission of the European Communities v Hellenic Republic* [2002] E.C.R. I-3879; Case 183/00 *Sanchez v Medicina Asturiana SA* [2002] E.C.R. I-3901 (ECJ, April 25, 2002); Case C-402/03, *Skov AEG and Bilka v Mikkelsen* [2006] 2 C.M.L.R. 16 (ECJ, January 10, 2006). For an assessment of the working of the Directive and discussion of areas where further reform may be needed, see the *Report From the Commission on the Application of Directive 85/374 on Liability for Defective Products*, COM (2000) 893 final.

[87] Whether it does in fact implement it has been a matter of dispute so far as the wording of s.4(1)(e) is concerned: see below, para.14–089.

[88] see Case C-91/92 *Faccini Dori v Recreb* [1994] E.C.R. I-3325, para.26; also, Arnull, 26 E.L. Rev. 213 (2001), commenting on the approach of Burton J. in *A v National Blood Authority* [2001] 3 All E.R. 289.

[89] A notable example is the expression "put into circulation", which appears throughout the Directive: see Case C-203/99 *Veedfald v Arhus Amtskommune* [2001] E.C.R. I-3569 (applying Art. 7(a)) and Case C-127/04 *O'Byrne v Sanofi Pasteur MSD Ltd and Sanofi Pasteur SA* [2006] 2 C.M.L.R. 24 (ECJ, Febuary 9, 2006) (applying Art. 11).

other matters.[90] Two general points should also be noted. First, the liability imposed is additional to, and does not operate in derogation of, liability which might arise under some other head, for example in contract.[91] The second and related point is that if, for whatever reason, a claim cannot be made under the Act,[92] it may still be possible to claim in, for example, the tort of negligence or in contract.

14–082 **Products within the scope of the Act.** Part I of the Act covers virtually all products,[93] including component parts and raw materials. In its original version it excluded, as had been permitted by the Directive, game and what may be called primary agricultural produce,[94] that is, produce which had not undergone an industrial process. This exclusion has since been removed[95] so that such products are now within the scope of the strict liability regime. It is likely that particular difficulties will arise in the case of other types of products, including pharmaceutical, medical,[96] chemical and building products, cigarettes, intellectual products including products associated with the computer[97] and aerospace industries.

14–083 **Persons subject to liability.** By section 2(1) of the Act, where any damage is caused wholly or partly by a defect in a product, liability is imposed on every person who falls within section 2(2). Section 2(2)(a) refers to the producer[98] of the product and no doubt in most cases his will

---

[90] For more detailed discussion of product liability see, in addition to the standard works on the law of tort, Miller and Goldberg, *Product Liability* (2004); Whittaker, *Liability for Products* (2005); Howells (ed.), *The Law of Product Liability* (2000); Stapleton, *Product Liability* (1994); Clark, *Product Liability* (1989); Miller, *Product Liability and Safety Encyclopaedia* (1979–2006); also Stapleton in Cane and Stapleton (eds.), *Essays for Patrick Atiyah* (1991), Ch.11.

[91] s.2(6).

[92] *e.g.* because the defective product was first supplied by its producer before the Act came into force (s.50(7)), or because of the operation of limitation periods (see below, paras 14–092—14–093).

[93] Defined by s.1(2) as "any goods or electricity". By s.45 "goods" includes "substances, growing crops and things comprised in land by virtue of being attached to it and any ship, aircraft or vehicle." The supply of water through the mains would also be included: see *AB v Southwest Water Services Ltd* [1993] Q.B. 507. As to blood and blood products, see *A v National Blood Authority* [2001] 3 All E.R. 289, below, paras 14–086, 14–089.

[94] Defined by s.1(2) as "any produce of the soil, of stockfarming or of fisheries." See also s.6(8), preserving the operation of the Nuclear Installations Act 1965, s.12.

[95] By the Consumer Protection Act 1987 (Product Liability) (Modification) Order 2000 (SI 2000/2771), giving effect to Directive 1999/34/EC ([1999] O.J. L141/20).

[96] See Grubb (ed.), *Principles of Medical Law* (2nd ed.), Ch.15; Goldberg, *Causation and Risk in the Law of Torts: Scientific Evidence and Medicinal Product Liability* (1999); Ferguson, *Drug Injuries and the Pursuit of Compensation* (1996); Howells (ed.), *Product Liability, Insurance, and the Pharmaceutical Industry* (1991); Goldberg and Lonbay (eds), *Pharmaceutical Medicine, Biotechnology and European Law* (2000); Newdick, 101 L.Q.R. 405 (1985); also Teff, 20 McGill L.J. 102 (1974); Howells and Mildred, 65 M.L.R. 95 (2002); Goldberg, 10 Med.L.Rev.165 (2002).

[97] Whittaker, 105 L.Q.R. 125 (1989); Stapleton, 9 *Tel Aviv University Studies in Law* 147 (1989). See also *St Albans City and District Council v International Computers Ltd* [1995] F.S.R. 686 (Scott Baker J.), [1996] 4 All E.R. 481, CA.

[98] Broadly, this means those who manufacture or win or abstract products, or who process them in such a way as to change their essential characteristics: see s.1(2).

be the sole liability under the Act. However, liability may also be imposed on persons who, by putting their name on the product or using a trade or other distinguishing mark in relation to it, have held themselves out to be the producer[99]; and on those who have imported the product into a Member State from a place outside the Member States in order to supply it in the course of their business.[1] There is a further complex provision in section 2(3) which is intended to facilitate recovery in the case of "anonymous" or generic goods which do not reveal the identity of the producer, or importer, or carry an own-brander's name. The solution is to impose a provisional liability on a mere supplier[2] who has been unable to comply with a request made by the person who suffered the damage[3] to identify a person to whom section 2(2) applies in relation to the product. Alternatively, the mere supplier (*e.g.* a retailer or hirer-out of DIY goods) may avoid liability under the Act by identifying the person who supplied the product to him (*e.g.* a wholesaler).[4] Frequently, the effect of these provisions will be such that several persons (*e.g.* the producer of a component and of a finished product and perhaps an own-brander) will be subject to liability. Their liability to the injured person will then be joint and several[5] and as against that person, or a dependant or relative of such a person, it cannot be limited or excluded.[6]

The definition of a defect.[7] As is made clear by Article 4 of the Directive, the injured person is "required to prove the damage, the defect and the causal relationship between defect and damage". However, it remains unclear whether this entails proving with some degree of specificity the precise respect in which the product is alleged to be defective.[8] More generally, the experience of the United States of America[9] strongly suggests that when strict liability is imposed attention will focus increasingly on the meaning of the words "defect" or "defective." This is particularly so when the defect alleged is one of design or inadequate warning, as opposed to production. The definition in section 3 of the 1987 Act is linked closely to the types of damage which are within the scope of the Act.[10] Its central 14–084

---

[99] s.2(2)(b).
[1] s.2(2)(c).
[2] In this context, see s.1(3).
[3] See also s.6(2).
[4] s.2(3)(c).
[5] s.2(5). Provisions for obtaining a contribution or indemnity are governed by the Civil Liability (Contribution) Act 1978.
[6] s.7. Liability *inter se* will depend on other factors, notably the Unfair Contract Terms Act 1977: see, in particular, s.6(2), above, para.13–083.
[7] See Miller and Goldberg, *Product Liability* (2004), Chs. 10–12; Howells in Howells (ed.), *The Law of Product Liability* (2000), paras 4.121–4.167; Stapleton, *Product Liability* (1994), Ch.10; Clark, 48 M.L.R. 325 (1985); Newdick, 104 L.Q.R. 288 (1987); Stapleton, 6 O.J.L.S. 392 (1986); 34 Tex.Int.L.J. 45 (1999), 39 Washburn L.J. 363 (2000); Griffiths [1987] J.B.L. 222; Stoppa, 12 L.S. 210 (1992); Hodges, 117 L.Q.R. 528 (2001).
[8] Some cases suggest that it does: see (*e.g.*) *Richardson v LRC Products Ltd* [2000] Lloyd's Rep. Med. 280 (Ian Kennedy, J.); *Foster v Biosil* (2000) 59 B.M.L.R. 178 (Cherie Booth, Q.C. sitting in the Central London County Court).
[9] See, above, paras 14–078—14–079.
[10] See s.5 and below, para.14–087.

feature is that "the safety of the product is not such as persons generally are entitled to expect."[11] By section 3(2) all the circumstances must be taken into account when determining whether this standard has been met. However, certain circumstances are mentioned specifically. These include: "the manner in which, and purposes for which, the product has been marketed ... and any instructions for, or warnings with respect to, doing or refraining from doing anything with or in relation to the product."[12] Whether warnings or instructions are necessary or sufficient will depend on a variety of factors.[13] Probably the most important include the degree of danger, and the location and explicitness of such warnings or instructions in relation to the risk. The two further specified circumstances are: (i) what might reasonably be expected to be done with or in relation to the product and (ii) the time when the product was supplied by its producer to another.[14] The former takes account of the fact that most products are capable of causing harm if misused, but are not necessarily "defective" as a result. The possibility of a reduction of damages on the ground of contributory negligence is available in an appropriate case.[15] The last designated circumstance takes account of the fact that product safety standards will change (and usually increase) over the years. The matter should be judged by reference to the standard which pertained when the product was supplied by its producer. This may be higher than the standard when the product was designed or indeed manufactured. Conversely, however, defendants should not be prejudiced by the fact that safety standards have risen between the time of supply and injury.[16]

14–085 In addition to the circumstances specified in section 3(2), further circumstances will often be relevant. These may include such matters as whether the danger was hidden or obvious, and whether the product complied, particularly in matters of design, specifications and warnings, with any relevant safety standards, including British Standards. Although

---

[11] s.3(1). Hence if a person is unusually sensitive or prone to some unusual reaction he will not (necessarily) recover, although a warning may still be appropriate. Similar issues arise under the Sale of Goods Act 1979, s.14: see, *e.g. Griffiths v Peter Conway Ltd* [1939] 1 All E.R. 685; *Slater v Finning Ltd* [1996] 3 All E.R. 398, above, para.11–057.

[12] s.3(2)(a).

[13] Clark [1983] J.B.L. 130; similar issues arise under the Sale of Goods Act 1979, s.14: see *Wormell v RHM Agricultural (East)* [1987] 1 W.L.R. 1091, reversing on the facts [1986] 1 W.L.R. 336, above, para.11–039. For modern examples, see *Buchan v Ortho Pharmaceutical (Canada) Ltd* (1986) 25 D.L.R. (4th) 658 (Ont. CA); *Dow Corning Corp. v Hollis* (1996) 129 D.L.R. (4th) 609 (Can.Sup.Ct.); *Worsley v Tambrands Ltd* [2000] P.I.Q.R. P 95 (Ebsworth J.)

[14] s.3(2)(b) and (c).

[15] s.6(4). The Law Reform (Contributory Negligence) Act 1945 will apply.

[16] A point which is reinforced by the closing words of s.3: "nothing in this section shall require a defect to be inferred from the fact alone that the safety of a product which is supplied after that time is greater than the safety of the product in question." For a duty to warn of subsequently discovered defects, see *Rivtow Marine Ltd v Washington Iron Works* (1973) 40 D.L.R. (3d.) 530 (Can. Sup. Ct.); *E Hobbs (Farms) Ltd v Baxenden Chemical Co. Ltd* [1992] 1 Lloyd's Rep. 55 and, in general, Miller and Goldberg, *op. cit.*, paras 14–116—14–123.

compliance is not a complete defence,[17] a court may need little persuading that detailed modern standards (especially when they are embodied in a statutory instrument)[18] are strongly indicative of the level of safety which persons generally are entitled to expect.[19] In other cases (of which pharmaceuticals are often good examples) the issue may depend on a very careful balancing of the drawbacks and benefits associated with the product.

The issue of defectiveness was considered by Burton J. against the background of tragic circumstances in *A v National Blood Authority*.[20] The claimants had been infected with hepatitis C through blood transfusions or blood products, usually in the course of undergoing surgery. The source of the infection was not contamination by an outside agent, but came, rather, from a donor's blood. In the relevant period the risk of infection was known to the medical profession in general terms, but impossible to avoid in any given case—whether because the virus had not been identified or, at a later stage, because it was undetectable through a screening test. Burton J. held that persons generally were entitled to expect that blood would be free from what was, in effect, an unavoidable risk and that "avoidability of the harmful characteristic" was not a relevant circumstance to take into account when determining whether a product was defective.[21] A cover to be attached to a child's pushchair by an elasticated buckle was also held to be defective in *Abouzaid v Mothercare (UK) Ltd*[22] even though the danger of the attachment snapping back had not previously been contemplated or appeared in accident statistics.[23] Such cases illustrate the important practical consequences of strict liability under the 1987 Act. 14–086

Types of damage or loss covered. The 1987 Act does not cover all types of damage or loss which may be caused by a defective product. Where the Act does not apply it may still be possible to claim under some other head, for example the tort of negligence.[24] The effect of section 5(1) is, broadly speaking, that strict liability is imposed in respect of "death or personal 14–087

---

[17] *cf.* the "presumption of conformity" with the "general safety requirement" of the General Product Safety Regulations 2005 (SI 2005/1803), reg. 6(1) and (2); and note also the other factors (including standards) which are stated to be relevant to the issue of conformity (reg. 6 (3) and (4)).

[18] As with safety regulations made under s.11 of the Act (below, para.14–115), for example those covering cosmetic products.

[19] *cf. Budden v BP Oil and Shell Oil* (1980) S.J. 376 (lead content of petrol and compliance with Control of Pollution Regulations).

[20] [2001] 3 All E.R. 289. See Howells and Mildred, 65 M.L.R. 95 (2002); Hodges, 117 L.Q.R. 528 (2001); Goldberg, 10 Med. L. Rev. 165 (2002).

[21] The infected blood was classified as a "non-standard" product in the sense of one which had not been produced as intended. *Quaere*, however, whether such matters as the avoidability, impracticability, cost or difficulty of avoiding danger can be ignored when determining whether a "standard" product is defective in design?

[22] [2002] All E.R. (D) 2436; *The Times*, February 20, 2001 (the "Cosytoes" case).

[23] An elder brother's retina was badly damaged; *cf. Richardson v LRC Products Ltd* [2000] Lloyd's Rep. Med. 280 (bursting condom leading to pregnancy: no liability); *B (a Child) v McDonald's Restaurants Ltd* [2002] EWHC 490 (burns from scalding coffee: no liability).

[24] See above, paras 14–061, 14–076.

injury[25] or any loss[26] of or damage to any property (including land)." However, important limitations are imposed in respect of loss of or damage to property. In particular, liability will not be incurred under section 2 for "any loss of or damage to any property which, at the time it is lost or damaged is not—(a) of a description of property ordinarily intended for private use, occupation or consumption; and (b) intended by the person suffering the loss or damage mainly for his own private use, occupation or consumption."[27] Furthermore, even claims in respect of damage to or loss of consumer property cannot be brought under the Act if the amount which would otherwise be awarded does not exceed £275.[28] Claims in respect of pure financial loss are similarly not covered and nowadays are most unlikely to succeed at common law even on proof of negligence.[29] Finally, section 5(2) provides that liability will not be incurred under section 2 where the defect in the product causes the loss of or damage to the product itself. Nor will it be incurred (*e.g.* by a component producer) in respect of the loss of or any damage to the whole or any part of any product (*e.g.* a car) which has been supplied with the product in question (*e.g.* a defective tyre or carburettor) comprised in it.[30] The prospects of recovery in the tort of negligence in any such case are, at best, doubtful.[31]

14–088 **Defences available.** Section 4 of the Act makes provision for some six defences which mitigate the strict liability otherwise imposed. Most are relatively uncontroversial. Thus by section 4(1)(a) it is a defence to prove that the defect is attributable to compliance with a requirement imposed by or under any enactment or with any Community obligation. Section 4(1)(b) provides a defence on proof that the defendant did not at any time supply[32] the product to another, while section 4(1)(c) provides a defence on showing that any such supply was otherwise than in the course of a business.[33] A further defence in section 4(1)(d) is based on proving that the defect did not exist in the product at "the relevant time" which, broadly speaking, is

[25] Defined by s.45(1) to include "any disease and any other impairment of a person's physical or mental condition", a form of words which would include psychiatric harm. See also s.6(3) which refers to the Congenital Disabilities (Civil Liability) Act 1976.
[26] *cf.* Art. 9(b) of the Directive "damage to, or destruction of, any item of property."
[27] s.5(3).
[28] s.5(4). There is no maximum limit on liability, *e.g.* for design defects, although the Directive permits this: Art. 16.1.
[29] See, above, para.12–126.
[30] *Aliter*, where the defective component was bought subsequently as a replacement part, provided always that s.5(3) and (4) are satisfied.
[31] See, generally, *Murphy v Brentwood District Council* [1990] 3 W.L.R. 414, *Nitrigin Eireann Teoranta v Inco Alloys Ltd* [1992] 1 W.L.R. 498; Miller and Goldberg, *Product Liability* (2004), paras 16–32–16–94 and above, para.12–126.
[32] See s.46. The equivalent provision in Art. 7(a) of the Directive confers a defence on proving that the producer did not "put the product into circulation". This expression has been discussed (without throwing any real light on its meaning) in Case C-203/99 *Veedfald v Arhus Amtskommune* [2001] E.C.R. I-3569; see Taschner, 39 C.M.L. Rev. (2002) 385; also, below para.14–092, n.53.
[33] By s.4(1)(c)(ii) it must further be proved that the defendant is not within s.2(2) and, if he is, is so by virtue only of things done otherwise than with a view to profit. As to "business," see s.45(1).

the time of supply.[34] The defence is unlikely to assist manufacturers when, for example, foreign objects are found in bottles or tins, but it may be more helpful when they can plausibly suggest that the defect was caused by a lack of servicing or incorrect installation by a third party.

A much more controversial defence is contained in section 4(1)(e) which is available on proving that "the state of scientific and technical knowledge at the relevant time was not such that a producer of products of the same description as the product in question might be expected to have discovered the defect if it had existed in his products while they were under his control." This is variously described as the "development risks" or the "state of the art" defence, and it is derived from an optional provision in the Directive.[35] The wording of the defence differs from that of the Directive[36] and it has been argued that it does so in a way which is significantly more favourable to manufacturers. The issue has been considered by the European Court of Justice which was not satisfied that there had been a failure to implement the Directive,[37] noting, in particular, the interpretative obligation imposed by section 1(1) of the Act[38] and the lack of any case law which might indicate non-implementation. In this context it is of interest to note that in the *National Blood Authority* case[39] Burton J. concentrated on the wording of the Directive, rather than on that of the Act. He concluded that the defence was inapplicable where the existence of the generic defect was known (or should have been known through accessible information) and yet in the then state of scientific and technical knowledge was undetectable in any given case. Less controversially, the defence also failed in *Abouzaid v Mothercare (UK) Ltd*[40] since the propensity of elastic to snap back was a matter of common knowledge. Such decisions indicate that the defence will be construed narrowly,[41] and it should be noted that the burden is on the defendant to establish it.[42] 14–089

---

[34] See s.4(2) which, however, makes special provision both for electricity and (in subs. (2)(b)) for a person who is not within s.2(2).

[35] See Arts 7(e) and 15.1(b). For general discussion of the defence, see (*e.g.*) Miller and Goldberg, *Product Liability* (2004), paras 13–25–13–105; Newdick, 47 C.L.J. 455 (1988) and 20 Anglo-Am.L.R. 309 (1992); Stapleton, *Product Liability* (1994), pp.236–242; 34 Texas Int. L.J. 45 (1999), 53 S.Carolina L.Rev. 1225 (2002) and 6 O.J.L.S. 392 (1986); Hodges, 61 M.L.R. 560 (1998); Howells in Howells (ed.) *The Law of Product Liability* (2000), paras 4–234—4–250; Howells and Mildred, 65 M.L.R. 95 (2002), 65 Tenn. L. Rev. 985 (1998).

[36] This requires the producer to prove "that the state of scientific and technical knowledge at the time when he put the product into circulation was not such as to enable the existence of the defect to be discovered": Art. 7(e).

[37] Case C–300/95 *European Commission v UK* [1997] E.C.R. 1–2649, ECJ.

[38] This provides that: "This Part shall have effect for the purpose of making such provision as is necessary in order to comply with the product liability Directive and shall be construed accordingly."

[39] *A. v National Blood Authority* [2001] 3 All E.R. 289, above, para.14–086.

[40] [2000] All E.R. (D) 2436; *The Times*, February 20, 2001, above, para.14–086.

[41] See also the much-cited "German Bottle case" May 9, 1995, NJW 1995, 2162 (German Federal Sup.Ct.) (exploding mineral water bottle). There is also a major underlying issue of when hunches and fears become "knowledge" so as to prevent the defence from applying. Examples from the past include asbestos and cigarettes and one can only guess at which current fears will prove to be well-grounded. See, generally, Miller and Goldberg, *Product Liability* (2004), paras 13–76–13–105.

[42] *cf.* the position in the tort of negligence: above, para.14–061.

14–090 The final defence of section 4(1)(f) benefits producers of components. It is available on proving that the defect constituted a defect in a product ("the subsequent product") in which the product in question was incorporated and was "wholly attributable" to the design of that product or to compliance with instructions given by its producer. Anything less than this would, in principle, lead to joint and several liability.[43]

14–091 **Causation and other matters.** The introduction of strict liability under the 1987 Act does not, of course, relieve the claimant of the need to prove that the allegedly defective product actually caused or materially contributed to the damage which is the subject of the claim. Issues of causation and remoteness of damage are apt to arise in many areas of the law of tort.[44] However, they can be particularly difficult in the area covered by Part I of the Act.[45] A modern example is provided by the pertussis vaccine litigation where, after lengthy submissions of evidence, it was not established that the vaccine caused permanent brain damage in young children.[46]

14–092 A further barrier to recovery may arise through limitation and cut-off periods. The Act establishes[47] a three-year limitation period in which to begin proceedings. It provides that an action shall not be brought under Part I "after the expiration of the period of three years from whichever is the later of (a) the date on which the cause of action accrued; and (b) the date of knowledge of the injured person or, in the case of loss of or damage to property, the date of knowledge[48] of the plaintiff or (if earlier) of any person in whom his cause of action was previously vested."[49] In the case of personal injuries and death, actions for damages for negligence are subject to a similar three-year limitation period[50] but the general time limit in the case of property damage is six years.[51] Hence it may be open to a claimant to sue in negligence when time-barred under the Act. Actions brought under Part I of the Act are also subject to an overriding 10-year cut-off

---

[43] s.2(5), above, para.14–083.
[44] See, generally, Markesinis & Deakin's, *Tort Law* (5th ed.), pp.185–213; *Street on Torts* (11th ed.), Ch.14; *Winfield & Jolowicz on Tort* (16th ed.), Ch.6.
[45] See Miller and Goldberg, *Product Liability* (2004), paras 17–01–17–97; Goldberg, *Causation and Risk in the Law of Torts: Scientific Evidence and Medicinal Product Liability* (1999); and in Howells (ed.), *The Law of Product Liability* (2000), Ch.5.
[46] See *Loveday v Renton*, [1990] 1 Med. L.R.117, *The Times*, March 31, 1988 and, generally, Ferguson, *Drug Injuries and the Pursuit of Compensation* (1996), Ch.9; Goldberg, 3 J.S.S.L. 100 (1996) (vaccine damage); 25 Anglo-Am.L.R. 286 (1996) (diethylstilbestrol); 4 Med.L.R 32 (1996) (debendox). Further examples of claims which have failed through inability to establish a causative link include *Reay v British Nuclear Fuels*; *Hope v BNFL* [1994] 5 Med. L.R.1 (paternal preconception irradiation and childhood leukaemia); *Davis and Doherty v Balfour Kilpatrick* [2002] EWCA Civ 736 (radio frequency emissions and radiation sickness).
[47] Through s.6 and Sch.1, inserting s.11A into the Limitation Act 1980.
[48] See Consumer Protection Act 1987, s.5(5)–(8).
[49] Limitation Act 1980, s.11A(4). The cause of action accrues only when damage occurs: see *Pirelli General Cable Works v Oscar Faber and Partners* [1983] 2 W.L.R. 6; *Nitrigin Eireann Teoranta v Inco Alloys Ltd* [1992] 1 W.L.R. 498. For the position where personal injury leads to death, see also subs. (5)–(7).
[50] Limitation Act 1980, s.11(4).
[51] *ibid.* s.14A(4), inserted by the Latent Damage Act 1986, s.1.

period which operates to extinguish any right of action even though such a right may not have accrued.[52] This generally runs from the time when the defendant supplied the product to another.[53] This may be important when products have a potentially long life-span or, as in the case of some pharmaceuticals, the capacity for causing harm many years after they are supplied. In the case of personal injuries and death, there is no equivalent provision covering actions in the tort of negligence. However, an overriding 15-year time limit operates for negligence actions not involving such injuries.[54]

It should be remembered that Part I does not have retrospective effect. It will apply only to products which were supplied by their producer after the Act came into force on March 1, 1988.[55] Raw materials and component parts will often have been supplied before the finished products in which they are comprised. Hence it is still possible, albeit increasingly unlikely, that one may see cases in which producers of finished products are liable under the Act without the producer of the defective component part being subject to a similar joint and several liability.[56] **14–093**

Finally, it may be noted that although Part I of the 1987 Act has now been in force for some years, it is only relatively recently that it has started to generate the case law which many had expected. Some of the possible reasons for this are discussed in the National Consumer Council Report, *Unsafe Products*, published in November 1995.

(k) *Civil Liability for Breach of Statutory Duty*

Rights directly conferred. Various statutes seek to prohibit unacceptable trade practices, or to secure acceptable ones, and many are directed at consumer situations. The main technique adopted is the creation of **14–094**

---

[52] Limitation Act 1980, s.11A(3). As to the substitution of a new party after the expiry of the 10-year time limit, see *Horne-Roberts v Smith Kline Beecham Plc* [2002] I W.L.R. 1662, CA (applying the Limitation Act 1980, s.35(3) and CPR r.19.5). The European Court of Justice in Case C-127/04 *O'Byrne v Sanofi Pasteur MSD Ltd and Sanofi Pasteur SA* [2006] 2 C.M.L.R. 24 has held, when construing the equivalent provision in Art. 11 of the Directive, that usually it is a matter for national law to determine the conditions in accordance with which one party may be substituted for another.

[53] This usually being the "relevant time" within the meaning of s.4(2) of the Consumer Protection Act 1987. As to "supply," see s.46. Note, however, that Art. 11 of the Directive refers to "the date on which the producer *put into circulation* the actual product which caused the damage . . ." (emphasis supplied). In its decision in the *O'Byrne* case (above, n.52) the ECJ ruled that a product is put into circulation when it is taken out of the manufacturing process operated by the producer and enters a marketing process in the form in which it is offered to the public in order to be used or consumed.

[54] Limitation Act 1980, s.14B, inserted by the Latent Damage Act 1986, s.1.

[55] Consumer Protection Act 1987, s.50(7). For the commencement date, see the Consumer Protection Act 1987 (Commencement No. 1) Order 1987 (SI 1987/1680).

[56] Under s.2(5). Similarly, the 10-year cut-off point (above) may benefit suppliers of defective components and raw materials without benefiting producers of the finished products in which they are comprised.

offences. But sometimes such a statute directly provides that civil rights arise in favour of the consumer. An example is the Agriculture Act 1970, Part IV of which regulates the sale of fertilisers and feeding stuffs, and which by section 72 imposes a warranty of fitness (which cannot be excluded) on certain sales of feeding stuffs.[57] It seems, however, that where a right of action is not specifically conferred (as it is by this Act), a statute imposing a penalty is assumed to do that alone and not by implication to raise an action for breach of statutory duty.[58]

14–095 **Consumer Protection Act 1987.** An important modern example of a statute which does confer a right of action is to be found in the Consumer Protection Act 1987. As is noted in the section on the criminal law,[59] section 11 of this Act enables the Secretary of State to make safety regulations for the purposes of securing, inter alia, that goods are safe. Section 12 makes it an offence to contravene such regulations as by supplying, or offering, or agreeing, etc. to supply non-complying goods. Moreover, section 41(1) provides that an obligation imposed on a person by safety regulations is a duty owed by him to any other person who may be affected by a failure to perform the obligation[60] and, subject to any provision to the contrary in the regulations, actionable as such, subject to the defences and other incidents applying to actions for breach of statutory duty.[61] Agreements are void in so far as they would have the effect of excluding or restricting such an obligation, or liability for its breach.[62] It should be noted that these actions may lie in favour of persons who were

---

[57] Feeding stuffs are now defined to include stuffs for oral feeding to pet animals as well as to farmed creatures: see the relevant definition in s.66(1) of the 1970 Act, as substituted by the Feeding Stuffs Regulations 2000 (SI 2000/2481), reg. 20(1)(a). See, as to the application of s.2(2) of the Fertilisers and Feeding Stuffs Act 1926 (now superseded by s.72(1) of the Agriculture Act 1970), *Henry Kendall & Sons v William Lillico & Sons Ltd* [1969] 2 A.C. 31.

[58] See *Badham v Lambs Ltd* [1946] K.B. 45 (road traffic legislation); *Square v Model Farm Dairies (Bournemouth) Ltd* [1939] 2 K.B. 365 (food and drugs legislation). *Cf. Read v Croydon Corporation* [1938] 4 All E.R. 631 (water infected by typhoid: right of action conferred on ratepayer but not his family). See also Fair Trading Act 1973, s.26, (below, para.14–126). For a general survey, see Markesinis and Deakin's *Tort Law* (5th ed.), pp.363–374. For a survey of new forms of the tort of breach of statutory duty, see Stanton, 120 L.Q.R. 324 (2004).

[59] Below, para.14–115.

[60] Note that this applies only where there has been a contravention of safety regulations. It has no application in the event of non-compliance with a prohibition notice or a notice to warn (s.13), or with a suspension notice (s.14) (see s.41(2). Similarly, contravention of the various provisions of the General Product Safety Regulations 2005 (SI 2005/1803) does not confer a civil remedy (see reg. 42). See further, below, paras 14–114 *et seq*.

[61] A standard "due diligence" defence is contained in s.39 of the Act (below, para.14–108). It is not clear whether or not establishing this defence would bar the civil action. See *Harrison v National Coal Board* [1950] 1 K.B. 466 at 476, 477; [1951] A.C. 639 at 657–658; Glanville Williams, 23 M.L.R. 233 at 243 (1960); *Restatement, Second, Torts*, paras 286 and 288A and comments. The question is discussed by Cane, 3 J. Products Liability 215 (1980), who also discusses problems of causation and contributory negligence. For a provision which is similar to s.41(1), see the Health and Safety at Work, etc. Act 1974, s.47(2).

[62] Consumer Protection Act 1987, s.41(4).

not privy to the original transaction, *e.g.* a member of the family of the purchaser of a defective article who is injured by it[63] and that liability is not confined to manufacturers.

Rights indirectly conferred. Sometimes a statute requires some sort of statement as to goods to be made (under criminal penalties) and then imposes civil liability for the untruth of the statement. Thus the Agriculture Act 1970, Pt IV, referred to above, requires by section 68 the giving of a "statutory statement" on the sale of fertilisers and feeding stuffs, containing certain particulars, and provides that it has effect as a warranty (which cannot be excluded) that the particulars contained in it are correct; related provisions as to marking, use of expressions with meanings prescribed by regulation and claims that certain attributes are present are to be found in sections 69 to 71. Again, the Plant Varieties and Seeds Act 1964 permits the making of regulations requiring the giving of a statutory statement and providing for civil liability (which cannot be excluded) on it if it is incorrect (ss.16, 17). 14–096

Illegality affecting contract. Sometimes the failure to comply with statutory requirements on a sale has been held to affect the contract with illegality, so that a seller who did not comply with his duties might be penalised at civil law by being unable to sue for the price. The buyer would, however, be able to sue for breach of warranty. Thus in *Anderson Ltd v Daniel*[64] it was held that a seller of a substance to be used as fertiliser who did not deliver the statutory statement required by the Fertilisers and Feeding Stuffs Act 1906 (an earlier counterpart of Part IV of the Agriculture Act 1970) could not enforce the contract. Present policy, however, tends to be hostile to this technique. Thus the Agriculture Act 1970 provides in respect of two of the duties imposed by Part IV that failure to comply with the duties "shall not invalidate a contract of sale"[65]; section 65 of the Road Traffic Act 1988 (which makes it an offence to supply certain vehicles which do not comply with specified safety requirements) provides that nothing in the section "shall affect the validity of a contract or any rights arising under or in relation to a contract."[66] Similar provisions appear in the Plant Varieties and Seeds Act 1964,[67] the Trade Descriptions Act 1968,[68] the Fair Trading Act 1973[69] and the Consumer Protection Act 1987.[70] 14–097

---

63 *cf.* above, paras 14–018, 14–019.
64 [1924] 1 K.B. 138. See also *B and B Viennese Fashions v Losane* [1952] 1 All E.R. 909; *cf. Marles v Philip Trant & Sons* [1954] 1 Q.B. 29 (successful action by buyer); above, para.3–030. But *cf. St John Shipping Corp. v Joseph Rank Ltd* [1957] 1 Q.B. 267. See further, Enonchong, *Illegal Transactions* (1998), Ch.15; Treitel, *The Law of Contract* (11th ed.), Ch.11, esp. pp.480–512; Law Commission Consultation Paper (No. 154), *Illegal Transactions: The Effect of Illegality on Contracts and Trusts* (1999) and above, paras 3–027 *et seq.*
65 ss.68(6), 71(4).
66 s.65(4).
67 s.17(5).
68 s.35; below, para.14–112.
69 s.26; below, para.14–126.
70 s.41(3).

3. THE CONSUMER'S REMEDIES

14–098 **Importance of remedies.**[71] However satisfactory they may appear on paper, legal rights are of little value unless it is practicable to enforce them. This is conspicuously true in the case of consumers, who may find the legal process too expensive, disconcerting and uncertain. Although the subject of procedure and remedies is outside the scope of this book, brief reference is therefore made, for the sake of completeness, to some of the factors affecting the enforcement of the consumer's private rights.

14–099 **Advice and complaints.** Consumers may obtain advice from a number of sources including Citizens' Advice Bureaux, Law Centres, and often from the Trading Standards Department (or equivalent) of the local authority.[72] At the national level, their interests are also promoted by such organisations as the National Consumer Council and the Consumers' Association. Codes of practice of particular trade associations frequently provide channels and procedures for complaints and conciliation.

14–100 **Arbitration.**[73] Particular contracts may provide for resolution of disputes by arbitration. Codes of practice of trade associations may also do so, and may be incorporated into a contract of sale. These constitute agreements to arbitrate made in advance of the arising of a dispute. Clauses whereby parties agree to submit present or future differences to arbitration are not affected by the Unfair Contract Terms Act 1977.[74] However, protection was accorded to consumers by the Consumer Arbitration Agreement Act 1988. This Act was repealed by the Arbitration Act 1996[75] which introduced an alternative method of control[76] by extending the Unfair Terms in Consumer Contracts Regulations[77] to a term which constitutes an arbitration agreement. For this purpose an "arbitration agreement" means an agreement to

---

[71] Cranston's *Consumers and the Law* (3rd ed.), pp.102–139; Harvey and Parry, *The Law of Consumer Protection and Fair Trading* (6th ed.), pp.55–65, 227–245; Miller, Harvey and Parry, *Consumer and Trading Law: Text, Cases and Materials* (1998), Chs 8 and 9; Genn, *Paths to Justice* (1999); *Ordinary Justice* (National Consumer Council, 1989); *Consumer Redress Mechanisms* (OFT, 1991); *Consumer Dissatisfaction* (OFT, 1996); Commission of the European Communities, *Green Paper on Access of Consumers to Justice and the Settlement of Consumer Disputes in the Single Market* (Com. (93) 576 final) and *Action Plan on Consumer Access to Justice and the Settlement of Consumer Disputes in the Internal Market* (Com. (96) 13 final).

[72] Baldwin, 8 C.J.Q. 24 (1989).

[73] *Chitty on Contracts* (29th ed.), Vol. 2, Ch.32, esp. 32–013.

[74] s.13(2): above, para.13–069.

[75] s.107(2), Sch.4. The Act came into force on January 31, 1997: see the Arbitration Act 1996 (Commencement No. 1) Order 1996, (SI 1996/3146), Art. 3.

[76] See s.89(1).

[77] Originally the 1994 Regulations (SI 1994/3159), but they have been superseded by SI 1999/2083, as amended by SI 2001/1186, SI 2003/3182, SI 2004/2095 and SI 2006/523. Note also that the "grey list" of terms which may be considered "unfair" includes a reference to ones which exclude or hinder the consumer's right to take legal action, etc. "particularly by requiring the consumer to take disputes exclusively to arbitration not covered by legal provisions": see reg. 5(5) and Sch.2, para.1(q), above, para.14–036.

submit to arbitration present or future disputes or differences (whether or not contractual).[78] Section 91(1) of the Act provides that: "A term which constitutes an arbitration agreement is unfair for the purposes of the Regulations so far as it relates to a claim for a pecuniary remedy which does not exceed" a modest amount to be specified by order.[79] The implication is that it will not then be binding on the consumer.[80] Subject to this, arbitration agreements are binding under general principles, although they remain under the overall control of the court which cannot be excluded.[81] The court must stay legal proceedings brought in breach of a valid arbitration clause[82] and has extensive supervisory powers over arbitral proceedings.[83] Arbitration awards can be enforced in the county or High Court as appropriate. Many codes of practice provide for such procedures: to reduce expense the arbitration is often on the basis of written evidence only. There may be a small fee, but usually there is no liability for costs.[84] Although the point is not clear beyond all doubt, such voluntary arrangements do not appear to fall within section 91 of the 1996 Act and indeed there is no apparent reason why they should do so.

Small claims proceedings. In many jurisdictions special small claims courts have been set up, which may use procedures, have powers and follow principles different from those applicable in ordinary civil litigation.[85] In English law the nearest equivalent was the county court small claims (previously arbitration) scheme[86] which was set up in 1973 in order "to meet the case, so far as it was valid, for a small claims court."[87] It was revised in 1981[88] and again, following the recommendations of the Civil Justice Review, in 1991,[89] and most recently in the aftermath of Lord 14–101

[78] s.89(2). By s.90 the Regulations apply where the consumer is a legal person as they apply where the consumer is a natural person. *Cf.* the definition of "consumer" in reg. 3(1) of the 1999 Regulations.
[79] The amount so specified is £5,000: see the Unfair Arbitration Agreements (Specified Amount) Order 1999, (SI 1999/2167).
[80] See reg. 8(1) of the 1999 Regulations.
[81] *Doleman & Sons v Osset Corp.* [1912] 3 K.B. 257. In principle, and subject to the 1996 Act and the 1999 Regulations, an agreement that the existence of an arbitral award is a condition precedent to any right of action under the contract is valid and effective: see *Scott v Avery* (1865) 5 H.L.C. 811; also *Ford v Clarksons Holidays Ltd* [1971] 1 W.L.R. 1412.
[82] Under the Arbitration Act 1996, ss.9. *Cf.* s.86, which has not been, and is unlikely to be, brought into force.
[83] See in general the Arbitration Act 1996.
[84] For discussion and evaluation see *Redress Procedures under Codes of Practice* (OFT, 1981); *Raising Standards of Consumer Care: Progressing Beyond Codes of Practice* (OFT, 1998); also Thomas [1988] C.J.Q. 206.
[85] See Cranston's *Consumers and the Law* (3rd ed.), pp.110–120; Ison, 35 M.L.R. 18 (1972); Turner, 9 Anglo-Am. L.Rev. 150 (1980); Whelan, *Small Claims Courts: A Comparative Study* (1990).
[86] See the County Courts Act 1984, s.64; CCR, Ord. 19.
[87] See 123 N.L.J. 215 (1973).
[88] See Thomas, 131 N.L.J. 429 (1981).
[89] Cmnd. 394 (1988), paras 159–162.

Woolf's reforms to the civil justice system.[90] The overall position is now governed by Part 27 of the Civil Procedure Rules and the so-called Small Claims Track which it established. In broad terms this is applicable where claims are for not more than £5,000, except that there is a lower limit of £1,000 where the claim is for damages for personal injuries or in the case of housing repairs.[91] Obviously, the general limit in cases not involving personal injuries is sufficiently high to cover the vast majority of consumer transactions. The procedure limits the ability to hold preliminary hearings[92] and provides that the conduct of hearings should be informal and without the application of the strict rules of evidence. Also, evidence need not be taken on oath, cross-examination may be limited and reasons must be given for the decision reached.[93] Similarly the power to award costs is very limited and covers only such matters as the fixed costs of issuing the claim, costs which are attributable to the unreasonable behaviour of the other party, court fees, enforcement costs, and limited sums to cover any travel expenses and loss of earnings incurred by the party or a witness.[94] In general, costs are not awarded in respect of legal advice or assistance, since the system has been specifically designed with litigants in person in mind, although there is a limited exception where proceedings include a claim for an injunction or for an order of specific performance.[95] Although the system is conceived as being for the benefit of consumers, there is nothing to prevent a business using the procedure as claimant, nor is there any restriction on legal representation.[96] In a recent report on the operation of the procedure the House of Commons Constitutional Affairs Committee concluded[97] that the system generally works well in providing litigants with a low cost and good quality procedure. The main deficiencies were identified as including the lack of adequate IT facilities, problems in listing, the low claims limit in cases involving personal injury and housing disrepair and the very long-standing problems of enforcing judgments.

14–102 **Civil litigation.** In cases where consumer litigation falls outside the small claims track (and presumably these will almost always involve claims for personal injury) the allocation of proceedings between the county court and

---

[90] See *Access to Justice: Interim Report on the Civil Justice System in England and Wales* (1995); also Lord Woolf's Final Report (1996). For discussion of small claims from a variety of perspectives, see Baldwin, *Small Claims in the County Courts in England and Wales* (1997); *Handling Small Claims in the County Courts* (National Audit Office, 1996); Applebey, 7 C.J.Q. 294 (1988); House of Commons Constitutional Affairs Committee, First Report of Session 2005–06, *The courts: small claims* (HC 519) (December, 2005).

[91] CPR, r.26.6.

[92] Rule 27.6.

[93] Rule 27.8, which states: "The court may adopt any method of proceeding at a hearing that it considers to be fair". On not allowing cross-examination, *cf. Chilton v Saga Holidays* [1986] 1 All E.R. 841.

[94] Rule 27.14.

[95] Rule 27.14 (2)(b).

[96] See, generally, Thomas, 1 C.J.Q. 52 (1982).

[97] See First Report of Session 2005–06, *The courts: small claims* (HC 519) (December, 2005)

the High Court is now principally controlled by an Order[98] made under section 1 of the Courts and Legal Services Act 1990. The general scheme is that actions in respect of personal injuries may only be commenced in the High Court if the financial value of the claim is £50,000 or more.[99] In other cases a claim for money in which county courts have jurisdiction may be commenced in the High Court only if the financial value of the claim is more than £15,000.[1] Furthermore, a claim with an estimated value of less than £50,000 will generally be transferred to a county court,[2] and one with a higher estimated value may be so transferred. Thereafter, the important point of distinction associated with the Civil Procedure Rules is between the "fast" and the "multi" track approaches, the former usually being appropriate (in order to keep costs at a level proportionate to the amount in dispute) where the claim has a financial value of not more than £15,000.[3] At least in the case of county courts, general efforts have been made to make it easier for a litigant to act in person.[4]

Class and group actions. The loss suffered by individual consumers from breach of contract or some other civil wrong committed by a seller, distributor or manufacturer may be slight; it may also be the case that the profit made by the manufacturer from his breach of duty far exceeds any loss recoverable from him. In addition, there will be situations in which numerous claimants have suffered broadly similar damage, whether through a common disaster or because they claim to have been injured by the same defect in a product, for example a drug or chemical. In such cases class actions may be brought in some jurisdictions, especially the United States, whereby a representative plaintiff or plaintiffs can recover damages for the whole class of consumers who could in principle sue.[5] Such actions are hedged about with restrictions, and may be difficult to finance except where this is possible on a contingency fee basis. In some countries such actions 14–103

---

[98] See the High Court and County Courts Jurisdiction Order 1991 (SI 1991/724) as amended by SI 1993/1407, SI 1995/205, SI 1996/3141, SI 1999/1014, SI 2001/1387, SI 2001/2685 and SI 2005/587.

[99] Art. 5.1, as substituted by SI 1999/1014, art. 6.

[1] Art. 4A, inserted by SI 1999/1014, art. 5.

[2] CPR Pt 29: Practice Direction 29–2.2.

[3] CPR r.26.6 (4) and (5). General matters relevant to the allocation to the appropriate track are listed in r. 26.7 and 26.8. The rules applicable to the two tracks are stated in Pt 28 (fast track) and Pt 29 (multi-track), respectively.

[4] *e.g.* Litigants in Person (Costs and Expenses) Act 1975; Applebey, 16 C.J.Q. 127 (1997).

[5] See Cranston's *Consumers and the Law* (3rd ed.), pp.120–133; Miller, Harvey and Parry, *Consumer and Trading Law: Text, Cases and Materials* (1998), pp.458–497; Jolowicz [1983] C.L.J. 222; 3 *Legal Studies* 295 (1983); Uff, 5 C.J.Q. 50 (1986); Glenn, 6 O.J.L.S. 262 (1986); Ontario Law Reform Commission, *Report on Class Actions* (1982); Australian Law Reform Commission, Discussion Paper No. 11 (1979); *Report of the Review Body on Civil Justice* (Cmnd. 394 (1988)), paras 274–276; Report of the National Consumer Council on "Group Actions" (1989); Mildred in Miller (ed.) *Product Liability and Safety Encyclopaedia*, Div. III A; *Group Actions Made Easier*, A Report of the Law Society's Civil Litigation Committee (1995); *Access to Justice* (HMSO, 1996) (The Final Report of the Woolf Committee), Ch.17; Hodges, *Multi-Party Actions* (2000); Mulheron, *The Class Action in Common Law System*: *A Comparative Perspective* (2005).

may be brought by consumer organisations or public agencies.[6] In England and Wales the court had the power to allow a representative action[7]; but it was by no means clear that such an action could lead to an award of damages, at least in typical situations involving consumers.[8] The problems were to some extent overcome, particularly in cases involving drugs (*e.g.* Opren) tranquillisers and the like, by adopting practical solutions based on steering committees and lead cases.[9]

14–104 Since May 2000 the previous representative action has been superseded by provisions for a Group Litigation Order under the new Civil Procedure Rules.[10] The background to such an order (known as a GLO) is the case management of claims which give rise to common or related issues of law or fact in circumstances where there are or are likely to be a number of claims giving rise to such issues.[11] A register is established,[12] a managing judge is appointed, and a judgment is binding on all who are on the register, unless the court orders otherwise.[13] The court may direct that litigation may proceed via a test claim[14] and there are provisions for the sharing of costs in group actions.[15] The detailed provisions are beyond the scope of this work.

14–105 **Conditional fee agreements.** Another prominent feature of certain types of litigation in the United States is the contingent fee under which the plaintiff's (claimant's) lawyer takes an agreed percentage of the damages if he wins the case but makes no charge if he loses. Such agreements are not enforceable in English law.[16] However, section 58 of the Courts and Legal Services Act 1990, as substituted by section 27(1) of the Access to Justice Act 1999, makes provision for conditional fee agreements.[17] Broadly

---

[6] See Tur, 2 *Legal Studies* 135 (1982); Fisch, 27 Am.J.Comp.L. 51 (1979); *e.g.* Trade Practice Act 1996 (B.C.); Consumer Affairs Act 1972–1978 (Vic.). The power accorded to certain consumer organisations to seek injunctions under the Unfair Terms in Consumer Contracts Regulations 1999 (SI 1999/2083), as amended by SI 2001/1186, SI 2003/3182, SI 2004/2095 and SI 2006/523 and the Part 8 procedures of the Enterprise Act, 2002 do not extend to a power to seek damages.

[7] See RSC, Ord. 15, r.12.

[8] See *Markt & Co. Ltd v Knight S.S. Co. Ltd* [1910] 2 K.B. 1021; *cf. Prudential Assurance Co. Ltd v Newman Industries Ltd* [1981] Ch.257; *E.M.I. Records Ltd v Riley* [1981] 1 W.L.R. 923; *Irish Shipping Ltd v Commercial Union Assurance Co. Plc* [1990] 2 W.L.R. 117; *Naken v General Motors of Canada Ltd* (1977) 92 D.L.R. (3d) 100.

[9] See Mildred in Miller (ed.) *Product Liability and Safety Encyclopaedia*, Div. III A.

[10] See the Civil Procedure (Amendment) Rules 2000 (SI 2000/221). For discussion in the context of product liability and other claims, see Mildred in Miller (ed.), *Product Liability and Safety Encyclopaedia*, Div. III A, paras [243] *et seq.*

[11] CPR Pt 19 III (Group Litigation), rr.19.10 and 19.11.

[12] Rule 19.11(2)(a).

[13] Rule 19.12(1)(a).

[14] Rule 19.13(b).

[15] CPR Pt 48, r.48.6A.

[16] For general discussion, see the Green Paper on *Contingency Fees* (Cmnd. 571 (1989)); Scott, 8 C.J.Q. 97 (1989).

[17] s.58 has been amended (along with s.58A) by the Secretary of State for Constitutional Affairs Order 2003 (SI 2003/1887), art. 9, Sch.2.

speaking, these are written agreements between advocates or litigators and their clients which provide for fees and expenses, or any part of them, to be payable only in specified circumstances, *e.g.* if the claim is successful. They may also provide for the fee to be subject to a percentage increase in specified circumstances. By section 58(1) a conditional fee agreement which satisfies all the conditions specified in section 58 shall not be unenforceable by reason only of its being such an agreement, but agreements which do not so comply generally are unenforceable.[18] Certain proceedings cannot be the subject of an enforceable conditional fee agreement, namely criminal proceedings and specified family proceedings.[19] Otherwise conditional fee agreements are permissible in other proceedings and they may provide for a success fee.[20] Where they do so provide the relevant percentage increase must be stated[21] and it must not exceed the maximum permitted amount,[22] which is currently 100 per cent.[23] Originally such matters as the contents of conditional fees agreements and the information to be given before they were made were subject to conditions which were stipulated by regulations.[24] However, these proved to be unduly complex and unnecessary and they have since been revoked[25] so as to leave such matters to control by primary legislation and the legal profession.

Powers of Criminal Courts (Sentencing) Act 2000. Under section 130(1) of the Powers of Criminal Courts (Sentencing) Act 2000 a court before whom a person is convicted of an offence, instead of or in addition to dealing with him in any other way, may, on application or otherwise, make an order requiring him to pay compensation for any personal injury, loss or damage resulting from that offence or any other offence which is taken into consideration.[26] It may also order him to make payments for funeral expenses or bereavement[27] in respect of a death resulting from any such 14–106

[18] There is an exception (see s.58(5)) for agreements within the Solicitors Act 1974, s.57.
[19] See s.58A of the 1990 Act which was added by the Access to Justice Act 1999, s.27(1).
[20] See the Conditional Fee Agreements Order 2000 (SI 2000/823), art. 3, specifying proceedings for the purposes of s.58(4)(a) of the 1990 Act. For a decision discussing when a "success fee" is reasonable, see *Atack v Lee* [2006] 1 W.L.R. 2643. Criminal proceedings under the Environmental Protection Act 1990, s.82, may be the subject of a conditional fee agreement, but may not provide for a success fee.
[21] Courts and Legal Services Act 1990, s.58(4)(b).
[22] See s.58(4)(c).
[23] Conditional Fee Agreements Order 2000 (SI 2000/823), art. 4.
[24] See the Conditional Fee Agreements Regulations 2000 (SI 2000/692), the Collective Conditional Fee Agreements Regulations 2000 (SI 2000/2988), the Conditional Fee Agreements (Miscellaneous Amendments) Regulations 2003 (SI 2003/1240) and the Conditional Fee Agreements (Miscellaneous Amendments) (No. 2) Regulations 2003 (SI 2003/2344) (collectively known as the CFA Regulations).
[25] See the Conditional Fee Agreements (Revocation) Regulations 2005 (SI 2005/2305) reg. 2. However the CFA Regulations continues to apply to agreements entered into before November 1, 2005: *ibid.* reg. 3(1).
[26] This does not include offences which have been admitted but not charged or taken into account: *R. v Crutchley and Tonks* (1994) 15 Cr.App.R.(S.) 627. See also ss.132 and 133 for appeals and review of compensation orders.
[27] See s.130(1)(b).

offence, other than a death attributable to an accident arising out of the presence of a motor vehicle on a road.[28] Broadly similar provisions were previously contained in section 35 of the Powers of Criminal Courts Act 1973 which has been repealed.[29]

14–107 The power to make a compensation order (which is not of course confined to consumer situations, but may prove of value to consumers) is exercisable by magistrates' courts and Crown Courts, though the jurisdiction of the former is limited to £5,000 for each offence of which the accused is convicted.[30] There is no set procedure and the court may even make such an order of its own motion. It must give reasons if an order is not made.[31] The amount is such as the court considers appropriate having regard to any evidence and to any representations that are made by or on behalf of the accused or the prosecutor.[32] In making an order the offender's means must be taken into account, so far as they appear or are known to the court,[33] and, where the offender has insufficient means to pay both an appropriate fine and appropriate compensation, preference must be given to the latter.[34] The power is applicable where an offence has been committed, even though there would be no civil liability,[35] *e.g.* in the case of misleading advertising, which might be an offence under the Trade Descriptions Act 1968[36] but might well not constitute a contractual promise or actionable representation.[37] Fine questions of causation will not be taken into account[38]; and the court may make assessments where the evidence is scanty or incomplete.[39] But it may not do so unless the right itself is clear.[40] Where civil proceedings have been settled it is not appropriate to make an order in respect of costs payable by the buyer.[41] Provision is also made for the effect of a compensation order on a subsequent award of damages in civil proceedings. Such damages are now to be assessed without regard to the

---

28 *ibid.* For other provisions relevant to injury, loss or damage arising in such circumstances, see s.130(6) to (8); see also s.130(5) for offences under the Theft Act 1968.

29 Leading cases decided under the 1973 Act included *R. v Inwood* (1974) 60 Cr.App.R. 70; *R. v Miller* (1979) 68 Cr.App.R. 56; *R. v Amey* [1983] 1 W.L.R. 346; *R. v Chorley Justices, ex p. Jones, The Times,* March 24, 1990; *R. v Godfrey* (1994) 15 Cr.App.R.(S.) 536; *R. v Palmer* (1994) 15 Cr.App.R.(S.) 550; see also Atiyah [1979] Crim.L.Rev. 504; Vennard, *ibid.*, 510.

30 Powers of Criminal Courts (Sentencing) Act 2000, s.131(1).

31 *ibid.*, s.130(3).

32 s.130(4).

33 s.130(11).

34 s.130(12). Where the offender is without means it is recognised that there is no point making a compensation order: (see *R. v Goodall* [2002] EWCA Crim 511, citing *R. v Jorge* [1999] 2 Cr.App.R. (S) 7.

35 *R. v Chappell* (1984) 80 Cr.App.R. 31.

36 Below, para.14–112.

37 Above, paras 10–005, 10–006. See *Chidwick v Beer* [1974] R.T.R. 415 ("excellent condition throughout"); *Furniss v Scholes, ibid.* p.133.

38 *R. v Thomson Holidays Ltd* [1974] Q.B. 592; *Bond v Chief Constable of Kent* [1983] 1 W.L.R. 40.

39 *R. v Horsham JJ., ex p. Richards* [1985] 1 W.L.R. 986 at 993.

40 *R. v Horsham JJ., above; R. v Chappell* (1984) 80 Cr.App.R. 31 at 35.

41 *Hammertons Cars Ltd v Redbridge London BC* [1974] 1 W.L.R. 484.

order. However, the claimant may only recover a sum equal to any amount by which they exceed such compensation and any portion of the compensation which he fails to recover.[42]

4. CRIMINAL LAW

Consumer protection by the criminal law. It will be apparent from the foregoing that the prospect of obtaining redress by a civil action is often an unsatisfactory one: the cost of preparing the case, producing the evidence and enforcing the judgment deters most private persons (though perhaps not most traders) with small claims, who tend to think that their protection should come from some public body. This has long been recognised, and a measure of consumer protection is provided by various statutes and regulations, most of which impose some form of criminal penalty for breach of duties imposed. Enforcement is typically by local weights and measures authorities or, in the case of the Food Safety Act 1990, food authorities established by section 5 of that Act. Many of the statutes permit the making of subordinate legislation creating or amplifying offences or controls. No more can be done here than indicate the common form provisions usually found in such consumer protection statutes. First, most of the offences thus created are ones of both strict and vicarious liability. Proof of *mens rea* is not required.[43] However, such strict liability is usually tempered by a "due diligence" defence. A standard example is section 39(1) of the Consumer Protection Act 1987, which provides that it shall be a defence for a person to show[44] that "he took all reasonable steps and exercised all due diligence" to avoid committing an offence. Section 39(2) makes provision for the common case in which the defence involves an allegation that the commission of the offence was "due (a) to the act or default of another; or (b) to reliance on information given by another." In any such case the defence cannot be relied upon, without the leave of the court, unless the prosecutor has been given notice seven clear days before the hearing. Such notice must give "such information identifying or assisting in the identification of the 14–108

[42] Powers of Criminal Courts (Sentencing) Act 2000, s.134.

[43] For a helpful discussion of the policy underlying such regulatory offences, see Cartwright, *Consumer Protection and the Criminal Law* (2001); *Chilvers v Rayner* [1984] 1 W.L.R. 328 (Robert Goff, L.J.). A notable example of an offence requiring proof of *mens rea* is the Trade Descriptions Act 1968, s.14, below, para.14–113. See also Tench, *Towards a Middle System of Law* (1981); Cranston, *Regulating Business: Law and Consumer Agencies* (1979); Miller, Harvey and Parry, *Consumer and Trading Law: Text, Cases and Materials* (1998), Chs 12 and 15.

[44] The onus is thus on the defendant. It may be discharged by proving the specified elements on the balance of probabilities: see *R. v Carr-Briant* [1943] K.B. 607. However, it is now possible, if unlikely, that by virtue of Art. 6 of the European Convention for the Protection of Human Rights and Fundamental Freedoms and the Human Rights Act 1998, s.3, such reverse onus provisions will be read as imposing only a lesser evidential burden on the defendant: see, generally, *R. v Lambert* [2001] UKHL 37; [2002] 2 A.C. 545, HL and *Sheldrake v DPP (Att-GenÆs Reference No. 4 of 2002)* [2004] UKHL 43; [2005] 1 A.C. 264; also, Cross and Tapper on *Evidence* (10th ed., 2004), Ch.III.

person who committed the act or default or gave the information as is in the possession of the person serving the notice at the time he serves it."[45] Similar provisions are to be found in other statutes.[46] Further common features of such statutes include provisions dealing with enforcement (powers of entry, search, seizure and offences of obstruction),[47] the liability of corporations and their officers[48] and with time limits for prosecution.[49] Another common provision is to be seen in the following example taken from section 20 of the Food Safety Act 1990. This provides that: "Where the commission by any person of an offence under any of the preceding provisions of this Part is due to an act or default of some other person, that other person shall be guilty of the offence; and a person may be charged with and convicted of the offence by virtue of this section whether or not proceedings are taken against the first-mentioned person."[50] The purpose of this "by-pass" or third-party procedure is to facilitate enforcement and the conviction of third parties whose act or default caused the commission of an offence by "the first-mentioned person."[51] However, the precise wording of this common form provision may vary, thus leading to uncertainty as to who may be convicted. The equivalent provision in section 40(1) of the Consumer Protection Act 1987 uses the expression "due to the act or default committed by some other person in the course of any business of his." In *R. v Warwickshire County Council, ex p. Johnson*[52] the House of Lords held that this did not include a branch manager of a major retailing group, but was limited, rather, to persons who owned or had a controlling interest in the company. On the other hand, section 23 of the Trade Descriptions Act 1968 simply refers to "the act of default of some other person" and it has been held that this may include a private individual.[53]

14–109 The principal statutes to which attention should be drawn are the Food Safety Act 1990, the Weights and Measures Act 1985, the Trade Descriptions Act 1968, and the Consumer Protection Act 1987.

---

[45] s.39(3).

[46] See, *e.g.* Trade Descriptions Act 1968, s.24; Weights and Measures Act 1985, s.35(1); Food Safety Act 1990, s.21(1) and (5)—supplemented by subss. (2), (3) and (4), modified by SI 2004/3279, reg. 7 and applied by numerous specific provisions relating to food. See, generally; Weatherill [1990] J.B.L. 36; Parry [1995] Crim.L.R. 695.

[47] See, *e.g.* Trade Descriptions Act 1968, ss.28, 29; Fair Trading Act 1973, ss.29, 30; Consumer Protection Act 1987, ss.29, 32; Food Safety Act 1990, ss.32, 33.

[48] See, *e.g.* Trade Descriptions Act 1968, s.20; Fair Trading Act 1973, s.132; Consumer Protection Act 1987, s.40(2); Food Safety Act 1990, s.36, modified by SI 2004/3279, reg. 7 and applied by numerous specific provisions relating to food.

[49] See, *e.g.* Trade Descriptions Act 1968, s.19; Fair Trading Act 1973, s.129; Food Safety Act 1990, s.34. In the absence of specific provisions, the general provisions of the Magistrates' Courts Act 1980, s.127(1) will apply.

[50] See also, *e.g.* Trade Descriptions Act 1968, s.23; Fair Trading Act 1973, s.24; Consumer Protection Act 1987, s.40(1).

[51] For the relationship between such provisions and the "due diligence" defence, see *Coupe v Guyett* [1973] 1 W.L.R. 669.

[52] [1993] 2 W.L.R. 1; see Miller, *All E.R.Rev. 1993*, pp.86–88.

[53] *Olgeirsson v Kitching* [1986] 1 W.L.R. 304. See, generally Cartwright, 59 M.L.R. 225 (1996).

The Food Safety Act 1990.[54] The Food Safety Act 1990 repealed and replaced earlier legislation, notably much of the Food Act 1984. The main provisions are to be found in Part II (sections 7–26), as amended, by, inter alia, the Food Standards Act 1999.[55] This both creates and largely re-enacts offences previously contained in the 1984 Act and empowers the Secretary of State to make regulations for inter alia, general food safety and consumer protection,[56] special provisions for particular foods,[57] and for the registration and licensing of food premises.[58] Considerable use has been made of these extensive enabling powers. Section 7 re-enacts the substance of a previous prohibition[59] against rendering food injurious to health by adding or abstracting articles or constituent parts with intent that the food should be sold for human consumption.[60] By section 8 it is an offence to sell[61] food which does not comply with food safety requirements as being unsafe within the meaning of Article 14 of Regulation (EC) No. 178/2002.[62] Section 14 re-enacts a long-standing prohibition[63] against selling to the purchaser's prejudice food which is not of the nature or substance or quality demanded, whilst section 15 creates offences based on falsely describing or presenting food.[64] Part II also contains important provisions covering the inspection and seizure of suspected food (section 9), the service of improvement notices (section 10) and prohibition orders (section 11) on proprietors of food businesses. There are provisions also for emergency prohibition notices and orders (section 12) and for the Secretary of State to issue emergency control orders (section 13). Overall, the powers are very extensive, as may be thought appropriate in an area where there is such an obvious need for consumer protection. 14–110

---

[54] See White Paper, *Food Safety: Protecting the Consumer* (Cmnd. 732, 1989); *Butterworths Law of Food and Drugs*; Practical Food Law Manual (Sweet & Maxwell); also *Halsbury's Statutes* (2005 Reissue), vol. 19, pp.1147 *et seq.*; Harvey and Parry, *Law of Consumer Protection and Fair Trading* (6th ed.), pp.429–443; Scott, 53 M.L.R. 785 (1990); Bradgate and Howells [1991] J.B.L. 320.

[55] s.40(1), Sch.5. See also the General Food Regulations 2004 (SI 2004/3279) which provide for the enforcement of certain provisions of Regulation (EC) No. 178/2002 ([2002] O.J. L31/1) laying down the general principles and requirements of food law, establishing the European Food Safety Authority and laying down procedures in matters of food safety; and the Food Safety Act 1990 (Amendment) Regulations 2004 (SI 2004/2990).

[56] s.16. Regulations may also be made to implement EC Directives (s.17).

[57] s.18.

[58] s.19.

[59] Previously contained in s.11 of the 1984 Act.

[60] s.7 of the 1990 Act has been amended by SI 2004/3279, reg. 9.

[61] The word "sell" is given an extended meaning by s.2.

[62] See the amendment introduced by SI 2004/3279, reg. 10. Article 14(2) provides that: "Food shall be deemed to be unsafe if it is considered to be: (a) injurious to health; (b) unfit for human consumption." Various factors which are relevant in making this assessment are listed in Art. 14.3-14.9.

[63] Previously contained in s.2 of the 1984 Act.

[64] Previously contained in s.6 of the 1984 Act. Further offences linked to contravention of or failure to comply with certain provisions of Regulation (EC) No. 178/2002 are provided for by SI 2004/3279, regs 4 and 5.

14–111 **The Weights and Measures Act 1985.**[65] The Weights and Measures Act 1985 consolidates a large body of legislation which formed perhaps the oldest major instance of public consumer protection. The principal Acts were those of 1963, 1976 and 1979. Part I lays down the units of measurement and makes provision as to the standards of measurement. Part II regulates weighing and measuring for trade, prescribing the units of measurement which are lawful for use for trade (a phrase widely defined by section 7), providing for control of weighing and measuring equipment and providing penalties for misuse of equipment, use of inaccurate equipment and failure to use approved equipment. It is under this part of the Act that, for example, beer for consumption on the seller's premises is normally served in a stamped glass: section 11(2) provides that "No person shall use any [weighing or measuring] equipment ... unless that article ... has been passed by an inspector as fit for such use and, except as otherwise expressly provided by or under this Act, bears a stamp indicating that it has been so passed ...ö Part III deals with public weighing and measuring equipment. Part IV deals with "Regulation of transactions in goods", and it is here that the most obvious consumer protection is to be found. Section 21 enacts four Schedules which regulate the sale of sand and other ballast, solid fuel, miscellaneous goods other than foods, and composite goods and collections of articles. Section 22(1) empowers the Secretary of State[66] to require by order that goods are only sold by quantity expressed in specified measures, that the quantity is marked on prepacked goods, and that the quantity of goods sold is in other cases made known to the buyer. The most conspicuous sections in the context of consumer protection are perhaps section 28, which creates an offence of delivering or causing to be delivered to a buyer a lesser quantity than that purported to be sold, and section 29, which creates an offence of making a misrepresentation as to the quantity of goods or doing any other act calculated to mislead a person buying or selling the goods as to the quantity thereof. In a related area the Prices Act 1974, section 4, as amended by the Price Commission Act 1977, section 16, empowers the Secretary of State to make orders for securing that prices are indicated on or in relation to goods which are to be sold retail.[67] A similar provision covers services.[68] Until recently relatively few goods were covered. Examples included food and drink sold and consumed on the premises,[69] and petrol.[70] More recently, the Price Marking Order 2004[71] which replaces a similar Order of 1999[72] imposes a much more general obligation in that, subject to limited exceptions,[73] "where a trader indicates that any product is

---

[65] O'Keefe, *Law of Weights and Measures* (2nd ed.); Harvey and Parry, *Law of Consumer Protection and Fair Trading* (6th ed.), pp.443–459.
[66] Originally the Board of Trade: at present the relevant Minister is the Secretary of State for Trade and Industry.
[67] s.4(1)(a).
[68] s.4(1)(b).
[69] Price Marking (Food and Drink Services) Order 2003, (SI 2003/2283).
[70] Price Marking (Petrol) Order 1980 (SI 1980/1121), as amended. See also the Price Marking Order 1991, (SI 1991/1382), as amended.
[71] SI 2004/102.
[72] SI 1999/3042.
[73] See arts 3 and 4(2).

or may be for sale to a consumer, he shall indicate the selling price of that product in accordance with the provisions of this Order."[74] The Order which requires inter alia that the unit price be clearly stated[75] seeks to give effect to an EC Directive.[76]

The Trade Descriptions Act 1968.[77] The Trade Descriptions Act 1968 is one of the most comprehensive measures of general consumer protection. It supersedes the Merchandise Marks Acts 1887–1953, which were principally directed at passing off and were regarded as unsatisfactory; though it should be noted that they, unlike the newer Act, conferred civil remedies in certain situations. Section 1 creates the principal offences of applying in the course of a trade or business[78] a false trade description to goods, or supplying or offering to supply goods to which a false trade description is applied. The notion of "trade description" is extremely widely defined by section 2, covering such things as quantity, size, gauge, method of manufacture, composition, fitness for purpose, strength, behaviour, accuracy, "any physical characteristics not included in the preceding paragraphs", testing by any person and the results thereof, approval by any person, place or date of manufacture, and "other history, including previous ownership or use". A false trade description is one false "to a material degree" and includes one that is misleading, this being defined in various ways (s.3). Applying a trade description includes the making of oral statements (s.4)[79] and may also include the publication of advertisements (s.5); a false trade description may be applied by a buyer.[80] Disclaimers (*e.g.* as to odometer readings on cars) will, if sufficiently clear,[81] prevent the offence of supplying or offering to supply goods to which a false description is applied[82] being 14–112

---

[74] See art. 4(1).
[75] See arts 5 and 7.
[76] Directive 1998/6/EC ([1998] O.J. L80/27).
[77] Bragg, *Trade Descriptions* (1991); *Butterworths Trading and Consumer Law*, Div. 3; Harvey and Parry, *Law of Consumer Protection and Fair Trading* (6th ed.), Ch.12; *Review of the Trade Descriptions Act 1968*, Cmnd. 6628 (1976). The principal Act is amended by various statutes: in particular, fresh provisions are made as to precious metals by the Hallmarking Act 1973 and regulations made thereunder.
[78] See *Davies v Sumner* [1984] 1 W.L.R. 1301 *cf.* in a different context *Stevenson v Rogers* [1999] Q.B. 1028 (Sale of Goods Act 1979, s.14), and *R & B Customs Brokers Co. Ltd v United Dominion Trust Ltd* [1988] 1 W.L.R. 321 (Unfair Contract Terms Act 1977, s.12).
[79] This can cover statements too vague to constitute operative representations under the civil law: *e.g. Chidwick v Beer* [1974] R.T.R. 415 ("in excellent condition throughout"); *Furniss v Scholes* [1974] R.T.R. 133 ("showroom condition throughout").
[80] *Fletcher v Budgen* [1974] 1 W.L.R. 1056; *cf. Wycombe Marsh Garages Ltd v Fowler* [1972] 1 W.L.R. 1156.
[81] See *Norman v Bennett* [1974] 1 W.L.R. 1229; *Zawadski v Sleigh* [1975] R.T.R. 113; *R. v Hammertons Cars Ltd* [1976] 1 W.L.R. 1243; *Waltham Forest LBC v TG Wheatley (Central Garage) Ltd (No.2)* [1978] R.T.R. 333; *Corfield v Starr* [1981] R.T.R. 380; *R. v Bull* 160 J.P. 24 (1996); *R. v Gregory* 1998 WL 1670525; *Farrand v Lazarus* [2002] EWHC 226; [2002] 3 All E.R. 175. (obligation to disclose known mileage: use of pro forma blanket disclaimer ineffective).
[82] But not the offence of applying the false description: *Newman v Hackney LBC* [1982] RTR 296; *R. v Southwood* [1987] 1 W.L.R. 1361; *Telford and Wrekin Council v Jordan* (2001) 165 J.P. 107.

committed: in this connection they are unaffected by the Unfair Contract Terms Act 1977 and not likely to be regarded as "unfair terms" within the meaning of the Unfair Terms in Consumer Contracts Regulations 1999.[83] Section 7 empowers the Secretary of State[84] to make orders assigning meanings to expressions; section 8 empowers him to require that goods are marked or accompanied by information or instructions; and section 9 empowers him to require that certain information is given in advertisements.[85]

14–113 Further important provisions are contained in section 14(1) of the principal Act which makes it an offence "for any person in the course of any trade or business—(a) to make a statement which he knows to be false; or (b) recklessly to make a statement which is false" as to certain specified matters. These include the provision, or nature or time or manner of supply of any services, accommodation or facilities. This section, which unusually requires proof of *mens rea*,[86] is particularly important as a means of controlling false statements in holiday brochures.[87] However, it has given rise to considerable difficulty in distinguishing between false statements of fact (which are covered) and simple unfulfilled promises as to the future provision of services which are not.[88] In a related area the Property Misdescriptions Act 1991 has been enacted to prohibit the making of false or misleading statements about a prescribed matter[89] in the course of an estate agency or a property development business.

14–114 **Consumer Protection Act 1987.**[90] Part I of the Consumer Protection Act 1987 (product liability) has been discussed in an earlier section.[91] Part II of the Act contains further important provisions. For the most part, these are

---

[83] SI 1999/2083, above, paras 14–030 *et seq*.

[84] Originally the Board of Trade. At present the relevant Minister is the Secretary of State for Trade and Industry.

[85] See Trade Descriptions (Sealskin Goods) (Information) Order 1980 (SI 1980/1150).

[86] *cf.* above, para.14–108. As to the potential overlap between ss.1 (goods) and 14 (services), see *Formula One Autocentres Ltd v Birmingham City Council* [1999] R.T.R. 195.

[87] *Wings Ltd v Ellis* [1985] A.C. 272 is a leading case. For further cases, see *R. v Piper* 160 J.P. 116 (1996); *Hotel Plan Ltd v Tameside MBC* [2001] EWHC Admin 154; *R. v Killian* [2002] EWCA Crim 404, (2002) 166 J.P. 169.

[88] See, *e.g. Breed v Cluett* [1970] 2 Q.B. 459; *Sunair Holidays Ltd v Dodd* [1970] 1 W.L.R. 1037, *R. v Sunair Holidays Ltd* [1974] 1 W.L.R. 1105, *British Airways Board v Taylor* [1976] 1 W.L.R. 13; *R. v Avro* (1993) 12 Tr.L.R. 83; *Lewin v Barratt Homes Ltd* [2000] Crim.L.R. 323.

[89] A "prescribed matter" is any matter relating to land which is specified in an order made by the Secretary of State: s.1(5)(d). See the Property Misdescriptions (Specified Matters) Order 1992 (SI 1992/2834). For a case applying the Act, see *Dacre Son & Hartley Ltd v North Yorkshire Trading Standards* [2004] EWHC (Admin) 2783, (2005) 169 J.P. 59.

[90] Miller, *Product Liability and Safety Encyclopaedia* (1979–2006), Div. IV; Howells, *Consumer Product Safety* (1998); Cartwright, "The Regulation of Product Safety" in Howells (ed.), *The Law of Product Liability* (2000), Ch.9 and *Consumer Protection and the Criminal Law* (2001), Ch.5; Miller and Goldberg, *Product Liability* (2004), Ch.19; Hodges, *European Regulation of Consumer Product Safety* (2005).

[91] Above, paras 14–080 *et seq*.

not new,[92] but rather they consolidate powers conferred by earlier statutes. Thus the Consumer Protection Acts 1961 and 1971[93] conferred on the Secretary of State powers to make regulations imposing, in respect of any prescribed class of goods, requirements as to composition or contents, design, construction, finish or packing in order to prevent or reduce risk of death or personal injury, and also to impose requirements as to marking.[94] It then created limited offences of selling, or having in possession for the purpose of selling, goods which contravened such regulations and component parts intended for such goods which if embodied in the goods would cause a breach of such regulations.[95] Although these Acts have been repealed, regulations made under the 1961 Act continue in force as if they were safety regulations made under section 11 of the 1987 Act.[96] It became apparent that the power to make such regulations was inadequate and that it needed to be supplemented by a power to act quickly so as to prevent the distribution of goods which were clearly unsafe. Such powers were conferred by the Consumer Safety Act 1978,[97] the main provisions of which were later taken over by the Consumer Protection Act 1987.

Safety regulations and the general safety requirement. The Consumer Protection Act 1987, section 11, confers on the Secretary of State powers to make regulations[98] for the purposes of securing (a) that goods are safe; (b) that goods which are unsafe (or would be unsafe in the hands of persons of a particular description) are not made available to persons generally or, as the case may be, to persons of that description; and (c) that appropriate information is provided and inappropriate information is not provided in respect of goods.[99] In particular, such regulations may contain provision with respect to the composition or contents, design, construction, finish or packing of goods[1] or they may require that goods satisfy certain specified standards[2] or are tested or inspected in prescribed ways.[3] By section 11(2)(j) 14–115

[92] A notable exception is the general safety requirement of s.10: see below, para.14–116 (since repealed and replaced by the General Product Safety Regulations 2005, SI 2005/1803, below, paras 14–119 *et seq*).
[93] The 1961 Act was amended as to accessories and due diligence by the Consumer Protection Act 1971.
[94] s.1.
[95] s.2.
[96] See the Consumer Protection Act 1987 (Commencement No. 1) Order 1987 (SI 1987/1680), arts 6 to 9. The limitation to sale or possessing for sale was removed by art. 8, so that the offence is now based on the wider notion of supplying goods.
[97] For the background, see *Consumer Safety: a consultative document*, Cmnd. 6398 (1976). The Act was amended by the Consumer Safety (Amendment) Act 1986.
[98] Usually, there is a requirement of consultation under s.11(5). In *R. v Secretary of State for Health, ex p. United States Tobacco International Inc.* [1992] Q.B. 353 failure to consult led to the Oral Snuff (Safety) Regulations 1989 (SI 1989/2347) being declared void following an application for judicial review. Subsequently they were replaced by the Tobacco for Oral Use (Safety) Regulations 1992 (SI 1992/3134). Consultation is not required where the regulations are of no more than 12 months' duration.
[99] s.11(1)(a)–(c).
[1] s.11(2)(a).
[2] s.11(2)(f).
[3] s.11(2)(g).

regulations may also (and typically will) prohibit persons from supplying,[4] or offering or agreeing to supply, or exposing or possessing for supply, specified goods and component parts and raw materials for such goods. A contravention of such a prohibition is an offence under section 12 and, as has been noted, a civil action will also lie.[5] A considerable number of regulations has now been made under section 11 and its immediate predecessor, section 1 of the Consumer Protection Act 1961,[6] or under an equivalent provision and in order to implement the requirements of EC Directives.[7] A comprehensive list of such regulations may be found elsewhere,[8] but the more important cover the following goods: filament lamps for vehicles,[9] pedal bicycles,[10] gas catalytic heaters,[11] asbestos products,[12] nightwear,[13] pushchairs,[14] bunk beds,[15] furniture and furnishings,[16] ceramic ware,[17] food imitations,[18] all-terrain motor vehicles,[19] tobacco products,[20] construction products,[21] fireguards for heating appliances,[22] simple pressure vessels,[23] machinery,[24] personal protective equipment,[25] medical devices,[26] imitation dummies,[27] electric plugs and sockets,[28] certain

---

[4] Comprehensively defined in s.46.

[5] s.41(1), see above, para.14–095.

[6] Regulations made under the 1978 Act continue in force notwithstanding the repeal of that Act by the Consumer Protection Act 1987, s.48(3) and Sch.5.

[7] They will then also be made or, as the case may be, made exclusively under the European Communities Act 1972, s.2(2). The notion of "safety" brings in further measures not entirely directed at consumers nor at sales. Examples include health and safety regulations made under the Health and Safety at Work Act 1974, s.15: see, *e.g.* the Chemicals (Hazard Information and Packaging for Supply) Regulations 2002 (SI 2002/1689), as amended and the Asbestos (Prohibitions) Regulations 1992 (SI 1992/3067), as amended. Further important examples include the Materials and Articles in Contact with Food (England) Regulations 2005 (SI 2005/898), and the Plastic Materials and Articles in Contact with Food (England) Regulations 2006 (SI 2006/1401).

[8] See, *e.g.* Miller, *Product Liability and Safety Encyclopaedia* (1979–2006), Div. IV, which contains the relevant texts.

[9] SI 1982/444.

[10] SI 2003/1101.

[11] SI 1984/1802, as amended by SI 1987/1979.

[12] SI 1985/2042, as amended by SI 1987/1979 and SI 1992/3067, as amended by SI 1999/2373, SI 1999/2977 and SI 2003/1889.

[13] SI 1985/2043, as amended by SI 1987/286.

[14] SI 1985/2047.

[15] SI 1987/1337.

[16] SI 1988/1324, as amended by SI 1989/2358 and SI 1993/207.

[17] SI 2006/1179.

[18] SI 1989/1291.

[19] SI 1989/2288.

[20] SI 2002/3041. See also SI 2004/765, SI 2004/1277 and SI 2004/1824.

[21] SI 1991/1620, as amended by SI 1994/3051.

[22] SI 1991/2693, See also SI 1995/1629.

[23] SI 1991/2749, as amended by SI 1994/3098.

[24] SI 1992/3073, as amended by SI 1994/2063 and SI 2005/831.

[25] SI 2002/1144.

[26] SI 2002/618, as amended by SI 2003/1400, SI 2003/1697 and SI 2005/2909.

[27] SI 1993/2923.

[28] SI 1994/1768.

dangerous substances and preparations,[29] motor vehicle tyres,[30] electrical equipment,[31] toys,[32] rubber teats and dummies,[33] gas appliances,[34] recreational craft[35] cosmetic products,[36] lifts,[37] fireworks,[38] wheeled child conveyances,[39] packaging,[40] pencils and graphic instruments,[41] cigarette lighter refills,[42] pressure equipment,[43] road vehicle brake linings[44] pressure systems,[45] dangerous substances and preparations (Nickel),[46] biocidal products[47] and blood.[48]

Important though these provisions are, they suffer from the limitation of being specific as to the goods to which they apply. A further and relatively innovatory provision was contained in section 10 of the 1987 Act which made it an offence to supply, etc.[49] any consumer goods[50] which fail to comply with the general safety requirement[51] by not being "reasonably safe"[52] having regard to all the circumstances, including certain designated circumstances. As will be noted later,[53] section 10 was largely superseded by the General Product Safety Regulations 1994,[54] although it remained in force until October 1, 2005 when it was repealed by the General Product Safety Regulations 2005.[55] These new Regulations cover a somewhat more 14–116

---

[29] SI 1994/2844, as amended by SI 1994/3247, SI 1996/2635, SI 1999/2084, SI 1999/3193, SI 2000/2897, SI 2002/1770, SI 2002/3010 and SI 2004/1417.
[30] SI 1994/3117, as amended by SI 1996/3227, SI 1997/815, SI 2003/1316 and SI 2003/2762.
[31] SI 1994/3260.
[32] SI 1995/204.
[33] SI 1995/1012.
[34] SI 1995/1629.
[35] SI 2004/1464, as amended by SI 2004/3201.
[36] SI 2004/2152, as amended by SI 2004/2361, SI 2004/2988, SI 2005/1815, SI 2005/3346 and SI 2006/1198.
[37] SI 1997/831, as amended by SI 2005/831.
[38] SI 2004/1836, as amended by SI 2004/3262.
[39] SI 1997/2866.
[40] SI 2003/1941, as amended by SI 2004/1188.
[41] SI 1998/2406.
[42] SI 1999/1884.
[43] SI 1999/2001, as amended by SI 2002/1267.
[44] SI 1999/2978, as amended by SI 2003/3314.
[45] SI 2000/128, as amended by SI 2004/568.
[46] SI 2005/2001.
[47] SI 2001/880, as amended by SI 2003/429 and SI 2005/2451.
[48] SI 2005/50, as amended by SI 2005/1098 and SI 2005/2898.
[49] "Supply" is comprehensively defined by s.46 of the Act. It was similarly an offence to offer or agree to supply, or expose or possess for supply: s.10(1)(b), (c).
[50] Defined by s.10(7) to mean "any goods which are ordinarily intended for private use or consumption," not being excluded goods within s.10(7)(a) to (f). Such excluded goods include aircraft, motor vehicles, controlled drugs and tobacco.
[51] The idea was raised in the White Paper, *The Safety of Goods*, Cmnd. 9302 (1984). A similar provision is contained in the Health and Safety at Work, etc. Act 1974, s.6.
[52] The word "safe" is defined by s.19 in terms of there being no risk, or no risk apart from one reduced to a minimum, of death or personal injury.
[53] Below, para.14–119.
[54] SI 1994/2328, as amended by SI 1994/3144.
[55] SI 2005/1803, reg. 46(2).

extensive ground than section 10 and indeed than the earlier 1994 version which is similarly revoked.[56]

14–117 **Prohibition notices and notices to warn.** The Consumer Protection Act 1987, section 13, confers further important powers on the Secretary of State.[57] Thus he may serve a "prohibition notice" on any person prohibiting that person from supplying, etc. any relevant goods[58] which the Secretary of State considers are unsafe and which are described in the notice.[59] Similarly he may serve a "notice to warn" on any person requiring that person to publish a warning about any relevant goods which the Secretary of State considers are unsafe and which are described in the notice.[60] Non-compliance with either type of notice is a criminal offence. Such provisions are clearly important, although rarely used in practice, as a way of dealing with unsafe goods which have found their way into the chain of distribution.

14–118 **Suspension notices and forfeiture.** There will be occasions when an enforcement authority has reasonable grounds for suspecting that a safety provision[61] has been contravened in relation to goods. By section 14 of the Consumer Protection Act 1987 the authority may then serve a "suspension notice" prohibiting the person on whom it is served from supplying, etc. the goods.[62] Such a notice may have a maximum duration of six months,[63] and compensation may be payable if a safety provision has not, in the result, been contravened.[64] There are provisions for appeals against suspension notices.[65] Section 16 of the 1987 Act empowers an enforcement authority to apply to a magistrates' court for an order for the forfeiture of goods on the ground that there has been a contravention in relation to the goods of a safety provision.[66]

---

[56] See SI 2005/1803, reg. 1(2).
[57] The powers were previously contained in the Consumer Safety Act 1978, s.3. They should be read in conjunction with Sch.2.
[58] As to which, see s.13(6).
[59] s.13(1)(a). Note, however, the limit imposed by s.13(7), which was added by the General Product Safety Regulations 2005 (SI 2005/1803), reg. 46(4). This provides that: "A notice may not be given under this section in respect of any aspect of the safety of goods, or any risk or category of risk associated with goods, concerning which provision is contained in the General Product Safety Regulations 2005."
[60] s.13(1)(b). For an attempt by a local authority to circumvent the requirements as to "notices to warn" by a Press release, see *R. v Liverpool City Council, ex p. Baby Products Association Ltd*, *The Times*, December 1, 1999 (baby walkers). The Divisional Court ruled this to be unlawful.
[61] Defined by s.45(1) (as amended by SI 2005/1803, reg. 46(7)) to mean a provision of safety regulations (s.11), a prohibition notice (s.13) or a suspension notice (s.14).
[62] Such a provision was previously contained in the Consumer Safety (Amendment) Act 1986, s.3.
[63] s.14(1).
[64] s.14(7).
[65] s.15. Almost invariably a suspension notice should be challenged by way of appeal and not judicial review: see *R. v Birmingham City Council, ex p. Ferrero Ltd* [1993] 1 All E.R. 530.
[66] Such a provision was previously contained in the Consumer Safety (Amendment) Act 1986, s.6. As to "safety provision", see above, n.61.

The General Product Safety Regulations 2005.[67] As was noted above,[68] these Regulations, which implement a European Community Directive,[69] replace the General Product Safety Regulations 1994[70] and also repeal the "general safety requirement" of section 10 of the Consumer Protection Act 1987.[71] The Regulations define the word "product" broadly[72]—so as to include products which are new, used or reconditioned[73] and those which are "intended for consumers or likely, under reasonably foreseeable conditions, to be used by consumers even if not intended for them".[74] They also cover products that are "supplied or made available to consumers for their own use in the context of providing a service".[75] Of course, many products (*e.g.* toys and cosmetics) are covered by specific sectoral directives which are then transposed into domestic law.[76] In such cases the general scheme is that the 2005 Regulations apply only to the aspects and risks not covered by the specific requirements.[77] To that extent the Regulations have only a residual role to play in ensuring product safety.[78] 14–119

The central obligation imposed by regulation 5(1) requires that: "No producer shall place a product on the market unless it is a safe product."[79] For this purpose the word "producer" is defined broadly to include 14–120

---

[67] SI 2005/1803.
[68] Above, para.14–116.
[69] Directive 2001/95/EC ([2002] O.J. L11/4) of the European Parliament and of the Council on general product safety (the GPS Directive). For discussion, see (*e.g.*) Miller and Goldberg, *Product Liability* (2004), paras 19.19–19.43; Miller, *Product Liability and Safety Encyclopaedia* (1979–2006), Div. IV, paras [9943—9990]; Fairgrieve and Howells, 69 M.L.R. 59 (2006); also various DTI Consultation Documents, including *Transposing the revised General Product Safety Directive* (2001) and *Consultation on proposals to implement Directive 2001/95/EC on general product safety (GPSD)* (December, 2004).
[70] SI 1994/2328, as amended by SI 1994/3144. These Regulations were based on and implemented Council Directive 1992/59/EEC ([1992] O.J. L228/24) on general product safety.
[71] See above, para.14–116.
[72] Reg 2.
[73] However, there is a defence for second-hand products supplied as antiques (reg. 30) and special provision is made for products supplied for repair or reconditioning prior to use (reg. 4).
[74] This addresses the issue of product migration where products intended for use by professionals are in practice also used by private individuals, *e.g.* in the course of DIY activities. Power tools are often cited in this context.
[75] Examples include a washing machine being "made available" to consumers in a launderette or an exercise machine in a fitness centre, but not equipment used by service providers themselves to supply a service to consumers (*e.g.* a train or a coach). *Cf.* the less extensive definition of "product" in reg. 2(1) of the 1994 Regulations.
[76] For examples, see above, para.14–115.
[77] Reg. 3 (1) and (2).
[78] However, even in the case of detailed sectoral directives the residual role will be important, notably in relation to the power to require the recall of unsafe products (see reg. 15 and below, para.14–122.
[79] See also reg. 5(4) which covers the "supply" (as defined in reg. 2) of products which are not safe products. There are further provisions (see reg. 5(2) and (3)) covering preparatory acts (*e.g.* offering or agreeing to place such a product on the market etc. or exposing or possessing it for such a purpose). For penalties, see reg. 20(1)–(3). A standard "due diligence" defence is contained in reg. 29.

manufacturers, own-branders, persons who recondition products and other professionals in the supply chain in so far as their activities may affect the safety properties of a product. Where the manufacturer is not established in a Member State the "producer" is his representative who is so established, or, if there is no such person, the importer of the product from a state that is not a Member State into a Member State.[80] A "safe product" is defined as one which "under normal or reasonably foreseeable conditions of use including duration and, where applicable, putting into service, installation and maintenance requirements, does not present any risk or only the minimum risks compatible with the product's use, considered to be acceptable and consistent with a high level of protection for the safety and health of persons."[81] In determining whether this standard has been achieved various matters must be taken into account, including the characteristics and presentation of the product and the category of consumers at risk when using it, particularly children and the elderly.[82] Producers are also subject to other obligations, including the provision of relevant information to consumers and the requirement to notify enforcement authorities of known risks associated with products which they have placed on the market or supplied.[83]

14–121 Although the above discussion is concerned with "producers", a person who is not a "producer" may none the less attract liability as a "distributor", who for this purpose is defined to mean "a professional in the supply chain whose activity does not affect the safety properties of a product."[84] A standard example is a retailer selling on a boxed item of electrical equipment. The principal obligation in any such case is to act with due care in order to help ensure compliance with applicable safety requirements.[85] In particular, a "distributor" must not supply, etc. a product which he knows is, or should have presumed to be, a dangerous product.[86] There are further obligations, including participating in monitoring the safety of products which have been placed on the market and notifying enforcement authorities of risks to consumers known to be associated with products which the distributor has placed on the market or supplied.[87]

14–122 A significant feature of the new General Product Safety Regulations 2005[88] is that, unlike their predecessor,[89] they contain their own detailed enforcement provisions. These cover not only standard powers of carrying

---

[80] See reg. 2.
[81] *ibid.* In turn, a "dangerous product" is defined as "a product other than a safe product"; *ibid.*
[82] *ibid.* See also reg. 6, which contains a limited presumption of conformity where a product complies with mandatory health and safety requirements or with certain national UK standards and makes further reference to other relevant factors, including recommendations of the European Commission and codes of good practice.
[83] See, respectively, regs 7 and 9.
[84] See reg. 2.
[85] Reg. 8(1).
[86] Reg. 8(1)(a).
[87] See, respectively, regs 8(1)(b) and 9. For penalties, see reg. 20(1)–(3). A standard "due diligence" defence is contained in reg. 29.
[88] SI 2005/1803.
[89] SI 1994/2328.

out test purchases and of entry into premises and the search and seizure of products and records, etc.,[90] but also powers which build on, but go beyond, those contained in Part II of the Consumer Protection Act 1987.[91] Thus in relation to dangerous products there are powers to serve "suspension notices", "requirements to mark" and "to warn", to serve "withdrawal notices" and to apply for an order for the forfeiture of a product.[92] However, the most important and controversial measure is a power to serve a "recall notice" where an enforcement authority has reasonable grounds for believing that a product is a dangerous product and that it has already been supplied or made available to consumers.[93] It is envisaged that the power will be used only as a last resort and where alternative means are insufficient to safeguard consumers.[94] As is well known, products are frequently recalled by producers on a voluntary basis, whether as a result of newspaper advertisements or more direct means of communication. Mandatory recall is, however, a significant new power to have in reserve.

Finally, Part 4 of the General Product Safety Regulations 2005 contains important provisions, the purpose of which is to implement Articles 11, 12 and 13 of the General Product Safety Directive. In broad outline, the general scheme is for enforcement authorities to inform the Secretary of State of product-related risks which have been notified to them[95] and, where appropriate, for the Secretary of State to pass the information on to the competent authorities in Members States where the product in question is or has been marketed or otherwise supplied to consumers.[96] Obligations are also imposed on enforcement authorities to notify the Secretary of State of measures taken to restrict the placing on the market of products or to require their withdrawal or recall and the Secretary of State must in turn notify the European Commission.[97] In the event of a "serious risk",[98] **14–123**

---

[90] See reg. 21 (test purchases), reg. 22 (entry and search, etc.) and reg. 23 (supplemental provisions); also reg. 24 (obstruction of officers), reg. 25 (appeals against detention of products and records), reg. 26 (compensation for seizure and detention), reg. 27 (recovery of expenses of enforcement) and reg. 28 (power of Secretary of State to obtain information).

[91] See above, paras 14–117—14–118

[92] See reg. 11 (suspension notices), reg. 12 (requirements to mark), reg. 13 (requirements to warn), reg. 14 (withdrawal notices) and reg. 18 (forfeiture); also reg. 16 (supplementary provisions relating to safety notices), reg. 17 (appeals against safety notices) and reg. 20(4) (offences). An important difference is that under the 1987 Act, s.13, the power to serve prohibition notices and notices to warn is reserved to the Secretary of State, whereas the 2005 Regulations confer powers on enforcement authorities (as defined in reg. 10).

[93] Reg. 15. For provisions as to the payment of compensation where the product is not in the result dangerous, see reg. 16(6) and for appeals, see reg. 17.

[94] See reg. 15(4) and (5). The point is made explicitly in Art. 8.2 of the GPS Directive. For discussion of product recalls, see Cartwright in Howells (ed.) *The Law of Product Liability* (2000), paras 9.66–9.70 and [2006] L.M.C.L.Q. 231.

[95] See reg. 33(1). For the obligation of producers and distributors to notify an enforcement authority, see reg. 9(1). Guidelines for the notification of dangerous consumer products to the competent authorities of the Member States are to be found in Commission Decision 2004/905/EC of December 14, 2004.

[96] Reg. 33(1).

[97] Reg. 33(2)–(4).

[98] Defined by reg. 2 as "a serious risk including one the effects of which are not immediate, requiring rapid intervention."

notification to the Commission must be through the Community Rapid Information System, known as "RAPAX".[99] Although it is primarily a matter for individual Member States to take appropriate measures with regard to dangerous products located within their territory, Article 13 of the Directive provides for situations in which such states differ in their approach to dealing with the risks posed by products. In the event of a serious risk, where urgent action is required and not forthcoming, the Commission may as a last resort adopt a decision to require Member States to take measures from among those listed in Article 8(1)(b)–(f).[1] This includes banning the marketing of products and ordering their withdrawal and recall. Prior consultation with Member States is required and in general the decision is valid for a period not exceeding one year, which may, however, be extended.[2] By Article 13(3) "Export from the Community of dangerous products which have been the subject of [such as decision] shall be prohibited unless the decision provides otherwise."[3]

14–124 **Misleading price indications.** Part III of the Consumer Protection Act 1987 is concerned with an entirely different area from the safety provisions outlined above. It replaces earlier legislation dealing with the vexed problem of so-called "bargain offers".[4] The basic offence is contained in section 20(1) and it is committed by a person who "in the course of any business of his . . . gives (by any means whatever) to any consumers an indication which is misleading as to the price at which any goods, services, accommodation or facilities are available (whether generally or from particular persons)."[5] The key word "misleading" is extensively defined in section 21. Section 25 enables the Secretary of State to approve codes of practice for purposes which include the giving of practical guidance with respect to the requirements of section 20.[6] Non-compliance or compliance with such a code may be relied upon in proceedings as tending to show that a price indication was or was not misleading.[7] Section 26 is also important as enabling the Secretary of State to make regulations, for example to prohibit a price indication from referring to prescribed matters or to require information or explanations to be given.[8]

---

[99] Reg. 33(5). See also Art. 10 and Recital 25 of the GPS Directive.

[1] See Art. 13(1) and Recitals 30, 31 and 32 of the GPS Directive; also reg. 35.

[2] There is no time limit where the decision concerns specific, individually identified products or batches of products: (see Art. 13.2).

[3] For implementation of this provision, see reg. 35(4).

[4] The legislation was of considerable complexity: see the Trade Descriptions Act 1968, s.11, and the Price Marking (Bargain Offers) Order 1979 (SI 1979/364), as amended.

[5] For an important case decided under s.20, see *R. v Warwickshire County Council, ex p. Johnson* [1993] A.C. 583; and see Miller, *All E.R. Rev.* 1993, pp.86–88.

[6] See the Consumer Protection (Code of Practice for Traders on Price Indications) Approval Order 2005 (SI 2005/2705), approving the Code of Practice for Traders on Price Indications.

[7] s.25(2).

[8] See the Price Indications (Method of Payment) Regulations 1991 (SI 1991/199); the Price Indications (Bureaux de Change) (No. 2) Regulations 1992 (SI 1992/737); and the Price Indications (Resale of Tickets) Regulations 1994 (SI 1994/3248); Bragg, 51 M.L.R. 210 (1988).

5. Administrative Protection

The Fair Trading Act 1973 and the Enterprise Act 2002.[9] The Fair Trading Act 1973 created the office of Director-General of Fair Trading[10] and conferred upon the holder considerable powers, a number of which concerned the protection of consumers against unfair trading practices. The office of Director-General was abolished by the Enterprise Act 2002[11] and the corresponding functions were transferred to the Office of Fair Trading or OFT.[12] The principal functions of the OFT include the acquisition of information, the provision of information etc. to the public, the provision of information and advice to Ministers, etc. and the promoting of good practice in the carrying out of activities which may affect the economic interests of consumers in the United Kingdom.[13] The powers discussed in this section are, for convenience, referred to as affording administrative protection to the consumer. However, it will be seen that some of them involve the setting in motion of normal legal mechanisms and techniques and that some are now shared with other public bodies and indeed consumer organisations. There are also important functions and powers in connection with what may be broadly termed uncompetitive trade practices, for example, mergers and cartels, but these are not discussed here. 14–125

Special procedure for delegated legislation. The Fair Trading Act 1973 set up a body called the Consumer Protection Advisory Committee[14] and created a special procedure for making orders[15] to prohibit consumer trade practices[16] which were adversely affecting the economic interests of consumers in the United Kingdom.[17] However, the procedure was very 14–126

---

[9] Harvey and Parry, *The Law of Consumer Protection and Fair Trading* (6th ed.), Ch.11; *Butterworths Trading and Consumer Law*, Div. 1. See also Borrie, *The Development of Consumer Law and Policy—Bold Spirits and Timorous Souls* (1984); [1978] J.B.L. 317.

[10] s.1.

[11] s.2(2).

[12] s.2(1).

[13] See, respectively, ss.5, 6 and 7. Annual plans must be drawn up (s.3) and annual reports must be made (s.4). For discussion of consumer codes, see below, para.14–137.

[14] s.3.

[15] The orders made under s.22(2) of the Act were subject to the affirmative resolution procedure (s.22(4)). A more general power to make recommendations was contained in s.2(3).

[16] Defined by s.13 as "any practice which is for the time being carried on in connection with the supply of goods (whether by way of sale or otherwise) to consumers or in connection with the supply of services for consumers and which relates—(a) to the terms or conditions (whether as to price or otherwise) on or subject to which goods or services are or are sought to be supplied, or (b) to the manner in which those terms or conditions are communicated to persons to whom goods are or are sought to be supplied or for whom services are or are sought to be supplied, or (c) to promotion (by advertising, labelling or marking of goods, canvassing or otherwise) of the supply of goods or of the supply of services, or (d) to methods of salesmanship employed in dealing with consumers, or (e) to the way in which goods are packed or otherwise got up for the purpose of being supplied, or (f) to methods of demanding or securing payment for goods or services supplied."

[17] s.13. There were certain exceptions: see s.16 and Sch.5.

protracted and tightly circumscribed and soon fell into desuetude before being eventually abolished by section 10 of the Enterprise Act 2002. The abolition was, however, without prejudice to the continuing operation of orders which had already been made and offences created,[18] namely: the Mail Order Transactions (Information) Order 1976;[19] the Consumer Transactions (Restrictions on Statements) Order 1976[20] as amended by the Consumer Transactions (Restrictions on Statements) (Amendment) Order 1978;[21] and the Business Advertisements (Disclosure) Order 1977.[22] The first such order has since been revoked and replaced by the Consumer Protection (Distance Selling) Regulations 2000.[23]

14–127 **Super-complaints to OFT.** A new and innovatory provision in section 11 of the Enterprise Act 2002 enables a designated consumer body[24] to complain to the OFT that any feature, or combination of features, of a market in the United Kingdom for goods or services is or appears to be significantly harming the interests of consumers. In any such case the OFT must publish a response stating how it proposes to deal with the complaint and what actions, if any, it proposes to take.[25] Examples of such complaints include one made by the National Association of Citizens Advice Bureaux in relation to doorstep selling[26] and one made by the Consumers' Association (now Which?) in relation to the care homes sector.[27]

14–128 **Enforcement of consumer legislation.** The enacting of delegated legislation and the creation of a mechanism for making "Super-complaints" which were outlined above[28] are not designed to enable enforcement agencies to target individual traders who are repeatedly in breach of criminal or civil obligations or otherwise acting in a way which is detrimental to the interests of consumers. Rather, they are of more general application. However, a means of controlling such persistent offenders has been available for some time. The original procedures were set out in Part III (sections 34 to 42) of the Fair Trading Act 1973. These applied where it appeared to the Direction-General of Fair Trading that a person had in the course of a

---

[18] See the Enterprise Act 2002, s.10(2)(a). Nor, indeed, the power to revoke them: s.10(2)(b). The associated offences and enforcement provision of ss.23–33 of the 1973 Act accordingly remain in force.
[19] SI 1976/1812.
[20] SI 1976/1813.
[21] SI 1978/127.
[22] SI 1977/1918.
[23] SI 2000/2334, reg. 2.
[24] By s.11(5) this means "a body designated by the Secretary of State by order". The list of such bodies is contained in the Schedule to the Enterprise Act 2002 (Bodies Designated to make Super-complaints) Order 2004, (SI 2004/1517), as substituted by SI 2005/2340, art. 2(2) and amended by SI 2005/2468. It includes the National Consumer Council, the Consumers Association and the National Association of Citizens Advice Bureaux.
[25] s.11(2). See also the Enterprise Act 2002 (Super-Complaints to Regulators) Order 2003 (SI 2003/1368).
[26] See *Butterworths Consumer Law Bulletin*, Issue No. 195, December, 2002, p.4.
[27] See *Butterworths Consumer Law Bulletin*, Issue No. 225, June, 2005, p.3.
[28] Above, paras 14–126 and 14–127.

business persisted in a course of conduct which was detrimental to the interests of consumers and unfair to consumers. In that event, the Director-General might seek a written assurance from the person concerned that he would refrain from such a course of conduct.[29] If the assurance was not forthcoming, or was given but not observed, then an application for an injunction could be made to the High Court or a county court and breach of any such order, or undertaking given in lieu, would be punishable as a contempt of court.[30] The power, although apparently quite broadly expressed, was limited in a number of important respects. In particular, there had to be an element of "persistence" in the offending conduct and the Director-General could not proceed without first having used his "best endeavours" to obtain a "satisfactory written assurance"[31] that the relevant conduct would cease. Also, the notion of conduct which was "unfair to consumers" was limited to breaches of the criminal or civil law.[32]

The Stop Now Orders (EC Directive) Regulations 2001. The above procedures of Part III of the Fair Trading Act 1973 were significantly enhanced by the introduction of the Stop Now Orders (EC Directive) Regulations 2001[33] which gave effect to Directive 1998/27/EC on injunctions for the protection of consumer interests (the "Injunctions Directive").[34] The Regulations applied only to "Community infringements", that is, acts which were contrary to designated Directives as transposed into the internal legal order of a Member State and which harmed the collective interests of consumers included in the Directives.[35] In relation to such infringements, a new and less restrictive set of procedures was introduced by the Regulations[36] and other qualified bodies or entities were given the power to initiate proceedings.[37] 14–129

[29] s.34. The Director might publicise the assurance by a press release (see *R. v Director-General of Fair Trading, ex p. FH Taylor & Co. Ltd* [1981] I.C.R. 292.

[30] s.37.

[31] s.34(1).

[32] s.34(2) and (3). Hence there was no power to act where the element of "unfairness" lay in the use of contract terms which could not have been relied on by virtue of the Unfair Contract Terms Act 1977 (above, paras 13–062 *et seq.*), unless, of course, use of such a term was also a criminal offence (see below, para.14–142). The limitation was largely overcome by procedures established under the Unfair Terms in Consumer Contracts Regulations of 1994 and 1999 (see, respectively, SI 1994/3159, reg. 8, and SI 1999/2083, regs 10–15; also, above, para.14–040).

[33] SI 2001/1422.

[34] [1998] O.J. L166/51.

[35] See reg. 2(1). Relevant UK laws were listed in reg. 2(3) and the corresponding Directives in Sch.1.

[36] See reg. 3 and Sch.2.

[37] See Sch.2, para.1. The definition of a "qualified entity" was contained in reg. 2(1). It included public UK qualified entities (as listed in Sch.3), qualified entities from other Member States (reg. 2(1)) and other UK qualified entities whose purpose is to protect the collective interests of consumers and which meet specified criteria (reg. 4).

14–130 **Enterprise Act 2002, Part 8.** The Enterprise Act 2002 repeals Part III (sections 34 to 42) of the Fair Trading Act 1973 and revokes the Stop Now Orders (EC Directive) Regulations 2001,[38] replacing them with the new Part 8 (sections 210 to 236) procedures and enforcement provisions.[39] These provide a mechanism for bringing to an end "domestic" and "Community" infringements[40] which are harming the collective interests of consumers.

14–131 **The definitions of "consumer".** Section 210 of the 2002 Act defines the word "consumer" in a way which distinguishes between the two categories of infringements noted above. In relation to domestic infringements, a consumer is "an individual"[41] to whom goods or services are supplied or sought to be supplied in the course of a business carried on by the person supplying or seeking to supply them[42] and who receives or seeks to receive the goods of services otherwise than in the course of a business carried on by him, or with a view to carrying on a business but not in the course of a business carried on by him.[43] It is immaterial whether the person supplying etc. the goods or services has a place of business in the United Kingdom.[44] In the case of a "Community infringement", a "consumer" is a person (not necessarily an "individual"), who is a consumer for the purposes of the Injunctions Directive and the relevant listed Directive.[45] There is no complete uniformity of definitions in the various Directives, although in general a "consumer" is a natural person who acts for purposes outside his trade, business or profession.

14–132 **Domestic infringements.** Section 211(1) of the Enterprise Act 2002 defines a "domestic infringement" as "an act or omission which—(a) is done or made by a person in the course of a business, (b) falls within subsection (2), and (c) harms the collective interests of consumers in the United Kingdom". In other words, the infringement must harm, or create a

---

[38] See s.278 and Sch.26; also the Enterprise Act 2002 (Commencement No. 3, Transitional and Transitory Provisions and Savings) Order 2003, (SI 2003/1397), art. 2 and Sch., bringing the changes into force with effect from June 20, 2003.
[39] For general guidance issued by the OFT in relation to Pt 8, see *Investigation, consulting and enforcing: An OFT guide to Part 8 of the Enterprise Act; Enforcement of consumer protection legislation: Guidance on Part 8 of the Enterprise Act*, June 2003.
[40] As to which, see further, below, paras 14–132—14–133.
[41] The word "individual" appears to be synonymous with a "natural person", which is the expression frequently used in EC Directives (see (*e.g.*) Joined Cases C-541/99 and C-542/99 *Cape Snc v Idealservice Srl; Idealservice MN RE SAS v MAI Srl* [2001] E.C.R. I-9049 (ECJ), interpreting Art. 2(b) of Directive 93/13/EEC on unfair terms in consumer contracts as excluding companies. Partnerships would also be excluded.
[42] s.210(2) and (3).
[43] s.210(4). Hence an individual may be a "consumer" (and so within the protective framework of Pt 8) when acquiring goods or services with a view to starting a business (perhaps as a home-worker or an aspiring author), but not when carrying on a business. For the definition of "business", see s.210(8).
[44] s.210(5)
[45] s.210(6) The relevant Directives are as specified in Sch.13 See further, below, para.14–133.

risk of harm to, the public generally or at least that sector of the public which buys or may buy the goods or services in question. Although there is no requirement that the offending conduct be "persistent",[46] a degree of regularity would in practice have to be present before the "collective interests of consumers" could be said to be affected. Section 211(2) requires that the relevant act or omission be specified by the Secretary of State by order and meet the broadly expressed criteria of section 211(2)(a)–(g). The Enterprise Act 2002 (Part 8 Domestic Infringements) Order 2003)[47] contains a long list of enactments in respect of which acts or omissions may constitute "domestic infringements". These include not only such specific measures as the Trade Descriptions Act 1968, the Unfair Contract Terms Act 1977 and the Sale of Goods Act 1979, but also more generally worded provisions covering "An act done or omission made in breach of contract for the supply of goods or services to a consumer [or] in breach of a duty of care owed to a consumer under the law of tort or delict of negligence."

Community infringements. Section 212(1) of the Act defines a "Community infringement" as "an act or omission which harms the collective interests of consumers[48] and which—(a) contravenes a listed Directive[49] as given effect by the laws, regulations or administrative provisions of an EEA State,[50] or (b) contravenes such laws, regulations or administrative provisions which provide additional permitted protections."[51] By section 222(3) the Secretary of State may by order specify the corresponding laws of the United Kingdom and this was done in the Enterprise Act 2002 (Part 8 Community Infringements Specified UK Laws) Order 2003.[52] The relevant "listed Directives" are set out in Schedule 13 to the 2002 Act[53] and the corresponding UK laws are as stated in the Schedule to the 2003 Order. The lists are lengthy and detailed and cover such areas as misleading advertising,[54] contracts negotiated away from business premises,[55] consumer 14–133

[46] *Cf.* the requirement in Pt III of the Fair Trading Act 1973, above, para.14–128.
[47] SI 2003/1593.
[48] Note that this is not limited to consumers in the UK.
[49] See s.210(7) and Sch.13. The list builds on the one previously contained in the Stop Now Orders (EC Directive) Regulations 2001 (SI 2001/1422), above, para.14–129.
[50] See s.212(5).
[51] Such additional permitted protection may exist where the relevant Directive is one of minimum harmonisation, as with Directive 1999/44/EC on certain aspects of the sale of consumer goods and associated guarantees.
[52] SI 2003/1374, as amended by SI 2005/2418.
[53] As amended by SI 2003/1374, art. 2 (since superseded by SI 2005/2759, reg. 4, Sch., para.19) and the Financial Services (Distance Marketing) Regulations 2004 (SI 2004/2095), reg. 26.
[54] See Directive 1984/450/EEC ([1984]) O.J. L250/17) and the corresponding provision in the Control of Misleading Advertisements Regulations 1988 (SI 1988/915). Comparative advertising is not covered.
[55] See Directive 1985/577/EEC ([1985] O.J. L372/31) and the corresponding provisions in the Consumer Protection (Cancellation of Contracts Concluded Away from Business Premises) Regulations 1987 (SI 1987/2117), as amended.

credit,[56] package travel, package holidays and package tours,[57] unfair terms in consumer contracts,[58] timeshares,[59] distance selling,[60] aspects of the sale of consumer goods and associated guarantees,[61] and the distance marketing of consumer financial services.[62]

14–134 Section 213 of the Act establishes the various categories of "enforcers" for the purposes of the Part 8 provisions. They are "general enforcers" (notably the OFT and local weights and measures authorities)[63] and enforcers which have been designated by order as having as one of their purposes the protection of the collective interests of consumers.[64] This category of "designated enforcers" comprises both independent public bodies[65] and private organisations which meet designated criteria and enforcers may be designated in respect of all infringements or such infringements as may be specified.[66] The final category is a "Community enforcer", that is a body which is neither a general enforcer nor a designated enforcer but which is a qualified entity for the purposes of the Injunctions Directive[67] and listed as such in the *Official Journal of the European Communities*.[68] There are also provisions for enabling enforcers

---

[56] See Directive 1987/102/EEC ([1987] O.J. L43/48), as amended, and the corresponding provisions in the Consumer Credit Act 1974 and secondary legislation made thereunder (not including consumer hire agreements and ss.137–140 (extortionate credit bargains)).
[57] See Directive 1990/314/EEC ([1990] O.J. L158/59) and the corresponding provisions in the Package Travel, Package Holidays and Package Tours Regulations 1992 (SI 1992/3288), as amended.
[58] See Directive 1993/13/EEC ([1993] O.J. L95/29) and the corresponding provisions in the Unfair Terms in Consumer Contracts Regulations 1999 (SI 1999/2083), as amended.
[59] See Directive 1994/47/EC (O.J. L280/83) and the corresponding provisions in the Timeshares Act 1992 and secondary legislation made thereunder (not including its application to timeshare accommodation in caravans).
[60] See Directive 1997/7/EC ([1997] O.J. L144/19) and the corresponding provisions in the Consumer Protection (Distance Selling) Regulations 2000 (SI 2000/2334).
[61] See Directive 1999/44/EC ([1999] O.J. L171/12) and the corresponding provisions which were introduced by the Sale and Supply of Goods to Consumers Regulations 2002 (SI 2002/3045).
[62] See Directive 2002/65/EC ([2002] O.J. L271/16) and the corresponding provisions in the Financial Services (Distance Marketing) Regulations 2004 (SI 2004/2095).
[63] s.213(1). General enforcers may apply for an enforcement order in respect of any infringement (s.215(2)).
[64] s.213(2). Designated enforcers may apply for an enforcement order in respect of an infringement to which the designation relates (s.215(3)).
[65] s.213(3).
[66] s.213(6). The Enterprise Act 2002 (Part 8 Designated Enforcers: Criteria for Designation, Designation of Public Bodies as Designated Enforcers and Transitional Provisions) Order 2003 (SI 2003/1399) designates the relevant public bodies including utility and other industry regulators (art. 5 and Sch.) and establishes criteria for designating non-public bodies (arts 3 and 4). See also SI 2004/935 (designation of the Financial Services Authority) and SI 2005/917 (designation of the Consumers, Association).
[67] That is, Directive 98/27/EC (O.J. L166/51). Community enforcers may apply for an enforcement order in respect of a Community infringement (s.215(4)).
[68] s.213(5). For the bodies so listed, see the Commission Communication concerning Article 4(3) of Directive 98/27/EC printed in O.J. C39 of 16.2.2006, pp.2–38.

to take proceedings in other EEA States and for cooperating with Community enforcers.[69] This may be important when a trader is operating from another EEA State but in such a way as to harm the collective interests of consumers in the United Kingdom.[70]

Where an enforcer contemplates bringing proceedings for an enforcement order the usual requirement is one of trying to achieve the cessation, non-repetition or, in the case of a Community infringement, the non-occurrence of the infringement through an appropriate consultation with the apparent offender.[71] Attempts to achieve cessation may be dispensed with where the OFT thinks that an application for an order should be made "without delay"[72] and, in any event, the period of grace will expire within 14 days after the request for consultation is received.[73] Applications for an enforcement order may be made to the High Court or a county court[74] and are subject to a significant amount of control in the form of directions by the OFT,[75] one purpose of which is to prevent multiple applications in respect of the same infringement in different parts of the country. The court may make an order where it finds that the person named in the application has engaged in the conduct which constitutes the infringement or, in the case of a Community infringement, is likely to do so.[76] Breach of such an order will attract the usual sanctions of the law of contempt. **14–135**

In general, it may be said that the Part 8 procedures are helpful in establishing a new framework to deal with persons who are in breach of criminal or civil obligations and who thereby harm the collective interests of consumers. However, the procedures are not free from complexity, not least because of the central distinction which is taken between "domestic infringements" and "Community infringements" falling within the scope of the Injunctions Directive.[77] As a further complication, the new procedures **14–136**

---

[69] s.221.

[70] Hence the OFT has used its cross-border enforcement powers to secure binding undertakings preventing a Dutch marketing company from publishing and distributing misleading mailings to UK residents (see *Butterworths Consumer Law Bulletin*, Issue No. 225, June, 2005, p.4).

[71] s.214(1)(a). The OFT must also be consulted where it is not the enforcer (s.214(b)).

[72] s.214(3).

[73] s.214(4)(a). Or seven days in the case of an application for an interim enforcement order (s.214(4)(b)).

[74] s.215(5)(a). No doubt in practice it will be a county court.

[75] s.216 which does not, however, prevent an application for an enforcement order being made by a Community enforcer (s.216(6)).

[76] s.217(1) and (2). There are provisions also for interim enforcement orders (s.218) and for accepting undertakings in lieu of an order (s.219). For enforcement orders against bodies corporate and accessories, see ss.222 and 223. For an example of an interim enforcement order being made both against a company and its directors, see *Office of Fair Trading v MB Designs (Scotland) Ltd* 2005 S.L.T. 691 (Outer House: Lord Drummond Young). The decision also confirms the important point that it is permissible to have regard to conduct which occurred before the Part 8 provisions came into force.

[77] For "domestic" and "Community" infringements, see, respectively, above, paras

overlap with more specific sources according powers to apply for injunctions, notably in the area of unfair contract terms, misleading advertising and distance selling.[78] Again, whilst the OFT (previously the Director-General of Fair Trading) is able to act under all these enactments there is no common list of others who may do so.

14–137 **Codes of practice; advice to consumers.** For many years the Office of Fair Trading and its Director-General have encouraged relevant trade associations to prepare and disseminate to their members' codes of practice for guidance in safeguarding and promoting the interests of consumers in the United Kingdom. Indeed, under the Fair Trading Act 1973 the Director General was under a duty to provide such encouragement.[79] Codes have been produced in many sectors of industry, including the motor industry, electrical and electronic appliances, footwear distributors and such services as laundry, glass and glazing and holidays.[80] Originally, the Director-General did not have any formal power to approve or validate a code. However, this has now changed as a result of the new provisions in section 8 of the Enterprise Act 2002 under which the OFT may make arrangements for approving consumer codes and, in accordance with such arrangements, give its approval to or withdraw its approval from any consumer code. In pursuance of this power the OFT has developed a two-stage process of approval with an initial preliminary approval being followed by a period of monitoring the operation of the code in practice.[81] Codes have been approved in such areas as the sale of new cars, vehicle repairs, direct selling, travel agents and estate agency.[82] Of course there are limits to what

14–132 and 14–133. Linked to this it will also be necessary to ensure that in respect of Community-based legislation the enforcement procedures comply with Regulation (EC) No. 2006/2004 on cooperation between national authorities responsible for the enforcement of consumer protection laws ([2004] O.J. L364/1). The Regulation applies from December 29, 2005 and it covers the Directives and Regulations listed in its Annex.

[78] See, respectively, the Unfair Terms in Consumer Contracts Regulations 1999 (SI 1999/2083, as amended by SI 2001/1186, S.I 2003/3182, SI 2004/2095 and SI 2006/523), reg. 12 and Sch.l; Control of Misleading Advertising Regulations 1988 (SI 1988/915), reg. 5; and the Consumer Protection (Distance Selling) Regulations 2000 (SI 2000/2334, as amended), reg. 27.

[79] s.124(3). See Borrie [1980] J.B.L. 315; Page [1980] J.B.L. 24; Pickering and Cousins, *European Journal of Marketing*, 31 (1982, No.6); Harvey and Parry, *Law of Consumer Protection and Fair Trading* (6th ed.), Ch.11, pp.360–379; Cranston's *Consumers and the Law* (3rd ed.), Ch.2, pp.42–51; *Voluntary Codes of Practice: A consultation paper* (OFT, 1996); *Raising Standards of Consumer Care: Progressing Beyond Codes of Practice* (OFT, Feb. 1998); *Modern Markets: Confident Consumers* (Cm. 4410) (1999).

[80] A selection of codes is printed in *Butterworths Trading and Consumer Law*, Div. 1; see also Harvey and Parry, *op. cit.*, pp.364–376.

[81] See *Core Criteria for Consumer Codes of Practice* (OFT, 390) (May, 2002).

[82] See the OFT publication *Fair Trading*, Issue 39, November, 2004, p.1 (noting the approval of the codes produced by the Society of Motor Manufacturers and Traders and the Vehicle Builders and Repairers Association Ltd (VBRA); also *Butterworths Consumer Law Bulletin*, No. 222, March, 2005, p.3 (Direct Selling Association Code of Practice), *Butterworths Consumer Law Bulletin* No. 230, November 2005, p.2 (which contains a list of such approved codes and makes reference to the OFT logo).

can be achieved through such codes. Sanctions for non-compliance may not be fully effective and less-reputable traders may not in any event belong to the association which draws up the code; but there are indications that the codes have reduced the number of consumer complaints and that they provide significant protection to consumers, especially in areas which do not lend themselves to a stricter form of regulation through the criminal or civil law.[83] The 2002 Act (and its predecessor) also empowers the OFT to publish information and advice to the public and to Ministers[84] and this power has been extensively exercised over the years.

Controlling other trade practices. The Office of Fair Trading also has extensive powers which enable it to exercise a less direct control over consumer protection measures. First, it has a key role under the Competition Act 1998 and the Enterprise Act 2002 in investigating and taking enforcement proceedings against agreements or practices which prevent, restrict or distort competition within the United Kingdom. Secondly, it has important functions regarding the granting of licences under the Consumer Credit Act 1974[85] and the revoking of licences granted to traders who by virtue of the trade practices in which they indulge appear unfit to hold a licence. Trading without a licence when one is required is an offence.[86] Similar possibilities of indirect control are contained in the Estate Agents Act 1979 which enables the making of an order prohibiting unfit persons from doing estate agency work.[87] In addition, the Secretary of State may by order declare a practice to be "undesirable" in relation to estate agency work.[88] An estate agent who engages in such a practice may then be prohibited from doing estate agency work under the provisions noted above. **14–138**

In relatively recent years there has been considerable discussion as to whether it would be appropriate to adopt a broadly-based provision to control trading malpractices.[89] Such provisions exist in some other common **14–139**

---

[83] Indeed, even the European Commission Green Paper, *European Union Consumer Protection* (COM (2001) 531 final) recognises (see para.4.4) that many problems are not suitable for regulatory action and effective self-regulation is more appropriate.

[84] See the Enterprise Act 2002, ss.6 and 7.

[85] Below, para.14–146. As to the significance of these powers, see Borrie, *The Development of Consumer Law and Policy—Bold Spirits and Timorous Souls* (1984), Ch.4. See also Borrie [1982] J.B.L. 91.

[86] Consumer Credit Act 1974, s.39. See (*e.g.*) *R. v Curr* (1980) 2 Cr.App.Rep. (S.) 153, CA (12 months' prison; £2,400 fine).

[87] s.3. Provisions for "warning orders" are contained in s.4. See, generally, Bragg, 55 M.L.R. 368 (1992); also *Antonelli v Secretary of State for Trade and Industry* [1998] Q.B. 948 (offences committed abroad and prior to commencement of 1979 Act may be taken into account). Examples of this power being used are noted in *Butterworths Consumer Law Bulletin* No. 226, July 2005, p.5 (Nottingham agent) and No. 227, August 2005, p.4 (Buckinghamshire agent). The operation of such orders is stayed pending any appeal.

[88] s.3(1)(d). See the Estate Agents (Undesirable Practices) (No. 2) Order 1991 (SI 1991/1032), and the Estate Agents (Specified Offences) (No. 2) Order 1991 (SI 1991/1091), as amended by SI 1992/2833.

[89] See Borrie, *The Development of Consumer Law and Policy—Bold Spirits and Timorous Souls* (1984), Ch.4, pp.74–77; *A General Duty to Trade Fairly: A Discussion Paper* (OFT, 1986); *Report by the Director-General of Fair Trading on Trading Malpractices* (1990); Borrie, 107 L.Q.R. 559 (1991); Harland, 111 L.Q.R. 100 (1995).

law jurisdictions, usually being linked to notions of deceptive, misleading or unconscionable practices.[90] A possible technique is to supplement a general clause with non-exhaustive lists of practices falling within it. The idea was advanced in a European Commission Green Paper on *European Union Consumer Protection*[91] and it has since been carried forward in Directive 2005/29/EC concerning unfair business-to-consumer commercial practices (the "Unfair Commercial Practices Directive").[92] The general scheme of the Directive is to prohibit "unfair commercial practices" which are defined to mean a practice which is "contrary to the requirements of professional diligence" and which "materially distorts or is likely to materially distort the economic behaviour with regard to the product of the average consumer whom it reaches or to whom it is addressed, or of the average member of the group when a commercial practice is directed to a particular group of consumers".[93] A broad distinction is taken between "misleading" and "aggressive" practices and there is a lengthy list of commercial practices which are in all circumstances considered to be unfair. Member States must adopt any provisions which are necessary to comply with the Directive and then apply them by December 12, 2007. This may require some considerable reshaping of English law.

6. INDIRECT PROTECTION

14–140 **Advertising control.** Various statutes impose control on advertising. The Broadcasting Act 1990[94] imposes a duty on the Independent Television Commission to draw up a code of advertising standards and secure compliance with it. Statutes may prohibit or empower the prohibition of the advertising of certain types of medicinal product or medical equipment, for example the Medicines Act 1968.[95] The Energy Act 1976[96] requires the provision of specified information as to relevant official tests in promotional literature referring to fuel consumption of passenger cars, and makes further provision regarding the giving of information as to such tests. There are many statutory provisions as to labelling and packaging.[97] The Consumer Credit Act 1974 contains provisions which control advertising.[98] There is also a voluntary code of practice, the British Code of Advertising Practice, administered by a non-statutory body, the Advertising Standards Authority. A more recent and wider-ranging example is to be found in the

---

[90] For an excellent (if now dated) survey, see Belobaba, 15 Osgood Hall L.J. 327 (1977). See also Australian Trade Practices Act 1974 (Cth.) (as amended), Pt. V; Skapinker and Carter, 113 L.Q.R. 294 (1997).
[91] COM (2001) 531 final, esp. paras 4.1 and 4.2.
[92] [2005] O.J. L149/22. For discussion, see Twigg-Flesner, 121 L.Q.R. 386 (2005); Stuyck, Terryn and Van Dyck, 43 C.M.L. Rev. 107 (2006).
[93] Art. 2.
[94] s.9.
[95] Pt VI.
[96] s.15(3).
[97] *e.g.* in the Food Safety Act 1990, the Medicines Act 1968 and the Weights and Measures Act 1985.
[98] Below, para.14–155.

Control of Misleading Advertisements Regulations 1988[99] made under section 2(2) of the European Communities Act 1972.[1] This requires the Office of Fair Trading (previously the Director-General of Fair Trading to consider complaints (other than frivolous or vexatious ones) about misleading advertisements.[2] However, before doing so the complainant may be required to establish that appropriate means of dealing with the complaint have been tried and found inadequate in the circumstances.[3] Such means might include complaining to, for example, the Advertising Standards Authority or a local trading standards department. The OFT is also empowered to bring proceedings for an injunction to prevent the publication of an advertisement which it considers misleading.[4] Any such injunction may be granted on such terms as the court thinks fit.[5] Contravention of laws concerning advertising may also constitute both a domestic and a Community infringement, thus leaving open the possibility of proceeding under the Part 8 provisions of the Enterprise Act 2002,[6] which have superseded Part III of the Fair Trading Act 1973 and the Stop Now Orders (EC Directive) Regulations 2001.[7]

Control of specific trading practices.[8] Various statutes regulate trading practices (including those involving advertising) which could be conducted in a harmful way. Self-explanatory examples are the Trading Representations (Disabled Persons) Acts 1958 and 1972 and the Mock Auctions Act 1961. Part XI of the Fair Trading Act 1973 empowers the making of regulations regarding "pyramid selling" and similar trading schemes.[9] Section 40 of the Administration of Justice Act 1970 makes it an offence to 14–141

[99] SI 1988/915 as amended, notably by the Control of Misleading Advertisements (Amendment) Regulations 2000 (SI 2000/914) and the Control of Misleading Advertisements (Amendment) Regulations 2003 (SI 2003/3183).

[1] The regulations implement Council Directive No. 1984/450/EEC ([1984] O.J. L 250/17) relating to misleading advertisements; and see also in relation to comparative advertising Directive 1997/55/EC ([1997] L290/18) and Directive 2005/29/EC ([2005] O.J. L149/37), Art. 14. For a leading case applying the Regulations, see *Director General of Fair Trading v Tobyward Ltd* [1989] 2 All E.R. 266. For a reference to the banning of misleading advertisements for Citra-Slim "slimming" tablets, see *Butterworths Consumer Law Bulletin*, No. 119, August 1996, p.2.

[2] Reg. 4. The Office of Communications established by the Office of Communications Act 2002, s.1(1) (OFCOM) is under a similar duty to consider complaints in relation to licensed services (reg. 8, as amended by SI 2003/3183, reg. 3).

[3] Reg. 4(3).

[4] Reg. 5. As to the control by OFCOM, see reg. 9, as amended by SI 2003/3183, reg. 4.

[5] Reg. 6(1). The relevant court is the High Court in relation to England, Wales and Northern Ireland and the Court of Session in relation to Scotland: reg. 2(1).

[6] For "domestic infringements", see s.211 of the Act and the Enterprise Act 2002 (Part 8 Domestic Infringements) Order 2003 (SI 2003/1593), art. 2 and Sch. For "Community infringements", see s.212 of the Act; also, Sch.13, and the Enterprise Act 2002 (Part 8 Community Infringements Specified UK Laws) Order 2003 (SI 2003/1374)) art.3 and Sch. (except comparative advertising). See, generally, above, paras 14–130—14–136.

[7] SI 2001/1422. See reg. 2(1) and (3)(a) and Sch.1, para.1.

[8] See Cranston's *Consumers and the Law* (3rd ed.), pp.418–424.

[9] See s.119 of the Act; the Trading Schemes Regulations 1997 (SI 1997/30) and the Trading Schemes (Exclusion) Regulations 1997 (SI 1997/31).

harass debtors in specified ways (*e.g.* by falsely representing that criminal proceedings lie in respect of failure to pay). Some practices are controlled by statutory instrument. For example, the Business Advertisements (Disclosure) Order 1977[10] made under section 22 of the Fair Trading Act 1973 provides that a person seeking to sell goods in the course of a business shall not publish an advertisement indicating that goods are for sale which is likely to induce consumers to buy unless it is reasonably clear from the contents of the advertisement, its format or size, the place or manner of publication or otherwise, that the goods are to be sold in the course of a business. This is to prevent, for example, the placing of several advertisements in a publication by a business seller, each of which separately gives the impression that a private seller is involved; with the result that the buyer may be unaware that the various legal restrictions on, and terms implied into, sale in the course of a business are applicable.[11]

14–142 **Consumer Protection (Restrictions on Statements) Order 1976.**[12] This Order, again made under the Fair Trading Act 1973,[13] prohibits persons who in the course of a business sell goods to consumers or supply them under hire purchase transactions from purporting by notices, advertisements or statements on or with goods to apply terms which are void[14] by virtue of section 6 of the Unfair Contract Terms Act 1977.[15] It also prohibits them from supplying statements about the consumer's rights against the supplier relating to quality, fitness or description[16] without at the same time notifying the consumer that his statutory rights are unaffected; and a similar restriction is placed on third parties, *e.g.* manufacturers and wholesalers, who supply goods intended or expected to be the subject of a consumer transaction where the goods bear or are in a container bearing a statement about the obligations accepted by that third party.[17]

---

[10] SI 1977/1918.

[11] For an unusually restrictive approach to this provision, see *Blakemore v Bellamy* [1983] R.T.R. 303.

[12] SI 1976/1813; as amended (to take account of the changes introduced by the Unfair Contract Terms Act 1977) by Consumer Protection (Restrictions on Statements) (Amendment) Order 1978 (SI 1978/127).

[13] Above, para.14–126.

[14] Section 6 does not in fact make any term void, though its predecessor the Supply of Goods (Implied Terms) Act 1973 had done so (see s.4, amending s.55 of the Sale of Goods Act 1893). It simply provides that in a consumer sale the obligations contained in ss.13, 14 and 15 of the Act cannot be excluded or restricted by reference to any contract term: above para.13–084. Hence at least where a term contains an unobjectionable part, it is arguable that no offence can be committed under the Act.

[15] In *Hughes v Hall* [1981] R.T.R. 430 the phrase "sold as seen and inspected" in the sale of a second-hand car was held to involve an offence. But in *Cavendish-Woodhouse Ltd v Marley* (1984) 82 L.G.R. 376 the phrase "bought as seen" in the sale of furniture was held not to do so. See above, para.13–067. Curiously, there is no similar provision for terms which are "void" by virtue of, for example, s.2(1), above, para.13–092 or s.7(2), above, para.13–085.

[16] Arising under ss.13 to 15 of the Sale of Goods Act 1979, and protected by s.6 of the Unfair Contract Terms Act 1977.

[17] The statutory rights would normally be against the actual seller: but see also Unfair Contract Terms Act 1977, s.5, above, para.14–069, which relates to manufacturers' guarantees.

7. CONSUMER CREDIT TRANSACTIONS

Consumer Credit Act 1974. A wide-ranging system of control over consumer credit transactions and over those whose business it is to provide consumer credit is exercised by the Consumer Credit Act 1974. Most of the Act became operative on May 19, 1985,[18] and from that day the existing provisions of the Moneylenders Acts 1900 to 1927[19] and the Hire-Purchase Act 1965[20] were repealed.[21] At the time of writing, significant modifications to some of the provisions of the 1974 Act are awaited pending the bringing into force of the Consumer Credit Act 2006.[22] These are noted in the relevant parts of the text which follows. However, it is anticipated that the provisions of the new Act will be brought into force only gradually over a period of time and hence that, even in areas which are affected by the new legislation, the old law will remain important for some time to come.[23] Unless specifically exempted by the 1974 Act[24] or order made under the Act,[25] any agreement made between an individual[26] ("the debtor") and any other person ("the creditor") by which the creditor provides the debtor with credit[27] not exceeding £25,000[28] is a regulated agreement for the 14–143

---

[18] Certain sections of the Act were, however, brought into force before that date. Moreover, some sections are retrospective and apply to an agreement "whenever made" or to an agreement made before May 19, 1985, where the agreement would have been a regulated agreement if made on that day. See Sch.3.

[19] But the repeal did not affect agreements made with, or any loans made by or security taken by, a moneylender before May 19, 1985: see art. 6(3) of SI 1983/1551 (c. 44), below.

[20] In respect of hire-purchase, conditional sale and credit sale agreements falling within the 1965 Act and made before May 19, 1985: see art. 6(1), (2) of SI 1983/1551 (c. 44), below.

[21] Consumer Credit Act 1974 (Commencement No. 8) Order 1983 (SI 1983/1551).

[22] For some of the background to the new provisions, see the DTI White Paper, *Fair, Clear and Competitive: The Consumer Credit Market in the 21st Century* (Cm. 6040, December, 2003); also Lomnicka, [2004] J.B.L. 129. Further reform may be required once proposals at the EU level have been agreed (see the second revised proposal relating to consumer credit COM (2005) final of October 7, 2005). For the background to the 1974 Act, see the *Report of the Committee on Consumer Credit* (Cmnd. 4596, March, 1971) (the Crowther Committee Report).

[23] Orders will be made under s.71(2) of the Act. The first such order was made on June 10, 2006: see the Consumer Credit Act 2006 (Commencement No.1) Order 2006 (SI 2006/1508). Transitional provisions and savings are contained in s.69 and Sch.3.

[24] s.16, as amended.

[25] Consumer Credit (Exempt Agreements) Order 1989, (SI 1989/869), as amended by SI 1989/1841, SI 1989/2337, SI 1991/1393, SI 1991/1949, SI 1991/2844, SI 1993/346, SI 1993/2922, SI 1994/2420, SI 1995/1250, SI 1995/2914, SI 1996/1445, SI 1996/3081, SI 1999/1956 and SI 2006/1273. For firms from other EEA Member States exercising their "European passport", see the Financial Services and Markets Act 2000, ss. 31(1)(b), (c) and Schs 3, 4. Note also *ibid.*, ss. 194, 203 (as amended by SI 2000/2952, reg. 8(2)), 204.

[26] Defined in s.189(1) to include "a partnership or other unincorporated body of persons not consisting entirely of bodies corporate".

[27] Defined in ss.9(1), 189(1).

[28] The financial limit was raised from £5,000 to £15,000 from May 20, 1985, by the Consumer Credit (Increase of Monetary Limits) Order 1983 (SI 1983/1878) and to £25,000 from May 1, 1998, by the Consumer Credit (Increase of Monetary Limits) (Amendment) Order 1998 (SI 1998/996).

purposes of the Act.[29] An agreement may be a regulated agreement even though credit is provided for business purposes, for example, to a sole trader or partnership. Subject to the financial limit, the criterion is, not the purpose of the credit, but the status of the debtor, *i.e.* whether or not the debtor is a body corporate. An agreement may be a regulated agreement even though the creditor does not carry on the business of providing credit.[30]

14–144 Under the new provisions the financial limit will be removed, but the effect of this is reduced in a number of important respects. First, the definition of an "individual" is narrowed so that it will include a partnership only if it consists of two or three persons not all of whom are bodies corporate.[31] Thus, large and even medium-sized partnerships will be outside the scope of the Act's protection. Secondly, the new provisions empower the Secretary of State to make an order providing that the Act will not regulate a consumer credit or hire agreement where the debtor or hirer is a natural person who agrees to forego the protection of the Act and is, in effect, certified as being of "high net worth".[32] Thirdly, there will be a general exemption from the regulation of the Act for consumer credit and hire agreements exceeding £25,000 where the agreement is entered into by the debtor or hirer wholly or predominantly for the purposes of a business carried on, or intended to be carried on, by him.[33] Thus, the £25,000 limit will remain important in this context.

The 1974 Act is a most complex piece of legislation and is supplemented by a large number of statutory instruments of even greater complexity.

14–145 **Outline of control.** The 1974 Act makes provision for the form and content of regulated agreements[34] and of security instruments,[35] for example, guarantees and indemnities,[36] given in respect of regulated agreements, and for the supply of copies to the debtor and sureties.[37] In some circumstances the credit agreement will be subject to a "cooling-off period" during which

---

[29] s.8.

[30] Certain sections of the Act do not, however, apply to a "non-commercial agreement", defined in s.189(1) as a consumer credit agreement not made by the creditor in the course of a business carried on by him.

[31] s.1, amending the previous definition in s.189(1) of the 1974 Act (above, n.26). The definition will continue to include an unincorporated body of persons which does not consist entirely of bodies corporate and is not a partnership.

[32] s.3 inserting a new s.16A.

[33] s.4 inserting a new s.16B.

[34] ss.60, 61; Consumer Credit (Agreements) Regulations 1983 (SI 1983/1553), as amended by SI 1984/1600, SI 1985/666, SI 1988/2047, SI 1999/3177, SI 2001/3649, SI 2004/1482, SI 2004/2619 and SI 2004/3236. See also the Consumer Credit (Disclosure of Information) Regulations 2004 (SI 2004/1481) made under s.55 of the Act.

[35] s.105.

[36] Consumer Credit (Guarantees and Indemnities) Regulations 1983 (SI 1983/1556), as amended by SI 2004/3236.

[37] ss.62–64, 105; Consumer Credit (Cancellation Notices and Copies of Documents) Regulations 1983 (SI 1983/1557), as amended by SI 1984/1108, SI 1985/666, SI 1988/2047, SI 1989/591, SI 2004/2619 and SI 2004/3236.

it may be cancelled by the debtor.[38] Restrictions are placed upon the power of the creditor to enforce a regulated agreement, to terminate it or to exercise his rights under the agreement in the event of the debtor's default.[39] The debtor has a statutory right to settle the agreement early if he so wishes,[40] and upon early settlement he becomes entitled to a rebate of future interest and charges.[41] The county court[42] is given wide discretionary powers to control regulated agreements,[43] including the power to make a "time order" whereby a debtor will be permitted to pay any sum owed by him by such instalments and at such times as the court, having regard to his means, considers reasonable, or to remedy any other breach of the agreement within such period as the court may specify.[44] The debtor is also entitled, while the agreement continues, upon request and the payment of £1[45] to a copy of the agreement and a statement of his account with the creditor.[46] The Consumer Credit Act 2006 contains further provisions as to annual statements which must be provided by creditors both in fixed sum and running account credit agreements.[47]

Licensing. A licence is required to carry on a consumer credit business,[48] 14–146
that is to say, any business so far as it comprises or relates to the provision of credit under regulated consumer credit agreements.[49] Unlicensed trading not only attracts a criminal penalty[50] but renders any regulated agreement

---

[38] ss.67–73. See above, para.14–045.

[39] ss.76, 87, 98; Consumer Credit (Enforcement, Default and Termination Notices) Regulations 1983 (SI 1983/1561), as amended by SI 1984/1109 and SI 2004/3237. Further detailed provisions relating to default under regulated agreements and notice of sums in arrears are contained in the Consumer Credit Act 2006, ss.8–14, which, when fully in force, will add new ss.86A to 86F and amend s.88. See also ss.90–92, 93, 126. S.127(3) of the Act which in certain circumstances prevents the making of enforcement orders under s.65(1) (improperly executed agreements) has been challenged as being incompatible with Art. 6 of the European Convention on Human Rights, but this challenge was rejected (at least in the case of a loan under £25,000), *obiter* by the House of Lords in *Wilson v Secretary of State for Trade and Industry* [2003] UKHL 40, [2004] 1 A.C. 816. Nonetheless, s.15 of the Consumer Credit Act 2006, will, when in force, repeal s.127(3) and allow enforcement at the discretion of the court.

[40] ss.94, 96.

[41] s.95; Consumer Credit (Early Settlement) Regulations 2004 (SI 2004 No.1483), as amended by SI 2004/2619. See also s.97; Consumer Credit (Settlement Information) Regulations 1983 (SI 1983/1564), as amended by SI 2004/1483.

[42] Actions to enforce a regulated agreement must be brought in the county court: s.141.

[43] Part IX (ss.127–144).

[44] s.129.

[45] Raised by SI 1998/997.

[46] ss.77, 78. See also ss.107, 108 (information to sureties) and s.78(4); Consumer Credit (Running-Account Credit Information) Regulations 1983 (SI 1983/1570) (periodic information under running-account credit agreements), as amended by SI 2004/3236.

[47] ss.6 and 7, adding a new s.77A and amending s.78 of the 1974 Act.

[48] s.21(1). See, generally, Borrie [1982] J.B.L. 91. As to the meaning of "business" in this context, see *R. v Marshall* (1990) 90 Cr.App.R. 73.

[49] s.189(1), (2).

[50] s.39(1). See also the Financial Services and Markets Act 2000, s.31, Sch.3, para.15(3).

made when the creditor is unlicensed unenforceable against the debtor in the absence of an order made by the Office of Fair Trading (OFT).[51] A licence is also required to carry on an ancillary credit business,[52] *e.g.* credit-brokerage.[53] A regulated agreement made on an introduction by an unlicensed credit-broker is similarly unenforceable against the debtor except upon an order of the OFT.[54] The licence must be specifically extended if it is to cover canvassing off trade premises.[55] Further detailed provisions introducing a general overhauling of the licensing system and the OFT's enforcement powers and extending the jurisdiction of the Financial Ombudsman Service set up under the Financial Services and Markets Act 2000[56] to consumer credit disputes are contained in the Consumer Credit Act 2006.[57]

14–147 **Hire-purchase and conditional sale.** The draftsman of the Act has formulated many of its provisions by reference to a new and complex terminology. Both hire-purchase[58] and conditional sale[59] agreements are for "fixed-sum" credit.[60] Unlike the Hire-Purchase Act 1965, where the limit was calculated by reference to the total sum payable under the agreement by the hirer or buyer, the £25,000 limit of the 1974 Act is calculated by reference to the balance financed, *i.e.* the total sum less the credit charges and any initial deposit.[61] A regulated hire-purchase or conditional sale agreement is a debtor-creditor-supplier agreement[62] for restricted-use credit,[63] whether the creditor is the supplier of the goods or a finance company which has purchased the goods from the supplier. Most of the general provisions of the Act apply to hire-purchase and conditional sale agreements, but there are also special provisions which govern such agreements.[64]

[51] s.40; see also SI 1992/3218, reg. 61(1) and (4) and SI 1995/3275, reg. 38(1).
[52] ss.145, 147. As to s.147(1), see also the Financial Services and Markets Act 2000, s.31, Sch.3, para.15(3).
[53] s.145(2).
[54] s.149; see also SI 1992/3218, reg. 61(3) and (4) and SI 1995/3275, reg. 38(3).
[55] s.23(3).
[56] See s.225(4) and Sch.17.
[57] See, generally, ss.23 to 64 and Schs. 1 and 2. Note, in particular, s.29 of the 2006 Act which will substitute s.25(2) of the 1974 Act and add s.25(2A) and (2B) so that, when considering an applicant's fitness to hold a licence, the OFT must have regard, *inter alia*, to practices which appear to the OFT to involve "irresponsible lending" (see s.25(2A)(e)).
[58] Defined in s.189(1).
[59] Defined in s.189(1).
[60] s.10(1)(b).
[61] ss.8(2), 9(3), (4). For a recent decision involving s.9(4) of the Act (items entering into the total charge for credit not to be treated as credit), see *Wilson v Robertsons (London) Ltd* [2005] EWHC 1425 (Ch.), [2006] 1 W.L.R. 1248.
[62] s.12(a).
[63] s.11(1)(a).
[64] *e.g.* ss.90, 99, 100, 129, 133, 134.

Credit-sale. A regulated credit-sale agreement[65] is similarly a debtor-creditor-supplier agreement[66] for restricted-use credit.[67] It is usually, but not invariably, for fixed-sum credit,[68] and in such case the £25,000 limit is again calculated by reference to the balance financed. A credit-sale agreement may, however, be an agreement for running-account credit,[69] as in the case of shop "budget" or "option" or "subscription" accounts, where payments made by the customer "top-up" the account, *i.e. pro tanto* restore it. In the case of running-account credit, the £25,000 limit is calculated by reference to the credit limit imposed.[70]A credit-sale agreement for fixed-sum credit is not regulated if the number of payments to be made by the debtor does not exceed four and those payments are required to be made within a period not exceeding 12 months beginning with the date of the agreement,[71] and an agreement for running-account credit is not regulated if payments are to be made by the debtor in relation to specified periods (*e.g.* monthly) and the whole amount of the credit provided in such period must be repaid by a single payment.[72] These exemptions will, as a general rule, place ordinary trade credit arrangements outside the regulating provisions of the Act notwithstanding that the person purchasing goods on credit is an individual and the credit provided is less than £25,000. 14–148

Credit cards, etc. Credit card agreements, whether entered into with the supplier of the goods (*e.g.* where the credit card is issued by a retail shop or store) or with a separate credit card company, are normally[73] regulated agreements and are normally[74]debtor-creditor-supplier[75] agreements for the provision of restricted-use[76] running-account[77] credit. Check and voucher trading agreements are also, as a general rule,[78] regulated by the Act. The credit card, check or voucher issued will be a "credit-token" for the purposes of the Act,[79] which makes special (and additional) provision for the content of credit-tokens and credit-token agreements.[80] In particular, 14–149

---

65 Defined in s.189(1).
66 s.12(a).
67 s.11(1)(a).
68 s.10(1)(b).
69 s.10(1)(a).
70 s.10(3)(a). But see s.10(3)(b).
71 Consumer Credit (Exempt Agreements) Order 1989 (SI 1989/869), art. 3(1)(a)(i).
72 *ibid.*, art. 3(1)(a)(ii).
73 But see Consumer Credit (Exempt Agreements) Order 1989 (SI 1989/869), art. 3(1)(a)(ii), which exempts, *e.g.* American Express, Diners' Club and certain shop accounts, where payment must be made in a single sum.
74 It is otherwise if the card may be used to obtain cash, see Sch.2, Pt II, Example 16.
75 s.12(a), (b).
76 s.11(1)(a), (b).
77 s.10(1)(a).
78 *cf.* s.17.
79 s.14.
80 ss.51, 63(4), 64(2), 66, 70(5), 84, 85, 171(4), 179; Consumer Credit (Agreements) Regulations 1983 (SI 1983/1553), Sch.2, Pt I, para.17, as substituted by SI 2004/1482, reg. 11 and amended by SI 2004/3236, art. 4; Consumer Credit (Credit-Token Agreements) Regulations 1983 (SI 1983/1555); Consumer Credit (Cancellation Notices and Copies of Documents) Regulations 1983 (SI 1983/1557), reg. 8.

there are considerable safeguards in the event of misuse both generally[81] and especially in the case of distance contracts.[82]

14–150 **Protection of the Act.** The protection afforded to the consumer by the Act is both extensive and intricate, and reference should be made to specialised commentaries.[83] Not only the credit agreement may be affected, but transactions connected with the credit agreement ("linked transactions"),[84] *e.g.* a sale of goods which is effected by means of a credit card issued to the buyer by a credit card company, or, in certain circumstances, a contract of sale of goods which is financed in whole or in part by a loan advanced to the buyer for that purpose.[85] The Act also seeks to promote "truth in lending" by disclosure of the "APR", *i.e.* the true annual percentage rate of interest or charge, to the debtor.[86] And extortionate credit bargains, for example, where the rate of interest or charge is grossly exorbitant, may be re-opened by the court whatever the amount of the credit.[87]

14–151 One of the more important changes to be introduced through the Consumer Credit Act 2006 is the repeal of the provisions covering extortionate credit bargains and their replacement by provisions which are based on the test of an "unfair relationship".[88] For this purpose a

---

[81] See the Consumer Credit Act 1974, s.84, as amended by the Consumer Credit Act (Further Increases of Monetary Amounts) Order 1998 (SI 1998/997) (maximum £50 limit).

[82] Consumer Protection (Distance Selling) Regulations 2000 (SI 2000/2334), reg. 21(5) and Financial Services (Distance Marketing) Regulations 2004 (SI 2004/2095), reg. 14(4) (both amending s.84 so that there is no liability for misuse of credit card in distance contracts covered by these Regulations).

[83] See Guest and Lloyd, *Encyclopedia of Consumer Credit Law* (1975); Goode, *Consumer Credit Legislation* (1977). Both of these works contain the regulations made under the Act. See also *Butterworths Trading and Consumer Law*, Div. 4; Harvey and Parry, *Law of Consumer Protection and Fair Trading* (6th ed.), Ch.10.

[84] s.19. But see Consumer Credit (Linked Transactions) (Exemptions) Regulations 1983 (SI 1983/1560).

[85] s.19(1)(b).

[86] ss.20, 44, 52, 60; Consumer Credit (Total Charge for Credit) Regulations 1980 (SI 1980/51), as amended by SI 1985/1192, SI 1989/596 and SI 1999/3177; Consumer Credit (Advertisements) Regulations 2004 (SI 2004/1484), as amended by SI 2004/2619; Consumer Credit (Agreements) Regulations 1983 (SI 1983/1553), as amended by SI 1984/1600, SI 1985/666, SI 1988/2047, SI 1999/3177, SI 2001/3649, SI 2004/1482, SI 2004/2619 and SI 2004/3236.

[87] ss.137–140. See *Ketley Ltd v Scott* [1981] I.C.R. 241; *Davies v Directloans Ltd* [1986] 1 W.L.R. 823; *Coldunell Ltd v Gallon* [1986] Q.B. 1184; *Castle Phillips Finance Co. v Williams* (1986) unreported, C.A.T./284); *Woodstead Finance Ltd v Petrou, The Times*, January 23, 1986, CA; *Falco Finance Ltd v Michael Gough* (1999) 17 Tr.L.R. 526; *Paragon Finance Plc v Staunton* [2001] EWCA Civ 1466; [2001] 2 All E.R. (Comm.) 1025; Harvey and Parry, *Law of Consumer Protection and Fair Trading* (6th ed.), pp.335–339; *Unjust Credit Transactions* (OFT, 1991); *Extortionate Credit in the UK: A report to the DTI* (June 1999); *Discussion Paper on the Extortionate Credit Provisions in the Consumer Credit Act 1974* (DTI, 2000); *Tackling loan sharks and more: Consultation Document on Modernising The Consumer Credit Act 1974* (DTI, 2001) (*www.dti.gov.uk/CACP/ca/consultation/loanshark.htm*).

[88] See s.70 and Sch.4 (prospectively repealing ss.137–140 of the 1974 Act) and ss.19–22 introducing the new provisions as ss.140A to 140D.

relationship may be unfair to the debtor because of one or more of the following: (i) any of the terms of the agreement or a related agreement, (ii) the way in which the creditor has exercised or enforced rights under the agreement or any related agreement, (iii) any other thing done (or not done) by, or on behalf of, the creditor (either occurring before or after the making of the agreement or any related agreement). In determining whether a relationship is unfair a court may take account of such matters as it considers relevant.[89] It is significant that in making its assessment the court is not limited to considering the terms of the agreement, but may also look at post-contractual behaviour or the way that rights against the debtor have been exercised or enforced. If it considers that the relationship is unfair it may re-open the agreement and exercise a wide range of powers such as ordering the repayment of sums paid or reducing or disallowing sums which would otherwise be payable.

Implied terms. The conditions and warranties as to title, quality, fitness for purpose and correspondence with description and sample implied in hire-purchase agreements are those set out in the Supply of Goods (Implied Terms) Act 1973[90] and in conditional sale and credit-sale agreements those set out in the Sale of Goods Act 1979.[91] They are not limited to agreements falling within the Consumer Credit Act 1974. Such implied undertakings can be excluded or restricted only to the extent permitted by the Unfair Contract Terms Act 1977.[92] 14–152

Liability of creditor for acts of supplier. In many hire-purchase, conditional sale or credit-sale transactions, the goods are offered or exposed for sale by a dealer, but the credit agreement is entered into by the hirer or buyer with a finance house which purchases the goods from the dealer and then lets or sells the goods on credit. By section 56 of the Consumer Credit Act 1974, "antecedent negotiations"[93] conducted by the dealer (who is a credit-broker)[94] in relation to the goods sold or proposed to be sold by him to the creditor before forming the subject-matter of a regulated hire-purchase, conditional sale or credit-sale agreement, are deemed to be conducted by him in the capacity of agent of the creditor as well as in his actual capacity.[95] The creditor will therefore be liable for any misrepresentation made or express undertaking given by the dealer in respect of the goods,[96] and cannot contract out of this deemed agency.[97] 14–153

---

[89] Unlike s.138, there is no statement of matters to which the court must have regard or of other matters which might be considered relevant.

[90] ss.8–11. S.10 of the Act (implied terms as to quality, etc.) has been amended by the Sale and Supply of Goods to Consumers Regulations 2002 (SI 2002/3045), reg. 13 to incorporate a provision which is equivalent to the new s.14(2D) to (2F) of the 1979 Act (see above, paras 11–033 and 14–010). However, given the nature of the contract of hire-purchase, there is no equivalent of the new Part 5A remedies of that Act.

[91] ss.12–15.

[92] See above, para.13–083. Note that the Unfair Contract Terms Act 1977, s.6, covers contracts of hire-purchase as well as of sale.

[93] s.56(1), (4).

[94] Defined in ss.145(2), 189(1).

[95] s.56(1)(b), (2).

[96] s.56(4).

[97] s.56(3).

14–154 A creditor may also provide or agree to provide credit to a debtor under a regulated agreement in order to enable the debtor to purchase goods from a dealer. If the credit agreement is a restricted-use agreement[98] and is made by the creditor under pre-existing arrangements,[99] or in contemplation of future arrangements[1] between himself and the dealer ("the supplier"),[2] as is the case, for example, where goods are supplied upon production of a credit card issued by a credit card company, then section 56 of the 1974 Act will similarly render the creditor liable for misrepresentations made or express undertakings given by the supplier.[3] Similar liability is imposed, for example, where a finance company advances a loan to finance the purchase of goods from a supplier with whom it has arrangements to this effect.[4] In addition, under section 75 of the Act, in these situations, if the debtor has, in relation to a transaction financed by a regulated agreement, a claim against the supplier in respect of misrepresentation or breach of contract, he has (with certain exceptions)[5] a like claim against the creditor, who, with the supplier, is jointly and severally liable to him.[6] Thus if goods are purchased with a credit card or with a loan pursuant to such an arrangement as is mentioned above, and the goods are not of satisfactory quality or are unfit for their purpose, the buyer can claim damages or other monetary compensation[7] from the credit card company or the finance company, as they are jointly and severally liable to him. In principle, this provision should be particularly helpful where the immediate supplier of the goods or services is insolvent. However, it has caused difficulty in a number of respects. These include doubts as to the legal position where a card was first acquired before the coming into force of section 75 on July 1, 1977, as to the position in so-called "four-party transactions" where the credit card company does not have what is termed a "merchant acquirer agreement" with the trader or supplier, and in the case of transactions which are made abroad. In some such cases a limited voluntary liability has been accepted.[8] The second and third of these areas of doubt were considered by Gloster, J. and subsequently by the Court of Appeal in *Office of Fair Trading v Lloyds TSB Bank Plc*.[9] It was held that

---

[98] s.11.

[99] ss.187, 189(1).

[1] *ibid.*

[2] A "debtor-creditor-supplier agreement" falling within s.12(b).

[3] s.56(1)(c), (2).

[4] *ibid.*

[5] s.75(3). The most important is that s.75 does not apply to a claim so far as it relates to any single item to which the supplier has attached a cash price not exceeding £100 or more than £30,000.

[6] s.75(1). For the creditor's indemnity from the supplier, see s.75(2).

[7] Contrast *United Dominions Trust v Taylor*, 1980 S.L.T. (Sh.Ct.) 28.

[8] See, generally, *Connected Lender Liability—A Review by the Director General of Fair Trading* (OFT, March 1994); *Connected Lender Liability—A second report by the Director General of Fair Trading* (OFT, May 1995); *Connected Lender Liability in United Kingdom Consumer Credit Law, A Consultation Document* (DTI, December 1995). On the problem concerning transactions abroad, see Gidney, 146 N.L.J. 762 (1996).

[9] [2004] EWHC (Comm), [2005] 1 All E.R. 843; on appeal [2006] EWCA Civ 268, [2006] 2 W.L.R 290.

the connected-lender liability of section 75 applied to four-party transactions, no less than to the traditional three-party transactions involving only the credit card company, the debtor and the supplier from whom the debtor uses the card to buys goods or services[10]; The Court of Appeal further held, overruling the decision of Gloster, J. on this point, that section 75 applied to all transactions entered into using credit cards under consumer credit agreements regulated by the 1974 Act, whether they were entered into in the United Kingdom or elsewhere. There were no exemptions for transactions made abroad or otherwise containing a foreign element.

Advertisements and enforcement. The advertising of consumer credit is regulated by sections 43 to 47 of the Consumer Credit Act 1974 and by the Consumer Credit (Advertisements) Regulations 2004.[11] These Regulations impose detailed requirements concerning the form and content of advertisements which relate to the provision of credit and the hiring of goods and they also contain a list of items of information for inclusion in credit advertisements and in hire advertisements. The details are beyond the scope of this book. 14–155

So far as general issues of enforcement are concerned, all breaches of the Act and of provisions in statutory instruments made thereunder are subject to the "domestic infringement" procedures of Part 8 of the Enterprise Act 2002[12] and, with the exception of consumer hire agreements and the provisions of sections 137–140 relating to extortionate credit bargains,[13] they are also subject to the "Community infringement" procedures of Part 8 of the 2002 Act.[14] 14–156

---

[10] See also *Bank of Scotland v Alfred Truman* [2005] EWHC 583, [2005] C.C.L.R. 3.
[11] SI 2004/1484, as amended by SI 2004/2619. See *Coventry City Council v Lazarus* [1996] C.C.L.R. 5; also, Consumer Credit (Exempt Advertisements) Order 1985 (SI 1985/621).
[12] See s.211 of the Act and the Enterprise Act 2002 (Part 8 Domestic Infringements) Order 2003 (SI 2003/1593), art. 2 and Sch.); above, para.14–132.
[13] See above, para.14–150.
[14] See s.212 of the Act and the Enterprise Act 2002 (Part 8 Community Infringements Specified UK Laws Order 2003 (SI 2003/1374), Art. 3 and Sch.); above, para.14–133 and, more generally, paras 14–130—14–136. In this respect the procedures have superseded the Stop Now Orders (EC Directive) Regulations 2001 (SI 2001/1422).

Part Six

REMEDIES

Chapter 15

THE SELLER'S REMEDIES AFFECTING THE GOODS

	PARA.
1. Introduction	15–001
(a) Remedies of unpaid seller	15–001
(b) Definition of "seller"	15–013
(c) When seller is "unpaid"	15–016
(d) Insolvency	15–024
2. Lien	15–028
(a) In general	15–028
(b) When the lien arises	15–030
(c) Effect of the lien	15–043
(d) Termination of the lien	15–045
3. Stoppage in transit	15–061
(a) In general	15–061
(b) Duration of transit	15–066
(c) Exercise of the right of stoppage	15–085
4. Sub-sales and other subsequent transactions	15–092
5. Resale	15–101
(a) Introduction	15–101
(b) Termination of contract upon buyer's repudiation or breach	15–107
(c) Statutory resale of perishable goods or upon giving notice	15–119
(d) Express right to resell	15–128
(e) The method of reselling	15–131
(f) Forfeiture of deposits or other prepayments	15–132

1. Introduction

(a) *Remedies of Unpaid Seller*

Summary of remedies against the goods.[1] It is provided by section 39(1) of the Sale of Goods Act 1979 that: "Subject to this[2] and any other Act,[3] notwithstanding that the property[4] in the goods may have passed to the buyer, the unpaid seller of goods, as such, has by implication of law—(a) a lien on the goods or right to retain[5] them for the price while he is in possession of them[6]; (b) in case of the insolvency[7] of the buyer, a right of stopping the goods in transit after he has parted with the possession of them[8]; (c) a right of resale as limited by this Act."[9] **15–001**

---

[1] For the rights of a seller in Scotland to attach, see s.40.
[2] The provisions of the Act which are directly relevant are ss.24, 25 and 41–48; see also s.55.
[3] See below, para.15–009.
[4] Defined in s.61(1): see above, paras 5–001 *et seq.*
[5] The "right to retain" is a term of Scots law.
[6] Below, paras 15–028 *et seq.*
[7] On the definition of "insolvent", see s.61(4); below, paras 15–024—15–027.
[8] s.44: below, paras 15–061 *et seq.* In the 1893 Act, and in most common law cases on the topic, the Latin phrase "stoppage *in transitu*" is used. The 1979 Act uses the English version "in transit".
[9] The provision referred to is s.48(3): *Ward (RV) Ltd v Bignall* [1967] 1 Q.B. 534 at 549.

Although the unpaid seller's normal remedy is to sue the buyer for the price[10] or for damages for non-acceptance,[11] the law gives him some remedies in respect of the goods themselves, analogous to a form of security for payment of the price. These remedies can be regarded as a type of self-help or extra-judicial remedy by which the seller gains better protection for his interests than he would by merely pursuing a claim for money: they reduce the risk of his being only an unsecured general creditor of the buyer, should the latter become bankrupt. By exercising these remedies, the unpaid seller in effect secures a form of preference over the general creditors of a bankrupt buyer.[12] The remedies are not derived from the ordinary law of contract: their historical origin is the law merchant.[13] They are known as "real" remedies, since they depend on, and are directed against, the *res*, the goods themselves; they are to be contrasted with "personal" remedies, such as a money claim for the price or for damages, which may be brought only against the parties to the contract, or their personal representatives, and which do not depend on the exact location, or possession of the goods.[14]

These remedies against the goods themselves arise "by implication of law" under section 39(1) and can therefore be excluded or varied by express agreement, or by the course of dealing between the parties, or by a usage binding on both parties to the contract.[15] In another chapter of this work,[16] there is a full discussion of *Romalpa* clauses, under which the seller retains the property in the goods until he has been fully paid. By express agreement these clauses provide the unpaid seller with a form of "security" over the goods which is more extensive than that provided in section 39(1) above, and which he will therefore use, wherever possible, in preference to the statutory remedies.[17]

Each separate section of this chapter considers one of the statutory remedies in detail; these introductory paragraphs give only a brief outline of them.

15–002 **Lien and stoppage in transit.** The remedies of lien and stoppage in transit are designed to give protection to an unpaid seller so long as the goods have not reached the actual possession of the buyer or his agent.

[10] See s.49 (below, para.16–001).
[11] See s.50 (below, para.16–060).
[12] See below, paras 15–027, 15–037.
[13] See below, para.15–061. The present law on the real remedies is critically reviewed in a report by the Ontario Law Reform Commission: *Report on Sale of Goods*, Vol. II, pp.406–416.
[14] Another contrast with the remedies against the goods is that there may be a claim for damages against the buyer even when the seller is not an "unpaid seller" within s.38(1). Personal remedies depend on a breach of contract by the buyer, but the real remedies do not necessarily do so.
[15] s.55 (above, paras 1–013—1–015).
[16] Above, paras 5–141 *et seq.*
[17] The creation of a security recognised at law requires the debtor to have both ownership and possession (actual or constructive) of the goods: *Armour v Thyssen Edelstahlwerke AG* [1991] 2 A.C. 339 at 353, HL. Since under a "retention of title" clause the buyer has no title to the goods until payment of the price, the buyer does not, by such a clause, create what the law recognises as a security over the goods in favour of the seller: *ibid.*, at p.353.

Although the property in the goods (which will include at least a conditional right to possession, if not the immediate right to possession of the goods) may have passed to the buyer,[18] until the buyer actually obtains (personally or through an agent) physical control over the goods, his right to possession is defeasible[19] on several conditions so long as the price remains unpaid. Insolvency[20] of the buyer is the main condition which will prevent the buyer from exercising his claim to obtain possession of the goods: "if the purchaser becomes openly insolvent before the delivery actually takes place, then the law does not compel the vendor to deliver to an insolvent purchaser."[21] Where the buyer becomes insolvent while the goods are still subject to the control of the unpaid seller or his agent, the seller is, by virtue of his right of lien,[22] entitled to retain possession of them until the price is paid. If the buyer becomes insolvent while the goods are still in the control of a carrier and before the buyer or his agent obtains delivery of them, the seller may, by giving notice to the carrier, prevent delivery to the buyer and direct redelivery to himself or his agent: this is the right of stoppage in transit, which enables the unpaid seller to resume possession of the goods and to retain them until the price is paid.[23] Although the right of stoppage is limited to the situation of the buyer becoming insolvent, the right of lien also extends[24] to the situations where payment is to be made prior to, or concurrently with delivery,[25] or where a period of credit has expired without payment of the price,[26] and the goods are still in the control of the seller or his agent. However, many of the earlier cases fail to distinguish the seller's right of lien from his right of stoppage; but although they share some similarities, the detailed rules of each vary considerably.

Resale by the seller. The mere exercise by an unpaid seller of his right of lien or of stoppage in transit does not terminate the contract of sale,[27] but by retaining or re-acquiring possession, the seller puts himself in a position where he is able to resell the goods and to deliver them to a new buyer. The unpaid seller who has exercised either the right of lien or of stoppage is given[28] the power to pass to the new buyer a good title to the goods, so that the resale will divest the original buyer of the title which he may have had. As against the original buyer, the legal right to resell the goods when the price is not paid under the original contract[29] depends on one of the 15–003

[18] s.39(1).

[19] This word is taken from the language of Bayley J. in a leading decision before the Act, *Bloxam v Sanders* (1825) 4 B. & C. 941 at 948 (the buyer's "right to possession . . . is liable to be defeated if he becomes insolvent before he obtains possession").

[20] For the definition of "insolvent" see s.61(4): below, paras 15–024—15–027.

[21] *Gunn v Bolckow, Vaughan & Co.* (1875) L.R. 10 Ch.App. 491 at 501.

[22] ss.41–43 (below, paras 15–028 *et seq.*).

[23] ss.44–46 (below, paras 15–061 *et seq.*).

[24] By s.41(1) (below, para.15–028).

[25] s.28 (above, para.8–004).

[26] This includes the dishonour of a negotiable instrument given as conditional payment of the price: s.38(1)(b): below, paras 15–018—15–020.

[27] s.48(1) (below, para.15–101).

[28] By s.48(2) (below, para.15–102).

[29] The right of resale is not, however, necessarily limited to an "unpaid seller".

following[30]: (1) an express term in that contract[31]; or (2) the failure of the original buyer to pay the price within a reasonable time after he receives a notice of the seller's intention to resell or where the goods are perishable[32]; or (3) the unpaid seller terminating the contract on the ground that the buyer has repudiated his obligations under it.[33]

Although in practice the unpaid seller will need to be in possession of the goods before he can effectively exercise his right to resell them, there may be some circumstances in which his entitlement to immediate possession of the goods will be a sufficient basis for his right to resell.[34] When the unpaid seller resells under his right to do so, the effect of his reselling is to terminate the original contract of sale,[35] and if the property in the goods had previously passed to the original buyer, to revest the property in himself in order to pass it to the new buyer.[36] Until the unpaid seller terminates the original contract of sale by reselling or otherwise, the buyer or his trustee in bankruptcy (and probably a sub-buyer) may pay the price to the seller and thereby terminate his right to retain the goods.[37]

15–004 **The "right" compared with the "power" to act.** When section 39(1) speaks of the "right" of the seller to do an act, it is primarily a right as against the original buyer which is envisaged, *i.e.* the entitlement of the seller to do the act in question without committing a breach of his contract with, or other legal wrong against, the original buyer. However, the "right" of the seller to do the act will sometimes also be a legal entitlement to do the relevant act as against third persons, *e.g.* in the case of stoppage in transit, as against the carrier.[38] The "right" of the seller under section 39 will also include his power to do the act in question, that is, his legal ability to bring about the specified legal result. Thus, under the "right of resale as limited by this Act" (section 39(1)(c)), it is provided by a later section (48(2)) that the unpaid seller is empowered, under a resale in certain circumstances, to confer a good title on the new buyer, as against the original buyer; but this provision is drafted in such a way as to leave open the possibility that although the new buyer may acquire a title valid as against the original buyer, the seller may thereby be committing a breach of his contractual obligations towards the original buyer and thus be liable to him in damages.

15–005 **Effect on third parties.** The remedies of the unpaid seller against the goods are not affected by the fact that the buyer has resold the goods to a sub-buyer, or made some other disposition of the goods to a third person. The rights of the unpaid seller therefore in principle prevail over those of a

---

30 There may be two further instances: see below, para.15–105.
31 s.48(4) (below, paras 15–128—15–129).
32 s.48(3) (below, paras 15–119 *et seq.*).
33 See below, paras 15–107—15–116.
34 See below, paras 15–124—15–125.
35 Provided that the contract had not already been validly terminated.
36 See below, paras 15–127—15–128.
37 See below, paras 15–027, 15–037, 15–072.
38 See below, para.15–088.

sub-buyer (although this rule is subject to a number of exceptions[39]). Furthermore, these remedies against the goods may be exercised in such a way as to affect third parties (*viz.* persons who are not parties to the contract of sale or claiming under such a party). The title of the claimant to bring proceedings for wrongful interference based on trespass to goods must, and that based on conversion may, be founded on the claimant's being in possession of the goods at the time of the defendant's interference with the goods.[40] The title of the claimant to bring proceedings for wrongful interference in respect of conversion may also be based on the claimant's right to the immediate possession of the goods at the time of the defendant's refusal to return the goods, or his interference with them.[41] Since the exercise of the remedies against the goods set out in section 39 may determine the issues of who has possession of the goods and who is entitled to possess them, it may affect the entitlement of both the seller and the buyer to bring proceedings for wrongful interference with the goods against third parties.[42] For instance, the liability of the carrier of the goods to an action of this kind may be affected by the seller's exercise of his right of stoppage in transit.[43]

Right to sue for the price is independent. The right of the seller to sue for the price of the goods is independent of his remedies against the goods and may arise before actual delivery of the goods to the buyer.[44] Indeed, the Act provides[45] that the seller does not lose his lien merely because he has obtained judgment for the price, thus emphasising that "paid" in the definition of "unpaid seller" (section 38(1)) means "actually paid"; only by satisfying the judgment will the buyer "pay" the price to a seller who has obtained a judgment for the price. On the other hand, the seller's right to sue for the price will often arise in circumstances in which he may no longer exercise any remedy against the goods themselves. **15–006**

Use of cases before 1893. On many aspects of the seller's remedies against the goods, the only decisions which can be cited are ones before the enactment of the Sale of Goods Act 1893. Although that Act (and the 1979 consolidating Act) in this part does closely follow the previous common law, it must be remembered that the proper approach is to give full weight to the natural meaning of the statute itself[46]: unless the meaning of a provision is doubtful, it will be unnecessary to rely on the previous common law.[47] But in this chapter extensive reference is made to the pre–1893 cases, **15–007**

---

[39] s.47 (below, paras 15–092 *et seq.*, where the exceptions to this rule are examined).
[40] *Clerk and Lindsell on Torts* (19th ed.), paras 17–40 *et seq.*, 17–128.
[41] *Clerk and Lindsell, op. cit.*, paras 17–58 *et seq.*
[42] See below, paras 16–089, 17–105, 17–106. The action for detinue was abolished by s.2(1) of the Torts (Interference with Goods) Act 1977.
[43] See s.46(4) (below, para.15–088).
[44] See s.49 (below, para.16–021).
[45] s.43(2). (This subsection, it is submitted, should also apply when the unpaid seller has resumed possession by exercising his right of stoppage in transit: see below, para.15–059.)
[46] *Bank of England v Vagliano* [1891] A.C. 107 at 145 (a decision on the Bills of Exchange Act 1882). See further on this point, above, para.1–002.
[47] *Wallis v Pratt and Haynes* [1911] A.C. 394 at 398.

because they often provide the only available illustrations of how the statutory rules work in practice.

15–008 **Agency.**[48] An agent who has actual or ostensible authority from the unpaid seller may exercise on his behalf the seller's remedies against the goods.[49] The doctrine of ratification will also apply; so where an agent without actual authority from the seller to do so, purported to exercise the right of stoppage in transit on the seller's behalf, the seller was entitled subsequently to ratify the purported agent's act,[50] provided[51] that his ratification was made at a time when he was still entitled to exercise the right himself.[52]

15–009 **Other relevant statutes.** Section 39(1) begins with the words "Subject to this and any other Act," the unpaid seller may exercise the real remedies. The other statute most directly relevant is the Factors Act 1889, some of whose provisions are repeated in the Sale of Goods Act 1979 in substantially the same form. Thus, section 47(2)[53] of the Sale of Goods Act 1979 is substantially the same as section 10 of the Factors Act 1889; and sections 24 and 25[54] of the Sale of Goods Act 1979 reproduce, with minor omissions and changes in language, sections 8 and 9 of the Factors Act 1889. Other sections of the Factors Act 1889 deal with dispositions by mercantile agents (sections 2 *et seq.*), which might also be relevant. There are certain other statutes, such as the Bills of Sale Act 1878 and the Carriage of Goods by Sea Act 1992, which, in particular circumstances, may affect the seller's exercise of his remedies against the goods.

15–010 **Remedies of seller who retains the property in the goods.** Section 39(2) of the 1979 Act enacts: "Where the property in goods has not passed to the buyer, the unpaid seller has (in addition to his other remedies)[55] a right of withholding delivery similar to and co-extensive with his rights of lien or retention and stoppage in transit where the property has passed to the buyer." The purpose of this subsection[56] is to bring into line the law on the seller's right to retain the goods pending payment of the price in the two possible situations which could arise in respect of the property in the goods. A lien is a right to retain possession of goods owned by another person,[57] and the unpaid seller's "lien" is therefore an appropriate term when the

[48] See below, para.15–013 (on s.38(2)) for circumstances where the agent may act in his own name and on his own behalf.
[49] *Whitehead v Anderson* (1842) 9 M. & W. 518 (stoppage in transit).
[50] *Hutchings v Nunes* (1863) 1 Moo.P.C.(N.S.) 243; *Bird v Brown* (1850) 4 Exch. 786.
[51] This proviso is in accordance with a general principle of agency: *Bowstead and Reynolds on Agency* (17th ed.), paras 2–060—2–066.
[52] *Viz.* before the transit terminated. See below, paras 15–066 *et seq.* on the duration of the transit.
[53] Below, paras 15–097—15–099.
[54] Above, paras 7–055—7–086.
[55] *e.g.* s.49 (below, paras 16–001 *et seq.*); s.50 (below, paras 16–060 *et seq.*).
[56] The position in the Act in which this subsection is placed is criticised by Cohen, 19 L.Q.R. 114–115 (1903).
[57] See below, para.15–028.

property in the goods has already passed to the buyer before the seller claims to retain possession of the goods.[58] When, however, the property in the goods is not to pass until a future event[59] (*e.g.* upon payment[60]), the seller is claiming to retain, pending payment of the price, goods in which he still has the property. Even before the 1893 Act, the courts recognised that the unpaid seller who retained the property in the goods was entitled to refuse to deliver them until the buyer paid him the price.[61] Thus, in a contract to deliver unascertained goods by instalments over a future period, the property in the goods in a particular instalment will normally not pass until the goods are "unconditionally appropriated" to that instalment[62]: but in such a case, it was held that the unpaid seller enjoyed a right to withhold delivery since "it would be strange if the right of a vendor who had agreed to deliver goods by instalments were less than that of a vendor who had sold specific goods."[63] Hence, one result of section 39(2) is that in an instalment contract the seller may usually[64] "withhold delivery" of future instalments until he is paid for instalments already delivered to the buyer. In a case concerning an instalment contract,[65] Atkin L.J. said[66]: "Where the property has not passed the buyer is unconcerned with the vendor's possession of the goods until the time has come for delivery . . . I think that one object of section 41 [which confers the seller's lien] is to protect a vendor from incurring expense in manufacturing or acquiring goods payment for which remains justly in doubt."

The "right" of withholding delivery under section 39(2) is a right as against the buyer, *viz.* an entitlement to withhold delivery without committing a breach of the contract. Before the property passes to the buyer, the seller, as owner of the goods, clearly enjoys the legal power to withhold delivery from the buyer.[67] In contrast to section 39(1)(c),[68] however, the draftsman did not include either a right or a power of resale under section 39(2) because he considered it unnecessary when the seller retained the property in the goods.[69] But although at common law the seller who retained the property would have the *power* to pass a good title to a third person, it would not necessarily be a *right* or entitlement to do so as against **15–011**

58 *Lickbarrow v Mason* (1793) 6 East 21 at 24n. (". . . it is a contradiction in terms to say a man has a lien upon his own goods . . .").
59 See above, paras 5–030 *et seq.*
60 See above, paras 5–021, 5–135. *Cf.* retention of title clauses (above, paras 5–141 *et seq.*).
61 *e.g. Bellamy v Davey* [1891] 3 Ch. 540.
62 s.18, r.5 (above, paras 5–068 *et seq.*).
63 *Ex p.Chalmers* (1873) L.R. 8 Ch.App. 289 at 293 (following *Griffiths v Perry* (1859) 1 E. & E. 680 at 688). See further below, para.15–042. *Cf.* below, para.15–017 (the parties may apportion the price between the instalments).
64 The contract may, however, be "severable" into separate contracts: see below, para.15–042.
65 *Longbottom (H) & Co. Ltd v Bass, Walker & Co.* [1922] W.N. 245 (see below, para.15–042).
66 *ibid.*, at p.246.
67 On the distinction between "right" and "power", see above, para.15–004.
68 Above, para.15–001.
69 See below, para.15–102.

the original buyer (*i.e.* without breach of the original contract).[70] It could not have been the intention of the draftsman that the unpaid seller who retained the property in the goods should not be entitled, as against the original buyer, to resell under the provisions of section 48(3),[71] when he would have been so entitled if the property had passed to the buyer.[72] Although a right of resale is not mentioned in section 39(2), section 48(3) can be interpreted as applicable to cases where the property has not passed to the buyer, as well as to those where it has; the subsection is not expressly limited to the latter case, and the enactment that "the unpaid seller may re-sell the goods" is enough to confer the right to resell which is omitted from section 39(2). In a case in the Court of Appeal,[73] Diplock L.J. said, by way of *obiter dictum*, that the right of resale is given by section 48(3)[74] whether or not the property in the goods has passed to the buyer.[75] "The seller cannot have greater rights of resale if the property has already passed to the buyer than those which he would have if the property had remained in him."[76]

15–012 **Goods not yet allocated to the contract.** If, under an agreement to sell[77] "future goods"[78] or "unascertained goods",[79] the seller has not yet obliged himself to deliver any particular goods to the buyer, he is obviously under no contractual obligation towards the buyer in regard to any goods subject to his control which happen to fit the contractual description, or which he has in mind to use in order to perform his obligations to the buyer.[80] Since such goods have not been attached to the particular contract, the seller's right and power over them is in no way restricted by the contract, and his rights over them are therefore wider than rights which would be "similar to and coextensive with his rights of lien . . . and stoppage in transit where the property has passed to the buyer" (section 39(2)). As section 39(2) is obviously intended to confer rights on the unpaid seller, it is submitted that it should not be interpreted so as to restrict any of his rights arising under common law rules.[81]

---

[70] *Cf.* s.24 (the power of a seller, who continues in possession after the sale, to transfer his title to a third person: it is clear that although the transferee may acquire a good title under this provision, the seller may thereby be in breach of his contractual obligations towards the original buyer. See above, paras 7–055—7–068).
[71] See below, paras 15–102—15–127.
[72] Atiyah, *Sale of Goods* (11th ed.), p.451.
[73] *Ward (RV) Ltd v Bignall* [1967] 1 Q.B. 534.
[74] Below, paras 15–119 *et seq.*
[75] *Ward (RV) Ltd v Bignall*, above, at p.545.
[76] *ibid.*
[77] s.2(5) (above, paras 1–025—1–028).
[78] s.61(1) (see above, para.1–100).
[79] s.16 (above, paras 1–113—1–119, 5–059 *et seq.*). *Cf.* s.18, r. 5(1) (above, paras 5–068 *et seq.*).
[80] *Cf. Carlos Federspiel & Co. SA v Charles Twigg & Co. Ltd* [1957] 1 Lloyd's Rep. 240 (below, para.20–071; also above, para.5–080).
[81] See the saving provisions of s.62(2) (above, para.1–007). (It is submitted that the argument in the text is not "inconsistent with the provisions of" the Act within the meaning of s.62(2)).

(b) *Definition of "Seller"*

Extended meaning of "seller". Section 38(2) extends the meaning of "seller" as follows: "In this Part of this Act 'seller' includes any person who is in the position of a seller, as, for instance, an agent of the seller to whom the bill of lading has been indorsed, or a consignor or agent who has himself paid (or is directly responsible for) the price." The term "seller" is defined for the Act as a whole by section 61(1): "'Seller' means a person who sells or agrees to sell goods." The person who "agrees to sell" will include a buyer who resells the goods before the property in the goods has passed to him.[82] For the purposes of the real remedies in Part V of the Act, which are set out in section 39,[83] the extended meaning of "seller" in section 38(2) gives a wider group of persons the opportunity of protecting their interests when they have not been paid. Those who are "in the position of a seller" are illustrated by the subsection itself, and these illustrations will no doubt be used by the courts as analogies for other cases.[84] 15–013

The main illustration is that of the agent who has himself paid the price to the seller.[85] Subsection (2) covers the agent who has made himself "directly" or personally responsible for the price. This situation was dealt with by decisions before the 1893 Act on the position of a commission agent who accepted an order to obtain goods for his principal on the understanding that the agent would buy the goods in his own name and then consign them to the principal. By buying in his own name, the commission agent pledged his own credit when buying the goods, and not the credit of his principal[86]: he was thus treated as a seller of the goods to his principal and was held to be entitled to exercise the right of stoppage in transit when his principal became insolvent during the course of transit of the goods.[87] Although before the Sale of Goods Act 1893 the courts laid down these rules for the remedy of stoppage in transit,[88] it is clear that under section 38(2) such an agent would, whenever the remedies were appropriate in the circumstances, also be entitled to exercise the other real remedies set out in section 39.

There are further circumstances in which an agent of the seller may exercise one of the real remedies. It was held in an early[89] decision[90] that

---

82 *Jenkyns v Usborne* (1844) 7 M. & G. 678 at 698–699 (buyer who resold is entitled, as against the insolvent sub-buyer, to stop the goods in transit).

83 Above, para.15–001.

84 See also below, paras 18–229—18–233.

85 *Imperial Bank v London and St Katherine Docks Co.* (1877) 5 Ch.D. 195. See *Bowstead and Reynolds on Agency* (17th ed.), paras 7–099—7–101.

86 *Feise v Wray* (1802) 3 East 93; *ex p. Miles* (1885) 15 Q.B.D. 39 at 42.

87 *Ireland v Livingston* (1872) L.R. 5 H.L. 395 at 408–409; *Cassaboglou v Gibb* (1883) 11 Q.B.D. 797 at 804, 806–807 (following *Feise v Wray*, above).

88 See below, para.15–065. In *Cassaboglou v Gibb*, above, the Court of Appeal held that for other purposes, such as assessing damages in the principal's claim against the agent, the relationship between them is not treated as that of seller and buyer.

89 Even before the Bills of Lading Act 1855 (which is now replaced by the Carriage of Goods by Sea Act 1992).

90 *Morison v Gray* (1824) 2 Bing. 260. (This was an action of trover, on which point reference should now be made to *Burgos v Nascimento* (1908) 100 L.T. 71 and to the Torts (Interference with Goods) Act 1977).

the transfer of a bill of lading from the seller to his agent could give the right to the possession of the goods to the agent,[91] which would entitle the agent to exercise in his own name the right of stoppage in transit. Section 38(2) now expressly classifies as a "seller" "an agent of the seller to whom the bill of lading has been indorsed".

15–014 **Surety.** At common law before the 1893 Act, a surety for the payment of the price under the contract of sale had no right to exercise the remedy of stoppage in transit against the goods.[92] It is submitted that a surety for the buyer is, when he has paid the seller, a "person who is in the position of a seller" within the meaning of subsection (2) above.[93] Before the buyer has defaulted in paying the price, the surety has only a contingent liability to pay the price[94]; but after payment he is subrogated to the rights of the seller against the defaulting buyer.[95]

15–015 **Rejection of goods by buyer.** The term "seller" in section 38(2) does not extend to a buyer who has a claim against the seller for repayment of the price.[96] So where the buyer paid the price to the seller, but later, and justifiably, rejected the goods, he could not claim a lien to retain the goods until the seller repaid him the price.[97] If the buyer who has paid the price wishes to reject the goods on the ground that they are not in accordance with the contractual description, he is dependent on the solvency of the seller for his recovery of the price[98]: the buyer's rejection of the goods revests the property in the seller and leaves the buyer with only a personal claim against the seller.

(c) *When Seller is "Unpaid"*

15–016 **Definition of unpaid seller.** Section 38(1) of the Act provides: "The seller of goods is an unpaid seller within the meaning of this Act—

(a) when the whole of the price has not been paid[99] or tendered[1];

---

[91] On the effect of the transfer of a bill of lading, see above, para.7–013; below, paras 18–062 *et seq*., esp. 18–089.
[92] *Siffken v Wray* (1805) 6 East 371.
[93] The Mercantile Law Amendment Act 1856, s.5, may also lead to the same result: *Imperial Bank v London and St Katherine Docks Co.*, above. (*Sed quaere* whether the right of lien or stoppage is a "security" within this section: it may, however, be covered by the wide words "shall be entitled to stand in the place of the creditor, and to use all the remedies . . . of the creditor." See Benjamin, *Sale of Personal Property* (8th ed.), pp.882–883.) See also *Chitty on Contracts* (29th ed.), Vol. 2, para.44–126.
[94] Chitty, *op. cit.*, Vol. 2, paras 44–001, 44–013.
[95] Chitty, *op. cit.*, Vol. 2, para.44–125.
[96] *J. L. Lyons & Co. Ltd v May and Baker Ltd.* [1923] 1 K.B. 685.
[97] *ibid.*
[98] This is the reason given in *Kwei Tek Chao v British Traders and Shippers Ltd* [1954] 2 Q.B. 459 at 483, for the buyer not rejecting the goods after he had paid the price.
[99] Below, para.15–017.
[1] Below, paras 15–022—15–023.

(b) when a bill of exchange or other negotiable instrument has been received as conditional payment, and the condition on which it was received has not been fulfilled by reason of the dishonour of the instrument or otherwise."[2]

The word "seller" is given an extended meaning by subsection (2) of the same section.[3] The various aspects of subsection 38(1) are examined in the succeeding paragraphs.

Payment of the price. Section 38(1)(a), when it refers to the condition that "the whole of the price has not been paid or tendered", must be construed in the light of the general principles governing payment of the price,[4] which have already been examined in Chapter 9. The seller can be "unpaid" within the meaning of section 38(1) despite the fact that payment of the price is, according to the terms of the contract, not yet due. When the buyer becomes insolvent,[5] the unpaid seller is entitled to exercise his right of lien[6] over any[7] goods not yet delivered to the buyer, or his right of stoppage in transit so long as the goods are in the course of transit[8]; and the fact that the price is not yet payable,[9] or that a negotiable instrument given by the buyer has not yet matured,[10] will not prevent the exercise of these remedies. Thus, the meaning of section 38(1)(a) is that the whole of the price has not *in fact* been paid or tendered to the seller, whether or not payment is due according to the contract.[11] During a period of credit, or during the currency of a negotiable instrument taken for the price, the seller is taken to have waived[12] his right to a lien, but he is nevertheless an unpaid seller. 15–017

At common law, payment of part of the price did not prevent the seller from exercising his right of stoppage in transit,[13] and section 38(1)(a) clearly extends this rule to the other real remedies.[14] However, although section 38(1)(a) speaks of the "whole" of the price, the price may be apportioned where the goods are to be delivered by separate instalments and to be paid for separately[15]; in these circumstances, the unpaid seller's remedies must be treated separately with respect to each instalment.[16]

---

[2] Above, paras 9–030—9–031.
[3] Above, paras 15–013—15–014.
[4] On the price, see ss.2(1), 8 and 9 (above, paras 2–044—2–052); on the buyer's duty to pay the price, see ss.27 and 28 (above, paras 9–021 *et seq.*).
[5] See s.61(4) (below, paras 15–024—15–027).
[6] s.41(1)(c).
[7] s.42 (below, paras 15–041—15–042).
[8] ss.44 and 45 (below, paras 15–061 *et seq.*).
[9] Below, paras 15–033—15–035.
[10] See below, para.15–018.
[11] s.41(1)(b) implies that during the period of credit the seller is nevertheless "unpaid": see below, paras 15–033—15–035. S.43(2) (which provides that a right of lien is not lost by the seller's obtaining a judgment for the price) also indicates that "paid" in s.38(1)(a) means "actually paid".
[12] See below, paras 15–033—15–036.
[13] *Hodgson v Loy* (1797) 7 T.R. 440; *Feise v Wray* (1802) 3 East 93 at 102; *Van Casteel v Booker* (1848) 2 Exch. 691 at 702.
[14] Even, it is submitted, to the right of resale under s.48(3).
[15] See below, paras 15–041—15–042.
[16] *ibid.*

15–018 **Payment by negotiable instrument.** Section 38(1)(b) of the Act is set out above,[17] and is in accordance with the position at common law: *viz.* that when, according to the contract, payment is to be made by means of a negotiable instrument, *e.g.* by the buyer's acceptance of the seller's drafts, both the right to sue under the contract and the seller's lien revive if the buyer's acceptance is dishonoured[18]; during the currency of the instrument, the seller's remedies are suspended[19] if (as is usual) the seller's acceptance of the instrument was only conditional payment, *i.e.* conditional on the instrument being honoured at maturity.[20] The circumstances in which a negotiable instrument is taken as absolute payment have already been considered.[21] In the case of an absolute payment by negotiable instrument, the only remedy of the seller is to sue the buyer on the instrument: he cannot sue for the price,[22] and therefore cannot exercise the real remedies as he is not an unpaid seller within the meaning of section 38(1).

15–019 **Insolvency of buyer during the currency of a bill of exchange.** Although as a general rule the seller has no lien, and no right to sue for the price, during the currency of a bill of exchange given as conditional payment of the price,[23] these remedies of the seller revive[24] if the buyer becomes insolvent.[25] (The words "or otherwise" in section 38(1)(b) refer to the buyer's insolvency.) The remedy of stoppage in transit also arises when the buyer becomes insolvent,[26] and the fact that the buyer had accepted a bill of exchange which was still current would not prevent the exercise of the right of stoppage.[27]

15–020 **Negotiation of a bill.** The fact that the seller, who has taken a bill of exchange as conditional payment, has negotiated the bill to a third person, does not alter the rule that there has been only a conditional payment of the price, because the seller may have to take up the bill.[28] The seller's remedy is therefore suspended while the instrument is outstanding in the hands of a third party.[29] Thus, when the bill, after being negotiated, is dishonoured while it is in the hands of a third person, the seller's remedies revive, *e.g.* his right to sue for the price and his lien as unpaid seller.[30]

---

[17] Above, para.15–016.
[18] *Gunn v Bolckow, Vaughan & Co.* (1875) L.R. 10 Ch.App. 491 at 501 (dishonour by nonpayment: *a fortiori* in the case of non-acceptance of the draft). See further the authorities cited above, para.9–030, n.53.
[19] Unless the buyer becomes insolvent: below, para.15–019.
[20] Above, para.9–020.
[21] Above, para.9–031.
[22] *Sayer v Wagstaff* (1844) 5 Beav. 415 at 423–424; see above, para.9–031.
[23] Above, para.15–018.
[24] The seller's lien will revive only if the other conditions for a lien are satisfied: in particular, that the goods have not yet been delivered to the buyer or his agent (see below, paras 15–038, 15–039, 15–049).
[25] *Gunn v Bolckow, Vaughan & Co.*, above, at p.501.
[26] s.44 (below, para.15–061).
[27] *Gunn v Bolckow, Vaughan & Co.*, above, at p.501.
[28] *Gunn v Bolckow, Vaughan & Co.*, above, at p.503.
[29] *Re a Debtor* [1908] 1 K.B. 344. (See the further authorities cited above, para.9–030, n.53).
[30] *Gunn v Bolckow, Vaughan & Co.*, above, at p.503. *Cf. Bunney v Poyntz* (1833) 2 L.J.K.B. 55 (see below, para.15–036).

Payment by banker's commercial credit. Where by the contract the buyer is obliged to pay the price by arranging for a banker's commercial credit to be opened in favour of the seller, the opening of the credit is normally only conditional payment.[31] If the banker defaults in honouring the credit, the seller may claim payment of the price directly from the buyer,[32] and the seller's remedies against the goods revive. 15–021

Tender of the price. In the case of all three remedies against the goods the relevant section specifies "until payment or tender of the price,"[33] or uses the verbs "pay or tender the price,"[34] to indicate the purpose of the remedies and the circumstances justifying them. The general principles of the law on tender of money to pay a debt should be sought elsewhere.[35] For a valid tender, the full[36] amount of the price must be tendered; the tender must be in legal currency[37] (unless the seller waives[38] his right to legal tender and is willing to accept another form of payment, *e.g.* a cheque[39]); and the tender must be unconditional.[40] But a valid tender may be made by an agent of the buyer, and to an agent of the seller, provided that the agent has actual or ostensible authority from his principal to pay, or to receive, the price.[41] 15–022

The effect of a valid tender of the price is that it prevents the seller from exercising any of his remedies against the goods under section 39 of the Act,[42] since he is no longer an "unpaid seller" within section 38(1).[43] But a valid tender does not discharge the buyer's obligation to pay the price[44]: it merely prevents the seller from claiming interest or damages for any loss or expenses arising after the tender.[45]

---

[31] *Alan (WJ) & Co. Ltd v El Nasr Export and Import Co.* [1972] 2 Q.B. 189 at 209–212, 221; *Man (ED & F) Ltd v Nigerian Sweets & Confectionery Co. Ltd* [1977] 2 Lloyd's Rep. 50. See below, paras 23–097—23–098.

[32] *Newman Industries Ltd v Indo-British Industries Ltd* [1956] 2 Lloyd's Rep. 219 at 236 (revsd. on another ground: [1957] 1 Lloyd's Rep. 211); *Soproma SpA v Marine and Animal By-products Corporation* [1966] 1 Lloyd's Rep. 367 at 386. For further details, see below, para.23–098.

[33] Lien: s.41(1); stoppage in transit: s.44.

[34] Resale: s.48(3) (". . . and the buyer does not within a reasonable time pay or tender the price . . . ").

[35] *Chitty on Contracts* (29th ed.), Vol. 1, paras 21–083—21–096. See also above, para.9–028.

[36] Chitty, *op. cit.*, para.21–085.

[37] Coinage Act 1971, s.2; Currency and Bank Notes Act 1954, s.1(2) and (6); Currency Act 1983, s.1(3). See Chitty, *op. cit.* para.21–086

[38] Chitty, *op. cit.*, paras 21–087—21–088.

[39] *Cubitt v Gamble* (1919) 35 T.L.R. 223; *Cohen v Roche* [1927] 1 K.B. 169 at 180 (below, para.15–023).

[40] Chitty, *op. cit.*, paras 21–091—21–092.

[41] Chitty, *op. cit.*, paras 21–094—21–095; *Bowstead and Reynolds on Agency* (17th ed.), paras 3–005, 3–021—3–023.

[42] The seller may nevertheless have a right of resale on another basis (see below, para.15–105).

[43] The position was the same before the Act: a valid tender of the price, even if made after the date when payment was due, divested the seller of his lien: *Martindale v Smith* (1841) 1 Q.B. 389.

[44] See below, para.16–017.

[45] Below, para.16–017.

15–023 **Waiver of tender.** If the seller waives[46] tender of the price by the buyer, he will be estopped from claiming subsequently that he is an "unpaid seller" for the purpose of exercising remedies under section 39. In *Cohen v Roche*,[47] the seller was held[48] to have "waived a formal legal tender" when the buyer's agent offered the seller a cheque for the price, but it was refused on a ground which challenged the validity of the contract. McCardie J. inferred waiver from the facts that the buyer was "willing to pay the price" and that the seller "did not object to the cheque as a cheque, inasmuch as the [buyer's] credit was perfectly good"[49]; and he assumed "that waiver of tender will produce the same result as actual tender in divesting a [seller] of his right to assert a vendor's lien."[50]

(d) *Insolvency*

15–024 **Definition of insolvency.**[51] Section 61(4) provides a definition of insolvency[52]: "A person is deemed to be insolvent within the meaning of this Act if he has either ceased to pay his debts in the ordinary course of business, or he cannot pay his debts as they become due." This definition is of crucial importance for two of the remedies against the goods: the right of stoppage in transit arises only upon the buyer's insolvency,[53] while in the case of the unpaid seller's lien, it is one of the three alternative situations which justify the seller's retention of the goods.[54]

There appears to have been only one reported case[55] since the 1893 Act in which the definition in section 61(4) has been interpreted. The courts are therefore likely to look for analogies elsewhere, but caution is necessary in using other cases where the word "insolvent" has been interpreted, since the meaning of the word may depend on the context of the relevant rule or clause: it is not essential that the word "insolvent" should bear the same meaning throughout the law.[56] Thus, the word "insolvent" has often been construed, "both in private instruments and upon the construction of a statute, to apply to a person labouring under a general disability to pay his just debts in the ordinary course of trade and business."[57] When a clause in

---

46 Chitty, *op. cit.*, paras 21–087—21–088.
47 [1927] 1 K.B. 169.
48 *ibid.*, at p.180.
49 *ibid.*
50 *ibid.*
51 See also above, paras 3–045—3–049, 5–005; and below, para.15–108.
52 This definition is required by ss.41 and 44 (in addition to s.39). The definition no longer refers to "an act of bankruptcy"; the words omitted were repealed by the Insolvency Act 1985, s.235(3), and Sch.10, Pt. III.
53 s.44 (below, para.15–061).
54 s.41(1) (below, para.15–028).
55 *The Feliciana* (1915) 59 S.J. 546, below.
56 *Cf.* the grounds on which a bankruptcy order may be made: ". . . a debt which the debtor appears either to be unable to pay or to have no reasonable prospect of being able to pay" (ss.267(2), and 271(1) of the Insolvency Act 1986: see the tests provided in s.268).
57 *R. v Saddlers' Co.* (1863) 10 H.L.C. 404 at 425 (*per* Willes J., on the construction of a by-law of a corporation: the actual decision of the House of Lords depended on the particular context and wording of the by-law).

a contract is to take effect upon the "insolvency" of a party, the ordinary meaning of the word has been held to be "an incapability of paying the party's just debts,"[58] or "a general inability to pay debts".[59] The phrase found in the cases,[60] "in the ordinary course of business" has been included in the definition in section 61(4), and shows that a special reason for a failure to pay debts may prevent the debtor being held to be "insolvent" within the definition, *e.g.* if an alien enemy failed to meet an acceptance because of the outbreak of war.[61]

Special considerations have arisen when the question is the effect of the buyer's alleged insolvency upon the contract of sale. If the buyer declares that he is insolvent this does not of itself terminate the contract[62]: but he may make the declaration in such circumstances as to show that he cannot, or does not intend to, perform his side of the contract, in which case the seller may treat the declaration as a repudiation and terminate the contract.[63] In this context, the Court of Appeal has held[64] that the mere fact that a debtor calls a meeting of his creditors, or some of them, need not necessarily imply that he is insolvent: the debtor may merely be discussing his need for more capital or for more credit, or the possibility that he may have to wind up an unprofitable business.[65] Mere suspicion of the buyer's insolvency is insufficient[66]: "there must be something, at all events, like proved or admitted insolvency, or circumstances shewing beyond all doubt that they were insolvent . . . in this sense—that there was a tacit or practical declaration that they would not be ready and willing to meet their engagements when their engagements became due."[67] 15–025

The buyer's own statements in documents or correspondence may be strong evidence against him. Thus, where, under a trust in a will in favour of a beneficiary until he should (*inter alia*) become "insolvent", the beneficiary executed a composition deed for the benefit of his creditors which contained a recital that he was unable to pay his debts in full, it was held that the recital proved his insolvency at that time.[68]

The time when the buyer becomes insolvent. The time when the buyer becomes insolvent may be a problem in stoppage in transit. If the seller stops the goods in the course of their transit, he takes the risk of being 15–026

[58] *Parker v Gossage* (1835) 2 C.M. & R. 617 at 620.
[59] *Biddlecombe v Bond* (1835) 4 A. & E. 332 at 337. (It is not restricted to a person who actually becomes "bankrupt" within the meaning of the Insolvency Act 1986: *ibid.* (referring to the Insolvent Debtors Act 1820).)
[60] *e.g.* in *R. v Saddlers' Co.*, above.
[61] *The Feliciana* (1915) 59 S.J. 546 at 547 (*obiter*: the goods were seized as prize before the seller purported to give notice of stoppage).
[62] *Ex p.Chalmers* (1873) L.R. 8 Ch.App. 289 at 293–294; *Mess v Duffus* (1901) 6 Com.Cas. 165 at 167. See above, para.8–086.
[63] *Mess v Duffus*, above. On this point, see below, para.15–108.
[64] *Re Phoenix Bessemer Steel Co.* (1876) 4 Ch.D. 108.
[65] *ibid.*, at p.120.
[66] *ibid.*, at p.120.
[67] *ibid.*, at pp.120–121, *per* James L.J. At p.122, Bramwell J.A. said that insolvency (for the purpose of justifying the seller's rescission (*i.e.* termination) of the contract) "ought to be an inability to pay, avowed either in act or in word, and a consequent intention on the part of the indebted company not to pay their debts."
[68] *Billson v Crofts* (1873) L.R. 15 Eq. 314.

unable to prove the buyer's insolvency[69]; at common law, however, the stoppage was held to be valid if the buyer became insolvent before the expected termination of the transit, even where it later appeared that he was not insolvent at the time of the stoppage.[70] Although section 44, in its literal interpretation, may appear to require the buyer's insolvency to be contemporaneous with the seller's exercise of the right of stoppage, it is submitted that it is possible to interpret the section so as to enable a retroactive justification of a premature stoppage, in line with the previous common law.[71]

15–027 **Bankruptcy.** The Sale of Goods Act 1979 lays down, in section 62(1), that: "The rules in bankruptcy relating to contracts of sale apply to those contracts, notwithstanding anything in this Act." The fact that the buyer has become bankrupt does not of itself terminate the contract, but the buyer's trustee in bankruptcy may exercise his power to disclaim onerous property, including any unprofitable contract.[72] The buyer's trustee in bankruptcy (and, probably, a sub-buyer of the same goods bought from the buyer) is entitled to choose to fulfil the original contract by paying the price in cash to the seller within a reasonable time of the buyer's default in payment.[73] If, however, the goods are still in transit because a bankrupt or insolvent buyer refused to take delivery of the goods from the seller or the carrier, the seller may still have the opportunity of exercising his right of lien or of stoppage in transit, and thus of gaining priority over the general creditors of the buyer.[74]

2. LIEN

(a) *In General*

15–028 **Seller's right to retain possession.** Section 41(1) of the Sale of Goods Act 1979 enacts that: "Subject to this Act,[75] the unpaid seller[76] of goods who is in possession of them is entitled to retain possession of them until payment or tender of the price in the following cases:—(a) where the goods have been sold without any stipulation as to credit; (b) where the goods

---

[69] *The Tigress* (1863) 32 L.J.P.M. & A. 97 at 101 (below, para.15–085).
[70] *The Constantia* (1807) 6 C.Rob.Adm.R. 321 at 326.
[71] This submission is supported by the words "he may resume possession of the goods *as long as* they are in course of transit" (s.44: italics supplied).
[72] Insolvency Act 1986, ss.315–321. See above, paras 3–045—3–049; also Muir Hunter on *Personal Insolvency* (1987–2005) paras 3–2000 *et seq.*
[73] *Ex p. Stapleton* (1879) 10 Ch.D. 586 at 590. *Cf.* Insolvency Act 1986, ss.311(5) and 314; and Sch.5; *Cf.* also *Kemp v Falk* (1882) L.R. 7 App.Cas. 573 at 578.
[74] *Ex p.Cooper* (1879) 11 Ch.D. 68 at 73. See below, paras 15–037, 15–072, 15–081.
[75] s.42 (part delivery: below, paras 15–041—15–042); s.43 (termination of lien: below, paras 15–045 *et seq.*); s.47 (disposition by buyer: below, paras 15–060, 15–092 *et seq.*); s.48 (right of resale: below, paras 15–119 *et seq.*) and s.55 (express agreement: below, para.15–031).
[76] The definition of "unpaid seller" is found in s.38: see above, paras 15–016—15–023 and below, para.15–042.

have been sold on credit but the term of credit has expired; (c) where the buyer becomes insolvent."

An early definition[77] of a lien is as follows: "A lien is a right in one man to retain that which is in his possession belonging to another, till certain demands of him the person in possession are satisfied."[78] But the unpaid seller's lien[79] is a special or particular lien, which arises only in the precise circumstances specified by the Act; it is not a general lien for all debts due from the buyer to the seller. Apart from an express term in the contract of sale,[80] the seller's only right of lien arises under the Act and the seller cannot rely on the equitable principle of a vendor's lien.[81] The gist of the unpaid seller's lien is his entitlement to retain the goods until the buyer has paid or tendered[82] the whole[83] of the price[84]; his lien is therefore a qualification on his duty to deliver the goods to the buyer.[85]

The right to be paid is independent of the existence of a lien: a "lien is an additional security given to the person who has to be paid; but he has a right to be paid besides and independently of his lien."[86]

The advantage of the lien is that when the buyer becomes bankrupt the seller is not treated equally with the general creditors: he receives preference by being able to retain the goods themselves. The seller will in practice exercise his right of lien as a first step towards exercising a right of resale[87]; the fact that he is in possession of the goods at the time of the resale, and thus able to deliver the goods to the second buyer will greatly facilitate his reselling, even though it may not always be legally necessary for the seller to be in possession of the goods to enable him to resell.[88]

The unpaid seller's lien arises whether the sale is of specific goods or an executory contract to supply unascertained goods, *e.g.* by instalments over a future period[89]; in the case of unascertained goods, the lien will arise when the goods have been ascertained.[90]

Right to withhold delivery when seller retains the property. By section 39(2), "Where the property in goods has not passed to the buyer, the unpaid seller has (in addition to his other remedies) a right of withholding 15–029

---

77 The Act does not define a lien. On the general law of lien, see Silvertown, *The Law of Lien* (1988).
78 *Hammonds v Barclay* (1802) 2 East 227 at 235 (factor's lien). For a later discussion of the nature of a lien, see Fletcher Moulton L.J.'s dissenting judgment in *Lord's Trustee v G.E. Ry* [1908] 2 K.B. 54 at 61–73. (The House of Lords allowed the appeal: *G.E. Ry v Lord's Trustee* [1909] A.C. 109).
79 On the history of the seller's lien, see *Blackburn on Sale* (1st ed.), p.318.
80 Below, paras 15–031, 15–053.
81 *Transport and General Credit Corporation Ltd v Morgan* [1939] 2 All E.R. 17 at 25.
82 When the buyer tenders payment of the price to the seller, the latter's right of lien over the goods is terminated: *Martindale v Smith* (1841) 1 Q.B. 389 at 396. (See also s.41(1): ". . . until payment or tender of the price . . .")
83 s.38(1)(a) (above, paras 15–016—15–017).
84 On the common law before the Act, see *Miles v Gorton* (1834) 2 Cr. & M. 504 at 511.
85 s.27 (above, paras 8–001 *et seq.*).
86 *The Eider* [1893] P. 119 at 131. See above, para.15–006.
87 See below, paras 15–101 *et seq.*
88 Below, paras 15–123—15–124.
89 *Griffiths v Perry* (1859) 1 E. & E. 680; *Ex p. Chalmers* (1873) L.R. 8 Ch.App. 289.
90 See above, paras 5–059 *et seq.*

delivery similar to and co-extensive with his rights of lien or retention and stoppage in transit where the property has passed to the buyer."[91] A lien, *stricto sensu*, can arise only when the property held belongs to another[92]; hence, the "right of withholding delivery" exercised by the unpaid seller over goods in which he still has the property, is a quasi-lien.[93] Thus, in a case before the 1893 Act, *Ex p. Chalmers*,[94] goods were sold on the terms of instalment deliveries each month, with payment in cash 14 days after each delivery. After the November (the penultimate) delivery, the price for that delivery was not paid and the buyer became insolvent.[95] It was held that the seller was entitled to withhold delivery of the December delivery until the price of both the November and December deliveries was tendered to him. This quasi-lien arose despite the fact that the property in the goods to be delivered in December remained with the seller, since it would not pass to the buyer until the delivery was actually made.[96]

(b) *When the Lien Arises*

15–030 **In general.** The seller's lien arises if the following conditions are satisfied:

(1) The seller is "unpaid"[97];
(2) The goods have been sold without any stipulation as to credit,[98] or the stipulated period of credit has expired,[99] or the buyer has become insolvent[1]; and
(3) The seller is in possession[2] of the goods or part[3] of them.

15–031 **Special terms in the contract.** Section 55(1) provides that any right which arises under the contract by implication of law may be negatived or varied by express agreement or by the course of dealing between the parties or by usage.[4] Thus, if the contract between the parties expressly creates a

---

[91] See above, para.15–010.
[92] *Hammonds v Barclay* (1802) 2 East 227 at 235 (factor's lien); *Nippon Yusen Kaisha v Ramjiban Serowgee* [1938] A.C. 429 at 444.
[93] See above, para.15–010. *Cf.* the retention of the property under a retention of title clause: above paras 5–141 *et seq*.
[94] (1873) L.R. 8 Ch.App. 289. (See also below, para.15–042.)
[95] In these circumstances, the conduct of the buyer may justify the seller in the belief that the buyer intends to abandon the contract on his insolvency, so that the seller could terminate the contract: *Morgan v Bain* (1874) L.R. 10 C.P. 15. (See further below, para.15–108.)
[96] See also *Farmeloe v Bain* (1876) 1 C.P.D. 445 (Since the goods were unascertained, property had not passed to the buyer, and the seller's right was therefore to withhold delivery and, after the 1893 Act, would fall within s.39(2).)
[97] s.38(1) (above, paras 15–016—15–023).
[98] Below, para.15–032.
[99] Below, para.15–035.
[1] Below, para.15–037.
[2] s.41(1) (below, para.15–038).
[3] s.42 (below, paras 15–041—15–042).
[4] See above, paras 1–013—1–015. For an illustration of usage, see *Field v Lelean* (1861) 6 H. & N. 617 (below, para.15–034).

lien or other form of security for the price, the express terms will prevail over, and therefore exclude, the statutory implication of a lien,[5] at least to the extent of any inconsistency with the express terms.[6]

Sale not on credit. The first circumstance in which the unpaid seller is given a lien by section 41(1) is "(a) where the goods have been sold without any stipulation as to credit." This rule was clearly established at common law.[7] In these circumstances, section 28 applies, so as to make the obligation of the seller to deliver the goods to the buyer dependent upon the readiness and willingness of the buyer to pay the price in exchange for possession of the goods.[8] Thus, the seller's obligation to deliver is made consistent with his entitlement to a lien until the price is paid or tendered. 15–032

Sale on credit terms. It is only the "unpaid seller" who enjoys a lien by virtue of section 41(1). The definition of "unpaid seller" in section 38(1)[9] when read into section 41(1), shows that a requirement for the exercise of the lien is that payment of the price must either be due, or the buyer must be insolvent. The question when payment is due depends on the terms of the contract.[10] Where the contract allows the buyer a period of credit[11] the seller waives his lien for that period,[12] and does not become an unpaid seller entitled to a lien until the period of the credit has expired,[13] or the buyer becomes insolvent.[14] The question whether the unpaid seller is entitled to exercise a lien if he wrongfully refuses to deliver the goods to the buyer who is entitled to credit, is considered below.[15] 15–033

The granting of "credit" does not necessarily mean that the seller is willing to deliver the goods before payment. Although section 41(1)(a) expressly permits a lien where the goods were sold without any stipulation as to credit, it is submitted that this does not imply that no lien can arise where there is such a stipulation but it is clear that the parties intended delivery to be dependent on payment. Thus in the early case of *Bloxam v Sanders*,[16] it was said[17]: "If goods are sold upon credit, *and nothing is agreed* 15–034

---

[5] *Re Leith's Estate* (1866) L.R. 1 P.C. 296. *Cf.* the effect of a retention of title clause: above, paras 5–141 *et seq.*
[6] *ibid.*, at pp.307, 308. *Cf.* on the question as to the inconsistency between an innkeeper's accepting security from his guest and the continuance of his lien on the guest's goods, *Angus v McLachlan* (1883) 23 Ch.D. 330.
[7] *Bloxam v Sanders* (1825) 4 B. & C. 941 at 948; *Miles v Gorton* (1834) 2 Cr. & M. 504 at 511.
[8] See above, para.8–004.
[9] See above, paras 15–016—15–023.
[10] See Ch.9, above.
[11] See above, paras 9–061—9–067.
[12] *Spartali v Benecke* (1850) 10 C.B. 212 at 223. The normal implication is that the buyer is immediately entitled to delivery without making payment: *ibid.*
[13] s.41(1)(b) (below, para.15–035).
[14] s.41(1)(c) (below, para.15–037).
[15] Below, para.15–039.
[16] (1825) 4 B. & C. 941.
[17] *ibid.*, at p.948 (italics supplied). See also *Miles v Gorton* (1834) 2 Cr. & M. 504 at 511 ("and nothing is specified as to delivery or payment").

upon as to the time of delivering the goods, the vendee is immediately entitled to the possession, and the right of possession and the right of property vest at once in him." It is submitted that this statement implies that the mere fact that the seller has allowed a period of credit need not mean that he has agreed to deliver the goods before he has received payment[18]: it should depend on the intention of the parties as revealed in the terms of the contract[19] whether the seller is entitled to retain possession of the goods in situations falling outside the provisions of section 41(1). Thus, in the case of a sale of mining shares made between brokers, a usage was proved among dealers in mining shares that delivery was to take place concurrently with payment, even though credit for a specified time was fixed in the contract.[20] The granting of credit, therefore, may mean merely that the seller is not insisting on immediate payment of the price; it need not imply that the seller is prepared to deliver the goods immediately without payment.

15–035 **Revival of lien after period of credit has expired.** By section 41(1)(b) it is provided that the seller's lien also arises "where the goods have been sold on credit but the term of the credit has expired." This provision follows the common law.[21] For the lien to arise the goods must remain in the possession of the seller until the period of the credit has expired: in other words, the buyer, though normally[22] entitled to claim delivery during the period of credit, must not in fact have taken delivery of the goods. "The sale on credit no doubt releases the lien until the credit expires, but it then revives again. . . . [The sellers] would have no lien for their money during the period of credit; but this was only a temporary waiver of the lien."[23] The lien will revive, after the period of credit has expired, whether or not the buyer is then insolvent.

15–036 **Acceptance of a negotiable instrument.** Where the buyer is given credit for the period of a bill of exchange or other negotiable instrument given by him to the seller in payment of the price, the seller's lien is waived[24] for that period, since acceptance of a negotiable instrument is normally treated as conditional payment.[25] But if, before the goods are delivered to the buyer, the negotiable instrument is dishonoured,[26] or the buyer becomes insol-

---

[18] See also Atiyah, *The Sale of Goods* (11th ed.), p.453. It is submitted that the wide statement in *Poulton and Son v Anglo-American Oil Co. Ltd* (1910) 27 T.L.R. 38 at 39 (quoted below, para.15–035) was made without consideration of the possibility of an express or implied term dealing with the time for delivery in a sale on credit.
[19] *cf.* the opening words of s.28: "Unless otherwise agreed" (above, para.8–004).
[20] *Field v Lelean* (1861) 6 H. & N. 617.
[21] *New v Swain* (1828) 1 Dans. & L. 193; *Bunney v Poyntz* (1833) 4 B. & Ad. 568 at 569.
[22] Above, para.15–034.
[23] *Poulton and Son v Anglo-American Oil Co. Ltd ante*, at p.39 (on appeal (1911) 27 T.L.R. 216).
[24] On waiver, see s.43(1)(c) (below, para.15–056).
[25] s.38(1)(b) (see above, para.15–018). *Cf. Horncastle v Farran* (1820) 3 B. & Ald. 497 (carrier's lien); *Hewison v Guthrie* (1836) 2 Bing.N.C. 755 at 759 (broker's lien).
[26] *Miles v Gorton* (1834) 2 Cr. & M. 504 at 512; *Gunn v Bolckow, Vaughan & Co.* (1875) L.R. 10 Ch.App. 491 at 501.

vent,[27] the seller's lien[28] will revive, so that he may retain the goods until he is paid.[29] In a case[30] before the 1893 Act, Wightman J. said: "As long as the bills were running they may be taken to have been prima facie payment, but they were dishonoured before the iron was delivered, and in that case I have no doubt that the vendor's lien attaches, and that he may retain his goods until he is paid." The lien revives upon dishonour of a bill given in payment of the price despite the fact that the dishonour occurred after the seller had, during the period of the buyer's solvency, committed a breach of his obligations under the contract (*e.g.* by failure to deliver part of the goods[31]). In these circumstances the buyer has a cause of action, but the seller has his lien for payment of the whole of the price,[32] which will be taken into account in assessing the buyer's damages for the seller's breach[33]; the buyer (or his trustee in bankruptcy) will, therefore, be entitled to only nominal damages for the seller's failure to deliver, unless the value of the goods at the time of the seller's breach was higher than the contract price.[34]

But if the seller (or his agent) accepted a negotiable instrument as payment, and then negotiated it without recourse, *i.e.* without making himself liable, he has converted the conditional payment into an absolute payment and cannot thereafter claim to exercise his lien.[35]

Buyer's insolvency. The mere fact that the buyer becomes insolvent or even bankrupt[36] does not terminate the contract of sale,[37] nor does it necessarily amount to a repudiation[38] of the contract by the buyer.[39] These rules are the background for the third situation in section 41(1), namely, "(c) where the buyer becomes insolvent".[40] The seller thereupon has a right of lien despite the fact that a stipulated period of credit has not yet 15–037

[27] *Miles v Gorton*, above, at pp.512, 514; *Gunn v Bolckow, Vaughan & Co.*, above, at p.501. (If the buyer becomes insolvent, it is likely that the bill will be dishonoured when it is due.)
[28] It may be that it is not a right to a lien *stricto sensu* because the lien had been waived by the granting of credit; but it is a right of withholding delivery analogous to a lien: *Griffiths v Perry* (1859) 1 E. & E. 680 at 688.
[29] *Valpy v Oakeley* (1851) 20 L.J.Q.B. 380; *Griffiths v Perry*, above. The lien arises whether or not it was a sale of specific goods: *ibid*.
[30] *Valpy v Oakeley*, above, at pp.382–383.
[31] *Valpy v Oakeley*, above; *Griffiths v Perry*, above.
[32] *ibid*.
[33] *ibid*.
[34] *ibid*.
[35] *Bunney v Poyntz* (1833) 2 L.J.K.B. 55. (See all the reports: 1 N. & M. 229; 4 B. & Ad. 568.) In this case, the transactions after the seller accepted the negotiable instrument showed that the seller had, through his agent, been paid: Benjamin, *Sale of Personal Property* (8th ed.), pp.844–845. *Cf. Re J. Defries & Sons Ltd* [1909] 2 Ch. 423 at 429.
[36] See above, para.15–027. But the buyer's trustee in bankruptcy may exercise his right to disclaim onerous property including any unprofitable contract: Insolvency Act 1986, ss.315–321.
[37] *Mess v Duffus* (1901) 6 Com.Cas. 165. See above, para.15–025; below, para.15–108.
[38] On the effect of repudiation, see below, para.15–108.
[39] *Re Phoenix Bessemer Steel Co.* (1876) 4 Ch.D. 108; *Ex p. Chalmers* (1873) L.R. 8 Ch.App. 289. See further above, paras 15–024—15–027; below, para.15–108.
[40] Defined in s.61(4) (see above, para.15–024).

expired[41]: this means that if the goods have not left the possession of the unpaid seller (even though the buyer, having been given credit, was normally[42] entitled to immediate delivery) the seller may exercise his right of lien against the buyer (or the assignees of the buyer) if the buyer becomes insolvent.[43] In these circumstances the seller can retain the goods until the buyer, or his trustee in bankruptcy,[44] pays the whole price. Thus, unless full payment is made, the seller's power of retention enables him to avoid the alternative of proving in the bankruptcy for the price: "if the purchaser becomes openly insolvent before the delivery actually takes place, then the law does not compel the vendor to deliver to an insolvent purchaser."[45] The buyer's trustee in bankruptcy may elect to fulfil the contract by paying the price in cash within a reasonable time[46]; dicta also suggest that a sub-buyer might have the same election.[47]

15–038 **Possession of the goods.** The unpaid seller's right of lien depends on his being in "possession"[48] of the goods at the time he exercises his right of lien. The lien entitles the seller to retain possession, but not to regain possession of the goods after he has given it up.[49] The meaning of possession[50] depends on the purpose of the particular rule in question,[51] and a seller's "possession" for the purpose of a claim to a lien may be different from that required for other types of lien.[52] Thus, in one case,[53] a carrier's lien was held to continue despite the fact that the consignee was permitted a measure of control over the goods (*viz.* unloading and stacking them) while they remained on the carrier's premises and under the general control of the carrier. This case supports the general proposition that a seller will continue in possession for the purpose of maintaining his lien, so long as the buyer has been given only restricted control of the goods, subject to the general control of the seller.[54] Thus the seller may give a

---

[41] s.41(1)(c). This was the law before the Act: *Ex p.Chalmers*, above; *Gunn v Bolckow, Vaughan & Co.* (1875) L.R. 10 Ch.App. 491 at 501; *Grice v Richardson* (1877) L.R. 3 App.Cas. 319.
[42] See above, paras 15–033—15–034.
[43] *Grice v Richardson*, above.
[44] *Ex p. Stapleton* (1879) 10 Ch.D. 586 at 590; *Ex p.Chalmers*, above, at p.294 (above, para.15–027).
[45] *Gunn v Bolckow, Vaughan & Co.*, above, at p.501.
[46] *Ex p. Stapleton*, above, at p.590.
[47] *Ex p. Stapleton*, above, at p.590. *Cf. Kemp v Falk* (1882) L.R. 7 App.Cas. 573 at 578.
[48] s.41(1).
[49] *Jeffcott v Andrew Motors Ltd* [1960] N.Z.L.R. 721, CA. *Cf.* the position where the buyer has unlawfully acquired possession, below, para.15–055. The exercise of the right of stoppage in transit may enable the seller to regain possession of the goods: see below, paras 15–061 *et seq.*
[50] The term is not defined in the Sale of Goods Act 1979. But *Cf.* the definition in s.1(2) of the Factors Act 1889; and the decisions under s.43(1)(b) (below, para.15–049).
[51] Harris, *Oxford Essays in Jurisprudence* (1961, ed. Guest), p.69.
[52] *GE Ry v Lord's Trustee* [1909] A.C. 109 at 115. (See also the dissenting judgment of Fletcher Moulton L.J. in the court below: *Lord's Trustee v GE Ry* [1908] 2 K.B. 54 at 71 (". . . such possession . . . as was necessary to maintain their lien.")
[53] *G.E. Ry v Lord's Trustee*, above.
[54] *Cf. Valpy v Gibson* (1847) 4 C.B. 836 (below, para.15–054).

measure of control to the buyer, without allowing the buyer such exclusive control over them as to amount to "possession" in the buyer which terminates the seller's lien.[55] In an old case[56] the seller retained his lien by maintaining his general control over the goods through his retention of the key of the premises, while allowing the buyer to lock up the goods in a container within the premises. But the question depends on the intention of the parties: if the seller allows the buyer to retain the keys of a room on the seller's premises, and gives the buyer a licence to enter his premises to remove the goods at any time, possession may be held to be with the buyer.[57] In another case,[58] a merchant bought a growing crop of potatoes and his employees handled the crop by lifting and pitting them on the farmer's land. The contract provided that the farmer was to cart the potatoes to the railway station. It was held that although property in the potatoes had passed on the lifting,[59] the farmer retained possession of them (and, therefore, his lien as unpaid seller) while they remained on his farm.

15–039 There are many other cases where the seller has not been held to have given possession to the buyer although he has permitted the buyer to do some act in relation to the goods while they remain under the general control of the seller, *e.g.* marking them[60] or packing them in his (the buyer's) own containers.[61] But the extent of the buyer's control is a question of degree to be decided by the court: thus, where timber was in the possession of a wharfinger, but the seller allowed the buyer to measure it, to mark it with his initials and to spend money in having it squared, it was held that possession had passed to the buyer.[62]

The fact that the buyer pays the seller warehousing charges in respect of the goods while they remain on the seller's premises does not prevent the seller from retaining his possession of the goods and exercising his lien as unpaid seller.[63] In these circumstances, the seller may act in the dual role of seller and warehouseman,[64] but the Act provides that the seller's lien is not

---

[55] s.43(1)(b) (below, para.15–049). For analogies, see *Albermarle Supply Co. Ltd v Hind & Co.* [1928] 1 K.B. 307 (continuance of repairer's lien over taxicabs which were allowed to ply for hire by day, on condition that they were returned to the repairer's garage each night); *Wallace v Woodgate* (1824) Ry. & Moo. 193 (below, para.15–055); *Reeves v Capper* (1838) 5 Bing.N.C. 136; *North Western Bank v Poynter, Son and Macdonalds* [1895] A.C. 56 (pledge); *Caldwell v Sumpters* [1972] Ch.478 (solicitors' lien over the title deeds of a former client was not lost by sending them to the client's present solicitors with the request that they should hold them to the first solicitors' order) and *Cf.* below, para.15–054.
[56] *Milgate v Kebble* (1841) 3 M. & G. 100.
[57] *Cf. Wrightson v McArthur and Hutchisons (1919) Ltd* [1921] 2 K.B. 807.
[58] *Paton's Trustees v Finlayson*, 1923 S.C. 872.
[59] See above, paras 5–023—5–024.
[60] *Dixon v Yates* (1833) 5 B. & Ad. 313.
[61] *Goodall v Skelton* (1794) 2 H.Bl. 316; *Boulter v Arnott* (1833) 1 Cr. & M. 333. See also *Milgate v Kebble*, above, and *Cf. Holderness v Shackels* (1828) 8 B. & C. 612.
[62] *Cooper v Bill* (1865) 3 H. & C. 722. See also *Tansley v Turner* (1835) 2 Bing.N.C. 151.
[63] *Miles v Gorton* (1834) 2 Cr. & M. 504 at 513, 514; *Grice v Richardson* (1877) L.R. 3 App.Cas. 319 at 323–324.
[64] *Grice v Richardson*, above.

lost by the fact that the seller holds the goods as agent or bailee for the buyer.[65]

If the buyer is entitled to delivery of the goods without paying the price, because the goods are sold on credit terms,[66] a wrongful refusal by the unpaid seller to deliver the goods to the buyer should, it is submitted, debar the seller from exercising his lien if the buyer should later become insolvent. A wrongful refusal by a carrier to deliver the goods to the buyer or his agent terminates the unpaid seller's right to stop the goods in transit,[67] and this should be an analogy for the seller's own wrongful refusal to deliver.

15–040 **Lien exists despite seller's attornment to the buyer.** Section 41(2) provides that: "The seller may exercise his lien or right of retention notwithstanding that he is in possession of the goods as agent or bailee or custodier for the buyer."[68] This alters the previous common law on the point, under which the seller lost his lien if he attorned[69] to the buyer, *viz.* acknowledged to the buyer that he held the goods as bailee for the buyer, and on account of the buyer.[70] As a result of the Act, the seller may exercise his lien until the price is fully paid, despite the fact that he acknowledges that he retains possession of the goods sold in the capacity of bailee to the buyer.[71] However, the fact that the seller no longer holds the goods in his capacity as seller, but as the buyer's agent or bailee, may be evidence that he has waived his lien.[72] Furthermore, so long as any period of credit granted to the buyer for payment of the price is running, the seller who holds as the buyer's bailee will normally[73] be bound to deliver the goods to the buyer upon demand.

The mere fact that the buyer agrees to pay warehouse charges for goods retained by the unpaid seller on his premises does not mean that the seller has lost either his possession or his lien.[74]

15–041 **Part delivery.** By section 42: "Where an unpaid seller has made part delivery[75] of the goods, he may exercise his lien or right of retention on the remainder, unless such part delivery has been made under such circum-

---

[65] s.41(2) (below, para.15–040).

[66] See above, para.15–033.

[67] s.45(6). See below, para.15–083. *Cf.* below, para.15–055.

[68] In *United Plastics Ltd v Reliance Electric (N.Z.) Ltd* [1977] 2 N.Z.L.R. 125, it was held that the corresponding section in the New Zealand Act applied only where the seller had never parted with possession of the goods.

[69] On attornment, see above, para.8–012; below, paras 15–040, 15–052, 15–075, 15–077—15–078, 15–096.

[70] *Cusack v Robinson* (1860) 1 B. & S. 299 at 308. At common law, however, the unpaid seller's lien revived, despite the seller's holding as bailee, if the buyer became insolvent: *Gunn v Bolckow, Vaughan & Co.* (1875) L.R. 10 Ch.App. 491 at 501, 503. See also *Townley v Crump* (1835) 4 A. & E. 58.

[71] *Poulton & Son v Anglo-American Oil Co. Ltd* (1911) 27 T.L.R. 216. The delivery of a document of title to the goods may bring s.47(2) into operation: see below, para.15–097.

[72] On waiver, see s.43(1)(c) (below, para.15–056).

[73] See above, para.15–034.

[74] *Miles v Gorton* (1834) 2 Cr. & M. 504 at 513, 514; *Grice v Richardson* (1877) L.R. 3 App.Cas. 319 at 323–324.

[75] For the rules on delivery, see s.27 (above, paras 8–001 *et seq.*).

stances as to show an agreement to waive the lien or right of retention."[76] Waiver is a method of terminating[77] the seller's lien, and this provision in section 42 is merely one illustration of the principle of waiver. There is a similar rule[78] in section 45(7) dealing with the right of stoppage in transit, and the decisions under that provision[79] may be relevant to the interpretation of section 42. In an old case,[80] the buyer of a parcel of hay asked for, and was granted, the seller's permission to take away part of it: it was held not to be a delivery of the whole since "the intention of both parties was to separate the part delivered from the residue."[81] In a later case of stoppage in transit, before the House of Lords, Lord Blackburn said: "Then it is said that the delivery of a part is a delivery of the whole. It may be a delivery of the whole. In agreeing for the delivery of goods with a person you are not bound to take an actual corporeal delivery of the whole in order to constitute such a delivery, and it may very well be that the delivery of a part of the goods is sufficient to afford strong evidence that it is intended as a delivery of the whole. If both parties intend it as a delivery of the whole, then it is a delivery of the whole; but if either of the parties does not intend it as a delivery of the whole, if either of them dissents, then it is not a delivery of the whole."[82] The onus is on the buyer, who claims that the seller has lost his lien, to show that it was the intention of the parties that the part delivery should constitute a delivery of the whole.[83]

The position may be different when the goods are in the possession of a third person.[84] If the seller's bailee attorns[85] to the buyer there is a constructive transfer of possession to the buyer[86] so that, despite an actual delivery of part only to the buyer, the rule in section 42 does not apply.[87]

Instalment contracts. Where there is a contract for the sale of a specified quantity of goods by instalments, the presumption is that it is an indivisible or entire contract, so that the seller may exercise his lien over any part of the goods not yet delivered, if any part[88] of the total price is 15–042

[76] This section sets out what was the position at common law: *Dixon v Yates* (1833) 5 B. & Ad. 313 at 341–342; *Bunney v Poyntz* (1833) 4 B. & Ad. 568; *Miles v Gorton*, above, at p.513; *Kemp v Falk* (1882) L.R. 7 App.Cas. 573 at 586.
[77] s.43(1)(c) (below, para.15–056).
[78] But s.45(7) does not use the language of waiver; instead it provides: ". . . unless such part delivery has been made under such circumstances as to show an agreement to give up possession of the whole of the goods."
[79] See below, para.15–084.
[80] *Bunney v Poyntz*, above.
[81] *ibid.*, at p.571.
[82] *Kemp v Falk*, above, at p.586.
[83] *Ex p. Cooper* (1879) 11 Ch.D. 68 at 73 (a case of stoppage in transit).
[84] *Miles v Gorton*, above, at pp.509–510.
[85] On attornment, see above, paras 8–012, 15–040; below, paras 15–052, 15–075, 15–077—15–078, 15–096.
[86] Even where the seller continues, for a period, to be liable for the warehouse charges: *Hammond v Anderson* (1803) 1 B. & P.N.R. 69. See above, para.15–039.
[87] *Hammond v Anderson*, above (as explained in *Ex p. Cooper*, above, 74–75).
[88] By s.38(1)(a), the seller is unpaid unless the whole of the price has been paid or tendered (above, paras 15–016—15–023).

unpaid.[89] In *Ex p. Chalmers*,[90] the position following the insolvency of a buyer under an instalment contract was examined: "in such a case the seller, notwithstanding he may have agreed to allow credit for the goods, is not bound to deliver any more goods under the contract until the price of the goods not yet delivered is tendered to him; and that, if a debt is due to him for goods already delivered, he is entitled to refuse to deliver any more till he is paid the debt due for those already delivered, as well as the price of those still to be delivered.[91]. . . it would be strange if the right of a vendor, who had agreed to deliver goods by instalments were less than that of a vendor who had sold specific goods."[92]

But if the contract is severable, in the sense that there are to be separate deliveries of specified instalments, with a separate payment to be made for each delivery, each delivery will be treated for the purposes of the seller's lien as if it were a separate contract[93]; in these circumstances, no lien can be exercised by the seller in regard to a particular instalment of the goods for which payment has been made,[94] and the lien can be exercised only over goods forming part of an instalment which has not been paid for.[95] Thus, if such an instalment has been paid for, it must be delivered despite the fact that the buyer has become insolvent.[96]

(c) *Effect of the Lien*

15–043 **Effect of the lien.** The contract of sale subsists during the period when the goods are detained by the seller under his lien since the mere exercise of the lien does not involve rescission (in the sense of termination) of the contract.[97] Although the exercise of his lien may often result later in the exercise by the unpaid seller of a power to resell the goods, the power of retention under the lien does not itself give the seller any property in the goods.[98] "The buyer, or those who stand in his place, may still obtain the right of possession if they pay or tender the price, or they may still act upon

---

[89] *Ex p. Chalmers* (1873) L.R. 8 Ch.App. 289; *Longbottom & Co. Ltd v Bass, Walker & Co.* [1922] W.N. 245. (See the quotation from this case, above, para.15–010). *Re Grainex Canada Ltd* (1987) 34 D.L.R. (4th) 646 (Brit.Col. CA).

[90] Above. (See also above, para.15–029).

[91] (1873) L.R. 8 Ch.App. 289 at 291.

[92] *ibid.*, at p.293.

[93] *Longbottom & Co. Ltd v Bass, Walker & Co.*, above, at p.246. However, a contract may be divisible despite the fact that it does not provide for delivery by instalments (which is dealt with by s.31(2), (above, paras 8–077 *et seq.*)): *ibid*.

[94] *Merchant Banking Co. of London v Phoenix Bessemer Steel Co.* (1877) 5 Ch.D. 205 at 219–220; *Longbottom & Co. Ltd v Bass, Walker & Co.*, above.

[95] An express term in the contract itself, however, may entitle the seller to exercise a general lien over any goods of the buyer in the seller's possession.

[96] *Merchant Banking Co. of London v Phoenix Bessemer Steel Co.*, above; *Longbottom & Co. Ltd v Bass, Walker & Co.*, above.

[97] s.48(1) (below, para.15–101).

[98] During the exercise of the lien, however, the seller's possession of the goods will support an action for wrongful interference with the goods (conversion or trespass): *Nippon Yusen Kaisha v Ramjiban Serowgee* [1938] A.C. 429 at 445. *Cf. Lord's Trustee v G.E. Ry* [1908] 2 K.B. 54 at 63–64 (a carrier's lien); (on appeal [1909] A.C. 109 (above, para.15–038)).

their right of property if anything unwarrantable is done to that right."[99] The right of the seller, as against the original buyer, to resell the goods must be derived from another source, such as section 48(3) of the Act, or an express power in the contract of sale.[1] But the fact that the unpaid seller is in possession of the goods by virtue of his lien will greatly facilitate[2] any resale, by enabling the seller to deliver the goods to a second buyer. If the unpaid seller resells while exercising his right of lien, the second buyer acquires a good title to the goods as against the original buyer.[3] This rule, however, does not mean that such a resale is justifiable as between the seller and the original buyer; if the seller had no right to resell, as distinct from a power to pass a good title to a second buyer upon a resale, he will be liable in damages to the original buyer.[4]

Extent of the lien. The extent of the lien is limited to the price[5]: the seller is not entitled[6] to exercise his lien so as to claim from the buyer his expenses for detaining the goods until the price is paid, because during the period of the lien the seller is detaining the goods for his own benefit.[7] The seller's remedy against the buyer for these expenses will be a claim for damages if he can establish a ground for such a claim.[8] If, however, there is an agreement that such expenses are to be treated as part of the price, the lien will extend to the amount of the expenses.[9] **15–044**

(d) *Termination of the Lien*

In general. By section 43 of the Act it is provided that: **15–045**

"(1) The unpaid seller of goods loses his lien or right of retention inrespect of them—

(a) when he delivers the goods to a carrier, or other bailee or custodier for the purpose of transmission to the buyer without reserving the right of disposal of the goods;

---

[99] *Bloxam v Sanders* (1825) 4 B. & C. 941 at 949 (cited with approval in *Ex p. Chalmers* (1873) L.R. 8 Ch.App. 289 at 292).
[1] See below, para.15–105.
[2] But it may not be necessary for the seller to be in possession before he can validly resell, see below, paras 15–124—15–125.
[3] s.48(2) (below, para.15–102).
[4] *Bloxam v Sanders*, above, at p.949. (See below, para.15–104).
[5] This is implied by s.41(1), and by s.39(1)(a) ("a lien on the goods . . . for the price"). *Cf.* a banker's lien: below, paras 22–139—22–145.
[6] Apart from an express term in the contract: *Miles v Gorton* (1834) 2 Cr. & M. 504 at 513.
[7] *Somes v British Empire Shipping Co.* (1860) 8 H.L.C. 338 (a case on a repairer's lien) (distinguished by the HL in *China Pacific SA v Food Corporation of India* [1982] A.C. 939 at 962–3 (gratuitous bailment following salvage: owner benefited from the expenditure which was incurred *before* he demanded redelivery of the goods.))
[8] *Bloxam v Sanders*, above, at p.950. *Cf.* s.37 (above, para.9–009). *Cf.* also *Hartley v Hitchcock* (1816) 1 Stark. 408 (repairer's lien).
[9] *cf. Winks v Hassall* (1829) 9 B. & C. 372 (agreement to pay duty on the goods in addition to the price).

(b) when the buyer or his agent lawfully obtains possession of the goods;
(c) by waiver of the lien or right of retention."[10]

Section 43(1) is not an exhaustive statement of the circumstances in which the seller's lien is lost. For instance, the seller will, of course, lose his right of lien if the whole of the price is paid or tendered[11] to him, since he then ceases to be an "unpaid" seller within the meaning of section 38(1).[12]

15–046 **Delivery to a carrier or bailee for the buyer.** Paragraph (a) of section 43(1), above, enacts the ordinary rule at common law that a delivery of the goods to a carrier[13] for conveyance to the buyer is prima facie deemed to be[14] a delivery of possession to the buyer which terminates the seller's lien.[15] Where, however, there are special circumstances, as where the seller contracts to deliver the goods to the buyer at a particular destination, the carrier may be treated as the seller's agent.[16] Where the goods are shipped under a bill of lading, possession of the goods is treated as having been transferred to the buyer or his agent when the bill has been endorsed and delivered to him.[17]

15–047 **Reservation of the right of disposal.** The power to reserve the right of disposal of the goods is contained in section 19, and is fully examined elsewhere in this work.[18] The normal rule where goods are shipped is that the seller reserves the right of disposal when he takes a bill of lading[19] on shipment which makes the goods deliverable to the order of himself or of his agent.[20] Such a reservation reserves the right to possession of the goods as well as the right of property, since possession of the bill of lading is

[10] For definitions of "unpaid seller", "buyer", and "delivery", see ss.38 (above, paras 15–013 *et seq.*, 15–016 *et seq.*) and 61(1) (above, para.8–002).
[11] The lien is lost even if the seller declines to receive the money which is tendered in payment of the price: *Martindale v Smith* (1841) 1 Q.B. 389 at 396. (See above, paras 15–022—15–023).
[12] Above, paras 15–016 *et seq.*
[13] On delivery to a carrier, see s.32 (above, paras 8–014—8–015).
[14] By s.32(1), delivery to a carrier is prima facie deemed to be delivery to the buyer (above, para.8–014; below, para.20–012).
[15] *Bolton v Lancs and Yorks Ry* (1886) L.R. 1 C.P. 431 at 439; *Badische Anilin und Soda Fabrik v Basle Chemical Works* [1898] A.C. 200 (for this purpose "the post office is simply a carrier of parcels like any other carrier", *ibid.* at p.204; but *cf. Postmaster-General v WH Jones & Co. (London) Ltd* [1957] N.Z.L.R. 829).
[16] This was the rule at common law, and it is not altered by the Act: *Dunlop v Lambert* (1839) 6 Cl. & F. 600; *Badische* case, above, at pp.207, 209. (See above, para.8–014; and below, paras 21–014 *et seq.*).
[17] *Sanders Bros v Maclean* (1883) 11 Q.B.D. 327 at 341; *The Prinz Adalbert* [1917] A.C. 586 at 589. There is no need for an attornment by the carrier to the buyer: see above, paras 8–008, 8–013; below, para.18–089. See generally below, paras 18–063 *et seq.*
[18] Above, paras 5–131 *et seq.*; below, paras 18–211 *et seq.*, 20–075 *et seq. cf.* retention of title clauses (*Romalpa* clauses): above, paras 5–141 *et seq.*
[19] Or a mate's receipt pending the issue of the bill of lading: see below, paras 18–163—18–168.
[20] s.19(2) (see above, para.5–137).

treated as constructive possession of the goods: it is only by endorsement and delivery of the bill of lading that possession of the goods is constructively transferred to the buyer or his agent.[21]

Right of stoppage in transit. Although, under section 43(1)(a), the seller loses his lien when he delivers the goods to a carrier for transmission to the buyer (without reserving the right of disposal), he may still exercise the separate right of stoppage in transit if the buyer becomes insolvent[22]: the effect of such stoppage is that his lien revives.[23] Because their effects are similar, the right of lien and the right of stoppage in transit are sometimes treated as the same in cases of the buyer's insolvency. But it should be remembered that the unpaid seller's lien can also be exercised in circumstances other than the buyer's insolvency.[24] 15–048

Buyer or his agent obtaining possession. The second situation under which the seller's lien is lost under section 43(1) is "(b) when the buyer or his agent lawfully obtains possession of the goods." Although the property in the goods, including the right to possess them, may pass to the buyer immediately upon the making of the contract of sale,[25] possession of the goods does not pass merely upon the making of the contract. Delivery[26] of some kind is required to pass possession to the buyer or his agent, unless the buyer was, before the sale, in possession of the goods as bailee of the seller[27]: in the latter situation the assent of the seller that, as from the formation of the contract, the buyer shall hold for himself would amount to a delivery to the buyer.[28] (It should be noted, however, that by section 41(2), the seller may exercise his right of lien notwithstanding that he is in possession of the goods as bailee for the buyer.[29]) Although possession of the goods may have passed to the buyer or his agent, so as to terminate the unpaid seller's statutory right to a lien, the contract itself may create a special right in the seller analogous to a lien.[30] The transfer of a bill of lading (by endorsement and delivery) from the seller to the buyer will pass constructive possession of the goods to the buyer so as to terminate the unpaid seller's lien.[31] 15–049

---

[21] Above, para.15–046.
[22] See below, paras 15–061 *et seq.*
[23] See below, paras 15–062, 15–088.
[24] See s.41(1) (above, para.15–028).
[25] See s.18, r.1 (above, para.5–017).
[26] See Ch.8, above. Where delivery and payment of the price are to be contemporaneous, the seller will intend to retain his lien (and so intend not to complete delivery) until payment: *Kidman v Patterson* (1887) 8 N.S.W.L.R. (L.) 290.
[27] A special term in the contract might, of course, govern the situation (s.55). See the analogous situation in *Dodsley v Varley* (1840) 12 A. & E. 632 (below, para.15–053). *Cf.* also a symbolic or constructive delivery in a sale and leaseback transaction: *Michael Gerson (Leasing) Ltd v Wilkinson* [2000] Q.B. 514.
[28] Above, para.8–011. *Cf.* the analogous situation with a *donatio mortis causa: Cain v Moon* [1896] 2 Q.B. 283.
[29] Above, para.15–040.
[30] See below, para.15–053.
[31] Above, para.15–046. But the right of stoppage in transit may be exercised by the unpaid seller if the buyer becomes insolvent before the transit terminates: see below, paras 15–061 *et seq.*

In the discussion[32] of the word "possession" in section 41(1), cases have been cited to support the proposition that the seller's possession for the purpose of maintaining his lien may continue despite the fact that the buyer has been given a measure of control over the goods or temporary possession of them for a limited and specific purpose[33]: these cases are also relevant to the interpretation of section 43(1)(b).[34] Assistance in the interpretation of section 43(1)(b) may also be found in the decisions on the termination of transit for the purpose of the right of stoppage in transit. Thus, decisions on section 45(1) (". . . until the buyer or his agent in that behalf takes delivery of them . . ."),[35] and on section 45(2) ("If the buyer or his agent . . . obtains delivery of the goods . . .")[36] are relevant, since the definition of "delivery" in section 61(1) reads: "voluntary transfer of possession from one person to another."[37]

15–050 **Analogies from decisions under the Statute of Frauds.** There are reported decisions[38] on what constituted an actual receipt by the buyer within the (now repealed) provision of the Statute of Frauds,[39] and these have some relevance to the interpretation of section 43(1), as the test for an actual receipt has been used to determine when the seller loses his right of lien. "The principle is that there cannot be an actual receipt by the vendee so long as the goods continue in the possession of the seller, as unpaid vendor, so as to preserve his lien."[40] There are at least[41] two differences, however, between the buyer's acquisition of possession which puts an end to the seller's lien, and the former rules under the Statute of Frauds[42]: first, "acceptance" of the goods and actual receipt of part of them were sufficient to satisfy the Statute, whereas the unpaid seller's lien would normally still continue in respect of the undelivered part[43]; secondly, the seller is entitled, by section 41(2)[44] to continue to exercise his right of lien despite the fact that he has agreed to hold the goods as agent or bailee for the buyer.[45] The old cases must therefore be read in the light of these differences.

15–051 **Part delivery.** The delivery of part only of the goods sold does not normally preclude the unpaid seller from exercising his right of lien over the remainder of the goods which continue in his possession.[46]

---

[32] Above, paras 15–038—15–039.
[33] See in particular the following cases, the facts of which have been summarised in para.15–038, above: *Paton's Trustees v Finlayson*, 1923 S.C. 872; *GE Ry v Lord's Trustee* [1909] A.C. 109; *Milgate v Kebble* (1841) 3 M. & G. 100.
[34] See especially *Cooper v Bill* (1865) 3 H. & C. 722 (above, para.15–039); *Tansley v Turner* (1835) 2 Bing.N.C. 151. *Cf.* below, para.15–054.
[35] Below, paras 15–068—15–073.
[36] Below, paras 15–074—15–076.
[37] See Ch.8 entitled "Delivery".
[38] See Benjamin, *Sale of Personal Property* (8th ed.), pp.207 *et seq.*
[39] Later s.4 of the Sale of Goods Act 1893 (now repealed).
[40] *Cusack v Robinson* (1861) 1 B. & S. 299 at 308. See also *Baldey v Parker* (1823) 2 B. & C. 37 at 44.
[41] See also *Boulter v Arnott* (1833) 1 Cr. & M. 333 at 335.
[42] Or the former s.4 of the Sale of Goods Act 1893.
[43] See above, paras 15–041—15–042.
[44] See above, para.15–040.
[45] On the former law, see *Bill v Bament* (1841) 9 M. & W. 36 at 41.
[46] See s.42 (above, paras 15–041—15–042).

Attornment and delivery orders.[47] The seller will also lose possession, and thus his lien as unpaid seller, whenever a third person who is in possession of the goods as the seller's bailee, attorns to the buyer.[48] Thus, where the warehousemen who hold the goods accept the seller's order and attorn to the sub-buyers of the goods, by acknowledging that they hold the goods for the sub-buyers, the right to possession passes to the sub-buyers, and the seller's right of lien is lost despite the buyer's insolvency.[49] But the fact that a delivery note or order[50] for goods stored in a warehouse is handed to the buyer does not normally give the buyer possession until the warehouseman attorns to the buyer[51]: until then the seller's lien continues. 15–052

Express creation of a right analogous to a lien. Even where the goods have passed into the possession of the buyer, the contract itself may create a special right in the seller which is analogous to a lien.[52] Thus, in one case the goods were delivered to a warehouse employed by the buyer, but the course of dealing[53] was that the goods were to remain there until they were paid for.[54] The seller was held to have "a special interest. . . growing out of his original ownership, independent of the actual possession, and consistent with the property being in the [buyer]."[55] 15–053

Later possession of the seller for a different purpose. In *Valpy v Gibson*[56] the goods had come into the possession of the buyer's agents, who subsequently delivered them to the sellers to be repacked: it was held that the lien was lost by the first delivery, and that the seller's later possession was for a limited purpose: it could not, without the buyer's agreement, create a new lien for the price.[57] 15–054

Lien not lost by the buyer's wrongful taking of the goods. Section 43(1)(b) refers to the buyer or his agent "lawfully" obtaining possession of the goods, and it can therefore be inferred that a wrongful taking of the 15–055

---

[47] See the decisions on s.45(3) (below, paras 15–077—15–078; also above, para.15–040, and below, para.15–096).
[48] s.29(4), (above, para.8–012).
[49] *Hawes v Watson* (1824) 2 B. & C. 540. The same result follows when the warehouseman attorns to the buyer himself: *Harman v Anderson* (1809) 2 Camp. 243; *Capital and Counties Bank Ltd v Warriner* (1896) 12 T.L.R. 216.
[50] On delivery orders in general, see above, para.8–013; below, paras 18–169 *et seq.*
[51] *M'Ewan and Sons v Smith* (1849) 2 H.L.C. 309; and s.29(4) (see above, para.8–012; below, para.18–174).
[52] In New Zealand, an express power for the seller to retake possession upon the buyer's default has been interpreted to allow the unpaid seller's lien to revive: *Bines v Sankey* [1958] N.Z.L.R. 886 at 895–896. But *cf. United Plastics Ltd v Reliance Electric (NZ) Ltd* [1977] 2 N.Z.L.R. 125. *Cf.* also a special agreement conferring a right of lien for agistment: *Richards v Symons* (1845) 8 Q.B. 90. *Cf.* also retention of title clauses (above, para.5–141 *et seq.*).
[53] s.55 allows such provisions to apply.
[54] *Dodsley v Varley* (1840) 12 A. & E. 632.
[55] *ibid.*, at p.634. *Cf. Howes v Ball* (1827) 7 B. & C. 481 (commented on in *Sewell v Burdick* (1884) 10 App.Cas. 74 at 96); *Re Hamilton Young & Co.* [1905] 2 K.B. 772.
[56] (1847) 4 C.B. 836. *Cf.* below, para.15–069.
[57] *ibid.*, at p.865. See, to the same effect, *United Plastics Ltd v Reliance Electric (NZ) Ltd*, above (goods returned for repair). *Cf.* the similar rule in the case of a repairer's lien: *Pennington v Reliance Motor Works Ltd* [1923] 1 K.B. 127; and in the case of pledge: *North Western Bank v Poynter* [1895] A.C. 56. *Cf.* also above, para.15–038, n.55.

goods by the buyer or his agent (*viz.* without the seller's consent[58]) will not terminate the seller's lien.[59] In an old case,[60] a livery-stable keeper sold horses but, by express agreement with the buyer, he had a lien over them for the expense of continuing to keep them in his stables. The buyer was permitted to use the horses, and one day he fraudulently removed them to other stables. It was held that the livery-stable keeper was entitled to retake[61] the horses (but without using force), and that his lien revived when he reacquired possession. Similarly, the "accidental or improper removal" by a debtor of deeds deposited as security in a deed box belonging to creditors has been held not to alter the validity of the lien over the deeds to secure a debt due to the creditors.[62] It would appear to follow from these cases that the buyer who is wrongfully in possession cannot pass a good title to a third person free from the seller's lien, unless section 47(2)[63] applies.

15–056 **Waiver of lien.** The third method of termination of the unpaid seller's lien specified in section 43(1) is: "(c) by waiver of the lien. . ." Waiver can occur in many ways: the right of lien may be waived at the outset, when the contract is formed, or subsequently, during the performance of the contract. Waiver of the lien at the time the contract was made is illustrated by the giving of credit which waives the lien, at least until the period of credit has expired[64]: and the lien will also be treated as waived during the currency of a bill of exchange which the seller has taken for the price.[65] Section 43(1)(c), above, deals with a waiver subsequent to the making of the contract, since it is assumed by the heading to the whole section, "Termination", and the words "loses his lien" at the beginning of subsection (1), that the lien had previously been in existence.[66] The seller may waive his lien by assenting to a sub-sale,[67] or by dealing with the goods in a manner inconsistent with the lien,[68] or by making a new arrangement with the buyer which is inconsistent with the continuance of his lien.[69] A lien may be lost if

[58] In *Jeffcott v Andrew Motors Ltd* [1960] N.Z.L.R. 721 at 730, two judges considered that "unlawfully" might mean "the seller must have been deprived of possession by an unlawful removal of such a nature as to negative consent." On the question of the seller's consent, see s.25(1) (above, paras 7–069 *et seq.*).

[59] *cf.* s.45(2) and (6) on stoppage in transit (below, paras 15–074, 15–083).

[60] *Wallace v Woodgate* (1824) Ry & Moo. 193 (followed in *Jeffcott v Andrew Motors Ltd*, above).

[61] In *Jeffcott v Andrew Motors Ltd*, above, at p.732, one judge said that the court cannot order return of the goods to the seller, because the lien gives the seller a defence, not a cause of action; and that the lien revives only if the seller actually recovers possession.

[62] *Mason v Morley* (1865) 11 Jur.(N.S.) 459 at 461. (It was also said that the same position would hold if the removal had been by a stranger: *ibid.*)

[63] Below, paras 15–097—15–099.

[64] s.41(1)(b) (above, paras 15–033—15–035).

[65] *cf.* s.38(1)(b) (above, paras 15–018—15–021). *Cf.* also *Horncastle v Farran* (1820) 3 B. & Ad. 497 (loss of lien for freight by accepting and negotiating a bill of exchange).

[66] Thus there is no need to argue, as does Benjamin, *Sale of Personal Property* (8th ed.), p.853, that s.43(1)(c) should be read "subject to" s.41(1)(b) and (c).

[67] Below, paras 15–060, 15–092—15–096.

[68] Below, para.15–057.

[69] Below, para.15–058. But obtaining a judgment for the price does not lead to loss of the lien: s.43(2) (below, para.15–059).

the seller refuses to deliver the goods on some ground other than the buyer's failure to pay or tender the price, or on some ground other than his right of lien.[70] In these circumstances, the buyer is released from his obligation to pay or tender the price before the lien is lost.[71]

Seller's dealing inconsistent with the lien. The seller's lien will also cease where the seller deals with the goods in a manner inconsistent with the continuance of his lien, which is a mere right to retain possession of them.[72] Thus, where the seller wrongfully resells[73] or himself consumes[74] the goods, he cannot justify such an act of conversion by relying on his lien as unpaid seller,[75] nor can he defend the buyer's claim on the ground that the price has not been paid or tendered to him before the action was brought.[76] However, in proceedings for wrongful interference with the goods based on conversion the buyer is entitled to recover from the seller only the loss he has suffered, *viz.* the value of the goods at the time of the conversion, less the price (or part of it) which he has not paid.[77] 15–057

New arrangement inconsistent with the lien. In a case dealing with a lien on a member's shares in a company, it was held "that a right of lien may be discharged by a new arrangement between creditor and debtor, the terms of which are incompatible with its retention, or by any other arrangement which sufficiently indicates the intention of the parties that the right shall no longer be enforced."[78] So where a seller takes security for the price from the buyer, the terms of the security may be inconsistent with the continuance of a lien. The seller would also have waived his lien if, after having refused to sell on credit terms at the time the contract was made, he later allowed the buyer to take possession before he had paid the price.[79] 15–058

Lien survives a judgment for the price. By section 43(2) of the Act, it is provided that "An unpaid seller of goods who has a lien or right of retention in respect of them does not lose his lien or right of retention by reason only that he has obtained judgment or decree for the price of the goods." The action for the price is dealt with elsewhere.[80] The point of 15–059

---

[70] *Boardman v Sill* (1808) 1 Camp. 410(n) (a claim for a lien for warehouse charges: approved (*obiter*) in *Yungmann v Briesemann* (1892) 67 L.T. 642 at 644); *Weeks v Goode* (1859) 6 C.B.(N.S.) 367. *Cf. White v Garnier* (1824) 2 Bing. 23 (no waiver of lien for work done on chattels).

[71] *cf. Kerford v Mondel* (1859) 28 L.J.Ex. 303 (lien for freight).

[72] *Gurr v Cuthbert* (1843) 12 L.J.Ex. 309.

[73] *Chinery v Viall* (1860) 5 H. & N. 288.

[74] *Gurr v Cuthbert*, above.

[75] *cf.* the similar rule in the case of an innkeeper's lien: *Mulliner v Florence* (1878) 3 Q.B.D. 484 at 489, 494.

[76] *Chinery v Viall*, above. *Cf. Jones v Tarleton* (1842) 9 M. & W. 674 (carrier's lien). The position is different in the case of a pledge: *Yungmann v Briesemann*, above, at p.644.

[77] *Chinery v Viall*, above. On this point, see below, para.17–106.

[78] *Bank of Africa Ltd v Salisbury Gold Mining Co. Ltd* [1892] A.C. 281 at 284. *Cf. Clifford Harris & Co. v Solland International Ltd* [2005] EWHC 141 (Ch), [2005] 2 All E.R. 334.

[79] *ibid.*

[80] See s.49 (below, paras 16–001 *et seq.*).

section 43(2) is that only full satisfaction of a judgment[81] for the price can amount to payment so as to defeat the seller's lien.[82] But if the seller causes the goods to be taken in execution by the sheriff, he loses his lien, because the sheriff must have possession in order to sell.[83]

Section 43(2) presumably applies when the seller has resumed possession of the goods by exercising his right of stoppage in transit. The language of section 44 on the right of stoppage[84] does not include the word "lien" which is found in section 43(2), but the words "resume possession" (s.44) seem to indicate that the seller is then in the same position, as regards his lien, as if he had not lost possession. Section 43(2) itself speaks of the unpaid seller having a "lien" or "right of retention," and although the phrase "right of retention" is probably included in the subsection as the appropriate term of Scots law, it could also be interpreted as including a reference to section 44 which provides that the unpaid seller, upon exercising his right of stoppage, "may retain them until payment or tender of the price."

15–060 **Effect of sub-sales and other dispositions.** The fact that the buyer has resold the goods to a sub-buyer, or agreed to pledge them or disposed of them in some other way, will not deprive the unpaid seller of his lien,[85] even where he knows of the sub-sale or other disposition, or knows that the sub-buyer has paid the buyer.[86] There are, however, a number of special circumstances in which the unpaid seller's right of lien will be lost or adversely affected by a sub-sale or other disposition of the goods: these are discussed elsewhere in this work, and the following is merely a brief summary. The seller will lose his lien if he assents[87] to the sub-sale or other disposition (*e.g.* by accepting the buyer's delivery order in favour of the sub-buyer, without giving the sub-buyer notice of his claim to a lien or contingent lien).[88] However, where the goods which are the subject-matter of the sale are held by a bailee as agent for the seller (*e.g.* a warehouseman holding on the seller's order) the mere fact that the seller gives to the bailee notice of the sub-sale does not amount to a waiver of the lien.[89]

But the unpaid seller will lose his right of lien when the bailee attorns to the buyer, although, until this has happened, and despite the handing of a delivery order to the buyer, the seller may stop delivery or attornment to the buyer or his sub-buyer.[90] The seller will also lose his lien if a sub-buyer

---

81 It is not clear whether the lien would cover the costs of the judgment as well as the judgment debt itself (the price). See, above, para.15–044.

82 The position was the same before the Act: *Houlditch v Desanges* (1818) 2 Stark. 337; *Scrivener v GN Ry* (1871) 19 W.R. 388.

83 *Jacobs v Latour* (1828) 5 Bing. 130. (The case concerned a stablekeeper and trainer's lien.)

84 See below, paras 15–061 *et seq.*

85 s.47(1), (below, paras 15–092 *et seq.*).

86 *M'Ewan and Sons v Smith* (1849) 2 H.L.C. 309. Nor can the fact that the unpaid seller has knowledge of a sub-sale be used to found an estoppel, so as to prevent him from setting up his lien: *Poulton and Son v Anglo-American Oil Co. Ltd* (1910) 27 T.L.R. 38 at 39.

87 s.47(1) (examined in detail, below, paras 15–092—15–096).

88 *Pearson v Dawson* (1858) E.B. & E. 448.

89 *Poulton and Son v Anglo-American Oil Co. Ltd*, above.

90 *M'Ewan and Sons v Smith*, above. On attornment, see above, paras 8–012, 15–040, 15–052; below, paras 15–077—15–078, 15–096.

or pledgee receives in good faith and for value a document of title to the goods which has been lawfully transferred to the buyer[91]; or if the sub-buyer or pledgee receives, in good faith and without notice of the seller's lien, the goods themselves or a document of title to the goods, provided that possession of the goods or document was obtained by the buyer with the seller's consent.[92]

3. STOPPAGE IN TRANSIT

(a) *In General*

Right of stoppage in transit. Section 44 of the Sale of Goods Act 1979 provides: "Subject to this Act,[93] when the buyer of goods becomes insolvent[94] the unpaid seller[95] who has parted with the possession of the goods has the right of stopping them in transit, that is to say, he may resume possession of the goods as long as they are in course of transit,[96] and may retain them until payment or tender of the price."[97] The doctrine of stoppage in transit was accepted by the House of Lords in 1793 in *Lickbarrow v Mason*.[98] It is said to have derived from the custom of merchants,[99] but earlier this century the right of stoppage in transit was referred to as an equitable right.[1] It is now based on the Act, which provides that the right of stoppage arises "by implication of law"[2]; this provision leads to the result that the right of stoppage may be negatived or varied by express agreement between the parties or by the course of dealing between them, or by usage.[3] 15–061

---

[91] s.47(2) (below, paras 15–97—15–099).
[92] s.25 (above, paras 7–069 *et seq.*).
[93] ss.45–47, and 55.
[94] Defined in s.61(4): see above, paras 15–024 *et seq.* The time when the buyer becomes insolvent is examined, above, para.15–026.
[95] See s.38 (above, paras 15–016—15–023).
[96] See s.45 (below, paras 15–066 *et seq.*).
[97] On the price, and its payment, see ss.8, 27 and 28 (above, paras 2–044—2–052, 9–021 *et seq.*).
[98] (1793) 4 Bro.Parl.Cas. 57; 6 East 22(n) (upholding (1787) 2 T.R. 63). The first reported case on stoppage in transit is *Wiseman v Vandeputt* (1690) 2 Vern. 203. The history of the doctrine is reviewed by Lord Abinger C.B. in *Gibson v Carruthers* (1841) 8 M. & W. 321 at 337 *et seq.*; see also *Booth SS Co. Ltd v Cargo Fleet Iron Co. Ltd* [1916] 2 K.B. 570. (In the 1893 Act, and in the common law cases before that Act, the Latin phrase "stoppage *in transitu*" was used. The 1979 Act uses the English phrase "in transit").
[99] *Kendall v Marshall Stevens & Co.* (1883) 11 Q.B.D. 356 at 364, 368. A similar right exists in civil law systems, and the English right may have derived from them.
[1] *Nippon Yusen Kaisha v Ramjiban Serowgee* [1938] A.C. 429 at 450. (The context of the statement is the rule that the transfer by the buyer of a bill of lading to a bona fide indorsee for value will prevent the unpaid seller from exercising his right of stoppage: see s.47(2) (below, paras 15–097 *et seq.*, 18–086.)
[2] s.39(1).
[3] s.55 (above, paras 1–013—1–015).

15–062 **Purpose of the right of stoppage.** As soon as the unpaid seller delivers the goods to a carrier for transmission to the buyer he normally[4] loses his right of lien, but he may, by exercising his right of stoppage, resume[5] his lien if the buyer becomes insolvent while the goods are still in transit. The main purpose of the right of stoppage is to enable the unpaid seller, by resuming his lien, to gain priority (in regard to the goods) over the general creditors of an insolvent buyer who becomes bankrupt.[6] By stopping the goods in the course of their transit, the seller puts the carrier under an obligation to redeliver the goods to him,[7] and thereby reacquires the right to possession of the goods. But the exercise of the right of stoppage does not of itself terminate the contract of sale[8]: it merely prevents the buyer from obtaining possession of the goods, and puts the seller in a position in which he can effectively exercise his statutory power of resale.[9] In the normal situation, the seller may, after giving notice to the buyer of his intention to do so, resell the goods if the buyer fails to pay the price within a reasonable time after the notice.[10] But if the buyer (or his trustee in bankruptcy[11]) tenders the whole price while the seller retains the goods, and before the seller terminates the contract by reselling the goods or otherwise, the seller is bound to accept the price[12] and to redeliver or redispatch[13] the goods to the buyer (or his trustee).

The unpaid seller's right of stoppage in transit arises solely upon the buyer's insolvency, unlike his right of lien, which may also arise in other circumstances.[14] The definition of "insolvent" found in section 61(4) has already been examined.[15] Partial payment of the price does not prevent the seller from exercising the right of stoppage in regard to the balance of the price[16]; nor does his acceptance of a negotiable instrument as conditional payment.[17] But the practical importance of the right of stoppage in transit

---

[4] See s.43(1)(a) (above, para.15–046).
[5] Or acquire a lien, if he did not have a right of lien under s.41(1) before the delivery of the goods to the carrier.
[6] *cf.* retention of title clauses, above, paras 5–141 *et seq.*
[7] s.46(4) (below, para.15–088).
[8] s.48(1) (below, para.15–101).
[9] s.48(3) (below, paras 15–119 *et seq.*).
[10] s.48(3). There are also other circumstances in which the seller may pass a good title to the goods to a second buyer (see below, paras 15–102—15–103).
[11] See above, para.15–027.
[12] See the wording of s.44 ("may retain them until payment or tender of the price"). The seller would not be bound to accept the price if he had justifiably terminated the contract on the ground of the buyer's breach (see below, paras 15–107—15–111).
[13] The buyer may have to pay the extra expense involved in the second carriage to him.
[14] s.41(1) (above, paras 15–028 *et seq.*). *Cf.* the consignor's more extensive right of stoppage in international carriage of goods; below, paras 21–055—21–057, 21–062—21–064, 21–069—21–071, 21–103.
[15] Above, paras 15–024—15–027.
[16] *i.e.* he may retain the goods until the balance of the price has been paid or tendered. See, on the definition of an "unpaid seller", s.38(1)(a) ("when the whole of the price has not been paid or tendered") (above, paras 15–016—15–017). This was the common law before the Act: *Hodgson v Loy* (1797) 7 T.R. 440.
[17] s.38(1)(b) (above, paras 15–018—15–021). See also above, para.9–030. This was the common law before the Act: *Feise v Wray* (1802) 3 East 93.

has greatly diminished with the development of more sophisticated methods of payment, particularly the use of banker's commercial credits[18] when the parties carry on business in different countries, and with the development of new forms of security, such as retention of title clauses.[19] Where a bank is in possession of the documents of title to the goods until payment, it is in a position to protect both the seller and itself if the buyer becomes insolvent; and since the buyer will not be able to get the documents unless he pays the issuing bank, he cannot obtain the goods without payment.

The effect of the passing of property. The right of stoppage in transit is exercised despite the fact that property in the goods has passed to the buyer,[20] as is explained in the following passage from an early case[21]: "If the seller has despatched the goods to the buyer, and insolvency occurs, he has a right, in virtue of his original ownership, to stop them in transit. Why? Because the property is vested in the buyer so as to subject him to the risk of any accident; but he has not an indefeasible right to the possession, and his insolvency, without payment of the price, defeats that right." 15–063

The right of stoppage in transit arises *stricto sensu* only[22] when the property in the goods has passed to the buyer[23]; so long as the seller remains the owner of the goods, he may withhold delivery to the buyer by virtue of his ownership. "Unless the property passed, there would be no need of the right of stopping *in transitu*. The only effect of the property passing is, that from that time the goods are at the risk of the buyer. But it by no means follows that the buyer is to have possession unless he is prepared to pay for the goods."[24] However, section 39(2) gives the unpaid seller, in situations where the property in the goods has not passed to the buyer,[25] "a right of withholding delivery similar to and co-extensive with his rights of lien or retention and stoppage in transit where the property has passed to the buyer."[26] As owner, the unpaid seller enjoys the legal power to stop the goods, and this subsection gives him the right to do so as against the buyer.

---

[18] See below, paras 23–001 *et seq*. Similarly, many modern contracts stipulate that payment is to be made against documents, as a result of which the seller retains the property in the goods until payment is made (see below, paras 18–208 *et seq*.).

[19] Above, paras 5–141 *et seq*.

[20] s.39(1) (". . . notwithstanding that the property in the goods may have passed to the buyer . . .") (above, para.15–001).

[21] *Bloxam v Sanders* (1825) 4 B. & C. 941 at 948 (cited with approval in *Ex p.Chalmers* (1873) L.R. 8 Ch.App. 289 at 291–292).

[22] *Lickbarrow v Mason* (1793) 6 East 22 at 27(n). (For other references to this case see above, para.15–061, n.98); *Gibson v Carruthers* (1841) 8 M. & W. 321.

[23] On the passing of property, see above, paras 5–001 *et seq*. By s.28 (above, para.8–004) delivery of the goods and payment of the price are normally concurrent conditions.

[24] *Bolton v Lancs & Yorks Ry* (1886) L.R. 1 C.P. 431 at 439.

[25] This may include the situation when the seller has retained a right of disposal over the goods, in accordance with s.19 (above, paras 5–131 *et seq*.; below, paras 18–211 *et seq*., 20–075 *et seq*.).

[26] This is merely declaratory of the previous law: *Griffiths v Perry* (1859) 1 E. & E. 680 at 688; *Ex p. Chalmers*, above, at p.292. On s.39(2), see above, paras 15–010—15–012.

15–064 **Justification of the doctrine.** The justification for the doctrine has varied. In 1761[27] it was said to be a right founded upon the plain reason that one man's goods (*i.e.* those of the unpaid seller) should not be applied to the payment of another man's debts (*i.e.* to pay the general creditors of the insolvent buyer).[28] This reason, however, is not convincing, since it involves giving preferential protection to one creditor,[29] despite the fact that he has allowed the debtor to acquire the property in the goods on credit. In 1825, the justification put foward was that the seller's delivery to the carrier was only a conditional delivery of possession to the buyer, *viz.* provided that the buyer remained solvent up to the time he obtained actual possession of the goods from the carrier.[30] This seems a more defensible ground and is in line with the statutory rules defining the duration of transit[31]: so long as the goods are in the possession of a middleman, who intervenes between the seller's loss of possession and the buyer's acquisition of possession, the seller retains this limited right to prevent actual delivery to the buyer.

15–065 **Who is entitled to exercise the right.** The right of stoppage in transit belongs to the seller in his capacity as seller of the goods: it does not depend on his having previously enjoyed the right of lien over the goods, since it is not a revival of that lien.[32] The definition of seller in the Act[33] includes one who agrees to sell: thus a buyer who resells the goods before the property in the goods has passed to him may exercise the right of stoppage as against the sub-buyer.[34]

The right of stoppage has also been extended to some quasi-sellers: by section 38(2) the term "seller" in this Part of the Act "includes any person who is in the position of a seller, as, for instance, an agent of the seller to whom the bill of lading has been indorsed, or a consignor or agent who has himself paid (or is directly responsible for) the price."[35] A person who was only a surety for the payment of the price had no right at common law to stop the goods in transit.[36] But now, under the Act, a surety of the buyer who has paid the seller is, it is submitted, a "person who is in the position of a seller", and thus entitled to exercise the right of stoppage.[37]

---

[27] *D'Aquila v Lambert* (1761) 1 Amb. 399 at 400 (quoted in *Booth SS Co. Ltd v Cargo Fleet Iron Co. Ltd* [1916] 2 K.B. 570 at 580).
[28] *cf. Kendall v Marshall, Stevens & Co. Ltd* (1883) 11 Q.B.D. 356 at 364 ("It is not founded on any ethical principle".).
[29] See the criticism of Atiyah, *The Sale of Goods* (3rd ed.), p.193, who quotes the analogy of a beneficiary who is entitled to trace trust property into the hands of a person who receives it, and thus is entitled to preference over the general creditors of that person. (This passage is omitted from later editions.)
[30] *Bloxam v Sanders* (1825) 4 B. & C. 941 at 948 (see the quotation, above, para.15–063).
[31] s.45 (below, paras 15–066 *et seq.*).
[32] Nor does a right of stoppage belong to other persons (*i.e.* other than a seller) who previously had a lien over the goods, *e.g.* a repairer.
[33] s.61(1) (above, paras 1–025 *et seq.*).
[34] *Jenkyns v Usborne* (1844) 7 M. & G. 678 at 698–699.
[35] See above, paras 15–013—15–014. The "agent who has himself paid . . . the price" is illustrated by *Imperial Bank v London and St Katherine Docks Co.* (1877) 5 Ch.D. 195.
[36] *Siffken v Wray* (1805) 6 East 371.
[37] See above, para.15–014.

Obviously, the seller's agent may exercise the right of stoppage on his behalf.[38] Where the right was exercised by a purported agent who lacked actual authority to do so, the seller may subsequently ratify the agent's act, provided the ratification is before the transit terminates,[39] *e.g.* by the buyer's valid demand for delivery.[40] An agent may, however, act in his own name in certain circumstances. Thus, the endorsement and delivery of a bill of lading from the seller to his agent gives the right to the possession of the goods to the agent, so that he may exercise the right of stoppage in transit in his own name.[41] Similarly, a commission agent may accept an order to obtain goods for his principal by buying them in his own name[42] and consigning them to him: such an agent is treated as a seller[43] of the goods to his principal and may exercise the right of stoppage in transit if the principal becomes insolvent.[44]

(b) *Duration of Transit*

Introduction. Section 45 contains seven subsections setting out various rules on the duration of transit for the purposes of the unpaid seller's right of stoppage.[45] These rules are a codification of the common law on the subject, and reflect the following principle: "The essential feature of a stoppage *in transitu*. . . is, that the goods should be at the time in the possession of a middleman, or of some person intervening between the vendor who has parted with and the purchaser who has not yet received them."[46] The whole of section 45 indicates that the carrier "middleman" must be independent of both the seller and the buyer, in the sense that he is not acting exclusively as the agent of one of them, even though he may have been appointed by only one of them[47]: if the carrier is the agent of the seller, the latter retains possession for the purpose of exercising his lien; whereas, if the carrier is the agent of the buyer, the transit is deemed to have terminated when the seller delivered the goods to the carrier. 15–066

---

[38] *Whitehead v Anderson* (1842) 9 M. & W. 518.

[39] *Hutchings v Nunes* (1863) 1 Moo.P.C.(N.S.) 243; *Bird v Brown* (1850) 4 Exch.786. (Under the general law of agency, the principal may ratify only if he was competent at the time of the ratification to do the act in question: *Bowstead and Reynolds on Agency* (17th ed.), paras 2–048, 2–060 *et seq.*

[40] See s.45(6) (below, para.15–083).

[41] See above, para.15–046, nn.16 and 17.

[42] This means that the agent pledges his own (and not his principal's) credit when buying the goods: *Feise v Wray* (1802) 3 East 93; *Ex p. Miles* (1885) 15 Q.B.D. 39 at 42.

[43] At least for the purpose of the remedy of stoppage in transit: *Cassaboglou v Gibb, below*. (Under s.38(2), his remedies under the Act will now include the three "real" remedies in s.39(1).)

[44] *Ireland v Livingston* (1872) L.R. 5 H.L. 395 at 408–409; *Cassaboglou v Gibb* (1883) 11 Q.B.D. 797 at 804, 806–807 (following *Feise v Wray*, above).

[45] The concept of goods in transit may be different in the conflict of laws (see below, paras 25–183—25–188).

[46] *Schotsmans v Lancs & Yorks Ry* (1867) L.R. 2 Ch.App. 332 at 338.

[47] Thus the mere fact that the carrier was appointed by the buyer does not mean that transit ended when the delivery was made to the carrier: *Bethell v Clark* (1888) 20 Q.B.D. 615 at 617.

"Transit" under section 45 does not mean that the goods must be actually moving at the relevant time: several subsections indicate that the goods may be stationary but still in transit in the sense that they are still in the possession of the carrier.

15–067 **Transfer of bill of lading to the buyer.** The transfer of a bill of lading by the seller to the buyer (or his agent) does not in itself terminate the transit for the purposes of stoppage in transit[48]: provided that possession of the goods was intended by the parties to pass directly from the seller to the carrier, and to be received by him as carrier (*i.e.* purely in his capacity as such and not as agent of the buyer), the transit as between the buyer and seller will continue.[49] Thus, where goods were delivered to a ship on this basis, it was held to be irrelevant to the continuance of the transit that the buyer had obtained a bill of lading in which he was named as consignor or as consignee.[50] Where, however, the buyer receives a bill of lading from the seller, and subsequently transfers the bill to a sub-buyer or pledgee,[51] the unpaid seller's right of stoppage in transit will normally be lost (or, in the case of pledge, made subject to the pledgee's rights).[52]

The duration of transit is a question which is entirely distinct from the passing of property.[53] "When the goods have not been delivered to the purchaser or to any agent of his to hold for him otherwise than as a carrier, but are still in the hands of the carrier as such and for the purposes of the transit, then, although such carrier was the purchaser's agent to accept delivery so as to pass the property, nevertheless the goods are *in transitu* and may be stopped."[54]

15–068 **Transit continues until buyer takes delivery.** By section 45(1) it is provided: "Goods are deemed to be in course of transit from the time when they are delivered to a carrier or other bailee[55] or custodier[56] for the purpose of transmission to the buyer, until the buyer or his agent in that behalf takes delivery[57] of them from the carrier or other bailee or custodier."[58] The buyer may take delivery personally or through an agent instructed to take delivery on his behalf. Thus, transit as between the seller and the buyer terminates when agents instructed by the buyer receive the

---

48 *Schotsmans v Lancs & Yorks Ry*, above, at p.337. See below, paras 15–092, 18–086.
49 *Lyons v Hoffnung* (1890) 15 App.Cas. 391.
50 *ibid.* (The buyer obtained the bill of lading directly from the carrier.)
51 On trust receipts, see below, paras 18–235 *et seq.*
52 s.47(2) (see below, paras 15–097—15–098).
53 On the passing of property, see above, paras 5–001 *et seq.*
54 *Bethell v Clark* (1888) 20 Q.B.D. 615 at 617 (see further, above, para.15–048).
55 These words would include a carrier by air: see McNair, *Law of the Air* (3rd ed.), pp.161–163 (s.45(1) of the 1893 Act read ". . . a carrier *by land or water* or other bailee . . .").
56 The Scottish term for bailee.
57 Defined in s.61(1) (above, para.8–002). Although the buyer may have taken delivery of the goods, the seller may still, through the reservation of the right of disposal, have rights over them. (See above, para.15–047; below, paras 18–211 *et seq.*, paras 20–075 *et seq.*).
58 See Todd [1978] J.B.L. 39.

goods to be held at the buyer's disposal,[59] and it is immaterial that the buyer has instructed his agents to forward the goods to another destination.[60] The relevant transit is that between the seller and the buyer: once the goods have reached the possession of the buyer or his agent, the transit for this purpose cannot commence again merely because, on the buyer's instructions,[61] the goods are sent on a further journey to another destination.[62] The transit continues when the delivery is to agents "whose sole duty it is to transmit the goods"[63]; nor is it relevant that the buyer nominated the carrier,[64] as would often be the case under an f.o.b. contract.[65]

The duration or extent of the transit will normally depend on the interpretation of the particular words used in the contract or in the directions of the buyer to the seller.[66] Thus, where the order for goods said: "Please deliver the ten hogshead of hollow ware to the *Darling Downs*, to Melbourne, loading in the East India Docks here," it was held[67] that the transit continued until the goods reached Melbourne: no fresh directions from the buyer were needed[68] as the ultimate destination had been specified by the buyer.[69] So long as the seller knows he is delivering to a carrier, who receives them in that capacity,[70] the right of stoppage arises despite the fact that the buyer had not informed the seller of the ultimate destination of the goods.[71] Thus, the seller has the right of stoppage even where he has fulfilled his obligations to put the goods on board under an f.o.b. contract,[72] as the shipowner is "a mere intermediary."[73] Delivery to a **15–069**

---

[59] *Bethell v Clark* (1888) 20 Q.B.D. 615 at 620 (". . . for the purpose of holding them for the purchaser or awaiting further orders"). For illustrations, see *Leeds v Wright* (1803) 3 B. & P. 320; *Scott v Pettit* (1803) 3 B. & P. 469.
[60] *Kendal v Marshall Stevens & Co.* (1883) 11 Q.B.D. 356. (See below, para.15–080.)
[61] In *Kendal v Marshall Stevens & Co.*, above, at pp.365, 368, it was held that it was immaterial whether the buyer's instructions to his agent were given before or after the buyer's order to the seller to deliver them to the agent.
[62] *Dixon v Baldwen* (1804) 5 East 175.
[63] *Bethell v Clark*, above, at p.619. For illustrations, see *Smith v Goss* (1808) 1 Camp. 282; *Coates v Railton* (1827) 6 B. & C. 422.
[64] *Ex p. Rosevear China Clay Co.* (1879) 11 Ch.D. 560; *Bethell v Clark*, above, at p.617.
[65] See below, para.20–135.
[66] For illustrations, see *Jackson v Nichol* (1839) 5 Bing.(N.C.) 508; *Ex p. Watson* (1877) 5 Ch.D. 35 (as explained in *Ex p.Miles* (1885) 15 Q.B.D. 39 at 46, 47); *Kemp v Ismay, Imrie & Co.* (1909) 100 L.T. 996.
[67] *Bethell v Clark*, above.
[68] *cf. Valpy v Gibson* (1847) 4 C.B. 837 at 865 (goods received by buyer's shipping agents, who had no authority to forward the goods until they received the buyer's order to do so); *Ex p. Miles*, above, at p.46 (". . . without the necessity of any new order from the purchaser").
[69] *Coates v Railton*, above.
[70] *viz.* as an intermediary between the seller and the buyer (see above, paras 15–066, 15–067).
[71] *Ex p. Rosevear China Clay Co.*, above.
[72] *ibid.*
[73] *ibid.*, at p.568.

ship[74] is "an indication that the goods were to go on a voyage"[75] and it is obvious that the ship is not the ultimate destination of the goods.[76]

15–070 The question whether delivery has been taken may depend on the buyer's intention to take delivery[77]: thus, where a buyer gave an order to land the goods at a particular wharf, but did not intend to use it as a "place of final deposit," where he would deal with the goods, sell them, or send them later to a further destination, it was held that the transit had not terminated.[78] The buyer may obtain constructive delivery[79] if the carrier attorns to him[80]; but, in the absence of attornment, the buyer will not obtain possession by his act of marking the goods or by taking samples of them, while they remain in the carrier's possession,[81] nor will he normally obtain delivery of the whole consignment by taking possession of part only.[82] Where the goods have to be weighed at their destination, in order to ascertain the freight payable on them, there will be no delivery to the consignee until the goods have been weighed and either the freight has been paid, or an agreement[83] made between the carrier and the consignee that the goods are to be held for the latter but subject to the lien for freight.[84] A carrier will often not intend to deliver the goods until the freight has been paid.[85]

15–071 **Delivery to the buyer's agent.** The words "his agent in that behalf" (section 45(1)) mean a person appointed for taking the goods on delivery on behalf of the buyer.[86] If the only destination given by the buyer to the seller is a firm of shipping agents employed by the buyer, transit ends when the goods reach them[87]; the fact[88] that the buyer has independently instructed the agents to forward the goods elsewhere does not continue the transit so as to enable the seller to stop the goods.[89]

---

[74] The position is different where it is the buyer's ship (see below, para.15–073).
[75] *Kendal v Marshall Stevens & Co.* (1883) 11 Q.B.D. 356 at 367.
[76] For the right of stoppage in f.o.b. and c.i.f. contracts, see below, paras 19–220, 20–141. See also above, para.15–062, n.14.
[77] Even though that intention may not have been communicated to the seller or to the warehouseman: *James v Griffin* (1837) 2 M. & W. 623.
[78] *James v Griffin*, above. See also s.45(4) and *Bolton v Lancs and Yorks Ry* (1866) L.R. 1 C.P. 431 (below, para.15–081). *Cf. Fairfax v Illawarra Steam Navigation Co.* (1872) 11 S.C.R. (N.S.W.) 103.
[79] *cf.* the symbolic or constructive delivery in a sale and leaseback transaction: *Michael Gerson (Leasing) Ltd v Wilkinson* [2000] Q.B. 514.
[80] See below, paras 15–077—15–078, 15–096.
[81] *Whitehead v Anderson* (1842) 9 M. & W. 518 at 535.
[82] See below, para.15–084.
[83] On such an agreement, see below, para.15–079.
[84] *Crawshay v Eades* (1823) 1 B. & C. 181.
[85] *Edwards v Brewer* (1837) 2 M. & W. 375. *Cf. Allan v Gripper* (1832) 2 C. & J. 218 (carrier acted as warehouseman until the buyer or his customers wanted the goods, although the carrier would not deliver to anyone until his charges were paid).
[86] *Jobson v Eppenheim & Co.* (1905) 21 T.L.R. 468 at 469.
[87] *Jobson v Eppenheim & Co.*, above.
[88] Even where this is known to the seller: *Jobson v Eppenheim & Co.*, above.
[89] *ibid.*

Effect of buyer's bankruptcy. The bankruptcy of the buyer does not itself constitute a rescission or termination of the contract[90]: thus, where possession of the goods is taken by the buyer (or his agent) after his bankruptcy,[91] or by his trustee in bankruptcy,[92] the delivery will terminate the transit and prevent the seller from exercising his right of stoppage. However, the bankrupt buyer or his agent will preserve the seller's right if he refuses to accept delivery of the goods.[93] 15–072

Delivery to the buyer's ship. Transit prima facie comes to an end[94] when goods are shipped by the seller on a ship belonging to the buyer,[95] even though the ship is employed as a general trader[96]; thus, delivery to the buyer is obvious where his ship is about to sail on a mercantile adventure or "a roving voyage".[97] However, even delivery aboard a ship owned or chartered[98] by the buyer will not amount to a delivery which terminates the transit if the seller takes in his name a bill of lading for the goods to be delivered "unto order or assigns"[99]; in this situation the master of the ship is only an agent to carry the goods since the seller has reserved the right of disposal over the goods.[1] Similarly, a seller may preserve his right of stoppage in the case of a delivery to a ship under an f.o.b. contract if, pending the issue of the bill of lading, he takes a mate's receipt acknowledging that the goods are shipped on account of the seller.[2] 15–073

Delivery before the appointed destination. Section 45(2) provides: "If the buyer or his agent in that behalf obtains delivery of the goods before their arrival at the appointed destination, the transit is at an end." The buyer, by taking delivery in the course of transit at a place before the goods 15–074

---

[90] See above, paras 3–045—3–049, 15–027.
[91] *Scott v Pettit* (1803) 3 B. & P. 469.
[92] *Ellis v Hunt* (1789) 3 T.R. 464.
[93] *Ex p. Cooper* (1879) 11 Ch.D. 68 at 73. See s.45(4) (below, para.15–081). On the question whether the unpaid seller's repudiation of the contract of sale constitutes a fraudulent preference in his favour, and the effect this might have on the right of stoppage, see *Re O'Sullivan* (1892) 61 L.J.Q.B. 228; *Re Johnson* (1908) 99 L.T. 305.
[94] This proposition may have to give way to the parties' intention: *Merchant Banking Co. v Phoenix Bessemer Steel Co.* (1877) 5 Ch.D. 205 at 219.
[95] *Van Casteel v Booker* (1848) 2 Exch.691 at 699, 708; *Berndtson v Strang* (1867) 4 Eq. 481 at 488–489; (on appeal) (1868) L.R. 3 Ch.App. 588; *Ex p. Francis & Co. Ltd* (1887) 56 L.T. 577. On the question of delivery to a ship chartered by the buyer, see s.45(5) (below, para.15–082).
[96] *Schotsmans v Lancs and Yorks Ry* (1867) L.R. 2 Ch.App. 332. The position may be different if the seller did not know that the ship belonged to the buyer: *ibid.*, at p.335.
[97] *Berndtson v Strang*, above, at pp.490, 491.
[98] See s.45(5) (below, para.15–082).
[99] *Van Casteel v Booker*, above, at pp.699, 708–709; *Berndtson v Strang*, above.
[1] s.19(2) (see above, para.5–137; below, para.18–214). The seller in this situation may often have retained the property in the goods, so that he is not limited to a right of stoppage in transit and can give directions to the carrier irrespective of the buyer's insolvency (see below, paras 18–211 *et seq.*).
[2] *Craven v Ryder* (1816) 6 Taunt. 433; *Ruck v Hatfield* (1822) 5 B. & A. 632. *Cf. Cowasjee v Thompson* (1845) 5 Moo.P.C. 165. On mate's receipts in general, see below, para.18–163.

arrive at their designated destination, may thus terminate the seller's right of stoppage in transit.[3] It is a general rule that, in the absence of special terms in the contract of carriage, the consignee may demand the goods from the carrier at a place en route to the designated destination.[4] So, where a seller sued a railway company for failure to deliver the goods in accordance with the contract of carriage, Pollock C.B. said[5]: "It is clear that a consignee may receive the goods at any stage of the journey; and though the consignor directs the carrier to deliver them at a particular place, there is no contract by the carrier to deliver at that place and not elsewhere. The contract is to deliver there unless the consignee shall require the goods to be delivered at another place. Here, the wheat was delivered at the place where the consignee desired it to be delivered, and therefore the carrier is not liable." However, in modern conditions it may often be impossible or impracticable for the carrier to deliver the goods to the consignee at any place en route to the appointed destination.[6] The terms of the contract of carriage may expressly or by implication deny the consignee the right to demand the goods before arrival at that destination.[7]

There is earlier authority for the view that the buyer could put an end to the transit by taking possession of the goods without the consent of the carrier, although this might be actionable at the suit of the carrier.[8] But by section 45(6),[9] the transit is deemed to be at an end when the carrier wrongfully refuses to deliver the goods to the buyer or his agent; and section 45(1) provides that transit ends when the buyer "takes delivery", which is defined[10] as meaning "voluntary transfer of possession from one person to another." It is therefore submitted that the buyer's tortious acquisition of possession without the carrier's consent should not terminate the transit.[11]

15–075 **Attornment by carrier before arrival of goods.** In one case, the original transit was interrupted by the buyers sending instructions to the carriers to hold the goods at an intermediate stage: since the carriers attorned to the buyers, by advising them that the goods were held pending further orders from them, the original transit was held to be terminated, and the seller's

[3] For an illustration of this rule after the 1893 Act, see *Johann Plischke und Sohne GmbH v Allison Brothers Ltd* [1936] 2 All E.R. 1009. The common law before the Act was to the same effect: *Whitehead v Anderson* (1842) 9 M. & W. 518 at 534. *Cf. L and NW Ry v Bartlett* (1861) 7 H. & N. 400.
[4] *Cork Distilleries Co. v GS and W Ry* (1874) L.R. 7 H.L. 269. *Cf.* below, para.15–087.
[5] *L and NW Ry v Bartlett*, above, at pp.407–408. This passage holds that it is not a breach of contract against the consignor, and does not necessarily mean that the consignee may demand the goods at a place other than the agreed destination.
[6] On the problems of container transport, see below, paras 21–072 *et seq.*
[7] See below, paras 21–069—21–071.
[8] *Whitehead v Anderson*, above, at p.534.
[9] Below, para.15–083.
[10] By s.61(1).
[11] *cf.* s.43(1)(b) (the unpaid seller's lien is lost when the buyer *lawfully* obtains possession of the goods: see above, para.15–055. See also Todd [1978] J.B.L. 39 at 43–44).

right to stop was thereby lost.[12] The carrier, however, is not bound to attorn to the buyer in such circumstances.[13]

Agent of buyer taking early delivery. For section 45(2) to apply, the agent of the buyer must have authority to take early delivery: "his agent in that behalf" means an agent with authority to take delivery at a place other than the appointed destination.[14] Thus, carriers who were employed generally to carry the buyer's goods from a railway station were held not to have implied authority to accept delivery on the buyer's behalf at the station.[15] 15–076

Acknowledgment to the buyer. Section 45(3) provides: "If, after the arrival of the goods at the appointed destination,[16] the carrier or other bailee or custodier acknowledges to the buyer or his agent that he holds the goods on his behalf and continues in possession of them as bailee or custodier for the buyer or his agent, the transit is at an end, and it is immaterial that a further destination for the goods may have been indicated by the buyer." This subsection deals with an acknowledgment by the carrier to the buyer which creates the relationship of bailment between them. Such an acknowledgment is an illustration of the doctrine of attornment,[17] which is often associated with the concept of estoppel: a bailee who acknowledges to the claimant that the claimant has title to[18] a chattel is estopped at common law from denying the claimant's title and becomes the bailee of the claimant.[19] The subsection codifies the common law before the 1893 Act; thus, it was said in 1866: "A carrier may and often does become a warehouseman for the consignee; but that must be by virtue of some contract or course of dealing between them, that, when arrived at their destination, the character of the carrier shall cease, and that of warehouseman supervene."[20] The buyer's request to the carrier to hold the goods in the carrier's warehouse pending further instructions from the buyer is strong evidence that the carrier thereupon becomes the buyer's agent and transit ends.[21] 15–077

---

[12] *Reddall v Union Castle Mail SS Co. Ltd* (1914) 84 L.J.K.B. 360 (the carrier charged the buyer warehouse rent from the date of the buyer's interception). On attornment, see below, paras 15–077—15–078, 15–096.

[13] *Jackson v Nichol* (1839) 5 Bing.(N.C.) 508.

[14] *Mechan & Sons, Ltd v NE Ry*, 1911 S.C. 1348 at 1357–1358.

[15] *ibid.*

[16] See below, para.15–080.

[17] *Chitty on Contracts* (29th ed.), Vol. 2, para.33–030.

[18] By s.8(1) of the Torts (Interference with Goods) Act 1977 a bailee may now set up the title of a third person in reply to the bailor's demand for redelivery of the chattel: see Chitty, *op. cit.*, Vol. 2, paras 33–015—33–016.

[19] *Henderson & Co. v Williams* [1895] 1 Q.B. 521; *Dublin City Distillery Ltd v Doherty* [1914] A.C. 823 at 847–848. See above, paras 5–065, 7–008 *et seq.*

[20] *Bolton v Lancs and Yorks Ry* (1866) L.R. 1 C.P. 431 at 438. See also *Ex p.Cooper* (1879) 11 Ch.D. 68 at 78.

[21] *Johann Plischke und Sohne GmbH v Allison Brothers Ltd* [1936] 2 All E.R. 1009. (This construction was not precluded by the fact that the contract provided for "Freehouse, London", *i.e.* that the seller would pay charges on the goods until delivered at the buyer's premises in London.)

15–078 **Assent of both parties required.** It is essential that the carrier should clearly consent to hold the goods as warehouseman for the buyer, so that he alters his previous character as carrier[22]: thus, silence on the part of the master of a ship, when the buyer or his agent claims to take constructive possession of goods while they are still on board ship, will not normally lead to an inference of consent.[23] Nor has attornment been inferred from a statement made by a ship's officer that the goods will be delivered to the buyer when sufficient of the cargo has been unloaded to enable the goods in question to be moved[24]: the carrier had not "entered into a new agreement to keep the goods for the [buyer] distinct from that originally entered into by him to convey them to their place of destination pursuant to the bill of lading."[25]

The carrier cannot himself change his character to that of warehouseman or agent for the buyer to hold the goods: the buyer must assent to the alteration[26] but his assent may be inferred from his silence and delay, *e.g.* after the carrier sends the buyer a notice that he will hold the goods as warehouseman and charge rent to the buyer.[27] Attornment, however, cannot be inferred from the mere fact that the carrier has notified the buyer that he is ready to deliver the goods.[28]

15–079 **Lien of the carrier.** The carrier may change his character to that of warehouseman despite the fact that he insists on his lien over the goods until the freight on them has been paid,[29] since there may be an agreement between the carrier and the buyer that the carrier should, while retaining his lien for the freight, hold the goods as agent for the buyer.[30] But the insistence of the carrier or his agent that he intends to hold the goods until the whole of the freight on them has been paid is in itself a strong indication that he continues to hold as carrier.[31]

15–080 **"Appointed destination" and "further destination".** The words "appointed destination" in subsection (3) refer to the place at which the goods are to be delivered according to the provisions of the contract of sale.[32] The concept of "place", however, needs further elaboration: "In

---

22 *Whitehead v Anderson* (1842) 9 M. & W. 518. The carrier's refusal to deliver to the buyer obviously prevents constructive delivery to the buyer: *Jackson v Nichol* (1839) 5 Bing.(N.C.) 508. (But transit is deemed to be at an end: s.45(6) (below, para.15–083).)
23 *Whitehead v Anderson*, above.
24 *Coventry v Gladstone* (1868) L.R. 6 Eq. 44.
25 *ibid.*, at p.50.
26 *Bolton v Lancs and Yorks Ry*, above; *Ex p.Barrow* (1877) 6 Ch.D. 783 at 789 (". . . until the buyer does something to evince an intention of possessing them . . .").
27 *Taylor v GE Ry* (1901) 17 T.L.R. 394; *Ex p. Catling* (1873) 29 L.T. 431.
28 *Mechan & Sons Ltd v NE Ry*, 1911 S.C. 1348 at 1359.
29 *Kemp v Falk* (1882) 7 App.Cas. 573 at 584.
30 *ibid.*
31 *ibid.*, at p.584; *Crawshay v Eades* (1823) 1 B. & C. 181; *Ex p. Barrow*, above, at p.789; *Ex p.Cooper*, above, at pp.72–73, 74, 76 (delivery of part after payment of part of the freight). *Cf. Whitehead v Anderson*, above, at pp.535–536. On the carrier's lien, see further, below, para.15–089.
32 *Mechan & Sons Ltd v NE Ry*, above, at pp.1356, 1358.

business 'destination' means that you must give not only the name of the place to which, but also the name of the person to whom, goods are to be sent."[33] The final part of subsection (3) provides that "it is immaterial that a further destination for the goods may have been indicated by the buyer." Thus, even where the seller knows that the buyer intends to send the goods on to a further place, this is not sufficient to prevent termination of the transit.[34] The transit as between seller and buyer will continue only where there is "an actual bargain between the buyer and the seller that the goods should go straight to the [ultimate destination]."[35] The law on this point was explained by Lord Esher M.R. in *Bethell v Clark*[36]: "Where the transit is a transit which has been caused either by the terms of the contract or by the directions of the purchaser to the vendor, the right of stoppage *in transitu* exists; but, if the goods are not in the hands of the carrier by reason either of the terms of the contract or of the directions of the purchaser to the vendor, but are *in transitu* afterwards in consequence of fresh directions given by the purchaser for a new transit, then such transit is no part of the original transit, and the right to stop is gone. So also, if the purchaser gives orders that the goods shall be sent to a particular place, there to be kept till he gives fresh orders as to their destination to a new carrier, the original transit is at an end when they have reached that place, and any further transit is a fresh and independent transit."

Rejection of the goods by the buyer. Section 45 further provides: "(4) If the goods are rejected by the buyer, and the carrier or other bailee or custodier continues in possession of them, the transit is not deemed to be at an end, even if the seller has refused to receive them back." The buyer may expressly[37] refuse to receive the goods, and this refusal will preserve the seller's right to stop the goods.[38] The question of rejection will often depend on the intention of the consignee: if he has no intention of taking possession, the transit is not at an end, despite the fact that the carrier intended to deliver the goods.[39] "The arrival which is to divest the vendor's right of stoppage *in transitu* must be such as that the buyer has taken actual or constructive possession of the goods; and that cannot be so long as he repudiates them."[40] Thus, a bankrupt buyer (or his agent), by refusing to take delivery of the goods, may give the unpaid seller the opportunity to exercise his right of stoppage in order to gain priority over the general creditors of the buyer.[41] If, however, the buyer had previously assented to the carrier's attornment to him (under section 45(3)[42]), it is submitted that 15–081

[33] *Ex p. Miles* (1885) 15 Q.B.D. 39 at 45.
[34] *Kendal v Marshall, Stevens & Co.* (1883) 11 Q.B.D. 356 (above, para.15–068).
[35] *Ex p. Miles*, above, at p.47 (referring to *Ex p. Watson* (1877) 5 Ch.D. 35). See also *Rodger v Comptoir D'Escompte de Paris* (1869) L.R. 2 P.C. 393.
[36] (1888) 20 Q.B.D. 615 at 617.
[37] *Bolton v Lancs and Yorks Ry* (1866) L.R. 1 C.P. 431.
[38] *cf.* the need for the buyer's intention to take "delivery": *James v Griffin* (1837) 2 M. & W. 623 (above, para.15–070).
[39] *Bolton v Lancs and Yorks Ry*, above, at p.438.
[40] *ibid.*, at p.440.
[41] *Ex p. Cooper* (1879) 11 Ch.D. 68 at 73 (see above, paras 15–027, 15–072).
[42] Above, para.15–077.

it would be too late for the buyer then to reject the goods so as to prevent the termination of transit under section 45(4).[43]

15–082 **Delivery to ship chartered by the buyer.** Section 45 continues: "(5) When goods are delivered to a ship chartered by the buyer it is a question depending on the circumstances of the particular case whether they are in the possession of the master as a carrier or as agent to the buyer." The question whether a ship chartered by the buyer is to be treated as the buyer's own ship depends on the intention of the parties shown by the terms of the charterparty and particularly by the form of the bill of lading: in whose name and to whose order was it made out?[44] In *Berndtson v Strang*[45] Lord Cairns L.C. indicated that the proper test to apply is whether the master of the ship is an employee of the owner or of the buyer as charterer. If the charterer is "owner for the voyage" because it is a charter by demise,[46] he is in possession of the ship and the master and crew are treated as his employees.[47] In this situation, delivery to the ship of goods bought by the charterer divests the unpaid seller of his right of stoppage in transit, unless the bill of lading is in a form which retains the seller's control. The position was extensively reviewed in *Berndtson v Strang*,[48] where the seller delivered to a ship chartered by the buyer, but took a bill of lading for the goods to be delivered to his "order or assigns"[49]: it was held that this form of bill of lading interposed the master of the ship, as carrier, between the seller and the buyer so as to preserve the seller's right of stoppage during the voyage.[50] Where, however, the charterparty is not a demise, the master is a mere carrier—the employee of the shipowner and not the agent of the charterer—and the transit is not terminated by delivery to the ship: hence, the unpaid seller retains his right of stoppage.

15–083 **Carrier's wrongful refusal to deliver.** Section 45(6) provides that: "Where the carrier or other bailee or custodier wrongfully refuses to deliver the goods to the buyer or his agent in that behalf, the transit is deemed to be at an end."[51] Section 45(1)[52] deals with a voluntary transfer of possession to the buyer or his agent, whereas this subsection deals with the carrier's wrongful refusal to deliver. Now "delivery" involves more than the arrival of the goods at their destination: the buyer or his agent must "take

[43] Todd [1978] J.B.L. 39 at 41. (At p.42, this writer speculates whether "continues in possession" in s.45(4) could refer to the time from which he receives the rejected goods from the buyer. *Sed quaere*.)
[44] See below, paras 20–077 *et seq*., 18–214 *et seq*.
[45] (1868) L.R. 3 Ch.App. 588.
[46] Which is a type of "lease" of the ship. See *Scrutton on Charterparties and Bills of Lading* (20th ed.), pp.59 *et seq*.
[47] *ibid*.
[48] (1867) 4 Eq. 481; on appeal, (1868) L.R. 3 Ch.App. 588.
[49] In *Ex p. Rosevear China Clay Co.* (1879) 11 Ch.D. 560, although delivery had been made to a ship chartered by the buyer, the stoppage was made before any bill of lading had been signed.
[50] See further on this point, above, para.15–073.
[51] This was the law before the 1893 Act: *Bird v Brown* (1850) 4 Exch.786.
[52] Discussed above, paras 15–068—15–073.

delivery".[53] This subsection therefore provides that the unpaid seller's right of stoppage terminates if the buyer or his agent is ready and willing to take delivery but the carrier wrongfully refuses to deliver. "Wrongfully" assumes that the carrier is bound to deliver to the buyer in accordance with the contract of carriage, and that the carrier has no legal justification for refusing to deliver, *e.g.* that he has no lien over the goods for unpaid freight[54] or demurrage, and that no valid notice of stoppage in transit has previously reached him. The carrier, however, is not bound to attorn to the buyer if the latter demands, in the course of transit, that the carrier should thereafter hold on behalf of the buyer[55]: thus the carrier's refusal in these circumstances will not be treated as wrongful.[56]

Delivery of part of the goods. Subsection (7) of section 45 provides: "Where part delivery of the goods has been made to the buyer or his agent in that behalf, the remainder of the goods may be stopped in transit, unless such part delivery has been made under such circumstances as to show an agreement to give up possession of the whole of the goods." This rule embodies the common law before the 1893 Act,[57] and is similar to the rule in section 42 dealing with the unpaid seller's right of lien,[58] so that the decisions under that section will be relevant to the interpretation of this subsection. The way the rule is expressed in the subsection shows that normally it will be difficult to prove that both parties intended delivery of part to be treated as delivery of the whole.[59] The fact that freight charges have not yet been paid may show that delivery of part of the goods was not intended to be constructive delivery of the whole, because it may be assumed that the carrier would not deliver the whole until all his freight charges have been paid.[60] The facts, however, may show that there was an intention on the part of both[61] parties that delivery of part of the consignment was to be treated as delivery of the whole[62]: "where a purchaser taking part shows an intention, acquiesced in by the carrier, to receive and take possession of the whole, that is a constructive possession of the whole by the acquiescence of both parties."[63] Thus, where the goods 15–084

[53] Above, para.15–070.
[54] See below, para.15–089.
[55] *Jackson v Nichol* (1839) 5 Bing. (N.C.) 508 (above, para.15–075). The case held that the transit was not terminated by the buyer's demand, which implies that the carrier was not obliged to comply with it.
[56] *ibid.* This is analogous to the rule that the seller who exercises his right of stoppage cannot demand that the carrier should deliver the goods to him anywhere except at the contractual destination: see below, para.15–087.
[57] *Jones v Jones* (1841) 8 M. & W. 431; *Tanner v Scovell* (1845) 14 M. & W. 28; *Bolton v Lancs and Yorks Ry* (1866) L.R. 1 C.P. 431 at 440; *Ex p. Cooper* (1879) 11 Ch.D. 68; *Kemp v Falk* (1882) 7 App.Cas. 573 at 579, 586.
[58] Above, paras 15–041—15–042.
[59] *Mechan & Sons Ltd v N.E. Ry*, 1911 S.C. 1348 at 1358.
[60] *Ex p. Cooper*, above (the carrier has a lien for the unpaid freight).
[61] *Kemp v Falk*, above, at p.586. (See the quotation, above, para.15–041.)
[62] *Jones v Jones*, above. (The consignee was an assignee for the benefit of creditors, which indicated an intention to take possession of the whole, for the purpose of distribution among the creditors, at the first opportunity.)
[63] *Ex p. Cooper*, above, at p.77. See also *Tanner v Scovell*, above, at pp.36, 38.

constitute one entire machine, and the consignee is permitted to take an essential part of it, that transfer might amount to transfer of the whole machine.[64]

Although the carrier may have delivered only part of the goods to the buyer, transit may have terminated on the ground that the carrier attorned to the consignee by undertaking to hold the goods for him: in this situation he has altered his position from that of mere carrier.[65] The transit "is not at an end until the carrier, by agreement between himself and the consignee, undertakes to hold the goods for the consignee, not as carrier, but as his agent."[66]

(c) *Exercise of the Right of Stoppage*

15–085 **Methods of exercising right of stoppage.** It is provided by section 46: "(1) The unpaid seller may exercise his right of stoppage in transit either by taking actual possession of the goods or by giving notice of his claim to the carrier or other bailee or custodier in whose possession the goods are. (2) The notice may be given either to the person in actual possession of the goods or to his principal. (3) If given to the principal, the notice is ineffective unless given at such time and under such circumstances that the principal, by the exercise of reasonable diligence, may communicate it to his servant or agent in time to prevent a delivery to the buyer." At common law no particular formality was necessary to exercise the right of stoppage[67]; and the use of the word "may" in the first sentence of section 46(1) suggests that the two alternative methods mentioned are not the only valid methods of stopping the goods. The seller takes the risk of the stoppage being unjustified,[68] so that the carrier is not concerned to investigate the facts to see whether the seller is justified in stopping the goods[69]; the carrier must give effect to the stoppage as soon as he is satisfied that it is the seller who claims the goods.[70] So a shipowner can give effect to a stoppage without requiring the seller to show that the bill of lading has not been transferred by the buyer to a third person.[71] The carrier, however, need not give effect to a stoppage if he is aware of a legal defect in the seller's claim.[72] If he is uncertain as to his position he can always protect himself by interpleading.[73]

---

64 *Ex p. Cooper*, above, at pp.75–76.
65 See s.45(3) and the cases cited above, paras 15–077—15–078. *Cf.* also above, para.15–075.
66 *Ex p. Cooper*, above, at p.78.
67 *Snee v Prescot* (1753) 1 Atk. 245 at 250; *Litt v Cowley* (1816) 7 Taunt. 169.
68 *The Tigress* (1863) 32 L.J.P.M. & A. 97 at 101.
69 *The Tigress*, above, at p.101. See also s.46(4) (". . . the carrier . . . must redeliver . . ."). If the seller acts without justification, *e.g.* if the buyer is not insolvent, the buyer's remedy is a claim for damages against the seller: *The Constantia* (1807) 6 C.Rob.Adm.R. 321 at 326. (The seller is still bound to deliver to the buyer, who apparently has no claim against the carrier.)
70 *The Tigress*, above, at p.101.
71 *ibid.* (On the effect of such a transfer, see below, paras 15–097—15–099.)
72 *ibid.* (But *cf.* the word "must" in s.46(4).)
73 *ibid.*, at p.102; *Bethell v Clark* (1888) 20 Q.B.D. 615.

The seller must countermand delivery to the buyer; usually it will be sufficient for him to notify the carrier that he is claiming as seller to stop the goods, and either that they should not be delivered to the buyer,[74] or that they should be held by the carrier subject to the seller's orders.[75] For instance, a notice to the consignee that he is to "hold proceeds subject to order" of the seller is not a direction that possession of the goods is to be withheld, and this is not a valid stoppage.[76] The seller's notice may be given with the full agreement of the buyer[77]; the buyer may be concerned to protect the unpaid seller's interests, which he can do by refusing to accept delivery of the goods.[78]

Notice must be given to "the person who has the immediate custody of the goods."[79] Thus, when the goods are on board a ship, notice to a shipowner at his office is not in itself sufficient, because he is not personally in possession of the goods: but the shipowner is under a duty to communicate the notice to the master of the ship.[80] It is doubtful whether notice to the consignee of the goods is sufficient.[81] If the person who gives notice of stoppage purports to act on behalf of the seller, he must have authority to do so.[82]

Notice to the carrier's principal. The provisions of section 46(3) as to notice to the carrier's principal follow the common law.[83] Thus, notice may be given to a shipowner, who is best placed to communicate with the master of the ship: at common law, the shipowner who received such notice was under an obligation to communicate with the master with reasonable diligence,[84] and the Act appears to imply that the principal is under such a duty. If the principal is under such a duty, he would be liable[85] to the seller if he failed in his duty so that the goods were delivered to the insolvent buyer. 15–086

Effect on the contract of carriage.[86] The stoppage, according to the view of Scrutton J.,[87] does not entitle the seller to demand actual possession during the transit against the will of the carrier, or to direct the carrier to deliver to him except at the contractual destination: the carrier is not 15–087

---

[74] *e.g. Booth SS Co. Ltd v Cargo Fleet Iron Co. Ltd* [1916] 2 K.B. 570 at 592.
[75] *e.g.* by the seller demanding the bills of lading from the shipowner when the latter holds them as security for the unpaid freight: *Ex p. Watson* (1877) 5 Ch.D. 35.
[76] *Phelps, Stokes & Co. v Comber* (1885) 29 Ch.D. 813 at 821–822, 824.
[77] *Nicholls v Le Feuvre* (1835) 2 Bing.N.C. 81.
[78] *Ex p. Cooper* (1879) 11 Ch.D. 68 at 73 (above, para.15–027). The buyer's intention to take delivery is an essential element in taking delivery: see s.45(1) and (4) (above, paras 15–070, 15–081).
[79] *Whitehead v Anderson* (1842) 9 M. & W. 518 at 534.
[80] See below, para.15–086.
[81] *Phelps, Stokes & Co. v Comber* (1885) 29 Ch.D. 813 at 822, 826.
[82] *Whitehead v Anderson*, above, at p.534. See further above, para.15–065.
[83] *Whitehead v Anderson*, above, at p.534.
[84] *Kemp v Falk* (1882) 7 App.Cas. 573 at 585–586.
[85] Either in conversion, or (*semble*) for breach of duty under s.60 of the Act (see below, para.16–094).
[86] See also, on the question of the carrier's lien, below, para.15–089.
[87] *Booth SS Co. Ltd v Cargo Fleet Iron Co. Ltd* [1916] 2 K.B. 570 at 600–601.

obliged during the transit to unload other goods to get at those which have been stopped. The only effect on the contract of affreightment is that delivery to the consignee at the port of destination is prevented, and the seller may direct other delivery there.[88] However, it is frequently convenient to the carrier to redeliver to the seller before the goods are carried to the contractual destination, but it is prudent for him to do so only under an indemnity from the seller.[89]

15–088 **Duties of the parties after notice is given.** By section 46(4): "When notice of stoppage in transit is given by the seller to the carrier or other bailee or custodier in possession of the goods, he must redeliver the goods to, or according to the directions of, the seller; and the expenses of the redelivery must be borne by the seller." This subsection again represents the common law before the 1893 Act.[90] The carrier is bound to act on the notice of stoppage[91]: if he disregards a valid notice, and delivers the goods to the consignee, *e.g.* by mistake,[92] he is liable to the seller for conversion,[93] since by the notice the seller resumes the right to possession of the goods.[94] Refusal of the carrier to deliver upon demand being made by the seller would also be evidence of conversion.[95] Other remedies of the seller may include an injunction,[96] or Admiralty proceedings if the goods are in the possession of a shipowner.[97]

The seller has the power not only to countermand delivery to the buyer, but also to order delivery to himself or to his order.[98] The exercise of the seller's power places the seller[99] under a direct obligation to the carrier either to take delivery or to give him directions for delivery.[1] Thus the correlative of the seller's right to stop is his duty to the carrier who is unable to deliver to the consignee: in order to regain actual possession of the goods, the seller must pay any unpaid freight due to the carrier,[2] and if

---

[88] *ibid.*

[89] *ibid.*

[90] *The Tigress* (1863) 32 L.J.P.M. & A. 97. *Cf.* the consignor's extensive rights of stoppage as against the carrier in the international carriage of goods (above, para.15–062, n.14).

[91] If the carrier is under any reasonable doubt as to who is entitled to the goods, he may interplead: *Wilson v Anderton* (1830) 1 B. & A. 450; *The Tigress*, above, at p.102; *Bethell v Clark* (1888) 20 Q.B.D. 615. See also above, para.15–085, n.69.

[92] *Litt v Cowley* (1816) 7 Taunt. 169. (This case is no longer authority on the question of revesting of title: see now s.48(1) (below, para.15–101).)

[93] *The Tigress*, above; *Mechan & Sons Ltd v NE Ry*, 1911 S.C. 1348. The action will fall under s.60 (below, para.16–094) and is classified as an action in tort, not in contract: *Pontifex v Midland Ry* (1877) 3 Q.B.D. 23; it will be governed by the Torts (Interference with Goods) Act 1977.

[94] See s.44 (see above, para.15–061, below, para.15–091. *Cf.* below, para.15–089).

[95] *Wilson v Anderton*, above, at p.456; *The Tigress*, above, at p.102.

[96] *Schotsmans v Lancs and Yorks Ry* (1867) L.R. 2 Ch.App. 332 at 340.

[97] *The Tigress*, above. (A proceeding by the seller to recover, by arrest of the ship, damages for refusal to deliver goods to him.)

[98] s.46(4). See also *The Tigress*, above; *United States Steel Products Co. v GW Ry* [1916] 1 A.C. 189 at 203.

[99] Even where he is not a party to the contract of affreightment: *Booth SS Co. v Cargo Fleet Iron Co.* [1916] 2 K.B. 570.

[1] *ibid.*

[2] *Booth SS Co. v Cargo Fleet Iron Co.*, above, at pp.583, 588.

he fails to do so, he must pay damages to the carrier for the amount of the freight.[3] Similarly, if the seller fails to give directions to the carrier after the stoppage, he will be liable to the carrier in damages for expenses, such as demurrage or landing charges[4]; the seller cannot make the carrier bear the expense of exercising the seller's lien for the benefit of the seller.[5] If the seller by his notice of stoppage prevents the carrier from completing the journey, the damages may amount to the freight for the whole journey.[6]

Lien of the carrier. In order to regain possession of the goods, the seller must discharge the carrier's lien for any unpaid freight due to the carrier[7]; the carrier has a lien on the goods for this freight, but this is a particular lien confined to the carrier's charges in respect of the carriage of those particular goods.[8] This lien has priority over the seller's right of stoppage, which in turn has priority over any general lien on the goods which the consignment contract may give the carrier in respect of sums owing to him from the consignee under other transactions.[9] Clear provision in the consignment contract could, however, bind the seller to postpone his lien to the general lien of the carrier in these circumstances.[10] 15–089

No stoppage against insurance money. Since the right of stoppage is a right exercisable only against the goods themselves, the unpaid seller has no right against money paid or payable to the buyer under a policy of insurance for damage suffered by the goods in course of transit.[11] (The same principle prevents the unpaid seller from using his right of stoppage in transit, after the actual transit has ended, to intercept the price due to be paid to the buyer under a sub-sale of the same goods.[12]) But it has been held in New York that, where the carrier has sold the goods to meet his freight charges, the unpaid seller's right of stoppage can attach to the balance of the proceeds of the sale.[13] 15–090

---

[3] *Booth SS Co. v Cargo Fleet Iron Co.*, above. See also below, para.20–141. (S.62(2) preserves the common law, save in so far as it is inconsistent with the provisions of the Act.)

[4] *Booth SS Co. v Cargo Fleet Iron Co.*, above. See also the last sentence of s.46(4); and *cf. Somes v British Empire Shipping Co.* (1860) 8 H.L.C. 338; *cf.* also *China Pacific SA v Food Corporation of India* [1982] A.C. 939 at 962–963 (see above, para.15–044, n.7).

[5] *Booth SS Co. v Cargo Fleet Iron Co.*, above, at p.602.

[6] *Booth SS Co. v Cargo Fleet Iron Co.*, above, at pp.584–585, 603; *Stewart v Rogerson* (1871) L.R. 6 C.P. 424.

[7] *Booth SS Co. v Cargo Fleet Iron Co.*, above, at pp.583, 588. The lien must be discharged whether it is a common law lien for freight on delivery or a contractual lien for advance freight: *ibid.*, at p.599.

[8] *United States Steel Products Co. v G.W. Ry*, above, at pp.196, 211.

[9] *United States Steel Products Co. v G.W. Ry*, above; *Oppenheim v Russell* (1802) 3 Bos. & P. 42; *Nicholls v Le Feuvre* (1835) 2 Bing.N.C. 81 (shipping agent's general lien).

[10] *United States Steel Products Co. v G.W. Ry*, above, at pp.198, 204, 209.

[11] *Berndtson v Strang* (1868) L.R. 3 Ch.App. 588 at 591. See also *Latham v Chartered Bank of India* (1873) 17 Eq. 205 at 216. *Cf. Phelps, Stokes & Co. v Comber* (1885) 29 Ch.D. 813 (above, para.15–085, n.76).

[12] See below, para.15–100.

[13] *Northern Grain Co. v Wiffler* (1918) 223 N.Y. 169. (It was held on the facts that the goods had not been delivered to the buyer.) *Cf.* below, para.15–100.

15–091 **The effect of stoppage.** By section 48(1), it is provided that: "Subject to this section, a contract of sale is not rescinded[14] by the mere exercise by an unpaid seller of his right of lien or retention or stoppage in transit."[15] This was the position at common law.[16] The effect of exercising the right of stoppage is that the seller "may resume possession of the goods"[17] and thereby regain his lien as unpaid seller,[18] which entitles him to retain the goods until the price is paid or tendered[19]: the seller regains the position he was in before he delivered the goods to the carrier. But the seller's resumed possession is more than a mere lien, because the unpaid seller, under the circumstances set out in section 48, may resell the goods and claim damages from the buyer for any loss caused by the breach of contract.[20]

4. SUB-SALES AND OTHER SUBSEQUENT TRANSACTIONS

15–092 **Sub-sale by buyer.** Section 47(1) of the Act provides: "Subject to this Act, the unpaid seller's right of lien or retention or stoppage in transit is not affected by any sale or other disposition of the goods which the buyer may have made, unless the seller has assented to it."[21] Thus, the fact that the seller knows of a sub-sale, or knows that the sub-buyer has paid the buyer, will not deprive the seller of his lien,[22] nor can such knowledge be used to found an estoppel so as to prevent the seller from setting up his lien.[23] An important exception to subsection (1) is, however, found in subsection (2)[24] which concerns the transfer of a document of title: for instance, the mere indorsement of a bill of lading by the seller to the buyer does not preclude the exercise of the right of stoppage in transit,[25] but, by virtue of subsection (2), when the buyer subsequently transfers the bill of lading to a sub-buyer or a pledgee, the seller's right is lost or (in the case of a pledge) made subject to that of the pledgee. "Subject to this Act" refers[26] to section 25 (on the sale and delivery to a third person by a buyer in possession[27]) and to section 55 (express agreement of the parties[28]) as well

---

[14] The word "rescinded" in s.48(1) must mean "treated as discharged by the seller," or "terminated by the seller."
[15] See below, para.15–101
[16] *Kemp v Falk* (1882) 7 App.Cas 573 at 581.
[17] s.44. This means that the seller acquires "the right to possession of the goods": *Booth SS Co. Ltd v Cargo Fleet Iron Co.* [1916] 2 K.B. 570 at 581. But the seller does not reacquire the property in the goods. *Cf.* also above, para.15–089.
[18] See above, paras 15–028 *et seq.*
[19] s.44. (See above, para.15–061.)
[20] See below, paras 15–119 *et seq.*
[21] See also above, para.1–018.
[22] *M'Ewan and Sons v Smith* (1849) 2 H.L.C. 309.
[23] *Poulton and Son v Anglo-American Oil Co. Ltd* (1910) 27 T.L.R. 38 at 39.
[24] See below, paras 15–097 *et seq.* In the 1893 Act, the provision now contained in s.47(2) was the proviso to s.47, and is referred to as such in the cases.
[25] *The Tigress* (1863) 32 L.J.P.M. & A. 97; *Ex p. Golding Davis & Co. Ltd* (1880) 13 Ch.D. 628 at 633. On the rules applicable to a bill of lading, see further below, paras 18–012 *et seq.*, especially paras 18–086—18–089.
[26] Possibly there is also a reference to s.62(2), which permits attornment to be recognised: see below, para.15–096.
[27] See above, paras 7–069 *et seq.* (s.9 of the Factors Act 1889 is substantially identical with s.25).
[28] See above, paras 1–013—1–015.

as to subsection (2) of section 47.[29] Thus, section 47 is not the only section of the Act which sets out circumstances in which the rights of lien and stoppage may be defeated by a sub-sale or subsequent transaction.[30]

Seller's assent to a sub-sale.[31] The provisions of section 47(1) are to the same effect as the previous common law.[32] In *Merchant Banking Co. v Phoenix Bessemer Steel Co.*[33] the sellers were held to have assented to the buyers dealing with the goods, because the sellers had issued to the buyers a warrant which was (by custom) treated as a representation that the goods were free from any seller's lien. The warrant provided: "The undermentioned iron will not be delivered to any party but the holder of this warrant . . . Iron deliverable (f.o.b.) to [X.Y.] or to their assigns by indorsement hereon." Jessel M.R. treated the case on the basis that the seller's act in issuing the warrants led to the loss of both his lien and his right of stoppage. He said[34] that "any man who gives this warrant understands that it shall pass from hand to hand for value by indorsement, and that the indorsee is to have the goods free from any vendor's claim for purchase-money . . . if he chooses to issue it in this shape he tells all the trade that they may safely deal on the faith of that warrant. . . ." 15–093

After the passing of the 1893 Act, the meaning of the seller's assent to the sub-sale was considered in *Mordaunt Brothers v British Oil and Cake Mills Ltd.*[35] In this case, the practice of sellers of oil was to retain possession until they received a delivery order signed by the buyer. The buyer resold the oil, and signed delivery orders[36] in favour of the sub-buyer, who sent them to the sellers with an endorsement such as "Please wait our orders." The sellers received the delivery orders (sometimes without comment, and sometimes saying that they were "in order") and made entries in their books to the effect that the sub-buyer was the person to whom deliveries were to be made. When the buyer stopped paying the sellers, the latter claimed to retain the oil under their lien. In regard to the sub-buyer's reliance on section 47, Pickford J. held[37] that ". . . the assent which affects the unpaid seller's right of lien must be such an assent as in the circumstances shews that the seller intends to renounce his rights against the goods. It is not enough to shew that the fact of a sub-contract has been brought to his notice and that he has assented to it merely in the sense of 15–094

---

[29] Below, paras 15–097 *et seq.*
[30] *Cahn and Mayer v Pockett's Bristol Channel Steam Packet Co. Ltd* [1899] 1 Q.B. 643 at 664–665.
[31] *Blackburn on Sale* (1st ed.), p.271.
[32] See *Stoveld v Hughes* (1811) 14 East 308 (seller allowed the sub-buyer to mark the goods); *Pearson v Dawson* (1858) E.B. & E. 448 (attornment: see below, para.15–096 for this and other cases).
[33] (1877) 5 Ch.D. 205.
[34] *ibid.*, at p.215.
[35] [1910] 2 K.B. 502.
[36] *cf.* a wharfinger's certificate that the goods are ready for delivery: *Gunn v Bolckow Vaughan* (1875) L.R. 10 Ch.App. 491. On delivery orders, see below, paras 18–169 *et seq.*
[37] *Mordaunt Brothers v British Oil and Cake Mills Ltd*, above, at p.507.

acknowledging the receipt of the information. . . Such an assent would imply no intention of making delivery to a sub-purchaser until payment was made under the original contract. The assent contemplated by section 47. . . means an assent given in such circumstances as shew that the unpaid seller intends that the sub-contract shall be carried out irrespective of the terms of the original contract." On the facts of the case, he held that the sellers' statements that the delivery orders were "in order" simply meant that, subject to the terms of the original contract, delivery would be made to the sub-buyer instead of to the buyer; their statements and acts did not mean that they were giving up their right to a lien if the price remained unpaid.

15–095 The "assent" provision was further examined in *Mount (DF) Ltd v Jay and Jay (Provisions) Co. Ltd.*[38] The sellers sold cartons in the possession of a wharfinger to the buyer for resale to two of the buyer's customers; the sellers agreed with the buyer that the price should be paid by the buyer out of the money received from the sub-sales. The sellers made out delivery orders in favour of the buyer, and gave them to the buyer, who indorsed them "Please transfer to our sub-order" and sent them to the wharfinger. The buyer sold some of the cartons to a sub-buyer and gave him a delivery order. The sub-buyer paid the buyer but the buyer failed to pay the original sellers, who purported to terminate their contract and wrote to the wharfinger cancelling the delivery orders. Salmon J. held[39] that the sellers had assented to the sale of the cartons to the sub-buyers within the meaning of section 47: "They knew that [the buyer] could only pay for them out of the money he obtained from his customers, and that he could only obtain the money he obtained from his customers against delivery orders in favour of those customers. In my view, the true inference is that the [sellers] assented to [the buyer] reselling the goods, in the sense that they intended to renounce their rights against the goods and to take the risk of [the buyer's] honesty."[40] The result of applying the section was that the original sellers could not exercise their rights as unpaid sellers in respect of the goods. In the same case[41] it was held[42] that section 47 could apply to a sale of unascertained goods, although it might in some circumstances be easier for the court to infer assent in the case of a sale of specific goods,[43] *i.e.* that the seller has assumed the position of holding the specific goods for the sub-buyer.[44]

---

[38] [1960] 1 Q.B. 159.
[39] Following *Mordaunt Brothers v British Oil and Cake Mills Ltd*, above, at p.507.
[40] [1960] 1 Q.B. 159 at 167. (It should be noted that in this case the seller's assent was given in anticipation of subsequent sub-sales.)
[41] *Mount (DF) Ltd v Jay and Jay (Provisions) Co. Ltd*, above.
[42] *ibid.*, at pp.167–168 (following dicta in *Mordaunt Brothers v British Oil and Cake Mills Ltd*, above, at pp.506–507). But see above, para.1–015, n.89.
[43] *Mount (DF) Ltd v Jay and Jay (Provisions) Co. Ltd*, above, at pp.167–168.
[44] *Mordaunt Brothers v British Oil and Cake Mills Ltd*, above, at p.506.

Attornment.[45] Where the unpaid seller who retains possession of the goods attorns to the sub-buyer, by acknowledging to the sub-buyer that he holds the goods on behalf of the sub-buyer, or to his order[46] (*e.g.* by accepting the buyer's delivery order in favour of the sub-buyer)[47] he has obviously assented to the sub-sale within the meaning of section 47(1).[48] The same principle applies where the seller accepts a delivery order in favour of a sub-buyer in respect of a certain quantity of goods held in bulk in his warehouse: the seller is estopped from denying the sub-buyer's title (*vis-a'-vis* himself[49]) despite the fact that a specific part of the bulk has not been appropriated to the sub-buyer.[50] The attornment in favour of the sub-buyer is binding on the unpaid seller even where the sub-buyer has not paid the buyer the price under the sub-sale.[51] 15–096

Transfer of document of title. By section 47(2): "Where a document of title to goods has been lawfully transferred[52] to any person as buyer or owner of the goods, and that person transfers the document to a person who takes it in good faith[53] and for valuable consideration,[54] then—(a) if the last-mentioned transfer was by way of sale the unpaid seller's right of lien or retention or stoppage in transit is defeated, and (b) if the last-mentioned transfer was made by way of pledge or other disposition for value, the unpaid seller's right of lien or retention or stoppage in transit can only be exercised subject to the rights of the transferee." (The corresponding provision in the 1893 Act was "the proviso to section 47", and is referred to as such in the reported cases.) Section 10 of the Factors Act 1889 is substantially identical with section 47(2) of the Sale of Goods Act 1979 (apart from the additional reference to cases of pledge in subsection 47(2)(b)). The meaning of "document of title" is fully examined elsewhere in this work[55] and so is not examined in detail here. This section will deal with only those points which relate particularly to section 47(2) and which 15–097

---

[45] See *Blackburn on Sale* (1st ed.), p.162; above, paras 8–012, 15–040, 15–052, 15–077—15–078.
[46] And without notice to the sub-buyer of his claim to a lien (or to a contingent lien) over the goods in respect of the unpaid price: *Pearson v Dawson* (1858) E.B. & E. 448.
[47] *Pearson v Dawson*, above.
[48] The same principle applies where it is the seller's warehouseman who attorns to the sub-buyer: *Hawes v Watson* (1824) 2 B. & C. 540.
[49] The seller may, however, defend a claim by reference to a third party who has a better title than himself: see s.8 of the Torts (Interference with Goods) Act 1977.
[50] *Woodley v Coventry* (1863) 2 H. & C. 164; *Knights v Wiffen* (1870) L.R. 5 Q.B. 660. See above, paras 5–065, 7–008 *et seq.* On the passing of property in an undivided share in a larger bulk, see Nicol, 42 M.L.R. 129 (1979) and the Sale of Goods (Amendment) Act 1995; above, paras 5–109—5–130.
[51] *Knights v Wiffen*, above, at p.666 (following *Gillett v Hill* (1834) 2 C. & M. 530).
[52] On the meaning of "lawfully transferred" see s.61(1) ("delivery") (above, para.8–002) and s.11 of the Factors Act 1889. (These two provisions must be read together: *Cahn and Mayer v Pockett's Bristol Channel Steam Packet Co. Ltd* [1899] 1 Q.B. 643 at 665 (below, para.18–087).)
[53] On the meaning of "good faith", see s.61(3), discussed above, paras 7–044, 7–086.
[54] See above, paras 7–040, 7–080; below, para.18–088.
[55] See s.62(1); and s.1(4) of the Factors Act 1889 (above, paras 7–012, 7–036, 7–070, 7–072; below, paras 18–006 *et seq.*).

are not fully treated elsewhere.[56] The person who transfers the document of title to the buyer may himself create the document (*e.g.* a delivery order); it is therefore unnecessary that he should have received it from a third person before he can "transfer" it within the meaning of subsection (2).[57] So when sellers gave a delivery order to a buyer for part of a consignment of seed, and the buyer indorsed the order to sub-buyers who took in good faith and for value, it was held that the order was a document of title whose transfer terminated the seller's right to a lien.[58]

To satisfy subsection (2) the document of title need not be one in respect of specific goods[59]; it is submitted (although there is no authority on the point) that the document of title need not relate to ascertained goods, but could relate to an unascertained part of a larger quantity of ascertained goods.[60]

15–098 **The same document must be transferred.** It has been said *obiter* that the words of subsection (2) confine it to cases where a document of title is transferred to the buyer and the same document is then transferred to the sub-buyer or transferee.[61] Thus, where the original seller gave delivery orders to the buyer, who (instead of endorsing them over to the sub-buyer) sent them to the warehouseman and gave fresh delivery orders to the sub-buyer, the latter was not protected by the subsection.[62] This construction leads to "a very artificial result" but is said to be unavoidable in the light of the plain language of subsection (2).[63] Although section 25[64] overlaps with subsection (2) of section 47, its language has been said to be "less rigorous", so that it is not limited to cases where the buyer transfers the same document as that which is in his possession with the consent of the seller.[65]

15–099 **Pledge.**[66] Section 47(2)(b) also covers a mortgage or pledge of a document of title, but in this situation the unpaid seller may still derive some advantage from exercising his right of stoppage, since his rights are merely postponed to those of the mortgagee or pledgee. The common law before the Act was to the same effect. Thus, where a bill of lading[67] for goods in

[56] *e.g.* in relation to bills of lading (below, paras 18–063 *et seq.*), and to s.25 (above, paras 7–069—7–086).
[57] *Ant. Jurgens Margarinefabrieken v Louis Dreyfus & Co.* [1914] 3 K.B. 40.
[58] *Ant. Jurgens Margarinefabrieken v Louis Dreyfus & Co.*, above.
[59] *Capital and Counties Bank Ltd v Warriner* (1896) 1 Com.Cas. 314 (above, para.7–072); *Ant. Jurgens Margarinefabrieken v Louis Dreyfus & Co.*, above, at p.45.
[60] See the Sale of Goods (Amendment) Act 1995 (above, paras 5–109 *et seq.*). *Cf.* s.16 (above, paras 5–059 *et seq.*). *Cf.* also above, para.5–065.
[61] *Mount (DF) Ltd v Jay and Jay (Provisions) Co. Ltd* [1960] 1 Q.B. 159 at 168.
[62] *ibid.*
[63] *ibid.*, at p.168.
[64] See above, paras 7–069 *et seq.*
[65] *Mount (DF) Ltd v Jay and Jay (Provisions) Co. Ltd*, above, at p.169. (See above, para.15–095.) For a critical review of this decision, see Borrie, 23 M.L.R. 100 (1960).
[66] On the meaning of "pledge", see s.1(5) of the Factors Act 1889 (above, para.7–049). A mercantile agent also has power to pledge goods or documents of title in his possession as security: ss.2–4 of the Factors Act 1889 (above, paras 7–031—7–054).
[67] Bills of lading are examined in detail below, paras 18–012 *et seq.*

transit has been endorsed by the buyer to a third person to secure a loan to the buyer, the unpaid seller has a claim in equity to stop the goods, subject to the mortgage: subject to repayment of the loan,[68] the seller has a right to the surplus of the proceeds of the goods in preference to the general creditors of the buyer.[69] "The unpaid vendor's right, except so far as the interest had passed by the pledging of the bill of lading to the pledgee. . . enabled the unpaid vendor in equity to stop in transitu everything which was not covered by that pledge."[70] The unpaid seller's right of stoppage would similarly be defeated *pro tanto* whenever a document of title was transferred for some other particular or limited purpose analogous to a pledge.

Stoppage in respect of price payable under sub-sale. A principle similar to that applied in the pledge cases has been applied in *Ex p. Golding Davis & Co. Ltd*[71] where a buyer resold the goods while the transit continued, but the sub-buyer had not yet paid the price under the sub-sale. On the ground that the seller has an equitable right to stop the goods in transit "except in so far as it is necessary to give effect to interests which other persons have acquired for value",[72] the Court of Appeal allowed the seller (who had given notice of stoppage before the transit ended) to intercept the unpaid purchase price due from the sub-buyer and to take from it the full price due to him as original seller, leaving only the balance to the buyer. The actual result, which was designed to protect the interests of the sub-buyer, can be justified on the basis that proper notice of stoppage had been given to the carrier and to the buyer before transit had ended.[73] Thus, only the method of implementing the right of stoppage was novel.[74] But some of the reasoning in the Court of Appeal could be taken as wide enough to apply to the situation where, although the unpaid seller has lost his right of stoppage, he has attempted to "stop" the price due under the sub-sale before it has been actually paid by the sub-buyer to the buyer. This wide reasoning seems to have been accepted in a later Court of Appeal decision,[75] but it was seriously doubted in the House of Lords in the same case (where the appeal turned on a different point).[76] Although the doubts[77] were *obiter dicta*,[78] it is submitted that they should be followed. Lord 15–100

[68] The pledgee may claim repayment of only the loan in respect of which the document of title was specifically pledged: *Spalding v Ruding, below*.
[69] *Kemp v Falk* (1882) 7 App.Cas. 573 at 576–577 (upholding *Re Westzinthus* (1833) 5 B. & A. 817, and *Spalding v Ruding* (1843) 6 Beav. 376, affirmed (1846) 15 L.J.Ch.375). See also below, paras 15–100, 18–086).
[70] *Kemp v Falk*, above, at p.582.
[71] (1880) 13 Ch.D. 628 (see below, para.18–086).
[72] *ibid.*, at p.638.
[73] Although the bill of lading had been made out in the name of the sub-buyer, it had not been transferred to him by the buyer (see above, para.15–097; below, para.18–086).
[74] There seems to be no difficulty in accepting this as a convenient method of implementing a valid stoppage: *Kemp v Falk* (1882) 7 App.Cas. 573 at 578.
[75] *Ex p. Falk* (1880) 14 Ch.D. 446.
[76] *Kemp v Falk*, above (the facts on which the Court of Appeal decided the case were modified by a supplementary statement laid before the House of Lords).
[77] *ibid.*, at p.577.
[78] *ibid.*, at pp.581, 588.

Selborne L.C. said[79]: "I assent entirely to the proposition that where the sub-purchasers get a good title as against the right of stoppage *in transitu* there can be no stoppage in transitu as against the purchase-money payable by them to their vendor. . . it is not consistent with my idea of the right of stoppage *in transitu* that it should apply to anything except to the goods which are *in transitu*."[80] This is in accordance with the traditional view,[81] which is that the purpose of the right is to enable the unpaid seller to resume his lien over the goods themselves.[82] Nothing in section 47[83] suggests that where the unpaid seller has lost his right of stoppage over the actual goods he may nevertheless intercept the unpaid price due from the sub-buyer to the buyer. Furthermore, there is an analogy in the rule that the unpaid seller has no power to exercise a right of stoppage in transit against the insurance money payable to the buyer in respect of damage to the goods in the course of transit.[84]

5. RESALE

(a) *Introduction*

15–101 **Contract not rescinded by exercise of lien or stoppage.** Section 48(1) provides: "Subject to this section, a contract of sale[85] is not rescinded by the mere exercise by an unpaid seller[86] of his right of lien[87] or retention or stoppage in transit."[88] The unpaid seller who exercises these rights is, in the first place, attempting to enforce the contract by obtaining a form of security for the performance of the buyer's duty to pay the price; he is entitled to retain possession only until payment or tender of the price. The unpaid seller who does not expect the price to be paid, however, is preparing the ground for the more radical remedies of termination of the contract and resale. But it is only by taking further steps that the seller can "rescind" in the sense of terminate further performance of the contract.[89] The circumstances in which the seller is entitled to terminate the contract are discussed below.[90] The important effect of section 48(1) is that where the property in the goods has passed to the buyer, the exercise of the lien or of the right of stoppage does not in itself revest the property in the seller;

79 *ibid.*, at pp.577–578.
80 To the same effect are dicta in *Hugill v Masker* (1889) 22 Q.B.D. 364 at 368–369.
81 *cf. Berndtson v Strang* (1868) L.R. 3 Ch.App. 588 at 591.
82 s.44 (above, para.15–061).
83 Nor in s.25; nor in s.9 of the Factors Act 1889.
84 Above, para.15–090.
85 For "contract of sale", see ss.2(1) and 61(1) (above, para.1–025).
86 See s.38 (above, paras 15–016—15–023).
87 Above, paras 15–028 *et seq.*
88 Above, paras 15–061 *et seq.*
89 s.48(1) uses the term "rescinded" (as does s.48(4)) but the more usual terms now are "terminate" or "treat the contract as discharged." For the consequences of such termination, see below, paras 15–110—15–111.
90 See below, paras 15–107—15–110, 15–127, 15–128.

the property is revested in the seller only[91] when he validly terminates the contract, by reselling[92] or otherwise.

Diplock L.J. has suggested[93] that section 48(1) was necessary to ensure that where there was a fixed date for delivery of the goods, the seller's failure to deliver in the course of his exercise of his lien or right of stoppage in transit does not discharge either party from their respective obligations to deliver upon tender of the price, or to accept the goods and to pay for them.

Power of the seller to pass a good title to a second buyer. The seller has the power to transfer a good title to the goods to a second buyer in several situations, in some of which he does not have, as against the original buyer, the right to resell the goods.[94] Where the seller has the power to pass a good title, but not the right to resell, the second buyer from the seller will obtain a good title to the goods (to the exclusion of the original buyer) but the seller will be liable in damages to the original buyer for breach of contract.[95] In a resale, the seller has the power to pass to a second buyer a good title to the goods in the following three situations: 15–102

(1) When, at the time of the resale, he has the property in the goods. In this situation, although the seller has agreed to sell to the buyer, the property in the goods has not yet passed to the buyer. As owner, the seller can transfer a good title to a new buyer under a second contract of sale,[96] although his act in doing so may amount to a breach of his contract with the first buyer.[97] The situation where the seller has the property in the goods at the time of the resale is not mentioned in section 48,[98] whereas section 48(2) confers an express power on the unpaid seller in circumstances where the property has passed to the buyer.[99] It is submitted that it is implicit in section 48 that, when the property remains in him, the seller has power to pass a good title to the second buyer under a resale.[1]

(2) Under section 24[2] a seller who has transferred the property in the goods to the buyer, but nevertheless continues in possession of them, or of the documents of title to them, can pass a good title in the goods to a third party.[3] Although the resale may be wrongful as against the original buyer,

---

[91] The need for s.48(2) (below, para.15–102) arises from the fact that the unpaid seller who has exercised his right of lien or of stoppage in transit may attempt to resell in circumstances in which he has not reacquired the property in the goods.
[92] See s.48(2), (3) and (4) (below, paras 15–102, 15–107, 15–119, 15–128).
[93] *Ward (R.V.) Ltd v Bignall* [1967] 1 Q.B. 534 at 549.
[94] On the right to resell, see below, para.15–105; on the contrast between "power" and "right", see above, para.15–004.
[95] The seller may also be liable in tort if the property in the goods has passed to the original buyer (see below, para.17–106).
[96] *Lickbarrow v Mason* (1793) 6 East 21 at 24n–25n; *Wait v Baker* (1848) 2 Exch.1. *Cf.* retention of title under a *Romalpa* clause: above, paras 5–141 *et seq.*
[97] *Wait v Baker*, above, at p.10.
[98] Nor in s.39(2). See the discussion of s.39(2) (above, paras 15–010—15–011).
[99] See *infra*, sub-para.(3) of this paragraph.
[1] *Ward (R.V.) Ltd v Bignall* [1967] 1 Q.B. 534 at 545. See above, paras 15–010—15–011.
[2] s.8 of the Factors Act 1889 is similar (but even wider in its terms).
[3] Discussed above, paras 7–055 *et seq.*

who may therefore sue the seller for damages, the seller who resells in the circumstances set out in section 24 will confer on the second buyer a title which is valid as against the original buyer.

(3) Even where the property in the goods has passed to the original buyer, the seller has power, by reselling, to pass a good title to a second buyer where he has exercised his right of lien or of stoppage in transit. This is provided by section 48(2): "Where an unpaid seller who has exercised his right of lien or retention or stoppage in transit re-sells the goods, the buyer acquires a good title to them as against the original buyer." This subsection may in some circumstances confer on the seller a wider power to pass a good title upon a resale than either of the two powers already considered. The effect of the subsection is that the title of the second buyer is good as against the original buyer,[4] whether or not the seller, as against the original buyer,[5] had a right of resale.[6] The second buyer would, at common law, obtain a good title only if the seller retained or had reacquired property in the goods at the time of the resale[7]: subsection (2) has effect when the property in the goods has passed to the original buyer by the time of the resale, and confers a good title on the second buyer whenever the seller was in possession of the goods (or entitled, as against the original buyer,[8] to the immediate possession of them[9]) under his right of lien or of stoppage in transit. The subsection assumes that the seller who has, in the past, validly exercised his right of lien or stoppage, continues in possession, with the right to possession as against the original buyer, up to the time of the resale. But if, between the valid exercise of the right of lien or stoppage and the resale, an event occurred which divested the seller of his right to retain possession (*e.g.* payment or tender of the price), it could not have been intended by the draftsman that section 48(2) should apply.[10]

It should be remembered that the mere exercise by an unpaid seller of his right of lien or of stoppage in transit does not terminate the contract of sale[11]; nor does a wrongful resale terminate the contract, even where the second buyer obtains a good title under section 48(2).

15–103 **Comparison of statutory powers of resale: sections 24 and 48(2).** As section 48(2) above is not the only statutory power under which the seller can pass a good title to the second buyer, it should be contrasted with

[4] Who therefore could not sue the second buyer for trespass or conversion. The limitation in the subsection "as against the original buyer" is included because the original seller's own title to the goods may be inferior to that of a third party. See above, para.7–066.

[5] *cf.* s.48(3) which gives the unpaid seller a right of resale as against the original buyer (below, paras 15–119 *et seq.*).

[6] *Ward (RV) Ltd v Bignall* [1967] 1 Q.B. 534 at 549.

[7] On transfer of title in general, see ss.12, and 21–26 (above, paras 4–002 *et seq.*, 5–001 *et seq.*).

[8] A carrier in possession of the goods may be entitled to a lien (see above, para.15–089).

[9] See above, para.15–088; below, para.15–125. It is submitted that, if the seller has wrongfully refused to deliver the goods to the buyer, s.48(2) does not apply to a resale by the seller while he in fact retains possession (see above, para.15–039).

[10] Although s.24 may apply (above, paras 7–055 *et seq.*).

[11] s.48(1) (above, para.15–101).

section 24 (the "seller in possession" provision considered in the preceding paragraph). In some respects, section 48(2) is wider, since the following requirements of section 24 are *not* required for the application of section 48(2): first, the seller must continue or be in possession of the goods or of the documents of title to the goods; secondly, the transaction must be completed by "the delivery or transfer . . . of the goods or documents of title" to the second buyer; thirdly, the second buyer must receive the goods or documents of title "in good faith and without notice of the previous sale." In contradistinction with section 24, therefore, the seller may confer a valid title on the second buyer under section 48(2) where he is not in possession of the goods or documents of title, but has validly exercised his right of stoppage in transit so that he is entitled (as against the original buyer) to immediate possession of the goods[12]; secondly, under section 48(2) there can be a valid sale to the second buyer (in the sense that the property in the goods has passed to him) even before the seller has delivered or transferred possession of the goods or documents of title to him; and thirdly, the seller's power to confer a good title on the second buyer under section 48(2) does not depend on the second buyer receiving the goods "in good faith and without notice of the previous sale," so that a second buyer may actually know of the original sale before he buys the goods from the seller. On the other hand, it has been suggested in an earlier chapter[13] that a seller who resumes possession of the goods by lawfully exercising his right of stoppage in transit could pass, by virtue of section 24, a good title under a resale, even though he might not be protected by section 48(2). An important difference between sections 48(2) and 24 is that under the former, but not under the latter, the original buyer must be in default in paying or tendering the price, so that the seller is an "unpaid seller" within the meaning of section 38(1).[14] However, despite the differences mentioned in this paragraph, in many situations the power to pass a good title under section 48(2) will overlap with that under section 24.

Wrongful resale. The operation of section 48(2) is not dependent on the seller having a right, as against the original buyer, to resell. Thus, even where the seller purports to resell under section 48(3),[15] but the notice of intention to resell which he gives to the original buyer is held to be too short to constitute "a reasonable time" within the subsection, the second buyer will obtain a title valid as against the original buyer, if section 48(2) applies. The seller, however, will be liable in damages to the original buyer if he had no right to resell, as distinct from a power of transferring a good title[16]; the buyer's damages for the seller's breach of contract will be assessed on ordinary principles.[17] Although in the cases on a wrongful resale by the seller the only remedy mentioned is the original buyer's right to claim damages for breach of contract, there is a possibility that when the 15–104

[12] s.46(4) (above, para.15–088).
[13] See above, para.7–060, n.75.
[14] Above, paras 15–016 *et seq.*
[15] Below, paras 15–119 *et seq.*
[16] *Bloxam v Sanders* (1825) 4 B. & C. 941 at 949.
[17] See below, para.17–106.

seller wrongfully resells, and passes a title to the second buyer which is valid as against the original buyer, the latter could "waive" the claim in damages for breach of contract so as to claim instead on the basis that the seller should be treated as if he were selling as the buyer's agent[18] and on his account.[19] This would be a principle analogous to "waiver of tort"[20] and would enable the original buyer to claim from the seller the actual price paid under the second contract instead of unliquidated damages; the advantages from the original buyer's point of view might be that the price under the resale may be higher than the market price, and that, since the claim would be for a liquidated sum, it would avoid some of the difficulties in claiming damages.[21] A wrongful sale under sections 24 or 48(2) could be treated as a conversion, a tort which can be waived in favour of a claim in restitution to the actual proceeds of the chattel converted and sold by the tortfeasor.[22]

15–105 **Right of the seller to resell.** Despite the fact that the seller may have the power to transfer a good title in the goods to a second buyer,[23] he may not have, as against the original buyer, the right to resell, *viz.* the power to transfer such a title without committing any breach of his contract with, or any tort against, the original buyer.[24] His right to resell as against the original buyer arises in any of the following situations:

(1) The seller obviously has a right of resale, as against the original buyer, if he has, in the original contract, expressly reserved the right to resell in the event of the original buyer's default. This situation is recognised by section 48(4), which deals with the consequences of resale in these circumstances.[25]

(2) By section 48(3) the unpaid seller is given a right of resale if the goods are of a perishable nature.[26]

(3) By the same subsection (3), the unpaid seller may resell if he gives notice to the buyer of his intention to resell and the buyer fails within a reasonable time thereafter to pay the price.[27]

(4) Where the buyer repudiates his obligations under the contract or commits a fundamental breach, the seller is entitled at common law to terminate the contract and to deal with the goods as their owner. These rules are examined in detail below.[28]

(5) Where there is a contract to sell unascertained or future goods by description, but the seller has not yet assumed any obligation to deliver

---

[18] The agency is purely fictitious, a device to open the way to a special remedy.

[19] The buyer would, of course, have to pay the seller the price under the original contract.

[20] Goff and Jones, *The Law of Restitution* (6th ed.), paras 36–001 *et seq.; Chitty on Contracts* (29th ed.), Vol. 1, paras 29–141—29–150.

[21] See below, para.16–004.

[22] *Lamine v Dorrell* (1705) 2 Ld.Raym. 1216.

[23] See above, para.15–102.

[24] On the distinction between "power" and "right," see above, para.15–004.

[25] See below, paras 15–128—15–129.

[26] Below, paras 15–119—15–121.

[27] Below, paras 15–119, 15–123—15–127.

[28] Below, paras 15–107—15–118.

particular goods, he is entitled to deal as owner with any goods of his which happen to meet the description.[29] Until the seller has appropriated particular goods to the contract,[30] he is obviously entitled to sell any goods to which he has title.[31]

(6) Possibly, where the seller can act as an "agent of necessity" on behalf of the buyer. This is considered in the next paragraph.

Agency of necessity.[32] There is no direct authority on the question whether the seller who is in possession of the goods may, in cases of urgency, sell them on behalf of the buyer as an "agent of necessity". In a case where an agent, without orders, sold goods belonging to his principal,[33] the principles laid down for an agent were wide enough to be possibly applicable to a seller; if they did so apply,[34] the seller would have to show his inability to communicate with the buyer, that there was an actual and definite commercial necessity,[35] and that he acted bona fide in the interests of the buyer.[36] The width of the alleged principles has been disapproved by Scrutton L.J.,[37] and the modern cases where bailees have sought to rely on an agency of necessity[38] also suggest that the courts are unlikely to extend the doctrine to a seller who wishes to resell in an emergency.[39] **15–106**

(b) *Termination of Contract upon Buyer's Repudiation or Breach*

Repudiation by the buyer entitling the seller to terminate the contract. If the buyer repudiates his obligations under the contract, the seller is entitled to accept the repudiation, viz. to treat the contract as "rescinded" or terminated[40] and to deal with the goods as their owner.[41] The general law **15–107**

---

[29] This situation is mentioned for the sake of completeness, although it is not a right, as against the original buyer, to resell particular goods, as in the other situations listed in this paragraph.
[30] s.18, r.5 (above, paras 5–068 *et seq.*).
[31] See above, paras 5–080, 15–012; also below, para.20–071.
[32] See *Bowstead and Reynolds on Agency* (17th ed.), paras 3–007, 4–001—4–012; Goff and Jones, *The Law of Restitution* (6th ed.), paras 17–001 *et seq.*
[33] *Prager v Blatspiel, Stamp and Heacock Ltd* [1924] 1 K.B. 566 (on the facts the sale was held to be neither necessary nor made bona fide).
[34] *cf.* s.21(2)(b).
[35] *cf.* the statutory right to sell "perishable goods": s.48(3) (below, paras 15–119—15–122) and the bailee's power of sale under ss.12 and 13 of the Torts (Interference with Goods) Act 1977.
[36] *Prager v Blatspiel, Stamp and Heacock Ltd*, above.
[37] *Jebara v Ottoman Bank* [1927] 2 K.B. 254 at 270–272 (reversed by the House of Lords on grounds not affecting these dicta: [1928] A.C. 269). See also *Re Banque des Marchands de Moscou* [1952] 1 All E.R. 1269 at 1278.
[38] *Sachs v Miklos* [1948] 2 K.B. 23; *Munro v Willmott* [1949] 1 K.B. 295.
[39] *cf. China Pacific SA v Food Corporation of India* [1982] A.C. 939 at 958, 964–966.
[40] "Rescission" for misrepresentation has different legal consequences from "rescission" or termination for breach or upon repudiation: see above, paras 12–002 *et seq.*
[41] *Cornwall v Henson* [1900] 2 Ch. 298 (a contract for the sale of land). For an illustration of the same principle being applied to the sale of goods, see *Compagnie de Renflouement, etc. v W. Seymour Plant Sales & Hire Ltd* [1981] 2 Lloyd's Rep. 466 at 482 (Seller who accepted buyer's repudiation held entitled to resell to a third party.) See below, para.15–112.

of contract determines when the buyer has acted in such a way as to repudiate his obligations[42]; the relevant principles have already been examined in connection with a wrongful neglect or refusal of the buyer to take delivery of the goods, or to pay for separate instalments.[43] The buyer must show by his actions, or his failure to fulfil his obligations, that he intended to abandon the contract[44]: "the breach of one stipulation does not necessarily carry with it even an implication of an intention to repudiate the whole contract."[45] So the buyer's breach of one obligation under a contract for the sale of goods by separate deliveries of instalments may not be a repudiation by the buyer[46]; if the buyer merely fails to pay for one instalment, this will not normally "evince an intention to be no longer bound by the contract,"[47]as is recognised by section 31(2) of the Act.[48]

15–108 **Insolvency.**[49] The buyer will be treated as having repudiated the contract if he becomes insolvent, and informs the seller of his insolvency in circumstances which show that he is unable or unwilling to pay the price of the goods.[50] So where the buyer becomes bankrupt[51] before the seller has parted with possession of the goods, this amounts to notice to the seller that the buyer is unable to pay the price and thus has repudiated his obligations.[52] But a mere declaration of insolvency by a party to a contract will not, on its own,[53] amount to a repudiation of his obligations, since he may still intend to perform and have a reasonable expectation of his ability in the future to do so.[54]

15–109 **Fundamental breach by the buyer.** The seller is entitled to terminate the contract (under principles similar to those which apply when the buyer repudiates his obligation) where the buyer has committed a fundamental breach of his contractual obligations.[55] The Act, however, provides that,

---

[42] See *Chitty on Contracts* (29th ed.), Vol. 1, paras 24–001 *et seq.*.

[43] See above, paras 8–078—8–081, 9–010.

[44] *e.g. Bloomer v Bernstein* (1874) L.R. 9 C.P. 588.

[45] *Cornwall v Henson*, above, at pp.303–304 (citing *Mersey Steel and Iron Co. Ltd v Naylor, Benzon & Co.* (1884) L.R. 9 App.Cas. 434). *Cf. Decro-Wall International SA v Practitioners in Marketing Ltd* [1971] 1 W.L.R. 361.

[46] See s.31(2) (above, paras 8–077—8–078).

[47] *Mersey Steel and Iron Co. Ltd v Naylor, Benzon & Co.*, above, at p.444.

[48] Above, para.8–077.

[49] See above, paras 15–024—15–027.

[50] *Re Phoenix Bessemer Steel Co.* (1876) 4 Ch.D. 108 (see the quotation, above, para.15–025); *Ex p. Stapleton* (1879) 10 Ch.D. 586; *Morgan v Bain* (1874) L.R. 10 C.P. 15; *Mess v Duffus* (1901) 6 Com.Cas. 165.

[51] On bankruptcy, see above, para.15–027.

[52] *Ex p. Stapleton*, above. (The trustee in bankruptcy has a reasonable time within which to decide whether or not to fulfil the contract by paying the price: *ibid.*, at p.590.) See also *Lawrence v Knowles* (1839) 5 Bing.N.C. 399.

[53] A special term in the contract may entitle the other party to rescind or terminate the contract upon the occurrence of such an event, *e.g.* suspension of payment: *Shipton, Anderson & Co. (1927) Ltd v Micks, Lambert & Co.* [1936] 2 All E.R. 1032.

[54] *Mess v Duffus*, above.

[55] See above, paras 8–078—8–081, 13–042 *et seq. Cf.* the buyer's right to treat the contract as repudiated by the seller's breach of a "condition": s.11 (above, paras 10–026—10–028).

unless a different situation appears from the terms of the contract, the buyer's failure to pay the price on the date fixed for payment is not a breach which entitles the seller to terminate the contract,[56] as a claim for interest is the seller's normal remedy for late payment.[57] However, a repeated failure to pay the price when the seller demands payment on several occasions, would, it is submitted, amount to a breach sufficiently serious to entitle the seller to terminate the contract.[58] Similarly, in a contract involving an overseas sale, the seller may be entitled to terminate the contract if the buyer fails to comply with the precise method of payment specified in the contract.[59]

The Act contains general provisions dealing with the entitlement of the buyer to treat the contract as repudiated by the seller,[60] but no similar general[61] provisions dealing with the reverse situation of the seller's entitlement to treat the contract as repudiated by the buyer.[62] In a contract in which the buyer undertakes other important obligations in addition to payment of the price, the seller may terminate the contract on the ground of the buyer's breach of one of these obligations, despite the fact that the buyer has paid the price; in other words, the common law right of the seller to treat the contract as discharged may arise although the statutory right of resale under section 48(3) does not arise because the seller is not "unpaid" within section 38(1).[63] Some inferences may[64] be drawn from the rule for damages for non-acceptance in section 50(3), which is that where there is an available market for the goods the seller's damages for the wrongful refusal of the buyer to accept and pay for the goods are prima facie the difference between the contract price and the market or current price at the time fixed in the contract for delivery.[65] This rule implies a "duty" on the seller to mitigate his loss, following the refusal of the buyer to accept and pay for the goods, by reselling in the market immediately, on the day of the breach, or, at least, on the next business day following the breach.[66] This in turn implies that a breach of the buyer's duty to accept and pay for the goods is a repudiation which entitles the seller to resell without complying with the provisions for giving notice under section 48(3).[67]

---

[56] s.10(1) (above, para.9–051).
[57] Below, paras 16–007—16–012. In relation to c.i.f. contracts, see below, para.19–207.
[58] This is termination under a common law right, quite apart from the statutory right of resale under s.48(3) (below, paras 15–119 *et seq.*). *Cf. Decro-Wall International SA v Practitioners in Marketing Ltd* [1971] 1 W.L.R. 361.
[59] See below, para.19–207.
[60] ss.11 and 53(1).
[61] ss.10(1) and 31(2) deal only with specific circumstances. *Cf.* s.50(3) discussed below.
[62] s.11(4) by referring to "a ground for rejecting the goods," indicates that it is intended to cover only the buyer's remedies, like s.11(2).
[63] See above, paras 15–016—15–023.
[64] But the section does not necessarily imply these conclusions.
[65] See below, paras 16–061 *et seq.*
[66] See below, paras 16–066, 17–008.
[67] On s.48(3), see below, paras 15–119 *et seq.*

15–110 **Alternative remedies of the seller.** Where the buyer has repudiated his obligations or committed a fundamental breach of his obligations in the sense discussed in the preceding paragraph, the seller has the option[68] either of affirming the contract, or of treating it as discharged in the sense of refusing further performance. If he "rescinds" the contract in this sense,[69] the result is that, as from the time of the termination, he is released from any obligation to perform his remaining contractual duties.[70] The seller can no longer sue the buyer for the price,[71] but the contract remains alive[72] for the purpose of assessing the seller's right of action for damages for the buyer's breach,[73] and for purposes incidental thereto.[74]

15–111 **Affirmation of the contract by the seller.** If the seller affirms the contract, it continues in full force for both parties,[75] and each is entitled to hold the other to the due performance of his remaining obligations.[76] But if the seller is unable to complete the performance of his obligations under the contract without the co-operation of the buyer, he must treat the contract as repudiated by the buyer and sue for damages.[77]

15–112 **Right of the seller to resell following termination for buyer's breach.** The cases on the sale of goods give little guidance on the consequences which the seller's termination of the contract, following the buyer's repudiation or breach, has upon the seller's right to resell or his power to pass a good title in the goods to the second buyer. Where a contract for the sale of land is validly terminated by the vendor on account of the purchaser's repudiation or default in completion, the vendor is entitled to deal with the property as owner and to resell[78]; he may retain the whole of the proceeds of the resale (even when he sells at a higher price[79]) and either

---

[68] *Mersey Steel and Iron Co. Ltd v Naylor, Benzon & Co.*, above, at p.440; *Michael v Hart & Co.* [1902] 1 K.B. 482 at 490. On the general principle, see *White and Carter (Councils) Ltd v McGregor* [1962] A.C. 413.
[69] See above, para.15–101, n.89.
[70] *Honck v Muller* (1881) 7 Q.B.D. 92; *Boston Deep Sea Fishing and Ice Co. v Ansell* (1888) 39 Ch.D. 339 at 364–365; *Heyman v Darwins Ltd* [1942] A.C. 356 at 399. See above, paras 8–082, 9–017.
[71] *Chinery v Viall* (1860) 5 H. & N. 288. See below, para.16–015.
[72] *cf.* the consequences of rescission for misrepresentation (above, para.12–003 *et seq.*).
[73] *Michael v Hart & Co.*, above, at p.490; *Johnstone v Milling* (1886) 16 Q.B.D. 460 at 467; *Moschi v Lep Air Services Ltd* [1973] A.C. 331; *Berger & Co. Inc. v Gill & Duffus SA* [1984] A.C. 382 at 390. *Cf. Johnson v Agnew* [1980] A.C. 367.
[74] *e.g.* an arbitration clause: *Heyman v Darwins Ltd*, above. See *Chitty on Contracts* (29th ed.), Vol. 1, paras 24–047—24–051. On the effect of termination for breach upon an exemption clause, see above, paras 13–042 *et seq.*
[75] So that the buyer could take advantage of any supervening circumstances which discharged his obligations, *e.g.* frustration: *Avery v Bowden* (1855) 5 E. & B. 714; (1856) 6 E. & B. 953; *Johnstone v Milling*, above, at p.470.
[76] *Suisse Atlantique Société d'Armement Maritime SA v NV Rotterdamsche Kolen Centrale* [1967] 1 A.C. 361 at 395, 419, 437–438 (see above, paras 9–018—9–019).
[77] *White and Carter (Councils) Ltd v McGregor* [1962] A.C. 413 at 430, 432, 439 (see below, para.16–022).
[78] *Cornwall v Henson* [1900] 2 Ch. 298 (vendor held not entitled to terminate the contract). See above, para.15–107.
[79] *Ex p. Hunter* (1801) 6 Ves.Jun. 94 at 97.

(a) claim from the original purchaser any difference between the original price and that under the resale,[80] after giving credit for any deposit paid; or (b) forfeit the deposit.[81] These principles are derived from the decided cases, and do not depend on any express terms in the contract; indeed, the power of resale derived from the restoration of the rights of ownership is independent of a power of resale expressly reserved in the contract of sale in the event of the purchaser's default[82]: even if the contract contains such an express power, the vendor may terminate the contract and resell as owner.[83]

A New Zealand case[84] holds that exactly the same principles apply to the seller's termination of a contract for the sale of goods: that at common law (and quite apart from the provisions of the Sale of Goods Act) the seller's acceptance of the buyer's repudiation revests the property in the seller so that he can resell as owner.[85] (This was a case where the buyer voluntarily returned possession of the goods to the seller[86] who was, therefore, in possession of the goods at the time of the resale.[87]) However, after the property in the goods has passed to the buyer, he can pass a good title to a third person,[88] and it is, therefore, submitted that it would be too late for the seller to purport to terminate the original contract if the buyer had already transferred the property in the goods to a third person.[89] Where the seller resells under his common law rights as owner of the goods following his termination of the original contract, he can keep the whole proceeds of the resale and either forfeit the deposit[90] paid by the buyer, or sue for damages for any net deficiency after giving credit for the deposit paid.[91]

If these principles from the cases on contracts for the sale of land can be carried over to contracts for the sale of goods, the seller who justifiably terminates the contract on the ground of the original buyer's repudiation or 15–113

---

[80] *Noble v Edwards* (1877) 5 Ch.D. 378 at 385 (appeal allowed on a different point: *ibid.*, at pp.393–394).
[81] *Howe v Smith* (1884) 27 Ch.D. 89 at 104–105 (vendor remained in possession). On the forfeiture of deposits, see below, paras 15–132—15–133.
[82] *Howe v Smith*, above, at p.105.
[83] *ibid.; Hall v Burnell* [1911] 2 Ch. 551 at 555. See also *Shipton, Anderson & Co. (1927) Ltd v Micks, Lambert & Co.* [1936] 2 All E.R. 1032.
[84] *Commission Car Sales (Hastings) Ltd v Saul* [1957] N.Z.L.R. 144 at 146 (following *Howe v Smith*, above).
[85] As owner the unpaid seller may, of course, keep the goods for his own use instead of reselling.
[86] See also *Worcester Works Finance Ltd v Cooden Engineering Co. Ltd* [1972] 1 Q.B. 210 (above, para.7–059) where the seller, with the buyer's consent, retook possession of the goods from the buyer, after the buyer had failed to honour the cheque given for the price.
[87] On the question whether the seller must be in possession of the goods at the time of the resale, see below, paras 15–124—15–125.
[88] See above, para.5–004.
[89] *cf.* s.23 (above, paras 7–021—7–030).
[90] On the difference between a deposit and a part payment of the price, see *Reid Motors Ltd v Wood* [1978] 1 N.Z.L.R. 319 at 325–329.
[91] *Commission Car Sales (Hastings) Ltd v Saul*, above, at p.146 (following the similar principles in the case of a sale of land in *Howe v Smith*, above, at pp.104–105). An earlier Canadian case is to the same effect: *McCowan v Bowles* [1923] 3 D.L.R. 756.

breach is entitled to resell whether or not the property in the goods has passed to the original buyer. If the property in the goods has not passed to the original buyer, the seller already has the power to pass a good title to a second buyer under a resale,[92] and his justifiable termination of the original contract, following the original buyer's repudiation or breach, will give him the right to resell as against the original buyer. Authority for this may be found in cases concerned with a *Romalpa* clause, under which, until full payment of the price, the seller retains the ownership of goods delivered to the buyer[93]; it is the view of the Court of Appeal that, where the seller accepts the buyer's repudiation of such a contract, he may resell the goods "as owner . . . uninhibited by any contractual restrictions": he would then sell the goods on his own account and retain any profit on the resale.[94] Although there is no need for the property to be *revested* in the seller in this situation, it is submitted that the power to resell following an accepted repudiation is the same whether the property remains with the seller or is revested in him. Where the property in the goods had passed to the original buyer before the seller terminated the original contract, the seller's action in terminating it (when he chooses to accept the buyer's repudiation, or to treat the buyer's breach as a ground for termination) will automatically revest the property in the goods in the seller (at least when the seller is in possession of the goods).[95] Upon the revesting of the property, the seller becomes entitled to the immediate possession of the goods, and can resell as absolute owner.[96] In the New Zealand case[97] mentioned above, the buyer after repudiating his obligations had returned the goods to the seller, who had accepted their return[98]; but the principle of termination for repudiation or breach should not be limited to cases of a voluntary return of the goods by the buyer.

The following paragraphs examine the different situations which could arise.

15–114 **Possession with buyer, but property still with seller.** The first situation is where the seller has retained the property in the goods, but has allowed the buyer to take delivery of them. If the seller is entitled to terminate the contract on account of the buyer's repudiation or breach, can he retake the goods or is he entitled to claim the immediate return of possession? In two cases where the goods had been delivered to the buyer but the property in them remained with the unpaid seller, it was held that a seizure of them by the seller operated as a "rescission" or termination of the contract and that

---

[92] See above, para.15–102.

[93] See above, paras 5–141 *et seq*.

[94] *Clough Mill Ltd v Martin* [1985] 1 W.L.R. 111 at 117–118, 122. (But the seller would then be bound to repay any part of the price already paid by the buyer.) *Cf. Armour v Thyssen Edelstahlwerke AG* [1991] 2 A.C. 339 at 353.

[95] On the question of possession, see below, paras 15–124—15–125.

[96] This position was accepted (without discussion) by the judge in *Compagnie de Renflouement, etc. v W. Seymour Plant Sales & Hire Ltd* [1981] 2 Lloyd's Rep. 466 at 482. As absolute owner, of course, the seller may keep the goods for his own use instead of reselling.

[97] *Commission Car Sales (Hastings) Ltd v Saul*, above.

[98] See also above, para.15–112, n.86.

this applied even where the seizure was made under an express power in the contract to do so upon the buyer's default.[99] (The consequence of holding that the contract had been terminated was that the seller could not sue to recover the balance of the price, but was relegated to a claim for damages for breach of contract.)[1] But where an administration order has been made (or a petition for an order presented) leave of the court is needed to enforce certain clauses entitling the seller to retake possession.[2]

No express power to retake. It is not clear whether the unpaid seller of goods who retains the property in them, despite the fact that possession of them has been given to the buyer, may be justified at common law (apart from an express power in the contract[3]) in retaking the goods upon the buyer's default.[4] It may be legitimate to take a further[5] analogy from the law on contracts for the sale of land. In such contracts, where the purchaser has been let into possession pending completion, and he commits a breach of contract entitling the vendor to terminate the contract, the vendor who chooses to terminate is entitled[6] to be reinstated in possession of the land.[7] The vendor, upon the termination, resumes his former position as full owner of the land,[8] and enjoys the power of disposition over it: hence he can resell.[9] 15–115

If the foregoing principles can be carried over to contracts for the sale of goods, it means that the seller who retains the property in the goods, despite the fact that the buyer has been given possession of them, may terminate the contract if the buyer repudiates or commits a fundamental breach; and, upon the termination, the seller resumes the immediate right to possession of the goods, and is entitled to resell as well as to recover

---

99 *Hewison v Ricketts* (1894) 63 L.J.Q.B. 711; *Att-Gen v Pritchard* (1928) 97 L.J.K.B. 561. (*Cf.* retention of title clauses which entitle the unpaid seller to retain the property in the goods, and to recover the goods (or even the proceeds of resale of the goods): above, paras 5–141 *et seq.*) The situation is different in the case of a contract to let out goods on hire, with only an option to purchase: *Brooks v Beirnstein* [1909] 1 K.B. 98.

1 *Att-Gen v Pritchard*, above.

2 See above, paras 5–162—5–163.

3 Under a retention of title clause (see above, paras 5–141 *et seq.*) it is usually provided that the seller may retake possession of the goods.

4 In *Keetley v Quinton Pty Ltd* (1991) 4 W.A.R. 133 it was held that the seller was not entitled to retake the goods in these circumstances (unless there was express power to do so conferred by the contract).

5 *cf.* the borrowing of principles from contracts for the sale of land in above, paras 15–112—15–113.

6 In equity (see the cases in the following note) or at law: *Williams on Vendor and Purchaser* (4th ed.), pp.1004–1005.

7 *Clark v Wallis* (1866) 35 Beav. 460. *Cf. King v King* (1833) 1 My. & K. 442; *Hope v Hope* (1856) 22 Beav. 351 at 365. See Williams, *op. cit.*, pp.1004–1005, 1009. *Cf.* also Misrepresentation Act 1967, s.1(b) (below, para.15–118).

8 But the vendor is not entitled to charge the purchaser with an occupation rent for any part of the premises which he occupied himself: *Hutchings v Humphreys* (1885) 54 L.J.Ch.650 at 652. (But the purchaser must account to the vendor for rents received by him from others: *Clark v Wallis*, above.)

9 *Howe v Smith* (1884) 27 Ch.D. 89 at 105 (the vendor remained in possession throughout, both at the time of the termination and at the time of the resale of the land).

possession from the original buyer.[10] If the seller who terminates the contract has the immediate right to possession of the goods as against the original buyer, he should be entitled to resell before he actually resumes possession of the goods, although if he does so, he will run the risk that he will not be able to give the second buyer actual possession of the goods.[11]

15–116 **Specific restitution of the goods.** The seller's remedy when he seeks specific restitution of his goods from the buyer will be based on section 3 of the Torts (Interference with Goods) Act 1977.[12] Under section 3(2)(a) of this Act the claimant, in proceedings for wrongful interference with goods against a person who is in possession or in control of the goods, may seek an order for delivery of the goods which does not give the defendant the alternative[13] of retaining them on payment of their value as assessed by the court.[14] But the court has a discretion to make such an order for delivery[15] and is unlikely to order specific restitution of the chattel if it is an ordinary article of commerce of no special value or interest and in respect of which damages would be an adequate remedy.[16] It may, however, be a special reason[17] justifying an order for specific restitution of a chattel that the claimant is a seller who has validly terminated the original contract of sale and has validly resold the chattel to a second buyer; but in these circumstances it is submitted that the order should be made only if the chattel is of some unique or special value to the second buyer.[18]

---

[10] Under a retention of title clause (see above, paras 5–141 *et seq.*) it has been assumed, without reference to any specific power to retake possession, that the seller may accept the buyer's repudiation and recover possession: *Clough Mill Ltd v Martin* [1985] 1 W.L.R. 111 at 118–119, 122 (above, para.15–113).

[11] Note also that the buyer in possession with the consent of the seller may pass a good title to a third person: s.25 (see below, para.15–126 and above, paras 7–069 *et seq.*).

[12] s.3 was derived from the old action of detinue (now abolished by s.2(1) of the 1977 Act) which was reviewed by Diplock L.J. in *General and Finance Facilities Ltd v Cooks Cars (Romford) Ltd* [1963] 1 W.L.R. 644 at 650–651. See also below, para.17–105.

[13] The alternative order is covered by s.3(2)(b) of the 1977 Act.

[14] CPR, Sch.1, RSC Ord. 45, r.4(1). *Cf.* s.52 (below, paras 17–096 *et seq.*). See *Hymas v Ogden* [1905] 1 K.B. 246.

[15] s.3(3)(b), (4) and (6) of the 1977 Act. Under s.3(6) the court may fix terms on which specific restitution is to be made: see (before the Act) *Peruvian Guano Co. v Dreyfus Bros* [1892] A.C. 166 at 176; *Greenwood v Bennett* [1973] 1 Q.B. 195 (claimant given specific restitution, subject to his compensating the defendant for the latter's expense in improving the goods at a time when he honestly believed he was their owner (not a sale of goods case)); and *Thomas v Robinson* [1977] 1 N.Z.L.R. 385. See (before the Act), Weir [1973] C.L.J. 23; 36 M.L.R. 89 (1973); and Birks [1974] C.L.P. 13 at 19 *et seq.* See also Goff and Jones, *The Law of Restitution* (6th ed.), paras 1–024, 6–009—6–014.

[16] *Whiteley Ltd v Hilt* [1918] 2 K.B. 808 at 819; *Cohen v Roche* [1927] 1 K.B. 169 at 181. *Cf.* specific performance (below, paras 17–096 *et seq.*).

[17] *Cohen v Roche*, above, at p.181 ("no grounds exist for any special order for delivery").

[18] *cf.* below, para.17–099.

15–117 **No power at common law to terminate the contract or to retake where both property and possession in the buyer.** Where, following the contract of sale, the buyer has both possession of, and the property[19] in, the goods, any retaking of the goods by the unpaid seller will (except in cases of fraud or misrepresentation)[20] be a conversion against the buyer.[21] In the cases which support this proposition, the seller did not purport, prior to the retaking, to terminate the contract of sale on the ground that the buyer had repudiated his obligations under the contract or had committed a fundamental breach. Would it have made any difference if he had done so?[22] It is submitted that, although direct authority is lacking,[23] the assumption behind these cases is that, once the seller has lost both his possession and his right of stoppage in transit, and has transferred the property in the goods to the buyer, he has no remedy against the goods themselves, and his only remedy is a claim for the price or for damages under the contract.[24] The assumption behind the statutory rules on the unpaid seller's rights of lien[25] or of stoppage in transit[26] is that if the property has passed to the buyer and the goods themselves have reached the actual possession of the buyer or his agent,[27] the unpaid seller has no further remedy against the goods[28]; if the seller had a common law power of revesting the property in himself by terminating the contract even where the buyer had lawfully obtained both the property in, and possession of, the goods, the statutory restrictions on

---

[19] *cf.* retention of title clauses, under which the unpaid seller retains the property in the goods until full payment has been made: above, paras 5–141 *et seq.*

[20] See below, para.15–118.

[21] *Page v Cowasjee Eduljee* (1866) L.R. 1 P.C. 127. See also *Stephens v Wilkinson* (1831) 2 B. & A. 320, 327; *Gillard v Brittan* (1841) 8 M. & W. 575; *Re Humberston* (1846) De G. 262. See further below, para.17–106. The seller's seizure may also be a breach of s.12(2)(b) (above, para.4–025): *Healing (Sales) Pty Ltd v Inglis Electrix Pty Ltd* (1968) 42 A.L.J.R. 280.

[22] In *Page v Cowasjee Eduljee*, above, at p.145, there is a suggestion to this effect: "If, when the [buyer] declined to pay the balance of the purchase money, and altogether repudiated the agreement, the [seller] had taken him at his word, and resumed possession without anything more being said, the case might have been different." There is no further discussion of this point in the case, but this sentence seems to envisage a termination by agreement.

[23] There is a further dictum in *Page v Cowasjee Eduljee*, above, at p.145: "There is no case to be found in the Books where, after a sale and complete delivery of a chattel, and the price not paid, the vendor's taking the property out of the purchaser's possession has been held to amount to a rescission of the contract." *Cf. Worcester Works Finance Ltd v Cooden Engineering Co. Ltd* [1972] 1 Q.B. 210 (above, para.7–059) where the seller, after the buyer's cheque for the price had been dishonoured, repossessed the goods; the Court of Appeal emphasised that this was done with the consent of the buyer and thus amounted to a voluntary transfer of title back to the seller in return for the seller's waiver of his claim on the cheque: *ibid.*, at pp.218, 219, 220.

[24] An express power in the contract might entitle the seller to retake or to resell in these circumstances (see *Bines v Sankey* [1958] N.Z.L.R. 886; below, para.15–129) but the Bills of Sale Act 1878 might then apply: see above, paras 1–016—1–017.

[25] Above, paras 15–028 *et seq.*

[26] Above, paras 15–061 *et seq.*

[27] s.43(1)(b); s.45(1), (2) and (3).

[28] It is implicit in the decision in *Healing (Sales) Pty Ltd v Inglis Electrix Pty Ltd* (1968) 42 A.L.J.R. 280, that the seller cannot enforce his right to the price by seizing the goods from a buyer who has both the property in, and possession of the goods.

the remedies of lien and stoppage could be easily evaded. Benjamin[29] considered that: "Whenever the property has passed and the goods have reached the actual possession of the buyer, the seller's *sole* remedy is by personal action. He stands in the position of any other creditor to whom the buyer may owe a debt; all special remedies in his favour *qua* seller are gone."

15–118 **Revesting of property in other circumstances.** It seems anomalous that the seller's termination of the contract on the ground of the buyer's repudiation or fundamental breach will not revest the property in him if the buyer had both possession of, and the property in, the goods before the termination, whereas, in two other apparently similar situations, the property in the goods will revest in the seller, namely, when the buyer validly rejects the goods,[30] or the seller or buyer "rescinds"[31] the contract on the ground that the other's misrepresentation induced him to enter the contract. Where a contract of sale of goods is voidable by the seller for the fraud of the buyer, a retaking of the goods by the seller without the knowledge of the buyer (but before a resale to an innocent sub-buyer) rescinds the contract and revests the property in the goods in the seller[32]: the retaking is treated as an unequivocal act of election to rescind the contract.[33] By statute,[34] the seller could now, even in the case of innocent misrepresentation, rescind the contract despite the fact that it has been "performed" by the passing of property to the buyer; the *restitutio in integrum* following such rescission would involve the revesting of the property in the seller even where the buyer had both the property and possession. However, it could be argued that the buyer's rejection of the goods is a voluntary and deliberate act by the person in whom the property is then vested; and that, for historical reasons, the remedy of rescission for misrepresentation has developed separately from the remedy of termination or rescission for breach.

The Act provides that in some circumstances where the buyer has "accepted" the goods, he cannot reject them, even though the seller has broken a "condition" or fundamental term.[35] The courts may think that, on

[29] Benjamin, *Sale of Personal Property* (8th ed.), p.829. The same passage from the 7th ed., p.864, was cited with approval in *Gallagher v Shilcock* [1949] 2 K.B. 765 at 770 (which has been overruled on other points: see below, para.15–127, n.99.)
[30] *Kwei Tek Chao v British Traders and Shippers Ltd* [1954] 2 Q.B. 459 at 487; *McDougall v Aeromarine of Emsworth Ltd* [1958] 1 W.L.R. 1126 at 1130. See above, para.12–064.
[31] This use of this word has different consequences in the context of misrepresentation from those when the contract is "rescinded" in the sense of terminated by the innocent party upon the other party's repudiation or fundamental breach.
[32] *Car and Universal Finance Co. Ltd v Caldwell* [1965] 1 Q.B. 525 at 551, 554, 558 (the analogy with termination for breach ("repudiation") was not accepted by the Lords Justices in another respect: *ibid.*, at pp.550, 556, 559); *Newtons of Wembley Ltd v Williams* [1965] 1 Q.B. 560 at 571.
[33] *Car and Universal Finance Co. Ltd v Caldwell*, above.
[34] Misrepresentation Act 1967, s.1(b). (The court has a discretion to award damages in lieu of rescission: s.2(2).) See above, paras 12–004—12–010.
[35] s.11(4) (see above, paras 12–038 *et seq.*). See also above, paras 12–024 *et seq.*

a reciprocal basis,[36] the seller should be unable to terminate the contract for the buyer's breach if the seller has transferred to the buyer both the property in, and possession of, the goods.[37]

(c) *Statutory Resale of Perishable Goods or Upon Giving Notice*

Statutory right of resale. Section 48(3) provides that: "Where the goods are of a perishable nature, or where the unpaid seller gives notice to the buyer of his intention to resell, and the buyer does not within a reasonable time pay or tender the price,[38] the unpaid seller may resell the goods and recover from the original buyer damages for any loss occasioned by his breach of contract." This subsection gives the seller a right[39] of resale as against the original buyer, and thus goes beyond subsection (2) which merely confers on the new buyer a title which is good as against the original buyer.[40] The definition of "unpaid seller"[41] shows that the seller may have a right to resell[42] even where part of the price has been paid; but if the seller resells when he has received part payment of the price he may be under an obligation to repay to the buyer any sum which was not intended to be a deposit[43] to be forfeited upon the buyer's default.[44] If, however, the price has been apportioned by the contract to different sections of the goods sold, and is payable separately for each section, the right of resale will arise only in respect of the section for which the price has not been paid as agreed.[45] 15–119

Although section 48(3) permits the unpaid seller to terminate[46] the contract and resell the goods, it is open to the unpaid seller under his

---

[36] It might be argued to the contrary that the fact that s.11(4) is limited to breaches of a condition by the seller indicates that no similar rule was intended in the case of a breach of "condition" by the buyer.

[37] Other possible analogies are the rules that the property in the goods sold passed by delivery of the goods to an infant buyer where the contract was void under the Infants Relief Act 1874: *Stocks v Wilson* [1913] 2 K.B. 235 at 246 (property may possibly have passed even without delivery: *Watts v Seymour* [1967] 2 Q.B. 647 at 654), and that under an illegal contract of sale, the property in the goods also passes upon delivery to the buyer: *Singh v Ali* [1960] A.C. 167 (or even where the contract has been "executed" without the buyer himself taking possession of the goods, *e.g.* by the seller making delivery direct to a third person who takes the goods under a hire-purchase agreement with the buyer: *Belvoir Finance Co. Ltd v Stapleton* [1971] 1 Q.B. 210).

[38] On the price, see ss.2(1) and 8 (above, paras 2–044—2–052); on the buyer's duty to pay the price, see ss.27 and 28 (above, paras 9–021 *et seq.*).

[39] Under s.12(1) there is, unless the circumstances show a different intention, an implied condition in the contract of sale on the part of the seller that he has a right to sell the goods (see above, paras 4–002 *et seq.*).

[40] See above, para.15–102.

[41] s.38(1)(a) ("when the whole of the price has not been paid or tendered") (see above, paras 15–016—15–023).

[42] s.39(1)(c) confers the right in general terms, while s.48(3), above, specifies the right in detail.

[43] On forfeiture of deposits, see below, paras 15–132—15–133.

[44] On the buyer's remedy in this situation, see below, paras 16–038—16–042. The seller may have a counterclaim for damages.

[45] *cf.* on severable contracts (above, para.15–042).

[46] See below, para.15–127.

common law rights[47] to terminate the contract and not to resell, but to keep the goods for his own use. Under his common law right to terminate the contract for the buyer's fundamental breach or repudiation,[48] the seller may be entitled to terminate for a breach other than a failure to pay the price; section 48(3), however, is limited to the "unpaid seller", as defined by section 38(1), and does not envisage breaches of other important obligations which the buyer may have undertaken in a complex arrangement.

The method of reselling, when the seller exercises his right of reselling under section 48(3), is considered below.[49]

15–120 **Resale of perishable goods.**[50] The assumption behind the part of section 48(3) dealing with perishable goods is that the seller retains possession of the perishable goods[51] and is only willing (and contractually obliged) to deliver the goods to the buyer in return for contemporaneous payment.[52] Goods will be "perishable" within the meaning of the subsection when they are likely to deteriorate physically as time elapses,[53] and also, it is submitted, when they are likely to deteriorate in a commercial sense so as to become unmerchantable,[54] *viz.* when "it is not dealt with by business people as the thing which it originally was."[55] A likely deterioration in the value of the goods, through a fall in market price, would not, it is submitted, make the goods "perishable"[56] (although in these circumstances the court has power to order the sale of goods in dispute).[57]

15–121 Where the goods are perishable, Benjamin argued[58] that the further condition set out in section 48(3) applied, *viz.* "and the buyer does not within a reasonable time pay or tender the price." This would mean that after the time fixed for payment of the price of perishable goods, the defaulting buyer would still have "a reasonable time" to pay before the seller could resell[59] (although the perishable nature of the goods might

[47] When the buyer has repudiated the contract or committed a fundamental breach of his obligations (see above, paras 15–107—15–116).
[48] See above, paras 15–107—15–116.
[49] Below, para.15–131.
[50] *cf.* the power to sell any perishable goods in a bankrupt's estate: Insolvency Act 1986, s.287(2)(b).
[51] But see below, paras 15–124—15–125 on the question whether the seller who is not in possession of the goods may resell under the subsection.
[52] See s.28 (above, para.8–004).
[53] *e.g.* potatoes are "a perishable commodity" in the sense that if they are held too long they become rotten: *Sharp v Christmas* (1892) 8 T.L.R. 687 at 688. *Cf.* the discussion of the meaning of the word "perish" in ss.6 and 7 (above, paras 1–124—1–134, 6–029—6–034).
[54] *cf.* on the concept of the goods having changed in nature in a commercial sense: *Asfar & Co. v Blundell* [1896] 1 Q.B. 123; *Duthie v Hilton* (1868) L.R. 4 C.P. 138 (cement, after being submerged, had ceased to be "cement"); *Dakin v Oxley* (1864) 15 C.B.(N.S.) 646 (entitlement of carrier to freight when goods are delivered in a damaged state).
[55] *Asfar & Co. v Blundell*, above, at p.128.
[56] But see dicta to the contrary in *Maclean v Dunn* (1828) 4 Bing. 722 at 728, 729.
[57] CPR, 25.1(1)(c)(v).
[58] Benjamin, *Sale of Personal Property* (8th ed.), p.947. (Sutton on *Sales and Consumer Law* (4th ed.), p.620 agrees.)
[59] The position of the commas in the subsection ("where . . . or where . . . to resell, and the buyer") appears to support this interpretation.

make that time relatively short). On this interpretation of the section, failure to pay within a reasonable time applies both to perishable goods and to cases where the seller gives notice of his intention to resell.[60] There are difficulties with this interpretation: from what point of time is "a reasonable time" to be measured in the case of perishable goods? When the seller gives notice of his intention to resell under the second limb of the subsection, the "reasonable time" will run from the time when notice was given to the buyer.[61] But it is obvious from the subsection that no notice of intention to resell is needed where the goods are perishable, and, in this situation, the only point from which a reasonable time could be measured would be the time fixed by the contract for payment of the price; if no time was fixed, a reasonable time could be measured from the time the contract was made. However, under the ordinary law of contract,[62] time is of the essence of the contract whenever the circumstances of the contract or the nature of the subject-matter indicate that the fixed time must be exactly complied with, *e.g.* in "mercantile contracts",[63] such as a contract for the sale of goods where a time is fixed for delivery.[64]

Although, by section 10(1),[65] stipulations as to time of payment are not deemed to be of the essence "unless a different intention appears from the terms of the contract," it is submitted that the sale of perishable goods does indicate a different intention, since the resale value of the goods will depend on how quickly the resale is made[66]; and that where delivery of perishable goods is a concurrent condition with payment of the price,[67] the buyer's failure to be "ready and willing to pay the price in exchange for possession of the goods"[68] at the fixed time is not merely a failure to pay, but also a failure to accept delivery on the agreed conditions. These submissions lead to a different interpretation of section 48(3) on this point. It could be the purpose of the subsection, in the case of a contract relating to perishable goods, to make time of the essence of the contract,[69] at least when payment and delivery are concurrent conditions,[70] so that, upon the **15–122**

---

[60] The question of what amounts to a reasonable time is discussed, below, para.15–122.

[61] Below, para.15–122. S.48(3) does not require the seller to notify the buyer of his intention to resell perishable goods.

[62] See Chitty (29th ed.), Vol. 1, paras 21–011—21–015.

[63] *Reuter, Hufeland & Co. v Sala & Co.* (1879) 4 C.P.D. 239 at 249; *Sharp v Christmas* (1892) 8 T.L.R. 687 at 688. *Cf. Bunge Corporation, New York v Tradax Export SA, Panama* [1981] 1 W.L.R. 711 at 729 (*cf.* at p.716) (HL); *Scandinavian Trading Tanker Co. AB v Flota Petrolera Ecuatoriana (The Scaptrade)* [1983] 2 A.C. 694 at 703–704.

[64] *Hartley v Hymans* [1920] 3 K.B. 475 at 484.

[65] See above, para.9–051.

[66] *cf. Hare v Nicoll* [1966] 2 Q.B. 130 at 142, 146 (time for payment held to be of the essence in a contract for the sale of shares liable to fluctuate in value).

[67] s.28 (above, para.8–004).

[68] s.28.

[69] *cf.* a case before the Act: *Sharp v Christmas*, above, at p.688, where the time for the buyer to take delivery of potatoes ("a perishable commodity") was held to be of the essence of the contract.

[70] s.28 (above, para.8–004). *Cf.* the position under a c.i.f. contract (below, para.19–207).

buyer's failure to pay on the stipulated date, the seller is immediately entitled to resell. (If no time for payment was stipulated, the provision for payment "within a reasonable time" would make sense even in the case of perishable goods.)

15–123 **Resale upon giving notice to the buyer.** The second aspect of section 48(3) applies irrespective of the nature of the goods. Unless a different intention appears from the terms of the contract, a stipulation as to time of payment is not deemed to be of the essence of a contract of sale,[71] and therefore failure by the buyer to pay at the stipulated time does not entitle the unpaid seller to treat the contract as repudiated; such a seller would, apart from subsection (3), continue under an obligation to deliver the goods[72] if the original buyer tendered the price at any time. Subsection (3) of section 48 enables the unpaid seller, by giving notice, to make payment within a reasonable time thereafter to be of the essence of the contract, so that failure to pay within a reasonable time after notice will entitle the seller to treat the contract as repudiated: he can then terminate the original contract and resell the goods. This is in line with the general law of contract.[73]

The question of what is a reasonable time is a question of fact.[74] Where notice is required under section 48(3), the calculation of "a reasonable time" will run from the date the notice was given. If the notice itself specifies a time by which payment should be made in order to avert a resale, the reasonableness of the period allowed by the seller will depend partly on whether there had been delay on the buyer's part before the notice was given.[75] The reasonableness of a time fixed by the notice must be judged at the time when it is given.[76]

15–124 **The seller's power of resale when he is out of possession.** There is a number of judicial statements which assume that the unpaid seller's statutory power of resale under section 48(3) may be validly exercised only where the seller is in possession of the goods at the time of the resale.[77] It

---

[71] s.10(1) (above, para.9–051).

[72] If the property in the goods had passed to the original buyer, the seller would, apart from s.48(3), be liable to him in conversion if he resold the goods.

[73] See Chitty (29th ed.), Vol. 1, para.21–014 *et seq.*.

[74] s.59 (above, para.8–037). For an illustration of what amounts to a reasonable time, see *Gallagher v Shilcock* [1949] 2 K.B. 765 at 770 (which has been overruled on other points by *Ward (R.V.) Ltd v Bignall* [1967] 1 Q.B. 534 (below, para.15–127)). *Cf. Hick v Raymond & Reid* [1893] A.C. 22 (delay attributable to causes beyond a party's control to be taken into account in deciding what is a "reasonable time").

[75] *cf. Charles Rickards Ltd v Oppenhaim* [1950] 1 K.B. 616 at 624 (which is not a case on the interpretation of s.48(3) but on a similar common law rule). *Cf.* also *Compton v Bagley* [1892] 1 Ch. 313 at 320–321 (sale of land: reasonable time to deliver an abstract of title).

[76] *cf. Charles Rickards Ltd v Oppenhaim*, above, at pp.624–625.

[77] In *Ward (RV) Ltd v Bignall* [1967] 1 Q.B. 534 at 545, Diplock L.J. criticises the opinion that the right of resale arises only where the seller has exercised his right of lien or of stoppage in transit; but he does so on the ground (which takes the strict view of a "lien": above, paras 15–010, 15–029), that the seller who retains the

has been submitted earlier that (except in cases of an express power of resale or of rescission for misrepresentation) the unpaid seller finally loses all of his remedies against the goods, including his right of resale under section 48(3), when the property has passed to the buyer and the goods have reached his actual possession.[78] But it is submitted that a seller has the right and the power to pass a good title to a second buyer under a resale, not only at common law,[79] but also under section 48(3) where, at the time of the resale, he has either: (a) the property in the goods[80]; or (b) possession of the goods[81]; or (c) the immediate right to possession as against the original buyer. The first ground has already been examined; if the seller has the property in the goods, but the buyer is in possession, the seller may be able to retake the goods, or recover possession from him by legal action,[82] so as to be in a position to deliver the goods to the second buyer.

The second ground, that the seller has retained or resumed possession of the goods, was obviously the main basis of the seller's power of resale which the draftsman of section 48(3) had in mind,[83] and it has received judicial support.[84] A major purpose of the remedies of lien[85] and stoppage in transit[86] is to give the seller possession of the goods so that he can effectively exercise his right of resale. The second buyer may well be unwilling to enter into a contract to buy the goods if he knows that the seller is not in possession of them and is merely relying on the third ground, *viz.* his legal right to obtain possession of them from the original buyer; there would be added reluctance to buy if the prospective second buyer align knew that the goods were in the possession of a defaulting original buyer, who might return them only under legal compulsion. The third ground is examined in the following paragraph.

Revesting of the immediate right to possession. A seller who is out of possession of the goods (because they are in the possession of the buyer or his agent, or of a carrier or third person) may resume the immediate right 15–125

property in the goods, and has withheld delivery under s.39(2), may also resell under s.48(3). The whole passage assumes that the seller must be in possession at the time of the resale. In the New Zealand case of *Commission Car Sales (Hastings) Ltd v Saul* [1957] N.Z.L.R. 144 at 146, it was held that the statutory right of resale under a section corresponding to s.48(3) of the U.K. Act was given only to sellers who had never lost possession of the goods sold.

78 Above, para.15–117.

79 See above, paras 15–112—15–113.

80 Above, paras 15–010—15–011, 15–102, 15–114.

81 Viz. possession which is lawful as against the original buyer, *e.g.* not acquired by a tortious retaking from the original buyer (see below, paras 17–105—17–106).

82 See above, paras 15–115—15–116.

83 It is a significant fact that s.48(3) immediately follows s.48(2) which confers on the unpaid seller a power of passing a good title to the second buyer where the seller has exercised his right of lien or stoppage in transit.

84 See n.77, above.

85 See above, paras 15–002, 15–003, 15–028, 15–043.

86 See above, paras 15–002, 15–003, 15–062.

to possession of them in several ways[87]: (1) where the buyer is in possession, but the seller retains the property, by the seller's terminating the contract on the ground of the buyer's repudiation or fundamental breach[88]; (2) where the contract is rescinded by either party on the ground of the other's misrepresentation[89]; (3) where the seller exercises his right of stoppage in transit[90]; or (4) where an express term in the contract empowers the seller to retake, or to resell, the goods in specified circumstances.[91] It is submitted that where the seller has acquired or resumed the immediate right to possess the goods, he has the power to sell them under section 48(3), although, if he resells before acquiring actual possession, he may run the risk[92] of being unable to deliver the goods to the second buyer at the time fixed for delivery.

15–126 **Power of buyer in possession to pass a good title.** Where the buyer, with the consent of the seller, obtains possession of the goods, or of the documents of title to the goods, and the buyer continues in possession after the seller has terminated the contract of sale on the ground of the buyer's repudiation or breach, the buyer has the power (but not, as against the seller, the right) to transfer a good title to the goods to a third party if the conditions of section 25 are satisfied.[93] Accordingly, the seller who is entitled to the immediate possession of the goods from the buyer under the circumstances examined in the preceding paragraph, may find that under this subsection he has lost his property in the goods to a third party.

15–127 **Resale terminates the original contract.** Although section 48(3) does not expressly provide that the original contract is terminated by the resale,[94] the Court of Appeal has decided that, by exercising the statutory right of resale under the subsection, the seller thereby "rescinds" or terminates the original contract but may sue the original buyer for damages.[95] Sellers L.J. said that "under subsection (3) no such provision of rescission [as in subsection (4)] is necessary, for if an unpaid seller resells, he puts it out of his power to perform his contract and his action is inconsistent with a subsisting sale to the original buyer."[96] The result of this interpretation of subsection (3) is that the seller who resells under section 48 cannot thereafter sue the buyer for the original price (even though he is willing to

---

[87] This is not intended to be an exhaustive list: *e.g.* the seller's right to immediate possession may also arise where the contract is held void for mistake (*Chitty on Contracts* (29th ed.), Vol. 1, para.5–008) or in some instances of illegality (Chitty, *op. cit.*, paras 16–172 *et seq.*).

[88] See above, paras 15–107—15–116.

[89] But in this situation, the court has a discretion to award damages in lieu of rescission: Misrepresentation Act 1967, s.2(2). See above, paras 12–004—12–010.

[90] See above, paras 15–085, 15–088.

[91] See s.48(4) (below, paras 15–128—15–129). For an illustration of such a clause, see above, paras 5–141 *et seq.* (retention of title clauses).

[92] See also the risk of losing title under s.25 (below, para.15–126).

[93] *Newtons of Wembley Ltd v Williams* [1965] 1 Q.B. 560. See above, para.7–076.

[94] Unlike subs. (4) of s.48 (below, paras 15–128—15–129).

[95] *Ward (RV) Ltd v Bignall* [1967] 1 Q.B. 534. The claim for damages will be under s.50 (see below, paras 15–127, 16–060 *et seq.*).

[96] *Ward (RV) Ltd v Bignall*, above, at p.543 (see also at p.548).

give the buyer credit against the price for the net proceeds of the resale); the seller is relegated by the subsection to his claim for damages for non-acceptance under section 50.[97] A further implication of subsection (3) is that the termination of the contract divests the original buyer of his property in the goods if the property had passed to him before the termination.[98] The practical result is that the seller is not account able to the buyer for any profit above the original contract price which he makes on the resale[99]; nor has the buyer a right of action against a seller who does not act with reasonable care in making the resale. However, if the seller sues the buyer for damages, the rules of mitigation will reduce the assessment of the seller's loss if he failed to take reasonable steps to mitigate his loss following the buyer's breach of contract. It is submitted that a resale at a lower price than the seller ought reasonably to have obtained on the resale will constitute a failure to mitigate.[1]

Where the unpaid seller is entitled to resell, but resells only part of the goods which he contracted to sell under the original contract, he thereby puts it out of his power to perform his contractual obligation to deliver the whole of the goods to the buyer, and thus is deemed to have terminated the original contract.[2]

The question of the forfeiture of any deposit paid by the buyer is considered below.[3]

(d) *Express Right to Resell*

Express reservation of the right of resale.[4] Section 48(4) of the Act provides: "Where the seller expressly reserves the right of re-sale in case the buyer should make default, and on the buyer making default resells the goods, the original contract of sale is rescinded but without prejudice to any claim the seller may have for damages." The effect of the seller's reselling under an express right and power to do so in the contract is that the contract is terminated so that the property in the goods revests in the seller (if it had previously passed to the buyer) who then resells as owner. The subsection, by providing that the original contract is "rescinded"[5] excludes an interpretation which might otherwise be placed on an express right of resale, *viz.* that when the property in the goods has already passed to the 15–128

[97] *Ward (RV) Ltd v Bignall*, above. (See below, para.16–015). Even before the Act, it was clear at common law that, where the seller resold following the buyer's refusal to take the goods, he could (even in the absence of a specific clause in the contract empowering him to do so) recover as damages from the buyer the loss, if any, on the resale, which loss would normally be the difference between the two prices: *Maclean v Dunn and Watkins* (1828) 4 Bing. 722.

[98] *Ward (RV) Ltd v Bignall*, above.

[99] In this, as well as in other respects, the decision in *Gallagher v Shilcock* [1949] 2 K.B. 765, has been overruled by *Ward (RV) Ltd v Bignall*, above.

[1] See below, para.16–052.

[2] *Ward (RV) Ltd v Bignall*, above, at p.550.

[3] Below, paras 15–132—15–133.

[4] On retention of title clauses, see above, paras 5–141 *et seq. Cf.* an express power in the contract permitting the buyer to repurchase elsewhere (below, para.17–001).

[5] In the sense of "terminated," see above, para.15–101, n.89.

buyer, the seller resells as agent for the buyer.[6] The consequence of the provision that the original contract is terminated by the resale is that the seller is entitled to retain any profit which he may make on the resale above the price in the original contract.[7] If, however, the seller can resell only at a loss, the original buyer is, by this subsection, liable to pay "damages", viz. the amount by which the contract price exceeds the resale price, and the expenses of the resale.[8]

Subsection (4) of section 48 enacts the common law. In *Lamond v Davall*,[9] the goods were sold on the express condition that, if the price was not paid at the fixed time, the seller could resell them, and the buyer would be liable for any loss on resale. It was held that ". . . a power of resale implies a power of annulling the first sale, and that, therefore, the first sale is on a condition, and not absolute." The court's reasoning was that if the seller was held to be the agent of the defaulting buyer, he might find himself in difficulty[10] (*e.g.* he might be liable to the buyer for any profit he made on the resale); and, further, that there would be injustice to the buyer if he was held liable for the full price which he agreed to pay, despite the facts that he could not obtain delivery of the goods, and that the seller had obtained the full price under the resale.[11] Thus, at common law, the rule was that the seller terminated the first contract by the resale,[12] so that the original buyer was no longer liable to pay the price,[13] although he remained liable in damages for the difference between the two prices (if any) and the extra expenses incurred by the seller in the course of the resale.[14] These rules still apply after the enactment of the 1893 Act, although they are now based on subsection (4) of section 48 of the 1979 Act.

15–129 **Conditions necessary for the exercise of an express right of resale.** The meaning of "default" in section 48(4) will depend on the construction of the words used in the clause of the contract which confers the right of resale; it will, therefore, not necessarily coincide with any concept of default under the Act itself. Subsection (4) is limited to a power of resale "in case the buyer should make default", but it is submitted that it would be possible for the parties to agree to an express right which arose upon an occurrence not involving the buyer's "default" and in circumstances where the whole of the price had in fact been paid.[15] (The consequences of exercising an express right wider than the right envisaged by subsection (4) should, it is submitted,[16] be the same as under subsection (4), *viz.* termination of the

[6] *Ward (RV) Ltd v Bignall* [1967] 1 Q.B. 534 at 551.
[7] The same is true of resale under s.48(3) (see above, para.15–127).
[8] See below, paras 16–060 *et seq.*, 16–086—16–088.
[9] (1847) 9 Q.B. 1030.
[10] *ibid.*, at pp.1031–1032.
[11] *ibid.*, at p.1032.
[12] The old-fashioned phrase used in *Lamond v Davall*, above, at p.1032, was: "the sale is conditioned to be void in case of default."
[13] *Hore v Milner* (1797) Peake 58n.
[14] *Lamond v Davall*, above.
[15] *cf.* s.48(3) where the seller may resell only if he is "unpaid" within s.38(1).
[16] *cf.* the interpretation put upon s.48(3), despite any express mention of rescission or termination (above, para.15–127).

contract, so that the seller resells as owner and may retain the proceeds of the resale.[17])

An express right to resell may be much wider than the statutory right of resale under section 48(3)[18] in many ways: for instance, the right of resale may be conferred upon the seller where the goods have been delivered to the buyer, and even where the buyer has both the property in the goods and possession of them.[19] If the seller complies with the terms of his express right to resell, the resale will be valid as against the original buyer despite the absence of the conditions which would entitle the seller to resell under his statutory right of resale. Thus, under subsection (4), the seller need not be an "unpaid seller" within the meaning of section 38[20]; nor need the seller notify the buyer of his intention to resell, unless the contract so provides.[21]

The same rules hold good when a relevant usage of trade confers a right of resale upon the seller.[22]

Common law remedies as an alternative. Where the contract confers an express right of resale or of repurchase on the innocent party following a default by the other party, the former may pursue his ordinary remedies at common law without complying with the terms of the special remedy conferred by the contract.[23] It is submitted that, in the same way, the seller could exercise his statutory right of resale under section 48(3) without relying on his contractual right to resell. But he could not exercise a common law or statutory remedy if the terms of the special contractual remedy indicate that it is to be the exclusive remedy for the default in question. 15–130

(e) *The Method of Reselling*

The method of reselling. Neither the Act[24] nor the common law provides authority on the question of the method of exercising the seller's right to resell.[25] It therefore seems that the seller is free to sell to anyone he chooses, and that he is under no restriction as to the price he obtains, or whether the sale is by public auction or made privately, without advertise- 15–131

---

[17] See *Lamond v Davall* (1847) 9 Q.B. 1030 (before the 1893 Act: above, para.15–128).

[18] Above, paras 15–119 *et seq.*

[19] But a document recording the contract might then fall within the scope of the Bills of Sale Act 1878 (see above, paras 1–016—1–017). *Cf.* the situation under s.48(3) (above, paras 15–117, 15–119).

[20] Above, paras 15–016—15–023.

[21] *cf.* s.48(3) (above, para.15–123). It might be implied in the terms of an express power that the seller should notify the buyer.

[22] *Re Tate* (1841) 2 Mont.D. & De G. 170.

[23] *Shipton, Anderson & Co. (1927) Ltd v Micks, Lambert & Co.* [1936] 2 All E.R. 1032. *Cf.* the same rule for contracts for the sale of land: *Howe v Smith* (1884) 27 Ch.D. 89 at 105 (above, para.15–112).

[24] *cf.* the Uniform Commercial Code which expressly regulates the method of exercising the seller's right of resale: s.2–706.

[25] The exercise of an express power to resell may be restricted by the terms of the contract.

ment. He is under no obligation to the buyer to act reasonably in deciding whether or not to resell; but if he acts unreasonably the rules of mitigation may limit the damages which he can recover from the original buyer following the resale. A seller cannot recover damages for loss caused by the buyer's breach of contract if the seller could have avoided the loss by taking reasonable steps,[26] and it is submitted that if the seller unreasonably resold at a price lower than he should have obtained, the damages recoverable from the original buyer should be assessed as the difference between the contract price and the price he ought reasonably to have obtained.[27]

At common law, unlike under section 48(3), the seller is under no obligation to inform the buyer of his intention to resell. Even under section 48(3), it seems that the seller is not obliged to inform the buyer of the proposed date or method of reselling.

(f) *Forfeiture of Deposits or Other Prepayments*

15–132 **Forfeiture of deposits.** Whether the seller resells under his common law rights,[28] under his statutory right (section 48(3)),[29] or under an express power to resell and to sue for any deficiency on the resale, it is submitted that the same rules apply to the forfeiture of deposits or other prepayments made by the buyer. "A deposit, if nothing more is said about it, is, according to the ordinary interpretation of business men, a security for completion of the purchase."[30] In a case on a deposit in a sale of land, the Privy Council has held that the amount of the deposit must be "reasonable".[31] It is submitted that the same principle applies to deposits in the sale of goods; an unreasonable deposit might also be an "unfair term" in a consumer contract.[32] The seller is bound to bring the deposit into account if he sues the buyer for damages, since he cannot allege a net deficiency without taking the deposit into account.[33] If, however, the seller makes no claim for damages under the original contract, he is entitled to keep all the proceeds of the resale and to forfeit the deposit paid by the defaulting

[26] *Chitty on Contracts* (29th ed.), Vol. 1, paras 26–092 *et seq.*; see below, paras 16–052—16–058.
[27] *cf.* below, paras 16–075, 17–004, 17–018.
[28] See above, paras 15–107—15–117.
[29] In *Gallagher v Shilcock* [1949] 2 K.B. 765, after the seller had resold the goods, the original buyer was held to be entitled to recover the deposit which he had paid. But this decision was based on the assumption that a resale under s.48(3) did not involve a termination of the first contract of sale: since the Court of Appeal has later rejected this view of the subsection (above, para.15–127) it is submitted that in these circumstances, the deposit paid by the original buyer should not be recoverable, but that the general rules on deposits set out in the text above should be applied.
[30] *Howe v Smith* (1884) 27 Ch.D. 89 at 98.
[31] *Workers Trust and Merchant Bank Ltd v Dojap Investments Ltd* [1993] A.C. 573 (25 per cent deposit held unreasonable).
[32] The Unfair Terms in Consumer Contracts Regulations 1999 (above, paras 13–103, 14–030 *et seq.*).
[33] *Commission Car Sales (Hastings) Ltd v Saul* [1957] N.Z.L.R. 144 at 146.

original buyer.[34] In a case dealing with a contract for the sale of land, Fry L.J. said[35]: "But in my opinion there has been such default as justifies the vendor in treating the contract as rescinded; it affords the vendor an alternative remedy, so that he may either affirm the contract and sell under this clause [an express power to resell] or rescind the contract and sell under his absolute title. If he act under the clause, he must bring the deposit into account in his claim for the deficiency: if he sell as owner, he may retain the deposit, but loses[36] his claim for the deficiency under the clause in question." The buyer may "trade in" other goods to the seller in lieu of a monetary deposit, and it may be the intention of the parties that these goods are to be treated in exactly the same way as a payment of money by way of deposit.[37]

Where the buyer fails to pay the agreed deposit, and the seller later accepts the buyer's repudiation of the contract, the seller may recover damages measured at the amount of the deposit.[38]

If the principles set out above are correct, they lead to the odd result that the defaulting buyer's position depends on the arbitrary choice of the seller: if the seller chooses to resell, he is entitled to retain the deposit paid by the original buyer, as well as the price paid under the second contract; whereas, if the seller chooses not to resell, but sues the buyer for damages, he must give the buyer credit for the amount of the deposit paid by him. The seller would also have to give credit for the deposit paid if, following a resale at a loss, he sued the original buyer for damages. Although these rules seem anomalous[39] they are the same in the case of sales of land[40]; they may seem to be contrary to the spirit of the rules on penalties,[41] but the rules on deposits have always been treated as independent of the rules governing a contractual stipulation for the payment of a sum of money by the guilty party after, and on account of, his breach of contract.[42] **15–133**

---

[34] *Commission Car Sales (Hastings) Ltd v Saul*, above, at p.146 (following the principles laid down in cases on contracts for the sale of land: *Ockenden v Henly* (1858) E.B. & E. 485; *Howe v Smith*, above, at pp.104–105; *Shuttleworth v Clews* [1910] 1 Ch. 176). See *Chitty on Contracts* (29th ed.), Vol. 1, para.29–064—29–065. *Cf.* the proposals of the Law Commission's Working Paper No. 61 (1975), paras 49–67.

[35] *Howe v Smith*, above, at p.105.

[36] The seller "loses" this claim only in the sense that he cannot *both* forfeit the deposit and sue for damages for the deficiency as if no deposit had been paid.

[37] *Commission Car Sales (Hastings) Ltd v Saul*, above, at p.145.

[38] *Damon Compania Naviera SA v Hapag-Lloyd International SA* [1985] 1 W.L.R. 435. If only part of the deposit has been paid by the buyer, the seller should, in principle, be entitled to recover the balance of the deposit due to him. See *Hinton v Sparkes* (1868) L.R. 3 C.P. 161 at 166 (sale of land); but *cf. Lowe v Hope* [1970] 1 Ch. 94 (sale of land); *Johnson v Jones* [1972] N.Z.L.R. 313 at 318 (an express forfeiture clause).

[39] See the criticism of Finnemore J. in *Gallagher v Shilcock* [1949] 2 K.B. 765 at 771 (overruled on another point (above, para.15–127) by *Ward (RV) Ltd v Bignall* [1967] 1 Q.B. 534; in the Court of Appeal nothing was said about the deposit).

[40] *Williams on Vendor and Purchaser* (4th ed.), pp.1007 (n. (e)), 1011.

[41] See below, paras 16–032 *et seq.*

[42] *cf.*, however, the decision of the Privy Council where the deposit in a sale of land was unreasonable in amount: *Workers Trust and Merchant Bank Ltd v Dojap Investments Ltd* [1993] A.C. 573. (See above, para.15–132, text at n.31.)

15–134 **Forfeiture of other prepayments.**[43] Where the contract provides[44] that a sum of money already paid shall be forfeited upon breach by the party who paid it, it may be relevant to consider the equitable jurisdiction of the court to intervene to grant the defaulting party relief against forfeiture of a proprietary or possessory right.[45] Since the jurisdiction extends to granting relief in respect of interests in personal property,[46] it will apply to the sale of goods[47]; but the relief granted may be limited to an extension of time in which the buyer may fulfil his obligations under the contract.[48] The jurisdiction is most unlikely to be applied to forfeiture of a sum of money designated as a reasonable "deposit"[49]; the cases where it has been considered have been concerned, not with "deposits",but with payments under contracts such as contracts of hire,[50] or to purchase by instalment payments.[51]

[43] The Consumer Credit Act 1974 (above, para.14–143 *et seq.*) may possibly govern some contractual provisions of this type: see ss.137–140 (on extortionate credit bargains). The Unfair Terms in Consumer Contracts Regulations 1999 may also apply: see above, paras 13–103, 14–030 *et seq*.

[44] For the position where there is no forfeiture clause in the contract, see below, para.16–040.

[45] See below, para.16–038; *Scandinavian Trading Tanker Co. AB v Flota Petrolera Ecuatoriana (The Scaptrade)* [1983] 2 A.C. 694; *Sport Internationaal Bussum BV v Inter-Footwear Ltd* [1984] 1 W.L.R. 776; *BICC Plc v Burndy Corporation* [1985] Ch.232.

[46] *BICC Plc v Burndy Corporation*, above (patent rights).

[47] Two earlier authorities did concern the sale of goods: *Stockloser v Johnson* [1954] 1 Q.B. 476 (see below, para.16–038); *Starside Properties Ltd v Mustapha* [1974] 1 W.L.R. 816 (see below, para.16–039).

[48] *BICC Plc v Burndy Corporation*, above; *Starside Properties Ltd v Mustapha*, above. *Cf. Jobson v Johnson* [1989] 1 All E.R. 621. For other factors which the court will take into account, see below, paras 16–038—16–039.

[49] Unless the size of the "deposit" in relation to the total price indicates that it is really a part payment of the price: *Reid Motors Ltd v Wood* [1978] 1 N.Z.L.R. 319 at 325–329. *Cf.* para.15–132 text at n.31.

[50] *The Scaptrade*, above.

[51] *e.g. Stockloser v Johnson*, above; *Starside Properties Ltd v Mustapha*, above.

Chapter 16

OTHER REMEDIES OF THE SELLER

	PARA.
1. The claim for the price	16–001
(a) In general	16–001
(b) Interest	16–007
(c) Wrongful failure to pay the price	16–014
(d) Entitlement to sue for the price	16–021
(i) Where the property has passed to the buyer	16–021
(ii) Price payable on "a day certain"	16–025
(iii) Other claims for the price	16–028
(e) Claims for consequential loss	16–030
2. General rules on damages	16–031
(a) Introduction	16–031
(b) Liquidated damages and penalties	16–032
(c) Remoteness of damage and causation	16–043
(d) Mitigation of damage	16–052
3. The seller's claim for damages	16–060
(a) Damages for non-acceptance	16–060
(b) An available market	16–062
(c) The absence of an available market	16–077
(d) Anticipatory breach	16–080
(e) Special cases	16–083
(f) Consequential losses and expenses	16–085
4. Miscellaneous remedies	16–089

1. The Claim for the Price

(a) *In General*

Introduction. The seller's claim to the agreed price and to damages for breach of contract by the buyer are personal remedies which he may exercise in addition to the real remedies already discussed[1]; the exercise of the latter remedies gives the seller additional security for his personal remedies.[2] Section 49 of the Act sets out the circumstances in which the seller may bring an action for the price[3]: the buyer must have made default in paying the price[4] and either the property must have passed to the buyer,[5] or the price must have been due "on a day certain irrespective of delivery".[6] **16–001**

---

[1] Above, Ch.15. See especially para.15–006.
[2] On the difference between real and personal remedies, see above, para.15–001.
[3] On the history of the action for the price of goods, see *Colley v Overseas Exporters* [1921] 3 K.B. 302 at 309–310. S.49(1) is quoted below, para.16–021, and s.49(2) below, para.16–025.
[4] Below, paras 16–014 *et seq.*
[5] s.49(1) (below, paras 16–021 *et seq.*).
[6] s.49(2) (below, paras 16–025 *et seq.*).

There may also be other situations (outside the scope of section 49) in which the terms of the contract entitle the seller to sue for the price.[7] The seller's entitlement to sue for the price depends on the contract continuing in force,[8] and, where the goods have not been delivered to the buyer, on the continuing ability and willingness of the seller to deliver the goods to the buyer in accordance with the contract.[9] The seller must give credit for the deposit paid (if any)[10] and the buyer may have a set-off for damages for breach of warranty by the seller.[11] The seller may be entitled to claim separately the instalments of the price payable at fixed times.[12] In addition to recovering the price itself, the seller may be able to obtain interest on the price,[13] and (possibly) consequential damages.[14]

Where, although the property in the goods has not passed to the buyer, the seller is entitled to sue for the price, the question may arise whether the property passes as a result of the seller's action in suing for the price, or in recovering judgment for it: this question is considered in an earlier chapter.[15]

16–002 **Reduction of the price.** The new Part 5A of the Act gives new, additional remedies to a buyer who deals as consumer: where the goods are not in conformity with the contract at the time of delivery, one of the new remedies given to the consumer is "an appropriate reduction of the price". This, and the other new remedies, are examined above in Chapter 12.[15a]

16–003 **Modification of statutory remedy.**[16] Section 49 does not in terms provide that it is to be read subject to any express provision of the contract itself, but it is submitted that, to the extent of any inconsistency between them, the contract should prevail over section 49.[17] It appears to be the underlying philosophy of the Act that the parties are free, by the express terms of the contract, to define their rights and duties, unless they are either illegal under common law rules or ousted by a peremptory enactment. Although this same freedom may not extend to all remedies,[18] it will

---

[7] Below, para.16–028.
[8] On the effect of termination by the seller, see below, para.16–015.
[9] *Maclean v Dunn and Watkins* (1828) 6 L.J.(O.S.)C.P. 184. (It "is clear . . . that, to entitle the vendor to recover against the purchaser the full amount of the price agreed to be paid for the articles in the first instance, he must show that they continue in his possession ready to be delivered": *ibid.*, at p.190.). Thus, where at the time the goods were lost or damaged the risk was on the seller, despite the fact that the property in the goods had passed to the buyer (see above, para.6–001), it is submitted that the seller could not sue for the price. *Cf.* below, para.16–020.
[10] Below, para.16–014.
[11] s.53(1)(*a*): below, paras 17–047—17–049.
[12] Below, paras 16–005, 16–027, 16–028.
[13] Below, paras 16–006 *et seq*.
[14] Below, para.16–030.
[15] Above, para.5–021.
[15a] Above, paras 12–088 *et seq.* (see also below para.20–120).
[16] On exclusion or exemption clauses, see above, Ch.13.
[17] *cf.* s.55 (above, paras 1–013—1–015). See also the explanation of *Workman, Clark & Co. Ltd v Lloyd Brazileno* [1908] 1 K.B. 968, below, in, para.19–212.
[18] See, in relation to s.52, below, para.17–096.

extend to the parties' ability to specify when the seller may sue for the price.[19] Section 49 itself gives prominence to the terms of the contract ("(1) . . . under a contract of sale . . . according to the terms of the contract, . . . (2) . . . under a contract of sale . . ."). It is submitted later that the terms of the contract may entitle the seller to sue for the price even where section 49 does not apply[20]; the present submission is that the terms of the contract may modify the operation of section 49.

Distinction between a claim for the price and a claim for damages. An action for the price of goods sold is a claim for a debt, *i.e.* a claim for a definite sum of money fixed by the contract as payable by the buyer in return for the performance of a specified obligation by the seller or upon the occurrence of a specified condition. Damages may be claimed from the buyer who has broken his contractual obligation in some way other than by failure to pay the price. The practical relevance of the distinction is that rules on damages do not apply to a claim for the price, *e.g.* the seller need only prove that the price is due according to the terms of the particular contract[21]; there is no need for him to prove any actual loss suffered by him[22] as a result[23] of the buyer's failure to pay; the whole concept of the remoteness of damage[24] is therefore irrelevant; the law on penalties does not apply to the price[25]; and the claimant's "duty" to mitigate his loss does not generally apply.[26] 16–004

Although in many situations the "commercial man" will not be interested in the difference between an action for the price and one for damages, as "he will get complete redress whether he proceeds by the one course or the other,"[27] there are circumstances in which the distinction is vital.[28] For instance, if the seller is entitled to claim the price, he will not be adversely affected by his failure to resell at the market price at the date of the buyer's breach,[29] since, subject to some possible qualifications,[30] the "duty" to mitigate affects only a claim to damages.[31]

If the seller claims the price, the court or arbitrator may nevertheless award him damages if it holds that this is his correct remedy.[32]

---

[19] The price is a debt: see below, para.16–004. The freedom of the parties to specify when a debt is to be due was upheld by the House of Lords in *White and Carter (Councils) Ltd v McGregor* [1962] A.C. 413 (see below, para.16–059).
[20] Below, paras 16–028—16–029.
[21] See s.49(1) and (2) (below, paras 16–021 *et seq.*); and below, paras 16–028—16–029.
[22] Below, para.16–031.
[23] Below, para.16–049.
[24] Below, paras 16–043 *et seq.*
[25] Below, para.16–035. See *Chitty on Contracts* (29th ed.), Vol. 1, para.26–118.
[26] Below, para.16–052.
[27] *Napier (FE) v Dexters Ltd* (1926) 26 Ll.L.R. 184 at 185.
[28] See below, paras 16–036, 16–059. *Cf. Jervis v Harris* [1996] Ch. 195.
[29] s.50(3) (below, paras 16–060 *et seq.*) .
[30] See below, para.16–059, text at n.67. See also Treitel, *The Law of Contract* (11th ed.), pp.1016–1019.
[31] *White and Carter (Councils) Ltd v McGregor* [1962] A.C. 413 (see below, paras 16–059, 19–215, 20–126).
[32] *Mediterranean and Eastern Export Co. Ltd v Fortress Fabrics (Manchester) Ltd* [1948] 2 All E.R. 186 (an arbitration case).

16–005 **Payment of the price by instalments.** The distinction between a claim for the price and a claim for damages will apply when the contract provides for the price to be paid by instalments spread over a period: a claim for arrears of instalments already due is a claim in debt quite distinct from a claim for damages for breach of the contract as a whole.[33] It has been decided in cases of the hire of chattels where payments were due by instalments, that a claim in respect of the prospective loss of instalments due in the future cannot be a claim for a debt, but must be a claim for damages,[34] which is subject to the ordinary rules on damages.[35] It is submitted that the same position would hold in the sale of goods where the price was payable by instalments due at dates in the future, subsequent to the date of the judgment.

16–006 **Debts due in foreign currencies.** Questions arising from a debt calculable in a foreign currency are considered in a later chapter.[36]

(b) *Interest*

16–007 **Power to award interest.**[37] Section 54 of the Act provides that: "Nothing in this Act shall affect the right of the buyer or the seller to recover interest or special damages in any case where by law interest or special damages may be recoverable. . .". At common law,[38] interest was payable on a debt, such as the price of goods sold, only where there was contractual provision for it to be paid[39]; the courts were sometimes prepared to infer an

---

[33] *Workman, Clark & Co. Ltd v Lloyd Brazileno* [1908] 1 K.B. 968 (below, para.16–027). See also *Overstone Ltd v Shipway* [1962] 1 W.L.R. 117 at 123, 129 (a hire purchase case); *Yeoman Credit Ltd v Waragowski* [1961] 1 W.L.R. 1124 (a hire purchase case).

[34] *Interoffice Telephones Ltd v Robert Freeman Co. Ltd* [1958] 1 Q.B. 190; *Robophone Facilities Ltd v Blank* [1966] 1 W.L.R. 1428; *Lombard North Central Plc v Butterworth* [1987] Q.B. 527. *Cf. Yeoman Credit Ltd v Waragowski*, above. Where the contract contains an "acceleration" clause, making the remaining total payable upon default in paying any instalment, the amount may be recoverable as a debt: below, para.16–029. *Cf. White and Carter (Councils) Ltd v McGregor*, above.

[35] Thus, an allowance must be made for a discount on account of the earlier payment of a lump sum to be received under the judgment for damages, in lieu of the instalments which would have been spread over a future period: *Interoffice Telephones Ltd v Robert Freeman Co. Ltd*, above; *Overstone Ltd v Shipway*, above; *Robophone Facilities Ltd v Blank*, above.

[36] Below, paras 25–193—25–194.

[37] See *McGregor on Damages* (17th ed.), Ch.15; Chitty, *op. cit.*, Vol. 1, paras 26–144 *et seq.*, Vol. 2, paras 38–248 *et seq.* See The Law Commission's Report on Interest (Cmnd. 7229) (1978: Law Com.No. 88).

[38] *cf.* the practice of the court in its equitable jurisdiction: *Wallersteiner v Moir (No. 2)* [1975] Q.B. 373 at 388, 406; *O'Sullivan v Management Agency and Music Ltd* [1985] Q.B. 428. In *Westdeutsche Landesbank Girozentrale v Islington London BC* [1996] A.C. 669 the HL held that in equity compound interest may be awarded only in cases of fraud or against a trustee (or other person in a fiduciary position) in respect of profits improperly made by him.

[39] Or where a bill of exchange was dishonoured (which is now covered by s.57 of the Bills of Exchange Act 1882; in the enactment of general powers to award interest (discussed *below*), this provision has been preserved: s.3(1)(c) of the Law Reform (Miscellaneous Provisions) Act 1934; s.35A(8) of the Supreme Court Act 1981; and s.69(7) of the County Courts Act 1984).

agreement to pay interest on the price of goods sold where this could be based on the course of dealing between the parties[40] or a relevant trade usage.[41] The House of Lords[42] has upheld the rule[43] that the common law does not permit the award of interest by way of general damages for delay in payment of a debt beyond the date when it was contractually due; but special damages may be recovered in respect of interest paid by the claimant as the result of the defendant's breach of contract, if the second rule of remoteness laid down in *Hadley v Baxendale*[44] is satisfied.[45]

The High Court[46] and the county court[47] are now empowered by separate statutes,[48] in proceedings for the recovery of a debt or damages,[49] to include "in any sum for which judgment is given" simple interest[50]; subject to any rules of court,[51] the court is given a discretion[52] to fix the rate of interest,[53] to decide whether the interest should be on "all or any part of" the debt or

[40] *Re Anglesey* [1901] 2 Ch. 548. See also *Great Western Insurance Co. v Cunliffe* (1874) L.R. 9 Ch. 525; *Re Duncan & Co.* [1905] 1 Ch. 307.
[41] *Ikin v Bradley* (1818) 8 Taunt. 250; *Page v Newman* (1829) 9 B. & C. 378 at 381.
[42] *President of India v La Pintada Compania Navigacion SA* [1985] A.C. 104 (which was further considered by the HL in *President of India v Lips Maritime Corporation* [1988] A.C. 395). See Mann, (1985) 101 L.Q.R. 30.
[43] The first decision of the HL upholding the rule was *London, Chatham and Dover Railway Co. v South Eastern Railway Co.* [1893] A.C. 429.
[44] (1854) 9 Ex. 341 (see below, para.16–046).
[45] *President of India v La Pintada Compania Navigacion SA*, above, at pp.125–127 (approving the decision in *Wadsworth v Lydall* [1981] 1 W.L.R. 598 where, as the result of the defendant's failure to pay money when it was due, the claimant had actually incurred interest charges in obtaining finance from another source). See also *Bacon v Cooper (Metals) Ltd* [1982] 1 All E.R. 397; and *The Borag* [1981] 1 W.L.R. 274 (amount of interest charges held to be unreasonable).
[46] By s.35A of the Supreme Court Act 1981 (which was inserted by s.15 and Sch.1 to the Administration of Justice Act 1982). For the power given to arbitrators, see *below*, para.16–012.
[47] By s.69 of the County Courts Act 1984. S.3 of the Law Reform (Miscellaneous Provisions) Act 1934 which is examined in the 2nd edition of this work (paras 1276–1277) remains in force for courts of record other than the High Court and County Court.
[48] The new statutory provisions were the result of the Law Commission's Report on Interest (1978) (No. 88, Cmnd. 7229).
[49] The House of Lords held that the words "any debt or damages" in s.3(1) of the 1934 Act, above, "are very wide, so that they cover any sum of money which is recoverable by one party from another, either at common law or in equity or under a statute of the kind here concerned" (viz. the Law Reform (Frustrated Contracts) Act 1943): *BP Exploration Co. (Libya) Ltd v Hunt (No. 2)* [1983] 2 A.C. 352 at 373. This statement should also apply to ss.35A and 69 of the present Act, above.
[50] For interest on judgment debts and arbitration awards, see below, paras 16–012, 16–013. On compound interest in equity, see above para.16–007, n.38.
[51] See *below*, at nn. 53, 64 and 69.
[52] Interest should be awarded only on money which has been wrongfully withheld: *Business Computers Ltd v Anglo-African Leasing Ltd* [1977] 1 W.L.R. 578 at 587–588.
[53] By CPR, Part 12, r.6, where a claim for interest on a specified sum is made under s.35A or s.69 (above) at a rate no higher than that payable on judgment debts at the date when the claim form was issued, a default judgment may include the amount of interest to the date of judgment. By CPR, Pt 36, r.22, a claimant's Pt 36 offer to accept a sum of money or a Pt 36 payment notice (for a payment into court) will, unless it indicates to the contrary, be treated as inclusive of all interest until the last date on which it could be accepted without needing the court's permission.

damages, and for "all or any part of the period between the date when the cause of action arose" and either the date of payment (of any sum paid before judgment) or the date of judgment.[54] The claimant[55] is also entitled (subject to a similar[56] judicial discretion as to the rate of interest, the period for which it is payable, and whether it should be on all or only part of the debt or damages) to the award of simple interest where the defendant pays the whole of a debt to the claimant after proceedings for its recovery were instituted but before the judgment.[57] Where an action has been brought for damages for breach of contract, payment of the amount claimed prior to the hearing does not extinguish the cause of action[58]: hence, when the payment does not include interest on the amount claimed, the court can still award the damages and interest under the statute.[59] (It should be noted, however, that neither enactment[60] entitles a creditor to claim interest in respect of a debt paid late but before any proceedings for its recovery have begun.[61])

Both statutes provide that interest in respect of a debt must not be awarded "for a period during which, for whatever reason, interest on the debt already runs."[62] Hence, if the contract itself fixes interest, the court has no power to fix any different rate. Both enactments also provide that the interest may be calculated at different rates in respect of different periods.[63] Any claim for interest, whether under the statutory provisions or otherwise, must be specifically pleaded.[64]

16–008 Where the buyer failed to pay the price of goods sold and delivered to him, interest has been awarded "on the simple commercial basis that if the money had been paid at the appropriate commercial time, the other side would have had the use of it."[65] The buyer's breach of contract deprived the seller of the opportunity to put the money to work. Where the seller failed to deliver the goods, the buyer's damages should include interest on the

---

54 Subs.(1) of ss.35A and 69 respectively.

55 Defined as the person seeking the debt or damages: s.35A(7) and s.69(6) respectively.

56 As in subs.(1), above.

57 Subs.(3) of ss.35A and 69 respectively.

58 The payment merely gives rise to an equitable set-off which could be used as a potential crossclaim: *Edmunds v Lloyd Italico, etc. SpA* [1986] 1 W.L.R. 492 at 495.

59 *ibid.* (The defendant could resist any attempt to levy execution on the judgment which failed to give credit for the amount already paid: *ibid.*)

60 See nn. 46 and 47, above.

61 *IM Properties Plc v Cape & Dalgleish (a firm)* [1999] Q.B. 297. (This rule applies to late payment of the whole or part of a debt and also to a sum paid as damages before the commencement of proceedings). In *President of India v La Pintada Compania Navigacion SA*, above, the House of Lords called for further legislation to remedy this gap in the law.

62 Subs.35A(4) and 69(4) respectively. (See below, para.16–009).

63 s.35A(6) and s.69(5) respectively.

64 CPR, Part 16.4(2): the claimant must give details of the legal basis of the claim and, where a specified amount of money is claimed, the percentage rate claimed, the date from which it is claimed, the total amount claimed up to the date of calculation, and the daily rate at which interest accrues after that date.

65 *Kemp v Tolland* [1956] 2 Lloyd's Rep. 681 at 691. *Cf. Marsh v Jones* (1889) 40 Ch.D. 563.

normal measure of damages, *viz.* the difference between the contract price and the market price at the date fixed for delivery.[66] Special rules[67] apply to the award of interest on damages in respect of death or personal injuries: it is difficult to conceive of these provisions applying to a seller's claim, but they will apply to a buyer's claim.[68]

In business contexts, the rate of interest to be awarded by the court[69] should reflect the current commercial rates.[70] It is the practice of the Commercial Court[71] to award interest at the base rate prevailing from time to time plus one per cent[72]; but this is only a presumption which can be displaced if its application would be unfair to either party.[73]

Difficulties have arisen over the exercise of the court's discretion to award interest on damages when the claimant had covered the loss in question by insurance. In one case,[74] the Court of Appeal was prepared to award interest on damages for the period after the claimants were in fact indemnified by their insurers in respect of the loss. The court implied a term into the contract of insurance, to the effect that the claimants could retain any interest awarded which accrued before the insurers paid the claimants, but that any interest for a later period must go to the insurers.

Interest due as of right. The general statutory powers to award interest which have been examined in the preceding paragraphs do not apply where interest is payable under the terms of the contract itself[75] or under some 16–009

[66] *Panchaud Frères v Pagnan and Fratelli* [1974] 1 Lloyd's Rep. 394 at 411, 414.
[67] s.35A(2) of the Supreme Court Act 1981; s.69(2) of the County Courts Act 1984. See McGregor on *Damages* (17th ed.), paras 15–046 *et seq.*.
[68] Below, para.17–072.
[69] By s.35A(5) of the Supreme Court Act 1981, the rate of interest which the High Court may award under s.35A may by rules of court be fixed by reference to the rate fixed from time to time under s.17 of the Judgments Act 1838 (see below, para.16–013) or by reference to a rate for which any other enactment provides. See above, n.53.
[70] *cf. The Mecca* [1968] P. 665 at 672. See also below, para.16–009. For the rate of interest on a judgment given in a foreign currency, see *Miliangos v George Frank (Textiles) Ltd (No. 2)* [1977] Q.B. 489; and Bowles and Phillips, 39 M.L.R. 196 (1976).
[71] The same rule has been followed in the case of damages in tort for loss of chattels: *Metal Box Co. Ltd v Currys Ltd* [1988] 1 W.L.R. 175 at 182–183.
[72] *Polish SS Co. v Atlantic Maritime Co.* [1985] Q.B. 41 at 66–67; *Shearson Lehman Hutton Inc. v Maclaine Watson & Co. Ltd (No. 2)* [1990] 3 All E.R. 723 at 732–733. (The court did not accept the contention that the rate should be the LIBOR (London Inter-Bank Offer Rate) plus one-eighth).
[73] The *Shearson Lehman* case, above, at p.733. Evidence is admissible as to the rate at which persons with the general attributes of the claimant could have borrowed the money: *ibid.; Tate & Lyle Food and Distribution Ltd v Greater London Council* [1982] 1 W.L.R. 149 at 154–155.
[74] *Cousins (H) & Co. Ltd v D and C Carriers Ltd* [1971] 2 Q.B. 230.
[75] For illustrations, see Chitty, *op. cit.*, Vol. 2, paras 38–248 *et seq.* Ss.137–140 of the Consumer Credit Act 1974 enable the court to re-open certain transactions where the rate of interest is "grossly exorbitant" (*cf.* ss.244 and 343 of the Insolvency Act 1986.)

other special provision.[76] Thus, where the contract of sale itself[77] entitles the seller to claim interest on the price, the seller is not dependent on the exercise of the court's discretion and the court can award interest only at the rate specified in the contract. A suitably worded contractual clause may fix interest to run beyond judgment for the debt.[78] It is not an "unfair term"[79] in a loan agreement that interest at the contractual rate would be charged until payment after (as well as before) any judgment.[80]

16–010 **Interest on commercial debts.** Interest is payable on certain debts under a term implied into contracts by the Late Payment of Commercial Debts (Interest) Act 1998. The Act applies to "a contract for the supply of goods or services"[81] where both parties are acting in the course of a business.[82] It is an implied[83] term in any such contract that any "qualifying debt"[84] created by the contract carries simple interest (called "statutory interest" in the Act).[85] The rate of statutory interest (or the formula for calculating it) is to be prescribed by order of the Secretary of State.[86]

16–011 **Period and rate of statutory interest.** Where the parties agree a date for payment of the debt, statutory interest starts to run on the next day[87]; but when the debt relates to an obligation to make an advance payment,[88] the

---

[76] By s.35A(4) of the Supreme Court Act 1981 and s.69(4) of the County Courts Act 1984, the court must not award interest in respect of a debt "for a period during which, for whatever reason, interest on the debt already runs."

[77] A course of dealing between the parties, or the custom or usages of a particular trade, may lead to an implied term that the seller may charge interest on the price: see above, para.16–007 nn. 40 and 41.

[78] *Economic Assurance Society v Usborne* [1902] A.C. 147.

[79] Under the Unfair Terms in Consumer Contracts Regulations 1999 see above, paras 13–103, 14–030 *et seq.*

[80] *Director General of Fair Trading v First National Bank Plc* [2002] A.C. 481.

[81] Defined by s.2(2), (3) and (4). (Some other relevant definitions are found in s.16). Certain contracts are excepted by s.2(5): consumer credit agreements; mortgages, pledges, charges or other securities; s.12 makes provision for the conflict of laws.

[82] s.2(1). The meaning of "business" includes a profession and the activities of any government department or local or public authority (s.2(7)). Initially, only businesses with 50 or fewer employees were entitled to claim under the Act: SI 1998/2479, Art. 2(2); see also SI 1998/2481. By the Late Payment of Commercial Debts (Interest) Act 1998 (Commencement No.5) Order 2002 (SI 2002/1673) the provisions of the Act apply to businesses of all sizes and to the public sector.

[83] In cases where the contract provides "a substantial remedy" (as defined in s.9) for late payment of the debt, s.1(3) and Pt II of the Act (ss.7–10) permit the parties to oust or vary the right to statutory interest conferred by s.1(1).

[84] As defined by s.3(1). S.3(2) and (3) exclude debts where any other enactment or any rule of law confers a right to interest or to charge interest. By s.13, the Act applies to a qualifying debt despite any assignment of the debt or the transfer of the duty to pay it, or any change in the identity of the parties, whether by assignment, operation of law or otherwise.

[85] s.1(1).

[86] s.6. The current rate is fixed at 8 per cent over the official dealing rate of the Bank of England: SI 2002/1675. In addition to interest fixed, sums are payable as "compensation arising out of late payment" (SI 2002/1674).

[87] s.4(3). The agreed date "may depend on the happening of an event or the failure of an event to happen": s.4(3). S.14 extends the application of the Unfair Contract Terms Act 1977 to a contract term postponing the time when a qualifying debt would otherwise arise.

[88] ss.4(4) and 11.

debt is treated as created on the day when the supplier's obligation is performed.[89] In other cases, statutory interest runs after the period of 30 days from the performance of the obligation to which the debt relates[90]; or from the day when the purchaser has notice of the amount of the debt.[91] Statutory interest ceases to run when the interest would cease to run if it were carried under an express contract term.[92] But statutory interest does not run for any period where "by reason of any conduct of the supplier",[93] "the interests of justice require".[94]

Arbitration awards. At common law an arbitrator has no power to award general damages in respect of interest on debts paid late,[95] but power is now granted by statute. It is provided[96] that (unless the parties agree otherwise) the arbitral tribunal may award simple or compound interest from such date at such rates and with such rests as it considers meets the justice of the case. Such interest may be awarded on the whole or any part of (a) the amount awarded in respect of any period up to the award; and (b) any amount which was claimed in the arbitration and outstanding at the commencement of the arbitral proceedings, but was paid before the award was made in respect of any period up to the date of payment.[97] This power granted to arbitrators is similar to that granted to courts, but is wider in that compound interest may be awarded[98]; as in the case of the judicial power, it does not entitle a creditor to claim interest on a debt which was paid late but before the reference to arbitration was made.[99] 16–012

Interest on judgment debts and arbitration awards. A special enactment prescribes the rate of interest on a High Court judgment debt[1]: the current 16–013

[89] s.11(3). S.11(4) to (7) prescribe detailed rules on advance payments in respect of part performance or the hire of goods.
[90] s.4(5)(a).
[91] If the amount is unascertained, the 30-day period runs from the day when the purchaser has notice of the sum claimed: s.4(5)(b).
[92] s.4(7).
[93] s.5(1). "Conduct" includes any act or omission (s.5(5)) and may be relevant whether it occurs before or after the time when the debt is created (s.5(4)).
[94] s.5(1) and (2). By s.5(3) a reduced rate of statutory interest may apply if "the interests of justice require". For possible analogies, see above, para.14–034 on " unfairness", and above, paras 13–086 *et seq.* on "reasonableness".
[95] *President of India v La Pintada Compania Navigacion SA* [1985] A.C. 104. See above, para.16–007. (In the same case it was held that the Admiralty jurisdiction does not extend to the award of interest on debts already paid, nor to the award of compound interest).
[96] s.49 of the Arbitration Act 1996. By s.49(6) the provisions in s.49 do not affect any other power of the tribunal to award interest.
[97] s.49(3) of the 1996 Act.
[98] *cf.* above, para.16–007, text at n.38.
[99] See the *President of India* case, above.
[1] s.17 of the Judgments Act 1838 (as amended by s.44 of the Administration of Justice Act 1970, which empowers the making of an order amending the rate of interest in s.17). On the time of entering up a judgment, see *Parsons v Mather & Platt Ltd* [1977] 1 W.L.R. 855 (approved by CA in *Erven Warnink BV v J Townend & Sons (Hull) Ltd* [1982] 3 All E.R. 312). County court judgments for not less than

rate is fixed from time to time by statutory instrument.[2] An arbitral tribunal has discretion to award simple or compound interest from the date of the award (or any later date) until payment; it has discretion to fix the rates of interest and the rests (if any).[3]

The rate of interest on a judgment debt is fixed at the rate in force at the time the judgment was entered up: it does not fluctuate in accordance with later statutory instruments made before the judgment is satisfied.[4]

(c) *Wrongful Failure to pay the Price*

16–014 **Definition of "price" and allowance for deposit.** Section 49, above, assumes the definition of the "price" which is found elsewhere in the Act.[5] Even where the buyer has made default in paying the price at the fixed time, the seller must give him credit for the deposit paid if he sues the buyer for the price under section 49.[6] If, on the other hand, the seller resells the goods and does not sue the buyer for damages, he may retain both the price he receives under the resale and the deposit paid by the defaulting buyer under the first sale.[7]

16–015 **No claim for the price after termination of the contract by the seller.** When the property has not passed to the buyer[8] the seller has the right to resell the goods,[9] if he chooses to terminate the contract upon the buyer's breach. If the seller, following the buyer's repudiation or fundamental breach, does terminate the contract, the seller is released from any further obligation under the contract[10]; and this, in turn, means that the seller can no longer sue the buyer for the price, but is relegated to his claim for damages.[11]

£5,000 (with some exceptions) will carry interest at the same rate specified for the time being under s.17 of the Judgments Act 1838: County Courts (Interest on Judgment Debts) Order 1991 (No. 1184). By SI 1998/2400 (L.9) county court judgments in respect of qualifying debts under the Late Payment of Commercial Debts (Interest) Act 1998 (see above, para.16–010) are included in the 1991 Order.

[2] The Judgment Debts (Rate of Interest) Order 1993 (SI 1993/564) fixes a rate of 8 per cent.

[3] s.49(4) of the Arbitration Act 1996.

[4] *Rocco Giuseppe & Figli v Tradax Export SA*, [1984] 1 W.L.R. 742.

[5] ss.2(1), 8 and 9. (above, paras 2–044—2–052).

[6] *Gallagher v Shilcock* [1949] 2 K.B. 765 at 771. (This case has been overruled on other points by *Ward (RV) Ltd v Bignall* [1967] 1 Q.B. 534 (above, para.15–127).

[7] Above, paras 15–132—15–133.

[8] There are special circumstances in which the seller may be able to resell even after the property in the goods has passed to the buyer: see above, para.15–102.

[9] Above, paras 15–105, 15–107, 15–116.

[10] Above, para.15–110. The seller is thus not obliged to accept a subsequent tender of the price.

[11] *Chinery v Viall* (1860) 5 H. & N. 288; *Att.-Gen. v Pritchard* (1928) 97 L.J.K.B. 561 (above, para.15–114). See also above, para.15–128. The seller, however, has no power to terminate the contract (so as to retake the goods) if both property and possession are with the buyer: see above, para.15–117.

Wrongful neglect or refusal to pay. The question whether the buyer has wrongfully neglected or refused to pay the price[12] depends on his duty to pay,[13] which is not the same question as whether the seller is entitled to bring an action for the price, because other conditions must also be satisfied for such an action to lie.[14] Even where the seller is otherwise entitled to sue for the price, the buyer's neglect or refusal to pay the price must be "wrongful" before he is liable to an action for the price. Since the terms of the contract will specify when payment is due, the meaning of "wrongful" must be gathered from those terms[15]; thus, where the contract entitles the buyer to a period of credit, he will not be liable to an action for the price until that period has expired.[16] The buyer may similarly show that his failure to pay the price is not "wrongful" where the seller has waived[17] the time for payment fixed by the contract. **16–016**

There is no need for the seller to make a special request to the buyer to pay the price when it is due, since, in the absence of any special term in the contract,[18] it is the duty of a debtor to tender the amount of the debt to his creditor[19] without waiting for a demand.[20] The parties are free to fix whatever terms they please as to the order in which delivery and payment of the price are to be made[21]; and the provisions of the contract dealing with payment will obviously prevail over the sections of the Act on payment, since the latter are intended to apply only in the absence of any contrary intention of the parties revealed in the terms of their contract. Where payment of the price is a concurrent condition with delivery of the goods to the buyer, the seller may be entitled to sue for the price (provided the property in the goods has passed to the buyer)[22] if he proves that he is ready and willing to deliver the goods upon payment of the price[23]; until actual payment he is entitled to exercise the unpaid seller's lien.[24] Similarly,

---

[12] s.49(1) and (2) (". . . wrongfully neglects or refuses to pay . . .").
[13] ss.27 and 28 (above, paras 9–021 *et seq.*); on the duty to pay the price under c.i.f. and f.o.b. contracts, see below, paras 19–075 *et seq.*, 20–055 *et seq.*
[14] Either the property must have passed (s.49(1)) or the price must be payable on "a day certain" (s.49(2)), or the terms of the contract must otherwise entitle the seller to claim the price in the particular circumstances (above, para.16–001); below, paras 16–028—16–029.
[15] See above, Ch.9 on Payment. On the time for payment, see s.10(1) (above, para.9–051) and s.28 (above, para.8–004); on the position where there is no term which expressly fixes the time for payment, see above, para.9–057.
[16] *Ferguson v Carrington* (1829) 9 B. & C. 59; *Strutt v Smith* (1834) 1 Cr.M. & R. 312. The seller may not be bound by his willingness, expressed after the sale but not as a term of the contract, to allow time for payment: *De Symons v Minchwich* (1795) 1 Esp. 430; on waiver, see n.17, below.
[17] See above, para.9–055.
[18] For the duty to pay on demand or upon notice, see above, para.9–059.
[19] Provided the creditor is in England: *cf. Fessard v Mugnier* (1865) 18 C.B.(N.S.) 286.
[20] *Walton v Mascall* (1844) 13 M. & W. 452 at 458; *Robey & Co. v Snaefell Mining Co. Ltd* (1887) 20 Q.B.D. 152. *Cf. Thompson v Palmer* [1893] 2 Q.B. 80.
[21] *Calcutta and Burmah Steam Navigation Co. v De Mattos* (1863) 32 L.J.Q.B. 322 at 328.
[22] See below, paras 16–021 *et seq.*
[23] s.28 (above, para.8–004).
[24] s.43(2) (above, para.15–059). See also above, para.15–016.

the seller must show that he has performed, or offered to perform, any other conditions precedent to payment of the price.[25]

It may, of course, be agreed between the parties that payment of the price is to be made in a special way and not by the delivery of cash, *e.g.* if it is agreed, upon a settlement of accounts which leaves a balance due to one party, that the balance should go to the credit of that party in future transactions between the parties.[26]

Where payment is to be made in a special way the seller cannot sue for the price as an ordinary debt.[27] Thus, if it is agreed that the price of the goods should be an item in settlements of accounts between the parties at stated intervals, the seller can sue only by showing a settlement of accounts on which the balance is in his favour.[28]

16–017 **The effect of tender.** The effect of a successful plea of tender is that it does not discharge the obligation of the buyer to pay the price[29]; but if the seller later sues for the price, the buyer, by paying the money into court, and by proving the tender and his continued willingness to pay the price since the tender,[30] will prevent the seller from recovering any interest or damages for costs or expenses[31] arising after the tender.[32] A valid tender of the price will, however, terminate the seller's rights to exercise his remedies against the goods (*viz.* lien, stoppage in transit, or resale).[33]

16–018 **Payment by negotiable instrument.** If payment is made, under the terms of the contract, by means of a negotiable instrument, the payment is prima facie conditional upon the instrument being honoured when it is due.[34] During the currency of the instrument, therefore, the seller's right to sue for the price is suspended.[35] In special circumstances, however, the seller may take a negotiable instrument as absolute payment, so that his only remedy will be on the instrument.[36] If, under the contract, the buyer is to pay the price by a negotiable instrument which is to be payable at a future date, but the buyer wrongfully fails to give the instrument, the seller cannot

---

[25] On the seller's duty under s.34 to allow the buyer to examine the goods, see above, para.12–039.
[26] *Smith v Winter* (1852) 12 C.B. 487. *Cf.* above, para.9–041.
[27] *Garey v Pyke* (1839) 10 A. & E. 512. *Cf. Smith v Winter*, above (no balance was due to the seller).
[28] *Garey v Pyke*, above.
[29] Chitty, *op. cit.*, Vol. 1, paras 21–083—21–096.
[30] *Dixon v Clark* (1848) 5 C.B. 365 at 377.
[31] *e.g.* the expense of storing the goods. *Cf.* s.37 (above, para.9–009; below, para.16–088).
[32] The seller would also be liable to pay the buyer his costs of defending an unnecessary action for the price, on the grounds that the seller should not have sued him: *Dixon v Clark*, above, at p.377; *Griffith v Ystradyfodwg School Board* (1890) 24 Q.B.D. 307.
[33] After a valid tender, the seller is no longer "unpaid" (s.38(1)) and, therefore, is not entitled to exercise the remedies specified in s.39. See above, paras 15–022—15–023.
[34] Above, para.9–030. (*Cf.* s.38(1)(b).)
[35] Above, para.9–030.
[36] Above, para.9–031.

recover the price before the date when the instrument would have been due.[37] If a negotiable instrument is given for part of the price, the seller cannot obtain judgment for the whole price unless the instrument has been dishonoured.[38]

Payment by banker's commercial credit. Where the contract requires payment to be made by banker's commercial credit,[39] the statutory rules on an action for the price will not usually be relied on by the seller, because he will be better protected by the credit.[40] But an action for the price may still be brought by the seller where he fails to obtain payment through the credit,[41] unless the credit was intended to be the exclusive source of payment. 16–019

Previous breach by seller. The buyer's failure to pay the price may be justified on the ground that the seller had previously broken his contractual obligation in such a way as to disentitle him to the price, *e.g.* by failure to deliver, or by delivering defective goods[42] or the wrong quantity. Similarly, the seller cannot claim the price from the buyer if it turns out that the seller has no title to the goods.[43] But the buyer may be liable to pay the price if, before the goods were delivered to him, they perished while the risk was on him (the buyer).[44] 16–020

A previous breach of contract by the seller may not, however, be sufficiently serious as to relieve the buyer of his entire obligation to pay the price: in these circumstances the buyer may rely on a set-off against the seller[45] or may bring a counterclaim for damages. Section 53(1) of the Act provides (*inter alia*) that where there is a breach of warranty by the seller, the buyer "may—(a) set up against the seller the breach of warranty in diminution or extinction of the price."[46]

---

[37] *Helps v Winterbottom* (1831) 2 B. & Ad. 431.

[38] *Bolt and Nut (Tipton) Ltd v Rowlands, Nicholls & Co. Ltd* [1964] 2 Q.B. 10.

[39] See below, Ch.23 on Documentary Credits.

[40] If the seller complies with the requirements of the credit, he will be entitled to enforce it even where the buyer wrongfully rejects the goods: below, para.23–139.

[41] *Newman Industries Ltd v Indo-British Industries Ltd* [1956] 2 Lloyd's Rep. 219 at 236 (revsd. on a different ground: [1957] 1 Lloyd's Rep. 211); *Saffron v Société Minie're Cafrika* (1958) 100 C.L.R. 231 at 244–245; *Alan (W.J.) & Co. Ltd v El Nasr Export and Import Co.* [1972] 2 Q.B. 189 at 209–212, 221 (see below, paras 23–097—23–098); *Man (ED & F) Ltd v Nigerian Sweets & Confectionery Co. Ltd* [1977] 2 Lloyd's Rep. 50 (see below, para.23–098).

[42] *Wayne's Merthyr Steam Coal and Iron Co. v Morewood* (1877) 46 L.J.Q.B. 746; *Underwood Ltd v Burgh Castle Brick and Cement Syndicate* [1922] 1 K.B. 123 at 343 (goods damaged in process of loading before property passed to the buyer: below, para.21–043).

[43] *Dickenson v Naul* (1833) 4 B. & Ad. 638; *Allen v Hopkins* (1844) 13 M. & W. 94. (Although this decision is based also on the fact that the buyer had had to pay the value of the goods to the true owner it is submitted that the principle need not be so limited.) See above, para.7–001.

[44] Above, para.9–056; see also Sealy [1972 B] Camb.L.J. 225 at 237–238. *Aliter*, if the risk was on the seller: above, para.16–001, n.9.

[45] *cf. Berger & Co. Inc. v Gill & Duffus SA* [1984] A.C. 382 at 392 (below, para.16–061).

[46] See also s.53(4) (below, para.17–049) and, on reduction in price, s. 48C (above, paras 12–088 *et seq.*, 16–002).

(d) *Entitlement to Sue for the Price*

(i) *Where the Property has Passed to the Buyer*

16–021 **Action for price when property has passed.** Section 49(1) provides that: "Where, under a contract of sale, the property in the goods has passed to the buyer and he wrongfully neglects or refuses[47] to pay for the goods according to the terms of the contract, the seller may maintain an action against him for the price of the goods."[48] This section depends on the rules for the passing of the property in the goods to the buyer, which are examined at length in an earlier chapter.[49] The property may pass to the buyer before delivery[50] of the goods to him, and before his acceptance[51] of the goods; hence, in some circumstances the price may be claimed under section 49(1) even where the buyer refuses to accept the goods.[52] On the other hand, the fact that delivery[53] of the goods has been made will not, on its own, support a claim for the price; nor can the seller sue for the price if he has terminated the contract of sale.[54] There are many cases before the 1893 Act which illustrate the proposition that, where there is no specific term of the contract dealing with the time when the price is to be paid, the seller cannot sue for the price until the property in the goods has passed to the buyer.[55]

16–022 More modern illustrations concern f.o.b. contracts. Since under an f.o.b. contract property does not pass before shipment,[56] the seller may sue for the price[57] only after he has put the goods on board[58]; even after shipment, however, the seller may have reserved a right of disposal, in which case he

---

47 "Wrongful neglect or refusal" to pay is considered above, paras 16–014—16–020.
48 This section follows the previous common law: *Scott v England* (1844) 14 L.J.Q.B. 43. See also *Studdy v Sanders* (1826) 5 B. & C. 628. For definitions in the section, see s.61(1).
49 Ch.5.
50 *e.g. Scott v England*, above. On delivery, see above, Ch.8.
51 On acceptance, see above, paras 9–002 *et seq.*
52 Alternatively, the seller may in these circumstances claim damages for non-acceptance under s.50(1) (below, paras 16–060 *et seq.*).
53 Delivery is normally concurrent with payment of the price: s.28 (see above, para.8–004).
54 Above, para.16–015. If the property (but not possession) had already passed to the buyer, the termination of the contract by the seller will revest the property in him: above, paras 15–107—15–110. But if the buyer has both the property in, and possession of the goods, the seller is not able to "terminate" the contract for failure to pay the price (so as to entitle him to retake the goods): see above, para.15–117. *Cf.* severable contracts, above, para.15–042.
55 *e.g. Atkinson v Bell* (1828) 8 B. & C. 277; *Boswell v Kilborn and Morrill* (1862) 15 Moo.P.C. 309. The seller may, however, obtain a declaratory judgment to the effect that the buyer is bound to pay the price upon the seller's fulfilling his obligations: see below, para.16–092.
56 Below, para.20–071.
57 Or, part of the price, if the buyer's breach prevented shipment of the rest of the goods: below, para.20–127.
58 *Green v Sichel* (1860) 7 C.B.(N.S.) 747; *Henderson and Glass v Radmore & Co.* (1922) 10 Ll.L.R. 727; see below, para.20–126.

may sue for the price only if he has waived his right of disposal.[59] If the seller ships the goods after the buyer has wrongfully repudiated an f.o.b. contract, his claim against the buyer is only for damages[60]; but it is submitted later[61] that this rule may need revision in the light of the proposition, accepted by the House of Lords in *White and Carter* (*Councils*) *Ltd v McGregor*,[62] that a party who, after the other's repudiation, can complete performance of his obligations without the co-operation of the other, may sue for the sum agreed to be paid for his performance. This case did not concern the sale of goods,[63] and it should be noted that it was said by Lord Keith (dissenting in the same case) that where unascertained or future goods[64] are the subject-matter of the contract, and the buyer repudiates his obligation before the goods have been appropriated to the contract (or refuses his assent to appropriation), the seller can claim only damages; he cannot ignore the repudiation, perform his obligation and claim the full price.[65]

Wrongful prevention of passing of property. Where the property in the goods has not passed to the buyer, no action for the price can be brought under section 49(1),[66] despite the fact that it is a wrongful act of the buyer which prevents the passing of the property.[67] Thus, where the buyer under an f.o.b. contract failed (in breach of his contractual obligation) to designate an effective ship, the seller's remedy was not a claim for the price but a claim for damages for non-acceptance,[68] because the property in the goods could not pass until the goods were actually put on board a ship.[69] Similarly, where the buyer under a c.i.f. contract wrongfully refused to take up the shipping documents when the seller tendered them the seller's only remedy was to sue for damages: he could not sue for the price, because the property in the goods had not passed to the buyer.[70] These cases should be contrasted with an appeal from Scotland to the House of Lords, where a machine had been delivered to the buyer, who was bound to keep and pay for it, unless it failed on a stipulated test to do specified work. The buyer neglected to put the machine to this test, but it was held that the seller 16–023

---

59 See below, para.20–128.

60 *Nortier (A A) & Co. v Wm. Maclean Sons & Co.* (1921) 9 Ll.L.R. 192 (below, para.20–126).

61 Below, para.20–126.

62 [1962] A.C. 413 (below, para.16–059).

63 *cf. Anglo-African Shipping Co. of New York Inc. v J. Mortner Ltd* [1962] 1 Lloyd's Rep. 81 at 94 (on appeal, *ibid.* at p.610, no mention was made of *White and Carter's* case): see below, para.16–059.

64 For definitions, see above, paras 1–101 *et seq.*, 1–113—1–119, 5–059 *et seq.*

65 *White and Carter (Councils) Ltd v McGregor*, above, at p.437. See also *Hounslow London Borough Council v Twickenham Garden Developments Ltd* [1971] Ch. 233 at 251–254; and the other cases cited below, para.16–059.

66 See, however, s.49(2) (below, para.16–025).

67 *Stein, Forbes & Co. v County Tailoring Co.* (1916) 86 L.J.K.B. 448; *Colley v Overseas Exporters* [1921] 3 K.B. 302.

68 Under s.50(1) (below, paras 16–060 *et seq.*).

69 *Colley v Overseas Exporters*, above (see below, paras 20–071, 20–126—20–128).

70 *Stein, Forbes & Co. v County Tailoring Co.*, above. (It was also held that the price was not payable "on a day certain" within s.49(2): see below, para.16–026).

could recover the price: the buyer's own failure to give it a fair test according to the contract relieved the seller of having to prove that the condition did not apply.[71] This case may be distinguished from those discussed earlier on the ground that the specific goods had been delivered by the seller to the buyer, so that the property had apparently passed[72]; it was a condition subsequent or a "resolutive condition",[73] and "a clear distinction exists between cases where the default of the buyer has occurred after the property has passed and cases where that default has been before the property has passed."[74]

16–024 **Estoppel and waiver.** In special circumstances, the doctrine of estoppel by conduct may operate to prevent the buyer from disputing the fact that the property has passed to him[75]; but the buyer's breach of contract will not of itself establish such an estoppel.[76]

It may be possible for the seller to waive a stipulation in his favour, so that property in the goods passes to the buyer at an earlier time than the contract stipulated, *e.g.* if the contract provides for payment of the price against the shipping documents, the seller may waive the benefit of this provision and thus allow the property to pass upon shipment; in these circumstances the seller may sue for the price.[77]

(ii) *Price Payable on "a Day Certain"*

16–025 **Action for price due on "a day certain".** The second situation in which the seller may claim the price is where the contract specially provides that the price is to be paid on a fixed date irrespective both of delivery to the buyer and of the passing of property. Section 49(2) provides that "Where, under a contract of sale, the price is payable on a day certain irrespective of delivery[78] and the buyer wrongfully neglects or refuses to pay such price, the seller may maintain an action for the price, although the property in the goods has not passed and the goods have not been appropriated to the contract." Section 49(2) is based on *Dunlop v Grote*,[79] where the contract, after requiring payment in cash for every ton of iron delivered as requested, provided that "if the delivery of the said iron should not be required before . . . 30 April", payment was to be made on that date. The sellers were held to be entitled under this clause to sue for the price of the part of the iron

---

[71] *Mackay v Dick* (1881) L.R. 6 App.Cas. 251. See also *Studdy v Sanders* (1826) 5 B. & C. 628 at 639.
[72] Under the relevant Scots law.
[73] *Colley v Overseas Exporters* [1921] 3 K.B. 302 at 307–308. See above, para.5–043.
[74] *Colley v Overseas Exporters*, above, at p.310.
[75] *Colley v Overseas Exporters*, above, at pp.311–312. *Cf.* above, paras 7–008 *et seq.; Knights v Wiffen* (1870) L.R. 5 Q.B. 660 (estoppel preventing seller from denying that property had passed: above, paras 5–065, 15–096).
[76] *Colley v Overseas Exporters*, above, at pp.311–312.
[77] *Napier (F E) v Dexters Ltd* (1926) 26 Ll.L.R. 62 at 63–64; 184, 187–188 (see below, para.20–128). See also *Henderson and Glass v Radmore & Co.* (1922) 10 Ll.L.R. 727 at 728.
[78] "Delivery" is defined in s.61(1). See above, paras 8–002 *et seq.*
[79] (1845) 2 Car. & K. 153.

which they were ready and willing to deliver but had not actually delivered by that date.

Price due on a contingent event. In *Shell-Mex Ltd v Elton Cop Dyeing Co. Ltd*[80] the meaning of "a day certain" in this provision was held to be "a time specified in the contract not depending on a future or contingent event."[81] The case concerned a contract for sale of oil to be delivered by instalments, at the request of the buyer, but the buyer repudiated the contract after only part had been delivered. Property in the remainder of the oil had not passed to the buyer, as there had not been a specific appropriation of the bulk.[82] A clause in the contract provided: "sellers have the right at any time to invoice to buyers the due quantities of oil not taken up, and to demand payment of the invoice amounts . . ." Wright J. held that this clause did not specify "a time certain"; it did "not in terms say that the buyers have to pay the invoice price as a debt at any specified time, or on delivery of the invoice, or at any specified time after delivery. What is invoiced under clause 15 is still the price payable under the contract, which includes the sellers' services in actually delivering the goods to the buyers' works."[83] Thus, the sellers' only remedy was in damages. The same approach to the interpretation of section 49(2) is found in overseas sales. In a c.i.f. contract, where payment was to be made by "Net cash against documents on arrival of the steamer", it was held[84] that the seller could not claim the price when the buyer wrongfully refused to take up the shipping documents; the property in the goods had not passed,[85] and the price was not payable "on a day certain irrespective of delivery." Atkin J. said that "On the contrary, it is payable expressly against delivery"[86] of the documents; in these circumstances, the seller's only remedy is a claim for damages.[87] The same rule is found in a case where goods were sold c. & f. to be paid for by cash against documents, but the buyer refused to pay against the documents; it was held that the seller could not sue for the price, because it was not payable "on a day certain" within section 49(2).[88] 16–026

In a later case, goods were sold on terms of "prompt cash against invoice": it was held by a Scottish court that this was not "on a day certain", which "must mean something of the nature of a fixed date . . . The date of

[80] (1928) 34 Com.Cas. 39.
[81] *ibid.*, at p.43 (citing *The Merchant Shipping Co. Ltd v Armitage* (1873) L.R. 9 Q.B. 99 at 114). See also *Muller, Maclean & Co. v Leslie and Anderson* (1921) 8 Ll.L.R. 328 at 330–331 (see below, para.19–214).
[82] Above, paras 5–061 *et seq.*
[83] (1928) 34 Com.Cas. 39 at 45 (distinguishing *Dunlop v Grote*, above).
[84] *Stein, Forbes & Co. v County Tailoring Co.* (1916) 86 L.J.K.B. 448 (see also below, para.19–214). *Cf.* below, para.16–028.
[85] So s.49(1) was inapplicable.
[86] (1916) 86 L.J.K.B. 448. (An earlier case, *Polenghi v Dried Milk Co. Ltd* (1904) 10 Com.Cas. 42, is inconsistent with this view: see below, paras 19–213—19–214).
[87] *Nortier (A. A.) & Co. v Wm. Maclean Sons & Co.* (1921) 9 Ll.L.R. 192 at 194; *Colley v Overseas Exporters* [1921] 3 K.B. 302 at 311; *Shell-Mex Ltd v Elton Cop Dyeing Co. Ltd* (1928) 34 Com.Cas. 39 at 44; *Tradax Internacional SA v Goldschmidt SA* [1977] 2 Lloyd's Rep. 604 at 614.
[88] *Muller, Maclean & Co. v Leslie and Anderson* (1921) 8 Ll.L.R. 328 at 330–331 (below, para.19–214).

the receipt of the invoice leaves it open to the seller to make the price payable at any time either before or after delivery of the goods. The buyer under such a stipulation can have no certainty as to when the price is to be required of him."[89]

16–027 **Meaning of "a day certain".** It is submitted, on the basis of these decisions, that the better view is that a day can be "certain" under section 49(2) only if it is fixed in advance by the contract in such a way that it can be determined independently of the action of either party or of any third person.[90] If, for example, an instalment of the price becomes due when the seller has reached a specified stage in the construction of the goods, it is submitted that the instalment should not be held to be "payable on a day certain" within the meaning of this subsection.[91] But dicta in the Court of Appeal[92] cast doubt on this submission: the contract was for the sale of a ship to be built by the seller, and it was held that section 49(2) could apply to claims for instalments of the price due to be paid on different dates, as well as to a claim for the full price of the goods.[93] But although the judgments do not discuss the meaning of "a day certain" in the subsection, they assume that the seller could sue for instalments falling due as he reached the specified stages of construction of the ship, *e.g.* when the keel was laid.[94] If the subsection does apply when the date for payment is ascertained in the course of the performance of the contract, it will enable the seller to recover the price in many cases where the property in the goods has not passed to the buyer; but this appears to be inconsistent with the purpose of section 50(1), which assumes that the normal[95] remedy when the property has not passed[96] is a claim for damages for non-acceptance.[97]

(iii) *Other Claims for the Price*

16–028 **Action for the price outside section 49.** There are a number of judicial statements which assume that section 49, above, provides an exhaustive statement of the circumstances in which the seller may sue for the price.[98]

---

[89] *Henderson and Keay Ltd v A M Carmichael Ltd*, 1956 S.L.T. (Notes) 58.
[90] This submission is consistent with that contained in para.19–212, below, to the effect that s.49(2) was intended to apply only to cases in which a specific date for payment, irrespective of delivery, was actually mentioned in the contract itself or was at any rate precisely ascertainable at the time of the contract.
[91] *cf.* Atiyah, *The Sale of Goods* (11th ed.), pp.482–486.
[92] *Workman, Clark & Co. Ltd v Lloyd Brazileno* [1908] 1 K.B. 968 at 977, 978, 981. *Cf.* s.31 (above, paras 8–064 *et seq.*).
[93] *ibid.* See above, para.16–005. *Cf. Hyundai Heavy Industries Co. Ltd v Papadopoulos* [1980] 1 W.L.R. 1129 (contract for building or manufacture *and* sale).
[94] Some doubts were later expressed by two members of the court: see below, para.19–212, n.54.
[95] See, however, below, paras 16–028—16–029.
[96] s.50(1) (on the seller's claim for damages) applies "Where the buyer wrongfully neglects or refuses to accept and pay for the goods. . . ."
[97] See below, paras 16–060 *et seq.*
[98] *Stein, Forbes & Co. v County Tailoring Co.* (1916) 86 L.J.K.B. 448; *Colley v Overseas Exporters* [1921] 3 K.B. 302 at 310 ("I have searched in vain for authority to

However, it is submitted that the seller should be entitled to sue for the price whenever the terms of the contract expressly or impliedly so provide[99]; and that, by the terms of the contract, the time fixed for payment need not be related either to delivery or to the passing of property.[1] Thus section 28 provides that it is only in the absence of contrary agreement that the seller must be ready and willing to give possession of the goods to the buyer in exchange for the price, and that the buyer must be ready and willing to pay the price in exchange for the goods.[2] That the parties may validly specify when the price may be recovered by action is supported by the analogy from the decisions upholding the validity of retention of title clauses providing that, despite delivery of the goods to the buyer, the seller is to retain the property in the goods until the price has been fully paid.[3]

The contract may provide that the price is to be paid before delivery is made (*e.g.* "net cash before delivery"[4]) and that property is to pass only upon delivery.[5] The implication of these provisions is that the price must be paid on demand[6] or within a reasonable time,[7] and thus it has been held in Australia that the seller may sue for the price,[8] although neither the property has passed, nor is there a "day certain" for payment of the price (*i.e.* neither subsection of section 49 applies).[9] The cases discussed in

---

the contrary.") The decision in *Muller, Maclean & Co. v Leslie and Anderson* (1921) 8 Ll.L.R. 328 at 330–331 (below, para.19–214) implicitly supports these cases on this point. See also *Plaimar Ltd v Waters Trading Co. Ltd* (1945) 72 C.L.R. 304 at 318 (below, para.19–215); *cf. Martin v Hogan* (1917) 24 C.L.R. 234. Lord Keith, in a dissenting speech in *White and Carter (Councils) Ltd v McGregor* [1962] A.C. 413 at 437, says that the seller may sue for the price "only in two cases" (*sc.* those specified in s.49). (The estoppel cases would be treated as merely an exception: see above, para.16–024.)

99 The terms must permit the seller to recover the price by action, and not merely specify when the price is payable: the buyer's duty to pay the price is not identical with the seller's entitlement to sue for the price. See below, para.19–211. *Cf.* above, para.16–016.

1 See above, paras 16–003, and 16–027. A wide interpretation of the words "a day certain" in s.49(2), as accepted in dicta in the CA in *Workman, Clark & Co. Ltd v Lloyd Brazileno* [1908] 1 K.B. 968 at 977, 978, 981 (above, para.16–027, n.94) would reach a similar result. It is noteworthy that s.49 gives the parties a wide measure of freedom to specify by their contract when the property is to pass, or to fix "a day certain", and thus to permit an action for the price. The argument suggested in the text is consistent with this wide freedom of the parties: *cf. White and Carter (Councils) Ltd v McGregor* [1962] A.C. 413 (above, para.16–004; below, para.16–059); *Armour v Thyssen Edelstahlwerke AG* [1991] 2 A.C. 339; *Polenghi v Dried Milk Co. Ltd* (1904) 10 Com.Cas. 42 (below, paras 19–212—19–214).

2 See above, para.8–004. See also above, para.16–003.

3 *Armour v Thyssen Edelstahlwerke AG*, above; *Clough Mill Ltd v Martin* [1985] 1 W.L.R. 111. See above, paras 5–141 *et seq.*

4 *Minister of Supply and Development v Servicemen's Co-op. Joinery Manufacturers Ltd* (1951) 82 C.L.R. 621. (By such a provision, the seller aims at ensuring that he is completely protected against the buyer's failure to pay the price.)

5 *ibid.*, at p.636.

6 *ibid.*, at p.636.

7 *ibid.*, at p.642 (*cf.* the view of the dissenting judge at p.644).

8 *ibid.*, at pp.636, 642.

9 Retention of title clauses (see above, paras 5–141 *et seq.*) often provide that the seller may maintain an action for the price, notwithstanding that the property in the goods will not pass until full payment of the price has been made.

paragraph 16–029 also give some support to the view that section 49 is not an exhaustive[10] statement of the right to sue for the price.[11]

Under the Vienna Convention on Contracts for the International Sale of Goods[12] no express restrictions are imposed on the seller's entitlement to sue for the price.[13]

16–029 **Payment by instalments.**[14] Another illustration of the seller being entitled to sue for the price outside the scope of section 49 may be found in the type of conditional sale agreement,[15] where it is agreed that until all the instalments are paid, the goods remain the property of the seller; and that upon default in payment of an instalment or upon the occurrence of a certain event (*e.g.* the bankruptcy of the buyer) the total amount is to become payable.[16] Subject to the legislative protection afforded in the case of "conditional sale agreements" which are consumer credit agreements,[17] the seller would appear to be entitled to sue for the full price under the terms of this type of contract,[18] although neither section 49(1) nor 49(2) applies. For instance, the House of Lords has treated as an agreement to sell a contract for the "hire" of an engine, which provided that upon payment in full of the instalments of "rent" the engine should become the property of the hirer.[19] Lord Herschell L.C. held that the provision that property was not to pass until the full purchase money was paid was "a perfectly lawful agreement".[20] The contract further provided that if the instalments were not paid when due, or if the "hirer" became bankrupt, the owners could elect either to sue for the remainder of the instalments at once, or to resume possession of the engine. Lord Herschell said that in the former case "the debt due is the balance of the price, the purchaser keeping the goods"[21]: this statement clearly assumes that the owners would be

---

[10] *cf.* on the scope of s.52 of the Act, the statement in *Re Wait* [1927] 1 Ch. 606 at 630 (below, para.17–096).

[11] See also Sealy [1972 B] Camb.L.J. 225 at 238. It is however, arguable that to increase the scope of the action for the price has the undesirable effect of limiting the scope of the mitigation rules: see below, paras 19–215, 20–130; but *cf.* below, para.16–059. *Cf.* also the Uniform Commercial Code, s.2–709(1)(b).

[12] See above, para.1–024.

[13] But see below, para.19–215, n.68, for some implicit restrictions.

[14] See also above, paras 16–005, 16–029.

[15] *cf.* the definition of conditional sale agreement in the Consumer Credit Act 1974, s.189(1). The buyer is bound to buy the goods, and thus the arrangement is not one of hire-purchase: Goode, *Consumer Credit Law and Practice* (2001) paras 11.121–11.123.

[16] *McEntire v Crossley Bros Ltd* [1895] A.C. 457, below; *Sandford v Dairy Supplies Ltd* [1941] N.Z.L.R. 141.

[17] Consumer Credit Act 1974. See above, paras 1–019 *et seq.*, 1–052.

[18] Provided that the buyer had taken delivery of the goods: *Sandford v Dairy Supplies Ltd*, above. The seller's decision to sue for the full price (*i.e.* the remainder of the instalments) means that the seller is affirming the contract, and is willing to allow the property to pass upon payment: *McEntire v Crossley Bros Ltd*, above, at p.464.

[19] *McEntire v Crossley Bros Ltd*, above. *Cf. Armour v Thyssen Edelstahlwerke AG* [1991] 2 A.C. 339.

[20] *McEntire v Crossley Bros Ltd*, above, at p.463. On the question when the property in the goods passes in this type of contract, see above, para.5–026.

[21] *ibid.*, at p.465. (The other speeches concurred in the speech of the Lord Chancellor, without making reference to this particular point.)

entitled to sue for the balance in circumstances in which neither subsection of section 49 would apply, but it is not a definite opinion on the point.[22]

(e) *Claims for Consequential Loss*

Claim for consequential loss in addition to the price. The seller may wish to claim damages in addition to his claim for the agreed price, on the ground that the buyer's failure to pay the price at the agreed time caused consequential loss to the seller. Although a claim for interest may arise under the terms of the contract itself,[23] or by statute,[24] the position at common law is that only nominal damages are recoverable for the mere failure to pay an agreed sum of money on the due date.[25] Thus, the common law does not permit the award of interest by way of general damages for delay in payment of a debt beyond the date when it was contractually due.[26] But, if the second rule of remoteness in *Hadley v Baxendale*[27] is satisfied, special damages may be recovered for interest paid and other expenses incurred by the creditor in arranging alternative finance as the result of the debtor's failure to pay a debt on the fixed date.[28] 16–030

Apart from loss caused by his not receiving the price when expected, the seller may be entitled to claim damages for expenses incurred by him,[29] *e.g.* for storage during the buyer's delay in taking delivery, or for his own "care and custody of the goods" during such delay.[30]

2. GENERAL RULES ON DAMAGES

(a) *Introduction*

General rules for the assessment of damages. A detailed examination of the general rules for the assessment of damages for breach of contract must 16–031

[22] See also above, paras 5–021, 5–141 *et seq.*, on clauses which make the passing of property conditional on actual payment of the price.
[23] *Chitty on Contracts* (29th ed.), Vol. 2, paras 38–248—38–249; above, para.16–009.
[24] See above, para.16–007.
[25] *London, Chatham and Dover Railway Co. v South Eastern Railway* [1893] A.C. 429; *President of India v La Pintada Compania Navigacion SA* [1985] A.C. 104. See Chitty, *op. cit.*, Vol. 1, paras 26–089, 26–144; *McGregor on Damages* (17th ed.), paras 25–001 *et seq*. See the criticism of the rule by Jessel M.R. in *Wallis v Smith* (1882) 21 Ch.D. 243 at 257.
[26] See the *President of India* case, above.
[27] (1854) 9 Exch. 341 (see above, para.16–046).
[28] *Wadsworth v Lydall* [1981] 1 W.L.R. 598 (which was approved by the House of Lords in the *President of India* case, above, at pp.125–127.) In some cases substantial damages have been awarded where the contractual promise was interpreted as an undertaking to maintain the claimant's financial credit: *Wilson v United Counties Bank* [1920] A.C. 102.
[29] See below, paras 16–086—16–088. See also *Wadsworth v Lydall*, above.
[30] s.37 (above, para.9–009; below, para.16–088).

be sought elsewhere.[31] In this work, the general principles on damages will be summarised and examined in detail only to the extent that they have been applied to contracts for the sale of goods. Accordingly, this section does not examine matters such as appeals against the assessment of damages,[32] the liability of damages to tax or the effect of tax liability on assessment of damages.[33] The rules discussed in this section are applicable both to the seller's and to the buyer's claim for damages.

Damages for breach of contract are a compensation to the innocent party for the damage, loss or injury he has suffered through that breach: he is, as far as money can do it, to be placed in the same position as if the contract had been performed. Damages are primarily intended to give him the value of the promised performance of which the breach deprives him,[34] which has been called the claimant's "expectation interest",[35] *e.g.* his expectation of making a profit or receiving a benefit through the transaction (subject however, to his compliance with the mitigation rules[36]). The claimant may also have a "reliance interest" which should be protected by the award of damages: this interest relates to the expense or loss which the claimant has himself incurred in reliance on the expected performance of the contractual promise made by the defendant and which is wasted by the breach.[37] This "reliance interest" is illustrated by many cases in the sale of goods,[38] in one of which the Court of Appeal has discussed whether the claimant can recover *both* his expected profit *and* the expenses he has incurred in reliance on the defendant's promise.[39] Subject to the rules of mitigation,[40] the claimant is, however, entirely free to elect between a claim for lost profits or one for wasted expenditure.[41] The claimant may sometimes have a claim in restitution, which can be more valuable than one for damages.[42]

---

[31] Chitty, *op. cit.*, Vol. 1, Ch.26; *McGregor on Damages* (17th ed.), Chs 1–10, 12–18; Waddams, *The Law of Damages* (3rd ed.). For a comparison between the Common Law and the Civil Law, see Treitel, *Remedies for Breach of Contract* (1988) Chs IV to VII. On the question of a claim for damages which are calculable in a foreign currency, see below, paras 25–193—25–194.

[32] Chitty, *op. cit.*, para.26–027; McGregor, *op. cit.*, Ch.45.

[33] Chitty, *op. cit.*, paras 26–134—26–143; McGregor, *op. cit.*, Ch.14.

[34] *Robinson v Harman* (1848) 1 Exch. 850 at 855; *Wertheim v Chicoutimi Pulp Co.* [1911] A.C. 301 at 307; *British Westinghouse Electric Co. Ltd v Underground Electric Rys* [1912] A.C. 673 at 689; *Watts & Co. Ltd v Mitsui & Co. Ltd* [1917] A.C. 227 at 241; *Banco de Portugal v Waterlow & Sons Ltd* [1932] A.C. 452 at 474; *Monarch S.S. Co. Ltd v Karlshamns Oljefabriker (A/B)* [1949] A.C. 196 at 220–221; *Czarnikow (C.) Ltd v Koufos* [1969] 1 A.C. 350 at 414; *Johnson v Agnew* [1980] A.C. 367 at 400. The courts adopt a "net loss" approach, in which the gains made by the claimant as a result of the breach (*e.g.* expenditure avoided) must be set off against his losses arising from the breach: *Westwood v Secretary of State for Employment* [1985] A.C. 20 at 44.

[35] Fuller and Perdue, 46 Yale L.J. 52 at 373 (1937).

[36] See below, paras 16–052.

[37] *ibid.* See also Owen, 4 Oxford J.L.S. 393 (1984).

[38] Below, paras 17–046, 17–063, 17–064, 17–070.

[39] *Cullinane v British "Rema" Manufacturing Co.* [1954] 1 Q.B. 292 (discussed below, para.17–070).

[40] See below, paras 16–052 *et seq.*

[41] *CCC Films (London) Ltd v Impact Quadrant Films Ltd* [1985] Q.B. 16 at 30–32 (interpreting the *Cullinane* case, above, at p.303; and *Anglia Television Ltd v Reed* [1972] 1 Q.B. 60 at 63). The claimant need not show that he cannot prove any loss

Recent cases have recognized the "performance interest" of the promisee[43] as where the discretionary remedy of specific performance[44] forces the promisor to do exactly what he has undertaken to do. But the restitutionary remedy (an account of profits) granted by the House of Lords in *Attorney-General v Blake*[45] provides a monetary remedy to protect the promisee's interest in performance of the promise. However, apart from specific performance, the performance interest is unlikely to be protected in the sale of goods, where under the rules of mitigation,[46] substitute performance from a third party is usually available, with the result that the promisee's damages are usually assessed at much less than the full value which the promised performance would have given to the promisee.[47]

(b) *Liquidated Damages and Penalties*[48]

Clauses fixing sums payable upon breach. This and the following paragraphs deal with the common law, but there may be statutory provisions applicable to similar terms in a contract.[49] The terms of the contract may provide that, in the event of a breach,[50] one party shall pay to the other a specified sum of money[51]: but the sum will be classified as either a penalty (which is irrecoverable) or liquidated damages (which are recoverable).[52] If the amount was fixed as a deterrent to ensure that the promise was not broken, the courts hold that this is a penalty and that the promisee should receive by way of damages only that sum which will compensate him for his actual loss.[53] The test for liquidated damages is that 16–032

---

of net profits, or that any such loss would be small; but the defendant may show that the expenditure would not have been recouped from the claimant's expected gross return: *ibid*.

[42] See below, paras 17–090—17–092.

[43] *Att-Gen v Blake* [2001] 1 A.C. 268; *Experience Hendrix LLC v PPX Enterprises Inc. and Edward Chaplin* [2003] EWCA Civ. 323, [2003] 1 All E.R. (Comm) 830. See Chitty. *op. cit.* paras 26–020—26–026.

[44] Below, para.17–096.

[45] Above.

[46] Below, paras 16–052.

[47] Campbell and Harris, 22 (2002) J. Leg. Studies 208; Campbell 67 (2004) M.L.R. 817.

[48] The Law Commission, in Working Paper No. 61 (1975), has made tentative proposals for reform of the law on this topic.

[49] See below, paras 16–041, 16–042.

[50] See below, para.16–036.

[51] The CA has held that the law on penalties also applies to a clause which, upon breach, obliges the contract-breaker to transfer property: *Jobson v Johnson* [1989] 1 W.L.R. 1026.

[52] The purpose of fixing such a sum is to facilitate recovery of compensation without the difficulty and expense of proving actual damage: *Clydebank Engineering and Shipbuilding Co. Ltd v Don Jose Ramos Yzquierdo y Castaneda* [1905] A.C. 6 at 11. There may also be losses likely to be suffered by the innocent party which do not fall within the test for remoteness of damage (below, paras 16–043 *et seq.*): *Robert Stewart & Sons Ltd v Carapanayoti & Co. Ltd* [1962] 1 W.L.R. 34 at 39.

[53] The strict legal position, according to the CA, is that the promisee may sue on the penal clause, but that "it will not be enforced . . . beyond the sum which represents [his] actual loss": *Jobson v Johnson*, above, p.1040.

the sum is (or does not exceed) "a genuine pre-estimate of damage,"[54] whereas a penalty is not a genuine pre-estimate, but rather "a payment of money stipulated as *in terrorem*" of the contract-breaker.[55] The question is one "of construction to be decided upon the terms and inherent circumstances of each particular contract, judged of at the time of the making of the contract, not as at the time of the breach"[56]; but the precise words used by the parties are not conclusive.[57] Where the parties fix a graduated system of sums which depend on the relative seriousness of the expected breach, *e.g.* so much per week for delay in performance,[58] or so much according to the number of items in question,[59] it is likely to be upheld as liquidated damages.

16–033 The fact that the loss or damage would be difficult to assess with precision strengthens the presumption that the parties have made a genuine attempt to pre-estimate it and to overcome the difficulties of proof.[60] Thus, where the retail price of an article was about one shilling, the sum of £15 was upheld as liquidated damages due to the manufacturer in respect of each sale of the article at a price lower than that fixed in a resale price-maintenance agreement.[61] The parties may fix a sum as liquidated damages in the event of one specific breach, and leave the claimant to sue for unliquidated damages if other types of breach occur.[62]

---

[54] *Dunlop Pneumatic Tyre Co. Ltd v New Garage and Motor Co. Ltd* [1915] A.C. 79 at 86–88 (the whole passage is the *locus classicus*).

[55] *Clydebank Engineering and Shipbuilding Co. Ltd* case, above. See also *Bridge v Campbell Discount Co. Ltd* [1962] A.C. 600 at 622; *Cameron-Head v Cameron & Co.*, 1919 S.C. 627; *Photo Production Ltd v Securicor Transport Ltd* [1980] A.C. 827 at 850. According to the Privy Council, the law on penalties "is designed for the sole purpose of providing relief against oppression": *Philips Hong Kong Ltd v Att-Gen of Hong Kong* (1993) 61 Build. L.R. 49 at 58.

[56] *Dunlop Pneumatic Tyre Co.* case, above, at pp.86–87; *Public Works Commissioner v Hills* [1906] A.C. 368 at 376; *Webster v Bosanquet* [1912] A.C. 394. The courts have developed a number of presumptions to help in the construction of these clauses: *Dunlop Pneumatic Tyre Co.* case, above, at pp.87–88. See *Chitty on Contracts* (29th ed.), Vol. 1, para.26–110.

[57] *Dunlop Pneumatic Tyre Co.* case, above, at p.86; *Willson v Love* [1896] 1 Q.B. 626 at 630. See *Alder v Moore* [1961] 2 Q.B. 57 at 65; *Robert Stewart & Sons Ltd v Carapanayoti & Co. Ltd*, above.

[58] *Clydebank Engineering and Shipbuilding Co. Ltd* case, above. See also *Law v Redditch Local Board* [1892] 1 Q.B. 127; *Cellulose Acetate Silk Co. Ltd v Widnes Foundry* (1925) *Ltd* [1933] A.C. 20. *Cf. Suisse Atlantique Société d'Armement Maritime v NV Rotterdamsche Kolen Centrale* [1967] 1 A.C. 361 (demurrage clause).

[59] *Elphinstone v Monkland Iron and Coal Co.* (1886) 11 App.Cas. 332; *Diestal v Stevenson* [1906] 2 K.B. 345.

[60] *Dunlop Pneumatic Tyre Co. Ltd* case, above; *English Hop Growers Ltd v Dering* [1928] 2 K.B. 174; *Robophone Facilities Ltd v Blank* [1966] 1 W.L.R. 1428 at 1447.

[61] *Imperial Tobacco Co. Ltd v Parslay* [1936] 2 All E.R. 515.

[62] *e.g. Aktieselskabet Reidar v Arcos Ltd* [1927] 1 K.B. 352. An agreed damages clause does not bar the remedy of rejection of the goods: above, para.13–036. The claimant may, in appropriate circumstances, obtain an injunction instead of enforcing the liquidated damages clause: but he cannot have both an injunction and liquidated damages in respect of a single breach: *Sainter v Ferguson* (1849) 1 Mac. & G. 286; *Carnes v Nesbitt* (1862) 7 H. & N. 778; *General Accident Insurance Co. v Noel* [1902] 1 K.B. 377. *Cf. Imperial Tobacco Co. Ltd v Parslay*, above (injunction granted and damages awarded for different breaches).

Single sum payable upon different breaches. The mere fact that the same sum is made payable upon the breach of several contractual obligations of varying importance is by no means conclusive,[63] since it may be that the sum is not disproportionate to the least important of these obligations and therefore represents a genuine attempt at an agreed estimate of likely loss.[64] In *Dunlop Pneumatic Tyre Co. Ltd v New Garage and Motor Co. Ltd*,[65] dealers in tyres agreed not to resell any tyres bought from the manufacturers to any private customers at less than the manufacturers' current list prices, nor to supply them to persons whose supplies the manufacturers had decided to suspend, nor to exhibit or export them without the manufacturers' consent; they also agreed to pay £5 by way of liquidated damages for every tyre sold or offered in breach of the agreement. It was held by the House of Lords that the £5 was not a penalty and was therefore recoverable as liquidated damages.[66] However, this decision should be contrasted with *Ford Motor Co. v Armstrong*,[67] where a retailer in a similar case agreed to pay £250 as "the agreed damage which the manufacturer will sustain" upon the breach of any one of several covenants (similar to those in the *Dunlop* case, above), and the Court of Appeal, by a majority, held that this was a penalty: it was an arbitrary and substantial sum, and was payable for various breaches differing in kind, some of which might cause only trifling damage. 16–034

The scope of the law on penalties. If the contract fixes a sum (a debt) which is payable in return for performance of the other party's obligation, the sum cannot be a penalty.[68] Similarly, the House of Lords has held that the law as to penalties is not applicable to a clause providing for payment of money upon the happening of a specified event other than a breach of a contractual duty owed by the contemplated payor to the contemplated payee.[69] Thus, the law on penalties did not apply to a contractual undertaking by the defendants to reimburse the claimants the amount paid by them to third parties under a guarantee (even where the claimants' obligation to meet the guarantee arose in the event of breach by the defendants of contractual duties owed to other parties).[70] Although this case concerned a guarantee, their Lordships' limitation on the scope of the law on penalties was expressed in such wide terms that it would prevent 16–035

---

[63] *cf. Dunlop Pneumatic Tyre Co. Ltd* case above, at p.87 (proposition 4(c)).

[64] *Wallis v Smith* (1882) 21 Ch.D. 243; *Pye v British Automobile Commercial Syndicate Ltd* [1906] 1 K.B. 425.

[65] [1915] A.C. 79.

[66] The House of Lords took the view that the £5 did not apply to the second and third obligations (not to sell to prohibited person, and not to exhibit without permission).

[67] (1915) 31 T.L.R. 267.

[68] *White and Carter (Councils) Ltd v McGregor* [1962] A.C. 413 at 427 (below, para.16–059). The contrast between a debt and liquidated damages is drawn by the HL in *President of India v Lips Maritime Corporation* [1988] A.C. 395 at 422–423, 424. But see Law Commission Working Paper No. 61 (1975) paras 17–26.

[69] *Export Credit Guarantee Department v Universal Oil Products Co.* [1983] 1 W.L.R. 399.

[70] *ibid.* But there may be a "disguised penalty clause": *Interfoto Picture Library Ltd v Stiletto Visual Programmes Ltd* [1988] 1 All E.R. 348 at 358.

many other clauses[71] from being subject to that law, *e.g.* a clause under a hire-purchase agreement which permitted the hirer at his option to terminate the hiring prematurely, but which obliged him thereupon to pay a sum by way of agreed compensation for "depreciation" of the chattel.[72] But it seems unfortunate that the law on penalties may protect the person who deliberately breaks his contractual obligations, but not the honest man who terminates the contract (under an express power to do so) when he finds that he is unable to fulfil his remaining obligations.[73]

The law on penalties may apply to an obligation to transfer property to the innocent party,[74] but it does not apply, as such, to "forfeiture" clauses, in respect of which a limited form of relief may be available.[75] But the law on penalties may apply to a clause which entitles the innocent party to withhold a payment which would otherwise be due to the contract-breaker.[76] An express power to terminate the contract following breach of a term classified as a condition[77] entitles the innocent party both to terminate and to sue for damages for loss of the contract as a whole,[78] not simply for loss suffered through any breaches up to the date of the termination[79]: the law on penalties does not apply to such a clause.[80]

16–036 **Clauses limiting liability.** The parties may fix a limit[81] to the damages recoverable for a breach of their contract,[82] and may fix a definite sum for the same purpose.[83] If the parties could foresee (at the time of making the contract) that the loss caused by a breach was likely to exceed the sum fixed

[71] The death or bankruptcy of a party might be another event, not constituting a breach, upon which money is to be paid.

[72] *Campbell Discount Co. Ltd v Bridge* [1961] 1 Q.B. 445 (on appeal a different view was taken of the facts: [1962] A.C. 600; but four of their Lordships *obiter* considered the issue. It is unfortunate that the short speech in the *Export Credit Guarantee* case, above, made no attempt to discuss these opinions.) *Cf. Adler v Moore* [1961] 2 Q.B. 57 (repayment of money paid by insurers on the basis of an undertaking to repay it in specified circumstances).

[73] Statutory controls may, however, apply, *e.g.* the Consumer Credit Act 1974, ss.99 and 100. See also below, para.16–041.

[74] See above, para.16–032, n.51; *cf. Forestry Commission of NSW v Stefanetto* (1976) 133 C.L.R. 507.

[75] Below, paras 16–038—16–039. On "acceleration" clauses, see Chitty, *op. cit.*, para.26–122.

[76] *Gilbert Ash (Northern) Ltd v Modern Engineering (Bristol) Ltd* [1974] A.C. 689.

[77] *Viz.* where *any* breach of the term entitles the innocent party to terminate, *e.g.* a clause making compliance with time "of the essence".

[78] *Viz.* in respect of all the outstanding obligations of the contract breaker.

[79] *Lombard North Central Plc v Butterworth* [1987] Q.B. 527. See Treitel [1987] L.M.C.L.Q. 143; Beale (1988) 104 L.Q.R. 355; and Chitty, *op. cit.*, para.27–123.

[80] The *Lombard* case, above. Agreed damages clauses do not bar the remedy of rejection of the goods. Above, para.13–036.

[81] For clauses excluding liability, see above, Ch.13.

[82] See above, para.13–036.

[83] *Cellulose Acetate Silk Co. Ltd v Widnes Foundry (1925) Ltd* [1933] A.C. 20. Such clauses may be subject to the provisions of the Unfair Contract Terms Act 1977 (above, paras 13–036, 13–062 *et seq.*). See *St Albans City Council v International Computers Ltd* [1996] 4 All E.R. 481.

as damages, the courts may construe[84] the clause as one placing an agreed limitation on the extent of the liability of the contract-breaker.[85]

16–037 **"Invoicing back" clauses.** The express terms of the contract may not only exclude or limit the innocent party's right to claim damages for breach of contract,[86] but may also provide other provisions intended to apply in the event of a breach. Subject to the law as to penalties,[87] and to the provisions of the Unfair Contract Terms Act 1977,[88] the courts will enforce these terms, despite the unexpected results which may occur. In one case,[89] a clause in a contract for the sale of goods provided that if the sellers made default in shipping, the contract should "be closed by invoicing back the goods" at the closing price fixed by the London Corn Trade Association. The sellers failed to ship, and the Association declared a closing price, which, because of a fall in market price, was lower than the contract price, so that a balance was due in favour of the sellers. Nevertheless, the Court of Appeal enforced the clause, despite the fact that the sellers were the party in default.[90] But an "invoicing back" clause may not be interpreted as the exclusive remedy,[91] *e.g.* the clause may not prevent the buyer obtaining damages for his loss of profits,[92] and the judges have interpreted such clauses restrictively.[93] An "invoicing back" clause may also allow a percent-

[84] *cf.* the rule that the effect of an exemption clause depends on the construction of the contract: *Suisse Atlantique Société d'Armement Maritime v NV Rotterdamsche Kolen Centrale* [1967] 1 A.C. 361 (above, paras 13–045—13–047); *Photo Production Ltd v Securicor Transport Ltd* [1980] A.C. 827 (above, paras 13–047 *et seq.*).

[85] *Cellulose Acetate Silk Co. Ltd v Widnes Foundry (1925) Ltd*, above. *Cf. Diestal v Stevenson* [1906] 2 K.B. 345; *Biggin & Co. Ltd v Permanite Ltd* [1951] 1 K.B. 422 at 436 (reversed on another ground [1951] 2 K.B. 314); *Elphinstone v Monkland Iron and Coal Co.* (1886) 11 App.Cas. 332 at 346. (There is a special rule applicable for such clauses in charter-parties: *Wall v Rederiaktiebolaget Luggude* [1915] 3 K.B. 66 (approved by the House of Lords in *Watts, Watts & Co. Ltd v Mitsui & Co. Ltd* [1917] A.C. 277); but *cf.* the *Suisse Atlantique* case, above.)

[86] On exemption clauses, see Ch.13, above.

[87] Above, paras 16–032 *et seq.*

[88] See above, paras 13–008, 13–062 *et seq.* Invoicing back clauses are not likely to affect consumer contracts: below, para.16–041.

[89] *Lancaster v J F Turner & Co. Ltd* [1924] 2 K.B. 222 (Scrutton L.J. dissenting); followed in *Adair (J F) & Co. Ltd v Birnbaum* [1939] 2 K.B. 149 (and the earlier case noted *ibid.*, at p.173); *Podar Trading Co. Ltd v François Tagher* [1949] 2 All E.R. 62; *Cf. Laing, Son & Co. Ltd v Eastcheap Dried Fruit Co. Ltd* [1961] 2 Lloyd's Rep. 277.

[90] Some clauses are drafted differently and avoid this difficulty, *e.g.* the clause may apply only to the defaulting buyer, and only if the market price has fallen: *Alexandria Cotton and Trading Co. (Sudan) Ltd v Cotton Co. of Ethiopia Ltd* [1963] 1 Lloyd's Rep. 576.

[91] *Roth, Schmidt & Co. v D Nagase & Co. Ltd* (1920) 2 Ll.L.R. 36 (CA: the clause did not expressly exclude the right to reject the goods or to recover damages upon rejection).

[92] *Re Bourgeois and Wilson Holgate & Co.* (1920) 25 Com.Cas. 260 (the Court of Appeal decided in this case that the seller in these circumstances could not enforce the clause against the buyer).

[93] One judge has held that the interpretation of a clause which requires damages to be paid *to* the defaulting party is contrary to "natural justice": *Cassir, Moore & Co. Ltd v Eastcheap Dried Fruit Co.* [1962] 1 Lloyd's Rep. 400 at 402. See also the qualifications suggested in *Lancaster v J F Turner & Co. Ltd*, above, at p.231; *Adair (J F) & Co. Ltd v Birnbaum*, above, at p.169.

age of the market price to be added to, or deducted from, the price, which if reasonable, will be upheld as liquidated damages covering items of loss not covered by the price alone.[94]

16–038 **Purchase by instalments and pre-payment of price.** This, and the following paragraph, deal with the law apart from the Consumer Credit Act 1974[95] and the Unfair Terms in Consumer Contracts Regulations 1999.[96] A contract may, instead of fixing a sum to be paid upon breach, provide that a sum or sums already paid by the buyer (but not intended to be a deposit[97]) shall be forfeited[98] upon breach by the buyer.[99] For many years, the courts have been willing to grant relief against the "forfeiture" of a leasehold interest,[1] and against the "forfeiture" of instalments already paid under a contract to purchase land by instalment payments.[2] There is now a jurisdiction to grant a limited type of relief against "forfeiture" in a wider range of situations, including the sale of goods.[3] In *Stockloser v Johnson*[4] there was a provision, in a contract to purchase plant and machinery by instalment payments, that upon default by the buyer, the seller might rescind the contract and forfeit the instalments already paid. The majority of the Court of Appeal held that the court has an equitable jurisdiction to relieve against forfeiture of such instalments, even after termination of the contract, if in the actual circumstances of the case the clause was penal[5] and it would be oppressive and unconscionable for the seller to retain all the instalments. In cases not involving the sale of goods, the House of Lords has now upheld the jurisdiction to relieve against forfeiture, but limited it

---

94 *Robert Stewart & Sons Ltd v Carapanayoti & Co. Ltd* [1962] 1 W.L.R. 34.

95 See below, para.16–042.

96 See below para.16–041.

97 If the sum is a deposit paid by the buyer (*viz.* a sum intended to be received by the seller as a security for the completion of the purchase by the buyer) it will be assumed that it is intended to be forfeited to the seller if the buyer defaults: *Howe v Smith* (1884) 27 Ch.D. 89 at 97–98 (sale of land). See further above, paras 15–132—15–133.

98 The payee "forfeits" the sum when he retains it for his own beneficial use, having released himself from any further obligations under the contract by terminating it on account of the payer's breach.

99 A similar type of clause is one which entitles the innocent party to the re-transfer of property which, under the terms of the contract, he had previously transferred to the contract-breaker: *Jobson v Johnson* [1989] 1 W.L.R. 1026.

1 *Shiloh Spinners Ltd v Harding* [1973] A.C. 691. See also s.146 of the Law of Property Act 1925.

2 *Re Dagenham (Thames) Dock Co.* (1873) L.R. 8 Ch.App. 1022; *John H. Kilmer v British Columbia Orchard Lands Ltd* [1913] A.C. 319; *Steedman v Drinkle* [1916] 1 A.C. 275; *Mussen v Van Diemen's Land Co.* [1938] Ch. 253. See Lang 100 L.Q.R. 427 (1984); Chitty, *op. cit.*, para.26–128.

3 There were a number of cases concerning contracts for the sale of land where the equitable principle was accepted: *Re Dagenham (Thames) Dock Co.*, above; *Steedman v Drinkle*, above; *Mussen v Van Diemen's Land Co.*, above.

4 [1954] 1 Q.B. 476.

5 ". . . the forfeiture clause must be of a penal nature, in this sense, that the sum forfeited must be out of all proportion to the damage . . .": [1954] 1 Q.B. 476 at 490. (The test should be "*expected* damage," judged in the light of the circumstances at the time of making the contract: see above, para.16–032, text at n.56). But see now, below para.16–041.

to contracts concerning the transfer or creation of proprietary or possessory rights[6]; the Court of Appeal has granted relief (in the form of an extension of time within which a payment could be made by the defendant) in a commercial contract involving "forfeiture" of patent rights,[7] holding that the jurisdiction extends to relief in respect of interests in personal property.[8] Under the equitable principle the court will seldom do more than give the contract-breaker more time in which to pay the sum he had failed to pay on time: if he then pays within the time fixed by the court he will not forfeit the right which the contract made subject to forfeiture.[9] However, the Court of Appeal has granted another type of relief against a clause which required the contract-breaker, upon breach, to retransfer some property to the innocent party: the innocent party was given the option of accepting a sale of the property by the court, so that he could receive out of the proceeds the amount of his actual loss, leaving any balance to go to the contract-breaker.[10] Although in a sale of goods case the buyer's readiness and willingness to produce the balance of the purchase-money is not a condition precedent for relief,[11] the court will not be easily satisfied that the seller's conduct is unconscionable, especially where the buyer has had the use or benefit of the subject-matter of the contract over a period.[12] On the facts of *Stockloser v Johnson*, above, although the majority of the court treated the clause as penal, they did not think that the seller's conduct in retaining £4,750 out of the £11,000 price in one contract, and £3,500 out of the £11,000 price on another, was unconscionable, because the buyer had already received substantial benefits in the form of royalties.[13]

The courts will be more reluctant to allow recovery of money already paid by the party later in breach (*i.e.* affirmative relief) than to deny recovery of a sum agreed to be payable upon breach by the contract- **16–039**

---

[6] *Scandinavian Trading Tanker Co. AB v Flota Petrolera Ecuatoriana (The Scaptrade)* [1983] 2 A.C. 694 (shipowner's withdrawal of the vessel for failure to make punctual payment of hire under a time charter); *Sport Internationaal Bussum BV v Inter-Footwear Ltd* [1984] 1 W.L.R. 776 (forfeiture of "mere contractual licences" to use trade marks). See also *The Laconia* [1977] A.C. 850 at 869–870, 873–874, 878, 887. *Cf. Legione v Hateley* (1983) 46 A.L.R. 1 (High Ct. of Aust.).

[7] *BICC p.l.c. v Burndy Corporation* [1985] Ch. 232 (extension of time granted).

[8] *ibid.*, at p.252 (followed in *On Demand Information Plc v Michael Gerson (Finance) Plc* [2002] UKHL 13, [2003] 1 A.C. 368 (it is not a purely contractual right where the lessee is entitled to indefinite possession of chattels so long as he makes hire payments: *ibid.*). See also para.16–039, text at n.19.

[9] Occasionally, the court has ordered the return to the contract-breaker of money previously paid to the innocent party, subject to payment of damages for the actual loss caused by the breach: *Public Works Commissioner v Hills* [1906] A.C. 368.

[10] *Jobson v Johnson* [1989] 1 W.L.R. 1026. The other option offered to the innocent party was to accept an order for specific performance (*i.e.* to compel re-transfer of the property) if a court-directed inquiry showed that the present value of the property did not exceed the innocent party's actual loss.

[11] *Starside Properties Ltd v Mustapha* [1974] 1 W.L.R. 816.

[12] *Stockloser v Johnson*, above. (Whether the seller's conduct is unconscionable or not must be judged as at the time of the suit: *ibid.* at pp.488, 492); *Campbell Discount Co. Ltd v Bridge* [1961] 1 Q.B. 445 (appeal allowed on a different view of the facts: [1962] A.C. 600.)

[13] [1954] 1 Q.B. 476 at 484, 492. *Cf.* below para.16–041.

breaker (*i.e.* negative relief) or to give more time to the party in breach.[14] Several cases,[15] however, indicate that the courts are very reluctant to exercise the equitable jurisdiction, and there is no reported case in which the principle has been positively applied to grant relief to a buyer of goods. In a case at first instance relief was denied to the hirer of a caravan, although the terms of the contract were "hideously harsh",[16] because the owner had not been guilty of any fraud, sharp practice or unconscionable conduct at the time of entering into the contract. But the Court of Appeal has accepted that if, under a contract to purchase by instalment payments, the purchaser defaulted in payment of an instalment of the price, the court has jurisdiction in a proper case to relieve the buyer against forfeiture of the instalments already paid, by granting an extension of time to him within which he could pay.[17] One of the conditions before equitable relief may be granted is that the forfeiture clause was inserted in order "to secure a stated result which can effectively be attained when the matter comes before the court, and where the forfeiture provision is added by way of security for the production of that result."[18] Possession of chattels by a lessee under a finance lease is capable of attracting relief against forfeiture; the sale of the chattels under an interim order of the court does not prejudice the granting of relief, since the proceeds of sale stand in the place of the chattels.[19]

16–040 **Recovery of instalments in the absence of a forfeiture clause.** If in a contract for sale there is no such forfeiture clause as has been discussed in the preceding paragraph, and the seller terminates the contract upon the buyer's default, the buyer may recover any prepayment or instalments in part payment of the price, subject to a counterclaim by the seller for damages for the breach of contract.[20] Thus, in one case, despite the buyer's

---

[14] *Starside Properties Ltd v Mustapha*, above. However, in a case on the forfeiture of a "deposit", the Privy Council has equated a "forfeiture" clause with a "penalty" clause (the deposit was unreasonable in amount): *Workers Trust and Merchant Bank Ltd v Dojap Investments Ltd* [1993] A.C. 573.

[15] *Campbell Discount Co. Ltd v Bridge* [1961] 1 Q.B. 445, CA (in the House of Lords their Lordships did not advert to this point: [1962] A.C. 600); *Galbraith v Mitchenhall Estates Ltd* [1965] 2 Q.B. 473 (which is strongly criticised by *McGregor on Damages* (17th ed.), paras 13–086—13–088).

[16] *Galbraith v Mitchenhall Estates Ltd*, above, at p.480.

[17] *Starside Properties Ltd v Mustapha*, above (see 37 M.L.R. 705 (1974); [1974] C.L.J. 209). An extension of time was the remedy granted in the *BICC* case, above, n.7.

[18] *Shiloh Spinners Ltd v Harding* [1973] A.C. 691 at 723 (as interpreted in the *Sport Internationaal Bussum* case, above, at p.785 and in the case cited in n.19).

[19] *On Demand Information Plc v Michael Gerson (Finance) Plc* [2002] UKHL 13, [2003] 1 A.C. 368 (it did not matter that the lessee could not be restored to possession: relief was given by ordering the proportions in which the parties were entitled to the proceeds of sale).

[20] On the sale of goods: *Dies v British and International Mining and Finance Corporation Ltd* [1939] 1 K.B. 724 (distinguished in *Hyundai Heavy Industries Co. Ltd v Papadopoulos* [1980] 1 W.L.R. 1129 (HL: shipbuilding contract)); *Stockloser v Johnson* [1954] 1 Q.B. 476 at 483, 489–490. For analogous cases on the sale of land, see *Palmer v Temple* (1839) 9 A. & E. 508; *Mayson v Clouet* [1924] A.C. 980, PC; *Williams on Vendor and Purchaser* (4th ed.), p.1006. *Cf. Rover International Ltd v Cannon Film Sales Ltd* [1989] 1 W.L.R. 912 at 930–932, 936–937.

repudiation of his contract to buy goods, he was held to be entitled to recover a substantial prepayment (not in the nature of a deposit)[21] made by him, subject to a deduction in respect of the actual loss suffered by the seller through the breach of contract: the court held that if it permitted the whole prepayment to be retained by the seller, it would be permitting the retention of a penalty, not liquidated damages.[22] This decision has been distinguished by two of their Lordships in the House of Lords[23] on the ground that it concerned a sale of existing goods where no expenditure was intended to be incurred by the seller in reliance on the advance payment. It has been persuasively argued[24] that the question should depend on the construction of the clause in the contract requiring the advance payment: was the right to retain the payment intended to be conditional upon performance by the payee of his obligations, or was it intended to be a security for performance of the payer's obligations?

The Unfair Terms in Consumer Contracts Regulations 1999.[25] These regulations provide that in a contract between a business and a consumer an "unfair term" will not be binding on the consumer.[26] The Regulations give illustrations of terms which will *prima facie* be regarded as unfair: relevant to clauses fixing damages is "(e) requiring any consumer who fails to fulfil his obligation to pay a disproportionately high sum in compensation." So a consumer will be able to appeal to this standard, as well as to the common law on penalties. 16–041

The Consumer Credit Act 1974. A few of the problems created by contractual provisions requiring payments on the occurrence of specified events will be governed by the Consumer Credit Act 1974.[27] For instance, section 100(1) provides that where a debtor under (*inter alia*) a regulated conditional sale agreement[28] has exercised his statutory power to terminate the agreement, he shall be liable to pay the difference between the sums already paid or payable by him and one-half of the total price; but by section 100(3) the court may order payment of a smaller sum if that would be equal to the loss sustained by the creditor. The court is also empowered to reopen a credit agreement "on the ground that the credit bargain was extortionate",[29] and may set aside the whole or part of any obligation 16–042

---

[21] See above, paras 15–132—15–133.
[22] *Dies v British and International Mining and Finance Corporation Ltd*, above.
[23] *Hyundai Heavy Industries Co. Ltd v Papadopoulos* above, at pp.1142–1143, 1147–1148. (The contract in this case was for work and material supplied in the course of building a ship, and so it was treated as analogous to a building contract.)
[24] Beatson (1981) 97 L.Q.R. 389. See also *McDonald v Dennys Lascelles Ltd* (1933) 48 C.L.R. 457 at 477; and the *Fibrosa* case [1943] A.C. 32 at 65.
[25] SI 1999/2083 (replacing SI 1994/3159).
[26] See above, paras 13–103, 14–030 *et seq.*
[27] See paras 14–143 *et seq.* But the Act does not deal with provisions for the forfeiture of instalments already paid.
[28] Definitions of these agreements are examined above in paras 14–147, 14–148.
[29] ss.137–140. (s.138(1) provides *inter alia* that a credit bargain is extortionate if it requires the debtor to make payments (whether conditionally, or on certain contingencies) which are grossly exorbitant.) These provisions do not apply where the debtor is a body corporate.

imposed on the debtor, or may require the creditor to repay the whole or part of any sum paid by the debtor.[30] This Act will therefore cover some of the situations which arise in practice, and the common law and equitable rules will not need to be applied.

(c) *Remoteness of Damage and Causation*

16–043 **Remoteness of damage.** The Sale of Goods Act 1979 lays down the basic principle for remoteness of damage in language derived from the leading case of *Hadley v Baxendale*[31] where the main proposition was: "Where two parties have made a contract which one of them has broken, the damages which the other party ought to receive in respect of such breach of contract should be such as may fairly and reasonably be considered either as arising naturally, *i.e.* according to the usual course of things, from such breach of contract itself, or such as may reasonably be supposed to have been in the contemplation of both parties, at the time they made the contract, as the probable result of the breach of it."[32] In the Act, the language of section 50(2) is: "The measure of damages is the estimated loss directly and naturally resulting,[33] in the ordinary course of events, from the buyer's breach of contract."[34]

The principles in *Hadley v Baxendale*, above, have been interpreted and restated in the Court of Appeal in 1949[35] and in 1978,[36] and in the House of Lords in 1967. The language used in the latter case, *Koufos v C Czarnikow Ltd*,[37] has departed somewhat from the language used in the Act (*e.g.* the word "directly" is not used, and some emphasis is placed on the "reasonable contemplation" of the parties), but it is submitted that the courts, when interpreting the Act, will be strongly influenced by the common law on remoteness of damage. Although their Lordships did not agree upon a common formula,[38] their slightly differing formulations of the common law principle for remoteness of damage in contract are still based on *Hadley v Baxendale*, above. Lord Reid said that Alderson B. in *Hadley v Baxendale* "clearly meant that a result which will happen in the great majority[39] of

---

[30] s.139(2).

[31] (1854) 9 Exch. 341. (For a discussion of this case, see Chitty, *op. cit.*, Vol. 1, paras 26–045 *et seq.*; *McGregor on Damages* (17th ed.), paras 6–146 *et seq.*).

[32] (1854) 9 Exch. 341 at 354 (*per* Alderson B.).

[33] On causation, see below, para.16–049.

[34] A similar provision in s.51(2) is enacted for the seller's breach. See below, paras 17–021 *et seq.*

[35] *Victoria Laundry (Windsor) Ltd v Newman Industries Ltd* [1949] 2 K.B. 528 (below, paras 17–040—17–041). (Some of the propositions in this case were cited with approval in *East Ham Corporation v Bernard Sunley & Sons Ltd* [1966] A.C. 406 at 440, 445, 450–451, as well as in *Koufos v C Czarnikow Ltd*, below.).

[36] *Parsons (H.) (Livestock) Ltd v Uttley Ingham & Co. Ltd* [1978] Q.B. 791. See also *Brown v KMR Services Ltd* [1995] 4 All E.R. 598 at 621, 642–643; *Kpohraror v Woolwich Building Society* [1996] 4 All E.R. 119.

[37] [1969] 1 A.C. 350. (The case is also known as "*The Heron II.*")

[38] Lords Morris (p.399), Hodson (pp.410–411) and Pearce (pp.414, 415, 417) gave general approval to the propositions of the Court of Appeal in the *Victoria Laundry* case, above; but Lord Reid (pp.389, 390) rejected parts of these propositions. See *Aruna Mills Ltd v Dhanrajmal Gobindram* [1968] 1 Q.B. 655 at 668.

[39] Lord Hodson [1969] 1 A.C. 350 at 411, also adopted the expression used in *Hadley v Baxendale*, above, "in the great multitude of cases": (1854) 9 Exch. 341 at 355, 356.

cases should fairly and reasonably be regarded as having been in the contemplation of the parties, but that a result which, though foreseeable as a substantial possibility, would only happen in a small minority of cases should not be regarded as having been in their contemplation."[40] Lord Reid continued: "The crucial question is whether, on the information available to the defendant when the contract was made, he should, or the reasonable man in his position would, have realised that such loss was sufficiently likely to result from the breach of contract to make it proper to hold that the loss flowed naturally from the breach or that loss of that kind should have been within his contemplation."[41] Lord Upjohn stated "the broad rule as follows: What was in the assumed contemplation of both parties acting as reasonable men in the light of the general or special facts (as the case may be) known to both parties in regard to damages as the result of a breach of contract."[42]

It is irrelevant that the potential contract-breaker could not contemplate, at the time the contract was made, the occurrence of the particular breach he would later commit; the test of remoteness *assumes* contemplation of the actual breach, and looks at the consequences of the breach.[43] Moreover, ". . . the party who has suffered damage does not have to show that the contract-breaker ought to have contemplated, as being not unlikely, the precise detail of the damage or the precise manner of its happening. It is enough if he should have contemplated that damage *of that kind* is not unlikely."[44] If the parties ought to have contemplated a particular type of loss ("head of damage") they need not have contemplated the extent of that loss.[45]

It is submitted that the statements of the common law set out in the preceding paragraphs may be used to elucidate the meaning of "directly and naturally resulting, in the ordinary course of events," found in sections

---

[40] [1969] 1 A.C. 350 at 384. Both Lords Reid and Upjohn criticised the words "foreseeable" or "reasonably foreseeable" in the *Victoria Laundry* formulations: *ibid.*, at pp.389, 423; Lord Upjohn, at pp.422–423, expressly preferred "contemplate" or "contemplation" for cases in contract, and these are the words used by Lord Reid at pp.384, 385.

[41] *ibid.*, at p.385.

[42] *ibid.*, at p.424.

[43] *Christopher Hill Ltd v Ashington Piggeries Ltd* [1969] 3 All E.R. 1496 at 1523 (CA, interpreting *Koufos v C Czarnikow Ltd*, above; the House of Lords reversed the decision on other grounds, without discussing the *Koufos* decision: [1972] A.C. 441); *Parsons (H) (Livestock) Ltd v Uttley Ingham & Co. Ltd*, above.

[44] *Christopher Hill Ltd v Ashington Piggeries Ltd*, above, at p.1524, CA; *Brown v KMR Services Ltd* [1995] 4 All E.R. 598 at 621; *Kpohraror v Woolwich Building Society* [1996] 4 All E.R. 119. See also *Koufos v C. Czarnikow Ltd*, above, at p.417 (Alderson B. in *Hadley v Baxendale* "was thinking of causation and type of consequence . . .": *per* Lord Pearce). The categorisation of loss into "types" or "kinds" is illustrated by *Balfour Beatty Construction (Scotland) Ltd v Scottish Power Plc* 1994 S.L.T. 807, HL.

[45] *Parsons (H) (Livestock) Ltd v Uttley Ingham & Co. Ltd*, above, at pp.804, 813. *Cf. Wroth v Tyler*, above, at pp.60–62 (on the "second rule" in *Hadley v Baxendale*, above). But see the cases on loss of profits, below, paras 17–040—17–042; and *cf. South Australia Asset Management Corporation v York Montague Ltd* [1997] A.C. 191; *Vacwell Engineering Co. Ltd v BDH Chemicals Ltd* [1971] 1 Q.B. 88.

50(2) and 51(2) of the Act.[46] The detailed examination of the cases decided under these sections will be found in later paragraphs.[47]

16–044 **The degree of probability.** The Sale of Goods Act 1979, in sections 50(2) and 51(2), above, does not give much guidance on the question of how likely a type of loss must be to satisfy the statutory test, and it is submitted that, in this respect also, the common law cases are persuasive authorities. What was in the contemplation of reasonable men obviously depends on the relevant degree of likelihood that the particular kind of loss may occur, and this issue was extensively discussed in *Koufos v C Czarnikow Ltd*, above. Lord Reid used "the words 'not unlikely' as denoting a degree of probability considerably less than an even chance but nevertheless not very unusual and easily foreseeable."[48] Although Lord Morris thought it unnecessary to choose any one phrase[49] he used "not unlikely to occur",[50] with "liable to result" as an alternative[51]; Lord Hodson accepted the latter phrase.[52] Both Lords Pearce[53] and Upjohn[54] adopted the words "a real danger" or "a serious possibility".[55]

16–045 **Imputed knowledge.** The main illustration of the principle of imputed knowledge is that, as recognised by the Act,[56] in contracts for the sale of goods, the defendant is taken to have known that the market price and the supply and demand of the market may change.[57] Usually, the imputed knowledge of the contract-breaker will be at least as great as (if not greater than) his actual knowledge. Thus, it is necessary to consider the actual knowledge[58] of the defendant only where he would not have been liable without that knowledge.

Lord Wright[59] has said that the test for imputed knowledge is "what reasonable business men must be taken to have contemplated as the natural

---

[46] The words "arising naturally" used in *Hadley v Baxendale*, above, were criticised by Lord Sumner in *Weld-Blundell v Stephens* [1920] A.C. 956 at 983.
[47] Below, paras 16–077—16–079, 17–021 *et seq*.
[48] [1969] 1 A.C. 350 at 383. (See also his statement at p.388: "a very substantial degree of probability").
[49] *ibid*., at pp.397, 400.
[50] *ibid*., at p.406.
[51] *ibid*., at p.406. ("Liable to result" was also one of the phrases accepted in the *Victoria Laundry* case, [1949] 2 K.B. 528 at 540.)
[52] [1969] 1 A.C. 350 at 410–411. (But Lord Reid, at p.389, rejected this phrase.)
[53] *ibid*., at p.415.
[54] *ibid*., at p.425.
[55] The *Victoria Laundry* case, above, at p.540, also accepted "a real danger" or "a serious possibility." See also *Parsons (H) (Livestock) Ltd v Uttley Ingham & Co. Ltd* [1978] Q.B. 791 at 807 ("What is meant by a 'serious possibility' is . . . ultimately a question of fact"). The two phrases accepted by Lords Pearce and Upjohn were rejected by Lord Reid (at p.390 of the *Koufos* case), who also rejected "foreseeable as a real possibility" (at p.385). Four of their Lordships agreed that the colloquialism "on the cards" should not be used: *ibid*., at pp.390, 399, 415, 425. (This was yet another phrase used in the *Victoria Laundry* case, above, at p.540.)
[56] ss.50(3) and 51(3) (below, paras 16–061 *et seq*.; paras 17–001 *et seq*.).
[57] *Interoffice Telephones Ltd v Robert Freeman Co. Ltd* [1958] 1 Q.B. 190 at 202. The same holds for contracts for the carriage of goods: *Koufos v C Czarnikow Ltd* [1969] 1 A.C. 350.
[58] See below, para.16–046.
[59] *Monarch Steamship Co. Ltd v Karlshamns Oljefabriker (A/B)* [1949] A.C. 196 at 224.

and probable result if the contract was broken. As reasonable business men, each must be taken to understand the ordinary practices and exigencies of the other's trade or business." Thus, a buyer or seller of goods normally knows more about the other's business than the carrier of goods knows about the business of the consignor or the consignee,[60] or than the seller of land knows about the intentions of the purchaser to use it in a particular way.[61] Another illustration of imputed knowledge is where the seller delays in delivering a profit-earning chattel: the buyer can normally claim loss of profits during the period of the delay.[62] The seller's knowledge that his breach is not unlikely to cause the buyer loss of profits is greater in the case of a profit-earning chattel which is an integral whole than it is for part of the whole.[63]

Actual knowledge of special circumstances. The so-called second rule in *Hadley v Baxendale*, above, applies when the loss (the "type or kind of loss"[64]) caused by the breach of contract is greater than, or different from, what it would have been in "normal" circumstances. The rule is that ". . . if the special circumstances under which the contract was actually made were communicated by the plaintiffs to the defendants, and thus known to both parties, the damages resulting from the breach of such a contract, which they would reasonably contemplate, would be the amount of injury which would ordinarily follow from a breach of contract under these special circumstances so known and communicated."[65] This "second rule" is not expressly incorporated in the Sale of Goods Act 1979, but it is submitted that it is impliedly accepted by the wording of section 54: "Nothing in this Act affects the right of the buyer or the seller to recover . . . special damages in any case where by law . . . special damages may be recoverable. . ." 16–046

Where actual knowledge of the contract-breaker is relied upon to make him liable for abnormal losses caused by the breach, it must be shown that he had that knowledge at the time the contract was made.[66] It is submitted that mere knowledge of the special circumstances is an insufficient basis for

[60] *Koufos v C. Czarnikow Ltd*, above, at p.424; *Victoria Laundry (Windsor) Ltd v Newman Industries Ltd* [1949] 2 K.B. 528 at 537.

[61] *Diamond v Campbell-Jones* [1961] Ch. 22 at 35–36.

[62] See below, paras 17–040—17–043.

[63] *Victoria Laundry (Windsor) Ltd v Newman Industries Ltd*, above, at pp.543–544. (See below, paras 17–040—17–041).

[64] *Wroth v Tyler* [1974] Ch. 30 at 61; It is unnecessary for the parties to have contemplated the *extent* of the loss, provided it falls within the contemplated *type* of loss: *ibid.*, at pp.60–62. *Jackson v Royal Bank of Scotland* [2005] UKHL 3, [2005] 1 W.L.R. 377 at [36]. But *cf.* cases on loss of profits, (below, paras 17–040—17–042); and the case on the limitation of a negligent valuer's liability, *South Australia Asset Management Corporation v York Montague Ltd* [1997] A.C. 191.

[65] (1854) 9 Exch. 341 at 354–355. See also *Wroth v Tyler*, above, at pp.60–62; *Jackson v Royal Bank of Scotland*, above, at [46–49].

[66] *Victoria Laundry (Windsor) Ltd v Newman Industries Ltd*, above, at p.539 (Proposition 3); *Jackson v Royal Bank of Scotland* [2005] UKHL 3, [2005] 1 W.L.R 377, at [35–36]. See also *Hydraulic Engineering Co. Ltd v McHaffie Goslett & Co.* (1878) 4 Q.B.D. 670 at 676. *Cf. Kellman v Watts* [1963] V.L.R. 396 (knowledge acquired *after* contract made).

holding the contract-breaker liable under the second rule in *Hadley v Baxendale*.[67] It has been said that: "The knowledge must be brought home to the party sought to be charged, under such circumstances that he must know that the person he contracts with reasonably believes that he accepts the contract with the special condition attached to it . . ."[68] But it is submitted that it is too stringent a test to require an express or implied term of the contract making the potential contract-breaker liable for the unusual loss resulting from the special circumstances known to him.[69] The defendant, despite his actual knowledge of special circumstances, should not be liable for an unusual loss if either (a) it was clear from all the circumstances that the defendant—to the knowledge of the claimant—did not wish to accept the risk of the unusual loss[70]; or (b) it was clear from all the circumstances that a reasonable man in the defendant's position would not, despite his knowledge of the special circumstances, have accepted the risk of the unusual loss.[71] It is essential that there should be communication of the special circumstances by or on behalf of the claimant to the defendant or his agent so as to show that the claimant thought it important that the defendant should know which other matters depended on his fulfilment of the contract; these facts may, in appropriate circumstances, lead to the inference that the defendant, as a reasonable man, was (by making this contract) implicitly accepting the risk of this unusual loss to the claimant.[72] The cases on sub-sales, considered in a later chapter, provide a good illustration of this principle.[73]

Sometimes, actual knowledge of special circumstances may operate in favour of the contract-breaker, *e.g.* if the parties knew that the extent of the buyer's loss from breach would be the amount of his liability to his sub-

---

[67] *Horne v Midland Ry* (1873) L.R. 8 C.P. 136 at 139, 141, 145, 146–147 (*cf.* at first instance (1872) L.R. 7 C.P. 583 at 591–592); *Elbinger Aktiengesellschaft v Armstrong* (1874) L.R. 9 Q.B. 473 at 478; *Victoria Laundry (Windsor) Ltd v Newman Industries Ltd*, above, at p.538. *Cf. Patrick v Russo-British Grain Export Co. Ltd* [1927] 2 K.B. 535 at 540.

[68] *British Columbia, etc., Saw Mill Co. Ltd v Nettleship* (1868) L.R. 3 C.P. 499 at 509. (But see the CA's criticism of this approach in *GKN Centrax Gears Ltd v Matbro Ltd* [1976] 2 Lloyd's Rep. 555 at 574, 579–580).

[69] *Koufos v C Czarnikow Ltd* [1969] 1 A.C. 350 at 422; *Satef-Huttenes Albertus SpA v Paloma Tercera Shipping Co. SA* [1981] 1 Lloyd's Rep. 175 at 183–184.

[70] With knowledge of the special circumstances, the defendant has the opportunity to protect himself by an exemption clause, or to increase the price he seeks for accepting a higher than usual risk.

[71] See the formulation in the *Satef-Huttenes* case, above, at pp.183, 184. *Cf. Robophone Facilities Ltd v Blank* [1966] 1 W.L.R. 1428 at 1437, 1448; *Koufos v C Czarnikow Ltd*, above, at p.385.

[72] *Muhammad Issa el Sheikh Ahmad v Ali* [1947] A.C. 414 at 427 (impecuniosity of one party: see below, para.16–054); *Trans Trust SPRL v Danubian Trading Co. Ltd* [1952] 2 Q.B. 297; *Panalpina International Transport Ltd v Densil Underwear Ltd* [1981] 1 Lloyd's Rep. 187 at 191; *Wadsworth v Lydall* [1981] 1 W.L.R. 598 (upheld by HL in *The President of India* case [1985] A.C. 104 at 125–127). *Cf. Aruna Mills Ltd v Dhanrajmal Gobindram* [1968] 1 Q.B. 655 (risk of devaluation of Indian rupee was in the contemplation of the parties: see below, para.17–046).

[73] Below, paras 17–028—17–036, 17–044—17–045, 17–076—17–084. See also above, para.16–007, text at n.45.

buyer, but the latter in fact makes no claim against the buyer.[74]"Of course the extension of the horizon need not always *increase* the damages; it might introduce a knowledge of particular circumstances, *e.g.* a sub-contract, which show that the plaintiff would in fact suffer *less* damage than a more limited view of the circumstances might lead one to expect."[75]

Non-pecuniary losses. Although damages for breach of contract normally relate to financial loss, non-pecuniary losses may be recovered if they were within the contemplation of the parties as not unlikely to result from the breach. If the defendant's breach of contract caused physical injury to the claimant himself,[76] or to his property,[77] the claimant may recover damages for that injury, provided the test for remoteness is satisfied. Damages for personal injury caused by breach of contract may include compensation for pain and suffering, and loss of amenity, as well as loss of earnings, which are normal heads of damages in the assessment of damages in tort for such injuries. Similarly, where the breach of contract involves the claimant in substantial physical inconvenience or discomfort, the defendant will be liable in damages,[78] but this will seldom arise in the sale of goods. A further development allows the award of damages for "loss of amenity" when an important purpose of the contract was to provide that amenity to the claimant.[79] **16–047**

No exemplary damages may be awarded for breach of contract, nor may damages in contract be awarded for the claimant's mental distress, annoyance, frustration or loss of reputation caused by the breach of contract.[80] The House of Lords has re-affirmed that damages for anguish, anxiety and frustration caused to the claimant by the breach of contract cannot be awarded in an ordinary contract.[81]

---

[74] *Biggin & Co. Ltd v Permanite Ltd* [1951] 1 K.B. 422 at 436 (below, para.17–081); the actual decision in this case was reversed on another ground: [1951] 2 K.B. 314 (see below, para.17–078) See also *Bence Graphics International Ltd v Fasson UK Ltd* [1998] Q.B. 87 (below, paras 17–058, 17–082).

[75] *Koufos v C Czarnikow Ltd* [1969] 1 A.C. 350 at 416 (*per* Lord Pearce).

[76] *Wren v Holt* [1903] 1 K.B. 610; *Grant v Australian Knitting Mills Ltd* [1936] A.C. 85; *Godley v Perry* [1960] 1 W.L.R. 9. See below, para.17–072.

[77] *Henry Kendall & Sons v William Lillico & Sons Ltd* [1969] 2 A.C. 31; *Parsons (H) (Livestock) Ltd v Uttley, Ingham & Co. Ltd* [1978] Q.B. 791. See below, paras 17–073—17–074.

[78] *Burton v Pinkerton* (1867) L.R. 2 Ex. 340 at 349–351; *Hobbs v LSW Ry* (1875) L.R. 10 Q.B. 111; *Bailey v Bullock* [1950] 2 All E.R. 1167; *Perry v Sidney Phillips & Son* [1982] 1 W.L.R. 1297; *Watts v Morrow* [1991] 1 W.L.R. 1421 at 1439–43, 1445–46, CA; *Farley v Skinner* [2001] UKHL 49; [2002] 2 A.C. 732 (below, paras 16–048, 17–071).

[79] Below, paras 16–048, 17–071.

[80] *Addis v Gramophone Co. Ltd* [1909] A.C. 488 (wrongful dismissal of an employee). But see *Malik v BCCI* [1998] A.C. 20. In *Eastwood v Magnox Electric Plc* [2004] UKHL 35, [2005] 1 A.C. 503. Lord Nicholls said (at [11]) that if the facts of *Addis* occurred today, the claimant would have a remedy at common law for breach of contract. See Chitty, *op. cit.*, para.26–074—26–078.

[81] *Johnson v Gore Wood & Co.* [2002] 2 A.C. 1 *Johnson v Unisys Ltd* [2001] UKHL 13; [2003] 1 A.C 518; and *Farley v Skinner*, above. (There are a few exceptions to the *Addis* principle which are recognised in these cases, but most are unlikely to apply to contracts for the sale of goods); *Hayes v James and Charles Dodd* [1990] 2 All E.R. 815, CA.

16–048 **Loss of amenity.** The House of Lords[82] has accepted that damages may be awarded for the loss of amenity suffered by the claimant where an important purpose of the contract was to give him a subjective, even idiosyncratic, pleasure or amenity. The loss of a personal, subjective benefit which the claimant expected from performance of the contract may not be measured by market value.[83] It is possible that a buyer might be able to establish such a loss.[84]

16–049 **Causation.** The word "resulting" in sections 50(2) and 51(2), above, assumes that there is a causal link between the "loss" and the "breach of contract" in question. Although the legal principles of causation have been developed mainly in cases of tort, they are also applicable to cases of contract.[85] The defendant's breach of contract must have been the "effective" or "dominant" cause of the claimant's loss; the application of this test depends on the court's common sense.[86]

The voluntary act of a third person who, with knowledge of the relevant circumstances,[87] intervened between the breach of contract by the defendant and the loss suffered by the claimant, will normally break the causal link between the breach and the loss,[88] except where the defendant's contractual duty was to take care to prevent such an intervening act.[89] An intervening act of the claimant, if it is unreasonable in the circumstances,[90] may also break the causal link between the breach and the loss.[91] So where the defendant builders failed, in breach of their contract, to supply the claimant (an independent contractor) with adequate equipment, *viz.* a step-ladder, and the claimant attempted to work on a makeshift trestle, it was held that the cause of his fall was his own voluntary choice to use unsuitable equipment, not the breach of contract.[92] In another case, the buyer, having discovered that a machine supplied to him was defective, arranged for

---

[82] *Ruxley Electronics and Construction Ltd v Forsyth* [1996] 1 A.C. 344 (swimming pool not constructed to the specified depth); *Farley v Skinner*, above.

[83] See Harris, Ogus and Phillips (1979) 95 L.Q.R. 581 (on the "consumer surplus") cited in the *Ruxley* case, above, at p.360 and in *Farley v Skinner*, above, at p.748.

[84] See below, para.17–071.

[85] *McGregor on Damages* (17th ed.), paras 6–126—6–143; Hart and Honoré, *Causation in the Law* (2nd ed.) Ch.11; *Chitty on Contracts* (29th ed.), Vol. 1, paras 26–029—26–041.

[86] *Galoo Ltd v Bright Grahame Murray* [1994] 1 W.L.R. 1360 at 1374–1375, CA.

[87] *cf. East Ham Corporation v Bernard Sunley & Sons Ltd* [1966] A.C. 406 (architect's certificate).

[88] *Weld-Blundell v Stephens* [1920] A.C. 956.

[89] *London Joint Stock Bank Ltd v Macmillan* [1918] A.C. 777; *Stansbie v Troman* [1948] 2 K.B. 48.

[90] *cf.* the doctrine of mitigation (below, paras 16–052 *et seq.*) and contributory negligence (below, para.16–051). On the question of the claimant's intervening negligence, see *Lambert v Lewis* [1982] A.C. 225 (below, para.17–059).

[91] *Compania Naviera Maropan SA v Bowaters Lloyd Pulp and Paper Mills Ltd* [1955] 2 Q.B. 68 (nomination of unsafe port), approved by the Privy Council in *Reardon Smith Line Ltd v Australian Wheat Board* [1956] A.C. 266 at 282–283.

[92] *Quinn v Burch Bros (Builders) Ltd* [1966] 2 Q.B. 370. (It was held that the breach of contract merely gave the claimant the opportunity to injure himself by using unsuitable equipment.) *Cf. Vacwell Engineering Co. Ltd v B D H Chemicals Ltd* [1971] 1 Q.B. 88.

repairs; his unreasonable failure to inspect the repair before using the machine was held to be the cause of the subsequent explosion.[93]

An intervening event which could reasonably be expected by the parties at the time the contract was made will not excuse the contract-breaker from liability for loss caused by the combined operation of the breach of contract and the intervening event.[94] Similarly, the contract-breaker is liable for the loss suffered by the claimant where the breach of contract is only one of two causes, which were of equal efficacy and combined to produce the loss.[95] But where the contract-breaker could have exercised a contractual option to terminate performance of the contract, the assessment of damages will be made on the basis that he would have done so.[96]

Loss of chance. The claimant may claim that, if the defendant had not 16–050
committed a breach of contract, he would have had a specific opportunity to obtain a benefit (or avoid a loss). If the hypothetical consequence would have depended on how the claimant himself would have acted, he must prove (on the balance of probabilities) that he would acted in the relevant way.[97] If the hypothetical consequnce would have depended on how a third party would have acted, the claimant must prove (on the balance probabilities)[98] that, in the absence of the breach, there was a "real" or "substantial" chance that the third party would have acted in a particular way so as to benefit the claimant: the chance is evaluated (usually as a percentage) and the damages for the lost benefit are discounted by reference to that percentage.[99]

Loss of a chance may also be relevant when a loss of profits depends on many speculative factors (and not on the loss of a specific opportunity). So (subject to the rules on remoteness) the defendant's breach of contract may cause the claimant to lose future profits from "repeat orders" from his previous customers.[1] Cases on the sale of goods illustrate this principle.[2]

Contributory negligence. The Law Reform (Contributory Negligence) 16–051
Act 1945 permits apportionment of loss by the reduction of the claimant's damages where he "suffers damage as the result partly of his own fault and

---

[93] *Beoco Ltd v Alfa Laval Co Ltd* [1995] Q.B. 137, CA. It is submitted that a failure to mitigate would have been a better explanation.

[94] *Monarch Steamship Co. Ltd v Karlshamns Oljefabriker (A/B)* [1949] A.C. 196 (unseaworthy ship delayed until war broke out); *The Wilhelm* (1866) 14 L.T. 636.

[95] *Heskell v Continental Express Ltd* [1950] 1 All E.R. 1033 at 1047–1048; *Banque Keyser Ullmann SA v Skandia (U.K.) Insurance Co. Ltd* [1990] Q.B. 665 at 813–814 (the decision of the HL did not deal with this point: [1991] 2 A.C. 249). *Cf.* s.1(1) of the Civil Liability (Contribution) Act 1978.

[96] *The Mihalis Angelos* [1971] 1 Q.B. 164.

[97] *Allied Maples Group Ltd v Simmons and Simmons* [1995] 1 W.L.R. 1602, C.A. (not a sale of goods case).

[98] *North Sea Energy Holdings NV v Petroleum Authority of Thailand* [1999] All E.R. (Comm) 173, 187, C.A.

[99] The *Allied Maples* case above. See Chitty, *op. cit.*, paras 26–039—26–040.

[1] *Jackson v Royal Bank of Scotland* [2005] UKHL 3, [2005] 1 W.L.R. 377 (HL, not a sale of goods case). The period of time for which the loss should be assessed is until the question whether any loss has been sustained has become "too speculative to permit the making of any award" (*ibid.*, at [37]).

[2] Below, paras 17–034,17–069.

partly of the fault of any other person"[3]; the definition in the Act of "fault" as (*inter alia*) "negligence" raises the question whether a defendant guilty of a breach of contract can take advantage of this provision if the claimant has himself contributed to causing his loss by some "fault" on his part.[4] This situation could easily arise where a buyer is injured when using defective goods.[5] The Court of Appeal has held[6] that the Act applies only in the special situation where the claim in contract is founded on an act or omission by the defendant which would also (even in the absence of any contract) have given rise to liability in tort.[7] In this situation it would be anomalous if the claimant could avoid the apportionment provisions of the Act by the simple device of suing only in contract. The Court of Appeal decided that in any other situation the Act should not apply to a claim in contract[8]; if it did apply, it would mean that a defendant who committed a breach of his contractual obligation without fault would be in a worse position than one who committed it through fault (*viz.* negligently).[9] So where the defendant undertook a strict contractual duty irrespective of reasonable care, contributory negligence could not be pleaded.[10]

Even where the Act does not apply to claims in contract, there are many situations where conduct of the claimant which would have constituted contributory negligence under the Act will bar his recovery on the ground of his failure to mitigate,[11] or his failure to prove causation—his own carelessness may be held to be the sole cause of the loss.[12] In an

---

[3] s.1(1). At common law, the plaintiff's contributory negligence was a complete defence in an action in tort; the defence had never been applied (*eo nomine*) in an action in contract before 1945: see the discussion in Glanville Williams, *Joint Torts and Contributory Negligence* (1951), pp.214–222.

[4] *cf. Grein v Imperial Airways Ltd* [1937] 1 K.B. 50 at 88, 92 ("act, neglect or default" now in the Fatal Accidents Act 1976 includes "negligent breach of contract," a phrase which was criticised in *Quinn v Burch Bros (Builders) Ltd* [1966] 2 Q.B. 370 at 379).

[5] See below, para.17–072.

[6] *Forsikringsaktieselskabet Vesta v Butcher* [1989] A.C. 852 at 860–867, 875, 879 (in the decision of the HL, contributory negligence was not dealt with); *Tennant Radiant Heat Ltd v Warrington Development Corp.* [1988] 1 E.G. L.R. 41, CA; *Bank of Nova Scotia v Hellenic Mutual War Risks Association (Bermuda) Ltd* [1989] 3 All E.R. 628 at 672; *Barclays Bank Plc v Fairclough Building Ltd* [1995] Q.B. 214. But the High Court of Australia has not followed the decision in *Vesta v Butcher*, above; *Astley v Austrust Ltd* [1999] Lloyd's Rep. P.N. 753.

[7] Since the CA decision in *Vesta v Butcher*, above, concurrent liability in contract and in the tort of negligence has been recognised by the House of Lords even in cases where the claimant claims purely financial loss: *Henderson v Merrett* [1995] 2 A.C. 145.

[8] *Forsikringsaktieselskabet Vesta v Butcher, above; Barclays Bank Plc v Fairclough Building Ltd, above; Tennant Radiant Heat Ltd v Warrington Development Corp.*, above. The Law Commission, in its Report No. 219 (1994) entitled *Contributory Negligence as a Defence in Contract*, makes provisional proposals for changing the law.

[9] Glanville Williams, *op. cit.*, 214–215, 328, 330; Swanton (1981) 55 A.L.J. 278; Chandler (1989) 40 N.I.L.Q. 152; Anderson [1987] L.M.C.L.Q. 10.

[10] *Barclays Bank Plc v Fairclough Building Ltd*, above.

[11] Below, paras 16–052 *et seq.* For an illustration see *Lambert v Lewis* [1982] A.C. 225 (below, para.17–059).

[12] Above, para.16–049.

appropriate case, the court may make an apportionment in its finding on causation.[13]

(d) *Mitigation of Damage*[14]

No recovery for loss which should have been avoided. The rules of mitigation of damage are closely associated with the "market price" rules found in sections 50(3) and 51(3) of the Act.[15] The rules deal with three aspects: first, the claimant cannot recover for loss caused by the defendant's breach of contract where the claimant could have avoided or minimised the loss by taking reasonable steps. This "avoidable loss" rule[16] "debars" the claimant "from claiming any part of the damage which is due to his neglect to take such steps",[17] and the onus of proof is on the defendant, who must show that the claimant ought, as a reasonable man, to have taken certain steps to mitigate his loss.[18] But since the defendant is a wrongdoer, in breach of his contractual obligation, the standard imposed on the claimant is not a high one. Thus, the claimant is not "under any obligation to do anything other than in the ordinary course of business"[19]; nor need he take risks with his money[20] in attempting to mitigate nor take a step which might endanger his own commercial reputation[21]; nor need he sacrifice any of his property or rights in order to mitigate the loss caused by the defendant's breach.[22] 16–052

---

[13] *Tennant Radiant Heat Ltd v Warrington Development Corp.*, above. But see the doubt expressed in the *Bank of Nova Scotia v Hellenic Mutual*, above, at p.672; Bennett (1984–85) 4 Litigation 195 at 197.

[14] See *McGregor on Damages* (17th ed.), paras 7–001 *et seq.; Chitty on Contracts, op. cit.*, Vol. 1, paras 26–092 *et seq.*

[15] Which are examined, below, paras 16–061 *et seq.*, 17–004 *et seq.*

[16] The claimant is not under a "duty" to mitigate: the rule simply places a restriction on the damages recoverable by him: *Darbishire v Warran* [1963] 1 W.L.R. 1067 at 1075; *The Solholt* [1983] 1 Lloyd's Rep. 605 at 608, CA.

[17] *British Westinghouse Electric and Manufacturing Co. Ltd v Underground Electric Rys* [1912] A.C. 673 at 689 (for the facts, see below, para.17–056). The claimant is debarred from recovering only the *net* gain from his mitigating action *viz.* he may set off against the substitute profits the reasonable expenses incurred in making them: *Westwood v Secretary of State for Employment* [1985] A.C. 20 at 44.

[18] *Roper v Johnson* (1873) L.R. 8 C.P. 167; *Pilkington v Wood* [1953] Ch. 770.

[19] *Dunkirk Colliery Co. v Lever* (1878) 9 Ch.D. 20 at 25 (approved by Lord Haldane in *British Westinghouse Electric and Manufacturing Co. Ltd v Underground Electric Rys*, above, at p.689). See also *Banco de Portugal v Waterlow* [1932] A.C. 452 at 506. *Cf.* below, paras 17–026—17–027.

[20] *Jewelowski v Propp* [1944] K.B. 510; *Lesters Leather and Skin Co. v Home and Overseas Brokers* (1948) 64 T.L.R. 569 (below, para.17–005). *Cf.* the duty of the buyer to purchase substitute goods if the seller defaults, which will, of course, involve the buyer in expenditure (below, paras 17–001 *et seq.*).

[21] *e.g.* by enforcing sub-contracts: *James Finlay & Co. Ltd v NV Kwik Hoo Tong HM* [1929] 1 K.B. 400 (below, para.17–027: seller's breach); *Banco de Portugal v Waterlow*, above (which also, at p.471, supports the proposition that the claimant need not act so as to injure innocent persons); *London and South of England Building Society v Stone* [1983] 3 All E.R. 105. *Cf. Pilkington v Wood*, above (no duty to embark on complicated litigation against a third party).

[22] *Elliott Steam Tug Co. v Shipping Controller* [1922] 1 K.B. 127 at 140–141. *Cf. Weir (Andrew) & Co. v Dobell & Co.* [1916] 1 K.B. 722.

In the sale of goods, this principle of mitigation is a foundation of the normal rule for the measure of damages which requires the innocent party to act immediately upon the breach, and buy or sell in the market, if there is an available market.[23] A similar principle applies when the defendant repudiates his obligations before the time fixed for performance, and the claimant accepts the repudiation as a breach.[24] Even in the absence of an available market, the innocent party must act reasonably to mitigate his loss,[25] *e.g.* by the seller trying to find another buyer.[26]

The opportunity to mitigate the loss may arise through an offer made by the contract-breaker: if the claimant unreasonably refuses to accept the offer he will have failed to mitigate his loss.[27]

16–053 **The time for mitigating action.** The time when the claimant should have mitigated may depend on when he discovered or ought to have discovered that the defendant had broken his contractual obligation.[28] So, as soon as the claimant discovers that an item supplied to him by the defendant is unsafe because it is defective (in breach of the contract) he cannot continue to use it at the defendant's risk: he must either make it safe or replace it, since he cannot recover damages from the defendant for any loss which arose after he discovered[29] the defect but which he could reasonably have avoided by taking remedial steps.[30] After he knows (or ought to have known) of the breach, the claimant still has a reasonable time, depending on all the circumstances, before he must decide how to mitigate.[31] In the case of damages for the cost of repairs or reinstatement, it may be reasonable for the claimant to delay getting the repairs or remedial work done so long as there is a reasonable chance that the defendant will repair or cure the defect[32]; or until the time when the defendant has accepted liability or been held liable.[33]

---

[23] ss.50(3) and 51(3) (below, paras 16–061 *et seq.*, 17–001 *et seq.*).

[24] Below, paras 16–080—16–081, 17–013—17–015.

[25] Below, paras 16–077—16–078. *Cf.* below, paras 17–023—17–027.

[26] *Charter v Sullivan* [1957] 2 Q.B. 117 (discussed below, para.16–065). *Cf.* the obligation of the buyer to try to find similar goods from another source (below, paras 17–023—17–027).

[27] *Payzu Ltd v Saunders* [1919] 2 K.B. 581 (seller in breach: below, para.17–026); *Houndsditch Warehouse Co. Ltd v Waltex Ltd* [1944] K.B. 579 (seller in breach: below, para.17–026). *Cf. Heaven and Kesterton Ltd v Establissements François Albiac & Cie* [1956] 2 Lloyd's Rep. 316 (buyer who rejects defective goods is not obliged to accept them when offered by the seller in mitigation); *ABD (Metals and Waste) Ltd v Anglo-Chemical and Ore Co. Ltd* [1955] 2 Lloyd's Rep. 456; *Harlow and Jones Ltd v Panex (International) Ltd* [1967] 2 Lloyd's Rep. 509. *Cf.* also *Sotiros Shipping Inc. and Aeco Maritime S A v Sameiet Solholt (The "Solholt")* [1983] 1 Lloyd's Rep. 605 (buyer who cancelled contract for delay in delivery could have avoided his loss by repurchasing from the seller at the original price); Bridge 105 L.Q.R. 398 (1989).

[28] *East Ham Corporation v Bernard Sunley & Sons Ltd* [1966] A.C. 406; *Van den Hurck v R Martens & Co. Ltd* [1920] 1 K.B. 850 (below, para.17–054).

[29] It is submitted that the same result should follow as soon as the claimant *ought* to have discovered the defect: below, paras 17–060—17–061).

[30] *Lambert v Lewis* [1982] A.C. 225 (below, para.17–059).

[31] *Sharpe (C) & Co. Ltd v Nosawa* [1917] 2 K.B. 814 at 821; *Asamera Oil Corp. Ltd v Sea Oil & General Corp.* (1978) 89 D.L.R. (3d) 1 (Sup.Ct. of Canada). See also below, paras 17–007, 17–067.

[32] *Radford v De Froberville* [1977] 1 W.L.R. 1262.

[33] *Alcoa Minerals of Jamaica Inc. v Broderick* [2002] 1 A.C. 371, PC (a tort case).

Impecuniosity of the claimant. In a tort case,[34] the House of Lords has held that impecuniosity could be relevant when it was reasonably foreseeable that an impecunious claimant might reasonably incur higher expense in mitigating than would an ordinary claimant who had the resources to pay for a cheaper form of mitigation. In contract, however, the claimant's impecuniosity will be relevant it it falls within the defendant's reasonable contemplation (at the time of contracting) as not unlikely to affect the claimant's ability to mitigate after a breach of the particular undertaking *viz.* that the claimant would be likely to incur greater than usual expense (or higher than normal interest charges) in a reasonable attempt to mitigate. In the *Monarch SS* case[35] Lord Wright said, with reference to an earlier House of Lords' decision,[36] that "damages consequent on impecuniosity were held not too remote because . . . the loss was such as might reasonably be expected to be in the contemplation of the parties as likely to flow from breach of the obligation undertaken." 16–054

It will be difficult for the claimant to satisfy this test unless he can prove that the defendant actually knew of the claimant's impecuniosity (see the following paragraph). No reported case in the sale of goods yet applies this test in the absense of such actual knowledge. The market price rule is fundamental to the sale of goods: if the seller fails to deliver, the buyer's damages are prima facie the difference between the contract price and the market price at the date of the breach.[37] The rule assumes that the buyer should be able to finance the purchase of substitute goods at the time of the breach, even though he may not receive the damages until much later. The rule works reasonably well if he retains the balance of the price and there has not been a substantial rise in the market price. But the buyer's lack of financial resources could prevent his purchase of a substitute if he had paid the price (or a substantial deposit) in advance, or if the rise in price has been substantial. But to date none of these factors has prevented the application of the prime facie rule.[38]

Actual knowledge of the claimant's impecuniosity. Under the second rule in *Hadley v Baxendale*[39] the claimant's impecuniosity could be a "special circumstance" if, with actual knowledge of it, the contract-breaker could contemplate that the claimant could mitigate his loss caused by the breach only by incurring greater expense than would be incurred by a financially secure person. The claimant must act "reasonably" in his mitigating actions but what is reasonable for a claimant known to be impecunious may be different from the case of a person with financial resources. Most of the cases[40] supporting this principle do not concern the 16–055

---

[34] *Lagden v O'Connor* [2003] UKHL 64, [2004] 1 A.C. 1067.
[35] *Monarch Steamship Co. Ltd v A/B Karlshamns Oljefabriker* [1949] A.C. 196 at 224.
[36] *Muhammad Issa el Sheikh Ahmad v Ali* [1947] A.C. 427.
[37] Below, para.17–004.
[38] Below, paras 17–004—17–007.
[39] (1854) 9 Exch. 341 (above para.16–046).
[40] *Wadsworth v Lydall* [1981] 1 W.L.R. 598; *Bacon v Cooper* [1982] 1 All E.R. 397; *Wroth v Tyler* [1974] Ch. 30. In *Compania Financiera "Soleada" SA v Hamoor Tanker Corporation Inc.* [1981] 1 W.L.R. 274 the principle was accepted by the Court of Appeal but not applied on the facts. See Chitty, *op. cit.* Supplement, paras 26–095B—26–095D.

sale of goods. But in *Trans Trust SPRL v Danubian Trading Co. Ltd*[41] the buyers undertook that a confirmed credit was to be opened forthwith in favour of the firm from which the sellers were obtaining the goods. The buyers knew that the sellers were not in a position themselves to open the necessary credit. The Court of Appeal held that the loss due to this impecuniosity was not too remote because it was within the reasonable contemplation of the parties as likely to flow from the buyer's breach of contract in failing to obtain the credit.

Actual knowledge of the buyer's lack of resources has been treated as relevant to the purchase of a house[42]; and the seller's decision to re-sell quickly because he was short of liquid resources was held to be reasonable mitigation in a sale of goods case.[43]

16–056 **No recovery for loss which is in fact avoided.** The second rule of mitigation is that if the claimant in fact avoids or mitigates his potential loss consequent upon the defendant's breach, he cannot recover for such avoided loss,[44] even though the steps he took were more than could be reasonably required of him under the first (the "avoidable loss") rule.[45] One illustration of this rule is discussed later, *viz.* where the seller resells immediately upon the buyer's breach, but at a price higher than the market price.[46] But if the seller could, but does not, resell immediately, and the market price later rises, the increased price which the seller obtains on his actual resale is not taken into account to reduce the damages payable by the buyer: the seller chooses to retain the goods at his own risk, and the benefit does not arise directly[47] from his acting in mitigation.[48] The benefit to the claimant must arise *out of*[49] his attempts to mitigate his potential loss resulting from the breach: if it arises from his actions which were independent of his mitigating steps, it should not lead to a reduction in his damages.[50]

---

[41] [1952] 2 Q.B. 297.
[42] *Wroth v Tyler*, above.
[43] *Robbins of Putney Ltd v Meek* [1971] R.T.R. 345.
[44] The claimant's actual loss is assessed by taking account of all the items in his notional "profit and loss" calculation for the whole transaction: *Westwood v Secretary of State for Employment* [1985] A.C. 20 at 44.
[45] *British Westinghouse Electric and Manufacturing Co. Ltd v Underground Electric Rys* [1912] A.C. 673 at 689, 690 (see below, para.17–075). *Cf.* below, para.16–059. See also *Erie County Natural Gas and Fuel Co. Ltd v Carroll* [1911] A.C. 105 (below, para.17–023); *Hill v Showell* (1918) 87 L.J.K.B. 1106. *Cf. Harbutt's "Plasticine" Ltd v Wayne Tank and Pump Co. Ltd* [1970] 1 Q.B. 447 at 467–468, 473, 475–476 (see *infra*, n.51, where it is noted that the case has been overruled on another point).
[46] Below, paras 16–075—16–076. *Cf. Melachrino v Nickoll and Knight* [1920] 1 K.B. 693 at 698 (below, para.17–015).
[47] *cf. Jebsen v East and West India Dock Co.* (1875) L.R. 10 C.P. 300.
[48] *Campbell Mostyn (Provisions) Ltd v Barnett Trading Co.* [1954] 1 Lloyd's Rep. 65 (below, para.16–076) (distinguished in *Pagnan (R) & Fratelli v Corbisa Industrial Agropacuaria Limitada* [1970] 1 W.L.R. 1306: see below, para.17–020). See also *Jones v Just* (1868) L.R. 3 Q.B. 197 (breach by seller but loss avoided by buyer when market price later rose); *Jamal v Moolla Dawood* [1916] 1 A.C. 175 (below, para.16–076, n.10).
[49] The *British Westinghouse* case, above, at p.689.
[50] *Hussey v Eels* [1990] 2 Q.B. 227 (sale of land); *Mobil North Sea Ltd v PJ Pipe and Valve Co.* [2001] EWCA Civ 741; [2001] 2 All E.R. (Comm.) 289.

However, a contract-breaker cannot have the damages reduced in respect of advantages gained by the claimant from wholly independent transactions,[51] as, for example, from a sum due to the claimant under an insurance policy.[52] So where the claimant, by another contract with a third party entered into *before* the defendant's breach of his contract with the claimant, has made an arrangement which should or does in fact prevent loss to the claimant from the defendant's breach, the defendant cannot rely on that other contract to reduce his damages[53]; it is an extraneous circumstance, *res inter alios acta*.

Release of resources for other uses.[54] If the seller was to manufacture an item to the buyer's specification, he may terminate the contract when the buyer commits an anticipatory breach by repudiating the contract before the item is manufactured. The termination will release for redeployment the resources which the seller-manufacturer would otherwise have devoted to performance of the contract, *e.g.* his equipment and labour. Although the seller may not be able to find another buyer for a similar item, he will not wish to keep his resources idle but will seek to switch them to another use. If the seller makes a profit from another use of the same resources, the buyer will claim that it is a substitute profit to be set against his liability to the seller for damages. This claim should succeed only if the seller could not have performed the second contract but for[55] the buyer's breach of the first contract, and if the seller used the same equipment and labour as he would have done in performing the first contract.[56] If the seller in 16–057

[51] See below, paras 17–019—17–020, 17–028. *Cf. Lavarack v Woods of Colchester* [1967] 1 Q.B. 278; *Harbutt's "Plasticine" Ltd v Wayne Tank and Pump Co. Ltd* [1970] 1 Q.B. 447 at 468, 473, 476 (overruled on another point: *Photo Productions Ltd v Securicor Transport Ltd* [1980] A.C. 827); *Hussey v Eels*, above.

[52] *Bradburn v GW Ry* (1874) L.R. 10 Ex. 1.

[53] *Haviland v Long* [1952] 2 Q.B. 80 at 84. See also *Joyner v Weeks* [1891] 2 Q.B. 31 (below, para.17–019); *Slater v Hoyle and Smith* [1920] 2 K.B. 11 (buyer of defective goods able to avoid loss on sub-sale; the contrary decision of the Privy Council in *Wertheim v Chicoutimi Pulp Co.* [1911] A.C. 301 (below, paras 17–038, 17–058) seems to be wrong). See below, paras 17–057, 17–058.

[54] The arguments in this paragraph are developed more fully in Chitty, *op. cit.*, paras 26–103—26–104.

[55] The causal test should be (1) that the seller used substantially the same resources as he would have done in the first contract, and (2) that the opportunity for the seller to use them in the new activity would not have arisen *but for* the defendant's breach of contract, that is, it was the breach alone which released them for the alternative use. For instance, in *Hill v Showell* (1918) 87 L.J.K.B. 1106 at 1108, the breach enabled the claimant to execute other profitable orders: it led to "the situation in which his machinery was rendered *free by reason of the breach* . . ." (italics supplied).

[56] *Hill v Showell*, above. However, it is submitted that the assessment should not deprive someone in the seller's position of all incentive to redeploy: some incentive would remain if the court did not deduct the whole of the substitute profit but left him to enjoy some of it as a reward for his initiative in seeking the alternative use. *Cf.* the *British Westinghouse* case [1912] A.C. 673 (below, para.17–056) where the House of Lords held that the *whole* of the benefit of the mitigating action of the claimant could be used to reduce the damages payable by the defendant, even though the claimant would not have been obliged under the "avoidable loss" rule to take that action.

performing the second contract used only part of the resources released by the buyer's breach, or if he used different skills, it is submitted that allowance for this different input of resources should be made by deduction of only part of the substituted profit.[57]

16–058 **Recovery of loss or expense incurred while attempting to mitigate.** The third rule of mitigation is that the claimant may recover any loss or expense incurred by him in the course of a reasonable attempt to mitigate his loss following the defendant's breach, even where the mitigating steps in fact lead to greater loss.[58] This rule is necessary to protect the claimant who makes an attempt to comply with his "duty" to mitigate under the first rule (para.16–052 above).

16–059 **No duty to mitigate where a debt is claimed.** In *White and Carter (Councils) Ltd v McGregor*,[59] the House of Lords appears to have decided, by necessary implication,[60] that the rules as to mitigation do not apply to a claim for a debt due under a contract in return for the claimant's performance of his obligation; such a claim is distinct from one for damages for breach of contract.[61] It was not a case of the sale of goods, and it is not clear how far the principle may extend to the sale of goods.[62] Under the contract the claimant agreed to manufacture and display advertisement plates for the defendant; the claimant refused to accept the defendant's anticipatory repudiation of the contract[63] and was able to complete the performance of his own contractual obligations without the co-operation of the defendant; the majority of their Lordships held that the claimant could recover the full amount due for his performance. The circumstances were unusual in that there was nothing which the defendant had to do or accept in order to enable the claimant to complete his performance, and this may prevent the principle from applying to ordinary contracts for the sale of goods.[64] But in one case[65] where, before the goods were shipped across the

---

[57] Some support for this is found in *Lavarack v Woods of Colchester Ltd* [1967] 1 Q.B. 278 (a wrongful dismissal case).

[58] *Wilson v United Counties Bank* [1920] A.C. 102 at 125; *Lloyds and Scottish Finance Ltd v Modern Cars and Caravans (Kingston) Ltd* [1966] 1 Q.B. 764 at 782–783. See also the quotations from *Erie County Natural Gas and Fuel Co. Ltd v Carroll* [1911] A.C. 105 in para.17–023, below. *Cf. Le Blanche v L.N.W. Ry* (1876) 1 C.P.D. 286; *Quinn v Burch Bros (Builders) Ltd* [1966] 2 Q.B. 370. *Cf.* also below, para.17–015 (text to n.22).

[59] [1962] A.C. 413. (See above, para.16–004; see also below, paras 19–215, 20–126).

[60] Since the majority must be taken to have rejected the view of two of their Lordships in the minority who thought that the claimant should have mitigated his loss by discontinuing his performance of the contract: *ibid.*, at pp.433, 439.

[61] See above, paras 16–004 *et seq.*

[62] *cf.* Lord Keith (dissenting), *ibid.*, at p.437 (above, para.16–022).

[63] The innocent party is under no obligation to accept the anticipatory repudiation as a breach of contract: see above, para.12–021; below, paras 16–080—16–082, 17–013—17–016.

[64] *cf.* Lord Keith (dissenting): *ibid.*, at p.437.

[65] *Anglo-African Shipping Co. of New York Inc. v J Mortner Ltd* [1962] 1 Lloyd's Rep. 81 at 94; on appeal, *ibid.*, at p.610, no mention was made of *White and Carter's* case in the judgments (the majority in the CA treated the claimants as shipping agents rather than as sellers).

Atlantic, the buyers notified their shipping agents in New York (who had bought the goods from the suppliers on behalf of the buyers) that they would not accept the goods, it was held (following the *White and Carter* case, above) that there was no duty on the agents to mitigate by not shipping the goods; Megaw J. said it was "an instance which tends to show the practical justice of that decision of their Lordships' House."[66] However, in the *White and Carter* case, above, Lord Reid (one of the majority) suggested[67] that the courts may not allow a contractor to complete his performance (despite a repudiation by the other party) if the contractor had no legitimate interest, financial or otherwise, in performing his side of the contract. In cases concerning charterparties, this limitation has been accepted by the Court of Appeal[68] and applied at first instance.[69] But, apart from this limitation, the principle laid down in the *White and Carter* case does not follow the policy of the mitigation rules, which appears to be the avoidance of wasted resources and effort in the community.[70] If the property in the goods sold can pass to the buyer without any act or consent on his part, the seller may be able to continue his performance of his side of the contract, despite the buyer's anticipatory repudiation, so that the seller completes the stage of performance at which the parties intend[71] the property to pass to the buyer[72]; thereupon, the seller is entitled under section 49(1)[73] to sue for the price if the buyer "wrongfully neglects or refuses to pay for the goods." (The price may also be payable under the provisions of the contract *before* the property in the goods passes to the buyer,[74] and in this situation also the seller may be able to complete the stage of the contractual performance at which the price becomes payable without any concurrence or act of acceptance by the buyer.) If, however, the property in the goods is to pass only upon delivery to, and acceptance by, the buyer,[75] this will involve the concurrence of the buyer, so that the seller will not be able to complete the performance of his obligations, so as to become entitled to the price, without the voluntary cooperation of the buyer[76]: thus, the seller in this situation will not be able to take advantage of the principle in the *White and Carter* case.

---

[66] *ibid.*, at p.94.

[67] At p.431. On American law, see the American Law Institute's *Restatement of the Law of Contracts*, s.338, especially Comment (c).

[68] *Attica Sea Carriers Corporation v Ferrostaal Poseidon Bulk Reederei GmbH (The Puerto Buitrago)* [1976] 1 Lloyd's Rep. 250 at 254–256; *The Odenfeld* [1978] 2 Lloyd's Rep. 357.

[69] *Clea Shipping Corporation v Bulk Oil International Ltd (The Alaskan Trader)* [1984] 1 All E.R. 129.

[70] See [1962] Camb.L.J. 12 at 213; 78 L.Q.R. 263 (1962); 25 M.L.R. 364 (1962); Treitel, *The Law of Contract* (11th ed.), pp.1016–1019.

[71] Intention is the basic test for the time when property is to pass: see above, Ch.5, and, in particular, paras 5–016, 5–026, 5–030.

[72] *e.g.* by shipment of the goods under a normal f.o.b. contract (below, paras 20–070—20–073); or by delivery of the goods to a carrier (s.32(1): above, para.8–014).

[73] Above, paras 16–021 *et seq.*

[74] Above, paras 16–025—16–029.

[75] *e.g.* where delivery is to be made "on request" or "as required" (above, para.8–039).

[76] *cf. Hounslow London Borough Council v Twickenham Garden Developments Ltd* [1971] Ch. 233 at 251–254 (building contract); see also *The Alaskan Trader*, above, at p.133.

3. THE SELLER'S CLAIM FOR DAMAGES

(a) *Damages for Non-acceptance*

16–060 **Introduction.** Where the property in the goods has not passed to the buyer, the seller's normal remedy in most circumstances[77] is an action for damages: for damages for non-acceptance under section 50(1), for consequential losses or expenses under section 54,[78] or for losses or expenses under section 37.[79] Section 50(1) provides that: "Where the buyer wrongfully neglects or refuses to accept and pay for the goods, the seller may maintain an action against him for damages for non-acceptance." This subsection is wide enough to cover non-acceptance when the property has already passed to the buyer, in which case it allows damages for non-acceptance as an alternative remedy to a claim for the price.[80] But the advantages of suing for the price as a debt clearly outweigh those of suing for unliquidated damages for non-acceptance.[81] If, however, there is some doubt as to whether the property in the goods has passed to the buyer, the seller who sues for the price when the buyer has not taken delivery of the goods runs the risk that the court may hold that property had not passed to the buyer: in this event, it follows that the seller's only remedy is a claim for damages for non-acceptance, and that the seller would be expected to mitigate his loss (*e.g.* by reselling) as from the date when the buyer should have accepted the goods. So long as the seller is claiming the price, he must hold the goods available for delivery to the buyer when the buyer pays the price,[82] but his failure to resell may lead to a reduction in his damages if it is later held that he was not entitled to the price. If the seller resells when he is entitled to do so, he is treated as having terminated the contract so that his only claim against the buyer is for damages.[83] If he attempts to resell, this may be taken as an acceptance of the buyer's repudiation of his obligations under the contract, in which case the seller is also relegated to his claim in damages.[84]

Section 50(1) is based on wrongful neglect or refusal by the buyer to pay the price, which has been considered above in relation to the action for the price,[85] and on wrongful neglect or refusal to accept the goods, which has been examined in an earlier chapter.[86]

---

[77] Except where s.49(2) applies, or there is a special term in the contract: see above, paras 16–025 *et seq.*, 16–028—16–029.
[78] Below, paras 16–085—16–087.
[79] Above, para.9–009; below, para.16–088. There are also other sections which entitle the seller to claim damages, *e.g.* s.48(3) and (4) (See above, paras 15–119 *et seq.*; 15–128 *et seq.*).
[80] On a claim for the price, see above, paras 16–021 *et seq.*
[81] Above, paras 16–004, 16–036, 16–059.
[82] Or, whenever the buyer is entitled by the terms of the contract to take delivery.
[83] *Ward (R V) Ltd v Bignall* [1967] 1 Q.B. 534 (above, para.15–127). If the property had already passed to the buyer, the seller's action in reselling revests the property in himself so that it passes to the second buyer: *ibid.*
[84] Above, paras 15–110, 16–015.
[85] Above, paras 16–014—16–020.
[86] Above, paras 9–001 *et seq.*

Normal measure of damages for non-acceptance. Section 50 of the Act lays down the following rules for the assessment of damages for non-acceptance[87]: ". . . (2) The measure of damages is the estimated loss directly and naturally resulting, in the ordinary course of events, from the buyer's breach of contract. (3) Where there is an available market for the goods in question the measure of damages is prima facie to be ascertained by the difference between the contract price and the market or current price at the time or times when the goods ought to have been accepted or (if no time was fixed for acceptance) at the time of the refusal to accept." Section 50(2) uses the language of the first rule in *Hadley v Baxendale*,[88] which does not depend on the buyer's actual knowledge of special circumstances (the second rule in that case[89]). The development of the common law since section 50(2) was first enacted in 1893 has already been considered,[90] and it has been submitted that the later common law decisions may be used to aid the interpretation of the current subsection.[91] Section 50(2) comes into operation either where there is no available market (within the meaning of section 50(3))[92] or where the "prima facie" rule in section 50(3) is deemed to be inapplicable.[93] In a case dealing with the assessment of the buyer's damages for breach of warranty (section 53), the Court of Appeal said[94] that the basic rule is section 53(2), the provision enacting the first rule in *Hadley v Baxendale*, which corresponds to section 50(2); and that the "market value" rule in section 53(3), which corresponds to section 50(3), should not apply if it would give the buyer "more than his true loss". If the analogy of this decision is followed it may lead to courts being more willing than in the past not to apply the other "prima facie" rules in sections 50(3) and 51(3) which are based on the market price at the time of the breach.[95] 16–061

The following paragraphs examine, first, the "available market" rule, and then the measure of damages in other situations where section 50(2) is applicable, as for instance, where the seller claims for the loss of the profits he expected to make under the contract.[96]

The sellers' damages for the buyers' refusal to accept the goods (or the documents representing the goods) may be reduced "by any sum which the buyers could establish they would have been entitled to set up in diminution of the contract price" as the result of any *previous* breach by the sellers.[97]

---

[87] s.50(1) (above, para.16–060) gives the entitlement to sue.
[88] (1854) 9 Exch. 341 (above, para.16–043).
[89] Above, para.16–046.
[90] Above, paras 16–043 *et seq.*
[91] Above, para.16–043.
[92] For the meaning of "available market", see below, paras 16–062 *et seq.*
[93] *e.g.* below, paras 16–064—16–065. *Cf.* below, para.17–002, n.18.
[94] *Bence Graphics International Ltd v Fasson U.K. Ltd* [1998] Q.B. 87. (See below, paras 17–058, 17–082.)
[95] *e.g.* (on s.50(3)) *Bem Dis A. Turk Ticaret S/A TR v International Agri Trade Co. Ltd* [1999] 1 All E.R. (Comm.) 619, CA.
[96] Below, para.16–085.
[97] *Berger & Co. Inc. v Gill & Duffus SA* [1984] A.C. 382 at 392.

(b) *An Available Market*

16–062 **The prima facie rule: the market price.** The normal rule stated in section 50(3) incorporates the common law established before the Act,[98] *viz.* when the buyer fails both to pay the price and to accept the goods, the seller's damages are calculated by deducting from the contract price the market price at the time and place[99] fixed by the contract for acceptance.[1] The doctrine of mitigation[2] is one of the bases of this principle: it is assumed that with this additional amount of money the seller could, by selling in the market at the current price, put himself into the same financial position he would have been in had the contract been performed according to its terms.[3] The ensuing paragraphs discuss the different aspects of the market price rule.

16–063 **Suggested tests for an "available market".**[4] An early view was that an available market is some place (*e.g.* an exchange) where the goods in question can be sold[5]; a later view was that it "means a particular level of trade"[6] in a particular locality; another that it refers to a sufficient demand for the goods "to absorb readily all the goods that were thrust on it"[7]; another that it means a situation where the current price for the goods may fluctuate according to supply and demand[8] (which rules out the situation "where the goods can only be sold at a fixed retail price"[9]); and another that ". . . there must be sufficient traders who are in touch with each other. . ."[10]

Cases about sales at a fixed retail price have considered the meaning of an "available market": these are discussed in the following paragraphs, and a submission as to its meaning is made below in paragraphs 16–066 *et seq.*

---

[98] *Barrow v Arnaud* (1846) 8 Q.B. 595 at 610.
[99] Below, paras 16–067, 16–068, 16–071.
[1] The existence or absence of an available market need not be specifically contemplated by the parties: *Coastal (Bermuda) Petroleum Ltd v VTT Vulcan Petroleum SA (No. 2) (The "Marine Star")* [1994] 2 Lloyd's Rep. 629.
[2] Above, paras 16–052 *et seq*.
[3] But if s.50(3) applies, the claimant need not satisfy the requirements of reasonable mitigation: *Shearson Lehman Hutton Inc. v Maclaine Watson & Co. Ltd (No.*2) [1990] 3 All E.R. 723 at 726.
[4] See Waters, 36 Can.Bar Rev. 360 (1958); Lawson, 43 A.L.J. 52 at 106 (1969).
[5] *Dunkirk Colliery Co. Ltd v Lever* (1878) 9 Ch.D. 20 at 25 (an *obiter dictum*, made prior to the 1893 Act, which was not expressly accepted by the other Lords Justices; followed in *Thompson (WL) Ltd v Robinson (Gunmakers) Ltd* [1955] Ch. 177).
[6] *Heskell v Continental Express Ltd* [1950] 1 All E.R. 1033 at 1056 ("A market for this purpose means more than a particular place. It also means a particular level of trade"). See also *The Arpad* [1934] P. 189 at 191 ("Market means buyers and sellers"); *ibid.*, at p.202.
[7] *Thompson (W L) Ltd v Robinson (Gunmakers) Ltd*, above, at p.187. (See on this case, below, para.16–064.)
[8] *Charter v Sullivan* [1957] 2 Q.B. 117 at 128. (See below, para.16–065.)
[9] *ibid*.
[10] *ABD (Metals and Waste) Ltd v Anglo Chemical and Ore Co. Ltd* [1955] 2 Lloyd's Rep. 456 at 466 (followed in the *Shearson Lehman* case, above, at p.730).

A fixed retail price. A problem has arisen in deciding whether there can be an "available market" when the relevant goods can be sold only at a fixed retail price. It has been considered in two cases[11] where, after the buyer defaulted, the seller was able to resell only at the same fixed price: in both cases the court held that the same result would follow whether or not there was an available market, so that a definite decision on the meaning of the term was not necessary. The result of the two decisions is that if the seller had the ability and the opportunity to make a profit for every buyer he could find (because the supply of the goods exceeded or was equal to the demand) he is entitled to the loss of profits on the sale to the defaulting buyer.[12] But if the demand for the goods exceeded the supply, so that the seller could readily sell every item he could obtain from the manufacturers, he is not entitled to loss of profits on the first sale when he made the same profit on a substituted sale following the first buyer's default.[13] 16–064

The former situation is illustrated by *Thompson (WL) Ltd v Robinson (Gunmakers) Ltd*.[14] The claimants, car dealers, agreed to sell a new Vanguard car to the defendants, at the retail price fixed by the manufacturers. On the defendant's refusal to accept the car, the claimants persuaded the wholesale suppliers to take the car back. Although there was no difference between the current retail price and the contract price, Upjohn J. awarded damages for the loss of profit on the sale. There was no shortage of Vanguard cars to meet all immediate demands in the locality: since a substituted buyer could not be found readily, the judge thought that there was not an available market.[15] He followed an earlier dictum,[16] but said[17]: "Had the matter been *res integra* I think that I should have found that an 'available market' merely means that the situation in the particular trade in the particular area was such that the particular goods could freely be sold, and that there was a demand sufficient to absorb readily all the goods that were thrust on it, so that if a purchaser defaulted, the goods in question could readily be disposed of."[18] In any event, since the market price rule in section 50(3) was only a "prima facie" rule, the judge held that it did not apply where it was clearly foreseeable by the parties that the rule would not compensate the seller for his loss of profit if the buyer defaulted.[19] If the second buyer was an additional customer of the seller, and not merely a substituted customer, and the seller had the ability and the opportunity of

---

[11] *Thompson (WL) Ltd v Robinson (Gunmakers) Ltd*, above; *Charter v Sullivan*, above.

[12] *Thompson (WL) Ltd v Robinson (Gunmakers) Ltd*, above (following *Re Vic Mill Ltd* [1913] 1 Ch. 465 (below, para.16–079)).

[13] *Charter v Sullivan*, above (below, para.16–065).

[14] Above.

[15] *ibid.*, at p.187.

[16] *Dunkirk Colliery Co. v Lever* (1878) 9 Ch.D. 20 at 25. See para.15–063, n.5, above.

[17] [1955] Ch. 177 at 187.

[18] Accepted by Sellers J. in *ABD (Metals & Waste) Ltd v Anglo-Chemical and Ore Co. Ltd*, above, p.466. *Cf. Lazenby Garages Ltd v Wright* [1976] 1 W.L.R. 459 (There is no "available market" for a unique item like a second-hand car.)

[19] [1955] Ch. 177 at 188. Had the seller not been a dealer, but a private person selling his own vehicle, the position would have been different. *Cf.* above para.16–061, text at n.94.

making two profits on the two transactions, he is entitled to damages for his loss of the first profit when the first buyer defaults.[20]

16–065 The second situation, where the demand for the goods in question exceeds the supply, occurred in *Charter v Sullivan*.[21] The defendant refused to accept delivery of a Hillman Minx car which he had agreed to buy from the claimant, a car dealer, at the fixed retail price. Within 10 days the claimant resold the car to another buyer at the same price. As the evidence showed that the claimant could always find a buyer for every Hillman Minx car he could get from the manufacturers, the Court of Appeal refused to allow him to recover more than nominal damages: he made the same number of sales (and therefore the same number of fixed profits) as he would have done if the defendant had performed his contractual obligation; hence it was a substituted, not an additional sale, because the seller had the ability to make only one sale and one profit. Although the court considered that it was immaterial whether or not there was an "available market", Jenkins L.J. said[22]: ". . . I doubt if there can be an available market for particular goods in any sense relevant to section 50(3) of the Sale of Goods Act 1893,[23] unless those goods are available for sale in the market at the market or current price in the sense of the price, whatever it may be, fixed by reference to supply and demand as the price at which a purchaser for the goods in question can be found, be it greater or less than or equal to the contract price. The language of section 50(3)[24] seems to me to postulate that in the cases to which it applies there will, or may, be a difference between the contract price and the market or current price, which cannot be so where the goods can only be sold at a fixed retail price."[25] Sellers L.J.[26] thought that "it must at least be a market in which the seller could, if he wished, sell the goods left on his hands."

16–066 **The meaning of "available market".**[27] It is submitted that the courts are likely to eschew formal limitations on the meaning of "available market",[28] especially in the light of the fact that the concept provides only a prima

---

[20] *Re Vic Mill Ltd*, above. *Cf. Interoffice Telephones Ltd v Robert Freeman* [1958] 1 Q.B. 190 (hire of telephone equipment).
[21] [1957] 2 Q.B. 117.
[22] *ibid.*, at p.128.
[23] Apart from minor, stylistic changes, s.50(3) of the 1979 Act is the same as s.50(3) of the 1893 Act.
[24] It should be noted that on the facts of the case Jenkins L.J. reached the same result by the application of the general principle of s.50(2) (*viz.* nominal damages) as he would have done by applying s.50(3) had he thought that there had been an available market.
[25] To the same effect see *Eclipse Motors Pty Ltd v Nixon* [1940] V.L.R. 49. *Cf. Marshall & Co. v Nicoll & Son*, 1919 S.C. 244 at 253.
[26] [1957] 2 Q.B. 117 at 133 (see also below, para.16–067).
[27] For the various tests suggested in the cases, see above, para.16–063.
[28] *Charrington & Co. Ltd v Wooder* [1914] A.C. 71 at 82 ("market" is "a term of no fixed legal significance": *per* Lord Dunedin). See also *Charter v Sullivan* [1957] 2 Q.B. 117 at 128; and *ABD (Metals and Waste) Ltd v Anglo-Chemical Ore Co. Ltd* [1955] 2 Lloyd's Rep. 456 at 466 ("It is not necessary to establish a market that it should have a fixed place or building").

facie measure of damages which need not be applied whenever there is some justification for not doing so.[29] The availability of buyers and sellers, and their ready capacity to supply or to absorb the relevant goods[30] is the basic concept of an "available market": it is submitted that there is no need to add to this the test of a price liable to fluctuations in accordance with supply and demand, as occurs in official exchanges or certain commodity markets. A fixed market price may render section 50(3) ineffective as a ground for substantial damages, but it should not make the term "available market" inapplicable.[31] A fluctuating market price indicates the existence of an available market, but it should not be a necessary test: "there must be sufficient traders, who are in touch with each other."[32]

The word "available" should be given both a temporal[33] and a geographical[34] meaning: the buyers or sellers should be immediately accessible[35] and within a reasonable distance of the place where the breach of contract occurs.

The temporal test of availability. The "ready" or "immediate" accessibil- **16–067**
ity to substitute buyers or sellers should not be taken too literally. In *Charter v Sullivan*[36] the Court of Appeal found that the demand for the goods exceeded the supply, but (apart from the question of a fixed retail price[37]) Sellers L.J. held that the fact that the resale of a car was made some seven to ten days after the breach prevented there being an available market: "there was no immediate buyer".[38] It is submitted[39] that the temporal test should be one of a reasonable time after the breach, given the nature of the goods in question[40] and the business situation of the claimant; and that the opinion of Sellers L.J. is wrong on this point. With many types

---

[29] See above, para.16–061, esp. nn. 93, 94.
[30] *Marshall & Co. v Nicoll & Son*, 1919 S.C. 244 at 253 (affirmed 1919 S.C. (HL) at p.129); *Thompson (W L) Ltd v Robinson (Gunmakers) Ltd*, above, at p.187 (cited above in para.16–064). *Cf. Lazenby Garages Ltd v Wright* [1976] 1 W.L.R. 459 (above, para.16–064, n.18).
[31] Waters, 36 Can.Bar Rev. 360 at 371 (1958); Lawson, 43 A.L.J. 106 at 110 (1969) ("The essential nature of a market requires potentially speedy buyers or sellers"). *Cf. McGregor on Damages* (17th ed.), paras 20–108—20–110.
[32] *ABD (Metals and Waste) Ltd v Anglo-Chemical Ore Co. Ltd*, above, at p.466 (followed in *Shearson Lehman Hutton Inc. v Maclaine Watson & Co. Ltd (No. 2)* [1990] 3 All E.R. 723 at 730: "sufficient traders potentially in touch with each other to evidence a market in which the actual or notional seller could if he wished sell the goods." So "if the seller actually offers the goods for sale there is no available market unless there is one actual buyer on that day at a fair price": *ibid.*).
[33] See below, para.16–067.
[34] See below, para.16–068.
[35] So that there is the possibility of an immediate sale and purchase: Lawson, 43 A.L.J. 52 at 54 (1969).
[36] [1957] 2 Q.B. 117.
[37] Considered above, para.16–065.
[38] [1957] 2 Q.B. 117 at 133–134. *Cf. Lesters Leather and Skin Co. v Home and Overseas Brokers Ltd* (1948) 64 T.L.R. 569 (8 or 9 months' delay in obtaining substitute goods: see below, para.17–005).
[39] This submission is "consistent with the effect of the *Garnac Grain* case" (see below, para.16–069) but it is not based on any express reference to "a reasonable time after breach" in any case: the *Shearson Lehman (No. 2)* case, above, p.730.
[40] *e.g.* perishables or durable goods.

of goods there would need to be the possibility of an immediate resale or new purchase before the test would be satisfied; but this test permits some flexibility in the particular circumstances. In the case of the sale of 10,000 tonnes of gasoline the judge held that there could be an available market where the seller could have disposed of the gasoline in smaller cargo loads of 1,000 to 3,000 tonnes over a period of about two weeks from the buyer's breach.[41] With some types (or quantities) of goods, negotiations with potential buyers would take several days to achieve a sale: in these circumstances, the market price should be fixed on the assumption that the hypothetical seller had begun to negotiate sufficiently far ahead to enable a sale to be made on the day in question.[42] It is most unlikely that there will be an available market where the goods in question have been (or were to be) specially manufactured to suit the particular requirements of the buyer[43]: the chance of resale of such goods within a reasonable time after the breach is too limited and fortuitous.

16–068 **The extent of the market area.** Since an innocent party's damages, following a breach of contract, are assessed on the basis that he should have taken reasonable steps to mitigate his loss, the question arises whether the concept of "market" extends to places other than the place of delivery.[44] James L.J., in discussing the meaning of "available market" in a case where the buyer refused to accept coal he had bought, said that the sellers "might have sent it in waggons somewhere else, where they could sell it, just as they sell corn on the Exchange, or cotton at Liverpool: that is to say, that there was a fair market where they could have found a purchaser either by themselves or through some agent at some particular place."[45] Thus, it has been assumed that where the seller's business area was the East Riding of Yorkshire, that was the area in which he should seek a substitute buyer.[46] It

---

[41] *Petrotrade Inc. v Stinnes Handel GmbH* [1995] 1 Lloyd's Rep. 142. *Cf.* The *Garnac Grain* case [1968] A.C. 1130 at 1138 (below, paras 16–069, 17–005).

[42] The *Shearson Lehman (No. 2)* case, above, p.731. A similar result would be reached by assuming, for sales concluded some days later, that the price had remained constant since the day in question: *ibid.*, at p.731. These assumptions are consistent with the *Garnac Grain* case (below, para.16–069).

[43] *Elbinger Actien Gesellschaft v Armstrong* (1874) 9 Q.B. 473 at 476–477; *Hinde v Liddell* (1875) 10 Q.B. 265 at 269. *Cf. Borries v Hutchinson* (1865) 18 C.B.(N.S.) 445 at 447; *Re Vic Mill Ltd* [1913] 1 Ch. 183 at 187 (on appeal, *ibid.*, at pp.465, 472–473). It is submitted that the decision of the Court of Session in *Marshall & Co. v Nicoll & Son*, 1919 S.C. 244 on this point is wrong, and that the dissenting judgment of Lord Salvesen is to be preferred: *ibid.*, at p.256 (failure to deliver steel which was not kept in stock but made to specification); the House of Lords, 1919 S.C.(HL) 129, divided evenly on this point, two of their Lordships expressing no opinion.

[44] It is submitted that *Wertheim v Chicoutimi Pulp Co.* [1911] A.C. 301 (below, para.17–039: delayed delivery) which is often cited in this connection, really concerns the question of reaching a market *value* in one place by basing the calculation on the market price elsewhere; it did not decide that the latter place constituted an available market.

[45] *Dunkirk Colliery Co. v Lever* (1878) 9 Ch.D. 20 at 25.

[46] *Thompson (W L) Ltd v Robinson (Gunmakers) Ltd* [1955] Ch. 177. *Cf. Lesters Leather and Skin Co. v Home and Overseas Brokers Ltd* (1948) 64 T.L.R. 569 (seller's breach: see below, para.17–005). Lawson submits that the courts should take account of the areas in which a dealer-seller or a dealer-buyer is permitted to operate by his contract of appointment: 43 A.L.J. 52 at 62 (1969).

is submitted that the test is one of reasonableness,[47] in the light of the time,[48] expense[49] and trouble involved.[50]

Other relevant factors. The size of the alleged market will be relevant to the decision whether it is an available market: thus, a few sales of small quantities of the relevant goods will not constitute an available market.[51] The House of Lords (in a case of a seller's breach) has been willing to accept that there could be a market in which to buy 15,000 tons of lard where the only purchases which could be made were of smaller quantities (up to 2,000 tons at a time) and spread over a period[52]; but the period must, it is submitted, be reasonable from the claimant's point of view.[53] Similarly, a seller who cannot find a substitute buyer for a large quantity of goods may have to mitigate by dividing it into separate sales of quantities which are readily saleable.[54] **16–069**

The fact that the price in the alleged market is out of line with the normal price at other times or places may indicate that it is not an available market: a very high or a very low price may[55] indicate that there is either a scarcity or glut[56] of the relevant goods.[57] But the fact that the market price is seriously affected by governmental intervention (*e.g.* the sudden imposition of import restrictions) does not prevent there being an available market.[58]

A "black" market, where the goods are bought and sold surreptitiously to evade contractual restrictions (*e.g.* restrictions on price or supplies) may nevertheless be an available market for the purposes of the Act.[59] It is,

---

47 *Kwei Tek Chao v British Traders and Shippers Ltd* [1954] 2 Q.B. 459 at 499; *Lesters Leather and Skin Co. v Home and Overseas Brokers Ltd*, above (seller's breach).

48 See above, para.16–067.

49 See above, para.16–052, text at n.22.

50 *cf. Ströms Brucks Aktie Bolag v Hutchison* [1905] A.C. 515 (breach of charterparty: claimants recovered cost of transporting the substitute goods to the contractual place of delivery).

51 *Kwei Tek Chao v British Traders and Shippers Ltd*, above, at p.498. *Cf.* the umpire's finding in *Koufos v Czarnikow (C.) Ltd* [1969] 1 A.C. 350 at 354 (". . . regularly bought and sold in large quantities at prices which were published").

52 *Garnac Grain Co. Inc. v H M F Faure and Fairclough Ltd* [1968] A.C. 1130 at 1138 (see below, para.17–005); *Cf.* (in the CA) [1966] 1 Q.B. 650 at 687.

53 See below, para.17–005.

54 *Tredegar Iron and Coal Co. v Gielgud* (1883) 1 Cab. & El. 27. In the case of the sale of 10,000 tonnes of gasoline it was held that there could be an available market where the seller could have disposed of the gasoline in smaller cargo loads of 1,000 to 3,000 tonnes over a period of about two weeks from the buyer's breach: *Petrotrade Inc. v Stinnes Handel GmbH* [1995] 1 Lloyd's Rep. 142.

55 But not necessarily: *Bradley & Sons Ltd v Colonial and Continental Trading Ltd* [1964] 2 Lloyd's Rep. 52 at 64 ("You do not do away with an existing market merely by proving that prices fall . . . disastrously").

56 *Kwei Tek Chao v British Traders and Shippers Ltd*, above, at p.498 (". . . there was no market in the ordinary sense . . . the market had gone to pieces"); *Campbell Mostyn (Provisions) Ltd v Barnett Trading Co.* [1954] 1 Lloyd's Rep. 65 at 69.

57 *cf. O'Hanlan v GW Ry* (1865) 6 B. & S. 484 at 494 (". . . there are no persons from whom such goods can be bought at the place except at an excessive price . . .": the case concerned a claim against a carrier for non-delivery).

58 *Campbell Mostyn (Provisions) Ltd v Barnett Trading Co.*, above.

59 *Mouat v Betts Motors Ltd* [1959] A.C. 71; *British Motor Trade Association v Gilbert* [1951] 2 All E.R. 641. (These decisions imply that the buyers were entitled to mitigate by themselves going into the black market to buy a substitute.)

however, doubtful whether a black market where the goods are available in breach of statutory controls would be treated similarly, since the seller cannot be required to mitigate his loss by committing a breach of the law.

16–070 **The relevant "market".** Normally, the concept of "available market" should be the same, whether the defaulting party is the buyer or the seller.[60] But the claimant's position could be crucial: if he is a seller, the issue is the availability of alternative buyers; whereas if he is a buyer, it is the availability of alternative sellers.[61] The selling, not the buying, price is relevant in one situation, but not necessarily the other, and vice versa[62]; for instance, it may be relevant, in the case of the innocent buyer who has received the goods, to know the price at which he could *sell* them.[63] The available market is that available to the innocent party in the circumstances in which he is placed by the breach.[64] But there are other types of market relationships which may be relevant,[65] *e.g.* between wholesaler and retailer, retailer and private buyer, as the prices for the goods in question may vary according to the particular relationship. In *Heskell v Continental Express Ltd*[66] Devlin J. said: "In this case I am concerned with the market price as between an exporter and an importer at Teheran,"[67] thus holding that the relevant market relationship is that in which the claimant and defendant are involved.[68] However, if the claimant cannot find a relevant market for the goods, he may try any reasonable alternative market relationship, *e.g.* in the case of a breach by the seller, if there is no wholesale market at the relevant place, the innocent buyer may be acting reasonably in buying in the retail market.[69]

The question which market is relevant creates problems in f.o.b. contracts, which are examined in a later chapter.[70] If at the relevant time the

---

[60] Lawson, 43 A.L.J. 106 at 113 (1969).
[61] *Kwei Tek Chao v British Traders and Shippers Ltd*, above, at p.497; *C. Czarnikow Ltd v Bunge & Co. Ltd* [1987] 1 Lloyd's Rep. 202 at 205. The difference is referred to in *The Arpad* [1934] P. 189 at 211; and in *Dominion Motors Ltd v Grieves* [1936] N.Z.L.R. 766 at 771.
[62] *Kwei Tek Chao v British Traders and Shippers Ltd*, above, at pp.497–498 (". . . the relevance of the buying price [depends] upon the fact that the buyer has not got the goods. . . . Therefore he has to buy").
[63] *ibid.*
[64] But the individual characteristics of the claimant (*e.g.* his personal skill in negotiating) are not relevant: the *Shearson Lehman* case, above, p.726.
[65] The parties may in their contract agree which market is to be the relevant one for fixing the market value: *Orchard v Simpson* (1857) 2 C.B.(N.S.) 299.
[66] [1950] 1 All E.R. 1033.
[67] *ibid.*, at p.1050. See also *Rice v Baxendale* (1861) 7 H. & N. 96 at 100.
[68] *cf. Charrington & Co. Ltd v Wooder* [1914] A.C. 71, where the House of Lords held that a contractual provision for the "fair market price" for beer meant, in the circumstances, the market for tied public houses and not that for free houses. *Cf.* also *James Buchanan & Co. Ltd v Babco Forwarding & Shipping (U.K.) Ltd* [1978] A.C. 141 (there may be different market prices for the same type of goods depending on whether the goods are intended for export or not).
[69] This seems to be inferred in *O'Hanlan v GW Ry* (1865) 6 B. & S. 484 at 494. *Cf. Zemel v Commercial Warehouses* (1945) 40 A. (2d) 642 (a case on conversion).
[70] Below, paras 20–133—20–135. *Cf.* below, para.19–216.

goods in question are in transit, the relevant market is that for similar goods in the same situation.[71]

16–071 **The relevant time for the market price.**[72] Section 50(3) provides that "the market or current price" is to be taken "at the time or times when the goods ought to have been accepted or (if no time was fixed for acceptance) at the time of the refusal to accept."[73] The contract itself will normally fix the exact time for acceptance.[74] A time fixed by reference to the happening of an event (*e.g.* the arrival of a ship) has been held to be a fixed time for the purposes of section 51(3)[75] and it is submitted that the same position should apply to section 50(3).

Where the contract fixes a period during which delivery and acceptance are to be made, the time when the goods ought to have been accepted is the time, within the stipulated period, when the goods were actually tendered to the buyer by the seller.[76] Where the contract provides that delivery is to be made by separate deliveries of part of the goods at stated times or intervals, the damages in respect of the buyer's failure to accept an instalment must be calculated by reference to the market price prevailing at the time fixed for delivery of that instalment.[77]

The question of the relevant time at which the market price is to be taken raises problems in regard to f.o.b. contracts, which are discussed in a later chapter.[78] In the case of a c.i.f. contract, the time will normally be the time fixed for acceptance of the documents, or the time of refusal to accept them.[79]

16–072 **"No time. . . fixed for acceptance".** The final provision in section 50(3) deals with cases of the buyer's refusal to accept delivery of the goods when tendered by the seller under a contract which did not fix a time for

---

[71] So when the goods in question are afloat at the relevant time, bound for a specified port, the reference to "the market price . . . for similar goods" in the contract is to goods of the same description and situated as the contractual goods were (afloat and bound for that port) or to goods which could be delivered about the time when the goods afloat could reasonably be expected to arrive at the port: *Esteve Trading Corporation v Agropec International (The Golden Rio)* [1990] 2 Lloyd's Rep. 273 (see below, paras 20–134—20–135).

[72] See also above, para.16–067.

[73] *cf.* the similar rule in s.51(3).

[74] See above, para.9–005. Since the seller will normally know of the buyer's refusal to accept on the day he tenders delivery of the goods, he will in most cases (where there is an available market for the goods) be able to find a substitute buyer on the same day: in such circumstances, the question discussed below (in the second para.of the text in para.17–008) will not arise.

[75] *Melachrino v Nickoll and Knight* [1920] 1 K.B. 693 at 696 (below, paras 17–008, 17–015). (This was a decision on s.51(3) of the 1893 Act, which was in substance the same as s.51(3) of the 1979 Act.).

[76] *cf.* the same rule in cases of non-delivery, where the latest time within the period is taken for assessing damages against the defaulting seller: *Leigh v Paterson* (1818) 8 Taunt. 540 at 541 (below, para.17–008). See also below, para.20–115, 20–135.

[77] s.50(3), above. There appear to be no reported cases directly in point, but the cases on the buyer's damages for non-delivery under an instalment contract are analogous: *Brown v Muller* (1872) L.R. 7 Ex. 319; *Roper v Johnson* (1873) L.R. 8 C.P. 167 (below, para.17–008).

[78] Below, paras 20–133—20–135.

[79] Below, para.19–216.

acceptance: in these circumstances, the prima facie rule for the assessment of damages is based on the market price "at the time of the refusal to accept." But the calculation of the market price at the time of the buyer's "refusal to accept" in terms of section 50(3) does not apply to an anticipatory breach by the buyer, *viz.* a repudiation by him of his obligations under the contract at a time earlier than would be reasonable for delivery and acceptance of the goods, when no definite time had been fixed. The measure of damages in these circumstances is considered later.[80]

A Divisional Court has held[81] that a contract for delivery within a reasonable time is not a contract with a fixed time for acceptance of the goods within the scope of section 51(3) (breach by the seller).[82] In the Court of Appeal,[83] opinions were expressly reserved on the point,[84] but Atkin L.J. thought that some meaning could be given to the second limb of the subsection: "It seems to me that a meaning could be given to the words 'if no time was fixed,' by reading them as referring to a contract such as to deliver goods on demand or to deliver goods as required by the purchaser."[85] The Privy Council, in a case on breach by the seller, doubted whether any meaning could be given to the words.[86] Although section 50(3) covers breach by the buyer, it is submitted that the same considerations should apply to the interpretation of the phrase "if no time was fixed" in section 50(3).

16–073 **Postponement of time fixed for delivery.** Where the buyer requests and obtains the seller's consent to waive[87] the time for delivery fixed by the contract, but he fails to accept the goods when the seller tenders them at the substituted time (or within the extended period), the calculation of the seller's damages will be made on the basis of the market price at the substituted time (or at the last day of the extended period)[88]; if the seller agreed to waive the original delivery date but no definite date or period was substituted by agreement, the calculation of damages will be made at the market price at a reasonable time after the last request by the buyer for postponement of delivery, or at the date when the seller refused to give any further time.[89]

Where the request for postponement of the agreed delivery date came from the seller, and at first the buyer agreed to waive delivery at that date

---

[80] Below, paras 16–080—16–082.

[81] *Millett v Van Heek & Co.* [1920] 3 K.B. 535 (seller's breach: see below, para.17–010); *Melachrino v Nickoll and Knight* [1920] 1 K.B. 693 at 696 (seller's breach: see below, para.17–010, n.88).

[82] Below, para.17–010.

[83] [1921] 2 K.B. 369.

[84] The appeal was dismissed on other grounds, *viz.* that s.51(3) did not apply to an anticipatory breach (see below, para.17–014).

[85] [1921] 2 K.B. 369 at 378. See further below, para.17–010 esp. n.86.

[86] *Tai Hing Cotton Mill Ltd v Kamsing Knitting Factory* [1979] A.C. 91 at 104 (see below, para.17–010).

[87] On waiver, see above, paras 8–030, 8–069, 8–070.

[88] *Hickman v Haynes* (1875) 10 C.P. 598 at 607 (following the similar rule in the case of the seller's failure to deliver: *Ogle v Vane* (1868) L.R. 3 Q.B. 272 (below, para.17–010)).

[89] *Hickman v Haynes*, above. (This case was mentioned with approval by the House of Lords in *Johnson v Agnew* [1980] A.C. 367 at 401).

but later repudiated his obligations in breach of the contract,[90] the damages should be calculated on the basis of the market price at the time of the buyer's repudiation.[91]

16–074 **Proof of "the market or current price".** For a buyer, faced with a breach of contract by the seller, the relevant market price is normally[92] the *buying* price[93]; for the seller, it is the *selling* price on the market. The individual characteristics of the claimant, such as his personal ability to negotiate sales, are irrelevant: "the subsection contemplates a hypothetical sale by a hypothetical seller of the amount in question of the goods in question."[94] If there is proof of the market price at the date of the buyer's breach[95] the actual price obtained by the seller upon his reselling the goods at a later[96] date is irrelevant to the assessment of damages, whether the resale price is higher or lower than the market price.[97] But where normal proof of the market price of the goods is not available (*viz.* by reference to published or recorded prices of deals at the relevant date) the court may accept other evidence, *e.g.* proof of the price at which the seller in fact resold the goods to a new buyer,[98] or of an offer for the goods received by the seller,[99] or proof of compromises in other disputes relating to the market value of similar goods at the same time.[1] However, there will be no evidential value from the price obtained by the seller under an actual resale if the terms of the resale are different in an important respect from those of the original sale, *e.g.* where a horse sold originally with a warranty is resold after the first buyer's default, at a lower price but without the warranty.[2]

---

90 Even where the ground for his repudiation is the seller's inability or unwillingness to deliver at the contractual date for delivery: *Hartley v Hymans* [1920] 3 K.B. 475.

91 *Hartley v Hymans*, above, at p.496 (following the similar rule in the case of the seller's failure to deliver: *Tyers v Rosedale and Ferryhill Co.* (1875) L.R. 10 Ex. 195 (below, para.17–012)). In *Hartley v Hymans*, above, the market price had fallen heavily between the contractual date for delivery and the date of the buyer's repudiation; but the judgment is very brief on the question of the assessment of damages.

92 But see *Kwei Tek Chao v British Traders and Shippers Ltd* [1954] 2 Q.B. 459 at 497–498 (above, para.16–070, n.62).

93 This is a result of the rules of mitigation, and is the position under the case law before the Act: *Barrow v Arnaud* (1846) 8 Q.B. 595.

94 The *Shearson Lehman* case, (No. 2) [1990] 3 All E.R. 723 at 726.

95 The court may infer the approximate market price on a given date from evidence that there was a steady decline in that price between an earlier and a later date: *Tai Hing Cotton Mill Ltd v Kamsing Knitting Factory* [1979] A.C. 91 at 106.

96 *cf.* below, para.16–075.

97 *Campbell Mostyn (Provisions) Ltd v Barnett Trading Co.* [1954] 1 Lloyd's Rep. 65 (below, para.16–076).

98 *Maclean v Dunn* (1828) 4 Bing. 722 at 729; *Ex p.Stapleton* (1879) 10 Ch.D. 586 at 590 ("the damages for the breach are plainly, if the market is falling, the difference between the contract price and the price obtained on the resale"). In these cases there was no indication that the resale prices were not identical with the market prices.

99 The seller may be able to establish the "current price" by seeking several offers for the goods from prospective buyers, with a view to accepting the best price obtainable.

1 *Hong Guan & Co. Ltd v R Jumabhoy & Sons Ltd* [1960] A.C. 684 at 703–704 (seller's breach: below, para.17–018).

2 *Macklin v Newbury Sanitary Laundry* (1919) 63 S.J. 337. *Cf. Aryeh v Lawrence Kostoris & Son Ltd* [1967] 1 Lloyd's Rep. 63 at 73 (below, para.17–018).

16–075 **Resale at a price lower or higher than the market or current price.** If there is an available market, but the seller immediately resells at *less* than the market or current price, he will be unable to recover the difference between the contract price and the actual resale price: the reasonable seller would have obtained the market price on the resale.[3] However, a difficulty arises if the seller more than fulfils his duty to take reasonable steps to mitigate loss, *viz.* if he resells at a price higher than the prevailing price. It is a rule of the doctrine of mitigation that if the claimant has in fact avoided loss resulting from the defendant's breach of contract, he cannot recover damages in respect of his potential loss.[4] "When in the course of his business [the claimant] has taken action arising out of the transaction, which action has diminished his loss, the effect in actual diminution of the loss he has suffered may be taken into account even though there was no duty on him to act."[5] If the seller has, at the date of the buyer's breach, only the one set of the relevant goods, *viz.* the set left on his hands following the buyer's breach, the price (higher than the market price) which he actually receives by reselling *immediately* is a direct consequence of the buyer's breach, and should be taken into account in assessing the seller's damages. The seller should recover only his actual loss,[6] *viz.* the difference between the contract price and the actual resale price, since, but for the breach, he would not have had the opportunity of reselling.[7] If, on the other hand, the seller had, at the date of the breach, further supplies of the relevant goods, a resale of only some of his stock at a higher than market or current price could not necessarily be attributed to the buyer's breach and, in these circumstances, the seller should be entitled to the normal measure of damages under section 50(3).[8]

16–076 Although there is no authority directly in point to support the submissions just made, inferences may be drawn from cases where the seller chooses to retain the goods for a period, instead of reselling them in the market immediately following the buyer's breach. The Court of Appeal[9] has held that if the seller subsequently resells the goods at a gain because the market price rises after the date of the breach, the enhanced price received by the seller does not reduce his damages, which are still to be determined by the difference between the contract price and the market price on the date of the breach. By retaining the goods after that date the seller is taking on himself the risk of fluctuations in the market price: if the price later fell,

---

[3] Above, para.16–052; s.50(3).
[4] Above, para.16–056.
[5] *British Westinghouse Electric and Manufacturing Co. Ltd v Underground Electric Rys* [1912] A.C. 673 at 689 (for the facts of the case, see below, para.17–056).
[6] His "actual loss" may include the expenses of reselling. *Cf. Westwood v Secretary of State for Employment* [1985] A.C. 20 at 44.
[7] Atiyah, *The Sale of Goods* (11th ed.), p.491–492; Fridman, *Sale of Goods in Canada* (4th ed.), pp.363–364. *Cf. Pagnan (R.) & Fratelli v Corbisa Industrial Agropacuaria* [1970] 1 W.L.R. 1306 (below, para.17–020).
[8] *cf.* the similar problem in *Charter v Sullivan* [1957] 2 Q.B. 117 (above, para.16–065); *Re Vic Mill Ltd* [1913] 1 Ch. 465 (below, para.16–079). *Cf.* also below, para.17–019.
[9] *Campbell Mostyn (Provisions) Ltd v Barnett Trading Co.* [1954] 1 Lloyd's Rep. 65.

the buyer would not be liable for the seller's additional loss, and, correspondingly, the seller is entitled to the gain if the price later rises.[10] There should be symmetry of risk. From this reasoning it may be inferred that if the seller does not take a chance on later fluctuations in the market price, but chooses to sell the one set of goods immediately upon the breach and happens to obtain a price higher than the market price at that time, his damages should be limited to his actual loss.[11]

(c) *The Absence of an Available Market*

Damages where there is no available market. If section 50(3) does not apply, because there is no available market, the court is thrown back on the general principle enunciated in section 50(2): "... the estimated loss directly and naturally resulting, in the ordinary course of events, from the buyer's breach of contract." The main rule should be that the seller's loss is the difference between the contract price and the value of the goods to the seller at the time and place of the breach,[12] and any relevant evidence may be admissible to prove this value.[13] If, despite the absence of an available market, the seller has in fact been able eventually to find a substitute buyer, the resale price may be evidence to fix the seller's loss, if the terms of the resale are substantially similar to those in the original sale.[14] 16–077

Even where there is no available market within section 50(3), the seller's damages will be assessed on the basis that he should have acted reasonably in mitigating his loss[15]: he may be able to persuade his own seller to take back the goods, in which case his damages against the defaulting buyer will be the contract price less the price payable under the contract under which he bought the goods.[16] Where the physical goods cannot be immediately resold, it may be reasonable for the seller (*e.g.* when prices are falling) to resell in a "terminal" or "futures" market, which is a mechanism by which he can insulate himself from future changes in market values.[17]

---

[10] The Court of Appeal in the *Campbell Mostyn* case, above, followed the reasoning of the Privy Council in *Jamal v Moolla Dawood* [1916] 1 A.C. 175 at 179 ("If the seller retains the shares after the breach the speculation as to the way the market will subsequently go is the speculation of the seller, not of the buyer"). See also *Koch Marine Inc. v D'Amica Societa di Navigazione ARL (The Elena D'Amico)* [1980] 1 Lloyd's Rep. 75 at 87–90.

[11] *cf.* the situation when the buyer resells the goods *before* the date of the seller's breach: below, para.17–028. *Cf.* above, para.16–074, text at n.94.

[12] *Harlow and Jones Ltd v Panex (International) Ltd* [1967] 2 Lloyd's Rep. 509 at 530. (This measure of damages will give the seller the profit which he expected to make under the contract.)

[13] *cf.* on s.51(2), below, paras 17–021—17–022.

[14] *Harlow and Jones Ltd v Panex (International) Ltd*, above; *Lazenby Garages Ltd v Wright* [1976] 1 W.L.R. 459 (seller able to find a substitute buyer for a second-hand car at a higher price: no damages awarded). For illustrations, see *Robbins of Putney Ltd v Meek* [1971] R.T.R. 345; and above, para.16–070, text at n.69.

[15] *Gebruder Metelmann GmbH & Co. KG v NBR (London) Ltd* [1984] 1 Lloyd's Rep. 614. The seller need not accept the buyer's offer to take the goods at a reduced price: *Harlow and Jones Ltd v Panex (International) Ltd*, above, at pp.530, 531. On the "duty" to mitigate, see above, para.16–052.

[16] *Harlow and Jones Ltd v Panex (International) Ltd*, above, at p.531.

[17] *The Gebruder Metelmann* case, above.

16–078 **Adaptation of goods for resale.** If there is no available market for the goods in their condition at the time of the buyer's failure to accept them,[18] the seller is entitled to deal with the goods "in any reasonable way",[19] *e.g.* by adapting them to suit another customer. The seller's damages will then include the cost of the adaptation, as well as the loss of profit on the first sale.[20] However, in these circumstances, the question arises whether the seller is not only entitled to, but should, under his "duty" to mitigate,[21] spend money to adapt them to make them suitable for resale. Although the seller need not incur speculative expenditure,[22] there may be circumstances in which it would be reasonable for the seller to incur a limited amount of expenditure to adapt the goods in such a way as to make them readily saleable.[23]

16–079 **Recovery of loss of profits despite resale.** A difficulty arises where the seller, despite the absence of an available market, claims the loss of profits on the abortive sale on the ground that the second buyer was an additional, not a substituted, buyer: *i.e.* the seller is claiming that he would have made the second profit on the second sale even if the first buyer had not defaulted. The test is whether the seller had the ability and the opportunity to make the two separate profits[24]: if the seller had fulfilled the first contract, would he have been able to fulfil the second contract as well? If so, he is entitled to recover from the defaulting buyer his loss of profit on the first contract.[25] The burden of proof lies on the defaulting buyer to show that the seller could not have earned the second profit but for his breach of the first contract.[26]

(d) *Anticipatory Breach*

16–080 **Anticipatory breach by the buyer.**[27] Where the buyer commits an anticipatory breach by repudiating his obligation to take delivery of the goods before the date fixed for delivery, the seller has an option[28]: he may either

[18] Or at the time when the seller accepts the buyer's anticipatory repudiation: below, para.16–081.
[19] *Re Vic Mill Ltd* [1913] 1 Ch. 465 at 473.
[20] *ibid.*, at pp.473, 474. *Cf. below,* paras 17–023—17–024.
[21] Above, para.16–052.
[22] *cf. Jewelowski v Propp* [1944] K.B. 510.
[23] *cf.* below, paras 17–023—17–025.
[24] *Re Vic Mill Ltd* [1913] 1 Ch. 465; *Hill & Sons v Edwin Showell & Sons Ltd* (1918) 87 L.J.K.B. 1106, HL. *Cf. Lazenby Garages Ltd v Wright* [1976] 1 W.L.R. 459 (above, para.16–077, n.14).
[25] *Re Vic Mill Ltd*, above, at pp.472, 474. *Cf. Charter v Sullivan* [1957] 2 Q.B. 117 at 130 (above, para.16–065).
[26] *Hill & Sons v Edwin Showell & Sons Ltd*, above, at pp.1108, 1114. See *Thompson (WL) Ltd v Robinson (Gunmakers) Ltd* [1955] Ch. 177 (above, para.16–064).
[27] See above, paras 8–078—8–089, 9–010—9–020; George [1971] J.B.L. 109. *Cf.* the analogous situation of an anticipatory breach by the seller: below, paras 17–013—17–016.
[28] The seller is not obliged to act "reasonably" in exercising this choice: *Tredegar Iron and Coal Co. (Ltd) v Hawthorn Bros & Co.* (1902) 18 T.L.R. 716 at 716–717; *White and Carter (Councils) Ltd v McGregor* [1962] A.C. 413.

accept the repudiation and so treat it forthwith as a discharge of the primary obligations of the parties, or he may continue to treat the contract as binding and thus not accept the repudiation as a discharge.[29]

Acceptance of the buyer's anticipatory repudiation. If the seller accepts the buyer's anticipatory repudiation, he may sue immediately for damages for breach of contract; but in those situations in which there is an available market for the goods,[30] the relevant date for ascertaining the market price remains prima facie (and subject to any requirement of mitigation) the date fixed for delivery, since that is when the contract ought to be performed.[31] If the action is heard before the date for delivery arrives, the court should attempt to estimate what the market price is likely to be at that future date. The seller cannot advance the relevant date for ascertaining the market price merely by exercising his option to accept the anticipatory breach: a lower market price at the time of repudiation should not increase the damages.[32] Thus, it is submitted that the provision in section 50(3) that, when no time is fixed for acceptance, damages should be assessed by reference to the market price "at the time of the refusal to accept" should not apply to an anticipatory breach by the buyer.[33] 16–081

But the rules of mitigation[34] may override this rule. If the seller does accept the buyer's anticipatory repudiation, his damages will be assessed on the basis that he took reasonable steps to mitigate his loss.[35] Where the seller should have mitigated by reselling,[36] the relevant market price is that

---

[29] *Fercometal SARL v Mediterranean Shipping Co. SA* [1989] A.C. 788.

[30] See above, paras 16–062 *et seq.*

[31] *Frost v Knight* (1872) L.R. 7 Ex. 111 at 113; *Melachrino v Nickoll and Knight* [1920] 1 K.B. 693 (seller's anticipatory repudiation: see below, para.17–014); *Millett v Van Heeck* [1920] 3 K.B. 535; [1921] 2 K.B. 369, CA. It is submitted that the statement by Mathew L.J. in *Tredegar Iron and Coal Co. (Ltd) v Hawthorn Bros & Co.*, above, at p.717, that "the damages were to be calculated as on the date of the acceptance of the repudiation—as if the contract had then run out," is incorrect. (See further on this point nn. 37 and 38, below, and *cf.* the analogous cases on the seller's anticipatory repudiation, below, para.17–014). On the question of discounting sums due in the future, see below, para.17–014, n.10.

[32] *Melachrino v Nickoll and Knight*, above.

[33] *cf.* below, para.17–014 (seller's anticipatory repudiation).

[34] See above, paras 16–052 *et seq.*

[35] *Roth & Co. v Taysen Townsend & Co.* (1895) 73 L.T. 628 at 629–630 (affirmed on appeal (1896) 12 T.L.R. 211 at 212); *Tredegar Iron and Coal Co. (Ltd) v Hawthorn Bros & Co.*, above; *Sudan Import and Export Co. (Khartoum) Ltd v Société Générale de Compensation* [1958] 1 Lloyd's Rep. 310 at 316. The rule is similar in the case of the buyer's acceptance of the seller's anticipatory repudiation: *Melachrino v Nickoll and Knight* [1920] 1 K.B. 693 at 697; *Garnac Grain Co. Inc. v H M F Faure and Fairclough Ltd* [1966] 1 Q.B. 650 at 687 (on appeal [1968] A.C. 1130 at 1140) (see below, para.17–015, for other analogous cases on the seller's anticipatory repudiation).

[36] The onus of proof is on the buyer: *Cf.* the analogous cases where the seller is in default: *Roper v Johnson* (1873) L.R. 8 C.P. 167; *Garnac Grain Co. Inc. v H M F Faure and Fairclough Ltd* [1968] A.C. 1130 (below, para.17–015).

existing at the date he ought reasonably to have resold,[37] not that at the date of the repudiation, nor that at the date when the repudiation is accepted.[38] If the market price is falling after the time the seller accepted the repudiation, it will normally be reasonable for the seller to resell immediately, so that he will be unable to recover the difference between the price on the date he ought to have resold[39] and the price on the date when he actually resold.

16–082 **Buyer's anticipatory repudiation not accepted.** The seller is not bound to accept an anticipatory repudiation by the buyer.[40] He may continue to treat the contract as binding on both himself and the buyer, and wait until the date fixed for delivery before he tenders the goods: if the buyer then fails to accept the goods, the seller thereupon has a "duty" to mitigate his loss by taking reasonable steps (*viz.* in normal circumstances by reselling forthwith).[41] Where there is an available market for the goods, the relevant market price will be that at the date fixed for delivery[42]: if the seller did not accept the buyer's anticipatory repudiation, a higher or a lower market price at the date of the repudiation, or at any date during the period up to the date fixed for delivery, is irrelevant, because the rules of mitigation do not apply until the date of the actual breach.[43] Thus, when the market is

---

[37] *Melachrino v Nickoll and Knight*, above, at pp.697, 699; *Sudan Import and Export Co. (Khartoum) Ltd v Société Générale de Compensation*, above, at p.316 (". . . you arrive at the sum of damage by ascertaining what the loss would be to the sellers by non-performance on the performance date, Sept. 30, looking back, however, to Sept. 20 [the date of the seller's acceptance of the buyer's repudiation] to see whether that loss ought to be reduced by steps which the sellers could reasonably have taken, *from and after* the last-mentioned date, in mitigation" (italics supplied)). *Cf.* below, para.17–015 (duty to mitigate following acceptance of the seller's anticipatory repudiation), especially *Kaines (U.K.) Ltd v Österreichische Warrenhandelsgessellschaft, etc.* [1993] 2 Lloyd's Rep. 1 at 11, 12.).

[38] Although the date of the seller's acceptance of the repudiation may be the date when he ought to have resold (*e.g.* if there was an available market), it will not always be the same date. (It is therefore submitted that the statement in *Roth & Co. v Taysen Townsend & Co.*, above, and in *Tredegar Iron and Coal Co. (Ltd) v Hawthorn Bros & Co.*, above, at p.717, that the relevant date is the date of the seller's acceptance of the repudiation, is misleading, as are the similar statements in *Sudan Import and Export Co. (Khartoum) Ltd v Société Générale de Compensation* [1957] 2 Lloyd's Rep. 528 at 538 ("the market price on the day when repudiation is accepted"); *Cf.* the statement in the CA [1958] 1 Lloyd's Rep. 310 at 316 (cited in n.37, above); *Cf.* also *Gebruder Metelmann GmbH & Co. v NBR (London) Ltd* [1984] 1 Lloyd's Rep. 614 at 630.

[39] *Melachrino v Nickoll and Knight*, above, at pp.697, 699.

[40] *Frost v Knight*, above (approved in *Fercometal SARL v Mediterranean Shipping Co. SA* [1989] A.C. 788); *White and Carter (Councils) Ltd v McGregor* [1962] A.C. 413; *Sudan Import and Export Co. (Khartoum) Ltd v SG de Compensation* [1958] 1 Lloyd's Rep. 310.

[41] See below, para.20–140 for an illustration of this rule in the case of an f.o.b. contract.

[42] *Tredegar Iron and Coal Co. (Ltd) v Hawthorn Bros & Co.* (1902) 18 T.L.R. 716. (The earlier case of *Phillpotts v Evans* (1839) 5 M. & W. 475 is to the same effect.) *Cf. Tai Hing Cotton Mill Ltd v Kamsing Knitting Factory* [1979] A.C. 91 at 102, 105 (below, para.17–010).

[43] *White and Carter (Councils) Ltd v McGregor*, above; *Tredegar Iron and Coal Co. (Ltd) v Hawthorn Bros & Co.*, above. See below, paras 20–135, 20–140.

falling, the seller is entitled, if he chooses, to wait until the time fixed for the buyer's acceptance, despite the seller's knowledge that the amount of damages payable by the buyer is likely to increase during the interval. Of course, during the interval the contract is kept alive for the benefit of *both* parties[44]: the buyer may change his mind and accept the goods when tendered[45]; or the seller may decide to accept the repudiation (before it has been retracted by the buyer) whereupon the seller's "duty" to mitigate will arise forthwith, with the consequence that the damages will be calculated by reference to the market price at the date when the seller ought reasonably to have resold following his acceptance of the repudiation[46]; or the obligations of the parties may be determined by the occurrence of a frustrating event[47]; or the buyer may exercise a right under the contract to cancel it.[48]

(e) *Special Cases*

Damages following resale under statutory or express power. Where the unpaid seller has resold the goods under section 48(3) or 48(4),[49] the seller cannot claim the price from the original buyer[50]: he is relegated to his claim for damages "comparable to a claim for damages for non-acceptance" under section 50 "where the property never has passed."[51] The seller's damages will be: (a) the difference between the original contract price (less any deposit[52] paid) and the price obtained on the resale (provided that it was not less than either the market price[53] or a reasonable price[54]); and (b) any expenses reasonably incurred by the seller as a result of the buyer's breach of contract or in connection with the resale (*e.g.* reasonable advertising expenses).[55] 16–083

Other special cases. In other chapters of this work there will be found discussions of the question of assessing the seller's damages in particular circumstances.[56] Thus, in Chapter 9 there is an examination of the 16–084

---

44 The *Fercometal* case, above, at p.805.
45 In which case, the buyer is not in breach of his contractual obligations, since his earlier repudiation is a "mere nullity" when not accepted by the seller: *Phillpotts v Evans*, above, at p.477; *White and Carter (Councils) Ltd v McGregor*, above, at p.444.
46 Above, para.16–081.
47 Above, paras 6–034 *et seq.*; the *Fercometal* case above, at pp.800, 805.
48 The *Fercometal* case, above.
49 See above, paras 15–119—15–131. (Under these subsections the seller may resell despite the fact that the property had previously passed to the buyer.)
50 Where the property in the goods has passed to the buyer, the resale revests the property in the seller: *Ward (RV) Ltd v Bignall* [1967] 1 Q.B. 534 (see above, para.15–127).
51 *ibid.*, at p.544.
52 On the position in regard to the deposit if the seller does not claim damages, see above, paras 15–132—15–133.
53 If there was an available market: s.50(3) (above, paras 16–062 *et seq.*). On the position if there was no available market, see above, paras 16–077 *et seq.*
54 See above, para.16–077. If the seller resold for less than either the market price or a reasonable price, he can recover only the difference between the original contract price and the market price or the price he ought to have obtained on the resale.
55 *Ward (RV) Ltd v Bignall*, above. See below, para.16–087.
56 On damages for failure to pay the agreed deposit, see above, para.15–132.

assessment of damages upon the failure of the buyer to give a bill of exchange[57]; in Chapters 19 and 20, of damages for breaches of f.o.b. and c.i.f. contracts[58]; and, in Chapter 23, of damages for the failure of the buyer to open a documentary credit,[59] and of damages for the refusal of a banker to accept a draft in accordance with a documentary credit.[60]

(f) *Consequential Losses and Expenses*

16–085 **Loss of profits.** Loss of profit which the seller expected to make on the sale is a regular head of damages for non-acceptance under section 50. The seller's loss of profits may fall under either the first rule of *Hadley v Baxendale*[61] (imputed knowledge)[62] or the second rule (actual knowledge of special circumstances).[63] The various situations in which the seller may recover damages for his loss of profits have been examined separately in preceding sections[64]: where the prima facie rule of the market price in section 50(3) is not applicable because the dealer-seller's supply of the goods exceeded the demand[65]; where there is no available market[66]; or where, although there was no available market, the seller managed to find a second buyer who was an additional, not a substituted, buyer (in the sense that the seller could have made two separate profits on the two sales).[67]

16–086 **Incidental losses and expenses.** Section 54 preserves the right of both the buyer and the seller to recover "special damages".[68] Consequential losses and expenses are often claimed by the buyer[69] but seldom by the seller who normally has not made other arrangements which both depend on the fulfilment of the contract and also involve losses or expenses which were within the reasonable contemplation of the parties at the time the contract was made.[70] The seller's normal loss when the buyer fails to pay the price on the agreed date is the loss of the use of the money: for this type of loss, the seller may claim interest[71] but not general damages.[72]

The seller may claim his reasonable expenses on resale,[73] storage and other charges when the buyer delays in taking delivery of the goods,[74] and

---

[57] Above, para.9–062, n.74.
[58] Below, paras 19–153 *et seq.*; 19–207 *et seq.*; 20–110 *et seq.*; 20–127 *et seq.*
[59] Below, para.23–105.
[60] Below, para.23–168.
[61] (1854) 9 Exch. 341 (above, para.16–043).
[62] Above, para.16–045.
[63] Above, para.16–046.
[64] In addition to the cross-references given below, see above, paras 15–126, 15–127.
[65] *Thompson (WL) Ltd v Robinson (Gunmakers) Ltd* [1955] Ch. 177 (above, para.16–064).
[66] Above, paras 16–077 *et seq.*
[67] *Re Vic Mill Ltd* [1913] 1 Ch. 465; *Hill & Sons v Edwin Showell & Sons Ltd* (1918) 87 L.J.K.B. 1106, HL; see above, para.16–079.
[68] Above, para.16–046.
[69] See below, paras 17–036, 17–045, 17–061—17–062.
[70] On remoteness of damage, see above, paras 16–043 *et seq.*
[71] Considered above, in paras 16–007—16–012.
[72] See above, para.16–030.
[73] Below, para.16–087, *cf.* below, para.20–132.
[74] Below, para.16–088; *Vitol SA v Phibro Energy AG (The Mathraki)* [1990] 2 Lloyd's Rep. 84 (buyer's breach caused seller to become liable in damages to the carrier).

any other loss or expense which satisfies the tests of causation[75] and remoteness.[76] The seller's claim does not depend on whether or not the property in the goods has passed to the buyer, and may lie in addition to his claim to the price.[77] The principles underlying the cases on the buyer's claim for consequential losses or expenses[78] will, it is submitted, apply by analogy to similar claims made by the seller. It may even be possible, in special circumstances, for the seller to recover damages in respect of expenses incurred by him prior to, but in anticipation of, the making of the contract.[79]

Expenses in reselling. Where the seller, immediately upon the buyer's failure to accept the goods, resells at the market price, he will be entitled to recover damages in respect of any expenses reasonably incurred in effecting the resale.[80] Similarly, where the unpaid seller has resold the goods under section 48(3) or 48(4)[81] he may claim his reasonable expenses: section 48(3) expressly entitles the seller to "recover from the original buyer damages for any loss occasioned by his breach of contract."[82] The seller's loss, in addition to the difference between the contract price and any lower price received from the second buyer,[83] will include his incidental expenses in finding the second buyer, *e.g.* advertising costs[84] and storage charges.[85] 16–087

Storage and charges for care of the goods. Section 37, which is considered elsewhere,[86] entitles the seller to make claims arising from the storage of the goods. The main application of the section is where the property in the goods has passed to the buyer, who nevertheless neglects, in breach of his obligation, to take delivery of them: although the seller's main remedy in these circumstances is an action for the price,[87] he may in addition claim for losses and expenses under section 37.[88] However, where the seller sues, not for the price, but for damages for non-acceptance, his claim for 16–088

---

75 Above, para.16–049.
76 Above, paras 16–043 *et seq.; e.g.* cancellation expenses: *Bem Dis A. Turk Ticaret S/A TR v International Agri Trade Co. Ltd* [1999] 1 All E.R. (Comm) 619.
77 Above, para.16–030.
78 Below, paras 17–036, 17–045, 17–061—17–062.
79 *Anglia Television Ltd v Reed* [1972] 1 Q.B. 60 (discussed below, para.17–064).
80 This is accepted by s.48(3), *infra*, in the case of resale under that subsection: see *Ward (RV) Ltd v Bignall* [1967] 1 Q.B. 534 (above, para.16–083). It is also supported by an established rule of mitigation: see above, para.16–058.
81 Above, paras 15–119 *et seq.*, paras 15–128 *et seq.*
82 s.48(4), dealing with an express right of resale, speaks of the seller's claim for "damages", without adding the last nine words of s.48(3): but it is submitted that the meaning given to the word "damages" should be the same in both subsections.
83 Above, para.16–083.
84 *Ward (RV) Ltd v Bignall* [1967] 1 Q.B. 534.
85 Subject, of course, to the seller's "duty" to act reasonably in mitigating his loss: above, para.16–052. On the recovery of the cost of adapting the goods for resale, see above, para.16–078.
86 See above, para.9–009.
87 Above, paras 16–001 *et seq.*
88 On the buyer's expenses when the seller delays in making delivery, see below, para.17–046.

damages[89] will include the categories of losses and expenses envisaged by section 37.[90]

4. MISCELLANEOUS REMEDIES

16–089 **Recovery of possession, or damages for conversion.** Although the seller may have delivered the goods to the buyer, he may be entitled to recover possession from the buyer under an express term of the contract[91]; or where, before the property in the goods has passed to the buyer, he justifiably terminates the contract on account of the buyer's breach.[92] When the buyer has possession of the goods but not the property in them, he is the bailee of the seller who may be entitled, either under the terms of the contract or under the ordinary law of contract, to determine the bailment and demand the immediate return of the goods, if the buyer commits a breach of his obligations under the contract.[93] The appropriate remedies are the proprietary ones for chattels under the law of torts,[94] *viz.* proceedings for wrongful interference with the goods in which the claimant seeks an order for specific delivery of the goods,[95] or for damages for conversion when the buyer has dealt with the goods in a manner which denies the seller's title to them. Similarly, when the seller retains the property in the goods, he may be entitled, on the basis of his immediate right to possession of the goods, to bring proceedings for wrongful interference to obtain an order for specific delivery or damages[96] for conversion against a stranger who wrongfully interferes with the goods while they are in the possession of the buyer, or who wrongfully detains them after taking them out of the possession of the buyer. The unpaid seller[97] who is in possession of the goods as a result of his having exercised his right of lien[98] or of stoppage in transit[99] may bring proceedings for wrongful interference with the goods against a stranger; and the unpaid seller who is immediately entitled to possession of the goods by virtue of his having stopped the goods in transit may bring such proceedings against the carrier or other bailee who fails to comply with the seller's instructions,[1] or against a stranger who detains or interferes with the goods.

---

[89] Under ss.50 and 54 (above, paras 16–060, 16–086).
[90] Although it is possible that both s.50 and s.37 apply to such a case, the courts have not distinguished between them when a claim for damages lies under s.50.
[91] *McEntire v Crossley Bros* [1895] A.C. 457 at 464; and above, para.15–114; *Cf.* s.52 (below, para.16–093).
[92] See above, paras 15–107—15–116. In this situation, the seller's continuing property in the goods entitles him to bring proceedings for wrongful interference against the buyer.
[93] On fundamental breach, see above, paras 8–078—8–081, 13–042 *et seq.*, 15–109.
[94] *e.g. Bishop v Shillito* (1818) 2 B. & A. 329n. (conversion); *Rew v Payne, Douthwaite & Co.* (1885) 53 L.T. 932. *Cf.* below, paras 17–105—17–106.
[95] Under s.3(2)(a) of the Torts (Interference with Goods) Act 1977. See above, para.15–116.
[96] *ibid*.
[97] For definition, see above, paras 15–016 *et seq.*
[98] Above, paras 15–028 *et seq.*
[99] Above, paras 15–061 *et seq.* See also above, para.15–005.
[1] s.46(4) (above, para.15–088).

Mistake and misrepresentation. The seller may have a remedy to recover the goods where he has parted with possession of them under an apparent contract which is void *ab initio* for mistake[2]: no property in the goods passes under such a contract, and the "seller" may recover the goods (by virtue of his right to possession) from either the "buyer" or from anyone who has acquired them through the "buyer", including even a bona fide purchaser for value from the "buyer".[3] Where by fraud or misrepresentation the buyer has induced the seller to enter into the contract, the seller may have the remedies of damages and/or rescission of the contract, either at common law[4] or under the Misrepresentation Act 1967.[5] 16–090

Forfeiture of deposits or of prepayments. The seller's right to forfeit a deposit paid by the buyer is examined under the section on resale,[6] and his right to forfeit instalments of the price or other prepayments made by the buyer before his breach of contract, in the section on liquidated damages and penalties.[7] 16–091

Declarations. The seller may in appropriate circumstances obtain a declaration setting out his legal rights against the buyer.[8] For instance, although the seller who retains the property in the goods cannot normally sue for the price,[9] he may obtain a declaration that the buyer is bound to pay the price upon the seller's fulfilling his obligations, *e.g.* upon tender of the shipping documents.[10] But the Court of Appeal[11] has decided that a declaration of indemnity should not be made where, as a result of the buyer's breach of contract, a third party (*e.g.* the supplier to the seller) has a potential claim against the seller: if that liability is not too remote a head of loss in the seller's action against the buyer, the proper course is for the court to reserve that head of damages.[12] 16–092

---

[2] See above, paras 3–011—3–026; *Chitty on Contracts* (29th ed.), Vol. 1, paras 5–001 *et seq.*

[3] *Cundy v Lindsay* (1878) 3 App.Cas. 459; *Ingram v Little* [1961] 1 Q.B. 31.

[4] *cf.* above, paras 12–002—12–016, 12–121—12–127.

[5] *cf.* above, paras 12–004—12–010, 12–014—12–016, 12–119—12–120.

[6] Above, paras 15–132—15–133.

[7] Above, paras 16–038—16–042.

[8] *e.g. Household Machines Ltd v Cosmos Exporters Ltd* [1947] K.B. 217 (buyer granted a declaration, below, para.17–104); but on the use of the remedy in a case of indemnity, see *Trans Trust SPRL v Danubian Trading Co. Ltd* [1952] 2 Q.B. 297 (*infra*); in the latter case, however, the Court of Appeal did not object in principle to the use of the remedy of a declaration between buyer and seller. See Zamir and Woolf, *The Declaratory Judgment* (3rd ed.), esp. Ch. 4; and below, para.17–104 (buyer's claim).

[9] s.49(1) (above, para.16–021); but he may be entitled to do so under s.49(2) (above, para.16–025) or an express term in the contract (above, para.16–028).

[10] *Polenghi Brothers v Dried Milk Co. Ltd* (1904) 10 Com.Cas. 42 (below, paras 19–212—19–214). The court has a discretion to make a negative declaration, *e.g.* to the effect that the claimant is not liable to the defendant in respect of a certain matter: *Messier-Dowty Ltd v Sabena SA* [2000] 1 W.L.R. 2040, CA.

[11] *Trans Trust SPRL v Danubian Trading Co. Ltd*, above. (On the ground that the head of loss was too remote the CA reversed the decision of the judge below to grant the seller a declaration of indemnity.)

[12] *ibid.* (See further, below, para.17–104, n.42). *Cf. Deeny v Gooda Walker Ltd (No. 3)* [1995] 4 All E.R. 289.

16–093 **Specific performance and injunctions.** Section 52, which entitles the court to make an order for the specific performance of the contract, has been said to refer only to claims by the buyer[13] and not by the seller.[14] Normally, the seller's action for the price[15] will have an effect similar[16] to that of an order for specific performance: if the buyer is compelled to pay the price, he will be induced to take delivery of the goods, and if he delays in taking delivery, the seller may claim for storage and other expenses.[17] In appropriate cases, however, the seller may be able to obtain an injunction to prevent the buyer from breaking his contractual obligations, *e.g.* under an exclusive purchasing agreement.[18]

16–094 **Special remedies.** The seller may have special remedies where he has taken a negotiable instrument[19] or a documentary credit[20] for the price, or an export credit guarantee[21]; or where the contract contains an arbitration clause.[22] It should also be noted that section 60 of the Act provides that "Where a right, duty or liability is declared by this Act, it may (unless otherwise provided by this Act) be enforced by action."[23] It is suggested by Chalmers[24] that the purpose of this section is to ensure that a breach of a mandatory provision of the Act should not, in the absence of express provision for its enforcement, be treated as a criminal offence.[25]

---

[13] See below, paras 17–096—17–100.
[14] *Shell-Mex Ltd v Elton Cop Dyeing Co. Ltd* (1928) 34 Com.Cas. 39 at 46. (On the wording of the section, it is just possible to argue that the section could apply to the seller's claim to recover the goods (above, para.16–089).) See also *Elliott v Pierson* [1948] 1 All E.R. 939 at 942; Treitel [1966] J.B.L. 211 at 229–230.
[15] Above, paras 16–001 *et seq.*
[16] But not identical: *e.g.* if the seller is entitled to the price, the court has no *discretion* whether or not to give judgment for the price.
[17] See above, para.16–088.
[18] *Metropolitan Electric Supply Co. Ltd v Ginder* [1901] 2 Ch. 799 (see below, para.17–102; and Sharpe, *Injunctions and Specific Performance* (3rd ed.) paras 9.130–9.200).
[19] Above, paras 9–030—9–031. See also below, paras 22–031 *et seq.*
[20] Below, Ch.23, esp. paras 23–171—23–172.
[21] Below, Ch.24.
[22] *Chitty on Contracts* (29th ed.), Vol. II, Ch.32.
[23] s.60 replaces s.57 of the 1893 Act. The normal meaning of "action" is extended by s.61(1).
[24] *Sale of Goods Act 1893* (18th ed.), p.261.
[25] *Stephen's Digest of Criminal Law* (9th ed.), Art. 152.

CHAPTER 17

THE REMEDIES OF THE BUYER

	PARA.
1. Damages for non-delivery	17–001
(a) In general	17–001
(b) An available market	17–004
(i) The relevant market	17–005
(ii) The time for taking the market price	17–008
(iii) Anticipatory repudiation	17–013
(iv) The market price	17–017
(c) The absence of an available market	17–021
(d) Resale by the buyer	17–028
(e) Consequential losses	17–037
2. Damages for delay in delivery	17–038
(a) In general	17–038
(b) Loss of profit	17–040
(c) Resale by the buyer	17–044
(d) Extra or wasted expenditure	17–046
3. Damages for defective quality	17–047
(a) In general	17–047
(b) Diminution in value	17–051
(c) Losses other than diminution in value	17–059
(i) The buyer's actual or imputed knowledge of the defect	17–059
(ii) Additional or wasted expenditure	17–062
(iii) Loss of profit	17–066
(iv) Loss of amenity	17–071
(v) Physical injury to the buyer or his property	17–072
(vi) Compensation paid to a stranger	17–075
(vii) Compensation paid to a sub-buyer	17–076
(viii) Compensation paid in a chain of sub-sales	17–081
4. Other claims for damages	17–086
5. Repayment of the price or advance payments	17–090
6. Remedies other than claims to money	17–093
(a) Termination of the contract and rejection of the goods	17–093
(b) Rescission by the consumer	17–094
(c) Remedies for other invalidating causes	17–095
(d) Specific performance for delivery of the goods	17–096
(e) Specific performance for repairs or replacement granted to a consumer	17–101
(f) Injunctions and declarations	17–102
(g) Proprietary claims to possession or damages	17–105
(h) Criminal sanctions and extra-legal remedies	17–107

1. DAMAGES FOR NON-DELIVERY

(a) *In General*

Introduction. General principles of the law on damages have been considered in Chapter 16.[1] For the buyer's claim for damages for non-delivery, section 51 of the Act lays down the following rules: 17–001

[1] Above, paras 16–031—16–059.

"(1) Where the seller wrongfully neglects or refuses to deliver the goods to the buyer, the buyer may maintain an action against the seller for damages for non-delivery.

(2) The measure of damages is the estimated loss directly and naturally resulting, in the ordinary course of events, from the seller's breach of contract.

(3) Where there is an available market for the goods in question the measure of damages is prima facie to be ascertained by the difference between the contract price and the market or current price of the goods at the time or times when they ought to have been delivered, or (if no time was fixed) at the time of the refusal to deliver."

As with section 50(2),[2] the provisions of section 51(2) are in the terms of the first rule in *Hadley v Baxendale*[3] which have been examined in Chapter 16.[4] However, the assessment of the buyer's damages is not always restricted to the provisions of section 51, since by section 54,[5] the buyer also has his rights to recover interest[6] and special damages, *e.g.* for unusual loss resulting from special circumstances known to the contract-breaker,[7] or, in certain circumstances, loss of profits under a resale.[8] A clause in the contract may permit the buyer, upon the seller's default, to repurchase elsewhere, and to claim any loss from the seller.[9]

17–002 The buyer may claim damages for non-delivery even where the property in the goods has passed to the buyer[10]; but, whether or not the property in the goods has passed to the buyer, his damages for the seller's failure to deliver should be assessed on the same basis. If the buyer sues for wrongful interference with the goods seeking an order for specific delivery of goods in which he has the property,[11] the court has a discretion to award damages in lieu of judgment ordering specific delivery; when the court does not order specific delivery, it is submitted that the buyer's damages should be assessed on the same basis as if the claim was for damages for breach of contract under section 51.[12]

Section 51(1) applies where the seller "wrongfully" neglects or refuses to deliver the goods. The meaning of "wrongfully" depends on the precise

---

[2] Above, paras 16–060 *et seq*.
[3] (1854) 9 Exch. 341.
[4] Above, paras 16–043 *et seq*.
[5] Above, paras 16–007, 16–046, 16–086.
[6] Above, paras 16–007.
[7] Above, para.16–046; below, para.17–037.
[8] Below, paras 17–028—17–036.
[9] It was held in *Simmonds v Millar & Co.* (1898) 15 T.L.R. 100 that, in making such a repurchase, the buyer is not acting as the seller's agent: hence, the seller cannot claim any profit arising from the fact that the buyer was able to repurchase at a price lower than the contract price.
[10] *cf.* the appropriate remedy of the seller (above, paras 16–021 *et seq*., 16–060).
[11] See below, para.17–105. *Cf.* below, paras 17–096—17–100.
[12] Below, para.17–105. Thus, the damages may exceed the current value of the goods: *cf.* damages for consequential loss following late delivery (below, paras 17–040—17–046.)

obligation of the seller under the contract, which has been examined in an earlier chapter.[13] In assessing damages for breach of contract it must be assumed that the defendant would act, if entitled to do so under the contract, in the way least favourable to the claimant.[14] "A defendant is not liable in damages for not doing that which he is not bound to do."[15] Accordingly, the minimum legal obligation of the seller is the basis for assessing damages against him for failure to deliver the goods.[16] Thus, where the contract was for "200 tons, 5 per cent more or less", the margin was held to be at the seller's option and the damages were assessed on the basis of failure to deliver 190 tons.[17]

Section 51(2) applies either where there is no available market (within the meaning of section 51(3)) or where the "prima facie" rule in section 51(3) is deemed to be inapplicable.[18] For this reason, section 51(3) will be considered first, and section 51(2), which applies in the absence of an available market or when the "prima facie" rule should not be applied, afterwards.[19]

Special remedies for the consumer. Under the new Part 5A of the Act, where the goods fail to conform to the contract at the time of delivery, the buyer who deals as a consumer is given a number of new remedies in addition to the traditional remedies of damages or specific performance: an order requiring the seller to repair or replace the goods; or a reduction of the purchase price; or rescission of the contract. These new remedies are examined above in Chapter 12. 17–003

(b) *An Available Market*

Damages where there is an available market. Section 51(3) spells out the normal application of the rule in section 51(2) to the situation where there is "an available market" for the goods.[20] The normal measure of 17–004

---

[13] Above, paras 8–001 *et seq*.

[14] *cf. Edwards v Society of Graphical and Allied Trades* [1971] Ch. 354 at 380; *Withers v General Theatre Corporation Ltd* [1933] 2 K.B. 536 at 548–550 (not on sale of goods). *Cf.* below, para.17–008, text at n.58.

[15] *Abrahams v Herbert Reiach Ltd* [1922] 1 K.B. 477 at 482; *Lavarack v Woods of Colchester Ltd* [1967] 1 Q.B. 278 at 293; *The Mihalis Angelos* [1971] 1 Q.B. 164 at 196, 202–203, 209–210 (the assumed contract-breaker had an option to terminate the contract; damages were assessed on the basis that he would have exercised the option.)

[16] *Cockburn v Alexander* (1848) 6 C.B. 791 at 814.

[17] *Re Thornett and Fehr and Yuills Ltd* [1921] 1 K.B. 219 at 229–230. *Cf. Bunge Corporation, New York v Tradax Export SA, Panama* [1981] 1 W.L.R. 711 (HL: damages assessed in respect of the minimum quantity which the buyers were obliged to take). *Cf.* also *Paula Lee Ltd v Robert Zehil & Co. Ltd* [1983] 2 All E.R. 390 (not a sale of goods).

[18] See below, paras 17–007, 17–021 *et seq.*, *e.g. Pagnan (R) & Fratelli v Corbisa Industrial Agropacuaria* [1970] 1 W.L.R. 1306 (below, para.17–020). *Cf.* s.50(2) and (3) (see above, paras 16–060 *et seq.*, 16–077—16–079).

[19] Below, paras 17–021 *et seq*.

[20] Following the common law before the Act: *Barrow v Arnaud* (1846) 8 Q.B. 595 at 609–610. *Cf.* s.50(3) (above, paras 16–061 *et seq.*). On the question of a "market" in relation to c.i.f. contracts, see below, paras 19–176, 19–186, 19–201.

damages when the seller[21] fails to deliver the goods is the difference between (a) the market price of the relevant goods at the time[22] fixed for delivery and at the place[23] fixed for delivery,[24] and (b) the contract price.[25] (The subsection assumes that the buyer has not previously paid the price to the seller: if he has, the damages must also cover the price.)[26] One of the grounds for this measure of damages is the rules of mitigation (which have been discussed elsewhere[27]) since section 51(3) assumes that the reasonable buyer should have gone into the market, immediately following the seller's breach of contract, and bought substitute goods. With the amount of money designated by section 51(3), the buyer should therefore be in the same financial position as he would have been in if the seller had performed his contractual obligation to deliver.[28]

Despite the absence of proof of loss caused by a breach of contract, nominal damages are always recoverable by the innocent party to signify the fact of the other's breach[29]: thus, when section 51(3) applies, and the market price at the time of the breach is the same as, or less than, the contract price, the buyer is still entitled to nominal damages.[30]

Many of the problems which may arise in the interpretation of section 51(3) are almost identical with those under section 50(3), which have been discussed in Chapter 16.[31] The present section will therefore deal only with aspects which are peculiar to the buyer's claim for damages for non-delivery.

(i) *The Relevant Market*

17–005 **An available market for the buyer.** The meaning of the term "an available market" has been discussed at length in Chapter 16, to which reference should be made.[32] In general, the same factors should be relevant in deciding whether there is such a market from the buyer's point of view

---

[21] By analogy, the same measure of damages has been used when an auctioneer at an auction expressed to be "without reserve" is liable to the highest bidder under a collateral contract that he would sell to that bidder: *Barry v Davies (trading as Heathcote Ball & Co.)* [2000] 1 W.L.R. 1962, CA (the goods were new.) (See above, para.2–005.)
[22] Below, para.17–008.
[23] Above, para.16–068.
[24] *Aryeh v Lawrence Kostoris & Son Ltd* [1967] 1 Lloyd's Rep. 63 at 73.
[25] On the ascertainment of the price, see above, paras 2–044—2–052, 9–021, *et seq.*
[26] See also below, para.17–009.
[27] Above, paras 16–052 *et seq.*
[28] The purpose for which the buyer wanted the goods is normally irrelevant: hence, where the buyer is a non-profit-making organisation the ordinary rule still applies: *Diamond Cutting Works Federation Ltd v Triefus & Co. Ltd* [1956] 1 Lloyd's Rep. 216 at 227.
[29] *Marzetti v Williams* (1830) 1 B. & Ad. 415; *The Mediana* [1900] A.C. 113 at 116.
[30] *Erie County Natural Gas and Fuel Co. Ltd v Carroll* [1911] A.C. 105 at 117–118 (PC, citing *Valpy v Oakeley* (1851) 16 Q.B. 941; and *Griffiths v Perry* (1859) 1 E. & E. 680). *Cf. Charter v Sullivan* [1957] 2 Q.B. 117 (above, para.16–065: nominal damages awarded to the seller).
[31] Above, paras 16–061 *et seq.*
[32] Above, paras 16–062—16–076.

(section 51(3)) as from the seller's (section 50(3)). The reported decisions draw no distinction between the meaning of "an available market" in the two subsections,[33] although it is obvious that in the one the question is the availability of substitute sellers and, in the other, the availability of substitute buyers.[34] The buyer is naturally concerned with an available market in the sense of his ability to *buy* substitute goods, *i.e.* the ready capacity of willing sellers to supply quickly goods of the relevant category.[35] The question is whether there was a sufficient number of sellers to meet readily all demands from prospective buyers.[36] Thus, if the demand for the goods exceeds the supply, so that some prospective buyers are unable to obtain the goods they wish, the rule in section 51(3) will not apply.[37] An excessive price may show that the supply of the goods is insufficient to constitute an "available market".[38]

The willing sellers should be immediately[39] accessible to the buyer, and within a reasonable distance of the place fixed by the contract for delivery.[40] The question whether the buyer, in order to comply with the rules of mitigation, should buy substitute goods available in a market at a distance from the contractual place of delivery, depends on a test of what was reasonable from the buyer's point of view.[41] Similarly, it is submitted[42] that the temporal test of availability should be satisfied if substitute goods are available for delivery to the buyer a reasonable time after the seller's breach; what is a reasonable time will depend on the nature of the goods in question and the business situation of the buyer.[43] Where the buyer needed to obtain 15,000 tons of lard for immediate delivery in the United Kingdom, the House of Lords apparently accepted[44] that there could be an available market from the buyer's point of view when he could buy in the USA, for delivery to ports for shipment to the United Kingdom, smaller

---

33 Lawson, 43 A.L.J. 106 at 113 (1969).

34 For authority, see above, para.16–070, nn.61 and 62.

35 Above, paras 16–066—16–072. On the question whether there is an "available market" for goods afloat which are sold by reference to a particular set of shipping documents, see below, para.19–176.

36 *cf.* above, paras 16–064—16–066.

37 *cf. Charter v Sullivan* [1957] 2 Q.B. 117 (the opposite case, where the buyer defaulted in this situation: above, para.16–065).

38 *cf. O'Hanlan v G.W. Ry* (1865) 6 B. & S. 484 at 494.

39 See above, para.16–067.

40 On the extent of the market area, see above, para.16–068. On the question *which* market is relevant when damages are assessed for breach of a seller's obligations under a c.i.f. contract, see below, para.19–186.

41 *Garnac Grain Co. Inc. v H. M. F. Faure and Fairclough Ltd*, below; *Lesters Leather and Skin Co. Ltd v Home and Overseas Brokers Ltd*, below. See above, paras 16–067—16–069; and *cf. Hasell v Bagot, Shakes and Lewis Ltd* (1911) 13 C.L.R. 374.

42 Following the similar submission made in the case of s.50(3) (above, para.16–067). But see the point made in n.39 to that para.)

43 See, however, *Shearson Lehman Hutton Inc. v Maclaine Watson & Co. Ltd* (*No.* 2) [1990] 3 All E.R. 723 (below). *Cf. Charter v Sullivan*, above, at pp.133–134 (discussed above, para.16–067).

44 *Garnac Grain Co. Inc. v HMF Faure and Fairclough Ltd* [1968] A.C. 1130 at 1138 (*cf.* above, para.16–069). *Cf.* the different opinion in the same case in the CA: [1966] 1 Q.B. 650 at 687. *Cf.* also *Petrotrade Inc. v Stinnes Handel GmbH* [1995] 1 Lloyd's Rep. 142 (above, para.16–069, n.54).

quantities separately (up to 2,000 tons at a time) and spread over a period.[45] Similarly, with some types or quantities of goods, negotiations with potential sellers might take several days: in these circumstances, the market price should be fixed on the assumption that the hypothetical purchaser had begun to negotiate sufficiently far ahead to enable a purchase to be made on the day in question.[46] In another case, where the sellers failed to deliver goods of merchantable quality[47] at a United Kingdom port, the Court of Appeal held[48] that the fact that there was a market for the purchase of similar goods in India did not impose on the buyers a "duty" to mitigate by ordering substitute goods from India. The reasons given for this ruling were that the substitute goods would reach England too late, *viz.* about eight months after the delivery date in the contract, and that the buyers could not be under a duty to buy from "some unknown seller in India."[49]

17-006 If the goods were to be manufactured specially to suit the particular requirements or specifications of the buyer it is most unlikely that there would be an available market in which he could buy suitable substitute goods.[50] Where goods are in short supply, so that retail sellers have agreed to a fixed price for selling the goods, a "black market" operating in defiance of contractual obligations has been treated as relevant to fix the market price when that is the only source of substitute goods available to the disappointed buyer.[51]

17-007 **Where the "prima facie" rule should not apply.** Section 51(3) is only a "prima facie" rule, and will not apply when the parties ought, at the time of making the contract, to have contemplated as reasonable men[52] that the rule would not compensate the buyer for his loss, should the seller fail to deliver.[53] In a case dealing with the assessment of the buyer's damages for breach of warranty (section 53) the Court of Appeal said[54] that the basic rule is section 53(2), the provision enacting the first rule in *Hadley v Baxendale*, which corresponds to section 51(2); and that the "market value" rule in section 53(3), which corresponds to section 51(3), should not apply if it would give the buyer "more than his true loss". If the analogy of this decision is followed it may lead to courts being more willing than in the

---

45 It is submitted that the period must be reasonable from the buyer's point of view (see above, para.16-069).

46 The *Shearson Lehman* case, above, p.731 (seller's claim: breach by buyer). This assumption is consistent with the *Garnac Grain* case, above.

47 The buyers justifiably rejected the goods which the sellers tendered.

48 *Lesters Leather and Skin Co. Ltd v Home and Overseas Brokers Ltd* (1948) 64 T.L.R. 569 (snake-skins). See below, para.19-186.

49 *ibid.* at p.569.

50 See the authorities cited above, para.16-067, n.43.

51 *Mouatt v Betts Motors Ltd* [1959] A.C. 71; *British Motor Trade Association v Gilbert* [1951] 2 All E.R. 641. See above, para.16-069.

52 See above, paras 16-043—16-045.

53 *cf.* on the analogous s.50(3): *Thompson (W L) Ltd v Robinson (Gunmakers) Ltd* [1955] Ch. 177 (above, para.16-064).

54 *Bence Graphics International Ltd v Fasson UK Ltd* [1998] Q.B. 87. (See below, paras 17-058, 17-082).

past not to apply the other "prima facie" rules in sections 50(3) and 51(3) which are based on the market price at the time of the breach. Section 51(3) will not apply if it is inappropriate in special circumstances, as where, following negotiations with the seller after his breach, the buyer finally accepted the same goods from the seller at a price lower than the market price either at the date of the breach or at the date of the final agreement.[55]

(ii) *The Time for taking the Market Price*

Relevant time for the market price. Section 51(3) specifies the time at which the market price is to be taken in assessing damages as "the time or times when [the goods] ought to have been delivered or (if no time was fixed) at the time of the refusal to deliver." The provisions of the contract must be looked at to determine whether a time has been fixed for delivery of the goods, and, if so, the exact time for delivery.[56] When the contract specifies that delivery is to be made by separate instalments at different times, the market price for each instalment is taken separately at the date when the particular instalment should have been delivered.[57] Where the contract fixes a period within which the seller is to make delivery of the goods, the time for fixing the market price in the event of non-delivery is the last possible time within that period: the seller is entitled to tender delivery to the buyer up till that moment.[58] If negotiations for purchase of the goods in question might take several days, the market price should be fixed on the assumption that negotiations had begun earlier so as to enable the purchase to be completed on the day in question.[59] It has also been held that a time is "fixed" for the purposes of section 51(3) if it is fixed by reference to the happening of a future event, *e.g.* the arrival of a ship at a certain destination.[60] 17–008

If the obligation imposed on the seller is to deliver the goods on a fixed date, it may be assumed that he has the whole of the usual business hours of that day in which to make delivery.[61] In the absence of the seller's repudiation of his obligation to deliver, the buyer may not know until the close of the usual business hours on that day whether the seller has neglected to deliver, and it will then be impracticable for the buyer to buy substitute goods in the market on that day. It is submitted that in these circumstances the relevant time for taking the market price under section 51(3) should be the first practical opportunity which the buyer reasonably[62]

---

[55] *Pagnan (R.) & Fratelli v Corbisa Industrial Agropacuaria* [1970] 1 W.L.R. 1306 (below, para.17–020).

[56] Above, paras 8–025—8–043. The contract itself may also specify the time by reference to which the damages are to be assessed: see below, para.19–181.

[57] *Brown v Muller* (1872) L.R. 7 Ex. 319; *Roper v Johnson* (1873) L.R. 8 C.P. 167; *Re Voss* (1873) L.R. 16 Eq. 155.

[58] *Leigh v Paterson* (1818) 8 Taunt. 540 at 541. See above, para.16–071. *Cf.* above, para.17–002.

[59] *Shearson Lehman Hutton Inc. v Maclaine Watson & Co. Ltd (No.* 2) [1990] 3 All E.R. 723.

[60] *Melachrino v Nickoll and Knight* [1920] 1 K.B. 693 at 696.

[61] *Roper v Johnson*, above, at p.179 (". . . there is no breach until that day has passed.") *Cf. Leigh v Paterson*, above. *Cf.* also s.29(5) (above, para.8–041).

[62] The "duty" to mitigate implied in s.51(3) only requires the buyer to take reasonable steps to mitigate his loss following the seller's breach of contract (see above, para.16–052).

had to buy in the market, *e.g.* normally on the next business day.[63] In one case, where the buyer accepted the seller's anticipatory repudiation, the time when the buyer should have bought substitute goods was held to be either during the five hours of trading (on the same day) left after the buyer's acceptance of the repudiation, or on the next day.[64] In another (House of Lords) case, Lord Wilberforce accepted (*obiter*) that "the common law, and prima facie, s.51 of the Act, provide for damages to be ascertained by reference to the price as on the last day for performance".[65] The case concerned a special clause in the contract that "damages shall be based upon the actual or estimated value of the goods on the date of default",[66] which was interpreted by the majority of their Lordships as meaning the day immediately following the last day for performance, since that was the first day on which the buyer could "buy in on the market"[67]; ". . . this seems . . . to accord with commercial reality and business sense."[68] "To hold that if the buyer does not buy in he can recover damages based on the price of [in this case] July 10—*i.e.* a day before he could have bought—would create injustices. . ."[69] It is difficult to understand why this reasoning should not in appropriate circumstances apply to the interpretation of section 51(3). Since section 51(3) is only a prima facie rule, the market price should be taken at the date when, on the facts of the particular case, the buyer could have bought substitute goods.

If the contract requires the seller to deliver the goods after transporting them to a specified destination, it is the normal[70] rule that the time and place of the final destination are the time and place which are relevant for fixing the relevant market price.[71] In later chapters of this work there is

---

[63] *Roper v Johnson*, above, at p.179; *Gainsford v Carroll* (1824) 2 B. & C. 624 at 625 (the buyer "might have purchased" similar goods "the very day after the contract was broken"); *Shearson Lehman Hutton Inc. v Maclaine Watson & Co. Ltd* (*No.* 2) [1990] 3 All E.R. 723 at 727 (". . . the time for delivery expired at midnight on March 12, so that March 13 would have been the first date on which [the claimants] could have sold . . ."). *Cf.* also *Gelmini v Moriggia* [1913] 2 K.B. 549 (duty to pay on a certain day: the cause of action is complete on the following day).

[64] *Kaines (UK) Ltd v Osterreischische Warrenhandelsgesellschaft, etc*. [1993] 2 Lloyd's Rep. 1 at 11, 12.

[65] *Bremer Handelsgesellschaft mbH v Vanden Avenne-Izegem PVBA* [1978] 2 Lloyd's Rep. 109 at 117. (Two members of the CA in a previous case had also assumed *obiter* that "the time" in s.51(3) means "the last day for performance": *Toepfer* (*Alfred C.*) *v. Peter Cremer* [1975] 2 Lloyd's Rep. 118 at 124, 128).

[66] The full clause is found in the report of the decision below: [1977] 1 Lloyd's Rep. 133. See below, para.19–181.

[67] The *Bremer* case, above, at pp.117, 129, 131. (*Cf.* Viscount Dilhorne dissenting at p.122: "I see no reason to construe 'date of default' as meaning 'date in default'"). On the interpretation of this clause, the majority of their Lordships in the HL disagreed with the CA in the *Toepfer* case, above, at pp.124–125, 126.

[68] The *Bremer* case, above, at p.129, *per* Lord Salmon.

[69] *ibid.*, at p.117. See *C Czarnikow Ltd v Bunge & Co. Ltd* [1987] 1 Lloyd's Rep. 202 at 205; see also below, para.19–181, n.24.

[70] *cf. van den Hurk v R Martens & Co. Ltd* [1920] 1 K.B. 850 (the parties knew that the goods could not be examined until the time they finally reached the sub-buyer: see below, para.17–054).

[71] *Melachrino v Nickoll and Knight* [1920] 1 K.B. 693; *ABD* (*Metals and Waste*) *Ltd v Anglo Chemical and Ore Co. Ltd* [1955] 2 Lloyd's Rep. 456 at 466. See also below, para.21–031.

discussion of the question of the time when the market value should be taken when the seller commits a breach of a c.i.f. contract,[72] or of an f.o.b. contract.[73]

17–009 **Damages when price paid in advance.** It could possibly be argued[74] that the time specified in section 51(3) is not appropriate when the buyer has paid the price to the seller in advance of the time fixed for delivery, and the market price rises between the time when the seller fails to deliver and the judgment in favour of the buyer. The buyer might say that only the amount of the higher market value at the time of judgment would put him into the same financial position as he would have been in if there had been no breach by the seller: since he has already paid the price, his financial position at the date of the seller's breach is to that extent worse[75] than the normal situation where the price would be paid only if delivery were made.[76] Although some support for this argument may be found in old decisions on the defendants' failure to replace stock[77] and in an early case on the sale of goods,[78] in another early case on sale of goods[79] the court refused to follow the cases on the purchase of stock and thus refused to award the buyer damages in respect of the higher market price at the date of its judgment. It is submitted that the latter case should be followed, since the buyer should normally be able to borrow to finance a purchase in the market at the time of the seller's breach.[80]

17–010 **No time fixed for delivery.** The second limb of section 51(3), that when no time was fixed for delivery of the goods, the market price is to be taken at the time of the seller's refusal to deliver, does not apply to an anticipatory repudiation by the seller.[81] A Divisional Court has decided[82] that a contract for delivery of the goods within a reasonable time is not a contract with a fixed time for delivery within section 51(3); but the Court of Appeal in the same case dismissed the appeal on other grounds[83] and

---

72 Below, paras 19–176—19–186 (where there is a full examination of *C Sharpe & Co. Ltd v Nosawa* [1917] 2 K.B. 814).
73 Below, paras 20–114—20–116.
74 In *Aronson v Mologa Holzindustrie AG* (1927) 32 Com.Cas. 276 at 289–291, Atkin L.J. treats the question as open.
75 *Startup v Cortazzi* (1835) 2 C.M. & R. 165 (as the buyers "had already parted with their money, they were not then in a situation to purchase other seed": *ibid.*, at p.169). On the possible relevance of the buyer's financial position, see above, paras 16–054—16–055.
76 s.28 (above, para.8–004).
77 *Shepherd v Johnson* (1802) 2 East 211; *McArthur v Seaforth* (1810) 2 Taunt. 257. See *McGregor on Damages* (17th ed.), paras 24–012—24–014.
78 *Gainsford v Carroll* (1824) 2 B. & C. 624 (because the buyer still had the money intended to be used for the price, the higher market price at the time of judgment was held to be irrelevant).
79 *Startup v Cortazzi*, above.
80 The court could consider an award of interest on the price, whether it is recovered by way of restitution or as part of the damages: see above, para.16–007.
81 *Tai Hing Cotton Mill Ltd v Kamsing Knitting Factory* [1979] A.C. 91, PC. On this question, see below, paras 17–013 *et seq.*, where the assessment of damages in this situation is examined. See also below, para.19–179.
82 *Millett v Van Heek & Co.* [1920] 3 K.B. 535. *Cf.* above, para.16–072 (on s.50(3)).
83 *Viz.* that s.51(3) does not apply to an anticipatory breach by the seller (below, para.17–014).

expressly reserved its opinion on this point in the decision of the Divisional Court.[84] It is not clear to which circumstances the second limb of section 51(3) may apply. The Privy Council has even said that: "It may well be . . . that the enactment was introduced into the subsection without consideration in depth of the juristic position, and that on analysis it proves, exceptionally, to have no content whatever. It would be surprising if the first limb of one and the same subsection were intended to be a specific application of the general principle in the preceding subsection, [s.51(2)] and the second limb to be a radical departure from it."[85] It is submitted that the only natural application of the concluding words of section 51(3), in the context of the words "the refusal to deliver", would be to a contract where the seller was to deliver at the request of the buyer[86]; and that where delivery is to be made within a reasonable time of the making of the contract,[87] the relevant market price should not necessarily be that prevailing at the date of the seller's refusal to deliver (which may in some circumstances be an anticipatory refusal) but at the time, perhaps later than the refusal, when it would have been reasonable for the seller to deliver.[88]

17–011 **Postponement at seller's request of time fixed for delivery.** The assessment of damages when the time fixed for delivery has been postponed by the parties depends on whose request led to the postponement.[89] If it was at the seller's request,[90] but he fails to deliver the goods at or before the postponed date of delivery, the breach occurs at the latter date[91] and the damages should be assessed on the basis of the market price at that date.[92] If there was a simple waiver by the buyer of the date fixed for delivery, without a specific date being substituted, a reasonable time (presumably

---

[84] [1921] 2 K.B. 369.

[85] *Tai Hing Cotton Mill Ltd v Kamsing Knitting Factory*, above, at p.104.

[86] See the dictum of Atkin L.J., quoted above, para.16–072. However in *Tai Hing Cotton Mill Ltd v Kamsing Knitting Factory*, above, at p.104, the PC said that once a demand had been made by the buyer "in accordance with the contract", it "would fix the time for delivery" (so bringing the case under the first limb of s.51(3)).

[87] Or from some other fixed point of time.

[88] *Tai Hing Cotton Mill Ltd v Kamsing Knitting Factory*, above. *Cf.* the *obiter dictum* in *Melachrino v Nickoll and Knight* [1920] 1 K.B. 693 at 696 (". . . when s.51 speaks of no time being fixed for delivery it refers to those contracts in which no mention of time is made and which therefore are to be performed within the indefinite period known as a reasonable time under the circumstances").

[89] *cf.* the analogous situation in assessing the seller's damages (above, para.16–073).

[90] Which normally means for his benefit.

[91] If a period was fixed within which the postponed delivery was to take place, the last day of the period should be taken: *Ogle v Vane* (1868) L.R. 3 Q.B. 272. *Cf. Leigh v Paterson* (1818) 8 Taunt. 540 at 541 (above, para.17–007).

[92] *Ogle v Vane*, above (This decision was mentioned with approval by the House of Lords in *Johnson v Agnew* [1980] A.C. 367 at 401); *Blackburn Bobbin Co. Ltd v T W. Allen & Sons Ltd* [1918] 1 K.B. 540 at 553–554 (affirmed on another ground: [1918] 2 K.B. 467); *Sheik Mohammad Habib Ullah v Bird & Co.* (1921) 37 T.L.R. 405 at 406 (PC accepting the principles in *Tyers v Rosedale and Ferryhill Iron Co. Ltd* (1875) L.R. 10 Ex. 195, where the buyer requested postponement; see below, para.17–012); *Johnson Matthey Bankers Ltd v The State Trading Corporation of India Ltd* [1984] 1 Lloyd's Rep. 427 at 436–438. *Cf.* above, para.16–073.

calculated from the due date[93]) is taken as the new date for delivery.[94] These rules apply only where there is a definite request by the seller for the postponement, and a promise by him that he will deliver at the postponed date or within the postponed period: mere forbearance by the buyer from insisting upon delivery upon the original contractual date for delivery will not entitle him to claim damages on the basis of a higher market price at a later date.[95]

Postponement of delivery at buyer's request. If the request for postponement of the delivery date was made by the buyer, and the seller agreed to the postponement but later repudiated his obligation to deliver, this repudiation will constitute a breach by the seller[96] so that the damages should be calculated by reference to the market price at the date of the seller's repudiation.[97] If the delivery date was postponed indefinitely at the request of the buyer, he cannot without notice call on the seller to deliver immediately; but the buyer may give notice fixing the date for delivery a reasonable time thereafter.[98] If the original arrangement was for delivery by instalments over a period, the postponement may have the effect of postponing the period of delivery, so that when the buyer requests the seller to deliver, he is bound to commence a new period of deliveries by instalments of the same amounts and at the same intervals as originally fixed.[99] 17–012

After granting a postponement of delivery to a definite date, the seller cannot refuse to deliver on the ground that the buyer was unable or unwilling to take delivery on the original date fixed for delivery: however, he may,[1] by giving reasonable notice to the buyer that he retracts his agreement to the postponement, oblige the buyer to accept the goods upon the expiry of that notice.[2]

---

[93] However, in *Ogle v Vane*, above, it was suggested that in this situation the damages should be assessed at a reasonable period after the time when the buyer agreed to the postponement. *Cf.* above, para.16–073.

[94] *Sheik Mohammad Habib Ullah v Bird & Co.*, above, at p.406.

[95] *Re Voss* (1873) L.R. 16 Eq. 155 (distinguishing *Ogle v Vane*, above). The buyers had in fact bought some substitute goods in the market at the dates when the seller failed to deliver instalments, and this fact contradicted the alleged postponement of delivery dates by consent. *Cf. Johnson v Agnew*, above.

[96] *Tyers v Rosedale and Ferryhill Iron Co. Ltd*, above. *Cf. Hartley v Hymans* [1920] 3 K.B. 475 (above, para.16–073).

[97] *Tyers v Rosedale and Ferryhill Iron Co. Ltd*, above. (But the decision of the court is not definite on this point: the obligation was to deliver by instalments, and the postponed period of the instalments would have extended beyond the date of the seller's repudiation.) On the time for taking the market price in a case of anticipatory repudiation, see below, paras 17–014—17–016).

[98] *ibid.*, at p.199 (*obiter*). See also on waiver, above, para.8–030.

[99] *ibid.*

[1] Unless there has been a binding variation of the contract of sale, *e.g.* supported by consideration.

[2] See above, para.8–030.

(iii) *Anticipatory Repudiation*[3]

17–013 **The seller's anticipatory repudiation.** The rules for the seller's anticipatory repudiation correspond with those for the buyer's anticipatory repudiation.[4] Where the seller, before the date fixed for delivery of the goods, repudiates his liability under the contract, the buyer has a choice[5]: he may either accept the repudiation as a breach and immediately sue for damages, or he may refuse to accept the repudiation and continue to treat the seller as bound by his contractual obligations.[6]

17–014 **Acceptance of the seller's anticipatory repudiation.** Where the buyer chooses the first alternative, and treats the repudiation as an immediate breach of contract, the relevant date for taking the market price[7] is, prima facie, and subject to the rules on mitigation,[8] the due date for delivery—not the date of the repudiation nor the date of the buyer's acceptance of the repudiation.[9] If the buyer's claim is heard before the date for delivery arrives, the court must attempt to estimate what the market price is likely to be at that date,[10] *e.g.* by taking into account the current trend of the market. The provision in section 51(3) that "if no time was fixed" for delivery, the relevant market price is taken "at the time of the refusal to deliver" does not apply to an anticipatory breach by the seller,[11] (*e.g.* when the seller's obligation was to deliver within a reasonable time).

17–015 **The rules on mitigation.** However, the "duty" to mitigate[12] is imposed on the buyer as soon as he accepts the seller's anticipatory repudiation, and this "duty" may override the prima facie rule stated in the preceding paragraph: the buyer's damages will be assessed on the basis that, following

---

[3] See above, paras 8–078—8–082, 9–010—9–020; George [1971] J.B.L. 109.
[4] Above, paras 16–080—16–082.
[5] *Fercometal S.A.R.L. v Mediterranean Shipping Co. SA* [1989] A.C. 788; the *Kaines* case, below, n.13. *Cf.* above, para.16–082, n.40.
[6] The buyer is not bound to act "reasonably" in choosing between his alternative courses of action (see above, para.16–080, n.28).
[7] *s.c.* in the situation where there is an available market in which to buy similar goods (see above, paras 16–062 *et seq.*).
[8] Below, para.17–015.
[9] *Garnac Grain Co. Inc. v HMF Faure and Fairclough Ltd* [1968] A.C. 1130 at 1140; *Tai Hing Cotton Mill Ltd v Kamsing Knitting Factory* [1979] A.C. 91 at 102. (The PC in this case was not asked to consider whether any "duty" to mitigate arose: see below, para.17–015, n.15). The earlier authorities were *Roper v Johnson* (1873) L.R. 8 C.P. 167; and *Melachrino v Nickoll and Knight* [1920] 1 K.B. 693 at 699.
[10] *Melachrino v Nickoll and Knight*, above, at p.699; *Millett v Van Heek & Co.* [1921] 2 K.B. 369 (CA affirmed [1920] 3 K.B. 535); *Roper v Johnson*, above. *Cf. The Mihalis Angelos* [1971] 1 Q.B. 164; and see above, para.16–081, n.31. A discount should be made in respect of any accelerated receipt (through the damages award) of any sum due in the future: *cf. Lavarack v Woods of Colchester Ltd* [1967] 1 Q.B. 278.
[11] *Tai Hing Cotton Mill Ltd v Kamsing Knitting Factory*, above (following *Millett v Van Heek & Co.*, above.) *Cf.* above, para.17–010; below, para.20–116. See the similar submission in respect of s.50(3) (above, para.16–081).
[12] See above, paras 16–052 *et seq.* It is not strictly a "duty": the buyer's damages are assessed on the basis that he should have acted reasonably so as to mitigate his loss.

his acceptance of the repudiation, he should have taken reasonable steps to reduce his loss, *e.g.* by buying substitute goods in the market.[13] The onus of proof is on the contract-breaker, the seller, to show that the buyer ought reasonably to have bought substitute goods at a time earlier than the date fixed for delivery under the contract[14]; if the seller fails to produce evidence to show that the buyer should have repurchased in the market, the buyer's damages should be calculated with reference to the market price at the due date for delivery.[15] But where the seller can prove that the buyer should reasonably have mitigated his loss by repurchasing before the due date, the relevant market price is that existing at the date the buyer ought reasonably[16] to have bought the substitute goods.[17] (Neither the price at the date of the repudiation, nor that at the date when the repudiation is accepted, is strictly relevant.[18]) If the market price was rising after the date when the repudiation was accepted, it would normally have been reasonable that the buyer should have bought in the market immediately, and if he failed to do so, he will be unable to recover as damages the difference between the lower price on the date he ought to have bought and the higher price on the date when he in fact bought substitute goods.[19]

However, if the buyer accepts the anticipatory repudiation but does not in fact mitigate by repurchasing in the market when he ought reasonably to have done so, the market price may fall between that date and the date fixed for delivery: it has been held that in these circumstances the buyer's damages will be assessed by reference to the lower price at the later date.[20] This rule is said to avoid placing the buyer in a better position than he

---

[13] *Kaines (UK) Ltd v Osterreichische Warrenhandelsgessellschaft, etc.* [1993] 2 Lloyd's Rep. 1 at 11, 12; *Melachrino v Nickoll and Knight*, above, at p.697; *Garnac Grain Co. Inc. v HMF Faure and Fairclough Ltd* [1966] 1 Q.B. 650 at 687 (on appeal [1968] A.C. 1130 at 1140). See the similar rule upon the buyer's anticipatory repudiation (above, para.16–081, n.35).

[14] *Roper v Johnson* (1873) L.R. 8 C.P. 167; *Garnac Grain Co. Inc. v HMF Faure and Fairclough Ltd* [1968] A.C. 1130.

[15] *Roper v Johnson*, above; *Garnac Grain Co. Inc. v HMF Faure and Fairclough Ltd*, above, at p.1140; *Tai Hing Cotton Mill Ltd v Kamsing Knitting Factory*, above, at p.105. (The seller in this case did not argue that the buyer should have mitigated by buying in the market between the date he accepted the seller's repudiation, and the date when delivery could have been required under the contract: the market price was falling between the two dates.)

[16] The buyer is allowed a "reasonable time" after his acceptance of the seller's breach before he must repurchase. So when the buyer accepted the seller's anticipatory repudiation, he should have bought in either during the five hours of trading left on the same day (after his acceptance) or on the next day: *Kaines (U.K.) Ltd v Osterreichische Warrenhandelsgessellschaft, etc.* [1993] 2 Lloyd's Rep. 1 at 11, 12. *Cf. Tredegar Iron and Coal Co. (Ltd) v Hawthorn Bros & Co.* (1902) 18 T.L.R. 716 (buyer's anticipatory breach: above, para.16–081, n.38).

[17] *Melachrino v Nickoll and Knight*, above, at pp.697, 699. See the similar rule for the buyer's anticipatory repudiation (above, para.16–081, n.37); and also below, para.19–179.

[18] See the analogous submissions made above, para.16–081, in n.38.

[19] *Melachrino v Nickoll and Knight*, above, at pp.697, 699.

[20] This was the actual decision in *Melachrino v Nickoll and Knight*, above, at p.698 (although the judgment contains many other propositions cited in this paragraph). *Cf. Tai Hing Cotton Mill Ltd v Kamsing Knitting Factory*, above, at p.1059 (see n.15, above).

would have been in if the contract had been performed[21]; thus, if the market price falls, the buyer's damages will be reduced, whereas if the price rises, the damages will be restricted to the lower price prevailing when he ought to have repurchased.

If the buyer reasonably attempts to mitigate by buying substitute goods in the market, he is entitled to have his damages assessed by reference to the market price at the date of the repurchase, despite the fact that the market price happened to be lower by the time the due date for delivery arrived.[22]

17–016 **Seller's anticipatory repudiation not accepted.** If the buyer chooses the second alternative[23] and does not accept the seller's anticipatory repudiation, it is treated as a "nullity"[24] and the contract continues to bind both parties[25]: the buyer will then await the date fixed for delivery, and the seller will commit a breach of contract only if he then fails to deliver. Thus, the seller may change his mind before the due date and (without breach of contract) fulfil his contractual obligation by delivering on that date[26]; or the contract may be terminated without a breach by the seller, *e.g.* by the seller exercising a right under the contract to cancel it[27]; by frustration[28] or by a fundamental breach by the buyer which justifies the seller in terminating the contract.[29] The "duty" on the buyer to mitigate his loss by taking reasonable steps arises only upon the seller's breach: thus, in the case of an unaccepted anticipatory repudiation by the seller, the buyer is bound to seek substitute goods in an available market immediately when the breach actually occurs, but not earlier, and his damages are assessed with reference to the market price at the date of the breach.[30] The buyer's damages for non-delivery at the due date cannot be reduced because the market price was lower at the date of the repudiation (or at any date between the repudiation and the due date for delivery[31]). When the market price is

---

[21] [1920] 1 K.B. 693 at 698–699. The propositions accepted in *The Mihalis Angelos* [1971] 1 Q.B. 164 lend some support, by way of analogy, to this conclusion.
[22] *Melachrino v Nickoll and Knight*, above, at pp.697, 699. The proposition in the text is in accord with the rules of mitigation (above, para.16–058). *Cf. Roth & Co. v Taysen Townsend & Co.* (1896) 12 T.L.R. 211 (buyer's anticipatory refusal to accept: above, para.16–081).
[23] See above, para.17–013.
[24] *Phillpotts v Evans* (1839) 5 M. & W. 475 at 477; *White and Carter (Councils) Ltd v McGregor* [1962] A.C. 413 at 444.
[25] *Fercometal SARL v Mediterranean Shipping Co. SA* [1989] A.C. 788.
[26] *Leigh v Paterson* (1818) 8 Taunt. 540.
[27] *cf.* the *Fercometal* case, above.
[28] Above, paras 6–034 *et seq.*; *Avery v Bowden* (1855) 5 E. & B. 714 (affirmed (1856) 6 E. & B. 953); the *Fercometal* case, above, pp.800, 805.
[29] Above, para.15–109.
[30] *Leigh v Paterson*, above (damages assessed by reference to the market price on the last day of the period fixed for delivery); *Brown v Muller* (1872) L.R. 7 Ex. 319 (delivery due by separate instalments: damages assessed as the total of the differences between the contract price and the market price for each instalment on the last day of the period in which delivery of that instalment was to be made); *Tai Hing Cotton Mill Ltd v Kamsing Knitting Factory* [1979] A.C. 91 at 104. See also the explanation of *C. Sharpe & Co. Ltd v Nosawa* [1917] 2 K.B. 814, below, para.19–179.
[31] *Tredegar Iron and Coal Co. (Ltd) v. Hawthorn Bros & Co.* (1902) 18 T.L.R. 716 (anticipatory repudiation by the buyer: see above, para.16–082).

likely to rise, the buyer may refuse to accept the seller's repudiation, and wait until the due date while the market price rises.[32] During the interval, the buyer may at any time decide to accept the seller's repudiation (provided it has not been retracted by the seller), whereupon his "duty" to mitigate will arise so that his damages will be assessed by reference to the market price at the date when he ought reasonably to have bought substitute goods.

(iv) *The Market Price*

The relevant prices. The ascertainment of the contract price has already been examined,[33] as has the question of the market price[34]; the same principles apply whether the seller is claiming damages for failure to accept, or the buyer damages for failure to deliver. The relevant market price will, however, depend on who is claiming damages: when the buyer is claiming under section 51(3), the relevant price is the *buying* price at which the buyer could obtain equivalent goods.[35] The relevant market price may also depend on the relevant market relationship, *e.g.* whether between wholesaler and retailer, or between retailer and private buyer, or any other relationship.[36] 17–017

In *Williams Bros. v Ed T Agius Ltd*,[37] the House of Lords held that where there is evidence of the market price at the date of the seller's breach, the buyer's damages for non-delivery cannot be reduced by reference to the fact that he had actually resold goods of the same description at a price lower than what happened to be the market price at the time fixed for delivery. In these circumstances, the buyer is entitled to fulfil his obligations under the sub-contract by buying equivalent goods in the market at the price current at the time of non-delivery. If the sub-sale was of the identical goods bought by the buyer from the defaulting seller, the buyer's damages are nevertheless assessed with reference to the market price, since the buyer's liability in damages to the sub-buyer might easily exceed the price in the sub-sale.[38]

Relevant evidence of the market price. Where normal proof of the market price at the date of the seller's breach is not available,[39] other evidence may be relied upon, *e.g.* the price at which a sub-buyer had agreed 17–018

---

[32] *Leigh v Paterson*, above; *Brown v Muller*, above.
[33] Above, paras 2–044—2–052.
[34] Above, para.16–074.
[35] Above, para.16–070, nn.61 and 62.
[36] Above, para.16–070.
[37] [1914] A.C. 510. (For the facts, see below, para.17–032; the difficulties of reconciling this case with *Re R and H Hall Ltd and WH Pim (Junior) & Co.'s Arbitration* [1928] All E.R. Rep. 763 (see below, paras 17–030—17–033) do not involve the question discussed in this paragraph, which concerns a sub-sale at a lower price: those difficulties concern a sub-sale at a higher price than the market price at the date of the breach.)
[38] [1914] A.C. 510 at 523. But *cf.* the willingness of the CA not to apply the prima facie "market value" rule in section 53(3): *Bence Graphics International Ltd v Fasson UK Ltd* [1998] Q.B. 87. (See below paras 17–058, 17–082.)
[39] See above, para.16–074.

to take the goods from the buyer,[40] or the price in an offer to buy from a third party, or the amount paid by the buyer in compromising disputes relating to the market value of similar goods at the relevant time.[41] The court may also infer the approximate market price on a given date from evidence that there was a steady decline in that price between an earlier and a later date.[42] But the price under a sub-sale with a different place of delivery from that in the sale may not be sufficient evidence of the market price relevant to the sale[43]; nor will the price under the sub-sale be relevant evidence if its terms were different from those in the sale.[44]

17–019 **Substitute goods bought at less than market price.** Where there is normal proof of the market price at the place and date fixed for delivery, damages for non-delivery should be calculated by reference to that price despite the fact that the buyer in fact succeeded in obtaining substitute goods at a price lower than that price, or even at no cost to himself (*e.g.* by gift).[45] It is submitted that the prima facie rule in section 51(3) should apply even where the buyer bought the substitute goods immediately[46] upon the seller's failure to deliver, since it cannot be said that the buyer's opportunity to buy at the bargain price arose only[47] because of the seller's breach: even if the seller had fulfilled his obligation by delivering the promised goods, the buyer could also have bought the other goods at the lower price.[48] "The person whose breach of contract has caused damage is not the less liable because the damage has been made good, or its effect compensated by an extraneous event of such a kind that if it had operated the other way it would not have increased his legal liability."[49]

17–020 **Substitute goods bought later at less than market price.** If the buyer does not buy substitute goods in the market immediately following the seller's failure to deliver, his damages should be assessed by reference to

[40] The normal rule is that the price fixed in a sub-sale is irrelevant (see above, para.17–017; below, paras 17–028, 17–036).
[41] *Hong Guan & Co. Ltd v R Jumabhoy & Sons Ltd* [1960] A.C. 684 at 703–704. (The Privy Council accepted "as a matter of business common sense . . . the inference that no settlement would have been negotiated . . . on the basis of paying more than the difference between the contract price and the current or market price at the time of non-delivery": *ibid.*)
[42] *Tai Hing Cotton Mill Ltd v Kamsing Knitting Factory* [1979] A.C. 91 at 106.
[43] *Aryeh v Lawrence Kostoris & Son Ltd* [1967] 1 Lloyd's Rep. 63 at 72–73.
[44] *ibid.*, at p.73. *Cf. Macklin v Newbury Sanitary Laundry* (1919) 63 S.J. 337 (buyer's breach: above, para.16–074).
[45] *cf.* above, paras 16–056, 16–075, 16–076. It is submitted that *Erie County Natural Gas and Fuel Co. Ltd v Carroll* [1911] A.C. 105 (discussed below, para.17–024) is not inconsistent with the proposition in the text, since it concerned a different situation, *viz.* the cost of obtaining, in the absence of an available market, an alternative source of *producing* the article (gas) which the seller failed to supply.
[46] *cf. Campbell Mostyn (Provisions) Ltd v Barnett Trading Co.* [1954] 1 Lloyd's Rep. 65 (above, paras 16–075, 16–076).
[47] *cf.* the submission made above, para.16–075 in the analogous case of a defaulting buyer where the seller has only the *one* set of goods to sell. See also above, para.16–056.
[48] But *cf.* the decision in *Bence Graphics International Ltd v Fasson UK Ltd* [1998] Q.B. 87, CA. (See below paras 17–058, 17–082). *Cf.* also *Pagnan (R.) & Fratelli v Corbisa Industrial Agropacuaria* [1970] 1 W.L.R. 1306 (below, para.17–020).
[49] *Joyner v Weeks* [1891] 2 Q.B. 31 at 34.

the market price at that date despite the fact that the buyer later bought substitute goods at a lower price. By not repurchasing immediately, the buyer was speculating on the future level of the market price and thus accepted the risk of fluctuations in that price: if the price later rose, the buyer could not claim the extra price from the seller, and the buyer should therefore be entitled to the benefit of any subsequent fall in the price.[50] The position may be different if the buyer later bought the *same* goods from the seller at a price lower than the market price. In one case,[51] the buyer justifiably rejected the goods on the ground of their defective quality. There were continuous negotiations between the parties following this rejection, leading to the buyer finally accepting the same goods from the seller at a reduced price. The Court of Appeal held[52] that the market price rule in section 51(3) did not apply: the buyer had suffered no loss since the price at which he obtained the goods was less than the market price for similar goods at the date[53] of the seller's breach of contract. The final purchase "formed part of a continuous dealing" and was not "an independent or disconnected transaction."[54]

(c) *The Absence of an Available Market*

Damages for non-delivery in the absence of an available market. If there was no available market[55] for goods of the contractual description at the time and place of the seller's failure to deliver (*e.g.* because the goods were to be specially manufactured[56]) the buyer's damages must be assessed under the general rule of section 51(2): "The measure of damages is the estimated loss directly and naturally resulting, in the ordinary course of events, from the seller's breach of contract." The assessment must be made on the basis 17–021

---

[50] This reasoning is supported by the analogous case of the buyer's breach: *Campbell Mostyn (Provisions) Ltd v Barnett Trading Co.*, above; *Jamal v Moolla Dawood* [1916] 1 A.C. 175 at 179 (on which cases, see above, para.16–076).

[51] *Pagnan (R) & Fratelli v Corbisa Industrial Agropacuaria* [1970] 1 W.L.R. 1306 (distinguished in *Mobil North Sea Ltd v PJ Pipe & Valve Co.* [2001] 2 All E.R. (Comm.) 289). *Cf.* the *Bence Graphics* case, above.

[52] Distinguishing *Campbell Mostyn (Provisions) Ltd v Barnett Trading Co.*, above (above, para.16–076. The rule in s.51(3) is only a prima facie one: see above, para.17–007.

[53] Megaw L.J. based his judgment on the ground that the final price was less than the *then*—prevailing market price: [1970] 1 W.L.R. 1306 at 1317; but it is submitted that the correct date is that stated in the text above.

[54] [1970] 1 W.L.R. 1306 at 1315. (These words were used in *British Westinghouse Electric and Manufacturing Co. Ltd v Underground Electric Rys* [1912] A.C. 673 at 689: on which see below, para.17–056). The decision in *Pagnan* would not preclude a claim for any consequential loss caused by the delay between the date for delivery fixed in the original contract and the date of actual delivery under the new arrangements.

[55] The meaning of "an available market" is discussed above, paras 16–062 *et seq*.

[56] *Hinde v Liddell* (1875) L.R. 10 Q.B. 265 (below, para.17–023). The effect of governmental regulation of the market may also mean that there is no available market in which the buyer can obtain substitute goods: *J Leavey & Co. Ltd v Geo H Hirst & Co. Ltd* [1944] K.B. 24 at 28.

of the value[57] of the contract goods at the time and place of the breach[58] which may be ascertained by any relevant evidence, such as the cost of the nearest equivalent[59] or a resale price,[60] or the profits which the buyer would have made had he acquired the goods and manufactured them into other articles, as the seller knew that he intended to do.[61]

17–022 **Resale price in the absence of an available market.** If there is no market for the goods, but the buyer has in fact resold them, the price under the resale may be put in evidence in order to show "the real value of the goods", despite the fact that the seller did not know of the resale.[62] In *The Arpad*,[63] the buyers were consignees under a bill of lading who sued the shipowner in respect of a shortage of delivery in the cargo of wheat shipped under the bill of lading. The buyers could not procure in the market at the port of delivery any wheat in accordance with the sample identifying the subject-matter of their contract, and therefore they were unable to fulfil their sub-contracts (which used the same description). Although the case concerned damages for breach of a contract of carriage, the judgments treat the situation as "closely analogous" to that of a seller's failure to deliver.[64] The majority[65] of the Court of Appeal held that where there was no market for the goods at the port of delivery, the value of the goods must be ascertained by other evidence, which might include evidence of the price at which the consignee (the buyer) had resold the goods[66]; but the price at which he had in fact resold the goods five months earlier was not satisfactory evidence of their value at the time of the failure to deliver.[67]

17–023 **Cost of procuring the nearest equivalent.** The "duty" to mitigate[68] lies upon the buyer even where there is no available market for the purchase of goods of the contractual description. The buyer's damages will be assessed on the basis that he should have taken reasonable steps to mitigate his loss, and where the seller fails to deliver, the buyer may[69] be able to buy

---

[57] It has been argued that the "value" of goods for which no substitutes are available may, in appropriate circumstances, include an element of subjective or idiosyncratic value: Harris, Ogus and Phillips, 95 L.Q.R. 581 (1979) (which was cited with approval in *Ruxley Electronics and Construction Ltd v Forsyth* [1996] 1 A.C. 344 at 360 and in *Farley v Skinner* [2001] UKHL 49; [2002] 2 A.C. 732 at 748).
[58] *Borries v Hutchinson* (1865) 18 C.B.(N.S.) 445 at 465; *Elbinger Actien-Gesellschaft v Armstrong* (1874) L.R. 9 Q.B. 473 at 476; *Hinde v Liddell*, above (below, para.17–023). *Cf.* on s.50(2) (above, para.16–077).
[59] Below, para.17–023.
[60] *The Arpad* [1934] P. 189 (below, para.17–022).
[61] *J Leavey & Co. Ltd v George H Hirst & Co. Ltd* [1944] K.B. 24 at 29.
[62] *Grébert-Borgnis v J & W Nugent* (1885) 15 Q.B.D. 85 at 89–90.
[63] [1934] P. 189.
[64] *ibid.*, at p.223. (See also p.233.)
[65] Scrutton L.J. dissented on the issue of assessing the damages in tort.
[66] *ibid.*, at pp.210, 219–221, 230.
[67] *ibid.*, at p.210 (". . . contracts . . . made at a date far removed from the date of the breach of contract have to be neglected . . .": p.212).
[68] See above, paras 16–052 *et seq.*
[69] The question whether the buyer is *obliged* to buy substitute goods is considered, below, para.17–025.

substitute goods from another source: in these circumstances, the price at which he reasonably[70] bought them will be the basis for assessing his damages under the general principle of section 51(2).[71] Provided that the buyer's mitigating action was reasonable in all the circumstances,[72] he may recover as damages the reasonable cost of obtaining goods which are the nearest available equivalent in quality and price to goods of the contractual description.[73] The nearest equivalent may be of superior quality and so higher in price than the contract goods[74]: thus, where the seller promised to deliver diamonds at 24s.6d. per carat, the buyer was found not to have acted unreasonably in buying substitutes at 40s.[75] In another case, where the defendants failed, in breach of contract, to supply gas to the claimants, the Privy Council[76] used the following words to approve of the claimants' acts to mitigate their loss: "They chose to perform on behalf of the defendants, in a reasonable way, that contract for them and to obtain from an independent source a sufficient quantity of gas, similar as near as might be in character and quality to that which they were entitled to receive. In such cases it is well established that the measure of damages is the cost[77] of procuring the substituted article, not at all the price at which the substituted article when procured could have been sold by the person who has procured it."[78]

In another case the seller failed to deliver Finnish timber, and the nearest substitute which the buyer could obtain was some English timber which was more expensive to cut and involved more waste in cutting: the buyer was held to be entitled to claim the extra cost.[79] Provided the buyer acted

[70] The buyer has a reasonable time to decide whether or not to buy substitute goods: *C. Sharpe & Co. Ltd v Nosawa* [1917] 2 K.B. 814 at 820 (see below, paras 19–177—19–186).

[71] *cf.* the similar rule in the case of a seller's claim for damages (above, paras 16–077—16–078).

[72] *Hinde v Liddell* (1875) L.R. 10 Q.B. 265 at 268, 270; *Erie County Natural Gas and Fuel Co. Ltd v Carroll* [1911] A.C. 105 at 117. *Cf. Le Blanche v LNW Ry* (1876) 1 C.P.D. 286 at 302.

[73] *Hinde v Liddell*, above. (Damages were assessed as the difference between the price paid for the substitute goods and the contract price: but Field J. said (at p.270) that if the buyer "had derived any benefit from the advance in price. I should hesitate before I said he could recover the whole of the difference"). See also *Blackburn Bobbin Co. Ltd v TW Allen & Sons Ltd* [1918] 1 K.B. 540 at 554 (the appeal was decided on another ground: [1918] 2 K.B. 467); *C Sharpe & Co. Ltd v Nosawa*, above, at p.820. *Cf.* above, para.16–078.

[74] *Hinde v Liddell*, above. *Cf. Intertradex SA v Lesieur-Tourteaux SARL* [1978] 2 Lloyd's Rep. 509 at 519 ("If they were significantly better or worse, it might be necessary to make some allowance either way as the case should require . . .").

[75] *Diamond Cutting Works v Treifus* [1956] 1 Lloyd's Rep. 216. *Cf. Le Blanche v LNW Ry*, above.

[76] *Erie County Natural Gas and Fuel Co. Ltd v Carroll*, above. (See below, para.17–024.)

[77] "It may well be that if several reasonable but abortive attempts had been made to procure this gas the cost of these would have been properly treated as part of the cost of ultimately obtaining it . . .": *ibid.*, at p.119.

[78] *ibid.*, at p.117.

[79] *Blackburn Bobbin Co. Ltd v TW Allen & Sons Ltd*, above, at p.554. (This was an alternative basis for calculating the damages (for the other alternative see above, para.17–011); the appeal was decided on the issue of frustration, and the assessment of damages was not considered: [1918] 2 K.B. 467.)

reasonably in his mitigating action, he may also claim the extra expense of adapting the substitute goods to suit his requirements, to the extent that goods of the contractual description would suit these requirements.[80] However, it will normally be unreasonable for the buyer to order the manufacture of substitute goods, where none are readily available.[81] So where the sale of a 14-year-old ship expressly included a "spare propeller" but there was none, the Court of Appeal upheld the decision of the arbitrator that its commercial value on the ship was no more than its scrap value: it would have been unreasonable to order one to be specially manufactured.[82]

17–024 **Extra profit through reselling the substitute.** The courts are anxious to prevent the buyer from receiving an extra benefit at the seller's expense. If the substitute goods bought by the buyer were later resold by him at an extra profit because they were of better quality or higher value than goods of the contractual description, the extra profit must be set off against the cost of buying the substitute goods if the buyer claims that cost from the defaulting seller.[83] In *Erie County Natural Gas and Fuel Co. Ltd v Carroll*,[84] the claimants were entitled, under a contract of sale to the defendants of some "gas leases," to receive from the defendants a supply of gas[85] sufficient to operate the claimants' plant. The defendants failed to supply the gas, whereupon the claimants spent $58,297 in procuring gas from other sources and constructing works to bring the substitute gas to their plant. Later the claimants sold these substitute sources and works for $75,000. The Privy Council held that when the claimants sued to recover as damages (for failure to supply the gas) the cost of procuring the substitute gas, there should be deducted from this cost the price obtained in the sale of the substitute sources and works.[86] Thus, only nominal damages were awarded to the claimants: if the defendants were to pay for the cost of the substitute works "they must get credit for the sum for which these works, after having supplied the gas, were sold, otherwise the claimants would make by the defendant's breach of contract a profit equal to the price obtained on

[80] *Blackburn Bobbin Co. Ltd v TW Allen & Sons Ltd*, above, at p.554. *Cf.* above, para.16–078.
[81] *Elbinger Actien-Gesellschaft v Armstrong* (1874) L.R. 9 Q.B. 473.
[82] *Sealace Shipping Co. Ltd v Oceanvoice Ltd* (*The Alecos M*) [1991] 1 Lloyd's Rep. 120, (criticised by Treitel, 107 L.Q.R. 364 (1991) but approved by Lord Lloyd of Berwick in *Ruxley Electronics and Construction Ltd v Forsyth* [1996] 1 A.C. 344 at 371–372). But *cf.* the position where part of a machine is essential, as in *Bacon v Cooper (Metals) Ltd* [1982] 1 All E.R. 397 (as a result of breach of contract, a partly-used working part had to be replaced with a new part which would last longer). See above, para.17–023.
[83] *Hinde v Liddell*, above, at p.270 (dictum quoted above, para.17–023, n.73, on the position where the buyer of substitute goods at a higher price is able to obtain a higher price from his sub-buyer).
[84] [1911] A.C. 105.
[85] On the question whether gas can be "goods", see above, para.1–087.
[86] The question whether general price-inflation caused the increase in the value of the substitute sources and works (since the date they were procured) was not raised in this case. If the increase was due only to general price-inflation, it is submitted that the decision was wrong.

sale."[87] There seems to have been no time limit to the defendants' obligation to supply the claimants with gas: thus, if the claimants had not sold the substitute works before suing for damages they could presumably have recovered the whole of the cost of the substitute works without any deduction for their potential, saleable value. It is submitted that the *Erie* case concerned the purchase of an alternative *source* of producing the substitute article, and thus cannot be treated as a direct authority on the question of directly purchasing substitute *goods* as near in quality as possible to those of the contractual description.

If the buyer acts reasonably in buying "near equivalent" goods for his own use (and not for resale nor for the purpose of making a profit through using them),[88] it is submitted that he should not be compelled, by a reduction in his damages for their cost, to "pay for" an extra benefit to himself because of some advantage which the substitute goods have over those of the contractual description.[89]

Is the buyer obliged to buy the nearest equivalent? Where there is no available market for goods of the contractual description, the question may arise whether the buyer's damages are to be assessed on the basis that, although he did not do so, he ought reasonably to have gone into the market and bought goods as near as possible in quality and price to the contractual goods.[90] In one case[91] the judge assumed that the buyer should have done this, but the point was not elaborated. The buyer is not obliged under the rules of mitigation to accept from the seller goods which do not conform with the specifications of the contract,[92] and it would seem to follow that his damages should not be assessed on the basis that he should have bought near equivalent goods from third parties in order to mitigate his loss.[93] If the buyer had resold goods of the same contractual description, his sub-buyer would be entitled to reject the near equivalent goods if the buyer tendered them in fulfilment of the sub-contract, and it would therefore be unfair to compel the buyer to accept them under the main contract. 17–025

---

[87] *ibid.*, at p.119. *Cf. British Westinghouse Electric and Manufacturing Co. Ltd v Underground Electric Rys* [1912] A.C. 673 (below, para.17–056).

[88] *cf. British Westinghouse Electric and Manufacturing Co. Ltd v Underground Electric Rys*, above (below, para.17–056).

[89] *cf. Harbutt's "Plasticine" Ltd v Wayne Tank and Pump Co. Ltd* [1970] 1 Q.B. 447, where the defendant's breach of contract caused the destruction of a building; the owners acted reasonably both in deciding to rebuild and in choosing the plan for the new building, and it was held that the defendants were not entitled to a reduction in damages (consisting of the actual cost of rebuilding) on account of the "betterment" enjoyed by the owners in having a new building in place of the old one: but a reduction would be made for any extra accommodation or an improvement going beyond replacement. (The decision in *Harbutt's* case has been overruled on another point: *Photo Production Ltd v Securicor Transport Ltd* [1980] A.C. 827.)

[90] *cf.* the obligation of a wrongfully dismissed employee to accept a reasonable opportunity for alternative employment, although it would never be an *exact* substitute for the post from which he was dismissed: see *Chitty on Contracts* (29th ed.), Vol. 2, para.39–193—39–194.

[91] *C Sharpe & Co. Ltd v Nosawa* [1917] 2 K.B. 814 at 820 (below, paras 19–177—19–186). See also below, para.17–056.

[92] Below, para.17–026.

[93] *cf.* above, paras, 16–054—16–055.

17–026 **Offers by the seller to mitigate his breach.** The rules of mitigation do not oblige the buyer to accept from the seller goods which do not conform with the contractual standard and which he is therefore entitled to reject.[94] Thus, where the buyer properly rejects goods on the ground of their defective quality, he is not obliged to accept them when the seller offers them in mitigation of his breach of contract.[95] However, the buyer's damages may be calculated on the basis that he should have accepted a reasonable offer by the seller[96] to mitigate his breach by supplying goods which are in fact up to the contractual standard, but are to be delivered on different terms so far as the timing and method of payment are concerned.[97] In *Payzu Ltd v Saunders*,[98] the contract was for delivery of the goods by instalments, with payment for each instalment to be made within one month of each delivery. When the buyers failed to pay for the first instalment the sellers purported to terminate the contract on the ground that the buyers had repudiated their obligations, but this termination was held not to be justified; thus, the sellers were themselves in breach. After their purported termination, they offered to continue deliveries in accordance with the contract if the buyers would pay cash against each delivery. Due to the war-time conditions, the buyers could not obtain similar goods from any other source, and the Court of Appeal held that it would have been reasonable for the buyers to have accepted the seller's bona fide offer and thus to have mitigated their loss. The market price of the goods later rose, but the buyers were debarred from recovering damages for the further loss caused by their neglect to take this reasonable step in mitigation, even though the offer was made by the contract-breaker.[99] It should be noted that there was no question of the goods not measuring up to the contractual standard, nor of the seller's ability and willingness to fulfil the terms of his offer in mitigation.[1]

17–027 **The buyer's "duty" to mitigate in other circumstances.** The seller may allege that the buyer should have mitigated in circumstances not dealt with by the preceding paragraphs. However, the standard of reasonableness to be applied to the decision of the innocent buyer is not a high one: "The law

[94] Above, para.12–027—12–028, below, para.19–184.

[95] *Heaven and Kesterton Ltd v Etablissements François Albiac & Cie* [1956] 2 Lloyd's Rep. 316 at 321. *Cf.* the position where the buyer in fact accepts the defective goods from the seller at a reduced price: *Pagnan (R) & Fratelli v Corbisa Industrial Agropacuaria* [1970] 1 W.L.R. 1306 (above, para.17–020).

[96] Even where the seller fails to take the initiative, it may be reasonable for the buyer to minimise his loss by offering to repurchase the goods at a later date, but at the original price: *Sotiros Shipping Inc. and Aeco Maritime SA v Sameiet Solholt* (*The "Solholt"*) [1983] 1 Lloyd's Rep. 605 (buyer had cancelled the contract on the ground of delay in delivery. The hypothetical offer by the buyer would have been without prejudice to his claim for damages for the delay).

[97] *Payzu Ltd v Saunders* [1919] 2 K.B. 581; *Heaven and Kesterton Ltd v Etablissements François Albiac & Cie*, above, at p.321.

[98] Above. *Cf.* the criticism of Bridge 105 L.Q.R. 398 (1989).

[99] *cf. Houndsditch Warehouse Co. Ltd v Waltex Ltd* [1944] K.B. 579 (genuine offer by seller to accept return of goods which buyer alleged not to correspond with sample).

[1] *e.g.* where the seller refused to "guarantee" a substituted delivery date: *ABD (Metals and Waste) Ltd v Anglo-Chemical & Ore Co. Ltd* [1955] 2 Lloyd's Rep. 456.

is satisfied if the party placed in a difficult situation by reason of the breach of a duty owed to him has acted reasonably in the adoption of remedial measures and he will not be held disentitled to recover the cost of such measures merely because the party in breach can suggest that other measures less burdensome to him could have been taken."[2] It is a question of fact, depending on the circumstances of the particular case, whether the claimant acted reasonably.[3] Thus, where the seller tendered to the buyer a bill of lading which was not accurately dated, but the buyer could nevertheless have legally compelled his sub-buyers to accept the goods, the Court of Appeal held that the buyer was not in breach of the rules of mitigation when he refused to enforce the sub-contracts because to do so in the circumstances would injure his commercial reputation by giving him a bad name in the trade.[4]

(d) *Resale by the Buyer*

Relevance of sub-contracts. Where a market price at the date of the seller's breach is ascertainable, a higher or lower price at which the buyer has resold the goods to a sub-buyer is generally irrelevant to the assessment of damages for the seller's failure to deliver: the damages are to be calculated on the basis of the market price of similar goods at the date (and place) of the failure to deliver.[5] Thus, the seller cannot take advantage of the fact that the buyer, following the seller's failure to deliver, fulfilled his obligations under a resale by using other goods, and thereby made a greater profit on the resale than he would have done if the seller had not broken the contract.[6] In one case, where the seller failed to deliver timber, the Privy Council said that "had the [seller] supplied the timber the [buyers] would have made their profits and would have still had the other timber to sell, upon which they were entitled to make such profit as they could."[7] The market price of the timber on the due date for delivery was therefore taken as the basis for assessing damages. 17–028

---

[2] *Banco de Portugal v Waterlow & Sons Ltd* [1932] A.C. 452 at 506 (a contract case, but not on sale of goods). *Cf. Moore v DER Ltd* [1971] 1 W.L.R. 1476 (a tort case involving loss of the claimant's motor car).

[3] *Payzu Ltd v Saunders*, above, at pp.588, 589; *Lesters Leather and Skin Co. Ltd v Home and Overseas Brokers Ltd* (1948) 64 T.L.R. 569 (above, para.17–005); *The Solholt*, above.

[4] *James Finlay & Co. Ltd v NV Kwik Hoo Tong HM* [1929] 1 K.B. 400 at 410, 415, 418.

[5] *Williams Bros Ltd v Ed T Agius Ltd* [1914] A.C. 510 (above, para.17–017; below, para.17–032, approving *Rodocanachi v Milburn* (1886) 18 Q.B.D. 67, where the contract was for carriage of goods); *James Finlay & Co. Ltd v NV Kwik Hoo Tong HM* [1929] 1 K.B. 400 at 411; *The Arpad* [1934] P.189 at 214, 223, 230; *Kwei Tek Chao v British Traders and Shippers Ltd* [1954] 2 Q.B. 459 at 489–490.

[6] *Sheik Mohammad Habib Ullah v Bird & Co.* (1921) 37 T.L.R. 405, PC. But *cf.* the willingness of the CA not to apply the prima facie "market value" rule in section 53(3): *Bence Graphics International Ltd v Fasson UK Ltd* [1998] Q.B. 87. (See below, paras 17–058, 17–082.)

[7] *Sheik Mohammad*'s case, above, at p.407. (*Cf.* where the seller, upon the buyer's refusal to accept, does not resell in the market immediately, but retains the goods and thus speculates on the future market price: above, para.16–076.)

In the exceptional cases where the seller is liable for loss of profits or expenses under the sub-sale, his liability is based on the parties' reasonable contemplation of the consequences of a breach of the contract,[8] which depends on the knowledge, actual or imputed, of the seller at the time of the contract.[9]

17–029 **Loss on a resale where there is an available market.** The buyer may have contracted to sell to his sub-buyer the very same goods as he bought from the seller, or he may have fixed the same delivery date in the contract of resale as in the original contract.[10] In these two situations, when the seller fails to deliver on the due date, the buyer cannot, despite the presence of an available market, avoid loss under the contract of resale: but the buyer can recover damages for that loss only where the seller should have contemplated, at the time the original contract was made, both that the buyer was, or was probably,[11] buying for resale,[12] and that the buyer could perform his obligations under a contract of resale only by delivering the same goods.[13] "If . . . the sub-sale is of the selfsame thing . . . then ex hypothesi the default of the seller in the original sale is going to bring about an enforced default on the part of the original buyer and subsequent seller."[14] The mere fact that sub-sales may be within the reasonable contemplation of the parties at the time the contract is made does not oust the market price rule.[15] Normally, when the seller knows[16] that the buyer is a trader buying for the purposes of resale, the seller will be able to contemplate that, if he fails to deliver, the buyer will be able to buy substitute goods in the market in order to fulfil his contracts of resale.[17]

---

[8] *Biggin & Co. Ltd v Permanite Ltd* [1951] 1 K.B. 422 at 435–436.
[9] See above, paras 16–043—16–046.
[10] *Patrick v Russo-British Grain Export Co. Ltd* [1927] 2 K.B. 535 at 541; *Kwei Tek Chao v British Traders and Shippers Ltd*, above, at pp.489–490.
[11] See below, para.17–030.
[12] Or that the buyer has already entered into an existing sub-contract and was buying in order to fulfil that particular contract: *Aryeh v Lawrence Kostoris & Son Ltd* [1967] 1 Lloyd's Rep. 63 at 68.
[13] *Re R. and H Hall Ltd and WH Pim (Junior) & Co.'s Arbitration* [1928] All E.R.Rep. 763 (see below, paras 17–030 *et seq.*); *Kwei Tek Chao v British Traders and Shippers Ltd*, above, at pp.489–490; *Aryeh v Lawrence Kostoris & Son Ltd*, above, at pp.67–68, 72; and see above, para.16–046. *Cf. Biggin & Co. Ltd v Permanite Ltd*, above, at pp.436 (below, para.17–082).
[14] *Williams Bros v Ed. T. Agius Ltd* [1914] A.C. 510 at 523 (below, para.17–032). See also *The Arpad* [1934] P. 189 at 215 ("If the court is dealing with a case in which the sub-sale is a sale of the selfsame thing, that involves the fact that there is no market in which the thing sold can be bought, but only a market in which it can be sold").
[15] Where the buyer is a trader, most sellers would be able to contemplate that possibility: *The Arpad*, above, at p.230; *Kwei Tek Chao v British Traders and Shippers Ltd*, above, at p.489. But *cf.* the willingness of the CA not to apply the prima facie "market value" rule in section 53(3): *Bence Graphics International Ltd v Fasson UK Ltd* [1998] Q.B. 87. (See below paras 17–058, 17–082.)
[16] Or ought reasonably to have contemplated.
[17] *Kwei Tek Chao v British Traders and Shippers Ltd*, above, at p.489; *Aryeh v Lawrence Kostoris & Son Ltd*, above, at pp.67–68. See also *Williams v Reynolds* (1865) 6 B. & S. 495.

Hall v Pim. For loss of profits under a sub-sale to be recoverable, the first part of the test requires proof of the seller's actual or imputed knowledge. The buyer may be able to prove that the seller knew, at the time of contracting, that the buyer definitely intended to resell.[18] But actual knowledge of a definite intention is not essential: the buyer may also recover loss of profits under a resale where the seller should have known that it was "probable" that the buyer would resell.[19] In *Re R and H Hall Ltd and W H Pim (Junior) & Co.'s Arbitration*,[20] the buyers bought (at 51s.9d. a quarter) an unascertained[21] cargo of 7,000 tons of Australian wheat under a c.i.f. contract,[22] which contained clauses expressly recognising that the buyer might resell during the voyage.[23] The market price rose after the contract was made, and the buyers resold to a sub-buyer at a higher price (56s.9d.); later the sub-buyer resold, at a yet higher price (59s.3d.), back to the buyers.[24] When the ship[25] arrived, the sellers failed to deliver (having previously sold the cargo to a different buyer) and the market price had fallen to 53s.9d. a quarter. The sellers were prepared to pay as damages the difference between the contract price and the market price on the date of the ship's arrival, but the buyers claimed[26] the 5s. a quarter difference between the contract price and the price at which they had resold.[27] The House of Lords held that the terms of contract showed "that it was contemplated that the cargo might be passed on by way of sub-sale if the buyer did not choose to keep it for himself, and that the seller in such a case contracted to put the buyer in a position to fulfil his sub-contracts if he entered into them."[28] The probability of reselling was thought by three of their Lordships to be immaterial when the contract expressly contemplated the buyer's right to resell.[29] But two of their Lordships accepted that the buyer could recover loss of profits under a sub-contract which the parties 17–030

[18] *e.g. Frank Mott & Co. Ltd v Muller & Co. (London) Ltd* (1922) 13 Ll.L.R. 492; *Household Machines Ltd v Cosmos Exporters Ltd* [1947] K.B. 217 at 219.

[19] *Re R and H Hall Ltd and WH Pim (Junior) & Co.'s Arbitration*, above; *Patrick v Russo-British Grain Export Co. Ltd* [1927] 2 K.B. 535 at 540 (". . . it is enough if both parties contemplate that the buyer will probably resell and the seller is content to take the risk"). *Cf.* above, para.16–044.

[20] [1928] All E.R.Rep. 763.

[21] The particular cargo was, according to the terms of the contract, to be identified by the seller's nomination before a certain date: thus the House of Lords was able to treat it as a "specific cargo": *ibid.* at pp.765, 768, 769, 771, 772, 774.

[22] See below, paras 19–001 *et seq.*, for the nature of such a contract.

[23] This type of contract might, depending on the circumstances, be one where the sub-buyers are "identified" as third parties intended to have an enforceable claim against the seller under the Contracts (Rights of Third Parties) Act 1999: see, above, para.2–026; below, paras 17–080, 18–005.

[24] The buyers were actually agents and were acting for different principals in the third contract: *ibid.* at p.773.

[25] Whose cargo the sellers had appropriated to the original contract.

[26] The buyers also claimed a declaration that they were entitled to recover all damages payable by them to their sub-buyers as a result of their inability to deliver to the sub-buyers (see below, para.17–036).

[27] The sellers contended that the damages should be only 2s. a quarter (the difference between the contract price and the market price on the ship's arrival).

[28] [1928] All E.R.Rep. 763 at 765 (*per* Viscount Haldane).

[29] *ibid.*, at pp.765, 766, 768.

ought reasonably to have contemplated "will probably be made".[30] It was a common practice in the trade to resell cargoes while still afloat, and for there to be successive resales (a "string of contracts"). The arbitrators had found that the chances of the cargo being resold as such and of the buyers actually taking delivery of it were "about equal," and it was held that this satisfied the "probable" test.[31] It was also contemplated by the parties that any resale would be of an identifiable or named cargo, which meant that the buyers would necessarily be in default under the sub-contract if the sellers failed to deliver under the original contract.[32]

17–031 **Terms of resale must be reasonable and usual.** In *Hall v Pim*, above, the House of Lords limited the original seller's liability to loss of normal profits under a resale made on usual terms.[33] The sub-contracts "must have been entered into before the time of delivery [under the original contract] and they must be contracts in accordance with the market, not extravagant and unusual bargains."[34] In a later case,[35] where the seller had actual knowledge of the buyer's intention to resell, the buyer recovered less than his actual loss of profit under the resale: the resale price was 12 per cent above the original contract price, but the buyer was awarded only 10 per cent of that price in respect of his loss of profit, because "the percentage claimed . . . is too high."[36] The same limitation to normal profits under usual contracts is found in decisions on the buyer's claim for loss of profits when the seller delays in making delivery.[37]

17–032 **Criticism of Hall v Pim.** The decision in *Hall v Pim* was subsequently criticised in the Court of Appeal,[38] where it was said to be dependent on the special fact that the contract expressly provided for resale. But it is

---

[30] *ibid.*, at pp.766, 767 ("The principle is not to be confined to a sub-contract already actually made at the date of the original contract": *ibid.*, at p.766). At p.769, Lord Shaw spoke of "a sub-contract which, in the ordinary course of business, was not unlikely to be made . . ." (See also at p.770.)
[31] *ibid.*, at p.767.
[32] *ibid.*, at pp.766, 768, 769, 771.
[33] *cf. Horne v Midland Ry* (1872) L.R. 7 C.P. 583; (1873) L.R. 8 C.P. 131 (delayed delivery under contract of carriage; an unusually high price under the resale was not within the contemplation of the parties); and see *The Arpad* [1934] P.189 at 201.
[34] [1928] All E.R. Rep. 763 at 767. "It is not suggested that these prices were out of the ordinary course of business" (*s.c.* the prices in the resales): *ibid.* at p.768. On the facts of the case, the sub-contracts were in the same form as the original contract: *ibid.* at pp.768, 773.
[35] *Household Machines Ltd v Cosmos Exporters Ltd* [1947] K.B. 217 (no available market for the goods).
[36] *ibid.*, at p.219. (This was applied in *Coastal International Trading Ltd v Maroil AG* [1988] 1 Lloyd's Rep. 92 at 96.)
[37] *Victoria Laundry (Windsor) Ltd v Newman Industries Ltd* [1949] 2 K.B. 528 (see below, para.17–040).
[38] *James Finlay & Co. Ltd v NV Kwik Hoo Tong HM* [1929] 1 K.B. 400 at 410–412, 417–418. (*Cf.* at p.415, where Greer L.J. approved the decision.) It is, however, significant that in *Koufos v C Czarnikow Ltd* [1969] 1 A.C. 350, the House of Lords frequently referred to statements made in *Hall v Pim* on the general question of remoteness of damage in contract, without any suggestion of disapproval of the actual decision in the case: *ibid.*, at pp.387–388, 405–406, 410, 414, 424.

submitted that the fact that the contract itself contemplated resales of the identical cargo merely excluded the rules of mitigation: the seller could not maintain that the buyer should have mitigated by repurchasing similar goods in the market at the date of the breach. Thus, it is submitted that, even in the absence of such express reference, the propositions in the case should be treated as authoritative on the question of how likely a resale of the identical subject-matter must be in order to satisfy the test of being within the reasonable contemplation of the parties.

It has been suggested[39] that there is a difficulty in reconciling *Hall v Pim*, above, with *Williams Bros v Ed T Agius Ltd.*[40] In the latter case, the sellers sold an unascertained cargo of coal to the buyers at 16s.3d. per ton, to be shipped in November; in October, the buyers resold to Ghiron at 19s. a ton, who in November resold to the original sellers at 20s. a ton. The sellers failed to deliver the coal, and at the date of the breach the market price was 23s.6d. a ton. The buyers claimed as damages the difference between the contract price (16s.3d.) and the market price at the breach (23s.6d.), but the sellers argued that the buyers were entitled only to the difference between the contract price and the resale price of 19s. The resale was not "for the identical article which was the subject of the principal sale",[41] although the buyers intended to fulfil the contract of resale by the cargo to be received from the sellers. Since the buyers were entitled to fulfil their contract of resale by buying in the market at the date of the breach, the House of Lords held[42] that the correct measure of damages was the difference between the contract price and the market price at the date of the breach.[43] Lord Dunedin said[44]: "The buyer never gets them [the goods], and he is entitled to be put in the position in which he would have stood if he had got them at the due date. That position is the position of the man who has goods at the market price of the day—and barring special circumstances, the defaulting seller is neither mulct in damages for the extra profit which the buyer would have got owing to a forward resale at over the market price,[45] nor can he take the benefit of the fact that the buyer has made a forward sale at under the market price."

It is submitted that *Hall v. Pim* can be distinguished from *Williams v Agius* on the ground that the original contract of sale in *Hall v Pim* contemplated that the buyer might resell the identical cargo, so that he would necessarily be in default under the sub-sale if the seller failed to deliver under the original sale[46]; whereas in *Williams v Agius* the buyer 17–033

---

39 *James Finlay & Co. Ltd v NV Kwik Hoo Tong HM*, above, at pp.410, 415, 417.
40 [1914] A.C. 510. (See also above, para.17–017.)
41 *ibid.*, at p.523; *The Arpad* [1934] P. 189 at 214, 215.
42 The House of Lords also held that the buyers had not assigned their contractual rights to Ghiron, nor had Ghiron in turn assigned them to the original sellers. (Assignment had been the basis of the decision of the majority in the Court of Appeal: (1913) 108 L.T. 906).
43 Their Lordships followed *Rodocanachi v Milburn* (1886) 18 Q.B.D. 67 ("That case rests on the sound ground that it is immaterial what the buyer is intending to do with the purchased goods": [1914] A.C. 510 at 530–531).
44 [1914] A.C. 510 at 522–523.
45 For which the case of *GW Ry v Redmayne* (1866) L.R. 1 C.P. 329 was quoted.
46 See above, para.17–029.

could reasonably, under the rules of mitigation, have gone into the market to purchase a substitute. A further distinction is that in *Hall v Pim* the buyer (the innocent party), by reference to a higher resale price, claimed as damages a *larger* sum than "the market price at the breach" test would have given him; whereas in *Williams v Agius* the innocent buyer claimed damages on the basis of this, the normal test, but the defaulting seller argued that the buyer was entitled only to a reduced sum because the resale price happened to be *lower* than the market price at breach.[47]

17–034 **Loss of general custom (or of "repeat orders").** Where at the time they made their contract, it was within the reasonable contemplation of the parties that defects in the goods supplied by the seller (in breach of his warranty as to their quality) might lead to sub-buyers (customers of the buyer) withdrawing their custom from the buyer, damages have been awarded for loss of profits on "repeat orders" from the sub-buyers.[48] It is submitted that a similar principle should apply where the seller's failure to deliver causes the buyer a general loss of custom which was within the reasonable contemplation of the parties at the time of contracting.[49] A similar principle has been accepted by the House of Lords in the case of a breach of obligation to maintain confidence, which led to the claimant losing future profits from "repeat orders" from his previous customers.[50]

17–035 **Loss of profits on resale: no available market.** If there was no market for the goods in question but the seller knew,[51] or ought to have known,[52] that the buyer bought the goods with a view to resale, the buyer is entitled to his loss of profit on the resale when the seller fails to deliver the goods.[53] Thus,

---

47 But *cf.* the willingness of the CA not to apply the prima facie "market value" rule in section 53(3): *Bence Graphics International Ltd v Fasson U.K. Ltd* [1998] Q.B. 87. (See below, paras 17–058, 17–082.) In cases on damages for defective quality, it has been held that in some circumstances the buyer's liability in damages to his sub-buyer may restrict the seller's liability: *ibid.*; *Biggin & Co. Ltd v Permanite Ltd* [1951] 1 K.B. 422 at 436 (see the quotation from this case, below, para.17–082). (The appeal was decided on a different point: below, para.17–078.)

48 *GKN Centrax Gears Ltd v Matbro Ltd* [1976] 2 Lloyd's Rep. 555 at 573–574, 579–580 (not following *Simon v Pawsons and Leafs Ltd* (1933) 38 Com.Cas. 151 at 158). See below, paras 17–043, 17–069.

49 On the question of the evidence to establish a general loss of custom, see below, para.17–069.

50 *Jackson v Royal Bank of Scotland* [2005] UKHL 3, [2005] 1 W.L.R. 377 (not a sale of goods case). *Cf.* below para.17–069.

51 *e.g. Frank Mott & Co. Ltd v Muller & Co. (London) Ltd* (1922) 13 Ll.L.R. 492. See also *Grébert-Borgnis v J and W Nugent* (1885) 15 Q.B.D. 85 at 89.

52 *Patrick v Russo-British Grain Export Co. Ltd* [1927] 2 K.B. 535 at 541 (". . . when the resale is contemplated by both parties as a thing that will probably occur in the ordinary course of business."). See above, paras 17–029—17–030.

53 *Patrick v Russo-British Export Co. Ltd*, above, at p.541; *Household Machines Ltd v Cosmos Exports Ltd* [1947] K.B. 217 at 219; *J. Leavey & Co. Ltd v George H Hirst & Co. Ltd* [1944] K.B. 24 (seller knew that buyer bought materials for manufacturing overcoats: loss of profits awarded to buyer). See also *Satef-Huttenes Albertus SpA v Paloma Tercera Shipping Co. SA (The Pegase)* [1981] 1 Lloyd's Rep. 175 at 183–4; and *Coastal (Bermuda) Petroleum Ltd v VTT Vulcan Petroleum SA (No. 2) (The "Marine Star")* [1994] 2 Lloyd's Rep. 629.

if the goods were to be specially manufactured for the buyer, and the seller knew that they were to be resold by him, the buyer's loss of profit is the measure of damages when the seller fails to deliver[54]: the seller is taken to know that similar goods cannot be bought in the market. For the buyer to be entitled to claim his loss of profits under this principle, the sub-contract must be of a usual type,[55] and the profit must be reasonable in amount.[56]

Damages payable by the buyer to the sub-buyer. In *Re R and H Hall Ltd and W H Pim (Junior) & Co.'s Arbitration*[57] discussed above,[58] the House of Lords held that in the circumstances in which the original buyer was entitled to recover the loss of profits on a resale which he was prevented from earning by the seller's failure to deliver,[59] he was also entitled to recover the loss which he incurred as a result of being made liable in damages to his sub-buyer for breach of the terms of the contract of resale.[60] The one loss was said to be "the corollary of the other".[61] In *Grébert-Borgnis v J and W Nugent*[62] the seller had actual knowledge, at the time of contracting, that the buyer had already sold the goods on the same terms (except as to price) to a sub-buyer in France, and that the buyer was purchasing the goods in order to fulfil that contract. The Court of Appeal awarded the buyer damages[63] in respect of the compensation which the buyer had been compelled to pay to the sub-buyer in proceedings in France. The amount of the award made by the French court was held not "necessarily"[64] to be the sum which should be awarded to the buyer in the English suit, but it was said that the English court might find "that in all probability the French court did that which was reasonable."[65] This decision should, it is submitted, be preferred to the earlier decision in *Borries v* 17–036

---

[54] *Kwei Tek Chao v British Traders and Shippers Ltd* [1954] 2 Q.B. 459 at 489. See also above, para.17–030, n.23.

[55] *Re R and H Hall Ltd and W H Pim (Junior) & Co.'s Arbitration* [1928] All E.R.Rep. 763 at 767, 768 (above, paras 17–030—17–033); *Coastal International Trading Ltd v Maroil AG* [1988] 1 Lloyd's Rep. 92.

[56] *Household Machines Ltd v Cosmos Exporters Ltd*, above, at p.219 (damages awarded for 10 per cent profit although resale price based on 12 per cent profit: above, para.17–031).

[57] [1928] All E.R.Rep. 763.

[58] Above, paras 17–030—17–033.

[59] Above, paras 17–029—17–034.

[60] [1928] All E.R.Rep. 763 at 767, 769. *Cf.* the analogous cases where the goods are of defective quality (below, paras 17–076 *et seq.*), where there is authority on the recovery of the amount paid by the buyer to his sub-buyer in a reasonable settlement out of court: see para.17–078).

[61] *ibid.*, at p.767 (citing as authority *Grébert-Borgnis v J and W Nugent* (1885) 15 Q.B.D. 85). The breach of the original contract must have been the cause of the breach of the contract of resale.

[62] Above (following *Elbinger Actien-Gesellschaft v Armstrong* (1874) L.R. 9 Q.B. 473: below, para.17–045).

[63] In addition to the buyer's loss of profit under the contract of resale (above, para.17–035).

[64] (1885) 15 Q.B.D. 85 at 93.

[65] *ibid.*, at p.92. (See also p.94.) The seller would not be liable in respect of unusual clauses in the contract of resale, of which he had no knowledge, *e.g.* a penalty clause: *ibid.*, at p.90.

Hutchinson[66] where, despite the seller's actual knowledge that the buyer intended to resell to a sub-buyer in Russia, the court refused to award the buyer as damages for the seller's failure to deliver, the amount which the buyer had paid the sub-buyer for breach of the sub-contract.[67]

Where the buyer can recover damages in respect of compensation paid to his sub-buyer, he may also recover costs incurred by him in defending a claim made by his sub-buyer; but such costs will be recoverable only if it was reasonable for the buyer to defend, *e.g.* if the sub-buyer's claim was excessive in amount.[68]

The buyer may be entitled to substantial damages from the seller even before he has discharged his liability to the sub-buyer by payment.[69] If the sub-buyer has not claimed damages from the buyer by the time the buyer's claim against the original seller is being decided by the court, the buyer may be entitled to a declaration of indemnity in respect of the sub-buyer's potential claim[70]; or the court may reserve this item of the buyer's claim for assessment of damages if and when the sub-buyer's claim is met by the buyer.[71]

(e) *Consequential Losses*

17–037 **Consequential and incidental losses incurred by the buyer.** Where the seller fails to deliver the goods, but there is an available market, the buyer should be able, by buying substitute goods, to avoid consequential losses flowing from the seller's breach.[72] There may, however, be some incidental expenses which the buyer incurs in buying substitute goods, such as extra expenses in transport or handling: these are recoverable as part of the buyer's damages,[73] in addition to the measure of damages in section 51(3).[74]

In the absence of an available market, however, the buyer may often wish to claim consequential losses such as: extra expenses incurred by him, *e.g.* in adapting the nearest equivalent goods which he can obtain[75]; or the loss of profits he would have made under a contract of resale[76]; or the loss of

---

[66] (1865) 18 C.B.(N.S.) 445.

[67] *cf.* the ground for distinction suggested in *Grébert-Borgnis v J and W Nugent*, above, at p.90 (existence of an unusual clause; but at p.94, Bowen L.J. thought that the two decisions might not be reconcilable).

[68] *cf. Agius v Great Western Colliery Co.* [1899] 1 Q.B. 413 at 420 (analogous case where seller delayed delivery: below, para.17–045); and the analogous cases where the goods were defective in quality (below, paras 17–077, 17–084). On the assessment of such costs see below para.17–077, n.33.

[69] *Total Liban SA v Vitol Energy SA* [2001] Q.B. 643. But various techniques are available to prevent any "windfall" recovery by the buyer; *ibid*.

[70] *Household Machines Ltd v Cosmos Exporters Ltd* [1947] 1 K.B. 217. (Doubt was expressed about this remedy in the Court of Appeal in *Trans Trust SPRL v Danubian Trading Co.* [1952] 2 Q.B. 297 at 303, 307 (seller's claim against buyer: see above, para.16–092; below, para.17–104).

[71] *Trans Trust SPRL v Danubian Trading Co.*, above. *Cf. Deeny v Gooda Walker Ltd (No. 3)* [1995] 4 All E.R. 289; *Total Liban SA v Vitol Energy SA*, above.

[72] *Peterson v Ayre* (1853) 13 C.B. 353 at 365.

[73] s.54 (above, para.16–046).

[74] Above, paras 17–001 *et seq.*

[75] Above, para.17–023.

[76] Above, para.17–035.

profits which he would have made had the goods been delivered so that he could manufacture them into different articles, as the seller knew he intended to do[77]; or the damages he paid to a sub-buyer.[78] In some circumstances the buyer may claim both loss of profits and the extra expenses incurred by him which are wasted as a result of the seller's breach of contract, but the courts will be careful to avoid overlapping of different heads of loss.[79]

Loss of profits which would have been derived by the buyer from the use of a profit-earning chattel (or part of such a chattel) is a possible head of damages for non-delivery, but the reported cases on this type of loss concern delayed delivery and are discussed below.[80] The principles of these cases may, it is submitted, be carried over to cases of non-delivery, subject to the buyer's "duty" to mitigate his loss; when it is clear to the buyer that the failure of the seller to deliver is not merely a delay in delivery, his "duty" to repurchase elsewhere may perhaps be higher than when the buyer reasonably believes that the seller will ultimately deliver the goods.

2. DAMAGES FOR DELAY IN DELIVERY

(a) *In General*

Delay in delivery. The Act contains no provision which expressly provides for the assessment of the buyer's damages when the seller fails to deliver on the date fixed for delivery, but the buyer accepts delivery of the goods from the seller at a later date.[81] Where there is an available market for the goods, the usual measure of the buyer's damages[82]is the difference between (a) their market value at the time and place[83] fixed by the terms of the contract for delivery, and (b) their market value at the time when (and the place where[84]) the goods are in fact delivered to the buyer.[85] Apart from **17–038**

[77] Above, para.17–021.
[78] Above, para.17–036. The costs of a reasonable defence by the buyer are also recoverable (see above, para.17–036, n.68).
[79] See below, paras 17–044, 17–046, 17–067—17–070.
[80] Below, paras 17–040—17–042.
[81] The case probably falls under the general provisions of s.53(2) (below, para.17–047): *Taylor & Sons Ltd v Bank of Athens* (1922) 91 L.J.K.B. 776 at 778. *Cf.* s.54 (above, para.16–046).
[82] This is the same as in cases of delay in the carriage of goods by sea: see *Koufos v C Czarnikow Ltd* [1969] 1 A.C. 350 at 400, 407, 417–418. (*Cf.* at pp.392–393, where Lord Reid left open the question whether the rule was the same in sale of goods, and at p.427, where Lord Upjohn thought that with delay in carriage of goods, "it all depends on the circumstances" whether "the market price measures the damage", and that "different considerations apply to cases between buyer and seller.")
[83] *Aryeh v Lawrence Kostoris & Son Ltd* [1967] 1 Lloyd's Rep. 63 at 73.
[84] In the cases in the next footnote, the place is assumed to be the same place as in (a). *Cf.* para.17–039, n.98 below; and below, para.17–051, n.90.
[85] *Addax Ltd v Arcadia Petroleum Ltd* [2000] 1 Lloyd's Rep. 493. See also the statements in *Borries v Hutchinson* (1865) 18 C.B.(N.S.) 445 at 465 (We must . . . ascertain what was the value of the article contracted for at the time it ought to have

consequential losses, such as extra expenses[86] or loss of profits,[87] this sum should put the buyer into the financial position he would have been in if the seller had fulfilled his contractual obligation. The buyer will, of course, be liable to pay the agreed price for the goods, and if he has not paid it before or upon delivery, his claim for damages will be by way of counterclaim. Where there is an available market for the goods within section 51(3), that subsection and the rules of mitigation[88] would normally require the buyer to repurchase in the market immediately[89] following the date of the seller's breach in failing to deliver in accordance with the contract, but it can be argued that the seller, by tendering the goods to the buyer at a later date, has estopped himself from taking up this position.

Where there is no available market for the goods, the court may use any relevant test to arrive at the "value" of the goods at the time fixed for delivery and at the actual date of delivery.[90] Thus, when the goods were to be delivered at Hull, whence the buyer (to the seller's knowledge) intended to send them to a sub-buyer on the continent, the value was said to be dependent on the relative cost of freight and insurance on the transport to the Russian destination at the different times. This cost was greater at the time when the goods were delivered than at the earlier time when they should have been delivered, and the buyer was entitled to the extra cost as damages for the seller's delay.[91] Another case of seasonal changes occurred when a shipbuilder failed to deliver a ship for the Australian trade on the due date in August (the high season for freight rates) but delivered it the following March when the rate for freight to Australia was low; the buyer was held to be entitled to damages which (in the absence of other evidence as to market values at the two times) were calculated by taking the profits which the ship would have made on a first voyage in August–September and deducting the profits actually made on her first voyage in May–June.[92]

17–039 **Irrelevance of resale price.** The relevance of different types of evidence of the market values at the due date for delivery and at the actual date of delivery will be the same as in cases of non-delivery,[93] or of breach of

---

been and at the time when it actually was delivered"; quoted with approval in *Elbinger Actien-Gesellschaft v Armstrong* (1874) L.R. 9 Q.B. 473 at 477 (where there was no available market) which was in turn approved by Lord Pearce (obiter) in *Koufos v C. Czarnikow Ltd*, above, at pp.417–418); *Taylor & Sons Ltd v Bank of Athens*, above (no difference in value between locust beans shipped in August and those shipped in September: see below, paras 19–189 *et seq*. See also n.82, above; *cf. Fletcher v Tayleur* (1855) 17 C.B. 21, below.

[86] *e.g.* extra freight and insurance incurred by the buyer: *Borries v Hutchinson*, above. (See also below, paras 17–044—17–046.)

[87] Below, paras 17–040—17–043.

[88] Above, paras 16–052 *et seq.*

[89] See above, para.17–008.

[90] *cf. Contigroup Companies Inc. v Glencore A.G* [2004] EWHC 2750 (Comm), [2005] 1 Lloyd's Rep. 241.

[91] *Borries v Hutchinson*, above.

[92] *Fletcher v Tayleur*, above. (The buyer did not claim the whole of his lost profits on the voyage, or voyages, missed between August and March: *cf.* below, paras 17–040—17–042.)

[93] Above, paras 17–005—17–008, 17–017—17–018.

warranty.[94] Thus, except in the absence of other evidence of market value, the contract price does not indicate the market price at either date nor does the price under a resale of the goods to a sub-buyer.[95] Whether the resale price is higher or lower than the market price at the date of actual delivery, the buyer's damages should be calculated exclusively by reference to the market prices at the due date and at the actual date, since the buyer could have bought other goods to fulfil his obligations under the sub-contract and the market price of the goods delivered late by the seller would then be relevant to those goods left on his hands at that date. This proposition is supported by Scrutton L.J. in *Slater v Hoyle & Smith Ltd*[96] who criticised the inconsistent decision of the Privy Council in *Wertheim v Chicoutimi Pulp Co.*[97] where the seller made late delivery of a quantity of wood pulp bought by the buyer at 25s. a ton. The market price of the pulp was 70s. a ton at the port of delivery on the date fixed for delivery (November 1900), but by the time of the actual delivery (June 1901) the market price had fallen to 42s.6d. a ton.[98] Under various sub-sales (some made before the original contract, and some later, but before the ultimate delivery by the seller) the buyer resold the pulp at a price of 65s. a ton. The buyer was able to fulfil these sub-contracts[99] and when he sued the original seller for damages for late delivery, the Privy Council assessed them as the difference between (a) the market value at the port of delivery at the due date for delivery, and (b) the actual price obtained on their resale. (On the facts, this formula gave the buyer 5s. a ton damages.) Lord Atkinson said that the market value at actual delivery was "presumed to be the true value of the goods to the purchaser. . ." but that this presumption was rebutted if "the real value of the goods to him is proved by the very fact of this sale [the resale] to be more than market value. . ."[1] He also thought that it would be "against all justice" if the buyer was "to be permitted to make a profit by the breach of contract" and to be "compensated for a loss he never suffered."[2] But the buyer was not bound to fulfil the sub-contracts by delivering the specific goods which he received under the original contract[3]: if he had procured substitute goods to fulfil the sub-contracts, he would then have had the goods delivered late by the seller on his hands at the date of actual delivery,

---

94 Below, paras 17–052—17–054.
95 *cf.* above, paras 17–017—17–018.
96 [1920] 2 K.B. 11 at 23–24 (below, paras 17–057—17–058).
97 [1911] A.C. 301.
98 On a precise statement of the facts, 13s. a ton for the cost of transport would need to be deducted from both these figures, since the Privy Council treated the market price at Manchester (where the buyer, following his regular practice, intended to send the goods) as sufficient evidence of the market value at the port of delivery, Chicoutimi, after deduction of the cost of carriage between the two places: *ibid.*, at pp.316–317.
99 The reason is not given in the report, but various reasons are possible, *e.g.* the dates for delivery under the sub-contracts may have been after the date of actual delivery by the seller, or the sub-buyers may have agreed to postpone the dates of delivery under their contracts.
1 [1911] A.C. 301 at 307–308.
2 *ibid.*, at p.308.
3 *cf. R. and H. Hall Ltd and W. H. Pim (Junior) & Co.'s Arbitration* [1928] All E.R.Rep. 763 (above, paras 17–030—17–033).

in which event the market price at that date would obviously have been the relevant basis for assessing his damages.[4] It was the choice of the buyer not to procure substitute goods at the date of the original breach which led to his ultimate profit[5]: the buyer was not obliged to accept late delivery under the original contract, and it cannot be said that by accepting late delivery he had waived his right to claim damages on the normal basis. However, the approach adopted in *Slater v Hoyle and Smith Ltd*, above, has itself been criticised by the Court of Appeal in an analogous situation[6], which may lead to acceptance of the *Wertheim* decision.[7]

(b) *Loss of Profit*

17–040 **Loss of profit caused by delay in delivery.** Where the seller makes a late delivery of a profit-earning chattel,[8] the buyer may (in the absence of an available market for such a chattel[9]) recover damages for loss of use, based on the normal use made of such a chattel, not on an exceptional use unknown to the seller.[10] The buyer's claim is for "user profits," *viz.* the loss of profits which he would have made from use of the goods during the period after the goods should have been delivered until the actual date of delivery.[11]

---

[4] *Slater v Hoyle and Smith Ltd*, above, at pp.23–24.

[5] *cf.* the analogous position in *Campbell Mostyn* (*Provisions*) *Ltd v Barnett Trading Co. Ltd* [1954] 1 Lloyd's Rep. 65 (above, para.16–076).

[6] In a case on damages for defective quality; *Bence Graphics International Ltd v Fasson UK Ltd* [1998] Q.B. 87 (At p.994, Auld L.J. approves the *Wertheim* decision). See the discussion of this case below, paras 17–058, 17–082.

[7] Lord Dunedin in *Williams Brothers v Ed. T. Agius Ltd* [1914] A.C. 510 at 522, approved of the decision. (*Cf.* Lord Atkinson at p.529.) *Cf.* also *Koufos v C Czarnikow Ltd* [1969] 1 A.C. 350 at 427. Waddams, *The Law of Damages* (3rd ed.), paras 1.1920—1.1940, defends the decision. The reasoning in *Pagnan* (*R*) *& Fratelli v Corbisa Industrial Agropacuaria* [1970] 1 W.L.R. 1306 (above, para.17–020), which concerns a different situation, may lend some support to the *Wertheim* decision.

[8] Or part of a profit-earning chattel: *Victoria Laundry* (*Windsor*) *Ltd v Newman Industries Ltd* [1949] 2 K.B. 528 at 543–544; *Elbinger Actien-Gesellschaft v Armstrong* (1874) L.R. 9 Q.B. 473 at 477 (see below, para.17–045).

[9] Where there is an available market, the buyer should normally be able to avoid loss of profits by immediately purchasing or hiring a substitute. *Cf. Smeed v Foord* (1859) 1 E & E 602 (buyer did not hire a substitute threshing machine because seller assured him that he would deliver forthwith).

[10] *Victoria Laundry* (*Windsor*) *Ltd v Newman Industries Ltd*, above. See also *Cory v Thames Ironworks and Shipbuilding Co. Ltd* (1868) L.R. 3 Q.B. 181 (below, para.17–042). The rule is similar for delay in a contract to repair a chattel: *Re Trent and Humber Co.* (1869) L.R. 8 Eq. 94. ("If a profit would arise from a chattel, and it is left with a tradesman for repair, and detained by him beyond the stipulated time, the measure of damages is prima facie the sum which would have been earned in the ordinary course of employment of the chattel in the time": *ibid.*, at p.117.); or for a carrier's delay: *Satef-Huttenes Albertus SpA v Paloma Tercera Shipping Co. SA* (*The Pegase*) [1981] 1 Lloyd's Rep. 175. *Cf. Contigroup Companies Inc. v Glencore A.G* [2004] EWHC 2750(Comm), [2005] 1 Lloyd's Rep. 241 (loss of profits under contract of resale).

[11] *Steam Herring Fleet Ltd v VS Richards & Co. Ltd* (1901) 17 T.L.R. 731. *Cf. Watson v Gray* (1900) 16 T.L.R. 308 (when seller delayed delivery of plates needed by the buyer, a bargebuilder, to build barges, no damages were awarded for "the loss of business generally" during the delay: a brief judgment); *Fletcher v Tayleur* (1855) 17 C.B. 21.

In *Victoria Laundry (Windsor) Ltd v Newman Industries Ltd*[12] the claimants were launderers and dyers who wished to expand their business by installing a larger boiler. The defendants were engineers who agreed to sell them a large boiler, and it was later agreed that delivery was to be fixed for June 5, 1946. While the boiler was being dismantled for delivery it was damaged, and delivery to the claimants was not made until November 8, 1946. The claimants sued for damages for delay in delivery[13] and claimed loss of profits in respect of: (1) the large number of new customers they could have taken on had the boiler been installed on the due date; and (2) the amount which they could have earned under special "highly lucrative", dyeing contracts with the Ministry of Supply. The defendants knew that the claimants were launderers and that they wanted the boiler for immediate use; the Court of Appeal held that with such knowledge the reasonable man could have foreseen that delay in delivery would lead to some loss of business (and therefore loss of profits) though he would not have foreseen the loss of profits under the special contracts with the Ministry, since these were special circumstances not within the defendant's actual knowledge. Hence the claimants could not recover the actual loss they had incurred under these contracts, but only the normal loss of business in respect of dyeing and laundering contracts to be reasonably expected.

Delayed delivery of part of a machine. The Court of Appeal found no difficulty in allowing recovery of lost profits when the seller delayed delivery of only a part of a profit-earning complex[14]: provided the seller should have contemplated that delay would cause loss of profits, he was liable for such loss. "The fact that a part only is involved is only significant in so far as it bears on the capacity of the supplier to foresee the consequences of non-delivery. If it is clear from the nature of the part (or the supplier of it is informed) that its non-delivery will have the same effect as non-delivery of the whole, his liability will be the same as if he had defaulted in delivering the whole."[15] Some of the earlier cases where the defendant was held not to be liable for loss of profits caused by the delayed delivery of part of a machine concerned contracts of carriage[16] and "a carrier commonly knows less than a seller about the purposes for which the buyer or consignee needs the goods, or about other 'special circumstances' which may cause excep- 17–041

[12] [1949] 2 K.B. 528. (The language in which the judgment was expressed may need to be modified in the light of *Koufos v C Czarnikow Ltd* [1969] 1 A.C. 350 (above, paras 16–043—16–045), but their Lordships appear to have accepted that the *Victoria Laundry* case was correctly decided even on the basis of their slightly different formulation of the remoteness test: *ibid.* at pp.389, 399, 414, 415.)

[13] A similar boiler was not readily available in the market.

[14] The earlier cases concerned delay in delivery of ships or vessels which clearly were intended to earn profits for their owners, *e.g. Cory v Thames Ironworks Co.*, above; *Re Trent and Humber Co.*, above; *Steam Herring Fleet Ltd v VS Richards & Co. Ltd*, above; or some essential part of a ship, *e.g. Wilson v General Screw Colliery Co.* (1877) 37 L.T. 789 (propeller shaft); *Saint Line Ltd v Richardsons Westgarth & Co. Ltd* [1940] 2 K.B. 99 at 104–105 (engines).

[15] [1949] 2 K.B. 528 at 543–544.

[16] *Hadley v Baxendale* (1854) 8 Exch. 341; *British Columbia etc. Saw Mill Co. Ltd v Nettleship* (1868) L.R. 3 C.P. 499; *Horne v Midland Ry* (1873) L.R. 8 C.P. 131.

tional loss if due delivery is withheld"[17]; others concerned the buyer's loss of profit on a resale of a whole into which the buyer intended to incorporate the part.[18]

17–042 **Contemplated loss as a limit on liability.** In *Cory v Thames Ironworks and Shipbuilding Co. Ltd*[19] coal merchants bought the hull of a floating boom derrick from the sellers, who finally delivered it six months later. The normal use of the hull would have been as a coal store, but the buyers (unknown to the sellers) intended to use it for a new method of transferring coal from colliers to barges. The buyers did not claim as damages for their loss of profits caused by the delay the profits which they would have made from their intended use of the hull, but only £420, which would have been their loss of profits had they intended to use the hull as a coal store. The court rejected the seller's argument that the damages should be nominal and awarded the £420. Some loss of profits from delay was within the reasonable contemplation of the parties at the time the contract was made, and the buyers actually lost profits through the delay; but their recovery was limited to the extent of the profits which would have been made through the method of using the hull which the seller could reasonably have contemplated. It should be noted that the court did not hold that no loss of the foreseeable type in fact occurred merely because the buyers did not intend to earn profits by the normal use of the hull; the buyers intended to earn profits by its use,[20] and they had actually lost greater profits than they claimed.[21]

17–043 **Loss of general custom (or of "repeat orders").** Where, at the time they made their contract, it was within the reasonable contemplation of the parties that defects in the goods supplied by the seller (in breach of his warranty as to their quality) might lead to sub-buyers (customers of the buyer) withdrawing their custom from the buyer, damages may be awarded for loss of profits on "repeat orders" from the sub-buyers.[22] It is submitted that a similar principle should apply to the analogous situation where the seller's delay in delivery causes loss of general custom to the buyer.[23] A

[17] *Victoria Laundry (Windsor) Ltd v Newman Industries Ltd*, above, at p.537. See also *Heskell v Continental Express Ltd* [1950] 1 All E.R. 1033 at 1049.
[18] Below, para.17–044.
[19] (1868) L.R. 3 Q.B. 181. See the analysis of the case in *Victoria Laundry (Windsor) Ltd v Newman Industries Ltd*, above, at p.538.
[20] "The [claimants] intended to apply it in their trade, but to the special purpose of transhipping coals; the defendants believed that the [claimants] would apply it to the purpose of their trade, but as a coal store": *ibid.*, at p.187.
[21] *cf. Elbinger Actien-Gesellschaft v Armstrong* (1874) L.R. 9 Q.B. 473 at 477 (below, para.17–045: delay in delivering a set of wheels to be incorporated into a wagon would mean "that the [claimants], if they meant the waggon for their own use, or their customers, if the waggon was bespoke, would be deprived of the use of a waggon for a period equal to that for which the set of wheels was delayed": note the acceptance of alternative uses).
[22] *GKN Centrax Gears Ltd v Matbro Ltd* [1976] 2 Lloyd's Rep. 555 at 573–574, 577, 579–580. See above, para.17–034, below, para.17–069. On loss of profits on a resale of the same goods, see below, para.17–044.
[23] *cf.* above para.17–040, n.11. On the question of the evidence to establish such loss, see below, para.17–069.

similar principle has been accepted by the House of Lords in the case of a breach of obligation to maintain confidence, which led to the claimant losing future profits from "repeat orders" from his previous customers.[24]

(c) *Resale by the Buyer*

17–044 **Loss on a resale.** As in the analogous situation where the seller fails to deliver,[25] the general rule is that the buyer cannot recover his loss of profits under a contract of resale when the seller makes a late delivery under the original contract. The seller cannot, in normal circumstances, reasonably contemplate loss under a resale as a result of delay in delivering goods which are readily available in the market.[26] Where, however, the seller actually[27] contemplated a resale by the buyer, the seller will be liable for the buyer's loss of profits under the contract of resale caused by the seller's failure to deliver on time.[28] Thus, where the seller knew[29] that the buyer required the article for the particular purpose of using it as a part in the manufacture of a machine being sold to the sub-buyer, the seller was held to be liable to the buyer for his loss of profits[30] when, due to the seller's delay in delivering the part, the sub-buyer refused to accept late delivery of the machine.[31] In addition to his loss of profits on the resale, the buyer was held to be entitled to his expenditure wasted[32] by the seller's breach of contract (less the value of the incomplete machine left on the hands of the buyer as the result of the breach).[33] It is submitted that the buyer should not recover his *gross* profit (*viz.* gross receipts) as well as his wasted expenses, but that there would not be double recovery if the buyer is given his *net* loss of profits (*viz.* after allowing for the expenses of earning the profits) and any expenses rendered useless by the seller's breach.[34] The delay may cause extra expenses to the buyer without also causing loss of profits. Thus, where the delay meant that the buyer had to send the goods

---

[24] *Jackson v Royal Bank of Scotland* [2005] UKHL 3, [2005] 1 W.L.R. 377 (not a sale of goods case). *Cf.* below para.17–069.

[25] Above, para.17–028.

[26] *cf. Portman v Middleton* (1858) 4 C.B.(N.S.) 322 (buyer needed article in order to fulfil a contract to repair a third party's machine: the seller did not know of this contract, and thus was not liable when his delay in delivery caused the buyer's breach of it).

[27] By analogy with the cases on non-delivery (see above, paras 17–029—17–030), the same proposition should apply when the seller "ought" to have contemplated a resale as "probable".

[28] *Hydraulic Engineering Co. Ltd v McHaffie Goslett & Co.* (1878) 4 Q.B.D. 670.

[29] At the time of contracting: *ibid.*, at p.676 (in fact, the sub-buyer introduced the buyer to the seller).

[30] "They are entitled to recover . . . the loss of their reasonable profit": *ibid.*, at p.675.

[31] *Hydraulic Engineering Co. Ltd v McHaffie Goslett & Co.*, above. (The seller knew the date when the completed machine was to be delivered to the sub-buyer, and he also knew that the sub-buyer might refuse to take the machine if the buyer did not deliver it on time.)

[32] *e.g.* the cost of the paint necessary to preserve the incomplete machine left in the buyer's hands. See below, para.17–046.

[33] (1878) 4 Q.B.D. 670 at 675, 676.

[34] See below, paras 17–046 n.53, 17–070.

to his foreign sub-buyer at a season in the year when both freight and insurance were higher than at the time fixed for delivery by the seller, the buyer was held to be entitled to recover the extra expense.[35]

17–045 Where the seller contemplated a resale (or ought to have done so) but delays delivery till after the due date,[36] he will be liable to the buyer in respect of the latter's liability in damages to his sub-buyer caused by the seller's delay.[37] In *Elbinger Actien-Gesellschaft v Armstrong*[38] the seller agreed to supply the buyers with 666 sets of wheels and axles. The seller knew[39] that the buyers were under a contract to deliver wagons to a railway company, and that the buyers intended to incorporate the wheels and axles in the wagons.[40] The seller delivered the first 100 sets late, with the result[41] that the buyers were in default in supplying the completed wagons to the railway company, and had to pay the latter part of a sum specified under the sub-contract as damages for delay.[42] The buyers were, at a minimum, entitled to "reasonable compensation for the loss of the use of the waggons"[43] during the delay, but the court was willing to include "the probable liability of the [claimants] to damages by reason of the breach through the defendant's default of that contract to which, as both parties knew, the defendant's contract with the [claimants] was subsidiary."[44] The court did not think that the buyer was entitled (in the absence of the seller's knowledge of the provisions of the liquidated damages clause) to recover the exact sum paid to the sub-buyer as compensation for delay; but on the particular facts of the case, the award of this sum by a jury was upheld.

It is only when he acts reasonably that the buyer can recover his costs incurred in defending a claim brought against him by his sub-buyer.[45] If he has no real ground for defence, the buyer cannot recover his costs from the

---

[35] *Borries v Hutchinson* (1865) 18 C.B.(N.S.) 445 (The seller knew, at the time of contracting, that the buyer intended to resell to a sub-buyer "on the continent" although he did not know until later the exact destination of the goods.)

[36] The proposition in the text assumes that the seller could reasonably contemplate that his delay would lead to the buyer being in breach under the contract of resale.

[37] *Elbinger Actien-Gesellschaft v Armstrong* (1874) L.R. 9 Q.B. 473 at 479; *Hydraulic Engineering Co. Ltd v McHaffie Goslett & Co.*, above, at pp.674, 677; *Agius v Great Western Colliery Co.* [1899] 1 Q.B. 413 (the sellers had actual knowledge of the buyer's intention to resell); *Contigroup Companies Inc. v Glencore A.G* [2004] EWHC 2750 (Comm), [2005] 1 Lloyd's Rep. 241.

[38] (1874) L.R. 9 Q.B. 473.

[39] *cf. Portman v Middleton* (1858) 4 C.B.(N.S.) 322 (above, para.17–044, n.26).

[40] The seller had not been told of the exact delivery dates specified in the contract of resale. The situation where the seller knew that the buyers were already contracted to deliver to a sub-buyer might, depending on the circumstances, in future give the sub-buyer a claim against the seller under the Contracts (Rights of Third Parties) Act 1999. See above, para.2–026, below, paras 17–080, 18–005.

[41] The buyers were unable to obtain substitute sets of wheels and axles.

[42] The seller had not been told of the amounts specified in the liquidated damages clause.

[43] (1874) L.R. 9 Q.B. 473 at 477.

[44] *ibid.*, at p.479.

[45] *Agius v Great Western Colliery Co.*, above, (following *Hammond & Co. v Bussey* (1887) 20 Q.B.D. 79). *Cf.* above, para.17–036; below, paras 17–077, 17–084. On the assessment of the costs, see below, para.17–077, n.33).

seller who delays in delivery under the original contract. Where, however, the sub-buyer makes an exorbitant claim for damages, it will be reasonable for the buyer (and in the interests of the defaulting seller[46]) to defend in order "to ensure that . . . the damages recovered should not be extravagant."[47]

(d) *Extra or Wasted Expenditure*

Claims for extra expenses or wasted expenditure. As a head of loss separate from loss of user profits, the buyer may claim[48] damages for the extra expenses which he has incurred as a result of not having the goods delivered on time.[49] The expenses must be such as were within the reasonable contemplation of the parties, at the time the contract was made, as not unlikely to result from a delay in delivery,[50] and this will often depend on the seller's knowledge of the type of business conducted by the buyer, and the purpose for which he knew, or ought to have known, that the buyer intended to use the goods.[51] Thus, when the sellers delayed delivery of a crane to buyers who were importers of timber, the court awarded the extra cost of man-handling timber at the buyers' wharf, but not the cost of extra congestion on the wharf nor of diverting ships elsewhere.[52] Similarly, when a shipbuilder was due to deliver three fishing vessels on a specified date and the buyers engaged crews of fishermen for them, they were entitled to claim the wages paid to the crews during the period of delay until the vessels were actually delivered to them.[53] 17–046

The extra expense caused by the seller's breach may relate even to the price itself. In one case,[54] the price in a c.i.f. contract was expressed in Indian rupees, and there was provision for a variation in price if the rate of exchange altered between the date of the contract and the date when

---

[46] *Agius v Great Western Colliery Co.*, above, at pp.419, 422, 424.

[47] *ibid.*, at p.420. On the facts of the case, the buyer had asked the seller to take over the defence of the claim, but the seller had refused to do so. In many circumstances, such a request to the seller will assist the buyer in showing that his action in defending was reasonable.

[48] The cases on delayed delivery do not discuss the question whether the buyer may claim both his loss of user profits and his wasted expenses but in *Hydraulic Engineering Co. Ltd v McHaffie Goslett & Co.* (1878) 4 Q.B.D. 670 (above, para.17–044) and in *Steam Herring Fleet Ltd v V. S. Richards & Co. Ltd* (1901) 17 T.L.R. 731, below, the buyer was awarded both. See further, below, para.17–070.

[49] *Smeed v Foord* (1859) 1 E. & E. 602; *Hydraulic Engineering Co. Ltd v McHaffie Goslett & Co.*, above; *Watson v Gray* (1900) 16 T.L.R. 308; *John M. Henderson & Co. Ltd v Montague L. Meyer Ltd* (1941) 46 Com.Cas. 209.

[50] *John M Henderson & Co. Ltd v Montague L. Meyer Ltd*, above, at p.219. The amount of the wasted expenditure which the buyer may claim should not exceed the gross return which the buyer expected to make: see below, para.17–063.

[51] *Smeed v Foord*, above; *John M Henderson & Co. Ltd v Montague L Meyer Ltd*, above.

[52] *John M Henderson & Co. Ltd v Montague L Meyer Ltd*, above, at pp.219–220.

[53] *Steam Herring Fleet Ltd v V. S. Richards & Co. Ltd*, above (the claim for the wasted expenditure on wages was in addition to the loss of profits which the buyers would have made during the period of the delay). See also *Waters v Towers* (1853) 8 Exch. 401; *Saint Line Ltd v Richardsons Westgarth & Co. Ltd* [1940] 2 K.B. 99 at 105.

[54] *Aruna Mills Ltd v Dhanrajmal Gobindram* [1968] 1 Q.B. 655.

payment had to be made, upon tender of the bill of lading. It was held that since the parties actually contemplated revaluation between the date of the contract and the date of payment as a serious possibility they must be assumed to have contemplated that late delivery by the sellers was liable to cause loss to the buyers in that they had to pay an increased price to the sellers.[55]

3. DAMAGES FOR DEFECTIVE QUALITY

(a) *In General*

17–047 **Introduction.** Section 53 of the Act prescribes[56] the measure of damages for breach of warranty, *viz.* a contractual undertaking which is not, or cannot be, treated by the buyer as a ground for rejecting the goods:

"(1) Where there is a breach of warranty by the seller, or where the buyer elects (or is compelled) to treat any breach of a condition on the part of the seller as a breach of warranty,[57] the buyer is not by reason only of such breach of warranty entitled to reject the goods; but he may—(a) set up against the seller the breach of warranty in diminution or extinction of the price, or (b) maintain an action against the seller for damages for the breach of warranty.

(2) The measure of damages for breach of warranty is the estimated loss directly and naturally resulting, in the ordinary course of events, from the breach of warranty.

(3) In the case of breach of warranty of quality such loss is prima facie the difference between the value of the goods at the time of delivery to the buyer and the value they would have had if they had fulfilled the warranty.

(4) The fact that the buyer has set up the breach of warranty in diminution or extincton of the price does not prevent him from maintaining an action for the same breach of warranty if he has suffered further damage."

Subsection 53(2) lays down the basic rule in terms of *Hadley v Baxendale*[58]; the Court of Appeal has emphasised the importance of section 53(2) as "the starting point",[59] holding that the prima facie rule in section

---

[55] The case was referred back to the arbitrators in order for them to ascertain whether the buyers would have been able to pay for the goods before the revaluation, if the sellers had not been guilty of delay.

[56] s.53(5) relates only to Scots law and is therefore not reproduced here.

[57] See above, paras 12–037, 12–038. S.53(1) speaks of a "warranty," whereas ss.13–15 imply "conditions" as to quality. Before *Wallis, Son and Wells v Pratt and Haynes* [1911] A.C. 394, the view may have been taken that when the buyer claims damages for breach of a condition, it should be treated as breach of a warranty.

[58] (1854) 9 Exch. 341 (the first rule: see above, para.16–043); *H Parsons (Livestock) Ltd v Uttley Ingham & Co. Ltd* [1978] Q.B. 791 at 800, 807.

[59] *Bence Graphics International Ltd v Fasson UK Ltd* [1998] Q.B. 87 at 102. (See below para.17–058, 17–082.) See also *Louis Dreyfus Trading Ltd v Reliance Trading Ltd* [2004] EWHC 525 (Comm), [2004] 2 Lloyd's Rep. 243.

53(3) should not be applied if it would give the buyer "more than his true loss".[60] In addition to damages under section 53(2), special damages may be recovered under section 54 in respect of loss suffered by the buyer as the result of special circumstances known to the seller at the time the contract was made.[61] By section 54, the buyer's right to recover interest is also preserved.[62]

Where the buyer is entitled to and does reject the goods on the ground that they do not measure up to the contractual description or standard, the buyer's damages are assessed on the basis that the seller has failed to deliver the goods (section 51), as discussed previously.[63] The present section of this chapter covers all breaches of sections 13, 14 and 15 of the Act[64]and any other breach of a contractual undertaking about the condition or attributes of the goods to be delivered.[65] Section 53(3) is stated to be the measure of damages for breach of a warranty as to the quality of the goods, but it is submitted that a similar measure would apply to breaches of other undertakings, such as those relating to the fitness of the goods for a particular purpose,[66] or to the description of the goods.[67]

The application of section 53(3) to international contracts for the sale of goods is discussed below.[68]

New remedies for the consumer-buyer. Under the new Part 5A of the Act, the buyer who deals as a consumer is given four new remedies where the goods are not in conformity with the contract at the time of delivery. The consumer's remedies include repair, replacement, price reduction[69] or rescission of the contract. Where the buyer who complains of defective quality is a consumer, his remedies under Part 5A are likely to be more advantageous to him than those under section 53 of the Sale of Goods Act. These new remedies are examined in detail in Chapter 12 earlier in this book.[70] 17–048

Breach of warranty as defence to action for the price.[71] Subsections (1)(a) and (4) of section 53 follow the law before the 1893 Act, as laid down 17–049

---

[60] The facts of the case are summarised below, para.17–058.

[61] The second rule in *Hadley v Baxendale*, above (see above, para.16–046). The fact that ss.53(2) and 54 are based on *Hadley v Baxendale* is accepted in *Bostock & Co. Ltd v Nicholson & Sons Ltd* [1904] 1 K.B. 725 at 735–736.

[62] On interest, see above, paras 16–007—16–013.

[63] Above, paras 17–001 *et seq*.

[64] Discussed above, paras 11–001 *et seq*.

[65] Damages for breaches of terms relating to the seller's title, the buyer's quiet possession, or freedom from charges or encumbrances (s.12) are considered elsewhere: see above, Ch.4; below, para.17–087.

[66] s.14(3) (above, paras 11–051 *et seq*.).

[67] s.13 (above, paras 11–001 *et seq*.).

[68] Below, paras 19–188 *et seq*.

[69] See below, para.17–050.

[70] Above, paras 12–071 *et seq*.

[71] When the seller claims *damages*, the buyer may, of course, claim a set-off of damages for the seller's *previous* breach of contract: *Berger & Co. Inc. v Gill & Duffus SA* [1984] A.C. 382 at 392 (see above, para.16–061).

in *Mondel v Steel*.[72] A ship was built for the buyer, but when the seller sued for the price the buyer set up as a defence the seller's breach of an express warranty as to quality. The buyer's damages were calculated at this stage by reference to the difference between the actual value of the ship at the date of delivery, and what it would have been worth if built to the contractual standard.[73] Later, the buyer sued for further damages for the cost of repairs to the ship, and it was held, with reference to the earlier case, that it was "competent for [the buyer] . . . simply to defend himself by showing how much less the subject-matter of the action was worth, by reason of the breach of contract; and to the extent that he obtains, or is capable of obtaining,[74] an abatement of price on that account, he must be considered as having received satisfaction for the breach of contract, and is precluded from recovering in another action to that extent; but no more."[75] Section 53(4) supplements the propositions in *Mondel v Steel*, above, by making it clear that the buyer is not precluded from bringing a separate action for damages for the same breach of warranty "if he has suffered further damage." It is not clear whether the word "further" relates to fresh damage suffered after the first action was disposed of, or to damage which was not taken into account when assessing the extent of the reduction in the price in the first action. *Mondel v Steel* suggests the latter interpretation, but the former is probably the more normal meaning of the word "further".[76]

But the buyer is not *bound* to set up the breach of warranty by way of defence when the seller sues for the price: the fact that the buyer has paid the full price or that the seller has recovered the full price by action against the buyer, does not prevent the buyer from subsequently bringing a separate action against the seller for breach of warranty.[77] One reason for this rule is that the existence or extent of the defect in the goods may not become apparent to the buyer until after he has paid the price claimed by the seller.[78] It is submitted that, by a term of the contract, the buyer may agree to waive his right to a set-off against the price[79]; but such a term may

---

[72] (1841) 8 M. & W. 858. See also *Poulton v Lattimore* (1829) 9 B. & C. 259 (none of the price recovered by the seller—nor was the buyer obliged to return the goods before setting up the breach of warranty as a defence). The meaning of set-off is examined in *BICC Plc v Burndy Corporation* [1985] Ch. 232 at 247–251, 254–259 (not a sale of goods case); in *British Anzani (Felixstowe) Ltd v International Marine Management (UK) Ltd* [1980] Q.B. 637 (landlord and tenant): in *Axel Johnson Petroleum AB v MG Mineral Group AG* [1992] 1 W.L.R. 270.

[73] (1841) 8 M & W 858 at 872.

[74] These words were interpreted in *Davis v Hedges* (1871) L.R. 6 Q.B. 687.

[75] (1841) 8 M & W 858 at 871–872.

[76] Another possible meaning could be that "further" refers to a sum "over and above" the price (at least in cases where the breach of warranty had been set up in "extinction" of the price).

[77] See the analogous case of a building contract: *Davis v Hedges* (1871) L.R. 6 Q.B. 687 (the sale of goods case is expressly said to be the same: *ibid.*, at p.690). S.53(4) inferentially supports this proposition.

[78] *Davis v Hedges*, above, at pp.690–691.

[79] *cf. Hongkong and Shanghai Banking Corporation v Kloeckner & Co. AG* [1990] 2 Q.B. 514 (not a sale of goods case) and *Connaught Restaurants Ltd v Indoor Leisure Ltd* [1994] 4 All E.R. 834 (obligation to pay rent "without any deduction" did not preclude equitable right of set off).

be invalid under the Unfair Contract Terms Act 1977[80] or under the Unfair Terms in Consumer Contract Regulations 1999.[81]

Where the seller sues to enforce a negotiable instrument which the buyer has given in respect of the price, the buyer cannot set off a claim for damages for breach of warranty but must counter-claim by a separate action.[82] Nor can the buyer defend by way of set-off where the claim against him arises, not from breach of the contract of sale, but from breach of a different contract, *e.g.* a mortgage back to the seller of the ship sold to the buyer.[83]

Reduction in price for a consumer. A reduction in price may be a remedy for a consumer who bought goods which were not in conformity with the contract when delivered to him.[84] Part 5A of the Act provides new remedies of repair, replacement and rescission which have been examined earlier in this book[85] but that of reduction in price deserves consideration in parallel with section 53(1)(a) and (4) on diminution or extinction of the price.[86] The buyer's action to reduce the price was previously unknown to English law and it is not yet clear how the "reduction of the price" will be assessed.[87] 17–050

(b) *Diminution in Value*

Damages for diminution in market value. As is illustrated by the rule in section 53(3) for "breach of warranty of quality",[88] the usual or "prima facie" measure of damages for breach of the seller's contractual undertaking as to the quality or condition of the goods is the difference between: (a) the value of the goods if they complied with the undertaking, measured at the time[89] and place[90] of delivery; and (b) the actual value of the goods, in 17–051

---

80 Above, paras 13–062 *et seq.*
81 Above, paras 12–077 *et seq.*
82 *Cebora SNC v SIP (Industrial Products) Ltd* [1976] 1 Lloyd's Rep. 271. *Cf. Nova (Jersey) Knit Ltd v Kammgarn Spinnerei GmbH* [1977] 1 W.L.R. 713; *James Lamont & Co. Ltd v Hyland Ltd (No.* 2) [1950] 1 All E.R. 929 (contract for repair of a ship); *All Trades Distributors Ltd v Agencies Kaufman Ltd* (1969) 113 S.J. 995.
83 *Bow, McLachlan & Co. Ltd v Ship "Camosun"* [1909] A.C. 597 at 610–613.
84 Above, paras 12–091 *et seq.*
85 Above, paras 12–076 *et seq.*
86 Above, para.17–049.
87 See above, paras 12–091 *et seq.*
88 "Quality of goods" includes "their state or condition" and various aspects are included: see s.14(2B) of the Act (inserted by s.1 of the Sale and Supply of Goods Act 1994) (above, para.11–026). S.53(2), however, is not limited to breaches of warranties of quality.
89 See above, paras 8–025 *et seq.*, 17–008 *et seq.* If the delivery is delayed (by the seller) beyond the contractual date for delivery, the actual date of delivery is the relevant time.
90 See above, paras 8–018 *et seq.* S.53(3) refers only to the time of delivery, but it is submitted that, in accordance with the rule for the market price in cases of non-delivery or delayed delivery (above, paras 17–004—17–005, 17–038), the contractual place for delivery is also relevant to the ascertainment of the market value of the goods: (see also below, para.19–201). But *cf.* the dictum in *Aryeh v Lawrence Kostoris & Son Ltd* [1967] 1 Lloyd's Rep. 63 at 73.

their actual condition, at the same time and place.[91] With the sum of money which amounts to this difference, the buyer should (so far as the *value* of the defective goods is concerned)[92] be put into the financial position he would have been in if the seller had complied with his undertaking. The measure prescribed by section 53(3) assumes that the buyer has paid the seller the full price for the goods and is bringing an action or claim against the seller for damages for breach of his contractual undertaking (section 53(1)(b)); if the buyer has not paid the price, his claim for damages may be used by him as a set-off against the seller's claim for the price (section 53(1)(a)).[93]

The rule as to the measure of damages in section 53(3) is based on cases decided prior to the 1893 Act.[94] The Court of Appeal has emphasised that the subsection provides only a "prima facie" rule, which should not be applied where it would give the buyer "more than his true loss".[95] The court said that subsection 53(2) was "the starting point".[96] Apart from this, subsection 53(3) is not often applied on its own because there may be consequential losses or injuries caused by the defective goods,[97] in respect of which the buyer may also be claiming damages.[98] The buyer may also have a claim for damages for "loss of amenity" despite the fact that the seller's breach of contract did not lead to any diminution in the market value of the goods.[99]

17–052 **Ascertaining the value of goods complying with the contract.** The problem of fixing the market value[1] of the goods is similar to that arising in the case of damages for non-delivery or delayed delivery,[2] and the cases on market value decided under sections 50(3) and 51(3) should be applicable to the interpretation of section 53(3).[3] Similarly, the problem of fixing a value for the goods in the absence of an available market for them has already been considered.[4]

In the absence of other evidence as to the market value of goods which comply with the contractual description and quality, some courts have taken

---

[91] Thus, (a) alone measures the damages if the defective goods which are delivered have no market value at the time of delivery: *Bridge v Wain* (1816) 1 Stark. 504.
[92] As to loss of profits, or other consequential losses, see below, paras 17–066 *et seq*.
[93] The fact that the buyer has paid the price to the seller makes no difference to the measure of damages: *Loder v Kekule* (1857) 3 C.B.(N.S.) 128.
[94] *e.g. Loder v Kekule*, above, at pp.139–140; *Dingle v Hare* (1859) 7 C.B.(N.S.) 145; *Jones v Just* (1868) L.R. 3 Q.B. 197 (below, para.17–054). For cases after the Act, see the following paragraphs.
[95] *Bence Graphics International Ltd v Fasson U.K. Ltd* [1998] Q.B. 87 at 102 (see below, para.17–058). The *Bence Graphics* case was applied by the CA in *Bem Dis A Turk Ticaret S/A v International Agri Trade Co. Ltd* [1999] 1 All E.R. (Comm) 619.
[96] *Bence Graphics*, above, at p.102.
[97] See below, paras 17–059—17–084.
[98] See the analogous situation with a building contract: *Davis v Hedges* (1871) L.R. 6 Q.B. 687 at 691.
[99] See below, para.17–071.
[1] The relevant "market value" will depend on the circumstances: see above, paras 16–070, 17–005.
[2] Above, paras 17–005—17–008, 17–017—17–018, 17–038—17–039.
[3] See above, paras 16–062—16–076.
[4] Above, paras 16–077—16–079, 17–021—17–027.

the contract price as evidence of the "value" of the goods.[5] But the correct measure according to section 53(3), is the value "at the time of delivery to the buyer", which should be taken when it is shown to be different from the contract price.[6] The price at which the buyer had previously resold the goods is normally irrelevant to the ascertainment of their value at the time of delivery to the buyer[7]; but, in the absence of other evidence, the price at which a sub-buyer had agreed to buy the goods from the buyer before the defect was discovered may be some evidence of their market value,[8] as may the price at which an offer for the goods was made by a third person.[9]

Ascertaining the value of the goods actually delivered. The second value to be ascertained is that of the defective goods which were actually delivered by the seller. Normally, there is no market in the ordinary sense for damaged or defective goods,[10] and thus other evidence is frequently needed to fix the value of the goods at the time and place[11] of delivery. This value may be evidenced by the price at which the buyer has been able to resell the goods to a sub-buyer who has knowledge of their defective condition.[12] "If the actual damaged goods are sold with all faults, good evidence can be obtained of the difference in value . . . "[13] But the court is unlikely to place reliance on the evidence of third persons ("hypothetical buyers") as to what they would have paid for goods "which they never saw and of whose defects they have learnt only at secondhand."[14] The value of defective goods will depend on the nature of the defect, or the extent of the damage to the goods. "It is a common practice in the commercial world to deal with this type of case by way of a price allowance; and claims for damaged goods are constantly met to the satisfaction of both parties by the fixing of an allowance by an adjuster or some person skilled in the trade. I 17–053

---

[5] *Dingle v Hare* (1859) 29 L.J.C.P. 143 (the judgment takes the measure of damages as "the difference of value between the article as delivered and the article as warranted," but the contract price was assumed to be the latter value (at p.148); the headn. to the report of the case in (1859) 7 C.B.(N.S.) 145, refers to the contract price); *Minster Trust Ltd v Traps Tractors Ltd* [1954] 3 All E.R. 136 at 156.

[6] *Loder v Kekule*, above; *Slater v Hoyle and Smith Ltd* [1920] 2 K.B. 11 at 17, 18 (". . . the contract price does not directly enter into the calculation at all" (*ibid.*, at p.18), though "it may be an element in assessing the value": *ibid.*, at p.17).

[7] *Slater v Hoyle and Smith Ltd*, above (below, para.17–057). See the same rule in the case of damages for non-delivery or delayed delivery: above, paras 17–028—17–036, 17–044—17–045. But *cf.* the willingness of the CA not to apply the prima facie "market value" rule in section 53(3): *Bence Graphics International Ltd v Fasson UK Ltd* [1998] Q.B. 87. (See below, paras 17–058, 17–082.)

[8] As suggested in *Clare v Maynard* (1837) 6 A. & E. 519.

[9] *Cox v Walker* (1835) 6 A. & E. 523n.

[10] *Biggin & Co. Ltd v Permanite Ltd* [1951] 1 K.B. 422 at 438. (The appeal was allowed, but on a different ground: [1951] 2 K.B. 314 (see below, para.17–078.)) There may, however, be a market for goods which are not up to sample, or not fit for a particular purpose.

[11] See above, para.17–051, n.90.

[12] *Cox v Walker*, above. *Cf.* the court's attempt at assessing such a price: *Jackson v Chrysler Acceptances Ltd* [1978] R.T.R. 474.

[13] *Biggin & Co. Ltd v Permanite Ltd*, above, at p.438.

[14] *ibid.*, at p.439.

think that that is a method which can legitimately be followed by the court where no more precise method of calculation presents itself."[15]

17–054 **The relevant time for ascertaining values.** Section 53(3) speaks of the value of the goods "at the time of delivery to the buyer". In *Jones v Just*,[16] a case before the 1893 Act, the buyers bought "fair current Manilla hemp", but the sellers, in breach of their contract,[17] delivered damaged hemp. After the date of the contract the market price rose, so that the buyers were able to resell the damaged hemp at a price nearly equal to the contract price. But it was held that the buyers were entitled to damages assessed as the difference between the value of the damaged hemp when it arrived, and the value at the same date of hemp up to the contractual standard. The buyer was entitled to the rise in the market price between the contract and the delivery, and the court treated as irrelevant the price at which the buyer had actually resold the goods at a date later than the date of delivery.[18] Section 53(3) clearly accepts this position. If there were separate deliveries, the measure of damages in section 53(3) should be applied separately to each delivery.[19]

Section 53(3) lays down only a "prima facie" rule, from which the court may depart in appropriate circumstances.[20] For instance, the time when the actual value of the goods in their defective state is assessed may be postponed until the defect is discovered.[21] Similarly, when the seller knows that the buyer intends to resell the goods to a sub-buyer at another place, and that the goods will not be examined until they reach the sub-buyer (*e.g.* because they are packaged), the date at which the latter examines the goods may be the date at which the market price should be taken to assess the buyer's damages for the defective condition of the goods.[22] A warranty as to quality may relate to the future[23] (*e.g.* that seed will produce a certain crop) so that there can be no question of the buyer's opportunity to resell the defective goods until the defect becomes apparent at a later date. The market value test should not be applied until the future event is

---

[15] *ibid.*, at p.439 (at p.440, the court assessed such an allowance at 15 per cent of the purchase price). See also *Cehave NV v Bremer Handelsgesellschaft mbH* (*The Hansa Nord*) [1976] Q.B. 44 at 63.
[16] (1868) L.R. 3 Q.B. 197.
[17] The case was mainly concerned with the terms to be implied in the contract.
[18] *cf. Campbell Mostyn* (*Provisions*) *Ltd v Barnett Trading Co.* [1954] 1 Lloyd's Rep. 65 (above, paras 16–056, 16–076). *Cf.* also *Pagnan* (*R.*) *& Fratelli v Corbisa Industrial Agropacuaria* [1970] 1 W.L.R. 1306 (above, para.17–020).
[19] *Slater v Hoyle and Smith Ltd*, above, at p.19 (the judge at first instance had used "a general average," and Scrutton L.J. agreed that the precise measure would have been "an almost impossible task": *ibid.*, at p.19).
[20] *Bence Graphics International Ltd v Fasson UK Ltd* [1998] Q.B. 87 (CA: see below, paras 17–058, 17–082).
[21] *Naughton v O'Callaghan* [1990] 3 All E.R. 191.
[22] *Van den Hurk v Martens* (*R*) *& Co. Ltd* [1920] 1 K.B. 850. See above, para.12–043. *Cf.* the similar ruling in *Kwei Tek Chao v British Traders Ltd* [1954] 2 Q.B. 459 (below, paras 19–191, 19–201). Normally, the place of delivery is the place for examination of the goods under s.34(2): see above, para.12–043; below, paras 19–216, 20–108—20–110, 20–116. On the question of the "time of delivery" in a c.i.f. contract, see below, paras 19–157, 19–201.
[23] See above, para.10–021.

known,[24] since section 53(3) assumes that the buyer could immediately resell the defective goods in the market. Where, however, the seller, by his negotiations with the buyer, delayed the resale of the defective goods for a period after delivery to the buyer and discovery of the defect, the price at the date of the resale was taken as the value of the goods which were delivered by the seller.[25]

Cost of remedying the defect.[26] Where the market value of the defective goods cannot be ascertained, because there was no market in which they could be disposed of, damages may be awarded on the basis of the cost of bringing the goods up to the contractual standard which would make them saleable.[27] This is similar to the position where the seller fails to deliver the goods, and there is no available market in which to buy substitute goods: the buyer may buy the nearest equivalent goods which are available, and recover as damages both the cost of procuring them and the cost of adapting them to meet the contractual standards.[28] 17–055

Cost of buying substitute goods.[29] In some circumstances the buyer may be entitled to claim, as damages for defective quality, the cost of buying substitute goods to perform the function intended to be performed by the contractual goods.[30] The House of Lords, in *British Westinghouse Electric and Manufacturing Co. Ltd v Underground Electric Railways Co. of London Ltd*,[31] accepted that the cost of substitute machines could be awarded, but held that the damages should take account of any extra profit to the buyer resulting from the replacement of the defective machines. The seller agreed to deliver and erect steam turbines of a specified kilowatt capacity. The turbines were delivered but the buyers complained that they failed to comply with the contractual provisions with respect to economy and steam consumption. Several years later, after experience of the defective supply of power from the seller's turbines, the buyers decided that they would replace the seller's turbines with eight new turbines of a different manufacturer, which were an improved type and of a greater kilowatt capacity than the seller's. The arbitrator found that the superiority of the newer machines was so great in efficiency and in economy of working expenses that it would have been to the buyers' pecuniary advantage to have replaced the seller's machines by them even if the seller's machines had complied with all the contractual specifications. The House of Lords held that the buyers' action 17–056

[24] *Ashworth v Wells* (1898) 14 T.L.R. 227 (below, para.17–066).
[25] *Loder v Kekule* (1857) 3 C.B.(N.S.) 128 at 140.
[26] A consumer may now have the further remedies of repair or replacement: see above, paras 12–076 *et seq*.
[27] *Minster Trust Ltd v Traps Tractors Ltd* [1954] 3 All E.R. 136 at 156. (The judge also allowed damages for the consequent loss of profits during the period when the machines were being overhauled.) The cost of repairs to the goods was also accepted as a basis for damages in *Mondel v Steel* (1841) 8 M. & W. 858 at 872 (above, para.17–049). *Cf.* above, para.17–023, n.73.
[28] Above, paras 17–023—17–025.
[29] See above, n.26.
[30] *cf.* above, paras 17–023—17–025.
[31] [1912] A.C. 673.

in replacing the obsolete machines "formed part of a continuous dealing with the situation in which they found themselves, and was not an independent or disconnected transaction"[32]; that it was "a reasonable and prudent course quite naturally arising out of the circumstances in which [they were] placed by the breach"[33]; and that, even though they may not have been under a duty to mitigate their loss in this way, when their action had in fact diminished their loss, their claim for damages for the cost of installing the newer turbines must take account of the extra profit (including the saving of expenses) resulting from this action.[34] Since this extra profit exceeded the cost of the substitute, the buyers could not recover the cost.[35] If, however, the buyers did not claim either the cost of buying substitute goods or their loss of profits, but only the normal measure of damages, the buyers' claim could not be reduced by reference to the rules of mitigation. This normal measure, according to section 53(3), is the difference between the value of the goods actually delivered at the time of delivery and the value they would have had if they had answered to the contractual undertaking as to their quality. If the buyers in the *British Westinghouse* case had claimed this measure of damages, their claim could not have been reduced by the seller's proving that at a later date it would have become more economical to discard their machines and to use the improved type.[36]

Where the buyer claims damages for his loss of profit[37] or other consequential losses[38] caused by the defective quality of the goods delivered by the seller, the seller may show that the buyer ought reasonably[39] to have mitigated his loss by acquiring substitute goods.[40]

17–057 **Buyer performing sub-contract despite seller's breach.** Where the seller delivers defective goods, but the buyer is nevertheless able to perform a sub-contract by delivering the goods to his sub-buyer, the question arises whether the buyer's damages against the seller should be reduced by taking this into account. Until recently *Slater v Hoyle and Smith Ltd*[41] was the leading authority. In this case the buyer bought cotton from the seller in order to fulfil another contract which the buyer had already made with a

[32] *ibid.*, at p.692.
[33] *ibid.*, at p.691.
[34] *cf. Erie County Natural Gas and Fuel Co. Ltd v Carroll* [1911] A.C. 105 (discussed above, para.17–024); *Nadreph Ltd v Willmett & Co.* [1978] 1 W.L.R. 1537 (not a sale of goods case). *Cf.* also *Hussey v Eels* [1990] 2 Q.B. 227 (sale of land).
[35] The buyers did recover damages for extra expenses incurred up to the time they acquired the substitute (below, para.17–062).
[36] But *cf.* the willingness of the CA not to apply the prima facie "market value" rule in section 53(3): *Bence Graphics International Ltd v Fasson UK Ltd* [1998] Q.B. 87. (See below, para.17–058, 17–082.)
[37] See below, paras 17–066—17–070.
[38] Below, paras 17–062—17–065.
[39] Although this would involve the buyer in considerable extra expense if he had already paid the price of the defective goods. Normally, the rules of mitigation do not oblige the innocent party to incur heavy expenditure (see above, paras 16–052, 17–025).
[40] *British Westinghouse* case, above.
[41] [1920] 2 K.B. 11.

sub-buyer.[42] The seller delivered cloth which was not up to the contractual quality, but the buyer was able to perform the sub-contract by delivering the same cloth.[43] The sub-buyer paid the full price under the sub-contract and when the buyer sued the seller for damages, the seller submitted, first, that the resale price should be taken instead of the market value of the cloth at the time it was delivered,[44] and, secondly, that the buyer had not in fact suffered any loss because he received the same resale price as he would have done if the seller had not been in breach. The Court of Appeal, however, awarded the buyer damages assessed at the normal measure, *viz.* the difference between (a) the market price, at the time and place of delivery, of cloth up to the contractual quality, and (b) the market price, at the time and place of delivery, of the cloth actually delivered. Scrutton L.J. said that "If the buyer is lucky enough, for reasons with which the seller has nothing to do, to get his goods through on the sub-contract without a claim against him,[45] this on principle cannot affect his claim against the seller any more than the fact that he had to pay very large damages on his sub-contract would affect his original seller."[46]

But in *Bence Graphics International Ltd v Fasson UK Ltd*[47] the Court of Appeal in 1996 has not followed the approach in *Slater's* case. In *Bence's* case, both parties contemplated: (a) that the buyer would, after manufacturing the goods into another product, sell the latter to others; and (b) that the measure of damages for defects in the goods should be the extent of the buyer's liability (if any) to those others resulting from the defect. In *Bence's* case the court accepted that its approach was contrary to *Slater's* case, which "should be reconsidered": Auld L.J. said that in the latter case the court wrongly overlooked the basic rule in section 53(2) as to what would have been in the ordinary and natural contemplation of the parties in a commercial contract—that the buyer could well be prejudiced in his onward dealing with the goods if they were defective.[48] In *Slater's* case the buyer did not use the goods in manufacturing them into another product, but this does not appear to be a sufficient ground for distinguishing between the cases. However, it is possible to distinguish *Slater's* case on the ground that, on the facts, the parties did not contemplate that if the goods were 17–058

[42] The description of the cloth was not identical with that in the original contract.

[43] The sub-buyer had made complaints but had not rejected the goods: *ibid.*, at p.19. The Court of Appeal assumed that the buyer would not have to pay damages to his sub-buyer: *sed quaere*.

[44] The resale price per yard was higher than the market price of the inferior cloth at the time of delivery.

[45] The same result might occur where an exemption clause in the sub-contract protects the original buyer.

[46] *ibid.*, at p.23. The buyers were not obliged to deliver to the sub-buyer the goods which they bought from the original seller, and in fact some of the goods which they delivered to the sub-buyer came from a different source.

[47] [1998] Q.B. 87 (see below, paras 17–082, 17–083). See also *Louis Dreyfus Trading Ltd v Reliance Trading Ltd* [2004] EWHC 525 (Comm) [2004] 2 Lloyd's Rep. 243 (parties contemplated sale of the same goods to the sub-buyer under a specific contract).

[48] [1998] Q.B. 87 at p.105.

defective, the extent of the buyer's liability towards his sub-buyer should be the measure of damages payable by the seller.[49]

The authority of *Slater's* case has thus been seriously undermined, and there is uncertainty as to the current law where the sub-buyer makes no claim against the buyer, despite the fact that the seller delivered defective goods to the buyer.[50] The reasoning in *Slater's* case also appears to be in conflict with that in *Wertheim v Chicoutimi Pulp Co.*,[51] a case of delay in delivery of the goods which is examined and criticised in an earlier section of this chapter.[52] In *Wertheim's* case the Privy Council took account of the fact that the buyer had been able to fulfil his sub-contracts,[53] despite the seller's delay in delivery, and, since the resale prices were higher than the market price at the actual time of delivery, damages were assessed at the difference between (a) the market price at the time and place fixed for delivery, and (b) the resale prices.

(c) *Losses other than Diminution in Value*

(i) *The Buyer's Actual or Imputed Knowledge of the Defect*

17–059 **The buyer's actual knowledge of the defect.** Where the seller delivers goods which fail to meet the contractual description or standard, the buyer may not immediately discover the defect or the failure of the goods to satisfy the description.[54] As soon as the buyer knows of the defect, he will be unable to recover damages for any further or consequential loss which he ought reasonably to have avoided by taking remedial or precautionary steps.[55] The buyer is not justified in continuing to rely on the seller's warranty after he knows that the goods are defective in that respect. In *Lambert v Lewis*,[56] where a buyer bought a trailer coupling, the House of Lords held that the warranty[57] that it was reasonably fit for towing trailers would continue in effect for a reasonable time after delivery, so long as it remained in the same apparent state as that in which it was delivered (apart from normal wear and tear). But as soon as the buyer learned[58] that the

---

[49] In *Bence Graphics*, however, the majority of the Court of Appeal limited the buyer's damages by reference to the use which the sellers *believed* the buyer intended to make of the goods. (The buyer could have used other material).

[50] But see the criticism of *Bence Graphics* by Treitel, 113 L.Q.R. 188 (1997) summarised below, para.17–082, nn. 71, 74, 75. See also Hawes, 121 L.Q.R. 389 (2005) (commenting on a New Zealand case which followed *Bence Graphics*).

[51] [1911] A.C. 301. In *Bence Graphics*, above, at pp.103–105, Auld L.J. approved the *Wertheim* decision.

[52] Above, para.17–039.

[53] For possible reasons for the buyer's ability to do so, see above, para.17–039, n.99.

[54] The consumer's new remedies under Pt 5A of the Act are available where the lack of conformity of the goods with the contract becomes manifest within two years of delivery: see above, paras 12–076 *et seq*.

[55] This principle is implicit in the decision of the House of Lords in *Lambert v Lewis* [1982] A.C. 225 (below). See also *British Oil and Cake Co. Ltd v Burstall & Co.* (1923) 39 T.L.R. 406 at 407; *Hammond & Co. v Bussey* (1887) 20 Q.B.D. 79 at 86.

[56] Above.

[57] Under s.14(1) of the 1893 Act (see now s.14(3) of the 1979 Act).

[58] On the question whether the buyer *ought* reasonably to have known of the missing handle, see below, para.17–060.

handle of the locking mechanism of the coupling was missing, he could no longer rely on the seller's warranty to excuse him from making his own examination to see if it was still safe to use.[59] The buyer was held liable[60] to third parties injured when the trailer broke away, but he could not recover from the seller the damages paid to them, because his reliance on the warranty was no longer justified.

After the buyer knows of the defect, he cannot, by reselling the goods to a third person, increase the original seller's liability by holding him liable for the buyer's own responsibility towards his sub-buyer.[61] If the buyer acquired knowledge of the defect at a time when the goods were already in the hands of the sub-buyer, he ought to have notified the sub-buyer if the latter could take reasonable steps to avoid further loss or injury.[62]

The buyer's failure to discover the defect. The buyer is not debarred from claiming damages merely because he did not make a thorough examination of the goods delivered by the seller to see whether they complied with the contract. Where the defect is not patent or obvious, he may, for a reasonable time after delivery,[63] rely on the seller's contractual undertaking as to quality or description.[64] Where copra cake was sold to the buyers for the purpose of being used as cattle food, the buyers were held to be entitled to recover from the sellers the compensation paid to the sub-buyers,[65] despite the fact that the buyers had not examined the goods before delivering them to the sub-buyers.[66] "The buyers were entitled, if they chose, without being guilty of negligence or unreasonable conduct, to rely on their contract[67] with the sellers rather than to rely on any precautions of their own."[68] Roche J. held that only an expert analyst could have discovered the poisonous admixture in the copra cake, and that it was not reasonable to expect the buyer to pay for such an examination. In two 17–060

---

[59] It is the rules of mitigation (above, paras 16–052—16–058) which prevent the buyer from continuing to rely on the warranty once he knows of the defect: his claim for damages will be assessed on the basis that thereafter he should have taken reasonable steps to minimise his loss.

[60] On the ground of his negligence in continuing to use the coupling without having it examined: see below, para.17–060.

[61] *Biggin & Co. Ltd v Permanite Ltd* [1951] 1 K.B. 422 at 435 (the appeal was decided on another point; see below, para.17–078). See also *Dobell (GC) & Co. Ltd v Barber and Garratt* [1931] 1 K.B. 219 at 238 (see also Greer L.J., dissenting, at pp.246–247).

[62] *Biggin & Co. Ltd v Permanite Ltd*, above, at p.435. (See further, below, para.17–079).

[63] *Lambert v Lewis*, above.

[64] *Pinnock Bros v Lewis and Peat Ltd* [1923] 1 K.B. 690; *British Oil and Cake Co. Ltd v Burstall & Co.*, above, at p.407; *Lambert v Lewis*, above, at pp.275–276. *Cf. Dobell (G.C.) & Co. Ltd v Barber and Garratt*, above. *Cf.* above, para.10–019.

[65] On this aspect of the case, see below, paras 17–076, 17–081.

[66] *Pinnock Bros v Lewis and Peat Ltd*, above; *British Oil and Cake Co. Ltd v Burstall & Co.*, above.

[67] *Viz.*, that the goods should comply with the description.

[68] *Pinnock Bros v Lewis and Peat Ltd*, above, at p.698. See also *Smith v Johnson* (1899) 15 T.L.R. 179 at 180; *Wagstaff v Short-horn Dairy Co.* (1884) Cab. & Ell. 324 ("If you think that [the buyers] acted reasonably in not examining them before planting . . .").

analogous cases[69] (not on the sale of goods), despite a failure to examine the goods supplied by the defendant for the use of the claimant and his employees, the claimant was held to be entitled to recover from the defendant, as damages for the latter's breach of warranty that the goods were reasonably fit for use, the damages paid by the claimant to his employee injured by the defective goods.[70] In each case the claimant was held to be entitled to rely on the defendant's fulfilment of his contractual undertaking, despite the fact that the claimant's own liability towards the injured man was based on his negligence *vis-à-vis* him in failing to see that the equipment was reasonably safe.[71] The House of Lords, in upholding this principle,[72] approved the following limitation: ". . . in a case where A has been held liable to X, a stranger, for negligent failure to take a certain precaution, he may recover over from someone with whom he has a contract only if by that contract the other contracting party has warranted that he *need not*—there is no necessity—take the very precaution for the failure to take which he has been held liable in law to [X]."

The decision of the House of Lords in *Lambert v Lewis*, in paragraph 17–059 above, was based on the buyer's actual knowledge that part of the locking mechanism of the coupling was missing: this knowledge put him on enquiry so that he should have conducted his own examination of the coupling to see if it was still safe to use it.[73] The decision was thus based partly on the buyer's actual knowledge, and partly on his imputed knowledge. Although their Lordships did not expressly consider the situation where the buyer ought, as a reasonable person, to have discovered that part of the mechanism was missing (and thus been put on enquiry), it is submitted that the fact that a reasonable[74] buyer would have been put on enquiry should be sufficient to prevent the seller's contractual liability for loss subsequently arising which could have been reasonably avoided by such a reasonable buyer.[75] This submission derives some support from the

[69] *Mowbray v Merryweather* [1894] 2 Q.B. 640 at 644, 646, 647 (below, para.17–075); *Scott v Foley, Aikman & Co.* (1899) 16 T.L.R. 55.

[70] This question is considered below, para.17–075.

[71] *Mowbray v Merryweather*, above, was cited with approval by the House of Lords in *Lambert v Lewis*, above, (para.17–059) at pp.275–276 ("up to [a reasonable time after delivery] the farmer would have had the right to rely on the dealers' warranty as excusing him from making his own examination of the coupling to see if it were safe": *ibid.*, at p.276). *Cf.* the difference of opinion between the majority of the CA and Greer L.J. (dissenting) in *Dobell (GC) & Co. Ltd v Barber and Garratt* [1931] 1 K.B. 219.

[72] *Lambert v Lewis*, above, at p.276.

[73] *ibid.*, at p.277.

[74] The standard of reasonableness in this situation should not be high *cf.* above, para.16–052. See also n.78, below.

[75] Under the rules of mitigation (above, paras 16–052—16–058). When the innocent party *ought* reasonably to have known of the breach he ought to have taken reasonable steps to avoid or minimise the loss arising from the breach: see above, para.16–053.

decision itself[76]; some from *dicta* in earlier cases[77]; and some from analogous rules about examination of the goods.[78]

Defect discoverable only by use of the goods. Sometimes the seller knows that there are some possible defects in the goods which can be discovered only by the buyer, or the ultimate buyer, actually using them.[79] Thus, the presence of a deleterious substance in a fur skin collar could not be discovered until it was worn and the defect shown by the injury to the skin of the wearer.[80] Similarly, the fact that coal supplied under a contract for use as steam-coal on steamers was not reasonably fit for the purpose "was not a fact which would be patent to the [buyers] on inspection of the coal; it could only be found out when it came to be used, which was not by the [buyers] but by their sub-vendees."[81] And where seed of inferior quality is delivered to a farmer, the fact of the inferior quality may not become apparent until the crop has been grown.[82] In these circumstances, there can be no question of the buyer failing to discover the defect before the use of the goods reveals it. 17–061

(ii) *Additional or Wasted Expenditure*

Other additional or wasted expenses. In addition to the particular items of expenditure mentioned in other paragraphs of this section,[83] the buyer may recover from the seller the reasonable amount of any expenses which have been wasted, or which he has reasonably incurred, as a result of the seller's breach. Such recovery is possible where it was within the reasonable contemplation of the parties, at the time of making the contract, that the 17–062

---

[76] The appellant's argument included several references to imputed knowledge; the decision itself was based partly on imputed knowledge: see above. The speech of Lord Diplock also referred to the coupling being "in an obviously damaged state" (p.276) which suggests an objective test.

[77] *e.g.* where the defect was "not patent" or "obvious": see para.17–060, n.64, above; and below, para.17–061.

[78] s.14(2C)(b): there is no implied condition of satisfactory quality where the buyer examines the goods before the contract is made, as regards defects which that examination ought to reveal (above, para.11–026); and s.15(2)(c) (". . . any defect . . . which would not be apparent on reasonable examination of the sample").

[79] *Kasler and Cohen v Slavouski* [1928] 1 K.B. 78, 85–86; *Bence Graphics International Ltd v Fasson UK Ltd* [1998] Q.B. 87 (CA: see below, para.17–082). See also *Lambert v Lewis*, above; and above para.17–059, n.54.

[80] *Kasler and Cohen v Slavouski*, above, at p.84.

[81] *Hammond & Co. v Bussey* (1887) 20 Q.B.D. 79, 86. (On the same page, Lord Esher M.R. assumes that the case would be different if the defect had been "patent on inspection" by the buyers before the sub-sale.)

[82] *Wagstaff v Short-horn Dairy Co.* (1884) Cab. & Ell. 324. See the facts of *George Mitchell (Chesterhall) Ltd v Finney Lock Seeds Ltd* [1983] 2 A.C. 803, where the House of Lords' decision is based on the assumption that the farmer was entitled to recover all his costs wasted in cultivating the worthless crop, as well as the net profit he would have made from a successful crop: see below, para.17–070.

[83] *e.g.* the cost of remedying the defect (above, para.17–055); the cost of acquiring a substitute (above, para.17–056); the cost of remedying physical injury to the claimant's person or property (below, para.17–072—17–074). See also below, para.20–119.

buyer was not unlikely to have wasted expenditure, or to incur additional expenses if the seller delivered defective goods in breach of his undertaking as to their description or quality.[84] Thus, where defective steam turbines were delivered, it was not disputed that the buyers could recover damages for the extra coal consumption and labour due to the defects in the machines during the period of their use.[85] In another case,[86] the seller knew that the buyer intended to send the goods to an American sub-buyer, who rejected them on the ground of their defective quality and shipped them back to England.[87] The buyer was held to be entitled to recover from the defaulting seller the freight both ways across the Atlantic, and the customs duty paid in New York.[88] The freight of the return voyage was an additional expense to the buyer, caused by the seller's breach of contract; the freight on the outward voyage was an expense which was wasted[89] as a result of the breach—it would have been an item in the buyer's calculation of the price to be charged to his sub-buyer and which he would have received if the seller had not broken the contract. The buyer was awarded, in addition to the freight, his loss of profit under the sub-sale[90]; provided that this loss was calculated as his *net* loss of profit after allowing for the cost of the freight which was presumably included in the price, there was no double recovery.[91]

17–063 **Expenditure incurred in reliance on the contract.** Incidental expenditure may be incurred by the buyer in reliance on the seller's promise to deliver goods which meet the contractual description or standard. Provided the buyer's expenditure was within the reasonable contemplation of the parties at the time of making the contract, he may recover damages in respect of this expenditure if it has been rendered futile by the seller's breach of contract.[92] But the buyer can recover his wasted expenditure only to the extent that it would have been covered by the gross return which he would

---

[84] *Smith v Johnson* (1899) 15 T.L.R. 179 (mortar supplied by a builder was below standard; it was used for a building which the local authority later condemned as unsafe, and the owner recovered from the builder the cost of pulling it down and of rebuilding; he also recovered damages for loss of ground-rent). See *Chitty on Contracts* (29th ed.), Vol. 1, paras 26–063—26–070.

[85] *British Westinghouse Electric and Manufacturing Co. Ltd v Underground Electric Railways Co. of London Ltd* [1912] A.C. 673 at 683. (In fact the buyers later replaced the defective turbines with a newer, more efficient, model: see above, para.17–056).

[86] *Molling & Co. v Dean & Son Ltd* (1901) 18 T.L.R. 217.

[87] It was held that the expected place of examination of the goods was in America.

[88] The buyer did not return all the goods to the seller and thus the case is not a simple one of non-delivery following rejection.

[89] It is an illustration of "reliance expenditure" (see below, para.17–063).

[90] See below, para.17–068.

[91] See below, para.17–070 on the question of recovery of lost profits in addition to wasted expenditure.

[92] Illustrations of this type of recovery are *Cullinane v British "Rema" Manufacturing Co. Ltd* [1954] 1 Q.B. 292 (discussed below, para.17–070); *Molling & Co. v Dean & Son Ltd* (1901) 18 T.L.R. 217 (in respect of the freight *to* New York: see above, para.17–062); *Richard Holden Ltd v Bostock & Co. Ltd* (1902) 18 T.L.R. 317 (below, para.17–066); *Bostock & Co. Ltd v Nicholson & Sons Ltd* [1904] 1 K.B. 725 (below, paras 17–066, also 17–074, 17–076). See also above, para.12–040 and, on pre-contract expenditure, below, para.17–064.

have made from his use of the goods if the seller had fully performed his contract[93]; the onus of proof is on the seller to show[94] that the buyer would not have recouped all of his expenditure if the contract had been fully performed by the seller.[95]

It is unsettled how far the buyer can recover damages in respect of both his "expectation interest" (the profit or gain which he expected to receive from performance of the contract but which was prevented by the seller's breach of contract) and of his "reliance interest" (wasted expenditure).[96] But it is clear that the buyer may recover one or the other[97] and that he is free to elect between them: if he claims his wasted expenditure, he need not show that he cannot prove his loss of expected profits.[98] Where, however, there is an available market in which the buyer could buy substitute goods, a claim for wasted expenditure will not be possible if the court holds that the "prima facie" rule in section 53(3)[99] is the proper measure of damages.

Pre-contract expenditure. In a case not concerning the sale of goods, the Court of Appeal has held[1] that the innocent party, following a breach by the other party to a contract, can claim his wasted expenditure incurred in anticipation of the making of the contract, provided that the expenditure would have been within the reasonable contemplation of the parties as likely[2] to be wasted if the contract was broken. In a case[3] where a seller wrongfully failed to convey land to the purchaser, it was held that the purchaser's damages could include some expenditure incurred prior to the contract, *e.g.* his legal costs for the contract, and "the cost of performing an act required to be done by the contract notwithstanding that the act is performed in anticipation of the execution of the contract."[4] If, for example, the buyer is a manufacturer who intends to use the raw materials he buys for the purpose of making his products, his factory is a going concern with many overhead costs already incurred before the making of any individual contract to buy raw materials. Unless there is an available market in which he can buy substitute goods, he should, in lieu of claiming loss of profits, be entitled to recover his wasted overhead and similar expenses if the seller delivers defective materials. 17–064

---

93 *C. & P. Haulage v Middleton* [1983] 1 W.L.R. 1461 at 1468; *C.C.C. Films (London) Ltd v Impact Quadrant Films Ltd* [1985] 1 Q.B. 16 at 32. (These are not sale of goods cases). The sentence in the text refers only to wasted expenditure which the claimant intended to recoup from the gross return.

94 On a balance of probabilities.

95 *C.C.C. Films (London) Ltd v Impact Quadrant Films Ltd*, above, at pp.39–40. In the absence of such proof, it will be assumed in favour of the buyer that he would have recouped his expenditure: *ibid.*

96 See the discussion below, para.17–070. The distinction between the two types of interest is made by Fuller and Perdue, 46 Yale L.J. 52 at 373 (1937). See also above, para.16–031.

97 See below, para.17–070.

98 *C.C.C. Films (London) Ltd v Impact Quadrant Films Ltd*, above.

99 See above, paras 17–047, 17–051 *et seq.*

1 *Anglia Television Ltd v Reed* [1972] 1 Q.B. 60.

2 According to *Koufos v C. Czarnikow Ltd* [1969] 1 A.C. 350, the test should be "not unlikely" or a "serious possibility". (See above, para.16–044.)

3 *Lloyd v Stanbury* [1971] 1 W.L.R. 535.

4 *ibid.*, at p.546.

17–065 **Fines paid by the buyer.** If it was within the reasonable contemplation of the parties at the time of making the contract that the buyer might be prosecuted if the goods supplied by the seller were defective,[5] *e.g.* food unfit for human consumption,[6] the buyer (in the absence of fault on his part) has been held entitled to recover from the seller both the fine and the costs of his defence.[7] If, however, the buyer's own negligence led, at least partly, to the imposition of the fine, it has been said that the buyer is not entitled to recover damages in respect of it.[8] However, a number of later cases[9] have raised the issue of public policy. In these it has been said that if the punishment inflicted by a criminal court is personal to the offender, the civil courts should not entertain an action by the offender to recover an indemnity against the consequences of that punishment.[10]

It is submitted that the issue should turn on whether or not the buyer was guilty of *mens rea*[11]: if he was not, the court should be willing to award him damages in respect of a fine imposed on him. The question of the buyer's negligence should, it is submitted, be dealt with in the same way as where a third party makes a claim against the buyer.[12]

If the buyer is acquitted, he may recover his costs in defending a prosecution resulting from the seller's breach of warranty, since public policy is not in question.[13]

(iii) *Loss of Profit*

17–066 **The buyer's loss of profit.**[14] Where, at the time of making the contract, the seller knew, or ought reasonably to have contemplated, that the buyer intended to use the goods to produce a profit,[15] and that a breach of the seller's undertaking as to description or quality of the goods would impede that profit-making, the buyer may recover damages for his loss of profits

---

[5] In breach of the seller's contractual undertaking as to description or condition of the goods.

[6] But see s.21 of the Food Safety Act 1990 (defence that offence was due to the act or default of another person).

[7] *Cointat v Myham & Son* [1913] 2 K.B. 220 (reversed on question of warranty: (1914) 30 T.L.R. 282). *Cf. Crage v Fry* (1903) 67 J.P. 240 (no evidence as to what influenced the court in imposing the fine). In *Marles v Philip Trant & Sons Ltd* [1954] 1 Q.B. 29 at 39–40, there is a dictum of Denning L.J. which accepts that these cases were correctly decided.

[8] *Cointat v Myham & Son*, above, at p.222.

[9] *Leslie (R) Ltd v Reliable Advertising and Addressing Agency* [1915] 1 K.B. 652; *Proops v Chaplin (WH) & Co.* (1920) 37 T.L.R. 112 at 114; *Askey v Golden Wine Co. Ltd* [1948] 2 All E.R. 35 (only the third case concerned the sale of goods).

[10] See also *Payne v Ministry of Food* (1953) 103 L.J. 141.

[11] There was *mens rea* in the claimant in both *Leslie (R.) Ltd v Reliable Advertising and Addressing Agency Ltd*, above, and *Askey v Golden Wine Co. Ltd*, above.

[12] See above, para.17–060. (If, however, the ground for the buyer's conviction was his own negligence, it is submitted that he should not be entitled to recover damages in respect of the fine.)

[13] *Proops v Chaplin (WH) & Co.*, above.

[14] For loss of profits under a sub-sale see below, para.17–068. For a general loss of custom, see below, para.17–069.

[15] The seller must have actual or imputed knowledge of the category of use intended by the buyer: *Bunting v Tory*, below.

caused by the breach.[16] In one case,[17] brewers bought sugar for making beer, but the sugar was poisoned with arsenic. The brewers were able to recover the market value of the beer in their stock which had to be destroyed, and the court expressly recognised that this market value would include the brewers' profits in making the beer, as well as their costs of production. In another case, a farmer bought seed potatoes of a specified type, but those delivered were mixed with an inferior type. When a crop of mixed potatoes resulted, the farmer's damages were assessed as the difference between (a) the market value of the normal crop which would have resulted if the seed potatoes had complied with the contractual description; and (b) the value of the mixed crop actually grown.[18]

Where there are several different uses to which the buyer might put the goods, the seller will be liable for the buyer's loss of profits in respect of a particular category of use only when the seller knew, or ought reasonably to have contemplated, that the buyer intended that category of use.[19] In one case[20] a bull was sold at an auction to a farmer who hoped to improve his butterfat production and who relied on a warranty in the auction catalogue that tests of the milk of the bull's dam had averaged a certain percentage of butterfat content. The farmer discovered three years later that this statement was incorrect and he sued to recover the resulting loss in value of every calf sired by the bull during these years. The court, however, refused to award damages beyond those specified in section 53(3),[21] because the seller had not known that the buyer intended to use the bull for breeding, and there were other purposes for which the buyer may have bought it, *viz.* for resale at a profit. However, it was found to be "likely" that the buyer was "buying it for breeding purposes",[22] and the decision is therefore hard to reconcile with cases where the buyer was claiming damages for physical loss caused by a particular use of the defective goods. In these cases, the buyer may recover if the category of use to which the buyer put the goods was *one* of the possible uses within the reasonable contemplation of the seller.[23] It is submitted that the same should apply when the buyer claims loss of profits caused by defective goods.

---

[16] See, in addition to the cases cited below: *Ashworth v Wells* (1898) 14 T.L.R. 227 (orchid sold warranted to flower white but two years later it flowered an ordinary purple, which was commercially worth little).

[17] *Richard Holden Ltd v Bostock & Co. Ltd* (1902) 18 T.L.R. 317.

[18] *Wagstaff v Shorthorn Dairy Co.* (1884) Cab. & Ell. 324. See also *Randall v Raper* (1858) E.B. & E. 84; and the facts of *Wallis, Son and Wells v Pratt and Haynes* [1910] 2 K.B. 1003 (on appeal [1911] A.C. 394) where the sub-buyer had grown inferior seeds, and his damages appear to have been assessed on the above basis).

[19] On the parties' reasonable contemplation of the *type* or *kind* of loss in question, see above, para.16–043.

[20] *Bunting v Tory* (1948) 64 T.L.R. 353.

[21] The difference between the actual value of the bull at the time of delivery, and its value if it had complied with the warranty—the auction price would be prima facie evidence of the latter (see above, para.17–052).

[22] *ibid.*, at p.354.

[23] *e.g. Bostock & Co. Ltd v Nicholson & Sons Ltd* [1904] 1 K.B. 725 at 736–739 ("sulphuric acid is used for a great variety of purposes; . . . the use of the acid for food products cannot be said to be other than a well-recognised and ordinary use": *ibid.*, at p.736); *Henry Kendall & Sons v William Lillico & Sons Ltd* [1969] 2 A.C. 31 (feeding stuffs sold as fit for all farm stock, which might be used for cattle, for

17–067 **Warranty as to profit-earning capacity.** Where the goods sold were a profit-earning machine,[24] which the seller undertook would perform in a specified manner or at a specified rate, the buyer may claim (subject to his "duty" to take reasonable steps to mitigate his loss) his loss of profits caused by the failure of the machine to perform as warranted.[25] Thus in the *Cullinane* case[26] where the seller warranted that a clay-pulverising machine had a certain productive capacity, but the machine failed to achieve this, the Court of Appeal held that the buyer was entitled to recover his net[27] loss of profits during the normal commercial life[28] of the machine.[29] "The plant having been supplied in contemplation by both parties that it should be used by the plaintiff in the commercial production of pulverised clay, the case is one in which the plaintiff can claim as damages for the breach of warranty the loss of the profit he can show that he would have made if the plant had been as warranted."[30] This means that the buyer is not limited to the amount of damages specified by the "prima facie" rule in section 53(3), *viz.* the difference between the market value (at the time of delivery) of the actual machine on the basis of its limited capacity, and its market value had it performed as specified.

But any claim for loss of profits must be considered in the light of the rules of mitigation: for a period after delivery it may be reasonable for the buyer to use the machine to see if it meets the warranty, but as soon as a reasonable buyer would have replaced the defective machine with one which functioned properly or efficiently, the buyer should not be entitled[31] to claim for any further loss of profits.[32] Only if no suitable replacement can reasonably be found should the buyer's claim for loss of profits extend over the full period of the original machine's expected life.[33] Similarly, damages claimed for loss of profits over the entire period of the machine's expected

---

poultry, or (as the ultimate buyer intended to use it) for pheasants and partridges). See further above, para.16–041; below, para.17–077. *Cf.* on a range of purposes for the goods, *Ashington Piggeries Ltd v Christopher Hill Ltd* [1972] A.C. 441 (claim against the third party under s.14: see above, paras 11–055, 11–060).

[24] Or part thereof: *cf.* above, para.17–041 for authority in an analogous situation.

[25] *cf.* the buyer's claim for loss of profits when the seller delays delivery of a profit-earning chattel (above, paras 17–040—17–042).

[26] *Cullinane v British "Rema" Manufacturing Co. Ltd* [1954] 1 Q.B. 292. (The case is discussed in more detail below, para.17–070, since the main issue was whether the buyer could claim both his wasted expenditure and his loss of profits.)

[27] *Viz.* after deducting from his expected gross profits (or gross receipts) the necessary expenditure in earning it.

[28] The expected useful life of the machine was 10 years, but the buyer limited his claim to only three years (*ibid.*, at pp.306–307) because he was also claiming his wasted expenditure (see below, para.17–070).

[29] [1954] 1 Q.B. 292 at 303, 308 (at p.315 Morris L.J., dissenting, accepted this proposition).

[30] *ibid.*, at p.308.

[31] Unless any replacement which he could reasonably acquire could not produce at the rate warranted by the defaulting seller.

[32] *British Westinghouse Electric and Manufacturing Co. Ltd v Underground Electric Railways Co. of London Ltd* [1912] A.C. 673 (above, para.17–056); *Cullinane v British "Rema" Manufacturing Co. Ltd*, above, at pp.314, 316. See also *McKenny v Drummond and Dvoretsky* (1926) 29 W.A.R. 6; and *cf. Lambert v Lewis* [1982] A.C. 225 (above, para.17–059—17–060).

[33] Macleod [1970] J.B.L. 19 at 26.

life should be reduced by the court if the buyer ought reasonably to have taken other steps to mitigate his loss caused by the breach of warranty, *e.g.* if he should have cut his losses by stopping the use of the machine. In the *Cullinane* case, above, it was held that the buyer did not act unreasonably in continuing to use the machine after he knew that its performance was defective.[34]

If the buyer replaces a defective machine supplied by the seller, extra profits made by the buyer from using the substitute machine must be taken into account in assessing his claim for damages for the cost of the substitute machine.[35]

Loss of profits or additional expenditure under a sub-sale. Where the seller knew that the buyer intended to resell the goods, and ought reasonably to have contemplated that a breach of his contractual undertaking as to the description or condition of the goods would be not unlikely to cause the buyer to lose the profit he hoped to make under the sub-sale,[36] the buyer may recover damages in respect of such a loss of profits caused by a breach of the seller's undertaking.[37] Similarly, where brewers bought sugar for use in manufacturing beer, and it was later discovered that the sugar contained arsenic, the brewers were held to be entitled to recover from the sellers the cost of printing and advertising notices to their customers advising them that there must be a change of brewing materials.[38] The brewers had reasonably incurred this expense in order to minimise any possible loss of business. 17–068

Loss of general custom (or of "repeat orders"). Where, at the time they made their contract, it was within the reasonable contemplation of the parties that defects in the goods supplied by the seller (in breach of his undertaking as to their quality) might lead to sub-buyers (customers of the buyer) withdrawing their custom from the buyer, damages may be awarded for loss of profits on "repeat orders" from the sub-buyers.[39] (A similar principle has been accepted by the House of Lords in the case of a breach of obligation to maintain confidence, which led to the claimant losing future profits from "repeat orders" from his previous customers.[40]) When 17–069

---

[34] [1954] 1 Q.B. 292 at 314, 316. *Cf. Lambert v Lewis* above.

[35] *British Westinghouse Electric and Manufacturing Co. Ltd v Underground Electric Railways Co. of London Ltd*, above (discussed above, para.17–056).

[36] Or under potential sub-sales: see *Richard Holden Ltd v Bostock & Co. Ltd* (1902) 18 T.L.R. 317 (above, para.17–066).

[37] *Molling & Co. v Dean & Son Ltd* (1901) 18 T.L.R. 217 at 218. The position is the same in the analogous cases of the seller's failure to deliver or his delay in delivery (see above, paras 17–029—17–035, 17–040—17–042).

[38] *Richard Holden Ltd v Bostock & Co. Ltd*, above.

[39] *GKN Centrax Gears Ltd v Matbro Ltd* [1976] 2 Lloyd's Rep. 555 at 573–574, 577, 579–580 (not following *Simon v Pawsons and Leafs Ltd* (1933) 38 Com.Cas. 151 at 158). See also *Aerial Advertising v Batchelor's Peas* [1938] 2 All E.R. 788. *Cf. Cointat v Myham & Son* [1913] 2 K.B. 220 (reversed on another point (1914) 30 T.L.R. 282): see above, para.17–063; *cf.* also *Amstrad Plc v Seagate Technology Inc.* (1998) 86 B.L.R. 34. *Cf.* above, para.17–068.

[40] *Jackson v Royal Bank of Scotland* [2005] UKHL 3, [2005] 1 W.L.R. 377 (not a sale of goods case), *cf.* above, para.17–043.

some customers give evidence that they would have given repeat orders but for the breach of warranty, the damages are not limited in amount to the loss of custom from those customers: the court may draw inferences as to the probable total loss of business.[41]

17–070 **Claims for both wasted expenses and loss of profits.** Difficult problems arise from a split claim for damages which is based partly on the expenses incurred by the claimant which the breach renders useless, and partly on the loss of profits caused by the breach. In *Cullinane v British "Rema" Manufacturing Co. Ltd*,[42] the claimant purchased a clay-pulverising machine from the defendant, who warranted that it would function at a certain rate. When it failed to do so, the claimant claimed damages: first, for his net capital loss or expenditure incurred (*viz.* the price paid for the machine, the cost of its housing and ancillary plant, plus interest thereon, *less* the residual value of the machine and plant in their actual condition at the time of the claim); and, secondly, for his loss of profits[43] for the three years up to the hearing of the case (*viz.* the estimated net profit for those years, after deducting interest on capital, depreciation, maintenance and other expenses). The useful commercial life of the machine was expected to be ten years, but in his pleading the claimant limited his claim for loss of profits to three years.[44] The majority of the Court of Appeal held that the claimant could not claim both his capital loss (expenditure incurred) and his loss of gross profits[45]: they were concerned that the claimant should not make a double recovery. In their opinion, the claimant must elect[46] between these two claims, and either seek to be put back into the position he would have been in if the contract had not been made (*viz.* recover his net outlay, his "reliance expenditure")[47] or, alternatively, claim what he would have received if the contract had been fully performed (*viz.* the gross profit he would have received if the machine had functioned in accordance with the contractual warranty[48]).

It is submitted that the position taken by the majority in this case is confusing[49]: their concern to avoid double recovery led them to overlook

[41] *GKN Centrax Gears Ltd v Matbro Ltd*, above, at p.578.

[42] [1954] 1 Q.B. 292 (criticised by Macleod [1970] J.B.L. 19; and Street, *Principles of the Law of Damages* (1962), pp.242–245).

[43] It was clear that the buyer's loss of profits was within the reasonable contemplation of the parties, within the test in *Koufos v C. Czarnikow Ltd* [1969] 1 A.C. 350 (above, paras 16–043—16–046). On the buyer's claim for loss of profits, see above, para.17–067.

[44] On the "duty" to mitigate in these circumstances, see above, paras 16–052, 17–067.

[45] [1954] 1 Q.B. 292 at 302, 303, 308, 311, 312.

[46] *cf.* cases not on the sale of goods: *Anglia Television Ltd v Reed* [1972] 1 Q.B. 60; *CCC Films (London) Ltd v Impact Quadrant Films Ltd* [1985] 1 Q.B. 16.

[47] Street, *op. cit.*, p.244. (This would be the only basis of the buyer's claim if no loss of profits was within the reasonable contemplation of the parties, or if any loss of profits would be impossible to quantify: *cf. McRae v Commonwealth Disposals Commission* (1951) 84 C.L.R. 377.)

[48] On the assumption, of course, that the buyer had already paid the agreed price.

[49] It may be that the case turned on the way in which the claimant pleaded, *i.e.* it could possibly be inferred from the pleadings that all the expected profits would have arisen in the first three years.

the fact that a *net* loss of profit can be calculated in such a way as to avoid overlapping with the wasted capital expenditure. They were correct in holding that the *gross* profit expected to be earned by the machine during its useful life would include the expected return of the capital expenditure incurred by the buyer. But, as Morris L.J. pointed out,[50] the claimant was not claiming his expected gross profits, but his net profit calculated after a deduction of depreciation, which represented the return to the buyer of the capital element; therefore, his claim for his net capital outlay did not overlap with his claim for loss of net profits.[51] It is submitted that the view of Morris L.J. is to be preferred, and that a split claim should be permitted so long as the calculations show that no overlapping occurs in the different heads of claim.[52] But the Court of Appeal, in a later case, again said that the claimant must choose between a claim for wasted expenses and a claim for loss of profits,[53] and that he cannot claim both.[54] Yet it is interesting to note that in a case where defective seed was supplied to a farmer with the result that the crop failed, the leading speech in the House of Lords approved (obiter) the inclusion in the damages of "all the costs incurred . . . in the cultivation of the worthless crop as well as the profit [the farmer] would have expected to make from a successful crop if proper seeds had been supplied."[55]

In cases not concerned with the sale of goods, it has been held that the claimant may recover damages for his wasted expenditure incurred in reliance on the contract only to the extent that it would have been covered by the gross profits (the gross return) which the claimant would have made if the contract had been fully performed.[56] But in this situation, the onus of proof is on the defendant to show, on the balance of probabilities, that the expenditure would not have been recouped: in the absence of such proof, it will be assumed in favour of the claimant that he would have recouped his expenditure from the gross return which he expected to receive from full performance of the contract.[57] This limitation should also apply to a split claim: even if the claimant claims both his wasted capital expenditure and

---

[50] [1954] 1 Q.B. 292 at 315, 317–318.

[51] Macleod [1970] J.B.L. 19. The distinction between gross and net profits is recognised in *CCC Films (London) Ltd v Impact Quadrant Films Ltd*, above, at p.32.

[52] *TC Industrial Plant Pty Ltd v Robert's Queensland Pty Ltd* [1964] A.L.R. 1083. See also Street, *op. cit.*, at p.245. It is noteworthy that split claims, partly for expenses wasted by the breach, and partly for loss of profits, were allowed in two earlier cases at first instance (neither of which was referred to in the *Cullinane* case, above): *Foaminol Laboratories v British Artid Plastics* [1941] 2 All E.R. 393; and *Molling & Co. v Dean & Son Ltd* (1901) 18 T.L.R. 217 (discussed above, para.17–062). *Cf.* above, para.17–046, n.48.

[53] *Anglia Television Ltd v Reed* [1972] 1 Q.B. 60 (not a sale of goods case).

[54] *ibid.*, at pp.63–64, where the *Cullinane* case, above, was relied upon. See also *CCC Films (London) Ltd v Impact Quadrant Films Ltd*, above.

[55] *George Mitchell (Chesterfield) Ltd v Finney Seeds Ltd* [1983] 2 A.C. 803 at 812 (the reference to "profit" should be to "net profit").

[56] *C & P Haulage v Middleton* [1983] 1 W.L.R. 1461 at 1468; *CCC Films (London) Ltd v Impact Quadrant Films Ltd*, above, at p.32. *Cf.* the view of Lord Evershed in the *Cullinane* case, above, at p.306. (The sentence in the text refers only to expenditure which the buyer intended to recoup from his gross return, not to additional expenditure incurred by the buyer after, and as a result of, the breach.)

[57] *CCC Films (London) Ltd v Impact Quadrant Films Ltd*, above, at pp.39–40.

his net loss of profits, which is calculated so as not to overlap with the expenditure, it should nevertheless be open to the defendant to prove the gross profits which the claimant could have expected, which amount would then be the ceiling on the total damages recoverable for the split claim.

(iv) *Loss of Amenity*

17–071 **Loss of amenity.** The House of Lords has upheld the award of damages for "loss of amenity" where an important object[58] of the contract was to give pleasure, relaxation or peace of mind. The development began with the "holiday"[59] and "wedding photograph"[60] cases, but it was extended by the House of Lords in *Farley v Skinner*[61] to a survey report on a house. The intending purchaser asked his surveyor to report whether the property would be seriously affected by aircraft noise. As the result of his failure to take reasonable care, the surveyor's written report was inaccurate on this point, with the result that the purchaser's pleasure, relaxation and peace of mind when living in the property were seriously impaired. The award of £10,000 damages for "loss of amenity" was upheld, even though the market value of the property, after taking account of the noise, was not less than the price paid by the purchaser. The breach of contract caused an individualistic loss recognised by the law, because the surveyor had accepted an obligation to take care in responding to the inquiry about noise. The principle in *Farley v Skinner* could apply to a specific contractual undertaking about the goods given by the seller, especially when it was given in response to a specific request by the intending buyer. "Loss of amenity" damages were first recognised by the House of Lords in *Ruxley Electronics and Construction Ltd v Forsyth*[62] where the owner of the property was awarded £2,500 because the depth of the swimming pool built for him by the defendant was one-and-a-half feet less deep than the depth specified in the contract. Although it would be unreasonable to give the owner the cost of rebuilding the pool to the proper depth, and the market value of the property was not diminished by the actual depth, nevertheless the owner had lost the "pleasurable amenity" for which he had contracted.[63] No reported case has awarded damages for loss of amenity to a buyer of goods, but the analogy is now provided by the purchase or construction cases dealing with land.

---

[58] The House of Lords held that it need not be the sole or principal object of the contract.

[59] *Jarvis v Swans Tours Ltd* [1973] Q.B. 233.

[60] *Diesen v Samson* 1971 S.L.T. (Sh. Ct.) 49.

[61] [2001] UKHL 49; [2002] 2 A.C. 732.

[62] [1996] A.C. 344.

[63] In economic terms, the owner had a "consumer surplus" beyond the cost to him of building the pool to the specified depth: it was a subjective, even idiosyncratic benefit to him to have that depth in his pool—an advantage not measured by any increase in the market value of his property. See Harris, Ogus and Phillips, 95 L.Q.R. 581 (1979) (cited in *Ruxley*, above, at p.360 and in *Farley v Skinner*, above, at p.748).

(v) *Physical Injury to the Buyer or his Property*

Physical injury to the buyer, his family or his property. If it was in the reasonable contemplation of the parties, at the time of making the contract, that the seller's breach of his contractual undertaking as to quality or description was not unlikely to cause[64] physical injury to the buyer's person,[65] or property,[66] the buyer may recover damages[67] for such injury.[68] The type or kind of loss in question must have been within the reasonable contemplation of the parties.[69] Thus, where food is sold for human consumption, the buyer may obviously recover damages for his illness caused by its defective condition.[70] Where the buyer of woollen underwear contracted dermatitis through the defective condition of the garment he recovered substantial damages from the retailers for breach of the statutory condition imposed by section 14 of the Act.[71] The prima facie rule under section 53(3)[72] would merely have given the buyer the difference in value between the defective garment and a similar one of merchantable quality.[73] Where personal injury or death is caused by the seller's breach, the damages may include compensation for pain and suffering, disfigurement, loss of faculty,[74] as well as loss of earnings, which are normal heads of damages in the assessment of damages in tort for personal injuries or death. (There may often be concurrent liability in tort, but the advantage[75] in suing in contract is that the claimant may not have to prove the negligence of the defendant.) 17–072

Where it was within the reasonable contemplation of the parties that the goods sold to the buyer would be used by members[76] of the buyer's family, and that a defect in them was not unlikely to cause injury to them, the

---

[64] The buyer will not be able to continue to rely on the undertaking after he knows that the goods are defective: see above, para.17–059. On the effect of the buyer's negligent failure to discover the defect, see above, para.17–060.

[65] In addition to the cases cited below, see *Geddling v Marsh* [1920] 1 K.B. 668; *Morelli v Fitch & Gibbons* [1928] 2 K.B. 636; *Andrews v Hopkinson* [1957] 1 Q.B. 229.

[66] See below, paras 17–073, 17–074.

[67] Special rules apply to the award of interest on such damages (see above, para.16–008, n.67).

[68] See below, para.17–074 for the situation where the defective goods cause injury to a third person or his property, and the buyer is compelled to compensate the third person.

[69] See above, para.16–043.

[70] *Wren v Holt* [1903] 1 K.B. 610.

[71] *Grant v Australian Knitting Mills Ltd* [1936] A.C. 85. (The relevant provision was s.14 of the South Australian Act, which was identical with s.14 of the United Kingdom 1893 Act at the time of the case.)

[72] See above, paras 17–047, 17–051, *et seq.*

[73] See also *Godley v Perry* [1960] 1 W.L.R. 9 (buyer recovered £2,500 damages for the loss of an eye caused by the breaking of a defective catapult bought for sixpence). The relevant standard in s.14(2) is now "satisfactory quality": see above, para.11–026.

[74] *Godley v Perry*, above, at p.13.

[75] There may, of course, be disadvantages, *e.g.* a narrower test for remoteness of damage than in tort: see *The Wagon Mound* (*No.*2) [1967] 1 A.C. 617.

[76] These cases concern wives of buyers, but it is submitted that at least the children of the buyer should also be covered by the principle.

buyer is entitled to recover damages for any pecuniary loss (such as expenses) caused to him by such injury.[77] So where food for human consumption was sold to the buyer and eaten by his wife who died as a result, the buyer recovered damages for the medical and funeral expenses he had paid, and for the loss of his wife's services which led to his employing extra servants.[78] But it should be noted that under the Contracts (Rights of Third Parties) Act 1999[79] members of the buyer's family may be sufficiently "identified" as third parties intended to have conferred on them the benefit of a term of the contract, so as to be entitled to enforce that term directly against the seller. The Act appears to create a presumption rebuttable by the promisor (the seller): "if the term purports to confer a benefit on him"[80] (the third party) it will be presumed that the term was to be enforceable by the third party unless the seller can rebut the apparent intention.[81]

17–073 **Damage to the goods caused by their defective condition.** The defective condition of the goods may cause further physical deterioration or damage to the goods themselves. Although the market value specified by section 53(3) may take account of expected physical loss to the goods, there may be cases where the buyer can recover more, *e.g.* where a motor-vehicle supplied with defective brakes is damaged in a collision caused by the defect.

17–074 **Damage to other property of the buyer.** Where it was within the reasonable contemplation of the parties that a defect in the goods bought by the buyer was not unlikely to cause loss of, or damage to, other property belonging to the buyer,[82] his damages may include compensation for this loss or injury.[83] In *Bostock & Co. Ltd v Nicholson & Sons Ltd*[84] the sellers sold by description "sulphuric acid commercially free from arsenic". In breach of the condition implied by section 13 of the Act[85] the sellers

---

[77] *Priest v Last* [1903] 2 K.B. 148; *Frost v Aylesbury Dairy Co. Ltd* [1905] 1 K.B. 608; *Jackson v Watson & Sons* [1909] 2 K.B. 193; *Square v Model Farm Dairies (Bournemouth) Ltd* [1939] 2 K.B. 365 at 374. *Cf.* the recovery of damages in respect of loss suffered by third parties, *Linden Gardens Trust Ltd v Lenesta Sludge Disposals Ltd* [1994] 1 A.C. 85; *Darlington BC v Wiltshier Northern Ltd* [1995] 1 W.L.R. 68; *Alfred McAlpine Construction Ltd v Panatown Ltd* [2001] 1 A.C. 518.

[78] *Jackson v Watson & Sons*, above (CA) at p.207 (the buyer's entitlement was limited to "pecuniary damage").

[79] The Act is summarised below, para.18–005. See also below, para.17–080.

[80] s.1(1)(b).

[81] s.1(2).

[82] The parties should have been able, as reasonable men, to contemplate the *type* or *kind* of loss in question: *Parsons (H) (Livestock) Ltd v Uttley Ingham & Co. Ltd* [1978] Q.B. 791 at 804, 813 (see above, para.16–043.)

[83] *Borradaile v Brunton* (1818) 8 Taunt. 535 (defective anchor cable caused loss of the anchor); *Randall v Newson* (1877) 2 Q.B.D. 102 (pole for a carriage broke in use, frightening the horses, which were injured: the court was prepared to allow damages to be awarded by a jury for the cost of a new pole and the injury to the horses); *Wilson v Rickett Cockerell & Co. Ltd* [1954] 1 Q.B. 598 (coalite exploded when burning in grate causing damage to the room and furniture); *Parsons (H) (Livestock) Ltd v Uttley Ingham & Co. Ltd*, above.

[84] [1904] 1 K.B. 725.

[85] See above, paras 11–001 *et seq*.

delivered some impure acid containing arsenic, which the buyers used for making brewing sugar for sale to brewers for making beer. The damages awarded for breach of the condition that the goods supplied should correspond with the description covered two items: the price paid by the buyers, since the acid supplied was worthless to them, and the value of the other ingredients wasted by being mixed with the poisonous acid.[86] Again, where the sellers installed a defective heating system, which caught fire and destroyed the buyer's factory, the replacement cost of a new factory was held to be the measure of damages.[87]

Where the seller of a cow knew, or ought to have known, that the buyer was a farmer, and that the cow was likely to be placed with others in a herd, he was taken to have contemplated that if the cow had an infectious disease (contrary to his warranty) it was not unlikely to be communicated to other cows. Hence, the buyer's damages covered the value of all his cows which died as a result.[88] So where game farmers bought compounded meal for feeding to their pheasants and many chicks died and others grew up stunted because the meal contained a toxic substance, the farmers recovered damages for the loss of the birds and the reduced value of the survivors.[89]

If the other property was damaged in the course of the use made of the goods by the buyer, the category of use in question must be one which was within the reasonable contemplation of the parties as a not unlikely use of the goods. If there are several categories of ordinary or common use, the buyer may recover damages if his use of the goods was within one of these categories,[90] even though it may not have been the main type of use.[91] Loss of, or damage to, other property resulting from a special use of the defective goods made by the buyer can lead to liability upon the seller only where he was told, before the making of the contract, that the buyer intended to use them in this way.[92]

---

[86] [1904] 1 K.B. 725 at 741–742. On the refusal to award to the buyers the compensation payable by the buyers to the brewers, see below, para.17–076.

[87] *Harbutt's "Plasticine" Ltd v Wayne Tank and Pump Co. Ltd* [1970] 1 Q.B. 447. (No reduction was made in the damages for "betterment" because a new factory was more modern than the old one: *ibid.*, at pp.468, 473, 476 (see above, para.17–024, n.89) where the overruling of the case on another point is noted).

[88] *Smith v Green* (1875) 1 C.P.D. 92 (warranty that it was free from foot and mouth disease). *Cf.* the cases where it was the sub-buyer's animals which were injured by defective cattle food (below, para.17–081).

[89] *Henry Kendall & Sons v William Lillico & Sons Ltd* [1969] 2 A.C. 31. (The decision of the House of Lords assumes that the game farmers were entitled to recover damages for these losses.) See also *Parsons (H) (Livestock) Ltd v Uttley Ingham & Co. Ltd*, above (defective hopper caused food to become mouldy, which was fed to pigs.)

[90] *Bostock & Co. Ltd v Nicholson & Sons Ltd*, above (one of the ordinary uses of the acid sold was for making brewer's sugar, which was the use intended by the buyer).

[91] *Henry Kendall & Sons v William Lillico & Sons Ltd*, above (groundnut extraction supplied for making compounds for feeding farm stock, which might be used for cattle, for poultry or (as the ultimate buyer intended to use it) for pheasants and partridges). *Cf. Bunting v Tory* (1948) 64 T.L.R. 353 (above, para.17–066). *Cf.* also *Ashington Piggeries Ltd v Christopher Hill, Ltd* [1972] A.C. 441 (claim against the third party under s.14: see above, paras 11–055, 11–060).

[92] See above, para.16–046.

(vi) *Compensation Paid to a Stranger*

17–075 **Compensation paid to a stranger (other than a sub-buyer[93]).** It may have been within the reasonable contemplation of the parties at the time of making the contract that: (a) if the goods were defective, a third person (or his property) was not unlikely to be injured as a result of the defect; and (b) as a result the buyer was not unlikely to be held legally liable to compensate the third party for his injury or loss. In these circumstances, if such an injury[94] occurs, and the defect was in breach of the seller's contractual obligations to the buyer, the latter may recover as damages from the seller the damages and costs paid to the third party,[95] and the buyer's own costs incurred in reasonably defending the third party's claim.[96] The legal basis of the buyer's liability towards the stranger is normally under the law of torts,[97] but it could be under a contract, *e.g.* a contract of employment. In an analogous case[98] of a contract to unload a ship, the shipowner supplied a defective chain to the claimant stevedoring firm. The shipowner impliedly warranted the chain to be reasonably fit for use by stevedores[99] but it broke and injured a stevedore employed by the claimants. The claimants recovered from the shipowner, as damages for his breach of warranty, the damages paid by them to the injured man. (Nowadays, the employee's claim against the buyer of defective goods which injured him might be brought under the tort of negligence, or for a tort of strict liability,[1] or for breach of an implied term in the contract of employment.[2] Earlier paragraphs in this chapter have examined the effect on the seller's liability of the buyer's discovery of, or his negligent failure to discover, the defect in the goods.[3])

In an analogous situation,[4] the buyer has been held entitled to recover a reasonable amount which he has paid to the sub-buyer in a reasonable

---

93 This paragraph does not concern sub-buyers, on which see below, paras 17–076—17–079.

94 All the cases under this heading have involved physical injury to the stranger or his property.

95 *Lambert v Lewis* [1982] A.C. 225. (The principle was approved by the HL though not applied: see above, paras 17–059, 17–060). The previous cases were not on sale of goods but on contracts where chattels were to be supplied for the use of the claimant and others: *Mowbray v Merryweather* [1895] 2 Q.B. 640, below (approved by HL in *Lambert v Lewis*, above); *Scott v Foley, Aikman & Co.* (1899) 16 T.L.R. 55 (breach of a warranty as to the condition of appliances on a ship). *Cf. Hadley v Droitwich Construction Co. Ltd* [1968] 1 W.L.R. 37.

96 *Scott v Foley, Aikman & Co.*, above, at p.56. The buyer's own costs are taxed on the standard basis: *British Racing Drivers' Club Ltd v Hextall Erskine & Co.* [1996] 3 All E.R. 667 at 685–691 (not a sale of goods case).

97 *Lambert v Lewis*, above; *Mowbray v Merryweather*, above; *Scott v Foley, Aikman & Co.*, above.

98 *Mowbray v Merryweather*, above.

99 The claimants were held to have been entitled not to examine the chain but to rely on the warranty: *ibid.*, at pp.644, 646, 647. (On this aspect, see above, paras 17–060—17–061).

1 *e.g.* under the, Factories Act 1961, or under the Employers Liability (Defective Equipment) Act 1969.

2 *Matthews v Kuwait Bechtel Corporation* [1959] 2 Q.B. 57.

3 See above, paras 17–059—17–061.

4 The buyer's liability to pay compensation in a series of "string contracts".

settlement out of court,[5] and it is submitted that the same should apply in the present situation.[6] There must, of course, be evidence proving the buyer's liability towards the injured stranger.[7]

If the buyer has acted reasonably in defending the stranger's claim against him, he may recover the costs[8] paid to the third party[9] and his own costs.[10] The test of reasonableness will depend on all the circumstances,[11] such as the legal ground of the stranger's claim, and whether the amount of the claim is excessive[12]; for instance, it will seldom be reasonable to incur the costs of an appeal which turns out to be unsuccessful.[13] If the conditions set out at the beginning of this paragraph are satisfied, the buyer may recover from the seller the costs incurred by the buyer in successfully defending a claim brought against him by a stranger as a result of the seller's breach of contract.[14]

(vii) *Compensation Paid to a Sub-buyer*

Compensation paid by the buyer to a sub-buyer.[15] This paragraph is concerned with the situation where the seller was in breach of his contractual undertaking as to the description or condition of the goods and it was within the reasonable contemplation of the parties, at the time of making the contract,[16] that[17]: (a) the buyer would, or probably[18] would, 17–076

---

[5] See below, para.17–078.

[6] In *Mowbray v Merryweather*, above, the sum claimed had been paid to the injured workman in a settlement out of court. (A "reasonable" settlement depends on many factors: see below, para.17–078).

[7] *cf. Kiddle & Son v Lovett* (1885) 16 Q.B.D. 605 (an analogous case where the defendants were under a contractual obligation to supply a working platform for the use of the claimant's workmen).

[8] Taxed on the standard basis.

[9] *Mowbray v Merryweather*, above, at p.646.

[10] The standard basis of taxation applies to the assessment of these costs: *British Racing Drivers' Club Ltd v Hextall Erskine & Co.* [1996] 3 All E.R. 667 (not a sale of goods case).

[11] *Scott v Foley, Aikman & Co.*, above. See also below, paras 17–077, 17–084.

[12] *cf.* above, para.17–045.

[13] *cf. Vogan v Oulton* (1899) 81 L.T. 435 (a case of hire).

[14] This is supported by an analogous case where the claimant's lorry was negligently repaired by the defendants: *Britannia Hygienic Laundry Co. Ltd v John I Thorneycroft & Co. Ltd* (1925) 41 T.L.R. 667 (reversed by the CA on a different view of the facts: (1926) 42 T.L.R. 198). The successful defence in this case is reported as *Phillips v Britannia Hygienic Laundry Co. Ltd* [1923] 1 K.B. 539; and [1923] 2 K.B. 832, CA.

[15] The sub-buyer may possibly have a direct claim against the seller: see below, paras 17–080, 18–005.

[16] See above, para.16–043.

[17] The composite propositions in the first two sentences of this paragraph are supported by the cases cited in the following footnotes. In particular, the propositions are supported by the judgment of Bowen L.J. in *Hammond & Co. v Bussey* (1887) 20 Q.B.D. 79 at 94–95 (a passage cited with approval by the CA in *Biggin & Co. Ltd v Permanite Ltd* [1951] 2 K.B. 314 at 318–319).

[18] *Hammond & Co. v Bussey*, above, at p.89 (". . . a sub-contract . . . which will probably be made . . . a sub-contract which within the knowledge of the defendant was in the ordinary course of business sure to be made." See also at p.88 (". . . sub-contract likely to be made")).

resell the goods to a sub-buyer; and (b) that the contract of sub-sale would, or probably would, contain the same,[19] or a similar,[20] contractual undertaking as to the description or condition of the goods; and (c) that it was not unlikely[21] that a breach of the seller's undertaking would cause the buyer to be in breach of his undertaking to the sub-buyer who would claim damages from the buyer for the loss or damage he suffered. If loss or injury occurs in these circumstances, the buyer who has paid damages and costs to his sub-buyer for breach of the undertaking in the sub-sale may recover this amount from the seller, together with his own costs in reasonably defending the sub-buyer's claim, as damages for the seller's breach of the original contract.[22] The main illustrations of this principle are the cases[23] where there was a chain of sub-sales longer than the single sub-sale envisaged in this paragraph, and the cases[24] where the seller admitted his liability to pay the damages paid to the sub-buyer but contested his liability to pay the costs incurred by the buyer.[25] There is, however, one case where the buyer failed in such a claim. In *Bostock & Co. Ltd v Nicholson & Sons Ltd*[26] where the buyers were supplied with impure acid which they used for making brewing sugar for sale to brewers for making beer,[27] it was held that the buyers could not recover from the sellers the compensation payable by the buyers to the brewers. The judgment was brief and unsatisfactory on this point, since it proceeded on the fallacious ground that no "special circumstances"[28] were communicated to the seller by the buyer.[29] It is submitted that, in the light of the later cases cited in this, and a later[30] paragraph, this case is no longer authoritative in this respect.

---

[19] As in *Hammond & Co. v Bussey*, above ("substantially the same description": at p.80 (statement of facts)).

[20] The possibility of a "similar" warranty leading to recovery of damages by the buyer was mentioned (*obiter*) in *Hammond & Co. v Bussey*, above, at pp.89, 96. See further the discussion below, para.17–083.

[21] In *Hammond & Co. v Bussey*, above, reference was made at p.93 to the parties' reasonable contemplation that "the highly probable result of a breach" of the original undertaking would be a lawsuit between the buyers and their sub-buyers. But it is submitted that the "not unlikely" test is now the correct one (see above, para.16–044).

[22] In some situations, the buyer's damages may be *restricted* by reference to the extent of the buyer's liability towards his sub-buyer (see below, para.17–082.)

[23] *e.g. Pinnock Bros v Lewis and Peat Ltd* [1923] 1 K.B. 690 (below, para.17–081); *Dobell (GC) & Co. Ltd v Barber and Garratt* [1931] 1 K.B. 219 (statutory warranty as to quality implied into the successive sales). See further below, para.17–081. (The cases before *Hadley v Baxendale* (1854) 9 Exch. 341 (see above, para.16–043) are no longer reliable, according to *Hammond & Co. v Bussey*, above, at p.91.)

[24] *e.g. Hammond & Co. v Bussey*, above.

[25] For other cases, see below, para.17–077.

[26] [1904] 1 K.B. 725.

[27] Which was one of the ordinary uses for the acid: see the fuller statement of facts (above, para.17–074).

[28] In terms of the second rule in *Hadley v Baxendale* (1854) 9 Exch. 341 (above, para.16–046): see [1904] 1 K.B. 725 at 736.

[29] [1904] 1 K.B. 725 at 742.

[30] Below, para.17–081.

17–077 **Costs paid or payable by the buyer.** If, in the circumstances set out in the first sentence of the preceding paragraph,[31] the buyer has, as a result of the defect in the goods, reasonably incurred costs in defending a claim brought against him by a sub-buyer, he may recover from the seller both the reasonable costs paid or payable to the successful sub-buyer[32] and also his own reasonable costs of his defence.[33] The test of reasonableness in incurring the costs is the crucial one,[34] which depends on the particular circumstances of the case,[35] judged as at the time when the buyer had to decide how to act.[36] The seller is likely to be in a better position than the buyer to answer the allegations of a sub-buyer that the goods are defective or do not meet the contractual standard[37]; thus, if the buyer notifies the seller that the sub-buyer is claiming damages from him (the buyer), but the seller, after saying that the sub-buyer's claim is unfounded, refuses to assist in defending it, the buyer's action in incurring costs to defend is likely to be held to have been reasonable[38]: "... the reasonable course to be pursued by the [buyers] might be that they should not at once submit to the claim but that, unless they could get information from the [seller] that there was really no defence, they should defend the action."[39]

If, before he incurred costs in defending the sub-buyer's claim, the buyer could himself have ascertained whether the goods complied with the contract, he will not be acting reasonably in defending, *e.g.* where the sub-buyer returned a horse to the buyer on the ground that it did not comply with a warranty of soundness.[40]

17–078 **Settlement out of court.** The buyer need not defend the sub-buyer's claim to the point of a judgment against him. If he reasonably settled the sub-buyer's claim out of court, he may recover as damages from the seller a

---

31 *Hammond & Co. v Bussey* (1887) 20 Q.B.D. 79, cited in support of that sentence, was a case where the seller contested his liability to pay the costs paid by the buyer to the sub-buyer while admitting his liability to pay the damages paid to the sub-buyer.

32 *Hammond & Co. v Bussey*, above; *Pinnock Bros v Peat and Lewis Ltd* [1923] 1 K.B. 690 at 698; *Sidney Bennett Ltd v Kreeger* (1925) 41 T.L.R. 609. See the similar position where there is a chain of sub-sales (below, para.17–084).

33 The standard basis of taxation is now the proper basis for the recovery of the claimant's costs incurred in litigation with a third party: *British Racing Drivers' Club Ltd v Hextall Erskine & Co.* [1996] 3 All E.R. 667 (not a sale of goods case). This basis replaces the previous rule laid down in *Sidney Bennett Ltd v Kreeger*, above; *Biggin & Co. Ltd v Permanite Ltd* [1951] 1 K.B. 422 at 430.

34 *Hammond & Co. v Bussey*, above.

35 *ibid.*, at pp.92, 98. *Cf.* above, para.17–075.

36 *Kasler and Cohen v Slavouski* [1928] 1 K.B. 78 at 87 (a case concerning costs in a chain of sub-sales: see below, para.17–084).

37 *Hammond & Co. v Bussey*, above, at p.95.

38 *ibid.*, at pp.87, 95–96. See also *Sidney Bennett Ltd v Kreeger*, above.

39 *Hammond & Co. v Bussey*, above, at p.90. (The buyers should "pay without contest if it was unreasonable to defend the action": *ibid.* at p.100.) *Cf. Kasler and Cohen v Slavouski*, above, at pp.87–89 (below, para.17–084).

40 *Wrightup v Chamberlain* (1839) 7 Scott 598. See also *Baxendale v London Chatham and Dover Ry* (1874) L.R. 10 Ex. 35, as explained in *Hammond & Co. v Bussey*, above, at pp.92, 99, 102.

reasonable amount paid under such settlement[41]: if litigation between the buyer and sub-buyer should have been in the contemplation of the parties, so should reasonable settlements.[42] The fact that the settlement was made under legal advice is relevant to its reasonableness.[43] The onus of proof is on the buyer to establish a prima facie case that the settlement was reasonable,[44] but it is open to the seller to attempt to show that the buyer was not liable to pay anything to the sub-buyer[45] or to produce new evidence or new factors to show that the sum paid was not reasonable.[46] In addition to the damages paid under the settlement, the buyer will recover his reasonable costs.[47]

17–079 **Knowledge of the defect.** Where the buyer, before reselling the goods, discovered[48] the defect in their description or condition, he cannot pass on to his seller any liability which he thereafter incurred towards his sub-buyer in respect of that defect.[49] Where the buyer acquired knowledge of the defect after making the contract of sub-sale but he could, by passing on the knowledge to his sub-buyer, reduce his liability towards the sub-buyer,[50] the buyer cannot recover any damages from his seller in respect of the loss incurred by the sub-buyer which could have been avoided by communicating the knowledge to him.[51] Thus, "if the knowledge of the defects comes to [the buyer] after the sale to the outside party, and if, by passing on that knowledge to the outside party, he can diminish his liability to that party, he is bound to do so."[52]

---

[41] *Biggin & Co. Ltd v Permanite Ltd* [1951] 2 K.B. 314 (reversing the decision below, on which see below, paras 17–079, 17–082). *Cf. Grébert-Borgnis v JW Nugent* (1885) 15 Q.B.D. 85 (above, para.17–036).

[42] *Biggin & Co. Ltd v Permanite Ltd*, above, at p.322. (It is also implicit in this case that it may be reasonable for the buyer to submit his dispute with the sub-buyer to arbitration.)

[43] *ibid.*, at pp.321, 325. The reasonableness of a settlement must be judged in the light of the facts available at the time it was made: *General Feeds Inc. Panama v Slobodna Plovidba Yugoslavia* [1999] 1 Lloyd's Rep. 688.

[44] *Biggin & Co. Ltd v Permanite Ltd*, above, at pp.324–325.

[45] *ibid.*, at p.320 (citing *Kiddle v Lovett* (1885) 16 Q.B.D. 605). No matter how reasonable a settlement may appear to the parties it does not determine the liability of a third party: *P & O Developments Ltd v Guy's and St Thomas' NHS Trust* (1998) 62 Con. L.R. 38 (not a sale of goods case).

[46] *Biggin & Co. Ltd v Permanite Ltd*, above, at pp.321, 325.

[47] By analogy from the position in para.17–077 above. If the amount of the costs is disputed, they should be taxed on the standard basis: see *British Racing Drivers' Club Ltd v Hextall Erskine & Co.* [1996[3 All E.R. 667 (not a sale of goods case).

[48] *cf.* above, para.17–059. The effect on the seller's liability of the buyer's *negligence* in failing to discover the defect in the goods is considered above, para.17–060.

[49] *British Oil and Cake Co. Ltd v Burstall & Co.* (1923) 39 T.L.R. 406 at 407; *Dobell (GC) & Co. Ltd v Barber and Garratt* [1931] 1 K.B. 219 at 238 (*cf.* at pp.246–247); *Biggin & Co. Ltd v Permanite Ltd*, above, at p.435. *Cf. Lambert v Lewis* [1982] A.C. 225. See also above, para.17–059.

[50] The sub-buyer would thereupon come under a "duty" towards the buyer to take reasonable steps to mitigate his loss caused by the defect.

[51] *Biggin & Co. Ltd v Permanite Ltd*, above, at pp.431, 435.

[52] *ibid.*

17–080 **A direct claim by the sub-buyer against the seller.** Under the Contracts (Rights of Third Parties) Act 1999[53] a sub-buyer as a "third party" may be able to enforce[54] a term in the main contract between the seller and the buyer if *either* the contract expressly provides that he may; *or* the term purports to confer a benefit on him and he is sufficiently "identified" (*e.g.* as a sub-buyer, an agent or employee of the buyer). But the contract may show that the third party was not intended to be entitled to enforce the term. The 1999 Act might apply where the buyer has already agreed to sell the goods to the sub-buyer, and the seller knows that the buyer is buying the goods in order to fulfil that contract.[55] Similarly, the seller may know that the buyer was, or was probably buying for resale, and that the buyer could perform his obligations under any contract of resale only by delivering the same goods.[56] In these situations, it is possible that the contract between the buyer and the seller might expressly entitle the sub-buyer to enforce an obligation on the seller (*e.g.* to deliver to the sub-buyer's premises) or might "purport to confer" such a benefit on the sub-buyer.

(viii) *Compensation Paid in a Chain of Sub-sales*

17–081 **Compensation paid to sub-buyers in a series of "string contracts".**[57] This paragraph is concerned with the situation where the seller was in breach of his contractual undertaking as to the description or condition of the goods, and it was within the reasonable contemplation of the parties, at the time of making the contract, that: (a) the buyer intended[58] to resell, or probably[59] would, and that his sub-buyer would probably resell, and so on, so that there would be a series of sub-sales or "string contracts" of the same goods; and (b) that each contract in the series would, or probably would, contain the same[60] or a similar,[61] contractual undertaking as to description or condition of the goods; and (c) that it was not unlikely that a breach of the seller's undertaking would cause the buyer and each sub-buyer in the series to be in breach of his undertaking to his own buyer; and (d) that it was not unlikely[62] that, in the case of such a breach, the ultimate buyers would recover damages from their sellers, so that liability would in turn be passed

---

[53] See above, para.2–026; below, para.18–005.
[54] As far as remedies are concerned, the third party is treated as a party to the contract: s.5(1).
[55] *e.g. Slater v Hoyle and Smith Ltd* [1920] 2 K.B. 11: see above, para.17–057.
[56] See above, para.17–030.
[57] See below, para.17–085.
[58] *e.g. Dobell (GC) & Co. v Barber and Garratt* [1931] 1 K.B. 219 at 231; *Biggin & Co. Ltd v Permanite Ltd* [1951] 1 K.B. 422 at 431 (reversed by the CA on another ground: [1951] 2 K.B. 314 (see above, para.17–078)).
[59] See above, para.17–076, n.18.
[60] *e.g. Kasler & Cohen v Slavouski* [1928] 1 K.B. 78 at 85. In *Dobell (GC) & Co. v Barber and Garratt*, above, the warranty was the same because it was implied by statute and "contracting out" was forbidden.
[61] See below, para.17–083.
[62] Or "a serious possibility": *Biggin & Co. Ltd v Permanite Ltd*, above, at p.428.

up the chain of sellers and buyers.[63] In these circumstances, the buyer who has paid to his sub-buyer damages and costs for breach of the undertaking in the first contract of sub-sale (which the sub-buyer claimed from the buyer, as the result of similar payments of compensation between successive sub-buyers down the chain) may recover the amount paid by him to the sub-buyer,[64] together with his own costs[65] in reasonably defending the sub-buyer's claim against him; the damages and costs paid or incurred by the buyer are taken as the measure of damages for the seller's breach of the original contract.[66]

In *Pinnock Bros v Lewis and Peat Ltd*,[67] the buyers bought East African copra cake, which they resold to sub-buyers who manufactured the cake into feeding materials for cattle. The copra cake was later found to contain an admixture which made it poisonous for cattle. The court found "that it was within the contemplation of the parties that this copra cake should be used . . . for cattle food and nothing else."[68] The farmers whose cattle fell ill claimed damages from the dealers, who claimed against the sub-buyers: the buyers were held to be entitled to recover from the original seller the damages and costs which they had had to pay to the sub-buyers. A similar result was reached in a case[69] where there was a warranty as to quality implied by statute into each of a series of sales of linseed cake sold for use as food for cattle. The farmers whose cattle were injured by eating the contaminated cake recovered from the dealers who sold to them; the dealers in turn recovered from the buyers, who successfully sued the sellers for the amounts paid to the dealers.

17–082 **Damages limited by reference to sub-sale.** In the situation of a chain of sales of the same goods, the buyer may sometimes be precluded from relying on the normal rule for the assessment of damages laid down by

[63] *Biggin & Co. Ltd v Permanite Ltd*, above, at pp.431–432. ("I do not think that the application of the principle is to be determined by the number of links in the chain. If what happened at the end was within the contemplation of the parties, I do not think it matters how long the chain is": *ibid.*, at p.432.) See also *Kasler and Cohen v Slavouski*, above, at pp.85, 87 (although this case was a contest over costs of the various parties down the chain (see below, para.17–084), it is a good illustration of the propositions contained in the first two sentences of the text of this paragraph). *Cf.* chain transactions involving breaches of s.12(1) (above, paras 4–014—4–017, 4–029).

[64] *Pinnock Bros v Lewis and Peat Ltd* [1923] 1 K.B. 690; *Dobell (GC) & Co. v Barber and Garratt*, above; *Biggin & Co. Ltd v Permanite Ltd*, above and below. The buyer's claim is subject to the limitations examined, above, para.17–079.

[65] See below, para.17–084.

[66] Para.43–460 in Chitty, *op. cit.* (which is virtually identical with the first paragraph of the present para.17–081—the same editor being responsible for both paragraphs) was cited in *Louis Dreyfus Trading Ltd v Reliance Trading Ltd* [2004] EWHC 525 (Comm), [2004] 2 Lloyd's Rep. 243 at [24].

[67] Above.

[68] *Pinnock Bros v Lewis and Peat Ltd*, above, at p.697 (distinguishing, on the facts, *Bostock & Co. Ltd v Nicholson & Sons Ltd* [1904] 1 K.B. 725 (above, paras 17–074, 17–076)).

[69] *Dobell (GC) & Co. Ltd v Barber and Garratt*, above. The main aspects of the case were concerned with the interpretation of the Fertilisers and Feeding Stuffs Act 1926, *e.g.* s.2(2) prevented "contracting out" of the warranty and thus defeated a clause in the contract providing that the sellers accepted no responsibility for the analysis. See also above, para.16–045.

section 53(3) (*viz.* the difference between the value of the goods in their defective state at delivery, and their value if they complied with the warranty).[70] The Court of Appeal has approved[71] the approach of Devlin J. in *Biggin & Co. Ltd v Permanite Ltd*[72] who held that where the subsale was within the contemplation of the parties, the original buyer's damages must be assessed by reference to it, whether he likes it or not. Knowledge of the defect in the goods might well reduce the market value of the goods, but if it is the original buyer's "liability to the ultimate user that is contemplated as the measure of damage and if in fact it is used without injurious results so that no such liability arises, the [original buyer] could not claim the difference in market value, and say that the subsale must be disregarded[73] . . . The liability for physical damage remains the primary measure of liability contemplated by the parties."[74] So in *Bence Graphics International Ltd v Fasson U.K. Ltd*,[75] the seller knew that the buyer would sell on to others (after manufacturing the goods into another product); the Court of Appeal held that the parties contemplated that the measure of damages for defects in the goods should be the extent of the buyer's liability (if any) to those others resulting from the defect.

Variations in descriptions or undertakings. The question whether the contractual undertakings as to the description or condition of the goods in the string contracts must be the same as in the original contract has caused difficulty in the cases. Scrutton L.J.[76] considered that, where there is "a chain of sales and sub-sales," then "in order to make a sum recovered for breach of the last contract in the chain the measure of damages for a similar breach of a contract higher up in the chain, it is essential that the contracts along the chain connecting them should be the same. Where, as here, the earlier contracts are for the sale of goods under one description, and that not an ordinary trade description, and at some link in the chain 17–083

[70] Above, paras 17–047 *et seq.*

[71] *Bence Graphics International Ltd v Fasson UK Ltd* [1998] Q.B. 87 (see above, para.17–058). In this case, the CA departed from the decision of the CA in *Slater v Hoyle and Smith Ltd* [1920] 2 K.B. 11 (above, para.17–057). But in (1997) 113 L.Q.R. 188 Treitel strongly supports the decision in *Slater v Hayle* and criticises the decision in *Bence Graphics*, on the ground that when the buyer is not seeking damages for consequential loss (*e.g.* arising under a resale) but claiming the "difference in value" (under s. 53(3)) the remoteness rules are not relevant. See also Hawes, (2005) 121 L.Q.R. 389 (commenting on a New Zealand case which followed *Bence Graphics*).

[72] [1951] 1 K.B. 422 (reversed on appeal on a different ground: see above, para.17–078).

[73] *ibid.*, at p.436. See also *Louis Dreyfus Trading Ltd v Reliance Trading Ltd* [2004] EWHC 525 (Comm), [2004] 2 Lloyd's Rep. 243.

[74] The *Bence Graphics* case, above, at p.437. Treitel (see n.71, above, argues that *Biggin v Permanite* was a "consequential loss" case where the remoteness rules were relevant. See also *Koufos v C Czarnikow Ltd* [1969] 1 A.C. 350 at 416 (quoted above, para.16–046).

[75] Above. Treitel (see n.71, above) argues that the buyer was not contractually bound to use the goods received from the seller to fulfil its obligations to its customers; so that it was not a "consequential loss" case. See also Hawes, cited in note 71 above.

[76] *Dexters Ltd v Hill Crest Oil Co. (Bradford) Ltd* [1926] 1 K.B. 348.

the description varies, and becomes a well-known trade description, I find it difficult to hold that the amount recovered for a breach of the last contract in the chain can be made the measure of damages for a breach of the first."[77] (The description of the goods in the original contract was "dark cotton seed grease as per sample No. 9536", whereas in the ultimate sub-contracts the description was "black cotton seed grease".[78]) However, in an earlier case,[79] despite some difference in the contracts in the chain,[80] the original buyer was able to recover from the original seller. In *Biggin & Co. Ltd v Permanite Ltd*,[81] Devlin J. considered what degree of variation in description would break the chain. He said[82]: "If the variation to a description is such that it is impossible to say whether the injury that ultimately results would have flowed from the breach of the original warranty, the parties must as reasonable men be presumed to have put the liability for the injury outside their contemplation as a measure of compensation. If this is, as I believe, the nature of the principle, it must be applied very differently according to whether the injury for which the defendant is being asked to pay is a market loss or physical damage. In the former case[83] . . . any variation that is more than a matter of words is likely to be fatal, because there is no way of telling its effect on the market value. In the latter case the nature of the physical damage will show whether the variation was material or not." It is submitted that this passage states the correct principle. If one of the buyers in the chain added to the description of the goods sold to him, or varied the undertaking as to their condition, the original seller should still be liable for the loss or injury suffered by the ultimate buyer if it was caused by a defect in the goods covered both by the original seller's description or undertaking and also by the descriptions or undertakings in all the intervening contracts.[84] As Devlin J. put it[85] ". . . the

---

[77] *ibid.*, at p.359 (*obiter dicta*; the judge said he was "not expressing a final opinion on this point").

[78] On the facts, however, it is not clear whether the amount awarded in the earlier arbitration between sub-buyers lower in the chain of sales depended on the fact that a different description was used in the ultimate sub-contract: *ibid.*, at pp.357, 359.

[79] *British Oil and Cake Co. Ltd v Burstall & Co.* (1923) 39 T.L.R. 406 (". . . the article supplied was not the contract article at all." This case should therefore be regarded as falling under the heading of a contractual description of the goods sold rather than a contractual undertaking as to their quality.)

[80] *ibid.*, at p.407.

[81] [1951] 1 K.B. 422 at 433–434 (reversed by the CA on a different point: [1951] 2 K.B. 314 (see above, para.17–078)).

[82] The learned judge expressly adopted the principle laid down by Scrutton L.J., above: [1951] 1 K.B. 422 at 433.

[83] As illustrated by *Dexters Ltd v Hill Crest Oil Co. (Bradford) Ltd*, above, n.76.

[84] *cf. Pinnock Bros v Lewis and Peat Ltd* [1923] 1 K.B. 690 (see above, para.17–081) where the sellers argued that they were not liable to the buyers in respect of their liability towards the sub-buyers, because there was an exemption clause in the sub-contract relating to latent defects; but it was held that the sellers were liable, because "the cause for complaint" fell outside both this clause and a differently-worded exemption clause in the original contract: *ibid.*, at pp.696–697, 698–699.

[85] *Biggin & Co. Ltd v Permanite Ltd* [1951] 1 K.B. 422 at 434. (On the facts of the case, it was found that the original manufacturers of the material were not liable under this principle because the buyers from them passed on the warranty without the qualification originally attached to it, and added to it a further warranty: *ibid.*, at pp.434–435.)

test will be whether [the penultimate buyer] could show that the whole of its liabilities to [the ultimate buyer] arose from the failure of the [goods] to behave as warranted by" the original sellers. In another case,[86] Auld L.J. said ". . . there appears to have been no material differences between the contracts in the chain which would have put damage claimed at any point in the chain outside the imputed contemplation of the buyer and seller. . .".

Costs paid or payable to sub-buyers lower in the chain. Following the proposition set out above[87] for the recovery of the costs incurred by the buyer in reasonably defending his sub-buyer's claim against him, the buyer who is liable to his sub-buyer in respect of a chain of sub-sales[88] may recover, as part of his damages from the seller, the total costs[89] incurred both by himself and also by the sub-buyers lower in the chain, provided each acted reasonably in incurring the costs.[90] Reasonableness depends on the circumstances at the time each buyer had to decide how to act[91]; at each link in the chain, the question must be asked whether it was reasonable for that person to put up "the amount of resistance" which he did to the attempt to pass liability up the chain of sellers.[92] But ". . . it must be reasonable for anyone before submitting to a liability of this kind to see a solicitor and have advice."[93] Thus, where the original seller knew that the buyer, a wholesale furrier, bought dyed rabbit skins for the purpose of making them into fur collars, and there were four further sub-sales before the ultimate buyer (who intended to wear it) bought a coat with one of the collars, it was held that the original buyer could recover from the original seller the costs as well as the damages paid by the ultimate seller to the ultimate buyer who developed "fur dermatitis" through wearing the collar.[94] The original seller was also held liable for the reasonable costs of each of the intervening parties in the chain who had paid the claim of his immediate sub-buyer without putting up a defence.[95] 17–084

---

[86] *Bence Graphics International Ltd v Fasson UK Ltd* [1998] Q.B. 87 at 107. (At pp.106–107, Auld L.J. approved the tests propounded by Devlin J. in the passages quoted in this paragraph.) (See above, para.17–058).
[87] Above, para.17–077.
[88] In the circumstances set out in the preceding paragraphs.
[89] Including each party's own reasonable costs taxed on the standard basis (on which see above, para.17–077, n.33) and the taxed costs paid to the next person in the chain. *Cf.* the similar situation where there is a breach of the implied condition as to title in a chain of sub-sales: *Butterworth v Kingsway Motors* [1954] 1 W.L.R. 1286 at 1297–1300 (above, paras 4–014—4–017); *Bowmaker (Commercial) Ltd v Day* [1965] 1 W.L.R. 1396. See also above, para.4–029.
[90] *Kasler & Cohen v Slavouski* [1928] 1 K.B. 78; *Godley v Perry* [1960] 1 W.L.R. 9 at 16–17. Costs were also passed up the chain of sellers in *Pinnock Bros v Lewis and Peat Ltd* [1923] 1 K.B. 690 (above, para.17–081).
[91] *Kasler & Cohen v Slavouski*, above, at p.87. *Cf.* the cases cited above, para.17–077.
[92] *Kasler & Cohen v Slavouski*, above, at p.89.
[93] *ibid.*, at p.89.
[94] *Kasler & Cohen v Slavouski*, above. The skins were not fit for the purpose of being made into fur collars for coats: see s.14(3) (above, paras 11–051 *et seq.*).
[95] *ibid.*, at p.89. (The costs actually paid by the intervening sub-buyers exceeded the £5 5s. allowed by the judge—they amounted in one case to £45 and in another to £21—but it must be assumed that the judge considered that these sums were more than reasonable.)

17–085 **Contracts (Rights of Third Parties) Act 1999.** This Act opens up the possibility that sub-buyers in a chain of sub-sales might be sufficiently "identified" as third parties intended to receive the benefit of the seller's undertaking as to the description or condition of the goods. If the conditions laid down in the Act are fulfilled[96] a sub-buyer may be entitled to enforce the undertaking directly against the original seller.

4. OTHER CLAIMS FOR DAMAGES

17–086 **Damages for breach of undertaking as to title.** Chapter 4 of this work examines the assessment of damages for the seller's breach of the implied condition that he has a right to sell the goods,[97] for the seller's breach of the implied warranty that the buyer shall have quiet possession of the goods,[98] and for breach of the implied warranty that the goods are free from encumbrances.[99]

17–087 **Damages for loss of the right to reject.** The assessment of damages when the buyer claims that the seller's breach prevented the buyer from rejecting the goods, or from rejecting the documents for the goods,[1] is discussed in a later chapter.[2]

17–088 **Damages for breach of other obligations imposed by the Act.** In addition to the claims for damages already dealt with in this chapter, there are other actions which could arise under the Act, but where there is a dearth of authority on the question of assessing the damages, *e.g.* damages for preventing a third party from making a valuation of the goods to fix the price (section 9(2)).[3] In such cases the general law on damages would apply, either by virtue of sections 54[4] or 62(2)[5] or (in the case of breach of warranty) of section 53(2).[6] The common law rules on causation,[7] remoteness of damage,[8] and mitigation[9] would be the main guidelines in the assessment of damages in such cases.

17–089 **Damages for deceit, misrepresentation or negligence.** Earlier chapters have dealt with the assessment of damages in various instances of the seller's fraud,[10] *e.g.* his selling when he knew that he had no right to sell the

[96] See above, paras 2–026, 17–080; below para.18–005.
[97] Above, paras 4–002 *et seq.*
[98] Above, paras 4–025 *et seq.*
[99] Above, para.4–023.
[1] *e.g.* where the seller sends a falsely-dated bill of lading.
[2] Below, paras 19–187 *et seq.*
[3] See above, para.2–049. See also s.60 (above, para.16–094).
[4] Above, para.16–046.
[5] Above, paras 1–007—1–011.
[6] Above, paras 17–047 *et seq.*
[7] Above, para.16–049.
[8] Above, paras 16–043—16–046.
[9] Above, paras 16–052—16–058.
[10] Above, paras 3–008—3–009.

goods,[11] or where the seller by a fraudulent misrepresentation induced the buyer to enter the contract.[12] Remedies for misrepresentation have also been examined elsewhere. If the buyer was induced to enter the contract by the seller's misrepresentation, he may be able to rescind the contract,[13] or to claim damages in lieu of rescission.[14] The seller is under a strict liability not to make a misrepresentation which he did not on reasonable grounds believe to be true.[15] In special circumstances, the buyer may also have a claim in the tort of negligence against the seller,[16] or for breach of the seller's statutory duty.[17]

5. REPAYMENT OF THE PRICE OR ADVANCE PAYMENTS

Restitution: recovery of money paid to the seller. Section 54 of the Act provides that: "Nothing in this Act affects the right of the buyer . . . to recover money paid where the consideration for the payment of it has failed." The claim referred to in this provision is one in restitution[18] where the claimant has failed to receive the benefit of the other party's performance[19]: "subject always to special provisions in a contract, payments on account of a purchase price are recoverable if the consideration for which that price is paid wholly fails."[20] Thus, the buyer has a claim in restitution to recover the price he has paid to the seller if the seller, in breach of his obligation under section 12(1),[21] failed to pass a good title to the goods sold.[22] The "consideration" for the payment of the price is treated as the transfer of the property in the goods to the buyer, and the buyer may sue in restitution to recover the price on the ground of a total failure of consideration, despite the fact that he enjoyed some use[23] of the 17–090

---

[11] Above, para.4–022.
[12] Above, para.12–012.
[13] Above, paras 12–003—12–009.
[14] Misrepresentation Act 1967, s.2(2). See above, paras 12–004—12–010.
[15] Misrepresentation Act 1967, s.2(1). See *Howard Marine and Dredging Co. Ltd v A Ogden & Sons (Excavations) Ltd* [1978] Q.B. 574 at 596, 601; and above, paras 12–014—12–016.
[16] See above, paras 12–013, 12–121—12–127. *Cf.* products liability above, paras 14–061 *et seq.*
[17] See above, paras 14–094 *et seq.*
[18] Goff and Jones, *The Law of Restitution* (6th ed.), 19–001—19–013, 20–007 *et seq.; Chitty on Contracts* (29th ed.), Vol. 1, paras 29–054—29–066.
[19] Actual "performance of the promise" is the sense in which "consideration" is used in this context: *Fibrosa Spolka Akcyjna v Fairbairn Lawson Combe Barbour Ltd* [1943] A.C. 32 at 48, 61, 72 (". . . the failure of consideration which justifies repayment is a failure in the contract performance": *ibid.*, at p.72).
[20] *ibid.*, at p.75 (quoting *Ockenden v Henly* (1858) E.B. & E. 485 at 492). See also below, para.20–109, text at n.44.
[21] Above, paras 4–002 *et seq.*
[22] *Rowland v Divall* [1923] 2 K.B. 500. See the examination and criticism of this case, above, paras 4–006 *et seq.*, where further authorities are cited; and Treitel, *Law of Contract* (11th ed.) pp.1053–1056.
[23] When "rescission" is the remedy of a consumer for non-conforming goods, under s.48C(3) of the Act any reimbursement to the consumer may take account of the use of the goods he has had since they were delivered to him: see above, para.12–097.

goods.[24] Similarly, if the seller failed to deliver the goods, or delivered goods which the buyer was entitled to, and did reject, the buyer may recover the deposit he paid to the seller.[25]

Where, after the buyer has paid the price (or part of it) to the seller, the seller fails to deliver the goods or the buyer justifiably rejects them,[26] he may either sue for damages, or for restitution of the money paid to the seller.[27] If he sues for damages, the assessment should take account of the amount paid to the seller,[28] but he will have to prove his actual loss, and will be subject to all the rules on damages, such as remoteness of damage and the rules of mitigation. If he sues for restitution, he can avoid the rules on damages,[29] since his claim is for return of the precise sum of money which he paid to the seller, but he must terminate the contract.[30] This type of claim is discussed in an earlier chapter.[31]

17–091 **Divisible contracts.** "If a divisible part of a contract has wholly failed, and part of the consideration can be attributed to that part, that portion of the money so paid can be recovered."[32] In one case, where the buyer ordered and paid for a specified tonnage of goods at a price of "18s. per cwt.", but it was discovered later that less than the specified tonnage had been shipped, it was held that the buyer could recover the sum overpaid,[33] *viz.* the excess in the price beyond the amount due (at the contractual rate)

---

[24] *Rowland v Divall*, above. *Cf. Yeoman Credit Ltd v Apps* [1962] 2 Q.B. 508 (accumulation of defects in a vehicle constituted breach of a fundamental term: but some use of the vehicle prevented a total failure of "consideration"); *cf.* also *Barber v NSW Bank Plc* [1996] 1 W.L.R. 641; see above, paras 12–067—12–068, 13–050—13–051. See the Law Commission's Report No. 160 (1987) paras 6.1–6.5.

[25] *Fitt v Cassanet* (1842) 4 M. & G. 898 (wrongful resale of the goods by the seller: the buyer also recovered damages for non-delivery).

[26] On rejection, see above, paras 12–027 *et seq.* The buyer has no lien over the goods for repayment of the price (see above, para.15–015).

[27] *e.g. Comptoir D'Achat et De Vente du Boerenbond Belge SA v Luis de Ridder Limitada* (*The Julia*) [1949] A.C. 293 (contract for sale and delivery ex ship: price recovered when outbreak of war prevented delivery: see below, para.21–018); *Fibrosa Spolka Akcyjna v Fairbairn Lawson Combe Barbour Ltd*, above (another frustration case, where part of the price had been paid in advance: see above, para.6–039).

[28] Above, para.12–067; *Bostock & Co. Ltd v Nicholson & Sons Ltd* [1904] 1 K.B. 725 at 741 (whole price included in the damages).

[29] By receiving repayment of the full price, the buyer may sometimes recover more than he would if damages were assessed under the ordinary rules, *e.g.* where the market price of the goods had fallen after the making of the contract. Often, however, a claim to damages will lead to recovery of a greater sum: *Mason v Burningham* [1949] 2 K.B. 545 (above, para.4–026) where the buyer received as damages for breach of s.12 both the amount of the price and the amount spent by her on overhauling the goods.

[30] *Yeoman Credit Ltd v Apps* [1962] 2 Q.B. 508 (above, paras 12–067—12–068, 13–050—13–051).

[31] Above, paras 12–067—12–068. *Cf.* below, para.19–215.

[32] *Fibrosa* case, above, at p.77. Apportionment may not be limited to cases where the intention of the parties is to make the contract divisible: *Goss v Chilcott* [1996] A.C. 788 at 798.

[33] *Devaux v Conolly* (1849) 8 C.B. 640. See also *Biggerstaff v Rowatt's Wharf Ltd* [1896] 2 Ch. 93; *Behrend & Co. Ltd v Produce Brokers Co. Ltd* [1920] 3 K.B. 530; *Ebrahim Dawood Ltd v Heath Ltd* [1961] 2 Lloyd's Rep. 512. See above, para.8–046.

for the goods which were delivered.[34] Where delivery is to be made by instalments,[35] the contract would probably be held to be divisible in this sense.

Recovery of advance payments by a buyer in default. In Chapter 16 there is some discussion of two situations where a defaulting buyer may be able to claim restitution of advance payments made to the seller. Where the seller justifiably terminates the contract after the buyer has paid him the price (or part of it not intended to be a deposit), the buyer may, in the absence of a forfeiture clause in the contract, recover the price or prepayment from the seller, subject to a right of set-off or counterclaim by the seller for damages.[36] Secondly, the buyer may possibly be entitled to some relief despite the fact that the contract expressly provides that sums already paid to the seller are to be forfeited upon default by the buyer.[37] 17–092

6. Remedies Other Than Claims to Money

(a) *Termination of the Contract and Rejection of the Goods*

Termination of the contract. Where the seller repudiates his obligations under the contract, or commits a fundamental breach of contract or a breach of condition, the buyer may choose to treat the contract as terminated and sue for damages. The right to treat the contract as discharged is examined elsewhere[38]; it will include the buyer's right to reject the goods, whether or not the property in the goods had previously passed to him.[39] Where the buyer justifiably rejects the goods, he can treat the seller's failure to deliver goods in conformity with the contract as a simple case of failure to deliver, and the buyer's damages will be assessed in accordance with section 51.[40] The provisions of section 51 are wide enough[41] to entitle the buyer to recover any additional expenses[42] which he has incurred as a result of the seller's breach, *e.g.* if the seller refuses to take the goods back, the buyer may claim the expenses of storing them until the seller does take redelivery[43] or until the buyer can reasonably resell them. 17–093

(b) *Rescission by the Consumer*

Consumer's remedy of rescission. Under the new Part 5A of the Act, where goods which are not in conformity with the contract are delivered to a consumer, one of his new remedies is to "have the contract rescinded". 17–094

---

[34] Above, para.12–069; *cf.* above, para.13–034.
[35] Above, paras 8–064 *et seq.*
[36] Above, para.16–040.
[37] Above, paras 16–037—16–042.
[38] See above, paras 12–018 *et seq.*
[39] Above, paras 12–027 *et seq.*; 12–064. In the case of f.o.b. or c.i.f. contracts, there may be a right to reject the documents which is separate from the right to reject the goods: below, paras 19–144 *et seq.*, 20–105 *et seq.*
[40] Discussed above, paras 17–001 *et seq.*
[41] s.51(3) provides only a "prima facie" rule.
[42] Above, para.17–037.
[43] See s.36 (above, para.12–065).

His entitlement to this remedy and its consequences are examined in Chapter 12.[44]

(c) *Remedies for Other Invalidating Causes*

17–095 **Illegality, mistake, misrepresentation or frustration.** An earlier chapter considers the remedies of the parties where the contract of sale is illegal,[45] or was entered into as the result of a mistake.[46] The remedy of rescission of the contract on the ground of misrepresentation is also discussed elsewhere,[47] as are the legal consequences of frustration.[48]

(d) *Specific Performance for Delivery of the Goods*[49]

17–096 **Introduction.** This section examines the traditional type of "specific performance" under section 52, which is an order of the court requiring the seller to deliver the goods to the buyer in conformity with the terms of the contract. Under the new Part 5A of the Act, there is now a new and different type of "specific performance" which is an order requiring the seller to repair or replace goods delivered to a consumer-buyer which are not in conformity with the contract (this remedy is examined elsewhere).[50] Section 52 of the Act provides that "(1) In any action for breach of contract to deliver specific or ascertained goods the court may, if it thinks fit, on the plaintiff's[51] application, by its judgment or decree direct that the contract shall be performed specifically, without giving the defendant the option of retaining the goods on payment of damages. (2) The plaintiff's application may be made at any time before judgment or decree. (3) The judgment or decree may be unconditional, or on such terms and conditions as to damages, payment of the price and otherwise as seem just to the court."[52] Before the Act, the remedy of specific performance was an equitable one,[53] and the courts have used the cases in equity to guide their use of section

[44] Paras, 12–088—12–089, 12–097 *et seq.*
[45] Ch.3, above, paras 3–027 *et seq.*
[46] Ch.3, above, paras 3–011 *et seq.*
[47] Above, paras 12–003 *et seq.*
[48] Above, paras 6–058 *et seq.*; below, para.20–104.
[49] Treitel [1966] J.B.L. 211; Sharpe, *Injunctions and Specific Performance* (3rd ed.), paras 8–230—8–510; Jones and Goodhart, *Specific Performance* (2nd ed.), pp.143–154. Spry, *The Principles of Equitable Remedies* (6th ed.), Ch.3. On specific performance in the international sale of goods, see below, paras 19–204, 20–121. On the question whether the seller can claim this remedy, see above, para.16–094.
[50] Ch.12, para.12–076. See also Harris (2003), 119 L.Q.R. 541
[51] If a third party is entitled to enforce a term of the contract under the Contracts (Rights of Third Parties) Act 1999, he may claim any remedy which would be available to him if he were a party: see above, para.17–080; below, para.18–005.
[52] Subsection (4), which refers to Scots law, is omitted. S.52 of the 1893 Act superseded s.2 of the Mercantile Law Amendment Act 1856 (which was repealed by s.60 of the 1893 Act). See above, paras 1–007—1–011.
[53] Details must be sought in standard works on equity: Fry, *Specific Performance of Contracts* (6th ed.), esp. pp.36–41; Snell's *Equity* (31st ed.), Ch.40; Ashburner's *Principles of Equity* (2nd ed.), pp.382–408.

52.[54] Atkin L.J. has said that after the 1893 Act, "in contracts for the sale of goods the only remedy by way of specific performance is the statutory remedy."[55] If the court makes an order for specific performance, the buyer will receive the goods themselves in the same way as the seller's right of stoppage in transit[56] entitles the seller to recover possession of the goods. An order for specific performance is the buyer's counterpart of judgment in the seller's action for the price,[57] in that the other party to the contract for sale is ordered to perform his promise according to its actual terms.[58] The implementation of section 52 is covered by the Civil Procedure Rules, which provide that a judgment or order for the delivery of goods which does not give the defendant the alternative of paying the assessed value of the goods may be enforced by a "writ of specific delivery" without alternative provision for recovery of the assessed value of the goods.[59]

"Specific or ascertained goods". Section 52, *above*, empowers the making of an order of specific performance only where the goods to be delivered by the defaulting seller are "specific or ascertained". "Specific goods" are defined[60] by section 61(1) as "goods identified and agreed on at the time a contract of sale is made and includes an undivided share, specified as a fraction or percentage, of goods identified and agreed on as aforesaid."[61] This definition has been examined in Chapter 1.[62] In accordance with this definition, the Privy Council held that an order for specific performance could not be made where the seller agreed to supply all the coal that might be required for the buyers' steel works.[63] But the 1995 extension[64] of the definition means that if a bulk (such as the cargo of a ship) was identified and agreed upon when the contract was made, an order of specific performance may be made under section 52 in respect of a fraction or percentage of the bulk. But where the part sold is a specified quantity to be taken from an identified bulk (*e.g.* 500 tons out of a cargo of 1,000 tons) it appears that no order can be made, because the goods are not "specific" in terms of the new definition, and they remain unascertained.[65] 17–097

54 *e.g. Re Wait* [1927] 1 Ch. 606 (below, para.17–097); and see above, paras 1–010—1–011; below, para.19–204.

55 *Re Wait*, above, at p.630. See above, paras 1–007—1–011. *Cf.* s.60 (above, para.16–094).

56 Above, paras 15–061 *et seq.*

57 Above, paras 16–001 *et seq.*

58 The buyer may be estopped from seeking an order for specific performance after he has elected to accept damages in lieu thereof: *Meng Leong Development Pte. Ltd v Jip Hong Trading Co. Pte. Ltd* [1985] A.C. 511.

59 CPR, Sch.1, RSC Ord. 45, r.4(1).

60 "Unless the context or subject-matter otherwise requires": s.61(1).

61 The words in the definition which follow "made" were added by s.2(d) of the Sale of Goods (Amendment) Act 1995. See the discussion above, paras 5–109—5–127.

62 See above, paras 1–113—1–119.

63 *Dominion Coal Co. Ltd v Dominion Iron and Steel Co. Ltd* [1909] A.C. 293 at 311. For an examination of the problems of enforcing long-term supply contracts, see Sharpe, *op. cit.*, paras 8–390—8–510, 9–130—9–200.

64 See n.61 above.

65 Under the new s.20A(2) of the 1979 Act (as inserted by s.1(3) of the 1995 Act) the buyer of the specified quantity may become the owner in common of the bulk, but the opening words of s.20A(1) refer to such goods as "a specified quantity of unascertained goods". See above, paras 5–109—5–127.

"Ascertained[66] goods", according to Atkin L.J. in *Re Wait*,[67] "probably means identified in accordance with the agreement after the time a contract of sale is made", *i.e.* goods which were unascertained[68] at the time the contract was made.[69] In another case, the judge ruled that "ascertained" in section 52 "means that the individuality of the goods must in some way be found out, and when it is, then the goods have been ascertained."[70] In the latter case the contract was for the sale of ten bales of Hessian bags, and the invoice sent by the seller after the making of the contract referred to ten out of a particular parcel of 45 bags: the judge held that this was insufficient ascertainment of the goods for the purposes of section 52. In the important case of *Re Wait*,[71] the majority of the Court of Appeal held that no order for specific performance should be made of a sub-contract to sell 500 tons out of a consignment of 1,000 tons of wheat bought by the seller, because the 500 tons were neither specific nor ascertained goods. One judge spoke of "clearly specific goods in a specific place, identified and ascertained as the subject-matter of the contract."[72] The new definition of "specific goods" above does not cover the facts of *Re Wait* since there was no specified "fraction or percentage" of the identified consignment.

17–098 **Claims when the property has passed.** Provided that the goods are specific or ascertained, section 52 applies whether or not the property in the goods has passed to the buyer.[73] However, instead of asking for an order under section 52, the buyer who has the property in the goods may, in proceedings for wrongful interference with goods under section 3 of the Torts (Interference with Goods) Act 1977, seek an order for delivery of the goods which does not give the defendant the alternative of retaining them on payment of their value as assessed by the court.[74] But the court has a discretion whether or not to make such an order[75]: "the power of the Court . . . rests upon a footing which fully accords with section 52 of the Sale of Goods Act, 1893",[76] since the court has a similar discretion not to order the

---

[66] Above, para.1–118.
[67] [1927] 1 Ch. 606 at 630.
[68] See the three categories of unascertained goods distinguished above, para.1–117. See also above, para.5–060.
[69] *cf.* ss.16, 17 (above, paras 5–059 *et seq.*).
[70] *Thames Sack and Bag Co. Ltd v Knowles & Co. Ltd* (1918) 88 L.J.K.B. 585 at 588 (following *Gillett v Hill* (1834) 3 L.J.Ex. 145 at 147). *Cf. Laurie and Morewood v Dudin & Sons* [1926] 1 K.B. 223 (CA: no appropriation by a warehouseman of 200 quarters of maize out of a bulk of 618 quarters: see above, paras 5–061, 5–109—5–127).
[71] [1927] 1 Ch. 606. (For a fuller statement of the facts, see above, para.1–108, and below, para.19–204.) The argument that there was an equitable assignment of the 500 tons is considered above, para.1–108. (The dissenting judge, at p.656, held that s.52 included "the enforcement of a specific equitable assignment or lien.")
[72] *ibid.*, at p.618. On the facts of *Re Wait* an order of specific performance would have given the buyer priority over general creditors in the seller's bankruptcy.
[73] *James Jones & Sons Ltd v Tankerville* [1909] 2 Ch. 440 at 445; *Re Wait*, above, at p.617; *Cohen v Roche* [1927] 1 K.B. 169 at 180.
[74] s.3(2)(a). See *Cohen v Roche*, above, at pp.179–180. *Cf.* above, para.15–116 and below, para.17–105.
[75] s.3(3)(b), (4) and (6) of the 1977 Act. See *Howard E. Perry & Co. Ltd v British Railways Board* [1980] 1 W.L.R. 1375 at 1382–1383 (not a sale of goods case).
[76] *Cohen v Roche*, above, at p.181 (quoting *Whiteley Ltd v Hilt* [1918] 2 K.B. 808 at 819 (an action of detinue in a hire-purchase case)).

specific delivery of "ordinary articles of commerce and of no special value or interest"[77] and where "no grounds exist for any special order for delivery."[78]

The types of goods for which the remedy is appropriate. The equitable remedy of specific performance before the Act was discretionary[79] and a wide discretion is conferred on the court by section 52, above (". . . may, if it thinks fit . . ."). "Courts of equity did not decree specific performance in contracts for the sale of commodities which could be ordinarily obtained in the market[80] where damages were a sufficient remedy."[81] Thus, before the Act, specific performance could be granted to compel sellers to transfer rare or unique articles such as a jewel,[82] china vases,[83] particular stones from Old Westminster Bridge,[84] and, in some cases, chattels which (although not unique) possessed a special value to the claimant.[85] After the 1893 Act, similar orders have been made in several cases. In *Behnke v Bede Shipping Co. Ltd*[86] it was held that a ship was a specific chattel within the Act, in respect of which an order for specific performance could be made.[87] Wright J. took account of the fact that the ship in question "was of peculiar and practically unique value to" the buyer[88]; that the buyer wanted the ship for immediate use,[89] and that damages would not be an adequate remedy.[90] In another case, an order was made for the specific delivery of an ornamental door designed by the famous architect Adam.[91] 17–099

---

77 *Cohen v Roche*, above, at pp.180–181.
78 *Cohen v Roche*, above, at p.181. (The old action of detinue was abolished by s.2(1) of the 1977 Act.)
79 See Fry, *Specific Performance of Contracts* (6th ed.), pp.36–41.
80 "Ordinary mercantile commodities": *Re Wait*, above, at p.633.
81 *Re Wait* [1927] 1 Ch. 606 at 630. ("Possibly the statutory remedy [s.52] was intended to be available even in those cases": *ibid.*) See Treitel [1966] J.B.L. 211. The wider use of specific performance in the sale of goods is discussed in *Butler v Countrywide Finance Ltd* [1993] 3 N.Z.L.R. 623.
82 *Pearne v Lisle* (1749) Amb. 75 at 77.
83 *Falcke v Gray* (1859) 4 Drew. 651 at 658.
84 *Thorn v Commissioners of Public Works* (1863) 32 Beav. 490.
85 Fry, *op. cit.*, p.39, citing *North v Great Northern Ry* (1860) 2 Giff. 64 at 69 (an injunction case: see below, para.17–102, n.22). On the "special value to the plaintiff", see Harris, Ogus and Phillips, 95 L.Q.R. 581 (1979); and *cf. Ruxley Electronics and Construction Ltd v Forsyth* [1996] 1 A.C. 344 (above, para.16–048); *Farley v Skinner* [2001] UKHL 49; [2002] 2 A.C. 732 above, para.17–071). See also *Behnke v Bede Shipping Co. Ltd* [1927] 1 K.B. 649 at 661 (quoted below).
86 Above.
87 *Allseas International Management Ltd v Panroy Bulk Transport SA* [1985] 1 Lloyd's Rep. 370. See also *C.N. Marine Inc. v Stena Line A/B* (*The Stena Nautica*) (*No.* 2) [1982] 2 Lloyd's Rep. 336 at 341, 348–349; *Eximenco Handels AG v Partrederiet Oro Chief* (*The "Oro Chief"*) [1983] 2 Lloyd's Rep. 509 at 521.
88 *Behnke v Bede Shipping Co. Ltd*, above, at p.661. There was probably only one other comparable ship, which was not available.
89 *cf.* a case where the buyer merely intended to resell at a profit: *Cohen v Roche* [1927] 1 K.B. 169 at 179–181 (quoted *infra*).
90 *Behnke v Bede Shipping Co. Ltd*, above, at p.661.
91 *Phillips v Lamdin* [1949] 2 K.B. 33 at 41–42. In Australia, an order has been made in respect of a taxi-cab to which a taxi-cab licence was attached: *Dougan v Ley* (1946) 71 C.L.R. 142.

But no order should be made if the goods sold were "of a very ordinary description" and were not alleged to be "peculiar" in the sense that similar goods could not be obtained elsewhere.[92] (The fact that there would be a delay in obtaining a comparable item from another manufacturer does not justify an order being made.[93]) An order for specific performance was refused when the buyer had purchased "ordinary Hepplewhite furniture" which "possessed no special features at all" and which the buyer intended for resale at a profit.[94] The mere fact that the contract of sale is for delivery of goods by stated instalments should not justify the making of an order for their specific delivery to the buyer.[95] But it has recently been argued that English courts should be willing to follow United States practice in granting (where appropriate) specific performance of contracts to sell all the seller's output or to satisfy all the buyer's requirements.[96]

17–100 **Discretion of the court.** The provisions of section 52, above, confer a wide discretion on the court[97] to decide whether or not to make an order of specific performance. In addition to considering the type of goods in question,[98] the court is entitled to look at all the circumstances of the case[99] including the conduct of both the buyer[1] and the seller,[2] and to consider the hardship which an order would inflict on the seller.[3] But in cases on the sale of land it has been held that inadequacy of the price is not a ground for refusing an order,[4] and it is submitted that the same should apply to sale of

---

[92] *Fothergill v Rowland* (1873) L.R. 17 Eq. 132 at 139. See also *Re Clarke* (1887) 36 Ch.D. 348 at 352; and *Whiteley Ltd v Hilt* [1918] 2 K.B. 808 at 819 (a hire-purchase case). *Cf. Lingen v Simpson* (1824) 1 S. & S. 600 (order for delivery of pattern books as agreed by the partners upon dissolution of the partnership).
[93] *Société des Industries Metallurgiques SA v The Bronx Engineering Co. Ltd* [1975] 1 Lloyd's Rep. 465. But *cf. Sky Petroleum Ltd v VIP Petroleum Ltd* [1974] 1 W.L.R. 576 (interlocutory injunction granted to protect the claimant's supply of scarce goods).
[94] *Cohen v Roche*, above, at pp.179–181. (On the claim in tort, see above, para.17–098).
[95] Fry, *op. cit.*, p.41. See Treitel [1966] J.B.L. 211 at 224–225.
[96] Jones and Goodhart, *Specific Performance* (2nd ed.), pp.148–149. See also Sharpe, *op. cit.*, paras 8-390—8-510, 9-130—9-200.
[97] By the Arbitration Act 1996, s.48(5)(b), an arbitrator may order specific performance of a contract not relating to an interest in land.
[98] Above, para.17–099.
[99] Fry, *op. cit.*, Pt III. The defence of set-off is available on a claim for non-money relief (such as specific performance) which itself arises upon non-payment of money: *BICC Plc v Burndy Corporation* [1985] Ch. 232.
[1] "He who comes into equity must come with clean hands." Thus, it would be relevant for the court to know whether there had been any default by the buyer (Snell, *op. cit.*, para.15–36); whether he had delayed unreasonably in seeking the remedy (Snell, *ibid.*, para.15–38); whether there had been misrepresentation by the buyer (Snell, *ibid.*, para.15–30).
[2] *e.g.* whether the seller had entered into the contract as the result of a mistake. See above, paras 3–011 *et seq.*
[3] The authorities for the latter part of this proposition are not sale of goods cases: *Tamplin v James* (1880) 15 Ch.D. 215 at 221; *Stewart v Kennedy* (1890) 15 App.Cas. 75 at 105. See Snell, *op. cit.*, para.15–32(c)(2).
[4] *Coles v Trecothick* (1804) 9 Ves. 234 at 246; *Sullivan v Jacob* (1828) 1 Moll. 472 at 477.

goods.[5] If the seller becomes insolvent after he has received the price from the buyer but before he has delivered the goods, an order for specific performance will give the buyer priority over other creditors of the seller by taking the goods out of the seller's estate: for this reason, an order is unlikely to be made in these circumstances.[6] Since the court has such a wide discretion under section 52, the buyer should always ask for damages in the alternative.[7]

By subsection (3) of section 52, the court when making an order for specific performance also has a wide discretion to impose conditions: "The judgment . . . may be unconditional, or on such terms and conditions as to damages, payment of the price and otherwise as seem just to the court." Thus, the buyer may be ordered to pay the price into court as a condition of the order being made against the seller.[8] Another illustration of the terms on which an order may be made is *Re Wait*,[9] where the court of first instance made an order in favour of sub-buyers upon payment of their share in the freight of the consignment. In ordering the specific performance of a contract to sell shares, the House of Lords required the buyer to pay interest on the purchase price which he had been entitled to retain pending the order.[10]

(e) *Specific Performance for Repair or Replacement Granted to a Consumer*

Repair or replacement of goods. Under the new Part 5A of the Act, the court may grant a new type of order to a consumer to whom goods were delivered which were not in conformity with the contract. Section 48E(2) empowers the court to make an order requiring "specific performance" by the seller of his obligation to repair or replace the goods. This power is examined above in Chapter 12.[11] 17–101

---

[5] *cf. Falcke v Gray* (1859) 4 Drew. 651 at 664–665 (specific performance denied when parties had not been on an equal footing).

[6] See *Re Wait* [1927] 1 Ch. 606 at 640. See Jones and Goodhart, *op. cit.*, pp.150–152. *Cf. Anders Utkilens Rederi A/S v O/Y Lovisa Stevedoring Co. A/B (The Golfstraum)* [1985] 2 All E.R. 669 at 674.

[7] As was done in *Dominion Coal Co. Ltd v Dominion Iron and Steel Co. Ltd* [1909] A.C. 293 (above, para.17–097). See also *Cohen v Roche* [1927] 1 K.B. 169 at 179. However, the House of Lords has held that the court cannot, in its equitable jurisdiction under Lord Cairns' Act (Chancery Amendment Act 1858), when awarding damages in lieu of specific performance or injunction, assess the damages on any new basis: *Johnson v Agnew* [1980] A.C. 367 at 400. Thus, in a sale of goods case, damages under Lord Cairns' Act could not be assessed on a more generous basis than is permitted under either the Sale of Goods Act or the common law: *cf. Wroth v Tyler* [1974] Ch. 30 at 57–60 (sale of land).

[8] *Hart v Herwig* (1873) L.R. 8 Ch.App. 860 at 864 (a similar injunction case: see below, para.17–102). *Cf. Langen and Wind Ltd v Bell* [1972] Ch. 685 (specific performance of agreement to transfer shares granted subject to a lien to protect the transferor against non-payment of the price of the shares).

[9] [1926] Ch. 962 at 972. The CA, however, did not consider this, as it held that no order should have been made: [1927] 1 Ch. 606 (see above, para.17–097).

[10] *Harvela Investments Ltd v Royal Trust Company of Canada (CI) Ltd* [1986] A.C. 207.

[11] Above paras 12–076 *et seq.*

(f) *Injunctions and Declarations*[12]

17–102 **Injunction.** Whereas specific performance is a remedy for the positive promise of the seller to deliver the goods, the remedy of an injunction is usually the order of the court restraining the breach of a purely negative promise by the seller.[13] Like specific performance,[14] an injunction is an equitable remedy,[15] but, unlike specific performance, it is not expressly referred to in the Act.[16] Section 62(2) preserves "the rules of common law" except where inconsistent with the express provisions of the Act, and it has been suggested earlier[17] that the rules of equity are included in this phrase. The court may use an injunction in support of an order for specific performance. In *Behnke v Bede Shipping Co. Ltd*,[18] in addition to making the order for specific performance against the sellers, as set out in an earlier paragraph,[19] the court also granted an injunction restraining the sellers from parting with the ship to anyone but the buyer.[20] Similarly, the court has power by injunction to prevent a specific chattel from being removed out of the jurisdiction until a question relating to the chattel has been decided by the court.[21] So where the buyer sought specific performance of the sale to him of a German ship, which was in an English port, the court restrained the seller and the master of the ship from removing her, so that she could be delivered under the contract if the court later so ordered.[22] In some circumstances an injunction may be granted which has much the same effect as an order of specific performance.[23] Thus, where the goods sold to the buyer are on the land of the seller, and the contract gives the buyer a right to enter the land to remove the goods, the court may grant an injunction to restrain the seller from preventing the due execution of the contract.[24]

---

[12] See above, para.17–096, n.51.
[13] The order of the court must define clearly what should or should not be done by the seller.
[14] Above, paras 17–096—17–100.
[15] *Kerr on Injunctions* (6th ed.), pp.409 *et seq.*; Sharpe, *Injunctions and Specific Performance* (3rd ed.), Pt I; Spry, *The Principles of Equitable Remedies* (6th ed.), Chs 4 and 5; Ashburner's *Principles of Equity* (2nd ed.), pp.384–387; Snell's *Equity* (31st ed.), Ch.16; *Doherty v Allman* (1878) 3 App.Cas. 709 at 719–721.
[16] *cf.* s.60 (above, para.16–094).
[17] Above, paras 1–007—1–011.
[18] [1927] 1 K.B. 649.
[19] Above, para.17–099.
[20] [1927] 1 K.B. 649 at 662. The Privy Council in *Dominion Coal Co. Ltd v Dominion Iron and Steel Co. Ltd* [1909] A.C. 293 at 310 (above, para.17–097) envisaged the granting of an injunction to prevent the sellers from discriminating against the buyers in the selection of the quality of the coal to be supplied to the buyers.
[21] *Hart v Herwig* (1873) L.R. 8 Ch.App. 860.
[22] *ibid. Cf. North v Great Northern Ry* (1860) 2 Giff. 64 (claimant hired coal wagons of special value to him; railway company could be restrained from selling them).
[23] *cf. Astro Exito Navegacion SA v Southland Enterprises (No. 2)* [1983] 2 A.C. 787 (injunction to buyers to sign document needed by sellers to comply with letter of credit; Master of Supreme Court to sign if buyers failed to do so).
[24] *James Jones & Sons Ltd v Tankerville* [1909] 2 Ch. 440 (timber growing on the seller's land: by s.61(1) "goods" are defined as including industrial growing crops which are to be severed under the contract of sale: see above, paras 1–090—1–094).

Normally, the court has a discretion whether or not to grant an injunction.[25] However, it is said that the court has no option but to grant an injunction to restrain the breach of a negative contractual undertaking.[26] In one case of a contract to sell all the seller's output over a two-year period, the court granted an injunction to enforce the seller's express undertaking not to sell similar goods during the period to any other manufacturer than the buyer.[27]

In another case, where the buyer agreed to take from the seller at a fixed price per unit *all* the electricity required for his premises for not less than five years, the buyer was restrained by injunction from taking it from any other supplier.[28] The buyer had agreed that if he took electricity, he would take it from the seller.[29] But an affirmative obligation will not be enforced by injunction merely because it implies a negative obligation: where a colliery agreed to sell to the buyer all the coal produced for five years, an injunction was not granted to prevent the colliery from being sold to third parties within the five years.[30] The contract was held to be in a category which the court would not order the seller specifically to perform,[31] and the court was unwilling to enforce specific performance "by a roundabout method".[32]

Repair or replacement of non-conforming goods. Under the new Part 5A of the Act, (above, para.12–071) the court may grant the consumer an order of "specific performance" requiring the seller to repair or replace the goods, which is an order similar to a mandatory injunction. This remedy is examined elsewhere.[33] 17–103

---

[25] Snell, *op. cit.*, paras 16–16; *James Jones & Sons Ltd v Tankerville*, above, at pp.445–446 (a sale of goods case). On the question of Lord Cairns' Act, see above, para.17–100, n.7.

[26] Snell, *op. cit.*, para.16–15 (2) (quoting *Doherty v Allman* (1878) 3 App.Cas. 709 at 720).

[27] *Donnell v Bennet* (1883) 22 Ch.D. 835. (The restraint of trade doctrine will apply to such contracts: see above, paras 3–034—3–039.)

[28] *Metropolitan Electric Supply Co. Ltd v Ginder* [1901] 2 Ch. 799. See also *Foley v Classique Coaches Ltd* [1934] 2 K.B. 1; *Servais Bouchard v Prince's Hall Restaurant* (1904) 20 T.L.R. 574. *Cf.* an injunction to enforce a "tied-house" covenant under which the publican agrees to take all his beer from one brewer: *Catt v Tourle* (1869) L.R. 4 Ch.App. 654 ("the exclusive right of supplying all ale"); and an injunction to enforce a "solus agreement": *Esso Petroleum Co. Ltd v Harper's Garage (Stourport) Ltd* [1968] A.C. 269 (see further, above, para.3–038). See also Sharpe, *Injunctions and Specific Performance* (3rd ed.), paras 8–390—8–510, 9–130—9–200.

[29] [1901] 2 Ch. 799, 806. (By "necessary implication" the buyer had agreed not to take it from others: *ibid.*) See Kerr, *op. cit.*, pp.457 *et seq. Cf. Bower v Bantam Investments Ltd* [1972] 1 W.L.R. 1120.

[30] *Fothergill v Rowland* (1873) L.R. 17 Eq. 132.

[31] It was "a simple contract for the sale of a chattel of a very ordinary description not alleged to be a peculiar coal, or coal that cannot be got elsewhere": *ibid.*, at p.139.

[32] *ibid.*, at p.140; *cf. Sky Petroleum Ltd v VIP Petroleum Ltd* [1974] 1 W.L.R. 576 (interlocutory injunction). *Cf.* also *Smith v Peters* (1875) L.R. 20 Eq. 511 (sale of a public-house and of the furniture at a valuation to be made by a named valuer: mandatory injunction granted to compel the vendor to allow the valuer to enter the house to value the furniture. See s.9(2): above, paras 2–049—2–052).

[33] Above paras 12–076 *et seq.*

17–104 **Declaration.**[34] In appropriate circumstances, the buyer may obtain a declaration setting out his legal rights against the seller.[35] A declaration may be made before any breach of contract has occurred, and may thus guide the parties in the implementation of a contract whose performance is spread over a long period.[36] For instance, the buyer may ask the court to determine whether he is still bound by the contract, or whether he is entitled to repudiate his remaining obligations.[37] If it would serve a useful purpose, the court may in its discretion make a negative declaration, *e.g.* to the effect that the claimant is not liable to the defendant in respect of a certain matter.[38] Even where the defendant is liable to pay damages, the claimant may claim only a declaration that the defendant was in breach of contract and that the damages for the loss caused by the breach of contract amounted to a stated sum.[39] In one case,[40] the buyers obtained against the sellers, who had committed a breach of their obligations to deliver, both an award of damages for their loss of profits, and also a declaration of indemnity that the buyers were entitled to recover from the sellers such damages as the buyers might be held liable to pay (as a result of the seller's breach) in respect of their legal liability to a sub-buyer.[41] However, the Court of Appeal, in another case,[42] has said that the proper course in this situation is for the court to reserve that head of damages.

(g) *Proprietary Claims to Possession or Damages*

17–105 **Claims for possession or damages for conversion.** Where the property in the goods and the immediate right to possession[43] of them has passed to the buyer, he may bring against the seller a proprietary action for chattels

---

[34] See Zamir and Woolf, *The Declaratory Judgment* (3rd ed.), esp. Ch.4. See also above, para.16–092 (seller's claim for a declaration).

[35] Declaratory proceedings in the Commercial Court are often quicker and cheaper than arbitration: *Vantol (JH) Ltd v Fairclough Dodd & Jones Ltd* [1955] 1 W.L.R. 642 at 648 (approved by HL in the same case: [1957] 1 W.L.R. 136 at 137, 138, 144).

[36] *Spettabile Consorzio Veneziano di Armamento e Navigazione v Northumberland Shipbuilding Co. Ltd* (1919) 121 L.T. 628 at 635.

[37] The mere issue of the writ (now claim form) asking for such a declaration does not amount to a repudiation: see *Spettabile* case, above.

[38] *Messier-Dowty Ltd v Sabena SA* [2000] 1 W.L.R. 2040, CA.

[39] *Louis Dreyfus & Co. v Parnaso Cia. Naviera SA* [1959] 1 Q.B. 498; [1960] 2 Q.B. 49.

[40] *Household Machines Ltd v Cosmos Exporters Ltd* [1947] K.B. 217 (the sellers knew that the buyers were buying the goods with a view to resale: see also above, para.17–031).

[41] The amount of this liability was not ascertained at the time of the hearing between the buyer and seller. *Cf. Total Liban SA v Vitol Energy SA* [2001] Q.B. 643. (see above, para.17–036). On this type of liability, see above, para.17–076.

[42] *Trans Trust SPRL v Danubian Trading Co. Ltd* [1952] 2 Q.B. 297 (see above, para.16–092). But see the uncertainty which this decision has created: *British Electrical and Associated Industries (Cardiff) Ltd v Patley Pressings Ltd* [1953] 1 W.L.R. 280 at 284. *Cf. Deeny v Gooda Walker Ltd (No. 3)* [1995] 4 All E.R. 289.

[43] If the whole price has not been paid and the seller is in possession of the goods by virtue of his lien (above, paras 15–028 *et seq.*), the buyer does not have the immediate right to possession, and cannot sue in conversion a stranger who removes the goods from the seller's possession: *Lord v Price* (1874) L.R. 9 Ex. 54. (The court

under the law of torts, *viz.* proceedings for wrongful interference with the goods seeking an order for the specific delivery of the goods,[44] or an action for damages for conversion when the seller's detention of the goods amounts to a denial of the buyer's title to them.[45] The proceedings for wrongful interference do not always entitle the buyer to receive the actual goods because the court has a discretion not to order the specific delivery of a chattel.[46] The buyer will normally be better advised to sue the seller for a contractual remedy rather than for a remedy in tort, since a claim for certain consequential losses may be easier to establish in contract, and the courts are unwilling to award the buyer a higher measure of damages if he sues in tort rather than in contract.[47]

The buyer, by virtue of his immediate right to possession of the goods, may also be entitled to bring these tortious actions against strangers[48]: thus, he may recover the full value of the goods from a stranger who converts them by taking them out of the possession of the seller.[49]

Wrongful resale or retaking by the seller. In *Chinery v Viall*,[50] where the unpaid seller, without a right to resell,[51] wrongfully resold the goods at a time when the original buyer was entitled to possession of them[52] (the sale being on credit terms[53]), the seller was held liable to the original buyer for damages for non-delivery,[54] or for conversion.[55] But it was held that the damages for the conversion did not amount to the full value of the goods, because the buyer had not paid the price[56]: the buyer could recover only his 17–106

left open the question whether, by later paying or tendering the balance of the price to the seller, the buyer could, in his own name, sue the stranger in conversion, or whether he would be limited to an action in the name of the seller: *ibid.* at p.56.) *Quaere* whether the buyer could bring an action on the case for injury to his reversionary interest in the goods: *cf. Mears v L and SW Ry* (1862) 11 C.B.(N.S.) 850; and see *Bloxam v Sanders* (1825) 4 B. & C. 941 at 949.

44 See above, para.17–098; *cf.* specific performance, above, paras 17–096—17–100.

45 Above, paras 1–028, 16–089. *Cf.* above, para.15–005.

46 See above, paras 17–002, 17–098. *Cf.* above, para.15–116.

47 *Chinery v Viall* (1860) 5 H. & N. 288 at 294–295 (below, para.17–106); *Cohen v Roche* [1927] 1 K.B. 169 at 180 (above, para.17–098). See further, below, para.17–106 and *cf. The Arpad* [1934] P. 180 at 216–219, 233.

48 *e.g. Langton v Higgins* (1859) 4 H. & N. 402 (wrongful second sale by seller to second buyer); *Denny v Skelton* (1916) 115 L.T. 305 (part of a cargo taken mistakenly in the name of the wrong sub-buyer).

49 *Chinery v Viall*, above, at pp.295–296. (The assumption was that the seller, not being in default, could recover the price from the buyer, who could recover the value of the goods from the stranger.) *Cf.* n.43, above.

50 (1860) 5 H. & N. 288.

51 See above, para.15–105.

52 The seller had remained in possession of the goods after the original sale.

53 Even where the buyer had failed to pay the price on the date fixed by the contract, he would be entitled to possession of the goods if he tendered the price to the seller within a reasonable time and before the seller had justifiably resold or terminated the contract: *Martindale v Smith* (1841) 1 Q.B. 389. See also *Bloxam v Sanders* (1825) 4 B. & C. 941.

54 *Fitt v Cassanet* (1842) 4 M. & G. 898. See s.51 (above, paras 17–001 *et seq.*).

55 *Bloxam v Sanders*, above, at p.949.

56 Since he had not delivered the goods, the seller could not sue for the price: *Lamond v Davall* (1847) 9 Q.B. 1030 (above, paras 15–128, 16–020).

actual loss, which was the difference between the market price of the goods at the time of the conversion[57] and the contract price.[58]

Where the property in the goods has passed to the buyer,[59] and the seller has delivered them to him, but the price remains unpaid, the contract of sale is not terminated by the act of the seller in tortiously retaking the goods and reselling them.[60] In these circumstances, the seller still has his action for the price,[61] while the buyer (even where his failure to pay the price is a breach of contract) has an independent claim for conversion for the full value of the goods at the time of the retaking[62]: these are separate claims and although either could be used to found a counterclaim, neither is a defence to the other claim,[63] since one is a claim in debt, the other for unliquidated damages.[64]

(h) *Criminal Sanctions and Extra-legal Remedies*

17–107 **Other miscellaneous remedies.** The ways in which the buyer is protected by statutes designed to protect the consumer have been considered in Chapter 14. There are some statutes where the criminal sanction may not be the exclusive remedy of the aggrieved buyer, in that he could base a civil claim for damages on breach of the statute.[65] Chapter 14 also discusses a number of miscellaneous remedies of the buyer, including some which lie outside normal judicial procedure.[66]

---

[57] The basic measure of damages in conversion is the value of the item at the time of the conversion: (this measure applies even where the tortfeasor replaces the item at a later date—its value at that date should be deducted from its value at the time of conversion): *BBMM Finance* (*Hong Kong*) *Ltd v Eda Holdings Ltd* [1990] 1 W.L.R. 409, PC: (a case concerning shares).

[58] *Chinery v Viall*, above (applied in *Butler v Egg and Egg Pulp Marketing Board* (1996) 114 C.L.R. 185.) The position is the same in the case of a wrongful taking, sale or pledge by a pledgee: *Johnson v Stear* (1863) 15 C.B.(N.S.) 330; *Brierly v Kendall* (1852) 17 Q.B. 937; or a wrongful sale and purchase of goods held on hire-purchase terms: *Wickham Holdings Ltd v Brooke House Motors Ltd* [1967] 1 W.L.R. 295 (distinguished in *Chubb Cash Ltd v John Crilley & Son* [1983] 1 W.L.R. 599). See *McGregor on Damages* (17th ed.), paras 33–057—33–062; *Clerk and Lindsell on Torts* (19th ed.), paras 17–108—17–111. On waiver of tort, see above, paras 1–073, 15–104.

[59] *cf.* the position where the unpaid seller retains the property in the goods and is entitled to retake them upon the buyer's default (above, paras 15–114, 15–116).

[60] *Page v Cowasjee Eduljee* (1866) L.R. 1 P.C. 127. See above, para.15–117.

[61] Above, paras 16–021 *et seq.*

[62] *Stephens v Wilkinson* (1831) 2 B. & Ad. 320 at 327; *Page v Cowasjee Eduljee*, above, at p.147. See McGregor, *op. cit.*, para.33–061. The claim will be made by proceedings for wrongful interference under the Torts (Interference with Goods) Act 1977.

[63] *Page v Cowasjee Eduljee*, above; *Stephens v Wilkinson*, above; *Gillard v Brittan* (1841) 8 M. & W. 575; *Re Humberston* (1846) De G. 262.

[64] *Gillard v Brittan*, above.

[65] Above, paras 14–094 *et seq.*

[66] Above, paras 14–098 *et seq.*, 14–125 *et seq.*

Part Seven

OVERSEAS SALES

CHAPTER 18

OVERSEAS SALES IN GENERAL

	PARA.
1. Preliminary	18–001
2. Documents of title to goods	18–006
(a) Bills of lading	18–012
(i) Types of bills of lading	18–013
(ii) Bill of lading as a receipt	18–028
(iii) Bill of lading as a contractual document	18–047
(iv) Bill of lading as a document of title	18–062
(v) Contractual effects of transfer of bill of lading: introductory	18–096
(vi) Acquisition of contractual rights	18–102
(vii) Imposition of contractual liabilities	18–123
(viii) Destroyed and unascertained goods	18–135
(ix) Other techniques for the acquisition of contractual rights and imposition of contractual liabilities	18–138
(x) Liability in tort	18–148
(b) Sea waybills	18–152
(i) Transfer of contractual rights	18–153
(ii) Imposition of contractual liabilities	18–162
(c) Mate's receipts	18–163
(d) Delivery orders and warrants	18–169
(i) Common law definitions	18–170
(ii) Contractual effects at common law	18–173
(iii) Ship's delivery orders: statutory transfer of contractual rights	18–175
(iv) Ship's delivery orders: statutory imposition of contractual liabilities	18–189
(v) Whether delivery orders are documents of title	18–193
(e) Other documents	18–199
(f) Paperless transactions	18–202
3. Passing of property	18–208
4. Loss or deterioration in transit	18–243
(a) Commercial Sales	18–244
(b) Consumer Sales	18–259
5. Implied terms	18–265
(a) Description	18–266
(b) Fitness for purpose	18–274
(c) Non-rejection clauses	18–275
(d) Statutory restrictions on right to reject	18–284
6. Bulk shipments	18–285
(a) Shipping documents	18–286
(b) Passing of property	18–287
(c) Risk	18–300
7. Export and import licences	18–308
(a) Incidence of duty	18–309
(b) Standard of duty	18–313
(i) Implication of a term	18–314
(ii) Construction	18–317
(c) Content of the duty	18–319
(d) Effects of failure to obtain licence	18–323

(i) Absolute duty 18–325
(ii) Duty of diligence 18–327
8. Supervening prohibition of export or import 18–333
(a) Discharge by supervening prohibition 18–334
(b) Prohibition of export or import clauses 18–342
(i) Effects 18–342
(ii) Burden of proof 18–346
(iii) Partial prevention 18–353
(iv) Notice of supervening events 18–356

1. PRELIMINARY

18–001 **Overseas sales.** Overseas sales give rise to special problems mainly because there is often a long interval of time between the despatch of the goods and their arrival at the agreed or contemplated destination. During this period, the parties are exposed to three types of risk: financial, physical and legal. So far as the financial risk is concerned, the seller will want to obtain payment as early as possible and to retain some interest in the goods, at least by way of security, until he has received, or been adequately assured of receiving, payment. On the other hand, the buyer will not want to pay for goods, which he has not yet received, until he has acquired an interest in the goods on which he can rely in the event of the seller's insolvency before actual delivery of the goods. To a large extent these conflicting desires have been reconciled by the law relating to documents of title to goods, to the passing of property in goods in transit, and to the unpaid seller's rights against the goods.[1] The physical risks arise from the possibility that the goods may be lost or damaged, or may deteriorate, in transit. The legal responsibility for such loss may lie on the buyer or on the seller or on some third person, such as the carrier. As between buyer and seller, the allocation of this responsibility depends partly on the rules relating to risk, and partly on the obligations undertaken by the parties: for example as to the quality of the goods at the time of shipment, or as to packing. What has here been called the legal risk arises mainly because of governmental interference with the export or import of goods.[2]

The parties to a contract of sale will often make provision for allocating some or all of these risks. In general, freedom of contract prevails in this respect, so that effect will be given to such provisions. Often the parties use standard types of overseas sales, such as c.i.f. and f.o.b. contracts, to which certain legal incidents are attached unless a contrary intention appears. Such standard types of contract are discussed in Chapters 19, 20 and 21 but their operation cannot be fully understood without first considering certain general concepts and principles applicable to overseas sales of all kinds; and it is with these concepts and principles that this chapter is concerned.

18–002 **INCOTERMS.** An attempt to define the duties of the parties under c.i.f., f.o.b. and other standard types of sales has been made by the International

[1] As to the unpaid seller's rights against the goods, see above, Ch.15.
[2] Below, paras 18–308 *et seq*.

Chamber of Commerce in its publication entitled INCOTERMS.[3] These definitions are sometimes at variance with the rules of English law which are discussed in this and the following three chapters of this book. To the extent of such variance, these rules will be displaced if the parties make their contract subject to INCOTERMS,[4] but in most of the cases which have come before the English courts, buyers and sellers do not appear to have adopted this practice.

ULIS. The contracting parties may make their contract subject to the Uniform Law on the International Sale of Goods (ULIS) which applies only "if it has been chosen by the parties to the contract as the law of the contract."[5] In the English case-law, ULIS has been of little importance, having hardly ever (if at all) been chosen by the parties as the law applicable to their contract. Such importance as the Convention ever had is, moreover, likely to be diminished by the development to be described in paragraph 18–004 below. But there is one problem arising from ULIS which still calls for some discussion, namely the problem which arises because ULIS does not specifically deal with the legal effects of standard types of overseas sales (such as c.i.f. or f.o.b. contracts). It merely provides in Article 9(3) that "expressions, provisions or forms commonly used in commercial practice . . . shall be interpreted according to the meaning usually given to them in the trade concerned." Some of the provisions of ULIS may prima facie affect contracts of the standard types commonly used in overseas sales. These provisions might, if they applied to such contracts, lead to results different from those at present established in English law in the case of such sales. ULIS can, however, be excluded by contrary agreement, and Article 3 provides that such exclusion may be express or implied. This provision could give rise to a difficult question of construction where the parties make their contract on (for example) c.i.f. terms and also choose ULIS as the law applicable to the contract, and where, on the matter in dispute, ULIS conflicts with one of the normal incidents of a c.i.f. contract. In such a case it would be open to the court to hold that ULIS was *pro tanto* excluded if the predominant intention of the parties was to subject their contract to the normal incidents of a c.i.f. sale. **18–003**

The Vienna Convention.[6] The Vienna Convention on Contracts for the International Sale of Goods is intended to supersede ULIS, from which it differs in a number of significant respects. It has not been ratified by the United Kingdom, so that extended or detailed discussion of it in this book would be premature; but a number of general points relating to it merit some consideration here. First, it is (unlike ULIS) intended to apply to **18–004**

---

[3] The current version is INCOTERMS 2000, I.C.C. Brochure No. 560.

[4] *e.g.* in *The Albazero* [1977] A.C. 774: see p.782; *BV Oliehandel Jongkind v Coastal International Ltd* [1983] 2 Lloyd's Rep. 463; *The Forum Craftsman* [1985] 1 Lloyd's Rep. 291; *P & O Oil Trading Ltd v Scanoil AB (The Orient Prince)* [1985] 1 Lloyds's Rep. 389; *ERG Petroli SpA v Vitol SA (The Ballenita)* [1992] 2 Lloyd's Rep. 455; *Trasimex Holdings SA v Addax BV (The Red Sea)* [1999] 1 Lloyd's Rep. 610.

[5] Uniform Laws on International Sales Act 1967, s.1(3).

[6] Above, para.1–024.

contracts which fall within its scope,[7] even though it has not been chosen by the parties as the law applicable to the contract. The choice of the parties is, however, relevant in that they may "exclude the operation of this Convention or . . . derogate from or vary the effect of any of its provisions."[8] Secondly, the parties are bound by "any usage to which they have agreed"[9] and are "considered, unless otherwise agreed, to have impliedly made applicable to their contract . . . a usage of which the parties knew or ought to have known and which in international trade is widely known to, and regularly observed by, parties to contracts of the type involved in the particular trade concerned."[10] Usages are also to be taken into account in interpreting the contract.[11] The Convention, however, omits the reference contained in ULIS Article 9(3) to the interpretation of "expressions, provisions or forms . . . according to the meaning usually given to them in the trade concerned."[12] On the other hand, the Convention resembles ULIS in that it does not specifically deal with standard types of overseas sales (such as c.i.f. or f.o.b. contracts), while at the same time laying down general rules which, if applied to such contracts, would produce one of two effects. They would *either* produce results significantly different from those produced by the present English rules governing such sales, *or* (because of the lack of precision with which the Convention is drafted) cause considerable uncertainty on points on which the present rules of English law lead to clear and easily predictable results.[13] This uncertainty is a significant disadvantage of the Convention, and a ground for maintaining the present position of non-ratification by the United Kingdom. If the Convention were ratified, the question would arise whether the parties would be considered to have excluded it, or to have derogated from its terms, by contracting on, for example, c.i.f. or f.o.b. terms, especially if they had also expressly or by implication chosen English law as the law applicable to their contract. In relation to some aspects of such contracts (such as those defining the duties of the parties) the present English rules could be preserved as "practices" or "usages" relevant to the interpretation of the contract.[14] This approach is more questionable in relation to other aspects of the contracts (such as remedies, including rejection and rescission); and in relation to such issues the decision of the parties to adopt standard terms could, it is submitted, be regarded as a decision by them to exclude, or derogate from, the provisions of the Convention and to subject their contract to the well-known incidents which flow in English law from the use of such terms. Relevant provisions of the Convention will be discussed in footnotes in this and the following three chapters.

---

[7] See Arts 1–5.
[8] Art. 6.
[9] Art. 9(1).
[10] Art. 9(2).
[11] Art. 8(3).
[12] See above, para.18–003.
[13] *e.g.* the clear and immediate right under English law to reject defective documents would be replaced by the need either to establish "fundamental breach" or to set an additional period for curing the breach: see Arts 47 and 49(1) of the Convention. See further Feltham [1991] J.B.L. 413; Nicholas 105 L.Q.R. 201 (1989).
[14] Under Art. 8(3).

18–005 **Contracts (Rights of Third Parties) Act 1999.** In the law relating to documents of title to goods and to other aspects of overseas sales, problems often arise as to the effects of contracts on persons other than the immediate parties to them. At common law, the solutions to these problems depended on the doctrine of privity of contract; but that doctrine is subject to many exceptions and in the present context two statutory modifications of the doctrine are of particular importance. The first, contained in the Carriage of Goods by Sea Act 1992, applies in the restricted field of certain contracts for the carriage of goods by sea and is discussed later in this Chapter.[15] The second, of more general application, is contained in the Contracts (Rights of Third Parties) Act 1999[16] under which persons are in certain circumstances[17] entitled to enforce terms in contracts to which they are not parties. This Act has many repercussion in the law relating to overseas sales and will therefore call for discussion at a number of points in this Chapter and in Chapters 19 to 21. To lay the groundwork for these discussions, it will be convenient here to summarise those salient provisions of the Act which are of particular significance in the law relating to overseas sales.

(a) The Act amends but does not abolish the common law doctrine of privity of contract. In the words of the Law Commission's Report on which the Act is based, the effect of the Act will be to create "a general and wide-ranging exception to the third party rule but it [will leave] that rule intact for cases not covered by the statute."[18]

(b) The principal provision of the Act is contained in section 1 by which a third party (C) is entitled to enforce a term in a contract between the promisor (A) and the promisee (B) if the contract either "expressly provides that he may"[19] *or* "the term purports to confer a benefit on him"[20] unless (in the latter case) "it appears on a proper construction of the contract that the parties [*i.e.*, A and B] did not intend the term to be enforceable by"[21] C. It is also necessary for C to be "expressly identified in the contract by name or as a member of a class or as answering a particular description",[22] and C has no right to enforce a term "otherwise than subject to and in accordance with any other relevant terms of the contract"[23]; it is thus possible by such terms to exclude the operation of the Act. Where a contract term excludes or limits liability, references in the Act to C's

---

15 Below, paras 18–080 to 18–131, 18–152 to 18–162.
16 Implementing, with some changes, the Law Commission's Report on *Privity of Contract: Contract for the Benefit of Third Parties*, Law. Com. No. 242 (1996), (hereafter "Report"). The changes do not (except in relation to arbitration agreements, dealt with in s.8 of the Act) reflect any major departures from the policy of the recommendations in the Report. For a fuller account of the 1999 Act, see *Chitty on Contracts*, 29th ed. (2004) (hereafter "*Chitty*") paras 18–084 to 18–112.
17 Specified in s.1 of the 1999 Act.
18 Report, para.5.16 and see *ibid.* para.13.2. *Cf. Heaton v Axa Equity Law Life Assurance Society Plc* [2002] UKHL 15; [2002] 2 A.C. 392 at [9].
19 s.1(1)(a).
20 s.1(1)(b).
21 s.1(2).
22 s.1(3).
23 s.1(4).

"enforcing" the term are to be "construed as references to his availing himself of the exclusion or limitation" of liability.[24]

(c) The common law doctrine of privity is generally thought to have two limbs or branches: that C cannot take the *benefit* of a term of a contract between A and B, and that C cannot be *bound* by a term in such a contract. The exception created by the Act is to the first branch of the doctrine; it does not directly affect the second branch. In the context of the present discussion, C can be adversely affected by a term of a contract between A and B only where the right which C seeks to enforce against A is what may be called a derivative right, that is (for present purposes) a right under the contract between A and B. Suppose, for example, that A contracts with B to render services to C, and C seeks, in reliance on the 1999 Act, to enforce A's promise. In such an action, a term excluding or restricting A's liability for breach of the contract between A and B can be relied on by A against C.[25]

(d) Where C has a right under section 1 to enforce a term of a contract between A and B, then the right of A and B to rescind or vary the contract by agreement without the consent of C is limited but not altogether removed. The general principle, laid down in section 2, is that A and B lose the right to rescind or vary the contract by agreement if C has communicated his assent to the term to A or if A knows that C will rely on the term or if A can reasonably foresee that C has relied on the term and C has in fact relied on it[26]; but these conditions may be modified by the terms of the contract[27] and it is also open to the court to dispense with C's consent in specified conditions: *e.g.* where C's consent cannot be obtained because his whereabouts cannot reasonably be ascertained.[28]

(e) Section 3 of the Act contains an elaborate set of provisions designed to deal with the situation in which A seeks, in an action by C to enforce a term of the contract between A and B, to rely by way of defence or set-off on matters which would have been available to A if proceedings for the enforcement of the contract had been brought by B. The general principle is that A can so rely on such a matter against C if it "arises from or in connection with the contract [between A and B] and is relevant to the term."[29] Under this provision, A could, for example, rely as against C on a valid exemption clause or on B's repudiatory breach. The general principle applies also where "enforcement" by C takes the form of his reliance[30] on an exemption clause in the contract between A and B: he (C) cannot rely on the clause if it would not have protected him, had he been a party to that contract.[31] The general principle stated above can be modified by

---

[24] s.1(6).
[25] s.3(2). The Act does not affect problems such as those which arose in *Lord Strathcona SS Co. v Dominion Coal Co.* [1926] A.C. 108 or *Port Line Ltd v Ben Line Steamers Ltd* [1958] Q.B. 146.
[26] s.2(1).
[27] s.2(3).
[28] s.2(4), and see s.2(5).
[29] s.3(2).
[30] Under s.1(6) (above, at n.24).
[31] s.3(6) *e.g.* if the clause were invalid, or did not satisfy the requirement of reasonableness, under the Unfair Contract Terms Act 1977.

contrary agreement between A and B[32]; and provision is also made for A to be able to rely on defences and counterclaims against C which would not have been available to A against B but would have been available to A against C if C had been a party to the contract.[33]

(f) Section 6 of the Act lists a number of exceptions to the general principle of section 1 under which C can acquire the right to enforce against A a term of a contract between A and B. In some of the excepted cases, the common law rules as to contracts for the benefit of third parties will continue to apply, so that as a general rule the third party will acquire no rights. This is, for example, the effect of the provision in the Act that "Section 1 confers no right on a third party to enforce (a) any term of a contract of employment against an employee . . ."[34] In another group of excepted cases, C has, or can acquire, rights under the contract under other rules of law established independently of the Act. This second group of exceptions includes one which is of particular significance for the purposes of this and the following three Chapters of this book: namely that contained in subsection 6(5) ("the subsection 6(5) exception"), which refers to certain contracts for the carriage of goods by sea and to certain contracts for the international carriage of goods by rail, road and air. Third parties can acquire rights under such contracts by virtue of other legislation, such as the Carriage of Goods by Sea Act 1992, in conditions there specified; and the carefully regulated schemes of such legislation could be disrupted if third parties (such as consignees of goods) could under the 1999 Act acquire rights to enforce terms of contracts of carriage to which they were not original parties in circumstances other than those specified in such other legislation.

(g) The third party is not deprived by the 1999 Act of any rights which he may have apart from its provisions. This is the effect of subsection 7(1) by which "Section 1 does not affect any right or remedy of a third party that exists or is available apart from this Act." Although the reference here is only to "section 1", it follows that many other provisions of the Act will likewise not apply where C's rights or remedies arise apart from the Act. In particular, section 2 of the Act applies only "where a third party has a right *under section 1* to enforce a term of the contract" and section 3 applies only "where, *in reliance on section 1*, proceedings for the enforcement of a term of a contract are brought by a third party." The rules contained in section 2 as to rescission and variation by agreement between the contracting parties, and those contained in section 3 as to defences and related matters available to the promisor, will therefore not apply where the third party seeks to enforce a term (including an exemption clause) apart from the Act. This point is of considerable significance where the third party can assert rights both under the Act and apart from its provisions[35]: in such a case the third party could, by bringing his claim apart from the Act, avoid the restrictions imposed by it on claims made under it.

---

[32] s.3(3).
[33] s.3(4).
[34] s.6(3)(a).
[35] *e.g.*, on facts such as those of *Nisshin Shipping Co. Ltd v Cleaves* [2003] EWHC 2602; [2004] 1 Lloyd's Rep. 38.

(h) The common law doctrine of privity does not prevent the promisee from enforcing a contract made for the benefit of a third party; and this position is preserved by section 4 of the Act.[36] For our purpose, a point of particular importance is that the promisee may be able to recover damages in respect of the third party's loss.[37] Obviously, however, the promisor should not in such a case be made liable for the same loss both to the promisee and to the third party; and the Act therefore directs the court in such a case to "reduce any award to the third party to such extent as it thinks appropriate to take account of the sum recovered by the promisee."[38]

2. DOCUMENTS OF TITLE TO GOODS[39]

18–006 **Meaning of "documents of title to goods".** In English law, the expression "document of title to goods" is used in two senses: a traditional narrow common law sense and a broader statutory sense. Recent authority[40] gives some support to the view that, even at common law, the expression may be used in more than one sense; and proposed legislation will, if made in its present form, give rise to a new category of documents of title for the purposes of that legislation.

18–007 **The traditional common law sense: "negotiability" or "transferability".** There is no authoritative definition of "document of title" at common law, but it is submitted that in its original or traditional meaning the phrase refers to a document, the transfer of which operates as a transfer of the constructive possession of the goods covered by the document[41] and may, if

---

36 See below, para.20–069. B could, for example, still claim specific performance in favour of C, as in *Beswick v Beswick* [1968] A.C. 58.

37 *e.g.*, under the so-called rule in *Dunlop v Lambert* (1839) 6 Cl. & F. 600, discussed in para.18–114, below.

38 s.5.

39 Purchase, *Documents of Title to Goods* (1931); Bools, *The Bill of Lading: A Document of Title* (1997). The Vienna Convention on Contracts for the International Sale of Goods (above, para.1–024) does not use the expression "document of title to goods"; this is because the Convention is not generally concerned with "the effect which the contract may have on the property in the goods sold": Art. 4(b). The Convention does treat separately the seller's duty to "deliver the goods and hand over any documents relating to the goods": Art. 30. Other references to documents are in Art. 32(1) (identification of goods by reference to "shipping documents"); Art. 34 (time and place of handing over of documents); Art. 58(1) and (2) (payment against documents); Art. 67 (retention of documents by seller not to affect risk); Art. 68 (risk passing on handing over of goods to carrier who issues documents); and Art. 71 (seller's right of stoppage not affected by buyer's holding of "a document which entitles him to obtain" the goods). Only the last of these provisions has any significance in the context of what would in English law be regarded as the proprietary aspects of dealings with documents of title.

40 see below, para.18–008.

41 *cf.* the references to "symbolical" and "constructive" delivery in *Sanders Bros v Maclean & Co.* (1883) 11 Q.B.D. 327 at p.341; *E Clemens Horst Co. v Biddell Bros* [1911] 1 K.B. 934 at p.957, per Kennedy L.J., whose dissenting judgment was upheld on appeal [1912] A.C. 18; *Hispanica de Petroles SA v Vencedora Oceanica Navegacion SA (The Kapetan Markos NL) (No. 2)* [1987] 2 Lloyd's Rep. 327 at p.340, and *The Future Express* [1992] 2 Lloyd's Rep. 79 at p.100, *affirmed* [1993] 2 Lloyd's Rep. 542.

so intended[42] operate as a transfer of the property in them. This concept of a document of title to goods is based on, or derived from, *Lickbarrow v Mason*[43] where the court recognised a custom of merchants that a bill of lading by which goods were stated to have been "shipped by any person or persons to be delivered to order or assigns"[44] was "negotiable and transferable"[45] by indorsement and delivery. We shall see that the description of such a bill as "negotiable", though common in commercial practice and in judicial discussion, is not strictly accurate,[46] but the quality of being "transferable" lies at the heart of the traditional common law concept of a bill of lading as a document which enables the holder, by transferring the bill, to transfer his property in the underlying goods to the transferee.

Similarly, a pledge of the bill can operate as a pledge of the goods.[47] At common law there is no other class of documents which is recognised as a document of title in this sense,[48] though the characteristics of such a document are conferred by a number of local Acts of Parliament on certain dock and warehouse warrants.[49] It is, moreover, possible for other kinds of documents to become documents of title in the common law sense by proof of a mercantile custom to that effect.[50] In one case[51] such a custom was proved in relation to warrants for the delivery of steel to named persons "or their assigns by endorsement thereon"; and in another the Privy Council was prepared to recognise such a custom in relation to certain mate's receipts.[52] But a document which belongs to a class of documents which, by virtue of such a custom, are "transferable" at common law will be deprived of that quality of transferability if it is marked "not transferable" or "not negotiable". The mate's receipts in the Privy Council case just referred to[53] were so marked and were therefore held not to be documents of title in the traditional common law sense.

Documents which have to be produced to obtain delivery of the goods. There is also support, especially in recent authority relating to "straight" bills of lading, which make the goods deliverable, not to order or 18–008

[42] See *JI MacWilliam Co. Inc. v Mediterranean Shipping Co. SA (The Rafaela S)* [2005] UKHL 11, [2005] 2 A.C. 423 at [69].
[43] (1787) 2 T.R. 63; reversed (1790) 1 H.Bl. 357, but restored by the House of Lords (1793) 2 H.Bl. 211, ordering a *venire de novo*; for the special verdict at the second trial, see (1794) 5 T.R. 683; for the judgment of Buller J. advising the House of Lords, above, see *Newsom v Thornton* (1805) 6 East 17 at 20n.
[44] (1794) 5 T.R. 683 at p.685.
[45] *ibid*.
[46] See below, para.18–084.
[47] *Official Assignee of Madras v Mercantile Bank of India Ltd* [1935] A.C. 53, at p.60; below, para.18–197. For statutory provisions extending this rule to certain documents which are not documents of title at common law, see below, para.18–198.
[48] *Official Assignee of Madras v Mercantile Bank of India Ltd*, above, at p.60.
[49] Below, para.18–198.
[50] See *Kum v Wah Tat Bank Ltd* [1971] 1 Lloyd's Rep. 439.
[51] *Merchant Banking Co. of London v Phoenix Bessemer Steel Co.* (1877) 5 Ch.D. 205.
[52] *Kum v Wah Tat Bank Ltd*, above; below, para.18–166.
[53] At n.50 above.

assigns, but simply to a named consignee,[54] for a different concept of a "document of title" to goods. Under this concept, a document falls into this category simply if it has to be produced to the carrier (or other bailee) by the person claiming delivery of the goods from the carrier or other bailee.[55] This concept of a document of title is distinct from that of a "negotiable" or "transferable" document of title.[56] The distinction is most clearly illustrated by the case of a document which expressly provides that it must be produced by the person claiming delivery of the goods but which is also marked "not negotiable" or "not transferable". Such a document would clearly not be a "document of title" in the traditional sense[57] based on, or derived from, *Lickbarrow v Mason*; but it equally clearly would be a "document of title" if that expression were used to refer to any document which had to be produced by the person claiming delivery of the goods. There may not be any compelling reason why a document of the latter kind should not be called a "document of title"; but the use of the same expression to refer to both of the types of documents here described is, with respect, unfortunate as a potential source of confusion. Clarity of discussion would be promoted by a terminology which reflected the differences, not only in the legal natures of the two types of documents, but also in the commercial purposes which they served. For reasons to be more fully discussed later in this Chapter,[58] it is submitted that such clarity would best be achieved by using the expression "document of title" *in the common law sense* to refer only to a document which has the quality of "negotiability" (or "transferability") described above.[59] An alternative possibility would be to describe documents of this kind as "negotiable" or "transferable" documents of title and documents which merely have to be produced to obtain delivery of the goods as "non-negotiable" or "non-transferable" documents of title. There seems, however, to be no point in the latter classification since its only consequence as a matter of common law would be to restate the quality or characteristic which the document must have to bring it within the class.

---

[54] See the discussion of such "straight" bills in paras 18–018, 18–067 *et seq.; Parsons Corp v C.V. Scheepvaartonderneming Happy Ranger (The Happy Ranger*) [2002] EWCA Civ 694, [2002] 2 All E.R. (Comm.) 24 (where the bill was not of the kind described in the text above), *J.I. MacWilliam Co. Inc. v Mediterranean Shipping Co. SA (The Rafaela S)* [2003] EWCA Civ 556, [2004] Q.B. 702, affirmed [2005] UKHL 11, [2005] 2 A.C. 423. The question discussed in these cases was whether such a bill was a "bill of lading or any similar document of title" within Art. I(b) of the Hague or Hague-Visby Rules.

[55] *cf. Niru Battery Manufacturing Co., Milestone Trading Ltd* [2003] EWCA Civ 1446, [2004] 1 Lloyd's Rep 344 at [9] (warehouse warranty "effectively documents of title" as delivery of the goods could only be obtained against presentation of the warrants).

[56] *cf. The Rafaela S* [2005] UKHL 11, [2005] 2 A.C. 423 at [21], below para.18–074 and the proposed legislation discussed in para.18–010 below, distinguishing between documents of title and "negotiable" documents of title.

[57] See above, para.18–007 at n.45.

[58] Below, paras 18–067 *et seq.*

[59] *cf. The Rafaela S*, above n.54, [2005] UKHL 11, [2005] 2 A.C. 423 at [22] per Lord Bingham ("The question before the House is not whether a straight bill is a document of title at common law").

The statutory definition: Factors Act 1889, section 1(4). The statutory definition of "document of title to goods" is contained in s.1(4) of the Factors Act 1889, and is incorporated by reference into the Sale of Goods Act 1979 by section 61(1) of the the latter Act. This definition falls into two parts. The first lists a number of kinds of documents; this list includes not only bills of lading but also (*inter alia*) delivery orders and warrants, which are not documents of title in the common law sense[60] unless a custom to that effect is proved in relation to the particular type of order or warrant in question. The second part of the definition consists of a general description of documents *not* included in the first part but "used in the ordinary course of business as proof of the possession or control of goods" or for certain other specified purposes; this part of the definition raises the issue of fact whether the document in question is used for any of the specified purposes. We shall see that such an issue can arise in relation to a number of documents commonly used in international trade.[61] Where a document falls within the statutory, but not within the traditional common law definition discussed in para.18–007 above, its transfer does not at common law[62] operate to transfer constructive possession to the transferee. It is submitted that this is also, for reasons to be given later in this Chapter,[63] true of a document which falls within the alternative common law concept of a "document of title" discussed in paragraph 18–008 above, but in relation to which no custom is proved making the class of documents to which it belongs "negotiable" or "transferable". The transfer of a document which falls within the statutory definition (whether or not it also falls within the traditional common law definition) may, however, result in a transfer of title in the goods to the transferee, even though the transferor was not owner, under one of the statutory exceptions to the general principle that *nemo dat quod non habet*.[64] 18–009

Proposed further legislative definition. A further definition of "document of title" is given in the Draft Company Security Regulations annexed to the Law Commission's Report on Company Security Interests.[65] A detailed discussion of this topic is beyond the scope of this Chapter. It suffices here to say that the main[66] purpose of the Report and of the Draft Regulations is to set up a scheme for the electronic[67] registration of charges 18–010

[60] Below, para.18–193; in this chapter we are concerned only with "documents of title" relevant to overseas sales. For warehouse-keepers' certificates within the statutory definition, see above, para.7–036.

[61] Below, paras 18–167 (mate's receipts), 21–054, 20–061, 21–068.

[62] For special statutory provisions giving this effect to certain documents which do not fall within the traditional common law definition, see para.18–007 at n.49.

[63] Below, paras 18–067 *et seq.*, especially paras 18–074, 18–075.

[64] See especially Factors Act 1889, ss.2, 8, 9 and 10; Sale of Goods Act 1979, ss.24–26, 47.

[65] Law Com. No. 296 (2005), hereafter "Report", to which the Draft Regulations are annexed as Appendix A.

[66] The Report and the Draft Regulations also deal with sales of "receivables", *i.e.* of money obligations as defined in Draft Reg.2(3).

[67] For the electronic nature of the Register, see Report paras 1.9, 3.69–3.71 and the first paragraph of the Introduction to the Draft Regulations. It is evidently envisaged that this matter will be dealt with in Rules to be made by the Registrar: see Explanatory Note to Draft Reg.5.

created by companies.[68] The registration requirement does not extend to a pledge of goods where the goods are in the possession of the creditor[69]; and such possession may be actual or constructive. It could be constructive where the goods are in the actual possession of a third party bailee who has issued a document of title in respect of them and it is this document, rather than the good themselves, which is in the pledgee's possession.[70] Thus the Report and the Draft Regulations envisage the possibility that there may be a "pledge of . . . a negotiable document of title to goods".[71] Liens which arise by operation of law are not subject to the registration requirement and retain the priority which they have apart from the scheme[72]; but contractual liens (*i.e.* those which by contract give the creditor rights more extensive than those which he would have under the general law relating to liens) constitute charges which are subject to the requirement of registration.[73]

It seems that the unpaid seller's lien as defined by the Sale of Goods Act 1979 will be regarded as one which arises by operation of law.[74] The point is significant because a seller who delivers the goods to a carrier or other bailee for the purpose of transmission of the buyer may retain his lien by reserving the right of disposal of the goods[75]; and such a reservation may be effected by his retention of a document of title relating to the goods.[76]

It is for the purposes of the proposed registration scheme that the Draft Regulations define "document of title" to mean "a document written on paper issued by or addressed to a bailee—(a) which covers goods in the bailee's possession that are identified or are unascertained portions of an identified mass, and (b) in which it is stated that the goods identified in it will be delivered to a named person, or to the transferee of that person, or to bearer or to the order of a named person".[77] This definition is wider in scope than the common law concept of a "negotiable" or "transferable" document of title[78] in that it extends to documents issued by any bailee, while the only class of documents within the common law concept consists of certain bills of lading which by the custom of merchants are "negotiable and transferable"[79]; and it is wider even than the statutory definition in

---

[68] See Draft Regs 2 and 3. It is envisaged that the scheme will apply also to Limited Liability Partnerships: see Report, para.3.8.

[69] Report, para.3.17; for some modification of this requirement where negotiable documents on goods are released by the creditor to the debtor under a Trust Receipt, see Report, para.3.25, Draft Reg. 22; below para.18–238.

[70] For the traditional concept of a document of title in the common law sense as one, the transfer of which transfers constructive possession of the goods, see above, para.18–007.

[71] Draft Reg.22(2)(a); Report, para.3.25.

[72] Draft Regs 4(1), 31; Report, paras 3.26, 3.27.

[73] Report, paras 3.28, 3.29.

[74] The point is not entirely clear since the contract of sale may be its express terms reserve the seller's lien until payment.

[75] Sale of Goods Act 1979, ss.39(1)(a), 41–43.

[76] *ibid*. S.43(1)(a); for reservation of the right of disposal under s.43(1), see above, para.15–047, and, in the context of overseas sales generally, below paras 18–211 *et seq*.

[77] Draft Reg. 42 ("document of title").

[78] Above para.18–007.

[79] *ibid*.; and see below, para.18–075.

Thank you for purchasing **Benjamin's Sale of Goods, 7th edition.**

Don't miss important updates

So that you have all the latest information, **Benjamin's Sale of Goods** is supplemented regularly. Sign up today for a Standing Order to ensure you receive the updating supplements as soon as they publish.

Setting up your Standing Order with Sweet & Maxwell is hassle-free. Simply complete and return this FREEPOST card and we'll do the rest. Your Standing Order can be countermanded at any time by notifying Sweet & Maxwell.

Alternatively, if you have purchased your copy of **Benjamin's Sale of Goods** from a bookshop or other supplier, please ask your supplier to ensure that you are registered to receive the supplements.

☐ Please enter my Standing Order for updating supplements, to be invoiced on publication unless countermanded.

☐ Please enter my Standing Order for future editions and updating supplements, to be invoiced on publication unless countermanded.

Name: ____________________

Job Title: ____________________

Organisation: ____________________

Address: ____________________

____

____

Postcode: ____________________

Telephone: ____________________

Email: ____________________

S&M account number: (if known) ____________________

Signed: ____________________ Date: ____________________

LBU1903

NO STAMP
REQUIRED
WITHIN U.K.

SWEET & MAXWELL
FREEPOST
PO BOX 2000
ANDOVER
SP10 9AH

section 1(4) of the Factors Act 1889[80] in that a document can fall within it without falling either within the list of documents given in section 1(4) or satisfying the requirement of being "used in the ordinary course of business as proof of the possession or control of goods".[81] But it is significant that in their substantive provisions (as opposed to those which define terms) the Draft Regulations invariably couple the expression "document of title" with the word "negotiable"[82]; and that they make no attempt to define the expression "negotiable document of title" or to explain what it is that may give the quality of a "negotiability" to a document of title to goods. By contrast, in the context of documents which evidence rights to the payment of *money* the Draft Regulations do provide a definition of the expression "negotiable instrument".[83] One can only assume that the omission of any explanation in the Draft Regulations of the quality of "negotiability" in relation to a document of title to goods is deliberate and that the question whether any class of documents or any particular document has this quality will continue to be determined as a matter of common law in accordance with the principles discussed in this Chapter.[84] The use of the word "negotiable" in this context indeed gives rise to the difficulty that in English law even bills of lading, to which that word is commonly applied, are not "negotiable" in the full sense of the word[85]; and it seems that the Draft Regulations use "negotiable" in what has been called its "popular" sense.[86] The important point is that the effect of dealings with such documents (in particular with bills of lading) will not be subjected to the proposed scheme for the registration of company security interests: the Draft Regulations provide that nothing in them "affects the right of a transferee of . . . (b) a . . . negotiable document of title"[87]. The underlying policy of this provision is explained in the Report: "It is vital to ensure . . . that the transferability of . . . negotiable documents of title is not compromised by the scheme"[88]. Equally, the scheme does not affect the proprietary effects that can follow as a matter of common law from the retention of such documents by a seller of goods, *e.g.* where a contract of sale provides for payment of the price against documents. A provision of this kind can operate as a kind of rudimentary retention of title clause; and such clauses are not to be covered by the proposed registration scheme but are to be the subject of further work to be undertaken by the Law Commission.[89] The important point for the purpose of this Chapter is that the common law rules by which dealings with bills of lading can reserve, create or transfer security interests[90] in the

---

[80] Above, para.18–009.
[81] Words quoted from Factors Act 1889, s.1(4).
[82] Draft Regs 22(2)(a) and (b), 28(2) and 30(1); an apparent exception is the "tailpiece" to Draft Reg. 22(2), but here the phrase "the document of title" merely refers back to the phrase "a negotiable document of title" used twice in the preceding part of Draft Reg. 22(2). Hence the exception is more apparent than real.
[83] Draft Reg. 42 ("negotiable instrument").
[84] See especially above para.18–007, below, paras 18–062, 18–067 to 18–077.
[85] See below, para.18–084.
[86] See *ibid.*, n.58.
[87] Draft Reg. 30.
[88] Report, para.3.222.
[89] Report, paras 1.14, 1.29.
[90] See below, paras 18–212 *et seq.*

goods will remain in force and that such dealings will not be subject to the requirement of registration under the proposed scheme. It would be impracticable to impose such a requirement in the case of dealings with goods afloat, which may be bought and sold many times while they are in transit.

18–011 **Scope of discussion.** The ensuing discussion deals with a number of types of documents which are, or may be, documents of title in the senses given to that expression either at common law or by legislation. Significant changes in the law relating to some such documents have been made by the Carriage of Goods by Sea Act 1992,[91] but that Act has no effect, in relation to any documents issued before it came into force on September 16, 1992.[92] Problems arising out of documents issued before that date will therefore continue to be governed in part by rules which are now obsolete. For a full discussion of such rules (where they still apply) reference should be made to the fourth edition of this book.[93] In the discussion that follows, the pre-1992 law will be considered only to the extent *either* that this is necessary for an understanding of the 1992 Act *or* that, in cases which are not covered by that Act, the previously established common law continues to apply.

The 1992 Act deals only with *contractual* rights and liabilities. It does not in terms deal with the transfer of *possessory or proprietary* rights in the goods covered by the document in question.[94] In other words, it does not deal with the question whether that document is a document of title in either the statutory or the common law sense. The question whether the Act may have an indirect bearing on that question in relation to ship's delivery orders will be considered in paragraph 18–195 below.

(a) *Bills of Lading*

18–012 **Bills of Lading.** A bill of lading is a document issued by or on behalf of a carrier of goods by sea[95] to the person (usually known as the shipper) with whom he has contracted for the carriage of goods. Such a document has three functions. First, it is a receipt: *i.e.* it is evidence that the goods

[91] Implementing the Law Commissions' Report on *Rights of Suit in Respect of Carriage of Goods by Sea* (Law Com. No. 196, Scot. Law Com. No. 130 (1991)).
[92] Carriage of Goods by Sea Act 1992, s.6(3).
[93] See especially paras 18–028, 18–029, 18–031, 18–040, 18–041.
[94] *Borealis AB v Stargas Ltd (The Berge Sisar)* [2001] UKHL 17, [2002] 1 A.C. 205 at [31]; *Primetrade AG v Ythan Ltd (The Ythan)* [2006] EWHC 2399 (Comm.), [2006] 1 All E.R. 367 at [70].
[95] It is doubtful whether a boat bill for the carriage of goods by inland waterway is in English law regarded as a bill of lading: *Bryans v Nix* (1839) 4 M. & W. 775. The U.C.P. distinguish between a "Marine/Ocean Bill of Lading" (Art. 23) and an "Inland Waterway Transport Document" (Art. 28). In the United States, "bill of lading" includes documents evidencing the receipt of goods for "shipment" by sea, land or air: see U.C.C., s.1–201(6); in its 2001 version (not yet widely adopted) there is no reference to the mode of carriage; and the expression "ocean bill of lading" is used to refer to what in England is known simply as a bill of lading. As to Indian Railway Receipts, see below, para.18–167, n.71.

described in it have been received by the carrier, or actually shipped; secondly, it is a contractual document: *i.e.* it is evidence of, or contains, a contract of carriage and it provides a mechanism for the transfer of rights arising under that contract to, and for the imposition of liabilities arising under it on, persons who were not original parties to that contract; and thirdly (where certain requirements to be discussed later in this Chapter[96] are satisfied) it is a document of title to the goods both in the common law and in the statutory senses.[97] In this book our main concern is with the third of these functions; but some account must be given of the other two, as they also affect the relations of buyer and seller.

(i) *Types of Bills of Lading*

Person to whom the goods are to be delivered. A bill of lading may indicate to whom the goods are to be delivered at the agreed destination in one of three ways; and the manner in which this is done provides the basis for distinguishing between bearer bills, order bills and straight consigned (or "non-negotiable" bills); the latter resemble, but appear to be distinguishable from, sea waybills.[98] For the purposes of the Carriage of Goods by Sea Act 1992 a sea waybill is "not a bill of lading"[99]; but it does not follow that for other legal purposes the expression "bill of lading" can refer only to bearer and order bills. For example, a contract of sale might require a buyer to pay "against bill of lading" (without qualification); and it would be a question of construction whether this phrase could cover a straight or "non-negotiable" bill or a sea waybill. Similarly, the fact that a sea waybill is "not a bill of lading" for the purposes of the Carriage of Goods by Sea Act 1992 does not preclude the possibility of such a document's being a "bill of lading" for the purposes of section 1(4) of the Factors Act 1889 and hence of the Sale of Goods Act 1979,[1] or for those of the Hague-Visby Rules, which have the force of law by virtue of the Carriage of Goods by Sea Act 1971.[2] **18–013**

Bearer bills. A bearer bill is one that does not name the person to whom the goods are to be delivered: it simply makes them deliverable to bearer,[3] *i.e.* to the person who has possession of the bill. **18–014**

Order bills. An order bill is one which provides for delivery of the goods to be made to the order of a person named in the bill.[4] Such bills are of two kinds. The first provides for delivery of the goods to a named consignee or **18–015**

[96] See especially paras 18–063, 18–067—18–080, below.

[97] Above, para.18–009.

[98] See Carriage of Goods by Sea Act 1992, s.1(3); *The Chitral* [2000] 1 Lloyd's Rep. 529 at p.532; below, para.18–018.

[99] Carriage of Goods by Sea Act 1992, s.1(3).

[1] Sale of Goods Act 1979, s.61(1) (definition of "document of title to goods").

[2] *J.I. MacWilliam Co. Inc. v Mediterranean Shipping Co. SA (The Rafaela S)* [2005] UKHL 11, [2005] 2 A.C. 423; below, para.18–074.

[3] For recognition of this possibility, see Carriage of Goods by Sea Act 1992, ss1(2)(a), 5(2)(b).

[4] For use of the expression "order bill", *cf.* the American Federal Bills of Lading Act 1916, s.3, now superseded by 49 U.S.C. §80103(a)(1)(A), calling such bills "negotiable;" for use of this word in the present context, see below, para.18–084.

to his "order or assigns"[5] (or contains in some part of the bill[6] similar words importing transferability).[7] The second simply makes the goods deliverable "to order or assigns" (or, again, contains similar words of transferability) without naming the consignee. The first kind of order bill is said to be made out to the order of the consignee, for on the face of the bill it is the consignee who is entitled to order the goods to be delivered to someone other than himself; he can do this by transferring the bill[8]; and the process can bc repeated by successive transferees until the bill is "accomplished" by delivery of the goods to the person entitled to the delivery. Where an order bill is of the second kind, no person is on the face of the bill entitled to give such orders and it is the shipper who is entitled to transfer the bill and so to direct the carrier to deliver the goods to the transferee: accordingly, such bills are said to be made out to shipper's order.[9] A bill may contain conflicting indications on the question of its transferability: for example, it may in its "consignee box" simply give the name of the consignee, contain words importing transferability in one of its other provisions and be marked "not transferable" or "not negotiable". It would then be a question of construction which of these indications prevailed. The court would probably attach greater importance to typed or handwritten provisions than to the printed terms of a standard form bill.[10]

18–016 **Methods of transferring bearer and order bills.** Transfer of a bearer bill is effected by delivery; and where an order bill makes the goods deliverable to a named consignee or order it can likewise be transferred by delivery to

[5] The mere use of the word "assigns" does not suffice to make a bill an order bill; *e.g.* where on its face the bill makes it clear that further words in the box designating the consignee are required to give it the characteristics of such a bill: *The Chitral* [2000] 1 Lloyd's Rep. 529 at p.532.

[6] The words importing transferability need not be immediately adjacent to the name of the consignee; the bill may be an order bill if they are contained in some other part of it: *Parsons Corporation v CV Sheepvaartonderneming The Happy Ranger (The Happy Ranger)* [2002] EWCA Civ 694, [2002] 2 All E.R. (Comm.) 24 at [29]; below para.18–019.

[7] The assumption apparently made in *Union Industrielle et Martime v Petrosul International Ltd (The Roseline)* [1987] 1 Lloyd's Rep. 18 at 22, that a bill cannot be an order bill merely because it names a consignee is, with respect, unfounded. The crucial feature of an order bill is that it makes the goods deliverable to a person's order: it is contrasted with a "straight bill" which makes the goods deliverable simply to a named person without further words of transferability: contrast in the United States, 49 U.S.C. §80103(a)(1)(A) with *ibid.* §80103(b)(1) and U.C.C. §7–104(1) with *ibid.* §7–104(2); in the revised 2003 version of U.C.C. Art. 7 (at the time of writing adopted in only eight States) these provisions are re-numbered §7–104(a) and 7–104(b). The bill in *The Roseline* was an "order", rather than a "straight", bill: the goods were "consigned to Order" of the buyer's bank.

[8] For methods of transferring bills, see below, para.18–016.

[9] *Laemthong International Lines Co. Ltd v Artis (The Laemthong Glory) (No.2)* [2005] EWHC 519, [2005] 1 W.L.R. 688 at [6].

[10] On the analogy of *Homburg Houtimport BV v Agrosin Private Ltd (The Starsin)* [2003] UKHL 12, [2004] 1 A.C. 783, where the question was not whether the bill was an order bill, but who were the parties to it.

that consignee:[11] there is no legal need[12] for the shipper in such a case to indorse the bill to the consignee as by its terms the goods are already deliverable to the order of the consignee. But where the person to whom goods are deliverable under an order bill wishes to transfer the bill to another, the transfer must be effected by indorsement[13] by the transferor and delivery of the bill to the transferee. The indorsement may be to the order of the transferee by name or in blank. Where the indorsement is to the named transferee, a subsequent transfer generally requires a further indorsement by the original indorsee. But there is an exception to this requirement where an original indorsement by X was mistakenly made to Y when X intended to make it to Z. In one such case, Y simply returned the bill to X who wrote "void" over the indorsement to Y and then indorsed the bill to Z; and the latter indorsement was said to be effective.[14] Where the bill of lading is indorsed in blank, no further indorsement, but only delivery, is normally required for subsequent transfers.[15] But it has been held in Singapore[16] that this rule is subject to an exception where a bill which has been indorsed in blank and delivered to a transferee, A, is then further transferred to B, not by simple delivery, but by delivery coupled with A's filling in of B's name onto the blank indorsement.[17] Any further transfer of the bill then requires B's indorsement, so that a simple redelivery of the bill to A is not an effective transfer; nor is the transfer made effective by A's writing or stamping the word "cancelled" over his

---

[11] Such delivery entitles the consignee to claim the goods from the carrier, even though he may do so as agent of the transferor, as in *Leigh & Sillavan v Aliakmon Shipping Co. Ltd (The Aliakmon)* [1986] A.C. 785. As the transferee in that case took delivery of the goods as the transferor's agent, property in the goods did not pass to him as a result of the transfer: this seems to be the force of the statement at p.818 that "the bill of lading never was negotiated by the sellers to the buyers." See further below, para.18–065, n.92.

[12] *JI MacWilliam Co. Inc. v Mediterranean Shipping Co. SA (The Rafaela S)* [2003] EWCA Civ 556, [2004] Q.B. 702 at [106] and [2005] UKHL 11, [2005] 2 A.C. 423 at [6]. The decided cases provide examples of indorsements of bills to buyers to whose order the goods were expressed to be deliverable: *e.g. Leigh and Sillavan Ltd v Aliakmon Shipping Co. Ltd (The Aliakmon)* [1986] A.C. 785 (see below, para.18–065 n.92); *East West Corp v DKBS 1912 AF A/S* [2003] EWCA Civ 83, [2003] Q.B. 1509 at [3], [5], [18]. Such cases may reflect a commercial practice to indorse bills to consignees when there is no legal need to do so. *Cf. ibid.* at [16], referring only to "the express consignment . . . to the banks followed by the delivery of such bills to such banks" but not to the shippers' indorsements.

[13] Or, according to *Dick v Lumsden* (1793) Peake 250 and *Meyer v Sharpe* (1813) 5 Taunt. 74 by an undertaking to indorse. As to indorsement, see further below, para.18–215.

[14] *Aegean Sea Traders Corp. v Repsol Petroleo SA (The Aegean Sea)* [1998] 2 Lloyd's Rep. 39 at p.61.

[15] *Keppel Tatlee Bank Ltd v Bandung Shipping Private Ltd* [2003], 1 Lloyd's Rep 619 at [20]; *cf. Primetrade AG v Ythan Ltd (The Ythan)* [2005] EWHC 2399 (Comm), [2006] 1 All E.R. 367 at [19], [80], describing such bills as bearer bills.

[16] *Keppel Tatlee Bank Ltd v Bandung Shipping Private Ltd*, above n.15; the actual decision is concerned with the effect of the dealing with the bills (described in the text above) for the purposes of the Singapore version of the Carriage of Goods by Sea Act 1992; but the statement of principle summarised above seems to be of general application.

[17] A "filled in the name of [B] . . . onto the blank indorsement . . ." (at [9]).

original indorsement to B; to make it effective, an indorsement by B is required. To put the point in another way, the bill loses its quality of being blank indorsed once any transfer of it is made to a named consignee.

An order bill normally retains the quality of transferability until the contract of carriage of which it is evidence, or which it contains, is performed. It is not necessarily performed merely because the goods have arrived at the destination and have there been discharged from the ship. It remains in force, even though the goods have been deposited in a warehouse at the destination, so long as the carrier's lien for freight subsists,[18] or, even where there is no such lien, if the goods have been deposited in the warehouse to the order of the carrier and not to the order of the consignee.[19]

18–017 **Requirement of presentation of bearer or order bill.** Delivery of goods covered by a bearer or by an order bill can be claimed, and must be made, only against presentation of the bill. This rule is more fully discussed in para.18–063 below.

18–018 **Straight (or "non-negotiable") bills and sea waybills.** A straight bill of lading is one which makes the goods deliverable to a named consignee[20] and either contains no words (such as "to order or assigns") importing transferability or contains words (such as "not transferable" or "not negotiable"[21]) negativing transferability. Under a straight bill, the goods are therefore, by its terms, "deliverable to the named consignee and (subject to the shipper's ability to redirect the goods) to no other".[22] The current trend in English legal discussions to refer to such documents as "straight" bills[23] appears to be derived from American legislation which formerly used this terminology[24] but now refers to them as "nonnegotiable".[25] Commercial practice also commonly refers to such documents as "not negotiable"[26] or "non-negotiable"; these expressions are somewhat misleading in the con-

---

[18] *Barber v Meyerstein* (1870) L.R. 4 H.L. 317.

[19] *Barclays Bank Ltd v Commissioners of Customs and Excise* [1963] 1 Lloyd's Rep. 81; *cf. Port Jackson Stevedoring Pty v Salmond and Spraggon (Australia) Pty (The New York Star)* [1981] 1 W.L.R. 138.

[20] *JI MacWilliam Co. Inc. v Mediterranean Shipping Co. SA (The Rafaela S)* [2005] UKHL 11, [2005] 2 A.C. 423 at [1], [59]. For the shipper's right to redirect, see below, para.18–025.

[21] *Mobil Shipping & Transportation Co. v Shell Eastern Petroleum plc (The Mobil Courage)* [1987] 2 Lloyd's Rep. 655 at 659.

[22] *The Rafaela S* [2003] EWCA Civ 556, [2004] Q.B. 702 at [1] per Rix L.J., whose judgment was approved in the House of Lords, above n.20 at [20], [24] and [51].

[23] *e.g.* Law Com. No. 196, Scot. Law Com. No. 130 para.2.50 and Part *IV, passim; The Chitral* [2000] 1 Lloyd's Rep. 529 at p. 532; *(The Rafaela S)* above, nn. 20 and 22 *Parsons Corporation v CV Scheepvaartonderneming "The Happy Ranger" (The Happy Ranger)* [2002] EWCA Civ 694 [2002] 2 All E.R. (Comm.) 24 at [21], [27]; below, para.18–152.

[24] Federal Bills of Lading Act (the Pomerene Act) 1916, s.2.

[25] 49 USC §80103 (b) (1994), replacing the Pomerene Act, above, n.24.

[26] See, for example, the wording of the bill of lading in *The Rafaela S* ("not negotiable unless 'ORDER OF'"); *cf.* in an analogous context, U.C.P. 500 Art. 24 ("non-negotiable sea waybill").

text of English law in that they suggest that order or bearer bills (with which straight bills are contrasted) are negotiable in the legal sense, while in English law they lack the full characteristics of negotiability.[27] The essential respect in which straight bills differ from order and bearer bills is that straight bills are not transferable by indorsement (where necessary[28]) and delivery.[29] Two things follow. First, *the consignee* named in a straight bill cannot, by purporting to transfer it in this way to another person, confer any right to the delivery of the goods on, or impose on the carrier any legal obligation to deliver the goods to, that other person. Secondly, *the shipper* cannot oblige the carrier to deliver the goods to a person other than the named consignee merely by indorsing and delivering the bill to that other person: the shipper may be entitled to redirect the goods[30] by giving notice to the carrier, but he cannot confer rights on a person other than the named consignee by transfer of the bill. Both these points follow from the fact that the carrier's promise in the contract contained in or evidenced by a straight bill is simply one to deliver the goods to the named consignee, as opposed to one to deliver to the order of the person originally entitled to delivery (or, in the case of a bearer bill, to bearer). Two further questions relating to the legal nature of straight bills will be discussed later in this Chapter. These are whether delivery of the goods must, and may only, be made by the carrier against production by the consignee of the straight bill[31]; and whether such a bill is a document of title in the traditional common law sense.[32]

The legal nature of sea waybills[33] in a number of important respects resembles that of straight bills of lading. First, such waybills provide for the goods to be delivered simply to a named (or identified) person and not to such a person "or order or assigns". They are therefore not transferable or "negotiable": this point is often made clear by their being marked "not negotiable". Secondly, for the purposes of the Carriage of Goods by Sea Act 1992, the expression "bill of lading" does not include "a document which is incapable of transfer either by indorsement or, as a bearer bill, by delivery without indorsement".[34] These words exclude both types of documents, so that for the purpose of the 1992 Act straight bills are treated as sea waybills[35]; and since it is part of the definition of a "sea waybill" in that Act that a sea waybill is not a "bill of lading",[36] it follows that for the

---

[27] See below, para.18–084.
[28] Indorsement is obviously not necessary for the transfer of a bearer bill and is not always necessary for the transfer of an order bill: see above, para.18–016.
[29] *The Rafaela S* [2005] UKHL 11 [2005] 2 A.C. 423 at [1] ("not transferable by endorsement"), [58] ("not transferable").
[30] Below, para.18–025.
[31] Below, paras 18–069 to 18–072.
[32] Below, paras 18–074 to 18–078.
[33] See Law Commission Report, above n.23, especially Part V (c); Williams [1979] L.M.C.L.Q. 279; Mustill [1989] L.M.C.L.Q. 47; Debattista, *ibid.* 403.
[34] Carriage of Goods by Sea Act 1992, s.1(2)(a).
[35] *The Chitral* [2000] 1 Lloyd's Rep. 529 at p. 532; *Parsons Corp. v CV Scheepvaartonderneming Happy Ranger (The Happy Ranger)* [2002] EWCA Civ 694, [2002] 2 All E.R. (Comm.) 24 at [30]; *cf. JI MacWilliam Co. Inc. v Mediterranean Shipping Co. SA (The Rafaela S)* [2005] UKHL 11, [2005] 2 A.C. 423 at [22], [50].
[36] Carriage of Goods by Sea Act 1992, s.1(3); below, para.18–155.

purposes of that Act a straight bill is also not a "bill of lading". But it does not follow that non-transferable carriage documents (whether they are straight bills or sea waybills) cannot be bills of lading for any legal purpose whatsoever. The definitions and distinctions just quoted apply only for the purposes of the Acts in which they occur and not for the purposes of other legislation or of rules of common law or where a question arises as to the meaning of the phrase "bill of lading" in a contract. For example, the fact that a document which has the characteristics of a sea waybill (and is therefore not a bill of lading) for the purposes of the Carriage of Goods by Sea Act 1992 does not preclude the possibility of such a document's being regarded as a "bill of lading" for the purposes of section 1(4) of the Factors Act 1889 and hence of the Sale of Goods Act 1979[37]; and there seems to be little doubt that a straight bill would be so regarded. The Carriage of Goods by Sea Act 1971, while not using the expression "sea waybill" contrasts bills of lading with "non-negotiable" receipts containing or evidencing contracts for the carriage of goods by sea.[38] Such documents are not, in the absence of express provisions in them, subject to the Hague-Visby Rules,[39] but a straight bill is a "bill of lading or any similar document of title" within them and so subject to their provisions.[40] As a matter of common law, two further possible distinctions between sea waybills and straight bills will be discussed later in this Chapter. The first of these is whether the carrier must, and may only, deliver the goods against production of a document of either type[41]; the second is whether either type of document is a document of title at common law.[42]

18–019 **Borderline cases.** In simple terms, a bill making the goods deliverable "to X or order" (or "order or assigns") is an order bill while a carriage document making them deliverable simply "to X" is not and so cannot be transferred by indorsement (where necessary[43]) and delivery. But it is also possible for a document to be so worded as to be a straight bill or a sea waybill (and not an order bill) even though it provides for the goods to be delivered to a named consignee "or his assigns." In *The Chitral*[44] a bill of lading made out in these terms also stated "in the printed box for naming the consignee 'if order state notify party'."[45] No such statement was made and it was held that the bill was not an order bill but that it was a "straight consigned" bill "or alternatively in the language of the Carriage of Goods by Sea Act 1992 a 'sea waybill'."[46] It does not follow from this decision that a bill making goods deliverable to a named consignee "or assigns" is necessarily incapable of being an order bill: in *The Chitral* the printed terms

[37] See Sale of Goods Act 1979, s.61(1) (definition of "documents of title to goods").
[38] Carriage of Goods by Sea Act 1971, s.1(6)(b).
[39] *ibid.*; and see below, para.21–105.
[40] *JI MacWilliam Co. Inc. v Mediterranean Shipping Co. SA (The Rafaela S)* [2005] UKHL 11, [2005] 2 A.C. 423, below para.18–067.
[41] Below, paras 18–069 to 18–072.
[42] Below, paras 18–074 to 18–078.
[43] See above, para.18–016.
[44] [2000] 1 Lloyd's Rep. 529.
[45] *ibid.* p.533.
[46] *ibid.* p.532.

of the document which was capable of being used either as a straight or as an order bill[47] expressly imposed a further requirement[48] before it could take effect as a bill of the latter kind. Conversely, a bill which contains no such further requirement and which identifies the consignee simply by name can be an order bill if, in another part of the bill, it provides for the goods to be deliverable to the consignee or to his assigns.[49]

Distinction between straight bills and sea waybills. The dictum from *The Chitral* quoted in paragraph 18–019 above[50] indicates that the expressions "straight consigned bill" and "sea waybill" are for the purposes of the Carriage of Goods by Sea Act 1992 merely two ways of referring to the same type of sea carriage document, namely to one which makes the goods deliverable to a named person, as opposed to one which makes them deliverable to bearer or to the order of the shipper or of a named consignee. For the purposes of the 1992 Act, indeed, neither a straight bill nor a sea waybill is a "bill of lading" at all,[51] but this point does not preclude the possibility that one or both of them may be so regarded for the purposes of other legislation, or for the purposes of rules of common law. For such purposes, it is, moreover, arguable that the law may attach different consequences, or attribute different legal characteristics to the two types of documents: it may, for example, require a person who claims delivery of the goods to produce the document if it is a straight bill but not if it is a sea waybill; and it may in some contexts treat the former but not the latter as (in some sense) a "document of title". These possibilities will be discussed later in this Chapter,[52] and they give rise to the question how, in the case of a bill which is neither an order nor a bearer bill, the distinction between a straight bill and a sea waybill is to be drawn. The central feature which straight bills and sea waybills have in common (and which distinguishes them from bearer and order bills) is that they make the goods deliverable simply to a named consignee (as opposed to bearer or to the order of such a named consignee or of the shipper); and it is perhaps for this reason that the Law Commissions regarded the two as "much the same type of document".[53] Where a carriage document exhibits this feature, it is far from clear what *further* feature it must have (or lack) that could provide the basis for saying that it was (or was not) a straight bill rather than a sea waybill. Clearly, the possible legal *effects* of the distinction[54] cannot provide such a basis since these effects are the consequence rather than the basis of the distinction. It seems that in drawing the distinction the 18–020

---

47 For criticism of the practice of issuing such "dual purpose" documents:, see *The Rafaela S*, above n.40, [2003] EWCA Civ 556, [2004] Q.B. 702 at [146], quoted in para.18–071 below at n.94.

48 *i.e.*, that stated at n.45. *Cf.* the terms of the carriage document in *The Rafaela S*, above, n.40.

49 *Parsons Corporation v C.V. Scheepvaartonderneming "The Happy Ranger" (The Happy Ranger)* [2002] EWCA Civ. 694, [2002] 2 All E.R. (Comm.), 24 at [29].

50 At n.46, above.

51 Law Com. No. 186, Scot. Law Com. 130, paras 2.50, 5.6 and 5.7.

52 Below, paras 18–067 to 18–078.

53 See para.2.50 of the Report referred to in n.51 above.

54 Above, after n.51.

courts will be influenced by two factors. The first is the way in which the document describes itself; for although "the court is not bound by the label",[55] it will at the same time be "slow to reject the description which the document bears", particularly where it is the issuer of the document who seeks to reject the label which he has himself attached to it.[56] The second is the wording and form of a document which makes the goods deliverable simply to a named consignee. It will be a straight bill (rather than a sea waybill) if it "uses the terminology of a bill of lading",[57] "contains the kinds of clauses . . . commonly found in a bill of lading"[58] which would be "entirely meaningless"[59] in the case of a sea waybill and if, following the traditional practice[60] applicable to bills of lading, it is issued in a set of more than one original document.[61] In borderline cases, where some but not all of these conditions were satisfied, these tests could lead to considerable uncertainty with regard to the classification of a particular document; but it has been said that, in most cases, they are unlikely to give rise to difficulties in practice.[62]

18–021 **Shipper's right to redirect goods: order bills.** Even where the bill is made out to the order of a named consignee, the shipper may, nevertheless, be entitled to direct the carrier to deliver the goods to another person. Thus, in *The Lycaon*[63] a seller shipped goods under a bill of lading naming the buyer as consignee; and it was held that the seller was entitled (no property in the goods having passed to the buyer) to divert the goods from the buyer by indorsing the bill of lading by way of pledge to a bank.[64] The shipper's right to redirect the goods to someone other than the originally named consignee may be compared with the "right of disposition" (or "disposal") or the "right to modify the contract of carriage" given to a consignor under the conventions (to be discussed in Chapter 21) which regulate the international carriage of goods by air, road and rail.[65] As a matter of law, the right to redirect the goods is based on the fact that the consignee is not a not prima facie[66] party to the contract of carriage contained in or evidenced by the bill of lading. The right to redirect the

[55] *JI MacWilliam Co. Inc. v Mediterranean Shipping Co. SA (The Rafaela S)* [2005] UKHL 11, [2005] 2 A.C. 423 at [5], [55]; *cf.* UCP 500, Arts 23(a), 24(a) ("however named").
[56] *The Rafaela S*, above n.56, at [5]; *cf.* at [58].
[57] *ibid*.
[58] *ibid*.
[59] *ibid*., at [5].
[60] See para.18–090, below.
[61] *The Rafaela S*, above n.56 at [5]; see also the judgment of Rix LJ in the court below [2003] EWCA Civ 556, [2004] Q.B. 702 at [138]; this judgement was expressly approved in the House of Lords, above n.56 at [20], [24] and [51].
[62] See *The Rafaela S*, above n.56, at [46] ("No trader, insurer or banker would assimilate the two").
[63] *Elder Dempster Lines v Zaki Ishag (The Lycaon)* [1983] 2 Lloyd's Rep. 548.
[64] *ibid*., at pp.550, 555.
[65] Below, paras 21–055, 21–062, 21–069.
[66] *i.e.*, unless the shipper has acted as the consignee's agent in making the contract of carriage: see below paras 19–091, 20–003, 20–008, 20–059—20–067; *East West Corp. v DKBS 1912 AF A/S* [2003] EWCA Civ 83, [2003] Q.B. 1509 at [34].

goods may, however, be limited at common law by the factors discussed in paragraphs 18–022 and 18–023 below; and it is also necessary to discuss the impact on this right of the Contracts (Rights of Third Parties) Act 1999.

Shipper's right to redirect limited by terms of contract of carriage. In *The Lycaon*, it was a matter of indifference to the carrier whether the goods were to be delivered to the buyer or to the pledgee; so that the contract of carriage could readily be construed as one by which the carier undertook to deliver the goods to the named consignee (the buyer) or as the shipper might direct. The question arises whether this construction would be adopted even where the carrier did have an interest in the delivery of the goods to the consignee named in the bill of lading. This was the position in *Mitchell v Ede*,[67] where goods were shipped on the defendant's ship *Thisbe* by one Mackenzie, who was indebted both to the defendant and to the claimant. The bill of lading, signed by the master, named the defendant as consignee (but not as carrier). Two days after the bill of lading had been issued, Mackenzie endorsed it to the claimant, and it was held that the claimant, not the defendant, was entitled to the goods. Lord Denman regarded it as a question of construction whether Mackenzie was entitled to divert the goods from the consignee originally named in the bill. He said: "As between the owner or shipper of the goods and the captain it [the bill of lading] fixes and determines the duty of the latter as to the person to whom it is (*at that time*) the pleasure of the former that the goods should be delivered. But there is nothing final or irrevocable in its nature. The owner of the goods may change his purpose, at any rate before the delivery of the goods themselves or of the bill of lading to the party named in it, and may order the delivery to be to some other person, to B instead of to A."[68] Two special features of the case should be noted. First, it appears from the opening sentence of the passage just quoted that Lord Denman regarded the bill of lading as containing, or evidencing, a contract between Mackenzie and *the captain*, who had himself no direct interest in the delivery of the goods to the consignee named in the bill. Secondly, he regarded the *Thisbe* as simply a general ship,[69] and not as one sent out by the defendant for the purpose of taking delivery of the goods in discharge of Mackenzie's debt to the defendant. If (as would now be usual) the contract contained in or evidenced by the bill of lading were made with *the carrier*, and if the carrier could show that he had an interest in delivery of the goods to the consignee named in the bill, then it is submitted that the bill should not be construed so as to entitle the shipper unilaterally to divert the goods from the named consignee to another person. But normally the carrier would have no such interest, so that the construction adopted in *The Lycaon*[70] would be applied. 18–022

---

[67] (1840) 11 Ad. & El. 888.

[68] *ibid.*, at p.903, applied in *The Lycaon*, above, n.63 at p.555. The rule is a special application of the general principle that a contract by which A promises B to render some performance to C may, on its true construction, be one to perform in favour of C *or as B may direct*: see *Tradigrain SA v King Diamond Mines Ltd (The Spiros C)* [2000] 2 Lloyd's Rep. 319 at p.331, where the principle is stated in relation to a promise by A to B to pay money to C.

[69] (1840) 11 Ad. & El. 888 at p.905.

[70] Above, n.63.

The carriage operation may be governed by more than one contract: *e.g.* where A's ship is chartered by B and a bill of lading covering goods in that ship is issued or transferred to C so as to constitute a contract between A and C.[71] The right of either B or C to redirect the goods can then be limited by the terms of either contract.[72]

18–023 **Loss of shipper's right to redirect by transfer of rights to consignee.** In *Mitchell v Ede* the shipper's power to substitute one consignee for another was said to be exercisable "at any rate before the delivery of the goods themselves or of the bill of lading to the party named in it"[73] (*i.e.* as consignee). Redirecting the goods after their delivery to the named consignee is scarcely a practical possibility; and loss of shipper's right to redirect the goods after delivery of the bill of lading was presumably based on the theory that, as a consequence of such delivery, the consignee obtained constructive possession of the goods,[74] and could obtain the property in them if the transfer of the bill was made with that intention.[75] The shipper would, it is submitted, also lose his right to redirect the goods once his rights under the contract of carriage had been transferred to the consignee, for once this had happened the whole basis of the right to redirect the goods (as explained in paragraph 18–022 above) would have disappeared. This possibility was not considered in *Mitchell v Ede*, which was decided before the Bills of Lading Act 1855 had first provided for the transfer of rights under the contract of carriage from a shipper to a consignee or transferee. Under section 1 of the 1855 Act, one situation in which such a transfer of contractual rights to a consignee named in the bill of lading could take place was that in which property in the goods had passed to the consignee "upon or by reason of such consignment." This could happen before delivery of the bill of lading to the consignee[76]; and where the shipper's rights under the contract had in this way been transferred to the consignee, it is submitted that the shipper could no longer substitute another consignee for the one named in the bill of lading, even if the goods or the bill had not yet been delivered to the named consignee, for in such a case the shipper would no longer have had any rights under the contract of carriage.[77] The transfer of contractual rights is now governed by the Carriage of Goods by Sea Act 1992,[78] under which such a transfer no longer takes place merely because the property in the goods has been passed to the consignee: where he relies on a bill of lading

[71] Below, paras 18–051 *et seq.*, 18–127.
[72] *Merit Shipping Co. Inc. v TK Boesen A/S (The Goodpal)* [2000] 1 Lloyd's Rep. 639 at p.643.
[73] (1840) 11 Ad. & El. 888 at p.903.
[74] Above, para.18–007.
[75] *ibid*.
[76] *e.g.* if the goods had been paid for or credit has been given: see *Enichem Anic SpA v Ampelos Shipping Co. Ltd (The Delfini)* [1990] 1 Lloyd's Rep. 252; *Anonima Petroli Italiana SpA v Marlucidex Armadora SA (The Filiatra Legacy)* [1991] 2 Lloyd's Rep. 337.
[77] *cf. Guarantee Trust of New York v Van den Berghs* (1925) 22 Ll. L. Rep. 447 at p.455.
[78] Below, para.18–102 *et seq.*

as the mechanism of transfer, he must be the lawful holder of the bill[79] and thus have acquired possession of it.[80] Goods may, however, be shipped under a bill of lading to a named consignee and the consignee may acquire rights under the contract of carriage otherwise than by becoming the lawful holder of the bill: *e.g.* by being the person to whom delivery is to be made in accordance with the terms of a ship's delivery order.[81] In such a case, it is submitted that the shipper, no longer having any contractual rights under the contract of carriage in relation to the goods covered by the order,[82] would not be entitled to divert the goods away from the originally named consignee.

Contracts (Rights of Third Parties) Act 1999. Under the rules stated in paragraphs 18–021 to 18–023 above, a shipper of goods on bill of lading terms may, even though the bill makes the goods deliverable to a named consignee, nevertheless be entitled to direct the carrier to deliver those goods to another person. Whether he is in fact so entitled depends on the construction of the bill, which may be a contract to deliver the goods *either* to the order of the named consignee *or* (more usually) to the order of that named consignee or to *such other person as the shipper may direct*; and even if the bill on its true construction bears the latter meaning a point may come when the shipper can no longer redirect the goods. 18–024

It is submitted that there are two reasons why these rules are not affected by the Contracts (Rights of Third Parties) Act 1999. First, where the contract of carriage is contained in or evidenced by a bill of lading, the case will fall within the subsection 6(5) exception[83] to that Act, by which rights under such a contract cannot be acquired by a third party by virtue of the Act. Secondly, even where the subsection 6(5) exception does not apply, *e.g.* because the contract of carriage is contained in a charterparty (and so not within the exception[84]), the shipper would not be precluded from redirecting the goods by the provision of section 2 of the 1999 Act which prevents the contracting parties from extinguishing or altering the third party's rights by varying the contract by subsequent agreement. If the contract on its true construction is one to deliver to A or as the shipper may direct, it is not *varied* by the shipper's directing the carrier to deliver the goods to B: such delivery is merely performance of the contract in accordance with its terms. Moreover a contract of this kind probably does not confer any rights on A under section 1 of the 1999 Act, for the power to divert the goods to another person would indicate that the parties did not intend the term providing for delivery of the goods to be enforceable by A,[85] or that any right to delivery which he might at one time have had was "subject to"[86] the shipper's power to order delivery to be made to another person.

---

[79] Carriage of Goods by Sea Act 1992, s.2(1)(a).
[80] *ibid.*, s.5(2).
[81] *ibid.*, s.2(1)(c).
[82] *ibid.*, s.2(5).
[83] See above, para.18–005, sub-paragraph (f).
[84] See 1999 Act. s.6(6) and (7).
[85] *ibid.*, s.1(2).
[86] *ibid.*, s.1(4).

18–025 **Right to redirect goods: straight bills and sea waybills.** The reasoning of *The Lycaon*[87] and *Mitchell v Ede*[88] can apply to a straight bill or sea waybill in the sense that the shipper may, before the carrier has delivered the goods to the named consignee, direct the carrier to deliver them to some other person.[89] Prima facie the carrier would be bound to give effect to such an order since normally the contract would be construed as one to deliver to the named consignee or to such other person as the shipper might direct.[90]

There are, however, two significant differences between the right to redirect goods under a document of the present kind and the similar right which exists where goods are shipped under an order bill. First, it follows from the reasoning in paragraph 18–018 above that, in the case of a straight bill, a sea waybill or a similar document, the shipper cannot exercise the right to redirect by merely indorsing the document and delivering it to the newly designated consignee: he must notify the carrier that delivery is to be made to that consignee, rather than to the one originally specified in the document. Secondly, the rule by which the shipper's right to redirect is lost under an order bill on the consignee's acquiring rights under the contract of carriage[91] could not now be applied to sea waybills (which here include straight bills[92]) without making the right to redirect nugatory, for under the Carriage of Goods by Sea Act 1992 rights under the contract of carriage can be acquired by the consignee as soon as the contract is made.[93] The Act therefore expressly preserves the shipper's right to redirect the goods where the contract is on its true construction one to deliver the goods to the consignee named in the sea waybill or as the shipper may direct.[94]

18–026 **Contracts (Rights of Third Parties) Act 1999.** A contract contained in or evidenced by a sea waybill (as defined by the Carriage of Goods by Sea Act 1992) is a "contract for the carriage of goods by sea" within the Contracts (Rights of Third Parties) Act 1999.[95] The reasoning of paragraph 18–124 above therefore applies to such a contract no less than to one contained in or evidenced by a bill of lading. It follows from that reasoning that the consignee named in a sea waybill acquires no rights under the 1999 Act, so that the shipper's right to redirect goods shipped under a sea waybill is not affected by that Act.

18–027 **"Shipped" and "received" bills.** A "shipped" bill of lading is one which states that goods have been shipped, *i.e.* put on board the carrying ship. Usually it will also state the date of shipment. It may be a valid document

[87] [1983] 2 Lloyd's Rep. 548.
[88] (1840) 11 Ad. & El. 888.
[89] *cf.* Carriage of Goods by Sea Act 1992, ss.1(3)(b), and 5(3).
[90] *cf.* above, para.18–022; for the possibility of displacing the prima facie construction stated in the text above, see *Carver on Bills of Lading*, 2nd ed. (2005) para.1–019.
[91] Above, para.18–023.
[92] See above, para. 18–018.
[93] s.2(1)(b); below, para.18–153.
[94] s.2(5) below, paras 18–113, 18–160; *East West Corp. v DKBS 1912* [2002] 1 All E.R. (Comm.) 676 at [23], affirmed, without reference to this point, [2003] EWCA Civ 83, [2003] Q.B. 1509.
[95] Contracts (Rights of Third Parties) Act 1999, s.6(6).

even though the quantity of goods shipped was originally left blank and is later correctly inserted by the shipper.[96] A bill of lading which contains a false statement as to the date of shipment is defective, in the sense that the buyer can reject it,[97] but it is not, merely on account of that falsity, an utter nullity.[98]

The expression "received bill of lading" is capable of referring to documents of several kinds. Most obviously, it refers to a document which states that the goods specified in it have been received by the carrier for shipment on a named ship; or that they have been so received and are intended to be shipped on that ship. Another type of received bill also states that the goods have been received by the carrier, but differs from the type just described in that it indicates that the goods have been so received for shipment *either* on a named ship or on some other, unspecified vessel.[99] Yet another kind of document is one which indicates that the goods are in the possession, not of the carrier, but of another person (*e.g.* a warehouseman), that they are held by that person "at the disposal of" the carrier or of his agent, and that they are intended to be shipped on a named ship. In such a case, it is hard to see that there has been any *receipt* of the goods by the carrier at all, and the view[1] that such a document is a received bill of lading is, with respect, open to question. The answer to this question was of little importance at common law; but it now determines whether the document is one to which the provisions of the Carriage of Goods by Sea Act 1992 apply, so far as they relate to bills of lading. References in the Act to a bill of lading "include references to a received for shipment bill of lading"[2]; but it is left to the courts to determine what is meant, in this definition, by the phrase "received for shipment". Prima facie these words would not seem to cover a document which merely indicated that goods were intended to be shipped by the carrier issuing the document, without also indicating their receipt by that carrier.

Under the 1992 Act, a received bill of lading can be used to transfer contractual rights to a lawful holder of it[3]; contractual liabilities under it can be imposed on such a transferee of it[4]; and it can give rise to conclusive evidence, in favour of the lawful holder of the bill, of the receipt of goods for shipment.[5] But from the point of view of a transferee of a bill of lading (such as a buyer of the goods covered by it) a "received" bill remains in

---

[96] *Cowdenbeath Coal Co. Ltd v Clydesdale Bank Ltd* (1895) 22 R. (Ct. of Sess.) 682.
[97] Below, para.19–035.
[98] *ibid.* and see below, para.18–028. The statement in *Motis Exports Ltd v Dampskibsselskapet AF 1912* [2000] 1 Lloyd's Rep. 211 at p. 216 that a forged bill of lading "is in the eyes of the law an utter nullity" refers to the different type of forgery: *i.e.*, to the case in which the goods stated in the bill to have been shipped were never shipped at all.
[99] As in *Diamond Alkali Export Corp. v Fl. Bourgeois* [1921] 3 K.B. 443; *cf. The Marlborough Hill* [1921] 1 A.C. 444; see below, para.18–079 for the form of the bills of lading in these two cases.
[1] Expressed in *Ishag v Allied Bank International* [1981] 1 Lloyd's Rep. 92, as to which see below, para.18–079.
[2] s.1(2)(b).
[3] s.2.
[4] s.3.
[5] s.4.

several respects a less satisfactory document than a "shipped" bill. It provides him with no evidence of the fact of actual shipment; it may fail to give him the "continuous documentary cover" to which he is entitled under a c.i.f. contract[6]; and it may leave him in ignorance of the date of actual shipment.[7] It is also doubtful whether a "received" bill is a document of title in the traditional common law sense.[8] If, after a "received" bill has been issued, the goods are shipped, this fact may be noted by, or on behalf of, the carrier on the bill, which can then become a shipped bill with effect from the date of shipment specified in the notation.[9]

(ii) *Bill of Lading as a Receipt*

18–028 **Bill of lading as evidence of facts stated in it.** A bill of lading is evidence of the facts stated in it, so that a shipped bill is evidence that the goods described in it have been shipped,[10] and of the date of shipment as stated in the bill.[11] A received bill which states that the goods have been received by the carrier is similarly evidence of that fact. A statement in the bill that the goods were shipped, or received, in apparent good order and condition is likewise evidence of the external condition of the goods at the time of shipment or receipt.[12] Similar effect is given to a statement as to the quantity, weight or number of the goods.[13] Such evidentiary effect of the bill may be negatived by its express terms: *e.g.* by a "weight, number and quantity unknown" clause.[14] At common law, a bill of lading is only prima facie evidence of these matters.[15] Thus a carrier who fails to deliver the quantity of goods stated in the bill of lading to have been shipped will not be liable to the shipper, if he can prove that only the smaller quantity which he has delivered was actually received or shipped; and similarly he will not be liable in respect of damage to goods stated in the bill to have been shipped in good condition, if he can prove that they had in fact been already damaged at the time of shipment. This rule, however, normally

---

[6] *Yelo v S M Machado Ltd* [1952] 1 Lloyd's Rep. 183 at 192; below, para.19–027.
[7] *cf.* below, para.18–079 and 18–267.
[8] Below, para.18–279, *i.e.*, in the sense described in para.18–007 above.
[9] Carriage of Goods by Sea Act 1971, Sch., Art. III, r.7; *cf.* U.C.P., 500, Arts 23(a)(ii), 24(a)(ii), 25(iv); *Westpac Banking Corp. v South Carolina National Bank* [1986] 1 Lloyd's Rep. 311; *semble*, the position is the same at common law.
[10] *Smith v Bedouin Steam Navigation Co.* [1896] A.C. 70.
[11] *J Aron & Co. (Inc.) v Comptoir Wegimont* [1921] 3 K.B. 435 at p.437.
[12] *The Peter der Grosse* (1875) 1 P.D. 414; Carriage of Goods by Sea Act 1971, Sch., Art. III, rr. 3(c) and 4. For the standard of the carrier's duty with respect to the accuracy of such statements, see *The David Agmashenebeli* [2002] EWHC 104 (Comm.), [2002] 2 All E.R. (Comm.) 806 and *Carver on Bills of Lading*, 2nd ed. (2005) paras 2–005, 9–163.
[13] Carriage of Goods by Sea Act 1971, Sch., Art. III, rr. 3(b) and 4.
[14] For the construction of such provisions in a bill of lading, see for example *New Chinese Antimony Co. Ltd v Ocean SS Co. Ltd* [1917] 2 K.B. 644; *Canadian Dominion Sugar Ltd v Canadian National (West Indies) Steamships Ltd* [1947] A.C. 46; *Carver on Bills of Lading* (2nd ed., 2005), paras 2–002 to 2–004.
[15] *J Aron & Co. (Inc.) v Comptoir Wegimont* [1921] 3 K.B. 435 at p.437, rejecting the earlier view stated in *Bowes v Shand* (1877) 2 App.Cas. 455 at p.481 that a statement in the bill of lading as to the date of shipment was "conclusive" evidence.

applies only between carrier and shipper. As against an indorsee of the bill, the carrier may be estopped from denying the truth of statements in it to the effect (for example) that the goods were shipped in apparent good order and condition,[16] or that they were shipped under deck[17] or that they were shipped on the date of shipment given in the bill of lading.[18]

Statements made without authority: common law. The carrier will be liable on the basis of such an estoppel only if the statement was made either by him or by some person with his authority. It has been held that the master of a ship has no actual or apparent authority to make a statement as to the commercial quality[19] (as opposed to the external condition[20]) of the goods, so that if such a statement is shown to be false the carrier is not liable either in contract[21] to the original shipper or by way of estoppel to an indorsee of the bill. This is a reasonable position since carriers who carry a wide range of goods cannot be expected to attest to the commercial quality of any particular consignment. But in *Grant v Norway*[22] it was further held that the master of a ship had no authority to sign a shipped bill of lading for goods which had not been put on board and that the carrier was therefore not liable to an indorsee of a bill of lading, signed by the master, stating goods to have been shipped when in fact no such shipment had been made. This result was open to the criticism that statements as to the fact of shipment, or as to the quantity of goods shipped, are precisely of the kind to which the carrier can be expected to attest, so that it is reasonable for a transferee to rely on them. The rule was also out of keeping with subsequently developed views of the nature of vicarious liability.[23] These 18–029

---

[16] *Compania Naviera Vasconzada v Churchill & Sim* [1906] 1 K.B. 237; *Silver v Ocean SS Co.* [1930] 1 K.B. 416; *Oceanfocus Shipping Ltd v Hyundai Merchant Marine Co. Ltd (The Hawk)* [1999] 1 Lloyd's Rep. 176 at p.185.

[17] *The Nea Tyhi* [1982] 1 Lloyd's Rep. 606 (disapproved on another point, in *Leigh & Sillavan Ltd v Aliakmon Shipping Co. Ltd (The Aliakmon)* [1986] A.C. 785).

[18] *The Saudi Crown* [1986] 1 Lloyd's Rep. 261; for the carrier's liability for his agent's fraudulent statement as to the date of shipment, see also *Standard Chartered Bank v Pakistan National Shipping Corp.* [1995] 2 Lloyd's Rep. 365; *Standard Chartered Bank v Pakistan National Shipping Corp. (No. 2)* [2000] 1 Lloyd's Rep. 218, varied, but not on the issue of the *carrier's* liability, [2002] UKHL 43, [2003] 1 A.C. 959 (see below para.18–046) for the measure of damages in this case, see *Standard Chartered Bank v Pakistan National Shipping Corp. (No. 3)* [2001] EWCA Civ. 55; [2001] 1 All E.R. (Comm.) 822; for rejection of the defence of contributory negligence, see *Standard Chartered Bank v Pakistan National Shipping Co. (No. 4)* [2001] Q.B. 617. In the House of Lords, the carrier's appeal on this aspect of the case was withdrawn: [2002] UKHL 43, [2003] 1 A.C. 959, at [5], [7].

[19] *Cox, Patterson & Co. v Bruce & Co.* (1886) 18 Q.B.D. 147.

[20] See *Compania Naviera Vasconzada v Churchill & Sim* [1906] 1 K.B. 237; *Silver v Ocean SS Co.* [1930] 1 K.B. 416.

[21] Below, para.18–030 at n.31.

[22] (1851) 10 C.B. 665; *Cf. A/S Iverans Rederei v KG MS Holstencruiser Seeschiffahrtsgesellschaft mbH & Co. (The Holstencruiser)* [1992] 2 Lloyd's Rep. 378 at p.385.

[23] See generally Reynolds, 83 L.Q.R. 189 (1967); *cf. The Nea Tyhi* [1982] 1 Lloyd's Rep. 606 at p.610 (as to which see below n.26); *Homburg Houtimport BV v Agrosin Private Ltd (The Starsin)* [2000] 1 Lloyd's Rep. 85 at p.97 (as to which see below n.26); *Alimport v Soubert Shipping Co. Ltd* [2000] 2 Lloyd's Rep. 447 at p.448; and

criticisms have led to some restrictions of the scope of the rule at common law: it has, for example, been held not to apply to false statements as to the date of shipment,[24] or to statements that goods had been shipped under deck, when they had actually been shipped on deck[25] or to the issue of a clean bill against mate's receipts which are claused.[26] Further attempts to reverse or modify the rule by legislation will be discussed in paragraphs 18–032 to 18–044 below.

18–030 **Effects of false statement as to shipment or receipt between shipper and carrier.** The difficulties arising from *Grant v Norway*[27] were exacerbated by a number of further rules which determined the effects of false statements as to the fact of shipment or receipt between putative shipper and carrier; it will be convenient to refer to these parties as shipper and carrier even though these expressions are not entirely accurate where nothing is shipped or carried.

There are three reasons why false statements as to the fact of shipment do not make the carrier liable to the shipper in contract. First, the principle that the master has no authority to issue a bill of lading in respect of unshipped goods can apply between shipper and carrier no less than between indorsee and carrier.[28] Secondly, the mere issue of a bill of lading (even if signed by the carrier personally or with his express authority) does not give rise to a contract of carriage. In the words of Devlin J. in *Heskell v Continental Express Ltd* "in many cases. . . . no [such] contract is concluded until the goods are loaded or accepted for loading",[29] though it is now increasingly common for shipper and carrier to enter into "an antecedent contract in the terms of the booking note."[30] And thirdly, it has been said that "the words shipped in apparent order and condition are not words of contract in the sense of a promise" but are merely "an affirmation of fact."[31] This has been said also to be the sole effect of a statement as to the

the discussion of the scope of vicarious liability in *Lister v Hesley Hall Ltd* [2001] UKHL 22; [2001] A.C. 215.

[24] *The Saudi Crown* [1986] 1 Lloyd's Rep. 261. No question of lack of authority arose in the *Standard Chartered Bank* cases cited in n.18 above.

[25] *The Nea Tyhi* [1982] 1 Lloyd's Rep. 604 (disapproved on another point in *Leigh & Sillavan Ltd v Aliakmon Shipping Co. Ltd* [1986] A.C. 785).

[26] *Homburg Houtimport BV v Agrosin Private Ltd (The Starsin)* [2000] 1 Lloyd's Rep. 85 at p.96 per Colman J., whose decision was eventually affirmed without reference to the present point: [2003] UKHL 12, [2004] 1 A.C. 715, below paras 18–127, 18–181. *Oceanfocus Shipping Ltd v Hyundai Merchant Marine Co. Ltd (The Hawk)* [1999] 1 Lloyd's Rep. 176 at pp.187–188; an apparently contrary dictum in *Sunrise Maritime Inc. v Uvisco Ltd (The Hector)* [1998] 2 Lloyd's Rep. 287 at p.298 was doubted in *Alimport v Soubert Shipping Co. Ltd* [2000] 2 Lloyd's Rep. 447 at p.448, but may perhaps be distinguished on the ground that it refers, not to the apparent authority of the *master* to sign on behalf of the ship owner, but to a charterer's authority so to sign.

[27] (1851) 10 C.B. 665.

[28] *Leduc v Ward* (1888) 20 Q.B.D. 475 at p.479.

[29] [1950] 1 All E.R. 1033 at p.1037.

[30] *Gulf Steel Co. Ltd v Al Khalifa Shipping Co. (The Anwar al Sabar)* [1980] 2 Lloyd's Rep. 261 at p.263; and see below, para.18–047.

[31] *Compania Naviera Vasconzada v Churchill & Sim* [1906] 1 K.B. 237 at p.247; *Silver v Ocean SS Co.* [1930] 1 K.B. 416 at p.439; *The Hawk*, above n.26, [1999] 1 Lloyd's Rep. 176 at p.185. *Semble*, this reasoning would not bar the shipper's claim where a contract could be established *aliunde* (*e.g.* in the way indicated at n.30, above).

quantity of goods shipped[32]; and the same principle seems to apply to a statement as to the fact of shipment where no goods at all were shipped.

It is more problematical whether such a statement, if expressly authorised or made personally by the carrier, would make the carrier liable to the shipper by estoppel. A number of difficulties would face a shipper trying to substantiate such a claim. First, he might suffer no prejudice where the goods, instead of being shipped, simply remained at the port of shipment and were there restored to him. Secondly, even if he did suffer prejudice,[33] he might be driven, in trying to found a claim based on estoppel, to take mutually contradictory positions. This difficulty arose in *Heskell's*[34] case, where a seller on what were substantially c.i.f. terms obtained a bill of lading which was later rejected by his buyer because no goods had ever been shipped. The seller's claim against the carrier was not one for failing to deliver the goods at the agreed destination (since the seller was not responsible for such delivery)[35]; it was one for failing to ship them and so to make a contract of carriage. The claim failed because it required the seller to allege simultaneously that the goods had been shipped (so as to give rise to the contract of carriage) and that they had not been shipped (so as to establish a breach of that contract). The situation would be different where the shipper was claiming damages for non-delivery at the destination (since the positions that the goods had been *shipped* but that they had not been *delivered* are not mutually inconsistent); but such a claim would face the difficulty that an estoppel by representation does not give rise to a cause of action.[36] To overcome this difficulty, the shipper would have to show that a contract had been established otherwise than by shipment: *e.g.*, by an antecedent reservation of space. If this could be established, the shipper might have a claim based on estoppel at common law, even where he was not a person who could rely on the statutory estoppel now contained in section 4 of the Carriage of Goods by Sea Act 1992.[37]

A third question is whether the carrier may be liable in tort in respect of a false statement made in a bill of lading, signed by the master or by some other agent of his, as to the fact of shipment. It may be that the signer would be so liable,[38] but the carrier would not be vicariously liable for the agent's tort since such liability arises only if the person signing the bill has done so within the scope of his authority,[39] and under the rule in *Grant v Norway* the signer has no authority to sign a bill of lading in respect of goods which have not been shipped.

---

[32] *V/O Rasnoimport v Guthrie & Co.* [1966] 1 Lloyd's Rep. 1 at p.7.

[33] *e.g.* by reason of incurring liability to his buyer in consequence of the falsity of the statement in the bill: this was the position in *Heskell's* case, above, n.29.

[34] Above, n.29.

[35] Below, paras 19–002, 19–072.

[36] *Low v Bouverie* [1891] 3 Ch. 82; *The Anemone* [1987] 1 Lloyd's Rep. 546 at p.557. For a possible qualification of this principle, see *Azov Shipping Co. v Baltic Shipping Co.* [1999] 2 Lloyd's Rep. 159 at pp.175–176, where, however, no reference was made to *Low v Bouverie*, above. Similar difficulty arises from more tentative suggestions in *Thornton Springer v NEM Insurance Ltd* [2000] 2 All E.R. 489 at p.519 (where the type of estoppel under discussion was estoppel by convention); and see *Chitty on Contracts*, 29th ed. (2004), para.3–098.

[37] See below, paras 18–036, 18–043.

[38] Below, para.18–045.

[39] *Armagas v Mundogas SA (The Ocean Frost)* [1986] A.C. 717 at p.781.

18–031 **False statements as to quantity.** At common law, the rule in *Grant v Norway*[40] applies not only in cases of total non-shipment, but also where the bill of lading represents a greater quantity of goods to have been shipped than has in fact been shipped. The falsity of the statement will not, in this type of case, prevent the formation of a contract of carriage since for this purpose shipment of *some* goods suffices. But the false statement as to quantity will not make the carrier liable in contract since the words of quantity lack contractual force,[41] while the rule in *Grant v Norway* will prevent the operation of a common law estoppel against the carrier in respect of statements made by the master. Such an estoppel could, however, operate against the carrier in respect of statements made with his express authority or by him personally: the cause of action would not be based on the estoppel but on the contract which had arisen from part shipment.[42] It seems that the common law estoppel could be available not only to an indorsee but also to the shipper[43]: in the latter respect, its scope could again be wider than that of section 4 of the Carriage of Goods by Sea Act 1992.[44]

18–032 **Modifications and mitigation of the common law rule.** A number of attempts have been made both by legislation and at common law, to alleviate the hardship which might be caused by the rule in *Grant v Norway*[45] to the transferee of a bill of lading. In English law[46] these have, at least until recently, had only a limited measure of success; the reason for this fact appears to be that they have attacked the *result* in *Grant v Norway*, rather than the *reasoning* on which it was based. They have not, in other words, sought to alter the rule that the master (or other agent of the carrier) has no authority to sign a bill of lading in respect of goods not on board. Recent legislation has accepted that position but has sought nevertheless to make the *carrier* liable for the false statement in spite of the fact that the bill was signed without his authority, while the common law has in certain circumstances imposed liability on the *signer* precisely because he had no authority to sign the bill.

18–033 **Bills of Lading Act 1855, section 3.** Legislative attempts to modify the rule began with section 3 of the Bills of Lading Act 1855 by which a bill of lading representing goods to have been shipped on board a vessel was in

---

40 (1851) 10 C.B. 665, above, para.18–029.

41 *V/O Rasnoimport v Guthrie & Co. Ltd* [1966] 1 Lloyd's Rep. 1 at p.7; the reason for this rule is the same as that given in para.18–030 above, at n.31.

42 *Rasnoimport*, case, above, at p.66.

43 The objection that he would have to take mutually inconsistent positions (*Heskell's* case [1950] 1 All E.R. 1033 at p.1044, above, para.18–030) would not apply as the contract would be established by part shipment.

44 Below, para.18–042.

45 (1851) 10 C.B. 665; above, para.18–029.

46 In the United States, the rule in *Grant v Norway*, above n.40, was followed by the Supreme Court in *Friedlander v Texas, etc. R Co.* 130 U.S. 416 at p.424 (1889) and *Missouri & Pacific R Co. v McFadden* 154 U.S. 155 at pp. 161, 163 (1893); but the rule is generally regarded as having been reversed by the Federal Bills of Lading Act 1916 (the Pomerene Act), s.2, now replaced by 49 U.S.C. §80113(a) (1994), though only in respect of "order" (now called "nonnegotiable") bills: *Chesapeake & OR Co. v State National Bank of Maysville* 133 S.W. 2d 511 (1939).

the hands of a consignee or indorsee for valuable consideration "conclusive evidence of such shipment as against the master or other person signing the same, notwithstanding that such goods or some part thereof may not have been so shipped". Detailed discussion of this now repealed[47] section is no longer necessary; but a better understanding of the provisions which have replaced it will be promoted by a brief description of its three main defects. The first of these was that the section applied only against the person who had signed the bill, so that, where the master or some other agent had on behalf of the carrier signed a bill falsely stating goods to have been shipped, that statement was not conclusive evidence *against the carrier*.[48] It had this effect only where the form of the signature was such as to amount to the personal signature of the carrier himself.[49] Secondly, where the signature was not that of the carrier himself, the fact that the bill was conclusive evidence of the fact of shipment against the signer was of little avail to the consignee or indorsee since any contractual or bailment relationship which would have arisen, if the facts of which the bill was conclusive evidence had been true, would have been with the *carrier*. Hence, where the bill of lading was signed by the *master*, the fact that *he* was precluded by section 3 from denying the fact of shipment would not of itself give rise to any cause of action against him. Thirdly, section 3 referred only to shipped bills of lading and so did not extend to received bills.[50]

Hague-Visby Rules, Article III.4. The second legislative provision which may affect the rule in *Grant v Norway*[51] applies where the false statement is contained in a bill of lading which is governed by the Hague-Visby Rules.[52] This provision, unlike section 3 of the Bills of Lading Act 1855, is of more than merely historical interest; for, while the 1855 Act has been repealed by the Carriage of Goods by Sea Act 1992, section 5(5) of that Act expressly states that its preceding provisions are to have effect without prejudice to the application of the Hague-Visby Rules. The effect of section 5(5) will be considered in paragraph 18–044 below. 18–034

Where a contract of carriage is governed by the Hague-Visby Rules, Article III.3 of those Rules requires the carrier, on demand of the shipper, to issue to the shipper a bill of lading. The bill must (among other things) show (a) the leading marks necessary for the identification of the goods, as furnished by the shipper; (b) the number of packages or the quantity or weight, as furnished by the shipper; and (c) the apparent order and condition of the goods. The first sentence of Article III.4 then provides that "such bill of lading shall be prima facie evidence of the receipt by the carrier of the goods therein described in accordance with paragraph 3(a),

---

47 Carriage of Goods by Sea Act 1992, s.6(2).
48 *e.g. V/O Rasnoimport v Guthrie & Co. Ltd* [1966] 1 Lloyd's Rep. 1.
49 See *Heskell v Continental Express Ltd* [1950] 1 All E.R. 1033 at p.1044 ("on a bill signed by [the shipowner]"); *cf. Parsons v New Zealand Shipping Co.* [1901] 1 K.B. 548 at pp.555, 562, where the signature was treated as that of the carrier personally. ("signed by the defendants".)
50 *Diamond Alkali Export Corp. v Fl Bourgeois* [1921] 3 K.B. 443 at p.450.
51 (1851) 10 C.B. 665; above, para.18–029.
52 Carriage of Goods by Sea Act 1971, Sch.

(b) and (c)." This resembles the common law effect of such statements, leaving it open to the carrier to prove (for example) that the goods were not of the apparent condition specified in the bill, or to rely on a provision in it of the weight, number and quantity unknown type.[53] The second sentence of Article III.4, however, goes on to provide that "proof to the contrary shall not be admissible when the bill of lading has been transferred to a third party acting in good faith." This again resembles the common law estoppel available to an indorsee, but it only precludes the carrier from denying facts of which the bill is prima facie evidence by virtue of the first sentence of Article III.4, *i.e.* facts which he is required to state under subparagraphs (a), (b) and (c) of Article III.3. The important point, in the present context, is that under a combination of subparagraph (b) and the second sentence of Article III.4 a false statement as to the *quantity* of goods received by the carrier will give rise to an estoppel against the carrier. But it does not seem that such an estoppel will arise where no goods at all have been received by the issuer of the bill, for in such a case the mis-statement in the bill can scarcely be described as one as to the *quantity* received. Moreover, the Rules make the bill evidence of receipt of the goods only by "the carrier" and they define this expression to mean the owner or charterer of a ship "who enters into a contract of carriage with the shipper."[54] Where no goods have been shipped or received for shipment, the mere issue of a bill of lading does not suffice to create a contract of carriage.[55] Hence, unless such a contract can be established *aliunde*,[56] it still seems to be open to the issuer of the bill of lading in such a case to show that he was not "the carrier" within Rules. He is therefore not precluded by the second sentence of Article III.4 from establishing the fact of non-shipment or from invoking the common law rule that the master has no authority to sign a bill of lading in respect of goods which have not been put on board.[57] Even if the shipowner can be said to have entered into a contract of carriage[58] and so to be "the carrier", the Hague-Visby Rules only make the bill of lading evidence of the *receipt* of the goods, and not of their *shipment* or of the terms of the contract of carriage. Where the goods have not been shipped, the shipowner may be liable as bailee by reason of being unable to deny that he received the goods, but if the goods were to have been shipped by their seller in performance of a contract of sale, the

---

[53] See above, para.18–028; *Noble Resources Ltd v Cavalier Shipping Corp. (The Atlas)* [1996] 1 Lloyd's Rep. 642; *River Gurara (Cargo-owners) v Nigerian Shipping Line Ltd (The River Gurara)* [1998] Q.B. 610 at pp.625–626; *Agrosin Pte Ltd v Highway Shipping Ltd (The Mata K)* [1998] 2 Lloyd's Rep. 614.

[54] Art. 1(a); *cf.* also Art. I(b).

[55] See above, para.18–030.

[56] *ibid*.

[57] *Grant v Norway*, above, n.51; a dictum in *Albacruz (Cargo Owners) v Albazero (Owners) (The Albazero)* [1977] A.C. 774 at p.847 states that a holder for value of the bill "has the benefit of an estoppel . . . that the bill of lading is conclusive evidence against the shipowner of the shipment of the goods described in it." From the context it seems more probable that this was intended to paraphrase s.3 of the Bills of Lading Act 1855 than to overrule *Grant v Norway*, which was not cited to the House of Lords. The correctness of *Grant v Norway* was left open in *Hindley v East Indian Produce Co. Ltd* [1973] 2 Lloyd's Rep. 515 at p.519.

[58] Above, para.18–030.

hypothetical bailment would normally be between *shipper* (*i.e.* the seller) and carrier[59] (so that it would not confer any rights on the buyer as transferee of the bill); and the carrier's liability as bailee might well yield a different measure of damages from liability for failing, in breach of a contract of carriage, to deliver the goods at the destination specified in the bill of lading.[60]

Article III.4, sea waybills and straight bills. The Hague-Visby Rules have the force of law in relation not only to bills of lading but also to "any receipt which is a non-negotiable document marked as such if the contract contained in or evidenced by it is a contract for the carriage of goods by sea which expressly provides that the Rules are to govern the contract as if the receipt were a bill of lading."[61] Under this provision, a sea waybill can be governed by the Rules if it expressly so provides. But the Rules apply to such documents subject to "any necessary modifications", one of which is that the second sentence of Article III.4 does not apply to them.[62] In other words, if a document of this kind states the matters specified in Article III.3 (a) to (c) (paraphrased in paragraph 18–034 above), the statement is no more than prima facie evidence of them: the rule making evidence to the contrary inadmissible where the document has been "transferred to a third party acting in good faith" does not apply. Indeed, the very concept of a "transfer" of a document of the present kind is hard to reconcile with its "non-negotiable" character.[63] **18–035**

It is an open question whether conclusive evidence provision in the second sentence of Article III. 4 applies to a straight bill of lading. The House of Lords has held that such a document is a "bill of lading or any

[59] See *Leigh and Sillavan Ltd v Aliakmon Shipping Co. Ltd (The Aliakmon)* [1986] A.C. 785 at p.818; for a possible reconciliation of an apparent conflict between this passage and one in *Borealis AB v Stargas Ltd (The Berge Sisar)* [2001] UKHL 17, [2002] 2 A.C. 205 at [18], see *East West Corp v DKBS 1912 AF A/S* [2003] EWCA Civ 83, [2003] Q.B. 1509 at [34–35], below, para.18–065. A buyer who was named as consignee could, exceptionally be the bailor if, in making the bill of lading contract, the seller had acted as his agent (see below, para.18–065); but this reasoning would hardly ever, if at all, apply where the buyer was indorsee of the bill: see *Carver on Bills of Lading*, 2nd ed. (2005), paras 7–037 to 7–039. See also *Compania Portorafti Commerciale SA v Ultramar Panama Inc. (The Captain Gregos) (No. 2)* [1990] 2 Lloyd's Rep. 394 at p.400.

[60] Prima facie, the measure of damages for breach of a contract of carriage would be based on the value of the goods at the destination, while that for breach of duty as a bailee would be based on their value at the place of the supposed receipt. A carrier may also be liable for damages for delay, *e.g.* where goods are shipped in a later ship than that specified in the bill of lading. See *Playing Cards (Malaysian) Sdn. Bhd. v China Mutual Navigation Co. Ltd* [1980] 12 M.L.J. 182 (where such liability was excluded by the terms of the bill of lading).

[61] Carriage of Goods by Sea Act 1971, s.1(6)(b). For conflicting decisions on the question whether s.1(6)(b) can apply where the words "as if it were a bill of lading" do not occur in the document, see *McCarren & Co. Ltd v Humber International Transport Ltd (The Vechscroon)* [1982] 1 Lloyd's Rep. 301 and *Browner International Ltd v Monarch Shipping Co. Ltd (The European Enterprise)* [1989] 2 Lloyd's Rep. 185.

[62] Carriage of Goods by Sea Act 1971, s.1(6)(b).

[63] Above, para.18–018; below para.18–077. In the present context, "non-negotiable" *means* "not transferable": *cf.* below, para.18–084.

similar document of title" for the purposes of the Hague-Visby Rules and the Carriage of Goods by Sea Act 1971[64] and in this respect the Act contrasts documents which fall within this description (and hence straight bills) with non-negotiable receipts (such as sea waybills) which contain or evidence contracts for the carriage of goods by sea.[65] This contrast gives some support to the view that the conclusive evidence provision of Article III.4 can apply to straight bills. On the other hand, a straight bill may contain words to the effect that it is not "negotiable" (*i.e.* not transferable),[66] or be by its nature not transferable,[67] and so have at least some of the characteristics of a non-negotiable receipt.[68] The concept of such a document's having been "transferred to a third party" within Article III.4 therefore gives rise to obvious difficulty.[69]

18–036 **Carriage of Goods by Sea Act 1992, section 4.** This section provides that "a bill of lading which (a) represents goods to have been shipped on board a vessel or to have been received for shipment on board a vessel; and (b) has been signed by the master of the vessel or by a person who was not the master but had the express, implied or apparent authority of the carrier to sign bills of lading, shall, in favour of a person who has become the lawful holder of the bill, be conclusive evidence against the carrier of the shipment of the goods or, as the case may be, of their receipt for shipment."

There is no doubt that this provision was intended to reverse the result of *Grant v Norway*,[70] *i.e.* to make the carrier liable to an indorsee to whom the bill has been transferred, and (presumably) to a consignee named in the bill to whom the bill has been transferred. It is no longer relevant that the signer had no authority to sign the particular bill because he had done so in respect of goods which had not been shipped: it is enough for him to be either the master or a person having authority to sign bills in general. The section applies in terms not only to shipped, but also to received, bills.

The first requirement of section 4 is that the bill must be one which "represents" the goods to have been shipped or received for shipment. In *The Mata K*[71–72] a bill of lading in a box marked "Shipper's Description" described the goods as "Muriate of Potash" and gave the figure of "11,000 MT" under "Gross Weight", while another box marked "Shipped" contained the words "Weight, measure, quality, condition, contents and value unknown." In accordance with the rule stated in paragraph 18–028 above, Clarke J. held that this "unknown" clause negatived any representation that 11,000 tons had been shipped so that, on a claim for short delivery, the carrier was not precluded by section 4 from relying on evidence that a smaller quantity had in fact been shipped. The question whether such a

[64] *JI MacWilliam Co. Inc. v Mediterranean Shipping Co. SA (The Rafaela S)* [2005] UKHL 11, [2005] 2 A.C. 423 at [1], [35], referring to s.1(4) of the 1971 Act.
[65] See 1971 Act, ss 1(4), 1(6)(b).
[66] See below, paras 18–076, 18–084.
[67] See below para.18–077; *cf. The Rafaela S*, above n.64, at [58].
[68] Within s.1(6)(b) of the 1971 Act.
[69] See para.18–073.
[70] Law Com. 196, Scot. Law Com. 130, paras 4.7, 7.1(5); and see below at n.39.
[71–72] *Agrosin Pte Ltd v Highway Shipping Co. Ltd (The Mata K)* [1998] 2 Lloyd's Rep. 614.

clause prevents statements in a bill from taking effect as representations depends on the construction of the clause: for example, a statement as to the *number* of items shipped would not be deprived of its force as a representation by a "*weight* unknown" clause.[73] It is also arguable that section 4 could apply, in spite of the presence of an "unknown" clause, where no goods at all belonging to the shipper had been shipped since such a clause could be said, as a matter of construction, not to cover total non-shipment.

Assuming that the statement as to the fact and quantity of goods shipped or received does amount to a representation, then the situation most obviously covered by section 4 is that in which (i) A issues a bill of lading signed in accordance with the requirements of the section to B (often a seller of goods), stating goods to have been shipped, when in fact none have been shipped; (ii) the bill makes the goods deliverable *either* to the order of C (often the buyer of the goods), *or* to the order of B and is endorsed by him to C, *or* to bearer; and (iii) the bill is delivered to C, who takes it in good faith, *i.e.* not knowing that no goods have been shipped. C is then the "lawful holder" of the bill which in favour of C is conclusive evidence against A of the fact that the goods were shipped. But if this were all it would fall short of establishing a cause of action in favour of C against A since C is not an original party to any contract with A; nor can C establish a bailment relationship with A since, even on the hypothesis that goods had been shipped, the bailor would normally be B, not C, and this would be so even if at some later stage property in the hypothetical goods would have passed to C.[74] The alternative argument open to C is that the rights under the contract between A and B have been transferred to him, on his having become lawful holder of the bill, by virtue of section 2 of the Act.[75] This in turn depends on there having been a "contract of carriage" between A and B, for it is rights of suit under this contract which are "transferred to and vested in [C] . . . as if he had been a party to that contract."[76] If, in consequence of the fact of non-shipment, no such contract had come into existence,[77] it is arguable that nothing could be transferred to C by virtue of section 2. But the effect of section 4 is to preclude A from denying the fact of shipment and the legislative intention appears to have been to give to C a cause of action against A on the hypothetical contract of carriage, which would have come into being, if goods had been shipped, even though no such contract may exist in fact. This may amount to basing a cause of action on what is in substance an estoppel (even though that word is not used in section 4) and is best regarded as a statutory exception to the general rule that estoppel by representation does not give rise to a cause of action.[78]

---

73 See *Att.-Gen. of Ceylon v Scindia Navigation Co. of India* [1962] A.C. 60.

74 *Leigh and Sillavan Ltd v Aliakmon Shipping Co. Ltd (The Aliakmon)* [1986] A.C. 785 at p.818; *Compania Portorafti Commerciale SA v Ultramar Panama Inc. (The Captain Gregos) (No.2)* [1990] 2 Lloyd's Rep. 395 at p.404 and see above, para.18–034, n.59, below, para 18–065.

75 Below, para.18–102.

76 Carriage of Goods by Sea Act 1992, s.2(1): and see the definition of "contract of carriage" in s.5(1).

77 Above, para.18–030.

78 Above, para.18–030 at n.36.

It is finally arguable that, where no goods have been shipped, there is no person who answers to the description of the "carrier", within section 4, against whom the bill is conclusive evidence, but acceptance of this argument would largely defeat the object of the section, which was to reverse the result in *Grant v Norway*[79]: it would restrict the operation of the section to cases in which there had either been shipment or receipt of part of the goods represented to have been shipped, or in which a contract of carriage was established *aliunde*.[80] It is submitted that "carrier" in section 4 need not be interpreted to refer exclusively to a person who has entered into a contract of carriage. The word could also refer to a person who is named or described in the bill of lading as the carrier and who therefore has undertaken to carry the hypothetical goods, even though that undertaking may lack contractual force by reason of the non-shipment or non-receipt of the goods; or perhaps to the person who would be the carrier of the goods if the facts of which the bill were conclusive evidence were true. There may be an element of circularity in the second of these interpretations; but unless one of them is adopted section 4 will to a considerable extent fail to achieve its purpose, as indicated by its legislative history.

18–037 **Bill signed by carrier personally.** Section 3 of the Bills of Lading Act 1855 was defective in that it made the bill conclusive evidence of the fact of shipment only "against the Master or other Person signing the same" and that such conclusive evidence was of no avail to the transferee where (as was often the case) there was no cause of action against that person since he was neither a party to any contract of carriage, nor normally a party to any bailment, which would have arisen if the goods had been shipped.[81] Section 4 of the 1992 Act appears to suffer from a somewhat similar, though no doubt in practice less significant, defect. It in terms deals *only* with the cases in which the bill has been "signed by the master . . . or by a person who . . . had the express, implied or apparent authority of the carrier to sign bills of lading."[82] A signature by the carrier himself does not fall within either of these descriptions, unless he happens to be the master; for a person can hardly be said to confer "authority" to sign bills of lading on himself. The case of a bill of lading signed by the carrier personally therefore does not appear to be covered by section 4. No doubt the practical importance of this point is reduced by the fact that most carriers nowadays are corporations which normally act through agents. But the law does recognise the concept of a document which is executed by a

[79] (1851) 10 C.B. 665, above, para.18–029, Law Commissions' Report (above, n.70) paras 4.7, 7.1(5); there is no reference to the point in the speech made by Lord Goff when introducing the Bill which became the Act in the House of Lords (538 H.L. Deb. Col. 73), but the point is made clear in his speech on his first introduction of the Bill (535 H.L. Deb. at Col. 233), which on that occasion failed to become law because of the dissolution of Parliament in 1992.
[80] See above, para.18–030; below, para.18–047.
[81] Above, paras 18–033 and 18–036, at n.74.
[82] s.4(b).

corporation itself, as opposed to being executed on its behalf,[83] and section 4 would appear not to apply to a bill of lading which was signed in the first of these two ways. Such a case would, indeed, fall within Article III.4 of the Hague-Visby Rules, where these governed the bill: this provision in terms refers to a bill issued by "the carrier or the master or agent of the carrier."[84] But, as we saw in paragraph 18–034 above, Article III.4 is subject to a number of limitations which will often make the position of a transferee less favourable under it than it would be under section 4 of the 1992 Act. Where the bill is signed by the carrier personally, the falsity of the statement may, finally, give rise to liability at common law. One possible basis of such liability is estoppel by representation; but, although the reasoning of *Grant v Norway*[85] would not stand in the way of holding the carrier so liable (since no question of authority to sign on behalf of the carrier could arise where he had personally signed the bill), the estoppel would not at common law create a cause of action and so would not help the consignee or indorsee where no contract of carriage had come into existence because no goods at all had been shipped.[86] Even in such a case, however, a carrier who had personally signed the bill could be liable in tort for fraud or negligence, in accordance with the principles to be discussed in paragraph 18–045.

Received bill of lading. Section 4 applies to received, no less than to shipped bills. This follows from the reference in the opening words of the section to "a bill of lading which represents goods to have been shipped on board a vessel or to have been received for shipment on board a vessel."[87] A bill of the latter kind is, if appropriately signed[88] is, in favour of a lawful holder, conclusive evidence of the "receipt for shipment" of the goods. This provision gives rise to a number of problems. The first is to what kinds of bills section 4, so far as it relates to received bills, applies. It will be recalled that the expression "received bill" is used in more than one sense.[89] In its most obvious sense, it refers to a bill which states that the goods have been received by the carrier for shipment in a ship named in the bill, and section 4 clearly applies to documents of this kind. It is more doubtful whether the section applies to a bill which states that the goods have been received for shipment but does not name the ship or enable her to be identified when the document is issued: *e.g.* to one which merely states the goods to have 18–038

[83] See *Newborne v Sensolid (Great Britain) Ltd* [1954] 1 Q.B. 45; *Cotronic (UK) Ltd v Dezonie (t/a Wendaland Builders Ltd)* [1991] B.C.L.C. 721. The bill in *Parsons v New Zealand Shipping Co.* appears to have been signed in this way: *i.e.* by the defendant's manager but in such a way as to make the signature that of the defendants themselves: see [1901] 1 K.B. 548 at pp.550, 555. See also *Meridian Global Fund Management Asia Ltd v Securities Commission* [1995] 2 A.C. 500 at pp.506–507 for the concept of an act done by a company itself, as distinct from one done on its behalf.

[84] Art. III.3, to which Art. III.4 refers.

[85] Above, para.18–029.

[86] See above, para.18–030.

[87] Carriage of Goods by Sea Act 1992, s.4(a).

[88] *i.e.* in accordance with s.4(b), above, para.18–036.

[89] Above, para.18–027.

been received for shipment "in the next available vessel." The doubt arises because the words "on board a vessel" occur twice in section 4. First, they occur after the word "shipped", where they most naturally mean "on board a *named* (or otherwise identified) vessel": they cannot here refer simply to the fact that the goods have been placed on board *some ship*, as opposed to some other means of transport (such as a train or a lorry); for to give them this meaning would turn them into mere surplusage, since in English law the word "shipped" already means "put on board a ship".[90] Secondly, they occur after the phrase "received for shipment", where their meaning is less clear. Prima facie one would suppose that they meant the same thing in both places, so that a bill stating that the goods had been received for shipment but not naming or otherwise identifying the proposed carrying ship would not be one representing the goods to have been "received for shipment on board a vessel". It follows that section 4 would not apply to such a bill. An intermediate type of document is that used in the *Diamond Alkali* case,[91] where the bill stated that the goods had been "received . . . to be transported by the *SS Anglia* . . . or failing shipment by said steamer in and upon a following steamer . . ." The case for arguing that section 4 applies to such a document would seem to be stronger than it is in relation to a bill which gave no indication at all of the name or identity of the proposed carrying ship. A final possibility is that the bill may name the proposed carrying ship but fail to indicate that the carrier has received the goods. This was the position in *Ishag v Allied Bank International*[92] where the goods were in two warehouses, at some distance from the ship[93] and warehouse receipts relating to them were surrendered by the shipper's agents to the carrier's agents, who issued what purported to be a bill of lading, stating that the consignment was "at the disposal of the [ship's] agents and that the same is intended to be shipped . . . with MS *Lycaon* . . ." Although there is, no doubt, some elasticity in the word "received", it is submitted that the requirement of receipt would not be satisfied where (as in *Ishag's* case) the carrier had no more than (at the most) a contractual right of call on the warehouseman to deliver the goods to him. It follows that the so-called bill of lading in *Ishag's* case would not be one which, in the words of section 4, had represented "goods . . . to have been received for shipment on board a vessel."

The second problem which arises from the application of section 4 to "received" bills is to determine the precise effect of the section in relation to such bills. The question, in other words, is: what follows from the rule that such a bill is "conclusive evidence" of the receipt for shipment of the goods? We have noted in paragraph 18–030 above that in some cases at least the contract of carriage is concluded only on actual shipment of the goods.[94] Where this is the position (or would be the position, if the goods had been shipped), then the fact that the bill was conclusive evidence of the

[90] Below, para.18–268.
[91] *Diamond Alkali Export Corp. v Fl. Bourgeois* [1921] 3 K.B. 443.
[92] [1981] 1 Lloyd's Rep. 92.
[93] One of the warehouses was not even in the same country as the port of intended (and eventual) shipment under another bill of lading.
[94] *Heskell v Continental Express Ltd* [1950] 1 All E.R. 1022 at p.1037.

receipt of the goods would not make the carrier liable to the lawful holder in contract; it would simply preclude the carrier from denying that he was bailee of the goods represented to have been so shipped. That bailment would, as already noted, normally be one in which the bailor was the shipper[95] so that it seems that the transferee of the bill would acquire no rights under it, unless he was the consignee named in the bill and the shipper had, in making the bill of lading contract, acted as his agent[96]; while the shipper could not rely on section 4 unless he could be said to fall within the definition of "lawful holder", a point to be discussed in paragraph 18–042 below. Even if that were the case, the rights under the bailment would differ from those under the hypothetical contract of carriage: the position in this respect would be similar to that under the Hague-Visby Rules Article III.4, discussed in paragraph 18–034 above. The difficulties just discussed would not arise if the contract of carriage could be established *aliunde, i.e.* apart from even the receipt of the goods,[97] or where the contract was concluded as soon as the goods were received[98] (as opposed to when they were shipped). It may for this purpose be significant that section 4 makes the bill conclusive evidence of the "receipt *for shipment*" of the goods, while Article III.4 merely makes them conclusive evidence of "the receipt by the carrier of the goods". It can be argued that "receipt for shipment" (in section 4) carries stronger contractual overtones than mere "receipt" in Article III.4, and that "received for shipment" in the section should be interpreted to mean "received under a contract of (or for) carriage". Such an interpretation of section 4 would avoid the difficulties discussed in the present paragraph by making the carrier liable to the lawful holder in contract under a "received", just as much as under a "shipped", bill.

Section 4 and false statements as to quantity. The difficulties discussed in paragraphs 18–036 and 18–038 above do not arise where some goods have been shipped but the bill represents a greater quantity to have been shipped. The fact that some goods have been shipped is sufficient to give rise to a contract of carriage (even where no such contract can be established *aliunde*[99]); and the fact that the bill is, as against the carrier, conclusive evidence of the shipment of "the goods" (*i.e.* of those represented to have been shipped) suffices to make him liable to the lawful holder for breach of that contract. The position is less clear where some goods have been shipped and the bill represents a greater quantity to have been "*received* for shipment on board a vessel." But if (as has been suggested in paragraph 18–038) this phrase means "received under a contract", then the 18–039

[95] Above, paras 18–034 and 18–036.
[96] See above, para.18–034 n.59 and below, para.18–065, where it will be submitted that where the shipper is a seller who has not been paid and the consignee is the buyer, the seller is more likely to have made the contract of carriage on his own behalf as principal.
[97] Above, para.18–030; below para.18–047.
[98] This is one of the alternatives stated in the dictum from *Heskell's* case referred to in n.94 above.
[99] See n.97 above.

carrier would again, in consequence of section 4, be liable to the holder for breach of that contract.

18–040 **Sea waybills, straight bills and section 4.** We have seen in paragraph 18–035 that the conclusive evidence provision in the second sentence of Article III.4 of the Hague-Visby Rules does not apply to a sea waybill,[1] and the same is true of section 4 of the Carriage of Goods by Sea Act 1992. The section applies only where the representation is contained in a "bill of lading" and this expression does not include a document which is "incapable of transfer by indorsement or, as a bearer bill, by delivery without indorsement"; while for the purposes of the 1992 Act it is part of the definition of a sea waybill that it is a document "which is not a bill of lading".[2] It follows from these provisions that for the purposes of the 1992 Act a straight bill of lading is treated in the same way as a sea waybill,[3] that such a bill is not for those purposes a "bill of lading" and that section 4 does not apply to it. Moreover, section 4 applies only in favour of the "lawful holder" of a bill, and the expression "lawful holder" is used and defined in the Act only in relation to bills of lading.[4] Two things follow from this restriction on the operation of section 4. First, statements in a sea waybill as to the fact of shipment or receipt, or as to the quantity of goods shipped or received, are no more than prima facie evidence, which can be rebutted by the carrier. Secondly, the reasoning of *Grant v Norway*[5] is not affected by section 4 in relation to such documents: that is, the master or other agent of the carrier has no authority to sign a sea waybill for goods that have not been shipped. As already noted,[6] neither section 4 nor any of the other legislative modifications of *Grant v Norway* have attacked the *reasoning* of that case; they have sought to reverse only its result.

The fact that section 4 has not affected the reasoning of *Grant v Norway* does not, indeed, lead inevitably to the conclusion that that reasoning would be applied to a sea waybill. The courts have shown themselves reluctant to extend the rule in *Grant v Norway*, and its application to sea waybills would no doubt involve some such extension. The restrictions on the scope of the rule have, however, been based on rational distinctions: *e.g.* on that between lack of authority to sign for unshipped goods and authority to make representations as to apparent order and condition,[7] date of shipment,[8] and shipment under deck.[9] These distinctions relate to the type of fact stated in the document rather than to the type of document in which the statement is contained. There seems to be no rational basis for distinguishing for the present purpose between bills of lading and sea waybills, where the fact stated in either type of document is the same: if the

---

1 For the legal nature of sea waybills, see above, para.18–018.
2 Carriage of Goods by Sea Act 1992, s.1(2)(a) and (3).
3 Above, para.18–018.
4 *e.g.* (apart from s.4) in s.2(1)(a), s.2(2) and s.5(2).
5 (1851) 10 C.B. 665, above, para.18–029.
6 Above, para.18–032.
7 See *Compania Naviera Vasconzada v Churchill & Sim* [1906] 1 K.B. 237.
8 *The Saudi Crown* [1986] 1 Lloyd's Rep. 261.
9 *The Nea Tyhi* [1982] 1 Lloyd's Rep. 606.

master or other agent has no authority to sign for goods not shipped under the former, he must equally lack authority to sign for goods not shipped under the latter.

The principle of *Heskell v Continental Express*[10] also appears to apply to sea waybills, so that the mere statement in such a document that goods have been shipped, when that is not the case, will not give rise to a contract of carriage, or to an estoppel operating against the putative carrier in favour of the putative shipper. The lack of such a contract is an additional reason why the false statement as to the fact of shipment cannot confer rights on the consignee. It follows from the continued applicability to sea waybills of the reasoning of *Grant v Norway* and of *Heskell's* case that the question of the carrier's liability[11] for false statements as to the fact of shipment made in a sea waybill by his agents will continue to be governed by the common law rules stated in paragraphs 18–029 to 18–031 above.

Delivery orders and section 4. Delivery orders are clearly not covered by section 4, but false statements in them can give rise to problems analogous to those which have been discussed in this chapter in relation to bills of lading and sea waybills. We shall see that rights under contracts for the carriage of goods by sea can be transferred by means of a ship's delivery order,[12] and the master of a ship on which goods are alleged, or believed, to have been shipped may issue such an order in respect of goods which had never been shipped or which had been shipped but which were no longer on board when the order was issued; and the question can then arise whether the carrier is liable in respect of such statements. 18–041

If no goods have been shipped, then it seems that, the principle stated in *Heskell v Continental Express Ltd*[13] may well prevent any contract of carriage from coming into being. Where this is the position, the order would not be a "ship's delivery order" within the 1992 Act, even if it contained an undertaking by the carrier to deliver the goods, for it could not be given "under or for the purposes of a contract for the carriage of the goods to which [it] relates",[14] there being *ex hypothesi* no such contract. If a contract for the carriage of the goods had been established *aliunde*[15] the order could be a ship's delivery order and so could prima facie transfer rights under the contract of carriage to the person identified in it as the person to whom delivery of the goods to which it related was to be made.[16] Whether such rights were in fact transferred would then depend on whether the false statement in the order was governed by the rule in *Grant v Norway*.[17] There appears to be no authority on this point. One possible view is that, if the master has no authority to sign a bill of lading in respect of

10 [1950] 1 All E.R. 1033, above, para.18–030.

11 For possible liability of the *signer* (including the carrier himself where he signed the document personally), see below, para.18–045.

12 Carriage of Goods by Sea Act 1992, s.2(1)(c); below, para.18–175.

13 [1950] 1 All E.R. 1033, above, para.18–030.

14 Carriage of Goods by Sea Act 1992 s.1(4)(a); below, para.18–176.

15 Above, para.18–030: after n.29; below, para.18–047 the contract could, for example, be made by advance reservation of shipping space.

16 Under Carriage of Goods by Sea Act 1992, s.2(1)(c).; below, para.18–175.

17 (1851) 10 C.B. 665; above, para.18–029.

goods which have not been put on board, then it should follow that he had no authority to issue a ship's delivery order in respect of such goods. The question in either case relates to the extent of the master's authority, and the principle of *Grant v Norway* is that he has no authority to bind the shipowner by untrue statements as to the fact of shipment. Indeed, the argument for applying this principle to a ship's delivery order is in one significant respect stronger than that for applying it to a bill of lading; for, even though ship's delivery orders have achieved a degree of transferability under the Carriage of Goods by Sea Act 1992,[18] they are not fully transferable in the same way as bills of lading,[19] *i.e.* by indorsement (where necessary) and delivery. Hence a false statement as to the fact of shipment in a ship's delivery order is *less* likely (than such a statement in a bill of lading) to prejudice third parties. On the other hand, it can be argued that the rule in *Grant v Norway* has been subjected to much adverse criticism[20]; that, in the context in which it was first formulated, its effect has been reversed by statute[21]; that before this reversal the courts were reluctant to extend it; and that it should therefore not be applied to documents which differ from bills of lading in that they neither contain nor evidence a contract of carriage. In this respect, ship's delivery orders differ from sea waybills,[22] so that the argument for applying the principle of *Grant v Norway* to such orders appears to be weaker than that put forward in relation to the application of this principle to sea waybills in paragraph 18–040 above.

The argument just put for applying the principle in *Grant v Norway* is even weaker where the goods to which the order relates had originally been shipped but were no longer on board the ship when the order was issued. In such a case a contract of carriage clearly came into being at the latest when the goods were shipped, so that no difficulty arises under the principle stated in *Heskell's* case[23]; and to apply the rule in *Grant v Norway* here would involve a double extension of the rule: both to documents and to statements of a kind not originally covered by it. The rule is unlikely to be extended in this way, so that, even if the contract of carriage had been discharged by previous delivery of the goods to another person (than the person named in the order) who was authorised to receive them, the carrier could be liable by estoppel on the ground of the false statement impliedly made in the undertaking to deliver the goods which was contained in the order. Of course, if the previous delivery was made to a person *not* authorised to receive the goods, then the carrier would be in breach of the contract of carriage and the person to whom the promise contained in the order was made would be entitled under the Carriage of Goods by Sea Act 1992[24] to claim damages from the carrier in respect of that breach. This

[18] See ss.2(1)(c) and 5(3); below, paras 18–175, 18–182.
[19] See Carriage of Goods by Sea Act 1992, s.1(2)(a) for the meaning of "bill of lading".
[20] Above, para.18–029.
[21] *i.e.* by Carriage of Goods by Sea Act 1992, s.4; above, para.18–036.
[22] Including, in the context of the 1992 Act, straight bills: above, para.18–018.
[23] Above, n.13.
[24] s.2(1)(c).

would also be true where the reason why the goods were no longer on board was that they had been lost as a result of some other breach of the contract of carriage.

Who can rely on section 4. Section 4 makes the bill of lading conclusive evidence of the fact of shipment or receipt "in favour of a person who has become the lawful holder of the bill." The definition of "holder" in section 5 of the 1992 Act is more fully discussed in paragraph 18–104. Here it suffices to say that two elements must be satisfied to make a person "holder."[25] First, he must have possession of the bill. Secondly, he must be either (a) the consignee; or (b) an indorsee to whom the bill has been delivered or a person to whom a bearer bill has been delivered; or (c) a person who would have satisfied either requirement (a) or (b) if the transfer had not occurred after the bill had been "spent."[26] Assuming that a person is the holder of the bill, he will be the "lawful" holder if he became the holder of the bill in good faith[27]: in the present context, this would normally require him not to be aware, when he acquired possession of the bill, of the fact of non-shipment or non-receipt. 18–042

In the normal case, the holder of the bill will be a person (other than the putative shipper) to whom the bill has been transferred. This was the position in *Grant v Norway* and the purpose of section 4 was to reverse the result of that case, so that where A issues a bill of lading to B who transfers it to C, then C can (if the requirements of the section are satisfied) rely on the bill as conclusive evidence against A of a statement in it that the goods represented to have been shipped or received were indeed shipped or received. The section also clearly applies in favour of persons to whom further transfers are made after the original transfer: *e.g.* by C to D, and so forth. In all these situations, the person relying on section 4 will be someone other than B, the person named in the bill as the original shipper; and the further question arises whether the section can apply also in favour of that shipper. Three situations call for discussion.

The first is that in which goods are shipped by B to his own order (or simply "to order" in which case the bill is interpreted as making the goods deliverable to his order). In such a case B may *be* the holder, but he would not (in the terminology of section 4) have "*become*" the holder: this word appears to refer to *change* in the person who becomes the holder after the original issue of the bill to B. The second is that in which B sells the goods to C who is both a buyer and a seller in a string of contracts which becomes a circle on the eventual resale of the goods to B. Here B re-acquires possession, not as shipper, but in his capacity as ultimate buyer; and it is submitted that he can rely on section 4 so long as he becomes holder of the bill (on its retransfer to him) in good faith. The third situation is that in which B sells the goods represented to have been shipped to C who rejects the documents on the ground that no such goods had been shipped. Here again B would re-acquire possession of the bill, not as shipper, but as the

---

[25] Carriage of Goods by Sea Act 1992, s.5(2).

[26] See below, para.18–113.

[27] Carriage of Goods by Sea Act 1992, s.5(2) below, para.18–105.

seller under his contract with C; but as by the time that he so "becomes" holder of the bill he will know that no goods have been shipped, it seems that he will not have become holder in good faith and so for this reason be unable to rely on section 4. This reasoning would, however, not apply where C's rejection was grounded, not on the fact that no goods had been shipped, but on the ground that the documents were dated outside the shipment period. In such a case, B would have "become" the holder of the bill and would be able to satisfy the requirements of good faith if, at the time of the rejection, he was unaware of the fact of non-shipment. It should finally be noted that the difficulties here discussed do not arise under Article III.4 of the Hague-Visby Rules since this provision does not specify in whose favour, or against whom, it operates.

18–043 **Statement about shipped or received goods.** Section 4 applies to false representations as to the fact of shipment and as to the quantity of goods shipped; it does not apply to statements *about* the goods, such as statements about their commercial quality or about their apparent order and condition. The distinction between statements as to the fact of shipment and statements about goods can, however, become blurred in borderline cases. If a bill of lading stated that peas had been shipped when the goods in fact shipped were beans, the case would be one of non-shipment of peas so that section 4 could apply; but in less clear cases it may be hard to tell whether the difference between what is shipped and what is stated to have been shipped falls into this category. It would seem that section 4 would apply if the difference is such that the goods tendered at the end of the transit cannot be identified as the goods stated to have been shipped,[28] or if, though such identification was possible, there was an essential difference between the goods shipped and those stated to have been shipped.[29]

18–044 **Carriage of Goods by Sea Act 1992, section 5(5).** This subsection provides that "The preceding provisions of this Act shall have effect without prejudice to the application, in relation to any case, of the rules (the Hague-Visby Rules) which for the time being have the force of law by virtue of section 1 of the Carriage of Goods by Sea Act 1971." The object of this subsection is to regulate the relationship between section 4 of the 1992 Act and Article III.4 of the Hague-Visby Rules; but the effect of the subsection on that relationship is not entirely clear. The principle underlying section 5(5) appears to be that, where a document is governed by the

[28] See *Parsons v New Zealand Shipping Co.* [1901] 1 K.B. 548 where a similar problem arose under s.3 of the Bills of Lading Act 1855 and where the goods delivered *could* be identified as those shipped. For the facts of this case, see below, para.19–146.

[29] *e.g.*, on facts such as those in *Egyptian International Foreign Trade Co. v Soplex Wholesale Supplies Ltd (The Raffaella)* [1984] 2 Lloyd's Rep. 102: see *ibid.* p.116; on appeal the point was said to give rise to "difficult questions": [1985] 2 Lloyd's Rep. 36 at p.39. For *The Raffaella* see further para.19–035, below.

Hague-Visby Rules, the outcome will be determined by those Rules, rather than by section 4.[30]

Neither Section 4 nor Article III.4 applies its "conclusive evidence" provision to sea waybills,[31] but Section 4 may have a narrower scope than Article III.4 in that straight bills of lading are treated as sea waybills for the purposes of the 1992 Act[32] so that section 4 does not apply to them[33]; while it has been held that a straight bill is a "bill of lading or any similar document of title" for the purposes of the 1971 Act and the Hague-Visby Rules[34]; hence it is arguable that such a bill is covered by the "conclusive evidence" provision of Article III.4 of the Rules.[35] On the other hand, section 4 has a potentially wider scope than Article III.4 in that the section can apply to bills which are governed by English law but are not subject to the Hague-Visby Rules because they fall outside the limits laid down in Article X of the Rules.

Where no goods are shipped, Article III.4 of the Rules may not apply since in such a case no "contract of carriage"[36] would arise (unless such a contract can be established *aliunde*).[37] Section 4, on the other hand, can apply even though no contract of carriage can be so established.

Article III.4 makes the bill conclusive evidence only of the *receipt* of the goods; section 4 can make it conclusive evidence of their *shipment*. It may have this effect even if the bill is governed by the Rules since this would not *restrict* their scope and so be "without prejudice" to them.

Section 4 makes the bill conclusive evidence only of the receipt or shipment of the goods. Article III.4 makes it conclusive evidence of certain other representations about the goods.

Article III.4 will prevail where its effect is *wider* than that of section 4: *e.g.* where the bill is signed by the carrier personally (and not by an agent)[38] or where it is not a transferee of the bill but the shipper who seeks to rely on the bill as conclusive evidence or (perhaps) where the false statement is contained in a straight bill.[39]

---

[30] *cf.* Law Com. No. 196, Scot. Law Com. No. 130 para.4.8 ("It is not our remit to reform the Hague- Visby Rules") and para.4.12 ("We have no mandate to alter the Hague-Visby Rules"). There is no reference to the point in the speech made by Lord Goff on either of the two occasions on which he introduced the Bill which was to become the 1992 Act in the House of Lords: see 538 H.L. Deb. Col. 73 and 535 H.L. Deb. 230.

[31] Above, paras 18–035, 18–040.

[32] Above, para.18–018; Carriage of Goods by Sea Act 1992, s.1(2)(a), 1(3).

[33] Above, para.18–040.

[34] *JI MacWilliam Co. Inc. v Mediterranean Shipping Co. SA (The Rafaela S)* [2005] UKHL 11, [2005] 2 A.C. 423.

[35] The point is an open one since a straight bill may contain words to the effect that it is not "negotiable" (*i.e.* not transferable: see below, para.18–084) or be by its nature not transferable: see below, para.18–074). Such a bill could therefore, in the terminology of the 1971 Act, fall within either s.1(4) (bill of lading) or s.1(6)(b) (non-negotiable receipt containing or evidencing a contract of carriage). The concept of a straight bill's being "transferred to a third party" within Article III.4 of the Rules also gives rise to difficulty: see above, para.18–035, below, para.18–074.

[36] Carriage of Goods by Sea Act 1971, Sch. Art. I(a) and (b), above, para.18–034.

[37] Above, para.18–030.

[38] See above, para.18–037.

[39] See above, at n.35.

18–045 **Liability of the signer.** The party prejudiced by a false statement as to the fact of shipment or receipt may wish to pursue his remedy, not against the carrier, but against the person who signed the bill. This possibility may arise either because the party prejudiced has no remedy under section 4 of the 1992 Act or under Article III.4 of the Hague-Visby Rules, or because that party has some practical reason for preferring to pursue his remedy against the signer.

The possibility of holding the signer liable in cases of fraud was recognised in *Grant v Norway* itself[40]; and, while the possibility of making him liable for negligence at common law was at one time dismissed,[41] that possibility now exists[42] in the light of developments in the law relating to liability for negligent misrepresentation in and after *Hedley Byrne & Co. Ltd v Heller & Partners Ltd.*[43] The question whether such a claim can succeed will depend in each case on the application of the principles which now determine whether the circumstances give rise to a duty of care,[44] and on whether that duty has been broken. No general answer can be given to these questions[45]; but it may be relevant to note that, since *Hedley Byrne's* case, a claim for negligence at common law has, in one case of the kind here under discussion, been rejected.[46] There will usually be no claim against the signer under section 2(1) of the Misrepresentation Act 1967 since a person who acts as agent is not liable under that subsection.[47]

Where the signer acts as agent he is not normally liable in contract to the shipper or to a transferee of the bill of lading since his contractual relationship is likely to be, not with these parties, but only with the carrier[48]; and even though it is possible for an agent to undertake personal contractual liability to a third party, that possibility is likely in the present context to be negatived by the form of the signature.[49] Even if this difficulty could be overcome, there would be the further point that statements in a

---

[40] (1851) 10 C.B. 665, above para.18–029.
[41] *Heskell v Continental Express Ltd* [1950] 1 All E.R. 1033 at pp.1041–1042.
[42] *Hedley Byrne & Co. Ltd v Heller & Partners Ltd* [1964] A.C. 465 at p.532.
[43] Above.
[44] *Smith v Eric S Bush* [1990] 1 A.C. 831, *Caparo Industries Plc v Dickman* [1990] 2 A.C. 605 at pp.617–618, *Marc Rich & Co. AG v Bishop Rock Marine Co. Ltd (The Nicholas H)* [1996] 1 A.C. 211 at p.236; *Williams v Natural Life Health Foods Ltd* [1998] 1 W.L.R. 830 at pp.835–838 where the agent was held not to owe a duty of care to the representee merely because the relationship between the latter and the principal was held to be such as to impose such a duty on the principal. This reasoning does not apply where the agent knows the representation to be false since in such a case all the requirements of the agent's liability *in deceit* are satisfied, there being then no further duty of care requirement: *Standard Chartered Bank v Pakistan National Shipping Corp* [2002] UKHL 43, [2003] 1 A.C. 959 at [21], [22], [41].
[45] *F Rudolf A. Oetker v IFA Internationale Frachtagentur (The Almak)* [1985] 1 Lloyd's Rep. 557 at p.560; for further discussion, see *Carver on Bills of Lading* (2nd ed., 2005) paras 2–040 to 2–043.
[46] *VO Rasnoimport v Guthrie & Co. Ltd* [1966] 1 Lloyd's Rep. 1, where it is not clear whether the negligence claim was dismissed because the defendants owed no duty of care or because, even if they owed such a duty, they were not in breach of it.
[47] *Resolute Maritime Inc. v Nippon Kayi Kyokai (The Skopas)* [1983] 1 W.L.R. 857. For possible liability of the agent in deceit, See above n.44.
[48] *Heskell v Continental Express Ltd* [1950] 1 All E.R. 1033.
[49] On the principle of such cases as *Mahony v Kekule* (1854) 14 C.B. 390.

bill of lading as to the quantity of goods shipped are "not . . . words of contract" but are "at most an affirmation of fact or a representation".[50] The further possibility of holding the signer liable on a collateral contract[51] is likewise likely to fail for want of contractual intention, particularly in view of the stringency with which the courts have applied that requirement to implied contracts.[52] Liability in contract could, however, arise where the signer acted in an ambiguous or dual capacity: *e.g.* as a freight forwarder who acted not only as agent of shipper or of carrier (or of both) but also as a person who undertook responsibility as principal to procure the making and performance of a contract for the carriage of goods.[53]

Where the signer purported to act as agent but lacked authority, he could also, if the want of authority caused loss to the third party,[54] be liable to the third party for breach of implied warranty of authority[55]; such liability is strict.[56] It is open to question, however, whether such a claim is now available against the agent where his principal, the carrier, is liable under section 4 of the 1992 Act. In such a case it is now arguable that the agent should not be liable for breach of the warranty, since in spite of this breach the principal (the carrier) would be liable to the third party, so that the breach would cause the third party no loss.[57]

Liability for other false representations Liability may arise at common law in respect of many false statements to which the rule in *Grant v Norway* does not apply: for example, to representations as to the time of shipment,[58] and such liability may fall not only on the carrier but also on other persons involved in the making of the statement. In *Standard Chartered Bank v National Shipping Corp. of Pakistan*,[59] for example, a seller of goods persuaded the agent of the carrier to antedate a bill of lading so as to **18–046**

---

[50] *VO Rasnoimport v Guthrie & Co. Ltd* [1966] 1 Lloyd's Rep. 1 at p.7; above, para.18–030.

[51] For such liability of an auctioneer, see *Woolfe v Horne* (1877) 2 Q.B.D. 755.

[52] A trend going back to *Heilbut Symons & Co. v Buckleton* [1913] A.C. 30 at p.47; see, more recently, *Blackpool and Fylde Aero Club v Blackpool BC* [1990] 1 W.L.R. 1195 at p.1202; *cf. The Aramis* [1989] 1 Lloyd's Rep. 213; below, para.18–142; *Baird Textile Holdings v Marks & Spencer Plc* [2001] EWCA Civ 274, [2002] 2 All E.R. (Comm.) 737 at [20], [21], [30], [62].

[53] *cf.* below, para.21–073.

[54] See *Heskell v Continental Express Ltd* [1950] 1 All E.R. 1033, where this requirement was not satisfied since, even if the agent had been authorised to sign the bill, no contract of carriage would have come into existence.

[55] *e.g. VO Rasnoimport v Guthrie & Co. Ltd* [1966] 1 Lloyd's Rep. 1.

[56] *Collen v Wright* (1857) 8 E. & B. 647; *Starkey v Bank of England* [1903] A.C. 114; *Yonge v Toynbee* [1910] 1 K.B. 215.

[57] On the principle of *Rainbow v Howkins* [1904] 2 K.B. 322 (agent not liable for breach of the implied warranty where the principal was liable on the basis of apparent authority); for the purpose of this principle, the decisive point should be *that* (rather than *why*) the principal is liable.

[58] See para.18–029 above.

[59] [1995] 2 Lloyd's Rep. 365; *ibid. (No.2)* [2000] 1 Lloyd's Rep. 218 (CA), reversed [2002] UKHL 32, [2003] 1 A.C. 959 insofar as the Court of Appeal had held that the seller's managing director was not liable in deceit and holding that contributory negligence was no defence to liability in deceit; on this point, see also *ibid. (No. 4)* [2001] Q.B. 617.

enable the seller to claim payment under a letter of credit; and such payment was made by the confirming bank to which the bill had been indorsed. It was held that the bank was entitled to damages in deceit from the carrier, the carrier's agent who had signed the bill knowing that the date of shipment given in it was false, the seller and the seller's managing director who, with the same knowledge, had forwarded the bill to the bank stating that it was one of the documents required by the credit.[60] Although the case is directly concerned only with a fraudulent statement about the date of shipment, there is no reason to suppose that the same rules would not apply to other statements about the goods which were known to be false[61] and which had caused loss to persons who had acted in reliance on them. Where the statement relates to the fact of shipment, the *carrier* would at common law be protected by the rule in *Grant v Norway*[62] but this rule would not protect the *signer* of the bill from liability in deceit,[63] nor would it protect persons such as the seller or managing director in the *Standard Chartered Bank* case.

(iii) *Bill of Lading as a Contractual Document*

18–047 **Bill of lading as evidence of contract of carriage.** It is often said that a bill of lading is not itself a contract of carriage, or does not contain a contract of carriage,[64] but is only evidence of its terms; and in a number of senses this is no doubt true. The contract of carriage is "in the vast majority of cases"[65] made before the issue of the bill of lading. It may be made when the goods are shipped, or when they are tendered for shipment and accepted for loading,[66] or (now more commonly) by previous arrangement between shipper and carrier[67]; while the bill of lading may not be issued

[60] To make agents of the carrier liable in *negligence*, it would be necessary to show that the agents owed a duty of care to the representee; but there is no such requirement where the agent is guilty of *fraud:* see *Carver on Bills of Lading*, 2nd ed. (2005), para.2–043.

[61] *e.g.*, statements of the kind discussed in para.18–028 above.

[62] See above para.18–029.

[63] See above para.18–045 at n.40.

[64] *Crooks & Co. v Allan* (1879) 5 Q.B.D. 38 at p.40; *Hansson v Hamel and Horley Ltd* [1922] 2 A.C. 36 at p.47; *Heskell v Continental Express Ltd* [1950] 1 All E.R. 1033 at p.1043; *The Ardennes* [1951] 1 K.B. 55 at p.60; *Partenreederei M/S Heidberg v Grosvenor Grain & Feed Co. Ltd (The Heidberg)* [1994] 2 Lloyd's Rep. 287 at 310 (overruled on another point in *Through Transport Mutual Insurance v New India Assurance Co. Ltd* [2005] EWCA Civ 1589, [2005] 1 Lloyd's Rep. 67); *Datec Electronics Holdings Ltd v United Parcels Ltd* [2003] EWCA Civ 1418, [2006] 1 Lloyd's Rep. 279 at [15], [16] (carriage by road).

[65] *Pyrene Co. Ltd v Scindia Navigation Co. Ltd* [1954] 2 Q.B. 402 at p.414; *JI MacWilliam Co. Inc. v Mediterranean Shipping Co. SA (The Rafaela S)* [2005] UKHL 11, [2005] 2 A.C. 423 at [38]; *Evergreen Marine Corp. v Aldgate Warehouse (Wholesale) Ltd* [2003] EWHC 667 (Comm.), [2003] 2 Lloyd's Rep. 579 at [29].

[66] *Heskell v Continental Express Ltd*, above, at p.1037 ("loaded or accepted for loading"); *cf. ibid.*, p.1041; *Playing Cards (Malaysia) Sdn. Bhd. v China Mutual Navigation Co. Ltd* [1980] 2 M.L.J. 182 at p.183.

[67] *The Ardennes*, above; *Pyrene Co. Ltd v Scindia Navigation Co. Ltd*, above, at p.424; *Anglo Overseas Transport Ltd v Titan Industrial Corp.* [1959] 2 Lloyd's Rep. 152 at

until after the ship has sailed.[68] Conversely, if goods were not in fact shipped and no contract for their carriage had been made independently of actual shipment, no contract of carriage would arise merely because a bill of lading had been issued.[69] As the bill of lading is not the contract of carriage but only evidence of its terms, a person who accepts a bill which the carrier hands to him does not "necessarily and without regard to the circumstances bind himself to abide by all its stipulations."[70] Thus, if the bill of lading is handed over after the making of the contract of carriage and contains an exemption clause not originally agreed on, that clause might not form part of the contract[71] unless the original contract was made "subject to the exceptions of our bills of lading",[72] or unless the clause was incorporated by course of dealing between the parties[73] or by trade custom or usage,[74] or unless the parties intended their original contract to be superseded[75] by one on the terms of the bill of lading. An antecedent "contract of carriage" may also provide for the incorporation into that contract of a bill of lading to be issued in pursuance of it; and on the issue of the bill both the antecedent contract and the bill may have contractual force.[76]

Where a shipment is covered both by a charterparty and by a bill of lading, the bill of lading may not be even evidence of the contract of carriage, but be a mere receipt: this possibility is discussed in paragraphs 18–051 and 18–053 below.

Bill of lading as a contract of carriage. Against the statements cited in paragraph 18–047 can be set a number of others which refer to a bill of lading as the contract of carriage, or to the contract of carriage "contained 18–048

p.159; *Gulf Steel Co. Ltd v Al Khalifa Shipping Co. (The Anwar al Sabar)* [1980] 2 Lloyd's Rep. 261 at p.263 ("antecedent contract in terms of the booking note"); *MSC Mediterranean Shipping Co. SA v BRE Metro Ltd* [1985] 2 Lloyd's Rep. 239 at p.240 ("contract of affreightment contained in a liner booking note"); *A Meredith Jones & Co. Ltd v Vangemar (The Apostolis) (No. 2)* [2000] 2 Lloyd's Rep. 337, where the booking note was evidently regarded as having contractual force; *Parsons Corporation v CV Scheepvaartonderneming Happy Ranger (The Happy Ranger)* [2002] EWCA Civ 694, [2002] 2 All E.R. (Comm.) 24; *cf. Sewell v Burdick* (1884) 10 App.Cas. 74 at p.105; *Sea Calm Shipping Co. SA v Chantiers Navals de L'Esterels (The Uhenbels)* [1986] 2 Lloyd's Rep. 294; contrast *Ngo Chew Hong Edible Oils Pte. Ltd v Scindia Steam Navigation Co. Ltd (The Jalamohan)* [1988] 1 Lloyd's Rep. 443 (fixture note between different parties than shipper and carrier not the contract); *Nelson Pine Industries, Ltd v Seatrans New Zealand Ltd* (*The Pembroke*) [1995] 2 Lloyd's Rep. 290 (New Zealand High Court); *Jarl Trä AB v Convoys Ltd* [2003] EWHC 1988, [2003] 2 Lloyd's Rep. 459.

68 See *Pyrene Co. Ltd v Scindia Navigation Co. Ltd*, above.

69 *Heskell v Continental Express Ltd* [1950] 1 All E.R. 1033; above, para.18–030: *Jarl Trä AB v Convoys Ltd* [2003] EWHC 1488, [2003] 2 Lloyd's Rep. 453.

70 *Crooks & Co. v Allan* (1879) 5 Q.B.D. 38 at pp.40–41.

71 On the principle of *Olley v Marlborough Court Ltd* [1949] 1 K.B. 532.

72 *Armour & Co. Ltd v Leopold Walford (London) Ltd* [1921] 3 K.B. 473.

73 On the principle stated in *Hardwick Game Farm v Suffolk Agricultural, etc., Association* [1969] A.C. 31 at pp.90, 104, 105, 113, 130.

74 On the principle in *British Crane Hire Corp. v Ipswich Plant Hire* [1975] Q.B. 303.

75 *cf. Sunrise Maritime Inc. v Uvisco Ltd (The Hector)* [1998] 2 Lloyd's Rep. 287 at p.299 ("supersedes"); doubted on another point in *Alimport v Soubert Shipping Co. Ltd* [2002], Lloyd's Rep. 447.

76 As in *The Happy Ranger* [2002] EWCA Civ 694, [2002] 2 All E.R. (Comm.) 24, above n.67.

in the bill of lading"[77]. These expressions, however, for the most part[78] occur in the context of the relationship which is said to spring up,[79] on the indorsement of the bill of lading, between the carrier and the indorsee of the bill. The position appears to be that, between these parties, the bill of lading is the contract of carriage and not merely evidence of its terms; or that it is the "only evidence"[80] of the contract between them or that the contract between carrier and transferee "consists only"[81] of the terms of the bill of lading. Even when the general rule is stated, that a bill of lading is only evidence of the contract, or a mere receipt, this is commonly qualified by saying that it is otherwise between shipowner and indorsee,[82] or that between these parties the bill of lading is the contract of carriage.[83] Thus in the hands of a buyer to whom a bill of lading has been transferred by the seller the bill of lading will normally be the contract of carriage[84]; and its terms will, in the absence of any contrary provision in it,[85] prevail over those of any previous contractual arrangement relating to the carriage of the goods, made between the shipowner and the shipper, or a person acting on

---

[77] *Van Casteel v Booker* (1848) 2 Ex. 691 at p.708; *Lecky & Co. Ltd v Ogilvy, Gillanders & Co.* (1897) 3 Com.Cas. 29 at pp.35, 37; *Hain SS Co. Ltd v Tate & Lyle Ltd* (1936) 41 Com.Cas. 350 at pp.357, 364; *JI MacWilliam Co. Inc. v Mediterranean Shipping Co. SA (The Rafaela S)* [2005] UKHL 11, [2005] 2 A.C. 423 at [37] ("containing the contract of carriage"), but contrast *ibid.* at [39] ("a memorandum of the terms of the contract of carriage. . ."); in *Glyn, Mills, Currie & Co. v East & West India Dock Co.* (1882) 7 App.Cas. 591 at p.596, Lord Selborne, more equivocally, says that the purpose of the bill of lading is "to express the terms of the contract"; more recently, it has become common to refer to documents "containing or evidencing" a contract of carriage: *e.g. SIAT di dal Ferro v Tradax Overseas SA* [1980] 1 Lloyd's Rep. 53 at p.63; Carriage of Goods by Sea Act 1971, s.1(6)(a); Carriage of Goods by Sea Act 1992, s.5(1).

[78] Not always: for example, in *Leduc v Ward* (1888) 20 Q.B.D. 475 at pp.478–480 Lord Esher M.R.'s statement that "the writing [in the bill of lading] is the only evidence of the contract" refers to the position between shipper and carrier; *cf. ibid.* at p.485, *per* Lopes L.J.

[79] See *Hain SS Co. v Tate & Lyle* (1936) 41 Com. Cas. 350 at p.356; *Rudolph A. Oetker v IFA Internationale Frachtagentur AG (The Almak)* [1985] 1 Lloyd's Rep. 557 at p.560. See further para.18–111, below.

[80] *George Kallis (Manufacturers) Ltd v Success Insurance Ltd* [1985] 2 Lloyd's Rep. 8 at p.11.

[81] *Partenreederei M/S Heidberg v Grosvenor Grain & Feed Co. Ltd (The Heidberg)* [1994] 1 Lloyd's Rep. 287 at p.310, as to which all above, para 18–047 n.64.

[82] *e.g. Leduc v Ward* (1888) 20 Q.B.D. 475 at 480; *cf. Delaurier & Co. v James Wyllie* (1889) 17 R. (Ct. of Sess.) 167 at p.193; *The Ardennes* [1951] 1 K.B. 55 at p.60; *Government of Swaziland Central Transport Administration v Leila Maritime Co. Ltd (The Leila)* [1985] 2 Lloyd's Rep. 172 at p.177; *The Al Battani* [1993] 2 Lloyd's Rep. 219 at p.222.

[83] *Leduc v Ward*, above. at p.484, *per* Fry L.J.; *Tradigrain SA v King Diamond Shipping SA (The Spiros C)* [2000] 2 Lloyd's Rep. 319 at p.327.

[84] *George Kallis (Manufacturers) Ltd v Success Insurance Ltd* [1985] 2 Lloyd's Rep. 8 at p.11.

[85] For an example of such contrary provision, see *Parsons Corporation v CV Scheepvaartonderneming Happy Ranger (The Happy Ranger)* [2002] EWC Civ 694, [2002] 2 All E.R. (Comm.) 24 where both the antecedent contract and the bill of lading provided that, in case of conflict between the two documents, the terms of the former should prevail. The issue in that case arose between shipper and carrier and was whether the contract between these parties was subjected to the Hague-Visby Rules.

the shipper's behalf. In one case, terms for the carriage of onions from Egypt had been agreed between carriers and a body which acted on behalf of exporters and was known as the Supreme Onion Shipping Committee; but the carriers issued bills of lading containing terms which differed from those so negotiated. These bills of lading were later indorsed to the buyers, and it was held that the buyers' rights under the contracts of carriage were governed by the bills of lading and not by the terms negotiated by the Committee.[86] The terms of the bill of lading will likewise (unless otherwise agreed[87]) prevail, between carrier and transferee, over any variations of those terms that may have been agreed between carrier and shipper after the issue of the bill.[88]

Terms of the bill of lading contract. Whether the bill of lading contains, or is only evidence of, the contract of carriage, the terms of that contract are to be determined in accordance with the general principles of the law of contract. They may be set out in the bill *in extenso*, or the bill may incorporate by reference terms set out elsewhere: for example (where a so-called "short form" bill is used) in the carrier's usual conditions of contracting.[89] Where the same carriage operation is governed both by a bill of lading and by a charterparty, the bill may provide for the incorporation into it of charterparty terms. The courts have traditionally adopted a somewhat restrictive approach to the interpretation of bill of lading clauses purporting by general words to incorporate charterparty terms into bill of lading contracts.[90] 18–049

The general principles of the law of contract also determine whether a statement in a bill of lading amounts to a contractual promise or merely to a representation of fact. In accordance with these principles,[91] it has for example, been held that words in a bill of lading which state that goods have been shipped,[92] or that they were when shipped in apparent good order and condition, were not "words of contract in the sense of a promise" but only affirmations of fact.[93]

Conflict between bill of lading and charterparty terms. As noted in paragraph 18–049 above, goods may be shipped by a seller or his supplier under one or more charterparties, as well as under bills of lading which are later transferred to the buyer. A number of problems can then arise, not from attempts to *incorporate* charterparty terms into the bills of lading, but 18–050

---

[86] *The El Amria and the El Minia* [1982] 2 Lloyd's Rep. 28.
[87] See above, at n.85.
[88] *Leduc v Ward* (1888) 20 Q.B.D. 475 at p.484, *per* Fry L.J.; *Tradigrain SA v King Diamond Shipping SA (The Spiros C)* [2000] 2 Lloyd's Rep. 319 at p.327.
[89] See Williams [1979] L.M.C.L.Q. 297; for an illustration, see *Jarl Trä AB v Convoys Ltd* [2003] EWHC 1488, [2003] 2 Lloyd's Rep. 459.
[90] *e.g. TW Thomas & Co. Ltd v Portsea Shipping Co. Ltd* [1912] A.C. 1; *Miramar Maritime Corp. v Holborn Oil Trading Ltd (The Miramar)* [1984] A.C. 617; *Skips A/S Nordheim v Syrian Petroleum Co. Ltd (The Varenna)* [1984] Q.B. 559; *Carver on Bills of Lading* (2nd ed., 2005), paras 3–012 *et seq.*
[91] See Treitel, *The Law of Contract*, (11th ed.) pp.352–357.
[92] See above, para.18–030.
[93] *Companía Naviera Vasconzada v Churchill & Sim* (1906) 1 K.B. 237 at p.247.

from a simple *conflict* between the charterparty terms and those of the bill of lading.

18–051 **Bill of lading issued to charterer.** First, goods may be shipped in a ship chartered by the shipper directly from the shipowner. In that case any bill of lading issued by or on behalf of the shipowner prima facie operates, as between shipowner and charterer, as a mere receipt. It is evidence of the facts stated in it, such as the receipt of the goods by the shipowner, the time of shipment and the apparent order and condition of the goods.[94] It may also be a document of title to the goods. But it is not evidence of the terms of a contract of carriage between shipper and shipowner, for that contract will be contained in the charterparty. If the bill of lading conflicts with the charterparty, the latter will normally prevail as the original contract of carriage. It is, indeed, open to the shipper and shipowner expressly[95] to provide that the terms of the bill of lading are to supersede those of the charterparty; but the point of the normal or prima facie rule is that the bill of lading will not be regarded as a subsequent contract varying the charterparty merely because of a conflict between the two documents.[96]

18–052 **Bill of lading transferred by charterer.** Secondly, the case put in paragraph 18–051 above may be varied by supposing that the bill of lading has been indorsed to a third party, *e.g.* by the shipper to his buyer. Between that third party and the carrier, the bill of lading will normally be the contract of carriage[97]; and its terms will prevail over those of a charterparty between shipowner and shipper except to the extent that the charterparty terms are effectively incorporated by reference into the bill of lading.[98] The terms of the bill of lading will also prevail over those of the charterparty as between the shipowner and a person to whom the bill of lading has been transferred, not as indorsee, but as consignee.[99]

---

94 Above, para.18–028.
95 *Rodocanachi, Sons & Co. v Milburn Bros* (1886) 18 Q.B.D. 67 at pp.75, 78 ("express provision").
96 *Rodocanachi, Sons & Co. v Milburn Bros*, above, at p.79; *Sewell v Burdick* (1884) 10 App.Cas. 74 at p.105; *Leduc v Ward* (1888) 20 Q.B.D. 475 at p.479; *Tagart, Beaton & Co. v James Fisher & Sons* [1903] 1 K.B. 391 as explained in *Molthes RA v Ellerman's Wilson Line Ltd* [1927] 1 K.B. 710 at p.716; *President of India v Metcalfe Shipping Co. Ltd (The Dunelmia)* [1970] 1 Q.B. 289 at pp.305, 308; *Aktieselskabet de Danske Sukkerfabrikker v Bajmar Compania Naviera SA (The Torrenia)* [1983] 2 Lloyd's Rep. 210 at p.216; *Trade Star Line Corp. v Mitsui & Co. Ltd (The Arctic Trader)* [1996] 2 Lloyd's Rep. 449 at p.455; *cf. The Ardennes* [1951] 1 K.B. 55 at p.60; *The Al Battani* [1993] 2 Lloyd's Rep. 219 at p.222. And see below, para.19–037, n.84. For difficulties arising in this connection from *Gullischen v Stewart* (1884) 13 Q.B.D. 317, see *Carver on Bills of Lading* (2nd ed., 2005), paras 5–043, 5–044.
97 Above, para.18–048; *The Arctic Trader*, above, at p.455.
98 Above, para.18–049; below, para.19–041.
99 *Compania Commercial Naviera San Martin SA v China National Foreign Trade Transportation Corp. (The Costanza M)* [1981] 2 Lloyd's Rep. 148 at p.150; *Skips A/S Nordheim v Syrian Petroleum Co. Ltd (The Varenna)* [1984] Q.B. 599, (where the action was brought both against the original shipper and against the consignee, and Donaldson M.R. therefore referred at p.615 to the contract "contained in, or evidenced by the bill of lading." The shipper took no part in the proceedings).

Bill of lading transferred to charterer. Thirdly, goods may be sold and shipped by a seller on a ship chartered by the buyer for the purpose of taking delivery of the goods under the contract of sale. If the seller takes a bill of lading in his own name and to his own order, the terms of that bill of lading would prima facie govern the contractual relations between seller and carrier.[1] That prima facie rule could be excluded by showing that, in taking out the bill, the seller had acted as agent for the buyer (or for some other person named as consignee in the bill). One fact tending to support the existence of such an agency relationship would be that property and risk had passed to the buyer on shipment, but it is submitted that this fact is far from decisive since it does not necessarily deprive the seller of his interest in the due performance of the contract of carriage.[2] Even if the seller had acted as agent for the purpose of making the buyer a party to the contract of carriage, it would not follow that the seller's own rights and liabilities under the contract were excluded: the situation might well be one in which, exceptionally, both principal and agent were entitled and liable under the contract.[3] 18–053

Where the prima facie rule stated above applies (so that the bill of lading terms govern the contractual relationship between seller and carrier), and the seller, in performance of the contract of sale, later transfers the bill of lading to the buyer (who has chartered the carrying ship), then the bill does not, in the hands of the buyer, become the contract of carriage, for that contract is contained in the charterparty between buyer and shipowner.[4] Hence the general principle[5] that, in the hands of an indorsee, the terms of the bill of lading prevail over those of the charterparty will not apply; if there is a conflict between the two documents, the terms of the charterparty will govern the relations between buyer and shipowner.

The rule just stated is based on the assumption that the ship has been chartered by the buyer for the purpose of the performance of the very

---

[1] According to *Union Industrielle et Maritime v Petrosul International Ltd (The Roseline)* [1987] 1 Lloyd's Rep. 18, there is no contractual relationship at all between the seller and the carrier if, in such a case, the bill is not made out to the order of the seller but names the buyer's bank as the consignee to whose order the goods were to be delivered (see above, para.18–015, n.7); but this may, with respect, be doubted. Prima facie the bill in such a case is evidence of a contract between the person named as shipper and the carrier for delivery to the consignee to whose order the bill is made out, or to such other person as the seller may direct (above, paras 18–021—18–023). In *Spiliada Maritime Corp. v Cansulex Ltd* [1987] 1 Lloyd's Rep. 1 at p.5 Lord Goff says that "there is doubt whether a similar conclusion [to that reached in *The Roseline*] would be reached in English law"; he refers *ibid.* to an unreported (and unnamed) contrary decision of Mustill J. The reference may well be to the subsequently reported case of *The Athenasia Comninos and George Chr. Lemos* (1979) [1990] 1 Lloyd's Rep. 277.

[2] *e.g.* if the buyer failed to pay, or if he (rightfully or wrongfully) rejected the goods.

[3] See *Bowstead and Reynolds on Agency* (18th ed.), Art. 98.

[4] *President of India v Metcalfe Shipping Co. (The Dunelmia)* [1970] 1 Q.B. 289, following *Love & Stewart Ltd v Rowtor S.S. Co. Ltd* [1916] 2 A.C. 527; *The Athenasia Comninos and George Chr. Lemos* (1979) [1990] 1 Lloyd's Rep. 277 at p.281. There is no reference to this point in *SA Sucre Export v Northern River Shipping Ltd* [1994] 2 Lloyd's Rep. 266, perhaps because the terms of the charterparty on the point in question (delivery to order) were for the purpose in question not materially different from those of the bill of lading.

[5] See above, para.18–052.

contract in pursuance of which the shipment is made: for example, where the sale is on f.o.b. terms and the buyer has chartered the ship for the purpose of taking delivery under that contract.[6] The position is different where there is no connection between the charterparty and the transaction in pursuance of which the bill of lading is transferred to the charterer: *e.g.* where a shipper of goods borrows money from a person who happens to be charterer of the carrying ship and then indorses the bill of lading to that charterer by way of security for the loan. In one such case,[7] the relations between the indorsee and the shipowners with regard to the shipment of the goods were held to be governed by the bill of lading since this was "a separate contract . . . independent of the charterparty".[8] Such reasoning might also apply where goods were sold on c.i.f. terms and the bill of lading was transferred in pursuance of that contract to a buyer who happened to be the charterer of the carrying ship but had not entered into the charterparty for the purpose of taking delivery under the subsequent contract of sale. The issue in cases of the kind here under discussion is one of contractual intention. Shipowner and charterer are likely to intend their contractual relations with regard to the shipment of the goods to be governed by the charterparty where the ship was chartered for the very purpose of receiving those goods; but such an inference is unlikely to arise where that shipment was not within their contemplation when the charterparty was concluded.

Rights under the bill of lading may also pass to a charterer, not by transfer of the bill of lading, but by the process of an assignment[9] of the rights of the shipper or of the transferee of the bill to the charterer.[10]

18–054 **Charterparty between others.** There may be a charterparty to which no person entitled and liable under the bill of lading is a party. For example, a ship may be chartered by her owner to a charterer and then sub-chartered by the charterer to a shipper, to whom a bill of lading may later be issued by the shipowner. There being, in such a case, no charterparty between shipowner and shipper, the bill of lading is regarded as "evidencing a contract of carriage between the shipowners and cargo-owners".[11] Hence

---

[6] As in *The Dunelmia*, above, n.4.

[7] *Calcutta SS Co. Ltd v Andrew Weir & Co.* [1910] 1 K.B. 759.

[8] *The Dunelmia*, above, at p.306.

[9] See para.18–147, below.

[10] See *Agrosin Pte. Ltd v Highway Shipping Co. Ltd (The Mata K)* [1998] 2 Lloyd's Rep. 614 at p.616; *Eridiana SpA v Rudolf A Oetker (The Fjord Wind)* [1999] 1 Lloyd's Rep. 307 at p.335, affirmed without reference to this point [2000] 2 Lloyd's Rep. 191; the charterer in the latter case took delivery of goods but the bill of lading was not transferred to him.

[11] *Bangladesh Chemical Industries Corp. v Henry Stephens Shipping Co. Ltd (The SLS Everest)* [1981] 2 Lloyd's Rep. 389 at p.391; *Heinrich Hanno & Co. BV v Fairlight Shipping Co. Ltd (The Kostas K)* [1985] 1 Lloyd's Rep. 231 at pp.235–236. *Cf. Continental Fertiliser Co. Ltd v Pionier Shipping Co. Ltd (The Pionier)* [1995] 1 Lloyd's Rep. 223; *Indian SS Co. Ltd v Louis Dreyfus Sugar Ltd (The Indian Reliance)* [1997] 1 Lloyd's Rep. 52 (where it appears at p.54 that the bills were owner's bills); *Sunrise Maritime Inc. v Uvisco Ltd (The Hector)* [1998] 2 Lloyd's Rep. 287 at p.289, where the actual decision was that there was *no* contract between the shipowner and the holder of the bill of lading; *The Hector* was doubted on another point in *Alimport v Soubert Shipping Co. Ltd* [2000] 2 Lloyd's Rep. 447 (see above, para.18–029, n.26).

the terms of the bill of lading will prevail over those of the charter[12] and sub-charter.[13] The position is the same where there is a charter but no sub-charter and the shipowner simply issues a bill of lading to a shipper other than the charterer.[14] Some of the authorities which support these propositions were concerned only with the relations between a shipowner on the one hand and, on the other, a person who had become entitled and liable under the bill of lading as indorsee or consignee.[15] They could therefore be regarded simply as applications of the rule that, as between such persons and the shipowner, the bill of lading was the contract of carriage.[16] But they could also be explained on the additional ground that, in them, there was no charterparty that governed the relations between shipowner and shipper. Where this is the case, the bill of lading is the *only* evidence of any contract of carriage between these parties, so that, even in the hands of the shipper, the terms of the bill of lading should prevail over those of the charterparties.[17] This reasoning would, however, not apply where the ship was first chartered to a charterer and then sub-chartered by him to the shipper, to whom a bill of lading was then issued by or on behalf of the *charterer*, in such a way as to indicate that the charterer (rather than the shipowner) was to be the party entitled and liable under the bill.[18] In such a case the bill of lading would not purport to record any contract between shipper and shipowner[19]; while between charterer and shipper the contract of carriage would be contained in the sub-charter, so that the bill of lading would prima facie be a mere receipt. Hence between charterer and shipper the terms of the sub-charter would prevail over those of the bill of lading[20]; but if the shipper then transferred the bill of lading, the terms of the bill would govern the contractual relations between charterer and transferee.

---

[12] Since neither the shipper nor the indorsee nor the consignee of the bill of lading will on the facts stated be a party to this contract.

[13] Since the shipowner will not be a party to this contract.

[14] *e.g. Skips A/S Nordheim v Syrian Petroleum Co. Ltd (The Varenna)* [1984] Q.B. 599.

[15] *i.e.* those cited in nn. 11 and 14, above.

[16] Above, para.18–052 at n.97.

[17] *Turner v Haji Goolam Mahommed Azam* [1904] A.C. 826.

[18] See *The Venezuela* [1980] 1 Lloyd's Rep. 393; *Homburg Houtimport BV v Agrosin Private Ltd (The Starsin)* [2003] UKHL 12, [2004] 1 A.C. 785. Even where the bill of lading indicates that the shipowner is to be liable as carrier, the charterer may by his conduct be estopped from denying liability under it: see *Pacol Ltd v Trade Lines Ltd (The Henrik Sif)* [1982] 1 Lloyd's Rep. 456. Some doubt as to the correctness of the decision in *The Henrik Sif* was expressed by Webster J. (who had decided the case) in *Shearson Lehman Hutton Inc. v MacLaine Watson & Co. Ltd* [1989] 2 Lloyd's Rep. 570 at pp. 596, 604, though the decision was approved on another point in *The Stolt Loyalty* [1993] 2 Lloyd's Rep. 281 at pp.289–291 (*affd.* without reference to this point [1995] 1 Lloyd's Rep. 599; and evidently treated as good law, though distinguished, in *Rafsanjan Pistachio Producers Co-operative v Bank Leumi (UK) Plc* [1992] 1 Lloyd's Rep. 513 at p.542). See also Treitel, *The Law of Contract* (11th ed.), pp.106–107.

[19] *The Forum Craftsman* [1985] 1 Lloyd's Rep. 291, where it followed that the shipowner could not rely on the bill of lading against a transferee of the bill of lading.

[20] The authorities cited in para.18–051, n.96, seem to govern this situation.

18–055 **Contracts (Rights of Third Parties) Act 1999.** It will be recalled[21] that section 1 of this Act entitles a person (the third party) in specified circumstances to enforce a term of a contract to which he is not a party; but that, by virtue of the subsection 6(5) exception, no such right is conferred on the third party in the case of a "contract for the carriage of goods by sea." This expression does not include a contract by way of charterparty but does include a bill of lading contract.[22] The question therefore arises whether, or to what extent, the subsection 6(5) exception applies where the carriage operation is the subject both of a charterparty and of a bill of lading. In answering this question, it will be necessary to refer again to some of the rules stated and distinctions drawn in paragraphs 18–050 to 18–053 above. Two situations call for discussion.

18–056 **Bill of lading issued to charterer.** The first situation is that in which goods are shipped by the shipper on a ship which the shipper has chartered from the shipowner. A bill of lading is then issued by the shipowner to the shipper. At this stage, the bill of lading is between shipper and shipowner a mere receipt and does not contain or evidence a contract for the carriage of the goods.[23] Hence the subsection 6(5) exception does not apply (there being no "contract for the carriage of goods by sea" within the 1999 Act) so that a third party can acquire the right to enforce a term of the charterparty under section 1 of the 1999 Act. Such rights could, for example, be acquired by a broker to whom commission was to be paid under a term of the charterparty (but who was not a party to it)[24] or by a third party to whom under that contract the shipowner had promised to deliver the goods. But if the bill of lading is then transferred to another third party who becomes a lawful holder of it, rights of suit under the bill of lading can be acquired by that third party, as transferee of the bill, by virtue of the Carriage of Goods by Sea Act 1992, section 2(1).[25] At this stage, therefore, there is a "contract for the carriage of goods by sea" within the 1999 Act so that the subsection 6(5) exception would seem to apply; and this point could be significant where the rights of the transferee were, under the bill of lading, less favourable to him than his rights as a third party under the charterparty. Could he then assert the latter rights by virtue of section 1 of the 1999 Act in preference to his rights as transferee under the 1992 Act? At first sight, it might appear that he could rely on section 2(1) of the 1999 Act, by which the contracting parties cannot, in the circumstances specified in the subsection, without his consent vary his right under section 1 so as to extinguish or alter that right. But it is submitted that this argument would not prevail since section 2(1) of the 1999 Act applies only to a variation "by agreement" between the parties; and in the case put the variation occurs not by such agreement, but by operation of law on the transfer of the bill of

---

[21] Above, para.18–005.
[22] This follows from the definitions in ss.6(6) and (7) of the 1999 Act.
[23] Above, para.18–051.
[24] *e.g. Less Affiéteurs Réunis SA v Leopold Walford (London) Ltd* [1919] A.C. 801; *Nisshin Shipping Co. Ltd v Cleaves & Co. Ltd* [2003] EWHC 2602, [2004] 1 Lloyd's Rep. 38.
[25] Below, para.18–102.

lading. This conclusion can also be supported by the further argument that, in the case put, the transfer of the bill of lading must be within the contemplation of the parties to the charterparty and therefore it should be an implied term of the charterparty that any rights conferred by it on the third party should be superseded by rights acquired by the third party on the transfer to him of the bill of lading. That implied term would limit or exclude any right which a third party might, but for that term,[26] have under section 1 of the 1999 Act, to enforce a term of the charterparty.

Bill of lading transferred to charterer. The second situation is that in which goods are shipped under a bill of lading which is later transferred to the charterer of the ship. Before the transfer of the bill of lading, there is clearly a "contract for the carriage of goods by sea" within the subsection 6(5) exception to the 1999 Act, so that no rights of enforcement under section 1 are conferred on the transferee. After the transfer of the bill of lading, a further distinction was drawn at common law (and continues to be drawn after the Carriage of Goods by Sea Act 1992)[27] between two types of case. The first was that in which the transferee had chartered the carrying ship for the very purpose of taking delivery of the goods from the shipper: *e.g.* where the transferee was a buyer on f.o.b. terms and had chartered the ship in order to perform his duty to take delivery under that contract. In such a case, the bill of lading normally becomes in the transferee's hands a mere receipt and the contractual relations between him and the shipowner are governed by the charterparty.[28] Hence at this stage there is no longer a "contract for the carriage of goods by sea" within the subsection 6(5) exception, so that rights under the charterparty can be conferred on a "third party" by section 1 of the 1999 Act. No such rights can, however, be conferred on the transferee of the bill of lading since he is, *ex hypothesi*, a party to the contract contained in the charterparty and so not a "third party" to that contract within section 1 of the 1999 Act.[29] It is, however, conceivable that the *transferor* of the bill of lading might seek to assert rights *under the charterparty: e.g.* in respect of damage to goods which were still at his risk when damaged. If he could satisfy the requirements of section 1, then he would not be precluded (in the present type of case) from making such a claim under that section by the subsection 6(5) exception. The second type of case is that in which there is no connection between the charterparty and the transaction in pursuance of which the bill of lading was transferred: in a case of this kind, the bill of lading (in respect of the shipment in question) governs not only the relations between shipper and carrier but also those between carrier and transferee.[30] Thus there is for the purpose of the subsection 6(5) exception a "contract for the carriage of goods by sea" throughout and no right to enforce any term of that contract could be conferred on any third party by section 1 of the 1999 Act. This 18–057

[26] 1999 Act, s.1(4) ("subject to"); *cf.* below, para.20–060.
[27] Above, para.18–053, below, para.18–111.
[28] As in *The Dunelmia* [1970] 1 Q.B. 289, above, para.18–053.
[29] This follows from s.1(1) of the 1999 Act.
[30] As in *Calcutta SS Co. Ltd v Andrew Weir & Co.* [1910] 1 K.B. 759, above para.18–053.

reasoning could, for example, apply where goods were sold afloat on c.i.f. terms to a buyer who happened to be the charterer of the carrying ship and to whom the bill of lading covering the goods sold was transferred by the seller.

18–058 **Exemption and limitation clauses.** For the avoidance of doubt, it should finally be repeated that the subsection 6(5) exception does not prevent any third party from availing himself of an exclusion or limitation clause in the contract of carriage,[31] so that nothing in the immediately foregoing discussion applies where a third party seeks to invoke such a clause.

18–059 **Deviation.** A carrier is said to deviate when he departs from the agreed route, or if no route is expressly mentioned in the contract of carriage, when he departs from the usual route.[32] Unjustifiable deviation is a breach of a fundamental term of the contract of carriage, and it has been held to deprive the carrier of the benefit of any exemptions from, or limitations of, liability to which he would otherwise have been entitled under the express terms of the contract[33] or under terms incorporated in the contract by statute.[34] Exemptions and limitations available to the carrier, not by force of contract but by force of statute, may survive deviation; whether they do so survive depends on the construction of the statute.[35] It has further been said that deviation "displaces the contract"[36] of carriage, so that the other party is relieved from his obligation to perform its terms.[37] These effects of

---

[31] See the concluding words of s.6(5).

[32] See *Frenkel v MacAndrews & Co. Ltd* [1929] A.C. 545; *Reardon Smith Line Ltd v Black Sea, etc. Insurance Co. Ltd* [1939] A.C. 562; delay may also amount to deviation according to dicta in *Brandt v Liverpool, etc. Steam Navigation Co.* [1924] 1 K.B. 575 at pp.597, 601.

[33] *e.g. Joseph Thorley Ltd v Orchis SS Co. Ltd* [1907] 1 K.B. 660.

[34] *e.g. Stag Line Ltd v Foscolo, Mango & Co. Ltd* [1932] A.C. 328 decided under the Carriage of Goods by Sea Act 1924 (now repealed). For the position under the Carriage of Goods by Sea Act 1971, s.1(2), see next note.

[35] See *Kenya Railways v Antares Co. Pte. Ltd (The Antares) (No. 2)* [1987] 1 Lloyd's Rep. 424, where the carrier was entitled to rely on the time-bar provided by Art. III.6 of the Hague-Visby Rules, which by virtue of Carriage of Goods by Sea Act 1971, s.1(2), have "the force of law". The court stressed that Art. III.6 discharged the carrier from all liability "whatsoever" after expiry of the time-bar. This word does not occur in Art. IV 5, which lays down financial limits governing the carrier's liability "in any event". It has been held that, by virtue of this phrase, the carrier's limitation of liability is not displaced merely by reason of his having committed the serious breach of carrying the goods on (rather than under) deck: *Daewoo Heavy Industries Ltd v Klipriver Shipping Ltd. (The Kapitan Petko Voivoda)* [2003] EWCA Civ. 451, [2003] 1 All E.R. (Comm.) 801, overruling *Wibau Maschinenfabrik Hartman SA v Mackinon Mackenzie & Co. (The Chanda)* [1989] 2 Lloyd's Rep. 494. *The Antares*, above, was likewise a case of unauthorised carriage on deck, which was formerly regarded as analogous to deviation in its effect on exemption and limitation clauses; the analogy appears not to have survived *The Kapitan Petko Voivoda*, above. For further discussion of these cases in the context of container transport, see below, paras 21–090, to 21–093.

[36] *Joseph Thorley Ltd v Orchis S.S. Co. Ltd*, above, n.33 at p.667.

[37] *Hain SS Co. Ltd v Tate & Lyle Ltd* (1936) 41 Com.Cas. 350 at p.356.

deviation appear to have been based[38] on the danger that the owner of the goods may lose the benefit of insurance on the goods when the ship deviates.[39] It is an open question whether the cases which specify these effects of deviation have survived the rejection by the House of Lords of the substantive doctrine of fundamental breach.[40] One view is that they have so survived, being regarded as *sui generis*,[41] by reason of their historical and commercial background. Another view is that they merely illustrate the general principle of the law of contract, that the effect of exemption clauses depends on the true construction of the contract of carriage.[42] On the latter view, the special effects of deviation, described above, would yield to sufficiently clear contrary provisions in that contract. Detailed discussion of deviation is beyond the scope of this book[43]; here it is necessary only to consider the position of an indorsee of a bill of lading in cases in which there has been a deviation, and the effect of deviation between buyer and seller.

Effects of deviation between carrier and indorsee of bill of lading. The principles which govern the effects of deviation apply, not only between the original parties to the contract of carriage, but also between the carrier and an indorsee of a bill of lading.[44] But where the bill of lading is indorsed, difficulties may arise if the original party to the contract of carriage has "waived" the deviation. In *Hain SS Co. Ltd v Tate & Lyle Ltd*[45] a c.i.f. seller of sugar chartered a ship to carry the sugar to England. Bills of lading were issued to him, which he indorsed to the buyer, who took them without 18–060

---

[38] For criticism, see *Farr v Hain SS Co.*, 121 F.2d. 940 at p.944, (1941) a case arising from the same facts as *Hain SS Co. Ltd v Tate & Lyle Ltd*, above.

[39] *Hain SS Co. Ltd v Tate & Lyle Ltd,* above n.37, at p. 354. Insurance cover is lost "*as from the time of deviation*": Marine Insurance Act 1906, s.46()1). This wording closely resembles part of s.33(3) of the Act, which provides that, in case of breach by the insured of a "warranty" (as defined in that subsection), "the insurer is discharged from liability *as from the date of the breach of warranty*". He is so discharged automatically, without any election on his part: *Bank of Nova Scotia v Hellenic Mutual War Risks Association (Bermuda) Ltd (The Good Luck)* [1992] 1 A.C. 233. It seems reasonable to deduce that, in the event of deviation, insurance cover likewise ceases automatically at the time of the deviation; and this point helps to account for the common law effects of deviation on exemption and limitation clauses on contracts for the carriage of goods by sea. In fact, the owner of the goods may be protected by a policy under which he is "held covered in case of deviation at a premium to be arranged" (*Hain SS Co. Ltd v Tate & Lyle Ltd*, above, at p.355). Even such a policy will not adequately protect the goods owner if the insurer "arranges" the premium at an amount equal to the loss, as in *Vincentelli v Rowlett* (1911) 16 Com.Cas. 310. *Quaere* whether, where the deviation is merely slight or technical, this method of "arranging" the premium is consistent with Marine Insurance Act 1906, s.31(2), under which such a premium must be reasonable.

[40] *Daewoo Heavy Industries Ltd v Klipriver Shipping Ltd. (The Kapitan Petko Voivoda)* [2003] EWCA Civ. 451, [2003] 1 All E.R. (Comm.) 801; above paras 13–047, 13–049.

[41] *Photo Production Ltd v Securicor Transport Ltd* [1980] A.C. 827 at p.845; *cf. ibid.* at p.850.

[42] *Treitel*, pp.225, *et seq.*

[43] See *Carver on Bills of Lading* (2nd ed., 2005) especially paras 9–036 *et seq*.

[44] *Evans, Sons & Co. v Cunard SS Co. Ltd* (1902) 18 T.L.R. 374.

[45] (1936) 41 Com.Cas. 350.

notice of the fact that the ship had previously deviated. It was held that the deviation gave the indorsee of the bill of lading the same right to rescind the contract of carriage as it had originally given to the charterer; and that this right of the indorsee was not affected by the fact that the charterer had waived the breach and so lost his right to rescind. Although the case is, strictly speaking, concerned only with the effect of waiver by a charterer on the position of an indorsee of the bill of lading, the position would seem to be the same if the original shipper was not a charterer but only the holder of a bill of lading.[46] Of course the indorsee may himself waive the breach, but it is submitted that he will not be deemed to have waived it merely because he had notice of the deviation when he took up the bill. For he may be bound to take up the bill by a contract of sale[47]; and this would negative any inference of waiver which might otherwise be drawn from taking up the bill of lading with notice of the deviation.[48] The rule that waiver of deviation by the shipper does not prejudice the rights of an indorsee of the bill is not affected by the Carriage of Goods by Sea Act 1992.[49]

18–061 **Effect of deviation between buyer and seller.** A buyer of goods under a c.i.f. contract is not entitled, as against the seller, to reject shipping documents merely because the ship has deviated. So long as the seller tenders the proper and usual shipping documents he is entitled to be paid, and the buyer must seek his remedy against the carrier.[50] This rule applies even though the buyer is entitled under the contract of sale only to a delivery order,[51] so that he may have difficulty in actually asserting his remedy against the carrier.[52] The c.i.f. buyer is, however, entitled to reject the bill of lading if it contains such wide liberties to deviate as to make it an improper shipping document.[53] If the buyer takes up such a document knowing that it is improper, he may be taken to have waived the seller's breach in tendering the document[54]; but it does not follow that he will also have waived any breach for which the carrier may be held liable by reason of the court's narrow construction of a deviation clause.[55]

---

[46] This view is supported by the reference in *Hain SS Co. Ltd v Tate & Lyle Ltd*, above, at p.364 to *Leduc v Ward* (1888) 20 Q.B.D. 475, where the shipper was not a charterer and the indorsee of the bill of lading was not affected by the shipper's knowledge that the ship *would* deviate.
[47] Below, para.18–061.
[48] *cf.* the argument, accepted in the context of estoppel in *Cremer v General Carriers SA* [1974] 1 W.L.R. 341 at p.351, that the carrier could not rely on a contract of sale to which he was not a party.
[49] Below, para.18–109.
[50] *Shipton, Anderson & Co. v John Weston & Co.* (1922) 10 Ll.L.R. 762; *Burstall v Grimsdale* (1906) 11 Com.Cas. 280 at p.291.
[51] As in *Burstall v Grimsdale*, above.
[52] Especially if the order is not a "ship's delivery order": see below, paras 18–171, 18–175.
[53] Below, para.19–033.
[54] *Shipton, Anderson & Co. v John Weston & Co.*, above, n.50.
[55] *e.g. Glynn v Margetson* [1893] A.C. 351.

(iv) *Bill of Lading as a Document of Title*

Introductory. Earlier in this Chapter, we saw that the expression "document of title of goods" was used in a variety of senses.[56] The leading distinction is between the common law and the statutory sense, but we also saw that there is recent judicial support for using the expression even at common law in more than one sense.[57] In its first, or traditional, sense, it refers to a document which is "negotiable and transferable".[58] The distinctive feature of such a document is that it can perform what may be called a conveyancing function, in that its transfer can operate as a transfer of the constructive possession of the goods, and, if so intended, of the property in them.[59] In the ensuing discussion, the expression "document of title in the common law sense" will, unless suitably qualified, be used in this traditional sense. In a second sense, the expression appears to have been used to refer simply to a document which must, as a matter of law, be produced to the carrier (or other bailee) by a person claiming delivery of the goods.[60] It will be submitted below[61] that a document is not, merely by reason of having to be so produced, capable of performing the conveyancing function (described above) of a document of title in the common law sense. 18–062

Distinctions between various types of bills of lading wer drawn earlier in this chapter[62] and the first topic here to be discussed is which of these types of bills are, and which types of bills are not, documents of title in the common law sense.[63] It will be necessary after discussing their status as such,[64] to consider whether bills of lading which are *not* documents of title in the common law sense may nevertheless be such documents in the statutory sense.[65]

Shipped bill made out to bearer or order. A bill of lading which states that goods have been shipped on board and which is either a bearer or an order bill,[66] is a document of title relating to those goods.[67] It is regarded as the symbol of the goods,[68] so that possession of the bill gives its possessor constructive possession of the goods. No doubt this position reflects the commercial need to provide a mechanism for dealing with cargoes afloat while they are "necessarily incapable of physical delivery."[69] It follows from this characteristic of such a bill[70] that the carrier must normally[71] deliver the 18–063

[56] Above, paras 18–006 to 18–009.
[57] Above, paras 18–007, 18–008.
[58] Above, para.18–007.
[59] *ibid.*
[60] Above, para.18–008.
[61] Below, paras 18–074, 18–075.
[62] See above, paras 18–014 to 18–020.
[63] See above, para.18–007.
[64] Below, paras 18–063 to 18–080.
[65] Below, para.18–083; for the statutory sense of "document of title", see above, para.18–009.
[66] Above, paras 18–014, 18–015.
[67] Above, para.18–007.
[68] *Sanders Bros v Maclean* (1883) 11 Q.B.D. 327 at p.341; *The Prinz Adalbert* [1917] A.C. 586 at p.589. *Cf.* above, para.18–007, n.41.
[69] *Sanders Bros v Maclean* (1883) 11 Q.B.D. 327 at p.341.
[70] Below, para 18–075 at n.56.
[71] Not if there has been a wrongful misappropriation of the bill: below, para.18–085.

goods, and deliver them only to the person in possession of the bill, whether as original shipper or as transferee of the bill by indorsement (where necessary) and delivery.[72] The carrier is not bound to deliver the goods except on production of the bill[73]; and is liable to the holder of the bill if he wrongfully delivers the goods to anyone else.[74] Delivery to such other persons is wrongful even if made against a forged bill of lading in circumstances in which the fact that the bill was not genuine was not known or reasonably apparent to the carrier.[75] In view of this application of the general rule, the suggestion that this rule does not apply where "it is proved to the carrier's reasonable satisfaction that the person seeking the goods is entitled to possession of them and there is some reasonable explanation of what has become of the bill of lading"[76] has been rightly doubted[77]; for it is hard to see why a carrier should be protected by a reasonable belief in the validity of a claim or demand for the goods induced by representations extrinsic to the bill presented to him which turn out to be false, if he is not protected by a reasonable belief in the genuineness of the bill. The general rule may, however, not apply where delivery without the bill is required or authorised by law at the port of discharge or by a custom prevailing there.[78] In the United States, it has been held that the rule can be excluded by the terms of the contract of carriage[79]; and in England there is also some

---

[72] See above, para.18–016.

[73] *Trucks & Spares Ltd v Maritime Agencies Ltd* [1951] 2 All E.R. 982; *Sze Hai Tong Bank Ltd v Rambler Cycle Co. Ltd* [1959] A.C. 576; *Parsons Corporation v CV Scheepvaartonderneming The Happy Ranger (The Happy Ranger)* [2002] EWCA Civ. 694, [2002] 2 All E.R. (Comm.) 24 at [27]; *Barclays Bank Ltd v Commissioners of Customs and Excise* [1963] 1 Lloyd's Rep. 81 at p.89; *aliter* if property has passed without transfer of the bill of lading (as in *Meyer v Sharpe* (1813) 5 Taunt. 74 and *Nathan v Giles* (1814) 5 Taunt. 558, below, para.18–216) and the owner has discharged any lien which the carrier may have; or if a seller has transferred the bill of lading to the buyer and has then exercised his right of stoppage in transit (above, para.15–088).

[74] *Bristol & W. of England Bank v Midland Ry Co.* [1891] 2 Q.B. 653; *Sze Hai Tong Bank Ltd v Rambler Cycle Co. Ltd*, above; *Chabbra Corp. Pte. Ltd v Jag Shakti (The Jag Shakti)* [1986] A.C. 337 at p.345; *Glebe Island Terminals Pty Ltd v Continental Seagram Pty Ltd (The Antwerpen)* [1994] 1 Lloyd's Rep. 213 at p.247; *SA Sucre Export v Northern River Shipping Ltd (The Sormovskiy 3068)* [1994] 2 Lloyd's Rep. 266; *Kuwait Petroleum Corp. v I & D Oil Carriers Ltd (The Houda)* [1994] 2 Lloyd's Rep. 541; *MB Pyramid Sound NV v Briese Schiffahrts GmbH (The Ines)* [1995] 2 Lloyd's Rep. 144 at pp.151–152; *Center Optical (Hong Kong) Ltd v Jardine Transport Services Ltd* [2001] 2 Lloyd's Rep. 678; *East West Corp v DKBS 1912 AF A/S* [2003] EWCA Civ 83, [2003] Q.B. 1509 at [60]; *cf. Frans Maas (UK) Ltd v Sun Alliance & London Insurance Plc* [2004] 1 Lloyd's Rep. 484 at [45].

[75] *Motis Export Ltd v Dampskilbsselskapet AF 1912* [2000] 1 Lloyd's Rep. 211.

[76] *The Sormovskiy 3056*, above, n.74, at p.272.

[77] *East West* case, above n.74, at [41]. Further ground for doubt is provided by *Kuwait Petroleum Corp. v I & D Oil Carriers Ltd (The Houda)* [1994] 2 Lloyd's Rep. 541, where the general rule is stated without qualification. See also *East West Corp. v DKBS 1912* [2002] EWHC 83 (Comm.); [2002] 1 All E.R. (Comm.) 676 at [128], preferring the *Motis Export* case, above, n.75 to the view stated in *The Sormovskiy*, above at n.74.

[78] *The Sormovskiy 3065*, above, n.74 at p.275; *East West* case, at first instance [2002] EWHC 83 (Comm.), [2002] 1 All E.R. (Comm.) at [132]–[133], affirmed without reference to this point [2003] EWCA Civ 83, [2003] Q.B. 1509.

[79] *Chilewish Partners v MV Alligator Fortune* [1994] 2 Lloyd's Rep. 314.

judicial support for the view that "an appropriately worded clause" could protect the shipowner from liability for delivering goods against a forged bill of lading to a person who was not entitled to them.[80] Where the ship arrives before the bill of lading, the carrier may, to avoid delays in unloading, agree to deliver the goods to the person claiming to be entitled to them, without production of the bill,[81] against a letter of indemnity (*e.g.* from a bank); the purpose of such a letter is to protect the carrier if it should turn out that the bill is in fact held by someone with a better right to it, or to the goods, than that of the person to whom delivery has been made. An alternative possible method for avoiding such delays is to arrange for one part of a set of bills of lading to be carried on the ship and to be handed at the destination to the consignee, so as to enable him to claim delivery.[82] Both these practices are based on the assumption that in law delivery can be claimed, and can be claimed only, by the holder of the bill. A buyer of goods can also avoid the need to produce a bill of lading by contracting for delivery ex ship,[83] so as to impose the duty of getting the goods out of the ship on the seller.[84]

Since *Lickbarrow v Mason*[85] it has also been settled that the transfer of a bill of lading will operate to transfer the transferor's property in the goods, if the transfer was made with that intention.[86] Transfer of a bill of lading may operate as a transfer of constructive possession of the goods even though the property in the goods has already passed from transferor to transferee.[87] Thus it may operate as a delivery under a contract of sale even after property has passed from seller to buyer.

The statement that a shipped order or bearer bill is a document of title assumes that the goods have indeed been shipped. A bill of lading which falsely states that goods have been shipped, when in fact none have been shipped, is not a document of title; for in such a case there are no underlying goods.[88]

---

[80] *Motis Export Ltd v Dampskilbsselskapet AF 1912* [2000] 1 Lloyd's Rep. 211 at p.217, where Mance L.J. said that there was no dispute on the point; but the clause in that case was not sufficiently clear to produce this result.

[81] For the practice of delivering oil cargoes without production of the bill of lading (or even of a letter of indemnity) see *A/S Hansens Tangens Rederi III v Total Transport Corp. (The Sagona)* [1984] 1 Lloyd's Rep. 194 at p.203; and see next note.

[82] See *Mobil Shipping & Transportation Co. v Shell Eastern Petroleum (Pte.) Ltd* (*The Mobil Courage*) [1987] 2 Lloyd's Rep. 655, where such an arrangement was made (pursuant to a practice of the oil industry) but not implemented.

[83] For this practice in the oil trade (so as to relieve the buyer from liability for pollution) see *Aegean Sea Traders Corp. v Repsol Petroleo SA (The Aegean Sea)* [1998] 2 Lloyd's Rep. 39 at p.64.

[84] Below, para.21–014.

[85] See above, para.18–007, n.43 for full references.

[86] *Lickbarrow v Mason*, above; *Thompson v Dominy* (1845) 14 M. & W. 403; *J.I. MacWilliam Inc. v Mediterranean Shipping Co. SA (The Rafaela S)* [2005] UKHL, [2005] 2 A.C. 423 at [69]; above, para.18–007; below, paras 18–089, 18–221—18–224.

[87] *Ilyssia Compania Naviera SA v Ahmed Abdul-Qawi Bamaodah (The Elli 2)* [1985] 1 Lloyd's Rep. 107 at p.115.

[88] *Hindley v East Indian Produce Co.* [1973] 2 Lloyd's Rep. 515 at p.519.

18–064 **Legal basis.** An explanation of the rule that delivery of "endorsed bills of lading" could amount to delivery of goods was given in *The Berge Sisar* by Lord Hobhouse who there said that the rule was "an application of the principles of bailment and attornment".[89] Two aspects of this explanation call for comment: the "bailment" and the "attornment" aspect.

18–065 **Bailment.** The bailment aspect is explained in the following further passage from Lord Hobhouse's speech in *The Berge Sisar*: "The bill of lading acknowledges the receipt of the goods from the shipper for carriage to a destination and delivery there to the consignee. It therefore evidences a bailment with the carrier who has issued the bill of lading as the bailee *and the consignee as bailor*."[90] The difficulty lies in the words here italicised since they appear to be inconsistent with part of the reasoning of *The Aliakmon*[91] (to which no reference was made in *The Berge Sisar*). In *The Aliakmon* goods were shipped on behalf of sellers under a bill of lading which named the buyers of the goods as consignees and was sent to them[92]; but the argument that there was a bailment relationship between the buyers and the carriers was rejected, Lord Brandon saying that "[the] only bailment was one by the sellers to the shipowner."[93] This statement forms part of the *ratio decidendi* of *The Aliakmon*, but the same cannot be said of Lord Hobhouse's statement in *The Berge Sisar* where no issue of bailment was argued or decided[94] and the passages quoted above merely form part of

---

[89] *Borealis AB v Stargas Ltd (The Berge Sisar)* [2001] UKHL 17 at [18]; [2002] 1 A.C. 205.
[90] *ibid.*, italics supplied.
[91] *Leigh & Sillavan Ltd v Aliakmon Shipping Co. Ltd (The Aliakmon)* [1986] A.C. 785.
[92] The exact position with regard to the bill of lading is not entirely clear from the reports but appears to have been as follows: (1) The shippers appear to have been the sellers' suppliers who "in shipping the goods were acting as agents of the sellers" ([1986] A.C. 785 at p.808). (2) The bill of lading "showed.. . the consignees as the buyers" (*ibid.*). (3) Since the bill named the buyers as consignees, there was strictly no need to *indorse* it to the buyers (above, para.18–016) but it seems that it was so indorsed: see Lord Brandon's reference to "the endorsement of the bill of lading": [1986] A.C. 785 at p.809; and see [1983] 1 Lloyd's Rep. 203 at pp.206, 207; [1985] Q.B. 350 at pp.363, 368. (4) The bill was also "sent . . . to the buyers": [1986] A.C. 785 at p.808. (5) Lord Brandon said ([1986] A.C. 785 at p.818) that "the bill of lading never was negotiated to the buyers". The meaning of this statement is not entirely clear in view of the references, quoted above, to the "endorsement" of the bill to the buyers and to its having been "sent" to them. The phrase "never negotiated" may refer to the fact that property did not pass to the buyers in consequence of the endorsement: see below, para.18–213.
[93] [1986] A.C. 785 at p.818.
[94] If the transferee of the bill of lading, whose liability was in issue in *The Berge Sisar*, above, n.80, had indeed been the bailor of the cargo, then it would have been arguable that he owed a duty to the carrier (the bailee) at common law as bailor in respect of the dangerous nature of the goods; and that this duty, and the consequent imposition of liability on the consignee, were not subject to the requirements of the Carriage of Goods by Sea Act 1992, which were held in that case not to have been satisfied: see below, paras 18–126, 18–131, 18–132. No attempt was made to rely on any such point. It would have been an implausible one for policy reasons similar to those given by Lord Brandon in *The Aliakmon*, above n.91, at p.818 where he said

an account of the "Genesis"[95] of the Carriage of Goods by Sea Act 1992. This point may have some weight when the apparent conflict between Lord Brandon's view (that the bailor is the shipper, or the shipper's principal) and Lord Hobhouse's view (that the bailor is the consignee named in the bill) comes to be resolved.

One way of resolving the apparent conflict is to say that it is the consignee who is the bailor where the shipper has in taking the bill of lading in his own name but to the order of the consignee acted as agent of the consignee, while it is the consignor (*i.e.*, the shipper) who is the bailor where "the consignor in delivering the goods to the carrier was acting as principal on his own account, with property and risk remaining in him during carriage."[96] In *The Albazero*,[97] Lord Diplock suggested that there was a presumption to the former effect; but that presumption is likely to be rebutted, or simply not to arise, where, as in *The Aliakmon*,[98] the bill is taken out and dealt with under an underlying contract of sale so as to protect the seller's security interest in the goods. More recently, in the *East West* case it was said that "where the named consignees were FOB buyers. . . a shipper may readily, indeed normally, be regarded as agent for a named consignee in making the relevant bill of lading contract",[99] and Lord Hobhouse's statement in *The Berge Sisar* (quoted above[1]) was explained as having been made in such a context. This explanation gives rise to a number of difficulties. The first relates to the facts of *The Berge Sisar* since the terms of the FOB contracts (especially as to the passing of property and risk) under which the goods were originally sold are not given in the report, though under the subsale to the claimants (on CFR terms) property and risk were to pass "at ship's manifold at the loading port."[2] Of the five bills of lading issued in *The Berge Sisar*, three named banks as consignees[3]; and Lord Hobhouse conjectured that the bills were so made out because the named consignees "were the bankers through whom the relevant buyers were to pay"[4] the price to the original sellers, who were named as shippers in the bills. In the *East West* case,[5] by contrast, sellers had also taken bills naming themselves as shippers and banks in Chile (the country of destination) as consignees. But it was held that the sellers "were at all times acting for themselves and the Chilean banks as their agents" (for the sole purpose of collecting the price[6]) so that the sellers (as

---

that, if the argument that the buyers/consignees were bailors was correct, then "there would never have been any need for the Bills of Lading Act 1855 . . ." The point, though (with respect) convincing in the context, may be overstated in the sense that rights in contract may be more extensive than rights in bailment: see below, para.18–115 after n.90.

95 [2002] 2 A.C. 205, before [18].

96 *East West Corp v DKBS 1912 AF A/S* [2003] EWCA Civ 83, [2003] Q.B. 1509 at [34].

97 [1977] A.C. 774 at p.842.

98 Above, n.91.

99 Above, n.96 at [34].

1 Above, n.90.

2 *The Berge Sisar*, above n.89, at [7].

3 *ibid*. at [10].

4 *ibid*. at [11].

5 Above, n.96.

6 The Chilean banks had not provided finance for the sale and so had no interest in looking to the goods as security: see *East West* Case, above n.96, at [3].

shippers) "were the original bailors."[7] The other two bills of lading in *The Berge Sisar*[8] appear to have been made out to the order of the buyers under the original FOB contracts and so raise the general question whether a seller under such a contract should be presumed to have acted as the buyer's agent in taking out a bill of lading naming himself as shipper, merely by virtue of the fact that the bill made the goods deliverable to the order of the buyer. For reasons to be further discussed in Chapter 20,[9] it is respectfully submitted that no such presumption should arise where at the time of shipment property remained in the seller (typically because the price had not been paid[10]); that, in such a case, a seller who takes a bill of lading naming himself as shipper is, on the contrary, to be regarded as having done so with a view to retaining his property in the goods and his right to redirect them; and that the retention of those rights by a seller named a shipper is, even where the bill names the buyer as consignee, more consistent with Lord Brandon's view, that it is the shipper who is bailor,[11] than with Lord Hobhouse's view that, in such cases the role of bailor of the goods to the carrier is occupied by the consignee.[12]

Further difficulty arises from Lord Hobhouse's earlier reference to "endorsed bills of lading"[13] since this phrase is capable of referring (a) to a bill made out simply "to order" and then indorsed to a person other than the shipper and (b) to a bill made out to the order of a named consignee (X) and indorsed by X to Y. In the first of these cases, no-one except the shipper can be the original bailor; in the second there is authority for the view that the indorsement does not, of itself, give rise to the relationship of bailor and bailee between Y and the carrier.[14] Further facts, such as an attornment by the carrier to Y (typically at the end of the transit) would have to be proved to establish such a relationship.[15]

---

[7] *ibid.* at [35].
[8] Above, n.89.
[9] Below, para.20–008.
[10] See below, paras 20–077, 20–082; *Evergreen Marine Corp. v Aldgate Warehouse (Wholesale) Ltd* [2003] EWHC 667 (Comm.), [2003] 2 Lloyd's Rep. 597 at [30].
[11] See above at n.93.
[12] See above at n.90.
[13] [2002] 2 A.C. 205, [18], sentence following the citation from the Bills of Lading Act 1855. See also [2002] 2 A.C. 205 at [31] ("right of the holder of the endorsed bill of lading to the possession of the goods as bailor . . .").
[14] *Compania Portorafti Commerciale SA v Ultramar Panama Inc. (The Captain Gregos) (No. 2)* [1990] 2 Lloyd's Rep. 395 at pp.404–405 (claim against PEAG); an apparently contrary dictum of Dillon L.J. in *Hispanica de Petroleos SA v Vencedora Navegaceon SA (The Kapetan Markos NL) (No. 2)* [1987] 2 Lloyd's Rep. 321 at p.340 gives rise to difficulty precisely because of its apparent inconsistency with Lord Brandon's view in *The Aliakmon*, above at n.93. A similar difficulty arises from the reasoning of *Sonicare International v East Anglia Freight Terminals Ltd* [1997] 2 Lloyd's Rep. 48 at p.53. In *The Kapetan Markos NL (No. 2)* the existence of the relevant bailment was "not seriously disputed" (at p.332) and Mustill L.J. did not regard such a relationship as necessary for the decision (*ibid.*).
[15] *The Captain Gregos (No. 2)*, above at p.406 (claim against BP). In *Homburg Houtimport BV v Agrosin Private Ltd (The Starsin)* [2003] UKHL 12, [2004] 1 A.C. 715 at [133] Lord Hobhouse refers to "the shippers" as parties to the bailment (as bailors) while at [137] he treats "the claimant cargo owners" as being potentially entitled "to hold the shipowners liable as bailors." The claimants were indorsees of bills from the shippers.

Attornment. The reference in the passage from *The Berge Sisar* quoted in paragraph 18–064 above to "attornment"[16] give rise to two further, perhaps related, questions: first, how the attornment is effected and secondly whether (or why) it is necessary. 18–066

The answer to the first question appears to be that the source of the attornment is the "receipt of the goods from the shipper . . . for delivery [at the agreed destination] to the consignee".[17] The difficulty with this explanation is that the undertaking to deliver the goods to the consignee is given, not to the consignee, but to the shipper and so can scarcely be regarded as an undertaking to the consignee, which is the type of undertaking that would be required to constitute an attornment to him. It is even harder to find an attornment where the bill does not name a consignee but is simply made out "to order" and later indorsed to a person of whose identity or existence the carrier is unaware at the time of the indorsement; or, even where the bill names the consignee, to find an attornment in favour of the person to whom that consignee has later transferred the bill. Lord Hobhouse's statement that, in such cases, "the law merchant recognised the attornment as transferable"[18] seems to be the equivalent of treating the "attornment" as a legal device or fiction.[19] Where a bill is indorsed many times before actual delivery of the goods, it is scarcely realistic to regard the carrier as having attorned to each transferee in the chain; yet as a matter of law there is no doubt that each of them in succession has constructive possession of the goods. There may indeed be an actual attornment to the ultimate transferee of the bill at a *later* stage than that of the transfer of the bill: *e.g.* on its presentation to the carrier coupled with a request, assented to by him, for delivery of the goods.[20] But this is an actual attornment,[21]

---

[16] At n.89, above.

[17] At n.90, above.

[18] [2002] 2 A.C. 205 at [18]. The "law merchant" here seems to refer to the custom of merchants recognised in *Lickbarrow v Mason* (1794) 5 T.R. 683 (above, para.18–007). Strictly speaking that custom refers to order *bills of lading*, and not to any *attornment*, as "transferable." The phrase "transferable attornment" in *East West Corp. v DKBS 1912 AF A/S* [2003[EWCA Civ 83, [2003] Q.B. 1509 at [42] appears to be derived from Lord Hobhouse's statement cited in the text above. The concept is based on the custom referred to above. It does not apply merely because a document makes goods deliverable to a named person "or assigns by endorsement hereon": see *Dublin Distillery Ltd v Doherty* [1914] A.C. 823, where a delivery warrant contained these words but constructive possession of the goods was said at pp.847–848 to pass only on actual attornment by the bailee. Lord Hobhouse's further statement in *Homburg Houtimport BV v Agrosin Private Ltd (The Starsin)* [2003] UKHL 12, [2004] 1 A.C. 715 at [136] that "no attornment by the sub-bailee was necessary" was made in a context different from that of the question of the transfer of constructive possession. The statement is part of a discussion whether, and subject to what terms, the sub-bailee was liable to the bailor in respect of loss of or damage to the goods.

[19] *cf. The Future Express* [1992] 2 Lloyd's Rep. 79 at p.12, affirmed without reference to this point [1993] 2 Lloyd's Rep. 542.

[20] *cf. Compania Portorafti Commerciale SA v Ultramar Panama Inc. (The Captain Gregos) (No. 2)* [1990] 2 Lloyd's Rep. 395 (claim by BP to whom the carrier had attorned on presentation of letters of indemnity).

[21] It is to such an actual attornment that Lord Brandon seems to refer in *The Aliakmon* [1986] A.C. 785 at p.818 when he says that "the bill of lading was never

quite distinct from any process by which constructive possession of the goods is transferred by dealings with the bill of which the carrier is likely to be unaware.

In answering the question whether (or why) the carrier's attornment should be regarded as necessary, it is convenient to begin by considering the case in which a document relating to goods in the possession of a bailee is *not* a document of title in the common law sense.[22] In such a case, the mere transfer of the document does not transfer constructive possession of the goods to the transferee of the document: such a consequence would follow only from the bailee's attornment to the transferee, and from his fresh attornment to any subsequent transferee. This rule would, for example, apply where a delivery order was issued in respect of goods in a warehouse.[23] But where a document *is* a document of title in the common law sense, it has not hitherto been thought that the transfer of constructive possession of the goods to the transferee of the document is subject to any further requirement of attornment by the bailee; indeed, when, in *Lickbarrow v Mason*,[24] bills of lading were first recognised as having the characteristics of such documents, it would, as a practical matter, have been impossible to procure such an attornment while the goods were in transit. There is no reference to the need for any attornment (in the form of an undertaking by the carrier to the transferee of the bill) in the passage from the judgment of Bowen L.J. in *Sanders Bros v Maclean & Co.*[25] cited in the part of Lord Hobhouse's speech in *The Berge Sisar*[26] here under discussion. Bowen L.J. based the rule that "indorsement and delivery of the bill of lading operates as a symbolical delivery of the cargo" simply on the practical consideration that "[a] cargo at sea while in the hands of the carrier is necessarily incapable of physical delivery."[27] The only other authority said in *The Berge Sisar* to support the view that the transfer of constructive possession of the goods by transfer of the bill was based on "attornment" is *Dublin City Distillery Ltd v Doherty.*[28] In that case, Lord Atkinson does indeed refer to the need for an attornment by the bailee.[29] But he does so in relation to a delivery order or warrant, where attornment is necessary precisely because (as Lord Sumner points out[30]) such a document is "not shewn by any mercantile custom to be a symbol of the goods, as an indorsed bill of lading is for goods at sea"—*i.e.* because such an order is *not* a document of title in

negotiated to the buyers *and* no attornment by the shipowners ever took place" (italics supplied). It seems from this statement that "negotiation" of the bill would not itself have been regarded as giving rise to such an attornment.

22 For this sense, see above, para.18–007.

23 See the *Dublin Distillery* case, above n.18 and below, n.28; and below, paras 18–173, 18–174.

24 (1787) 2 T.R. 63; for full references, see above, para.18–007, n.43.

25 (1883) 11 Q.B.D. 327 at p.341.

26 [2001] 2 All E.R. 193, [18].

27 Above para.18–063 at n.69.

28 [1914] A.C. 823.

29 *ibid.*, p.847.

30 *ibid.*, p.865.

the common law sense.[31] If this is why attornment is necessary where the document is *not* a document of title in that sense (or where it is doubtful whether it is a document of this kind[32]), then it does not follow from that reasoning that there is any requirement of actual attornment for the transfer of constructive possession to the transferee of goods covered by a document which (like an order or bearer bill of lading) is a document of title in that sense.

Whether "straight" or "non-negotiable" bills, or sea waybills are documents of title. The nature of "straight" (or "non-negotiable") bills of lading and of sea waybills has been discussed in paragraph 18–018 above. Our present concern is with the question whether such bills or waybills are documents of title in the common law sense described in paragraphs 18–007 and 18–062 above. The custom of merchants, by virtue of which bills of lading were found in *Lickbarrow v Mason*[33] to be documents of title in that sense, referred only to order bills, perhaps because at the time of that decision bills of lading were usually in that form, making the goods deliverable to the order or assigns of a named consignee or, if no such consignee were named, to the order or assigns of the shipper. When, nearly 100 years later, the Privy Council was faced in *Henderson v Comptoir d'Escompte de Paris*[34] with a bill which simply named the consignee, "omitting the usual words 'or order or assigns'",[35] Sir Robert Collier assumed that the bill was "not a negotiable instrument."[36] He gave, as his reason for this assumption, that "the general view of the mercantile world has been for some time that, in order to make bills of lading negotiable, some words such as 'or order or assigns' must be in them."[37] A bill which did not contain such words was described as "very odd and unusual"[38] by Scrutton L.J. in a case in which he found it "unnecessary to determine whether such a bill of lading is or is not a negotiable instrument".[39] There is little doubt that in these statements the word "negotiable"[40] is used to refer to the characteristics which a document has if it is a document of title in the 18–067

---

[31] See also *Kum v Wah Tat Bank Ltd* [1971] 1 Lloyd's Rep. 439, where the discussion of attornment comes (at p.445) *after* the conclusion that the mate's receipt in that case was *not* a document of title. Delivery to the carrier was there held to amount to delivery to the consignee because it was so intended by the shipper: *cf. Evans v Nicholl* (1841) 3 M. & G. 614, 4 Scott's N.R. 43 and *Bryans v Nix* (1839) 4 M. & W. 775, where the court did not find it necessary to decide whether the "boat bill" for carriage by inland waterway was a "bill of lading". Neither of these two cases has any bearing on the question whether transfer of the documents in question could operate as a transfer of constructive possession.

[32] As in *Bryans v Nix*, above, n.31.

[33] (1794) 5 T.R. 683; for full references, see above, para.18–007, n.43.

[34] (1873) L.R. 5 P.C. 253.

[35] *ibid*. at p.255.

[36] *ibid*. at p.260.

[37] *ibid*. at pp.259–260.

[38] *Thrige v United Shipping Co. Ltd* (1924) 18 Ll. L. Rep. 6 at p.8; *cf. JI MacWilliam Co. Inc. v Mediterranean Shipping Co. SA (The Rafaela S)* [2005] UKHL 11, [2005] 2 A.C. 423 at [43] (order bills used in the "vast preponderance of transactions") and [60] (straight bills said to be "highly unusual, to say the least").

[39] *Thrige v United Shipping Co. Ltd.* (1924) 18 Ll. L. Rep. 6 at p.8.

[40] The usage is common, if not strictly accurate: see below, para.18–084.

common law sense.[41] It is also clear that a document which would have those characteristics by virtue of a custom proved in relation to documents of the class to which it belongs can be deprived of those characteristics by being marked "not negotiable"[42]; and it seems to follow that a bill of lading which was so marked would not be a document of title in the common law sense. The "general view" referred to by the Privy Council in the dictum quoted above[43] was also accepted by the Law Commissions who, in the Report which led to the passing of the Carriage of Goods by Sea Act 1992, stated that a straight bill was "not a document of title at common law"[44]; indeed for the purposes of the 1992 Act, sea carriage documents which simply make goods deliverable to a named person are not bills of lading at all but are sea waybills.[45] Such waybills are also not documents of title in the common law sense[46]; and the line of demarcation between them and straight bills of lading is by no means easy to draw.[47] All these factors gave support to the general view that straight bills of lading were not documents of title in the common law sense.[48] But this view has recently been doubted by the Court of Appeal in *The Happy Ranger*[49] and *The Rafaela S*[50]; the latter decision has been affirmed by the House of Lords with specific approval of the reasoning of Rix L.J. and Jacob J in the Court of Appeal.[51] That approval does not, however, provide a conclusive answer to the present question, whether a straight bill is a document of title in the common law sense, since neither case directly raised the issue whether dealings with a straight bill could give rise to the possessory and proprietary consequences which follow from the characteristics of an order bill as a document of title in the common law sense. The issue in each case was

---

[41] See above, paras 18–007, 18–062.
[42] See *Kum v Wah Tat Bank Ltd.* [1971] 1 Lloyd's Rep. 439, below para.18–166.
[43] Above, at n.37.
[44] Law Com. No. 196, Scot. Law Com. No. 130, para.2.50; this view had also been accepted at first instance in *East West Corp. v DKBS 1912 AF A/S* [2002] EWHC 83 (Comm.), [2002] 1 All E.R. (Comm.) 276 at [23], [24], affirmed without reference to the point [2003] EWCA Civ 83, [2003] Q.B. 1509 and in *JI MacWilliam Co. Inc. v Mediterranean Shipping Co. SA (The Rafaela S)*, [2002] EWHC 593, [2002] Lloyd's Rep. 403 at [23], [24], revsd. [2003] EWCA Civ. 556, [2004] Q.B. 702 and [2005] UKHL 11, [2005] 2 A.C. 423, discussed in paras 18–071 *et seq.*; for comment in the House of Lords on the view of the Law Commissions see below, para 18–074 at n.38.
[45] See *The Chitral* [2000] 1 Lloyd's Rep. 529 at p.533, above, para.18–018.
[46] Law Commissions' Report, above, n.44, para.5.6; *J.I. MacWilliam Co. Inc. v Mediterranean Shipping Co. SA (The Rafaela S)* [2005] UKHL 11, [2005] 2 A.C. 423 at [46]; *Browner International Ltd. v Monarch Shipping Co. Ltd. (The European Enterprise)* [1989] 2 Lloyd's Rep. 185 at p.188.
[47] Above, para 18–018; below, para.18–083.
[48] It is arguable that "straight" or "non-negotiable" bills and sea waybills could be documents of title in the statutory sense discussed in para.18–009 above: see para.18–083 below. If the bill of lading in *Henderson's* case (above n.34) was a document of title in the statutory sense, then the actual decision could now be based on Sale of Goods Act 1979, s.25(1).
[49] *Parsons Corp. v CV Scheepvaartonderneming Happy Ranger (The Happy Ranger)* [2002] EWCA Civ. 694, [2002] 2 All E.R. (Comm.) 24 (where the bill was held to be an order bill).
[50] Above, n.44.
[51] [2005] UKHL 11, [2005] 2 A.C. 423 at [3], [20], [24], and [51].

whether a straight bill was a "bill of lading or any similar document of title" within Article I(b) of the Hague-Visby Rules so as to subject the contract contained in or evidenced by it to the contractual regime of those Rules.[52] The point is made particularly clear in *The Rafaela S* by Lord Bingham when he says that "the question before the House is not whether a straight bill is a document of title at common law but whether it is a 'bill of lading or any similar document of title' for the purposes of the Hague and Hague-Visby Rules"[53]; and Lord Steyn similarly says[54] that the latter was the "sole issue" before the House. Lord Roger also says that "in substance the appeal turns on the proper interpretation of article I(b) of the Hague Rules . . ."[55] and bases his decision on the point that the straight bill in that case was a "bill of lading" within this article.[56] He adds that the words "similar document of title" were intended to extend, rather than to narrow, the meaning of "bill of lading" in the Rules[57]; that they do not refer to "the document having any effect in relation to the title to the goods"; and that they "should be understood as applying to any document which entitles the holder to have the goods carried by sea".[58]

Under an order bill, the goods are deliverable to the order of a named consignee or (if no consignee is named) to the order of the shipper. Such an order is typically given by indorsement of the bill.[59] An order bill being a document of title in the common law sense, such an indorsement, followed by delivery of the bill to the indorsee, transfers the constructive possession of the goods to the indorsee; and this process can be repeated by further transfers, likewise effected by indorsement and delivery.[60] It follows, not only that the indorsee is entitled to delivery of the goods from the carrier, but also that the indorsee can, by virtue of the indorsement, acquire a security interest in the goods as against persons to whom the goods are (after the transfer of the bill to the indorsee) delivered. These consequences follow whether or not the conditions for the transfer of *contractual* rights against the carrier (now laid down in the Carriage of Goods by Sea Act 1992)[61] are satisfied. As a matter of history, English common law recognised order bills as a mechanism for the transfer of proprietary or possessory rights[62] long before legislation made it possible to use them as a mechanism for the transfer of contractual rights.[63] Moreover, 18–068

[52] See below, paras 18–074, 21–106.
[53] [2005] UKHL 11, [2005] 2 A.C. 423 at [22].
[54] *ibid*. at [35].
[55] *ibid*. at [54].
[56] *ibid*. at [64], [65].
[57] *ibid*. at [57]; *cf*. at [43], per Lord Steyn.
[58] *ibid*. at [75].
[59] Above, para.18–016. No indorsement is necessary (1) for the transfer of the bill to the named consignee to whose order the goods are deliverable by its terms; or (2) after the bill has been indorsed in blank: *ibid*..
[60] Above, para.18–016.
[61] Below, paras 18–101 *et seq*.
[62] *Lickbarrow v Mason* (1794) 5 T.R. 683; for full references, see above, para.18–007, n.43.
[63] Bills of Lading Act 1855, below para.18–100.

in the case of an order bill, the carrier could not tell who was entitled to possession of the goods without examining the bill to see what indorsements it contained.[64] It followed that the carrier was not bound to deliver the goods except on production of the bill; and that he would be liable for misdelivery if he delivered the goods without such production to someone other than the person entitled to them by virtue of a previous transfer of the bill.[65]

18–069 **Do straight bills have to be produced?** The reasoning in paragraph 18–068 above cannot in terms apply where the contract of carriage is covered by a straight bill, that is, one by which the goods are deliverable, not to the order of any person, but simply to the named consignee.[66] Such a bill "requires delivery of the goods to the named consignee and . . . to no other"[67] and is "not transferable by endorsement"[68] The carrier thus does not have to see the bill to determine the identity of the person entitled to delivery of the goods; nor can the identity of that person be changed by any purported indorsement of the bill. It is true that where goods are shipped under a straight bill, the shipper (and sometimes the consignee) has, subject to certain restrictions, the right to redirect the goods. These points are discussed in paragraphs 18–021 to 18–026 above. But this right must be exercised by notice to the carrier, to be given (prima facie) by the shipper and not by the named consignee. Even if the bill provided for the exercise of the right by the consignee,[69] notice to the carrier would still have to be given, in this case by the consignee. If, on the true construction of the bill, the right were exercisable by a mere indorsement by the consignee, then the true nature of the bill, however it described itself, would be that of an order bill.[70]

18–070 The question then arises whether, granted that the carrier does not need to see a straight bill in order to determine who is entitled to delivery of the goods,[71] delivery of goods shipped under a straight bill can be claimed, and must be made, only on production of the bill. The starting point for a discussion of this question is that there is no general principle in the law of

[64] *JI MacWilliam Co. Inc. v Mediterranean Shipping Co. SA (The Rafaela S)* [2003] EWCA Civ 556, [2004] Q.B. 702 at [99], and [2005] UKHL 11, [2005] 2 A.C. 423 at [6].
[65] Above, para.18–063.
[66] *JI MacWilliam Co. Inc. v Mediterranean Shipping Co. SA (The Rafaela S)* [2005] UKHL 11, [2005] 2 A.C. 423 at [1].
[67] *JI MacWilliam Co. Inc. v Mediterranean Shipping Co. SA (The Rafaela S)* [2003] EWCA Civ. 556, [2004] Q.B. 702, at [1], affirmed [2005] UKHL 11, [2005] 2 A.C. 423.
[68] *The Rafaela S,* above, n.60, [2005] UKHL 11, [2005] 2 A. C. 423 at [1], per Lord Bingham; Lord Roger at [58] says, more generally, that such a bill is "not transferable"; contrast Lord Steyn at [46], saying that such a bill is "transferable only to the named consignee", but "transferable" here refers to the delivery of the bill and not to any mechanism for changing the identity of the person entitled to delivery of the goods.
[69] See *Carver on Bills of Lading*, 2nd ed. (2005), para.1–017.
[70] *ibid*.
[71] Above, para.18–069.

carriage that the consignee named in the contract of carriage can claim delivery only on production of the carriage document, or of any other document.[72] Prima facie, a contract by which a bailee (A) of goods promises the bailor (B) to deliver the goods to a third party (C) is performed by such delivery without the need for C to produce any document containing or evidencing the contract of bailment; this is true whether A is a carrier or some other kind of bailee. The requirement of the production of an order bill by C is best regarded as an exception to this general principle. The exception is justified by the practical consideration that, without seeing such a bill, A cannot be sure that C is indeed entitled to delivery of the goods, and therefore of getting a good discharge by delivery of the goods to C[73]; and this reasoning does not apply where the bill is a straight bill.[74] Such a bill simply contains or evidences a contract by which A promises B to deliver the goods to C and under such a contract A gets a good discharge by making such delivery unless the goods have been effectively redirected.[75] Such redirection requires notice to be given to A who is therefore not at risk of being unable to determine (without seeing the bill) whether delivery is to be made to C or to someone else. In the United States, this position is made clear by legislation which provides that the carrier "may deliver" the goods to a consignee named in what was formerly called a "straight" and is now called a "nonnegotiable" bill[76] without any requirement of the consignee's being in possession of the bill. In the words of a leading treatise, in the case of a "straight" bill, "the carrier normally discharges its duty by delivering the goods to the named consignee; the consignee need not produce the bill or even be in possession of it; the piece of paper on which the contract is written is of no importance in itself."[77] The general rule to this effect is further supported by the generally accepted position that, where the contract of carriage is contained in or evidenced by a sea waybill, the carrier can safely (and must) deliver the goods to the named consignee without production of the waybill.[78] The view that the general principle stated above[79] applies in the case of a straight bill, so that a straight bill does not have to be produced by the named consignee on claiming delivery of the goods, has also been taken in Hong Kong.[80]

---

[72] There is, for example, no such requirement in the case of a contract of carriage covered by a sea waybill: see below, n.86. Nor is it necessary under the Conventions governing international carriage by air, road or rail to produce the carriage document in order to claim delivery: see below, paras 21–053, 21–061, 21–068; and such documents are not documents of title.
[73] Above, para.18–068.
[74] Above para.18–069.
[75] Above, para.18–025.
[76] Federal Bills of Lading Act 1916 (the Pomerence Act), s.9; now replaced by USC §80110(b) (1994).
[77] *Gilmore and Black on Admiralty*, 2nd ed., para.3–4.
[78] Law Commissions, Report on *Rights of Suit in Respect of Contracts for the Carriage of Goods by Sea*, Law Com. No. 196, Scot. Law Com. No. 130 (1991), para.5.7; *The Rafaela S*, above, n.64, [2003] EWCA Civ 556, [2004] Q.B. 702 at [138] approved [2005] UKHL 11, [2005] 2 A.C. 423 at [24] and see *ibid.* at [46].
[79] At n.72.
[80] *The Brij* [2001] 1 Lloyd's Rep. 431 at p.434 (Hong Kong High Court).

18–071 Nevertheless, the weight of current judicial opinion seems to favour the view that the consignee named in a straight bill is entitled to delivery of the goods only on production or presentation of the bill to the carrier. Since the reasoning which justifies this requirement in the case of an order bill (*i.e.* that "until such a bill is presented the carrier will not know the identify of the party entitled to delivery"[81]) does not apply in the case of a straight bill, some other legal or practical reason for the requirement must be found to take such a case out of the principle of the law of carriage of goods that, in general, there is *no* requirement that the person claiming delivery of the goods must present the carriage document to the carrier.[82] One such reason is that "the shipper will not wish to part with the original bill of lading to the consignee or buyer until that party has paid [for the goods], and requiring production of the bill is the most effective way of ensuring that the consignee or buyer who has not paid cannot obtain delivery."[83] This is, with respect, true; for, even though delivery of the goods will not necessarily pass the property in the goods to a buyer who has not paid for them,[84] the seller may well encounter greater practical difficulty in enforcing his proprietary rights in goods which have been delivered to the buyer than he would if they were still in the hands of the carrier.[85] The difficulty with this rationale of the requirement of production of a straight bill is that it can apply equally where goods have been shipped by a seller to a buyer under a sea waybill; and it is accepted that in such a case delivery can be claimed by the named consignee from the carrier without production of the waybill.[86] This is also the position under the Conventions relating to international carriage of goods by air, road or rail.[87] *The Rafaela S* contains a survey of "the law in certain leading maritime jurisdictions",[88] the purpose

---

[81] *JI MacWilliam Co. Inc. v Mediterranean Shipping Co. SA (The Rafaela S)* [2005] UKHL 11, [2005] 2 A.C. 423 at [6].

[82] Above para.18–070 at n.72.

[83] *JI MacWilliam Co. Inc. v Mediterranean Shipping Co. SA (The Rafaela S)* [2005] UKHL 11, [2005] 2 A.C. 423 at [6]; *cf.* [2003] EWCA Civ 556, [2004] Q.B. 702 at [145], approved [2005] UKHL 11, [2005] 2 A.C. 423 at [24].

[84] See, for example, *Cheetham & Co Ltd. v Thornham Spinning Co. Ltd* [1964] 2 Lloyd's Rep. 17; *Ginzberg v Barrow Haematite Steel Co. Ltd.* [1966] 1 Lloyd's Rep. 343; below, paras 19–102, 19–103.

[85] This may have been the forensic reason why, in the Singapore case of *Voss v APL Co. Pte Ltd* [2002] 2 Lloyd's Rep. 707, the shipper/seller brought his action against the carrier who had delivered the goods to a buyer/consignee named in a straight bill without production of the bill. The claim succeeded on the ground that the delivery was wrongful. As the buyer had not paid, it is unlikely that the property had passed to him under the contract of sale, and as the buyer is not stated in the report to have been insolvent, it is not clear why the seller did not pursue his remedy against the buyer either under the contract of sale or by virtue of still being owner of the goods.

[86] Law Commission's Report, above n.78, paras 2.50, 5.7; *cf. JI MacWilliam Co. Inc. v Mediterranean Shipping Co. SA (The Rafaela S)* [2005] UKHL 11, [2005] 2 A.C. 423 [46]. For further discussion of possible justifications for requiring a straight bill to be produced by the person claiming delivery, see Treitel, (2003) 119 L.Q.R. 608 at pp.615–618, commenting on the decision of the Court of Appeal in *The Rafaela S* [2003] EWCA Civ 556, [2004] Q.B. 702.

[87] See above, para.18–070, n.72.

[88] *JI MacWilliam Co. Inc. v Mediterranean Shipping Co. SA (The Rafaela S)* [2005] UKHL 11, [2005] 2 A.C. 423 at [12]–[15].

of which was not to answer the present question (whether straight bills had to be produced) but rather to make the points that such bills were "a familiar mercantile phenomenon in the early 1920s",[89] when the Hague Rules were being drafted, and that this would tend to support the view that the Rules were intended to apply to them.[90] But for our present purpose the survey is inconclusive since it shows that production of a straight bill was not necessary in the United States[91] but was necessary in Germany, France and Scandinavia; and it is impossible from the survey to tell which of these views had the greater degree of commercial importance.

Probably, the most convincing rationale for the requirement of production of straight bills lies in the terms of such documents. This line of reasoning can be illustrated by cases in which the parties make use of hybrid or "dual purpose" forms of carriage documents which can, according to the way in which blanks in them are filled in, be used either as order or as straight bills.[92] This was described in *The Rafaela S*[93] as "an unfortunate development" inviting "error and litigation"[94] and obscuring the distinction between bills of lading and sea waybills.[95] In that case, a bill of lading contained the words "Consignee: BL not negotiable unless 'ORDER OF'"; and the bill merely gave the name of the consignee without adding the words "order of". It was thus a straight bill but a requirement that delivery was to be made only against its production was imposed by a provision in its attestation clause which stated that "One of the Bills of Lading [issued in a set of three] must be surrendered duly endorsed[96] in exchange for the goods . . ." In *The Rafaela S*, the requirement of production of the straight bill was thus imposed by one of the express terms of the bill; but dicta in the case extend the requirement beyond this situation. Thus Lord Bingham said that he would "if it were necessary to do so, hold that production of the bill is a necessary pre-condition of requiring delivery even if there is no express provision to that effect."[97] Cases of the kind contemplated in this statement can be explained on the ground that, even in the absence of an *express* term to that effect, a term to the same effect can be *implied*. This

---

[89] *ibid.* at [16].
[90] *ibid*.
[91] See above, para.18–070.
[92] *The Chitral* [2000] 2 Lloyd's Rep. 529; *Parsons Corp. v CV Scheepvaartondernem-ing Happy Ranger (The Happy Ranger)* [2002] EWCA Civ. 694, [2002] 2 All E.R. (Comm.) 24; *JI MacWilliam Co. Inc. v Mediterranean Shipping Co. SA (The Rafaela S)* [2005] UKHL 11, [2005] 2 A.C. 423 affirming [2003] EWCA Civ 556, [2004] Q.B. 702.
[93] Above, n.92, [2003] EWCA Civ 556 at [146].
[94] *The Rafaela S*, above n.92, [2003] EWCA Civ 556, [2004] Q.B. 702 at [146], approved on appeal [2005] UKHL 11, [2005] 2 A.C. 423 at [24].
[95] *The Rafaela S*, above, n.93, at [146] per Rix L.J.: "Carriers should not use bill of lading forms if they want to invite shippers to enter into sea waybill type of contracts."
[96] Although the words "duly endorsed" could not strictly apply where the document was filled in as a straight bill, they were held not to exclude the operation of the rest of the term in the attestation clause requiring surrender of the document to the carrier: see [2005] UKHL 11, [2005] 2 A.C. 423 at [6], [45].
[97] [2005] UKHL 11, [2005] 2 A.C. 423 at [20], expressing his agreement with Rix L.J. [2003] EWCA Civ 556, [2004] Q.B. 702 at [145].

appears from the statement of Lord Steyn that "In any event the issue of a set of three bills of lading, with the provision that 'one being accomplished, the others to stand void' necessarily implies that delivery will only be made against presentation of the bill of lading."[98] This reasoning can, however, give rise to difficulty where the terms of the document appear to negative the implication: thus if the term requiring production of the document were expressed to apply only where it was filled in so as to create an order bill, then an implication that the term should apply also where the document was filled in as a straight bill would fail for inconsistency with the express term. This would be so whether the term was alleged to be one implied in fact[99] or one implied in law.[1] Probably the implication would be regarded as falling into the latter category[2] and the question whether such an implication is indeed inconsistent with an express term of the contract is one that can give rise to considerable difficulty.[3] The difficulty can be illustrated by reference to the Singapore case of *Voss v APL Co. Pte Ltd*[4] where a "dual purpose" bill contained a term which was similar to that referred to by Lord Steyn in the passage quoted above[5] but differed from it in providing that "upon surrender to the carrier of one *negotiable* bill properly endorsed, all others to stand void"; and the bill actually issued was completed so as to be a straight bill.[6] It was held that the carrier was liable to the shipper for delivering the goods to the named consignee without production of the bill[7]; and in *The Rafaela S* the case is cited with apparent approval by Lord Bingham[8] and expressly approved by Lord Steyn in the sentence immediately following that quoted above.[9] It seems reasonable to infer from this that, in Lord Steyn's view, the case illustrated the process of implication that he had just described. It can be argued that the implication was not excluded by the reference in the clause quoted above to "negotiable" bills since this did not expressly *restrict* the requirement of production to such bill.

18–072 **Conclusion on requirement of production.** It is submitted (not without some hesitation) that the best explanation for the requirement of production of a straight bill by the named consignee, when claiming delivery of the goods, is that the requirement is based on an express or implied term in the bill to that effect. This seems to be a safer explanation than those based on

---

98 [2005] UKHL 11, [2005] 2 A.C. 423 at [45].
99 See, *e.g. Duke of Westminster v Guild* [1985] Q.B. 688 at p.700.
1 See, *e.g. Eagle Star Life Insurance Co. Ltd v Griggs and Miles* [1998] 1 Lloyd's Rep. 256.
2 For the distinction between terms implied in fact and terms implied in law, see *Treitel* at pp.207–208.
3 See, *e.g. Johnstone v Bloomsbury Health Authority* [1992] 1 Q.B. 333, where there was a difference of judicial opinion on such a point.
4 [2002] 2 Lloyd's Rep. 707.
5 At n.98 above.
6 It provided "Non-Negotiable Unless Consigned to Order" and named the consignee without adding the words "to Order".
7 See also above, n.98.
8 At [21].
9 Above, at n.98.

considerations of convenience to the shipper or the carrier, since the rejection of the requirement in the United States[10] is not there alleged to have been a source of inconvenience. Where, however, a straight bill is issued on a form which contains the normal terms of an order bill, with the exception only of words importing transferability, then English law will normally regard the requirement of production of the bill as having been imposed by its express or implied terms. As this seems to be the usual practice with regard to the issue of straight bills, the discussion that follows, of the question whether straight bills are documents of title in the common law sense,[11] will be based on the assumption that such bills do have to be produced to the carrier by the named consignee on claiming delivery.

For the avoidance of doubt, it should be added that the preceding discussion is concerned with the question whether the carrier may, and must, make delivery to the consignee named in a straight bill only on production of the bill. It is not concerned with the question whether rights of suit under the contract of carriage have been transferred to that consignee by virtue of the Carriage of Goods by Sea Act 1992. For the purposes of this Act, a straight bill is clearly not a "bill of lading" since it is not capable of being transferred either "by indorsement" or "as a bearer bill without indorsement"[12]; it is treated for these purposes as a sea waybill.[13] It follows from section 2(1)(b) of the Act that rights under the contract of carriage are vested in the consignee simply by virtue of his being "the person to whom delivery of the goods is to be made *in accordance with that contract*".[14] Hence for this purpose the consignee prima facie need not have possession of, let alone produce, a straight bill; and this is so even though, in accordance with common law rules discussed in paragraphs 18–071 and 18–072 above, the carrier is bound and entitled to deliver the goods only against production of the bill. If, however, that common law rule is (as was submitted in paragraph 18–072 above) based on an express or implied term imposing the requirement of production of the bill, then the question whether such production was also necessary for the acquisition of contractual rights by virtue of section 2(1)(b) would depend on whether the words of that provision which have been italicised above[15] refer only to the *identity* of the person to whom delivery is to be made or also to the *conditions* in which it is to be made. Comparison with other provisions in section 2 of the 1992 Act seems to support the former view,[16] so that a 18–073

---

[10] See para.18–070 above.
[11] Above, paras 18–007, 18–062.
[12] Carriage of Goods by Sea Act 1992, s.1(2)(a); a bill made out to bearer cannot be a straight bill.
[13] See above, para.18–018.
[14] Carriage of Goods by Sea Act 1992, S. 2(1)(b); and see n.16, below.
[15] At n.14.
[16] *i.e.* those relating to the transfer of contractual rights by the use of a ship's delivery order. Here s.2(1)(c) of the Act uses the phrase "*in accordance* with the undertaking contained in the order" to identify the person to whom delivery is to be made while s.2(3)(a) uses the phrase "subject to the terms of the order" to refer to other requirements (such as production of the order) that may be imposed by the terms of the order. The second of these phrases is not replicated in the provisions of the Act relating to sea waybills, an expression which, in the Act, includes straight bills (see above, para.18–018).

consignee could acquire contractual rights without having to produce the document. The point would, for example, be significant where the named consignee was claiming, not delivery of the goods (*e.g.* because they had been lost), but only damages for breach of the contract of carriage. The common law rule requiring production of a straight bill also applies where the question is not whether the consignee has acquired rights against the carrier, but whether the carrier is liable to the shipper for having delivered the goods to the consignee without production of the bill.[17]

18–074 **Document of title function?** It is now generally agreed that a document cannot be a document of title in the common law sense[18] unless it has to be produced to the carrier by the person claiming delivery of the goods.[19] But the fact that there is such a requirement of production in the case of a straight bill[20] does not conclude the question whether a straight bill is a document of title in that sense; for while the existence of the requirement is no doubt a *necessary*, it does not follow that it is also a *sufficient*, condition of a document's falling within that class. A discussion of that question concerns what we have called the "conveyancing" function of a bill of lading[21]: *i.e.* the capacity of its transfer to operate as a transfer of the constructive possession of the goods and of the property in them if so intended. No issue of that kind arose in *The Rafaela S*[22] where the question whether a straight bill was a document of title was discussed in the entirely different context of the issue whether such a bill was a "bill of lading or any similar document of title" within Article I(b) of the Hague-Visby Rules, so as to subject the contract of carriage contained in or evidenced by the bill to those Rules, which are primarily concerned with the *contents* of the carrier's obligations under that contract. The distinction between the two questions is made clear by Lord Bingham's statement in *The Rafaela S* that "the question before the House is not whether a straight bill is a document of title at common law."[23] The question that was before the House had nothing to do with the "conveyancing" function of the straight bill issued in that case. The actual decision was that the bill was a "bill of lading or any similar document of title" within the Rules so that the carrier's duties under the contract of carriage and the extent to which his liability under it was limited was governed by them. For this purpose, there is no good policy reason for distinguishing between order bills and straight bills[24]; but the

---

[17] As in *Voss v APL Co. Pte Ltd* [2002] 2 Lloyd's Rep. 707, above para.18–071.
[18] See above, paras 18–007, 18–062.
[19] See, for example, *The Maheno* [1977] 1 Lloyd's Rep. 81 (Supreme Court of New Zealand).
[20] Above, paras 18–071 to 18–072.
[21] Above, para.18–062.
[22] *JI MacWilliam Co. Inc. v Mediterranean Shipping Co. SA (The Rafaela S)* [2005] UKHL 11, [2005] 2 A.C. 423, above, para.18–071.
[23] *JI MacWilliam Co. Inc. v Mediterranean Shipping Co. SA (The Rafaela S)* [2005] UKHL 11, [2005] 2 A.C. 423 at [22].
[24] *ibid*. at [49]; the point is further supported by Carriage of Goods by Sea Act 1971, s.1(6)(b), by which the Rules can be made applicable by appropriate words to a contract for the carriage of goods by sea contained in or evidenced by a "non-negotiable" receipt.

decision does not conclude the question whether a straight bill can perform the "conveyancing" function of a bill of lading at common law since the Rules have no concern with the *transfer* of rights under that contract,[25] let alone with the transfer of the constructive possession of, or property in, the goods. There would be no inconsistency in holding that such a bill was a "document of title" for the purpose of attracting the operation of the Rules but that it could not perform the "conveyancing" function that can be performed by an order bill at common law. The two issues raise entirely different policy considerations. Indeed, it is far from clear why the Rules use the expression "document of title" for the purpose of defining the scope of their contractual regime[26]: the use of the phrase in Article I(b) of the Rules may be regarded as unfortunate; and it is interesting to note that their ancestor, the American Harter Act 1893, at this point uses the more neutral expression "similar transport document."[27]

The difficulty of determining whether, for the purpose the "conveyancing" function, with which we are here concerned, a straight bill of lading is a "document of title" is increased by the fact that, as was noted earlier in this Chapter, this expression seems recently to have been used, even as a matter of common law, in more than one sense.[28] The point is reflected in Lord Bingham's statement in *The Rafaela S* that "The main characteristics of a bill of lading[29] . . . were its negotiability *and* its recognition as a document of title, requiring presentation to obtain delivery of the cargo. While a straight bill lacked the first of these characteristics, there was no reason to infer that the parties intended to do away with the other also."[30] It has been suggested above that "negotiability" (in the sense of transferability[31]) is the distinguishing characteristic of a document of title in the traditional common law sense.[32] In the case of an order bill, the requirement of presentation followed as a matter of law from its "negotiability",[33] while in the case of a straight bill the same requirement followed from the terms (express or implied) of the document.[34] Hence a straight bill could possess the second of the two characteristics to which Lord Bingham refers, while it "lacked the first of these characteristics", *i.e.* that of "negotiability".

---

[25] Article III.4 distinguishes between the evidentiary force of certain statements about the goods in the bill as against (a) the shipper and (b) a bona fide transferee of the bill. But this provision is concerned with the *receipt* function of the bill (see above, paras 18–029, 18–034) and not with the transfer of rights under the contract of carriage.

[26] The interesting discussion of this point in *The Rafaela S* [2003] EWCA Civ. 556, [2004] Q.B. 702 provides no clear answer to this question.

[27] For legislation using other terminology, see aso *Carver on Bills of Lading*, 2nd ed. (2005) para.9–099.

[28] See above, paras 18–006, 18–008.

[29] The reference is evidently to an order or bearer bill.

[30] *JI MacWilliam Co. Inc. v Mediterranean Shipping Co. SA (The Rafaela S)* [2005] UKHL 11, [2005] 2 A.C. 423 at [21] italics supplied, paraphrasing with apparent approval a passage from the Singapore case of *Voss v APL Co. Pte Ltd* [2002] 2 Lloyd's Rep. 707 at [48].

[31] See para.18–084 below.

[32] Above paras 18–007 and 18–062.

[33] Below, para.18–075 at n.56.

[34] Above, para.18–071.

Use of the phrase "document of title" to refer to a document possessing only the second characteristic may, with respect, be entirely appropriate in the context of the question which arose in *The Rafaela S*, whether a straight bill was a "bill of lading or any similar document of title" for the purpose of attracting the contractual regime of the Hague-Visby Rules.[35] But in the context of the present question, whether a straight bill can perform the "conveyancing" function that can be performed by an order bill, the expression is more commonly used to refer to a document possessing both these characteristics and so to exclude straight bills. That seems to be the sense in which it was used by the Law Commissions in the Report which led to the passing of the Carriage of Goods by Sea Act 1992.[36] This states,[37] (in a passage which Lord Bingham says "must command respect"[38]) that a straight bill "is not a document of title at common law" but also appears to take the view that such a bill must be presented to the ship to obtain delivery of the goods.[39] The same view is, it is submitted, reflected in the passage from *The Rafaela S* quoted above,[40] according to which a straight bill is not "negotiable"[41] merely by reason of having to be presented to the carrier by the consignee on claiming delivery of the goods. It is further reflected in Lord Roger's statement in that case that such a bill is "not transferable"[42]; and it is this quality of "negotiability" (or transferability) which is an essential part of the traditional common law concept[43] of an order bill as a document of title. If the expression "document of title" were used to refer to all documents which had to be produced by the person claiming delivery of the goods, then it would be necessary to distinguish between "documents of title" *simpliciter* and "documents of title" which were "negotiable". Such a distinction is indeed used in the United States,[44] but there it is part of a scheme by which an order or bearer bill is truly negotiable[45] (in the sense in which in English law it is not[46]). The same distinction is also implicit in the draft legislation on Company Security Interests discussed in paragraph 18–010 above; and it may also be appropriate in other legislative contexts, such as that which arose in *The*

---

[35] See above, at n.24.
[36] *Rights of Suit in Respect of Contracts for the Goods by Sea,* Law Com. No. 196, Scot. Law Com. No. 130 (1991).
[37] At para.2.50.
[38] *The Rafaela S*, above n.30, at [22]; in the Court of Appeal (above, n.26) some doubt as to the correctness of para.2.50 of the Report is expressed by Peter Gibson L.J. and it may be significant that the approval of the judgments in the Court of Appeal in [2005] UKHL 22, [2005] A.C. 423 at [24] extends only to the judgments of Rix L.J. and Jacob J.
[39] This can be inferred from the statement in para.2.50 of the Report that a straight bill will "resemble a sea waybill apart from the fact that a sea waybill will not normally be presented to claim delivery."
[40] Above, at n.30.
[41] *i.e.* not transferable: see para.18–084 below.
[42] At [54]; *cf. ibid.* at [1] per Lord Bingham ("not transferable by endorsement").
[43] Above, paras 18–007, 18–062.
[44] UCC §7–104.
[45] See the Comment to UCC §7–502 and *cf.* Federal Bills of Lading Act 1916 (the Pomerene Act) §§31 and 32, now replaced by USC §§80105 and 80103(b)(1)(B).
[46] See para.18–084 below.

Rafaela S.[47] But it would be a novelty when applied to the common law concept of a document of title[48]; and in the context of the question which kinds of bills of lading are documents of title within that concept there seems to be no merit in such a novelty, which may, on the contrary, lead to terminological confusion. It is respectfully submitted that discussions of the common law concept of a document of title, and in particular of the "conveyancing" function of such documents, have been primarily concerned with their quality of "negotiability (or transferability): that is, they have referred to the point that any person to whom the document has been indorsed (where indorsement is required[49]) and delivered acquires, by virtue of such a transfer of the document, the constructive possession of, and, if so intended, the property in, the goods.

Requirement of proof of custom. In English law, the history of the concept of a "negotiable" (*i.e.* transferable) document of title is usually thought to begin with *Lickbarrow v Mason*[50] where the concept was based on proof of mercantile custom relating to order bills. Proof of custom for this purpose was also assumed to be necessary in a number of 19th century cases, in which attempts were made, sometimes with success and sometimes without, to establish that certain other documents, such as delivery orders[51] or mate's receipts,[52] were documents of title in this sense at common law.[53] The same assumption was made by Lord Devlin in *Kum v Wah Tat Bank Ltd.*,[54] where certain mate's receipts were recognised as being potentially documents of title by virtue of a mercantile custom proved in relation to them; though the custom was held not to apply to the receipts in question since they were marked "not negotiable". Conversely, the status of "negotiable" documents (of title) has been denied to other mate's receipts precisely because the requirements of a valid custom in relation to them were not established.[55] It seems to follow that the requirement of production of the document is, as a matter of history, not the cause, but the consequence,[56] of its being recognised as a "negotiable" document of title; and that the cause of its being recognised as such lies in the proof of mercantile custom. Such proof has, at least until now, been regarded as essential before a document or class of documents will be recognised as having the characteristics of a "negotiable" document of title in the 18–075

[47] See above, para.18–074 after nn. 22 and 23.
[48] Above, para.18–007 and 18–062.
[49] See above, para.18–016.
[50] (1794) 5 T.R. 683; for full references see above, para.18–007, n.43.
[51] *Merchant Banking Co. of London v Phoenix Bessemer Steel Co.* (1877) 5 Ch.D. 205; for the required of proof of custom, see also *Dublin City Distillery C v Doherty* [1914] A.C. 823 at p.865.
[52] See below, para.18–166 at n.61.
[53] Some delivery orders are document of title by special statute: see below, para.18–198.
[54] [1971] 1 Lloyd's Rep. 439.
[55] See below, para.18–166 at n.58.
[56] *Motis Exports Ltd v Dampskibsselskapet AF 1912* [2000] 1 Lloyd's Rep. 211 at p.216, stating that the rule requiring production of the bill "*stems from* the negotiable nature of the bill of lading" (italics supplied).

common law sense[57] and the phrase "document of title", without more, has been taken to refer to a document of this kind. It is true that cases such as those referred to above[58] do not in terms state that a document can be recognised as a document of title (in this sense) by virtue *only* of proof of mercantile custom,[59] but there are, it is submitted, good reasons of policy for insisting on this requirement. Recognition of a document as a "negotiable" document of title no doubt confers advantages or privileges on persons who deal with such documents; but if it can have this effect it must follow that it can equally prejudice third parties who deal with, or have an interest in, the underlying goods. In the law of Prize, the interests of such third parties prevail even where the document in question *is* a "negotiable" document of title in the common law sense. Hence for the purposes of that branch of the law, property cannot pass merely by dealings with shipping documents: the object of this rule is to guard against the risk that the rights of belligerents might be too easily defeated by paper transfers.[60] Ordinary third parties are exposed to this risk where the dealings are with "negotiable" documents of title; and the requirement of proof of mercantile custom, satisfying the usual requirements of being notorious, certain and reasonable,[61] does provide such third parties with a degree of protection. It is submitted that the courts should be slow to reduce that protection by removing the requirement of proof of custom.[62]

18–076 **Documents expressed to be not negotiable.** Even where a document belongs to a class in relation to which a mercantile custom is proved, making documents within the class "negotiable" documents of title in the common law sense, the particular document in question may be deprived of that characteristic by its terms, *e.g.* by being marked "not negotiable", as in *Kum v Wah Tat Bank Ltd*.[63] This rule can give rise to a problem of classification where a straight bill of lading is created because a dual purpose document[64] is filled in by inserting the name of the consignee

---

[57] The point is not discussed by the House of Lords in *JI MacWilliam Co. Inc. v Mediterranean Shipping Co. SA (The Rafaela S)* [2005] UKHL 11, [2005] 2 A.C. 423 since in that case the issue whether a straight bill was a document of title in the common law sense was not before the House: see at [22]. It is merely said at [9] that "the custom found in the leading case of *Lickbarrow v Mason* . . . related to the negotiability and transferability of an order bill." In the Court of Appeal ([2003] EWCA Civ 556, [2004] Q.B. 702) *Lickbarrow v Mason* is referred to only in a quotation at [79] from *Kum v Wah Tat Bank Ltd* [1971] 1 Lloyd's Rep. 439 at p.446.

[58] At nn. 50–54.

[59] Our concern here is with the requirements imposed by the common law. The further possibility that legislation can confer on a document the same characteristics as those of a document of title at common law, is illustrated by the examples given in para.18–198 below.

[60] Below, para.18–242.

[61] For these requirements, see *Chitty on Contracts*, 29th ed., paras 12–129, 13–018.

[62] *cf* the Law Commissions' Report, cited in n.36 above, para.5.4 ("While it is possible for other documents to become documents of title by proof of custom, the courts have not been eager to extend the number of such documents"); and the rule that a document cannot become a (truly) negotiable instrument except on proof of such a mercantile custom: see *Chitty*, 29th ed., para.34–006.

[63] [1971] 1 Lloyd's Rep. 439; see above after n.54.

[64] See para.18–075 above.

without the addition (whether in the consignee box or elsewhere in the bill[65]) of the words "or order", or of similar words importing transferability. This was the position in *The Rafaela S*[66] where the "consignee box" was headed "Consignee: BL not negotiable unless 'ORDER OF'". The effect of failing to insert these last two words was therefore the same as if the bill had been marked "not negotiable". Hence, on the reasoning of *Kum v Wah Tat Bank Ltd.*,[67] the bill in *The Rafaela S* would not be a "negotiable" document of title in the common law sense even if a straight bill not containing these words were, by proof of custom to that effect, capable of being such a document.

"Transferability". For the purpose of the present discussion, the crucial difference between an order bill and a straight bill is that goods covered by the former are deliverable to any person to whom the bill has been duly transferred by indorsement (where necessary) and delivery, while goods covered by the latter are deliverable only to the named consignee (unless they have been redirected to someone else by notice to the carrier).[68] This distinction is sometimes expressed by saying that an order bill is "transferable" while a straight bill is not. In *The Rafaela S*, however, the Court of Appeal accepted the argument of counsel[69] that a straight bill *can* be "transferred" though only once, *i.e.* to the named consignee. In the words of Rix L.J., "although a [straight bill] cannot be transferred more than once, for it is not *negotiable*, it can be transferred by delivery (just like a classic bill) to the named consignee."[70] One difficulty with this statement is that the word "negotiable" in this context is not used in its strict legal sense. It merely means "transferable"[71] and there would at first sight seem to be an element of contradiction in saying that "although . . . it [a straight bill] is not *transferable*, it can be transferred . . .", even once. The apparent contradiction can be resolved only by arguing that "transferable" in relation to an order bill is used to refer to a group of *legal consequences* which follow from the delivery of the document (duly endorsed where necessary), while in the case of a straight bill it is used to refer to that *delivery itself*. In the case of an order bill, delivery of the document is part of the legal machinery (1) under the Carriage of Goods by Sea Act 1992, for transfer- 18–077

---

[65] See *The Happy Ranger* [2002] EWCA Civ. 694, [2002] 2 All E.R. (Comm.) 24, above para.18–019 at n.49.
[66] *JI MacWilliam Co. Inc. v Mediterranean Shipping Co. SA (The Rafaela S)* [2005] UKHL 11, [2005] 2 A.C. 423; *cf. Voss v APL Co. Pte Ltd* [2002] 2 Lloyd's Rep. 707; see above, 18–071 at n.4.
[67] Above, para.18–076 n.54.
[68] *The Rafaela S*, above n.66, at [1].
[69] *The Rafaela S*, above n.66, at [32].
[70] *ibid.*, at [137], italics supplied. In the House of Lords, [2005] UKHL 11, [2005] 2 A.C. 423, this paragraph of Rix L.J.'s judgment was one of those specifically approved by Lord Bingham at [24] wile Lord Steyn at [46] makes a substantially similar point when he says that "a straight bill is only transferable to a named consignee and not generally." Lord Roger, on the other hand, says at [58] that, by the printed terms of the document in that case "the default position is that it is not transferable: it becomes transferable only if the shipper chooses to add the words 'or order' after the consignee."
[71] See below, para.18–084.

ring contractual rights; and (2) at common law for transferring constructive possession of the goods, and property in them if so intended. It is the second of these consequences which follows from the status of order bills as "negotiable" documents of title. In the case of a straight bill, delivery of the document is not necessary for the transfer of contractual rights.[72] Nor can one argue that because such a bill can be "transferred" once, in the sense of being delivered to the named consignee, it can therefore transfer constructive possession of the goods to him. It can have this effect only if it is a "negotiable" document of title in the common law sense, so that the argument assumes the very point in issue: *i.e.* that a straight bill is such a document, for only then would delivery of the document amount to constructive delivery of the goods. Of course if the relationship of shipper and consignee were that of seller and buyer, or that of pledgor and pledge, then constructive possession of the goods and proprietary interests in them might pass (as in *Kum v Wah Tat Bank Ltd*)[73] on the ground that the shipper had delivered the goods to the carrier as bailee for the named consignee. But such a transfer of constructive possession would result from dealings with *the goods* rather than from any transfer of the documents; and it could so result even if (as in that case) the document was *not* a document of title in the common law sense.

18–078 **Summary of conclusions.** Until recently, the general view was that straight bills were not documents of title in the common law sense[74]; that is, that they were not "negotiable" documents in the sense of being transferable; and it is submitted that this view should prevail. The reasons for this submission are set out in the paras 18–067 to 18–077 above; they may be summarised as follows. First, although the weight of judicial opinion is that a straight bill must be produced by the named consignee when claiming delivery of the goods,[75] the existence of this requirement is not a sufficient (though it is now a necessary) condition of such a bill's having the characteristics of a "negotiable" document of title to goods in the common law sense. It is necessary, in addition, to prove a mercantile custom relating to such bills, of the same kind as that proved in *Lickbarrow v Mason* in relation to order bills.[76] Secondly, even if such a custom were proved in relation to straight bills as a class, a particular bill would be deprived of those characteristics by being expressly or by implication marked "not negotiable"[77]: this possibility is illustrated by some of the forms of "dual purpose" bills considered in the preceding discussion.[78] Thirdly, nothing in that discussion precludes the possibility that straight bills may be "documents of title" in the statutory sense given to that term by section 1(4) of

---

[72] Straight bills are sea waybills for the purposes of the 1992 Act (see para.18–018 above) and the transfer of contractual rights arising under them does not require the delivery of the document to the named consignee (see below, para.18–153).
[73] [1977] 1 Lloyd's Rep. 439; below, para.18–166.
[74] Above, para.18–067.
[75] Above, paras 18–069 to 18–072.
[76] Above, para.18–073.
[77] Above, para.18–076.
[78] As in the *Voss* case, above para.18–071 and *The Rafaela S*, above paras 18–071 and 18–076 at n.66.

the Factors Act 1889[79] or that they may fall within that expression where it is used for purposes other than their "conveyancing" function: *e.g.* for the purpose of subjecting contracts contained in or evidenced by them to the contractual regime of the Hague or Hague-Visby Rules.[80]

Whether received bills are documents of title. The custom recognised in *Lickbarrow v Mason*,[81] by virtue of which bills of lading are documents of title, refers only to shipped bills of lading and it is uncertain whether received bills or other similar documents are documents of title in the common law sense.[82] In *The Marlborough Hill*[83] a bill of lading provided that goods had been "received for shipment by the sailing vessel called the *Marlborough Hill*, or by some other vessel owned or operated by"[84] the shipowners. The Privy Council described the bill as "negotiable",[85] presumably intending thereby to indicate that it was a document of title. But the only question actually before the Privy Council was whether the document was a "bill of lading" within section 6 of the Admiralty Court Act 1861 (which then governed aspects of admiralty jurisdiction). No reference was made to the terms of the custom proved in *Lickbarrow v Mason*, which is restricted to shipped bills.[86] The view that the bill was a document of title can perhaps be supported on the ground that it was issued in New York, where the use of such received bills was customary and where they are regarded as documents of title.[87] 18–079

The Privy Council's view of the legal nature of the bill of lading in *The Marlborough Hill* was criticised in *Diamond Alkali Export Corp. v Fl Bourgeois*,[88] where the bill of lading was for goods "received in apparent good order and condition . . . to be transported by the SS. *Anglia* . . . or failing shipment by said steamer in and upon a following steamer."[89] McCardie J. held that this document did not fall within the custom recognised in *Lickbarrow v Mason* and it follows that he cannot have regarded it as a document of title. It is true that the only point actually decided in the *Diamond Alkali* case was that the "received" bill was not a good tender under a c.i.f. contract; but one practical reason why a c.i.f.

---

[79] See para.18–083 below.
[80] See para.18–074 above.
[81] See above, para.18–007, n.43 for full references.
[82] The question was said to be an open one in *MB Pyramid Sound NV v Briese Schiffahrts GmbH (The Ines)* [1993] 2 Lloyd's Rep. 492; for further proceedings, see [1995] 2 Lloyd's Rep. 144.
[83] [1921] 1 A.C. 444.
[84] *ibid.*, p.452.
[85] *ibid.*, p.452; "negotiable" not strictly accurate: below, para.18–084. The Carriage of Goods by Sea Act 1992 applies to received bills (s.1(2)(b)) but does not deal with the question whether they are documents of title: see above, para.18–011.
[86] Above, para.18–007.
[87] Uniform Bills of Lading Act 1909, s.1; see now UCC, §§1–201(6) and (15) (1–201(16) in the not yet widely adopted 2001 version), 7–102(1)(e), 7–104 (7–104(a) in the 2003 version, as to which see above, para.18–015, n.7); 49 U.S.C. Ch.801 (1994) does not contain any definition of "document of title" but leaves the nature of such a document to be inferred from §80105a.
[88] [1921] 3 K.B. 443.
[89] *ibid.*, p.446.

buyer is likely to object to such a document is precisely that it lacks the characteristics of a document of title.[90]

In *Ishag v Allied Bank International*[91] goods in two warehouses (one in Germany and the other in Holland) had been sold by a German seller to a buyer in The Central African Republic. Warehouse receipts relating to the goods were surrendered by the seller's forwarding agents to sub-agents of the ship in exchange for a document issued in January 1980 and purporting to be a "bill of lading". It stated that "the above mentioned consignment is at the disposal of [the ship's sub-agents] and that the same is intended to be shipped in one lot with MS *Lycaon* from Bremen to Douala."[92] The goods were later shipped on the *Lycaon* and in February a second "shipped" bill of lading was issued in respect of them to the seller's forwarding agents, who undertook not to part with it, but who broke that undertaking and transferred the February bill to the seller's bank in order to obtain payments of freight which they had made or for which they were liable. Meanwhile the January "bill of lading" had been pledged by the seller as security for a loan. It was held that the pledge was valid at law as the January "bill of lading" was a document of title; or alternatively that the pledge was effective as an equitable pledge by deposit of documents. The first ground for the decision was based on *The Marlborough Hill*[93]; but no reference was made to the criticisms of that decision in the *Diamond Alkali*[94] case. In one respect, indeed, the January "bill of lading" came closer to a traditional bill of lading than the documents considered in the two earlier cases: it unequivocally named the ship and did not give the carrier the option to carry the goods on a substitute ship. But in two other, and it seems more significant, respects the January "bill of lading" differed strikingly from even a received bill of lading. First, it did not state that the goods had been received by the carrier but only that they were "at the disposal" of the carrier's sub-agents: in the context, these words could mean no more than that the sub-agents had (or thought they had) a contractual right to call upon the warehousemen to deliver the goods.[95] Secondly, it merely said that the goods were "intended to be shipped"[96] on the *Lycaon*, without indicating any physical proximity between the goods and the ship; indeed, one of the warehouses in which the goods were stored was not even in the same country as the port of shipment. In these circumstances, it is straining language to say that the goods had been "received for shipment" on the *Lycaon*; and the view that the January "bill of lading" was a document of title is, with respect, open to doubt. The doubt is strengthened by the facts of *Ishag's* case where two sets of documents, both purporting to be original bills of lading covering the same goods, came into of the hands

[90] See below, para.19–030.
[91] [1981] 1 Lloyd's Rep. 92.
[92] *ibid.*, p.97.
[93] Above, n.083.
[94] Above, n.088.
[95] *cf.* below, para.18–174.
[96] For this reason it would not have been acceptable to a bank under a documentary credit calling for tender of a "Marine/Ocean" bill of lading: U.C.P. 500 Art. 23(a)(ii); *cf.* Art. 25(a)(iv); under Art. 24(a)(ii) the position would be the same where the credit called for "a non-negotiable sea waybill".

of different holders, each of whom claimed the goods. The master declined to deliver to either holder and carried the goods back to the port of shipment. The carrier's claim against the pledgee for "return freight" was dismissed as "it was clearly wrong that two sets of what looked like original bills of lading should have been allowed to be in circulation at the same time."[97]

It is submitted that, as a matter of legal principle, a "received" bill should be regarded as a document of title in the common law sense only if a custom to that effect can be established.[98] This follows from the view that, at common law, the only way in which documents can become documents of title is by proof of such custom,[99] and from the fact that the custom recognised in *Lickbarrow v Mason* extends only to "shipped" and not to "received" bills.[1] There is, moreover, a practical reason for distinguishing, for this purpose, between shipped and received bills. Once goods have been shipped, it is impossible or extremely difficult for the shipper or consignee to deal with them physically and it was this impossibility or extreme difficulty which originally led to the recognition of shipped bills of lading as documents of title.[2] There is no such impossibility or extreme difficulty in dealing with goods before they have been shipped, and correspondingly less need to regard documents relating to them as documents of title. On the other hand, refusal to recognise received bills as documents of title need not hamper dealings in such goods once they have been shipped, since it is then a simple matter to turn the received into a shipped bill by a notation recording the fact of shipment.[3] If this process had been adopted in *Ishag v Allied Bank International*, much of the confusion that arose in that case could have been avoided and the need for litigation reduced.[4]

Whether spent bills are documents of title. A bill of lading is "spent" or "exhausted" when the goods covered by it have been delivered to the person entitled to delivery under the bill.[5] 18–080

[97] *Elder Dempster Lines v Zaki Ishag (The Lycaon)* [1983] 2 Lloyd's Rep. 548 at 552. See further para.18–095, below.

[98] It may be relevant that received bills are not acceptable to banks under UCP 500, Art. 23(a)(ii); *cf. ibid.* Art. 24(a)(ii), applying the same requirement of shipment to "non-negotiable" sea waybills.

[99] Above, para.18–075 below, para.18–201.

[1] Above, para.18–007.

[2] *cf. Sanders Bros v Maclean* (1883) 11 Q.B.D. 327 at p.341 (cargoes afloat "necessarily incapable of physical delivery").

[3] Above, para.18–029. The UCP provisions cited in n.96, above, allow for this possibility.

[4] At least the second action (above, n.97) could have been avoided.

[5] Above, paras 18–015, 18–016; *Barber v Meyerstein* (1874) L.R. 4 H.L. 317 at pp.329–330; *London Joint Stock Bank v British Amsterdam Maritime Agency* (1910) 104 L.T. 143; *Hayman & Son v M'Lintock* 1907 S.C. 936 at p.951. A bill is not "spent" by reason of delivery of the goods to a person *not* entitled to the delivery: see *The Future Express*, below n.14; *East West Corp. v DKBS 1912* [2002] EWHC 83 (Comm.), [2002] 1 All E.R. (Comm.) 676 at [39], affirmed [2003] EWCA Civ 83, [2003] Q.B. 1509 where this point was not pursued: see at [19]. The question whether the bill was "spent" arose in the *East West* case, in the context of the transfer of *contractual* (not of *possessory or proprietary*) rights: see below, para.18–113.

The concept of a "spent" bill of lading is used in law for two distinct, though related, purposes. The first such purpose is to determine whether such a bill is a document of title to the goods. This question can, for example, arise where the document is transferred by way of pledge as security for a loan: if the bill is at the time of its transfer "spent", then it is arguable that its transfer cannot have the effect of transferring constructive possession to the person claiming to be the pledgee of the underlying goods. Questions of this kind can arise between persons other than carrier and shipper (or consignee) and are not in principle connected with the transfer of contractual rights under the contract of carriage.[6] The second purpose for which the concept is used is that of determining whether a person other than the original shipper can acquire rights against, or incur liabilities to, the carrier under the contract of carriage. This question will be discussed in paragraphs 18–113 and 18–131 below. It arises because the Carriage of Goods by Sea Act 1992 has created exceptions to the general rule, stated in section 2(2) of the Act, that rights of suit do not pass to a person who becomes the lawful holder of a bill of lading when "possession of the bill no longer gives a right (*as against the carrier*) to possession of the goods . . ."[7] The phrase here italicised seems, from the context, to indicate that the "right" referred to is the *contractual* right to have the goods delivered and this is not necessarily the same as the *constructive possession* of the goods which can be transferred, by transfer of the bill and by virtue of the bill's status as a document of title, from one holder of the bill to another, *e.g.* from seller to buyer or from pledgor to pledge. The two purposes here described are, however, related in that, because the bill is a document of title in the common law sense, it imposes on the carrier a duty to deliver the goods to the person in possession of it[8] (the holder), though at common law any contractual duty to do so was owed to the shipper rather than to the holder; and by statute the latter person would now also, by virtue of having become the lawful holder of the bill, have vested in him "all rights of suit under the contract of carriage as if he had been a party to that contract."[9] But as a matter of history the common law concept of an order bill as a document of title antedates the transferability of contractual rights by means of such a bill,[10] so that the transfer of such a bill could, before the Bills of Lading Act 1855, operate as a transfer of constructive possession of the goods even though it could not then operate as a transfer of contractual rights. Conversely, between 1855 and 1992,[11] a consignee named in a bill of lading could acquire contractual rights under it without ever having had possession of the bill.[12] It seems, therefore, that a bill of

[6] *e.g. Barber v Meyerstein* (1870) LR 4 HL 317, below para.18–091.
[7] Below, para.18–113.
[8] Above, para.18–063.
[9] Carriage of Goods by Sea Act 1992, s.2(1).
[10] See above, para.18–068. The concept of the bill of lading as a document of title, goes back to at least 1794: see *Lickbarrow v Mason* above, para.18–007, n.43; that of a bill as a document by means of which contractual rights could be transferred was not recognised in English law until the Bills of Lading Act 1855, below, para.18–100.
[11] When the Bills of Lading Act 1855 was repealed and superseded by the Carriage of Goods by Sea Act 1992.
[12] Bills of Lading Act, 1855, s.1, below, para.18–100 so far as it refers to the contractual rights vested in a consignee by virtue of the consignment.

lading can still be a document of title whether or not the carrier's contractual duty (originally owed to the shipper) to deliver the goods was legally enforceable by the holder of the bill. If so, the questions whether a bill is a document of title and whether the transfer of it vests contractual rights in the transferee remain distinct, so that the exceptions created by the 1992 Act to the general rule that a spent bill cannot be used to transfer contractual rights are not directly relevant to the status of such a bill as a document of title. The 1992 Act, it must be repeated, deals only with the transfer of contractual rights.

The question whether a spent bill is a document of title may, however, depend on the continued enforceability *by someone* of the carrier's promise to deliver the goods and it is this point which gives rise to problems with regard to the status of a spent bill as a document of title. Once the carrier has delivered the goods to the person entitled to delivery under the bill, his obligation in that respect is discharged by performance and therefore ceases to exist.[13] It would at first sight seem to follow that the reason for regarding the bill as a document of title likewise falls away at this point. In the normal case, indeed, the bill will be surrendered to the carrier when such delivery is made and no question will arise as to its continuing to be a document of title to the goods. But such a question can arise where the bill is not available when the ship reaches the agreed destination and delivery is there made against letters of indemnity. In *The Future Express*[14] the goods were delivered against letters of indemnity; and as they were so delivered to a person *not* entitled to them under the terms of the contract of carriage, the bill was not "exhausted" by the delivery. The question whether an "exhausted" bill could continue to be a document of title therefore did not strictly arise, but at first instance Judge Diamond Q.C. said that he would be "reluctant to hold that a bill of lading becomes exhausted as a document of title once the carrier has delivered the goods against an indemnity to a person authorized to receive delivery."[15] Such a conclusion would, in his view, "greatly detract from the value of bills of lading as documents of title to goods, would diminish their value to bankers and other persons who have to rely on them for security and would facilitate fraud."[16] No doubt the view that a "spent" bill can continue to operate as a document of title will have the result of protecting banks and other persons who part with money on the faith of the document; but if such persons are protected it follows that persons who deal in the actual goods may be correspondingly prejudiced.[17] Suppose, for example, that A, to whose order the goods have been shipped, obtains delivery of the goods from the carrier under a letter of indemnity, sells the goods to B and then pledges the bill to C. Here both B and C are innocent victims of A's fraud and there is no very obvious reason for giving C the priority over B which C would have[18] if the bill

[13] *cf.* above, at n.7.
[14] [1992] 2 Lloyd's Rep. 79, *affd.* without reference to this point [1993] 2 Lloyd's Rep. 542.
[15] [1992] 2 Lloyd's Rep. 79 at p.99.
[16] *ibid.*
[17] *cf.* above, para.18–075.
[18] Under Sale of Goods Act 1979, s.24 (good faith on C's part is assumed).

remained a document of title after delivery of the goods to B. Indeed, the need for giving C such priority is reduced now that, so long as he took his pledge in good faith, he has a remedy against the carrier even though the bill was "spent" when it was transferred to him.[19] The carrier will in turn have a remedy under the letter of indemnity against A, though if this consists only of a personal undertaking by A, it is likely to be of little value where A was guilty of fraud. The view that a "spent" or "exhausted" bill can remain a document of title is also a potential source of uncertainty since it would give rise to the question for how long after the delivery of the goods the bill would retain this quality; and this is a question which could depend on facts which are extrinsic to the document and to which persons dealing with it are unlikely to have access. On balance, it is submitted that the better view is that "spent" bills should not be regarded as documents of title.[20]

18–081 **"Negotiability as against the ship".** As noted in para.18–080 above, the question whether a "spent" bill is a document of title is distinct[21] from the question of the carrier's contractual liability where goods covered by a bill of lading are delivered to A (who is entitled to the delivery) and the bill then gets into the hands of B who claims delivery of the same goods from the carrier. Where this happens because the bill is part of a set, the carrier can rely on the usual provision in the bill that, when one part is accomplished (by delivery to A) the others are to stand void[22]; the carrier would be liable to B only if A were *not* a person entitled to delivery. The position would appear to be the same where a bill containing such a protective provision was a single bill, as opposed to one of a set. In the United States legislation expressly provides that a carrier who fails to take and cancel a bill after the goods have been delivered is liable to a person to whom the bill is later transferred in good faith and for value[23]; and that he is similarly liable if after part of the goods have been delivered he fails to make a notation of this fact on the bill. The rights of B against the carrier under the rules just stated of English or American law are personal rights only. If the carrier and the person to whom the goods have been wrongfully delivered are both insolvent, B will be able to rely on a right of property or security interest (*e.g.* by way of pledge) only if the bill, at the time of its transfer to him, was still a document of title, that is if (in accordance with the submission made above), it was at the time not yet "spent". The concept of what has been called "negotiability [of bills of lading] as against

[19] Carriage of Goods by Sea Act 1992, ss.2(2), 5(2) below, para.18–113. On the facts of *The Future Express*, above, n.14, it is doubtful whether the transferee of the bill of lading could now satisfy the requirement of "good faith".
[20] *cf. Hayman & Son v M'Lintock*, above, n.5; *Seconsar Far East Ltd v Bank Markazi Jomhouri Islami* [1997] 2 Lloyd's Reps. 89 at p.97: "The bills of lading were worthless as security because the [goods] were delivered without them." (The delivery was made to the consignees entitled to it); *Borealis AB v Stargas Ltd (The Berge Sisar)* [2001] UKHL 17, [2002] 2 A.C. 205 at [27].
[21] *cf.* above, para.18–011.
[22] See below, para.18–090.
[23] USC §80111(c), formerly Federal Bills of Lading Act 1916 (the Pomerene Act), s.11.

the ship"[24] should, it is submitted, be understood in this sense: that is, as referring to the question whether a person may, by virtue of the transfer of a "spent" bill, acquire personal rights (of the kind described above) against the carrier, as opposed to constructive possession of, or property in, the goods. This submission is supported by the context in which the phrase has been used: that is, in the context of the transfer of *contractual* rights by means of the transfer of bills of lading,[25] and it seems not implausible to conjecture that the words "as against the ship" reflect the words "as against the carrier"[26] which are used in the provision of the Carriage of Goods by Sea Act 1992 which specifies one of the circumstances in which *contractual* rights can be acquired by the transferee of a "spent" bill of lading.

Bill discharged otherwise than by performance. The reason why a bill of lading is said to be "spent" or "exhausted" by delivery of the goods to the person entitled to such delivery in accordance with its terms[27] is that the delivery discharges the carrier's obligation, with respect to the delivery, by performance. The further questions can then arise, whether the bill may similarly become "spent" where that obligation is discharged or varied in some other way: for example, by agreement between the parties to the contract of carriage. In one case,[28] an agreement was made between carriers and shippers (to resolve a dispute between them) by which two out of a set[29] of three bills of lading which had been issued to the shippers were to be presented by them to the carriers, marked "accomplished" and returned to the shippers, to whom the carriers then began to deliver the goods. It was said that the "obvious purpose" of so marking the bills "was to indicate that their function as negotiable documents of title whereby the holder was entitled to obtain delivery from the ship was thereupon exhausted."[30] The point actually decided in this case was that the buyers of the goods, into whose hands the bills of lading had come, had not thereby acquired any *contractual* rights against the carriers.[31] But it seems that when, in accordance with the agreement between carriers and shippers, the bills were marked "accomplished" they were also deprived of their characteristic, as documents of title in the sense here under discussion, of providing a mechanism by which their transfer could operate as a transfer of proprietary or possessory rights in the goods. There is, it is submitted, no doctrinal 18–082

[24] *The David Agmashenbeli* [2002] EWHC 104 (Comm.), [2002] 2 All E.R. (Comm.) 806 at [196].
[25] Contrast *ibid*. at [197], discussing *Barber v Meyerstein* (1870) LR 4 HL 317, where the contest was between successive pledges and the issue was whether at the time of the second pledge the bills were still documents of title in the sense discussed in paras 18–007 and 18–062 above.
[26] Carriage of Goods by Sea Act 1992, s.2(2); and see s.5(2)(c), below, para.18–113.
[27] See above, para.18–080 at n.5.
[28] *The David Agmashenebeli* [2002] EWHC 104 (Comm.), [2002] 2 All E.R. (Comm.) 806.
[29] See below, para.18–090 n.90.
[30] *The David Agmashenebeli*, above n.28, at [51].
[31] See below, para.18–113. *Cf.* the references in *The David Agmashenebeli*, above n.24, at [196] and [202] to negotiability "against the ship" (see above, para.18–081) and the discussion of Carriage of Goods by Sea Act 1992 at paras [203–207] of the judgment.

or practical objection to allowing the original parties to deprive a bill of its document of title function by subsequent agreement. They can clearly do so *ab initio* by marking a document 'not negotiable'[32] and it should be equally open to them to achieve the same result *ex post facto* by marking the bill 'accomplished' (or using words to the like effect). Nor, so long as the agreement is recorded in some such way on the face of the document, will third parties by prejudiced by allowing it so to take effect.

The contract of carriage may also be discharged in ways other than by performance or agreement: *e.g.* by frustration or by repudiatory breach of one party accepted by the other. There appears to be no direct authority on the question whether such events also deprive the bill of lading of its characteristic as a document of title. In the case of frustration, it is established that a c.i.f. buyer is entitled to reject a bill of lading which has been frustrated on the ground that its continued performance would as a result of supervening events involve trading with the enemy.[33] The reason given for this result is that after the occurrence of these events the buyer would not get any *contractual* rights against the carrier[34]; but the outcome could also be justified on the ground that in those circumstances the transfer of the bill of lading no longer amounted to a constructive delivery of the goods to the buyer. This would of course also be true where the contract of carriage was frustrated by loss of the ship, but it is well settled that such loss after appropriation but before tender of documents does not relieve the buyer from his duty to pay.[35] This result follows, however, from the nature of a c.i.f. contract, or from the rules as to the passing of risk under such a contract.[36] It therefore sheds no light on the question whether a frustrated bill of lading can be a document of title. The case of a repudiatory breach by one party accepted by the other can be illustrated by supposing that the carrier has deviated and the shipper has accepted this breach as bringing the contract to an end.[37] Plainly, such acceptance does not deprive the shipper of his right to claim the goods at the end of the transit (assuming them to have survived the effects of the deviation). But it seems that this right arises by virtue of shipper's ownership of the goods, or by virtue of the bailment of them by him to the carrier. It can no longer be based on the defunct contract, the primary obligations of which are discharged by acceptance of the breach. That being so, it is arguable that, in the words of Bowen L.J.'s well-known metaphor, the document in which that contract was contained, or by which it was evidenced, can no longer function as the key to the warehouse.[38] The practical difficulty in cases of

---

[32] Above, para.18–076.
[33] Below, para.19–036.
[34] *Arnhold Karberg & Co. v Blythe Green Jourdain & Co.* [1916] 1 KB 495 at p.506; *cf. Duncan Fox & Co. v Schrempft and Bonke* [1915] 3 K.B. 355.
[35] Below, paras 19–001, 19–059, 19–080.
[36] Below, para.19–110.
[37] Example based on *Hain SS Co. Ltd. v Tate & Lyle Ltd.* (1936) All Com. Cas. 350, above, para.18–060.
[38] *Sanders Bros v Maclean & Co.* (1883) 11 Q.B.D. 327 at p.341.

discharge by frustration or by acceptance of a repudiatory breach is that the events giving rise to such discharge are unlikely to be recorded on the face of the bill so that a transferee who in good faith advances money in exchange for the bill is likely to be prejudiced if such events deprive the bill of its legal nature as a document of title. In the case of discharge by frustration, this difficulty may be mitigated by the fact that the events giving rise to such discharge are often matters of public notoriety; but this reasoning will only rarely apply to the case of an accepted repudiatory breach. The question whether a bill of lading which has been discharged by frustration or acceptance of a breach thus gives rise to difficult issues of principle (which might suggest that such a bill should no longer be a document of title[39]) and policy (which might favour the opposite conclusion). There may be no general solution to this problem; the resolution of the conflict may well depend on the way in which the opposing claims have arisen in each particular case.[40]

Bills of lading as documents of title in the statutory sense. There is no doubt that a bill of lading which is a document of title in the common law sense is also a document of title in the statutory sense given to that expression in section 1(4) of the Factors Act, 1889[41]; but the question whether a bill of lading which is not a document of title in the common law sense can nevertheless be one in the statutory sense gives rise to more difficulty. The words "any bill of lading" in the first part of the definition of document of title in section 1(4)[42] are perfectly general and would seem to be capable of including a "received" bill even though such a bill is (at least probably) not a document of title in the common law sense.[43] It is similarly arguable that a "straight" or "non-negotiable" bill is a "bill of lading" within the first part of the statutory definition, even though it is not a document of title in the common law sense.[44] 18–083

The legal nature of sea waybills resembles that of straight or "non-negotiable" bills of lading[45] but further difficulty as to their status arises from the part of the definition of a sea waybill, in section 1(3) of the Carriage of Goods by Sea Act 1992, by which such a document is "not a bill of lading". This definition, however, applies only for the purposes of that

---

[39] There is obvious difficulty in the concept of a document of title to non-existent goods. This difficulty is not dispelled by the possibility that contractual rights of suit in respect of such goods may be transferred by virtue of Carriage of Goods by Sea Act 1992 (see below, para.18–136); for the Act does not deal with the function of bills of lading as documents of title (see above, para.18–011).

[40] The argument advanced in relation to the facts of *The Future Express* after n.16 above does not necessarily apply where the bill is discharged otherwise than by physical delivery of the goods to one of the parties claiming an interest in them.

[41] Above, para.18–009.

[42] Above, para.18–009.

[43] Above, para.18–079.

[44] See above, para.18–078. The proposed legislative definition of "document of title" in the Draft Company Security Regulations (above, para.18–010) is also wide enough to include documents which are not documents of title in the common law sense. A document which is a document of title in that sense would seem to be a "negotiable document of title" within these Draft Regulations.

[45] Above, para.18–018; *The Chitral* [2000] 1 Lloyd's Rep. 529.

Act and is there used only in the context of the transfer of contractual rights and the imposition of contractual liabilities which arise under a contract for the carriage of goods by sea contained in or evidenced by a sea waybill. The 1992 Act does not deal with the question whether a person can transfer a better title than he himself has to the goods covered by the document and it is for the purpose of answering this question that the statutory definition of "document of title" was framed in the Factors Act 1889. The definition of "sea waybill" in the 1992 Act therefore does not conclude the question whether such a document could be a "bill of lading" within the first part of the definition of "document of title" in the 1889 Act; or (if a negative answer were given to that question) whether a sea waybill could, as a matter of fact, satisfy the requirements of the second part of that definition.[46]

Somewhat similar difficulties can arise with regard to "spent" bills of lading, which are probably not documents of title in the common law sense.[47] The Carriage of Goods by Sea Act 1992 does regard such documents as bills of lading for the purposes of the transfer of contractual rights[48] and the imposition of contractual liabilities.[49] But it does not follow that a spent bill should be regarded as a document of title for the purposes of section 1(4) of the Factors Act 1889. It is, on the contrary, arguable that after the goods covered by the bill of lading have been delivered by the carrier to the person entitled to them, thus turning the bill into a "spent" one,[50] then the bill should be regarded as having become extinct and so as being no longer capable of being used so as to enable a transferor of it to confer a better title than he himself had on the transferee[51]; and that the same reasoning should apply where the bill has become extinct for one of the other reasons discussed in para.18–082 above.

18–084 **Whether bill of lading negotiable.** A bill of lading which satisfies the requirements of a document of title at common law possesses one of the attributes of negotiability, *viz.* that it is transferable by indorsement (where necessary) and delivery. Statements to the effect that a bill of lading is "negotiable"[52]

---

[46] See above, para.18–009.
[47] Above, para.18–080.
[48] ss.2(2) and 5(2)(c), below, para.18–131.
[49] ss. 2(2), 3(1)(c) and 5(2)(c); below, para.18–113.
[50] Above, para.18–080.
[51] Above, para.18–080.
[52] *Pease v Gloahec (The Marie Joseph)* (1866) L.R. 1 P.C. 219 at p.227; *Rodger v Comptoir d'Escompte de Paris* (1869) L.R. 2 P.C. 393 at pp.405–406; *Barber v Meyerstein* (1870) L.R. 4 H.L. 317 at p.337; *Cowdenbeath Coal Co. Ltd v Clydesdale Bank Ltd* (1895) 22 R. (Ct. of Sess.) 682; *Thomas v Portsea* [1912] A.C. 1 at pp.6, 9, 11; *The Merak* [1964] 2 Lloyd's Rep. 527 at pp.531, 534; *Mobil Shipping & Transportation Co. v Shell Eastern Petroleum (Pte) Ltd (The Mobil Courage)* [1987] 2 Lloyd's Rep. 655 at p.658; *Federal Bulk Carriers Inc. v C Itoh Ltd (The Federal Bulker)* [1989] 1 Lloyd's Rep. 103 at p.105; *Kuwait Petroleum Corp. v I & D Oil Carriers Ltd (The Houda)* [1994] 2 Lloyd's Rep. 541 at p.556; *OK Petroleum AB v Vitol Energy SA* [1995] 2 Lloyd's Rep. 160 at 162; *Excess Insurance Co. Ltd v Mander* [1997] 2 Lloyd's Rep. 119 at pp.123, 125; *Sunrise Maritime Inc. v Uvisco Ltd (The Hector)* [1998] 2 Lloyd's Rep. 287 at p.293; *Motis Exports Ltd v Dampskibsselskapet*

(or that it has been "negotiated"[53]) may be taken to refer to this attribute of transferability alone. Thus it has been said that in *Lickbarrow v Mason*[54] "the word 'negotiable' was not used in the sense in which it is used as applicable to a bill of exchange, but as passing the property in goods only."[55] There are, in particular, two legal attributes of bills of exchange as negotiable instruments which are not shared by bills of lading. The first is that the transferee of a bill of lading as a general rule acquires only such interest as the transferor had, and does not take free from defects in the transferor's title.[56] And, secondly, the rules governing the consideration for the transfer of a bill of exchange do not apply to the transfer of a bill of lading.[57] For these reasons the general view is that a bill of lading is not a truly negotiable instrument in the full legal sense.[58] When a bill of lading is described as "negotiable", what is meant is that it is *transferable*[59]: in other words, the point of the description is to exclude sea waybills,[60] bills or copies expressly marked "not transferable" or "not negotiable", and probably other straight bills.[61]

Defects in transferor's title. The general rule was stated by Lord Campbell C.J. in *Gurney v Behrend*[62]: "Although the shipper may have indorsed in blank a bill of lading deliverable to his assigns, his right is not 18–085

AF 1912 [2000] 1 Lloyd's Rep. 211 at p.216; *Tradigrain SA v King Diamond Shipping SA (The Spiros C)* [2000] 2 Lloyd's Rep. 319 at p.328; *Delos (Cargo Owners) v Delos Shipping Ltd (The Delos)* [2001] 1 All E.R. (Comm.) 763 at p.768; *The David Agmashenebeli* [2003] EWHC 104 (Comm.), [2002] 2 All E.R. (Comm.) 86 at [105]. The Draft Regulations referred to in n.44 above also use the expression "negotiable document of title" (Regs 22(2), 28(2) and 30(g)).

53 *The Aramis* [1989] 1 Lloyd's Rep. 213 at 231.

54 For full references see above, para.18–007, n.43.

55 *Thompson v Dominy* (1845) 14 M. & W. 403 at p.408.

56 Below, para.18–085.

57 Below, para.18–088.

58 *Waring v Cox* (1808) 1 Camp. 369 at p.370; *Gurney v Behrend* (1854) 3 E. & B. 622 at pp.633–634; *Dracachi v Anglo-Egyptian Navigation Co.* (1868) L.R. 3 C.P. 190 at p.192; *Nippon Yusen Kaisha v Ramjiban Serowgee* [1938] A.C. 429 at p.449; *Heskell v Continental Express Ltd* [1950] 1 All E.R. 1033 at p.1042: bill of lading described as negotiable only "in the popular sense"; *Parsons Corporation v CV Scheepvaartonderneming The Happy Ranger (The Happy Ranger)* [2002] EWCA Civ. 694 at [27] ("colloquially . . . described as . . . negotiable"); *JI MacWilliam Co. Inc. v Mediterranean Shipping Co. SA (The Rafaela S)* [2003] EWCA Civ 556, [2004] Q.B. 702 at [1] ("traditionally but idiosyncratically referred to as 'negotiability'"), and [2005] UKHL 11, [2005] 2 A.C. 423 at [3] ("negotiable" said to be "somewhat inaccurate.") *Bateman v Green* (1867) I.R. 2 C.L. 166 at p.197. For the position in the United States of America, (where bearer and order bills of lading are truly negotiable) see UCC, s.7–104, 7–502, 7–503; 49 USC §§80104, 80105 and see nn. 63 and 64, below.

59 See *Kum v Wah Tat Bank Ltd* [1971] 1 Lloyd's Rep. 439 at p.446 ("'Negotiable' when used in relation to a bill of lading means transferable"); *cf. The Rafaela S*, above, n.58, [2005] UKHL 11, [2005] 2 A.C. 423 at [37] ("negotiability" in this context used "in a special sense" to mean that the document is "transferable by endorsement").

60 Above, para.18–018.

61 For straight bills, see above, para.18–018; for the view that such bills are "transferable once only", see above, para.18–077.

62 (1854) 3 E. & B. 622.

affected by an appropriation of it without his authority. If it be stolen from him, or transferred without his authority, a subsequent bona fide transferee for value cannot make title under it, as against the shipper of the goods. The bill of lading only represents the goods: and, in this instance, the transfer of the symbol does not operate more than a transfer of what is represented."[63] The position is similar where it is not the bill but the goods which are stolen. The owner of such goods is not deprived of his title to them merely because the thief has shipped the goods, obtained a bill of lading, and transferred the bill to a third party who took it in good faith.[64]

18–086 **Stoppage in transit.** This principle stated in *Gurney v Behrend*[65] was, however, subject at common law to the exception that a lawful transferee of a bill of lading could, by making a further transfer to a bona fide transferee, confer on the latter a title free from the shipper's right of stoppage in transit[66]: this rule accounts for the description of bills of lading as negotiable instruments "against stoppage *in transitu* only".[67] The exception is now contained in section 10 of the Factors Act 1889 and in section 47(2) of the Sale of Goods Act 1979.[68] To bring the exception into operation, the bill of lading must have been lawfully transferred to A who must then transfer it to B who must take it in good faith and for value. Thus it does not apply where goods are sold and then resold and a bill of lading in the name of and to the order of the sub-buyer is issued to the buyer and handed by him to his trustee in bankruptcy[69]: there is, in such a case, no "transfer" of the bill of lading to the sub-buyer. The original transfer must be lawful: this excludes cases in which it was obtained by fraud,[70] but not cases in which a bill lawfully obtained was retained in breach of contract.[71] A transfer by way of pledge may (if the other requirements of the exception are satisfied) defeat the right of stoppage,[72] but only to the extent of the

---

[63] *ibid.*, at p.634. The position is different in the United States where a transferee of a "negotiable" bill of lading can acquire a good title even from a transferor who has acquired the bill by theft: 49 USC §80104(b), UCC §7–502(2) (§.7–502(b) in the 2003 version, as to which see above, para.18–015 n.7.

[64] *Finlay v Liverpool and Great Western SS Co. Ltd* (1870) 23 L.T. 251. In such a case, the position is the *same* in the United States: *Kendall Produce Inc. v Terminal Warehouse Transfer Co.* 145 A. 511 (1929); UCC §7–503(1) (§7–503 (a) in the 2003 version, as to which see above, para.18–015 n.7; 49 USC §80105(a)(1)(A).

[65] (1862) 3 E. & B. 622 above, para.18–085.

[66] *Lickbarrow v Mason* (1787). T.R. 63 (for full references see above, para.18–007, n.43); *Pease v Gloahec, The Marie Joseph* (1866) L.R. 1 P.C. 219; *The Argentina* (1867) L.R. 1 Ad. & E. 370.

[67] *Fuentes v Montis* (1868) L.R. 3 C.P. 268 at p.276.

[68] ULIS, (above, para.1–024) Art. 73(3) contains a similar rule, but the Vienna Convention on Contracts for the International Sale of Goods (above, para.1–024) Art. 71(2) deals only with rights in the goods between buyer and seller: it says nothing about the effect of a transfer of documents on the right of stoppage against the transferee.

[69] *Ex p. Golding, Davis & Co. Ltd* (1880) 13 Ch.D. 628; doubted on another point in *Kemp v Falk* (1882) 2 L.R. 7 App.Cas. 573 at pp.581, 588.

[70] *Schuster v McKellar* (1857) 7 El. & Bl. 704.

[71] *Cahn & Mayer v Pockett's Bristol Channel Steam Packet Co.* [1899] 1 Q.B. 643; below, para.18–087.

[72] *e.g. Cowdenbeath Coal Co. Ltd v Clydesdale Bank Ltd* (1895) 22 R. (Ct. of Sess.) 682.

pledge: the right of stoppage "remains, in Equity at all events, as it was before, subject to a charge in favour of the indorsee of the bill of lading."[73] Where the pledgee of a bill of lading from a buyer of goods also holds other goods as security from that buyer, it has been held that the pledgee must have recourse to those goods (even though they had been bought from other sellers and not paid for) before the goods covered by the bill of lading, in respect of which the seller of those goods had purported to exercise a right of stoppage in transit.[74]

The right of stoppage is sometimes described as an equitable right,[75] and the rule stated in the preceding paragraph may likewise defeat other equitable rights of the shipper, such as an equitable lien claimed by virtue of the terms of the contract of sale. This was decided in *Nippon Yusen Kaisha v Ramjiban Serowgee*, where Lord Wright said[76]: "It is true generally that a bill of lading is not a negotiable instrument in the sense that a bill of exchange is and that the transferee of a bill of lading does not get a better title than his transferor. But while that is true of title in law, it cannot be asserted of equitable rights."

Transferee obtaining good title by statute. Further exceptions to the principle that a transferee of a bill of lading takes no better title than his transferor were created by the Factors Acts. The exceptions concerning transfers by buyers and sellers are now contained in sections 8 and 9 of the Factors Act 1889 and in sections 24 and 25 of the Sale of Goods Act 1979, under which a seller in possession of a bill of lading, and a buyer in possession of a bill of lading with the consent of the seller, may be able to confer a better title than he himself had. Under these provisions the transfer of the bill of lading would merely have the same effect as if it had been authorised by the owner of the goods,[77] and a transfer so authorised would not necessarily defeat the right of stoppage in transit. It was therefore necessary to make the special provisions already mentioned[78] which preserve the common law rule as to the effect of a transfer of a bill of lading on the right of stoppage. The operation of both sets of provisions is illustrated by *Cahn & Mayer v Pockett's Bristol Channel Steam Packet Co. Ltd*[79] where copper was sold on c.i.f. terms and an equivalent quantity was resold by the buyer to a sub-buyer. The copper was shipped by the seller and the bill of lading, indorsed in blank, was forwarded to the buyer, together with a draft for the price. The buyer failed to accept the draft so that the property in the copper did not pass to him[80] but he sent the bill of lading to his sub-buyer who paid for it in good faith. It was held that the 18–087

[73] *Kemp v Falk* (1882) 7 App.Cas. 573 at pp.576–577; *Spalding v Ruding* (1843) 6 Beav. 376, affirmed (1846) 15 L.J.Ch.374. Sale of Goods Act 1979, s.47(2)(b) restates this rule.
[74] *In the matter of Westzinthus* (1833) 5 B. & Ad. 817.
[75] *Nippon Yusen Kaisha v Ramjiban Serowgee* [1938] A.C. 429 at p.450.
[76] *ibid.* at p.449; *cf. Meyer v Sharpe* (1813) 5 Taunt. 74.
[77] So far as s.25 is concerned, this rule is imported as a result of Factors Act 1889, s.2.
[78] Factors Act 1889, s.10; Sale of Goods Act 1979, s.47(2) (above, para.18–086).
[79] [1899] 1 Q.B. 643.
[80] Sale of Goods Act 1979, s.19(3); above, para.5–138, below, para.18–221.

sub-buyer obtained a good title to the copper under section 25[81] in spite of the fact that, at the time of the resale to him, the buyer was not yet in possession of the bill of lading. And the seller's right of stoppage in transit was barred under section 47(2)[82]: the bill had been "lawfully transferred" to the buyer even though he had not performed the conditions on which the transfer was made.

18–088 **Consideration for the transfer of a bill of lading.** The transfer of a bill of lading does not pass property or title, or bar the right of stoppage in transit, unless value is given for the transfer.[83] Thus it has been held that the indorsement of a bill of lading to an agent solely with a view to enabling him to collect or store the goods did not pass any property to the agent.[84] One reason for this result was that the agent had not given any consideration for the transfer; another was that the transfer was not made with the intention of transferring property.[85] There appears to be no support in the authorities for any presumption that value has been given for an indorsement of a bill of lading. There are conflicting decisions on the question whether past consideration amounts to "value" for the transfer of a bill of lading.[86] Where the transfer is made in consideration of an antecedent debt, the transferee's forbearance to enforce the debt will generally be sufficient "value"[87] for this purpose.[88] There is no authority on the question whether a transfer of a bill of lading made without consideration can vest the *contractual* rights under the bill in the transferee. The Carriage of Goods by Sea Act 1992, which now deals with the transfer of such contractual rights, contains no reference to any requirement of consideration for this purpose and gives some support to the view that there is no such requirement.[89] In

---

[81] And Factors Act 1889, s.9.
[82] And Factors Act 1889, s.10.
[83] *Coxe v Harden* (1803) 4 East 211 at p.217; *Waring v Cox* (1808) 1 Camp. 369; *Rodger v Comptoir d'Escompte de Paris* (1869) L.R. 2 P.C. 393; *Burgos v Nascimento* (1909) 100 L.T. 71 doubting statements in *Morison v Gray* (1824) 2 Bing. 260; and see below, n.84.
[84] *Coxe v Harden* (1803) 4 East 211; *Waring v Cox* (1808) 1 Camp. 369; *Burgos v Nascimento* (1909) 100 L.T. 71, where it is said at pp.73–74 that the statement in *Morison v Gray* (1824) 2 Bing. 260 at 261 (to the effect that the agent obtains a "special property" in such circumstance) does not represent the general rule.
[85] *Burgos v Nascimento ubi* above; following *Sewell v Burdick* (1884) 10 App.Cas. 74 (on such facts, see now Carriage of Goods by Sea Act 1992, ss.2, 3, below paras 18–102, 18–123, 18–129). It is not clear whether the gratuitous transfer of a bill of lading might operate by way of gift, if so intended. An attempt to make a gift of goods afloat in this way might fail under the rule in *Cochrane v Moore* (1890) 25 Q.B.D. 57 under which *actual* (and not merely constructive) delivery is required to perfect a gift of a chattel not made by deed of gift. *Cf.* below, after n.90, for shipments made by way of gift.
[86] Contrast *Newsom v Thornton* (1805) 6 East 17 and *Rodger v Comptoir d'Escompte de Paris* (1869) L.R. 2 P.C. 393 with the authorities cited in n.89, below.
[87] Under the principle of *Alliance Bank v Broom* (1864) 2 Dr. & Sm. 289.
[88] *Chartered Bank of India v Henderson* (1874) L.R. 5 P.C. 501; *The Emilien Marie* (1875) 44 L.J.Adm. 9; *Leask v Scott* (1877) 2 Q.B.D. 376. But if a transfer for such consideration were made by a mercantile agent by way of pledge the transferee's rights would be limited by Factors Act 1889, s.4 (above, para.7–050).
[89] See ss.2(1)(a) and 5(2)(a).

dealing with such transfers to holders of "spent" bills, it refers to transactions "effected in pursuance of any contractual *or other* arrangements"[90]; and the words here italicised are capable of referring to transactions by way of gift (*e.g.* to an overseas charity).

Transfer of property by transfer of bill of lading. The transfer of a bill of lading operates to transfer the transferor's property in the goods to the transferee if the transfer was made with that intention[91]; but no property is transferred in the absence of such intention[92] though the transfer of a bill of lading for value is prima facie evidence of intention to pass the property.[93] Since the effect of the transfer depends on the intention of the parties, it has been said that "whether or not the transfer of a bill of lading transfers the property in goods is always a question of fact with the answer depending on the nature of the agreement under which the transfer takes place."[94] The intention of the parties may likewise control the extent of the interest which passes to the transferee by virtue of the transfer. Thus if the transfer is by way of pledge or security, the transferee will only have a "special property" or security interest in the goods[95] while the general property will remain unaffected by the transfer of the bill. The intention of the parties may also be to pass the property subject to certain conditions, generally as to payment. The extent to which effect will be given to his intention in this way to restrict the passing of property will be further discussed below.[96] 18–089

Bills in sets. Bills of lading are commonly issued in sets of three or four identical parts; each of these parts is an original carriage document, states the number of parts and usually concludes with words such as "one of which being accomplished, the others shall stand void." The objects of this practice were to facilitate dealings in cargoes afloat at a time when communications were slow, and to guard against the risk of loss of a single part.[97] As long ago as 1882 Lord Blackburn criticised the practice in the 18–090

---

[90] s.2(2)(a).

[91] *Lickbarrow v Mason* (1787) 2 T.R. 64; for full references see above, para.18–007, n.7; *Thompson v Dominy* (1845) 14 M. & W. 403; *cf. Leigh & Sillavan v Aliakmon Shipping Co. Ltd (The Aliakmon)* [1986] A.C. 785, below, para.18–149.

[92] *Burgos v Nascimento* (1908) 100 L.T. 71; *Yangtsze Insurance Association v Luckmanjee* [1918] A.C. 585 at p.589 (bill of lading delivered under an ex ship contract "given as a delivery order"; below, para.21–020 at n.84); *cf. Kaukomarkkinat O/Y v Elbe Transport-Union GmbH (The Kelo)* [1985] 2 Lloyd's Rep. 85 at p.87 *East West Corp. v DKBS 1912 AF A/S* [2003] EWCA Civ 83, [2003] Q.B. 1509 at [3] (bills of lading transferred by sellers to their banks, not to create any security interest in favour of the banks, but solely to enable the banks to collect the price from the buyers on behalf of the sellers).

[93] *Dracachi v Anglo-Egyptian Navigation Co.* (1868) L.R. 3 C.P. 190.

[94] *JI MacWilliam Co. Inc. v Mediterranean Shipping Co. SA (The Rafaela S)* [2005] UKHL 11, [2005] 2 A.C. 423 at [69], per Lord Roger.

[95] *Hibbert v Carter* (1787) 1 T.R. 745; *Sewell v Burdick* (1884) 10 App.Cas. 74; *Brandt v Liverpool, etc., Steam Navigation Co.* [1924] 1 K.B. 575.

[96] Below, paras 18–211—18–225.

[97] *Sanders Bros v Maclean & Co.* (1883) 11 Q.B.D. 327 at p.341.

light of the speed of communication then available.[98] But it has continued[99] and it gives rise to a number of problems. These are discussed in paragraphs 18–091 to 18–094 below.

18–091 **Competing pledges.** First, several parts of the same set may be pledged successively to a number of persons for more than the goods are worth. Here the general rule, laid down in *Barber v Meyerstein*,[1] is that successive pledgees rank in the order in which they took their pledges; though it is possible for a subsequent pledgee to obtain priority over an earlier one under the Factors Act 1889.[2] This would, however, only be the case if the subsequent pledgee took his pledge from a person in possession of one of the parts of the set with the consent of the "owner" who, for this purpose, would appear to be, or at any rate to include, the earlier transferee, even though he was only a pledgee.[3] Thus the rule that successive pledgees rank in order of time is unlikely to be displaced by the operation of the Factors Act.

18–092 **Delivery by carrier against part of a set.** Secondly, the goods may actually be delivered by the carrier (or by a warehouseman in the position of a carrier) against one part of a set, in ignorance of the fact that another part had previously been transferred to another person, who would therefore have priority under the rule in *Barber v Meyerstein*.[4] In *Glyn Mills Currie & Co. v East & West India Dock Co.*[5] sugar was shipped from Jamaica under a set of three bills of lading in the usual form[6] making the sugar deliverable to the order of Cottam & Co., who indorsed the first part to a bank as security for a loan. The sugar was later deposited in the defendants' warehouse on terms authorising them to deliver it to "the holders of the bills of lading." Cottam & Co. brought the second part of the set to the defendants and were entered in the defendants' books as owner. The defendants then in good faith and without notice of the bank's claim delivered the sugar to one Williams against delivery orders signed by Cottam & Co. On the insolvency of Cottam & Co. it was held that the defendants, who stood in the same position as the carrier, were not liable to the bank: they were protected by the provision in the bills of lading that,

---

[98] *Glyn Mills Currie & Co. v East & West India Dock Co.* (1882) 7 App.Cas. 591 at p.605. *Cf.* restrictions on the practice imposed in the United States by 49 USC §80112, formerly Federal Bills of Lading Act 1916, s.4; UCC s.7–304.

[99] The "three original bills of lading out of three" referred to in *The David Agmashenebeli* [2002] EWHC 104 (Comm.), [2002] 2 All E.R. (Comm.) 806 at [51] appear to have been three parts of one set. The way in which these documents were dealt with (*ibid.* at [51]) and the reasoning at [202–204] seem to support this assumption. So, indeed, does the use of the singular pronoun ("it") to refer back to "bills of lading" in the last two sentences of [196].

[1] (1870) L.R. 4 H.L. 317.

[2] Especially under ss.2, 8 and 9 (see above, Ch.7).

[3] See *Lloyds Bank Ltd v Bank of America* [1938] 2 K.B. 147.

[4] Above, para.18–091.

[5] (1882) 7 App.Cas. 591.

[6] See above, para.18–090.

one part being accomplished, the others were to stand void.[7] The House of Lords was in this case concerned only with the position between the bank as pledgee and the defendants, who stood in the position of the carrier. It was said that the bank could still seek redress "from any one who may illegally have obtained possession of their goods."[8] In other words, the position between the bank and Williams would depend on the principles stated in paragraph 18–091 above. If a similar situation arose today, the bank would be likely to safeguard its rights against the carrier by insisting on a full set of bills of lading[9] or by giving notice to the carrier of its rights as pledgee of part of the set.

Part delivery. For the purpose of the rule stated in paragraph 18–092 above, a bill of lading is prima facie "accomplished" only when delivery has been made of *all* the goods which the carrier has in the bill undertaken to deliver. The authorities do not cover the situation in which only *part* of the goods has been delivered: *e.g.* the situation that would have arisen in the *Glynn Mills* case[10] if the defendants had been notified of the bank's claim when they had delivered only part of the sugar to Williams and had then refused to deliver the rest of it to him. Although in such a case the bill of lading would not have been fully "accomplished" and so not have been "void", it is submitted that it should be regarded as "accomplished" *pro tanto*, so that the defendants should not be liable in respect of such part of the sugar as they had in good faith delivered to Williams before getting notice of the bank's claim. This view derives some support from an alternative reason given by Lord Blackburn for the decision in the *Glynn Mills* case, which was that, under the general law relating to the assignment of choses in action, the defendants were entitled to perform in favour of their creditor (Cottam & Co) until they received notice of assignment of the rights under the bill to the bank.[11] The point could be one of considerable practical importance where the bill covers a large bulk cargo and the process of discharging it extends over several weeks.[12] 18–093

Tender to buyer of less than a full set. Thirdly, a buyer might object to tender of less than a full set of bills of lading, in view of the commercial risks to which such tender might expose him under the rule in *Glyn Mills Currie & Co. v East & West India Dock Co.*[13] It was however held in *Sanders Bros v Maclean & Co.*[14] that the buyer is not entitled to reject such a tender unless, *before* it was made, another part of the bill had been transferred to a third party. The result of such previous transfer would be that the tender to 18–094

---

[7] For an alternative reason for the decision, see below, para.18–093.
[8] (1882) 7 App.Cas. 591 at pp.603–604; *cf. Sanders Bros v Maclean* (1883) 11 Q.B.D. 327 at p.334.
[9] *cf.* UCP 500 Art. 23(iv) below, para.23–219.
[10] Above, at n.5.
[11] (1882) 7 App. Cas. 591 at p.613.
[12] As, for example, in *The David Agmashenebeli* [2002] EWHC 104 (Comm.), [2002] 2 All E.R. (Comm.) 806.
[13] Above, para.18–092.
[14] (1883) 11 Q.B.D. 327 (c.i.f. contract); *cf. Cederberg v Borries, Craig & Co.* (1885) 2 T.L.R. 201 (f.o.b. contract).

the buyer would not be "effectual"[15] as it would be incapable of transferring the property to him.[16] But the buyer cannot, under the rule in *Sanders Bros v Maclean & Co.*, reject tender of part of the set merely because some later dealing with the other parts may deprive him of his title to the goods[17] and of his rights against the carrier.[18] The buyer can protect himself against these risks by stipulating for delivery of a full set of bills of lading.

18–095 **More than one set of bills of lading.** The rule stated in paragraph 18–091 above applies where a carrier issues a single set of bills of lading consisting of several original parts. It does not apply where he adopts the dangerous practice[19] of issuing two sets of carriage documents each of which purports to be an original set of bills of lading relating to the same consignment.[20] In such a case it seems that the carrier can be contractually liable under both sets of bills of lading; and expenses incurred by him as a result of the difficulty in which he thus finds himself cannot be recovered from the holder of either set.[21] Whether the rules stated in paragraphs 18–091 and 18–094 apply to such a case depends on the characteristics of the documents. If they are both documents of title in the common law sense,[22] it is submitted that those rules should apply, so that successive pledges of the two sets would rank in order of creation, and tender of either set would be good under a contract of sale; but the qualifications to which those rules are subject in the case of dealings with parts of a single set would apply (*mutatis mutandis*) to dealings with one of several sets of bills of lading. If one of the sets of carriage documents is a document of title while the other is not, it is submitted that the rules stated in paragraphs 18–091 and 18–094 would not apply. Instead, a pledge of the set that was a document of title would prevail over a pledge of the set that did not have this characteristic; and prima facie only the set that was a document

---

[15] (1883) 11 Q.B.D. 327 at p.339; below, para.19–037.
[16] Because of the rule in *Barber v Meyerstein* (above, para.18–091).
[17] Under Sale of Goods Act 1979, s.24 (above, para.7–053).
[18] Under the rule in *Glynn Mills, Currie & Co. v East & West India Dock Co.* (above, para.18–092).
[19] See *Noble Resources Ltd v Cavalier Shipping Corp. (The Atlas)* [1996] 2 Lloyd's Rep. 642 at p.644 describing the practice as "fraught with danger." *Cf.* also *SIAT di del Ferro v Tradax Overseas SA* [1980] 1 Lloyd's Rep. 53; below, para.18–286. Contrast *Guaranty Trust of New York v Van den Berghs* (1925) 22 Ll. L. Rep. 447 at p.455 (no objection to cancellation of one set of bills followed by the issue of a new set before the first had come into the possession of, or property had passed to, the consignee named in the first set); *The Brij* [2001] 1 Lloyd's Rep. 431 where the existence of one set of bills which were documents of title was said at p.434 to be one reason why the parties could not have regarded another set as such documents and therefore classifying the latter as straight bills (above, para.18–018) which, in the view of the Hong Kong Court, were not documents of title in the traditional common law sense (above, paras 18–007, 18–062). For the question whether straight bills are documents of title in that sense, see above, paras 18–069 to 18–077.
[20] See *Elder Dempster Lines v Zaki Ishag (The Lycaon)* [1983] 2 Lloyd's Rep. 548.
[21] *ibid.*; above, para.18–079.
[22] As was said to be the case in *Ishag v Allied Bank International* [1981] 1 Lloyd's Rep. 92 (doubted on this point in para.18–079, above). For the concept of a document of title in the common law sense, above paras 18–007 and 18–062.

of title would constitute a good tender under a contract of sale where such a contract stipulated for a tender of "documents" or "shipping documents" without qualification.

(v) *Contractual Effects of Transfer of Bill of Lading: Introductory*

Goods deliverable to a third party. Where a bill of lading made the goods deliverable to a person other than the shipper, or was transferred to such a person, then that person prima facie acquired no rights under the contract of carriage, and was not subject to any liabilities under it, because he was not a party to that contract. This position may look like a straightforward application of the doctrine of privity of contract,[23] but that doctrine is by no means the sole source of the difficulty of creating a contractual nexus between the transferee of the bill and the carrier. The difficulty had arisen before the doctrine of privity was firmly recognised as a legal principle[24] and it persisted even in common law systems which rejected that doctrine[25] but nevertheless found it necessary to deal with the present problem by legislation.[26] It was, and is, difficult to regard remote transferees of a bill of lading as third party beneficiaries; and even a consignee named in the bill could not be so regarded in view of the fragility of his rights under the rule in *Mitchell v Ede*.[27] Moreover, in the bill of lading context, the law is concerned, not only with the acquisition of rights by, but also with the imposition of liabilities on, third parties; while a third party beneficiary doctrine (to the extent to which it is recognised by law) is concerned only with the former topic. The acquisition of rights under the contract of carriage by, and the imposition of liabilities under that contract on, persons such as transferees of the bill has therefore since 1855[28] been dealt with by special legislation and is now dealt with by the Carriage of Goods by Sea Act 1992. This position is preserved after the creation of a "general and wide-ranging exception"[29] to the common law doctrine of privity of contract by the Contracts (Rights of Third Parties) Act 1999; for, by reason of what we have called the subsection 6(5) exception,[30] section 1 of that Act confers no rights on a third party in the case of a "contract for the carriage of goods by sea", an expression which refers (*inter alia*) to a contract contained in or evidenced by a bill of lading.[31] The subsection 6(5) exception likewise applies to contracts for the international carriage of 18–096

[23] It appears to be so regarded by Lord Lloyd in *Effort Shipping Co. Ltd v Linden Management SA (The Giannis K)* [1998] A.C. 605 at p.616.
[24] The recognition of the doctrine is generally associated with *Tweddle v Atkinson* (1861) 1 B. & S. 393; see *Chitty on Contracts* (29th ed.), paras 18–019 to 18–020.
[25] *e.g.* in the United States of America, where *Lawrence v Fox* (1859) 20 N.Y. 268 marked the beginning of the recognition of the law of third party beneficiaries.
[26] *e.g.* Federal Bills of Lading Act 1916 (the Pomerene Act), s.31(b), now replaced by 49 USC §80105(a)(2); Uniform Bills of Lading Act, s.32, now replaced by UCC §7–502 1(d) and in the 2003 version (above, para.18–015, n.7 by para.7–502(a)(4)).
[27] (1840) 11 Ad. & E. 888, above, para.18–021.
[28] Bills of Lading Act 1855, below, para.18–100.
[29] Above, para.18–005, sub-paragraph (a).
[30] Above, para.18–005, sub-paragraph (f).
[31] s.6(6)(a); and see s.6(7)(a).

goods by air, road or rail which are governed by the Conventions to be discussed in Chapter 21.[32] A number of questions concerning the scope of the subsection 6(5) exception will, indeed, call for discussion in the following account of the Carriage of Goods by Sea Act 1992; but the principle is that the 1999 Act does not displace the rules contained in the 1992 Act which specify when third parties can acquire rights of suit under contracts of carriage dealt with by the latter Act. Nor does the 1999 Act affect the general common law rule that a contract cannot impose liabilities on third parties. In other words, the answer to the questions when (for example) the transferee of a bill of lading can acquire rights or incur liabilities under the contract of carriage depends primarily on the relevant provisions of the 1992 Act.

18–097 **Agency and assignment.** The answer to the questions put at the end of paragraph 18–096 above does not, however, depend exclusively on the provisions of the 1992 Act since, even apart from them, the common law doctrine of privity of contract was, and remains, subject to significant exceptions, some of which could apply in the present context. For example, a consignee could acquire rights and become subject to liabilities under a contract of carriage which had been made by the shipper as his agent.[33] But this reasoning is unlikely to apply where, when the contract of carriage is made by a seller of goods, he contemplates that the bill of lading will pass through many hands under "string" contracts, or that it will be pledged to a bank. A second exception to the doctrine of privity is assignment, which though ineffective at common law, can take effect in equity and under section 136(1) of the Law of Property Act 1925. We shall see that the ordinary process of assignment is sometimes used to transfer a shipper's contractual rights under a bill of lading[34]; but the mere transfer of a bill of lading did not operate as such an assignment[35]; and even an express assignment of the benefit of the contract does not, for a number of reasons, provide a satisfactory solution to the present problem. For one thing, it was often hard to give to the debtor (*i.e.* in the present context, to the carrier)

[32] s.6(5)(b); and see s.6(8) as amended by Railways (Convention on International Carriage by Rail) Regulations 2005, SI 2005/2092, Reg. 9(2) and Sch. 3, para.3. For these Conventions, see below, paras 21–051, 21–058, 21–065.

[33] *e.g. Anderson v Clark* (1824) 2 Bing. 20; *cf.*; where the consignee is owner of the goods, *Texas Instruments Ltd v Nason (Europe) Ltd* [1991] 1 Lloyd's Rep. 146; but in overseas sales property will generally pass only *after* shipment, on payment against tender of documents: below, paras 18–209, 18–216, 19–103 and 20–082. The fact that the bill of lading names a person other than the shipper as consignee may support an inference that the shipper made the contract as agent for that person: see *Borealis AB v Stargas Ltd (The Berge Sisar)* [2001] UKHL 17, [2002] 2 A.C. 205 at [18], as explained in *East West Corp. v DKBS 1912 AF A/S* [2003] EWCA Civ 83, [2003] Q.B. 1509 at [34], where the point is made in the context of the law of bailment. But this fact is far from decisive for that purpose: the cases on the shipper's right to redirect the goods (above, para.18–021) are based on the assumption that, in spite of the consignee's being named in the bill, the contract of carriage is between shipper and carrier.

[34] Below, para.18–147.

[35] *Thomson v Dominy* (1845) 14 M. & W. 403 at pp.405, 407; *Howard v Shepherd* (1850) 9 C.B. 297 at p.319.

the notice of the assignment which was desirable in the case of an equitable, and is essential in the case of a statutory, assignment[36]; for another, an assignee takes "subject to equities"[37] and so might find that his rights were restricted by terms agreed between carrier and shipper but not apparent on the face of the bill.[38] Nor could assignment impose any liabilities on the transferee since, while the law recognises the assignment of *rights*, it does not as a general rule recognise any corresponding concept of "assignment of liabilities".[39]

General common law rule. The general common law position, therefore, was that the transferee of a bill of lading (or the consignee, if he was not also the shipper) could not claim damages from the carrier for breach of contract in failing to deliver the goods[40] nor was he liable to the carrier for freight[41] or other charges due under the contract of carriage. Nor could he sue the carrier on the ground of bailment since that relationship normally[42] existed only between carrier and shipper.[43] A new bailment between carrier and consignee could come into existence only by virtue of an attornment by the carrier, and a mere promise by the carrier to the *shipper* to deliver the 18–098

---

36 See Treitel, *The Law of Contract* (11th ed.), pp.681–682.

37 Law of Property Act 1925, s.136(1); *Mangles v Dixon* (1852) 3 H.L.C. 702 at p.731.

38 This would have been the position in *Leduc v Ward* (1888) 20 Q.B.D. 475 (above, para.18–048) if that case had been one of ordinary assignment.

39 See Treitel, *The Law of Contract* (11th ed.), p.701.

40 *Thompson v Dominy* (1845) 14 M. & W. 403; *Howard v Shepherd* (1850) 9 C.B. 297.

41 *Sanders v Vanzeller* (1843) 4 Q.B. 260.

42 There might be an exception where the consignee was already owner of the goods when they were shipped so that the shipper was acting as his agent when shipping them; but in that case the consignee would be a party to the contract of carriage: See above at n.33. A wider view of the scope of bailment reasoning was taken by Dillon L.J. in *Hispanica de Petroleos SA v Vencedora Oceanica Navegacion SA (The Kapetan Markos NL) (No. 2)* [1987] 2 Lloyd's Rep. 321; but this is hard to reconcile with the first two of the authorities cited in n.43, below. For rights of the *shipper* in bailment after he has lost his contractual rights against the carrier by transfer of the bill, see *East West Corp. v DKBS 1912* [2003] EWCA Civ 83, [2003] Q.B. 1509, below para.18–115; our present concern is with the relationship (at common law) between the carrier and the consignee named in, or the transferee of, the bill of lading.

43 Above, para.18–065. *Leigh and Sillavan Ltd v Aliakmon Shipping Co. Ltd (The Aliakmon)* [1986] A.C. 785 at p.818; *Compania Portorafti Commerciale SA v Ultramar Panama Inc. (The Captain Gregos) (No. 2)* [1990] 2 Lloyd's Rep. 395 at 404; for the difficulty of reconciling these statements with *Borealis AB v Stargas Ltd (The Berge Sisar)* [2001] UKHL 11, [2002] 2 A.C. 205 at [18], according to which the bailment is between carrier and consignee, see above, para.18–065. If the latter view is explicable on the ground that the shipper had acted as the consignee's agent in making the shipment (see the *East West* case, above, at [34]) then the consignee would, by virtue of such agency, be a party to the contract of carriage and be entitled and liable under it on that ground. A relationship of bailor and sub-bailee may also arise between the *shipper* and a person to whom the carrier has sub-contracted the carriage operation, even though there is no contract between the shipper and that person: See *Elder Dempster & Co. v Paterson Zochonis & Co.* [1924] A.C. 522; *KH Enterprise v Pioneer Container (The Pioneer Container)* [1994] 2 A.C. 324; *The Mahkutai* [1996] A.C. 650; *Carver on Bills of Lading* (2nd ed., 2005), Ch.7; but this reasoning would not at common law give any rights to the *transferee* of the bill of lading.

goods to the consignee's (or a fortiori, to the shipper's) order could not be regarded as such an attornment.[44]

18–099 **Common law mitigations.** These common law rules were, before legislation intervened, mitigated in two ways. First, the transferee or consignee might acquire a right to sue the carrier in tort if the transferor was owner and if property had passed to the transferee.[45] Secondly, the carrier might acquire rights (and immunities) against the transferee or consignee, or become contractually liable to him, if the transferee or consignee presented the bill of lading to the carrier with a request for delivery of the goods and the goods were delivered to him in response to such request. Such facts could provide evidence of a new implied contract between the person so requesting delivery and the carrier, incorporating by reference the terms of the bill of lading.[46] These possibilities have survived the legislation by virtue of which rights can be conferred and liabilities imposed on transferees of bills of lading; and they will be more fully discussed in paragraphs 18–138 to 18–151 below. But they did not suffice to produce satisfactory solutions to the problems here to be discussed. Tort reasoning could serve only to make the carrier *liable* to, without normally giving him any *rights against*, the transferee; and, while the implied contract device was not open to this objection, it could fail for other reasons to produce a satisfactory solution: most commonly for want of the requisite contractual intention.

18–100 **The Bills of Lading Act 1855.** The common law having failed to provide a satisfactory solution to the present problem, it became necessary to make legislative provision for the acquisition of contractual rights by, and the imposition of contractual liabilities on, the consignee named in, or the transferee of, a bill of lading. Such provision was first made by the Bills of Lading Act 1855, but this Act was itself found to be unsatisfactory, so that it was eventually repealed[47] and superseded by the Carriage of Goods by Sea Act 1992. Some account of the main features of the 1855 Act is, however, necessary for an understanding of the provisions of the 1992 Act. Under section 1 of the 1855 Act, "Every consignee of goods named in a bill of lading, and every endorsee of a bill of lading, to whom the property in the goods therein mentioned shall pass upon or by reason of such consignment or endorsement, shall have transferred to and vested in him all rights of suit, and be subject to the same liabilities in respect of such goods as if the contract contained in the bill of lading had been made with himself." The two most significant features of this legislative scheme were that (i) the passing of contractual rights was linked to the transfer of property and (ii) the imposition of contractual liabilities on the consignee or indorsee was

---

[44] *The Future Express* [1993] 2 Lloyd's Rep. 542 at p.550; above, para.18–066.
[45] See *Howard v Shepherd*, above, where this condition was not satisfied, so that an action of trover against the carrier failed. As to negligence, see below, paras 18–149 *et seq.*
[46] *Cock v Taylor* (1811) 13 East 399; *Stindt v Roberts* (1848) 17 L.J.Q.B. 166; *cf. Young v Moeller* (1855) 5 E. & B. 755; below, paras 18–138 *et seq.*
[47] Carriage of Goods by Sea Act 1992, s.6(2).

linked to, and occurred at the same time as, the acquisition by that person of contractual rights. The consequence of the first of these features was that a person who had bought the goods from the shipper would not acquire rights under the bill of lading contract, even though property had at some stage passed to him, where the passing of property had already taken place before the bill was transferred to him, or where it passed to him after, and not "by reason of", such transfer.[48] This may be described as the "property gap" in section 1 of the 1855 Act. That gap was widened by the further requirement that, to satisfy section 1, property must pass to the transferee of the bill before the bill was "accomplished."[49] The second main feature of section 1 (*i.e.* the link between the imposition of contractual liabilities and the acquisition of contractual rights) was another potential source of hardship, in that there was at one time a risk that liabilities might be incurred by persons to whom goods were consigned or bills of lading indorsed merely by way of security. This point was met by adopting a narrow construction of the Act. Section 1 required "the property" to have passed; and in *Sewell v Burdick*[50] the House of Lords held that this meant *the* (general) property in the goods and not a special property in them. It followed that a bank to which bills of lading had been indorsed by way of pledge did not, by reason of such indorsement, become liable under the section to pay the freight or other charges due under the bills on the goods. This outcome is generally regarded as having served the interests of commercial convenience, since it is unlikely that, as between pledgor and pledgee, it is the intention of the parties that the liabilities of the pledgor to the carrier in respect of goods held as security are to be imposed on the pledgee.[51] On the other hand, if the goods had been damaged as a result of the carrier's breach of contract so as to impair the pledgee's security, the bank would, under the reasoning of *Sewell v Burdick* have fallen into what we have called the "property gap" and so would have had no rights under section 1[52]; it would have had to rely on the somewhat fragile device of an implied contract of the type to be discussed in paragraphs 18–138 to 18–144. Arguments of convenience or policy could therefore be used to support both a broad and a narrow interpretation of the Act: the former to widen the range of situations in which rights could be acquired by transferees of the bill, and the latter to avoid the imposition of liabilities where such imposition was commercially undesirable.

Carriage of Goods by Sea Act 1992. The Carriage of Goods by Sea Act 1992 avoids this dilemma by severing the two links made by the 1855 Act between (i) transfer of rights and passing of property, and (ii) transfer of 18–101

---

[48] *The Aramis* [1989] 1 Lloyd's Rep. 213; *Enichem Amic SpA v Ampelos Shipping Co. Ltd (The Delfini)* [1990] 1 Lloyd's Rep. 252; *Leigh & Sillavan Ltd v Aliakmon Shipping Co. Ltd (The Aliakmon)* [1986] A.C. 785.

[49] *The Aliakmon*, above.

[50] (1884) 10 App. Cas. 74; *The Future Express* [1993] 2 Lloyd's Rep. 542 (where the transactions in question occurred before the coming into force of the Carriage of Goods by Sea Act 1992).

[51] *Borealis AB v Stargas Ltd (The Berge Sisar)* [2001] UKHL 17, [2002] 2 A.C. 205 at [22], [27], [31].

[52] See *Brandt v Liverpool, etc. Steam Navigation Co.* [1924] 1 K.B. 575, where the bank's claim succeeded on the ground of an "implied contract" of the kind discussed in para.18–139, below.

rights and imposition of liabilities.[53] The 1992 Act, indeed, maintains some connection between the latter two consequences,[54] but it does not link them in the way in which this was done by the 1855 Act. Under the 1992 Act, the acquisition of contractual rights by virtue of its provisions is a *necessary* condition of the imposition of contractual liabilities,[55] but it is not a sufficient condition: at least one of a number of further circumstances[56] has to be established before the acquirer of rights is also subjected to liabilities. For a full discussion of the 1992 Act, reference should be made to works on bills of lading.[57] The account that follows is intended to deal only with those aspects of the Act which are of particular importance to buyers and sellers of goods carried under documents to which the 1992 Act applies.

The 1992 Act deals with the transfer of contractual rights and the imposition of contractual liabilities by the use of three types of documents: bills of lading, sea waybills and ship's delivery orders.[58] It implements a Report on this topic issued in 1991 by the English and Scottish Law Commissions.[59] Our concern in the immediately following discussion is with bills of lading; the other two types of documents will be discussed later in this Chapter.[60] Where the document with which the parties deal does *not* fall within any of the three types dealt with by the Act (*e.g.* where the document is a delivery order which does not fall within the statutory definition of a "ship's delivery order"[61]) the questions of transfer of contractual rights and imposition of contractual liabilities continue to be governed at common law by the general principle that such rights are not transferred, nor are such liabilities imposed, by transfer of the document.[62] Of course the common law principle would in such a case be subject to the qualifications discussed elsewhere in this Chapter: for example, the holder of the document might acquire contractual rights or be subjected to contractual liabilities where dealings with, or in reliance on, the document gave rise to an implied contract.[63] He could also acquire rights under the Contracts (Rights of Third Parties) Act 1999 where the requirements of section 1 of that Act were satisfied.[64] The case would not fall within what we have called "the subsection 6(5) exception"[65] to that Act since this exception applies only (in relation to carriage of goods by sea) where the document in question is a bill of lading, sea waybill or ship's delivery order within the Carriage of Goods by Sea Act 1992.[66] The 1999 Act, however,

---

[53] *The Berge Sisar*, above, n.51, at [27].
[54] See s.3 of the 1992 Act, below, paras 18–123, 18–125.
[55] Carriage of Goods by Sea Act 1992, s.3(1).
[56] *i.e.* those specified in s.3(1)(a)–(c), below, paras 18–126, 18–129, 18–131.
[57] *e.g. Carver on Bills of Lading* (2nd ed., 2005) especially Chs 5 and 8.
[58] 1992 Act, s.1(1).
[59] Rights of Suit in Respect of Carriage of Goods by Sea, Law Com. No. 196, Scot. Law Com. No. 130 (1991); for an authoritative account of the "genesis" of the 1992 Act, see *Borealis AB v Stargas Ltd (The Berge Sisar)* [2001] UKHL 17, [2002] 2 A.C. 205 at [18] *et seq*.
[60] Below, paras 18–153 *et seq*; 18–175 *et seq*.
[61] Carriage of Goods by Sea Act 1992, s.1(d), below, para.18–176.
[62] Above, para.18–098.
[63] Below, para.18–138.
[64] Above, para.18–005.
[65] *ibid*.
[66] Contracts (Rights of Third Parties) Act 1999, s.6(6) and (7).

while enabling a person to acquire *rights* under a contract to which he is not a party, does not subject him to *liabilities* under the contract, though he might be required to discharge a liability as a condition of the exercise of the right[67]: *e.g.* to discharge a carrier's lien if he wished to assert his right to delivery of the goods.

(vi) *Acquisition of Contractual Rights*[68]

Carriage of Goods by Sea Act 1992, section 2(1)(a). The main rule with regard to the transfer of contractual rights by the use of bills of lading is contained in section 2(1) of the 1992 Act by which "a person who becomes (a) the lawful holder of a bill of lading. . . . shall (by virtue of becoming the holder of the bill. . .) have transferred to and vested in him all rights of suit under the contract of carriage as if he had been a party to that contract." It is no longer necessary for the holder to show that the property in the underlying goods has passed to him upon or by reason of his having become the lawful holder, or at all; and the reasoning of many earlier cases is now obsolete to the extent that these cases hold that contractual rights had not been transferred because the property had not passed[69] to the transferee, or because it had passed too early or too late. 18–102

Meaning of "bill of lading". The 1992 Act does not define "bill of lading" but it does give two pieces of information about the meaning of this expression. First, section 1(2)(a) tells us that references in the Act to bills of lading "do not include references to a document which is incapable of transfer, either by indorsement or, as a bearer bill, by delivery without indorsement." The purpose of this provision appears to be to restrict the meaning of "bill of lading" to order bills and bearer bills.[70] Although section 1(2)(a) appears to contrast "indorsement" with "delivery", the Act elsewhere makes it clear that completion of an "indorsement" requires "delivery" of the bill.[71] It is also possible for an order bill to be indorsed in blank before being delivered to a first transferee. Subsequent transfers of the bill can then be effected by delivery alone, without the need for any further indorsement, except where, on the occasion of an intermediate transfer, a personal indorsement has been written on the bill.[72]. 18–103

Secondly, section 1(2)(b) provides that references to a bill of lading "include references to a received for shipment bill of lading". We have

---

[67] See Law Com. No. 242 (1996), paras 10.24 to 10.32.

[68] For further details, see *Carver on Bills of Lading* (2nd ed., 2005), paras 5–013 to 5–107.

[69] *e.g.* in *Brandt v Liverpool, etc., Steam Navigation Co. Ltd* [1924] 1 K.B. 575 (below, para.18–139) the claimants could now sue on the bill of lading contract under s.2(1)(a) of the 1992 Act and would not need to rely on the implied contract which they established in that case.

[70] Above, paras 18–014, 18–015. A "straight" bill or a sea waybill is thus not a "bill of lading" within the Act: see above, para.18–018.

[71] s.5(2)(b); *cf.* Bills of Exchange Act 1882, s.31(3).

[72] *Keppel Tatlee Bank v Bandung Shipping Private Ltd* [2003] 1 Lloyd's Rep. 619, above para.18–016.

seen[73] that the expression "received bill" is used in a number of senses. Of these, section 2(1)(a) would apply to a bill which stated that the goods had been received by the carrier for shipment on a named ship or on a ship capable of being identified when the bill was issued as the ship in which the carrier had contracted to carry them. But section 2(1)(a) would not apply to a document which merely stated that goods which were not in the carrier's possession were held to his order[74] or to a bill which stated that the goods had been received but did not identify the ship on which they were to be carried or which did identify that ship but gave the carrier the option of carrying the goods on another ship.[75]

18–104 **Lawful holder.** To acquire rights under section 2(1)(a), a person must have become the "lawful holder" of the bill. Section 5(2) provides that a person can be the "holder" of a bill in the following three situations[76]: if he has possession of it and (a) is the consignee identified in the bill; or (b) his possession is "the result of the completion, by delivery of the bill, of any indorsement of the bill, or, in the case of a bearer bill, of any other transfer of the bill"; or (c) he acquires possession of a bill after it has become "spent" in circumstances to be more fully discussed in paragraph 18–113 below, or after the goods covered by it have been destroyed, *e.g.* by the explosion and sinking of the ship on which they were being carried.[77] For the purpose of the second of these alternatives, "delivery" requires more than merely sending the bill to the transferee: there must also be an intention on the part of the transferor to deliver the bill to the recipient and an intention on the latter's part to accept delivery.[78] Where goods are shipped by A under a bill making them deliverable to the order of B, then the mere delivery of the bill will make B the lawful holder of the bill. But its redelivery to A will not of itself make A the lawful holder: for this purpose the bill must be indorsed, as well as redelivered, by B to A.[79] Delivery of a blank indorsed bill without further indorsement would fall within the

[73] Above, para.18–027.
[74] *i.e.* a document of the kind illustrated by the "January bills of lading" in *Ishag v Allied Bank International* [1981] 1 Lloyd's Rep. 92, above, para.18–079.
[75] *i.e.* a document of the type illustrated by the bill tendered in the *Diamond Alkali* case, [1921] 3 K.B. 443, above, para.18–038, where the same point is discussed in the context of s.4 of the 1992 Act; to the extent that that discussion is based on the fact that in s.4 the phrase "on board a vessel", qualifies both "shipped" and "received", it is inapplicable in the present context of s.2(1)(a).
[76] s.5(2).
[77] See *Primetrade AG v Ythan Ltd (The Ythan)* [2005] EWHC 2399 (Comm.), [2006] 1 All E.R. 367 at [71].
[78] *Aegean Sea Traders Corp. v Repsol Petroleo SA (The Aegean Sea)* [1998] 2 Lloyd's Rep. 39, where the actual issue was whether the alleged transferee had incurred *liabilities* under the bill. The case reflects the reluctance of the courts to impose liabilities on bill of lading transferees for conduct of shippers for which the transferees bear no responsibility: see below, para.18–123 and *Borealis AB v Stargas Ltd (The Berge Sisar)* [2001] UKHL 17, [2002] 1 A.C. 215, below paras 18–126, 18–131 adopting in that context a strict interpretation of the requirement of taking or demanding delivery *of the goods*.
[79] *East West Corp. v DKBS 1912* [2002] EWHC 83 (Comm.), [2002] 1 All E.R. (Comm.) 676 at [39]-[41]; on appeal, the claim based on redelivery of the bill was not pursued: [2003] EWCA Civ 83, [2003] Q.B. 1509 at [19].

second of the above alternatives: it would do so on the ground either that such delivery amounted to the completion of the original indorsement, or that, on being blank indorsed, the bill became a bearer bill.[80] According to *The Ythan*,[81] a person's acquisition of possession of the bill in any of the circumstances specified in section 5(2), though clearly under that subsection a necessary, is not a sufficient, condition of that person's becoming the "holder" of a bill. In that case, bills of lading covering goods which had been destroyed after shipment were transferred to an insurance agent[82] acting on behalf of a buyer to whom the risk had passed;[83] and the cargo underwriters agreed to settle the buyer's claim in respect of this loss "upon receipt of a full set of bills of lading". It was held that the buyer had not become the "holder" of the bills on their transfer to the buyer's insurance agent because that transfer "had nothing to do with the normal course of trading a bearer bill of lading"[84]: its purpose was "solely to enable [the buyer] to collect from the underwriter once the casualty had taken place and the insurance settlement had been made."[85] There is no direct support in the wording of the Act for this further requirement (of the transfer's being made "in the normal course of trading" bills of lading); nor is it clear exactly why that requirement was regarded as not having been satisfied.[86]

Where a bill names several persons as consignee in succession,[87] it seems that any of them can, if in possession of the bill, be its holder. It seems that contractual rights can be acquired by a person who is holder of the bill as agent for another. This was the position in *The Aliakmon*[88] where a bill of lading was in sent to a buyer who was named in it as consignee and who, being unable to pay for the goods in accordance with the contract of sale, agreed to take delivery of them on behalf of the seller. It has been said that such a case would now be covered by the 1992 Act[89]; and this seems to mean that the buyer could now sue the carrier in contract as holder of this bill. It is submitted that this view does not exclude the possibility of such

---

80 *Primetrade AG v Ythan Ltd (The Ythan)* [2005] EWHC 2399 (Comm.), [2006] 1 All E.R. 367 at [19], [80].

81 Above, n.80.

82 Transfer of possession to the agent seems to have been regarded as transfer to the principal (the buyer): *cf.* below at n.90.

83 See *The Ythan*, above n.80 at [19].

84 *ibid.* at [80].

85 *ibid.*

86 The underwriters may have wanted the transfer to enable them to make a claim against the carrier. If so, it is hard to see why the transmission of the bills of lading to them via the buyer or his agent was not "normal". The reluctance of the court to hold that the buyer was the "holder" of the bill may, at least in part, be explicable on the ground that the actual issue was not whether the buyer was entitled to enforce the contract of carriage (to which he was not an original party) but whether he was liable for loss of the ship caused by allegedly dangerous cargo shipped, not by him, but by his supplier: *cf.* below, para.18–123.

87 As in *K/S A/S Seateam Co. v Iraq National Oil Co. (The Sevonia Team)* [1983] 2 Lloyd's Rep. 641.

88 *Leigh and Sillavan Ltd v Aliakmon Shipping Co. Ltd (The Aliakmon)* [1986] A.C. 785.

89 *White v Jones* [1995] 2 A.C. 207 at p.265.

rights being also acquired by the principal,[90] so long as the bill does not name the agent as consignee or bear a *personal* indorsement to him.[91]

18–105 **Good faith.** A person who has become the "holder" of a bill of lading can acquire rights by virtue of section 2(1)(a) only if he has become the "lawful" holder and the latter requirement is satisfied "wherever he has become the holder of the bill in good faith."[92] The concept of good faith, which is not defined in the Act,[93] is that of "honest conduct".[94] This would, for example, be negatived when the holder had acquired possession of the bill by fraud or by theft or from a previous holder who, to his knowledge, had so acquired it. It is also arguable that a buyer would not have acted in good faith where he had acquired possession of the bill from the seller without complying with the conditions (typically as to payment) which, under the contract of sale, entitled him to such possession.[95] A number of further problems relating to good faith remain as yet unresolved. These include[96] the question whether the requirement can be satisfied if, to the holder's knowledge, the transfer amounts to a civil wrong committed by the transferor on a third party; or if, again to the holder's knowledge, the bill does not contain the true terms of the contract of carriage or contains representations about the goods which are untrue.

18–106 **What is transferred.** Section 2(1) of the 1992 Act provides that the lawful holder of a bill of lading "shall . . . have transferred to and vested in him all rights of suit under the contract of carriage as if he had been a party to that contract." The rights of the holder will therefore in general be the same as those of the shipper.[97] But section 5(1) of the Act defines "the contract of carriage" to mean "the contract contained in or evidenced by" the bill; and it follows from these words that the rights of the holder may in some respects differ from those of the transferor.[98]

One possibility is that the bill may not accurately state the terms of the contract of carriage. For example, where that contract permits deviation but this fact is not stated in the bill and the transferee is unaware of it, then the carrier will not be entitled to rely on the liberty to deviate against the transferee.[99] Conversely, where the bill contains such a liberty on its face,

---

90 This is assumed in *The Ythan*, above n.80, where the actual decision was that the principal was *not* the "holder".
91 See s.5(2)(b); *East West Corp. v DKBS 1912 AF A/S* [2003] EWCA Civ 83, [2003] Q.B. 1509 at [16]–[17].
92 s.5(2).
93 Contrast Bills of Exchange Act 1882, s.90; Sale of Goods Act 1979, s.61(3).
94 *Aegean Sea Traders Corp. v Repsol Petroleo SA (The Aegean Sea)* [1998] 2 Lloyd's Rep. 39 at p.60.
95 This may be the reason why the claimant was found not to have become the lawful holder of the bill in the Australian case of *Ahmad v Mitsui OK Lines Ltd (ARBN 008 311 831)* [2005] F.C.A. 731; the judgment at [68] is not explicit as to the court's reason for its conclusion.
96 See *Carver on Bills of Lading* (2nd ed., 2005), paras 5–024, 5–025.
97 See *Jindal Iron & Steel Co. Ltd. v Islamic Solidarity Shipping Co. Jordan Inc. (The Jordan II)* [2003] EWCA Civ 144, [2003] 1 All E.R. (Comm.) 747 at [44], affirmed without reference to this point [2004] UKHL 49, [2005] 1 W.L.R. 363.
98 See Carver, *op. cit*., paras 5–027 to 5–039.
99 Example based on *Leduc v Ward* (1888) 20 Q.B.D. 475.

the transferee will not be able to rely on an agreement not to exercise it made between shipper and carrier.[1] If, however, the bill were eventually transferred back to the shipper in performance of a "circle" contract, it is submitted that the relationship between that shipper and the carrier would be governed by the terms of the contract of carriage as actually agreed between these parties.[2]

Other factors affecting shipper's rights. Under the rules discussed in paragraph 18–106 above, the transferee of a bill of lading may in some cases acquire greater contractual rights than are vested in the shipper. This position may be contrasted with the general rule that the transferor cannot transfer greater *proprietary* rights than he himself has.[3] It also gives rise to the question whether there are any situations, other than that discussed in paragraph 18–106, in which the transferee's contractual rights are greater than those of the original shipper. 18–107

One possibility is that no contract was concluded, *e.g.* for want of correspondence of offer and acceptance. In such a case there would be no "contract of carriage"[4] on which section 2(1) could operate. The same would be true if no contract had come into existence because of mistake or lack of capacity; and if the contract had been induced by the shipper's fraud, the wording of section 2(1)[5] would appear to allow the carrier to rely on that fraud as against the transferee. Where no contract has come into existence because no goods were shipped,[6] the transferee may have a remedy under section 4 of the Act even though no rights are transferred to him by virtue of section 2(1). The question whether cross-claims which the carrier may have against the shipper can be set up against the transferee gives rise to many difficulties; these await judicial determination.[7]

Estoppel available to transferee. Where a bill of lading contains a false statement as to the order and condition of the goods, that statement can at common law give rise to an estoppel in favour of the transferee against the carrier[8]; and it can have this effect even though no such estoppel is available to the shipper: *e.g.* because he knew of the falsity of the statement when the bill was issued or was himself responsible for the defects in or damage to the goods which the statement concealed.[9] There is nothing in 18–108

---

[1] Example based on *SS Ardennes (Owners of Cargo) v SS Ardennes* [1951] K.B. 55, where the actual decision was that the carrier was liable in respect of the deviation to *the shipper*.
[2] The fiction in s.2(1)(a) ("as if he had been a party") is inappropriate in the case of a person who actually is a party to the contract of carriage.
[3] Above, paras 18–084, 18–085.
[4] As defined by s.5(1).
[5] "As he had been a party to that contract."
[6] See *Heskell v Continental Express Ltd* [1950] 1 All E.R. 1033, above, para.18–030.
[7] For some suggested answers, see *Carver, op. cit.*, paras 5–031, 5–032.
[8] Above, para.18–028.
[9] As in *Brandt v Liverpool, etc. Steam Navigation Co. Ltd* [1924] 1 K.B. 575, where the transferee successfully relied on an implied contract of the kind described in para.18–139, below and was able to invoke the estoppel. On the facts of the case the transferee would now have a claim under s.2(1) of the 1992 Act.

section 2(1) to exclude such an estoppel so that the transferee can still rely on it at common law.

18–109 **Waiver of shipper's right to rescind for breach.** In discussing the effects of deviation, we have seen[10] that waiver of the deviation by the shipper does not as a matter of common law prejudicially affect the transferee of the bill: *i.e.* where the shipper has (while the transferee has not) elected to affirm the contract, rather than to rescind it on account of the breach. There is nothing in section 2(1) of the 1992 Act to alter this common law rule, which appears also to extend to waiver by the shipper of other breaches (than deviation) by the carrier.

18–110 **Bill of lading transferred by charterer.** We saw in paragraph 18–051 above that, where a bill of lading was issued to a shipper who was also the charterer of the carrying ship, the bill of lading was, between shipper and carrier, normally a mere receipt; it neither contained nor evidenced the contract of carriage between them, this being contained in the charterparty. Nevertheless, it was accepted before 1992 that the transfer of the bill to an indorsee[11] or to the consignee[12] gave rise to a contractual relationship between carrier and transferee of the terms of the bill of lading. There is nothing in the legislative history of the 1992 Act to indicate any intention to change this position[13] which was, and is, not easy to explain precisely because in the case put *no* contract of carriage is "contained in or evidenced by"[14] the bill of lading. The explanation usually given before the 1992 Act was that a new contract "sprang up"[15] when the bill was transferred. Exactly why or how such a contract should "spring up" at the time of the transfer between parties who were not at this stage in contact with each other is not altogether clear; perhaps the best explanation (if it can be regarded as one) is that such a contract was a legal device, invented to avoid what would otherwise be a commercially inconvenient result. At any rate, the argument that a new contract springs up is no weaker now (under the 1992 Act) than it was before that Act. The further question arises whether that contract is to be regarded as arising by virtue of the Act or at common law. The practical importance of this point is that the 1992

---

[10] Above, paras 18–059, 18–060.

[11] *Leduc v Ward* (1888) 20 Q.B.D. 475 at p.479; *The Al Battani* [1993] 2 Lloyd's Rep. 219 at p.222; *Trade Star Line Corp. v Mitsui & Co. Ltd (The Arctic Trader)*]1996] 2 Lloyd's Rep. 449 at p.455. Since on transfer by the charterer the bill acquires the status of a contractual document, it becomes at this stage capable of being a good tender under a c.i.f. contract: below, para.19–037 at n.84.

[12] *Compania Commercial Naviera San Martin SA v China National Foreign Trade Transportation Corp. (The Costanza M)* [1981] 2 Lloyd's Rep. 148 at p.150; *Skips A/S Nordheim v Syrian Petroleum Co. Ltd (The Varenna)* [1984] Q.B. 599, (where the action was brought both against the original shipper and against the consignee, and Donaldson M.R. therefore referred at p.615 to the contract "contained in, or evidenced by the bill of lading." The shipper took no part in the proceedings).

[13] See Law Com. No. 196, Scot. Law Com. No. 130, paras 2.54 (1991).

[14] Carriage of Goods by Sea Act 1992, s.2(1).

[15] See *Hain SS Co. v Tate & Lyle Ltd* (1936) 41 Com. Cas. 350 at p.356; *Rudolph A. Oetker v IFA Internationale Frachtagentur AG (The Almak)* [1985] 1 Lloyd's Rep. 557 at p.560.

Act links certain further consequences (other than the mere transfer of rights) to the transfer's having taken place *by virtue of section 2(1)*, so that such consequences would not follow if rights were acquired by the transferee by virtue of a common law principle operating outside the Act. Some such consequences do appear to be intended to apply to the present situation: *e.g.* the rules relating to "spent" bills[16] and the rules relating to the imposition of liabilities on the transferee.[17] For these purposes, it would certainly be convenient to regard the holder as having acquired his rights by virtue of section 2(1) rather than under a new contract arising at common law.

Bill of lading transferred to charterer. In paragraph 18–053 we considered the situation in which A's ship was chartered by B, goods were shipped in her by C under a bill of lading containing or evidencing a contract between A and C, and that bill of lading was later transferred by C to B. The position before the 1992 Act was that, if B had chartered the ship for the very purpose of taking delivery of the goods from C (*e.g.* under an f.o.b. contract), then the contractual relations between B and A continued to be governed by the charterparty, the bill of lading operating in such a case as a mere receipt.[18] If, on the other hand, there was no connection between the charterparty and the transaction in pursuance of which the bill was transferred to B, then the contractual relations between B and A were (in respect of the shipment in question) governed by the bill of lading.[19] The distinction between the two situations was that in the first it was inferred that A and B intended their relations to be governed by the charterparty but that in the second no such inference could be drawn as the subsequent transaction was not in their contemplation when they entered into the charterparty. The 1992 Act is not intended to alter the position established by these cases.[20] Thus even though a charterer to whom a bill of lading is indorsed may fall literally within the words of section 2(1), it remains open to the courts to hold that carrier and charterer intended their relations to be governed by the charterparty rather than by the bill of lading. Whether such an inference is to be drawn will continue to be governed by the factors which were relevant to such an issue before the 1992 Act. 18–111

Contracts (Rights of Third Parties) Act 1999. The impact of this Act on the situations discussed in paragraphs 18–110 and 18–111 above has been considered earlier in this Chapter.[21] 18–112

Spent bill of lading. Before 1992, contractual rights were not transferred to a person who satisfied the requirements (then in force[22]) for the transfer 18–113

[16] Carriage of Goods by Sea Act 1992, s.2(2); *cf.* also s.2(4).
[17] *ibid.*, s.3.
[18] *President of India v Metcalfe Shipping Co. Ltd (The Dunelmia)* [1970] 1 Q.B. 289.
[19] *Calcutta SS Co. Ltd v Andrew Weir & Co.* [1910] 1 K.B. 759.
[20] See Law Com. No. 196, Scot. Law Com. No. 130 para.2.53 (1991).
[21] Above, paras 18–055 and 18–056.
[22] Bills of Lading Act 1855; above, para.18–100.

of such rights only after the bill was "spent"[23] or "accomplished", usually[24] by delivery of the goods by the carrier to a person entitled to such delivery under the bill.[25] Under this rule, the ultimate buyer in a "string" of contracts might, because of inevitable delays in transmission of the bill, fail to acquire any contractual rights against the carrier. On the other hand, if a buyer could, after transfer of the bill and delivery of the goods to him, by making a further transfer of the bill, vest contractual rights under it in the transferee, then the rule under which champertous agreements are illegal might be evaded. The 1992 Act therefore modifies,[26] but does not abolish, the former rule that contractual rights could not be transferred by the use of a "spent" bill.

Section 2(2) of the 1992 Act deals with the situation in which "when a person becomes the lawful holder of the bill of lading, possession of the bill no longer gives a right (as against the carrier) to possession of the goods to which the bill relates."[27] The subsection provides that, in such a case, that person "shall not have any rights transferred to him by virtue of [section 2(1)] unless he becomes the holder of the bill" in one of two circumstances specified in section 2(2). The effect of this double negative is that, as a general rule, the holder of a spent bill acquires no contractual rights by virtue of section 2(1) against the carrier[28] but that he does acquire such rights in the two exceptional cases. Section 2(2) operates as a qualified exception to section 2(1), so that, where one of the exceptions applies,[29] rights are acquired by virtue of the latter subsection.

---

[23] *Leigh & Sillavan Ltd v Aliakmon Shipping Co. Ltd (The Aliakmon)* [1986] A.C. 785; *Compania Portorafti Commerciale SA v Ultramar Panama Inc. (The Captain Gregos) (No. 2)* [1990] 2 Lloyd's Rep. 395.

[24] For other ways in which a bill of lading may become "spent", see above, para.18–082, and below, n.28.

[25] See *Barber v Meyerstein* (1870) L.R. 4 H.L. 317 at p.330; *Enichem Anic SpA v Ampelos Shipping Co. Ltd (The Delfini)* [1990] 1 Lloyd's Rep. 252 at p.269; above, 18–080.

[26] Law Com. No. 196, Scot. Law Com. 130, paras 2.44 (1991).

[27] For the part of the definition of "holder" to include this situation, see s.5(2)(c). This part of the definition applies, not only where the bill has become "spent" for the reason given at n.25 above, but also where the goods are "lost for ever" when the ship on which they are being carried explodes and sinks, as in *Primetrade AG v Ythan Ltd (The Ythan)* [2005] EWHC 2399 (Comm.), [2006] 1 All E.R. 367 (at [71]). The holder of the bill may then have a right to *damages* against the carrier, but there cannot be a right to the *possession* of goods which no longer exist: *ibid.*, at [68], [70].

[28] *e.g. The David Agmashenebeli* [2002] EWHC 104 (Comm.), [2002] 2 All E.R. (Comm.) 806, where the bills in question became spent, not by delivery of the goods to the person entitled to such delivery, but when, in pursuance of an agreement between the original parties to the contract of carriage "the bills were presented to the shipowners' representatives, were indorsed 'Accomplished' and the shipowners agreed to instruct the master to deliver in accordance with the instructions of (the shippers') representative" (at [204]).

[29] Section 2(2) has been held not to apply where the bill of lading was sent back without indorsement by the consignee to the shipper after the goods had been delivered by the carrier to a person *not* entitled to them since in such a case the bill is not spent (see above, para.18–080): *East West Corp. v DKBS 1912* [2002] 1 All E.R. (Comm.) 676 at [39]–[42]. On appeal, the claim based on delivery of the bill was not pursued. [2003] EWCA Civ 83, [2003] Q.B. 1509 at [10].

The first of the exceptions, stated in section 2(2)(a), arises where a person becomes holder of the bill "by virtue of a transaction effected in pursuance of any contractual or other arrangements made before the time when such a right to possession [*i.e.* of the goods] ceased to attach to possession of the bill." The word "transaction" here seems to refer to the process of transferring the bill,[30] while the words "contractual or other arrangements" refer to the reason or cause for the transfer.[31] The "transaction" takes place (*ex hypothesi*) *after* the bill has become spent; the "contractual or other arrangements" must take place *before* that time.[32] The typical situation covered by this exception is that in which goods are sold afloat to a buyer in a "string" of contracts but he does not get possession of the bill until after the goods have been delivered to him. Where a contract of sale is made before but varied after the bill became spent, the outcome depends on the extent of the variation. If the varied contract differs in such "important respects" from the original one as to amount to a "new contract",[33] then that new contract will become the "contractual arrangement" for the purpose of section 2(2)(a) and no rights under the contract of carriage will be acquitted by the buyer by virtue of the transfer to him of the spent bill.[34]

The second exception, stated in section 2(2)(b), arises where a person becomes holder of the bill "as a result of the rejection to that person by another person of goods or documents delivered to the other person in pursuance of any such arrangements." This exception would typically apply where goods were sold by a shipper, the goods were delivered to the buyer without surrender of the bill (*e.g.* against a letter of indemnity), the bill of lading was transferred to the buyer, and he then rejected the goods and the documents, normally for breach of condition. In spite of the words "rejection. . . . of goods or documents", the present exception would not apply where only the goods (but not the documents) were rejected to the seller, for in that case the seller could not be the "holder" of the bill.[35] The exception could, however, apply where it was only the documents but not the goods which were rejected (*e.g.* because the defect in the goods had caused such serious deterioration that they had ceased to exist as a commercial entity.[36])

---

[30] *Primetrade AG v Ythan Ltd (The Ythan)* [2005] EWHC 2399 (Comm.), [2006] 1 All E.R. 367 at [66].
[31] *ibid.* at [84].
[32] See *Borealis AB v Stargas Ltd (The Berge Sisar)* [2001] UKHL 17, [2002] 2 A.C. 205 at [31], where the actual decision was that, for reasons discussed in para.18–131 below, the transferee was not *liable* on the bill. *Cf. Primetrade AG v Ythan Ltd (The Ythan)* [2005] EWHC 2399 (Comm.), [2006] 1 All E.R. 367 at [68]. The actual decision was that the alleged transferee had not acquired rights of suit under the bill as he had not become the "holder" of it (see above, para.18–104); and that therefore, for the reason given in para.18–121 below, he had not incurred any liability under it.
[33] *The David Agmashenebeli* [2002] EWHC 104 (Comm.), [2002] 2 All E.R. (Comm.) 806 at [206].
[34] *ibid.* at [207]; it is not clear from the report whether the bill was ever transferred to the buyer.
[35] See s.5(2) of the 1992 Act.
[36] Example based on *Mash & Murrell Ltd v Joseph I Emanuel Ltd* [1962] 1 W.L.R. 16.

18–114 **Rights of original shipper.** At common law, transfer of a bill of lading did not operate as a transfer of contractual rights, so that the original shipper retained these rights under the bill. He could therefore sue the carrier for breach of that contract; and under what has become (rightly or wrongly) known as the rule in *Dunlop v Lambert*[37] he could do so though the loss caused by the carrier's breach was suffered, not by him, but by the transferee.[38] This would typically be the position where the relationship of shipper and transferee was that of seller and buyer of the goods covered by the bill and risk had passed under the contract of sale between them to the buyer. The shipper could then sue the carrier for breach of the contract of carriage and recover damages in respect of the transferee's loss,[39] by way of exception to the general common law rule that a claimant could recover damages only in respect of his own loss.[40] The practical justification for this exception was that the transferee of the bill (*i.e.* the buyer of the goods) would be unlikely to have acquired any contractual rights[41] against the carrier, so that, if a substantial remedy were denied to the shipper, there would be no effective remedy against the carrier even in respect of a plain and uncontested breach. The exception has been rationalised on the ground that, since the carrier must have contemplated that property in the goods might be transferred to third parties after the making of the contract of carriage, the shipper must be treated in law as having made the contract of carriage for the benefit of all persons who might after the making of that contract acquire an interest in the goods.[42] This rationalisation has been extended beyond contracts for the carriage of goods by sea: *e.g.* to a case

---

[37] (1839) 9 Cl. & F. 600 at pp.626–627. For a full discussion of this case, see the speech of Lord Clyde in *Alfred McAlpine Construction Ltd v Panatown Ltd* [2001] 1 A.C. 518 at p.523 *et seq*., doubting whether the so-called "rule in *Dunlop v Lambert*" is actually supported by the decision in that case, but recognising that the existence of the rule is supported by other authorities, in particular by *Albacruz (Cargo Owners) v Albazero (Owners) (The Albazero)* [1977] A.C. 774; for antecedents of the rule, see *Joseph v Knox* (1813) 3 Camp. 320. It will be convenient in the present discussion to continue to refer to the rule by its traditional name.

[38] The rule has been said to apply only if at the time of the contract it was "in the actual contemplation of the parties that an identified third party or a third party who was a member of an identified class might suffer damage in the event of a breach of contract": *Rolls Royce Power Engineering Plc v Ricardo Consulting Engineers Ltd* [2003] EWHC 2871 (T.C.C.), [2004] 2 All E.R. (Comm.) 129 at [124]. When (as in the situation described in the text above) the third party was the transferee of a bill of lading, this requirement would normally be satisfied.

[39] For the destination of these damages, see below at n.52.

[40] See *The Albazero*, above, n.37, at p.846; *Woodar Investment Development Ltd v Wimpey Construction Co. Ltd* [1980] 1 W.L.R. 277. For the purpose of this rule, a party's "own loss" includes expenses paid by his agent which he is liable, as principal, to reimburse to the agent: *Eridiana SpA v Rudolf A Oetker (The Fjord Wind)* [1999] 1 Lloyd's Rep. 307, affirmed without reference to this point [2000] 2 Lloyd's Rep. 192. The events giving rise to this litigation occurred before the coming into force of Carriage of Goods by Sea Act 1992 so that no question arose under s.2(4) of this Act (below, para.18–119).

[41] He would now have a right of action in tort if he could prove damage to the goods caused by the carrier's negligence at a time when property had passed to him: *Karlshamns Oljefabriker v Export Navigation Corp. (The Elafi)* [1981] 2 Lloyd's Rep. 679; and see below, paras 18–148 to 18–150.

[42] *The Albazero*, above, n.37 at p.847.

where A contracted with B to do building work on B's land in circumstances in which A could foresee that the land would be transferred to C and that C would not acquire rights under the building contract because that contract prohibited assignment of B's rights under it without the consent of A.[43] It was held that B could recover substantial damages in respect of loss suffered by C as a result of A's breach of contract. Yet a further extension of the rule in *Dunlop v Lambert* was made in a case[44] in which A contracted with B to do building work on land already belonging to C and in which it was held that A's breach gave B a right to substantial damages[45] in respect of loss suffered by C, even though no *transfer* of the property to C was made or contemplated. It remains to be seen whether this extension of the rule will be applied to contracts for the carriage of goods by sea: *i.e.* whether the rule in *Dunlop v Lambert* will be applied where the goods already belonged to the third party when they were shipped. Even if the rule were not applied in cases of this kind, the third party may on such facts have a direct claim against the carrier on the ground that the shipper acted as his agent in making the contract of carriage.[46] But it is settled that the rule does not apply where the third party has acquired his own contractual rights against the carrier by virtue of the transfer of the bill of lading to the third party[47]; and in the building contract cases the promisee's claim for damages in respect of the third party's loss has similarly been rejected where the latter has his own contractual right against the building contractor in respect of the breach under a separate contract between these parties.[48] In such cases, the rule in *Dunlop v Lambert* does not apply "because it was not needed"[49]; this restriction on the scope of the rule will be more fully discussed in paragraph 18–116 below. In cases which do fall within the rationale of the rule in *Dunlop v Lambert*, that rule can still apply where for some reason contractual rights have *not* been transferred (now by virtue of section 2(1) of the 1992 Act) to the person who has suffered the loss: *e.g.* where goods were shipped under

---

[43] *Linden Gardens Trust v Lenesta Sludge Disposals Ltd* [1994] A.C. 85.

[44] *Darlington v Wiltshier Northern Ltd* [1995] 1 W.L.R. 68; this extension appears to have been approved by Lords Clyde and Jauncey, two members of the majority in *Alfred McAlpine Construction Ltd v Panatown Ltd* [2001] 1 A.C. 518; neither of them regarded the actual or prospective transfer of the subject-matter of the building contract from the promisee to the third party as an essential requirement of the promisee's right to recover substantial damages in respect of the third party's loss (under the present exception to the general rule that the victim of a breach of contract can recover damages only in respect of his own loss): see *ibid.* pp.531, 566. For further discussion of these building contract cases, see *Chitty on Contracts* 29th ed. (2004) paras 18–051 to 18–059.

[45] The right had been assigned by B to C who, as assignee, could not recover more than B could have done; hence, although the action was brought by C, it was necessary to decide how much B could have recovered.

[46] Above, para.18–097 at n.33; contrast above para.18–065 after n.9.

[47] *The Albazero*, above, n.37.

[48] *Alfred McAlpine Construction Ltd v Panatown Ltd* [2001] 1 A.C. 518.

[49] *ibid.*, at p.575; *The Albazero,* above n.37, at pp.847–848.

a bill of lading which was never delivered to the buyer[50] or which was delivered to him without a requisite indorsement. In such a case, the shipper could therefore recover damages in respect of the buyer's loss.[51] The damages recovered by the shipper in such a case must be held by him for the transferee, *i.e.* for the buyer who has suffered the loss.[52]

The common law rule that contractual rights could not be transferred by transfer of a bill of lading was first altered by section 1 of the Bills of Lading Act 1855, and the word "transferred" in that section was interpreted to mean that, once these rights became vested in the consignee or indorsee, they were no longer available to the original shipper.[53] The Carriage of Goods by Sea Act 1992 in section 2(1) likewise provides that rights of suit under the contract of carriage are "transferred" to the lawful holder, but it does not rely on this word alone to produce the consequence that the shipper loses his rights under that contract as a result of the transfer. The Act expressly provides in section 2(5) that, where rights are transferred by virtue of section 2(1), that transfer "shall extinguish any entitlement to those rights which derives (a) where that document is a bill of lading, from a person's having been an original party to the contract of carriage."[54] The common law rule under which the shipper retained his rights of action under the bill of lading contract accordingly no longer applies where those rights have been transferred by virtue of section 2(1). The common law rule is thus restricted to cases in which *no* rights are transferred to the third party: *e.g.* where the bill is never transferred, or where it lacks a requisite indorsement, or where it is simply lost in transmission so that the prospective transferee never acquires possession of it.[55] It is also theoretically possible for a shipper to lose his rights (even where rights are not transferred by virtue of section 2(1)) if he makes an equitable or statutory assignment of his rights under the contract of carriage[56]; but this machinery is only rarely used for the purpose of transferring the shipper's rights under such a contract.

---

[50] As in *Sanix Ace*, below, n.52 where there was only one bill of lading but there were 11 buyers, each of whom received only a *copy* (as opposed to one of a number of original parts of a bill issued in a set: see above, para.18–090). The example in the text assumes that no other document capable of transferring rights under s.2(1) (such as a ship's delivery order) has come into existence.

[51] Such a case would not fall within s.2(4) of the 1992 Act (below, para.18–119) since this subsection only enables a transferee of rights under the contract of carriage to recover damages in respect of a third party's loss: it does not enable the original shipper to do this.

[52] *The Albazero* [1977] A.C. 774 at p.845; *Obestain Inc. v National Mineral Development Corp. (The Sanix Ace)* [1987] 1 Lloyd's Rep. 465 (claim under charterparty); *O'Sullivan v Williams* [1992] 3 All E.R. 385 at p.387, discussing *The Winkfield* [1902] P. 42.

[53] *Sewell v Burdick* (1884) 10 App. Cas. 74 at p.84: *Mitsui & Co. Ltd v Flota Mercante Grancolombiana SA (The Ciudad de Pasto and the Ciudad de Neiva)* [1988] 1 W.L.R. 1145 at p.1148; *cf. Short v Simpson* (1866) L.R. 1 C.P. 248.

[54] In *Borealis AB v Stargas Ltd (The Berge Sisar)* [1999] Q.B. 863 at p.883 (affirmed without reference to this point [2001] UKHL 17, [2002] 2 A.C. 205) Millett L.J. doubted whether this provision was "strictly necessary" since the extinction of the transferor's right was "the inevitable consequence of the mechanism of transfer."

[55] See *The Albazero* [1977] A.C. 774, overruling *Gardano & Giamperi v Greek Petroleum George Mamidakis & Co.* [1962] 1 W.L.R. 40, so far as *contra*.

[56] See below, para.18–147.

The foregoing discussion of the original shipper's contractual rights against the carrier is based on the assumption that the only contract between these parties is the contract contained in or evidenced by the bill of lading. This is "the contract of carriage" to which alone (by virtue of the statutory definition of that phrase[57]) subsections 2(1) and 2(5) apply. There may also be some *other* contract between shipper and carrier and rights under any such other contract are neither transferred by virtue of section 2(1) nor extinguished by section 2(5). One possibility is that the shipment may be made under some antecedent arrangement between carrier and shipper, *e.g.* under a reservation of shipping space having contractual effect.[58] The subsequent issue of a bill of lading in respect of a shipment made in pursuance of such an arrangement is likely to be regarded as a novation, superseding the original contractual arrangement and so (at common law) as extinguishing the rights and liabilities of both parties under that arrangement. A second possibility is that the shipper may charter a ship and that a bill of lading may be issued to him by the shipowner and be later transferred by him, *e.g.* to a buyer, to whom contractual rights are transferred by virtue of section 2(1)(a) of the 1992 Act on his having become the lawful holder of the bill.[59] But between shipper and shipowner the bill of lading operates as a mere receipt and does not contain or evidence a contract of carriage. The only contract between these parties is that contained in the charterparty,[60] and since this contract does not fall within the definition of "contract of carriage" in the 1992 Act,[61] rights under it are neither transferred by virtue of section 2(1) nor extinguished under section 2(5). The status of such rights therefore continues to be governed at common law by the principles which are discussed in paragraph 18–116 below. These apply, not only where the bill of lading is issued directly to the charterer, but also where it is originally issued to another person who has shipped the goods and is then transferred to the charterer in circumstances in which it is, between charterer and carrier, a mere receipt.[62]

Original shipper's rights independent of contract. The shipper may, 18–115
after transfer of the bill and consequent loss of his rights under the contract of carriage,[63] be able to found his claim on some basis other than that contract. This possibility is illustrated by the *East West* case,[64] where sellers of goods which had been sold on c.o.d. terms shipped them under bills of lading making them deliverable to the order of the sellers' banks. The bills were indorsed by the sellers,[65] and sent to the banks simply to enable the banks to collect the price; the banks acquired no security interest in the

[57] Carriage of Goods by Sea Act 1992, s.5(1), above, para.18–106.
[58] See above, paras 18–030, 18–047.
[59] Above, para.18–110.
[60] Above, para.18–051.
[61] See s.5(1).
[62] *e.g. President of India v Metcalfe Shipping Co. Ltd (The Dunelmia)* [1970] 1 Q.B. 289, above, para.18–053.
[63] Carriage of Goods by Sea Act 1992, ss.2(1)(a) and 2(5).
[64] *East West Corp. v DKBS 1912 AF A/S* [2003] EWCA Civ 83, [2003] Q.B. 1509.
[65] Unnecessarily, it seems: see para.18–016, above.

goods, property in which remained at all relevant times in the sellers.[66] The goods were delivered on behalf of the carriers to the buyers without production of the bills of lading and so, as a practical matter,[67] lost to the sellers. The delivery no doubt amounted to a breach of the contract of carriage, but the sellers had lost their rights under the contract when these rights were transferred to their banks on the transfer to those banks of the bills of lading.[68] The sellers' claim for damages against the carriers for the loss which the sellers had suffered by reason of the misdelivery was allowed by the Court of Appeal as one which arose "in bailment" and therefore "[did] not depend on contract".[69] Under the original contract of carriage, the bailment was from the sellers to the carriers[70] and the relationship of bailor and bailee between these parties had not been brought to an end by the transfer of the rights of suit under the bill of lading contracts. The 1992 Act did not affect "rights in bailment" where there was "no intention to pass any possessory rights"[71]; and even if the banks had acquired possessory rights in the goods (as they might have done by virtue of the transfer to them bills of lading which were documents of title at common law[72]), such "rights in bailment"[73] would not have vested *exclusively* in them since they "were never more than agents at will of the [sellers]"[74] who therefore retained their rights in bailment by virtue of having of having the immediate right to possession of the goods. This reasoning is based on the special facts of the *East West* case in which the sole function of the banks to whom the bills were transferred was to act as the sellers' agents for the purpose of collecting the price.[75] It would not extend to the situation in which the bills had been transferred to a bank by way of security since in such a case the sellers would not have had an immediate right to possession so long as the debt secured by the transfer remained unpaid. Nor would it have applied if the bill had been transferred to buyers to whom credit had been given by the sellers since in such a case transfer of the bill would in all probability have had the effect of passing property and depriving the sellers of their lien. In such cases, the carriers might nevertheless have been liable to the sellers for the misdelivery on one of two other grounds.

The first such ground would be that the misdelivery had caused the "loss of. . .[the sellers'] reversionary interests in the goods";, and such a claim would (apart from not depending on an immediate right to possession) be

---

[66] *East West case,* above n.64, at [3]
[67] *ibid.* at [62] stating that it was "wholly impractical for the [sellers] to recover these goods . . . from "the buyers". It is not clear why the sellers could not have recovered the price or damages for wrongful failure to pay it from the buyers, who are not stated in the report to have been insolvent.
[68] Carriage of Goods by Sea Act 1992, s.2(1)(a) and (5).
[69] *East West* case, above n.64, at [24]; *cf.* at [30] ("non-contractual liability of a bailee").
[70] *ibid.*, at [35]; *cf.* above para.18–065.
[71] *East West* case, above n.64, at [45].
[72] See above paras 18–007, 18–062; the point is not explicitly discussed in the *East West* case above n.64.
[73] *East West* case, above n.64 at [37].
[74] *ibid.*, at [49(b)].
[75] *ibid.*, at [3], [35]

"determined by the same principles as govern a claim in bailment."[76] In particular, the "doctrine of bailment on terms"[77] would limit such claims, so that shippers could not, by formulating their claim in this way, escape from exclusions or limitations of liability to which they had agreed under the contract of carriage.

The second possible ground of liability would be that the carriers were in breach of "an ordinary duty of care"[78] or (in other words) of a "purely tortious duty",[79] not arising from bailment or interference with a reversionary proprietary interest. It was on this second ground that the carriers had been held liable at first instance,[80] and on appeal it was unnecessary to express a concluded view on the point as the carriers had been held liable on the bailment (or analogous) reasoning discussed above. But Mance L.J. saw "a formidable impediment to the recognition of any purely tortious duty" independent of "duties in or paralleling those owed in bailment."[81] This impediment was that "purely tortious" duties were not subject to the doctrine of bailment on terms and so their imposition might deprive the carrier of the contractual protection of bill of lading exclusions and limitations. This objection has prevailed where tort claims were made against carriers, in respect of damage to the goods, caused by breach of the contract of carriage, by persons who were never parties to that contract[82]; and the sellers' claim in the *East West* case may be regarded as analogous to such a third party claim in that, after the transfer of the bills of lading, the sellers no longer had any rights under the contract of carriage.[83] Their claim, indeed, differed from third party claims of the kind described above in that, as original parties to the bills, they had (or must be taken to have) agreed to the terms of the bills, while third parties cannot be assumed to have done so. But this difference strengthens, rather than weakens, the case for rejecting a claim a tort claim by the sellers independent of both contract and bailment, and for holding that the only non-contractual claim available to them should be one that was subject to the doctrine of bailment on terms, since both the crucial requirements of the doctrine were satisfied. These requirements were (1) "the voluntary taking into possession [by the carrier] of another's goods on terms qualifying the taker's responsibility towards the owner or other person entitled to immediate possession"[84] and (2) the consent of that person [the shipper] to those terms.[85] Hence the rights of the shippers after they had lost their rights under the contract of

---

[76] *ibid.*, at [49(c)], *cf.*[32]. For the requirement of "actual and permanent injury" to the reversionary interest, see *ibid* at [31]. In *HSBC Rail (UK) Ltd v Network Rail Infrastructure Ltd* [2005] EWCA Civ 1437, [2006] 1 All E.R. 343 this requirement was not satisfied as the bailor had been fully compensated for his loss by the bailee.
[77] *East West* case, above n.64 at [32]; *cf.* para.18–049 below after n.69 for the significance of this point in a bill of lading context.
[78] *East West* case, above n.64, at [50].
[79] *ibid.*
[80] [2002] EWHC 83 (Comm.), [2002] 1 All E.R. (Comm.) 676 at [59]–[60].
[81] [2003] EWCA Civ. 83, [2003] Q.B. 1509, at [50].
[82] See below, para.18–049 at n.64.
[83] Above at n.68.
[84] *East West* case, above n.64, at [69].
[85] See *KH Enterprise v Pioneer Container (The Pioneer Container)* [1994] 2 A.C. 324.

carriage continued to be "subject to the same terms."[86] The reference in this passage appears to be to terms "qualifying"[87] the carriers' liability: it does not seem that the concept of bailment on terms would have entitled the shippers to claim the benefit of positive duties, going beyond those imposed at common law on a bailee, as opposed to terms "qualifying" the bailee's normal duties as such. Thus it seems unlikely that the doctrine of bailment on terms would have entitled shippers who had lost their rights under the contract to recover (for example) damages for delay (amounting to a breach of that contract) in completing the contract voyage.

The submission just made seems to be in accord with the legislative policy underlying the provisions of the 1992 Act by which the transferor of the bill, by reason of the transfer, loses his rights of suit under it.[88] The policy is stated in the Report of the Law Commisssions which led to the Act: "if a person who transfers a bill of lading were to retain rights, it would enable him to undermine the security of the new holder by anticipatory action, in addition to exposing the carrier to inconsistent claims."[89] It seems that "rights" here mean "rights of suit under the contract of carriage"; for the Law Commissions, in a passage relied on in the *East West* case, also say that there was "nothing in our recommendation to prevent the seller suing in tort by reason of being the owner of the goods."[90] The first of these statements would prevent a former holder of the bill from enforcing what we have called positive duties arising from the contract of carriage; the second would merely leave in being the rights of the shipper as owner of the goods.

18–116 **Rights of charterer after transfer of bill of lading.** The leading modern authority on the common law position is *The Albazero*,[91] where crude oil was shipped on the defendant's ship, which had been time-chartered by the claimant. The shipment was made in pursuance of an f.o.b. contract under which the claimant was the buyer. A bill of lading was issued by the defendant in which the claimant's supplier was named as shipper and the claimant as consignee. The claimant then sold the oil on c.i.f. terms to one of its associated companies, to which property in the goods passed on transfer of the bill, and that company later paid the price of the oil against an invoice.[92] The ship and the oil were lost by reason of the carrier's assumed breach of contract, and the claim for the value of the oil was

---

[86] *East West* case, above n.64, at [69]; the actual decision was that there were no relevant terms in the bills of lading which protected the carriers: see *ibid.* at [81], [86(vi)].
[87] *ibid.*, at [69].
[88] s.2(1) and 2(5)(a).
[89] Law Com. No. 196, Scot Law Com. No. 130, para 2–34 (iii), cited in *Keppel Tatlee Bank Ltd. v Bandung Shippimg Pte. Ltd.* [2003] 1 Lloyd's Rep. 619 at [27] in support of the view that the contract rights of the transferor were extinguished.
[90] Law Commissions' Report, above n.89, cited in the *East West* case [2003] EWCA Civ. 83, [2003] Q.B. 1509 at [46] in support of the view that the owner's rights in the bailment survived his transfer of the bill.
[91] *Albacruz (Cargo Owners) v Albazero (Owners) (the Albazero)* [1977] A.C. 774.
[92] See the report of the decision at first instance [1974] 2 All E.R. 906 at p.926; [1977] A.C. 774 at p.779.

brought after the one year period[93] for bringing claims for breach of the bill of lading contract had expired but before the expiry of the limitation period for claims under the charterparty. The House of Lords rejected the claim on the ground that it fell within the general principle of the law of contract, that the victim of a breach of contract could recover damages only for his own loss, and not for loss suffered by a third party.[94] That principle was indeed subject to exceptions and qualifications, and the exception potentially applicable in the present context was the so-called rule in *Dunlop v Lambert*.[95] This exception applied, not only where the contract between the claimant and carrier was on bill of lading terms, but also where it was contained in a charterparty.[96] But it did not apply, (because it was no longer needed[97]) where the third party who had suffered loss was, by the operation of the Bills of Lading Act 1855, brought into a direct contractual relationship with the carrier; nor would it now apply where such a relationship had been brought into existence as a result of the operation of the 1992 Act. To apply the exception to such cases would amount to an extension of it "to cases in which there are two contracts with the carrier covering the same carriage and under one of them there is privity of contract between the person who actually sustains the loss and the carrier by whose breach of that contract it was caused."[98] In the present context, it follows that if conduct of the carrier (A) amounts to a breach both of a charterparty with B and of a bill of lading contract with C (who had become the lawful holder of the bill), then A is at common law liable for substantial damages to B only if the breach has caused loss to B, and not merely because it has caused loss to C (but not to B). It seems that the reasoning of *The Albazero* would also apply where the contractual relationship between A and C arose, not by virtue of the transfer of rights under the statutory provision for such transfer now contained in section 2(1) of the 1992 Act, but where C had acquired contractual rights against A by virtue of an implied contract of the kind discussed in paragraph 18–139 below, or where C could recover his loss from A by suing in tort.[99] Here, too, there is no need to allow B to recover substantial damages from A in respect of C's loss since C has his own independent rights against A.

A significant aspect of *The Albazero* was that the claimant company (the charterer) had resold the oil on c.i.f. terms, and so was not responsible for the safe arrival of the oil at the destination specified in the c.i.f. contract: it was responsible only for making an effective contract for the carriage of the goods to that destination and for tendering the requisite shipping documents to the buyer.[1] Risk had moreover passed to the c.i.f buyer on or as

---

[93] Under Art. III.6 of the Hague Rules, now superseded in England by Carriage of Goods by Sea Act 1971, Sch. (the Hague-Visby Rules) Art. III.6.
[94] Above, para.18–114 at n.40.
[95] (1839) 6 Cl. & F. 600 at pp.626–627, as to which see above, para.18–114, n.37.
[96] *cf. Obestain Inc. v National Mineral Development Corp. (The Sanix Ace)* [1971] 1 Lloyd's Rep. 465, below at n.8.
[97] See above, para.18–114 at n.49.
[98] *The Albazero* [1977] A.C. 774 at p.847.
[99] *Riyad Bank v Ahli United Arab Bank (UK) Plc* [2005] EWHC 279 (Comm.), [2005] 2 Lloyd's Rep. 409 at [173].
[1] See below, paras 19–002, 19–072; it is assumed that the seller has not actively prevented delivery: see below, para.19–073.

from shipment,[2] so that the subsequent perishing of the goods did not affect the buyer's duty to pay the price, and this duty had in fact been performed. The position would have been different if the sale by the claimant had been a "c.i.f. contract with variations"[3] under which the amount payable by the buyer depended on the quantity of goods which actually arrived[4] or which provided that the contract was to be void if the ship carrying the goods were lost.[5] Such terms leave the risk of loss during transit with the seller; and if the sale by the claimant in *The Albazero* had included a term of this kind, then the loss resulting from the carrier's breach would have been suffered by the claimant who could therefore have been entitled to substantial damages in respect of his *own* loss for breach of the charter-party.[6] A similar possibility would have arisen if the contract of sale had contained an undertaking on the part of the seller as to the time of the arrival of the goods at the agreed destination; such an undertaking is unusual in a c.i.f. contract, but by no means unknown, especially in the oil trade.[7] If the charterparty had required the ship to go directly to the port of discharge but the bill of lading had contained a liberty to call at intermediate ports, and that liberty had been exercised, then it is submitted that the seller could, as charterer, have recovered substantial damages for breach of the charterparty if the resulting delay had led to his being in breach of the c.i.f. contract and so liable to the buyer in damages, or for the return of the price if the buyer had exercised his right to reject the goods on account of that breach.

The reasoning of *The Albazero* was also held to be inapplicable in *The Sanix Ace*.[8] Goods were shipped in bulk, in pursuance of an f.o.b. contract, on a ship which had been chartered by the claimants who became owners of the goods on shipment and to whom the bill of lading, originally made out to the order of their bank,[9] was later transferred.[10] They resold the goods to 11 end-users to whom risk passed on shipment and who paid the price in full, but to whom property could not, as the law then stood,[11] pass as the goods sold to each of them were specified quantities forming undifferentiated parts of a bulk. Nor was the bill of lading indorsed to any of the end-users, each of whom simply received a copy of the single bill which covered the whole shipment. The goods having been damaged in transit by unseaworthiness amounting to a breach by the shipowner of the contract

---

[2] Below, para.19–110.
[3] *The Gabbiano* [1940] P. 166 at p.174; below, para.19–006.
[4] See *Calcutta, etc., SN Co. v De Mattos* (1863) 32 L.J. Q.B. 332; 33 L.J. Q.B. 214; *Dupont v British South Africa Co.* (1901) 18 J.L.R. 24; *Arnhold Karberg & Co. v Blythe, Green Jourdain & Co.* [1915] 2 K.B. 495; *Krohn & Co. v Mitsui & Co. Europe GmbH* [1978] 2 Lloyd's Rep. 419 (c.&.f. contract).
[5] *Karinjee Javinjee & Co. v William F. Malcolm & Co.* (1926) 25 Ll.L. Rep. 28; *Re Denbigh Cowan & Co. and R. Atcherley & Co.* (1921) 90 L.J. Q.B. 836.
[6] *cf. Den of Airlie Co. Ltd v Mitsui & Co.* (1910–1911) 17 Com.Cas 16 (where the contract was described at p.122 as a "basis delivered" contract).
[7] See below, para.19–074.
[8] *Obestain Inc. v National Mineral Development Corp. Ltd (The Sanix Ace)* [1987] 1 Lloyd's Rep. 465.
[9] *ibid.*, p.467.
[10] *ibid.*, p.470.
[11] See now Sale of Goods Act 1979, s.20A.

contained in the charterparty, it was held that the claimants could recover substantial damages from the shipowner in respect of that loss, even though it had been suffered, not by them, but by the end-users; and that those damages were to be held for the account of the end-users. In reaching this conclusion, Hobhouse J. chiefly emphasised the fact that the claimants had remained owners[12] of the goods, and this would on similar facts no longer be true now that a buyer of a specified quantity of unascertained goods which form part of an identified bulk can acquire property in an undivided share in that bulk.[13] No doubt this change in the law would now enable the end-users to sue the carrier in tort on proof of negligence[14]; but they would still have no right of action against him for breach of the contract of carriage since no bill of lading was ever transferred to them, nor was any other document capable of transferring rights under that contract (such as a ship's delivery order[15]) issued in respect of the shipment. It is submitted that the charterer's claim for damages for breach of the charterparty (to be held on behalf of the end-users) should still succeed on such facts, even though property could now be acquired by the end-users. One reason given for the decision in *The Sanix Ace* was that, if the carriers were not liable to the charterers for substantial damages, there would be "no-one who could recover substantial damages from the carriers"[16]; and this would be just as true where the *only* cause of action against the carriers was in contract and the reason for the end-users' inability to bring such a claim against the carriers was that they were not original parties, to, or transferees of rights under, any contract with the carriers.

Contracts (Rights of Third Parties) Act 1999.[17] Under section 1 of this Act, a person (the third party) can, in circumstances described earlier in this Chapter,[18] acquire the right to enforce a term of a contract to which he is not a party. Section 4 of the Act provides that "Section 1 does not affect any right of the promisee to enforce any term of the contract": these words preserve (*inter alia*) the right of the promisee in certain exceptional cases[19] to recover damages in respect of the third party's loss.[20] One such 18–117

[12] For the right of an owner to recover damages in respect of loss suffered by others, see also *Eridiana SpA v Rudolf A Oetker (The Fjord Wind)* [1999] 1 Lloyd's Rep. 307, affirmed without reference to this point [2000] 2 Lloyd's Rep. 192. The point arose here in the different context of the extent of the rights of a bill of lading holder to damages for breach of the contract of carriage before the coming into force of the Carriage of Goods by Sea Act 1992.

[13] Sale of Goods Act 1979, s.20A below, paras 18–293 *et seq*.

[14] The requirement, stated in *The Aliakmon* [1986] A.C. 785 at p.809 (below, para.18–149), that the claimant in such an action must have "either the legal ownership or a possessory title to the property concerned" would, on the facts of *The Sanix Ace*, above, now be satisfied.

[15] See Carriage of Goods by Sea Act 1992, s.2(1)(c), below, para.18–175.

[16] [1987] 1 Lloyd's Rep. 465 at p.470.

[17] For further discussion of the impact of this Act on the present situation, see *Carver on Bills of Lading* 2nd ed., (2005), paras 5–070 to 5–073.

[18] Above, para.18–005.

[19] See generally *Chitty on Contracts*, 29th ed. (2004) paras 18–047 to 18–063.

[20] For safeguards against the promisor's being made liable twice over see s.5 of the 1999 Act above, para.18–005, below, n.33.

exceptional case arises under the so-called rule in *Dunlop v Lambert*,[21] as interpreted and restricted in *The Albazero*.[22] Under that rule, which is discussed in paragraphs 18–114 and 18–116 above, a shipper of goods can recover damages for breach of contract from the carrier in respect of loss of or damage to goods even though the resulting prejudice is suffered, not by the shipper but by the consignee, so long as the consignee has not been brought into a direct contractual relationship with the carrier, typically by becoming the transferee of the bill of lading. Our present concern is with the impact of the 1999 Act on the justification for, and scope of, this rule. In particular, it will be necessary to consider what we have called the subsection 6(5) exception,[23] which states that section 1 of the 1999 Act confers no rights on a third party in the case of a "contract for the carriage of goods by sea." A contract contained in or evidenced by a bill of lading is, while a charterparty is not, a "contract for the carriage of goods by sea" within the 1999 Act.[24]

Where the contract between shipper and carrier is contained in or evidenced by a bill of lading, the case will fall within the subsection 6(5) exception, so that section 1 of the 1999 Act can confer no rights on the consignee. Where, however, that contract is contained in a charterparty between shipper and carrier, the case will not fall within the subsection 6(5) exception, since a charterparty is not a "contract for the carriage of goods by sea" within the 1999 Act.[25] This would be so even if the carrier had issued a bill of lading to the charterer since between these parties the bill of lading would be a mere receipt.[26] If the shipper then transferred the bill of lading to a third party (typically a buyer of the goods from him), rights *under the charterparty* would not be transferred or extinguished by virtue of the 1992 Act.[27] It is, however, possible for the third party to have acquired a right to enforce a term of the charterparty against the carrier under section 1 of the 1999 Act; and in that event the reasoning of *The Albazero* would seem to preclude the operation of the rule in *Dunlop v Lambert*. That reasoning admittedly is in terms concerned only with the situation in which the third party has acquired rights under the contract of carriage as transferee of the bill of lading. But the underlying rationale of the *Albazero* restriction on the scope of the rule in *Dunlop v Lambert* is simply *that* the third party has acquired contractual rights against the carrier: not *how* (*i.e.* by what legal mechanism) he has acquired them. The shipper would then have no right to recover damages from the carrier in respect of the third party's loss: this would follow, not merely because rights had been conferred on the third party under section 1 of the 1999 Act, but because the acquisition of such rights had brought into operation the common law reasoning of *The Albazero*. Where that reasoning applies, the shipper's

---

[21] Above, para.18–114.
[22] Above, para.18–116.
[23] Above, para.18–005.
[24] Above, para.18–055.
[25] This follows from s.6(6) and (7) of the 1999 Act.
[26] Above, para.18–052.
[27] *i.e.* s.2(1) and 2(5) of the 1992 Act would not apply to rights under the charterparty.

rights would not be preserved by section 4 of the 1999 Act even if the shipper's rights had originally arisen under a bill of lading contract.

The 1999 Act might also affect the situation in which the bill of lading containing or evidencing the contract of carriage was later transferred *to* the charterer of the carrying ship. This was the position in *The Sanix Ace*,[28] discussed in paragraph 18–116 above. It will be recalled that one reason given in that case for allowing the charterer to recover damages in respect of the third parties' loss was that, if the carriers were not liable to the charterer for substantial damages, there would be "no-one who could recover substantial damages from the carriers".[29] It has been suggested above[30] that, under the 1999 Act, a case of this kind would not fall within the subsection 6(5) exception, so that there would be a possibility of the end-users' acquiring rights to enforce a term of the charterparty under section 1 of that Act. Whether the end-users could have satisfied the requirements of section 1 of the 1999 Act is not at all clear[31]; but if they could have done so the case would now appear to fall within the *Albazero* exception[32] to the rule in *Dunlop v Lambert*.[33]

Rights of intermediate transferee. The situation here to be considered is that in which goods are shipped by A under a bill of lading which he transfers to B who then transfers it to C. If each of these transfers is made in circumstances vesting rights in the transferee, by virtue of section 2(1) of the 1992 Act, then section 2(5) (which extinguishes the contractual rights of the transferor)[34] operates in relation to the second transfer no less than in relation to the first. In the case put, A's rights under the bill of lading as an original party to the contract of carriage are extinguished by section 2(5)(a), while the rights under that contract which had been vested in B by virtue of section 2(1) are extinguished by section 2(5)(b).[35] **18–118**

An intermediate transferee, no less than an original shipper, may be the charterer of the carrying ship. For example goods may be sold by A to B on f.o.b. terms, shipped (as in *The Dunelmia*)[36] on board a ship chartered by B under a bill of lading issued to A as shipper; and the goods may then be sold afloat by B to C on c.i.f. terms. The bill of lading may in such a case be

---

[28] *Obestain Inc. v National Mineral Development Corp. (The Sanix Ace)* [1987] 1 Lloyd's Rep. 465.

[29] *ibid.*, p.480.

[30] Above, para.18–056. The charterer in *The Sanix Ace* was an f.o.b. buyer who had chartered the ship for the purpose of taking delivery from his supplier, so that the bill of lading became in his hands a mere receipt: above, para.18–052 at n.97.

[31] It does not appear from the report whether the requirements stated in para.18–005, sub-para. (b) were satisfied.

[32] Above, para.18–116 after n.97.

[33] The above suggestion is not negatived by s.5 of the 1999 Act which provides against double recovery where the promisee and third party each has a cause of action against the promisor. This section does not specify when or to what extent the promisee has such a cause of action: the answer to that question depends, in the situation here under discussion, on the reasoning of *The Albazero*.

[34] Above, para.18–114.

[35] *Keepel Tatlee Bank v Banding Shipping Plc Ltd* [2003] 1 Lloyd's Rep. 619 (Singapore Court of Appeal), discussed, para.18–016 above.

[36] [1970] 1 Q.B. 289.

transferred first by A to B and then by B to C. Section 2(5)(b) would not apply in this situation since in the hands of B the bill would be a mere receipt, so that rights under it would not be transferred to B by virtue of section 2(1); nor would section 2(5)(a) apply since the charterparty is not "the contract of carriage" within the 1992 Act.[37] Nor, for the reasons given in paragraph 18–114 above, would the transfer of the bill from B to C extinguish B's rights under the charterparty.

18–119 **Loss suffered by person other than lawful holder.** Section 2(4) of the 1992 Act deals with the situation in which rights under the contract of carriage are transferred to A by virtue of section 2(1), but the loss resulting from a breach of that contract is suffered by B. The subsection provides that "where, in the case of any document to which this Act applies—(a) a person with any interest or right in or in relation to goods to which the document relates sustains loss or damage in consequence of a breach of the contract of carriage; but (b) subsection (1) above operates in relation to that document so that rights of suit in respect of that breach are vested in another person, the other person shall be entitled to exercise those rights for the benefit of the person who sustained the loss or damage to the same extent as they could have been exercised if they had been vested in the person for whose benefit they are exercised." The purpose of this subsection is to avoid the consequences which might, but for the subsection, flow from the general principle of English law[38] that damages in a contractual action can be recovered only in respect of the claimant's own loss.[39] That general principle was also subject to exceptions at common law,[40] and these exceptions could still apply in the present context even in cases which did not fall squarely within section 2(4).[41]

Section 2(4) would most obviously apply where the bill of lading had been transferred to a person other than the owner of the goods at whose risk they were when they were damaged: *e.g.* where the transferee was the owner's agent, or a bank which had financed the transaction and been reimbursed by its customer and so had suffered no loss as a result of a breach by the carrier of the contract of carriage. It is also possible to imagine situations of somewhat greater complexity which could fall within section 2(4). The subsection could, for example, apply where B shipped

[37] See the definition of "contract of carriage" in s.5(1): this restricts the meaning of the phrase (in the example given in the text above) to the contract contained in or evidenced by a bill of lading or in a sea way bill.

[38] Above, para.18–114.

[39] This appears to be what is meant by the Law Commissions' somewhat puzzling statement in Law Com. No. 196, Scot Law Com. No. 130, para.2.8 that, but for s.2(4) "the decision in *The Albazero* [1977] A.C. 774 [above, para.18–116], could prevent those holders of bills of lading who do not themselves sustain loss from recovering anything other than nominal damages." The reason for the actual result in *The Albazero* was that the claimants had transferred the bill of lading so as to vest contractual rights in the transferee; and where this is done by a person whose only contract with the carrier is on bill of lading terms, that person's rights under the contract of carriage will be extinguished under s.2(5) of the 1992 Act.

[40] Above, para.18–114.

[41] Below, para.18–120 at n.61.

goods under a bill of lading, sold them to A on c.i.f. terms of the kind which make the amount payable dependent on the quantity of goods that arrived,[42] and transferred the bill of lading to A.[43] At this stage, rights under the contract of carriage would be transferred from B to A and B's rights under the contract of carriage would be extinguished, but if some of the goods were lost as a result of the carrier's breach of contract, that loss would fall on B rather than on A. The subsection could also apply where B was not an original shipper but a sub-buyer from A (the lawful holder): *e.g.* where goods which had been shipped by X were sold to A to whom rights under the bill of lading were transferred on his becoming the lawful holder, A then sold the goods to B under an orthodox c.i.f. contract under which risk passed to B on or as from shipment, but contractual rights under the bill of lading were not transferred to B because the bill had not been delivered to him[44] or because it lacked a requisite indorsement. Here again, if the goods were lost as a result of the carrier's breach of the contract of carriage, the loss would fall on B rather than on A. In both these situations A would (if the other requirements of section 2(4) were satisfied) be entitled to exercise his right under the contract of carriage for the benefit of B.

On the other hand, section 2(4) would not apply where A was the original shipper under the bill of lading, for in that case his rights under the contract of carriage would have been acquired as an original party to the contract of carriage and not (as required by section 2(4)(b)) by virtue of section 2(1). Hence if, in such a case, loss resulting from breach of the contract were suffered by B, and B had acquired no rights under the contract of carriage, the case would be governed by the common law rule in *Dunlop v Lambert*[45] stated in paragraph 18–114 above. Under that rule A could (as under section 2(4)) recover damages in respect of B's loss, and would be required to hold those damages for B; but his entitlement (and duty to hold the damages so recovered for B) would not be subject to any of the restrictions which section 2(4) may impose[46] on A's entitlement to sue for the benefit of B. Nor would section 2(4) apply where A's claim was made, not under a bill of lading, but under a charterparty, as in *The Albazero* and *The Sanix Ace*, discussed in paragraph 18–116 above. On facts such as those in *The Albazero*, a further reason why section 2(4) could not now apply was that the charterer, to whom the bill of lading had been transferred, had then in turn transferred it to the sub-buyer, so that any rights which the charterer may have had as transferee of the bill of lading would have been extinguished.[47] And on the facts of both these cases it is (to say the least) likely that the bills of lading, having been transferred to charterers, were in the hands of those charterers mere receipts.[48] If so, no

---

[42] See below, para.19–006 *cf.* above, para.18–116 at nn. 3, 4.
[43] *e.g. R & W Paul Ltd v National SS Co. Ltd* (1937) 59 Ll. L.R. 28.
[44] *cf. Obestain Inc. v National Mineral Development Corp. (The Sanix Ace)* [1987] 1 Lloyd's Rep. 465, above, para.18–116.
[45] (1839) 6 Cl. & F. 600 at pp.626–627.
[46] See paras 18–120 and 18–121, below.
[47] Under Carriage of Goods by Sea Act 1992, s.2(5), above, para.18–114.
[48] See above, para.18–053, 18–118; the facts of the two cases are closer to those in *President of India v Metcalfe Shipping Co. Ltd (The Dunelmia)* [1970] 1 Q.B. 289 than to those of *Calcutta S.S. Co. Ltd v Andrew Weir & Co.* [1910] 1 K.B. 759.

rights of suit under them would now be vested in the charterers (as lawful holders of the bills) by virtue of section 2(1), and consequently the requirements of section 2(4) would not be satisfied.

18–120 **"Any interest or right in or in relation to goods".** Section 2(4)(a) describes the person for whose benefit the action can be brought as "a person with any interest or right in or in relation to goods to which the document relates." The question therefore arises what is meant by the phrase "any interest or right in or in relation to goods." Where a person who has no rights against the carrier in contract seeks to recover damages in tort, that person must have "either the legal ownership of or a possessory title to the property concerned at the time when the loss or damage occurred",[49] or when the cause of action in respect of it accrued.[50] In particular it is for this purpose *not* sufficient that the claimant had a contractual right to have the goods delivered to him or that the goods were at his risk.[51] Section 2(4)(a) appears to be satisfied where the goods have been contractually appropriated to a contract of sale, in the sense that the seller has bound himself to deliver those particular goods, even though there has been no "proprietary" appropriation, *i.e.* even though the goods have not been unconditionally appropriated to the contract so as to pass the property in them.[52] It is less clear whether the mere fact that goods are at the risk of the person for whose benefit the action is brought gives that person an "interest or right in or in relation to goods". Two situations call for discussion.

First, risk has passed to the buyer but the bill of lading remains in the hands of the seller (and no other document[53] has been issued in relation to the goods which is capable, by virtue of section 2(1), of transferring contractual rights to the buyer). In such a situation, the fact that the goods are at the buyer's risk appears at first sight to come closer to imposing a *duty* on the buyer in relation to them (*i.e.* one to pay the price) than to conferring an "interest or right in or in relation to" them. It is, indeed, arguable that a person has an "interest" in goods whenever he suffers loss as a result of their having been lost, damaged or delayed in transit in consequence of the carrier's breach. But it seems that section 2(4)(a) requires the person for whose benefit the action is brought to have the "interest or right" *and* to suffer loss; for if it were sufficient for him to suffer loss the reference to "interest or right" would be mere surplusage. In many cases of overseas sales, risk no doubt passes on contractual appropriation by shipment[54]; and where such an appropriation has taken place the buyer will have an "interest" in the goods in consequence of that

---

[49] *Leigh and Sillavan Ltd v Aliakmon Shipping Co. Ltd (The Aliakmon)* [1986] A.C. 785 at p.809, and see below, para.18–149.
[50] See below, para.18–149 at n.55.
[51] *The Aliakmon*, above, *Margarine Union GmbH v Cambay Prince SS Ltd (The Wear Breeze)* [1969] 1 Q.B. 619.
[52] For the distinction between these two types of "appropriation" see below, para.18–210.
[53] *e.g.* a ship's delivery order: see s.2(1)(c), below, para.18–175.
[54] Below, paras 18–210, 18–244.

appropriation, so that the question here put will not arise. But where goods are sold afloat on c.i.f. terms risk can pass retrospectively as from shipment and so can be on the buyer *before* contractual appropriation.[55] At this stage, it is hard to see that the buyer has any "interest or right in or in relation to" the goods. There can also be difficulty in satisfying this requirement where the goods are a specified quantity of unascertained goods forming part of an identified bulk cargo. It is true that property can now pass to the buyer in an undivided share of such goods, but only if he has paid the whole or part of the price[56]; and where he has not made any such payment it is again not clear whether he has an "interest or right in relation to" any goods. Nor, indeed, since in the case put the goods are "unascertained" is it clear which are the "goods to which the document relates".

Secondly, risk remains on the seller but the bill of lading has been transferred to the buyer. This is an unusual situation (since normally risk will pass on shipment) but it can nevertheless arise: *e.g.* in the type of c.i.f. contract, already discussed,[57] in which the amount payable depends on the quantity of goods which arrive. If payment is not due or made till after arrival of the goods, the seller is likely to remain owner till then,[58] and that fact would clearly satisfy the requirement of section 2(4)(a). But payment may be due and made against documents, with a provision for price-adjustment depending on the outturn; and in such a case it is again hard to see what "interest" the seller has in or in relation to the goods. In other words, the same difficulties arise here as those considered in the case of a buyer who has merely the risk.

Section 2(4) does not make it clear at what time the person for whose benefit the action is to be brought must have the "interest or right". The common law tort rule, stated above, requires the claimant to have a legal ownership or a possessory title "at the time when the loss or damage occurred" or when the cause of action in respect of it occurred.[59] Section 2(4) does not in terms impose a similar temporal requirement, but the subsection does seem to be based on the assumption that such a requirement must be satisfied.

Where section 2(4) does not apply because B has no "right or interest", or because he has acquired it too late, it may still be possible for A to recover damages in respect of B's loss under the common law exceptions to the general rule that a party can recover damages only in respect of his own loss. In particular, he may be able to do so under the so-called rule in *Dunlop v Lambert*[60] which has, since the passing of the 1992 Act been significantly extended by the courts beyond its original scope.[61]

Extent of rights exercisable. Where rights are "vested"[62] in A by virtue of section 2(1), "those rights" can, in the circumstances specified in section 2(4), be exercised by A for the benefit of B "to the same extent as they 18–121

[55] Below, para.19–110, for limitations on the scope of this principle, see below, para.19–113.
[56] Sale of Goods Act 1979, s.20A, below paras 18–293, 18–295.
[57] Above, paras 18–116 at n.4.
[58] Below, paras 19–098, 19–103.
[59] Above, at nn. 49, 50.
[60] (1839) 6 Cl. & F. 600 at pp.626–627, above, para.18–114.
[61] Above, para.18–114.
[62] s.2(4)(b).

could have been exercised if they had been vested in the person for whose benefit they are exercised",[63] *i.e.* in B as if he had been a party to the contract of carriage.[64] The assumption (or fiction) that B is a party to the contract of carriage (when actually he is not) most obviously covers the case where B is not and never has been a party to that contract. This would be the position where (assuming the other requirements[65] of section 2(4) to have been satisfied) B was a buyer of goods covered by a bill of lading, of which A (the seller) had become the lawful holder, and that bill had not yet been transferred to B. It could also cover the case in which B *was* originally a party to the contract of carriage but his rights under it had been extinguished[66]: *e.g.* where (again assuming that the other requirements of section 2(4) had been satisfied) B was a seller of goods covered by a bill of lading originally issued or previously transferred to him, and that bill had been transferred by B to A, the buyer. In the first of these situations, it is clear from the wording of section 2(4) that the damages which A can recover for B's benefit are subject to the terms of the bill of lading contract and to statutory defences and limits of liability such as those provided by the Hague-Visby Rules.[67] This is also normally true in the second of our two situations, where B was originally a party to the contract of carriage but has lost his rights under it by transferring the bill to A. But in this type of case it is possible for the original contract between the carrier and B to be on different terms from the contract between the carrier and A; and the result of the difference may be to make B's rights against the carrier under the original contract either more or less extensive than those acquired by A in consequence of the transfer of the bill. It is submitted that where (for example) B's rights under the contract of carriage were restricted by a term extrinsic to the bill of lading,[68] then there would be no reason for allowing A (who would not be bound by the term) to recover damages (under section 2(4)) for the benefit of B which B could not have recovered himself if he had not transferred the bill to A. In the converse case, in which B's rights under the bill were by reason of some extrinsic term *more* extensive than those transferred to A,[69] there is some support in the concluding words of the subsection for the view that A could recover the amount that B himself could (but for the transfer to A) have recovered, even though this exceeds the amount that A could have recovered, had he been suing for his own benefit.

18–122 **No duty to sue for benefit of another.** Where section 2(4) applies, it provides that A, the person who has acquired rights of suit by virtue of section 2(1), "shall be *entitled* to exercise those rights for the benefit of" B,

[63] s.2(4), "tailpiece."
[64] This follows from the use (twice) of the word "vested" in s.2(4) and from the cross-reference in that subsection to s.2(1).
[65] *i.e.* those specified in s.2(4)(a), discussed in paras 18–119, 18–120, above.
[66] Under s.2(5), above, para.18–114.
[67] *cf.* the Hague-Visby Rules (Carriage of Goods by Sea Act 1971, Sch.) Art. IV bis (1) for a similar idea.
[68] Above, para.18–106.
[69] *ibid*.

the person who has suffered the loss. The subsection does not *require* A to exercise those rights for the benefit of B, or at all; it shares this feature with other rules of common law (including the so-called rule in *Dunlop v Lambert*)[70] under which a contracting party can, exceptionally, recover damages in respect, not of his own loss, but in respect of loss suffered by a third party.[71] Nor does section 2(4) (or any other provision of the Act) provide machinery by which B can compel A to exercise those rights. It is possible for such machinery to be provided by the contract between A and B which gives rise to B's "interest or right in or in relation to [the] goods".[72] This is obviously more probable where B is the buyer of goods from A than in the converse situation of a sale by B to A. Contracts of sale commonly require a seller to transfer rights under a contract of carriage to the buyer,[73] and it would be only a slight extension of this duty to require the seller to exercise rights under section 2(4) for the benefit of the buyer. It is much less common for contracts of sale to require the buyer to transfer rights under a contract of carriage to the seller. At the most the seller might become bound and possibly entitled *vis-à-vis* the carrier by terms agreed between buyer and carrier, on the basis of a separate implied contract,[74] but this concept cannot readily be extended so as to impose on the buyer a duty to exercise rights for the benefit of the seller. A seller who wished to compel the buyer to do this should therefore make express provision to this effect in the contract of sale.

(vii) *Imposition of Contractual Liabilities*[75]

Introductory. As noted in paragraph 18–100 above, section 1 of the Bills of Lading Act 1855 had the effect that a consignee or indorsee of a bill of lading had liabilities under the bill imposed on him at the same time as that at which he acquired rights under it. For two reasons, the Carriage of Goods by Sea Act 1992 breaks this link between the acquisition of rights and the imposition of liabilities. First, there is no necessary connection between the two processes, as the analogy of the general law relating to the assignment of choses in action[76] shows: an assignee of a chose in action is not liable on a contract merely because he has acquired rights under it.[77] Secondly, by closing the "property gap"[78] the 1992 Act has greatly extended the range of persons who can acquire rights under bills of lading, having, in 18–123

[70] (1839) 6 Cl. & F. 600 at pp.626–627, above, para.18–114; *White v Jones* [1995] 2 A.C. 207 at pp.266–267.
[71] See *Gurtner v Circuit* [1968] 2 Q.B. 587 at p.596; *Chitty on Contracts*, 29th ed., paras 18–064 to 18–071.
[72] s.2(4)(a).
[73] This is one consequence of the duty incumbent on a c.i.f. seller to transfer a bill of lading to the buyer: see below, para.19–025.
[74] *cf. Pyrene Co. Ltd v Scindia Navigation Co. Ltd* [1954] 2 Q.B. 402.
[75] See *Carver on Bills of Lading*, 2nd ed. (2005), paras 5–084 to 5–103.
[76] *Cf East West Corp v DKBS 1912 AF A/S* [2003] EWCA Civ 83, [2003] Q.B. 1509 at [57] ("the statutory assignments worked by the 1992 Act").
[77] *e.g. Young v Kitchin* (1878) 3 Ex. D. 127; *The Trident Beauty* [1994] 1 W.L.R. 161 at pp.165, 170.
[78] Above, para.18–100, 18–101.

particular, included among such persons those who have become lawful holders of bills only by way of security. If the link between acquisition of rights and imposition of liabilities had been maintained, the undesirable consequence[79] would have followed that such persons would, merely by virtue of having in this way become secured creditors, have been subjected to liabilities under the bill. In broad terms, the solution adopted by the 1992 Act is that a person is not liable under the contract contained in or evidenced by the bill of lading merely because rights under it have been transferred to him on his becoming the lawful holder of the bill: he becomes liable only if in addition he takes or claims the benefit of that contract. It is this "principle of mutuality"[80] which underlies, and governs the interpretation of, the provisions of the Act under which liabilities can be incurred by the transferee of a bill of lading. Since those liabilities may "particularly when alleged dangerous goods are concerned"[81] be extensive, and may result from breaches of the contract of carriage by a shipper for whose conduct the transferee is not responsible,[82] the conditions in which such liabilities may be incurred by transferees by virtue of the Act have been strictly interpreted against the carrier. The authorities show a somewhat greater readiness to hold a transferee liable for failure to perform conditions on which his entitlement to receive performance from the carrier depends: *e.g.* for freight and perhaps certain other charges payable at the point of delivery.[83]

18–124 **Carriage of Goods by Sea Act 1992, section 3(1).** This subsection provides: "Where subsection (1) of section 2 of this Act operates in relation to any document to which this Act applies and the person in whom rights are vested by virtue of that subsection—(a) takes or demands delivery from the carrier of any of the goods to which the document relates; (b) makes a claim under the contract of carriage against the carrier in respect of any of those goods; or (c) is a person who, at a time before those rights were vested in him, took or demanded delivery from the carrier of any of those goods, that person shall (by virtue of taking or demanding delivery or making the claim or, in a case falling within paragraph (c) above, of having the rights vested in him) become subject to the same liabilities under that contract as if he had been a party to that contract." It follows that liabilities will be incurred under this subsection only if two requirements are satisfied: first, the holder must have acquired rights by virtue of section 2(1); and secondly one of the circumstances described in paragraphs (a), (b) or (c) of section 3(1) must have occurred.

---

[79] Below, para.18–129.

[80] *Borealis AB v Stargas Ltd (The Berge Sisar)* [2001] UKHL 17, [2002] 2 A.C. 205 at [31].

[81] *ibid.* at [33].

[82] As in *The Berge Sisar*, above n.82 and in *Primetrade AG v Ythan Ltd (The Ythan)* [2005] EWHC 2399, [2006] 1 All E.R. 367.

[83] As in *Compania Commercial v China National Foreign Trade Transportation Corp (The Costanza M)* [1981] 2 Lloyd's Rep. 147 and *K/S A/S Seateam a Co. v Iraq National Oil Co. (The Sevonia Team)* [1983] 2 Lloyd's Rep. 641. American law reaches a substaintially similar result: it does not impose liabilities on the transferee but protects the carrier by giving him a lien against the transferee for his charges: 49 USC §80109; UCC §7–307. See further *Carver on Bills of Lading*, 2nd ed. (2005) para.5–009.

Rights must have been acquired by virtue of section 2(1). Liabilities are incurred by virtue of section 3(1) only by a person in whom contractual rights are vested by virtue of section 2(1), *i.e.* (in the case of a bill of lading) by a person who has become the lawful holder of the bill. Liabilities would therefore not be incurred by virtue of section 3(1) where *no* rights had been transferred by virtue of section 2(1): *e.g.* where the bill lacked a requisite indorsement, where it had never come into the possession of the person to whom it was sent because it was lost in transmission,[84] where for some other reason the alleged transferee had not become the "holder" of the bill,[85] or where the bill was transferred to the charterer of the carrying ship in circumstances making it, in his hands, a mere receipt.[86] In such cases, the person with possession of the bill, or the person to whom it was sent, might nevertheless take or demand delivery or make a claim under the contract of carriage. His taking or demanding delivery might give rise to an implied contract of the kind to be discussed in paragraph 18–139 below, and under such an implied contract he could incur liabilities as well as acquire rights; but no liabilities would be incurred under section 3(1). The point could be of practical importance since the implied contract might impose less extensive liabilities than section 3(1): the extent of the liabilities would be governed by the implied contract and not by the fiction that the defendant "had been a party to" the original contract of carriage.[87] It does not, moreover, seem that any such contract could be implied where *no* delivery had been taken nor any demand for delivery of the goods had been made: *e.g.* where they had in breach of contract been lost, destroyed or misdelivered by the carrier. If in such a case a claim under the contract of carriage were made by a person who had *not* acquired any rights by virtue of section 2(1), then no liabilities would be imposed on the claimant either under section 3(1) or at common law. 18–125

Taking or demanding delivery. The reference in section 3(1)(a) to a person who "takes . . . delivery" is clearly to one who takes actual or physical possession of the goods and not to the constructive possession obtained by the transferee of a bill of lading as a result of the transfer.[88] Delivery involves the "voluntary transfer of possession"[89] (from the carrier to the holder of the bill) in circumstances in which the holder's conduct is such as to "amount to an election [by the holder] to avail himself of . . . 18–126

---

[84] In such cases the person in question would not have become the "holder" of the bill: see s.5(2); *cf. Aegean Sea Traders Corp. v Repsol Petroleo SA (The Aegean Sea)* [1998] 2 Lloyd's Rep. 39; above, para.18–104.
[85] As in *Primetrade AG v Ythan Ltd (The Ythan)* [2005] EWHC 2399 (Comm.), [2006] 1 All E.R. 367: see above, para.18–104.
[86] As in *The Athenasia Comninos and George Chr. Lemos* (1979) [1990] 1 Lloyd's Rep. 277 at p.281 (claim against C.E.G.B., who appear to have been sub-charterers).
[87] Thus liability in respect of shipment of dangerous goods by the original shipper could be incurred under s.3(1) (though the courts appear to be reluctant to reach such a conclusion: see *Borealis AB v Stargas Ltd (The Berge Sisar)* [2001] UKHL 17, [2002] 2 A.C. 205, at [31]) but probably not under the implied contract: contrast below, para.18–133 after n.51 with below, para.18–143 at n.19.
[88] Above, para.18–063.
[89] *Borealis AB v Stragas Ltd (The Berge Sisar)* above, n.87 at [32].

[his] contractual rights against the carrier."[90] It requires "more than just co-operating in the discharge of the cargo from the vessel",[91] so that the requirement is not satisfied by the holder's merely providing berthing facilities[92] or by his receiving "routine samples"[93] to enable him to determine whether he is bound to accept the bulk from which they are taken. A "demand" for delivery must likewise be such as to provide evidence of the holder's election to avail himself of his rights against the carrier.[94] In accordance with the judicial policy of construing section 3 strictly against the carrier,[95] it has further been held that the demand involves more than an informal request or invitation. To satisfy the requirement, there must be "a formal demand made to the carrier or his agent asserting the contractual right as endorsee of the bill to have the carrier deliver the goods to him."[96] The contrast in section 3(1)(a) between *taking* and *demanding* delivery indicates that liabilities may be incurred by a holder who demands delivery even though the carrier does not comply with the demand. Where the carrier has a legal justification for not complying with the demand, the outcome may be that the holder incurrs liability by reason of having made the demand, even though the right which he has acquired by virtue of section 2(1) is no more than an empty one. The justice of making the holder liable in such circumstances is questionable; and such a result could perhaps be avoided by relying on the principle, adopted in construing the phrase "demanded delivery" in section 3(1)(c),[97] that "a rightly rejected demand for delivery by one who is not entitled to delivery is an act devoid of legal significance"[98] and therefore does not subject the person making such a "demand" to liability by virtue of section 3.

Section 3(1)(a) merely requires the holder to have taken or demanded delivery: it does not in terms require him to have done so in the exercise or purported exercise of rights "under the contract of carriage". This phrase occurs in section 3(1)(b), to be discussed in paragraph 18–129 below, but is significantly absent from section 3(1)(a). The reference in the dictum quoted above[99] to a "formal demand", asserting "the contractual right" of the indorsee of the bill of lading to delivery of the goods, gives rise to the question whether the holder of the bill to whom such a contractual right had been transferred could avoid liability by basing the "formal demand" on some other legal ground, such as his title to the goods. Probably such a course of action would be regarded as a mere subterfuge and would fail, in

---

[90] *ibid.*, at [36]; *cf. Primetrade AG v Ythan Ltd (The Ythan)* [2005] EWHC 2399 (Comm.), [2006] 1 All E.R. 367 at [94]; the assumption in this part of the judgement is that the actual ground for the decision (that the alleged transferee of the bill had not aquired rights, and therefore could not incur liabilities, under it: see above, para.18–125) "might be wrong" (at [91]).
[91] *The Berge Sisar*, above n.87 at [36].
[92] *ibid.*
[93] *ibid.*, at [5], [38].
[94] *ibid.*
[95] Above, para.18–123.
[96] *The Berge Sisar*, above, n.87, at [33].
[97] See below, para.18–131.
[98] *The Berge Sisar*, above n.87, at [35].
[99] Above, at n.96.

spite of the judicial tendency noted above[1] to construe section 3 strictly against the carrier. It is also uncertain whether liability is incurred where the demand is rejected and then not pursued by the holder who had originally made it.[2]

Where the bill of lading has not reached the buyer by the time of arrival of the goods, delivery may be made against a letter of indemnity given by either buyer or seller. The mere giving of such a letter does not amount to a "demand" within section 3(1)(a), whether the promise contained in the letter is to indemnify the carrier if he delivers the goods to the person making that promise[3] or to another person.[4] In the former case, actual delivery in response to the letter could give rise to an implied contract of the kind discussed in paragraphs 18–138 to 18–144 below.[5]

From the carrier. For the purpose of section 3(1), delivery must be taken or demanded "from the carrier". This phrase most obviously covers the case in which delivery is taken or demanded directly from the carrier. But it is submitted that it would also cover the case where the goods were collected from a warehouse into which the goods had been deposited to the carrier's order.[6] On the other hand, where oil from a tanker which had foundered was delivered to the defendants by salvors acting under government orders authorised by legislation, it was held that there had been no delivery "from the carrier".[7] 18–127

Where A's ship is time or voyage chartered by B and goods are carried in her under a bill of lading issued to C, the contract contained in or evidenced by the bill may be between A and C[8] or between B and C.[9] In the former case, A is no doubt "the carrier" within section 3; in the latter it is arguable that both A and B answer to that description: A because he performs the carriage operation and B because he has contracted with C that it should be performed.

The goods. The goods of which delivery is taken or demanded must be "substantially the same"[10] as those shipped. This requirement was, for example, not satisfied where the goods shipped consisted of a cargo of oil but those delivered consisted of a parcel of oil salvaged after the carrying ship had sunk.[10a] Section 3(1)(a) is satisfied if delivery is taken "of any of 18–128

---

[1] See para.18–123 after n.82.

[2] *The Berge Sisar*, above, n.87, at [34].

[3] *Aegean Sea Traders Corp. v Repsol Petroleo SA (The Aegean Sea)* [1998] 2 Lloyd's Rep. 39 at p.62.

[4] *The Berge Sisar*, above, n.87, at [38].

[5] *cf.* below, para.18–140.

[6] *Barclays Bank Ltd v Commissioners of Customs & Excise* [1963] 1 Lloyd's Rep. 81; *cf. Port Jackson Stevedoring Pty v Salmond and Spraggon (Australia) Pty (The New York Star)* [1981] 1 W.L.R. 138.

[7] *The Aegean Sea*, above, n.3 at p.62.

[8] *e.g. The Rewia* [1991] 2 Lloyd's Rep. 325.

[9] *e.g. Homburt Houtimport BV v Agrosin Private Ltd (The Starsin)* [2003] UKHL 12, [2004] A.C. 785; and see *Carver on Bills of Lading* (2nd ed., 2005), paras 4–028 *et seq.*

[10] *Aegean Sea Traders Corp. v Repsol Petroleo SA (The Aegean Sea)* [1998] 2 Lloyd's Rep. 39 at p.63, invoking the analogy of *Asfar v Blundell* [1896] 1 Q.B. 123.

[10a] *The Aegean Sea*, above n.10.

the goods" to which the bill relates. The potential injustice of holding the transferee fully liable where he takes delivery of only part of the goods (especially in circumstances in which the carrier is not liable for failure to deliver the rest of the shipment) is however mitigated by the strict construction of the requirement of "delivery" described in paragraph 18–126 above. In particular, a holder will not be regarded as having demanded delivery merely because he has asked for "routine samples"[11] so as to be able to determine whether he is bound to accept the bulk from which they were taken.

18–129 **Making a claim under the contract of carriage.** Under section 3(1)(b), liabilities are imposed on a holder who has acquired contractual rights by virtue of section 2(1) if he "makes a claim under the contract of carriage against the carrier in respect of any of [the] goods" to which the bill of lading relates: *e.g.* where no goods were delivered, or even demanded (because they were known to have perished). The phrase "makes a claim" is (like the phrase "demands delivery") strictly construed so as to give effect to the policy underlying section 3.[12] It requires more than merely "expressing a view in the course of a meeting or a letter"[13]; and refers to "a formal claim against the carrier asserting a legal liability of the carrier under the contract of carriage to the holder of the bill of lading."[14] But it seems that the holder may incur liability by virtue of section 3(1)(b) even though the claim that he makes turns out to be unfounded. Although a rightly rejected "demand" is, for the purposes of section 3(1)(a) and (c), "devoid of legal significance", the same is not true of a claim which fails, since it is the nature of a "claim" that its outcome is in law uncertain.[15] The requirement that the claim must be made "under the contract of carriage" is expressly stated in section 3(1)(b), which in this respect differs from section 3(1)(a). But it is submitted that the holder should not be able to avoid liability, even under section 3(1)(b),[16] merely by framing his claim against the carrier in tort where the facts constituting the tort also amounted to a breach of the contract of carriage. Cases of this kind would probably be held to fall within the general principle that a claim in tort is not available where there is a contract between the claimant and the defendant and that contract is intended exclusively to regulate the relations between the parties.[17]

---

[11] *Borealis AB v Stargas Ltd (The Berge Sisar)* [2001] 1 A.C. 205 at [5], [38].
[12] Above, para.18–123.
[13] *Borealis AB v Stargas Ltd (The Berge Sisar)* above, n.11 at [33]. *Cf. Primetrade AG v Ythan Ltd (The Ythan)* [2005] EWHC 2399 (Comm.), [2006] 1 All E.R. 367 at [98]–[104]: a request for security for a cargo claim made by an agent of the still unnamed cargo owner who had not yet become "holder" of the bill *held* not to amount to the making of a claim by that owner. For the assumption made in this part of the judgment (that the cargo owner later become the "holder" of the bill) see above, para.18–126 n.90.
[14] *The Berge Sisar*, above n.11, at [33].
[15] *ibid.*, at [35]; see above para.18–102, below, para.18–131.
[16] For a similar problem under s.3(1)(a), see above, para.18–126.
[17] See *Greater Nottingham Co-operative Society Ltd v Cementation Piling & Foundations Ltd* [1989] Q.B. 71; *Red Sea Tankers Ltd v Papachristides (The Hellespont Ardent)* [1997] 2 Lloyd's Rep. 547; the qualification of this principle in *Henderson v Merrett Syndicates Ltd* [1994] 2 A.C. 145 would not, it is submitted, apply in the present context: see *ibid.*, p.194; below, para.18–151 at n.2.

Questions as to the identity of "the carrier" can arise under section 3(1)(b) (no less than under section 3(1)(a)) where goods are carried in a chartered ship[18]. Where the contract of carriage is between shipper and charterer but a claim is made by the transferee of the bill against the shipowner, that claim will not be "under the contract of carriage" since there is no contract between these parties. Even where there is a contractual relationship between them, it will not always be clear whether the claim is made "under" that contract. This difficulty may be illustrated by reference to the facts of *Sewell v Burdick*[19] where goods were shipped to Russia and the bill of lading was transferred by way of security to a bank in circumstances that would now make the bank the "lawful holder" of the bill and vest contractual rights in it.[20] The goods were sold by the Russian authorities at the destination to pay customs duties and other charges and the bank made a claim, not for delivery of the goods, but for payment to it of part of the proceeds of sale, *i.e.* of the amount by which these exceeded the freight due to the carrier. The sale, however, yielded no more than was due to the Russian authorities for their charges, and the carrier brought an action against the bank for the freight due on the bill of lading. The actual decision was that the bank was not liable for the freight as "the" (general) property in the goods had not passed to it. This result was generally approved on the ground that it would be commercially inconvenient to make banks liable on bills of lading where those bills had been transferred to them merely by way of security; and it was certainly not an object of the 1992 Act to reverse that result: indeed, to do so was said to be "commercially undesirable."[21] The actual reasoning of the case is obsolete now that the 1992 Act has closed the "property gap" in section 1 of the Bills of Lading Act 1855 and has broken the former link between the transfer of rights and the imposition of liabilities. The question that would now arise, on similar facts,[22] is whether the banks' claim for the proceeds of the sale would be a "claim under the contract of carriage" within section 3(1)(b). On the one hand, it can be argued that no such claim would have come into existence if no contract of carriage had been made, for it was only under this contract that the carrier had dealt with the goods in such a way as to provide any basis for a claim by the bank; and that the claim would therefore fall within section 3(1)(b). On the other hand, so to regard the bank's claim would to a considerable extent defeat the legislative policy of preserving the result in *Sewell v Burdick*,[23] and this is a point on which the courts would be justified in taking the legislative history of the Act into account when interpreting the provision here under consideration.

---

[18] *cf.* above, para.18–127.
[19] (1884) 10 App.Cas. 74.
[20] At the time when *Sewell v Burdick*, above, was decided, no rights were acquired under the bill of lading by the bank, since the case fell into the "property gap" of the scheme created by the Bills of Lading Act 1855, above, para.18–100.
[21] Law Com. No. 186, Scot. Law Com. No. 130, para.3.3 (1991).
[22] A fact that might cause some additional complications under the 1992 Act was that the bank had indorsed the bill to their agent at the port of discharge, with instructions to protect their interests.
[23] Above, at n.21.

18–130 **Claims under section 2(4).** Where this subsection applies,[24] it enables A, the holder of a bill of lading who has acquired rights by virtue of section 2(1), to make a claim under the contract of carriage for the benefit of another person, B, who has suffered loss in consequence of a breach of the contract of carriage. The liability which can arise under section 3(1)(b) from A's making such a claim will be imposed on him and not on B. It is however open to A to avoid this apparently incongruous result. Section 2(4) does not oblige him to exercise his rights under section 2(1) for the benefit of B so that, on being requested by B so to exercise those rights, A can make it a condition of so doing that B will indemnify him against any liability which A may in consequence of such exercise incur under the contract of carriage.

18–131 **Holder of spent bill.** Just as contractual rights can be vested in a person who has become the holder of a "spent" bill,[25] so the holder of such a bill can incur liabilities under the contract of carriage. Section 3(1)(c) provides that such liabilities can be incurred by the holder (subject to the overriding requirement[26] of his having had contractual rights vested in him by virtue of section 2(1)), if he was "a person who, at a time before those rights were vested in him, took or demanded delivery from the carrier of any of those goods" (*i.e.* the goods covered by the bill). This provision will typically apply where there is some delay in the transmission of the bill so that it is not available when the carrying ship reaches the contractual destination and the goods are there delivered (usually against a letter of indemnity) to the person who later becomes the ultimate holder of the bill.[27] Such a case falls within the words "took . . . delivery" but section 3(1)(c) also applies where a person who later became holder of the bill "demanded delivery". Since that person cannot, before becoming holder of the bill, have acquired contractual rights under the bill by virtue of section 2(1), "demand" in section 3(1)(c) cannot be used in the same sense as that in which it is used in section 3(1)(a), *i.e.* to refer to the assertion of "the contractual right as endorsee of the bill of lading to have the carrier deliver the goods to him."[28] A person who has not yet got possession of the bill has *no* such right,[29] so that the carrier is entitled to reject his demand for delivery and "a rightly rejected demand for delivery by one who is not entitled to delivery is an act devoid of legal significance".[30] Hence it is unlikely that section 3(1)(c) will apply where there has been no actual delivery[31]; effect could be given to the words "or demanded" only by arguing that they did not here have the same meaning as in section 3(1)(a) but referred to a demand having some legal basis other than the contract of carriage, for

[24] Above, paras 18–119 *et seq.*
[25] Above, para.18–113.
[26] Above, para.18–125.
[27] As, for example, in *Enichem Anic SpA v Ampelos Shipping Co. Ltd (The Delfini)* [1990] 1 Lloyd's Rep. 252.
[28] *Borealis AB v Stargas Ltd (The Berge Sisar)* [2001] UKHL 17, [2002] 2 A.C. 205 at [33], above, para.18–126.
[29] See Carriage of Goods by Sea Act 1992, s.5(2).
[30] *The Berge Sisar*, above, n.28, at [35]; above, para.18–126.
[31] *The Berge Sisar*, above n.28, at [35].

example to a demand based on the ownership of the goods. Even if this argument were accepted, a person would not, by merely "co-operating [with the carrier] in discharge of the vessel",[32] have demanded (any more than he would by such acts have taken[33]) delivery. In *The Berge Sisar*[34] buyers of propane directed the carrying ship to their import jetty, took routine samples which showed the cargo to have been contaminated and therefore refused to allow the cargo to be discharged into their terminal. This conduct was held to "fall a long way short of amounting to any demand"[35] for delivery so that no liability was incurred by the buyers by virtue of section 3(1)(c) even though the bills of lading were transferred to them (after the goods had been discharged at another port) so as to vest rights under the contract of carriage in them by virtue of section 2(1).

Liability is incurred under section 3(1)(c) only where the holder of a "spent" bill "took or demanded delivery" of the goods covered by the bill. There is nothing in section 3(1)(c) which corresponds to section 3(1)(b) under which liabilities are imposed on a holder who "makes a claim under the contract of carriage".[36] The reason for this difference between paragraphs (b) and (c) may be that, *before* contractual rights were vested in the person who later became holder of the bill, that person could not in law make "a claim under the contract of carriage".[37] There is, indeed, the practical possibility that a buyer at the end of a string of sales might know that the goods had been lost, destroyed or mis-delivered in consequence of the carrier's breach. That buyer might make a formal claim under the contract of carriage against the carrier before the bill had come into his hands and then become the holder of it so as to acquire contractual rights under it by virtue of section 2(1). Such a case would not appear to fall within section 3(1)(c).

Liability of intermediate transferee. A person may acquire contractual rights and incur contractual liabilities under a bill of lading by virtue of becoming the lawful holder of it[38] and (for example) demanding delivery of the goods[39]; and he may then, before taking delivery, make a further transfer of the bill (*e.g.* to his sub-buyer) and so lose the contractual rights previously vested in him. Under the Bills of Lading Act 1855, it had been held to be "clearly repugnant to one's notions of justice"[40] that an intermediate transferee should remain liable under the bill after he had, on the further transfer, lost his contractual rights under it, and that it was only "the assignee who receives the cargo"[41] who was or remained liable under 18–132

[32] *ibid.*, at [36].
[33] Above, para.18–126.
[34] Above, n.28; Treitel [2001] L.M.C.L.Q. 344.
[35] *The Berge Sisar*, above, n.28, at [38].
[36] Above, para.18–129.
[37] See above, para.18–129 at n.14.
[38] Carriage of Goods by Sea Act 1992, s.2(1)(a).
[39] *ibid.*, s.3(1)(a).
[40] *Smurthwaite v Wilkins* (1862) 11 C.B. (N.S.) 842 at p.849; the argument was stronger under the 1855 Act than it is under the 1992 Act since under the former Act liabilities were incurred automatically on the acquisition of rights, without the need for any further acts on the part of the transferee.
[41] *Smurthwaite v Wilkins*, above, at p.848.

the bill. In *The Berge Sisar*[42] the actual decision was that the intermediate transferee had never incurred liability under the bill[43]; but it was further held that the mere fact that such a transferee has at some stage incurred liability (*e.g.* by demanding delivery) does not leave him with that liability after he has made a further transfer of the bill[44] and so lost the rights previously vested in him by virtue of the transfer to him.[45] It is submitted that this position causes no injustice to the carrier who will have rights under the contract of carriage against the ultimate transferee who takes delivery of the goods[46] and against the original shipper.[47] The intermediate transferee would also no longer be "the person in whom rights *are vested*"[48] by virtue of section 2(1). The present tense ("are vested") suggests that a person is liable only if those rights are *still* vested when he takes or demands delivery or makes a claim under the contract of carriage.

18–133 **Extent of liability.** Section 3(1) provides that, where the conditions specified in the subsection are satisfied, the person who has acquired rights by virtue of section 2(1) "shall" . . . become subject to the same liabilities under . . . [the contract of carriage[49]] as if he had been a party to that contract." Under this subsection, the transferee is treated as if he had been a party to the contract of carriage and incurs all liabilities which would on that assumption have rested on him: for example, liability for freight, for demurrage at either end of the transit, and for loss or damage suffered by the carrier by reason of the fact that the goods were dangerous when shipped.[50] The justification for imposing such extensive liabilities on the transferee is that he is no longer liable *merely* by virtue of having acquired rights under the contract. He is liable only if he takes active steps to enforce or to obtain the benefit of the contract[51]; and these requirements have been strictly interpreted against the carrier.[52] In making the holder liable "as if he had been a party to" the original contract of carriage, section 3(1) gives rise to problems (similar to those discussed in relation to section 2(1)[53]

[42] *Borealis AB v Stargas Ltd (The Berge Sisar)* [2001] UKHL 17, [2001] 2 A.C. 205.
[43] Above, para.18–131.
[44] *The Berge Sisar*, above n.42, at [45]. Other circumstances could lead to a different result: *e.g.* the fact that the conduct by virtue of which liability had been incurred was "irreversible" (such as taking actual delivery of the goods from the carrier): see the decision of the majority of the Court of Appeal in *The Berge Sisar* [1999] Q.B. 863 at pp.884–885; Reynolds [1999] L.M.C.L.Q. 161.
[45] Carriage of Goods by Sea Act 1992, s.2(5).
[46] *ibid.*, s.3(1)(a).
[47] *ibid.*, s.3(3).
[48] *ibid.*, s.3(1).
[49] ". . . that contract" in the "tailpiece" of s.3(1) refers back to "the contract of carriage" in s.3(1)(b).
[50] See Law Com. No. 196, Scot. Law Com. No. 130, paras 3.22, 7.20 (1991). Thus on the facts of *Brandt v Liverpool, etc., Steam Navigation Co. Ltd* [1924] 1 K.B. 575 the claimants would now be liable under s.3(1) in respect of any loss which may have been suffered by the carrier in consequence of the shipper's breach in shipping the goods in such a state that some of them had to be unloaded.
[51] *i.e.* taking or demanding delivery or making a claim under the contract of carriage.
[52] See above, paras 18–123, 18–126, 18–129 and 18–131.
[53] Above, para.18–106.

which arise where extrinsic terms, not incorporated in the bill of lading, may have been agreed between shipper and carrier. These would not govern the liabilities of the holder, whether their effect was to increase or to reduce the liability of the shipper.[54] Conversely, extrinsic terms agreed between carrier and holder could no doubt prevail over the terms of the bill, whether by way of variation or of waiver or by way of promissory estoppel.

Liabilities of original contracting parties. At common law, an original shipper[55] remained liable on the bill of lading contract even though another person, such as the holder of a bill of lading, also became liable under a new implied contract of the type to be discussed in paragraphs 18–138 to 18–144 below.[56] Section 3(3) of the 1992 Act confirms the common law position by providing that "this section, so far as it imposes liabilities under any contract on any person, shall be without prejudice to the liabilities under the contract of any person as an original party to the contract" (*i.e.* the contract contained in or evidenced by the bill of lading[57]). Section 3 thus preserves the liabilities of the original shipper under the contract of carriage. It is capable of referring also to the liabilities of the carrier, but such liabilities to the original shipper, or to any intermediate transferees, will be extinguished on the transfer by such persons of the bill of lading to the ultimate transferee.[58] 18–134

(viii) *Destroyed and Unascertained Goods*

Carriage of Goods by Sea Act 1992, section 5(4). This subsection provides that "[w]ithout prejudice to sections 2(2) and 4 above, nothing in this Act shall preclude its operation in relation to a case where the goods to which a document relates—(a) cease to exist after the issue of the document; or (b) cannot be identified (whether because they are mixed with other goods or for any other reason); and references in this Act to the goods to which a document relates shall be construed accordingly." 18–135

Goods which cease to exist. Section 5(4)(a) refers to goods "which cease to exist *after* the issue of the document". It seems to follow that, in general, no rights can be acquired (or liabilities imposed) by virtue of the 1992 Act in respect of goods which have already ceased to exist *before* the issue of 18–136

[54] *cf.* above, paras 18–048, 18–106.
[55] It is here assumed that the original shipper has made the contract of carriage as principal and not as agent for the transferee of the bill. This would normally be the position where the relationship between these parties was that of seller and buyer of the goods covered by the bill: see above; para.18–097, n.33.
[56] This position was preserved under the Bills of Lading Act 1855: see *Fox v Nott* (1861) 6 H. & N. 630; *The Athenasia Comninos and George Chr. Lemos* [1990] 1 Lloyd's Rep. 277 at p.281; *Effort Shipping Co. Ltd v Linden Management SA (The Giannis NK)* [1998] A.C. 605.
[57] "The contract" in s.3(3) clearly refers back to "the contract of carriage" in s.3(1) and (2).
[58] s.2(5).

the document: *e.g.* where a ship's delivery order[59] or a bill of lading[60] was issued in respect of goods after they had been washed overboard and in ignorance of this fact. There is, however, nothing in section 5(4) to prevent the carrier from being liable in such cases at common law: for example, where a ship's delivery order was issued by a carrier in favour of a third party after the goods covered by the order had already been lost as a result of the carrier's breach of the contract of carriage between carrier and shipper.[61]

It is submitted that the words "cease to exist" in section 5(4) should not be restricted to cases in which the goods have suffered total physical annihilation (if such a thing is possible). Goods should be regarded as having "ceased to exist" when they have ceased permanently to be available for the purpose of the performance of the contract. Analogies taken from the common law doctrine of frustration,[62] the doctrine of constructive total loss in insurance law[63] and the interpretation of the word "perished" in sections 6 and 7 of the Sale of Goods Act 1979[64] all support this view. Some of these analogies also suggest that goods should be regarded as having "ceased to exist" if they have been stolen[65] and cannot be traced or recovered by their true owner.

Section 5(4) is expressed to operate "without prejudice to sections 2(2) and 4 above." It is clear that section 4 can apply even though the goods have "ceased to exist" *before* the issue of the document: *e.g.* where they were stolen before or during shipment.[66] To exclude cases of antecedent destruction or theft from section 4 would partly defeat the purpose of that section, which was designed to deal with *inter alia* cases of this kind. The purpose of the reference in section 5(4) to section 2(2) is at first sight less clear. The main object of section 2(2) was to enable a person, in the circumstances specified in the subsection,[67] to acquire rights of suit under the contract of carriage even though he became the "holder" of the bill of lading after it was "spent", typically by delivery of the goods to a person entitled to their delivery.[68] In cases of such delivery, the goods cannot have "ceased to exist" after the bill was issued and before the contract of carriage was discharged by performance. But section 2(2) can also apply where the goods are not delivered to anyone but are simply destroyed, *e.g.*

---

[59] Below, para.18–175 *et seq.*

[60] The bill of lading may not be issued until after the ship has sailed; see above, para.18–047 n.65.

[61] Above, para.18–041.

[62] See Treitel, *Frustration and Force Majeure*, 2nd ed. (2004) paras 3–005, 3–006.

[63] See *Moss v Smith* (1850) 9 C.B. 94 at p.103.

[64] Above, paras 1–126 to 1–128, 6–035; Treitel, *Frustration and Force Majeure*, 2nd ed. (2004) para.3–016.

[65] *Barrow Lane & Ballard v Phillips & Co. Ltd* [1929] 1 K.B. 574.

[66] As in *V/O Rasnoimport v Guthrie & Co. Ltd* [1966] 1 Lloyd's Rep. 1.

[67] See below, para.18–113.

[68] Law Commissions' Report on *Rights of Suit in Respect of Carriage of Goods by Sea,* Law Com. 196, Scot. Law Com. 130 (1991), paras 2.42–2.44, 7.3. For the possibility of a bill's becoming "spent" in other ways, *e.g.* by frustration, see above, para.18–082.

where the ship on which they are being carried sinks[69]; and one consequence of the reference in section 5(4) to section 2(2) is that nothing in section 5(4) restricts the right of a holder, in cases of such destruction, to invoke section 2(2) and so, in the circumstances specified by it, to acquire rights under the contract of carriage.[70] In particular, section 5(4)(a) applies only where goods cease to exist "*after* the issue of the" bill of lading but this restriction does not apply where the holder has a claim under the contract of carriage by virtue of section 2(2). Bills of lading may not be issued until after the ship has sailed[71] and the goods may be destroyed after the ship has sailed but before the bill is issued by a carrier who, when he issued the bill, was unaware of the destruction of the goods.

Goods which "cannot be identified". Under this part of section 5(4) rights can be acquired and liabilities imposed by virtue of the Act in respect of goods which form an undifferentiated part of an identified bulk cargo. 18–137

Such goods must be divided into two categories. The first consists of goods which are described as forming a fraction or percentage of an identified bulk. For the purposes of the Sale of Goods Act 1979, such goods can fall within the definition of "specific goods"[72] and where this is the case it can be argued that they *can* be identified, so that it is not necessary to have recourse to section 5(4) to bring them within the 1992 Act. The second category consists of goods which form a specified quantity out of a bulk which has been identified either in the contract or by subsequent agreement between the parties. A buyer of goods in the second category can acquire ownership in common of such a bulk,[73] but he can do so, not because the goods are regarded as ascertained, but in spite of the fact that the goods are unascertained.[74] Such goods are therefore goods which "cannot be identified" and the 1992 Act can apply to them by virtue of section 5(4). The subsection cannot, however, apply to goods which "cannot be identified" simply because they are purely generic goods, for the assumption on which it is based is that the goods are goods to which a document (to which the Act applies) "relates"; and this requirement can be satisfied only if the document indicates the receipt or shipment of the goods in question and so takes them out of the category of purely generic goods.

Of the documents covered by the 1992 Act, those most commonly issued in respect of goods which are unidentified because they form specified

---

[69] As in *Primetrade AG v Ythan Ltd* (*The Ythan)* [2005] EWHC 2399 (Comm.), [2006] 1 All E.R. 367. See also the Draft Bill attached to the Report cited in n.68 above, Explanatory Notes to Clause 2, subsection (2) and to Clause 5, subsection (4). These subsections were enacted as ss.2(2) and 5(4) of the Carriage of Goods by Sea Act 1992. If the sinking of the ship were or resulted from a frustrating event, then the contract of carriage would be discharged with effect from the time of the casualty; but the holder of the bill of lading might (subject to the Law Reform (Frustrated Contracts) Act 1943) retain an interest in asserting rights which had accrued before that time.

[70] See *Primetrade AG v Ythan Ltd (The Ythan)* [2005] EWHC 2399 (Comm.), [2006] 1 All E.R. 367 at [69].

[71] See above, para.18–047 at n.65.

[72] Sale of Goods Act 1979, s.61(1), definition of "specific goods".

[73] Sale of Goods Act 1979, s.20A(2).

[74] See *ibid.*, s.20A(1) ("quantity of unascertained goods").

quantities out of bulk cargoes[75] are ship's delivery orders; and the transfer of contractual rights by the use of such orders in cases of this kind will be discussed in paragraphs 18–175 to 18–188 below. The reference in section 5(4) to "goods which cannot be identified" could also apply to goods covered by bills of lading: *e.g.* where ten bills of lading, each covering 1000 tons, are issued in respect of a bulk shipment of 10,000 tons. The provisions of the Act which limit the rights and liabilities of a person to whom part of a bulk cargo is to be delivered under a ship's delivery order[76] do not apply to this situation; but it does not follow that the holder of one of the bills of lading would be entitled or liable in respect of the whole shipment. The holder is (assuming the other requirements of sections 2(1) and 3(1) to be satisfied) entitled and liable "as if he had been a party to that contract,"[77] and "that contract" in this context refers to the contract contained in or evidenced by the bill of lading of which he has become the lawful holder. Thus in our example the holder can acquire rights and be subject to liabilities only in respect of the 1,000 tons covered by the bill of which he had become holder.

(ix) *Other Techniques for the Acquisition of Contractual Rights and Imposition of Contractual Liabilities*

18–138 **Implied contract.** Neither the Bills of Lading Act 1855 nor the Carriage of Goods by Sea Act 1992 has abolished the common law rule by which a new contract might arise as a result of a request for delivery of the goods made to the carrier, and complied with by him, against presentation of the bill of lading.[78] The 1992 Act will in practice make recourse to the implied contract device less frequent since this Act has greatly increased the range of cases in which holders of bills of lading and persons to whom delivery is to be made under sea waybills or ship's delivery orders can become entitled, and liable, under a contract of carriage to which they are not original parties. In particular, the implied contract device will no longer be needed in cases which fell within the "property gap" of the 1855 Act,[79] now that that gap has been closed by the 1992 Act. But it is still possible for situations to arise, to which the 1992 Act will not extend: for example, delivery may be taken by a buyer under a letter of indemnity,[80] or under a delivery order other than a ship's delivery order as defined by that Act,[81] no other carriage document being transferred to him or identifying him as the person to whom delivery is to be made; goods may be sold after a bill of lading has become "spent"[82] and the bill may then be transferred to, and

[75] Sales of fractions or percentages of cargoes do not, if the reported cases are any guide, seem to be common.
[76] ss.2(3), 3(2).
[77] ss.2(1) "tailpiece," 3(1) "tailpiece."
[78] Above, para.18–099.
[79] Above, para.18–100.
[80] As in *Compania Portorafti Commerciale SA v Ultramar Panama Inc. (The Captain Gregos) (No. 2)* [1990] 2 Lloyd's Rep. 395, below, para.18–142.
[81] Below, para.18–176 *et seq.*
[82] So that the case would not be covered by Carriage of Goods by Sea Act 1992, s.2(2), above, para.18–113.

delivery of the goods be claimed by, the buyer; the goods may be delivered to a buyer against a bill of lading which has not been indorsed, or properly indorsed, to him[83]; or such delivery may be made against a bill of lading which is governed by a system of law in which the transferee would not, by virtue of the transfer, be entitled under, or bound by, the bill of lading contract, and the alleged implied contract may be governed by English law. The circumstances in which the implied contract can arise therefore still require discussion, even though many of the authorities on which that discussion is based would, now that the "property gap" has been closed,[84] be differently decided, or decided in the same way but on different grounds.

Delivery of goods against bill of lading. The implied contract most obviously arises where the carrier delivers the goods to the person presenting the bill of lading, in exchange for the bill and for payment of freight or other charges. This was the position in *Brandt v Liverpool, etc. Steam Navigation Co.*,[85] the leading case from which this type of implied contract takes its name. In that case a person to whom goods had been consigned as pledgee presented the bill of lading, paid the freight and took delivery of the goods. Because of the "property gap" in the Bills of Lading Act 1855, no contractual rights under the bill of lading contract were transferred to the pledgee, but it was held that he was entitled to recover damages from the carrier (in respect of damage to the goods) for breach of the new contract which arose on receipt of the goods and payment of freight. Now that the "property gap" has been closed by the Carriage of Goods by Sea Act 1992, the pledgee would on such facts acquire rights under the contract of carriage by virtue of section 2(1) of that Act; but this would not be the case where the bill named another person as consignee and had not been indorsed to the person presenting it to the carrier: *e.g.* where delivery was made to a buyer on presentation of a bill naming the buyer's bank as consignee.[86] The implied contract can not only confer rights, but also impose liabilities, on the person to whom delivery is made: for example, it can make him liable for freight and (where appropriate) demurrage in accordance with the terms of the bill of lading. It can also benefit the carrier in other ways: *e.g.* by giving him the protection of exceptions from and limitations of liability contained in the bill of lading. The implied contract can, moreover, have retrospective effect in that it can include terms of the bill of lading contract which refer to acts done before 18–139

---

[83] See below at n.86.

[84] See para.18–101 above.

[85] [1924] 1 K.B. 575; *cf. R & W Paul Ltd v National SS Co. Ltd* (1937) 59 Ll.L.R. 28; *The Subro Valour* [1995] 1 Lloyd's Rep. 509 at p.519; contrast *Mitsui & Co. Ltd v Flota Mercante Grancolombiana SA (The Ciudad de Pasto and the Ciudad de Neiva)* [1988] 1 W.L.R. 1145, where no implied contract arose as there was no evidence of the circumstances in which delivery from the ship was obtained by the buyer. Where such an implied contract arises, the transferee of the bill has the benefit of the estoppels described in para.18–028, above even though the transfer does not vest contractual rights in him under the legislation governing the contractual effects of such transfers: see *Brandt's* case, above, at p.596.

[86] As in *Compania Continental del Peru v Evelpis Shipping Corp. (The Agia Skepi)* [1992] 2 Lloyd's Rep. 467.

the "new contract" was formed: *e.g.* in *Brandt's* case it made the carrier liable for delays arising at the point of shipment. In the court's view, this retrospective operation of the implied contract was in accordance with the intention of the parties: just as the carrier would want the protection of the bill in respect of acts done before the formation of the new contract, so he should be bound by the stipulations of the bill in respect of such acts. We shall see that the intention of the parties can also limit the retrospective operation of the new contract.[87]

It is an essential feature of the implied contract that the carrier must have delivered (or been asked to deliver) *the goods* to the other party to the alleged contract. In *Sewell v Burdick*[88] the goods had been sold and it was held that the bank did not become liable for freight under an implied contract merely by claiming to be entitled, as a pledgee, to the *proceeds of sale*.[89] *A fortiori* there will be no implied contract where no delivery is claimed by, or made to, the holder of a bill of lading to whom rights had not been transferred by virtue of the transfer of the bill. Thus where delivery was made against a letter of indemnity to a buyer no implied contract arose between the carrier and *the seller* to whom the bill of lading had been transferred by an earlier seller in the chain.[90]

A buyer who has a claim against the carrier for short delivery or for nondelivery under an implied contract of the present kind is entitled, as against the carrier, to the full value of the goods even though he may in part have been compensated by the seller for this loss.[91]

18–140 **Presentation of documents other than bill of lading.** One of the circumstances that gave rise to the implied contract in *Brandt v Liverpool, etc. Steam Navigation Co.*[92] was the presentation of the bill of lading; but this is not an essential requirement of such a contract. Thus an implied contract on bill of lading terms can arise where a buyer who cannot present the bill of lading when claiming the goods (*e.g.* because the bill is still in the hands of his bank) instead obtains delivery by giving the carrier a guarantee that the bill of lading will be presented: this is sufficient to indicate that the delivery of the goods is to be on the terms of the bill of lading.[93] The position is the same where the buyer obtains delivery on presentation to the carrier of a ship's delivery order, which (even though it may not be such an order within the 1992 Act[94]) refers to the bill of lading.[95]

---

[87] Below, para.18–143 at n.19.
[88] (1884) 10 App.Cas. 74; above, para.18–129.
[89] A similar point can arise under Carriage of Goods by Sea Act 1992, s.3(1): see above, para.18–129.
[90] *Compania Portorafti Commerciale SA v Ultramar Panama Inc. (The Captain Gregos) (No. 2)* [1990] 2 Lloyd's Rep. 295 at p.403 (so far as it relates to PEAG's claim).
[91] *The Aramis* [1989] 1 Lloyd's Rep. 213 at p.226, following *Paul v National S.S. Co. Ltd* (1937) 59 Ll.L.R. 28.
[92] [1924] 1 K.B. 575.
[93] *Ilyssia Compania Naviera SA v Ahmed Abdul-Qawi Bamaodah (The Elli 2)* [1985] 1 Lloyd's Rep. 107.
[94] See the discussion of *Peter Cremer GmbH v General Carriers SA (The Donna Mari)* [1974] 1 W.L.R. 341, in para.18–183, below.
[95] As in the *Cremer* case above; below, para.18–174.

Consideration. Consideration for the respective promises constituting the implied contract gives rise, in the normal case, to little difficulty: the consideration for the carrier's promise would be the payment of freight or other charges, while the consideration for the other party's promise would be the delivery of the goods or the release of the carrier's lien.[96] The fact that the carrier was already bound by his contract with a third party (*i.e.* the shipper) to make the delivery would not prevent such delivery from constituting consideration for the other party's promise.[97] Payment of freight is not, however, necessary to constitute consideration for the carrier's promise: thus the implied contract can arise even where freight has been prepaid, so long as consideration for the carrier's undertakings is provided in some other way, *e.g.* by the buyer's making some other payment (such as demurrage) or by promising to do so.[98] A further possibility is to say that, as the implied contract incorporates by reference at least some[99] of the terms of the bill of lading, the requirement of consideration is satisfied because under these terms each party makes promises to the other. These mutual promises can constitute consideration[1] so long as at the time of the conclusion of the implied contract at least one of them on each side remains unperformed. It is, finally, arguable that the cargo-owner can provide consideration in that, by claiming delivery, he gives the carrier the opportunity of performing his contract with the shipper and so of being discharged from liability under that contract.[2] **18–141**

Contractual intention. The fact that no payment at all is made or to be made by the person presenting the bill of lading may lead the court to infer that there was no contractual intention and hence no implied contract.[3] This was held to be the position in *The Aramis*,[4] where bills of lading were presented to the ship, and delivery of the goods was requested, on behalf of two buyers of goods to whom the bills had been transferred, but who had acquired no contractual rights against the carrier by virtue of the transfer.[5] Freight had been prepaid and no other sum remained payable or was paid **18–142**

---

[96] *Scotson v Pegg* (1861) 6 H. & N. 295.

[97] *New Zealand Shipping Co. Ltd v AM Satterthwaite & Co. Ltd (The Eurymedon)* [1975] A.C. 154. Insofar as a dictum in *Halifax BS v Edell* [1992] Ch.436 at p.454 suggests the contrary, it cannot be reconciled with the now generally accepted view that performance of a contractual duty owed to a third party can constitute consideration.

[98] *The Elli 2*, above n.93, at p.115.

[99] As noted above in para.18–127, the implied contract may retrospectively incorporate some bill of lading terms, but it does not incorporate them all: see *The Athenasia Comninos and George Chr. Lemnos* (1979) [1990] 1 Lloyd's Rep. 277, below, para.18–143 at n.19.

[1] See *The Aramis* [1989] 1 Lloyd's Rep. 213 at p.225 ("bundle of rights and duties which the parties would respectively obtain and accept").

[2] On a principle analogous to that of such cases as *Charnock v Liverpool Corporation* [1968] 1 W.L.R. 1498.

[3] *Kaukomarkkinat O/Y v Elbe Transport-Union GmbH (The Kelo)* [1985] 2 Lloyd's Rep. 85 at p.88.

[4] [1989] 1 Lloyd's Rep. 213; Treitel [1989] L.M.C.L.Q. 162.

[5] Because of the "property gap" in the Bills of Lading Act 1855 (above, para.18–100).

by the buyers in respect of the cargo; one of them received only a small proportion of the goods; no delivery at all was made to the other. It was held that no contract could be implied since the conduct of the parties was readily explicable on the ground that they were respectively seeking, or agreeing to render, performance of an earlier contract (*i.e.* that between shipper and carrier) which obliged the carrier to deliver the goods to the holders of the bills. Accordingly, that conduct did not give rise to the inference that the buyers were intending to make an offer to enter into a *new* contract, or that the carrier had intended to accept such an offer. Similar objections could, however, be levelled at other applications of the implied contract as a legal device, which has sometimes been used to good effect in situations which (for similar reasons to those given in *The Aramis*) cannot be explained in terms of a strict or schematic analysis of offer, acceptance and contractual intention.[6] In *The Aramis* the Court of Appeal seemed to recognise that its decision had led to a commercially inconvenient result[7]; and on similar facts that result would now probably be reversed in the sense that the buyers would acquire rights under the contract of carriage by virtue of section 2(1) of the Carriage of Goods by Sea Act 1992.[8] But inconvenience similar to that described in *The Aramis* could still arise in a situation not covered by the Act: *e.g.* where the bill had not come into the possession of the buyer or where it lacked a requisite indorsement.

In *The Captain Gregos (No. 2)*[9] the carrier delivered the goods under a letter of indemnity to a buyer to whom property had passed before delivery but to whom the bills of lading were never transferred at all. It was held that an implied contract had arisen between the carrier and the buyer, so that the carrier was protected by the terms of the bill of lading. *The Aramis* was distinguished[10] on the grounds that the buyer in *The Captain Gregos (No. 2)* was already owner at the time of discharge and that he had consented to carriage on the bill of lading terms. Perhaps the facts that the buyer did not present a bill of lading, and that the letter of indemnity emanated from an affiliate of the seller, can also be regarded as significant in relation to the issue of contractual intention: these facts would support the argument that in delivering the goods to the buyer the carrier was not merely intending to perform a pre-existing contractual obligation owed under the bill to the shipper, to deliver the goods to the buyer.

On the other hand, the mere fact that the arrangements between carrier and bill of lading holder do go beyond the obligations imposed by the bill

---

[6] *e.g. The Satanita* [1895] P. 248, affirmed, *sub nom. Clarke v Dunraven* [1897] A.C. 59; *Pyrene Co. Ltd v Scindia Navigation Co. Ltd* [1954] 2 Q.B. 402; *New Zealand Shipping Co. Ltd v AM Satterthwaite & Co. Ltd (The Eurymedon)* [1975] A.C. 154.

[7] See [1989] 1 Lloyd's Rep. 213 at p.225 (recognising "the good sense and commercial convenience" of the decision of Evans J. at first instance, which was reversed on appeal).

[8] The point is not entirely clear since any rights which might now be acquired by the buyers by virtue of s.2(1) might also be lost under s.2(5) by reason of the further indorsement by their agents referred to on pp.216–217 of the report; the purpose of this indorsement is far from clear. It should also be noted that the bills were in the hands, not of the buyers, but of their agents: *cf.* above, para.18–104.

[9] [1990] 2 Lloyd's Rep. 395 (so far as it relates to BP's claim).

[10] *ibid.*, p.403.

of lading will not of itself suffice to give rise to an implied contract. This appears from *The Gudermes*[11] where it had become necessary for a cargo of oil to be transhipped before it could be unloaded since the vessel on which the oil had originally been shipped lacked facilities for heating it. The owners of the cargo claimed the cost of the trans-shipment under an implied contract but their claim was rejected since the alleged implication was one of fact[12] and could succeed only if what the parties had done was "consistent only with there being a new contract and inconsistent with there being no such contract".[13] This very strict test had not been satisfied since the alleged implied contract was on the terms, not merely of the bill of lading, but also of the arrangement relating to trans-shipment; and when this arrangement was made the shipowners had expressly refused to bear the expenses of that operation. The bill of lading in this case had been indorsed to the claimants[14] so that prima facie they would now have rights of suit under the bill of lading transferred to them by virtue of section 2(1)(a) of the Carriage of Goods by Sea Act 1992. But it is not obvious that this would enable them to recover the costs of the trans-shipment since this operation appears to have been carried out, not under the bill of lading, but under a subsequent agreement between the claimants and the shipowner. The alleged resulting "hybrid"[15] contract, which was on the terms partly of the bill of lading and partly of the subsequent arrangement, would not appear to be "the contract of carriage"[16] within section 2(1), so that the claim would still have to be based on an implied contract, and would presumably fail for want of contractual intention. Perhaps this difficulty could be overcome by arguing that the ship was unseaworthy or that the shipowner had failed properly to care for the cargo and that the cargo owners' claim was therefore based exclusively on breach[17] of the bill of lading contract. It would be irrelevant for the purpose of this argument that the shippers had agreed with the carriers that the cargo did not require to be heated; for such an extrinsic term would not bind an indorsee of the bill of lading who had no notice of the term.[18]

Scope of the implied contract. Even where it is clear that some implied contract has arisen, the requirement of contractual intention may limit the scope of that contract. Thus there is authority for the view that the person presenting the bill of lading and claiming delivery would not, under the implied contract, incur any liability which might have rested on the shipper 18–143

[11] *Mitsui & Co. v Novorossiysk Shipping Co. (The Gudermes)* [1993] 1 Lloyd's Rep. 311.
[12] *ibid.*, p.318.
[13] *ibid.*, p.320; *Eridiana SpA v Rudolf A. Oetker (The Fjord Wind)* [1999] 1 Lloyd's Rep. 307 at p.336, affirmed without reference to this point [2000] 2 Lloyd's Rep. 191.
[14] But the indorsement did not transfer contractual rights under Bills of Lading Act 1855, s.1 because of the "property gap" in that legislation (above, para.18–100).
[15] [1993] 1 Lloyd's Rep. 311 at 321.
[16] See the definition in Carriage of Goods by Sea Act 1992, s.5(1).
[17] *i.e.* under Art. III.1 and 2 of the Hague-Visby Rules, to which the bill of lading was expressed to be subject.
[18] Above, para.18–048.

by reason of his having shipped dangerous goods.[19] This restriction on the scope of the implied contract has been justified on the ground that the intention of the parties is assumed to be that the obligations created by the implied contract should extend only to "those rights and obligations which concern the carriage and delivery of the goods and payment therefor".[20]

18–144 **Delivery taken as agent for another.** A further limitation on the principle of *Brandt v Liverpool, etc., Steam Navigation Co.* is that receipt of the goods on presentation of the bill of lading will not give rise to an inference of a new contract between the carrier and the person presenting the bill of lading or other document, if that person, in receiving the goods, acted on behalf of another. In *The Aliakmon*[21] sellers delivered a bill of lading[22] to their buyers, who presented it to the carriers, paid discharging costs, promised to pay import duty on behalf of the sellers, and asked for the goods to be deposited in a warehouse "to the sole order of the sellers". It was held that no implied contract arose between the carriers and the buyers since, in taking delivery, the buyers had acted throughout as agents of the sellers. On the facts of *The Aliakmon*, it is probable that the buyers would now acquire contractual rights under the bill of lading by virtue of section 2(1) of the Carriage of Goods by Sea Act, 1992[23]; the bill was in their possession,[24] named them as consignees[25] and was (unnecessarily, it seems[26]) indorsed to them.[27] But the reasoning of the case on the implied contract point could still apply on slightly different facts: *e.g.* if the seller were named as consignee and delivered the bill, without indorsement, to the buyer.

18–145 **Contracts (Rights of Third Parties) Act 1999.** Section 7 of this Act preserves "any right or remedy of a third party that exists or is available apart from this Act." One group of such rights or remedies are those arising, in favour of a person who is not a party to the bill of lading contract, out of an implied *Brandt v Liverpool* contract. Two points must be made in discussing the relationship between such a contract and the 1999 Act.

The first is that a *Brandt v Liverpool* contract is not contained in or evidenced by a bill of lading and is therefore not itself a "contract for the

[19] *The Athenasia Comninos and George Chr. Lemos* (1972) [1990] 1 Lloyd's Rep. 277 at p.281.
[20] *ibid.*
[21] *Leigh & Sillavan Ltd v Aliakmon Shipping Co. Ltd (The Aliakmon)* [1985] Q.B. 350; affirmed without further discussion of this point [1986] A.C. 785.
[22] Naming the sellers' suppliers as shippers, and the buyers as consignees: See above, para.18–065, n.92.
[23] *White v Jones* [1995] 2 A.C. 207 at p.265; above, para.18–104.
[24] The fact that it was in their possession as agents would not of itself precluded the acquisition by them of contractual rights by virtue of s.2(1): see above, para.18–104.
[25] See [1985] Q.B. 350 at p.360.
[26] Above, para.18–016.
[27] [1985] Q.B. 350 at p.363; [1986] A.C. 785 at p.809; the point is not free from doubt since Lord Brandon also said (*ibid.*, p.818) that "the bill of lading was never negotiated by the sellers to the buyers." See above, para.18–065, n.92.

carriage of goods by sea" within the definition of that phrase in the 1999 Act.[28] It follows that the implied contract is not (though the antecedent bill of lading contract is) within what we have called the subsection 6(5) exception,[29] by which section 1 confers no rights on a third party "in the case of . . . a contract for the carriage of goods by sea".

The second point, however, is that section 1 of the 1999 Act does not apply to the implied contract for the more fundamental reason that this contract is a direct contract between the carrier and the person receiving (or claiming) delivery. Hence neither of them is a "third party" within the 1999 Act, *i.e.* "a person who is not a party to a contract". It is true that the receiver is not a party to the bill of lading contract, but the term which he is seeking to enforce is a term, not of that contract, but of the implied contract; while the carrier is a party to both these contracts. The parties' rights under the implied contract therefore continue to be enforceable at common law and are not subject to the provisions of the 1999 Act.

Other implied or collateral contracts. Our sole concern in paragraphs 18–138 to 18–145 has been with one type of implied contract, namely that which can arise between a carrier of goods and a person claiming delivery of them on presentation of a bill of lading or of some other document containing a reference to the bill. It is possible for implied or collateral contracts on bill of lading terms to arise between different parties,[30] and in different circumstances, at least if the normal requirements of offer and acceptance, consideration and contractual intention are satisfied. In one case,[31] goods belonging to the claimant were loaded on the defendant's ship in pursuance of a charterparty between the defendant and a third party; and a bill of lading covering these goods was later indorsed to the claimant. The indorsement did not at the time transfer contractual rights to the claimant because of the "property gap" in the Bills of Lading Act 1855[32]; and the argument that there was a collateral contract between the claimant and the defendant was rejected on the ground that there was no identifiable offer and acceptance, nor any evidence of contractual intention.[33] 18–146

Transfer by assignment. The benefit of the contract contained in or evidenced by a bill of lading may be transferred, apart from the Carriage of Goods by Sea Act 1992, under the general law relating to the assignment of choses in action.[34] Three situations call for discussion. 18–147

[28] See ss.6(6) and (7) of the Act.
[29] Above, para.18–005, sub-para.(f).
[30] *e.g. Pyrene Co. Ltd v Scindia Navigation Co. Ltd* [1954] 2 Q.B. p.402, as explained in *Scruttons Ltd v Midland Silicones Ltd* [1962] A.C. 446 at p. 471; *AM Satterthwaite & Co. Ltd v New Zealand Shipping Co. Ltd (The Eurymedon)* [1975] A.C. 154.
[31] *Hispanica de Petroleos SA v Vencedora Oceanica Navegacion SA (The Kapetan Markos NL) (No. 2)* [1987] 2 Lloyd's Rep. 323; *cf. Compania Portorafti Commerciale SA v Ultramar Panama Inc. (The Captain Grego) (No. 2)* [1990] 2 Lloyd's Rep. 395.
[32] Above, para.18–100; on similar facts rights under the contract of carriage would now be transferred to the claimant by virtue of Carriage of Goods by Sea Act 1992, s.2(1).
[33] [1987] 2 Lloyd's Rep. 323 at p.331. But the claimant had a right of action, as owner, in tort.
[34] Above, para.3–043.

First, a bill of lading may be transferred in circumstances not giving the transferee any rights by virtue of section 2(1) of the Carriage of Goods by Sea Act 1992 (*e.g.* because the bill lacks a requisite indorsement) and the transferor may subsequently execute an instrument amounting to an assignment of his rights under the bill to the transferee and satisfying the requirements of a statutory assignment of a chose in action, as set out in section 136(1) of the Law of Property Act 1925. In such circumstances, the transferee could sue the carrier, by virtue of the assignment, for breach of the contract of carriage.[35] As the assignee's title is based solely on the assignment, he can enforce only such rights as the assignor himself had. An assignee from the original shipper would therefore not have the benefit of the estoppels that are normally available to the transferee of a bill of lading[36] (but not to the shipper) in respect of misstatements in the bill; but such a misstatement could give him a cause of action against the person responsible for it in tort for misrepresentation.[37]

Secondly, a bill of lading may be transferred in circumstances not giving the transferee any rights by virtue of section 2(1) of the Carriage of Goods by Sea Act 1992; and the transferee may argue that the mere transfer of the bill of lading, without the execution of any further instrument, operated as an assignment to him (in equity or under section 136(1) of the Law of Property Act 1925) of the benefit of the contract of carriage. If such an argument were to succeed, the transferee would acquire rights under the bill of lading contract in spite of the fact that the requirements of section 2(1) of the 1992 Act had not been satisfied; though he would not become liable on that contract by taking or demanding delivery of the goods, or by making a claim under the contract,[38] since the ordinary process of assignment transfers only rights and not liabilities.[39] The argument perhaps derives some support from the distinction referred to in *Sewell v Burdick* between a "personal" indorsement and an indorsement "in blank", and the suggestion that a "personal" indorsement of a bill of lading might give rise to the inference that "a title by assignment . . . was meant to pass to the indorsee . . ."[40] But there seems to be no case before the Bills of Lading Act 1855 in which the mere transfer of a bill of lading (even by a "personal" indorsement) was held to amount in equity to an assignment of

[35] *Kaukomarkkinat O/Y v Elbe Transport-Union GmbH (The Kelo)* [1985] 2 Lloyd's Rep. 85, where the transferee had not acquired rights under the Bills of Lading Act 1855 because he fell into the "property gap" (above, para.18–100).

[36] Above, para.18–028. Not being, in our example, the "lawful holder" of the bill within s.5(2)(b) of the 1992 Act, the assignee could not rely on s.4 of that Act.

[37] See *The Saudi Crown* [1986] 1 Lloyd's Rep. 261; *cf. Standard Chartered Bank v Pakistan National Shipping Corp.* [1995] 2 Lloyd's Rep. 365; [1998] 1 Lloyd's Rep. 656; *id. (No.2)* [2001] 1 Lloyd's Rep. 218, varied [2002] UKHL 43, [2003] 1 A.C. 959 (carrier and various other persons responsible for the misrepresentation held liable on deceit to a bank paying the beneficiary of a letter of credit in reliance on false date of shipment in the bill: see para.18–045 above); for liability for false statements in the bill, see generally paras 18–028 to 18–046 above and below, para.19–196.

[38] Carriage of Goods by Sea Act 1992, s.3(1)(a) and (b).

[39] *The Trident Beauty* [1994] 1 W.L.R. 161 at pp.165, 170; Treitel, *The Law of Contract* (11th ed.), p.701. For exceptions (some of which could apply in the present context) see *ibid.*, pp.701–706.

[40] (1884) 10 App.Cas. 74 at p.83.

the benefit of the contract of carriage; and in *Brandt v Liverpool, etc. Steam Navigation Co. Ltd*, Scrutton L.J. said without qualification that "before the Bills of Lading Act 1855 . . . the indorsement of the bill of lading . . . did not assign the contract contained therein."[41] It is submitted that this represents the present position and that the mere transfer of a bill of lading would not now be regarded as an equitable assignment since it is not intended as such.[42] Moreover, if the transfer could not take effect as an assignment in equity before the Judicature Act 1873, then it probably cannot operate as a statutory assignment under section 136(1) of the Law of Property Act 1925.[43] Even if it could so operate, the requirement that a statutory assignment must be "by writing" would not, it is submitted, be satisfied merely by the indorsement of the bill of lading; *a fortiori* it would not be satisfied where the transfer was effected without indorsement, *e.g.* in the case of a bearer bill or of one that had, before the transfer, been indorsed in blank.[44] Finally, the requirement that written notice of the assignment must be given to the debtor (*i.e.* the carrier) in order to constitute a statutory assignment is unlikely to be satisfied in the case of a transfer of a bill of lading.

Thirdly, an attempt might be made to assign the benefit of the contract of carriage without transferring the bill of lading. It is submitted that it would be most undesirable to allow such a transaction to take effect as a statutory assignment so as to entitle the assignee to claim delivery of the goods[45]; for if this were possible a shipper could assign his rights under the bill of lading to one person and then transfer it to another as lawful holder, with the result that the carrier could be exposed to conflicting claims from the assignee and a holder of the bill of lading.

(x) *Liability in Tort*

Whether buyer from shipper can sue carrier in tort for negligence. Goods may be shipped under a bill of lading, sold by the shipper and then damaged in transit as a result of the carrier's breach of the contract contained in or evidenced by the bill of lading. Since goods in transit are often, under overseas sales, at the buyer's risk,[46] the buyer is 18–148

---

[41] [1924] 1 K.B. 575 at p.594.

[42] For the requirement of such an intention, see *William Brandt's Sons & Co. v Dunlop Rubber Co.* [1905] A.C. 462.

[43] *Torkington v Magee* [1902] 2 K.B. 427 at p.430 (actual decision reversed on another ground [1903] 1 K.B. 644). There is no reference in Law of Property Act 1925, s.136 to bills of lading, though there is a reference in subs. (2) to policies of insurance made assignable by Policies of Assurance Act 1867.

[44] See above, paras 18–014, 18–016.

[45] In *The Kelo* (above, n.35) the bill of lading was in the hands of the assignee and the goods had been discharged, so that the bill was accomplished. All that was assigned was the right to sue the carrier in respect of damage to the cargo. In *Eridiana SpA v Rudolf A Oetker (The Fjord Wind)* [1999] 1 Lloyd's Rep. 307, affirmed without reference to this point [2000] 2 Lloyd's Rep. 191, the assignment was similarly of rights to damages in respect of expenses of trans-shipment incurred by reason of the unseaworthiness of the carrying ship.

[46] Below, paras 18–244, 19–110, 20–088.

likely to be the party principally interested in pursuing a claim against the carrier in respect of such damage. But, for various reasons, the buyer may not have acquired any contractual rights against the carrier by virtue of the Carriage of Goods by Sea Act 1992[47]; and the circumstances may be such that no implied contract of the kind described in paragraphs 18–138 to 18–144 above can arise. Where the buyer has no claim in contract, he may seek to hold the carrier liable in tort for damage suffered by the goods in transit, assuming it to have been caused by the negligence of the carrier, or of persons for whose acts or omissions the carrier is vicariously liable.

18–149 **Buyer having no proprietary interest in the goods.** In *The Wear Breeze*[48] goods which had been sold on c.i.f. terms were damaged in transit after the risk, but before the property, in them had passed to the buyer. No bill of lading or other document capable of giving the buyer contractual rights against the carrier had been transferred to the buyer.[49] An action by the buyer against the carrier in tort for negligence in damaging the goods was dismissed on the ground that such a claim could not be maintained by a person who was neither the owner of the goods, nor entitled to immediate possession of them, when the damage occurred. This case was followed in *The Aliakmon*[50] where risk had passed to c. & f. buyers on shipment,[51] but property did not pass to them until they had paid the price,[52] long after the goods had been delivered to them. Nor, as the law then stood, were rights under the contract of carriage transferred to the buyers when the bill of lading, which named them as consignees, was transmitted to them.[53] The House of Lords unanimously held that the buyers had no claim against the carriers in tort for negligently damaging the goods in transit, while they were at the buyers' risk. Such a claim in tort was available only to a person who "had either the legal ownership of or a possessory title to the property

---

[47] See above, para.18–138. *Cf.* also *The Seven Pioneer* [2001] 2 Lloyd's Rep. 57 (below n.50), where the consignee had failed to acquire contractual rights under the foreign law which governed the bill of lading.

[48] *Margarine Union GmbH v Cambay Prince SS Co. Ltd (The Wear Breeze)* [1969] 1 Q.B. 619; the reasoning of this case was followed in *Karlshamns Oljefabriker v Eastport Navigation Corp. (The Elafi)* [1982] 1 All E.R. 208 at pp.211–212 (where the tort claim succeeded on the ground that property *had* passed to the buyer at the relevant time).

[49] This would, on the same facts, still be true as the delivery orders against which the buyer paid were not "ship's delivery orders" within Carriage of Goods by Sea Act 1992, s.1(4); below, para.18–176.

[50] [1986] A.C. 785, overruling *Schiffahrt & Kohlen GmbH v Chelsea Maritime Ltd (The Irene's Success)* [1981] 2 Lloyd's Rep. 635, and disapproving a dictum in *The Nea Tyhi* [1982] 1 Lloyd's Rep. 606 at p.612. Treitel [1986] L.M.C.L.Q. 294; Markesinis, 103 L.Q.R. 354 at pp.384–390 (1987); Tettenborn [1987] J.B.L. 12. *The Aliakmon* was followed in New Zealand in *The Seven Pioneer* [2001] 2 Lloyd's Rep. 57 referring also to other common law jurisdictions taking the same view.

[51] Below, paras 19–110, 21–013.

[52] Below, para.18–213, 18–216.

[53] They fell within the "property gap" of the Bills of Lading Act 1855, above, para.18–100. On similar facts, the buyers would now probably acquire rights under the contract of carriage by virtue of s.2(1)(a) of the Carriage of Goods by Sea Act 1992; see *White v Jones* [1995] 2 A.C. 207 at p.265; above, para.18–104.

concerned at the time when the loss or damage occurred"[54] or, where the loss is caused by a continuing process, at the time when the cause of action in respect of it first accrued.[55] Since property had not passed to the buyer at the relevant time, the requirement of "legal ownership" was clearly not satisfied[56]; nor was any attempt made to argue that the buyers had a "possessory title" to the goods at any relevant time. It seems clear that they had no such title at that time; for in this context "possessory title" seems to refer to either actual possession[57] or an immediate right to such possession.[58] The goods were in the actual possession of the carrier, some of whose charges remained unpaid so that the buyers were not entitled to immediate actual possession of the goods even though the bill of lading had been delivered to them; and, as between buyers and sellers, the goods were subject to the sellers' right of withholding delivery.[59] Nor had the buyers acquired any equitable interest in the goods by virtue of the appropriation of the goods to the contract[60]; and even the acquisition of such an interest would not have entitled them to sue the carrier in tort without joining the

---

[54] [1986] A.C. 785 at p.809. For the suggestion that the principle may have been qualified by Latent Damage Act 1986, s.3, see Griew, 136 N.L.J. 1201 (1986); but there is no hint in the legislative history of this section that such a change (in the present context) was intended. The point was left open in *Homburg Houtimport BV v Agrosin Private Ltd (The Starsin)* [2001] EWCA Civ. 56, [2001] 1 Lloyd's Rep. 437 at [119]–[128] (*per* Rix L.J., dissenting, but not on this point), [134], [202], [203]; the point was not discussed on appeal to the House of Lords: [2003] UKHL 12, [2004], 1 A.C. 715. The suggested qualification could, in any event, apply only where the damage was still latent when the claimant became owner; and this was not the position in *The Aliakmon*. For another possible qualification of the *Aliakmon* principle, not applicable in the present context, see *Virgo Steamship Co. SA v Skaarup Shipping Corp. (The Kapetan Georgis)* [1988] 1 Lloyd's Rep. 352, holding that, where A's breach of contract with B causes physical harm to B's property and gives rise to liability on the part of C to indemnify B, A may be liable in tort to C.

[55] *Homburg Houtimport BV v Agrosin Private Ltd (The Starsin)* [2001] EWCA Civ. 56, [2001] 1 Lloyd's Rep. 437 at [96] (*per* Rix L.J., whose judgment was affirmed by the House of Lords [2003] UKHL 12, [2004] 1 A.C. 715 at [40], [64], [96], [131]. It is not sufficient for the claimant to show that damage flowing from a cause of action which had arisen before he had become owner of the goods continued to accrue after that event.

[56] *cf. Mitsui & Co. Ltd v Flota Mercante Grancolombiana SA (The Ciudad de Pasto and the Ciudad de Neiva)* [1988] 1 W.L.R. 1145, and *The Seven Pioneer* [2001] 1 Lloyd's Rep. 57; in both these cases, tort claims by f.o.b. buyers against carriers failed because property had not passed to the buyers for the reasons stated in paras 20–082, 20–083 below.

[57] *e.g.* as bailee: see *O'Sullivan v Williams* [1992] 3 All E.R. 385 at p.387, referring to *The Aliakmon*, above, n.50.

[58] *e.g.* as bailor: *The Hamburg Star* [1994] 1 Lloyd's Rep. 399 at pp.403–405; a bailor of goods may have a sufficient possessory title for the present purpose even after his rights under their contract of carriage have become extinct by reason of the transfer by him of the bill of lading containing or evidencing that contract: see *East West Corp. v DKBS 1912 AF A/S* [2003] EWCA Civ 83, [2003] Q.B. 1509, above para.18–114. See also *Transcontainer Express Ltd v Custodian Security Ltd* [1988] 1 Lloyd's Rep. 120 at p.138, where the question whether a right to possession sufficed for the present purpose was left open.

[59] Sale of Goods Act 1979, ss.39(2), 43(1)(a); the sellers had never abandoned their right of disposal.

[60] *The Aliakmon*, above, n.50, [1986] A.C. 785 at p.812; *MCC Proceeds Inc. v Lehman Bros International (Europe)* [1998] 4 All E.R. 675 at pp.700–701.

legal owners of the goods (*i.e.* the sellers) as parties to the action.[61] Having no proprietary or possessory rights in the goods, the buyers were simply in the position of persons whose contractual rights to the goods against the seller had been adversely affected by the negligence of the carrier in damaging the goods; and many authorities establish that prejudice of this kind is not sufficient to give rise to a cause of action in negligence.[62]

A further reason for the decision in *The Aliakmon* was that the bill of lading expressly incorporated the Hague Rules[63] which, on the one hand, impose certain responsibilities and liabilities on a carrier under a contract for the carriage of goods by sea, and, on the other hand, give the carrier the benefit of certain immunities from, and limitations of, liability. To have held the carrier liable to the buyers in tort would have led to the undesirable result of subjecting him to a standard of liability similar to that imposed by the Rules, while depriving him of their protection.[64] In cases of this kind, it would therefore be inconsistent with the contractual structure to allow the buyer to make a claim in tort against the carrier.[65] Counsel for the buyers sought to meet this objection by arguing that the terms of the contract of carriage, including the Rules, were relevant in defining or qualifying the duty of care owed by the carrier to the buyers in tort; but the House of Lords rejected the argument for the reason given by Sir John Donaldson M.R. in the Court of Appeal, *viz.* that the intricate scheme of

---

[61] *The Aliakmon*, above, n.50. And see below, para.19–101.

[62] See *Candlewood Navigation Corp. Ltd v Mitsui OSK Lines Ltd (The Mineral Transporter)* [1986] A.C. 1, reviewing earlier cases.

[63] Below, para.21–047.

[64] Under the Conventions relating to the international carriage of goods by air, an owner of goods may have a right in tort against the carrier without depriving the latter of the protection of the Convention. Such protection may be retained by interpreting the relevant Convention so as either (i) to restrict the categories of persons entitled to sue the carrier to those specified in the Convention (*e.g.* as consignor or consignee, or as principals of the persons so specified) or (ii) to allow claims based on title to the goods (irrespective of contract) to be brought against the carrier only subject to the "scheme of liability" imposed by the Convention: see *Sidhu v British Airways Plc* [1997] A.C. 430 at pp.442–443, discussing *Gatewhite Ltd v Iberia Lineas de Espanea Sociedad* [1990] 1 Q.B. 326; *Herd v Clyde Helicopters* [1997] A.C. 473; *Western Digital Corp. v British Airways Plc* [2001] Q.B. 733 at pp.752, 755, 769; *cf. Re Deep Vein Thrombosis and Air Travel Group Litigation* [2005] UKHL 72, [2006] 1 All E.R. 786 at [3], [27], [29] and [62] for the exclusive nature of the remedy under the amended Warsaw Convention in cases of personal injury. The reasoning outlined in this note is based on the terms of the relevant Convention and there are no similar terms in the Hague (or Hague-Visby) Rules which could support a similar conclusion in cases of carriage by sea governed by those Rules.

[65] This would not be the kind of "unusual situation" in which it was held in *Henderson v Merrett Syndicates Ltd* [1995] 2 A.C. 145 at p.195 that A can be liable in tort to C for economic loss suffered by C in consequence of A's breach of his contract with B; *cf.* the express approval, *ibid.*, of *Simaan General Contracting Co. v Pilkington Glass Ltd* [1988] Q.B. 758 and especially at pp.782–783. For the same reasons, the view expressed in *Holt v Payne Shillington* (1996) B.L.R. 51, that a tortious duty in a contractual relationship may be wider than that arising out of the contract, would not be likely to apply in the present context; the tort claim in this case failed on the pleadings.

the Rules could not be "synthesised into a standard of care".[66] Nor could the carriers rely by analogy on the suggestion made by Lord Roskill in another context, that the tortious duty of care owed by a building sub-contractor to the building owner might be limited by a "relevant exclusion clause in the main contract"[67]; for that suggestion presupposed that the

---

[66] [1985] Q.B. 350 at p.360; approved [1986] A.C. 785 at p.818. Similar reasoning led to the rejection of a tort claim by a cargo-owner against a classification society (whose alleged negligence had led to the loss of the ship and the cargo) in *Marc Rich & Co. AG v Bishop Rock Marine Co. Ltd (The Nicholas H)* [1996] 1 A.C. 211, where success of the claim would have enabled the cargo owner to circumvent the tonnage limitation laid down in the international Convention to which effect is given by Merchant Shipping Act 1979, s.17 and SCh.4. Since classification societies would be likely to pass this liability on to the shipowners, the practical effect of holding the societies liable would be to deprive shipowners of the benefit of the Convention. *Cf. Reeman v Department of Transport* [1997] 2 Lloyd's Rep. 648; contrast *Perrett v Collins* [1998] 2 Lloyd's Rep. 255, where the policy reasons (stated above) for the decision in *The Nicholas H*, above, were held not to protect an aircraft inspection society from liability for *personal* injury.

[67] *Junior Books Ltd v Veitchi Co. Ltd* [1983] 1 A.C. 520 at p.546. This part of the Lord Roskill's reasoning does not seem to be affected by subsequent cases restricting the scope of the actual decision in the *Junior Books* case, *e.g. Aswan Engineering Establishment Co. v Lupdine Ltd* [1987] 1 W.L.R. 1; *Simaan General Contracting Co. v Pilkington Glass Ltd (No. 2)* [1988] Q.B. 758; *D & F Estates Ltd v Church Commissioners for England* [1989] A.C. 177; *cf. Murphy v Brentwood DC* [1991] 2 A.C. 398 at pp.466, 469; *Saipem SpA v Dredging VO 2 BV (The Volvox Hollandia) (No. 2)* [1993] 2 Lloyd's Rep. 315 at p.322. Those cases were not concerned with the effects of exemption clauses but with the problem whether a claimant could recover damages in tort in respect of pure economic loss suffered by him as a result of the breach of a contract to which he was not a party. The suggestion in *Muirhead v Industrial Tank Specialities Ltd* [1986] Q.B. 507 at p.525, that Lord Roskill intended to refer to an exclusion clause in the sub-contract, may, with respect, be doubted since in such a case the party prejudiced by the clause (*i.e.* the owner) would not have assented to it, as he would have done in Lord Roskill's example. A number of later cases have followed Lord Roskill's suggestion in the terms in which it was made: *Southern Water Authority v Carey* [1985] 2 All E.R. 1077; *Norwich CC v Harvey* [1989] 1 W.L.R. 828; *Pacific Associates Inc. v Baxter* [1990] 1 Q.B. 993. An exclusion clause in the sub-contract should only (if at all) be available to the sub-contractor against the owner where the latter had assented to it: for the requirement of such assent, see *Henderson v Merrett Syndicates Ltd* [1995] 2 A.C. 145, at p.196, where the word "authorised" may indicate that the main contractor acted as the (building) owner's agent for the purpose of creating privity of contract between the owner and the sub-contractor so as to bind the owner by an exemption clause in the sub-contract. In the absence of privity of contract, most modern authorities hold that the owner is bound by exclusion clauses in a sub-contract to which he has assented only if the relationship between him and the sub-contractor is that of bailor and sub-bailee: see below, at nn. 68 and 69. In *White v Jones* [1995] 2 A.C. 207 the tort liability of a solicitor, engaged by a testator to draw up a will, to beneficiaries who suffer loss in consequence of the solicitor's negligence in failing to give effect to the testator's instructions was said by Lord Goff at p.268 to be "subject to any term in the contract between the solicitor and the testator which may exclude or restrict the solicitor's liability to the testator in tort." This suggestion gives rise to the difficulty that the disappointed beneficiaries would, under it, be adversely affected by a contractual term to which they have *not* consented; and it is significant that Lord Nolan at p.294 leaves the point open. The suggestion may be explicable by reference to the special nature of the "disappointed beneficiary" cases, (and of closely analogous cases, such as *Gorham v British Telecommunications Plc* [2000] 1

exclusion clause was contained in a contract to which the claimant was a party, while here the Rules formed part of a contract to which the claimant was a stranger.[68] Nor, finally could the buyers rely on the argument that any tort liability of the carriers to them would be qualified by the Rules on the ground that the circumstances in which the carriers had received the goods constituted a bailment on terms, since there was no such bailment between the *buyers* and the carriers: "The only bailment of the goods was one by the sellers to the shipowners."[69] Such an argument based on bailment might succeed if the buyers had become owners of the goods *before* shipment and would be one way of preserving the protection of the Rules for the carrier where, under the principles stated in *The Aliakmon*, the buyer did have a tort claim by virtue of his legal ownership of the goods.[70]

In *The Aliakmon*, the House of Lords was concerned only with a bill of lading which incorporated the Hague Rules, and not with one that was governed by the amended version of those Rules known as the Hague-Visby Rules,[71] which have the force of law in the United Kingdom.[72] The defences and limits of liability provided for in those Rules are expressed to apply "in any action against the carrier in respect of loss or damage to the goods covered by a contract of carriage whether the action be founded in contract or in tort."[73] It has been suggested that these words would make the Hague-Visby Rules applicable to a tort claim by someone who is not a party to the contract of carriage[74]; so that, in a case like *The Aliakmon*, it

---

W.L.R. 2129) and it is submitted that it cannot be used to support the argument that a cargo-owner should be bound by exclusions or restrictions of liability to which he has not assented and which are contained in a contract of carriage to which he is not a party.

[68] [1986] A.C. 785 at p.817 where Lord Brandon first doubted whether an exclusion clause can be relevant if contained "in a contract to which the plaintiff is a party but the defendant is not"; and then said that Lord Roskill's suggestion was not "a convincing legal basis for qualifying a legal duty of care owed by A to B by reference to a contract to which A is, but B is not, a party." Since in the second of Lord Brandon's sentences A is the defendant, it may be that the first should read "in a contract to which the defendant is a party but the plaintiff is not"; and this is the converse of the situation that Lord Roskill seems to have had in mind in the dictum in the *Junior Books* case cited at n.67, above. Lord Brandon's views on this point in *The Aliakmon*, above, were in turn questioned in *Pacific Associates Inc. v Baxter* [1990] 1 Q.B. 993 at p.1038.

[69] [1986] A.C. 785 at p.818. Hence the buyers would not be bound by exemptions or limitations in the contract of carriage on the principle of bailment on terms stated in cases such cases as *Morris v CW Martin Ltd* [1966] 1 Q.B. 716 at p.729; *cf. Compania Portorafti Commerciale SA v Ultramar Panama Inc. (The Captain Gregos) (No. 2)* [1990] 2 Lloyd's Rep. 395 (claim by PEAG). For the question whether the principle applies only where there is a relationship of bailor and bailee (or sub-bailee) between the carrier and the person alleged to be bound by terms in a contract to which he is not a party, see *Carver on Bills of Lading*, 2nd ed. (2005) paras 7–100 to 7–103. For the difficulty of reconciling the view of Lord Brandon in the statement quoted in the text above (that the bailor was the seller) with that of Lord Hobhouse in *Borealis AB v Stagas Ltd (The Berge Sisar)* [2001] UKHL 17, [2002] 1 A.C. 205 AT [31] (that the bailor was the consignee) see above, para.18–065.

[70] For this and other possible ways of preserving such protection, see para.18–150.

[71] Below, para.21–047 below, after n.86.

[72] Carriage of Goods by Sea Act 1971, s.1(2); these Rules are set out in the Schedule to that Act.

[73] *ibid.*, Art. 4 bis (1).

[74] See Diamond [1978] L.M.C.L.Q. 225 at pp.248–249.

would be possible to hold the carrier liable to the buyers in tort without depriving the carrier of the benefit of the Rules. But the better view is that the words quoted merely mean that a person who *is a party* to the contract of carriage cannot improve his position by disregarding the contract and suing in tort.[75] As the buyer in *The Aliakmon* was not a party to the contract of carriage, a tort claim by him would therefore not have been subject to the Rules and would, if upheld, have deprived the carrier of the protection of the Rules. It is accordingly submitted that the reasoning of *The Aliakmon* applies whether the contract of carriage is governed by the Hague, or by the Hague-Visby Rules.

The result of *The Aliakmon*, therefore, is that a buyer has no claim against the carrier in tort for negligently damaging the goods in transit before property, or an immediate right to possession, has passed to the buyer: it is not enough for the buyer to show that the resulting loss will fall on him because the goods, when damaged, were already at his risk. In most situations (including probably that which arose in *The Aliakmon* itself),[76] the buyer will not now be prejudiced by this state of the law, as he will acquire contractual rights against the carrier by virtue of the Carriage of Goods by Sea Act 1992.[77] But where this is not the case,[78] the buyer should protect himself[79] by stipulating that the seller should either exercise his contractual right against the carrier,[80] in respect of loss of or damage to the goods in transit, for the buyer's account, or transfer such rights to the buyer by assignment.[81] Provided that these steps are taken, the buyer will not be prejudiced by his lack of a tort claim for negligence against the carrier where he has neither a proprietary nor a possessory right to the goods at the relevant time.[82] He will not, indeed, then have the benefit of estoppels available to a transferee in respect of false statements in the bill of lading[83]; but such statements will make the person responsible for them liable to him in tort for misrepresentation,[84] and may also make the seller liable to him for breach of the contract of sale.[85]

---

[75] *Compania Portorafti Commerciale SA v Ultramar Panama Inc. (The Captain Gregos)* [1990] 1 Lloyd's Rep. 310 at p.318, approving Scrutton on *Charterparties and Bills of Lading* (20th ed.), p.454.

[76] See above, n.53.

[77] Above, para.18–102 *et seq.*; above, at n.53.

[78] See, *e.g.* above, n.49.

[79] As the buyer in *The Aliakmon* could have done: see [1986] A.C. 785 at p.819.

[80] The goods in *The Aliakmon* had been shipped by the sellers' suppliers who had, for this purpose, acted as the sellers' agents.

[81] Above, para.18–147.

[82] Above, at nn. 54, 55.

[83] See *The Aliakmon* [1985] Q.B. 350 at p.360; *cf.* above, para.18–028; such estoppels are also available to a transferee of the bill under an implied contract on the principle of paras 18–138 *et seq.*, above: see above, para.18–139, n.85.

[84] *The Saudi Crown* [1986] 1 Lloyd's Rep. 261; and see above, para.18–147, n.37.

[85] Below, paras 19–035, 19–038; in *The Aliakmon*, the variation of the contract may have relieved the seller from such liability as it turned the contract "in effect" into an ex-warehouse contract: [1986] A.C. 785 at p.809.

18–150 **Third party with proprietary or possessory interest.** The above discussion is concerned with the relationship between a carrier and a person who has *not* become owner of the goods and who has not acquired contractual rights against the carrier by virtue of section 2 of the Carriage of Goods by Sea Act 1992. It is, however, also possible for a buyer to have become owner and nevertheless not have acquired contractual rights against the carrier: *e.g.* because the only document capable of vesting such rights in him was a bill of lading, and no transfer of the bill was ever made to him. In such a case the buyer may have a claim in tort as owner if the carrier has negligently damaged the goods.[86] Of course, the terms of the contract of carriage will be relevant in determining the extent of the duty (if any) owed by the carrier to the cargo-owner: *e.g.* he is unlikely to owe any duty to heat the cargo if the contract is one to carry the goods in a ship without heating facilities.[87] A further possibility is that goods already owned by A before shipment are shipped with A's authorisation by B on C's ship under a contract made between B and C. In such circumstances, B may be A's agent for the purpose of creating privity of contract between and A and C,[88] or at least for the limited purpose of binding A by the exclusions from, or limitations of, liability available to C under the contract between B and C.[89] But even if B is not A's agent for either of these purposes, and there is accordingly no privity of contract between A and C, such facts can give rise to the relationship of bailor and bailee between A and B, and that of bailor and sub-bailee between A and C. Two things follow: first, that C may be liable to A in tort for breach of his duty as sub-bailee, and secondly that C may be able to rely against A on the terms of the contract between C and B if the terms of the sub-bailment have been authorised by A.[90] The relationship of bailor and bailee may also arise between A and C, even though A was not a party to the original bailment, where C later attorns to A and in this way gives rise to a new bailment between them.[91] But where goods are shipped by B on C's ship under a bill of lading consigning them to A, no bailment relationship arises between A and C merely by virtue of

---

[86] See *Anonima Petroli Italiana SpA v Marlucidez Armadora SA (The Filiatra Legacy)* [1991] 2 Lloyd's Rep. 337 (where the claim was for short delivery but failed as the buyer was unable to show that the carrier was responsible for the shortage).
[87] See *Mitsui & Co. Ltd v Novorossiysk Shipping Co. (The Gudermes)* [1993] 1 Lloyd's Rep. 311 at p.326.
[88] *Sandeman Coprimar SA v Transitos y Transportes Intergrales SL* [2003] EWCA Civ 113, [2003] Q.B. 1270 at [63].
[89] See *The Kite* [1938] P. 164 at p.181; *Norfolk Southern Railway Co v James N Kirby Pty Ltd* 125 S. Ct. 395 at 399 (2004) (US Supreme Court).
[90] *Hispanica de Petroleos SA v Vencedora Oceanica Navegacion SA (The Kapetan Markos NL) (No. 2)* [1987] 2 Lloyd's Rep. 321 at p.340, applying the principle stated in *Morris v CW Martin & Sons Ltd* [1966] 1 Q.B. 716 at p.729; *KH Enterprise v Pioneer Container (The Pioneer Container)* [1994] 2 A.C. 324. *Spectra International Plc v Hayesoak Ltd* [1997] 1 Lloyd's Rep. 153 (revsd. on another point [1998] 1 Lloyd's Rep. 162); and see *Lotus Cars Ltd v Southampton Cargo Handling Plc (The Rigoletto)* [2000] 2 Lloyd's Rep. 532; *The Mahkutai* [1996] A.C. 650 at pp.667–668 (where the actual question was not whether A was *bound* by a term in the contract between B and C, but whether C was entitled to the *benefit* of a term in the contract between A and B); *Carver on Bills of Lading* (2nd ed., 2005), paras 7–092 *et seq*.
[91] *Compania Portorafti Commerciale SA v Ultramar Panama Inc. (The Captain Gregos) (No.2)* [1990] 2 Lloyd's Rep. 395 at p.406 (claim by BP).

such shipment: it is normally the shipper and not the consignee who in such a case is the bailor.[92] It is submitted that this is, *a fortiori*, true where A is not the consignee named in the bill as the person to whose order the goods are to be delivered, but is a person to whom a bill made out to the order of another consignee (or of the shipper) has been indorsed.[93]

Where goods are shipped by their owner, that shipper's rights under the contract of carriage may then be lost by his transferring the bill to a lawful holder in whom those rights will be vested in consequence of the transfer.[94] The shipper will thus be placed in a position analogous to that of a third party, but he may nevertheless retain a right of action against the carrier based on the bailment relationship which arose between these parties at the time of the shipment.[95]

Concurrent liability in contract and tort. The preceding discussion is 18–151 based on the assumption that there is *no* contractual relationship between buyer and carrier. The further question arises whether the buyer can recover damages in tort from the carrier even where there is a contractual relationship between them: *e.g.* where the buyer is the shipper of the goods (as he may be where he has bought the goods on f.o.b. terms[96]) or where he has become the lawful holder of the bill of lading[97] (as will often be the case where he has bought the goods on c.i.f. terms[98]). In such cases there may well be concurrent liability in contract and tort: indeed, the provision of the Hague-Visby Rules, quoted above,[99] are based on this assumption. There is likely, for example, to be such concurrent liability where the duty arising under the contract (and alleged to have been broken) is no different from the corresponding tort duty.[1] But there will be no liability in tort where the imposition of the tort duty would be "so inconsistent with the applicable contract that, in accordance with ordinary principles, the parties must be taken to have agreed that the tortious remedy is to be limited or excluded."[2] For example, it is submitted that, where the contract between buyer and carrier was governed by the Hague Rules, the buyer should not be able to deprive the carrier of the exceptions and limitations of those Rules simply by framing his claim in tort; and that this is so even though

---

[92] *ibid.*, p.404; *Leigh and Sillavan Ltd v Aliakmon Shipping Co. Ltd (The Aliakmon)* [1986] A.C. 785 at p.818, per Lord Brandon, quoted in para.18–149 above at n.69; for the difficulty of reconciling this statement with the view of Lord Hobhouse in *Borealis AB v Stargas Ltd (The Berge Sisar)* [2001] UKHL 17, [2002] 1 A.C. 205 at [31], see above, para.18–065.

[93] See para.18–065 above, especially at n.14; and see *Carver on Bills of Lading*, 2nd ed. (2005) paras 7–036 to 7–041, 7–105 to 7–107.

[94] Carriage of Goods by Sea Act 1992, s.2(5)(a).

[95] *East West Corp. v DKBS 1912 AF A/S* [2003] EWCA Civ 83, [2003] Q.B. 1509; and see above para.18–115 for the extent of this right in bailment.

[96] See below, para.20–003.

[97] And so have acquired rights under the contract of carriage by virtue of Carriage of Goods by Sea Act 1992, s.2(1)(a), above, para.18–102.

[98] In consequence of the performance of the seller's duty to tender documents, including (prima facie) a bill of lading: below, paras 19–024, 19–025, 19–059.

[99] Art. IV bis (i), above para.18–149 at n.73.

[1] *Henderson v Merrett Syndicates Ltd* [1995] 2 A.C. 145 at p.193.

[2] *ibid.*, p.194; and see above para.18–149, n.65.

the Hague Rules lack the express provision to this effect which is now contained in the Hague-Visby Rules.[3]

(b) *Sea Waybills*

18–152 **Legal nature of sea waybills.** Sea waybills have a number of features in common with bills of lading. They contain or evidence contracts of carriage and they are receipts for the goods, though the "conclusive evidence" provisions of Article III.4 of the Hague-Visby Rules and of section 4 of the Carriage of Goods by Sea Act 1992 do not apply to them.[4] Their issue where no goods have been shipped does not (any more than the issue of a bill of lading in such circumstances) give rise to a contract of carriage or to an estoppel against the carrier.[5] Their legal nature resembles that of straight bills of lading; and, although the two types of documents appear to be regarded as commercially distinct, straight bills are treated as sea waybills for the purposes of the 1992 Act.[6] Sea waybills are not documents of title in the traditional common law sense,[7] though it is arguable that they may fall within the statutory definition of such documents.[8] All these aspects of the law relating to sea waybills have been discussed in earlier sections of this Chapter.[9] Our present concern is with their use as a mechanism for the transfer of rights under the contract of carriage to, and for the imposition of liabilities under that contract on, persons other than the original parties to it.[10]

(i) *Transfer of Contractual Rights*

18–153 **Carriage of Goods by Sea Act 1992, section 2(1)(b).** This paragraph provides that "a person who becomes . . . the person who (without being an original party to the contract of carriage) is the person to whom delivery of the goods to which a sea waybill relates is to be made by the carrier in accordance with that contract . . . shall (by virtue of becoming . . . the person to whom delivery is to be made) have transferred to and vested in him all rights of suit under the contract of carriage as if he had been a party to that contract." In relation to a sea waybill, "the contract of carriage" means "the contract contained in or evidenced by that . . . waybill."[11] The transfer of contractual rights under a sea waybill differs from the transfer of such rights under a bill of lading in that it is effected without transfer of possession of the document: the person identified as consignee in a sea

---

[3] Above, at n.99.
[4] See paras 18–035 and 18–040, above.
[5] *cf. Heskell v Continental Express Ltd* [1950] 1 All E.R. 1033, para.18–030 above.
[6] See para.18–018 above.
[7] See above para.18–067, at n.46; for that traditional common law sense, see paras 18–007, 18–062
[8] See para.18–083, above.
[9] See nn. 4 to 7, above.
[10] For a fuller discussion, see *Carver on Bills of Lading* (2nd ed., 2005), paras 8–002 to 8–016.
[11] s.5(1).

waybill does not need to become the holder, or lawful holder, of it to acquire contractual rights against the carrier by virtue of it. This legal difference between the two types of documents reflects the commercial practice relating to sea waybills. Unlike order and bearer bills of lading, sea waybills are not transferred to consignees and do not need to be produced in order to obtain delivery of the goods: the practice is for carriers to deliver the goods to the named consignee simply on proof of identity.[12] Indeed, the very fact that goods will be so delivered has been relied upon to show that the document under which they are shipped is not a bill of lading.[13]

Definition of "sea waybill". Section 1(3) of the 1992 Act provides that references in the Act to a sea waybill are "references to any document which is not a bill of lading but—(a) is such a receipt for goods as contains or evidences a contract for the carriage of goods by sea; and (b) identifies the person to whom delivery of the goods is to be made by the carrier in accordance with that contract." This definition must be supplemented by the definition of "the contract of carriage" in section 5(1) (quoted in paragraph 18–153 above), and by section 5(3) which provides that references in the Act "to a person's being identified in a document include references to his being identified by a description which allows for the identity of the person in question to be varied, in accordance with the terms of the document, after its issue; and the reference in section 1(3)(b) of this Act to a document's identifying a person shall be construed accordingly." A number of points in these definitions call for discussion; they are considered in paragraphs 18–155 to 18–158 below. **18–154**

"Not a bill of lading". This phrase seems to refer to the characteristic of a bill of lading which makes such a document transferable by indorsement (where necessary) and delivery. That is, it means that a document must be incapable of such transfer[14] if it is to be a sea waybill. Accordingly, a document making goods deliverable "to A or order" would be a bill of lading but one making them deliverable simply "to A" would be a sea waybill within s.1(3). Even in the case of a sea waybill, however, it is possible for the identity of the person named in it as consignee to be "varied, in accordance with the terms of the document, after its issue".[15] The question whether such a term prevented the document from being a sea waybill depends on how or by whom the identity of the consignee could be varied. If delivery were to be made "to A or order" the document would be a bill of lading since the variation could be effected by indorsement by the consignee (A) without prior notice to the carrier. If, on the other hand, **18–155**

[12] Law Com. No. 196, Scot. Law Com. No. 130 (1991), para.5.7; above, para.18–018. Straight bills of lading are sea waybills for the purposes of the 1992 Act (see above, para.18–152) but generally contain terms (express or implied) requiring their production by the named consignee when he claims delivery of the goods: see above, para.18–071.

[13] See *The Maheno* [1977] 1 Lloyd's Rep. 81.

[14] *cf.* Carriage of Goods by Sea Act 1992, s.1(2)(a).

[15] *ibid.*, s.5(3).

delivery were to be made "to A or as *the shipper* may direct", then the document would be a sea waybill and the variation could be effected only by notice by the shipper. If the document provided for delivery "to A or as A might direct", then it would be a bill of lading if, on its true construction, it meant that the identity of the consignee could be varied simply by indorsement; but it would be a sea waybill if the variation could be effected only by notice to the carrier. Obviously in borderline cases the distinction between the two types of documents can give rise to difficult questions of construction: for example, we have seen that a document may be a sea waybill even though it provides for delivery of the goods to a named consignee "or assigns" if it also contains words indicating that some further requirement must be satisfied to give it the characteristic of transferability by indorsement and delivery, and if that requirement is not in fact satisfied.[16]

18–156 **"Receipt for the goods."** The "receipt" to which this part of the definition[17] refers must, it is submitted, be a receipt by or on behalf of the carrier. It suffices that the document indicates receipt; there is no need for it to indicate shipment, or even (as in the case of a bill of lading) receipt "*for shipment*".[18]

18–157 **"Contains or evidences a contract for the carriage of goods by sea".** We have seen that similar words are used in relation to bills of lading and that in this context it was commonly held that, between the original parties, the bill was no more than evidence of the terms of the contract of carriage, while between carrier and transferee of the bill it contained the contract.[19] A somewhat similar possibility can now arise in relation to a sea waybill since the 1992 Act seems to envisage[20] that the rights of the named consignee may differ from those of the shipper. But the rationale of the common law rule that, in the hands of the transferee, a bill of lading "contained" the contract of carriage, was that the transferee of the bill must be entitled to rely on the terms of the document against which he had paid the price of the goods covered by it. This rationale scarcely applies in the case of a sea waybill, under which contractual rights can be acquired by the consignee named in it without any delivery of it to him, so that he may be as unaware of the terms contained in it as of any extrinsic terms agreed between the original parties.

Where goods are shipped in a ship chartered by the shipper, any further document issued to him in relation to them would be a mere receipt[21] and so could not fall within the statutory definition of a sea waybill, though purporting to be such. Nor could the document change its character on

---

[16] *The Chitral* [2000] 1 Lloyd's Rep. 529; above, para.18–019.
[17] s.1(3)(a).
[18] See s.1(2)(b).
[19] Above, paras 18–047, 18–048.
[20] See the words "as if he had been a party to that contract" in the "tailpiece" to s.2(1) of the 1992 Act.
[21] Above, paras 18–051, 18–110.

transfer, as a bill of lading can,[22] since there is no such concept or practice as the transfer of a sea waybill. There is also the converse possibility of a ship's being chartered by an f.o.b. buyer in which goods are shipped by the seller under a sea waybill naming the charterer as consignee.[23] Such a document could certainly fall within the statutory definition of a sea waybill but it is submitted that the buyer's contractual rights against the carrier would be governed by the terms of the charterparty rather than by those of the sea waybill.[24]

"By the carrier". The question who is "the carrier" can give rise to difficulties, particularly where goods are carried in a chartered ship. These difficulties are discussed in relation to bills of lading in paragraph 18–127 above; and that discussion applies *mutatis mutandis* to carriage under sea waybills. 18–158

"Spent" documents. Since rights under the contract of carriage can be vested in a sea waybill consignee without his having acquired possession of the waybill,[25] the problem of "spent" documents does not normally arise in relation to sea waybills; and section 2(2) (which deals with these problems in relation to bills of lading[26]) does not apply to them.[27] But an analogous problem could arise where A, the sea waybill consignee, sold the goods in transit to B and the shipper at A's request directed the carrier to deliver the goods to B.[28] The carrier might make such delivery against a letter of indemnity from A or B before the shipper's direction to make such delivery had reached him; and it is arguable that, when the direction did reach him, rights under the contract of carriage would be vested in B.[29] 18–159

Rights of original shipper. Section 2(1), refers to rights of suit being "transferred" to the person to whom delivery is to be made under a sea waybill, If full force were given to the word "transferred", then A (the shipper) would lose his rights under the contract of carriage when C (the consignee) acquired such rights; and since in our example the contract contained in or evidenced by the sea waybill from its inception provided for delivery to C, it might seem at first sight to follow that A lost his rights under the contract as soon as it was made. Quite apart from the logical difficulty of such a concept, the reasoning would also give rise to the practically undesirable consequence of depriving A of the rights which a shipper has at common law of redirecting the goods; and we have seen[30] 18–160

---

22 Above, para.18–052.
23 Example based on *President of India v Metcalfe Shipping Co. Ltd (The Dunelmia)* [1970] 1 Q.B. 289, above, paras 18–053, 18–111, where the document in question was a bill of lading.
24 As in *The Dunelmia*, above, n.23.
25 s.2(1)(b); above, para.18–153.
26 Above, para.18–113.
27 s.2(2) contains no reference to sea waybills.
28 For preservation of the shipper's common law right to redirect the goods, see above, para.18–025.
29 By virtue of ss.2(1)(b) and 5(3).
30 Above, para.18–025; *cf.* above, para.18–114.

that the Act preserves this right by providing in section 2(5) that the operation of section 2(1) "shall be without prejudice to any rights which derive from a person's having been an original party to the contract contained in, or evidenced by, a sea waybill." It seems that these words could similarly apply where the goods were damaged by the carrier (in breach of the contract of carriage) when they were at the risk of the shipper or at the risk partly of the shipper and partly of the consignee.[31]

18–161 **Change in consignee.** Section 2(5) preserves only the rights of the original sea waybill shipper. If the sea waybill makes the goods deliverable to A and the shipper validly redirects the goods to B,[32] then rights under the contract of carriage become vested in B[33] and the rights under that contract formerly vested in A[34] become extinct.[35]

(ii) *Imposition of Contractual Liabilities*

18–162 **Carriage of Goods by Sea Act 1992, section 3.** This section applies in the same way where the contract of carriage is contained in or evidenced by a sea waybill as it does where that contract is contained in or evidenced by a bill of lading.[36] That is, a person in whom rights under the contract are vested by virtue of section 2(1), because he is the person to whom delivery of the goods is to be made under a sea waybill, will also become subject to liabilities if he takes or demands delivery of the goods from the carrier or if he makes a claim against the carrier under the contract of carriage in respect of any of those goods.[37] It is even possible (if unlikely) for the section 3(1)(c), which relates to "spent" documents,[38] to apply to carriage under a sea waybill: circumstances in which this can occur are described in paragraph 18–159 above. The rule that the original shipper remains liable under the contract[39] also applies to shipments under sea waybills.

The problems to which section 3 gives rise have been discussed in relation to bills of lading in paragraphs 18–123 to 18–134 above. That discussion is, *mutatis mutandis*, applicable to shipments under sea waybills.

(c) *Mate's Receipts*

18–163 **Nature of mate's receipt.** A mate's receipt is a document issued, on the receipt or shipment of goods, by or on behalf of the shipowner. It

---

[31] *e.g.* in the case of a c.i.f. contract "with variations" of the kind described in para.18–119 above and para.19–006, below; or under Sale of Goods Act 1979 s.33, below, para.18–249.
[32] Above, para.18–025; s.5(3).
[33] s.2(1)(b).
[34] By virtue of s.2(1)(b).
[35] s.2(5)(b).
[36] Of the documents dealt with by the 1992 Act, only ship's delivery orders receive special treatment in s.3: see s.3(2), below, para.18–190.
[37] s.3(1)(a) and (b).
[38] Above, para.18–131.
[39] s.3(3).

acknowledges his receipt of the goods[40] and states their quantity and condition, and it may also state the name of the shipper or owner of the goods. Mate's receipts are preliminary or temporary receipts for the goods which may later be presented to the shipowner or his agent in exchange for bills of lading. Four aspects of such documents call for discussion here: their function as receipts, the question whether they are contractual documents, the question whether they are documents of title to the goods covered by them and the related question of their use for the purpose of securing payment for those goods.

Receipt function. A mate's receipt has been described as a "simple receipt"[41]; as such, it is "not ordinarily anything more than evidence that the goods have been received on board."[42] It is also commonly evidence as to the condition of the goods at the time of the receipt[43]; and this fact can give rise to problems where in this respect there is a discrepancy between the words of the mate's receipt and those of the subsequently issued bill of lading. In one case,[44] the mate's receipt was claused with respect to the condition of the goods while the bill of lading stated them to have been received in good order and condition but also contained words which on their true construction made it subject to the terms of the receipt. It was held that the bill of lading did not give rise to the estoppel with respect to the condition of the goods which normally arises on the issue of a clean bill of lading in favour of an indorsee.[45] It seems, however, that such an estoppel could have arisen if the bill had *not* contained the words making it subject to the terms of the receipt.[46] **18–164**

Where the receipt contains a false statement, *e.g.* as to the apparent order and condition of the goods, the shipowner will not be liable for breach of contract to a shipper who knows the truth but has instigated the making of the statement: thus there will be no such liability where the shipper has persuaded the master to issue a mate's receipt stating that the goods were shipped in apparent good order and condition when they were known by the shipper to be damaged or contaminated.[47] Nor will the shipowner be so liable to a charterer who has suffered loss because of the falsity of the statement if the shipper was a sub-charterer who acted as the

---

[40] In *A/S Inverans Rederei v KG MS Holstencruiser Seeschiffahrtsgesellschaft mbH & Co. (The Holstencruiser)* [1992] 2 Lloyd's Rep. 378 a "container stuffing report" was held not to be a "mate's receipt" within the meaning of the charterparty in that case.

[41] *Naviera Mogor SA v Soc. Metallurgique de Normandie (The Nogar Marin)* [1988] 1 Lloyd's Rep. 412 at p.420.

[42] *Kum v Wah Tat Bank Ltd* [1971] 1 Lloyd's Rep. 439 at p.442.

[43] For the standard of the carrier's duty with regard to the accuracy of such statements, see *The David Agmashenebeli* [2004] EWHC 104 (Comm.), [2002] 2 All E.R. (Comm.) 806; *Carver on Bills of Lading*, 2nd ed. (2005) paras 2–005, 9–163.

[44] *Canadian & Dominion Sugar Co. Ltd v Canadian National (West Indies) Steamships Ltd* [1947] A.C. 46.

[45] For this estoppel, see para.18–028, above.

[46] See *Oceanfocus Shipping Ltd v Hyundai Merchant Marine Co. Ltd (The Hawk)* [1991] 1 Lloyd's Rep. 176 at pp.187–188.

[47] *Trade Star Line Corp. v Mitsui & Co. Ltd (The Arctic Trader)* [1996] 2 Lloyd's Rep. 449 at pp.458–459.

charterer's agent in persuading the master to issue such a false mate's receipt, for in such a case the shipper's knowledge of the true condition of the goods will be attributed to the charterer.[48] But it seems that the shipowner could be liable in respect of such false statements to other parties, for example to an f.o.b. buyer who had paid against the mate's receipt[49] in reliance on the statement and in ignorance of the true condition of the goods when they were shipped. The same principles could apply to other false statements in the mate's receipt, though where the statement related to the fact of shipment no liability to third parties could arise under section 4 of the Carriage of Goods by Sea Act 1992 since that Act does not apply to mate's receipts[50] and liability at common law would, in the present state of the authorities, appear to be excluded on the principle of *Grant v Norway*.[51]

18–165 **Contractual function.** A mate's receipt has been described as a chose in action,[52] but it is not a contract of carriage.[53] It has been suggested that a mate's receipt may be "the best evidence" of the terms of such a contract until the issue of the bill of lading,[54] though such evidence is more likely to be found in the booking note or similar document which comes into being as a result of a reservation of cargo space before the receipt of the goods by the carrier.[55] Before the Carriage of Goods by Sea Act 1992 a mate's receipt was not regarded as a document by means of which contractual rights against the carrier could be transferred to, or created in favour of, third parties[56]; nor is it included in the list of documents to which that Act applies.[57] It follows that a mate's receipt cannot be used as a mechanism for the statutory transfer of contractual rights or imposition of contractual liabilities arising under the bill of lading contract which will normally come into being after the issue of such a receipt. Nor (although the point does not seem to have been decided) is it likely that the transfer or purported

---

[48] This was the point actually decided in *The Arctic Trader*, above.
[49] *e.g.* in the third of the types of f.o.b. contracts described by Devlin J. in *Pyrene Co. Ltd v Scindia Navigation Co. Ltd* [1954] 2 Q.B. 402 at p.424, below, para.20–003; *cf. The Arctic Trader*, above, at p.455.
[50] *cf. The Hawk*, above, n.40, [1999] 1 Lloyd's Rep. 176 at p.185.
[51] (1851) 10 C.B. 665, above, para.18–029.
[52] *Hathesing v Laing* (1873) L.R. 17 Eq. 92 at p.103.
[53] *AR Brown, McFarlane & Co. v Shaw Lovell & Sons and Walker Potts* (1921) 7 Ll. L.R. 36 at p.37; *cf. Trade Star Line Corp. v Mitsui & Co. Ltd (The Arctic Trader)* [1996] 2 Lloyd's Rep. 449 at p.458.
[54] *Sunrise Maritime Inc. v Uvisco Ltd (The Hector)* [1998] 2 Lloyd's Rep. 287 at p.299; though it is with respect, open to question whether the suggestion is supported by the passage on which it relies from *Nippon Yusen Kaisha v Ramjiban Serowgee* [1938] A.C. 429 at pp.445–446. This passage describes a mate's receipt as (a) a receipt and (b) a document binding the shipowner to deliver the bill of lading to a shipper who is owner of the goods and has "contracted for freight". *The Hector* was approved on another point in *Homburg Houtimport BV v Agrosin Private Ltd (The Starsin)* [2003] UKHL 17, [2004] 1 A.C. 715. When the bill of lading is issued, its terms will normally supersede those of the mate's receipt: see *Transpacific Eternity SA v Kanematsu Corp. (The Antares III)* [2002] 1 Lloyd's Rep. 233 at p.236.
[55] See para.18–047, above.
[56] *Naviera Mogor SA v Soc. Metallurgique de Normandie (The Nogar Marin)* [1988] 1 Lloyd's Rep. 412 at p.420.
[57] See Carriage of Goods by Sea Act 1992, s.1(1).

transfer of a mate's receipt would be regarded as an equitable or statutory assignment of rights under that contract or under any antecedent contract between carrier and shipper which may have arisen by virtue of a previous reservation of shipping space.

Mate's receipts generally not documents of title in the traditional common law sense. A mate's receipt is not normally a document of title[58] in the traditional common law sense.[59] A practical reason for this rule is that, if mate's receipts were documents of title, then on the subsequent issue of a bill of lading the undesirable result could follow of there being two documents of title in relation to the same goods[60]; though no such difficulty would arise if the normal practice were followed of issuing the bill of lading only on surrender of the mate's receipt. 18–166

By way of exception to the general rule just stated, a mate's receipt can become a document of title in the common law sense on proof of a custom to that effect. Such a custom was proved in *Kum v Wah Tat Bank Ltd*[61] in relation to mate's receipts in favour of a named consignee in the trade between Sarawak and Singapore, this trade being, on the evidence in that case, for the most part conducted by the use of such receipts and without bills of lading. The Privy Council however held that the custom did not apply to the particular receipt in question since this was marked "not negotiable"[62] so that the custom was inconsistent with the express terms of the receipt. The bank named in the receipt as consignee (which had advanced money to finance the shipment) nevertheless obtained a good pledge over goods, which were shipped under the terms of the mate's receipt so naming it, on the ground that such shipment of the goods amounted to a delivery of the goods to the bank. But if the receipt had named some other person as consignee, then a transfer or purported transfer of the receipt to the bank would not have given the bank any interest in the goods as pledgee. This would also be the position in the absence of evidence of any custom such as that proved in *Kum v Wah Tat Bank Ltd*, since, apart from such evidence, the mate's receipt would not have been a document of title in the traditional common law sense.[63] Some further support for this view is provided by the fact that mate's receipts are not mentioned in the Uniform Customs and Practice for Documentary Credits (UCP)[64] as documents acceptable to banks under documentary credits.[65]

---

[58] *FE Napier v Dexters Ltd* (1926) 26 Ll.L.R. 184 at p.189; *Nippon Yusen Kaisha v Ramjiban Serowgee* [1938] A.C. 429 at p.445; in *Hathesing v Laing* (1873) L.R. 92 at p.105 a custom of the port of Bombay that mate's receipts were "negotiable" (see p.96) was rejected as "against common sense" since captains of foreign ships could not be aware of it.

[59] Above, paras 18–007, 18–062.

[60] *Kum v Wah Tat Bank Ltd* [1971] 1 Lloyd's Rep. 439 at p.446.

[61] Above.

[62] Meaning, in this context, "not transferable": see above, para.18–084.

[63] See above, paras 18–007, 18–062, 18–075.

[64] For judicial reliance on the U.C.P. as evidence of commercial practice, *cf. Homburg Houtimport BV v Agrosin Private Ltd (The Starsin)* [2003] UKHL 17, [2004] 1 A.C. 715 at [16], [47], [77], [126] and [128].

[65] Too much should not, however, be made of this point since some documents acceptable to banks are plainly not documents of title in any sense: *e.g.* courier and post receipts which may be accepted under U.C.P., Art. 29.

18–167 **Whether mate's receipts documents of title in the statutory sense.** A mate's receipt can, in spite of not being a document of title in the traditional common law sense,[66] give the person in possession of it some degree of control over the goods to which it refers. This possibility arises because prima facie the person in possession of a mate's receipt in which he is named as shipper is entitled to the bill of lading[67]; and the carrier is normally neither bound nor entitled to deliver the bill of lading to anyone else.[68] For this reason mate's receipts are sometimes held as a form of security for the price under contracts which provide for payment against mate's receipt.[69] This might suggest that mate's receipts may (in the words of section 1(4) of the Factors Act 1889) be "used in the ordinary course of business as proof of the . . . control of goods" and that they may therefore be documents of title in the statutory sense.[70] The point seems never to have been raised in England; and the question whether mate's receipts are so used in the ordinary course of business seems to be one of fact.[71] Judicial statements that mate's receipts are not "documents of title"[72] are perfectly general and not confined to the common law sense of the phrase. But they occur in the context of the passing of property between buyer and seller, on which the statutory definition of "document of title" has no bearing; and they therefore do not conclude the question whether mate's receipts may be "documents of title" within the statutory definition.

18–168 **Use of mate's receipt as security for payment.** Since a mate's receipt may give a seller some degree of control over the goods,[73] it is possible for him to reserve the "right of disposal"[74] by having the receipt made out in his own name as shipper: in this way, he can prevent the passing of property in the goods until payment in exchange for the receipt.[75] But there are also dangers in relying on such a document as a method of securing payment of the price. For "if the mate's receipt acknowledges receipt from a shipper other than the person who actually receives the mate's receipt, and in

---

[66] See above, para.18–166.
[67] *Nippon Yusen Kaisha v Ramjiban Serowgee* [1938] A.C. 429 at p.445.
[68] *Falk v Fletcher* (1865) 18 C.B. (N.S.) 403; *cf. Ruck v Hatfield* (1822) 5 B. & Ald. 632 at p.634. Under Carriage of Goods by Sea Act 1971, Sch., art. III, r.3, the carrier is bound to issue a bill of lading "on demand of the shipper" and "to the shipper," who will usually be the person in possession of any mate's receipt relating to the goods.
[69] See the terms of the contracts in *FE Napier v Dexters Ltd* (1926) 26 L1.L.R. 62; *ibid.* at p.184; *AR Brown, McFarlane & Co. v C Shaw Lovell & Sons and Walter Potts & Co.* (1921) 7 Ll.L.R. 36; *Nippon Yusen Kaisha v Ramjiban Serowgee* [1938] A.C. 429; below, para.18–168.
[70] Above, para.18–009.
[71] *cf. Ramdas Vithaldas Dubar v S Amerchand* (1916) 85 L.J.P.C. 214; L.R. 43 Ind. App. 164 (Indian railway receipts: these are expressly included in the statutory definition of documents of title in Indian Sale of Goods Act 1930, s.2(4); *cf.* also, as to such receipts, *Official Assignee of Madras v Mercantile Bank of India Ltd* [1935] A.C. 53).
[72] Above, para.18–166, n.58.
[73] Above, para.18–167.
[74] Within Sale of Goods Act 1979, s.18, rule 5(2): see below, para.18–211.
[75] *Falk v Fletcher* (1865) 18 C.B. (N.S.) 403, below, para.18–228; contrast *FE Napier v Dexters Ltd* (1926) 26 Ll.L. Rep. 62 and 184, below, para.20–076.

particular if the property is in that shipper and the shipper has contracted for the freight, the shipowner will prima facie be entitled and indeed bound to deliver the bill of lading to that person."[76] Thus in *Nippon Yusen Kaisha v Ramjiban Serowgee*[77] goods were sold f.a.s.[78] Calcutta on the terms that the sellers' lien for the price was to subsist until payment in full, so long as the sellers were in possession of mate's receipts. The goods were delivered by the sellers' suppliers alongside a ship on which the buyers had booked space; and mate's receipts were issued naming the buyers as shippers. While these receipts were in the possession of the sellers, the shipowners issued bills of lading to the buyers; these were subsequently transferred for value to a third party, to whom the shipowners delivered the goods. It was held that the shipowners were under no liability to the sellers for having issued bills of lading to the buyers without requiring production of mate's receipts, as the buyers were not only the owners of the goods (property having passed on delivery alongside[79]) but also the persons named as shippers in the mate's receipts. It made no difference that the contract under which the shipowners had accepted the goods for carriage[80] provided that bills of lading were not to be issued except on presentation of mate's receipts. This provision was solely for the protection of the shipowner and could be waived by him[81]: although he was not bound to issue bills of lading to the buyers without presentation of mate's receipts, he had committed no wrong against the sellers by so issuing the bills. The position will be the same, though the mate's receipt is in the seller's name, if the buyer is by custom regarded as the shipper, and if the property has passed to him, *e.g.* on his acceptance of a draft for the price.[82] The seller can, however, improve his position by giving notice to the shipowner not to issue a bill of lading except to the person who has actually delivered the goods, even though he was not named as the shipper in the mate's receipt. According to the Privy Council in the *Nippon Yusen Kaisha* case, the shipowner would not be at liberty to disregard such a notice.[83]

(d) *Delivery Orders and Warrants*

Introductory. The use of delivery orders in overseas sales is common **18–169**
where bulk cargoes are split into more parcels than there are bills of lading. We shall see that this practice gives rise to considerable difficulties[84]; but it is to be preferred to the dangerous practice[85] of procuring substitute bills of lading, after the issue of the original one, for quantities corresponding with

[76] *Nippon Yusen Kaisha v Ramjiban Serowgee* [1938] A.C. 429 at pp.445–446.
[77] Above; and see below, para.18–212.
[78] Below, para.21–010.
[79] Below, para.18–228.
[80] Evidently, the buyer's booking of shipping space was regarded as having contractual force.
[81] *Nippon Yusen Kaisha v Ramjiban Serowgee* [1938] A.C. 429 at p.448.
[82] *Cowasjee v Thompson* (1845) 5 Moo.P.C. 165.
[83] [1938] A.C. 429 at p.446.
[84] Below, paras 18–285 to 18–307.
[85] *Noble Resources Ltd v Cavalier Shipping Corp. (The Atlas)* [1996] 1 Lloyd's Rep. 642 at p.644 ("fraught with danger"); above, para.18–095.

those sold to each of the buyers.[86] Delivery orders may also be used to expedite the performance of contracts where bills of lading representing the goods are delayed in transmission.

The use of delivery orders gives rise to at least three groups of legal problems. The first is whether the particular document tendered for the purpose of performing a contract of sale is in conformity with that contract. This a question of construction, to be answered in accordance with the common law principles discussed in paragraphs 18–170 to 18–172 below. The second problem is whether, and if so in what circumstances, the person in whose favour the document is made out can acquire contractual rights and become subject to contractual liabilities under the contract of carriage in pursuance of which the document was issued. In answering this question, a distinction must be drawn between documents which do not, and those which do, fall within the definition of "ship's delivery order" given in the Carriage of Goods by Sea Act 1992.[87] The contractual effects of documents which do not fall within this definition depend on the common law rules discussed in paragraphs 18–173 and 18–174 below; while the contractual effects of documents which do fall within this definition are specified in those provisions of the 1992 Act (and of the Contracts (Rights of Third Parties) Act 1999) which are discussed in paragraphs 18–175 to 18–192 below. Great care is needed in approaching terminological issues relating to the two problems so far described. It is by no means inconceivable (though it may be unlikely) for a document to be a good tender under a contract of sale which calls for a "ship's delivery order" in spite of the fact that it does not satisfy all the requirements of the statutory definition of that expression in the 1992 Act. The third problem (or group of problems) is whether documents of the kind here under discussion are documents of title in the common law or statutory sense: this is discussed in paragraphs 18–193 to 18–198 below.

(i) *Common Law Definitions*

18–170 **Delivery orders and warrants.** The term "delivery order" is used to describe documents of various kinds. In its most obvious sense, it refers to an order given by an owner of goods to a person in possession of them, *e.g.* as carrier or warehouseman, directing the latter to deliver the goods to the person named in the order. However, the term is not one of art and is also used in a number of other senses. Thus it may be used to refer to a document issued by a person in possession of goods stating that he will deliver the goods to a named person, or to a named person or his assignee, or to the holder: such a document is sometimes referred to as a "delivery warrant". The term "delivery order" may, again, refer to an order addressed to a person who is not in possession of the goods at all, but who is expected to acquire possession or some other kind of control: thus it may refer to an order by a seller of goods given to his agent at the port of

[86] *SIAT di del Ferro v Tradax Overseas SA* [1978] 2 Lloyd's Rep. 470, affirmed [1980] 1 Lloyd's Rep. 53; below, para.19–034.
[87] s.1(4), below, para.18–176.

destination, directing the agent to deliver the goods, when they arrive, or to cause them to be delivered, to some person there, *e.g.* to the buyer,[88] or simply to some person to be nominated by the seller.[89] It cannot be said that any of these meanings is the "correct" one; and where a contract calls for tender of, or payment against, a "delivery order" the question in which sense that expression is used is one of construction in each case.

Ship's delivery order. Similarly, the meaning of the expression "ship's delivery order" depends, at common law, on the context in which it occurs. 18–171
In *Colin & Shields v W Weddel & Co.*[90] a c.i.f. contract provided for payment on presentation of documents, which were to include, *inter alia*, "ship's delivery order (the latter to be countersigned by banker, shipbroker, captain, or mate if so required) . . . Should bill of lading and/or insurance policy not be supplied, buyers to be put in the same position as if they had been in possession of such documents." The order which was tendered had been signed by the shipowner; it was addressed to the Master Porter at the docks where the goods had been delivered, and authorised him to deliver the goods to the person named in the order, who was the buyer. This was held not to be a "ship's delivery order" within the meaning of the contract of sale. The object of the parties to that contract was to put the buyer as nearly as possible into the position in which he would have been, had he been given a bill of lading.[91] A delivery order addressed *to* the shipowner and countersigned by him or on his behalf would have approximated to some extent to this position in that it might have given the buyer *some* rights against the shipowner by reason of the inference of attornment which could be drawn from the shipowner's countersignature or from his subsequent words or conduct.[92] The delivery order which was tendered was one which had been given *by* the shipowner and was addressed to a third party: it gave the buyer no rights against the shipowner at all. But it should not be thought that an order issued *by* the shipowner is less likely to be a ship's delivery order than one addressed *to* him. The contrary is the case: thus where a contract uses the words, "ship's delivery order", they may refer to a document (in the nature of a delivery warrant[93]) issued by the shipowner promising to deliver goods from the ship to a named person or to the holder of such order.[94]

The essential feature of a ship's delivery order is that the document should give the person in whose favour it is issued some rights (probably of

---

88 As in *The Julia* [1949] A.C. 293.

89 *Waren Import Gesellschaft Krohn & Co. v Internationale Graanhandel Thegra NV* [1975] 1 Lloyd's Rep. 146.

90 [1952] 2 All E.R. 337 (below, para.18–172).

91 *cf. Cremer v General Carriers SA* [1974] 1 W.L.R. 341 at p.350.

92 *cf.* below, paras 18–172, 18–174. Apart from such attornment, it is submitted that (notwithstanding apparently contrary dicta in *Colin & Shields v W Weddel & Co.*, above, at pp.342, 343) an order addressed *to* the shipowner would not, merely by reason of being so addressed, be a "ship's delivery order".

93 See above, para.18–170.

94 This seems to be the sense in which Roskill J. used the expression in *Margarine Union GmbH v Cambay Prince SS Co. Ltd (The Wear Breeze)* [1969] 1 Q.B. 219 at p.231.

a contractual nature) against the ship.[95] It most obviously has this effect where it is issued by or on behalf of the shipowner and contains, expressly or by necessary implication, a promise by him to the person to whom it is issued or transferred (*i.e.* usually to the buyer of the goods) to deliver the goods to that person. It is submitted that so long as the document contains some such promise, it may be a ship's delivery order even though it is not issued by the shipowner, but is addressed to him and attorned to by him.[96] If no such promise can be inferred, the document is unlikely to be a "ship's delivery order"; for it will then fail in its (presumptively intended) object of putting the buyer as nearly as possible into the position in which he would have been, had he received a bill of lading. In *Colin & Shields v W Weddel & Co.*[97] the order was not a "ship's delivery order" because it contained no such promise by the shipowner, but only an authority from him to the bailee in actual possession of the goods to deliver them up to the buyer, in whose favour the order had been issued. Similarly, an order addressed by a charterer or sub-charterer to the chief officer of the ship, directing him to deliver the goods to the holder of the order, but not attorned to by or on behalf of the shipowner is not a "ship's delivery order".[98] The same is true of an order issued by a charterer on behalf of the shipowner and addressed to the charterer's agent at the port of destination, directing him to deliver the goods to the order of a seller of goods: such a document contains no *undertaking* by the shipowner to deliver; and, even if such an undertaking could be spelled out, it would not be one in favour of the buyer.[99] Nor is a document issued by a time charterer (not acting on behalf of the shipowner) in the form of a bill of lading a "ship's delivery order" since it does not purport to be such and imposes no obligations on the shipowner.[1]

Similar principles determine the meaning of the expression "ship's release". This may mean an order *by* the ship addressed to a third person, for example to one in whose warehouse the goods have been stored[2]; or an undertaking by the ship to deliver the goods, given either by attornment to a delivery order addressed *to* the ship, or by a document in the nature of a delivery warrant.[3]

---

[95] *Waren Import Gesellschaft Krohn & Co. v Internationale Graanhandel Thegra NV* [1975] 1 Lloyd's Rep. 146 at pp.154–155, explaining *Cremer v General Carriers SA* [1974] 1 W.L.R. 341 at p.350.

[96] According to a dictum in *Waren Import Gesellschaft Krohn & Co. v Internationale Graanhandel Thegra NV* [1975] 1 Lloyd's Rep. 146 at p.155 the document must be issued (or reissued) by the shipowner *and* contain a promise of the kind described in the text; but it is submitted that the second of these elements should be regarded as the crucial one.

[97] [1952] 2 All E.R. 337; above, n.90.

[98] *Margarine Union GmbH v Cambay Prince SS Co. Ltd (The Wear Breeze)*, above, n.94.

[99] *Waren Import Gesellschaft Krohn & Co. v Internationale Graanhandel Thegra NV* [1975] 1 Lloyd's Rep. 146.

[1] *SIAT di del Ferro v Tradax Overseas SA* [1978] 2 Lloyd's Rep. 470; *affd.*, without express reference to this point [1980] 1 Lloyd's Rep. 53.

[2] As in *Colin & Shields v Weddel & Co.* [1952] 2 All E.R. 337.

[3] See *Heilbert, Symons & Co. Ltd v Harvey, Christie-Miller & Co.* (1922) 12 Ll.L.R. 455 where the term "ship's release" was used in one of these two senses; for delivery warrants, see above, para.18–170.

Countersigned delivery orders. Contracts of sale which call for or permit the tender of delivery orders sometimes require these to be countersigned or certified by certain named or designated persons,[4] *e.g.* by a banker or ship-broker, or by the master or the mate. The object of this requirement is presumably to make the signer, or the person on whose behalf he signs, contractually liable on the delivery order, though it is by no means clear whether a mere countersignature actually produces this effect. If a third party's liability is desired, it is safer to stipulate for this expressly, *e.g.* by requiring a guarantee or a letter of indemnity. 18–172

(ii) *Contractual Effects at Common Law*

Contractual effects of issue of delivery order. A may have goods in B's warehouse and issue to C an order calling on B to deliver the goods to C. If B refuses to deliver the goods to C, one question that may arise is whether C has any remedy against A. This depends on the intention of the persons giving and receiving the order.[5] The issue of the delivery order may amount either to a promise by A to C to procure the delivery of the goods; or only to an authority given by A to B to deliver the goods to C.[6] If the order amounts to a promise which is intended to be binding and is supported by consideration, it will give rise to a contract between A and C. 18–173

If a seller gives a delivery order to his buyer, and the warehouseman refuses to deliver or attorn, the buyer is entitled to damages from the seller for breach of the contract of sale and need not prove any separate contract arising from the giving and receipt of the delivery order. Such a contract would only have to be proved if the buyer sought a remedy against a person (other than the seller) who had issued the delivery order, *e.g.* if it had been issued to the buyer by a person to whom the seller had pledged the goods.[7]

Effects of attornment to a delivery order. If, in the example given at the beginning of paragraph 18–173, the warehouseman B either attorns to C or issues a warrant in C's favour or in some other way makes a promise to C, he may be under some liability to C in the event of his failing to deliver the goods. Such liability may be based either on contract or on estoppel. 18–174

So far as contract is concerned, attornment or the issue of a warrant is prima facie a promise to C; and the questions are whether there is contractual intention and consideration to turn the promise into a contract. Consideration may easily be provided, *e.g.* if under the terms of the delivery order or warrant the holder undertakes to pay, or if he actually pays, the warehouseman's charges. Where the goods are in the possession of a

---

[4] *e.g Colin & Shields v Weddel & Co.* [1952] 2 All E.R. 337 (above, para.18–171); *John Martin of London Ltd v A E Taylor & Co. Ltd* [1953] 2 Lloyd's Rep. 589; *Olearia Tirrena SpA v NV Algemeene Oliehandel (The Osterbek)* [1972] 2 Lloyd's Rep. 341; *Cremer v General Carriers SA* [1974] 1 W.L.R. 341; *Waren Import Gesellschaft Krohn v Internationale Graanhandel Thegra NV* [1975] 1 Lloyd's Rep. 146.

[5] *Alicia Hosiery Ltd v Brown, Shipley & Co. Ltd* [1970] 1 Q.B. 195.

[6] *ibid*.

[7] *ibid.* (the buyer's claim against the pledgee failed for lack of proof of contractual intention).

carrier who attorns or issues a document in the nature of a warrant or ship's delivery order, the further question arises whether the terms of the resulting contract can be said to incorporate by reference the terms of the contract under which the goods are carried. In one case involving a "ship's release" this was held not to be the case. Bailhache J. said: "All that the ship's release does is to bind the shipowner to hand over to the person to whom the release is given the goods which are mentioned in the release: but it does not make the shipowner liable for any acts of negligence on his part in the carriage of the goods from the port of loading to the port of destination."[8] More recently, however, in *Cremer v General Carriers SA*[9] two ship's delivery orders were issued to the holder of a bill of lading covering a bulk shipment of broken tapioca roots, so as to enable him to dispose of part of the shipment to a buyer. He transferred one of the orders to the buyer who presented it to the carrier and paid the freight on the portion of the goods to which the order related. It was held that there was a contract[10] between the buyer and the carrier under which the latter could be made liable in respect of damage to the goods. The contract was on the same terms as that evidenced by, or contained in, the bill of lading, which was expressly incorporated by reference in the delivery order. The earlier decision of Bailhache J. can be distinguished on the ground that, in that case, there was no such incorporation. This is also likely to be the position where the delivery order is attorned to by the shipowner, but the bill of lading contains or evidences a contract of carriage, not between the shipper and the shipowner, but between the shipper and a charterer or sub-charterer of the ship[11]; for it is implausible to suggest that, by attorning to the delivery order, the shipowner agreed to be bound by terms of a contract to which he was a stranger and of the contents of which he was unaware. In cases in which the terms of the bill of lading are not incorporated, it remains true that the delivery order will confer "some rights against the person in possession of the goods, even though falling short of the rights conferred by the transfer of the bill of lading."[12] Where the bill of lading terms are incorporated in the delivery order, the person entitled to delivery under it will, with respect to contractual rights against the carrier, be in as good a position as if he had been a transferee of a bill of lading. With regard to contractual liabilities, he may also on presenting the delivery order and claiming the goods, be taken to have made an offer to the carrier to enter into an implied contract incorporating at least some of the terms of the contract of carriage[13]; and he can, on the carrier's acceptance of that offer (*e.g.* by delivering the goods), not only acquire rights, but also incur liabilities under that contract.

---

[8] *Heilbert, Symonds & Co. Ltd v Harvey, Christie-Miller & Co.* (1922) 12 Ll.L.R. 455 at p.457; *cf. Colin & Shields v Weddel & Co.* [1952] 2 All E.R. 337 at p.343.
[9] [1974] 1 W.L.R. 341. The question how this case would now be decided under the Carriage of Goods by Sea Act 1992 is discussed in para.18–183, below.
[10] On the analogy of *Brandt v Liverpool, etc. Steam Navigation Co.* [1924] 1 K.B. 575, above, para.18–139.
[11] As in *Margarine Union GmbH v Cambay Prince SS Co. Ltd (The Wear Breeze)* [1969] 1 Q.B. 219 (see p.231); *cf.* above, para.18–171.
[12] *Waren Import Gesellschaft Krohn & Co. v Internationale Graanhandel Thegra NV* [1975] 1 Lloyd's Rep. 146 at p.154.
[13] Above, paras 18–138, 18–139.

So far as estoppel is concerned, it is well settled that an estoppel by representation cannot be founded on a promise, but only on a statement of fact.[14] Prima facie, therefore, the promise to deliver contained in the attornment to a delivery order or in the issue of a warrant or of a ship's delivery order does not give rise to any such estoppel; nor does the so-called doctrine of promissory estoppel apply, as the situation here under discussion concerns the creation of new rights and not the variation or abrogation of existing ones.[15] But if a warehouseman in a delivery warrant makes statements of fact which are untrue (*e.g.* that the goods are in his warehouse, or that they are in good condition, when they are not) he may be estopped from denying the truth of such statements.[16] A similar estoppel may operate against a carrier who issues a delivery order (or warrant) indicating that the goods were shipped in good condition. Where such an order induces action in reliance on the statement (for example, by causing a buyer to pay for the goods against the order[17]) the carrier will be estopped from relying on the defence that the goods were not damaged through his breach of contract but were already defective at the time of shipment.[18] It would seem that a carrier or other bailee could be similarly liable if he expressly or by clear implication made a statement about the condition of the goods in an attornment to a delivery order.[19] But such liability will normally[20] arise only if there is some positive act of attornment: the mere receipt by a warehouseman of a delivery order without either objection or acknowledgement on his part is not sufficient to raise an estoppel against him.[21]

(iii) *Ship's Delivery Orders: Statutory Transfer of Contractual Rights*[22]

Carriage of Goods by Sea Act 1992. Section 2(1)(c) provides that "a person who becomes . . . the person to whom delivery of the goods to which a ship's delivery order relates is to be made in accordance with the 18–175

[14] *Jorden v Money* (1854) 5 H.L.Cas. 185; *Roebuck v Mungovin* [1994] 2 A.C. 224 at p.235.
[15] See *Chitty on Contracts* (29th ed.), para.3–098.
[16] See *Coventry, Shepperd & Co. v GE Ry* (1883) 11 Q.B.D. 776; *cf. Alicia Hosiery Ltd v Brown Shipley & Co. Ltd* [1970] 1 Q.B. 195 at p.206; *Griswold v Haven* 25 N.Y. 595 (1862); *Maynegrain Pty Ltd v Compafina Bank* [1982] 2 N.S.W.R. 141 (reversed on other grounds (1984) 58 A.L.J.R. 389, PC).
[17] The fact that the buyer is already bound by his contract with the seller to make such payment does not preclude him from showing that, as against the carrier, he relied on the terms of the delivery order: *Cremer v General Carriers SA* [1974] 1 W.L.R. 341; it only prevents him from relying on a presumption of such reliance: *ibid.* p.352, explaining *The Skarp* [1935] P. 134. For false statements in ship's delivery orders as to the fact of shipment, see above, para.18–041.
[18] *Cremer v General Carriers SA*, above.
[19] The dictum from the *Alicia Hosiery* case referred to in n.16 is not inconsistent with this view: it only rules out liability based on estoppel on the part of the person *issuing* the delivery order (not on the part of the person *attorning* to it).
[20] Inactivity may sometimes amount to breach of a duty to speak: *e.g. Vitol SA v Norelf Ltd* [1996] A.C. 800 at p.812: but it is unlikely that such a duty will arise in the context here under discussion.
[21] *Laurie & Morewood v Dudin & Sons* [1926] 1 K.B. 223.
[22] For a fuller account, see *Carver on Bills of Lading* (2nd ed., 2005), paras 8–035 to 8–054.

undertaking contained in the order, shall (by virtue of becoming . . . the person to whom delivery is to be made) have transferred to and vested in him all rights of suit under the contract of carriage as if he had been a party to that contract." In relation to a ship's delivery order, "the contract of carriage" means "the contract under or for the purposes of which the undertaking contained in the order is given"[23]; this definition must be read together with the definition of "ship's delivery order" to be considered in and after paragraph 18–176 below. As a matter of law, the transfer of contractual rights under a ship's delivery order differs from the transfer of such rights under a bill of lading[24] (and resembles such transfer under a sea waybill[25]) in that it can be effected without transfer of possession of the document: the person identified in the order as the person to whom delivery is to be made does not need to become the holder or lawful holder of the document in order to acquire contractual rights against the carrier by virtue of it. In the case of ship's delivery orders, however, this principle is subject to section 2(3)(a),[26] by which rights vested in any person by virtue of section 2(1) in relation to a ship's delivery order "shall be so vested subject to the terms of the order". Those terms may provide that the carrier will deliver the goods in question only against, or on presentation of, the order; and if the order contains such terms, then it seems that contractual rights can be acquired only by a person with possession of the order. The contractual effects of delivery orders which do *not* fall within the statutory definition of "ship's delivery order" continue to be governed by the rules of common law discussed in paragraphs 18–173 and 18–174 above.

18–176 **Definition of "ship's delivery order".** Section 1(4) of the 1992 Act provides that references in the Act to a ship's delivery order are "references to any document which is neither a bill of lading nor a sea waybill but contains an undertaking which—(a) is given under or for the purposes of a contract for the carriage[27] by sea of the goods to which the document relates, or of goods which include those goods; and (b) is an undertaking by the carrier to a person identified in the document to deliver the goods to which the document relates to that person." References in the Act "to a person's being identified in a document include references to his being identified by a description which allows for the identity of the person in question to be varied, in accordance with the terms of the document, after its issue."[28] In discussing these definitions[29] it will be helpful to begin with the standard situation in which A ships goods in bulk on B's ship under a single bill of lading and then sells part of those goods to C. Delivery to C will usually be secured by means of a delivery order; and if that order contains an undertaking by B to C to deliver goods shipped under the bill

---

[23] s.5(1).
[24] Above, paras 18–102, 18–104.
[25] Above, para.18–153.
[26] Where the order relates to only part of the goods covered by the contract of carriage, the principle is also subject to s.2(3)(b): see para.18–185 below.
[27] As defined by s.5(1), above, para.18–175.
[28] s.5(3).
[29] Below, paras 18–177 to 18–183.

of lading to C, then that order is likely to be a ship's delivery order and to transfer to C at least some of A's rights under his contract of carriage with B. Such a transfer can take place even though the goods form an undifferentiated part of an identified bulk.[30]

"Neither a bill of lading nor a sea waybill". The main differences between these types of documents and ship's delivery orders are that bills of lading and sea waybills are receipts for the goods and contain or evidence contracts of carriage.[31] A ship's delivery order has neither of these characteristics: it is not a receipt but an undertaking to deliver[32]; and although it is "given under or for the purposes of"[33] a contract of carriage it does not contain or evidence such a contract. 18–177

A ship's delivery order is also distinguishable from a bill of lading within the 1992 Act[34] in that prima facie such an order is not transferable by indorsement (where necessary) and delivery. The express terms of such an order may indeed purport to make a ship's delivery order transferable in this way: *e.g.* where B's undertaking in the order is expressed to be to deliver the goods "to C or order" or "to bearer".[35] If in the first of these cases C indorsed and delivered the order to D, or if in the second he simply delivered it to D, then D would become the "person identified"[36] in the order as the person to whom delivery was to be made. But an order in these terms would still differ from a bill of lading in that it would not be a receipt for the goods or contain or evidence a contract of carriage; and that it would not be a document of title in the traditional[37] common law sense.[38]

"Contains an undertaking". To be a ship's delivery order within section 1(4), the document must "contain" an undertaking by the carrier (B). This requirement is most obviously satisfied where B issues a document in which he undertakes to deliver the goods to C. Where the document originates as a request from the shipper (A) to the carrier (B) to deliver the goods to C, a ship's delivery order may come in to existence by virtue of a written attornment by B to C. It may be necessary to regard that order as consisting of two documents (the attornment incorporating the request by reference) if only one of them refers to the contract of carriage between A and B. An oral attornment would not suffice since no "document" would "contain" it. 18–178

"Given under or for the purposes of a contract for the carriage [of the goods] by sea".[39] This requirement is most obviously satisfied where the document expressly refers to the contract under which the goods are 18–179

---

[30] s.5(4), above, para.18–137.
[31] ss.1(3)(a), 5(1).
[32] s.1(4).
[33] ss.1(4)(a), 5(1).
[34] See s.1(2)(a), above, para.18–103.
[35] *cf.* the terms of the order (not connected with carriage by sea) in *Sterns Ltd v Vickers Ltd* [1923] 1 K.B. 78.
[36] ss.1(4)(b), 5(3). But such a case would give rise to the further problems discussed in para.18–182, below.
[37] See above, paras 18–007, 18–062.
[38] See below, paras 18–193, 18–195.
[39] ss.1(4)(a), 5(1).

carried: *e.g.* where it incorporates by reference the terms of the bill of lading issued by the carrier in respect of the shipment.[40] Where the document contains no such reference, it is arguable that it might be linked to the contract of carriage by extrinsic evidence. Where the document can be linked with the contract of carriage either by its express terms or by extrinsic evidence, a further question could arise as to the extent to which the order was intended to incorporate the terms of the contract of carriage. This would be a question of the shipowner's contractual intention, similar to that which could arise at common law.[41]

The "contract for the carriage [of the goods] by sea" to which the definition refers will normally be contained in or evidenced by a bill of lading but there is nothing in the statutory language[42] to rule out the possibility of its being contained in or evidenced by a sea waybill or even of its being contained in a voyage charterparty.[43]

18–180 **"Of goods which include those goods".**[44] This phrase covers the situation in which A ships a quantity of goods in bulk under a single bill of lading and, having sold part of the goods to C, performs the contract of sale by tendering a delivery order in respect of that part to C. Such a document can be a ship's delivery order even though it relates only to a part of the shipment and even though the goods covered by the order form an undifferentiated part of the bulk shipment so that, when the order is issued, the part to which the order relates cannot be identified.[45]

18–181 **"An undertaking by the carrier".**[46] The crucial feature of a ship's delivery order is that it must contain an undertaking by the carrier. This requirement would clearly not be satisfied where the order took the form merely of a request by the shipper addressed to his own agent[47] or even to the carrier, or of a direction issued by the carrier to a warehouseman holding the goods on the carrier's behalf.[48] In a number of cases discussed in paragraph 18–171, documents have been held not to be "ship's delivery orders" at common law precisely because they contained no undertakings by the carrier (or no undertakings to the relevant person).[49] It is submitted that these documents would likewise not fall within the statutory definition

---

[40] As in *Cremer v General Carriers SA* [1974] 1 All E.R. 1; the question whether the order in that case would now be a ship's delivery order is discussed in para.18–183, below.

[41] *Heilbert, Symons & Co. Ltd v Harvey, Christie-Miller & Co.* (1992) 12 Ll.L.R. 455 at p.457; above, para.18–174.

[42] The definition of "the contract of carriage", as applied to a ship's delivery order, in s.5(1)(b) contains no reference to a bill of lading.

[43] There is, however, no reference to the second of these possibilities in Law Com. No. 196, Scot. Law Com. 130 (1991) paras 5.25 to 5.31.

[44] s.1(4)(a).

[45] s.5(4)(b), above, para.18–137.

[46] s.1(4)(b).

[47] As in *The Julia* [1949] A.C. 293.

[48] As in *Colin & Shields v W Weddel & Co.* [1952] 2 All E.R. 337.

[49] See the authorities cited in para.18–171, above, nn. 97–1.

of a ship's delivery order, for the statutory requirement of an undertaking by the carrier appears to be derived from the corresponding common law concept. It is true that the common law concept of a ship's delivery order was developed largely in the context of the question whether the order was good tender between seller and buyer; and an order is not necessarily such a good tender merely because it is a ship's delivery order within the statutory definition.[50] But an important aspect of the common law concept lies in the capacity of the document to give rise to contractual rights against the carrier, and this is also the purpose of the statutory definition of a ship's delivery order.

The undertaking must be one given "by the carrier"; and here (as elsewhere)[51] difficulties can arise in identifying that person, particularly if goods are shipped in a chartered ship. An order issued by the charterer would not be issued by "the carrier" if the contract of carriage were between shipper and shipowner.[52] If the contract of carriage were between shipper and charterer,[53] it is arguable that both charterer and shipowner were "the carrier"[54] so that an order issued by either of them could be a "ship's delivery order" within section 1(4).

Person to whom the undertaking must be given. Section 1(4)(b) requires 18–182
the undertaking to be given "to a person identified in the document" and to be one "to deliver the goods . . . to that person". It follows from these words that the person to whom the undertaking is given and the person to whom delivery is to be made must be *the same* person. Thus if A ships goods on B's ship and B gives an undertaking to C to deliver the goods or some of them to C (*e.g.* because C has bought the goods from A), then the document can be a ship's delivery order; but a document could not be a ship's delivery order if B gave an undertaking to A to deliver the goods to C. An undertaking given by B to A to deliver the goods to A or A's order could be a ship's delivery order for the purposes of the Act[55] even though it was not at common law a ship's delivery order for the purpose of enabling A to tender it under a c.i.f. sale of the goods to C: in the context of such a sale, the document must contain an undertaking to make delivery to the buyer.[56]

The above requirement of section 1(4)(b) must further be considered together with section 5(3) under which "References in this Act to a person's being identified in a document include references to his being identified by a description which allows for the identity of the person in question to be varied, in accordance with the terms of the document, after its issue." This subsection is intended to cover the case where a document

---

[50] Below, para.18–182; *cf.* above, para.18–170.

[51] Above, paras 18–036, 18–127.

[52] See *The Rewia* [1991] 2 Lloyd's Rep. 325.

[53] As in *Homburg Houtimpoit BV v Agrosin Private Ltd (The Starsin)* [2003] UKHL 12, [2004] 1 A.C. 715, above para.18–127.

[54] *cf.* above, para.18–127.

[55] And so transfer contractual rights to C if A gave the requisite direction.

[56] See *Waren Import Gesellschaft Krohn & Co. v Internationale Graanhandel Thegra NV* [1975] 1 Lloyd's Rep. 146, above, para.18–171; below, para.19–024.

makes goods deliverable "to C or order"[57] and it could presumably apply whether, under the terms of the document, the order was to be given by C or by A. If the document provided that the order was to be given by C, and C ordered delivery to be made to D (*e.g.* because D was a sub-buyer from C), then the document would become one which contained an undertaking by B given to C to deliver the goods to D. This would appear not to satisfy section 1(4)(b), since the person to whom the undertaking was given would not be the same person as the person to whom delivery was to be made. Hence the document, though originally a ship's delivery order, would cease to be one when C ordered delivery to be made to D. This inconvenient conclusion can, however, be avoided by providing in the document that a change in the identity of the person to whom delivery was to be made should also have the effect of changing the identity of the person to whom the undertaking was given.[58]

18–183 **Cremer v General Carriers.** The difficulty of determining whether a particular document is a "ship's delivery order" within the 1992 Act is well illustrated by the facts (so far as they are reported) of *Cremer v General Carriers SA*,[59] where a c.i.f. seller had, for the purpose of performing part of his obligations under the contract of sale, obtained a delivery order making the goods deliverable to his order and relating to part of a larger quantity covered by a bill of lading. The seller "presented the delivery order . . . to"[60] the buyer, who was held to have a cause of action against the carrier on an implied contract of the kind discussed in paragraphs 18–114 and 18–140 above. Kerr J. evidently regarded the order as a "ship's delivery order"[61] in the common law sense[62]; and the questions would now arise whether the document fell within the definition of such an order given in section 1(4) of the 1992 Act, and whether it would transfer any rights under the contract of carriage to the buyer by virtue of section 2(1). These questions are hard to answer, particularly because the precise terms of the order are not given in the report. Kerr J.'s description of a ship's delivery order as one "issued by the shipowner's agents addressed to the master or chief officer or other persons authorising delivery to the holder or to the order of a named person"[63] would certainly not fit the statutory definition, for such an order would not contain any undertaking by the carrier. However, the order is also stated to have "incorporated all the terms of the bill of lading"[64]; and so it must have contained, at least by reference, an undertaking by the carrier to deliver the goods. That undertaking, however, was addressed to and given in favour of the seller; and his having merely "presented" the order to the buyer would not of itself now give the buyer

[57] See Explanatory Notes to Cl. 5(3) of the Bill attached to Law Com. No. 196, Scot. Law Com. 130 (1991); this Bill was enacted, without alterations, as the 1992 Act.
[58] ss.1(4) and 5(3) make it possible to vary the identity of either or both of these persons.
[59] [1974] 1 W.L.R. 341; see also above, para.18–171.
[60] [1974] 1 W.L.R. 341 at p.346.
[61] See *ibid.*, p.349.
[62] Above, para.18–171.
[63] [1974] 1 W.L.R. 341 at p.349.
[64] *ibid.*, p.346.

any rights against the carrier under the contract of carriage. For this purpose, the buyer would need, in addition, to show that the identity of the person to whom delivery was to be made[65] had been varied[66] (most probably by an appropriate indorsement)[67] so that he had replaced the seller as that person.

Operation of section 2(1)(c). It will be convenient to discuss the operation of section 2(1)(c) by reverting to the example in which A ships goods on B's ship under a bill of lading containing or evidencing a contract of carriage between A and B, and then induces B to issue a ship's delivery order to C making the goods deliverable to C. The effect of section 2(1)(c) in such a case is that C has "transferred to and vested in him all rights of suit under the contract of carriage as if he had been a party to that contract". That is, C is treated as if he had been a party to the bill of lading contract.[68] 18–184

The above example is based on the assumption that the bill of lading contains or evidences the contract of carriage between A and B. But this will not be the position where A has chartered B's ship and B issues a bill of lading in respect of the shipment to A. In such a case the bill of lading will, as between A and B, be a mere receipt, the contract of carriage between them being contained in the charterparty.[69] If B issues a delivery order to C (typically in respect of part of the goods) naming C as the person to whom delivery is to be made, then the order can vest contractual rights in C by virtue of section 2(1)(c); and those rights will prima facie be governed by the charterparty, this being the only "contract of carriage"[70] between A and B. Yet this might be regarded as likely to mislead C if the order referred to the bill of lading, especially where the terms of the bill differed from those of the charterparty. It is arguable that, if C had obtained delivery of the goods against presentation of the order, B could be bound by the terms of the bill of lading on the ground of an implied contract,[71] or that, if C had in some other way relied on the reference in the order to the bill, B might be estopped from denying that C's rights under section 2(1)(c) were governed by the terms of the bill.

Since contractual rights can be vested in the consignee named in a ship's delivery order without his having acquired possession of the order,[72] there is in principle no obstacle to the transfer of such rights to him where the order is "spent" in the sense of reaching him only after the goods have been delivered to him. Problems with regard to "spent" orders could, however, arise where the order provided that delivery was to be made only against production of the order[73] but delivery was in fact made to the

---

[65] s.1(4)(b).
[66] s.5(3).
[67] Above, para.18–182.
[68] Above, para.18–175.
[69] Above, paras 18–051, 18–110.
[70] See s.5(1)(b).
[71] Analogous to the type of implied contract discussed in paras 18–138 *et seq*.
[72] Above, para.18–175.
[73] Effect would be given to such a provision under s.2(3)(a), above, para.18–175.

consignee without such production (probably against a letter of indemnity) and the order came into his possession at a later time. It is submitted that he could acquire contractual rights against the carrier since he would be "the person . . . to whom delivery [was] *to be* made in accordance with the undertaking contained in the order"[74] even though it was not actually made in accordance with its terms.[75]

18–185 **Ship's delivery order relating to part of a shipment.** Ship's delivery orders are commonly used to split up large bulk shipments among several buyers. Section 2(3)(b) of the 1992 Act deals with this situation by providing that "the rights vested in any person by virtue of the operation of [section 2(1)] in relation to a ship's delivery order . . . where the goods to which the order relates form part only of the goods to which the contract of carriage relates, shall be confined to rights in respect of the goods to which the order relates". Such rights are acquired notwithstanding the fact that the part to which the order relates constitutes an undifferentiated part of a larger bulk[76]; and if several ship's delivery orders are issued, rights of suit are vested *pro rata* in each of the persons to whom delivery is to be made under those orders.[77] This position could prejudice a carrier who had, or alleged that he had, a defence to all the claims: he would have to make good that defence in each action brought under each of the delivery orders. To avoid this inconvenience, the court could perhaps, under the Civil Procedure Rules, order the other potential claimants to be joined to the action on the ground that their presence was "desirable . . . so that the court can resolve all matters in dispute in the proceedings".[78]

18–186 **Rights of original shipper and bill of lading holders.** Where contractual rights are transferred by virtue of section 2(1) through the operation of a ship's delivery order, then section 2(5) provides that the transfer "shall be without prejudice to any rights deriving otherwise than from the previous operation of [section 2(1)] in relation to that order." It follows that section 2(1) does not deprive the original shipper of his rights under the original contract of carriage, whether that contract is contained in a charterparty or is contained in or evidenced by a bill of lading. In the latter case, at least, this point is unlikely to be a source of difficulty where the whole of a bulk shipment is split up by the use of a number of ship's delivery orders, since the carrier is likely to issue such orders only against surrender of the bill of lading.[79] But this solution would not be available if a carrier of 1,000 tons under a single bill of lading were to issue a delivery order for 250 tons without obtaining the surrender of the bill of lading. The effect of section 2(5) would be to preserve the whole of the original shipper's rights even though rights in respect of 250 tons had vested in the person entitled to

---

74 s.2(1)(c).
75 See s.2(3)(a), above, n.73.
76 s.5(4), above, paras 18–135, 18–137.
77 This follows from the joint operation of ss.2(3)(b) and 5(4)(b).
78 CPR r.19(2)(2)(a).
79 Law Com. No. 196, Scot. Law Com. No. 130, explanatory note to clause 2(5) of the Draft Bill attached to the Report.

delivery under the ship's delivery order. Similarly, any rights which the original shipper might have against the carrier under a charterparty covering the whole bulk could be preserved by section 2(5), even if the bill of lading had been surrendered. Clearly, however, the carrier would not be liable twice over in respect of the 250 tons: such duplication would be avoided by applying the general common law principle that the claimant in a contractual action is entitled to damages only in respect of his own loss.[80] That principle would also apply if the above example was varied by supposing that the original shipper had, after the issue of the ship's delivery order, transferred the bill of lading to a lawful holder who had in consequence of the transfer acquired rights under the contract of carriage by virtue of section 2(1)(a).

The example given in the preceding paragraph may be further varied by supposing that the original shipper (A) had first transferred the bill of lading to a lawful holder (C) and that C had then induced the carrier (B) to issue a ship's delivery order in respect of 250 out of the 1,000 tons in favour of D. In such a case, A's rights as an original party to the bill of lading contract would have been extinguished under section 2(5)(a), and C's rights would remain in force since those rights are derived "otherwise than from the previous operation of [section 2(1)] in relation to that order". They are indeed derived from the previous operation of section 2(1), but from that operation in relation to the bill of lading, not in relation to the ship's delivery order.[81] Again, however, for the reason given in the preceding paragraph, it is submitted that the carrier would not be liable twice over in respect of the 250 tons.

Change in consignee. We saw in paragraph 18–182 above that under section 5(3) it was possible for the identity of the person to whom delivery was to be made under a ship's delivery order to be changed after the issue of the order: *e.g.* by the substitution of D for C in accordance with the terms of an order originally made out in favour of C, or by the delivery by C to D of an order made out to bearer. Two consequences follow: D acquires contractual rights against the carrier by virtue of section 2(1)(c); and rights previously so acquired by C are extinguished by virtue of section 2(5)(b). If, in ignorance of the substitution of D for C, the carrier delivers the goods to C, he will be liable to D. It is therefore advisable for the carrier to provide in the order that delivery of the goods to which the order relates will be made only on presentation of it. Without such a provision, the carrier has no means of ensuring that the person claiming delivery is indeed entitled to it; for section 5(3), which makes it possible to substitute D for C as the person to whom delivery is to be made, does not itself require notice of the substitution to be given to the carrier who had 18–187

---

[80] We are not here concerned with exceptions to that principle, such as those discussed in paras 18–114, 18–116 and 18–119, above.

[81] For the same reason, s.2(5)(b) (above, para.18–118), which refers to "the previous operation of [s.2(1)] in relation to that document", would not, in the case put, extinguish C's rights: "that document" must here mean the ship's delivery order, and C's rights are derived from the previous operation of s.2(1) in relation to the bill of lading.

originally issued the order in favour of C. In the case of bills of lading and sea waybills, the nature of the document ensures that the carrier will receive notice of such substitutions.[82] In the case of a ship's delivery order this is not the case, so that the carrier will need to rely for this purpose on the express provisions of the document.

18–188 **Contracts (Rights of Third Parties) Act 1999.** Under section 1 of this Act, a term of a contract can, in the circumstances specified in the section, be enforced by a person (the third party) who is not a party to the contract; but under what we have called the subsection 6(5) exception,[83] no such right of enforcement is conferred on a third party in the case of a "contract for the carriage of goods by sea". By virtue of the statutory definition of this phrase, the exception applies, not only where a third party seeks to enforce a term of a contract contained in or evidenced by a bill of lading or a sea waybill,[84] but also where he bases his claim on a contract of carriage "under or for the purposes of which there is given an undertaking which is contained in a ship's delivery order".[85] The expression "ship's delivery order" here has the same meaning as in the Carriage of Goods by Sea Act 1992.[86] The point of excepting this situation from section 1 of the 1999 Act is to ensure that the acquisition of contractual rights by the "person identified"[87] in a ship's delivery order is to be governed by section 2(1)(c) of the 1992 Act[88] and not by the 1999 Act.

The typical situation in which delivery orders are used to secure delivery of goods to a person who is not a party to the contract of carriage is that in which goods are shipped in bulk on A's ship by B who then sells part of the bulk to C (and no doubt other parts of it to D, E, etc.). In such a case, there will or may be two contracts with the carrier. The first is the contract between A and B, which will typically be one contained in or evidenced by a bill of lading though it could also be one contained in or evidenced by a sea waybill.[89] It is this contract which is excepted by subsection 6(5) from the scope of section 1 of the 1999 Act. The second contract which may arise is one between A and C by reason of A's having in the order given an "undertaking" to C to deliver the goods to C. If there is acceptance of this undertaking by, and consideration moving from, C, and contractual intention, then the undertaking will amount to a direct contract between A and C.[90] *This* contract is not in terms within the subsection 6(5) exception, which applies, in the case of a ship's delivery order, only to the contract "under or for the purposes of which"[91] the undertaking contained in the order was given and not to any other contract which may be contained in,

---

[82] See above, paras 18–016, 18–018, 18–021, 18–025.
[83] Above, para.18–005, sub-paragraph (f).
[84] 1999 Act, s.6(6)(a).
[85] *ibid.*, s.6(6)(b).
[86] *ibid.*, s.6(7)(a).
[87] 1992 Act, s.1(4)(b).
[88] Above, para.18–175.
[89] For the further possibility that this contract may be contained in a charterparty, see para.18–179, above.
[90] Above, para.18–173.
[91] 1999 Act, s.6(6)(b).

or arise by reason of, the terms of the order itself. But section 1 of the 1999 Act will not apply to the enforcement by C of the latter contract since in this contract C is not a "third party" within the 1999 Act: this expression refers to "a person who is *not* a party to a contract" (*i.e.* to the contract, the enforcement of a term of which is sought), and in the case put C *is* a party to that contract. Since the direct contract between A and C may by express or implied reference incorporate some of the terms of the contract of carriage between A and B, C may thus indirectly acquire rights originally conferred on B by that contract. This result will, however, follow as a matter of common law and not by virtue of the 1999 Act.

The subsection 6(5) exception is, in cases where its operation depends on the giving of a delivery order, expressed to apply only where that order is a "ship's delivery order"[92] as defined by the 1992 Act. Where the order is one which does *not* fall within this definition (*e.g.* because it contains no undertaking by A[93]), the contract "under or for the purposes of which" it was given may well itself be contained in or evidenced by a bill of lading, and then *that* contract will fall within the subsection 6(5) exception. But this will not be true of any contract which may arise at common law from conduct after the issue of the order, *e.g.* from A's attornment to C.[94] The contractual effects of such an order will therefore not be affected by the 1992 Act; nor, in the case just put, will C's right to enforce the contract resulting from the attornment be governed by section 1 of the 1999 Act since C would be a party to that contract and hence not a "third party" within section 1.

An order may fail to qualify as a "ship's delivery order", not only where it "contains" no undertaking by the carrier at all, but also where it does contain such an undertaking but this undertaking is addressed (so to speak) to the wrong person. An order which contained an undertaking by A (the carrier) addressed to B (the shipper) to deliver the goods to C (the consignee) would not be a "ship's delivery order" within the definition of this expression in the 1992 Act, for that definition requires the person to whom the undertaking is given to be the *same* person as the person to whom the goods were to be delivered.[95] If such an order had contractual force between A and B, then that contract would not be within the subsection 6(5) exception since the only delivery orders to which that exception refers are "ship's delivery orders" and since the exception applies only to the contract "under or for the purposes of which"[96] the undertaking contained in the order was given. Any contract between A and B contained in, or arising under, the order itself could then fall within section 1 of the 1999 Act since it would be a contract between these parties which purported to confer a benefit on C. That contract could, moreover, incorporate by express or implied reference at least some of the terms of the contract of carriage contained in or evidenced by the bill of lading issued by A to B. In this way terms of that contract could, notwithstanding

92 1999 Act, s.6(6) and (7).
93 See above, para.18–178.
94 Above, para.18–174.
95 s.1(4); above, para.18–182.
96 1999 Act, s6(6)(b).

the fact that the bill of lading contract fell within the subsection 6(5) exception, become enforceable by a third party under section 1 of the 1999 Act.

(iv) *Ship's Delivery Orders: Statutory Imposition of Contractual Liabilities*

18–189 **Carriage of Goods by Sea Act 1992, section 3.** The conditions which must be satisfied for the imposition of liabilities in respect of goods covered by a ship's delivery order are set out in section 3 of the Carriage of Goods by Sea Act 1992: they are similar to those which must be satisfied in the case of goods covered by a bill of lading or by a sea waybill. Thus a person in whom rights are vested by virtue of section 2(1) because he is the person to whom delivery is to be made under a ship's delivery order also becomes subject to liabilities if he takes or demands delivery from the carrier of any of the goods to which the order relates or if he makes a claim against the carrier under the contract of carriage in respect of any of those goods.[97] It is also possible for a person to acquire rights by virtue of section 2(1) under a "spent" ship's delivery order[98]; and that person could then also incur liabilities under the contract of carriage.[99]

18–190 **Ship's delivery order relating to part of a shipment.** Section 3(2) provides that where a ship's delivery order relates only to part of the goods covered by the contract of carriage, the liabilities imposed by virtue of section 3 "shall exclude liabilities in respect of any goods to which the order does not relate". Thus if A ships 1,000 tons on B's ship and a ship's delivery order is issued to C in respect of 250 tons, and C takes delivery of that quantity, then C will not be liable for more than one quarter of the freight. It would not, however, be appropriate to apply this simple mathematical formula to all liabilities which C may incur under the contract of carriage. For example, the extent to which C was liable for demurrage might more appropriately depend on the extent to which C was responsible for the delay in respect of which liability for demurrage was incurred. The words of section 3(2) (quoted above) appear to be sufficiently flexible to permit such a solution.

18–191 **Liability of other parties.** The original shipper remains liable under the contract of carriage[1]; and this rule applies even though liabilities have also been incurred by another person in respect of goods covered by a ship's delivery order. A further possibility arises where 1,000 tons of goods are shipped by A on B's ship under a bill of lading which A transfers to C who then procures the issue of a ship's delivery order to D in respect of 250 tons. In such a case, C and D will incur liabilities under the contract of carriage if they take or demand delivery or make a claim under the contract of carriage[2] and A will remain liable under that contract.[3] D will be liable

[97] s.3(1)(a) and (b).
[98] See above, para.18–184.
[99] s.3(1)(c), above, para.18–131.
[1] s.3(3).
[2] s.3(1).
[3] s.3(3).

only in respect of the 250 tons[4]; but there is no corresponding restriction on C's liability. C becomes subject under section 3(1) to "the same liabilities" as if he had been a party to the original contract; he becomes so liable if he takes or demands delivery "of *any* of the goods"; and the restriction on liability contained in section 3(2)[5] applies only in favour of a person to whom delivery is to be made under a ship's delivery order. Hence it does not protect C even if he receives (in the event) no more than part delivery under the bill of lading.

Other problems arising from section 3. Other problems to which section 3 gives rise have been discussed in relation to bills of lading in paragraphs 18–123 to 18–134 above. That discussion, is *mutatis mutandis*, applicable to shipments or parts of shipments in respect of which ship's delivery orders are issued. 18–192

(v) *Whether Delivery Orders are Documents of Title*

Delivery order not a document of title at common law. A delivery order is not a document of title[6] in the traditional common law sense[7] of being "negotiable" (*i.e.* transferable)[8] unless a custom to that effect is proved in relation to the particular kind of delivery order in question.[9] In the absence of such proof of custom, two separate but related rules at common law determine its operation. The first is that if A, the owner of goods in B's warehouse, orders B to deliver the goods to C, the mere issue of the order by A will not transfer constructive possession, or amount to a delivery, to C.[10] There is no delivery until B attorns to C, *i.e.* acknowledges to C that he holds the goods on his behalf.[11] Where the relationship between A and C is that of buyer and seller this rule is now stated in section 29(4) of the Sale of Goods Act.[12] Attornment requires a positive act; mere failure to repudiate a delivery order will not suffice.[13] If in our example B were to issue a 18–193

[4] s.3(2).
[5] Above, para.18–190.
[6] *The Julia* [1949] A.C. 283 at p.316; *cf. Maynegrain Pty Ltd v Compafina Bank* (1984) 58 A.L.J.R. 389 at p.393, PC (warehouse receipt); Law Com. No. 196, Scot. Law.
[7] See above, paras 18–007, 18–062.
[8] See above para.18–084.
[9] *Dublin City Distillery Ltd v Doherty* [1914] A.C. 823 at p.865; for a case in which such a custom was proved, see *Merchant Banking Co. of London v Phoenix Bessemer Steel Co.* (1877) 5 Ch.D. 205.
[10] *cf. M'Ewan v Smith* (1849) 2 H.L.C. 309. Here the seller gave the buyer a delivery order addressed, not to the warehouseman, but to the seller's own agent, who later gave a delivery order to a sub-buyer. It was held that possession had not passed by virtue of either order.
[11] *Dublin City Distillery Ltd v Doherty*, above, at pp.843, 847. 848; *Farina v Howe* (1846) 16 M & W. 119 at p.123.
[12] Above, para.8–012. The point is not affected by the change in the definition of "delivery" in s.61(1) as amended by Sale of Goods (Amendment) Act 1995, s.2(d): that change applies only for the purposes of ss.20A and 20B, which deal with transfer of property.
[13] *Laurie & Morewood v Dudin & Sons* [1926] 1 K.B. 223.

delivery warrant in favour of C, this would presumably amount of itself to attornment.[14] The second rule is that if the delivery order or warrant is after attornment further transferred by the person in whose favour it was issued[15] (*i.e.* if in our example C transfers it to D) a fresh attornment by the person in possession (B) will be required to transfer constructive possession to the transferee (D).

Delivery warrants sometimes contain words which could be construed as a purported attornment in advance to any transferee. For example, in *Sterns Ltd v Vickers Ltd*[16] such a warrant made a quantity of oil "deliverable to Messrs. Stern Ltd or assignees only against this warrant duly indorsed . . . This warrant is the only document issued as a legal symbol of the goods." It may be that the purpose of words such as these is to give the warrants in which they are contained the characteristics of documents of title at common law.[17] But it has been submitted in paragraph 18–075 above that, at common law, a document can become a "negotiable" (*i.e.* transferable)[18] document of title only by virtue of proof of a mercantile custom to this effect; and it follows from the reasoning on which this submission is based that a document cannot acquire the characteristic of this kind of transferability merely by virtue of the intention of the parties to it, or of one of them, as expressed in its terms. It has, indeed, been said that "A warehouse warrant is a special kind of document constituting a document of title to the goods which a delivery order is not"[19]; but it is submitted that this statement, so far as it relates to warrants, can be explained in one of two ways. The first possibility is to say that it must be understood to refer to warrants which have acquired the characteristic of transferability by proof of mercantile custom or under the special legislation discussed in paragraph 18–198 below. The second possibility arises because, even as a matter of common law, the expression "document of title" to goods has been used in more than one sense. In its traditional sense,[20] it refers to a document which is "negotiable" (*i.e.* transferable)[21]; but it is also sometimes used to refer to documents merely because they have to be produced to the bailor by the person claiming delivery of the goods.[22] In this sense a warehouse warrants have been described as "effectively documents of title",[23] apparently because delivery of the goods could only be obtained against presentation of the warrants.[24] There is no doubt that this requirement of production or presentation can be imposed by the terms of the document[25];

[14] As in *Sterns Ltd v Vickers Ltd* [1923] 1 K.B. 78.
[15] As in *Laurie & Morewood v Dudin & Sons*, above.
[16] [1923] 1 K.B. 78; and see below, para.18–300.
[17] *cf.* the terms of the delivery order in *Inglis v Robertson* [1898] A.C. 616 at p.620.
[18] See above, para.18–084.
[19] *Alicia Hosiery Ltd v Brown Shipley & Co. Ltd* [1970] 1 Q.B. 195 at p.205.
[20] See above, paras 18–007, 18–062.
[21] See above, para.18–084.
[22] See above, para.18–008.
[23] *Niru Battery Manufacturing Co. v Milestone Trading Ltd* [2003] EWCA Civ 1446, [2004] 1 Lloyd's Rep.334 at [9]; the word "effectively" may indicate that the expression "document of title" is not here being used in its usual sense.
[24] *ibid.*
[25] See the discussion of this aspect of straight bills of lading in paras 18–071 and 18–072 above.

but it does not follow from the existence of the requirement that the document is "negotiable" (*i.e.* transferable) so as to make it a document of title in the traditional common law sense.[26] In other words, it does not follow merely from the existence of such a requirement that the transfer of the document operates as a transfer of the constructive possession of the goods.

It is arguable that words in a delivery order or warrant which indicate that the goods will be delivered to any lawful holder of the document may give rise to an estoppel against the issuer and in favour of the holder. The difficulties which stand in the way of making the issuer liable on the basis of such an estoppel have been considered in paragraph 18–174 above. Here it is only necessary to say that, even if those difficulties could be overcome, the effect of the estoppel might be to make the issuer liable to the holder, but it would not follow from this that the document had the characteristics of a document of title in the traditional common law sense. The question whether the document has these characteristics is most likely to arise where the dispute is between the holder of the document and a third party who claims to have acquired an interest in the goods by some route which does not involve any dealing with that document: *e.g.* where goods are claimed by C as transferee of a delivery order or warrant and by D as transferee of a bill of lading relating to the same goods. In such a case, it is submitted that D would not be affected by any estoppel which might operate in favour of C against the issuer of the delivery order or warrant; for D would not have made, or have been privy to the making of, the representation on which the estoppel is alleged to be based, nor would D derive the title that he claims through the maker of the representation. The relative rights of C and D would then depend on the general principle that *nemo dat quod non habet*, subject to the exceptions to that principle which are discussed in Chapter 7 of this book. If no such exception were applicable, D's interest in the goods would prevail over C's precisely because D held a document of title while C did not. This position would not be affected by any remedy which C might have, against the issuer of the delivery order or warrant, on the basis of an estoppel arising from the terms of that document.

It might be thought that where a delivery order was issued or transferred, property (as well as constructive possession) passed on, and not before, attornment. A number of cases decided before the Sale of Goods (Amendment) Act 1995 might at first sight have seemed to give support to this view. In the cases in question,[27] the delivery order related to a specified quantity forming an undifferentiated part of an identified bulk, so that property could not formerly pass before the goods were ascertained[28]; and **18–194**

[26] See the discussion of this aspect of straight bills of lading in paras 18–074 and 18–075 above.
[27] *e.g. Laurie & Morewood v Dudin & Sons* [1926] 1 K.B. 223; *Wardar's (Import & Export) Ltd v W Norwood & Sons Ltd* [1968] 2 Q.B. 663; *Margarine Union GmbH v Cambay Prince SS Co. Ltd (The Wear Breeze)* [1969] 1 Q.B. 219; *Cremer v General Carriers SA* [1974] 1 W.L.R. 341; *Waren Import Gesellschaft Krohn & Co. v Internationale Graanhandel Thegra NV* [1975] 1 Lloyd's Rep. 146.
[28] Sale of Goods Act 1979, s.16, before its amendment by Sale of Goods (Amendment) Act 1995, s.1(1).

attornment might often take place at the same time as ascertainment: *i.e.* when the carrier separated the quantity covered by the order from the bulk and acknowledged that he held it for the person designated in the delivery order. Property in an individed share in such goods can now pass under a contract of sale, even before ascertainment, to the extent that payment has been made.[29] It follows that attornment is no longer necessary to bring about such passing of property. Nor is it sufficient for this purpose: no property will pass on attornment, even where part of the price has been paid, if the contract of sale provides that it is to pass only on payment in full, or if the seller in some other way reserves the right of disposal until payment.[30] Attornment is relevant to the transfer of possession to the person designated in the delivery order; and there is no necessary connection between this transfer of possession and the passing of property.

18–195 **Ship's delivery orders under Carriage of Goods by Sea Act 1992.** In discussing the transfer of contractual rights by means of ship's delivery orders, we saw that the 1992 Act envisages the *transfer* of a ship's delivery order, in the sense that a number of persons can acquire contractual rights under it in succession. If, for example, such an order provides for goods to be delivered to C or to C's order (or to bearer), and if C orders delivery to be made to D (or hands a bearer delivery order to D), then D is sufficiently identified as the person to whom delivery is to be made[31] and contractual rights against the carrier which had previously been vested in C,[32] will be transferred to D,[33] C's rights becoming extinct.[34] In this way, the order can be used to transfer contractual rights even though, at common law, the order is not a document of title and so cannot transfer possession without the carrier's attornment to the transferee.[35] The 1992 Act does not appear to alter this common law rule: it is concerned, not with the question whether the documents to which it refers are documents of title, but only with the transfer of contractual rights and the imposition of contractual liabilities. It is, however, arguable that the two issues are connected indirectly. If, in our example, contractual rights against the carrier were transferred by means of the transfer of the order from C to D, those rights would include the right to demand delivery of the underlying goods. The transfer of such a right might be regarded as relevant if an attempt were now made to establish a mercantile custom that ship's delivery orders within the 1992 Act were documents of title in the common law sense. The mere fact that such orders now provide a mechanism for the transfer of contractual rights cannot, however, be regarded as a decisive factor for this

---

[29] Sale of Goods Act 1979, s.20A, discussed, in relation to overseas sales, in paras 18–293 *et seq.*, below.

[30] *cf. Shepherd v Harrison* (1871) L.R. 5 H.L. 116, where the buyer's agent obtained a delivery order from the ship but property was held not to have passed on the principle now contained in Sale of Goods Act 1979, s.19(3); above, para.5–138; below, para.18–221.

[31] Carriage of Goods by Sea Act 1992, ss.1(4), 5(3), above, paras 18–182, 18–187.

[32] *ibid.*, s.2(1)(c).

[33] *ibid.*

[34] *ibid.*, s.2(5)(b).

[35] Above, para.18–193.

purpose. It is significant in this context to recall that bills of lading were recognised as documents of title *before* their transfer was capable of transferring contractual rights[36]: this shows that, as a matter of history, constructive possession may be transferred without contractual rights. Conversely, it is generally agreed that air and land carriage documents are not recognised as documents of title (in the common law sense)[37] in England even though they can confer contractual rights (including the right to demand delivery of the underlying goods) on persons who are named in them as consignees but are not parties to the original contract of carriage[38]; and even though the transfer of such documents appears to be envisaged by at least some of the relevant international Conventions.[39] Thus it is clear that a carriage document which confers contractual rights to delivery of the goods is by no means necessarily a document of title in the traditional common law sense.[40] The operation of ship's delivery orders under the 1992 Act, moreover, differs in one crucial respect from the operation of bills of lading. A person who claims, by virtue of that Act, to have acquired contractual rights under a ship's delivery order will not (unless the order in terms so provides[41]) need to show that the order has been transferred to him or that he has become the holder, or the lawful holder, of the order: all that he will have to show is that he is identified as the person to whom delivery is to be made under the order.[42] Even after the 1992 Act, a ship's delivery order as there defined, may therefore lack one of the requirements of a document of title in the common law sense, *i.e.* the requirement that it must be produced by the person claiming delivery of the goods covered by it. Such a requirement may indeed be imposed by an express term of the order; and the rights under the contract of carriage will then, by virtue of the Act, be transferred only if that requirement is satisfied.[43] But the Act deals only with the transfer of contractual (as opposed to possessory or proprietary) rights; and so the fact that the requirement is imposed by a term of the order will not, of itself, give the order the characteristics of a "negotiable" (*i.e.* transferable)[44] document of title at common law. The submission made in paragraph 18–075 above, that a document can acquire those characteristics only on proof of a mercantile custom to that effect, applies also in the present context.

Delivery order a document of title in the statutory sense. Although a delivery order is not (in the absence of proof of a mercantile custom) a document of title at common law,[45] it is a "warrant or order for the delivery of goods" within the statutory definition of "document of title" in section 1(4) of the Factors Act 1889,[46] which applies for the purpose of the Sale of 18–196

[36] Above, paras 18–007, 18–063, 18–068, 18–100.
[37] Below, paras 21–053, 21–061, 21–068.
[38] Below, paras 21–052, 21–060, 21–066.
[39] Below, para.21–052.
[40] See above, paras 18–007, 18–062.
[41] s.2(3)(a), above, para.18–175.
[42] s.1(4)(b), 2(1)(c), 5(3).
[43] 1992 Act, s.2(1)(c) ("in accordance with the terms of the order").
[44] See para.18–084 above.
[45] Above, para.18–193.
[46] Above, para.18–009.

Goods Act 1979. But this in no way affects the principle that, as between buyer and seller, constructive possession of goods in the actual possession of a third party will be transferred only by the third party, attornment, and not by the issue or transfer of a delivery order.[47] It is true that section 29(4) of the 1979 Act, after stating the requirement of such attornment, concludes with the words that "nothing in this section affects the operation of the issue or transfer of any document of title to goods." But for the purpose of this provision, one has first to ask what the effect of the issue or transfer of the document of title in question would have been, apart from the words quoted. Thus if the document were an order or bearer bill of lading, its transfer would at common law operate as a transfer of constructive possession without any actual attornment[48]; while if the document were a delivery order, its transfer would not at common law operate as a transfer of constructive possession without such attornment. The effect of the concluding words of section 29(4) is to preserve both these rules.

18–197 The fact that a delivery order is a "document of title" within the Factors Act 1889 and the Sale of Goods Act 1979 does, however, mean that a delivery order may be used to transfer title under some of the exceptions to the general principle that *nemo dat quod non habet*. This topic is discussed in Chapter 7; here it is necessary only to stress that such transfer of title does not require any attornment by the person in possession.[49] Moreover, under section 3 of the Factors Act 1889 a pledge of the documents of title, if made by a mercantile agent, is deemed to be a pledge of the goods.[50] It follows, paradoxically, that "a mercantile agent can do that which the real owner cannot do, that is, obtain a loan on the security of a pledge of the goods by a pledge of the documents, without giving notice of the pledge to the warehouseman . . . and obtaining the latter's attornment to the change of possession."[51] Similarly, if A sells goods to B and gives[52] B a delivery order to which there has been no attornment, there will be no delivery of the goods between A and B; but if B transfers the delivery order to C, title may be acquired by C[53] even if B has not become owner, and, if B has become owner, C may take free from A's right, lien or right of stoppage in transit.[54]

The same goods may be covered by one or more delivery orders and by a set of bills of lading, so that there may be many documents of title (in the statutory sense) concerning the goods.

---

[47] See above, para.18–193.
[48] See above, para.18–066.
[49] *Official Assignee of Madras v Mercantile Bank of India Ltd* [1935] A.C. 53 at p.60.
[50] See *Inglis v Robertson* [1898] A.C. 616.
[51] *Official Assignee of Madras v Mercantile Bank of India*, above, at p.60.
[52] This is a "transfer" within Sale of Goods Act 1979, s.47(2): *Ant Jurgens Margarinefabrieken v Louis Dreyfus & Co.* [1914] 3 K.B. 40.
[53] Under Sale of Goods Act 1979, s.25(1). According to *D F Mount Ltd v Jay & Jay (Provisions) Co. Ltd* [1960] 1 Q.B. 159 this subsection applies even where B does not transfer *the* delivery order which he has received but issues a fresh delivery order on the warehouseman in favour of C. See above, para.7–062.
[54] Sale of Goods Act 1979, s.47(2); above, para.18–063.

Statutory dock and warehouse warrants. Special provision with regard to dock and warehouse warrants are contained in a number of local Acts of Parliament. Thus under section 146(4) of the Port of London Act 1968 certain dock warrants "shall be transferable by endorsement[55] and shall entitle the person named therein or the last endorsee thereof to the delivery of the goods specified therein and the goods so specified shall for all purposes be deemed to be his property."[56] The effect of these words is clearly to give such warrants the quality of transferability of documents of title in the traditional common law sense[57]; but they go even beyond this. Thus it seems that property passes by indorsement and delivery of such warrants notwithstanding any attempt to reserve the right of disposal; and that such warrants are negotiable in the sense that an indorsee takes free from any defects in the transferor's title. It is remarkable that the section does not expressly require the indorsee to have taken the instrument for value or in good faith; but probably such requirements would be implied. 18–198

(e) *Other Documents*

Air waybills, cargo receipts and consignment notes. The question whether air waybills, cargo receipts and consignment notes, issued on international carriage of goods by air, road and rail, are documents of title is discussed in Chapter 21.[58] 18–199

Multimodal transport documents. The question whether multimodal transport documents are documents of title is discussed in Chapter 21.[59] 18–200

Self-styled "documents of title". A document can become a document of title in the above statutory sense only by being either included in the list of such documents given in the legislation or by belonging to a class of documents there described. It has further been submitted earlier in this chapter that a document will not be recognised as a document of title in the traditional common law sense[60] (of a document, the transfer of which operates as a transfer of the constructive possession of the goods covered by it)[61] except on proof of a mercantile custom, satisfying the usual requirements of being notorious, certain and reasonable.[62] These requirements give some degree of protection to third parties, who may deal in good faith with the goods, against the prejudice which they might suffer if a new type of document were given the characteristics of a transferable 18–201

---

[55] And, presumably, delivery.
[56] *cf.* Mersey Docks Consolidation Act 1858, s.200; Trafford Park Act 1904, ss.33, 34; Liverpool Mineral and Metal Storage Co. Ltd (Delivery Warrants) Act 1921, ss.3, 4.
[57] See above, para.18–007, 18–062.
[58] Below, paras 21–053, 21–054, 21–061, 21–068.
[59] Below, paras 21–079, 21–083.
[60] See above paras 18–006 to 18–009 for the distinction between the common law and statutory senses of "document of title".
[61] See above, paras 18–007, 18–062.
[62] Above, para.18–075; *Chitty on Contracts*, 29th ed., paras 12–129, 13–018.

document of title at common law. If this reasoning restricts the power of the courts to give a document these characteristics, it should a *fortiori* restrict the power of the parties to do so by private contract. The requirement of proof of custom for this purpose may be compared with the analogous rule that a document cannot become a negotiable instrument by the will of the parties: it can acquire this characteristic only by custom or by statute.[63]

A fortiori, a document is not a document of title at common law merely because it describes itself as a "document of title", or in similar words, *e.g.* as a "certificate of title".[64] A distinction must be drawn between two possible effects of such a document: it may *transfer title* (in the sense of property) between the parties, or it may purport to be a *document of title*. The first effect can be achieved (so long as the goods are specific or ascertained[65] or are a specified quantity forming part of an identified bulk) merely by virtue of the intention of the parties.[66] The second effect cannot be achieved merely because the parties so intend: it requires proof of mercantile custom or legislation. Documents which by their terms are intended to produce only the first of the two effects described above are clearly not documents of title in the traditional common law sense referred to above[67] and cannot, it is submitted, even be used as evidence of a custom that they should be so regarded. Such a document would have to be one which entitled its transferee to possession of the goods in question[68]; and a document which did no more than to describe a named holder or addressee as owner of the goods would not even purport to confer any rights to possession on a person to whom it was, or purported to be, transferred.

As noted earlier in this Chapter[69] there is support, especially in some recent cases,[70] for the view that, even at common law, the expression "document of title" may be used to refer to a document simply because it has to be produced to the bailee in possession of the goods by the person claiming delivery of them. Two points must be made about this usage. The first is that the requirement of production can be, and commonly is, imposed by the terms of the document,[71] so that it is no doubt possible for a

[63] *ibid.* para.34–006. The analogy is not exact since bills of lading, though documents of title in the common law sense, are not strictly "negotiable": see para.18–084 above. But the policy reason for restricting the right of private parties to create negotiable instruments at will apply equally to transferable documents of title: this reason is that such freedom could, in relation to both types of documents, operate to the prejudice of third parties: see above para.18–075.
[64] As in *Re London Wine Co. (Shippers)* [1986] P.C.C. 121.
[65] Sale of Goods Act 1979, ss.16 and 20A, and s.61(1) (definition of "specific goods"). In *Re London Wine Co. (Shippers)*, above, the goods were not ascertained and did not form part of an identified bulk.
[66] Sale of Goods Act 1979, s.17.
[67] See above at, n.61.
[68] *cf. The Maheno* [1977] 1 Lloyd's Rep. 81, below, para.21–081.
[69] See above paras 18–008, 18–074.
[70] Especially in *JI MacWilliam Co. Inc. v Mediterranean Shipping Co. SA (The Rafaela S)* [2005] UKHL 11, [2005] 2 A.C 423 affirming [2003] EWCA Civ 556, [2004] Q.B. 702 and approving the judgment of Rix L.J. in the Court of Appeal
[71] See the discussion of this aspect of the straight bills of lading in para.18–071 above.

document to become a document of title *in this sense* by the will of the parties, or of one of them, as expressed in the document. The second, and in the present context the more important, point is that a document does not acquire the characteristic of "negotiability" (*i.e.* of transferability)[72] merely because it has to be produced to obtain delivery of the goods: proof of mercantile custom is necessary for this purpose.[73] The power of the parties to impose such a requirement of production is therefore not open to the objection on the ground of policy[74] which stands in the way of allowing them at will to create "negotiable" documents of title to goods; for that requirement does not, while the quality of "negotiability" may, operate to the prejudice of third parties who deal in good faith with the goods.

(f) *Paperless Transactions*

Carriage of Goods by Sea Act 1992, section 1(5). This subsection[75] **18–202**
enables the Secretary of State to make provision by statutory instrument "for the application of this Act to cases where an electronic communications network[76] or any other information technology[77] is used for effecting transactions corresponding to (a) the issue of a document to which this Act applies; (b) the indorsement, delivery or other transfer of such a document; or (c) the doing of anything else in relation to such a document." Section 5(1) defines "information technology" to include "any computer or other technology by means of which information or other matter may be recorded or communicated without being reduced to documentary form". It is therefore possible, for the purposes of the Act, for such information or other matter to constitute a "document" without being in "documentary form": *i.e.* even though it does not take the form of written characters recorded in a medium (now almost invariably paper) which can be passed from hand to hand.[78]

The phrase "electronic bill of lading" is sometimes used[79] to refer to a non-documentary document which is or may be intended to perform the functions traditionally performed by bills written or printed on paper. It is obvious that many practical and legal difficulties can arise in applying to electronic bills such concepts as the "delivery" or "indorsement" or "possession" of the document and in determining who is or has become the "holder" of it.[80] Problems of a similar nature can arise in relation to other

---

[72] See para.18–084 above.
[73] See below, paras 18–074 and 18–075.
[74] Above, after n.63; and see above, para.18–075.
[75] As amended by Telecommunications Act 2003, Sch. 17, para. 119.
[76] As defined by s.1(5), referring to Telecommunications Act 1984; see s.4 of the latter Act.
[77] See the definition in s.5(1), quoted below. The repeal of part of this definition by Communications Act 2003, Sch.19, para.1 does not affect the words quoted in the above text.
[78] *cf.* the definition of "document" in Civil Evidence Act 1995, s.13 and in Police Act 1996, s.81(3); *Victor Chandler International Ltd v Customs & Excise Commissioners* [2000] 1 W.L.R. 1296.
[79] *e.g.* Faber [1996] L.M.C.L.Q. 232.
[80] See, *e.g.* Carriage of Goods by Sea Act 1992, for use of those expressions.

"documents" than bills of lading to which the Act applies, such as ship's delivery orders and sea waybills.[81] Section 1(5) recognises that such problems are more appropriately to be resolved by delegated legislation, than by either primary legislation or judge-made law, since the rules required for this purpose must be capable of quick and clear adaptation in response to technological change.

18–203 **Problems beyond the scope of section 1(5).** Problems of the kind discussed in paragraph 18–202 above are by no means confined to aspects of the subject which are covered by the 1992 Act. That Act deals mainly with the transfer of contractual rights to, and the imposition of contractual liabilities on, persons, other than the original parties to the contract of carriage. It follows that the power to make regulations conferred by section 1(5) of the Act cannot be used to resolve the further legal difficulties which can arise from the use of "electronic bills" as documents of title in the traditional sense,[82] *e.g.* from their use for the purpose of transferring possession, of passing property (if so intended), of creating security and of determining priorities between competing interests in goods on the insolvency of buyer or seller. Such problems, too, await legislative solution, perhaps to be based on international agreement. These problems appear to be significantly harder to solve than those which arise from paperless transactions in money since money is (or has become) a more abstract concept than goods. The existence of such difficulties has, if the reported cases are any guide, so far inhibited the use of paperless carriage documents for the purposes with which this chapter and the following three chapters of this book are concerned. At the present stage of development, detailed speculation as to how the law might adapt the present rules on these topics to transactions which dispense with documents of the traditional kind would therefore appear to be premature. An attempt to deal with some[83] of the resulting problems, not as a matter of general law, but by private contract, is discussed in paragraph 18–204 below.

18–204 **Contractual solutions.** In the absence of legislative solutions of the kind discussed in paragraphs 18–202 and 18–203 above, attempts may be made to resolve some of the problems arising from "electronic bills" by means of what amounts to a multilateral contract. One example of such an approach is the Bolero Rule Book, issued in 1999, which contains the terms of such a contract between users of such instruments *inter se* and also with the association which has been set up to administer an "electronic bill of lading" system. No attempt can be made here to provide a full analysis of the complex provisions of this lengthy document. But reference should be made to the two salient respects in which the "bill of lading" to which it refers lacks the features of a traditional paper bill of lading.[84] These are,

---

[81] See *ibid.*, s.1(1).

[82] See above, para.18–007, 18–062.

[83] By no means all: *e.g.* not with the adaptation of the rules governing c.i.f. or f.o.b. sales to transactions involving "electronic bills of lading".

[84] For this reason the Law Commission has said that such "electronic bills of lading" are "not true equivalents" (to paper bills of lading) and that "it is more accurate to refer to them as "electronic contracts for carriage": Law Commission Paper on *Electronic Commerce, Formal Requirements in Electronic Transactions* (December 2001) para.4.7; and see below, at n.87.

first, the function of a traditional bill as a document of title and, secondly, the use of such a bill as a mechanism for the transfer of contractual rights. For both these purposes, legal consequences flow, in the case of paper bills, from the *transfer of possession* of the document: at common law, the document of title function means that such transfer of possession operates as a transfer of the constructive possession of the goods; while under the Carriage of Goods by Sea Act 1992 the transfer of contractual rights under the bill of lading contract requires the transferee to have become the holder of the bill and this again requires him to have acquired possession of the document.[85] This concept of the transfer of possession cannot be applied, except by way of somewhat inexact metaphor, to electronic documents; for even if their transmission could be said to give the recipient of the electronic message a kind of possession of them, it would not of itself deprive the sender of such possession. The transmission of a paper document, by contrast, not only gives the recipient possession of it but necessarily deprives the sender of that possession. The only qualification of this statement in the present context arises under the rules relating to bills in sets[86] but if these rules were applied in the present context it would, in effect, become impossible in the case of an electronic bill, to transfer a full set of bills since one part of the set would remain with the transferor. It is the need for the transfer not only to give possession of the document to the transferee, but also to deprive the transferor of such possession, that seems to underlie the Law Commission's view that "documents of title are limited to paper documents".[87]

It is the above aspect of *transfer* of *possession* of the bill of lading which lies at the heart of the concept of an order or bearer bill of lading as a document of title in the common law sense,[88] under which the transfer of possession of the bill not only has the legal effect of transferring the constructive possession of the underlying goods from the transferor to the transferee of the bill, but has this effect without any need to communicate with, or to obtain the assent of, the carrier. The acquisition of possession of such a bill by the transferee is likewise an essential requirement for the transfer of contractual rights under the contract of carriage to him by virtue of the Carriage of Goods by Sea Act 1992; and again where the requirements of the Act are satisfied such rights will be vested in the transferee

---

[85] Carriage of Goods by Sea Act 1992, s.5(2)(a).

[86] Above, paras 18–090 to 18–094.

[87] Law Commission, Consultative Report on *Company Security Interests,* Law Com. No.176 (2004), para.3.20 and the definition of "document of title" in reg.2 (1) of the Draft regulations, appended to the Report; this definition begins by stating that such a document means "a document written on paper. . .". The same words are used in the definition of "document of title" in reg.42 of the Draft Regulations appended to the Law Commission's final Report on *Company Security Interests* (Law Com. No.296, 2005), above para.18–010. In the United States, the 2003 version of UCC Art. 7 (see above, para.18–015, n.7) attempts to solve the problem described in the text above by introducing a new concept of "control" of an electronic document of title: see §7–106; but it makes no attempt to define "control". Comment 3 to §7–106 simply "leaves to the market place the development of sufficient technologies and business practices that will meet the "test" of "control".

[88] Above, paras 18–007, 18–062.

without the need to comply with any further requirements which might exist for their transfer under the general law relating to the assignment or choses an action (such as notice to the debtor, *i.e.* in this context, the carrier) or to the creation of new rights by way of novation, requiring the consent of all three parties involved in the process, *i.e.* of creditor (shipper) debtor (carrier) and third party (transferee). The Bolero "bill of lading" does not have either of these distinctive characteristics of a traditional bill of lading: under the Rule Book, constructive possession of the goods is to be transferred by a form of attornment by the carrier; and contractual rights are not strictly transferred at all but are to be acquired by the third party by a form of novation. These processes are necessarily subject to the risks of, for example, delays, omissions or faults in the transmission of electronic messages, and of events such as intervening insolvency or loss of capacity, making them (to say the least) less robust than the transfer of constructive possession and of contractual rights which follow without the need for any further steps in the case of the transfer of possession of paper bills, as described above. The need for the bailee's attornment to achieve a transfer of the constructive possession of the goods will also prevent the use of this kind of electronic bill of lading from being evidence of any mercantile custom giving it the characteristics of a document of title in the traditional common law sense.[89] Nor would the multilateral contract between users *inter se* and with the association confer contractual rights on persons who were not members of the association: at common law, this would follow from the doctrine of privity of contract; and no rights would be acquired under the Contracts (Rights of Third Parties) Act 1999 since there is nothing in the contract to satisfy the requirement of that Act that the third party must be "identified".[90] *A fortiori* the contract could not impose obligations on third parties. For all these reasons, a legislative solution to the problem of electronic bills is to be preferred. The Carriage of Goods by Sea Act 1992 envisages such a solution for the use of such instruments as a mechanism by which contractual rights can be vested in transferees, contractual liabilities imposed on them, and certain estoppels created in their favour. Further legislation would be necessary to give electronic bills the characteristics of documents of title in the traditional common law sense.

18–205 **Electronic bills as documents of title in the statutory sense.** So far as it relates to the status of an electronic bill as a "document of title", the preceding discussion is concerned with the common law sense of that expression, *i.e.* with the quality of "negotiability" (in the sense of transferability) which is accorded at common law to order and bearer bills.[91] It does not, therefore, conclude the question whether an electronic bill may not be a "document of title" in the statutory sense[92] given to that expression

[89] See above, paras 18–007, 18–062.
[90] Accordingly, s.1(3) of the 1999 Act (above, para.18–005 sub-paragraph (b)) would not be satisfied.
[91] Above, paras 18–007, 18–062, 18–063.
[92] Above, paras 18–009, 18–083.

by section 1(4) of the Factors Act 1889.[93] There is no difficulty in regarding an electronic bill as a "document"[94]; and, even if it is not a bill of lading within the first part of the definition in section 1(4),[95] it may fall within the second part of that definition if it is "used in the ordinary course of business as proof of the possession or control of goods" or for any of the other purposes specified in the subsection.[96] If one of these requirements were satisfied, a further difficulty would, however, arise under the provisions of the Sale of Goods Act 1979 which enable a person, by use of a document of title within the statutory definition, to transfer a better title than he himself has. This difficulty is that the relevant sections[97] of the Act require for this purpose either the delivery of the goods (which is not in question here) or[98] the "transfer" of a document of title; and the use here of the word "transfer" gives rise to a difficulty, similar to that discussed above[99] in relation to the "transfer" (for other purposes) of an electronic bill of lading: *i.e.* that, even if "possession" of such a "document" were acquired by the transferee, it would not, merely by virtue of an electronic transmission, be lost by the transferor. A possible resolution of this difficulty in the present context may be that there is judicial support for the view that a non-owner who is in possession of a delivery order can transfer title even though the delivery order which he uses for that purpose is not the same document as that originally in his possession but is a fresh delivery order issued by him to the transferee.[1] An analogous application of this rule to electronic bills of lading would enable a person to whom such a document had been electronically transmitted to acquire a better title than the transmitter's even though the transmission had not deprived the latter of "possession" of the bill.

Sea waybills and ship's delivery orders. The difficulties discussed in paragraph 18–204 in relation to electronic bills of lading do not arise in the same form in relation to the possible use in future of electronic sea waybills or ship's delivery orders. Even paper documents of this kind are not documents of title in the traditional common law sense[2] so that no question as to their "transfer" arises with regard to the acquisition of constructive possession of the underlying goods. Ship's delivery orders are, however, and sea waybills may be, documents of title in the statutory sense[3]; and with regard to transfer of title by the use of electronic documents of this kind the reasoning in paragraph 18–205 above[4] appears, *mutatis mutandis*, to apply. With regard to the use of electronic sea waybills and ship's delivery orders 18–206

---

[93] Law Commission, *Electronic Commerce: Formal Requirements in Electronic Transactions* (December 2001), paras 5.7, 5.8.
[94] Above, para.18–202, n.78.
[95] Above, para.18–009.
[96] *ibid.*
[97] ss.24, 25(1) and 47(1).
[98] Above, paras 7–062, 7–077.
[99] See above, para.18–204 after n.85.
[1] See *Mount Ltd v Jay & Jay (Provisions) Ltd* [1960] 1 Q.B. 159.
[2] Above, paras 18–067, 18–074, 18–075, 18–193 to 18–195.
[3] Above, paras 18–083, 18–196 to 18–197.
[4] Above, para.18–205.

as mechanisms for the transfer of *contractual* rights, it should be recalled that rights under the contract of carriage can be transferred by means of paper documents of these kinds *without* any transfer of the document in question.[5] In relation to such documents, the difficulties which are discussed in paragraph 18–204 with regard to the transfer of contractual rights by means of electronic bills of lading therefore will not normally arise. They could in theory arise in relation to a ship's delivery order since contractual rights can be transferred to a person by means of such a document only "subject to the terms of the order"[6]; and these terms may require possession of the order to have been transferred to that person. This theoretical possibility can, however, be disregarded since it is highly unlikely that parties who wish to use an electronic document for the present purpose will choose to subject that process to a requirement, compliance with which is, as a practical matter, impossible.

18–207 **Straight bills.** So far it relates to sea waybills, most of the reasoning in paragraph 18–206 above would apply also to straight bills. For the purposes of the Carriage of Goods by Sea Act 1992, straight bills are treated in the same way as, or are, sea waybills.[7] Hence the difficulties which have been discussed in paragraph 18–204 above with regard to the transfer of contractual rights by means of electronic order or bearer bills would not apply to electronic straight bills, any more than they apply to electronic sea waybills. Straight bills also resemble sea waybills in not being "negotiable" (*i.e.* transferable)[8] documents of title[9] in the common law sense[10]; and it is for this reason, rather than because of the difficulty of making a "transfer" of an electronic document,[11] that an electronic straight bill could not be used to transfer the constructive possession of the goods covered by it. An electronic straight bill could be a document of title in the statutory sense by virtue of being a "bill of lading" within section 1(4) of the Factors Act 1889; and although this reasoning probably would not apply to an electronic sea waybill, such a document could fall within the second part of the definition of "document of title"[12] within the subsection. This would, indeed, be true whether either type of document were in paper or in electronic form.[13]

3. PASSING OF PROPERTY

18–208 **In general.** The rules which govern the passing of property in certain particular types of overseas sales will be discussed in relation to these contracts in Chapters 19, 20 and 21. But there are some principles with

---

[5] Above, paras 18–153, 18–175.
[6] Carriage of Goods by Sea Act 1992, s.2(3)(a); above, para.18–175.
[7] See above, para.18–018 at n.35.
[8] See above, para.18–084.
[9] See above paras 18–067 (sea waybills); 18–074, 18–075 (straight bills).
[10] See above, paras 18–007, 18–062.
[11] See above, para.18–204.
[12] For the two parts of the definition of "document of title" in Factors Act 1889, s.1(4), see above para.18–009.
[13] *ibid.*

respect to the passing of property in overseas sales which are best discussed in this introductory Chapter as they are not confined to any one type of overseas sale; and as in some of the cases it is far from clear exactly which type of contract was involved. Problems with regard to the passing of property in overseas sales arise most frequently in order to determine whether the goods can, in effect, be treated as security for payment of the price; though they also arise in other contexts, *e.g.* in determining whether the action for the price can be brought[14] and whether a party to the contract of sale who has no rights in contract against the carrier can sue the carrier in tort for negligently damaging the goods[15]; and they may also be relevant in determining the measure of damages.[16] In overseas sales the passing of property is of relatively little importance in determining the incidence of risk, which is commonly separated from the passing of property,[17] or at any rate governed by independent rules.

Overseas sales are often sales of unascertained goods, though they may be sales of specific goods, *e.g.* where a particular Shetland pony is sold on c.i.f. terms[18] or where the sale is of the entire cargo of a particular ship[19] or of goods already afloat and identified by reference to some particular bill of lading. Where the sale is of goods which are unascertained in the sense of being simply generic goods,[20] property cannot pass until the goods are ascertained[21]; and, even where the goods are specific, property will not normally pass under an overseas sale when the contract is made.[22] The courts, in cases involving overseas sales, often stress the general rule that property passes when it is intended to pass[23]; and they make considerable efforts to determine this intention, although it has been said that "the intention in this regard by the parties is seldom or never capable of proof".[24] The law appears to start with the assumption that a seller of goods in transit will not normally wish to part with the property in the goods so long as he needs it as security for payment of the price. The suggestion[25] that such a seller has adequate security for the payment of the price by reason of his rights of lien or stoppage in transit has not been accepted by the courts[26]; and their refusal to accept it is based on a realistic 18–209

---

14 Above, para.16–001; below, paras 19–211, 19–215, 20–126, 20–130.
15 Above, para.18–149.
16 *Joseph (D.) v. Ralph Wood & Co.* [1951] W.N. 224.
17 See below, para.18–244.
18 *Wiehe v Dennis Bros* (1913) 29 T.L.R. 250.
19 *e.g. Couturier v Hastie* (1856) 5 H.L.C. 673.
20 For goods which are unascertained in the sense of forming an undifferentiated part of an identified bulk, see below, para.18–293 *et seq.*
21 Sale of Goods Act 1979, s.16; *Re Goldcorp Exchange Ltd* [1995] 1 A.C. 74, a decision that would not be affected by Sale of Goods Act 1979, s.20A (as inserted by Sale and Supply of Goods Act 1994, s.1) since the bulk of which the goods formed part was never "identified" in accordance with s.20A(1).
22 *i.e.* s.18, r.1, will rarely apply to such sales.
23 Sale of Goods Act 1979, s.17.
24 *Ross T Smyth & Co. Ltd v T D Bailey, Son & Co.* [1940] 3 All E.R. 60 at p.67.
25 In *The Parchim* [1918] A.C. 157 at pp.170–171; below, para.20–080.
26 See *James v The Commonwealth* (1939) 62 C.L.R. 339 at pp.379, 385; and see next note.

appreciation of modern methods of financing overseas sales. A bank willing to advance money on the security of property in goods would be much less ready to accept the somewhat perilous security of the rights of lien or stoppage.[27] These rights may be useful, in the last resort, when other means of securing payment have failed; but it is unlikely that a bank (or consequently a seller wanting to raise money on the security of shipping documents) would intend to rely solely on them. In overseas sales, there is, therefore, a fairly strong presumption that the seller does not intend to part with property until he has either been paid or been given an adequate assurance of payment.[28] Of course the presumption may be rebutted: for example, by the fact that buyer and seller are associated companies (so that the seller does not need security for payment),[29] by the fact that the contract expressly provides for credit, by the fact that credit is in fact given by delivery of the goods before payment,[30] or by the fact that the contract expressly provides for property to pass on the occurrence of some event other than payment.[31] In the oil trade, sale contracts sometimes provide for property and risk to pass as the oil passes the flange connection between the delivery hose and the vessel's permanent cargo intake manifold.[32] The fact that many such contracts are made between a relatively small number of companies, well known to each other, presumably reduces the importance which sellers normally attach to the security provided by the retention of shipping documents.

---

[27] *Arnhold Karberg & Co. v Blythe, Green, Jourdain & Co.* [1915] 1 K.B. 495; *Stein Forbes & Co. v County Tailoring Co.* (1916) 115 L.T. 215 at p.217; *Ross T Smyth & Co. Ltd v T. D. Bailey, Son & Co.* [1940] 3 All E.R. 60 at p.67; *The Future Express* [1993] 2 Lloyd's Rep. 542 at p.547. But see *Sale Continuation Ltd v Austin Taylor & Co.* [1968] 2 Q.B. 849 where the bank appears to have accepted a pledge of documents from the seller after the property had passed to the buyer. Perhaps the fate of the bank suggests that this was not good business practice.

[28] Below, paras 19–103, 20–082; *Ishag v Allied Bank International* [1981] 1 Lloyd's Rep. 92 at p.97; *Elder Dempster Lines v Zaki Ishag (The Lycaon)* [1983] 2 Lloyds Rep. 548 at 555; *Mitsui & Co. Ltd v Flota Mercante Grancolombiana (The Ciudad de Pasto and the Ciudad de Neiva)* [1988] 1 W.L.R. 1145 at p.1153; *The Montana* [1990] 1 Lloyd's Rep. 402; *M. B. Pyramid Sound NV v Briese Schiffahrts GmbH (The Ines)* [1995] 2 Lloyd's Rep. 144 at p.156.

[29] *The Albazero* [1977] A.C. 774; below, para.19–103, n.48.

[30] *Anonima Petroli Italiana SpA v Marlucidez Armadora SA (The Filiatra Legacy)* [1991] 2 Lloyd's Rep. 337, below, para.18–219; *cf. The Future Express* [1993] 2 Lloyd's Rep. 542, below, para.18–220.

[31] *e.g. Primetrade AG v Ythan Ltd (The Ythan)* [2005] EWHC 2399 (Comm.), [2006] 1 All E.R. 367 at [19] ("risk of loss and title were agreed to pass from the sellers to the buyers as the material passed the ship's rail at the loading port.") Payment was to be by irrevocable letter of credit; for the relevance of this point to the passing of property, see below, para.18–218).

[32] See, *e.g. Compania Portorafti Commerciale SA v Ultramar Panama Inc. (The Captain Gregos) (No. 2)* [1990] 2 Lloyd's Rep. 395; *Marimpex Mineralöl Handelsgesellschaft mbH v Louis Dreyfus et Cie Mineralöl GmbH* [1995] 1 Lloyd's Rep. 167 and *Vitol SA v Norelf Ltd (The Santa Clara)* [1993] 2 Lloyd's Rep. 301 at p.302 *revsd.* [1995] 2 Lloyd's Rep. 128 but restored [1996] A.C. 800; contrast *The Surf City* [1995] 2 Lloyd's Rep. 242 at p.245, where risk was to pass at the point described in the text but property only on tender of documents (*sc.* against payment).

Appropriation. In relation to a contract for the sale of unascertained goods, the term "appropriation" is used in several senses.[33] First it is used in what may be called a "contractual" sense: in this sense a seller is said to "appropriate" goods to the contract when he does an act which binds him contractually to deliver those goods[34] under the contract. Appropriation in this sense depends primarily on the intention of the seller.[35] Secondly, the word is used in what may be called a "proprietary" sense: this is found in section 18, rule 5(1) of the Sale of Goods Act 1979, which provides that (unless a different intention appears) property under a contract for the sale of unascertained goods passes when goods of the contract description and in a deliverable state are "unconditionally appropriated" to the contract. Under rule 5(1), such unconditional appropriation requires the assent of both parties,[36] so that it is arguable that the buyer may, by refusing his assent, be able to prevent the passing of property.[37] But in many cases the buyer's assent to the appropriation is considered to be given in advance[38]: it "does not mean expressed assent, but simply that the appropriation has been made in the manner contemplated by the parties."[39] Thus, where the buyer has given his consent in advance, both kinds of appropriation depend on the intention of the seller; but for the purpose of passing of property he must intend not merely to bind himself contractually to deliver a particular parcel of goods, but to appropriate those goods "unconditionally" to the contract. The question what acts may constitute "appropriation" is discussed in general terms in Chapter 5 and in relation to particular types of overseas sales in Chapters 19 and 20.[40] An appropriation may be conditional in many ways; but in relation to overseas sales the rule that the seller must intend to appropriate the goods "unconditionally" refers primarily to the requirement that he must do so without reserving "control"[41] or the "right of disposal"[42] of the goods. This requirement is discussed in the following paragraphs. 18–210

---

[33] *Wait v Baker* (1848) 2 Exch.1; *Produce Brokers Co. Ltd v Olympia Oil & Cake Co. Ltd* [1917] 1 K.B. 320; *Ross T Smyth & Co. Ltd v T D Bailey, Son & Co.* [1940] 3 All E.R. 60 at p.66; *Empresa Exportadora de Azucar v Industria Azucarera Nacional SA (The Playa Larga)* [1983] 2 Lloyd's Rep. 171 at p.186.

[34] Or the documents relating to them.

[35] See below, paras 19–015, 19–016; *Wait v Baker* (1848) 2 ExCh.1 at pp.8–9.

[36] *Carlos Federspiel & Co. SA v Charles Twigg & Co. SA* [1957] 1 Lloyd's Rep. 240 at p.255. *Cf. The Ciudad de Pasto and the Ciudad de Neiva*, above, n.28, at p.1153 ("common intention of the parties").

[37] *White & Carter (Councils) Ltd v McGregor* [1962] A.C. 413 at p.437, *per* Lord Keith, dissenting. Where the passing of property is deferred because the seller has reserved the "right of disposal", he may be able to waive this right (below, para.18–224), in which case property may pass to a buyer who may in a sense be unwilling to receive it; though it is arguable that he is only unwilling to perform the conditions on which property is to pass.

[38] *Carlos Federspiel & Co. SA v Charles Twigg & Co. SA* [1957] 1 Lloyd's Rep. 240 at p.255; *James v The Commonwealth* (1939) 62 C.L.R. 339 at p.377.

[39] *Nippon Yusen Kaisha v Ramjiban Serowgee* [1938] A.C. 429 at pp.443–444.

[40] Above, paras 5–068 *et seq.*; below, paras 19–100 *et seq.*, 20–070 *et seq.*

[41] See *Falk v Fletcher* (1865) 18 C.B.(N.S.) 403.

[42] See *Bruce v Wait* (1837) 3 M. & W. 15 (where there was appropriation in the "contractual" but not in the "proprietary" sense).

18–211 **Reservation of right of disposal.** Under section 18, rule 5(2) of the Sale of Goods Act 1979, a seller who delivers the goods to a carrier for transmission to the buyer is to be taken to have unconditionally appropriated them to the contract if he does not "reserve the right of disposal"[43]; and section 19(1) provides that the seller may by the terms of the contract or of the appropriation reserve the right of disposal until certain conditions are fulfilled. The most common condition is in effect that payment to the seller shall be made, or adequately assured. Section 19(2) deals with the reservation of the right of disposal by the way in which the shipping documents are made out[44] and section 19(3) with the passing of property as a result of the tender of a "documentary bill" of exchange.[45] In overseas sales, the passing of property thus depends primarily on the provisions of the contract, the form of the shipping documents, and the way in which the documents have been dealt with.

18–212 **Provisions of the contract.** Under section 19(1), the question whether the seller has reserved a right of disposal depends, in the first place, on any relevant provisions in the contract. Thus the contract may expressly provide that the property is to remain in the seller until payment of the price of the goods sold,[45a] or of other goods sold by the seller to the buyer under earlier or later contracts[46]; and there is no doubt that effect will be given at common law and under the 1979 Act to such a provision as between buyer and seller, and as between the seller and a third party to whom documents of title are transferred with notice of the seller's rights under the contract.[47] Similarly, a provision in the contract for payment by "cash against documents" will commonly prevent property from passing, even though the documents have been transferred, until the price is paid.[48] Difficulties begin to arise where the contract contains apparently conflicting provisions. Thus in *Nippon Yusen Kaisha v Ramjiban Serowgee*[49] the contract provided for payment by cash against mate's receipts, and this provision would, had it stood alone, have postponed the passing of property until such payment.[50] But the contract went on to provide that so long as the mate's receipts were in the possession of the seller, his lien was to subsist until payment in full; and this clause supported the conclusion that the property had passed before payment, for the seller could not have a lien over goods which were

---

[43] *e.g. Badische Anilin und Soda Fabrik v Basle Chemical Works* [1898] A.C. 200.
[44] Below, para.18–214.
[45] Below, para.18–221.
[45a] *e.g. Stora Enso OYJ v Port of Dundee* [2006] CSOH 40, *The Times*, April 11, 2006.
[46] See *Aluminium Industrie Vaassen BV v Romalpa Aluminium Ltd* [1976] 1 W.L.R. 676; above, para.5–141.
[47] *Bateman v Green* (1867) I.R. 2 C.L. 166.
[48] Below, para.19–088; *cf. Re Shipton Anderson & Co. and Harrison Bros* [1915] 3 K.B. 676. Such a provision in a contract of sale, by virtue of which the seller retains property until the goods are paid for, will not be subject to the requirement of registration under the proposed scheme for the registration of company security interests set out in the Law Commission's Report on *Company Security Interests,* Law Com. No.296 (2005): see paras 1–14 and 1–29 of the Report and above, para.18–010 at n.89.
[49] [1938] A.C. 429; and see above, para.18–048; below, para.18–228.
[50] [1938] A.C. 429 at p.444.

his own property. In *Barton, Thompson & Co. v Vigers Bros*[51] the contract provided for payment by approved acceptance at three months from the date of bill of lading, in exchange for shipping documents; and continued: "Property in goods to be deemed for all purposes, except retention of vendor's lien for unpaid price, to have passed to buyer when goods put on board." The buyer refused to accept the draft or pay for the goods; and the actual decision was that he was not entitled to retain, or deal with, the shipping documents. Dicta in the case suggest that the property in the goods had not passed to the buyer[52] though it does not seem that these dicta were necessary for the decision. To the extent to which the opinions expressed in these two cases conflict, one can only say that the passing of property is a question of intention in each case.

Subsequent agreement varying the contract. In *The Aliakmon*[53] a c. & f. contract provided for payment to be made 180 days after bill of lading date, by bill of exchange indorsed by the buyer's bank in exchange for the bill of lading. The goods were duly shipped by the sellers' suppliers under a bill of lading naming the buyers as consignees. The buyers being, however, unable to procure their bank's indorsement to the bill of exchange, the parties agreed to a variation of the contract of sale, under which the sellers sent the bill of lading to the buyers, who in return undertook to present it to the ship, to take delivery of the goods as agents of the sellers, to warehouse the goods to the sole order of the sellers and to notify them in advance of any resales of the goods. Under the original contract, property would no doubt have passed on delivery of the bill of lading to the buyers, against the indorsed bill of exchange: the sellers would have been regarded as having given credit for the stipulated period, and to have looked to the bank (rather than to the goods) as security for payment.[54] But the subsequent variation of the contract indicated that the sellers intended to retain their right of disposal within section 19(1) of the Act, so that property remained in the sellers until payment of the price[55] in spite of the delivery of the bill of lading to the buyers. 18–213

Form of bill of lading. Where a seller ships goods in pursuance of a contract of sale, he may take a bill of lading to his own order, or to the order of his agent, or to the buyer's order.[56] By section 19(2) of the Sale of Goods Act 1979, a seller is prima facie taken to reserve the right of disposal where goods are shipped and the bill of lading makes the goods deliverable to the order of the seller or his agent. If the bill is taken in this form, 18–214

---

[51] (1906) 19 Com.Cas. 175.
[52] See the references to *Shepherd v Harrison* (1871) L.R. 5 H.L. 116 and to Sale of Goods Act 1893 (now 1979), s.19(3), in (1906) 19 Com.Cas. 175 at 176.
[53] *Leigh & Sillavan Ltd v Aliakmon Shipping Co. Ltd (The Aliakmon)* [1986] A.C. 785; and see above, para.18–065 n.92.
[54] *cf.* below, paras 18–216, 18–218, 18–222.
[55] *The Aliakmon*, above n.53, at p.809.
[56] Above, para.18–015; for similar distinctions in relation to mate's receipts, see below, para.18–228. The possibilities mentioned in the text are not exhaustive: for example a documentary credit may require the bill to be made out to the order of the bank.

shipment will therefore not be an "unconditional appropriation"[57] so that the property will not pass merely by virtue of the shipment. This rule may apply even though the goods are shipped on a ship owned by the buyer[58] but it did not apply, on such facts, where the master of the ship was only induced to sign a bill of lading to the order of the seller by the seller's representation that the form of the bill was immaterial.[59] Although it has been said that the taking of a bill of lading to the seller's order is "nearly conclusive evidence"[60] that property did not pass on shipment, there is no absolute rule of law to that effect. Before the original enactment (in 1893) of section 19(2) it was held to be a question for the jury whether the taking of a bill of lading in this form was evidence of intention "to preserve the right of the unpaid vendor until some further act was done"[61]; and although section 19(2) creates a presumption that the seller has such an intention, the presumption is a rebuttable one. The subsequent conduct of the seller may be relevant to his intention at the time of shipment: thus transfer of the bill of lading to the buyer otherwise than against payment may negative the inference that the seller originally intended to reserve the right of disposal by taking a bill of lading to his own order.[62] The presumption created by section 19(2) does not apply where the bill of lading is made out to the order of the buyer[63]; but the mere fact that the bill of lading is made out in this way will not suffice to pass property on shipment if the bill is so dealt with as to show an intention on the part of the seller to retain the right of disposal: *e.g.* if he sends such a bill to his own agent with instructions to deliver it up to the buyer only against payment[64]; or if, though the buyer is named as consignee, the parties later agree that the goods are to remain at the disposal of the seller even after the bill has been sent to the buyer[65]; or if the contract provides for payment in exchange for or "on receipt of" (shipping) documents[66]; or if other circumstances indicate that the seller intended to reserve his right of disposal.[67]

---

[57] Within Sale of Goods Act 1979, s.18, r.5(2).
[58] *Turner v Trustees of the Liverpool Docks* (1851) 6 Exch. 543.
[59] *Ogle v Atkinson* (1814) 5 Taunt. 759.
[60] *Jenkyns v Brown* (1849) 14 Q.B. 496 at 502.
[61] *Van Casteel v Booker* (1848) 2 Exch.691 at 709. In *Coxe v Harden* (1803) 4 East 211 a bill of lading to the order of the seller was sent unindorsed to the buyer who managed to get delivery from the ship; and it was held that property had passed on delivery: *sed quaere*.
[62] *Van Casteel v Booker* (1848) 2 Exch.691; *Joyce v Swann* (1864) 17 C.B.(N.S.) 84; and *cf. The Parchim* [1918] A.C. 157 discussed below, para.20–080.
[63] See *Mitsui & Co. Ltd v Flota Mercante Grancolombiana SA (The Ciudad de Pasto and the Ciudad de Neiva)* [1988] 1 W.L.R. 1145 at pp. 1153–1154; *The Seven Pioneer* [2001] 2 Lloyd's Rep. 57 at [34] (High Court of New Zealand).
[64] *Sheridan v New Quay Co.* (1858) 4 C.B.(N.S.) 618.
[65] *Leigh & Sillavan Ltd v Aliakmon Shipping Co. Ltd (The Aliakmon)* [1986] A.C. 785 (where the goods were shipped by the seller's supplier who delivered the bill of lading to the seller who later delivered it to the buyer in circumstances described in para.18–213, above).
[66] As in *The Seven Pioneer*, above n.63, at [35].
[67] *Ishag v Allied Bank International* [1980] 1 Lloyd's Rep. 92 at p. 97; *Elder Dempster Lines v Zaki Ishag (The Lycaon)* [1983] 2 Lloyd's Rep. 548 at p. 555.

Subsequent dealings with shipping documents. Dealings with shipping documents may be evidence of the intention of the seller at the time of shipment[68]; but they more frequently have the effect of passing property after shipment. **18–215**

A bill of lading making the goods deliverable to the seller's order may be indorsed to the buyer, or indorsed in blank for the purpose of transmission to the buyer. In spite of a dictum to the contrary,[69] it seems clear that property does not pass *merely* by indorsement of the bill of lading. Such indorsement, if for value, is at most prima facie evidence of passing of property[70]; but further inferences of intention to pass property may be drawn from subsequent dealings with the bill.

Transmission of bill of lading to the buyer, to an agent or to a bank. If the bill of lading is indorsed in blank, or to the buyer's order, and sent directly to the buyer, then the property may, and often[71] will, pass to the buyer. Even where the bill of lading is not properly indorsed, an undertaking to procure a proper indorsement appears to be capable of passing the property.[72] But property will not pass if a contrary intention appears from the terms of the contract or from the circumstances in which the bill was sent. Thus the property would not pass if the contract expressly provided that it was to remain in the seller until payment, or for "cash against documents"; if the bill of lading was sent, together with a demand for payment, and payment was not made within a reasonable time[73]; or if the bill of lading was attached to a bill of exchange drawn on the buyer for the price.[74] In *The Aliakmon*[75] it was similarly held that property did not pass on transmission of the bill of lading to the buyers who had not yet paid the price because buyers and sellers had expressly agreed that the buyers were to take delivery of the goods from the ship solely as agents of the sellers and to warehouse them to the sole order of the sellers. **18–216**

One way in which a seller can preserve his property in the goods after parting with the bill is by sending it, not directly to the buyer, but to his own

---

[68] Above, para.18–214.

[69] *R & W Paul Ltd v National S.S. Co. Ltd* (1937) 59 Ll.L.R. 28 at p. 32 (where it is also said at p.33 that "the absolute property is transferred by virtue of the Bills of Lading Act 1855"—a statement so patently wrong as to cast doubt on the accuracy of the report at this point. As the buyer had in fact paid the price and received both the documents and the goods, there could scarcely be any doubt that property had passed).

[70] *Dracachi v Anglo-Egyptian Navigation Co.* (1868) L.R. 3 C.P. 190 (above, para.18–089).

[71] *Wilmshurst v Bowker* (1841) 10 L.J.C.P. 161; (1844) 7 Man. & G. 882; *Key v Cotesworth* (1852) 7 Ex. 595; *König v Brandt* (1901) 84 L.T. 748; *cf. Walley v Montgomery* (1803) 3 East 584.

[72] *Dick v Lumsden* (1793) Peake 250; *Meyer v Sharpe* (1813) 5 Taunt. 74 (where the interest of the holder of the unindorsed bill was said to be only equitable); *Nathan v Giles* (1814) 5 Taunt. 557.

[73] See below, para.19–103.

[74] Above, para.18–212; below, paras 18–221 *et seq.*

[75] *Leigh & Sillavan Ltd v Aliakmon Shipping Co. Ltd (The Aliakmon)* [1986] A.C. 785; above, para.18–213.

agent with instructions to present it in exchange for payment.[76] Where this course is adopted, the general result is that no property passes either to the agent[77] or to the buyer[78] until payment[79] or until the occurrence of such other conditions as may be specified in the contract in pursuance of which the transfer was made[80]; but if the agent has advanced money on the security of the goods he may obtain a special property in them as pledgee.[81] Where a bill of lading is transferred by the seller to a bank for the sole purpose of enabling the bank on the seller's behalf to collect the price from the buyer, the property in the goods remains in the seller until payment and no interest by way of security passes by virtue of the transfer to the bank.[82] Even where a bill of lading is transferred to a bank as security for an advance, the bank will normally acquire only a special property as pledgee, that being the intention of the parties.[83] Where a special property is in this way transferred to an agent or to a bank, the general property will normally remain in the seller[84] until payment.[85] This rule may, however, be displaced by proof of contrary intention: thus the general property may vest in the buyer by virtue of the terms of an invoice from which an intention to transfer it may be inferred.[86]

18–217 **Seller having other security for payment.** Property may also vest in the buyer if the seller is assured of payment even though the buyer may fail to pay, *e.g.* if the contract provides for payment by a bill of exchange endorsed by the buyer's bank (so as to make the bank liable on the bill) in return for the bill of lading,[87] or if the buyer has provided a bank guarantee before shipment.[88] In such cases the seller has little further interest in retaining the

---

[76] *Key v Cotesworth* (1852) 7 Exch. 595 at p.607; *König v Brandt* (1901) 84 L.T. 748 at p.753; *cf. Cahn & Mayer v Pockett's Bristol Channel Steam Packet Co. Ltd* [1899] 1 Q.B. 643 at p.661. "Payment" in this context does not necessarily mean payment in cash: see *The Argentina* (1867) L.R. 1 Ad. & E. 370.

[77] *Patten v Thompson* (1816) 5 M. & S. 350; *Burgos v Nascimento* (1908) 100 L.T. 71.

[78] *James v The Commonwealth* (1939) 62 C.L.R. 339.

[79] Below, para.18–226.

[80] *e.g.* acceptance of a bill of exchange: *cf.* below, para.18–223.

[81] *Jenkyns v Brown* (1849) 14 Q.B. 496.

[82] *East West Corp. v DKBS 1912 AF A/S* [2003] EWCA Civ 83, [2003] Q.B. 1509 at [3], [42].

[83] *Sewell v Burdick* (1884) 10 App.Cas. 74; *cf. Hibbert v Carter* (1787) 1 T.R. 745; *Guaranty Trust Co. of New York v Hannay* [1918] 2 K.B. 623 at pp.631, 653.

[84] *The Orteric* [1920] A.C. 724.

[85] *Empresa Exportadora de Azucar v Industria Azucarera Nacional SA (The Playa Larga)* [1983] 2 Lloyd's Rep. 171 at 186; *P S Chellaram & Co. Ltd v China Ocean Shipping Co.* [1989] 1 Lloyd's Rep. 413, revsd. on other grounds [1991] 1 Lloyd's Rep. 493.

[86] *Jenkyns v Brown* (1849) 14 Q.B. 496; *cf. Walley v Montgomery* (1803) 3 East 584.

[87] The property would have passed on presentation of such a bill of exchange in *Leigh & Sillavan Ltd v Aliakmon Shipping Co. Ltd (The Aliakmon)* [1986] A.C. 785 if the contract had not been varied: see above, para.18–213.

[88] Some importance was attached to this fact in *Enichem Anic SpA v Ampelos Shipping Co. Ltd (The Delfini)* [1990] 1 Lloyd's Rep. 252, below, para.19–102; *cf. Noble Resources Ltd v Cavalier Shipping Corp. (The Atlas)* [1996] 1 Lloyd's Rep. 642 at p.644, where property under an f.o.b. contract of barter was held to have passed on shipment, even though the bank guarantee required by the contract had not been given.

general property in the goods. Where, on the other hand, the seller has merely discounted a bill of exchange drawn on the buyer for the price, the general property remains in the seller at least until the buyer accepts the bill. In such a case the seller, being liable to the discounting bank as drawer of the bill, has an interest in retaining the property of the goods until that liability is discharged.[89]

Payment by documentary credit. A further situation in which it is arguable that the seller does not intend to retain the right of disposal (and hence the property in the goods) is that in which the contract provides for payment by documentary credit. A number of dicta support the view that, in such cases, the seller relies on the bank's promise, rather than on his right of property in the goods, as security for payment of the price.[90] This view may derive some further support from a case in which property under such a contract was held not to have passed at the relevant time[91] precisely because the bank had not yet made any binding promise to the seller[92]; and from one[93] in which the fact that the buyer had provided a standby letter of credit[94] helped to support the view that property had passed before the buyer had actually paid the price. On the other hand, the fact that the seller, as beneficiary under a documentary credit, holds an enforceable promise from a bank does not by any means invariably support the inference that the seller no longer intends to retain property. Thus it has been said that "even the most copper-bottomed letter of credit sometimes fails to produce payment" and that a seller who holds a letter of credit "will nevertheless often retain the property in his goods until he has presented the documents and obtained payment."[95] The only conclusion which can, in the present state of the authorities, be drawn from these conflicting dicta, is that the issue of a letter of credit is relevant, but not decisive, to the seller's intention to transfer property. Where it is so relevant, the question exactly when property passes is, furthermore, an open one. It would not normally pass when the credit is issued, for at that stage the goods would often be unascertained, and it would not be clear whether the documents which the seller proposed to tender would be accepted by the bank as being in conformity with the credit. At the other extreme, there is obviously no reason why property should not pass on payment. The difficult case is that in which the bank has accepted the documents against a time draft. In such a case property may pass on the bank's acceptance of the draft, by analogy 18–218

[89] *The Prinz Adalbert* [1917] A.C. 586; *cf. The Glenroy* [1945] A.C. 124; below, para.19–103.
[90] *The Dirigo* [1919] P. 204 at p.221; *Sale Continuation Ltd v Austin Taylor & Co.* [1968] 2 Q.B. 849; *cf Davy Offshore Ltd v Emerald Field Contracting Ltd* [1992] 2 Lloyd's Rep. 142 at p.156.
[91] Below, para.18–242.
[92] *The Kronprinsessan Margareta* [1921] 1 A.C. 486 at p.514.
[93] *Anonima Petroli Italiana SpA v Marlucidez Armadora SA (The Filiatra Legacy)* [1991] 2 Lloyd's Rep. 337.
[94] Below, paras 23–050, 23–039 *et seq.*
[95] *Mitsui & Co. Ltd v Flota Mercante Grancolombiana SA (The Ciudad de Pasto and the Ciudad de Neiva)* [1988] 1 W.L.R. 1145 at p.1153; *cf. The Glenroy* [1945] A.C. 124 at 145 ("the bank might fail").

with the rules relating to documentary bills, to be discussed in paragraphs 18–221 to 18–225 below. A seller who parts with documents against such a draft can be regarded as giving credit[96] and so displacing the prima facie rule[97] that property passes only on payment. The case for taking this view is (to put the matter at its lowest) no weaker where the draft is accepted by a bank under a documentary credit, than it is where the draft is accepted by the buyer himself under a documentary bill.

18–219 **Subsequent dealings with the goods.** The rules which link the passing of property to the way in which the shipping documents are made out, and dealt with, are based on the traditional assumption that, in order to obtain delivery of the goods from the carrier, the buyer must present a bill of lading made out to his order or to bearer, or duly indorsed to him or in blank. Where this assumption is negatived by the facts, it may well be more appropriate to look to dealings with the goods themselves as evidence of the seller's intention to give up the right of disposal and so to transfer property. In *The Filiatra Legacy*[98] a c.i.f. contract for the sale of oil provided that payment was to be made "within 30 days of bill of lading date" and that the payment was to be "supported by" a standby letter of credit, which was duly opened. The voyage was described as a "short" one[99]; an expression which in the context refers to one which was likely to be accomplished before transmission of the shipping documents to the buyers. The voyage was in fact so accomplished, and the sellers (to whose order the oil was deliverable by the terms of the bill of lading) directed the carrier to deliver it to the buyers against a letter of indemnity. It was, moreover, contemplated that the oil might be refined and resold before payment. In these circumstances it was held that credit had been given[1] and that property had passed at the latest when discharge of the cargo began, even though at that stage the buyers had not paid the price. It should, however, be emphasised that the inference that credit has been given is by no means invariably to be drawn merely from the fact that, in order to save time or expense, delivery is made before payment against shipping documents.[2] In *The Filiatra Legacy* the inference was drawn from a combination of this fact, the payment term of the contract, and the contemplated speedy use and resale of the subject-matter of the contract.

18–220 **Other evidence of intention to pass property before payment.** Even where the seller has not relied on the personal credit of the buyer, there may be other evidence of intention to pass property before payment; and

---

96 *cf. Davy Offshore Ltd v Emerald Field Contracting Ltd* [1992] 2 Lloyd's Rep. 145 at p.156 ("when [the sellers are] equipped to operate the letter of credit, or . . . when they present the documents to the bank").

97 Above, para.18–209.

98 *Anonima Petroli Italiana SpA v Marlucidez Armadora SA (The Filiatra Legacy)* [1991] 2 Lloyd's Rep. 337.

99 *ibid.*, at p.342.

1 In the court's view, the provision as to payment "within 30 days of bill of lading date" was one by which "the contract . . . provided for credit" (at p.343); such a provision might, alternatively, be one specifying the time of tender of, and payment against, documents, as in *Toepfer v Lenersan- Poortman NV* [1980] 1 Lloyd's Rep. 143. See further para.19–103, below.

2 See below, paras 19–102, 19–103.

this possibility is illustrated by *The Future Express*.[3] Wheat had been sold on c. & f. terms under a contract which provided for payment by letter of credit, which was duly opened. The seller agreed with the buyer[4] to delay presentation of documents to the bank, so as to enable the buyer in turn to delay reimbursing the bank while obtaining delivery of the goods from the carrier against a letter of indemnity.[5] The seller subsequently obtained payment from the bank against documents (including bills of lading), and the bank sued the carrier in conversion[6] for having wrongfully delivered the goods to the buyer, who had become insolvent. The bank's claim against the carrier failed on the ground that, when the seller delivered the documents to the bank, property had already passed to the buyer, so that the seller could no longer create a valid pledge in favour of the bank: the seller's ability to do this had been "frustrated by the willingness of [the seller] to facilitate [the buyer's] fraud"[7]; and this willingness showed that the seller had agreed to pass property to the buyer before presenting the documents to the bank and so obtaining payment.

Documentary bill of exchange. A "documentary bill" is a bill of exchange to which shipping documents are attached. Where a contract of sale provides for payment by acceptance of seller's draft in exchange for shipping documents, the seller may send to the buyer a bill of exchange together with the bill of lading, and possibly other shipping documents, in order to obtain the buyer's acceptance of the bill of exchange. In such a case the buyer is under a contractual obligation to accept the bill of exchange; and in addition section 19(3) of the Sale of Goods Act 1979 provides that "the buyer is bound to return the bill of lading if he does not honour the bill of exchange, and if he wrongfully retains the bill of lading the property in the goods does not pass to him." If the buyer refuses to accept a bill of exchange sent to him in these circumstances the property in the goods does not pass to him[8]; and he is not entitled to retain or deal with the bill of lading[9]; or to impose conditions as to its return: *e.g.* he is not entitled, as a condition of returning the bill of lading, to insist on repayment of any freight which he may have paid.[10] The same rules apply 18–221

---

[3] [1993] 2 Lloyd's Rep. 542.

[4] Nominally the buyer was a foreign government but in substance he was an individual who throughout this account is referred to as the buyer.

[5] An action by the bank against *the seller* was brought in Switzerland; the outcome of this action is not stated in the report cited in n.3, above.

[6] The bank could not sue the carrier as transferee of the bill of lading for breach of the contract contained or evidenced in the bill because, being only a pledgee, it fell into the "property gap" in the Bills of Lading Act 1855, s.1, above, para.18–100. Now the bank would have a right of action against the carrier in contract by virtue of Carriage of Goods by Sea Act 1992, s.2(1)(a) and (2), but only if it had become holder of the bill of lading in good faith: s.5(2). In view of the bank's agreement to accept "stale" documents, and of its acceptance of the documents after the goods had, to its knowledge, been discharged, there must be some doubt as to whether this requirement would now be satisfied.

[7] [1993] 2 Lloyd's Rep. 542 at p.548.

[8] *Shepherd v Harrison* (1871) L.R. 5 H.L. 116; *The Miramichi* [1915] P. 71 at p.78.

[9] *Barton, Thompson & Co. v Vigers Bros* (1906) 19 Com.Cas. 175.

[10] *Rew v Payne, Douthwaite & Co.* (1886) 53 L.T. 932.

where the bill of exchange is drawn, not on the buyer, but on a person nominated by him, and not accepted by that person[11]; and where the documents are presented, not by the seller, but by a bank with which the seller has discounted the bill of exchange.[12] Such cases may not be directly within section 19(3) but are governed by the same principle at common law. Where the documents are presented by a person (other than the seller) who has advanced money on them, that person is, as against the buyer, entitled by virtue of his special property to possession of the documents[13] if the buyer does not accept the bill of exchange. The above principles apply only where payment is to be made by bill of exchange and that bill is sent to the buyer together with the bill of lading. Thus where payment was to be by banker's draft, to be remitted on receipt of bill of lading, it was held that property passed on transfer of the bill of lading, the sending of the draft being a "condition subsequent"[14]; and similarly property was held to have passed where the seller's draft did not accompany the bill of lading, which had been made out to seller's order, indorsed in blank and sent independently to the buyer.[15] Property may also pass irrespective of the terms of the bill of lading and of any dealings with it. Thus where the intention of the parties was that property should pass on shipment, refusal by the buyer to accept a "documentary bill" would not prevent that intention from taking effect.[16]

18–222 The provision of section 19(3) with respect to the passing of property is negative in terms, *i.e.* it says that the property will *not* pass if the buyer "wrongfully retains[17] the bill of lading". It is, however, equally true that the property *will* pass (unless there is evidence of contrary intention) if the buyer does accept and pay the bill of exchange in accordance with the contract,[18] or if he offers to accept it and this offer is wrongfully rejected by the seller.[19]

18–223 Section 19(3) says that the buyer must return the bill of lading if he "does not honour the bill of exchange". A bill of exchange may be dishonoured in two ways, by non-acceptance and by non-payment[20]; and section 19(3) does not expressly say which of these kinds of dishonour it contemplates. The reasoning of the Privy Council in *The Prinz Adalbert*,[21] however, suggests that it is dishonour by non-acceptance which is the crucial factor in

---

[11] *Brandt v Bowlby* (1831) 2 B. & Ad. 932.
[12] See *The Prinz Adalbert* [1917] A.C. 586; below, para.18–223.
[13] *Rew v Payne, Douthwaite & Co.*, above, n.10.
[14] *Wilmshurst v Bowker* (1844) 7 Man. & G. 882 at p.892.
[15] *Key v Cotesworth* (1852) 7 Exch. 595; *cf. Danish Dairies Co-operative Society v Midland Ry* (1892) 8 T.L.R. 212.
[16] *Ogle v Atkinson* (1814) 5 Taunt. 759.
[17] If he does not obtain it at all, the property will normally not pass by reason of the principles stated in paras 18–214, 18–216, above.
[18] *The Prinz Adalbert* [1917] A.C. 586; and see below, para.18–223.
[19] As in *Walley v Montgomery* (1803) 3 East 584, where the seller's agent demanded cash to which the seller was not entitled under the contract at this stage.
[20] Bills of Exchange Act 1882, ss.42, 47.
[21] [1917] A.C. 586.

preventing the passing of property. In that case Lord Sumner considered the position of a banker who, having discounted a draft accompanied by a bill of lading, parts with the bill of lading on acceptance of the draft. "The inference," he said, "is that he [the banker] is satisfied to part with his security in consideration of getting this further party's liability on the bill [of exchange]."[22] If this is true of the banker in the case put, it is presumably also true of a seller who presents the documentary bill directly for the buyer's acceptance; and this view is supported by a further quotation from the same case: "If the shipper, being then owner of the goods, authorizes and directs the banker . . . to surrender the bill of lading against *acceptance* of the draft, it is natural to infer that he intends to transfer the ownership when this is done, but intends also to remain the owner until this has been done . . . ."[23] A seller who wants to retain the property until the draft is actually paid can include a stipulation to this effect in the contract,[24] or achieve the same result by providing that payment must be by cash against bill of lading.[25]

It is arguable that the requirements of section 19(3), which prevent the passing of property, are wholly for the benefit of the seller, and that they can therefore be waived by him, with the result that the property may pass although they are not complied with. There is certainly support for the view that a stipulation for payment by cash against documents can be waived with this result by the seller[26]; though a stipulation for payment by documentary bill could be distinguished on the ground that it might afford the buyer credit and therefore be partly for his benefit. In any event the seller cannot, it is submitted, both retain his right of disposal and argue that the property has nevertheless passed because this happens to be to his advantage. In other words, he may sometimes be able to waive his right of disposal, but he cannot waive the rule that property does not pass so long as he retains the right of disposal.[27] **18–224**

Section 19(3) is concerned with the passing of property between buyer and seller. A buyer who fails to accept a "documentary bill" may, although property has not passed to him, be able to transfer title under some exception to the principle *nemo dat quod non habet*. Such a buyer is in possession of the bill of lading "with the consent of the seller" within section 25 of the Sale of Goods Act 1979; and he is also a person to whom the bill of lading has been "lawfully transferred" within section 47(2) of the Act.[28] A seller who wishes to protect himself against the risk of losing his **18–225**

---

[22] *ibid.*, at p.589.
[23] *ibid.*, at pp.589–590; *cf. Berndtson v Strang* (1868) L.R. 3 Ch.App. 588 at p.590; below, para.20–085.
[24] See *Bateman v Green* (1867) I.R. 2 C.L. 166. The words "to secure acceptance *or payment*" in s.19(3) would cover this situation.
[25] *Sheridan v New Quay Co.* (1858) 4 C.B.(N.S.) 618; *Moakes v Nicolson* (1865) 19 C.B.(N.S.) 290 (the actual decision would now be different under Sale of Goods Act 1979, s.25).
[26] *F E Napier v Dexters Ltd* (1926) 26 Ll.L.R. 62 at 64; *ibid.*, pp.184, 187–188.
[27] *cf.* below, para.20–128.
[28] *Cahn & Mayer v Pockett's Bristol Channel Steam Packet Co. Ltd* [1899] 1 Q.B. 643 (above, para.18–087).

title by the buyer's dealing with the bill of lading can do so by sending the bill to his own agent with a view to securing acceptance of the bill of exchange.[29]

18–226 **Effect of payment of, or offer to pay, the price.** Where payment is actually made in full on presentation of documents, property will normally pass to the buyer.[30] Once an offer to pay has been made, its wrongful rejection by or on behalf of the seller has the same effect.[31] Where the contract provides for payment by acceptance of a bill of exchange, property may pass on such acceptance,[32] even though the seller wrongfully refuses the buyer's offer to pay in this form and insists on cash.[33] But in *Jenkyns v Brown*[34] the buyer's offer to pay bills of exchange on the day on which they were due could not be accepted because the bills were temporarily unavailable. The buyer was asked to call again the next day but failed to do so, and did not thereafter accept or pay the bills. It was held that, although property had passed by virtue of previous dealings, the buyer was not entitled to possession of the goods.

18–227 **Bill of lading obtained by fraud.** In *Schuster v McKellar*[35] goods were shipped by a seller on a ship on which space had been reserved by the buyer[36]; and a mate's receipt was issued to the seller. This was to be "redeemed" by the buyer, who instead by fraud induced the captain to issue a bill of lading to him (naming him as shipper), which he indorsed to a third party. It was held that property remained in the seller, who had no intention to relinquish it before redemption of the mate's receipt. Nor would a buyer who had obtained a bill of lading in this way be in a position to transfer title, since he would not be a person who was in possession of the bill of lading with the consent of the seller,[37] nor one to whom the bill had been lawfully transferred.[38] The suggestion in the same case[39] that the

---

[29] [1899] 1 Q.B. at 661; *cf.* above, para.18–216.

[30] *James v The Commonwealth* (1939) 62 C.L.R. 339 (first case); contrast *Mitsui & Co. Ltd v Flota Mercante Grancolombiana SA (The Ciudad de Pasto and the Ciudad de Neiva)* [1988] 1 W.L.R. 1145 (where property was held not to have passed on payment of part only of the price).

[31] *Mirabita v Imperial Ottoman Bank* (1878) 3 Ex.D. 164 at p.171. *Cf.* below, para.20–084. For conflicting dicta on the question whether tender of the price *after* wrongful repudiation by the seller can pass property, see *City Motors v Southern Aerial Super Services* (1961) 106 C.L.R. 477 at pp.485–486, 487–490.

[32] *Ex p. Brett, In Re Howe* (1871) L.R. 6 Ch.App. 838; a dictum at p.840 requires payment but this does not appear to have been made.

[33] *Walley v Montgomery* (1803) 3 East 584.

[34] (1849) 14 Q.B. 496.

[35] (1857) 7 El. & Bl. 704.

[36] For the purpose of the case it made no difference that the relationship of consignor and consignee could be described as that of agent and principal: *cf.* below, para.18–229.

[37] Within Sale of Goods Act 1979, s.25. The case could not be one in which the *seller* could be said to have given his *de facto* consent in spite of the fraud (see above, para.7–074) since the fraud was practised on the *captain*, the seller knowing nothing of the circumstances in which the bill of lading had been obtained. Nor (as shipping space had been reserved by the buyer) could the captain be regarded as agent of the seller for the purpose in question.

[38] Within Sale of Goods Act 1979, s.47(2).

[39] (1857) 7 El. & Bl. 704 at p.721.

fraudulent person would be able to give a bona fide assignee for value rights against the carrier at the time gave rise to some difficulty because of the "property gap" in the Bills of Lading Act 1855[40] would have prevented the "assignee" from acquiring contractual rights against the carrier. Under the Carriage of Goods by Sea Act 1992, it seems that the fraud of the person named in the bill as the shipper would in principle provide the carrier with a defence to an action on the contract of carriage.[41] Perhaps in a case of this kind the holder could rely on an estoppel against the carrier which would preclude the latter from denying that the goods had been shipped by the fraudulent person.

Mate's receipts. The retention by a seller of a mate's receipt in his own name as shipper may be evidence of his intention to retain property after shipment. In *Falk v Fletcher*[42] a seller took a mate's receipt in his own name and the jury found that he had done so with the intention to retain "control" over the property, which therefore did not pass. It was held that the question had been properly left to the jury, and Willes J. added that it had been correctly answered by them. On the other hand, in *FE Napier v Dexters Ltd*[43] a contract provided for payment by "cash against mate's receipt". The seller obtained a wharf receipt in the buyer's name and transmitted it to the buyer. It was held that, although the stipulation as to payment might prima facie indicate an intention to reserve the right of disposal, the intention was negatived by the fact that the receipt was taken in the buyer's name and had been transmitted to him. And in *Nippon Yusen Kaisha v Ramjiban Serowgee*[44] it was held that even the seller's possession of mate's receipts naming the buyer as shipper did not prevent the passing of property under a contract which provided for payment against mate's receipts. That decision was, however, based on the special terms of the contract[45]; but for these it is submitted that the seller's retention of the mate's receipts would at the very least have been evidence of intention to retain the right of disposal, so as to prevent the passing of property until payment against those receipts. **18–228**

Shipments by and to agents. The relationship between shipper and consignee may not be that of seller and buyer but that of agent and principal. The general rule in such a case, stated in *Hathesing v Laing*[46] and *Ex p. Banner*,[47] is that the goods become (as between shipper and consignee) the property of the principal as soon as they are consigned to him. In *Jenkyns v Brown* it was said that the general rule did not apply where the agents had paid "with their own money" for the goods, which **18–229**

---

[40] Above, para.18–100.
[41] Above, para.18–107.
[42] (1865) 18 C.B.(N.S.) 403; *cf.* *Craven v Ryder* (1816) 6 Taunt. 433 ("lighterman's receipts").
[43] (1926) 26 Ll.L.R. 62; *ibid.*, p.184; below, para.20–076.
[44] [1938] A.C. 429.
[45] Above, para.18–212.
[46] (1873) L.R. 17 Eq. 92 at p.101.
[47] (1876) 2 Ch.D. 278 at p.287.

then "became their property".[48] It is not clear just what is meant here by the agent's "own money", for the general rule has certainly been applied even where the agent had not been put into funds by his principal before the purchase and consignment.[49] Perhaps *Jenkyns v Brown* can be explained as a case in which the shipper was both an agent and a seller.[50] Even where the shipper is purely an agent, he may initially have a lien on the goods for the price; but he will lose this if he ships the goods and takes the mate's receipts[51] or bill of lading[52] in the name of the principal as shipper. It makes no difference in such a case that the agent draws on the principal for the price of the goods, and that the principal fails to accept the bill of exchange.[53] The agent can however protect his rights if he takes a bill of lading making the goods deliverable to his own order and transmits it to his own agent with directions not to hand it over to the principal unless the bill of exchange is accepted. It was said in *Ex p. Banner* that "The right of an agent in such a case over the goods, as against his principal, is the same as that of a vendor against a purchaser."[54] As this statement follows the supposition that the goods have become the property of the principal, it seems to refer to the agent's lien: it is this lien which is protected by the form of the bill of lading and the manner of its presentation to the principal. An agent who fails in this way to protect his lien may still have a right to stop the goods in transit, analogous to that of an unpaid seller.[55]

18–230 In *Ex p. Banner* the court also recognised a general rule that "every person who consigns goods to another has a right to give directions how the goods are to be disposed of . . . and that a consignee to whom such directions are given must dispose of the goods in the way directed or else return them."[56] A disposition which contravened such a direction would therefore not operate to pass property to the transferee, though it might transfer title under one of the exceptions to *nemo dat quod non habet*. The rule was held to be inapplicable on the facts of the case as the directions given to the consignee only told him how to dispose of the *proceeds* of the goods; and it seems in any case to be restricted to the situation where the directions accompany the original consignment, *i.e.* where goods are consigned on the terms that they are to be applied for a particular purpose.[57]

18–231 Where goods are consigned by a principal to an agent for sale, the general rule is that, as between principal and agent, the property remains in the principal; but the agent is entitled to apply the proceeds of the goods in

---

48 (1849) 14 Q.B.D. 496 at p.502. The property was said at p.503 to have passed by subsequent dealings subject to the reservation of a "special property" until actual payment.
49 As in *Hathesing v Laing*, above, and *Ex p. Banner*, above.
50 Below, para.18–232.
51 *Hathesing v Laing*, above.
52 *Ex p. Banner*, above.
53 *Ex p. Banner*, above; *cf. Anderson v Clark* (1824) 2 Bing. 20.
54 (1876) 2 Ch.D. 278 at p.287.
55 *ibid.*, at p.288; *cf.* Sale of Goods Act 1979, s.38(2), above, para.15–013.
56 (1876) 2 Ch.D. 278 at p.289.
57 *Tooke v Hollingworth* (1793) 5 T.R. 215, the only authority cited in *Ex p. Banner* in support of the proposition quoted above, was such a case.

repaying to himself any advances which he may have made to the principal in respect of the goods.[58]

18–232 **"Agents" in fact sellers or buyers.** The principles stated in paragraphs 18–229 to 18–231 above assume that the relationship of the parties is clearly identifiable as that of principal and agent, as opposed to that of buyer and seller; but this assumption may be ill-founded.[59] In a number of 19th century cases, "agents" in one country were for many purposes regarded as sellers to, or buyers from, "principals" in another. In *Ireland v Livingston*[60] diverging views were expressed on the question whether the relation between a commission agent abroad and his English principal, to whom he shipped goods, was that of principal and agent or of buyer and seller. One view was that the relationship was that of principal and agent[61]; another that the agent might in some respects be treated as seller, *e.g.* for the purpose of stoppage in transit[62]; another that "after the goods were shipped a relation like that of vendor and vendee might arise"[63] and yet another that a commission agent who, "in thus executing an order, ships goods to his principal, is in contemplation of law a vendor to him."[64] In many cases the shipper "filled the joint character of vendor and agent to the vendee"[65] and where this was the case the passing of property depended on the rules normally applicable between buyer and seller.[66] These rules were certainly not displaced merely because the shipper was to be remunerated by a commission.[67] It is, finally, possible for the relationship of the parties to change its nature by reason of a variation of the contract between them. This was the position in *The Aliakmon*[68] where the consignee named in a bill of lading was originally intended to take delivery of the goods as buyer but later agreed to do so as agent of the seller and to warehouse them to the sole order of the seller. In these circumstances it was held that no property passed to the buyer on delivery to him of the bill of lading.

18–233 It should be stressed that the discussion in the preceding paragraphs is concerned with the effect of the relationship of the parties on the passing of property and on the shipper's rights of lien and stoppage. It is not concerned with the question who can sue and be sued on the contract of

[58] *Ex p. Banner* (1876) 2 Ch.D. 278 at p.286.
[59] The problem of classification persists: see, for example, *AMB Imballagi Plastici SRL v Pacflex Ltd* [1992] 2 All E.R. (Comm.) 249.
[60] (1871) L.R. 5 H.L. 395; and see generally Bowstead and Reynolds on *Agency* (18th ed.), para.1–032.
[61] (1871) L.R. 5 H.L. 395 at p.412; *cf. Anglo-African Shipping Co. of New York Inc. v J Mortner & Co. Ltd* [1962] 1 Lloyd's Rep. 610.
[62] (1871) L.R. 5 H.L. 395 at p.416.
[63] *ibid.*, at p.405.
[64] *ibid.*, at p.408.
[65] *Falk v Fletcher* (1865) 18 C.B.(N.S.) 403 at p.410.
[66] *cf. The Prinz Adalbert* [1917] A.C. 586, where it was suggested (at p.590) that it was immaterial whether the relation of the parties was that of principal and agent or buyer and seller.
[67] *e.g. Schuster v McKellar* (1857) 7 El. & Bl. 704.
[68] [1986] A.C. 785; above, para.18–213.

sale or on the contract of carriage[69]; nor with the question whether the agent may be able to transfer title to a third party.

18–234 **Hypothecation of bills of lading.** A mere agreement to transfer bills of lading by way of security (or hypothecation of them) does not transfer property in the goods at law, though it was held before the original enactment of the Sale of Goods Act in 1893 that such an agreement could, by reason of its specific enforceability, operate to pass an equitable interest or charge.[70] As between the immediate parties to such an agreement, the equitable charge is good without notice to the person in actual possession of the goods[71]: it is treated, for this purpose, like an equitable assignment of a chose in action, which is valid between assignor and assignee without notice to the debtor.[72] On the same analogy, notice would be required to protect the creditor's equitable right against later incumbrancers.[73]

In *Re Wait*, Atkin L.J. said that the rules stated in the Sale of Goods Act "for the transfer of property as between seller and buyer . . . appear to be complete and exclusive statements of the legal relations both in law and in equity."[74] But this statement refers only to the passing of property between seller and buyer. It has, as Atkin L.J. added, "no relevance when one is considering rights legal or equitable which may come into existence dehors the contract of sale"[75]; and subsequent dicta in the Privy Council recognise the possibility of creating equitable charges in favour of third parties by letters of hypothecation.[76] Of course an agreement to hypothecate bills of lading may be, and no doubt commonly is, followed or accompanied by their actual transfer.

18–235 **Trust receipts.** Where bills of lading are held, generally by a bank, as security for an advance, it is often necessary for the debtor (often a buyer of the goods) to sell the goods in order to obtain the funds required to repay the advance. This need may be satisfied, and the interests of the bank to a large extent protected, by the use of trust receipts. These documents are by no means uniform in content, but their essential features are as follows.

---

[69] As to these questions, see, for example, *Anderson v Clark* (1824) 2 Bing. 20; *Depperman v Hubbersty* (1852) 17 Q.B. 766; *Rew v Payne, Douthwaite & Co.* (1886) 53 L.T. 932; *Teheran-Europe Co. Ltd v S T Belton (Tractors) Ltd* [1968] 2 Q.B. 545; Reynolds, 85 L.Q.R. 92 (1969); *cf. Tudor Marine Ltd v Tradax Exports* [1976] 2 Lloyd's Rep. 135.

[70] *Lutscher v Comptoir d'Escompte de Paris* (1876) 1 Q.B.D. 709; and see generally *Swiss Bank Corp. v Lloyd's Bank Ltd* [1982] A.C. 584 (below, para.18–236, n.79).

[71] *Official Assignee of Madras v Mercantile Bank of India* [1935] A.C. 53 at p.68.

[72] *Gorringe v Irwell India Rubber, etc. Works* (1886) 34 Ch.D. 128; *Re Trytel* [1952] 2 T.L.R. 32; for the effect of failure to give notice between assignee and debtor, see *Warner Bros Records Inc. v Rollgreen Ltd* [1976] Q.B. 430; *Herkules Piling v Tilbury Construction* (1992) 61 Build. L.R. 107 at p.119.

[73] See Treitel, *The Law of Contract*, (11th ed., 2003), p.682.

[74] [1927] 1 Ch. 606 at p.636; and see below, para.19–101.

[75] [1927] 1 Ch. 606 at p.636.

[76] *Official Assignee of Madras v Mercantile Bank of India* [1935] A.C. 53 at p.68; *cf.* the recognition of an equitable *seller's* lien in *Nippon Yusen Kaisha v Ramjiban Serowgee* [1938] A.C. 429 at 444, suggesting that the provisions of the Sale of Goods Act are (contrary to the view of Atkin L.J. in *Re Wait*, above at n.74) not exclusive.

They provide for the release by the bank of the bills of lading to the debtor as trustee for the bank, and authorise him to sell the documents or the goods on behalf of the bank. The debtor, for his part, undertakes to hold the goods and their proceeds in trust for the bank, and to remit the proceeds to the bank, at least up to the amount of the advance.[77] Under such a document, the bank is protected against the debtor's insolvency, though not against his dishonesty.

So far as protection against the debtor's insolvency is concerned, it was held in *North Western Bank v Poynter*[78] that a bank which parts with bills of lading under a trust receipt retains its interest as pledgee in the goods and in their proceeds. On the insolvency of the pledgor, the bank was therefore entitled to proceeds of sale[79] (which had not yet been paid over to the pledgor) in preference to the pledgor's general creditors. It seems that the bank would equally have been entitled to the proceeds if they had been paid over to the pledgor; and that it would also have been entitled to the goods if they had still been in his possession.[80] **18–236**

A trust receipt does not protect the bank against the dishonesty of the pledgor if he sells the goods and *misappropriates the proceeds* by disposing of them otherwise than in accordance with the terms of the trust receipt. In such a case the bank normally has nothing except a personal claim against the pledgor[81]; though it could no doubt assert a proprietary claim to any traceable product of the misappropriated proceeds in the hands of the pledgor and of anyone except a bona fide purchaser for value.[82] The bank, having authorised the sale, would certainly not have any claim *to the goods*, the property in which would have passed to the person who had bought from the pledgor. **18–237**

The bank's position is not likely to be any better where the pledgor has made an *unauthorised disposition of the goods*. In *Lloyd's Bank Ltd v Bank of America*[83] bills of lading were pledged to the claimants under letters of hypothecation empowering the claimants to sell the documents or the

[77] *cf. Aluminium Industrie Vaassen BV v Romalpa Aluminium Ltd* [1976] 1 W.L.R. 676 (above, para.5–141) where the provisions of clause 13 of the contract in many ways resembled those of a trust receipt; *cf.* also below, para.18–238, n.91.

[78] [1895] A.C. 56 at pp.64–68; *cf. Official Assignee of Madras v Mercantile Bank of India* [1935] A.C. 53 (pledge of Indian railway receipts having for the present purpose by statute the characteristics of bills of lading: see above, para.18–167, n.71).

[79] This entitlement appears to be a legal one based on the pledge. It is to be distinguished from the equitable interest that may arise where A promises to pay a debt due to B out of the proceeds of specific property of which A is the legal owner. For a discussion of this equitable interest, see *Swiss Bank Corp. v Lloyd's Bank Ltd* [1982] A.C. 584 (where on the facts there was no such promise by A).

[80] There was formerly an exception to this rule where the pledgor was bankrupt and the goods were in his "reputed ownership" within Bankruptcy Act 1914, s.38(c); but the reputed ownership doctrine was abolished by the repeal of that Act and the redefinition of the bankrupt's estate in Insolvency Act 1986, s.283.

[81] *Lloyds Bank Ltd v Bank of America* [1938] 2 K.B. 147 at p.166.

[82] See generally Goff & Jones, *The Law of Restitution* (6th ed., 2002), Ch.2.

[83] Above, n.81, and see above, para.7–037.

goods as if they were absolute owners. The documents were released to the pledgors under a trust receipt and were, in breach of the terms of the trust receipt, pledged with the defendants who received them in good faith. On the pledgors' insolvency it was held that the pledge to the defendants was effective against the claimants under section 2(1) of the Factors Act 1889. It was scarcely disputed that the pledgors had acted as mercantile agents; but it was argued that, as they were themselves owners of the goods, section 2(1) could not apply, as it requires the mercantile agent to be in possession of the documents "with the consent of the owner". The Court of Appeal rejected this argument holding that "owner" in section 2(1) meant "the person who would be in a position to give express authority with regard to the dealing in question"[84]; that, as the pledgor was not in that position, he could not "by himself constitute what is described as owner"[85]; and that the subsection was not excluded merely because the incidents of ownership were divided between the pledgor and the claimants. Thus the claimants were treated as "owners"[86] for the purposes of the subsection, so that their consent to the possession of the documents was treated as the relevant one. The same result was also based, more narrowly, on the terms of the letter of hypothecation which gave the bank "power . . . to exercise all the rights of ownership over the goods"[87]; but it seems that the court would have been content to base its decision on the first, broader, ground alone.

18–238 Trust receipts do not need to be registered as bills of sale. One reason for this is that they are exempted by section 4 of the Bills of Sale Act 1878 from the requirement of registration as "documents used in the ordinary course of business as proof of possession or control of goods".[88] Another is that a trust receipt does not of itself confer any charge: the bank's rights as pledgee do not arise under the trust receipt, but under the original pledge.[89] Nor, if the pledgor is a company registered in Great Britain, does the trust receipt require registration under the Companies Act 1985 as a charge on the book debts of the company.[90] The receipt generally creates no charge on debts but simply enables the bank to realise a charge on goods which existed before.[91] Of course this argument presupposes the validity or

[84] [1938] 2 K.B. 147 at p.161.
[85] *ibid.*, at p.162.
[86] Contrast the treatment of the pledgee for the purposes of s.1 of the Bills of Lading Act 1855 in *Sewell v Burdick* (1884) 10 App.Cas. 74 (above, para.18–100).
[87] [1938] 2 K.B. 147 at p.164.
[88] *Re Young, Hamilton & Co.* [1905] 2 K.B. 772, where the right of the bank to an injunction to restrain dealings inconsistent with the terms of the trust receipt was said to give "control." And see Bills of Sale Act 1891.
[89] *Re David Allester Ltd* [1922] 2 Ch. 211, where the actual decision was based on words in Companies Act 1948, s.95 which are no longer to be found in the corresponding provisions of Companies Act 1985, ss.395 and 396, as inserted by Companies Act 1989, s.93. For further effects of these 1989 amendments, see above, para.5–143.
[90] Under Companies Act 1985, s.396(1)(c)(iii).
[91] *Re David Allester Ltd*, above. Nor does it seem that the receipt, or the pre-existing charge, would require registration as a floating charge under Companies Act 1985, s.396(1)(e), as the cases discussed in the present paragraph concern charges over

effectiveness of the prior charge on goods. Thus where a seller hypothecated bills of lading relating to goods, the property in which had already passed to the buyer, this was held to amount to a hypothecation of the proceeds of the sale only and thus to a charge on book debts[92]; and similar reasoning would presumably apply to the subsequent release under a trust receipt of documents originally deposited in similar circumstances.

Under the Law Commission's proposed scheme for the registration of company security interests,[93] the bank's original pledge of the bill of lading will not be subject to the requirement of registration.[94] But if the bank releases a "negotiable document of title" to the debtor for specified purposes, such as the sale of the goods, then the bank's pledge will be treated as a charge which must be registered within 15 days, unless the document is returned or the proceeds of sale are transferred to the pledgee bank within that period.[95]

In the above discussion of trust receipts, it has so far been assumed that the banker to whom documents of title are pledged has either made the advance for which they are pledged, or that he has accepted a draft for such an advance and that there is no reason to suppose that he will not honour his acceptance by payment. If, however, documents are released under a trust receipt and the banker fails to perform, or repudiates, his obligation to pay, the further question arises whether such failure affects the obligation of a person who has received documents under a trust receipt to remit the proceeds of sale to the bank in accordance with the terms of the receipt. In *Sale Continuation Ltd v Austin Taylor & Co. Ltd*[96] it was held that in such circumstances an agent of the seller to whom the documents were released was justified in remitting the proceeds (which he had received from the buyer) to the seller instead of to the bank. The court went "behind the face"[97] of the trust receipt and held that the bank's repudiation of the contract of pledge entitled the seller to cancel that contract; and, just as this would enable the seller to reclaim the thing pledged, so it entitled him to its proceeds. The decision has been criticised on the ground that, by parting with the documents and thus transferring the property in the goods to the buyer, the seller must have been content to be treated as an unsecured creditor and to rely on the bank's promise as his primary assurance of 18–239

specific assets. Contrast such cases as *Re Bond Worth* [1980] Ch.228 and *Borden (UK) Ltd v Scottish Timber Products Ltd* [1981] Ch.25, discussed in paras 5–144 to 5–149, above. Nor would the charge appear to be registrable as a "charge on goods" within s.396(1)(b) as that provision excepts charges "under which the chargee is entitled to possession either of the goods or of a document of title to them". This exception does not apply where "the chargee is entitled to take possession in case of default or on the occurrence of some other event" (s.396(2)(c)) but in the case under consideration the entitlement arises, not by virtue of such default or event, but by virtue of the original pledge.

[92] *Ladenburg v Goodwin Ferreira & Co. Ltd* [1912] 3 K.B. 275, discussed in *Re David Allester*, above.

[93] Law Com. No.296 (2005), above para.18–010.

[94] See Law Com. No.296 (2005), para.3.17.

[95] *ibid.*, para.3.25; Draft Regulations attached to the above Report, Reg. 22(2) and (3).

[96] [1968] 2 Q.B. 849.

[97] *ibid.*, at p.861.

receiving payment.[98] But it is doubtful whether property would now be regarded as having passed (without payment) in such circumstances. It is also an open question whether the principle of the case would apply in the more usual case where documents are pledged by a seller and released to the *buyer*. On the one hand it could be argued that in such a case the repudiation of the bank's obligation to the seller could not affect its rights under the trust receipt against the buyer. But it is submitted that, if (as would generally be the case) the bank had also made a contract with the buyer to pay the seller, breach of that contract could prejudice the buyer by creating or reviving a personal liability on his part to pay the price[99] and if it had this effect the principle of looking "behind the face" of the trust receipt should equally apply.

18–240 **Romalpa clauses.**[1] A contract of sale may provide that property is to remain in the seller not only until the goods sold have been paid for, but until any other sums due from the buyer to the seller (*e.g.* under earlier or later sales) have been paid.[2] A bank taking a pledge of documents relating to goods under the principal contract may well find its security impaired by reason of such a clause, even though it has paid in full for the goods represented by those documents.[3]

---

[98] Gutteridge & Megrah, *Law Relating to Bankers Commercial Credits* (7th ed.), pp.43–45, below, paras 23–099 to 23–101.

[99] See *Saffron v Soc Minie're Cafrika* (1958) 100 C.L.R. 231; below, para.23–098.

[1] *Aluminium Industrie Vaassen BV v Romalpa Aluminium Ltd* [1976] 1 W.L.R. 676, discussed above, paras 5–141 *et seq*.

[2] Title retention clauses are not covered by the proposed scheme for the registration of company security interests set out in the Law Commission's Report on *Company Security Interests,* Law Com. No.296 (2005), above para.18–010; such clauses are to be the subject of further work by the Commission: see paras 1.14 and 1–29 of the Report. In its earlier Consultative Report on *Company Security Interests* (Consultation Paper No.176 (2004) para.2.135(2) the Law Commission had provisionally recommended that "title-retention devices that have a security purpose" should be brought within the scheme." This provisional recommendation appeared to include *Romalpa* clauses (see Law Commission Consultation Paper No.164 (2002) para 7.24); but the Law Commission's further paper on *Company Security Interests: Developing a Final Scheme* (April, 2005) para.1.4 stated that the scheme was not to apply to "simple retention of the title clauses." The distinction between title retention devices "that have a security purpose" and "simple retention of title clauses" would, if this distinction were to prevail, apparently be left to the courts: *cf.* Law Commission Consultation Paper No.164 (2002) paras 5.11, 5.12. For the purposes of the present Chapter and Chapters 19–21 of this book, the important point is that the proposed registration scheme does not apply to provisions in a contract of sale, such as one requiring payment against documents, by which the seller reserved the right of disposal and so prevented property from passing before payment had been made in full.

[3] It seems that the bank could not rely on Sale of Goods Act 1979, s.24, since the case would not be one in which the seller had "sold" the goods (but one in which he had agreed to sell them); nor on s.25 as in the normal case of a bank's taking the pledge under a banker's commercial credit, the documents would not be delivered or transferred to the bank by the buyer (but by the seller). *A fortiori*, the bank could not rely on these sections where it had notice of the clause. The bank might be able to rely on an estoppel against the seller if it could show (1) that, by presenting the documents and claiming payment, the seller had unequivocally represented that he had no intention of invoking the clause against the bank, and (2) that it (the bank) had relied on that representation by making the payment.

Bill of exchange drawn against goods. Bills of exchange drawn on buyers to whom goods have been shipped, or on agents to whom goods have been consigned for sale, may specify that they are drawn against a particular cargo, or against a particular parcel of goods. Such a bill may be payable, or transferred, to a third party who does not also hold the bill of lading. If the bill of exchange is not accepted, or not paid, such a third party will not (save in the most exceptional circumstances) have any rights against the goods. The mere drawing of a bill of exchange against the goods will not give a lien[4]: the practice is only an inducement to the drawee to accept. "A mercantile man who intended to have a lien on a cargo expects to have the bill of lading annexed; if there is no bill of lading annexed he only expects to get the security of the bill [of exchange] itself."[5] The position is the same where the bill of lading was originally in the hands of the third party but is surrendered by him on acceptance of the bill of exchange under a letter of credit in accordance with terms of the credit known to the third party when he acquired the bill of exchange.[6] 18–241

Special Prize rules. A number of leading cases on the passing of property under overseas sales are Prize cases[7] in which the question was whether property in goods which were seized as Prize had, at the relevant time, passed from or to an enemy subject. 18–242

For the purpose of the law of Prize, property cannot pass *from* an enemy merely by dealings with the shipping documents[8]: this rule is based on the danger that if property could be so pass the rights of belligerents might be too easily defeated by paper transfers. To avoid condemnation of goods bought from an enemy, the neutral buyer[9] will therefore have to show that property passed before the ship sailed.[10]

The rule that property cannot (for Prize purposes) pass merely by dealings with shipping documents does not apply to the converse case of a sale by a neutral seller *to* an enemy. Here the normal rules as to the transfer of property in goods afloat determine whether the goods became the property of an enemy subject at the relevant date. Neutral claimants must show that the goods remained their property at the time of seizure and at the time at which "they came into Court to prove a claim as owners".[11]

---

[4] *Robey & Co.'s Perseverance Ironworks v Ollier* (1872) L.R. 7 Ch.App. 695; *Brown, Shipley & Co. v Kough* (1885) 29 Ch.D. 848; *König v Brandt* (1901) 84 L.T. 748; *Frith v Forbes* (1826) 4 De G.F. & J. 409, *contra* was doubted in *Brown, Shipley & Co. v Kough*, above, and explained as turning on its special facts in *Robey & Co.'s Perseverance Ironworks v Ollier*, above and *Ex p. Dever* (1884) 13 Q.B.D. 766.

[5] *Robey & Co.'s Perseverance Ironworks v Ollier*, above, at p.699.

[6] *Ex p. Dever*, above.

[7] See n.11 below. Such cases are not necessarily conclusive authorities on the passing of property in other contexts.

[8] *The Dirigo* [1919] P. 204 at p.220; *The Kronprinsessan Margareta* [1921] 1 A.C. 486.

[9] A British buyer might be in additional difficulty on account of the rules which prohibit trading with the enemy.

[10] *The Dirigo*, above, at pp.220–224; *cf. The Parchim* [1918] A.C. 157.

[11] *The Prinz Adalbert* [1917] A.C. 586 at p.591.

4. LOSS OR DETERIORATION IN TRANSIT

18–243 **In general.** The problem of the loss or deterioration of the goods in transit must be analysed partly in terms of the obligations of the parties as to quality, packing, shipment, etc.; and partly in terms of risk. These notions are closely related, as the incidence of risk depends, under some provisions of the Sale of Goods Act 1979, on the due performance by buyer and seller of certain of their obligations under the contract.

Typically overseas sales on c.i.f., and other terms discussed in this Part of this book will be between corporate entities each of which acts in the course of a business. Our concern in paragraphs 18–244 to 18–258 below will be with rules relating to loss or deterioration in transit as they apply to overseas sales between such parties. It is, however, also possible for the buyer in an overseas sale to deal as consumer and, as a result of amendments to the Sale of Goods Act 1979 made in 2003, certain effects of loss or deterioration in transit, where the buyer so deals, are now governed by special rules. These are discussed in paragraphs 18–259 to 18–264 below.

(a) *Commercial Sales*

18–244 **Risk in overseas sales.** The general rule that risk passes with property[12] is often excluded in overseas sales, in which it is common for risk to pass on or as from shipment[13] and for property to pass only at some later point, generally when payment is made in exchange for the shipping documents.[14] On the other hand, some of the exceptions to the general rule which are stated in the Sale of Goods Act do apply to overseas sales in the sense that they may alter the point at which the risk would otherwise pass by virtue of

---

[12] Sale of Goods Act 1979, s.20(1) (above, para.6–002).

[13] Below, paras 19–104, 20–088. *Cf.* the Vienna Convention on Contracts for the International Sale of Goods (above, para.1–024), Art. 69(1), stating the general rule that risk passes to the buyer "when he takes over the goods". However, overseas sales are more likely to be governed by the rule stated in Art. 67(1) under which (in the circumstances there specified) risk passes when the seller hands the goods over to a carrier (see further, below, para.21–101, n.51); if the goods are already in transit when sold, Art. 68 provides that risk passes from the time of the conclusion of the contract, or "if the circumstances so indicate" from the time of the handing over of the goods to the carrier.

[14] Below, paras 19–110, 20–088; though in the oil trade the express contractual terms of the kind described in para.18–209 above, often unite the passing of property and risk. There seems, with respect, to be no foundation for the assumption, apparently made in *Stora Enso OYJ v Port of Dundee* [2006] CSOH 40, *The Times*, April 11, 2006, at [19] that a contractual provision, to the effect that property was not to pass until payment in full, also delayed the passing risk until such payment had been made. No issue as to the passing of risk arose in that case; the issue was whether the unpaid seller had title to sue a warehouseman (who had negligently damaged the goods) in tort. For this purpose, retention of ownership by the seller (by virtue of the contractual provision referred to above) would suffice: see above, para.18–148. The sale was on "C.I.P" (Carriage and Insurance Paid) terms, under which the seller had paid for insurance; and this fact would tend to negative the retention of risk by him once the insurance cover had taken effect, even though the property was still in him: *cf.* below, para.19–110.

the express terms of the contract, or by virtue of the incidents attached by law to a particular type of overseas sale. Thus where the sale is of a type under which risk would normally pass on shipment, it may pass before shipment if shipment is delayed by the fault of the buyer,[15] or after shipment if delivery is delayed by the fault of the seller.[16] Similarly, the normal incidence of risk under an overseas sale may be displaced if one of the parties to the sale commits a breach of his duties as bailee for the other.[17]

A number of exceptions to the general rule that risk passes with property are of special importance in relation to overseas sales. These are contained in sections 32 and 33 of the Sale of Goods Act 1979 and are discussed in paragraphs 18–245 to 18–252.

Seller's duty to make a reasonable contract of carriage. Section 32(1) provides that "Where, in pursuance of a contract of sale, the seller is authorised or required to send the goods to the buyer" delivery of the goods to a carrier for the purpose of transmission to the buyer is prima facie deemed to be a delivery to the buyer.[18] Subsection (2) then provides, with reference to the cases contemplated by subsection (1),[19] that "Unless otherwise authorised by the buyer, the seller must make such contract with the carrier on behalf of the buyer as may be reasonable . . ."; if he fails to do so "and the goods are lost or damaged in the course of transit, the buyer may decline to treat the delivery to the carrier as a delivery to himself or may hold the seller responsible in damages."[20] Of course if the seller is contractually bound to make a contract of carriage (as he is under a c.i.f. contract and may be under an f.o.b. contract) his failure to make such a 18–245

---

[15] Sale of Goods Act 1979, s.20(2); it is assumed in *J & J Cunningham Ltd v Robert A Munro Ltd* (1922) 28 Com.Cas. 42 that this provision could apply to an f.o.b. contract, though there was in fact no delay caused by the buyer's fault. A dictum in *Colley v Overseas Exporters* [1921] 3 K.B. 302 at p.307 is contrary to the proposition in the text, but the only question in that case was as to the passing of property; and it is submitted that the reference to risk was made *per incuriam* in disregard of what is now s.20(2). *Cf.* the Vienna Convention on Contracts for the International Sale of Goods (above, para.1–024), Art. 69(1), by which risk passes to the buyer if he fails to take over the goods in due time after the goods have been placed at his disposal and the failure amounts to a breach of contract; and Art. 69(2), by which, if the goods were to be taken over at a place other than the seller's place of business, risk passes when delivery is due and the buyer knows that the goods have been placed at his disposal at the agreed place.

[16] See *Gatoil International Inc. v Tradax Petroleum Ltd (The Rio Sun)* [1985] 1 Lloyd's Rep. 350 at p.362 (c.i.f. seller wrongfully interfering with performance of cariage: see below, para.19–073); below, para.19–121. *Cf.* Vienna Convention on Contracts for the International Sale of Goods (above, para.1–024), Art. 70 preserving the buyer's remedies, notwithstanding the passing of risk, where the seller is guilty of a "fundamental breach" (defined in Art. 25: see below, para.18–267, n.38).

[17] s.20(3); applied to a c.i.f. contract in *Wiehe v Dennis Bros* (1913) 29 T.L.R. 250.

[18] *cf.* Vienna Convention on Contracts for the International Sale of Goods (above, para.1–024), Art. 31(a).

[19] See *Wimble Sons & Co. v Rosenberg* [1913] 3 K.B. 743 (below, para.18–247) for the view that subss. (2) and (3) of s.32 are in the nature of provisos to subs. (1).

[20] *cf.* Vienna Convention on Contracts for the International Sale of Goods (above, para.1–024), Art. 32(2).

contract on the terms specified in the contract of sale, or, if no terms are so specified, on the terms usual in the trade, will amount to a breach of the contract of sale, leading to inability to tender proper documents and justifying rejection on that ground.[21] But the provisions of section 32(2) apply even where there is no contractual obligation on the seller to make a contract of carriage—where he is merely "authorised" but not "required" to send the goods to the buyer.[22] The subsection has no application where the contract of carriage is made by the buyer, as under certain f.o.b. contracts.[23] But under some f.o.b. contracts the seller makes the contract of carriage; and, in such cases, section 32(2) can apply even, it seems, although the buyer is a party to the contract of carriage,[24] or rights under that contract are transferred to and vested in him as if he had been a party to it.[25] Where an f.o.b. seller makes the contract of carriage, section 32(2) can apply in spite of the fact that the goods are prima facie deemed to have been "delivered" to the buyer on shipment,[26] for the seller may still be authorised or required to "send" the goods to the buyer even after there has been such a "delivery" to the buyer.[27] Section 32(2) is not restricted to any particular kind of contract of carriage: it applies whether the contract made by the seller is for the carriage of the goods by land, sea or air, or by any combination of the three. What is a reasonable contract appears to depend on what is usual in the trade in question. In one case the seller had the option of sending the goods either at carrier's or owner's (*i.e.* buyer's) risk; and it was held that he had not made a reasonable contract by choosing the latter method.[28]

18–246 **Seller's duty to give notice enabling the buyer to insure.** Section 32(3) of the Act, which is derived from Scots law,[29] provides that "Unless otherwise agreed, where goods are sent by the seller to the buyer by a route involving

---

[21] Below, paras 19–024, 20–020.

[22] Contrast Vienna Convention on Contracts for the International Sale of Goods (above, para.1–024), Art. 32(2) which applies only "if the seller is *bound* to arrange for carriage of the goods".

[23] *e.g. Pyrene Co. Ltd v Scindia Navigation Co. Ltd* [1954] 2 Q.B. 402; and see below, paras 20–002 to 20–007 for the various kinds of f.o.b. contracts.

[24] The buyer may be a party to the contract of carriage (1) because he is named as shipper in the bill of lading: see below, para.20–003; and below, paras 20–059 to 20–069 for discussion of contractual relations between c.i.f. buyer and seller on the one hand and carrier on the other: see below, paras 19–090 to 19–097; or (2) because, although the seller is named as shipper in the bill of lading, he has made the contract of carriage as the buyer's agent: see *East West Corp v DKBS 1912 AF A/S* [2003] EWCA Civ 83, [2003] Q.B. 1509 at [34] and, in a case of carriage by road, *Texas Instruments Ltd v Nason (Europe) Ltd* [1991] 1 Lloyd's Rep. 146, where the seller was regarded as the buyer's agent in making the contract of carriage because property had passed to the buyer before that contract was made. In cases of c.i.f. and f.o.b. sales property is unlikely to have passed before that stage: see further para.20–008 below.

[25] By virtue of Carriage of Goods by Sea Act 1992, s.2(1).

[26] Under Sale of Goods Act 1979, s.32(1), above.

[27] *cf.* the meaning of "sent" in s.32(3): below, para.18–248.

[28] *T Young & Sons v Hobson & Partners* (1949) 65 T.L.R. 365.

[29] *Wimble, Sons & Co. v Rosenberg* [1913] 3 K.B. 743 at p.761; *Arnot v Stewart* (1817) 5 Dow.App. Cas. 274; *Fleet Bros v Morrison* (1854) 16 D. 1122; *Hastie & Hutchinson v Campbell & Dunn* (1857) 19 D. 557.

sea transit, under circumstances in which it is usual to insure, the seller must give such notice to the buyer as may enable him to insure them during their sea transit; and, if the seller fails to do so, the goods are at his risk during such sea transit". As the expression "sea transit" occurs three times it is hard to avoid the conclusion that the subsection is restricted to cases in which the goods are carried by sea. The suggestion[30] that it would apply where the goods are carried by air and it is usual to insure can perhaps be supported as an analogous extension of the subsection as a matter of common law[31]; and if it were accepted it could perhaps also be applied to cases of combined carriage, for example by road and sea.[32]

In *Wimble, Sons & Co. v Rosenberg & Sons*[33] a majority of the Court of Appeal held that section 32(3) applied to an f.o.b. contract under which the seller shipped the goods to a destination named by the buyer on a ship which had been selected by the seller: the goods were being "sent" to the buyer while the sea transit lasted, even though they had been "delivered" to him on shipment.[34] But a notice to enable the buyer to insure need not be given by the seller if under the terms of the contract of sale the seller is himself under an obligation to insure. Such terms amount to a contrary agreement, ousting subsection (3). It follows that the subsection does not normally[35] apply to a c.i.f. contract since under such a contract the seller is bound to insure[36]; nor would it seem to apply to an f.o.b. contract under which the seller had agreed to arrange for insurance for the buyer's account.[37] And the subsection would be irrelevant where goods are sold on terms (such as ex ship terms) under which they are in any event at the seller's risk during transit.[38] **18–247**

The seller need not give notice under section 32(3) if the buyer already has enough information to be able to insure. This was held to be the position in *Wimble, Sons & Co. v Rosenberg & Sons*,[39] where the buyer **18–248**

---

[30] Schmitthoff, *Sale of Goods* (2nd ed.), p.136.

[31] The fact that the subsection is based on Scots law should not cause any insuperable difficulty. The cases on which the subsection is based (above, n.29) happen to be cases of sea carriage, but this fact was not stressed in them.

[32] Below, para.21–101. *Cf.* Vienna Convention on Contracts for the International Sale of Goods (above, para.1–024), Art. 32(3), which is not restricted to any particular kind of carriage but which only requires the seller to give the buyer the requisite information "at the buyer's request".

[33] [1913] 3 K.B. 743 (Hamilton L.J. dissenting on this point); followed with some reluctance in *Northern Steel & Hardware Co. Ltd v John Batt & Co. (London) Ltd* (1917) 33 T.L.R. 516.

[34] Below, para.20–012. *Semble*, the same reasoning would apply under Vienna Convention on Contracts for the International Sale of Goods (above, para.1–024), Art. 32(3).

[35] Below, para.19–124, discussing the normal rule and a possible exception to it.

[36] *Law & Bonar Ltd v British American Tobacco Co.* [1916] 2 K.B. 605; below, para.19–042. Similarly, Vienna Convention on Contracts for the International Sale of Goods (above, para.1–024), Art. 32(3) applies only "If the seller is not bound to effect insurance." "*Semble*, Sale of Goods Act 1979, s.32(3) could apply to a c. & f. contract.

[37] As, for example, in *NV Handel My J Smits Import-Export v English Exporters (London) Ltd* [1957] 1 Lloyd's Rep. 517; and see below, para.20–007.

[38] Below, para.21–020.

[39] [1913] 3 K.B. 743 (Vaughan Williams L.J. dissenting on this point).

already knew the particulars of the goods, the port of loading and the port of discharge. He therefore needed no further notice to "enable" him to insure: for this purpose it was not necessary for him to know the name of the ship or its sailing date. In view of this part of the decision, subsection (3) is not likely to apply very frequently to f.o.b. contracts, for under such contracts the buyer is normally under a duty to nominate the ship.[40]

It is clear from the reasoning in *Wimble, Sons & Co. v Rosenberg & Sons* that the "sea transit" referred to in the subsection means the transit from the port of loading to the port of discharge. Whether the goods were being "sent by the seller to the buyer" during this "sea transit" will often depend on factors similar to those which determine whether goods are in transit for the purpose of the right of stoppage in transit.[41] Thus if goods were delivered to an agent of the buyer, or to the buyer himself, at the port of loading and transmitted to the port of discharge as a result of an order given by the buyer or his agent[42] there would be no duty to give notice to insure: the case would not be one where the goods were "sent *by the seller* to the buyer" for the relevant part of the sea transit. "Sent" means dispatched or forwarded[43] and the act of dispatching or forwarding the goods would be that of the buyer or his agent. But it is possible to imagine cases in which the goods are in the course of "sea transit" from seller to buyer for the purposes of section 32(3) even though they are no longer in transit for the purpose of the seller's right of stoppage in transit: for example, where the seller delivered the goods to a carrier, not as such, but as agent of the buyer.[44] Similarly, the fact that the buyer obtains possession of the goods "before their arrival at the appointed destination" puts an end to the seller's right of stoppage in transit[45] but does not, it is submitted, affect the scope of the duty under section 32(3); for this duty arises, at the latest, at the time of shipment, and probably arises at such time as will enable the buyer to insure the goods from the beginning of the sea transit, at least where it is reasonably practicable to give notice by this time.

The effect of the seller's failure to make a reasonable contract of carriage is stated in section 32(2)[46] to be that "the buyer may decline to treat the delivery to the carrier as a delivery to himself, or may hold the seller responsible in damages." Section 32(3) does not give the buyer this choice in cases of the seller's failure to give notice enabling the buyer to insure: it simply provides that if the required notice is not given "the goods shall be deemed to be at his [the seller's] risk during such sea transit." The reason for this distinction between the subsections is not easy to see.

18–249 **Necessary deterioration in transit.** Section 33 provides that "Where the seller of goods agrees to deliver them at his own risk at a place other than that where they are when sold, the buyer must nevertheless (unless

---

[40] Below, para.20–042; the facts of *Wimble, Sons & Co. v Rosenberg & Sons* are, from this point of view, somewhat unusual.
[41] Sale of Goods Act 1979, s.45 (above, paras 15–066 *et seq.*).
[42] *cf. Dixon v Baldwen* (1804) 5 East 175; *Valpy v Gibson* (1847) 4 C.B. 837; *Kendall v Marshall Stevens & Co.* (1883) 11 Q.B.D. 356.
[43] *Wimble, Sons & Co. v Rosenberg* [1913] 3 K.B. 743.
[44] Sale of Goods Act 1979, s.45(5) (see above, para.15–082).
[45] *ibid.*, s.45(2) (see above, para.15–074).
[46] Above, para.18–245.

otherwise agreed) take any risk of deterioration in the goods necessarily incident to the course of transit." This must be read together with section 29(2),[47] by which, in the absence of express agreement, the place of delivery is the seller's place of business, or, where the goods are specific and are to the knowledge of the parties in another place when the contract is made, the place where the goods are. Section 33 may apply where the goods are to be delivered at the seller's place of business, if that is not where they are when they are sold; though its more normal application would be to a case in which they are to be sent from the seller's (or his supplier's) place of business to a place nominated by the buyer. The section gives rise to many problems.

"Transit". The first of these is the meaning of "transit" in the section. 18–250
At first sight it is the transit between the place where the goods are when they are sold and the place at which the seller agrees to deliver the goods. This is clear enough when the seller agrees himself to perform the entire operation of delivery; but what if he agrees to forward the goods by an independent carrier? Prima facie delivery to such a carrier is deemed to be a delivery to the buyer.[48] The more extended meaning of "transit" in section 32(3)[49] is based on the use in that subsection of the expression "sent", as interpreted in *Wimble, Sons & Co. v Rosenberg & Sons*[50]; and this interpretation cannot be applied to section 33, which begins with the words "Where the seller of goods agrees to *deliver* them . . ." The use of the word "deliver" (as opposed to "send") may seem to support the view that the transit ceases on delivery to the independent carrier; but it is hard to suppose that it was intended to limit the scope of the section in this way. More probably, "deliver" was intended in this context to refer to actual delivery to the buyer as opposed to delivery to a carrier which is only "prima facie deemed to be a delivery . . . to the buyer".[51]

Necessary and extraordinary deterioriation. The second problem is what 18–251
is meant by the opening phrase of section 33: "Where the seller of goods agrees to deliver them at his own risk . . ." The phrase most obviously covers cases in which the seller agrees to bear the risk during transit when it would normally be on the buyer, either under the rules as to risk contained in the Sale of Goods Act or under rules as to risk developed at common law in relation to certain types of contracts (such as c.i.f. and f.o.b. contracts). The effect of the section is to limit the scope of such an agreement by splitting the risk of deterioration during transit so that the seller bears the risk of what may be called "extraordinary" deterioration, that is, deterioration due to some accident or casualty, while the buyer bears the risk of what may be called "necessary" deterioration, that is, deterioration which any goods of the contract description must necessarily suffer in the course of the contemplated transit.[52] However, this rule is in

---

[47] Above, para.8–019.
[48] Sale of Goods Act 1979, s.32(1) (above, para.18–245).
[49] Above, para.18–247.
[50] [1913] 3 K.B. 743; above, para.18–247.
[51] Sale of Goods Act 1979, s.32(1).
[52] It is assumed here that the deterioration is not due to the seller's breach of contract: as to this see below, para.18–254 *et seq.*, and, in particular, para.18–255.

turn subject to contrary agreement,[53] so that if the seller's agreement to bear the risk during transit is, on its true construction, an agreement to bear the *whole* risk, he would bear the risk of both "necessary" and "extraordinary" deterioration. This would be the position if the seller undertook that the goods should be of a certain quality at their destination.

The opening phrase of section 33 may also cover the case in which the seller agrees to deliver the goods at a distant place in circumstances in which they would, under the normal rules as to risk, be at his risk during transit. It was held before the Act that in such a case the risk of necessary deterioration during transit was on the buyer[54]; and even if such a case is not within section 33 there is, it is submitted, nothing in the Act to alter this common law rule.[55]

18–252 Section 33 has in any event a restricted scope in overseas sales. Under c.i.f.and f.o.b. contracts the goods are normally at the buyer's risk during transit and the seller does not in practice agree to deliver them at his own risk so that he is not responsible for deterioration in transit.[56] Of course the goods may nevertheless *be* at his risk by virtue of section 32(2) or (3); and if the opening words of section 33 do apply where the goods are at the seller's risk under the general law (and not by special agreement) section 33 would put the risk of "necessary" deterioration in such a case on the buyer. It would also (on this assumption) have this effect in the case of an ex ship contract.[57] But probably the same result would follow at common law[58] even if section 33 were held not to apply to such a case. On the other hand, a seller who agreed to deliver goods at a specified destination and undertook that they should be of a particular quality on arrival there would be responsible for all (including "necessary") deterioration in transit.[59]

18–253 The above rules as to "necessary" deterioration assume that such deterioration is not due to the seller's breach of contract. The seller's contractual obligations as to quality during (and to some extent after) transit are discussed in paragraphs 18–255 to 18–257.

18–254 **Deterioration due to seller's breach of contract.** For the purpose of this discussion a distinction must be drawn between defects in existence at the time of sale and subsequent deterioration. The seller's responsibility for the former depends on his express or implied undertakings as to quality which generally refer to the quality of the goods at the time of sale,[60] while the

[53] s.33 only applies "unless otherwise agreed".
[54] *Bull v Robison* (1854) 10 Exch. 342.
[55] As a matter of principle it is hard to see why this rule should be restricted to goods *in transit* and not extend to goods which are bound to deteriorate while in store.
[56] *Shipton, Anderson & Co. v John Weston & Co.* (1922) 10 Ll.L.R. 762 (c.i.f. contract); *Broome v Pardess Co-operative Society of Orangegrowers Ltd* [1940] 1 All E.R. 603 (f.o.b. contract).
[57] Below, para.21–020.
[58] *i.e.* under the rule in *Bull v Robison*, above n.54.
[59] Below, para.21–020.
[60] See, *e.g. A B Kemp Ltd v Tolland* [1956] 2 Lloyd's Rep. 681 at p.684, where Devlin J. referred to the implied undertaking under what is now s.14(3) of the Sale of Goods Act 1979 as "speaking about the time of the sale and about the condition of the goods at the time of sale."

effect of subsequent deterioration is generally determined by the rules as to risk. The distinction is however blurred by two factors. First the seller may, and in overseas sales often does, give undertakings as to quality which refer to a time other than that of sale. For example, a c.i.f. seller normally undertakes that the goods are of the contract quality at the time of shipment.[61] He is normally not concerned with what happens to the goods on the voyage[62]: that is a matter of risk, and the risk is usually on the buyer after shipment. Secondly, a defect in the goods existing at the time to which the seller's undertaking as to quality relates may only become apparent at some later time; and if deterioration is caused by such a defect the seller will be liable for breach of his undertaking as to quality: he will not be able to rely on the fact that the risk had passed to the buyer before the deterioration became apparent, or indeed before it occurred. This possibility is discussed in paragraphs 18–255 to 18–257 below.

Implied undertaking that goods can endure normal transit. In *Mash & Murrell Ltd v Joseph I. Emanuel Ltd* Diplock J. said: "When goods are sold under a contract such as a c.i.f. contract, or f.o.b. contract, which involves transit before use, there is an implied warranty not merely that they shall be merchantable[63] at the time they are put on the vessel, but that they shall be in such a state that they can endure the normal journey and be in a merchantable condition on arrival"[64]; and for a reasonable time thereafter to allow for disposal,[65] or use, as the case may be. Similar statements have been made in a number of other cases[66] which show that the implied "warranty"[67] is not restricted to c.i.f. and f.o.b. contracts, but applies to all cases in which transit before disposal or use is within the contemplation of the parties. The seller's undertaking of fitness for a particular purpose[68] 18–255

[61] *Cordova Land Co. Ltd v Victor Bros* [1966] 1 W.L.R. 793; *Shipton, Anderson & Co. v John Weston & Co.* (1922) 10 Ll.L.R. 762 at p.763; *Oleificio Zucchi v Northern Sales Ltd* [1965] 2 Lloyd's Rep. 496 at p.518; The Vienna Convention on Contracts for the International Sale of Goods (above, para.1–024), Art. 36(1) reaches substantially the same result by providing that the seller's undertakings as to conformity of the goods to the contract relate to the time at which the risk passes: *i.e.* (in cases of the kind here under discussion) when the goods are handed over to the first carrier (Art. 67(1)).

[62] *Shipton, Anderson & Co. v John Weston & Co.* (1922) 10 Ll.L.R. 762 at p.763.

[63] *i.e.* under Sale of Goods Act 1979, s.14(2) (above, para.11–026) before its amendment by Sale and Supply of Goods Act 1994, s.1(1), substituting "satisfactory" for "merchantable:" see below at n.33.

[64] [1961] 1 W.L.R. 862 at p.865; below, para.18–33; Sassoon, 28 M.L.R. 180 at p.189 (1965); [1962] J.B.L. 351.

[65] [1961] 1 W.L.R. 862 at p.867: this refers to the case where the goods are bought for resale.

[66] *Ollett v Jordan* [1918] 2 K.B. 41 at p.45, discussing *Beer v Walker* (1877) 46 L.J.C.P. 677; *Evanghelinos v Anderson* (1920) 4 Ll.L.R. 17 at p.18; *H Glynn (Covent Garden) Ltd v Wittleder* [1959] 2 Lloyd's Rep. 409 and see above, para.11–049.

[67] *Quaere* where the term is not rather a "condition" (in the sense in which that expression is used in ss.11–15 of the Sale of Goods Act 1979) than a "warranty" (as defined in s.61(1) of the Act). Lord Diplock has elsewhere used the expression "warranty" to refer to implied terms described in the Sale of Goods Act as "conditions": *Lambert v Lewis* [1982] A.C. 225 at pp.273, 276.

[68] Under Sale of Goods Act 1979, s.14(3) (above, para.11–051).

will, when it arises, have a similar scope.[69] In *A B Kemp Ltd v Tolland*[70] Devlin J. said that the effect of this implied undertaking (in relation to a sale of peaches) was that "the sellers warrant that the goods, at the time of sale,[71] are in such a condition that, unless that condition is unnaturally changed, they will, at the end of the normal period of journey . . . be still fit for human consumption." But the burden of proving that the goods were not in this condition lay on the buyers; and as they failed to discharge this burden it was held that they were liable for the price. In the above cases, the implied undertaking that the goods can endure normal transit was developed as a matter of common law, apart from the Sale of Goods Act. It is now also arguable that, where the undertaking is broken, the seller is in breach of the term implied under section 14(2) that the goods are of "satisfactory quality" because they lack the characteristic of "durability",[72] though the legislative history of the latter requirement indicates that it is concerned rather with the durability of goods in use than with the capacity of commercial commodities to endure normal transit.[73] The question whether the implied term here under discussion arises at common law or under section 14 is of some practical significance, in that the statutory restrictions on the buyer's rights to reject which are discussed in paragraph 18–284 below do not apply where the right to reject arises by reason of the breach of a term implied at common law.

The implied undertaking formulated in the *Mash & Murrell* case[74] is that the goods can endure *normal* transit. Thus where the goods deteriorated during a delay in transit due to the buyer's failure to nominate the destination within the time required by the contract,[75] it was held that the seller was not liable for the deterioration.[76] It is submitted that the position would be the same where the delay was due to some other cause for which the seller was not responsible.

18–256 **Time to which the undertaking relates.** The seller does not, under the principle stated in paragraph 18–255 above, give any implied undertaking as to the condition of the goods on arrival at the contemplated destination. His implied undertaking relates solely to their condition at some previous time, and to their capacity to survive normal transit. In overseas sales it commonly relates to the condition of the goods at the time of shipment,[77] and it is only broken if at that time they suffer from a defect making them

[69] This was an alternative basis for Diplock J.'s decision in *Mash & Murrell v Joseph I. Emanuel Ltd,* above, n.64.
[70] [1956] 2 Lloyd's Rep. 681 at p.685.
[71] The sale was not on c.i.f. or f.o.b. terms so that there was no question of the undertakings speaking from, *e.g.* the time of shipment: *cf.* above, para.18–254; below, para.19–111.
[72] Sale of Goods Act 1979, s.14(2) and (2B)(e).
[73] Law Com. No. 160, Scot. Law Com. No. 104 (1967), paras 2.14, 2.15, 3.47–3.61 do not refer to the *Mash and Murrell* type of case.
[74] Above, at n.64.
[75] See below, para.19–089.
[76] *Gatoil International Inc. v Tradax Petroleum Ltd (The Rio Sun)* [1985] 1 Lloyd's Rep. 350.
[77] See below, para.19–111.

unfit to stand the journey. Thus in *Mash & Murrell Ltd v Joseph I Emanuel Ltd*[78] itself, Cyprus potatoes were sold c. & f. Liverpool. They were sound when shipped but rotten on arrival. Three possible causes were suggested for the deterioration: fungus infection, wetting at or before the time of shipment, and poor ventilation during carriage. The seller would have been in breach of the implied undertaking stated by Diplock J.[79] if the rotting had been due to one of the first two causes. But the Court of Appeal[80] found as a fact that the cause of the rotting was poor ventilation; and, as this was a matter occurring after shipment, the seller was not liable for the deterioration. On such facts the buyers might have a claim against the carrier for breach of the contract of carriage; but they had none against the seller under the contract of sale.

Goods of a kind incapable of enduring transit. The implied undertaking that the goods can endure normal transit applies only where the goods are of a kind that could endure the transit; and it makes the seller liable if the particular goods sold suffered from some defect (not shared by other goods of that kind) which caused their deterioration. If some deterioration is necessarily incident to the normal transit of *all* goods of the kind in question the implied undertaking does not apply.[81] The position is the same where, although goods of the kind contracted for will not *necessarily* deteriorate in transit, there is a high risk known to both parties that they will do so.[82] In the last type of case the seller might, however, be liable if the buyer had made known to the seller the purpose for which the goods were required and if the buyer had reasonably relied on the seller's skill or judgment to select goods of a kind which could survive the transit.[83] 18–257

Other breaches by seller. A seller is liable for deterioration which is due to defective packing,[84] or to failure to load with due care and skill,[85] where under the contract packing or loading (as the case may be) is his responsibility. Where delivery is delayed as a result of the seller's breach of contract, he is liable for deterioration caused by such delay, and the goods are at his risk as regards any loss which might not have occurred but for such breach.[86] 18–258

---

78 [1961] 1 W.L.R. 862; reversed [1961] 2 Lloyd's Rep. 326.
79 Above, para.18–255.
80 [1961] 2 Lloyd's Rep. 326.
81 *e.g. Broome v Pardess Co-operative Society of Orangegrowers Ltd* [1940] 1 All E.R. 603.
82 *Bowden Bros & Co. Ltd v Little* (1907) 4 C.L.R. 1364; dicta at pp.1380–1381, 1386, 1391 suggesting that goods sold on c.i.f. terms need only be merchantable at the point of *shipment* are inconsistent with the English authorities cited in para.18–255, above.
83 *cf. George Wills & Sons Ltd v Thomas Brown & Sons* (1922) 12 Ll.L.R. 292.
84 *George Wills & Sons Ltd v Thomas Brown & Sons*, above; *Sime, Darby & Co. Ltd v Everitt & Co.* (1923) 14 Ll.L.R. 120.
85 *A Hamson & Son (London) Ltd v S Martin Johnson & Co. Ltd* [1953] 1 Lloyd's Rep. 553.
86 Sale of Goods Act 1979, s.20(2); *Gatoil International Inc. v Tradax Petroleum Ltd (The Rio Sun)* [1985] 1 Lloyd's Rep. 350 at p.362; below, para.19–121.

(b) *Consumer Sales*

18–259 **Buyer dealing as consumer.** In overseas commodity contracts of the kind with which this and the following three Chapters of this book are mainly concerned, the buyer is unlikely to "deal as consumer" within the Sale of Goods Act 1979, which incorporates by reference the definition of this expression in the Unfair Contract Terms Act 1977.[87] But the buyer in an overseas sale may exceptionally so deal: for example, where a Shetland pony was bought in England on c.i.f. terms as a gift for a foreign princess[88]; or where a car is bought on such terms by a buyer in one country from a seller in another and that buyer does not make the contract "in the course of a business" either because the car was bought for his own private use or because the buyer is a company not engaged in the motor trade which has bought the car for use by one of its directors and the purchase was not part of its *regular* course of business.[89] Such possibilities call for some discussion here of two of the amendments of the Sale of Goods Act 1979 made by the Sale and Supply of Goods to Consumers Regulations 2002, which are intended to implement Directive 1999/44/EC of the European Parliament and the Council.[90]

18–260 **New sections 20(4) and 32(4).** The first of the amendments here to be considered takes the form of the addition to section 20 of the 1979 Act of a new subsection (4). This provides that, where the buyer deals as consumer, subsections (1) to (3) of section 20 "must be ignored" and that "the goods remain at the seller's risk until they are delivered to the consumer." It will be recalled that subsection (1), under which risk passes (unless otherwise agreed) with property is often displaced in overseas sales on c.i.f. or f.o.b. terms,[91] so that the effect of ignoring it will, of itself, have little significance where the buyer in such a sale deals as consumer. The main difficulty arising from subsection (4) is to determine when, under such a sale, the goods are "delivered" to the consumer so as no longer to be at the seller's

---

[87] See s.61(5A); above, paras 13–071 *et seq*. A buyer may "deal as consumer" within the 1977 and 1979 Act even if the buyer is not an individual: see below, at n.89. This remains true even after the amendments to s.12 of the 1977 Act made by the Sale and Supply of Goods to Consumers Regulations 2002, SI 2002/3045 reg. 14: see above, paras 13–072, 13–077.

[88] As in *Wiehe v Dennis Bros* (1913) 29 T.L.R.250.

[89] As in *R & B Customers Brokers Ltd v United Dominion Trust Ltd* [1988] 1 W.L.R. 321. In *Voss v APL Co Pte Ltd* [2002] 2 Lloyd's Rep. 707 a German seller sold a single Mercedes car to a Korean buyer. It appears from the judgement of Judith Prakash J. at first instance at [1] that the sale was on c. & f. terms and that the buyer was a corporation but the report does not state whether the car was bought for resale or for use by one of the buyer's staff. The *R & B Customers Brokers* case would not survive the implementation of the Law Commissions' Report on *Unfair Terms in Contracts*, Law Com. No 192, Scot. Law Com No. 199 (2005) paras 3.23, 3.24; Draft Bill annexed to the Report, Clause 26(1)(a).

[90] O.J No. L 171, 7.7.99, p.12. The Articles of the Directive do not in terms refer to risk but may do so by implication in Art 2.1 which requires the seller to "deliver goods to the consumer which are in conformity with the contract": see above, para.6–014.

[91] See above, para.18–244.

risk. In attempting to answer this question, it is necessary to take account of the second of the two amendments of the 1979 Act, referred to above, which takes the form of the addition of a new subsection (4) to section 32 of the Act. This provides that, where the buyer deals as consumer, subsections (1) to (3), (the application of which to overseas sales is discussed in paragraphs 18–245 to 18–248 above) "must be ignored" but that "if in pursuance of a contract of sale the seller is authorised or required to send the goods to the buyer, delivery of the goods to the carrier is not delivery of the goods to the buyer."

It is clear from the new subsections 20(4) and 32(4) that risk does not pass to the consumer merely because the goods have been delivered to the carrier. Indeed this is true in the case of c.i.f. and f.o.b. sales even where the buyer does not deal as consumer: the general rule is that in such cases risk passes on or as from *shipment*,[92] which is or may be a distinct (and later) stage of the performance of the contract of sale from that of delivery to the carrier.[93] If, then , the goods are not "delivered" to the consumer when they are delivered to the carrier, the question arises when such delivery does take place where goods are sold on c.i.f. or f.o.b. terms.

"Delivery" in c.i.f. contracts. In the case of a sale on c.i.f. terms, a 18–261
distinction has been drawn between "three stages of delivery": "provisional delivery" on shipment, "symbolical delivery" on tender of documents and "complete delivery" on the handing over the goods to the buyer.[94] When the last of these stages is reached, there would clearly be a "delivery" within section 20(4), so that the goods are then no longer at the seller's risk. It seems probable, though the point is not directly answered by section 32(4),[95] that there would be no "delivery" within section 20(4) at the first stage (of shipment). The question whether there would be such a delivery at the second stage gives rise to more difficulty. Where the documents which are tendered include a duly indorsed order bill, or a bearer bill, the transfer of such a bill to the consumer would amount to a constructive or symbolical delivery of the goods to the buyer[96]; and it has been suggested in paragraph 6–013 above that a delivery of this kind may amount to a "delivery" for this purpose of section 20(4).[97] If so, the goods would no longer be at the seller's risk, under section 20(4), after such a bill had been transferred to the consumer. Indeed, the risk might then pass to the buyer with retrospective effect by virtue of the rule that risk under a c.i.f. contract can pass as from shipment.[98] This position would also be consistent with the

---

[92] See below, paras 19–110, 20–088.
[93] *cf.* the distinction between "shipped" and "received" bills of lading, discussed on para.18–027 above.
[94] See *Schmoll Fils & Co. v Scriven Bros & Co* (1924) 19 L1.L.Rep 118 at p.119, below para.19–072.
[95] Because s.32(4) refers only to "delivery of the goods to the carrier", which does not of itself amount to shipment.
[96] See para.18–063 above.
[97] The example of delivery of the contents of a safe deposit box by handing over the key, given in para.1–087 of the Special Supplement to the 6th edition of this book is reminiscent of Bowen L.J.'s well known statement in *Sanders Bros v Maclean & Co* (1883) 11 Q.B.D. 327 at p.341, likening an order bill to the key to a warehouse.
[98] See below, paras 19–110, 19–112.

rule that, under a c.i.f. contract, the buyer must pay the price even though the goods have been destroyed before tender of documents, at least where the destruction occurs after the goods have been (contractually) appropriated to the contract.[99] On the other hand, the view that risk can pass to the consumer on or by virtue of symbolical delivery is not free from difficulty. For one thing, it would apply only where the document tendered to the buyer in performance of the contract of sale was a "negotiable" (*i.e.* transferable)[1] document of title and it is hard to see why the buyer should be in a worse position with regard to the passing of risk in such a case than he would be where the document was not of this kind, *e.g.* where it was a straight bill, a sea waybill or a delivery order.[2] For another, the part of section32(4) which provides that section 32(3) must be ignored, so that the seller need not give the buyer notice enabling him to insure, seems to assume that the goods remain at the seller's risk for the whole of the transit. If risk could nevertheless pass on symbolical delivery by transfer of an order or a bearer bill, then a buyer who dealt as a consumer would, paradoxically, be in a worse position than one who did not so deal: the consumer would not be entitled to any notice enabling him to insure and failure to give such a notice would not postpone the passing of risk. The point is of little practical significance in relation to c.i.f. contracts since section 32(3) does not often apply them,[3] but it could be significant where goods were sold to a consumer on c. & f. terms.[4] The part of section 32(4) requiring section 32(2) to be ignored where the buyer deals as consumer does not appear to affect the common law rules which specify a c.i.f. (or c.& f.) seller's duty with regard to the making of the contract of carriage or with regard to the requirements of the bill of lading to be tendered by such a seller.[5]

18–262 **"Delivery" in f.o.b. contracts.** Where goods are sold on f.o.b. terms to a buyer who deals as consumer, it seems that the effects of section 20(4) and 32(4) will depend on the type of f.o.b. contract in question. The ways in which shipping arrangements can be made for the purpose of performing such a contract are fully discussed in Chapter 20[6]; here it suffices to distinguish between three types of cases.[7] The first is that in which all the shipping arrangements are made by the seller who takes a bill of lading in his own name and obtains payment against transfer of the bill "as in a c.i.f. contract".[8] Here the question when the goods are "delivered" to the buyer

[99] See below, para.19–080.
[1] See above, para.18–084.
[2] For the status of such documents see above, paras 18–075 (straight bills), 18–067 (sea waybills) and 18–193, 18–195 (delivery orders).
[3] Since the seller's obligation to provide insurance will normally be evidence of an agreement to exclude s.32(3): see above, para.18–247; below, para.19–124.
[4] See below, para.21–013.
[5] See below, paras 19–025 and 19–030.
[6] See below, paras 20–003 to 20–005.
[7] The following discussion is based on Devlin J.'s judgement in *Pyrene Co. Ltd v Scindia Navigation Co. Ltd* [1954] 2 Q.B. 402 at p.424.
[8] *ibid.*; in Devlin J.'s account, this is the second type of situation that may arise under an f.o.b. contract.

within section 20(4) (so as to be no longer at the seller's risk) seems to depend on the same reasoning as that discussed in paragraph 18–261 above in relation to c.i.f. contracts. It is irrelevant that the goods may still be in the process of being "sent" to the buyer even after they have been "delivered" to him.[9] The second situation is that in which no advance shipping arrangements are made and the seller simply puts the goods on board a ship nominated by the buyer and takes out the bill of lading in the buyer's name.[10] Here again there is probably no "delivery" to the buyer within section 20(4) merely because the goods have been *delivered* to the carrier, even though by *shipping* the goods on board, or having them shipped on board, the seller will perform his contractual duty of delivery.[11] The third situation is that in which all the shipping arrangements are made by the buyer, typically by reservation of shipping space on the carrying ship, and the seller delivers the goods to the carrier and has them put on board in exchange for a mate's receipt, which he then surrenders to the buyer to enable the buyer to obtain a bill of lading.[12] Section 32(4) declares in general terms that where the buyer deals as consumer "delivery of the goods to the carrier is not delivery of the goods to the buyer" and it seems at first sight to follow that these words apply to the third of the situations here described, so that risk remains with the seller under section 20(4) until the goods "are delivered to the consumer." Since in the case put there is no transfer of any document of title from the seller to the consumer, it would follow that the risk remained with the seller until the buyer acquired actual possession of the goods at the end of the transit. Yet this could be a wholly unreasonable conclusion since the destination of the goods is not necessarily or even normally a term of an f.o.b. contract[13] so that it would be open to the buyer in a case of the present kind to contract with the carrier for the carriage of the goods to a destination, the transit to which would expose them to perils wholly outside the contemplation of the seller at the time of the contract of sale. Indeed, it is possible for the buyer to resell the goods in transit (*e.g.* if, in the example given in paragraph 18–259 above, the director for whose use the car was intended had died and the company had no further use for it) and then the goods would never be "delivered to the consumer" (in the sense of passing into its physical possession) at all. It is not clear when, in such case, the goods would cease to be at the seller's risk under section 20(4) .One way of avoiding these difficulties would be to treat the third of the situations here discussed as analogous to the situation in which the buyer "sends his own transport to collect the goods"[14] and to argue that shipment of the goods under a bill of lading naming the buyer as shipper is delivery to the buyer himself, who then makes a bailment of the goods to the carrier.[15] There is some support for such a conclusion at

---

[9] See above, para.18–247.
[10] *Pyrene* case, above n.7, at p.424, where this is the first of the situations discussed by Devlin J.
[11] See below, para.20–012.
[12] *Pyrene* case above n.7, at p.424.
[13] See below, paras 20–021, 20–042.
[14] See, para.1–090 of the Special Supplement to the 6th edition of this book.
[15] See above, para.18–065.

common law in cases not governed by the Sale of Goods Act[16] and it is submitted that the common law reasoning could also apply in the present context as it is not inconsistent[17] with section 20(40) if the process of getting the goods into the hands of the carrier can be analysed as taking place in the two stages here described.

18–263 **Delivery delayed through consumer's fault: f.o.b. contracts.** Further difficulty can arise, in the case of an f.o.b. contract, from the fact that one of the provisions of section 20 which under section 20(4) "must be ignored" where the buyer deals as consumer is section 20(2), which deals with the situation in which delivery is delayed through the "fault" of either party and provides that the goods are then at the risk of the party at fault as regards any loss which might not have occurred but for such fault. Where the buyer does not deal as consumer, risk may, by virtue of section 20(2) pass before the usual time of shipment[18], but where the buyer does deal as consumer, the effect of ignoring section 20(2) appears to be that risk cannot pass before delivery to the consumer even where delivery is delayed by the consumer's fault, so that, if the goods deteriorated during the delay, the seller would be liable in respect of the deterioration. This result has been criticised as being "not . . . reasonable"[19] in the case of a domestic sale; and the criticism applies with at least equal force to overseas sales. The hardship to the seller is mitigated where the delay is due, or amounts to a breach of contract by the consumer, since the seller may then have a remedy in respect of that breach.[20] In the case of an f.o.b. contract, there is some support for the view that the seller may be entitled to damages in respect of deterioration of the goods even where the delay does not amount to a breach: *e.g.* where the buyer had indicated that he would take delivery on a specified day during the contractual shipment period but was not in fact ready to do so until a later day, still during the period, and the goods had deteriorated by reason of the seller's having acted in reliance on the buyer's original declaration.[21] It is arguable that such liability arises as a matter of common law, apart from section 20(2), and that it can therefore be imposed on an f.o.b. buyer who deals as consumer in spite of the fact that, where he so deals, section 20(4) requires section 20(2) to be ignored

18–264 **Exclusion implied contrary agreement.** Section 20(1) provides that the general rule (that risk passes with property) applies only "unless otherwise agreed" and it was noted in paragraph 18–244 above that this general rule is often displaced in overseas sales. The rules laid down by section 32(1)

---

[16] See the actual outcome in *Kum v Wah Tat Bank Ltd* [1971] 1 Lloyd's Rep. 439, above, para.18–166 (shipment of goods under a mate's receipt held to be delivery to the bank named as shipper in the receipt and so to create a pledge of the goods to the bank).
[17] Within Sale of Goods Act, s.62(2).
[18] See above, para.18–244 at n.15.
[19] Para.1–081 of the Supplement referred to in n.14 above.
[20] Above, para.6–015.
[21] *J and J Cunningham Ltd v Robert A Munro & Co. Ltd* (1922) 28 Com. Cas. 42 at p.46; below, para.20–092.

and (2) are likewise only prima facie rules; while section 32(3) applies only "unless otherwise agreed" and we have noted[22] that, in the case of a c.i.f. contract this subsection is generally displaced by the nature of such a contract, under which insurance must be provided by the seller. The rule is, in other words, displaced because the nature of a c.i.f. contract makes it inappropriate in the context of such a contract. Sections 20(4) and 32(4) do not purport to lay down rules which are only prima facie rules or which apply "unless otherwise agreed"; at least in so far as they provide that the preceding three subsections of the two sections "must be ignored", the two subsections appear to contain imperative or mandatory provisions. It has nevertheless been argued in paragraph 6–014 above that sections 20(4) and 32(4) could be displaced by an express term of the contract, at least if it passed the test of reasonableness under the Unfair Contract Terms Act 1977 or that of fairness under the Unfair Terms in Consumer Contracts Regulations 1999, or both these tests where the consumer was an individual.[23] If this view prevailed, it could further be argued that the two subsections could also be displaced by an implied term arising as a matter of law from the inappropriateness to specific types of contract, in particular to overseas sales on terms such as c.i.f. and f.o.b. terms. In the preceding discussion a number of illustrations have been given of such inappropriateness[24], and a drastic solution of the many difficulties to which this gives rise would be to say that the two subsections do not apply to, because they cannot sensibly operate in the context of, overseas sales on such standard terms, and because they must therefore be regarded as having been impliedly excluded by parties when they contract on such terms.

5. Implied Terms

In general. The terms implied in a contract of sale under sections 12 to 15 of the Sale of Goods Act apply to overseas sales.[25] These implied terms are discussed in Chapters 4 and 11; but something must be said here about 18–265

[22] Above, para.18–261.

[23] The cases cited in para.18–259, n.89 would not fall within the 1999 Regulations as the buyer was not an individual.

[24] *e.g.* the significance of shipment, rather than delivery to the carrier, in relation to risk (above, para.18–260 at n.92); the difficulty of determining which of the three stages of delivery in a c.i.f. contract is relevant for the purpose of s.20(4); the rule that a c.i.f. buyer must pay against documents even if after appropriation but before the tender of documents the goods have been destroyed (above, para.18–261 after n.98); the incongruity of holding that s.20(4) could be satisfied of the seller tendered a "negotiable" bill of lading but not if he tendered some other document (above, para.18–261 at n.1); the possibility that "ignoring" s.32(3) might leave a buyer who dealt as consumer in a worse position than one who did not so deal (*ibid.*, after n.2); the difficulty determining whether an f.o.b. seller, in performing his duty to deliver, has delivered the goods to the carrier (within s.32(4)) or to the buyer (above, para.18–262); and the injustice of leaving the goods at an f.o.b. seller's risk until the end of the transit when the seller may not know of the destination of the goods (*ibid.*, at n.13).

[25] *e.g. Marimpex Mineralöl Handelsgesellschaft mbH v Louis Dreyfus & Cie. Mineralöl GmbH* [1995] 1 Lloyd's Rep. 167. *Cf.* Vienna Convention on Contracts for the International Sale of Goods (above, para.1–024), Arts 35, 41 and 42.

the requirement in overseas sales that the goods must correspond to the contractual description, about the implied term as to fitness for a particular purpose, about non-rejection clauses and about statutory restrictions on the right to reject for breach of certain implied terms.

(a) *Description*

18–266 **Sale by description.** The requirement that goods must correspond with their description is a very strict one, in general entitling the buyer to reject for quite trivial discrepancies,[26] and to do so even though the failure of the seller to deliver goods of the contract description does not in the least prejudice the buyer.[27] To a considerable extent, the strictness of the requirement is due to the needs, real or imagined, of promoting commercial certainty in overseas sales; and indeed many of the cases on the subject concern such sales. Goods sold in one country for shipment to another may be resold many times before they reach their destination, and before most of the sellers and buyers in the chain have any opportunity of examining the goods to see whether they correspond with the description. The intermediate dealings are in fact with documents whose accuracy is thought by the courts to be of vital importance to the buyers.[28] The possibility of prejudice to a buyer from some inaccuracy in the documents if he has resold, or if he has raised money on the security of the documents or the goods, is one of the justifications mentioned in the cases for the requirement that the goods must correspond strictly with their description[29]; and it may also account for the wide notion of what forms part of the description in such cases. An indication of some judicial dissatisfaction with this state of the law was given by Lord Wilberforce when he described some of the relevant cases as "excessively technical and due for fresh examination in this House".[30] But he recognised that a "strict and technical view" might have to be taken "as regards the description of unascertained future goods (*e.g.* commodities) as to which each detail of the description may be assumed to be vital."[31] Most of the cases on overseas sales discussed in this and the following three chapters fall into this category, so that the wide notion of what forms part of the description, and the requirement of strict conformity of the goods and the documents to the contract, is likely to continue to apply to them even if the reconsideration suggested by Lord Wilberforce occurs.

Even in sales of commodities, the extensive rights of rejection which arise from the strict requirement that goods must correspond with their descrip-

[26] See below, para.18–284 for the effect on overseas sales of the statutory restrictions on the right to reject which were introduced by Sale and Supply of Goods Act 1994, s.4.
[27] *e.g. Arcos Ltd v Ronaasen & Son* [1933] A.C. 470 (c.i.f. contract), where the discrepancy did not make the goods unfit for the buyer's purpose.
[28] *Cehave NV v Bremer Handelsgesellschaft mbH (The Hansa Nord)* [1976] 1 Q.B. 44 at p.70 ("long been made sacrosanct by the highest authority").
[29] *e.g. Bowes v Shand* (1877) 2 App.Cas. 455 at p.463; *Re General Trading Co. and Van Stolk's Commissiehandel* (1911) 16 Com.Cas. 95 at p.101; *Re Moore and Landauer* [1921] 2 K.B. 519 at p.525.
[30] *Reardon Smith Line Ltd v Hansen Tangen* [1976] 1 W.L.R. 989 at p.998.
[31] *ibid*.

tion appear sometimes to have been regarded by businessmen with some disfavour.[32] Evidence of this view is provided by trade customs permitting some departure from the contractual description,[33] by express stipulations to this effect[34] and by clauses attempting to restrict rights of rejection where the goods do not correspond with the contractual description. Restrictive judicial interpretation of such non-rejection clauses may to a considerable extent have defeated their commercial purpose[35]; and their efficacy is in certain cases restricted by legislation.[36]

Time and place of shipment. In English law, it has been settled ever since the decision of the House of Lords in *Bowes v Shand*[37] that stipulations as to the time of shipment form part of the description of the goods, and that breach of such stipulations entitles the buyer to reject.[38] In that case 600 tons of Madras rice were sold on the terms that they were "to be shipped during the months of March and/or April 1874." The bulk of the rice[39] was put on board in February and four bills of lading were issued, 18–267

---

32 "The businessman does not like the idea of rejection": *per* Scrutton L.J. in *Montague L Meyer Ltd v Osakeyhtio Carelia Timber Co. Ltd* (1930) 36 Com.Cas. 17 at p.19.

33 *Montague L Meyer Ltd v Vigers Bros Ltd* (1939) 63 Ll.L.R. 10.

34 *Vigers Bros Ltd v Sanderson Bros* [1901] 1 Q.B. 608; *Arcos Ltd v Ronaasen & Son* [1933] A.C. 470 at p.479.

35 Below, paras 18–276 to 18–279.

36 Below, para.18–280 to 18–283.

37 (1877) 2 App.Cas. 455; *cf. Bowes v Chaleyer* (1923) 32 C.L.R. 159; *Phibro Energy AG v Nissho Iwai Corp. (The Homan Jade)* [1991] 1 Lloyd's Rep. 38 at p.42; *Coastal Bermuda Petroleum Ltd v VTT Vulcan Petroleum SA (The Marine Star) (No. 2)* [1994] 2 Lloyd's Rep. 629 at p.633 (revsd. on another point [1996] 2 Lloyd's Rep. 383); contrast, in the United States, *National Importing and Trading Co. Inc. v E A Bear & Co.* 155 N.E. 343 (1927).

38 Under the Vienna Convention on Contracts for the International Sale of Goods (above, para.1–024) breach of such a stipulation might be regarded *either* as failure to deliver on the agreed date (Art. 33(a)) or within the agreed period (Art. 33(b)) *or* as leading to lack of conformity with the contractual description (Art. 35(1)). Into whichever of these categories the breach may be considered to fall, Art. 49(1)(a) gives the buyer the right, in the case put, to "declare the contract avoided", but only if the breach is "fundamental". Under Art. 25, a breach "is fundamental if it results in such detriment to [the buyer] as substantially to deprive him of what he is entitled to expect under the contract, unless the [seller] did not foresee and a reasonable person of the same kind in the same circumstances would not have foreseen such a result." This position is much less favourable to the buyer than the automatic right of rejection given to him in cases of breach of a stipulation as to the time of shipment in English law under the rule in *Bowes v Shand*, above. It is also open to criticism on the ground that it is likely to lead to uncertainty since the open-textured nature of the definition in Art. 25 makes it hard to predict just when a breach will be regarded as "fundamental." In cases of non-delivery, this uncertainty is mitigated by Art. 49(1)(b), which gives the buyer the right to declare the contract avoided if (i) he gives the seller reasonable notice under Art. 47(1) requiring him to perform; and (ii) the seller fails to perform within the time specified in the notice or declares that he will not deliver within the time so fixed. This right of avoidance after expiry of a notice is derived from the German institution of the *Nachfrist*: see Treitel, *Remedies for Breach of Contract*, paras 245, 251. But under the Convention this right is not available in the cases of *late* or *defective* delivery with which cases like *Bowes v Shand* are concerned: the opening words of Art. 49(1)(b) make it available only "in case of *non-delivery*".

39 8,150 out of 8,200 bags.

three being dated in February and the fourth in March. It was held that the buyer was entitled to reject the shipment. Lord Blackburn said: "If the description of the article tendered is different in any respect it is not the article bargained for and the other party is not bound to take it."[40] Stipulations as to the place of shipment[41] and as to the time at which the goods are to be ready for shipment[42] are similarly part of the description of the goods. Indeed, for some purposes stipulations as to the time (and presumably as to the place) of shipment have been treated as "a good deal more than a mere description of the goods within section 13 of the Sale of Goods Act . . ."[43]

Where the contract provides that shipment is to be made and bills of lading are to be dated within a certain period, both these stipulations must be performed: thus where the goods were shipped within the contract period but the bills of lading were dated outside the period, it was held that the buyer was entitled to reject the goods.[44]

Where a shipment is made partly before and partly within the contract period, the buyer will normally be entitled to reject[45]; but he will not be so entitled if it can be shown that the contract on its true construction meant that shipment was to be *completed* within the contract period, at any rate if a substantial part of the goods was shipped and the bill of lading was dated within this period.[46] Shipment does not normally refer to the date of sailing, though it is of course possible for the parties to stipulate for sailing by a specified date.[47]

---

40 (1877) 2 App.Cas. 455 at p.480; *Aruna Mills Ltd v Dhanrajmal Gobindram* [1968] 1 Q.B. 655 at p.665.

41 *Montague L Meyer v Travaru A/BH. Cornelius of Gambleby* (1930) 46 T.L.R. 553 at p.554 (as to the mode of shipment, see below, para.18–272); *Aruna Mills Ltd v Dhanrajmal Gobindram*, above; *Petrotrade Inc. v Stinnes Handel GmbH* [1995] 1 Lloyd's Rep. 142. Under the Vienna Convention on Contracts for the International Sale of Goods (above, para.1–024) breach of such a stipulation might be regarded either as failure to deliver at the agreed place (see Art. 31) or as leading to lack of conformity with the contractual description (Art. 35(1)); the latter is the more plausible view where the contract states that the goods *have been* shipped at a particular place (as opposed to containing an undertaking that they *will be* so shipped). In either case, the buyer's rights of rejection are governed by the provisions of Art. 49(1)(a) and 25 discussed in n.38, above; the provisions of art. 49(1)(b) do not apply for the reason given in that note.

42 *Montague L Meyer Ltd v Osakeyhtio Carelia Timber Co. Ltd* (1930) 36 Com.Cas. 17.

43 *J Aron & Co. (Inc.) v. Comptoir Wegimont* [1921] 3 K.B. 435 at p.440; see below, para.18–276.

44 *Re General Trading Co. and Van Stolk's Commissiehandel* (1911) 16 Com.Cas. 95. The Vienna Convention on Contracts for the International Sale of Goods (above, para.1–024) does not deal with this situation. Art. 34 deals only with the time of handing over of the documents and with the seller's right in certain circumstances to cure a lack of conformity in the documents. The detailed provisions on lack of conformity in Art. 35 refer to *the goods* only and contain no reference to lack of conformity in the documents. In this respect they resemble Sale of Goods Act 1979, ss.13–15.

45 *Bowes v Shand* (1877) 2 App.Cas. 455.

46 *Alexander v Vanderzee* (1872) L.R. 7 C.P. 530, as explained in *Bowes v Shand*, above.

47 *cf. Bentsen v Taylor, Sons & Co. (No. 2)* [1893] 2 Q.B. 274 (charterparty); and see *Thalmann Frères v Texas Star Flour Mills* (1900) 5 Com.Cas. 321 (where "clearance not later than . . ." was held *not* to refer to the date of *sailing*).

When are goods "shipped"? In England the word "shipped" prima facie means "placed on board ship"; while in the United States it is used in a broader sense to refer to goods being placed on any means of transport, whether by sea, land or air.[48] The English meaning of the word is illustrated by *Mowbray Robinson & Co. v Rosser*[49] where a contract for the sale of timber provided for "shipment" in November. The goods were put on rail at the American seller's sawmill in November but were not put on board ship at New Orleans till January. It was held that the buyer was entitled to reject as there had been no "shipment" in November; and evidence of a trade custom that "shipment" meant putting the goods on rail was rejected as inconsistent with the contract.[50] Similarly, delivery of goods at the dock does not amount to shipment,[51] and where a contract called for rubber to be "shipped . . . by vessel or vessels. . . . from the East to New York" it was held that the buyer was entitled to reject goods carried by sea to Seattle and then forwarded by rail to New York, even though this was at the time a usual route for the carriage of such goods.[52] **18–268**

But words such as "shipped" or "shipment" will not invariably be interpreted in this narrow sense. In an old case, where a contract provided that the goods were to be "dispatched" by a certain date, it was held sufficient that they were placed in lighters by that date.[53] More recently a similar question arose where a licence under an EEC Regulation was issued, permitting the import of goods so long as they had been "shipped" by the end of 1979. Bingham J. said: "I would be inclined to define the transitive verb 'to ship' as Dr. Johnson did, 'to put into a ship,' adding only to 'ship' 'or other final conveyance.'"[54] On this view, goods would have been "shipped" for the purpose of the Regulation if they had been put on a lorry which was later put on a ship without the goods' being unloaded.[55] Such an interpretation seems (with respect) to be consistent with the purpose of the Regulation, in which no special significance appears to be attached to the commencement of transit *by sea*. It is arguable that the word "shipped" might be given a similar meaning when used in a contract of sale, particularly where the parties envisaged combined transport of the goods in a container. This aspect of the meaning of "shipment" is further considered in Chapter 21.[56]

---

[48] See UCC, s.1–201(6), above, para.18–012 n.95, and n.50, below.
[49] (1922) 91 L.J.K.B. 524.
[50] The decision no doubt surprised the American seller in view of the broader American meaning of "shipment:" *cf.* UCC, s.2–320, Comment 13 under which "shipment" by rail in the contractual shipment period would be "timely." Under proposals for amendment of Article 2 of the UCC (April 2003), s.2–320 is to be omitted.
[51] *J Aron & C Inc. v Comptoir Wegimont* [1921] 3 K.B. 435; *cf. Michel Frères SA v Kilkenny Woollen Mills (1929) Ltd* [1961] I.R. 157.
[52] *Re L Sutro & Co. and Heilbut Symons & Co.* [1917] 2 K.B. 348. Scrutton L.J. dissented and the correctness of the majority decision was left open in *Tsakiroglou v Noblee Thorl GmbH* [1962] A.C. 93 at p.113.
[53] *Busk v Spence* (1815) 4 Campb. 329.
[54] *Customs & Excise Commissioners v ApS Samex* [1983] 1 All E.R. 1042 at p.1051.
[55] This was not the position in the *Samex* case, above, where the goods were unloaded from the lorries at the docks.
[56] Below, para.21–096.

It is submitted that, where goods are shipped within the contract period in one vessel and transhipped outside that period in another, which carries them to the contractual destination, the time of shipment would be that of the original shipment.[57]

Assuming that goods have been loaded on or into a ship, the exact time of "shipment" (in the English sense) is traditionally taken to be the time when they cross the ship's rail; and this view still seems, in general, to prevail even though some doubts have been expressed as to the continuing significance of the "ship's rail" in this context.[58] Those doubts are most obviously justified in the case of bulk liquid cargoes (such as oil) which are not loaded across the ship's rail but are simply pumped into the ship. In contracts for the sale of such goods it is common to find contractual provisions for certain legal consequences which are normally associated with shipment (such as passing of property and risk[59]) to occur when the cargo passes the flange connection between the delivery hose and the vessel's permanent cargo intake manifold; and it seems likely that this would also be the time of shipment for the present purpose, *i.e.* for the purpose of the rule that a stipulation as to the time of shipment formed part of the description of the goods.

18–269 **Time of arrival of ship.** Statements as to the expected time of arrival of goods shipped on board a named ship may likewise form part of the description of the goods. In *Macpherson, Train & Co. Ltd v Howard Ross & Co. Ltd*[60] peaches were sold on ex store terms by a contract which provided: "Shipment and Destination. Afloat per *SS Moreton Bay* due London approximately 8th of June". This statement was based on an itinerary published by the owners of the *Moreton Bay*; but on the day before the sale they had published a revised itinerary stating that she was due in London on June 21, when she in fact arrived. It was held that the words "due London approximately 8th of June", though not constituting an absolute guarantee of arrival on that day, nevertheless formed part of the description of the goods[61]; and as at the time of the contract they were no longer true the buyers were entitled to reject.[62]

18–270 **Other statements about the ship.** Many other statements about the ship are treated as part of the description of the goods, or at any rate as statements the falsity of which justifies rejection.[63] Thus in one case it was

---

[57] *cf.* in another context, *The Anders Maersk* [1986] 1 Lloyd's Rep. 483 (High Court of Hong Kong).
[58] See below, para.20–089.
[59] *e.g.* below, paras 19–110, 20–071, 20–088.
[60] [1955] 1 W.L.R. 640.
[61] The assumption is that these statements serve to identify the goods: see below, para.18–273; above, para.11–014.
[62] *cf. SHV Gas Supply & Trading SAS v Naftomar Shipping & Trading Co Ltd Inc (The Azur Gaz)* [2005] EWHC 2528 (Comm.), [2006] 1 Lloyd's Rep. 163 at [53] (seller's estimate of time of arrival not given in good faith: see below, para.19–074). For rights of avoidance under the Vienna Convention on Contracts for the International Sale of Goods (above, para.1–024), see above, para.18–267, n.38.
[63] *cf.* para.18–267, n.43, above.

held that a seller of goods to be shipped "by sailer or sailers" could not perform by declaring a shipment on a steamer.[64] In another[65] rice was sold "per *Coldinghame* . . . now at Rangoon." The jury found that the truth of this statement was vital[66] to the buyer who was held entitled to reject the goods as the ship was not at Rangoon at the time of the contract. Similarly, where the contract calls for shipment on a ship that will sail "directly" to the destination specified in the contract of sale, the buyer can reject if the goods are shipped on a ship that is scheduled to call, and does call, at a number of intermediate ports.[67]

Provisions in contracts of sale requiring goods to be shipped in named ships which were stated in those contracts to be "expected ready to load" or "expected to load" or "due to sail" within a specified period have likewise been treated as part of the description of the goods,[68] even where the contract contained separate sections headed respectively "description" and "shipment" and the statement in question occurred in the latter section.[69] A term of this kind is not broken merely because the ship does not in fact load or sail within the specified time,[70] but it is broken if at the time of the contract of sale the seller does not hold the expectation honestly and on reasonable grounds.[71]

Goods "afloat", etc. A statement that goods are at the time of the contract "afloat" or already shipped is part of the description of the goods,[72] so that the seller will be in breach if at the time of the contract the goods have not yet been loaded[73] or if at that time they have already been discharged.[74] Similarly, where the contract states that the goods are "advised as already shipped" the seller will be in breach if his only advice is that the goods have been received for shipment, and if they have not at the time of the contract been actually shipped.[75] But if the seller had received advice of actual shipment and honestly and on reasonable grounds believed 18–271

64 *Ashmore & Son v CS Cox & Co.* [1899] 1 Q.B. 436.

65 *Oppenheim v Fraser* (1876) 34 L.T. 534, following *Behn v Burness* (1863) 3 B. & S. 751; *cf. Bentsen v Taylor, Sons & Co. (No. 2)* [1893] 2 Q.B. 274, where the right to rescind a charterparty on this ground was waived.

66 Hence the breach would prima facie be "fundamental" within Vienna Convention on Contracts for the International Sale of Goods (above, para.1–024), Art. 25 (and so give the buyer the right to declare the contract avoided under Art. 49(1)(a)).

67 *Bergerco USA v Vegoil Ltd* [1984] 1 Lloyd's Rep. 440.

68 *Finnish Govt (Ministry of Food) v H. Ford Ltd* (1921) 6 Ll.L.R. 188; *Sanday & Co. v Keighley, Maxted & Co.* (1922) 91 L.J.K.B. 624; *Foreman and Ellams Ltd v Blackburn* [1928] 2 K.B. 60; *Macpherson, Train & Co. Ltd v Howard Ross & Co. Ltd* [1955] 1 W.L.R. 640 at p.642.

69 *Foreman and Ellams Ltd v Blackburn*, above.

70 *Weis & Co. v Produce Brokers* (1921) 7 Ll.L.R. 211; *cf. Macpherson, Train & Co. Ltd v J Milhem & Sons (No. 2)* [1955] 2 Lloyd's Rep. 396 ("scheduled to sail": here the ship was late and the *seller's* claim that this discharged him failed).

71 *Sanday & Co. v Keighley, Maxted & Co.*, above, at p.625; *Weis & Co. v Produce Brokers*, above, at p.214; *cf. The Mihalis Angelos* [1971] 1 Q.B. 164 (charterparty).

72 *Macpherson, Train & Co. Ltd v Howard Ross & Co. Ltd* [1955] 1 W.L.R. 640 at p.642.

73 *Gorrissen v Perrin* (1857) 2 C.B.(N.S.) 681.

74 *Benabu & Co. v Produce Brokers Co. Ltd* (1921) 37 T.L.R. 609; *ibid.*, p.851.

75 *J Aron & Co. (Inc.) v Comptoir Wegimont* [1921] 3 K.B. 435.

that it was correct he could, it is submitted, have relied on the words "advised as" to show that he was not in breach: the analogy of the "expected ready to load" cases[76] would seem to support this view.[77]

Just as the contract may describe the goods as already loaded, so it may describe them as not yet loaded. Thus where a contract for the sale of frozen rabbits made on July 2 provided for "Shipment . . . per *Suffolk* due to sail during August" it was held that this referred to a future shipment, and that the buyer was entitled to reject rabbits already on board the *Suffolk* at the time of the contract.[78]

18–272 **Mode of shipment: "under deck."** Where a contract provides for shipment of the goods "under deck" this is part of the description of the goods; so that the buyer is entitled to reject if the goods, or part of them, are carried on deck.[79] If the contract provides that a specified part of the goods may be carried on deck, the buyer may similarly reject if more than that part is carried on deck.[80] The reason for these rules is no doubt that the buyer may not be protected either by insurance[81] or under the contract of carriage in respect of goods which are carried on deck.[82] Indeed the position seems to be that the buyer is entitled to reject goods carried on deck unless the contract of sale expressly permits such carriage. The "general proposition that the deck is not the place upon which to put cargo except by some special arrangement"[83] appears to apply as much to contracts of sale as to contracts of carriage.[84]

18–273 **Physical characteristics.** In *Christopher Hill Ltd v Ashington Piggeries Ltd*[85] the House of Lords held that words in a contract only formed part of the description of the goods where they served to *identify* the subject-matter

[76] Above, para.18–270.
[77] *cf. Gattorno v Adams* (1862) 12 C.B.(N.S.) 560, where the words of the contract were held to reflect the seller's doubt as to whether shipment had taken place.
[78] *Foreman & Ellams Ltd v Blackburn* [1928] 2 K.B. 60. For rights of avoidance under the Vienna Convention on Contracts for the International Sale of Goods see above, para.18–267, nn. 38, 41.
[79] *Montague L Meyer Ltd v Travaru A/BH. Cornelius of Gambleby* (1930) 46 T.L.R. 553; *White Sea Timber Trust Ltd v W W North Ltd* (1932) 49 T.L.R. 142 at p.143. For rights of avoidance under the Vienna Convention on Contracts for the International Sale of Goods, see above, para.18–267, n.38.
[80] *Messers Ltd v Morrison's Export Co.* [1939] 1 All E.R. 92.
[81] *cf.* above, para.18–059; below, para.21–090; below, n.82.
[82] The Hague-Visby Rules (below, para.21–047) do not apply to goods stated as being carried, and carried, on deck: Carriage of Goods by Sea Act 1971; Sch., art. 1(c), so that the carrier is free to exclude liability, but he is guilty of a breach if he carries the goods on deck without the previous consent of the shipper. For the effects of such a breach, see below, para.21–090.
[83] *Messers Ltd v Morrison's Export Co.*, above, at n.80. As to containers, see below, para.21–090.
[84] Our concern here is only with the question whether unauthorised carriage on deck is a breach of condition in the contract of sale. This question is distinct from the question, discussed in para.18–059 above, whether such carriage on deck amounts to, or has the effects of a wrongful deviation, depriving the carrier of the protection of the contract of carriage.
[85] [1972] A.C. 441.

of the sale; statements as to quality which did not serve this purpose were not part of the description of the goods. On the other hand, in *Reardon Smith Line Ltd v Hansen Tangen*[86] the House of Lords held that words which served *merely* to identify the subject-matter did not form part of the description if they simply amounted to a substitute for a name. To be *capable of forming* part of the description of the goods, it seems that the identifying words must refer to some quality or attribute of the subject-matter. Whether words containing such a reference *actually form* part of the description depends on the intention of the parties. This criterion was applied in *Ebrahim Dawood Ltd v Heath (Est. 1927) Ltd*,[87] where a c.i.f. contract for the sale of sheet steel provided: "Assorted over 6, 7, 8, 9 and 10 feet long. Assorted tonnage per size." McNair J. held that this was "quite plainly made part of the description of the goods."[88] In overseas sales a useful guide to the intention of the parties can often be found in the way in which the contract is set out. In *Montague L Meyer Ltd v Kivisto*[89] a contract for the sale of timber contained on its face a section headed "Specification" which referred to the number and dimensions of the goods sold; and on the back a series of "conditions," one of which was that the goods were to be "properly seasoned for shipment to the UK" They were not so seasoned and it was held that the statement that they were "properly seasoned" was not part of the description of the goods. Greer L.J. stressed that the contract was "divided intentionally into two parts" one of which (*i.e.* the "specification") "describes the thing sold" while the other (the "conditions" on the back) contained "terms binding on the parties with regard to the goods so described".[90] But the way in which the contract is set out is not decisive. On the one hand, terms which are not contained in the part of the contract headed "specification" or "description" may form part of the description of the goods.[91] On the other hand, the mere fact that the contract deals in one clause with matters clearly forming part of the description and in another with "quality" is not decisive to show that *all* statements about the goods occurring in the former clause are part of the description. In *Tradax Internacional SA v Goldschmidt SA*[92] the words "4 per cent foreign matters" in an f.o.b. contract for the sale of barley were held to amount only to an intermediate term, it being conceded that they did not form part of the description; while in *Tradax Export SA v European*

---

[86] [1976] 1 W.L.R. 989. For the distinction between "identification" and "identity", see also *Parsons v New Zealand Shipping Co.* [1901] 1 Q.B. 548, above, para.18–043, below, para.19–146.
[87] [1961] 2 Lloyd's Rep. 512; *cf.* (in domestic sales) *Harlingdon & Leinster Enterprises Ltd v Christopher Hull Fine Arts Ltd* [1991] 1 Q.B. 564.
[88] [1961] 2 Lloyd's Rep. 512 at p.518; the question whether it was part of the "description" here arose under a now repealed provision of the Sale of Goods Act 1979; see above, para.18–079.
[89] (1930) 142 L.T. 480.
[90] *ibid.*, at p.482.
[91] *e.g.* in *Foreman and Ellams Ltd v Blackburn* [1980] 2 K.B. 60 (above, para.18–270); and in *White Sea Timber Trust Ltd v W W North Ltd* (1932) 49 T.L.R. 142; 148 L.T. 263: in these cases a statement that goods were "already shipped" and a provision as to shipment under deck were held to be part of the description though not contained in the "description" or "specification".
[92] [1977] 2 Lloyd's Rep. 604.

Grain & Shipping Co.[93] the words "maximum 7.5 per cent fibre" in a c.i.f. contract for the sale of solvent extracted toasted soyabean meal were held to form part of the description. In both cases, the words quoted occurred in a part of the contract containing other statements that without question formed part of the description; and the contracts in both cases contained separate quality clauses. The difference in the results reached in the two cases can, perhaps, be accounted for on the ground that in the second there was evidence that fibre content was usually a matter for price adjustment in contracts for the sale of the commodity in question and that the specification of a maximum fibre content in such a contract was unusual. Hence the express reference to such content in a clause dealing with other matters of description provided evidence of the intention of the parties that the statement as to fibre content was intended to form part of the description. On the other hand express contractual provisions for price adjustment in the event of failure to conform with specified stipulations as to quality or quantity, would clearly indicate that those stipulations were not intended to take effect as conditions.[94]

(b) *Fitness for Purpose*

18–274 **Fitness for particular purpose.** Section 14(3)[95] of the Sale of Goods Act applies generally to overseas sales. It has, in particular, been regarded as applicable in a number of cases in which the buyer has relied on the seller's skill or judgment to supply goods capable of enduring a transit made known to the seller[96] or to pack them adequately for such a purpose.[97] On the other hand, there are two reasons why section 14(3) is less important in relation to overseas than to domestic sales. In the first place, where the "particular purpose" which is made known to the seller is that the goods are required for resale in the buyer's country, the court is unlikely to infer that the buyer relied on the seller's skill or judgment to supply goods suitable for that purpose. Normally in such a case the seller will know less than the buyer about market conditions in the latter's country, so that the buyer will be taken to have relied on his own knowledge of these conditions.[98] Secondly, many overseas sales are transactions, the nature of

---

[93] [1983] 2 Lloyd's Rep. 100 (where *Tradax Internacional SA v Goldschmidt SA*, above, was not cited); *cf. Vargas Pena Apezteguia y Cia. v Peter Cremer GmbH* [1987] 1 Lloyd's Rep. 394, where the words "Max 15% fat. If above 15% fat rejectable at buyer's option" put the buyer's right to reject beyond doubt when one of the shipping documents showed a fat content of 15.73%.

[94] As in *Charles E. Ford Ltd v AFEC Inc.* [1986] 2 Lloyd's Rep. 307.

[95] Above, para.11–051. *Cf.* Vienna Convention on Contracts for the International Sale of Goods (above, para.1–024), Art. 35(2)(b). For rights of avoidance under this Convention, see above, para.18–267, nn. 38, 41.

[96] *Mash & Murrell Ltd v Joseph I Emanuel Ltd* [1961] 1 W.L.R. 862, reversed [1961] 2 Lloyd's Rep. 326 (above, paras 18–255, 18–256); *A. B. Kemp Ltd v Tolland* [1956] 2 Lloyd's Rep. 681.

[97] *George Wills & Sons Ltd v Thomas Brown & Sons* (1922) 12 Ll.L.R. 292.

[98] *Teheran-Europe Co. Ltd v S T Belton (Tractors) Ltd* [1968] 2 Q.B. 554; Davies 85 L.Q.R. 74, 86 (1969); *cf. Sumner Permain & Co. v Webb & Co.* [1922] 1 K.B. 55, where a claim under s.14(2) failed on similar grounds.

which excludes the provisions of section 14(3). In *Henry Kendall & Son v William Lillico & Sons Ltd*[99] Lord Reid said: "If one merchant merely acquired from an importer by buying on c.i.f. documents goods from a normal source and then resold to another merchant by transfer of the c.i.f. documents before taking delivery, there might then be little or no reason to suppose that the former merchant had exercised or could have exercised any skill or judgment with regard to the quality of the goods or that the latter was relying on him. But that was not the position in this case."[1] The facts were that Brazilian groundnut extractions had been sold afloat under c.i.f. contracts. The seller knew that the buyer bought for resale to compounders of animal feeding stuffs. The goods were so resold, and compounded into meal which poisoned pheasants belonging to the ultimate buyer; the poisonous element was traced to the Brazilian groundnut extractions. A claim by the original buyer against the original seller succeeded under what is now section 14(3). Lord Reid, in holding that the case fell outside the general rule stated by him in the words quoted above, stressed that the goods had been acquired by the seller from a new source; that therefore "one would suppose . . . he must have exercised skill in deciding to buy them and put them on the market"; and that, on the evidence, the seller had recommended the goods to the buyer.[2] Lord Wilberforce stressed the fact that the buyer had never bought Brazilian groundnut extractions before[3]; while Lords Morris and Pearce simply held that on the evidence as a whole the buyer had relied on the seller's skill or judgment.[4] In the somewhat exceptional circumstances of the case, the subsection applied in spite of the fact that buyer and seller were members of the same trade association; although normally the seller would be able to rely on this fact as showing that the buyer had not reasonably relied on the seller's skill or judgment.[5]

(c) *Non-rejection Clauses*

In general.[6] Where goods do not comply with statements which are held to form part of the description, the seller may wish to rely on a non-rejection clause, that is, on a clause purporting to deprive the buyer of his right to reject, and limiting him to a right to damages.[7] In overseas sales the courts were, at common law, reluctant to allow the seller to rely on such a clause, particularly where he had not complied with the contractual stipulations as to the time, place or method of shipment. A non-rejection 18–275

[99] [1969] 2 A.C. 31.
[1] *ibid.*, at p.84; *cf.* p.124.
[2] *ibid.*, at p.84.
[3] *ibid.*, at p.125.
[4] *ibid.*, at pp.94–95; 116; Lord Guest disssented on this point.
[5] *cf. ibid.*, at p.125.
[6] See also above, para.13–032, and below, para.19–172 for clauses excluding the right to reject defective documents.
[7] A clause which merely specifies how *damages* are to be assessed will not bar *rejection: Roth, Schmidt & Co. v D Nagase & Co.* (1920) 2 Ll.L.R. 36 (invoicing back clause): see above, para.16–037. For certification clauses (which commonly bar all remedies) see above, para.13–040.

clause may also be ineffective under the Unfair Contract Terms Act 1977, but none of the limits imposed by that Act on the efficacy of contract terms which exclude or restrict liability or a remedy (such as rejection)[8] apply to contracts for the international supply of goods.[9] The Act is therefore of relatively small importance in relation to overseas sales. The same is true, for reasons to be discussed in paragraphs 18–282 and 18–283, of the Unfair Terms in Consumer Contracts Regulations 1999. Accordingly, we shall first consider the position at common law and then state the effects of the 1977 Act and of the 1999 Regulations on overseas sales.

18–276 **Effect of non-rejection clauses at common law.** In *J Aron & Co. (Inc.) v Comptoir Wegimont*[10] a contract for the sale of cocoa powder made on October 8 provided: "Shipment: . . . from U.S.A. ports during October, advised as already shipped." In fact the only advice the seller had received was that the powder had been received for shipment on October 8; and owing to a strike it was not actually shipped until November. It was held that the buyer could reject in spite of a clause in the contract which provided that the buyer should not be entitled to reject "whatever the difference of the shipment may be in value from the grade, type or description specified." McCardie J. said: "In one sense the time of shipment is part of the description of the goods . . . but . . . the express requirement of a contract that goods shall be shipped at a particular period is a good deal more than a mere description of the goods within section 13 of the Sale of Goods Act 1893. It is an express term of the contract independent of that which is generally known as the description of the goods. It is, I think, a condition precedent . . . that the goods shall be shipped as required by the contract."[11] The clause could have applied to "the description of the goods as actual articles of commerce",[12] and to statements as to their quality[13]; but it did not apply to "the non-fulfilment of a specific condition of the contract as to the month in which the goods were to be shipped."[14] The exact force of McCardie J.'s reference to the time of shipment as a "condition precedent" as distinct from "description . . . within section 13" (and hence from the implied "condition" there

[8] Unfair Contract Terms Act 1977, s.13(1)(b); *cf. Stewart Gill Ltd v Horatio Meyer & Co. Ltd* [1992] Q.B. 600 and *Schenkers Ltd v Overland Shoes Ltd* [1998] 1 Lloyd's Rep. 499 (clauses excluding set-off). Under the Draft Bill attached to the Law Commissions' Report on *Unfair Terms in Contracts.*, Law Com. No. 292, Scot. Law Com. No. 199 (2005) non-rejection clauses will be clauses "excluding or restricting liability" by virtue of Clause 30(1)(b) of the Bill.

[9] Unfair Contract Terms Act 1977, s.26(1): below, para.18–281, where s.26, and a proposal made in the Report referred to in n.8 above, to replace it by a less complex provision, are discussed.

[10] [1921] 3 K.B. 435; *cf. Re General Trading Co. Ltd and Van Stolk's Commissiehandel* (1911) 16 Com.Cas. 95.

[11] [1921] 3 K.B. 435 at p.440.

[12] [1921] 3 K.B. 435 at p.441.

[13] *ibid.; Montague L Meyer Ltd v Kivisto* (1930) 142 L.T. 480, where it is not clear to what extent the court relied on the non-rejection clause. The breach resulted in a depreciation of 10 per cent; and Scrutton L.J. said at p.481: "That seems to me to be peculiarly a case. .. for damages and not for rejection."

[14] [1921] 3 K.B. 435 at p.441.

stated) is far from clear. One possibility is that the former expression was used with reference to the *order* of performance (*i.e.* to indicate that the seller must ship within the specified period before any liability on the part of the buyer accrues) while the latter was used with reference to the *conformity* of the performance rendered with that promised (*i.e.* to indicate that the buyer can escape liability but only if he takes positive steps to disaffirm the contract).[15] The present status of McCardie J.'s views is, moreover, in doubt because those views resemble the subsequently developed doctrine of fundamental breach.[16] That doctrine is now regarded as a rule of construction only[17] and is less rigorously applied to clauses which merely limit, than to clauses which wholly exclude, liability.[18] It would seem that non-rejection clauses come closer to the first, than to the second, of these two types of clauses and that they would therefore be less restrictively construed than clauses which purported to exclude all liability. The question whether, in overseas sales, a non-rejection clause can apply to breaches of the term as to the time of shipment, or to other breaches which deprive the buyer of the substance of his bargain, is further discussed in paragraphs 18–277 to 18–279 below. Even words which are not, as a matter of construction, sufficiently clear to deprive the buyer of his right to reject on account of such breaches, may nevertheless bar his right to reject for other breaches of condition.[19]

The part of reasoning of McCardie J. in *J Aron & Co. (Inc.) v Comptoir Wegimont*,[20] quoted in paragraph 18–276 above, appears (as there noted) to be inconsistent with the now established view that the so-called doctrine of "fundamental breach" is a rule of construction only, and does not restrict the operation of exemption clauses as a matter of substantive law. It follows that a clause which clearly covered the breach of a stipulation as to the time, place or method of shipment, and excluded the right to reject for such a breach, could, at common law, take effect in accordance with its terms. The actual decision in *J Aron & Co. (Inc.) v Comptoir Wegimont*[21] can be explained as turning on the construction of the clause in that case, which, by coupling the word "description" with the words "grade" and "type", could be said to refer only to the physical characteristics of the goods[22] and so not to cover the date of shipment. **18–277**

---

[15] For judicial recognition of this distinction, see *State Trading Corporation of India v M Golodetz Ltd* [1989] 2 Lloyd's Rep. 277, esp. at pp.284–286; discussed by Treitel, 106 L.Q.R. 185 (1990); *Bank of Nova Scotia v Hellenic Mutual War Risks Assocn (The Good Luck)* [1992] 1 A.C. 233 at pp.262–263.
[16] Above, paras 13–042 *et seq.*
[17] *Photo Production Ltd v Securicor Transport Ltd* [1980] A.C. 827; *George Mitchell (Chesterhall) Ltd v Finney Lock Seeds Ltd* [1983] 2 A.C. 803.
[18] *Ailsa Craig Fishing Co. Ltd v Malvern Fishing Co.* [1983] 1 W.L.R. 964.
[19] *e.g.* those implied by virtue of the Sale of Goods Act 1979, ss.13–15: *cf.* below, para.18–278 at n.28.
[20] [1921] 3 K.B. 435 at p.440.
[21] [1921] 3 K.B. 435; no reference was made to this case in the two decisions of the House of Lords cited n.17, above.
[22] *cf.* the reference in [1921] 3 K.B. 435 at p.441 to "description of the goods themselves".

18–278 In *Vigers Bros v Sanderson Bros*[23] sawn laths of "about the specification stated below" were sold under two contracts. The shipments were found on arrival to contain in the one case 33 per cent of laths longer than those specified (and therefore difficult to resell), and in the other 60 per cent of laths shorter than those specified (and therefore practically worthless). It was held that the buyer could reject in spite of the fact that the contract provided: "Should any dispute arise under the stipulations of the contract, buyers shall not reject the goods . . ." Bigham J. said that the clause must be interpreted consistently with the main object of the contract, which was "to effect a sale . . . of two parcels of goods commercially within the description in the specification."[24] The case was subsequently described by Scrutton L.J. as one of "deliberate dishonesty"[25]; and he added that the non-rejection clause "must be reasonably interpreted; it does not mean that . . . if you have contracted to sell beans you may deliver peas; . . . you must deliver substantially what you have contracted to sell."[26] And Greer L.J. has said[27] that such a clause "must refer to a breach of condition[28]; because it is not wanted for breach of a warranty at all"; but that the clause would not apply where the goods were "not of the kind contracted for at all." It seems that the case would now be explained as an application of the rule of construction referred to in paragraph 18–276 above[29]: *i.e.* on the ground that the clause did not, on its true construction, cover the very serious breach which the seller had committed.

18–279 Non-rejection clauses sometimes provide that the buyer shall not reject the goods "herein specified"; and the contract may contain a separate section headed "specification". Where, in such a case, the goods differed substantially from their description in the "specification", it was held that they were not the goods "herein specified" and that a non-rejection clause did not apply.[30] Nor will such a clause prevent the buyer from rejecting the goods on grounds other than their failure to comply with the "specification"; for example on the ground that they were not shipped under deck as required by the contract[31] or that they were not shipped, or ready for shipment, within the required time.[32] Such a clause could, however, apply

---

23 [1901] 1 Q.B. 608.
24 *ibid.*, at p.611.
25 *Montague L Meyer Ltd v Osakeyhtio Carelia Timber Co. Ltd* (1930) 36 Com.Cas. 17 at p.20.
26 *ibid.*, at p.20.
27 *ibid.*, at p.27.
28 Or to breach of an intermediate term (above, para.10–033)—a category not recognised in 1930.
29 *cf. Thor Line AB v Alltrans Group of Canada (The TFL Prosperity)* [1984] 1 W.L.R. 48, where the clause in question was one purporting to limit a shipowner's liability.
30 *e.g. Montague L Meyer Ltd v Travaru A/BH. Cornelius of Gambleby* (1930) 46 T.L.R. 553; *cf. Beck & Co. v Szymanowski* [1924] A.C. 43, where similar reasoning was applied to a non-rejection clause in a case of short delivery.
31 *White Sea Timber Trust Ltd v W W North Ltd* (1932) 148 L.T. 263; 49 T.L.R. 142, above, para.18–272.
32 *Montague L Meyer Ltd v Osakeyhtio Carelia Timber Co.*, above, n.25; *Montague L. Meyer Ltd v Kivisto* (1930) 142 L.T. 480 at p.482.

where it is "doubtful whether the shipper has adhered sufficiently closely to the stipulation that the goods shall be of 'about' the specification length"[33]; and where the term broken does not form part of the specification or description of the goods, and is either a condition or an intermediate term.[34]

Unfair Contract Terms Act 1977.[35] Section 6 of this Act limits the validity of contract terms (including non-rejection clauses)[36] purporting to exclude or restrict liability for breach of the implied terms arising from sections 13 to 15 of the Sale of Goods Act. Such contract terms are completely ineffective as against a person dealing as consumer[37] and subject to the requirement of reasonableness as against a person dealing otherwise than as consumer.[38] Section 6 of the 1977 Act only limits the right to exclude or restrict liability for breach of the statutorily implied terms: it does not affect the validity of non-rejection clauses which are to operate in the event of (for example) short or late delivery. But in overseas sales a stipulation as to the time of shipment forms part of the description of the goods[39]; so that a non-rejection clause purporting to apply to such a stipulation may be ineffective, or subject to the requirement of reasonableness, under section 6 of the 1977 Act. Even a clause purporting to deprive a buyer of the right to reject on account of some other breach (such as short delivery) is subject to the requirement of reasonableness under section 3 of the 1977 Act where the buyer deals (i) as consumer; or (ii) "on the other's [*i.e.* the seller's] written standard terms of business." The latter phrase can apply to terms drafted by a trade association and incorporated in his terms of business by one of the parties to the contract who is,[40] while the other party is not, a member of the association. It is less clear whether the phrase also applies to the situation, common in overseas sales, where a contract is made on a form provided by a trade association of which *both* parties are members. 18–280

---

[33] *Vigers Bros v Sanderson Bros* [1901] 1 Q.B. 608 at p.611.

[34] *Montague L Meyer Ltd v Kivisto* (1930) 142 L.T. 480 (above, para.18–276). See above, para.10–023 as to warranties and above, para.10–033 as to intermediate terms.

[35] See generally paras 13–062 *et seq.*, above.

[36] Unfair Contract Terms Act 1977, s.13(1)(b),above, para.18–275, n.8.

[37] *ibid.*, s.6(2). For "dealing as consumer", see s.12(1), above, para.13–071.

[38] *ibid.*, s.6(3). Under the Draft Bill annexed to the Law Commissions' Report on *Unfair Terms in Contracts* (Law Com. No. 292, Scot. Law Com. No. 199 (2005)), s.6(2) of the 1977 Act is replicated by Clause 5(2) of the Draft Bill; s.6(3) is not replicated in Clause 10 of the Draft Bill since the buyer in a "business contract" is considered to be adequately protected by the general requirement, imposed by Clause 9, that a party to such a contract cannot rely on his written standard terms of business unless they are fair and reasonable. Clause 11, which imposes a requirement of fairness and reasonableness on certain non-negotiated terms in "small business contract", likewise contains no special reference to contracts for the sale of goods.

[39] Above, para.18–267.

[40] *e.g. Overseas Medical Supplies Ltd v Orient Trading Services Ltd* [1999] 2 Lloyd's Rep. 273.

The 1977 Act is not likely to be of great importance in relation to non-rejection clauses in overseas sales. The buyer under such a contract will not generally (though he may occasionally); [41] deal as consumer[42]; and where (as is more usual in overseas sales) the buyer does not so deal, the clause (even if it purports to exclude or restrict liability for breach of the terms implied by sections 13 to 15 of the Sale of Goods Act 1979) will not (under the 1977 Act) be wholly invalid but subject only to the requirement of reasonableness. The guidelines provided by the 1977 Act[43] for the application of that requirement under section 6[44] suggest that in many overseas sales the requirement will be satisfied. There is not usually any great disparity of bargaining power between such parties[45]; and where the contract is on trade-association terms, the customer will know or have ready means of knowledge of, the clause.[46] Although these factors are not decisive,[47] the test of reasonableness is, in such circumstances likely to lead to much the same results as the common law rules discussed in paragraphs 18–276 to 18–279 above.

18–281 **International Supply Contracts.** Even where the test of reasonableness would not be satisfied, the validity of the clause may not be affected by the 1977 Act, since section 26 provides that the limits imposed by the Act on the effectiveness of contract terms do not apply to certain inter-

---

[41] Under the Law Commissions' Report on *Unfair Terms in Contracts*, Law Com. No. 292, Scot. Law Com. No. 199 (2005) the possibility of an overseas sale's being a "consumer contract" is still further reduced by the requirements that the consumer must be an individual: see Clause 26(1)(a) of the Draft Bill attached to the Report. This requirement would exclude cases such as *R & B Customs Broker Ltd v United Dominion Trust Ltd* [1988] 1 W.L.R. 321 (above, para.18–259 n.89). On the other hand, there is, under the proposals in the Report, an increased chance that an overseas sale could be a "small business contract" so that "non-negotiated" terms in it would be subject to a requirement of fairness and reasonableness under Clause 11 of the Draft Bill: for the definition of "small business" and "small business contract", see Clauses 27 to 29.

[42] See above, para 18-259.

[43] Sch.2.

[44] Sch.2 does not apply for the purpose of s.3, but the court could take similar factors into account in determining reasonableness under that section: *Singer (UK) Ltd v Tees & Hartlepool Port Authority* [1988] 2 Lloyd's Rep. 164 at p.169; *Flamar Interocean Ltd v Denmac Ltd (The Flammar Pride)* [1990] 1 Lloyd's Rep. 434 at p.439.

[45] *cf.* Unfair Contract Terms Act 1977, Sch.2, para.(a); *Granville Oil & Chemicals Ltd v Davies Turner & Co. Ltd* [2003] EWCA Civ 570, [2003] 1 All E.R. (Comm.) 819 at [19].

[46] *ibid.*, para.(c); *cf. R W Green Ltd v Cade Bros Farms* [1978] 1 Lloyd's Rep. 602 at p.607, decided under Supply of Goods (Implied Terms) Act 1973, s.4(5), now superseded by Unfair Contract Terms Act 1977, s.6(3); *Schenkers Ltd v Overland Shoes Ltd* [1998] 1 Lloyd's Rep. 499 at p.507.

[47] See *George Mitchell (Chesterhall) Ltd v Finney Lock Seeds Ltd* [1983] 2 A.C. 803 at p.817 where the fact that an exception clause was "universally embodied in the terms of trade" (though not settled by a trade association) was described as "equivocal" and did not prevent the clause from being struck down for unreasonableness under the transitional provisions of Sale of Goods Act 1979, s.55(3) and Sch.1, para.11.

national supply contracts.[48] The definition of such contracts contains two elements.[49]

First, the contract must be one for the sale of goods[50] made by parties whose places of business (or, if they have none, whose habitual residences) are in the territories of different States. This requirement is satisfied when the places of business of the parties are, even though those of their agents are not, in different States.[51]

---

[48] These include not only contracts for the sale of goods but also other contracts (such as contracts of hire or exchange) under which the possession or ownership of goods passes: s.26(3)(a). Our sole concern here is with contracts for the sale of goods. On s.26 of the 1977 Act, see also above, para.13–099; below, para.25–090. For proposals for reform, see *Unfair Terms in Contracts*, Law Com. No. 292, Scot Law Com. No. 199 (2005) Part 7, distinguishing for the present purpose between "consumer" contracts, "business contracts" and "small business contracts". Under these proposals, certain statutory restrictions on the validity of the contract terms are not to apply to business or small business contracts "for the supply of goods to be delivered overseas" but will continue to apply to contracts "for the supply of goods in the UK whether the seller is in the UK or overseas" (Report, paras 7–57, 7–61). In the Draft Bill appended to the Report, the cases to which the statutory restrictions are not to apply are stated to be contracts "for the supply of goods where the supply is to be made to a place outside the United Kingdom" (cl.22 and Sch.3 para.8). These words are a potential source of difficulty in relation to standard types of overseas sales, such as c.i.f. and f.o.b. contracts. Where goods are sold on c.i.f. terms by the seller in the UK to a buyer in another country, the contractual destination of the goods may be in the latter country or in a third country and the contract may provide for tender of documents in any of those countries or in yet a fourth country. Although the seller performs his obligation to the deliver by the tender of documents (see para.19–002 below) it is probable that the place where "the supply is to be made" is the place specified as the destination in the contract. Where the sale is on f.o.b. terms, the contract will not normally specify a destination (see below, para.20–021 and n.52 below) and the place where the "supply is to be made " will depend on how the contract is, or is intended to be, performed. If the shipping arrangements are made or to be made, and the bill of lading is obtained or to be obtained by the buyer (as in the third of the situations discussed in para.20–003 below), then that place will probably be that of shipment or intended shipment, even though the seller knows that the goods are ultimately destined by the buyer for some other country. If, on the other hand, no advance shipping arrangements are made, or if such arrangements are made by the seller pursuant to the buyer's shipping instructions and the bill of lading is obtained by the seller (as in the first and second of the situations discussed in para.20–003 below), then the place where the " supply is or is to be made" may well be the place of destination named in the bill of lading, even though no destination is named in the contract. If the goods in question are never shipped, then it seems that the relevant "place" can only be that at which they ought to have been shipped. The situation is further complicated by the fact that goods may be sold on f.o.b. terms naming a place in one country as the place of shipment and then resold afloat on c.i.f. or similar terms (as in *Borealis AB v Stargas Ltd (The Berge Sisar)* [2001] UKHL 17, [2002] 1 A.C. 205). The place where "the supply is to be made" might then be in one country for the purpose of the first, and in another for that of the second, contract.

[49] s.26(3)(b) and (4). *Cf. Rasbora Ltd v JCL Marine Ltd* [1977] 1 Lloyd's Rep. 645 at p.652.

[50] A contract may be one of the sale of goods within s.26 although it also contains a service element (*e.g.* where the seller undertakes maintenance obligations with respect to the goods): see *Amiri Flight Authority v BAE Systems Ltd* [2003] EWCA Civ 1447, [2003] 2 Lloyd's Rep. 767.

[51] *Ocean Chemical Transport Inc. v Exnor Craggs Ltd* [2000] 1 Lloyd's Rep. 446 at pp.451–452.

Secondly, one of the following conditions must be satisfied, namely that:

(a) the goods are, at the time of the conclusion of the contract, in the course of carriage or will be carried, from the territory of one State to that of another; or

(b) the acts constituting the offer and acceptance have been done in the territories of different States; or

(c) the contract provides for the goods to be delivered to the territory of a State other than that within whose territory those acts were done.

It is important to stress that *both* elements of the definition must be satisfied. If two persons who carry on business in England made a contract for the sale of coffee to be shipped from Brazil c.i.f. London, the contract would not be an international supply contract, since the first element of the definition (that the parties must carry on business in different States) would not be satisfied. If the parties do carry on business in different States, the question whether any of the conditions (a) to (c) above have been satisfied can give rise to many difficulties. Suppose, for example, that goods are sold by an English seller to a French buyer under a contract made in England which provides for delivery f.o.b. London. The buyer intends to ship the goods to France, and the seller knows this, but it is not a term of the contract. Is this a case in which the goods "will be carried from the territory of one State to the territory of another?"[52] Again suppose that the offer to buy is posted in France and arrives in England: in which State is the act constituting the offer "done"?[53] A similar question can be raised in relation to the acceptance; and here the answer might depend on whether the contract was subject to English law (by which a posted acceptance generally takes effect on posting),[54] or to a foreign law (by which such an acceptance may take effect on its receipt by the offeror).[55] Yet a further problem is what is meant by "delivered"[56]; this may refer to delivery of the goods to a carrier, or to tender of documents, or to actual physical delivery of the goods to the buyer.[57] It would not be difficult to multiply examples and to

---

[52] Within Unfair Contract Terms Act 1977, s.26(4)(a). The *Amiri* case, above n.50 at [32] treats the contract in the case put above as falling within s.26(4)(a) if the sale was "on c.i.f. or f.o.b. terms." This point is, with respect, clear in the case of a c.i.f. contract, since such a contract invariably specifies the destination, but less clear where the sale is on f.o.b. terms since such a contract does not normally specify the destination of the goods: see below, para.20–021; for exceptions, see below, para.20–024. In the *Amiri* case itself, a contract for the sale of an aircraft to be delivered at Hatfield was held not to fall within s.26(4)(a) even though the seller knew that the aircraft was to be exported to the United Arab Emirates; and it is not easy to distinguish this case from one in which the contract provides for delivery f.o.b. a British port without giving an indication of the ultimate destination of the goods.

[53] Within Unfair Contract Terms Act 1977, s.26(4)(b); for similar problems in criminal law, see *Treacy v DPP* [1971] A.C. 537 (blackmail); *R v Baxter* [1972] 1 Q.B. 1 (attempting to obtain property by deception).

[54] Treitel, *The Law of Contract* (11th ed.), p.24.

[55] *e.g. Albeko Schuhmaschinen AG v The Kamborian Shoe Machine Co. Ltd* (1961) 111 L.J. 519.

[56] In Unfair Contract Terms Act 1977, s.26(4)(c). *Cf.* the discussion in para.18–261 above of what, in the context of the passing of risk to buyer who deals as a consumer, amounts (in overseas sales) to "delivery" for the purpose of Sale of Goods Act 1979, ss.20(4) and 32(4).

[57] *cf.* below, para.19–072.

point to some very curious distinctions which may arise from the statutory definition of international supply contracts. But the point is not worth labouring. Its practical importance will probably be small, since in overseas sales non-rejection (and other exemption) clauses which are valid at common law are likely to satisfy the requirement of reasonableness.

The reasonableness test imposed by sections 3 and 6 of the 1977 Act is also inapplicable where the contract is governed by the law of a part of the United Kingdom only by choice of the parties and would, but for that choice, have been governed by the law of some country outside the United Kingdom.[58] This limitation on the scope of the reasonableness test is of considerable importance in relation to overseas sales, since it is quite common for such contracts to be governed by English law only by choice of the parties.

Unfair Terms in Consumer Contracts Regulations 1999. These Regulations[59] apply to terms which have not been individually negotiated in contracts between consumers and commercial sellers or suppliers.[60] If such terms are unfair, they are not binding on the consumer.[61] The Regulations are highly unlikely to apply non- rejection clauses in overseas sales of the kind discussed in this Part in this book. Unlike the Unfair Contract Terms Act 1977, they apply *only* where one party to the contract is a "consumer"; and they will hardly ever apply to overseas sales for the simple reason that "consumer" in the Regulations refers only to a natural person,[62] while almost all contracts of the kind here under discussion are now made by corporations. It is also part of the definition of "consumer" in the Regulations that the person in question must, in making the contract, be "acting for purposes which are outside his business".[63] This makes the definition significantly narrower than that of "dealing as consumer" under the Unfair Contract Terms Act 1977.[64] In particular, a contract made by a party acting in the course of business would not be covered by the Regulations even though it fell within the definition of "dealing as consumer" within the Act on the ground that the contract was not made in 18–282

[58] Unfair Contract Terms Act 1977, s.27(1) (as amended by Contracts (Applicable Law) Act 1990, s.5 and Sch.4). Section 27(1) of the 1977 Act also makes inapplicable to such contracts a number of other provisions of the Act, with which the present discussion is not concerned. The Law Commissions' Report on *Unfair Terms in Contracts* (Law Com. No. 292, Scot. Law Com. 199 (2005) in paras 7.29 and 7.63 recommends that a provision replicating s.27(1) of the 1977 Act should be contained in the proposed new Unfair Contract Terms Bill in relation to business and small business contracts, but not in relation to consumer contracts.

[59] SI 1999/2083. Under the report referred to in n.58 above, the provisions of the Regulations will, in effect, be amalgamated with a reformed version of the 1977 Act, discussed in relation to overseas sales in paras 18–280 and 18–281 above.

[60] Reg. 4(1).

[61] Reg. 8(1).

[62] Reg. 3(1), definition of "consumer. In para 3.24 of the Report referred to in n.58 above the Law Commissions likewise recommend that, for the purposes of the proposed Unfair Contract Terms Act, "only natural persons should constitute consumers."

[63] Reg. 3(1).

[64] Unfair Contract Terms Act 1977, s.12(1); above, para.13–071.

the *regular* course of that business.[65] The older authorities do provide an example of a c.i.f. contract in which the buyer could be a "consumer" within the Regulations[66]; but in commodity contracts of the kind with which the present discussion is mainly concerned this possibility is so remote that it can safely be disregarded.

18–283 Unlike the 1977 Act, the 1999 Regulations contain no specific exception for international supply contracts; but the terms of at least some such contracts may fall within another exception to the Regulations. This is the exception which states that the Regulations do not apply to "contractual terms which reflect . . . the provisions or principles of international conventions to which the Member States or the Community are party".[67] This exception resembles a similar limitation on the scope of the 1977 Act,[68] but it is in two respects wider than that contained in the Act. First, it refers to conventions to which the Member States or the Community are party, while the Act refers only to international agreements to which the United Kingdom is a party. Secondly, the Regulations refer to "the provisions *or principles*" of such conventions, so that a term based on the principles of such a convention would not be governed by the Regulations, even though the contract in which the term was contained was not governed by the convention or was governed by the law of a country which had not ratified the convention. One relevant convention is the Vienna Convention on Contracts for the International Sale of Goods,[69] which some Member States have ratified, though the United Kingdom has not done so. If a contract governed by English law were by one of its terms (whether express or implied from, for example, course of dealing) made subject to the Vienna Convention, then it is submitted that any term in the contract which "reflected" the provisions of the Convention would, by virtue of the exception to the Regulations here described, not be subject to the Regulations. The point is not likely to be of major importance, since the consumer contracts to which the Regulations apply will only rarely, if ever, be governed by the Convention.[70] But if such a contract were governed by the Convention, then the parties would, under the terms of the Convention,

---

[65] See *R & B Customs Brokers Ltd v United Dominion Trust Ltd* [1988] 1 W.L.R. 321, above, para.18–280.

[66] *Wiehe v Dennis Bros* (1913) 29 T.L.R. 250.

[67] Reg. 4(2)(b); for the definition of "Member State" and "the Community", see reg. 3(1).

[68] s.29(1)(b). Paragraph 3.72 of the Report referred to in n.58 above replicates the exception here under discussion by referring simply to "an international convention", without specifying who the parties to the convention must be; but Sch.3, para.1(1)(b), of the Bill annexed to the Report refers to "an international convention to which the United Kingdom or European Community is a party." The Vienna Convention (above para.18–024) seems not to fall within Sch.3, para.1(1)(b).

[69] Above, para.1–024.

[70] See Art. 2(a) of the Vienna Convention; the reference in Art. 1 to the "places of business" of the "parties" (in the plural) may suggest that the Convention does not apply at all to a contract, one party to which is a "consumer" within the Regulations: for the purpose of the Regulations, that party must be "acting for purposes which are outside his trade, business or profession" (Reg. 3(1)), so that his place of business (within the Convention) would have no relevance to the contract.

be allowed to "derogate" from it or to vary its provisions[71] so that a seller could exclude or restrict a liability which, but for such derogation, would be imposed on him by the Convention. This appears to be one of the "principles" of the Convention, so that the Regulations would not apply to a term of this kind.

(d) *Statutory Restrictions on Right to Reject*

Sale of Goods Act 1979, section 15A. Statutory restrictions on a buyer's right to reject goods for breach of certain implied conditions are imposed by section 15A of the Sale of Goods Act 1979; similar restrictions on the buyer's right to reject goods for quantitative defects[72] are discussed, in the context of overseas sales, in paragraph 19–012 below. Section 15A applies where the seller is in breach of a condition[73] implied by section 13, 14 or 15 of the 1979 Act[74] and the buyer does not deal as consumer;[75] if, in such cases, "the breach is so slight that it would be unreasonable for [the buyer] to reject [the goods]",[76] then the breach is "not to be treated as a breach of condition but may be treated as a breach of warranty".[77] This statutory restriction on the buyer's right to reject will, however, be excluded if "a contrary intention appears in, or is to be implied from, the contract".[78] It applies only to breaches of *implied* terms (as opposed to *express* ones), only to breaches of the implied terms set out in sections 13 to 15 of the 1979 Act (and not, for example, to those set out in section 12) and only to breaches by the seller (and not to such breaches by the buyer as give the seller the right to rescind)[79]. 18–284

Section 15A is discussed generally in Chapter 11; our sole concern here is with its effect on overseas sales and in particular on the rule in *Bowes v Shand*,[80] that, where a contract provides for goods to be shipped within a specified period, the buyer is entitled to reject them if they are shipped outside that period. Under this rule, the fact that shipment was made by so much as a single day outside the shipment period can justify rejection. The results of its application may sometimes have been harsh to sellers,

---

[71] Art. 6 of the Convention.
[72] Sale of Goods Act 1979, s.30(2A).
[73] See Sale of Goods Act 1979, ss.13(1A), 14(6), 15(3).
[74] s.15A(1)(a).
[75] A c.i.f. buyer will not normally deal as consumer but may occasionally do so: see above, para.18–259. If he does so deal and the goods do not conform to the contract at the time of delivery, he has the "additional rights" specified in Pt 5A of the Sale of Goods Act 1979. One of these rights is the right to require the seller to repair or replace the non-conforming goods: Sale of Goods Act 1979, ss.48A(2)(a), 48B. If the buyer chooses to exercise this right, then he may not reject the goods until he has given the seller a reasonable time in which to repair or replace them: s.48D. There is, however, nothing in Pt 5A to compel the buyer to exercise the "additional right" to require repair or replacement; and if he chooses not to do so his right to reject the goods for breach of condition will not be restricted by s.48D.
[76] s.15A(1)(b).
[77] s.15A(1).
[78] s.15A(2).
[79] For examples of such breaches, see below, paras 19–207, 20–123 to 20–125.
[80] (1877) 2 App.Cas. 455, above, para.18–267.

especially where the rejection was motivated by the fact that the market has fallen rather than by the fact of late (or early) shipment.[81] But the rule has been justified in the interests of commercial certainty; for, where goods pass rapidly through many hands, it is important to be able to establish rights of rejection quickly[82] and without the need for each buyer to show to what extent (if at all) he was prejudiced by the breach. The Law Commissions, in the Report which led to the passing of section 15A, recognise this point, saying that "in many commercial situations it would be normal to infer an intention that any breach of a time clause, however slight, would justify rejection of the goods and termination of the contract. We do not expect our recommendations to have any effect on such time clauses."[83] Although section 15A contains no express savings for the right to reject for such breaches, a number of arguments can be advanced in favour of the view that the section has not restricted that right in cases of this kind. One is that, in overseas sales (especially in those on c.i.f. or f.o.b. terms) which specify a shipment period, the buyer's right to reject goods on the ground that they have been shipped outside the shipment period is so well established by authority and recognised in commercial practice, that, merely by entering into such a contract, the parties have provided evidence of a "contrary intention"[84] which, under the express words of section 15A, can exclude the operation of that section. A second argument is that, for some purposes at least, stipulations as to the time of shipment have been held to be "a good deal more than a mere description of the goods within section 13 of the Sale of Goods Act . . ."[85] This is true, in particular, for the purpose of determining whether a non-rejection clause applies to a breach of such a stipulation[86]; and section 15A could perhaps be described as a kind of statutory non-rejection clause. A third argument is that, if section 15A did restrict the buyer's right to reject for breach of a stipulation as to the time of shipment, then its operation in overseas sales would be curiously one-sided. We shall see that a seller is normally entitled to rescind an f.o.b. contract on account of the buyer's failure to perform his undertaking to nominate a ship capable of taking the goods on board within the contractual shipment period,[87] and section 15A does not in any way affect the remedies of the *seller*. Yet if the statutory restriction does not apply to the seller's right to rescind on account of the buyer's breach with regard to the time of *taking* delivery, then it is submitted that the buyer's right to reject for breach by the seller as to the time of performing one phase[88] of his duty to *make* delivery should likewise be free from this

[81] *cf.* the discussion of damages for loss of the right to reject in paras 19–187 *et seq.*, esp. at para.19–195.
[82] *cf. Hansson v Hamel & Horley Ltd* [1922] 2 A.C. 36 at p.46 (documents "have to be taken up or rejected promptly").
[83] Law Com. No. 160, Scot. Law Com. No. 104, para.4.24 (1987).
[84] s.15A(2).
[85] *J Aron & Co. (Inc.) v Comptoir Wegimont* [1921] 3 K.B. 435 at p.440; above, para.18–276.
[86] Above, paras 18–276 to 18–279.
[87] *e.g.* below, paras 20–029, 20–032, 20–046; *Bunge Corp. New York v Tradax Export SA* [1981] 1 W.L.R. 711.
[88] *cf.* below, para.19–072 for the three "stages of delivery" in a c.i.f. contract.

restriction. It is true that the buyer's breach in the case put is of an *express* term and that section 15A applies only to breaches of certain statutorily *implied* terms; but where a seller fails to ship goods within the contractual shipment period his breach could plausibly be said to fall into either of these categories.

The foregoing discussion has been concerned only with stipulations as to the *time* of performance; but in overseas sales statements relating to the *place* of shipment,[89] and many other statements about the ship or the goods[90] have likewise been held to be part of the description of the goods. The effect of the falsity of such statements has been discussed in paragraphs 18–269 to 18–272; and where (as is generally the case) their falsity gives the buyer a right to reject, it is submitted that, in overseas sales, that right should not be restricted by section 15A. This submission is again made in the interests of commercial certainty, and it can again be supported on the ground that parties to overseas sales on typical c.i.f. or f.o.b. terms must be taken to have impliedly agreed to exclude the statutory restriction on the right to reject.

The restrictive interpretation of section 15A which is here put forward is based on the requirements of commercial certainty; these are particularly strong in sales of commodities under which it is vital that decisions on matters of rejection should be capable of being taken quickly and with confidence. It is no answer to this point to say (as the Law Commissions did) that section 15A will not be "a major alteration to the law"[91] since it will only apply in a narrow range of cases. Certainty would nevertheless be seriously undermined if section 15A were not excluded (by contrary intention) from such cases; for the questions whether a defect was "slight" and whether it was "unreasonable" for the buyer to reject[92] necessarily involve value judgments, so that the parties, or their legal advisers, would find it hard in any particular case to predict whether rejection would be justified. In the present context, the requirements of certainty are traditionally regarded as more important than those of justice; and if parties to overseas sales wish to impose restrictions on the right to reject it is open to them to do so by means of non-rejection clauses which clearly and unequivocally cover the breach in question.[93]

6. BULK SHIPMENTS

In general. A number of problems arise from the sale of an undifferentiated part of a bulk, or the splitting up of a single consignment on resale to several buyers. These problems stem largely from the fact that goods forming an undifferentiated part of a bulk are often unascertained. In cases of overseas sales, such problems are particularly acute where the subject- 18–285

[89] Above, para.18–267.
[90] Above, paras 18–269 to 18–272.
[91] Law Commissions' Report (above, n.83), para.4.21.
[92] s.15A(1)(b).
[93] Above, para.18–277.

matter of the sale is a part of (even an identified) bulk shipment which is not split up[94] until some considerable time after the conclusion of the contract of sale; often the part of the bulk to which the contract relates will not be divided from the rest (and so become ascertained) until the arrival of the ship at the specified destination. By then the goods (or some of them) may have perished or deteriorated, or one of the parties may have become insolvent; and the rules which determine the effect of such events in cases where the goods are already ascertained at the relevant time cannot be applied without difficulty to cases where the goods are not so ascertained because the sale was of an undifferentiated part of a bulk shipment.

(a) *Shipping Documents*

18–286 **Tender of documents.** Where a contract provides for payment against shipping documents the buyer is not prima facie bound to accept, or pay on, tender of anything less than a bill of lading covering the contract goods and no others.[95] If there is only one bill of lading in respect of a bulk shipment, the seller cannot prima facie make a good tender of documents to a buyer of part of the shipment. One way of avoiding this difficulty is for the seller to take several bills of lading, each for a specified proportion of the cargo or for a specified amount out of the cargo.[96] It has been doubted whether a bill of lading "for an undistinguished part of a cargo" would be a good tender[97]; but such a tender would clearly be good if the contract expressly so provided.[98] It would also be good if a term to that effect could be implied, *e.g.* if the contract was for the sale of goods normally shipped in bulk and if the quantity sold was less than the amount that would normally constitute a full cargo.[99] But the practice of taking several bills of lading will only help if it is possible at the time of shipment to forecast the size of the lots in which the shipment will eventually be sold. In one case[1] a seller to whom a single bill of lading had been issued in respect of a whole bulk shipment attempted to solve the problem by procuring further bills for parts

[94] If the bulk shipment is physically split up into ascertained parts the following discussion does not apply to it. See *The Arpad* [1934] P. 189 at p.198 where there was a provision for storing the bulk shipment "as per plan" and this enabled "the specific wheat shipped to be identified". *Cf. Karlshamns Oljefabriker v Eastport Navigation Corp. (The Elafi)* [1981] 2 Lloyd's Rep. 679, where a c.i.f. contract required "bills of lading to identify the holds": a sale in respect of which such bills were tendered would be one of ascertained goods if the bill or bills related to the entire contents of one or more of a larger number of holds.

[95] *Heilbert, Symons & Co. Ltd v Harvey, Christie-Miller & Co.* (1922) 12 Ll.L.R. 455; below, paras 19–024, 19–036, 20–021.

[96] For this practice, see for example *Inglis v Stock* (1885) 10 App.Cas. 263; *Ross T. Smyth & Co. Ltd v T D Bailey, Son & Co.* [1940] 3 All E.R. 60.

[97] *Re Reinhold & Co. and Hansloh* (1896) 12 T.L.R. 422.

[98] *e.g. Dewar & Webb v Joseph Rank Ltd* (1923) 14 Ll.L.R. 393; see on this point 13 Ll.L.R. at 211.

[99] As in *Karlshamns Oljefabriker v Eastport Navigation Corp. (The Elafi)* [1981] 2 Lloyd's Rep. 679.

[1] *SIAT di del Ferro v Tradax Overseas SA* [1978] 2 Lloyd's Rep. 470; affirmed [1980] 1 Lloyd's Rep. 53.

of the same bulk, issued by the time charterer of the carrying ship and purporting to be (though in fact they were not) issued on behalf of the shipowners.[2] But the tender of such bills was held bad as they had not been issued either on behalf of the shipowner, or on shipment, or in the ordinary course of business.[3]

From the seller's point of view, a preferable course is to stipulate for the right to tender a delivery order as an alternative to a bill of lading.[4] Such tender will then be valid; but the practice is in turn less than wholly satisfactory from the buyer's point of view. If the order is not a "ship's delivery order" within the Carriage of Goods by Sea Act 1992,[5] the contractual rights (if any) which he will acquire against the carrier may be less advantageous than those which he would have acquired, if a bill of lading had been transferred to him[6]; and even if the order is a "ship's delivery order" within that Act, so that rights under the contract of carriage are vested in the buyer,[7] the order will still leave the buyer in ignorance of the (often crucial) fact of the date of shipment.[8] One possible way in which the buyer can protect himself against these disadvantages is by stipulating for a guarantee (for example from a bank) to hold him harmless against the consequences of taking a delivery order.[9] Buyers of parts of bulk shipments do sometimes pay against delivery orders and even invoices when they are not obliged to do so; but the reported cases[10] show that this practice exposes them to considerable risks.

(b) *Passing of Property*

Introduction. The law with regard to the passing of property in goods which, at the time of the contract of sale, formed an undifferentiated part of a bulk has been in part codified and in part significantly altered by the Sale of Goods (Amendment) Act 1995.[11] In the following discussion, it will be convenient (if perhaps not entirely accurate) to refer to the provisions of this Act as "the 1995 reforms." They are considered in detail in Chapter 5; 18–287

---

[2] [1978] 2 Lloyd's Rep. 470 at p.480. *Cf. Noble Resources Ltd v Cavalier Shipping Corp. (The Atlas)* [1996] 1 Lloyd's Rep. 642 at p.644, describing the practice of issuing such "switch" bills as "fraught with danger" since it gives opportunities for fraud.

[3] [1978] 2 Lloyd's Rep. 470 at p.493; [1980] 1 Lloyd's Rep. 53 at p.63; *cf.* below, para.19–034.

[4] *e.g. The Julia* [1949] A.C. 293. This is the method favoured in *SIAT di del Ferro v Tradax Overseas SA* [1978] 2 Lloyd's Rep. 470 at p.492; affirmed without reference to the point in [1980] 1 Lloyd's Rep. 53.

[5] s.1(4), above, para.18–176; the definition would not, for example, cover the order against which the buyer had paid in *The Julia* [1949] A.C. 293.

[6] *ibid*, at p.312; above, para.18–174.

[7] By virtue of Carriage of Goods by Sea Act 1992, s.2(1)(c), above, para.18–175.

[8] See above, para.18–267.

[9] *Heilbert, Symons & Co. Ltd v Harvey, Christie-Miller & Co.* (1922) 12 Ll.L.R. 455; *cf.* the provisions for countersignature discussed in para.18–172 above.

[10] *e.g. Re Wait* [1927] 1 Ch. 606; *Margarine Union GmbH v Cambay Prince SS Co. Ltd (The Wear Breeze)* [1969] 1 Q.B. 219; below, paras 18–299, 18–302.

[11] Implementing Law Com. No. 215, Scot. Law Com. No. 145 (Sale of Goods forming Part of a Bulk) (1993); Davenport [1986] L.M.C. L.Q. 4.

the discussion of them present chapter will deal only with the special problems to which they give rise in overseas sales.

Before the 1995 reforms, a contract for the sale of (for example) 500 out of the 1,000 tons of goods of a designated kind shipped or to be shipped in bulk on a named ship was (as indeed it still is) a contract for the sale of unascertained goods.[12] The 500 tons would normally remain unascertained until that quantity was separated from the bulk[13]; and the effect of section 16 of the Sale of Goods Act 1979 was that property could not pass to the buyer, even though he had paid the price in full,[14] before the goods become ascertained, normally by "final appropriation of the quantities sold at the port of destination".[15]

18–288 **Ascertainment by "exhaustion" or "consolidation".** The general rule that property could not pass before such "final appropriation" was, however, based on two assumptions: that the whole of the bulk cargo was to be carried to the same destination and that the rights to receive different parts of the cargo continued, on arrival at that destination, to be vested in different consignees. Where either of these assumptions was falsified, goods originally forming an undifferentiated part of a bulk shipment could become ascertained (and property in them could pass), before "final appropriation . . . at the port of destination",[16] by a process that has been described as "exhaustion"[17] or by one that may be called "consolidation."[18] There is ascertainment by "exhaustion" if, before the ship reaches her final destination, the rest of the bulk has been discharged at other ports, leaving on board only the quantity sold to the buyer at the final destination. The 1995 reforms have given statutory force to this principle by adding[19] two provisions to section 18, rule 5 of the Sale of Goods Act 1979.

The first of these new provisions is Rule 5(3), which deals with the situation "where there is a contract for the sale of a specified quantity of unascertained goods . . . forming part of a bulk which is identified either in the contract or by subsequent agreement between the parties." This would clearly cover a contract for the sale of a specified amount forming part of the cargo of a named ship; certain other problems relating to the scope of the new rule 5(3) in the context of overseas sales are discussed in paragraphs 18–294 and 18–295 below. The new rule goes on to provide that, when "the bulk is reduced to (or to less than) that [*i.e.* the specified] quantity, then, if the buyer . . . is the only buyer to whom goods are then due out of the bulk", two consequences follow: "(a) the "remaining goods" are to be taken as appropriated to that contract at the time when the bulk is

[12] *Re Wait* [1927] 1 Ch. 606.
[13] *Margarine Union GmbH v Cambay Prince SS Co. Ltd (The Wear Breeze)* [1969] 1 Q.B. 219 at pp.277–228; *cf. Wardar's (Import & Export) Co. Ltd v W Norwood & Sons Ltd* [1968] 2 Q.B. 663.
[14] Below, para.18–291.
[15] *Peter Cremer v Brinkers Groudstoffen NV* [1980] 2 Lloyd's Rep. 605 at p.608.
[16] *ibid*.
[17] *Karlshamns Oljefabriker v Eastport Navigation Co. (The Elafi)* [1981] 2 Lloyd's Rep. 679 at p.684.
[18] Below, at n.21.
[19] Sale of Goods (Amendments) Act 1995, s.1(2).

so reduced; and (b) the property in those goods then passes to that buyer." The second of these statements is, in the present context, slightly misleading since the whole of section 18 applies only (as the opening words of the section state) "unless a different intention appears". In overseas sales, the courts commonly infer from the terms of the contract and the surrounding circumstances an intention that property is not to pass until payment has been made or adequately assured[20]; and the mere fact that goods have been ascertained by exhaustion will not, it is submitted, displace that inference. It is significant that the new Rule 5(3)(a) refers to the goods being "appropriated" on exhaustion, rather than to their being (in the terminology of Rule 5(1)) *unconditionally* appropriated. It follows that the seller is contractually bound to deliver the "remaining goods" even though the passing of property is deferred until payment.

The second new provision is Rule 5(4), which extends the principle of ascertainment by exhaustion to the situation in which the buyer is entitled under separate contracts to undifferentiated parts of a bulk identified in accordance with Rule 5(3): *e.g.* where under each of two contracts he has bought 1,000 tons out of a bulk shipment of 5,000 tons. Exhaustion would occur when the bulk was reduced to 2,000 tons, provided that the buyer was then the only one to whom goods were due out of the shipment.

"Consolidation" is the converse of "exhaustion:" it takes place where a buyer of an undifferentiated part of a bulk cargo acquires the rest of the cargo from the person or persons previously entitled to it.[21] The two processes may be combined: *e.g.* if A and B each buy 1,000 tons out of a bulk cargo of 10,000 tons, the bulk is reduced to 2,000 tons or less by deliveries to other buyers and B then sells his 1,000 tons to A. The balance of the cargo is then ascertained so that property could have passed to A before the 1995 reforms and may now pass even though one or more of the conditions in which the relevant one of those reforms[22] operates are not satisfied.

Goods could, before the 1995 reforms become ascertained by "exhaustion" or "consolidation" only where the bulk itself was ascertained: there could be no such ascertainment where the contract left it open to the seller to fulfill his obligations under it by appropriating some shipment other than that in relation to which the "exhaustion" or "consolidation" was alleged to have occurred.[23] The new Rule 5(3) is similarly restricted by the requirement that the bulk must be identified in the contract or by subsequent agreement.[24]

The preceding discussion is based on the assumption that the whole of a bulk shipment is in the ownership of the seller and that parts of that bulk are sold, at least initially, to different buyers without any segregation of the parts so sold from that part of the bulk which remains in the ownership of the seller. This situation should be contrasted with *Re Stapylton Fletcher*

---

[20] Above, para.18–209; below, paras 19–098, 19–103, 20–070, 20–082.
[21] See *Karlshamns Oljefabriker v Eastport Navigation Co. (The Elafi)* [1981] 2 Lloyd's Rep. 679; *cf. Inglis v Stock* (1885) 10 App.Cas. 263.
[22] *i.e.* Sale of Goods Act 1979, s.20A, below, para.18–293.
[23] *Re London Wine Co. (Shippers)* [1986] P.C.C. 121 at 152; above, para.5–064.
[24] For a similar restriction on the scope of s.20A, see below, para.18–295.

Ltd[25] where wine was sold to various buyers and was on such sale removed from the seller's trading stock and separately held in bonded warehouses on behalf of the buyers as a group, but not so that any particular bottles or cases were marked with the names of individual buyers. It was held that the wine had become "ascertained" within section 16 and that property had passed to the buyers as tenants in common when the quantity bought by them was segregated from the wine which remained in the ownership of the seller. The transaction was regarded as having given rise to two separate, but related, contracts: one to sell, and another to store, the wine. Similar reasoning can in theory apply to an overseas sale: *e.g.* where undifferentiated parts of a bulk stored by the seller in a shore installation are sold to ten buyers and the whole quantity so sold is then removed from the shore installation and shipped in bulk by the seller under ten bills of lading covering the entire shipment and making the appropriate quantity deliverable to each buyer. In practice, however, the seller is likely to retain property in the goods shipped until he receives payment,[26] and his act of shipping the whole quantity will not amount to a segregation of goods destined for any one or more of the buyers from those parts of the whole remaining in his ownership until then; while conversely the buyers are unlikely to pay except in return for shipping documents. It is only where payment has been made before shipment that the reasoning of *Re Stapylton Fletcher Ltd* is likely to apply in the context of an overseas sale; but in such a case that reasoning would no longer be needed since the buyer would now be able to rely on section 20A of the Sale of Goods Act 1979, discussed (in relation to overseas sales) in paragraphs 18–293 to 18–299 below.[27] It is also unlikely that a c.i.f. sale would be regarded as constituting two contracts, *i.e.* one of sale and one for the carriage of the goods, particularly as one inclusive price covers both these elements.[28]

18–289 **Passing of property in undivided parts of a bulk shipment.** The 1995 reforms are based on a division (which probably antedates them) of contracts for the sale of undifferentiated parts of bulk shipments into two main groups.[29] The first consists of contracts in which the part sold is expressed as a fraction or percentage of the whole: *e.g.* half (or 50 per cent) of the cargo shipped in bulk on the *Peerless*. The second consists of contracts in which the part sold is expressed as a specified quantity out of the bulk: *e.g.* 500 tons out of the cargo of the *Peerless*, that cargo consisting of 1,000 tons. With regard to the first group, the 1995 reforms merely codify what was, or was believed to be, the previous law. With regard to the latter, those reforms make a fundamental change in the law: they make it possible for the buyer to acquire a proprietary interest in goods forming part of an

---

[25] [1994] 1 W.L.R. 1181.
[26] Above, para.18–186, and see above, n.20.
[27] Payment (which is a requirement for the operation of s.20A) is not a requirement of the reasoning of *Re Stapylton Fletcher Ltd*, above, though it was because payment had been made that the legal dispute in that case arose by reason of the insolvency of the seller.
[28] Below, para.19–001.
[29] For a possible overlap between the two groups, see below, para.18–294.

identified bulk, even though the goods remain unascertained. In either case, the rules which govern ascertainment of the amount sold by "exhaustion" or "consolidation",[30] and the consequent passing of property, can continue to apply.[31] When the goods are so ascertained the buyer can therefore acquire *sole* ownership in them, as opposed to the ownership in common which he can acquire under the 1995 reforms.[32]

Parts expressed as fractions of the bulk. Before the 1995 reforms, there 18–290
was some support for the view that, in the first of the examples given in paragraph 18–289 above, the contract was one for the sale of specific goods,[33] under which the buyer could acquire an undivided share in those goods. This view is confirmed by the 1995 reforms, in that "an undivided share in goods" is included in the definition of "goods" and "an undivided share, specified as a fraction or percentage, of goods identified and agreed on as aforesaid" (*i.e.* when the contract is made) is included in the definition of "specific goods."[34]

Property in the fraction or percentage (hereafter referred to as a fraction) bought can therefore pass when it is intended to pass, and in cases of overseas sales the most likely intention is that property will pass when payment is made, usually against shipping documents.[35] At this stage, the buyer will become owner in common with the seller, or with the other buyer or buyers of the remaining fraction or fractions of the cargo, of an undivided share in that cargo.[36] The buyer's ownership in common can presumably become sole ownership after the fraction or fractions which he has not bought are discharged from the ship so that only the fraction which he has bought remained on board. At this stage, he would become sole owner of that fraction by the process of "exhaustion", described in paragraph 18–288 above. It seems that for the purpose of these rules the goods must already have been shipped when the contract was made, so that a contract for the sale of half the cargo *to be* shipped in bulk on the *Peerless* would not be one for the sale of specific goods.[37] Property in such goods could certainly not pass before shipment, even if the parties had so intended and even if the goods had been paid for, since in such a case the goods sold would be simply unascertained (except where they were already ascertained in some other way: *e.g.* as "the cargo of the *Arpad*, to be transshipped into the *Peerless*" so as to constitute half the cargo of the latter). It seems that overseas sales of parts of shipments expressed as percentages or fractions are not common transactions, at least if the reported cases are any guide.

It is possible for a seller who is fraudulent, careless or forgetful to sell a number of fractions which together amount to more than the whole: *e.g.* to

---

[30] Above, para.18–288.
[31] This is implicit in the codification of the rules as to "exhaustion" in s.18 r.5(3) and (4), discussed in para.18–288 above.
[32] Below, paras 18–290, 18–293, 18–296.
[33] Above, paras 1–018, 1–116.
[34] Sale of Goods Act 1979, s.61(1) (definitions of "goods" and "specific goods").
[35] Above, para.18–209, below, paras 19–098, 19–103, 20–070 20–082.
[36] Law Com. No. 215, Scot. Law Com. No. 145, para.2.4 (1993).
[37] *cf. Kursell v Timber Operators and Contractors Ltd* [1927] 1 K.B. 298; above, para.5–022; and see below, para.18–294.

sell one quarter of a cargo to each of five buyers. The 1995 reforms may provide for this type of situation where *specified* but undifferentiated *quantities* are sold out of a single shipment: *e.g.* where five lots of 200 tons each are sold to different buyers out of an identified cargo of only 800 tons.[38] But these provisions do not apply where the quantities sold are expressed as *fractions*; and there seems to be no common law authority on how the cargo is to be allocated in such a case. One possibility would be to allocate the cargo in the chronological order of the various contracts; another would be to allocate it *pro rata*.[39] On balance, it seems probable that the first of these solutions would prevail[40] on the ground that when (in our example) the fifth quarter was sold the seller simply had nothing left to sell. It is arguable that this solution is liable to be displaced by the rules as to transfer of title discussed in Chapter 7, so that the buyer of the fifth quarter may obtain a good title under (for example) section 24 of the Sale of Goods Act 1979. It is, however, hard to see over which of the other four buyers the fifth would prevail, and even if this question could be satisfactorily answered it would merely push the problem back to the stage of having to decide how the remaining three quarters were to be allocated.

18–291 **Specified quantities forming part of bulk: before 1995.** Before the 1995 reforms, it was held that a contract for the sale of a specified quantity of goods forming an undifferentiated part of a larger bulk was one for the sale of unascertained goods; and it followed from section 16 of the Sale of Goods Act 1979 that property under such a contract could not pass until the goods were ascertained.[41] This was so even where the buyer had paid for the goods. Typically he would do so against tender of a delivery order; though occasionally he might do so against other documents, such as an invoice.[42] It made no difference for the present purpose whether the delivery order was issued by the seller to his own agent,[43] or by the ship or to the ship or (in the last case) whether it contained a promise by the carrier to deliver the specified quantity to the buyer, or whether the carrier had in some other way attorned to the buyer.[44] There was some support for the view that the position might be different where the buyer held a bill of lading. Thus in *Hayman v M'Lintock* Lord M'Laren said: "It is perfectly true that a delivery order is worthless as passing specific property until the goods have been ascertained, but that is exactly the distinction between the

---

[38] Sale of Goods Act 1979, s.20A(4); though this subsection is unlikely to be determinative in situations of the kind described in the text above: see above, para.5–121; *cf.* below, para.18–299.

[39] *cf.* below, paras 18–353, 18–354 (allocation of available supplies in case of supervening prohibition of export).

[40] *cf.* the discussion, in a different context, of an analogous problem in *Cox v Bankside* [1995] 2 Lloyd's Rep. 437 at pp.457, 467.

[41] *Re Wait* [1927] 1 Ch. 606.

[42] In *Re Wait*, above, payment was made against only an invoice.

[43] See *The Julia* [1949] A.C. 393.

[44] *Margarine Union GmbH v Cambay Prince SS Co. Ltd (The Wear Breeze)* [1969] 1 Q.B. 219; *Cremer v General Carriers SA* [1974] 1 W.L.R. 341; *Waren Import Gesellschaft Krohn & Co. v Internationale Graanhandel Thegra NV* [1975] 1 Lloyd's Rep. 146; *cf. Colin & Shields v W Weddel & Co.* [1952] 2 All E.R. 337.

effect of a delivery order for goods on shore and a bill of lading . . . We know that bills of lading are granted for portions of cargo in bulk which cannot, of course, be ascertained; and where bills of lading are granted[45] in these circumstances they must operate as a transfer of an unascertained quantity of goods on board the ship until delivery is made in terms of the obligation."[46] The actual decision, however, was that, while a delivery order given to a buyer in respect of an undifferentiated part of goods in a warehouse could not pass property under a contract of *sale*, a *pledge* of a bill of lading covering goods similarly situated did create a good security. If Lord M'Laren's dictum was intended to suggest that the transfer of a bill of lading covering such goods could pass the property under a contract of sale, it was, with respect, inconsistent with section 16 as it stood before the 1995 reforms[47]; and the dictum is best explained by reference to the context of a contract of pledge, to which section 16 does not apply. The point retains some significance since, if Lord M'Laren's dictum were interpreted as relating to sale, it would presumably have survived the 1995 reforms and be capable of applying even where some of the conditions specified in those reforms were not satisfied.

Payment in overseas sales is commonly made on tender of documents, so **18–292**
that it will often precede physical delivery of goods to the buyer. Where goods were shipped in bulk under a single bill of lading, and a specified quantity forming an undifferentiated part of the bulk was then sold and paid for against a delivery order or an invoice,[48] the position before the 1995 reforms was that, in the event of the seller's insolvency, the buyer was no more than an unsecured creditor.[49] He had no proprietary interest in the goods until they were ascertained,[50] either by being separated from the bulk or by "exhaustion" or by "consolidation"; nor does he normally have such an interest in the purchase price,[51] nor can he acquire such an interest in the price by rescinding the contract (the effect of rescission being simply to give him a personal claim to the return of an equivalent sum[52]); nor can he claim specific performance since, so long as the goods remain an undifferentiated part of the bulk, they are not "specific or ascertained" within section 52 of the Sale of Goods Act 1979.[53]

The fact that property in a specified quantity of goods forming an undifferentiated part of a bulk could not pass to the buyer also led to a number of further legal consequences. He could not recover damages from

---

[45] A misprint for "transferred"?
[46] 1906–1907 S.C. 936, 952.
[47] *cf. Peter Cremer v Brinkers Groudstoffen NV* [1980] 2 Lloyd's Rep. 605, where a c.i.f. buyer seems to have held a bill of lading covering an undifferentiated part of a bulk cargo (see p.606) and it was said at p.608 that property could pass only on "final appropriation of the quantities sold at the port of destination".
[48] Above, at n.42.
[49] *Re Wait* [1927] 1 Ch. 606.
[50] Sale of Goods Act 1979, s.16.
[51] *cf. Re Goldcorp Exchange Ltd* [1995] 1 A.C. 74, where the sale was not of goods forming part of an identified bulk but simply one of "generic goods" (p. 89).
[52] *ibid.*, p.102.
[53] Below, para.19–204.

the carrier in tort for negligently damaging the goods before he had become owner, even though the risk had already passed to him.[54] His failure to pay the price in accordance with the terms of the contract made him liable to an action for damages but not to an action for the price unless the contract provided for payment "on a day certain irrespective of delivery."[55] Two further legal consequences of the fact that property could not pass before ascertainment had been removed even before the 1995 reforms. First, this fact could prevent the buyer, as transferee of a bill of lading, from acquiring contractual rights against the carrier: this was the consequence of the "property gap" in the Bills of Lading Act 1855,[56] but under the Carriage of Goods by Sea Act 1992 the passing of property is no longer relevant to the acquisition of contractual rights by the transferee of the bill.[57] Secondly, the fact that property had not passed was relevant where the contract was one which obliged the seller to deliver the goods at the contractual destination and was frustrated before such delivery had been made. Since property had not passed and no delivery had been made, the buyer could then reclaim the price on the ground of total failure of consideration.[58] Under section 1(2)[59] of the Law Reform (Frustrated Contracts) Act 1943, such a claim can now be made even though the failure was not total (so that passing of property before delivery would not of itself bar the claim),[60] but the seller can exclude his liability to repay by an express or implied stipulation to that effect.[61]

18–293 **Sale of Goods Act 1979, section 20A.** The main object of the 1995 reforms was to improve the buyer's position where he had paid for a specified quantity of goods forming an undifferentiated part of an identified bulk and the seller then became insolvent before the goods for which the buyer had paid were ascertained.[62] The improvement was achieved by making section 16 of the Sale of Goods Act 1979 subject to a new section 20A, under which a buyer of a specified quantity of unascertained goods forming an undifferentiated part of an identified bulk can acquire a

---

[54] Above, para.18–149; in *Margarine Union GmbH v Cambay Prince SS Co. Ltd (The Wear Breeze)* [1969] 1 Q.B. 219 at p.223 and in *Leigh & Sillavan Ltd v Aliakmon Shipping Co. Ltd (The Aliakmon)* [1986] A.C. 785 at p.809, it was accepted that a "possessory title" would suffice to give the buyer a right of action in negligence; but such a title is unlikely to be in a buyer of an undifferentiated part of a bulk cargo.
[55] Sale of Goods Act 1979, s.49(2); below, paras 19–212, 20–129.
[56] Above, para.18–100.
[57] Above, para.18–101.
[58] *The Julia* [1949] A.C. 293.
[59] s.1(2) did not apply in *The Julia*, above, because the frustrating event took place before July 1, 1943: see s.2(1).
[60] *e.g.* where property has passed but there has been no delivery.
[61] Law Reform (Frustrated Contracts) Act 1943, s.2(3). Such a stipulation is not subject to the Unfair Contract Terms Act 1977, being "*authorised or* required by the express terms . . . of an enactment" within s.29(1)(a) of that Act; but it would be subject to the Draft Unfair Contract Terms Bill annexed to the Law Commissions' Report on *Unfair Terms in Contracts* (Law Com. No. 292, Scot. Law Com. No. 199 (2005), Sch.3 para 1(1)(a) of which excepts only contract terms "*required* by an enactment . . ."
[62] Law Com. No. 215, Scot. Law Com. No. 145 (1993), para.4.2; *cf. ibid.*, para.5.2.

proprietary interest in the bulk. Section 20A is discussed generally in Chapter 5; the discussion of it in the present Chapter is confined to the special problems to which it gives rise in the context of overseas sales.

Scope of the section. Section 20A applies only to contracts for the sale of a "specified quantity of unascertained goods". This phrase contains two requirements: the quantity must be specified and the goods must be unascertained. The structure of the Sale of Goods Act makes it impossible for goods at the same time to be specific and unascertained, so that a contract for the sale of specific goods cannot fall within section 20A. This point is potentially significant in the context of overseas sales since an undifferentiated part of a bulk cargo expressed as a fraction or percentage of the whole cargo can, after the 1995 reforms, fall within the statutory definition of specific goods.[63] For example, a contract for the sale of "half the cotton which has been shipped in bulk on the *Peerless*" would be one for the sale of specific goods and thus could not fall within section 20A: the passing of property in such goods would be governed by the law as it stood before 1995. On the other hand, a contract for the sale of "500 out of the 1,000 bales of cotton which have been shipped in bulk on the *Peerless*" would not be a contract for the sale of "specific goods" within the new statutory definition of that phrase, since the quantity sold is not expressed as a fraction or percentage of the whole; and such a case could fall within section 20A. 18–294

A contract for the sale of a fraction or percentage of a larger quantity of goods can, however, be one for the sale of specific goods only if the bulk of which the fraction or percentage forms part is itself specific, *i.e.* in the words of the statutory definition, if it is identified and agreed on when the contract is made.[64] It follows that a contract for the sale of "half the cotton to be shipped on the *Peerless* in October" would not be one for the sale of specific goods: in such a case, the receptacle may be identified and agreed upon when the contract is made, but the goods which form the bulk are not. The question then arises, whether such a contract could fall within section 20A. The wording of the section, as well as its legislative history, would seem to support a negative answer to this question. The words "a contract for the sale of a specified quantity" in section 20A(1) indicate that the quantity which is sold out of the bulk must be defined by, or at least discoverable from, the wording of the contract when the contract is made; and where the quantity contained in the bulk is itself unspecified, a fraction or percentage of it cannot be a "specified quantity". So far as the legislative history of the section is concerned, the Law Commissions evidently did not regard sales of fractions of a bulk as giving rise to a need for reform[65]; and Lord Mustill, when moving the Second Reading of what was to become the 1995 Act, said: "Section 20A(1) makes it clear that the contract must be one for the sale of a specified quantity of unascertained goods. That does not include a contract for the sale of a fraction or percentage of goods."[66] It

---

[63] Above, para.18–290.
[64] Sale of Goods Act 1979, s.61(1), definition of "specific goods".
[65] Law Com. No. 215, Scot. Law Com. No. 145 (1993), para.4.2; *cf.* para.5.2.
[66] (1995) H.L. Vol. 536, col. 1456.

follows from this statement that a contract for the sale of a fraction or percentage of a cargo which is not itself specific and which consists of an unspecified amount is governed by the pre–1995 law, so that the buyer, even if he pays in advance, cannot acquire any property in the subject-matter of the sale before the goods become ascertained. This might appear to be a gap in the 1995 legislative scheme, but there are two reasons why the gap is not a serious one. First, sales of this kind are rare[67]: the reported cases do not appear to provide a single example of the sale of a fraction or percentage of even a specific cargo, let alone one of a fraction or percentage of a cargo which is not specific. Secondly, a sale of this kind (if it were concluded) would involve a considerable element of risk-taking by the buyer, especially if he had agreed to pay a lump sum for an unknown quantity; and the risk of his being an unsecured creditor in respect of an advance payment is a comparatively minor one when set against the quantitative risk which, under such a contract, he has willingly accepted. It can, indeed, be argued that the Law Commissions' restriction of the scope of section 20A to specified quantities (as opposed to fractions or percentages) is based on the assumption that *all* sales of fractions or percentages can give the buyer a proprietary interest either under the law as it stood before the 1995 reforms, or (all the more readily) now that the point has been clarified by the extension of the statutory definition of "specific goods" so as to include fractions or percentages of a specific bulk[68]; and that the restriction ought not to prevail where the assumption on which it is based is false because the bulk is not itself specific. That, however, appears to be an argument about the legislative policy favoured by the Commissions, rather than one about the words used to implement the policy actually adopted, *i.e.* that of restricting section 20A to cases where the sale is of a "specified quantity".

A quantity may, of course, be "specified" without being expressed in so many words: *i.e.* by virtue of a formula which makes it possible to determine the precise amount sold. For example, it may be the custom of a particular trade to deal in "units" or "contracts" of (say) 50 tons, and a sale of "6 contracts [of such goods] out of the bulk cargo to be shipped on the *Peerless* in October" would be just as much a contract for the sale of a "specified quantity" as one for the sale of 300 tons of such goods out of that cargo. And just as the quantity may be specified by a process of multiplication, so it may be specified by a process of division. It follows that a contract for the sale of "half the cargo *of 600 tons* to be shipped on the *Peerless* in October" could fall within section 20A. In such a case, there is no more doubt about the quantity sold than there would be if the contract had been for "300 out of the 600 tons . . ."; and to give differing legal effects to the two contracts merely because the first expressed the quantity sold as a fraction of a specified amount would be drawing a distinction without a difference. A fraction or percentage of a bulk can therefore be a "specified quantity" where the quantity in the bulk is itself specified; but it is submitted that, where the quantity in the bulk is itself unspecified, then

[67] Law Com. No. 215, Scot. Law Com. No. 145 (1993), para.4.2.
[68] *ibid.*, para.5(2).

the quantity sold cannot become "specified" merely by being expressed as a fraction or percentage of that bulk.

Requirements of section 20A. The first condition, laid down in section 20A(1)(a), is that the goods "or some of them" must "form part of a bulk". The phrase "or some of them" is needed to cover the case in which the contract is for the sale, not only of goods forming part of the bulk but also of other goods: *e.g.* where it covers all the goods in one ship and 5,000 out of the 10,000 tons in another. "Bulk" means "a mass or collection of goods of the same kind which (a) is contained in a defined space or area; and (b) is such that any goods in the bulk are interchangeable with any other goods therein of the same number or quantity".[69] The definition fortunately avoids the difficult term "fungible goods".[70] The two characteristics of bulk goods are that they must be "of the same kind" as and "interchangeable with" other goods in the bulk. It is submitted that these characterisics depend on the intention of the parties and (in the absence of evidence of such intention) on commercial usage. Under these tests, goods may possess the required characteristics even though they are not, in a physical or objective sense, identical with each other: for example, a contract for the sale of 500 out of a cargo of 1,000 live sheep would be one for the sale of "part of a bulk".[71] The requirement that the mass or collection must be "contained in a defined space or area" gives rise to somewhat more difficulty. Obviously these words would cover the cargo of a named ship or some identified part of such a cargo such as goods shipped in a particular hold. In theory, "a defined space or area" could cover a much larger area than this but it is submitted that some limit must be placed on the phrase, so that it would not cover cases in which the contract merely defined the source from which the goods were to be taken by reference to some geographical area or to some country or region. For example, a contract for sale of "U.S. soyabeans to be shipped from the United States" would be one for the sale of generic goods rather than one for the sale of goods forming part of a bulk. 18–295

Secondly, section 20A(1)(a) requires the bulk to be "identified either in the contract or by subsequent agreement between the parties". These words most obviously cover such cases as that of a contract for the sale of 500 bales of cotton forming part of the 1,000 bales already shipped on the *Peerless*, and that of a contract for the sale of 500 bales of cotton in pursuance of which the seller, with the assent of the buyer, later shipped such goods as part of a larger bulk on the *Peerless*.[72] But it is less clear whether they would apply to the more common case in which identification

---

[69] Sale of Goods Act 1979, s.61(1), definition of "bulk", as inserted by Sale of Goods (Amendment) Act 1995, s.2(a).

[70] Above, paras 1–101, 1–120; Treitel, *Frustration and Force Majeure*, (2nd ed. 2004) paras 3–017, 3–018.

[71] *cf.* the illustration given by Lord Mustill when introducing the Second Reading of the Bill which became the Sale of Goods (Amendment) Act 1995: "100 of your sheep now on your farm at Blackacre": (1995) 563 H.L. Col. 1455.

[72] *cf.* the illustration given in Law Com. No. 215, Scot. Law Com. No. 145 para.4.5 (1993).

of the bulk takes place, not by "subsequent agreement between the parties" but simply by a notice (such as a notice of appropriation[73]) given by the seller. Where the contract requires the seller to give a notice of appropriation, it can be argued that the buyer has assented in advance to whatever appropriation the seller may make, so long as it satisfies the requirements of the contract; but even if this argument is accepted, the buyer's *advance* assent given in the contract can hardly be evidence of a "*subsequent* agreement". It is even harder to find evidence of subsequent agreement where the contract contains *no* provision as to notice of appropriation[74] and the seller, after the making of the contract, simply gives such a notice. So long as the notice is valid, the buyer has no choice in the matter: if the seller validly appropriates goods on the *Peerless I*, the buyer cannot object merely because he would have preferred goods on the *Peerless II*.[75] Such cases are hard to bring within the literal meaning of the words of section 20A(1)(a); it seems that they would be covered only if the courts were prepared to adopt a "purposive" construction of these words: *i.e.* by arguing that, if the section did not apply where the bulk was identified by a notice of appropriation, then the section would fail to deal with what is probably the single most significant mischief which it was intended to cure. So long as the bulk is "identified" in one of the ways here discussed, there is no further requirement in section 20A(1)(a) for it to have been in existence when the contract was made.[76] In this respect it differs from the statutory definition of specific goods, which does impose such a requirement. Thus a sale of "half the cotton to be shipped on the *Peerless*" would not be one of "specific goods" within the new definition of that expression[77]; but a sale of "500 out of the 1,000 bales of cotton to be shipped on the *Peerless*" could fall within section 20A.

The third condition which must be satisfied for section 20A to apply is stated in section 20A(1)(b): it is that the buyer must have "paid the price for some or all of the goods which are the subject of the contract and which form part of the bulk". This requirement follows from the main purpose of the 1995 reforms, which was to protect buyers in cases of this kind against the risk of the seller's insolvency. The effect of payment for only some of the goods is more fully considered in paragraph 18–297 below. Where the contract is for the sale of goods only some of which form part of the bulk, and the buyer pays part of the price due for all the goods sold, the question can arise, to which goods that payment is to be appropriated; such a question would presumably be settled by analogy to the rules stated in paragraph 9–046 above. Subject to this point, little difficulty arises in applying section 20A(1)(b) to payments in cash; but in overseas sales other methods of payment are commonly adopted: for example, payment may be by documentary credit[78] or by documentary bill.[79] Where the contract

---

[73] Below, paras 19–017 *et seq*.
[74] *cf.* below, para.19–023.
[75] *cf.* below, para.19–023.
[76] See, for example, the illustration given at n.72 above.
[77] Sale of Goods Act 1979, s.61(1), definition of "specific goods"; above, para.18–290.
[78] Below, Ch.23.
[79] Above, para.18–221.

provides for payment in one of these ways, property in ascertained goods can pass on acceptance of a draft by the bank or on acceptance of the bill of exchange by the buyer, even though that acceptance is subsequently dishonoured by non-payment[80]; but in the case of a contract for the sale of a specified quantity out of a bulk, if this method of payment is adopted, and fails, then it seems that the case would not be one in which "the buyer ha[d] paid the price" within section 20A(1)(b). The same may be literally true if payment under a documentary credit is made by the bank; but even if such a case is not literally one in which "the buyer has paid the price", it is clearly one in which payment had been made on his behalf, and such a payment should, it is submitted, suffice for the purpose of section 20A(1)(b).

Effects of the contract on property. The main legal effects, so far as property is concerned, of a contract for the sale of a specified quantity of unascertained goods forming part of an identified bulk are set out in section 20A(2). This provides that, where section 20A applies, then "(unless the parties agree otherwise) as soon as the conditions specified in paragraphs (a) and (b) of subsection (1) above[81] are met or at such later time as the parties may agree—(a) property in an undivided share in the bulk is transferred to the buyer, and (b) the buyer becomes an owner in common of the bulk." Thus if a contract is made for the sale of 500 out of the 1,000 bales of cotton shipped on the *Peerless* and the buyer pays for the 500 bales in full, he will acquire an undivided half[82] share in the 1,000 bales and become owner in common of the bulk; and in the event of the seller's insolvency he would, by reason of this proprietary interest, rank as a secured creditor. He would also, by virtue of that interest, be entitled to recover damages from the carrier in tort for negligently damaging the goods[83]: this could be a significant point if for some reason he had not acquired contractual rights against the carrier under the Carriage of Goods by Sea Act 1992[84] or otherwise. Under section 20A, the buyer's proprietary interest is acquired, not on the basis that the goods have become ascertained, but in spite of the fact that they remain unascertained. The section therefore does not affect the remedy of specific performance: this point is further discussed in paragraph 19–204 below. 18–296

If the buyer had not yet paid any part of the price, section 20A would not apply and the case would fall within section 16 as it stood before the 1995 reforms, so that no property could pass before ascertainment.[85] The fact that the buyer would thus be an unsecured creditor would be of relatively

---

[80] Above, paras 18–218, 18–223.
[81] These conditions are discussed in para.18–295, above.
[82] The size of the share is determined in accordance with s.20A(3), quoted in para.18–267, below. It is assumed at this stage that the full quantity of 1,000 tons has been shipped and that there is no shortage.
[83] He would have a "proprietary interest" for the purpose of the rule in *Leigh & Sillavan Ltd v Aliakmon Shipping Co. Ltd (The Aliakmon)* [1986] A.C. 785, above, para.18–149.
[84] *e.g.* if he had taken delivery under a delivery order not falling within the definition of a "ship's delivery order" given in Carriage of Goods by Sea Act 1992, s.1(4).
[85] Above, paras 18–287, 18–291.

little significance since he would not have parted with his money. On the other hand, he would not be entitled to recover damages from the carrier for negligently damaging the goods, even though the risk had passed to him so that he remained liable for the price.[86] His liability to the seller would, however, be in damages only: no property having passed (by reason of the non-payment) the action for the price would not be available against him unless the price was under the contract payable "on a day certain irrespective of delivery."[87] This requirement is unlikely to be satisfied in overseas sales, as these commonly provide for payment on tender of documents.[88]

18–297 **Part payment.** The situation which is likely to give rise to the greatest difficulty in the context of overseas sales is that in which the buyer has paid only part of the price: *e.g.* where he has bought 500 out of a cargo of 1,000 tons and has paid no more than half the agreed price of the 500 tons. In such a case, the general rule laid down in the 1995 reforms is that the buyer will (assuming that there was no shortage, *i.e.* that the cargo does indeed consist of 1,000 tons) acquire an undivided share in the bulk to the extent of one quarter of the bulk and become owner of the bulk in common. This follows from section 20A(3), by which the buyer's undivided share is "such share as the quantity of goods *paid for and* due to the buyer out of the bulk bears to the quantity of goods in the bulk". It makes no difference that the payment of half the price is not appropriated by the buyer to any particular quantity; for section 20A(6) provides that, for the purposes of section 20A, "payment of part of the price for any goods shall be treated as payment for a corresponding part of the goods". The application of this general rule in cases of overseas sales would, however, appear to give rise to an incongruous result. In such sales, the normal position is that property does not pass (because it is not intended to pass) until the price has been paid in full.[89] Thus if the buyer had bought an *entire* cargo and paid only half the price, or even three quarters of it, he would normally at this stage acquire no property at all; and it is at first sight hard to see why a buyer of an undifferentiated part of a bulk cargo should in this respect be in a better position than one who has bought the whole. One way of avoiding such incongruity is to rely on the fact that the general rule laid down in section 20A(2) (by which property in an undivided share is transferred to the buyer) can, by the express words of that provision, be excluded or varied by contrary agreement: the subsection applies only "unless the parties otherwise agree"; and the transfer of an undivided share may take place either on identification of the bulk and payment,[90] "or at such later time as the parties may agree". Where the sale is on c.i.f. or f.o.b. terms, an agreement to defer the transfer to the buyer of an undivided share could be inferred

[86] *The Aliakmon*, above, n.83.
[87] Sale of Goods Act 1979, s.49(2).
[88] Below, paras 19–212, 20–129.
[89] Above, para.18–209; below, paras 19–103, 20–082.
[90] *i.e.* (in the language of s.20A(2)) "as soon as the conditions specified in paragraph (a) and (b) of [s.20A(1)] are met."

from the well established rule that under such contracts property prima facie passes only on payment in full.[91]

The difficulty discussed in the preceding paragraph is (like so many legal difficulties) the product of a conflict of policies. The policy of the 1995 reforms is to protect the buyer against the risk of the insolvency of the seller; while the prima facie common law rule stated above[92] is based on the converse policy of protecting the seller against the risk of the insolvency of the buyer. The rule laid down by section 20A for cases of part payment can be regarded as a compromise between these two policies. In proportioning the buyer's proprietary interest to the amount of his payment, it satisfactorily protects each party against the risk of the other's insolvency. This statutory compromise applies in terms only where the specified quantity sold forms "*part of* a bulk"[93] and cannot therefore displace the common law rule which prima facie applies where the *whole* bulk is sold to the same buyer. It is, however, less clear whether the statutory compromise is likewise displaced by the common law rule that, where the sale is on c.i.f. or f.o.b. terms, property normally passes only on payment in full.[94] Section 20A(2) makes it clear that the statutory rule can be displaced by an express term of the contract; and it is submitted that it can equally well be displaced by an inference, based on the nature of the contract, as to the intention of the parties with regard to the passing of property. In the case of c.i.f. and f.o.b. contracts, the normal provision for payment against documents (or by documentary credit) is designed precisely to protect each party against the insolvency risks described above and is the basis for the rule that property under such contracts does not normally pass (because it is not intended to pass) until payment in full. It is submitted that, in the case of such contracts, this inference as to the intention of the parties as to the passing of property would, at least generally, be regarded as evidence of an agreement which, by virtue of section 20A(2), either excluded[95] the provisions of section 20A(3) with regard to the passing of property where the buyer[96] had paid only part of the price, or deferred[97] the passing of property until payment had been made in full.

Contrary agreement. Section 20A(2) applies "unless the parties agree otherwise" and provides that an undivided share in the goods is transferred once the bulk is identified and payment has been made "or at such *later* time as the parties may agree". It seems that the purpose of the first of these phrases is to enable the parties to exclude the operation of the subsection altogether (so that no property is transferred at all), while that of the second is to enable them to vary the time of the transfer of the 18–298

---

[91] *cf.* Law Com. No. 215, Scot. Law Com. No. 145, para.4.8 (1993): ". . . very often the parties would wish, and expect, the property to pass when the price was paid in exchange for documents."

[92] *i.e.* at nn. 89 and 91 above.

[93] Sale of Goods Act 1979, s.20A(1)(a).

[94] Above, at n.89.

[95] s.20A(2): "(unless the parties agree otherwise").

[96] *i.e.* one who had bought on c.i.f. or f.o.b. terms.

[97] s.20A(2): "or at such later time as the parties may agree".

undivided share to the buyer. But the second phrase deals only with their agreement that property is to pass at a time *later* than that specified in the subsection; while it is also possible for them to agree that it is to pass at an *earlier* time. For example, there may be a contract for the sale of 5,000 out of the cargo of 10,000 tons of oil to be shipped on a named tanker and the contract may provide that property and risk are to pass when the oil passes the tanker's inlet valve,[98] but that payment is to be made on tender of documents. It seems that effect could not be given under section 20A(2) to the contractual provision as to the passing of property, and that property in the 5,000 tons could only pass either (under the subsection) when the 5,000 tons were paid for, or (apart from the subsection) when the 5,000 tons became ascertained: *e.g.* by delivery or by "exhaustion".[99]

18–299 **Competing interests.** Before the 1995 reforms, the leading case which had established that property in an undifferentiated part of a bulk could not pass to the buyer was *Re Wait*.[1] In that case Wait had bought on c.i.f. terms 1,000 tons of wheat to be shipped on the *Challenger*. He then resold 500 tons of this cargo, also on c.i.f terms, to a sub-buyer, who paid the price of the 500 tons against only an invoice. Wait became bankrupt before the 500 tons were "ascertained", so that (as the law then stood) no property could have passed at this stage to the sub-buyer. Wait's trustee in bankruptcy claimed the whole cargo, and the sub-buyer, in order to obtain some security for the repayment of the price, argued that an equitable interest in, or lien on, the cargo had passed to him by virtue of the subsale. This argument was rejected[2] on the ground (stated by Atkin L.J.) that the recognition of such interests or liens could seriously inconvenience banks taking bills of lading for bulk shipments as security for advances.[3] Under the 1995 reforms, a similar difficulty would arise where a buyer of a specified quantity of unascertained goods forming an undifferentiated part of an identified bulk cargo had paid against an invoice and the seller had then pledged the bill of lading with a bank. The buyer would, if the conditions specified in section 20A[4] of the Sale of Goods Act 1979 were satisfied, acquire an undivided share in the cargo and become owner of it in common with the seller.[5] The 1995 reforms do to some extent deal with the difficulty raised by Atkin L.J. in *Re Wait*, in that the new section 20B(1) of the Sale of Goods Act 1979 provides that a person who has become owner in common of a bulk under section 20A shall be "deemed to have consented to . . . (b) any dealing with . . . goods in the bulk by any other person who is an owner in common of the bulk insofar as the goods fall

[98] For provisions of this kind in the oil trade, see above, para.18–209.
[99] Above, para.18–288.
[1] [1927] 1 Ch. 606.
[2] Disapproving dicta in *Hoare v Dresser* (1859) 7 H.L.C. 291 at pp.317–318: see [1927] 1 Ch. 606 at p.603; *Re London Wine Co. (Shipper)* [1986] P.C.C. 121 at p.152; *cf.* below, para.19–101.
[3] [1927] 1 Ch. 606 at p.640; in *Re Wait* the bill of lading had been "hypothecated" (above, para.18–234) to Wait's bank, but it was also in the possession of the bank: see *ibid*, at p.635. And see below, para.19–199.
[4] Above, para.18–295.
[5] s.20A(2).

within that owner's undivided share in the bulk at the time of the dealing . . ."[6] Under this provision, the buyer in our example would be deemed to have consented to the seller's dealing with the part of the cargo which had not been sold, so that a pledge of the bill of lading by the seller would be valid at least to this extent. Whether the pledge would also prevail over the buyer's proprietary interest in the part of the cargo sold to him would depend on the operation of the exceptions to the general rule that *nemo dat quod non habet*. For example, a bank which had taken a pledge from the seller of a bill of lading covering the whole bulk cargo would be able to rely on section 24 of the Sale of Goods Act 1979 if it had acted in good faith and without notice of the sale of part of the cargo. If the seller had disposed of *all* his interest in the bulk cargo to several buyers, each of an undifferentiated part, then the "deemed consent" provision of section 20B(1)(b) would not apply to a pledge of the bill of lading subsequently made by the seller since that provision applies only when the "dealing" is by one of the co-owners of the bulk, of whom the seller would no longer be one. Hence in such a case the pledgee would succeed only if he could rely on one of the exceptions to *nemo dat quod non habet*, such as section 24 of the 1979 Act.[7] The pledgee's position in this type of case is, in other words, similar to the position in which he would be, if the seller had sold the *whole* of the cargo to a single buyer who had paid against a document other than a bill of lading: this situation is more fully considered in Chapter 19.[8] The fact that undifferentiated parts were sold to several buyers is then relevant only to the issue of good faith: *e.g.* where the pledgee had notice of one or some of those sales but not of the other or others.

The foregoing discussion is concerned with the situation in which a single bill of lading is issued in respect of a bulk cargo and is then pledged after dealings have taken place with respect to specified quantitites forming undifferentiated parts of that cargo. It is also possible for more than one bill of lading to be issued in respect of such undifferentiated parts: *e.g.* for a shipper of 10,000 tons in bulk to take 10 bills of lading, each for an undifferentiated 1,000 tons out of the bulk. It will be recalled that one of the points decided in *Hayman v M'Lintock*[9] was that a pledge of such a bill of lading, covering an undifferentiated part of the bulk, could create a good security. The contract of pledge is not governed by the Sale of Goods Act 1979, so that section 16 of the Act would be no obstacle to the creation of such a security, nor would the requirements of section 20A have to be satisfied for this purpose. The reasoning of *Hayman v M'Lintock* is, however, suspect so far as it relates to sales[10] and it remains to be seen whether the decision, so far as it relates to pledges of bills of lading for undifferentiated parts of bulk cargoes, will be accepted in England.

A question of competing interests could also arise where a seller, after disposing of the whole of his interest in the bulk to two or more buyers, then purported to sell a further quantity out of the same bulk (or the whole

---

[6] s.20B(1)(b).
[7] *cf.* above, paras 5–121 to 5–123.
[8] Below, para.19–133.
[9] 1906–1907 S.C. 936; above, para.18–291.
[10] *ibid.*

of it) to a third buyer to whom he then transferred the bill of lading in performance of the contract of sale with him.[11] Since the seller would in such a case have disposed of all his interest in the bulk to the original buyers, the "deemed consent" provision of section 20B could not apply; but the later buyer could, like the pledgee in the example given above, prevail over the earlier ones if the bill of lading were transferred to him in circumstances in which the requirements of section 24 of the 1979 Act were satisfied.[12]

(c) *Risk*

18–300 **Loss or deterioration.** Risk in overseas sales is often separated from property, so that it would not be surprising if risk in part of a bulk shipment could pass to the buyer before property had passed: *e.g.* because the goods were not ascertained and the conditions laid down in Sale of Goods Act 1979, section 20A[13] had not been satisfied. Conversely, it is submitted that risk in such goods would not necessarily pass merely because the buyer had become owner in common of the bulk by virtue of that section. Risk may, indeed, pass even under a domestic sale of an undifferentiated part of a bulk in a store or warehouse. In *Sterns Ltd v Vickers Ltd*[14] there was a sale of 120,000 gallons of white oil out of a larger bulk of 200,000 gallons lying in tanks belonging to a wharf company. The seller obtained and delivered to the buyer a delivery warrant issued by the wharf company "For 120,000 gals. ex white oil in bulk deliverable to Messrs. Stern Ltd [the buyer] or assignees only against this warrant duly indorsed. This warrant is the only document issued as a legal symbol of the goods." It was held that risk had passed to the buyer even though the 120,000 gallons were not at the relevant time ascertained, so that, as the law then stood,[15] property could not pass to the buyer. Two reasons were given by the Court of Appeal for the decision, namely (1) that the seller had, by obtaining and handing over the delivery warrant, done all that he had undertaken to do[16]; and (2) that after the buyer had accepted the delivery warrant the seller had no further control over the goods and could do nothing to prevent their deterioration.[17] The decision was further said to turn on "special facts"[18] from which two further reasons for it (though not expressly given by the court) may be deduced. These are (3) that under the terms of the delivery warrant the buyer was to pay rent for storage,[19] so that he would have contractual remedies against the warehouseman for deterioration due to the latter's

---

[11] *cf.* above, paras 5–121 to 5–123.
[12] *cf.* above, para.18–290, discussing the sale of fractions amounting to more than the whole. Such a case is outside the scope of s.20B for the different reason that co-ownership by buyers of fractions does not arise "by virtue of section 20A", as is required by s.20B(1).
[13] Above, paras 18–293, 18–294.
[14] [1923] 1 K.B. 78 (see above, para.6–004).
[15] Above, para.18–287.
[16] [1923] 1 K.B. 78 at p.85.
[17] *ibid.*
[18] (1923) 92 L.J.K.B. 331 at p.335; 128 L.T. 402 at p.405.
[19] [1923] 1 K.B. 78 at pp.83, 85.

breach of contract; and (4) that by the terms of the warrant the warehouseman had attorned to the buyer.[20] The applicability of the rule in *Sterns Ltd v Vickers Ltd* to overseas sales depends to a considerable extent on which of these reasons is stressed; and a number of hypothetical situations will be considered in the following paragraphs to illustrate this point.

First, the example may be taken of goods which are sold on ordinary c.i.f. or f.o.b. terms and shipped in bulk under several bills of lading, each for an undifferentiated part of the bulk, one of which, covering the quantity sold, is transferred to the buyer. Assuming that freight has not been paid and that the buyer has taken or demanded delivery or made a claim under the bill of lading contract, the first three reasons for the decision in *Sterns Ltd v Vickers Ltd*[21] will apply in such a case; and it is submitted that the risk will pass without any attornment by the carrier. It is true that the rule by which transfers of bills of lading require no actual attornment[22] applies primarily to the transfer of possession and to the passing of property; but the result of the rule is that such attornment to the transferee of the bill does not in practice take place while the goods are in transit, so that failure so to attorn is not usually thought to produce any legal consequences. The argument so far presupposes that the bill of lading has been transferred before the loss or destruction of the goods; but the position appears to be the same even if the goods have already been lost or damaged at the time of the transfer. In *Inglis v Stock*[23] sugar was sold under f.o.b. contracts calling for payment in exchange for bills of lading. The sugar was shipped as an undifferentiated part of a larger bulk.[24] After the ship had been lost, bills of lading in respect of the quantity sold were tendered to the buyer, paid for, and transferred to him. The actual decision was that the buyer had an insurable interest in the goods. But it was also said in the Court of Appeal that the goods were at the buyer's risk from the time of shipment.[25] And in the House of Lords, Lord Blackburn similarly said that the seller "was entitled to recover the price in exchange for bills of lading, and it was no answer that the goods had perished at sea before the bill of lading was offered."[26] Thus it appears that risk in part of a bulk not only passes by transfer of the bill of lading in these cases, but passes at the normal time, that is, on shipment.[27] **18–301**

Secondly, the above example may be varied by supposing that part of the bulk is sold on c.i.f. terms which do not require the seller to tender a bill of lading, but give him the option of tendering a bill of lading or a delivery order and he elects to tender a delivery order[28]; or that the buyer in fact **18–302**

---

[20] See *ibid.*, at p.79 (*cf.* above, para.18–155).
[21] Above, para.18–300.
[22] Above, para.18–066.
[23] (1885) 10 App.Cas. 263.
[24] The rest of which, as it happened, was acquired by the same buyer: as to this, see above, para.18–288.
[25] (1884) 12 Q.B.D. 564 at pp.573, 577, 578.
[26] (1885) 10 App.Cas. 263 at p.273. As to the availability of the *action* for the price, see below, paras 19–211 *et seq.*, 20–126 *et seq.*
[27] Below, para.20–088. Or sometimes "as from" shipment where goods are shipped and then sold on c.i.f. terms: below, para.19–110.
[28] As in *The Julia* [1949] A.C. 293.

accepts a delivery order although he is not under the contract bound to do so.[29] The result in such a case might well depend on the form of delivery order tendered. If it was issued by the carrier to the buyer while the goods were still in the carrier's possession, all except the third of the reasons for the decision in *Sterns Ltd v. Vickers Ltd*[30] would apply; and even that third reason could apply if the order tendered were a "ship's delivery order" within the Carriage of Goods by Sea Act 1992, and if it identified the buyer as the person entitled to delivery of the goods.[31] It is submitted that risk would pass to the buyer where the order did give him a contractual remedy for deterioration against the carrier either by virtue of the 1992 Act or at common law under an implied contract.[32] Risk could pass even where the buyer had no such remedy against the carrier because no undertaking to him by the carrier was contained in the order. This was the position in *Margarine Union GmbH v Cambay Prince SS Co. Ltd (The Wear Breeze)*[33] where a c.i.f. seller tendered a delivery order, addressed by a sub-charterer to the chief officer of the ship, directing the latter to deliver the goods to the holder of the delivery order.[34] It was said that the risk of deterioration had passed; but it is not entirely clear from the relevant passages in the report whether the reference is to the normal rule that risk passes under a c.i.f. contract on *or as from* shipment.[35] Certainly counsel for the buyers argued that the risk had passed "retrospectively to the moment of shipment."[36] Roskill J. simply said that the risk passed "when the delivery orders were tendered to and accepted by the plaintiffs"[37] (*i.e.* the buyers). He did not in so many words say that the passing of risk was, in a case of this kind, to be given the normal retrospective effect. It is submitted that, once it is shown that risk in part of a bulk can pass by acceptance of a delivery order at all, it should be held to pass at the normal time for the type of contract in question, in accordance with the statements in *Inglis v Stock*.[38] The application in this situation of a different rule, as to the time of the passing of risk, would create uncertainty where the goods had deteriorated at some unknown point during the transit. The weakest case of all, from the seller's point of view, would be one in which the delivery order was addressed to the seller's own agent[39] while the goods were still in the possession of the carrier. In such a case the first of the reasons in *Sterns Ltd v Vickers Ltd*[40] might apply; but the second would not; nor would the "special facts" existing in that case be present. Dicta in *The Julia*[41] support

---

[29] As in *Margarine Union GmbH v Cambay Prince SS Co. Ltd (The Wear Breeze)* [1969] 1 Q.B. 219.
[30] Above, para.18–300.
[31] So that the buyer would acquire contractual rights against the carrier by virtue of s.2(1)(c) of the 1992 Act: above, para.18–175, and could incur contractual liabilities under s.3 of that Act, above, para.18–189.
[32] Above, para.18–140.
[33] [1969] 1 Q.B. 219.
[34] *ibid.*, at p.231.
[35] Below, para.19–110.
[36] [1969] 1 Q.B. 219 at p.234.
[37] *ibid.*, at pp.253–254; *cf.* p.252.
[38] Above, para.18–301.
[39] As in *The Julia* [1949] A.C. 293.
[40] Above, para.18–300.
[41] [1949] A.C. 293 at p.312.

the view that the risk would not pass merely because the buyer had accepted such a delivery order.

18–303 Thirdly, f.o.b. contracts may provide for payment against mate's receipts[42]; and a seller might make a bulk shipment for the purpose of satisfying several such contracts. If the buyer paid against the mate's receipt and obtained a bill of lading for an undifferentiated part of the cargo from the carrier, the reasoning of *Sterns Ltd v Vickers Ltd*[43] would clearly apply, so that the risk would pass at the latest on the issue of the bill of lading by the carrier to the buyer. It is submitted that the risk would also be on the buyer between shipment and the issue of the bill of lading. If risk can pass where the seller tenders and the buyer accepts an unattorned delivery order addressed by a sub-charterer to the chief officer of the ship,[44] it is hard to see why it should not pass where the seller tenders and the buyer accepts a mate's receipt; and if the tender is in accordance with the contract of sale, the risk should again be held to pass at the normal time (that is, on shipment) in accordance with the statements in *Inglis v Stock*.[45]

18–304 Fourthly, the contract of sale, though perhaps purporting to be a c.i.f. contract, is, on its true construction, a contract to deliver the goods at a named destination.[46] Here it is clear that risk does not pass simply by virtue of tender and acceptance of a delivery order addressed to the seller's own agent while the goods are still in the possession of the carrier. None of the reasons for the decision in *Sterns Ltd v Vickers Ltd*[47] would apply to such a case.[48] *A fortiori*, the mere sending of an invoice to the buyer will not pass the risk to him.[49] It is submitted that the same result would follow if the seller under such a contract tendered a delivery order addressed to the carrier and not attorned to, and hence containing no undertakings, by him[50]; but it is more doubtful whether risk would pass on attornment by the carrier. Probably it would not, as the seller would still have failed to do "all that [he] undertook to do",[51] *viz.* to deliver or to procure the delivery of the goods at the destination.

18–305 The submissions as to the passing of risk in parts of bulk shipments which have been put forward in the preceding paragraphs are, of course, subject to the overriding intention of the parties. Effect will clearly be given to express contractual provisions as to risk.[52] Similarly, the courts can give

---

42 Below, para.20–076.
43 Above, para.18–300.
44 As in *Margarine Union GmbH v Cambay Prince SS Co. Ltd (The Wear Breeze)* [1969] 1 Q.B. 219 (above, para.18–302).
45 Above, para.18–301.
46 See below, para.19–003.
47 Above, para.18–300.
48 *The Julia* [1949] A.C. 293 at pp.311–312.
49 See *Healy v Howlett & Sons* [1917] 1 K.B. 337.
50 Or perhaps if the seller were to hand over a bill of lading, though under such a contract this operates as a delivery order: see below, para.21–020.
51 *Sterns Ltd v Vickers Ltd* [1923] 1 K.B. 78 at p.85.
52 *e.g.* to the effect that the contract is (even though it is on c.i.f. terms) to be void should the goods not arrive, as in *Denbigh, Cowan & Co. v R Atcherley & Co.* (1921) 90 L.J.K.B. 836; *cf.* below, para.19–006.

effect to indications of intention not amounting to express agreements as to risk. Thus the fact that a buyer of part of a bulk receives not only a delivery order but also the benefit of insurance may be taken as an indication that the risk was intended to pass to him[53]; while the fact that no such benefit was transferred may indicate a contrary intention.[54]

18–306 **Deterioration or destruction of part of the goods.** There is little authority on the problems which may arise as between several buyers of undifferentiated parts of a bulk shipment where the bulk has deteriorated, or been destroyed, in part after the risk had passed to the buyers. One possible solution of these problems is to look for some act of "appropriation" (in the contractual sense[55]), allocating the deteriorated portion to a particular buyer.[56] Another possibility, illustrated by the terms of the contracts in some of the reported cases of this kind, is expressly to provide for *pro rata* division among the various buyers[57]; and a similar solution might be reached even without such express provision.[58] The *pro rata* solution derives some support from the fact that it is adopted by Sale of Goods Act 1979 section 20A(4) with regard to the passing of property in undifferentiated parts of a bulk which have been bought by several buyers. But that provision would not directly apply where one or more of the conditions required for the operation of section 20A were not satisfied: *e.g.* where the bulk had been identified otherwise than "in the contract or by subsequent agreement between the parties",[59] or where one or more of the buyers had not paid the price or any part of it.[60] *Pro rata* division would, in any event, apply only to the relative rights of the buyers *inter se* and on the assumption that the risk has passed to them. It has no application to their rights against the carrier. If the carrier made delivery to one buyer of the full quantity specified in his bill of lading or delivery order, he would probably not be liable to another buyer who in consequence failed to obtain

[53] As in *Margarine Union GmbH v Cambay Prince SS Co. Ltd (The Wear Breeze)* [1969] 1 Q.B. 219; see *ibid.*, at p.252.
[54] As in *The Julia* [1949] A.C. 293.
[55] Above, para.18–210.
[56] See *Karlshamns Oljefabriker v Eastport Navigation Corp. (The Elafi)* [1981] 2 Lloyd's Rep. 679 at p.686 (where "appropriation" is used both in its contractual and in its proprietary sense: see above, para.18–210).
[57] See *The Arpad* (1935) 51 Ll.L.R. 115 (for full references to this case, which was several times litigated, see below, para.19–100, n.9); *cf. Dewar & Webb v Joseph Rank Ltd* (1923) 13 Ll.L.R. 211; 14 Ll.L.R. 393.
[58] Apparently contrary dicta in *J Lauritzen AS v Wijsmuller BV (The Super Servant Two)* [1990] 1 Lloyd's Rep. 1 at p.10 refer to partial destruction as a possible ground of frustration, and are (it is submitted) inapplicable in the context of the present discussion, which is based on the assumption that risk has passed so that the seller is, for that reason, not liable in respect of the subsequent destruction of the goods. Nor can there be frustration by destruction which follows the passing of risk (see Treitel, *Frustration and Force Majeure*, 2nd ed. (2004), para.3–011), so that the general principle that frustration automatically brings about *total* discharge (*ibid.*, paras 15–003, 15–010) does not apply. *Cf.* below, paras 18–353, 18–354; and see Hudson, 31 M.L.R. 535 (1968), discussing similar problems in cases of frustration.
[59] s.20A(1)(a); for discussion of the question whether this covers identification by notice of appropriation, see above, para.18–295.
[60] s.20A(1)(b), above, para.18–295.

full delivery, unless of course the loss or deterioration was due to the carrier's breach of the contract of carriage. It would be unreasonable to impose a duty to apportion on the carrier, especially if (as would often be the case) the shortage did not become apparent until the last delivery was made. The remedy (if any) of the disappointed buyer should be against the one (or those) who had obtained delivery of more than his rateable share.

Buyer dealing as consumer. The parties to contracts for the sale of undifferentiated parts of bulk cargoes will commonly be corporate commodity traders, so that in cases of this kind the buyer will not normally deal as consumer. But the possibility of his doing so cannot be ruled out: he could, for example, so deal where he bought (say) 10 cases of wine for his domestic consumption and the wine formed part of a bulk shipment identified in the contract. Under section 20(4) of the Sale of Goods Act 1979, the wine would then "remain at the seller's risk" until it had been "delivered" to the buyer; and under section 32(4) delivery of it to the carrier would not be "delivery of the goods to the buyer" even if "in pursuance of the contract of sale the seller [was] authorised or required to send the goods to the buyer." In discussing the effects of these subsections in relation to overseas sales, we saw that many difficulties arose in determining when goods had been "delivered" within these subsections where the contract was on standard terms of overseas sales, such as c.i.f. or f.o.b. terms;[61] and that it was also an open question whether parties who had contracted on such terms could be regarded as having effectively excluded the two subsections by agreements.[62] Similar difficulties can arise where the goods form an undifferentiated part of a larger bulk. If in our example the sale had been on c.i.f. terms, the seller had given the buyer a notice appropriating to the contract 10 cases out of a larger quantity of wine shipped on the *Peerless* and then tendered documents relating to 10 cases so shipped to the buyer, the latter might well have to pay the price even though the whole shipment had been lost between the time of the appropriation and that of tender.[63] If the documents, tendered included a "negotiable" (*i.e.* transferable[64]) bill of lading there might, on transfer of the bill, be a "symbolical" or "constructive" delivery of goods to the buyer, and this might amount to a "delivery" within section 20(4)[65]; but this reasoning could not apply where (as is more likely in the case put) the seller tendered a delivery order, which would normally lack the quality of "negotiability".[66] In a case of the latter kind, the goods would often not be "delivered to the consumer"(so that the risk would remain on the seller) until the 10 cases were separated from the bulk; though the possibility of delivery being effected by the carrier's attornment to the buyer[67] (*e.g.* where the delivery order was a ship's delivery order) cannot be ruled out. In the 18–307

[61] See above, paras 18–259 to 18–263.
[62] See above, para.18–264.
[63] See below, para.19–080.
[64] See above, para.18–084.
[65] See above, para.18–261.
[66] See above, paras 18–193, 18–194.
[67] See Sale of Goods Act 1979, s.29(4).

present uncertain state of the law relating to the effects of sections 20(4) and 32(4) on overseas sales, their impact on the passing of risk where the goods sold on standard terms of such sales form an undifferentiated part of a bulk remains likewise uncertain. The outcome in cases of the present kind will depend partly on the immediately preceding discussion of risk in overseas sales of goods forming an undifferentiated part of a bulk[68] and partly on the discussion earlier in this chapter of risk in overseas sales where the buyer deals as consumer.[69]

7. EXPORT AND IMPORT LICENCES

18–308 **Introductory.** A number of problems arise where overseas sales are subject to export or import licensing requirements.[70] The first question is which party is bound, under the contract, to obtain the licence; the second is as to the standard of diligence which that party is required to exercise for this purpose; and the third concerns the effect of failure to obtain a licence. In this discussion it will initially be assumed that the licensing requirement exists at the time of the contract. The problems which arise where it is imposed after the making, but before the performance, of the contract will be discussed later in this chapter.[71]

(a) *Incidence of Duty*

18–309 **Whether licence to be obtained by buyer or seller.** The question which party is under a duty to obtain or apply for an export or import licence depends in the first instance on any express provision on the point in the contract,[72] or in any relevant legislation.[73] If the contract expressly puts the

---

[68] See above, paras 18–300 to 18–306.
[69] See above, paras 18–259 to 18–264.
[70] In English law, such licensing requirements exist by or under statute: see, for example, the Import of Goods (Control) Order 1954 (SI 1954/23) and the Export of Goods (Control) Order 1978 (SI 1978/796), both made under the Import, Export and Customs Powers (Defence) Act 1939. These Orders are voluminous and subject to frequent amendment, so that little purpose would be served by an attempt, in a work such as the present, to summarise their scope and effect. See also the Strategic Goods (Control) Order 1967 (SI 1967/983) made under the Emergency Laws (Re-enactment and Repeals) Act 1964.
[71] Below, paras 18–333—18–358.
[72] See, for example, *Austin, Baldwin & Co. v Wilfred Turner & Co. Ltd* (1920) 36 T.L.R. 769; *Pavia & Co. v Thurmann-Nielsen* [1952] 2 Q.B. 84; *C Czarnikow Ltd v Centrala Handlu Zagranicznego "Rolimpex"* [1979] A.C. 351; *Overseas Buyers Ltd v Granadex SA* [1980] 2 Lloyd's Rep. 608; *Atisa SA v Aztec AG* [1983] 2 Lloyd's Rep. 579; *Bangladesh Export Import Co. Ltd v Sucden Kerry SA* [1995] 1 Lloyd's Rep. 1, where it is tentatively suggested at p.6 that the effect of the relevant clause on its true construction was merely to relieve the seller from the duty, rather than to impose it on the buyer. The point may be that any duty of the buyer's had been *performed* by his obtaining a licence, which was later withdrawn: see below, para.18–322. *Semble* the duty of the buyer to obtain an export licence in *Maine Spinning Co. v Sutcliffe & Co.* (1917) 87 L.J.K.B. 382 and of the seller to obtain customs clearance in *Agricultores Federados Argentinos v Ampro SA* [1965] 2 Lloyd's Rep. 757 also arose under the express terms of the contracts; though this is not wholly clear from the reports.
[73] *Mitchell Cotts & Co. (Middle East) Ltd v Hairco Ltd* [1943] 2 All E.R. 552 at p.555.

duty on one of the parties, he will be liable in damages if he fails to perform it[74]; even if he has in the normal course of business left the necessary arrangements to the other party.[75] Where the contract simply provides for delivery "as soon as export licence in order" and does not specify who is to take steps to obtain it, the question whether such steps are to be taken by the buyer or by the seller depends on the same factors which apply where the contract contains no express provision as to licence at all.[76] In such cases there is no general rule, nor any set of rules putting the burden of obtaining a licence on one party or the other, according to the particular type of overseas sale involved. The law is now settled in this sense though, as will appear from the cases discussed in the following paragraph, there was formerly some doubt on the point.

In *H O Brandt & Co. v H N Morris & Co.*[77] aniline oil intended for export to the United States was sold f.o.b. Manchester. At the time of the sale aniline oil could be exported only under licence and no such licence was obtained. The buyers' claim for damages was rejected on the ground that the duty of obtaining an export licence lay on the buyers themselves and not on the sellers. Scrutton L.J. based this view in part on the duty of the buyers to provide "an effective ship, that is to say a ship which can legally carry the goods."[78] This might suggest that, as a general rule, under f.o.b. contracts export licences had to be obtained by the buyers. But Scrutton L.J. restricted his remarks to the duty of the buyers "in *this* f.o.b. contract"[79]; and Lord Reading C.J. stressed that "the facts which it was necessary to state when a licence had to be applied for were known to them [the buyers] and not to the defendants [the sellers]."[80] This aspect of the case was emphasised in *A V Pound & Co. Ltd v M W Hardy & Co. Inc.*[81] where turpentine was sold f.a.s. buyers' tanker at Lisbon. The buyers intended to ship the turpentine to an East German port and the sellers knew this. By Portuguese law turpentine could be exported only under licence and such licences could be obtained only by persons registered for this purpose by the Portuguese authorities. The buyers and the sellers were not, while the sellers' supplier was, so registered, but his application for a licence to export the turpentine to East Germany was refused. It was held that the buyers were not liable in damages as in these circumstances it was not their duty to apply for a Portuguese export licence. The House of Lords stressed that the sellers knew that the buyers wanted the goods for export to East Germany, and that only the sellers' supplier (whose identity had been deliberately withheld from the buyers) was in a position to apply for a 18–310

---

[74] *e.g. Austin, Baldwin & Co. v Wilfred Turner & Co. Ltd*, above.
[75] *Maine Spinning Co. v Sutcliffe & Co.*, above; but such conduct might be evidence of waiver by the other party.
[76] See *Peter Cassidy Seed Co. Ltd v Osuustukkukauppa Ltd* [1957] 1 W.L.R. 273, below, para.18–310 (where only the standard of duty was in issue: see below, para.18–313).
[77] [1917] 2 K.B. 784.
[78] *ibid.*, at p.798; below, para.20–043.
[79] [1917] 2 K.B. 789 at p.798 (italics supplied).
[80] *ibid.*, at p.795.
[81] [1956] A.C. 588.

licence. *H O Brandt & Co. v H N Morris & Co.*[82] did not lay down a general rule that under an f.o.b. or f.a.s. contract it was always the buyer who had to apply for an export licence. The duty in that case was on the buyer because he alone knew the full facts as to the destination of the goods, so that for practical purposes only he, and not the seller, was in a position to apply for the licence. The duty of applying for a licence would similarly be on the buyer where the sale was f.o.b. a British port but it was not known to the seller whether the goods were intended for export or for shipment coastwise to another British port.[83] On the other hand, "There might be a licence system based not on destination but on the proportion of a manufacturer's product to be sent out of the country. In such a case the facts necessary to be stated would be known to the producer and not to the buyer. It would seem obvious that in such a case it would be for the seller to apply."[84] In the later *Peter Cassidy* case, ant eggs were sold f.o.b. Helsinki to an English buyer by a Finnish seller, and the seller was held liable in damages on account of failure to obtain a Finnish export licence. Such licences were granted only to members of the Finnish Ant Egg Exporters' Association, and the seller, though not a member of the Association, had nevertheless assured the buyer that the grant of a licence was "merely a formality". It was conceded in these circumstances that the duty of applying for a licence was on the seller; and this concession was approved by Devlin J.[85] It has further been held that an f.o.b. seller who intends to appropriate to the contract goods originating from a country other than that of shipment is not excused by his inability to obtain a licence in the country of origin if the origin of the goods was not a term of the contract, nor within the contemplation of both parties, but was a matter of complete indifference to the buyer.[86] If any general statement can be based on this collection of cases, it is that the courts put the duty of obtaining a licence on buyer or seller according to which of them, in all the circumstances, is the better placed to obtain it.

18–311 Where goods are sold on c.i.f. or c. & f. terms by a seller in one country to a buyer in another, the duty of obtaining an export licence will often be on the seller while that of obtaining an import licence will be on the buyer.[87] This follows from the cases discussed in the preceding paragraph, as each party will normally be in a better position than the other to know and satisfy the legal requirements in his own country.[88] But there does not appear to be any absolute rule of law to this effect, and it is submitted that the position again depends in each case on the facts known to the parties, their opportunities for obtaining a licence, and the risks consciously

[82] [1917] 2 K.B. 784.
[83] *D. McMaster & Co. v Cox, McEwen & Co.*, 1921 S.C.(H.L.) 24.
[84] *A V Pound & Co. Ltd v M W Hardy & Co. Inc.* [1956] A.C. 588 at p.611.
[85] *Peter Cassidy Seed Co. Ltd v Osuustukkukauppa Ltd* [1957] 1 W.L.R. 273 at p.277. The actual decision turned on another point: see para.18–313, below.
[86] *Beves & Co. Ltd v Forkas* [1953] 1 Lloyd's Rep. 103.
[87] *e.g. Congimex Companhia Geral, etc. SARL v Tradax Export SA* [1983] 1 Lloyd's Rep. 250.
[88] *cf. K C Sethia Ltd v Partabmull Rameshwar* [1950] 1 All E.R. 51 (quota); affirmed [1951] 2 All E.R. 352n; [1951] 2 Lloyd's Rep. 89.

undertaken by them. Thus where goods are sold on c.i.f. terms by a seller to a buyer in the same country for export to another country it is perfectly possible for the buyer alone to know all the facts relevant to an application for an export licence, in which case it would be up to him to obtain the licence. Or the buyer might at the time of contracting consciously take the risk that a licence might not be granted, in which case he would not be entitled to damages if the licence was refused.[89] Conversely, it may be the c.i.f. seller's duty to obtain an import licence.[90] Dicta in one case suggest that a c.i.f. buyer is necessarily under the duty to obtain an import licence as soon as the bill of lading is transferred so as to pass the property to him[91]; and in another case it is, conversely, stated that the buyer is not under any such duty until tender of documents.[92] But it is submitted that such statements are not rigid rules of law and that they must be read subject to the principles laid down in *A V Pound & Co. Ltd v M W Hardy & Co. Inc.*[93] Those principles seem to be of general application, and not to be restricted to f.o.b. and f.a.s. contracts. It should be added that many of the cases on c.i.f. and c. & f. contracts concern the standard of duty (*i.e.* whether it is an absolute duty or only one to use due diligence)[94] and simply assume its incidence.[95]

Excuses for failure to obtain licence. The inability of one party to obtain an export or import licence, may be excused if it is due to the other contracting party's failure to co-operate with him in this respect. In *Kyprianou v Cyprus Textiles Ltd*[96] a seller of cottonseed to be shipped "from Syrian and/or Lebanese ports" intended, as the buyer knew, to ship from Syria. He was unable to get a Syrian export licence within the shipment period because the buyer had not provided him with a certificate, required by the Syrian authorities, that the goods would not be resold so as to reach Israel. It was held that the buyer was not entitled to damages as he had failed to perform his duty to cooperate[97] with the seller in getting the export licence. 18–312

[89] This was the view of Bailhache J. in *Re Anglo-Russian Merchant Traders and John Batt (London) Ltd* [1917] 2 K.B. 679 at p.682; his decision was reversed by the Court of Appeal *ibid.* on another ground: below, para.18–314.
[90] *J W Taylor & Co. v Landauer & Co.* [1940] 4 All E.R. 335.
[91] *Mitchell, Cotts & Co. (Middle East) Ltd v Hairco Ltd* [1943] 2 All E.R. 552 at pp.555, 556.
[92] *J W Taylor & Co. v Landauer & Co.*, above, at p.341.
[93] [1956] A.C. 588 (above, para.18–310).
[94] Below, paras 18–313 *et seq.*
[95] *e.g. Re Anglo-Russian Merchant Traders and John Batt & Co. (London) Ltd* [1917] 2 K.B. 679 as explained in *Partabmull Rameshwar v K C Sethia Ltd* [1950] 1 All E.R. 51 and [1951] 2 Lloyd's Rep. 89 (where the decision of the House of Lords is most fully reported); *Mitchell, Cotts & Co. (Middle East) Ltd v Hairco Ltd* [1943] 2 All E.R. 552.
[96] [1958] 2 Lloyd's Rep. 60; *cf. SCCMO (London) Ltd v Soc. Générale de Compensation* [1956] 1 Lloyd's Rep. 290.
[97] Contrast *North Sea Energy Holdings NV v Petroleum Authority of Thailand* [1999] 2 Lloyd's Rep. 483: f.o.b. buyer of oil not bound to supply seller with list of discharge ports so as to enable the seller to obtain a "confirmation" that the oil could be "supplied without restriction" to the buyer in the country of destination.

A party's failure to obtain a licence will also be excused if before such failure the other party to the contract has wrongfully repudiated it.[98] If the party failing to obtain the licence accepts that repudiation so as to rescind the contract, that party is entitled to damages, without having to show that he could have obtained a licence, had the other party not previously been guilty of the wrongful repudiation of the contract.[99]

(b) *Standard of Duty*

18–313 **Introductory.** Once it is determined which party is to obtain the licence, the next question is whether his duty in that respect is absolute or one of reasonable diligence only. This again depends in the first instance on any relevant terms in the contract. No doubt a guarantee by one party to obtain an export or import licence[1] would be held to impose an absolute duty. Such a duty was also held to arise where the contract provided for shipment "as soon as export licence in order", and the seller assured the buyer that the obtaining of the licence was "merely a formality".[2] On the other hand it is equally possible for a contract expressly to impose less stringent duties such as duties to use reasonable efforts or best endeavours.[3] The difficult cases are those in which the contract fails to specify the standard of duty. It may so fail either because it makes no reference to the need to obtain the licence or because, while making such a reference, it does not state whether the duty to obtain the licence is to be a duty of diligence or an absolute one. In the first of these types of cases, the question is whether any, and if so what, term can be implied, specifying the standard of duty; in the second, the standard of duty turns on the construction of the term which refers to the requirement of obtaining the licence.

(i) *Implication of a Term*

18–314 **General rule: duty of diligence.** Where the contract contains no express reference to the need for an export or import licence, the general or prima facie rule is that the party who is obliged to take steps to get any necessary

---

[98] *D H Bain v Field & Co.* (1920) 5 Ll.L.R. 16.

[99] On the principle of *British and Beningtons Ltd v N W Cachar Tea Co.* [1923] A.C. 48; see below, para.19–161.

[1] *Pavia & Co. v Thurmann-Nielsen* [1952] 2 Q.B. 84; [1951] W.N. 533; [1951] 2 All E.R. 866 at p.867; [1952] 1 Lloyd's Rep. 153; this point does not appear in the report in [1952] 2 Q.B. 84; *cf. Austin Baldwin & Co. v Wilfred Turner & Co. Ltd* (1920) 36 T.L.R. 769; *Thomas P. Gonzalez Corp. v Müller's Mühle, Müller GmbH* [1980] 1 Lloyd's Rep. 445 at p.449. And see *BS & N Ltd (BVI) v Micado Shipping Ltd (Malta) (The Seaflower)* [2000] 2 Lloyd's Rep. 37 and *id. (No. 2)* [2001] 1 Lloyd's Rep. 341, a charterparty case in which the duty imposed on a shipowner to obtain a third party's approval by a "guarantee" to this effect was evidently assumed to be strict; the actual points decided were (i) that failure to obtain the guarantee did not amount to a repudiation, but (ii) that it did amount to a breach of condition and so justified rescission by the charterer.

[2] *Peter Cassidy Seed Co. Ltd v Osuustukkukauppa Ltd* [1957] 1 W.L.R. 273.

[3] *e.g. Charles H Windschuegl Ltd v Alexander Pickering & Co. Ltd* (1950) 84 Ll.L.R. 89.

licence is in this respect under a duty to do no more than to exercise due diligence or to make reasonable efforts. This point was settled in *Re Anglo-Russian Merchant Traders and John Batt & Co. (London) Ltd*,[4] where 50 tons of aluminium were sold c. & f. Vladivostock. Buyer and seller were resident in England; both knew that aluminium could not be exported without licence. They also contemplated that the aluminium would be shipped from England, though a shipment from America would have been in accordance with the contract. The sellers applied for an export licence and it was refused. Before the end of the shipment period an order further forbade all dealing in aluminium (whether in the United Kingdom or not) without permit. The sellers never applied for such a permit, but it was found as a fact that, if such an application had been made, it would have been refused. The alternative of supplying American aluminium was therefore barred; and it was held that the sellers were not liable in damages for failing to ship. The contract contained no express reference to the need to get an export licence; and the only term which the court was prepared to imply was that the sellers should use their best endeavours[5] or reasonable diligence[6] to this end. It is hard to find in the judgments the exact reason why the court defined the seller's obligation to obtain a licence in this way; but no doubt the fact that both parties were at the time of contracting fully aware of the licensing requirement was an important factor in the decision. The general rule has also been explained on the ground that, where the contract makes no reference to the need to get a licence, the court will "only imply the least onerous obligation to give the contract business efficacy".[7]

General rule displaced by other terms of the contract. The general rule stated in paragraph 18–314 above may be displaced by other terms of the contract. Thus in one case[8] a contract contained elaborate provisions protecting the *seller* in the event of *force majeure* or prohibition of export, but contained no similar provisions protecting the *buyer* in case of prohibition of import. The court refused to imply a term that the buyer's duty to obtain an import licence was one of diligence and held that duty to be an absolute one. 18–315

General rule displaced by extraneous factors. The general rule, stated in paragraph 18–314 above may also be displaced by factors extraneous to the contract. In *K C Sethia (1944) Ltd v Partabmull Rameshwar*[9] c.i.f. sellers of 18–316

[4] [1917] 2 K.B. 679.
[5] *ibid.*, at p.686.
[6] *ibid.*, at p.689; in *A V Pound & Co. Ltd v M W Hardy & Co. Inc.* [1956] A.C. 588 (above, para.18–310) Lord Kilmuir said (at p.604) that it was up to the sellers to "do their best to obtain a licence" while Lord Simonds said (at p.606) that prima facie they had "unreservedly undertaken to deliver the goods f.a.s." Lord Somervell (at p.612) mentions both possible standards but does not decide between them. The standard of the seller's obligation was not in issue in that case.
[7] *Pagnan SpA v Tradax Ocean Transportation SA* [1987] 3 All E.R. 565 at p.572; *cf.*, in another context, *Gamerco SA v ICM/Fair Warning (Agency) Ltd* [1995] 1 W.L.R. 1226 at p.1231.
[8] *Congimex Companhia Geral, etc. v Tradax Export SA* [1981] 2 Lloyd's Rep. 687 at p.693, affirmed [1983] 1 Lloyd's Rep. 250 at p.254.
[9] [1950] 1 All E.R. 51; affirmed [1951] 2 All E.R. 352n; [1951] 2 Lloyd's Rep. 89.

Indian jute to Italian buyers failed to obtain an Indian "quota" for export to Italy. It was held that no term could be implied to relieve the sellers from their obligation to ship, and that they were liable in damages for failing to do so. The *Anglo-Russian Merchant Traders* case[10] was distinguished on a number of grounds. In that case it was agreed that *some* term must be implied to qualify the seller's duty, while there was no such agreement here. There was, moreover, a difference between a licensing and quota requirement: under a quota system it was possible to deal lawfully within the quota, while under a licensing requirement all dealings without licence were unlawful; and this made it "easy to imply a term to the effect that the transaction is subject to the necessary licence being obtained, for otherwise it would be manifest to both parties[11] that the transaction could not be carried out at all."[12] The final, and perhaps the most important, point was that in the *Anglo-Russian Merchant Traders* case the licensing system was, at the time of contract, a matter equally within the knowledge of both parties, while in the *KC Sethia* case the facts relevant to the working of the quota system were within the knowledge only of the sellers; they would (but the buyers did not) know the size of their quota, how much of it had been used up and other facts relevant to its operation. Thus the knowledge of the parties can determine not only the incidence[13] but also the stringency of the duties to obtain export or import licences or similar permits.

(ii) *Construction*

18–317 **Construction of term referring to the duty.** No difficulty arises in cases of the kind described in paragraph 18–313 above, in which one of the terms of the contract specifies the standard of duty; but where such a term merely refers to the need or duty to get a licence, without specifying the standard of duty, then that standard depends on the construction of the relevant term. Thus in the *Peter Cassidy*[14] case (the facts of which are stated in para. 18–310 above) the seller's assurance that the obtaining of the duty was "merely a formality" was held to affect not only the incidence, but also the standard, of the duty: its effect was to impose an absolute duty on the seller. The same conclusion was reached in *Pagnan SpA v Tradax Ocean Transportation SA*,[15] where a special typed condition in a contract for the sale of Thailand tapioca pellets provided "Sellers to provide for export certificate enabling buyers to obtain import licence into EEC . . ." As the clause did not in terms qualify the sellers' obligation or refer to due diligence, it was said to impose "an absolute obligation on the sellers to provide for the export certificate, save in so far as any other clause of the contract might modify the sellers' obligation or relieve him from the consequences of

[10] Above, para.18–314; see also the discussion of this case in *Walton* (*Grain and Shipping*) *Ltd v British Italian Shipping Co.* [1959] 1 Lloyd's Rep. 223 at pp.236–7; and *Coloniale Import-Export v Loumidis Sons* [1978] 2 Lloyd's Rep. 560 at p.562.
[11] Since both knew of the licensing requirements at the time of the contract.
[12] [1950] 1 All E.R. 51 at p.58.
[13] Above, paras 18–310, 18–311.
[14] [1957] 1 W.L.R. 273.
[15] [1987] 3 All E.R. 565.

breach."[16] In fact the sellers were so relieved by a prohibition of export clause since the cause of their failure to obtain the certificate was an event covered by that clause, *i.e.* a prohibition imposed by the Thai authorities. But they would have been liable if the cause of that failure had been simply a refusal on the part of those authorities to issue this particular certificate, without imposing any general prohibition of export.

In the *Pagnan* case, the prohibition clause provided the seller with a specific excuse, without otherwise directly affecting the standard of his duty. But in determining what standard is imposed by terms which specify the incidence of the duty, the courts will have regard to the contract as a whole and may therefore take into account prohibition and *force majeure* clauses in the contract. In one case, for example, the contract imposed a duty on the seller to obtain an export, and on the buyer to obtain an import, licence, and also contained a *force majeure* clause. The duty to obtain such licences seems to have been regarded as absolute,[17] since the *force majeure* clause expressly provided that failure to obtain the relevant licence should not be a ground for invoking that clause. But in another case[18] the *force majeure* clause contained no such provision, and it was held that the duty to obtain the licence (imposed by another term of the contract) was one of reasonable diligence only. The cases may be distinguished on the ground that the wording of the *force majeure* clause in the first case indicated an intention to impose absolute duties, while in the second the *force majeure* clause contained no such indication. In the absence of such an indication, the courts approach the question of construction (no less than that of implication) with an inclination towards applying the "less burdensome" standard where "both are equally open for selection".[19]

Contract "subject to licence". There may be no indication, either in the express terms of the contract,[20] or in the surrounding circumstances,[21] of the standard of duty incumbent on the party who is to obtain the licence, but the contract may be made expressly "subject to licence". Such words do not (like the words "subject to contract") prevent the formation of a binding contract. Their effect is "that there is introduced into the contract a condition that a licence must be obtained and that neither party will be liable to perform the duties under the contract unless the licence is obtained."[22] Where such words occur, the party who is (either by the express terms of the contract or under the rules stated in paragraphs 18–309 to 18–311 above) bound to apply for or obtain a licence must use reasonable endeavours to obtain the licence[23]; he obviously does not 18–318

[16] *ibid.*, at p.572.

[17] *C Czarnikow Ltd v Centrala Handlu Zagranicznego "Rolimpex"* [1979] A.C. 351 at p.371; *cf. Atisa SA v Aztec AG* [1983] 2 Lloyd's Rep. 579.

[18] *Coloniale Import-Export v Loumidis Sons* [1978] 2 Lloyd's Rep. 560 at p.562.

[19] *Pagnan SpA v Tradax Ocean Transportation SA* [1986] 2 Lloyd's Rep. 646 at p.652, affirmed [1987] 3 All E.R. 565.

[20] As in the *Pagnan* case [1987] 3 All E.R. 565, above, para.18–317.

[21] As in the *Peter Cassidy* case [1957] 1 W.L.R. 273, above, paras 18–310, 18–317.

[22] *Charles H Windschuegl Ltd v Alexander Pickering & Co. Ltd* (1950) 84 Ll.L.R. 89 at p.92.

[23] *ibid.*, at p.93; *Brauer & Co. (Great Britain) Ltd v James Clark (Brush Materials) Ltd* [1952] 2 All E.R. 497 at p.501.

warrant that one will be obtained.[24] It is in theory possible for the "condition" to be construed as not imposing any duty on either party to take steps to obtain the licence[25]; but in the absence of clear words to this effect it is submitted that a contract for the sale of goods "subject to" export or import licence is unlikely to be construed in this way.[26]

(c) *Content of the Duty*

18–319 **General.** Where the duty is an absolute one, no question can arise as to its content: the duty is one to obtain the licence. More difficulty arises where the duty is one to make reasonable efforts, and where the licence is obtained and then revoked.

18–320 **Duty to take reasonable steps.** Where a party is under a duty to take reasonable steps to obtain a licence, either because the contract expressly so provides[27] or because the court implies a term to that effect[28] or because the contract is "subject to licence"[29] he must normally show that he actually did take such steps. If he takes no steps at all, he will be liable unless he can discharge the "difficult burden" of showing that any steps which he could have taken (in the performance of his duty to take reasonable steps) would have been useless.[30] In the *Anglo-Russian Merchant Traders* case[31] the failure of the sellers to apply for a permit to deal in American aluminium did not put them in breach as there was a finding of fact that such an application would have been refused. The burden of proof on this issue is on the party on whom the duty lies and is a difficult one to discharge: it must be "quite clear" that the steps which were not (but should have been) taken would have been useless.[32]

18–321 What are reasonable steps for the present purpose depends on a variety of circumstances. The application for a licence must be made without undue delay after the conclusion of the contract.[33] A party may be required

---

[24] *cf. Walton (Grain & Shipping) Ltd v British Italian Trading Co.* [1959] 1 Lloyd's Rep. 223.

[25] *cf. Total Gas Marketing Ltd v Arco British* [1998] 2 Lloyd's Rep. 209, where it was conceded that a different contingent condition imposed no obligation on either party.

[26] *cf.* the regrets expressed at the result in the *Total Gas* case, above, at p.223 by Lord Hope.

[27] *e.g. Charles H Windschuegl Ltd v Alexander Pickering & Co. Ltd* (1950) 84 Ll.L.R. 89.

[28] Above, para.18–314.

[29] Above, para.18–318.

[30] *Charles H. Windschuegl* case, above, at p.95; *Overseas Buyers Ltd v Granadex SA* [1980] 2 Lloyd's Rep. 608 at p.612.

[31] [1917] 2 K.B. 679 (above, para.18–314).

[32] *Charles H Windschuegl Ltd v Alexander Pickering & Co. Ltd* (1950) 84 Ll.L.R. 89 at 95; *Soc. d'Avances Commerciales Ltd v A Besse & Co. Ltd* [1952] 1 Lloyd's Rep. 242; *Vidler & Co. (London) Ltd v R Silcock & Sons Ltd* [1960] 1 Lloyd's Rep. 509; *cf. J W Taylor & Co. v Landauer & Co.* [1940] 4 All E.R. 335; *Mitchell, Cotts & Co. (Middle East) Ltd v Hairco Ltd* [1943] 2 All E.R. 552; *Malik Co. v CETA* [1974] 2 Lloyd's Rep. 279; and see (in the context of failure to take steps to obtain planning permission) *Obagi v Stanborough Developments* (1995) 69 P. & C.R. 573.

[33] *Agroexport v Cie. Européene de Céreales* [1974] 1 Lloyd's Rep. 499; *Malik Co. v CETA* [1974] 2 Lloyd's Rep. 279.

to take steps to obtain a licence even though they involve considerable expense and turn the contract for him into an unprofitable one. In *Brauer & Co. (Great Britain) Ltd v James Clark (Brush Materials) Ltd*[34] Brazilian piassava was sold in February for February to July shipment on c.i.f. terms "subject to any Brazilian export licence." After the contract was made, the Brazilian authorities refused (in effect) to grant export licences unless the sellers paid their Brazilian suppliers some 25 per cent more than the amount which they would have received from the buyers under the contract of sale.[35] It was held that the sellers were not justified in refusing to ship. They could have obtained an export licence by paying their suppliers more and should have done so in performance of their duty to take all reasonable steps to obtain the licence. The mere fact that this would have turned the contract into a losing bargain for them was no excuse, since under a forward contract such as this the risk of increase in price between contract and shipment was on the sellers. On the other hand it was said that if the sellers could have obtained a licence only "on prohibitive terms or on terms entirely outside the contemplation of the parties"[36] they would not have been bound to do so in performance of their duty to take reasonable steps: they would not, for example, have been obliged for this purpose to comply with a requirement to pay the local suppliers 100 times the price which was due to them under the contract of sale.[37]

Revocation of licence. Once the licence has been obtained, the duty to obtain it is performed. The party under that duty is therefore not prima facie in breach if the licence is later revoked,[38] at least if the revocation is not due to that party's conduct or culpable omission. This rule appears to apply whether the duty is an absolute one or one of diligence.[39] The prima facie rule can be excluded by an express term of the contract[40]; and there is some support for the view that, even where the contract contains no such term, the party under the duty must make reasonable efforts to secure the restoration of the licence.[41] But in the absence of such a term the suggested additional duty appears to be inconsistent with the view that once the licence has been obtained the duty of the party required to obtain it has been performed; and it is submitted that a term imposing the additional duty is unlikely to be implied. 18–322

---

[34] [1952] 2 All E.R. 497; followed in *Beves & Co. Ltd v Farkas* [1953] 1 Lloyd's Rep. 103. *Cf. Exportelisa SA v Giuseppe Figli Soc. Coll.* [1978] 1 Lloyd's Rep. 433 (where there was no licensing requirement but the authorities in the country of origin were monopoly suppliers and raised their price above that for which the seller had agreed to sell to the buyer).

[35] The contract price per ton was £163 for one of the grades sold and £118 for the other. The Brazilian authorities required the sellers to pay the Brazilian suppliers £28 and £40 per ton respectively in excess of these prices.

[36] [1952] 2 All E.R. 497 at p.500; *cf. ibid.*, p.501.

[37] *ibid*, p.501.

[38] *C Czarnikow Ltd v Centala Handlu Zagranicznego "Rolimpex"* [1979] A.C. 351.

[39] The duty in the *Czarnikow* case, above, n.38, was an absolute one: see above, para.18–317.

[40] *Bangladesh Export Import Ltd v Sucden Kerry SA* [1995] 2 Lloyd's Rep. 1, below, para.18–331.

[41] *Provimi Hellas AE v Warinco AG* [1978] 1 Lloyd's Rep. 373.

(d) *Effects of Failure to Obtain Licence*

18–323 **Licensing requirement in existence at time of contracting.** The effects of failure to obtain a licence may vary according to whether the licensing requirement existed at the time of contracting or was imposed only after that time. Our present concern is with the former situation; supervening licensing requirements are discussed in paragraphs 18–333 to 18–341 below.

18–324 **Intention to perform without licence.** If it is the intention of the parties, or of one of them, to perform the contract without obtaining the necessary licence, or if it is in fact so performed, the contract is affected by illegality.[42] It will, consequently, be unenforceable by the guilty party,[43] and it may be unenforceable by either party.[44] More usually, in overseas sales, the parties intend, not to flout, but to comply with, the licensing requirement; and the legal problems which call for discussion here result from their inability to do so. The resolution of these problems depends on whether the party who is to obtain the licence has undertaken an absolute duty to do so or only one to make reasonable efforts to that end.[45]

(i) *Absolute Duty*

18–325 **Where the duty is absolute.** Where a party who is under an absolute duty[46] fails to obtain the licence, he is liable in damages.[47] So as to avoid a possible conflict with the rules relating to illegal contracts, this liability is said to be based on a collateral contract,[48] but the measure of damages appears to be the same as that for breach of the principal contract. The "collateral contract" reasoning makes it possible to apply the present rule to cases in which the illegality arises under English law, no less than where it arises under foreign law.[49] A further consequence of the failure to obtain the licence is that the party who gave the absolute undertaking cannot claim damages.[50] This results from his inability to perform a condition precedent

---

42 *e.g. J Dennis & Co. Ltd v Munn* [1949] 2 K.B. 327 (building licence); *Bigos v Bousted* [1951] 1 All E.R. 92 (Exchange Control).
43 Above, para.3–029.
44 *Re Mahmoud and Ispahani* [1921] 2 K.B. 716.
45 Above, paras 18–313 to 18–318.
46 Above, paras 18–313, 18–315 to 18–317.
47 *e.g. K C Sethia Ltd v Partabmull Rameshwar* [1950] 1 All E.R. 51; affirmed [1951] 2 All E.R. 352n; *Peter Cassidy Seed Co. Ltd v Osuustukkukauppa* [1957] 1 W.L.R. 273.
48 *Walton (Grain & Shipping) Ltd v British Italian Trading Co.* [1959] 1 Lloyd's Rep. 223 at p.236; *Johnson Matthey Bankers Ltd v The State Trading Corp. of India* [1984] 1 Lloyd's Rep. 427 at p.434; *Pagnan SpA v Tradax Ocean Transportation SA* [1987] 3 All E.R. 565 at p.577; the "collateral contract" explanation is said at p.576 to be inapplicable where at the time of contracting the parties had no reason to suppose that shipment would be unlawful, since in such a case there would be no intention to enter into the alleged collateral contract.
49 As in the cases cited in n.47, above.
50 See, *e.g. H O Brandt & Co. v H N Morris & Co. Ltd* [1917] 2 K.B. 784, above, para.18–310. The standard of diligence was not in issue in this case, but the rule stated in the text at this point applies irrespective of the standard of duty: *cf.* below at n.55.

to, or a concurrent condition of, the other party's liability. If, for example, a seller promises absolutely to obtain an export licence, and fails to secure one, he will be unable lawfully to deliver the goods in accordance with the contract and so fail to perform the concurrent condition of delivery under section 28 of the Sale of Goods Act.[51] If it is the buyer who promises, but fails, to obtain the licence, he can still perform the concurrent condition of payment under section 28, but performance of his promise to obtain the licence would no doubt be held to be a condition precedent of the seller's duty to deliver, if without such performance the seller could not lawfully perform his promise to deliver in accordance with the contract.

Contract not frustrated. The analysis in paragraph 18–325 above shows that, in cases of the present kind, failure to obtain the licence will not discharge the contract under the doctrine of frustration. The party under the duty to obtain the licence will remain liable even though the failure to obtain it was in no way due to his fault. The other party's position is not that he is discharged, but that performance from him never became due. 18–326

(ii) *Duty of Diligence*

Failure to make reasonable efforts. Where the duty is one to make reasonable efforts to obtain a licence,[52] and such efforts are not made, the party who ought to have made the efforts is liable in damages (unless he can show that the efforts, if made, would have been useless[53]) for breach of what is clearly a collateral undertaking to make them.[54] And he cannot claim damages from the other party for the reasons which bar such a claim in the case of failure to perform an absolute undertaking.[55] 18–327

Failure to obtain licence in spite of making reasonable efforts. Where the duty is one to make reasonable efforts but no licence is obtained in spite of the fact that such efforts have been made, the party under the duty is not liable for breach of it,[56] since the duty is not broken but performed. The further question then arises whether either party may nevertheless be liable for breach of some *other* duty alleged to have arisen under the contract. Where the contract is expressly "subject to licence", a negative answer has been given to this question, on the ground that it was an implied condition of the contract "that a licence must be obtained and that neither party will be liable to perform the duties under the contract unless the licence is obtained".[57] This seems to mean, not that the duties are discharged, but that they are prevented from arising because the grant of 18–328

---

[51] Above, para.8–004.
[52] Above, paras 18–313, 18–315, 18–318.
[53] Above, para.18–320.
[54] *e.g. Brauer & Co. (Great Britain) Ltd v James Clark (Brush Materials) Ltd* [1952] 2 All E.R. 497; above, para.18–321.
[55] *H O Brandt & Co. v H N Morris & Co. Ltd*, above, para.18–325, n.50.
[56] *Overseas Buyers Ltd v Grennadex SA* [1980] 2 Lloyd's Rep. 608.
[57] *Charles H Windschuegl Ltd v Alexander Pickering & Co. Ltd* (1950) 84 Ll.L.Rep. 89 at p.92 (above, para.18–318).

the licence was a condition precedent to their accrual. If the contract is not expressly "subject to licence", the question whether a claim can successfully be made for breach of such *other* duty under the contract is one of greater complexity. Such a claim may be made either by or against the party whose duty it was to make reasonable efforts to obtain the licence.

18–329 **Claim by party under the duty.** When such a claim is brought *by* that party, it will be dismissed if his failure to obtain the licence prevents him from performing a condition precedent to, or a concurrent condition of, the other party's liability. If, for example, a c.i.f. seller is, by reason of his failure to obtain an export licence, prevented from lawfully shipping goods (and hence from tendering documents) the buyer will not be bound to pay[58]; and if an f.o.b. buyer is prevented by such failure from providing an effective ship,[59] the seller will not be bound to deliver. But failure to obtain the licence will not necessarily prevent the party who is under the duty to make reasonable efforts to obtain it from performing such a condition precedent or concurrent condition. If, for example, a c.i.f. contract imposes a duty on the buyer to make reasonable efforts to obtain an import licence and these efforts prove unavailing, the buyer can still lawfully pay[60] and the seller may be bound to ship the goods since shipment may not be prevented or made unlawful by the lack of such a licence. It seems, therefore, that if, in such a case, the seller failed or refused to ship, the buyer could recover damages even though his efforts to obtain the licence had remained fruitless. The same principle might, at first sight, seem to apply where a seller on f.o.b. or f.a.s. terms failed, in spite of making reasonable efforts, to obtain an export licence; for this failure would not prevent him from delivering free on board or free alongside in the country of origin, and the buyer is not normally discharged from such a contract merely because his purpose of exporting the goods, or of exporting them to a particular country, had been defeated whether by failure to obtain a licence, supervening prohibition of export or some other supervening event; he would be discharged only if the export purpose formed a term of the contract.[61] Yet in *A V Pound & Co. Ltd v M W Hardy & Co. Inc.*[62] an f.a.s. seller's claim for damages in such circumstances was dismissed. The question mainly discussed in the House of Lords was whether the duty to make reasonable efforts to obtain an export licence was on the buyer or on the seller; and the dismissal of the seller's claim was considered to follow from the decision that the duty was not on the buyer (and was apparently regarded as incumbent on the seller.[63]) It therefore followed that the buyer

---

58 *e.g.* in *Re Anglo-Russian Merchant Traders and John Batt & Co. (London) Ltd* (above, para.18–314) there would have been no liability on the buyers.
59 Below, para.20–043.
60 The contract is not frustrated merely because the goods cannot be lawfully imported into the country of the port of destination named in the contract: *Congimex Companhia Geral, etc., SARL v Tradax Export SA* [1983] 1 Lloyd's Rep. 250, below, para.19–137.
61 Below, paras 18–335, 20–100, 20–101.
62 [1956] A.C. 588; above, para.18–310.
63 See below, para.18–331 at n.78.

was not liable for breach *of that duty*; but it is less clear why the buyer was not liable for breach of *other* duties, such as his duty to accept and pay for the goods against their delivery f.a.s. Lisbon. One possible explanation for this aspect of the case is that, even if contract was not expressly for export, it was nevertheless interpreted as such,[64] in the light of the seller's knowledge that the buyer intended to export the goods to East Germany; and, as no licence to export the goods to *any* country had been obtained by the end of the shipment period, the seller would, on this interpretation, have been unable lawfully to make delivery in accordance with the contract. An alternative possibility is that it was actually an express term of the contract that the goods should be capable of being legally exported to East Germany since the stipulation as to payment[65] referred to that country. If the contract was, expressly or by implication, one for the sale of goods for export (or for export to East Germany) the seller would be unable lawfully to deliver the goods in accordance with the contract. Such inability would amount to the failure of a concurrent condition of the buyer's duty to accept and pay; and this would explain Lord Simonds' statement that, without the necessary export licence, the contract "could not be performed".[66]

Claim against the party under the duty. A claim for breach of some *other* duty under the contract may be available against the party who was under the duty to make reasonable efforts to obtain a licence but failed to obtain one in spite of having made such efforts and having therefore performed that duty. Such a claim might, for example, be brought where a c.i.f. contract imposed a duty on the buyer to make reasonable efforts to obtain an import licence, and he failed, in spite of making such efforts, to obtain the licence. That failure would not prevent the seller from lawfully shipping goods and tendering shipping documents.[67] Hence it would not lead to any failure of condition precedent or concurrent condition on the seller's part, and prima facie the buyer would not be absolved from his duty to pay against documents.[68] Another possibility is that a c.i.f. contract might impose an obligation to make reasonable efforts to obtain an import licence on the *seller*.[69] If he failed (in spite of making such efforts) to obtain the licence, he could nevertheless still lawfully ship the goods, so that prima facie he would not be absolved from his duties to ship goods and tender 18–330

---

[64] *cf. Maine Spinning Co. v Sutcliffe* (1917) 87 L.J.K.B. 382; below, paras 20–010, 20–015.

[65] See [1956] A.C. 588 at p.590. The stipulation was in a covering letter sent by the seller with the contract form; it is not clear whether the letter was regarded as incorporated in the contract.

[66] [1956] 2 W.L.R. 683 at p.691, a passage which does not occur in the *Law Reports. Cf.* [1956] A.C. 588 at p.607 (where the obtaining of an export licence was said to be "a condition of delivery f.a.s.").

[67] Below, para.19–010.

[68] *Congimex Companhia Geral, etc. SARL v Tradax Export SA* [1983] 1 Lloyd's Rep. 250 at p.253; *cf. Bangladesh Export Import Co. Ltd v Sucden Kerry SA* [1995] 2 Lloyd's Rep. 1, where the contract provided for import licence "to be obtained by buyers" and it was obtained but then withdrawn.

[69] *JW Taylor & Co. v Landauer & Co.* [1940] 4 All E.R. 335.

documents: performance by him would not be illegal since it is no part of a c.i.f. seller's duty to ensure the actual delivery of the goods at the contractual destination.[70] It would thus seem to be open to the buyer to claim performance and to divert the goods elsewhere.[71] The seller would be discharged from his duties to ship and tender documents only in the unusual case in which the contract could be interpreted as giving rise to a duty to deliver the goods (at least if they were not lost in transit) at the destination named[72]: in that case the seller could argue that performance would involve participation in an attempt to do an unlawful act in the country of destination. A similar argument could (*mutatis mutandis*) be used to protect a seller on f.a.s. terms[73] who had undertaken to make reasonable efforts to obtain an export licence but had failed, in spite of making reasonable efforts, to obtain the licence.

A final possibility is that failure to obtain the licence might lead to frustration of the contract of sale: this possibility is discussed in the following paragraph.

18–331 **Whether contract frustrated.** The first point to be made in answering this question is the obvious one that failure to obtain a requisite licence can frustrate a contract only if it either prevents performance or makes it illegal or frustrates the common purpose of both parties. In the case of a c.i.f. contract, the failure of the buyer to obtain an import licence will not normally have any of these effects, since the import of the goods into the country of destination named in the contract is normally neither a term of the contract nor the common purpose of both parties, though it may be the purpose of the buyer.[74] But in *A V Pound & Co. Ltd v M W Hardy & Co. Inc.*[75] performance of an f.a.s. contract was (at least on one view of the facts[76]) prevented as a result of the failure to obtain an export licence. The only question actually before the House of Lords was whether the buyers were in breach, and this question was answered in the negative as it was not their duty to obtain a licence. That duty appears to have been on the sellers, but the nature of the duty and the sellers' liability for breach of it did not arise for decision, since a claim for damages by the buyers against the sellers was not pressed in the House of Lords. It was therefore unnecessary to decide whether the doctrine of frustration applied.[77] Lord Kilmuir did, however, say that "it was for the sellers to do their best[78] to obtain a licence . . . through the suppliers and, if they found that they could not, further performance of the contract was excused."[79] This seems to mean that further performance by *both* parties was excused; and this result could be

[70] *Manbré Saccharine Co. Ltd v Corn Products Ltd* [1919] 1 K.B. 198 at p.202 ("not by actual physical delivery of the goods. . ."); below, paras 19–001, 19–004, 19–072.
[71] *e.g.* on facts such as those in the *Congimex* case, above, n.68.
[72] See below, para.19–003; such a contract is probably not a true c.i.f. contract.
[73] As in *A V Pound & Co. Ltd v M W Hardy & Co. Inc.* [1956] A.C. 588.
[74] See para.18–330 above, and below, para.19–137.
[75] [1956] A.C. 588; above, paras 18–310, 18–329.
[76] Above, para.18–329.
[77] [1956] A.C. 588 at p.605.
[78] See above, para.18–314, n.6.
[79] [1956] A.C. 588 at p.604.

explained either on the grounds stated in paragraph 18–329 above or on the ground that the contract was frustrated.[80] It is submitted that the former is the more plausible explanation. The seller would be excused from "further performance" of his duty to make reasonable efforts to obtain a licence,[81] because he had *performed* that duty by making such efforts, not because its performance was prevented; while the buyer would be excused on the assumption that the seller could not lawfully deliver the goods in accordance with the contract,[82] and so would have been unable to perform a condition precedent to, or a concurrent condition of, the buyer's liability. It follows from the explanation here put forward that neither party would be entitled to make a claim under the Law Reform (Frustrated Contracts) Act 1943.

Where the contract is expressly "subject to licence"[83] failure to obtain a licence will not give rise to any liability so long as the party whose duty it was to obtain the licence had used reasonable diligence to that end.[84] But for a number of reasons the failure would not be a ground of frustration: the obligation to use reasonable diligence would have been *performed*; the other obligations of the contract would not have been *discharged*, but would have been *prevented from arising* by failure of condition precedent[85]; and even if the contract were regarded as having been discharged, such discharge would take place under the express term that the contract was "subject to licence" and not under the doctrine of frustration since this doctrine does not apply to events for which express and complete provision is made in the contract.[86]

Frustration may also be excluded by other terms of the contract. This is true not only where the term in question actually covers the event which has happened but also where the term, though not precisely covering that event, shows that the parties contemplated it and allocated the risk of its occurrence. Thus in one case[87] a c. & f. contract provided that "inability to *obtain* a licence shall not be justification for declaration of *force majeure*". An import licence was obtained by the buyer but later *revoked*, and one reason why this fact did not frustrate the contract was that the term showed that the lack of an import licence "was within the contemplation of the parties and was not to constitute a frustrating event".[88]

Frustration by revocation of licence? Even in the absence of a term of the kind discussed at the end of paragraph 18–331 above, it is submitted that a contract for the sale of goods would not normally be frustrated by the 18–332

[80] *cf. Walton (Grain & Shipping) Ltd v British Italian Trading Co.* [1959] 1 Lloyd's Rep. 223; *Johnson Matthey Bankers Ltd v The State Trading Corp. of India* [1984] 1 Lloyd's Rep. 427 at pp.429, 434.
[81] No claim was made for breach of any duty of the seller to deliver f.a.s. without licence (the buyer having no interest in claiming such delivery). *Semble* there was no such duty as the seller's duty was to deliver for export only: see above, para.18–329.
[82] See previous note.
[83] Above, para.18–318; *cf.* below, para.18–342.
[84] Above, para.18–318.
[85] Above, para.18–328.
[86] *Joseph Constantine SS Line v Imperial Smelting Co. Ltd* [1942] A.C. 154 at p.163; Treitel, *Frustration and Force Majeure*, 2nd ed. (2004), paras 12–002, 12–009.
[87] *Bangladesh Export Import Ltd v Sucden Kerry SA* [1995] 2 Lloyd's Rep. 1.
[88] *ibid.*, p.6.

revocation of the requisite licence. The reasons for this submission are the same as those given above[89]: obtaining the licence would have discharged the duty of the party who had obtained it by performance, and its revocation would lead to that party's inability to perform a condition of the accrual of the duty of the other party. There may, however, be some scope for application of the doctrine of frustration where the revocation of the licence is accompanied by an effective legal prohibition of the means of performing the particular contract in question. In a case involving, not the sale of goods, but the hire of a stadium for the purpose of giving a "rock concert" the use of the stadium for that purpose was "banned . . . and the permit for [that] use was revoked"[90], and this combination of circumstances was held to frustrate the contract for giving the concert. In the case of a contract for the sale of goods similar circumstances could perhaps give rise to frustration on the ground that they led, not only to inability to comply with an antecedent licensing requirement, but also to a supervening prohibition of export. As will be seen in paragraphs 18–335 to 18–340 below, such a prohibition may, though it will not commonly, frustrate a contract for the sale of goods.

7. Supervening Prohibition of Export or Import

18–333 **In general.** Performance of an overseas sale may be prevented or made illegal by a prohibition of export or import imposed after the conclusion of the contract and before breach. Such a prohibition does not make the contract illegal *ab initio*, but may discharge it under the doctrine of frustration, if the prohibition would have made the contract illegal, had it been in force when the contract was made.[91] The ground of discharge is not physical impossibility, but rather the consideration of public policy that parties should be given no incentive to perform contracts affected by supervening illegality. The prohibition may be absolute, permanently affecting all goods of a specified description. It may, on the other hand, be only temporary; or partial, in that it may except certain categories of goods which would, but for the exception, fall within the prohibited class[92]; or qualified, in that it may merely prohibit the export or import without licence of goods which were not previously subject to any such restriction.

(a) *Discharge by Supervening Prohibition*

18–334 **Supervening prohibition as a ground of frustration.** Whether a supervening prohibition of export or import discharges a contract depends on the normal requirements of the doctrine of frustration.

---

[89] See above, para.18–329.
[90] *Gamerco SA v ICM Fair Warning (Agency) Ltd* [1995] 1 W.L.R. 1226 at p.1233.
[91] *e.g. not* in circumstances such as those which arose in *St John Shipping Corp. v Joseph Rank Ltd* [1957] 1 Q.B. 267.
[92] See, for example, the prohibition imposed in the soyabean meal cases, below, para.18–348.

18–335 **The illegality must prevent performance.** In the present context, the first such requirement is that the prohibition must "prevent" performance of the contract in the sense of actually making the performance illegal. It is not sufficient for a buyer to show that his intention to export the goods from the country in which they were, or were to be delivered to him, or to import them into a particular country, cannot be lawfully carried out, if that export or import purpose was not a term of the contract.[93] Nor, conversely, can the seller rely as a ground of frustration on a prohibition of export imposed by the country from which he intended to obtain the goods if it was not a term of the contract that they should come from a source in that country.[94] Even a contract which does so provide will not be discharged if it provides for delivery f.o.b. (for export) *or* in a warehouse at a port in the country imposing the prohibition.[95] In this respect, the prohibition of export or import cases differ from those in which the cause of illegality is the rule against trading with the enemy in time of war. In such cases, it is enough to frustrate the contract that the parties contemplated that the goods were to be taken from an enemy source.[96] This rule may be justified by the strong need to deter trading with an enemy in time of war. Prohibition of export or import can only frustrate the contract if the contract actually provides that the goods are to be exported from, or imported into, the country which has imposed the prohibition.[97]

18–336 **Temporary interference with performance.** Assuming that the requirement just stated is satisfied, the question whether the prohibition actually frustrates the contract depends on the extent to which the prohibition interferes with the performance of the contract. For example, if the prohibition is of only limited duration, the question may arise whether the delay in performance occasioned by it is sufficiently serious to turn performance, when it again becomes legally possible, into one that is "as a matter of business a totally different thing"[98] from that originally undertaken.

---

[93] *D McMaster & Co. v Cox, McEwen & Co.*, 1921 S.C.(H.L.) 24; *Maine v Lyons* (1913) 15 C.L.R. 671; *Congimex SARL (Lisbon) v Continental Grain Export Corp. (New York)* [1979] 2 Lloyd's Rep. 346; *cf. Congimex Companhia Geral, etc., SARL v Tradax Export SA* [1983] 1 Lloyd's Rep. 250, a case of change of government policy (below, para.18–340) where the plea of frustration failed on grounds stated in para.19–137 below; *Austin Baldwin & Co. v Wilfred Turner & Co. Ltd* (1920) 36 T.L.R. 769 (below, para.20–016); *Bangladesh Export Import Co v Sucden Kerry SA* [1995] 2 Lloyd's Rep 1, where frustration was also excluded by the express term of the contract discussed in para.18–331 above; contrast *Maine Spinning Co. v Sutcliffe & Co.* (1918) 87 L.J.K.B. 382 (where the contract on its true construction did provide that the goods were to be exported: below, paras 20–010, 20–015); the position seems to have been the same in *A V Pound & Co. v M W Hardy Inc.* [1956] A.C. 588: see above, para.18–329, n.65. *Edward Grey & Co. v Tolme and Runge* (1915) 31 T.L.R. 551 is hard to reconcile with the other authorities cited in this note: see Treitel, *Frustration and Force Majeure* 2nd ed.(2004), para.7–029.

[94] *Beves & Co. Ltd v Farkas* [1953] 1 Lloyd's Rep. 103.

[95] *Smith, Coney & Barrett v Becker, Gray & Co.* [1916] 2 Ch. 86.

[96] *Re Badische Co. Ltd* [1921] 2 Ch. 331.

[97] As in *Andrew Millar & Co. Ltd v Taylor & Co. Ltd* [1916] 1 K.B. 402 (where frustration was excluded for reasons to be discussed in para.18–336 below) and in *C Czarnikow Ltd v Centrala Handlu Zagranicznego "Rolimpex"* [1979] A.C. 351 (where the contract was discharged under an express *force majeure* provision).

[98] *Bank Line Ltd v Arthur Capel & Co.* [1919] A.C. 435 at p.460.

A case which gives rise to some difficulty in this connection is *Andrew Millar & Co. Ltd v Taylor & Co. Ltd.*[99] It was there held that an embargo on the export of confectionery imposed by Royal Proclamation on the outbreak of war in 1914 did not frustrate a sale of such goods, f.o.b. Liverpool for export to Morocco, as the embargo was only temporary, and had been withdrawn by a subsequent Proclamation only 15 days after it had been imposed and before the end of the normal delivery period. Warrington L.J. said: "If . . . the performance of a contract becomes impossible by reason of its illegality, then both parties to the contract are discharged. But they are only discharged because the performance of the contract has become impossible."[1] He added that there would have been "no question . . . that the performance of the contract had become impossible"[2] if the illegality had consisted in trading with the enemy; but he distinguished between illegality arising from a state of war "the duration of which it is impossible to foresee" and illegality arising "from an act of the Executive Government"[3] when that act had been revoked before the end of the period fixed for performance. At first sight, these observations are open to the objection that supervening illegality discharges a contract on the ground of public policy stated in paragraph 18–333 above and not on the ground of impossibility. This view is supported by the cases in which contracts have been frustrated because their performance after the outbreak of war would have involved trading with the enemy.[4] In such cases, the contracts are discharged by supervening illegality even though it may be physically possible to perform them by sending the goods through a neutral country to the destination specified in the contract. The distinction drawn by Warrington L.J. can, however, be supported on the ground that the policy considerations which underlie the prohibition against trading with the enemy are of exceptional strength[5] and that the need to deter contravention is greater in the case of this prohibition than in the case of a prohibition of export or import.

Andrew Millar & Co. Ltd v Taylor & Co. Ltd[6] also gives rise to difficulty in relation to the general principle that the applicability of the doctrine of frustration is to be judged by reference to the time at which the (allegedly) frustrating event occurs. If at that time a reasonable person would conclude that performance would be prevented, the contract may be frustrated even though there is a subsequent, unexpected turn of events making performance once again possible.[7] So far as *Andrew Millar & Co. Ltd v Taylor & Co. Ltd* is inconsistent with this principle, it has been criticised in the House of Lords.[8] The case can, however, be explained, on the ground that the principle of looking to the time of the occurrence of the allegedly

[99] [1916] 1 K.B. 403.
[1] *ibid.*, at p.415.
[2] *ibid.*, at p.416.
[3] *ibid.*
[4] *e.g. Fibrosa Spolka Akcyjna v Fairbairn Lawson Combe, Barbour Ltd* [1943] A.C. 32.
[5] *cf.* above, para.18–335, after n.96.
[6] [1916] 1 K.B. 403.
[7] *e.g. Embiricos v Sydney Reid & Co.* [1914] 3 K.B. 45.
[8] *Watts, Watts & Co. Ltd v Mitsui & Co. Ltd* [1917] 2 A.C. 227 at p.245.

frustrating event has to be modified where the event is of such a nature that a reasonable view of its effect on the contract cannot be formed immediately on its occurrence. If, for example, the event is one that may cause either slight or serious interference with performance, it is "necessary to wait upon events"[9] until it becomes possible to form a reasonable view on the question whether the interference likely to result will be sufficiently serious to frustrate the contract. In *Andrew Millar & Co. Ltd v Taylor & Co. Ltd* the seller can be said to have acted "with undue precipitation"[10]: in the circumstances,[11] it was not probable, when the embargo was imposed, that it would last sufficiently long to frustrate the contract.

Qualified prohibition. Where a supervening prohibition is qualified (*i.e.* where it makes the previously unrestricted export or import of goods subject to a licensing requirement) the contract is not automatically discharged. The court may in such a case impose on one of the parties a duty to make reasonable efforts to obtain the licence.[12] The question which party was bound to make such efforts would depend on factors similar to those discussed in relation to licensing requirements in existence at the time of contracting.[13] So far as the standard of duty is concerned, it is theoretically possible for the court to regard the contract as imposing an absolute duty; but in the case of a supervening prohibition this possibility is a remote one.[14] Assuming, then, that the duty is one to make reasonable efforts, the party under the duty will be able to rely on the prohibition as a ground of discharge only if he can show that he has made such efforts, or that reasonable efforts to obtain the licence would have proved unavailing.[15] It is not enough for him to show that he reasonably believed that the **18–337**

---

[9] *Pioneer Shipping Ltd v BTP Tioxide Ltd (The Nema)* [1982] A.C. 724 at p.753; *cf. Kodros Shipping Corp. of Monrovia v Empresa Cubana de Fletes of Havana, Cuba (The Evia)* (No.2) [1983] 1 A.C. 736; *International Sea Tankers Inc. v Hemisphere Shipping Co. Ltd (The Wenjiang) (No.* 2) [1983] 1 Lloyd's Rep. 400; *Vinava Shipping Co. v Finlivet AG (The Chrysalis)* [1983] 1 W.L.R. 1469; Treitel, *Frustration and Force Majeure*, 2nd ed. (2004) para.9–008.

[10] *Atlantic Maritime Co. Inc. v Gibbon* [1954] 1 Q.B. 105 at p.114.

[11] The embargo had been imposed during the first two weeks of the war, when no view as to its duration could safely be formed.

[12] *e.g. Dalmia Dairy Industries Ltd v National Bank of Pakistan* [1978] 2 Lloyd's Rep. 223 at p.253 (affirmed *ibid.* on different grounds); *cf.* the cases in which such a duty was imposed under contracts containing "prohibition of export" clauses cited below, para.18–345, n.62.

[13] Above, paras 18–309 to 18–311.

[14] The absolute duty imposed by clause 21 of the contract in *C Czarnikow Ltd v Centrala Handlu Zagranicznego "Rolimpex" Ltd* [1979] A.C. 351 at p.371 (above, para.18–317) was there expressly confined to the situation in which the licensing requirement was already in force at the time of contracting, thus perhaps reflecting a commercial viewpoint that such a stringent duty is inappropriate in cases of supervening impossibility. *Cf. Empresa Exportadora de Azucar v Industria Azucarera Nacional SA (The Playa Larga)* [1983] 2 Lloyd's Rep. 171 at p.191, where the embargo was supervening and unqualified and the Court of Appeal held that (in the absence of "clear words" to that effect) no absolute warranty that performance would be lawful (*cf.* above, paras 18–315 to 18–317) should be implied.

[15] *cf.* above, para.18–320. One of the prohibitions in the *Anglo-Russian Merchant Traders* case [1917] 2 K.B. 679 (above, paras 18–314, 18–320) was a qualified *supervening* one.

licence would probably be refused, if such efforts were to be made.[16] To this extent cases of qualified prohibitions constitute a further modification[17] of the general principle[18] of looking at the probabilities at the time of the supervening event in order to determine whether it frustrates the contract. But the contract may be frustrated on other grounds; if so, the duty to make reasonable efforts will be discharged, along with the other duties under the frustrated contract.[19]

18–338 **Partial prohibition.** Where the prohibition is partial,[20] the contract is not discharged but the prohibition may *pro tanto* excuse performance. If, for example, the prohibition merely restricts the amount which a seller is allowed to export to 40 per cent. of any quantity which he has contracted to sell, he must supply that amount but is excused from supplying the remaining 60 per cent. In this respect, the effect of the prohibition is the same as that of physical impossibility caused by (for example) the partial failure of a specified crop.[21] The excuse is subject to the same restrictions that limit it in cases of physical impossibility. Thus it would not be available where inability to supply the full contract quantity is due to the seller's "fault"; for example, where his failure to obtain a licence for the full amount is due to his breach of duty to take reasonable steps to obtain a licence,[22] or to some other culpable act or omission on his part.[23] These restrictions are analogous to the principle which prevents a party from relying on frustration where it was "self-induced."[24] The seller would also be liable if the contract was simply one for the sale of unascertained goods by description and goods of that description were available to him from a source not affected by the prohibition.[25]

18–339 **Foreign prohibition.** Where prohibition of export or import is imposed by a foreign law, it may likewise frustrate the contract. This conclusion can be based on an implied term that the law of the foreign country will "not be so altered as to prevent the contract from being fulfilled",[26] or on physical

[16] *Dalmia Dairy Industries Ltd v National Bank of Pakistan* [1978] 2 Lloyd's Rep. 223 at p.253 (affirmed *ibid.* on different grounds).
[17] In addition to that noted in para.18–336 above, at n.9.
[18] Above, para.18–336 at n.7.
[19] *Nile Co. for the Export of Agricultural Crops v H & J M Bennett (Commodities) Ltd* [1986] 1 Lloyd's Rep. 555 at p.582, where the contract was frustrated on the ground stated in para.20–102, below.
[20] Above, para.18–333; below, para.18–348.
[21] *H R & S Sainsbury Ltd v Street* [1972] 1 W.L.R. 834. The buyer need not normally accept the smaller quantity: Sale of Goods Act 1979, s.30(1); see also below, para.18–355.
[22] *cf.* above, paras 18–320, 18–321.
[23] *e.g.* if the seller's failure to obtain a licence was due to his criminal contravention of the prohibition on another occasion.
[24] Below, para.18–341.
[25] As, for example, in those of the "soyabean cases" in which the seller was unable to identify the "relevant shipper" (below, para.18–350).
[26] *Soc. Co-operative Suisse des Céréales etc. v La Plata Cereal Co. SA* (1947) 80 Ll.L.R. 530 at p.542; doubted on this point in *Atisa SA v Aztec AG* [1983] 2 Lloyd's Rep. 579 at p.586.

impossibility if this in fact results from the prohibition; or on a rule of law that a contract will be discharged by supervening illegality under the law of the place of performance.[27] The basis of discharge in such cases does not appear to be the principle of public policy which justifies discharge on the ground of supervening illegality by English law[28]; though an analogous principle may require that contracting parties be deprived of the incentive to do an illegal act in a friendly foreign country.[29]

Supervening and antecedent prohibitions. The distinction between supervening and antecedent prohibitions tends to become blurred where the prohibition is a qualified one, that is, one which only prevents the export or import of goods without licence. If in such cases a licence is refused after the conclusion of the contract, it is possible to look upon the refusal as a supervening event (even though the licensing requirement was already in existence at the time of contracting) and so to argue that the refusal is a ground of discharge under the doctrine of frustration. It is, however, submitted that the discharge in this type of case is not, in general, based on frustration but on the principles discussed in paragraphs 18–323 to 18–331 above. If the party under a duty to obtain the licence fails, in spite of exercising due diligence, to secure one, further performance may, indeed, be excused to the extent stated in those paragraphs. But this result follows from the fact that that duty is *performed*, or from failure of a condition *precedent*,[30] or of a concurrent condition; while the doctrine of frustration, to the extent to which it can be said to depend on an implied term, operates by virtue of an implied condition *subsequent* which discharges both parties when performance is *prevented*. Moreover, in cases of antecedent qualified prohibition, the refusal of a licence is not necessarily a ground of discharge, for a party may be liable on an absolute collateral undertaking to obtain a licence.[31] It is most unlikely that such an undertaking would be held to exist where the prohibition was first imposed after the time of contracting.[32] 18–340

There is, however, one situation in which it is plausible to argue that refusal of a licence may discharge a contract by frustration even though the licensing requirement was already in force at the time of contracting. This is the situation in which up to that time licences have been granted as a

---

[27] *Soc. Co-operative* case, above, at p.543, relying on the analogy of *Ralli Bros v Compania Naviera Sota y Aznar* [1920] 2 K.B. 287 (below, para.25–119), though this was not a case of the *total* discharge that results from frustration: see Treitel, *Frustration and Force Majeure*, 2nd ed. (2004), para.8–030; *cf. Walton (Grain and Shipping) Ltd v British Italian Trading Co.* [1959] 1 Lloyd's Rep. 223 at p.236; *C. Czarnikow Ltd v Centrala Handlu Zagranicznego "Rolimpex"* [1979] A.C. 351 at p.362; *Empresa Exportadora de Azucar v Industria Azucarera Nacional SA (The Playa Larga)* [1983] 1 Lloyd's Rep. 171; *Nile Co. for the Export of Agricultural Crops v H & J M Bennett (Commodities) Ltd* [1986] 1 Lloyd's Rep. 555.

[28] Above, paras 18–333, 18–335.

[29] See generally para.25–119, below.

[30] *Walton* (*Grain & Shipping*) *Co. Ltd v British Italian Trading Co. Ltd* [1959] 1 Lloyd's Rep. 223 at p.236.

[31] Above, paras 18–313, 18–315 to 18–317, 18–325.

[32] Above, para.18–337.

matter of course,[33] but there is then a change of government policy as a result of which licences are refused, or only issued subject to new restrictions, so that the contract cannot lawfully be performed. There is authority for the view that a contract can be frustrated by the refusal of a licence in such circumstances[34]; and this rule could apply to a case involving the refusal of export or import licences where the issue of such licences is after the time of contracting made subject to new and unexpected restrictions.[35] Similarly, refusal of a licence in such circumstances can bring a prohibition of export clause into operation.[36] It should be emphasised that, while a change of government policy of the kind here described *may* discharge the contract, it will not necessarily have this effect. In particular, the party whose performance is affected by the change may, after it, still be under a duty to take reasonable steps to obtain the requisite licence.[37] Nor will a seller be discharged merely because he has entered into the contract in the expectation of receiving a supply of the goods in question from a foreign government which has, as a result of a change of its policy, simply broken its contract with him.[38] The seller's remedy is to enforce such rights as he may have under the supply contract; if he has no such rights, his failure to make an effective supply contract is no ground for relieving him from liability to the buyer.

There is, finally, the possibility that a licensing requirement is in force at the time of contracting, and that legislation enacted after the time of contracting changes that requirement by the imposition of additional conditions for the issue of a licence. It seems, that, in such a case, the combined prohibitions will be regarded as subsequent.[39]

18–341 **Self-induced frustration.** The doctrine of frustration operates in cases of prohibition of export or import subject to the usual restrictions. One of these is that a party cannot rely on frustration which is "self-induced".[40] It may be so induced either by the act or by the omission of the party seeking to rely on it.

The first possibility is illustrated by the situation in which a foreign government, having entered into a contract of sale, then imposes the

---

[33] *cf.* the illustrations given in *C. Czarnikow Ltd v Centrala Handlu Zagranicznego "Rolimpex"* [1979] A.C. 351 at p.372 (dog and television licences).

[34] *Maritime National Fish Ltd v Ocean Trawlers Ltd* [1935] A.C. 524 (where the actual decision was that the contract was not discharged because the frustration was "self-induced").

[35] *cf. Beves & Co. Ltd v Farkas* [1953] 1 Lloyd's Rep. 103 (where the plea of frustration failed as it was not a term of the contract that the goods were to come from the country, whose government discontinued its previous practice of issuing licences); *Congimex Companhia Geral, etc. SARL v Tradax Export SA* [1983] 1 Lloyd's Rep. 250 (where the plea of frustration failed on grounds stated in para.19–137, below); *Johnson Matthey Bankers Ltd v The State Trading Corp. of India* [1984] 1 Lloyd's Rep. 427 at p.429.

[36] *Pancommerce SA v Veecheema BV* [1983] 2 Lloyd's Rep. 304 (where this defence failed on grounds stated in para.18–353, below).

[37] Above, para.18–337.

[38] *Atisa SA v Aztec AG* [1983] 2 Lloyd's Rep. 579.

[39] *e.g. Nile Co. for the Export of Agricultural Products v H & J M Bennett (Commodities) Ltd* [1986] 1 Lloyd's Rep. 555.

[40] *Bank Line Ltd v Arthur Capel & Co.* [1919] A.C. 435 at p.452.

relevant prohibition. This fact may prevent that government, as a contracting party, from relying on the prohibition as a ground of discharge[41]; but the mere fact that the contracting party is a state trading organisation in the country whose government has imposed the prohibition will not prevent that party from relying on the prohibition as a ground of frustration.[42] Where the prohibition is a domestic (English) one, the prohibition may excuse even the public body imposing it on the ground that a contract previously made by such a body should not be allowed to prevent it from performing an essential governmental function[43]; and it is at least arguable that a similar principle may be recognised in relation to prohibitions imposed by foreign governmental authorities.

Frustration may be self-induced by reason of a party's omission where the prohibition is a qualified one, subjecting the previously free movement of goods to a licensing requirement. In such cases one of the parties may come under a duty to take reasonable steps to procure a licence; and his failure to take such steps will normally deprive him of the defence of frustration.[44]

(b) *Prohibition of Export or Import Clauses*[45]

(i) *Effects*

Relation to frustration. As a general rule, the doctrine of frustration is excluded if the contract makes express and full provision for a supervening event which might, but for such a provision, discharge it.[46] In the case of discharge by supervening illegality, there is an exception to this rule. A contract which becomes illegal because its performance would, as a result of war, involve trading with the enemy is discharged even if it expressly provides that it is, in the events which have happened, only to be suspended.[47] The reason for this exception is that to uphold the suspension would be contrary to the public policy which requires the complete abrogation of commercial relations with the enemy in time of war.[48] Such reasoning does not apply to clauses in contracts which provide that, in the event of prohibition of export or import, performance shall be suspended for a specified period and the contract regarded as cancelled or as void if by the end of that period the prohibition has not been revoked. Clauses of this 18–342

[41] See *Prodexport v E D & F Man Ltd* [1972] 1 All E.R. 355.
[42] *C Czarnikow Ltd v Centrala Handlu Zagranicznego "Rolimpex"* [1979] A.C. 351; *Empressa Exportadora de Azucar v Industria Azucarera Nacional SA (The Playa Larga)* [1983] 1 Lloyd's Rep. 171.
[43] *William Cory & Son Ltd v London Corporation* [1951] 2 K.B. 476; *Chitty on Contracts* (29th ed.), Vol. 1, para.10–022.
[44] *cf. Malik v CETA* [1974] 2 Lloyd's Rep. 279 (where such failure precluded reliance on a "prohibition of export" clause). The position would be different if it were shown that reasonable efforts to obtain a licence would have proved unavailing: *cf.* above, para.18–320.
[45] See further below, paras 19–034 to 19–038 and 20–103; and above, para.8–088.
[46] Treitel, *Frustration and Force Majeure* 2nd ed.(2004), para.12–002.
[47] *Ertel Bieber & Co. v Rio Tinto Co. Ltd* [1918] A.C. 260.
[48] *ibid.*, at p.286.

kind are not opposed to the policy of the prohibition but rather give effect to that policy. They are in principle valid[49]; and have the practical advantage of enabling the parties to know in advance exactly when (if at all) the contract has come, or can be brought, to an end.

A prohibition of export or import clause may either give one of the parties the option to cancel the contract, or provide for its automatic termination. A clause of the latter kind has been described as a "contractual frustration clause".[50] The point of this description, however, is simply that one effect of the clause is the same as that of frustration under the general law, *i.e.* to lead to automatic discharge of the contract, without any act or election of either party. The clause can come into operation whether or not the interference with performance, which results from the prohibition, is sufficiently serious to lead to frustration as a matter of general common law. Even if the interference is such that it would (apart from the clause) frustrate the contract, discharge will take place under the clause, and not under the doctrine of frustration, since that doctrine does not apply where express provision is made in the contract for the supervening event.[51] Hence it seems that the resulting situation will not be governed by the Law Reform (Frustrated Contracts) Act 1943.[52] The doctrine of frustration, and the 1943 Act, could, however, apply where the clause, though literally applicable to the circumstances arising as a result of the prohibition, is held on its true construction not to apply to them.[53]

18–343 **Scope.** Clauses of the kind described in paragraph 18–342 above can apply both where the embargo is imposed after the sale, and also where the "prohibition" is the result of failure (not amounting to a breach of contract) to obtain a licence under a licensing requirement in existence at the time of the contract.[54]

18–344 **Construction.** The only perfectly general statement which can safely be made about the operation of prohibition of export or import clauses is that their effect depends in each case on the words used and is therefore a

[49] Such clauses would not be subject to the Unfair Contract Terms Act 1977 since they are clauses defining duties rather than exemption clauses within s.13 of that Act. Nor would they normally be open to attack under the Unfair Terms in Consumer Contracts Regulations 1999, since these will hardly ever apply to contracts of the kind here under consideration (above, para.18–282) and since a term operating only in circumstances beyond the control of one of the parties would not normally be unfair. Under Clause 9 of the Draft Bill annexed to the Law Commissions' Report on *Unfair Terms in Contracts*, Law Com. No. 292, Scot. Law Com. No. 199 (2005) such terms, even in business contracts, will be subject to the requirement of fairness and reasonableness; but if the term operates only in circumstances beyond the control of the party relying on it, that requirement is, again, likely to be satisfied. Clause 9 of the Draft Bill applies to terms generally and is not restricted to exemption clauses.

[50] *Bremer Handelsgesellschaft mbH v Vanden Avenne-Izegem PVBA* [1978] 2 Lloyd's Rep. 109 at p.112.

[51] *Agrokor AG v Tradigrain SA* [2000] 1 Lloyd's Rep. 497 at p.504.

[52] Treitel, *Frustration and Force Majeure* 2nd ed. (2004), para.12–019.

[53] This appears to be the explanation for the alternative ground of decision in *Walton (Grain & Shipping) Ltd v British Italian Trading Co.* [1959] 1 Lloyd's Rep. 223 at p.236.

[54] *e.g. Walton (Grain & Shipping) Ltd v British Italian Trading Co.* [1959] 1 Lloyd's Rep. 223.

matter of construction. There may be a tendency of the courts to construe such a clause narrowly, against the party relying on it, but there is no absolute rule of law to this effect. Thus if a clause excuses a seller should he fail to ship "*by reason of*" specified events, the seller must show a causal connection between the occurrence of such events and his failure to perform[55]; but no such causal connection need be shown if the clause allows a seller to cancel "*in case of* prohibition of export".[56] Similarly, a seller cannot rely on a clause which applies only where specified events "*prevent*" performance if, in spite of the prohibition, an alternative source of supply remained available to him[57]; but the availability of such an alternative would not preclude reliance on a clause which applied on the occurrence of specified events "*hindering*" performance.[58] The discussion that follows is for the most part concerned with cases in which the clause did require a causal connection between the specified event and the failure of performance and did require the effect of that event to be that performance was prevented; and the discussion will (except where otherwise indicated) be based on these assumptions.

Effective prohibition. The party claiming to be discharged under such a clause must show that there was an effective prohibition, and not a merely technical one. To be "effective" for this purpose, the prohibition must prevent the seller from exporting goods of the contract description[59] within the shipment period. Thus a seller cannot rely on the clause if the prohibition is imposed only for a short time and then withdrawn[60]; or if the prohibition is only against shipment without licence and the seller has within the shipment period obtained a licence,[61] or if his failure to obtain one is a breach of his obligation to take reasonable steps to that end[62]; or if the embargo is not an absolute one but is subject to exceptions (*e.g.* if it does not apply to goods already loaded on an exporting vessel) and the seller could have appropriated to the contract goods at his disposal which fell within such an exception,[63] or within an extension of such an exception **18–345**

---

[55] *cf. P.J. van der Zijden Wildhandel NV v Tucker & Cross Ltd* [1975] 2 Lloyd's Rep. 240, below, para.19–141 (*force majeure* clause); *Hoechong Products Ltd v Cargill Hong Kong Ltd* [1995] 1 W.L.R. 407.

[56] *Ford & Son (Oldham) Ltd v Henry Leetham & Sons Ltd* (1915) 21 Com.Cas 55.

[57] This was the position in the soyabean cases discussed in paras 18–348 *et seq. cf.* also *Agrokor AG v Tradigrain SA* [2000] 1 Lloyd's Rep. 497.

[58] *Tennants (Lancashire) Ltd v CS Wilson & Co. Ltd* [1917] A.C. 495.

[59] See *Soc Co-operative Suisse des Céréales etc. v La Plata Cereal Co. SA* (1947) 80 Ll.L.R. 530.

[60] *Samuel Sanday & Co. v Cox, McEuen & Co.* (1922) 10 Ll.L.R. 459 at p.460; *cf. Andrew Millar & Co. Ltd v Taylor & Co. Ltd* [1916] 1 K.B. 402 (above, para.18–336) where the same principle was applied in determining the issue of frustration.

[61] *Samuel Sanday & Co. v Cox, McEuen & Co.* (1921) 10 Ll.L.R. 459.

[62] *Joseph Pyke & Son (Liverpool) Ltd v Richard Cornelius & Co.* [1955] 2 Lloyd's Rep. 747; *Vidler & Co. (London) Ltd v R Silcock & Sons Ltd* [1960] 1 Lloyd's Rep. 509; *Agroexport v Cie Européenne de Céréales* [1974] 1 Lloyd's Rep. 499; *Malik Co. v CETA* [1974] 2 Lloyd's Rep. 279; contrast *Provimi Hellas AE v Warinco AG* [1978] 1 Lloyd's Rep. 373 (where a reasonable effort had been made to have a revoked licence restored).

[63] *e.g. Bremer Handelsgesellschaft mbH v C Mackprang Jr* [1979] 1 Lloyd's Rep. 221; and see below, para.18–349.

made, within the shipment period, by the authorities of the country of origin[64]; or if the prohibition only prevents shipment from the one particular port from which the seller had intended to ship, without affecting the possibility of shipment from other ports designated as shipment ports by the contract[65]; or if the prohibition applies only to goods to be taken from the country intended by the seller, leaving it open to him to fulfil his contractual obligations by shipping goods taken from elsewhere[66]; or if the prohibition only prevents the seller from acquiring the goods from his intended supplier but leaves it open to him to acquire goods of the contract description (though at a price higher than that to be paid by the buyer[67]) from the foreign government imposing the embargo.[68] The seller will not be able to rely on a prohibition of export clause if the authorities of the country of origin indicate in advance that the export of goods of the contract description will definitely be prohibited from a future date within the shipment period, for it will then be the seller's duty to ship in the part of the period falling before that date.[69] But where those authorities merely indicate that an embargo *may* be imposed, there is no such duty, so that the imposition of the embargo during the shipment period will, if all other necessary conditions are satisfied, bring a prohibition of export clause into operation.[70]

As a general rule, a c.i.f. seller will not be excused by a prohibition of export clause merely because he was prevented by prohibition of export from shipping the goods which he had intended to appropriate to the contract; for other goods may be available to him for the purpose of performance. Thus if, before the embargo was imposed, the seller had already shipped other goods of the contract description, and had not appropriated those goods to any other contract, he must appropriate them to the contract in question.[71] Other goods may also be available where they had been shipped by others[72] before the embargo was imposed. Where this is the case, the general rule is that the seller must, so long as it is possible for him to do so, acquire such other goods and appropriate them to the contract.[73] Even if this is not possible, he will not be excused if the embargo

---

64 *Raiffeisen Hauptgenossenschaft v Louis Dreyfus & Co.* [1981] 1 Lloyd's Rep. 345.
65 *Warinco AG v Fritz Mauthner* [1978] 1 Lloyd's Rep. 151; *cf. The Furness Bridge* [1977] 2 Lloyd's Rep. 367.
66 *Agrokor AG v Tradigrain SA* [2000] 1 Lloyd's Rep. 497.
67 *cf.* above, para.18–321.
68 *Exportelisa SA v Guiseppe & Figli Soc Coll* [1978] 1 Lloyd's Rep. 433 (f.o.b. contract).
69 *Ross T Smyth & Co. Ltd (Liverpool) v W N Lindsay (Leith)* [1953] 1 W.L.R. 1280; *cf.* below, para.19–013.
70 *Tradax Export SA v André & Cie.* [1976] 1 Lloyd's Rep. 416 at p.426; *Continental Grain Export Corp. v STM Grain Ltd* [1979] 2 Lloyd's Rep. 460 at pp.474–475.
71 See the authorities cited in para.18–349, below, n.99.
72 Obviously this possibility would be excluded where the contract was for the sale of goods to be *shipped by the seller: cf. Fairclough Dodd & Jones Ltd v J H Vantol Ltd* [1957] 1 W.L.R. 136.
73 Below, paras 19–011, 19–037; *cf. Joseph Pyke & Son (Liverpool) Ltd v Richard Cornelius & Co.* [1955] 2 Lloyd's Rep. 747, where there was in such circumstances a finding of fact that performance was not impossible, so that the general question of law did not arise.

was only partial[74] and if he could have acquired other goods of the contract description which were not covered by the prohibition and were therefore available for lawful export in performance of the contract.[75] But there are exceptions to the rule requiring a c.i.f. seller to buy goods already afloat (or excepted from the embargo) where the export of the goods which he had intended to appropriate to the contract was prevented. These exceptions are discussed in Chapter 19[76]; where they apply, the seller is not precluded from relying on a prohibition of export clause merely because it was theoretically possible for him to acquire goods afloat[77] or excepted goods.[78] *A fortiori* he could rely on the clause where the contract was for the sale of specific or ascertained goods the export of which was prevented; or where it was a term of the contract that the goods should come from the country imposing the prohibition and the only available substitutes were goods afloat which had originated in another country.

The foregoing account of the operation of prohibition of export clauses is based on the assumption that the seller is to perform by shipping or appropriating goods. But an original obligation of this kind may be converted into an obligation to pay money, *e.g.* by a "circle clause" providing that if, as a result of sales and resales, a "circle" was established, the transaction should be settled by a monetary adjustment and failure to deliver shipping documents should no longer be a breach. Where such a "circle" was established and export of goods of the contract description was *later* prohibited, it was held that the seller could not rely on a prohibition of export clause.[79]

Findings by an arbitrator on the question whether performance has been made impossible by prohibition of export (for the purpose of clauses of the kind here under discussion) have been held to be findings of "fact"[80]; but they give rise to issues of law where the arbitrator's conclusion on the point is inconsistent with the totality of the facts found by him.[81]

(ii) *Burden of Proof*

Burden on party relying on clause. The party (usually the seller) who seeks to rely on a "prohibition of export" clause must prove the facts required to bring the clause into operation.[82] For example, if the clause 18–346

[74] Above, paras 18–333, 18–338.

[75] See *Bremer Handelsgesellschaft mbH v C Mackprang Jr* [1979] 1 Lloyd's Rep. 221; below, para.18–349.

[76] Below, para.19–141.

[77] *Bremer Handelsgesellschaft mbH v C Mackprang Jr*, above.

[78] *Bunge SA v Kruse* [1979] 1 Lloyd's Rep. 279; affirmed [1980] 2 Lloyd's Rep. 142 on other grounds.

[79] *Tradax Export SA v Rocco Guiseppe & Figli* [1981] 1 Lloyd's Rep. 353, not following *Tradax v Carapelli* [1977] 2 Lloyd's Rep. 157 on this point.

[80] *Joseph Pyke & Son (Liverpool) Ltd v Richard Cornelius & Co.*, above n.73; *cf. Produce Brokers Co. Ltd v Weiss* (1918) 118 L.T. 111; 87 L.J.K.B. 472 (there are considerable divergences between these reports).

[81] *e.g. Soc Co-operative Suisse des Céréales etc. v La Plata Cereal Co. SA* (1947) 80 Ll.L.R. 530.

[82] *Tradax Export SA v André & Cie.* [1976] 1 Lloyd's Rep. 416; *Thomas P. Gonzalez Corp. v Müller's Mühle, Müller GmbH* [1980] 1 Lloyd's Rep. 445.

protects the seller in the event of "prohibition of export . . . preventing fulfilment",[83] then the seller must prove the existence of the embargo and that it prevented him from performing his part of the contract.[84] The ensuing discussion will deal mainly with clauses containing words of this kind: others which impose less exacting requirements will be considered in paragraph 18–352 below.

18–347 **Where the embargo is absolute.** If the seller relies on an absolute embargo covering the entire shipment period, he must show that such an embargo was imposed; but it is not necessary for him to show that he could have performed but for the embargo: *i.e.* that, when the embargo was imposed, he had goods of the contract description available and a ship to carry them.[85] Indeed, even if the buyer can show that the seller did not at that time have such goods or shipping space available, this is not sufficient to make the seller liable[86]; for he would (but for the embargo) have been entitled to ship later in the shipment period,[87] at least if the exact time of shipment during that period was at his, rather than at the buyer's, option[88]; and after the imposition of the embargo it would be pointless for him to continue his efforts to procure goods and make shipping arrangements in accordance with the contract. It has, indeed, been suggested that, if *the buyer* can show that the seller could not at any time during the shipment period have performed, then the buyer should be entitled to damages.[89] But there is no actual decision to this effect; and the analogy of the rule which applies where the seller relies on the common law doctrine of frustration suggests that, as a matter of substantive law, and quite apart from any question of burden of proof, the seller should not be liable in such a case.[90]

We saw in paragraph 18–345 above that a seller will not be excused by a prohibition clause of the kind here under consideration where, before the embargo was imposed, he had already shipped goods of the contract description and had not, when the embargo took effect, yet appropriated those goods to another contract. In such a case a seller who wishes to rely

---

[83] See below, para.18–348, after n.93.

[84] *Tradax Export SA v André & Cie*, above, at p.425; *Avimex SA v Dewulf & Cie.* [1979] 2 Lloyd's Rep. 57; *Raiffeisen Hauptgenossenschaft v Louis Dreyfus & Co. Ltd* [1981] 1 Lloyd's Rep. 345; and see above, paras 18–344 at n.55 and above, 18–345. Such a clause may go on to provide *how* the causal connection between the embargo and the failure to perform must be established: *e.g.* by specifying the documentation to be provided for this purpose, as in *Hoechong Products Ltd v Cargill Hong Kong Ltd* [1995] 1 W.L.R. 404.

[85] *Tradax Export SA v André & Cie.*, above, at pp.425, 427; so far as *contra*, a dictum in the same case at p.423 was disapproved in *Bremer Handelsgesellschaft mbH v Vanden Avenne-Izegem PVBA* [1978] 2 Lloyd's Rep. 109 at pp.114, 121; *Bremer Handelsgesellschaft mbH v C Mackprang Jr* [1979] 1 Lloyd's Rep. 221 at p.229.

[86] See authorities cited in previous note.

[87] Above, para.18–345; below, para.19–013.

[88] Under an f.o.b. contract, the time of shipment is prima facie at the buyer's option, but this prima facie rule can be displaced by the terms of the contract: see below, paras 20–030, 20–035, and 20–047 to 20–049.

[89] *Bremer Handelsgesellschaft mbH v C Mackprang Jr* [1979] 1 Lloyd's Rep. 221 at pp.227–228.

[90] *cf. Avery v Bowden* (1855) 5 E. & B. 714.

on the clause has the burden of proving that no such unappropriated goods afloat are available to him.[91]

Where the embargo is partial. The position is more complex where the embargo is only a partial one, from which certain categories of goods of the contract description are excepted. This situation arose when, in 1973, the United States authorities imposed an embargo on the export of soyabean meal. Warning that such an embargo might be imposed was given by an official bulletin of June 13. A further bulletin of June 27, imposed the embargo, by providing that no soyabean meal could be exported unless it fell within one of two "loopholes": the embargo did not apply to goods already on a lighter destined for an exporting vessel, or to goods for which loading aboard an exporting vessel had actually commenced.[92] On July 2, a further bulletin introduced a licensing system which provided for the issue of licences for 40 per cent of quantities outstanding under existing contracts; but between June 27 and July 2, the embargo was subject only to the two "loopholes". In a number of cases,[93] the question arose what the seller had to show to bring himself within a "prohibition" clause in a standard form contract prepared by a trade association,[94] on which contracts for June shipment of soyabean meal had been made. The clause provided that the contract was to be cancelled in case of "prohibition of export . . . preventing fulfilment . . ." of the contract; and the cases support a number of propositions with regard to burden of proof. 18–348

Seller must show that no excepted goods available. The general rule stated in paragraph 18–347 above in discussing absolute embargoes also applies where the embargo is partial, *i.e.* the seller does not have to show that he could have performed but for the embargo.[95] Nor, it is submitted, would he be deprived of the protection of the clause merely because *the buyer* proved that he (the seller) could *not* have performed, even if there had been no embargo: the reasoning which supports this submission in the case of an absolute embargo[96] is equally applicable where the embargo is partial. But the requirement that the seller must show that it was the embargo which prevented performance does impose an additional requirement in the case of a partial embargo: it requires the seller not only to show 18–349

---

[91] Below, para.18–349, n.99.

[92] For the later creation by the United States authorities of a third "loophole", see *André & Cie. v Tradax Export SA* [1983] 1 Lloyd's Rep. 254.

[93] The reported cases on this subject were said in *Bremer Handelsgesellschaft mbH v Westzucker GmbH (No. 3)* [1989] 1 Lloyd's Rep. 198 at p.199 (affirmed [1989] 1 Lloyd's Rep. 582) to number 45 and to represent no more than "the tip of a massive iceberg". It is one of the peculiarities of this line of cases that they were all litigated in England even though the events giving rise to them, and most of the parties, had no connection with this country.

[94] Grain and Feed Trade Association (or GAFTA) Form 100. For a revised version of the clause, see below, para.18–352; for the legal consequences of the eventual lifting of the embargo, see below, para.19–141.

[95] *Bremer Handelsgesellschaft mbH v Vanden Avenne-Izegem PVBA* [1978] 2 Lloyd's Rep. 109; *Tradax Export SA v Cook Industries Inc.* [1982] 1 Lloyd's Rep. 385.

[96] Above, para.18–347.

that the embargo has been imposed but also to "close the loopholes", *i.e.* to show that no goods of the contract description were available to him within one of the two "loopholes" to which the embargo was subject.[97] He must also (as in the case of an absolute embargo[98]) show that no unappropriated goods afloat were available to him, *i.e.* that he had not already shipped goods of the contract description before the embargo was imposed or, if he had shipped such goods, that he had not before then appropriated them to any other contract.[99] These propositions are analogous[1] to the rules which apply as a matter of general common law (*i.e.* apart from a prohibition of export clause) where performance of a contract is alleged to have been prevented by a frustrating event. In such a case, the party failing to perform is excused without having to show that, but for the event, he could have performed.[2] But he is only excused if the event did indeed prevent performance; so that, if the contract could have been performed in a number of different ways, he would not be excused by an event making only some of these methods of performance impossible.[3]

In *Bremer Handelsgesellschaft mbH v Vanden Avenne-Izegem PVBA*[4] the House of Lords affirmed the first of the above propositions, *i.e.* that the seller need not show that he could, but for the embargo, have shipped goods in accordance with the contract. But in that case it was found[5] or conceded[6] that the "loopholes" were not available to the seller; and later

---

[97] *Tradax Export SA v André & Cie.* [1976] 1 Lloyd's Rep. 416; *Continental Grain Export Corp. v STM Grain Ltd* [1979] 2 Lloyd's Rep. 460; *Tradax Export SA v Cook Industries Inc.* [1982] 1 Lloyd's Rep. 385; *Bremer Handelsgesellschaft mbH v Raiffeisen Hauptgenossenschaft* [1982] 1 Lloyd's Rep. 210, affirmed *ibid.*, p.599; *Bremer Handelsgesellschaft mbH v Continental Grain Co.* [1983] 1 Lloyd's Rep. 269 at p.283.

[98] Above, para.18–347.

[99] *Continental Grain Export Corp. v S.T.M. Grain Ltd* [1979] 2 Lloyd's Rep. 460 at p.473; *Cook Industries Inc. v Meunerie Liègeois* [1981] 1 Lloyd's Rep. 359 at p.366; *Bremer Handelsgesellschaft mbH v Continental Grain Co.* [1983] 1 Lloyd's Rep. 269 at p.283; *cf. Bremer Handelsgesellschaft mbH v Westzucker GmbH (No. 2)* [1981] 2 Lloyd's Rep. 130 (where this point was not open on appeal, not having been taken by the buyers in the court below); *Tradax Export SA v Cook Industries Inc.* [1982] 1 Lloyd's Rep. 385 (where the buyer was allowed to take the point on appeal for the first time as the law relating to it was not clarified until after the original hearing); *André & Cie. SA v Tradax Export SA* [1983] 1 Lloyd's Rep. 254 (where the seller succeeded in discharging the burden of proof on this point).

[1] For use of the analogy, see *Continental Grain Export Corp. v STM Grain Ltd* [1979] 2 Lloyd's Rep. 460 at p.471.

[2] *e.g. Avery v Bowden* (1855) 5 E. & B. 714.

[3] *e.g. The Furness Bridge* [1977] 2 Lloyd's Rep. 367; *Warinco AG v Fritz Mauthner* [1978] 1 Lloyd's Rep. 151.

[4] [1978] 2 Lloyd's Rep. 109 at pp.114, 121. The buyer accordingly lost his claim against the seller; but in later proceedings the buyer was held liable to his sub-buyer as he could not identify the seller as the "relevant shipper" (below, para.18–350): *Vanden Avenne-Izegem PVBA v Finagrain SA* [1985] 2 Lloyd's Rep. 99.

[5] [1978] 2 Lloyd's Rep. 109 at pp.112, 118, 129.

[6] See *ibid.*, at p.122; *Bremer Handelsgesellschaft mbH v C Mackprang Jr* [1979] 1 Lloyd's Rep. 221 at pp.223, 227.

cases[7] make it clear that the decision of the House of Lords has not affected the rule requiring the seller to show that goods within the "loopholes" were not available to him.[8]

18–350 **Goods to be shipped by person other than seller.** The rules stated in paragraph 18–349 above apply where the seller intended himself to ship the goods. Further complications can arise (and did arise in many of the soya-bean cases) where the seller occupies (or claims that he occupies) an intermediate position between a prospective shipper and the buyer in a "string" of contracts. The burden of proof which lies on the seller in such cases is complex and was in practice only rarely discharged.

In the first place, the burden (in cases of this kind) is on the seller first to "trace the string back to the relevant shipper",[9]—a task that can prove extremely difficult where no goods were ever shipped; for in such a case the obvious method of identifying the relevant shipper (*i.e.* by notices of appropriation[10] passed down the string) is plainly not available.[11] Although the question whether the seller has identified the relevant shipper has been described as one of "fact",[12] the cases yield a number of helpful guidelines on the issue. A seller who is not himself a shipper will clearly be unable to identify the relevant shipper if he simply contracts to sell goods of a particular kind and does not also contract to acquire goods of the contract description from a supplier[13]; for in such circumstances it has been said that "the chain of contracts leading back to the shippers failed at its very first link."[14] Assuming that there is a series of supply (as well as sale) contracts, one possible way of tracing the string back to the relevant shipper is by means of notices[15] claiming excuse under the prohibition clause[16]; but this is

---

[7] *Bremer Handelsgesellschaft mbH v C Mackprang Jr* [1979] 1 Lloyd's Rep. 221; *Avimex SA v Dewulf & Cie.* [1979] 1 Lloyd's Rep. 57 at p.58; *André & Cie. v Ets. Michel Blanc & Fils* [1979] 2 Lloyd's Rep. 427; *Bunge SA v Deutsche Conti-Handelsgesellschaft mbH* [1979] 2 Lloyd's Rep. 435; *Bremer Handelsgesellschaft mbH v Westzucker GmbH (No. 2)* [1981] 2 Lloyd's Rep. 130.

[8] *cf.* also *Joseph Pyke & Sons (Liverpool) Ltd v Richard Cornelius & Co.* [1955] 2 Lloyd's Rep. 747; *Continental Grain Export Corp. v STM Grain Ltd* [1979] 2 Lloyd's Rep. 460 at p.471 (where the "prohibition of export" clause was on terms substantially similar to those of the corresponding clause of GAFTA Form 100).

[9] *Bremer Handelsgesellschaft mbH v C Mackprang Jr* [1981] 1 Lloyd's Rep. 292 at p.297; The case concerns the "force majeure" clause in GAFTA Form 100, but the same principle applies to the "prohibition" clause: see *Cook Industries Inc. v Meunerie Liègeois SA* [1981] 1 Lloyd's Rep. 359; *Bremer Handelsgesellschaft mbH v Continental Grain Co.* [1983] 1 Lloyd's Rep. 269 at p.293. The seller succeeded on this point in *Bunge AG v Fuga AG* [1980] 2 Lloyd's Rep. 513 (though he failed on another: see below, para.18–357, n.80) and in *Tradax Export SA v Cook Industries SA* [1982] 1 Lloyd's Rep. 385 (though he failed on another: above, n.97).

[10] See below, para.19–017 as to notices of appropriation under c.i.f. contracts.

[11] *Cook Industries Inc. v Meunerie Liègeois SA* [1981] 1 Lloyd's Rep. 359 at p.365; *Bremer Handelsgesellschaft mbH v C Mackprang Jr* [1981] 1 Lloyd's Rep. 292 at p.297.

[12] *Deutsche Conti-Handelsgesellschaft mbH v Bremer Handelsgesellschaft mbH* [1984] 1 Lloyd's Rep. 447 at p.449, 450; *cf. European Grain & Shipping Ltd v Peter Cremer* [1982] 1 Lloyd's Rep. 211.

[13] *Avimex SA v Dewulf & Cie.* [1979] 2 Lloyd's Rep. 57.

[14] *Bunge AG v Fuga AG* [1980] 2 Lloyd's Rep. 513 at p.520.

[15] See below, para.18–356.

[16] *Cook Industries Inc. v Meunerie Liègeois SA* [1981] 1 Lloyd's Rep. 359 at p.365.

not of itself sufficient. A person is not identified as the relevant shipper merely because the seller, *after* the embargo has been imposed, gives a notice appropriating goods shipped by that person[17]; nor does the mere fact that the seller appropriates in part fulfilment of the contract goods shipped by a particular shipper necessarily identify that shipper as the relevant one for the balance of the quantity sold[18]; nor can the seller identify himself as the relevant shipper merely by giving notice claiming excuse under the prohibition clause.[19] In holding that a seller had failed to identify either himself or a third person as relevant shipper, the courts have in a number of cases stressed that the seller was not bound to appropriate to his contract with the buyer goods shipped by himself or the alleged shipper but retained complete freedom to appropriate goods shipped by another.[20] It seems to follow from this reasoning that the shipper must be named or capable of being identified[21] so as to oblige the seller (either by the contract or by a notice of appropriation) to tender goods, or documents relating to goods, shipped by that shipper: it is not enough for the seller to show merely that he intended to appropriate those goods in performance of his obligations under the contract of sale.[22] If the seller cannot identify the relevant shipper, the string is incomplete: the situation is simply one where the seller (or his immediate or remote supplier) intends at some stage between the time of contracting and that fixed for performance to acquire goods of the contract description from an as yet undesignated shipper. In such a case the seller cannot rely on a prohibition clause merely because the embargo has been imposed.[23]

If the seller can show that there was a complete string and if he can identify the relevant shipper, he must next establish that that shipper was, by reason of the embargo, prevented from performing his obligations under the supply contract between himself and the next person in the string. It follows that the seller must show that the relevant shipper had no goods available to him which were either within the "loopholes" or had already been shipped before the embargo was imposed but had not yet been appropriated to any other contract.[24] If there is more than one relevant

---

[17] *Bremer Handelsgesellschaft mbH v C Mackprang Jr* [1981] 1 Lloyd's Rep. 292.

[18] *Bremer Handelsgesellschaft mbH v Deutsche Conti-Handelsgesellschaft mbH* [1984] 1 Lloyd's Rep. 397; *Deutsche Conti-Handelsgesellschaft mbH v Bremer Handelsgesellschaft mbH* [1984] 1 Lloyd's Rep. 447.

[19] *Bremer Handelsgesellschaft mbH v Continental Grain Co.* [1983] 1 Lloyd's Rep 269 at p.290.

[20] *Bremer Handelsgesellschaft mbH v Bunge Corp.* [1983] 1 Lloyd's Rep. 476 at p.481; *Deutsche Conti-Handelsgesellschaft mbH v Bremer Handelsgesellschaft mbH* [1984] 1 Lloyd's Rep. 447 at p.449.

[21] See *Bunge AG v Fuga AG* [1980] 2 Lloyd's Rep. 513 at p.520.

[22] See *Deutsche Conti-Handelsgesellschaft mbH v Bremer Handelsgesellschaft mbH* [1984] 1 Lloyd's Rep. 447 at p.449; *Vanden Avenne-Izegem PVBA v Finagrain SA* [1985] 2 Lloyd's Rep. 99.

[23] *Bunge SA v Deutsche Conti-Handelsgesellschaft* [1979] 2 Lloyd's Rep. 435; *Bunge SA v Deutsche Conti-Handelsgesellschaft (No. 2)* [1980] 1 Lloyd's Rep. 352; *Bremer Handelsgesellschaft mbH v Westzucker GmbH* [1981] 1 Lloyd's Rep 207; *Bunge SA v Compagnie Européenne de Céréales* [1982] 1 Lloyd's Rep. 307.

[24] Above, para.18–349; *Cook Industries Inc. v Meunerie Liègeois* [1981] 1 Lloyd's Rep. 359; *Bremer Handelsgesellschaft mbH v Continental Grain Co.* [1983] 1 Lloyd's Rep. 269 at 283; *Bremer Handelsgesellschaft mbH v Bunge Corp.* [1983] 1 Lloyd's Rep. 476 at p.481 (where the seller failed to identify the "relevant shipper").

shipper, the seller must show that no such goods were available to any of those shippers.[25] The burden of proof on all these issues is on the seller: hence if he adduces no evidence as to the availability of such goods to the relevant shipper, he will be liable for breach of the contract of sale.[26] It may seem hard on a seller thus to hold him liable for failing to provide evidence that no goods within the "loopholes" were available to a third person (the relevant shipper).[27] But the result of putting the burden on the buyer to prove that goods *were* available within the "loopholes" might be to "make a breach of contract too easy."[28] The buyer would have no better access than the seller to facts relating to the availability of goods within the "loopholes" to the relevant shipper; and if the buyer failed to adduce such proof but goods within the "loopholes" were in fact available, the seller would profit from the embargo by being able to dispose of those goods at a price enhanced by it.[29]

There is, at least in theory, another way in which a seller may be protected by a prohibition clause. The possibility has been judicially recognised that he could be so protected, even though he had failed to identify the relevant shipper, if he could show that no goods of the contract description could have been shipped within the "loopholes" by any possibly relevant shipper, and that no such goods were already afloat (and not appropriated to any other contract) when the embargo was imposed[30]; but there appears to be no reported case in which a seller has succeeded in discharging the difficult task of proving a multiple negative proposition of this kind.

Burden of proof and substantive duties. In the case of a partial embargo, such as one which is subject to "loopholes"[31] a distinction must be drawn between two questions. The first is the question of fact whether the seller or relevant shipper had available to him goods which he could have appropriated to the contract: *e.g.*, because they fell within the "loopholes", so that their shipment was not prevented by the embargo, or because they had been shipped by the seller or by the relevant shipper before the embargo took effect and had not been appropriated to another contract. It is in relation to such questions of fact that the rules as to burden of proof stated in paragraphs 18–346 to 18–350 above apply. The second question is one of law and relates to the substantive duties of the seller, assuming that 18–351

[25] *Cook Industries v Tradax Export SA* [1985] 2 Lloyd's Rep. 454.
[26] *Bremer Handelsgesellschaft mbH v C Mackprang Jr* [1979] 1 Lloyd's Rep. 221.
[27] [1979] 1 Lloyd's Rep. 221 at p.230, *per* Shaw L.J.
[28] *ibid.*, at p.226, *per* Stephenson L.J.
[29] *ibid.*, at p.224, *per* Lord Denning M.R. The argument is perhaps too strongly stated, since if the seller actually pursued this course the buyer would have little difficulty in discharging any burden of proof with regard to the "loopholes" which the law might impose on him.
[30] This possibility is recognised in *Cook Industries Inc. v Meunerie Liègeois* [1981] 1 Lloyd's Rep. 359 at p.363 and in *Bremer Handelsgesellschaft mbH v Westzucker GmbH (No. 3)* [1989] 1 Lloyd's Rep. 582, where the seller's attempt to prove these facts failed.
[31] As in the case of the United States embargo on the export of soyabean meal: above, para.18–348.

he can discharge the burden of proving that no goods of the contract description were at his or at the relevant shipper's disposal for the purpose of performing the contract. This question is whether the seller is then bound to acquire goods of the contract description from some other source: *e.g.* by buying goods which had already been shipped before the embargo took effect, or (in the case of a partial embargo) goods excepted from the embargo. If, under the rules stated elsewhere in this book,[32] the seller is under *no* duty to make a substitute purchase,[33] the availability of an alternative source of supply becomes irrelevant, so that no issue as to burden of proof can arise in respect of it.[34] If he is under such a duty,[35] the burden of proving that no such goods could have been obtained will, once again, be on the seller; and the burden will be extremely hard to discharge since it would require him to show that no unappropriated goods of the contract description were available to *any* shipper or could be acquired afloat.

18–352 **Other less exacting requirements.** The soyabean cases discussed above illustrate the difficulties which faced sellers who sought to rely on prohibition and similar clauses which applied only where the sellers could show that performance had been "prevented" by the supervening event. It was, for example, often impossible for them to discharge the burden of tracing the string back to the "relevant shipper"[36] and that of "closing the loopholes."[37] It was probably with reference to these difficulties that prohibitions of export were said to have been "a seller's nightmare".[38] The source of these difficulties in the soyabean cases lay in the words "preventing . . . fulfilment" in the prohibition clause of the standard trade association form of contract used in those cases[39]; and it was with a view to improving the seller's position that this clause was later redrafted. In its revised version it applied in case of a prohibition or of an executive act of the government of the country of origin "restricting export whether partially or otherwise"; and it provided that "such restriction shall be deemed by both parties to apply to this contract and to the extent of such total or partial restriction to prevent fulfilment whether by shipment or by any other means whatsoever". Taken literally, these words might be thought to have been intended to apply irrespective of any causal connection[40] between the prohibition and

[32] Above, para.18–345, below, paras 19–011, 19–141.
[33] *e.g.* where the case falls within an exception to the general rule requiring a c.i.f. seller who is prevented from shipping goods to acquire them afloat: see references in n.32 above.
[34] *Bunge SA v Kruse* [1979] 1 Lloyd's Rep. 279 (affirmed on other grounds [1980] 2 Lloyd's Rep. 142) was doubted in *Bremer Handelsgesellschaft mbH v C Mackprang Jr* [1979] 1 Lloyd's Rep. 221 at 228 so far as it can be interpreted as laying down a rule as to burden of proof. For criticism of the case so far as it lays down a rule of substance, see below, para.19–141.
[35] See *Bunge SA v Deutsche Conti-Handelsgellschaft mbH* [1979] 2 Lloyd's Rep. 435; below, para.19–141.
[36] Above, para.18–350.
[37] Above, para.18–349.
[38] *Pancommerce SA v Veecheema BV* [1983] 2 Lloyd's Rep. 304 at p.307.
[39] Grain and Feed Trade Association Form 100 Clause 21.
[40] *cf.* above, para.18–344.

the seller's non-fulfilment. But in *Pancommerce SA v Veecheema BV*[41] the Court of Appeal rejected the argument that the sellers could rely on this provision merely because a prohibition had been imposed, when in fact that prohibition had not prevented them from performing. In reaching this conclusion the court seems to have been influenced by the possibility that, if the sellers' argument had prevailed, they would have been entitled to cancel their contract with the buyers, even though they were in fact able to perform it, and so to take advantage of the rise in the market price of the goods which had resulted from the export prohibition.[42] Sir John Donaldson M.R. said that, to adopt the seller's construction of the clause would convert prohibition of export from a "seller's nightmare . . . into a seller's dream".[43] But there is no reason in principle why a clause should not (if sufficiently clear in its wording) entitle the seller to refuse to perform on the occurrence of a specified event even though the event does not in fact affect his ability to perform at all. The case which supports this view[44] is not now commonly relied on, but it appears to be a correct application of the overriding principle that the operation of such clauses depends ultimately on the wording of the particular clause in each case. General policies (such as that stated in the *Pancommerce* case) may influence, but cannot in the last resort determine, decisions on such questions of construction.

(iii) *Partial Prevention*

Allocation of available supplies.[45] A seller may enter into a number of contracts containing prohibition of export (or similar) clauses and may, find that, under exceptions to a partial embargo, he has available for export a quantity of goods sufficient to fulfil one or some of these contracts, but not all. In such a case[46] it seems that no single buyer can complain if the seller divides the available goods *pro rata* among the various buyers.[47] It has further been suggested that the seller is bound to divide the available goods, so that each buyer is entitled to his *pro rata* share.[48] The first of these 18–353

[41] Above n.38; for another aspect of this case, see below, para.18–353.

[42] This was not in fact the motive for the seller's seeking to rely on the clause in the *Pancommerce* case.

[43] [1983] 2 Lloyd's Rep. 304 at p.307; *cf. Tennants (Lancashire) v CS Wilson Ltd* [1917] A.C. 495.

[44] *Ford & Sons (Oldham) Ltd v Henry Leetham & Sons Ltd* (1921) Com.Cas. 55, above, para.18–344.

[45] See generally Treitel, *Frustration and Force Majeure* 2nd ed. (2004), paras 5–017 to 5–032.

[46] Where he has *no* goods available, questions of allocation of the quantity that he might have had available, if he had not been in breach, do not arise: *Bremer Handelsgesellschaft mbH v Contintental Grain Co.* [1983] 1 Lloyd's Rep. 269 at p.293.

[47] *Bremer Handelsgesellschaft mbH v Vanden Avenne-Izegem PVBA* [1978] 2 Lloyd's Rep. 109 at pp.115, 128, 131 (where the exact method of allocation to be adopted is left open); *cf. Tennants (Lancashire) Ltd v C S Wilson Ltd* [1917] A.C. 495 at pp.511–512.

[48] *Bremer Handelsgesellschaft mbH v C Mackprang Jr* [1979] 1 Lloyd's Rep. 221 at pp.221 to 224; the question is left open in *Continental Grain Export Corp. v STM Grain Ltd* [1979] 2 Lloyd's Rep. 460 at p.473.

rules simply states, negatively, that no buyer is entitled to the whole; the second affirmatively states that each buyer is entitled to his share. For the purpose of the second rule, the order of transactions may, however, also be relevant. Thus in a case in which a seller relied not on a prohibition of export, but on a *force majeure*, clause, it was held that he had acted properly in allocating the whole of his available supply to a buyer whose contract antedated that between the seller and another claimant.[49] Whether the claims of the various buyers are, as between them, to be settled on a *pro rata* or temporal basis thus remains uncertain. Probably the overriding test is whether the seller acted reasonably in allocating the available supplies.[50] In deciding the issue of reasonableness, the court could also have regard to other circumstances than the order in which the contracts were made: *e.g.* that the quantity available was so small that apportionment between purchasers would not make commercial sense.[51]

The possible solutions discussed above are based on the assumption that the seller has entered into binding contracts with more than one buyer for total amounts exceeding the quantity that he is allowed (under the exceptions to the embargo) to export. Where a seller has a binding contract with only one buyer and a non-contractual arrangement with another (*e.g.* to give the latter the "first refusal" of a specified amount) the principle of *pro rata* division does not apply. Thus if the seller is allowed to export only enough to satisfy the buyer with whom he has entered into the binding contract, the whole of that amount must be allocated to that buyer.[52] Nor, *a fortiori*, can the seller rely on a partial embargo as an excuse for not performing his contract with the buyer so as to keep quantities available under exceptions to the embargo for his own purposes; for to allow him to do this would enable him to benefit at the buyer's expense from the rising market price likely to result from the embargo.[53]

18–354 **Scope of principle of allocation.** Our concern in paragraph 18–353 has been with the effect of partial prevention of performance on the operation of express contractual provisions which excuse a seller in the specified events which have occurred. The judicial statements which support the principle of allocation of available supplies all occur in cases of this kind, and not in cases in which the seller relies on the common law doctrine of

---

[49] *Intertradex SA v Lesieur Torteaux SARL* [1978] 2 Lloyd's Rep. 509; *cf.* above, para.6–053. It is assumed that the clause gives some protection to the seller; if not (and if there is no frustration) he is liable to all the buyers, as in *Hong Guan & Co. v R Jumabhoy* [1960] A.C. 684, below, para.19–140.

[50] *Continental Grain Export Corp. v STM Grain Ltd* [1979] 2 Lloyd's Rep. 460 at p.473; *Bremer Handelsgesellschaft mbH v Continental Grain Co.* [1983] 1 Lloyd's Rep. 269 at p.292 (where the seller had no excuse as he had failed to identify the "relevant shipper": above, para.18–350).

[51] [1983] 1 Lloyd's Rep. 269 at p.293.

[52] *Pancommerce SA v Veecheema BV* [1983] 2 Lloyd's Rep. 304 (not following UCC, s.2–615(b), which allows the seller to take into account "regular customers not then under contract").

[53] Under UCC, s.2–615(b) the seller can also take into account "his own requirements for further manufacture" but *not* for resale. English law would give the buyer priority in both cases; this follows *a fortiori* from the *Pancommerce* case, above.

frustration. In cases of the latter kind, there are or may be two difficulties in applying the principle of allocation.[54] One is that frustration is said to lead to automatic total discharge,[55] while allocation of supplies would amount to modification of the contracts. It is, however, possible to point to many possible mitigations of the rule of automatic total discharge[56] and the possibility that the courts might create a further such exception in the present context should not (it is submitted) be wholly ruled out. A second difficulty is that allocation may be regarded as an "election" by the seller, so as to bring into operation the rule that a party cannot rely on frustration which is "self-induced".[57] It is submitted that this objection, too, should not be regarded as conclusive. It could be met by arguing that the method of allocation (whether on a pro rata or temporal basis, or by reference to the standard of reasonableness) is laid down by law[58]: if so, the allocation does not result from the election of the seller. A further possible approach is to say that the seller can rely on partial embargo, not as a ground of frustration, but as a partial excuse for non-performance. It seems that such an excuse is available where a physical shortage, occurring without the fault of the seller, prevents him from fully performing a contract with a single buyer.[59] It is submitted that there is no compelling reason why this principle should not apply where a shortage of supply results from an export embargo, and where contracts have been made with more than one buyer.

A seller cannot rely on the principle of allocation where there is at the relevant time *no* shortage of supply. Thus in one case the principle was held not to apply where the seller had merely decided to divert to another contract a cargo which he had originally appropriated to the buyer and the alleged difficulties of finding a substitute cargo for the buyer arose only after the seller had taken this step.[60]

Effect of partial embargo on liability of buyer. Most of the reported cases arising out of partial embargoes concern the liability of the seller, who cannot rely on the prohibition clause with regard to quantities not affected by the embargo: *e.g.* in the soyabean cases he would not be protected by the clause with regard to the 40 per cent. which he was permitted to export.[61] The buyer, on the other hand, would not be bound to accept the smaller quantity[62]; but he would be bound to accept the full contract quantity if the seller was able to obtain it under an exception to the embargo or from a **18–355**

---

[54] *J Lauritzen AS v Wijsmuller BV (The Super Servant Two)* [1989] 1 Lloyd's Rep. 148 at p.158; [1990] 1 Lloyd's Rep. 1 at p.8.
[55] *e.g. Hirji Mulji v Cheong Yue SS Co. Ltd* [1926] A.C. 497 at p.505.
[56] *e.g.* in cases of "divisible contracts"; see *Stubbs v Holywell Ry* (1867) L.R. 2 Ex. 311; or of "self-induced" frustration: see *F C Shepherd & Co. v Jerrom* [1987] Q.B. 301; and see generally Treitel, *Frustration and Force Majeure* 2nd ed. (2004), paras 15–013—15–041.
[57] *Bank Line Ltd v Arthur Capel Ltd* [1919] A.C. 434 at p.452.
[58] Above, para.18–353, nn. 49, 50.
[59] See *HR & S Sainsbury Ltd v Street* [1972] 1 W.L.R. 834; above, para.6–038.
[60] *Coastal (Bermuda) Petroleum Ltd v VTT Vulcan Petroleum SA (The Marine Star)* [1993] 1 Lloyd's Rep. 329.
[61] *cf.* above, para.18–338.
[62] Sale of Goods Act 1979, s.30(1).

source not affected by it. In one of the soyabean cases,[63] the sellers tendered documents in respect of 40 per cent of the contract quantity "in total fulfilment of 40 per cent", and the buyers accepted this tender. It later turned out that the sellers were able to ship the remaining 60 per cent and it was held that there had been no variation of the contract but only a statement by the sellers of their mistaken belief as to the effect of the embargo. Hence the buyers were liable to accept the balance of 60 per cent of the goods.

(iv) *Notice of Supervening Events*

18–356 **Requirements as to notice, etc.** A seller who wishes to rely on a prohibition of export or *force majeure* clause[64] may, by the terms of the clause, be obliged to take certain preliminary steps: *e.g.* to give written notice to the buyer within a stipulated time indicating from which port or ports he had intended to ship, stating that such shipment is likely to be prevented and specifying the cause of such prevention.[65] Clearly, the party wishing to rely on the clause cannot rely on it if he simply fails to give the notice; but greater difficulty arises where he gives a notice which is defective, in that it fails in some way to comply with the contractual requirements. Two questions then arise: the first relates to the legal effects of defects in the notice and the second to waiver of those defects.

18–357 **Defects in the notice.** The first of the above questions has arisen in a number of cases in which the notice was defective in being out of time. The issue in these cases was whether the contractual requirement as to the timing of the notice was a condition or an intermediate term.[66] If it was a condition, the seller could not rely on the clause and so was liable for non-delivery; if it was an intermediate term, he could rely on the clause (unless the delay seriously prejudiced the buyer) but he was liable in damages, not for non-delivery, but in respect of the loss suffered by the buyer in consequence of the seller's delay in giving the notice. The question whether the contractual requirement as to the time of giving notice is a condition or an intermediate term[67] depends, as Lord Wilberforce said in *Bremer*

[63] *André & Cie v Cook Industries Inc.* [1987] 2 Lloyd's Rep. 463.
[64] As to *force majeure* clauses, see further below, paras 19–138, 19–139.
[65] For the effect of a notice relating to only part of the quantity sold, see *Bremer Handelsgesellschaft mbH v Archer Daniels Midland International SA* [1981] 2 Lloyd's Rep. 483.
[66] See generally, para.10–033, above.
[67] A third possibility is that the term relating to the timing of the notice may be neither a condition nor an intermediate term, but a term the breach of which gives rise only to a right to damages, even if the breach causes serious prejudice to the injured party. In *Friends Provident Life & Pensions Ltd v Sirius International Insurance* [2005] EWCA Civ. 601, [2005] All E.R. (Comm.) 145 this was held to be the sole effect of a term in an insurance contract requiring notice of claims to be given "immediately" on the occurrence of specified events; see also *Ronson International v Patrick* [2005] EWHC 1767 (HC), [2005] 2 All E.R. (Comm.) 453 at [38]–[41]. The cases discussed in para.18–357 provide no illustration of such a classification of a provision in a contract for the sale of goods requiring notice of supervening events to be given by a party seeking to invoke a clause specifying the effect of such events on the obligations of the parties.

Handelsgesellschaft mbH v Vanden Avenne-Izegem PVBA on three factors: "(i) the form of the clause itself, (ii) the relation of the clause to the contract as a whole, (iii) general considerations of law."[68] In the present context, two such general considerations or trends are of particular significance. The first is the judicial reluctance[69] to classify terms as conditions where the parties themselves have not clearly expressed them as such and where they have not been previously so classified by statute or by judicial decision.[70] The second, countervailing, trend relates to stipulations as to the time of performance: these have been commonly (though not invariably[71]) classified as conditions where they specify a date by, or time within, which the stipulated acts were to be done.[72] Such a classification promotes certainty: in the present context, it enables the buyer to know precisely when the seller's failure to comply with the requirement (*e.g.* as to giving notice) will prevent the seller from relying on the clause and so put him in breach. But such certainty is not attainable where the terms of the clause neither specify, nor make it possible to determine, the *precise* time at which the notice is to be given; and a term of this kind is unlikely to be treated as a condition.[73] The distinction between the two types of terms is illustrated by two provisions in the contract considered by the House of Lords in *Bremer Handelsgesellschaft mbH v Vanden Avenne-Izegem PVBA*. The first formed part of a prohibition of export clause; it required the sellers to "advise buyers without delay" of any prohibition making shipment impossible. This was held to be an intermediate term only,[74] so that failure to give the required notice "without delay" did not prevent the sellers from

---

[68] [1978] 2 Lloyd's Rep. 109 at p. 113.

[69] *e.g. Cehave NV v Bremer Handelsgesellschaft mbH (The Hansa Nord)* [1976] Q.B. 44; *Tradax Internacional SA v Goldschmidt SA* [1977] 2 Lloyd's Rep. 604 at p.612; the trend is recognised in *Bunge Corp. New York v Tradax Export SA* [1981] W.L.R. 711 at pp. 715, 727, though not applied in that case: see text at n.72 below, and below, paras 19–061 to 19–064, 20–032.

[70] [1978] 2 Lloyd's Rep. 109 at pp.113, 121.

[71] *State Trading Corp. of India v M Golodetz Ltd* [1989] 2 Lloyd's Rep. 277; *ERG Petroli SpA v Vitol SA (The Ballenita)* [1992] 2 Lloyd's Rep. 455; *Torvald Klaveness A/S v Arni Maritime Corp. (The Gregos)* [1994] 1 W.L.R. 1465 at p.1475; *Universal Bulk Carriers Ltd v André & Cie* [2001] EWCA Civ. 588, [2001] 2 Lloyd's Rep. 65.

[72] *e.g. Bunge Corp. v Tradax Export SA* [1981] 1 W.L.R. 711; *Compagnie Commerciale Sucres et Denrées v C Czarnikow Ltd (The Naxos)* [1990] 1 W.L.R. 1337; *B S & N Ltd BVI v Micado Shipping Ltd (Malta) (No.2) (The Seaflower)* [2001] 1 All E.R. (Comm.) 240.

[73] See *Tradax Export SA v Italgrani di Francesco Ambrosio* [1986] 1 Lloyd's Rep. 112 at p. 120; *Alfred McAlpine Plc v BAI (Run-off) Ltd* [2000] 1 Lloyd's Rep. 437; *SHV Gas Supply & Trading SAS v Naftomar Shipping & Trading Co Ltd Inc (The Azur Gaz)* [2005] EWHC 2528 (Comm.), [2006] 1 Lloyd's Rep. 163 at [39]; in this case, adequate notice was given: *ibid.* at [38]. Contrast *Société Italo-Belge pour le Commerce et l'Industrie v Palm Vegetable Oils (Malaysia) Sdn. Bhd. (The Post Chaser)* [1981] 2 Lloyd's Rep. 695 at p. 700 (criticised on this point in para.19–064, below).

[74] [1978] 2 Lloyd's Rep. 109; applied on this point in *Bunge SA v Kruse* [1979] 1 Lloyd's Rep. 279 (affirmed on other grounds [1980] 2 Lloyd's Rep. 142); *Bremer Handelsgesellschaft mbH v Westzucker GmbH* [1981] 1 Lloyd's Rep. 207; *Bremer Handelsgesellschaft mbH v Westzucker GmbH (No. 2)* [1981] 1 Lloyd's Rep. 214 at p.222, affirmed [1981] 2 Lloyd's Rep. 130; *Bremer Handelsgesellschaft mbH v Finagrain, etc. SA* [1981] 2 Lloyd's Rep. 259.

relying on the clause: it would have had this effect only if the resulting delay had caused serious prejudice to the buyer. The term was not expressly made a condition and could in this respect be contrasted with other provisions in the contract which were so drafted as to take effect as conditions. Nor would certainty be significantly promoted by classifying the term as a condition, since the phrase "without delay" was inherently vague: it raised "questions of degree",[75] and therefore did not enable the buyer to tell *exactly* when the seller was in default. The second stipulation formed part of a *force majeure* clause in the same contract; it provided that notice of certain events delaying shipment was to be given within seven days of their occurrence; and that a further notice was to be given claiming an extension of the shipment period "not later than two business days after the last day of the contract period of shipment". The clause went on to give the buyer an option to cancel by notice to be received by the seller, again by a precisely specified day, and to provide exactly when the contract was to be considered void, in default of the exercise of this option. It was held that the stipulation as to the time at which notice claiming the extension must be given was a condition. Unlike the prohibition clause, it specified fixed days for the giving of the various notices. It was a "complete regulatory code" and "accurate compliance with its stipulations" was "essential to avoid commercial confusion in view of the possibility of there being long strings of buyers and sellers."[76]

Most of the cases on this topic are concerned with notices which are out of time, but the notice may also be defective in some other way. For example, in *Bremer Handelsgesellschaft mbH v Vanden Avenne-Izegem PVBA*[77] the notice under the *force majeure* clause was defective, not only because it was late, but also because it failed with sufficient certainty to specify the intended port or ports of shipment. This breach, too, appears to have been regarded as one of condition, probably because it formed part of the same "complete regulatory code" as the provisions as to the time of giving notice. Where the clause contains no such "code" covering more than one requirement, the question whether any particular requirement is a condition or an intermediate term will depend on the general principles of the law of contract on which the distinction between these two categories of terms is based.[78] In particular, it is submitted, it will depend on the words in which the requirement is expressed and (if these are equivocal) on the importance which the party to whom the notice is given may be supposed to have attached to compliance with the requirement in question.[79]

Where the notice is alleged to be in some way defective, it is usually the buyer who takes this point for the purpose of holding the seller liable. But sometimes, paradoxically, it is the seller who will seek to rely on defects in

---

[75] *The Naxos*, above, n.72, at p.1347.
[76] [1978] 2 Lloyd's Rep. 109 at p.116; *Berg & Son Ltd v Vanden Avenne-Izegem PVBA* [1977] 1 Lloyd's Rep. 500 (where the seller's notice claiming extension was defective in failing to specify the port of intended shipment; contrast on this point *Alfred C Toepfer v Peter Cremer* [1975] 2 Lloyd's Rep. 118).
[77] [1978] 2 Lloyd's Rep. 109.
[78] See Treitel, *The Law of Contract* (11th ed.), pp.795–800.
[79] *ibid.*, p.800.

the notice; for such defects may alter the time of breach in a way that benefits him on a fluctuating market. As a general rule, the seller cannot impugn the validity of his own notice if that notice is accepted as good by the buyer.[80] It is only if the buyer treats the notice as bad that the seller, too, can rely on defects in it, to the extent that it is to his advantage to do so.[81]

Waiver of defects in the notice. Even where the notice is defective in a way that amounts to a breach of condition, the seller may nevertheless be entitled to rely on the prohibition or *force majeure* clause if the buyer has waived the breach. It is well known that "waiver" is used in several senses,[82] of which two are relevant here. In the first of these, it refers to the abandonment of a right; in the second to an election between remedies, *i.e.* between enforcing the contract and rescinding it on account of the breach.[83] The context in which waiver falls to be considered here is that of a supervening event which results in a failure on the part of the seller to deliver, and usually in an increase in the market price of the goods. In these circumstances the buyer will wish to enforce his rights under the contract, rather than to rescind or terminate it. If he has "waived" the seller's failure to comply with the requirements of the clause, then the seller will be able to rely on the clause as an excuse for not performing his obligations under the contract. It follows that "waiver" is here used to refer to the abandonment by the buyer of his right to delivery (or to damages for non-delivery), and not to the process of election between remedies which would arise if the buyer were seeking, not to enforce the contract, but to rescind it. The distinction is important since the conditions which must be satisfied for the operation of the two types of waiver, though similar, are not identical.[84] 18–358

To give rise to waiver in the sense of the abandonment of a right, the buyer must in the first place unequivocally represent that he is not objecting to the defects in the notice[85]; and the seller must rely on that representation so as to make it inequitable[86] for the buyer to insist on his strict legal rights to full performance of the contract by reason of the defect in the notice.[87] It has been held that the first of these requirements was not satisfied where

[80] *Alfred C Toepfer v Peter Cremer* [1975] 2 Lloyd's Rep. 118 at 123, 128; *Bunge AG v Fuga AG* [1980] 2 Lloyd's Rep. 513 (these cases concerned *force majeure* clauses).

[81] As in *Avimex SA v Dewulf & Cie* [1979] 2 Lloyd's Rep. 57 (where the buyer relied on defects in the seller's notice invoking a *force majeure* clause on the issue of liability, though not on the issue of damages).

[82] See Treitel, *The Law of Contract* (11th ed.), pp.811–813.

[83] *Glencore Grain Ltd v Flacker Shipping Ltd (The Happy Day)* [2002] EWCA Civ 1068, [2002] 2 Lloyd's Rep. 487 at [64]–[65].

[84] Treitel above, n.82, pp.813–816 *Motor Oil Hellas (Corinth) Refineries SA v Shipping Corp. of India (The Kanchenjunga)* [1990] 1 Lloyd's Rep. 391 at p. 399; *Oliver Ashworth (Holdings) Ltd v Ballard (Kent) Ltd* [2000] Ch.12 at p. 28.

[85] Treitel, above, n.82, at pp.107–109, stating this requirement for so-called "promissory estoppel"; an expression now often used interchangeably with this kind of "waiver": see below at n.94 and 95.

[86] Merely furnishing documents in proof of *force majeure* was held not to be sufficient to satisfy this requirement in *Bremer Handelsgesellschaft mbH v Deutsche Conti-Handelsgesellschaft mbH* [1983] 1 Lloyd's Rep. 689.

[87] *Bremer Handelsgesellschaft mbH v Bunge Corp.* [1983] 1 Lloyd's Rep. 476.

the notice, though actually defective, was good on its face and the buyer had no means of knowing that it was defective.[88] This may seem to support a separate requirement that the buyer must have been aware of the defect in the notice at the time of the alleged waiver. But knowledge of the breach is not a separate requirement of this type of waiver[89] (though it is a requirement of waiver in the sense of election between remedies[90]). The decisions under consideration can best be explained on the ground that, if the defective notice is good on its face, the buyer's apparent acceptance of it cannot be regarded as an unequivocal representation that he will not rely on defects in it which are latent, and certainly cannot be reasonably understood in this sense by the seller who gave the notice.

The operation of the kind of waiver here under consideration is illustrated by *Bremer Handelsgesellschaft mbH v Vanden Avenne-Izegem PVBA*,[91] where the seller gave a notice, which was out of time, claiming an extension of the shipment period. The buyer, while objecting to the quantity of goods specified in the notice, did not raise any point as to its being out of time. He continued to press for delivery in the extended period and during it the seller made efforts to appropriate goods to the contract. It was held that the buyer had waived the seller's breach in giving notice out of time.[92] Such a result may also be explained on the grounds of estoppel or promissory estoppel[93]; indeed, in the context of abandonment of rights, the expressions "waiver" and "promissory estoppel" are now often used interchangeably[94] and have been described as "two ways of saying exactly the same thing".[95] In whatever way the rule may be described, a buyer is not

---

[88] *Avimex SA v Dewulf & Cie.* [1979] 2 Lloyd's Rep. 57 at pp. 67–68; *Cook Industries v Tradax Export SA* [1985] 2 Lloyd's Rep. 454.

[89] *The Kanchenjunga*, above, n.84, at p.399.

[90] *Peyman v Lanjani* [1985] Ch. 457.

[91] [1978] 2 Lloyd's Rep. 109; *cf. Intertradex SA v Lesieur-Torteaux SARL* [1978] 2 Lloyd's Rep. 509; *Bremer Handelsgesellschaft mbH v C Mackprang Jr* [1979] 1 Lloyd's Rep. 221.

[92] The case was described in *Glencore Grain Ltd v Flacker Shipping Ltd (The Happy Day)* [2002] EWCA Civ 1068, [2002] 2 Lloyd's Rep. 487 at [64] as one of "waiver by election" (*sc.* of remedies) but the description may, with respect, be doubted. The buyer in *Bremer v Vanden* was seeking to enforce the contract of sale and so could have had no interest in rescinding (as opposed to affirming) it. The issue was not whether he had lost his right to rescind by election between remedies but whether he had abandoned his right to delivery (or to damages for non-delivery).

[93] *Bremer Handelsgesellschaft mbH v Finagrain, etc. SA* [1981] 2 Lloyd's Rep. 259 at p.263.

[94] See Treitel, *The Law of Contract*, (11th ed.) p.117.

[95] *Prosper Homes v Hambro's Bank Executor and Trustee Co.* (1979) 39 P. & C.R. 395 at p.401. In *Glencore Grain Ltd v Flacker Shipper Ltd (The Happy Day)* [2002] EWCA Civ 1068, [2002] 2 Lloyd's Rep. 487 the two doctrines are described as "closely associated" (at [67]) but nevertheless distinct in that "waiver looks principally to the position and conduct of the person who is said to have waived his rights" while estoppel "looks chiefly at the position of the person relying on the estoppel" (at [64]). The guarded nature of the latter statement, however, shows that the distinction is far from clear-cut. Waiver in the sense of election between remedies is certainly distinct from estoppel in that such waiver requires no action in reliance by the person invoking it: see Treitel, *The Law of Contract,* (11th ed.), p.814; but waiver in the sense of abandonment of a right does require such action in reliance: *ibid.*, p.109. Our present concern is with the latter kind of waiver.

prevented by it from relying on a defect in the notice merely because he fails to object to the notice on account of the defect when he first receives the notice[96]; or merely because he calls for proof of *force majeure* after receipt of the notice[97]; or merely because, after receipt of the notice, he accepts an appropriation of part of the quantity sold (which the seller was allowed to export under an exception to the embargo).[98] In none of these cases is there any "unequivocal representation" by the buyer that he is treating the notice as valid and does not intend to rely on the defect in it; and even if there is such a representation the argument that the defect in the notice has been waived will still fail if the seller's alleged action in reliance consists of some act (such as applying for an export licence) that he would have done anyway, even if the representation had not been made.[99]

[96] *V Berg & Sons Ltd v Vanden Avenne-Izegem PVBA* [1977] 1 Lloyd's Rep. 499; *cf. Bunge SA v Companie Euopéenne de Céréales* [1983] 1 Lloyd's Rep. 307, where the sellers' defence failed, not because of defects in the notice, but because he could not identify the "relevant shipper": above, para.18–350.
[97] *Bremer Handelsgesellschaft v Deutsche Conti-Handelsgesellschaft mbH* [1983] 1 Lloyd's Rep. 339.
[98] *Bremer Handelsgesellschaft mbH v Bunge Corp.* [1983] 1 Lloyd's Rep. 476.
[99] *ibid.*

Chapter 19

C.I.F. CONTRACTS

	PARA.
1. Nature of a c.i.f. contract	19–001
2. Duties of the seller	19–010
(a) Shipment and appropriation	19–011
(b) The shipping documents	19–024
(i) The bill of lading	19–025
(ii) Insurance	19–042
(iii) The invoice	19–053
(iv) Other documents	19–058
(c) Tender of documents	19–059
(d) Duties with respect to delivery	19–072
3. Duties of the buyer	19–075
(a) Payment of the price	19–075
(b) Other duties	19–089
4. Contractual relations with carrier	19–090
5. Passing of property	19–098
6. Risk	19–110
7. Frustration	19–124
(a) Possible causes of frustration	19–124
(b) Provisions for supervening events	19–138
(c) Effects of frustration	19–143
8. Remedies of the buyer	19–144
(a) Rejection	19–144
(b) Damages for non-delivery	19–175
(c) Damages for defective delivery: in general	19–187
(i) Defect in goods alone	19–189
(ii) Defects in the documents and in the goods	19–190
(iii) Defect in the documents alone	19–198
(iv) Assessment of market loss damages	19–201
(v) Analogy of negligent valuation cases?	19–202
(d) Defective delivery: consumer sales	19–203
(e) Specific performance and injunction	19–204
9. Remedies of the seller	19–207
(a) Rescission	19–207
(b) Action for the price	19–211
(c) Action for damages	19–216
(d) Rights against the goods	19–220

1. Nature of a C.I.F. Contract

Importance of tender of documents. A c.i.f. contract is an agreement to sell[1] goods at an inclusive price covering the cost of the goods, insurance and freight. The essential feature of such a contract is that a seller, having 19–001

---

[1] See *Henry Kendall & Son v William Lillico & Sons Ltd* [1969] 2 A.C. 31 (where, however, such a contract was held to be a "sale" within Fertilisers and Feeding Stuffs Act 1926, s.2(2); see now Agriculture Act 1970, s.72).

shipped, or bought afloat, goods in accordance with the contract, can (and must) fulfil his part of the bargain by tendering to the buyer the proper shipping documents[2]: if he does this, he is not in breach even though the goods have been lost before such tender.[3] In the event of such loss the buyer must nevertheless pay the price on tender of the documents,[4] and his remedies, if any, will be against the carrier or against the underwriter,[5] but not against the seller on the contract of sale.

19–002 The statement that the seller performs his obligations by tendering documents assumes that he has previously shipped, or bought afloat, goods in accordance with the contract. His failure to do this may lead to inability to tender proper shipping documents; and it has been held that it is then the failure to ship, or buy afloat, which is the real or substantial breach.[6] If, on the other hand, the seller *has* shipped goods in the country of origin, but fails to prepare proper shipping documents, then that failure will lead to his inability to tender documents in the country specified in the contract for such tender; and in such a case the "principal breach" occurs in the latter country.[7]

It follows from the statement that the seller performs his part of the bargain by tendering documents, that he is not obliged actually to deliver the goods at the agreed destination[8]; he is only under a negative duty not to prevent the goods from being delivered to the buyer at that destination, by (for example) diverting them elsewhere, or by ordering the carrier not to deliver them to the buyer.[9] If the contract does impose an affirmative obligation on the seller to deliver the goods at the agreed destination, or in respect of their discharge there,[10] it is not a c.i.f. contract even though the letters "c.i.f." occur in the contract. The question whether a contract obliges the seller to deliver goods or only to tender documents depends on the construction of the contract as a whole. Thus, on the one hand, it has been said that "Not every contract which is expressed to be a c.i.f. contract is such."[11] On the other hand, a contract for the sale of goods "*delivered*

---

[2] *Manbré Saccharine Co. Ltd v Corn Products Co. Ltd* [1919] 1 K.B. 198 at p.202.
[3] Below, paras 19–002, 19–059.
[4] Below, paras 19–059, 19–080.
[5] *Ireland v Livingston* (1871) L.R. 5 H.L. 395 at p.407. These remedies may yield a different measure of recovery from remedies against the seller.
[6] *Johnson v Taylor Bros* [1920] A.C. 144; below, para.19–008. *Cf.* Vienna Convention on Contracts for the International Sale of Goods (above, para.1–024, Arts 30, 32(1) and 34.
[7] *Union Transport Plc v Continental Lines SA* [1991] 2 Lloyd's Rep. 49 at p.51, affirmed without reference to this point [1992] 1 W.L.R. 15.
[8] *Parker v Schuller* (1901) 17 T.L.R. 299; *cf. Bowden Bros & Co. Ltd v Little* (1907) 4 C.L.R. 1364; as to deterioration in transit see above, paras 18–243 *et seq.*
[9] *Peter Cremer v Brinkers Groudstoffen NV* [1980] 2 Lloyd's Rep. 605; *Empresa Exportadora de Azucar v Industria Azucarera Nacional SA* (*The Playa Larga*) [1983] 2 Lloyd's Rep. 171; *Gatoil International Inc. v Tradax Petroleum Ltd* (*The Rio Sun*) [1985] 1 Lloyd's Rep. 351; *Etablissements Soules et Cie v Intertradex SA* [1991] 1 Lloyd's Rep. 379 at 386; *Birkett Sperling & Co. v Engholm & Co.* (1871) 10 M (Ct. of Sess.) 170 at p.174; below, paras 19–008, 19–073.
[10] *Soon Hua Seng Co. Ltd v Glencore Grain Ltd* [1996] 1 Lloyd's Rep. 398 at p.401.
[11] *The Julia* [1949] A.C. 293 at p.309; *Manbré Saccharine Co. Ltd v Corn Products Co. Ltd* [1919] 1 K.B. 198; *Gardano and Giampieri v Greek Petroleum Co.* [1962] 1 W.L.R. 40; as to this case, see para.18–114, n.55.

Harburgh, cost freight and insurance" has been held to be a c.i.f. contract, so that the seller's obligations were performed by tender of documents even though the goods did not arrive.[12]

A contract which gives the seller the option of tendering documents *or* goods is not a c.i.f. contract, so that a contract on such terms does not oblige the seller to tender documents.[13] Conversely, a true c.i.f. contract does not give the seller this option: he *must* tender documents and cannot perform by instead tendering goods alone, even though they may be of the contract description.[14] Nor, if shipment to the c.i.f. destination becomes impossible or illegal, can the seller be required to deliver the goods at some other place.[15]

Provisions for tender of delivery order. In the ordinary case of a c.i.f. contract, the documents to be tendered will include a bill of lading.[16] But the contract may expressly stipulate for tender of a delivery order, or give the seller the option of tendering a delivery order; and it is a question of construction, depending in particular on the form of delivery order contemplated by the parties, whether a contract of this kind is one for the delivery of goods at the agreed destination, or a c.i.f. contract. The mere fact that the contract allows the seller to substitute a delivery order for a bill of lading does not, as a general rule, import any obligation to deliver the actual goods so as to prevent the contract from being a true c.i.f. contract.[17] But in *The Julia*[18] a contract for the sale of rye "c.i.f. Antwerp" gave the seller the option of tendering bills of lading or delivery orders. The seller shipped rye in bulk and tendered a delivery order in respect of a quantity smaller than the entire shipment; this order was directed to the seller's agent at Antwerp and was merely a preliminary step in a complicated procedure for securing the release of the goods.[19] It was held that the contract was not a c.i.f. contract but one for the delivery of the goods at Antwerp, and, as the goods were not so delivered, there was a total failure of consideration.[20] This was the case even though the contract provided for payment in exchange for the documents. The House of Lords laid stress on the fact that the seller in fact purported to perform by tendering a delivery 19–003

[12] *Tregelles v Sewell* (1862) 7 H. & N. 574.

[13] *Holland Colombo Trading Soc. Ltd v Alawdeen* [1954] 2 Lloyd's Rep. 45; *cf.* below, para.19–059.

[14] *Harper v Hochstim* 278 F. 102 (1921); *cf. Manbré Saccharine Co. Ltd v Corn Products Co. Ltd* [1919] 2 K.B. 198 at p.202 ("by delivery of documents and not by the actual physical delivery of goods"). The rules that the buyer is entitled to continuous documentary cover whether he needs it or not (below, para.19–027) and to an insurance policy even though the goods arrive safely (below, para.19–042) seem to be based on the same principle.

[15] See below, para.19–072 at n.95.

[16] Below, para.19–024.

[17] *Re Denbigh Cowan & Co. and R Atcherley & Co.* (1921) 90 L.J.K.B. 836.

[18] [1949] A.C. 293.

[19] See *ibid.*, at p.311.

[20] Contrast *Calcutta etc. Steam Navigation Co. v De Mattos* (1863) 32 L.J.Q.B. 322; 33 L.J.Q.B. 214 (where, the contract being a true c.i.f. contract, a similar claim to recover money paid against documents failed). And see below, paras 21–015, 21–016.

order, and on the form of the delivery order tendered. It was, in particular, significant that this order was of such a kind that it required further acts to be done by or on behalf of the seller at the port of destination in order to secure delivery of the goods to the buyer; a more normal delivery order addressed to, or issued by, the carrier would not have imposed any such requirement and would not have deprived the contract of its nature as a c.i.f. contract.[21] If, moreover, the seller in *The Julia* had chosen to tender a bill of lading he would, it seems, have been held to have performed his obligations. The contract was therefore a c.i.f. or delivery contract at the option of the seller and its true nature could not be determined until that option had been exercised.

19–004 **Provision as to destination.** A contract may be a c.i.f. contract even though the destination specified in it is not merely a port but a particular point (such as a wharf or terminal) within that port. Such a provision in a c.i.f. contract merely obliges the seller to make, or procure, a contract for the carriage of the goods to that point: it does not oblige him to deliver them there.[22]

19–005 **Provision for performance guarantee.** A contract on c.i.f. terms may stipulate for the tender of the normal shipping documents but go on to provide that, if some of these documents are "missing", the buyer must nevertheless pay if in lieu of such documents the seller provides a performance guarantee[23] or a letter of indemnity against missing documents.[24] In spite of the fact that the buyer may, when such a clause comes into operation, find himself without any remedy against the carrier or the underwriter, the contract retains many of the basic features of a c.i.f. contract: for example, the characteristics of the bill of lading to be tendered under the contract are determined in accordance with the rules to be discussed later in this chapter.[25]

19–006 **Provisions affecting risk.** A contract may be a c.i.f. contract although it postpones the *time* of payment either wholly or in part until arrival or delivery of the goods,[26] thus varying the normal rule that the buyer must

---

[21] See above, para.18–170; below, para.19–024.

[22] See, *e.g. Marshall Knott & Barker Ltd v Arcos Ltd* (1933) 44 L. LL. Rep. 384 (below para.19–031); *American Sugar Refining Co. v Page* 16 F.2d 662 (1927); *Warner Bros & Co. Ltd v Israel* 101 F. 2d 59 (1939). For the seller's duty not to prevent delivery at the contractual destination, see above, para.19–002, below, paras 19–008, 19–075.

[23] *e.g. SIAT di dal Ferro v Tradax Overseas SA* [1980] 1 Lloyd's Rep. 53.

[24] *e.g. Enichem Anic SpA v Ampelos Shipping Co. Ltd* (*The Delfini*) [1990] 1 Lloyd's Rep. 252.

[25] Below, paras 19–026 to 19–040, and esp. paras 19–031, 19–034, 19–038.

[26] *Calcutta, etc. Steam Navigation Co. v De Mattos*, above; n.20 *Dupont v British South Africa Co.* (1901) 18 T.L.R. 24; *Arnhold Karberg & Co. v Blythe, Green, Jourdain & Co.* [1916] 1 K.B. 495; *Stein, Forbes & Co. v County Tailoring Co.* (1916) 115 L.T. 215; *Plaimar Ltd v Waters Trading Co. Ltd* (1945) 72 C.L.R. 304; *cf. Houlder Bros & Co. Ltd v Commissioners of Public Works* [1908] A.C. 276 at p.280 where this type of contract was said not to be a "normal c.i.f. contract".

pay on tender of documents[27]; and although it makes the amount payable depend on the quantity of goods which actually arrive,[28] or provides that the contract is to be void if the ship carrying the goods is lost.[29] The effect of such provisions is to some extent to leave the risk of loss, which under a normal c.i.f. contract passes to the buyer on or as from shipment,[30] with the seller during transit. For this reason Lord Merriman P. said in *The Gabbiano* that a provision of this kind was "inappropriate to a c.i.f. contract proper."[31] But he added that the contract might "remain a c.i.f. contract with variations"; for, if the circumstances thus provided for did not arise, the contract "would, in normal conditions, be performed according to its tenor as an ordinary c.i.f. contract." Here again the question whether the contract is to be regarded as a c.i.f. contract cannot be finally determined when the contract is made, but may depend on subsequent events. A contract providing for payment on arrival of the goods could, moreover, retain the characteristics of a c.i.f. contract, in defining the obligations of the seller, though not those of the buyer: that is, if the goods or part of them failed to arrive as a result of some accident or of some breach of the contract of carriage, the seller would not, for that reason alone,[32] be in breach of the contract of sale: the failure of the goods to arrive would merely provide the buyer with an excuse for not paying the price against documents. Such a clause may also be narrowly construed. It has, for example, been said that a clause by which the amount to be paid was to be based on "full outturn weight at port of destination" would apply only in respect of "weight differences arising in . . . ordinary circumstances"[33] (such as evaporation during the voyage) and not where the goods were lost through an accident during the voyage. The contract therefore retained its character as a c.i.f. contract. On the other hand a contract putting the whole

---

[27] Below, para.19–075.

[28] *Calcutta, etc. SN Co. v De Mattos* (1863) 32 L.J.Q.B. 322; 33 L.J.Q.B. 214; *Dupont v British South Africa Co.*, above; *Arnhold Karberg & Co. v Blythe, Green, Jourdain & Co.* [1915] 2 K.B. 370 at pp.379–380 (c.i.f. contract "with . . . variation"); affirmed [1916] 1 K.B. 495; *Warner Bros & Co. Ltd v Israel* 101 F.2d 59 (1939); *cf.* the contract in *The Aramis* [1989] 1 Lloyd's Rep. 213; contrast *The Julia* [1949] A.C. 293, where one reason why the contract was held not to be a c.i.f. contract was that the seller was "to pay for deficiency in Bill of Lading weights"; *Produce Brokers New Company (1924) Ltd v Wray, Sanderson & Co. Ltd* (1931) 39 Ll.L.R. 257, where the price depended on "delivered weight"; *Krohn & Co. v Mitsui & Co. Europe GmbH* [1978] 2 Lloyd's Rep. 419 (c. & f. contract); and see below, para.19–119.

[29] *Karinjee Javinjee & Co. v William F. Malcolm & Co.* (1926) 25 Ll.L.R. 28; *Re Denbigh Cowan & Co. and R. Atcherley & Co.* (1921) 90 L.J.K.B. 836.

[30] Below, para.19–110.

[31] [1940] P. 166 at p.174; *Houlder Bros & Co. Ltd v Commissioners of Public Works* [1908] A.C. 276 at p.291; *Peter Cremer v Brinkers Groudstoffen NV* [1980] 2 Lloyd's Rep. 605 at p.606 ("rather hybrid c.i.f. contract"); *Congimex Companhia Geral, etc. SARL v Tradax Export SA* [1983] 1 Lloyd's Rep. 250 at p.252 ("not a classic c.i.f. contract").

[32] For the position where the failure of the goods to reach the agreed destination results from the seller's interference with the contract of carriage, see below, paras 19–008, 19–073.

[33] *Soon Hua Seng Co. Ltd v Glencore Grain Ltd* [1996] 1 Lloyd's Rep. 398 at p.405; the buyer however escaped liability as proper shipping documents had not been tendered: see below, para.19–027.

risk (of deterioration as well as of loss) on the seller until actual delivery is probably not a c.i.f. contract.[34]

19–007 **Passing of property.** In *The Julia* Lord Simonds said that it was a "salient characteristic" of a c.i.f. contract "that the property not only may but must pass by delivery of the documents against which payment is made."[35] This characteristic is, however, not peculiar to c.i.f. contracts. A contract might provide for passing of property on delivery of documents against payment, and also oblige the seller to deliver the actual goods. Such a contract would not be a c.i.f. contract. Conversely, a contract may be a c.i.f. contract even though property passes before delivery of documents or payment; *e.g.* (occasionally) on shipment[36]; and even though property does not pass on such delivery or on payment.[37]

19–008 **Whether sale of goods or documents.** It has from time to time been said that a c.i.f. contract is not a sale of goods but a sale of documents.[38] This view is based on the rule that a c.i.f. seller, who has shipped or bought afloat goods in accordance with the contract, performs his part of the bargain by tender of documents; and on the fact that c.i.f. contracts often provide for payment in exchange for the documents. What the buyer buys, on this view, are the rights of action against the carrier and the underwriter, evidenced by, or contained in, the shipping documents[39]; in other words he buys not goods, but things in action. If this were so, c.i.f. contracts would not be governed by the Sale of Goods Act at all, since things in action are not goods.[40] This conclusion would not, perhaps, be as startling as might at first sight appear since in the case of c.i.f. contracts the provisions of the Act are very frequently excluded by contrary agreement, whether express or inferred from the nature of the transaction.

Although the statement that a c.i.f. contract is a sale of documents "contains more than a grain of truth"[41] it is "not wholly true".[42] The prevailing view is that a c.i.f. contract is not a sale of documents but a sale of goods[43] or a contract for the sale of goods to be performed by delivery of

---

[34] Below, para.19–119.
[35] [1949] A.C. 293 at p.317.
[36] Below, para.19–099; *The Albazero* [1977] A.C. 774 at pp.794, 840; above, para.18–209.
[37] See, for example, below, para.19–104.
[38] *e.g.*, in *Arnhold Karberg & Co. v Blythe, Green, Jourdain & Co.* [1915] 2 K.B. 379 at p.388; affirmed [1916] 1 K.B. 495.
[39] *Lloyd v Fleming* (1872) L.R. 7 Q.B. 299 at p.303.
[40] Sale of Goods Act 1979, s.61(1) ("goods"). *Cf.* Vienna Convention on Contracts for the International Sale of Goods (above, para.1–024), Art. 2(d).
[41] *SIAT di del Ferro v Tradax Overseas SA* [1978] 2 Lloyd's Rep. 470 at p.495; affirmed [1980] 1 Lloyd's Rep. 53; *cf. Soules CAF v PT Transcap of Indonesia* [1999] 1 Lloyd's Rep. 917 at p.918 ("essentially a documentary transaction").
[42] *SIAT* case [1978] 2 Lloyd's Rep. 470 at p.495; *cf. Warner Bros & Co. Ltd v Israel* 101 F.2d 59, at p.60 ("an unduly broad generalisation").
[43] *Ross T Smyth & Co. Ltd v TD Bailey, Sons & Co.* [1940] 3 All E.R. 60 at p.68; *The Gabbiano* [1940] P. 166 at p.174.

documents,[44] or "a contract for the sale of documents representing goods"[45] (and not merely rights of action). It has been said that the difference between the two views "is one of phrase only"[46] but there may be cases in which it cannot be dismissed so lightly. Thus if the agreed destination of the goods becomes, after the making of the contract, enemy territory, the contract may be discharged by supervening illegality even though the documents were to be tendered in England.[47] Again, where a seller fails to ship goods of the contract description, this, and not his consequent inability to tender documents, is the "substantial breach", so that if he fails abroad to ship goods under a contract providing for shipment of the goods to, or tender of documents in, this country the "substantial breach" does not take place in this country.[48] Similarly, if no goods have been shipped but the seller nevertheless tenders documents good on their face, he is in breach even though those documents may give the buyer a right of action against the carrier.[49] The seller is similarly in breach if, having shipped goods to the c.i.f. destination, he then interferes with the performance of the contract of carriage, *e.g.* by ordering the ship to carry them to a place other than that destination[50]; or by ordering her to leave that destination without having delivered the goods to the buyer[51]; or by simply ordering her (in purported exercise of an unjustified lien) not to make such delivery.[52] In all these cases, the seller, as well as the carrier, is in breach; for a c.i.f. contract "contemplates that the [buyer][53] is to get physical possession of the goods through the contract of carriage that it is the seller's duty to arrange." Again, a c.i.f. contract may specify the rate at which the goods are to be discharged and provide that the buyer is to pay demurrage[54] to the seller if that rate is not attained: under such a provision the buyer owes a duty to

---

[44] *Arnhold Karberg & Co. v Blythe, Green, Jourdain & Co.* [1916] 1 K.B. 495 at p.510; *Hindley & Co. Ltd v East Indian Produce Co. Ltd* [1973] 2 Lloyd's Rep. 515 (c. & f. contract); *Trasimex Holdings SA v Addax BV* [1999] 1 Lloyd's Rep. 28 at p.32.

[45] *Congimex Companhia Geral, etc. SARL v Tradax Export SA* [1983] 1 Lloyd's Rep. 250 at p.253; *Bangladesh Export Import Co. Ltd v Sucden Kerry SA* [1995] 2 Lloyd's Rep. 1 at p.5 (c. & f. contract) *Cargill International SA v Bangladesh Sugar & Food Industries Corp.* [1996] 4 All E.R. 563 at p.565, affirmed [1998] 1 W.L.R. 461.

[46] *Manbré Saccharine Co. Ltd v Corn Products Co. Ltd* [1919] 1 K.B. 198 at p.203; *cf. Malmberg v H & J Evans & Co.* (1924) 30 Com.Cas. 107 at p.112.

[47] *Duncan, Fox & Co. v Schrempft & Bonke* [1915] 1 K.B. 365; 3 K.B. 355; below, para.19–136.

[48] *Wancke v Wingren* (1889) 58 L.J.Q.B. 519; *Parker v Schuller* (1901) 17 T.L.R. 299; *Johnson v Taylor Bros* [1920] A.C. 144; *Seaver v Lindsay Light Co.* 135 N.E. 329 (1922); above, para.19–002.

[49] *Hindley & Co. Ltd v East Indian Produce Co. Ltd* [1973] 2 Lloyd's Rep. 515 (c. & f. contract). There would now be a right of action against the carrier on the facts of this case if the requirements of Carriage of Goods by Sea Act 1992 (above paras 18–036 and 18–102 *et seq.*) were satisfied.

[50] *Peter Cremer v Brinkers Groudstoffen NV* [1980] 2 Lloyd's Rep. 605; below, para.19–073.

[51] *Empresa Exportadora de Azucar v Industria Azucarera Nacional SA* (*The Playa Larga*) [1983] 2 Lloyd's Rep. 171 (c. & f. contract).

[52] *Gatoil International Inc. v Tradax Petroleum Ltd* (*The Rio Sun*) [1985] 1 Lloyd's Rep. 351.

[53] *The Playa Larga*, above, at p.180. The report at this point has "seller"—an obvious misprint for "buyer." *Cf. The Rio Sun*, above n.52, at p.362.

[54] Below, para.19–088.

the seller (and not merely to the carrier) with regard to the time taken in unloading the goods.[55] It is also possible for the seller to give a contractual undertaking as to the time of the arrival of the goods at the c.i.f. destination. He could then be in breach if the goods arrived there after the stipulated time.[56] All these rules suggest that the transaction is, in essence, a sale of goods; and the same view is perhaps also supported by the rule that a c.i.f. contract for the sale of specific goods is void if at the time of the contract the goods had perished, even though there was in existence at that time a set of shipping documents including a valid policy of insurance on the goods.[57]

19–009 **Provisions as to freight and insurance.** In the normal c.i.f. contract, the seller charges an inclusive price covering the cost of the goods, freight and insurance. If under the contract of carriage the freight is payable at the destination, it may in fact be paid by the buyer; but in that case it is simply deducted by the buyer from the price.[58] As between buyer and seller, responsibility for the cost of freight and insurance is the seller's: thus any increase in freight or insurance rates must be borne by the seller[59] and any decrease enures for his benefit. But these are not essential features of a c.i.f. contract. Thus a contract may be a c.i.f. contract even though it provides that variations in freight or insurance rates are for the buyer's account[60] or if this result is held to follow from a stipulation in the contract that freight is "payable on discharge", this being interpreted as an undertaking by the buyer "to discharge the freight, whatever it might be"[61]; or if the contract gives the buyer a choice of destinations and makes the freight charge, and hence the total amount payable by the buyer, depend on which destination he selects[62]; or if the contract provides that the buyer is to be liable for such demurrage as the seller may have to pay to the carrier.[63]

---

[55] See *Etablissements Soules et Cie. v Intertradex SA* [1991] 1 Lloyd's Rep. 379.
[56] See *Cargill International SA v Bangladesh Sugar & Food Industries Corp.* [1998] 1 W.L.R. 461 at p.465. On the other hand, the c.i.f. seller would not, it is submitted, be in breach of his undertaking as to the *time* of arrival if, as a result of some casualty (not due to any failure on his part to make a proper contract of carriage) the goods never arrived at all: see below, para.19–074.
[57] *Couturier v Hastie* (1856) 5 H.L.C. 673; Sale of Goods Act 1979, s.6 (above, para.1–124).
[58] See the form of invoice described in *Ireland v Livingston* (1872) L.R. 5 H.L. 395 at p.407; below, para.19–053.
[59] *Houlder Bros & Co. Ltd v Commissioners of Public Works* [1908] A.C. 276 at p.290; *Oulu Osakayetio v Arnold Laver & Co.* [1940] 1 K.B. 750.
[60] *Acetylene Corp. of GB v Canada Carbide Co.* (1921) 6 Ll.L.R. 410 at p.468; reversed. on the issue of frustration (1922) 8 Ll.L.R. 456, CA; *Colin & Shields v Weddel & Co.* [1952] 2 All E.R. 337; *Plaimar Ltd v Waters Trading Co.* (1945) 72 C.L.R. 304; *D. I. Henry Ltd v Wilhelm C Clasen* [1973] 1 Lloyd's Rep. 159 ("Cape surcharge for buyer's account"). But by virtue of a provision of this kind the seller is entitled to charge the buyer only for increases in normal rates and not for the extra expense of, *e.g.* insuring shipment on a belligerent ship: *Oulu Osakayetio v Arnold Laver & Co.*, above, n.59.
[61] *Modiano Bros & Sons v Bailey & Sons Ltd* (1933) 47 Ll.L.R. 134.
[62] As in *Tsakiroglou & Co. Ltd v Transgrains SA* [1958] 1 Lloyd's Rep. 562; *Gatoil International Inc. v Tradax Petroleum Ltd (The Rio Sun)* [1985] 1 Lloyd's Rep. 351.
[63] See *Bunge AG v Giuseppe Rocco & Figli* [1973] 2 Lloyd's Rep. 152; *Malozzi v Carapelli SpA* [1976] 1 Lloyd's Rep. 407; below, para.19–088.

Even a contract by which insurance was "to be covered by seller for buyer's account" has been described as a "modified c.i.f. contract"[64]: it was, presumably, not a c. & f. contract[65] because the seller was obliged to insure, though the whole cost of insurance had to be borne by the buyer.

Thus variations in the normal rules as to the cost of freight and insurance do not necessarily destroy the character of the contract as a c.i.f. contract. But if they are suficiently far-reaching they may have this effect. In *The Parchim*[66] German sellers chartered a ship to carry a cargo of nitrate from Chile to a European port. They sold the cargo to Dutch buyers at a stated price "cost and freight Channel . . . Insurance to be covered by the sellers . . . and the buyer has to accept the policy of insurance against payment of premium and costs." The contract went on to provide that "The buyers have to take over the charter"; that if they made use of the option to cancel contained in the charter they would have to ship the goods by another vessel; that "any freight difference pro or contra is for account of the buyers", and that, if the ship were lost after part of the goods had been loaded, the contract was to be "cancelled for the balance". Under these provisions, the buyer had to pay for insurance effected by the seller; in certain events the buyer had to ship the goods and take the risk of fluctuations in freight rates; and loss of part of the goods after shipment could relieve him from liability. None of these consequences would normally follow from a sale on c.i.f. terms; and their cumulative effect was said to be that the contract was "not an ordinary c.i.f. contract" and that it had "far more of the characteristics of a contract f.o.b. Taltal [the Chilean port] than it had of a contract c.i.f. European port."[67]

2. DUTIES OF THE SELLER

In general.[68] The duties of a c.i.f. seller are, first to ship (or procure a shipment of) goods in accordance with the contract and, where necessary, to appropriate such goods to the contract; secondly to procure or prepare the proper shipping documents; and thirdly to tender these documents to the buyer, or as the buyer directs. He is not under any duty to ensure the 19–010

---

[64] *Colin & Shields v Weddel & Co.* [1952] 2 All E.R. 337 at p.342.
[65] Below, para.21–012.
[66] [1918] A.C. 157; and see below, para.20–008.
[67] [1918] A.C. 157 at p.163.
[68] For general statements of a c.i.f. seller's duties, see *E. Clemens Horst Co. v Biddell Bros* [1911] 1 K.B. 214 at p.220 (reversed. [1911] 1 K.B. 934 but restored [1912] A.C. 18); *Johnson v Taylor Bros* [1920] A.C. 144 at p.155; (where "six things" seems to be a misprint for "five things": see *Petrofina SA v Aut Ltd* (*The Maersk Nimrod*) [1991] 1 Lloyd's Rep. 269 at p.272); *Shipton, Anderson & Co. v John Weston & Co.* (1922) 10 Ll.L.R. 762 at p.763; *Ross T Smyth & Co. Ltd v TD Bailey, Sons & Co.* [1940] 3 All E.R. 60 at p.68; *The Julia* [1949] A.C. 293 at p.308; *SIAT di del Ferro v Tradax Overseas SA* [1978] 2 Lloyd's Rep. 470 at p.492; affirmed [1980] 1 Lloyd's Rep. 53; *Gatoil International Inc. v Tradax Petroleum Ltd* (*The Rio Sun*) [1985] 1 Lloyd's Rep. 351 at p.357. The Vienna Convention on Contracts for the International Sale of Goods (above, para.1–024) contains no statement of any special duties which arise where goods are sold on c.i.f. terms.

actual physical delivery of the goods at the c.i.f. destination; though he is under a duty not to take active steps to prevent such delivery.[69]

(a) *Shipment and Appropriation*

19–011 **Seller's duty to ship or buy afloat.** The seller's duty to ship may be performed by actually shipping goods, by allocating such goods which he has already shipped,[70] or by buying such goods afloat.[71] If performance in one or more (but not all) of these ways becomes impossible, the general rule is that the seller must perform in any one of them that remains possible. Thus if shipment by the seller is prevented through some cause beyond his control, the general rule is that he must buy goods already afloat and appropriate them to the contract. An exception to the seller's duty to buy afloat in such circumstances is discussed later in this chapter.[72] Sometimes the terms of the contract may exclude the possibility of performance by appropriating goods already shipped by someone other than the seller, *e.g.* where the sale is of goods to be shipped, or to be manufactured, by the seller.[73]

19–012 **Conforming goods.** The first requirement is that the goods must be of the contract description; this is considered in general terms in Chapter 11.[74] Certain factors of special importance in overseas sales are mentioned in Chapter 18[75]; in particular, statements as to the time of shipment are regarded as part of the description in such sales.[76] The shipment must secondly be of the contract quality: this is prima facie determined by reference to the time of shipment[77] though there is in some cases an

---

[69] Below, para.19–073.

[70] *Shipton, Anderson & Co. v John Weston & Co.*, above; *Ross T. Smyth & Co. Ltd v TD Bailey, Sons & Co.*, above.

[71] *JH Vantol Ltd v Fairclough, Dodd & Jones Ltd* [1955] 1 W.L.R. 642 at p.646 (rvsd. *ibid.* 1302 but restored [1957] 1 W.L.R. 136). A sale of goods afloat on a *named* ship has been said now to be a "rare phenomenon": *Eurico SpA v Philipp Brothers (The Epaphus)* [1986] 2 Lloyd's Rep. 387 at p.389, [1987] 2 Lloyd's Rep. 215 at p.222, *per* Croom-Johnson L.J. (dissenting).

[72] Below, para.19–141.

[73] As in *Johnson v Taylor Bros* [1920] A.C. 144.

[74] Above, paras 11–001 *et seq.*

[75] Above, paras 18–265 *et seq.*

[76] Above, para.18–267.

[77] *H Glynn (Covent Garden) Ltd v Wittleder* [1959] 2 Lloyd's Rep. 409. It is possible, if uncommon, for a c.i.f. buyer to "deal as consumer" within the Sale of Goods Act 1979: see above, para.18–259. A buyer who so deals has the "additional rights" specified in Pt 5A of the Act if "the goods do not conform to the contract of sale at the time of delivery." These rights are discussed in Chapter 12 above. For the difficulty of determining the meaning of "delivery" in the context of a c.i.f. sale, see above, para.18–261. Probably the requirement of conformity "at the time of delivery" for the purposes of Pt 5A would not, in the case of a c.i.f. contract, refer to the time of shipment. The question whether it would refer to the time of symbolical delivery by tender of documents or to complete (physical) delivery of the goods would seem to depend on considerations similar to those discussed in para.18–261 above. For the possibility of excluding the "additional rights" conferred by Pt 5A by contrary agreement, see above, para.12–117 above. For the possibility that a term excluding these rights may be implied from the nature of a c.i.f. contract, *cf.* the reasoning of para.18–264 above.

implied undertaking that the goods are at the time of shipment in such a condition that they can survive normal transit.[78] Thirdly, the shipment must be of the correct quantity.[79] If it is not, the buyer is not deprived of his right to the full quantity sold merely because he accepts the smaller quantity shipped.[80] He is also entitled to reject the quantity tendered,[81] unless the discrepancy is trifling[82] or unless, as will commonly be the case, the seller has stipulated for a margin. Such a margin must not be exceeded.[83]

In 1994, the Sale of Goods Act 1979 was amended by the addition of a new section 30(2A) under which a buyer who does not deal as consumer[84] may not reject goods where the quantity delivered is less or more than that contracted for if the discrepancy is "so slight that it would be unreasonable for him to do so" (*i.e.* to reject). These words resemble those of section 15A, which imposes statutory restrictions on the buyer's right to reject for breach of certain implied conditions[85]; it will be recalled that section 15A will not apply where "a contrary intention appears in, or is to be implied from"[86] the contract. Section 30(2A) is similarly (and perhaps somewhat more broadly) "subject to any usage of trade, special agreement, or course of dealing between the parties."[87] The fact that the sale is on c.i.f. terms can, it is submitted, be regarded as evidence of a usage of trade, and the fact that the contract stipulates for a margin as a "special agreement", so as to restrict the operation of section 30(2A) in relation to c.i.f. contracts. The first part of this submission derives support from the rule that the documents which the seller is required to tender under such a contract must cover "the goods contracted to be sold and no others".[88] The right to reject *documents* covering the wrong quantity is not in terms affected by section 30(2A) at all, and there is no doubt that, having rejected the documents,

---

[78] Above, paras 18–255 to 18–257.

[79] *Re Keighley Maxsted & Co. and Bryant, Durant & Co. (No.2)* (1894) 70 L.T. 155; *Harland and Wolff Ltd v Burstall & Son* (1901) 6 Com.Cas. 113; *Payne and Routh v Lillico & Sons* (1920) 36 T.L.R. 569; *cf. Donald H Scott v Barclays Bank Ltd* [1923] 2 K.B. 1; *Cobec Brazilian Trading & Warehousing Corp. v Alfred C Toepfer* [1983] 2 Lloyd's Rep. 386.

[80] *Finagrain v Kruse* [1976] 2 Lloyd's Rep. 508.

[81] See cases cited in n.79, above.

[82] *Shipton, Anderson & Co. v Weil Bros & Co.* [1912] 1 K.B. 574 (excess of 55 lbs over 4,950 tons); *cf. Tamvaco v Lucas (No.2)* (1861) 1 B. & S. 185; (1865) 3 B. & S. 89 (slight deficiency in amount of insurance not a ground of rejection); contrast *Payne & Routh v Lillico & Sons* (1920) 36 T.L.R. 569 (excess of 2 over 4,000 tons a "serious amount").

[83] *Tamvaco v Lucas (No.1)* (1859) 1 E. & E. 581; unless the excess is trifling: see n.82, above.

[84] If a c.i.f. buyer deals as consumer (see above, n.77) and chooses to exercise one of his "additional rights" under Pt 5A of the Act, then this right to reject delivery of the wrong quantity may, in effect, be suspended. This possibility arises where in case of short delivery (which can amount to non-conformity by virtue of being a breach of an express term: see s.48F) the buyer requires the seller to "repair" or "replace" the goods, *i.e.* to make good the deficiency (see ss.48A(2)(a), 48B(1), above, paras 12–076, 12–077). The buyer cannot then reject the short delivery until he has given the seller a reasonable time in which to effect the "repair" or "replacement": s.48D.

[85] Above, para.18–284.

[86] s.15A(2).

[87] s.30(5).

[88] *The Julia* [1949] A.C. 293 at p.301; below, para.19–032.

the buyer would be entitled to reject the goods.[89] If the documents did not disclose the discrepancy and had been accepted, it is submitted that section 30(2A) should not affect the buyer's right to reject the goods on the ground that the quantity delivered was not in accordance with the contract. This submission is based on the considerations of commercial certainty which justify a narrow construction of section 15A in the context of overseas sales[90]: these considerations apply (*mutatis mutandis*) with equal force to quantitative as to qualitative breaches in contracts of this kind.

19–013 **Shipment period.** The contract may define the shipment period in various ways. It may provide that the goods are to be shipped, or that they have been shipped, within specified limits of time; it may, alternatively, provide for tender of a bill of lading dated within certain limits of time: such provisions have been interpreted as requiring shipment within the time stated.[91] Where shipment was begun outside the contract period, but was completed, *and the bills of lading were dated*, within it, this was regarded a shipment in accordance within the contract.[92] But in *Bowes v Shand*[93] a contract for the sale of rice provided for shipment "during the month of March and/or April". Most of the rice[94] was put on board in February and the rest in March; of the four bills of lading issued, three bore February dates and one a March date. This was held to be a February shipment. Loosely worded provisions as to shipment sometimes give rise to difficult questions of construction. A contract calling for shipment in "September or October" has been held to provide a single shipment period, so that a seller who had lawful excuse for not shipping in September was nevertheless liable for failing to ship in October.[95] And where a contract called for shipment from June 1, 1960, but gave the buyer the option to postpone shipment until June 1, 1961, it was held that the shipment period ended on the latter date: the court rejected the argument that a new shipment period began to run from that time.[96] A stipulation in a c.i.f. contract for a "laycan" period[97] does not amount to one specifying a shipment period, so that failure to ship the goods within the specified "laycan" period does not, of itself, justify the buyer's rejection of the goods.[98] If the contract specifies

[89] *cf.* below, para.19–147.
[90] Above, para.18–284.
[91] *Suzuki & Co. v Burgett and Newsam* (1922) 10 Ll.L.R. 223 (for a fuller statement of the facts see 8 Ll.L.R. 495); *Dewar and Webb v Joseph Rank Ltd* (1923) 14 Ll.L.R. 393.
[92] *Alexander v Vanderzee* (1872) L.R. 7 C.P. 530.
[93] (1877) 2 App.Cas. 455.
[94] 8,150 out of 8,200 bags.
[95] *Charles H. Windschuegl Ltd v Alexander Pickering & Co. Ltd* (1950) 84 Ll.L.R. 89 at p.94.
[96] *Alexandria Cotton and Trading Co. (Sudan) Ltd v Cotton Co. of Ethiopia Ltd* [1963] 1 Lloyd's Rep. 576.
[97] See *SHV Gas Supply & Trading SAS v Naftomar Shipping & Trading Co Ltd Inc (The Azur Gaz)* [2005] EWHC 2528 (Comm.), [2006] 1 Lloyd's Rep. 163. In the context of charterparties, "laycan" refers to the commencement of the laydays and the date after which the charter can be cancelled if the vessel has not by then arrived: see *ibid*. at [9], pointing out that "the expression does not fit . . . easily into the confines of a cif contract".
[98] *ibid.*, at [20].

a "laycan" period, but not a shipment period, it will therefore contain no express provision as to the time of shipment. A contract which specifies no such time will however be regarded as containing an implied term requiring the seller to ship the goods within a reasonable time.[99] This term has been described as a condition,[1] with the result that, where the seller was in breach of it, the buyer would be entitled to reject the goods.

Once the shipment period has been ascertained, it is sometimes said that the seller has the whole of that period for shipment.[2] Thus in the normal case the option as to the exact time of shipment within the period is the seller's, so that he is entitled to ship at any time during the period.[3] If before the end of the period an event occurs which prevents shipment, or makes it unlawful, the seller is accordingly not in breach for having failed to ship in the earlier part of the period when shipment was still possible and lawful.[4] But if it becomes clear during the period that shipment *will* be prevented for part of it, the seller is bound to ship during the part of it in which shipment remains possible and lawful. Thus where a contract for the sale of Sicilian horsebeans c.i.f. Glasgow provided for shipment in October or November, and the Italian authorities announced on October 20, that the export of such goods would be prohibited[5] from November 1, it was held that the seller, who had not yet shipped when the announcement was made, was bound to ship between October 20 and 31.[6] The position is different where the authorities of the country of origin merely indicate during the shipment period that an export embargo *may* be imposed. In one case of this kind, it was held that such an announcement did not abridge the shipment period, so that the seller was not in breach for having failed to ship between the announcement and the later imposition of the embargo during the shipment period.[7]

---

[99] *ibid.*, at [23].

[1] *ibid.*, at [27]. The classification of the implied term as a condition is, perhaps, open to question as such a classification of a term which specifies no precise time can scarcely promote certainty, which is one of the main objects of classifying a term as a condition: *cf.* above, para.18–357, below, para.19–064. For the actual ground on which the buyer was entitled to reject in *The Azur Gaz*, see below, para.19–074.

[2] *Re Anglo-Russian Merchant Traders and John Batt & Co.* (London) *Ltd* [1917] 2 K.B. 679 at p.688; *cf.* Vienna Convention on Contracts for the International Sale of Goods (above, para.1–024), Art. 33(b).

[3] The rule can be regarded as an application of the general principle that a contract which provides for alternative methods of performance is likely to be construed as giving the choice between those methods to promisor; for this principle, see *Mora Shipping Inc. v Axa Corporate Solutions Assurance SA* [2005] EWCA Civ. 1069, [2005] 2 Lloyd's Rep. 769 at [40]–[44].

[4] *Re Anglo-Russian Merchant Traders and John Batt & Co.* (*London*) *Ltd* [1917] 2 K.B. 679.

[5] Except under licence, which was not obtained.

[6] *Ross T Smyth & Co. Ltd* (*Liverpool*) *v W. N. Lindsay Ltd* (*Leith*) [1953] 1 W.L.R. 1280; *cf. Charles H Windschuegl v Alexander Pickering & Co. Ltd* (1950) 84 Ll.L.R. 89; and above, para.18–345.

[7] *Tradax Export SA v André & Cie.* [1976] 1 Lloyd's Rep. 416 at p.426; above, para.18–345.

19–014 **Sale "subject to shipment".** A contract which is "subject to shipment" may give the seller an option whether to ship or not[8]; but if the seller does actually make a shipment he must allocate the shipped goods to the contract "at any rate if they have not been shipped in fulfilment of other contracts."[9] The courts are however somewhat reluctant to interpret "subject to shipment" clauses in such a way as to give the seller a completely free choice in the matter.[10] Thus where the contract referred to shipment by a supplier from whom the seller intended to buy the goods, and contained the words "shipment prompt . . . subject to shipment", it was held that the seller was bound to ensure that the necessary shipment would take place.[11] Similarly, a contract "subject to *force majeure* and shipment" has been held to excuse the seller only in the event of inability to secure a shipment of the contract description, and not to give him an option whether to ship or not.[12] If the seller in such a case is able to secure such a shipment, he is not excused from his obligation to perform a particular contract merely because he has been unable to ship a suficient quantity to satisfy other contracts for the sale of goods of the same description.[13]

19–015 **Appropriation.** Where the contract is for the sale of unascertained goods, the seller is bound to appropriate goods of the contract description to the contract. "Appropriation" is used in several senses.[14] Here we are not concerned with the "proprietary" sense of the word (*i.e.* with the "unconditional appropriation" which is required to pass the property in goods), but with its "contractual" sense, *i.e.* with the appropriation by which a seller of unascertained goods binds himself contractually to deliver particular goods (or goods from a specified source), or the documents representing them. There can be an appropriation in this sense even though the goods remain "unascertained" in the sense of forming an undifferentiated part of a larger bulk.[15] Thus if a seller of 500 quarters of wheat appropriates part of a larger cargo on a named ship he becomes contractually bound to deliver 500 quarters, or documents representing that amount, out of that particular cargo.

---

[8] *e.g. Hollis Bros & Co. Ltd v White Sea Timber Trust Ltd* [1936] 3 All E.R. 895 at p.900.

[9] *ibid.*, at p.900.

[10] If the clause were so interpreted, it seems that the seller would be under no "contractual obligation" at all, so that the clause would not be subject to the requirement of reasonableness under Unfair Contract Terms Act 1977, s.3(1) and (2)(b)(ii). In any event, the Act does not apply to "international supply contracts": see s.26, discussed in para.18–281, above; and see above, para.18–281 n.48 for proposals for reform. If the clause were interpreted so as to leave performance to the seller's discretion, this very fact could make it an unfair term within the Unfair Terms in Consumer Contracts Regulations 1999, SI 1999/2083 (see Sch.2 para.1(c)); but these Regulations may, but will not often, apply to contracts of the kind here under consideration: above, para.18–259.

[11] *Star Public Saw Mill Co. v Robert Bruce & Co. Ltd* (1923) 17 Ll.L.R. 7.

[12] *Hong Guan & Co. Ltd v R Jumabhoy* [1960] A.C. 684. below, para.19–140.

[13] *ibid.*

[14] Above, paras 5–069, 18–210.

[15] Such goods remain "unascertained" even though property in an undivided share in the bulk can pass to the buyer: see Sale of Goods Act 1979, s.20A(1).

Time of appropriation. In discussing various meanings of "appropriation" in *Wait v Baker*, Parke B. said: "it may mean a selection on the part of the vendor, where he has the right to choose the article which he has to supply in performance of his contract. . . ."[16] In the normal case of a c.i.f. sale of unascertained goods, the seller would have this "right to choose"; and the difficult question is exactly when he has exercised it. Where the contract expressly provides that the seller is to give a notice of appropriation,[17] it would no doubt be inferred that he had not irrevocably made the "selection" until he had given the notice. But where the contract says nothing about appropriation, it is not at all clear whether a seller can be said, in the "contractual" sense, to have appropriated goods to the contract by some act of which notice has not been given to the buyer. There are, in particular, conflicting dicta on the question whether a seller can be taken to have appropriated goods to the contract by the mere act of shipping them. On the one hand Dixon J. has said that a seller "in shipping a definite parcel of goods in performance of a contract for the sale of unascertained goods by description ascertains the goods and prima facie he appropriates them to the contract."[18] But this prima facie rule may be displaced, for example, by showing that the shipment had been made in fulfilment of another contract.[19] A different approach was adopted by Scrutton L.J. when he said that "The mere shipment of the cargo does not appropriate it to the contract"[20]; and the context indicates that something more, in the nature of a notice to the buyer, would be required.[21] These statements seem to be applicable to c.i.f. contracts, though the cases from which they are taken were not concerned with such contracts. The position appears to be that shipment may amount to appropriation: for example, where the contract provides for shipment on a named ship and goods of the contract description are shipped on that ship[22]; or where there is other evidence of the seller's intention that the shipment was intended by him to be made "in performance of the contract".[23] But the court will not lightly draw the inference of appropriation (in the "contractual" sense) from the mere fact 19–016

---

[16] (1848) 2 Exch. 1 at p.8 (the sale was on f.o.b. terms).

[17] Below, para.19–017.

[18] *James v The Commonwealth* (1939) 62 C.L.R. 339 at p.377; the same assumption seems to underlie *Plaimar Ltd v Waters Trading Co. Ltd* (1945) 72 C.L.R. 304; *cf. The Gabbiano* [1940] P. 166 at p.175.

[19] *Hollis Bros & Co. Ltd v White Sea Timber Trust Ltd* [1936] 3 All E.R. 895 at p.900.

[20] *Produce Brokers Co. Ltd v Olympia Oil and Cake Co. Ltd* [1917] 1 K.B. 320 at pp.320 to 329; *cf. Empresa Exportadora de Azucar v Industria Azucarera Nacional SA* (*The Playa Larga*) [1983] 2 Lloyd's Rep. 171 at p.186.

[21] *cf.* the assumption in *C. Groom Ltd v Barber* [1915] 1 K.B. 316 at p.324 that there was no appropriation though the goods had been shipped; but the reference seems to be to "appropriation" in the "proprietary" sense: see below, para.19–082. In *Clemens E Horst Co. v Biddell Bros* [1911] 1 K.B. 934 at pp.934 to 956 shipment was said to amount to appropriation even for the purpose of passing of property but it is now generally accepted that the appropriation may not at the stage of shipment be unconditional for this purpose: below, para.19–100.

[22] See *Hoare v Dresser* (1859) 7 H.L.Cas. 290; for criticism of the view that such appropriation passed an "equitable title" see *Re Wait* [1927] 1 Ch. 606. *Cf.* below, para.19–101.

[23] *James v The Commonwealth* (1939) 62 C.L.R. 339 at p.377.

that the seller has shipped goods of the contract description, so that such a shipment will not generally bind the seller to tender those particular goods to the buyer.[24] What has been said about shipment applies equally to a purchase by the seller of goods afloat, for the purpose of performing the seller's obligations to the buyer under the original sale.

19–017 **Notice of appropriation.** The contract of sale may expressly require the seller to give a notice of appropriation, or to "declare" a shipment made under the contract, or to give a "notice of nomination" (*i.e.* one declaring the name of the ship carrying the goods which he has appropriated to the contract).[25] One object of such a requirement is to give the buyer advance notice of the shipment so as to make it possible for him to contract to resell the goods before shipping documents are actually tendered to him. Even where the buyer does not intend to resell the goods, a "notice of nomination" may be important to him (*e.g.* in the oil business) to enable him to make the necessary berthing and discharging arrangements.[26] Because of the importance of the receipt of notices of these kinds, the provisions of the contract with respect to the giving of such notices must be strictly complied with; if they are not complied with, the buyer is generally[27] entitled to reject the documents and the goods.[28]

19–018 **Time of notice.** The notice must be sent off within the time stipulated in the contract[29]; and where the contract provided that the notice must be "given" within seven days from the date of the bill of lading this was held to mean that it must actually reach the buyer within that time, as the object of the notice was to enable him to deal speedily with the goods.[30] On the other hand, where the contract provided that the notice must (a) be given by cable and (b) reach the buyer within a stipulated time, it was held that the buyer could not reject on the ground that the notice was sent by airmail, as it had nevertheless reached him within the stipulated time.[31] Where the contract specifies a day on which the notice must be given, the seller prima

---

[24] See *Harland and Wolff Ltd v Burstall & Son* (1901) 6 Com.Cas. 113 at p.116.
[25] See *Transpetrol Ltd v Transol Olieprodukten Nederland BV* [1989] 1 Lloyd's Rep. 309; *Vitol SA v Phibro Energy AG*) (*The Mathraki*) [1990] 2 Lloyd's Rep. 84.
[26] This appears to have been the purpose of the requirement in the cases cited in n.25, above.
[27] For an exception, see below, para.19–018 at n.36.
[28] *Kleinjan & Holst NV Rotterdam v Bremer Handelsgesellschaft mbH Hamburg* [1972] 2 Lloyd's Rep. 11; and see paras 19–018 and 19–019 below; *cf.* a dictum in *Produce Brokers Ltd v Weiss* (1918) 118 L.J. 111 at p.115 (where the right to reject was not directly in issue) describing a stipulation as to the time for giving a provisional invoice (a document in the nature of a notice of appropriation: below, para.19–057) as "a vital term of the bargain."
[29] *Graves v Legg* (1854) 9 Exch. 709; *cf. Bunge GmbH v CCV Landbouwbelang GA* [1980] 1 Lloyd's Rep. 458 (below, para.19–208).
[30] *Cie Continentale d'Importation v Handelsvertretung der Union der Russian Soviet Republic in Deutschland* (1928) 138 L.T. 663. Contrast the interpretation of "giving" a notice invoking a *force majeure* clause in *Bremer Handelsgesellschaft mbH v Vanden-Avenne-Izegem PVBA* [1978] 2 Lloyd's Rep. 109 at p.116.
[31] *Daulatram Rameshwarlall v European Grain and Shipping Ltd* [1971] 1 Lloyd's Rep. 368.

facie has the whole of that day for giving the notice, so that a notice given after the close of business hours is valid[32]; but this prima facie rule can be displaced by a contrary term in the contract, whether express or implied (*e.g.* by custom[33]). The contract may specify, not a day on, but an interval within, which the notice may be given but fail to specify the point from which the interval is to be calculated: for example, by simply requiring the seller to give "3 working days' notice of nomination". It seems that such a requirement is satisfied where the notice precedes the end of the delivery period by three days, even though it does not precede the estimated arrival time of the ship by more than two days.[34] The buyer can avoid any inconvenience which this interpretation may cause to him by cxpressly stipulating that the notice must be given by at least a specified number of days before the arrival of the ship.[35] In one case,[36] a c.i.f. contract for the sale of gasoil required the seller to give such a notice "Latest 3 . . . working days prior to vessel arrival"; and the notice actually given preceded the arrival of the vessel by only two days. The seller was accordingly in breach but it was held that the term broken was only a warranty or an intermediate term, rather than a condition, so that the buyer's remedy was to be based simply on the loss caused by the fact that the notice was late and not on the theory that the breach gave him a right to reject. The explanation for this unusual result is that it was the practice of the parties to accept late nominations with an adjustment of laytime so that the vessel would be deemed to have arrived at the end of the contractual notice period.[37] In these special circumstances, it was no doubt in accordance with "the clear intention of the parties"[38] that the breach should not give rise to a right to reject; but in the absence of such circumstance the normal rule would apply, giving the buyer the right to reject on account of defects in the notice.

Sometimes the contract does not specify an exact time by, or interval within, which the notice is to be given but merely indicates the need for promptness in general terms, *e.g.* by providing that the notice is to be given "as soon as possible after vessel's sailing". In one case,[39] a provision containing these words was classified as a condition, so that failure to comply with it was held to justify rejection. Such a classification of a term which, because of its inherent vagueness, did not enable the buyer to tell precisely when the notice was due, could scarcely promote the certainty which the classification of a term as a condition is meant to achieve[40]; but

---

[32] *Vitol SA v Phibro Energy AG* (*The Mathraki*) [1990] 2 Lloyd's Rep. 84.
[33] In *The Mathraki*, above, n.32 an attempt to prove such a custom failed.
[34] *The Mathraki*, above, n.32 disagreeing on this point with *Transpetrol Ltd v Transol Olieproduckten Nederland BV* [1989] 1 Lloyd's Rep. 309.
[35] *e.g. Nova Petroleum International Establishment v Tricon Trading Ltd* [1989] 1 Lloyd's Rep. 312 ("minimum 2 working days' notice of vessels' arrival").
[36] *ERG Petroli SpA v Vitol SA (The Ballenita)* [1992] 2 Lloyd's Rep. 455.
[37] *ibid.*, p.464.
[38] *ibid.*, p.465.
[39] *Société Italo-Belge pour le Commerce et l'Industrie v Palm & Vegetable Oils* (*Malaysia*) *Sdn. Bhd.* (*The Post Chaser*) [1981] 2 Lloyd's Rep. 695; in this respect going beyond *Graves v Legg* (1854) 9 Ex. 709: see para.21–025, below; for criticism, see para.19–064, below.
[40] See below, para.19–064.

the actual decision can be justified by reference to the commercial importance to the buyer of receiving the notice promptly, so as to enable him to deal speedily with the goods.

19–019 **Other requirements of notice.** The notice must be given to the person indicated in the contract: if this is the buyer's agent in one country, notice given to the buyer himself in another is defective.[41] The notice must accurately state the particulars required by the contract,[42] which usually include the ship's name, the date of the bill of lading and a statement of the kind and quantity of the goods shipped. If the notice does not state the required particulars, it is immaterial that another document sent later (but not itself amounting to a valid notice of appropriation) does state them.[43] If on the other hand the notice does correctly state the particulars required by the contract, the buyer cannot reject it merely because it also contains further information which is inaccurate. Thus where the notice wrongly stated the bill of lading number (which the contract did not require it to state) it was held that the buyers could not reject merely on that ground.[44] A different position "would or might have arisen" if the mistake had had "some prejudicial effect in relation to the buyers"[45], *e.g.* if they had resold by reference to the incorrect number. Even a mistake as to one of the contractually required particulars will not justify rejection if the contract indicates that accuracy with respect to it is not vital, *e.g.* where the contract requires the notice to state "the date or the presumed date of the Bill of Lading which shall be for information only and shall not be binding."[46]

Where two notices are sent one of which contains insufficient particulars while the other contains qualifications inconsistent with the contract, the two cannot be combined to form a single valid notice.[47]

19–020 **Waiver of defects in notice.** A notice of appropriation may indicate on its face that the goods to which it refers are not of the contract description, *e.g.* that they have been shipped outside the shipment period. If the buyer nevertheless accepts such a notice, he may be taken to have waived the defects in it and so to have lost his right to reject it. However, he will not have lost this right if he accepts the notice expressly subject to a reservation of his rights.[48] Even where there was no such reservation, it was held that a buyer had not lost his right to reject the notice merely by a delay of two days before rejecting it, spent in ascertaining that the notice was not acceptable to his sub-buyer.[49] A buyer who accepts a notice of appropria-

---

[41] *Luis de Ridder SA v André & Cie. SA (Lausanne)* [1941] 1 All E.R. 380.
[42] *Dalgety & Co. Ltd v TG Bradfield & Co. Ltd* (1930) 35 Com.Cas. 213; *Kleinjan & Holst NV Rotterdam v Bremer Handelsgesellschaft mbH Hamburg* [1972] 2 Lloyd's Rep. 11.
[43] *Cie Continentale d'Importation v Handelsvertretung der Union der Soviet Russian Republic in Deutschland* (1928) 138 L.T. 663.
[44] *Bremer Handelsgesellschaft mbH v Toepfer* [1980] 2 Lloyd's Rep. 43.
[45] *ibid.*, at p.49.
[46] As in *Bremer Handelsgesellschaft mbH v Toepfer*, above, at p.46.
[47] *Aure v Van Cauwenberghe & Fils* [1938] 2 All E.R. 300.
[48] *Bremer Handelsgesellschaft mbH v Deutsche Conti-Handelsgesellschaft mbH* [1983] 2 Lloyd's Rep. 45 (first and third notice).
[49] *ibid.* (fourth notice).

tion reserving his rights may later go further by taking up and paying against shipping documents.[50] The question whether he has thereby lost his right to reject those documents, or the goods, is discussed later in this chapter.[51]

Withdrawal of notice. A seller may give a notice of appropriation which is valid, but may wish to withdraw it on the ground that it did not relate to the goods which he in fact intended to appropriate to the contract. It is submitted that the notice could not be withdrawn[52] at least if the buyer had acted in reliance on it. The point can be put beyond doubt by stipulating in the contract that "A valid notice of appropriation when once given shall not be withdrawn."[53] So long as the notice complies in all respects with the requirements of the contract, it is "valid", within the meaning of such a stipulation, even though it does not accurately reflect the seller's state of mind. Hence it cannot be withdrawn or even amended except to the extent that the contract allows amendment, *e.g.* for errors in transmission for which the seller is not responsible,[54] or where a c.i.f. sale provides for delivery by a ship "to be nominated or substitute". In a case of the latter kind,[55] the seller had originally nominated a ship which was not in accordance with the requirements of the contract and it was held that he was entitled to nominate a second ship which did comply with those requirements.[56] He would not, in such a case, be estopped from making the substitution merely because the buyer had acted in reliance on the original nomination,[57] for the term quoted above would normally preclude the mere making of that nomination from amounting to a representation that no substitution would be made. An estoppel could arise only if the seller had in some other way indicated that he would not exercise his power of substitution. Where the *contract* does not allow for withdrawal or amendment of the notice, the general view is that a power to withdraw or amend the notice cannot be reserved by the terms of the *notice, e.g.* by a term in the notice indicating that the seller is appropriating goods on board a named ship "or better name".[58] The authorities which support this view 19–021

---

[50] *ibid.* (documents relating to goods covered by the first notice).

[51] Below, paras 19–151 to 19–152.

[52] *Borrowman, Phillips & Co. v Free & Hollis* (1878) 4 Q.B.D. 500 at p.504; *cf. Coastal (Bermuda) Petroleum Ltd v VTT Petroleum SA (The Marine Star)* [1993] 1 Lloyd's Rep. 329 at p.332.

[53] As in *Dalgety & Co. Ltd v TG Bradfield & Co. Ltd* (1930) 35 Com.Cas. 213 *Grain Union SA Antwerp v Hans Larson AS Aalborg* (1933) 38 Com.Cas. 261; *Ross T. Smyth & Co. Ltd v TD Bailey, Sons & Co.* [1940] 3 All E.R. 60; *Getreide Import Gesellschaft mbH v Itoh & Co. (America) Ltd* [1979] 1 Lloyd's Rep. 592.

[54] *Kleinjan & Holst NV Rotterdam v Bremer Handeslgesellschaft mbH Hamburg* [1972] 2 Lloyd's Rep. 11; *Waren Import Gesellschaft Krohn & Co. v Alfred C. Toepfer (The Vladimir Ilich)* [1975] 1 Lloyd's Rep. 322.

[55] *ERG Petroli SpA v Vitol SA (The Ballenita)* [1992] 2 Lloyd's Rep. 455 ("TBN or sub").

[56] For the question whether the notice of substitution was given in time, see above, para.19–018.

[57] *cf.* below, para.20–051.

[58] See the authorities cited in n.54, above.

were not cited in a case,[59] in which the contrary assumption seems to have been made, *i.e.* that a power to substitute could be reserved by the terms of the notice, even though no such power was reserved by the contract. But the only points there actually decided were that the seller had, by nominating "ship A/substitute" made an effective nomination of ship A and that he was not entitled simply to withdraw that nomination without making any substitution at all. An invalid notice does not bind either party; but if such a notice is followed by a valid notice within the contract period[60] the latter notice takes effect.

19–022 **Notice relating to non-existent goods.** So long as the notice complies on its face with the requirements of the contract, it is "valid" even though it relates to non-existent goods: for example, to goods alleged to have been, but not in fact, shipped on a particular ship, or on a non-existent ship.[61] "Validity depends upon form and timing and not upon substance or factual accuracy."[62] The notice "commits the seller to tender performance in that way"[63] (*i.e.* in the way specified in the notice). The contract will therefore become one which the seller will be unable to perform, so that he will be liable in damages, while the buyer will be entitled to rescind. If, however, the buyer treats a notice of this kind as *invalid*, he leaves it open to the seller to give a further notice of appropriation within the time fixed for performance. The buyer is then prima facie in breach of contract if he repudiates before expiry of that time.[64]

19–023 **Cases in which notice must be given.** In describing the characteristics of a c.i.f. contract, Lord Wright has said: "The seller has to ship or acquire after that shipment the contract goods, as to which, if unascertained, he is generally required to give a notice of appropriation."[65] This statement is taken from a case in which the contract contained express provisions as to notice of appropriation; and it is submitted that it refers only to such a situation: in other words it means that a c.i.f. seller "generally" has to give notice because the contract will generally contain a provision to that effect.

---

[59] *Coastal (Bermuda) Petroleum Ltd v VTT Vulcan Petroleum SA (The Marine Star)* [1993] 1 Lloyd's Rep. 329; for further proceedings in this case, see [1994] 2 Lloyd's Rep. 629.

[60] As in *Borrowman, Phillips & Co. v Free and Hollis* and *Getreide Import Gesellschaft mbH v Itoh & Co. (America) Ltd*, above, nn. 52 and 53.

[61] See the authorities cited in n.54, above.

[62] *Waren Import Gesellschaft Krohn & Co. v Alfred C Toepfer* (*The Vladimir Ilich*) [1975] 1 Lloyd's Rep. 322 at p.329; *cf. Grain Union SA Antwerp v Hans Larson AS Aalborg* (1933) 35 Com.Cas. 261.

[63] *PT Putrabali v Fratelli de Lorenzi SNC* (unrep., October 15, 2001) per Moore-Bick J., cited in *PT Putrabali Adyamulia v Société Est Epices (The Intan v 360A SN)* [2003] 2 Lloyd's Rep. 700 at [9].

[64] *Waren Import Gesellschaft Krohn & Co. v Alfred C Toepfer* (*The Vladimir Ilich*) [1975] 1 Lloyd's Rep. 322 at p.329.

[65] *Ross T Smyth & Co. Ltd v TD Bailey, Son & Co.* [1940] 3 All E.R. 60 at p.68.

Where the contract is silent on the point, the seller is not, it is submitted, bound to give notice of appropriation.[66]

(b) *The Shipping Documents*

In general. The shipping documents are those documents which a seller is required to tender as a condition of obtaining payment.[67] In the absence of any contrary provision in the contract, or of a relevant trade usage or custom, a c.i.f. seller is bound to tender three such documents: a bill of lading,[68] a policy of insurance[69] and an invoice.[70] 19–024

Contractual variations of these requirements are in fact quite common. The contract may, for example, substitute a delivery order for a bill of lading, or a certificate for a policy of insurance, or call for additional documents such as inspection certificates,[71] or performance guarantees.[72] Such contractual variations are, however, interpreted against the background of the obligations prima facie resting on a c.i.f. seller under the general law. Thus where a c.i.f. contract provided for payment "against documents or delivery order" it was held that this entitled the seller only to substitute a delivery order for a bill of lading; and that it therefore did not relieve him from his obligation to tender a policy of insurance.[73] Similarly, where a c.i.f. contract gives a seller an option to tender a delivery order instead of a bill of lading, this provision "should prima facie be interpreted as intended to confer upon the buyer control over the goods covered by the delivery order, even though falling short of ownership, and also some right against the person in possession of the goods, even though falling short of the rights conferred by transfer of the bill of lading."[74] Accordingly, where a c.i.f. contract required the seller to tender a bill of lading or ship's delivery order,[75] it was not sufficient for him to tender a document containing or giving rise to no promise by the carrier to deliver the goods, or one containing only a promise to deliver the goods to the seller (or his order) but not to the buyer.[76]

---

66 See, for example, *C Groom Ltd v Barber* [1915] 1 K.B. 316; *Empresa Exportadora de Azucar v Industria Azucarera Nacional SA* (*The Playa Larga*) [1983] 2 Lloyd's Rep. 171 at p.185. Contrast Vienna Convention on Contracts for the International Sale of Goods (above, para.1–024), Art. 32(1), requiring the seller to give "notice of the consignment" where the goods have been handed over to a carrier but have not been "clearly identified to the contract."

67 For the distinction between shipping documents and other documents or notices which the seller may be required to provide, see below, para.19–058.

68 See *Heilbert, Symons & Co. Ltd v Harvey, Christie-Miller & Co.* (1922) 12 Ll.L.R. 455; below, paras 19–025 to 19–040; for the question whether a charterparty must also be tendered see below, para.19–041.

69 Below, paras 19–042 to 19–052.

70 Below, paras 19–053 to 19–057.

71 *e.g. Re Reinhold & Co. and Hansloh* (1896) 12 T.L.R. 422.

72 Above, para.19–005.

73 *Re Denbigh Cowan & Co. and R Atcherley & Co.* (1921) 90 L.J.K.B. 836.

74 *Waren Import Gesellschaft Krohn & Co. v Internationale Graanhandel Thegra NV* [1975] 1 Lloyd's Rep. 146 at p.154. *Cf.* above, paras 18–171, 18–174, 18–175 *et seq.*, and, as to insurance documents, below, para.19–048.

75 See above, para.18–171 for the common law sense of this expression.

76 *Waren Import Gesellschaft Krohn & Co. v Internationale Graanhandel Thegra* [1975] 1 Lloyd's Rep. 146 at p.155.

Customary variations are also common, particularly in relation to the characteristics of the individual shipping documents. The seller must, and need only, tender such documents as are "usual and customary".[77] This is subject to the qualification that such documents must not be "fundamentally inconsistent" with "the character of the documents which must in point of law have been tendered".[78] The qualification is illustrated by a case[79] in which the seller tendered a defective bill of lading[80] and relied on a custom to the effect that the defect could be cured by his providing a guarantee against adverse consequences of the defect. It was held that the buyer was not required to accept the guarantee in place of a conforming bill of lading since such a requirement would be "fundamentally inconsistent with the nature of a c.i.f. contract"[81] in that it would purport to replace the buyer's remedy against the carrier with nothing but a further promise from the seller.

(i) *The Bill of Lading*[82]

19–025 **Duty of seller in relation to contract of affreightment.** A c.i.f. seller must make or procure a proper contract of affreightment,[83] and procure a proper bill of lading. These are, strictly speaking, separate duties, for the duty to make or procure a proper contract of affreightment would exist even though the seller was, by the terms of the contract, only bound to tender a delivery order; and might exist even though the contract of sale provided that shipping space was to be booked by the buyer.[84] But in the normal case, in which the seller is bound to make the shipping arrangements and to tender a bill of lading, the two duties are so closely related as to be virtually identical; for the question whether the seller has made a proper contract of affreightment will depend on the form and content of the bill of lading, and on the circumstances in which it was issued. The two duties will therefore be considered together in the following discussion.

---

77 *Burstall v Grimsdale* (1906) 11 Com.Cas. 280 at p.289; *National Bank of Egypt v Hannevig's Bank Ltd* (1919) 1 Ll.L.R. 69; 3 *Legal Decisions affecting Bankers*, at p.214; *TW Ranson Ltd v Manufacture d'Engrais* (1922) 13 Ll.L.R. 205; *NV Arnold Otto Meyer v Aune* [1939] 3 All E.R. 168; *Ceval Alimentos SA v Agrimpex Trading Co. Ltd (The Northern Progress) (No.2)* [1996] 2 Lloyd's Rep. 319 at p.328.

78 *Burstall v Grimsdale*, above, at p.289.

79 *Soules CAF v PT Transcap of Indonesia* [1999] 1 Lloyd's Rep. 917.

80 The bill did not comply with the requirement stated in para.19–039, below.

81 [1999] 1 Lloyd's Rep. 917 at p.921.

82 See generally on bills of lading, above, paras 18–012 *et seq.*

83 Sale of Goods Act 1979, s.32(2); (as to which, in the context of c.i.f. sales, see also paras 18–260 and 18–261 above); *Houlder Bros & Co. Ltd v Commissioner of Public Works* [1908] A.C. 276 at 290; *Tsakiroglou & Co. v Noblee Thorl GmbH* [1962] A.C. 93; Vienna Convention on Contracts for the International Sale of Goods (above, para.1–024), Art. 32(2).

84 As in *Krohn & Co. v Mitsui & Co. Europe GmbH* [1978] 2 Lloyd's Rep. 419. The mere "booking" of space by the buyer might be non-contractual: *Heskell v Continental Express Ltd* [1950] 1 All E.R. 1033; if so, the seller would still be responsible for ensuring that the terms of the contract of carriage made it a proper contract of affreightment. *cf.* above, para.18–030.

Normal requirements as to bill of lading.[85] The bill of lading must normally be in a transferable form[86]; provide continuous documentary cover; state that the goods have been actually shipped, and not merely that they have been received for shipment; provide for the carriage of the goods to the agreed destination by the agreed or customary route; be issued "on shipment"; be "genuine"; cover the goods sold and no others; be "valid and effective"; and be "clean". The first of these requirements does not call for further discussion here[87]; the others will be considered in the following paragraphs. They are of course subject to the terms of the contract and to any relevant custom or usage.[88] 19–026

Continuous documentary cover. The principle of continuous documentary cover was stated by Lord Sumner in *Hansson v Hamel and Horley Ltd*: a c.i.f. seller must "cover the buyer by procuring and tendering documents which will be available for his protection from shipment to destination."[89] In that case cod guano was sold c.i.f. Kobe or Yokohama, to be shipped from Norway in March/April 1920. The goods were shipped in April from the Norwegian port of Braatvag on the *Kiev* and carried to Hamburg where they were transhipped into the *Atlas Maru*. The owners of the latter ship on May 5 signed a so-called "Through Bill of Lading" by which the goods were stated to have been shipped on the *Kiev* "lying in or off the port of Braatvag and bound for Hamburg for trans-shipment into the *Atlas Maru* . . . to be delivered at the port of Yokohama . . .". It was held that this bill of lading did not provide "continuous documentary cover" since under it the owners of the *Atlas Maru* were under no contractual responsibility in respect of the carriage of the goods from Braatvag to Hamburg.[90] Lord Sumner said that the bill "though called a through bill . . . is not really so. It is the contract of the subsequent carrier only, without any complementary provisions to bind the prior carrier."[91] The bill would have been a real "through bill" if the owners of the *Atlas Maru* had taken responsibility for the shipment of the goods from Braatvag to Yokohama; and although no opinion was expressed by Lord Sumner on the effect of tender of such a bill,[92] it would at any rate seem to satisfy the requirement of continuous documentary cover. The question whether tender of the *Kiev* bill of lading, 19–027

---

85 For similar requirements under documentary credits, see below, paras 23–218 *et seq*.
86 *Soproma SpA v Marine & Animal By-Products Corp.* [1966] 1 Lloyd's Rep. 367 (above, paras 18–014, 18–015).
87 See above, paras 18–013—18–018.
88 Above, para.19–024.
89 [1922] 2 A.C. 36 at pp.44–45.
90 *cf. Landauer & Co. v Craven & Speeding* [1912] 2 K.B. 94; *Suzuki & Co. v Burgett & Newsam* (1921) 8 Ll.L.R. 495; (1922) 10 Ll.L.R. 223; *Holland Colombo Trading Co. Ltd v Alawdeen* [1954] 2 Lloyd's Rep. 45 (where the contract was held not to be a c.i.f. contract). Lord Sumner's earlier and apparently contrary decision in *Cox, McEuen & Co. v Malcolm & Co.* [1912] 2 K.B. 107 n.was explained by him in *Hansson v Hamel & Horley Ltd* [1922] 2 A.C. 36 at pp.49–50 after having been doubted by Scrutton J. in *Landauer & Co. v Craven & Speeding* [1912] 2 K.B. 94 at pp.104–105.
91 [1922] 2 A.C. 36 at p.46.
92 See *ibid*., at p.48.

together with the *Atlas Maru* bill, would have cured the defect in the tender of the latter bill was also left open.[93] It is possible that even such tender might have left a gap in the documentary cover at the point of transhipment: that is, between the times at which the goods were unloaded from the *Kiev* and put on board the *Atlas Maru*. The seller could have met the buyer's objections by providing in the contract of sale for shipment from Hamburg and tendering a bill of lading covering the carriage of the goods on the *Atlas Maru* from that port.[94] In such a case any loss of or damage to the goods before they reached Hamburg would have been at the seller's risk.[95]

The points between which documentary cover has to be provided are determined by reference to relevant provisions in the contract of sale. For example, in one case[96] goods were sold "c. & f. liner terms Rotterdam" and the expression "liner terms" meant that the responsibility for discharge was to be that of the carriers.[97] The sellers tendered a bill of lading which contained terms under which that responsibility could rest, not on the carriers but on the sellers (or on the buyers with a right of recourse against the sellers). This was held to be a bad tender as it left "the buyers without documentary protection or rights against the carriers in respect of the discharging operation."[98]

The buyer is entitled to continuous documentary cover whether he actually needs it or not. It would not have helped the seller in *Hansson v Hamel and Horley Ltd* to have been able to show that the goods were not in fact damaged on the *Kiev* or at all.[99] The reason for this rule is that the buyer may not, at the time when the documents are tendered, have the means of knowing anything about the physical condition of the goods; and he needs to know at that time what his rights against the carrier will be in case the goods have been damaged.

19–028 **Liberty to tranship and transhipment.** It has been said that the buyer is not deprived of continuous documentary cover merely because the bill of lading contains a liberty to tranship, if that liberty has not in fact been exercised.[1] As a general principle,[2] this statement gives rise to some difficulty; for, as Lord Sumner said in *Hansson v Hamel and Horley Ltd*, the shipping documents "have to be taken up or rejected promptly"[3]; and a buyer (or banker) to whom such a bill is tendered may have no means of knowing at the time of tender whether the goods have actually been transhipped. The position would be different where the goods had in fact

[93] *ibid.*, at p.46.
[94] *ibid.*, at p.48.
[95] Below, para.19–110.
[96] *Soon Hua Seng Co. Ltd v Glencore Grain Co. Ltd* [1996] 1 Lloyd's Rep. 398.
[97] See *Ceval International Ltd v Cefetra BV* [1996] 1 Lloyd's Rep. 464.
[98] *Soon Hua Seng Co. Ltd v Glencore Grain Co. Ltd*, above, at p.401.
[99] *Landauer & Co. v Craven & Speeding* [1912] 2 K.B. 94.
[1] *Soproma SpA v Marine and Animal By-Products Corp.* [1966] 1 Lloyd's Rep. 367 at p.388.
[2] *i.e.* subject to contrary provisions in the contract, and to custom: below, para.19–029.
[3] [1922] A.C. 36 at p.46.

been transhipped and the bill of lading *either* contained no liberty to tranship *or* was in such terms that one of the carriers was responsible for the whole of the carriage and for any loss or damage to the goods at the point of transhipment.[4] In such cases the buyer would, if the goods were lost or damaged, have a remedy against at least one of the carriers for breach of the contract of carriage.[5] Thus the requirement of continuous documentary cover would be satisfied and the buyer would not be entitled to object to the documents merely on account of the transhipment.[6] A bill of lading containing a liberty to tranship might also be a good shipping document by custom.

Relaxation of requirement of continuous documentary cover. The requirement of continuous documentary cover may be varied by the terms of the contract of sale, or by the customs or usages of the relevant trade. Thus where it is customary to ship goods by coastal or river steamers to a port for ocean shipment, and to tender the ocean bills of lading only, such a tender is good under a c.i.f. contract.[7] The custom may require the seller expressly to reserve power to tranship in the contract of sale, in which event the buyer will be entitled to reject the documents on account of transhipment if no such reservation was made.[8] 19–029

Shipped and received bills. Prima facie the seller must obtain a bill of lading which states that the goods have actually been shipped[9] and not merely that they have been received for shipment.[10] One reason for this rule is that a "received" bill probably lacks the characteristics of a document of title in the traditional common law sense,[11] so that such a bill would be an unsatisfactory security for the buyer. A second reason for the rule is that a "received" bill might fail to provide the buyer with "continuous documentary cover". This could be the position where a "received" bill provided that the shipowner was to be liable only in respect of goods actually shipped on board[12] and they were damaged while being loaded; though where the bill made the shipowner liable on the terms of the contract of carriage from the 19–030

---

[4] As in *Mayhew Foods Ltd v Overseas Containers Ltd* [1984] 1 Lloyd's Rep. 317.

[5] *e.g. The Berkshire* [1974] 1 Lloyd's Rep. 185.

[6] For a similar rule in cases of deviation see above, para.18–061; below, para.19–033.

[7] *N.V. Arnold Otto Meyer v Aune* [1939] 3 All E.R. 168; *cf. Burstall v Grimsdale* (1906) 11 Com.Cas. 280; *Plaimar Ltd v Waters Trading Co. Ltd* (1945) 72 C.L.R. 304.

[8] *Fischel & Co. v Knowles* (1922) 12 Ll.L.R. 36.

[9] *Diamond Alkali Export Corp. v Fl. Bourgeois* [1921] 3 K.B. 443, where the bill of lading stated that the goods had been "received . . . to be transported on the *Anglia* . . . or failing shipment by said steamer in and upon a following steamer." The case therefore does not conclude the question whether the rule applies to a received bill which names the ship but gives *no* option to carry on another (unnamed) ship. Under U.C.P. 500 (below, para.23–013), Art. 23(ii) a shipped bill must be tendered under a documentary credit which calls for an ocean bill of lading; *cf.*, in the case of a credit calling for a "non-negotiable sea waybill", Art. 24(ii).

[10] For the distinction between the two kinds of bills of lading see above, para.18–027.

[11] Above, para.18–079. For the contrary view, see *Ishag v Allied Bank International* [1981] 1 Lloyd's Rep. 92, discussed in para.18–079, above.

[12] *Yelo v SM Machado Ltd* [1952] 1 Lloyd's Rep. 183 at p.192 (f.o.b. contract).

time that the goods were received by him the objection to it would not be based on the lack of documentary cover.[13] A third reason for the rule requiring the seller to tender a "shipped" bill is that a received bill would leave the buyer in doubt as to the date of actual shipment, a point of crucial importance in overseas sales.[14] On the other hand, a received bill resembles a shipped bill in that rights under the contract of carriage contained in or evidenced by a received bill can be acquired by the lawful holder of it by virtue of section 2(1) of the Carriage of Goods by Sea Act 1992, and liabilities under that contract can be imposed on the lawful holder in the conditions specified in section 3 of that Act.[15] The lawful holder also has the protection of section 4 of the 1992 Act in the sense that representations in a received bill as to the fact of receipt for shipment are conclusive evidence of such receipt (though not, of course, of shipment).[16]

A document which originates as a received bill can become a shipped bill if, after the goods have been shipped, this fact is noted by or on behalf of the carrier on the bill.[17] Once this has been done, the bill will be a good tender under a c.i.f. contract.[18] Even where no such notation has been made, tender of a "received", or of a "shipped or received", bill will be good if it is usual in the trade[19] or in accordance with the normal course of dealings between the parties.[20]

19–031 **Destination.** The bill of lading must provide for the carriage of the goods to the destination specified in the contract of sale[21]: if the bill of lading does not satisfy this requirement, the seller is in breach even though the actual contract of carriage made by him did provide for carriage to that destination.[22] A bill of lading may fail to satisfy this requirement, even though it is expressed to be for the delivery of the goods at the c.i.f. destination, if it does not oblige the carrier to deliver them there, *e.g.* if the

---

[13] See *Weis & Co. v Produce Brokers* (1921) 7 Ll.L.R. 211.
[14] Above, para.18–267.
[15] These consequences follow from s.1(2)(b); above, para.18–103.
[16] s.4(a); above, para.18–038.
[17] Above, para.18–027.
[18] *cf.* U.C.P. 500, Art. 23(ii); *cf.* Art. 24(ii) (sea waybill).
[19] *United Baltic Corp. v Burgett and Newsam* (1921) 8 Ll.L.R. 190. But even in such a case the buyer can still reject the goods if in fact they are not shipped within the shipment period: *Suzuki & Co. v Burgett and Newsam* (1922) 10 Ll.L.R. 223.
[20] *Weis & Co. v Produce Brokers*, above n.13.
[21] *Acmé Wood Flooring Co. Ltd v Sutherland, Innes & Co. Ltd* (1904) 9 Com.Cas. 170; *Marshall, Knott & Barker Ltd v Arcos Ltd* (1933) 44 Ll.L.R. 384; *Colin and Shields v Weddel & Co.* [1952] 2 All E.R. 337; *SIAT di dal Ferro v Tradax Overseas SA* [1980] 1 Lloyd's Rep. 53 (c.i.f. destination Venice; bills of lading with destination "Ancona/Ravenna" held a bad tender); *cf. Ceval Alimentos SA v Agrimpex Trading Co. Ltd (The Northern Progress) (No.2)* [1996] 2 Lloyd's Rep. 319 (tender held bad where bill of lading apparently incorporated charterparty term which required sellers, as charterers, in specified events to divert the carrying ship to a destination other than that specified in the contract of sale). *cf. Sargant & Sons v East Asiatic Co. Ltd* (1915) 85 L.J.K.B. 277, where the requirement was waived.
[22] *Lecky & Co. Ltd v Ogilvy Gillanders & Co.* (1897) 3 Com.Cas. 29; *SIAT di dal Ferro v Tradax Overseas SA* [1980] 1 Lloyd's Rep. 53 (c.i.f. destination Venice; bills of lading with destination "as per charterparty" held a bad tender where charterparty destination was Venice *or* Ravenna).

obligation to deliver is qualified by the words "or so near as the ship can safely get" and she cannot safely get to the particular wharf named as the destination in the contract of sale.[23] Similarly, if the contract provides for delivery of the goods at any one of a range of ports to be selected by the buyer, the seller must arrange for them to be shipped on board a ship which can enter the particular port selected by the buyer: it is not enough for him to show that she could have entered other ports within the contractual range, nor is the buyer's choice of ports restricted to such ports as the ship could have entered.[24] Similarly, where the contract provides for delivery at one of a number of named ports, a bill of lading is defective if it provides for delivery at a range of ports wider (or presumably narrower) than that specified in the contract.[25] Tender of a bill of lading is, however, good in spite of the fact that the bill contains a qualification with respect to the destination which is not expressed in the contract of sale, if that qualification is one which would in any event have been implied.[26] Tender of a bill of lading which obliges the carrier to carry the goods to the c.i.f. destination is good even though the carrier is prevented from discharging the goods there by some supervening event for which the seller is not responsible, *e.g.* if, after the time of contracting, "a sudden storm had silted up the harbour there",[27] or the port had become strikebound or the authorities of the country of destination had imposed a prohibition of import[28] or the discharge of the goods there had become otherwise illegal. This follows from the nature of a c.i.f. contract, under which the seller is not obliged to ensure delivery of the goods at the c.i.f. destination.[29]

Route of shipment. The contract of sale may specify the route of shipment, in which case it would seem, on principle, that the seller is bound to obtain a bill of lading for shipment by that route.[30] Thus where peas were sold c. & f. Bombay and the contract required the ship to sail directly to Bombay, it was held that the buyer could reject on the ground that the ship was scheduled to call, and did call, at a number of intermediate ports.[31] The crucial point was that the bill of lading did not (while the contract of sale did) require the ship to go directly to Bombay: the failure of the bill in this respect to comply with the contract of sale would, it is submitted, have justified rejection even if the ship had not in fact called at any of the 19–032

---

23 *Marshall, Knott and Barker Ltd v Arcos Ltd*, above n.21.
24 *Eurico SpA v Phillipp Brothers (The Epaphus)* [1987] 2 Lloyd's Rep. 215.
25 *Soules CAF v PT Transcap of Indonesia* [1999] 1 Lloyd's Rep. 917.
26 *Re Goodbody & Co. and Balfour Williamson & Co.* (1900) 82 L.T. 484 (c.i.f. destination "any safe port in the UK"; bill of lading to "any safe port in the UK (Manchester excepted)" *held* good as Manchester was not, in a commercial sense, a "safe port").
27 *Eurico SpA v Phillipp Brothers (The Epaphus)* [1987] 2 Lloyd's Rep. 215 at p.220.
28 *Congimex Companhia Geral, etc., SARL v Tradax Export SA* [1983] 1 Lloyd's Rep. 250
29 Above, para.19–002.
30 *cf. Re L. Sutro & Co. and Heilbut, Symons & Co.* [1917] 2 K.B. 348, where the Court of Appeal was not divided on the principle but on the construction of the contract. The actual decision may require consideration: *Tsakiroglou & Co. Ltd v Noblee Thorl GmbH* [1962] A.C. 93 at 113.
31 *Bergerco USA v Vegoil Ltd* [1984] 1 Lloyd's Rep. 440.

intermediate ports. This is because shipping documents "have to be taken up or rejected promptly"[32]: the practical considerations which govern the right to reject in the somewhat analogous case of transhipment[33] apply also in the present context.

More usually, the route of shipment will be a matter of indifference to the buyer and will not be specifically laid down in the contract of sale; and in such a case the court will not imply a term that a particular route must be used, merely because both parties contemplated that it would be used.[34] The only term which the court may imply is that the seller will ship the goods by the route which is usual and customary at the time, not of the contract of sale, but of the shipment.[35] If at that time there is no "usual and customary" route, the seller must ship the goods by any route that is reasonable and practicable.[36] Under these rules the route of shipment is not necessarily the most direct route.[37]

19–033 **Deviation clauses.** Assuming that the route of shipment has been determined in accordance with the rules stated in paragraph 19–032 above, objection may nevertheless be taken to a bill of lading on the ground that it contains deviation or similar clauses permitting the carrier to depart from that route. Thus in one case a bill of lading contained a clause in words "so wide that the ship might have called anywhere she liked, and almost gone round the world before she came to the port of discharge."[38] This would have justified rejection by the buyer if he had not on the facts waived the right to reject. It is submitted that this rule would apply even though the court would, as a matter of construction, cut down the clause, so as not to defeat the main object of the contract of carriage.[39] Once again it is important to stress that the shipping documents "have to be taken up or rejected promptly"[40] and this would not be possible if, on tender of documents, the buyer (or his bank) had to resolve such difficult questions of construction. It is submitted that if the buyer is entitled to object to the bill of lading on account of a deviation clause he can do so whether or not the ship has actually deviated, since he may have no means of knowing this at the time of tender of documents. It must be emphasised that our concern at this point is with *deviation clauses*, and not with *actual deviation*. If the bill of lading contains no objectionable deviation clause, the buyer is not

---

[32] *Hansson v Hamel & Horley Ltd* [1922] A.C. 36 at p.46.
[33] Above, para.19–028.
[34] *Tsakiroglou & Co. v Noblee Thorl GmbH* [1962] A.C. 93.
[35] *ibid.*
[36] *ibid.*, at pp.113–114, 127, 133 criticising dicta in *Re L. Sutro & Co. and Heilbut, Symons & Co.* [1917] 2 K.B. 348.
[37] *cf.* the similar rule in cases concerned with the question whether departure from the agreed route amounts to deviation: *Evans, Sons & Co. v Cunard SS Co. Ltd* (1902) 18 T.L.R. 374; *Frenkel v MacAndrews & Co. Ltd* [1929] A.C. 545; *Reardon Smith Line Ltd v Black Sea and Baltic General Insurance Co. Ltd* [1939] A.C. 562.
[38] *Shipton, Anderson & Co. v John Western & Co.* (1922) 10 Ll.L.R. 762 at p.763; *cf. Spillers Ltd v JW Mitchell Ltd* (1929) 33 Ll.L.R. 89 (bill of lading referring to "the deviation clause" ineffective because of the uncertainty thus introduced).
[39] As in *Glynn v Margetson* [1893] A.C. 351.
[40] *Hansson v Hamel and Horley Ltd* [1922] 2 A.C. 36 at p.46.

entitled to reject it merely because the ship has in fact wrongfully deviated. In such a case the buyer has a remedy against the carrier for breach of the contract of carriage; and the seller is not responsible for this breach.[41]

The rule that a bill of lading may be rejected on account of a deviation clause is again subject to contrary custom or usage. Thus in *Burstall v Grimsdale*[42] tender of a bill of lading containing a deviation clause was held good, whether or not the ship had actually deviated, as the bill was "usual and customary" in the trade in question, and not inconsistent with the express terms of the contract of sale. It is now common for a bill of lading to contain a deviation clause; and it seems probable that such a bill would (for the purpose of a c.i.f. contract) be a good shipping document by custom, unless *either* the clause was drafted in such wide terms as to make it unusual, *or* the contract of sale expressly required the contract of carriage to provide for "direct" shipment to the destination named, *i.e.* for shipment without deviation even to an intermediate port on the general route to that destination.[43]

To be issued on shipment. The bill of lading must be issued "on shipment".[44] This does not mean that it must be issued at the precise time of shipment[45]: it probably means no more than that the bill of lading must be issued without undue delay and in accordance with the usual course of business, under which bills of lading may not be issued until some days after the ship has sailed.[46] Where several bills of lading are issued in respect of a single bulk shipment, "there is no obligation to issue bills of lading hold by hold".[47] Hence tender of a bill issued within a reasonable time of completion of loading is good even though the particular bill relates to a part of the bulk shipped well before the end of that time. On the other hand, once a single bill of lading had been issued in respect of a bulk shipment, further bills issued later by a time charterer (not acting on behalf of the shipowner) in respect of parts of the same bulk, for the purpose of enabling the seller to split up the bulk among several buyers,[48] were held not to have been issued on shipment or in the ordinary course of business[49]; so that the tender of such bills was bad. The same conclusion was reached where the bill of lading was issued as much as seven weeks after shipment[50]; and where a bill of lading was issued only 13 days after shipment, the shipment having taken place in another country and the goods having in the meantime been transhipped.[51] 19–034

[41] Above, para.18–061.
[42] (1906) 11 Com.Cas. 280.
[43] *Bergerco USA v Vegoil Ltd* [1984] 1 Lloyd's Rep. 440, above, para.19–032.
[44] *Hansson v Hamel and Horley Ltd* [1922] 2 A.C. 36 at p.46; *Landauer & Co. v Craven and Speeding* [1912] 2 K.B. 94 at p.105.
[45] *Hansson v Hamel and Horley* [1922] 2 A.C. 36 at p.47.
[46] *ibid.*; *cf.* above, para.18–047.
[47] *M. Golodetz & Co. Inc. v Czarnikow Rionda Inc.* (*The Galatia*) [1980] 1 W.L.R. 495 at p.512.
[48] Above, para.18–286.
[49] *SIAT di del Ferro v Tradax Overseas SA* [1978] 2 Lloyd's Rep. 470 at p.493; affirmed [1980] 1 Lloyd's Rep. 53.
[50] *Foreman and Ellams Ltd v Blackburn* [1928] 2 K.B. 60.
[51] *Hansson v Hamel and Horley Ltd* [1922] 2 A.C. 36.

19–035 **Genuine bill of lading.** The bill of lading must be "genuine".[52] A bill of lading issued in respect of goods which have never been shipped,[53] or one which contains a false date of shipment is a bad tender under a c.i.f. contract[54]; and the same would be true of a bill of lading containing some other forgery, such as a forged signature by or on behalf of the carrier.[55] A bill of lading which falsely represents goods to have been shipped, when no such goods have been shipped in fact, is a bad tender under a c.i.f. contract even though the carrier is liable to the buyer in respect of the false statement,[56] *e.g.* under section 4 of the Carriage of Goods by Sea Act 1992,[57] or in deceit.[58] A bill of lading is also a bad tender if, before tender, shipper and carrier have agreed that the goods are to be carried to some destination other than that stated in the bill; for in such a case the bill would be "false in that [it] purported to represent a contract which had been privately varied".[59] It seems that such a bill of lading is a bad tender by reason of its falsity even though the carrier might not, as against the transferee, be able to rely on the "private" variation[60] and so be liable for failing to carry the goods to the destination stated in the bill. It is submitted that a bill of lading would, *a fortiori*, not be genuine if it were issued after shipper and carrier had agreed to rescind the contract of carriage and the goods had been unloaded from the ship on which they were to have been carried.[61]

Where a bill of lading is not "genuine", the buyer is entitled to reject it. But the further question arises whether, if he pays against such a bill, the buyer has a restitutionary right against the seller for the return of that payment. In *Kwei Tek Chao v British Traders and Shippers Ltd*[62] a buyer paid against a bill of lading which stated that goods had been shipped in October, when in fact they had been shipped on November 3 (outside the shipment period specified in the contract of sale). It was held that the buyer could not recover back the payment as having been made on a consideration which had totally failed; for the bill of lading, though not genuine, was

---

[52] *James Finlay & Co. Ltd v Kwik Hoo Tong* [1929] 1 K.B. 400 at p.408.
[53] *Hindley & Co. Ltd v East Indian Produce Co. Ltd* [1973] 2 Lloyd's Rep. 515 (c. & f. contract).
[54] *James Finlay & Co. Ltd v NV Kwik Hoo Tong HM* [1929] 1 K.B. 400; *Kwei Tek Chao v British Traders and Shippers Ltd* [1954] 2 Q.B. 459.
[55] But a bank transferring such a bill on payment does not warrant its genuineness: below, para.23–191; *Leather v Simpson* (1871) L.R. 11 Eq. 398; *Baxter v Chapman* (1873) 29 L.T. 642; *Guaranty Trust Co. of NY v Hannay* [1918] 2 K.B. 623.
[56] This point is implicit in *Hindley & Co. Ltd v East Indian Produce Co. Ltd*, above, n.53, where it was assumed that the bill made the carrier liable in respect of the false statement under German law.
[57] Above, para.18–036.
[58] Above, para.18–045 (if the carrier is the signer).
[59] *Empresa Exportadora de Azucar v Industria Azucarera Nacional SA* (*The Playa Larga*) [1983] 1 Lloyd's Rep. 171 at p.184 (where the point arose under a letter of credit).
[60] *cf.* above, para.18–048.
[61] As in *The Forum Craftsman* [1985] 1 Lloyd's Rep. 291 (where the sale was on f.o.b. terms and no issue arose between buyer and seller).
[62] [1954] 2 K.B. 459.

not an utter nullity.[63] This decision may be contrasted with that in *The Raffaella*[64] where a bill of lading was alleged to represent cement shipped on the *Raffaella* in May 1979 at Constantza for Port Said. In fact the cement had been shipped elsewhere a year earlier (when the ship bore a different name), had not then been destined for Port Said, and was, by the time of tender, much deteriorated. Legatt J. described the bill of lading as "a sham piece of paper"[65]; and held that money paid on behalf of the buyer against the bill could be recovered back by the buyer as having been paid under a mistake of fact. The two cases can be reconciled[66] on the ground that the forgery in the first case related only to a single (though important) characteristic of a shipment which had undoubtedly been made, while in the second it went "to the whole or to the essence of the instrument"[67] in the sense that no shipment of the kind described in the bill of lading had ever been made at all. The fact that the buyer might have a remedy against *the carrier* in respect of the false statement[68] should not, it is submitted, affect his remedy against *the seller* for the recovery of money paid under a mistake.

Quantity. The bill of lading must be for the quantity of goods sold[69] and for those goods only: it must not cover more goods, or other goods of a different description.[70] This rule is distinct from the rule relating to shipment of the correct quantity.[71] In one case[72] a contract for the sale of 3,000 tons of grain gave the sellers the option of shipping more, the excess to remain for seller's account. The seller shipped a greater quantity in bulk and it was held that, even though the seller had committed no breach by *shipping* more, the buyers were entitled to bills of lading for the contract quantity. The statutory restrictions on the buyer's right to reject where the seller delivers the wrong "quantity of *goods*"[73] do not (insofar as they apply at all to c.i.f. contracts[74]) appear to extend to the situation in which the 19–036

---

63 *cf. Lombard Finance Ltd v Brookplain Trading Ltd* [1991] 1 W.L.R. 271 at p.277; *Transpacific Discovery SA v Cargill International SA (The Elpa)* [2001] 2 Lloyd's Rep. 596.

64 *Egyptian International Foreign Trade Co. v Soplex Wholesale Supplies (The Raffaella)* [1984] 1 Lloyd's Rep. 102, affirmed on other grounds [1985] 2 Lloyd's Rep. 36, where the point discussed in the text above was said at p.39 to give rise to "difficult questions".

65 [1984] 1 Lloyd's Rep. 102 at p.116.

66 The *Kwei Tek Chao* case (above, n.62) was not cited in *The Raffaella* (above, n.64).

67 *Kwei Tek Chao* case, above, at p.476.

68 Above at n.57 and 58.

69 *Tamvaco v Lucas (No.1)* (1859) 1 E. & E. 581; *Re Keighley Maxtead & Co. and Bryant, Durant & Co. (No.2)* (1894) 70 L.T. 155. Where goods are shipped in bulk and several bills of lading are issued, they must all be tendered: *Gatoil International Inc. v Tradax Petroleum Ltd (The Rio Sun)* [1985] 1 Lloyd's Rep. 351 at p.362; and they must be for the full quantity sold: *Cobec Brazilian Trading & Warehousing Corp. v Alfred C Toepfer* [1983] 2 Lloyd's Rep. 386.

70 *The Julia* [1949] A.C. 293 at p.301.

71 Above, para.19–012.

72 *Re Keighley Maxtead & Co. and Bryant, Durant & Co. (No.2)*, above n.69.

73 Sale of Goods Act 1979 s.30(2A); above, para.19–012.

74 *ibid.*

seller tenders *documents* which are not in conformity with the contract because they relate to the wrong quantity.

19–037 **The bill of lading must be "valid and effective".**[75] The buyer is, as a general rule, entitled to "a bill of lading which is still [*i.e.* at the time of tender] a subsisting contract of affreightment."[76] This requirement was not satisfied in *Arnhold Karberg & Co. v Blythe Green Jourdain & Co.*[77] English sellers sold horsebeans to English buyers c.i.f. Naples, to be paid for in London in exchange for bills of lading and policies of insurance.[78] The goods were shipped on a German ship and German bills of lading were issued. Before tender of documents, the contracts of carriage contained in, or evidenced by, these bills of lading were frustrated by supervening illegality on the outbreak of war in 1914; and it was held that the buyers were entitled to reject the bills. On the other hand, a buyer is not entitled to reject a bill of lading merely on the ground that the goods cannot be discharged at the destination named in it because the authorities there have refused to allow the import of such goods.[79] This will not of itself frustrate the contract of carriage, which may entitle the consignee to redirect the goods to another destination,[80] or entitle the carrier to divert them to another destination if unloading at the destination named becomes impossible for reasons beyond his control.[81]

The rule that the buyer is entitled to a bill of lading which is "valid and effective" does not mean that the buyer must have a good claim under the bill of lading. So long as the bill was originally valid and remains a subsisting contract at the time of tender, it is immaterial that it contains provisions exempting the carrier from liability in the events which have happened.[82] This is true even though the bill of lading was originally a mere receipt (*e.g.* because it was issued to the seller in respect of goods shipped in a ship chartered by him).[83] It is enough that the bill is capable, on transfer to the buyer, of constituting or evidencing an effective contract of carriage between him and the carrier.[84]

---

[75] *Arnhold Karberg & Co. v Blythe, Green, Jourdain & Co.* [1916] 1 K.B. 495 at p.506.
[76] *ibid.*, at p.509. See, however, an *obiter dictum* in *Palmco Shipping Inc. v Continental Ore Corp.* [1970] 2 Lloyd's Rep. 21 at p.31, suggesting that a seller could make a good tender of documents even though the contract of carriage had been frustrated by closure of the agreed route (as to which *cf.* below, para.19–127).
[77] Above, n.75; *cf. Landauer v Asser* [1905] 2 K.B. 184; *Duncan, Fox & Co. v Schrempft and Bonke* [1915] 3 K.B. 355.
[78] Or in certain other events, not relevant here.
[79] *Congimex Companhia Geral, etc. SARL v Tradax Export SA* [1983] 1 Lloyd's Rep. 250.
[80] *ibid*; below, para.19–137.
[81] See the decision at first instance in the *Congimex* case, above, [1981] 2 Lloyd's Rep. 687 at p.694, referring to *G. H. Renton & Co. Ltd v Palmyra Trading Corp. of Panama* [1957] A.C. 149.
[82] *M. Golodetz & Co. Inc. v Czarnikow Rionda Co. Inc.* (*The Galatia*) [1980] 1 W.L.R. 495 at p.511.
[83] Above, para.18–051.
[84] In *M. Golodetz & Co. Inc. v Czarnikow Rionda Co. Inc.* (*The Galatia*) [1980] 1 W.L.R. 495 the bill of lading was issued to the seller, who was charterer of the

The requirement that the bill must be "effective" is subject to an important qualification. If the goods are destroyed after shipment a c.i.f. seller can (and indeed must[85]) perform his obligations by tendering the documents[86] "although there cannot be a more complete frustration for the purposes of a contract of carriage than the destruction of its subject-matter."[87] The qualification also applies where the goods have not actually been destroyed but have become unavailable to the parties in some other way, *e.g.* by enemy seizure or requisition.[88] In *Re Weis & Co.*[89] bean oil was sold c.i.f. Antwerp. At the time of tender of documents, the ship carrying the goods had been seized by hostile German forces, but Antwerp was still in Belgian hands. It was held that the tender was good, as at the time of tender the bill of lading was not affected by illegality. The position would have been different if at the time of tender Antwerp had fallen and so had become an enemy port.[90]

Where a bill of lading is issued in a set of several parts,[91] one part is not "effective" if, before it is tendered, the goods have already been delivered to the holder of another part[92]; for on such delivery the bill is "accomplished" and the contract contained in or evidenced by it is discharged by performance.

Clean bill. Where a banker's commercial credit calls for tender of a bill of lading, the general rule is that this means a clean bill of lading.[93] In one case it was held that, as the relevant parties knew that in the circumstances of the case it was not possible for the seller to obtain clean bills, the bank was justified in paying against bills which were not clean.[94] It would seem that a custom or usage to pay against bills which are not clean would have the same effects, but in view of the practice of banks to stipulate for "clean" bills[95] it is unlikely that such a custom could now be proved. The principles developed in these banking cases with regard to the requirement of a clean bill of lading apply equally to the position between c.i.f. buyer 19–038

---

carrying ship; and was transferred to the buyer, who accepted it subject to a reservation of his rights. *Semble* it would have been "effective" even if the buyer had rejected it, so that it would have remained in the seller's hands as a mere receipt and would not have acquired the status of a contractual document (*cf.* above, para.18–051).

[85] *Manbré Saccharine Co. Ltd v Corn Products Co. Ltd* [1919] 1 K.B. 198.

[86] Above, para.19–001; *e.g. C. Groom Ltd v Barber* [1915] 1 K.B. 316; below, para.19–080.

[87] *Baxter Fell & Co. Ltd v Galbraith and Grant Ltd* (1941) 70 Ll.L.R. 142 at p.148. It is assumed that the destruction is not due to the carrier's breach of contract.

[88] See *Luis de Ridder Ltd v André & Cie SA* (*Lausanne*) [1941] 1 All E.R. 380 where the seller's claim failed on other grounds (above, para.19–019).

[89] [1916] 1 K.B. 346.

[90] *cf. Landauer v Asser* [1905] 2 K.B. 184.

[91] Above, para.18–090.

[92] Above, para.18–094.

[93] Below, para.23–221; *British Imex Industries Ltd v Midland Bank Ltd* [1958] 1 Q.B. 542.

[94] *cf. National Bank of Egypt v Hannevig's Bank Ltd* (1919) 1 Ll.L.R. 69; 3 *Legal Decisions Affecting Bankers* at p.213.

[95] U.C.P. 500, Art. 32.

and seller.[96] The seller would of course have to tender a clean bill of lading where the contract expressly so provided.[97]

The expression "clean bill of lading" has not been exhaustively defined, but Salmon J. has said: "I incline to the view . . . that a clean bill of lading is one that does not contain any reservation as to the apparent good order or condition of the goods, or the packing"[98]; the reservation may be contained in another document (such as a mate's receipt) and incorporated in the bill by reference.[99] The time to which the reservation must relate to prevent the bill of lading from being clean is that of shipment. In *The Galatia*[1] a bill of lading stated that the goods had been shipped in apparent good order and condition but bore a notation that they had been (subsequently) discharged, at the port of loading, because they had been "damaged by fire and/or water used to extinguish fire". This notation did not, as a matter of law, prevent the bill from being clean, as it did not contain anything "to qualify the admission that the goods were in apparent good order and condition at the time of shipment".[2] Thus a buyer is not normally entitled to reject a bill of lading merely because it indicates post-shipment damage. His remedies in respect of such damage are normally provided by the contract of carriage or by insurance.[3]

In *The Galatia* the notation recording post-shipment damage evidently gave rise to considerable difficulty in dealing with the bill of lading. If there had been evidence of a trade custom or usage by which a bill with such a notation was treated as unclean, it would have been so treated by the court.[4] Megaw L.J. accepted the argument that such evidence would have prevented the bill from being "a document that would ordinarily and properly have been accepted in the trade as being an appropriate document."[5] Thus a bill of lading may be unclean *either* as a matter of law (if it indicates pre-shipment damage) *or* by custom (even though the damage that it indicates is stated to have occurred after shipment). Megaw L.J.'s statement is, indeed, not restricted to indications in the bill of lading *as to the condition of the goods*; but the right to reject for other departures from customary requirements appears to be an application rather of the general principle that a bill of lading must be "usual and customary"[6] than of the specific rule that the bill must be "clean".

---

[96] 3 *Legal Decisions Affecting Bankers*, at p.214.

[97] As, for example, in *M. Golodetz & Co. Inc. v Czarnikow-Rionda Inc. (The Galatia)* [1980] 1 W.L.R. 495.

[98] *British Imex Industries Ltd v Midland Bank Ltd*, above, at p.551; *cf. Canadian & Dominion Sugar Co. Ltd. v Canadian National (West Indies) Steamships Ltd* [1947] A.C. 46 at p.54; *Sea Success Maritime Inc. v African Maritime Carriers Ltd* [2005] EWHC 1542, [2005] 2 All E.R. (Comm.) 441 at [11]–[14], [16], [24], [26]; U.C.P. 500, Art. 32(a).

[99] As in the *Canadian & Dominion Sugar* case, above, where the issue arose between a c.i.f. buyer and the carrier.

[1] *M. Golodetz & Co. Inc. v Czarnikow Rionda Inc.* (*The Galatia*) [1980] 1 W.L.R. 495; *The Forum Craftsman* [1985] 1 Lloyd's Rep. 291.

[2] [1980] 1 W.L.R. 495 at p.518.

[3] In *The Galatia*; above, the buyer may have had no such rights. The sale was on c. & f. terms (below, para.21–012) and the buyer had failed to effect insurance, while the carrier may have been protected by exceptions in the contract of carriage.

[4] [1980] 1 W.L.R. 495 at pp.510, 519.

[5] *ibid.*, at p.519; *cf. Hansson v Hamel & Horley Ltd* [1922] A.C. 36 at p.46.

[6] Above, para.19–024.

A bill is not unclean merely because it contains the qualification "weight, quantity, condition, contents and value unknown"[7]; nor merely because it contains an unusual provision purporting to limit or exclude the carrier's liability.[8]

Freight. There is no general rule requiring a c.i.f. seller to provide a freight prepaid bill of lading[9]; this appears from the form of the invoice (described in para.19–053 below) in which freight payable at the destination is deducted from the c.i.f. price. If, however, the seller invoices the buyer for the full c.i.f. price, without any such deduction, then he must tender a bill under which the buyer is not liable for payment, or further payment, of freight to the carrier on delivery of the goods. Thus where, together with such an invoice, the seller tendered a bill providing that freight was to be "payable as per charterparty", it was held that the tender was bad since it left "wide open the possibility that the shipowner would demand freight at the discharge port."[10] 19–039

Alterations and erasures. In *Re Salomon & Co. and Naudszus*[11] a c.i.f. seller of wheat tendered a bill of lading and an inspection certificate which had originally stated that the wheat had been loaded in holds 2 and 3 of the ship, but which had been later altered to show that the wheat had been loaded in holds 3 and 4. The alterations were made before the bill was issued and before the inspection certificate was put into circulation; and the seller also tendered a certificate of insurance, which had not been altered, and which stated that the wheat had been loaded in holds 3 and 4. Arbitrators held that the buyers were not entitled to reject; and, the Divisional Court[12] being equally divided, this decision stood. It is however submitted that the contrary view of Phillimore J. is to be preferred. For, as the learned judge said, "In this class of cases, a man specially requires a good marketable title. He is probably dealing largely on borrowed money, and he is possibly buying to sell again. In either case he requires not only documents that would satisfy him but documents which he can compel others to take as being satisfactory."[13] This view was approved in *SIAT di dal Ferro v Tradax Overseas SA*[14] where a bill of lading which did not originally provide for shipment to the destination named in the contract of sale was altered to indicate that destination after the goods had in fact arrived there. It was held that the buyer need not accept such an altered bill, as there was no evidence of any authority to make the alteration on behalf of the carrier and as, in any case, the buyer was entitled to documents evidencing a contract of carriage which provided *from the time of shipment* (and not from the time of a later variation) for the carriage of 19–040

---

[7] *The Galatia*, above.
[8] *British Imex Industries Ltd v Midland Bank Ltd* [1958] 1 Q.B. 542 at p.551.
[9] *Soules CAF v P.T. Transcap of Indonesia* [1999] 1 Lloyd's Rep. 917 at p.921.
[10] *ibid*.
[11] (1899) 81 L.T. 325.
[12] Darling and Phillimore JJ.
[13] (1899) 81 L.T. 325 at p.329.
[14] [1978] 2 Lloyd's Rep. 470; affirmed [1980] 1 Lloyd's Rep. 53.

the goods to the destination specified in the contract of sale.[15] It has, however, been suggested that the buyer might be bound to accept an altered bill where the alteration merely corrected a "minor clerical error".[16]

19–041 **Whether charterparty must be tendered.** To judge from the reported cases, it seems in the nineteenth century to have been a not uncommon practice to tender charterparties as well as bills of lading[17]; and the charterparty is listed as one of the documents which the seller is required to tender in Blackburn J.'s summary of the obligations of a c.i.f. seller in *Ireland v Livingston*.[18] The case for requiring tender of the charterparty is particularly strong where the bill of lading purports to incorporate the terms of the charterparty.[19] For the effect of such words is that some at least of the terms of the charterparty will be incorporated into the bill of lading,[20] and so affect the legal position of a buyer to whom the bill of lading has been transferred.[21] Without the charterparty the buyer may well be unable to determine his precise legal relationship with the carrier.[22] In the case of insurance documents an objection has successfully been raised on similar grounds to the tender of a certificate issued subject to the terms of the policy[23]; though these cases may be distinguished from those in which bills of lading are issued which provide for the incorporation of charterparty terms, by reason of the somewhat limited effect of such provisions.[24]

---

[15] *SIAT di dal Ferro v Tradax Overseas SA* [1980] 1 Lloyd's Rep. 53 at p.64.
[16] [1978] 2 Lloyd's Rep. 470 at p.493.
[17] *e.g. Covas v Bingham* (1853) 2 E. & B. 836; *Vernede v Weber* (1856) 1 H. & N. 311; *Simonds v Braddon* (1857) 2 C.B. 324; *Delaurier & Co. v James Wyllie & Co.* (1889) 17 R. (Ct. of Sess.) 167; *cf. Rew v Payne, Douthwaite & Co.* (1886) 53 L.T. 933 (where the buyer asked to see the charterparty).
[18] (1872) L.R. 5 H.L. 395 at p.406; for his earlier similar view, see *Tamvaco v Lucas (No. 2)* (1861) 1 B. & S. 185 at p.206, and *cf. ibid.*, at p.201.
[19] Or where the buyer is to "adopt" it, as in *Wancke v Wingren* (1889) 58 L.J.Q.B. 519.
[20] *Carver on Bills of Lading* (2nd ed., 2005), paras 3–012 *et seq.*; for narrow construction of general words in bills of lading incorporating charterparty terms, see, *e.g. TW Thomas & Co. Ltd v Portsea Shipping Co. Ltd* [1912] A.C. 1; *Skips A/S Nordheim v Syrian Petroleum Co. Ltd (The Varenna)* [1984] Q.B. 599; *Miramar Maritime Corp. v Holborn Oil Trading Ltd (The Miramar)* [1984] A.C. 676; *Federal Bulk Carriers Inc. v C. Itoh Ltd (The Federal Bulker)* [1989] 1 Lloyd's Rep. 103; *Balli Trading Ltd v Afalona Shipping Co. Ltd (The Coral)* [1993] 1 Lloyd's Rep. 1; *Tradigrain SA v King Diamond Shipping SA (The Spiros C)* [2000] 2 Lloyd's Rep. 319 at p.355; for *conflicts* between bill of lading and charterparty terms, see above, paras 18–050 to 18–054. For attempts directly to incorporate such terms into c.i.f. contracts, see *OK Petroleum A.B. v Vitol Energy* SA [1995] 2 Lloyd's Rep. 160 at 165; *Ceval Alimentos SA v Agrimpex Trading Co. Ltd (The Northern Progress) (No. 2)* [1996] 2 Lloyd's Rep. 319 at pp.328–329.
[21] Above, paras 18–050 to 18–054.
[22] See, for example, *Marshall, Knott and Barker Ltd v Arcos Ltd* (1933) 44 Ll.L.Rep. 384 (where the terms of the charterparty were the source of the trouble). Contrast *Welex A.G. v Rosa Maritime Ltd (The Epsilon Rosa)* [2003] EWCA Civ. 938, [2003] 2 Lloyd's Rep. 509 where the sale contract "permitted the sellers to tender bills of lading incorporating the terms of any charterparty without any obligation to provide a copy of such charter" (at [3]). The bill of lading was held to have incorporated a charterparty arbitration clause.
[23] *Donald H. Scott Ltd v Barclays Bank Ltd* [1923] 2 K.B. 1; below, para.19–047.
[24] See above, n.20.

In *Finska Cellulosaforenigen v Westfield Paper Co. Ltd*[25] a c.i.f. seller tendered a bill of lading which contained the words "All conditions and exceptions as per charterparty". It was held that the seller was not obliged to tender the charterparty "in the circumstances of this case".[26] These were that there had been a long course of dealing between the parties on the terms of a standard form of charterparty, which was well known to the buyer and which had been used in the transaction in question. The case leaves open the possibility that, but for such circumstances, the seller would have been obliged to tender the charterparty. Accordingly, a tender of bills of lading showing the destination to be "as per charterparty" was held to be bad as it did not enable the buyer to tell from the face of the bills whether they contained or evidenced a contract of carriage to the c.i.f. destination.[27] The principle appears to be that the charterparty must be tendered where this is necessary to enable the buyer to tell whether the tendered documents are in accordance with the requirements of the contract of sale. Where this is not necessary, the charterparty need not be tendered even though it is referred to in the bill of lading.[28] However, a requirement to tender the charterparty would cause considerable inconvenience where several bills of lading which had been issued under a single charterparty were transferred to different buyers. And there would be no point in imposing an obligation to tender the charterparty where the bill of lading did not purport to incorporate its terms. Such attempted incorporation may now be discouraged by the fact that banks under documentary credits will not accept bills of lading subject to the terms of a charterparty,[29] unless the credit expressly calls for or permits such bills.[30]

(ii) *Insurance*

In general. The principles which govern a seller's obligations in respect of insurance are in many ways analogous to those which determine his obligations in respect of the bill of lading. The seller is prima facie bound to tender a policy of insurance.[31] He does not perform his obligations by tendering some other document such as a certificate of insurance[32] or a broker's cover note[33] or a written statement that he holds the buyer "covered by insurance".[34] The policy must be assignable by indorsement 19–042

[25] [1940] 4 All E.R. 473.
[26] *ibid.*, at p.477.
[27] *SIAT di dal Ferro v Tradax Overseas SA* [1980] 1 Lloyd's Rep. 53 at p.63.
[28] *SIAT di dal Ferro v Tradax Overseas SA* [1978] 2 Lloyd's Rep. 470 at p.492; affirmed, above, n.20.
[29] See the custom proved in *Enrico Furst & Co. v WE Fischer Ltd* [1960] 2 Lloyd's Rep. 340; *cf.* U.C.P. 500, Arts 23(vi) and 24(vi) (sea waybills).
[30] *ibid.*, Art. 25.
[31] *Diamond Alkali Export Corp. v Fl Bourgeois* [1921] 3 K.B. 443.
[32] Below, para.19–047.
[33] *Wilson Holgate & Co. Ltd v Belgian Grain and Produce Co. Ltd* [1920] 2 K.B. 1; *Promos SA v European Grain & Shipping Ltd* [1979] 1 Lloyd's Rep. 375.
[34] *Manbré Saccharine Co. Ltd v Corn Products Co. Ltd* [1919] 1 K.B. 198. The statement at p.200 that "the *plaintiff* effected several policies of insurance" must be a mistake. The plaintiff was the buyer and it was the *sellers* who had effected the policies.

under section 50(3) of the Marine Insurance Act 1906, and not merely as an ordinary chose in action[35]; and it must be "effective" in the sense that it must be a valid contract: it may satisfy this requirement even though it does not cover the actual loss which has occurred.[36] An "honour" policy is not effective as it is not legally enforceable,[37] even though as a matter of business underwriters regularly pay on such policies. A policy which is voidable for misrepresentation or non-disclosure is not effective unless it has been affirmed by the underwriter.[38] The policy must cover the contract goods and no others[39]; and it must provide continuous cover from shipment to the c.i.f. destination specified in the contract.[40] The seller must tender the policy whether the buyer needs it or not: in other words, he must tender it even though the goods have actually arrived unharmed.[41] The reason for this rule is that the buyer will often be obliged to pay, or that he may want to resell the goods, while they are still afloat and before they can be examined.

19–043 **Usual policy.** In the absence of express provisions in the contract, the seller must tender such policy as is usual in the trade in question.[42] A policy insuring the goods against total loss only is not normally adequate.[43] If, in the circumstances surrounding a particular transaction, it is, as a matter of business, impossible to procure a policy which provides continuous cover, the seller need not procure such a policy but can perform his obligations by tendering such policy as is usual in the circumstances.[44] Conversely, the seller may, where it is usual to do so, be obliged to provide cover extending beyond the period between shipment and arrival at the c.i.f. destination, *e.g.* from warehouse to warehouse.[45]

It is not altogether clear at exactly what point of time the criterion of what is a "usual" policy is applied. In *C. Groom Ltd v Barber*[46] a policy not covering war risks was held to be a good tender and one reason for the decision was that *at the time of the contract of sale* it was not usual to cover war risks.[47] The case certainly shows that the time of tender of documents is

---

35 *Diamond Alkali Export Corp. v Fl. Bourgeois, above n.31.*
36 *C. Groom Ltd v Barber* [1915] 1 K.B. 316.
37 *Strass v Spillers and Bakers Ltd* [1911] 2 K.B. 759.
38 *Cantiere Meccanico Brindisino v Janson* (1912) 17 Com.Cas. 182 at p.332.
39 *Manbré Saccharine Export Corp. v Corn Products Ltd* [1919] 1 K.B. 198 at p.205; *John Martin of London Ltd v AE Taylor & Co. Ltd* [1953] 2 Lloyd's Rep. 589 at p.592; *cf. Hickox v Adams* (1876) 34 L.T. 404.
40 *London Tricotagefabrik v White & Meacham* [1975] 1 Lloyd's Rep. 384; *cf.* above, para.19–027.
41 *Orient Co. Ltd v Brekke Howlid* [1913] 1 K.B. 531.
42 *Burstall v Grimsdale* (1906) 11 Com.Cas. 280; *Ranson (T.W.) Ltd v Manufacture d'Engrais, etc.* (1922) 13 Ll.L.R. 205.
43 *Hickox v Adams* (1876) 34 L.T. 404; *cf. Borthwick v Bank of N.Z.* (1900) 6 Com.Cas. 1.
44 *Plaimar Ltd v Waters Trading Co. Ltd* (1945) 72 C.L.R. 304.
45 *e.g. Ide and Christie v Chalmers & White* (1900) 5 Com.Cas. 212.
46 [1915] 1 K.B. 316.
47 Another reason for the decision was that the contract contained the words "war risk for buyer's a/c". Contrast *Birkett Sperling & Co. v Engholm & Co.* (1871) 10 M. (Ct. of Sess.) 170 (where a usual policy was found to be one that did cover war risks).

not decisive; but it leaves open the question whether the relevant time is that of the sale or the time at which the policy of insurance was taken out. In *C. Groom Ltd v Barber* there was no interval between these two points; indeed the seller had himself bought identical goods afloat and it seems that the insurance had been effected before the sale between the parties to the litigation. In a subsequent case in which there may have been such an interval Rowlatt J. merely said that there was "no real evidence that it was usual to insure against war risk at any material time"[48]; but he did not indicate what the material time was. It is submitted that the criterion of what is usual should be applied at the time at which the insurance is effected.[49] Although there is no authority on the point, it is further submitted that the criterion should also be applied at the place at which the insurance is effected. For this purpose it must, however, be assumed that the seller does tender a policy. If he wishes to tender some other document, such as a certificate of insurance,[50] he must provide for this in the contract. He cannot rely merely on the fact that such tender is usual,[51] though what is usual may be relevant where there is genuine doubt as to whether a document which is described as a policy really is one.[52]

Foreign policy. Doubts have been expressed on the questions whether a foreign c.i.f. seller performs his obligations by tendering in England a policy which is valid in his own country, or whether the policy must also be valid and enforceable under English law[53]; and whether it must be expressed in sterling, where that is the currency in which payment under the contract of sale is to be made.[54] The answers to these questions would (in the absence of express provisions in the contract) depend on whether the foreign policy, or policy expressed in foreign currency, was a "usual" policy in the sense discussed in the preceding paragraph. It is submitted that it would not be unusual merely because it was valid only in the foreign country or expressed in a foreign currency.[55] 19–044

Provisions of the contract as to policy. The contract of sale may specify the type of policy to be taken out, and the extent and duration of the insurance cover to be provided. Thus the contract may expressly require the seller to insure against damage occurring before shipment,[56] or after 19–045

---

[48] *Law and Bonar Ltd v British American Tobacco Co. Ltd* [1916] 2 K.B. 605 at p.609; *semble* when the policy was effected it had not become usual to insure against war risks: see p.608.

[49] *cf.* above, para.19–032 as to the time for determining what is the usual route of shipment.

[50] Below, paras 19–047, 19–048.

[51] *e.g. Diamond Alkali Export Corp. v Fl Bourgeois* [1921] 3 K.B. 443.

[52] See *Malmberg v H & J Evans & Co.* (1924) 30 Com.Cas. 107.

[53] *ibid.*, at p.111; *cf. Donald H Scott Ltd v Barclays Bank Ltd* [1923] 2 K.B. 1 at pp.13, 16.

[54] *Donald H Scott Ltd v Barclays Bank Ltd*, above.

[55] The fact that the foreign currency was subject to exchange controls preventing transfer of the policy moneys to the buyer's country would, no doubt, be relevant to the issue of the "usualness" of the policy.

[56] *e.g. Reinhart & Co. v Joshua Hoyle & Sons Ltd* [1961] 1 Lloyd's Rep. 346.

discharge, or both.[57] The contract of sale may, similarly, require the insurance to be against "all risks" or "free from particular average" and so forth. For discussions of the meaning of such terms in the law of insurance, the reader is referred to works on that topic.[58] Here it is necessary only to make the point that a court, faced with such a term in a contract of sale, is concerned with the construction of that contract; and the court may conclude that the parties to the contract of sale did not use the term in the technical sense which it bears in the law of insurance. For example, in *Yuill v Scott-Robson*[59] a seller of cattle c.i.f. Durban undertook in the contract of sale to insure "against all risks". He took out an "all risks" policy but this did not cover the buyer's loss, which occurred when the authorities at Durban refused to allow the cattle to be landed.[60] It was held that the seller was liable in damages: his obligation to insure "against all risks" was not performed by taking out an "all risks" policy. On the other hand, in *Vincentelli v Rowlett*[61] a contract of sale provided "Insurance to be effected by [seller] all risks". The seller took out a policy covering "all risks by land or water" but not (for practical purposes) "any circumstances . . . which may cause a variation and/or entire alteration of the risk". The carrier, in breach of the contract of carriage, carried the goods on deck, where they were damaged; and the underwriters refused fully to compensate the buyer as the fact that the goods had been carried on deck constituted a variation of the risk. It was held that the buyer had no claim against the seller: on the true construction of the contract of sale, the parties had not intended that the seller should insure against losses arising "out of the sheer breaches of a contract of carriage made in proper form, with proper care, and with a well-known reputable line of shipowners".[62]

Where a contract provided for tender of an "approved insurance policy" this was held to mean a policy "to which no reasonable objection could be made, but which ought therefore to be approved".[63]

19–046 **Risks not covered.** So long as the seller tenders a policy which is usual, or in accordance with the express requirements of the contract, it is immaterial that the policy does not cover the loss which has actually occurred. If, for example, it was not usual at the time the policy was taken out to insure against war risks, a policy not providing such insurance can be validly tendered although the goods have been lost by war risks and although such risks were expressly excepted from the policy.[64] Nor is the seller in such a case normally bound to give the buyer notice to enable him to insure under section 32(3) of the Sale of Goods Act 1979[65]; for prima

[57] *e.g.* under a "warehouse to warehouse" clause.
[58] *e.g. MacGillivray on Insurace Law* (10th ed. 2003).
[59] [1908] 1 K.B. 270 (affg. [1907] 1 K.B. 685).
[60] This was not an "accidental cause" which is what is usually covered by an "all risks" policy: *British and Foreign Marine Insurance Co. Ltd v Gaunt* [1921] 2 A.C. 41.
[61] (1911) 16 Com.Cas. 310.
[62] *ibid.*, at p.320.
[63] *Donald H Scott Ltd v Barclays Bank Ltd* [1923] 2 K.B. 1; *cf. Hodgson v Davies* (1810) 2 Camp. 530 ("approved bill").
[64] *C Groom Ltd v Barber* [1915] 1 K.B. 316.
[65] Where the buyer deals as consumer, s.32(3) "must be ignored": see s.32(4), discussed in relation to overseas sales in paras 18–259 to 18–264 above.

facie a c.i.f. contract is considered, by reason of the seller's obligation to insure, to contain a contrary agreement ousting the provisions of the subsection.[66]

Certificate of insurance. A c.i.f. seller does not perform his obligations by procuring and tendering a certificate of insurance.[67] The form of such a certificate is variable; but its essential feature is that it certifies that the goods in question have been insured[68] under a policy to which reference is made in the certificate. Usually the certificate is expressed to be subject to the terms of the policy; and the main reason why tender of a certificate is insufficient is that the person to whom such a tender is made will be unable to determine from the certificate what the terms of the insurance are.[69] Other objections are that such certificates are not transferable by indorsement,[70] and that they may not give a right of action against the underwriters,[71] apparently as they do not comply with the formal requirements of section 22 of the Marine Insurance Act 1906, by which a contract of marine insurance is inadmissible in evidence unless embodied in a policy.[72] Of course a document may be a policy even though it does not contain all the terms of the insurance, but incorporates by reference certain Institute Clauses[73]; and it may be that a document of this kind would be a good tender whether it was called a "policy" or a "certificate". Perhaps the view that American certificates are "accepted in this country as policies"[74] can be explained, in some cases, on this ground. But in *Donald H Scott Ltd v Barclays Bank Ltd*[75] it was held that an American certificate could not be tendered in place of a policy under a banker's commercial credit. Atkin L.J. said that the document did not "contain on the face of it the terms of the actual contract of insurance or the risks against which the insuring company 19–047

---

[66] *Law and Bonar Ltd v British American Tobacco Co. Ltd* [1916] 2 K.B. 605 (above, para.18–247; for exceptional cases in which a c.i.f. seller may be required to give notice under s.32(3), see below, para.19–117).

[67] *Maine Spinning Co. v Sutcliffe & Co.* (1917) 87 L.J.K.B. 382; *Diamond Alkali Export Corp. v Fl. Bourgeois* [1921] 3 K.B. 443; *Donald H Scott Ltd v Barclays Bank Ltd* [1923] 2 K.B. 1; *cf. Koskas v Standard Marine Insurance Co. Ltd* (1927) 32 Com.Cas. 160.

[68] The seller warrants the truth of such a statement: *AC Harper & Co. Ltd v Mackechnie & Co. Ltd* [1925] 2 K.B. 423.

[69] *Diamond Alkali Export Corp. v Fl Bourgeois*, above; *Donald H Scott Ltd v Barclays Bank Ltd above*, at pp.12–13, 15 and 17.

[70] Under Marine Insurance Act 1906, s.50(3): see *Diamond Alkali Export Corp. v Fl Bourgeois*, above.

[71] *Wilson Holgate & Co. Ltd v Belgian Grain and Produce Co. Ltd* [1920] 2 K.B. 1 at p.9.

[72] See *Diamond Alkali Export Corp. v Fl Bourgeois*, above.

[73] See *Malmberg v H & J Evans & Co.* (1924) 30 Com.Cas. 107 at p.112.

[74] *Wilson Holgate & Co. Ltd v Belgian Grain and Produce Co. Ltd* [1920] 2 K.B. 1 at p.7. In the United States, tender of a certificate of insurance under a c.i.f. contract is good by custom: *Kunglig Jarnvagsstryelsen v Dexter & Carpenter Inc.* 290 F. 991 (1924); this position has been given legislative recognition in U.C.C., s.2–320 (2)(c), but Comment 9 excludes brokers' cover notes or certificates. In the amendments to U.C.C. Article 2 proposed by the American Law Institute in 2003, s.2–320 is to be deleted.

[75] [1923] 2 K.B. 1.

purports to secure the insured, and there are no means of ascertaining these terms except by reference to another document which is not tendered and is not within convenient reach for reference."[76]

19–048 **Contract permitting tender of documents other than policies.** The rule requiring tender of a policy is inconvenient where a bulk shipment covered by a single policy is sold in several lots, or where an exporter maintains a floating policy under which he makes declarations from time to time as shipments are made. For this reason the requirement is often relaxed by provisions[77] in the contract permitting tender of a certificate of insurance, or of some other document.[78] In such a case the seller is bound to tender a document of the kind described in the contract. The buyer "cannot be compelled to take a document something like that which he had agreed to take."[79] Where the contract simply calls for tender of a certificate of insurance, without going into further details, the certificate tendered must be in the "usual" form[80]; whether this requirement is satisfied depends on principles similar to those which apply in relation to policies.[81] The document tendered should, moreover, "provide as near as possible to the buyer the same protection and rights as he would get by a policy."[82] The essential points are that he should get rights against the underwriter and that the extent of these rights should be ascertainable by reference to an identified or identifiable policy, or perhaps in some other way, *e.g.* by reference to terms known in the trade. So long as these requirements are satisfied, it is not a fatal objection that the buyer is at the time of tender ignorant of the exact terms of the policy: this is "probably unavoidable in the ordinary course of trade".[83]

Where the contract does permit tender of a certificate of insurance, and that certificate refers to a policy, difficulties may arise from the fact that these two documents are not in perfect harmony. In *Koskas v Standard Marine Insurance Co. Ltd*[84] a c.i.f. buyer received a certificate which was expressed to represent, and take the place of, the policy. The policy

---

[76] At p.17. He added: "though even if it were I do not say that would invalidate the objection." It is perhaps significant that he omitted these last words when quoting the rest of the passage in *Malmberg v H & J Evans & Co.* (1924) 30 Com.Cas. 107 at pp.116–117.
[77] Such a provision may be implied from previous dealings but not if these were on different terms: *Manbré Saccharine Co. Ltd v Corn Products Co. Ltd* [1919] 1 K.B. 198.
[78] *John Martin of London Ltd v AE Taylor & Co. Ltd* [1953] 2 Lloyd's Rep. 589; *Promos SA v European Grain & Shipping Ltd* [1979] 1 Lloyd's Rep. 375. Under U.C.P. 500, Art. 34(d) insurance certificates are (though under Art. 34(c) brokers' cover notes are not) acceptable to banks under documentary credits.
[79] *Wilson Holgate & Co. Ltd v Belgian Grain and Produce Co. Ltd* [1920] 2 K.B. 1 at p.9.
[80] *Burstall v Grimsdale* (1906) 11 Com.Cas. 280.
[81] Above, para.19–044.
[82] *Promos SA v European Grain & Shipping Ltd* [1979] 1 Lloyd's Rep. 375 at p.387. *cf.* the rule applied where the contract permits tender of a delivery order instead of a bill of lading: above, paras 18–171, 19–024.
[83] *Promos* case, [1979] 1 Lloyd's Rep. 375 at p.387.
[84] (1927) 32 Com.Cas. 160.

contained a clause in small print requiring loss or damage to be reported "as soon as the goods are landed or the loss is known or expected"[85]; but the certificate contained no such clause. It was held that the buyer's rights were not restricted by the printed clause as the underwriter had not taken adequate steps to bring it to his attention. Similarly, in *De Monchy v Phoenix Insurance Co. of Hartford*[86] a time limit on claims was imposed by the policy and not by the certificate (which was again said to represent and take the place of the policy). It was again held that the buyer's right of action was not restricted by the time limit as it was contained only in the policy. The underwriter could have invoked that time limit only if he had given notice of it to the insured so as to incorporate it in the certificate; and he had not done so merely because the clause might "with diligence be found in the crazy patchwork of documents and clauses"[87] which constituted the policy. The issue in these cases was between the underwriter and the buyer; but after strongly criticising the insurance documents in *De Monchy's* case, Scrutton L.J. said: "The form of this certificate fully justifies the view. . . that some certificates may not be a good tender."[88] This seems to refer to the position between buyer and seller and suggests that tender of such an unsatisfactory certificate would be bad even if the contract of sale did permit tender of *a* certificate.

Transhipment and deviation. Events may occur after the issue of the policy which (in the absence of express provision in it to the contrary) entitle the underwriter to repudiate liability: for example, transhipment, deviation or carriage on deck. At first sight, tender of a policy after such events might appear to be bad, for the policy would be no more effective than one which was void *ab initio*, in the sense that no claim whatever could be made under it against the underwriter. But the actual result in such cases depends on the terms of the policy. 19–049

In *Belgian Grain and Produce Co. Ltd v Cox & Co. (France) Ltd*[89] objection was taken by a bank to tender of a policy on the ground that the goods had been transhipped. The objection was held to be groundless as a clause in the policy contained the words "Including all liberties as per contract of affreightment", and as transhipment was held to be such a

[85] The validity of such a clause, if incorporated, would not be affected by the Unfair Contract Terms Act 1977, since the relevant provisions of the Act do not apply to contracts of insurance: Sch.1, para.1(a). Nor is such validity likely to be affected by the Unfair Terms in Consumer Contracts Regulations 1999 since neither party to a contract of the kind here under discussion is likely to be a "consumer" within those Regulations: above, para.18–282. If, exceptionally, the person entitled to the benefit of the insurance were a "consumer", (see above, para.18–259) the clause could be "unfair" on the ground that it "hindered" that party's right to take legal action within Sch.2, para.1(q); *cf.* also Treitel, *The Law of Contract*, (11th ed., 2003), p.272; for proposals for reform, see Law Commissions' Report on *Unfair Terms in Contracts*, Law Com. No. 292, Scot. Law Com. No. 199 (2005) paras 3.80, 8.20, 8.54, 5.77, 8.64 and attached Draft Bill, Sch.3 para.3.
[86] (1928) 33 Com.Cas. 197.
[87] *ibid.*, at p.211.
[88] *ibid.*, at p.206.
[89] (1919) 1 Ll.L.R. 256; [1919] W.N. 308; following *Neale and Wilkinson v Rose* (1898) 3 Com.Cas. 236.

liberty. The reasoning suggests that a contrary conclusion would have been reached in the absence of this clause; and, although the case arose between seller and banker, there seems to be no ground for thinking that different principles would apply between buyer and seller. It is assumed that a contract of affreightment involving transhipment is a proper contract for the purposes of the contract of sale. If this is so, the seller must procure a contract of insurance which, so to speak, matches the contract of affreightment.

19–050 **Breach by carrier.** The seller may procure proper contracts of carriage and insurance, but the carrier may then break the contract of carriage by deviating or carrying the goods on deck. Prima facie the carrier thereby gives the underwriter the right to repudiate liability; and it is arguable that, as a result of this, the contract of insurance is no longer effective. But in two cases objections taken to insurance documents in such circumstances were rejected.[90] In each of these cases, the contract of insurance contained a provision by which the interest insured was to be held covered, in case of deviation or other circumstances altering the risk, at a premium to be fixed by the insurer, or to be arranged. These "held covered" clauses may be said to have kept the contracts of insurance alive as effective contracts. But they do not as a matter of business provide effective protection if the underwriter refuses to accept liability except at a premium amounting to the whole loss[91]; and the two decisions mentioned above are not based on the "held covered" clauses, but rather on the view that the seller was not, under the contract of sale, bound to insure against losses arising out of breaches of the contract of carriage.[92] In such cases the buyer's remedy is against the carrier and not against the seller for having tendered faulty documents. This view is not without its difficulties: in particular, a buyer who bargains for protection against certain risks by insurance may be in a less favourable position by having to look for redress in respect of them to the carrier.[93] On the other hand, convenience does seem to demand that breaches of the contract of carriage should not affect the effectiveness of insurance documents which were good when procured.[94] This point may be particularly important where there have been a number of successive sales of goods afloat, made in ignorance of breaches of the contract of carriage which would entitle the underwriter to repudiate liability if the policy contained no "held covered" clause. If the buyer does pay an additional premium under such a clause, it is arguable that he should be entitled, not to reject the documents, but to recover the amount of such a payment from the seller since under a c.i.f. contract it is the seller who is responsible for the cost of insurance[95]; but here again the better view is that, once the seller has procured a proper policy, he should not, by reason of later events for

[90] *Burstall v Grimsdale* (1906) 11 Com.Cas. 280; *Vincentelli v Rowlett* (1911) 16 Com.Cas. 310.
[91] As in *Vincentelli v Rowlett*, above n.90.
[92] *Vincentelli v Rowlett*, above.
[93] *cf. Vincentelli v Rowlett*, above, at p.320.
[94] *cf. Shipton Anderson & Co. v John Weston & Co.* (1922) 10 Ll.L.R. 762.
[95] Above, para.19–009.

which he is not responsible, be under any further responsibility in this respect. This argument is reinforced by the fact that the seller's only remedy in respect of having to make such an extra payment would be against the carrier; and in the case put the seller would have lost his right of action under the contract of carriage[96] against the carrier on transfer of the bill of lading to the buyer.[97]

Amount of insurance. This is normally specified in the contract of sale. If the contract provides for insurance at a stated percentage above the invoice or contract price, that c.i.f. price is, for this purpose, regarded as an "indivisible price"[98]: thus the policy must cover not only the cost of the goods and insurance, but also the freight even though this is payable on arrival and the goods do not arrive.[99] This rule can be excluded by a provision in the contract that insurance is to be "for invoice amount less freight when payable at the port of discharge".[1] If the contract simply provides for insurance, without specifying the amount, the seller is not bound to provide insurance against freight payable at destination and deducted from the price in the invoice,[2] as such freight is never at the buyer's risk.[3] **19–051**

The insurance must be for the proper amount determined in accordance with the above principles, though as between buyer and seller a minor deficiency may be disregarded.[4] Insurance in excess of the contract requirement does not of course vitiate the policy, as it is inconceivable that it can prejudice the buyer; but it does give rise to the problem whether it is the buyer or the seller who is entitled to the excess. As between these parties, the general rule is that the buyer is entitled to the excess whether the insurance was effected before[5] or after[6] the sale; but this rule can be displaced by a provision in the contract of sale that any excess over the required amount is to be for the seller's account.[7]

Assignment and insurable interest. Detailed discussions of the rules relating to assignment of marine policies and to insurable interest will be found in works on marine insurance. Here it is necessary only to say that a **19–052**

---

96 For the possibility that a seller who was also the shipper might have rights against the carrier apart from the contract of carriage (*e.g.* in bailment) see *East West Corp. v DKBS 1912 AF A/S* [2003] EWCA Civ. 83, [2003] Q.B 1509, above, para.18–115.

97 Carriage of Goods by Sea Act 1992, s.2(5); even if the buyer could sue the carrier in respect of the seller's loss under s.2(4), the seller could not compel him to do so: above, para.18–122. If at the time of the carrier's breach the seller remained owner of the goods (as he probably would until payment of the price: below, para.19–103), then s.2(4)(a) (above, para.18–100) would be satisfied.

98 *Loders & Nucoline Ltd v Bank of New Zealand* (1929) 33 Ll.L.R. 70 at p.74.

99 *Loders & Nucoline Ltd v Bank of New Zealand*, above.

1 *Ide and Christie v Chalmers and White* (1900) 5 Com.Cas. 212.

2 Below, para.19–053.

3 *Tamvaco v Lucas (No.2)* (1861) 1 B. & S. 185; (1862) 3 B. & S. 89; *cf. The Pantanassa* [1970] P. 187 (c. & f. contract); below, para.19–120.

4 *Tamvaco v Lucas (No.2)*, above: insurance for £3,600, being £24 10s. less than required.

5 *Ralli v Universal Marine Insurance Co.* (1862) 4 D. F. & J. 1; there is a contrary dictum in *Harland and Wolff v Burstall & Son* (1901) 6 Com.Cas. 113 at p.117.

6 *Landauer v Asser* [1905] 2 K.B. 184.

7 *Strass v Spillers and Bakers Ltd* [1911] 2 K.B. 759.

marine policy can be assigned after loss[8] and even though at the time of the loss the assignee had no interest in the subject-matter of the insurance.[9] These rules are obviously essential for the operation of a normal c.i.f. contract.

A converse rule may also be mentioned here. If after the making of the contract of sale, the seller takes out supplementary insurance on the buyer's behalf, and the buyer later rejects the documents, then the seller may sue on the policy.[10]

(iii) *The Invoice*

19–053 **Form of invoice.** It is the duty of the seller "to make out an invoice as described by Blackburn J. in *Ireland v Livingston*[11] or in some similar form."[12] Blackburn J.'s description of the invoice can only be understood in the light of the distinction, drawn by him in the same passage, between a c.i.f. sale and instructions to an agent to buy at a price to include cost, freight and insurance. "The invoice", he said, "is made out debiting the consignee with the agreed price (or the actual cost and commission, with premiums of insurance, and the freight, as the case may be), and giving him credit for the amount of the freight which he will have to pay to the shipowner on actual delivery . . ."[13] This form of invoice presupposes that the freight is payable at destination and would of course be inappropriate where the freight had been paid in advance. The invoice may state the cost of the goods, insurance and freight as separate items; but the c.i.f. price is nevertheless regarded as an "indivisible price".[14] In the situation described by Blackburn J., the freight thus remains part of the c.i.f. price for the goods in spite of the fact that it is deducted on the invoice from the amount payable to the seller. It is simply paid by the buyer to the carrier (instead of to the seller to enable the latter to pay the carrier) for the obvious reason of convenience that the buyer is, while the seller is not, likely to be present or represented at the port of destination.[15]

19–054 **Contents of invoice.** There is little authority on the degree of particularity with which the invoice must describe the goods. It seems that the invoice must at least contain sufficient particulars to enable the buyer to relate it to the subject-matter of contract of sale. On the other hand, the invoice need not "identify" the goods in the sense of making them specific or ascertained: thus it may relate to a specified quantity of goods forming undifferentiated part of a larger identified bulk. Nor does it seem essential

[8] *Lloyd v Fleming* (1872) L.R. 7 Q.B. 299.
[9] *J Aron & Co. (Inc.) v Miall* (1928) 98 L.J.K.B. 204.
[10] *Fooks v Smith* (1924) 30 Com.Cas. 97 at pp.101–102; also reported [1924] 2 K.B. 508, but not on this point.
[11] (1871) L.R. 5 H.L. 395 at pp.406–407.
[12] *E Clemens Horst Co. v Biddell Bros* [1911] 1 K.B. 214 at p.220; reversed. *ibid.*, at p.934 but restored [1912] A.C. 18.
[13] *Ireland v Livingston*, above, at p.406.
[14] Above, para.19–051.
[15] *cf.* above, para.19–009.

for the invoice to contain the full contractual description of the goods. In an Australian case[16] a seller of "150 bales first selection Liverpool wheat sacks" tendered an invoice for "150 bales Liverpool sacks". It was common ground[17] that it was not necessary to put the full contractual description into the invoice; and it seems that the buyer would not have been entitled to reject merely on account of the wording of the invoice. On the other hand, an invoice would be defective if it were actually at variance with the contract, for example, if it referred to a quantity of goods other than that sold.[18]

The contract of sale may expressly require the invoice to contain certain designated particulars; and failure to comply with such requirements would normally entitle the buyer to reject the documents. But this is not always the case. In *John Martin of London Ltd v AE Taylor & Co. Ltd*[19] the contract called for invoices "stating lodgement number and location of certificate of origin". The invoices did not give the lodgement number as the customs authorities had delayed the issue of such a number. It was held that the buyer was not entitled to reject the documents, the contract being interpreted to mean that the sellers would give the lodgement number when they received it.[20] 19–055

Liability for misstatements in invoice. The cases discussed in paragraphs 19–054 and 19–055 concern invoices from which information concerning the goods is simply omitted or which contain statements which are true but at variance with the contract. They do not directly touch the problem of the seller's liability for statements in an invoice which are actually false. A case which came close to raising this issue was one[21] in which a c.i.f. sale of oil provided that the price was to depend on viscosity and the seller issued an invoice stating that the price had been calculated in accordance with the contractual formula. This was held to be no more than a "representation . . . that the sellers had applied the price calculation machinery under the contract"[22] so that there was "no implied warranty [as to the accuracy of the invoice] analogous to that in respect of the contents of a bill of lading"[23] (*e.g.* as to the date of shipment[24]). The invoice contained no express statement as to viscosity; and it seems that any actual misstatement in this respect would have made the invoice defective and the sellers liable in respect of the misstatement. 19–056

---

16 *Henry Dean & Sons (Sydney) Ltd v O'Day* (1927) 39 C.L.R. 330, disapproved on another point in *Gill & Duffus SA v Berger & Co. Inc.* [1984] A.C. 382 (below, paras 19–163 to 19–165.)
17 *Henry Dean & Sons (Sydney) Ltd v O'Day*, above, at p.357.
18 *cf. Tamvaco v Lucas (No.1)* (1859) 1 E. & E. 581.
19 [1953] 2 Lloyd's Rep. 589.
20 *ibid.*, at p.592.
21 *Apioil Ltd v Kuwait Petroleum Italia SpA* [1995] 1 Lloyd's Rep. 124.
22 *ibid.*, at p.132.
23 *ibid.*, at p.133.
24 The reference at *ibid.*, p.132 to *James Finlay & Co. Ltd v NV Kwik Hoo Tong HM* [1929] 1 K.B. 400 suggests that the contrast is intended to be with this type of case, at least among others.

19–057 **Provisional invoice.** A contract of sale may call for a provisional invoice, giving the buyer advance information about the shipment before full tender of documents.[25] Sometimes, such a provisional invoice serves the commercial purpose of a notice of appropriation,[26] rather than that of the invoice (discussed in paras 19–053 to 19–056, above) which forms one of the shipping documents.[27] Sometimes a provisional invoice is given in addition to a notice of appropriation; it may then give further information about the goods and complete the process of appropriation in the contractual sense, that is, it may specify "the goods to which the contract attaches"[28] where the notice of appropriation has not been sufficiently precise for this purpose.

(iv) *Other Documents*

19–058 **Other documents.** The contract of sale may require the seller to tender additional documents, such as certificates of origin, quality or inspection (relating to the state of the goods at the time of shipment[29]), performance guarantees[30] licences or permits required in connection with the shipment,[31] or advance notice of the arrival of the ship on which the goods are carried at the port of destination.[32] Such requirements could also arise from custom or usage in the relevant trade.

Not all documents which the seller is required to provide in the course of the performance of the contract constitute "shipping documents", this expression being used to refer only to those documents which the seller is required to tender as a condition of obtaining payment. Some documents have to be provided well before payment is due: this is true of the notices of appropriation or provisional invoices, already discussed.[33] Other documents will not come into being until well after payment has become due: this is true where the contract provides that the quality of the goods *on discharge* is to be conclusively determined by a certificate issued by an independent third party at that time. Such a certificate (as distinct from one containing statements as to the quality of the goods at the time of shipment) "is not, and is indeed incapable of being, included among shipping documents which a seller is required to tender to his buyer in return for payment of the price under a contract of sale on ordinary c.i.f. terms."[34]

---

[25] See *Produce Brokers Ltd v Weiss* (1918) 118 L.T. 111; 87 L.J.K.B. 472 (there are considerable discrepancies between the two reports).
[26] Above, para.19–017; *e.g.* (*semble*) in *Produce Brokers Ltd v Weiss* (1918) 118 L.T. 111, discussed in para.19–180, below.
[27] *cf.* above, para.19–024; below, para.19–058.
[28] *Ross T Smyth & Co. Ltd v TD Bailey, Son & Co.* [1940] 3 All E.R. 60 at p.66; *cf.* above para.18–210.
[29] See below, para.19–076.
[30] Above, para.19–005; *State Trading Corp. of India v M Golodetz Ltd* [1989] 2 Lloyd's Rep. 277.
[31] Above, paras 18–309 *et seq.*
[32] See *Nova Petroleum International Establishment v Tricon Trading Ltd* [1989] 1 Lloyd's Rep. 312.
[33] Above, paras 19–017 to 19–019, 19–057.
[34] *Gill & Duffus SA v Berger & Co. Inc.* [1984] A.C. 382 at p.389.

(c) *Tender of Documents*

Duty to tender documents. Having procured the proper shipping documents[35] the seller must tender those documents to (or as directed by) the buyer. If the goods have been destroyed, or seized by an enemy, after the making of the contract, the c.i.f. seller is not bound to do *more* than tender the documents: that is, he is not bound to deliver the goods at the agreed destination.[36] It is equally true that, in such a case, the seller is not relieved from his obligation to tender documents merely because the goods have been destroyed or seized. This rule is important where the goods have been insured for an amount in excess of the contract price: its effect is that the seller is not entitled to keep this excess.[37] If the seller refuses to tender documents in respect of lost goods, he can also be made liable in damages for any further excess of the market price, at the time when tender was due, over the insured value.[38] 19–059

Time of tender. The seller's duty with regard to the time of tender depends in the first place on the terms of the contract. The cases fall into two main groups. The first, to be discussed in paragraphs 19–061 to 19–065, consists of cases in which the contract contains a stipulation as to the time of tender; the second, to be discussed in paragraphs 19–066 to 19–068, consists of cases in which the contract contains no such stipulation. 19–060

Stipulations as to the time of tender. Stipulation as to the time of tender are normally express terms of the contract, but such a stipulation may also be implied. The latter possibility is illustrated by a case[39] in which a c.i.f. contract expressly provided for *payment* against documents at a specified time and it was held that that time was also, by implication, the time at which the seller was obliged to *tender* the shipping documents. 19–061

Effects of failure to perform stipulations as to time of tender. Any such stipulation, express or implied, must of course be performed by the seller; but in the event of his failure to perform it, the further question will arise as to the effect of that failure. Does the fact that documents are tendered late 19–062

---

[35] At this stage, it is assumed that the seller has procured proper shipping documents. If he has not, *e.g.* because he has failed to ship the goods which he has contracted to sell, he cannot perform his part of the contract by buying similar goods at the destination and there tendering physical delivery of those goods to the buyer. This follows from the nature of a c.i.f. contract: see above, paras 19–002, 19–003.

[36] *Manbré Saccharine Co. Ltd v Corn Products Co. Ltd* [1919] 1 K.B. 198 at pp.202–203 (above, paras 19–001, 19–037). The Vienna Convention on Contracts for the International Sale of Goods (above, para.1–024), Art. 30 requires the seller both to deliver the goods and to hand over any documents relating to them; but delivery here refers to handing the goods over to the first carrier for transmission to the buyer: see Art. 31(a).

[37] *cf.* above, para.19–051.

[38] This was the actual result in *Manbré Saccharine Co. Ltd v Corn Products Co. Ltd*, above.

[39] *Toepfer v Lenersan-Poortman NV* [1980] 1 Lloyd's Rep. 143.

give rise only to a claim for damages, or does it also entitle the buyer to reject? The answer to this question depends, it is submitted, on a distinction between two types of stipulations: those which specify a *precise* time, such as a date or period or event at, within or before which tender must be made; and those in which the time mentioned in the stipulation is neither *precise* nor capable of being precisely ascertained (*e.g.* where tender is to be made "as soon as possible" after a specified event, or "without delay").

19–063 **Stipulations specifying precise time for tender.** One view is that failure to perform such a stipulation does not, of itself, justify rejection. This was, for example, said by Brett M.R. to be the position where a seller failed to perform an express term calling for tender of documents "before arrival" of the carrying ship.[40] More recently, however, it has been assumed that a buyer would be entitled to reject if the seller failed to comply with a contractual stipulation for tender of documents on arrival[41]; and in *Toepfer v Lenersan-Poortman NV*[42] it was held that a seller's failure to comply with a stipulation for tender of documents "not later than 20 days after date of Bill of Lading" entitled the buyer to reject. One ground for the decision was that stipulations as to the time of tender could not be distinguished from stipulations as to the time of shipment (the breach of which unquestionably justifies rejection).[43] The analogy between the two types of stipulation may not be exact; for a shipment period is precisely ascertained from the time of contracting; while the operation of a stipulation for tender "before arrival" or "20 days after date of Bill of Lading" depends on a future uncertain event, making it impossible to determine as soon as the contract has been made exactly when the seller will be bound to make, or when the buyer will be entitled to receive, tender. Nevertheless, the decision is in line with the principle that "broadly speaking, time will be considered of the essence in mercantile contracts."[44]

---

[40] *Sanders Bros v Maclean* (1883) 11 Q.B.D. 327 at p.336, the other members of the court expressed no concluded view on the point: see *Toepfer v Lenersan–Poortman NV* [1980] 1 Lloyd's Rep. 143 at p.148.

[41] *Cerealmangimi SpA v Toepfer (The Eurometal)* [1981] 1 Lloyd's Rep. 337 (where the right to reject was lost by waiver).

[42] [1980] 1 Lloyd's Rep. 143. *Cf. Cerealmangimi SpA v Toepfer (The Eurometal)* [1979] 2 Lloyd's Rep. 72 (for further proceedings in this case, see above, n.41). See also a dictum in *Produce Brokers Ltd v Weiss* (1918) 118 L.T. 111 at p.115 (where the right to reject was not directly in issue) that a stipulation as to the time for tender of a provisional invoice was "a vital term of the bargain."

[43] Above, para.18–267. *Cf.* also the rules that in a contract for the sale of goods stipulations as to the time of delivery are of the essence of the contract (above, para.8–025), and that for many purposes transfer of a bill of lading is treated as the equivalent of delivery of the goods (above, para.18–063). But in a c.i.f. contract there are "three stages of delivery" (below, para.19–072) and it is not clear that the rule making time of the essence applies to them all with equal force.

[44] *Bunge Corp. v Tradax Export SA* [1981] 1 W.L.R. 711 at p.716; and see *ibid.*, p.730 where Lord Roskill referred with approval to *Toepfer v Lenersan–Poortman NV*, above; *Hyundai Merchant Marine Co. Ltd v Karander Maritime Co. Ltd (The Niizura)* [1996] 2 Lloyd's Rep. 66 at p.71.

In accordance with this principle, courts normally[45] treat as conditions any stipulations in such contracts which specify a date or period for performance that is either fixed[46] by the terms of the contract or can be precisely ascertained[47] in accordance with those terms. The purpose of this approach is to promote certainty by enabling the buyer to know that he can safely reject if tender is made after the end of the fixed or ascertainable time: for example, in a case like *Toepfer v Lenersan-Poortman NV*[48] it will enable him at the time of tender immediately to tell, merely by reference to the bill of lading date and to his calendar, whether he has the right to reject the tender. Alternatively, the decision in that case can be explained on a narrower ground, as resting on the special terms of the contract. One of these obliged the buyer to take delivery as soon as the vessel was ready to discharge,[49] and he would have had obvious difficulties in performing this obligation unless he then had the shipping documents. Hence delay in tendering them might have operated to his prejudice, though in fact there cannot have been any such prejudice: the shipping documents had been tendered some two months before arrival of the ship (which had gone aground) so that delay in tendering the documents in no way impeded the buyer in performing his obligation to take delivery. Other terms of the contract, however, made it "a commodity contract with an elaborate time-table".[50] This called not only for payment within 20 days of date of bill of lading, but also for a notice of appropriation to be given within 14 days of that date. Such a notice was given on December 17 and must have stated the date of the bill of lading,[51] which had been issued on December 11. But documents were not tendered till the following February, nearly seven weeks after the date specified in the "elaborate time-table". By then, the buyer could reasonably have formed the view that the seller would be unable to tender documents, at least without serious delay; and the delay which had already occurred appears to have given rise to such uncertainty as to the seller's ability to perform as to justify rejection on that ground. These special terms and circumstances in *Toepfer v Lenersan-Poortman NV* leave open the possibility that the failure to comply with a stipulation as to the time of tender may not invariably give rise to a right to reject,[52] and in particular that it may not have this effect when it does not, or is not in the

---

45 For exceptions, see *State Trading Corp. of India v M Goldetz Ltd* [1989] 2 Lloyd's Rep. 277; *ERG Petroli SpA v Vitol SA (The Ballenita)* [1992] 2 Lloyd's Rep. 45; the point is left open in *Phibro Energy AG v Nissho Iwai Corp. (The Homan Jade)* [1991] 1 Lloyd's Rep. 38, below, para.20–034 and in *Torvald Klaveness A/S v Arni Maritime Corp. (The Gregos)* [1994] 1 W.L.R. 1465 (a charterparty case).

46 *e.g. Bowes v Shand* (1877) 2 App. Cas. 455 (above, para.18–267), *Bunge Corp. v Tradax Export SA* [1981] 1W.L.R. 711 (below, para.20–032).

47 *e.g.* "20 days after bill of lading," as in *Toepfer v Lenersan–Poortman NV* [1980] 1 Lloyd's Rep. 143, above, n.42; *cf. Compagnie Commerciale Sucres et Denrees v C. Czarnikow Ltd (The Naxos)* [1990] 1 W.L.R. 1337 (f.o.b. contract, below, para.20–033).

48 [1980] 1 Lloyd's Rep. 143.

49 [1980] 1 Lloyd's Rep. 143 at p.148.

50 [1978] 2 Lloyd's Rep. 555 at p.559 (*per* Donaldson J. at first instance).

51 As required by the contract: see [1980] 2 Lloyd's Rep. 143 at p.144; *cf.* above, para.19–019 as to contents of notices of appropriation.

52 [1978] 2 Lloyd's Rep. 555 at p.559 ("probably no rule of general application.")

commercial setting likely to, cause any, or any serious prejudice to the buyer.[53]

19–064 **Stipulation not specifying precise time of tender.** Our concern here is with stipulations as to the time of tender which do not precisely fix that time or enable it to be precisely ascertained. There is some conflict in the authorities on the question how time clauses of this kind are to be classified and consequently on the question whether their breach of itself gives rise to the right to reject. Two cases raising analogous questions may be contrasted. In the first, the House of Lords held that a stipulation requiring a c.i.f. seller to give notice "without delay" of circumstances entitling him to invoke a prohibition of export clause was an intermediate term only, so that delay in giving the notice did not prevent the clause from operating, but gave rise only to a claim for damages.[54] On the other hand, in a second, later, decision at first instance a stipulation requiring a c.i.f. seller to give notice of appropriation "as soon as possible after vessel's sailing" was classified as a condition so that its breach justified rejection of the notice.[55] It has been suggested that the two cases can be reconciled on the ground that the decision of the House of Lords was concerned with a stipulation governing the machinery of *termination*, while the later case was concerned with a stipulation governing the machinery of *performance*.[56] But it is, with respect, hard to see the force of this distinction,[57] since one important question in relation to each type of term is whether the breach of it entitles the injured party to terminate the contract; and it is submitted that neither type of term should be classified as a condition where it does not specify a fixed or precisely ascertainable date or period for performance.[58] Neither of

[53] Under the Vienna Convention on Contracts for the International Sale of Goods (above, para.1–024) the seller on the facts of the *Toepfer* case would no doubt have been in breach (Art. 34), but the buyer would have had a right of avoidance only if that breach had been "fundamental" (Art. 49(1)(a), below, para.19–144, n.99; above, para.18–267, n.38). This might depend on the length of the delay and so give rise to the very uncertainty which the Court of Appeal in that case was anxious to avoid.

[54] *Bremer Handelsgesellschaft mbH v Vanden Avenne-Izegem PVBA* [1978] 2 Lloyd's Rep. 109 (so far as it related to the notice under clause 21 of the contract) (above, para.18–357).

[55] *Société Italo-Belge pour le Commerce et l'Industrie v Palm & Vegetable Oils (Malaysia) Sdn. Bhd. (The Post Chaser)* [1981] 2 Lloyd's Rep. 695; in this respect going beyond *Graves v Legg* (1854) 9 Exch. 709 (below, para.21–025).

[56] *The Post Chaser*, above, n.55 at p.699.

[57] The difficulty of reconciling the two cases here under discussion is recognised in *Concordia Trading BV v Richo International Ltd* [1991] 1 Lloyd's Rep. 475 at p.481.

[58] *Tradax Export SA v Italgrani di Francesco Ambrosio* [1986] 1 Lloyd's Rep. 112 at p.120; *cf. Alfred McAlpine Plc v BAI (Run-off) Ltd* [2000] 1 Lloyd's Rep. 437 (notice of insurance claims to be given "as soon as possible"), and *Friend's Provident Life and Pensions Ltd v Sirius International Insurance* [2005] EWCA Civ. 601, [2005] 2 All E.R. (Comm.) 145 (clause requiring notice of insurance claim to be given "immediately" held to be neither a condition nor an intermediate term but to be a term, the breach of which gave rise *only* to a claim for damages); followed in *Ronson International Ltd v Patrick* [2005] EWHC 1767 (Q.B.), [2005] 2 All E.R. (Comm.) 453. Probably these cases are based on special policy considerations applicable only to insurance contracts so that their reasoning would not apply in the present context of delay in tendering shipping documents.

the two cases was, moreover, concerned with the effects of a seller's failure to tender *shipping documents*[59] in accordance with a contractual stipulation merely requiring tender to be made promptly, without precisely specifying the time for tender, or enabling it to be precisely ascertained. It is submitted that, where the stipulation is in this respect imprecise, then a delay in tendering documents that is only slight should not of itself justify rejection.[60] Such a rule would not run counter to the requirements of commercial certainty since the imprecise nature of the stipulation itself would make it impossible for the buyer to predict exactly when documents were to be tendered to him.

Buyer dealing as consumer. It is uncommon but not impossible for a c.i.f. buyer to deal as consumer.[61] Where he so deals and "the goods do not conform to the contract of sale at the time of delivery"[62] he has certain "additional rights" under Part 5A of the Sale of Goods Act 1979; one of these is the right in specified circumstances "to rescind the contract".[63] Goods "do not conform to the contract of sale" in a number of situations; one of these arises "if there is, in relation to the goods, a breach of an express term of the contract".[64] There is no need for the express term to be a condition. The question therefore arises whether, if a c.i.f. seller is in breach of an express term requiring him to tender documents "without delay" or "as soon as possible" after a specified event, the buyer can then "rescind" under Part 5A. One objection to his being able to do so is that Part 5A in terms deals only with non-conformity of the goods themselves and nowhere refers to non-conformity of documents. But this is also true of many other references in the Act to "goods" in provisions which have nevertheless been adapted, in the context of c.i.f. contracts, to documents. A more compelling objection to allowing a c.i.f. buyer to "rescind" under Part 5A for breach of an express term of the kind here under discussion is that Part 5A refers primarily to the quality or description of the goods themselves,[65] rather than to the time of their tender. The words "the goods do not conform to the contract at the time of delivery"[66] give some support to the view that the time of delivery itself is not a factor that can lead, for the purposes of Part 5A, to non-conformity of the goods to the contract; and if that Part can apply to documents, then the same reasoning can apply to a delay, in breach of the contract, in tendering the documents. 19–065

[59] A notice of appropriation is not a "shipping document" (above, para.19–058) and in *The Post Chaser*, above n.55, the contract did not fix any date for tender of shipping documents see p.699 of the report.
[60] *cf. Scandinavian Trading Co. A/B v Zodiac Petroleum SA (The Al Hofuf)* [1981] 1 Lloyd's Rep. 81 (f.o.b. contract; below, para.20–032).
[61] See above, para.18–259.
[62] Sale of Goods Act 1979, s.48A(1)(b).
[63] *ibid.*, s.48A(2)(b)(ii). For the circumstances in which this right to "rescind" arises, see s.48C(1)(b) and (2); below, para.19–144.
[64] *ibid.*, s.48F.
[65] This appears from the reference in s.48F to ss.13, 14 and 15 of the 1979 Act. It is arguable that the words "breach of an express term" (in s.48F) should be construed *eiusdem generis*.
[66] S.48A(1)(b). The words "in relation to the goods" in s.48F support the same view.

19–066 **No stipulation as to time of tender: documents to be tendered promptly.** Where the contract contains no provisions as to time of tender, the seller must take steps to tender the documents as soon as possible after the goods have been shipped[67] or (in the case of goods sold afloat) after the seller has "destined the cargo to the particular vendee or consignee."[68] Although the contrary has been suggested,[69] a c.i.f. seller appears, according to the older authorities, to be under no absolute obligation to tender the documents before the arrival of the ship.[70] However, the increased speed of modern communications is likely to have reduced the practical importance of this rule (if it exists) since a seller who failed (for example) to forward the documents by air would probably be in breach of his obligation to tender them with the required degree of promptness; and documents, so forwarded should (except where the sea transit was short) normally arrive before the ship.[71]

19–067 **"String" contracts.** Where shipping documents are passed down a "string" of buyers and sellers, they may, because of administrative delays, fail to reach the ultimate receiver until after the arrival of the ship; but that buyer may in practice get delivery of the goods against letters of indemnity, even though he is not yet in possession of the documents[72]; and the contract of sale may expressly provide for delivery to be made in this way.[73] In such cases, the seller is clearly under no duty to tender documents before arrival of the ship. String contracts, moreover, commonly contain express provisions as to the time at which documents must be tendered; and contracts

---

[67] *C Sharpe & Co. Ltd v Nosawa* [1917] 2 K. B. 814; *Borrowman, Phillips & Co. v Free & Hollis* (1878) 4 Q.B.D. 500 at p.504; *Gatoil International Inc. v Tradax Petroleum Ltd (The Rio Sun)* [1985] 1 Lloyd's Rep. 351 at p.357; *Birkett Sperling & Co. v Engholm & Co.* (1871) 10 M. (Ct. of Sess.) 170 at p.174 ("quam primum"). *Cf.* U.C.C., s.2–320(2)(e) (as to which see above, para.19–047 n.74), requiring documents to be tendered "with commercial promptness"; Comment 11 says that this phrase "expresses a more urgent need for action than that suggested by the phrase 'reasonable time'." This is also the position in English law: *cf.* the interpretation in *Bank of Nova Scotia v Hellenic Mutual War Risk Association (Bermuda) Ltd (The Good Luck)* [1992] A.C. 233 of an express contractual provision requiring a notice that a ship had ceased to be insured to be given "promptly" to the mortgagee of the ship.

[68] *Sanders Bros v Maclean & Co.* (1883) 11 Q.B.D. 327 at p.337; *Concordia Trading BV v Richo International Ltd* [1991] 1 Lloyd's Rep. 475 at p.476.

[69] *Re Salomon & Co. and Naudszus* (1889) 81 L.T. 325 at pp.326, 329.

[70] *Sanders Bros v Maclean & Co.*, above, at pp.336–337 (a passage treated with some reserve in *Toepfer v Lenerson-Poortman NV* [1980] 1 Lloyd's Rep. 143 at p.148); *cf. Barber v Taylor* (1839) 9 L.J. Ex. 21; if the proposition in the text is right, expenses of storage incurred between the arrival of the ship and tender of documents must be borne by the buyer so long as the seller has made all reasonable efforts to tender the documents as soon as possible after shipment.

[71] See, however, *Tradax Internacional SA v Goldschmidt SA* [1977] 2 Lloyd's Rep. 604 (where bills of lading reached an f.o.b. buyer at Ravenna after the arrival of the goods); and *Ginzberg v Barrow Haematite Steel Co. Ltd* [1966] 1 Lloyd's Rep. 343 (below, para.19–103).

[72] *e.g. Nile Co. for the Export of Agricultural Crops v H & JM Bennet* (*Commodities*) *Ltd* [1986] 1 Lloyd's Rep. 555.

[73] *e.g. Enichem Anic SpA v Ampelos Shipping Co. Ltd* (*The Defini*) [1990] 1 Lloyd's Rep. 252.

containing such provisions will be governed, not by the rules stated in paragraph 19–066, but by those stated in paragraphs 19–061 to 19–065, above.

Effect of failure to tender documents promptly. Where the contract contains no stipulation as to the time of tender, the further question arises whether the seller's failure to tender documents with the degree of despatch required by law justifies rejection or gives rise only to a claim for damages. In paragraph 19–064 above, it was submitted that failure to perform an express term requiring tender to be made "promptly", but not fixing a *precise* time of tender, should not, of itself, justify rejection. It is here further submitted that the position should be the same in cases of the present kind in which the contract does not fix a time for tender or indicate how it is to be ascertained and so merely imposes, as a matter of law, an obligation to act promptly; and that accordingly the buyer should not be entitled to reject merely on account of a slight delay in tendering documents, causing no serious prejudice to the buyer. Such a rule would not violate the needs of commercial certainty where the contract does not entitle the buyer to expect tender on a fixed or ascertainable day; for there is necessarily some elasticity in the rule of law requiring the seller to tender documents promptly where the contract makes no provision as to the time of tender. 19–068

Place of tender. Under section 29(2) of the Sale of Goods Act 1979, the place of delivery of goods is, subject to contrary agreement, the seller's place of business[74]; and it might be thought that tender of documents, being in some respects[75] the equivalent of delivery of the goods, is to be made at the same place. Conflicting views have been expressed on the question.[76] Dicta to the effect that the seller is bound to hand over,[77] tender[78] or deliver[79] shipping documents are quite neutral; they do not, with one exception,[80] make any express reference to the place of tender. Where the seller carries on business in one country and the buyer in another, which is also the country of destination, it would certainly be strange to apply the prima facie rule of section 29(2), under which the buyer would be bound to collect the bill of lading from the seller's premises. In such a case it would probably be held that tender need not be made at the seller's place of business, unless this was the normal course of dealing between the parties.[81] It would not however follow that tender was to be made at the buyer's place of business. The seller may forward the documents to his own agent in the 19–069

---

[74] *cf. Rein v Stein* [1892] 1 Q.B. 753; Vienna Convention on Contracts for the International Sale of Goods (above, para.1–024), Art. 31.
[75] See below, para.19–072.
[76] *Stein, Forbes & Co. v County Tailoring Co.* (1916) 115 L.T. 215 at p.216; *Johnson v Taylor Bros* [1920] A.C. 144 at p.156.
[77] *cf. Ireland v Livingston* (1872) L.R. 5 H.L. 385 at p.406.
[78] *E. Clemens Horst Co. v Biddell Bros* [1912] A.C. 18 at p.23.
[79] *C. Sharpe & Co. Ltd v Nosawa* [1917] 2 K.B. 814 at p.818.
[80] *Johnson v Taylor Bros*, above, at p.406.
[81] *Rein v Stein* [1892] 1 Q.B. 753 at p.758 (Lindley L.J.); contrast *ibid.*, at p.758 (Kay L.J.). The issue was as to the place of payment, not of tender of documents.

buyer's country with instructions to hold them until payment of the price: it would then probably be up to the buyer to collect the documents from the agent's premises, which would be the place of tender.[82] On the other hand, where payment is made through a bank in the seller's country, the place of tender might well be the premises of the bank. Problems as to the exact place of tender do not seem often to arise, though issues do occasionally arise for jurisdictional purposes as to the *country* in which tender is to be made. In most cases the country of tender will, by implication, be the country in which payment is to be made; and this is commonly specified in the contract.

19–070 **Person to whom tender is to be made.** Prima facie tender must be made to the buyer. But where a contract provides for payment by banker's commercial credit, the documents required by the credit must be tendered to the bank. If the seller tenders to the bank documents which do not comply with the terms of the credit, he cannot later make a valid tender to the buyer himself[83]; though he may have a cause of action against the buyer for damages for failing to provide a credit in accordance with the contract of sale,[84] or for the price if it is held that the credit is only the primary and not the sole source of payment,[85] and if the conditions in which an action for the price can be brought[86] are satisfied.

19–071 **Bad tender followed by good tender.** A seller who tenders defective documents is not in final or irrevocable default if the tender is made before the end of the time allowed for tender.[87] Within that time, it is open to the

[82] Unless, perhaps, the contract provided for payment by acceptance of the seller's draft on the buyer. In that case the buyer's place of business is the place at which the draft must be presented for acceptance and payment (Bills of Exchange Act 1882, s.41(1)(a) and s.45(4)(c)); and it would seem reasonable to require tender of the shipping documents at the same place.

[83] *Soproma SpA v Marine & Animal By-Products Corp.* [1966] 1 Lloyd's Rep. 367 at p.386.

[84] *ibid.*

[85] *Saffron v Soc. Minière Cafrika* (1858) 100 C.L.R. 231; *ED & F Man Ltd v Nigerian Sweets & Confectionery Co.* [1977] 2 Lloyd's Rep. 50 (c. & f. contract); below, para.23–098.

[86] Below, paras 19–211 *et seq.*

[87] *Empresa Exportadora de Azucar v Industria Azucarera Nacional SA* (*The Playa Larga*) [1983] 2 Lloyd's Rep. 171 at p.184; *Hyundai Merchant Marine Co. Ltd v Karander Maritime Co. Ltd (The Niizuru)* [1996] 2 Lloyd's Rep. 66 at p.70; *cf.* below, para.19–171. The above discussion is concerned with the seller's *liberty* to cure. A c.i.f. buyer will not normally, but may occasionally, deal as consumer (see above, para.18–259). Where the buyer so deals, the seller may be under a *duty*, at the request of the buyer, to repair or replace non-conforming goods within a reasonable time (Sale of Goods Act 1979, ss.48A(2)(a), 48B); "repair" means "to bring the goods into conformity with the contract" (s.61(1), "repair"). The question whether these provisions can apply to non-conformity of the documents (as opposed to the goods) is discussed in para.19–065 above. If they can so apply and the seller performs the duty to repair or replace by (at the buyer's request) making a fresh tender of conforming documents, then it must follow that the buyer would no longer be entitled to reject that tender; and the "reasonable time" within which the seller must repair or replace may extend beyond the time specified for tender in the

seller to offer to make another good tender; and, unless the original bad tender can be treated as a repudiation of the contract, the buyer is not entitled to reject such an offer. If he does reject it without lawful excuse he is liable in damages even though the subsequent good tender is never made.[88] Conversely, the seller is not in breach if, before the second tender can be made, the contract is frustrated[89]; or if the contract is rescinded by the seller on account of the buyer's repudiatory breach in rejecting the offer of the second tender.[90]

(d) *Duty with Respect to Delivery*

Three stages of delivery. In a c.i.f. contract, there are "three stages of delivery": a "provisional delivery" on shipment; a "symbolical delivery" on tender of documents; and a "complete delivery of the cargo" when the goods are handed over to the buyer at the destination.[91] The duties of the seller so far discussed relate to the first two of these stages; if the seller performs those duties he is not normally in breach merely because the third stage is not reached.[92] This follows from the nature of a c.i.f. contract[93] and from the rules as to risk as they apply to such a contract.[94] Having shipped proper goods and tendered proper documents, the seller is not normally concerned with what happens to the goods in transit: the buyer's remedies (if any) in respect of the failure of the goods to arrive are against the carrier or the underwriter, not against the seller. Conversely, if shipment of the goods to the c.i.f. destination becomes impossible or illegal, the seller cannot be required to deliver them at some other place. Thus in the *Fibrosa*[95] case machinery was sold c.i.f. Gdynia and it became illegal for the 19–072

---

contract. To this extent the seller's opportunity to cure defective performance under these provisions may have a wider scope than that of the rule stated in the text above. If the buyer requests repair or replacement, his right to reject is also restricted in that he must not exercise it until he has given the seller a reasonable time within which to replace or repair (Sale of Goods Act 1979, s.48D). But the buyer is not bound to request repair or replacement; and if he makes no such request, then any *liberty* to cure which the seller may have can be exercised only within the time allowed by the contract for tender.

88 *Borrowman Phillips & Co. v Free & Hollis* (1878) 4 Q.B.D. 500. *Cf.* Vienna Convention on Contracts for the International Sale of Goods (above, para.1–024), Art. 34, restricting the seller's right to "cure" the defective tender to cases in which the exercise of the right does not cause the buyer unreasonable inconvenience or expense, and preserving the buyer's right to damages in respect of any loss suffered in consequence of the original, defective, tender. The Convention gives the seller a similar right to remedy non-conformity in *the goods*: see Art. 37.

89 As in *Empresa Exportadora de Azucar v Industria Azucarera Nacional SA (The Playa Larga)* [1983] 2 Lloyd's Rep. 171 at p.184.

90 *cf.* below, para.19–170.

91 *Schmoll Fils & Co. v Scriven Bros & Co.* (1924) 19 Ll.L. Rep. 118 at p.119; and see below, para.19–156.

92 *Manbré Saccharine Co. Ltd v Corn Products Co. Ltd* [1919] 1 K.B. 198 at p.202 ("not by actual physical delivery of goods . . .").

93 Above, paras 19–001, 19–002.

94 Below, para.19–110.

95 *Fibrosa Spolka Akcyna v Fairbairn Lawson Combe Barbour Ltd* [1942] 1 K.B. 12 at pp.19–20 (Tucker J.) and pp.26–27 (C.A.), rvsd., with regard to the *effects* of frustration, [1943] A.C. 32.

sellers to ship the goods to the port when it was occupied by enemy forces in the Second World War. It was held that the buyers did not have the option of requiring the sellers to deliver the goods at the sellers' place of business in Leeds or at the then neutral port of Riga. The buyers' willingness to accept delivery at one of the these places therefore did not save the contract from being frustrated by the supervening illegality of shipment to Gdynia.

19–073 **Duty not to prevent "complete delivery".** It does not, however, follow that a seller who has performed his duties with respect to the first two stages of delivery cannot be in breach of a duty with respect to the third. The existence of such a duty was assumed in *Gill & Duffus SA v Berger & Co. Inc.*[96] where a c.i.f. seller rescinded after tender of documents had been wrongfully rejected by the buyer; and Lord Diplock said that the seller was, as a result of that rescission, relieved of "any further obligation to deliver to the buyers any of the goods that were the subject-matter of the contract".[97] This statement clearly refers to the third stage of "complete delivery" since this was the only aspect of the seller's "obligation to deliver" that remained unperformed after the second stage of tender of documents; and since it is contrasted by Lord Diplock with the first stage, *viz.* the seller's "obligation . . . to ship goods that were in conformity with the contract".[98] But the seller's duty at the third stage is not one to take positive steps to procure delivery of the goods to the buyer.[99] The duty is the purely negative one of not interfering with the contract of carriage so as to prevent the buyer from receiving the goods at the agreed destination. Thus the seller would be in breach of duty at the third stage if, having time-chartered the carrying ship, he ordered her to a port other than that stated as the destination of the goods in the contract of sale and in the contract of carriage[1]; or if, after the goods had arrived at that destination, he ordered the carrier not to deliver them to the buyer.[2] The seller may also, at the third stage, be in breach of the implied warranty of quiet possession under section 12(2) of the Sale of

[96] [1984] A.C. 382; below, para.19–163.
[97] [1984] A.C. 382 at p.391; *cf. ibid.*, at pp.394, 395–396.
[98] *ibid.*, at p.390.
[99] Above, n.92.
[1] A suggestion for which Mocatta J. thought there was "much to be said": *Peter Cremer v Brinkers Groudstoffen NV* [1980] 2 Lloyd's Rep. 605 at p.608; and which was accepted as good law by the Court of Appeal in *Empresa Exportadora de Azucar v Industria Azucarera Nacional SA* (*The Playa Larga*) [1983] 2 Lloyd's Rep. 171 at p.180 (though on the facts an implied term to this effect was rejected as the buyer was already adequately protected by the warranty implied under Sale of Goods Act 1979, s.12(2): see text at n.3); *Ceval Alimentos SA v Agrimpex Trading Co. Ltd (The Northern Progress) (No.2)* [1996] 2 Lloyd's Rep. 319, where the actual decision seems to have been based on the sellers' breach in tendering a bill of lading which permitted carriage to a destination other than that specified in the contract of sale (above, para.19–031); but it was also said at p.332 that, if the bill had been in conformity with the contract, the buyers could have relied on "the different breach of the sellers' wrongful interference with the voyage" to the destination specified in the contract of sale.
[2] *Gatoil International Inc. v Tradax Petroleum Ltd* (*The Rio Sun*) [1985] 1 Lloyd's Rep. 351 at p.362.

Goods Act 1979 if, after tender of documents and payment, he prevents the carrier from actually delivering the goods to the buyer.[3]

Time of "complete delivery". Traditionally, c.i.f. contracts specify the time by, or period within, which the goods are to be shipped or documents are to be tendered, but they do not specify the time of the actual delivery of the goods at the contractual destination. This traditional approach is still reflected in a number of recent decisions, even though it may become inappropriate in relation to dealings in certain commodities (such as oil) where the time of arrival may be of crucial importance to a buyer who has to make advance arrangements for the provision of terminal facilities needed for the reception of the goods.[4] Stipulations as to the time of arrival have therefore become increasingly common in c.i.f. contracts; though they tend still to be interpreted against the background of the traditional assumption that the seller normally gives no undertaking as to that time. Thus in one case[5] a c.i.f. contract provided for "delivery February 15/March 15. Basis Rotterdam", and also gave the buyer the option of choosing other discharging ports within a specified range. The buyer selected one such port and it was held that he was not entitled to reject the goods on the ground that they arrived there on March 16. Prima facie, a c.i.f. seller gives no undertaking as to the time of "complete delivery"[6]; and the provision in question merely meant that the seller had to load the ship in time to enable her to discharge at Rotterdam within the specified period; and on this interpretation of the contract a seller who so loaded would perform his obligation with respect to the time of delivery, even though the actual delivery of the goods at the contractual destination was delayed by circumstances for which he was not responsible.[7] Practical considerations of the kind described above may, however, make it important for the buyer to know, not merely when the goods are to be shipped, but also when they will, or are likely to, arrive. This need of the buyer's can be met by clear words in the contract requiring the seller to give an undertaking as to the time of the "complete delivery" of the goods: for example where the seller expressly promised to ensure the arrival of the goods at the contractual destination before a specified date "positively".[8] The position was the same where a c.i.f. contract provided for "delivery February 15–28" and required the sellers to give "minimum two working days' notice of vessel's arrival. . ." The sellers were held to be in breach (and the buyers entitled to 19–074

---

[3] *The Playa Larga*, above n.1, at p.180. Later amendments of s.12(2) have not affected the point.

[4] *cf.*, for a discussion of similar problems which can arise as to the time of shipment in f.o.b. contracts, *Phibro Energy AG v Nissho Iwai Corp.* (*The Honam Jade*) [1991] 1 Lloyd's Rep. 38, below, 20–034.

[5] *P & O Trading Ltd v Scanoil Ltd* (*The Orient Prince*) [1985] 1 Lloyd's Rep. 389.

[6] *Vitol SA v Esso Australia Ltd* (*The Wise*) [1989] 2 Lloyd's Rep. 451 at p.454; *E.R.G. Petroli SpA v Vitol SA (The Ballenita)* [1992] 2 Lloyd's Rep. 455 at p.464.

[7] *e.g.* the carrier's breach of contract or excepted perils in the contract of carriage; but the seller would be responsible for delays due to his unjustified interference with the contract of carriage. *Cf.* below, paras 20–037, 21–030.

[8] *Cargill International SA v Bangladesh Sugar & Food Industries* [1998] 1 W.L.R. 461 at p.465.

reject) by reason of the facts that the sellers had given the notice of arrival less than two days before the end of the delivery period and that they had indicated on the last day of that period that the vessel was not expected to arrive until after its expiry.[9] A similar conclusion was reached where a c.i.f. contract did not specify a shipment period but did give an estimate of the times at which the goods were expected to arrive at either of the two possible ports of destination named in the contract. This estimate was given because the buyer was, as the seller knew, in urgent need of the goods to enable the buyer to supply them to a sub-buyer; and this urgency was reflected in the price payable by the buyer to the seller. The seller was unable to ship the goods until after the estimated arrival times, and it was held that the buyer was entitled to terminate the contract as the seller's estimate of the arrival dates had not been made in good faith.[10]

3. DUTIES OF THE BUYER

(a) *Payment of the Price*

19–075 **Duty to pay price on tender of documents.** Under section 28 of the Sale of Goods Act 1979, the general rule is that delivery and payment are concurrent conditions; but this rule can be excluded by contrary agreement. In the case of a c.i.f. contract, the duty to pay prima facie arises on tender of shipping documents; but the parties can vary this rule, *e.g.* by providing for payment against letter of indemnity, should shipping documents not be available at the time at which they ought to be tendered.[11]

It is arguable that the prima facie rule, obliging the buyer to pay against shipping documents, is an application of the general rule in section 28, as tender of a bill of lading amounts to tender of constructive possession of the goods.[12] But this reasoning will not cover all cases; for the c.i.f. buyer is bound to pay on tender of documents even though these do not include a bill of lading but only, for example, a delivery order.[13] The better view therefore is that a c.i.f. contract contains an agreement excluding section 28.[14] Normally, this agreement will be express,[15] as where the contract

---

[9] *Nova Petroleum International Establishment v Tricon Trading Ltd* [1989] 1 Lloyd's Rep. 312; *cf. Michael J Warde v Feedex International Inc.* [1985] 2 Lloyd's Rep. 289 at pp.292, 293 (where the contract specified both a shipment period and an arrival date); and see above, paras 18–275, 19–016.

[10] *SHV Gas Supply & Trading SAS v Naftomar Shipping & Trading Co Ltd Inc (The Azur Gaz)* [2005] EWHC 2528 (Comm.), [2006] 1 Lloyd's Rep. 163 at [53].

[11] *e.g. Enichem Anic SpA v Ampelos Shipping Co. Ltd (The Delfini)* [1990] 1 Lloyd's Rep. 252.

[12] Above, para.18–063.

[13] Above, para.19–003. *Cf. Polenghi v Dried Milk Co. Ltd* (1904) 10 Com.Cas. 42 (shipping or railway documents).

[14] Under the Vienna Convention on Contracts for the International Sale of Goods (above, para.1–024), Art. 58(1) (first sentence) the duty to pay arises "when the seller places either the goods or the documents controlling their disposition at the buyer's disposal", unless some other time for payment is specified.

[15] *cf.* Vienna Convention on Contracts for the International Sale of Goods (above, para.1–024), Art. 58(1), second sentence.

provides for payment "against" or "in exchange for" or "on presentation of" shipping documents. But the agreement may also be implied from the nature of a c.i.f. contract: thus the duty to pay arises on tender of documents even where a c.i.f. contract simply provides "terms net cash".[16] Where such a contract did expressly provide for "cash against documents" a custom that payment was not to be made until arrival of the ship was rejected as inconsistent with the contract.[17] The effect of a provision in the contract for "payment against documents on arrival of steamer"[18] appears to be that the duty to pay arises on tender of documents, though the time of payment is postponed until arrival of the steamer.[19] Stronger words are needed to negative the duty to pay against documents.[20] Once the duty to pay on tender of documents is established, it is not negatived by a provision in the contract that the exact amount payable is to depend on the quantity of goods landed: such a provision is merely the basis for a subsequent adjustment of the price.[21]

The rule that the duty to pay arises on tender of documents has two important consequences. These are discussed in paragraphs 19–076 to 19–084 below.

No right of examination before payment. A c.i.f. buyer must pay against documents: he is not entitled to refuse to pay until he has examined the goods[22] for the purpose of determining whether the bulk corresponds with the sample[23] or whether the goods are otherwise of the contract description, quality or quantity. If the buyer insists on examination of the goods before payment, the seller is entitled to refuse to ship.[24] The rule is based on considerations of commercial convenience: if the buyer were not bound to 19–076

[16] *E Clemens Horst Co. v Biddell Bros* [1912] A.C. 18.
[17] *JW Elliott & Co. v Candor Manufacturing Co.* (1920) 3 Ll.L.R. 105.
[18] As in *Stein, Forbes & Co. v County Tailoring Co.* (1916) 115 L.T. 215.
[19] *cf. Fragano v Long* (1825) 4 B. & C. 219 at p.222, where a stipulation for payment three months from arrival was said only to define the period of credit. For the distinction between the times at which sums due under contract are respectively *earned* and *payable, cf. Bank of Boston Connecticut v European Grain & Shipping Ltd* (*The Dominique*) [1989] A.C. 1056.
[20] See below, para.19–081.
[21] *Plaimar Ltd v Waters Trading Co. Ltd* (1945) 72 C.L.R. 304 at p.314; *Soon Hua Seng Co. Ltd v Glencore Grain Co. Ltd* [1996] 1 Lloyd's Rep. 398.
[22] *E. Clemens Horst Co. v Biddell Bros* [1912] A.C. 18. The same rule is stated in ULIS (above, para.1–024), Art. 72(2) where it constitutes an exception the general rule that the buyer is not bound to pay the price until he has had an opportunity to examine the goods: Arts 71, 72(1). The Vienna Convention on Contracts for the International Sale of Goods (above, para.1–024) states the same general rule in Art. 58(3) and subjects it to a less precisely defined exception: "unless the procedures for delivery or payment agreed upon by the parties are inconsistent with his [*i.e.* the buyer's] having such an opportunity [*i.e.* to examine the goods]". The exact scope of this exception is obscure. It would clearly apply where the contract specified a *date* for payment before the arrival of the ship. It is submitted that it should also apply in the ordinary case of a c.i.f. contract (under which payment is due under Art. 58(1) against documents) since in such a case it is normal for the documents to arrive before the goods (even though this is not necessarily the case). In other words, it is submitted that the position under the Convention is the same as that in English law.
[23] *Polenghi v Dried Milk Co. Ltd* (1904) 10 Com.Cas. 42.
[24] *E Clemens Horst Co. v Biddell Bros* [1912] A.C. 18.

pay till after he had examined the goods, the seller would *either* have to provide inspection facilities at the place of destination (which is likely to be distant from his place of business) *or* allow the buyer to have the shipping documents before payment (in order to obtain the release of the goods for inspection) and so run the risk of prejudicing the security which retention of the documents until payment is normally intended to provide.[25] To give the buyer the right to inspect the goods before payment would also be impracticable where (as often happens with commodity sales) the goods pass rapidly through many hands while they are still afloat. The buyer, on the other hand, can protect himself against the risk to which the rule exposes him by stipulating that the shipping documents are to include an inspection certificate, or a certificate of quality: in this way the buyer obtains the views of an independent third party as to the quality and condition of the goods at the time of shipment. Because of the importance to the buyer of such a certificate, the task of inspection cannot be delegated: hence the certificate is ineffective if it is issued, or if the inspection is made, by a person or body other than the one nominated for this purpose in the contract.[26] That person is unlikely to be in any contractual relationship with the buyer but nevertheless owes a duty of care to the buyer with respect to the accuracy of statements about the goods in the certificate; breach of this duty can give rise to liability in tort.[27]

19–077 **Duty to pay though goods not in conformity with contract.** The buyer must, as a general rule, pay against conforming documents even though the goods are not in conformity with the contract, and even though he knows or rightly suspects that this is the case.[28] The fact that he has paid against documents will not, however, deprive him of his other remedies (than withholding the price) in respect of the non-conformity: he is prima facie[29] entitled to damages and may be entitled to reject the goods,[30] and consequently to the return of the price. The exact legal consequences of the buyer's failure or refusal to pay in such circumstances are further discussed in paragraphs 19–163 to 19–166 below.

19–078 **Exceptions.** The rule requiring the buyer to pay against conforming documents even though the goods are not in accordance with the contract is subject to one, and may be subject to two, exceptions. First, the rule does

[25] *E Clemens Horst Co. v Biddell Bros* [1911] 1 K.B. 934 at p.959 (*per* Kennedy L.J. dissenting, whose judgment was approved by the House of Lords: [1912] A.C. 18).
[26] *Kollerich & Cie. SA v State Trading Corp. of India* [1980] 2 Lloyd's Rep. 32 (f.o.b. contract).
[27] *Niru Battery Manufacturing Co v Milestone Trading Ltd* [2003] EWCA Civ. 1446, [2004] 1 Lloyd's Rep. 344; *AIC Ltd v ITS Testing Services (UK) Ltd* [2005] EWHC 2122, [2006] 1 Lloyd's Rep 1, where the issuer of the certificate was held liable for breach a of duty of care in both contract and tort and also in deceit.
[28] *Gill & Duffus SA v Berger & Co. Inc.* [1984] A.C. 382 (below, para.19–163).
[29] The right to damages may be excluded by a term of the contract: *e.g.* by the "certification clause" in *Gill & Duffus SA v Berger & Co. Inc.* [1984] A.C. 382, below, para.19–163.
[30] If the buyer deals as consumer (see above, para.18–259), he seems also to be entitled under Pt 5A of the Sale of Goods Act 1979 to "additional rights" such as reduction of the purchase price or rescission of the contract: see ss.48A(2)(b), 48C; for the question whether these provisions apply to non-conformity in documents (as opposed to goods) see above, para.19–065.

not apply in "cases of fraud"[31], *e.g.* where the seller has tendered documents knowing that they contained false statements of fact about the date of shipment or about other aspects of the description or about the quality of the goods, and the buyer would have been entitled to reject the documents if they had stated the truth with regard to those matters. Secondly, it may not apply where the goods that are actually shipped differ fundamentally from those that have been sold, *e.g.* where the contract is for the sale of peas and the documents tendered relate to goods that are in fact beans.[32] The second exception is a narrow one, for generally, if the case is of this kind, the buyer will be justified in refusing to pay on another ground, *e.g.* on the ground that the seller was guilty of fraud in shipping beans and tendering documents relating to peas; or on the ground that the documents were not "genuine" in describing beans as peas.[33] But the seller might not himself be guilty of fraud, *e.g.* where he was one of a string of buyers and sellers and had in good faith passed on documents handed to him by his supplier[34]; and the bill of lading might be "genuine", in spite of the misdescription, where the difference between the goods shipped and those described in the bill of lading was not such as would appear from the sort of examination that the carrier could reasonably be expected to make,[35] *e.g.* where cases containing beans were labelled peas and described in the bill of lading as "said to contain peas". In the United States, the buyer's duty to pay against conforming documents appears not to extend to cases of this kind[36]; and the position may be the same in English law.

Conformity of the documents. The buyer is only bound to pay against documents which are in accordance with the requirements of the contract. **19–079**
Documents may fail to conform with those requirements in two ways. First, the documents may on their face indicate that they are not in accordance with the contract, *e.g.* where the bill of lading is not "clean", or where it states that the goods have been shipped outside the shipment period. Secondly, the documents may be latently defective, *e.g.* where the bill of lading is not "genuine"[37] because it contains a false date of shipment. Dicta in the House of Lords, to the effect that the buyer is in breach if he fails to pay "upon presentation . . . of shipping documents which *on their face* conform to those called for by the contract"[38] may at first sight seem to suggest that a buyer is bound to pay against documents which, though good on their face, are not "genuine". But this would be inconsistent with the

[31] *Gill & Duffus SA v Berger Co. Inc.*, above n.29, at p.390; for some of the difficulties arising from the concept of "fraud", see *Armitage v Nurse* [1998] Ch. 241 at p.251.
[32] *Gill & Duffus SA v Berger Co. Inc.*, above, at p.390.
[33] Above, para.19–035.
[34] *cf. Hindley & Co. Ltd v East Indian Produce Co. Ltd* [1973] 2 Lloyd's Rep. 515 (where a bill of lading was issued though no goods of the kind described in it had been shipped at all).
[35] *cf. Cox, Patterson & Co. v Bruce & Co.* (1886) 18 Q.B.D. 147.
[36] U.C.C., s.2–320, Comment 12. For the proposed deletion of s.2-320, see above, para.19–047, n.74.
[37] Above, para.19–035.
[38] *Gill & Duffus SA v Berger & Co. Inc.* [1984] A.C. 382 at p.390 (italics supplied).

established view that where such documents are tendered the buyer has *two* rights of rejection,[39] being entitled to reject both the documents and the goods. It is submitted that the dicta requiring the buyer to pay against documents which "on their face conform to the requirements of a c.i.f. contract"[40] should be interpreted more narrowly, to refer to the situation in which the documents are genuine but simply fail to reveal a defect in the goods which shipping documents would not ordinarily be expected to disclose on their face, *e.g.* where a bill of lading contained no misstatements but failed to disclose that the goods were not up to sample. In such a case, the buyer must pay against documents and seek his remedy later in respect of defects in the goods; but where the documents, though good on their face, are not genuine, the buyer's refusal to pay against documents would not be wrongful.[41]

19–080 **Goods lost in transit.** Just as the loss, destruction or enemy seizure of the goods after shipment does not discharge the seller from his obligation to tender documents,[42] so these events do not relieve the buyer from his obligation to pay the price.[43] The remedy of the buyer (if any) in such cases is against the carrier for breach of the contract of carriage, or against the underwriter on the policy of insurance. But the buyer is bound to pay the price on tender of documents even though he has no claim either against the carrier, because the goods were lost through some cause for which the carrier was not responsible, or against the underwriter because they were lost by a peril not insured against.[44] In *C Groom Ltd v Barber*[45] 100 bales of Hessian cloth were sold on June 8, 1914 by one London merchant to another, for shipment from Calcutta c.i.f. London; the contract provided that war risks were for the buyer's account. The seller on the day of the sale bought an equivalent quantity, of which 25 bales were later shipped by the seller's suppliers on the *City of Winchester*. On August 3, 1914 (shortly before the outbreak of war), the seller wrote to the buyer informing him that war risks were not covered. The *City of Winchester* was captured by a

---

[39] Below, para.19–144.
[40] *Gill & Duffus SA v Berger & Co. Inc.* [1984] A.C. 382 at p.391.
[41] See *Kwei Tek Chao v British Traders & Shippers Ltd* [1954] 2 Q.B. 459 at p.480, a decision referred to with approval in the *Gill & Duffus* case, above, at p.395 (where the rights to reject the documents and the goods are referred to as "separate and successive").
[42] Above, paras 19–001, 19–059.
[43] *C Groom Ltd v Barber* [1915] 1 K.B. 316; *Arnhold Karberg & Co. v Blythe, Green, Jourdain & Co.* [1916] 1 K.B. 495 at p.510; *Ross T Smyth & Co. Ltd v TD Bailey, Son & Co.* [1940] 3 All E.R. 60 at pp.69–70; *cf. Law and Bonar Ltd v British American Tobacco Co. Ltd* [1916] 2 K.B. 605; *M Golodetz & Co. Inc. v Czarnikow Rionda Co. Inc.* (*The Galatia*) [1980] 1 W.L.R. 495 (where the contract expressly provided for payment, "ship lost or not lost"); *Leigh & Sillavan Ltd v Aliakmon Shipping Co. Ltd* (*The Aliakmon*) [1986] A.C. 785 at p.808. See also above, para.19–001 , 19–006, 19–037, and 19–124; below. Where the buyer deals as consumer (see above, para.18–259), the goods "remain at the seller's risk until they are delivered to the consumer": Sale of Goods Act 1979, s.20(4). For the difficulties which can arise in applying this subsection to c.i.f. contracts, see above, paras 18–260 to 18–264.
[44] *Law and Bonar v British American Tobacco Co. Ltd*, above; *Manbré Saccharine Co. Ltd v Corn Products Co. Ltd* [1919] 1 K.B. 198 at p.203.
[45] [1915] 1 K.B. 316.

German cruiser on August 6 and sunk. Later, on August 20, the seller in London tendered an invoice, and was admittedly able to tender the other documents, relating to the 25 bales. The next day, news of the loss of the *City of Winchester* reached London. It was held that the buyer was bound to pay the price, even though he had no right of action either against the carrier or against the underwriter.[46] The position would have been the same if at the time of tender of documents the seller had known that the ship had been sunk.[47]

Provision in the contract as to loss. The buyer's duty to pay in spite of the loss of the goods can be excluded by the provisions of the contract. A provision merely for payment "against documents on arrival of steamer"[48] will probably not have this effect, being construed as a stipulation as to the time of payment only.[49] Thus if the ship is lost payment will have to be made against documents when she would normally have arrived.[50] On the other hand, where the contract provided for payment of half the price against documents and the other half on delivery of the goods at the agreed destination, it was held that the seller had a valid claim only in respect of such part of the goods as actually arrived.[51] The general rule that the buyer must pay on tender of documents is most clearly excluded by a provision that "should the goods or any portion thereof not arrive from loss of vessel . . . this contract to be void". The effect of such a provision is that after loss the seller is not bound to tender, nor the buyer to accept, the documents. But once performance has been completed by the buyer's taking up the documents, the seller cannot rely on the provision to claim that he, and not the buyer, is entitled to the benefit of the insurance.[52] 19–081

Can seller appropriate goods already lost? A c.i.f. buyer is clearly bound to pay the price where goods are sold, appropriated to the contract, and then lost before tender of documents.[53] On the other hand, he is not bound 19–082

---

[46] Clause 4 of the contract of sale provided that, should the goods not arrive from loss of the vessel, tender of an insurance policy and other documents "*which will enable the buyer to recover* the amount of the insurance . . . shall be deemed a good tender of the goods so not arriving." In spite of what is said at p.325, this seems (by reason of the words here italicised) to go beyond the normal requirements of a c.i.f. contract; but in effect clause 4 was construed subject to the war risks provision in the contract.

[47] *Manbré Saccharine Co. Ltd v Corn Products Ltd*, above. For the position under the Vienna Convention on Contracts for the International Sale of Goods (above, para.1–024), see *infra*, nn. 53, 54 and below, para.19–083, n.82).

[48] As in *Stein, Forbes & Co. v County Tailoring Co.* (1916) 115 L.T. 215.

[49] Above, para.19–075.

[50] *cf. Fragano v Long* (1825) 4 B. & C. 219. The actual dispute in that case was between buyer and carrier.

[51] *Dupont v British South Africa Co.* (1901) 18 T.L.R. 24; *cf. Polenghi v Dried Milk Co. Ltd* (1904) 10 Com.Cas. 42.

[52] *Karinjee Javinjee & Co. v William F Malcolm & Co.* (1926) 25 Ll.L.R. 28; and see above, para.19–006.

[53] Above, para.19–080. The position is the same under the provisions as to the passing of risk in the Vienna Convention on Contracts for the International Sale of Goods (above, para.1–024) both where the contract is for the sale of goods to be shipped (Art. 67) and where it is for the sale of goods afloat (Art. 68). See further n.54, *infra* and below, para.19–083, n.82.

to pay where the goods which the seller has purported to appropriate to the contract had already been lost at the time of contracting, at any rate where they are specific.[54] There is, however, an intermediate situation which gives rise to a difficult problem which has never been squarely faced in the cases. This arises where goods are lost after the conclusion of the contract but before a purported appropriation. Is the seller in such a case entitled to appropriate the goods which have already been lost, or must the appropriation have been made *before* the loss? C.i.f. contracts are often sales of goods which are unascertained in the sense of being simply generic goods; and where such goods are sold otherwise than on c.i.f. terms, the general rule is that a seller who has not yet appropriated any goods to the contract is not entitled to rely on the fact that the particular goods which he *intended* to appropriate to the contract have been destroyed. If his intention in this respect is defeated, he must appropriate other goods of the contract description to the contract.[55] Prima facie this principle would appear to apply where goods which a c.i.f. seller intends to appropriate to the contract are lost before he has done so. Yet in *C Groom Ltd v Barber*[56] (the facts of which are stated in paragraph 19–080 above) Atkin J. assumed that there had been no appropriation; and he said: "The seller must be in a position to pass property by the bill of lading if the goods are in existence, but he need not have appropriated the particular goods in the particular bill of lading until the moment of tender."[57] The reference to property in the opening words of this passage suggests that Atkin J. had in mind "appropriation" in its "proprietary" sense,[58] and this would not normally take place under a c.i.f. contract until documents had been tendered by the seller and taken up by the buyer.[59] But the question raised by the case was whether the seller had "appropriated" the goods in the "contractual" sense of

[54] *Couturier v Hastie* (1856) 5 H.L.C. 673. The same rule would apply if the goods were not specific or ascertained because they consisted of a specified quantity forming an undifferentiated part of a larger bulk, the whole of which was destroyed: see above, para.1–124; and *cf.* below, para.19–113. The position is generally the same under Vienna Convention on Contracts for the International Sale of Goods (above, para.1–024), Art. 68, first sentence (risk passing from the time of the conclusion of the contract); but under Art. 68 second sentence risk may pass from the time when the goods were handed over to the first carrier "if the circumstances so indicate." The meaning of this phrase is obscure; it refers most obviously to special agreement excluding the normal rule stated in Art. 68, first sentence; but it could also refer to the rule that under a c.i.f. contract risk can pass as from *shipment* (below, para.19–110), and extend that rule so that risk can pass from *delivery to the carrier*. Even if such "circumstances" are present, the third sentence of Art. 68 would probably, on facts such as those in *Couturier v Hastie*, lead to the same result as that reached in that case: it puts the risk on the seller if at the time of contracting he "knew or ought to have known that the goods had been lost and did not disclose this to the buyer." The English cases do not seem to regard the seller's knowledge, or means of knowledge, as relevant in the present context.

[55] Above, paras 6–004, 6–041.

[56] [1915] 1 K.B. 316.

[57] At p.324; *cf. Arnhold Karberg & Co. v Blythe, Green, Jourdain & Co.* [1915] 2 K.B. 379 at p.387 (affirmed [1916] 1 K.B. 495).

[58] For the various senses of "appropriation" see above, paras 18–210, 19–015, 19–016.

[59] Below, para.19–103.

binding himself contractually to deliver particular goods or goods forming an undifferentiated part of a particular bulk cargo, or to deliver documents relating to such goods. An "appropriation" of this kind depends, as we have seen,[60] primarily on the intention of the seller (who must not merely intend to deliver the goods or documents relating to them, but to bind himself contractually to do so); and in *C Groom Ltd v Barber*[61] there was evidence in the correspondence[62] relating to insurance, that the seller had appropriated *some* shipment (and it seems likely that he intended to appropriate *the* shipment which was lost) to the contract. In this sense, therefore, he could be said to have "appropriated" the goods on the *City of Winchester* before they were lost. Even such evidence was lacking in *Manbreé Saccharine Corporation v Corn Products Ltd*[63] where the first communication concerning the shipment was sent off by the sellers after the ship had been sunk; and it was held that the buyer would not have been entitled to reject proper documents[64] on the ground that the goods had been lost "prior to *actual tender* of documents".[65] The question whether the goods had been lost before *appropriation* was not discussed; and it may be possible to infer from certain passages in the report,[66] that this question did not arise as the case was one in which the seller had bound himself contractually to deliver the particular goods or documents relating to them, simply by the act of shipping the goods in performance of the contract.[67] In the absence of clear authority to the contrary, it is submitted that a c.i.f. seller of unascertained generic goods is not entitled to the price, if the goods have been lost in transit, unless at the time of loss he had appropriated them to the contract in the sense of binding himself contractually to deliver, or tender documents relating to, the particular goods which have been lost, or to a quantity out of the particular bulk of which they form a part. For the reasons stated in paragraph 19–083 below, there seems to be no good ground why this rule, which normally applies to sales of unascertained goods, should not apply to c.i.f. contracts.

Balance of convenience. In *Re Olympia Oil and Cake Co. and Produce Brokers Co.*[68] a contract for the sale of 6,000 tons of soyabeans provided that particulars of shipment were "to be declared by original sellers", and that "in case of resales, copy of original appropriation to be accepted by buyers . . ." The sellers bought an equivalent amount from their suppliers who declared a shipment on the *Canterbury*, and the sellers appropriated **19–083**

---

[60] Above, para.18–210.
[61] Above, n.56.
[62] *i.e.* the seller's letter of August 3: see above, para.19–080.
[63] [1919] 1 K.B. 198.
[64] In fact, the seller failed to tender a proper insurance document: see above, para.19–042.
[65] [1919] 1 K.B. 198 at p.203 (italics supplied).
[66] *e.g.* at p.203: "If the vendor fulfils his contract by shipping the appropriate goods . . ." For other dicta referring, in this context, to "appropriation" by shipment see, for example, *Arnhold Karberg & Co. v Blythe, Green, Jourdain & Co.* [1915] 2 K.B. 379 at pp.387–388; affirmed [1916] 1 K.B. 495.
[67] Above, para.19–016.
[68] [1915] 1 K.B. 233; reversed. on proof of contrary custom [1916] 1 A.C. 314.

this shipment to their contract with the buyers after the *Canterbury* had, to their knowledge, been lost. The Divisional Court held that the appropriation after knowledge of the loss was not an effective one. The decision was later doubted by Scrutton L.J., who said[69]: "My own strong impression is that on the true meaning of this contract . . . where a seller under the contract has received an appropriation from an original buyer,[70] this clause binds the buyer under that contract to accept the declaration whether the cargo is lost or not." This criticism is based on the particular terms of the contract and not on any general principle as to the effectiveness of appropriation after loss. In view of this, and of the fact that the contract was, in spite of a dictum to the contrary,[71] not a c.i.f. contract,[72] neither the decision of the Divisional Court nor the subsequent criticisms of it afford any safe guide to the solution of the general problem of the effectiveness of appropriation after loss under c.i.f. contracts. Rowlatt J. pointed out that to allow appropriation after loss might lead to some strange results. "Pushed to its logical conclusion, this would involve that the person in whose hands the ship was lost could afterwards enter into a contract to sell a cargo, and, if the price fell, buy a cargo and tender it and pocket the difference; and, if the price rose, tender the lost ship and escape from the speculation without loss."[73] Although the dictum refers to the case of goods lost before the conclusion of the contract, exactly the same result would follow if a c.i.f. seller had, as a matter of law, a general right to appropriate goods after loss. To be able to sell on c.i.f. terms, he would have to be in a position to pass on the benefit of an insurance policy. Hence if the market rose (or if the policy did not cover the loss)[74] he would appropriate and tender the lost shipment. But he would not be bound to do this, so that, if the market fell and the policy did cover the loss, he could buy another shipment below the contract price, tender that, and claim the insurance (which would normally be based on the contract price[75]) on the original (lost) shipment.[76] It was this possibility that Rowlatt J. sought to eliminate in the passage quoted.

A c.i.f. seller may, of course, also suffer hardship through *not* being entitled to appropriate goods already lost: for example, a seller in a "string" of contracts might be liable to his supplier for goods appropriated by the latter *before* loss, without being able to acquire any rights against the buyer by passing on that appropriation *after* loss. But he can expressly guard

[69] *Produce Brokers Co. Ltd v Olympia Oil Co. Ltd* [1917] 1 K.B. 320 at pp.329–330; *cf. Clark v Cox, McEuen & Co.* [1921] 1 K.B. 139 at pp.142–143, 146.
[70] *Sic.* "Seller" would make better sense and the reports in 33 T.L.R. 95 at p.96 and [1916–1917] All E.R. Rep. 753 at p.756 are to this effect.
[71] [1915] 1 K.B. 233 at p.237.
[72] *Manbré Saccharine Co. Ltd v Corn Products Co. Ltd* [1919] 1 K.B. 198 at p.201; *Clark v Cox, McEuen & Co.*, above n.69, at p.142.
[73] [1915] 1 K.B. 233 at p.239, Rowlatt J. contemplates the sale of "a cargo"—not of "the cargo", which would be specific goods.
[74] *e.g.* because war risks were excluded: *cf.* above, para.19–046.
[75] Above, para.19–051.
[76] It is true that any seller of unascertained goods could, in a falling market, buy goods other than those which he had originally intended to tender, and tender those other goods; but where the goods which he had originally intended to tender had *not* been destroyed he would have no incentive to do so, since he would then be left holding those goods and thus suffer the market loss in respect of them.

against such a risk by the terms of his contract with the buyer, *e.g.* by a provision to the effect that, if the goods were lost before the seller had given a notice of appropriation, the seller was nevertheless (after such notice) to tender shipping documents and the buyer to pay.[77] This seems also to have been the purpose of the provision in the *Olympia Oil* case,[78] that a copy of the original appropriation was to be accepted by the buyers; and so far as the interpretation of the actual contract is concerned the view of Scrutton L.J. is, with respect, to be preferred to the decision of the Divisional Court. The contract in *C Groom Ltd v Barber*[79] contained a similar provision.[80] Any hardship which the buyer may then suffer in consequence of having to pay for lost goods can in turn be alleviated by provisions in the contract excluding his liability to pay where the vessel carrying the goods is lost.[81] There being thus well-known ways of allocating the risk of such loss by the terms of the contract, it is submitted that the balance of convenience does not, in the absence of such express provisions for the benefit of either party, favour any general rule allowing appropriation after loss under c.i.f. contracts.[82]

Appropriation of deteriorated goods. The remarks of Rowlatt J. quoted in paragraph 19–083 above apply only where a seller purports to appropriate goods which have been lost. Where the goods have merely deteriorated after shipment but before appropriation, the seller is entitled to appropriate the deteriorated goods in reliance on the rule that the risk of deterioration 19–084

---

[77] As in *PT Putrabi Adyamulia v Société Est Epices (The Intan 6 V 360A SN)* [2003] 2 Lloyd's Rep. 700 (see clause 11 of the contract, set out at [7]; the sale was on c.i.f. terms).

[78] [1915] 1 K.B. 233, above, n.68.

[79] [1915] 1 K.B. 316.

[80] Clause 5.

[81] See above, para.19–081 after n.51.

[82] *Contra*, Feltham [1975] J.B.L. 273, arguing that appropriation after loss should be permissible so long as at the time of contracting the seller did not both know of the loss and intend to appropriate the lost goods to the contract. The Vienna Convention on Contracts for the International Sale of Goods (above, para.1–024) distinguishes for the present purpose between cases in which the goods have at the time of contracting not yet been handed over to the first carrier and those in which they are at that time already "in transit." In the first situation, risk cannot pass until the goods have been "clearly identified to the contract" (Art. 67(2)): this excludes the possibility of appropriation after loss. In the second, risk generally passes to the buyer "from the conclusion of the contract" (Art. 68, first sentence) and may "if the circumstances so indicate" pass even earlier, *viz.* from the time when the goods were handed over to the carrier (Art. 68, second sentence). Under Art. 68, there is no requirement of prior "identification". It follows that where the goods are already afloat at the time of contracting the seller can appropriate goods subsequently lost. For the position where the goods sold in transit were lost *before* the time of contracting and the seller at that time knew or ought to have known of the loss, see Art. 68, third sentence (above, para.19–082, n.54). In the United States, U.C.C., s.2–509 Comment 2 makes appropriation after loss ineffective "aside from special agreement". This phrase seems to refer to provisions of the kind discussed at n.80 above; the Comment is not reproduced in the proposed (2003) version of U.C.C Art. 2. Under the Vienna Convention, such a provision would be effective by virtue of Art. 6 to "derogate from or vary" the requirement of "identification" stated in Art. 67(2) above.

generally passes on *or as from* shipment[83] under a c.i.f. contract. There are two practical considerations which justify this difference in the rules relating to lost and deteriorated goods. In the first place, where goods have merely deteriorated after shipment but before appropriation, the situation described by Rowlatt J. would not arise. If the market fell, the seller would be left with the original cargo, which would itself have declined in value by reason of the fall in the market. In respect of this loss, the seller would not be covered by insurance: this would extend only to the loss resulting from the deterioration. Thus the situation would not be one in which he was proof against loss whether the market rose or fell. Secondly, the time at which goods are lost is generally easier to establish than that of deterioration, which is commonly not discovered till after the goods have arrived at their destination. It will often be impossible to show whether the deterioration occurred before or after appropriation; so that a rule to the effect that a c.i.f. seller could not appropriate goods which had already deteriorated would be open to the objection that it would give rise to insurmountable difficulties of proof.

19–085 **Time of payment.** Although normally payment is due on tender of documents, the time of payment may be deferred by the terms of the contract, *e.g.* until arrival of steamer.[84] Conversely, the time may be accelerated, *e.g.* by a provision that payment is to be made against a letter of indemnity in case of delay in obtaining the documents.[85] Even where the contract contains no express stipulation as to time of payment, the buyer is not in breach merely because he does not pay immediately on tender of documents. It is enough for him to pay within a reasonable time of such tender.[86] Where the contract provides for payment by banker's commercial credit, problems may arise as to the time when the credit is to be made available.[87] These are discussed in Chapter 23.

19–086 **Place of payment.** According to a dictum in *Rein v Stein*[88] payment must be made at the seller's place of business, on the principle that a debtor must seek out his creditor. But this is probably not an inflexible rule in the case of c.i.f. contracts. Problems as to the precise place of payment under such contracts do not seem to be common; though problems may arise for

---

[83] Below, paras 19–110, 19–112; as to risk of total loss, see para.19–113. Arts 67 and 68 of the Vienna Convention on Contracts for the International Sale of Goods (above, para.1–024), apply to cases of deterioration no less than to cases of loss; but in practice the third sentence of Art. 68 (which leaves the risk of goods sold in transit on the seller where at the time of contracting he knew or ought to have known that the goods had been lost or damaged) is unlikely to apply to cases of mere deterioration since the seller will usually have no knowledge (actual or imputed) of deterioration before the end of the transit.

[84] Above, paras 19–069, 19–074.

[85] As in *Gatoil International Inc. v Tradax Petroleum Ltd* (*The Rio Sun*) [1985] 1 Lloyd's Rep. 351; *Enichem Anic SpA v Ampelos Shipping Co. Ltd* (*The Delfini*) [1990] 1 Lloyd's Rep. 252.

[86] *Ryan v Ridley* (1902) 8 Com.Cas. 105.

[87] Below, para.23–088.

[88] [1892] 1 Q.B. 753 at p.758.

jurisdictional purposes as to the country in which payment is to be made.[89] For these purposes the factors already considered in relation to the place of tender of documents[90] are, it is submitted, also applicable (*mutatis mutandis*) to the place of payment.

Method of payment. Contractual stipulations as to the method of payment must, as a general rule, be strictly performed.[91] This is, for example, true where the contract stipulates for payment by banker's commercial credit: strict compliance is required with the contractual stipulations as to the type of credit to be provided, and as to the time and place at which it is to be provided.[92] The same would be true where the buyer undertook to provide a bank guarantee by a specified time, or on the occurrence of a specified event.[93] 19–087

Other payments to be made by buyer. A c.i.f. buyer may, by the terms of the contract, be obliged to pay for items which do not, strictly speaking, form part of the price, such as demurrage,[94] the cost of stevedoring, or import duty.[95] Such undertakings are often be construed as promises to indemnify the seller.[96] Thus where the buyer undertook to pay to the seller demurrage "as per charterparty" or "at the rates indicated in the charterparty" it was held that he was under no liability if by the terms of the charterparty the seller was not liable for demurrage[97]; and where he undertook to pay "the cost of stevedoring" this was held to mean such part of that cost as is not borne by the ship.[98] But a provision in the contract of sale for payment of demurrage "as per charter-party" may also give rise to "an independent and free standing right"[99] to such a payment; and where this was the position it was held that the buyer could not rely as against the seller on an "ancillary"[1] provision in the charterparty, such as a term 19–088

---

[89] See above, para.19–008. For the currency in which payment must be made, see below, paras 25–165 *et seq*.

[90] Above, para.19–069.

[91] *cf.* below, para.19–207, and see *ibid.* for qualifications of the rule in case of trivial discrepancies between the credit required by the contract of sale and that actually provided.

[92] Below, paras 23–083 *et seq.*; *Nichimen Corp. v Gatoil Overseas Inc.* [1987] 2 Lloyd's Rep. 46.

[93] *e.g. Enichem Anic SpA v Ampelos Shipping Co. Ltd (the Delfini)* [1990] 1 Lloyd's Rep. 252 (bank guarantee to be opened not later than nomination of vessel).

[94] As in *R Pagnan & F. lli v Lebanese Organisation for International Commerce (The Caloric)* [1981] 2 Lloyd's Rep. 675.

[95] *cf. American Commerce Co. Ltd v Frederick Boehm Ltd* (1919) 35 T.L.R. 224.

[96] *cf. D I Henry Ltd v Wilhelm G. Clasen* [1973] 1 Lloyd's Rep. 159.

[97] *Suzuki & Co. v Companhia Mercantile Internacional* (1921) 8 Ll.L.R. 174; 9 Ll.L.R. 171; *Malozzi v Carapelli SpA* [1976] 1 Lloyd's Rep. 407 (but on such facts the buyer might be liable in damages for delay).

[98] *White v Williams* [1912] A.C. 814.

[99] *OK Petroleum AB v Vitol Energy SA* [1995] 2 Lloyd's Rep. 160 at p.164.

[1] *ibid.*, p.168, where it was also said that the charterparty was concluded only *after* the contract of sale; but this is often the position where goods are sold on c.i.f. terms and is therefore not the decisive factor in precluding the incorporation into the sale contract of charterparty terms: see *Ceval Alimentos SA v Agrimpex Trading Co. Ltd (The Northern Progress) (No.2)* [1996] 2 Lloyd's Rep. 319 at p.327 (where incorporation of a charterparty term into the contract of sale failed on the different ground that the term in question would have allowed tender of a bill of lading that was not "usual" and "customary" within the rule stated in para.19–024, above.

limiting the time within which notice of claims for demurrage had to be given. The question whether the demurrage provisions in the sale contract "operate by way of indemnity [to the seller] or give rise to an independent obligation"[2] is one of construction in each case, depending "on the context and wording of particular provisions."[3] Factors supporting the "independent obligation" view are that the contract of sale was made "independently of and without knowledge of the charterparty"[4] and that the contract covered several shipments, likely to be made under different charterparties. Where an undertaking to pay demurrage gives rise to such an independent right, it may on its true construction provide either more, or less, than an indemnity. Thus on the one hand in *Houlder Brothers & Co. Ltd v Commissioners of Public Works*[5] the buyer undertook in the contract of sale to pay demurrage to the seller at a specified rate. It was held that he was bound to pay at that rate even though the rate at which the seller had to pay demurrage to the carrier was lower. On the other hand, in *Etablissements Soules et Cie. v Intertradex SA*[6] a c.i.f contract specified the rate at which the goods were to be discharged and went on to provide for demurrage at a specified daily rate, without making any reference to the charterparty. It was held that, on the true construction of this provision, demurrage began to run against the buyer under the contract of sale only from the time when the vessel berthed, even though it might have begun to run against the seller as charterer under the charterparty from the earlier time of the vessel's arrival at the port of discharge. Similarly, demurrage will not be payable by the buyer at the charterparty rate if the contract of sale expressly provides that he is to pay demurrage at a *maximum* rate which is below that specified in the charterparty.[7] Nor is demurrage payable by the buyer if the delay in unloading is due to the seller's breach of the contract of sale, *e.g.* in providing a ship which cannot enter the port of discharge specified in that contract without first being lightened.[8]

Where a c.i.f. contract provided for the buyer to pay demurrage "to the extent that the same can be recovered from" the terminal operator at the port of destination (to whom the goods had been resold) the contract was held to impose a duty on the buyer so to recover the demurrage.[9] The buyer was accordingly held liable to the seller for the demurrage, in spite of having failed, after only "desultory"[10] efforts, to recover it from the terminal operator.

---

[2] *Fal Oil Co. Ltd. v Petronas Trading Corp (The Devon)* [2004] EWCA Civ. 822, [2004] 2 Lloyd's Rep. 282 at [27].
[3] *ibid.*, at [42]; in this case there was a difference of judicial opinion on the point.
[4] *ibid.*, at [43].
[5] [1908] A.C. 276; *cf. French Government v S Sanday & Co. Ltd* (1923) 16 Ll.L.R. 238; and see *S L Sethia Liners Ltd v State Trading Corp. of India* [1986] 1 Lloyd's Rep. 31 and *R. Pagnan & Fratelli v Finagrain* (*The Adolph Leonhart*) [1986] 2 Lloyd's Rep. 395 for similar problems under f.o.b. contracts.
[6] [1991] 1 Lloyd's Rep. 379.
[7] *Gill & Duffus SA v Rionda Futures Ltd* [1994] 2 Lloyd's Rep. 67.
[8] *Eurico SpA v Philipp Brothers* (*The Epaphus*) [1987] 2 Lloyd's Rep. 387.
[9] *Galaxy Energy International Ltd v Bayoil SA* [2001] 1 All E.R. (Comm.) 289.
[10] *ibid.*, at 291, [7].

(b) *Other Duties*

19–089 **Other duties imposed by contract.** A c.i.f. contract may impose various other duties on the buyer. For example, it may impose on him a duty to discharge the cargo at a specified rate; and failure to perform this duty will make him liable to the seller for any demurrage which the latter has to pay in consequence of the delay.[11]

Where a c.i.f. contract specifies several possible destinations, the buyer must notify the seller of his choice of destination. Normally the notice must reach the seller within a reasonable time before the beginning of the shipment period, so as to enable the seller to ship the goods (if he so wishes) on the first day of that period.[12] But the strictness of this requirement was modified where the seller had already chartered a ship to carry the goods and the choice of destinations given to the buyer under the contract of sale was no wider than that given to the seller under the charterparty. In these circumstances it was held that the buyer need only notify the seller of his choice of destination within such time that the vessel could go without delay straight to that destination.[13] If the buyer fails to notify the seller of his choice of destination within the time required by these rules, the seller is entitled to rescind the contract.[14] If the buyer makes a choice which is invalid because the chosen port has become an enemy port, a subsequent valid declaration, made in time, will be effective.[15]

In general, duties to be performed by the buyer before the goods can be shipped must prima facie be performed before the beginning of the shipment period; but where a c.i.f. contract for the sale of iron to be shipped in May and June required the buyer to give the specification "in the beginning of May" it was held that performance of this duty before the middle of May was in time; and that the seller was accordingly not entitled to refuse to ship.[16]

Any duties to which the buyer may be subject with respect to the rate at which the goods are to be discharged is normally owed to the carrier, *e.g.* where the buyer acquires rights and becomes subject to liabilities under the contract of carriage by virtue of the Carriage of Goods by Sea Act 1992,[17] or under an implied contract at common law.[18] Where the buyer's liability to the carrier is incurred as a result of the seller's failure to perform one of his obligations under the contract of sale, the buyer is prima facie entitled to recover from the seller any payments which he has to make the carrier (*e.g.* by way of demurrage). But there would be no such entitlement where the buyer had himself failed to perform a condition precedent to the per-

---

[11] *Acada Chemicals Ltd v Empresa Nacional Pesquera SA* [1994] 1 Lloyd's Rep. 428.

[12] *Tsakiroglou & Co. Ltd v Transgrains SA* [1958] 1 Lloyd's Rep. 562; *cf.* above, para.19–013.

[13] *Gatoil International Inc. v Tradax Petroleum Ltd* (*The Rio Sun*) [1985] 1 Lloyd's Rep. 351 at p.359.

[14] See *The Rio Sun*, n.13, above.

[15] *Hindley & Co. Ltd v General Fibre Co. Ltd* [1940] 2 K.B. 517.

[16] *Kidston & Co. v Monceau Ironworks Co. Ltd* (1902) 7 Com.Cas. 82.

[17] Above, paras 18–102, *et seq.*

[18] Above, paras 18–138, *et seq.*

formance of the obligation in question by the seller,[19] *e.g.* where the delay resulted from the buyer's failure to perform a stipulation as to the time at which a letter of credit was to be provided by him.[20] It is, finally, possible for a c.i.f. contract to provide that a duty to unload the goods within a stipulated time is to be owed by the buyer to the seller and so to be enforceable by the seller by way either of unliquidated damages or of demurrage.[21]

4. CONTRACTUAL RELATIONS WITH CARRIER

19–090 **Introductory.** Two questions concerning the contractual relations of the parties to a c.i.f. contract with the carrier of the goods form the subject-matter of the following discussion. The first is whether it is the seller or the buyer who is an original party to the contract of carriage (or to some other related contract) with the carrier. The second is what the effect is on this original contractual relationship of the seller's tender of, and the buyer's taking up, documents in the performance of their duties under the contract of sale; it will here be assumed that those documents include a bill of lading. This second question is one of considerable complexity as the answers to it may depend partly on the Carriage of Goods by Sea Act 1992 and partly on the Contracts (Rights of Third Parties) Act 1999. In particular, a number of problems arise under the 1999 Act from what we have called the subsection 6(5) exception[22] in the latter Act.

19–091 **Seller named as shipper.** In the case of a c.i.f. sale, the original contract of carriage contained in or evidenced by the bill of lading will normally be between seller and carrier or, where goods are sold afloat, between a previous shipper and the carrier. Indeed, in the case of such a sale afloat, there can be no question of the buyer's being an original party to that contract since at the time of its conclusion and in all probability at the time of the issue of the bill of lading the buyer's identity will not be known. The buyer will then acquire rights under the contract of carriage in one of the ways discussed in Chapter 18, *i.e.* typically by becoming the lawful holder of the bill of lading[23]; or by being the person identified as the person to whom the carrier has undertaken to deliver the goods in a ship's delivery order given under or for the purposes of the bill of lading contract[24]; or, where the contract of carriage is contained in or evidenced by a sea waybill, as the person to whom delivery under that contract is to be made.[25] There is the further possibility of the seller's having acted as agent for the buyer so that

[19] Such a situation is more likely to arise where the sale is on f.o.b., than where it is on c.i.f., terms: see *Kronos Worldwide Ltd v Sempra Oil Trading SARL* [2004] EWCA Civ. 3, [2004] 1 All E.R. (Comm.) 915, below para.20–019.
[20] As in the *Kronos* case, above n.19.
[21] *Establissements Soules et Cie. v Intertradex SA* [1991] 1 Lloyd's Rep. 379.
[22] Above, para.18–005 sub-paragraph (f).
[23] Carriage of Goods by Sea Act 1992, s.2(1)(a).
[24] *ibid.*, s.2(1)(c).
[25] *ibid.*, s.2(1)(b).

the latter, though not named as a party to the contract of carriage, becomes a party to it.[26] But this reasoning would be hard to apply to the case of a sale afloat (since in such a case the identity of the buyer will at the relevant time be unknown, so that it will be highly unlikely that the seller intended to act on his behalf, even as an undisclosed principal). Even if the sale is of goods to be shipped to a buyer whose identity is known at the time of shipment, one circumstance which can give rise to an inference of agency for the present purpose will normally be absent. That circumstance is the fact that the property in the goods to be carried is—when the contract of carriage is made—vested, not in the shipper named in the bill, but in another person (typically the consignee).[27] This will not normally be the position under a c.i.f. contract, under which, as a general rule, property passes only when the buyer pays the price on tender of documents.[28] To avoid confusion, it should be emphasised that our present concern is with the identification of the original party to the contract of carriage who occupies that role by virtue of being the *shipper* under that contract. A person is not an original party to the contract of carriage by virtue of being named in the bill of lading as the *consignee* to whose order the goods are to be delivered.[29] This point is made clear by the rule that the mere fact of a person's being so named does not deprive the shipper of the right to redirect the goods to another person[30]; and this rule applies also where goods are shipped under a sea waybill.[31]

Contracts (Rights of Third Parties) Act 1999. In the normal case of a c.i.f. contract, the situation is that described in paragraph 19–091 above, so that it is the seller who is the original party to the contract of carriage; the buyer will later acquire rights under that contract by virtue of the operation of the Carriage of Goods by Sea Act 1992. Such a case falls squarely within the subsection 6(5) exception[32] to the 1999 Act. This subsection provides that "Section 1 confers no rights on the third party in the case of (a) a contract for the carriage of goods by sea . . .".[33] The last eight words refer in the first place to a contract which is "contained in or evidenced by a bill of lading"[34]—an expression which here has "the same meaning as in the Carriage of Goods by Sea Act 1992".[35] The same definition applies (*mutatis mutandis*) where the contract of carriage is contained in or evidenced by a 19–092

[26] *cf.* above, para.18–065.
[27] See *Texas Instruments Ltd v Nason (Europe) Ltd* [1991] 1 Lloyd's Rep. 146 where the fact that the consignee was owner of the goods was relied on to support the inference that the consignor had acted as the consignee's agent for the purpose of making a contract for the carriage of the goods by land.
[28] Below, paras 19–118, 19–123.
[29] See (in the case of f.o.b. contracts) para.20–067, below.
[30] *i.e.*, under the rule in *Mitchell v Ede* (1840) 1 Ad & El.888, above, paras 18–021 to 18–024.
[31] Above paras 18–025 to 18–026.
[32] Above, para.18–005, sub-paragraph (f).
[33] Subsection 6(5)(a).
[34] Subsection 6(6)(a) ("or a corresponding electronic transaction": see Carriage of Goods by Sea Act 1992, s.1(5)).
[35] 1999 Act, subsection 6(7)(a); the 1992 Act (above) does not actually *define* "bill of lading".

sea waybill which identifies the buyer as the person to whom delivery is to be made[36] and where the contract of carriage is one under or for the purposes of which a "ship's delivery order" is given, *e.g.* where the seller, for the purpose of performing his obligations under the contract of sale, procures such an order (as defined by the 1992 Act) identifying the buyer as the person to whom the carrier has undertaken to deliver the goods.[37] In all these cases, the buyer will get rights of suit against the carrier under the contract of carriage if the requirements laid down in the 1992 Act for the acquisition of such rights are satisfied.[38] If those requirements are not satisfied, he will not get any such rights either under the 1992 Act or under section 1 of the 1999 Act. Equally, the extinction, by the virtue of section 2(5) of the 1992 Act, of the seller's rights as an original party to the contract of carriage (on their transfer to the buyer) is not affected by section 4 of the 1999 Act[39]: the effect of the latter section is that "section 1" of the 1999 Act (*i.e.* the acquisition of rights by the third party *under that section*) will not affect the promisee's rights of enforcement. This provision therefore does not apply where "section 1" is excluded (by subsection 6(5)) and the third party has acquired rights under the contract of carriage by virtue of some *other* rules of law (such as those contained in the 1992 Act).

19–093 **Other person named as shipper.** It is possible, if unusual, for a bill of lading issued in respect of goods sold on c.i.f. terms to name the buyer as shipper. The reported cases contain few examples of this practice and no judicial discussion of the legal relationships which flow from it. One example of it is provided by *Hansson v Hamel & Horley Ltd*,[40] where the buyers were named as shippers in the bill of lading "in accordance with a stipulation they had made"[41]—presumably in the contract of sale. The purpose of this stipulation is far from clear and was not in issue in *Hansson's* case. In two respects, naming the buyers as shippers placed them in a better position than that in which they would have been in the more usual situation in which the bill named the sellers as shippers: being original parties to the bill, they could have asserted rights against the carrier under the contract contained in or evidenced by it without having to show that the conditions for the transfer of such rights (then laid down in the Bills of Lading Act 1855) were satisfied[42]; and under a bill which named the buyer as shipper, the seller would not have the normal shipper's right to redirect

---

[36] 1999 Act, subsections 6(5), 6(6)(a), 6(7)(a) and 1992 Act, ss.1(3), 5(3). For "corresponding electronic transactions", see n.34 above.
[37] 1999 Act, subsections 6(5), 6(6)(b), 6(7)(a) and 1992 Act, ss.1(4), 5(3). For "corresponding electronic transactions", see n.34 above.
[38] For a full discussion of these requirements, see above, paras 18–101 *et seq*.
[39] See above para.18–005, sub-paragraph (h).
[40] [1922] 2 A.C. 36.
[41] *ibid.*, p.43.
[42] In particular, they were not affected by the "property gap" in the Bills of Lading Act 1855, s.1 (above, para.18–100); and, although this gap has now been closed by the Carriage of Goods by Sea Act 1992 (above, para.18–101) it could still be to the buyer's advantage not to be affected by the restrictions placed by the 1992 Act on the acquisition of rights under the contract of carriage by a person who is not an original party to that contract.

the goods.[43] In another respect, the position of the buyers was less favourable than it would have been if they had been transferees of the bill from a seller named in it as shipper: as Lord Sumner pointed out, since the buyers were named as shippers "no question arises of any estoppel as against the carriers in favour of persons taking the bill of lading by endorsement and on the faith of the statements recited in it".[44] It is, in fact, not at all easy to see why a c.i.f. buyer should wish to have the bill made out in his own name as shipper. This form of bill of lading certainly does not amount to a relinquishment by the seller of his "right of disposal"[45] so as to result in the passing of property to the buyer. Lord Sumner refers in this context to the point that "the insertion of the consignee's name in the bill of lading" does not negative the intention of the seller to reserve the "jus disponendi"[46]; though the case to which he refers in this context[47] was one in which the consignee's name was so inserted, not as that of the shipper, but as that of the person to whose order delivery of the goods was to be made. A buyer may well wish to have the bill made out in the latter way so as to facilitate subsales, but the insertion of his name *as shipper* is scarcely necessary for this purpose. The balance of advantage to the buyer in being named as shipper is far from clear; and perhaps this is one reason why bills of lading taken out for the purpose of performing c.i.f. contracts do not seem commonly to be made out in this way.

Rejection of bill not naming seller as shipper. The bill of lading in *Hansson's* case was rejected by the buyers on the ground that it did not provide the continuous documentary cover to which they were entitled under the c.i.f. contract.[48] This rejection was held to have been justified, though later a compromise was reached by which the buyers took up the shipping documents "relating to the bulk of the goods".[49] From the decision of the House of Lords it is, however, clear that the buyers were not bound to take up any of the documents and the discussion that follows will be based on the assumption that they had maintained their original rejection of them all. The question could then have arisen on what legal basis the sellers could have maintained an action against the carriers for any breach of the contract of carriage.[50] As the law then stood, they could certainly not have done so as indorsees of the bill; for even if there had been such an indorsement, the requirement of section 1 of the Bills of Lading Act 1855 that, in order for the indorsement to transfer contractual rights, property 19–094

[43] Above, para.19–091 at n.30.
[44] [1922] 2 A.C. 36 at p.44; for such estoppels (the scope of which has been considerably extended by legislation since *Hansson's* case) see above, paras 18–028 *et seq*.
[45] Within Sale of Goods Act 1979, s.18, r. 5: see above, para.19–100; *cf.* above, para.18–214.
[46] [1922] 2 A.C. 36 at p.43.
[47] *The Kronprinsessan Margareta* [1921] 1 A.C. 486 at p.515 (referred to by Lord Sumner, above, n.46 at p.43, under its alternative name of *The Parana*).
[48] Above, para.19–027.
[49] [1922] 1 A.C. 36 at p.39.
[50] This question did not in fact arise, there being no allegation of any breach by the carriers.

must pass to the transferee upon or by reason of the indorsement would not have been satisfied: the goods not having been paid for, property would have remained in the sellers throughout and would not have passed to the sellers at any relevant stage.[51] Nor is it likely that, if the bare facts stated in the report of *Hansson's* case occurred now, contractual rights against the carrier would be transferred to the seller under the Carriage of Goods by Sea Act 1992, since the mere rejection of the bill of lading would not make the seller the "lawful holder" of it in the absence of its either naming him as consignee or being indorsed to him[52]; and nothing in the report indicates that either of these conditions was satisfied.

If one of them *were* satisfied and the seller had become the "lawful holder" of the bill, rights under the contract of carriage would be transferred to him by virtue of subsections 2(1) and 2(2)(b) of the 1992 Act; but he would have no rights under the 1999 Act since, the contract of carriage being contained in or evidenced by a bill of lading, the case would fall within the subsection 6(5) exception.[53] This would, moreover, also be the position even where the seller had acquired no rights by virtue of the 1992 Act because he had not become the "lawful holder" of the bill: the case would still fall within the subsection 6(5) exception in the 1999 Act so that the seller could not make any claim under section 1 of that Act even in the somewhat unlikely event of his being able to satisfy the requirements of that section.[54]

19–095 **C.i.f. contract "with variations".** Problems similar to those discussed in paragraph 19–094 above could arise if the seller for some other reason had an interest in enforcing the contract of carriage against the carrier: for example, if the contract of sale were a "c.i.f. contract with variations"[55] under which the amount payable to him by the buyer depended on the quantity of goods which arrived at the destination specified in the contract of sale, or under which the sale contract was to become void if the ship carrying the goods were lost en route to that destination. Such provisions in effect leave the risk of loss with the seller (contrary to the general rule that risk passes on or as from shipment)[56]; and the seller may wish to hold the carrier liable for the loss that he thus has to bear. He will not be able to assert his claim in tort for negligence if property has passed to the buyer before the loss,[57] typically on payment against documents[58]; and a claim in bailment will be, to say the least, problematical since the bill of lading, in the case put,[59] will be in the buyer's name and hence acknowledge receipt

[51] Below, paras 19–098, 19–103.
[52] See 1992 Act, ss.2(1)(a), 5(2)(a) and (b).
[53] Above para.18–005, sub-paragraph (f).
[54] The seller is unlikely to be able to satisfy the requirement, stated in s.1(3) of the 1999 Act, of being "expressly identified" in the contract.
[55] Above, para.19–006, nn. 28, 31.
[56] Below, para.19–110.
[57] *Leigh & Sillavan Ltd v Aliakmon Shipping Co. Ltd (The Aliakmon)* [1986] A.C. 785.
[58] Below, paras 19–098, 19–099.
[59] The discussion above is still based on the assumption that, as in *Hansson v Hamel & Horley Ltd* [1922] 2 A.C., above para.19–093, the bill of lading names the *buyer* as shipper.

of the goods from the buyer, making him (rather than the seller) the bailor, even though the actual delivery of the goods to the carrier may have been made by the seller.[60] The seller may therefore wish to make his claim in contract and he would have considerable difficulty in making good such a claim under the 1992 Act if only part of the goods had been lost, for in such a case the buyer would be likely to retain the bill or to have surrendered it to the carrier when claiming delivery of the (remaining) goods, so that the seller would not be the "lawful holder" of it within section 2(1). But the contract of carriage would nevertheless be contained in or evidenced by a bill of lading and so fall within the subsection 6(5) exception to the 1999 Act, so that the seller would have no claim under that Act, even if he could satisfy the requirements of its section 1 by arguing that he was a member of a class expressly identified[61] in the bill by virtue of the words "or order" (or similar expressions). One possibility would be for the seller to argue that an implied contract arose when he presented, and the carrier accepted, the goods for loading.[62] This possibility is further discussed in paragraph 19–097 below. Here it suffices to say that such an implied contract would not fall within the subsection 6(5) exception. If the seller cannot establish any such implied contract (for example, because he cannot prove the requisite contractual intention on the part of the carrier),[63] then the seller's best course would be to induce the buyer to make a claim against the carrier under section 2(4) of the 1992 Act, though it is an open question whether the seller would have an "interest or right in relation to goods" merely because they were at his risk.[64] If this question were answered in the negative, the seller would have no remedy either under the 1992 Act or under the 1999 Act. His position could be more favourable if the goods had been wholly destroyed as a result of the carrier's breach. In such a case, the buyer would have no interest in retaining the bill of lading and might well be willing to transfer it to the seller, making him its lawful holder and thus giving him rights of suit under section 2(1) of the 1992 Act. Since there would have been no delivery of the goods to the person entitled to them,[65] it is submitted that the bill would not (at the time of the transfer) be a "spent" bill so that the seller would have a right of action on the bill even though the case did not fall within either of the two exceptions, stated in section 2(2) of the 1992 Act, to the general rule that no such rights are transferred to the holder of a "spent" bill. The result would be that the seller's rights would not be subject to the restrictions imposed by the 1999 Act on the rights of third parties arising under it.

---

[60] The bailor would prima facie be the person named as shipper in the bill, though if that person had acted as the consignee's agent in making the contract of carriage, then it would be the consignee who would occupy the position of bailor: see above, para.18–065. In *Hansson's* case, above n.50, the bill named the buyer as shipper and made the goods deliverable "to Order . . ." without naming any consignee. In these circumstances, it is not plausible to argue that the buyer had shipped the goods as agent of the seller; the converse is the more plausible view.

[61] Within subsection 1(3) of the 1999 Act.

[62] *cf. Elder Dempster & Co v Paterson Zochonis & Co* [1924] A.C. 522.

[63] *cf.* in the context of another type of implied contract, para.18–142 above.

[64] Above, para.18–120.

[65] *cf.* above, para.18–080.

19–096 The significance of the points made in paragraphs 19–094 and 19–095 above is twofold. First, the conditions in which a transferee of a bill can acquire rights under the 1992 Act differ from those in which a third party can acquire rights under the 1999 Act: for example, a person may become the "lawful holder" of a bill of lading for the purposes of section 2 of the 1992 Act without being "expressly identified" in the contract of carriage so as to satisfy section 1(3) of the 1999 Act. Secondly, the contents of the rights acquired under the 1992 Act may differ from those which a third party would acquire (but for the subsection 6(5) exception) under the 1999 Act. The point may be illustrated by reference to cases such as *Leduc v Ward*[66] and *The Ardennes*[67] in which the terms of the contract of carriage were varied by extrinsic agreement between shipper and carrier. In the former case, the bill of lading did not permit deviation but the shipper had acquiesced in the deviation which occurred, so that, against him, it was not a breach of contract. The transferee of the bill was nevertheless entitled to treat the deviation as a breach in respect of which he could recover damages. It seems that he would similarly be so entitled under the 1992 Act, at least so long as he did not know of the shipper's assent to the deviation.[68] If the case were not excepted from the 1999 Act and the claim were made under it, the carrier would be able to rely on the extrinsic agreement against the transferee as a "matter that arises from or in connection with the contract and is relevant to the term"[69] (*i.e.* to the term specifying the route). No doubt this difference between the 1992 Act and the 1999 Act is explicable, at least in part, on the ground that the transferability of bills of lading would be unduly hampered if a "matter" such as an extrinsic agreement between shipper and carrier were available as a defence against a bona fide transferee. The question exactly which defences against the shipper are available to the carrier against a transferee making a claim under the 1992 Act is a difficult and complex one which has been considered in Chapter 18.[70] The point to be emphasised here is that in this respect the position of the promisor (the carrier) is more favourable under the 1999 Act than it is under the 1992 Act.

19–097 **Antecedent contract.** The foregoing discussion shows that in the type of situation here under consideration a c.i.f. seller who is not an original party to the contract of carriage may fail to acquire contractual rights against the carrier (a) under the 1992 Act because the requirements of that Act are not satisfied (*e.g.* because the seller has not become the lawful holder of the bill) or (b) under the 1999 Act because, even if the requirements of section 1 of that Act are satisfied, the case falls within the subsection 6(5) exception. If the seller has suffered loss as a result of the carrier's breach of the contract of carriage, he may then seek to establish some other legal basis for asserting contractual rights against the carrier. One possible source

---

66 (1885) 20 Q.B.D. 475.
67 [1951] 1 K.B. 55.
68 Above, para.18–106.
69 1999 Act, subsection 3(2)(a).
70 See above, paras 18–106 to 18–109; and see *Carver on Bills of Lading* (2nd ed., 2005), paras 5–026—5–039.

of such rights is the antecedent contract which is likely to arise, in cases of the present kind, before the issue of the bill of lading. The seller will require the bill to be issued initially to himself (even if it names the buyer as shipper) since, unless he has possession of the bill, he will not be able to perform his duty under the c.i.f. contract to tender it to the buyer. Before such issue of the bill, the goods will have been presented by or on behalf of the seller to the carrier and the fact of their being so presented and accepted for carriage would seem to be capable of giving rise to an implied contract, inferred from the conduct of seller and carrier[71]; it is also arguable that it would give rise to a "bailment on terms"[72] which might be contractual or non-contractual in nature,[73] though this suggestion gives rise to the difficulty, noted above, that if the bill of lading acknowledged receipt of the goods from the buyer it would prima facie be the buyer, rather than the seller, who would be the bailor.[74] This fact would not, however, rule out the possibility of an antecedent implied *contract* between seller and carrier; and indeed such a contract may be made expressly. There was said to have been such an express contract in *Hansson's* case. The seller in that case had made a proposal to the carrier's agent to "book [the goods] for conveyance from Hamburg to Japan"; the agent then "altered the proposed contract"; these alterations were accepted by the seller; and the outcome of these negotiations was described by Lord Sumner as "a contract, partly expressed in a "Freight Contract" and partly in correspondence with [the shipowners' agent] for the conveyance of the [goods] from Hamburg to Japan on the terms, among others, that bills of lading should be signed in Hamburg . . ."[75] The exact terms of this antecedent contract are not stated in the report,[76] but the words "a contract . . . for the conveyance of the goods" suggest that this contract imposed at least some obligations on the carrier with respect, not only to the making of a further contract on bill of lading terms, but also with regard to the performance of the carriage operation. There is no way of telling whether in this respect the antecedent contract incorporated any, and if so which, terms of the bill of lading contract; but even if bill of lading terms were incorporated into the antecedent contract, this contract would not itself be a "bill of lading" within the 1992 Act or a "contract for the carriage of goods by sea" for the purposes of the subsection 6(5) exception to the 1999 Act.[77] The possibility of there being an antecedent contract between the carrier and one of the parties to the contract of sale and another, later, contract on bill of lading terms between

---

[71] On a principle analogous to that of *Brandt v Liverpool, etc. Steam Navigation Co. Ltd* [1924] 1 K.B. 575, above, para.18–139. For some difficulties in incorporating the bill of lading terms into an implied contract made at the stage of *shipment* (as opposed to that of *delivery*) see *Carver, op. cit.*, para.7–010.
[72] On the principle of *Elder Dempster & Co. v Paterson Zochonis & Co.* [1924] A.C. 522: see *Carver, op. cit.*, paras 7–005, 7–006.
[73] *ibid.*, paras 7–027 to 7–030.
[74] See above, para.19–095 at n.60.
[75] [1922] 2 A.C. 36 at p.43.
[76] It is not entirely clear whether the carrier's agent undertook that the goods would be carried, or whether his undertaking was merely to procure the making of a contract of carriage between carrier and buyer on bill of lading terms.
[77] See 1999 Act, s.6(6) and (7).

the carrier and the other party to the contract of sale more commonly arises where the sale is on f.o.b. terms. This type of situation is therefore more fully discussed in paragraph 20–060 below.

5. PASSING OF PROPERTY

19–098 **In general.** Goods sold under a c.i.f. contract may be specific, *e.g.* where the sale is of the cargo or of half the cargo, of a named ship. In such a case, property may pass as soon as the contract is made,[78] but usually this result will be negatived by the intention of the seller to retain the property until the price has been paid or at least until he has adequate assurance that it will be paid.[79] Once payment has been made, property in specific goods may pass under a c.i.f. contract, even before shipment.[80]

More commonly, c.i.f. contracts are contracts for the sale of goods which are unascertained for one of two reasons. First, the goods may simply be generic goods sold by description: *e.g.* "500 bales of cotton". In such a case, the general rule applies that no property can pass before ascertainment,[81] which does not normally[82] take place until contractual appropriation[83] on or after shipment.

Secondly, the goods may be unascertained because they are a specified quantity forming part of an identified bulk, *e.g.* 500 bales of the cargo of cotton shipped on the *Peerless*. In such a case, the rule that property cannot pass before ascertainment is subject to a statutory exception.[84] This exception, and the difficulties which arise in applying it to c.i.f. contracts, have been discussed in Chapter 18.[85]

Once the goods are ascertained (or fall within the statutory exception to the rule requiring them to be ascertained) the overriding rule is that property passes when intended to pass.[86] Under this rule, property may remain in the seller even after the goods have actually come into the possession of the buyer.[87] More generally, however, property under a c.i.f. contract will pass before physical delivery of the goods to the buyer, as a result of dealings with the shipping documents. The courts look to those

---

[78] Sale of Goods Act 1979, s.18, r. 1 (above, para.5–017).
[79] *cf. R V Ward Ltd v Bignall* [1967] 1 Q.B. 534 at p.545, quoted in para.5–018 above.
[80] See *Wiehe v Dennis Bros* (1913) 29 T.L.R. 250: in treating the seller as bailee for the buyer Scrutton J. must have assumed that the property had passed.
[81] Sale of Goods Act 1979, s.16; and see next note.
[82] For an exception, see *Redler Grain Silos Ltd v BICC Ltd* [1982] 1 Lloyd's Rep. 435, where a c. & f. contract was varied so as to provide for delivery to the buyer in the country of origin and for payment in advance of delivery; and property passed on such payment.
[83] Above, para.18–210, 19–015–19–017.
[84] Sale of Goods (Amendment) Act 1995, ss.1(1) and (3), amending Sale of Goods Act 1979, s.16 and inserting into that Act a new s.20A.
[85] Above, paras 18–293 *et seq.*
[86] *Sanders Bros v Maclean & Co.* (1883) 11 Q.B.D. 327 at p.341; Sale of Goods Act 1979, s.17(1) (above, para.5–016); and *cf.* s.20A(2).
[87] *Cheetham & Co. Ltd v Thornham Spinning Co. Ltd* [1964] 2 Lloyd's Rep. 17; *Ginzberg v Barrow Haematite Steel Co. Ltd* [1966] 1 Lloyd's Rep. 343.

dealings in order to determine whether the seller intended, on the one hand, unconditionally to appropriate the goods to the contract, or, on the other hand, to reserve the right of disposal. As the question of passing of property is one of "actual intention"[88] it is "impossible to lay down a general rule applicable to all c.i.f. contracts."[89] The courts look for indicia of intention in the terms of the contract of sale and in the subsequent conduct of the parties; and they have developed what amounts to a rebuttable presumption that the seller will not have intended to part with property until he has been paid or been adequately assured of payment.[90] The possible stages at which property may pass under a c.i.f. contract are discussed in the following paragraphs.

On shipment. In *E Clemens Horst Co. v Biddell Bros* Kennedy L.J., in a dissenting judgment which was approved on appeal in the House of Lords, twice said that property under a c.i.f. contract passed on shipment[91]: he said that it passed conditionally if the bill of lading was made out in favour of the seller, and unconditionally if the bill of lading was made out in favour of the buyer.[92] A similar possibility appears to have been envisaged by Lord Porter in *The Julia*, when he said that "The property may pass either on shipment or on tender (of documents)."[93] The view that property passes on shipment seems to be based on two lines of reasoning. The first, sometimes found in nineteenth century cases, is that property should be in the person at whose risk the goods are[94]; but this is of course the exact converse of the general rule as to the passing of risk now stated in section 20 of the Sale of Goods Act 1979, and the present position under a c.i.f. contract is that risk very commonly passes before property,[95] though the converse is hardly ever true. The second is that a seller is after shipment adequately protected by his rights of lien[96] and stoppage in transit; but such reasoning is no longer generally accepted in view of modern methods of financing c.i.f. sales.[97] It has also been criticised on the ground that the rights of lien and stoppage cannot influence the seller's intention as to passing of property unless he can be shown to have been aware of them.[98] Kennedy L.J.'s statement was therefore confined by Lord Wright in *Ross T Smyth & Co. Ltd v T D Bailey, Son & Co.*[99] to cases in which the seller had *not* reserved the right of 19–099

---

[88] *Ginzberg v Barrow Haematite Steel Co. Ltd* [1966] 1 Lloyd's Rep. 343 at p.353.
[89] *Stein, Forbes & Co. v County Tailoring Co.* (1916) 115 L.T. 215 at p.216.
[90] Above, para.18–209.
[91] [1911] 1 K.B. 934 at pp.956, 959; [1912] A.C. 18; *cf.* his earlier, similar view in *Dupont v British South Africa Co.* (1901) 18 T.L.R. 24 at p.25.
[92] By "in favour of" Kennedy L.J. seems to have meant "to the order of". *Cf.* above, para.18–015.
[93] [1949] A.C. 293 at p.309; *cf. Ilyssia Compania Naviera SA v Bamaodah* (*The Elli 2*) [1985] 1 Lloyd's Rep. 107 at p.115.
[94] *e.g. Castle v Playford* (1872) L.R. 7 Ex. 98; for similar reasoning see *The Parchim* [1918] A.C. 157 at p.169 (where the contract was not a true c.i.f. contract: above, para.19–009); and *cf.* a dictum in *M Golodetz & Co. Inc. v Czarnikow Rionda Co. Inc.* (*The Galatia*) [1980] 1 W.L.R. 495 at p.510, discussed in below, para.19–107.
[95] *The Surf City* [1995] 2 Lloyd's Rep. 242 at p.245.
[96] See *The Parchim*, above n.94, at p.171.
[97] Above, para.18–209.
[98] *The Kronprinsessan Margareta* [1921] 1 A.C. 486 at p.515.
[99] [1940] 3 All E.R. 60 at p.70; *cf. Baxter, Fell & Co. Ltd v Galbraith and Grant Ltd* (1941) 70 Ll.L.R. 142.

disposal; and the intention to reserve this right will generally[1] be inferred from retention of the shipping documents by the seller or his agent for presentation to obtain payment.[2] The property will certainly not pass to the buyer on shipment merely because the bill of lading makes the goods deliverable to the order of the buyer.[3] The inference that the seller intended to reserve the right of disposal is, of course, even stronger where the bill of lading makes the goods deliverable to the order of the seller[4] or to the order of his bank which has financed the transaction.[5] The result of all this is that, although property may theoretically pass on shipment, it will only do so in the rare cases in which the seller's intention to pass it at this point is clear.[6]

19–100 **On appropriation.** Property will not pass merely because the seller has appropriated goods to the contract in the "contractual" sense[7] of binding himself to deliver those goods (or documents relating to them) under the contract. Accordingly, Lord Wright has said that "The notice of appropriation under an ordinary c.i.f. contract is not intended to pass, and does not pass, the property."[8] At first sight, this statement is inconsistent with a dictum in *The Arpad*,[9] where a claim was made by a c.i.f. buyer against the carrier for short delivery. In holding that the buyer had a right of action, Langton J. said that property was intended to pass "at the normal time", namely when the goods were appropriated to the contract.[10] But it is submitted that "appropriated" is here used in its "proprietary" sense,[11] *i.e.* to refer to the "unconditional appropriation" necessary to pass the property, though admittedly on that view the dictum becomes unhelpful as

---

[1] Though not invariably: see *The Parchim* [1918] A.C. 157, discussed on this point below, para.20–080; *Albacruz (Cargo Owners) v Albazero (Owners) (The Albazero)* [1977] A.C. 774, below, para.19–103, n.48; *Anonima Petroli Italiani SpA v Marlucidez Armadora SA (The Filiatra Legacy)* [1991] 2 Lloyd's Rep. 337, above, para.18–219; *The Future Express* [1993] 2 Lloyd's Rep. 542; above, para.18–220.

[2] *Eastwood & Holt v Studer* (1926) 31 Com.Cas. 251; *East West Corp v DKBS 1912 AF/AS* [2003] EWCA Civ. 83, [2003] Q.B. 1509 at [3], where the sale was on c.o.d. terms.

[3] *The Kronprinsessan Margareta* [1921] A.C. 486; *cf. Hansson v Hamel and Horley Ltd* [1922] 2 A.C. 36 at p.43. It is open to the seller as shipper to order the carrier to deliver the goods to someone other than the consignee: see above, para.18–021.

[4] See Sale of Goods Act 1979, s.19(2), above, para.18–224; *The Charlotte* [1908] P. 206; *The Gabbiano* [1940] P. 166.

[5] *Stein Forbes & Co. v County Tailoring Co.* (1916) 115 L.T. 215.

[6] A dictum at first instance in *Anonima Petroli Italiani SpA v Marlucidez Armadora SA (The Filiatra Legacy)* [1990] 1 Lloyd's Rep. 354 at p.358 refers to shipment as one possible point at which property passed under a c.i.f. contract, but on appeal property was evidently regarded as having passed at a later stage: see [1991] 2 Lloyd's Rep. 337 at p.343. The latter view is, with respect, to be preferred since there was no indication that the seller had intended at the time of shipment to relinquish his right of disposal. For the passing of property in this case, see above, para.18–219.

[7] See above, paras 18–210, 19–015.

[8] *Ross T Smyth & Co. Ltd v T D Bailey, Son & Co.* [1940] 3 All E.R. 60 at p.66.

[9] (1933) 46 Ll.L.R. 182 (this case was several times litigated: see also 48 Ll.L.R. 202; [1934] P. 189 (49 Ll.L.R. 313); (1934) 50 Ll.L.R. 134; (1935) 51 Ll.L.R. 115).

[10] (1933) 46 Ll.L.R. 182 at p.188.

[11] Above, para.19–015.

it does not indicate when the appropriation becomes unconditional. The bills of lading had in fact been indorsed to the buyer, who had paid for the goods by the relevant date,[12] and there is nothing in the reports to suggest why the property should not have passed once these things had been done.

Equitable title. It has been suggested that, even though the legal title to goods does not pass on contractual appropriation, such appropriation may nevertheless pass an equitable title to the buyer.[13] But this suggestion has twice been judicially doubted on the ground that the rules laid down in the Sale of Goods Act as to the passing of property constitute "a complete code" which is "intended to comprise both the legal and the equitable title"[14]; and it is respectfully submitted that these doubts are, at least as a general rule,[15–16] well founded. Judicial statements to the effect that property does not pass on (contractual) appropriation under a c.i.f. contract are also quite general, drawing no distinction between legal and equitable property; and it is submitted that the reasons of convenience which restrict the availability of specific performance of c.i.f. sales of commodities[17] equally militate against the view that contractual appropriation of goods to such a contract can, in the normal case, pass an equitable title in the goods to the buyer in spite of the fact that the seller has retained the legal title by reserving the right of disposal. 19–101

On transfer of documents. The transfer of a bill of lading for value is prima facie evidence of intention to pass property[18] and it has accordingly been said by Bowen L.J. that property under a c.i.f. contract "passes by such indorsement and delivery".[19] This statement was cited with approval by Kennedy L.J. in the judgment to which reference has already been made[20]; and a somewhat similar view was expressed by Lord Porter when he referred to tender of documents as one possible point at which property passes.[21] Other cases contain statements to the effect that property passes on shipment and transfer of bills of lading[22]: these statements may be 19–102

---

[12] See [1934] P. 189.

[13] By counsel for the buyers in *Leigh & Sillavan Ltd v Aliakmon Shipping Co. Ltd* (*The Aliakmon*) [1986] A.C. 785; *cf.* above, para.18–149.

[14] *The Aliakmon*, above n.13, at p.812; *Re Wait* [1927] 1 Ch. 606 at pp.635–636; *cf. Re London Wine Co. (Shippers)* [1986] P.C.C. 121 at p.147; above, para.5–064.

[15–16] There may be an exception in the case of a specifically enforceable contract, but see *infra*, at n.17.

[17] Below, para.19–204.

[18] *Wilmshurst v Bowker* (1841) 10 L.J.C.P. 161; (1844) 7 M. & G. 882 (above, para.18–089).

[19] *Sanders Bros v Maclean & Co.* (1883) 11 Q.B.D. 327 at p.341; *cf. Karslhamns Oljefabriker v Eastport Navigation Corp.* (*The Elafi*) [1981] 2 Lloyd's Rep. 679 at p.686 ("upon the negotiation of the documents").

[20] *E Clemens Horst & Co. v Biddell Bros* [1911] 1 K.B. 934 at p.957 (above, para.19–099, n.91).

[21] *The Julia* [1949] A.C. 293 at p.309.

[22] *Calcutta, etc. Steam Navigation Co. v De Mattos* (1863) 32 L.J.Q.B. 329 at p.332; affirmed (1863) 33 L.J.Q.B. 214; *Delaurier & Co. v James Wyllie & Co.* (1889) 17 R. (Ct. of Sess.) 167 at pp.180–181.

explained to mean that shipment is necessary to ascertain the goods, and transfer of the bills of lading to show that the seller has given up his right of disposal.[23] Just as transfer of the bill of lading may thus pass the property, so retention of the bill may have the effect of negativing the intention to transfer property.[24] Thus in *Cheetham & Co. Ltd v Thornham Spinning Co. Ltd*,[25] c.i.f. sellers of cotton had expressly refused to give credit to the buyers; but they later, in order to save quay charges, agreed that the cotton should be sent to the buyers for warehousing at their mill. The sellers, however, retained the shipping documents, believing that they were thereby[26] retaining the legal title to the goods; and the buyers knew of this belief. It was held that the property had not passed as the conduct of the sellers in keeping the shipping documents negatived any intention to pass it. On the other hand, retention of the bill of lading is not *necessarily* evidence of intention to retain property. In *The Delfini*[27] c.i.f. buyers had opened a bank guarantee for payment before the goods were shipped, and had paid in full after actual delivery, which had been made under letters of indemnity as the bills of lading had not reached the destination by the time of the ship's arrival there. The only reason why the bills of lading were not transferred until later was that they had not yet come into the hands of the seller; and it was held that property had passed before the transfer of the bills.[28] The position is similar where the buyer actually pays against a delivery order: in such a case, property will almost certainly pass when he obtains possession of the goods[29] and may pass before (so long as the goods are ascertained[30] or form part of an identified bulk[31]) even though the seller retains the bill of lading. Indeed there is no reason in theory why the giving of a delivery order in respect of ascertained goods may not pass property in goods still afloat irrespective of payment[32] if the seller so intends; but the court would infer such intention only in the most exceptional circumstances. If the price has not been paid, property may not pass even by the transfer of a bill of lading; the conditions discussed in the following paragraph will normally have to be satisfied.

19–103 **On payment.** Dicta to the effect that property under a c.i.f. contract passes on tender of documents probably assume either that no right of disposal was reserved by the contract or the appropriation[33] or that the

---

[23] Above, para.18–211.
[24] See *Eastwood and Holt v Studer* (1926) 31 Com.Cas. 251.
[25] [1964] 2 Lloyd's Rep. 17.
[26] The bills of lading were in fact spent: *cf.* above, para.18–080.
[27] *Enichem Anic SpA v Ampelos Shipping Co. Ltd* (*The Delfini*) [1990] 1 Lloyd's Rep. 252; Treitel [1990] L.M.C. L.Q. 1.
[28] So that no contractual rights were transferred under Bills of Lading Act 1855, s.1: see above, para.18–100.
[29] See *Margarine Union GmbH v Cambay Prince SS Co. Ltd* (*The Wear Breeze*) [1969] 1 Q.B. 219.
[30] Sale of Goods Act 1979, s.16.
[31] For fractions, see the definition of "specific goods" in Sale of Goods Act 1979, s.61(1) and above, para.18–290; for specified quantities out of the bulk, see *ibid*; s.20A, above, para.18–293.
[32] Property in a specified quantity of *unascertained* goods which form part of an identified bulk cannot pass without payment under s.20A.
[33] See above, para.18–211.

conditions on which the appropriation was made have been fulfilled by the buyer: in other words, that the buyer has "taken up" the documents, by making (or offering to make[34]) payment,[35] or by accepting a draft for the price in accordance with the contract.[36] Where the contract provides for payment by cash against documents, the normal inference is that no property passes until the condition as to payment is satisfied.[37] In *Ginzberg v Barrow Haematite Steel Co. Ltd*[38] manganese ore was sold c.i.f. Birkenhead, to be paid for against documents including bills of lading. The goods arrived before the bills of lading and, to expedite matters, the seller sent the buyer a delivery order by means of which the buyer obtained actual possession of the goods. But the buyer did not pay, and, on his subsequent bankruptcy, it was held that the property in the goods had not passed to him. McNair J. said that the question of passing of property was "one of actual intention"[39]; and he relied both on the fact that it was the seller's practice never to sell on credit, and on the inference as to intention to pass property normally to be drawn in cases of c.i.f. contracts. On the latter point he said: "If the buyer takes the bills of lading and does not within a reasonable time[40] pay in accordance with the invoice accompanying the bills of lading, the property does not ordinarily pass."[41] One particular application of this principle is in cases of payment by a documentary bill (of exchange)[42] presented for payment either to the buyer himself[43] or to a bank under a letter of credit. In *The Glenroy*[44] payment was to be made by a bank under a letter of credit. The documents with a draft for the price were presented to the bank but the draft was not accepted or paid; and it was held that property had not passed. Lord Porter said that "in the normal case [of a c.i.f. contract] the property would not pass until the documents were taken up and paid for."[45] Nor, for reasons already discussed,[46] did it

---

[34] *cf.* above, para.18–226 and below, para.20–084 (f.o.b. contracts).
[35] *e.g. Karlshamns Oljefabriker v Eastport Navigation Corp.* (*The Elafi*) [1981] 2 Lloyd's Rep. 679 (where 95 per cent of the price was paid, in accordance with the contract, against documents covering *most* of the goods and property was held to have passed in *all* the goods, including a small quantity not covered by any documents).
[36] Merely giving the seller a promissory note was held not to amount to "payment" for this purpose in *Ishag v Allied Bank International* [1981] 1 Lloyd's Rep. 92, where the promissory note was that of a third party.
[37] *Ross T Smyth & Co. Ltd v T D Bailey, Son & Co.* [1940] 3 All E.R. 60 at p.67 ("Conditions stipulated *in the bill of lading*" appears to be a misprint for "conditions stipulated *in the contract of sale*"); *cf. Empresa Exportadora de Azucar v Industria Azucarera Nacional SA* (*The Playa Larga*) [1983] 2 Lloyd's Rep. 171 at p.186.
[38] [1966] 1 Lloyd's Rep. 343.
[39] At p.353.
[40] Above, para.19–085.
[41] [1966] 1 Lloyd's Rep. 343 at p.352; *cf. ibid.*, at p.353; *The Charlotte* [1908] P. 215 at p.216; *cf Huyton SA v Peter Cremer GmbH* [1999] 1 Lloyd's Rep. 620 at p.631 (f.o.b. contract providing for "cash on delivery").
[42] Above, para.18–221.
[43] As in *The Miramichi* [1915] P. 71; *The Derfflinger* (*No.2*) (1918) 118 L.T. 521.
[44] [1946] A.C. 124.
[45] *ibid.*, at p.134; *cf. Leigh & Sillavan Ltd v Aliakmon Shipping Co. Ltd* (*The Aliakmon*) [1986] A.C. 785 at p.808.
[46] Above, para.18–216.

make any difference that the seller had discounted the drafts with another bank.

These statements of McNair J. and Lord Porter refer to the normal case. As the passing of property depends on intention, it is perfectly possible for the property to pass where actual payment has not been made, *e.g.* on acceptance of a documentary bill which is payable at a future time and so indicates an intention to give credit to the buyer[47]; or where buyer and seller are associated companies and the sale is expressly on credit[48]; or where there are other indications of the seller's indication to give credit to the buyer. Such an indication may appear from the payment term of the contract of sale; but for this purpose it is submitted that credit would not be given merely because that term provided for payment within a specified number of days from the date of the bill of lading. The most likely effect of such a term is merely to fix the time at which the price is to be exchanged for the documents[49]: in this respect, such a term resembles one by which a future date is specified for delivery *against* payment, rather than one which provides for delivery *before* payment. In one case, indeed, a term in a c.i.f. contract calling for payment "within 30 days from bill of lading date provided that . . . usual shipping documents have reached the buyer. . . at least five days before due date" was said to have given the buyers a "thirty-day period of credit".[50] The view that credit was being given to the buyer can perhaps be supported on the ground that the payment term clearly envisaged receipt of the shipping documents five days before payment (though this would point to a credit period of five, rather than to one of 30, days). An alternative (and, it is submitted a more plausible) interpretation of the payment term is that the five-day interval between the buyer's receipt of shipping documents and payment merely specified the reasonable time[51] within which payment had to be made to effect the passing of property.

19–104 **Retention of property after payment.** Occasionally, a seller may have an interest in retaining property after payment in full. This possibility is illustrated by *The Gabbiano*,[52] where manganiferous ore was shipped in pursuance of a c.i.f. contract which stipulated that if, after loading, the ship was lost or for any reason unable to deliver the cargo or any part thereof, the quantity so undelivered should be written off the contract quantity.[53] It was held that the clause provided a "valid business reason for taking the bills of lading to the sellers' order"[54]; that this reason had not "in the circumstances of this case"[55] disappeared merely because the buyer had

[47] Above, para.18–223.
[48] This was the view of Brandon J. and the Court of Appeal in *The Albazero* [1977] A.C. 774; their decision was reversed on other grounds by the House of Lords, where the view that property had passed was accepted, and said at p.840 to depend on "facts . . . peculiar to the instant case".
[49] *e.g. Toepfer v Lenersan-Poortman NV* [1980] 1 Lloyd's Rep. 143.
[50] *Anonima Petroli Italiana SpA v Marlucidex Armadora SA (The Filiatra Legacy)* [1991] 2 Lloyd's Rep. 337 at pp.341, 343.
[51] Above, at n.40.
[52] [1940] P. 166.
[53] Thus it was a c.i.f. contract "with variations" (above, para.19–006).
[54] [1940] P. 166 at p.175.
[55] *ibid.*

elected to pay the price in full before shipment, though he was bound to pay only against shipping documents, which were never transferred to him; and that the property in the goods had not passed to him. The special circumstances justifying this conclusion were that the buyer had nominated Stettin (then in Germany) as the port of destination, and that the goods had been shipped on August 27, 1939, when war between the United Kingdom and Germany was imminent. On the outbreak of war, the goods were seized by the British authorities, and the point of the seller's claim that the property had not passed was to prevent the condemnation of the goods as contraband[56]; for their seizure could (under the clause referred to above) make him liable to repay the price to the buyer. The possibility that the goods might be condemned could well have been in the seller's mind at the time of shipment and so have affected his intention with regard to passing of property.

It is possible to think of other circumstances in which it might be in the seller's interest to argue that property had not passed (even after payment) where the risk remained in him by virtue of a provision that lost or undelivered goods should be written off. If the goods were lost, he might have to repay the price or part of it, but have difficulty in claiming damages from the carrier if the property in the goods had passed to the buyer. An action in tort would not be available to the seller (if he was no longer owner) merely because the goods were still at his risk[57]; nor could he sue on the contract contained in, or evidenced by, the bill of lading if the bill had been transferred to the buyer, since under the Carriage of Goods by Sea Act 1992 that transfer would extinguish his rights as an original party to the contract of carriage, or as a previous transferee of the bill of lading[58]; and the buyer's claim for the return of the price would not seem to be a "rejection of . . . goods or documents" so as to be capable of revesting those contractual rights in the seller under the provisions of the 1992 Act which apply to "spent" bills of lading.[59] If the goods had been shipped by the seller, then the seller might continue to have a right of action in bailment against the carrier.[60] That right might, however be less extensive than the seller's rights against the carrier for breach of the contract of carriage: the right of action in bailment would, in particular not extend to the enforcement of positive duties arising under the contract of carriage and going beyond those imposed by the general law on bailees.[61] A final possibility is that the buyer might be entitled to sue the carrier for the benefit of the seller by virtue of section 2(4) of the 1992 Act[62]; but the seller could not require him to do so unless such a requirement was imposed by the contract of sale.[63]

---

[56] *cf.* above, para.18–242.
[57] See above, para.18–149.
[58] Carriage of Goods by Sea Act 1992, s.2(5), above, para.18–114.
[59] *ibid.*, s.2(2)(b), above, para.18–113.
[60] *East West Corp. v DKBS 1912 AF A/S* [2003] EWCA Civ. 83, [2003] Q.B. 1509; above, para.18–115.
[61] *ibid.*, after n.89.
[62] This would depend on whether in the circumstances described the seller would have "any interest or right in relation to" the goods within s.2(4): see above, para.18–120.
[63] Above, para.18–122.

19–105 **On performance of other conditions.** Property may pass under a c.i.f. contract on transfer of documents accompanied by the performance of some other condition specified in the contract, *e.g.* by the buyer's acceptance of a documentary bill (of exchange)[64] or by the provision of a letter of credit or of some other form of undertaking from the buyer's bank to pay the price. Such provisions may (though they will not necessarily) indicate that the seller does not look to his property in the goods as security for payment of the price, but relies for such security rather on the buyer's promise in the bill of exchange or on the promise of the bank.[65]

19–106 **On dealings with the goods after shipment.** Property may pass by reason of dealings with the goods after shipment, in spite of the facts that shipping documents have not been transferred to the buyer and that he has not paid the price. This possibility has already been discussed: we have seen that property will not pass merely by delivery of the goods to the buyer without payment,[66] but that such delivery may have this effect where the circumstances exceptionally indicate that, by the delivery, the seller has given up his right of disposal.[67]

19–107 **As from shipment.** It has been suggested *obiter* that "As between seller and c.i.f. and c. & f. buyer, the property and risk normally pass on the negotiation of the bill of lading, but do so as from shipment."[68] There is, however, no support in any of the other authorities for the view that *property* can pass under such contracts *as from* shipment. This possibility is generally thought to exist only in relation to risk, the passing of which is not usually associated with the transfer of documents. It is submitted that the dictum quoted above runs together two rules: that property may pass on transfer of documents,[69] and that risk may pass as from shipment.[70] The first rule is inapplicable to the passing of risk, and the second inapplicable to the passing of property. To give retrospective effect to the passing of property, by holding that it could pass *as from* shipment, could prejudice third persons who had acquired an interest in the goods between shipment and the transfer of the documents to the buyer.

19–108 **Destroyed or lost goods.** A c.i.f. buyer may be bound to pay against documents even though the goods which are the subject-matter of the contract have been destroyed or lost,[71] or he may pay against documents in

---

[64] Above, para.18–221.
[65] Above, paras 18–218, 18–223.
[66] *e.g. Cheetham & Co. Ltd v Thornham Spinning Co. Ltd* [1964] 2 Lloyd's Rep. 17, above, para.19–102; *Ginzberg v Barrow Haematite Steel Co. Ltd* [1966] 1 Lloyd's Rep. 343, above, para.19–103.
[67] *e.g. Anonima Petroli Italiana SpA v Marlucidex Armadora SA* (*The Filiatra Legacy*) [1991] 2 Lloyd's Rep. 337 above, para.18–219; *The Future Express* [1993] 2 Lloyd's Rep. 542; above, para.18–220.
[68] *M. Golodetz & Co. Inc. v Czarnikow Rionda Inc.* (*The Galatia*) [1980] 1 W.L.R. 495 at p.510 (there is no reference to this point in the Court of Appeal, *ibid.*, pp.517 *et seq.*).
[69] Above, paras 19–097, 19–103.
[70] Below, para.19–110.
[71] Above, para.19–080: *e.g.* where the loss occurs after appropriation and before tender of documents.

ignorance of the fact that the goods have been destroyed or lost, even where he is not bound to do so.[72] The question then arises whether property in such goods can pass to the buyer on payment. Where the goods have literally ceased to exist, it makes no sense to say that the buyer can thereafter acquire the property in them; but goods may be lost without being destroyed, *e.g.* where they are stolen or misdelivered and cannot be traced. It is submitted that in such a case it makes no more sense, than it does in the case of goods which have been destroyed, to say that the buyer has become owner of the goods which the seller had, or purported to have, appropriated to the contract. On the contrary, there is authority for the view that goods which have been stolen and cannot be traced are for some purposes under the Sale of Goods Act 1979 treated as having "perished"[73]; and once they are so treated it is submitted that property in them can no longer pass to the buyer. The position would of course be different where the goods *were* traced after the theft or misdelivery[74]; but in such a case they would no longer be lost goods.

Revesting of property on rejection. If a buyer, having taken up the documents, later rejects the goods, property may revest in the seller. This possibility is further discussed below.[75] 19–109

6. RISK

Generally passes on or as from shipment. In *The Julia* Lord Porter said that risk, under a c.i.f. contract, "generally passes on shipment or as from shipment".[76] The risk is thus commonly separated from property[77]: the seller's obligation to cover the buyer by insurance from shipment[78] is regarded as evidence of agreement to exclude the general rule[79] that, where the buyer does not deal as a consumer,[80] risk passes with property. Our 19–110

---

[72] Above, paras 19–082 to 19–083: *e.g.* where the loss occurs before the making of the contract or (it is submitted) after contract but before appropriation.

[73] See *Barrow Lane & Ballard Ltd v Phillip Phillips & Co. Ltd* [1929] 1 K.B. 574, where goods which were stolen were held to have "perished" for the purpose of s.6 of the Act; and there seems to be no reason to suppose that the same would not be true for the purpose of s.7.

[74] The "vintage car" example discussed in *NSW Leather Co. Pty Ltd v Vanguard Insurance Co. Ltd* (1991) 25 N.S.W.L.R. 699 at p.712 is of this kind; but the actual case was concerned with *untraced* stolen goods and the view of the majority that property in such goods passed on payment is, with respect, open to doubt.

[75] Below, para.19–174.

[76] [1949] A.C. 293 at p.309; *E Clemens Horst Co. Ltd v Biddell Bros* [1911] 1 K.B. 934 at pp.956, 959; *Bowden Bros & Co. Ltd v Little* (1907) 4 C.L.R. 1364; *M. Golodetz & Co. Inc. v Czarnikow Rionda Co. Inc.* (*The Galatia*) [1980] 1 W.L.R. 495 at p.510, discussed above, para.19–107, and affirmed without reference to this point in [1980] 1 W.L.R. 517.

[77] *cf.* para.19–099, above.

[78] Above, para.19–042; *cf.* para.19–027 as to continuous documentary cover by the contract of carriage.

[79] Sale of Goods Act 1979, s.20(1) (above, para.6–002).

[80] For the position where the buyer does deal as consumer, see Sale of Goods Act 1979, ss.20(4) and 32(4), discussed in relation to overseas sales in paras 18–259 to 18–264 above and in para.19–123 below.

concern in paragraphs 19–111 to 19–122 will be with cases in which the buyer does not so deal. Lord Porter's statement contains two rules. Where the goods are sold and then shipped, the risk passes *on* shipment[81]; but where they are already afloat at the time of sale it is more apposite to refer to the risk as having passed *as from* shipment.[82] After considering the relation between these rules and the seller's undertakings as to quality, we shall discuss their application to cases first of deterioration, and secondly of total loss, of the goods.

19–111 **Seller's undertakings as to quality.** In a domestic sale, not on c.i.f. terms, in which the buyer does not deal as consumer, the seller's undertakings as to quality refer to the time of sale[83] (or, where the sale is of unascertained goods, to the time of contractual appropriation). The rules as to risk apply to deterioration which takes place after that time. In the case of a c.i.f. contract, however, the seller's undertakings as to quality refer to the time of *shipment*,[84] only subsequent deterioration being governed by the rules as to risk. Hence no question of risk arises in relation to nonconformity of the goods with the contract description at the time of shipment.[85] The rule that the c.i.f. seller's undertakings as to quality relate to the time of shipment must be understood in the light of the implied undertaking that the goods are fit to endure normal transit.[86] Although this undertaking relates to the condition of the goods at the time of shipment[87] it makes the seller responsible for deterioration which does not become apparent until later.

19–112 **Risk of deterioration.** Under the rules stated by Lord Porter in *The Julia*, and quoted in paragraph 19–110, the risk of deterioration will be on the buyer where the sequence of events is as follows:

---

[81] *Leigh & Sillavan Ltd v Aliakmon Shipping Co. Ltd* (*The Aliakmon*) [1986] A.C. 785 at p.808; *cf.* Vienna Convention on Contracts for the International Sale of Goods (above, para.1–024), Art. 67(1), first sentence (under which risk passes, not on shipment, but on the handing over of the goods to a carrier).

[82] *cf.* Vienna Convention on Contracts for the International Sale of Goods (above, para.1–024), Art. 68, second sentence ("from the time the goods were handed over to the carrier . . .").

[83] Above, para.18–254. The "additional rights" conferred on a buyer who deals as consumer by Pt 5A of the Sale of Goods Act 1979 arise "if . . . the goods do not conform to the contract at the time of *delivery*": s.48A(1)(b) and see s.48F for the meaning in Pt 5A of conformity with the contract. For the possibility of a c.i.f. buyer's dealing as consumer, see above, para.18–259; for the difficulty of determining when "delivery" occurs in such a case, see above, para.18–261.

[84] See above, paras 18–254, 19–012; *Oleificio Zucchi SpA v Northern Sales Ltd* [1965] 2 Lloyd's Rep. 496 at p.518; *Cordova Land Co. Ltd v Victor Bros* [1966] 1 W.L.R. 793. The Vienna Convention on Contracts for the International Sale of Goods (above, para.1–024) reaches a similar result by a different route. Art. 36(1) provides that the seller's undertakings as to quality refer to the time, not of sale, but to the passing of risk; and under Art. 67(1), first sentence, risk under a c.i.f contract normally passes "when the goods are handed over to the first carrier for transmission to the buyer in accordance with the contract of sale." This position is only similar to the English position, but not identical with it, since "handing over" of the goods to the carrier will usually precede *shipment*. For the position in English law where a c.i.f. buyer deals as consumer, see above, n.83.

[85] *Trasimex Holdings SA v Addax BV (The Red Sea)* [1999] 1 Lloyd's Rep. 28 at p.33.

[86] Above, para.18–255 to 18–257.

[87] Above, para.18–255.

(1) Goods are sold, shipped and then deteriorate: here the risk will have passed *on* shipment.

(2) Goods are shipped, deteriorate and are then sold: here the risk is on the buyer *as from* shipment. It passes *with retrospective effect* in the sense that the buyer bears the risk of deterioration which had already occurred when the contract of sale was made.

(3) Goods are shipped, a contract is made for the sale of goods of that description and the shipped goods are then appropriated to the contract: here the risk is on the buyer (a) without retrospective effect if the goods deteriorate *after* appropriation and (b) with some retrospective effect if they deteriorate after contract but *before* appropriation. In case (a) the risk can be said to have passed on contract or on later appropriation; in case (b) it can be said to have passed as from shipment, though it might be more accurate to say that it passed as from contract,[88] it being unnecessary in such a case to relate the retrospective effect back to the time of shipment. A further possible variant is that the appropriation may be made *by* the contract, *e.g.* where the contract specifies the cargo which in this way becomes the subject-matter of the sale. In such a case the risk of subsequent deterioration is on the buyer without retrospective effect and can be said to have passed to the buyer on contract or on appropriation by contract.

Risk of total loss. Lord Porter's statement in *The Julia*, quoted in paragraph 19–110 above, begins with the word "generally"; and, although the statement does not distinguish between risk of deterioration and risk of loss, it is submitted that the rules governing them differ in significant respects. This can be seen by taking the situations discussed in paragraph 19–112 and considering the effect in them of total loss, as opposed to deterioration. 19–113

(1) Goods are sold, shipped and then lost: the risk is on the buyer.[89] This is a simple application of the rule that risk passes *on* shipment.

(2) Goods are shipped, lost and are then sold: here risk is not on the buyer under a c.i.f. contract. In *Couturier v Hastie*[90] a cargo of corn on a named ship was sold on what were in substance c.i.f. terms[91] but had, unknown to the parties, ceased to exist as a commercial entity, before the time of the sale. It was held that the buyer was not in these circumstances bound to pay the price; and the decision is quite inconsistent with the view

---

[88] *cf.* Vienna Convention on Contracts for the International Sale of Goods (above, para.1–024), Art. 68, first sentence ("from the time of the conclusion of the contract").

[89] *e.g. Law & Bonar Ltd v British American Tobacco Co.* [1916] 2 K.B. 605.

[90] (1856) 5 H.L.C. 673 (above, para.1–134).

[91] The terms were "at 27s. per quarter free on board and including freight and insurance, to a safe port in the United Kingdom." The words "free on board" seem simply to mean that the goods had been shipped before the time of the sale. Clearly freight and insurance were for the seller's account, so that the words "free on board" did not prevent the contract from being a c.i.f. (as opposed to an f.o.b.) contract.

that the risk of loss under the c.i.f. contract had passed *as from* shipment.[92] The case concerns a sale of specific goods[93] but the reasoning would appear to apply equally to a sale of a specified quantity of unascertained goods forming an undifferentiated part of an identified bulk shipment, the whole of which had been destroyed before the contract was made.[94] The most difficult case is that of a sale of unascertained generic goods by description in which the particular shipment which the seller has purported to appropriate to the contract had already been lost when the contract was made. If, as has been submitted above,[95] a seller cannot appropriate such goods to a c.i.f. contract where they are lost after contract but before the purported appropriation, then it follows, *a fortiori*, that he cannot appropriate goods already lost at the time of sale. Hence it cannot be true that the risk of total loss necessarily passes *as from* shipment under a c.i.f. contract. For this purpose, total loss would include a total destruction of the commercial character of the shipment.[96] Partial loss, leading to a mere shortage, would be treated in the same way as deterioration, so that the risk of such loss would pass *as from* shipment.[97]

(3) Goods are shipped, a contract is made for the sale of goods of that description and the shipped goods are then appropriated to the contract. If those goods are lost *after* appropriation, the risk is no doubt on the buyer but it will have passed to him without retrospective effect; as in cases of deterioration, the risk in this situation is best described as having passed on contract or on the later appropriation. If the shipped goods are lost *before* the seller purports to appropriate them to the contract, it is submitted that

---

92 *cf.* Vienna Convention on Contracts for the International Sale of Goods (above, para.1–024), Art. 68, first sentence, under which risk in respect of goods sold in transit generally passes "from the time of the conclusion of the contract": this leads to the same result as that reached in *Couturier v Hastie*. Under Art. 68, second and third sentences, risk may exceptionally pass from the time the goods were "handed over to the carrier who issued the documents embodying the contract of carriage", but only if at the time of contracting the seller neither knew nor ought to have known of the previous loss; *semble* that the seller had such knowledge or means of knowledge in *Couturier v Hastie*, so that this part of Art. 68 would also lead to the same result as that reached by the House of Lords. For other problems arising from Art. 68 in the context of c.i.f. sales, see above, paras 19–082, n.54, 19–083, n.82.

93 So that now the contract would be void under s.6 of the Sale of Goods Act 1979, (above, para.1–124). This would now also be the case where the sale was of a fraction or percentage of an identified bulk cargo: see Sale of Goods Act 1979, s.61(1), definition of "specific goods".

94 See *Barrow Lane & Ballard Ltd v Phillip Phillips & Co.* [1929] 1 K.B. 574 at p.583.

95 Above, para.19–083.

96 *Asfar v Blundell* [1896] 1 Q.B. 123; *cf. Duthie v Hilton* (1870) L.R. 4 C.P. 138.

97 Contrast the position under the Vienna Convention on Contracts for the International Sale of Goods (above, para.1–024). Art. 68 (above, n.92) does not distinguish between loss and deterioration: the risk of both generally passes as from contract, so that the risk of pre-contract deterioration of goods sold in transit would generally be left with the seller (Art. 68, first sentence); but may exceptionally be on the buyer from the time of handing the goods over to the carrier "if the circumstances so indicate" (Art. 68 second sentence). This exception does not apply where the seller at the time of contracting knew or ought to have known of the deterioration (Art. 68 third sentence); but a c.i.f seller of "goods in transit" is unlikely at that time to have such knowledge or means of knowledge of mere deterioration (as opposed to total loss) of the goods.

the risk will not have passed to the buyer. This follows from the submission made above[98] that a c.i.f. seller is not entitled to appropriate goods already lost at the time of appropriation, and that the buyer is not bound to pay against such an appropriation. The discussion so far is based on the assumption that appropriation occurs *after* the contract. Appropriation may also be made *by* the contract, *e.g.* where goods are shipped and sold as a specific cargo. Here again the risk can be said to pass to the buyer on contract, or on appropriation by contract, where the goods are lost *after* the sale, but the risk will not have passed to the buyer if the goods were already destroyed *before* the contract was made.[99]

It follows from the discussion of cases (2) and (3) above that the concept of risk passing with retrospective effect "as from" shipment does not normally[1] apply where goods sold on c.i.f. terms have been totally lost.

Risk passing before shipment? Normally, risk under c.i.f. contract does not pass before shipment. But where specific goods are sold on c.i.f. terms and paid for before shipment, the property may pass before shipment[2]; and it is possible in such cases for the risk to pass with property. This assumption seems to have been made by Scrutton J. in *Wiehe v Dennis Bros*[3] where a Shetland pony which had been sold c.i.f. Rotterdam was paid for and injured before shipment. The actual decision, however, was that the seller was liable for the injury as he had broken his duty as bailee.[4] It is submitted that, in the rare cases in which property passes before shipment under a c.i.f. contract, the risk should nevertheless prima facie remain with the seller until shipment. The c.i.f. buyer's normal assumption is that the goods are at his risk when his insurance cover begins; and if that cover begins only on shipment (as is usually the case[5]), then this will be evidence of intention to exclude the general rule that risk passes with property.[6] 19–114

---

[98] Above, paras 19–081 to 19–082; *cf.* U.C.C., s.2–509, Comment 2. The position is different under the Vienna Convention on Contracts for the International Sale of Goods, Art. 68 of which provides that where goods are "sold in transit" (our present situation) risk generally passes as from contract, and may pass even earlier (*i.e.* as from the time when the goods are handed over to the carrier). Risk can therefore pass before appropriation. But this rule does not apply where the goods are shipped after contract: here Art. 67(2) provides that risk cannot pass before the goods are "identified" (*i.e.* in English terminology, contractually appropriated) to the contract.

[99] *Couturier v Hastie* (1856) 5 H.L.C. 673.

[1] For exceptions, see contractual provisions requiring buyers to pay against an appropriation even though the goods were lost before appropriation, as in *Re Olympia Oil and Cake Produce Brokers Co.* [1915] 1 K.B. 233, discussed in para.19–083, above.

[2] Above, para.19–098. Exceptionally, property may pass before shipment even under a contract for the sale of unascertained generic goods: see above, para.19–098, n.082.

[3] (1913) 29 T.L.R. 250. The buyer in this case might now be regarded as having dealt as consumer (see above, para.18–259); but no such concept was known to English Law at the time of the decision.

[4] Under Sale of Goods Act 1979, s.20(3); above, para.6–026; below, para.19–122.

[5] Above, para.19–042.

[6] *cf.* Vienna Convention on Contracts for the International Sale of Goods (above, para.1–024), Art. 67(1).

Risk may pass before shipment under a c.i.f. contract by virtue of an express provision to that effect, *e.g.* where the contract provides that risk is to pass as soon as the goods are alongside the exporting vessel.[7]

19–115 **Special rules as to risk in transit.** The Sale of Goods Act 1979 lays down a number of special rules as to risk during transit. These have been discussed in Chapter 18[8] and are, as the following further discussion will show, of little importance in relation to c.i.f. contracts.

19–116 **Reasonable contract of carriage.** There is, first, the requirement of section 32(2) of the Sale of Goods Act 1979 that a seller who is "authorised or required" to send the goods to the buyer must make a reasonable contract with the carrier.[9] This subsection can apply to a c.i.f. contract[10]; but under such a contract the seller is not merely "authorised or required" to send the goods to the buyer: he is contractually bound to make a proper contract of carriage.[11] If he fails to do so he will be in breach of the contract of sale and the buyer will be entitled to reject, so that no question of risk will arise.[12]

19–117 **Notice enabling buyer to insure.** There is secondly the duty of the seller under section 32(3) of the Sale of Goods Act 1979 to give notice to enable the buyer to insure.[13] This subsection does not normally apply to c.i.f. contracts under which the seller is himself under an obligation to insure, so that any duty to give notice to enable the buyer to insure is negatived[14] by implied contrary agreement.[15] In *Law & Bonar Ltd v British American*

---

[7] *M. Golodetz & Co. Inc. v Czarnikow Rionda Co. Inc.* (*The Galatia*) [1980] 1 W.L.R. 495.

[8] Above, paras 18–245 to 18–252.

[9] Above, para.18–245. *Cf.* Vienna Convention on Contracts for the International Sale of Goods (above, para.1–024), Art. 32(2).

[10] *Houlder Bros & Co. Ltd v Commissioners of Public Works* [1908] A.C. 276.

[11] Above, para.19–025.

[12] The Vienna Convention on Contracts for the International Sale of Goods (above, para.1–024), Art. 70 expressly provides that the rules as to the passing of risk, which are stated in Arts 67–69, "do not impair the remedies available to the buyer on account of" a breach which is "fundamental" (see Art. 25, above para.18–267, n.38); the seller's failure to make a reasonable contract of carriage may amount to such a breach under Art. 32(2). Art. 66 further has the effect that the buyer is discharged from liability to pay the price if the goods suffer loss or damage which "is due to an act or omission of the seller": there is no requirement of "fundamental breach" under Art. 66. Unlike Sale of Goods Act 1979, s.32(2), the provisions of Arts 66 and 70 quoted in this note seem to apply only where the seller's breach of duty under Art. 32(2) (above, n.9) is the cause of the loss or damage.

[13] Above, para.18–246. *Cf.* Vienna Convention Contracts for the International Sale of Goods (above, para.1–024), Art. 32(3). This provision differs from Sale of Goods Act 1979, s.32(3) in that it contains no express reference to risk, but its breach has repercussions on risk by virtue of the provisions of Arts 66 and 70 of the Convention, discussed in para.19–116, n.12, above.

[14] *cf.* Vienna Convention on Contracts for the International Sale of Goods, Art. 32(3) (above, para.1–024), under which the seller's duty to give notice enabling the buyer to insure applies only "If the seller is not bound to effect insurance in respect of the carriage of the goods . . ."

[15] Above, para.18–247.

Tobacco Co.[16] goods were sold on c.i.f. terms in May 1914 and shipped on July 20. It was not usual to insure against war risks at the time of the sale, nor, apparently, at the time when the policy of insurance was taken out. The policy excepted war risks and the goods were lost as a result of enemy action. Rowlatt J. held that the sellers were not bound, on or shortly before the outbreak of war on August 4, to give notice to the buyers to enable them to insure against war risks. The decision, though hard on the buyers, may be justified on the ground that a seller who has taken out a proper policy of insurance should be under no further responsibility in this respect by reason of a subsequent change of circumstances. Rowlatt J., however, left open the question whether section 32(3) might apply to a c.i.f. contract "made at a time when insurances other than those provided by the seller—*e.g.* against war risks—are usual."[17] Since the seller is prima facie bound to provide whatever insurance is usual,[18] the reference seems to be to a case in which a c.i.f. contract in some way restricted the seller's normal obligation with respect to insurance: for example, if such a contract, made in time of war, expressly provided that the seller was not to be responsible for covering war risks. The effect of such a provision might well be to rebut the inference of intention to exclude section 32(3), which is normally drawn from the fact that a c.i.f. seller is bound to provide insurance.

Necessary deterioration in transit. There is, thirdly, the special rule contained in section 33 of the Sale of Goods Act 1979, placing the risk of necessary deterioration in transit on the buyer though the seller "agrees to deliver the goods at his own risk".[19] There is little scope for this provision in relation to c.i.f. contracts, since under such contracts the whole risk is normally on the buyer during transit in any event. It is theoretically possible for a c.i.f. seller expressly to agree to deliver the goods at his own risk.[20] But if he did so, the contract would not properly speaking be a c.i.f. contract at all[21]; and for this reason such provisions in c.i.f. contracts are restrictively interpreted.[22] 19–118

Contractual provisions as to risk. A contract purporting to be on c.i.f. terms may expressly provide that the goods are to be at the seller's risk until their actual delivery. In *Law & Bonar v British American Tobacco Co. Ltd*[23] Rowlatt J. rejected a printed clause in these terms as repugnant to the nature of a c.i.f. contract. On the other hand, effect is commonly given to clauses which put, not the whole risk, but only the risk of (usually partial) loss, on the seller, *e.g.* by providing that the amount payable is to depend on the quantity of goods which actually arrives,[24] or that any quantity which 19–119

[16] [1916] 2 K.B. 605.
[17] *ibid.*, at p.609.
[18] Above, para.19–043.
[19] Above, para.18–249.
[20] Above, para.19–006.
[21] Above, para.19–006; below, para.19–119.
[22] Below, para.19–119.
[23] [1916] 2 K.B. 605.
[24] *e.g. Calcutta, etc. Steam Navigation Co. v De Mattos* (1863) 32 L.J.Q.B. 214; *Dupont v British South Africa Co.* (1901) 18 T.L.R. 24; *Houlder Bros & Co. Ltd v Commissioner of Public Works* [1908] A.C. 276.

cannot be delivered is to be written off the contract quantity.[25] Contracts containing such clauses are considered to remain c.i.f. contracts, though with variations.[26]

It is also possible for a c.i.f. contract expressly to provide that risk is to pass *before* shipment.[27]

19–120 **Risk of freight.** As freight is part of the c.i.f. price, it may be at the buyer's risk in the sense that he may have to pay the full price even though the goods do not arrive. This will, however, be the case only where the freight is payable in advance. Where it is payable at destination under the bill of lading or under the contract of sale or under both, it is not at the buyer's risk[28] in the sense that he will not have to pay it to the carrier if the goods do not arrive; nor will he have to pay it to the seller, as the amount of the freight will be deducted from the contract price in the invoice.[29] Where the freight is payable at destination under the contract of sale and under the bill of lading, it is not at the buyer's risk even though the goods were shipped under a charterparty entered into by the seller under which the freight was "earned on shipment of goods, ship lost or not lost"; and even though the seller has in fact paid such freight under the charterparty.[30]

19–121 **Delay in delivery.** Under section 20(2) of the Sale of Goods Act 1979, "where delivery has been delayed through the fault of either buyer or seller the goods are at the risk of the party at fault as regards any loss which might not have occurred but for such fault."[31] This subsection will not normally apply to c.i.f. contracts. The "delivery" to which it refers seems to be delivery of the goods[32]; and the c.i.f. seller is not under any obligation actually to deliver the goods at the agreed destination,[33] while delay in shipment beyond the contractual shipment period normally justifies rejection[34] and so makes the question of risk academic. Where tender of documents is delayed through the fault of the seller, he may be in breach of

---

[25] *The Gabbiano* [1940] P. 166.

[26] Above, para.19–006; *cf. Produce Brokers New Company (1924) Ltd v Wray, Sanderson & Co. Ltd* (1931) 39 T.L.R. 257: a contract which provided for a refund in case of short delivery was said at p.260 to be "of a mixed character".

[27] Above, para.19–114.

[28] *Tamvaco v Lucas (No. 2)* (1861) 1 B. & S. 185; (1862) 3 B. & S. 89; *The Pantanassa* [1970] P. 187 (c. & f. contract).

[29] Above, para.19–053.

[30] *The Pantanassa* [1970] P. 187.

[31] Under the Vienna Convention on Contracts for the International Sale of Goods (above, para.1–024), Arts 66 and 70 (above, para.19–116, n.12) the normal rules as to risk may be displaced where delay in *making* delivery is due to an act or omission of, or to a fundamental breach by, the *seller*. Neither of these provisions afford any remedy to the seller where delay in delivery is due to a breach of contract on the part of the *buyer* in taking delivery, but the buyer's wrongful failure to take delivery can lead to the passing of risk to the buyer under Art. 69(1) and (2).

[32] See *Demby Hamilton & Co. Ltd v Barden* [1949] 1 All E.R. 435. The same argument applies to Vienna Convention on Contracts for the International Sale of Goods (above, para.1–024), Art. 69(1) and (2), above, n.31.

[33] Above, paras 19–002, 19–072.

[34] Above, para.18–261.

contract[35]; and the result of this breach is often to entitle the buyer to reject,[36] though there may be cases in which it only entitles him to damages.[37] These remedies do not necessarily lead to the same results as section 20(2). Thus, on the one hand, where the buyer is entitled to reject a late tender he can do so even though the delay has caused him no loss at all; while in the cases in which his only remedy is in damages, these would be awarded only in respect of a loss which was caused by the breach (and not for one which merely might not have occurred but for the breach).

There are, however, exceptional circumstances in which section 20(2) can apply to a c.i.f. contract. A c.i.f. seller may commit a breach of the contract of sale by wrongfully interfering with the performance of the contract of carriage[38] and so causing delay in the actual delivery of the goods to the buyer. The risk due to such delay apppears to be on the seller (even after shipment) under section 20(2).[39] Conversely, the subsection could put the risk on the buyer before shipment, *e.g.* where a c.i.f. contract gave the buyer a choice of destinations and a delay in shipment resulted from his failure to notify the seller in time[40] of his choice of destination.

Seller's liability as bailee. Under section 20(3) of the Sale of Goods Act 1979 "nothing in this section affects the duties or liabilities of either seller or buyer as a bailee . . . of the other party."[41] This subsection will hardly ever apply to a c.i.f. contract since the seller will not normally be in possession of the goods after the property has passed. But such a situation could arise where the goods had been paid for before shipment; and in that event a c.i.f. seller may be held liable under the subsection.[42] 19–122

Buyer dealing as consumer. It is possible, if unusual, for a c.i.f. buyer to deal as consumer[43]; and subsection 20(4) of the Sale of Goods Act 1979 provides that, where the buyer so deals, then subsections 20(1) to 20(3) "must be ignored and the goods remain at the seller's risk until they are delivered to the consumer". The difficulties that can arise from this provision where a c.i.f. buyer deals as consumer are discussed in paragraphs 18–259 to 18–264 above. 19–123

Some of the special rules as to risk in transit discussed in paragraphs 19–115 to 19–119 above also do not apply, or apply with modifications, where

[35] Above, paras 19–164 to 19–170.
[36] Above, para.19–063.
[37] Above, paras 19–064, 19–068.
[38] Above, paras 19–073, 19–074.
[39] *Gatoil International Inc. v Tradax Petroleum Ltd* (*The Rio Sun*) [1985] 1 Lloyd's Rep. 351 at p.362.
[40] Above, para.19–100.
[41] The Vienna Convention on Contracts for the International Sale of Goods (above, para.1–024), imposes a similar duty on the seller in certain cases to take reasonable steps for the preservation of the goods if they are in his possession or control. The converse situation (of the buyer as bailee for the seller before risk has passed) is unlikely to arise under the Convention, since the risk passes to the buyer "when he takes over the goods" (Art. 69(1)) and under a c.i.f. contract is likely to pass to him even earlier under Arts 67 or 68 (above, paras 19–110, nn. 81, 82, 19–111, n.84, 19–112, n.86, 19–113, nn. 92, 97, 98).
[42] *Wiehe v Dennis Bros* (1913) 29 T.L.R. 250.
[43] See above, para.18–259.

the buyer deals as consumer. This follows from section 32(4) of the 1979 Act, by which, where the buyer so deals, subsections 32(2) and 32(3) "must be ignored". The disapplication of subsection 32(2) does not, however, affect the point that a c.i.f. seller is, quite apart from that subsection, contractually bound to make a proper contract of carriage.[44] This common law principle is not excluded by the fact of the buyer's having dealt as consumer; and if the seller has committed a breach of the contract of sale by failing to make such a contract of carriage, then the buyer will be entitled to reject; and if he does so no question of risk will arise.[45] The disapplication of section 32(3) could give rise to problems where the buyer dealt as consumer, particularly if "delivery" of goods sold to a consumer could, for the purposes of section 20(4), take place, in a c.i.f. contract, at the stage of "symbolical" delivery.[46] These problems have been discussed in paragraph 18–261 above. With regard to contractual provisions as to risk, it has, as was noted in paragraph 19–119 above, been suggested that an express provision in a contract of sale that the goods were to be at the seller's risk until their actual delivery to the buyer would be inconsistent with the nature of a c.i.f. contract. If this were so, and if "delivered" in subsection 20(4) referred to actual delivery of the goods, then it could be argued that, by reason of that subsection, there could be no such thing as a c.i.f. contract in which the buyer dealt as consumer. But this is probably too extreme a view. For one thing, the suggestion referred to above[47] cannot, as we have seen,[48] be accepted without qualification. For another, it is by no means clear that the word "delivered" in subsection 20(4) refers, in the case of a c.i.f. contract, to the stage of "complete"[49] or actual delivery of the goods to the buyer[50]; nor is it clear whether in the case of such a contract the subsection would be excluded by implied agreement.[51]

The deterioration in transit of goods sold on c.i.f. terms to a buyer who deals as consumer can also give rise to problems under Part 5A of the Sale of Goods Act 1979. This Part gives certain "additional rights" to a buyer who deals as consumer if "the goods do not conform to the contract at the time of delivery".[52] The exercise or attempted exercise of these rights could come into conflict with the common law principle that, in a c.i.f contract, the seller's undertaking as to the quality relate to the time of *shipment*. Whether the exercise of Part 5A rights actually does give rise to such a conflict depends, in the case of a c.i.f. sale to a buyer who deals as consumer, on the meaning of the phrase "time of delivery": *i.e.* on which of the "three stages of delivery"[53] in a c.i.f. contract it was, to which that the phrase referred. The meaning of the phrase in this context raises issues

---

[44] See above, para.19–116.
[45] *ibid.*
[46] Above, para.19–072.
[47] *i.e.* that made in para.19–119 above.
[48] *ibid.*
[49] See above, para.19–072.
[50] See above, para.18–261.
[51] See above, para.18–264.
[52] Sale of Goods Act 1979, s.48A(1)(b).
[53] See above, para.19–072.

similar to those discussed earlier in this book in relation to the meaning, in this context, of the word "delivered" in subsection 20(4) of the 1979 Act.[54]

7. FRUSTRATION

(a) *Possible Causes of Frustration*

19–124 **Destruction of goods after shipment.** Although the doctrine of frustration[55] applies to c.i.f. contracts, in practice its application to such contracts is very much restricted. Thus the most obvious cause of frustration in a domestic sale is the destruction of specific goods, or of an identified bulk of which the goods form a part[56]; but this will not generally frustrate a c.i.f. contract where the goods are destroyed after shipment. On the contrary, in such a case the seller remains bound to tender the shipping documents and the buyer to pay the price; and the same is true where a contract is made for the sale of unascertained generic goods and the goods which are appropriated to that contract on or after shipment are then destroyed.[57] Nor will destruction of specific goods after shipment normally avoid a c.i.f. contract under section 7 of the Sale of Goods Act 1979, as the risk will normally have passed on shipment or on contract.[58]

19–125 **Destruction of goods before shipment.** A c.i.f. contract for the sale of specific goods would presumably be frustrated, or avoided under section 7, if the goods were destroyed before shipment. If the contract were for the sale of a specified quantity of unascertained goods forming part of an identified bulk, or of unascertained goods to be taken from an identified source, it would likewise be frustrated if (without any default on the part of the seller) the bulk was destroyed or the source failed or became unavailable before shipment. A c.i.f. contract for the sale of unascertained generic goods would not be frustrated merely because goods which the seller had intended to appropriate to the contract were destroyed before shipment. But there are various other ways in which such a contract may be frustrated[59]; and these are discussed in the following paragraphs.

---

[54] See above, paras 18–259 to 18–264.

[55] For the relationship between the English doctrine of frustration and Art. 79 of the Vienna Convention on Contracts for the International Sale of Goods, see Treitel, *Frustration and Force Majeure* (1994), paras 6–043, 15–039.

[56] *cf. Howell v Coupland* (1876) 1 Q.B.D. 258 (above, para.6–038).

[57] Above, paras 19–001, 19–059, 19–080.

[58] Above, para.19–113. Where the buyer deals as consumer (see above, para.18–259) the goods "remain at the seller's risk until they are delivered to the consumer": Sale of Goods Act 1979, s.20(4). If "delivered" here refers to the stage of "complete delivery" (see above, para.18–261), then the destruction of the goods after shipment but before their actual delivery to the consumer could frustrate a c.i.f. contract. The buyer would then be released from his duty to pay and the seller from his duty to tender documents.

[59] *Acetylene Corp. of GB v Canada Carbide Co.* (1921) 6 Ll.L.R. 410 at pp.468, 472 where Rowlatt J. refused to accept that a contract for the sale of unascertained goods can never be frustrated (*sc.* by impossibility); the actual decision, that frustration was excluded by a provision in the contract for suspension if shipment was "hindered", was reversed on appeal (1922) 8 Ll.L.R. 456, CA; below, para.19–133.

19–126 **Stipulated method of performance impossible.** A c.i.f. contract may be frustrated if it provides for a method of performance which becomes impossible. In *Nickoll and Knight v Ashton, Edridge & Co.*[60] cottonseed was sold "to be shipped per steamship *Orlando* . . . during the month of January". Shipment on the *Orlando* in January became impossible because of the stranding of the ship; and the seller successfully claimed that the contract was frustrated.[61] The contract was for delivery of the cottonseed in the United Kingdom; but it seems that the contract would similarly have been discharged if it had been on c.i.f. terms and had provided for shipment on a particular ship within a designated period. Thus in an Australian case[62] a c.i.f. contract for the sale of onions provided for "shipment per P. & O. steamer sailing from Japan about the 8th September." Because of a strike, the P. & O. steamer which was to have sailed from Japan at about that time did not do so; and it was held that the seller was not liable for having failed to ship the goods in accordance with the contract.[63] In the *Nickoll and Knight* case itself, the crucial factor leading to frustration was that the contract was construed (by a majority of the Court of Appeal) as providing for performance *only* by the stipulated method. If that method had not been regarded as exclusive, the seller *might* have been bound to perform by shipping the goods on a different ship[64]; whether he *would* have been bound to do so would depend on whether such a different method of performance differed fundamentally from that called for by the express terms of the contract.[65]

The foregoing discussion is concerned only with a method of performance to be adopted by the *seller*. It seems that a c.i.f. contract could also be frustrated where impossibility affected a method of performance to be adopted by the *buyer*. This could, for example, be the position where the contract called for payment by a letter of credit to be opened by a named bank and that bank ceased to exist before the time for opening the credit had been reached. Whether the contract actually *was* frustrated would depend on whether payment through a different bank would impose fundamentally different risks or burdens on the parties.[66] The contract could also be frustrated where the authorities of the country of origin

---

[60] [1901] 2 K.B. 126.

[61] The claim was presumably made because the price of cottonseed had risen (see p.127 of the report), and seems to have had little merit. Its success enabled the seller to rely on the stranding of the ship as an excuse for escaping from a bad bargain.

[62] *Cornish & Co. v Kanematsu* (1913) 3 S.R. (N.S.W.) 83.

[63] The seller in this case was not relying on the supervening event to escape from the contract on a rising market (contrast the position in the *Nickoll and Knight* case [1901] 2 K.B. 126, as explained in n.61 above). In *Cornish & Co. v Kanematsu* the seller had offered to make alternative shipping arrangements. The buyer was not bound to accept this offer as it provided for shipment by a route other than that specified by the contract (see above, para.19–032) and he in fact rejected it. But in making it the seller did give the buyer the opportunity of acquiring the goods at the originally agreed price, notwithstanding the impossibility in the agreed method of performance.

[64] *cf.* in the United States, U.C.C., s.2–614(1); below, para.20–015.

[65] See below, para.19–127.

[66] See further Treitel, *Frustration and Force Majeure* (2nd ed. 2004), para.4–069.

prohibited the export of the goods unless a method of payment was adopted which differed fundamentally from that on which the parties had agreed, *e.g.* by requiring payment to be made *in advance* when the parties had agreed on payment against documents.[67]

Contemplated method of performance impossible. Where a c.i.f. contract does not in terms provide for a particular method of performance, but both parties merely contemplate that it will be used, the contract will not be frustrated merely because that method becomes impossible. In *Tsakiroglou & Co. v Noblee Thorl GmbH.*[68] Sudanese groundnuts were sold c.i.f. Hamburg for shipment from Port Sudan[69] during November/December 1956. At the time of the contract it was contemplated by both parties that shipment would be via the Suez Canal, but the Canal was blocked on November 2 and not reopened until well after the end of the shipment period. It was held that the contract was not frustrated. The contract did not expressly provide for the shipment of the goods via the Suez Canal; nor could any such term be implied since the actual route of shipment was a matter of indifference to the buyer. The seller could therefore have performed by procuring a contract for the carriage of the goods to Hamburg via the Cape of Good Hope. Although this method of performance would involve the seller in considerable additional expense it was not fundamentally different from that originally contemplated[70]; nor would it prejudice the buyer in any way. Any hardship which this result might be thought to have caused to the seller could have been avoided by contracting on different terms, *e.g.* by selling the goods f.o.b. port Sudan, or by providing that the extra cost of shipping the goods via the Cape should be borne by the buyer.[71] 19–127

In the *Tsakiroglou* case, Lord Simonds said: "It appears to me that it does not automatically follow that, because one term of the contract, *e.g.* that the goods shall be carried by a particular route, becomes impossible of performance, the whole contract is thereby abrogated."[72] This suggests that, even if the contract had expressly provided for shipment via Suez, it would not have been frustrated merely because shipment by that route became impossible. Frustration would have occurred only if shipment by the designated route was a matter of fundamental importance. No reference was made by any other member of the House of Lords to this point, which (in relation to a c.i.f. contract) is not free from difficulty. On the one hand, inability to perform a term of minor importance should not, as a matter of

---

[67] *Nile Co. for the Export of Agricultural Crops v H & JM Bennett (Commodities) Ltd* [1986] 1 Lloyd's Rep. 555 (f.o.b. contract).

[68] [1962] A.C. 93.

[69] It was found that Port Sudan was the intended port of shipment, even though the parties had, by mistake, used a form which stipulated for shipment from a *West* African port; see [1962] A.C. 93 at p.95.

[70] The extra cost of sending the goods via the Cape was £7 10s., while their market price had risen by £18 15s. above the contract price (see p.111 of the report). If the seller's plea had succeeded, it seems that he would have made a profit out of frustration; *cf.* n.61, above.

[71] As in *DI Henry v Wilhelm G Clasen* [1973] 1 Lloyd's Rep. 159.

[72] [1962] A.C. 93 at p.112.

general principle, frustrate a contract. On the other hand, if the contract of carriage does not comply with the express provisions as to the route of shipment contained in the contract of sale, it might seem that the buyer would be entitled to reject the documents[73]; and at first sight it is hard to see why the seller should be bound to procure a carriage document which the buyer could reject. Probably the reason why the buyer would not be entitled to reject in Lord Simonds' example is that the stipulated method of performance is assumed to be one that is not intended to be exclusive.

19–128 **Method contemplated by one party only.** A c.i.f. contract is not frustrated merely because the seller alone expected to use a method of performance which has become impossible. Thus in *Blackburn Bobbin Co. Ltd v T W Allen & Sons Ltd*[74] a seller of "Finland birch" intended to perform by supplying goods to be shipped straight from Finland. Such shipment became impossible because of wartime conditions. It was held that the contract was not frustrated as the buyer did not know, and had no reason to suppose, that this method of performance was contemplated by the seller: for all the buyer knew, the seller might have appropriated to the contract goods taken from stocks kept in this country. The contract in this case provided for delivery free on rail Hull, but it is submitted that the same principle would apply to a c.i.f. sale where it was the intention only of the seller that the goods should be taken from a particular foreign source, and that source became unavailable while other methods of performance remained open.[75] Similarly, a c.i.f. contract is not frustrated merely because the seller expects to receive the price in his own country by there selling a draft on the buyer and this expectation is defeated because wartime conditions make it impossible so to sell the draft.[76] Nor will such a contract be frustrated merely because the buyer is prevented from making use of a method of payment intended by him alone, *e.g.* where exchange control regulations in his own country prevent him from providing a letter of credit for payment to be made outside that country,[77] the sellers being "not in the least concerned as to the method by which the . . . buyers [were] to provide that letter of credit".[78]

19–129 **Alternatives.**[79] Where a contract imposes alternative obligations, it is not in general frustrated merely because performance of some of the alternatives becomes impossible or illegal, so long as performance of at least one of them remains possible and legal. One illustration of this principle is provided by the rule that a c.i.f. seller who is prevented from shipping goods of the contract description must (in general) perform by acquiring and appropriating to the contract goods which are already afloat.[80]

---

73 Above, para.19–032.
74 [1918] 2 K.B. 467.
75 *cf.* below, para.19–129.
76 *Re Comptoir Commercial Anversois and Power, Sons & Co.* [1920] 1 K.B. 868.
77 *Toprak Mahsulleri Offisi v Finagrain Cie. Commercile* [1979] 2 Lloyd's Rep. 98.
78 *ibid.*, 114.
79 See Treitel, *Frustration and Force Majeure* (2nd ed. 2004), Ch.10.
80 Above, para.19–011, *cf.* below, para.19–141.

Similarly, if a c.i.f. seller knows that shipment will definitely become impossible during part of the shipment period he is bound to ship during that part (if any) of the period in which shipment remains possible after he has acquired this knowledge.[81] And if a c.i.f. contract gives the buyer an option to choose between several ports of destination, the contract is not frustrated merely because one or some (but not all) of those ports become enemy ports.[82] This is so even if the buyer had originally, and without any intention that the contract was to be performed in an illegal way, declared an enemy port. Such a declaration is a nullity and leaves it open to the buyer to make a further, valid declaration within the contract period.[83]

Inability to ship. A c.i.f. seller of unascertained generic goods who does not, at the time of the sale, have goods of the contract description in stock cannot escape liability for breach merely because, as a result of being let down by his supplier,[84] or of market conditions, he is unable to procure goods to satisfy his obligations under the contract. That is not to say, however, that such a contract can never be frustrated by physical impossibility of performance. McCardie J. has said that "a bare and unqualified contract for the sale of unascertained goods" will not be frustrated in this way "unless most special facts compel an opposite implication".[85] This dictum raises the questions when such a contract is "bare and unqualified" and what kinds of "special facts" may "compel an opposite implication". In particular, where a c.i.f. contract for the sale of unascertained generic goods provides for shipment from a certain place within a certain time, can the contract be frustrated because the seller is prevented by unavailability of shipping space to make such a shipment? 19–130

In *Ashmore & Son v C S Cox & Co.*[86] 250 bales of Manila hemp were sold on c.i.f. terms,[87] "Shipment to be made from a port or ports in the Philippine Islands direct or indirect to London between May 1 and July 31, 1898, both inclusive." The sellers were unable, because of the Spanish-American war, to make such a shipment, though there had within the contract period been a shipment to Liverpool "of hemp which, had it been a shipment of the defendants [*i.e.* the sellers] would have satisfied the plaintiffs [*i.e.* the buyers]."[88] It was held that the sellers were in breach. One possible explanation for the decision is that there were in existence goods 19–131

---

[81] *Ross T Smyth & Co. Ltd (Liverpool) v WN Lindsay Ltd (Leith)* [1953] 1 W.L.R. 1280 (above, para.19–013).

[82] *Hindley & Co. Ltd v General Fibre Co. Ltd* [1940] 2 K.B. 517; *cf. The Furness Bridge* [1977] 2 Lloyd's Rep. 376.

[83] *Hindley & Co. Ltd v General Fibre Co. Ltd*, above.

[84] *Intertradex SA v Lesieur-Torteaux S.A.R.L.* [1978] 2 Lloyd's Rep. 509; *Atisa SA v Aztec AG* [1983] 2 Lloyd's Rep. 579 (f.o.b. contract). *Cf.* Vienna Convention on Contracts for the International Sale of Goods (above, para.1–024), Art. 79(2).

[85] *Blackburn Bobbin Co. Ltd v TW Allen & Sons Ltd* [1918] 1 K.B. 540 at p.550; affirmed [1918] 2 K.B. 467 (above, para.19–128); *cf. Intertradex SA v Lesieur-Torteaux SARL*, above, at p.515.

[86] [1899] 1 Q.B. p.436.

[87] See the reports in 68 L.J.Q.B. 75; 4 Com.Cas. 48.

[88] [1899] 1 Q.B. 436 at 438.

which the sellers might have been able to buy afloat to perform the contract; but the basis for the decision was that the seller's undertaking was an "absolute" one.[89] The decision has been both approved in the Court of Appeal[90] and doubted in three decisions at first instance.[91] But one of these decisions[92] was overruled by the House of Lords in the *Tsakiroglou* case[93] where no reference was made to *Ashmore & Son v C. S. Cox & Co.*; so that the present status of the decision is very much in doubt.

19–132 In *Lewis Emanuel & Son Ltd v Sammut*[94] 1,000 half sacks of Maltese new potatoes were sold on April 14, 1958 c.i.f. London, to be shipped from Malta "on or before" April 24, 1958. This was held to require shipment between April 14 and 24; and only one ship sailed from Malta between those dates. It was found that it was "not practicable or possible" to ship the potatoes on that ship, and there was no evidence that any potatoes of the contract description were on that ship, so that there was no possibility of buying such goods afloat and appropriating them to the contract. Nevertheless the seller was held liable in damages. Pearson J. said that a contract for the sale of unascertained goods could be frustrated.[95] But there was no frustration in the case before him as the parties had not bargained on the footing that the contract should be at an end if the seller could not get shipping space within the contract period. "The seller, being on an island, if he wants to export goods he must. . . make sure that shipping space is available before he commits himself to an absolute contract"[96]; alternatively, he must provide in the contract for the eventuality that space may not be available.

19–133 The result of these cases seems to be that unavailability of shipping space will not generally amount to frustration, but the possibility that it may in exceptional circumstances have this effect is not utterly excluded. A case which may illustrate this possibility is *Acetylene Co. of GB v Canada Carbide Co.*[97] which concerned a sale of carbide to be shipped from Canada, c.i.f. various United Kingdom ports. Deliveries were to commence in 1917, but at that time most of the available shipping space had been requisitioned by the government. The contract provided that performance should be sus-

[89] *ibid.*, at p.442; subject to an exclusion clause which was held, on construction, not to apply.
[90] *Blackburn Bobbin Co. Ltd v TW Allen & Sons Ltd* [1918] 2 K.B. 467 at p.470.
[91] *Carapanayoti v ET Green Ltd* [1959] 1 Q.B. 131 at p.137; *Albert D Gaon v Société Interprofessionelle des Oléagineux Fluides Alimentaires* [1959] 2 Lloyd's Rep. 39 at p.41 (there is no reference to this point in the report of the case in the *Law Reports*: [1960] 2 Q.B. 318); *Lewis Emanuel & Son Ltd v Sammut* [1959] 2 Lloyd's Rep. 629 at p.640.
[92] *Carapanayoti v ET Green Ltd*, above.
[93] [1962] A.C. 93, above, para.19–127.
[94] [1959] 2 Lloyd's Rep. 629; for the converse situation, see *Hills v Sughrue* (1846) 15 M. & W. 253 (ship available, but not goods).
[95] The authorities which he cited (*viz.* the *Carapanayoti*, *Gaon* and *Tsakiroglou* cases, above) show that he had in mind the possibility of frustration by physical interference with performance, and not merely by illegality.
[96] [1959] 2 Lloyd's Rep. 629 at p.642.
[97] (1922) 8 Ll.L.R. 456, CA.

pended if deliveries were "hindered"; and no claim was made by the buyer until 1920. By this time shipment was again possible but market conditions had radically changed. The Court of Appeal held that the suspension clause in the contract did not cover such a long delay; and that the seller was not liable for failing to ship in 1920. The result was that a c.i.f. contract for the sale of unascertained generic goods was held to have been frustrated as a result of the seller's inability to find shipping space.

Inability to effect insurance. The seller's inability to effect insurance seems to be governed by the same principles as inability to ship: that is, inability to insure would not normally frustrate the contract. This is *a fortiori* the case where the seller finds that he cannot insure against a risk which he is not bound to cover under the contract of sale, but which he wishes to cover to protect his own security interest in the goods. In *Re Comptoir Commercial Anversois and Power, Son & Co.*[98] a c.i.f. contract provided that, in the event of war, the sellers should have the right to cover war risks "if they think fit and are able" for the account of the buyers. On the outbreak of war the sellers were unable to cover these risks; and it was held that the contract was not frustrated. 19–134

Breakdown of diplomatic and commercial relations. In *The Playa Larga*[99] a contract was made for the sale of sugar c. & f. Chilean port; the seller was a Cuban state trading organisation and the buyer was controlled by a Chilean state trading organisation. Later, diplomatic relations between Chile and Cuba were severed and there was a complete breakdown of commercial relations between the two countries. Although these events did not make performance of the contract impossible, they were held to have frustrated it since, after them, there was no practical possibility that the contract would be implemented by either side. It is submitted that this conclusion depended on the exceptional circumstances that the breakdown in diplomatic and commercial relationships was between governments which controlled the entire trade between the two countries in question and that the parties to the contract of sale were state entities controlled by those governments. The decision would not support the view that a contract between two private parties would be discharged merely because its performance would involve trade between two countries which had ceased, before performance had been completed, to have diplomatic relations with each other. 19–135

Illegality: trading with the enemy. A c.i.f. contract may be frustrated by supervening illegality, for example if the port of destination named in the contract becomes an enemy port. In such a case the contract can be frustrated even though it contemplates eventual delivery of the goods to a place in neutral territory. Thus in *Fibrosa Spolka Akcyjna v Fairbairn, Lawson, Combe Barbour Ltd*[1] English manufacturers sold machinery to a 19–136

---

98 [1920] 1 K.B. 868.
99 *Empresa Exportadora de Azucar v Industria Azucarera Nacional SA* (*The Playa Larga*) [1983] 2 Lloyd's Rep. 171 at pp.187–188.
1 [1943] A.C. 32.

Polish company c.i.f. Gdynia. The contract was frustrated by the German occupation of Gdynia after the outbreak of war in 1939 even though the ultimate destination of the goods was Vilna which remained (so far as this country was concerned) in neutral territory until the summer of 1941. Where the contract is alleged to be frustrated because the port of destination has become an enemy port, the crucial date is that on which the documents are (or are to be) tendered. The contract is not frustrated merely because the port becomes an enemy port after tender of documents.[2] It would seem that a c.i.f. contract will also be frustrated if the goods appropriated to it are being carried on a ship which before tender of documents becomes an enemy ship.[3] Similarly, such a contract will be frustrated by illegality if it provides, or if the parties contemplate, that the goods are to be obtained from an enemy source.[4]

19–137 **Illegality: export or import prohibitions.** Another possible cause of illegality is supervening prohibition of export or import. This is discussed generally in Chapter 18; as is the question whether failure to obtain a licence under regulations already in existence at the time of the contract may amount to frustration.[5] But two aspects of this type of supervening event call for further discussion in the present chapter.

First, a prohibition of export may merely prevent a c.i.f. seller from *shipping* goods of the contract description. The question whether he must nevertheless *acquire, and tender, such goods already afloat* relates specifically to c.i.f. contracts, and is discussed in paragraph 19–141, below.

Secondly, a c.i.f. contract is not frustrated merely because the buyer's purpose of importing the goods into the country of the c.i.f. destination is defeated by a prohibition of import. In one case,[6] soyabean meal was sold c.i.f. Lisbon under a contract governed by English law and providing for payment in New York. It was held that the contract was not frustrated by a change of Portuguese Government policy,[7] as a result of which a licence to import the goods into Portugal was refused. This followed from the nature of a c.i.f. contract, which was not a contract to deliver the goods in Lisbon, but one to ship them under a contract of carriage with that destination.[8] It was therefore possible for the contract to be performed and for the buyer then to redirect the goods to another country. Such performance could, moreover, be rendered without violating Portuguese law,[9] even though the

[2] *In re Weis & Co. Ltd* [1916] 1 K.B. 346; the same was assumed in *The Julia* [1949] A.C. 293.

[3] *cf. Duncan Fox & Co. v Schrempft and Bonke* [1915] 3 K.B. 355 (where the contract was c.i.f. Hamburg *and* the ship was German; but it is submitted that either factor standing alone would have sufficed to frustrate the contract); as to tender of a bill of lading issued by an enemy shipowner, see above, para.19–036.

[4] *cf. Re Badische Co. Ltd* [1921] 2 Ch. 331; above, para.18–335.

[5] Above, paras 18–331 *et seq.*

[6] *Congimex Companhia Geral, etc. SARL v Tradax Export SA* [1983] 1 Lloyd's Rep. 250; *cf. L'Office National du Thé et du Sucre v Philippine Sugar Trading (London) Ltd* [1983] 1 Lloyd's Rep. 89.

[7] *cf.* above, para.18–340.

[8] Above, paras 19–001, 19–072.

[9] So far as this was relevant, the contract being governed by English law and the law of the place of payment being New York law. On the view taken by the court, Portuguese law was not the law of the place of delivery.

contract provided for weighing and sampling at Lisbon, since there was no finding that these acts (as opposed to the import of the goods) were illegal by Portuguese law. Performance being thus neither impossible nor illegal, the contract was not frustrated merely because the buyer's purpose of importing the goods into Portugal was defeated: "frustrated expectations and intentions of one party to a contract do not necessarily or indeed usually lead to the frustration of that contract".[10] In a later case[11] it was similarly held that a contract for the sale of sugar c. & f. Chittagong was not frustrated when the buyer's licence to import the sugar into Bangladesh was withdrawn. The contract did not oblige either the buyer to import the goods into that country or the seller to procure such import,[12] so that its performance had not become illegal by the law of the place of performance. The contract, moreover, expressly required the buyer to obtain an import licence and went on to provide that his inability to do so should "not be justification for declaration of force majeure". While this clause did not in terms cover the situation in which a licence was first granted and then withdrawn, it showed that the lack of a valid export licence "was within the contemplation of the parties"[13] and that the buyer was to bear the risk of not only inability to obtain a licence, but also of its withdrawal. Hence the contract was not discharged by the fact that the buyer's purpose of importing the goods into Bangladesh was defeated. *A fortiori*, a c.i.f. contract is not frustrated merely because the buyer's purpose of ultimately importing the goods into a country *other* than that of the c.i.f. destination is defeated by a prohibition of import imposed by that other country.[14]

(b) *Provisions for Supervening Events*

Provision for delays, etc.[15] C.i.f. contracts commonly make provision for delay in, or prevention of, performance resulting from various specified causes over which the parties have no control, such as strikes, war, hostilities, prohibition of export, blockade or *force majeure*[16]; or the contract may be "subject" to such events.[17] Clauses of this kind may provide for cancellation of the contract in the specified events[18]; or for an extension of the shipment period[19]; or (what amounts to the same thing) for a 19–138

---

[10] [1983] 1 Lloyd's Rep. 250 at p.253.
[11] *Bangladesh Export Import Co. Ltd v Sucden Kerry SA* [1995] 2 Lloyd's Rep. 1.
[12] Above, para.19–001, 19–002.
[13] [1995] 2 Lloyd's Rep. 1 at p.6.
[14] *Congimex SARL (Lisbon) v Continental Grain Export Corp. (New York)* [1979] 2 Lloyd's Rep. 346.
[15] *cf.* above, paras 18–342, 18–356; below, para.20–103.
[16] *e.g. Produce Brokers Ltd v Weiss* (1918) 118 L.T. 111; 87 L.J.K.B. 472 (prohibition of export, blockade or hostilities); *Blythe & Co. v Richards, Turpin & Co.* (1916) 114 L.T. 753 (war or any other cause over which the sellers have no control); *Fairclough, Dodd & Jones Ltd v JH Vantol Ltd* [1957] 1 W.L.R. 136 (prohibition of export or any other cause comprehended in the expression *force majeure*).
[17] *Hong Guan & Co. Ltd v R Jumabhoy* [1960] A.C. 684 (subject to *force majeure* and shipment; above, para.19–014); below para.19–140.
[18] *Produce Brokers Ltd v Weiss*, above; *cf. Hong Guan & Co. Ltd v R Jumabhoy*, above.
[19] *e.g. Koninklijke Bunge v Cie. Continentale d'Importation* [1973] 2 Lloyd's Rep. 44. For suspension as to part, see *Bremer Handelsgesellschaft mbH v Arthur Daniels Midland International SA* [1981] 2 Lloyd's Rep. 483.

suspension of the contract[20]; or for a period of suspension followed by cancellation at the end of it, if performance has not once again become possible.[21] Such cancellation may be at the option of one of the parties,[22] or it may follow automatically from the occurrence of the specified event.[23] A provision of this kind may operate as an excuse for non-performance; and it may exclude the doctrine of frustration.

19–139 **As excusing non-performance.** A provision of the kind described in paragraph 19–138 may give one party an excuse for non-performance in the specified events, whether or not those events would otherwise frustrate the contract. The exact effect of such provisions is governed by principles similar to those discussed in Chapter 18 in relation to prohibition of export or import clauses.[24] Thus the same rules as to burden of proof apply[25]; and the clause may, on its true construction, require the party relying on it (usually the seller) to show not only that the event has occurred, but also that it has prevented performance.[26]

19–140 **Construction of provisions for supervening events.** The courts tend to construe such clauses against the seller; and this tendency is illustrated by *Hong Guan & Co. Ltd v R. Jumabhoy*,[27] where a contract for the sale of 50 tons of cloves was made "subject to *force majeure* and shipment". The sellers succeeded in procuring a shipment of 50 tons, but not in shipping enough to satisfy all their contracts for the sale of cloves. It was held that the provision could not be construed to mean "subject to our shipping enough to satisfy all our contracts"[28] or "subject to our shipping 50 tons which we allocate to you"; and that the sellers, who had allocated the 50 tons to other buyers, were in breach. Similarly, where a c.i.f. contract provided for suspension, should the seller be prevented from shipping "under normal conditions", it was held that the seller was not excused merely by a steep rise in freight rates under the influence of war-time conditions[29]; where the clause provided for extension of the shipment

---

[20] *Blythe & Co. v Richards, Turpin & Co.* (1916) 114 L.T. 753.

[21] *e.g.* Grain and Feed Trade Association form 100, cl. 22, discussed in *Bremer Handelsgesellschaft mbH v Vanden Avenne-Izegem PVBA* [1978] 2 Lloyd's Rep. 109, above, para.18–357.

[22] See the clause referred to in n.21, above.

[23] See clause 21 of the form referred to in n.21, above; for a later variation of this clause, see above, para.18–352.

[24] Above, paras 18–342 to 18–358.

[25] Above, paras 18–346 to 18–351; *Avimex SA v Dewulf & Cie.* [1979] 2 Lloyd's Rep. 57; *cf. Huilerie L'Abelle v Société des Huileries du Niger* (*The Kastellon*) [1978] 2 Lloyd's Rep. 203, discussed below, para.19–197.

[26] See above, paras 18–345, 18–349; *Hoecheong Products Ltd v Cargill Hong Kong Ltd* [1995] 1 Lloyd's Rep. 584 at p.587.

[27] [1960] A.C. 684.

[28] Contrast *Bowring & Walker Pty Ltd v Jackson's Corio Meat Packing (1965) Pty Ltd* [1972] 1 N.S.W.R. 277, where "subject to export quota permit" was held to make the contract subject to the seller's obtaining permits sufficient to enable him to fulfil the contract with the buyer after having performed *previous* contracts *of which the buyer knew*.

[29] *Blythe & Co. v Richard Turpin & Co.* (1916) 114 L.T. 753; *S Instone & Co. Ltd v Speeding & Marshall* (1915) 32 T.L.R. 202; *Re Comptoir Commercial Anversois and Power, Son & Co.* [1920] 1 K.B. 868; a "prohibitive" rise in freight rates might bring such a provision into play: *cf.* above, para.18–321.

period, should shipment be prevented by strikes, the seller could not rely on it merely because grain elevators belonging to the shipper[30] were affected by strikes, other elevators in the port of shipment not being so affected[31]; and where the contract provided the seller with an excuse in the event of "mechanical breakdown" it was held that the clause would operate only if the breakdown was the sole cause of the seller's inability to deliver.[32] On the same principle, a seller cannot rely on a clause excusing his failure to deliver by reason of certain listed events (such as flood, fire or storm) or "any other causes beyond his control" merely because he is let down by the supplier from whom he expected to obtain the goods: he must show that the supervening event prevented him from procuring goods of the contract description from some other supplier.[33]

On the other hand, it should be stressed that the cases discussed in the preceding paragraph illustrate no more than a rule of construction. It is therefore possible for a clause on its true construction to protect a seller even though the events which have occurred have not prevented all possible methods of performance. Thus in *Fairclough, Dodd and Jones Ltd v J H Vantol Ltd*[34] a clause provided for extension of the shipment period by two months "should shipment be delayed" by certain specified causes. Even though those causes of delay only operated for part of the shipment period, it was held that the clause applied, so that the sellers were not in default, by reason of the delay so caused, and were excused by subsequent prohibition of export. Similarly, it has been said that, where the contract provided for shipment from a number of ports, the seller might, on the true construction of the clause, be protected by it even though he could not show that shipment from all ports within the permitted range was impossible.[35] In one such case the seller was held to be protected on showing that the ports through which he in fact would have shipped were strike-bound.[36]

---

[30] Who was not the seller but the first in a "chain" involving a number of buyers and sellers.

[31] *Koninklijke Bunge v Cie. Continentale d'Importation* [1973] 2 Lloyd's Rep. 44. Contrast *BTP Tioxide Ltd v Pioneer Shipping Ltd* (*The Nema*) [1982] A.C. 724 (frustration of charterparty by strike affecting entire loading port).

[32] *Intertradex SA v Lesieur-Torteaux SARL* [1978] 2 Lloyd's Rep. 509; *cf. Huilerie L'Abelle v Société des Huileries du Niger* (*The Kastellon*) [1978] 2 Lloyd's Rep. 203, discussed below, para.19–197.

[33] *PJ van der Zijden Wildhandel NV v Tucker & Cross Ltd* [1975] 2 Lloyd's Rep. 240; the default of the intended suppliers might bring the clause into operation if they were "monopoly suppliers"; *ibid.*, at p.241; *cf. Hoechong Products Ltd v Cargill Hong Kong Ltd* [1995] 1 Lloyd's Rep. 584 at p.587, where the sellers successfully relied on a "virtually identical" clause. But such default would not, of itself, frustrate the contract: *Atisa SA v Aztec AG* [1983] 2 Lloyd's Rep. 579 (f.o.b. contract). Nor would the mere fact that such a monopoly supplier had raised his price above that for which the seller had agreed to sell to the buyer enable the seller to rely on the clause: *Exportelisa SA v Giuseppe Figli Soc. Coll.* [1978] 1 Lloyd's Rep. 433 (f.o.b. contract); *cf.* above, para.18–321.

[34] [1957] 1 W.L.R. 136; *cf. European Grain and Shipping Ltd v J. H. Rayner & Co. Ltd* [1970] 2 Lloyd's Rep. 239.

[35] *Koninklijke Bunge v Cie. Continentale d'Importation* [1973] 2 Lloyd's Rep. 44 at p.51.

[36] *Sociedad Iberica de Molturacion SA v Tradax Export SA* [1978] 2 Lloyd's Rep. 545; contrast the *PJ van der Zijden Wildhandel* case, above, n.33.

In one case an arbitrator's finding that shipment had not been "prevented by hostilities" was treated as a finding of "fact" which the court could not reverse[37]; but the court added that the arbitrator had not misconstrued the contract. Where there is such misconstruction, the court has power to interfere, since the construction of the contract raises an issue of law.

A c.i.f. contract commonly gives the seller the right to give a notice nominating the ship from which delivery is to be made, and it may go on to give him the right to substitute a different ship for that named in his original notice. Once the seller has nominated ship A, he cannot rely on a *force majeure* clause on the ground that supervening events (even if they fall within the clause) have prevented him from giving effect to his desire to substitute another vessel for ship A[38]; for his "option to substitute is not an obligation at all but a right, and so falls completely outside the scope of the *force majeure* clause."[39]

19–141 **Effect of provision on duty to buy afloat.** Normally, a c.i.f. seller is bound to perform either by shipping goods of the contract description or by buying such goods already afloat.[40] If performance in the first of these ways is prevented, the second must be adopted[41]; so that normally a c.i.f. seller cannot rely on a clause, which is expressed to apply where *force majeure* or similar causes prevent performance, merely because shipment is prevented: he will be excused only if he was also prevented from buying goods afloat.[42] But this general rule was held not to apply in a number of cases arising out of the embargo imposed in June 1973 on the export of soyabean meal from the United States.[43] The contracts in those cases contained prohibition of export and *force majeure* clauses; many of the buyers had resold so that "string" or "circle" contracts were formed under which each seller "had already made arrangements to ship the goods by himself or some shipper higher up in the string".[44] The resulting "chains" of buyers and sellers commonly had 20 to 30 (and sometimes as many as 100) links.[45] The effect of the export embargo was to push prices up steeply,[46] so that buyers claimed damages from sellers who had failed to deliver, while sellers relied on prohibition and *force majeure* clauses in the contracts. It was held that

---

[37] *Produce Brokers Ltd v Weiss* (1918) 118 L.T. 111.
[38] *Coastal (Bermuda) Petroleum Ltd v VTT Vulcan Petroleum SA (The Marine Star)* [1993] 1 Lloyd's Rep. 329 (where in fact the supervening event did not fall within the clause, the seller's reason for withdrawing ship A being merely that he wanted to divert its cargo to another contract; for further proceedings in this case see [1996] 2 Lloyd's Rep. 383).
[39] [1993] 1 Lloyd's Rep. 329 at p.332.
[40] Above, para.19–011.
[41] *ibid.*; *Tradax Export SA v André & Cie.* [1976] 1 Lloyd's Rep. 416 at p.423.
[42] *Fairclough, Dodd & Jones Ltd v JH Vantol* [1957] 1 W.L.R. 136 at p.146 (referring to statements of McNair J. in [1955] 1 W.L.R. 642 at p.646); *Bremer Handelsgesellschaft mbH v Finagrain, etc. SA* [1981] 2 Lloyd's Rep. 259 at p.265).
[43] Above, para.18–348.
[44] *Tradax Export SA v André & Cie.*, above, at p.423.
[45] *Cook Industries Inc. v Meunerie Liègeois* [1981] 1 Lloyd's Rep. 359 at p.364.
[46] *Bremer Handelsgesellschaft mbH v Vanden-Avenne Izegem PVBA* [1978] 2 Lloyd's Rep. 109 at 122; and see [1977] 1 Lloyd's Rep. 133 at p.143.

the general rule, requiring a c.i.f. seller who was prevented from shipping to buy afloat, did not apply,[47] and the reason given for this exception to the general rule was that, in the circumstances which had arisen, it would not be clear which (or how many) of the sellers in the string was (or were) to do the buying afloat. If they all attempted to do so, the result would be that a large number of buyers would be chasing the relatively small quantity of soyabean meal left available (because already afloat) after the embargo,[48] thus creating an extreme pressure on prices, which would be driven up to "unheard-of levels",[49] so that no seller would be able to obtain goods of the contract description "by the exercise of any means reasonably open to him".[50] Similar reasoning was applied when the embargo was eventually lifted in September 1973 with regard to *future* contracts. It was held that sellers were not then bound to go into the market to procure the amounts that they had been unable to deliver under *existing* (pre-embargo) contracts which called for delivery in September; for to have required all sellers in a string of contracts to do this in the "limited market" for goods shipped in September would have driven prices up to "levels just as unheard of"[51] as those that would have been reached if such sellers had been obliged to buy afloat when the embargo was originally imposed.

The exact scope of the present exception to the c.i.f. seller's duty (if he cannot ship) to buy afloat is uncertain. One view is that "if shipment is prevented by *force majeure* the shipper is under no obligation to buy afloat"[52]; but if this is to be taken literally it is, with respect, too wide, and inconsistent with the authorities cited in paragraph 19–140 above.[53] A second view is that the exception is restricted to the particular facts (including the provisions of the contracts)[54] in the soyabean meal cases cited above, in one of which it was said that there was no duty to buy afloat "in circumstances such as the present"[55] and "in the context of this particular system of purchase and sale of goods."[56] This view is, in turn, probably too narrow. The justification for the exception suggests that the important factors for determining its scope are that the contract should specify the country of origin; that shipment from that country should be prevented (whether by prohibition of export or by *force majeure*); and that

---

[47] Though sellers were frequently liable on other grounds: see above, para.18–349, 18–351.

[48] *Bremer Handelsgesellschaft mbH v Vanden Avenne-Izegem PVBA* [1978] 2 Lloyd's Rep. 109 at p.115.

[49] *Tradax Export SA v André & Cie.*, above, at p.423; *Bremer Handelsgesellschaft mbH v Vanden Avenne Izegem PVBA* [1978] 2 Lloyd's Rep. 109 at pp.115, 125.

[50] *André & Cie. SA v Tradax Export SA* [1983] 1 Lloyd's Rep. 254 at p.258; *Continental Grain Export Corp. v STM Grain Ltd* [1979] 2 Lloyd's Rep. 460 at p.473.

[51] *Cook Industries v Tradax Export SA* [1983] 1 Lloyd's Rep. 327 at p.344; affirmed [1985] 2 Lloyd's Rep. 454.

[52] *Bremer Handelsgesellschaft mbH v Vanden Avenne-Izegem PVBA*, above n.49, at p.121.

[53] *e.g. PJ van der Zijden Wildhandel NV v Tucker & Cross Ltd* [1975] 2 Lloyd's Rep. 240.

[54] See *Warinco AG v Fritz Mautner* [1978] 1 Lloyd's Rep. 151 at p.154 (*per* Megaw L.J.).

[55] *Bremer Handelsgesellschaft mbH v Vanden Avenne-Izegem*, above n.49, at p.125.

[56] *ibid.*, at p.131.

the contract should be one of a "string" or "circle" of contracts, leading back to a relevant shipper[57] who, at the time of the contract in question, had made, or undertaken to make, arrangements to ship goods intended for appropriation to that contract.[58] It is in this situation that attempted performance of a duty to buy afloat could lead to the extreme pressure on prices which is said to justify the exception.

The exception has also been extended in one of the soyabean meal cases[59] so as to negative the seller's duty to buy goods which, though not beyond the reach of the export embargo because they were already afloat, were exempt from it by reason of the "loopholes"[60] to which the embargo was subject. Such an extension of the exception can be supported on the same grounds as those that have been advanced as justifications for the exception itself: attempts by all the sellers in a string to buy the limited quantity of available "loophole" goods would create an extreme pressure on prices. But the case in question does give rise to difficulty in that it further holds that the seller could rely on the exception without having to show that he was a seller in a "string" of contracts, or that he or a relevant shipper had (before the embargo was imposed) made arrangements for shipment of the goods. Insofar as the case lays down a rule as to burden of proof, it is inconsistent with later decisions which require a seller claiming excuse under the clause to trace the string back to a relevant shipper.[61] Insofar as it lays down a rule of substance, to the effect that a seller need not buy "loophole" goods even where his contract with the buyer is *not* one of a string of contracts, it is submitted that the case extends the instant exception too far.[62] Normally a seller of unascertained generic goods is not relieved (even by a *force majeure* or prohibition clause) from his duty to appropriate such goods of the contract description as may be available, merely because a particular source of supply intended by him (but not specified by the contract) has failed.[63] Prohibition of export or *force majeure* will commonly make performance more expensive for the seller, and normally (where an alternative method remains open to him) he has to bear this expense.[64] It is the extremity of the increase which accounts for

---

[57] Above, para.18–350.

[58] *Warinco AG v Fritz Mautner* [1978] 1 Lloyd's Rep. 151 at p.156 (*per* Bridge L.J.); *cf. ibid.* at p.154 (*per* Megaw L.J.); *Bunge SA v Deutsche Conti-Handelsgesellschaft mbH* [1979] 2 Lloyd's Rep. 435 at p.439; it is submitted that these views are to be preferred to the suggestion of Lord Denning M.R. in *Bremer Handelsgesellschaft mbH v Finagrain, etc. SA* [1981] 2 Lloyd's Rep. 259 at p.265, that *no* string need be established for the purpose of the exception.

[59] *Bunge SA v Kruse* [1979] 1 Lloyd's Rep. 279, affirmed on other grounds [1980] 2 Lloyd's Rep. 142 and referred to with apparent approval on this point in *Andrè & Cie. v Tradax Export SA* [1983] 1 Lloyd's Rep. 254 at p.267.

[60] Above, para.18–348.

[61] Above, para.18–350, *Bremer Handelsgesellschaft mbH v C Mackprang Jr.* [1979] 1 Lloyd's Rep. 221 at p.228.

[62] *cf. Bunge SA v Deutsche Conti-Handelsgesellschaft mbH*, above. In so far as *Bunge SA v Kruse*, above, lays down a rule as to burden of proof, it was doubted in *Bremer Handelsgesellschaft mbH v C Mackprang Jr.* [1979] 1 Lloyd's Rep. 221 at p.228; above, para.18–351.

[63] *Agrokor AG v Tradigrain SA* [2000] 1 Lloyd's Rep. 497 (f.o.b. contract).

[64] *e.g. PJ van der Zijden Wildhandel NV v Tucker & Cross Ltd* [1975] 2 Lloyd's Rep. 240; *cf.* above, para.19–140.

the exceptional rule applied where performance of "string" contracts is affected by an embargo interfering with previously made shipping arrangements; and it is submitted that the exception should be confined to cases of this kind.[65]

19–142 **As excluding frustration.** A prohibition, "*force majeure*" or similar clause may exclude frustration, on the general principle that the parties to a contract may expressly provide that the contract is not to be discharged but, for example, varied by suspending performance in events which would otherwise frustrate it.[66] But a clause of this kind will not exclude frustration if it is intended to deal only with temporary interruptions and the events which happen "strike at the contract as a whole and render performance . . . unthinkable".[67] Similarly, a provision for the suspension of the contract which does not specify the duration of the suspension will exclude frustration only where the suspension is for a reasonable time, and not where the period of suspension is so great "as to make the contract, if resumed, a different contract from the contract interrupted".[68] And a provision which specifies some obstacles to performance which might, but for the express terms of the contract, frustrate it does not prevent a party from relying on other obstacles as grounds of frustration.[69] Even where the clause provides for automatic cancellation of the contract on the occurrence of a specified event, the contract will, when that event occurs, be discharged under the clause and not under the general doctrine of frustration[70]; for discharge will follow on the occurrence of the event whether or not this would (but for the clause) have given rise to an interference with performance sufficiently serious to frustrate the contract. Where discharge takes place under an express provision of the contract, its effects will therefore not be governed by the Law Reform (Frustrated Contracts) Act 1943.[71]

A contract may be frustrated by supervening illegality even though it contains a provision purporting merely to suspend it in that event.[72] Thus a c.i.f. contract will be frustrated if the port of destination becomes an enemy port, even though the contract contains a provision that performance is to be suspended in the event of war.[73] Such a provision may be construed narrowly, so as to exclude reference to a war which will make the contract

---

[65] See the authorities cited in n.58, above.

[66] Treitel, *Frustration and Force Majeure* (2nd ed. 2004), para.12–002; *Agrokor AG v Tradigrain SA* [2000] 1 Lloyd's Rep. 497 at p.504 (f.o.b. contract); *Kuwait Supply Co. v Oyster Marine Management Inc. (The Safeer)* [1994] 1 Lloyd's Rep. 637 (charterparty).

[67] *Empresa Exportadora de Azucar v Industria Azucarera Nacional SA* (*The Playa Larga*) [1983] 2 Lloyd's Rep. 171 at p.189.

[68] *Acetylene Co. of G.B. v Canada Carbide Co.* (1922) 8 Ll.L.R. 456 at p.460, CA (above, para.19–133). *Fibrosa Spolka Akcyjna v Fairbairn, Lawson, Combe Barbour Ltd* [1943] A.C. 32.

[69] See *Intertradex SA v Lesieur-Torteaux S.A.R.L.* [1978] 2 Lloyd's Rep. 509 at p.515.

[70] *cf.* above, para.18–342.

[71] See s.2(3) of the 1943 Act; Treitel, *Frustration and Force Majeure* (2nd ed. 2004), para.12–019.

[72] *Ertel Bieber Co. v Rio Tinto Co. Ltd* [1918] A.C. 260.

[73] As in the *Fibrosa* case [1943] A.C. 32 at p.34.

illegal[74]; but, if it cannot be so construed, it is void on grounds of public policy.[75] In the case of other types of supervening illegality, provisions for suspension are, however, commonly treated as valid. This is, for example, the position where the cause of the illegality is supervening prohibition of export or import.[76] Clauses of this kind are not contrary to public policy[77] since they assume that the prohibition is going to be observed, and since the continuation of the contractual relationship between buyer and seller does not in the present group of cases have any tendency to subvert the purpose of the prohibition. By contrast, in the trading with the enemy cases the continuation of a contractual relationship with an enemy subject would have such a tendency.

(c) *Effects of Frustration*

19–143 **Effects of frustration.** The effects of frustrtion on contracts for the sale of goods are discussed generally in Chapter 6.[78] Here it is only necessary to point out that the powers of the court to order restitution and make allowance for expenses under the Law Reform (Frustrated Contracts) Act 1943 apply, in principle, to c.i.f. contracts. Indeed, the Act was passed partly as a result of the decision of the House of Lords in the *Fibrosa*[79] case, which concerned a contract of this kind. Thus if payment is due, or has actually been made, wholly or in part, in advance of tender of documents, and the contract is subsequently frustrated, the payment ceases to be due, or must be repaid, subject to the discretion of the court to allow the seller to recover or retain expenses under section 1(2) of the Act. It is an open question whether section 1(2) could apply where no actual payment had been made by, or become due from, the buyer, but where the seller had, before the time of discharge of the contract of sale, merely been notified by a bank of an irrevocable credit established by the buyer in pursuance of the contract of sale. If the subsection did not apply in such a case, the seller could not recover anything in respect of expenses incurred by him before the time of discharge; if the subsection did apply, it is not clear whether the seller's claim in respect of such expenses would be available against the buyer or against the bank.

Where section 1(2) does apply, payments made to the seller can now be recovered back although the failure of consideration is not total.[80] The expenses which the seller could retain or claim out of the sum which had been, or should have been, prepaid would include not only manufacturing costs, but also costs incurred in relation to shipment and insurance. Of

[74] *ibid.*, p.40; *Re Badische Co. Ltd* [1921] 2 Ch. 331.
[75] *Ertel Bieber & Co. v Rio Tinto Co. Ltd* [1918] A.C. 260.
[76] Above, para.18–342.
[77] *Johnson Matthey Bankers Ltd v State Trading Co. of India* [1984] 1 Lloyd's Rep. 427 at p.434.
[78] Above, paras 6–053, 6–058 to 6–071; and see Treitel, *Frustration and Force Majeure*, 2nd ed. (2004), Ch.15.
[79] [1943] A.C. 32.
[80] s.1(2) of the 1943 Act having, on this point, altered the previous law as laid down in the *Fibrosa* case [1943] A.C. 32.

course a payment made on tender of documents would not be recoverable merely because subsequent events prevented the goods from reaching the agreed destination. The reason for this is not merely, as it was before the Act, that the failure of consideration in such a case would not be total[81] but that the contract would not be frustrated by such an event[82]; and so the Act would not apply at all.

Part delivery before frustration might give rise to a claim for recovery in respect of a valuable benefit under section 1(3) of the Act; though it is more likely that the contract would be treated as severable so that payment at the contract rate would be recoverable by virtue of section 2(4). An irrevocable credit notified before frustration might conceivably be a "valuable benefit" to the seller within section 1(3), even if the seller had not actually drawn on it[83] but it seems unlikely that the court would make any award under section 1(3) in respect of such a "benefit". Section 2(5)(c) excepts from the Act certain contracts for the sale of specific goods which are avoided or frustrated by reason of the fact that the goods have perished. As the perishing of specific goods will avoid or frustrate a c.i.f. contract only if it occurs before shipment,[84] these exceptions are of relatively small importance for the purpose of this chapter.

Section 1(5)[85] lays down the general rule that, in considering whether any sum ought to be recovered or retained by any party to the contract under the foregoing provisions of section 1, the court shall not take into account any sums which have, by reason of the circumstances giving rise to the frustration, become payable to that party under any contract of insurance. But the subsection is subject to an exception which applies where "there was an obligation to insure imposed by an express term of the contract." A c.i.f. contract falls within this exception as it expressly imposes such an obligation to insure; and if such contract were frustrated the seller would be discharged from his obligation to tender documents. Hence any sums payable under the policy of insurance would be payable to the seller; and, as the general rule in section 1(5) would not apply, the court could take such sums into account in assessing any claims of the seller (*e.g.* in respect of expenses or valuable benefits) under subsections 1(2) and 1(3).[86]

---

[81] See *The Julia* [1949] A.C. 293 where the buyer's claim would have failed on this ground, had the contract been a true c.i.f. contract (above, para.19–003). The 1943 Act did not apply as the frustrating event took place before July 1, 1943: see s.2(1).
[82] See, *e.g.* above, para.19–136 at n.2. For a possible exception to the rule that the contract would not be frustrated in the circumstances described in the text above, see para.19–124 above, n.58 (buyer dealing as consumer).
[83] Once he did draw on it he would receive a "payment of money" within s.1(2) of the 1943 Act.
[84] Above, paras 19–124, 19–125. For the possibility that the contract may, exceptionally, be frustrated by the destruction of specific goods after shipment, see above, para.19–124 n.58 (buyer dealing as consumer).
[85] See above, para.6–070.
[86] See Treitel, *Frustration and Force Majeure,* (2nd ed 2004), para.15-080; for other problems arising from s.1(5), see *ibid.*, paras 15–079 to -15–082.

8. REMEDIES OF THE BUYER

(a) *Rejection*

19–144 **Two rights to reject.** The duties of a c.i.f. seller include a duty to ship (or buy afloat) goods in accordance with the contract, and a duty to tender proper shipping documents.[87] The seller may fail to perform one or both of these duties; and the buyer may have a right to reject in respect of any such failure. The same act or omission of the seller may lead to the breach of both duties. For example, where the goods are shipped outside the shipment period they will not correspond with the contract description[88]; and such late shipment will also generally lead to inability to tender proper shipping documents, either because the bill of lading will not be dated in accordance with the contract, or because it will not be "genuine".[89] In a case of the last kind, Devlin J. said that there were "successive breaches of different conditions committed one after the other", giving rise to "two rights to reject", namely "a right to reject documents, and a right to reject goods, and the two things are quite distinct."[90] It has, indeed, been suggested that "in another sense, much more realistic . . . they are both really breaches of the same condition, that is to say of shipment within the contract period."[91] But more recently Lord Diplock has referred to the

---

[87] Above, paras 19–010, *et seq. Cf. Hindley & Co. v East Indian Produce Co. Ltd* [1973] 2 Lloyd's Rep. 515 at p.517 (c. & f. contract).

[88] Above, para.18–267.

[89] Above, para.19–035.

[90] *Kwei Tek Chao v British Traders & Shippers Ltd* [1954] 2 Q.B. 459 at p.480; *cf. J Aron & Co. (Inc.) v Comptoir Wegimont* [1921] 3 K.B. 435 at p.439 (buyer entitled to reject "the documents and the goods"); *James Finlay & Co. Ltd v Kwik Hoo Tong* [1929] 1 K.B. 400 at p.414 (below, para.19–190); *Trasimex Holdings SA v Addax BV (The Red Sea)* [1999] 1 Lloyd's Rep. 28 at p.33 (buyer entitled to reject "non-conforming documents or non-conforming goods"). Art. 30 of the Vienna Convention on Contracts for the International Sale of Goods (above, para.1–024) likewise obliges the seller to "deliver the goods [and] hand over any documents relating to them". The buyer is entitled to declare the contract avoided in two sets of circumstances. First, he can do so under Art. 49(1)(a) if failure by the seller to perform *any* of his obligations amounts to a "fundamental breach" (as defined in Art. 25: see above, para.18–267, n.38). Secondly, he can do so under Art. 49(1)(b) "in cases of non-delivery" (even though the breach is not "fundamental") if the seller has *either* still not delivered the goods within an additional reasonable time fixed by the buyer (under Art. 47) requiring the seller to perform his obligations (*i.e.* to cure the breach) *or* declared that he would not do so. It is not clear whether "non-delivery" in Art. 49(1)(b) refers only to non-delivery of the goods or also to failure to tender documents. The doubt arises because the Convention appears in Arts 30–34 to distinguish between a duty to "deliver" goods and one to "hand over" documents. The distinction may not be significant, for the duty to "deliver" goods can be performed by "handing . . . over" the goods "to the first carrier for transmission to the buyer" (Art. 31(a); see also Art. 32(1)). This provision is actually inappropriate to a c.i.f. contract, in which the crucial time is not that of *handing over* the goods to the carrier, but that of *shipment* (above, paras 18–267, 19–012). Perhaps this position could be preserved under Art. 30, by which "delivery" must be made "as required *by the contract and* this Convention"; see also Art. 9, discussed in para.18–004 above.

[91] *Panchaud Frères SA v Et. General Grain Co.* [1970] 1 Lloyd's Rep. 53 at p.61.

buyer's rights to reject documents and to reject goods as "separate and successive rights"[92]; and this view is (with respect) to be preferred, in particular because, as Devlin J. has pointed out, the right to reject the goods is not necessarily impaired by acceptance of the documents[93]; and because the distinction is relevant as to damages.[94]

A c.i.f. buyer may sometimes, though he will not usually, deal as consumer.[95] If he so deals and if "the goods do not conform to the contract of sale at the time of delivery",[96] then he has certain "additional rights" under Part 5A of the Sale of Goods Act 1979. One of these is the right to require the seller to repair or replace the non-conforming goods,[97] subject to specified limitations.[98] Where these apply, or where the seller has failed to comply within a reasonable time with the buyer's requirement to repair or replace the goods, then the buyer has the right (under Part 5A) "to rescind the contract"[99] with regard to the non-conforming goods; and the practical effects of the exercise of this right are likely to resemble those of the exercise of the right to reject. In relation to c.i.f. contracts, the "right to rescind the contract" (in common with the other "additional rights") gives rise to two problems which have already been discussed in this and the preceding chapter of this book. The first is whether the right to "rescind" under Part 5A is available, not only where it is the *goods*, but also where it is the *documents*, which are not in conformity with the contract[1]; the second is to which of the "stages of delivery" in a c.i.f. contract the requirement of conformity "at the time of delivery" refers.[2] In view of these uncertainties, a c.i.f. buyer who deals as consumer may, in situations of the kind of which the following discussion is concerned, prefer to rely on the rights to reject which were available to him before, and remain available to him after,[3] the introduction of Part 5A.[4] The following discussion of the c.i.f. buyer's right to reject is (except where otherwise expressly indicated) based on the assumption that he has chosen to exercise the former rights to reject and not to rely on the "additional right" to "rescind" that may be available to him under Part 5A.

Right to reject goods. A c.i.f. buyer is generally bound to pay on tender of documents, before he has had an opportunity to examine the goods.[5] But if it turns out that the goods were not, when shipped, of the contract 19–145

---

92 *Gill & Duffus SA v Berger & Co. Inc.* [1984] A.C. 382 at p.395.

93 *Kwei Tek Chao v British Traders & Shippers Ltd above*, at p.482; below, para.19–191.

94 Below, paras 19–188 *et seq*.

95 See above, para.18–259.

96 Sale of Goods Act 1979, s.48A(1)(b).

97 *ibid.*, s.48B(1).

98 *ibid.*, s.48B(3). One of these limitations applies where repair or replacement are "impossible" (s.48B(3)(a)), as might be the case where the goods were not shipped within the shipment period specified in the c.i.f. contract and the non-conformity was not discovered until after that period had expired.

99 *ibid.*, ss.48A(2)(b)(i), 48C(1)(b).

1 See above, para.19–065.

2 See above, para.18–261.

3 This follows from the permissive wording ("may") of Sale of Goods Act 1979, s.48C(1).

4 By Sale and Supply of Goods to Consumers Regulations 2002, SI 2002/3045.

5 *E Clemens Horst Co. v Biddell Bros* [1912] A.C. 18 (above, para.19–076).

description,[6] or of the contract quantity, the buyer is entitled to reject them[7]; he also has this right if there was a qualitative defect in the goods amounting to a breach of a fundamental term or to a breach of condition, or to a breach of an intermediate term which causes him serious prejudice.[8] The buyer is entitled to reject the goods even though he has previously accepted documents which were perfectly in accordance with the contract. This would be the case, for example, where the goods suffered from some qualitative defect not apparent on the face of the documents: *e.g.* where they were not equal to sample, or where they had deteriorated in breach of the seller's implied undertaking that they could endure normal transit.[9] Similarly, in *Suzuki & Co. v Burgett and Newsam*[10] peas were sold under a c.i.f. contract which called for shipment by January 1920.[11] The seller tendered a "received for shipment" bill of lading (which was usual in the trade[12]) dated January 31, 1920. The goods had been received for shipment on that day, but were not actually shipped until February. It would seem that the bill of lading was in accordance with the contract, but the buyer was nevertheless entitled to reject the goods as they did not constitute a January shipment.

19–146 The buyer may also be entitled to reject the goods on account of the seller's breach of a stipulation as to the time of *arrival* of the goods at the contractual destination.[13]

A buyer can reject goods if they do not correspond with the contractual description even though their failure to do so does not cause him any loss.[14]

---

[6] *Tradimex Holdings SA v Addax BV (The Red Sea)* [1999] 1 Lloyd's Rep. 28.
[7] The statutory restrictions on the buyer's right to reject contained in Sale of Goods Act 1979, ss.15A and 30(2A) probably do not apply where goods sold on c.i.f. terms are not of the contract description or quantity: see above, paras 18–284, 19–012.
[8] *Polenghi v Dried Milk Co. Ltd* (1904) 10 Com.Cas. 42 at p.47; *E. Clemens Horst Co. v Biddell Bros* [1911] 1 K.B. 934 at p.960, *per* Kennedy L.J. whose judgment was affirmed by the House of Lords, above; *Cehave NV v Bremer Handelsgesellschaft mbH* (*The Hansa Nord*) [1976] Q.B. 44. If the buyer has dealt as consumer, he may (see above, para.19–144) also have the right to "rescind" the contract under Sale of Goods Act 1979 ss.48A(2)(b) and 48C(1)(b) for breach of an express term: see *ibid.*, s.48F. He may have this right even though the express term is neither a condition nor an intermediate term but is only a warranty. But the right to "rescind" is the effect subject to the discretion of the court which may in the case put refuse to allow rescission: see s.48E(3) and (4). Under the Vienna Convention on Contracts for the International Sale of Goods (above, para.1–024) the buyer's right to reject for defects of quality is limited to cases in which the breach is "fundamental": see Art. 49(1)(a) and n.90, above. The further right of avoidance on expiry of a reasonable notice fixed by the buyer given to him by Art. 41(1)(b) does not extend to cases of defective delivery: it exists only "in cases of non-delivery." And see above, para.18–267, nn. 38, and 41.
[9] Above, para.18–230.
[10] (1922) 10 Ll.L.R. 223 (for a fuller statement of the facts see (1921) 8 Ll.L.R. 495).
[11] (1922) 10 Ll.L.R. 223 at p.225.
[12] *ibid.*; for "received" bills, see above, para.18–027.
[13] *Nova Petroleum Establishment v Tricon Trading Ltd* [1989] 1 Lloyd's Rep. 312 at p.315; for stipulation as to the time of arrival, see above, para.19–092.
[14] *e.g. Arcos v Ronaasen & Son* [1933] A.C. 470. *Semble* such a breach would not be "fundamental" within Art. 25 of the Vienna Convention on Contracts for the International Sale of Goods and so would not give the buyer a right of avoidance under Art. 49(1)(a) (above, n.8). For the English position, see above, para.18–266.

The courts have, however, restricted the scope of this rule by narrowing the concept of the description of the goods. A statement may be part of the description of the goods if it serves to *identify* them, by reference to one or more of their essential qualities.[15] But an identifying statement will not be part of the description, so that its falsity will not entitle the buyer to reject, where it is a mere substitute for a name[16] and the subject-matter can be identified by other means. So long as such identification is possible, the position may be the same even where the statement is *not* a mere substitute for a name, at least if the misstatement is "immaterial" in the sense that it does not affect the value of the goods and is of no commercial significance. In *Parsons v. New Zealand Shipping Co.*[17] lamb carcases were stated in a bill of lading to bear the marks 488X and 622X, but the carcases tendered by the carrier to the indorsee of the bill in fact bore the marks 388X and 522X. A majority of the Court of Appeal held that the buyer could not, as against *the carrier*, reject the goods[18] since, in spite of the discrepancy between the marks on the bill and those on the goods, it was shown that the goods tendered were in fact the same as those shipped under the bill, and since the discrepancy was "immaterial" in that it did not affect the market value of the goods and was of no commercial significance to the indorsee.[19] It is, however, submitted that there is force in the dissenting view that the marks *were* material in enabling the buyer to tell exactly to which of the goods on the ship he was entitled. And if there had been a similar discrepancy between marks specified in a contract of sale and marks appearing on the goods it is submitted that the buyer should not be deprived, as against the *seller*, of his right to reject the goods merely because he had accepted documents, the marks on which corresponded with those in the contract of sale; for he might be put into a position of considerable difficulty if he had resold the goods, while they were still afloat, by reference to the marks in the contract of sale and on the documents.[20] *A fortiori* a buyer should not be required to accept documents, the marks on which did not correspond with those in the contract of sale, however "immaterial" the discrepancy might turn out to be. It is an important principle of the law relating to c.i.f.

---

[15] *Christopher Hill Ltd v Ashington Piggeries Ltd* [1972] A.C. 441 (above, para.18–273).

[16] *Reardon Smith Line Ltd v Hansen Tangen* [1976] 1 W.L.R. 989; above, para.18–273.

[17] [1901] 1 Q.B. 548; *cf. Bremer Handelsgesellschaft mbH v Toepfer* [1978] 1 Lloyd's Rep. 643 at p.651 (affirmed [1980] 2 Lloyd's Rep. 43 at p.49: notice of appropriation giving wrong bill of lading number); above, para.19–019.

[18] The motive for rejection seems to have been that the market had fallen, the damages for loss of the goods being, under the contract of carriage, based on the *invoice* price in the contract under which the indorsee had bought the goods from the shipper.

[19] The marks were part of a private code used by the shipper, in which the first digit referred to the day of the week on which the carcases in question had been frozen.

[20] This factor would have brought the *Parsons* case (had it arisen between buyer and seller) within the class of cases excepted by Lord Wilberforce from his criticism of the wide scope of the right to reject in sales by description (above, para.18–266): the sale would have been of "unascertained future goods (*e.g.* commodities) as to which each detail of the description may be assumed to be vital": *Reardon Smith Line Ltd v Hansen Tangen* [1976] 1 W.L.R. 989 at p.998.

contracts that documents "have to be taken up or rejected promptly"[21]; and such promptness could not be achieved if, in the situation here under consideration, the buyer had to investigate the "materiality" of the discrepancy before exercising his right to reject the documents.

19–147 **Right to reject documents.** A buyer is entitled to reject documents which are defective in the sense of failing to comply with the requirements stated earlier in this chapter[22]; for example, documents which do not contain, or evidence "a contract or contracts of carriage of the contractual goods from the contractual port of loading to the contractual destination."[23] Where the documents reveal a defect in the goods, the buyer may be entitled to reject them even though that defect would not, of itself, have justified rejection of the goods. For example, in *Cehave NV v Bremer Handelsgesellschaft mbH* (*The Hansa Nord*)[24] it was held that a c.i.f. buyer was not entitled to reject the goods on the ground that they were not "shipped in good condition", as required by the contract. The term that they should be so shipped was an intermediate term[25] and its breach had not caused the buyer sufficiently serious prejudice to justify rejection. But Roskill L.J. said that if the documents had been claused to indicate that the goods had not been shipped in good condition the buyer could have rejected.[26] In that case the seller would have been in breach of his duty to tender a "clean" bill of lading; and the right to reject on account of defects in documents had "long been made sacrosant by the highest authority".[27] Any defect in the documents suffices for this purpose: "the documentary requirements of the contract must be strictly complied with and the buyer is not obliged to evaluate how significant any documentary discrepancy may turn out to be."[28]

The position is, however, different, if the document which reveals a defect in the goods is not in itself a defective document. Thus a certificate of quality is not a defective document merely because it states that the goods contain a slightly higher percentage of impurities than is permitted by the contract.[29] It follows that such a statement in a certificate of quality will not, of itself, entitle the buyer to reject *the documents*. He will, indeed, be entitled to reject *the goods* if the certificate indicates that the goods suffer from a defect that amounts to a breach of condition (*e.g.* that the goods are not of the contract description[30]) and if *either* the goods actually

---

[21] *Hansson v Hamel & Horley Ltd* [1922] A.C. 36 at p.46.
[22] Above, paras 19–024 to 19–058.
[23] *SIAT di dal Ferro v Tradax Overseas SA* [1980] 1 Lloyd's Rep. 53 at p.63.
[24] [1976] Q.B. 44.
[25] Above, paras 10–033, 10–037.
[26] [1976] Q.B. 44 at p.70.
[27] *ibid.* The goods were in *apparent* good condition (see [1974] 2 Lloyd's Rep. 218); and it seems that the bills of lading did not contain any false statements so as to render them defective on the principle stated in para.19–035, above.
[28] *Soules CAF v PT Transcap of Indonesia* [1999] 1 Lloyd's Rep. 917 at p.919.
[29] *Tradax Internacional SA v Goldschmidt SA* [1977] 2 Lloyd's Rep. 604 (f.o.b. contract).
[30] In *Tradax Internacional SA v Goldschmidt SA*, above, it was "accepted that the provision as to impurities was not a part of the description" (at p.612 and *cf.* p.617; and see above, para.18–273); nor was any attempt made to rely on any condition implied under s.14 of the Sale of Goods Act 1979.

suffer from such a defect, *or* the certificate is conclusive as to their quality or description under a certification clause.[31] The defect in the goods being, in such a case, *apparent* on the face of the documents, and such as to justify rejection of the goods, the buyer is also entitled to reject the documents, not because they are in themselves defective, but because they reveal a defect in the goods which justifies rejection of the goods.[32]

A buyer is entitled to reject documents which do not comply with the contract even though the goods themselves are perfectly in accordance with the contract.[33] Thus if the contract provides that the goods are to be shipped, and the bills of lading are to be dated, in January the buyer can reject bills of lading dated in February, even though the goods were actually shipped in January.[34] Similarly, the buyer can reject a bill of lading for a quantity of goods in excess of the contractual limits, even though the goods actually shipped are within these limits.[35] Where the buyer thus has and exercises the right to reject the documents, it follows that he can also reject the goods.[36]

Missing documents. Documents may be defective in the sense that a bundle of documents tendered does not include all those required by the contract. If a c.i.f. seller tendered documents which did not include a bill of lading, or a full set of bills where this was required by the contract, or proper insurance documents, the buyer could no doubt reject the tender[37] (though he might have to accept a subsequent good tender.[38]) On the other hand where some less important document is missing from the bundle (for example, a counter-trade performance guarantee[39] or weight certificate) it has been held that the buyer cannot reject the tender unless failure to tender the missing document was "persisted in and amounted to a refusal".[40] The assumption is that the failure to tender the guarantee or certificate in question is not, of itself, a sufficiently serious breach to justify 19–148

---

[31] *Tradax Export SA v European Grain & Shipping Co.* [1983] 2 Lloyd's Rep. 100; above, para.18–273.

[32] The correctness of the position taken in the text above appears to have been assumed in *Vargas Pena Apeztieguia y Cia v Peter Cremer GmbH* [1987] 1 Lloyd's Rep. 394 at p.396, 398 where the buyer was entitled to reject documents which were not in themselves defective because they revealed a defect in the goods which justified rejection of the goods. The sale was on f.o.b. terms, but the principles applicable to c.i.f. contracts were relevant for the reason stated in para.20–106, below. The principle stated in para.19–163, below applies only where the defect in the goods is *not* apparent on the face of the documents.

[33] The position appears to be the same under the Vienna Convention on Contracts for the International Sale of Goods (above, para.1–024), Arts 30 and 49(1): see above, para.19–144, n.90.

[34] *Re General Trading Co. Ltd, and Van Stolk's Commissiehandel* (1911) 16 Com.Cas. 95.

[35] *Tamvaco v Lucas (No.1)* (1859) 1 E. & E. 581.

[36] *Shipton, Anderson & Co. v John Weston & Co.* (1922) 10 Ll.L.R. 762 at p.763.

[37] *e.g.* above, para.19–024, n.73.

[38] Above, para.19–071.

[39] *State Trading Corp. of India v M Golodetz Ltd* [1989] 2 Lloyd's Rep. 277.

[40] *Mantovani v Carapelli SpA* [1978] 2 Lloyd's Rep. 63 at p.72 (affirmed without reference to this point [1980] 1 Lloyd's Rep. 375). The case concerned an f.o.b. contract; but the same principle seems to apply to c.i.f. contracts.

rejection. Whether the failure to tender the missing document falls into the former or the latter class presumably depends (in the absence of express contractual provisions or previous classification by authority) on the commercial importance likely, in the court's view, to be attached to that document by the buyer.[41] These principles also determine the effects of the seller's failure to perform his obligations to give notices which are not included among the shipping documents.[42]

19–149 **When do the two rights to reject arise?** The right to reject defective documents obviously cannot be exercised before tender of documents; but it is less clear at which stage in the performance of the contract[43] the buyer becomes entitled to reject goods on the ground that they are defective (in the sense of not being in conformity with the contract). He cannot generally be entitled to reject the goods before tender of documents; for, if the documents are defective, and he rejects them, no question of rejection of the goods can ever arise, while, if the documents are in conformity with the contract, the buyer cannot, as a general rule, refuse to pay against them merely on account of a defect in the goods.[44] Lord Diplock has said that, where the documents are, but the goods are not, in conformity with the contract, the right to reject the goods "does not become exercisable until the seller has unconditionally appropriated the goods to the contract"[45]; and that this happens under a c.i.f. contract when the seller relinquishes his right of disposal "by . . . transferring the shipping documents to the buyers".[46] Although strictly speaking Lord Diplock's statement merely means that the goods *cannot* be rejected *before* transfer of documents, it seems from the context to be intended to mean that the buyer *can* reject the goods *at any time after* he has, as a result of the transfer of documents, become entitled to call for the delivery of the goods from the carrier, without any further act on the part of the seller. If this is right, the buyer's right to reject can arise before actual arrival of the goods, though in practice it will normally be exercised at (or shortly after) that time.

19–150 **Loss of the rights to reject: "waiver" or election.**[47] The rights to reject may be lost by waiver in the sense of an election between rem-

---

[41] *State Trading Corp. of India v M Golodetz Ltd* [1989] 2 Lloyd's Rep. 277.
[42] Above, para.19–058; *e.g. Nova Petroleum International Establishment v Tricon Trading Ltd* [1989] 1 Lloyd's Rep. 312.
[43] For the "three stages of delivery" in a c.i.f. contract, see above, para.19–072.
[44] Above, para.19–077; below, para.19–163.
[45] *Gill & Duffus SA v Berger & Co. Inc.* [1984] A.C. 382 at p.395.
[46] *ibid*.
[47] See generally, paras 12–034 *et seq.*, above. If the buyer has dealt as consumer (see above, para.18-259) and has required the seller to repair or replace non-conforming goods (Sale of Goods Act 1979, s.48B), then he cannot reject the goods until he has given the seller a reasonable time to effect repair or replacement: *ibid.*, s.48D. The buyer's right to "rescind the contract" under s.48C is similarly limited: see s.48C(2)(b); see also above, paras 12–106, 12–108 to 12–110. Under the Vienna Convention on Contracts for the International Sale of Goods (above, para.1–024) the general principle (contained in Art. 49(2)) is that the buyer's "right to declare the contract avoided" is lost by lapse of time. In the case of *late delivery*, such time runs from the buyer's becoming aware that delivery has been made: Art. 49(2)(a). In

edies[48] (also sometimes referred to as affirmation[49]), under certain analogous doctrines,[50] or by acceptance.[51] The type of waiver which gives rise to loss of the right to reject arises when the buyer unequivocally indicates that he will not exercise his right to reject. It is a requirement of this type of waiver that the buyer must be aware, not only of the facts which have given rise to the right to reject, but of the existence of the right itself.[52] Acceptance, on the other hand, can lead to loss of the right to reject even though the buyer is not *actually* aware of the right or of the facts giving rise to it—he need only have had a reasonable *opportunity* of examining the goods for the purpose of discovering whether they are in conformity with the contract.[53] Where the right to reject is lost by waiver or acceptance, the right to damages normally survives.[54]

Waiver is also used in another sense,[55] to refer to the situation in which the buyer relinquishes not merely his right to reject, but also his right to a part of the promised performance, or to damages for not receiving it.[56] One

---

the case of *any other breach* it runs *either* from the moment when the buyer knew or ought to have known of the breach (Art. 49(2)(b)(i)); *or*, where he has given a notice under Art. 47(1) requiring the seller to perform within a reasonable period, from the expiration of that period, or from the seller's declaration that he will not perform his obligations within that period: Art. 49(2)(b)(ii). As a general rule, the buyer also loses the right to avoid the contract if he cannot restore the goods in substantially the condition in which he received them: Art. 82. It is also relevant to note that the buyer loses all his rights to rely on non-conformity of the goods if he does not notify the seller of the lack of conformity within a reasonable time after he has, or ought to have discovered it: Art. 39(1); and in any event within two years of actual delivery (unless this period is extended by the contract): Art. 39(2). These rules lead to a loss of *all* of the buyer's remedies; but the requirement of Art. 39(1) seems also to be relevant for the purpose of the operation of Art. 49(2)(b)(i), above.

[48] See Sale of Goods Act 1979, s.11(2); see above, para.18–358; *Glencore Grain Ltd v Flacker Shipping Ltd (The Happy Day)* [2002] EWCA Civ. 1068, [2002] 2 All E.R. (Comm.) 896 at [68]; *cf. infra*, n.52.

[49] *Kwei Tek Chao v British Traders and Shippers Ltd* [1954] 2 Q.B. 459 at 477.

[50] See below, paras 19–151, 19–160.

[51] Sale of Goods Act 1979, s.11(4).

[52] *Peyman v Lanjani* [1985] Ch. 457; *Transatlantica de Commercio SA v Incrobasa Industrial & Commercio Brasileira SA* [1995] 1 Lloyd's Rep. 215 at pp.219–220 (f.o.b. contract); for the view that knowledge of the facts is sufficient, see *Cerealmangimi SpA v Toepfer* (*The Eurometal*) [1981] 1 Lloyd's Rep. 337 at p.341; and see below, para.19–151.

[53] Sale of Goods Act 1979, s.35(2) and (5); *cf.* also s.34.

[54] *e.g. Ets. Soules & Cie. v International Trade Development Co. Ltd* [1980] 1 Lloyd's Rep. 129. *Cf.* Vienna Convention on Contracts for the International Sale of Goods (above, para.1–024), Art. 83.

[55] See above, para.18–358; *Kammins Ballroom Ltd v Zenith Investments* (*Torquay*) *Ltd* [1971] A.C. 850 at pp.882–883; *State Trading Corp. of India v Cie Française d' Importation et de Distribution* [1983] 2 Lloyd's Rep. 679 at p.681; *Motor Oil Hellas* (*Corinth*) *Refineries SA v Shipping Corp. of India* (*The Kanchenjunga*) [1990] 1 Lloyd's Rep. 391 at 397–399; *Oliver Ashworth (Holdings) Ltd v Ballard (Kent) Ltd* [2000] Ch.12 at p.28; *The Happy Day*, above n.48, at [64]; and see the authorities cited in n.74, below.

[56] *e.g. Bremer Handelsgesellschaft mbH v C Mackprang Jr.*[1979] 1 Lloyd's Rep. 221 at p.224 (so far as it relates to the part of the goods shipped on July 17). *The Happy Day*, above n.48, et [64], [65], [67] Contrast *Finagrain v Kruse* [1976] 2 Lloyd's Rep. 508 (where acceptance of short delivery was held not to amount to waiver of the

way of establishing this kind of waiver is for the seller to show "a separate agreement, binding on the buyer by which he agreed to surrender the right to damages which automatically vested in him at the time of the breach."[57] Alternatively, the same result may be reached under the doctrines of estoppel or promissory estoppel.[58] This will be the position where the buyer has (a) made an unequivocal representation (whether expressly or by conduct) to the effect that he is relinquishing, not only his right to reject, but also his right to damages in respect of a particular breach, and, (b) before that representation has been withdrawn,[59] the seller has acted in reliance on it so as (c) to make it inequitable[60] for the buyer to go back on the representation.[61] The test of whether an unequivocal representation has been made is objective: "not what the buyers meant . . . but what the sellers reasonably understood them to mean".[62] It has been held that a c.i.f. buyer had not made the necessary "unequivocal representation" merely because his bank had paid against documents,[63] or because he had accepted non-conforming documents subject to a reservation of his rights,[64] or because he had simply failed to challenge the validity of a notice given by the seller claiming excuse under a *force majeure* clause,[65] or by asking for documentary proof of *force majeure* in spite of the invalidity of the notice.[66] Nor does a buyer, merely by accepting non-conforming documents in respect of part of the quantity sold, represent that he will not claim damages for failure to

---

buyer's right to the full contract quantity); and *Edm. JM Mertens & Co. PVBA v Vervoeder Import Export Vimex BV* [1979] 2 Lloyd's Rep. 372 (where there was held to be no waiver when buyers continued to press for performance, knowing that there was no real hope of obtaining it).

[57] *Kwei Tek Chao v British Traders & Shippers Ltd* [1954] 2 Q.B. 459 at p.477; *Bremer Handelsgesellschaft mbH v Westzucker GmbH (No. 2)* [1981] 1 Lloyd's Rep. 214 at p.222) affirmed [1981] 2 Lloyd's Rep. 130

[58] For a discussion of the relationship between waiver and estoppel, see *Glencore Grain Ltd v Flacker Shipping Ltd (The Happy Day)* [2002] EWCA Civ. 1068, [2002] 2 All E.R. (Comm.) 896 at [64]–[67].

[59] See *Bremer Handelsgesellschaft mbH v Raiffeisen Hauptgenossenschaft EG* [1982] 1 Lloyd's Rep. 599 (where the representation was withdrawn before such reliance).

[60] For cases in which this requirement was not satisfied, see *Société Italo-Belge pour le Commerce et l'Industrie v Palm & Vegetable Oils (Malaysia) Sdn Bhd. (The Post Chaser)* [1981] 2 Lloyd's Rep. 695; *Bremer Handelsgesellschaft mbH v Bunge Corp.* [1983] 1 Lloyd's Rep. 476 at p.484.

[61] *e.g. Bremer Handelsgesellschaft mbH v Vanden Avenne-Izegem PVBA* [1978] 2 Lloyd's Rep. 108, discussed above para.18–357; for cases in which the requirement of reliance by the seller was not satisfied see the authorities cited in nn. 66 and 67, and *Ets. Soules & Cie. v International Trade Developments Ltd* [1980] 1 Lloyd's Rep. 129; *Bremer Handelsgesellschaft mbH v Westzucker GmbH* [1981] 1 Lloyd's Rep. 207; *Cook Industries Inc. v Meunerie Liègeois SA* [1981] 1 Lloyd's Rep. 359; *Peter Cremer v Granaria BV* [1981] 2 Lloyd's Rep. 5831.

[62] *Bremer Handelsgesellschaft mbH v C Mackprang Jr.* [1981] 1 Lloyd's Rep. 292 at p.299.

[63] *Ets. Soules & Cie. v International Trade Developments Ltd* [1980] 1 Lloyd's Rep. 129.

[64] *Cook Industries Inc. v Meunerie Liègeois SA* [1981] 1 Lloyd's Rep. 359; *Peter Cremer v Granaria BV* [1981] 2 Lloyd's Rep. 583; *Bremer Handelsgesellschaft mbH v Deutsche Conti- Handelsgesellschaft mbH* [1983] 2 Lloyd's Rep. 45.

[65] *Bunge SA v Compagnie Europeenne de Céréales* [1982] 1 Lloyd's Rep. 307.

[66] *Bremer Handelsgesellschaft mbH v Deutsche Conti-Handelsgesellschaft mbH* [1983] 1 Lloyd's Rep. 689.

tender conforming documents in respect of the balance due under the contract.[67] Even where there had been an unequivocal representation, the requirement that the seller must have acted in reliance on it in such a way as to make it inequitable for the buyer to go back on the representation was not satisfied where the seller had done no more than produce (at the buyer's request) documentary evidence of *force majeure*,[68] or where he had simply done something that he would have done anyway, even if the representation had not been made.[69]

In many cases concerning c.i.f. contracts, a seller's claim that the buyer had waived, not only the right to reject, but also his right to further performance, or to damages, has failed because he was unable to satisfy the requirement of sufficient action in reliance.[70] That requirement need not be satisfied where the seller claims only that the buyer has waived his right to reject (and not his right to further performance, or to damages, as well[71]) though it is sometimes unnecessarily stated in relation to this type of waiver.[72] The confusion between the two processes is due partly to the use of the word "waiver" to describe them both, and partly to the fact that they have one important requirement in common, namely that of "some unequivocal representation by or on behalf of the buyers".[73] The confusion would be reduced by referring to the relinquishment of only the right to reject as an election (of remedies) and by reserving "waiver" for the

---

[67] *Bremer Handelsgesellschaft mbH v Westzucker GmbH* [1981] 1 Lloyd's Rep. 207; *Bremer Handelsgesellschaft mbH v Westzucker GmbH* (*No. 2*) [1981] 1 Lloyd's Rep. 214 at p.222, affirmed [1981] 2 Lloyd's Rep. 130; *Bremer Handelsgesellschaft mbH v Deutsche Conti- Handelsgesellschaft mbH* [1983] 2 Lloyd's Rep. 45. For the converse process of partial *rejection*, see below, para.19–158.

[68] *Bremer Handelsgesellschaft mbH v Deutsche Conti-Handelsgesellschaft mbH* [1983] 1 Lloyd's Rep. 689.

[69] *Bremer Handelsgesellschaft mbH v Bunge Corp.* [1983] 1 Lloyd's Rep. 476.

[70] See the cases cited in nn. 68 and 69, above and the cases, except the first, cited in n.61, above.

[71] *Edm. J Mertens PVBA v Veevoeder Import Export Vimex BV* [1979] 2 Lloyd's Rep. 372 at p.384; *Telfair Shipping Corp. v Athos Shipping Corp.* (*The Athos*) [1981] 2 Lloyd's Rep. 74 at pp.87–88, affirmed on this point [1983] 1 Lloyd's Rep. 127; *Scandinavian Trading Tanker Co. AB v Flota Petrolera Ecuatoriana* (*The Scaptrade*) [1981] 2 Lloyd's Rep. 425 at p.430, affirmed on this point [1983] Q.B. 529 and [1983] 2 A.C. 694); *Peter Cremer v Granaria BV* [1981] 2 Lloyd's Rep. 583 at p.589; *cf. Société Italo-Belge pour le Commerce et l'Industrie v Palm & Vegetable Oils* (*Malaysia*) *Sdn. Bhd.* (*The Post Chaser*) [1981] 2 Lloyd's Rep. 695 at p.702; *Peyman v Lanjani* [1985] Ch. 457 at p.494, 500, 734; *Sea Calm Shipping SA v Chantiers Naval de l'Esterel* (*The Uhenbels*) [1986] 2 Lloyd's Rep. 294 at p.297; *Motor Oil Hellas* (*Corinth*) *SA v Shipping Corp. of India* (*The Kanchenjunga*) [1990] 1 Lloyd's Rep. 391 at p.398.

[72] *e.g. Cerealmangimi SpA v Toepfer* (*The Eurometal*) [1981] 1 Lloyd's Rep. 337 at p.341; *cf. Bremer Handelsgesellschaft mbH v Finagrain* (*etc.*) *SA* [1981] 2 Lloyd's Rep. 259 at p.265; *Procter & Gamble Philippine Manufacturing Corp. v Peter Cremer GmbH* (*The Manila*) [1988] 3 All E.R. 843 at p.854; *Vitol SA v Esso Australia Ltd* (*The Wise*) [1989] 2 Lloyd's Rep. 451 at pp.460–461.

[73] *Cobec Brazilian Warehousing Co. v Alfred C. Toepfer* [1983] 2 Lloyd's Rep. 386 at p.392, where the requirement was not satisfied merely by reason of the buyers' saying, after they had received tender of a bill of lading for part of the quantity sold, that "to-day we need a full tender"; *The Happy Day*, above n.57, at [67].

situation in which the buyer gives up *all* his rights in respect of the breach.[74] It is with waiver in the first of these senses that the following discussion of the loss of the right to reject is concerned.

19–151 **Waiver and analogous doctrines.** Defects in a c.i.f. seller's performance may become apparent to the buyer well before actual delivery of the goods: for example, where the seller gives a notice of appropriation or tenders shipping documents, and the notice or the documents fail to comply with the requirements of the contract. If the buyer, though aware of the non-conformity,[75] takes up the documents without express reservation of his rights,[76] he will clearly have waived his right to reject the documents. This may be so even if the buyer accepts (or agrees to accept) the documents or the goods subject to a reservation of his rights, or "without prejudice".[77] The effect of such expressions may be to preserve merely his right to damages,[78] and possibly his rights in respect of *other* deliveries due at a later stage under the contract,[79] but not his right to reject the delivery in question.

A buyer who has knowingly accepted non-conforming documents cannot subsequently reject the goods where there is *either* a defect only in the documents (but none in the goods[80]) *or* where the defect in the goods is apparent on the face of the documents and is known to the buyer. In the latter case, the buyer will have waived his right to reject the goods by taking up the documents with knowledge of the defect in the goods.[81] If he takes up the documents in ignorance of facts giving him the right to reject, he will not be taken to have waived his right to reject the documents or the goods,[82] though he may have lost his right to reject by acceptance.[83]

Where a c.i.f. buyer, having taken up documents in ignorance of a defect giving him the right to reject either the documents or the goods or both,

[74] See *Kammins Ballroom Ltd v Zenith Investments (Torquay) Ltd* [1971] A.C. 850 at pp.882–883; *cf.* the use of "elect" and "waive" in Sale of Goods Act 1979, s.11(2); *Peyman v Lanjani* [1985] Ch. 457 at pp.493, 500.

[75] For the requirement of knowledge, see *Panchaud Frères SA v Etablissements General Grain Co.* [1971] 1 Lloyd's Rep. 53 at p.57; and *ibid.*, p.59, approving Roskill J.'s statement on this point ([1969] 2 Lloyd's Rep. 109 at p.124), while reversing his decision on other grounds: below, para.19–160.

[76] A mere reservation of rights will not preclude a finding of waiver, since this is based on an overall assessment of the injured party's conduct: see *Nichimen Corp. v Gatoil Overseas Inc.* [1987] 2 Lloyd's Rep. 46 at p.50 (a case of alleged waiver by the seller of the buyer's breach).

[77] *Vitol SA v Esso Australia Ltd (The Wise)* [1989] 2 Lloyd's Rep. 451.

[78] *cf. Peter Cremer v Granaria BV* [1981] 2 Lloyd's Rep. 583 at p.590.

[79] *e.g.* acceptance of part-delivery subject to a reservation of the buyer's rights would preserve his right to claim the balance of the goods due under the contract: *cf.* above, para.18–358.

[80] *e.g. Shipton Anderson & Co. v John Weston & Co.* (1922) 10 Ll.L.R. 762, where the bill of lading contained an unacceptably wide deviation clause (see above, para.19–033) but there was no defect in the goods; *cf. Procter & Gamble Philippine Manufacturing Corp. v Kurt A. Becher* [1988] 2 Lloyd's Rep. 21 (below, para.19–198), where rejection was not in issue.

[81] *Bremer Handelsgesellschaft mbH v Deutsche Conti-Handelsgesellschaft mbH* [1983] 2 Lloyd's Rep. 45 (the *Paul L. Russ* shipment).

[82] *Suzuki & Co. v Burgett and Newsam* (1921) 8 Ll.L.R. 495; (1922) 10 Ll.L.R. 223.

[83] Below, paras 19–153, 19–160.

later discovers the defect and then takes delivery of the goods, he will be taken to have waived his right to reject, not only the goods, but also the documents, on account of that defect. The position would be the same if the buyer learned of the facts giving rise to the right to reject after the goods have been delivered to him and with knowledge of those facts retained the goods.[84]

A number of dicta have cast some doubt on the requirement that the buyer must know of the defect before he can be said to have waived his right to reject.[85] But if the basis of such waiver is that the buyer is "taken to have affirmed" the contract,[86] it would seem that knowledge of the defect (or at least "obvious means of knowing it"[87]) and of the right to reject is essential before the buyer can be said to have waived the right to reject; and this view has been affirmed by the Court of Appeal.[88] Where the buyer has no such knowledge, he may, however, be precluded from rejecting on the different ground that he was estopped from denying that he had waived his right to do so. Like waiver of the right to reject, such estoppel requires an unequivocal representation on the part of the buyer.[89] But the two doctrines differ in that, while waiver of the right to reject requires such knowledge on the part of the buyer but no action in reliance on the part of the seller,[90] the converse is true of estoppel, *i.e.* it requires action in reliance by the seller but no such knowledge on the part of the buyer.[91] The buyer's conduct in taking up the shipping documents can amount to the representation required for the purpose of an estoppel if those documents on their face disclose the defect giving rise to the right to reject, even though the buyer has not actually become aware of the defect[92]; and such conduct may similarly amount to such a representation even where the buyer does not have such means of discovering the defect. This possibility is illustrated by *Bremer Handelsgesellschaft mbH v C. Mackprang Jr.*[93] where a c.i.f. seller gave a notice of appropriation which was defective in not having been

---

[84] *cf. Kwei Tek Chao v British Traders & Shippers Ltd* [1954] 2 Q.B. 459 at p.477.
[85] *Bremer Handelsgesellschaft mbH v C Mackprang Jr.* [1979] 1 Lloyd's Rep. 221 at pp.226, 230; *Avimex SA v Dewulf & Cie.* [1979] 2 Lloyd's Rep. 57 at p.67.
[86] *Kwei Tek Chao v British Traders & Shippers Ltd* [1954] 2 Q.B. 459 at p.457.
[87] *Bremer Handelsgesellschaft mbH v C. Mackprang Jr.*, above, at p.229, *per* Stephenson L.J. (dissenting).
[88] *Peyman v Lanjani* [1985] Ch. 457; above, para.19–150. *cf. Cobec Brazilian Trading & Warehousing Corp. v Alfred C. Toepfer* [1983] 2 Lloyd's Rep. 386 at 392; *Procter & Gamble Philippine Manufacturing Corp. v Peter Cremer GmbH & Co.* (*The Manila*) [1988] 3 All E.R. 843 at p.853; and, in other contexts, *Trustees of Henry Smith's Charity v Willson* [1983] Q.B. 316 at 328; *Haydenfayre Ltd v British National Insurance Society Ltd* [1984] 2 Lloyd's Rep. 393 at p.400; *Motor Oil Hellas (Corinth) SA v Shipping Corp. of India SA* (*The Kanchenjunga*) [1990] 1 Lloyd's Rep. 391 at p.398; *Transcatalana de Commercio SA v Incrobasa Industrial e Commercio Brasileira SA* [1995] 1 Lloyd's Rep. 215 at pp.219–220 (f.o.b. contract).
[89] See above, para.19–150 at n.73.
[90] Above, para.19–150
[91] *Peyman v Lanjani* [1985] Ch. 457 at p.495; *cf. The Kachenjunga*, above n.88, at p.399.
[92] As in *Panchaud Frères SA v Etablissements General Grain Co.* [1970] 1 Lloyd's Rep. 53 (but the requirement of action in reliance seems not to have been satisfied in that case: see below, para.19–160).
[93] [1979] 1 Lloyd's Rep. 221.

passed on in due time by a previous seller in a "string" of contracts. The buyer did not object to the notice when it was given; and there is (with respect) force in the view[94] that his failure to do so could not amount to waiver since at that time he neither knew of the defect nor had any more obvious means of knowing it than were available to the seller. A majority of the Court of Appeal nevertheless held that the buyer could not, when shipping documents were later tendered, rely on defects in the notice. This view appears to be based on the fact that the seller had acted in reliance on the belief (induced by the buyer's failure to object to the notice) that such tender would be accepted; and had so acted to his detriment in continuing (on a rising market) to make efforts to perform by procuring goods, or documents relating to them, for the purpose of tendering them to the buyer. It should be emphasised that buyer and seller were intermediate parties in a "string" of contracts and that the defect in the notice was due to the fault, not of the seller, but of an earlier party in the string. This fact, coupled with the seller's detrimental reliance, may justify the view that it would have been "unfair or unjust"[95] to allow the buyer to object at the time of tender of documents to the defect in the notice of appropriation. In the absence of such special facts, it is submitted that the buyer should not have been prevented from relying on the defect if he neither knew of it nor could have discovered it from the notice itself, and if means of discovering it were no more readily accessible to him than to the seller.

19–152 **Partial waiver.** A buyer may take up documents relating only to part of the goods sold, knowing that the documents are defective, *e.g.* because they indicate shipment outside the period specified in the contract. By taking up such documents the buyer loses his right to reject those documents and the goods to which they relate; but he does not, merely on that account, lose his right to reject other documents which relate to the rest of the goods sold and suffer from a similar defect.[96]

19–153 **Acceptance.** Under sections 34 and 35 of the Sale of Goods Act 1979, a buyer is deemed to have accepted goods (a) when he intimates to the seller that he has accepted them, or (b) when the goods have been delivered to him and he does any act in relation to them which is inconsistent with the ownership of the seller, or (c) when after the lapse of a reasonable time he retains the goods without intimating to the seller that he has rejected them. In the first two cases, the buyer is not deemed to have accepted the goods until he has had a reasonable opportunity of examining them for the purpose of ascertaining whether they are in conformity with the contract,[97]

94 Expressed by Stephenson L.J., dissenting.
95 [1979] 1 Lloyd's Rep. 221 at p.226, *per* Lord Denning M.R.
96 *Bremer Handelsgesellschaft mbH v Deutsche Conti-Handelsgesellschaft mbH* [1983] 2 Lloyd's Rep. 45; *cf. Peter Cremer v Granaria BV* [1981] 2 Lloyd's Rep. 583 at p.590 (acceptance of notice of appropriation with knowledge that it related to goods shipped late).
97 Sale of Goods Act 1979, s.35(1) and (2). A buyer who deals as consumer (see in the context of overseas sales, above, para.18–259) "cannot lose his right to rely on s.35(2) by agreement, waiver or otherwise": s.35(3), above, para.13–102.

and in the third the question whether he has had such an opportunity is material in determining whether a reasonable time has elapsed.[98] Intimation of acceptance and retention without intimating rejection do not (as such) call for further comment here[99]; but something must be said of acceptance by doing an act inconsistent with the ownership of the seller, and of separate acts of acceptance and opportunities of examination in relation to the documents and to the goods.

Act inconsistent with the ownership of the seller. In *Hardy & Co. v Hillerns and Fowler*[1] a c.i.f. buyer who had taken up the documents then resold part of the goods and delivered these to his sub-buyer. It was held that the resale and delivery of the goods by the buyer to the sub-buyer amounted to an "act inconsistent with the ownership of the seller"; but this part of the decision has been reversed by section 35(6)(b) of the Sale of Goods Act 1979, which provides that the buyer is not deemed to have accepted the goods merely[2] because he has delivered them to another person under a sale or other disposition. It was further held that the buyer's act had barred his right to reject the goods even though he had not at the time of the resale and delivery had an opportunity of examining the goods, and this part of the decision, too, has been reversed by the provisions of section 35[3] referred to in paragraph 19–153 above. These legislative changes, however, leave open the question whether a dealing with the documents (as opposed to one with the goods) may lead to a loss of the buyer's right to reject. Before the changes were made, it was said that a mere *pledge* of documents by a c.i.f. buyer would not be an "act inconsistent with the ownership of the seller"[4] and conflicting views were expressed on the question whether a *sale* of the documents followed by their transfer to the buyer amounted to such an act.[5] The importance of the point is reduced by the rule that such an act cannot amount to acceptance unless there has been an opportunity of examination; but the point could still arise where there had been such an opportunity and the defect was not actually discovered. Probably, the buyer would be regarded as having dealt with his own "conditional property" (acquired when he took up the documents) and so not to have done an "act inconsistent with the ownership of the *seller*", that is, with the seller's "reversionary interest"[6] in the goods, merely by dealing with the documents.[7] Even if he could be deemed to have accepted the documents by 19–154

---

[98] Sale of Goods Act 1979, s.35(4) and (5).
[99] See above, paras 12–045, 12–053.
[1] [1923] 2 K.B. 491.
[2] See below, n.8 and below, para.20–111.
[3] See above, at n.97.
[4] *Kwei Tek Chao v British Traders and Shippers Ltd* [1954] 2 Q.B. 459 at 485–486.
[5] See *ibid.*, at p.488.
[6] *ibid.*, at p.487.
[7] *cf.* below, para.19–174. Similarly, a buyer would not act inconsistently with the seller's "reversionary interest" (above at n.6) merely by insuring the goods: *Clegg v Olle Andersson* [2003] EWCA Civ. 320, [2003] 1 All E.R. (Comm.) 721 at [59]. The point could be relevant where the sale was on c. & f. terms and the buyer had insured (see below, para.21–012). Under a c.i.f. contract, the obligation to insure

such dealing, it is submitted that he would not be deemed to have accepted *the goods* unless he had actually dealt with the goods themselves in a way that was "inconsistent with the ownership of the seller."

In the situation just discussed, the buyer was not, at the time of the alleged acceptance, actually aware of the non-conformity which gave rise to the right to reject. Where the buyer was aware of such a non-conformity when he later resold the goods, this act of resale has been held to amount to an act inconsistent with the ownership of the seller, even (it seems) without any delivery of the goods to the sub-buyer: hence the right to reject was held to have been barred by acceptance, apparently of the documents.[8] It seems at least equally plausible to say that the right to reject had in such circumstances been lost by waiver.[9] There could, however, be no such waiver where the buyer did not know of the defect[10]; nor does the decision support the view that a mere dealing with documents (even by way of sale) could amount to an acceptance where at the time of the dealing the buyer had no such knowledge.

19–155 **Separate acts of acceptance in relation to documents and goods.** Section 35 is drafted on the assumption that it is the goods themselves which may be examined and are accepted[11]; and the section is not easy to apply to c.i.f. contracts, in which there are separate rights to reject the goods and the documents.[12] Acceptance of the documents and acceptance of the goods appear to be separate acts; and acceptance of the documents will not necessarily bar the right to reject the goods. Although the law on the point is far from clear, it seems that a distinction must be drawn between defects in the goods which are apparent on the face of the documents, and those which are not. Acceptance of documents will not of itself deprive the buyer of his right to reject the goods on account of a defect in them which is not apparent on the face of the documents: for example on account of the failure of the goods to conform with the contract description in a way that was not, and could not have been expected to have been,[13] revealed by the

---

normally rests on the seller so that the buyer would not need to insure. But he might wish to do so in exceptional circumstances: *e.g.* where at the relevant time it was not usual to insure against war risks and the buyer wished to cover himself against such risks: see above para.19–046 and *cf.* below para.19–117. Under a "classic" f.o.b. contract (below, para.20–002) a seller is likewise not bound to insure so that insurance, if any, is likely to be effected by the buyer.

[8] *Vargas Pena Apeztieguia y Cia v Peter Cremer GmbH* [1987] 1 Lloyd's Rep. 394 at p.398 ("must be taken to have accepted the documents"); *cf.* the reference on p.396 to the buyers' "right to reject the documents". *Semble*, the point would not be affected by Sale of Goods Act 1979, s.35(6)(b) (above at n.2): the word "merely" in that provision would seem to exclude the situation in which the seller deals with documents knowing of their non-conformity. The sale in the *Vargas Pena* case was on f.o.b terms, but the principles applicable to c.i.f contracts were relevant for the reasons stated in para.20–107, below.

[9] Above, para.19–150

[10] *ibid*.

[11] The same assumption underlies Art. 38(1) of the Vienna Convention on Contracts for the International Sale of Goods (above, para.1–024).

[12] Above, para.19–144.

[13] Under the rule in *Cox, Patterson & Co. v Bruce & Co.* (1866) 18 Q.B.D. 147, above para.18–029.

documents.[14] In such a case, there is no defect in the documents, so that there is only one right to reject, *i.e.* a right to reject the goods. If, on the other hand, there is a defect in both the goods and the documents, for example if the documents on their face indicate that the goods were shipped late, and the buyer, though aware of this defect in the documents, nevertheless accepts them without reservation of his rights, then he will have waived his right to reject the goods on the ground that they were shipped late[15]; and he may lose the right to reject the goods even though he has not read the documents,[16] so that he cannot strictly speaking be said to have waived the right to reject, since waiver requires actual knowledge of the existence of the right to reject.[17] On the other hand, the buyer could still reject the goods after accepting the documents if the goods suffered from a defect which did *not* appear on the face of the documents. Thus he could reject the goods (even after he had accepted the documents) on the ground of late shipment if the bill of lading was forged to show shipment within the contract period.[18] The buyer would also, it is submitted, be entitled to reject the goods, even though he had accepted documents which on their face showed that the goods were not in accordance with the contract, if he could show that the goods also suffered from *another* defect which was not apparent from inspection of the documents. This would be the position where, for example, the documents showed that the goods were shipped outside the contract period, but not that they failed to correspond with a sample.

Opportunity to examine documents and goods. Unlike waiver, acceptance does not require actual knowledge of the defect, but in general a buyer is not deemed to have accepted the goods until he has had a reasonable opportunity of examination.[19] In the case of a c.i.f. contract, that opportunity may relate either to the documents or to the goods or to both, according to the circumstances. Thus if the ground of rejection is late shipment, which could have been discovered from examining the documents, it is the opportunity of examining the documents which will be crucial, since no further examination of the goods would be of the slightest use "for the purpose of ascertaining whether they are in conformity with the contract".[20] Conversely, the opportunity of examining the goods will be crucial where the ground of rejection is a qualitative defect which is not, and cannot be, apparent on the face of the documents. Where the ground of rejection is late shipment and this is not apparent from inspecting either the documents or the goods, the provisions of the Act as to opportunity of 19–156

---

[14] *Trasimex Holdings SA v Addax BV (The Red Sea)* [1999] 1 Lloyd's Rep. 28 at 33 (where the actual claim was for damages, the buyer having treated the breach of condition as one of warranty).
[15] Above, para.19–151.
[16] Above, para.19–151; below, para.19–160.
[17] Above, paras 19–150, 19–151.
[18] See *Kwei Tek Chao v British Traders and Shippers Ltd* [1954] 2 Q.B. 459; in fact the buyer accepted the goods but the fact that he had at one time had a separate right to reject them was important in assessing damages: below, para.19–191.
[19] Above, para.19–153.
[20] Sale of Goods Act 1979, s.34.

examination are scarcely appropriate; but it seems that in such a case acceptance of the documents will not bar the right to reject the goods.[21]

19–157 **Delivery and examination.** Under section 35 of the Sale of Goods Act 1979, the question whether the buyer has lost his right to reject may depend on whether the goods have been delivered to him, and on whether he has had a reasonable opportunity of examining them. In a c.i.f. contract it has been said that there are "three stages of delivery": a "provisional delivery" on shipment; a "symbolical delivery" on tender of documents; and a "complete delivery of the cargo" when the goods are handed over to the buyer at the c.i.f. destination.[22] Although some dicta can be cited in favour of the view that one or another of these stages is "the" time of delivery,[23] the best view is that, for the present purpose, there is no single time of delivery. The buyer's opportunity of examining the *documents* arises at the second stage, when the documents are tendered; and his opportunity of examining the *goods* arises at the third stage of complete delivery[24] unless the contract expressly provides that he must examine the goods at the port of shipment.[25] The buyer is allowed a reasonable time after discharge for examining the goods and then a further reasonable time for deciding whether he intends to reject. Thus in one case it was held that the right to reject had not been lost where a c.i.f. buyer completed his examination of the goods seven days after discharge and rejected them after another four days.[26]

19–158 **Partial rejection.** Section 35A of the Sale of Goods Act 1979 deals with the situation in which the buyer "has the right to reject the goods by reason of a breach on the part of the seller that affects some or all of them". It provides that if, in such a case, the buyer accepts some of the goods, he does not thereby lose his right to reject the rest. The section may not literally apply to the case where a c.i.f. buyer has the right to reject documents even though there is no defect in the goods, *e.g.* where the documents indicate shipment outside the shipment period even though the goods were actually shipped within that period,[27] so that there is no "breach

---

[21] *Kwei Tek Chao v British Traders and Shippers Ltd*, above.

[22] *Schmoll Fils & Co. Inc. v Scriven Bros & Co.* (1924) 19 Ll.L.R. 118 at p.119; above, para.19–072.

[23] *Ströms Bruks A/B v John and Peter Hutchison* [1905] A.C. 515 at p.524 (shipment); *Kwei Tek Chao v British Shippers and Traders Ltd* [1954] 2 Q.B. 459 at p.487 (shipment); *Blythe & Co. v Richards, Turpin & Co.* (1916) 114 L.T. 753 (delivery at destination); *Lesters Leather and Skin Co. Ltd v Home and Overseas Brokers Ltd* (1949) 82 Ll.L.R. 203 at p.205 (delivery at destination).

[24] *Schmoll Fils & Co. Inc. v Scriven Bros & Co.* (1924) 19 Ll.L.R. 118; *Molling & Co. v Dean & Son (Ltd)* (1901) 18 T.L.R. 217 (criticised in *Hardy & Co. v Hillerns and Fowler* [1923] 2 K.B. 491 at p.497; but see now para.19–154 at nn. 2 and 3; *Bergerco USA v Vegoil Ltd* [1984] 1 Lloyd's Rep. 440; *Trasimex Holdings SA v Addax BV (The Red Sea)* [1999] 1 Lloyd's Rep. 28 at p.33. *Cf.* Vienna Convention on Contracts for the International Sale of Goods (above, para.1–024), Art. 38(2), under which examination of the goods "may be deferred until after the goods have arrived at their destination."

[25] *H Glynn (Covent Garden) Ltd v Wittleder* [1959] 2 Lloyd's Rep. 409.

[26] *Tradax Export SA v European Grain & Shipping Co.* [1983] 2 Lloyd's Rep. 100.

[27] As in *Re General Trading Co. Ltd and Van Stolk's Commissiehandel* (1910) 16 Com.Cas. 95, above, para.19–147.

on the part of the seller that affects some or all of them". Nevertheless, it is submitted that if, in such a case, the buyer accepted documents relating only to part of the goods sold, he would not thereby have lost the right to reject other documents. This submission is supported by the analogy of the rules relating to partial waiver[28] and by the fact that the principal provisions of the Act with regard to acceptance[29] are always taken to apply to acceptance of documents, even though in terms they refer only to acceptance of goods.

Rejection for wrong reason: general principle. It is a general principle of the law of contract that a person who refuses to perform a contract and gives a ground which does not justify the refusal, or no ground at all, may nevertheless subsequently rely on another ground, which does justify the refusal to perform, provided that that other ground in fact existed at the time of the refusal.[30] There is no reason to suppose that this principle does not apply to c.i.f. contracts. Thus if a c.i.f. buyer rejected goods on the ground that they were not shipped within the shipment period and failed to substantiate that ground, he might still be entitled to justify his rejection on the ground that the goods were not of the quality or description called for by the contract.[31] 19–159

Qualifications. The general principle stated in paragraph 19–159 is subject to a number of qualifications. 19–160

First, it will not apply "if the point which was not taken is one which if taken could have been put right."[32] Thus if, during the time spent in investigating and attempting to meet the buyer's groundless objection, the

---

[28] Above, para.19–152.
[29] *i.e.* s.35; (above, para.19–155).
[30] *Boston Deep Sea Fishing and Ice Co. v Ansell* (1888) 39 Ch.D. 339; *Taylor v Oakes, Roncoroni & Co.* (1922) 38 T.L.R. 349 at p.351 (affirmed *ibid.*, 517); *Heisler v Anglo-Dal Ltd* [1954] 1 W.L.R. 1273 at p.1277; *Cerealmangimi SpA v Toepfer (The Eurometal)* [1979] 2 Lloyd's Rep. 72 (and [1981] 1 Lloyd's Rep. 337); *Kydon Compania Naviera v National Westminster Bank Ltd (The Lena)* [1981] 1 Lloyd's Rep. 68 at p.79 (letter of credit); *Glencore Grain Rotterdam BV v LORICO* [1997] 2 Lloyd's Rep. 386 at pp.394–395; *Soules CAF v P.T. Transcap of Indonesia* [1999] 1 Lloyd's Rep. 917; *SHV Gas Supply & Trading SAS v Naftomar Shipping & Trading Co Ltd Inc (The Azur Gaz)* [2005] EWHC 2528 (Comm.), [2006] 1 Lloyd's Rep. 163 at [54]; and see below, para.19–209. Under the Vienna Convention on Contracts for the International Sale of Goods (above, para.1–024) the scope of this principle will be reduced since Art. 39(1) provides that the buyer "loses his right to rely on a lack of conformity of the goods if he does not give notice to the seller specifying the nature of the lack of conformity within a reasonable time after he has discovered it or ought to have discovered it." However, he can rely on an unspecified defect if at the time of rejection he had neither knowledge nor means of knowledge of it; this is so even if at that time he had given notice of another defect. Art. 39(1) also does not apply if the defect was one of which the seller "knew or could not have been unaware and which he did not disclose to the buyer": Art. 40. Nor does Art. 39(1) in terms apply to defects in the documents. In all these cases, the common law principle stated in the text can apply to a contract governed by the Convention.
[31] As in *Arcos Ltd v Ronaasen* [1933] A.C. 470; see 37 Com.Cas. 291 at pp.294–295 for some critical remarks by Scrutton L.J.
[32] *Heisler v Anglo-Dal Ltd* [1954] 1 W.L.R. 1273 at p.1277.

seller loses the opportunity of obtaining some essential document (to the lack of which the buyer had not originally objected), then the buyer cannot justify his original rejection on the ground that that document was not tendered.[33] Similarly, a buyer who fails to rely on the lateness of a notice of appropriation at the time when the notice was given cannot take the point in legal proceedings many years later if the seller could (had the point been raised when the notice was first given) have made another valid appropriation relating to another shipment, or if he could have validated the original appropriation, *e.g.* because the contract provided for extension of time in case of "proof of string".[34] On the other hand, the present qualification to the general principle stated in paragraph 19–159 does not apply where, at the time of refusal to perform, the time for putting "the point which was not taken . . . right" had already passed so that, within the contractual framework, it could no longer, if taken, have been put right. In such a case, therefore, the refusal is justified, even though the ground which justified it was not stated at the time of the refusal, so long as that ground existed at the time of the refusal.[35]

The general principle stated in paragraph 19–159 may secondly be excluded by the doctrines of estoppel or waiver if (1) the buyer's assertion of an invalid ground for rejection, or his failure to state a valid ground, amounts to a representation that he will not rely on grounds which he has failed to state; and (2) the seller acts on that representation to his detriment, *e.g.* by continuing to make efforts to perform.[36]

There is, thirdly, some support for the view that a c.i.f. buyer who fails, at the time of the rejection, to specify a valid ground for it, which existed at that time, may be precluded from later relying on that ground even though the seller could not have put the matter right if the point had been taken earlier, and even though the seller did not in any way change his position in consequence of the buyer's original failure to specify the valid ground of rejection. In *Panchaud Frères SA v Etablissements General Grain Co.*[37] a c.i.f. contract for the sale of maize provided for shipment in June/July 1965. A shipment was made in August and the fact of late shipment should have been apparent to the buyers (even though the bill of lading was falsely dated July 31) since the shipping documents tendered by the sellers included a certificate of quality which referred to samples drawn in August as having been drawn "concurrently with loading". The buyers took up the documents and paid the price without actually becoming aware of this point, and when the goods arrived they rejected them on account of defects for which the sellers were not responsible. Three years later the buyers claimed the return of the price, now relying for the first time on the fact of

[33] *ibid.*
[34] *André & Cie. v Cook Industries Inc.* [1987] 2 Lloyd's Rep. 463.
[35] *Glencore Grain Rotterdam BV v LORICO* [1997] 2 Lloyd's Rep. 386 at p.395.
[36] On the analogy of *Bremer Handelsgesellschaft mbH v C Mackprang Jr.* [1979] 1 Lloyd's Rep. 221 above, para.19–151; see also *The Lena*, above, n.30 at p.79 (where the requirements of representation and reliance were not satisfied) and *Glencore Grain Rotterdam v LORICO* [1997] 2 Lloyd's Rep. 386 at p.395 (where no reliance was placed on waiver or estoppel).
[37] [1970] 1 Lloyd's Rep. 55.

late shipment as justifying their original rejection of the goods. Their claim was dismissed, the court being no doubt impressed by the possible harshness of allowing the buyers to rely, at such a late stage, on an originally unstated ground for rejection which they could have discovered by a careful inspection of the shipping documents when these documents were originally tendered.[38] To allow the buyers to rely on that ground three years after it had arisen would, it was said, have been inconsistent with a "requirement of fair conduct".[39] But the vagueness of this requirement makes it very hard to say which cases will be governed by it and which by the general rule that a buyer can rely on an originally unstated ground for rejection.[40] Hence the *Panchaud Frères* case has been viewed with some scepticism.[41] It has been said that "no distinctive principle of law can be distilled from the . . . case"[42]; and that no "separate doctrine"[43] can be derived from it; and various other explanations of it have been put forward. One suggestion is that the buyers had waived[44] the right to reject; but in the actual judgments this suggestion was rightly rejected on the ground that the buyers did not know of the late shipment when they took up the documents.[45] Another suggestion is that the buyers' conduct gave rise to an estoppel or equitable estoppel[46]; but it is hard to see that the buyers' taking up the documents amounted to an unequivocal representation that they would not reject the goods or that, if it did, the sellers had relied on it[47]; and in the absence of such a representation and such reliance there could be no scope for either waiver or estoppel.[48] Certainly, the sellers lost no chance of curing the defect in their tender, for when that tender was made such cure was no longer possible. Probably the best explanation of the case

---

[38] In relation to defects in the goods, this point is intended to be met in the Vienna Convention on Contracts for the International Sale of Goods (above, para.1–024) by Art. 39(1), as to which see n.30, above.

[39] [1970] 1 Lloyd's Rep. 53 at p.59.

[40] Above, para.19–159.

[41] *Syros Shipping Co. SA v Elaghill Trading Co.* (*The Proodos C*) [1980] 2 Lloyd's Rep. 390 at p.392.

[42] *Procter & Gamble Philippine Manufacturing Corp. v Peter Cremer GmbH & Co.* (*The Manila*) [1988] 3 All E.R. 843 at p.852.

[43] *Glencore Grain Rotterdam BV v LORICO* [1997] 2 Lloyd's Rep. 386 at p.397.

[44] *V Berg & Son Ltd v Vanden-Avenne Izegem PVBA* [1977] 1 Lloyd's Rep. 499 at pp.502–503; *Intertradex SA v Lesieur Torteaux* [1978] 2 Lloyd's Rep. 509 at p.513; *Bremer Handelsgesellschaft mbH v C Mackprang Jr.* [1979] 1 Lloyd's Rep. 221 at p.225.

[45] [1970] 1 Lloyd's Rep. 53 at pp.57, 59; above, para.19–151, n.88.

[46] [1970] 1 Lloyd's Rep. 53 at p.56 ("estoppel by conduct"); *cf. Intertradex SA v Lesieur Torteaux* [1978] 2 Lloyd's Rep. 509 at p.515, describing the question as "not really one of waiver but one of equitable estoppel"; *Procter & Gamble Philippine Manufacturing Corp. v Peter Cremer GmbH & Co.* (*The Manila*) [1988] 3 All E.R. 843 at p.852 ("estoppel") and p.853 ("waiver/estoppel").

[47] *cf. Raiffeisen Hauptgenossenschaft v Louis Dreyfuss & Co. Ltd* [1981] 1 Lloyd's Rep. 345, where the *Panchaud Frères* case was held inapplicable precisely because the requirement of reliance was not satisfied. The same conclusion was reached in *The Manila*, above, n.46.

[48] *Glencore Grain Rotterdam BV v LORICO* [1997] 2 Lloyd's Rep. 386 at p.398 (f.o.b. contract).

is that the buyers lost their right to reject the documents by acceptance[49] when they took up, and paid against, the documents, and that they at the same time lost their right to reject the goods as the fact of late shipment, which would have justified rejection of the goods, was apparent on the face of the documents.[50] It follows from this explanation that the buyers could have relied on the fact of late shipment in later proceedings if they had *rejected* the documents, even though they had, at the time of such rejection, given an inadequate reason for it, or none at all.[51] It has also been held that the buyer could rely on the fact of late shipment where all the *shipping* documents agreed in stating a false date of shipment within the contract period and the fact of late shipment was ascertainable only from a survey report which was not one of the shipping documents called for by the contract but which was in fact supplied by the seller.[52]

19–161 **Ground of rejection must exist at time of rejection.** The ground of rejection on which subsequent reliance is placed must actually exist at the time of rejection.[53] It is not enough for the party who at the time of rejection gave an insufficient ground, or no ground at all, to show that a good ground for rejection might or would have arisen subsequently. Thus in *British and Beningtons Ltd v NW Cachar Tea Co.*[54] three contracts for the sale of tea were made, providing for delivery in London but not fixing any delivery dates. Delivery was therefore due within a reasonable time, and

---

[49] *BP Exploration Co. (Libya) Ltd v Hunt* [1979] 1 W.L.R. 783 at pp.810–811, affirmed without reference to this point [1983] A.C. 352; *Glencore Grain Rotterdam BV v LORICO* [1997] 2 Lloyd's Rep. 386 at p.396.

[50] Above, para.19–155.

[51] *cf. v Berg & Son Ltd v Vanden Avenne Izegem PVBA* [1977] 1 Lloyd's Rep. 499.

[52] *Procter & Gamble Philippine Manufacturing Corp. v Peter Cremer GmbH & Co.* (*The Manila*) [1988] 3 All E.R. 843; the fact that the sellers had not "acted on the faith of the buyer's conduct" was said at p.854 to be one ground for distinguishing the *Panchaud Frères* case; but no such action by the sellers was shown in the latter case. The shipment in *The Manila*, above, also gave rise to the litigation in *Procter & Gamble Philippine Manufacturing Corp. v Kurt A Becher* [1988] 2 Lloyd's Rep. 21, below, para.19–198.

[53] Under the Vienna Convention on Contracts for the International Sale of Goods (above, para.1–024) the position is different. If before the date for performance it is "clear" that A will commit a "fundamental breach" (defined in Art. 25: see above, para.18–267, n.38) B can declare the contract avoided, (Art. 72(1)), so long as, "if time allows," B gives A a notice permitting him "to provide adequate assurance of performance" (Art. 72(2)), but this requirement need not be satisfied where A has "declared that he will not perform his obligations" (Art. 72(3)). Exercise of the right of avoidance would give rise to a right to damages: see Art. 81(1). In English law, there would be no right to damages in the situations described in Art. 72(1) and (2); but there would be a right to rescind and to claim damages for anticipatory breach in the situation described in Art. 72(3). A less drastic remedy, which has no counterpart in English law, is provided by Art. 71(1): this is the right of a party to "suspend" performance of his own obligations if it becomes "apparent" that the other party will not perform a "substantial part" of his obligation as a result of "(a) a serious deficiency in his ability to perform or his credit-worthiness; or (b) his conduct in preparing to perform or in performing the contract." This provision might, in a case like the *British and Beningtons* case (*infra*, n.54), justify suspension by the buyers of their obligations to perform, but it would not justify the buyers' outright repudiation of the contract.

[54] [1923] A.C. 48.

before this had expired the buyers repudiated the contracts. It was held that they had thereby committed an anticipatory breach and that this had been accepted by the sellers. Hence the buyers were liable in damages: they could not rely, by way of defence, on the argument that the sellers had not shown that they would have been able to deliver in accordance with the contract, for by accepting the buyers' repudiation, the sellers had put an end to their own obligation to perform[55] so far as it fell due after the date of that acceptance. If the sellers had *not* accepted the buyers' repudiation, and had indeed been unable (as the buyers alleged) to deliver in time, the sellers would not have been discharged from their own obligation and their failure to perform that obligation would have justified the buyers' repudiation. Hence the sellers would not have been entitled to damages[56] and would, on the contrary, have been themselves liable in damages for failing to deliver in time.[57]

The buyers would, moreover, have been liable even if they had shown that the sellers *could not* have performed obligations which would, but for the sellers' acceptance of the buyer's wrongful repudiation, have fallen due *after* that acceptance. This is most obviously true where the sellers' inability to perform was *induced* by the buyers' wrongful repudiation[58], *e.g.* where the sellers were induced by the buyers' repudiation to abandon any attempts which they would (but for that repudiation) have made to perform their own obligations under the contract. In such a case it would be said that the buyers were estopped from relying on the sellers' inability to perform.[59] The position is the same where a buyer throughout insists on performance in a manner other than that stipulated by the contract, *e.g.* by demanding that the goods are to be shipped to a destination other than that specified in the contract. The seller is clearly not bound to perform in that way, nor is it open to the buyer to argue that the seller could not, in any event, have delivered in accordance with the contract, if "it was [the buyer's] insistence on non-contractual destination and not any conduct on the part of [the seller] that prevented the seller from delivering"[60] the goods.

If the sellers' inability to perform was *not* induced by the buyers' repudiation, proof by the buyers that the sellers could not have performed might sometimes be relevant as to damages[61] but even in such a case it would not justify the buyers' refusal to accept and pay (so as to entitle them to damages), unless the sellers' inability to perform was due to a prior

---

[55] This point is not affected by the fact that "ancillary" obligations may survive rescission (as in *Heyman v Darwins Ltd* [1942] A.C. 356) and that even obligations to perform may survive by virtue of an express term to that effect in the contract (as in *Harbinger UK Ltd v GE Information Services Ltd* [2000] 1 All E.R. (Comm.) 166).

[56] *cf. Fercometal SARL v MSC Mediterranean Shipping Co. SA* (*The Simona*) [1989] A.C. 788, a charterparty case: see below para.19–166, n.17.

[57] In *The Simona*, above, there was no question of the shipowner's being *liable* by reason of his failure to accept the charterer's repudiation, since the later arrival of the ship did not amount to a breach.

[58] As in *Bulk Oil (Zug) AG v Sun International Ltd* [1984] 1 Lloyd's Rep. 531 at pp.545–546; for earlier proceedings, see [1983] 1 Lloyd's Rep. 655.

[59] *cf. Fercometal SARL v Mediterranean Shipping Co. SA (The Simona)* [1989] A.C. 788 at pp.805–806.

[60] *Bulk Oil (Zug) AG v Sun International Ltd* [1984] 1 Lloyd's Rep. 531 at p.546.

[61] See below, para.19–166.

repudiatory breach on the part of the sellers, *i.e.* to one committed before the buyers' repudiation and justifying that repudiation.[62] Such a breach might be actual or anticipatory and might thus consist of conduct by which the sellers had disabled themselves from performing.[63] But where no prior repudiatory breach has been committed by the sellers, the buyers' repudiation will amount (as in the *British and Beningtons* case) to an anticipatory breach; and the sellers can rely on their acceptance of that breach as liberating them from their own duty to perform obligations which would (but for such acceptance) subsequently have fallen due.[64] It follows that even their proved inability to render such performance after that acceptance becomes irrelevant to the buyers' liability in damages for their wrongful repudiation.

An event *other* than the seller's prospective breach by reason of an inability to perform contractual obligations which would have fallen due after the seller's acceptance of the buyer's anticipatory breach can, however, be relevant to the buyer's liability in damages. This possibility is discussed in paragraph 19–166 below; it is illustrated by the situation in which the contract gives the buyer the right to cancel the contract on the occurrence of a specified event, not amounting to breach by the seller, such as the outbreak of a war of the kind specified by a cancelling clause in the contract.[65]

19–162 **Simultaneous breaches.** Both parties may simultaneously commit breaches, each of which would, standing alone, give a right to rescind to the other party. This could be the position where a c.i.f. contract required the buyer to open a letter of credit on a specified day and the seller to provide a performance guarantee on the same day and neither party performed its obligations. On the assumption that the terms imposing these obligations

---

[62] *e.g.*, *Soules CAF v PT Transcap of Indonesia* [1999] 1 Lloyd's Rep. 917. See also above, para.9–017 and *cf.* the similar rule applicable where a party relies on a prohibition or *force majeure* clause, stated in paras 18–347, 18–349 above. Dawson, 96 L.Q.R. 239 (1980) argues that the interpretation of the *British and Beningtons* case put forward in the text above is inconsistent with *Universal Cargo Carriers Corp. v Citati* [1957] 2 Q.B. 401. But the claim for damages discussed in that case was made *against* the party alleged to be unable to perform (the charterer), while in the *British and Beningtons* case the claim for damages was made *by* that party (the sellers). Moreover in the *Citati* case the charterer was already in breach (both actual and anticipatory) at the time of the shipowner's refusal to perform and the issue was whether that breach was sufficiently serious to justify the shipowner's rescission; while in the *British and Beningtons* case the sellers were not in breach at the time of the buyers' purported rescission. If the sellers had been guilty of the breach alleged (failure to deliver within the time stipulated in the contract), it would without doubt have justified rescission by the buyer: *cf.* above, para.18–267.

[63] A seller of unascertained generic goods does not so disable himself by selling part or all of his stock to a third party, since this does not prevent him from supplying the original buyer from another source: *Texaco Ltd v Eurogulf Shipping Co. Ltd* [1987] 2 Lloyd's Rep. 541.

[64] *cf. Gill & Duffus SA v Berger & Co. Inc.* [1984] A.C. 382, below, para.19–163.

[65] As in *Golden Strait Corporation v Nippon Yusen Kubishika Kaisha (The Golden Victory)* [2005] EWCA Civ. 1190, [2005] 2 Lloyd's Rep. 747 (time charterparty).

were both conditions of the contract, each party would then have a right to rescind the contract.[66]

19–163 **No right to reject documents merely on account of defects in the goods.** Under the rule stated in paragraph 19–161 above, it is crucial to know which party was the first to commit a repudiatory breach, and this question can give rise to particular difficulty where a c.i.f. seller is able to tender conforming documents in spite of the fact that the goods, when shipped, were defective in the sense of not being in accordance with the contract. Except where the seller was guilty of fraud or (probably) where the goods shipped differed fundamentally from those sold, the buyer must pay against conforming documents even though the goods suffered from a defect justifying their rejection[67]; in other words, a defect in the goods alone does not generally give the buyer the right to reject conforming documents. Authority for this proposition is provided by the decision of the House of Lords in *Gill & Duffus SA v Berger & Co. Inc.*[68] where 500 tonnes of Argentine Bolita beans were sold c.i.f. Le Havre. The contract provided for payment against documents and contained a "certification clause" which read "Quality final at port of discharge as per certificate of [G.S.C.], indicating that the quality of the lot is equal to the one of the sealed sample." The sellers duly shipped the full 500 tonnes but only 445 tonnes were originally discharged at Le Havre, the remaining 55 tonnes being overcarried to Rotterdam,[69] transhipped and later discharged at Le Havre. Before this had happened, the buyers had refused to pay against documents on the ground that these did not include the G.S.C. certificate. This was plainly a bad ground for refusing to pay as the certificate was not one of the shipping documents.[70] The sellers nevertheless obtained a certificate from G.S.C., stating that the parcel of 445 tonnes[71] was "equal to the samples previously sealed by us"; but when they retendered the documents together with this certificate, the buyers again rejected the tender. Thereupon, the sellers rescinded the contract and claimed damages, the market having apparently fallen. In the resulting arbitration proceedings, it was found that the goods did not correspond with the sealed samples or with the contract description[72]; but it was later held that, at least in relation to the 445 tonnes, the buyers were precluded from relying on this fact by the certification clause in the contract.[73] The House of Lords held the buyers

---

[66] *State Trading Corp. of India v M Golodetz Ltd* [1989] 2 Lloyd's Rep. 277, where the seller's breach was held *not* to be a breach of condition: Treitel, 106 L.Q.R. 105 (1990).
[67] Above, para.19–077.
[68] [1984] A.C. 382; Reynolds [1984] L.M.C.L.Q. 191; Treitel [1984] L.M.C.L.Q. 565.
[69] This was a matter for which the sellers (having arranged for shipment to Le Havre) were not responsible.
[70] Above, para.19–058.
[71] The fact that the certificate related to only 445 tonnes did not infringe the requirement that the shipping documents must relate to the full quantity sold (above, para.19–036) as the certificate was not one of the shipping documents (above, para.19–058) and those documents did relate to the full quantity sold.
[72] See [1982] 1 Lloyd's Rep. 101 at p.103; [1983] 2 Lloyd's Rep. 622 at p.625; [1984] A.C. 382 at p.396.
[73] On this point the House of Lords affirmed the decision of the courts below: see [1984] A.C. 382 at p.394.

liable in damages. One possible way of reaching this conclusion might have been to say that the documents were, and that the goods must be deemed (by reason of the certification clause) to have been, in accordance with the contract; this is the view that the Court of Appeal[74] would have taken if the G.S.C. certificate had related to the whole 500 tonnes. But in the House of Lords the buyers' liability was based on a broader ground. Lord Diplock[75] said that the certification clause did "not go to the buyers'[76] liability" but was "relevant only to the measure of damages."[77] The buyers were thus held liable in damages in spite of the fact that the goods were not (rather than because the goods were deemed to be) in conformity with the contract. Such non-conformity of the goods does not justify a c.i.f. buyer's rejection of documents which are in accordance with the contract: the buyer's remedies (if not excluded by the contract) are to claim damages in respect of the non conformity, or to reject the goods if their non-conformity is such as to justify rejection. If the buyer nevertheless refuses to pay against documents, he is himself in repudiatory breach, thus giving rise to a right on the part of the seller to rescind the contract and to claim damages.

19–164 At first sight this reasoning is hard to reconcile with the rule that the party who is the first to commit a repudiatory breach thereby gives the other the right to rescind[78]; for, by shipping goods the non-conformity of which amounted to a breach of condition,[79] the sellers might seem to have committed the first such breach, thus justifying the buyers' refusal to pay. That had been the view of two members of the High Court of Australia in *Henry Dean & Sons* (*Sydney*) *Ltd v O'Day Pty Ltd*,[80] where c.i.f. buyers had refused to pay against conforming documents representing goods which, when shipped, had not been of the contract description. Knox C.J. and Higgins J. held that the buyers were nevertheless entitled to damages: their refusal to pay was "justified by the result",[81] *i.e.* by the discovery that the goods were not of the contract description. This view was rejected in *Gill & Duffus SA v Berger & Co. Inc.* where Lord Diplock said that it was "not the law of England".[82] Hence, even if the first breach is the seller's (in shipping non-conforming goods), the buyer's repudiation is not justified. In the traditional common law terminology, the c.i.f. buyer's duty to pay against documents is an "independent covenant"[83] which must be performed in

---

74 [1983] 1 Lloyd's Rep. 623.

75 With whose speech all the other members of the House of Lords concurred.

76 [1984] 1 All E.R. 438 at p.444. In [1984] A.C. 382 at p.392 the phrase reads "does not go to *their* liability", but plainly the reference is to the liability of the buyers.

77 [1984] A.C. 382 at p.392.

78 Above, para.19–161.

79 *i.e.* under Sale of Goods Act 1979, ss.13 and 15: above, at n.72.

80 (1927) 39 C.L.R. 330, criticised on the present point in the 2nd edition of this work, para.1717.

81 At p.338, *per* Knox C.J.; Higgins J. took the same view (at pp.350–351). Starke J. decided for the buyers on the narrower ground that they had not unequivocally refused to pay against documents; Isaacs and Powers JJ. dissented.

82 [1984] A.C. 382 at p.392; *cf. ibid.*, p.396 rejecting as "wrong" a dictum of Robert Goff L.J. (dissenting) in the *Gill & Duffus* case [1983] 1 Lloyd's Rep. 622 at (*semble*) p.635 to the effect that a c.i.f. buyer can justify rejection of conforming documents on account of defects in the goods when shipped.

83 See, *e.g. Pordage v Cole* (1669) 1 Wms. Saund. 319; *Huntoon Co. v Kolynos* (*Inc.*) [1930] 1 Ch. 528; *The Odenfeld* [1978] 2 Lloyd's Rep. 357.

spite of the seller's earlier breach in shipping non-conforming goods; or, to put the same point in another way, the seller's breach in shipping non-conforming goods is not, at the stage of tender of documents, a repudiatory one. One can explain this rule on a number of practical grounds. It promotes certainty where (as often happens in commodity contracts) the documents pass through many hands while the goods are in transit and their physical state remains unknown. It further gives effect to the commercial risks taken by a buyer under a c.i.f. contract. The buyer's duty to pay without examining the goods[84] requires him to part with his money before he has any assurance about their conformity with the contract. The risk that the goods may not be of (for example) the stipulated quality is therefore taken by him to this extent, that he can only assert remedies in respect of defects in the goods by action (for the recovery of the price if he rejects the goods, or for damages if he does not reject), rather than by the (often more efficacious) method of withholding the price. To allow him to refuse to pay against conforming documents merely on account of a defect in the goods would therefore give him a degree of protection greater than that for which he had bargained when he bought on c.i.f. terms. The rule that non-conformity of the goods does not justify refusal to pay against conforming documents is also consistent with the rule that, under a documentary credit, a banker is not entitled to refuse to pay against documents on the ground that the goods do not conform with the contract of sale,[85] unless the seller is guilty of fraud[86]; and with the rule that, if the buyer accepts a bill of exchange for the price, he cannot rely on the non-conformity of the goods against a holder in due course.[87]

Gill & Duffus SA v Berger & Co. Inc. establishes that a c.i.f. buyer is not justified in rejecting documents merely because the seller has, before such rejection, committed a prior breach by shipping non-conforming goods. The exact remedies of the parties, in cases of this kind, depend on whether the seller exercises his right to rescind on account of the buyer's breach in refusing to pay against documents. These remedies are discussed in paragraphs 19–165 and 19–166 below.

Effects of wrongful rejection where the seller does not rescind. If the buyer wrongfully rejects documents on the ground that the goods are not in conformity with the contract, and the seller does not rescind, neither party is discharged from his primary obligations[88] and the seller remains in theory entitled to damages for the buyer's wrongful repudiation. But the buyer will be able to neutralise this liability by arguing that, on "complete delivery of the cargo"[89] he would have exercised his right to reject the goods and so 19–165

[84] Above, para.19–076.
[85] Below, para.23–139.
[86] Below, para.23–141; for the effect of such fraud between buyer and seller, see above, para.19–078.
[87] Below, para.22–062.
[88] *cf. Segap Garages Ltd v Gulf Oil (Great Britain) Ltd, The Times*, October 24, 1988; *Fercometal SARL v M. S. C. Mediterranean Shipping Co. SA (The Simona)* [1989] A.C. 789; Carter [1989] L.M.C.L.Q. 81; Marston [1988] C.L.J. 340.
[89] See n.12, *infra*.

become entitled to the return of the money that he ought to have paid on tender of documents. In this way, his rejection of the documents "may escape pecuniary consequences"[90]: it would cause the seller no loss and reduce his damages to a nominal amount.[91] This was the position in *Henry Dean & Sons (Sydney) Ltd v O'Day Pty Ltd*[92] where the seller had not rescinded and his claim for damages was rejected by the lower courts. No appeal as taken on this point to the High Court of Australia; nor did this aspect of the case draw any criticism in *Gill & Duffus SA v Berger & Co. Inc.*[93] where it was only the decision of the High Court to allow the *buyer's* claim which was regarded as wrong.[94] Alternatively, the buyer could claim damages for the seller's failure to ship conforming goods. But he could not claim such damages *and* reduce the seller's damages to a nominal amount by arguing that he would have rejected the goods; for the two positions are plainly inconsistent. These rights of the buyer are subject to the qualifications to be more fully discussed in paragraph 19–166 below: they may be excluded by the contract[95] or on the ground that the seller was induced by the buyer's repudiation to abstain from making any effort to cure his breach.[96]

---

[90] *Henry Dean & Sons* (*Sydney*) *Ltd v O'Day Pty Ltd* (1927) 39 C.L.R. 330 at p.340, *per* Isaacs J., who had dissented from the decision allowing the *buyer's* claim. *Cf. Charles E. Ford Ltd v AFEC Inc.* [1986] 2 Lloyd's Rep. 307, where the seller had not rescinded on account of the buyer's failure to pay against documents, and evidence of the non-conformity of the goods was held to be admissible; and *S N Kurkjian* (*Commodity Brokers*) *Ltd v Marketing Exchange for Africa Ltd* [1986] 2 Lloyd's Rep. 614, where the buyers would have been entitled to reject the goods as the sellers had not rescinded on account of the buyers' failure to pay against documents, but the buyers had abandoned their right to reject the goods by a subsequent variation agreement.

[91] On the analogy of the principles stated in *Maredelanto Compania Naviera v Bergbau Handel GmbH* (*The Mihalis Angelos*) [1971] 1 Q.B. 164 at pp.196–197, 201–203, 208–210. The present point is not affected by criticisms of part of the reasoning of *The Mihalis Angelos* in *Golden Strait Corp. v Nippon Yusen Kubishika Kaisha (The Golden Victory* [2005] EWHC 161 (Comm.), [2005] 1 All E.R. (Comm) 467 at [16]–[23] and, on appeal, [2005] EWCA Civ. 1190, [2005] 2 Lloyd's Rep. 747 at [18]–[21]. These relate to (1) the standard of proof of supervening events which may reduce or extinguish the injured party's right to damages and (2) to the time by reference to which the occurrence of such events must be proved (see above, para.19–161 and below para.19–166). No such issues would arise in the situation discussed in the text above. See also *Bremer Handelsgesellschaft mbH v JH Rayner & Co. Ltd* [1979] 2 Lloyd's Rep. 216 at p.224 (where there *was* sufficient evidence of the injured party's ability to perform); *Regent OHG. Aisenstadt und Barig v Francesco of Jermyn Street* [1981] 3 All E.R. 327 at p.335 (where the seller's breach was not sufficiently serious to justify rescission). According to a dictum in *Bunge Corp. v Vegetable Vitamin Foods* (*Private*) *Ltd* [1985] 1 Lloyd's Rep. 613 at p.620 the seller's damages are nominal only if the defect in the goods makes them worthless. But it is submitted that the buyer's case is not that *the goods* are worthless: it is that the seller's *right to have the goods accepted* is worthless because the buyer's option to reject them would certainly have been exercised.

[92] (1927) 39 C.L.R. 330.

[93] [1984] A.C. 382.

[94] Above, para.19–164.

[95] As by the certification clause in *Gill & Duffus SA v Berger & Co. Inc.* [1984] A.C. 382.

[96] See nn. 22 and 23 below; *cf. Bunge Corp. v Vegetable Vitamin Foods* (*Private*) *Ltd* [1985] 1 Lloyd's Rep. 613 at p.620 ("had there been no time for the sellers to have substituted another load").

Effects of wrongful rejection where seller rescinds. If the buyer wrongfully rejects documents on the ground that the goods are not in conformity with the contract, and the seller does rescind the contract, three consequences follow. First, "all primary obligations of the parties under the contract which [have] not yet been performed [are] terminated."[97] The reference here is to *future* obligations, *i.e.* to those which have not yet fallen due at the time of rescission. Primary obligations which have accrued before that time are not discharged by rescission[98] but in the present context that rule is of little importance with respect to the seller's remedies. Even if the *obligation* to pay the price has accrued on tender of documents (and thus before rescission), the *action* for the price is not normally available at this stage,[99] and could not, even if available, be brought by the seller if he retained the documents or the goods.[1] Hence the seller's only remedy will be by way of damages, in accordance with the discussion that follows. It is clear that the seller is liberated by the rescission from any further obligation with respect to the delivery of the goods.[2] 19–166

Secondly, the buyer is liable in damages for wrongful repudiation[3]: these are the equivalent of damages for non-acceptance and are prima facie the amount by which the contract price exceeds the market price[4] at the time of rescission.[5] The buyer cannot, where the seller *has* rescinded, neutralise such liability by relying on the argument available to him where the seller has *not* rescinded[6]; *i.e.* that the seller's rights against him were worthless as he would, if the goods had actually been delivered to him, have rejected them and so have become entitled to the return of the price that he ought to have paid on tender of documents.[7] When the seller has rescinded, such an argument will fail since the stage at which the buyer would have been entitled to reject the goods on account of the seller's breach in shipping defective goods would never be reached. Lord Diplock in *Gill & Duffus SA v Berger Co. Inc.* explains this point on the ground that rescission by the sellers relieved them from "any further obligation to deliver to the buyers

---

[97] *Gill & Duffus SA v Berger & Co. Inc.* [1984] A.C. 382 at p.390.

[98] For this general principle, see (for example), *Hyundai Shipbuilding & Heavy Industries Ltd v Pournaras* [1989] 2 Lloyd's Rep. 502; *Hyundai Shipbuilding & Heavy Industries Ltd v Papadopoulos* [1980] 1 W.L.R. 1129; *Bank of Boston Connecticut v European Grain & Shipping Ltd* (*The Dominique*) [1989] A.C. 1056; *Hurst v Bryk* [2002] 1 A.C. 185 at p.194.

[99] Below, paras 19–211 to 19–214.

[1] On the principle of *McDonald v Dennys Lascelles Ltd* (1933) 48 C.L.R. 457, cited with approval in *Johnson v Agnew* [1980] A.C. 367 at p.396 and in the second of the *Hyundai* cases cited in n.98, above, [1980] 1 W.L.R. 1129 at p.1141; followed in *Rover International Ltd v Cannon Films Ltd* [1989] 1 W.L.R. 912.

[2] For such further obligations, see *infra*, at nn. 11, 12.

[3] *Gill & Duffus SA v Berger & Co Inc.* [1984] A.C. 382 at p.390; *cf. State Trading Corp. of India v M. Golodetz Ltd* [1989] 2 Lloyd's Rep. 277 at p.287.

[4] Sale of Goods Act 1979, s.50(3) (below, para.19–216). Such a claim can be combined with rescission: *Johnson v Agnew* [1980] A.C. 637.

[5] *Semble* this, rather than the time of tender of documents, is the relevant date: *cf. Toprak Mahsulleri Ofisi v Finagrain Cie Commerciale* [1979] 2 Lloyd's Rep. 98 (a case of seller's breach).

[6] Above, para.19–165.

[7] Above, para.19–165, at nn. 89–90.

any of the goods that were the subject-matter of the contract."[8] This explanation at first sight gives rise to some difficulty, for a c.i.f. seller normally performs his duty to deliver by shipping goods and tendering documents,[9] so that he is not, having done these things, under any "further obligation to deliver . . . goods."[10] But even after shipment and tender of documents, a c.i.f. seller can still be under some duty with respect to delivery: in particular, he must not give orders to the carrier which will prevent or delay "complete delivery of the cargo"[11] to the buyer.[12] If, by rescinding the contract, he is relieved from that duty, no breach of it which might, but for the rescission, have justified rejection by the buyer can occur. Moreover, the very earliest time at which the buyer's right to reject the goods on account of the seller's breach can be exercised is after the buyer has become entitled to claim delivery of the goods by taking up the shipping documents[13]; and even this stage will not be reached where the buyer has wrongfully refused to pay against documents and the seller has rescinded on that ground.

The preceding discussion is based on the assumption that the buyer's only ground for rejecting the goods is an alleged breach by the seller (in actually delivering non-conforming goods) which, because of the seller's earlier rescission, can no longer occur.[14] Different considerations arise where the contract gives the buyer the right to cancel on the occurrence of a specified *event*, irrespective of the seller's *breach*.[15] In such a case, the event giving the buyer the right to cancel (and so to make the seller's rights against him worthless) can still occur even after the seller has, by rescinding, put an end to his duties under the contract; and if it is shown

[8] [1984] A.C. 382 at p.391.

[9] Above, paras 19–001, 19–010, 19–072.

[10] *e.g. Manbré Saccharine Co. Ltd v Corn Products Co. Ltd* [1919] 1 K.B. 198 at pp.202, 203.

[11] One of the "three stages of delivery" under a c.i.f. contract distinguished in *Schmoll Fils & Co. Inc. v Scriven Bros & Co.* (1924) 19 Ll.L.Rep. 118 at p.119 and discussed in para.19–072, above. Provisions in the contract for demurrage and dispatch, as in *Etablissements Soules et Cie. v Intertradex SA* [1991] 1 Lloyd's Rep. 379, may also indicate that the seller is under some duty at this stage; the actual decision was concerned with the duties of the buyer.

[12] Above, para.19–073.

[13] See *Gill & Duffus SA v Berger & Co. Inc.* [1984] A.C. 382 at p.395; above, para.19–149.

[14] On the seller's rescission (by acceptance of the buyer's wrongful repudiation) the seller's duty to perform comes to an end: *Photo Production Ltd v Securicor Transport Ltd* [1980] A.C. 827 at p.849; but such rescission does not relieve the buyer of his secondary liability in damages: see, for example, *Lep Air Services Ltd v Rolloswin Investments Ltd* [1973] A.C. 331 at p.350; and see generally Treitel, *The Law of Contract*, 11th ed. (2003) pp.849–855.

[15] *e.g.* under a cancelling clause: see *Maredelanto Compania Naviera v Bergbau Handel GmbH* (*The Mihalis Angelos*) [1971] 1 Q.B. 164 at pp.196–197, 201–203, 208–210, *cf. North Sea Energy Holding NV v Petroleum Authority of Thailand* [1999] 1 Lloyd's Rep. 483 at p.496 (f.o.b. buyer not liable for purported acceptance by seller of buyer's alleged repudiation where contract had become ineffective by reason of failure, without any default on the buyer's part, of a condition precedent); *Golden Strait Corporation v Nippon Yusen Kubishika Kaisha (The Golden Victory)* [2005] EWCA 1190, [2005] 2 Lloyd's Rep. 747, doubting dicta in *The Mihalis Angelos*: see above, para.19–165, n.91.

that the event did occur and that the buyer would, on its occurrence, have exercised his right to cancel,[16] then the seller will be entitled to no more than nominal damages.[17]

Thirdly, the seller remains liable in damages for *past* breaches, committed before he rescinded the contract but not justifying the buyer's repudiation: for example, for his failure "to ship goods that were in conformity with the contract."[18] The buyer's damages for that breach will be the loss that he would have suffered "if those goods had in fact been delivered to him",[19] *i.e.* prima facie the difference between the value of those goods and goods which were in accordance with the contract.[20] So long as the seller's *breach* in shipping non-conforming goods occurred *before* rescission, he may be liable for a *loss* that would have resulted *after* rescission. This explains the apparent oddity of saying that a seller who rescinds is under no further obligation to deliver but is nevertheless liable in damages assessed by reference to a hypothetical delivery assumed to have been made after rescission. The seller's liability in damages may, however, be excluded by the terms of the contract and was so excluded in *Gill & Duffus SA v Berger & Co. Inc.* by the certification clause. This is the point of the statement in that case that the clause was "relevant only to the

---

[16] In *Fercometal SARL v MSC Mediterranean Shipping Co SA (The Simona)* [1989] A.C. 788, a shipowner's claim for wrongful anticipatory repudiation by a charterer in cancelling too early failed in part because the shipowner had affirmed the contract and the charterer then again cancelled in time. From the emphasis placed on shipowner's affirmation; it can be inferred that his claim would have succeeded in full if, instead of affirming the charterparty, he had rescinded it. A possible way of reconciling this inference with dicta in the *Mihalis Angelos*, above n.15, is that there it was already certain at "the date of acceptance of the [assumed] repudiation" (at p.210, per Megaw LJ) that the events giving the alleged wrongdoer (in that case, the charterer) the right to cancel would occur, while there was no corresponding certainty in *The Simona*. The difficulty with this line of reasoning is that two later authorities have rejected the view that such certainty must exist at the time referred to above by Megaw LJ: *B.S. & N. Ltd BVI v Micado Shipping Ltd (The Seaflower)* [2002] 2 Lloyd's Rep. 37 at 44; *Golden Strait Corporation v Nippon Yusen Kubishika Kaisha (The Golden Victory)* [2005] EWCA Civ. 1190, [2005] 2 Lloyd's Rep. 747 at [15]–[18]. But in neither of these two cases was *The Simona* cited to the court, so that the outcome in cases of the kind described in the text above remains in some doubt. It should be added that the actual decision in *The Mihalis Angelos* above was that the charterers were not in breach at all as their repudiation was justified by the shipowner's earlier breach of condition.

[17] In the case of a long-term contract the effect of the prospective exercise of the buyer's right to cancel may be merely to make the contract, not worthless, but only less valuable to the seller, whose damages would then be reduced accordingly: *cf.* *The Golden Victory*, above n.16, a time charter case in which the war giving rise to the right to cancel broke out after part of the chartered period had elapsed. Similar reasoning could apply to a contract for the sale of goods which provided for delivery by instalments over a stipulated period.

[18] *Gill & Duffus SA v Berger & Co. Inc.*, above, at p.390 (where Lord Diplock seems to assume that such a breach had indeed occurred).

[19] *ibid.*, at p.392.

[20] Sale of Goods Act 1979, s.53(3); *cf.* [1984] A.C. 382 at p.396 (where the value of conforming goods is assumed to be equal to the price).

measure of damages".[21] The seller will also escape liability in damages if (a) the breach was one that he could have cured (*e.g.* by making a fresh shipment of conforming goods during the shipment period[22]) and (b) he was induced by the buyer's repudiation not to effect such cure.[23]

19–167 ***Braithwaite v Foreign Hardwood Co. Ltd.*** The question whether a buyer was justified in rejecting documents by his later discovery that defective goods had been shipped arose also in the controversial case of *Braithwaite v Foreign Hardwood Co. Ltd.*[24] A contract for the sale of 100 tons of rosewood logs on c.i.f. terms[25] provided that the goods were to be delivered in instalments, but did not specify the number or size of the instalments. The contract was made in November 1902 and called for a 1903 shipment. On October 5, 1903, the buyers repudiated the contract on the ground that the sellers had broken an alleged term that they would not ship rosewood to the buyers' competitors; but it was found that the contract contained no such term, so that the repudiation could not be justified on the ground given by the buyers. The sellers did not at this stage accept the repudiation. They had already (before October 5) shipped 63 tons of rosewood logs, and when the bill of lading for this shipment reached London their agents in England "informed the defendants [*i.e.* the buyers] that they were ready to hand . . . over [the bill of lading] in exchange for cash."[26] The buyers refused on October 30 to take up the bill of lading and pay for the goods, on the ground which they had already given on October 5. There is no record of any further communication between the parties in relation to the 63 tons. The ship carrying this instalment arrived in England on November 9, and at some unspecified time soon thereafter the sellers' agents put the consignment into the hands of a broker, who sold it on the market for less than the contract price.[27] A second instalment of about 37 tons[28] arrived in January 1904 and was likewise rejected by the buyers; and there was no question that the buyers were liable in damages for refusing to accept this instalment, once it was shown that the ground for rejection originally given by them on October 5 was a bad one. But in relation to the first instalment, the buyers argued that their rejection of it was justified by the fact that about 17 of the 63 tons were not of the contract description. At first instance, Kennedy J. said that if the buyers "had chosen to rely upon the defects in that cargo, they might have refused it as it stood"[29]; and a

[21] [1984] A.C. 382 at p.392. In the Court of Appeal, Robert Goff L.J. (dissenting) had relied on the certification clause (and on the fact that the buyers had failed to show that a certificate would not have been granted for the 55 tonnes not originally discharged at Le Havre) as to *liability*. That argument seems to have been accepted in the House of Lords as to *damages*: [1984] A.C. 382 at p.397.
[22] Above, para.19–071.
[23] Above, paras 19–160, 19–165; below, para.19–171.
[24] [1905] 2 K.B. 543.
[25] See below, para.19–168.
[26] [1905] 2 K.B. 543 at p.549.
[27] See the report in 74 L.J.K.B. 688 at p.694.
[28] 74 L.J.K.B. 688; 30 tons according to [1905] 2 K.B. 543.
[29] 92 L.T. 637 at p.640. It seems that the reference is to tender of *the goods*: *cf.* below, para.19–168.

majority of the Court of Appeal was prepared to assume the correctness of this view.[30] It was nevertheless held, both by Kennedy J. and by the Court of Appeal, that the buyers were liable in damages for refusing to accept the first (as well as the second) instalment. At first sight, this appears to be inconsistent with the rule that a buyer who gives a bad ground for rejecting can still justify his rejection by showing that a good ground did in fact exist[31]; and it is arguable that such a ground existed by reason of the seller's earlier breach in shipping non-conforming goods. There are three possible answers to this argument: that the seller had committed no such breach; that, if he had committed it, it was not repudiatory; and that the buyer was precluded by his conduct from relying on it. These possibilities are discussed in paragraphs 19–068 to 19–171 below.

No breach by seller. In *Taylor v Oakes, Roncoroni & Co.*[32] Greer J. explained *Braithwaite's* case by saying that the buyers did not, either on October 5 or on October 30 in fact have a ground for rejection as the sellers had never *actually tendered* either the documents or the goods: they had only *offered to tender* them; and "such an offer is not an actual breach of contract."[33] By refusing the sellers' offer before the sellers were in actual breach, the buyers have been said to have waived further performance by the sellers.[34] Similarly, Bankes L.J. in *Taylor's* case said "The decision in [*Braithwaite's* case] merely means that a buyer cannot justify his refusal of an *offer to deliver* goods under the contract by proving that, if he had not refused, the goods when delivered would not have been in accordance with the contract."[35] In further support of this view, it could be argued that even an actual tender of the 63 tons (including 17 tons which were not of the contract description) would not necessarily have been a good ground for the buyer's outright rejection of the whole instalment, since the contract did not specify either the size of the instalments or the exact delivery dates within the year-long contractual shipment period. If the buyers had objected, on tender, to the 17 non-conforming tons, one possible view is that the sellers could have selected the part of the consignment which was in accordance with the contract, and validly have retendered that part. This appears to be the point of Kennedy J.'s statement that the buyers might 19–168

---

30 [1905] 2 K.B. 543 at p.552 (*per* Collins M.R., with whom Cozens-Hardy, L.J. agreed).

31 See above paras 19–159, 19–161; *British and Beningtons Ltd v N W Cachar Tea Co.* [1923] A.C. 48 at 70 where Lord Sumner doubted *Braithwaite's* case, in which he had been counsel for the unsuccessful buyers; while the decision was supported by Scrutton and Atkin L.JJ. (who had been counsel for the successful sellers) in *Continental Contractors Ltd v Medway Oil & Storage Co. Ltd* (1925) Ll.L.R. 124 at pp.132, 133 (actual decision reversed (1926) 25 Ll.L.R. 288, the House of Lords holding that on the construction of the contract there only the seller, but not the buyer, was in breach). Lord Sumner's doubts were shared by Mocatta J. in *Scandinavian Trading Co. A/B v Zodiac Petroleum SA* (*The Al Hofuf*) [1981] 1 Lloyd's Rep. 81 at p.90.

32 (1922) 38 T.L.R. 349; affirmed *ibid.*, at p.517.

33 *ibid.*, at p.351; *cf. Continental Contractors Ltd v Medway Oil and Storage Co. Ltd* (1925) 23 Ll.L.R. 124 at p.132 (as to which see n.31, above).

34 *ibid.*, at p.134.

35 (1922) 38 T.L.R. 517 at p.518 (italics supplied).

have refused the consignment "if the other party had persisted in tendering it *as it stood*."[36] Nevertheless, there are difficulties in the way of explaining *Braithwaite's* case on the ground that at the time of the buyers' repudiation, the sellers were not in breach because they had never actually tendered the defective consignment. It is, indeed, clear that the *goods* comprised in it were never tendered, but the position with respect to the documents is less clear. According to the statement of facts in the *Law Reports*, the bill of lading was tendered,[37] but in his judgment Collins M.R. says that the sellers' agents informed the buyers that they "were ready to hand it over",[38] while Matthew L.J. says that the bill of lading "was tendered in proper form".[39] In the *Law Journal*, the Master of the Rolls is reported to have said that "the bill of lading for [the second] shipment *also* was tendered",[40] which suggests that he may have regarded the conduct of the agents in relation to the bill of lading for the first shipment as amounting to tender. And according to the *Law Times*, Collins M.R. actually said that when the bill of lading arrived the sellers' agents "informed the defendants of the fact and tendered it."[41] So, too, in the *British and Beningtons* case, Lord Atkinson refers to the bill of lading in *Braithwaite's* case as having been tendered.[42] Of course it could be argued that the sellers were not in breach, even if they did tender the bill of lading, as there was nothing wrong with the bill itself, which was a perfectly good shipping document. But the fact (mentioned in all but one of the reports[43]) that the sale was on c.i.f. terms makes it hard to sustain the argument[44] that the sellers could validly have retendered such part of the 63 tons as corresponded with the contract. The argument assumes that their obligation was to tender goods, while under a c.i.f. contract it was to tender documents,[45] and no bill of lading in respect of the "good" part of the shipment appears to have existed.[46]

19–169 **Breach by seller not repudiatory.** The sale in *Braithwaite's* case being on c.i.f. terms,[47] the seller was also under an obligation to ship goods of the contract description[48]; and the shipment of the first instalment, which took place before any repudiation by the buyers, appears to have involved a breach of that obligation. It is of course possible that, when the buyers first repudiated on October 5, the goods had not yet been appropriated to the contract,[49] in which case the sellers would not have been in breach on

---

36 Above at n.29; *cf. Taylor v Oakes, Roncoroni & Co.* (1922) 38 T.L.R. 349 at p.351.
37 [1905] 2 K.B. 543 at p.544.
38 *ibid.*, at p.549.
39 *ibid.*, at p.553.
40 74 L.J.K.B. 688 at p.691 (italics supplied).
41 92 L.T. 637 at p.640.
42 [1923] A.C. 49 at pp.64–65.
43 92 L.T. 637; 74 L.J.K.B. 688; 10 Com.Cas. 189; 21 T.L.R. 413; 10 M.L.C. 52; the exception is [1905] 2 K.B. 543.
44 Above, at n.36.
45 Above, paras 19–00, 19–059, 19–072.
46 *cf.* above, para.19–036.
47 Above, at n.43.
48 Above, para.19–012.
49 Above, para.19–016.

October 5. But it seems clear that the goods were appropriated to the contract at the latest on October 30, when the sellers' agents communicated with the buyers informing them that they were ready to hand over the bill of lading in exchange for payment. Once non-conforming goods had been appropriated, the sellers were, it is submitted, in breach of their obligation to ship goods of the contract description; and this breach clearly occurred before the buyers' second repudiation on October 30 and may have occurred before the buyers' first repudiation on October 5. It is thus clear that the sellers were in breach before the buyers' final repudiation. But, as the contract was on c.i.f. terms, that breach did not justify the buyers' repudiation; for it is now settled that a c.i.f. buyer cannot reject documents merely on account of a defect in the goods which would justify rejection of the goods.[50]

Effect of buyers' repudiation. If, in accordance with the discussion in paragraphs 19–168 to 19–169 above, the sellers were either not yet in breach, or not in repudiatory breach, at the time of the buyers' repudiation, then the sellers were entitled to accept the buyers' repudiation. On their doing so, they would have been relieved of any further obligation to tender documents or goods[51] and become entitled to damages based on the amount by which the contract price exceeded the market price; though they would also have been liable in damages by reason of the defects in the goods.[52] If, on the other hand, the sellers had *not* accepted the buyers' repudiation, then they would have been entitled to no more than nominal damages. They would in that event, not have been relieved of their own obligation with respect to the conformity of the goods. It would therefore have been open to the buyers to argue that, on the actual delivery of the non-conforming goods, they would have exercised their right to reject those *goods*; that the sellers would then have had to return to them any payment previously made against documents[53]; and that the sellers' right of action against the buyers for wrongful repudiation was of no value to the sellers. The crucial question therefore was whether the sellers had accepted the buyers' repudiation. In *The Simona*[54] (a charterparty case) *Braithwaite's* case was explained on the ground that the sellers there *had* accepted that repudiation; and Lord Ackner (with whom all the other members of the House of Lords agreed) said that, if there was no such acceptance,[55] then 19–170

---

[50] Above, paras 19–077, 19–163.

[51] *Continental Contractors Ltd v Medway Oil and Storage Co. Ltd* (1925) 23 Ll.L.R. 124 at p.132 (as to which see n.31, above).

[52] Above, para.19–166.

[53] As in the situation in which the buyers' repudiation takes the form of wrongful refusal to pay against documents on account of non-conformity of the goods: above, para.19–165. In *Braithwaite's* case the buyers' refusal to pay against documents was likewise wrongful, though the (unsubstantiated) ground for it was breach by the seller of another alleged term of the contract: above, para.19–167.

[54] *Fercometal SARL v MSC Mediterranean Shipping Co. SA (The Simona)* [1989] A.C. 788 at pp.803–805; *cf. British and Beningtons Ltd v N W Cachar Tea Co.* [1923] A.C. 48 at p.65 (*per* Lord Atkinson); *Esmail v J. Rosenthal & Sons Ltd* [1964] 2 Lloyd's Rep. 447 at p.466, affirmed [1965] 1 W.L.R. 1117.

[55] Collins M.R. in *Braithwaite's* case seems to have treated the sellers as not having accepted the buyers' repudiation: [1905] 2 K.B. 543 at p.551.

Braithwaite's case must be regarded as having been wrongly decided.[56] At first sight, there may seem to be some difficulty with this explanation of *Braithwaite's* case, in particular with regard to the time at which the sellers can be said to have accepted the repudiation. Clearly they had not done so at the time of the buyers' original repudiation on October 5, for they subsequently either tendered, or offered to tender, documents.[57] Even on October 30 the sellers did not accept the buyers' repudiation: at this time, they were still claiming payment of the price. The buyers' repudiation seems to have been accepted only at some time after the arrival of the goods on November 9, by the sale of the goods in the market,[58] and before this time the sellers seem to have appropriated the defective 63 tons to the contract so that before the time of the alleged acceptance of the repudiation they were themselves in breach. In a domestic sale, the sellers' acceptance of the buyers' repudiation might have been too late. But this was not true in *Braithwaite's* case, as the sale was on c.i.f. terms and the sellers' breach related only to the goods. It therefore did not justify the buyers' refusal to pay against documents.[59]

19–171 **Conduct of the buyer.** There is, moreover, a third explanation of *Braithwaite's* case, which would have applied even if the non-conformity of the 63 tons had justified the buyers' refusal to pay against the documents relating to that instalment. The general rule which allows a contracting party to rely on an unstated ground as a justification for his refusal to perform[60] is subject to an exception[61] (which was recognised in *The Simona*[62]) in cases of "estoppel" or "inducement", and this exception was, it was submitted, applicable in *Braithwaite's* case. Even if the sellers had not accepted the buyers' repudiation (or had not accepted it in time), and even if at the time of that repudiation the sellers were already in breach by reason of the non-conformity of the 63 tons, they were not yet *irrevocably* in breach: they might, if the buyers had rejected on account of the defective quality of the goods, have found another cargo exactly conforming to the contract "which

[56] In the Court of Appeal in *The Simona* [1987] 2 Lloyd's Rep. 236 at 244 Parker L.J. disapproved apparently contrary statements in *Bunge v Vegetable Vitamin Foods (Private) Ltd* [1985] 1 Lloyd's Rep. 613 at p.619. The importance attached to the seller's rescission by Lord Ackner in *The Simona* and by Lord Diplock in *Gill & Duffus SA v Berger & Co. Inc.* [1984] A.C. 382 (above, paras 19–163, 19–166) settles (so far as c.i.f. contracts are concerned) the point said in *Bulk Oil (Zug) AG v Sun International* [1984] 1 Lloyd's Rep. 531 at p.546 to have been "left open" in *Braithwaite's* case and in *British & Beningtons Ltd v North West Cachar Tea Co.* [1923] A.C. 48 at pp.72, 74, *i.e.* whether a seller who has *not* rescinded can recover substantial damages for the buyers' repudiation if at the time of that repudiation the seller had become wholly *and finally* disabled from performing. Where the buyers' repudiation takes the form of an unjustified refusal to pay against conforming documents on account of non-conformity of the goods, the seller has a right of action, but if he does not rescind on account of the repudiation, that right will be valueless for the reason given in para.19–165.

[57] Above, paras 19–167, 19–168.

[58] *The Simona*, above n.54, [1989] A.C. 788 at p.805.

[59] Above, para.19–163.

[60] Above, para.19–159.

[61] Above, para.19–160.

[62] [1989] A.C. 788 at pp.805–806.

[they] might duly have tendered and so have put [themselves] right."[63] They could have done this because of the general rule that, where a bad tender is followed within the contract period by a good tender, the latter must normally be accepted.[64] The buyers in *Braithwaite's* case could not rely on the sellers' failure to make a second, good, tender as this failure could be said to have been induced by their (the buyers') persistent allegation of an insufficient ground of repudiation; another way of putting the point is to say that the buyers were estopped from relying on the non-conformity of the sellers' tender,[65] or that they had waived any such breach.[66] In view of this conduct on the part of the buyers, it would have been unreasonable to expect the sellers to make further efforts to ship conforming goods in the remaining part of the shipment period.[67] *A fortiori*, the sellers could have recovered damages if the buyers' conduct had actually prevented them from making a shipment in accordance with the contract. A seller's right to damages in such a case does not depend on his acceptance of the buyer's repudiation as rescinding the contract,[68] for the right is based on the assumption that the seller would, but for the buyer's conduct, have *affirmed* the contract by making a fresh tender and so have performed his obligations under it. Nor can the buyer reduce the seller's damages by relying on defects in the tender if those defects could have been cured by a subsequent good tender[69] and if the seller was by the buyer's breach induced not to make such a tender or actually prevented from making it.[70]

Non-rejection clauses. The right to reject may be excluded, or limited as to time, by a non-rejection clause in the contract. Such clauses may refer simply to the right to reject *the goods*, and clauses of this kind have been discussed in relation to overseas sales in Chapter 18.[71] In a c.i.f. contract, a non-rejection clause may also exclude or limit the right to reject *the documents*, which is sometimes wider than the right to reject the goods 19–172

---

63 *British and Beningtons Ltd v NW Cachar Tea Co.* [1923] A.C. 48 at 71; *Empresa Exportadora de Azucar v Industria Azucarera Nacional SA* (*The Playa Larga*) [1983] 2 Lloyd's Rep. 171 at p.186.

64 Above, para.19–068.

65 *Fercometal SARL v MSC Mediterranean Shipping Co. SA* (*The Simona*) [1989] A.C. 788 at pp.805–806; *cf. Sheffield v Conran* (1987) 22 Con.L.R. 108 and the discussion of *The Simona*, above, by the High Court of Australia in *Foran v Wight* (1989) 168 C.L.R. 385, where a buyer of land was similarly induced by the seller's conduct not to take steps to raise the money needed to complete the purchase and was consequently held entitled to rely on the vendor's inability to complete and so to recover his deposit.

66 *cf. Tufton Associates Ltd v Dilmun Shipping* [1992] 1 Lloyd's Rep. 71 at p.80 (waiver of condition precedent).

67 *cf.* above, para.19–161, at n.58.

68 *Bulk Oil* (*Zug*) *AG v Sun International Ltd* [1984] 1 Lloyd's Rep. 531; for earlier proceedings see [1983] 1 Lloyd's Rep. 655.

69 Such cure was possible in *Braithwaite v Foreign Hardwood Co.* [1905] 2 K.B. 543 but not in *Gill & Duffus SA v Berger & Co. Inc.* [1984] A.C. 382 (above, para.19–163). For this reason it is submitted that there is no inconsistency between the two cases on the issue of damages, though the contrary is suggested by Carter, 101 L.Q.R. 167 (1985).

70 *cf.* above, paras 19–165, 19–166.

71 Above, paras 18–275 to 18–279.

themselves.[72] Such "documents clauses" are, like other non-rejection clauses, strictly construed against the seller. Thus in one case[73] the contract provided that, if the documents were defective, the buyer must nevertheless take them up if the seller *guaranteed performance* in accordance with the contract. It was held that the seller was not entitled to rely on the clause where he merely undertook to *indemnify the buyer against loss* resulting from defects in the documents.

19–173 **Statutory restriction on rights of rejection.** Section 15A of the Sale of Goods Act 1979 restricts the rights of a buyer who does not deal as consumer[74] to reject goods for breach of the statutorily implied terms as to correspondence with description and as to quality. These restrictions have been considered in relation to overseas sales in Chapter 18, where it was submitted that these restrictions probably did not apply to such contracts where the goods were not of the contract description.[75] A similar submission is made in the present Chapter with regard to the similar statutory restriction (contained in section 30(2A) of the 1979 Act) on the buyer's right to reject delivery of the wrong quantity.[76] All these submissions are concerned with rights of rejection arising by reason of the non-conformity of *the goods*. So far as quantitative discrepancies are concerned, it has already been argued that section 30(2A) does not apply where the seller tenders *documents* relating to the wrong quantity[77]; and it is submitted that section 15A is similarly inapplicable where the documents are defective for some other reason, *e.g.* because the bill of lading is not "genuine"[78] or because it is not "clean".[79] The seller in such a case may be in breach of an implied term, but the term is not implied by sections 13 to 15 of the Sale of Goods Act 1979, and section 15A applies *only* to breaches of these implied terms.[80] Even where the documents indicated shipment outside the shipment period (so that the seller would be in breach of the statutorily implied term as to correspondence with description with regard to the goods[81]), it is submitted that the section would not apply to the buyer's right to reject *the documents*. The c.i.f. buyer's right to reject documents has been described as "quite distinct",[82] and as "separate",[83] from his right to reject goods. Hence even if (contrary to the submission made in Chapter 18) section 15A did apply to the buyer's right to reject such *goods*, it would not apply to his right to reject the *documents* since it makes no reference to this separate right.

---

[72] Above, para.19–147.
[73] *SIAT di dal Ferro v Tradax Overseas SA* [1980] 1 Lloyd's Rep. 53.
[74] Where a c.i.f. buyer does deal as consumer, (see above, para.18–259) his right to reject the goods may be restricted by s.48D: see above, para.18–284 n.75.
[75] Above, para.18–284.
[76] Above, para.19–012.
[77] Above, para.19–037.
[78] Above, para.19–035.
[79] Above, para.19–038.
[80] s.15A(1)(a).
[81] Above, para.18–267.
[82] *Kwei Tek Chao v British Traders and Shippers Ltd* [1954] 2 Q.B. 459 at p.480; above, para.19–144.
[83] *Gill & Duffus SA v Berger Co. Inc.* [1984] A.C. 382 at p.395.

Effect of rejection on property. Where the buyer rejects the documents property will not normally pass to him; but where he accepts the documents and subsequently rejects *the goods* the property thereupon revests in the seller.[84] Meanwhile, the buyer has what has been called a "conditional property" in the goods, that is, a property subject to the "condition subsequent" that it will "revest if upon examination [the buyer] finds [the goods] to be not in accordance with the contract."[85] If the buyer, between accepting the documents and rejecting the goods, deals with the documents, he is taken to deal with this "conditional property" and not with the seller's "reversionary interest".[86] Thus such dealing is not an act "inconsistent with the ownership *of the seller*" so as to amount to an acceptance[87]; and, even if it were such a dealing, it would no longer[88] amount to an acceptance unless the buyer had been given the requisite opportunity of examination. Of course the buyer cannot generally[89] reject the goods unless he is able and willing to restore them to the seller. If the goods have been delivered to a third person in pursuance of a sale or pledge, this will no longer *ipso facto* deprive the buyer of his right to reject,[90] but he will not in fact be able to exercise that right unless he can regain possession of the goods so as to be able to restore them to the seller. 19–174

(b) *Damages for non delivery*

The market rule. Under section 51(1) of the Sale of Goods Act 1979, the buyer is entitled to damages for non-delivery "where the seller wrongfully neglects or refuses to deliver the goods". The general rule relating to such damages is stated in section 51(2) of the Sale of Goods Act 1979, under which the measure of damages is "the estimated loss directly and naturally resulting in the ordinary course of events" from the seller's breach. Section 51(3) goes on to provide that, where there is an available market, damages for non-delivery are prima facie "the difference between the contract price and the market or current price of the goods at the time or times when they ought to have been delivered or (if no time was fixed) at the time of the refusal to deliver."[91] This subsection gives rise to a number of special problems in relation to c.i.f. contracts. 19–175

---

[84] *Hardy & Co. v Hillerns and Fowler* [1923] 2 K.B. 491 at pp.496, 499 (actual decision reversed by statute: above, para.19–154); *Kwei Tek Chao v British Traders and Shippers Ltd* [1954] 2 Q.B. 459 at p.487; *Rosenthal & Sons Ltd v Esmail* [1965] 1 W.L.R. 1117 at p.1131; *Tradax Export SA v European Grain & Shipping Co.* [1983] 2 Lloyd's Rep. 100 at p.107.
[85] *Kwei Tek Chao* case, above, at p.487.
[86] *ibid.*
[87] Within Sale of Goods Act 1979, s.35.
[88] Above, para.19–154.
[89] Except where his inability to restore the goods is due to the seller's own breach (above, para.12–067). *Cf.* Vienna Convention on Contracts for the International Sale of Goods (above, para.1–024), Art. 82.
[90] Sale of Goods Act 1979, s.35(6)(b), above, para.19–154.
[91] The Vienna Convention on Contracts for the International Sale of Goods (above, para.1–024), Art. 45(1)(b) confers a general right to damages on the buyer in cases of failure by the seller to perform "any of his obligations." In the circumstances to

19–176 **Is there a "market"?** The first is whether there is a "market" for goods sold by reference to a particular set of shipping documents. Where the sale is of goods afloat and en route to a particular port or range of ports, this requirement will be satisfied only if there is a market in which *such* goods can be bought[92] and "it is not sufficient to show that there was a market for goods which belong to the same genus, but which were not of the contract description."[93] As the description may include the date of shipment[94] and other statements about the ship[95] the notion of a "market" in relation to c.i.f. contracts can be a restricted one.[96] Thus Scrutton L.J. has said that, where the goods were sold by reference to a bill of lading bearing a particular date, there was no market for goods of the contract description and that therefore the "market" rule did not apply.[97] It seems that there can similarly be no "market" for goods sold afloat on a named ship, though such a transaction has been said now to be a "rare phenomenon".[98] If there is no market, damages may be assessed by reference to an actual subsale, so long as this contains no unusual features which make the loss, or part of it, too remote.[99]

19–177 **Time when market is relevant.** Assuming that there is a "market", the next question is, at what time the market value is relevant for the purpose

---

be described below, damages are to be assessed by reference to the "current price" of the goods; this appears to be a reference to the market price. Under Art. 76(1), the difference between the contract price and the current price is the appropriate measure of damages where (a) the contract has been avoided; and (b) there is a "current price" (as defined by Art. 76(2): see below, para.19–186, n.47); and (c) the injured party has *not* actually made a reasonable substitute transaction. If that party *has* made such a substitute transaction (after avoiding the original contract) the damages are the difference between the contract price and the price in the substitute transaction: Art. 75. Other foreseeable loss is recoverable (whether or not the contract has been avoided) under Art. 74.

92 *Re Bourgeois and Wilson Holgate* (1920) 25 Com.Cas. 260.

93 *ibid.*, at p.281; *Coastal International Trading Ltd v Maroil AG* [1988] 1 Lloyd's Rep. 92 at p.95; *cf. Esteve Trading Corp. v Agropec International* (*The Golden Rio*) [1990] 2 Lloyd's Rep. 273, where a similar question arose under a "circle clause" in an f.o.b. contract.

94 Above, para.18–267.

95 Above, para.18–270; *cf.* also paras 18–271, 18–272.

96 *cf. Pagnan R. & Fratelli v Lebanese Organisation for International Commerce* (*The Caloric*) [1981] 2 Lloyd's Rep. 675; *Coastal (Bermuda) Petroleum Ltd v VTT Vulcan Marine Petroleum SA (The Marine Star) (No.2)* [1994] 2 Lloyd's Rep. 629 at p.634 (revsd on another point [1996] 2 Lloyd's Rep. 383); *Standard Chartered Bank v Pakistan National Shipping Co. (No.3)* [1999] 1 Lloyd's Rep. 747 at p.762, affirmed without reference to this point, [2001] EWCA Civ. 55 [2001] 1 All E.R. (Comm.) 822; *Bem dis A Turk Ticaret v International Agri Trade Co. (The Selda)* [1999] 1 Lloyd's Rep. 729 at p.733, where the same point arose on the buyer's breach under Sale of Goods Act 1979 s.50(3).

97 *Re Bourgeois and Wilson Holgate* (1920) 25 Com.Cas. 260 at p.281.

98 *Eurico SpA v Philipp Brothers* (*The Epaphus*) [1986] 2 Lloyd's Rep. 387 at p.389, affirmed [1987] 2 Lloyd's Rep. 215, where the same point was made at p.222 by Croom-Johnson L.J. (dissenting).

99 *Coastal International Trading Ltd v Maroil AG* [1988] 1 Lloyd's Rep. 92 (where part of the loss was too remote); *The Marine Star (No.2)*, above, n.96.

of assessing damages.[1] In a c.i.f. contract, the time when the goods "ought to have been delivered" refers prima facie to the time when documents should have been tendered[2]; but this prima facie rule may be excluded or modified by the provisions of the contract or by other relevant circumstances.

Time of tender of documents. In *C Sharpe & Co. Ltd v Nosawa*[3] a contract was made for the sale by sample of Japanese peas, June shipment, c.i.f. London at £10 15s. per ton. The sellers wrongfully refused to ship part of the goods and purported to cancel the contract; but this cancellation was not accepted by the buyers. If shipment had been made by the end of June, the documents would have arrived in London on about July 21, and the goods by the end of August. The price of Japanese peas in London was £12 per ton at the end of July and £17 10s. at the end of August. Atkin J. held that the buyers' damages were to be assessed with reference to the London market price at the end of July. For the purpose of a c.i.f. contract, the "time . . . when [the goods] ought to have been delivered" was the time at which the documents should have been tendered and not the time when the goods themselves should have arrived at the destination. If the buyers had been able to buy a June shipment in accordance with the sample on the day on which the shipping documents should have reached them, the cost of doing so would have been the basis for assessing damages. In fact they could not at that time obtain either the contract quantity, or a June shipment, or goods precisely up to the sample. In these circumstances Atkin J. held that the buyers ought, acting reasonably, to have made spot purchases of Japanese peas in London "as near in quality as possible to the goods which the defendants contracted to sell"[4]; that they had a "reasonable time to consider the position," *i.e.* whether or not to make such purchases; that that time had expired at the end of July; and that the damages were therefore the difference between the contract price and the spot price in the London market at the end of July. 19–178

Damages for anticipatory breach. As an authority on the interpretation of section 51(3), *C Sharpe & Co. Ltd v Nosawa* gives rise to a number of further difficulties. The reference in the subsection to "the time . . . when [the goods] ought to have been delivered" seems (as the following words "or (if no time was fixed)" indicate) to be a reference to a time fixed for delivery. In *C Sharpe & Co. Ltd v Nosawa*[5] there seems to have been no such time: certainly none was fixed for tender of documents. One possible way out of this difficulty is to say that where no time is "fixed for delivery" a term will be implied that the goods must be delivered within a reasonable time or, in the case of a c.i.f. contract, that documents must be tendered 19–179

[1] Under the Vienna Convention on Contracts for the International Sale of Goods (above, para.1–024), Art. 76(1) (above, n.91), the time at which the current price is relevant is that of the avoidance of the contract.
[2] Below, para.19–178.
[3] [1917] 2 K.B. 814.
[4] *ibid.*, at p.821.
[5] Above.

promptly after shipment[6]; and that damages will be assessed by reference to the market at the end of such time.[7] On this view it is at first sight hard to see what scope there is for the words of the subsection "if no time was fixed"; though it has been suggested that they could apply where the contract was to deliver on demand, or as required by the buyer.[8] Another possibility is to say that the damages ought to be assessed by reference to the time specified by the concluding words of section 51(3), namely, "the time of the refusal to deliver". But this view does not help to explain *C Sharpe & Co. Ltd v Nosawa*, for the seller had, by refusing to ship *before* the end of the shipment period, committed an anticipatory breach; and it has been held that the concluding words of section 51(3) do not apply to this kind of breach.[9] The general rule with regard to damages for anticipatory breach is that they are assessed by reference to the market price at the time when the goods ought to have been delivered, subject to the duty of the buyer to mitigate if he accepts the repudiation.[10] *C Sharpe & Co. Ltd v Nosawa*[11] is perhaps best regarded as an application of this rule; on this view the decision can be explained without any need for a strained interpretation of section 51(3). The buyer did not accept the seller's anticipatory breach. Hence he was entitled to wait until the seller should have delivered; and in the circumstances this meant that he was entitled to wait until tender of documents should have been made.

19–180 **Time of failure or refusal to appropriate goods.** The only question discussed in *C Sharpe & Co. Ltd v Nosawa*[12] was whether damages were to be assessed by reference to the time when the documents should have been tendered, as opposed to the time when the goods should have arrived. The sellers made a payment into court on the former basis, which was upheld. No earlier time was suggested by counsel or considered by Atkin J.; and it does not seem from any of the reports of the case that the contract required the sellers to give any notice of appropriation, or in some other way to notify the buyers, in advance of tender of documents, which particular goods they had appropriated to the contract. Where the contract does contain such a requirement, it has been held that damages are to be assessed by reference to the time at which the notice ought to have been given. In *Produce Brokers Ltd v Weiss*[13] a c.i.f. contract for the sale of

---

[6] Above, para.19–066.
[7] *Millet v Van Heek & Co.* [1921] 2 K.B. 369 at p.377 (where the contract was on f.o.b. terms).
[8] *ibid.*, at p.378.
[9] *Melachrino v Nickoll and Knight* [1920] 1 K.B. 693 at p.697; *Millet v Van Heek & Co.*, above, at p.375; *Tai Hing Cotton Mill Ltd v Kamsing Knitting Factory* [1979] A.C. 91. The "current price" rule stated in Art. 76 of the Vienna Convention on the International Sale of Goods (above, para.19–175, n.91) appears to apply to anticipatory as well as to actual breach. Arts 71 and 72 of the Convention, which deal with rights to suspend performance and to avoid the contract (and with certain related remedies) in cases of "anticipatory breach", lay down no special rules as to damages.
[10] For a fuller account, see above, paras 17–013 *et seq.*; below, para.20–116.
[11] [1917] 2 K.B. 814.
[12] [1917] 2 K.B. 184; above, para.19–178.
[13] (1918) 118 L.T. 111.

Japanese beans, February/March shipment, provided for payment against the "usual documents" and for the tender of a provisional invoice "not later than 30 running days from date of bill of lading." The seller failed to ship in February or March and McCardie J. held that the damages were to be assessed by reference to the market on the last day on which a provisional invoice should have been tendered, had shipment taken place by the end of the contract period.

This day was chosen as "a date upon which appropriation was to take place." It was also said to be "equivalent to the date for delivering shipping documents": this would bring the case within the prima facie rule laid down in section 51(3) of the Sale of Goods Act. But that rule is only a prima facie rule; and the better view seems to be that it was excluded by the provision of the contract as to the giving of a provisional invoice. It would similarly be excluded by a contractual provision requiring the seller to give a notice of appropriation within a fixed time from shipment[14] or from the date of the bill of lading, or "as soon as possible after vessel's sailing."[15] Two practical reasons may be given for assessing damages by reference to the date when such a notice should have been given rather than by reference to that on which the shipping documents should have been tendered. The latter date is, in the first place, often fortuitous, particularly where it was contemplated that the shipping documents (of which the notice of appropriation is not one[16]) were to pass through many hands before tender by the seller to the buyer. Secondly, the buyer can reasonably be expected to go into the market as soon as the seller commits a breach by failing, on the due date, to tender a provisional invoice, or to give a notice of appropriation. Such failure will often indicate that the seller will not be in a position to tender shipping documents when due and will entitle the buyer to rescind.[17] It would therefore be unreasonable to expect the buyer to wait until the date on which shipping documents should have been tendered, before going into the market to make a substitute purchase. In *C Sharpe & Co. Ltd v Nosawa*[18] no similar argument was open to the sellers. In the absence of a contractual provision calling for notice of appropriation, the sellers' first actual breach was in failing to tender the shipping documents. Their earlier repudiation constituted only an anticipatory breach; and it is well settled that the injured party does not need to accept such a breach, and that, if he does not do so, damages are to be assessed by reference to the market at the time of actual breach.[19] Where the contract calls for tender of a provisional invoice or for the giving of a notice of appropriation, the seller's failure to comply with that requirement constitutes an immediate actual breach.

The reasoning of *Produce Brokers Ltd v Weiss*[20] applies only where the seller's breach consists of failing to give a notice of appropriation or a

---

[14] See above, paras 19–017, 19–018 and the cases cited in para.19–180, n.24.
[15] As in *Société Italo-Belge pour le Commerce et l'Industrie v Palm & Vegetable Oils Malaysia Sdn. Bhd.* (*The Post Chaser*) [1981] 2 Lloyd's Rep. 695; above, paras 19–018, 19–064.
[16] Above, para.19–058.
[17] Above, para.19–064.
[18] Above.
[19] Above, para.19–179.
[20] (1918) 118 L.T. 111.

similar document to the buyer within the time allowed by the contract. If the seller duly gives such a notice and later fails to tender proper shipping documents, damages will be assessed by reference to the time when those documents ought to have been tendered,[21] in accordance with the rule stated in paragraph 19–178 above.

19–181 **Other time designated by the contract.** The contract may make its own provision for the time by reference to which damages are to be assessed: *e.g.* by providing that the damages "shall be based upon the actual or estimated value of the goods[22] on the date of default."[23] These words may refer to the date on which default is first made; or to the date on which the seller is in default; *i.e.* the first day after that by the end of which he ought to have performed. The first of these interpretations would accord with the rule laid down in section 51(3) of the Sale of Goods Act, being the last day on which the goods ought to have been (but were not) delivered. But since the seller has the whole of that day for performance, so that it is only on the following day that the buyer will in practice have the opportunity to buy against the seller, the prevailing view is that it is this latter day which constitutes the "date of default".[24] Where the contract provides for the giving of a notice of appropriation, the "default" will be the seller's failure to give the notice within the time required by the contract. The relevant day for assessing damages will accordingly be the first day after the end of the period in which the notice should have been given. It is assumed that the failure entitles the buyer to rescind and the expression "date of default" has accordingly been interpreted (in cases of such failure) to mean "the date on which the sellers failed to perform the obligation which entitled the buyers to determine the contract."[25] If, however the buyers continued after that date to press for performance and only brought the contract to an end at some later date, on account of the sellers' continuing refusal to perform the relevant obligation, then the buyers' damages would be assessed by reference to the latter date.[26] The cases on this subject are, once again[27]

---

[21] *Bremer Handelsgesellschaft mbH v Westzucker GmbH* [1981] 1 Lloyd's Rep. 207.

[22] *i.e.* the goods which have been appropriated to the contract (and not other similar goods): *R Pagnan & Fratelli v Lebanese Organisation for International Commerce* (*The Caloric*) [1981] 2 Lloyd's Rep. 675.

[23] As in GAFTA Form 100, cl. 26, discussed in the authorities cited in n.24, *infra*. A claim under this provision for the difference between the "default price" and the contract price has been held (for limitation purposes) to be one for unliquidated damages: *European Grain & Shipping Ltd v R & H Hall Plc* [1990] 2 Lloyd's Rep. 139.

[24] *Bremer Handelsgesellschaft mbH v Vanden Avenne-Izegem PVBA* [1978] 2 Lloyd's Rep. 109 at p.117 (*per* Lord Wilberforce, with whom Lord Keith agreed), p.129 (*per* Lord Salmon), disapproving *Toepfer v Cremer* [1975] 2 Lloyd's Rep. 118 (with which Lord Dilhorne, however, agreed: [1978] 2 Lloyd's Rep. 109 at p.122); *Bremer Handelsgesellschaft mbH v C Mackprang Jr.* [1979] 1 Lloyd's Rep. 221; *Avimex SA v Dewulf & Cie.* [1979] 2 Lloyd's Rep. 57; *Edm. J M Mertens & Co. PVBA v Veevoeder Export Vimex BV* [1979] 2 Lloyd's Rep. 372.

[25] *Fleming & Wendelen GmbH v Sanofi SA/AG* [2003] EWHC 561 (Comm.) [2003] 2 Lloyd's Rep. 475, at [62(4)].

[26] See *Toprak Mahsulleri Ofisi v Finagrain Compagnie Commerciale Agricole et Financière SA* [1979] 2 Lloyd's Rep. 98 at p.115.

[27] *cf.* above, para.19–179.

concerned with actual, as opposed to anticipatory breach, *i.e.* the seller's failure to give notice of appropriation by the end of the period within which the notice ought to have been given. This is one factor which appears to distinguish them from *C Sharpe & Co. Ltd v Nosawa*,[28] where the buyer was entitled, after the sellers' refusal to ship, to continue to press for performance, and may not have known, till the time when the documents should have arrived, that his efforts to induce the seller to ship by the end of the shipment period would turn out to be fruitless.

End of delivery period. According to one dictum, the relevant time for assessing damages for breach of a c.i.f. contract is "the last day of the delivery period."[29] It seems that "delivery period" here means "shipment period"; if so, the dictum is inconsistent with the authorities discussed in paragraphs 19–177 to 19–181 above. For this reason, it is respectfully submitted that the dictum is inappropriate to c. & f. and c.i.f. contracts, though it does correctly state a rule which applies to certain types of f.o.b. contracts.[30] 19–182

Other circumstances affecting the time for assessment. The prima facie rule that damages are assessed by reference to the time when goods "ought to have been delivered"[31] is simply an application of the general principle of the law of contract that damages are to be assessed by reference to the time of breach. That principle does not apply when, for some reason, it is not reasonable for the injured party to make a substitute contract at that time[32]; and this qualification of the principle applies to c.i.f. contracts. Thus if a c.i.f. buyer acts reasonably in continuing to press for performance after the time when documents should have been, but were not, tendered, damages will be assessed by reference, not to that time, but to the later time at which it became clear that there was no prospect of securing performance.[33] Similarly, if a c.i.f. buyer had paid against documents and later discovered that the goods were defective, and rejected them, damages would no doubt be assessed by reference to the date of rejection, and not by reference to the date of tender of documents.[34] 19–183

Duty to buy similar goods? A further difficulty arising from *C. Sharpe & Co. Ltd v Nosawa*[35] is the statement there made that the buyer should have gone into the July spot market and bought goods not of the exact quality required by the contract, but "as near in quality as possible to the goods the defendants contracted to sell."[36] If the sellers had tendered such goods the 19–184

---

[28] [1917] 2 K.B. 814; above, para.19–178.
[29] *Coastal International v Maroil AG* [1988] 1 Lloyd's Rep. 92 at p.96.
[30] Below, paras 20–115, 20–135.
[31] Sale of Goods Act 1979, s.51(3).
[32] *e.g. Johnson v Agnew* [1980] A.C. 367.
[33] *Johnson Matthey Bankers Ltd v The State Trading Corp. of India* [1984] 1 Lloyd's Rep. 427 at p.437.
[34] *cf. Toprak Mahsulleri Ofisi v Finagrain Cie. Commerciale* [1979] 2 Lloyd's Rep. 98.
[35] [1917] 2 K.B. 814; above, para.19–178.
[36] At p.821.

buyers could without any doubt have rejected them. A buyer is not, as a general rule, bound to mitigate his loss by accepting a tender that he would have been entitled to reject.[37] But if it would have been reasonable for him to accept such a tender in mitigation, he will not be entitled to damages in respect of loss resulting from his rejection of it.[38] If a c.i.f. buyer has resold the goods under the contract description, it might not be reasonable for him to purchase similar goods, whether from the seller or from another source: such a purchase might be useless if his sub-buyer could reject those goods (even if in practice he would be unlikely to do so on a rising market). However, these points were not raised in *C Sharpe & Co. Ltd v Nosawa*: the only question was whether the relevant market price was that at the end of July or that at the end of August. On slightly different facts (involving, for example, a subsale on a falling market) it might well be held that the market rule (which in any case is only a prima facie rule) was not applicable at all.[39]

19–185 **Breach occurring after tender of documents.** A c.i.f. seller may commit a breach after tender of documents, *e.g.* by directing the ship on which the goods have been loaded to a place other than the c.i.f. destination and so preventing physical delivery of the goods to the buyer.[40] In such a case the damages will be assessed by reference to the time at which the buyer, acting reasonably, should have made a substitute purchase.[41] Alternatively the seller's directions to the carrier may result merely in delay in the physical delivery of the goods. The buyer will then be entitled to damages for delay in delivery, *e.g.* in respect of any deterioration of the goods occasioned by the delay.[42]

19–186 **Place where market is relevant.** Various possible markets may be relevant for the purpose of assessing damages under a c.i.f. contract: for example the market at the place of origin, or at the destination, or at the place at which tender of documents is due, or at the place of the seller's refusal to deliver or to appropriate goods. An "available market" may exist in one or more of these places, but not in one or more of the others; and the prices in these markets may differ. In *C Sharpe & Co. Ltd v Nosawa*[43] the damages were assessed by reference to the London market; and it seems that this market was regarded as relevant because London was the place at which the documents should have been tendered. It is not wholly clear whether the court would have looked to the London market if the documents were to have been tendered in London but the destination of

[37] *Heaven and Kesterton Ltd v Et. Francois Albiac & Cie.* [1952] 2 Lloyd's Rep. 316; and see above, para.16–052.
[38] See *Sotiros Shipping Inc. v Sameiet Solholt* (*The Solholt*) [1983] 1 Lloyd's Rep. 605.
[39] *cf.* above, para.19–176.
[40] Above, para.19–073.
[41] *Empresa Exportadora de Azucar v Industria Azucarera Nacional SA* (*The Playa Larga*) [1983] 2 Lloyd's Rep. 171.
[42] *Gatoil International Inc. v Tradax Petroleum Ltd* (*The Rio Sun*) [1985] 1 Lloyd's Rep. 351.
[43] [1917] 2 K.B. 814; above, para.19–178.

the goods had been, for example, Lisbon. There is no suggestion in the case that the Japanese market was of any relevance, either as the market at the place of origin or as the market at the place of refusal to deliver (if indeed the refusal took place in Japan where the letter announcing it was posted, rather than in London, where it was received). The question whether the market at the place of origin is relevant was discussed in *Lesters Leather and Skin Co. Ltd v Home and Overseas Brokers Ltd*[44] where Indian snakeskins were sold c.i.f. UK port. The buyers justifiably rejected the goods on their arrival in London where there was at the time "no real market"[45] for them. The argument that the buyers could have bought against the sellers in India was rejected on the ground that a purchase of goods there after the arrival of the defective goods in London would not have enabled the buyers to get actual delivery of the goods "within a reasonable time after the date at which they ought to have got them."[46] Lord Goddard C.J. added that the position might be different if there was a market close at hand from which delivery could be obtained within a reasonable time. For example, if claret were sold c.i.f. London, to be shipped from Bordeaux, then the Bordeaux market might be relevant. Thus the position seems to be that prima facie the relevant market is that at the place of tender of documents[47]; but that this prima facie rule may be displaced if it is reasonable for the buyer to buy in some other market.[48] That other market is not necessarily the market at the place of origin or the market at the place of destination, if different from the place of tender of documents. Any market in which it is reasonable for the buyer to make a substitute purchase may be taken into account.[49]

---

[44] (1949) 82 Ll.L.R. 203.

[45] *ibid.*, at p.203.

[46] *ibid.*, at p.205.

[47] Under Art. 76(2) of the Vienna Convention on Contracts for the International Sale of Goods (above, para.1–024) "the current price is the price prevailing at the place where delivery should have been made. . ." In relation to a c.i.f contract, it is not clear to which of the "three stages of delivery" (above, para.19–072) this part of Art. 76(2) refers: *i.e.* whether it refers to handing the goods over to a carrier (*cf.* Art. 31(a)), or to tender of documents (*cf.* Art. 34), or to the physical delivery of the goods to the buyer. Art. 76(2) goes on to provide that, if there is *no* current price at the place of "delivery", the "price at such other place as serves as a reasonable substitute" may be taken into account. If the buyer *actually* makes a reasonable substitute contract, the damages will be assessed by reference to the price under that contract: Art. 75.

[48] *cf. Gebruder Metalmann GmbH v NBR (London) Ltd* [1984] 1 Lloyd's Rep. 614 (buyer's breach of f.o.b. contract).

[49] *cf. Att.-Gen. of the Republic of Ghana v Texaco Overseas Tankships Ltd (The Texaco Melbourne)* [1994] 1 Lloyd's Rep. 473 at pp.479–480, where the claim was made against a carrier and the actual decison was that damages could not be recovered by the shipper in respect of currency fluctuations after the date of breach.

(c) *Damages for Defective Delivery: in General*

19–187 **Defects in documents or in goods.** The general principles governing damages for defective delivery[50] apply to c.i.f. contracts, but special problems arise from the fact that the defect may be a defect in the goods, or in the documents, or in both. The relevant provisions of the Sale of Goods Act 1979 are section 53(2), under which damages for breach of warranty are "the estimated loss directly and naturally resulting, in the ordinary course of events, from the breach of warranty"; and section 53(3), which provides that "In the case of breach of warranty of quality" the prima facie measure of damages is "the difference between the value of the goods at the time of delivery to the buyer and the value they would have had if they had fulfilled the warranty."[51] The subsections apply not only to breach of a term which is a warranty *ab initio*, but also to breach of a condition which the seller elects, or is compelled, to treat as a breach of warranty,[52] and (presumably) where damages are claimed for breach of an intermediate term which is neither a condition nor a warranty.[53] Section 53(3) refers only to breach of a warranty of "quality". It has been said that the subsection does not apply where the breach is of a term which forms part of the

---

[50] *i.e.* delivery which is not in conformity with the contract, including short and delayed delivery: see *Gatoil International Inc. v Tradax Petroleum Ltd* (*The Rio Sun*) [1985] 1 Lloyd's Rep. 351; and damages for consequential loss: see *Marimpex Mineralöl Handelsgesellschaft mbH v Louis Dreyfus et Cie. Mineralöl GmBH* [1995] 1 Lloyd's Rep. 167.

[51] Art. 50 of the Vienna Convention on Contracts for the International Sale of Goods (above, para.1–024) provides that where "the goods do not conform to the contract" the buyer may "reduce the price" (whether or not it has been already paid) "in the same proportion as the value that the goods actually had at the time of delivery bears to the value that conforming goods actually delivered would have had at that time." This formula differs from the "difference in value" measure in Sale of Goods Act 1979, s.53(3) in that what is reduced under Art. 50 is *the price*, while what is awarded under s.53(3) is the difference in *value*, the price (as such) being irrelevant under s.53(3). If, for example, goods worth £60 were sold for £90 and their failure to conform to the contract reduced their value by one third, then the Art. 50 formula would yield £30 and the s.53(3) formula £20. If, on the other hand, the goods had been sold for £30, then the Art. 50 formula would yield £10 and the s.53(3) formula £20. The Art. 50 formula is based on a corresponding Civil Law concept: see, for example, German Civil Code (BGB) § 441(3). The assumption underlying Art. 50 is that the contract has not been avoided; on that assumption; the buyer is also entitled to damages for other loss insofar as the seller foresaw or ought to have foreseen it: Art. 74. If the contract has been avoided, the damages are assessed under Arts 75 and 76 (above, para.19–175, n.91). Arts 74 to 76 apply to *any* breach, whether it relates to the documents or to the goods. Art. 50, on the other hand, applies only "if *the goods* do not conform to the contract . . .:" *i.e.* it does not refer to defects in documents. In English law, the remedy of price reduction may also be available where the buyer deals as consumer and the goods do not conform to the contract at the "time of delivery": Sale of Goods Act 1979, ss.48A(1), 2(b)(i) and 48C(1)(a), discussed, in relation to c.i.f. contracts, in para.19–203 below. The price under these provisions is to be reduced "by an appropriate amount." This phrase is not explained in the Act and the question whether the "appropriate amount" is to be assessed by reference to the formula in s.53(3), or to that in Art. 50, or in some other way, is one that awaits determination.

[52] Sale of Goods Act 1979, s.53(1).

[53] Above, para.10–033.

description of the goods but has nothing to do with their quality, *e.g.* to breach of a stipulation as to the time of shipment,[54] and that damages for such a breach would be governed by section 53(2) rather than by section 53(3). The distinction between statements as to quality and statements which form part of the description is not, however, always clear cut[55]; and where a statement could fall into either category damages in respect of its falsity could be recovered under either subsection.

Where the defect in respect of which the damages are claimed is one of quality of the goods and is not apparent on the face of the documents, the "time of delivery" by reference to which damages are assessed under section 53(3) is (even in the case of a c.i.f. contract) the time at which the buyer takes delivery of the goods,[56] since it is only at this time that he has the opportunity of discovering the defect.[57]

Difference in value or market loss? The application of section 53(2) and (3) gives rise to difficulties in relation to c.i.f. contracts where the market value of the goods has fallen between the time of contracting and the time of tender of documents, but the value of the goods is not affected by the fact that they are not in conformity with the contract. In such a situation, the "difference in value" formula of section 53(3) will yield only nominal damages; and the same is true of the "loss . . . resulting . . . from the breach" formula of section 53(2), since the general fall in the market will not be the result of the non-conformity of the particular goods which have been appropriated to the contract. But if the buyer had been aware of the non-conformity in time he could, by exercising either of his rights to reject[58] have refused to pay or have recovered back any payment which he had made, and so have avoided the market loss. The question therefore arises whether he can recover that loss by way of damages where he has lost his chance to reject[59] before becoming aware of the breach.[60] In answering this question, three types of cases fall to be considered in paragraphs 19–189 to 19–201 below: first those in which there is a defect in the goods alone, secondly those in which there is a defect both in the documents and in the goods, and thirdly those in which there is a defect in the documents alone. The outcome in these cases turns on questions of causation, *i.e.* on whether the market loss "resulted from" or was "caused by" the seller's breach. This 19–188

[54] *Taylor v Bank of Athens* (1922) 27 Com.Cas. 142 at p.146.

[55] See, *e.g.* *Toepfer v Continental Grain Co.* [1974] 1 Lloyd's Rep. 11 at pp.13, 14, 15; above, para.11–016.

[56] *Marimpex Mineralöl Handelsgesellschaft mbH v Louis Dreyfus et Cie Mineralöl GmbH* [1995] 1 Lloyd's Rep. 167.

[57] *cf.* the similar rule which governs restrictions on the buyer's right to reject defective goods: above, para.19–157.

[58] For the c.i.f. buyer's two rights of rejection, see above, para.19–144.

[59] Whether as a matter of law or of business: see below, para.19–191.

[60] A similar problem can arise under the Vienna Convention on Contracts for the International Sale of Goods (above, para.1–024) since the "current price" basis of assessment applies only where the contract has been avoided: see Art. 76(1), above, para.19–175, n.91 Where the contract has not been avoided, Art. 74 requires the loss to have been suffered "as a consequence of the breach", while price reduction for defects in the goods is assessed under Art. 50 (above, n.51) on a "difference in value" basis.

reasoning must therefore be distinguished from that of a wholly different group of cases (not concerned with c.i.f. contracts) in which recovery of market loss damages is sometimes denied on grounds (to be discussed in para. 19–202, below) which have "nothing to do with questions of causation."[61]

(i) *Defect in the Goods Alone*

19–189 **Damages restricted to difference in value.** In *Taylor v Bank of Athens*[62] 500 tons of Cyprus beans were sold c.i.f. London for shipment in July and/or August. The goods were not shipped until September 6; and if the buyer had known this he would certainly have rejected the documents and the goods, since by the time of shipment the market value of the goods had fallen some £2,000 below the contract price. But he paid against delivery orders, having been assured by the seller that the bills of lading were dated August 31. This was indeed the case, and the seller had given the assurance in good faith, neither he nor anyone for whom he was responsible being aware of the fact that the bills had been falsely dated. The buyer claimed damages[63] and, there being no difference between the market value of an August and a September shipment, McCardie J. held that the damages were no more than nominal. He based this conclusion not on section 53(3), since the non-conformity related to the *description* of the goods rather than to their *quality*, but on section 53(2) as the loss attributable to the fall in the market value of the goods between the time of the contract and the time of the breach was not one "resulting. . . from the breach" as required by the latter subsection. The market loss was not recoverable as it had resulted "not from the breach of warranty but from an unfortunate or improvident bargain which the buyer may have made"[64]; in other words, the breach had not caused this loss. The decision has been approved in a number of later cases[65] and seems, with respect, to be correct in principle. There was no good reason for allowing the buyer to recover damages in respect of the market loss, since that loss was not caused by, or suffered as a result of, the seller's breach.

It is submitted that the rule in *Taylor v Bank of Athens* would also apply where the goods suffered from some qualitative defect which was not, and could not have been expected to be, apparent on the face of the documents: *e.g.* where the goods were not up to sample.[66] *A fortiori*, the buyer will recover no more than nominal damages where the goods suffer from such a defect and that defect is *revealed* by documents which are not in themselves defective. This was the position in the *Vargas Pena*[67] case where a contract

---

[61] *Nykredit Bank v Edward Erdman Group* [1997] 1 W.L.R. 1627 at p.1638.
[62] (1922) 27 Com.Cas. 142.
[63] He had resold the goods and so presumably had lost the right to reject them.
[64] (1922) 27 Com. Cas. 142 at p.147.
[65] Below, paras 19–190 to 19–193, 19–198.
[66] *cf.* above, para.19–145.
[67] *Vargas Peena Apeztieguia y Cia v Peter Cremer GmbH* [1987] 1 Lloyd's Rep. 394. The sale was on f.o.b terms but the principles applicable to c.i.f. contracts were relevant for the reasons stated in para.20–093, below. Most of the authorities discussed in the judgment concern c.i.f. contracts.

for the sale of cotton-seed expeller expressly gave the buyer the right to reject, if the goods should contain more than 15 per cent fat[68]; and the seller tendered an analysis certificate which showed the fat content to be 15.73 per cent. This fact did not make the certificate a defective document,[69] but merely one which revealed such a defect in the goods as would have justified their rejection. The buyers could, indeed have rejected the documents on the ground that they revealed such a defect in the goods,[70] but they nevertheless accepted the documents[71] and so lost their right[72] to reject the goods. It was held that they were entitled to no more than nominal damages since any further loss suffered by them on account of the difference between the contract and the lower resale price had not been caused by the sellers' breach.[73]

(ii) *Defects in the Documents and in the Goods*

Market loss recoverable. A number of cases show that damages in respect of the market loss could have been recovered in *Taylor v Bank of Athens*[74] if the seller had, instead of tendering delivery orders containing no mis-statements, tendered the falsely dated bills of lading; for in that case there would have been a defect not only in the goods but also in the documents. The significance of this point was first made clear in *James Finlay & Co. Ltd v Kwik Hoo Tong*[75] where sugar was sold c.i.f. Bombay, shipment to be made in September. The sugar was in fact shipped on October 1, but the bills of lading were falsely dated September 30. This was not discovered by the buyers until two years later[76]; and in the meantime the buyers had paid against documents, accepted the goods and so lost their right to reject them. It was held that the buyers were entitled to damages for loss suffered as a result of a fall in the market, even though there was no difference in value between an October and a September shipment. There were, in this case, two breaches. As Scrutton L.J. said: "It was a condition of the contract not only that the goods be shipped in September but that a genuine bill of lading should be delivered showing the right date of shipment."[77] The importance of this point was made clear by Greer L.J. when he said: "The judge has taken the view that the shippers [*i.e.* the sellers] promised to state truly in the bill of lading the date of shipment, and the respondents [*i.e.* the buyers] say that if that had been done they would have been entitled to reject the goods. By the breach of contract in sending forward a bill of lading containing a false statement, the plaintiffs 19–190

---

[68] Above, para.18–273, n.93.
[69] Above, para.19–142.
[70] *ibid.*
[71] Above, para.19–153.
[72] Above, para.19–151.
[73] [1987] 1 Lloyd's Rep. 394 at p.399 (where it is surmised that the market had fallen).
[74] (1922) 27 Com. Cas. 142, above para.19–189.
[75] [1929] 1 K.B. 400. For further facts in this case, see below, para.19–197.
[76] *Kwei Tek Chao v British Traders and Shippers Ltd* [1954] 2 Q.B. 459 at p.492.
[77] [1929] 1 K.B. 400 at p.409.

[*i.e.* the buyers] have been deprived *of that right*"[78] (*i.e.* of the right to reject the goods). In other words, the damages for the seller's breach in "sending forward" a falsely dated bill of lading included the loss suffered by the buyers in being deprived of the right to reject the goods.[79]

When a bill of lading is falsely dated, there will often be two breaches of this kind. *Taylor v Bank of Athens*[80] was distinguished by Greer L.J. in the *James Finlay* case on the ground that there the claim was not based upon a breach of contract in putting forward a bill of lading with the wrong date.[81] And he added: "I agree that if no question were involved of a distinct breach of contract by tendering a wrongly dated bill of lading the position would be quite different"[82] and that in such a case only nominal damages could be awarded.

19–191 The *James Finlay* case was applied and extended in *Kwei Tek Chao v British Traders Ltd*[83] where Rongalite C lumps were sold c.i.f. Hong Kong, shipment to be made by October 31, 1951. Shipment was in fact made on November 3, but the bills of lading were forged (without the complicity of the sellers) to show an October shipment. The sellers on November 10 presented the documents to the buyers' bank and two days later obtained payment of the price. The goods arrived in Hong Kong on December 17, 1951, by which time the buyers were aware of the actual date of shipment, but they nevertheless took possession of the goods on behalf of their bank, and paid off the bank on February 12, 1952. By April 1952 they were held to have affirmed the transaction. There was no difference in value between an October and a November shipment, but by December 17, the goods had become substantially worthless because of a collapse in the Hong Kong market for them[84] and this state of affairs continued at all subsequent material times. Devlin J. rejected the argument that the buyers were entitled to no more than nominal damages. He held that the principle of the *James Finlay*[85] case applied even if the buyers knew at the time of the arrival of the goods that they had a legal right to reject them, or if they then knew the facts on which such a right might be based.[86] He justified this

[78] *ibid.*, at p.413; *cf. Malozzi v Carapelli SpA* [1975] 1 Lloyd's Rep. 249 at p.256 (varied, without reference to this point, [1976] 1 Lloyd's Rep. 407).

[79] Such damages can be recovered not only in respect of market fluctuations but also (*e.g.*) in respect of storage charges; *Malozzi v Carapelli SpA*, above.

[80] (1922) 27 Com.Cas. 142 (above, para.19–189).

[81] [1929] 1 K.B. 400 at p.414.

[82] *ibid.*

[83] [1954] 2 Q.B. 459.

[84] There was no evidence of a market elsewhere: see p.499.

[85] [1929] 1 K.B. 400 (above, para.19–190).

[86] From the statement of facts at pp.462–463 and the judgment at pp.473–474 and 480 it is not clear exactly when the buyers became sufficiently aware of the true facts to enable them to exercise their right to reject. On p.493 Devlin J. expresses what seems to be his final view on the matter when he says that "the plaintiffs knew or ought to have known that they had a right to reject . . . not later than December 17, 1952." It is fairly obvious that "1952" here is a misprint for "1951", December 17, 1951, being "the date when the goods arrived" referred to in the previous paragraph of the report; and also the date given in the penultimate line of p.494. No relevant event in the case took place on December 17, 1952.

extension of the principle on the ground that a buyer who has paid against apparently conforming documents cannot as a matter of business be expected later to reject the goods which those documents represent, as this will turn him into an unsecured creditor for the amount which he had paid. Thus the buyers recovered substantial damages for breach of the sellers' obligation to tender a correctly dated bill of lading, since this breach had (whether as a matter of law or business) deprived them of their right or opportunity to reject the goods, and so of the opportunity to throw back on the sellers the loss due to the fall in the market. A similar argument was rejected in the later *Vargas Pena*[87] case, but the two cases are readily distinguishable. In the *Vargas Pena* case, the buyers, though not obliged to pay anything before tender of documents, had in fact paid 50 per cent of the price before then; the documents on their face[88] revealed the fact that the goods suffered from a defect which justified rejection; and the documents themselves were not defective.[89] It followed that, although the buyers may have found it "commercially impracticable"[90] to reject (in the sense that rejection would have left them without any security for the return of their advance payment), this position was not caused by the sellers' breach.[91] In the *Kwei Tek Chao* case, on the other hand, the buyers' difficulties (as described above) *were* the result of the sellers' breach, it being assumed that the buyers would not have paid if the documents had stated the true date of shipment.

Damages in respect of market loss were again awarded in *Kleinjan & Holst NV Rotterdam v Bremer Handelsgesellschaft mbH*.[92] In that case, c.i.f. sellers had given a notice of appropriation stating that the goods had been shipped on one ship (on which no such shipment had been made) and had then tendered documents relating to goods which had been shipped on a different ship. The buyers, as they were entitled to do,[93] objected to these documents, but, instead of rescinding the contract, they paid the price against the documents, "reserving our rights". The fact that the goods had been shipped on the second (rather than on the first) ship in no way affected their value; but by the time of tender of documents the market price of the goods had fallen below the contract price. It was held that the sellers were liable for the difference between the contract and the market price. Cooke J. followed the *James Finlay*[94] case and said that it had laid down "a general rule as to the measure of damages in cases where the sellers have broken a condition of the contract by failing to tender proper documents. The reasons why the buyers have not rescinded are immaterial. Whether they have been misled [as in the *James Finlay* case] or have **19–192**

---

[87] *Vargas Pena Apeztieguia y Cia v Peter Cremer GmbH* [1987] 1 Lloyd's Rep. 394; above, para.19-189.
[88] [1987] 1 Lloyd's Rep. 394 at p.396.
[89] See above, paras 19–147, 19–189.
[90] [1987] 1 Lloyd's Rep. 394 at p.398.
[91] *ibid.*, at p.399.
[92] [1972] 2 Lloyd's Rep. 11.
[93] Above, paras 19–017, 19–021.
[94] Above, para.19–190.

elected not to rescind with full knowledge of the facts [as in the *Kleinjan* case] the position is the same, namely, that if they had rescinded, they would not have had to pay a price (*viz.* the contract price) in excess of the market price of the goods at the time of the breach."[95] The difficulty with this reasoning is, however, that it can apply equally where the only thing of which the buyers complain is that the goods themselves are not in accordance with the contract. Here, too, the buyers would, if they had rescinded, not have had to pay the price. Yet the learned judge expressly approved the rule in *Taylor v Bank of Athens*[96] that, in such a case, the damages would be nominal if the value of the goods was not affected by the fact that the goods were not in accordance with the contract. The passage in the *Kleinjan* case quoted above was therefore rejected in a later decision at first instance,[97] the reasoning of which on this point has since been approved in the Court of Appeal where the same passage was described as "too wide".[98] The actual decision in the *Kleinjan* case is best explained on the grounds that the defect there affected *both* the documents *and* the goods; and that the buyers had paid against the defective documents only on the terms of a special agreement that, if they did not reject, they should be entitled to such damages as would put them into the same financial position as that in which they would have been, if they had exercised their undoubted right to reject the documents.[99]

19–193 The view that substantial damages for loss of the right to reject can be recovered when there is a defect both in the documents and in the goods is again supported by *The Kastellon*.[1] Groundnut oil was sold c.i.f. Marseilles, to be shipped in December 1974 or January 1975. It was in fact shipped on February 1 and 2, 1975, but the bills of lading were falsely dated January 31, as a result of "a covert initiative of the sellers' transit agent in Lagos."[2] Had the buyers known the true facts, they would have rejected, the market having fallen; and it was held that they were entitled to damages for loss of the right to reject, based on the difference between the contract and the market price. On the facts of the case there was, again, a defect both in the documents (as they were forged) and in the goods (as they were shipped out of time).

19–194 **Effect of statutory restrictions on right to reject.** The question arises whether the reasoning of the *James Finlay* case,[3] and of the cases which follow it, has been affected by section 15A of the Sale of Goods Act 1979;

[95] [1972] 2 Lloyd's Rep. 11 at p.22.
[96] Above, para.19–189.
[97] *Vargas Pena Apeztieguia y Cia v Peter Cremer GmbH* [1987] 1 Lloyd's Rep. 394 at p.399, as to which see above, para.19–189, n.67.
[98] *Procter & Gamble Philippine Manufacturing Corp. v Kurt A. Becher* [1987] 2 Lloyd's Rep. 21 at p.29, below, para.19–198.
[99] *Vargas Pena* case, above n.97, at p.399.
[1] *Huilerie L'Abelle v Société des Huileries du Niger* (*The Kastellon*) [1978] 2 Lloyd's Rep. 203.
[2] *ibid.*, at p.204.
[3] [1929] 1 K.B. 400; above, para.19–190.

this section provides that, if the buyer does not deal as consumer,[4] the breach of certain statutorily implied conditions[5] may be treated as a breach of warranty if it is so slight that it would be unreasonable for the buyer to reject the goods. The section does not say anything about the measure of damages for the hypothetical breach of warranty; but it can be argued that if, by virtue of the section, the buyer never had a right to reject the goods, then he would not be entitled to the market loss damages which were awarded in the *James Finlay* and later cases on the ground that he had been "deprived of that right".[6] It has however, been submitted in paragraph 18–284 above that section 15A does not affect the right of a buyer under an overseas sale to reject goods because they have been shipped outside the shipment period or because they in some other way fail to correspond with the contractual description. The cases in which "market loss" damages have been awarded to c.i.f. buyers on account of the seller's "double breach" are all of this kind; and if the submission that section 15A does not apply to them is accepted, then it follows that the section is not a bar to the award of market loss damages in such cases.

Evaluation. In *The Kastellon* Donaldson J. decided in favour of the buyers with regret "because there is little merit in the buyers' contentions."[7] The sellers were "reasonably aggrieved" that the buyers should take advantage of what the sellers regarded as a "legal technicality"[8]; for the oil arrived when expected and the buyers were not prejudiced by the fact that it was shipped a day or two after the end of a two-month shipment period. This factor is present in all the cases[9] in which damages based on a fall in the market have been recovered for loss of the right to reject. Such cases are, moreover, open to criticism on the ground that to award market loss damages to a buyer who has lost the right to reject amounts to putting him into the same financial position as that in which he would have been, if he had indeed rejected. Such a result in effect conflicts with the policy of the rules that limit the right to reject. 19–195

One possible argument for allowing a c.i.f. buyer to recover market loss damages in cases of the kind discussed in paragraphs 19–190 to 19–193 is that, in many such cases, the reason for his having lost the right to reject the goods is that an element of fraud is involved in the preparation of the defective documents.[10] Although the seller himself may be innocent of such 19–196

[4] If the buyer deals as consumer (see above, para.18–259), then his right to reject may be in effect suspended. This would be the position where he had exercised one of his "additional rights" under Pt 5A of the Sale of Goods Act 1979, *i.e.* his right to require the seller to replace or repair non-conforming goods (ss.48A(2)(a), 48B). He would then not be able to reject until he had given the seller a reasonable time in which to repair or replace the goods: s.48D. But there is nothing to compel the buyer to exercise his rights under Pt 5A and if he chooses to ignore those rights, then his right to reject for breach of condition is not restricted by s.48D.
[5] *i.e.* those implied by ss.13, 14 and 15 of the Sale of Goods Act 1979.
[6] [1929] 1 K.B. 400 at p.413; above, para.19–190.
[7] [1978] 2 Lloyd's Rep. 203 at p.207.
[8] *ibid.*, at p.204.
[9] *i.e.* those discussed in paras 19–190 to 19–193 above.
[10] As in the cases discussed in para.19–191, and para.19–193. For the *James Finlay* case [1929] 2 K.B. 400 see above, para.19–190 and below, para.19–197.

fraud, it may have been committed by someone for whose acts he is vicariously liable; and in such cases an award of substantial damages may be justified by the need to deter that fraud. Even where the fraud is not that of the seller,[11] or that of a person for whom he is vicariously liable, it has been suggested that it may be necessary to hold the seller liable for substantial damages in order to forge the first link in a chain of liability stretching back to the person who perpetrated the original fraud, so that that person should not "escape with impunity from the consequences of the fraud . . .".[12] But this justification of the buyer's right to recover substantial market loss damages from *the seller* may, with respect, be doubted, for no such chain of liability is necessary to reach the person who, or whose agent, made the fraudulent statement. Damages for deceit can be claimed from that person directly (without involving the seller) by a buyer who is deprived of the right to reject the goods because the bill of lading which has been indorsed to him contains a false statement: such damages would include loss suffered by reason of a fall in the market.[13] *A fortiori*, the "chain of liability" argument would not justify the award of substantial damages where there was no fraud (but only confusion) in the preparation of the shipping documents. This was the position in the *Kleinjan*[14] case, the result of which can perhaps be justified by to its tendency to encourage compromises. That justification would, however, be restricted to cases in which the buyer already knew of the defects in the documents and in the goods when he accepted the documents subject to a reservation of his rights.

19–197 The criticism of the law in *The Kastellon*,[15] and the difficulty of meeting that criticism by reference to the need to deter fraud,[16] raise the question whether the law may not have taken a wrong turning in the *James Finlay*[17] case. That case seems to illustrate the most commonly occurring situation,

---

[11] *e.g.* where the fraud is that of a loading broker (who is normally the agent of the carrier), as in *United City Merchants (Investments) Ltd v Royal Bank of Canada (The American Accord)* [1983] 1 A.C. 168.

[12] *Kwei Tek Chao v British Traders Ltd* [1954] 2 Q.B. 459 at p.484.

[13] *The Saudi Crown* [1986] 1 Lloyd's Rep. 261; *cf. DSW Silo- und Verwaltungsgesellschaft mbH v Owners of The Sennar (No.2)* [1985] 1 W.L.R. 490 (where the claim failed on other grounds); *Stanmore Wesson & Co. v Breen* (1886) 12 App.Cas. 698 (where the shipowner admitted liability to the indorsee and successfully claimed over against the master who had signed the misdated bill of lading); *Standard Chartered Bank v Pakistan National Shipping Corp.* [1995] 2 Lloyd's Rep. 365 (where a shipowner and his agent were held liable to a bank which had paid against a falsely dated bill of lading under a letter of credit; other aspects of this litigation are discussed in paras 18–028 n.18 and 18–046 above). The position is different where the buyer claims *as charterer* in respect of the misdating of a bill of lading which he himself (or a shipper for whom he is responsible) has presented for signature to the master. In such a case the shipowner does not impliedly promise that the date on the bill of lading is accurate: *Rudolph A. Oetker v IFA Internationale Frachtagentar AG* [1985] 1 Lloyd's Rep. 557.

[14] [1972] 2 Lloyd's Rep. 11, discussed above, para.19–192. Even the misdating of a bill of lading may be the result of an innocent mistake, as in *Mendala III Transport v Total Transport Corp.* [1993] 2 Lloyd's Rep. 41.

[15] [1978] 2 Lloyd's Rep. 203; above, paras 19–193, 19–195.

[16] Above, para.19–196.

[17] [1929] 1 K.B. 400; above, para.19–190.

so far as c.i.f. contracts are concerned: a falsely dated bill of lading will, more often than not, conceal a shipment outside the shipment period, so that the case will be one of a "double breach", *i.e.* one in which there is a defect both in the documents and in the goods. Yet one may, with respect, share the doubts expressed by Donaldson J.,[18] whether market loss damages should be recoverable in such cases against a wholly innocent seller. Where, indeed, the seller is guilty of some degree of culpable complicity in the misdating of the bill of lading, the award of such damages can be justified on tort principles, by reference to the seller's blameworthiness; and, in cases of fraud, it can further be justified by reference to its deterrent effect. It is unfortunate that this approach was not taken in the *James Finlay* case, where the judgments emphasise that no allegation of fraud was made against the sellers.[19] Those sellers had, indeed, not acted dishonestly in the sense that they had relied on a custom allowing them, in certain circumstances, to date bills of lading within the month in which the carrier had *agreed* to ship the goods, even though they were not actually shipped within that month. But, as the sellers failed to establish either the custom or the circumstances in which it could operate, Wright J. said at first instance that it was "almost inconceivable" that their breach in tendering falsely dated bills of lading could have been "other than designed"[20]; and on appeal Scrutton L.J. referred with evident disapproval to the "lax practice"[21] of misdating the bills of lading. No attempt was made in the *James Finlay* case to argue that a person may be liable in deceit, even though he has no dishonest intent, if he makes a statement which he knows to be untrue[22]; and it is now clear that an "intention to deceive" suffices for this purpose even though there is not "intention to defraud".[23] As the law stands, market loss damages are no doubt recoverable even from a wholly innocent seller in the "double breach" situations discussed in paragraphs 19–190 to 19–193 above[24]; but it is submitted that the law would be in a more satisfactory

---

[18] In *The Kastellon*; above, para.19–195, nn.7 and 8.

[19] [1928] 2 K.B. 604 at p.613; [1929] 1 K.B. 400 at p.412, ("Fraud was not alleged or proved"); *cf. ibid.*, at p.416 ("No fraud is imputed to the appellants," *i.e.* the sellers); *cf.* also the argument of counsel *ibid.*, at p.405 and *Kwei Tek Chao v British Traders & Shippers Ltd* [1954] 2 Q.B. 459 at pp.478, 484.

[20] [1928] 2 K.B. 604 at p.613.

[21] [1929] 1 K.B. 400 at p.408.

[22] See *Polhill v Walter* (1832) 2 B. & Ad. 114; *cf. Edgington v Fitzmaurice* (1885) 29 Ch.D. 459 at p.481.

[23] *Standard Chartered Bank v Pakistan National Shipping Corp.* [1995] 2 Lloyd's Rep. 365 at p.375; *Standard Chartered Bank v Pakistan National Shipping Corp. (No.2)* [2000] 1 Lloyd's Rep. 218 at p.221, reversed, but not on the point here under discussion [2002] UKHL 43, [2003] A.C. 959: see above, para.18–046. Hence the statements quoted in n.19, above that *fraud* was not alleged against the sellers in the *James Finlay* case do not preclude the possibility that liability for deceit can be incurred on such facts. The "dishonesty" said in *Thomas Witter Ltd v TBP Industries Ltd* [1996] 2 All E.R. 573 to be necessary for this purpose seems to be intended to exclude mere negligence and to refer to no more than an "intention to deceive": *cf. Armitage v Nurse* [1998] Ch. 241 at p.251; *KCB Bank v Industrial Steels (U.K.) Ltd* [2001] 1 Lloyd's Rep. 370 at p.374; *GE Commercial Finance Ltd v Gee* [2005], EWHC 2056 (Comm), [2006] 1 Lloyd's Rep. 337 at [97].

[24] In *Procter & Gamble Philippine Manufacturing Corp. v Kurt A Becher* [1988] 2

state if such damages were available only where the seller (or someone for whom he was responsible) was to blame for the false statements, or at least knew of their falsity at the time of tender of documents.

(iii) *Defect in the Documents Alone*

19–198 **Damages generally restricted to difference in value.** The situation in which there was a defect in the documents alone could arise where the goods were in all respects in accordance with the contract but the seller tendered, for example, a certificate of insurance when he should have tendered a policy[25]; or where the goods were in fact shipped within the shipment period but the bill of lading was not "genuine",[26] *e.g.* because it bore a false date of shipment.[27] This was the position in *Procter & Gamble Philippine Manufacturing Corp. v Kurt A. Becher*[28] where a c.i.f. contract had originally provided for shipment in January; and this period was later extended to the end of February. The sellers tendered a bill of lading which (without any complicity on their part) was misdated January 31, shipment having not been made until February 10. This tender could clearly have been rejected, either because the bill was not "genuine",[29] or because the sellers were in breach of an express term of the contract[30] requiring the bill to be "dated when the goods were actually on board." But the buyers paid 98 per cent of the price against documents and so lost the right to reject the documents by acceptance. They had, moreover, no right to reject the goods, as these were in conformity with the contract, having been shipped within the extended shipment period. Instead they resold the goods at a price well below the original contract price, the market having fallen; and they claimed this market loss as damages for the sellers' breach in tendering the falsely dated bill of lading. The Court of Appeal rejected the claim and held that the buyers were entitled to no more than nominal damages. The buyers could, indeed, have avoided the market loss, if they had known of the misdating of the bill when it was tendered, since they would in that event no doubt have rejected the bill (and consequently the goods[31]). But their

---

Lloyd's Rep. 21 (below, para.19–198) the actual decision was that market loss damages were not recoverable in respect of contracts of which the seller had committed only a single breach in tendering false documents; but no appeal was taken from the arbitrators' award of such damages in respect of another contract of which the seller had committed the double breach of tendering false documents and shipping goods out of time.

[25] See above, para.19–047.

[26] See above, para.19–035.

[27] As in *Re General Trading Co. Ltd and Van Stolk's Commissiehandel* (1910) 16 Com.Cas. 95 (above, para.19–147), where the defect was apparent on the face of the bill.

[28] [1988] 2 Lloyd's Rep. 21, affirming [1988] 1 Lloyd's Rep. 88; Treitel [1988] L.M.C.L.Q. 457.

[29] Above, para.19–035: see [1988] 2 Lloyd's Rep. 21 at p.29.

[30] GAFTA Form 100 Cl. 6: see [1988] 2 Lloyd's Rep. 21 at p.30.

[31] This would also have been the position in *The Kastellon* [1978] 2 Lloyd's Rep. 203 (above, para.19–193) if the sellers had been able to prove facts entitling them to invoke a *force majeure* clause, and so extend the shipment period beyond the date on which the goods were shipped. The reasoning of Donaldson J. indicates that, on such facts, the buyer's damages would have been no more than nominal.

position differed from that of the buyers in the *James Finlay*[32] case in a number of crucial respects. First, the falsity of the bill in the *Procter & Gamble* case did not conceal any further breach in relation to the goods, or deprive the buyers of any independent right to reject the goods, since the goods were in conformity with the contract. Secondly, the buyers in the *Procter & Gamble* case would not have been entitled to reject the documents, had the bill been correctly dated, while in the *James Finlay* case the buyers would in that event have been so entitled. Hence, if the bill of lading had been correctly dated, the buyers could have avoided the market loss in the *James Finlay* case, but not in the *Procter & Gamble* case. Since the purpose of awarding damages for breach of contract is to put the injured party into the position in which he would have been, if the contract had been performed (*i.e.* if the bill of lading had been correctly dated), it followed that market loss damages were not recoverable in the *Procter & Gamble* case: the buyers' market loss had not been caused by the breach, but by the fact that they were unaware of it at the crucial time.[33] That was also the position in *Taylor v Bank of Athens*,[34] where the damages were similarly no more than nominal. In both cases the sellers were guilty of only a single breach; and these cases establish that, in such "single breach" cases, market loss damages are, as a general rule,[35] not available to the buyer. Since the availability of such damages is open to the objections stated in paragraphs 19–195 to 19–197 above, this development in the law is, with respect, to be welcomed.

Other damages. Even where a c.i.f. seller's breach consisted only in tendering a false bill of lading, the buyer might in certain circumstances recover substantial damages for the seller's breach of contract. This might (in the words of Kerr L.J. in the *Procter & Gamble*[36] case) be the position where "a falsely dated bill of lading becomes effectively unmerchantable . . . once its true date is known", so that the buyer finds himself "'locked in' on a falling market" or unable to fulfil a previously concluded subsale.[37] A buyer who proved such facts could recover substantial damages, but they would differ from the "market loss" damages recovered in the cases described in paragraphs 19–190 to 19–193 above. Those damages would be based on market movements between the time of contracting and the time when the buyer resold the goods, or reasonably should have done so.[38] On the other hand, where the buyer was "'locked in' on a falling market" his damages would be based on market movements between the time when the buyer discovered of the truth and the time when he resold the goods; while where he lost a subsale they would be based on the subsale price, provided that this loss were not too remote. 19–199

[32] [1929] 1 K.B. 400; above, para.19–190.
[33] [1988] 2 Lloyd's Rep. 21 at p.32.
[34] (1922) 27 Com.Cas. 1242; above, para.19–189.
[35] For qualifications, see below, paras 19–199, 19–200.
[36] [1988] 2 Lloyd's Rep. 21; above, para.19–198.
[37] [1988] 2 Lloyd's Rep. 21 at p.30; *cf. ibid.*, at p.32.
[38] Below, para.19–201.

19–200 **Liability in tort.** In the *Procter & Gamble* case[39] there was "no claim based on fraud or misrepresentation"[40]; and it was said that "the position would . . . be entirely different if the sellers themselves had been involved in the false dating of the bill of lading and could therefore have been sued in fraud."[41] There would probably be no liability under section 2(1) of the Misrepresentation Act 1967 since that subsection applies "where a person has entered into a contract after a misrepresentation has been made to him . . ."; and the sequence of events here under discussion is the opposite of that described in the subsection: *i.e.* the misrepresentation is made after the conclusion of the contract, not to induce the contract, but in the course of its purported performance. Even a misrepresentation of the latter kind could, however, give rise to liability in tort at common law for deceit (or perhaps for negligence).[42] The object of the damages in such an action would be to put the buyer into the position in which he would have been, if the statement had not been made.[43] If, in the *Procter and Gamble* case, the seller had known that the bill of lading which he had obtained was misdated, the buyer would, in an action for deceit, thus have been entitled to be put into the position in which he would have been if the seller had not tendered that bill at all. On that assumption, the buyer could, in the tort action, recover back the price less the proceeds of any (reasonably concluded) resale. In other words, he could recover market loss damages against a seller who presented documents which he knew to be false, even though the goods were in conformity with the contract.

(iv) *Assessment of Market Loss Damages*

19–201 **Where and when value to be assessed.** Granted that a buyer can, where there is a defect both in the documents and in the goods,[44] recover market loss damages of the kind described in paragraphs 19–190 to 19–193 above, two further questions arise: which market is relevant for this purpose, and when? In the *Kwei Tek Chao* case Devlin J. referred throughout to the price in the market in which the goods could be disposed of at the c.i.f. destination, *i.e.* to the Hong Kong market; and this would normally be the relevant market since it would be the market in which the buyer's loss would be realised. But Devlin J. also said that there was no evidence of a market for the goods elsewhere[45]; and where there is such evidence the court might hold that the buyer should have realised his loss in that market, particularly if there is no market at the destination.

---

[39] [1988] 2 Lloyd's Rep. 21; above, para.19–198.
[40] [1988] 2 Lloyd's Rep. 21 at p.33. "Fraud" here refers to the tort of deceit: *cf. Armitage v Nurse* [1998] Ch. 241 at p.252.
[41] [1988] 2 Lloyd's Rep. 21 at p.28.
[42] The latter possibility would depend on whether, in the court's view, the relationship between buyer and seller gave rise to a duty of care in addition to the duties owed by the seller to the buyer under the contract of sale. *cf.* above, paras 18–150, 18–151.
[43] *e.g. Broome v Speak* [1903] 1 Ch. 586 at p.605, 623, affirmed *sub. nom Speak v Broome* [1904] A.C. 342; and see generally McGregor on *Damages* (17th ed.), para.41–002 (2003).
[44] Above, para.19–190 to 19–193.
[45] [1954] 2 Q.B. 459 at p.499.

On the question of the time at which the market is relevant, it is clear that, if the buyer knows of the defect in the documents at the time when they are tendered, the damages will be assessed by reference to that time. This was the position in the *Kleinjan* case.[46] In the *Kwei Tek Chao*[47] case, on the other hand, the buyers did not know of the defects in the documents when they were tendered, and the sellers' argument, that the damages should be assessed by reference to that time, was rejected by Devlin J.[48] In the *James Finlay* case[49] the time at which the market price was held to be relevant was the time at which the goods were actually resold[50] but there was in fact no difference between the market price at this time and at the time of tender of documents. In the *Kwei Tek Chao* case two further possibilities were put forward by counsel for the buyers: the time of actual delivery of the goods[51] and the time at which the buyers first became aware of their right to reject.[52] It was not necessary to decide between these possibilities because the buyers in fact knew or ought to have known of their right to reject by the time the goods arrived[53]; and because the market price did not in any event vary between the two dates suggested by counsel. But if the market declines between tender of the false documents and the buyer's discovery of his right to reject, he will in fact continue to suffer loss as a result of the falsity of the documents; and the damages should then be assessed by reference to the time at which the buyer became, or should reasonably have become, aware of the facts giving him the right to reject.

(v) *Analogy of Negligent Valuation Cases?*

Other grounds for denying recovery in respect of market loss. The reasoning of the cases discussed in paragraphs 19–189 to 19–197 must be distinguished from that of another line of cases in which lenders had suffered loss in consequence of a fall in the market value of the property on which their loans were secured and sought to recover damages in respect of such loss from a valuer who had negligently over-valued that property. In the *South Australia Asset Management* case[54] claims for such damages were rejected on the ground that the valuer was liable only for "those consequences which are attributable to that which made the act wrongful."[55] The application of this test depended on the definition or scope of the valuer's duty,[56] which was merely one to *provide information* to enable the 19–202

46 [1972] 2 Lloyd's Rep. 11; above, para.19–192.
47 [1954] 2 Q.B. 459; above, para.19–191.
48 It seems nevertheless to have been accepted by the arbitrators in *The Kastellon* [1978] 2 Lloyd's Rep. 203 (above, para.19–193); but before Donaldson J. no point appears to have been taken as to the time for assessment.
49 [1929] 1 K.B. 400; above, para.19–190.
50 *Kwei Tek Chao* case [1954] 2 Q.B. 459 at p.492.
51 *ibid.*, at p.491.
52 *ibid.*; according to [1954] 2 Lloyd's Rep. 114 at p.115 the second alternative was differently formulated as "the date when the plaintiffs lost the right of rejection."
53 Above, para.19–191, n.86.
54 *South Australia Asset Management Corp. v York Montague Ltd* [1997] A.C. 191.
55 *ibid.*, p.213.
56 *ibid.*, p.214, *per* Lord Hoffmann; *Platform Home Loans Ltd v Oyston Shipways Ltd* [2000] 2 A.C. 190 at p.208.

lenders to decide on their course of action; it was not one to *advise* as to the desirability or prudence of making the loan.[57] The principle of the case had "nothing to do with questions of causation or any limit or 'cap' imposed upon damages which would otherwise be recoverable."[58] By contrast, it was precisely with such questions of causation that the cases on damages for defective delivery under c.i.f. contracts were concerned. Thus the reason why in *Taylor v Bank of Athens*[59] the buyer recovered no more than nominal damages was that the fact of late shipment had not caused the buyer to suffer the market loss[60]; and the reason for the same result in the *Procter & Gamble*[61] case was that it was not the defect in the documents (but the buyer's ignorance of it at the crucial time) which caused the buyers to suffer the market loss.[62] In the double breach cases, on the other hand (such as the *James Finlay* case)[63] it was the defect in the documents which had caused the seller to suffer (in the sense of depriving him of a legal right to avoid) the market loss. There was not in any of these cases any question (as there had been in the *South Australia Asset Management* case)[64] as to the scope of the sellers' duties: these were, in all the defective delivery cases, to ship and appropriate conforming goods and to procure and tender conforming documents. For these reasons, it is submitted that the reasoning of the *South Australia Asset Management* case does not provide any independent explanation of, or justification for, the recoverability of market loss damages in the "double breach" cases,[65] or raise any questions about the irrecoverability of such damages in the single breach cases.[66] In the former group of cases, moreover, the seller was in breach of a contractual *undertaking* that the documents were in conformity with the contract, while a valuer gives no such undertaking as to the value of the subject-matter: he undertakes only to make the valuation with reasonable care.

(d) *Defective Delivery: Consumer Sales*

19–203 **Buyer dealing as consumer.** In the rare cases in which a c.i.f. buyer deals as consumer,[67] Part 5A of the Sale of Goods Act 1979 confers on the buyer certain "additional rights" where "the goods do not conform to the

[57] For the difficulty of distinguishing between a duty to provide information and one to advise, see *Aneco Reinsurance Underwriting Ltd v Johnson & Higgins Ltd*, [2001] UKHL 51, [2001] 2 All E.R. (Comm.) 929; in that case a broker's statement as to the availability of reinsurance cover was held, by implication, to contain advice to his client with regard to entering into a reinsurance treaty.
[58] *Nykredit Bank v Edward Erdman Group* [1997] 1 W.L.R. 1627 at p.1638, *per* Lord Hoffmann; *Platform Home Loans Ltd v Oyston Shipways Ltd*, above, at pp.208, 213.
[59] (1922) 27 Com. Cas. 142; above, para.19–189.
[60] See the reliance in that case at p.147 on the words "resulting . . . from" in Sale of Goods Act 1893 (now 1979) s.53(2).
[61] [1988] 2 Lloyd's Rep. 21.
[62] *ibid.*, at p.32; above, para.19–198 at n.33.
[63] [1929] 1 K.B. 400; above, para.19–190, 19–197.
[64] Above, n.54.
[65] Above, paras 19–190 to 19–197.
[66] Above, paras 19–189 and 19–198.
[67] See above, para.18–259.

contract of sale at the time of delivery."[68] The first, and perhaps the most important, point to be made about these rights is that there is nothing in Part 5A to compel the buyer to resort to them.[69] He can, if he so prefers, exercise his rights to reject in accordance with the law as it stood before the introduction of Part 5A in 2003.[70] If he chooses to do so, his rights to damages, including any right to damages for loss of the right to reject, will be governed by the rules stated in the preceding discussion of damages for defective delivery in commercial sales.[71]

If the buyer seeks to exercise the "additional rights" conferred on him by Part 5A, a number of questions which arise in relation to the applicability of that Part to c.i.f. sales have already been discussed. In the present context, the most important of these questions are whether the "additional rights" are excercisable, not only in respect of non-conformity of "the goods" themselves, but also in respect of non-conformity of the documents[72]; and what, in the context of a c.i.f. sale, constitutes "the time of delivery."[73] If an affirmative answer were to be given to the first of these questions, and if the answer to the second were that the relevant time were, or could be, that of shipment, then a number of questions, analogous to those discussed in paragraphs 19–187 to 19–201 above could arise in the context of the "additional rights" conferred on the buyer by Part 5A.

The two most significant of these rights in the present context are the buyer's rights under section 48C to require the seller "to reduce the price by an appropriate amount"[74] and his right "to rescind the contract with regard to [the non-conforming] goods."[75] With regard to the first of these rights, we have noted above that section 48C does not specify any formula for calculating the price reduction,[76] nor does it refer to any time by reference to which the "appropriate amount" is to be assessed; and if the reduction of the price is to be made in the proportion which the actual value of the goods bears to that which they would have had, if they had been in conformity with the contract,[77] then the question would arise, by reference to what time those values were to be assessed. The most plausible time is that of "delivery" but that statement is not a particularly helpful one in the case of a c.i.f. contract, in which there are "three stages of delivery".[78] If "delivery" here referred to the third stage,[79] *i.e.* to that of "complete delivery" then an element of market loss might be relevant to the

---

[68] Sales of Goods Act 1979, s.48A(1)(b).

[69] See the word "may" in ss.48B(1), 48C(1).

[70] By Sale and Supply of Goods to Consumers Regulations 2002, SI 2002/3045.

[71] An apparent exception to the proposition in the text is that Sale of Goods Act 1979 s.15A does not, by its terms, apply where the buyer deals as consumer; but it has been submitted in paras 18–284 and 19–173 above that the section is unlikely to apply to c.i.f. contracts even where the buyer does not so deal.

[72] See above, para.19–173.

[73] See above, para.18–261.

[74] s.48C(1)(a).

[75] s.48C(1)(b).

[76] Above, para.19–187 n.50.

[77] *ibid.*, discussing the remedy of price reduction under Art. 50 of the Vienna Convention on Contracts for the International Sale of Goods, (above, para.1–024).

[78] Above, para.19–072.

[79] See above, para.18–261.

assessment of the "appropriate amount". But that amount would not be the same as the "market loss" damages awarded in the "double breach" situations discussed above[80] since it would be assessed, not in respect of the buyer's loss of his right to reject, but simply in proportion to the reduction of the value of the goods. The buyer would not be able to escape entirely from the consequences of a bad bargain (or of one that had become bad for him): he would still have to pay a proportion of the agreed price. If that were, in financial terms, less favourable to him than "market loss" damages as discussed above, then it would be open to him to pursue the latter remedy.

The second of the consumer buyer's rights under section 48C, *i.e.* his right "to rescind the contract",[81] is in some respect more restricted than the right which he has, apart from Part 5A, to reject goods (typically for breach of condition). The right to rescind under section 48C arises only where the buyer "must not" require repair or replacement of the non-conforming goods because that remedy is either "impossible" or because that remedy is "disproportionate" to another which is available to him under Part 5A[82]; or where, after the buyer has required the seller to repair or replace the goods, the seller has failed to do so within a reasonable time.[83] It is also, in effect, subject to the discretion of the court to award another remedy available to him under that Part.[84] On the other hand, the right to "rescind" is wider than the right to reject (apart from Part 5A) in that there is nothing in Part 5A which corresponds to the loss of the right to reject (apart from that Part) by acceptance. The effect of these differences on the question of damages for defective delivery, and in particular on the question when "market loss" damages are recoverable, can be considered by referring back to the situations discussed above[85] in which the goods are not of the contract description, *e.g.* because they have been shipped outside the contractual shipment period or on a ship other than that specified in the contract or in the notice of appropriation. In such cases, there can be no question of "repairing" those goods (*i.e.* of bringing them into conformity with the contract[86]) or of replacing them, once the contractual shipment period has expired, as it normally will have done by the time of discovery of the breach. Repair or replacement being therefore impossible, the buyer will be able to rescind the contract, at least subject to the discretion of the court, described above.[87] He will then be entitled to the return of the price[88] and so be able to throw the market loss back on the seller without having to rely on the reasoning of the cases in which damages in respect of such loss is (or is not) recoverable under section 53 of the 1979 Act. If the buyer

---

[80] See above, paras 19–190 to 19–197.
[81] s.48C(1)(b).
[82] ss.48B(3), 48C(2)(a).
[83] ss.48B(2)(a), 48C(2)(b).
[84] s.48E.
[85] Above, paras 19–187 *et seq*.
[86] See the definition of "repair" in s.61(1).
[87] At n.84.
[88] Subject only to an allowance in respect of "the use he has had of the goods since they were delivered to him": s.48C(3); this point is unlikely to be significant in situations of the kind here under discussion.

nevertheless claims such damages under section 53, one possible argument against upholding the claim is that the buyer could have avoided the market loss by rescinding under Part 5A and that his failure to do so amounted to a failure to mitigate his loss. It is, however, submitted that this argument is less than compelling since the discretion of the court to refuse to allow rescission under Part 5A makes the availability of this remedy uncertain. The buyer's failure to seek rescission would therefore not amount to such failure to take reasonable steps to reduce his loss as is required to bring the mitigating rules into operation.

(d) *Specific Performance and Injunction*

Specific performance where goods specific or ascertained. Under section 52 of the Sale of Goods Act 1979 the court has a discretion to order specific performance "In any action for breach of contract to deliver specific or ascertained goods."[89] Such an order is analogous to a seller's action for the price[90] in that it gives the buyer exactly what he bargained for. But it is also analogous to the seller's rights against the goods[91] in that the order for specific performance will, if granted, entitle the buyer to the actual goods themselves. If the buyer has paid in advance and the seller has become insolvent, the effect of an order of specific performance will thus be to enable the buyer to take the goods out of the insolvent seller's estate in priority to other creditors, even though at the time of the seller's insolvency the property in the goods had not passed to the buyer. It is this aspect of 19–204

[89] The Vienna Convention on Contracts for the International Sale of Goods (above, para.1–024) gives the buyer a general right to "require performance by the seller of his obligations" (Art. 46(1)); a right to require "delivery of substitute goods" if the non-conformity of the goods delivered amounts to a "fundamental breach" (as defined in Art. 25, above, para.18–267, n.38) and if the buyer has made a formal request for a substitute (Art. 46(2)); and a right to require the seller to repair non-conforming goods, unless repair is in all the circumstances unreasonable (Art. 46(3)). The right to require performance does not apply where the buyer has resorted to an "inconsistent" remedy, *i.e.* where he has avoided the contract. The Convention does not in terms exclude the right to require performance on the ground that the buyer could, acting reasonably, have made a substitute contract, though this possibility might exclude the remedy on the ground that the Convention was to be interpreted so as to "promote . . . the observance of good faith in international trade" (Art. 7). The apparently wide availability of specific relief is, however, significantly restricted by Art. 28, which provides that, even where a party is entitled to "require performance", a court is "not bound" to order "specific performance" unless that remedy would be available "under its own law in respect of similar contracts not governed by the Convention." Thus in an action brought in England the court would not be *bound* to order specific performance in a case in which the remedy would not be available under English domestic law, but it would be *entitled* to do so where the contract was governed by the Convention. In this sense, the Convention would extend the powers of English courts to order specific enforcement of contracts for the international sale of goods.

[90] Below, paras 19–211 to 19–215.

[91] Below, para.19–220.

the matter which gives rise to particular problems in relation to c.i.f. contracts.[92]

In *Re Wait*[93] a c.i.f. buyer of 500 tons out of a bulk cargo of 1,000 tons of wheat to be shipped on the *Challenger* had paid (although he was not bound to do so) against an invoice. The seller was thus left in possession of the bill of lading which he hypothecated and delivered to his bank; he then became bankrupt before the 500 tons had been separated from the bulk, so that (as the law then stood) no property in them could have passed to the buyer. The buyer claimed specific performance: in substance this was a claim to look to 500 tons of the wheat as security for his advance payment. A majority of the Court of Appeal rejected the claim on the ground that the goods formed at all relevant times an undifferentiated part of a larger bulk and that they were therefore not "specific or ascertained" within section 52. Atkin L.J. stressed[94] that recognition of the equitable claim put forward by the buyer in *Re Wait* would seriously inconvenience banks taking bills of lading for bulk shipments as security for advances; for it could deprive such a bank of the security normally afforded by shipping documents dealt with in the ordinary course of business. Under the 1995 reforms to the Sale of Goods Act 1979, the buyer in a case like *Re Wait* could now acquire an undivided half share in the cargo and become owner of it in common with the seller[95]; and where he had acquired such ownership he would no longer need to seek specific performance in order to establish a proprietary interest in the 500 tons for which he had paid, so as to gain priority over unsecured creditors of the seller. But the 1995 reforms have not solved the problem of priorities which could on similar facts arise between the buyer of the 500 tons and a creditor of the seller who held the 500 tons or the whole bulk (or documents representing the goods) as security for the seller's indebtedness to him, as the bank did in *Re Wait*. The problem of priorities between such competing interests is discussed (in the context of overseas sales) in paragraph 18–299; the only further point to be made here is that where, under the rules there discussed, the secured creditor has priority over the buyer, then that priority cannot be displaced by an order of specific performance. Even though the buyer can now acquire property in a specified quantity of goods which form an undifferentiated part of an identified bulk, such goods remain unascertained,[96] so that the case would not be one under which the court had a discretion under section 52 to order specific performance.

[92] The Vienna Convention on Contracts for the International Sale of Goods (above, para.1–024) is not itself "concerned with . . . the effect which the contract may have on the property in the goods sold" (Art. 4(b)). But if an English court were to order specific performance under the wide empowering provisions of the Convention described in n.89, above, proprietary consequences could follow, not indeed from the *contract*, but from the *order of the court*.

[93] [1927] 1 Ch. 606 (above, para.18–299).

[94] At p.640. It is true that Lord Hanworth M.R. also said at p.617 that the seller's bankruptcy was legally irrelevant. *Cf.* also the view that specific enforceability does not necessarily give the buyer an equitable interest in the goods: *Re Stapylton Fletcher Ltd* [1994] 1 W.L.R. 1181 at p.1203.

[95] Sale of Goods Act 1979, s.20A, discussed in relation to overseas sales in paras 18–293, *et seq*.

[96] s.20A(1), above, applies "to a contract for the sale of a specified quantity of *unascertained* goods" where the conditions specified in the subsection are satisfied.

The reasoning in *Re Wait* is based on the fact that the goods were not "specific or ascertained". If the buyer were to buy *the whole* cargo of 1,000 tons to be shipped on a named ship, the goods would be "ascertained" once they were shipped; and if he were to buy *half* the cargo shipped on a named ship, or *50 per cent* of it, the goods would now be "specific".[97] In such cases the court would therefore have a discretion to order specific performance; and, in considering whether that discretion should be exercised, two possibilities which may arise in this type of case must be considered. First, the property may remain in the seller by virtue of his retention of the bill of lading.[98] In that case the policy considerations stated by Atkin L.J. apply as much as in *Re Wait* itself; so that the court, though having a discretion to order specific performance should, it is submitted, refuse to exercise it. The second (and more likely) possibility is that property would pass to the buyer by virtue of his payment, even though the documents against which he paid did not include a bill of lading.[99] Such passing of property would prima facie make it tortious for the seller to deal with the goods in a manner that was inconsistent with the buyer's ownership,[1] so that the seller could be restrained by injunction from delivering the goods to a third party,[2] and he could be ordered to deliver them to the buyer.[3] The passing of property would also give the buyer priority over unsecured creditors. But a bank to which a bill of lading had been pledged would still be protected: by the general rule that *nemo dat quod non habet* if the pledge had been made before the property had passed to the buyer; and by section 24 of the Sale of Goods Act 1979 if the pledge had been made thereafter, so long as the bank had acted in good faith and without notice of the sale. It is submitted that the court would not allow such protection to be impaired by ordering specific performance in favour of the buyer. The court could in its discretion either refuse to make such an order, or make it subject to the satisfaction of the claim of the pledgee.

Hypothecation of bills of lading. It has been noted previously[4] that an agreement to transfer bills of lading as security (or an hypothecation of them) may be specifically enforceable[5] but this rule does not seem ever to have been applied to a simple undertaking to deliver bills of lading under a contract of sale. 19–205

---

97 Sale of Goods Act 1979, s.61(1), definition of "specific goods"; such a transaction appears to be rare in overseas sales: *cf.* above, para.18–290.
98 Above, para.19–102.
99 Above, para.19–103.
1 The "deemed consent" provisions of Sale of Goods Act 1979, s.20B do not apply where undifferentiated parts of an identified bulk are specified as fractions or percentages; they apply only where the sale is of specified quantities out of such a bulk: see the reference to s.20A in s.20B(1). Section 20B is discussed in relation to overseas sales in para.18–299, above.
2 *Redler Grain Silos Ltd v BICC Ltd* [1982] 1 Lloyd's Rep. 435; it is assumed that (as in that case) the third party has no title to or interest in the goods superior to that of the buyer.
3 This is a matter for the discretion of the court under s.3(2) of the Torts (Interference with Goods) Act 1977.
4 Above, para.18–234 and see above, para.18–238.
5 *Lutscher v Comptoir d'Escompte de Paris* (1876) 1 Q.B.D. 709.

19–206 **Defective delivery of goods supplied to consumers.** The concept of specific performance in section 52 is that of a remedy for *non-delivery* of goods; but there is the further possibility that specific relief may be sought in respect of delivery which is defective in the sense that the goods delivered are not in conformity with the contract. This possibility is recognised by Part 5A of the Sale of Goods Act 1979, under which a buyer who deals as consumer may, "if the goods do not conform to the contract at the time of delivery",[6] require the seller to repair or replace them.[7] Specific performance is made available to enforce the seller's duty to comply with such a requirement,[8] though the limits imposed by the Act on the buyer's right to require repair or replacement make the availability of specific relief in cases of this kind consistent with a number of general rules restricting the availability of specific relief. Thus repair or replacement cannot be ordered if it is "impossible"[9]; one of those remedies cannot be ordered against the seller if it is "disproportionate" to the other,[10] and specific performance of the seller's duty to repair or replace cannot be ordered if another of the Part 5A remedies (*e.g.* price reduction[11]) is "appropriate",[12] *i.e.* more so than specific enforcement of the seller's duty to repair or replace. On the other hand, the rationale of ordering the seller to repair or replace is precisely that monetary compensation will often be an inadequate remedy to a consumer: *e.g.* where he has bought a complex appliance which malfunctions. It will be seen from this brief account that the policy considerations underlying the grant of, or restrictions on, specific relief in cases of defective delivery are wholly different from those that apply in cases of non-delivery, such as *Re Wait*.[13] They have nothing to do with the desire of a buyer who has paid for the defective goods to escape from the loss that he would suffer in the event of the seller's insolvency by looking to the goods as security for his claim. Indeed, in the normal case the buyer who claims repair or replacement will have acquired the property in the goods, so that his position in this respect cannot be improved by specifically ordering the seller to repair or replace non-conforming goods.

There are, however, a number of special considerations which may affect the availability or the exercise of the discretion to order specific performance of the seller's obligation to repair or replace non-confirming goods in the rare, but not unimaginable, situation in which the sale to the consumer is on c.i.f. terms.[14] The discretion exists[15] (like the consumer's

---

[6] Sale of Goods Act 1979, s.48A(1)(b).
[7] *ibid.*, ss.48A(2), 48B.
[8] *ibid.*, s.48E(2).
[9] *ibid.*, s.48B(3)(a); *cf.* the general principle that specific performance will not be ordered of an obligation which it is impossible to perform.
[10] *ibid.*, s.48B(3)(b).
[11] *ibid.*, s.48A(2)(b)(i), 48C(1)(a).
[12] *ibid.*, s.48E(3) and (4); *cf.* the general principle that specific performance will not be ordered where damages are an "adequate" remedy.
[13] Above, para.19–204.
[14] See above, para.18–259.
[15] Sale of Goods Act 1979, s.48E(2) refers to obligations imposed on the seller "by virtue of section 48B above" and that section deals only with repair or replacement of the goods.

right to require repair or replacement itself) only where the goods are not in conformity with the contract "at the time of delivery"[16] and, as already noted,[17] it is not clear to which of the three "stages of delivery"[18] in a c.i.f. contract the expression "time of delivery" refers. In particular, it is not clear whether the general rule that a c.i.f. seller's duty with respect to the quality of the goods here refers (in accordance with the general rule applicable to c.i.f. contracts) to the time of shipment,[19] or whether it refers to the time of "complete delivery"[20] to the consumer. If the latter view were adopted, it could have bearing on the availability of specific enforcement, particularly where this was sought of the seller's obligation to repair. The defect giving rise to this obligation is unlikely to become apparent before the goods have actually got into the buyer's hands; and by the time this has happened the goods may be far from the seller's place of business and in a country in which he has no facilities for effecting repair. In such a case, the court may be persuaded that the monetary remedy of price reduction, enabling the buyer in his own country to secure the necessary repair, is more appropriate[21] than specific enforcement of the seller's duty to repair. Even if no facilities for repair are available to the buyer in his own country, the court may conclude that undue hardship to the seller would result from compelling him to effect repair there and that "recission"[22] under Part 5A would be the more "appropriate" remedy.

9. REMEDIES OF THE SELLER

(a) *Rescission*

For buyer's failure to comply with stipulations as to payment. The seller's right to rescind is the counterpart of the buyer's right to reject.[23] In 19–207
c.i.f. contracts the seller's right to rescind most commonly arises where the buyer fails to comply with the stipulations of the contract with regard to the method or time of payment.[24] Thus the seller can rescind if the buyer

[16] Sale of Goods Act 1979, s.48A(1)(b).
[17] Above, para.18–261.
[18] Above, para.19–072.
[19] Above, para.19–111.
[20] Above, para.19–072.
[21] Within Sale of Goods Act 1979, s.48E(3) and (4).
[22] *ibid.*, s.48C(1)(b) and (2).
[23] It can also be compared (though the analogy is in some ways more remote) with the consumer's right to "rescind" under Sale of Goods Act 1979, ss.48A(2)(b)(ii) and 48C.
[24] Art. 53 of the Vienna Convention on Contracts for the International Sale of Goods (above, para.1–024) obliges the buyer "to pay the price for the goods and take delivery . . ." The seller is entitled to declare the contract avoided in two sets of circumstances. First, he can do so under Art. 64(1)(a) if failure by the buyer to perform *any* of his obligations amounts to a "fundamental breach" (as defined in Art. 25: see above, para.18–267, n.38). Secondly, he can do so under Art. 64(1)(b) (even though the breach is not "fundamental") if the buyer has failed to perform his obligations to pay the price or to take delivery as required by the contract and has

wrongfully refuses to pay on tender of documents[25] or if the buyer fails to comply with a requirement of the contract to provide a bank guarantee for payment,[26] or a confirmed credit[27] or if the buyer provides an unconfirmed credit when the contract calls for a confirmed credit.[28] A purely trivial failure to comply with a stipulation as to the method of payment will not, of itself, justify rescission by the seller.[29] But it is open to the parties to treat even a quite unimportant stipulation of this kind as a condition; and where the terms of the contract or the other circumstances of the case indicate that they have done so,[30] failure to comply with the stipulation will entitle the seller to rescind.

Under section 10(1) of the Sale of Goods Act 1979, stipulations as to the time of payment are not of the essence of the contract "unless a different intention appears from the terms of the contract." Hence mere delay in payment prima facie does not justify rescission by the seller. But in *Ryan v Ridley & Co.*[31] a cargo of codfish was sold c.i.f. Bari "payment to be made by cash in London in exchange for bill of lading and policy of insurance." A week after tender of these documents the buyer had failed to pay; and it was held that the seller was justified in rescinding as the buyer had not paid within reasonable time of tender of documents. One reason for the decision was that "the nature of the cargo demanded promptitude".[32] But Kennedy J. also said that the term broken by the buyer was "not merely one with

---

then also *either* failed to perform one (or both) of these obligations within an additional reasonable time fixed by the seller requiring the buyer to perform these obligations (under Art. 63(1)) *or* declared that he would not do so. In relation to a c.i.f. contract, the buyer's "obligation . . . to take delivery of the goods" presumably refers to the stage at which the goods are unloaded from the ship: *cf.* Art. 60(b) ("taking over the goods"). Normally a c.i.f. buyer owes no duty to the seller with respect to this stage, but such a duty may exceptionally be imposed on the buyer: see *Etablissements Soules et Cie. v Intertradex SA* [1991] 1 Lloyd's Rep. 379, above, para.19–088. Such provisions are, however, likely to be interpreted as providing the *only* remedy for a breach consisting merely of delay in unloading, and thus as excluding any right of avoidance on the part of the seller. The circumstances in which a seller may lose his rights of avoidance under the Convention are specified in Art. 64(2); they resemble (*mutatis mutandis*) those in which the buyer loses his correponding rights under Art. 49(2), as to which see above, para.19–150, n.47.

[25] *Gill & Duffus SA v Berger & Co. Inc.* [1984] A.C. 382; above, para.19–163.

[26] *Continental Contractors Ltd v Medway Oil and Storage Co.* (1925) 23 Ll.L.R. 55 at p.124 (reversed on other grounds 25 Ll.L.R. 288); *SCCMO (London) Ltd v Soc. Générale de Compensation* [1956] 1 Lloyd's Rep. 290 (neither of these cases concerned c.i.f. contracts, but the same principles would apply to such contracts).

[27] *Trans Trust SPRL v Danubian Trading Co.* [1952] 2 Q.B. 297; *cf. State Trading Corp. of India v M. Golodetz Ltd* [1989] 2 Lloyd's Rep. 277 (where this point was conceded).

[28] *Panoutsos v Raymond Hadley Corp. of NY* [1917] 2 K.B. 473; *Soproma SpA v Marine and Animal By-Products Corp.* [1966] 1 Lloyd's Rep. 367 (in these cases the sellers were precluded from rescinding by variation, waiver or estoppel).

[29] *Bunge Corp. v Vegetable Vitamin Foods (Private) Ltd* [1985] 1 Lloyd's Rep. 613 at p.616 (where the discrepancies were found in the arbitration proceedings to be "*de minimis*").

[30] *Michael J Warde v Feedex International Inc.* [1985] 2 Lloyd's Rep. 289 (buyer's duty to nominate bank by "at latest . . . 2nd March 1982" held to be a condition, though it gave seller no rights against the bank).

[31] (1902) 8 Com.Cas. 105.

[32] *ibid.*, at p.107.

regard to the time of payment. No property passed . . . till the condition . . . was performed—namely, until the defendants received the bill of lading and policy of insurance."[33] This suggests that section 10(1) will hardly ever apply to a stipulation for payment by cash against documents in a c.i.f. contract. It should, however, be remembered that prima facie the buyer's duty is to pay within a reasonable time of tender[34]: thus his mere failure to pay at the moment of tender will not justify rescission by the seller. Even where the buyer's failure to pay in time does not of itself entitle the seller to rescind, it normally does entitle him to give notice, under section 48(3) of the Act, of his intention to resell on the buyer's failure to pay within a reasonable time; and if the seller then resells, the original contract of sale is rescinded.[35] The position is the same if the seller resells under an express provision in the original contract entitling him to do so "in case the buyer should make default". This is laid down by section 48(4) which is not confined to default by non-payment. Rescission of the contract does not prevent the seller from claiming damages for the buyer's breach.[36]

For other breaches. The seller may also be entitled to rescind for other breaches: for example[37] where a buyer by instalments wrongfully refuses to accept and pay for goods in circumstances amounting to a repudiation by him of the whole contract. The principles which determine the effects of such refusal are discussed in Chapter 8[38]; they apply to c.i.f. contracts in the ordinary way. Thus the mere fact that a c.i.f. buyer has taken a position that is inconsistent with the contract will not of itself amount to a repudiation of the contract by him; for "a mere honest misapprehension, especially if open to correction, will not justify a charge of repudiation."[39] This principle was applied where a c.i.f. contract specified one period for giving a notice of appropriation if the seller was the original shipper of the goods and another (longer) period if he was a subsequent seller. The buyer declared the seller in default at the end of the first period, and it was held that, although this declaration was unjustified, it did not amount to a repudiation, and that, accordingly, the seller was not entitled to rescind.[40] 19–208

Rescission for wrong reason. The principle that a person who refuses to perform a contract on a ground that does not justify the refusal or on no ground at all, may nevertheless later rely on another ground which existed 19–209

---

33 *ibid.*

34 Above, para.19–085.

35 *R v Ward Ltd v Bignall* [1967] 1 Q.B. 534; above, para.15–126. The procedure set out in s.48(3) resembles that (described in n.24, above) of Vienna Convention on Contracts for the International Sale of Goods (above, para.1–024), Art. 64(1)(b).

36 Sale of Goods Act 1979, s.48(4) (above, para.15–119); the seller's right to damages is likewise preserved at common law in the other cases discussed in para.19–207. See *R v Ward Ltd v Bignall* [1967] 1 Q.B. 534; and the statements of general principle by Lord Wilberforce in *Johnson v Agnew* [1980] A.C. 367 at pp.394–398; 492–493 and by Lord Diplock in *Photo Production Ltd v Securicor Transport Ltd* [1980] A.C. 827 at pp.848–850.

37 For a further example, see above, para.19–089. *Cf.* Vienna Convention on Contracts for the International Sale of Goods (above, para.1–024), Art. 64(1)(a), above, para.19–207, n.24.

38 Above, paras 8–064 *et seq.*

39 *Alfred C Toepfer v Peter Cremer* [1975] 2 Lloyd's Rep. 118 at p.125.

40 *Bunge GmbH v CC v Landbouwbelang GA* [1980] 1 Lloyd's Rep. 458.

at the time of refusal and does justify the refusal has been discussed earlier in this chapter in relation to a c.i.f. buyer's right to reject on account of breaches of the contract of sale by the seller.[41] The same principle applies in relation to the exercise by the seller of the right to rescind an account of a repudiatory breach by the buyer,[42] and it is, in this context, subject *(mutantis mutandis)* to the same qualifications as those which apply in the case of breach by the seller. Thus it does not apply where the buyer's breach could, had the true ground for recission been stated at the time of rescission, have been cured in time; and it may be excluded by waiver or estoppel,[43] or analogous doctrines.[44]

19–210 **Ground of rescission must exist at the time of rescission.** In discussing the remedies of the buyer, we saw that rejection was justified only if the ground of rejection existed at the time of rejection[45]; and the same principle applies to rescission by the seller. Thus if a c.i.f. seller repudiates the contract on an inadequate ground, and the buyer accepts that repudiation, then the seller cannot justify the repudiation on the ground of the buyer's later failure to provide a letter of credit within the time allowed by the contract of sale[46]; for the buyer's acceptance of the repudiation will have liberated him from any duty of further performance.[47] This reasoning does not apply where the buyer does *not* accept the seller's repudiation, since in that case the obligations of both parties remain in force.[48] It follows that the seller in such a case will generally be entitled to rescind for the buyer's repudiatory breach committed after the seller's own repudiation, and to claim damages even if the buyer's subsequent breach is not repudiatory. This general rule is, however, subject to the significant qualification that it does not apply where the buyer's failure to perform was induced by the seller's own repudiation.[49]

(b) *Action for the Price*

19–211 **Where property has passed.** Under section 49(1) of the Sale of Goods Act 1979, an action for the price may be maintained "where . . . the property in the goods has passed to the buyer and he wrongfully neglects or refuses to pay for the goods according to the terms of the contract." This provision

[41] Above, para.19–159 *et seq*.
[42] *Stocznia Gdanska SA v Latvian Shipping Co. (No.3)* [2003] EWCA Civ. 889, [2002] 2 All E.R. (Comm.) 768 at [32]; *South Caribbean Trading v Trafigura BV* [2004] EWHC 2676, [2005] 1 Lloyd's Rep. 128 at [133].
[43] *South Caribbean* case, above n.42, at [133].
[44] See above, para.19–160.
[45] Above, para.19–161.
[46] *Bunge Corp. v Vegetable Vitamin Foods* (*Private*) *Ltd* [1985] 1 Lloyd's Rep. 613 at pp.618–620; the actual decision in that case was that the buyer had *not* committed any such breach.
[47] *cf.* the explanation of *Braithwaite v Foreign Hardwood Co.* [1905] 2 K.B. 543 given in *Fercometal SARL v Mediterranean Shipping Co. SA* (*The Simona*) [1989] A.C. 788, above, para.19–170.
[48] *cf. The Simona*, above, n.47.
[49] *cf.* above para.19–161.

gives rise to no special difficulty in relation to c.i.f. contracts. It would apply where the shipping documents had been transferred to the buyer so as to pass the property in the goods to him but actual payment had not been made. This would be the position where a documentary bill (of exchange)[50] had been accepted and not paid. In such a case there would be a wrongful neglect or refusal to pay, as acceptance of the bill is conditional payment only.[51] The question whether the buyer's neglect or refusal is wrongful depends on whether his *duty* to pay the price has arisen[52]; this question is quite separate from the question whether the *action* for the price can be maintained.[53]

Where property has not passed. Under section 49(2) of the Sale of Goods Act 1979, an action for the price may be maintained, even though the property in the goods has not passed and the goods have not been appropriated to the contract, "where . . . the price is payable on a day certain irrespective of delivery, and the buyer wrongfully neglects or refuses to pay such price." This subsection was probably intended to apply only to cases in which a date for payment was either specifically mentioned in the contract of sale or ascertainable at the time of the contract. There is, however, some authority for the view that the action for the price also lies when the price is, under the terms of the contract, payable on the occurrence of an event of uncertain date, *e.g.* when the keel of a boat which is the subject-matter of the sale is laid.[54] In the case of c.i.f. contracts, the price is often made payable on such an event, *viz*. on tender of documents; and there is some conflict of opinion on the question whether the seller can maintain an action for the price if the contract contains such a provision and the buyer wrongfully refuses to pay on tender of documents. 19–212

In *Polenghi v Dried Milk Co. Ltd.*[55] 500 tons of dried milk were sold by sample, c.i.f. London, payment to be made "in cash in London on arrival of the powders against shipping or railway documents." On arrival of the first instalment of two tons, the buyers took the position that they would not pay against documents unless they could first examine the bulk to see whether it corresponded with the sample. This refusal to pay was wrongful,[56] and it 19–213

---

[50] Above, para.18–221.
[51] Above, para.9–030. The seller may prefer to sue on the bill of exchange for the reasons stated in para.22–062, below.
[52] Above, paras 19–075 *et seq*.
[53] *cf. M Golodetz & Co. Inc. v Czarnikow Rionda Co. Inc.* (*The Galatia*) [1980] 1 W.L.R. 495 at p.515 (affirmed without reference to this point *ibid.*, at pp.517 *et seq*.). The two issues of *duty* to pay the price and availability of the *action* for the price appear, with respect, to be conflated in the argument reported in *Huyton SA v Peter Cremer GmbH* [1999] 1 Lloyd's Rep. 620 at p.630 (f.o.b. contract).
[54] *Workman Clark & Co. Ltd v Lloyd Brasileno* [1908] 1 K.B. 968. There is in fact some doubt as to whether this case is any authority on the interpretation of s.49(2). In the *Law Reports* only Lord Alverstone C.J. refers to s.49(2); Kennedy and Farwell L.J.J. refer simply to s.49. In the other reports these two Lords Justices also refer to s.49(2): 77 L.J.K.B. 953 at pp.959, 960; 99 L.T. 477 at pp.481, 482; 11 Asp.M.L.C. 126 at 129, 130. Either these other reports are inaccurate or the Lords Justices later deleted their reference to subs. (2). See also above, paras 16–026, 16–027.
[55] (1904) 10 Com.Cas. 42.
[56] Above, para.19–078.

was held that the sellers were entitled to a declaration that the buyers were bound under the contract to pay against documents. This form of relief was not, of course, an action for the price: it was simply a declaration that the duty to pay the price would arise from time to time as documents were tendered; and it was therefore unaffected by section 49. But the sellers also recovered judgment for the payment of £105 18s. 0d. due on tender of the documents relating to the two tons. This seems to be a judgment for the price, and it is hard to reconcile this part of the decision with the requirements of section 49(2).

19–214 *Polenghi's* case was not cited in *Stein Forbes & Co. v County Tailoring Co.*[57] where sheepskins were sold c.i.f. London or Liverpool, payment "net cash against documents on arrival of steamer." The goods were shipped in three shipments, and the buyer wrongfully refused to pay against the documents relating to the third shipment. Atkin J.[58] held that the seller was entitled to damages but that he could not maintain an action for the price. Property had not passed, nor was the price payable "on a day certain irrespective of delivery" within section 49(2). "On the contrary, it is payable expressly against delivery,"[59] that is, against delivery of the documents. In a later case a claim for damages by a c.i.f. seller against a buyer who had wrongfully rejected documents was said to be "the only possible claim" as the seller could not maintain an action for the price,[60] and the same view is supported by dicta in other cases not concerned with c.i.f. contracts.[61] The rule applies even though the contract merely provides for payment against documents and does not go on to stipulate (as in the *Stein Forbes* case) "on arrival of steamer" or of the goods. Thus in *Muller, MacLean & Co. v Anderson*[62] padlocks were sold c. & f. Bombay, to be paid for by cash against documents. The goods were duly shipped but the buyer refused to pay against documents on grounds which were untenable. It was held that, as the price was not payable "on a day certain irrespective of delivery", the seller could not maintain an action for the price, but was entitled only to damages. In accordance with these cases, it has been said that section 49(2) makes the action for the price available only where the price is payable "at a time specified in the contract not depending on a future or contingent event"[63]; and the tender of documents against which payment is to be made is such an event.

19–215 **Consequences of limits on action for the price.** The question whether the seller is entitled to recover the price, or only to recover damages, is of relatively small importance where the contract provides for payment by

[57] (1916) 115 L.T. 215.

[58] Atkin J. had, as counsel for the successful sellers in *Workman Clark & Co. v Lloyd Brasileno* [1908] 1 K.B. 968, above, n.54, relied on s.49(2): see p.973 of the report.

[59] (1916) 115 L.T. 215 at p.216.

[60] *AA Nortier & Co. v Wm. MacLean, Sons & Co.* (1921) 9 Ll.L.R. 192 at p.194.

[61] *Colley v Overseas Exporters* [1921] 3 K.B. 302 at pp.310, 311; *Muller, MacLean & Co. v Leslie Anderson* (1921) 8 Ll.L.R. 328 at p.330 (where "41" is a misprint for "49"); *Shell-Mex Ltd v Elton Cop Dyeing Co.* (1928) 34 Com.Cas. 39 at p.44.

[62] Above, n.61.

[63] *Shell-Mex Ltd v Elton Cop Dyeing Co.*, above, n.61, at p.44.

banker's commercial credit; for under such an arrangement a seller who complies with the requirements of the credit will generally receive the amount of the price even if the buyer wrongfully refuses to accept the goods.[64] The distinction between the two types of remedies may, however, be of practical importance in a number of situations.[65] First, it may be shown that the seller could have mitigated his loss by reselling the goods. Such proof can reduce the *damages* recoverable by the seller, but it would not affect his right to recover the full price, at any rate where he had, at the time of the buyer's repudiation, done all that he was under the contract required to do to become entitled to maintain the action for the price.[66] The effect of the rule in the *Stein Forbes*[67] case is thus to enlarge the scope of the mitigation principles,[68] by restricting the scope of the action for the

---

[64] But if the seller does not receive payment from the bank he may still be entitled to sue the buyer: see *Newman Industries Ltd v Indo-British Industries Ltd* [1956] 2 Lloyd's Rep. 219; *rvsd.* on the ground that the parties were never *ad idem*, [1957] 1 Lloyd's Rep. 211; *ED & F Man Ltd v Nigerian Sweets & Confectionery Co. Ltd* [1977] 2 Lloyd's Rep. 50 (c. & f. contract); *Saffron v Soc. Minière Cafrika* (1958) 100 C.L.R. 231 (the first and third of these cases concerned f.o.b. contracts but the same principles would apply to c.i.f. contracts). Whether the seller's remedy was an action for the price or one for damages would depend on the principles discussed in paras 19–211 to 19–214, above.

[65] See generally para.16–004, above.

[66] If he had not done this, a question whether he had a "legitimate interest" in persisting might arise under *White and Carter (Councils) Ltd v McGregor* [1962] A.C. 413 (above, para.16–022); and *cf. Attica Sea Carriers Corp. v Ferrostaal Poseidon Bulk Reederei (The Puerto Buitrago)* [1976] 1 Lloyd's Rep. 250; *Gator Shipping Corp. v Transatlantic Occidental Shipping Establishment (The Odenfeld)* [1978] 2 Lloyd's Rep. 357; *Clea Shipping Corp. v Bulk Oil International (The Alaskan Trader (No.2))* [1983] 2 Lloyd's Rep. 645, *Ocean Marine Navigation Ltd v Koch Carbon Inc (The Dynamic)* [2003] EWHC 1936 (Comm.), [2003] 2 Lloyd's Rep. 693 at [23]–[24]

[67] (1916) 115 L.T. 215 (above, para.19–214).

[68] The restrictions imposed on the availability of the action for the price by s.49 of the Sale of Goods Act 1979 have no direct counterpart in the Vienna Convention on Contracts for the International Sale of Goods (above, para.1–024). Art. 62 provides generally that the seller "may require the buyer to pay the price, take delivery or perform his other obligations . . ." From the last two words just quoted, it seems that the action for the price is regarded here as one for (specific) performance, since it is one in which the buyer claims the very performance bargained for. Art. 77 of the Convention recognises the mitigation principle, but only as a ground for reducing the injured party's damages. There are, however, three ways in which the seller's remedy by way of requiring the buyer to pay the price are, or may be, limited. First Art. 62 provides that the remedy is not available if the seller has resorted to an inconsistent remedy: this would be the position if he had avoided the contract. Secondly, since the remedy is regarded as a form of specific relief, its scope is limited by Art. 28 which provides that the court "is not bound to enter a judgment for specific performance unless it would do so under its own law in respect of similar contract of sale not governed by this Convention." Under this provision, an English court would be entitled to refuse to allow an action for the price (even though the contract was governed by the Convention) unless the case fell within s.49 of the Sale of Goods Act, though the court would not be *bound* to dismiss such an action in such circumstances. Thirdly, the remedy might be limited by reference to the general principle, stated in Art. 7(1) of the Convention, that, in interpreting the Convention, regard was to be had (*inter alia*) to "the observance of good faith in international trade." Under this provision, a seller who required payment when he could easily have resold the goods, and so have mitigated his loss, might be held not

price.[69] Again, where goods sold under a c.i.f. contract have been lost before property has passed, it is commonly said that the buyer is nevertheless bound to pay the price against documents[70]; but this is a statement merely of the buyer's *duty*: if the buyer wrongfully refuses to take up and pay against the documents, the only *remedy* available to the seller will be an action for damages.[71] Usually the measure of damages would be the contract price, that being the amount of the seller's loss. But where the seller had received the benefits of insurance effected by him in performance of his obligations under the contract the seller's loss would be less than the price,[72] and the damages would be reduced accordingly. If the seller claims the price when he is only entitled to damages, the court can nevertheless award him damages.[73]

(c) *Action for Damages*

19–216 **Damages for non-acceptance: the market rule.** Under section 50(1) of the Sale of Goods Act 1979, the seller is entitled to damages for non-acceptance "where the buyer wrongfully neglects or refuses to accept and pay for the goods."[74] By subsection (2), the measure of damages is "the estimated loss directly and naturally resulting in the ordinary course of events from the buyer's breach of contract"; and by subsection (3), where there is an available market for the goods, the measure of damages is prima facie "the difference between the contract price and the market or current price at the time or times when the goods ought to have been accepted, or (if no time was fixed for acceptance) at the time of the refusal to accept."[75] The concept of a "market" for goods sold on c.i.f. terms is here, as in the case of a seller's breach,[76] a somewhat restricted one: it has, for example,

to have acted in good faith, and his claim for the price might be rejected on this ground.

[69] In the *Stein Forbes* case (1916) 115 L.T. 215 (above, para.19–214) the seller could without undue difficulty have resold the goods (which were simply generic goods sold by description), and so have mitigated his loss. By contrast, in the *Workman Clark* case [1908] 1 K.B. 968 (above, para.19–212, n.54) it would have been considerably more difficult for the seller to resell a boat which had been partly built to the buyer's specifications. This practical point may account for the difference in the results reached in the two cases which, on the wording of Sale of Goods Act 1979, s.49, are not easy to reconcile.

[70] Above, paras 19–075, 19–080.

[71] *Plaimar Ltd v Waters Trading Co. Ltd* (1945) 72 C.L.R. 304 at p.318.

[72] *Plaimar Ltd v Waters Trading Co. Ltd*, above.

[73] *Mediterranean and Eastern Export Co. Ltd v Fortress Fabrics (Manchester) Ltd* [1948] 2 All E.R. 186.

[74] *cf.* The Vienna Convention on Contracts for the International Sale of Goods (above, para.1–024); Art. 61(1)(b) confers a general right to damages on the seller in cases of failure by the buyer to perform "any of his obligations . . ."

[75] Under the Vienna Convention on Contracts for the International Sale of Goods (above, para.1–024) the rules as to assessment of damages, whether by reference to the "current price" (Art. 76), or to a substitute transaction (Art. 75), or otherwise, where the contract has not been avoided (Art. 74), apply in the same way to a seller's as to a buyer's claim. The effect of the relevant provision is stated in para.19–175, n.91, above.

[76] Above, para.19–176.

been held that there was no "market" within subsection 50(3) for manioc or tapioca to be shipped *to specified ports*; and there would similarly be no such market for goods shipped or to be shipped *on a named ship*.[77]

In the case of a c.i.f. contract, the acceptance referred to in section 50(1) is probably, by analogy to the similar rules in cases of non-delivery,[78] the acceptance of the shipping documents, and not of the goods themselves.[79] Accordingly, the time at which the market price is relevant for the purpose of assessing damages is the time (if any) fixed for acceptance of the documents or if no such time is fixed the time of the buyer's refusal to accept and pay against documents.[80] If at that time there is a market for goods afloat at the place where the documents should have been accepted, that would prima facie be the market by reference to which damages are to be assessed.[81] But this is by no means an invariable rule and it is submitted that any other market in which it would be reasonable for the seller to dispose of the goods would be relevant if there was no market where the documents should have been accepted.[82] If there is no market for goods afloat, the market at the destination will be the relevant one,[83] since that will be that market in which the seller will normally dispose of the goods; and if at the time of the buyer's breach the goods are still afloat the time at which that market is relevant will be the time of the arrival of the goods or such reasonable time thereafter as is needed by the seller for disposing of the goods.

---

[77] *Bem Dis A Turk Ticaret S/A TR v International Agri Trade Co. (The Selda)* [1999] 1 Lloyd's Rep. 729 at p.733.

[78] Above, paras 19–177, 19–178. A buyer's groundless objection to a notice of appropriation (which is not one of the shipping documents: see above, paras 19–024, 19–058) would not amount to an actual breach by him, so that the date of such an objection would not be relevant on the analogy of the rule stated in para.19–179, above. At most such an objection could amount to an anticipatory breach, as to which see para.19–217, below.

[79] Though the buyer may be liable under s.37 for refusing to take delivery of the goods: below, para.19–219; above, para.19–088.

[80] *cf. John Martin of London Ltd v AE Taylor & Co. Ltd* [1953] 2 Lloyd's Rep. 589 (where nothing seems to have turned on the distinction between rejecting the documents and rejecting the goods).

[81] Under the Vienna Convention on Contracts for the International Sale of Goods (above, para.1–024), Art. 76(2), the relevant "current price" is that prevailing at the "place of delivery." For the difficulty of applying these words to c.i.f. contracts, see above, para.19–186, n.47.

[82] *cf. Gebruder Metalman GmbH v NBR (London) Ltd* [1984] 1 Lloyd's Rep. 614 (f.o.b. contract). Under Vienna Convention on Contracts for the International Sale of Goods (above, para.1–024), Art. 76(2), if there is no "current price" at the "place of delivery", then "the price at such other place as serves as a reasonable substitute . . ." is to be taken into account.

[83] *cf. Muller, MacLean & Co. v Leslie Anderson* (1921) 8 Ll.L.R. 328 (c. & f. contract); *Aryeh v Lawrence Kostoris & Son Ltd* [1967] 1 Lloyd's Rep. 63 at p.71; *Bem Dis A Turk Ticaret S/A TR v International Agri Trade Co. (The Selda)* [1999] 1 Lloyd's Rep. 729 at p.732, where the market rule did not apply for the reason given at n.77, above. The position might be different if at the time of the buyer's breach the goods had not yet been shipped: *cf.* below, para.20–135.

19–217 **Anticipatory breach.** Where a c.i.f. buyer commits an anticipatory breach by wrongfully repudiating the contract before payment is due,[84] the seller will be immediately entitled to damages if he accepts the repudiation. He may accept it either by expressly communicating the acceptance to the buyer, or by conduct or even by inactivity which is apparent to the buyer and which unequivocally indicates that the seller regards the contract as at an end. In one case,[85] for example, a c.i.f. seller took no steps, after the buyer's wrongful repudiation, to perform his undertaking to tender the bill of lading promptly after loading; and a finding that he had accepted the repudiation was upheld by the House of Lords. If, on the other hand, the seller does not accept the repudiation, he will not normally be entitled to damages before the end of the period fixed for the buyer's performance, since before such acceptance and within that period it would normally[86] be open to the buyer to withdraw the repudiation. Section 50(3) does not seem, any more than section 51(3), to govern the assessment of damages for anticipatory breach. The rules on this point which have been discussed in relation to a seller's anticipatory breach[87] apply *mutatis mutandis* in the present context.

19–218 **Other damages for non-acceptance.** Damages for non-acceptance may include consequential loss, so long as this is not too remote.[88] The buyer is under a duty not only to pay, but also to accept the documents; and if his refusal to perform the latter duty exposes the seller to liabilities in respect of duties owed to the carrier which, as between buyer and seller, should have been performed by the buyer, then the seller is entitled to recover any loss so occasioned as damages for non-acceptance: for example, he may be entitled to recover from the buyer damages for detention of the ship for which he becomes liable to the carrier in consequence of the buyer's breach[89]; or, if the goods are not shipped in consequence of the buyer's repudiatory breach, the seller may be entitled to recover from the buyer any charges which the seller has to pay to the prospective carrier on cancellation of the charterparty into which the seller had entered with a view to shipping the goods.[90]

19–219 **Damages for not taking delivery.** Under section 37 of the Sale of Goods Act 1979, a buyer may be made liable for any loss occasioned by his neglect or refusal to take delivery of the goods "When the seller is ready and

[84] *e.g.* by wrongfully rejecting a notice of appropriation: see above, n.78.
[85] *Vitol SA v Norelf Ltd (The Santa Clara)* [1996] A.C. 800. The case was treated in the lower courts as one of anticipatory breach but, except in quotations from the judgments of those courts, no reference to this aspect of the case was made in the House of Lords.
[86] *i.e.* subject to qualifications similar to those discussed (in cases of a seller's breach) in para.19–160, above.
[87] Above, para.19–179; *cf.* below, paras 20–116, 20–140. For the position under the Vienna Convention on Contracts for the International Sale of Goods, see above, para.19–179, n.9.
[88] Above, paras 16–043 *et seq. Cf.* Vienna Convention on Contracts for the International Sale of Goods (above, para.1–024), Art. 74.
[89] *e.g. Vitol SA v Phibro Energy AG* (*The Mathraki*) [1990] 2 Lloyd's Rep. 84.
[90] *Bem Dis A Turk Ticaret S/A TR v International Agri Trade Ltd (The Selda)* [1999] 1 Lloyd's Rep. 416.

willing to deliver the goods, and requests the buyer to take delivery." This section is hard to apply directly to c.i.f. contracts, for the buyer's refusal *to take delivery of the documents* will hardly ever cause the seller any loss,[91] though his refusal to *accept* them might do so. But the principle of section 37 might be applied by analogy to a case in which the buyer had "accepted" and paid for the documents and then failed to take delivery of the goods from the carrier or had delayed in taking such delivery. If, as a result, the seller, in his capacity as shipper of the goods, is held liable under the contract of carriage to the carrier,[92] *e.g.* for demurrage (which may exceed the price) he may need a further remedy in the nature of an action against the buyer for neglecting or refusing to take delivery.[93] It is also possible for a c.i.f. contract to contain stipulations as to the rate at which the goods are to be discharged and expressly to provide that the buyer is to pay demurrage to the seller if the buyer should fail to discharge at the stipulated rate.[94] Such a payment can be regarded as liquidated damages for neglecting to take delivery in accordance with the contract.

(d) *Rights against the Goods*

Seller's rights against the goods. The unpaid seller's rights of lien and stoppage in transit, his right of withholding delivery, and the seller's right of resale are discussed in Chapter 15.[95] In the case of a c.i.f. contract, these rights are of little importance, since the seller will usually look to the shipping documents (by means of which he reserves the right of disposal) as security for payment of the price, rather than to the actual goods themselves. If the seller has parted with the documents but has not actually been paid,[96] he can still as a last resort rely on his rights against the goods, though he runs the risk that these rights may be defeated by subsequent dealings with the documents.[97] The right of resale is available to a c.i.f. seller in the ordinary way. Although the wording of the Act gives rise to some difficulty on the point[98] it is now clear that the right is available whether or not the property in the goods has passed to the buyer.[99] In the 19–220

[91] Taking delivery of a bill of lading would be necessary to confer rights under the contract of carriage on the buyer by virtue of Carriage of Goods by Sea Act 1992, s.2(1)(a) and 5(2); but the acquisition of such rights would not exonerate the seller from liability as an original party to that contract: *ibid.*, s.3(3). Where the seller is not the original shipper but is himself a transferee of the bill, the buyer's refusal to take delivery of the bill will not of itself expose the seller to liability under the contract of carriage: *ibid*, s.3(1).

[92] See Carriage of Goods by Sea Act 1992, s.3(3).

[93] *cf.* above, paras 19–088, 19–089.

[94] See *Etablissement Soules et Cie. v Intertradex SA* [1991] 1 Lloyd's Rep. 379; above, para.19–088.

[95] *cf.* Vienna Convention on Contracts for the International Sale of Goods (above, para.1–024), Arts 71(2) and 88, for rights analogous to those of stoppage and resale.

[96] *e.g.* if he has parted with documents in exchange for a draft accepted but not yet paid as in *Schotsmans v Lancashire and Yorkshire Ry Co.* (1867) L.R. 2 Ch.App. 332 (f.o.b. contract).

[97] Sale of Goods Act 1979, s.47(2); and see *Schotsmans v Lancashire and Yorkshire Ry Co.*, above.

[98] There is no reference in s.39(2) to the right of resale: see above, para.15–010.

[99] Above, para.15–013.

case of a c.i.f. sale, the passing of property after shipment is generally delayed because the seller has reserved the "right of disposal" over the goods. But it seems that this reservation does not of itself give a right of resale, in the sense of entitling the seller to resell without breach of contract[1]; though if before the property has passed he rescinds the contract on account of the buyer's breach he may be entitled to resell as owner at common law.[2] Subject to this possibility, the c.i.f. seller's right of resale is, like any other seller's, exercisable only "as limited by"[3] the Act.

[1] Above, para.15–004.
[2] Above, para.15–007.
[3] s.39(1)(c).

CHAPTER 20

F.O.B. CONTRACTS

	PARA.
1. Definition and classification	20–001
2. Duties of the seller	20–011
(a) Delivery free on board	20–012
(b) Shipping documents	20–020
(c) Shipping space	20–028
(d) Time of shipment	20–029
(e) Conformity of the goods	20–038
(f) Insurance	20–039
(g) Other duties	20–040
3. Duties of the buyer	20–041
(a) Shipping instructions	20–042
(b) Payment of the price	20–055
4. Contractual relations with carrier	20–059
5. Passing of property	20–070
6. Risk	20–088
7. Frustration	20–095
8. Remedies of the buyer	20–105
(a) Rejection	20–105
(b) Action for damages	20–114
(c) Specific performance	20–121
9. Remedies of the seller	20–123
(a) Rescission	20–123
(b) Action for an agreed sum	20–126
(i) Action for the price	20–126
(ii) Action for carrying charges	20–131
(c) Action for damages	20–133
(d) Rights against the goods	20–141

1. DEFINITION AND CLASSIFICATION

Definition. The f.o.b. contract has, in the words of Devlin J.,[1] become "a flexible instrument", so much so that no really satisfactory definition of such a contract is possible. The central idea is that the seller is bound at his expense to place the goods "free on board" a ship for transmission to the buyer.[2] The expression "free on board" does not merely "condition the constituent elements of the price"[3]; it generally performs the more important function of expressing the obligations of the parties "additional to the bare bargain of purchase and sale".[4] In particular, it defines the obligations **20–001**

[1] *Pyrene Co. Ltd v Scindia Navigation Co. Ltd* [1954] 2 Q.B. 402 at 424.
[2] *Stock v Inglis* (1884) 12 Q.B.D. 564 at 573; *J Raymond Wilson & Co. Ltd v Norman Scatchard Ltd* (1944) 77 Ll.L.R. 373 at 374.
[3] *Wimble Sons & Co. v Rosenberg* [1913] 3 K.B. 743 at 756; *cf. John Elton & Co. Ltd v Chas Page & Co. Ltd* (1920) 4 Ll.L.R. 226.
[4] *Wimble Sons & Co. v Rosenberg*, above, at p.756.

which arise in connection with the transmission of the goods from the seller to the buyer. An f.o.b. seller is not, in the absence of contrary stipulations in the contract,[5] bound to find shipping space for the goods[6] or to insure them; and the cost of carriage and insurance, even if these items are procured by the seller, is normally for the buyer's account.[7]

F.o.b. contracts are sometimes divided into certain broad categories or classes, which depend on the duties undertaken by the parties in particular cases. Since these duties depend on the terms of each individual contract, the categories are almost infinitely variable. Some attempt must, however, be made to define the so-called "classic" f.o.b. contract, since such a definition will indicate, in broad terms, the duties of the parties to an f.o.b. contract in the absence of special agreement. Variations from the "classic" f.o.b. contract may go so far that the contract cannot properly be called an f.o.b. contract at all, so that, for example, the rules which normally govern passing of property and risk under an f.o.b. contract may not apply to the transaction. For this reason f.o.b. contracts must be distinguished from analogous transactions.

20–002 **The "classic" f.o.b. contract: relative duties of buyer and seller.** The "classic" f.o.b. contract was described in *Wimble, Sons & Co. v Rosenberg.*[8] Its essential features are that the seller must at his own expense put the goods on board a ship which has to be nominated or designated by the buyer. The seller is not bound to reserve shipping space in advance nor to bear any expense of shipment which arises after the goods have been put on board. When these features are said to be the mark of a "classic" f.o.b. contract, stress is placed on the relative duties of buyer and seller in relation to shipment.

20–003 **The "classic" f.o.b. contract: relations of buyer and seller with carrier.** A different feature of a "classic" f.o.b. contract was stressed in *Pyrene Co. Ltd v Scindia Navigation Co. Ltd*[9] and is based on the relations which may arise between buyer and seller on the one hand and the carrier on the other. In that case Devlin J. distinguished between three types of case.[10] He referred first to the "classic" type of f.o.b. contract (in which the seller puts the goods on board a ship nominated by the buyer) and said: "In such a case the seller is directly a party to the contract of carriage at least until he takes out the bill of lading in the buyer's name."[11] Of course he will, *a fortiori*, normally[12] be a party to the contract of carriage if he takes out the

[5] Below, paras 20–028, 20–039.
[6] *Ian Stach Ltd v Baker Bosley Ltd* [1958] 2 Q.B. 130 at 139.
[7] *The Parchim* [1918] A.C. 157 at 164; below, para.20–008.
[8] Above, n.3, at p.757; [1913] 1 K.B. 279 at 282; *cf. Saffron v Soc. Minière Cafrika* (1958) 100 C.L.R. 231 at 241; *Scandinavian Trading Co. A/B v Zodiac Petroleum SA (The Al Hofuf)* [1981] 1 Lloyd's Rep. 81 at 84.
[9] [1954] 2 Q.B. 402 at 424.
[10] For further discussion of these and a number of other situations which may arise in the performance of an f.o.b. contract, and of the effects of the Contracts (Rights of Third Parties) Act 1999 on these situations, see below, paras 20–059 to 20–067.
[11] See below, after n.17.
[12] i.e., unless the seller has acted as the buyer's agent in making the contract of carriage (see below para.20–008), where it will be submitted that no such inference of agency can be drawn merely from the fact that the bill makes the goods deliverable to the order of the buyer.

bill of lading in his own name. Devlin J. contrasted this first "classic" type with a second and a third type of f.o.b. contract. In the second type, "the seller is asked to make the necessary arrangements [for shipping][13]; and the contract may then provide for his taking the bill of lading[14] in his own name and obtaining payment against the transfer, as in a c.i.f. contract." Here again it is the seller who is the original party to the contract of carriage, the buyer normally acquiring rights under that contract only on the transfer to him of the bill.[15] *A fortiori*, where no bill of lading is ever issued, the buyer is not a party to any contract with the carrier merely by virtue of being named as consignee in a booking note having contractual force[16] between seller and carrier.[17] It seems that, for the purpose of the distinction between the first two types of f.o.b. contracts, the person in whose *name* the bill of lading is taken out is the person who is named in it as *shipper*, rather than the person named in it as the *consignee* to whom, or to whose order, the goods are to be delivered.[18] In the third type, the shipping arrangements are made by the buyer, or by the buyer's forwarding agent, who books space on the carrying ship, and "the seller discharges his duty by putting the goods on board, getting the mate's receipt and handing it to the forwarding agent to enable him to obtain the bill of lading."

There is no difficulty in seeing that the contract in the second of the above types is not a "classic" f.o.b. contract, as the seller undertakes the additional duty of making arrangements for shipping. But the distinction between the first and third type of case, and in particular the view that the third type is not a "classic" f.o.b. contract, requires a different explanation. It appears to be implicit in the distinction between the first and third types that an f.o.b. contract is only of the "classic" type if the seller at some stage makes a contract, with the carrier, for the carriage of the goods. He makes such a contract in the first but not in the third case and this is one of the distinctions between them. A second distinction is that the seller in the first, but not in the third, type of contract at some stage holds (and perhaps is bound to procure) a bill of lading, though it may be in the buyer's name; and this, too, is sometimes regarded as an essential feature of a "classic" f.o.b. contract. Thus Dixon C.J. has said: "In what has been called the 'classic' type of f.o.b. contract it is the duty of the seller both to put the goods on board and to procure a bill of lading . . . ."[19] He added ". . . but this is not always the case" and illustrates the qualification by referring to Devlin J.'s third type of case, which he, too, regards as not being a "classic" f.o.b. contract. Hamilton L.J. has similarly said that under an "ordinary

---

[13] For an illustration of this kind of f.o.b. contract, see *The El Amria and The El Minia* [1982] 2 Lloyd's Rep. 28.

[14] Or for his chartering the ship on which the goods are to be carried, as in *Satef-Huttenes Albertus SpA v Paloma Tercera Shipping Co. SA* (*The Pegase*) [1981] 1 Lloyd's Rep. 175.

[15] Above, para.18–102.

[16] Above, para.18–047.

[17] *Hanjin Shipping Co. Ltd v Procter & Gamble (Philippines) Ltd* [1997] 2 Lloyd's Rep. 341.

[18] See above, paras 18–013 *et seq.*; below, paras 20–005, 20–008, 20–026.

[19] *Saffron v Soc. Minière Cafrika*, above, at p.241; *cf. Pyrene Co. Ltd v Scindia Navigation Co. Ltd*, above, n.9, at p.424.

f.o.b. contract" (which seems to mean the same thing as a "classic" f.o.b. contract) the seller "puts the goods safely on board, pays the charge of doing so, and, for the buyer's protection, but not under a mandate to send, gives up possession of them to the ship only upon the terms of a reasonable and ordinary bill of lading."[20] It appears from these statements that a contract in Devlin J.'s third category, under which the seller merely puts the buyer into a position to obtain a bill of lading by handing him a mate's receipt or similar document,[21] is not a "classic" f.o.b. contract. Yet it is by no means universally agreed that only contracts within Devlin J.'s first category are "classic" f.o.b. contracts. Thus Diplock J. has referred to a contract as a "classic f.o.b. contract in which the buyer has the right and the responsibility of selecting the port, of *making arrangements for shipping* and choosing the date of shipment."[22] Since "making arrangements for shipping" goes well beyond the mere nomination of a ship, such a contract seems to fall within the third, rather than the first, of Devlin J.'s categories; and the view that it is a "classic" f.o.b. contract is also hard to reconcile with *Wimble, Sons & Co. v Rosenberg*[23] where the contract was regarded as an "ordinary" f.o.b. contract even though the buyer made no "arrangements" for shipping but merely instructed the seller to put the goods on board some ship bound for a named port.

20–004 It may be that the difference of opinion described above reflects a change in commercial practice. The view that a "classic" f.o.b. contract is one under which the seller is an original party to the contract of carriage and procures a bill of lading is based on two assumptions. The first is that the buyer is not in fact able to make a contract of carriage with a ship at a distant place: all he can do is to instruct the seller to get the goods on board a nominated or designated[24] ship. The second, is "that the ship nominated will be willing to load any goods brought down to the berth or at least those of which she is notified."[25] In modern conditions both these assumptions may be false, so that one of the parties to the contract of sale may have to reserve shipping space in advance, and prima facie that party will be the buyer.[26] The result of these developments may be that Devlin J.'s third category has in fact become more common than the first; and this may be the basis for the view that the third category is now aptly described as the "classic" type. But as yet the weight of authority does not support this usage; and in the rest of this chapter the expression "classic f.o.b. contract" will be used to refer to the first of the three categories described by Devlin J.

20–005 Yet another feature of a "classic" f.o.b. contract, mentioned by Devlin J. in the *Pyrene* case is that the seller takes out the bill of lading "in the buyer's name."[27] The assumption is that the seller, having made the

[20] *Wimble Sons & Co. v Rosenberg* [1913] 3 K.B. 743 at 756 (dissenting).
[21] *e.g.* the weight certificate in *Saffron v Soc. Minière Cafrika*, above.
[22] *Ian Stach Ltd v Baker Bosley Ltd* [1958] 2 Q.B. 130 at 139 (italics supplied).
[23] [1913] 3 K.B. 743.
[24] Below, para.20–042.
[25] *Pyrene Co. Ltd v Scindia Navigation Co. Ltd* [1954] 2 Q.B. 402 at 424.
[26] Below, paras 20–008, p 20–028.
[27] [1954] 2 Q.B. 402 at 424; *cf.* below, paras 20–020 and 20–026.

contract of carriage and shipped the goods, has become entitled as against the carrier to a bill of lading. He then asks the shipowner to issue to him a bill of lading in which the buyer is named as shipper even though the seller has in fact shipped the goods. This is sometimes regarded as the normal position under an f.o.b. contract.[28] But it is perfectly possible for an f.o.b. seller without breach of contract to take out a bill of lading in his *own* name, so that he (and not the buyer) is named as shipper.[29] This is so even where the goods are shipped on a vessel chartered for this purpose by the buyer.[30]

Principal features of "classic" f.o.b. contract summarised. In the light of the foregoing discussion, it seems that the principal characteristics of a "classic" f.o.b. contract are as follows. First, the seller is not obliged to make advance arrangements for shipping the goods nor to bear any expense beyond that of putting the goods on board. Secondly, the seller at or before the moment of putting the goods on board becomes a party to the contract of carriage. Thirdly, the seller may be bound to procure a bill of lading on the terms usual in the trade, but it does not seem that he is necessarily bound to take out the bill of lading in the buyer's name. 20–006

F.o.b. contract with additional duties. An f.o.b. contract may impose on a seller duties in addition to those undertaken by him under a "classic" f.o.b. contract. Thus it may impose on him liability for expenses beyond those of putting the goods on board (such as dock and harbour dues and port rates[31]) as well as the duty of finding shipping space[32] or of doing his best to that end,[33] or of effecting insurance.[34] In such cases the seller's duties in relation to shipment and insurance are analogous to those of a c.i.f. seller; but the contract is distinguishable from a c.i.f. contract in that the cost of freight and insurance are for the buyer's account. This will be so even if the seller is under the contract of carriage or of insurance liable to pay these sums to the carrier or to the underwriter or to both. As between the parties to the contract of sale the buyer bears the ultimate responsibility for these payments, and he takes the risk of any variation in, for example, freight rates which may occur between the time of sale and the making of the contract of affreightment.[35] 20–007

---

[28] *Cowas-jee v Thompson* (1845) 5 Moo.P.C. 165 at 173–174; *A. R. Brown, McFarlane & Co. v C Shaw Lovell & Sons and Walter Potts & Co.* (1921) 7 Ll.L.R. 36 at 37; and *cf.* below, para.20–020.

[29] Below, para.20–026.

[30] As in *The Tromp* [1921] P. 337 and *President of India v Metcalfe SS Co. Ltd* (*The Dunelmia*) [1970] 1 Q.B. 289. *Cf.* below, para.20–026.

[31] As in *Pyrene Co. Ltd v Scindia Navigation Co. Ltd* [1954] 2 Q.B. 402.

[32] As in *Gabarron v Kreeft* (1875) L.R. 10 Ex. 274; *Board of Trade* (*Minister of Materials*) *v Steel Bros & Co. Ltd* [1952] 1 Lloyd's Rep. 87; *Warin and Craven v Forrester* (1876) 4 R. (Ct. of Sess.) 190; *cf. Wimble, Sons & Co. v Rosenberg* [1913] 1 K.B. 279 at 283 (actual decision rvsd. [1913] 3 K.B. 743).

[33] *NV Handel My J Smits Import-Export v English Exporters* (*London*) *Ltd* [1957] 1 Lloyd's Rep. 517; below, para.20–044.

[34] As in *Carlos Federspiel & Co. SA v Charles Twigg & Co. Ltd* [1957] 1 Lloyd's Rep. 240.

[35] *The Parchim* [1918] A.C. 157 at 164; *cf.* the contract in the *Carlos Federspiel* case, above.

20–008 **F.o.b. contracts distinguished from c.i.f. contracts.** The essential distinction between a c.i.f. contract and an f.o.b. contract with additional duties, under which the seller is bound to make arrangements for the carriage of the goods and to insure them, is that stated in paragraph 20–007 above, namely that the cost of freight and insurance is under an f.o.b. contract for the buyer's account, though it may be initially paid by the seller. Under a normal[36] c.i.f. contract the seller cannot recover these charges as such from the buyer, so that it is he and not the buyer who bears the risk of any variations in the cost of these items. It has been suggested that the contract is an f.o.b. contract if the seller makes the contracts of affreightment and insurance as agent of the buyer, and is only an f.o.b. contract if he makes these contracts in this capacity.[37] An f.o.b. seller may, for example, be regarded as having so made the contract of carriage where he takes out the bill of lading in the buyer's name as shipper. There is also judicial support for the view that, where an f.o.b. seller takes out a bill of lading in his own name as shipper, but making the goods deliverable to the order of the buyer, then the "shipper may readily, indeed normally, be regarded as agent for a named consignee in making the relevant bill of lading contract".[38] This may, for example, be the position where property and risk have passed to the buyer on shipment[39] and the price has been paid (or payment of it has been adequately secured) so that the seller has no personal interest in the performance of the contract of carriage nor any reason for retaining control of the goods as security for payment of the price. In discussing the concept of a "classic" f.o.b. contract, we saw that it was open to f.o.b. seller to take out the bill of lading either in the buyer's or in his own name as shipper.[40] If the seller intends to act as the buyer's agent in taking out the bill of lading, the obvious way of giving effect to this intention is to deal in the first of these two ways; and the fact that this method of dealing is open to him tends to support the view that, where he chooses not to adopt it, but to take out the bill in his own name as shipper, he does so with the intention of becoming a principal party to the bill of lading contract. The crucial point, it is submitted, is whether the seller has any commercial interest in being a principal party to that contract. The example given above,[41] in which the property and risk have passed to the buyer on shipment, may be contrasted

---

[36] For exceptions, see above, para.19–009.
[37] Sassoon, *C.I.F. and F.O.B. Contracts* (4th ed., 1984), para.513. *Cf. Warin and Craven v Forrester* (1876) 4 R. (Ct. of Sess.) 190 at 193 (where the Lord President added: "I am not sure that this has any great bearing on the case"); *cf.* a dictum in *Sunrise Maritime Inc. v Uvisco Ltd (the Hector)* [1998] 2 Lloyd's Rep. 287 at 299 which regards the f.o.b. seller as making a contract of carriage on mate's receipt terms as agent for the buyer; but the contract in question was not of the "additional duties" variety: it fell within the *third* of the categories described in para.20–003 above. For the further question whether a mate's receipt has the force of a contract of carriage, see above, para.18–165.
[38] *East West Corp. v DKBS 1912 AF A/S* [2003] EWCA Civ. 83, [2003] Q.B. 1509 at [34]
[39] *cf.* in case of carriage by road, *Texas Instruments Ltd v Nason (Europe) Cargo Ltd* [1991] 1 Lloyd's Rep. 146; and, in case of carriage by air, *Western Digital Corp. v British Airways plc* [2001] Q.B. 733 at 752.
[40] See above, para.20–003.
[41] At n.39. above.

with the situation in which the property has not passed by the time of shipment, typically because at that time the goods have not been paid for.[42] The seller will then have an interest in the performance of the contract of carriage and in the goods; and if he takes out the bill of lading in his own name as shipper, it then becomes implausible to regard him as having made the contract of carriage as agent of the buyer. On the contrary, if he takes the bill of lading in his own name so as to hold it as security for payment, or to preserve his right to redirect the goods, he should *prima facie* be regarded as being a principal party to the bill of lading contract. In one case,[43] factors of this kind account for the conclusion that COD sellers had acted as principals in taking out bills of lading in their own names as shippers and consigned to the order of banks who acted as their agents in the country of destination for the sole purpose of collecting payment. The seller's commercial interest in retaining control of the goods until payment would have supported the same conclusion if the sale had been on f.o.b. terms and had named the buyers as consignees, particularly as the fact of the buyers' being so named would not have deprived the sellers of their right to redirect the goods. It follows that there is no inflexible rule that an f.o.b. seller has acted as the buyer's agent in making the contract of carriage merely by reason of having taken out a bill of lading which names the buyer as consignee. The question whether a seller who has taken such a bill of lading in his own name as shipper has in so doing acted on his own behalf (as principal) or as the buyer's agent "depends upon the analysis of the terms, e.g. of any contract of sale between the consignor [i.e. the seller] and the consignee [i.e. the buyer]."[44] If, as is often the case where the sale is on f.o.b. terms, the property passes at a later stage than that of shipment,[45] then it is submitted that the seller should not be regarded as making the contract of carriage exclusively as agent of the buyer. In particular, if he takes the bill of lading in his own name so as to hold it as security for payment,[46] he should prima facie be regarded as being a principal party to the bill of lading contract.[47]

A contract of sale under which the seller is required to arrange for the carriage of the goods and insurance, but in which the cost of these items is expressed to be for the buyer's account, may be an f.o.b. contract even

---

[42] See below, paras 20–077, 20-082.
[43] The *East West* case, above n.38.
[44] *East West Corporation v DKBS 1912 AF A/S* [2003] EWCA Civ. 83, [2003] Q.B. 1509 at [35]; above, paras 18–065, 18–115.
[45] See below, paras 20–070 et seq.
[46] See below, para.20–026.
[47] *Evergreen Marine Corp v Aldgate Warehouse (Wholesale) Ltd* [2003] EWHC 667 (Comm.), [2003] 2 Lloyd's Rep. 597 where the bills of lading named the manufacturer who was the f.o.b. seller's supplier as shipper, a bank in the country of origin as consignee and the buyer as a notify party. It was held that the buyer was not an original party to the contract of carriage; merely by virtue of having made a "special freight agreement" with the carrier governing the *rate* of freight; and that, as the bills were never indorsed to the buyer, he had not become a party to that contract; *cf. Center Optical (Hong Kong) Ltd v Jardine Transport Services Ltd* [2001] 2 Lloyd's Rep. 678 (Hong Kong High Court). So far as *contra, Union Industrielle et Maritime v Petrosul International Ltd* (*The Roseline*) [1987] 1 Lloyd's Rep. 18 is doubted in para.18–053, n.1, above.

though it contains a reference to the "approximate c.i.f. charge".[48] It may also be an f.o.b. contract even though the term "f.o.b." is not used, and even though the price is said to be calculated on a c. & f. or on a c.i.f. basis. Thus in *The Parchim*[49] a contract was made for the sale of nitrate to be shipped from Taltal in Chile at "9s. 1d. per cwt. cost and freight Channel". Insurance was to be covered by the sellers but to be paid for by the buyers. A ship for the carriage of the goods was chartered by the sellers, but the contract of sale provided that the buyers had to take over the charter; that, if they exercised an option contained in the charter to cancel it, they would have to ship the goods by another ship; and that, in that event "any freight difference *pro* or *contra*" was for their account. It was held that the contract had "far more of the characteristics of a contract f.o.b. Taltal than it has of a contract c.i.f. European port."[50]

20–009 **Effects of distinction between f.o.b. and c.i.f. contracts.** The distinction between these two types of contracts is important in determining the method of calculating the price,[51] the passing of property and risk, and the methods in which the parties can perform their obligations under the contract. It would seem to follow from the nature of an f.o.b. contract that the seller (even if, like a c.i.f. seller, he has undertaken to arrange for carriage and insurance) must actually ship goods in accordance with the contract. This does not mean that the seller must ship personally: he can perfectly well procure the shipment to be made by a supplier on his behalf. What he cannot do is to tender documents in respect of goods already afloat, or a shipment made by a third party after and without reference to the contract, and subsequently appropriated by the seller.[52] " 'Sales afloat' in practice are synonymous with c.i.f. and c. & f. contracts."[53] Under such contracts, goods may be appropriated to the contract after shipment; but in the case of an f.o.b. contract such appropriation[54] must be made by (or before) shipment.[55] This is the natural meaning of the obligation to deliver free on board. If the seller could appropriate to an f.o.b. contract goods shipped by another person, considerable difficulty might also arise in adequately covering the buyer's interest by insurance.

---

48 As in *Carlos Federspiel & Co. SA v Charles Twigg & Co. Ltd* [1957] 1 Lloyd's Rep. 240.
49 [1918] A.C. 157.
50 *ibid.*, at p.164; above, para.19–009.
51 *NV Handel My J. Smits Import-Export v English Exporters* (*London*) *Ltd* [1957] 1 Lloyd's Rep. 517 at 521; *cf.* the arbitrator's finding in *John Elton & Co. Ltd v Chas. Page & Co. Ltd* (1920) 4 Ll.L.R. 226.
52 In *Martin v Hogan* (1917) 24 C.L.R. 234, Isaacs, Higgins and Rich JJ. in the High Court of Australia took this view, while the other three members of the court held that, on the pleadings, the point was not open to the buyer. As a result of this equal division, the decision of the lower court in favour of the seller stood; but it is submitted that the view of Isaacs, Higgins and Rich JJ. (especially at pp.257–259) is to be preferred.
53 *Esteve Trading Corp. v Agropec International* (*The Golden Rio*) [1990] 2 Lloyd's Rep. 273 at 276.
54 In the "contractual" sense (above, para.18–210), so that the seller becomes bound to deliver those goods under the contract: *cf.* above, paras 19–015, 19–016.
55 *The Golden Rio*, above, n.45, at p.276.

F.o.b. contract distinguished from contract to deliver at dock, or alongside.[56] An f.o.b. contract must further be distinguished from a contract to deliver goods simply at the port of shipment. Under a contract of the latter kind the seller is not bound to put the goods on board, nor is the buyer bound to nominate an effective ship.[57] If the contract is on f.o.b. terms, a buyer who fails to nominate an effective ship is not entitled to claim damages for nondelivery[58]; and the distinction between an f.o.b. contract and one simply to deliver at the port of shipment may also be relevant in determining where the buyer should have examined the goods so that he may be deemed to have accepted them.[59] The distinction turns on the construction of the term as to delivery. In *Maine Spinning Co. v Sutcliffe & Co.*[60] a contract for the sale of wool for export was made "subject to the embargo being removed . . . Delivery Liverpool". Previous correspondence had referred to the sale as being "f.o.b. Liverpool". Bailhache J. held that, as the goods were intended for export, "delivery Liverpool" meant "delivery in the way in which goods are delivered at Liverpool, where they are delivered for export at Liverpool, namely 'delivery f.o.b. Liverpool'."[61] 20–010

An intermediate position is illustrated by an f.a.s. contract, under which the seller undertakes to deliver goods "free alongside" a ship nominated by the buyer.[62] The main distinction between such a contract and an f.o.b. contract is that under an f.a.s. contract the seller is not bound to bear the expense of putting the goods on board. The buyer is, as under an f.o.b. contract, bound to give shipping instructions, but any requirement that the instructions must be "effective" would have to be interpreted somewhat differently in relation to an f.a.s. contract than in relation to an f.o.b. contract.[63] The test of "effectiveness" under an f.a.s. contract would be whether the seller could get the goods "alongside"—and not, as under an f.o.b. contract, whether he could get them on board.

2. Duties of the Seller

In general. The duties of an f.o.b. seller are hard to state in general terms, for the obvious reason that they vary according to the type of f.o.b. contract in question. A further difficulty in discussing the duties of the seller results from the fact that shipment under an f.o.b. contract is in many respects a collaborative enterprise, involving co-operation between buyer and seller. It follows that there can be no neat separation between 20–011

---

56 *cf.* below, para.21–010.
57 See below, paras 20–042, 20–043 for this duty under an f.o.b. contract.
58 *Maine Spinning Co. v Sutcliffe & Co.* (1918) 87 L.J.K.B. 382. *John Elton & Co. Ltd v Chas. Page & Co. Ltd* (1920) 4 Ll.L.R. 226; and see below, para.20–015.
59 *J W Schofield & Sons v Rownson, Drew and Clydesdale Ltd* (1922) 10 Ll.L.R. 480; *cf.* below, paras 20–108 to 20–110.
60 (1918) 87 L.J.K.B. 382.
61 *ibid.*, at p.383; see further below, para.20–015.
62 Below, para.21–010.
63 As to this see below, paras 20–042, 20–043.

discussions of the duties of the two parties, so that, in discussing the duties of the seller reference necessarily has to be made to those of the buyer; and conversely. Subject to these difficulties it can, however, be said that the principal duties normally undertaken by an f.o.b. seller are to put goods which conform with the contract on board ship in accordance with the shipping instructions (if any) received from the buyer, and to bear the expense of doing so.[64] Additional duties may, of course, be undertaken by the contract.

(a) *Delivery Free on Board*

20–012 **Duty to put goods on board.** It is the duty of an f.o.b. seller to put the goods on board a ship nominated or designated by the buyer. Under section 32(1)[65] of the Sale of Goods Act 1979 the seller is, by performing this duty, prima facie deemed to have delivered the goods to the buyer[66]; but it must be emphasised that a mere "delivery of the goods to a carrier" within that subsection is not sufficient to discharge the seller's duty under an f.o.b. contract, since he must not merely deliver the goods to the carrier but actually put them on board the ship.[67] The place at which the goods are thus delivered is considered to be the place of performance under an f.o.b. contract.[68] For the purpose of the rules relating to stoppage in transit, the delivery which is made by placing the goods on board may only be constructive delivery. Thus in the normal case, where possession of the goods is taken by the carrier as such, and not as agent of the buyer, the seller's right of stoppage in transit will remain in existence after the goods have been placed on board.[69]

Under an ordinary f.o.b. contract, the seller's duty to deliver, or to tender delivery, arises only after the buyer has nominated or designated the ship. Thus if the buyer fails to give shipping instructions or to give them within the required time, or to give shipping instructions which are effective, the seller is not liable in damages for non-delivery[70]; and this may be so even though the seller could not in fact have delivered the goods if proper shipping instructions had been given to him within the contract period.[71]

---

64 *Henderson and Glass v Radmore & Co.* (1922) 10 Ll.L.R. 727; *J Raymond Wilson & Co. Ltd v Norman Scatchard Ltd* (1944) 77 Ll.L.R. 373 at 374.

65 Above, para.18–245. S.32(4) provides that s.32(1) "must be ignored" where the buyer deals as consumer; for this possibility, see above para.18–259. A rule similar to that laid down by s.32(1) is contained in Art. 31(a) of the Vienna Convention on Contracts for the International Sale of Goods (above, para.1–024).

66 See *Wimble, Sons & Co. v Rosenberg* [1913] 3 K.B. 743; *cf. Badische Anilin und Soda Fabrik v Basle Chemical Works* [1898] A.C. 200.

67 Similarly, an f.o.b. seller would not discharge his duty to deliver by merely "handing the goods over to the first carrier for transmission to the buyer" within Art. 31(a) of the Vienna Convention on Contracts for the International Sale of Goods (above, para.1–024), since this provision contains no reference to actual shipment.

68 *Benaim & Co. v L. S. Debono* [1924] A.C. 514.

69 Sale of Goods Act 1979, s.45(5); *Ex p. Rosevear China Clay Co.* (1879) 11 Ch.D. 560 (above, para.15–082).

70 Below, paras 20–029, 20–036, 20–042.

71 See *Forrestt & Son Ltd v Aramayo* (1900) 83 L.T. 335 (below, para.20–049).

Carrier's failure to load. Goods may be delivered by the seller to a carrier for the purpose of being loaded in pursuance of an f.o.b. contract, but the carrier may fail or refuse to take the goods on board. Under a "classic" f.o.b. contract,[72] it is submitted that the seller would not be in breach by reason of such failure to get the goods on board; on the contrary, it would be the buyer who would be in breach, since his shipping instructions would not be "effective".[73] The position would be different where the contract of sale required the seller to make the shipping arrangements by reserving space in advance[74]: in such a case he might be in breach[75] if the carrier failed to load the goods; but he would have a remedy over against the carrier if the carrier failed to load the goods, and if the advance shipping arrangements had contractual force.[76] The most difficult situation is that in which all the shipping arrangements are made by the buyer, who reserves shipping space in advance, so that no contract of carriage is made between the carrier and the seller.[77] It has been suggested that if, in such a case, the carrier fails or refuses to take the goods on board, the seller is in breach of the contract of sale even though the failure to get the goods on board is entirely the fault of the carrier and in no way due to lack of diligence on the part of the seller; but that in such a case the seller may have a remedy over against the carrier.[78] Special circumstances[79] may justify the inference that the carrier had agreed to take the goods on board when they were presented for loading by the seller, and hence the implication of a contract between seller and carrier even though the shipping arrangements were made by the buyer. But normally the carrier's refusal to take the goods on board would negative, and his failure to do so would scarcely support, such an inference, and an alternative (and, it is submitted, a preferable) view is that in this type of case it is, again, not the seller, but rather the buyer, who is in breach of the contract of sale, since the shipping instructions would not be "effective".[80] If this is the correct analysis, the seller will not need any remedy over against the carrier; and the availability to the buyer of a remedy against the carrier would depend on whether the buyer's reservation of shipping space had given rise to any contract between him and the carrier.[81] 20–013

---

72 Above, paras 20–002 to 20–006.
73 Below, para.20–043.
74 *i.e.* where it fell into the second of the categories described by Devlin J. in *Pyrene Co. Ltd v Scindia Navigation Co. Ltd* [1954] 2 Q.B. 402 at 424, above, para.20–003.
75 Either of his duty to put the goods on board or of a duty to make effective shipping arrangements.
76 Above, para.18–047; *cf.* 18–030.
77 *i.e.* where the contract falls into the third of the categories described by Devlin J. in the *Pyrene Co. Ltd v Scindia Navigation Co. Ltd* [1954] 2 Q.B. 402 at 424, above, para.20–003.
78 *Pyrene Co. Ltd v Scindia Navigation Co. Ltd* [1954] 2 Q.B. 402 at 425; now to be explained on the ground of implied contract *Scruttons Ltd v Midland Silicones Ltd* [1962] A.C. 446 at 471.
79 Such as those in the *Pyrene* case, above, n.78, where the goods in question formed part of a larger consignment, the rest of which had been taken on board by the carrier: see below, paras 20–062, 20–066; *Scruttons Ltd v Midland Silicones Ltd* [1962] A.C. 447 at 471.
80 Below, para.20–043.
81 Above, para.18–047.

20–014 **Place of delivery.** An f.o.b. contract will normally indicate the port of shipment, either by naming it or by stating which party has the right to name it.[82] The place of delivery may also be defined more narrowly, as a particular wharf within a port.[83] An f.o.b. contract which contains no indication at all as to the place of delivery may be void for uncertainty: thus it has been said that an agreement simply to ship goods f.o.b. is not, "in the absence of any stipulation express or implied as to the port of shipment . . . , sufficiently certain to be enforced in a court of law".[84] The court may, however, resolve the uncertainty by interpreting the contract to mean "f.o.b. at the seller's place of business".[85] And where the contract specifies a range of ports, without stating which party is to select the port from which shipment is to be made, it is not void for uncertainty: on the contrary, the buyer is both entitled and bound to make the selection. This was, for example, held to be the position where goods were sold "f.o.b. stowed good Danish port".[86]

Once the place of delivery has been determined in accordance with the rules stated above, the seller is bound to put the goods on board the named or designated ship at that place. He is not bound[87] to deliver at a port other than that designated; and where delivery is to be made at a particular wharf he is not liable for any additional expense caused by the inability of the nominated ship to get to that wharf.[88] It would seem that the seller could, in such a case, strictly speaking, refuse to deliver at all.[89]

Just as the seller is not bound to deliver at a place other than that specified in the contract as the place of shipment, so he is not entitled to do so.[90] In one case,[91] contract for the sale of gasoline called for delivery to be made f.o.b. Antwerp and the seller, being unable to make such delivery within the contract period, offered instead to deliver the goods at Flushing,

---

[82] As in *Ian Stach Ltd v Baker Bosley Ltd* [1958] 2 Q.B. 130 (buyer's option) and *Bunge Corp. v Tradax Export SA* [1981] 1 W.L.R. 711 (seller's option). For stipulations as to the time by which the option must be exercised, see *Gill & Duffus SA v Société pour l'Exportation des Sucres* [1986] 1 Lloyd's Rep. 322, below, para.20–045.

[83] As in *Hecht, Pfeiffer (London) Ltd v Sophus Berendsen (London) Ltd* (1929) 33 Ll.L.R. 157; *Miserochi & Co. SpA v Agricultures Federados Argentinos* [1982] 1 Lloyd's Rep. 202 (below, para.20–045).

[84] *Cumming & Co. Ltd v Ince* (1982) 28 C.L.R. 508 at 512.

[85] As in *Sutherland v Allhusen* (1866) 14 L.T. 666 (where the point was not argued). *Cf.* Vienna Convention on Contracts for the International Sale of Goods (above, para.1–024), Art. 31(c).

[86] *David T Boyd & Co. Ltd v Louis Louca* [1973] 1 Lloyd's Rep. 209; *cf. Pagnan SpA v Feed Products Ltd* [1987] 2 Lloyd's Rep. 601 at 612. Contrast the position in a contract for delivery f.o.t. (below, para. 21–042) in a named country but specifying no place of delivery within that country. In *Bulk Trading Corp. Ltd v Zenziper Grains and Foodstuffs* [2001] 1 Lloyd's Rep. 357, the duty to specify that place was held to be on the *seller* since it was he who had made all the arrangements with the ship on which the goods were to be carried to the country of destination.

[87] *Forrestt & Son Ltd v Aramayo* (1900) 83 L.T. 335; below, para.20–049.

[88] *Hecht, Pfeiffer (London) Ltd v Sophus Berendsen (London) Ltd*, above, n.83.

[89] Below, para.20–015.

[90] See *Peter Turnbull & Co. Pty Ltd v Mundas Trading Co. (Australia) Ltd* (1953–54) 90 C.L.R. 235; *Transcatalana de Commercio SA v Incrobasa Industrial e Commercial Brazileira SA* [1995] 1 Lloyd's Rep. 215.

[91] *Petrotrade Inc. v Stinnes Handel GmbH* [1995] 1 Lloyd's Rep. 142.

which was closer than Antwerp to the point at which the ship on which the goods were to be shipped was waiting, so that delivery at Flushing would presumably have saved the buyer expense. It was held that the buyer was nevertheless justified in rejecting the seller's offer since the stipulation as to the place of shipment was a condition (being part of the description of the goods[92]) and was moreover a term of vital importance to the buyer since it was his duty to make contractual arrangements[93] with the carrier to take the goods on board at that place. The second of these reasons would not apply where the f.o.b. contract was one under which shipping arrangements were to be made by the seller; but even in such a case a stipulation as to the place of shipment would still form part of the description of the goods and its breach could seriously prejudice a buyer who had resold under the same description.[94] Hence even in such a case it is submitted that the buyer would be justified in rejecting for breach of that stipulation.

Seller not normally bound to deliver except on board. The seller's duty being to put the goods on board, he is not normally bound to deliver in any other way. Thus in *Maine Spinning Co. v Sutcliffe & Co.*[95] a contract for the sale of wool for export was held on its true construction to provide for delivery "f.o.b. Liverpool". Such delivery could not legally be made because the seller's application for an export licence was refused; and it was held that the seller was not liable[96] for failing to deliver simply at Liverpool. Bailhache J. rejected the buyers' argument that they could waive the provision for delivery f.o.b. Liverpool and take delivery in some other way. "A term of the contract as to the mode of delivery is not entirely for the benefit of either party to the contract and neither party can waive it without the consent of the other."[97] It might, at first sight, be thought that a buyer who was ready to accept delivery otherwise than on board simply saved the seller the trouble and expense of putting the goods on board; so that the seller would not be prejudiced by being asked to deliver short of the ship. In one case[98] a contract for the sale of cotton provided that the cotton was "to be taken from the quay" but the seller moved it from the quay to a warehouse. It was held that the buyers were not entitled to reject a tender of the goods from the ware house. Erle C.J. said: "Looking at the nature of the stipulation itself, I cannot see how it can be of any importance to the vendees whether they receive the cotton from the quay or from the 20–015

---

[92] Above, para.18–267.

[93] Reference seems here to be made to the third type of f.o.b. contract described in *Pyrene Co. Ltd v Scandia Navigation Co. Ltd* [1954] 2 Q.B. 402 at 424, and discussed in para.20–003, above.

[94] *Petrotrade Inc. v Stinnes Handel GmbH* [1995] 1 Lloyd's Rep. 142 at 149.

[95] (1918) 87 L.J.K.B. 382 (above, para.20–010). The same principle was applied *(mutatis mutandis)* to a c.i.f. contract in *Fibrosa Spolka Akcyna v Fairbairn Lawson Combe Barbour Ltd* [1942] 1 K.B. 12 at 20, and see *ibid.* at 26–27, reversed with regard to the *effects* of frustration [1943] A.C. 32.

[96] The contract was expressly "subject to the embargo being removed": above, para.20–010; for the effect of such a stipulation, see above, para.18–318.

[97] At pp.383–384; *cf. John Elton & Co. Ltd v Chas Page & Co. Ltd* (1920) 4 Ll.L.R. 226.

[98] *Neill v Whitworth* (1866) L.R. 1 C.P. 684, *affg.* (1865) 18 C.B.(N.S.) 435.

warehouse, providing the warehouse does not impose on them any additional expense or undue delay."[99] The case arose out of a contract on "arrival" terms[1] and the question it raised was whether the seller was entitled to make delivery at a point in the port of destination other than the point specified in the contract. But it has been suggested in the High Court of Australia that an f.o.b. buyer may similarly be entitled to elect to take delivery otherwise than on board ship, *e.g.* at the wharf or at the seller's warehouse "unless it can be shown that the seller thereby sustains some detriment"[2]; and in the United States damages have indeed been awarded against an f.o.b. seller who had refused to make such delivery when wartime conditions prevented him from putting the goods on board ship.[3] The seller may, however, suffer detriment by having to deliver short of the ship, in spite of the fact that by making such delivery he saves the expense of putting the goods on board. Thus it is arguable that, where supervening events prevent shipment and such prevention would release the seller from his obligation *to ship*, then, if the seller were required to *deliver short of the ship*, it would on a rising market be a "detriment" to him to lose the chance of relying on the supervening event as a ground of discharge. Similarly, it is a detriment for the seller to lose an export rebate or similar fiscal advantage by delivery otherwise than on board.[4] The seller may also have perfectly good commercial reasons for not wishing goods intended by him for export to be unexpectedly available for disposal by the buyer (perhaps in competition with the seller) on the home market. It is submitted that the burden of proving that the seller would not be prejudiced by having to deliver otherwise than on board is on the buyer; and that it could be discharged only in exceptional circumstances. Thus the buyer cannot normally demand delivery short of the ship; in this sense he cannot "waive" the contractual stipulation as to delivery. However, if the buyer asks for delivery short of the ship he can be said to have "waived" delivery f.o.b. in the sense that tender of delivery at the point requested by the buyer will amount to performance of the seller's duty to deliver the goods.[5]

20–016 **Special provision as to delivery.** A seller may be entitled or bound to deliver short of the ship if the contract expressly or by implication allows or requires him to do this. Thus the contract may give the buyer the option of taking delivery free on board or from barge alongside.[6] In one case[7] the contract expressly provided for delivery to the buyer's agent at the port of shipment, should any requisite licence not be obtained. It was held that the seller could perform by delivering to the agent, so that the buyer's inability to procure the requisite licence did not justify his refusal to accept the

[99] (1865) 18 C.B.(N.S.) 435 at 442.
[1] Below, paras 21–014, *et. seq*.
[2] *Cohen & Co. v Ockerby & Co. Ltd* (1917) 24 C.L.R. 288 at 299.
[3] *Meyer v Sullivan* 131 P. 847 (1919); *cf.* U.C.C., s.2–614(1) and Comment 1.
[4] As in *Wackerbarth v Masson* (1812) 3 Camp. 270.
[5] See *Henderson and Glass v Radmore & Co.* (1922) 10 Ll.L.R. 727, where in fact the seller failed to establish "waiver".
[6] As in *Hecht, Pfeiffer (London) Ltd v Sophus Berendsen (London) Ltd* (1929) 33 Ll.L.R. 157.
[7] *Austin, Baldwin & Co. v Wilfred Turner & Co. Ltd* (1920) 36 T.L.R. 769.

goods.[8] It seems that a local custom requiring or allowing a seller to deliver to a wharfinger would not be rejected as inconsistent with the contract.[9] And "The expression 'free on board' does not necessarily import that the goods should be put on board ship; it would be competent to the parties to prove that the goods were to be delivered somewhere else . . ."[10] – for example, at a railway station. In a Scottish case[11] a contract for the sale of sugar was made "f.o.b. Dunkirk or Antwerp . . . to be delivered at the port of shipment" within a named period. It was held that the sellers were obliged only to have the goods ready at the port of shipment within the contract period and were not in breach merely because the goods had not, within that period, been actually put on board ship. If the contract had not contained the words "to be delivered at the port of shipment", the seller's failure to put the goods on board within the shipment period would have been a breach and a ground on which the buyer could have rejected the goods.[12]

Seller's responsibility for safety of the goods. Under an f.o.b. contract, risk normally passes on shipment[13]; but the seller will be responsible for any subsequent loss of or damage to the goods which is due to his breach of contract. Thus he may in certain circumstances be liable for deterioration in transit[14]; and this is so, not only where the deterioration is due to a defect in the goods themselves, but also where it is due to some default of the seller in relation to the loading of the goods. The seller must see to it that the goods are loaded skilfully and carefully and he is liable for any loss resulting from his failure to do so, unless the failure consists merely in following the buyer's instructionsas to loading.[15] The seller is likewise liable in damages for any loss which results from his failure to pack the goods in accordance with the provisions of the contract.[16] And failure to pack the goods in such a way that they can with stand the contemplated voyage may amount to a breach of section 14(3) of the Sale of Goods Act 1979.[17] 20–017

---

[8] The buyers undertook to "attend to any and every requisite licence": *cf. above*, paras 18–313, 18–317.
[9] See *Henderson and Glass v Radmore & Co.* (1922) 10 Ll.L.R. 727, where, however, no such custom was proved. Proof of such a custom was an alternative ground for the decision in *Meyer v Sullivan*, above, n.3.
[10] *Sutherland v Allhusen* (1866) 14 L.T. 666 at 667. *Cf.* UCC, s.2–319(1)(c) ("f.o.b. vessel, *car or other vehicle*"). "F.o.b. vessel" is the American equivalent of the English "f.o.b".
[11] *Warin and Craven v Forrester* (1876) 4 R. (Ct. of Sess.) 190.
[12] Below, para.20–029.
[13] Below, para.20–086. For the position where the buyer deals as consumer, see above, paras 18–259 to 18–264; and below, para.20–094.
[14] Above, para.18–255.
[15] *A. Hamson & Son (London) Ltd v S. Martin Johnson & Co. Ltd* [1953] 1 Lloyd's Rep. 553.
[16] *Sime Darby & Co. Ltd v Everitt & Co.* (1923) 14 Ll.L.R. 120; *Board of Trade (Minister of Materials) v. Steel Bros & Co. Ltd* [1952] 1 Lloyd's Rep. 87. *Cf.* Vienna Convention on Contracts for the International Sale of Goods (above, para.1–024), Art. 35(1) ("packaged in the manner required by the contract").
[17] See *George Wills & Sons Ltd v Thomas Brown & Sons* (1922) 12 Ll.L.R. 292. Subsequent changes in the subsection have not affected the present point.

20–018 **Seller's responsibility for expenses.** Under a "classic" f.o.b. contract,[18] the seller is prima facie responsible for the cost of getting the goods over the ship's rail.[19] He is not responsible for any further expenses, such as the expenses of stowing the goods once they are on board[20] unless the contract is on "f.o.b. and stowed" terms.[21] If the contract contains no such term but the seller in fact pays charges of stowage, he is entitled to recover these from the buyer.[22] One would, conversely, expect the buyer to be able to recover from the seller any charges paid by the buyer, under his contract with the carrier, of getting the goods from the quay over the ship's rail. In a Scottish case[23] such a claim was dismissed on the ground that the seller, if called upon to pay the charges "would . . . have called on the owner of the ship to pay."[24] Lord Traynor said that, whether the contract was on f.o.b. or on f.a.s.[25] terms "the universal practice is that the ship undertakes the duty and the expense of putting the cargo from the quay or alongside into the hold of the vessel."[26] It is, however, submitted that two questions must be distinguished. The first is who bears the cost of loading as between shipper and carrier; and the second is who bears this cost as between f.o.b. buyer and seller?

As between shipper and carrier the traditional rule of English law differs from that stated by Lord Traynor. It is that the shipper has "to bring the cargo alongside . . . and to lift that cargo to the rail of the ship. It is then the duty of the shipowner to be ready to take such cargo on board and to stow it in the vessel".[27] This rule is, however, "somewhat out of keeping with modern methods"[28] under which the duties of the carrier may begin before the goods cross the ship's rail, either by the terms of the contract of carriage or by the custom of the port. If the carrier charges for the performance of such duties simply as part of the freight[29] the whole expense of loading will have to be borne by the shipper (*i.e.* under a "classic" f.o.b.

---

[18] Above, paras 20–002 to 20–006.
[19] *Att.-Gen. v Leopold Walford (London) Ltd* (1923) 14 Ll.L.R. 359; *Cowas-jee v Thompson* (1845) 5 Moo.P.C. 165 at 173; *Miserochi & Co. SpA v Agricultores Federados Argentinos* [1982] 2 Lloyd's Rep. 202 at 207.
[20] *Att.-Gen. v Leopold Walford (London) Ltd*, above.
[21] *e.g. David T Boyd & Co. Ltd v Louis Louca* [1973] 1 Lloyd's Rep. 209; *Cargill Inc. v Mapro Ltd (The Aegis Progress)* [1983] 2 Lloyd's Rep. 570; Reynolds [1994] L.M.C.L.Q. 119; and see the terms of the buyer's offer in *Hecht, Pfeiffer (London) Ltd v Sophus Berendsen (London) Ltd* (1929) 33 Ll.L.R. 157. *Cf. S. L. Sethia Liners Ltd v State Trading Corp. of India* [1985] 1 W.L.R. 1398 (f.o.b. contract making seller liable for demurrage at loading port).
[22] As in *Att.-Gen. v Leopold Walford (London) Ltd*, above.
[23] *Glengarnock Iron and Steel Co. Ltd v Henry G. Cooper & Co.* (1895) 22 R. (Ct. of Sess.) 672.
[24] At p.675.
[25] Below, para.21–010.
[26] At p.676.
[27] *Harris v Best* (1892) 68 L.T. 76 at 77; *Pyrene Co. Ltd v Scindia Navigation Co. Ltd* [1954] 2 Q.B. 402 at 417.
[28] Scrutton, *Charterparties and Bills of Lading* (20th ed.), p.170, n.29; *cf.* below, para.20–089.
[29] *Heskell v Continental Express Ltd* [1950] 1 All E.R. 1033 at 1041.

contract, by the buyer),[30] no part of the freight payable by the shipper being apportioned to that part of the loading operation which takes place before the goods cross the ship's rail. The position is obviously the same where the buyer is the shipper and the contract of carriage between him and the carrier expressly provides that the *whole* cost of loading *and stowing* is to be borne by the shipper.[31] If the contract of carriage was between seller as shipper and the carrier,[32] it seems that the effect of such a provision would (as between buyer and seller) be that the whole charge would fall on the seller, as part of the (unapportioned) cost of performing his duty to ship the goods. The position would be different where, under a contract of carriage, a *separate* charge is made for the part of the loading operation which takes place before the goods cross the ship's rail. That charge would, as between f.o.b. buyer and seller, fall on the seller who could not escape responsibility for it by showing that the buyer was the shipper and that, as between buyer (in his capacity as shipper) and carrier it had to be borne by the buyer.[33] The point can be put beyond doubt by expressly providing in the contract of sale that the cost of getting the goods to the ship's rail are to be for the seller's account. Such a provision can take effect even if *no* separate charge was made in the contract of carriage for this part of the loading operation, so long as the cost of performing it was practically apportionable.[34] Conversely, where the seller was shipper and by the terms of the contract of carriage had to pay a separate charge for stowage after the goods had crossed the ship's rail, he should be entitled to recover that charge from the buyer.

As between buyer and seller, any expenses, duties or charges payable before shipment have to be borne by the seller[35]; and duties and charges payable after shipment fall on the buyer.[36] Both limbs of this rule can be varied by the express terms of the contract, and by any relevant custom of the port of shipment.[37]

Demurrage. Where shipping arrangements are made by the buyer, liability for any demurrage which may be incurred falls, as between buyer and carrier, on the buyer alone. If such liability results from the seller's wrongful delay in shipping the goods, any payments made by the buyer in respect of it would appear to be recoverable by the buyer as damages from 20–019

[30] *i.e.*, in the first and third types of f.o.b. contracts described in the *Pyrene* case [1954] 2 Q.B. 402 at 424, above, para.20–003, in each of which the bill of lading will name the buyer as shipper.

[31] As in *The Panaghia Tinnou* [1986] 2 Lloyd's Rep. 586.

[32] *i.e.*, in the second type of f.o.b. contract described in the *Pyrene* case [1954] 2 Q.B. 402 at 424, above para.20–003.

[33] *W Siemon & Sons Ltd v Samuel Allen & Sons Ltd* [1925] Q.S.R. 269 at 273–275.

[34] *cf. Congimex Companhia Geral, etc, SARL v Tradax Export SA* [1981] 2 Lloyd's Rep. 687, affirmed [1983] 1 Lloyd's Rep. 250 and *Ceval International Ltd v Cefetra BV* [1996] 1 Lloyd's Rep. 467 (costs of *discharge* split at ship's rail under c.i.f. contract).

[35] See *Bowhill Coal Co. Ltd v Tobias* (1902) 5 F.(Ct. of Sess.) 262.

[36] Below, para.20–054.

[37] For an account of practices at ports, see *F.O.B. Vessel*, a publication of the British Association of Chambers of Commerce.

the seller; the buyer's right to recover such payments may be put beyond doubt by a provision in the contract of sale making the seller liable for demurrage.[38] Such a provision may merely require the seller to indemnify the buyer against any payments which he becomes liable to make, and actually makes, to the carrier; but if the provision specifies a rate of demurrage, either expressly or by reference to a form of charterparty, it may give rise to an independent obligation to pay at the specified rate, irrespective of the amount actually paid to the carrier by the buyer.[39] Whether the provision operates by way of indemnity or gives rise to an independent obligation appears (as in the case of a c.i.f. contract)[40] to be a matter of construction. Conversely, the provision may limit the seller's liability for delay to the specified amount of demurrage.[41]

Where the contract of sale requires payments to be made by irrevocable letter of credit, the buyer's provision of the credit it is a condition precedent to the seller's duty to perform any part of the loading operation. Hence until the letter of credit is provided laytime does not run against the seller under the contract of sale and the seller does not become liable for demurrage under that contract, even though the buyer may have become liable for demurrage under the charterparty by which he has chartered a ship for the purpose of taking delivery of the goods.[42]

(b) *Shipping Documents*

20–020 **Whether seller bound to obtain bill of lading.** Under a "classic" f.o.b. contract,[43] responsibility for making shipment is divided in the sense that the buyer is bound to nominate or designate the ship while the seller is, in the words of Devlin J. in *Pyrene Co. Ltd v Scindia Navigation Co. Ltd*,[44] bound "to put the goods on board for account of the buyer and procure a bill of lading in terms usual in the trade." But there is no invariable rule obliging the seller to obtain a bill of lading. In *Green v Sichel*[45] an f.o.b. seller shipped the goods with the intention of delivering them to the buyer and it was found that he had thereby placed them under the buyer's control. He requested the shipowner to issue a bill of lading in the buyer's name and to the buyer's order, but the shipowner refused to do this unless the seller prepaid freight. In an action for the price, it was held that the seller was not bound to prepay freight; nor even to obtain a bill of lading though

---

[38] *e.g. SL Sethia Liners Ltd v State Trading Corp. of India* [1986] 2 All E.R. 395; *Compagnie Commerciale Sucres et Denrées v C Czarnikow Ltd* (*The Naxos*) [1990] 1 W.L.R. 1337, reversing [1989] 2 Lloyd's Rep. 462; *cf. Fina Supply Ltd v Shell UK Ltd* (*The Poitu*) [1991] 1 Lloyd's Rep. 452.

[39] As in *R Pagnan & Fratelli v Finagrain etc.* (*The Adolph Leonhart*) [1986] 2 Lloyd's Rep. 395; *cf. S.L. Sethia Liners Ltd v State Trading Corp. of India*, above, n.38.

[40] See above, para.19–088.

[41] See *Richo International Ltd v Alfred C Toepfer International GmbH* (*The Bonde*) [1991] 1 Lloyd's Rep. 136.

[42] *Kronos Worldwide Ltd v Sempra Oil Trading SARL* [2004] EWCA Civ. 3, [2004] 1 A11 E.R. (Comm.) 915.

[43] Above, paras 20–002, 20–006.

[44] [1954] 2 Q.B. 402 at 424.

[45] (1860) 7 C.B.(N.S.) 747.

he had undertaken to do it "as a matter of courtesy".[46] The decision can be interpreted to mean either that an f.o.b. seller is not prima facie bound to obtain a bill of lading at all; or, more narrowly, that he is not bound to prepay freight in order to obtain it, responsibility for freight being the buyer's. The point will often be settled by the terms of the contract as to payment. Where the contract provides for payment against bill of lading,[47] an implication obviously arises that the seller is bound to procure a bill of lading, and to tender it in accordance with the terms of the contract as to payment.[48] Equally obviously, the seller will not be bound to procure a bill of lading where the contract provides for payment against some other document, such as a mate's receipt.[49]

Where the seller is bound to procure a bill of lading, he is not normally bound to procure one that states freight to have been prepaid since an f.o.b. seller is "expressly free of any obligation to pay freight".[50] He can be required to procure a freight prepaid bill only if the contract so provides or perhaps if "some other guaranteed payment mechanism is in place"[51] – *e.g.* if the buyer has provided a satisfactory bank guarantee for payment of the freight. Subject to express provisions in the contract which specify the type of document to be procured by the seller, the essential point would seem to be that the documents should prove actual shipment of the goods on board.[52] This could be sufficiently shown by a mate's receipt; but on the other hand, a "received for shipment" bill of lading would not normally suffice since it is not evidence of actual shipment.[53]

Form and kind of bill of lading. Where the seller is bound to obtain a bill of lading, the form or kind of bill which he must obtain depends, in the first place, on the terms of the contract; for example, he need not (as stated in para.20–020 above) normally obtain a "freight prepaid" bill unless the contract in terms requires him to do so. The terms of the contract may similarly specify other characteristics of the bill; if these terms provide no guidance, regard must be had to what is usual in the trade. If the terms of the contract do not help and there is no evidence of what is usual in the trade, the seller's duties with respect to tender of documents will, it seems, be governed by the same general rules as those which determine the duties in this respect of a c.i.f. seller,[54] so far as those rules are appropriate in the 20–021

[46] At p.749.
[47] *e.g. Yelo v S M Machado Ltd* [1952] 1 Lloyd's Rep. 183.
[48] *Inglis v Stock* (1885) 10 App.Cas. 263 at 271. For the view that the provisions of a payment clause may be "mutual", so as to define the obligations of the seller, *cf. Toepfer v Lenersan- Poortman NV* [1980] 1 Lloyd's Rep. 143 (c.i.f. contract); above, para.19–060.
[49] *e.g. Pyrene Co. Ltd v Scindia Navigation Co. Ltd* [1954] 2 Q.B. 402. *cf. Sunrise Maritime Inc. v Uvisco Ltd (The Hector)* [1998] 2 Lloyd's Rep. 287 at 299. Insofar as the same dictum further refers to a "contract of carriage made by the seller on the terms of the mate's receipt . . . on behalf of the buyer" it gives rise to the difficulties which have been discussed in paras 18–165 and 20–008, above.
[50] *Glencore Grain Rotterdam BV v LORICO* [1997] 2 Lloyd's Rep. 386 at 394.
[51] *ibid.*
[52] *Green v Sichel* (1860) 7 C.B.(N.S.) 747.
[53] *Yelo v S M Machado Ltd* [1952] 1 Lloyd's Rep. 183 at 192; above, para.18–027. *cf.* above, para.20–012.
[54] Above, paras 19–032 to 19–047.

context of an f.o.b. contract. Thus the bill of lading must be in transferable form; be a "shipped" (as opposed to a "received") bill[55]; be issued "on shipment"; be "genuine"[56]; cover the goods sold and no others; be "valid and effective"; and be "clean." The requirements that the bill of lading must provide continuous documentary cover and that it must provide for carriage to the agreed destination by the agreed or customary route are obviously subject to some modification in relation to f.o.b. contracts, since such contracts do not usually specify a destination or a route.[57] For the purpose of these requirements, the destination (if any) specified by the buyer in his shipping instructions will therefore normally be the relevant one. Since an f.o.b. contract will, on the other hand, specify the place of shipment, the bill of lading must state that the goods have been shipped from that place. It follows that, where the contract provides for payment against documents, the buyer need not pay if the bill of lading indicates shipment from some other place, even though the original shipment was in fact made at the place specified in the contract.[58] It has been said that the bill must not be claused to incorporate the terms of a charterparty[59]; but presumably tender of such a bill would be good between buyer and seller if the reference was to a standard form of charterparty previously in use between the parties (and hence well known to the buyer), or if the charterparty were tendered together with the bill of lading.[60]

20–022 **Time of tender.** An f.o.b. seller who undertakes to tender a bill of lading is not (any more than a c.i.f. seller[61]) under any absolute obligation to make the tender before the arrival of the goods at their intended destination[62]; though (like a c.i.f. seller) he is no doubt under a duty to tender the documents within such time as may be specified by the contract,[63] or, if no such time is specified, to tender them promptly or "forthwith, that is to say, with all reasonable despatch".[64] This should be taken to mean, not that the seller has a reasonable time within which to take steps to tender documents, but rather that he must act at once to take such steps as are necessary to ensure reasonable despatch.[65] For example, posting documents

[55] Above, para.20–020, n.53.
[56] See *United City Merchants Investments Ltd v Royal Bank of Canada* (*The American Accord*) [1983] 1 A.C. 168, where it was said at p.185 that a bill of lading showing a false date of shipment could have been rejected by an f.o.b. buyer, though (for reasons discussed in para.23–142, below) the falsity did not justify refusal of a bank to pay under an irrevocable and confirmed letter of credit; *NSW Leather Co. Pty Ltd v Vanguard Insurance Co. Ltd* (1991) 25 N.S.W.R. 699 at 709.
[57] For the possibility that an f.o.b. contract may, exceptionally, specify such matters, see below, para.20–042 (destination); *Hackfield v Castle* 198 P. 1041 (1921) (destination and route).
[58] *Mitsubishi Goshi Kaisha v J Aron & Co. Inc.* 16. F. 2d 185 (1926) *per* Learned Hand J.
[59] *Enrico Furst & Co. v W E Fischer Ltd* [1960] 2 Lloyd's Rep. 340 at 346.
[60] *cf. above*, para.19–041.
[61] *cf. above*, para.19–066.
[62] See *Tradax Internacional SA v Goldschmidt SA* [1977] 2 Lloyd's Rep. 604.
[63] Above, paras 19–062 to 19–064.
[64] *Concordia Trading BV v Richo International Ltd* [1991] 1 Lloyd's Rep. 475 at 479.
[65] *cf. above*, para.19–066; and (in another context) *Bank of Nova Scotia v Hellenic Mutual War Risk Association (Bermuda) Ltd* (*The Good Luck*) [1992] A.C. 233.

promptly may suffice, even though their despatch by special courier might have secured their earlier receipt by the buyer. For the purpose of deciding whether a seller has acted promptly, due allowance must, in the case of string contracts, be made for documents to be passed down the string.[66] If the seller fails to tender the documents promptly, his breach occurs when the documents should have been so tendered, rather than at the later time of the arrival of the carrying ship at the destination[67]; for although the buyer will not need the documents for the purpose of obtaining possession of the goods until such arrival, he has obvious commercial interests in having the documents before then: *e.g.* he may wish to use them for purposes of security or for the purpose of dealing with the goods. The seller's failure to comply with the rules governing the time of tender has, it seems, the same legal consequences as under a c.i.f. contract.[68]

Bills in a set. Where the seller is bound to tender a bill of lading and the bills are issued in a set[69] he is not bound to tender a full set, even if the contract provides for payment "in exchange for all the shipping documents".[70] Of course the position would be different if the contract expressly called for a "full set" of bills of lading. 20–023

Payment by banker's commercial credit. The fact that the contract calls for payment by banker's commercial credit is relevant in two ways to the extent of the seller's obligation with regard to obtaining and tendering shipping documents. In the first place, such a provision may be regarded as imposing a prima facie obligation on the seller to tender a bill of lading. Thus where an f.o.b. contract stipulated for payment by irrevocable letter of credit against (*inter alia*) a mate's receipt, this was said to be "in error, for there had been no oral agreement that the mate's receipt should be a good tender instead of the bills of lading".[71] Secondly, the terms of the credit may sometimes be looked at to determine exactly what documents the seller is obliged to tender under the contract of sale. Thus in *Yelo v S. M. Machado*[72] the contract of sale provided for payment by irrevocable credit and the credit when opened stipulated for shipped bills of lading. After the credit had been notified to the sellers, certain variations were made in the terms of the contract of sale; and the sellers at this stage raised no objection to the terms of the credit. It was held that (whatever may have been their obligation as expressed in the original contract of sale) they had become bound to tender shipped bills of lading. For this reason, in addition to those 20–024

[66] *Concordia Trading BV v Richo International Ltd* [1991] 1 Lloyd's Rep. 475 at 480.
[67] *ibid.*, at p.479, where it was the buyer who argued for the later date, the market having risen.
[68] See above, paras 19–062 to 19–068 as to the buyer's right of rejection in such cases.
[69] Above, paras 18–090 to 18–094.
[70] *Cederberg v Borries, Craig & Co.* (1885) 2 T.L.R. 201.
[71] *Enrico Furst & Co. v W E Fischer Ltd* [1960] 2 Lloyd's Rep. 340 at 344. A mate's receipt would be a less satisfactory security for the bank since it is not, while an order or bearer bill of lading is, a document of title in the traditional common law sense: above, paras 18–007, 18–062, 18–161.
[72] [1952] 1 Lloyd's Rep. 183.

already stated,[73] tender of received bills was bad. The case should be contrasted with *Glencore Grain Rotterdam BV v LORICO*[74] where a letter of credit notified to an f.o.b. seller required him to tender a bill of lading which stated that freight had been prepaid. The seller, being prima facie under no obligation to tender such a bill,[75] immediately objected to the requirement and it was held that he was not bound to comply with it, so that the buyer's continued insistence on a freight prepaid bill amounted to a repudiatory breach on the buyer's part.

20–025 Where the seller is obliged to procure and tender a bill of lading, he must tender such bill of lading as is usual in the trade; and the terms of the letter of credit may do no more than to spell out what the requirements of such a bill of lading are. If this is so, the seller cannot object that he is being asked to do more under the credit than under the express terms of the contract of sale.[76] But where the terms of the contract of sale and the credit actually conflict, the seller's obligations under the contract of sale would not, it is submitted, be increased merely because he failed to protest against the terms of the credit. Thus if the contract of sale called for payment against mate's receipt, the seller would not be bound under the contract of sale to provide a bill of lading merely because the credit so required and he failed to object. The effect of such failure to object could at most be to waive the seller's right to be paid against mate's receipt; but a variation of the contract would be necessary to impose on the seller an actual obligation to tender a bill of lading. Such a variation could be implied from the seller's conduct in relation to the non-conforming credit: for example from his drawing on it or asking it to be extended.[77]

20–026 **Bill of lading to seller's order.** In *Pyrene Co. Ltd v Scindia Navigation Co. Ltd* Devlin J. referred[78] to the practice under a "classic" f.o.b. contract[79] of the seller's taking out "the bill of lading in the buyer's name", *i.e.* naming the buyer as shipper, and (presumably) making the goods deliverable to the buyer's order. No doubt the bill must be in this form if the contract expressly so requires. But it was held in *Browne v Hare*[80] that f.o.b. sellers were not in breach of their undertaking to deliver the goods "free on board" merely because they had taken a bill of lading in their own name and to their own order. The reason given was that the form of the bill did not, in the circumstances, indicate an intention on the part of the sellers to retain ownership. In the Court of Exchequer, Pollock C.B. said that if the sellers "had taken the bill of lading in the terms in which it was made for the purpose of continuing the ownership and exercising dominion over the oil, they would in our opinion have broken their contract to ship the oil

[73] In paras 20–020 and 20–021, above.
[74] [1997] 2 Lloyd's Rep. 386.
[75] Above, para.20–020.
[76] *Enrico Furst & Co. v W E Fischer Ltd*, above n. 71.
[77] *W J Alan & Co. Ltd v El Nasr Export and Import Co.* [1972] 2 Q.B. 189.
[78] [1954] 2 Q.B. 402 at 424.
[79] Above, paras 20–002 to 20–006.
[80] (1858) 3 H. & N. 484; (1859) 4 H. & N. 822; below, para.20–078.

'free on board' and the property would not have passed to the [buyer]."[81] In the Exchequer Chamber, Erle J. said[82] that the question was whether the seller "shipped the goods in performance of his contract to place them 'free on board' or for the purpose of retaining control over them and continuing to be the owner, contrary to the contract as in the case of *Wait v Baker*".[83] However, the actual decision in *Browne v Hare* was concerned with the passing of risk (and thus, indirectly, of property), and not with the question whether the seller was in breach of his duty to deliver. The suggestion that an f.o.b. seller is in breach of contract merely because he takes out a bill of lading in such a form that property does not pass on shipment does not seem to have been adopted in any subsequent case[84]; and it is submitted that it is not law.[85] There is no necessary connection between delivery and passing of property; and a seller may perform his duty to deliver by shipping the goods without at the same time unconditionally appropriating them to the contract so as to pass the property.[86] If this were not possible, considerable difficulties could arise in the financing of f.o.b. sales.[87]

Other documents. Like a c.i.f. seller,[88] an f.o.b. seller may be bound to tender other documents such as a weight certificate[89] or an inspection certificate.[90] His duties in this respect depend on the terms of the contract, including terms which may be implied as a result of any relevant custom or usage. Here again,[91] the terms of a letter of credit may be relevant in determining the extent of the seller's obligations under the contract of sale. Thus in *Ficom SA v Sociedad Cadex Ltda.*[92] an f.o.b. contract did not specify what documents the seller was to tender but a letter of credit procured by the buyer required the seller to tender to the bank (*inter alia*) a certificate of quality. The seller by his conduct in subsequent negotiations showed that he had accepted this requirement. It was held that his failure to tender the certificate not only prevented him from recovering payment under the letter of credit but also justified the buyer in bringing the contract of sale to an end. It follows that the requirement of tendering a certificate of quality had become a term not only of the credit but also of the contract of sale. 20–027

---

[81] 3 H. & N. 484 at 498–499.
[82] 4 H. & N. 822 at 830.
[83] (1848) 2 Exch. 1.
[84] It is also inconsistent with *Wait v Baker*, above, n.83.
[85] See *Concordia Trading BV v Richco International Ltd* [1991] 1 Lloyd's Rep. 475 at 478 (stating that normally an f.o.b. seller will take a bill of lading to his own order).
[86] *Mitsui & Co. Ltd v Flota Mercante Grancolombiana SA* (*The Ciudad de Pasto and the Ciudad de Neiva*) [1988] 2 Lloyd's Rep. 208 at 213; *Frebold & Sturznickel* (*Trading as Panda OHG*) *v Circle Products Ltd* [1970] 1 Lloyd's Rep. 499 at 503; *cf. Evergreen Marine Corp. v Aldgate Warehouse (Wholesale) Ltd* [2003] EWHC 667 (Comm), [2003] 2 Lloyd's Rep. 597 at [30], [32].
[87] *cf. above*, para.18–209.
[88] Above, para.19–058.
[89] A possibility recognised, though negatived on the facts, in *Mantovani v Carapelli SpA* [1978] 2 Lloyd's Rep. 63 at 72 (affirmed without reference to this point [1980] 1 Lloyd's Rep. 375).
[90] As in *Tradax Internacional SA v Goldschmidt SA* [1977] 2 Lloyd's Rep. 604.
[91] Above, para.20–024.
[92] [1980] 2 Lloyd's Rep. 118.

(c) *Shipping Space*

20–028 **Duty to find shipping space.** The "classic" f.o.b. contract[93] is "probably . . . based on the assumption that the ship nominated will be willing to load any goods brought down to the berth or at least those of which she is notified".[94] In such a situation neither party has, strictly speaking, any duty to obtain or reserve shipping space. But the question who has such a duty has become increasingly important in modern conditions "when space often has to be booked well in advance".[95] The duty to reserve shipping space may, by the terms of the contract, be placed on the seller or on the buyer. In the absence of any contractual stipulation dealing with the matter, the duty lies on the buyer, but, as Diplock J. has said, "there are probably as many exceptions to the rule as there are examples of it".[96] In other words, sellers in fact quite commonly undertake to find shipping space, and also undertake other duties not arising out of a "classic" f.o.b. contract, such as to insure the goods and even to prepay freight.

The rule that an f.o.b. seller is (in the absence of a contrary stipulation) under no duty to reserve shipping space was criticised by Bailhache J. in *D. H Bain v Field & Co.*[97] so far as it related to f.o.b. sales of small parcels (as opposed to entire cargoes). In such cases, the buyer will often have no representative at the port of shipment, so that the task of finding shipping space will in fact be undertaken by the seller, and the theory that he "is acting merely in a friendly way or as an agent[98] for the buyer is . . . not in accordance with the commercial practice or the views of commercial men." Accordingly, the learned judge said[99]: "My own view is that in the case of small parcels sold f.o.b. it is the duty of the seller to take the necessary steps to provide the shipping accommodation." He admitted that this was "contrary to what is always held in these Courts"; but it seems that in cases of the kind contemplated by Bailhache J. the courts will rely on very slight indications of intention to hold that the seller has in fact undertaken to find shipping space. Thus in one case the situation under an f.o.b. contract was described as one "where the seller undertook to find the ship"[1] even though there was no express provision to that effect in the contract; and the only circumstances on which such an "undertaking" could be said to have been based were that the buyer had no representative at the port of shipment and that the seller had in past transactions arranged for shipment.

Where the seller expressly undertakes to find shipping space a further question may arise as to the standard of duty imposed by the contract. In

---

[93] Above, paras 20–002, 20–006.
[94] *Pyrene Co. Ltd v Scindia Navigation Co. Ltd* [1954] 2 Q.B. 402 at 424.
[95] *ibid.*
[96] *Ian Stach Ltd v Baker Bosley Ltd* [1958] 2 Q.B. 130 at 139.
[97] (1920) 3 Ll.L.R. 26 at 29; affirmed without reference to this point (1920) 5 Ll.L.R. 16.
[98] He may act as agent for the purpose of making the contract of carriage even though he is not obliged to find shipping space; but if he takes the bill of lading in his own name as shipper he will normally be taken to have done so as principal (see above, para.20–008).
[99] (1920) 3 Ll.L.R. 26 at 29.
[1] *Yelo v S M Machado* [1952] 1 Lloyd's Rep. 183 at 192.

one such case[2] it was held that the seller had, on the true construction of the contract, undertaken to do no more than to use his best endeavours, or to make all reasonable efforts, to find the shipping space.

(d) *Time of Shipment*

Time of shipment.[3] Under a "classic" f.o.b. contract[4] the seller is under no duty to ship until the buyer has given proper shipping instructions.[5] If such instructions have been given, the seller must ship the goods at the latest by the end of the period (if any) specified for shipment in the contract.[6] He may be bound to ship before the end of that period, as the ensuing discussion will show.[7] Even where the buyer has in fact undertaken the task of putting the goods on board (though he is not bound to do so) the seller must place the goods in such a position that the buyer can get them on board within the shipment period. In determining the extent of the shipment period, the court may take into account any relevant custom at the port of loading, at any rate where the contract provides for shipment "in accordance with the custom of the port".[8] If no shipment period is specified by the contract, the period may be fixed by the terms of the buyer's shipping instructions,[9] provided that those instructions allow the seller a reasonable time for shipping the goods. **20–029**

Failure to load within the contractual shipment period is (unless the contract otherwise provides[10]) a ground for rejection.[11] This rule is not affected by the statutory restrictions on the buyer's right to reject contained in Sale of Goods Act 1979, section 15A. Even if (contrary to the submissions made elsewhere in this book[12]) these restrictions can affect

---

[2] *Warin and Craven v Forrester* (1876) 4 R.(Ct. of Sess.) 190.

[3] For the buyer's duties in this respect, see below, para.20–046.

[4] Above, paras 20–002 to 20–006.

[5] Above, para.20–012, below, para.20–042.

[6] *Yelo v S M Machado* [1952] 1 Lloyd's Rep. 183; and see *All Russian Co-operative Society Ltd v Benjamin Smith & Sons* (1923) 14 Ll.L.R. 351.

[7] Below, paras 20–030, 20–032.

[8] As in *Einar Bugge A.S. v W. H. Bowater Ltd* (1925) 31 Com.Cas. 1.

[9] See below, para.20–051. *Cf. Shaw Macfarlane & Co. v Waddell & Sons* (1900) 2 F. (Ct. of Sess.) 1070, where the issue was whether the seller was bound to load after the end of the time specified in the buyer's notice.

[10] As in *Compagnie Commerciale Sucres et Denrées v C Czarnikow Ltd* (*The Naxos*) [1990] 1 W.L.R. 1337 and in *Phibco Energy Inc. v Coastal* (*Bermuda*) *Ltd* (*The Aragon*) (1987) [1991] 1 Lloyd's Rep. 61 note (liability for delay in loading limited to payment of demurrage).

[11] *Yelo v S M Machado* [1952] 1 Lloyd's Rep. 183; *Tradax Export SA v Italgrani di Francesco Ambrosio* [1986] 1 Lloyd's Rep. 112 at 117; *Petrotrade Inc. v Stinnes Handel GmbH* [1995] 1 Lloyd's Rep. 142 at 148; and see below, para.20–032. Under the Vienna Convention on Contracts for the International Sale of Goods (above, para.1–024), Art. 49(1)(a) the failure would only be a ground of rejection if the breach was "fundamental:" see above, para.18–267, n.38. It is important to note that the case would be one of *late* delivery and not one of *non*-delivery, and that the requirement of fundamental breach could not be circumvented by the mechanism of giving a notice requiring the seller to perform (Art. 47(1)) since failure to comply with such a notice gives rise to a right of avoidance only in cases of non-delivery (Art. 49(1)(b)).

[12] Above, paras 18–284, 19–173, below, para.20–038.

rights of rejection for breach of time stipulations in overseas sales on c.i.f. or f.o.b. terms, they do not apply to cases of the present kind since the seller's failure to load within the stipulated time is a breach, not of a term implied by sections 13 to 15 of the Act, but of an express term as to the time of shipment.[13] As an alternative to rejecting the goods, the buyer can affirm the contract and claim damages for loss occasioned by the delay. This may include demurrage which the buyer has to pay to the carrier in consequence of the delay[14]; and provisions in the contract of sale calling for the payment of a specified sum by way of "demurrage" may be enforced as liquidated damages clauses.[15]

Where the contract calls for shipment within a continuous period, *e.g.* during a specified month, the seller may be bound to ship before the end of that period. This depends on which party has the option as to the exact time, within the shipment period, at which the goods are to be shipped. As the following discussion shows, the option may be that of the buyer,[16] or that of the seller,[17] or it may in a sense be divided between the parties.[18]

20–030 **Time of shipment at buyer's option.** If the option is expressly given to the buyer, the general rule is that the seller is bound to ship within a reasonable time of receiving shipping instructions from the buyer[19]; but this rule may be displaced by express contractual provisions: *e.g.* by a term requiring the seller to load within a specified time of the receipt of the shipping instructions, or by one requiring him to have the goods ready for shipment at any time within the shipment period.[20]

If the contract does not state who has the option as to the time of shipment, the rule is that under a "classic" f.o.b. contract[21] the option is the

---

[13] Where an f.o.b. buyer deals as consumer (see above, para.18–259) his right to "rescind" the contract under Part 5A of the Sale of Goods Act 1979 extends to breach of an express term leading to failure of the goods "to conform to the contract of sale at the time of delivery" (Sale of Goods Act 1979, ss.48A(1)(b), 48A(2)(b)(ii) and 48C(1)(b) and (2)). This wording suggests that failure to comply with a stipulation as to the "time of delivery" does not of itself amount to non-conformity of the goods for the purposes of Part 5A. Hence the restriction imposed on such a buyer's right to reject where he requires the seller to repair or replace non-conforming goods (see s.48D(2)(a)) could not come into operation in the context of an f.o.b. seller's failure to load within the contractual shipment period. For various possible meanings of "time of delivery" in the case of an f.o.b. contract, see above, para.18–262.

[14] *J & J Cunningham Ltd v Robert A Munro & Co. Ltd* (1922) 28 Com.Cas. 42; and see *Einar Bugge AS v W H Bowater Ltd* (1925) 31 Com.Cas. 1, where on the facts the seller was not in breach; *cf. Compagnie Commerciale Sucres et Denrées v C Czarnikow Ltd* (*The Naxos*) [1990] 1 W.L.R. 1337 at 1341.

[15] *Trading Society Kwik-Hoo-Tong v Royal Commission on Sugar Supply* (1923) 16 Ll.L.R. 250; (1924) 19 Ll.L.R. 343.

[16] Below, paras 20–030, 20–047.

[17] Below, paras 20–035, 20–048.

[18] Below, paras 20–036, 20–049, 20–050.

[19] *Nordisk Oversoisk Handelsselskab A/S v Eriksen & Christensen* (1920) 5 Ll.L.R. 71.

[20] As in *Compagnie Commerciale Sucres et Denrées v C Czarnikow Ltd* (*The Naxos*) [1991] 1 W.L.R. 1337.

[21] Above, paras 20–002 to 20–006.

buyer's[22] who is normally entitled to call for shipment at any time during the period. The seller is correspondingly obliged to put the goods on board any ship nominated by the buyer which is capable of receiving shipment within the period.[23] This does not mean that the seller is bound to have the goods ready at the port of shipment for the whole of the period.[24] The buyer is bound to nominate a ship and to give notice of the nomination in good time to enable the seller to have the goods ready for shipment by the nominated ship.[25] This rule may be displaced by an express stipulation requiring the seller to have the goods ready for shipment at any time within the shipment period[26]; but such a stipulation is most unlikely to be found in a contract which does not state which party has the option as to the time of shipment.

Two further questions arise in cases of the kind described above: how much notice must the buyer give of the ship's readiness to load; and at what rate is the seller bound to load? The contract may be silent on these points or it may expressly provide for them.

Contract containing no provisions as to notice or rate of loading. Where the contract does not specify how much notice the buyer must give of the ship's readiness to load, or at what rate the seller is bound to load, the buyer must give adequate notice enabling the seller to get the goods on board within the shipment period; and the seller must then "load in a reasonable time and in the customary manner"[27]; and the question whether 20–031

[22] *Ian Stach Ltd v Baker Bosley Ltd* [1958] 2 Q.B. 130 at 142; *cf. Miserochi & Co. SpA v Agricultores Federados Argentinos* [1982] 1 Lloyd's Rep. 202 at 207 (where the buyer's option was said to result from a term of the contract stating merely that he was to "tender vessels between . . ." specified dates); As a general principle, a contract which provides for alternative methods of performance is likely to be constructed as giving the choice between these methods to the promisor (see *Mora Shipping Inc. v Axa Corporate Solutions Assurance SA* [2005] EWCA Civ. 1069, [2005] 2 Lloyd's Rep. 769 at [40]–[44]). But this principle is of no help in determining which party to a "classic" f.o.b. contract has the option as to the time of shipment since, with regard to this matter, each party makes a relevant promise: the seller one to provide the goods and the buyer one to provide the ship. The effect of Art. 33(b) of the Vienna Convention on Contracts for the International Sale of Goods (above, para.1–024) is to give the option as to the time of delivery to the seller "unless circumstances indicate that the buyer is to choose a date." The fact that the sale was on f.o.b. terms might well be such a "circumstance;" or it might import a "usage" binding the parties under Art. 9(2); or it might be evidence of an agreement to exclude the Convention or to derogate from or vary the provision of Art. 33(b) which gives the option as to the time of delivery to the seller; see Art. 6 and para.18–004, above. On any of these grounds, it is submitted that the position under the Convention would not differ from the common law position stated in the text above.

[23] The contract may contain an express provision to this effect, *e.g.* by specifying a "laycan" period (see *SHV Gas Supply & Trading SAS v Naftomar Shipping & Trading Co. Ltd Inc.* (*The Azur Gaz*) [2005] EWHC 2528 (Comm), [2006] 1 Lloyd's Rep. 163 at [9]; for the meaning of "laycan", see above, para.19–013 n.97).

[24] *Tradax Export SA v Italgrani di Francesco Ambrosio* [1986] 1 Lloyd's Rep. 112 at 118.

[25] *Harlow and Jones Ltd v Panex (International) Ltd* [1967] 2 Lloyd's Rep. 509 at 526.

[26] See above, at n.20.

[27] *Einar Bugge AS v W H Bowater Ltd* (1925) 31 Com.Cas. 1 at 9. It follows that failure to agree expressly on such a point does not leave an f.o.b. contract void for uncertainty: *Pagnan SpA v Feed Products Ltd* [1987] 2 Lloyd's Rep. 601 at 613.

the buyer has given adequate notice to the seller is one of fact. In *Agricultores Federados Argentinos v Ampro SA*[28] maize was sold under an f.o.b. contract calling for shipment from September 20 to 29. The buyers nominated a ship, and when it became clear that this ship would not be able to load by September 29, they, at 4 p.m. on that day, nominated a second ship and the arbitrators found that it was not "impossible for all the necessary arrangements to have been made to enable her to complete loading before midnight on the 29th of September." It was held that the sellers were liable in damages for failing to load the second ship. On the other hand, where an f.o.b. buyer nominated a ship which was not ready to load until two hours before the end of the last working day of the shipment period, it was held that the seller could have rejected the nomination because loading could not have been completed within those two hours. He had not waived his right to reject the nomination by loading part of the goods within the two available hours; and he was in any event not bound to go on loading after the end of the shipment period.[29]

Where the nomination is of a ship initially capable of loading all the goods sold within the shipment period, the seller must begin to load even though subsequent events make it impossible to complete the loading within the period; but here again he need not continue to load after the period has come to an end.[30] Nor is the seller bound to load if the nominated ship, though expected (when the nomination was made) to be ready to load within the shipment period, in fact only reaches the port of shipment after the end of that period.[31]

20–032 **Express provisions as to notice and rate of loading.** The rules stated in paragraph 20–031 above may leave the parties to an f.o.b. contract in considerable uncertainty as to their obligations under the contract with regard to the time of making and taking delivery. To avoid such uncertainty, the contract may provide how much notice of the ship's readiness to load must be given by the buyer,[32] and at what rate the seller is bound to load. In *Bunge Corp. v Tradax Export SA*[33] an f.o.b. contract provided for shipment in June at a U.S. Gulf port. The time of shipment (within the shipment period) was at the buyers' option, while the sellers had the option as to the port of shipment. The contract further provided that the buyers were to give "15 days pre-advice of readiness of steamer", and that the sellers were then to load at the rate of 2,000 tons per day. The House of

[28] [1965] 2 Lloyd's Rep. 157.

[29] *Bunge & Co. Ltd v Tradax England Ltd* [1975] 2 Lloyd's Rep. 235.

[30] *ibid.*, at p.239.

[31] *Olearia Tirrena SpA v NV Algemeene Oliehandel* (*The Osterbek*) [1972] 2 Lloyd's Rep. 341.

[32] Such a term may be implied by custom: see *Scandinavian Trading Co. A/B v Zodiac Petroleum SA* (*The Al Hofuf*) [1981] 1 Lloyd's Rep. 81.

[33] [1981] 1 W.L.R. 711; *cf. Bremer Handelsgesellschaft mbH v Rayner & Co.* [1978] 2 Lloyd's Rep. 73 at 81; reversed on other grounds [1979] 2 Lloyd's Rep. 216, but approved on this point in *Bunge Corp. v Tradax Export SA above*, at p.730; *Miserochi & Co. SpA v Agricultores Federados Argentinos* [1982] 1 Lloyd's Rep. 202; *Compagnie Commerciale Sucres et Denrées v C Czarnikow Ltd* (*The Naxos*) [1990] 1 W.L.R. 1337 (below, para.20–033).

Lords held that the buyers' notice had to be given at least 15 days before the last day on which the sellers had to begin to load if they were to be able to complete loading by the end of the shipment period at the rate of 2,000 tons per day.[34] The actual notice given by the buyers fell five days short of this requirement and it was further held that the sellers were on this ground justified in rescinding the contract. They did not have to show that the delay caused them serious (or any) prejudice; for the term specifying the length of the notice to be given by the buyers was a condition (as opposed to an intermediate or innominate term[35]). Two reasons were given for so classifying the term. The first was that, in the interests of certainty, stipulations which specified a precise time for performance were normally to be classified as conditions in commercial contracts.[36] This rule is well established in relation to stipulations as to the time of *making* delivery[37] and was here extended to one as to the time of *taking* delivery: in the present context this would promote certainty, for it would enable a seller to tell, immediately on receipt of the notice, whether the notice was adequate and so whether he was bound to load. Secondly, the House of Lords emphasised the close relation between the buyers' duty to give the notice and the sellers' duty to nominate the port. Until the buyers had given shipping instructions, the sellers would not, in practice, be in a position to nominate the port; and Lord Roskill therefore accepted the argument that "when a term has to be performed by one party as a condition precedent to the ability of the other party to perform another term, especially an essential term such as the nomination of a single loading port, the time for the performance of the former obligation will in general fall to be treated as a condition"[38]; and conversely the lack of interdependence between the obligations of the parties is sometimes relied on in support of the conclusion that the term is not a condition.[39] However, the factor of such interdependence is not conclusive either way, and a number of cases support the view that a term may be classified as a condition even in the absence of this factor.[40]

The seller's right to rescind for breach of the condition here described is not affected by the statutory restrictions on rights to reject contained in Sale of Goods Act 1979, sections 15A and 30(2A), since these restrictions apply only where it is the seller who is in breach and not to the converse situation, here under discussion, of a breach of condition by the buyer.[41]

---

[34] [1980] 1 Lloyd's Rep. 294 at 301, approved [1981] 1 W.L.R. 711 at 723.
[35] *cf. above*, para.18–267.
[36] *cf. above*, para.19–063; a possible qualification is discussed in para.20–034, below.
[37] Above, paras 18–267, 18–269, 19–063; for cases in which the contract does not specify a *precise* time, see above, para.19–064.
[38] [1981] 1 W.L.R. 711 at 729; all the other members of the House of Lords agreed with Lord Roskill.
[39] *Universal Bulk Carrier Ltd v Andre & Cie* [2001] EWCA Civ. 588; [2001] 2 Lloyd's Rep. 65 (voyage charterparty).
[40] *Greenwich Marine Inc. v Federal Commerce Navigation Co. Inc.* (*The Mavro Vetranic*) [1985] 1 Lloyd's Rep. 580 at 583; *Michael J Warde v Feedex International Inc.* [1985] 2 Lloyd's Rep. 289 at 298.
[41] This is also true of the restriction imposed by the Sale of Goods Act 1979, s.48D on the right of a buyer who deals a consumer to reject non-conforming goods(see above, para.18–284 n.75).

20–033 **Effect of seller's failure to load within required time.** We have seen that a seller's failure to load within the contractual shipment period is a ground of rejection.[42] But where the contract provides for shipment within a specified period at the buyers' option, the seller may be under a duty to load *before* the end of the shipment period (*e.g.* if the buyer calls for shipment early in that period)[43]; and he may also be under a duty to load at a rate specified in the contract.[44] Breach of these duties may make the seller liable in damages,[45] though mere failure to *begin* loading in accordance with the contract will not have this effect if, by loading more quickly than he was contractually bound to load, the seller nevertheless *completes* loading within the time allowed by the contract.[46] Nor does the mere fact that the seller has failed to comply with the requirements of the contract as to the commencement or rate of loading of itself entitle the buyer to reject: thus so long as the seller loaded, or was able to load, within the shipment period, the buyer could not reject merely because the seller failed to load within a reasonable time of receipt of shipping instructions, or merely because the seller failed to load at the stipulated rate.[47]

A right to rescind in such circumstances may, however, be conferred on the buyer by the express terms of the contract. In *The Naxos*[48] an f.o.b. contract for the sale of sugar, under which the time of shipment was at the buyers' option, required the buyers to give 14 days' notice of the ship's expected readiness to load; it further entitled the buyers, on giving such[49] notice, to call for delivery of the sugar "between the first and last days inclusive of the contract period"; and it also required the sellers to have "the sugar ready *at any time* within the contract period". The cumulative effect of these provisions was held to be that the sellers were obliged to have the goods ready immediately on the ship's presenting herself (after the required notice had been given) in readiness to load; and it was further held that the term requiring them to have the sugar ready "at any time within the contract period" was a condition, so that their failure to load immediately on the presentation of the ship justified rescission by the buyers, even before the end of the shipment period. One reason given for

---

[42] Above, para.20–029.

[43] Above, para.20–030.

[44] Above, para.20–032.

[45] These may be limited by the terms of the contract of sale to any demurrage for which the buyer is liable under the contract of carriage: this was the position in *Compagnie Commerciale Sucres et Denrées v C Czarnikow Ltd* (*The Naxos*) [1990] 1 W.L.R. 1337, where the buyer had the right to rescind for reasons stated after n.48 *infra; cf. Richo International Ltd v Alfred C Toepfer International GmbH* (*The Bonde*) [1991] 1 Lloyd's Rep. 136.

[46] *Kurt A Becher GmbH v Roplak Enterprises* (*The World Navigator*) [1991] 2 Lloyd's Rep. 23.

[47] *Tradax Export SA v Italgrani di Francesco Ambrosio* [1986] 1 Lloyd's Rep. 112 at 117.

[48] *Compagnie Commerciale Sucres et Denrées v C Czarnikow Ltd* (*The Naxos*) [1990] 1 W.L.R. 1337; Treitel [1991] L.M.C.L.Q. 147.

[49] Paragraph 2 of rule 14 of the London Refined Sugar Association was incorporated by reference into the contract; it merely required "reasonable notice", but this phrase was interpreted in the light of clause 7 of the contract which specified the period of notice as 14 days.

this conclusion was that prompt delivery was "of the utmost importance"[50] to the buyers. Another was that this classification promoted certainty for, although the contract did not actually specify a date by which loading had to begin, such a date could be determined without question in the light of subsequent events,[51] *viz.* the giving of the specified period of notice[52] and the declaration of ship's readiness to load. It is submitted that an f.o.b. buyer would, *a fortiori*, be entitled to rescind where the seller had failed to comply with a provision of the contract requiring him, not only to ship during the shipment period, but also to do so within a specified number of days after receipt (during that period) of the buyer's shipping instructions. Since such a provision would lay down a precise time-table for performance, it would properly be classified as a condition in accordance with the principles laid down in *Bunge Corp. v Tradax Export SA,*[53] so that *any* breach of it (and not only a serious one) would justify rejection. For the reasons already given in paragraph 20–029, the statutory restrictions on the buyer's right to reject contained in sections 15A and 30(2A) do not apply to cases of this kind.

Qualified buyer's option. An f.o.b. contract may expressly qualify the buyer's option as to the time of shipment, so as to take account of the fact that the time at which the goods are shipped is to a large extent within the control, not of buyer or seller, but of a third party, such as an oil terminal operator who reserves the right to allocate loading slots for particular shipments. Thus the contract may provide that the buyer's nomination is to be "subject to acceptance by . . . terminal operator"[54] and may go on to require the seller to notify the buyer of such acceptance or of an acceptance for a number of dates within the shipment period; the buyer can then either accept these dates or propose yet other loading days. In this way the exact time of shipment may be determined by further negotiations between buyer and seller after the time of contracting. To expedite this process, the contract may specify a time-limit within which the seller must notify the buyer of the terminal operator's acceptance of the buyer's nomination of a ship. Although stipulations as to the time of performance are prima facie conditions,[55] such a classification of terms requiring sellers to observe short time-limits for giving notices of the present kind can give rise to difficulties 20–034

[50] [1990] 1 W.L.R. 1337 at 1347; *cf. Société Italo-Belge pour le Commerce et l'Industrie v Palm & Vegetable Oils* (*Malaysia*) *Sdn. Bhd.* (*The Post Chaser*) [1981] 2 Lloyd's Rep. 695, above, para.19–018; criticised on another point above, para.19–064.

[51] *cf.* from this point of view, *Toepfer v Lenersan-Poortman NV* [1980] 1 Lloyd's Rep. 143 (above, para.19–063).

[52] Such certainty would not have been promoted if no period of notice had been specified; for in that case it would not have been clear to the sellers whether the notice was adequate and so whether they were bound to load the nominated ship: the term would have raised "questions of degree:" [1990] 1 W.L.R. 1337 at 1347; *cf.* above, paras 18–266, 19–064.

[53] [1981] 1 W.L.R. 711; above, para.20–032.

[54] As in *Phibro Energy AG v Nissho Iwai Corp.* (*The Homan Jade*) [1991] 1 Lloyd's Rep. 38.

[55] This is recognised in *The Homan Jade*, above, n.54 at p.45.

in the performance of string contracts, where it may in practice be impossible to pass the notice along the string within the specified time. In one case, for example, the contract required the seller to notify the buyer of the terminal operator's acceptance of the buyer's nomination within five days of the seller's receipt of the buyer's nomination. At first instance it was said that this stipulation was an innominate term,[56] rather than a condition, but that its breach gave the buyer the right to reject since the delay on the part of the seller was so long as to have "frustrated the commercial basis of the contract".[57] In the Court of Appeal some reservations were expressed about this reasoning, because of the "element of uncertainty"[58] which flowed from the classification of the term as an innominate one; but as the buyer's right to reject was not in doubt the Court was prepared to assume the correctness of the classification.

20–035 **Time of shipment at seller's option.** The contract may expressly or by implication give the seller the right to choose at which point in the shipment period the goods are to be shipped. In *Harlow and Jones Ltd v Panex (International) Ltd*[59] a contract for the sale of 10,000 tons of iron on f.o.b. terms provided for shipment "during August/September 1966, at the . . . suppliers' option." The sellers notified the buyers that 5,000 tons would be ready at the port of shipment "at the beginning of August, and our suppliers . . . request you to arrange a steamer for August". The buyers failed to make the requested shipping arrangements for this quantity; and it was held that this failure amounted to a breach, justifying the sellers in refusing to comply with a demand to guarantee, within 24 hours, the loading of the full 10,000 tons in August.[60] Under this contract the sellers had the option as to the time of shipment within the shipment period, even though it was the buyers who were obliged to provide the ship. Hence it was the sellers in this case who had the entire shipment period available for shipment – and, correspondingly, the buyers who were bound, on reasonable notice[61] that the goods were ready (or on such notice as might be specified by the contract), to arrange for shipment at such point in that period as was designated by the sellers. Similarly, where an f.o.b. contract for the sale of goods to be manufactured by the seller called for delivery "within four months" it was held that the seller was not bound to ship before the end of the four months.[62]

20–036 **Divided option as to time of shipment.** The possibility that the option as to the time of shipment may, in a sense, be divided between buyer and seller is discussed in paragraphs 20–049 and 20–050 below.

[56] *ibid.*
[57] *ibid.*, at p.49.
[58] *ibid.*, at p.58.
[59] [1967] 2 Lloyd's Rep. 509.
[60] The contract did not expressly provide for delivery by instalments. But the negotiations as to shipment had proceeded on the basis that there would be two shipments; and it was held that the buyers could not peremptorily insist on their right to a single shipment as they had "waived" this right: *cf. Charles Rickards Ltd v Oppenhaim* [1950] 1 K.B. 616.
[61] *Harlow & Jones Ltd v Pannex (International) Ltd* [1967] 2 Lloyd's Rep. 509 at 526.
[62] *Forrestt & Son Ltd v Aramayo* (1900) 83 L.T. 335; below, para.20–049.

Stipulations as to time of "delivery". Provisions as to the time of delivery in an f.o.b. contract are assumed to refer to the time of shipment and not to the time of arrival of the goods; and this may be so even though the provision in question contemplates the arrival of the goods by a certain time. Thus in *Frebold and Sturznickel (Trading as Panda OHG) v Circle Products Ltd*[63] German sellers sold toys to English buyers f.o.b. Continental port on the terms that the goods were to be delivered in time to catch the Christmas trade. The goods were shipped from Rotterdam and reached London on November 13; but, because of an oversight for which the sellers were not responsible, the buyers were not notified of the arrival of the goods until the following January 17. It was held that the sellers were not in breach as they had delivered the goods in accordance with the requirements of the contract by shipping them in such a way as would normally have resulted in their arrival in time for the Christmas trade. 20–037

(e) *Conformity of the Goods*

Duty to ship conforming goods. The goods shipped by the seller under an f.o.b. contract must be in conformity with the contract.[64] They must, in the first place, be of the contract description.[65] Certain special applications of this rule to overseas sales have been discussed in Chapter 18.[66] Where an f.o.b. contract is (on its true construction) one for the sale of goods originating in a particular country, the seller cannot perform by delivering goods of the same kind, but originating in another country.[67] A provision as to the time of shipment may form part of the description of the goods,[68] or at any rate be a term the breach of which entitles the buyer to reject.[69] The 20–038

---

[63] [1970] 1 Lloyd's Rep. 499; *cf.* Vienna Convention on Contracts for the International Sale of Goods (above, para.1–024), Art. 31(a), a provision not entirely appropriate to f.o.b. contracts as it refers to "handing the goods over to the.. . carrier," rather than to *shipment*.

[64] *cf.* Vienna Convention on Contracts for the International Sale of Goods (above, para.1–024), Art. 35. Where the buyer deals as consumer (see above, para.18–259) the requirement of conformity must, for the purposes of Part 5A of the Sale of Goods Act 1979, be satisfied "at the time of delivery" (s.42A(1)(b)). For various possible meanings of this phrase in the context of an f.o.b. contract, see above , para.18–262.

[65] *e.g. Scaliaris v E Ofverberg & Co.* (1921) 37 T.L.R. 307.

[66] Above, paras 18–266 to 18–273.

[67] *Schijveschuurder v Canon (Export) Ltd* [1952] 2 Lloyd's Rep. 196.

[68] *Wilson v Wright* (1937) 59 Ll.L.R. 86, following *Bowes v Shand* (1877) 2 App.Cas. 455; *cf. Yelo v S M Machado* [1952] 1 Lloyd's Rep. 183 at 192.

[69] Above, para.18–267. The Vienna Convention on Contracts for the International Sale of Goods (above, para.1–024) likewise gives the buyer the right to declare the contract avoided if the goods are not in conformity with the contract (see Art. 35), but only if the non-conformity "amounts to a fundamental breach of contract": see Art. 49(1)(a) and Art. 25 for the definition of "fundamental breach"; above, para.18–267, n.38. In cases of the present kind, the requirement of fundamental breach cannot be circumvented by the mechanism of giving the seller reasonable notice requiring him to perform, since failure to comply with such a notice gives rise to a right of avoidance only in cases of non-delivery: see Art. 49(1)(b).

goods must be of the contract quality and quantity[70] and must not be mixed with other goods.[71] The implied condition as to fitness for a particular purpose under section 14(3) of the Sale of Goods Act 1979 can apply to an f.o.b. contract: for example, the buyer may reasonably rely on the seller's skill or judgment with regard to the packing of the goods.[72] On the other hand an f.o.b. seller is not (any more than a c.i.f. seller[73]) normally responsible for matters affecting the saleability of the goods in the country of destination. In *Sumner Permain & Co. v Webb & Co.*[74] the defendants sold tonic water f.o.b. London, knowing that the buyers intended to resell it in Argentina. The tonic water contained salicylic acid, and, by a provision of Argentine law of which the defendants were assumed to be ignorant, the sale of food or drink containing such acid was prohibited. It was held that the defendants were not in breach of condition under what is now section 14(3) of the Sale of Goods Act 1979 as "the particular question whether these goods . . . were . . . compounded in such a way as to infringe the Argentine law is not a matter upon which it can be said that the buyer relied on the seller's judgment".[75] Nor was the seller liable for breach of the implied term as to what is now called "satisfactory" quality under section 14(2) of the Act, since "quality" did not include "the capability of the goods being lawfully resold according to the law of the country in which it is known that the sale would take place".[76]

For reasons discussed elsewhere in this book,[77] it is unlikely that a buyer's right to reject for breach of the seller's obligations with regard to the conformity of the goods with the contractual description or quantity will, in the case of an f.o.b. contract, be affected by the statutory restrictions on the right to reject which are contained in sections 15A and 30(2A) of the Sale of Goods Act 1979.[78]

(f) *Insurance*

20–039 **Insurance.** An f.o.b. seller is under no duty to insure for the benefit of the buyer unless the contract expressly (or by necessary implication) obliges him to do so; and even if he is bound to insure, the cost of insurance will be

---

70 *Smeaton, Hanscomb & Co. Ltd v Sassoon I Setty & Co. (No. 1)* [1953] 1 W.L.R. 1468; *J and J Cunningham Ltd v Robert A. Munro & Co. Ltd* (1922) 28 Com.Cas. 42 (seller who ships insufficient quantity may be liable to buyer for dead freight which the buyer has to pay to the carrier).

71 See *Imperial Ottoman Bank v Cowan* (1874) 31 L.T. 336 (where there was evidence of a new agreement that the buyer should not rely on this objection).

72 *George Wills & Sons Ltd v Thomas Brown & Sons* (1922) 12 Ll.L.R. 292.

73 Above, para.18–274.

74 [1922] 1 K.B. 55.

75 27 Com.Cas. 105 at 110; the discussion of s.14(1) (the precursor of the present s.14(3)) is not reported in the *Law Reports*.

76 [1922] 1 K.B. 55 at 60.

77 Above, paras 18–284, 19–173.

78 Where the buyer deals a consumer (see above, para.18–259) his right to reject may be restricted by s.48D of the Sale of Goods Act 1979 if he has required the seller to repair or replace non-conforming goods; but if he makes no such requirement his right to reject is not affected by s.48D. See further, in relation to overseas sales, above, para.18–284, n.75.

for the buyer's account. Where (as in a "classic" f.o.b. contract[79]) the seller is under no duty to insure, section 32(3) of the Sale of Goods Act 1979 may apply, so that in the circumstances specified in the subsection[80] the seller "must give such notice to the buyer as may enable him to insure [the goods] during their sea transit".[81] The only stated consequence of the seller's failure to give such notice is that "the goods shall be deemed to be at his risk during such sea transit". It does not seem that the subsection imposes a *contractual duty* to give notice to the buyer, for breach of which the buyer can reject or claim damages. Thus if the goods arrive safely the seller's failure to give notice will have no legal consequences; and this position should be contrasted with the consequences of a c.i.f. seller's failure to tender a proper policy of insurance.[82]

There is no authority on the nature and amount of insurance which an f.o.b. seller must supply when the contract does impose on him a duty to insure. In an f.o.b. contract of this kind, these matters are likely to be dealt with by express terms. In the absence of such contractual provisions the rules which determine the seller's obligations in this respect under a c.i.f. contract[83] could be applied by analogy. When (as is more usual) an f.o.b. contract imposes no duty on the seller to insure, each party is likely to insure his own interest. The seller's interest would normally terminate at the ship's rail[84] though it is arguable that he may retain an insurable interest in the goods even after property and risk have passed to the buyer, by virtue of the possibility that he may become entitled to stop the goods in transit.[85] Conversely, the buyer's interest normally commences when the goods cross the ship's rail since the risk normally passes to him at that point.[86]

Difficulty as to insurable interest is particularly acute where only a part of the goods sold is loaded and then destroyed. In *Colonial Insurance Co. of New Zealand v Adelaide Marine Insurance Co*,[87] a cargo of wheat was sold, to be loaded on a ship chartered by the buyers. After part of the wheat had been loaded, the ship and that part of the cargo were lost. It was held that the buyers had an insurable interest in that part, even though they might have become entitled to reject the part loaded "in the event of the sellers neglecting, without lawful excuse, to complete the supply".[88] The Privy

---

[79] Above, paras 20–002 to 20–006.
[80] Above, paras 18–246 *et seq*. Where the buyer deals as consumer (above, para.18–259) s.32(3) "must be ignored" (see s.32(4), discussed in relation to overseas sales in paras 18–262 above).
[81] *cf.* Vienna Convention on Contracts for the International Sale of Goods (above, para.1–024), Art. 32(3), which requires the seller to give the buyer the requisite information only "at the buyer's request."
[82] Above, para.19–042.
[83] Above, paras 19–042 to 19–052.
[84] See *W L R Traders Ltd v British and Northern Shipping Agency Ltd* [1955] 1 Lloyd's Rep. 554 (forwarding agent engaged by f.o.b. seller to arrange for shipment under no obligation to seller to insure).
[85] Schmitthoff, *The Export Trade* (10th ed.), para.19 014; Sassoon, *C.I.F. and F.O.B. Contracts* (4th ed.), para.670, citing *Moran, Galloway & Co. v Uzielli* [1905] 2 K.B. 555.
[86] Below, paras 20–088—20–090.
[87] (1886) 12 App.Cas. 128.
[88] At p.140.

Council stressed that the ship had been chartered by the buyers, that the sellers had nothing to do with the shipping documents, and that putting the wheat on board amounted to delivery to the buyers. The earlier decision in *Anderson v Morice*[89] was distinguished on these grounds. In that case a cargo of rice was sold on c. & f. terms. After part of it had been loaded the ship and that part were lost. It was held by the Exchequer Chamber that the buyers had no insurable interest until the loading was completed as the risk was not intended to pass, and the buyers had no sufficient interest in the preservation of the goods, until then.[90] Decisions on insurable interest in this type of situation are hard to predict so that the question which party effectively can (and, for his own benefit, should) insure is a difficult one to resolve; and the difficulty is increased by the possibility mentioned in the *Colonial Insurance* case that the buyer may be entitled to reject the part loaded and so, in effect, throw back the risk on the seller. Here again the seller may retain an interest in the goods even after property and risk have passed to the buyer; and it is arguable that he can insure this interest on a contingency basis so as to protect himself if the buyer fails to pay and the goods are lost or damaged.[91]

(g) *Other Duties*

20–040 **Other duties.** The parties are free to stipulate for the performance by the seller of other duties, *e.g.* he may be required to give a performance guarantee,[92] or to procure any documents which may be needed to obtain permission for the export of the goods.[93] The nature and extent of such additional duties depends entirely on the terms of each particular contract; and no useful purpose would be served by discussing them in detail.

3. DUTIES OF THE BUYER

20–041 **In general.** The principal duties of the buyer are to "name the vessel and to give shipping instructions in time to enable the seller to send forward the goods so that they can be shipped in accordance with the instructions"[94]; and to pay for the goods in accordance with the contract.

---

[89] (1875) L.R. 10 C.P. 609; on appeal the House of Lords was evenly divided: (1876) 1 App.Cas. 713.

[90] See *Sharp v Sphere Drake Insurance (The Moonacre)* [1992] 2 Lloyd's Rep. 501 at 511–512; *Glengate Properties Ltd v Norwich Union Fire Insurance Society* [1996] 2 All E.R. 487 at 498.

[91] See the references given in n.90, above.

[92] *Heisler v Anglo-Dal Ltd* [1954] 1 W.L.R. 1273.

[93] *Pagnan SpA v Tradax Ocean Transportation SA* [1987] 3 All E.R. 565; *Nile Co. for the Export of Agricultural Crops v H & J M Bennett (Commodities) Ltd* [1986] 1 Lloyd's Rep. 555 at 581; above, para.18–310.

[94] *Henderson and Glass v Radmore & Co.* (1922) 10 LL.L.R. 727; *Ian Stach Ltd v Baker Bosley Ltd* [1958] 2 K.B. 130 at 139; *Miserochi & Co. SpA v Agricultores Federados Argentinos* [1982] 1 Lloyd's Rep. 202 at 207; *Bunge AG v Sestostrad SA (The Athos C)* [1984] 1 Lloyd's Rep. 687 (where the duty was alleviated by the terms of the contract).

(a) *Shipping Instructions*

Duty to give shipping instructions. Unless the seller has undertaken the duty to find shipping space, an f.o.b. buyer is bound to give instructions with regard to the shipment of the goods.[95] The exact form of the shipping instructions depends on the terms of the contract: these may require the buyer to instruct the seller to put the goods on a particular ship; or on a ship bound for a particular port[96] or country[97]; or simply on the "next steamer".[98] The essential point is that the seller must be instructed, in accordance with any relevant terms of the contract, as to the way in which he can perform his duty to put the goods on board. If no shipping instructions are given, or if shipping instructions are not given within the time allowed by the contract,[99] the seller is not liable in damages for non-delivery[1]; and the buyer is liable in damages for non-acceptance.[2] **20–042**

Shipping instructions must be "effective". The instructions given by the buyer must be "effective" in the sense that it must be possible and lawful for the seller to comply with them.[3] Thus if the buyer nominates a particular ship, it must be capable of loading the goods within the shipment period.[4] A nomination which comes so late as to leave inadequate time for loading within that period is defective.[5] The same is true if the ship cannot lawfully load at the port of shipment named in the contract; and, where the contract names a range of ports and gives the option as to the port within **20–043**

---

[95] Above, para.20–029; *infra*, n.3; *Burch & Co. v Corry & Co.* [1920] N.Z.L.R. 69; *Fyffes Group Ltd v Reefer Express Lines Pty Ltd (The Kriti Rex)* [1996] 2 Lloyd's Rep. 171 at 196; *cf.* the buyer's duty under Art. 60(a) of the Vienna Convention on Contracts for the International Sale of Goods (above, para.1–024) of "doing all the acts which could reasonably be expected of him in order to enable the seller to make delivery".

[96] *Green v Sichel* (1860) 7 C.B.(N.S.) 747; *Wimble, Sons & Co. v Rosenberg* [1913] 3 K.B. 743. *Cf. Laing, Son & Co. Ltd v Eastcheap Dried Fruit Co.* [1961] 2 Lloyd's Rep. 277 (below, para.20–133, n.90).

[97] See *Port Sudan Cotton Co. v Govindaswamy Chettiar & Sons* [1977] 1 Lloyd's Rep. 166, reversed [1977] 2 Lloyd's Rep. 5 (where Donaldson J. held that the buyer was bound to nominate a ship with "destination India" but the Court of Appeal on the facts found that the destination did not form a term of the contract); *cf. Bulk Oil (Zug) AG v Sun International Ltd* [1984] 1 Lloyd's Rep. 531 ("Destination.. . in line with exporting Government's policy").

[98] *Wilson v Wright* (1937) 59 Ll.L.R. 86.

[99] Above, paras 20–029 to 20–035.

[1] *Armitage v Insole* (1850) 14 Q.B. 728; *Sutherland v Allhusen* (1866) 14 L.T. 666; *Soc. Cooperative Suisse des Céréales v La Plata Cereal Co. SA* (1947) 80 Ll.L.R. 530; *cf. Maine Spinning Co. v Sutcliffe & Co.* (1917) 87 L.J.K.B. 382 (above, paras 20–010, 20–015).

[2] *David T Boyd & Co. Ltd v Louis Louca* [1973] 1 Lloyd's Rep. 209.

[3] *Agricultores Federados Argentinos v Ampro SA* [1965] 2 Lloyd's Rep. 157 at 167; *cf. A v Pound & Co. Ltd v M W Hardy & Co. Inc.* [1956] A.C. 588 (above, paras 18–310, 18–329).

[4] *F E Napier v Dexters Ltd* (1926) 26 Ll.L.R. 62; *ibid.*, at p.184; for a similar rule with regard to the seller's duty to put the goods on board within the time allowed by the contract for loading, see above, para.20–029.

[5] *Bunge & Co. Ltd v Tradax England Ltd* [1975] 2 Lloyd's Rep. 235; above, para.20–032.

that range to the seller, if the ship cannot lawfully load at *any* of those ports.[6] If the buyer instructed the seller to load the goods on a ship bound for a particular port, the instructions would be insufficient if no ship bound for that destination were available at the port of shipment during the shipment period. The duty to give shipping instructions is sometimes referred to as synonymous with the duty to provide shipping space; but the two ideas would appear to be distinct. Instructions to ship on a particular ship may be perfectly adequate if the named ship can in fact take the goods, irrespective of the question whether the buyer has made advance arrangements to that effect with her owners. Indeed, under the "classic" f.o.b. contract[7] it is the seller who is an original party to the contract of carriage, and the assumption underlying this type of contract is that neither party has made any advance reservation of shipping space.[8] Similarly, a buyer who instructs the seller to ship the goods on a ship bound for a named port need not show that he has actually reserved space in advance on some ship bound for that port.[9] The buyer is, it is submitted, under a "duty to provide a ship", or shipping space, only if the contract expressly or by necessary implication requires him to do so.[10] If he has not reserved shipping space in advance, he runs the risk that his shipping instructions may turn out to be ineffective, but he does not commit any breach of contract so long as the seller is in fact able to ship the goods in accordance with those instructions. If, however, after the seller has tendered the goods for shipment, the nominated ship refuses or fails to take the goods on board, it is submitted that the nomination will normally be regarded as ineffective, whether or not the buyer has previously reserved space on that ship.[11]

A buyer who has nominated a ship which is capable of taking the goods on board may then also nominate the same ship to load other goods under another contract and that ship may not have the capacity to load the full quantity sold under both contracts. Such "overbooking" does not amount to a renunciation by the buyer of the first contract so as to amount to a repudiatory breach: it does not put it out of the buyer's power to perform that contract, but merely shows that he *might* not be able or willing to perform it.[12]

20–044 **Duty may be negatived by contract.** The buyer's duty to give shipping instructions may be negatived by the terms of the contract. Most obviously it will be negatived if a duty to obtain shipping space is placed by the

[6] *Richco International Ltd v Bunge & Co. AG* (*The New Prosper*) [1991] 2 Lloyd's Rep. 93; below, para.20–045.
[7] Above, para.20–003.
[8] As to the legal effect of such a reservation, see *Heskell v Continental Express Ltd* [1950] 1 All E.R. 1033; *The Ardennes*, [1951] 1 K.B. 55; above, para.18–047.
[9] *e.g. Wimble, Sons & Co. v Rosenberg* [1913] 3 K.B. 743.
[10] *e.g. J and J Cunningham Ltd v Robert A Munro & Co. Ltd* (1922) 28 Com.Cas. 42.
[11] *cf. above*, para.20–213.
[12] *Alfred C Toepfer International GmbH v Itex Itagrani Export SA* [1993] 1 Lloyd's Rep. 360.

contract on the seller.[13] In one case[14] the seller merely undertook to do his best to obtain shipping space, but failed in his attempts to do so. It was held that neither party was in breach: the seller had performed his duty to do his best, while the buyer's normal duty to give effective shipping instructions was negatived by the terms of the contract.

Place of shipment. The buyer must give instructions to ship from the agreed (or designated)[15] port of shipment, or from such place within the port of shipment as may have been agreed (or designated).[16] If the ship nominated by the buyer fails to get to that port or place, or if she cannot lawfully load there because she does not comply with the port's load restrictions,[17] the seller can refuse to load[18]; and if he does load any extra cost of loading incurred by reason of the ship's failure to get to that point must be borne by the buyer.[19] Where the contract provides for shipment at one (or more) of several ports, the right, and duty, to choose the port of shipment is the buyer's,[20] unless the contract expressly confers the choice of port on the seller.[21] In *Bunge Corp. v Tradax Export SA*,[22] the contract gave the seller the right to choose the port of shipment, but also required the buyer to give advance notice of readiness to load.[23] It was held that the seller was not bound to nominate the port until the buyer had given that notice. Where the contract gives the seller the right to indicate the berth within the specified port at which the goods are to be loaded, the buyer must get the vessel to the berth that the seller nominates.[24] It seems that the seller must act reasonably in nominating the berth (*e.g.* he must not nominate one at which delays are liable to occur because of congestion, when others which the ship could reach promptly are available).[25] But he is under no duty to ensure that a berth will be available as soon as the buyer nominates a ship: hence the cost of delay resulting from the unavailability of a berth at this stage will normally fall on the buyer.[26] If the contract does not specify which party is to nominate the berth, it is submitted that the right and duty of doing so are the buyer's.[27] 20–045

---

[13] Above, para.20–028.
[14] *NV Handel My J Smits Import-Export v English Exporters (London) Ltd* [1957] 1 Lloyd's Rep. 517.
[15] See above, para.20–014.
[16] *Hecht, Pfeiffer (London) Ltd v Sophus Berendsen (London) Ltd* (1929) 33 Ll.L.R. 157.
[17] *Richco International Ltd v Bunge & Co. AG (The New Prosper)* [1991] 2 Lloyd's Rep. 93.
[18] *The New Prosper*, above n.6.
[19] *Hecht Pfeiffer* case, above, n.16; above, para.20–014.
[20] *Ian Stach Ltd v Baker Bosley Ltd* [1958] 2 Q.B. 130 at 139; *David T. Boyd & Co. Ltd v Louis Louca* [1973] 1 Lloyd's Rep. 209; *cf. above*, para.20–014.
[21] *e.g. Cargill Inc. v Mapro Ltd (The Aegis Progress)* [1983] 2 Lloyd's Rep. 570; *cf. The New Prosper*, above, n.6.
[22] [1981] 1 W.L.R. 711.
[23] See above, para.20–032.
[24] *Miserochi & Co. SpA v Agricultores Federados Argentinos* [1982] 1 Lloyd's Rep. 202.
[25] *ibid.*, at p.209.
[26] *ibid.*
[27] This follows from the authorities cited in n.20, above.

An f.o.b. contract which gives an option to one of the parties as to the port of shipment may also specify the time by which that party must nominate the port. Failure to make the nomination within that time is a breach of condition and accordingly entitles the injured party to rescind the contract.[28]

20–046 **Time of shipment.** It is the duty of the buyer to nominate a ship capable of loading within the shipment period and to give reasonable notice of readiness to load, or such notice as may be required by the express terms of the contract.[29] Failure to give such notice as will enable the seller to load by the end of the shipment period, or to give notice within such time as is specified by the contract, makes the buyer liable in damages and entitles the seller to refuse to deliver, since the time of taking delivery[30] (no less than the time of shipment) is of the essence of an f.o.b. contract.[31] The severity of this rule may, however, be mitigated by a variety of contractual provisions. The cases illustrate four types of such provisions. (1) First, the contract may require the seller to make (and the buyer to take) delivery if the ship nominated by the buyer is ready to *begin* loading within the shipment period, even though she cannot complete the process before its end.[32] (2) Secondly, the contract may provide for the payment of demurrage if a ship is duly nominated by the buyer but arrives late; and this provision

---

[28] *Gill & Duffus SA v Société pour l'Exportation des Sucres SA* [1985] 1 Lloyd's Rep. 621, applying the principle of *Bunge Corp. v Tradax Export SA* [1981] 1 W.L.R. 711, above, para.20–032. In the *Gill & Duffus* case the term required the seller to make the nomination by a specified day "at the latest". These words "reinforced" (p. 325), but seem not to have been essential for, the classification of the term as a condition.

[29] Above, paras 20–031, 20–032.

[30] Above, para.20–032.

[31] *Soc. Co-operative Suisse des Céréales v La Plata Cereal Co. SA* (1947) 80 Ll.L.R. 530; *Olearia Tirrena SpA v NV Algemeene Oliehandel* (*The Osterbek*) [1972] 2 Lloyd's Rep. 341; *Bunge & Co. Ltd v Tradax England Ltd* [1975] 2 Lloyd's Rep. 235; *Bunge Corp. v Tradax Export SA* [1981] 1 W.L.R. 711. *Cf. Bremer Handelsgesellschaft mbH v J H Rayner & Co.* [1978] 2 Lloyd's Rep. 73 at 81 (*revsd.* on other grounds [1979] 2 Lloyd's Rep. 216 but approved on this point in *Bunge Corp. v Tradax Export SA* [1981] 1 W.L.R. 711 at 730); *Tradax Export SA v Italgrani di Francesco Ambrosio* [1986] 1 Lloyd's Rep. 112 at 117; above, para.20–032. The seller's right to declare the contract avoided under Art. 64 of the Vienna Convention on Contracts for the International Sale of Goods (above, para.1–024) arises where the buyer has (a) committed a "fundamental breach" (as defined in Art. 25 (above, para.18–267, n.38)) of any of his obligations or (b) failed to perform his obligations to accept or pay as required by the contract and has also failed to perform at least one of these obligations within an additional reasonable time fixed by the seller under Art. 63(1), or declared that he (the buyer) would not do so. Under these provisions, failure to comply with the contractual time-table does not of itself give the seller a right of avoidance. On the facts of *Bunge Corp. v Tradax Export SA* [1981] 1 W.L.R. 711, such a right might, however, arise under the Convention by reason of the finding that the term there broken was "of great or fundamental importance"; though that might be said to make merely the term, rather than the breach, fundamental. An alternative way of preserving the certainty of the English rule would be to rely on Arts 6 and 9 of the Convention: see above, para.18–004.

[32] This possibility is illustrated by the terms of the contract in *Compagnie Commerciale Sucres et Denrées v C Czarnikow Ltd* (*The Naxos*) [1990] 1 W.L.R. 1337, above, para.20–033.

may be interpreted to mean that such a payment is to be the seller's sole remedy in that event.[33] (3) A third, commonly found, provision is one giving the buyer an option to extend the shipment period by a further period specified in the contract, usually on condition of his paying "carrying charges" to the seller. Such charges are regarded as the price payable by the buyer for that option,[34] and not as damages for delay in taking delivery. Accordingly the charges are not penalties, even if it is clear that they will exceed the seller's loss.[35] They may be recoverable (where the buyer has exercised the option) even in respect of delays caused by the seller's failure to load at the rate specified in the contract: this was held to be the position where the seller's liability for such delay was limited by the contract to the payment of demurrage.[36] But no claim for carrying charges can be brought in respect of delays which occur after the contract has been terminated on account of the buyer's failure to present the ship within such time as will enable her to load within the shipment period. In one case[37] this was held to be the position even though the goods were subsequently loaded. The case gives rise to some difficulty since normally the contract would come to an end only on the seller's acceptance of the buyer's breach; and there is nothing in the report to indicate that such acceptance had taken place. (4) A fourth type of provision which may exclude the normal rule is one to the effect that the buyer should pay storage charges if, as a result of his failure to make a proper nomination, the goods are not shipped within the shipment period.[38] In such a case, the seller would be entitled to refuse to deliver only if the delay was so great as to occasion him serious prejudice. This would also, it is submitted, be the position where the contract failed to specify any time or period for shipment.[39]

Time of shipment at buyer's option. Where, as is usual, the contract specifies a shipment period, the option as to the time within that period at which the goods are to be shipped is prima facie the buyer's, who is normally entitled to the whole shipment period in the sense that he is not 20–047

[33] This was the effect of clause 9 of the contract in *The Naxos*, above.
[34] *Lusograin Commercio Internacional de Cereas Ltda. v Bunge AG* [1986] 2 Lloyd's Rep. 654 at 662.
[35] As in *Fratelli Moretti SpA v Nidera Handelscompagnie BV* [1980] 1 Lloyd's Rep. 534, affirmed [1981] 2 Lloyd's Rep. 47. *Cf. Thomas P Gonzales Corp. v F R Waring (International) Pty* [1980] 2 Lloyd's Rep. 160 (where the option whether to grant the extension was the seller's); *Toepfer v Sosimage SpA* [1980] 2 Lloyd's Rep. 397 at 402; *Miserochi & Co. SpA v Agricultores Federados Argentinos* [1982] 1 Lloyd's Rep. 202; *Richco International Ltd v Alfred C Toepfer International GmbH* (*The Bonde*) [1991] 1 Lloyd's Rep. 136 at 145.
[36] *Richco International Ltd v Alfred C Toepfer International GmbH* (*The Bonde*) [1991] 1 Lloyd's Rep. 136; for demurrage payable by the seller, see above, para.20–019.
[37] *Kurt A Becher GmbH & Co. v Voest Alpine Intertrading GmbH (The Rio Apa)* [1992] 2 Lloyd's Rep. 586.
[38] As in *The Osterbek*, above, n.31 (where the provision was disregarded as there were no appropriate storage facilities at the port of shipment) and *Toepfer v Sosimage SpA* [1980] 2 Lloyd's Rep. 397; *cf.* the terms of the contract in *R. Pagnan & Fratelli v NGJ Schouten NV* (*The Philipinas I*) [1973] 1 Lloyd's Rep. 349.
[39] *cf. above*, para.20–029.

bound to nominate a ship which can load before the end of the period. In *J J Cunningham Ltd v Robert A Munro & Co. Ltd*[40] bran was sold f.o.b. Rotterdam for shipment during October. The seller had the goods ready at Rotterdam on October 14, but the buyer was not able to nominate an effective ship until October 28. It was held that there was no breach of contract on the buyer's part, so that he was entitled to reject the bulk of the goods, which had deteriorated between October 14 and 28. His only duty was to nominate a ship at such time as would enable the seller to put the goods on board before the end of the shipment period. The position would, it is submitted be different if the ship nominated by the buyer arrived after the date specified in the nomination. In such a case the contract may expressly make the buyer liable for loss occasioned to the seller as a result of the delay,[41] and it is submitted that he should be so liable even in the absence of such an express provision. Nor, in the case put, should the buyer be entitled to reject the goods on account of their deterioration after the date given by him in his shipping instructions: this conclusion follows from the rules as to risk discussed in paragraph 20–092 below.

The buyer must notify his nomination of the ship so as to enable the seller to have the goods ready for shipment by that ship. The contract may expressly lay down how much notice is to be given.[42] In the absence of such a provision, the seller is entitled to such notice as will allow him a reasonable time to have the goods ready for shipment by the nominated ship.[43]

The buyer may be able to perform his duty to give shipping instructions only after some act has been done by the seller: for example, after the seller has given notice that the goods are ready for shipment. In such a case the general rule[44] is that the seller must give the required notice within a reasonable time before the beginning of the shipment period "so as to enable the buyer to ship from the very beginning of the shipment period."[45]

20–048 **Time of shipment at seller's option.** The rules stated in paragraphs 20–046 and 20–047 are based on the assumption that the buyer has the option as to the time of shipment; but that option may be the seller's.[46] In such a case it would seem that the buyer's duty to nominate an effective ship can arise only on notification by the seller that the goods are, or will be, ready for shipment at a designated time within the shipment period. Thus if the seller fails to give such notice, the general rule is that the buyer is not bound to give shipping instructions and that the seller is liable in damages. This rule will, however, be displaced where the seller's failure to give the notice is due to the deliberate conduct of the buyer in obstructing or

---

40 (1922) 28 Com.Cas. 42.

41 As in *Compagnie Commerciale Sucres et Denrées v C Czarnikow Ltd* (*The Naxos*) [1990] 1 W.L.R. 1337.

42 See above, para.20–032.

43 *Forrestt & Son Ltd v Aramayo* (1900) 83 L.T. 335 at 338.

44 It may be modified by provisions of the kind discussed in para.20–049, below, which divide the option as to the time of shipment between the parties.

45 *David T Boyd & Co. Ltd v Louis Louca* [1973] 1 Lloyd's Rep. 209 at 212.

46 Above, para.20–035.

preventing the seller from giving it. Thus where an f.o.b. buyer, wishing to escape from the contract, deliberately failed to pick up his telephone when the seller attempted to give the notice before the contractual deadline, it was the buyer (and not the seller) who was held to be in breach.[47]

Divided option as to time of shipment. The option as to the time of shipment may also in a sense be divided between the parties. This would be the position where the seller undertook to have the goods ready before the end of a specified period and to give notice when they were ready, but where the buyer then had the *whole* of the rest of that period available for shipment. If in such a case the seller failed to give notice that the goods were ready he would be liable in damages and the buyer would not (it is submitted[48]) be bound to give shipping instructions. Once the seller had given such notice, the buyer would be bound to give shipping instructions. If he failed to do so he would in turn be liable in damages and the seller would not be bound to deliver. But these rules may be displaced by the conduct of the parties, in particular where neither of them is able to comply with the contractual time-table for delivery. In *Forrestt & Son Ltd v Aramayo*[49] a contract was made to build a steam launch and to deliver it f.o.b. London by January 7, 1899. On the preceding December 12, the buyers asked the sellers to ship the launch at Liverpool on December 29 or at Hamburg on January 6. The sellers justifiably refused to make such shipment, and on December 14 the buyers wrote to the sellers, saying that, if the launch were not so shipped, there would be no further opportunity of shipment until April. The buyers subsequently nominated a ship which sailed on April 17. The launch was shipped on this ship, having been completed only in April, and in an action by the sellers for the price, the buyers counterclaimed for damages for delay in delivery. They argued that they were not bound to name a ship in January as the sellers could not have delivered the launch before April.[50] But the argument was rejected and the buyers' claim failed on the ground that they were not ready and willing to give shipping instructions in accordance with the contract. It may, at first sight, seem strange that the buyers should have been required to nominate a vessel which could load in accordance with the contract if they knew[51] that such a nomination would be perfectly useless. Probably their failure to give shipping instructions would not, of itself, have made them *liable* in damages: to resist such a claim they would have had to show no more than that the sellers had failed to give notice that the launch was ready for delivery,[52] in time for arrangements to be made for shipment to take place 20–049

[47] *Nissho Iwai Petroleum Co. Inc. v Cargill International SA* [1993] 1 Lloyd's Rep. 180. Contrast *North Sea Energy Holdings NV v Petroleum Authority of Thailand* [1999] 2 Lloyd's Rep. 418, where an f.o.b. contract was held not by implication to require the buyer to provide the seller with a list of ports of *discharge*.
[48] Below, para.20–050.
[49] (1900) 83 L.T. 335.
[50] See p.337. In line 5 of the argument of counsel for the appellants, "defendants" is an obvious misprint for "plaintiffs".
[51] This seems to have been assumed at p.338.
[52] Below, para.20–050.

before the end of the contract period.[53] But to *succeed* in a claim for damages, the buyers would have had to show one of two things. The first possible basis for such a claim would have been proof by the buyers that they were ready and willing to nominate a ship able to load in accordance with the contract. This was the only possibility considered in the judgments and it was obviously negatived by the facts. The second possibility would have been for the buyers to show that the sellers had indicated that they could not deliver the launch within the contract period. Later authority[54] supports the view that, if such an indication could have been treated by the buyers as an anticipatory breach and had been accepted by them as such, then they would have been entitled to damages without having to show that they could have nominated a ship able to load within the shipment period. On the facts, however, the buyers could not have established such an anticipatory breach. There was no express repudiation by the sellers of their obligation to deliver the launch in accordance with the contract. Nor could one be inferred from the mere fact that the launch was not ready for delivery until April; for this delay may well have been *induced* by the buyers' letter of December 14, stating that, if delivery were not made in accordance with their original instructions (which the sellers had justifiably rejected), then it could not be taken until April. In these circumstances, the sellers could in their turn have treated this letter as an anticipatory breach, rescinded the contract, and claimed damages from the buyers without having to show that they could (but for the delay induced by the letter of December 14) have delivered by January 7.[55] Proof by the *buyers* that (even if the delay had not been so induced) the sellers could *not* have made such delivery may sometimes[56] be relevant as to damages, but it would not absolve the buyers from liability, unless the sellers' inability to make the delivery was due to some breach on their part committed before December 14 and justifying rescission by the buyers.[57]

20–050 The judgments in *Forrestt & Son Ltd v Aramayo* are based on the assumption that the case was one in which, in accordance with the normal rule, the seller was under no obligation to deliver unless the buyer first nominated an effective ship. But the contract in that case was for goods to be manufactured by the seller, who was not bound to deliver before the end of the shipment period. In such a case it is submitted that the buyer is not bound to nominate a ship until he has been notified by the seller, within

---

[53] *cf. Tradax Export SA v Italgrani di Francesco Ambrosio* [1983] 2 Lloyd's Rep. 109 at 115 for a similar argument concerning the buyer's duty to give shipping instructions.

[54] *British and Beningtons Ltd v NW Cachar Tea Co.* [1923] A.C. 48; *Gill & Duffus SA v Berger & Co. Inc.* [1984] A.C. 382; above, paras 9–011 *et seq.*, 19–161, 19–163, 19–164.

[55] *cf. Peter Turnbull & Co. Pty Ltd v Mundus Trading Co. (Australia) Ltd* (1953–55) 90 C.L.R. 235, where a seller was held liable in damages in spite of the buyer's failure to give proper shipping instructions, since this failure was induced by the conduct of the seller.

[56] In particular, if the seller's inability gives the buyer the right to cancel *irrespective of breach* under an express provision of the contract: above, para.19–165.

[57] Above, paras 19–161, 19–165, 19–167.

that period, that the goods are ready for shipment[58]; a term to this effect should be implied to give business efficacy to the contract, for unless this were done the buyer might be legally obliged to make a perfectly useless nomination. But this argument would not affect the actual decision; for even if the seller had been under an obligation to give notice of readiness to deliver within the shipment period, this obligation would have been waived, in respect of time, by the buyer's letter of December 14.

Withdrawal of a nominated ship. A buyer who has the option as to the time of shipment may nominate a ship to load at one time in the shipment period, cancel that nomination and then substitute another ship to load at a later time, still within the shipment period. In one such case Widgery J. said[59] that the buyers must "provide a vessel which is capable of loading within the stipulated time, and if, as a matter of courtesy or convenience, the buyers inform the sellers that they propose to provide vessel A, I can see no reason in principle why they should not change their mind and provide vessel B at a later stage, always assuming that vessel B is provided within such time as to make it possible for her to fulfil the buyer's obligations under the contract". In the case in question, vessel A was nominated in the expectation that she would reach the port of loading within the shipment period and it was only when this expectation was falsified by unexpected delays that the buyers had substituted vessel B. Moreover, the interval between the estimated arrival of vessel A and the actual arrival of vessel B was only three days; the goods were not perishable; and there was no suggestion that the sellers had in any way acted in reliance on the nomination of vessel A or been prejudiced by the substitution of vessel B. The significance of the first of these factors was brought out in a later case[60] in which a buyer was required to nominate a vessel for loading at Milford Haven. Three days before the end of the shipment period he nominated a vessel which was then at Istanbul. It was held that he could not rely on the possibility of making a substitute nomination since the original nomination was not a "true and proper" one, but one which was "manifestly false" and "wholly artificial".[61] Even where no objection can be taken to the original nomination on this ground, it is questionable whether the buyer would be entitled to make a substitute nomination where the seller had acted in reliance on the original one. Suppose the buyer nominates a ship for loading on a day early in the shipment period and the seller acts in reliance on the nomination by getting 20–051

---

[58] *cf. above*, para.20–035. It does not follow that the option as to the time of shipment is wholly the seller's as the buyer may have the whole *rest* of the shipment period to ship the goods, after notice that they are ready: above, para.20–049.
[59] *Agricultores Federados Argentinos v Ampro SA* [1965] 2 Lloyd's Rep. 156 at 167 (above, para.20–031). Where the contract does *not* specify a shipment period, the terms of the buyer's shipping instructions seem to determine the contractual date of shipment (above para.20–029 at n.9); but Widgery J.'s dictum quoted in the text above assumes that this is not the case where the contract *does* specify a shipment period. The same assumption underlies the passage in *J & J Cunningham Ltd v Robert A. Munro Ltd* (1922) 28 Com.Cas. 42 at 46 referred to in n.62, *infra*.
[60] *Texaco Ltd v Eurogulf Shipping Co. Ltd* [1987] 2 Lloyd's Rep. 541.
[61] *ibid.*, at p.545.

the goods to the docks ready for shipment on that day. If the buyer could with impunity withdraw the ship and nominate another to load on a different day, much later in the shipment period, the seller could be gravely prejudiced: *e.g.* if he had to pay storage charges, or if the goods deteriorated. It has been suggested that the seller can recover damages for such loss though the precise legal basis for such a claim is by no means clear.[62]

The substitute nomination must, moreover, be itself valid, *i.e.* in accordance with the requirements of the contract. Thus in one case[63] the contract required the buyer to give the seller a "provisional notice of eight clear days of vessel's e.t.a.", and the buyer gave such notice in relation to vessel A. Less than eight days before the end of the shipment period it had turned out that vessel A would not arrive within the shipment period and the buyer purported to substitute vessel B. This substitution was ineffective since the eight days' notice required by the contract could no longer be given in relation to an arrival time of vessel B within the shipment period. *A fortiori*, a substitution would be invalid where it was made in breach of a restriction imposed by the contract: *e.g.* of a provision to the effect that a nomination once made could be withdrawn only in case of *force majeure*[64] and no event amounting to *force majeure* had occurred.

20–052 **Bad nomination followed by good.** Where a nomination which is not in accordance with the contract is followed by one which is in accordance with the contract, the second nomination is good and the seller is bound to load in accordance with it. Thus where the buyer nominated a ship to load at the wrong port and then (within the shipment period) nominated the same ship to load at the right port the second nomination was held good.[65] The same result was reached where the first nomination was of a ship expected ready to load on a specified day within the shipment period. She was delayed and the buyers nominated a second ship which was able to load on a later day but still within the shipment period; and it was held that the second nomination was good.[66] It is submitted, however, that the seller's liability to load a later ship is subject to the principle, discussed in the preceding paragraph, that the seller must be allowed some remedy if, as a result of having acted on reliance on the original nomination, he is prejudiced by the change of the date, within the shipment period, on which he is, by the later nomination, required to load.

20–053 **Ship "expected to arrive".** A buyer who buys on terms specifying a shipment period and arranges shipment by a ship which is only "expected ready to load" by the end of that period obviously runs a commercial risk.

---

[62] In *J J Cunningham Ltd v Robert A Munro & Co. Ltd* (1922) 28 Com.Cas. 42 at 46 Lord Hewart C.J. said that it was "not exactly estoppel" and based it on a principle analogous to that in *Hughes v Metropolitan Ry.* (1877) 2 App.Cas. 439, with the addition that the claimant must "suffer damage." Normally that principle would not in English law give rise to a cause of action but only to a defence: see Treitel, *The Law of Contract* (11th ed., 2003), pp.112–115.

[63] *Cargill UK Ltd v Continental UK Ltd* [1989] 2 Lloyd's Rep. 290.

[64] See the terms of the f.o.b. contract in *Alfred C. Toepfer International GmbH v Itex Itagrani Export SA* [1993] 1 Lloyd's Rep. 360.

[65] *Modern Transport Co. Ltd v Ternstrom and Roos* (1924) Ll.L.R. 345.

[66] *Agricultores Federados Argentinos v Ampro SA* [1965] 2 Lloyd's Rep. 157; *cf. Bremer Handelsgesellschaft mbH v J H Rayner & Co. Ltd* [1979] 2 Lloyd's Rep. 216.

Nomination of such a ship would not amount to compliance with the contract of sale if the ship failed to arrive within the shipment period; while such failure would not give the buyer any remedy against the carrier[67] so long as the latter had reasonable grounds for his stated expectation.[68] Indeed the buyer might well be liable to the shipowner for dead freight on account of the seller's justified refusal to load after the end of the shipment period. The buyer can protect himself by providing in the contract of sale for loading on a ship or ships "expected ready to load" so that a nomination of a ship expected ready to load within the named period would not be bad merely because the ship arrived after the end of the period.[69] Alternatively, the buyer can provide in the contract of carriage for the right to cancel that contract if the ship is not ready to load by the end of the shipment period laid down in the contract of sale: this will at least save him from being simultaneously in breach of two contracts through no fault of his own.

Expenses related to shipment. As between buyer and seller, any charges made by the carrier for operations taking place after the goods cross the ship's rail,[70] and any duties or other charges becoming payable after shipment, fall on the buyer. Thus the buyer is responsible for the cost of stowage once the goods are on board[71]; but not (for example) for export duty payable before shipment.[72] These statements refer only to the position between buyer and seller. Thus the cost of stowage may fall on the buyer as between buyer and seller, even though as between shipper and carrier it falls on the shipper (who, in some types of f.o.b. contracts,[73] may be the seller). The prima facie rule may also be varied by the contract of sale for example by a provision that export duty (irrespective of the time when it is payable) is for the buyer's account.[74] 20–054

(b) *Payment of the Price*

Payment. At this point we are concerned with the buyer's *duty to pay* the price; the circumstances in which this arises are not necessarily the same as those in which the seller can bring an *action for* the price.[75] Under section 20–055

[67] See *Finnish Government (Ministry of Food) v H. Ford & Co.* (1921) 6 Ll.L.R. 188.
[68] *Sanday v Keighley Maxted & Co.* (1922) 91 L.J.K.B. 624; *cf. The Mihalis Angelos* [1971] 1 Q.B. 164.
[69] *Finnish Government (Ministry of Food) v H. Ford & Co.*, above (where the actual decision was that the buyer could not in May nominate a ship as "expected ready to load" in February and/or March).
[70] Above, para.20–018.
[71] *Att.-Gen. v Leopold Walford (London) Ltd* (1923) 14 Ll.L.R. 359; *cf. Blandy Bros & Co. Ltd v Nello Simoni Ltd* [1963] 2 Lloyd's Rep. 24, affirmed *ibid.*, at p.393.
[72] *Bowhill Coal Co. Ltd v Tobias* (1902) 5 F.(Ct. of Sess.) 262.
[73] *i.e.* where the seller takes out the bill of lading "in his own name," as in the second of the types of f.o.b. contracts described in the *Pyrene* case [1954] 2 Q.B. 402 at 424, above, para.20–003.
[74] See *Cie. Continentale d'Importation Zurich SA v Ispahani Ltd* [1962] 1 Lloyd's Rep. 213.
[75] As to this, see below, paras 20–126 *et seq.*

28 of the Sale of Goods Act, 1979, "unless otherwise agreed . . . the buyer must be ready and willing to pay the price in exchange for possession of the goods".[76] Where the goods have been shipped and the bill of lading has been obtained by the seller, the price normally becomes payable on tender of the bill of lading, amounting to tender of constructive possession of the goods[77]; this result may be based either on an application of section 28, or on a contrary agreement ousting the section.[78] The contract may call for payment against bill of lading even where the goods are shipped on a ship chartered by the buyer.[79] Where all the shipping arrangements are made by the buyer (so that the bill of lading is never in the seller's hands) the contract is likely to call for payment against some other document evidencing delivery of the goods on board ship, such as a mate's receipt or similar document[80]; and it may also call for further documents (such as an invoice, a policy of insurance,[81] an inspection certificate, a certificate of origin, etc.) against which payment is to be made. The duty to pay arises on tender of all the documents against which payment is, under the terms of the contract, to be made. As in the case of a c.i.f. contract, not all documents to be produced or procured by the seller necessarily fall into his category.[82]

20–056 **Time and place of payment.** The time and place of payment are prima facie the time and place of tender of whatever documents are specified in the contract as those against which payment is to be made. The buyer is under no duty to pay except in accordance with such requirements. If the contract provides for payment against bill of lading, and the buyer becomes bankrupt before the goods are shipped, the seller is not entitled to refuse to ship on the ground that the buyer's trustee has not notified him, before shipment, of his intention to adopt the contract. The trustee is not bound to declare his intention in this respect until the time for payment under the contract arrives.[83] Special problems as to time and place of payment which

---

[76] Under the Vienna Convention on Contracts for the International Sale of Goods (above, para.1–024) the buyer must, unless otherwise agreed, pay the price "when the seller places either the goods or the documents controlling their disposition at the buyer's disposal": Art. 58(1). But Art. 58(3) provides that the buyer is not bound to pay the price "until he has had an opportunity to examine the goods, unless the procedures for delivery or payment agreed upon by the parties are inconsistent with his having such an opportunity." The precise effect of these words is far from clear, but it seems that a stipulation for payment against documents in an f.o.b. contract would normally give rise to such an inconsistency, at least where the buyer was not present, or represented, at the port of shipment.

[77] Above, para.18–063; *cf. Jack v Roberts and Gibson* (1865) 3 M.(Ct. of Sess.) 554. It is assumed that the bill of lading is an order or a bearer bill and thus a document of title in the traditional common law sense described in para.18–007 above.

[78] *cf. above*, para.19–075.

[79] *Gibson v Carruthers* (1841) 8 M. & W. 321.

[80] As in *F E Napier v Dexters Ltd* (1926) 26 Ll.L.R. 62; *ibid.*, at p.184 and *Pyrene Co. Ltd v Scindia Navigation Co. Ltd* [1954] 2 Q.B. 402 (where payment was actually made in advance).

[81] If the seller is bound to procure it.

[82] See the discussion of the meaning of the expression "shipping documents" in paras 19–024 and 19–058, above; this applies *mutatis mutandis* to f.o.b. contracts.

[83] *Gibson v Carruthers*, above n.79.

may arise where the contract provides for payment by documentary bill, other negotiable instrument or documentary credit are discussed elsewhere in this book.[84]

Excuses for failure to comply with stipulations as to payment. Failure to comply with the contractual stipulations as to payment may be excused by waiver on the seller's part, or by the seller's own breach of contract. This topic is discussed generally in Chapter 9,[85] and in relation to stipulations for payment by documentary credit in Chapter 23.[86] If such a credit is on terms different from those required by the contract of sale, but the seller nevertheless accepts it, he may thereby be held to have agreed to vary the buyer's original obligation, so that payment in accordance with the terms of the credit actually opened will give the buyer a good discharge.[87] 20–057

Effect of breach by seller. An f.o.b. seller may purport to cancel the contract on the ground that the buyer has allegedly failed to comply with a stipulation as to the time of payment. If there has in fact been no such failure, the attempt to cancel will normally amount to a repudiation of the contract in the sense of an expression of unwillingness to perform and to accept further performance. If the buyer accepts this repudiation, he is relieved from his obligation to comply thereafter with the requirements of the contract as to payment. The buyer may be relieved from this obligation even if he does not accept the repudiation, for the repudiation may have induced his nonpayment by making it clear that tender of payment would be refused. Failure to accept the repudiation entitles the seller to withdraw it within the contract period and then to demand performance; but it does not enable him to rely on the fact that the buyer has not made a useless tender of payment as an *ex post facto* justification of his own wrongful repudiation.[88] 20–058

Refusal by the seller to deliver may constitute a repudiation of the contract and if the repudiation takes place before his performance becomes due it will amount to an anticipatory breach. If accepted as such, it entitles the buyer to damages even though he cannot show that he could have performed the contractual stipulation as to payment[89]; though proof by the

---

[84] Above, paras 18–221 to 18–225; below, Chs 22 and 23.

[85] Above, paras 9–050, 9–055.

[86] Below, paras 23–095, 23–096.

[87] *W J Alan & Co. v El Nasr Export & Import Co.* [1972] 2 Q.B. 189; *cf.* above, para.20–024; *Shamsher Jute Mills v Sethia (London) Ltd* [1987] 1 Lloyd's Rep. 388 at 392.

[88] *Et. Chainbaux SARL v Harbormaster Ltd* [1955] 1 Lloyd's Rep. 303 at 310, discussing *Braithwaite v Foreign Hardwood Co. Ltd* [1905] 2 K.B. 543 (as to which see above, paras 19–167 to 19–171).

[89] On the principle of *British and Beningtons Ltd v N W Cachar Tea Co. Ltd* [1923] A.C. 48 and *Gill & Duffus SA v Berger & Co. Inc.* [1984] A.C. 382, above, paras 19–161 to 19–166. Apparently contrary statements in *Cohen & Co. v Ockerby & Co. Ltd* (1917) 24 C.L.R. 288 at 298, 302 and *Bowes v Chaleyer* (1923) 32 C.L.R. 159 at 169, 192 are restricted to the situation in which an anticipatory breach is *not* accepted. In *Cohen & Co. v Ockerby & Co. Ltd*, above, the dismissal of the f.o.b. buyer's claim was also based on the alternative ground that his demand for delivery short of the ship was unjustified; above, para.20–015.

seller that the buyer could not have performed may sometimes[90] be relevant as to damages, and even as to liability if the inability was due to a repudiatory breach on the buyer's part committed before the seller's repudiation.[91] Where the seller's refusal to deliver is *not* repudiatory, it seems that the buyer cannot *claim* damages without showing that he could have performed the stipulations of the contract as to payment. But even in such a case the buyer would not *be liable* for non-payment, so long as the seller maintained his refusal to deliver, if (as would normally be the case) that refusal amounted, or led, to a failure to perform a condition precedent to or a concurrent condition of the buyer's duty to accept and pay.

4. CONTRACTUAL RELATIONS WITH CARRIER

20–059 **Introductory.** In Chapter 19, a number of questions were considered concerning the contractual relations which could arise in the course of the performance of a c.i.f. contract between seller or buyer on the one hand and carrier on the other.[92] Our present concern is with similar questions which can arise where the sale is on f.o.b. terms. The starting point for this discussion lies in the distinction drawn by Devlin J. in *Pyrene Co. Ltd v Scindia Navigation Co Ltd*[93] between three ways in which arrangements may be made for the carriage of goods sold on such terms; and we shall see that the classification there adopted is by no means exhaustive. It is a feature of many of the situations here to be discussed that a contractual relationship may arise between, on the one hand, the buyer or seller and, on the other, the carrier *before* the issue of a bill of lading; and this fact gives rise to problems in determining the impact of the Contracts (Rights of Third Parties) Act 1999 ("the 1999 Act")[94] on these situations. These problems arise because the right of enforcement given to a third party by section 1 of the Act does not, because of the subsection 6(5)[95] exception, apply in the case of (*inter alia*) a "contract for the carriage of goods by sea". For our present purposes, it suffices to recall that this expression includes a contract of carriage "contained in or evidenced by a bill of lading".[96]

20–060 **No advance booking of shipping space.** It will be recalled that, in the first of the situations described by Devlin J. in the *Pyrene* case,[97] there is no antecedent reservation of space in the ship nominated by the buyer to receive the goods[98] and that the seller is said to be "directly a party to the

[90] In particular, if the buyer's inability gives the seller a right to cancel *irrespective of breach* under an express provision of the contract: above, para.19–166.
[91] Above, paras 9–017, 19–161; *cf.* para.20–049.
[92] Above, paras 19–090 *et seq.*
[93] [1954] 2 Q.B. 402 at 424, above, para.20–003.
[94] Above, para.18–005.
[95] *ibid.*, sub-paragraph (f).
[96] Contracts (Rights of Third Parties) Act 1999, ss.6(6)(a); "bill of lading" has the same meaning here as in Carriage of Goods by Sea Act 1992: Contracts (Rights of Third Parties) Act 1999, s.6(7)(a).
[97] Above, para.20–003.
[98] Above, para.20–004.

contract of carriage at least until he takes out the bill of lading in the buyer's name".[99] When the bill is so taken out, a new contract contained in or evidenced by the bill of lading will be created and the subsection 6(5) exception will apply to this contract, so that the acquisition of third party rights under it will be governed by the Carriage of Goods by Sea Act 1992 and not by the 1999 Act. This will be so whether the shipper named in the bill of lading is the buyer or the seller.[1] But the earlier contract between seller and carrier[2] is *not* contained in or evidenced by a bill of lading, having not only come into existence before the bill of lading contract, but being also (where the bill names the buyer as shipper) between different parties. Hence it does not fall within the definition of a "contract for the carriage of goods by sea" in the 1999 Act,[3] so that at first sight it is not within the subsection 6(5) exception, with the result that rights of enforcement under this earlier contract can, under subsection 1(1) of that Act, be conferred on a third party (such as, typically, the buyer). The fact that the original (pre-bill of lading) contract is between seller and carrier, while the new bill of lading contract is between buyer and carrier, can, however, give rise to difficulties under the 1999 Act if the terms of the new contract differ from those of the old: the difficulties arise from the general principle that, once a third party has acquired rights of enforcement under the 1999 Act, the contracting parties cannot, without the third party's consent, rescind or vary the contract by agreement so as to extinguish or alter those rights after one of the circumstances specified in subsection 2(1) of that Act has occurred.[4] The difficulties arise because the buyer may have acquired rights by virtue of the 1999 Act under the pre-bill of lading contract and because those rights may differ from those which he has under the later bill of lading contract, The general view hitherto has been that the relations between buyer and carrier are then governed by the terms of the latter contract alone; and there are, it is submitted, two ways of preserving this position under the 1999 Act. The first is to say that the buyer has consented (within subsection 2(1) of the 1999 Act) to the variation. He may not, indeed, have done so at the stage at which (in Devlin J.'s words) the seller "takes out" the bill of lading since at that stage the buyer is unlikely to be aware of its terms. But he can be said to have done so at the later stage at which the bill is tendered to, and accepted by, him against payment; or it could be argued that, by contracting on f.o.b. terms and nominating the ship, the buyer has consented in advance to the seller's taking out the bill of lading in (to quote Devlin J. again) "terms usual in the trade".[5] The second line of argument is to rely on subsection 1(4) of the 1999 Act, by which "This section does not confer any right on a third party to enforce a term of a contract otherwise than subject to and in accordance with any other relevant term of the

---

99 [1954] 2 Q.B. 402 at 424. The assumption made by Devlin J. is that the seller has, in making the preliminary contract of carriage, acted as principal an not as agent for the buyer; *cf.* above, para.20–008.

1 See above, para.20–005.

2 Above, at n.99; above, para.18–047.

3 See subsections 6(6) and (7).

4 See para.18–005 sub-paragraph (d), above.

5 [1954] 2 Q.B. 402 at 424.

contract". It can be argued that the pre-bill of lading contract is subject to an implied term that it is to be superseded by another contract when the bill of lading is "taken out" and that the contractual relations of all the relevant parties are then (so far as the carriage operation is concerned) to be governed by the terms of the bill of lading alone. Since the whole pre-bill of lading contract is (in the present situation) implied from conduct, there should be little difficulty in convincing the court that such a term is to be implied. The implication could be said to arise either in fact (under the "officious bystander" or "business efficacy" tests) or in law because such a term was one of the "legal incidents" of the "kind of contractual relationship" here under discussion.[6]

20–061 **Shipping arrangements made by seller.** In the second of the situations discussed by Devlin J. in the *Pyrene* case, the seller "is asked to make the necessary arrangements" and "takes the bill of lading in his own name" (*i.e.* as shipper) and later transfers the bill to the buyer "as in a c.i.f. contract". The seller would then normally be an original party to the bill of lading contract[7]; and for the purposes of the Contracts (Rights of Third Parties) Act 1999, the case would fall within the subsection 6(5) exception,[8] so that the acquisition of rights by the buyer under the bill of lading contract would be governed, not by that Act, but by section 2(1) of the Carriage of Goods by Sea Act 1992.[9] The extinction of the seller's rights under the contract of carriage would likewise be governed by section 2(5) of the 1992 Act[10]; those rights will not be preserved under section 4 of the 1999 Act. No reference is made by Devlin J. to any pre-bill of lading contract in this situation. If there were such a contract, it would be between the *same* parties as the bill of lading contract; and it is not likely that the requirements of the 1999 Act would be satisfied in relation to this contract so as to confer any rights of enforcement on the buyer (*e.g.* by virtue of his being named as the person to whom the goods were to be delivered under the bill of lading).[11] In the unlikely event of the seller's having made an antecedent contract with the carrier as the buyer's agent,[12] the buyer would be a party to it, so that there would be no question of the buyer's acquiring rights under it by virtue of section 1 of the 1999 Act.[13]

A variant of Devlin J.'s second situation is illustrated by *Hanjin Shipping Co. Ltd v Procter and Gamble Philippines Ltd*[14] where a cargo-booking

---

[6] For the distinction between these two types of implied contract, see Treitel, *The Law of Contract* (11th ed. 2003), pp.201, 206.
[7] See above, para.20–008; *cf. Evergreen Marine Corp. v Aldgate Warehouse (Aldgate) Ltd* [2003] EWHC 667 (Comm), [2003] Lloyd's Rep. 587 (f.o.b. buyer held not to be a party to the contract of carriage merely by reason of having made a "special freight agreement" with the carrier governing the rate of freight. The bill of lading named the sellers as shippers).
[8] Above, para.18–005, sub-paragraph (f).
[9] Above, para.18–102.
[10] Above, para.18–114.
[11] *cf.* below sentence after n.16; above, para.18–024.
[12] *cf.* above, para.20–008.
[13] This follows from the words "not a party" in s.1(1) of that Act.
[14] [1997] 2 Lloyd's Rep. 341.

contract was made by an f.o.b. seller's agent with the carrier's agent, naming the buyer's agent as the consignee to whom delivery was to be made. The seller having instructed the carrier to return the goods to the port of loading, no bill of lading was ever issued[15] and it was held that the only contract which had ever come into existence was the cargo-booking contract, to which the buyer was not a party. Under the Contracts (Rights of Third Parties) Act 1999, the subsection 6(5) exception could not apply to such a case (there being no "contract for the carriage of goods by sea" within that subsection[16]) and the question would now arise whether the cargo-booking contract could confer rights on the buyer under section 1 of that Act. The answer to this question would depend on factors analogous to those discussed in paragraph 18–024 above in relation to the effect of the 1999 Act on a shipper's right to divert goods away from a consignee named in the bill of lading. As we there saw, rights are unlikely to be acquired by a third party in such circumstances.

Shipping space reserved by buyer. The third of the situations discussed by Devlin J. in the *Pyrene* case[17] is that in which shipping space has been booked by the buyer's agent, and the goods are loaded by the seller who obtains a mate's receipt which he hands to the buyer's agent who then obtains a bill of lading in the buyer's name.[18] This is what may be called the normal sequence of events in the third situation; we shall see that there are many possible variations of it. The actual decision in the *Pyrene* case was that the seller was *bound* by some of the terms of the bill of lading even though this contained or evidenced a contract between buyer and carrier; and this aspect of the case is not affected by the Contracts (Rights of Third Parties) Act 1999.[19] But Devlin J. also said that the seller could acquire *rights* against the carrier, such as a right to damages if the carrier "sail[ed] off without loading the goods".[20] One possible basis for the acquisition of such rights by the seller was that an implied contract arose when the seller "by delivering the goods alongside . . . implicitly invited the shipowner to load and the shipowner implicity accepted that invitation".[21] On the special facts of the *Pyrene* case, to be described in paragraph 20–066 below, there is (with respect) much to be said for the inference of such an implied contract. But in the absence of such special facts no such inference of the shipowner's acceptance of the seller's invitation could be drawn merely from the fact that the carrier had refused (or failed) to take goods on board when presented for loading by the seller.[22] Another possible basis for the acquisition of rights by the seller, and apparently the one favoured by Devlin J., was the "wider principle"[23] that "a third party [*i.e.* the seller] 20–062

[15] *ibid.*, p.345.
[16] See Contracts (Rights of Third Parties) Act 1999, s.6(6).
[17] [1954] 2 Q.B. 402 at 424.
[18] The bill of lading in the *Pyrene* case above, named the buyer as shipper.
[19] Above, para.18–005, sub-paragraph (c).
[20] [1954] 2 Q.B. 402 at 425.
[21] *ibid.*, p.462; the actual decision in the *Pyrene* case was explained on this ground in *Scruttons Ltd v Midland Silicones Ltd* [1962] A.C. 446 at 471.
[22] *cf. above*, para.20–013.
[23] sc., than agency or implied contract.

takes those benefits of the contract [*i.e.* that between buyer and carrier] which appertain to his interest therein".[24] This view did not, as a matter of common law, survive the later reaffirmation of the common law doctrine of privity of contract[25]; but the question now arises whether, in a situation of this kind, rights against the carrier could be acquired by the seller by virtue of section 1 of the 1999 Act. In so far as the seller's claim was based on an implied contract between himself and the carrier, it would not be governed by the 1999 Act since section 1 confers rights only on "a person who is *not* a party to a contract". But this restriction would not prevent the seller from acquiring rights, by virtue of section 1, to enforce a term of some *other* contract between buyer and carrier, such as that which had arisen between these parties on the booking of cargo space. The question whether the seller had actually acquired such rights would depend on his being able to satisfy the other requirements of section 1 and on the operation of the subsection 6(5) exception. This would in turn depend on the course of dealing that followed the making of the cargo-booking contract between buyer and carrier. Four possibilities will be considered in paragraphs 20–063 to 20–066 below.

20–063 **No bill of lading issued.** The first possibility is that no bill of lading is ever issued because the goods are never shipped. In such a case, no "contract for the carriage of goods by sea" within subsection 6(5) of the 1999 Act comes into existence,[26] so that the rights (if any) of the seller to enforce a term of some other contract between buyer and carrier will be determined in accordance with section 1 of the 1999 Act.

20–064 **Received bill issued but goods not shipped.** The second possibility is that a received for shipment bill is issued but the goods are never shipped. If the statement that the goods had been so received was accurate, and if the goods had been received by the carrier *from the seller* for shipment, then the fact of such receipt might give some plausibility to the suggestion that an implied contract had arisen between carrier and seller, giving the latter a remedy at common law in respect of the carrier's later failure or refusal to ship. That contract would be distinct from the bill of lading contract which would, ex hypothesi,[27] be between buyer and carrier; and the contract contained in or evidenced by the received bill would fall within the definition of a "contract for the carriage of goods by sea" in subsection 6(5) of the 1999 Act.[28] Hence that subsection would prevent the buyer from asserting any rights under that contract by virtue of the 1999 Act; and it seems that any rights which he might have had under that Act as a third party to the pre-bill of lading contract between buyer and carrier would cease to exist as a term is likely to be implied into that contract by which it was to be superseded, and so cease to have effect, on the issue of the bill of lading.[29]

---

[24] [1954] 2 Q.B. 402 at 426.
[25] See especially *Scruttons Ltd v Midland Silicones Ltd* [1962] A.C. 446 at 471.
[26] This follows from subsections 6(6) and 6(7) of the 1999 Act.
[27] The hypothesis is that the buyer is a principal party to the bill of lading contract by virtue of being named as shipper in the bill (see above, para.20–062).
[28] This follows from subsections 6(6) and 6(7) of the 1999 Act, read together with Carriage of Goods by Sea Act 1992, s.1(2)(b).
[29] cf. above, para.20–060.

Shipped bill issued but goods not shipped. The third possibility is that a bill of lading is issued falsely stating that the goods had been shipped when this was not the case. The mere issue of a bill of lading containing such a false statement does not give rise to a contract of carriage,[30] though a carrier who issues such a bill may be liable to a lawful holder of the bill by virtue of section 4 of the 1992 Act (but probably not by virtue of Article III.4 of the Hague-Visby Rules).[31] Such liability, however, would arise by virtue of a statutory estoppel: *i.e.* not because there is a contract of carriage, but because the carrier is estopped from denying that there is one. In any event the seller could not rely on section 4 of the 1992 Act in the situation here under discussion since the bill has not been transferred to him; since, even if it had been so transferred, he would not be a "lawful holder" within section 4 if he knew that the goods had not been shipped[32]; and since section 4 is intended to give rise to claims in respect of non-delivery or short delivery, as opposed to claims in respect of damage caused by the carrier's failure to perform his contractual duty of care. If, then, there was *no* contract of carriage contained in or evidenced by the bill of lading, because no goods had been shipped, then the case would not fall within the subsection 6(5) exception. Any claims which the seller might have under section 1 of the 1999 Act as a third party to a pre-bill of lading contract between buyer and carrier would survive; though, as we have seen,[33] it is far from clear that he actually would have such claims. 20–065

Goods deleted from bill of lading covering larger shipment. The fourth possibility is illustrated by the *Pyrene* case itself where the subject-matter of the litigation was a fire-tender which had been sold together with other goods; the whole consignment was then presented by the seller to the carrier in pursuance of shipping arrangements which had been made by the buyer. The fire tender was dropped and damaged while being loaded; consequently it was not shipped; and the bill of lading, which had originally covered the whole proposed consignment "was issued to [the buyer's agent] . . . but with the fire tender deleted from it".[34] Such special circumstances can with considerable plausibility be said to support the inference of an implied contract between seller and carrier, extending even to the fire tender which was never shipped. That plausibility is made all the greater by the fact that the process of loading the fire tender had actually begun,[35] though it was never finished. In such special circumstances there is, with respect, considerable force in the view that the implied contract could have conferred on the seller contractual rights of the kind described in paragraph 20–062 above, *i.e.* rights to have the unshipped goods taken on board.[36] But where no such special circumstances are present it is submitted that no 20–066

---

[30] *Heskell v Continental Express Ltd* [1950] 1 All E.R. 1030; above, para.18–030.
[31] Above, paras 18–034, 18–036 to 18–039.
[32] Carriage of Goods by Sea Act 1992, s.5(2) ("in good faith").
[33] Above, para.20–061.
[34] [1954] 2 Q.B. 402 at 413.
[35] At this stage, what may previously have been a unilateral contract between carrier *and seller* could be said to have become bilateral.
[36] Above, para.20–013 at n.79.

contract between seller and carrier would arise merely because the seller had presented goods to the carrier for carriage pursuant to a booking of shipping space made by the buyer, and the carrier had then either refused or simply failed to take *any* of the goods on board. To give rise to an implied contract, *both* parties must so conduct themselves that an inference of agreement between them can be drawn, and a refusal by the carrier would negative, while a mere failure on his part would not support, such an inference.

Assuming that there is no implied contract between seller and carrier, the further question arises whether, in a case of the present kind, a claim could be made by the seller against the carrier under section 1 of the Contracts (Rights of Third Parties) Act 1999. One possible basis for such a claim could be that the pre-bill of lading contract between carrier and buyer, made by the reservation of shipping space, was capable of conferring rights on the seller as a third party under section 1 of the 1999 Act. The question then is whether the subsequent issue of the bill of lading, with the goods which were not shipped deleted from it, will preclude the application of section 1 by virtue of the subsection 6(5) exception. There is on such facts "*a* contract for the carriage of goods by sea"[37] within that subsection,[38] and the parties to that contract are the same as the parties to the pre-bill of lading contract under which (if no bill of lading had been issued) the third party might have acquired rights by virtue of section 1: both these contracts are between buyer and carrier. It is (with some hesitation) submitted that the applicability of the subsection 6(5) exception to facts such as those which actually occurred in the *Pyrene* case should depend on whether the subject-matter of the bill of lading contract was substantially the same as that of the pre-bill of lading contract. If it was, the subsection 6(5) exception should apply; if it was not, the seller's rights (if any) should depend on section 1.

20–067 **Shipping arrangements made by buyer; seller named as shipper.** The crucial feature of the third of the situations described by Devlin J.,[39] and of three of the variants of it already discussed,[40] is that the bill of lading in them is obtained by the buyer and names him as shipper. It is this last fact that prevents the seller from being a party to the contract of carriage, even if he does become a party to some other implied or collateral contract with the carrier. But there is a further possible situation which differs so radically from Devlin J.'s third situation as to constitute an independent fourth category. This situation is that in which the buyer books space on, or indeed charters, the carrying ship and the seller, after having the goods put on board, takes a bill of lading in his *own* name as shipper.[41] From the seller's point of view, two advantages may be gained in this way: first, the taking of a bill of lading in his own name is a more certain way than the retention by him of a mate's receipt of reserving the right of disposal[42] and

---

[37] *i.e.*, the contract contained in or evidence by the bill of lading, so far as it relates to goods not deleted from the bill and actually shipped.
[38] See 1999 Act, subsections 6(6) and (7).
[39] Above, para.20–062.
[40] Above, paras 20–064 to 20–066.
[41] As in *The Seven Pioneer* [2001] 2 Lloyd's Rep. 57 (High Court of New Zealand).
[42] See above, para.18–168 for the risks involved in this procedure of taking only a mate's receipt.

so of retaining property until payment[43]; and secondly he will under such a bill prima facie have the right to redirect the goods,[44] which he may wish to exercise in the event of the buyer's repudiatory breach of the contract of sale. These consequences follow from the fact that, where the seller takes out the bill in his own name as shipper, the normal position is that he is, and the buyer is not, an original party to the contract of carriage.[45] The buyer might, indeed, be such an original party where the seller could be regarded as having acted as the buyer's agent in taking out the bill of lading, even in the seller's name as shipper. Such an inference of agency might be drawn where property in the goods had passed to the buyer before shipment[46] or where it passed on shipment. But property under an f.o.b. contract hardly ever passes before shipment[47] and certainly does not pass before then merely because the price has been paid in full.[48] Even after shipment, the passing of property is normally deferred until payment of the price has been made against documents[49] which, in a case of the kind here under discussion, are likely to include the bill of lading. This position is likely to negative any inference that an f.o.b. seller who takes out a bill of lading in his own name as shipper does so as agent of the buyer.[50]

Contracts (Rights of Third Parties) Act 1999. In the situation discussed in paragraph 20–067 above, the transfer to the buyer of rights under the contract contained in or evidenced by the bill of lading will be governed by the Carriage of Goods by Sea Act 1992, section 2(1)[51]; no rights to enforce terms of this contract will be conferred on the buyer by virtue of section 1 of the Contracts (Rights of Third Parties) Act 1999 since the subsection 6(5) exception will apply to the bill of lading contract. The buyer will not need, and indeed will be unable,[52] to invoke the 1999 Act in relation to the antecedent contract (whether by way of cargo-booking or by way of charterparty) since he is an immediate party to it. The antecedent contract between buyer and carrier would not fall within the subsection 6(5) exception, so that this exception would not be a bar to a claim by the *seller* to enforce a term of that contract by virtue of section 1 of the 1999 Act. Such a claim would however, fail if (as seems likely) the bill of lading contract was intended to supersede any rights which an antecedent cargo-booking having contractual force might have purported to confer on the seller.[53] The subsection 6(5) exception would not, indeed, apply where the 20–068

---

[43] *ibid.*
[44] Above, para.18–021.
[45] *The Athenasia Comninos* (1979) [1990] 1 Lloyd's Rep. 277; so far as *contra, Union Industrelle et Maritime v Petrosul International (The Roseline)* [1987] 1 Lloyd's Rep. 18 is doubted in para.18–053 n.1, above.
[46] *cf. Texas Instruments Ltd v Nason (Europe) Ltd* [1991] 1 Lloyd's Rep. 146.
[47] Below, para.20–071.
[48] *ibid.*
[49] Below, para.20–082.
[50] *cf.* above, para.20–008.
[51] Above, para.18–080.
[52] See the words "person who is not a party to a contract" in s.1(1).
[53] On the reasoning of para.20–060, above insofar as it is based on s.1(4) of the 1999 Act.

bill of lading had no contractual force, *e.g.* because none of the goods stated in the bill to have been shipped had in fact been shipped.[54] A bill of lading which had no contractual force would, moreover, probably not supersede contract between buyer and carrier; and the subsection 6(5) exception would not apply to the antecedent contract since that contract would not be one "for the carriage of goods by sea" within the 1999 Act.[55] But it seems unlikely that the seller would, in the situation here under discussion, be able to satisfy either of the requirements of section 1 of that Act in relation to the antecedent contract[56] so that probably he would not have any rights under that section.

20–069 **Rights apart from 1999 Act.** Nothing in the foregoing discussion affects any rights or remedies which a person (such as the seller) might have apart from the 1999 Act: *e.g.* rights arising by virtue of agency, implied contract or other exceptions to the common law doctrine of privity. Any such rights or remedies are expressly preserved by subsection 7(1) of the 1999 Act.[57]

5. PASSING OF PROPERTY

20–070 **In general.** An f.o.b. contract may be for the sale of specific goods, in which case property may in theory pass as soon as the contract is made[58]; but such a conclusion is in practice most unlikely as the parties to such a contract will hardly ever intend the property to pass at this time.[59] More commonly the goods will be unascertained, and they may fall into this category either because they are a specified quantity of unascertained goods forming an undifferentiated part of an identified bulk or because they are simply generic goods sold by description. The first of these possibilities gives rise to many difficulties[60] where goods are sold on c.i.f. and c. & f. terms, since such sales are commonly made of goods afloat. This concept is, however, inapplicable to f.o.b. contracts,[61] under which goods must be appropriated to the contract by or before shipment. Hence the authorities on f.o.b. contracts do not deal with the problems which formerly arose from the rule that property could not pass so long as the goods consisted of a specified quantity which formed an undifferentiated part of an identified bulk. Such problems are now dealt with in Sale of Goods Act 1979 section 20A, the possible (if rare) application of which to f.o.b. contracts will be discussed in paragraph 20–086 below. The problems with which the

---

54 *Heskell v Continental Express Ltd* [1950] 1 All E.R. 1030; above, para.18–030.
55 See ss.6(6) and (7).
56 See ss.1(1)(c) and (b), above, para.18–005, sub-para.(b).
57 See above, para.18–005, sub-para.(h).
58 Sale of Goods Act 1979, s.18, r. 1 (above, para.5–017).
59 *cf.* above, para.19–098.
60 Above, paras 18–291 to 18–301.
61 Above, para.20–009. In *Inglis v Stock* (1885) 10 App.Cas. 263, affirmed (1894) 12 Q.B.D. 564 (below, para.20–086) questions arose as to insurable interest, and the passing of risk, in an undifferentiated part of a bulk cargo sold on f.o.b. terms; but the contracts of sale in that case were made *before* the goods were shipped.

authorities on f.o.b. contracts do deal with are those which arise from the rule that property in goods which are unascertained (in the sense of being simply generic goods sold by description) cannot pass before goods of the contract description and in a deliverable state are unconditionally appropriated to the contract.[62] The question whether goods are unconditionally appropriated to the contract depends on the intention of the parties[63]; and "appropriation"[64] is used both in a "contractual" and in a "proprietary" sense.[65] In the case of an f.o.b. contract goods are "appropriated" to a contract in the "contractual" sense (so that the seller is irrevocably bound to deliver those goods under the contract[66]) on shipment[67] at the latest.[68] Property under an f.o.b. contract cannot pass *before* such appropriation[69] and will pass if the goods have been shipped and there has also been a "proprietary" appropriation, *i.e.* one that is "unconditional" in the sense that the seller does not reserve the "right of disposal".[70] But often there will be no such "unconditional" appropriation on shipment, for the seller may, by the manner in which he deals with the shipping documents, indicate his intention to reserve the right of disposal. Thus two matters are usually considered in relation to the passing of property under an f.o.b. contract: shipment and dealings with documents.

Property does not pass before shipment. Property under an f.o.b. contract is sometimes said to pass on shipment[71]; but this is true only where the seller has not reserved the right of disposal. As an f.o.b. seller quite commonly does reserve the right of disposal even after shipment (*e.g.* by stipulating for payment by cash against documents[72]), it would be mislead- 20–071

---

[62] Sale of Goods Act 1979, s.18, r. 5 (above, para.5–068).

[63] Above, para.18–210.

[64] Above, paras 18–210, 19–100; *Wait v Baker* (1848) 2 Exch. 1 at 8.

[65] Above, para.18–210.

[66] *Carlos Federspiel & Co. SA v Charles Twigg & Co. Ltd* [1957] 1 Lloyd's Rep. 240 at 255.

[67] *Colonial Insurance Co. of New Zealand v Adelaide Marine Insurance Co.* (1886) 12 App.Cas. 128 at 137–138; *The Parchim* [1918] A.C. 157 at 168; *F E Napier v Dexters Ltd* (1926) 26 Ll.L.R. 62 at 63, affirmed *ibid.*, at p.184; *Safron v Soc. Minière Cafrika* (1958) 100 C.L.R. 231 at 242.

[68] *Esteve Trading Corp. v Agropec International* (*The Golden Rio*) [1990] 2 Lloyd's Rep. 273 at 276; above, para.20–009. There may be appropriation *in this sense* before shipment: see below, para.20–072.

[69] See *Carlos Federspiel & Co. SA v Charles Twigg & Co. Ltd* [1957] 1 Lloyd's Rep. 240 at 255; *Mitsui & Co. Ltd v Flota Mercante Grancolombiana SA* (*The Ciudad de Pasto and the Ciudad de Neiva*) [1988] 2 Lloyd's Rep. 208 at 212.

[70] Sale of Goods Act 1979, s.18 r.5(2); *The Parchim, above; A A Nortier & Co. v Wm. Maclean, Sons & Co.* (1921) 9 Ll.L.R. 192 (so far as it relates to the goods shipped under the Glasgow contract before the buyers' repudiation); *ex p. Rosevear China Clay Co.* (1879) 11 Ch.D. 560 at 569; *cf. The San Nicholas* [1976] 1 Lloyd's Rep. 8 (where the contract expressly provided that "the title . . . and the risk of loss shall pass to the buyers at the permanent hose connection"); *cf. Noble Resources Ltd v Cavalier Shipping Corp. (The Atlas)* [1996] 1 Lloyd's Rep. 642 at 644 (f.o.b. contract of barter).

[71] See the authorities discussed in paras 20–065 to 20–068 below and *Borealis AB v Stargas Ltd (The Berge Sisar)* [2001] UKHL 17, [2002] 2 A.C. 205 [23], but the statement is immediately qualified by a reference to what is plainly intended to be Sale of Goods Act 1979, s.18 r.5(2) and s.19(2).

[72] As in *Huyton SA v Peter Cremer GmbH* [1999] 1 Lloyd's Rep. 620.

ing to say that there was a general rule to the effect that property passes on shipment under an f.o.b. contract. It is more accurate to state the general rule negatively, that property does not pass before shipment.[73] This rule may apply even though the goods have been wholly paid for before shipment.[74] Thus in *Carlos Federspiel & Co. SA v Charles Twigg & Co. Ltd*[75] children's bicycles were sold f.o.b. United Kingdom port; freight and insurance were to be arranged by the seller, for the buyer's account. The goods were paid for and packed in cases marked with the buyer's name. Shipping instructions were given, but the goods were never shipped, nor even dispatched from the seller's works. On the seller's insolvency, the question arose whether property in the goods had passed to the buyer. Pearson J. said[76] that for the purpose of passing of property "a mere setting apart or selection of the seller of the goods which he expects to use in performance of the contract is not enough.[77] If that is all, he can change his mind and use those goods in performance of some other contract and use some other goods in performance of this contract. To constitute an appropriation of the goods to the contract, the parties must have had, or be reasonably supposed to have had, an intention to attach the contract irrevocably to those goods, so that those goods and no others are the subject of the sale and become the property of the buyer." He concluded that "usually, but not necessarily, the appropriating act is the last act to be performed by the seller."[78] Here the "important and decisive act"[79] remained to be done by the seller who was to send the goods to the port of shipment and have them shipped. Accordingly property had not passed. A further reason for this conclusion was the close connection between property and risk. The parties clearly did not intend the risk to pass before shipment and this was "*prima facie* an indication"[80] that property also should not pass before that point.

Risk may, of course, be separated from property, as commonly happens under a c.i.f. contract,[81] and under an f.o.b. contract in which the seller retains the property after shipment,[82] even though the risk may have passed on, or (in the case of a c.i.f. contract) as from, shipment. In such cases risk passes to the buyer before property, but passes only at a time when the buyer is likely to be protected by the contract of carriage and covered by insurance. It is much less common, because it would be commercially inconvenient, for property to pass before shipment, and so before risk. If

---

[73] *Colley v Overseas Exporters* [1921] 3 K.B. 302 at 307; *Henderson and Glass v Radmore & Co.* (1922) 10 Ll.L.R. 727; a dictum of Lord Dunedin in *D McMaster & Co. v Cox McEuen & Co.*, 1921 S.C.(H.L.) 24 at 28 may suggest that property passed before shipment, but was not necessary for the decision.
[74] *Gabarron v Kreeft* (1875) L.R. 10 Ex. 274 at 278.
[75] [1957] 1 Lloyd's Rep. 240.
[76] At p.255.
[77] But it may be in special circumstances as in *Demby Hamilton & Co. Ltd v Barden* [1949] 1 All E.R. 435.
[78] [1957] 1 Lloyd's Rep. 240 at 255.
[79] *ibid.*, at p.256.
[80] *ibid.*, at 255.
[81] Above, para.19–110.
[82] Below, para.20–077.

property did so pass, one of two views might be taken as to the effect of such passing of property on risk. The first is that the risk would pass to the buyer together with the property, by virtue of the prima facie rule to that effect, stated in section 20(1)[83] of the Sale of Goods Act 1979. This would be inconvenient as an f.o.b. buyer would not normally be protected by the contract of carriage or covered by insurance until after shipment. The second possible view is that the risk would remain on the seller, by virtue of the general rule that risk under an f.o.b. contract passes on shipment.[84] This would in turn be inconvenient; for if the goods were damaged or destroyed by a third party before shipment, the seller would not be entitled to claim the price; nor might he (if he were no longer owner) have any right of action against the third party in tort.[85] On either view, therefore, the passing of property before shipment is likely to lead to commercially undesirable results.

This may be the reason why the general rule that property does not pass before shipment is so hard to displace. In *Carlos Federspiel & Co. SA v Charles Twigg & Co. Ltd*[86] the goods had not been appropriated even in the "contractual" sense[87] of binding the seller to use any particular goods in performance of the contract. Moreover, the seller had come nowhere near to doing the decisive last act since the duty to make shipping arrangements was by the contract placed on the seller and the goods intended for the buyer had never left the seller's premises. But the general rule applies even in the absence of such circumstances. Thus in *Pyrene Co. Ltd v Scindia Navigation Co. Ltd*[88] a fire tender was sold f.o.b. London and paid for in advance (though the contract provided for payment against specified documents). The contract provided that freight was to be engaged by the buyer. Devlin J. said that in making the contract of carriage the buyer must to some extent be acting as agent of the seller: "For if the shipowner lifts the seller's goods from the dock without the seller's authority[89] he is guilty of conversion . . . ."[90] The implication is that, at the moment of lifting, the goods were still the seller's property. Yet for practical purposes no act, certainly no decisive act, remained at this stage to be done by the seller, since all the shipping arrangements were to be made by the buyer; and it is hardly credible that the seller could have intervened and substituted a different tender immediately before the lifting on board had commenced or (*a fortiori*) after this point but before the tender had crossed the ship's rail. It is submitted that the tender had been "appropriated" to the contract, in the "contractual" sense, so that the seller had become contractually bound 20–072

---

[83] s.20(1) "must be ignored" where the buyer deals a consumer (see s.20(4)), discussed in relation to f.o.b. contracts in paras 18–260 and 18–262 to 18–264 above and in para.20–094 below.
[84] Below, para.20–088.
[85] Above, para.18–149.
[86] [1957] 1 Lloyd's Rep. 240; above, para.20–071.
[87] Above, para.18–210.
[88] [1954] 2 Q.B. 402.
[89] *Quaere* whether a contract between seller and carrier is really necessary to confer such authority.
[90] At p.425. *Cf. ibid.*, at p.413, and see below, para.20–090.

to deliver it under the contract, before "shipment"[91]; and, as the tender had been paid for, it is hardly plausible to suggest that the seller had reserved the right of disposal. The view that the property had not passed is based on the difficulty of overcoming the general rule that property under an f.o.b. contract does not pass before shipment.

20–073 The rule that the property does not pass before shipment applies whether the fact that the goods are not shipped is due to the seller's default,[92] or to the carrier's default[93] or to the buyer's failure to give effective shipping instructions.[94] Where the buyer wrongfully repudiated the contract before completion of shipment, and the seller nevertheless continued to ship the remainder of the goods sold, it seems to have been assumed that the property in those goods did not pass[95] (so that the seller's remedy was in damages and not by way of an action for the price[96]). The assumption was apparently based on the fact that at the time of shipment the *buyer* no longer intended the property to pass. But the preferable view is that this is irrelevant as the buyer can be taken to have given his consent in advance "by the contract or otherwise"[97] to the unconditional appropriation[98] of the goods to the contract, so that the only relevant intention at the time of shipment was that of the seller.[99]

20–074 **Shipment of part.** Where the seller ships only part of the goods, the property in that part may pass if his inability to ship the whole is due to the buyer's failure to give proper shipping instructions[1] or if the ship on which the goods are being loaded is lost through a peril of the seas.[2] If failure to ship the whole is not due to the buyer's default, the buyer can reject the quantity shipped,[3] and if he does reject it the question of passing of

---

[91] *cf.* below, paras 20–089, 20–090 for the meaning of "shipment" for this purpose.
[92] As in the *Carlos Federspiel* case, above.
[93] As in the *Pyrene* case, above.
[94] *Colley v Overseas Exporters* [1921] 3 K.B. 302.
[95] *A A Nortier & Co. v Wm. Maclean, Sons & Co.* (1921) 9 Ll.L.R. 192 (so far as it relates to the goods not yet shipped under the Glasgow contract before the buyers' repudiation). *cf. above*, para.19–214, below, paras 20–126 to 20–128.
[96] See below, para.20–126 for criticism of this aspect of *A A Nortier & Co. v Wm. Maclean, Sons & Co.*, above.
[97] *Carlos Federspiel & Co. SA v Charles Twigg & Co. Ltd* [1957] 1 Lloyd's Rep. 240 at 256.
[98] The seller in *A A Nortier & Co. v Wm. Maclean, Sons & Co.*, above had clearly not reserved the right of disposal; for property in goods which had been shipped *before* the buyer's repudiation was held to have passed on shipment.
[99] *cf. above*, para.18–210, below, para.20–128. Sale of Goods Act 1979, s.18, rules 2 and 3 similarly require only notice to the buyer, and not his continuing consent.
[1] *F E Napier v Dexters Ltd* (1926) 26 Ll.L.R. 62 at 184.
[2] *Colonial Insurance Co. of New Zealand v Adelaide Marine Insurance Co.* (1886) 12 App.Cas. 128 at 140 (the actual decision turned not on passing of property but on insurable interest).
[3] Sale of Goods Act 1979, s.30(1) (above, para.8–045). The buyer's right to reject delivery of the wrong quantity is unlikely, in the case of an f.o.b. contract, to be restricted by s.30(2A): see above, para.19–012. S.30(2A) applies only where the buyer does not deal a consumer. Where he does so deal (see above, para.18–259),

property becomes academic for the purposes of risk and of the action for the price. But if either party had become insolvent it is submitted that the buyer (or, where the insolvent party was the buyer, the person or persons appointed to represent his estate) could rely on the shipment as passing the property to the buyer; provided, of course, that the seller had not reserved the right of disposal.

Form of and dealings with shipping documents. In determining whether a seller has reserved the right of disposal the court has regard to the terms of the contract, the terms of the appropriation, the way in which the shipping documents are made out, and the way in which the documents or the goods are dealt with.[4] It is impossible to lay down any hard and fast rules as to reservation of the rights of disposal; so much so that the question whether such a right of disposal has been reserved by an f.o.b. seller has been described as one of "fact".[5] There are, nevertheless, certain prima facie assumptions as to the reservation of the right of disposal under f.o.b. contracts. 20–075

Mate's receipts. Under an f.o.b. contract the shipping arrangements may be made by the buyer and the only shipping document in the seller's possession at any time may be a mate's receipt or similar document,[6] the bill of lading (if any) being issued directly to the buyer. In such a case the seller may be held to have reserved the right of disposal[7] if the mate's receipt is made out in his name and if "the ship will only act on a bill of lading, and will only give a bill of lading on a mate's receipt".[8] But in *F. E. Napier v Dexters Ltd*[9] an f.o.b. contract provided for payment by "cash against mate's receipt". The seller delivered the goods to the wharf named by the buyer and obtained a wharf receipt in the buyer's name; no mate's receipt or bill of lading was ever issued. The seller tendered the wharf receipt to the buyer together with a demand for the price. The arbitrator found that property had passed, and it was held that this conclusion was not wrong in law. The seller had not reserved the right of disposal by the form of the only relevant document in the case; nor was the passing of property prevented by the provision in the contract that payment was to be against mate's receipt. If this provision had the effect of reserving the right of disposal at all,[10] it was a provision wholly for the benefit of the seller which 20–076

---

shipment of part can amount to non-conformity of the goods for the purposes of Part 5A of the Sale of Goods Act 1979. The right of such a buyer to reject the short delivery may then, in effect, be suspended if he has required the seller to "repair or replace" the goods (see ss.48B ad 48D). But there is nothing in Part 5A to compel the buyer to seek repair or replacement; and if he chooses not to do so his right to reject under other provisions of the Act is not affected by Part 5A.

[4] Above, paras 18–211 *et seq*.

[5] *Browne v Hare* (1859) 4 H. & N. 822 at 830; *F E Napier v Dexters Ltd* (1926) 26 Ll.L.R. 62 at 63; *cf. ibid*., at pp.184, 187.

[6] *e.g.* a wharf receipt, as in *F E Napier v Dexters Ltd*, above.

[7] *cf. Craven v Ryder* (1816) 6 Taunt. 433.

[8] *F E Napier v Dexters Ltd*, above, at p.189.

[9] Above.

[10] The Court of Appeal did not think that it had this effect.

could be, and had been, waived by him,[11] presumably on tender of the receipt to the buyer. It is, however, uncommon for a seller who has reserved the right of disposal by stipulating for payment against documents to waive that right: it has, for example been held[12] that where the contract contained such a stipulation, there was no such waiver merely because the goods were delivered to the buyer without presentation of the bill of lading under an arrangement to which the seller was not a party. Normally, therefore the buyer's failure to pay on tender of documents will prevent the property from passing.[13]

20–077 **Bill of lading to seller's order.** By section 19(2) of the Sale of Goods Act 1979, a seller is prima facie to be taken to reserve the right of disposal "where goods are shipped, and by the bill of lading the goods are deliverable to the order of the seller or his agent." This subsection is based on a number of nineteenth century cases, some of which were concerned with f.o.b. contracts, in which the taking of a bill of lading in this form was regarded as evidence of intention on the part of the seller to reserve the right of disposal.[14] The suggestion[15] that section 19(2) does not apply to an f.o.b. contract would therefore seem to be historically unsound. It appears to be based on the view that a seller who reserves the right of disposal acts "contrary to the contract" and not "in performance of his contract to place them [the goods] 'free on board'."[16] But it has already been submitted that this view is incorrect,[17] and the prevailing view is that section 19(2) can apply to an f.o.b. contract.[18] Under such a contract the seller is not bound to pass the property in the goods at any particular time: he can perfectly well ship the goods "in performance of his contract" and so perform his duty to deliver without simultaneously making an *unconditional* appropriation so as to pass the property.[19] If this were not the case, considerable difficulties would arise in financing f.o.b. sales.

---

[11] On this point, see further para.20–128, below; where the contract requires payment against a bill of lading, it has been doubted whether this stipulation is wholly for the benefit of the seller (presumably because transfer of the bill would confer rights on the buyer): *Huyton SA v Peter Cremer GmbH* [1991] 1 Lloyd's Rep. 610 at 632.

[12] *Huyton SA v Peter Cremer GmbH*, above.

[13] Below, para.20–084.

[14] *Wait v Baker* (1848) 2 Exch. 1; *Turner v Trustees of the Liverpool Docks* (1851) 6 Exch. 543; *Ellershaw v Magniac* (1843) 6 Exch. 570, n.(*a*); *Gabarron v Kreeft* (1875) L.R. 10 Exch. 274; *cf. Gibson v Carruthers* (1841) 8 M. & W. 321 at 328; *Ogg v Shuter* (1875) 1 C.P.D. 47 at 50.

[15] In Carver, *Carriage by Sea* (13th ed.), para.1620.

[16] *Browne v Hare* (1859) 4 H. & N. 822 at 830. In *F E Napier v Dexters Ltd* (1926) 26 Ll.L.R. 184 at 189 Scrutton L.J. treats the question whether the right of disposal has been reserved as one of fact, and Roche J. at first instance (*ibid.*, at p.62) seems to assume that s.19(2) can apply to an f.o.b. contract. In *The Parchim* [1918] A.C. 157, s.19(2) is mentioned in the headnote and by counsel at p.159, but not by the Privy Council.

[17] Above, para.20–026.

[18] *Mitsui & Co. Ltd v Flota Mercante Grancolombiana SA* (*The Ciudad de Pasto and the Cuidad de Neiva*) [1988] 2 Lloyd's Rep. 208; *cf.* also *Concordia Trading BV v Richco International Ltd* [1991] 1 Lloyd's Rep. 475.

[19] *Wait v Baker* (1848) 2 Exch. 1 at 7–8; *cf. Continental Grain Co. v Islamic Republic of Iran Shipping Lines* (*The Iran Bohonar*) [1983] 2 Lloyd's Rep. 620 at 621.

Section 19(2), however, embodies only a prima facie rule; so that it is theoretically possible for property to pass on shipment despite the fact that the bill of lading made the goods deliverable to the seller's order. But where the buyer has not yet paid for goods shipped under such a bill this result would follow only in highly exceptional circumstances. The current view is that property normally passes only on payment in full[20]; and a number of earlier cases which at first sight may appear to support a different view are, it is submitted, explicable on other grounds. These cases are discussed in paragraphs 20–078 to 20–081 below.

In *Browne v Hare*[21] oil was sold f.o.b. Rotterdam to be paid for on delivery of bill of lading by a bill of exchange payable three months after date of shipment. The oil was shipped under a bill of lading making it deliverable to the order of the sellers, who immediately indorsed the bill of lading to the buyer and sent it to the broker who had negotiated the sale. The broker presented it to the buyer together with a draft for the price. The ship having been lost, the buyer returned the bill of lading to the broker and refused to accept the sellers' draft or to pay the price. It was held that the sellers were entitled to sue for the price as the property had passed on shipment. In the Court of Exchequer it was said that the sellers had no intention to "continue their ownership"[22] by taking the bill of lading to their own order: this (it was said) was shown by the fact that they had immediately indorsed the bill of lading and forwarded it to the buyer. But they had actually forwarded it to the broker and their conduct was at least equally consistent with the view that they had no intention of parting with such control over the goods as possession of the bill of lading, either in their own hands or in those of their agent,[23] gave them, unless and until the buyer accepted the draft for the price. The decision was affirmed in the Exchequer Chamber where it was said that the question, with what intention the sellers took the bill of lading to their own order, was one of fact.[24] The only principle which can be extracted from the decision is that property is not necessarily prevented from passing on shipment under an f.o.b. contract merely because the seller takes the bill of lading to his own order. **20–078**

In *The Sorfareren*[25] chrome ore was sold by English sellers to German buyers f.o.b. Pangoumene; half the price was to be paid on shipment and the other half on arrival at the port of discharge. The contract provided that insurance was to be effected by the buyers who were to hand the policy to the sellers; and that the bills of lading were to be made out to the order of the sellers. The goods were put on board a ship chartered by the buyers, under bills of lading made out to the order of the sellers. After the outbreak of the First World War the ship was captured and the cargo **20–079**

---

[20] Below, para.20–082.
[21] (1858) 3 H. & N. 484; (1859) 4 H. & N. 822.
[22] 3 H. & N. 484 at 498–499.
[23] Erle J. in 4 H. & N. 822 at 830 treats the broker as the sellers' agent.
[24] 4 H. & N. 822 at 830.
[25] (1916) 114 L.T. 46.

condemned as prize and sold. The sellers claimed the proceeds of this sale, but Evans P. rejected the claim on the ground that the property in the goods had passed to the German buyers on shipment. In his view the sellers had no intention to reserve a right of disposal: "Their holding of the bill of lading, and of the policies of insurance, did not preserve the property in them in the circumstances. Their object in obtaining and holding these documents was simply to secure greater protection for themselves for the payment of the balance."[26] But the best way of securing such protection would be to reserve the right of disposal so as to retain the property in the goods.[27] The decision is best explained as turning "on its own facts",[28] or on the ground that the sellers had shown that they did not intend to reserve the right of disposal; for in making their claim they had described themselves, not as owners of the cargo, but as persons "interested in the cargo to the extent of the unpaid balance".[29]

20–080 In *The Parchim*[30] German sellers sold a cargo of nitrate to Dutch buyers under a contract which was nominally a c.i.f. or c. & f. contract but which was said to have "more of the characteristics" of an f.o.b. contract.[31] The goods were shipped and bills of lading were taken by the sellers' agent in the sellers' name and to their order; at the time when he took the bills the agent did not know of the sale. Payment was due "ninety days after receipt of the first bill of lading, and to be paid by the buyers three days before maturity,[32] or in case of an earlier arrival already [*i.e.* of the *Parchim*] then against acceptance of the documents". The bills of lading were indorsed in blank by the sellers' agent and sent to the sellers' bank in Amsterdam. It was said that the bank held the bills of lading "as it were, *in medio*. On the one hand they were not to hand them over to the buyers without the money, but equally . . . they were to hold them until the due date, and not hand them back to the sellers unless and until the buyers made default in taking them up."[33] The buyers paid the price in ignorance of the fact that the ship had been seized and her cargo condemned as prize; and they claimed that the cargo should not have been condemned, since it was their (and hence neutral) property. For this purpose they had, under the relevant Prize rules,[34] to show that the property in the goods had passed by, at the latest, the time of shipment. In upholding the buyers' claim, Lord Parker relied principally on two points. First, the fact that risk had passed on shipment pointed "to the property having been intended to pass at that

[26] At p.48.
[27] Above, para.18–209; below, para.20–080.
[28] *Mitsui & Co. Ltd v Flota Mercante Grancolombiana SA* (*The Cuidad de Pasto and the Cuidad de Neiva*) [1988] 2 Lloyd's Rep. 208 at 214.
[29] (1916) 114 L.T. 46 at 48. If the sellers' claim had succeeded they would have recovered some £16,000 whereas under the contract no more than £4,000 was still due to them. The case was later compromised: see *The Parchim* [1918] A.C. 157 at 168.
[30] [1918] A.C. 157.
[31] At p.164 (above, para.20–088).
[32] A phrase described at p.166 as "a little perplexing".
[33] At p.167.
[34] Above, para.18–242.

time".[35] But he also quoted with approval[36] a dictum of Blackburn J. that property and risk were "not inseparable".[37] In *The Parchim* the contract made it clear that the risk passed to the buyers on shipment[38] so that there was no need for the seller to transfer the property at this stage so as to get rid of the risk. Secondly, Lord Parker relied on the way in which the seller had dealt with the shipping documents: this pointed "rather to a desire to support his lien than to a desire to retain the property or any *jus disponendi* incident to the property"[39]; and this inference was not negatived by the form in which the bills of lading were taken, as they were so taken by the sellers' agent without knowledge of the sale. With respect, it is submitted that this reasoning is no longer acceptable as a general rule. As Lord Wright has said in a case involving a c.i.f. contract which called for payment against documents: "In this course of business, the general property in the goods remains in the seller until he transfers the bills of lading. . . . The general property in the goods must be in the seller if he is to be able to pledge them. The whole system of commercial credits depends on the seller's ability to give a charge on the goods and the policies of insurance. A mere unpaid seller's lien would for obvious reasons be inadequate and unsatisfactory."[40] In another Prize case Lord Sumner said[41] that *The Parchim* had been "decided on very special facts" and did not "purport to lay down any general rule, that a particular mode of dealing with a bill of lading must, whenever it occurs and in whatever circumstances, always prove a particular intention". It is submitted that, in the absence of special cirumstances, an f.o.b. seller who sends bills of lading to his own bank with instructions not to hand them to the buyer except against payment will be taken to have reserved a right of disposal so as to prevent the passing of property.[42] Indeed, this much was admitted by Lord Parker in *The Parchim*; for he said that, where the seller dealt with the bill of lading so as to "secure the contract price", then "The prima facie presumption . . . appears to be that the property is to pass only on the performance by the buyer of his part of the contract and not forthwith subject to the seller's lien." But he added: "inasmuch, however, as the object to be attained, namely, securing the contract price, may be attained by the seller merely reserving a lien, the inference that the property is to pass on the performance of a

---

[35] At p.168.
[36] *ibid.*
[37] *Martineau v Kitching* (1872) L.R. 7 Q.B. 436 at 454.
[38] [1918] A.C. 157 at 168–169.
[39] At p.172.
[40] *Ross T Smyth & Co. Ltd v T D Bailey, Son & Co.* [1940] 3 All E.R. 60 at 68; and see above, para.18–219.
[41] *The Kronprinsessan Margareta* [1921] 1 A.C. 486 at 516–517, approved in *Ross T Smyth & Co. Ltd v T D Bailey, Son & Co.*, above, at p.68; *cf. Mitsui & Co. Ltd v Flota Mercante Grancolombiana SA* (*The Cuidad de Pasto and the Cuidad de Neiva*) [1988] 2 Lloyd's Rep. 208 at 214.
[42] See *James v The Commonwealth* (1939) 62 C.L.R. 339 at 384–385; *cf.* the New South Wales decision in *PS Chellaram & Co. Ltd v China Ocean Shipping Co.* [1989] 1 Lloyd's Rep. 413 at 421–422, reversed on other grounds [1991] 1 Lloyd's Rep. 493, but affirmed on the point that "title to the goods" remained in the seller (at p.495). *Cf. East West Corp v DKBS 1912 AF A/S* [2003] EWCA Civ 83, [2003] Q.B. 1509 at [3], where the sale was on c.o.d. terms; and see above, para.18–216.

condition only is necessarily somewhat weak, and may be rebutted by the other circumstances of the case".[43] It is submitted that (for the reasons given by Lord Wright) the inference would no longer be regarded as "somewhat weak"; and that it would be particularly hard to displace where the contract envisaged a pledge of the documents to a third party, such as a bank.

20–081 In *Frebold and Sturznickel (Trading as Panda OHG) v Circle Products Ltd*[44] an f.o.b. contract provided for payment through the sellers' bank by cash against documents; and the sellers instructed their agents not to part with the goods until they were paid for. Two members of the Court of Appeal said that in these circumstances property had passed on shipment.[45] But the only point which it was necessary to decide was whether the sellers had delivered the goods within the time allowed by the contract.[46] The passing of property was not in issue, and the terms of the contract and the conduct of the sellers would prima facie appear to indicate an intention to reserve the right of disposal, or at any rate an intention not to pass property on shipment. The view that the sellers intended only "to secure the contract price" and that they had done "nothing inconsistent with the intention to pass the property on shipment"[47] is, with respect, open to the same criticisms as those which have been levelled at similar statements in *The Parchim*[48]; and it is submitted that the better view is that property had not passed on shipment in the *Frebold* case.

20–082 What has above[49] been called the current view was taken in *The Ciudad de Pasto*,[50] where goods were shipped in pursuance of an f.o.b. contract under bills of lading making the goods deliverable to the seller's order. Eighty per cent. of the price had been paid by means of a letter of credit before shipment; it was not clear against what documents (if any) this payment had been made; no shipping documents could have been available at the time of the payment to provide the buyer with any effective security for the (advance) payment. It was held that the presumption created by section 19(2) had not been displaced, so that property had not passed to the buyer. This conclusion was regarded as giving effect to the "common intention"[51] of the parties. As the buyer had been content to pay 80 per cent of the price without security, no intention to acquire the property could be imputed to him before payment of the balance. So far as the intention of the seller was concerned, it was said that "In the ordinary way a seller will not wish to part with property in goods if they are shipped

---

43 [1918] A.C. 157 at 170–171.
44 [1970] 1 Lloyd's Rep. 499.
45 *ibid.*, at pp.504, 505.
46 Above, para.20–037.
47 [1970] 1 Lloyd's Rep. 499 at 505.
48 Above, para.20–080.
49 Above, para.20–077.
50 *Mitsui & Co. Ltd v Flota Mercante Grancolombiana SA* (*The Ciudad de Pasto and the Ciudad de Neiva*) [1988] 2 Lloyd's Rep. 208.
51 *ibid.*, at p.215.

overseas until he has been paid in full."[52] It is submitted that this statement must now be taken to represent the general rule where the seller takes a bill of lading to his own order, and that the statements as to passing of property made in the cases discussed in paragraphs 20–078 to 20–081 above are either no longer to be regarded as good law or to be explained by reference to the special circumstances of the cases in which those statements were made.

Bills of lading to buyer's order. The presumption in section 19(2) applies only where the goods are by the bill of lading deliverable to the order of the seller or his agent. It has been suggested[53] that the presumption may be displaced by naming the buyer as consignee; but it is respectfully submitted that, where this is done, the statutory presumption simply does not arise, and that a seller should not be taken to have given up his right of disposal merely because the bill is made out to the buyer's order.[54] This submission is based on the fact that retention even of such a bill of lading gives the seller considerable control over the goods; for the buyer is not normally entitled to demand delivery of the goods from the carrier without presenting the bill,[55] while the seller is normally entitled to direct the carrier to deliver the goods to a different consignee.[56] It therefore does not follow that property will pass on shipment merely because the bill of lading is made out to buyer's order. As Lord Sumner said in a case involving a c.i.f. contract: "in spite of the insertion of the consignee's (*i.e.* the buyer's) name in the bill of lading, the intention to reserve the *jus disponendi* to the seller till the documents are taken up is manifested by the way in which the transaction is carried through with regard to the presentation of the documents."[57] It is submitted that where the contract provides for payment against bill of lading the normal inference[58] would be that the seller had reserved a right of disposal until payment in accordance with the contract had been made.[59] 20–083

---

[52] *ibid; The Subro Valour* [1995] 1 Lloyd's Rep. 509 at 519; *Eridiana SpA v Rudolf A. Oetker (The Fjord Wind)* [1999] 1 Lloyd's Rep. 307 at 335, affirmed without reference to this point [2000] 2 Lloyd's Rep. 191; *Center Optical (Hong Kong) Ltd v Jardine Transport Services (Hong Kong) Ltd* [2001] 2 Lloyd's Rep. 678 at 683; *Evergreen Marine Corp. v Aldgate Warehouse (Wholesale) Ltd* [2003] EWCH 667 (Comm), [2003] 2 Lloyd's Rep. 597 at [30]–[33], where the bill named the seller' s suppliers as shippers, a "local bank" (at [32]) as consignee and the buyer as a "notify party". The relationship between the bank and the seller is not clear from the report.

[53] *Mitsui & Co. Ltd v Flota Mercante Grancolombiana SA* (*The Cuidad de Pasto and the Cuidad de Neiva*) [1988] 2 Lloyd's Rep. 208 at 215.

[54] The above submission was accepted in *The Seven Pioneer* [2001] 2 Lloyd's Rep. 57 at [34] (High Court of New Zealand).

[55] Above, para.18–063.

[56] Above, paras 18–021 *et seq.*

[57] *Hansson v Hamel and Horley Ltd* [1922] 2 A.C. 36 at 43; *cf. The Kronprinsessan Margareta* [1921] 1 A.C. 486 at 517.

[58] See above, para.20–082.

[59] See *Sheridan v New Quay Co.* (1858) 4 C.B.(N.S.) 618, where the sale seems to have been on f.o.b. terms and not "delivered Liverpool" as the headnote states, the reference to delivery at Liverpool being contained in the buyer's shipping instructions and not in the contract of sale. *Cf. The Seven Pioneer*, above n.54, where the contract of sale provided for payment in exchange for or "on receipt of [shipping] documents".

In *London Joint Stock Bank Ltd v British Amsterdam Maritime Agency Ltd*[60] oil was sold f.o.b. Amsterdam, put into drums belonging to the buyer, and shipped by the seller under a bill of lading making it deliverable to the buyer's order. It was agreed that the seller was to keep possession of the bill of lading until a draft for the price was actually paid. The ship's agents delivered the goods to the buyer even though the latter did not have the bill of lading and the agents were held liable in conversion to a bank to whom the seller had sold the draft and transferred possession of the bill of lading.[61] The effect of the arrangement between buyer and seller was said to be "that, notwithstanding the passing of the property, if the property had passed, the vendors were to have a lien upon the goods which they could give effect to by keeping, not possession of the goods, but possession of the bill of lading."[62] The suggestion that property had passed is thus very tentatively made; and, if accepted, may be explained by the special circumstance that the oil was put in the buyer's own drums. In any event, the view that the seller retained a lien after delivering the goods to the carrier can only be explained on the ground that he reserved some kind of "right of disposal"; for under section 43(1)(a) of the Act the unpaid seller's lien is lost "when he delivers the goods to a carrier . . . for the purpose of transmission to the buyer without reserving the right of disposal of the goods". Of course this presupposes that the property has passed (since a person cannot have a lien over his own goods)[63]; and it is arguable that there are two kinds of "right of disposal", one reserving property and the other a lien. But it is submitted that this distinction (if it exists) is too subtle to form the basis of any inference as to the intention of the seller with regard to the passing of property, particularly if the seller did not in fact know of his right of lien[64]; and that the natural inference, where the seller holds a bill of lading as security for payment of the price, is that he intends to remain owner until he receives payment and not merely to rely on the somewhat circumscribed right of an unpaid seller's lien. This inference is, it is submitted, particularly strong where the transaction is financed through banks.

20–084 **Subsequent dealings with documents.**[65] Where property in goods sold under an f.o.b. contract does not pass on shipment, it may, and often will, pass by virtue of some subsequent dealing with the shipping documents. Normally, where the seller reserves the right of disposal, he does so until the conditions of the contract as to payment are met[66]; and before they are

[60] (1910) 16 Com.Cas. 102; disapproved on the measure of damages in *Chabra Corp. Pte. Ltd v Jag Shakti* (*Owners*) (*The Jag Shakti*) [1986] A.C. 337 at 348.
[61] The bank also obtained the buyer's indorsement of the bill of lading, but only after the goods had been delivered to him. Possession of the bill of lading was never given to the buyer.
[62] (1910) 16 Com.Cas. 102 at 106.
[63] *Nippon Yusen Kaisha v Ramjiban Serowgee* [1938] A.C. 429 at 444 (above, para.18–212).
[64] *The Kronprinsessan Margareta* [1921] 1 A.C. 486 at 514–515.
[65] See generally above, paras 18–215, 18–216.
[66] *Mitsui & Co. Ltd v Flota Mercante Grancolombiana SA* (*The Ciudad de Pasto and Ciudad de Neiva*) [1988] 2 Lloyd's Rep. 208 at 214; *James v The Commonwealth* (1939) 62 C.L.R. 339 at 381.

met the property does not pass.[67] This may be so even though the goods have come into the possession of the buyer.[68]

In *Ogg v Shuter*[69] potatoes were sold under an f.o.b. contract which provided for payment by cash against bill of lading. The goods were shipped under a bill of lading making them deliverable to the order of the seller's agent. On tender of the bill of lading, the buyer, without justification, refused to pay for the goods; and it was held that property had not passed. Lord Cairns L.C. said that a seller who took a bill of lading in this form preserved "a hold over the goods until the bill of lading is handed over on the conditions being fulfilled, *or at least until the consignee is ready and willing and offers to* fulfil these conditions, and demands the bill of lading".[70] Some difficulty arises with the italicised part of his statement, as it is inconsistent with *Wait v Baker*.[71] In that case an f.o.b. seller who had shipped the goods under bills of lading to his own order wrongfully refused the buyer's offer to pay cash against bills of lading, and instead transferred the bill to a third party. It was held that property had not passed to the buyer. It had not passed by the original contract or on shipment, since at these stages the seller still reserved the right of disposal; nor was there at any subsequent stage an agreement on the part of the seller that the property should pass. On the contrary, "his object was to have the contract repudiated,[72] and thereby to free himself from all obligation to deliver the cargo".[73] In an unreported case[74] it was similarly held that where a seller had included a term in the appropriation which constituted a breach of contract the property did not pass. But it is hard to see why there should be any need for a second "agreement" on the part of the seller to pass the property; or why it is not sufficient for the buyer to satisfy the conditions laid down in the original contract or appropriation.[75] The decision in *Wait v Baker* was probably influenced by the court's desire to protect the rights of the third party to whom the bill of lading was indorsed. Now that such protection is afforded by section 8 of the Factors Act 1889 and by section 24 of the Sale of Goods Act 1979, the reasoning of *Wait v Baker* is no longer necessary for this purpose; and it is submitted that the view of Lord Cairns in *Ogg v Shuter*[76] is to be preferred.

---

[67] *ibid.*, at pp.384–385; *Huyton SA v Peter Cremer GmbH* [1999] 1 Lloyd's Rep. 620 at 631.

[68] As in *Tradax Internacional SA v Goldschmidt SA* [1977] 2 Lloyd's Rep. 604; and *London Joint Stock Bank Ltd v British Amsterdam Maritime Agency Ltd* (1910) 16 Com.Cas. 102, discussed in para.20–083, above. *Cf.* also above, paras 19–102, 19–103.

[69] (1875) 1 C.P.D. 47; the facts are more fully stated in 45 L.J.Q.B. 44.

[70] 1 C.P.D. 47 at 50 (italics supplied) and see above, para.18–226. *Cf. Gabarron v Kreeft* (1875) L.R. 10 Ex. 274; but in that case the goods in question do not seem ever to have been appropriated to the contract.

[71] (1848) 2 Exch. 1.

[72] As the market price had risen.

[73] (1848) 2 Exch. 1 at 9.

[74] Cited in *F E Napier v Dexters Ltd* (1926) 26 Ll.L.R. 62 at 64.

[75] *cf.* the position under s.18, r. 5(1), where the act of the seller can pass property by virtue of the buyer's advance agreement (above, paras 18–210, 20–073).

[76] Above, n.70.

20–085 Where an f.o.b. contract provides for payment by buyer's acceptances of seller's drafts, and, on obtaining such acceptances, the seller indorses bills of lading, originally made out to his order, to the buyer, the property thereupon passes even though the bill of exchange is subsequently dishonoured by nonpayment[77]; but the seller may still be able to stop the goods in transit.[78] On the other hand where a bill of lading to seller's order is indorsed by way of security to a bank to whom the seller has sold a draft on the buyer, and the draft is not paid, it has been said that the property remains in the seller, who in such circumstances "retains more than a mere lien upon the goods."[79]

20–086 **Goods forming part of a bulk.** Section 20A[80] of the Sale of Goods Act 1979 provides that, in certain circumstances, a buyer of a specified quantity of unascertained goods which form part of an identified bulk can acquire an undivided share in the bulk and become owner in common of the bulk. A situation in which the section could apply to an f.o.b. contract is illustrated by the facts of *Inglis v Stock*,[81] where the question was not whether property had passed to the buyer but whether he had an insurable interest in the goods.[82] In that case, A sold 200 tons of sugar to B who resold those 200 tons to C; A also sold a further 200 tons directly to C; and all these sales were on f.o.b. terms. After the contracts of sale had been made, 390 tons were shipped in bags on board a ship in which B and C had engaged space for such shipment. At this stage no division was made between the quantity sold directly to C and that sold to B and then resold to C. On this resale the 390 tons would now be regarded as having become ascertained by "consolidation",[83] so that property in the whole 390 tons could at this stage pass to C; but before the resale it could be argued that section 20A would now apply to the transactions since B and C had each entered into a "contract for the sale of a specified quantity of unascertained goods"[84] and that these formed part of a bulk which had been "identified . . . by subsequent agreement between the parties."[85] The inference of such an agreement could be drawn from the giving of shipping instructions by B and C and the act of A in putting the goods on board the ship in response to those instructions, the goods being at this stage appropriated to the contracts. The further requirement of section 20A, of the buyers' having "paid the price for some or all of the goods . . .",[86] was also satisfied, each

---

[77] *Berndston v Strang* (1868) L.R. 3 Ch.App. 588 at 590.
[78] *ibid*.
[79] *Turner v Trustees of the Liverpool Docks* (1851) 6 Exch. 543 at 569; for a possible contrary view, see *London Joint Stock Bank Ltd v British Amsterdam Maritime Agency Ltd* (1910) 16 Com.Cas. 102 at 106 (above, para.20–083); and see generally above, paras 18–215 *et seq*.
[80] Discussed generally in relation to overseas sales in paras 18–293 to 18–299.
[81] (1885) 10 App.Cas. 263.
[82] The actual decision was that the buyer referred to as "C" in the following discussion did have such an interest; *cf. above*, para.18–301.
[83] Above, para.18–288.
[84] s.20A(1).
[85] s.20A(1)(a).
[86] s.20A(1)(b).

buyer having paid the price in full, in compliance with a term of the contract calling for payment "by cash . . . in exchange for the bill of lading". For reasons given in Chapter 18, it is submitted that no property would have passed under section 20A to an f.o.b. buyer who had paid only a part of the price.[87]

If the reported cases are any guide, f.o.b. sellers do not often ship goods in bulk for the purpose of performing contracts with more than one buyer. This process appears to be much less common than that of dividing bulk shipments which are already afloat between two or more buyers on c.i.f. or c. & f. terms. In the case of an f.o.b. contract, the goods might indeed at the time of sale form part of an identified bulk in a warehouse or other shore installation. But in such a case property is most unlikely to pass before shipment, even if the goods have been paid for[88]; while goods shipped in fulfilment of a single contract will become ascertained on shipment so that there will be no scope for the operation of section 20A.[89] For all these reasons, the section will only rarely apply to f.o.b. contracts.

6. RISK

Introductory. Our main concern in this section is with the passing of risk under f.o.b. contracts where the buyer does not deal as consumer. This topic is the subject-matter of the discussion in paragraphs 20–088 to 20–093 below. It is also possible, if uncommon, for a buyer on f.o.b. terms to deal as consumer[90]; and the special rules which govern risk in cases of this kind are discussed in paragraphs 20–094 below. 20–087

Generally passes on shipment. The general[91] rule is that risk under an f.o.b. contract does not pass before shipment[92] so that until shipment it is on the seller[93]; and it passes to the buyer on shipment.[94] There is no scope 20–088

---

[87] Above, para.18–297.

[88] Above, para.20–071; this rule would prevail over s.20A by virtue of the parties' contrary agreements, see s.20A (2) and *cf.* above, para.18–298.

[89] See s.20A(1) (the subsection applies only to "unascertained goods").

[90] See above, para.18–259.

[91] For exceptions, see below, para.20–091 to 20–093.

[92] *Colley v Overseas Exporters* [1921] 3 K.B. 302.

[93] *e.g. J & J Cunningham Ltd v Robert A Munro & Co. Ltd* (1922) 28 Com.Cas. 42.

[94] *Stock v Inglis* (1884) 12 Q.B.D. 564 at 573, 575, 577; *Inglis v Stock* (1885) 10 App.Cas. 263 at 273; *The Parchim* [1918] A.C. 157 at 168 (above, paras 20–008, 20–080); *cf. Browne v Hare* (1858) 3 H. & N. 484; (1859) 4 H. & N. 822 (where the discussion is in terms of passing of property); *Broome v Pardess Co-operative Society of Orange Growers* [1940] 1 All E.R. 603; *J. Raymond Wilson & Co. Ltd v Norman Scatchard Ltd* (1944) 77 Ll.L.R. 373 at 374; *Glengarnock Iron and Steel Co. Ltd v Henry G Cooper & Co.* (1895) 22 R.(Ct. of Sess.) 672. Under the Vienna Convention on Contracts for the International Sale of Goods (above, para.1–024) the general or residual rule is that risk passes when the buyer "takes over the goods:" Art. 69(1): exactly when this point is reached under an f.o.b. contract would depend on the type of f.o.b. contract in question (see above, paras 20–002 to 20–007). Art. 67(1) of the

in the case of f.o.b. contracts for the rule applicable to c.i.f. contracts[95] that risk can pass "as from" shipment.[96] This rule presupposes that goods are first shipped and then sold; and this is a sequence which cannot occur under an f.o.b. contract since goods sold on f.o.b. terms must be appropriated to the contract by shipment at the latest.[97] The rule as to the passing of risk under f.o.b. contracts applies where the sale is of specific goods, where it is of goods which were originally unascertained because the contract was simply one for the sale of generic goods by description and goods of that description are appropriated to the contract on or before shipment and so become ascertained, and even in the apparently rare case[98] where such goods remain unascertained even after shipment because they are shipped as an undifferentiated part of a larger bulk.[99] Risk may pass on shipment even though property does not pass at this time, either because the seller reserves the right of disposal[1]; or because the goods at the time of shipment form an undifferentiated part of a larger bulk and have not been paid for[2];

Convention deals with cases in which "the contract of sale involves carriage of the goods", and it is far from clear whether these words are appropriate to refer to f.o.b. contracts since such contracts envisage, but do not provide for, carriage. Presumably the answer to this question depends on the circumstances in which delivery is made. Assuming that the particular f.o.b. contract is one to which Art. 67(1) does apply, it is next necessary to ask which of two rules contained in it governs the passing of risk under such contracts. The first rule applies where "the seller is not bound to hand [the goods] over at a particular place:" here risk passes when the seller hands the goods over to the first carrier for transmission to the buyer. The second rule applies where "the seller is bound to hand the goods over to a carrier at a particular place": here the risk "does not pass . . . . until the goods are handed over to the carrier at that place." The second of these rules is the more appropriate to an f.o.b. contract, since such a contract invariably specifies (or requires one party to specify) the place of shipment. Even under the second rule, however, risk can pass at an earlier point than under the English rule, for the handing over of the goods will often precede shipment. Such a result could be inconvenient as the buyer would be unlikely to be covered by insurance before shipment. One way of avoiding such an inconvenient result is to argue that the second of the two rules stated in Art. 67(1) merely specifies the *earliest* point at which risk can pass: risk "does *not* pass *until* the goods are handed over", etc. This can be contrasted with the wording of the first of the two rules: "risk passes . . . when the goods are handed over . . . ." Alternatively, it can be argued that, in an f.o.b. contract governed by English law, the Convention rules as to passing of risk would be displaced by contrary agreement (Art. 6) or by usage (Art. 9): see above, para.18–004.

[95] Above, para.19–110.

[96] *ibid.* In *The Subro Valour* [1995] 1 Lloyd's Rep. 501 at 519 col. 1 risk under an f.o.b. contract is said to pass "as from" shipment, but *ibid.* col. 2 correctly states that the risk had passed "on" shipment.

[97] Above, para.20–009. It follows that the rule laid down by Art. 68 of the Vienna Convention on Contracts for the International Sale of Goods (above, para.1–024), that risk "in respect of goods sold in transit passes to the buyer from the time of the conclusion of the contract," cannot apply to f.o.b. contracts.

[98] See above, para.20–086.

[99] See *Stock v Inglis*, above, n.71 (above, para.20–086).

[1] *Williams v Cohen* (1871) 25 L.T. 300 at 303; *James v The Commonwealth* (1939) 62 C.L.R. 339 at 385 (above, paras 20–075 *et seq.*).

[2] Above, para.20–086.

or for both these reasons. Where only part of the goods has been loaded the risk may pass as to that part.[3]

In *The Parchim*[4] the contract provided: "Should the ship be lost before the loading is completed, this contract is cancelled for that part of the cargo which is not yet laden." The Privy Council relied on this clause as an indication that the risk had passed on shipment. Indeed, the clause went further and absolved *both* parties from liability in respect of the part of the goods which was not yet loaded, and in respect of which the risk had therefore not yet passed.

Goods lost or damaged while being loaded. Most of the statements as to the passing of risk under f.o.b. contracts refer to the goods as being either on board or not on board, or as loaded or not yet loaded. They do not deal with the problem of loss of or damage to the goods during the actual process of loading. There is no reported case on the passing of risk between buyer and seller in this situation; but the problem arose between an f.o.b. seller and the carrier in *Pyrene Co. Ltd v Scindia Navigation Co. Ltd.*[5] In that case a fire tender which had been sold f.o.b. London was damaged through the fault of the carrier while being lifted on board. The damage occurred before the tender had crossed the ship's rail and the question was whether the shipowner was entitled to limit his liability under the Hague Rules (now superseded in England by the Hague-Visby Rules).[6] This depended in part on whether at the relevant time the goods were being "loaded on . . . the ship".[7] Counsel for the seller[8] argued that this was not the case. He treated "the word 'on' as having the same meaning as in 'free on board'; goods are loaded on the ship as soon as they are put across the ship's rail, which the tender never was"[9]; and he submitted that loading was "a joint operation, the shipper's duty being to lift the cargo to the rail of the ship . . . and the shipowner's to take it on board and stow it. . . ."[10] But Devlin J. held that the shipowner was protected by the Hague Rules. He said: "The division of loading into two parts is suited to more antiquated methods of loading than are now generally adopted and the ship's rail has lost much of its nineteenth-century significance.[11] Only the most enthusiastic lawyer could watch with satisfaction the spectacle of liabilities shifting uneasily as the cargo sways at the end of a derrick across a notional 20–089

---

[3] *Colonial Insurance Co. of New Zealand v Adelaide Marine Insurance Co.* (1886) 12 App.Cas. 128 (the actual decision turned on insurable interest); above, para.20–039.
[4] [1918] A.C. 157; above, paras 20–008, 20–080.
[5] [1954] 2 Q.B. 402.
[6] Below, para.21–047.
[7] See now Carriage of Goods by Sea Act 1971, Sch., Art. 1(e).
[8] Megaw Q.C.
[9] [1954] 2 Q.B. 402 at 414.
[10] *ibid.*, at p.414.
[11] But see above, para.20–018 at n.34 (cost of discharge split, under c.i.f. contract, at ship's rail) and *infra*, n.20. And see *Parsons Corporation v CV Scheepvaartondernem-ing Happy Ranger (The Happy Ranger)* [2001] 2 Lloyd's Rep. 530 when the relevant phrase was "shipped on deck" and the goods were damaged before they had "reached the deck" (at p.540), revsd. on other grounds [2002] EWCA Civ. 694, [2002] 2 All E.R. (Comm) 24.

perpendicular projecting from the ship's rail."[12] He held that "the operation of the [Hague] rules is determined by the limits of the contract of carriage by sea and not by any limits of time"[13]; that the parties were free to define their respective obligations as to "loading"; and that in the case before him the carrier's obligations in this respect had begun before the tender had crossed the ship's rail.

20–090 Devlin J. did not, in the *Pyrene* case, make any specific statement as to the passing of risk between buyer and seller. But it is arguable that his reasoning can be applied by analogy to this problem: in other words, that the question whether the goods have been "shipped" at any particular point (so as to pass the risk) depends on the division of duties with regard to shipment which the contract of sale makes between buyer and seller. This division is, of course, not necessarily the same as that between shipper and carrier: indeed it does not seem to have been the same in the *Pyrene* case itself, for it was there said that the property in the tender had not passed at the time when it was dropped and damaged.[14] As the price had by then been paid,[15] the most likely explanation for this is that the goods had not yet been "shipped" as between buyer and seller[16] even though, as between shipper (*i.e.* buyer) and carrier, the loading had begun. If this is correct, the risk in the tender would also not have passed at the time when it was dropped, and indeed the seller's action against the carrier seems to have been based on the assumption that this was the position. According to the traditional view, the risk would pass when the goods cross the ship's rail, as that is the point at which performance of the seller's duty to ship is completed.[17] But that duty may be enlarged or curtailed by the provisions of the contract of sale; and it is arguable that, where this is the case, the risk should pass, not when the goods cross the ship's rail, but whenever the seller's duty with respect to loading is performed. Thus if the sale were on "f.o.b. and stowed" terms the risk would on this view not pass until the goods were stowed. Conversely, it has been suggested that if the contract provided for payment against a "received" bill of lading, the seller's duty would, by implication, cease when the goods had been delivered to the carrier for shipment; and that the risk would pass at that point.[18] The view that the risk passes when the seller's duty with respect to loading is performed certainly looks less arbitrary than the traditional view that the risk passes when the goods cross the ship's rail. But it may also be less

---

[12] *ibid.*, at p.419; *cf. above*, para.20–018.

[13] [1954] 2 Q.B. 402 at 416; For approval of Devlin J.'s reasoning on this point, see *Jindal Iron & Steel Ltd v Islamic Solidarity Shipping Co. Jordan Inc. (The Jordan II)* [2004] UKHL 49 [2005] 1 W.L.R. 363; *cf. Fyffes Group Ltd v Reefer Express Line Pty Ltd (The Kriti Rex)* [1996] 2 Lloyd's Rep. 171 at 188.

[14] *Pyrene* case, above n.13 at pp.413, 425.

[15] *ibid.*, at p.424.

[16] Above, paras 20–071, 20–072.

[17] Above, paras 20–012, 20–018.

[18] Sassoon, *C.I.F. and F.O.B. Contracts* (4th ed.), para.577. This would appear to be the effect of Art. 67(1) of the Vienna Convention on Contracts for the International Sale of Goods (above, para.1–024), if that article applies to f.o.b. contracts: see above, para.20–088, n.94.

convenient since it may lead to a situation in which the risk can pass to the buyer before shipment, and hence before he is likely to be covered by insurance; or at least to considerable uncertainty as to which of the parties to the contract of sale should insure against loss or damage during that part of the process of loading in respect of which the carrier is entitled to the protection of the Hague, or Hague-Visby[19] Rules. The best way of avoiding this uncertainty is to specify the point at which risk is to pass by an express provision in the contract of sale.[20]

An alternative solution would be one by which (for the purpose of the passing of risk) the goods were "shipped", as between buyer and seller, as soon as the duties of the carrier with respect to loading had, as between carrier and shipper, begun. Under such a rule, the risk would pass at the point from which the carrier was protected by the Hague or Hague-Visby Rules; and this would have the advantage that only one of the parties to the contract of sale (*i.e.* the buyer) would need to insure the goods against loss or damage resulting from acts or omissions of the carrier for which the latter was not contractually liable. The suggested solution is, however, inconsistent with the assumptions underlying the *Pyrene* case[21]: these are that the carrier is protected by the contract of carriage as soon as performance of his duty to load has *begun*, but that the risk passes from seller to buyer only when performance of the seller's duty to load is *completed*.

Exceptions. The risk may remain, wholly or in part, on an f.o.b. seller after shipment in a number of situations which have in Chapter 18 been discussed in relation to the general problem of risk during transit. Thus the seller's duties to make a reasonable contract of carriage[22] and to give notice enabling the buyer to insure[23] can apply to an f.o.b. contract under which the contract of carriage is made by the seller; and one effect of breach of these duties is that the goods during transit remain at the seller's risk,[24] save, perhaps, to the extent that the risk of necessary deterioration in transit remains on the buyer.[25] The risk of deterioration will also be on the f.o.b. seller where he is in breach of his implied undertaking that the goods can endure normal transit[26] or of some other undertaking, *e.g.* as to packing or loading with due care and skill.[27] The whole risk may be on the seller if he ships the goods but at the same time demands a price higher than that 20–091

[19] Below, para.21–047.
[20] *e.g. The Forum Craftsman* [1985] 1 Lloyd's Rep. 291 (express contractual provision that risk should pass at ship's rail): *cf. above*, para.18–209, n.32 (express contractual provisions for property and risk to pass at inlet valve).
[21] [1954] 2 Q.B. 402.
[22] Sale of Goods Act 1979, s.32(2) (above, para.18–245).
[23] *ibid.*, s.32(3) (above, para.18–246).
[24] This is the sole effect stated in s.32(3); s.32(2) produces a similar effect by providing that the buyer can "decline to treat the delivery to the carrier as a delivery to himself" but adds that he may, alternatively, claim damages. *cf.* above, para.18–248.
[25] Sale of Goods Act 1979, s.33 (above, paras 18–249 to 18–252).
[26] Above, paras 18–255 to 18–257.
[27] Above, para.18–258.

agreed: in one such case the shipment was held not to be in accordance with the contract.[28]

20–092 Risk may conversely be on the buyer before shipment where delivery has been delayed through his fault.[29] This would be the position, for example, where a perishable cargo deteriorated because of the buyer's breach of contract in failing to give instructions for shipment within the contract period. The goods may also be at the buyer's risk before shipment even though he is not guilty of any actual breach of contract. This would be the position if the buyer had induced the seller to have the goods ready at the docks by telling him that the ship on which they were to be loaded would be there on a particular day during the contractual shipment period but she did not actually arrive until a later day, still within that period, and the goods had deteriorated by the time the ship arrived.[30] In such a case it has been said that, although "the purchaser may be entitled to reject when the goods are being placed over the ship's rail, yet the vendor may be entitled to recover damages in respect of the deterioration of the goods".[31] This is not quite the same as saying that the risk had passed (for in that case the purchaser would not be entitled to reject); but in practice it leads to much the same result.

20–093 The general rule as to the passing of risk under an f.o.b. contract[32] can also be varied by the terms of the contract. In *The Parchim* it was said that "The effect of the contract was to provide that on shipment, *or at all events upon notification of the shipment*, the cargo was to be at the risk of the buyers."[33] It is hard to see from the report upon what provision of the contract the words here italicised are based. They certainly cannot be based on any duty of the seller to give notice to enable the buyer to insure, since the contract provided for insurance to be covered by the sellers, though for the buyers' account. In a subsequent passage the cargo is said to have been "at the buyers' risk from the moment it was placed on board"[34]; and it seems unlikely that there was, in fact, any provision in the contract excluding the general rule that risk passes on shipment.

---

[28] *Williams v Cohen* (1871) 25 L.T. 300.

[29] Sale of Goods Act 1979, s.20(2). The subsection does not put the whole risk on the buyer in such a case, but only "the risk . . . as regards any loss which might not have occurred but for such fault." Under the Vienna Convention on Contracts for the International Sale of Goods (above, para.1–024) the normal rules as to risk may similarly be displaced where delay on the part of the seller is due to an act or omission of, or to a fundamental breach by, the *seller*: Arts 66 and 70. Neither of these provisions affords any remedy to the seller where delay in delivery is due to a breach of contract on the part of the *buyer* in taking delivery, but the buyer's wrongful failure to take delivery can lead to the passing of risk to the buyer under Art. 69(1) and (2) (above, paras 18–088, n.94, para.20–244, n.16).

[30] *J & J Cunningham Ltd v Robert A Munro & Co. Ltd* (1922) 28 Com.Cas. 42 at 46. There would be no breach by the buyer in such a case: see above, para.20–049, at n.53.

[31] *J & J Cunningham Ltd v Robert Munro & Co. Ltd*, above, at p.46.

[32] Above, para.20–088.

[33] [1918] A.C. 157 at 164 (italics supplied).

[34] *ibid.*, at p.168.

20–094 **Buyer dealing as consumer.** It is possible, if unusual, for an f.o.b. buyer to deal as consumer.[35] Two provisions of the Sale of Goods Act 1979 are relevant to the passing of risk when the buyer so deals. The first is section 20(4) which provides that, in such cases, subsections 20(1) to 20(3) "must be ignored and the goods remain at the seller's risk until they are delivered to the consumer". The second is section 32(4) which provides that, in such cases, subsections 32(1) to 32(3) "must be ignored, but if in pursuance of a contract of sale the seller is authorised or required to send the goods to the buyer, delivery of the goods to the carrier is not delivery of the goods to the buyer". The difficulties that can arise from those provisions where an f.o.b. buyer deals as consumer are discussed in Chapter 18,[36] where it is suggested that their operations may depend on which of the ways of making shipping arrangements is adopted. [37] Here it must be added that the two subsections may (a) displace the general rule that risk under an f.o.b. contract passes on shipment,[38] and (b) displace or modify the exceptions to that rule discussed in paragraphs 20–091 and 20–092 above. With regard to the first of these points, it must be recalled that where (as in the third of the situations described by Devlin J. in the *Pyrene* case[39]) shipping arrangements are made by the buyer, one possible view is that the goods are "delivered" to the buyer within section 20(4) where they are delivered to the carrier engaged by him.[40] Such delivery to the carrier does not, however, necessarily amount to *shipment* of the goods, so that in a case of this kind there would still be scope for the general rule that risk under an f.o.b. contract did not pass before, but passes on, shipment.[41] With regard to the second of the above points, it must be noted that subsection 32(4) disapplies only the preceding provisions of section 32 and does not affect common law rules which may overlap with them. For example, the disapplication of subsection 32(2) (which requires the seller to make a reasonable contract of carriage on behalf of the buyer) would not affect the seller's duty in the first of the situations described by Devlin J. in the *Pyrene* case to procure "a bill of lading in terms usual in the trade".[42] At common law, the general rule as to passing of risk under f.o.b. contracts can also be displaced by contrary agreement; and it was submitted in Chapter 18 that subsections 20(4) and 32(4) can also, subject to the Unfair Contract Terms Act 1977 and the Unfair Terms in Consumer Contracts Regulations 1999, be excluded by express or even by implied agreement.[43]

---

[35] See above, para.18–259.
[36] See above, paras 18–259—18–264.
[37] See above, para.18–262.
[38] See above, para.20–088.
[39] [1954] 2 Q.B. 402 at 424; see above, para.20–003.
[40] See above, para.18–262.
[41] See above, para.20–088. On facts such as those of the *Pyrene* case (above, n.39) it seems that the fire tender would be regarded as having been "delivered" to the carrier (see the statement of the facts of this case in paras 20–066 and 20–089 above) but the risk had not passed to the buyer because the tender had not been shipped.
[42] *Pyrene* case, above n.39, at 424.
[43] See above, para.18–264.

7. FRUSTRATION

20–095 **In general.** There are relatively few cases on frustration of f.o.b. contracts. Such as there are mostly concern prohibition of export or import, or failure to obtain export or import licences.[44] So far as the following discussion relates to other causes of frustration it is, for lack of authority, largely conjectural.[45]

20–096 **Destruction of goods after shipment.** If specific goods are sold on f.o.b. terms to a buyer who does not deal as consumer and destroyed after shipment, the contract will not be avoided under section 7 of the Sale of Goods Act 1979, since the risk will normally have passed on shipment.[46] Even where the risk remains, in the exceptional situations discussed in paragraphs 20–091 and 20–092 above, on the seller after shipment,[47] it is submitted that the contract would not be avoided under section 7. The reason for this submission is that the risk remains on the seller in these exceptional cases by reason of some breach of duty on his part. Destruction of the goods after shipment in such circumstances would therefore have the effect of relieving only the *buyer* from liability. The *seller* would remain liable on the principle that a party cannot rely on self-induced frustration.[48] Nor would an f.o.b. contract for the sale of specific goods be frustrated at common law[49] by the destruction of the goods after shipment, since the seller would have performed his principal obligation by delivering the goods free on board. This reasoning would equally apply where the contract was one for the sale of unascertained goods to which goods were appropriated by the shipment; and it would apply even where the goods were shipped as an undifferentiated part of a larger bulk so that they remained unascertained at the time of loss.[50] It would further apply even though the f.o.b. contract was one under which the seller was obliged to arrange for carriage and insurance on the buyer's behalf. Thus in all such cases not only is the buyer bound to pay the price (a result which would follow from the passing

[44] Above, paras 18–308 *et seq*.
[45] For the relationship between the English doctrine of frustration and Art. 79 of the Vienna Convention on Contracts for the International Sale of Goods (above, para.1–024), see Treitel, *Frustration and Force Majeure* 2nd ed. (2004), paras 6–048, 15–043.
[46] Above, para.20–088. When the buyer deals as consumer, the goods "remain at the seller's risk until they are delivered to the consumer" (Sale of Goods Act 1979, s.20(4)). The question when goods are "delivered" to the buyer where the sale is on f.o.b. terms depends on the way in which the shipping arrangements are made (see above, paras 18–262, 20–003) and on possible express or implied terms excluding s.20(4)(see above, para.18–264). If the effect of s.20(4) is to leave the risk with the seller after shipment, then the contract could be discharged under s.7 by the destruction of the goods at that stage.
[47] Above, para.20–091 to 20–092.
[48] Treitel, *Frustration and Force Majeure* (1994), Ch.14.
[49] *i.e.* apart from s.7.
[50] *Inglis v Stock* (1885) 10 App.Cas. 263 (above, para.18–301). S.20A of the Sale of Goods Act 1979 (added in 1995) has not affected the point that such goods *remain unascertained:* see s.20A(1).

of risk) but the seller also remains bound to perform such obligations (*e.g.* as to tender of documents) as remain outstanding at the time of the destruction of the goods.

Destruction of goods before shipment. An f.o.b. contract for the sale of specific goods could be frustrated or avoided under section 7 of the Act if the goods were destroyed before shipment, since at this stage the risk would not normally have passed to the buyer.[51] Risk may exceptionally pass to the buyer before shipment: this is the position where the shipment is delayed as a result of the buyer's fault.[52] In such a case, destruction of the goods before shipment would discharge the seller under the rules relating to risk, but the buyer would remain liable on the principle that a party cannot rely on self-induced frustration.[53] 20–097

An f.o.b. contract for the sale of a specified quantity of goods forming an undifferentiated part of an identified bulk, or of goods to be taken from an identified source, could likewise be frustrated if the bulk were destroyed, or if the source dried up, before shipment.[54] On the other hand, an f.o.b. contract for the sale of unascertained generic goods would not be frustrated merely because the goods which the seller intended to appropriate to the contract had been destroyed. But such a contract might be frustrated where a stipulated method of performance became impossible, or by supervening illegality. These possibilities are discussed below.

Method of performance impossible. As in the case of c.i.f. contracts,[55] a distinction must be drawn between methods of performance which are stipulated in the contract and those which are merely contemplated. An f.o.b. contract, might, for example, provide for shipment by a named ship and it seems that such a contract could be frustrated if, as a result of the stranding of the ship, it became impossible to ship the goods in her during the shipment period.[56] An f.o.b. contract can similarly be frustrated if the authorities of the country of origin prohibit the export of the goods unless the buyer adopts a method of payment which differs fundamentally from that specified in the contract: *e.g.* by requiring payment to be made *in advance* when the contract stipulated for payment against documents.[57] In the case of a c.i.f. contract it is, as we have seen, arguable that inability to 20–098

---

[51] Above, para.20–088.
[52] Sale of Goods Act 1979, s. 20(2); above, para.20–092. S.20(2) "must be ignored" where the buyer deals as consumer (s.20(4)). For difficulties arising from this part of s.20(4), where the sale is on f.o.b. terms, see above, para.18–263. Even if the result of ignoring s.20(2) were that the goods remained at the seller's risk, the destruction would still be due to the buyer's "fault" for the purpose of the rule that a party cannot rely on self-induced frustration (see above, at n.48).
[53] Above, n.48.
[54] On the principle of *Howell v Coupland* (1876) 1 Q.B.D. 258, above, paras 6–038, 6–051.
[55] See above, paras 19–126, 19–127.
[56] *cf. Nickoll and Knight v Ashton, Edridge & Co.* [1901] 2 K.B. 126 (above, para.19–126).
[57] *Nile Co. for the Export of Agricultural Crops v H & JM Bennett (Commodities) Ltd* [1986] 1 Lloyd's Rep. 555.

ship by the agreed route may in theory frustrate the contract.[58] But in the case of an f.o.b. contract this will be a cause of frustration only in exceptional circumstances,[59] since normally[60] the contract of sale will not, either expressly or by implication, specify any route of shipment. On the contrary, it is normally[61] a matter of indifference to the seller what the buyer intends to do with the goods once they have been placed free on board[62]: hence such a case will be governed by the principle that a contract is not frustrated by impossibility of a method of performance contemplated by one party only.[63] For the same reason, such a contract is not frustrated merely because the goods to be supplied under it were intended by the seller to be drawn from a particular source which became unavailable.[64] Thus an f.o.b. contract is not frustrated merely because the seller is let down by his supplier in the country of origin; and this is true even though that supplier is the government of that country and is (unknown to the buyer) the only exporter from there of goods of the contract description.[65] Nor, conversely, would an f.o.b. contract be frustrated merely because a method of payment which the buyer intended to use, but as to which the seller was indifferent, was prohibited by exchange control regulations in the buyer's country.[66]

20–099 **Alternatives.** An f.o.b. contract would not be frustrated merely because one or some of several alternative methods of performance became impossible while at least one remained possible: there is no reason to suppose that in this respect f.o.b. contracts are not, like c.i.f. contracts, governed by the general rule applicable to the frustration of contracts which impose alternative obligations.[67]

20–100 **Inability to ship.** We have seen that, as a general rule, inability to ship does not frustrate a c.i.f. contract, with the result that a seller who cannot find shipping space will be liable in damages for failing to ship.[68] It would seem that the same principle applies to f.o.b. contracts, though its effect in the case of a "classic" f.o.b. contract[69] will be to produce the opposite result, *viz.* that the buyer will be liable in damages for failing to give proper shipping instructions.[70] On the other hand, if it is the f.o.b. seller who has

[58] *cf. above*, para.19–127.
[59] As in *Hackfield v Castle* 198 P. 1041 (1921).
[60] The destination may be (though it rarely is) a term of an f.o.b. contract (above, para.20–021); and the same is true with regard to the route: see *Hackfield v Castle*, above, n.59 where an f.o.b. contract did specify the route.
[61] For an exception, see above, para.20–042, and see n.60, above.
[62] *SCCMO (London) Ltd v Soc. Générale de Compensation* [1956] 1 Lloyd's Rep. 290 at 299.
[63] *cf. above*, para.19–128.
[64] *Beves & Co. Ltd v Farkas* [1953] 1 Lloyd's Rep. 103.
[65] *Atisa SA v Aztec AG* [1983] 2 Lloyd's Rep. 579; above, para.18–340.
[66] *Toprak Mahsulleri Offsi v Finagrain Cie. Commerciale* [1979] 2 Lloyd's Rep. 98.
[67] *cf. above*, para.19–129.
[68] *cf. Lewis Emanuel & Son Ltd v Sammut* [1959] 2 Lloyd's Rep. 629 (above, para.19–132).
[69] Above, paras 20–002 to 20–006.
[70] *Baetjer v New England Alcohol Co.*, 66 N.E. 2d 798 (1946).

undertaken to find shipping space (and not merely to use his best endeavours to that end[71]), the result will be the same as in the case of a c.i.f. contract: *i.e.* the seller will be liable in damages if he cannot perform the undertaking.

Illegality. An f.o.b. contract may be frustrated by supervening illegality, for example if the port of shipment becomes an enemy port.[72] The mere fact that the buyer was prevented from exporting the goods to the destination intended by him because it became enemy territory would not frustrate the contract,[73] though the contract would be frustrated if that destination actually formed one of its terms.[74] More usually, an f.o.b. contract would not contain any term as to the destination. If, in such a case, the buyer instructed the seller to ship the goods to a destination which, before actual shipment, became enemy territory, it is submitted that the contract would not be frustrated and that the buyer would be both entitled and bound to give fresh shipping instructions. 20–101

Prohibition of export or import, etc. The questions whether, and in what circumstances, a contract can be frustrated by prohibition of export or import, or by failure to obtain an export or import licence, have been considered generally in Chapter 18.[75] In accordance with the principles there discussed, it seems that a supervening prohibition of export could frustrate an f.o.b. contract if it made shipment in accordance with the contract illegal. This was, for example, held to be the position where shipment was prohibited by the authorities of the country of origin unless the buyer, whose contractual obligation it was to pay against documents, instead paid (as required by those authorities) by confirmed documentary credit opened in advance.[76] 20–102

A supervening prohibition of export would not, however, frustrate an f.o.b. contract where the authorities of the country of origin had prohibited the export of the goods only to the particular country to which the buyer intended to ship the goods[77] (without affecting the legality of export to other countries), or if the contract could be performed without exporting the goods[78] (*e.g.* by shipping them coastwise); for, except in the unusual case in which the destination intended by the buyer forms a term of the contract,[79] that destination is not a matter with which an f.o.b. seller has any

[71] See above, paras 20–028, 20–044.
[72] *cf. above*, para.19–136.
[73] *cf. above*, para.20–098, at n.59.
[74] *cf. above*, para.18–335. *Quaere*, whether a *common* intention of buyer and seller (not giving rise to a contractual term) that the goods should be sent to such a destination would frustrate the contract, on the analogy of *Re Badische Co. Ltd* [1921] 2 Ch. 331, above, para.18–335, n.96.
[75] Above, paras 18–331, 18–334 *et seq.*
[76] *Nile Co. for the export of Agricultural Crops v H & J M Bennett (Commodities) Ltd* [1986] 1 Lloyd's Rep. 555 (where the illegality arose under foreign law).
[77] *Amtorg Trading Corp. v Miehle Printing Co. (of Delaware)* 206 F. 2d 103 (1953).
[78] This depends on the construction of the contract: *cf. Maine Spinning Co. v Sutcliffe & Co.* (1918) 87 L.J.K.B. 382 (above, para.20–015).
[79] *cf. above*, para.20–042, n.97.

concern. For the same reason, an f.o.b. contract would not normally be frustrated by a prohibition of import imposed by the country of destination intended by the buyer.[80] Such a prohibition could frustrate an f.o.b. contract only in the unusual case in which it was a term of the contract, that the goods should be imported into that country.[81]

20–103 **Provisions for delays, etc.** An f.o.b. contract may make provision for delay in, or prevention of, shipment resulting from causes (such as prohibition of export or import[82] or force majeure) over which the parties have no control. Similar provisions in c.i.f. contracts have been discussed in Chapter 19[83] and there is no reason to suppose that the principles there stated do not, where appropriate,[84] apply to f.o.b. contracts.[85]

20–104 **Effects of frustration.** The effects of frustration are dealt with in relation to sales of goods in general in Chapter 6.[86] Here it is necessary only to make a number of points about the impact on f.o.b. contracts of the Law Reform (Frustrated Contracts) Act 1943. Since the provisions of the Act which deal with restitution, release from liability to pay money and expenses[87] all refer to things which were, or should have been, done *before* the time of discharge, these provisions are likely to have a narrow scope in relation to f.o.b. contracts. For it is on the one hand unlikely that, under such a contract, payment will have become due (or been made) to the seller, or a valuable benefit conferred on the buyer, before shipment, and on the other hand virtually impossible for an f.o.b. contract to be frustrated after shipment. If, exceptionally, a payment has become due (or been made) before shipment and the contract is then frustrated, the payment ceases to be due (or must be repaid) subject to the discretion of the court to allow the seller to recover or retain expenses under section 1(2) of the Act. These expenses could include manufacturing costs and costs incurred in relation to the anticipated shipment. Payments due or made after shipment would not normally cease to be due or become recoverable as a result of subsequent events, as such events would not normally frustrate the contract. Part shipment before frustration might give rise to a claim for recovery of a valuable benefit under section 1(3), though if the contract is

80 *Swift Canadian Co. Ltd v Banet* 224 F. 2d 36 (1955); for a similar rule applicable to c.i.f. contracts, see above, para.19–137.

81 *cf. above*, para.20–042, n.97.

82 Above, paras 18–342 *et seq*.

83 *cf. above*, paras 19–138 *et seq*.

84 For example, the discussion in para.19–141 above, of the effect of such a provision on a c.i.f. seller's duty to buy afloat, would not be relevant in the context of f.o.b. contracts since an f.o.b. seller cannot perform his duty to ship by appropriating goods already afloat: see above, para.20–009.

85 See, for example, *Bache and Vig v Montague L. Meyer* (1921) 7 Ll.L.R. 63; *Exportelisa SA v Guiseppe & Figli Soc. Coll.* [1978] 1 Lloyd's Rep. 433; *Agrokor AG v Tradigrain SA* [2000] 1 Lloyd's Rep. 497; *cf. Maine Spinning Co. v Sutcliffe* (1918) 87 L.J.K.B. 382 (above, para.20–010: contract expressly "subject to the embargo being removed").

86 See generally, paras 6–058 *et seq.*, above; Treitel, *Frustration and Force Majeure* 2nd ed. (2004), Ch.15.

87 *i.e.* s. 1(2) and (3).

severable payment at the contract rate would be recoverable under section 2(4); alternatively it is arguable that the same result follows at common law from the passing of risk.[88] The Act does not apply to certain contracts for the sale of specific goods which are avoided or frustrated by reason of the fact that the goods have perished. This exception could apply to f.o.b. contracts where the goods perish before shipment[89] but is unlikely to apply where the goods perish after shipment since in the latter case the perishing of the goods will not normally frustrate the contract.[90]

The questions whether a documentary credit opened in pursuance of a c.i.f. contract constitutes either a "payment" within section 1(2) of the Act or a "valuable benefit" within section 1(3) have been discussed in Chapter 19[91] and the same considerations apply where the credit is opened in pursuance of an f.o.b. contract.

Section 1(5) of the Act provides that, in considering whether any sum ought to be recovered or retained by any party to the contract under the foregoing provisions of section 1, the court shall, as a general rule, not take into account any sums which have, by reason of the circumstances giving rise to frustration, become payable to that party under any contract of insurance. This subsection could apply to claims to recover or retain sums of money under subsections 1(2) and (3) made by either party to an f.o.b. contract. Subsection 1(5) is subject to an exception which applies where "there was an obligation to insure under the express terms of the contract". This exception would not normally apply to an f.o.b. contract since a "classic" f.o.b. contract would not contain any express term obliging either party to insure.[92] It is, however, arguable that the exception could apply to an f.o.b. with additional duties[93] which required the seller to effect insurance. It would seem that the seller is in such a case under "obligation to insure" even though the insurance may be taken out on behalf, or for the benefit, of the buyer, and even though, between buyer and seller, the cost of the insurance is for the buyer's account.[94]

8. REMEDIES OF THE BUYER

(a) *Rejection*

Right to reject the goods. An f.o.b. buyer has the normal right to reject the goods if they are defective in a way that amounts to a breach of a fundamental term, or to a breach of condition, or to a breach of an intermediate term which causes serious prejudice to the buyer[95]; or if the 20–105

---

[88] *Colonial Insurance Co. of New Zealand v Adelaide Marine Insurance Co.* (1886) 12 App.Cas. 128 (above, para.20–039).
[89] See above, para.20–097.
[90] See above, para.20–096 and (where the buyer deals as consumer) para.20–094, 20–096 n.46.
[91] paras 19–143, above.
[92] Above, para.20–001.
[93] Above, para.20–007.
[94] Above, paras 20–007, 20–008.
[95] Not if the breach of such a term causes no such prejudice: *Tradax Internacional SA v Goldschmidt SA* [1977] 2 Lloyd's Rep. 604; above, para.18–273.

goods are not of the agreed quantity. Breach by an f.o.b. seller of a provision in the contract as to the date or place[96] of shipment is a ground for rejection.[97] As already noted,[98] it is unlikely that a buyer's right to reject goods which are not of the contractual description or quantity will, in the case of an f.o.b. contract, be affected by the statutory restrictions on the right to reject which are contained in sections 15A and 30(2A) of the Sale of Goods Act 1979.

Sections 15A and 30(2A) do not apply where the buyer deals as consumer. Where the buyer does so deal,[99] he has certain "additional rights" under Part 5A of the Sale of Goods Act 1979. One such right is the right to require the seller to repair or replace goods which do not conform to the contract at the time of delivery.[1] If the buyer chooses to exercise this right, then he may not reject the goods until he has given the seller a reasonable time within which to repair or replace them.[2] The buyer is, however, under no legal compulsion to proceed under Part 5A, and can therefore avoid the restriction which it imposes on his right to reject by ignoring that Part and exercising his right to reject under the rules which governed that right before the addition (in 2003)[3] of Part 5A to the Act. Under that Part, a buyer who deals as consumer also has, in certain circumstances, a right to "rescind"[4] the contract with regard to non-conforming goods; this right is further discussed in paragraph 20–113 below. The discussion in paragraphs 20–106 to 20–112 deals with cases in which the buyer has not dealt as consumer.

---

[96] *Petrotrade Inc. v Stinnes Handel GmbH* [1995] 1 Lloyd's Rep. 142, above, para.20–014.

[97] *Yelo v S M Machado* [1952] 1 Lloyd's Rep. 183 at 192; above, para.20–029. Under the Vienna Convention on Contracts for the International Sale of Goods (above, para.1–024) the buyer is entitled to declare the contract avoided in two sets of circumstances. First, he can do so under Art. 49(1) (a) if failure by the seller to perform *any* of his obligations amounts to a "fundamental breach" (as defined by Art. 25: see above, para.18–267, n.38): this would apply to cases of delivery of non-conforming goods, in contravention of Art. 35. Secondly, the buyer can declare the contract avoided under Art. 49(1)(b) "in cases of non-delivery" (even though the breach is not "fundamental") if the seller has *either* still not delivered the goods within an additional reasonable time fixed by the buyer (under Art. 47) requiring the seller to perform his obligations (*i.e.* to cure the breach) *or* declared that he would not do so. Cases of late shipment, though amounting to breach of the seller's duty with respect of the time of delivery (in contravention of Art. 33) are not "cases of non-delivery" within Art. 49(1)(b) and so prima facie there is, in such cases, a right to declare the contract avoided only in cases of "fundamental breach." It is, however, arguable that in a f.o.b. contract governed by English law the wider right to reject under English law would be taken to have displaced the Convention rule by virtue of an agreement to this effect (Art. 6) or by usage (Art. 9): see above, para.18–004. For the buyer's further rights of avoidance under Art. 72 and of suspension under Art. 71(1), see above, para.19–161, n.53.

[98] Above, paras 18–284, 19–173, 20–038.

[99] See above, para.18–259.

[1] ss.48A(1)(b), 48A(2)(b)(i), 48B; for the meaning of "delivery" in f.o.b. contracts see above, para.18–262.

[2] s.48D.

[3] By Sale and Supply of Goods to Consumers Regulations 2002, SI 2002/3045.

[4] ss. 48A(2)(b)(ii), 48C(1)(b).

Right to reject documents. In the case of a c.i.f. contract there may be a right to reject the goods and a right to reject the documents; and the relation between these two rights gives rise to many difficulties.[5] Discussion of these problems is generally confined to c.i.f. contracts but it seems that they can arise also in relation to f.o.b. contracts, under which the seller may be obliged to procure and tender certain documents.[6] Thus in one case[7] an f.o.b. contract (as varied) provided that the goods were to be shipped by December 12 and that payment was to be made against "shipped" bills of lading. The seller tendered "received" bills of lading and was also unable to prove shipment by December 12. It was held that the buyer could reject on both these grounds. In another case, it was common ground that an f.o.b. buyer was entitled to reject shipping documents which included an analysis certificate revealing on its face a failure of the goods to conform to the contract in a way that amounted to a breach of condition.[8] It would seem that where an f.o.b. buyer has these two rights of rejection, the relationship between them is governed by the same principles as those which apply in the case of c.i.f. contracts.[9] These principles also determine whether a particular document is defective, and whether a seller's failure to tender some document called for by the contract, other than a bill of lading or mate's receipt—for example, a weight certificate—can justify rejection.[10] It is submitted that an f.o.b. buyer's right to reject non-conforming *documents* is not affected by the statutory restrictions imposed by sections 15A and 30(2A) on a buyer's right to reject nonconforming *goods*: and that the arguments which support this submission in the case of a c.i.f. contract[11] apply equally where the sale is on f.o.b. terms. 20–106

Loss of right to reject.[12] The right to reject may be lost in the usual ways, that is by waiver (or under certain analogous doctrines[13]) and by acceptance.[14] Loss of the right to reject does not of itself impair the right to damages; but if the buyer delays in giving the seller notice of a known 20–107

---

[5] Above, paras 19–144 *et seq*.
[6] Above, paras 20–020 to 20–027.
[7] *Yelo v S M Machado Ltd* [1952] 1 Lloyd's Rep. 183 (above, para.20–024).
[8] *Vargas Pena Apeztieguia y Cia v Peter Cremer GmbH* [1987] 1 Lloyd's Rep. 394; *cf. NSW Leather Co. Pty. Ltd v Vanguard Insurance Co. Ltd* (1991) 25 N.S.W.R. 699 at 709.
[9] Above, paras 19–128 *et seq*; for the right to reject documents under the Vienna Convention on Contracts for the International Sale of Goods (above, para.1–024), see above, para.19–044, n.90.
[10] See, for example, *Tradax International SA v Goldschmidt SA* [1977] 2 Lloyd's Rep. 604; *Mantovani v Carapelli SpA* [1978] 2 Lloyd's Rep. 63 (affirmed without reference to this point [1980] 1 Lloyd's Rep. 375); *Vargas Pena Apeztieguia y Cia v Peter Cremer GmbH* [1987] 1 Lloyd's Rep. 394; above, para.19–148.
[11] Above, para.19–173.
[12] For loss of the right to declare the contract avoided under the Vienna Convention on Contracts for the International Sale of Goods (above, para.1–024), see above, para.19–150, n.47 and *cf.* above, para.19–159, n.30.
[13] *cf. above*, paras 19–150, 19–160; Contrast *Petrotrade Inc. v Stinnes Handel GmbH* [1995] 1 Lloyd's Rep. 142, 151 (where the requirements of estoppel were not satisfied).
[14] Sale of Goods Act 1979, s.11(2) and (4). See for example, *Tradax International SA v Goldschmidt SA* [1977] 2 Lloyd's Rep. 604.

defect he may[15] be held to have waived the entire breach, or to have failed to perform his duty to mitigate. In such cases no damages, or only nominal damages, will be recoverable from the seller.[16]

Where the buyer has both a right to reject the goods and a right to reject the documents,[17] the principles governing loss of these rights would appear to be the same as those which apply to c.i.f. contracts.[18] Most of the reported cases on f.o.b. contracts assume that the buyer wishes to reject *the goods*; and raise the question whether he has lost that right by "acceptance". The buyer is deemed to have accepted the goods (a) when he intimates to the seller that he has accepted them, or (b) when the goods have been delivered to him and he does any act inconsistent with the ownership of the seller,[19] or (c) when after the lapse of a reasonable time he retains the goods without intimating to the seller that he has rejected them.[20] In the first two of these situations, the buyer is not deemed to have accepted the goods until he has had a reasonable opportunity of examining them for the purpose of ascertaining whether they are in conformity with the contract[21] and in the third the question whether he has had such an opportunity is material in determining whether a reasonable time has elapsed.[22] The question in all these situations is whether the buyer has had the *opportunity* of examining the goods, not whether he has examined them or has actually discovered the non-conformity. Under all these rules the point of examination may be of crucial importance in determining whether an f.o.b. buyer has lost the right to reject. Where the ground of rejection is that the *documents* are not in conformity with the contract, the point for examining them would seem to be the place where they are tendered, as under a c.i.f. contract.[23] The following discussion is concerned with the question at which point (for the purposes of the rules relating to "acceptance") an f.o.b. buyer ought to examine the *goods*.

20–108 **Point of examination: general rule.** The general rule, so far as domestic sales are concerned, was stated in *Perkins v Bell*[24] where barley was sold by sample, to be delivered at Theddingworth Station. A.L. Smith L.J. said that

---

[15] If the requirements of this type of waiver (stated in paras 19–150, 19–160, above) are satisfied.

[16] *Toepfer v Warinco AG* [1978] 2 Lloyd's Rep. 569.

[17] See above para.20–106.

[18] Above, paras 19–155 *et seq.*

[19] Under a "classic" f.o.b. contract (above, para.20–002) the buyer would be likely to insure the goods; but his doing so would not be an act inconsistent with the ownership of the seller. This follows from the reasoning of *Clegg v Olle Anderson* [2003] EWCA Civ 320, [2003] 1 All E.R. (Comm) 721 at [59] (see above, para.19–154 n.7).

[20] Sale of Goods Act 1979, s.35(1) and (4).

[21] *ibid.*, s.35(2) A buyer who deals as consumer (see above, para.18–259) "cannot lose his right to rely on [s.35(2)] by agreement, waiver or otherwise" (s.35(3), above, para.13–102).

[22] *ibid.*, s.35(5).

[23] Above, para.19–157.

[24] [1893] 1 Q.B. 193 (above, para.12–043); *Commercial Fibres (Ireland) Ltd v Zabaida* [1975] 1 Lloyd's Rep. 27 (where the contract between buyer and seller was a domestic sale, and the buyer had a representative at the place of delivery under that contract).

there was "a presumption . . . that the place of delivery is the place for inspection. To hold otherwise could be to expose the vendor to unknown risks, impossible of calculation, when the contract was entered into. The vendee might consign the barley not only to one, but to different subvendees, living in different places and at different distances from Theddingworth Station, and until arrival at these places the barley would be at the risk of the vendor."[25] But he also made it clear that the presumption could be rebutted, for he added "that the place for inspection need not necessarily be the place at which delivery is to be made."[26]

Application to f.o.b. contracts. An f.o.b. seller normally performs his duty to deliver the goods by shipping them; but, in relation to f.o.b. contracts, the presumption stated in *Perkins v Bell*[27] probably does not exist, or, if it exists, is more frequently rebutted than applied. Thus it has been said that "there was not. .. any general rule that an f.o.b. buyer must inspect the goods before they were put on board"[28] and an alleged custom to the contrary has been described as unreasonable.[29] But there is equally no "prima facie rule that [under an f.o.b. contract] the goods should be examined at the place of destination. . . . The question of whether there has been reasonable opportunity of examination before shipment where the goods are to be put free on board is a question to be decided in the particular case on its circumstances."[30] The mere fact that the buyer is to find shipping space is not decisive to show that the point for inspection is the point of shipment: in such a case acceptance of the goods by the carrier may be for the purpose of carriage only and "no acceptance at all of the goods as a delivery under the contract".[31] On the other hand the fact that the seller knows that the goods were intended for ultimate disposal at some particular destination is not decisive to show that the point of inspection is the destination of the goods.[32] In a case of this kind Bailhache J. has said: "To postpone the place for inspection it is necessary that there should be . . . two elements; the original vendor must know . . . that the goods are going further on, and the place at which he delivers must either be unsuitable in itself or the nature of the packing of the goods[33] must make inspection at that place unsuitable."[34] In the case of an f.o.b. contract the first element will generally be present,[35] and a third alternative must be 20–109

---

[25] [1893] 1 Q.B. 193 at 197.
[26] At p.196.
[27] Above, para.20–108.
[28] *Boks & Co. v J H Rayner & Co.* (1921) 37 T.L.R. 519 at 520 (affirmed *ibid.*, at p.800); *Bragg v Villanova* (1923) 40 T.L.R. 154.
[29] *Boks & Co. v J H Rayner & Co.*, above (where there was not, in fact, sufficient proof of the custom).
[30] *J W Schofield & Son v Rownson, Drew and Clydesdale Ltd* (1922) 10 Ll.L.R. 480 at 482.
[31] *Vigers Bros v Sanderson Bros* [1901] 1 Q.B. 608 at 612.
[32] *Saunt v Belcher and Gibbons* (1920) 26 Com.Cas. 115, where the contract was not on f.o.b. terms but for delivery at a wharf.
[33] See *Molling & Co. v Dean & Son Ltd* (1901) 18 T.L.R. 217; *Van den Hurk v R. Martens & Co. Ltd* [1920] 1 K.B. 850.
[34] *Saunt v Belcher & Gibbons* (1920) 26 Com.Cas. 115 at 120.
[35] An f.o.b. seller will normally know (in the words of Bailhache J. quoted at n.34 above) that "the goods are going further on", even if he does not know exactly *where* they are going(see above, para.20–021).

added to the second element: namely, that the place of shipment will not be the place for inspection if the buyer is in another country and has no representative at the place of shipment.[36] Even with this qualification, the place for inspection has in cases of f.o.b. contracts been postponed where the two elements mentioned by Bailhache J. have not been present.[37] In most of the reported cases on f.o.b. contracts the point of examination has been held to be, not the place of shipment, but the destination of the goods: that is, the place at which they actually get into the hands of the buyer[38] or into the hands of a sub-buyer to whom they are directly despatched.[39]

The reluctance of the courts to deprive an f.o.b. buyer of the right to reject on the ground that he might have examined the goods at the place of shipment is illustrated by two further rules. First, the burden of proving that the buyer had a reasonable opportunity of examining the goods at the point of shipment lies on the seller[40]; and unless there is an affirmative finding of fact to that effect the buyer will not be held to have accepted the goods merely because he failed to examine them at that point.[41] Secondly, the opportunity afforded to the buyer must be a "reasonable opportunity of examining the goods to see whether they were in accordance with the contract – not merely whether there was reasonable opportunity to have

[36] *e.g. Bragg v Villanova* (1923) 40 T.L.R. 154.

[37] *e.g. Boks & Co. v J H Rayner & Co.* (1921) 37 T.L.R. 800.

[38] *Scaliaris v E Ofverberg & Co.* (1921) 37 T.L.R. 307; *Boks & Co. v J H Rayner & Co.*, above; *Bragg v Villanova, above; Obaseki Bros v Reif & Son Ltd* [1952] 2 Lloyd's Rep. 364 at 367. The Vienna Convention on Contracts for the International Sale of Goods (above, para.1–024), Art. 38(1) requires the buyer to "cause the goods to be examined, within as short a period as is practicable." This examination may "if the contract involves carriage of the goods . . . be deferred until after the goods have arrived at their destination": Art. 38(2). It is far from clear whether an f.o.b. contract is one which "involves carriage of the goods": this would, presumably, depend on the circumstances in which delivery was made. The requirement of causing the goods to be examined is stated in Art. 38 in the context of the rule that the buyer loses *all* right to rely on lack of conformity of the goods if he fails to give notice to the seller specifying the lack of conformity within a reasonable time after he has discovered it or ought to have discovered it: Art. 39(1). But the requirement seems also to be relevant for the purpose of the narrower rule that the buyer loses the right to declare the contract avoided unless he does so within a reasonable time after he knew or ought to have known of the breach: Art. 49(2)(b)(i); *cf. above*, paras 19–150, n.47, 19–159, n.30.

[39] *Molling & Co. v Dean & Son Ltd* (1901) 18 T.L.R. 217; *James Southern & Co. v E Austin & Son* (1921) 6 Ll.L.R. 24; *J W Schofield & Son v Rownson, Drew and Clydesdale Ltd* (1922) 10 Ll.L.R. 480; *cf. Van den Hurk v R Martens & Co. Ltd* [1920] 1 K.B. 850 (where the question arose for the purpose of fixing the time for the assessment of damages). These cases were hard to reconcile with *Hardy & Co. v Hillerns and Fowler* [1923] 2 K.B. 490 under which the subsale and despatch of the goods amounted to an act inconsistent with the ownership of the seller and deprived the buyer of his right to reject. But their authority is revived now that such an act no longer deprives the buyer of the right to reject if he has not had an opportunity of examining the goods: see above, para.19–154. *Cf.* the rule laid down by Vienna Convention on Contracts for the International Sale of Goods (above, para.1–024), Art. 38(3).

[40] *J W Schofield & Son v Rownson, Drew and Clydesdale Ltd* (1922) 10 Ll.L.R. 480 at 482.

[41] *Boks & Co. v J H Rayner & Co.* (1921) 37 T.L.R. 800.

discovered the particular defect which is being sued for if it had been the only defect"[42]; but this rule does not apply where that defect is "so clear and so obvious"[43] that the buyer ought clearly to have discovered it.

Where an f.o.b. buyer lawfully rejects goods at their destination, he is entitled to recover the price, or any part of it, which he has paid before the arrival of the goods.[44]

20–110 Under the rules stated in paragraph 20–109, the courts appear strongly to favour the f.o.b. buyer's right of rejection, even though this can cause hardship to the seller who may have the goods thrown back on his hands at a distant place[45] of which he knew nothing at the time of sale; and at a time long after that at which the risk will normally have passed, so that he may no longer be covered by insurance. This is, of course, simply an acute instance of the hardship to the seller mentioned in *Perkins v Bell*.[46] The seller can attempt to protect himself against it by a non-rejection clause; but such clauses are subject to at least some of the restrictions which limit the effectiveness of exclusion clauses[47]: for example, such a clause may be construed so as not to defeat the main object of the contract.[48] The seller can also protect himself against loss or destruction of the goods by contingency insurance.[49]

---

[42] *J W Schofield & Son v Rownson, Drew and Clydesdale Ltd above*, at p.482.
[43] *ibid*.
[44] *Bragg v Villanova* (1923) 40 T.L.R. 154.
[45] *e.g. Service, Reeve & Co. (London) Ltd v Central Iron and Metal Co.* (1926) 24 Ll.L.R. 340.
[46] [1893] 1 Q.B. 193 at 197 (above, para.20–108). A similar hardship to the seller could arise under Part 5A of the Sale of Goods Act 1979. This Part confers certain "additional rights" on a buyer who deals as consumer (see above, para.18–259) if "the goods do not conform to the contract *at the time of the delivery*" (section 48A(1)(b)). If, in the case of an f.o.b. contract, that time were held to be the time when the goods came into the actual possession of the buyer at the end of the transit (see above, para.18–262), then hardship of the present kind could arise where the seller shipped conforming goods but those goods deteriorated during the voyage so that, at its end, they no longer to conformed to the contract. The very existence of the "additional rights", and so the seller's liability in respect of them, would, on this view, depend on the state of the goods at the end of the transit. The rule in *Perkins v Bell*, by contrast, is based on the assumption that the seller is in breach at the time of shipment, only the risk of subsequent deterioration being normally on the buyer. The effect of that rule is therefore not to give rise to any new rights in favour of the buyer; it is merely to define the circumstances in which one of his remedies (rejection), in respect of an undoubted breach, is barred. In this sense the hardship to the seller that could arise from the rule in *Perkins v Bell* is less severe that that which would arise under Part 5A if "the time of delivery" referred, in the case of an f.o.b. contract, to the time when the goods came into the actual possession of the buyer at the end of the transit.
[47] Above, paras 18–275 to 18–279. Such clauses fall within the definition of exemption clauses in Unfair Contract Terms Act 1977. That Act does not apply to international supply contracts but it is an open question whether a contract which calls for delivery f.o.b. at a British port falls within this category merely because the buyer intended to export the goods to a foreign country: see above, para.18–281.
[48] See *Vigers Bros v Sanderson Bros* [1901] 1 Q.B. 608 (where the terms of the sale closely resembled f.o.b. terms) (above, paras 18–276 to 18–279).
[49] Above, para.20–039.

20–111 **Act inconsistent with the ownership of the seller.** Before 1994, it had been held that an f.o.b buyer would generally[50] be regarded as having done an act consistent with the ownership of the seller if he resold the goods and forwarded them to the sub-buyer.[51] Under an amendment of the Sale of Goods Act made in that year,[52] a buyer is no longer deemed to have accepted the goods *merely* because they have been delivered to another person under a sub-sale or other disposition; the point of this amendment is that such a delivery no longer of itself amounts to an act inconsistent with the ownership of the seller. The amendment does not rule out the possibility that the delivery could, in combination with other circumstances, amount to such an act: for example, if the goods were sold on and delivered to a sub-buyer with full knowledge of the non-conformity giving rise to the right to reject under the original contract of sale. It seems that once the buyer has lost the right to reject by doing an act inconsistent with the ownership of the seller, then that right will not be revived merely because he later re-acquires possession of the goods and is therefore in a position to restore them to the seller.[53]

It has been said that an f.o.b. buyer who insures the goods and makes a claim for loss of some of them against the underwriter does not do an act inconsistent with the ownership of the seller as "the money could be applied in their place."[54]

20–112 **Other problems relating to rejection.** The problems of rejection for the wrong reason, of non-rejection clauses, of statutory restrictions on rights of rejection and of the effect of rejection on property, have been discussed in relation to c.i.f. contracts.[55] Broadly speaking the same principles apply to f.o.b. contracts[56] but this statement can only be made subject to a number of qualifications. Thus the explanation of *Braithwaite v Foreign Hardwood Co.*[57] given in *Taylor v Oakes, Roncoroni & Co.*[58] would not hold if the contract in the former case had been an f.o.b. contract, for in that case the shipment of non-conforming goods would have put the seller in repudiatory

---

[50] For exceptional circumstances see *Heilbutt v Hickson* (1872) L.R. 7 C.P. 438 as explained in *Jordeson & Co. v Stora Kopparbergs Bergslags Aktiebolag* (1931) 41 Ll.L.R. 201 at 205.

[51] *Benaim & Co. v L S Debono* [1924] A.C. 514; *Jordeson & Co. v Stora Kopparbergs Bergslags Aktiebolag,* above; above, para.19–154.

[52] Sale of Goods Act 1979, s.35(6)(b), as substituted by Sale and Supply of Goods Act 1994, s.2(1).

[53] As in the authorities cited in n.51, above, though the reasoning of those cases on the question whether the buyer had done an act inconsistent with the ownership of the seller is no longer tenable after the amendment of the 1979 Act referred to in n.52, above.

[54] *J S Robertson (Aust.) Pty Ltd v Martin* (1956) 94 C.L.R. 30 at 44.

[55] Above, para.19–159 *et seq*.

[56] See, *e.g. Glencore Grain Rotterdam BV v LORICO* [1997] 2 Lloyd's Rep. 386.

[57] [1905] 2 K.B. 543.

[58] (1922) 38 T.L.R. 349 at 351; *ibid.*, at pp.517 at 518 (above, paras 19–167 to 19–168); in *Taylor v Oakes, Roncoroni & Co.* the sale was on f.o.b. terms and the actual decision was that the buyer's breach in relation to a single instalment did not justify the seller's repudiation under s.31 of the Sale of Goods Act 1979 (above, para.8–077).

breach before the buyer's repudiation, which would therefore have been justified. And the rules as to the effect of rejection on property are to some extent concerned with the effects of dealings with bills of lading which would not apply where an f.o.b. contract was one under which no bill of lading was ever held by the seller.

Buyer dealing as consumer. An f.o.b. buyer may sometimes, though he will not usually, deal as consumer.[59] If he so deals and if "the goods do not conform to the contract at the time of delivery",[60] then he has certain "additional rights" under Part 5A of the Sale of Goods Act 1979. One of these is the right to "rescind the contract"[61] with regard to the non-conforming goods, in circumstances specified in Part 5A.[62] The practical effects of the exercise of this right are likely to resemble those of the exercise of the right to reject. In relation to f.o.b. contracts, the exercise of the right to "rescind" the contract gives rise to two problems which have already been discussed in Chapters 18 and 19 above. The first is whether the right to "rescind" under Part 5A is available, not only where it is the goods, but also where it is the *documents*, which are not in conformity with the contract,[63] the second is the meaning of "the time of delivery" where goods are sold on f.o.b. terms.[64] The right to "rescind" under Part 5A is in one respect wider than the right to reject under other provisions of the Act: it arises for breach, not only of condition, but also of any express term,[65] even though the term is neither a condition nor an intermediate term but is only a warranty. This advantage of the right to "rescind" may, however, be more apparent than real since the exercise of the right to rescind is, in effect, subject to the discretion of the court.[66] That discretion extends also to the situation where the buyer seeks to "rescind" under part 5A for breach of condition. The right to "rescind" under Part 5A is also not barred by "acceptance".[67] Where the buyer has a right to reject apart from Part 5A, and has not lost that right by "acceptance," he may therefore prefer to ignore Part 5A and to exercise his right to reject. In this way, he can gain two advantages: the right to reject is not subject to the discretion of the court[68] but is available as of right;[69] and the right is also not affected by the uncertainties (described above[70]) which may limit the scope of the right to rescind under part 5A. 20–113

A non-rejection clause may be so drafted as to exclude not only the right to reject but also to the right to "rescind" under Part 5A. Even if the

---

[59] See above, para.18–259.
[60] Sale of Goods Act 1979, s.48A(1)(b).
[61] *ibid.*, ss.48A(2)(b)(ii), 48C(1)(b).
[62] See *ibid.*, s.48C(2); above, para.20–105.
[63] See above, para.19–065.
[64] See above, para.18–262.
[65] See Sale of Goods Act 1979, s.48F.
[66] See *ibid.*, s.48E.
[67] *cf.* above, paras 12–109, 12–112.
[68] Under s.48E.
[69] ss.15A and 30(2A) are unlikely to apply where the sale is on f.o.b. terms (see above, paras 18–284, 20–033.
[70] At nn. 63 and 64.

contract is an international supply contract and so not subject to the Unfair Contract Terms Act 1977,[71] such a clause could, where the buyer deals as consumer, be subject to the Unfair Terms in Consumer Contracts Regulations 1999,[72] and so not bind the consumer if it is "unfair" within those Regulations.[73]

(b) *Action for Damages*

20–114 **In general.** The principles which govern the assessment of damages have been discussed in relation to c.i.f. contracts in Chapter 19[74]; and although some of these principles apply also to f.o.b. contracts, there are in this respect important differences, as well as similarities, between the two types of contract. Thus in the case of a c.i.f. sale the fact that the contract is for the sale of goods already afloat is sometimes relevant in assessing damages[75]; but as under an f.o.b. contract appropriation of the goods to the contract must take place, at the latest, by shipment,[76] this fact could not affect the damages for breach of such a contract.[77] Again, in the case of a c.i.f. contract damages for non-delivery may be assessed with reference to the time at which the documents should have been tendered, this being for the purpose of a c.i.f. contract the "time or times when [the goods] ought to have been delivered" within section 51(3) of the Sale of Goods Act 1979. In the case, at any rate, of a "classic" f.o.b. contract,[78] the time fixed for shipment would prima facie be the time when the goods ought to have been delivered, so that the reasoning of *C Sharpe & Co. Ltd v Nosawa*[79] would be inapplicable where such a contract was broken by the seller's failure to ship, though similar reasoning would govern the date of assessment where an f.o.b. seller's breach took the form, not of failure to ship, but of failure to tender shipping documents at the required time.[80]

20–115 **Damages for non-delivery: commercial sales.** Under section 51(3) of the Act these are, where there is an available market, prima facie "the difference between the contract price and the market or current price of the goods at the time or times when they ought to have been delivered, or (if no time was fixed) at the time of the refusal to deliver".[81] It is submitted

[71] See above, para.18–281.
[72] SI 1999/2083.
[73] *ibid.*, reg. 8(1).
[74] Above, paras 19–175 to 19–202.
[75] See above, para.19–176.
[76] Above, para.20–009.
[77] Hence the restriction on the scope of the "market" rule for the purpose of assessing damages (discussed in para.19–176, above) does not apply in the case of an f.o.b. contract, though a similar problem can arise where such a contract provides that a payment which is to be made, *e.g.* under a "circle clause", is to be assessed by reference to "the market price for similar goods", as in *Esteve Trading Corp. v Agropec International* (*The Golden Rio*) [1990] 2 Lloyd's Rep. 273.
[78] Above, paras 20–002 to 20–006.
[79] [1917] 2 K.B. 814 (above, para.19–178 *et seq*).
[80] See *Concordia Trading BV v Richco International Ltd* [1991] 1 Lloyd's Rep. 475; for the time of tender of documents under f.o.b. contracts, see above, para.20–022.
[81] For the position under the Vienna Convention on Contracts for the International Sale of Goods (above, para.1–024), see above, paras 19–175, n.91; 19–177, n.1; 19–186, n.47.

that, in the case of a "classic" f.o.b. contract,[82] the place at which the market is relevant is prima facie the place designated in the contract for shipment.[83] The damages would not be assessed by reference to the market value of the goods *on board* the nominated ship, since if the goods are not shipped by the end of the shipment period there is no market value for *such* goods: "once the shipment period is over there cannot be a market f.o.b. price for goods to be shipped during that period".[84]

It is further submitted that the "time . . . when [the goods] ought to have been delivered" (within section 51(3)) is the time when they ought to have been put free on board. Where the contract provides for shipment during a specified period, the time at which the goods ought to have been put on board will depend on which party had the option as to the time of shipment.[85] If the option was the buyer's, damages will be assessed by reference to the market at the time at which the goods ought to have been shipped in response to his shipping instructions. If the option was the seller's, and he designates a time for shipment, but then fails to ship, the buyer's damages will be assessed by reference to the market at that designated time. If the option was the seller's, and he fails to designate a time for shipment, one possible view is that damages should be assessed by reference to the market at that point in the shipment period which is most favourable to the seller,[86] it being presumed that he would have performed the contract in the way which would cause least expense to himself. But this view would give rise to too much uncertainty; and the preferable view is that damages should be assessed simply by reference to the market at the end of the shipment period.[87]

These prima facie rules are, however, liable to be displaced[88]; and may in particular be displaced in the case of an f.o.b. contract by which the seller undertakes to arrange for shipment and insurance on the buyer's account and in which the buyer agrees to pay in exchange for shipping documents.[89] Such a contract is in so many respects similar to a c.i.f. contract that it is arguable that the rules as to the time and place at which the market is relevant in cases of c.i.f. contracts[90] would apply to it.

---

[82] Above, paras 20–002 to 20–006; the rule stated in the text would apply to the first *and third* categories described in para.20–003.

[83] *cf.* Vienna Convention on Contracts for the International Sale of Goods (above, para.1–024), Art. 76(2) ("the place where delivery of the goods should have been made").

[84] *Esteve Trading Corp. v Agropec International (The Golden Rio)* [1990] 2 Lloyd's Rep. 273 at 276, where the claim was not for damages but for the amount due on "closing" of the contract under a "circle" clause.

[85] Above, paras 20–029 to 20–036, 20–046 to 20–050.

[86] On the principle of *Kay SN Co. Ltd v W & R Barnett Ltd* (1932) T.L.R. 440 (charterparty); *cf. above*, para.17–008.

[87] *cf. Phoebus D Kyprianou Coy. v Wm. H Pim Jr. & Co. Ltd* [1977] 2 Lloyd's Rep. 570 and below, para.20–135, for a similar rule where the seller claims damages.

[88] *cf. above*, para.19–183.

[89] *i.e.* where the contract falls into the second category described in para.20–003, above; see also para.20–007.

[90] Above, paras 19–177 to 19–186. In c.i.f. contracts the time of shipment is not for this purpose the time of "delivery."

20–116 **Damages for anticipatory breach.** The concluding words of section 51(3) provide that where no time is fixed for delivery, the damages are to be assessed by reference to the market "at the time of the refusal to deliver." It has been held that these words do not apply to an anticipatory breach of an f.o.b. contract[91] any more than to an anticipatory breach of a c.i.f. contract.[92] In other words in the case of an anticipatory breach of a contract in which no time was fixed for delivery, the damages are not assessed by reference to the market price at the time of the seller's refusal to ship. They are assessed by reference to the normal rule as to damages for an anticipatory breach: that is, by reference to the market price at the time when the goods ought to have been delivered[93] subject to the buyer's "duty to mitigate" by buying against the seller if[94] (but only if)[95] the buyer "accepts" the breach.[96] Performance of this "duty" requires him to buy against the seller within a reasonable time of such "acceptance" and the buyer's damages will be assessed by reference to the market at the end of that time.[97] Failure to perform the "duty to mitigate" does not give rise to any liability on the part of the buyer[98]: the only consequence of such failure is that he cannot recover damages in respect of any further increase in the market price after the time at which he ought to have bought against the seller. The "duty to mitigate" arises even if there is a "time fixed for delivery", *i.e.* even if the contract provides shipment within a fixed period; but if the buyer does not "accept" the breach he is not bound to buy against the seller before the time fixed for delivery[99] and he will be entitled to damages based on the market at that time,[1] or at the end of such a reasonable time thereafter as may be allowed to him for buying against the seller.[2]

20–117 **Other time designated by the contract.** An f.o.b. contract may make its own provisions as to the time by reference to which damages are to be assessed. Such provisions have been discussed in relation to c.i.f. contracts

[91] *Millett v Van Heek & Co.* [1921] 2 K.B. 369; *Tai Hing Cotton Mill Ltd v Kamsing Knitting Factory* [1979] A.C. 91. For the position under the Vienna Convention on Contracts for the International Sale of Goods (above, para.1–024), see above, para.19–179, n.9.
[92] Above, para.19–179.
[93] *Millett v Van Heek & Co.*, above; *Garnac Grain Co. Inc. v Faure and Fairclough Ltd* [1968] A.C. 1130 at 1140; *cf. Roper v Johnson* (1873) L.R. 8 C.P. 167.
[94] *cf. Roth & Co. v Taysen, Townsend & Co.* (1895) 1 Com.Cas. 240; *Sudan Import and Export Co. (Khartoum) Ltd v Soc. Générale de Compensation* [1958] 1 Lloyd's Rep. 310 (both cases of buyer's breach).
[95] *cf. Tredegar Iron and Coal Co. Ltd v Hawthorn Bros* (1902) 18 T.L.R. 716 (a case of buyer's breach).
[96] See generally, above, para.19–179 and below, para.20–140.
[97] *Tai Hing Cotton Mill Ltd v Kamsing Knitting Factory* [1979] A.C. 91; *cf. Kaines (UK) Ltd v Ostereichische Warenhandelsgesellschaft Austrowaren* [1993] 2 Lloyd's Rep. 1.
[98] *Sotiros Shipping Inc. v Sameiet Solholt (The Solholt)* [1983] 1 Lloyd's Rep. 605 at 608; *Sealace Shipping Co. Ltd v Oceanvoice Ltd (The Alecos M)* [1991] 1 Lloyd's Rep. 120 at 124.
[99] As to this time, see above, para.20–115.
[1] *Tredegar Iron and Coal Co. Ltd v Hawthorn Bros*, above, n.95; *Brooker, Dore & Co. v Keymer, Son & Co.* (1923) 15 Ll.L.R. 23; *cf. Brown v Muller* (1872) L.R. 7 Ex. 319.
[2] *cf. Tredegar Iron and Coal Co. Ltd v Hawthorn Bros*, above (where the seller was allowed such reasonable time for reselling on the buyer's breach).

in paragraph 19–181, above. The principles there stated apply equally to f.o.b. contracts.[3]

Damages for defective delivery. Where goods are delivered but the delivery is not in conformity with the contract, the general rule, stated in section 53(2), is that "the measure of damages for breach of warranty is the estimated loss directly and naturally resulting, in the ordinary course of events, from the breach of warranty." This rule would, for example, apply where the goods were not of the contract description and (at least by analogy) where there had been short or late delivery.[4] A special prima facie rule is laid down by section 53(3) "in the case of a breach of warranty of quality"[5]: here the prima facie measure of damages is "the difference between the value of the goods at the time of delivery to the buyer and the value they would have had if they had fulfilled the warranty".[6] Both subsections apply, not only to breach of a term which is a warranty *ab initio*, but also to a breach of condition which the seller elects or is compelled to treat as a breach of warranty[7] and (presumably, by analogy) to damages for breach of an intermediate term which is neither a condition or a warranty. **20–118**

In the case of an f.o.b. contract, it might be thought that "the time of delivery" for the purpose of section 53(3) was the time of shipment since it is by shipping the goods that the seller performs his duty to deliver.[8] But in one case[9] the prima facie rule stated in that subsection was displaced and it was held that the damages were to be assessed by reference to the market price at the time when the defect was discovered. Similarly, the damages have been assessed by reference to the market at the *place* where the defect was actually discovered[10] and this will often be the market at the destination of the goods rather than the market at the place of shipment.[11] Where the buyer had paid for freight and insurance, damages were based on c.i.f. values at destination in such a case, and not on f.o.b. values at the port of shipment.[12] Damages for late delivery may likewise be based on the market at the place of destination, at least if the seller knows the destination of the goods.[13]

An f.o.b. buyer may, like a c.i.f. buyer, have a right to reject either documents or goods or both[14]; and where he has lost one or both of these

---

[3] *Concordia Trading BV v Richco International Ltd* [1991] 1 Lloyd's Rep. 475 at 481.
[4] *cf.* above, para.19–187.
[5] See *ibid.* for the distinction in this context between quality and description.
[6] For the buyer's rights under the Vienna Convention on Contracts for the International Sale of Goods (above, para.1–024) to a price reduction and to damages see above, para.19–187, n.51.
[7] Sale of Goods Act 1979, s. 53(1).
[8] Above, para.20–012.
[9] *Van den Hurk v R Martens & Co. Ltd* [1920] 1 K.B. 850.
[10] *Van den Hurk v R Martens & Co. Ltd,* above; *Obaseki Bros v Reif & Son Ltd* [1952] 2 Lloyd's Rep. 364; in *George Wills & Sons Ltd v Thomas Brown & Sons* (1922) 12 Ll.L.R. 292 this basis of assessment was rejected and the buyer was awarded *the price* he had paid plus expenses; but no discussion as to damages is reported and the result is hard to defend on principle.
[11] *cf.* paras 20–109, 20–110, above.
[12] *Obaseki Bros v Reif & Son Ltd* [1952] 2 Lloyd's Rep. 364.
[13] *Joseph I Emanuel Ltd v Cardia and Savoca* [1958] 1 Lloyd's Rep. 121.
[14] Above, para.20–106.

rights (*e.g.* by acceptance) the question can arise whether he is entitled to recover damages in respect of the market loss which he could have avoided, if he had exercised the right to reject. This question has been discussed in relation to c.i.f. contracts in Chapter 19[15] and there is no reason to suppose that the principles which govern the answers to it in the case of such contracts do not apply also to f.o.b. contracts.[16]

20–119 **Consequential loss.** In addition to damages prima facie recoverable under the rules stated in section 51(3) in cases of non-delivery and in section 53(3) in cases of breach of warranty of quality, the buyer can recover damages for consequential loss.[17] These may include not only damages for loss of profits, in the usual way, but also the cost of carriage where the point of examination is the destination of the goods and they turn out on arrival there to be useless.[18] The buyer can also recover damages in respect of dead freight or demurrage[19] which he may have to pay to the carrier in consequence of the seller's breach. The seller is prima facie liable for demurrage even though the delays giving rise to it are occasioned by his supplier; but he can limit his liability for demurrage incurred in this way by providing that he is to be liable for demurrage only to the extent that he is able himself to recover it from his supplier.[20]

20–120 **Consumer's right to reduction of the price.** In the rare case in which an f.o.b. buyer deals as consumer,[21] Part 5A of the Sale of Goods Act 1979 confers on him certain "additional rights" if "the goods do not conform to the contract at the time of delivery".[22] One of these rights is the right to require the seller "to reduce the purchase price of the goods to the buyer by an appropriate amount".[23] There is no doubt that this right can arise in situations to which the "difference in value" principle stated in section 53(3) would also apply; but, unlike that subsection, Part 5A lays down no formula for calculating the "appropriate amount" of the price reduction available under it. One possibility is to apply the "difference in value" formula of section 53(3). Another possibility is to apply the formula stated in Article 50 of the Vienna Convention on Contracts for the International Sale of Goods[24]: this provides that where the goods do not conform to the contract, the buyer may "reduce the price . . . in the same proportion as the

---

[15] Above, para.19–188 to 19–200.
[16] See *Vargas Pena Apeztieguia y Cia v Peter Cremer GmbH* [1978] 1 Lloyd's Rep. 394, where a problem of this kind arose from an f.o.b. contract but most of the authorities discussed in the judgment concerned c.i.f. contracts. The claim for "market loss" damages failed for reasons stated in para.19–191, above.
[17] Such damages would be recoverable under ss. 51(2) and 53(2) as well as under analogous common law principles.
[18] *James Southern & Co. v E Austin & Son* (1921) 6 Ll.L.R. 24.
[19] *J & J Cunningham Ltd v Robert A Munro Ltd* (1922) 28 Com.Cas. 42; *Trading Society Kwik-Hoo-Tong v Royal Commission on Sugar Supply* (1923) 16 Ll.L.R. 250; (1924) 19 Ll.L.R. 343.
[20] *Socap International Ltd v Marc Rich & Co. AG* [1990] 2 Lloyd's Rep. 175.
[21] See above, para.18–259.
[22] Sale of Goods Act 1979, s.48A(1)(b).
[23] *ibid.*, ss.48A(2)(i), 48C(1)
[24] Above, para.1–024.

value that the goods actually delivered had at the time of delivery bears to the value that conforming goods would have had at that time". This formula differs from that in section 53(3) in that what is reduced under Article 50 is the *price,* which is irrelevant (as such) under the "difference in *value*" formula in section 53(3). The Article 50 formula would yield more than the section 53(3) formula if the goods had been sold for more, and less if they had been sold for less, than they were worth.[25] It is not clear which of these formulae, or what other formula, would be adopted for the purpose of assessing the "appropriate amount" of a price reduction under Part 5A. If that amount were less than that recoverable under section 53(3), then it would be open to the buyer to claim damages under that section; for there is nothing in Part 5A to compel him to exercise the "additional rights" conferred on him by that Part.[26]

The buyer's right to a price reduction arises, like his other "additional rights" under Part 5A, only if the goods do not conform to the contract "at the time of delivery"[27]; and we have seen that considerable difficulties arise in determining to which time this phrase refers where goods are sold on f.o.b. terms.[28] Where the buyer seeks a price reduction, Part 5A gives no guidance on the question, by reference to what time the "appropriate amount" is to be assessed. As noted above, Article 50 of the Vienna Convention refers in the context of price reduction to the "time of delivery" and this phrase is also used, in the context of "difference in value" damages, in section 53(3). In the latter context, that phrase has been interpreted in favour of the buyer so as to refer, not to the time of shipment (when the seller performs his duty to deliver) but not some later time such as that of the discovery of the defect in the goods.[29] The authorities which support this view may give some support to the adoption of a similar approach to the question, by reference to what time the "appropriate amount" of a price reduction under Part 5A should be assessed.

(c) *Specific Performance*

Specific performance. This remedy has been discussed in relation to c.i.f. contracts[30]; and it was pointed out that it would often be undesirable to grant specific performance to a buyer to whom property had not passed as this might prejudice third parties to whom the shipping documents had been pledged. Similar difficulties could arise in the case of f.o.b. contracts; and the discretion to order specific performance is unlikely to be exercised in the case of an f.o.b. contract for the sale of goods which are ordinary articles of commerce.[31] 20–121

---

[25] See the examples given above in para.19–187 n.51.
[26] See Sale of Goods Act 1979, s.48C(1) ("may").
[27] *ibid.*, s.48A(1)(b).
[28] See above, para.18–262, discussing the same phrase in Sale of Goods Act 1979, s.20(4) which, like Part 5A, was added to the Act by the Sale and Supply of Goods to Consumers Regulations 2002, SI 2002/3045.
[29] See above, para.20–118.
[30] Above, para.19–204, where the position under the Vienna Convention on Contracts for the International Sale of Goods (above, para.1–024) is stated in nn. 89 and 92.
[31] Above, para.17–099.

20–122 **Defective delivery to buyer dealing as consumer** An f.o.b. buyer may, though he will not commonly, deal as consumer.[32] Where he so deals, Part 5A of the Sale of Goods Act 1979 confers on him a number of "additional rights" if "the goods do not conform to the contract at the time of delivery".[33] One of these rights is to require the seller to repair or replace the non-conforming goods;[34] and the remedy of specific performance is made available to enforce the seller's duty to comply with such a requirement.[35] The possible limits on the scope of this remedy, particularly where the work of making the repairs would have to be done at a place far distant from the seller's place of business, have been discussed in relation to c.i.f. contracts[36] and that discussion applies, *mutatis mutundis*, to f.o.b. contracts.[37] In such cases, the court may conclude that other remedies available under Part 5A, such as price reduction or rescission are more appopriate[38] than specific relief.

9. REMEDIES OF THE SELLER

(a) *Rescission*

20–123 **Buyer's failure to comply with stipulations as to payment.** The seller is normally entitled to rescind an f.o.b. contract where the buyer fails to comply with a stipulation as to the time or method of payment.[39] The duties of the buyer in this respect are discussed elsewhere in this book[40] and the general rule is that any failure of the buyer, unless waived by the seller,[41] as to the time and place at which a credit must be opened, or a guarantee supplied, justifies rescission by the seller.[42] But it would seem that the rule is not utterly inflexible: thus where a contract obliged the buyer to provide a bank guarantee for payment it was held that the seller could not rescind because the buyer had, instead, provided an irrevocable credit.[43] In another case[44] the contract called for a credit to be opened in London and one was in fact opened in Geneva. This was said to make "no real commercial difference"[45]; but the decision that the sellers were not entitled to rescind

[32] See above, para.18–259.
[33] Sale of Goods Act 1979, s.48A(1)(b).
[34] *ibid.*, ss.48A(2)(a), 48B.
[35] *ibid.*, s.48E(2).
[36] Above, para.19–206.
[37] See Sale of Goods Act 1979, ss.48A(2)(b), 48C.
[38] See *ibid.*, s.48E(3) and (4).
[39] For the seller's right under the Vienna Convention on Contracts for the International Sale of Goods (above, para.1–024) to declare the contract avoided, see above, para.19–207, n.24; and see above, para.19–161, n.53.
[40] Above, paras 20–055, 20–056; below, para.23–083 *et seq.*
[41] Above, para.20–057; below, paras 23–095, 23–096.
[42] Below, para.23–083.
[43] *Sinason-Teicher Inter-American Grain Corp. v Oilcakes and Oilseeds Trading Co.* [1954] 1 W.L.R. 935; *ibid.*, at p.1394.
[44] *Enrico Furst & Co. v WE Fischer Ltd* [1960] 2 Lloyd's Rep. 340.
[45] *ibid.*, at p.348.

was based, so far as this ground for rescission was concerned, on the fact that they had waived their right to rely on the fact that the credit had not been opened in London.

Buyer's refusal to accept and pay. The seller may also be entitled to rescind where the buyer refuses to accept and pay for the goods.[46] This possibility requires no further comment here.[47] 20–124

Buyer's failure to give proper shipping instructions. Another situation in which the seller is entitled to rescind is that in which the buyer fails to give proper shipping instructions. For example, where the contract provided that at least 15 days' notice of readiness of steamer had to be given by the buyer, failure to give notice of the required length of time was held to justify rescission by the seller.[48] If the contract contains no provision as to the amount of notice to be given by the buyer, and the buyer nominates a ship which is not capable of loading within the contractual shipment period, the seller is prima facie[49] entitled to refuse to load[50]; and even if he begins to load on such a ship he is not bound to continue loading after that period has come to an end.[51] In the case of f.o.b. contracts, the law recognises an exception to the rule that the time of *taking* delivery is not prima facie of the essence of a contract for the sale of goods.[52] 20–125

(b) *Action for an Agreed Sum*

(i) *Action for the Price*

Where property has passed: on shipment. Under section 49(1) of the Sale of Goods Act 1979 the action for the price can be maintained "Where . . . the property in the goods has passed to the buyer and he wrongfully neglects or refuses to pay for the goods according to the terms of the contract."[53] As property under an f.o.b. contract does not (save in the most 20–126

---

[46] *e.g. Warinco AG v Samor SpA* [1979] 1 Lloyd's Rep. 450.
[47] *cf. above*, paras 9–010, 19–208.
[48] *Bunge Corp. v Tradax Export SA* [1981] 1 W.L.R. 711 (above, para.20–031); *cf. Bremer Handelsgesellschaft mbH v JH Rayner & Co. Ltd* [1979] 2 Lloyd's Rep. 216 at 224, 229. In the latter case, the seller's rescission was wrongful on the principle stated in para.20–049, above, as the buyers showed that they could have made a valid nomination within an extended shipment period. Under the Vienna Convention on Contracts for the International Sale of Goods (above, para.1–024) the buyer would in cases of this kind be in breach of his obligation to take delivery in that he would not have done "all the acts which could reasonably be expected of him in order to enable the seller to make delivery" (Art. 60(a)); and his breach would give the seller a right to declare the contract avoided in the circumstances set out in Art. 64(1), as to which see above, para.19–207, n.24.
[49] The prima facie rule can be excluded by the terms of the contract: see above, para.20–046.
[50] *Olearia Tirrena SpA v NV Algemeene Oliehandel* (*The Osterbek*) [1972] 2 Lloyd's Rep. 341; above, para.20–046.
[51] *Bunge & Co. Ltd v Tradax* (*England*) *Ltd* [1975] 2 Lloyd's Rep. 235.
[52] *Wolfe v Horne* (1877) 2 Q.B.D. 355; above, para.9–005.
[53] For the position under the Vienna Convention on Contracts for the International Sale of Goods (above, para.1–024), see above, para.19–215, n.68.

exceptional cases) pass before shipment,[54] it follows that the action for the price is not available if the goods have not been shipped,[55] even though the fact that they have not been shipped is due to the buyer's breach of contract in failing to give effective shipping instructions.[56] The action for the price is likewise not available if the property in the goods has not passed for some other reason: *e.g.* because of the buyer's wrongful refusal to take up documents by means of which the seller had reserved the right of disposal.[57] Of course in such cases the seller is entitled to damages. Conversely, the action for the price is available once the seller has put the goods on board without having reserved the right of disposal.[58] Where the buyer wrongfully repudiates the contract but the seller nevertheless proceeds to ship the goods in accordance with the buyer's shipping instructions, it has been held that the seller's remedy is in damages and not by way of action for the price.[59] It is doubtful to what extent this decision remains good law after the House of Lords held in *White and Carter (Councils) Ltd v McGregor*[60] that a party who continues performance of a contract after repudiation by the other may, in certain circumstances, be entitled to sue for the agreed sum. One such circumstance is that the injured party must be able to perform without any further co-operation from the party in breach[61]: in the case of an f.o.b. contract, this requirement would often be satisfied once the buyer had given effective shipping instructions. A second requirement is that the injured party must have a "legitimate interest"[62] in continuing performance. In the case of an f.o.b. contract the seller could have such an interest in shipping after the buyer's repudiation if he had, before that repudiation, undertaken responsibilities towards a carrier with respect to the shipment of the goods. In such circumstances an f.o.b. seller might therefore now be entitled to bring the action for the price.

20–127 **Part shipment.** Where part of the goods had been shipped and shipment of the rest was prevented by the buyer's breach, it was held that the seller was entitled to sue for the price of the part shipped.[63] In one case of this

---

[54] Above, para.20–071.
[55] *Henderson and Glass v Radmore & Co.* (1922) 10 Ll.L.R. 727.
[56] *Colley v Overseas Exporters* [1921] 3 K.B. 302; contrast *Burch & Co. v Corry & Co.* [1920] N.Z.L.R. 69, where there was no discussion as to the remedy.
[57] *Tradax Internacional SA v Goldschmidt SA* [1977] 2 Lloyd's Rep. 604.
[58] *Green v Sichel* (1860) 7 C.B.(N.S.) 747.
[59] *AA Nortier & Co. v Wm. Maclean, Sons & Co.* (1921) 9 Ll.L.R. 192 (so far as it relates to the part of the goods under the Glasgow contract not yet shipped at the time of the buyer's repudiation).
[60] [1962] A.C. 413; Lord Keith at p.43 said that in such a situation the seller could only claim damages; but this is an *obiter dictum* in a dissenting speech. *Cf. Attica Sea Carriers Corp. v Ferrostaal Poseidon Bulk Reederei (The Puerto Buitrago)* [1976] 1 Lloyd's Rep. 250; *The Odenfeld* [1978] 2 Lloyd's Rep. 357; *Clea Shipping Corp. v Bulk Oil International Ltd (The Alaskan Trader)* [1983] 2 Lloyd's Rep. 645; *Ocean Marine Navigation Ltd v Koch Carbon Inc. (The Dynamic)* [2003] EWHC 1936; [2003] 2 Lloyd's Rep. 693 at [23]–[24]; and see generally para.16–059, above.
[61] [1962] A.C. 413 at 431.
[62] [1962] A.C. 413 at 431. Under the Vienna Convention on Contracts for the International Sale of Goods (above, para.1–024) the "good faith" provision of Art. 7(1) (above, para.19–215, n.68) might support a similar requirement.
[63] *AA Nortier & Co. v Wm. Maclean, Sons & Co.*, above (so far as it relates to the part of the goods under the Glasgow contract already shipped at the time of the buyer's repudiation); *FE Napier v Dexters Ltd* (1926) 26 Ll.L.R. 62; *ibid.*, at p.184.

kind, the question was raised, and left open, whether the requirement that property must pass applies "where the seller is claiming the statutory right which is given to him"[64] by section 30(1) in cases of part delivery. With respect, section 30(1) is concerned, not with the seller's *action* for the price, but with the buyer's *duty* to pay the price, and this duty does not, in principle, depend on passing of property at all.[65]

Reservation of right of disposal. Where goods are shipped (and thus appropriated[66] to the contract) and the seller reserves the right of disposal,[67] property normally passes when the conditions on which the goods have been appropriated are satisfied: generally this will happen when the buyer pays the price or accepts a draft in accordance with the contract. If the draft is not paid, the seller can bring an action against the buyer, not only on the bill of exchange, but also for the price, so long, of course, as the buyer is not made liable twice over. But a further problem arises where the buyer without justification refuses to take up the documents or to perform some other condition on which the appropriation was made. Where the sale is on c.i.f. terms, it is well settled that the seller's remedy in such circumstances is in damages and not by way of action for the price. It is assumed that property has not passed, so that no action for the price lies under section 49(1); and the courts have held that the price is not payable "on a day certain irrespective of delivery" where it is, under the contract, payable against shipping documents.[68] But in *F.E. Napier v Dexters Ltd*[69] sweet fat was sold f.o.b. London, to be paid for by cash against mate's receipt. Most of the contract quantity was shipped, and the seller's failure to ship the rest was due to the buyer's breach in failing to give shipping instructions in time. The seller obtained a wharf receipt in the buyer's name, but the buyer refused to pay against that receipt and purported to reject the goods on grounds which were untenable. It was held that the seller was entitled to bring an action for the price of the goods shipped; and the decision of the Court of Appeal is based on the view that the seller had not in fact reserved the right of disposal, so that the property had passed on shipment. At first instance Roche J. had also said that a stipulation by which the seller reserved the right of disposal until certain conditions were fulfilled was wholly for the benefit of the seller and could be waived by him[70]; and this reasoning was approved by Bankes L.J. in the Court of Appeal.[71] Thus the seller may succeed in an action for the price by waiving his right of disposal; but it seems unlikely that he could similarly succeed in an action for the 20–128

---

64 *FE Napier v Dexters Ltd* (1926) 26 Ll.L.R. 184 at 187.
65 The leading section on the time when the duty to pay arises is s.28 which contains no reference to passing of property.
66 Above, paras 18–210, 20–009, 20–070.
67 Above, paras 18–211 *et seq*.
68 Above, paras 19–212 to 19–214.
69 (1926) 26 Ll.L.R. 62; *ibid.*, at p.184.
70 *ibid.*, at pp.63–64.
71 (1926) 26 Ll.L.R. 184 at 187–188; contrast the view of Lord Keith in *White and Carter (Councils) Ltd v McGregor* [1962] A.C. 413 at 437 (as to which, see n.60, above) and of Mance J. in *Huyton SA v Peter Cremer GmbH* [1999] 1 Lloyd's Rep. 620 at 632, above, para.20–076.

price of goods which (through no fault of his own) had not been shipped at all. For in such a case the property would have been prevented from passing, not by a provision in the contract which the seller could waive, but by a general rule of law that property does not pass before shipment; and it is by no means clear that this rule exists entirely for the benefit of the seller.[72]

20–129 **Where property has not passed.** Under section 49(2), an action for the price may be maintained "Where . . . the price is payable on a day certain irrespective of delivery and the buyer wrongfully neglects or refuses to pay such price." This subsection has been considered in relation to c.i.f. contracts; and the prevailing view is that a stipulation in such a contract for payment against documents is not one making the price "payable on a day certain irrespective of delivery."[73] There is no reason to suppose that this view does not apply also to f.o.b. contracts, so that if the buyer wrongfully refuses to pay on tender of documents (and if, as a result, no property passes to him) the seller is not entitled to bring an action for the price; his remedy is in damages.[74] A seller may, however, be entitled to bring the action for the price if he waives the benefit of the stipulation for payment against documents, so that property passes to the buyer[75]; but he cannot insist on performance of the stipulation so as to retain property in the goods and at the same time bring an action for the price. If he retains the property, he can at most obtain a declaration that the buyer is bound to pay the price.[76]

20–130 **Consequences of limits on actions for the price.** In *FE Napier v Dexters Ltd* Bankes L.J. said[77] that the question whether the seller's remedy was by way of an action for the price or by way of one for damages was "not of much interest to the commercial man" as he would "get complete redress whether he proceeds by the one course or the other." This may very often be true; and the question whether an action for the price can be brought will be largely academic where the contract provides for payment by banker's commercial credit. But it may be of some importance, even in such cases, if the agreed source of payment fails[78]; and where the contract does not provide for this method of payment the distinction does have a number

[72] In *Colley v Overseas Exporters* [1921] 3 K.B. 302 the possibility of waiver in such a situation is not even mentioned. *cf.* above, paras 20–070 to 20–073.
[73] Above, paras 19–212, 19–214.
[74] *Tradax Internacional SA v Goldschmidt SA* [1977] 2 Lloyd's Rep. 604. In *Martin v Hogan* (1917) 24 C.L.R. 234 Isaacs, Higgins and Powers JJ. took the view put forward in the text; and it is submitted that this view was correct even though the lower court's judgment, to the effect that the seller was entitled to recover the price, stood because three other judges held that on the pleadings it was not open to the buyer to argue that the seller had chosen the wrong remedy. The decision is not direct authority on the interpretation of s.49(2) since at the time the relevant jurisdiction (New South Wales) had not adopted the Sale of Goods Act.
[75] Above, para.20–128.
[76] *Polenghi v Dried Milk Co. Ltd* (1904) 10 Com.Cas. 42 (above, para.19–213).
[77] (1926) 26 Ll.L.R. 184 at 185.
[78] *Saffron v Soc. Minière Cafrika* (1958) 100 C.L.R. 231; *ED & F Man v Nigerian Sweets & Confectionery Co. Ltd* [1977] 2 Lloyd's Rep. 50; below, para.23–098.

of practical consequences. These have been discussed in Chapter 19 in relation to c.i.f. contracts[79] and the points there made apply equally to f.o.b. contracts.

(ii) *Action for Carrying Charge*

Nature of carrying charges. An f.o.b. contract may provide that the buyer is to be entitled to extend shipment period on payment of carrying charges.[80] If he exercises that right, the carrying charges are regarded as the price of an option to extend the shipment period, rather than as liquidated damages for delay in taking delivery.[81] In this respect, an action for the recovery of such charges therefore resembles the action for the price of the goods; but an action for carrying charges is obviously not subject to the restrictions (discussed above) which Sale of Goods Act 1979, section 49, imposes on the availability of the action for the price. 20–131

Effect of wrongful repudiation by buyer. Where an f.o.b. contract gives the buyer an option to extend the shipment period on payment of carrying charges, the buyer may exercise that option and then wrongfully repudiate the contract of sale before the end of the shipment period. Whether the seller can recover the agreed carrying charges in respect of the part of that period which follows the wrongful repudiation then depends on the scope of the principle laid down by the House of Lords in *White and Carter (Councils) v McGregor*.[82] 20–132

To bring that principle into play, two conditions must be satisfied[83]: first, the party claiming the agreed sum must be able to perform his part of the contract without the co-operation of the other, and secondly he must have a "legitimate interest"[84] in keeping the contract in force, rather than accepting the other party's repudiation. So far as the first requirement is concerned, it is submitted that the relevant contract for the present purpose is not the principal contract of sale but rather the accessory contract under which the buyer has the option to extend the shipment period. The former contract, indeed, cannot be performed without the co-operation of the buyer in giving shipping instructions[85]; but performance of the latter requires no such cooperation: all that the seller needs to do for the purpose of its performance is to hold himself ready to deliver. So far as the second requirement is concerned, it is submitted that the seller should not be taken to lack a "legitimate interest" merely because at the time of the repudiation the market price had moved above the contract price. Where the subject-matter of the sale is one which fluctuates rapidly in value, such a price movement could easily be reversed by the end of the shipment period; and,

---

[79] Above, para.19–215.
[80] Above, para.20–046.
[81] *ibid.*
[82] [1962] A.C. 413; above, para.20–126.
[83] Above, para.20–126; Treitel, *The Law of Contract* (11th ed.), pp.1013–1019.
[84] [1962] A.C. 413 at 431.
[85] The seller's only remedy for the buyer's wrongful failure to give such instructions is in damages: above, para.20–126 n.56.

as a general rule, certainty is best promoted by allowing the seller to hold the buyer to the extended shipment period chosen by the buyer. This is particularly true where the seller has in some way relied on the exercise of the buyer's option. Some support for these submissions is provided by *Lusograin Commercio de Cereas Ltda. v Bunge AG*,[86] where a buyer, having exercised the option to extend the shipment period on payment of carrying charges, then repudiated the contract of sale within the extended period. The sellers did not accept the repudiation and were entitled to recover the carrying charges for the whole of the extended period. The actual decision can, however, be explained on the narrow ground that the arbitrators had not found any facts relevant to the issue whether the sellers ought to have accepted the buyer's repudiation.

(c) *Action for Damages*

20–133 **Damages for non-acceptance: the market rule.** Section 50(1) of the Sale of Goods Act 1979 provides that the seller can bring an action for damages for non-acceptance "where the buyer wrongfully neglects or refuses to accept and pay for the goods".[87] By subsection (2), the measure of damages is "the estimated loss directly and naturally resulting, in the ordinary course of events, from the buyer's breach"; and by subsection (3), where there is an available market for the goods the measure of damages is prima facie "the difference between the contract price and the market or current price at the time or times when the goods ought to have been accepted or (if no time was fixed for acceptance) at the time of the refusal to accept". As in the case of c.i.f. contracts,[88] the rule that damages are to be assessed by reference to the market when the goods ought to have been accepted is only a prima facie one. Assessment may be by reference to some other time: *e.g.*, where the buyer repudiates, by reference to the time of the seller's acceptance of the buyer's repudiation.[89]

It is submitted that, in the case of an f.o.b. contract, the questions by reference to what market, and to what time, damages are to be assessed further depend on the terms of the contract and on the circumstances in which the non-acceptance occurs. If the contract provides that, in the event of default, damages are to be assessed by reference to the market "at the destination named" effect will be given to such a provision; and if no destination is named in such a contract the court can assess the damages by reference to the destination named in the buyer's shipping instructions.[90] In the absence of such a provision, the question which market is relevant depends on whether at the time of the buyer's breach the goods have been

---

[86] [1986] 2 Lloyd's Rep. 654.
[87] For the position under the Vienna Convention on Contracts for the International Sale of Goods (above, para.1–024), see above, para.19–216, nn.74, 75.
[88] *cf.* above, para.19–183 (seller's breach).
[89] *Gebruder Metalman GmbH & Co. KG v NBR* (*London*) *Ltd* [1984] 1 Lloyd's Rep. 614; *cf.* Vienna Convention on Contracts for the International Sale of Goods (above, para.1–024), Art. 76(1) ("at the time of avoidance").
[90] *Laing, Son & Co. Ltd v Eastcheap Dried Fruit Co.* [1961] 2 Lloyd's Rep. 277 (where the parties to an f.o.b. contract adapted a form designed for a c.i.f. contract).

shipped or not: these alternative possibilities are discussed in paragraphs 20–134 and 20–135 below.

Where the goods have been shipped. If the buyer's neglect or refusal to accept the goods takes place after the goods have been shipped (either to a destination named in the contract or, more usually,[91] to one indicated in the buyer's shipping instructions) the seller's damages will prima facie be assessed by reference to the market at the destination.[92] This rule is based on the assumption that there is no market for goods afloat of the contract description, so that it is at the destination that the seller will have to dispose of the goods. For this purpose it is immaterial that the contract was one under which the seller had arranged freight and insurance for the buyer's account, or that the buyer had agreed to pay against documents at some place other than the destination of the goods.[93] Thus, if there is a market both at the place of tender of documents and at the destination, the damages will prima facie be quantified by reference to the latter market; and it is submitted that the time at which that market is relevant is the time of the arrival of the goods (or as soon thereafter as they reasonably can be resold). If there is a market for goods afloat of the contract description, that market may be taken into account for the purpose of assessing damages, if it would be reasonable for the seller to dispose of the goods in that market. In relation to f.o.b. contracts, however, the concept of a market afloat gives rise to the practical difficulty that goods are not sold afloat on f.o.b terms.[94] The only market price for the goods afloat is therefore likely to be their c.i.f price.[95] The cost of freight and insurance would then have to be deducted from that market price for the purpose of assessing damages for breach of an f.o.b contract.[96] The market price would, moreover, have to be the market price of goods shipped on the particular ship on which the goods in question had been loaded, and not that of goods of the same kind but in free circulation.[97] Where the contract provides for payment against shipping documents, the market for goods afloat at the time and place of tender of documents would prima facie be the relevant one. But (as in the case of a c.i.f. contract)[98] this prima facie rule could be displaced if in all the circumstances it was reasonable for the seller to dispose of the goods in some other market. 20–134

Where the goods have not been shipped. If the buyer's breach occurs before shipment, for example if it consists of failure to give effective shipping instructions so that the goods are never shipped,[99] the goods will 20–135

---

[91] *i.e.*, where no destination is named in the contract (See above, para.20–021).

[92] *FE Napier v Dexters Ltd* (1926) 26 Ll.L.R. 62 at 64 ("Hamburg measure"); affirmed *ibid.*, 184 without reference to this point. Contrast Vienna Convention on Contracts for the International Sale of Goods (above, para.1–024), Art. 76(2) ("the place where delivery of the goods should have been made" or, if there is no market there "the price at such other place as serves as a reasonable substitute.").

[93] Contrast, above, para.19–216.

[94] Above, para.20–009.

[95] *cf. Esteve Trading Corp. v Agropec International* (*The Golden Rio*) [1990] 2 Lloyd's Rep. 273 at 277.

[96] *ibid.*

[97] *ibid., cf.* above, para.19–176.

[98] *cf.* above, para.19–216.

[99] As in *Colley v Overseas Exporters* [1921] 3 K.B. 302.

be left on the seller's hands at the place of intended shipment. The damages should therefore prima facie be based on the market at that place.[1] Here again a question may arise as to the time at which that market is relevant, particularly when an f.o.b. contract[2] calls for shipment during a specified period.[3] If the time of shipment is at the seller's option, and the seller gives notice requiring the buyer to have a ship ready by a named date, it is arguable that the relevant time should logically be the time at which such a ship should have been ready to take the goods; though the courts may in the interests of greater certainty look to the end of the shipment period.[4] If the time of shipment is at the buyer's option, he may at one point in the shipment period give shipping instructions which are ineffective; and if as a result of such instructions the seller suffers loss he can no doubt recover damages, *e.g.* in respect of storage charges or deterioration of the goods before shipment.[5] But such abortive shipping instructions do not put the buyer finally in breach, it being still open to him to give effective shipping instructions during the remainder of the shipment period; and the market may fluctuate during this time. It would seem that, if the buyer fails to give shipping instructions capable of taking effect by the end of the shipment period, this will constitute the final breach so that damages will be assessed by reference to the market at the end of the period.[6] In the interests of certainty, this date is regarded as the relevant one,[7] rather than the last date on which shipping instructions could have been given so as to enable the goods to be shipped by the end of the period.[8]

20–136 **Time for assessment specified by contract.** The rules as to time for assessment stated in paragraphs 20–134 and 20–135 above may be displaced by express provisions of the contract. This was said to be the position where an f.o.b contract gave the buyer the right to extend the shipment period for 60 days on payment of carrying charges[9] and went on to provide that the date of default was to be the "day after the last day for performance of the

---

[1] *cf.* Vienna Convention on Contracts for the International Sale of Goods (above, para.1–024), Art. 76(2), above, n.92.

[2] Such problems do not arise in connection with c.i.f. contracts since the shipment period does not in such contracts have any bearing on the time at which the goods ought to have been *accepted*.

[3] For the converse problem in cases of seller's breach, see above, para.20–115.

[4] See *Brooker, Dore & Co. v Keymer, Son & Co.* (1923) 15 Ll.L.R. 23; *Sudan Import and Export Co. (Khartoum) Ltd v Soc. Générale de Compensation* [1958] 1 Lloyd's Rep. 310; *Harlow and Jones Ltd v Panex (International) Ltd* [1967] 2 Lloyd's Rep. 509.

[5] *J & J Cunningham Ltd v Robert A Munro Ltd* (1922) 28 Com.Cas. 42 at 46 (above, paras 20–047, 20–092).

[6] *Phoebus D Kyprianou Coy. v Wm. H Pim Jr. & Co. Ltd* [1977] 2 Lloyd's Rep. 570 at 580, as to which see *Lusograin Comercio Internacional de Cereas Ltda. v Bunge AG* [1986] 2 Lloyd's Rep. 654 at 658.

[7] *Phoebus D Kyprianou Coy. v Wm. H Pim Jr. & Co. Ltd* [1977] 2 Lloyd's Rep. 570 at 580; *cf.* above, para.20–115.

[8] The suggestion made in para.20–115, above (that the seller may be presumed to wish to perform in the way which will cause least expense to himself) is inappropriate in the case of a buyer's breach since his obligation, to pay the price, remains a constant expense.

[9] Above, para.20–046.

buyer's main obligation [*i.e.* to provide a ship] taking into account the 60 day extension".[10] Damages were accordingly assessed by reference to the market at the end of the extended period. This seems not to differ from the result reached under the general common law in the absence of an express contractual provision, though the result was reached by a different route. Strictly speaking, it seems that the reasoning should have led to an assessment by reference to the market price on the day after the last day on which the buyer should have provided a ship capable of loading by the end of the extended shipment period,[11] but as loading could have been accomplished in only two days the difference between this time and that chosen by the court is probably of little significance.

Damages where there is no market for goods of the contract description. If there is no market, the measure of damages for non-acceptance is 20–137
"the difference between the contract price of the goods and the . . . value [at the end of the shipment period] of the goods to [the seller]"[12]; and this may be assessed by reference to a price at which the goods have in fact been resold by the seller. The same rule applies where, though there is a market for the commodity in question, there is no market at the relevant time for goods of the exact contract description, *e.g.* for goods shipped in the contractual shipment period.[13] The resale price will form the basis of assessment so long as the seller acted reasonably in reselling for that price.[14] If the buyer offers to take the goods for a price less than the contract price, the seller's damages will not be reduced on the ground that he failed to mitigate merely because he did not accept that offer.[15] Such a reduction will be made only if it was in all the circumstances reasonable to expect the seller to accept the buyer's offer.[16]

Other damages for non-acceptance. Damages for non-acceptance may 20–138
include consequential loss, so long as this is not too remote.[17] Any charges for freight and insurance incurred by the seller on the buyer's account would likewise be recoverable as damages for non-acceptance. Assuming that the shipment of the goods amounted to a delivery of the goods, such damages would (in the case of an f.o.b. contract)[18] appear to be damages for non-acceptance.

---

[10] *Lusograin Comercio Internacional de Cereas Ltda. v Bunge AG* [1986] 2 Lloyd's Rep. 654.
[11] *cf.* above, para.19–181.
[12] *Harlow and Jones Ltd v Panex (International) Ltd* [1967] 2 Lloyd's Rep. 509 at 530. This appears to be an application of the rule in Sale of Goods Act 1979, s.50(2).
[13] *e.g. Gebruder Metalman GmbH & Co. KG v NBR (London) Ltd* [1984] 1 Lloyd's Rep. 614.
[14] *ibid. Cf.* Vienna Convention on Contracts for the International Sale of Goods (above, para.1–024), Art. 75 (which can apply even if there is a market).
[15] *Harlow and Jones Ltd v Panex (International) Ltd*, above.
[16] *cf. Sotiros Shipping Inc. v Sameiet Solholt (The Solholt)* [1983] 1 Lloyd's Rep. 605 (seller's breach).
[17] Above, paras 16–043 *et seq. Cf.* Vienna Convention on Contracts for the International Sale of Goods (above, para.1–024), Art. 74.
[18] Contrast paras 19–216, 19–219 above (c.i.f. contract).

20–139 **Damages for not taking delivery.** Section 37 of the Sale of Goods Act 1979 makes the buyer liable for neglecting or refusing to take delivery where the seller is ready and willing to deliver the goods and requests the buyer to take delivery.[19] Such damages may be recoverable by an f.o.b. seller even though the buyer does accept the goods. If, for example, the seller has the option as to the time of shipment and gives the buyer notice that the goods are ready, the buyer may nominate a ship which is incapable of loading the goods within a reasonable time, but which does eventually load them within the contract period. In such a case any extra storage charges incurred by the seller as a result of the delay could be recovered under section 37.[20] Similarly, where the option as to the time of shipment is the buyer's and he gives shipping instructions but the ship is late, the seller may be entitled to damages if as a result of the delay he suffers loss[21]; and such a claim would most naturally fall under section 37. The distinction between damages for non-acceptance and damages under section 37 gives rise to theoretical difficulties; but where (as is commonly the case) non-acceptance involves neglect or refusal to take delivery the courts do not trouble to draw the distinction.

20–140 **Damages for anticipatory breach.** The rules already stated in relation to the damages recoverable by an f.o.b. buyer for the seller's anticipatory breach[22] apply *mutatis mutandis*, to the converse situation of an anticipatory breach committed by the buyer. Thus the concluding words of section 50(3) provide that, where no time is fixed for acceptance, damages for nonacceptance are to be assessed by reference to the market "at the time of the refusal to accept". Although there is no decision on the point, it seems that these words do not (any more than the corresponding words in section 51(3)[23]) apply to an anticipatory breach, in this case, by the buyer.[24] In other words, in the case of an anticipatory breach of a contract in which no time was fixed for acceptance, the damages are not assessed by reference to the market price at the time of the buyer's refusal to accept. They are assessed by reference to the market price when the goods ought to have been accepted,[25] subject to the seller's "duty to mitigate"[26] by selling against the buyer if,[27] but only if,[28] he "accepts" the breach. Once the seller has

[19] See above, paras 9–009, 16–088, 19–219.
[20] Above, para.19–219.
[21] *e.g. Addax Ltd v Arcadia Petroleum Ltd* [2000] 1 Lloyd's Rep. 493, where, by reason of the buyer's delay in taking delivery, the price, which under the contract depended on the bill of lading date, was lower than it would have been, if delivery had been taken on time.
[22] Above, para.20–116.
[23] *ibid.*
[24] Contrast Vienna Convention on Contracts for the International Sale of Goods (above, para.1–024), Art. 76, as to which see above para.19–179, n.9.
[25] *Garnac Grain Co. Inc. v Faure and Fairclough Ltd* [1968] A.C. 1130 at 1140; *Sudan Import and Export Co. (Khartoum) Ltd v Soc. Générale de Compensation* [1958] 1 Lloyd's Rep. 310; *cf. Roper v Johnson* (1873) L.R. 8 C.P. 167 (seller's breach); above, para.19–179 (c.i.f. contracts).
[26] See above, para.20–116, n.91.
[27] *Roth & Co. v Taysen, Townsend & Co.* (1895) 1 Com.Cas. 240; *Garnac Grain Co. Inc. v Faure and Fairclough Ltd*, above.
[28] *Tredegar Iron and Coal Co. Ltd v Hawthorn Bros & Co.* (1902) 18 T.L.R. 716.

"accepted" the breach, this "duty to mitigate" will arise even if the contract provides for shipment within a named period, and is thus one which (at least by implication) does fix a time at which the goods ought to have been accepted.[29] But if an f.o.b. seller does not "accept" the breach he is not bound to sell against the buyer before the time fixed for acceptance of the goods,[30] and is entitled to damages based on the market price at that time, or within such reasonable time thereafter as may be allowed to him[31] for reselling the goods.

(d) *Rights against the Goods*

Seller's rights against the goods. These are fully discussed in Chapter 15 and mentioned, in relation to c.i.f. contracts, in Chapter 19.[32] The unpaid seller's right of stoppage in transit is theoretically of somewhat greater importance in relation to f.o.b. than to c.i.f. contracts; for under an f.o.b. contract an unpaid seller may part with possession of the goods against only a mate's receipt,[33] which is not a document of title[34] in the traditional common law sense.[35] He therefore runs a greater risk than a c.i.f. seller (who commonly holds a bill of lading) of losing both the property in the goods and his lien.[36] In practice, however, this does not now seem to be a common situation since f.o.b. sellers often hold bills of lading and since even the retention of a mate's receipt in the seller's name can amount to a reservation of a right of disposal and so prevent property from passing before payment.[37] At any rate there are few modern reported cases in which an f.o.b. seller has had to rely on his right of stoppage. The right of resale is available to an f.o.b. seller in the ordinary way, whether or not the property in the goods has passed to the buyer.[38] 20–141

With regard to the right of stoppage, it should be noted that goods shipped under an f.o.b. contract generally remain in transit until they reach the destination to which they have been shipped[39] even though that destination is not known to the seller at the time of shipment.[40] The transit

---

[29] See *Roth & Co. v Taysen, Townsend & Co., above; Sudan Import and Export Co. (Khartoum) Ltd v Soc. Générale de Compensation* [1958] 1 Lloyd's Rep. 310.
[30] See above, para.20–135.
[31] *Tredegar Iron and Coal Co. Ltd v Hawthorn Bros & Co.* (1902) 18 T.L.R. 716; contrast *Warin and Craven v Forrester* (1876) 4 R.(Ct. of Sess.) 190 where the seller's delay in reselling was unreasonably long.
[32] Above, para.19–220. *Cf.* Vienna Convention on Contracts for the International Sale of Goods (above, para.1–024), Arts. 71(2) and 88.
[33] As in the third of the situations described by Devlin J. in *Pyrene Co. Ltd v Scindia Navigation Co. Ltd* [1954] 2 Q.B. 402 at 424, above, para.20–003.
[34] Above, para.18–166.
[35] See above, paras 18–007, 18–062.
[36] See *FE Napier v Dexters Ltd* (1926) 26 Ll.L. Rep. 62 at 184, above, para.20–076; *Nippon Yusen Kaisha v Ramjiban Serowgee* [1938] A.C. 429, above, para.18–168.
[37] See *Falk & Fletcher* (1865) 18 C.B.(N.S.) 403, above, para.18–168.
[38] Above, para.15–101.
[39] *Ruck v Hatfield* (1822) 5 B. & A. 632; *Berndtson v Strang* (1867) L.R. 4 Eq. 481 varied L.R. 3 Ch.App. 588; *Booth SS Co. Ltd v Cargo Fleet Iron Co. Ltd* [1916] 2 K.B. 570; *FW Kennedy & Co. v F Leyland & Co. Ltd* (1923) 16 Ll.L.R. 399.
[40] *Ex p. Rosevear China Clay Co.* (1879) 11 Ch.D. 560.

is at an end once the goods reach that destination and does not continue merely because the buyer redirects the goods to a further destination for the purpose of delivery to a sub-buyer.[41] If, on the facts, the goods are considered on shipment to have been delivered to the carrier, not as such, but as the buyer's agent, the transit will cease on shipment: for example, where the goods are shipped on a ship owned by the buyer under a bill of lading making them deliverable to his order.[42] Where the right of stoppage exists, it may be defeated by dealings with documents of title to the goods.[43]

An f.o.b. seller who exercises his right of stoppage will be entitled to take possession of the goods only if he discharges the carrier's lien for freight; and this is so even though he is not a party to the contract of carriage.[44] In *Booth SS Co. Ltd v Cargo Fleet Iron Co. Ltd*[45] the seller, in the exercise of his right of stoppage, ordered the carrier not to deliver the goods to the buyer, but he did not either give any other directions to the carrier, or himself claim possession of the goods. It was held that the seller was liable in "damages" to the carrier amounting to the freight which the carrier could have recovered from the buyer on delivery of the goods at the agreed destination. The liability of the seller is thus established but its legal nature is far from clear. It is probably a species of quasi-contractual or restitutionary liability, though some dicta in the case may suggest that it is based on tort.[46]

---

[41] *Ex p. Golding Davis & Co. Ltd* (1880) 13 Ch.D. 628.
[42] *Schotsman v Lancs and Yorks. Ry Co.* (1867) L.R. 2 Ch.App. 332; *cf. Cowas-jee v Thompson* (1845) 5 Moo.P.C. 165 as explained in *Berndtson v Strang* (1867) L.R. 4 Eq. 481 at 482 (varied L.R. 3 Ch.App. 588); *Cowdenbeath Coal Co. Ltd v Clydesdale Bank Ltd* (1895) 22 R.(Ct. of Sess.) 682 and Sale of Goods Act 1979, s.45(5) (ship chartered by buyer).
[43] Above, paras 18–086, 18–087; *e.g. Cowdenbeath Coal Co. Ltd v Clydesdale Bank Ltd*, above.
[44] see above, para.20–003.
[45] [1916] 2 K.B. 570.
[46] *e.g.* at pp.584, 603 (interference with contract). The seller was not an original party to the contract of carriage, nor was any document ever issued to which the Carriage of Goods by Sea Act 1992 could now apply. For the seller's liability to the carrier, see also para.15–088 above.

Chapter 21

OTHER SPECIAL TERMS AND PROVISIONS IN OVERSEAS SALES

	PARA.
1. Ex works or ex store contracts	21–002
2. F.a.s. contracts	21–010
3. C. & f. contracts	21–012
4. Ex ship and arrival contracts	21–014
5. Sale of a cargo	21–032
6. F.o.r. and f.o.t. contracts	21–042
7. Conventions on international carriage of goods	21–047
(a) International carriage of goods by air	21–051
(b) International carriage of goods by road	21–058
(c) International carriage of goods by rail	21–065
8. Container transport	21–072
(a) Introductory	21–072
(b) Multimodal transport document	21–075
(i) Contractual effects	21–076
(ii) Document of title function	21–079
(c) Liability of carrier	21–084
(i) Package or unit limitation	21–085
(ii) Carriage on deck	21–088
(d) Sale terms and container transport	21–094
(e) Provisions for mixed carriage	21–104

Introductory. Although overseas sales are most frequently concluded on c.i.f. or f.o.b. terms, the duties of the parties may be defined in various other ways. The points of delivery may vary from, at the one extreme, the seller's place of business to the buyer's at the other; and for convenience the terms of sale are in the present Chapter considered in this geographical order. Finally we shall consider certain special problems arising out of methods of carriage other than carriage by sea and out of container transport. **21–001**

1. Ex Works or Ex Store Contracts

Goods to be delivered from seller's works. This is not, in a sense, an overseas sale at all, but goods may be sold to an overseas buyer on the terms that they are to be delivered from the seller's works or store. In such a case the normal rule applies, that the place of delivery is the seller's place of business[1] and the seller performs his duty to deliver by allowing the buyer to collect the goods.[2] The expenses of and incidental to putting the **21–002**

---

[1] Sale of Goods Act 1979, s.29(2); *cf.* Vienna Convention on Contracts for the International Sale of Goods (above, para.1–024), under which Art. 31(c), together with Art. 30, would lead to the same result in the case of an ex store contract.
[2] Sale of Goods Act 1979, s.29(2); *cf.* s.61(1) ("delivery"); see above, paras 8–002, 8–005.

goods into a "deliverable state" must be borne by the seller[3]; he must provide such packing as is customary, including any special packing required for export if the goods are sold for export. This appears to follow from the definition of "deliverable state" in section 61(5) to mean "such a state that the buyer would under the contract be bound to take delivery of them [the goods]".[4] The seller must also notify the buyer when the goods are ready for collection and indicate where they are to be collected.[5]

21–003 **Passing of property and risk in ex works contracts.** Where a seller agrees to manufacture goods and deliver them from his own works, the contract is an agreement for the sale of unascertained, future goods. In cases of this kind, property will not normally pass until the goods are ascertained; and prima facie it then passes, in accordance with section 18, rule 5, when goods of the contract description are unconditionally appropriated to the contract by the seller with the consent of the buyer.[6] Such unconditional appropriation is normally deemed to have taken place when the seller "delivers" the goods to the buyer, *i.e.* when the buyer with the seller's permission takes them away; and the risk would normally pass at the same time.[7] A number of exceptions to these general rules are considered in paragraph 21–004 below.

21–004 Property may pass before delivery. Suppose, for example, that the seller manufactures the goods, packs them, labels them with the buyer's name and notifies the buyer that they are ready for collection. That could be an appropriation[8] of the goods by the seller; and it has been said that "if the buyer agrees to come and take them that is the assent to the appropriation".[9] It is also possible that "the buyer's assent to the appropriation is conferred in advance by the contract itself or otherwise"[10] and in such a case property (and consequently risk) may pass even if the buyer has not, after receiving notice that the goods are ready, agreed to collect them. It is

---

[3] *ibid.*, s.29(6); see above, para.8–005.
[4] *cf.* Vienna Convention on Contracts for the International Sale of Goods (above, para.1–024), Art. 35(2)(d).
[5] *Davies v McLean* (1873) 21 W.R. 264.
[6] r. 5(1); the concluding words ("or by the buyer with the consent of the seller") are inapposite in the context of an ex works contract.
[7] See *Wardar's (Import and Export) Co. Ltd v W Norwood & Sons Ltd* [1968] 2 Q.B. 663. Where the buyer deals as consumer, this would also be the time when the goods were "delivered to the consumer" within s.20(4), so that they would then be no longer at the seller's risk. The difficulties discussed in paras 18–259 to 18–264 in relation to the effects of s.20(4) on overseas sales are unlikely to arise where goods are sold on ex works or ex store contracts. Under the Vienna Convention on Contracts for the International Sale of Goods (above, para.1–024), an ex store contract would be governed by Art. 69(1), under which risk similarly passes to the buyer when he "takes over" the goods (or fails in breach of contract to do so).
[8] For the various senses of appropriation, see above, para.18–210; here the goods would be appropriated in the "contractual" sense that the seller would be bound to deliver them under the contract.
[9] *Carlos Federspiel & Co. SA v Charles Twigg & Co. Ltd* [1957] 1 Lloyd's Rep. 240 at 256.
[10] *ibid.*, at p.255.

not of course suggested that property will necessarily pass before delivery in such cases. As Diplock L.J. has said, "In modern times very little is needed to give rise to the inference that the property in specific goods is to pass only on delivery or payment."[11] The same would, it is submitted, be true where the contract was for the sale of unascertained goods which had later been appropriated to the contract; and the court would often infer that the seller intended to retain the property until delivery or payment or both. Thus in fact property is not likely to pass before delivery unless the price has been paid in advance. The property in goods sold on ex works terms can pass even before the goods become ascertained: for example, if the sale was of 500 telephones to be collected from the seller's warehouse. If the warehouse contained 10,000 telephones of the contract description, the 500 could form part of a bulk identified by the contract and on payment of the price the buyer would acquire an undivided share in the bulk and become owner in common of it.[12]

Where the contract is for the sale of specific goods, section 18, rules 1 to 3, will prima facie determine the passing of property. In view of the seller's obligation with regard to packaging, the operative rule will often be rule 2 which provides that if "the seller is bound to do something to the goods for the purpose of putting them into a deliverable state, the property does not pass until the thing is done, and the buyer has notice that it has been done." Again these rules are only prima facie rules and are likely to be displaced where delivery and payment have not taken place. **21–005**

Risk in ex works contracts will normally pass with property,[13] *i.e.* on delivery and payment; but the two may be separated. This could happen, for example, if property passed before the buyer had collected the goods, but the seller undertook to keep them insured until delivery; or where the buyer dealt as consumer.[14] Conversely, risk may pass without property where the sale is of a specified quantity of goods forming an undifferentiated part of an identified bulk and the buyer has not yet paid the price.[15] **21–006**

Goods to be delivered from third party's warehouse. An ex store or ex warehouse contract, may provide for delivery of the goods from a store or warehouse in which the goods are kept in the possession of a third person, the warehouseman. In such a case, the basic rule is laid down by section 29(4): "there is no delivery by seller to buyer unless and until the third person acknowledges to the buyer that he holds the goods on his behalf." Such acknowledgment will often result in passing of property and risk, though the passing of property is not necessarily connected with the **21–007**

---

[11] *R. v Ward Ltd v Bignall* [1967] 1 Q.B. 534 at 545.
[12] Sale of Goods Act 1979 s.20A, discussed in relation to overseas sales in paras 18–293 to 18–299 above.
[13] *cf. Leigh & Sillavan Ltd v Aliakmon Shipping Co. Ltd (The Aliakmon)* [1986] A.C. 785 at 809.
[14] Sale of Goods Act 1979, s.20(4), above para.21–003 n.7.
[15] *cf.* above, para.18–300. In the case put, no property could pass under Sale of Goods Act 1979, s.20A as payment had not been made.

"delivery" which takes place on acknowledgment. If the goods are specific or ascertained[16] and have been paid for, property may pass before the warehouseman attorns.

Where the contract is one for the sale of unascertained goods, property cannot normally pass before ascertainment.[17] In the case of a contract for the sale of a specified quantity of unascertained goods forming part of an identified bulk, ascertainment normally takes place when the quantity to which the buyer is entitled is separated from the bulk for the purpose of being delivered to him. But the goods may also become ascertained by "exhaustion" where the remainder of the bulk has previously been delivered to others, leaving in the warehouse only the quantity sold to the buyer[18]; or by the converse process (which may be described as "consolidation") where the buyer acquires the rest of the bulk from the person or persons previously entitled to it.[19] Property in a specified quantity of unascertained goods forming part of an identified bulk can pass even before ascertainment: once the goods have been paid for, the buyer can acquire an undivided share in the bulk and become owner of it in common.[20] Property can pass in any of these ways only where the bulk itself is ascertained: for example, it would not so pass where the seller had goods in several warehouses and could perform his contract by appropriating goods from one such source other than that in relation to which the alleged "exhaustion" or consolidation had occurred.[21] *A fortiori* property would not pass if the seller could perform from some other extraneous source. Once the goods are ascertained, property and risk normally pass on attornment[22]; but in exceptional circumstances risk in goods which form an undifferentiated part of a larger bulk may pass without property.[23]

21–008 **Delivery orders.** Where goods are in the possession of a third party, delivery is often effected through the medium of a delivery order. The operation and effect of such orders has been discussed in Chapter 18.[24]

---

16 Goods stored in a warehouse in bulk for several buyers (but segregated from the sellers' own goods) may be "ascertained" for the purpose of passing of property: *Re Stapylton Fletcher Ltd* [1994] 1 W.L.R. 1181, above, para.18–288.
17 Sale of Goods Act 1979, s.16 (above, 18–209).
18 *Wait & James v Midland Bank* (1926) 31 Com.Cas. 172; *cf. Karlshamns Oljefabriker v Eastport Navigation Corp. (The Elafi)* [1981] 2 Lloyd's Rep. 679 (goods forming part of a bulk cargo in a ship); Sale of Goods Act 1979, s.18 r. 5(3) and (4); above, para.18–288.
19 *cf. The Elafi*, above n.18 and *Inglis v Stock* (1885) 10 App.Cas. 263.
20 Sale of Goods Act 1979, s.20A, discussed (in relation to overseas sales) in paras 18–293 to 18–299 above.
21 *Re London Wine Co. (Shippers)* [1986] P.C.C. 121 at 152.
22 *Wardar's (Import Export) Co. Ltd v W. Norwood & Sons Ltd* [1968] Q.B. 663. For attornment, see Sale of Goods Act 1979, s.29(4); before the revision of the Act in 1979, this provision was contained in s.29(3): hence the reference to "s.29(3)" in the *Wardar* case at 671. *Quaere* whether such attornment amounts to "delivery" for the purpose of s.20(4), which provides that, where the buyer deals as consumer, "the goods remain at the seller's risk until they are delivered to the consumer".
23 *Sterns Ltd v Vickers Ltd* [1923] 1 K.B. 78 (above, para.18–300).
24 Above, paras 18–169 to 18–171.

21–009 **Liability of warehouseman.** A warehouseman who refuses to deliver goods to the person entitled to them, or who misdelivers them, may be liable for breach of contract,[25] or in tort for conversion. But if he delivers the goods, in accordance with the usual course of business, against one part of a set of bills of lading he is not liable in tort to a person to whom other parts of the same set have previously been transferred.[26]

2. F.A.S. Contract

21–010 **Duties of the parties.** An f.a.s. contract is one by which the seller undertakes to deliver goods free alongside a ship designated by the buyer. Such a contract has many features in common with an f.o.b. contract; the main difference between the two is that the point of delivery is earlier in an f.a.s. than in an f.o.b. contract; and this has various effects on the rights and duties of the parties. Under an f.a.s contract, "it is for the buyers to arrange for shipping space and . . . to what port and by what date the goods are to be brought to that place"[27] (*i.e.* the place of shipment). The seller is bound to bring the goods alongside the ship "that is, placed in possession of the shipowners".[28] He is not responsible (as between buyer and seller[29]) for the expense of putting the goods on board; and he will not at any time be a party to the contract of carriage.[30] It does not follow that the seller may not be contractually bound to see that the goods are put on board. An f.a.s (no less than an f.o.b.) seller may undertake duties in addition to those normally imposed by such a contract. But even if he does undertake additional duties in respect of loading, the expense of loading will nevertheless (as between buyer and seller) have to be borne by the buyer.[31]

21–011 **Property and risk.** Generally, goods sold under an f.a.s contract will be unascertained generic goods, and the passing of property will depend on unconditional appropriation to the contract. Goods are "appropriated" in the "contractual" sense[32] when the contract is irrevocably attached to them, though the appropriation may not be unconditional for the purpose of

---

[25] Above, para.18–174.

[26] *Glyn Mills & Co. v East and West Indian Dock Co.* (1882) 7 App.Cas. 591. In this case the warehouseman stood in the same position as the carrier by sea: above, para.18–092.

[27] *Anglo-African Shipping Co. of New York Inc. v J Mortner Ltd* [1962] 1 Lloyd's Rep. 81 at 92; affmd. [1962] 1 Lloyd's Rep. 610. *Semble*, the buyer is not obliged to make an advance reservation of shipping space unless the contract so provides: *cf.* above, para.20–028 (f.o.b. contracts).

[28] *Nippon Yusen Kaisha v Ramjiban Serowgee* [1938] A.C. 429 at 444. *Cf.* Vienna Convention on Contracts for the International Sale of Goods (above, para.1–024), Art. 31(a): "handing the goods over to the . . . carrier"—a phrase more appropriate in the context of an f.a.s. than of an f.o.b. contract, where *shipment* is required: above, paras 20–010, 20–012.

[29] For the positions between these parties and the carrier, see above, para.20–018.

[30] Contrast paras 20–003, 20–059 *et seq.*, above.

[31] *cf.* para.20–010, above.

[32] Above, para.18–210.

passing the property because the seller has reserved the right of disposal.[33] Under an f.a.s. contract, goods are commonly appropriated in the "contractual" sense on delivery alongside, and, if that appropriation is "unconditional", property[34] and risk[35] will pass at that point, before actual shipment. But property will not pass on delivery alongside if the seller has reserved the right of disposal[36]; and whether he has done so can give rise to difficult questions of construction and of fact. In *Nippon Yusen Kaisha v Ramjiban Serowgee*[37] bales of gunnies were sold f.a.s. Calcutta under contracts which provided by clause 3 that payment was to be made against mate's receipts and by clause 4 that, so long as the mate's receipts were in the possession of the sellers, the sellers' lien was to subsist until payment in full. The goods were put on board a ship on which the buyers had booked space; and mate's receipts, naming the buyers as shippers, were sent to the sellers' suppliers, who forwarded them to the sellers. Meanwhile the carriers had issued bills of lading to the buyers and eventually they delivered the goods to sub-buyers against the bills of lading. On the buyers' default in payment, it was held that the sellers had no cause of action in respect of this delivery against the carrier, as the property in the goods had passed on delivery alongside. Clause 3 of the contract would normally have prevented the passing of property until payment, but it had to be read together with clause 4, which indicated that property had passed before payment, since "a person cannot have a lien on his own goods".[38] It was said that the position would have been different if the sellers had taken the mate's receipt in their own (and not in the buyers') name.[39] The form of the mate's receipt could not alter the construction of the contract, but it could amount to a reservation of the right of disposal *by the terms of the appropriation*; and this

---

[33] Above, para.18–211.

[34] *Nippon Yusen Kaisha v Ramjiban Serowgee* [1938] A.C. 429 at 444.

[35] *Warin and Craven v Forrester* (1876) 4 R. (Ct. of Sess.) 190. Where the buyer deals as consumer (see above, para.18–259) "the goods at the seller's risk until they are delivered to the consumer" (s.20(4)). It is submitted that in case of an f.a.s. contract "delivery" to the consumer would, for the purpose of s.20(4), occur when the goods were delivered free alongside the ship designated by the buyer. The case would be analogous to that in which the buyer sends his own transport to collect the goods (*cf.* above, para.8–007); and it would be unreasonable to defer the passing of risk until the goods had reached their destination, since that destination would not be a term of the contract and the buyer could send the goods to a destination, the transit to which could expose them to perils wholly outside the contemplation of the seller at the time of the contract of sale (*cf.* above, para.18–262 at n.13). In the situation here under consideration, the seller would also no longer be "sending" the goods to the buyer after delivery alongside, so that s.32(4) (discussed in relation to overseas sales in paras 18–261 and 18–262 above) would not apply. The situation would not be covered by reasoning of *Wimble, Sons & Co. v Rosenberg* [1913] 3 K.B. 743, discussed in para.18–247 above. That reasoning applies to an f.o.b. contract under which the goods are shipped on a ship *selected by the seller*; that is not the position under f.a.s sales. For the possibility of excluding ss.20(4) and 32(4) by agreement, see above, para.18–264.

[36] *e.g.*, by taking a bill of lading to his own order, as in *Transpacific Eternity SA v Kanematsu Corp. (The Antares III)* [2002] 1 Lloyd's Rep. 233, holding that Sale of Goods Act 1979, s.19(2) (above, para.18–214) applies to f.a.s. contracts.

[37] [1938] A.C. 429.

[38] *ibid.*, at p.444.

[39] *ibid.*, at p.445.

would be sufficient to prevent the passing of property under section 19(1) of the Sale of Goods Act 1979. Where an f.a.s. seller thus retains the property after delivery alongside, he would at first sight appear also to retain the risk.[40] But this view would tend to produce commercially inconvenient results[41]; and it seems more probable that under these contracts (as under c.i.f. and f.o.b. contracts) the risk can pass notwithstanding the seller's reservation of the right of disposal.

3. C. & F. CONTRACTS

Duties of the parties. A c. & f. contract is an agreement to sell goods at an inclusive price covering their cost and freight to the agreed destination. With the obvious exception that the seller is not bound to insure, the duties of the parties are the same as under a c.i.f. contract. Generally, a c. & f. contract will simply omit reference to insurance. But it may require the seller to insure the goods at the buyer's request and for his account.[42] A c. & f. contract containing such a provision differs from a c.i.f. contract in that the buyer has to pay the cost of insurance, so that he and not the seller takes the risk of any variation in that cost. A c. & f. contract may, conversely, provide for insurance to be effected by the buyer, with a view to protecting the seller until the risk passes or until payment is made. A buyer who fails to effect such insurance is liable to the seller in damages for such sum as the seller could have recovered under the policy which should have been taken out.[43] Where the contract simply provides that insurance is to be effected by the buyer but fails to specify the extent of insurance coverage required, it has been held that the buyer's obligation to insure is co-extensive with that incumbent on a seller under a normal c.i.f. contract.[44] 21–012

Passing of property and risk. Property and risk under a c. & f. contract generally pass at the same time and in the same way as under a c.i.f. contract.[45] But there may be exceptions to this principle. Thus the duty of a seller to give notice to enable the buyer to insure, under section 32(3) of the Act,[46] does not generally apply to a c.i.f. contract, because the terms of such a contract, obliging the seller to insure, are evidence of contrary intention.[47] This reasoning obviously does not apply to a c. & f. contract 21–013

---

[40] By virtue of s.20(1).
[41] *cf.* above, para.20–071.
[42] *cf. Muller, McLean & Co. v Leslie Anderson* (1921) 8 Ll.L.R. 328.
[43] *M. Golodetz & Co. Inc. v Czarnikow Rionda Co. Inc. (The Galatia)* [1980] 1 W.L.R. 495 at 513–515; affirmed without reference to this point *ibid.*, p.517.
[44] *Reinhart Co. v Joshua Hoyle & Sons Ltd* [1961] 1 Lloyd's Rep. 346; above, paras 19–042 *et seq.*
[45] *The Kronprinsessan Margareta* [1921] 1 A.C. 486 (property); *Fuerst Day Lawson Ltd v Orion Insurance Co. Ltd* [1980] 1 Lloyd's Rep. 656 at 664 (risk); *Anderson v Morice* (1875) L.R. 10 C.P. 609; (1876) 1 App.Cas. 713 (risk—part shipment; *cf.* above, para.20–039); *The Pantanassa* [1970] P. 187 (risk of freight above, para.19–120).
[46] Above, paras 18–246 to 18–248.
[47] *Law and Bonar Ltd v American Tobacco Co. Ltd* [1916] 2 K.B. 605 (above, para.19–117).

which either contains no provisons as to insurance,[48] or requires the buyer to insure,[49] so that a c. & f. seller may well be under a duty to give the notice required by section 32(3), with consequent effects on risk.[50]

4. EX SHIP AND ARRIVAL CONTRACTS

21–014 **Definition.** An ex ship contract is one by which a seller is bound to procure the delivery of the goods from a ship (whether named or not) at an agreed destination. If the contract contains the name of the ship this, as well as any stipulation as to the time of arrival,[51] forms part of the description of the goods.[52] Under such a contract the seller is bound to deliver the goods at the agreed destination, *e.g.* at a named port[53] or from the seller's installations at a named port.[54] Such a contract may or may not be conditional on the arrival of the ship or the goods.[55] The seller's obligation under an ex ship contract is one to deliver the actual goods. Unlike a c.i.f. seller, he cannot perform his obligations by transferring shipping documents to the buyer[56]: in an ex ship contract, "The mere documents do not take the place of the goods."[57]

21–015 **Distinguished from c.i.f. contracts.** Other distinctions between ex ship and c.i.f. contracts have been discussed in Chapter 19.[58] In particular it will be recalled that a contract may be a c.i.f. contract even though the time of payment is postponed until arrival of the ship[59]; even though the amount to be paid depends on the quantity which arrives[60]; and even though the contract provides that it is to be void should the goods fail to arrive on account of one (or more) specified causes.[61] It is true that, in such cases, a

---

48 See above, para.21–012.
49 See above, para.21–012.
50 Where a c. & f. buyer deals as consumer (see above, para.18–259) s.32(3) "must be ignored": (s.32(4), discussed in relation to overseas sales in paras 18–260 and 18–261. Risk in such cases remains with the seller until the goods are "delivered to the consumer" (s.20(4)). For the meaning of this expression in context of a c. & f. contract, see above, para.18–261; for the possibility of excluding ss.20(4) and 32(4) by agreement, see above, para.18–264.
51 Below, para.21–030.
52 See *Macpherson, Train & Co. Ltd v Howard Ross & Co. Ltd* [1955] 1 W.L.R. 640 (above, para.18–041), where the sale was on ex store terms.
53 As in *The Julia* [1949] A.C. 293 (above, para.19–003). The position would be the same under the Vienna Convention on Contracts for the International Sale of Good (above, para.1–024): an ex ship contract being one in which the seller *was* bound to deliver the goods at a "particular place" within the opening words of Art. 31, none of the alternatives listed in Art. 31(a) to (c) would apply.
54 As in *Gardano Giampieri v Greek Petroleum Co.* [1962] 1 W.L.R. 40. As to this case, see para.18–114, n.55.
55 Below, paras 21–022 to 21–024.
56 *The Julia* [1949] A.C. 293 (above, para.19–003).
57 *Yangtsze Insurance Association Ltd v Lukmanjee* [1918] A.C. 585 at 589.
58 Above, paras 19–003, 19–006.
59 *Stein Forbes & Co. v County Tailoring Co.* (1916) 115 L.T. 215.
60 *Dupont v British South Africa Co.* (1901) 18 T.L.R. 24; *Arnhold Karberg & Co. v Blythe Green Jourdain & Co.* [1916] 1 K.B. 495.
61 As in *Re Denbigh Cowan & Co. and R Atcherley & Co.* (1921) 30 L.J.K.B. 836.

c.i.f. buyer may never be liable for the price, but the seller may remain bound to tender documents; and so long as he does this he will not be in breach by reason of non-delivery of the goods themselves. If, on the other hand, the sale is on ex ship or arrival terms the seller will be liable for non-delivery of the goods unless the contract was conditional on their arrival[62] or unless he can rely on frustration, or on an excuse for non-performance (such as a provision that the contract is to be "void if the goods do not arrive").[63]

A contract may be a c.i.f. contract although it provides for "delivery c.i.f." at a named port[64] or for goods to be "shipped to" a named port[65] or for tender by the seller of a delivery order instead of a bill of lading. But in *The Julia*[66] the terms of the contract, and the nature of the delivery order contemplated and given, led to the conclusion that the contract was "not a c.i.f. contract even in a modified form but a contract to deliver at Antwerp".[67] The result was that the contract was frustrated when delivery at Antwerp became illegal. Had the contract been a c.i.f. contract, the issue of supervening illegality would have been determined by reference to the time of tender of documents, regardless of subsequent events.[68] 21–016

Provision for payment against documents. An ex ship or delivery at destination contract may provide for payment "against documents"; but in such a contract a provision of this kind is not construed in the same way as it is in a c.i.f. contract.[69] In *Yangtsze Insurance Association v Lukmanjee*[70] teak logs were sold "ex ship, payment against documents".[71] After the logs had been unloaded, a gale drove them out to sea; and the question was whether the buyer could sue in respect of this loss on an insurance policy taken out by the seller. This raised (among other issues) the question whether the policy should have been tendered by the seller; and the Privy Council answered this question in the negative. In an ex-ship contract, the provision for payment against documents did not have the effect that it would have had in a c.i.f. contract, of obliging the seller to tender the policy. Lord Sumner said that the provision as to payment must be taken to refer to such documents as were appropriate to the contract,[72] and in the context of an ex ship contract it was not appropriate to require the seller to insure the goods during transit as they were, at this stage, at the seller's risk. The provision for payment against documents meant merely that the buyer was not bound to pay until the seller gave him "an effectual direction to the ship to deliver".[73] 21–017

---

62 Below, paras 21–022 to 21–024.
63 Below, para.21–022.
64 *Tregelles v Sewell* (1862) 7 H. & N. 574.
65 *Wancke v Wingren* (1889) 58 L.J.Q.B. 519.
66 [1949] A.C. 293 (above, para.19–003).
67 [1949] A.C. 293 at 312.
68 Above, para.19–136.
69 See above, paras 19–024, 19–075.
70 [1918] A.C. 585.
71 The statement in *J Aron & Co. (Inc.) v Miall* (1928) 34 Com.Cas. 18 at 21 that there was "no evidence that cash was against documents" in the *Yangtsze* case, above, is hard to follow.
72 [1918] A.C. 585 at 589.
73 *ibid*.

21–018 **Time of payment.** In the *Yangtsze* case[74] it was admitted that payment could not be demanded until the ship had arrived with the goods on board. The general rule that delivery and payment are concurrent conditions[75] applied; and the provision as to payment against documents merely enabled "payment to be made in a counting-house and in the ordinary course of business, without reference to the precise stage which the process of tumbling the logs into the water may happen to have reached".[76] The general rule may of course be varied; *e.g.* by providing for payment by "cash on first presentations of and in exchange for bills of lading and/or delivery orders".[77] But if the buyer pays before arrival in accordance with such terms and the goods subsequently fail to arrive, he is entitled to recover back the price as money paid on a total failure of consideration or under a frustrated contract[78] unless, exceptionally, property and risk had passed to the buyer before arrival.

21–019 **Landing charges.** Under a c.i.f. contract these must, unless the contract otherwise provides,[79] be borne by the buyer[80]; but under an ex ship or delivery at destination contract they have to be borne by the seller, in accordance with the normal rules relating to the expenses of delivery.[81]

21–020 **Property and risk.** Although there is no necessary connection between delivery and passing of property, the general rule is that property in goods sold on "ex ship" or "arrival" terms remains in the seller until, and may pass to the buyer when, the goods are delivered to the buyer; and that the risk passes at the same time.[82] Two aspects of this rule call for discussion here.

The first is that property and risk do not pass *before* delivery; and this aspect of the rule may apply even though the contract calls for payment against documents and the seller transfers a bill of lading to the buyer. Property passes by the transfer of a bill of lading only if the transfer was made with that intention[83]; and in the *Yangtsze* case, Lord Sumner said, with reference to an ex ship contract: "If an indorsed bill of lading is

[74] Above, para.21–017.
[75] Sale of Goods Act 1979, s.28 (above, para.8–004).
[76] [1918] A.C. 585 at 590.
[77] As in *The Julia* [1949] A.C. 293.
[78] In *The Julia*, above, n.77 it was admitted that, if the contract was for delivery at Antwerp, it had been frustrated. The Law Reform (Frustrated Contracts) Act 1943 was inapplicable as the date on which the contract was discharged was before that specified in s.2(1) of that Act.
[79] *e.g. Ceval International Ltd v Cefetra BV* [1996] 1 Lloyd's Rep. 651 (cost of discharge split between c.i.f. seller and buyer at ship's rail).
[80] See *Re Denbigh Cowan & Co. and R. Atcherley & Co.* (1921) 90 L.J.K.B. 836 at 841.
[81] Above, para.8–005.
[82] *cf. North of England Pure Oil-Cake Co. v Archangel Maritime Insurance Co.* (1875) L.R. 10 Q.B. 249 (insurable interest); above, paras 21–003, 21–007. Where the buyer deals as consumer, the rule that, "the goods remain at the seller's risk until they are delivered to the consumer" is laid down by the Sale of Goods Act 1979, s.20(4). Under the Vienna Convention on Contracts for the International Sale of Goods (above, para.1–024) risk would similarly pass on delivery: Art. 69(1).
[83] Above, para.18–071.

delivered to the buyer it is given as a delivery order and not with any intention of making him a party liable upon it[84] or of vesting him with the property in the goods by the mere delivery of the documents."[85] And he added in the same passage that the goods were "not at the buyer's risk during the voyage".[86] On the other hand, in *The Julia*[87] (where the contract was held to be one to deliver at Antwerp) Lord Simonds said that if the seller had tendered a bill of lading the property would have passed to the buyer.[88] Perhaps the explanation for this view is that the contract was ex facie a c.i.f. contract and was treated as such by the lower courts. It is true that the House of Lords finally held that the contract was not a c.i.f. contract; but if the submissions made in Chapter 19[89] are correct, the contract was a c.i.f. or delivery contract at the seller's option; and if he had tendered a bill of lading he would have turned it into a c.i.f. contract by adopting this method of performance.

The second aspect of the rule is that property may pass *on* delivery; but this will be true only where the seller has not reserved the right of disposal, normally until payment. If he has reserved such a right of disposal, property will pass only on payment.[90]

The general rule that risk passes only on delivery may likewise be displaced by contrary agreement. Thus in *Castle v Playford*[91] a contract was made by which the seller agreed to ship a quantity of ice and the buyer "to buy and receive the said ice on its arrival . . . and to pay for the same in cash on delivery at the rate of 20s. per ton weighed on board." The contract provided that the bills of lading should be forwarded "and upon receipt thereof the purchaser takes upon himself all risks". After receipt of the bills of lading, the ship and cargo were lost; and it was held that the risk and property in the goods had passed to the buyer when the loss occurred.[92] Another possibility is that the sale may originally be on terms (such as c.i.f. or c. & f. terms, under which risk has passed on shipment) and be later varied so as to be transformed into an ex ship contract. The risk of loss or 21–021

---

[84] Under Bills of Lading Act 1855, s.1, now repealed. Since the passing of Carriage of Goods by Sea Act 1992, the mere transfer of the bill of lading to the buyer would no longer make him liable under the bill (above, paras 18–101, 18–123), though his subsequent conduct could make him so liable by virtue of s.3 of that Act (above, para.18–124) or make him liable under an implied contract of the kind discussed in paras 18–138 to 18–144 above.

[85] *Yangtsze Insurance Association v Lukmanjee* [1918] A.C. 585 at 589.

[86] *ibid.; cf. Gardano Giampieri v Greek Petroleum Co.* [1962] 1 W.L.R. 40 (as to which see para.18–114, n.55); in *SS Den of Airlie Co. Ltd v Mitsui & Co.* (1911–12) 17 Com.Cas. 116 the question whether property passed under a "basis delivered" (at p.122) contract by transfer of bills of lading was left open.

[87] [1949] A.C. 293.

[88] *ibid.*, at p.315; *cf. Sheridan v New Quay Co.* (1858) 4 C.B.(N.S.) 618 where the sale seems to have been on f.o.b. terms (above, para.20–083, n.59).

[89] Above, para.19–003.

[90] *Leigh & Sillavan Ltd v Aliakmon Shipping Co. Ltd (The Aliakmon)* [1986] A.C. 785 at 809; the contract, as varied, had there become an ex warehouse contract, but there seems to be no reason why passing of property under an ex ship contract should not be governed by the same principle.

[91] (1872) L.R. 7 Ex. 98.

[92] See also *The Julia* [1949] A.C. 293 at 312.

deterioration in transit, which will then have passed to the buyer, will not revert to the seller merely by virtue of the change in the character of the contract.[93]

21–022 **Stipulations as to arrival.** Sales on ex ship or arrival terms may contain a variety of stipulations as to the arrival of the goods or the ship. Such stipulations were more common in the days of sail (when much uncertainty attended the movement of ships) than they are today; though they came back into vogue during the first World War[94] and may still be important with regard to the time of arrival.[95] The contract might, in the first place, provide for the sale of goods "to arrive" by, or "on arrival" of, a named ship. It has been said that in such cases there was "no sale"[96] if the goods did not arrive in the ship; and where the ship arrived without any goods of the contract description on board it was held that the seller was not liable.[97] But this was true only so long as the failure of the goods to arrive was "due to accidental circumstances and not due to any fraud on the part of the seller"[98]; for if there were such fraud the seller would be liable on the ground that a party cannot generally escape liability by reason of the non-occurrence of a contingent condition precedent if he has prevented its occurrence deliberately or in some way that was otherwise wrongful.[99] Under modern conditions failure to ship will often render the seller liable even if it does not amount to fraud.[1] It was also held that the seller was not liable if the contract provided that it should be void in certain contingencies, which occurred: *e.g.* if the ship should fail to arrive[2] or if the ship or the goods should be lost,[3] or if the ship should fail to arrive by a named date,[4] or if she should arrive without goods of the contract description on board.[5]

21–023 If the ship arrived with goods of the contract description on board but the quantity at the seller's disposal was less than that which he had agreed to sell, a number of possibilities call for consideration. First, the ship simply

---

93 *Leigh & Sillavan Ltd v Aliakmon Shipping Co. Ltd (The Aliakmon)* [1986] A.C. 785 at 809 as to which see above, n.90.

94 See *Barnett v Javeri & Co.* [1916] 2 K.B. 390.

95 Below, paras 21–029, 21–030.

96 *Hollis Bros & Co. Ltd v White Sea Timber Trust Ltd* [1936] 3 All E.R. 895 at 900; unless "sale" is here used in the technical sense given to it by s.1(4) of the Sale of Goods Act 1979 (*i.e.* contrasted with "agreement to sell") the statement that there is "no sale" (in the sense of "no contract") is not to be taken quite literally. If it were, *either* party could withdraw with impunity at any time and before the "arrival"; but in the *Hollis Bros* case at p.900 a sale on "to arrive" terms is said to leave it only "at the option of the *sellers* to ship or not to ship as they please." *Cf.* also below, para.21–024, n.11, and *Barnett v Javeri & Co.* [1916] 2 K.B. 390 (below, para.21–026) cited by counsel, but not in the judgment, in the *Hollis Bros* case.

97 *Boyd v Siffkin* (1809) 2 Camp. 326; *Johnson v Macdonald* (1842) 9 M. & W. 600.

98 *Hawes v Humble* (1809) 2 Camp. 327n.

99 See *Mackay v Dick* (1881) 6 App.Cas. 251; Treitel, *The Law of Contract* (11th ed., 2003), p.63.

1 Below, para.21–026.

2 *Lovatt v Hamilton* (1839) 5 M. & W. 639.

3 *Lovatt v Hamilton*, above; *Johnson v Macdonald*, above, n.97.

4 *Idle v Thornton* (1812) 3 Camp. 274.

5 *cf. Lovatt v Hamilton*, above. For the effect of failure to ship, see below, para.21–026.

contains a smaller quantity of goods than the seller contracted to sell: here the ordinary principles relating to non-arrival apply.[6] Secondly, the ship contains goods of the contract description and quantity but the goods or part of them have been consigned to third parties, so that the seller is not entitled to deal with them: here the seller is probably liable in damages[7] unless on its true construction the contract was only for such part of the cargo as was consigned to him. Thirdly, the ship contains goods of the contract description and quantity but the seller has allocated the goods to other buyers: here he would be prima facie liable to the disappointed buyer,[8] unless the contract indicated otherwise, as where it expressly provided that it was to be void "in case of . . . the vessel not having so much in after delivery of former contracts".[9]

The prima facie rule, then, was that, under contracts on "to arrive" or "on arrival" terms, the obligations of the parties to deliver and to pay were construed as conditional[10] on the arrival both of the ship, and of goods in her of the contract description and quantity.[11] But this construction was not invariably adopted. Thus where tallow was sold "to be delivered on the safe arrival of" a named ship, the seller's obligation was held to be conditional on the arrival of the ship only and not of the tallow in her.[12] And where the contract was for the sale of a stated quantity of goods "now on passage . . . and expected to arrive" by named ships, it was held that the seller had "warranted" that goods of the contract quantity had been shipped, though he might have been protected by the words "expected to arrive", had circumstances occurred after such shipment, preventing the arrival of the goods.[13] It is similarly a question of construction whether the seller gave an absolute undertaking that the shipment should be of the designated quality[14] or only undertook to deliver goods of that quality if such were shipped.[15] 21–024

Ship to be declared. Where the contract is for the sale of goods "to arrive" but no ship is named in the contract, the seller may be bound by the express terms of the contract to declare the name of the ship on which the 21–025

---

[6] *i.e.* those stated in paras 21–022 and 21–024.
[7] See *Fischel v Scott* (1854) 15 C.B. 69 (where no definite conclusion was reached).
[8] *cf. Hong Guan & Co. Ltd v R. Jumabhoy & Sons Ltd* [1960] A.C. 684 (sale "subject to shipment").
[9] As in *Lovatt v Hamilton* (1839) 5 M. & W. 639.
[10] *Johnson v Macdonald* (1842) 9 M. & W. 600 at 606.
[11] The description of such a contract as "conditional" was not, it is submitted, intended to mean that until the double condition occurred there was no contract, so that either party could withdraw, but only that until then neither party was bound to perform the respective obligations to deliver and to pay; see *Johnson v Macdonald*, above, at p.605 ("the language of the contract renders *the performance of* it conditional on a double event"); *cf.* above, para.19–014.
[12] *Hale v Rawson* (1858) 4 C.B.(N.S.) 85.
[13] *Gorrissen v Perrin* (1857) 2 C.B. 681.
[14] As in *Simond v Braddon* (1857) 2 C.B. 324 ("The cargo to consist of fair average Nicranzi rice").
[15] As in *Vernede v Weber* (1856) 1 H. & N. 311 (sale of Aracan Necrenzie rice "as shipped per *Minna* provided the same be shipped for seller's account").

goods are shipped or to be shipped. In *Graves v Legg*[16] wool was sold "to arrive . . . at Liverpool . . ."; the contract provided that the goods were "deliverable at Odessa during August . . . to be shipped with all despatch . . . the names of the vessels to be declared as soon as the wools were shipped". It was held that the stipulation requiring the seller to declare the vessels as soon as the goods were shipped (no less than that requiring the goods to be shipped with all despatch[17]) was a condition, so that its breach entitled the buyer to reject the goods.[18] This conclusion was based on the commercial importance of the stipulation to the buyer who (as the seller knew) was a dealer and had bought in a volatile market.[19] But if a ship is duly declared the buyer may be bound to accept the goods even though they arrive by other means. Thus in *Neill v Whitworth*[20] cotton was sold "to arrive from Calcutta to Liverpool . . . to be taken from the quay". The seller declared the names of two ships, one of which was wrecked. The cotton in her was saved, brought to Liverpool and tendered to the buyer. It was held that the buyer was not justified in rejecting this cotton.

21–026 **Failure to ship.** A seller may be in breach, notwithstanding a provision which protects him in the event of the goods' not arriving, if the reason why they do not arrive is that he has failed to ship any goods of the contract description. In *Barnett v Javeri & Co.*[21] hematine crystals were sold "ex Liverpool . . . subject to safe arrival". No goods of the contract description arrived because the sellers' source of supply failed; and it was held that the seller was liable in damages. Bailhache J. stressed that the contract did not name any particular ship and that it was subject to *safe* arrival. He said: "Under the contract the sellers' obligation is to ship the goods or get them so far under their control that they are put on board some ship or other. But, having shipped them, if any accident occurs in transit, then they are not liable for non-delivery."[22] In the older cases, contracts for the sale of goods "on arrival" or "to arrive" or "subject to arrival" in a *named* ship were rather construed as contracts to deliver such goods (if any) of the contract description as were shipped on that ship for the seller's account,[23] unless the contract contained words importing that such goods actually *had*

---

16 (1854) 9 Exch. 709.

17 This stipulation was admitted to be a condition by counsel for the sellers (Blackburn) and the concession was approved by Parke B. at p.717.

18 For reasons stated in para.18–284 above, this right to reject would not be affected by the statutory restrictions on the right to reject now contained in Sale of Goods Act 1979, s.15A.

19 *Graves v Legg* (1854) 9 Exch. 709 at 717. *Cf.* above, para.19–017; *Société Italo-Belge pour le Commerce et l'Industrie v Palm & Vegetable Oils Malaysia Sdn Bhd (The Post Chaser)* [1981] 2 Lloyd's Rep. 695 goes beyond *Graves v Legg*, above in classifying as a condition a term in a c.i.f. contract requiring a notice of appropriation to be given "as soon as *possible after* vessel's sailing." The stipulation in *Graves v Legg* (quoted above) made it possible to tell *precisely* (in the light of subsequent events) when the notice should have been given; this was not the case in *The Post Chaser*. *Cf.* above, para.19–064.

20 (1865) 18 C.B.(N.S.) 435, affirmed (1866) L.R. 1 C.P. 684.

21 [1916] 2 K.B. 390.

22 *ibid.*, at p.394.

23 Above, paras 21–022, 21–023.

been loaded on the ship.[24] The cases to this effect have never been disapproved,[25] but, having regard to the relatively greater speed of modern communications, it is submitted that similar contracts, if made nowadays, would probably be construed as importing an undertaking that goods of the contract description *would be* loaded on the named ship, even if the contract also contained words exonerating the seller if the goods did not arrive. Of course the seller will not be in breach if the goods are specific and are destroyed before shipment.[26]

There is some ambiguity in a contract for the sale of goods "to arrive" or "on arrival" by a named ship, and in a contract providing that it is to become void in case of "non-arrival". Such a provision may import a double contingency, *viz.* the arrival of the ship and the goods,[27] or only a single contingency: *viz.* the arrival of the ship, or that of the goods. If the ship arrives without the goods, the general rule is that the seller is not liable (so long as the goods have been shipped) merely because they are not on board on arrival; but if the contract is for delivery on the safe arrival of a named ship and can be satisfied by any goods (whether on that ship or not) the seller will be bound to deliver though only a single contingency (the arrival of the ship) has occurred.[28] It is also possible for the goods to arrive without the ship, *e.g.* where the ship is lost and the goods are saved and brought to the agreed destination by other means; or where the goods have been transhipped. In such cases the buyer may be bound to accept the goods if tendered at the agreed destination, or at a point more favourable to him than the agreed destination[29]; but it does not follow that the seller is bound to forward the goods to the agreed destination after loss of the ship[30] or to deliver goods which arrive in another ship after having been (without breach of contract) transhipped.[31] It is theoretically possible for the liability of the buyer to depend on a single contingency (the arrival of the goods) and for that of the seller under the same contract to depend on a double contingency (the arrival of the goods in the ship); though there is no actual decision to this effect. 21–027

Frustration. Even if, on the true construction of the contract, the seller has undertaken that the goods have been shipped, or that they will be shipped, or that they will be shipped and arrive, he may still be excused by 21–028

[24] Above, para.21–024.

[25] Indeed, a dictum in *Hollis Bros & Co. Ltd v White Sea Timber Trust Ltd* [1936] 3 All E.R. 895 at 900 (discussed above, para.21–022, n.96) can be interpreted as approving them.

[26] *Smith v Myers* (1871) L.R. 7 Q.B. 139 where the court also relied on a clause that the contract was to be void should shipment be prevented by "any circumstance or accident". See further below, para.21–028 for frustration; here we are concerned only with the definition of the seller's duty to deliver.

[27] *Johnson v Macdonald* (1842) 9 M. & W. 600.

[28] *Hale v Rawson* (1858) 4 C.B.(N.S.) 85.

[29] *cf. Neill v Whitworth* (1865) 18 C.B.(N.S.) 435; affirmed (1886) L.R. 1 C.P. 684 (above, para.20–015) where the ship was not named in the contract but declared later; *Wylie v Porah* (1907) 12 Com.Cas. 317.

[30] *Idle v Thornton* (1812) 3 Camp. 274.

[31] *Lovatt v Hamilton* (1835) 5 M. & W. 639.

the frustration of the contract, for example if delivery at the agreed destination becomes illegal. If the contract contains an undertaking that the goods will arrive, the destruction of generic goods appropriated to the contract will not, of itself, frustrate the contract.[32] But if the sale is of goods to arrive in a named ship which is lost the contract may well be frustrated.[33] If the contract is for the sale of specific goods which are lost before the risk has passed to the buyer, the contract will normally be avoided under section 7 of the Sale of Goods Act 1979. But if, exceptionally, the risk in such goods has passed to the buyer before they are lost,[34] he will be under an obligation to pay the price, though the seller's obligation to deliver is likely to be discharged.[35]

21–029 **Time of arrival.** If a contract for sale of goods "to arrive" contains no stipulation as to the time of arrival, the question arises whether any term as to arrival within a reasonable time (either of the contract or of the shipment) can be implied. In *Levi v Berk*[36] a cargo of guano was sold "expected to arrive per *Alert* at Hamburg". The buyers rejected the goods on a number of grounds, including late arrival. Although this ground was abandoned on appeal, Lord Esher M.R. said that no term could be implied that a ship should arrive "from the other end of the world"[37] within a reasonable time. But it is doubtful whether this statement would now be followed. In the first place, the *Alert* was a sailing ship; and Lord Esher's reasoning loses much of its force where the goods are carried in a ship driven by engine power. Secondly, the case was decided before the passing of the Sale of Goods Act, section 29(3) of which now provides that "Where . . . the seller is bound to send the goods to the buyer, but no time for sending them is fixed, the seller is bound to send them within a reasonable time." Unfortunately the subsection throughout uses the word "send" which, in another section of the Act,[38] has been held to refer to the transit *after* delivery by shipment in an f.o.b. contract.[39] This interpretation cannot be directly applied to an "arrival" contract, in which the transit *precedes* delivery; and it is an open question just which part of the operation of "sending" the seller is required by section 29(3) to perform within a reasonable time in contracts for the sale of goods "to arrive".

21–030 **Goods "expected to arrive" on a stated date.** The contract may provide that the goods are "expected to arrive" on or by a stated date, or that the goods will arrive at "about" a stated time,[40] or that they are on a ship which is due at the place of arrival on (or by) "approximately" a stated date.[41]

---

[32] Above, para.6–051.
[33] *cf. Nickoll and Knight v Ashton, Edridge & Co.* [1901] 2 K.B. 126; above, para.19–126
[34] Normally, risk under an arrival contract will not pass before the goods are delivered to the buyer: above, para.21–020.
[35] See above, paras 21–023, 21–024, 21–027.
[36] (1886) 2 T.L.R. 898.
[37] *ibid.*, at p.899.
[38] s.32(3).
[39] *Wimble, Sons & Co. v Rosenberg* [1913] 3 K.B. 743 (above, paras 18–246, 18–247).
[40] As in *Barnett v Javeri & Co.* [1916] 2 K.B. 390.
[41] *Macpherson, Train & Co. Ltd v Howard Ross & Co. Ltd* [1955] 1 W.L.R. 640 (where the sale was on ex store terms, the provision as to arrival being part of the description of the goods; *cf.* above, para.18–269).

Such words do not amount to a guarantee that the goods will arrive on or by that date, so that the seller is not liable in damages, nor can the buyer reject, merely because the goods arrive after the stated date has gone by.[42] On the other hand, the seller would be liable in damages, and the buyer entitled to reject, if the seller had no reasonable grounds for believing that the goods would arrive on or by the stated date[43]; and it would seem that the buyer would also be entitled to reject if the delay was so great as to frustrate his purpose[44] in entering into the contract. Even if the contract provides without qualification for delivery by a stated date, it does not follow that the seller will be liable in damages if the goods arrive after that date since it is possible, if unlikely, for the sole effect of the provisions to be to entitle the buyer to reject the goods in that event.[45] If the contract provides that it is to be "void" if the goods do not arrive by a stated date,[46] their failure to do so would discharge both parties, unless of course one of them was guilty of some other breach.

Time for assessing damages. A seller who is not liable in damages 21–031 merely because the goods have not arrived within an estimated time may nevertheless be liable for some other breach: for example, he may have failed without lawful excuse to ship goods of the contract description. In such a case the damages will prima facie be assessed by reference to the market at the estimated date of arrival.[47] But this prima facie rule may be displaced: for example, if the seller assures the buyer that the goods will arrive at a later date, but finally declares his inability to perform, then the damages may be assessed by reference to the market at the time of such declaration.[48] And if the seller had made a shipment but the quantity was insufficient to satisfy the buyer, it is submitted that damages would be assessed by reference to the market at the time when the ship arrived; for that would, in the circumstances, be "the time at which [the goods] ought to have been delivered" within section 51(3) of the Sale of Goods Act 1979.[49]

5. Sale of a Cargo

Meaning of sale of a cargo. A contract is a sale of "a cargo" only if it is 21–032 expressed to be such a sale. A contract for the sale of goods is not a sale of a cargo merely because goods of the contract description and quantity are

---

[42] *Macpherson, Train & Co. Ltd v Howard Ross & Co. Ltd*, above, at p.642.

[43] *ibid.; cf. Finnish Govt. (Ministry of Food) v H. Ford & Co. Ltd* (1921) 6 Ll.L.R. 188; *Sanday & Co. v Keighley Maxted* (1922) 91 L.J.K.B. 624 ("expected ready to load").

[44] *i.e.* his actual purpose, if known to the seller; or the purpose for which the goods might reasonably be supposed by the seller to have been required, if the buyer's actual purpose was not known to the seller.

[45] As in *Alewyn v Prior* (1826) Ry. & Mood. 406.

[46] As in *Idle v Thornton* (1812) 3 Camp. 274.

[47] *Barnett v Javeri & Co.* [1916] 2 K.B. 390 at 394. Contrast Vienna Convention on Contracts for the International Sale of Goods (above, para.1–024), Art. 76(1), making the time when the "current price" is relevant the time of the avoidance of the contract. *Cf.* also above, para.19–175, n.91.

[48] *Barnett v Javeri & Co.*, above, at pp.394–395.

[49] *cf. Hong Guan & Co. Ltd v R Jumabhoy & Sons Ltd* [1960] A.C. 684, above, para.19–140 (sale "subject to shipment").

loaded on a particular ship and happen to form its entire cargo.[50] A sale of a cargo may be made on any of the terms used for overseas sales, that is on c.i.f., f.o.b., ex ship and other terms already discussed. It may be a sale of a cargo already loaded at the time of the contract, in which case, if the ship is named (or otherwise designated), it will be a sale of specific goods[51]; or it may be a sale of a cargo to be loaded, in which case it will generally[52] be a sale of unascertained goods, which are likely to become ascertained on shipment.

21–033 **Cargo and words of quantity.** A contract for the sale of "a cargo" may contain an estimate of quantity; and there may be a discrepancy between the actual amount of the cargo and the amount indicated by the words of quantity. In such a case it has been said that "the governing word was 'cargo' and the buyer was bound to take the cargo whatever the quantity might be".[53] It follows from this rule that the buyer's rights of rejection under section 30 of the Sale of Goods Act 1979 do not extend to cases of this kind. But the rule would not apply if "something plainly showed the contrary to be intended"[54]: for example if the contract put an upper limit on the amount bought and sold and the cargo exceeded that amount.[55]

21–034 **Cargo generally means whole cargo.** The general rule is that "a cargo" means the whole or entire cargo, so that the buyer is neither bound to accept, nor entitled to demand, anything more or less. In *Kreuger v Blanck*[56] "a small cargo" of wood "in all about 60 cubic fathoms" was sold on c.i.f. terms. The seller chartered a ship on which 83 cubic fathoms were loaded, and tendered documents in respect of 60 cubic fathoms. It was held that the buyer was entitled to reject for he might be prejudiced as a result of not getting the whole cargo. He might, for example, have to pay freight on the whole (to discharge the shipowner's lien) in order to get delivery of the part tendered to him; he might be deprived of any right to give orders with regard to the destination of the ship which he would have had, if the whole cargo had been his[57]; he might find it inconvenient to have someone else's goods delivered at the same time as his own: for he might have bought the whole cargo so as to be "free from . . . the competition arising from other persons' goods being ready for sale, at the same place, and at the same time, with his"[58]; and there might be difficulties if part of the cargo had been damaged.

Since a sale of "a cargo" means the whole or entire cargo, such a sale does not give rise to the problems which have been discussed in Chapter 18,[59] as to passing of property in undifferentiated *parts* of bulk shipments.

---

[50] *Re Wait* [1927] 1 Ch. 606 at 626.

[51] As in *Couturier v Hastie* (1856) 5 H.L.C. 673; *HW Paul Ltd v WH Pim Junior & Co. Ltd* [1922] 2 K.B. 360 at 362.

[52] But not always: see *Smith v Myers* (1871) L.R. 7 Q.B. 139.

[53] *Levi v Berk* (1886) 2 T.L.R. 898 at 899; *Re Harrison and Micks, Lambert & Co.* [1917] 1 K.B. 755 (remainder of a cargo: below, para.21–038).

[54] *Levi v Berk*, above.

[55] As in *Borrowman v Drayton* (1876) 2 Ex.D. 15 (below, para.21–036); *cf. Re Harrison and Micks, Lambert & Co.*, above, at p.761.

[56] (1870) L.R. 5 Ex. 179.

[57] *Borrowman v Drayton*, above, at p.19.

[58] *ibid.*

[59] Above, paras 18–287 to 18–299.

21–035 In *Kreuger v Blanck*[60] the buyer would have been bound to accept tender of documents in respect of the 83 cubic fathoms as the governing word in the contract was "cargo", the words of quantity being words of estimate only.[61] If the cargo had consisted of less than 60 cubic fathoms he would likewise have been bound to accept the smaller amount[62]; and he would not have been entitled to damages if the actual outturn had been less than the estimate.[63] In that case, payment would have been due only for the amount actually delivered and at the contract rate; but it is also possible for the buyer to bind himself to pay in any event, in which case he will be liable for the full price even though less than the estimated quantity is delivered. In *Covas v Bingham*[64] a cargo of corn was sold "consisting of about 1,300 quarters . . . at the price of 30s. per quarter . . . The quantity to be taken from the bill of lading." The buyer paid on tender of a bill of lading for 1,667 quarters and sought to recover from the seller in respect of a shortage of 50 quarters on this quantity. The claim was rejected as "the cargo was to be sold and paid for according to the bill of lading, for better or for worse, whether the quantity should be more or less".[65]

21–036 Further difficulty arises where the sale is of a cargo but also contains a limit of quantity, beyond which the buyer is not bound to accept. In *Borrowman v Drayton*[66] a contract was made for the sale of "a cargo of from 2,500 to 3,000 barrels" of petroleum. The seller chartered a ship on which 3,300 barrels were loaded; and it was held that the buyer was not bound to accept *either* the whole cargo, as this was in excess of the quantity that he had ordered, *or* a quantity within the contractual limits, as this did not constitute an entire cargo. For reasons given in Chapter 19,[67] it is unlikely that the buyer's right to reject in cases of this kind would be subject to the restriction now contained in section 30(2A) of the Sale of Goods Act 1979.

21–037 **Exception.** The general rule that "a cargo" means the whole cargo is liable to cause hardship to the seller. In both *Kreuger v Blanck*[68] and *Borrowman v Drayton*[69] it enabled the buyer to reject the goods on a falling market without having to show that he had actually suffered any of the hypothetical hardships on which the rule is based.[70] Where the general rule operates in this way, the courts have sometimes been anxious to avoid its

---

[60] (1870) L.R. 5 Ex. 179; above, para.21–034.
[61] See above, para.21–033; and *Re Harrison and Micks, Lambert & Co.* [1917] 1 K.B. 755; below, para.21–038.
[62] *Levi v Berk* (1886) 2 T.L.R. 898.
[63] *Covas v Bingham* (1853) 2 E. & B. 836, *infra* at n.64.
[64] Above.
[65] (1853) 2 E. & B. 836 at 843. On such facts the buyer would now have a claim in respect of the shortage *against the carrier* if the requirements of s.4 of the Carriage of Goods by Sea Act 1992, above para.18–036, were satisfied.
[66] (1876) 2 Ex.D. 15.
[67] Above, para.19–012. A buyer of "a cargo" is so unlikely to deal as consumer that there is no need here to discuss the possibility that his right to reject may be suspended under s.48D of the Sale of Goods Act 1979.
[68] Above, para.21–034.
[69] Above, para.21–036.
[70] Above, para.21–034.

application. In *HW Paul Ltd v WH Pim Junior & Co. Ltd*[71] a contract was made on c.i.f. terms for the sale of "the cargo of . . . maize shipped . . . *per S.S. Rijn*, consisting of about 2,813 French tons, or what steamer carries as per bill of lading". In addition to the maize, there were 58 tons of tobacco on board the *Rijn*; and when the buyers discovered this they purported to reject the maize and claimed the return of the price, which had been paid against documents. Bailhache J. rejected their claim. He distinguished *Borrowman v Drayton* on the grounds that the contract in the present case was for the sale of a cargo already shipped, and so for specific goods; that there was no possibility of confusion between the tobacco and the maize; and that the tobacco was on board, not under any contract between the seller and the carrier, but without the knowledge, and in fraud, of the seller.

21–038 **Remainder of a cargo.** In *HW Paul Ltd v WH Pim Junior*[72] the court refused to allow the buyer to rely on the general rule, that "a cargo" means an entire cargo, since none of the reasons for the rule[73] applied, and the buyer's claim to reject was wholly unmeritorious. It is also possible for such a claim to be defeated by the *application* of the general rule, *e.g.* where the court refuses to allow a buyer to reject a cargo for some excess over the estimated quantity.[74] In such situations the courts are even prepared to extend the general rule. Thus in *Re Harrison and Micks, Lambert & Co.*[75] a contract was made for the sale of "the remainder *of a cargo*[76] (more or less about) 5,400 quarters" of wheat. The remainder of the cargo exceeded this amount by more than the customary margin and the buyer purported to reject the excess. It was held that he was not entitled to do so. The court applied the general rule[77] even though Bailhache J. admitted that some of the reasons which might induce a buyer to want a whole cargo[78] did not apply to a sale of the remainder of a cargo.

21–039 **Stipulation as to shipment.** In *Gattorno v Adams*[79] a contract was made on c.i.f. terms for the sale of a cargo of wheat "shipped per *Diletta Mimbella* . . . as per bill of lading dated September or October". At the time of the contract, the entire cargo had been shipped, and it was also stated in the bill of lading to have been shipped, though in fact at the date of the bill of

---

[71] [1922] 2 K.B. 360; more fully reported in 27 Com.Cas. 98.
[72] Above, para.21–037.
[73] Above, para.21–034.
[74] See para.21–033, above.
[75] [1917] 1 K.B. 755.
[76] The italicised words are not in the report in the *Law Reports* or in 22 Com.Cas. 273 but occur in 116 L.T. 606 at 607 and in 14 Asp.M.L.C. at p.76; *cf.* also 86 L.J.K.B. 573. *Semble*, a sale of "the remainder of a cargo" would not be one for the sale of a "specified quantity" of goods for the purpose of Sale of Goods Act 1979, s.20A(1) (above, paras 18–293, 18–294), so that no property could pass under such a contract until the goods had become ascertained; this would normally happen by "exhaustion" (above, para.18–288).
[77] Above, paras 21–034, 21–035.
[78] Above, para.21–034.
[79] (1862) 12 C.B.(N.S.) 560.

lading only part of the cargo was on board.[80] It was held that the buyer was not entitled to reject because the words of the contract made it clear that there was some doubt as to the exact date of shipment.[81] On the other hand, where the contract contained a definite statement as to the *position of the ship*, the buyer was entitled to reject for breach of this term, even though considerable latitude as to time of shipment was allowed by the contract.[82]

Damages. The actual decision in *Borrowman v Drayton*[83] was that the buyer was not bound to accept either more than the quantity contracted for, or less than a full cargo. It is not strictly accurate to say that "it was held . . . that the buyer was entitled to the whole of the cargo which was in fact carried".[84] This question did not arise for (as the market had fallen) the buyer in fact rejected and did not claim damages for non-delivery. If such a claim had been made, it is submitted that the assessment of damages should have been based on the contractual limits of quantity and not on the amount of the cargo. The latter would be the correct basis of assessment where the contract contained no limit of quantity; but where there is such limit beyond which the buyer is not bound to accept, that limit would seem, prima facie at least, to apply to the liability of both parties. In the circumstances of *Borrowman v Drayton*[85] the assessment should probably be based on the upper limit of quantity (more than that quantity having actually been shipped[86]); though it is possible to imagine circumstances (such as total failure to ship) in which the assessment would more appropriately be based on the lower limit on the principle that the seller may be presumed to intend to perform in the manner least burdensome to himself.[87] 21–040

---

[80] The rest was alongside in lighters and it was in accordance with the custom of the port to issue "shipped" bills of lading in respect of such goods. *Quaere* whether in these circumstances the bill of lading was "genuine" for the purpose of the rule stated in para.19–035, above. *Cf.* the somewhat similar custom alleged (but not proved) in *James Finlay & Co. Ltd v Kwik Hoo Tong* [1929] 1 K.B. 400 (above, para.19–197), where the bill of lading was held not to be "genuine."

[81] *cf. R and W Paul Ltd v WH Pim Junior & Co. Ltd* [1922] 2 K.B. 360 ("bills of lading dated about March 1921").

[82] *Oppenheim v Fraser* (1876) 34 L.T. 524.

[83] (1876) 2 Ex.D. 15 (above, para.21–036).

[84] *Re Harrison and Micks, Lambert & Co.* [1917] 1 K.B. 755 at 759.

[85] Above, n.83.

[86] Thus showing that the seller had elected to perform by delivering more than the minimum contractual quantity: *cf. Shipping Development Corp. SA v V/O Sojusneftexport (The Delian Spirit)* [1972] 1 Q.B. 103 at 111–112; *Shipping Co. of India Ltd v Naviera Letasa SA* [1976] 1 Lloyd's Rep. 132; *Toprak Mahsulleri Ofisi v Finagrain Cie. Commerciale* [1979] 2 Lloyd's Rep. 98.

[87] *cf. Re Thornett & Fehr and Yuills Ltd* [1921] 1 K.B. 219; *Phoebus D. Kyprianou Coy. v Wm. H. Pim Jr.* [1977] 2 Lloyd's Rep. 570 at 581, above, para.20–135 (buyer's breach); *Kay SN Co. Ltd v W & R Barnett Ltd* (1932) 48 T.L.R. 440 (voyage charterparty); *Santa Marta Bay Scheepvaart and Handelsmaatschappig NV v Scanbulk A/S (The Rijn)* [1981] 2 Lloyd's Rep. 267 (time charterparty); *Kurt A Becher GmbH v Roplak Enterprises (The World Navigator)* [1991] 2 Lloyd's Rep. 23 at 33 (alleged delay in loading).

21–041 **Destruction after part shipment.** Where goods are shipped in pursuance of a sale of a cargo and part of the goods is destroyed after shipment, problems may arise as to risk and insurable interest. The cases on this topic have been discussed in Chapter 20.[88]

6. F.O.R. AND F.O.T. CONTRACTS

21–042 **Duties of the parties.** An f.o.r. contract is a contract by which the seller undertakes at his expense to put the goods into the possession of a rail carrier (or, if the contract is on so-called f.o.t. terms,[89] to bear the expense of loading them on the railway or other truck), usually at a named place of departure, for transmission to the buyer. Such a contract is not void for uncertainty merely because it fails to name the place at which the goods are to be put into the possession of the carrier: the uncertainty is resolved by imposing on one of the parties the duty to specify that place. The question which party it is who is under that duty depends on the practical consideration whether "the mechanics of the contract [would] work better"[90] by imposing it on the seller than on the buyer. In one case,[91] the duty was held to be on the seller since the contract was for delivery f.o.t. in a country other than that of the origin of the goods and it was the seller who had made all the arrangements with the ship on which the goods had been carried to the country of destination. It follows from this reasoning that if it had been the buyer who had made those arrangements, then the duty to specify the place of delivery f.o.t. might well have been on him.[92]

The seller is bound to put the goods free on rail within the time fixed by the contract,[93] or, if no time is fixed, within a reasonable time.[94] He is also, under section 32(2) of the Sale of Goods Act 1979,[95] bound to make a reasonable contract with the carrier.[96] As delivery to the carrier is prima facie deemed to be a delivery to the buyer,[97] the latter is (unless the

---

[88] Above, para.20–039.
[89] *cf. Jarl Trä AB v Convoys Ltd* [2003] EWHC 1488, [2003] 2 Lloyd's Rep. 459: "F.O.M." (*i.e.* "free on motor") term.
[90] *Bulk Trading Corp. Ltd v Zenziper Grains and Feedstuffs Ltd* [2001] 1 Lloyd's Rep. 357 at 86.
[91] *Bulk Trading* case, above, n.90.
[92] As in the case of an f.o.b. contract: above, para.20–014.
[93] *Joseph I Emanuel Ltd v Cardia and Savoca* [1958] 1 Lloyd's Rep. 121.
[94] *Macauley v Horgan* [1925] 2 I.R. 1.
[95] Where the buyer deals as consumer (*cf.* above, para.18–259) s.32(2) "must be ignored": (s.32(4)), discussed, in relation to overseas sales, in para.18–260 above. But an f.o.r. contract may, as a matter of common law, and apart from s.32(2), impose on the seller a duty to make a reasonable contract of carriage: (*cf.* above, paras 18–261, 19–123 (c.i.f. contract).
[96] *Thomas Young & Sons Ltd v Hobson & Partners* (1949) 65 T.L.R. 365. *Cf.* Vienna Convention on Contracts for the International Sale of Goods (above, para.1–024), Art. 32(2).
[97] s.32(1). *Cf.* Vienna Convention on Contracts for the International Sale of Goods (above, para.1–024), Art. 31(a). Where the buyer deals as consumer (*cf.* above, para.18–259), Sale of Goods Act 1979, s.32(1) "must be ignored": s.32(4), discussed, in relation to overseas sales, in para.18–260 above.

contract otherwise provides) bound to pay at this point, or at least to be ready and willing to do so.[98] But a contrary agreement to pay at the destination, or at the buyer's place of business, may be implied from the course of dealing between the parties.[99]

Property and risk. Where the goods are specific, property may pass under section 18, rule 1, of the Sale of Goods Act 1979 even before the goods are put on rail. But in *Underwood Ltd v Burgh Castle Brick and Cement Syndicate*[1] a condensing machine was sold "to be delivered free on rail in London". At the time of the sale, the machine was embedded in a concrete floor and considerable expense had to be incurred in dismantling and moving it so that it could be loaded on the railway truck. The Court of Appeal held that "the proper inference to be drawn is that property was not to pass until the engine was safely placed on rail . . ."[2] Accordingly, the machine was still at the seller's risk[3] while it was being loaded on the railway truck; and as it was damaged in the process of loading the seller was not entitled to the price. Even after the goods are loaded, they will remain at the seller's risk if he has failed to make a reasonable contract of carriage, *e.g.* if he has sent the goods at owner's risk when it would have been reasonable to send them at carrier's risk.[4] 21–043

If the sale is of unascertained generic goods, the act of putting them on rail is likely to amount to an appropriation in the "contractual" sense[5] of indicating that those are the goods which the seller is bound under the contract to deliver; and that appropriation will be "unconditional" for the purpose of passing the property[6] if the seller has not reserved the "right of disposal".[7] The question whether there has been such an unconditional appropriation is here (as elsewhere)[8] one of intention; and if the contract provides for payment at some point after the goods have been put on rail the court would no doubt be ready to infer an intention to reserve the right of disposal until payment. It is however submitted that the mere retention 21–044

---

[98] Sale of Goods Act 1979, s.28; *Macauley v Horgan*, above, n.94.
[99] *King v Reedman* (1883) 49 L.T. 473.
[1] [1922] 1 K.B. 123; affirmed *ibid.*, at p.343.
[2] [1922] 1 K.B. 123 at 345.
[3] Under Art, 67(1), second sentence, of the Vienna Convention on Contracts for the International Sale of Goods (above, para.1–024), it seems that, on the facts of this case the risk would have passed when the goods were "handed over to the carrier" at that place" (*i.e.* London). In English law, where the buyer deals as consumer (*cf.* above, para.18–259) "the goods remain at the seller's risk until they are delivered to the consumer": (Sale of Goods Act 1979, s.20(4)). The difficulties that can arise in determining exactly when the goods are "delivered to the consumer" under an f.o.r. or f.o.t. contract resemble those which arise where the sale is on f.o.b. terms. These are discussed in paras 18–262 and 20–094 above, and the principles there stated appear to apply, *mutatis mutandis*, to f.o.r. and f.o.t. contacts.
[4] Sale of Goods Act 1979, s.32(2); (as to which, see n.95 above) *Thomas Young & Sons Ltd v Hobson & Partners*, above.
[5] Above, para.18–210.
[6] Sale of Goods Act 1979, s.18, r. 5(1).
[7] *ibid.*, s.18, r. 5(2).
[8] Above, paras 18–211 *et seq.*

by the seller of the rail consignment note[9] would not be evidence of intention to reserve the right of disposal save in the exceptional cases where the document has to be produced in order to obtain actual delivery of the goods from the carrier.[10] Nor, it is submitted, would an intention to reserve the right of disposal be inferred merely because the seller had under the contract of carriage or under some applicable international convention a right to modify the contract of carriage or a right of "disposition", or one to "dispose" of the goods.[11] It is true that, in the exercise of such a right, the seller may be able to recall the goods, or to order the railway to deliver them to some person other than the buyer. But the purpose of these rights is to regulate the relations of seller and carrier (or, where they are vested in the buyer, the relations of buyer and carrier) and not the relations of buyer and seller under the contract of sale. Moreover, such rights may pass to the buyer, quite irrespective of any act of the seller.[12] The existence of such rights would thus not normally be evidence of intention with regard to the passing of property.

21–045 **Place of inspection.** Prima facie the place at which the buyer must inspect the goods for the purpose of the rules relating to acceptance (and consequent loss of the right to reject) is the station at which the goods are to be put free on rail.[13] But it is submitted that this rule may well be inappropriate in cases of overseas sales, where goods are placed free on rail in one country for dispatch to a buyer in another.[14] In such cases the more flexible rules as to the place of inspection which have been developed in connection with f.o.b. contracts should be applied also to f.o.r. contracts.[15]

21–046 **Damages.** In two cases damages under f.o.r. contracts have been assessed with reference to the market at the place of destination, and not at the place where the goods were to be put free on rail.[16] If the goods are dispatched late, it seems that damages will be assessed by reference to the market at the destination at the time when the goods would have arrived there if they had been dispatched in time.[17] For the purpose of these rules it is enough if the seller knows or ought to have known of the destination to which the goods are to be sent. It seems unnecessary for the destination actually to be a term of the contract of sale.

---

[9] See, in cases of international carriage by rail, below, para.21–066.
[10] As in *Ramdas Vithaldas Durbar v S Amerchand & Co.* (1916) 85 L.J.P.C. 214; L.R. 43 Ind.App. 164 (Indian railway receipt, as to which see above, para.18–167, n.71; *cf.* below, (paras 21–053, 21–054, 21–061, 21–068).
[11] Below, paras 21–055, 21–062, 21–069.
[12] e.g. below, paras 21–055, 21–060.
[13] *Perkins v Bell* [1893] 1 Q.B. 193 (above, para.20–108).
[14] *e.g. Joseph I Emanuel Ltd v Cardia & Savoca* [1958] 1 Lloyd's Rep. 121.
[15] Above, paras 20–109, 20–110. For the position under the Vienna Convention on Contracts for the International Sale of Goods (above, para.1–024), see above, para.20–109, n.38.
[16] *Joseph I Emanuel Ltd v Cardia & Savoca*, above n.14; *Macauley v Horgan* [1925] 2 I.R. 1. Contrast Vienna Convention on Contracts for the International Sale of Goods (above, para.1–024), under Art. 76(2) of which the relevant "current price" is that of "the place where delivery of the goods should have been made."
[17] *cf. Joseph I Emanuel Ltd v Cardia & Savoca,* above n.14.

7. CONVENTIONS ON INTERNATIONAL CARRIAGE OF GOODS

In general. International carriage of goods is governed by a number of international conventions. Carriage of goods by sea was formerly governed by the Hague Rules[18]; a revised version of these Rules, known as the Hague-Visby Rules, now has the force of law in England under the Carriage of Goods by Sea Act 1971.[19] International carriage by air is governed by a number of Conventions based on the Warsaw Convention of 1929. This continues to apply in certain cases which are commonly, though perhaps not with strict accuracy, referred to as cases governed by "the unamended Warsaw Convention".[20] The 1929 Convention was amended at the Hague in 1955 and this version of it will here be referred to as "the 1955 amended Convention".[21] Further amendments were made to it at Montreal in 1975, the most significant of which were in Protocol 4 and are embodied in the "MP4 Convention"[22]; and again at Montreal in 1999 by the "Montreal Convention"[23]; it will be convenient in the text that follows to refer to this last Convention as "the 1999 Montreal Convention". All the above Conventions have the force of law in the United Kingdom.[24] Contracts for the carriage of goods by air are, in addition, regulated by the Carriage by Air (Supplementary Provisions) Act 1962,[25] giving effect to the 21–047

---

[18] Carriage of Goods by Sea Act 1924, Sch. The original version of the Rules remains in force in many countries, for example, in the United States of America (though subject to variations such as that noted in para.21–085, n.36, below).

[19] s.1(2); Schmitthoff [1971] J.B.L. 191; Zaphirou, *ibid.*, p.12; Diamond [1978] L.M.C.L.Q. 225; *Carver on Bills of Lading* (2nd ed., 2005), Ch.9. For a new Convention (not yet in force) known as the Hamburg Rules, see below, para.21–087, n.61; Carver, *op. cit.* paras 9–318, 9–319.

[20] For this usage, see Carriage by Air Acts (Application of Provisions) Order 2004, SI 2004/1899, headings before Art. 5, before Sch.2 Pt I and before Sch.2 Pt IIA Ch.1.

[21] For this usage, see SI 2004/1899 (above n.20) Art. 2, definition of "the 1955 amended Convention". Carriage by Air Act 1961, s.1(5)(a), as substituted by Carriage by Air Acts (Implementation of Montreal Convention 1999) Order 2002, SI 2002/263, Art. 2, refers to this version simply as "the Convention".

[22] For this usage, see SI 2004/1899 (above, n.20) Art. 2, definition of "the MP4 Convention"; Carriage by Air Act 1961, s.1(5)(b), as substituted by SI 2002/263 (above, n.21) refers to this version as "the Convention as amended". For further modifications also made at Montreal in 1975, affecting financial limits of liability which are not our concern in this book, see SI 2004/1899, Art. 6 and Sch.3.

[23] For this usage, see Carriage by Air Act 1961, s.1(5)(c), as substituted by SI 2002/263 (above, n.21).

[24] Carriage by Air Act 1961, s.1 gives the force of law to the three Conventions described in the text above as "the 1955 amended Convention", "the MP4 Convention" and "the 1999 Montreal Convention"; the text of these Conventions is set out in the Carriage by Air Act 1961, Schs 1 and 1A (as inserted by Carriage by Air Acts (Implementation of Protocol 4 of Montreal 1975) Order 1999, SI 1999/1312) and Sch.1B (as inserted by Carriage by Air Acts (Implementation of Montreal Convention 1999) Order 2002, SI 2002/263). The "unamended Warsaw Convention" (above, at n.20) retains the force of law by virtue of SI 2004/1899 (above, n.20) Art. 5; the text of this Convention is set out in SI 2004/1899, Sch.2 Pt IIA.

[25] As amended by Carriage by Air Acts (Implementation of Protocol No. 4 of Montreal, 1975) Order 1999 (SI 1999/1312). For the amended text of the Guadalajara Convention, see SI 2004/1899 (above. n.20) Sch.2 Part IIB and Sch.3 Part IIB.

Guadalajara Convention of 1961, which deals with the position of a carrier who performs the whole or part of a contract of carriage made by another carrier. International carriage of goods by road is governed by the Geneva or CMR[26] Convention, which has been given the force of law by the Carriage of Goods by Road Act 1965.[27] International carriage of goods by rail is governed by the CIM[28] Uniform Rules which form part of the Convention concerning International Carriage by Rail (or COTIF[29]); this Convention, as modified by the Vilnius Protocol of 1999,[30] has been given the force of law by the Railways (Convention on International Carriage by Rail) Regulations 2005.[31]

These Conventions do not necessarily apply to all international carriage, or to all international carriage originating in or destined for this country. For example, the Hague-Visby Rules do not apply unless the goods are carried under a "bill of lading or any similar document of title",[32] or under a contract contained in or evidenced by a "non-negotiable" receipt which expressly provides that the Rules are to govern the contract as if the receipt were a bill of lading[33]; the various versions of the Warsaw Convention referred to in the text above do not apply where the destination of the goods is in a state which is not a party to the relevant Convention[34] while the CMR Convention and the CIM Uniform Rules may not apply where part of the carriage is performed otherwise than by road or rail as the case may be[35]; though in such a case that part may be governed by one of the other Conventions. It is also possible for part of the carriage to be governed by one, and another part to be governed by another, of the Conventions. This possibility is discussed in paras 21–104 and 21–105 below.

21–048 The main purpose of all these Conventions is to regulate the relations between, on the one hand, the carriers and other persons engaged in the performance of the carriage, and, on the other, the consignor and the consignee of the goods. For detailed discussions of these matters, reference

[26] *Convention relative au contrat de transport internationale de Marchandises par Route.*

[27] As amended by Carriage of Goods by Air and Road Act 1979, which is only partly in force: see SI 2000/2768 and earlier Orders there listed; International Transport Conventions Act 1983, s.9 and Sch.2.

[28] *Convention Internationale concernant le transport de Marchandises par chemins de fer.*

[29] "Convention" concerning the "*Organisation intergouvernementale pour les Transports Internationale Ferroviaires.*"

[30] For the text of the modified Convention, see Cm 4873 (2000), where "the Uniform Rules Concerning the Contract of International Carriage of Goods by Rail (CIM)" are set out as Appendix B to the Convention. Art. 6(1)(b) of COTIF provides for international carriage of goods by rail to be governed by the CIM Uniform Rules. For the text of the now superseded Convention and Rules, see Cmnd. 8535 (1982), where the Rules are set out as Appendix B.

[31] SI 2005/2092, Reg.3. The Regulations were brought into force, with effect from July 1, 2006 and subject to certain reservations, by a notice published (pursuant to Reg.1) in the London, Edinburgh and Belfast Gazettes on July 3, 2006.

[32] Carriage of Goods by Sea Act 1971, Sch., Art. 1(b).

[33] *ibid.*, s.1(6)(b), as to which see further below, para.21–081, n.88.

[34] Below, para.21–051.

[35] Below, paras 20–058, 20–065.

should be made to works on carriage by sea, air and land.[36] The Conventions do not directly regulate the relations between consignor and consignee under any contract of sale which may exist between them. But the Conventions, and the legislation under which effect is given to them, do contain provisions which may have some bearing on the relationship of consignor and consignee under a contract of sale, or their relationship to third parties who have acquired an interest in the goods. These provisions concern the nature of the documents which must be issued in respect of the carriage and the "right of disposition" (or "disposal") or the "right to modify the contract of carriage" which both the consignor and the consignee may have under the Conventions.

International sales of goods to be carried by air, road or rail may in theory be made on any of the common terms. "Arrival" terms[37] would probably have much the same effects as those which are attributed to such terms in the case of seaborne trade. A contract may name an airport as the place of "shipment" under an f.o.b. contract,[38] or as the destination under a c.i.f. contract[39]; and the effects of such provisions would no doubt be determined, so far as appropriate, by analogy to the rules discussed in Chapters 19 and 20. But the analogy should not be pressed too far: in particular, the lack of proper documents of title would give rise to difficulties where the sale was on c.i.f. terms. **21–049**

Under the Conventions relating to international carriage of goods by air, road and rail, rights under the contract of carriage can be acquired by the consignee even though he is not an original party to the contract of carriage. In this respect, the position under these Conventions resembles that which can arise in relation to contracts for the carriage of goods by sea under the Carriage of Goods by Sea Act 1992; and the resemblance is carried further by the fact that contracts for the international carriage of goods by air, road and rail covered by the Conventions fall within the subsection 6(5) exception to the Contracts (Rights of Third Parties) Act 1999.[40] The acquisition of rights under such contracts by such third parties is therefore governed by the Conventions and not by the 1999 Act; though problems analogous to those discussed in Chapter 18 in relation to contracts for the carriage of goods by sea could arise also in the present context: *e.g.* where a contract governed by one of the Conventions had been preceded by a contractual arrangement not covered by that Convention and **21–050**

---

[36] *e.g.* Scrutton, *Charterparties and Bills of Lading* (20th ed.); *Carver on Bills of Lading* (2nd ed.,); Shawcross and Beaumont, *Air Law* (4th ed.); McNair, *Law of the Air* (3rd ed.); Kahn- Freund, *Law of Inland Transport* (4th ed.), pp.408–455; *Chitty on Contracts* (29th ed.), Vol. 2, Chs 35 and 36; Clarke, *International Carriage by Road: CMR* (4th ed.).
[37] Above, paras 21–014 *et seq.*
[38] See INCOTERMS (above, para.18–002) "FOB Airport."
[39] See *Johnson Matthey Bankers Ltd v The State Trading Corp. of India* [1984] 1 Lloyd's Rep. 427 ("c. & f. London airport"); Pal [1973] J.B.L. 9.
[40] Above, para.18–005, sub-paragraph (f); see 1999 Act ss.(5)(b) and 6(8) as amended by Railways (Convention on International Carriage by Rail) Regulations 2005, SI 2005/2092, Reg.9(2) and Sch.3, para.3.

it was arguable that this antecedent contract had conferred rights on the (prospective) consignee. The solution of such problems would, it is submitted be (*mutatis mutandis*) governed by similar reasoning to that which governs the similar problems which arise where a contract to which the Carriage of Goods by Sea Act 1992 applies is preceded by a contract relating to the carriage of the same goods but falling outside the scope of that Act.[41]

(a) *International Carriage of Goods by Air*

21–051 **Conventions.** The Carriage by Air Act 1961 (as amended) gives effect to the provisions of the 1955 amended Convention, the MP4 Convention and the 1999 Montreal Convention[42] "so far as they relate to the rights and liabilities of carriers, carriers' servants and agents, passengers, consignors and other persons".[43] The 1955 amended Convention and the MP4 Convention apply to international carriage; and this is defined to mean "carriage in which, according to the agreement between the parties, the place of departure and the place of destination, whether or not there be a break in the carriage or a transhipment, are situated either within the territories of two High Contracting Parties or within the territory of a single High Contracting Party if there is an agreed stopping place within the territory of another State, even if that State is not a High Contracting Party."[44] The 1999 Montreal Convention applies both to international and to "non-international"[45] carriage; the definition of "international carriage" in this Convention[46] is substantially similar[47] to that, quoted above,[48] which applies for the purposes of the 1955 amended Convention and the MP4 Convention.

The unamended Convention[49] also applies to "international carriage" which for this purpose is defined in similar[50] terms to those quoted above,[51] except that the territories referred to are those of States which are parties only to the unamended Warsaw Convention.[52] In other words, the "una-

[41] Above, paras 18–055 *et seq.*, 19–092 *et seq.*, 20–059 *et seq.*
[42] Above, para.21–047.
[43] Carriage by Air Act 1961, s.1(6), as substituted by Carriage by Air Acts Implementation of the Montreal Convention 1999) Order 2002, SI 2002/263, Art. 2.
[44] Carriage by Air Act 1961, Sch.1, Art. 1(2) and Sch.1A, Art. 1(2), as inserted by SI 1999/1312, above, para.21–047 n.24.
[45] See Carriage by Air (Application of Provisions) Order 2004, SI 2004/1899 heading to Art. 5 and to Sch.1. Our concern here is within international carriage.
[46] Carriage by Air Act 1961, Sch.1B as inserted by Carriage by Air Acts (Implementation of the Montreal Convention 1999) Order 2000, SI 2000/263, Art. 2(25).
[47] Not identical: the unamended Warsaw Convention, Art. 1(2) (as set out in SI 2004/1899) uses the term "contract" where the 1955 Amended Convention, Art. 2(2) (as set out in Carriage by Air Act 1961, Sch.1), the MP4 Convention, Art. 1(a) (as set out in carriage by Air Act 1961, Sch.1A) and the 1999 Montreal Convention. Art. 1(2) (as set out in Carriage by Air Act 1961, Sch.1B) use the term "agreement".
[48] At n.44.
[49] Above, para.21–047, n.20.
[50] The text is now set out in Carriage by A, (Application of Provisions) Order 2004, SI 2004/1899, Sch.2, Pt IIA.
[51] Above, at n.44.
[52] Unamended Convention (above, para.21–047, n.20), Art. 1(2).

mended Warsaw Convention" still applies to carriage between States which are parties only to the original Convention, and to carriage within such a State if there is an agreed stopping place outside it. It follows from these definitions that, if goods are to be carried from a State which is a party to the unamended Warsaw Convention to a State which is a party to both Conventions (or conversely), only the unamended Warsaw Convention would apply; and that if the goods are to be carried to or from a State which is not a party to either Convention, then neither would apply.

The Conventions also provide[53] for "combined carriage" performed partly by air and partly by some other mode of carriage. In such cases the Conventions apply to the part of the carriage performed by air, but only if that part of the carriage is "international carriage" within the above definitions.

Air waybills and cargo receipts. Under the unamended Warsaw and the 1955 amended Conventions, the carrier has the right to require the consignor to make out and hand over to him, and the consignor has the right to require the carrier to accept, a document formerly known, under the unamended Warsaw Convention,[54] as an air consignment note, and now known as an air waybill.[55] The MP4 Convention[56] and the 1999 Montreal Convention provide that an air waybill "shall be delivered"[57]; but, with the consent of the consignor, "any other means which would preserve a record of the carriage to be performed" may be substituted.[58] If this is done the carrier must, at the consignor's request, deliver to the consignor a "receipt for the cargo", permitting identification of the consignment and access to the "record of the carriage" mentioned above.[59] 21–052

An air waybill must be in three original parts.[60] The first part is marked "for the carrier" and signed by the consignor. The second part is marked "for the consignee": it is signed by the consignor and by the carrier; under the unamended Warsaw and 1955 amended Conventions, it travels with the goods.[61] The third part is signed by the carrier and handed to the consignor after the cargo has been accepted. The air waybill (or cargo receipt) is prima facie evidence of the conclusion of the contract, of the receipt of the cargo and of the conditions of the contract of carriage.[62] The carrier must

---

[53] Unamended Convention, 1955 amended Convention and MP4 Convention, Art. 31, 1999 Montreal Convention, Art. 38.

[54] Carriage by Air Act 1932, Sch.1, Art. 5.

[55] Art. 5 of the 1955 amended and unamended Warsaw Conventions (see above, para.21–047, n.20).

[56] Above, para.21–047, n.22.

[57] MP4 Convention, Art. 5(1): (1999) Montreal Convention Act. 4(1): these do not require the air waybill to be made out by the consignor.

[58] MP4 Convention, Art. 5(2) 1999 Montreal Convention, Act, 4(2).

[59] MP4 Convention, Art. 5(2); the 1999 Montreal Convention, Art. 4(2) uses similar, but not identical language.

[60] Art. 6 of the unamended Warsaw Convention, the 1955 amended Convention and the MP4 Convention, Art. 7 of the 1999 Montreal Convention. For the practice of issuing copies (in addition to the original parts) see *Victoria Fur Traders Ltd v Roadline UK Ltd* [1981] 1 Lloyd's Rep. 571.

[61] There is no such requirement in Art. 6(2) of the MP4 Convention (above, para.21–047, n.22).

[62] Art. 11(1) of all four Conventions.

notify the consignee of the arrival of the cargo at the place of destination,[63] and the consignee is, on such arrival, "entitled . . . to require the carrier to deliver the cargo to him, on payment of the charges due and on complying with the conditions of carriage set out in the air waybill."[64] Under the unamended Warsaw and 1955 amended Conventions (but not under the MP4 Convention or the 1999 Montreal Convention) the consignee is also entitled to require the carrier "to hand over to him the air waybill"[65] (*i.e.* the second part). Until the arrival of the goods at the place of destination (and even in certain circumstances thereafter[66]) the consignor has "the right to dispose of the cargo" by withdrawing or stopping it or by calling for it to be delivered to a person other than the person named (or originally designated) as consignee in the air waybill (or cargo receipt), or by requiring the cargo to be returned to the airport of departure.[67] The exercise of the "right of disposition"[68] by the consignor is not made expressly conditional on the production by him of the third part of the air waybill (or of the cargo receipt[69]); but Article 12(3)[70] provides that if the carrier obeys the instructions of the consignor without production of that part (or of the cargo receipt) he will be "liable, without prejudice to his right of recovery from the consignor, for any damage which may be caused thereby to any person who is lawfully in possession of that part of the air waybill" (or cargo receipt). This provision seems to envisage the possibility that the third part of the air waybill (or the cargo receipt) may have been transferred to a third person so as to confer rights on such a third person; and this possibility may also be reflected in the language of section 1(6) of the Carriage by Air Act 1961,[71] which refers to the rights and liabilities of certain persons concerned with the performance of the contract of carriage "and other persons." Article 15(3) of the 1955 amended Convention further provides that "Nothing in this Convention prevents the issue of a negotiable air waybill."[72] This provision is purely permissive; and so far as English law is concerned an air waybill would not be negotiable merely

---

[63] *ibid.*, Art. 13(2).
[64] *ibid.*, Art. 13(1).
[65] Art. 13(1) of the unamended Warsaw and 1955 amended Conventions.
[66] *ibid.*, Art. 12(4): if the consignee "declines to accept *the waybill or* the cargo, or if he cannot be communicated with, the consignor resumes his right of disposition." The italicised words are omitted from Art. 12(4) of the MP4 and 1999 Montreal Conventions.
[67] Art. 12(1) of all four Conventions. The wording of the MP4 and 1999 Montreal Conventions differs in various minor ways from that of the other two Conventions, but not so as to affect the substance of the position stated in the text above. The "right to dispose of the cargo" under the Conventions seems simply to be one to give instructions to the carrier. It should not be confused with the "right of disposal" the reservation of which prevents property from passing under s.18, r. 5, and s.19 of the Sale of Goods Act 1979; see para.21–055, below.
[68] Art. 12(1) of all four Conventions.
[69] Above, at n.59.
[70] Of all four Conventions (above para.21–047, nn.20–23). There are minor differences between the wording of Art. 12(3) in the 1999 Montreal Convention and in the other three Conventions.
[71] As substituted by the Carriage of Goods by Air Acts, (Implementation of the Montreal Convention 1999) Order 2002, SI 2002/263, Art. 2(1).
[72] See Beaumont [1957] J.B.L. 130.

because it was expressed to be so, since negotiability can be established only by statute or by mercantile usage.[73] The object of Article 15(3) was to set at rest doubts which had arisen under the unamended Convention whether, in view of the consignor's right of disposition, an air consignment note could be made negotiable. These doubts appeared to be ill-founded since that Convention provided (and the amended Convention provides) for the possibility of excluding the right of disposition.[74] Accordingly, Article 15(3) is not reproduced in the MP4 Convention or in the 1999 Montreal Convention.[75] In practice, air waybills are expressed to be not negotiable.

Whether air waybill or cargo receipt a document of title. It is generally agreed that an air waybill is not a document of title in the traditional common law sense,[76] so that transfer of the air waybill does not operate as transfer of constructive possession of the goods.[77] For an air waybill to become a document of title in this sense, it would be necessary to prove a mercantile custom by which transfer of an air waybill operated in this way.[78] In the reported cases, no attempt has ever been made to prove such a custom, and it is unlikely that such an attempt would succeed. For one thing, it is not necessary for the consignee to produce any of the parts of the air waybill to obtain possession of the goods: on the contrary, under the unamended Warsaw and the 1955 amended Conventions, the consignee's copy travels with the goods.[79] For another, there is, in view of the speed of air transport, relatively little commercial need to give this degree of transferability to air waybills: lack of such transferability does not impede dealings in the goods for very long (though it might affect the financing of sales of goods to be carried by air[80]). Even if a mercantile custom could be shown making air waybills transferable like order or bearer bills of lading, it would apply only to air waybills making the goods deliverable to bearer, or to a named consignee or order or assigns, or simply to order or assigns[81]; and in practice air waybills do not appear to be made out in this way. The 21–053

[73] *See cf.* above, paras 18–075, 18–201.
[74] Art. 15(2). See also Art. 15(2) of the MP4 and 1999 Montreal Conventions (above, para.21–052).
[75] Above, para.21–047, n.22 and 23. Art. 15(3) is also not reproduced in the revised version of the 1955 amended Convention that was to have superseded the text of that Convention (as set out in Sch.1 to the Carriage by Air Act 1961) on the coming into force of s.1 and Sch.1 of the Carriage by Air and Road Act 1979. These provisions of the 1979 Act have, however, not yet been brought into force.
[76] Above, para.18–007.
[77] McNair, *Law of the Air* (3rd ed.), p.181; Shawcross and Beaumont, *Air Law* (4th ed.), Vol. I, para.VII(177); Kahn-Freund, *Law of Inland Transport* (4th ed.), p.771.
[78] See above, para.18–075.
[79] Art. 6(2) of the unamended Warsaw and 1955 amended Conventions (above, para.21–047, n.20 and 21).
[80] The acceptability to banks of certain air carriage documents under UCP Art. 27 is not of itself evidence of a mercantile custom giving such documents the characteristics of a document of title in the traditional common law sense. Under Art. 29, banks may likewise accept certain courier and post receipts, but such receipts are plainly not documents of title in that sense.
[81] Above, paras 18–014; 18–015, 18–063, 18–075.

same arguments apply to cargo receipts governed by the MP4 and 1999 Montreal Conventions.[82]

21–054 It is however arguable that an air waybill (or cargo receipt) may be a "document of title" in the statutory sense given to that expression by section 1(4) of the Factors Act 1889 and hence within the Sale of Goods Act 1979.[83] Since such a document is not one of those enumerated in section 1(4), the question is whether it falls within the second part[84] of the definition in that subsection; *i.e.*, whether it can be described as "any other document used in the ordinary course of business as proof of the possession or control of goods, or authorising or purporting to authorise, either by endorsement or by delivery, the possessor of the document to receive the goods thereby represented". As the third part of the air waybill (or the cargo receipt[85]) will normally have to be produced by a consignor wishing to exercise his right of disposition, it is in a sense "used . . . as proof of the control of goods"; and this would be sufficient to make it a document of title within the subsection if it was so used "in the ordinary course of business". This is a question of fact.[86] It is of course a different question from the question whether transfer of an air waybill (or cargo receipt) operates, like the transfer of a bearer or order bill of lading, as a transfer of constructive possession of the goods. There would therefore be no inconsistency between saying that a mercantile custom to the latter effect was *not* established and saying that an air waybill (or cargo receipt) *was* used in the ordinary course of business as proof of the control of goods. There is no reported case in which the latter proposition has ever been proved. If it could be proved, it would not be necessary to establish anything about the effects of the transfer of an air waybill, within the concluding words of section 1(4),[87] as these refer to an alternative way in which a document may become a document of title within the statutory definition. It is in fact not at all clear what rights are conferred on a person to whom the third part of an air waybill (or a cargo receipt) may be transferred, as appears to be

---

[82] Above, para.21–052, n.59. There is, indeed, no provisions in these Conventions to the effect that cargo receipts must (like the consignee's copy of an airway bill) travel with the goods; but equally there is nothing in them to indicate that cargo receipts must be produced to obtain possession of the goods. Their functions, according to Art. 5(2) of the MP4 Convention and Art. 4(2) of the 1999 Montreal Convention, are merely to permit identification of the cargo and access to the "record of the carriage" contained in the receipt. Cargo receipts must under these Conventions be produced by a consignor wishing to exercise his "right of disposition", see Art. 12(3), below, para.21–055; but it does not follow that they have to be produced by the person claiming delivery of the goods.

[83] s.61(1); above, para.18–009; Chorley, 17 M.L.R. 487 at 488 (1954); McNair, *Law of the Air* (3rd ed.), p.183.

[84] See above, para.18–009.

[85] See Art. 12(3) of the MP4 and 1999 Montreal Conventions.

[86] See *Ramdas Vithaldas Durbar v S Amerchand & Co.* (1916) 85 L.J.P.C. 214; L.R. 43 Ind.App. 164, where certain Indian railway receipts were, on the facts, held to be documents of title within a statutory definition in terms similar to those of s.1(4) of the Factors Act 1889. *Cf.* also above, para.18–167, n.71.

[87] *i.e.* "or authorising or purporting to authorise, either by way of endorsement or by way of delivery, the possessor of the document to transfer or receive goods thereby represented."

envisaged by Article 12(3) of the Conventions. This provision does not explicitly give a right of disposition to such a third person; though he might be regarded as assignee of the consignor's right of disposition, and his possession of the third part of the air waybill (or of the cargo receipt) will at the very least impede the consignor's right of disposition. Of course if an air waybill (or cargo receipt) can be shown to be a document of title within section 1(4), the transferee may, as a matter of English law, acquire title under some of the relevant exceptions to *nemo dat quod non habet*: for example, under sections 24 or 25 of the Sale of Goods Act 1979.[88]

Right of disposition. Under the Conventions the consignor has a right to dispose of the cargo,[89] while the consignee has a right to require the carrier to deliver the cargo to him and, (under the unamended Warsaw and 1955 amended Conventions) to require the carrier to hand over to him the air waybill.[90] Except where the consignee refuses to accept the cargo (or, under the unamended Warsaw and 1955 amended Conventions, the air waybill), or cannot be found, the consignor's right ceases when the consignee's begins; that is, on arrival of the cargo at the place of destination.[91] Article 15(1) of the Conventions declares that these rights "do not affect either the relations of the consignor and[92] the consignee with each other or the mutual[93] relations of third parties whose rights are derived either from the consignor or from the consignee". The rights under the Conventions affect only the relations between consignor and carrier, and those between consignee and carrier. They do not affect the relations of consignor and consignee under any contract of sale between them; and they may pass from the consignor to the consignee as a result of events wholly outside the consignor's control.[94] Thus a seller will not be taken to have reserved the "right of disposal" under the Sale of Goods Act 1979, so as to prevent the passing of property to the buyer, merely because he has the "right to dispose of the cargo" under one of the Conventions; and a seller who exercises this right under the Conventions may well be liable to the buyer for breach of the contract of sale. And there are other possible conflicts between the rights under the Conventions and rights arising out of a contract of sale between consignor and consignee: these are discussed in paragraphs 21–056 and 21–057 below. 21–055

First, the consignor may exercise his right of disposition under the Conventions in circumstances amounting to a breach of the contract of sale, after the property has passed to the consignee, and even though the 21–056

---

[88] Above, paras 7–055, 7–069.
[89] Art. 12.
[90] Art. 13.
[91] Arts 12(4) and 13(1) of all four Conventions (above, para.21–047, nn.20–23).
[92] "And" according to the MP4 Convention (above, para.21–047, n.22); "or" according to the unamended Warsaw and 1955 amended Conventions. The former version is the correct one as it corresponds with "et" in the French text which prevails under Conventions (above, para.21–047): Carriage by Air Act 1961, s.1(8), as substituted by Carriage by Air Acts (Implementation of Montreal Convention 1999) Order 2002, SI 2002/263, Art. 2(1)); and see *Corocraft v Pan American Airways Inc.* [1969] 1 Q.B. 616.
[93] It is not clear which part of the French text at this point corresponds to "mutual."
[94] Above, para.21–052.

consignee is solvent, or has paid the price, so that the consignor has no right of stoppage in transit under the Sale of Goods Act 1979. In such a case the consignor is of course liable to the consignee for breach of the contract of sale. But it is submitted that the carrier is under no liability to the consignee, either in contract or in tort (for wrongful interference with goods), as by the Conventions, which have the force of law,[95] the carrier is bound to obey the orders of the consignor. It is true that this obligation is not expressly stated in the Conventions[96]; but it would seem that such an obligation must be implied from the provisions of the Conventions relating to the right to dispose of the cargo. The present submission is supported by the provision in the Conventions by which the consignee's right to require the carrier to deliver the cargo to the consignee is expressed to be subject to an exception which applies where the consignor has exercised the right to disposition conferred on the consignor by the Conventions.[97]

21–057 Secondly, it is possible for the consignor to have a right of stoppage in transit[98] under the Sale of Goods Act 1979 after his "right to dispose of the cargo" under the Conventions has ceased. This would happen if the consignee had not paid the price and was insolvent, and the goods had arrived at the place of destination but had not yet been delivered to the consignee. In such a situation, the right of stoppage would still be in the seller under section 45(1) of the Sale of Goods Act 1979, at least until the carrier acknowledged to the consignee that he held the goods on his behalf.[99] On the other hand, under the Conventions the consignee has the right (even before any such acknowledgment) to require the carrier to deliver the cargo to him, and (under the unamended Warsaw and 1955 amended Conventions) to hand him the air waybill[1]; and as soon as the consignee's right begins the consignor's right of disposition ceases.[2] It is therefore possible for the carrier to be faced with a notice of stoppage in transit from the consignor, on receipt of which he "must redeliver the goods to, or according to the directions of, the seller" under section 46(4) of the Sale of Goods Act 1979, and also with a notice requiring him to deliver the cargo to the consignee, which he must obey under the Conventions. It is submitted that the carrier would not be liable to the consignor if he obeyed the orders of the consignee. The Conventions, no less than the Sale of Goods Act, have the force of law[3]; and, to the extent of any conflict, the Conventions should prevail since they are specifically designed to regulate the relations arising out of the contract of carriage, while the Sale of Goods Act is intended primarily to regulate the relations

---

[95] See above, para.21–047.
[96] For the position under the CIM Uniform Rules, see below, para.21–070.
[97] Art. 13(1) of all four Conventions.
[98] Or an analogous right under Art. 71(2) of the Vienna Convention on Contracts for the International Sale of Goods (above, para.1–024).
[99] Sale of Goods Act 1979, s.45(3).
[1] Art. 13(1).
[2] Arts 12(4) and 13(1) of all four Conventions (above, para.21–047, nn.20–23).
[3] Above, para.21–047.

between buyer and seller. Hence the effect of the exercise of the right of disposition on the relations between consignor or consignee on the one hand,[4] and carrier on the other, should be governed by the Conventions; while the validity of the exercise of the right of stoppage between buyer and seller is governed by the Sale of Goods Act.

(b) *International Carriage of Goods by Road*

Scope of the CMR Convention. International carriage of goods by road is governed by the CMR Convention which is set out as the Schedule to the Carriage of Goods by Road Act 1965.[5] The Act gives the force of law to this Convention so far as its provisions "relate to the rights and liabilities of persons concerned in the carriage of goods by road under a contract to which the Convention applies".[6] These persons are[7] the sender of the goods, the consignee, the carrier or carriers[8] and their servants or agents[9] and "any person to whom the rights and liabilities of any of [these] persons . . . have passed (whether by assignment or assignation or by operation of law)". **21–058**

The Convention provides in Article 1(1) that it applies "to every contract for the carriage of goods by road in vehicles for reward, when the place of taking over of the goods and the place designated for delivery, as specified in the contract, are situated in two different countries, of which at least one is a Contracting country."[10] Article 2(1) envisages the possibility that goods may be carried partly by road and partly by some other means of transport.[11] It begins by providing that "Where the vehicle containing the goods is carried over part of the journey by sea, rail, inland waterways or air, and . . . *the goods are not unloaded from the vehicle*, this Convention shall nevertheless apply to the *whole* of the carriage." If the goods are unloaded during, for example, sea carriage the Convention would thus not apply to the sea carriage, but it may nevertheless apply to the road part of the carriage since a contract may be one "for the carriage of goods by road"

---

[4] *Semble*, the position would be the same if the seller exercised his right to "prevent the handing over of the goods to the buyer" under Art. 71(2) of the Vienna Convention on Contracts for the International Sale of Goods (above, para.1–024). This provision differs from Sale of Goods Act 1979, s.46(2), in that it "relates only to the rights in the goods between the buyer and the seller", and in that it makes no reference to the relations between either of them and the carrier. It would thus be irrelevant for the present purpose if the Vienna Convention were to be given the force of law in the United Kingdom. The position would then be that the sale Convention and the carriage Conventions would equally have the force of law; and in this situation the carriage Conventions would govern the rights between consignor and consignee on the one hand and carrier on the other.

[5] As amended by Carriage by Air and Road Act 1979: see above, para.21–047, n.17.

[6] Carriage of Goods by Road Act 1965, s.1(1).

[7] *ibid.*, s.14(2).

[8] Including successive carriers: see Art. 34 of the Convention.

[9] Art. 3.

[10] For power to certify who are contracting parties, see s.2 of the 1965 Act. Traffic between the UK and the Republic of Ireland is excluded by the Protocol of Signature.

[11] See Fitzpatrick [1968] J.B.L. 311; below, para.21–105.

even though it also provides for or permits part of the carriage operation to be, and that part is, carried out by some other means of transport.[12]

Where the goods are not unloaded during the sea carriage, so that the CMR Convention applies to the relation between sender and road carrier, there may nevertheless be a contract for the carriage by sea of the vehicle (and its contents) between the road carrier and the sea carrier; so that the relations between those two carriers are likely to be governed by the relevant Convention on carriage of goods by sea.[13]

21–059 Article 2(1) of the CMR Convention concludes with an elaborate proviso, the effect of which is best illustrated by assuming that the goods are carried partly by sea and not unloaded from the vehicle during the sea transit. In such a case the liability of the road carrier for loss which was caused during the sea carriage and which was not due to any act or omission of the road carrier, but which could have occurred only in the course of and by reason of the sea carriage, is to be determined, not by the CMR Convention, but in the same way as if a contract for the carriage "of the goods alone" (*i.e.* not including the vehicle) had been made between the sender of the goods and the sea carrier "in accordance with the conditions prescribed by law for the carriage of goods by" sea. These words are not particularly helpful, for the mere hypothesis that such a contract has been made does not enable one to tell whether the Hague-Visby Rules[14] apply. This would depend in the first place on whether the hypothetical contract was "covered by a bill of lading or any similar document of title, in so far as such document relates to the carriage of goods by sea".[15] The CMR Convention does require the contract to be confirmed by the making out of a consignment note[16]; and although this differs in content and effect from a maritime bill of lading, it may be that, for the purpose of the proviso to Article 2(1), the requirement of a consignment note would give rise to a presumption that the hypothetical contract of sea carriage would be covered by a bill of lading or any similar document of title. Of course the Hague-Visby Rules may still not apply, *e.g.* because the goods are stated as being, and are, carried on deck[17]; and there is also the possibility that the parties may have validly agreed to vary the rights and immunities of the carrier under the Rules.[18] Under Article 2 of the CMR Convention, it is

---

[12] *Quantum Corporation Inc. v Plane Trucking* [2002] EWCA Civ. 350 [2002] 1 W.L.R. 2678; below, para.21–076, n.60.

[13] As in *McCarren & Co. Ltd v Humber International Transport Ltd (The Vechscroon)* [1982] 1 Lloyd's Rep. 301, where the contract between the two carriers was governed by the Hague-Visby Rules by virtue of Carriage of Goods by Sea Act 1971, s.1(6)(b). Contrast, so far as incorporation of these Rules is concerned, *Browner International Ltd v Monarch Shipping Co. Ltd (The European Enterprise)* [1989] 2 Lloyd's Rep. 185; below, para.21–081, n.88.

[14] Above, para.21–047.

[15] Carriage of Goods by Sea Act 1971, Sch., art. 1(b). The *hypothetical* contract envisaged by CMR Convention Art. 2(1) could scarcely incorporate the Hague-Visby Rules by *express* reference under s.1(6)(b) of the 1971 Act.

[16] CMR Convention, Art. 4.

[17] Carriage of Goods by Sea Act 1971, Sch., Art. 1(c).

[18] See Hague-Visby Rules (above, para.21–047) Arts V and VI.

therefore necessary to ask what terms the parties would have agreed in the contract for the carriage of the goods by sea alone; and the carrier's liability will be determined by reference to this hypothetical contract.[19]

Consignment note. The CMR Convention provides that "the contract of carriage shall be confirmed by the making out of a consignment note."[20] This is to consist of three original copies signed by the sender and the carrier.[21] The first is to be handed to the sender, the second is to accompany the goods and the third is to be retained by the carrier. The consignment note is "prima facie evidence of the making of the contract of carriage, the conditions of the contract, and the receipt of the goods by the carrier".[22] In the normal case, the second copy of the consignment note will be handed to the consignee on delivery of the goods to him. After the arrival of the goods at their destination, the consignee is "entitled to require the carrier to deliver to him, against a receipt, the second copy of the consignment note and the goods".[23] While the goods are in transit, the sender has "the right to dispose of the goods"[24]; and he also has this right if the consignee "refuses the goods" after their arrival at the place designated for delivery.[25] In the exercise of this right, the sender can stop the goods in transit, change the place of delivery, or order the goods to be delivered to a different consignee. The sender's right of disposal ceases when the second copy of the consignment note is handed to the consignee, or when the consignee exercises the right, mentioned above,[26] to require the carrier to deliver the second copy of the consignment note to him[27]; and "from that time onwards the carrier shall obey the orders of the consignee".[28] The "right of disposal" will, moreover, be in the consignee if the sender makes an entry to that effect in the consignment note.[29] In order to exercise the right of disposal, the sender (except where the consignee has refused the goods) or the consignee (where the right is vested in him)[30] must produce 21–060

---

[19] *Thermo Engineers Ltd v Ferrymaster Ltd* [1981] 1 W.L.R. 1470.

[20] Carriage of Goods by Road Act 1965, Sch., Art. 4, which provides that the Convention can apply although no consignment note is issued: see *Gefco UK Ltd v Mason* [1998] 2 Lloyd's Rep. 585.

[21] Art. 5.

[22] Art. 9. For the weight of the presumption contained in Art. 9, contrast *Elektronska Industrija Oour TVA v Transped Oour Kintinentalna Spedicna* [1986] 1 Lloyd's Rep. 49 with *Texas Instruments Ltd v Nason (Europe) Ltd* [1991] 1 Lloyd's Rep. 146.

[23] Art. 13.

[24] Art. 12(1). This seems to mean simply that he has the right to give instructions to the carrier. Although also described in the Convention as a "right of disposal" (*e.g.* in Art. 12(3), (4) and (5)), it should not be confused with the "right of disposal" the reservation of which prevents property from passing under s.18, r. 5, and s.19 of the Sale of Goods Act 1979: see below, para.21–062.

[25] Art. 15(1).

[26] Above, n.24.

[27] Art. 12(2).

[28] *ibid.* Hence the statement that one of the primary purposes of the consignment note is "to enable the consignee to stop the goods in transit": *Gefco UK Ltd v Mason* [1998] 2 Lloyd's Rep. 585 at 590.

[29] Art. 12(3).

[30] Art. 15(1).

"the first copy of the consignment note on which the new instructions to the carrier have been entered".[31] It is further provided that "If in exercising his right of disposal the consignee has ordered the delivery of the goods to another person, that other person shall not be entitled to name other consignees."[32] There is no corresponding restriction where the sender exercises his right of disposal.

21–061 **Whether consignment note a document of title.** The CMR Convention contains no reference to the possibility of issuing a negotiable consignment note[33] or to the transfer of consignment notes to third parties; nor does it provide that the right of disposal can be excluded by agreement.[34] It seems probable that consignment notes would not be documents of title in the traditional common law sense.[35] In the last resort this is a question of fact, depending on proof of mercantile custom; but in deciding this question weight would no doubt be given to the fact that in the normal case there is no transfer of either the first or the second copy from the sender to the consignee; and that the consignee is not bound to produce the consignment note in order to claim the goods. It is true that on arrival of the goods the consignee is entitled to require the carrier to deliver the second copy to him. But the only consequences of such delivery are that it puts an end to the sender's right of disposal and that it obliges the carrier to obey the orders of the consignee. There is nothing to suggest that the acquisition of the second copy transfers constructive possession of the goods to the consignee, or that the second copy can itself be transferred once it has been delivered to the consignee. There is perhaps a slightly stronger case for arguing that the first copy is in a sense transferable if the consignment note contains an entry that the consignee shall have the right of disposal, for that right can be exercised only if the consignee obtains possession of the first copy. But even in this case transfer of the first copy would, it is submitted, at most transfer the right of disposal conferred by the Convention, and not constructive possession of the goods.

It is, again, arguable that the first copy of the consignment note is a document of title within section 1(4) of the Factors Act 1889 (and thus within the Sale of Goods Act 1979), on the ground that it is "used in the ordinary course of business as proof of the. . . control of goods". Here the same arguments apply as those which have already been considered in relation to air waybills (and cargo receipts issued by an air carrier)[36]; though

---

[31] Art. 12(5)(a).

[32] Art. 12(4).

[33] *cf.* the position under Art. 15(3) of the 1955 amended Convention relating to carriage of goods by air (above, para.21–052).

[34] Contrast the position under the Conventions relating to carriage by air: above, para.21–052.

[35] Above, para.18–007; Law Commission, *Electronic Commerce: Formal Requirements in Commercial Transactions* (December 2001), para.6.2. The acceptability to banks of certain road carriage documents under UCP Art. 28 is not of itself evidence of a mercantile custom giving such documents the characteristics of a document of title in the traditional common law sense (*cf.* above, para.21–053, n.80).

[36] Above, para.21–054.

the absence of any reference in the CMR Convention to the possibility of transfer of consignment notes to third parties would further weaken the argument that these documents are documents of title even within the statutory definition.

Rights of disposal. Under the CMR Convention the right of disposal is normally vested in the sender, while the consignee is entitled to require the carrier to deliver the second copy of the consignment note and the goods after arrival of the goods at the place designated for delivery.[37] In addition, the *consignee* has a right of disposal "from the time when the consignment note is drawn up, if the sender makes an entry to that effect in the consignment note"[38]; there is no corresponding provision in the Conventions relating to air carriage[39] or in the CIM Uniform Rules relating to rail carriage.[40] **21–062**

The CMR Convention does not contain any provision similar to Article 15(1) of the Conventions relating to air carriage by which the rights mentioned above do not affect the relations of the consignor and consignee with each other,[41] but it is nevertheless submitted that this is also the position under the CMR Convention. In other words, the rights of disposal, and the right to require the carrier to deliver the consignment note and the goods, affect only the relations between sender and carrier, and those between consignee and carrier, but not the relation of sender and consignee under any contract of sale between them. Thus a seller will not be taken to have reserved the "right of disposal" under the Sale of Goods Act 1979, so as to prevent the passing of property to the buyer, merely because he has a right of disposal under the CMR Convention; and the exercise of the right of disposal under that Convention may well amount to a breach of the contract of sale. This view is, it is submitted, supported by the general structure of the provisions in the CMR Convention relating to these rights, which deal only with the relationships between sender or consignee on the one hand and the carrier on the other; by the fact that the right of disposal may pass from the sender to the consignee as a result of events wholly outside the sender's control[42]; and by section 1(2) of the Carriage of Goods by Road Act 1965, which gives the force of law to the provisions of the Convention "so far as they relate to the rights and liabilities of persons concerned in the carriage of goods". In the context this can only mean rights and liabilities arising out of the carriage, and not all rights and liabilities whatsoever of such persons. It is, therefore, again necessary to consider possible conflicts between the rights under the Convention and rights arising under a contract of sale between sender and consignee.

First, the sender may exercise his right of disposal under the CMR Convention in circumstances amounting to a breach of the contract of sale, after the property has passed to the consignee and even though the **21–063**

[37] Above, para.21–060.
[38] Art. 12(3) of the CMR Convention.
[39] Above, para.21–055.
[40] Below, para.21–069.
[41] Above, para.21–055.
[42] Above, para.21–060.

consignee is solvent or has paid the price, so that the sender has no right of stoppage in transit under the Sale of Goods Act 1979. In such a case the sender is liable to the consignee for breach of the contract of sale, but it is submitted that the carrier is under no liability to the consignee. The reason for this submission is similar to, and indeed slightly stronger than, that given in relation to carriage by air,[43] namely, that the carrier is bound by the Convention, which has the force of law, to obey the orders of the sender. Again this obligation is not actually stated, but the CMR Convention does come very close to stating it. Article 12(2) provides that once the sender's right of disposal has ceased "the carrier shall obey the orders of the consignee". The natural inference is that previously he must obey the orders of the sender.

21–064 Secondly, it is possible for the sender to have a right of stoppage in transit under the Sale of Goods Act 1979 after his right of disposal under the CMR Convention has ceased. It is submitted that, in such a case, the carrier would not be liable to the sender if he obeyed the orders of the consignee. The reasons advanced for this submission in relation to carriage by air[44] again apply in cases arising under the CMR Convention, and are indeed reinforced in such cases by the explicit provision of the CMR Convention that, after the sender's right of disposal has ceased, "the carrier shall obey the orders of the consignee."[45] This provision does not in terms apply where the right of disposal was never in the sender at all, but was in the consignee from the beginning because there was an entry to that effect in the consignment note.[46] Analogous cases on the meaning of "transit" in the Sale of Goods Act, however, suggest that in this situation the sender would not have any right of stoppage in transit[47] so that there would not in fact be any conflict between rights under the Convention and those under the Act. The CMR Convention does not affect the validity of the exercise of the right of stoppage as between buyer and seller.

(c) *International Carriage of Goods by Rail*

21–065 **Scope of COTIF and the CIM Uniform Rules.** International carriage of goods by rail is governed by the Convention concerning International Carriage by Rail (or COTIF) which incorporates the CIM Uniform Rules and has been given the force of law in the United Kingdom by the Railways (Convention on International Carriage by Rail) Regulations 2005.[48] The CIM Uniform Rules apply (subject to certain exceptions[49]) to "every contract of carriage of goods by rail when the place of taking over the goods and the place for delivery are situated in different Member States"[50]

[43] Above, para.21–056.
[44] Above, para.21–057.
[45] Art. 12(2).
[46] Art. 12(3).
[47] Above, para.15–075; but contrast para.15–067.
[48] See above, para.21–047, n.31. COTIF Art. 6(2) makes the CIM Uniform Rules "an integral part of the Convention."
[49] CIM Uniform Rules, Art. 1(5).
[50] Art. 1(1); "Member States" refers to the parties to COTIF; see COTIF, Art. 1(1).

and, where the parties so agree, where those places "are situated in two States, at least one of which is a Member State."[51] The Uniform Rules can also apply, in specified circumstances, where a single contract for international carriage includes carriage by road or inland waterway in internal traffic of a Member State as a supplement to transfrontier carriage by rail; and where a single contract for international carriage includes carriage by sea or transfrontier carriage by inland waterway as a supplement to carriage by rail, so long as the carriage by sea or inland waterway is performed on services included in the list provided in COTIF Article 24(1).[52] In cases of "rail--sea carriage"[53] by services referred to in this Article, the carrier[54] is, if the relevant Member State requests a suitable note to be included in the list referred to above, entitled to certain additional exemptions[55] from liability[56] if he proves that the loss, damage or delay "occurred in the course of the journey by sea between the time when the goods were loaded on the ship and the time when they were unloaded from the ship."[57] The carrier is deprived of the benefit of these exemptions if the person entitled to bring the claim against the carrier[57a] proves that the loss, damage or delay is due to the fault of the carrier, the master, a mariner, the pilot or the carrier's servents.[57b]

Consignment note and duplicate of the consignment note. Under the CIM Uniform Rules, the contract of carriage "must be confirmed by a consignment note which accords with a uniform model"[58] and which contains particulars specified in the Rules[59]; the consignment note must be signed by the consignor and the carrier.[60] The Rules also provide for the issue of a "duplicate consignment note" on which the carrier "must certify the taking over of the goods"[61]; the carrier must then return the duplicate to the consignor.[62] It is envisaged that entries on the consignment note are to be made by or on behalf of the consignor.[63] The consignment note is "prima facie evidence of the conclusion and of the conditions of the contract."[64] At this stage, the consignment note remains in the possession 21–066

[51] CIM Uniform Rules, Art. 1(2).
[52] *ibid.*, Art. 1(3) and (4).
[53] *ibid.*, Art. 38(1).
[54] Defined in *ibid.*, Art. 3(a) as "the contractual carrier with whom the consignor has entered into the contract of carriage pursuant to these Uniform Rules." In cases of "rail-sea carriage" contemplated by Art. 38(1), "the carrier" is likely to be the initial rail carrier.
[55] *i.e.*, additional to those specified in *ibid.*, Arts 23(2) and (3).
[56] *ibid.*, Art. 38(1)(a)–(d).
[57] *ibid.*, Art. 38(2). These exemptions resemble those available to a carrier of goods by sea under the Hague-Visby Rules (above, para.21–047); a detailed comparison of the two sets of Rule is beyond the scope of this book.
[57a] See CIM Uniform Rules, Arts. 43, 44.
[57b] *ibid.*, Art. 38(3).
[58] Art. 6(2).
[59] See Art. 7(1).
[60] Art. 6(3).
[61] Art. 6(4).
[62] *ibid.*
[63] Art. 8.
[64] Art. 12(1).

of the carrier: this appears from the further requirement of the Rules that "the carrier must hand over the consignment note and deliver the goods at the place designated for delivery against receipt and payment of amounts due to the carrier according to the contract of carriage"[65] and from the provision that "after arrival of the goods at the place of destination, the consignee may ask the carrier to hand over the consignment note and deliver the goods to him."[66] The "person entitled" (*i.e.* typically the consignee[67]) may "refuse to accept the goods even when he has received the consignment note" pending examination of the goods to establish loss or damage.[68] It is thus envisaged that the consignee may acquire possession of the consignment note before the goods are delivered to him. The duplicate must be produced by the consignor if he wishes to exercise his right (to be further discussed below[69]) to "dispose of the goods and to modify the contract of carriage."[70] It must also be produced by him if he wishes to make a claim relating to the contract of carriage[71] or to bring an action based on the contract of carriage,[71a] unless (in either of these two situations) he can "produce an authorisation from the consignee [to make the claim or bring the action] or furnish proof that he consignee has refused to accept the goods."[71b]

21–067 The duplicate of the consignment note remains in the hands of the consignor; and this document is important in relation to the exercise of the consignor's right under the CIM Uniform Rules "to dispose of the goods and to modify the contract of carriage."[72] The distinction between these rights will be discussed in paragraph 21–069 below; our present concern is with the right to modify the contract of carriage, which is analogous to the right of disposition or disposal under the Conventions relating to international carriage of goods by air and road.[73] As the ensuing discussion will show, the right may be excercisable by the consignor or by the consignee. The consignor "may in particular ask the carrier" to discontinue the carriage of the goods, to delay their delivery, to deliver them to a consignee "different from the one entered on the consignment note" or to deliver them at a destination other than that entered on the consignment note.[74] The consignor's right to modify the contract is extinguished when the consignee has taken possession of the consignment note,[75] accepted the

[65] Art. 17(1).
[66] Art. 17(3).
[67] Unless the consignee has, and has duly exercised his right to modify the contract of carriage (see (Arts 17(3) and 18) by giving "instructions for the delivery of the goods to another person" (Art. 17(5)).
[68] Art. 17(4).
[69] Below, para.21–067.
[70] Art. 18(1).
[71] Art. 43(3).
[71a] Art. 44(5).
[71b] Arts 44(3), 44(5).
[72] CIM Uniform Rules, Art. 18(1).
[73] Above, paras 21–052, 21–060.
[74] CIM Uniform Rules, Art. 18(1)(a) to (d).
[75] *ibid.*, Art. 18(2)(a); for the consignee's right to possession of the consignment note after arrival of the goods at the destination, see *ibid.* Art. 17(3), above para.21–066 at n.66.

goods,[76] asked the carrier to hand over the consignment note and deliver the goods to him[77] or become entitled under the Rules[78] to give orders modifying the contract of carriage.[79] The Rules provide that the consignee has the right to modify the contract of carriage "from the time when the consignment note is drawn up, unless the consignor indicates to the contrary on the consignment note"[80]: and that from the time the consignee is thus entitled to modify the contract of carriage "the carrier shall comply with orders and instructions of the consignee."[81] The consignee may thus *have* the right to modify the contract of carriage at an early stage of the transport operation; but he may not be able to *exercise* this right since its exercise requires the person (whether the consignor or the consignee) who wishes to modify the contract to "produce to the carrier the duplicate of the consignment note on which the modifications have to be entered."[82]. The duplicate consignment note is issued to the consignor[83] and the Rules envisage its retention by him; for example, in the provision that, to make a claim "relating to" the contract of carriage and to bring an action against the carrier, the consignor "must produce the duplicate of the consignment note."[84] By contrast, where such a claim is made by the consignee, he "must produce the consignment note [not the duplicate] if it has been handed over to him."[85] It is the duplicate, not the consignment note, which the

---

[76] See CIM Uniform Rules, Art. 18(2)(b).
[77] *ibid.*, Art.18(2)(d); for the consignee's right to possession of the consignment note, see above n.75.
[78] See CIM Uniform Rules, Art. 18(3).
[79] *ibid.*, Art. 18(2)(d).
[80] *ibid.*, Art. 18(3). This provision gives rise to some difficulty since it might be thought to follow from it, and from Art. 18(2)(d) (above, n.79) that the consignor's right to modify the contract of carriage is extinguished at the very moment of its coming into existence: *i.e.*, as soon as the contract is made. The difficulty can perhaps in part be resolved by arguing that the contract of carriage can be made, on general principles of law of contract (*cf.* above para.18–042), before the consignment note is, in the words of Art. 18(3), "drawn up". Art. 6(2) gives some support to this view by requiring the contract of carriage to be "confirmed" by the consignment note, and by providing that its "absence . . . shall not affect the existence of validity of the contract which shall remain subject to the Uniform Rules." Thus before the consignment note is drawn up, the consignor may *have* the right to modify the contract of carriage, but he will not at this stage be able to *exercise* it since, before the consignment note is drawn up, there can be no duplicate of it, so that the consignor will not be able to comply with the requirement of producing the duplicate: see the words of Art. 19(1) quoted in the text below at n.82.
[81] CIM Uniform Rules, Art. 18(2)(d).
[82] Art. 19(1). Production of the duplicate consignment note by the consignor is also required by Arts 43(3) and 44(5) in the event of his making a claim relating to the contract of carriage or bringing an action on that contract; but such production is only one of the ways stated in those Articles of satisfying their requirements. By contrast, production of the duplicate consignment note is the only way in which the requirements of the exercise of the right to modify the contract of carriage can, under Art. 19(1), be satisfied. Art. 19(7), indeed, envisages that the carrier may implement such a modification without production of the duplicate; but it provides that, in that event, he is liable in damages to the originally named consignee.
[83] *ibid.*, Art 6(4).
[84] *ibid.*, Arts 43(3) and 44(5), as to which see n.82 above.
[85] *ibid.*, Art. 43(4). For the right of the consignee, to ask the carrier to "hand over the consignment note . . . to him," see Art. 17(3), above, para.21–066.

consignee needs to produce if he wishes to modify the contract of carriage; indeed, his taking possession of the consignment note is note is one of the circumstances in which the consignee's right to modify the contract of carriage is extinguished.[86] The consignee's right to modify the contract of carriage is also extinguished where he has accepted the goods,[87] asserted his rights to ask the carrier to hand over the consignment note and to deliver the goods to him[88] or if he has given instructions (to the carrier) for delivery of the goods to another person (than the consignee) and that person has asserted his rights to ask the carrier to hand over the consignment note and to deliver the goods to him.[89] If the consignee has given instructions for delivery of the goods to another person, then that person is not, in turn, entitled to modify the contract of carriage.[90–96] There is no corresponding restriction where the consignor exercises his right to modify the contract in favour of a third party.

21–068 **Whether consignment note or duplicate a document of title.** For reasons already stated in relation to international carriage of goods by air and road, the consignment note issued under the CIM Uniform Rules is not a document of title in the traditional common law sense.[97] Once the consignment note has been completed by entry of the required particulars[98] and signed by the consignor and the carrier,[99] it remains, while the goods are in transit, in the possession of the carrier; but once the goods have arrived at the place of destination, the consignee may obtain possession of it before he obtains delivery of the goods.[1] But the only legal consequences of his obtaining possession of the consignment note are to extinguish his,[2] as well as the consignor's,[3] right to modify the contract of carriage; to entitle the consignee to bring an action against the carrier based on the contract of carriage[4] and to deprive the consignor of the right to bring such an action[5]; and perhaps to entitle the carrier, as against the consignee, to outstanding charges.[6] The Rules do not provide for or envisage any transfer

---

[86] CIM Uniform Rules, Art. 18(4)(a).
[87] *ibid.*, Art. 18(4)(b).
[88] *ibid.*, Art 18(4)(c), referring to Art. 17(3).
[89] *ibid.*, Art 18(4)(d), again referring to Art. 17(3).
[90–96] *ibid.*, Art. 18(5).
[97] Above, para.18–007; and see above, paras 21–053, 21–061; Law Commission, *Electronic Commerce: Formal Requirements in Commercial Transactions* (December 2001), para.6.5. The acceptability to banks of certain rail carriage documents under UCP Art. 28 is not of itself evidence of a mercantile custom giving such documents the characteristics of a document of title in the traditional common law sense (*cf.* above, para.21–053, n.80).
[98] See Arts 6 and 7.
[99] Art. 6(3).
[1] See Arts 17(1) and (3), discussed in para.21–066, above.
[2] Art. 18(4)(a).
[3] Art. 18(2)(a).
[4] Art. 44(1)(b), 44(6). The right of the consignee is extinguished when the person designated by him as the person to whom delivery is to be made (see Art. 18(5)) has taken possession of the consignment note: Art. 44(2).
[5] Art. 44(1)(a) 1.
[6] Art. 17(1) requires the carrier to hand over the consignment note and deliver the

of the consignment note from the consignor to the consignee: it is from the carrier that the consignee obtains possession of the consignment note and his receipt of that note is not regarded as the equivalent of delivery of the goods.[7] Nor does such receipt enable the consignee to transfer the consignment note to (and so to confer rights on) a third person: on the contrary, the consignee's right to modify the contract of carriage is extinguished as soon as he has taken possession of the consignment note.[8] It follows from these features that the consignment note lacks the characteristics of a document of title in the common law sense[9] and also within section 1(4) of the Factors Act 1889 (and hence for the purposes of the Sale of Goods Act 1979). These conclusions are supported by Article 6(5) of the Rules, by which "the consignment note shall not have effect as a bill of lading."

Article 6(5) refers only to "the consignment note" and not to the duplicate consignment note.[10] It seems from the structure of the Rules that these are distinct documents[10a] so that they are not to be treated as equivalents of each other, in the way in which parts of a bill of lading issued in a set of several parts are so regarded.[10b] Under the Rules, the two documents perform different functions: the consignment note is not issued to the consignor but is kept during transit by the carrier, who must hand it over to the consignee at the end of the transit;[10c] while it is the duplicate which is handed to the consignor (forming his receipt for the goods[10d]) and is then of importance for the exercise of the right to modify the contract of carriage. The consignee does not need to produce the duplicate to the carrier to become entitled to delivery of the goods; he needs so to produce it only where he has, and wishes to exercise, the right to modify the contract of carriage.[10e] If the consignor sends the duplicate to the consignee, two

---

goods to the consignee "against payment of the amounts due according to the contract of carriage." It is not entirely clear whether the effect of these words is to *oblige* the consignee to pay these amounts or merely to make such payment a *condition* of his right under Art. 17(1) to have the consignment note handed over to him. Under Art. 10, the consignor is the person primarily liable for the carrier's charges under the contract of carriage.

[7] Art. 17(1) states the carrier's duties to "hand over the consignment note and deliver the goods" as separate duties.

[8] Art. 18(4)(a); under Art. 18(4)(c) and (d), the consignee's right to modify the contract of carriage may be extinguished before he has taken possession of the consignment note.

[9] This is true both of the traditional sense of the expression "document of title to goods" described in para.18–007 above and of the alternative sense described in para.18–008 above.

[10] The version of the CIM Uniform Rules which is superseded by the current version (see above, para.21–047 n. 30), Art 11(5) provided that "the *duplicate* shall not have effect . . . as a bill of lading." For a discussion of this provision, see para.21–068 of the 6th edition of this book.

[10a] See, for example, the reference in Art. 43(5) to the "consignment note, the duplicate and any other documents"; and the distinction drawn between the consignment note and the duplicate in Art. 43(3) and (4).

[10b] See above, para.18–090.

[10c] Art. 17(1), (3).

[10d] Art. 6(4).

[10e] Art. 19(1).

legal consequences follow. First, the consignor can no longer exercise his right to modify the contract of carriage as he can no longer "produce [the duplicate] to the carrier;"[10f] and if the carrier obeys the orders of the consignor "without requiring production [from the consignor] of the duplicate consignment note",[10g] then the carrier is liable in damages to the consignee "if the duplicate has been passed on to the consignee."[10h] Secondly, if the consignor has parted with possession of the duplicate, then he cannot, in general, make a claim under the contract of carriage since for this purpose he must "produce the duplicate of the consignment note" unless he is authorised by the consignee to make the claim or proves that the consignee has refused to accept the goods.[10i] Both the above consequence follow from the fact that the consignor has lost possession of the duplicate—not from the fact that the consignee has acquired it. There is nothing in the Rules to suggest that the transfer of the duplicate from the consignor to the consignee operates as a transfer between these parties of the constructive possession of the goods. It is thus clear from the nature of the duplicate, as here described, that the duplicate is not, any more than the consignment note itself, a document of title in the common law sense.[10j]

The possibility remains, however, that the duplicate may be a "document of title" within section 1(4) of the Factors Act 1889 (and thus within the Sale of Goods Act 1979). It is arguable that the duplicate is "used in the ordinary course of business as proof of the . . . control of goods" within section 1(4), as it must be produced by a consignor or a consignee wishing to exercise his right to modify the contract of carriage.[11] Possession of the duplicate does not, indeed, of itself give the consignee the right to modify the contract of carriage, since his right to do so may be excluded by contrary provision on the consignment note.[12–14] But even where the consignee's right to modify the contract of carriage is so excluded, his possession of the duplicate does enable him to prevent the consignor from exercising that right; while in the hands of the consignor possession of the duplicate (being essential to the exercise of the right to modify the contract), is certainly "proof of the . . . control of goods"; the question whether it is used as such "in the ordinary course of business" is one of fact.[15]

21–069 **Rights to modify the contract.** Under the CIM Uniform Rules, the consignor is "entitled to dispose of the goods and to modify the contract of carriage",[16] while the consignee has the "right to modify the contract of carriage"[17] in the circumstances described in paragraph 21–067 above.[18]

[10f] As required by Art. 19(1).
[10g] Art. 19(7): "requiring" here seems to mean "obtaining".
[10h] Art. 19(7).
[10i] Art. 43(3).
[10j] See above (para.21–068 nn.97 and 9).
[11] Art. 19(1).
[12–14] Art. 18(3).
[15] See *Ramdas Vithaldas Durbar v S. Amerchand & Co.* (1916) 85 L.J.P.C. 214; L.R. 43 Ind.App. 164 (above, para.18–167, n.71, and para.21–054, n.56).
[16] Art. 18(1).
[17] Art. 18(3).
[18] Above, para.21–067 at n.80.

From the wording of these provisions, it might at first sight be supposed that the (consignor's) right to "dispose of the goods" was distinct from his right to "modify the contract of carriage", only the latter right being available to the consignee. This impression may be reinforced by the fact that the provisions of the Rules which specify when the consignor's right to "modify the contract of carriage" is extinguished[18a] do not in terms apply to his right to "dispose of the goods." In fact, however, the *content* of the consignor's right under the Rules to "dispose of the goods" appears to be exactly the same as the content of his right to "modify the contract of carriage": it is a right to give orders to the carrier to perform that contract in specified ways at variance from those originally agreed in the contract of carriage between these parties.[18b] It is, in other words, a right to vary the contractual relationship between carrier and consignor. The phrase "right to dispose of the goods" may reflect an assumption that the consignor is, while the consignee is not, owner of the goods when they are handed over to the carrier for carriage. But this is by no means necessarily the case. The consignee may have become owner before this point, e.g. where he has bought goods and paid for them before the beginning of the carriage operation.[18c] If the consignee then resold the goods and ordered the carrier to deliver them to the sub-buyer[18d] it would make perfectly good sense to say that he had "disposed" of the goods as well as having "modified" the contract of carriage. But the Rules do not use the former expression when dealing with the consignee's right to give orders to the carrier,[18e] nor do they even specify the content of that right.[18f] The significant point, for the purpose of the ensuing discussion is that the Rules do not deal with the contractual or proprietary relations between the consignor and consignee, typically as seller and buyer of the goods. Their concern is with the contractual relations between either or both of these parties and the carrier. It is also relevant to the discussion that follows to recall that "once the goods have arrived at the place of destination, the consignee may ask the carrier to hand over the consignment note and to deliver the goods to him"[18g]; he has this right whether or not his right to modify the contract of carriage has been excluded by the terms of the consignment note.[18h] The Rules do not contain any provisions similar to Article 15(1) of the Conventions relating to carriage of goods by air[18i] by which the rights described above do not affect the relations of consignor and consignee with

---

[18a] See above, para.21–067.

[18b] The list of ways in which the consignor can modify the contract of carriage is set out in Art. 18(1). There is no corresponding list in Art. 18(3), which specifies the time from which the consignee has the right to modify that contract; but it is reasonable to assume that the list in Art. 18(1) applies to this situation.

[18c] See, for example, *Texas Instruments Ltd v Nason (Europe) Ltd* [1991] 1 Lloyd's Rep. 146 (a case of carriage by road).

[18d] A situation envisaged by CIM Uniform Rules, Art. 18(5).

[18e] In Art. 18(3).

[18f] See n. 18b above.

[18g] Art. 17(3), where "may" seems to mean "is entitled to."

[18h] See Art. 18(3) for the possibility of so excluding the consignee's right to modify the contract of carriage.

[18i] Above para.21–055.

each other; but it is submitted that this is also the position under the CIM Uniform Rules. In other words, the rights to modify the contract, and the rights to require the carrier to hand over the consignment note and deliver the goods, affect only the relations between consignor and consignee on the one hand and carrier on the other: they do not affect the relations of consignor and consignee under any contract of sale between them. It follows that a seller will not be taken to have reserved the "right of disposal" under the Sale of Goods Act 1979 (so as to prevent the passing of property) merely because under the Rules he has, as consignor, the right to modify the contract of carriage or to dispose of the goods.[19] The use in this context of the expression "right to modify the contract of carriage" plainly refers to the relations between, on the one hand, the consignor[19a] or the consignee[19b] and, on the other, the carrier; and, as has been submitted above,[19c] the consignor's right to "dispose of the goods" is similarly a right to vary the contractual relations between these parties. The consignee's right to require the carrier to hand over the consignment note and deliver the goods is clearly regarded in the CIM Uniform Rules as being similarly a right under that contract. It is therefore again necessary to consider two possible conflicts between the various rights arising under the CIM Uniform Rules and rights arising under a contract of sale between consignor and consignee.

21–070 First, the consignor might exercise his right to modify the contract in circumstances amounting to a breach of the contract of sale, after the property had passed to the consignee and even though the consignee was solvent or had actually paid the price, so that the consignor had no right of stoppage in transit under the Sale of Goods Act 1979. In such a case the consignor is liable to the consignee for breach of the contract of sale but it is submitted that the carrier is under no liability to the consignee. The reason for this submission is similar to that given for the same conclusion in relation to cases of international carriage of goods by air and road.[20] It is that under the CIM Uniform Rules, which have the force of law, the carrier is bound to obey the orders of the consignor so long as the consignor has, and has duly[21] exercised, the right to modify the contract of carriage.[22] It is

[19] Art. 18(1).

[19a] See Art. 18(1), referring to modification of the contract of carriage by the consignor.

[19b] See Art. 18(3), referring to modification of the contract of carriage by the consignee.

[19c] After n.18b above.

[20] See above, paras 21–056, 21–063.

[21] If the consignor has not *duly* exercised his right to modify the contract of carriage, the carrier may be liable in damages to the consignee for implementing the consignor's orders. This is the position under Art. 19(7) where the consignor has purported to modify the contract of carriage without producing the duplicate of the consignment note to the carrier.

[22] Art. 19 imposes various restrictions on the carrier's duty to comply with orders modifying the contract of carriage, whether they are given by the consignor or the consignee: *e.g.* that the carrying out of the orders must be "possible, lawful and reasonable to require at the time when the orders reach the person who is to carry them out" (Art. 19(3)) and that they "must not have the effect of splitting the consignment" (Art. 19(4)). The discussion in the text above is based on the assumption that none of these restrictions applies.

true that the carrier's obligation to obey the orders of the consignor in the exercise of his right to modify the contract of carriage is not expressly stated in the Rules, but they do come very close to stating it. Article 18(2)(d) states that, where the consignee has become entitled to modify the contract of carriage, then "from that time onwards, the carrier shall comply with the orders and instructions of the consignee." The natural inference is that, before that time, he must obey the orders of the consignor.[23]

Secondly, a consignor who has sold goods to the consignee may have a right of stoppage in transit under the Sale of Goods Act 1979 after his right to modify the contract of carriage under the CIM Uniform Rules has been extinguished and after this right has, under the Rules, passed to the consignee. This is, indeed, more likely to happen in cases of rail carriage than in the cases of air and road carriage already discussed[24] since under the CIM Uniform Rules the consignor's right to modify the contract of carriage may be extinguished at an early stage, namely, "from the time when the consignment note is drawn up, unless the consignor indicates to the contrary on the consignment note."[25–26] When the consignment note is drawn up, the goods may still be in transit for the purposes of the right of stoppage in transit, so that there may again be a conflict between the Sale of Goods Act and the CIM Uniform Rules. Under section 46(4) of the Act, a carrier who receives a notice of stoppage in transit may be obliged to deliver the goods "to, or according to the directions of, the seller", while under Article 18(2)(d) of the Rules, the carrier must "from that time onwards" (*i.e.* from the time when the consignment note is drawn up) "comply with the orders and instructions of the consignee" (*i.e.* in the case put, the buyer). The conflict cannot be resolved by relying on the rule that the transit under the Sale of Goods Act is at an end when the carrier acknowledges to the consignee that he holds the goods on his behalf[27]; for the seller may have given his notice of stoppage before any such acknowledgment has been given to the consignee while at the same time the seller's right as consignor to modify the contract of carriage under the Rules may have been extinguished because that right is vested in the consignee.[28] Nor can the conflict be resolved by relying on the rule, stated in section 45(6) of the Sale of Goods Act, that the transit is deemed to be at an end "where the carrier . . . wrongfully refuses to deliver the goods to the buyer . . .", for a refusal based on a valid notice of stoppage would not be wrongful; and the question, in the case put, is whether, or for what purposes, the notice of stoppage is valid. It is submitted that, in the case put, the carrier would not be liable to the consignor if it disregarded his notice of stoppage and instead obeyed the orders of the consignee. Two of the arguments in favour of this submission are the same as those advanced **21–071**

[23] In this respect, the position under the CIM Uniform Rules is more closely analogous to that under the CMR Convention (above, para.21–063) than to that under the air carriage Conventions (above, para.21–056).
[24] Above, paras 21–057, 21–064.
[25–26] Art. 18(2)(d) and (3).
[27] Sale of Goods Act 1979, s.45(3).
[28] CIM Uniform Rules, Art. 18(2)(d); above, para.21–067.

in relation to international carriage of goods, by air and by road[29]: that is, the Rules have the force of law; and they regulate the relations arising out of the contract of carriage. A third argument in favour of the view that the carrier is not liable to the consignor for failing to give effect to his notice of stoppage in transit is that the CIM Uniform Rules oblige the carrier to "comply with the orders and instructions of the consignee"[30] once the consignor's right to modify the contract of carriage has been extinguished on the acquisition of that right by the consignee. The Conventions relating to international carriage of goods by air and road contain no such express provision, so that in this respect the argument that the carrier is not, in the case put, liable to the consignor is stronger under the CIM Uniform Rules than it is under those other Conventions.

8. CONTAINER TRANSPORT[31]

(a) *Introductory*

21–072 **Forms of container transport.** The basic features of container transport are that goods are put into a container at an inland point; the container is then sealed and carried by road or rail to a sea port and put on board ship; at the end of the sea transit the container is unloaded and carried by road or rail to an inland destination where the container is opened and the goods are delivered to, or made availabe for collection by, the consignee. Container transport does not, of course, necessarily involve a combination of land and sea carriage; it may involve land and air carriage, sea and air carriage, or a combination of land, sea and air carriage. But as the combination of land and sea carriage is the most common, it will be made the basis of the following discussion. The container may be filled wholly with the goods of a single consignor, intended for a single consignee; or it may contain goods belonging to several consignors or destined for several consignees.

21–073 **Problems arising out of container transport.** Container transport gives rise to special problems partly because of the nature of the packaging provided by the container; and partly because it often involves what used to be called "combined",[32] but is now more commonly (if less elegantly)

---

[29] Above, paras 21–057, 21–064.

[30] CIM Uniform Rules, Art. 18(2)(d), 18(3); above, para.21–067 at n.81.

[31] de Wit, *Multimodal Transport* (1995); Gronfors [1967] J.B.L. 298; Angus, 14 McGill L.J. 395 (1968); Gottschalk, 3 Israel L.Rev. 578 (1968); Sassoon, 1 *Journal of Maritime Law and Commerce* 73 (1970); Schmetzer and Peavey, *ibid.*, p.203 (1970); Kee, 12 Malay L.Rev. 364 (1970); Lee Kew Chai [1970] 2 Malay L.J. xliii. Hickey, 45 Tulane L.Rev. 863 (1971); Bissell, *ibid.*, 902; Spitz, *ibid.*, 925. And see International Carriage of Perishable Foodstuffs Act 1976, s.19 for a definition of "container" for the purposes of that Act.

[32] See, *e.g.*, I.C.C. Uniform Rules for a Combined Transport Document, below para.21–082.

referred to as "multimodal"[33] transport of the kind described in paragraph 21–072 above. The most important of these problems concern the liabilities of the various parties engaged in carrying the goods, such as the sea carrier and the road or rail carriers at each end of the sea transit. Usually, the transport operation is carried out by several carriers, each performing one of its stages. It is also possible for one such carrier to make arrangements for the whole carriage, in which case he is sometimes referred to as the combined, or multimodal, transport operator. This expression is, however, also used to refer to a forwarding agent, who (generally on behalf of the owner of the goods[34]) makes arrangements for the multimodal carriage, without himself being a carrier.[35] Such a person may merely undertake to negotiate contracts between the consignor and the carrier or carriers involved in the multimodal transport operation[36]; but his undertaking may also go beyond this. Thus he may undertake that the goods will actually be carried[37]: in such a case the multimodal transport operator would be liable if the goods were not carried at all, but it seems that only the actual carrier would be liable if, in breach of the contract of carriage, the goods were lost or damaged while being carried by him. A multimodal transport operator who is not himself the carrier may, moreover, by issuing documents purporting to be, or to have the effect of, bills of lading, assume at least some of the responsibilities (and acquire some of the rights[38]) of a carrier.[39] It is also possible for a person to act as forwarding agent *and* carrier.[40] His liability in the latter capacity will normally be confined to the stage at which

---

[33] See, *e.g.*, UNCTAD/ICC Rules on Multimodal Transport, below para.21–082. UCP, Art. 26.

[34] *Jones v European Express* (1921) 90 L.J. 159; *Hair & Skin Co. Ltd v Norman Airfreight Carriers Ltd* [1974] 1 Lloyd's Rep. 442; *Western Digital Corp. v British Airways plc* [2001] Q.B. 733 at 743; occasionally forwarding agents act as principals: see *Hair & Skin Co.* case, above, at p.445; *Tetroc Ltd v Cross-Con (International) Ltd* [1983] 1 Lloyd's Rep. 192. In *Sonicare International Ltd v East Anglia Freight Terminals Ltd* [1997] 2 Lloyd's Rep. 48 a freight forwarder's "bill of lading" was regarded as capable of transfer; the underlying assumption seems to be that the freight forwarder had (unusually) acted as agent of *the carrier.*

[35] *e.g.* in *Chellaram & Sons (London) Ltd v Butlers Warehousing & Distribution Ltd* [1978] 2 Lloyd's Rep. 412; *cf.* the position of the second defendants in *Gallagher Ltd v BRS* [1974] 1 Lloyd's Rep. 400. See also *J Evans & Son (Portsmouth) Ltd v Andrea Merzario Ltd* [1976] 1 W.L.R. 1078 at 1082; below, paras 21–081, n.5, 21–089, n.75; *Sydney G. Jones Ltd v Martin Bencher Ltd* [1986] 1 Lloyd's Rep. 54 at 64; *Lukoil-Kalingradmorneft Plc v Tata Ltd* [1999] 2 Lloyd's Rep. 129 at 138.

[36] *e.g. The Maheno* [1977] 1 Lloyd's Rep. 81 ("freight consolidator" not liable for loss during sea carriage, but said to be liable if loss had occurred during the preceding land carriage).

[37] *Salsi v Jetspeed* [1977] 2 Lloyd's Rep. 57; *cf. Harlow & Jones Ltd v PJ Walker Shipping & Transport Ltd* [1986] 2 Lloyd's Rep. 141 at 144; *KH Enterprise v Pioneer Container (The Pioneer Container)* [1994] 2 A.C. 324. *cf. Royal and Sun Alliance Insurance Plc v MK Digital FZE (Cyprus) Ltd* [2005] EWHC 1408 (Comm) at [46].

[38] See *Britannia Distribution Co. Ltd v Factor Pace Ltd* [1998] 2 Lloyd's Rep. 420 at 423.

[39] *cf.* Carriage of Goods by Sea Act 1971, s.1(6)(b).

[40] See, for example, *Club Specialty (Overseas) Inc. v United Marine (1939) Ltd* [1971] 1 Lloyd's Rep. 482 at 485; *cf. Norwich Pharmacal Co. v Commissioners of Customs* [1974] A.C. 133 at 187; *Elektronska Industrija Oour TVA v Transped Oour Kintinentalnja Spedicna* [1986] 1 Lloyd's Rep. 49.

he acts as carrier[41]; but it is perfectly possible for him to give a contractual undertaking on account of the breach of which he will be liable for loss or damage occurring at some other stage of the multimodal transport operation.[42]

21–074 The liability of some (but not necessarily all) of the persons concerned with the making and performing of the contract or contracts of carriage may be regulated by various laws and Conventions,[43] imposing different standards of liability and different levels of limitation of liability[44] at different stages of the carriage; and, while this point does not directly affect the relations of buyer and seller, it is of obvious practical importance to them in determining what provisions should be made for insurance. The laws and Conventions applicable to the various stages of the carriage may also contain different requirements as to the form and contents of the carriage documents, and different provisions as to the legal nature of those documents, at the different stages of carriage.[45] This question of documentation may again affect the relations of buyer, seller and any banker involved in the financing of the sale. Proposals to harmonise these rules by an international convention on multimodal transport have not as yet been implemented by legislation.[46] A further problem affecting buyer and seller is that the common sale terms, such as c.i.f. and f.o.b. terms, assume breaks in the carriage at the points when the goods are loaded on, and discharged from, the carrying ship; and, as these assumptions are inappropriate in cases of multimodal container transport, the rules which determine, for example, the duties of the parties and the passing of property and risk under such sale terms require modification in cases of such transport.[47] The legal problems which can arise out of this form of transport between buyer and seller have as yet received little attention in the English authorities, so that the following account is more than usually speculative.

---

[41] As in *The Maheno*, above, n.36.

[42] *e.g. J Evans & Son (Portsmouth) Ltd v Andrea Merzario Ltd* [1976] 1 W.L.R. 1078 (liable for loss during sea carriage under a collateral contract).

[43] Above, para.21–047.

[44] In the American case of *The OOCL Bravery* [2000] 1 Lloyd's Rep. 394 the bill of lading provided that the sea carrier's liability was to be governed by the United States Carriage of Goods by Sea Act 1936 for the whole of the carriage so that the cargo-owner's claim was not affected by the (in the circumstances) lower limitation of liability applicable under the CMR Convention which governed the relations between the sea carrier and a land carrier under a contract which could not adversely affect the cargo-owner's rights as he was not a party to it. In the contrasting American case of *Norfolk Southern Railway Co. v James N Kirby Pty Ltd* 125 S.Ct. 385 (2004) the limitation of liability under the 1936 Act was available to the inland carrier of goods which, after having been carried for most of the contractual voyage by sea, were then carried for the final land "leg" by rail. The 1936 limitation was available to the rail carrier even though one of the *contracts* of carriage provided for a higher limitation for the final land "leg": but no question arose under any *Convention* with regard to this part of the carriage operation.

[45] For bills of lading, see above, paras 18–012 to 18–137; for air waybills (and cargo receipts) and road and rail consignment notes, see above, paras 21–052 to 21–054, 21–060, 21–061, 21–066, 21–067.

[46] Below, para.21–082.

[47] Below, paras 21–094 *et seq.*

(b) *Multimodal Transport Document*

Scope of discussion. Our concern in the following discussion will be with two questions concerning the function and legal nature of the carriage documents used in relation to multimodal transport. The first is whether such documents provide a mechanism for the transfer of contractual rights to, and the imposition of contractual liabilities on, persons who are not original parties to the contract of carriage. The second question is whether documents covering multimodal transport are documents of title. In discussing these questions, it will be necessary to distinguish between (a) cases in which the entire multimodal transport operation is covered by a single transport document (a multimodal transport document); and (b) cases in which separate carriage documents are issued for each stage of the multimodal transport operation. 21–075

(i) *Contractual Effects*

Application of Carriage of Goods by Sea Act 1992. The application of this Act to documents issued in relation to multimodal transport operations depends on the distinction drawn at the end of paragraph 21–075 above. 21–076

It is convenient first to consider the case in which the transport operation is governed by separate documents for each of its stages. In such a case, the transport document covering the sea carriage is likely to be an ordinary bill of lading[48] or sea waybill; and the 1992 Act will apply to it in accordance with the principles (and subject to the limitations) discussed elsewhere in this book.[49] If the document is a bill of lading and is issued when the goods are accepted at the first (inland) stage of the multimodal transport operation, then it cannot be a "shipped" bill of lading; whether it is a "received" bill so as to fall within the 1992 Act depends on the meaning of that expression in the Act.[50] Difficulty may (as already noted[51]) arise in this connection where the document states that the goods have been received, but not that they have been actually "received *for shipment*"[52] by the sea carrier: *e.g.* where it simply names the loading port without naming or otherwise identifying the carrying ship.[53] The difficulty can be overcome by making an "on board" notation on the document (so as to turn it into a "shipped" bill) at the time of shipment.

The second situation is that in which a single multimodal transport document is issued covering the whole of the transport operation from the

---

[48] See, *e.g. PS Chellaram & Co. Ltd v China Ocean Shipping Co. (The Zhi Jiang Kou)* [1991] 1 Lloyd's Rep. 493 (CA of N.S.W.); *A/S Iverans Rederei v KG MS Holstencruiser Schiffahrtsgesellschaft mbH & Co. (The Holstencruiser)* [1992] 2 Lloyd's Rep. 378; *Glebe Island Terminals Pty Ltd v Continental Seagram Pty Ltd (The Antwerpen)* [1994] 1 Lloyd's Rep. 213 (CA of N.S.W.).

[49] See above, paras 18–096 *et seq.* (bills of lading), 18–153 *et seq.* (sea waybills).

[50] Above, para.18–103.

[51] Above, paras 18–027, 18–038.

[52] Carriage of Goods by Sea Act 1992, s.1(2)(b).

[53] As in *Mayhew Foods Ltd v Overseas Containers Ltd* [1984] 1 Lloyd's Rep. 317; above, paras 18–027, 18–038.

inland point of origin via the seaports at which the goods are loaded on, and discharged from, the ship to the ultimate inland point of destination. The question then arises whether such a document is either a "bill of lading" or a "sea waybill" within the 1992 Act so as to be capable of becoming a mechanism for the transfer of contractual rights and the imposition of contractual liabilities under that Act.

If the document is in transferable form,[54] the fact that it does not state that the goods have been placed on board the ship which is to carry them does not prevent it from being a bill of lading within the Act, since the Act applies to received[55] no less than to shipped bills; though here again the point must be made that if the document merely specifies the intended place of shipment and does not designate the carrying ship or indicate receipt of the goods by the sea carrier, then it could not be a bill of lading within the meaning of the Act.[56] Even if these obstacles could be overcome, there is the further, and more fundamental, difficulty that the Act gives no comprehensive definition of the expression "bill of lading"; while in the English common law this expression has been used to refer only to a document containing or evidencing a contract for the carriage of goods *by sea.*[57] The 1992 Act gives no indication of any legislative intention to depart from this common law concept of a bill of lading as a sea carriage document. It would, moreover, be strange if "bill of lading" were not, while sea waybills and ship's delivery orders were (as the following discussion will show), restricted to documents relating to the carriage of goods by sea. The short title of the Act gives some support to the view that the meaning of all these expressions is so restricted in relation to all the documents to which the Act applies.[58]

If the multimodal transport document is not in transferable form, either because it is (as apparently such documents often are) marked "not negotiable" or because it makes the goods deliverable simply to a named consignee, then it cannot be a "bill of lading" within the 1992 Act[59]; and the question arises whether it can be a "sea waybill" for the purposes of that

---

[54] See r.2.6(a) of the UNCTAD/ICC Uniform Rules, discussed in para.21–082, below.

[55] Carriage of Goods by Sea Act 1992, s.1(2)(b).

[56] Above, paras 18–027, 18–038, 18–103.

[57] Above, para.18–012. In *Princes Buitoni Ltd v Hapag-Lloyd AG* [1991] 2 Lloyd's Rep. 383 a document covering land carriage at the end of the transit was called a "bill of lading" but no issue arose as to whether the document had the legal characteristics of a bill of lading.

[58] *i.e.* to bills of lading, sea waybills and ship's delivery orders: s.1(1). The point appears to be left open in Law Commissioner's Report on *Rights of Suit in Respect of Carriage of Goods by Sea*, Law Com. No.196, Scot. Law Com. No.130 (1991), on which the 1992 Act was based. In para.2.49 of that Report, it is suggested that multimodel transport documents are "capable of falling within [the] ambit" of the implementing legislation as received bills. But if (as seems to be the current practice) they are marked "not negotiable", or made out in favour of a named consignee (without the addition of words, such as "or order", importing transferability), then they would not be "bills of lading" within the 1992 Act since they would be "incapable of transfer either by endorsement or, as a bearer bill, by delivery without endorsement" within s.1(2)(a): see above, para.18–103.

[59] s.1(2)(a).

Act. It seems that a negative answer must be given to this question since the Act defines "sea waybill" as a document containing or evidencing a "contract for the carriage of goods *by sea*" and since this definition would seem to exclude a document containing or evidencing a contract for the carriage of goods partly by some other means of transport.[60] It follows that the machinery provided by the Act for the transfer of contractual rights to, and the imposition of contractual liabilities on, third parties would not operate in relation to "non-negotiable" multimodal transport documents.[61] Similar reasoning applies to any delivery orders that might be given in relation to goods carried under such documents: such orders could not be ship's delivery orders within the statutory definition since this requires the order to have been given "under or for the purposes of a contract for the carriage [of goods] *by sea*".[62] It is true that the definitions in the 1992 Act of sea waybills and ship's delivery orders do not in so many words refer to a contract for the carriage of goods *only* by sea; but it is submitted that the words "carriage . . . by sea" do not in their natural meaning refer to carriage partly by land. The point is obvious enough where only a small part of the carriage is by sea (as in the cross-Channel trade); although the point may seem to lose much of its force where the primary purpose of the contract is carriage by sea (as, for example, where the contract is for the carriage of goods from a port in Australia to an inland destination in England).[63] On balance, it is submitted that the proportion which the one mode of carriage bears to the other should not affect the natural meaning of the words "by sea". To allow it to do so would give rise to questions of degree and consequently to uncertainty.

A multimodal transport document which is not a bill of lading or sea waybill may, under the provisions for mixed carriage to be discussed in paragraphs 21–104 to 21–106 below, be wholly governed by one of the

---

[60] UCP Arts 23 and 25 treat "Marine/Ocean" bills of lading as distinct from "Multimodal Transport" documents. In *Quantum Corp. Inc. v Plane Trucking Ltd* [2002] EWCA Civ. 350, [2002] 1 W.L.R. 2673, a contract was made for the carriage of goods from Singapore to Dublin; the goods were carried from Singapore to Paris by air and then from Paris to Dublin by lorry. To the extent that the contract provided for or permitted carriage by lorry from Paris to Dublin, it was held to be a "contract of the carriage of goods by road" within the CMR Convention (above, para.21–058). The case is concerned with the interpretation of that Convention and its reasoning does not directly touch the present question (discussed in the text above): this question is whether, where a document contains or evidences the *whole* of the multimodel transport operation, that contract is one for the carriage of goods by sea.

[61] The point left open in the Law Commission's Report in the passage quoted in n.58 above is whether multimodel transport documents may fall within the(proposed) 1992 Act as received bills of lading. The question whether they may do so as sea waybills is not discussed either in that passage or in Part V of the Report, so far as it deals with the sea waybills.

[62] s.1(4)(a).

[63] *cf. Norfolk Southern Railway Co. v James N Kirby Pty Ltd* 125 S. Ct. 385 (2004) where the United States Supreme Court held that a contract for the carriage of goods from Sydney to an inland destination in the United States, 336 miles from the port of discharge (Savannah, Georgia), was a "maritime" contract for the purpose of giving the Federal Courts jurisdiction under Art. III, § 2 Cl 1 ("admiralty and maritime jurisdiction") of the United States Constitution.

Conventions on international carriage otherwise than by sea. The acquisition of contractual rights by, and the imposition of contractual liabilities on, third parties will then be governed by that Convention.

21–077 **Contracts (Rights of Third Parties) Act 1999.** Under section 1 of this Act, the right to enforce a term of a contract may, if specified requirements are satisfied, be conferred on a person who is not a party to the contract ("the third party")[64]; but this right is subject to what we have called the subsection 6(5) exception.[65] For the purpose of the present discussion, it is necessary to make the further point that this exception falls into two parts. The first part is contained in section 6(5)(a) which provides that no right is conferred by section 1 on the third party in the case of a "contract for the carriage of goods by sea".[66] The second part of the exception is contained in section 6(5)(b) which provides that no rights are conferred by section 1 on the third party under contracts for the carriage of goods by rail or road, or of cargo by air, which are governed by the international Conventions regulating these modes of transport referred to in paragraph 21–047 above and which have the force of law under other legislation. Our concern here is with the question whether these Conventions and the legislation giving them the force of law may bring multi-modal transport documents within the scope of the subsection 6(5) exception and so outside the scope of section 1 of the 1999 Act.

If, as has been submitted in paragraph 21–076 above, multimodal transport documents are not bills of lading or sea waybills within the Carriage of Goods by Sea Act 1992 since they do not contain or evidence contracts for the carriage of goods (wholly) "by sea", then the first part of the subsection 6(5) exception in the 1999 Act does not apply to them. It follows that a consignee named in such a document and containing a contract between shipper (or consignor) and carrier would not be precluded by this part of the exception from relying on section 1 of the 1999 Act so as to enforce a term of that contract as a third party. But he might be so precluded by the second part of the subsection 6(5) exception. It may be objected that, if a contract for the carriage of goods partly by sea and partly by land is not one for the carriage of the goods "by sea", then such a contract cannot be one for the carriage of goods "by rail" or "by road" either (or one for the carriage of cargo "by air"). But at least some such contracts may fall within the second part of the subsection 6(5) exception. This may be the position either because the relevant Conventions on road and rail carriage can apply to the whole of the multimodal transport operation even though part of it is carried out by some other mode of transport, such as carriage by sea[67]; or because one part of the carriage operation was governed by one of the transport Conventions to which

[64] Above, para.18–005.
[65] Above, para.18–005, sub-paragraph (f).
[66] For discussion of some of the other problems arising from this part of the subsection 6(5) exception, see above, paras 18–055, 18–056, 18–117, 18–145, 18–188, 19–092 *et seq.*, 20–059 *et seq.*, 21–050.
[67] CMR Convention, above, para.21–047, Art. 2(1); CIM Uniform Rules, above, para.21–047, Arts 1(4), 38(1); COTIF, above, para.21–047, Arts 24(1).

subsection 6(5) refers[68] while the rest of the carriage operation is governed by another of those Conventions.[69] The air carriage Conventions, moreover, apply in cases of "combined carriage" to that part of the carriage by air which is "international carriage" within those Conventions.[70] Where one of the carriage Conventions applies, the contract of carriage (or the relevant part of it) will (to that extent) fall within the second part of the subsection 6(5) exception so that the third party will have no right to enforce the contract (or that part of it) under section 1 of the 1999 Act. Such a right could, however, be conferred on the third party where the contract was one to which the Conventions did not apply (*e.g.* because their territorial requirements were not satisfied) and to which the Carriage of Goods by Sea Act 1992 also did not apply because the contract was, by reason of its multimodal nature, not one for the carriage of goods by sea.[71]

The 1999 Act does not impose liabilities under a contract on the third party merely because he has acquired rights under it, though the Act does entitle the promisor (*i.e.* in our context the carrier) to rely against the third party (typically the consignee) on certain matters that would have been available to the carrier by way of defence or set-off either against the promisee (the shipper or consignor) if the proceedings had been brought by him[72] or against the third party if the latter had been a party to the contract.[73] At common law, the third party could incur liabilities to the carrier under an implied contract[74]; and the carrier could rely against the third party on any lien available to him which amounted to a "proprietary or possessory" and not to a mere contractual right.[75]

A multimodal transport document which was not one of the classes of documents to which the Carriage of Goods by Sea Act 1992 applies might contain an express term purporting to make the provisions of that Act applicable to it. It is, however, submitted that such a term would extend the provisions of the Act to the document by way of contract and not as a

---

[68] See s.6(8) of the 1999 Act as amended by the Railways (Convention on International Carriage by Rail) Regulations 2005, SI 2005/2092 art.9(2) and Sch.3, para.3. The Carriage by Air (Application of Provisions) Order 1976, SI 1967/480, referred to in s.6(8)(c)(iii) of the 1999 Act has been revoked by the carriage by Air (Application of Provisions) Order 2004, SI 2004/1899, art. 9 and Sch.4.

[69] As in *Quantum Corp Inc v Plane Trucking Ltd* [2002] EWCA Civ 350, [2002] 1 W.L.R. 2678 (above, para.21–076 n.60), where part of the carriage was governed by the CMR Convention. In that case the other part was presumably governed by the relevant air carriage Convention, but if that part had not been covered by any of the Conventions or by a bill of lading, then the subsection 6(5) exception would seem to have been applicable to the road part of the carriage operation.

[70] Art. 31 of the unamended Warsaw Convention, the 1955 amended Convention and the MP4 Convention; Art. 38 of the 1999 Montreal Convention. For these Conventions, see above, para.21–047.

[71] This possibility is recognised in the Law Commission's Report on which the 1999 Act was based: Law Com. No.242 (1996) paras 12–14, n.20.

[72] Contracts (Rights of Third Parties) Act 1999, s.3(2).

[73] *ibid.*, s.3(4).

[74] Below, para.21–078. The fact that delivery was made without presentation of the document should not be an insuperable bar to the creation of such a contract, so long as the delivery was made with reference to the document.

[75] *Port Line Ltd v Ben Line Steamers Ltd* [1958] Q.B. 146 at 166; and see generally Treitel, *The Law of Contract* (11th ed.), pp.607–607, 622–625.

matter of law; for to give it the latter effect could enable it to impose liabilities on a third party without his consent and this is a concept which, apart from statute, is not recognised by English law. Hence such a document would not fall within the subsection 6(5) exception to the 1999 Act and rights could be acquired by a third party under, and subject to the provisions of, that Act or under some other exception to the doctrine of privity of contract which operated in the third party's favour.[76]

21–078 **Implied contract.** A person named as consignee in a multimodal transport document might acquire rights against, and incur liabilities to, a carrier under an implied contract of the kind discussed in paragraphs 18–138 to 18–144 above. The scope of this device is, however, limited in the present context in that it could apply only between the consignee and the carrier from whom delivery was taken, *i.e.* usually the last of the carriers involved in the multi-modal transport operation.

(ii) *Document of Title Function*

21–079 **Introduction.** In discussing the question whether documents issued in relation to multimodal transport are documents of title, reference must again be made to the distinction drawn in paragraph 21–075 above between cases in which the multimodal transport operation is covered by a series of documents and those in which a single document is issued covering the whole of that operation.

21–080 **Multimodal transport covered by a series of documents.** If a separate document is issued in respect of each of the stages of carriage[77] then the document relating to the sea carriage stage is capable of being a normal order or bearer bill of lading and so of being a document of title in both the traditional common law and in the statutory sense[78]; while the documents relating to the land carriage stages at either end of the transit are not documents of title in the common law sense,[79] though it is arguable that they may be documents of title in the statutory sense.[80] The practical difficulty with this type of documentation is that it may fail to provide the "continuous documentary cover" to which a buyer is entitled under a c.i.f. contract.[81] If, in the case of goods to be carried in a container under a multimodal transport operation, this cover is required to extend from inland point of origin to inland destination,[82] then there may be gaps in the cover when the goods are loaded on, and discharged from the ship, especially if at the first of these points they are taken off the land-carrying vehicle. For this and no doubt other reasons, it may be desirable to issue a single multimodal transport document.

---

[76] Contracts (Rights of Third Parties) Act 1999, s.7.
[77] See below, para.21–081, n.92.
[78] Above, paras 18–007, 18–062, 18–009.
[79] Above, paras 21–061; 18–068 below paras 21–081 at n.92.
[80] See the references in n.79, above; *cf.* below, para.21–083.
[81] Above, para.19–027.
[82] Below, para.21–095.

Multimodal transport covered by a single document. If a single multimodal transport document is issued, covering the whole of the multimodal transport operation, then that document may, for four reasons, lack the characteristics of a document of title in the traditional common law sense.[83] 21–081

First, it seems that such documents commonly make the goods deliverable to a named consignee without words (such as "or order") importing transferability. Hence they are at most straight bills of lading and, as has been submitted in Chapter 18, not documents of title in the traditional common law sense, in the absence of the proof of a mercantile custom giving them this characteristic.[84] The point that they do not have this characteristic is usually put beyond doubt by their being marked "not negotiable".[85]

Secondly, the document may be issued by a forwarding agent who is not a carrier and who acts on behalf of the consignor. This seems to be common in the case of a "mixed" container, containing goods of several consignors collected together by a "freight consolidator" to make up a full load, which is then packed into the container at the inland point of departure. When the container is shipped, a single bill of lading may be issued by the sea carrier *to* the forwarding agent[86]; but the documents issued *by* such an agent are not bills of lading since (unless the agent also fills the role of a loading broker) they are not issued by or on behalf of the sea carrier.[87] The fact that documents issued by forwarding agents are not documents of title is implicitly recognised by the Uniform Customs and Practice for Documentary Credits, under which banks will accept a transport document issued by a "freight forwarder" only if it indicates that the freight forwarder was acting as carrier or multimodal transport operator, or if it names the carrier or multimodal transport operator and is signed on his behalf by the freight forwarder as a named agent for the carrier or multimodal transport operator.[88] Sometimes *two* "combined transport bills of lading" (covering the entire carriage operation) are issued—one by the initial land carrier and one by the carrier by sea.[89] This

[83] Above, paras 18–007, 18–062.

[84] Above, para.18–075; for the possibility of establishing such a custom in relation to the multimodel transport documents, see below after n.6.

[85] See above, para.18–076.

[86] As in *The Maheno* [1977] 1 Lloyd's Rep. 81.

[87] Above, para.18–012; *The Maheno*, above.

[88] UCP 500 art. 30. Under the Carriage of Goods by Sea Act 1971, s.1(6)(b), such a document may be a receipt and be subject to the Hague-Visby Rules if it expressly provides that they are to govern the contract contained or evidenced in it "as if it were a bill of lading". There are conflicting decisions on the question whether s.1(6)(b) can apply where the words "as if it were a bill of lading" do not occur in the document: *McCarren & Co. Ltd v Humber International Transport Ltd (The Vechscroon)* [1982] 1 Lloyd's Rep. 301; *Browner International Ltd v Monarch Shipping Co. Ltd (The European Enterprise)* [1989] 2 Lloyd's Rep. 185. On either view, the use of this fiction in the Act clearly indicates that the document *is not* a bill of lading: *cf. The Maurice Desgagnes* [1977] 1 Lloyd's Rep. 290 where a carriage document issued by a "freight forwarder" was held not to be a bill of lading for the purposes of the Hague Rules. The Hague and Hague Visby Rules do not deal with what, in para.18–062 above, we have called the "conveyancing" function of carriage documents.

[89] As, for example in *Customs & Excise Commissioners v ApS Samex* [1983] 1 All E.R. 1042.

practice can lead to difficulties[90] where the two documents get into different hands; and it seems unlikely that the document issued by the land carrier would be regarded as a document of title in the traditional common law sense.[91]

Even if there is only a single combined transport document and it is issued by or on behalf of a carrier by sea, there is, thirdly, the question whether it should take on the characteristics of a land-carriage document (which is not a document of title in the common law sense)[92] or of a bill of lading (which is such a document if it complies with the requirements stated in paragraph 18–063 above). Where the sea transit forms the greater part of the total carriage undertaken, it may be tempting to attribute to the combined transport document the characteristics of a bill of lading; but the temptation is obviously less strong where the sea carriage form only a small part of the total carriage undertaken. Here again,[93] the point arises that it would scarcely be satisfactory to make the legal nature of the document depend on the proportion which the sea carriage bore to the land carriage. A bill of lading may be a document of title even though it provides for carriage *to* an inland destination,[94] or for overland carriage for part of the way[95]; but it is less clear that the same is true of a document which is not in origin a sea-carriage document at all. In an American case[96] a document purporting to be a bill of lading was accepted as such without comment even though it described both the place where the goods had been loaded on a truck *and* the port of shipment as the "port of loading"; but the case provides no guidance for the solution of similar problems in England, since in the United States carriage documents issued by land carriers are called "bills of lading"[97] and recognised as documents of title.[98]

A fourth difficulty arises from the fact that combined transport documents may be issued at the place and time at which the goods are packed into the container, and before the container is put on board the carrying

---

[90] Analogous to those that arose in *Ishag v Allied Bank International* [1981] 1 Lloyd's Rep. 92 and *Elder Dempster Lines v Zaki Ishag (The Lycaon)* [1983] 2 Lloyd's Rep. 548, above, para.18–079.
[91] *cf.* above, paras 21–061, 21–068.
[92] *cf.* above, paras 21–061, 21–068.
[93] *cf.* above, para.21–076.
[94] See *Johnson v Taylor Bros & Co. Ltd* [1920] A.C. 144.
[95] *e.g. Re L Sutro & Co. and Heilbut, Symons & Co.* [1917] 2 K.B. 348 where tender of such a document was held bad, not because of its nature, but because a majority of the Court of Appeal (Scrutton L.J. dissenting) took the view that the contract of sale required the goods to be carried by sea only. The correctness of this decision was left open in *Tsakiroglou & Co. Ltd v Noblee Thorl GmbH* [1962] A.C. 93. It would presumably not apply where the contract of sale provided for or permitted carriage by land for part of the transit: the reasoning of *Quantum Corp. Inc. v Plane Trucking Ltd* [2002] EWCA Civ. 350, [2002] 1 W.L.R. 2678, above, para.21–076, n.60, though not directly applicable to this situation, could be relied on by way of analogy.
[96] *Cameco Inc. v SS American Legion*, 514 F.2d 1291 (1974); [1975] 1 Lloyd's Rep. 295.
[97] UCC s.1–201(6). *Cf. The OOCL Bravery* [2000] 1 Lloyd's Rep. 394.
[98] UCC, s.1–201(15), s.1–206(16) in the 2002 edition (not yet widely adopted). In these respects, the U.C.C. did not change the previous law. As to Indian Railway Receipts, see above, para.18–167, n.71 and para.21–054, n.86.

ship. In that case, they can at most[99] be "received", rather than "shipped" bills of lading[1]; and only the latter are documents of title under the custom recognised in *Lickbarrow v Mason*.[2] This difficulty can be overcome, once the goods had been put on board, by making a notation to this effect on the combined transport document.[3]

In view of the above difficulties it seems that, in the present state of the authorities, a shipper who wanted to be sure of getting a document of title in the traditional common law sense[4] would need to obtain a separate bill of lading for the part of the transit involving carriage by sea.[5] The question whether multimodal carriage documents are documents of title (in that sense) is one which cannot yet be answered with certainty. The now common use of such documents, the increasing degree of their standardisation[6] may support the view that a custom, similar to that established in *Lickbarrow v Mason*,[7] exists in relation to such documents, at least where they are issued by, or on behalf of, sea carriers; but for the present it awaits judicial recognition. Perhaps the relative speed of container transport and the nature of most containerised cargoes (which are not usually sold afloat) account for the fact that such recognition has, as yet, not been sought.[8] To obtain that recognition, it would presumably also be necessary to show that delivery of the goods could be obtained on production of the document by any lawful holder of it.[9] In one case,[10] evidence that delivery could not have been so obtained led the New Zealand Supreme Court to doubt whether a "consignment note" issued by a "freight forwarder" was a valid document

---

[99] See above, para.18–027.

[1] See above, para.18–079. For the view that the date of "shipment" specified in a bill of lading should be the date on which the container was put on board, and not that on which the goods were placed in the container, see *United City Merchants (Investments) Ltd v Royal Bank of Canada (The American Accord)* [1979] 1 Lloyd's Rep. 267 at 273, reversed on other grounds [1983] 1 A.C. 168.

[2] Above, para.18–063. The point that "received" bills of lading are not documents of title in the common law sense is not affected by the Carriage of Goods by Sea Act 1992: see above, para.18–011.

[3] Above, paras 18–027, 18–079.

[4] Above, paras 18–007, 18–062.

[5] For this practice, see *J Evans & Sons (Portsmouth) Ltd v Andrea Merzario Ltd* [1976] 2 Lloyd's Rep. 165; *The Maheno* [1977] 1 Lloyd's Rep. 81; *Customs & Excise Commissioners v ApS Samex* [1983] 1 All E.R. 1043; *Neptune Orient Lines Ltd v JVC (UK) Ltd (The Chevalier Roze)* [1983] 2 Lloyd's Rep. 438 (showing that such a document will not cover land carriage at the destination unless it actually provides for such carriage, as in *The Elbe Maru* [1978] 1 Lloyd's Rep. 206); *PS Chellaram & Co. Ltd v China Ocean Shipping Co. (The Zhi Jiang Kou)* [1991] 1 Lloyd's Rep. 493 (New South Wales Court of Appeal). An alternative possibility is to use a dual purpose document which may be filled in so as to serve either as an ordinary bill of lading or as a multimodal transport document: see *Glebe Island Terminals Pty Ltd v Continental Seagram Pty Ltd (The Antwerpen)* [1994] 1 Lloyd's Rep. 213 (New South Wales Court of Appeal).

[6] *cf.* below, para.21–082.

[7] Above, paras 18–007, 18–075. The acceptability to banks of certain multimodal transport documents under UCP Art. 26 is not of itself evidence of a mercantile custom of the present kind (*cf.* above, para.21–053 n.80).

[8] *cf.* above, para.21–053.

[9] Above, para.18–063; *cf.* below, para.21–082.

[10] *The Maheno* [1977] 1 Lloyd's Rep. 81.

of title. Even if such a custom could be established in relation to multimodal transport documents as a class, it would not apply to any such document which was marked "not negotiable" or which contained other words to the same effect.[11] Multimodal transport documents appear commonly to be so marked, and this may in part account for the fact that no attempt has been made to establish a custom by virtue of which they would be recognized as documents of title in the traditional common law sense.

21–082 **The UNCTAD/I.C.C. Rules on Multimodal Transport.** In 1968 the International Maritime Committee issued a Draft Convention on Combined Transport, also known as the Tokyo Rules.[12] Further drafts followed,[13] culminating in a UN Convention on the International Multimodal Transport of Goods[14]; and Uniform Rules for a Combined Transport Document, drawn up by the International Chamber of Commerce, originally published in 1975[15], have now been superseded by the UNCTAD/ICC Rules for Multimodal Transport Documents.[16] These Rules do not have the force of law but may be incorporated in contracts for the multimodal carriage of goods.[17] So far as they conflict with applicable Conventions which do have the force of law,[18] (or with other rules law of which cannot be displaced by contract) the Rules must necessarily yield to such Conventions (or rules of law).[19] The Rules provide for the issue of a multimodal transport (or MT) document in either "negotiable"[20] or "non-negotiable"[21] form. If the document is issued in "negotiable" form, it has some of the characteristics of a bill of lading. For example, the Rules envisage the transfer of such a document, evidently by delivery if it is made out to bearer[22] and by endorsement and delivery if it is made out to order.[23] They also envisage that delivery of the goods is to be made against surrender of the document to the multimodal transport operator[24] and that, if it is issued in a set of more than one original, then the multimodal transport operator's undertaking is to deliver the goods against surrender of one original of the

[11] See above, para.18–076.
[12] I.M.C. Document CR-T-16 32, *Export*, June 1969, p.21.
[13] See, for example, 3 *Journal of Maritime Law and Commerce* 617 (1972); Massey, *ibid.*, 725; Ramberg [1968] J.B.L. 132. For recommendations made by a conference at Genoa under the chairmanship of Lord Diplock, see [1972] J.B.L. 269.
[14] United Nations Document TD/MT/Conf. 16 adopted on May 24, 1980.
[15] ICC Brochure No.273, reproduced in [1975] L.M.C.L.Q. 29; for a revised version see I.C.C. Publication No.298, reproduced in [1976] L.M.C.L.Q. 148.
[16] ICC Publication No.481; for a report of a working party leading to these Rules, see ICC Document No.321–34/1 (1990).
[17] As defined in r. 2.1.
[18] *e.g.* The Hague-Visby Rules, the CMR Convention and the CIM Uniform Rules: above, para.21–047, 21–058, 21–065.
[19] This is explicitly recognised in r. 13.
[20] r. 2.6(a). "Negotiable" here means "transferable." *Cf.* above, para.18–084.
[21] r. 2(6)(b).
[22] See r. 4.3(a).
[23] See r. 4.3(b).
[24] r. 4.3(a), (b) and (c); see r. 2.2 for the definition of "multimodal transport operator."

document.[25] These provisions of the Rules are concerned only with the definition of the person to whom the multimodal transport operator undertakes to deliver the goods. Both for this reason, and because the rules have the force only of contract and not of law, the fact of their incorporation in the multimodal transport contract will not of itself confer on the multimodal transport the characteristics of a document of title at common law[26]; though it might (if it became sufficiently widespread) be evidence of a custom having that effect.[27] Where the document is issued in a "non-negotiable" form, it resembles a sea way bill[28] in that delivery is to be made to the person named in it "upon proof of his identity", without any requirement of surrender of the document.[29] Such a "non-negotiable" document is clearly not a document of title in the common law sense.[30]

Document of title in the statutory sense. It is arguable that a single document covering the whole of the multimodal transport operation may be a document of title within section 1(4) of the Factors Act 1889[31] and hence for the purposes of the Sale of Goods Act 1979.[32] It will be recalled that that definition consists of two parts: a list of documents, followed by a general description of a further class of documents.[33] A multimodal transport document could fall within the first part of the definition as a "bill of lading" if it so described itself and if the definition were considered to be legally accurate. Alternatively, it could fall within the second part of the definition on proof that it was used in the ordinary course of business for any of the purposes there described. 21–083

(c) *Liability of Carrier*

In this book, our prime concern is with the relations between buyer and seller; but in cases of overseas sales these parties will, in regulating these relations, obviously have regard to the extent to which either of them, or both, can recover from the carrier in respect of loss of or damage to the goods in transit. The fact that the goods are carried in a container gives rise to a number of special problems. A full discussion of these will be found in works on the carriage of goods by sea;[34] but some reference to two of them must be made here. 21–084

---

[25] *ibid.*; *cf.* above, para.18–092.
[26] *cf.* above, paras 18–193, 18–201.
[27] *cf.* above, paras 18–007, 18–075, 18–166, 18–193, 18–200.
[28] *See* above, para.18–018.
[29] r. 2.6; *cf.* above, para.18–070.
[30] Above, para.18–076.
[31] Above, para.18–009.
[32] Sale of Goods Act 1979, s.61(1), definition of "document of title".
[33] Above, para.18–009.
[34] See *Carver on Bills of Lading*, (2nd ed. 2005) paras 9–255, *et seq.*

(i) *Package or Unit Limitation*

21–085 **Introduction.** Where a contract for the carriage of goods by sea is governed by the Hague or Hague-Visby Rules,[35] the liability of the carrier is limited to a stated sum "per package or unit"[36]; under the Hague-Visby Rules, there is an alternative limitation by reference to weight and the effective limitation is the higher of the two.[37] Where goods are carried in a container under a contract governed by the Hague Rules, it will therefore be important to know whether the container is to be treated as a single package, or whether individual boxes or cartons within the container are to be regarded as separate packages. The question is less likely to have practical importance where the contract of carriage is governed by the Hague-Visby Rules, under which the weight limitation may be sufficiently high to cover the whole loss even if the container is a single package[38]; but even under such a contract the "package or unit" limitation is obviously capable of yielding a higher measure of recovery than the limitation based on weight. The answer to the question whether a container is a single package can therefore bear on (for example) the extent of the insurance cover to be provided by a seller under a c.i.f. contract.[39]

21–086 **Hague Rules.** The question put in paragraph 21–085 above has been much litigated in the United States, where the Hague-Visby Rules have not been adopted. Four tests or guidelines have been formulated for the purpose of determining whether it is the container or each of the items packed within it which constitutes "the" package for the purpose of the Hague Rules. Under the first, the courts have regard to the question of who provided the container; the fact that it was provided by the shipper favours the view that it was "the" package,[40] while the fact that it was provided by the carrier makes it more likely that each box or carton within the container is a separate package.[41] The second test is to ask who packed the container:

---

[35] Above, para.21–047.
[36] Art. IV(5)(a); the US Carriage of Goods by Sea Act 1936 uses slightly different language: "per package . . . or, in case of goods not shipped in packages, per customary freight unit." The phrase "goods not shipped in packages" has been held to apply where the bill of lading stated that goods (such as bulk goods or large items) had been shipped in a container but made no reference to any separate packaging within the container. Hence in some such cases the carrier was protected only by the "freight unit" and not by the "package" limitation: *Binladen BSB Landscaping Inc. v NV Nedlloyd Rotterdam* 759 F.2d 1006 (1985); *Morris Graphics Inc. v Trans Freight Lines Inc.* [1990] A.M.C. 2764. But where the "freight unit" is the container (because freight is charged per container) the result will be the same as it would be if the container were the "package" see *SWE Corp. v TFL Freedom* 704 F.Supp. 380 (1989).
[37] Art. IV(5)(a).
[38] See *McCarren & Co. Ltd v Humber International Transport Ltd (The Vechscroon)* [1982] 1 Lloyd's Rep. 301 at 304.
[39] Above, para.19–051.
[40] *Standard Electrica SA v Hamburg Süd-amerikanische Dampfschiffahrts-Gesellschaft*, 375 F.2d. 943 (1967); [1967] 2 Lloyd's Rep. 193 (pallet prepared by shipper); *Re Norfolk, Baltimore & Carolina Line Inc.* 478 F.Supp. 383 (1979).
[41] *Inter American Foods Inc. v Co-ordinated Caribbean Transport Inc.*, 313 F.Supp. 1334 (1970) (trailer sent by carrier to collect the goods). *Mitsui & Co. Ltd v American Export Lines Inc.* 636 F.2d. 807 (1981).

it is more likely to be "the" package if it was packed and sealed by the shipper[42] than if it was packed by (or under the supervision of) the carrier.[43] The third is the so-called "functional package"[44] or "functional economics"[45] test: if the goods could safely have been carried in the packages in which they were packed before being placed in the container, without the additional protection provided by it, there is a presumption that each such package was a separate package. A fourth test is to have regard to the way in which the consignment was described in the bill of lading: if the bill listed or enumerated the items within the container, each of those items was a separate package[46]; if it did not do so, or if it did not refer to them as separate packages, the container was the package.[47] None of these tests, standing alone, is however regarded as decisive, so that the resulting American position is one of considerable uncertainty. This uncertainty is the product of a conflict between two policies. The first is one of reluctance to regard the container as a single package, since so to regard it is thought

---

[42] *Royal Typewriter Co. v M/V. Kulmerland (The Kulmerland)*, 346 F.Supp. 1019 (1972); [1973] 1 Lloyd's Rep. 318; for further proceedings, see n.45 *infra*; *Re Norfolk, Baltimore & Carolina Line Inc.* 478 F.Supp. 383 (1979). *Cf. Acme Import Pty Ltd v Companhia de Navegaceo Lloyd Brasiliero (The Esmarelda*) [1988] 1 Lloyd's Rep. 207, where a similar question arose in the Supreme Court of New South Wales for the purpose of the estoppel discussed in para.18–028, above.

[43] *Leather's Best Inc. v The "Mormaclynx"*, 451 F.2d. 800 (1971); [1971] 2 Lloyd's Rep. 476; *cf. Shinko Boeki Co. Ltd v SS Pioneer Moon*, 507 F.2d. 342 (1974); [1975] 1 Lloyd's Rep. 199; *Mitsui & Co. Ltd v American Export Lines Inc.* 636 F.2d. 807 (1981).

[44] See *Royal Typewriter Co. v MV Kulmerland*, above; *Cameco Inc. v SS American Legion*, 514 F.2d 1291 (1974); [1975] 1 Lloyd's Rep. 295; this test was rejected in *Matsushita Electric Corp. of America v SS Aegis Spirit*, 414 F.Supp. 894 (1976); [1977] 1 Lloyd's Rep. 93; *Yeramex International v The Tendo*, 1977 A.M.C. 1807 at 1834, where the "functional economics" test would have led to the same results as that reached by the court; and in *Mitsui & Co. Ltd v American Export Lines Inc.* 636 F.2d. 807 (1981). The latter group of cases is referred to with apparent approval by Phillips L.J. in *River Gurara (Cargo-Owners) v Nigerian National Shipping Line Ltd (The River Gurara)* [1998] Q.B. 610 at 620–622.

[45] *Royal Typewriter Co. v MV Kulmerland (The Kulmerland)* [1973] 2 Lloyd's Rep. 428 at 431; *The River Gurara*, above, n.44, [1998] Q.B. 610 at 620.

[46] *Leather's Best Inc. v The "Mormaclynx,"* above; *St. Paul Fire & Marine Ins. Co. v Sea-Land Service Inc.* 735 F.Supp. 129 (1990) and 745 F.Supp. 189 (1990); *Seguros "Illimani" SA v M/V Popi* 929 F.2d 89 (1991); *cf. Sperry Rand Corp. v Norddeutscher Lloyd* [1973] A.M.C. 1392; [1974] 1 Lloyd's Rep. 122; and, in other jurisdictions, *JA Johnston Co. Ltd v The Tindefjell* [1973] 2 Lloyd's Rep. 253; *PS Chellaram & Co. Ltd v China Ocean Shipping Co.* [1989] 1 Lloyd's Rep. 413 at 427 (reversed on other grounds [1991] 1 Lloyd's Rep. 493). This test may also determine what amounts to a "package" within the container: see *Mitsui & Co. Ltd v American Export Lines Inc.* 636 F.2d. 807 (1981).

[47] *Royal Typewriter Co. Inc. v MV Kulmerland*, above; *Rosenbruch v American Export Isbrandtsen Lines*, 357 F. Supp. 982 (1973); [1974] 1 Lloyd's Rep. 119; *Re Norfolk, Baltimore & Carolina Line Inc.*, above; *contra, Matsushita Electric Corp. of America v SS Aegis Spirit*, above. *Cf. Browner International Ltd v Monarch Shipping Co. Ltd (The European Enterprise)* [1989] 2 Lloyd's Rep. 185 (container and vehicle carrying it to be regarded as a single package or unit). The assumption that each enumerated package within the container constituted a separate package was also made in the American case of *The OOCL Bravery* [2000] 1 Lloyd's Rep. 394, when the bill of lading was governed by the United States Carriage of Goods Act 1936 (below, n.49).

to be contrary to the spirit of the Hague Rules,[48] which have the force of law in the United States.[49] The second, by way of contrast, asserts that the parties should be free to define what constitutes the "package", and so to allocate risks between themselves, by the way in which they describe the shipment in the bill of lading. This second policy has been favoured by a number of later authorities[50] according to which items within the container will only be regarded as "packages" within the Rules if in the bill of lading they are separately listed and described as separate packages. This test had been adopted at first instance in *The River Gurara*,[51] an English case in which the contract of carriage was governed by the Hague Rules.[52] The bill of lading in that case listed the number of packages stowed within the containers and Colman J.[53] held that each package so listed constituted a separate "package" within the Hague Rules. This reasoning was accepted on appeal by Hirst L.J.; but it was rejected by Phillips L.J., with whose judgment Mummery L.J. agreed. In their view the description of the consignment in the bill of lading was not decisive for the present purpose: the question was to be determined "by reference to the particulars of the cargo and its packaging as it is *proved to have been on loading*, not by reference to the *description in the bill of lading*".[54] That description was no more than prima facie evidence which could be displaced by proof that the number of packages was in fact different from that stated in the bill. The policy reason for this view is that stated above,[55] *i.e.* that to make the terms of the bill of lading decisive on the point would enable the carrier to impose "unrealistically low limits of liability"[56] by describing the container as the package; though on the facts of *The River Gurara* no such result would have followed since the bill listed the items within the containers so that the two approaches led to substantially the same conclusion.[57] The approach of the majority of the Court of Appeal is, as Phillips L.J. recognised, open to the objections that it was "inconvenient and [could] lead to uncertainty"[58]; and that it might also, where the container was

---

[48] *Matsushita Electric Corp. of America v SS Aegis Spirit*, above; *cf. Shinko Boeki Co. Ltd v SS Pioneer Moon*, 507 F.2d 342 (1974); [1975] 1 Lloyd's Rep. 199; *Commonwealth Petrochemicals Ltd v S.S. Puerto Rico*, 455 F. Supp. 310 (1978); *Yeramex International v The Tendo* 1977 A.M.C. 1807 at 1834.

[49] US Carriage of Goods by Sea Act, 46 U.S.C. §§1300 *et seq.*

[50] *Binladen BSB Landscaping Inc. v NV Nedlloyd Rotterdam* 759 F.2d 1006 at 1015–1016 (1985) (announcing this test prospectively); *Hayes-Leger Association Inc. v M/V Oriental Knight* (1985) 765 F. 2d 1076; *DWE Corp v TFL Freedom* 704 F.Supp. 380 (1989). *Norwich Union Fire Ins. v Lykes Bros S.S. Co.* 741 F.Supp. 1051 at 1057 (1990).

[51] *River Gurara (Cargo Owners) v Nigerian National Shipping Line Ltd (The River Gurara)* [1998] Q.B. 610.

[52] Because shipment was from a country in which the Hague Rules were in force.

[53] [1996] 2 Lloyd's Rep. 53.

[54] [1998] Q.B. 610 at 625; *cf. Center Optical Hong Kong Ltd v Jardine Transport Services (Hong Kong) Ltd* [2001] 2 Lloyd's Rep. 678 at 688 (Hong Kong High Court).

[55] At n.48.

[56] [1998] Q.B. 610 at 624.

[57] The appeal was dismissed, though for different reasons from those given by Colman J.

[58] [1998] Q.B. 610 at 625.

stuffed and sealed by the shipper, expose the shipowner to liability to the consignee for more "packages" than were listed in the bill of lading, the accuracy of which in this respect he had no means of checking; though in the event of being held so liable the carrier might have a remedy over against the shipper.[59] These objections, however, could not (in the view of the majority) "justify an interpretation which the [Hague] rules cannot bear",[60] having regard to their legislative policy as stated above.

Hague-Visby Rules. So far as container transport is concerned, the first aspect of legislative policy stated in paragraph 21–086 above no longer prevails under the Hague-Visby Rules which adopt what is in substance the fourth of the American tests stated above and that accepted by Colman J. and Hirst L.J. in *The River Gurara*. Article IV(5)(c) of these Rules provides that "where a container, pallet or similar article of transport is used to consolidate goods, the number of packages or units enumerated in the bill of lading as packed in such article of transport shall be deemed the number of packages or units for the purpose of this paragraph as far as these packages or units are concerned. Except as aforesaid, such article of transport shall be considered the package or unit."[61] A purely formal test is thus adopted, no attempt being made (as it is in some of the American decisions) to base the result on practical or functional considerations affecting particular transactions. The statutory test has the advantage of promoting certainty and of thus enabling the parties to make appropriate insurance arrangements. A similar test has been applied at common law in an English case in which the Hague-Visby Rules were expressly incorporated (in part) into a contract to which they would not otherwise have applied.[62] Effect was given to a provision by which the container, together with the vehicle on which it was carried, was to be regarded as a single package or unit.[63] 21–087

Article IV(5)(c) of the Hague-Visby Rules refers to "a container, pallet or similar article of transport". As the reported cases indicate, it sometimes happens that pallets consisting of a number of individual packages are placed into a container[64]; and that the bill of lading then describes the goods in words such as "one container containing 30 pallets". It would seem that in such a case the pallets would be the "packages" under the Hague-Visby Rules. The same conclusion has been reached, as a matter of common law, in a number of American cases.[65] If, however, the bill went on

---

[59] *ibid.*
[60] *ibid.*
[61] See Lord Diplock, *Journal of Maritime Law and Commerce* 525, 532–536; De Gurse, *ibid.*, 131. *Cf.* the "Hamburg Rules" (a Convention adopted by the United Nations Conference on Carriage of Goods by Sea at Hamburg on March 30, 1978, but not yet having the force of law), Art. 6(2)(a). For the text of these Rules, see [1978] L.M.C.L.Q. 439; for comment, see *Carver on Bills of Lading* (2nd ed., 2005) paras 9–318, 9–319.
[62] Below, para.21–106.
[63] *Browner International Ltd v Monarch Shipping Co. Ltd (The European Enterprise)* [1989] 2 Lloyd's Rep. 185.
[64] *e.g. DuPont de Nemours v SS Mormacvega*, 493 F.2d 97 (1974); [1974] 1 Lloyd's Rep. 296; *Cameco Inc. v SS American Legion* 514 F.2d 1291 (1974).
[65] See the case cited in n.64, above.

to list the number of individual packages in or on each pallet, then each such package *could* be a separate one for the purposes of the Rules.[66] Whether they *would* be so regarded depends, according to an Australian case,[67] on the further question whether such package or unit had, in the words of Art. IV(5)(c), been "enumerated . . . *as packed* in" the container. In that case the bill of lading stated the number of packages to be "1" (*i.e.* the container) and added that this was "said to contain: 200945 pieces posters and prints".[68] These words were held not to amount to an enumeration of the number of packages or units within the container since they did not "identify, or identify with any clarity, how or in what manner the articles of cargo have been made up into packages or units"[69] for the purposes of transport.[70] The statement of the number of items within the container therefore did not constitute an "enumeration of packages or units *as packed*"[71]; and, there being no such enumeration in the bill, the container was, by virtue of the concluding words of Article IV(5)(c), "the package or unit".

There is no authority on the question whether the container itself may be a separate package or unit. Under the Hamburg Rules[72] (which as yet do not have the force of law) it is to be so regarded when it is not supplied by the carrier.[73]

(ii) *Carriage on deck*

21–088 **Legal consequences.** Containers are often carried on deck, and this form of carriage traditionally has (or had) two legal consequences.

21–089 **Possible exclusion of Hague-Visby Rules.** The first is that the Hague or Hague-Visby Rules do not apply to "cargo which by the contract of carriage is stated as being carried on deck *and* is so carried".[74] Where these conditions are satisfied, the carrier is therefore not subject to the restrictions on freedom of contract imposed by the Rules. Hence he is free to exclude liability, *e.g.* by providing that the goods are "shipped on deck at shipper's risk".[75] Often, however, it is not possible for the carrier to tell in

---

[66] See *The River Gurara*, above n.51.

[67] *El Greco (Australia) Pty Ltd v Mediterranean Shipping Co. SA* [2004] FCAFC 202, [2004] 2 Lloyd's Rep. 537.

[68] *ibid.*, at [112]–[113] and see the copy of the bill of lading set out at the end of the report.

[69] *ibid.*, at [307]. The 200945 pieces are said at [111] to have been "made up into about 2,000 packages", but this fact is not stated in the bill of lading and no attempt was made to argue that "there were in the container, in fact, 2,000 packages" (at [246]).

[70] See *ibid.* At [284].

[71] *ibid.*, at [150].

[72] Above, n.61.

[73] Art. 6(2).

[74] Art. 1(c).

[75] As in *J Evans & Sons (Portsmouth) Ltd v Andrea Merzario Ltd* [1976] 1 W.L.R. 1078; *cf. Transocean Reederei GmbH v Euxine Shipping Co. (The Imvros)* [1999] 1 Lloyd's Rep. 848.

advance exactly which containers will be carried on, and which under, deck. In such a case the bill of lading may not *state* that the container is carried on deck, and, if the bill contains no such statement, then the fact that the container is carried on deck will not prevent the Hague or Hague-Visby Rules from governing the contract of carriage. Hence the right of the carrier to exclude or limit liability will be restricted by the Rules. The question whether the carrier is entitled, in respect of goods wrongfully carried on deck, to the exceptions and limitations of liability provided by the Rules, however, depends on the second possible legal consequence of carriage on deck.

Carriage on deck as breach of a fundamental term? This second consequence of wrongful carriage on deck is more controversial. Such carriage without the previous consent of the shipper was formerly regarded as the equivalent of deviation, and hence as breach of a fundamental term.[76] It follows from this view that the carrier is, under the common law rules of construction which apply where such breaches have been committed, prima facie[77] deprived of the benefit of exceptions and limitations of liability contained in the contract of carriage, in respect of goods carried on deck. In *The Kapitan Petko Voivoda* the Court of Appeal rejected this view, at least so far as the carrier's limitations of liability are concerned, and treated the question whether such limitations apply simply as one of construction of the contract.[78] Three further questions, however, call for discussion. 21–090

Effect of the breach under the Hague Rules. The first such question arises where the contract is governed by the Hague Rules and the carrier relies (in respect of loss of or damage to goods carried, without the previous consent of the shipper, on deck) on the time limit on claims, or on the "package or unit" limitation.[79] The Rules state that the carrier is not to be liable, after the expiry of the specified time limit (of one year), or for more than the stipulated amount per package or unit "in any event", and it has been held in England that these words make the time limit[80] or package 21–091

---

[76] *cf.* above, para.18–266 and para.18–059. No reference is made to this rule of common law in *Browner International Ltd v Monarch Shipping Co. Ltd (The European Enterprise)* [1989] 2 Lloyd's Rep. 185, where the goods were stated to have been carried "on the upper deck" of a cross-Channel ferry; this may refer to a covered-in area and not to the "deck" in the traditional sense. No point relating to carriage "on deck" seems to have been taken on behalf of the shipper.

[77] The prima facie rule can be displaced, *e.g.* by an express provision that deck cargo is to be carried at shipper's risk: see *Kuwait Maritime Transport Co. v Rickmers Linie KG (The Danah)* [1993] 1 Lloyd's Rep. 351 at 354.

[78] *Daewo Heavy Industries Ltd v Klipriver Shipping Ltd (The Kapitan Petko Voivoda)* [2003] EWCA Civ 451, [2003] 1 All E.R. (Comm) 801, affirming [2002] EWHC 1306, [2002] 2 All E.R. (Comm) 810, where Langley J. had at [27]–[28] distinguished, for this purpose, between *exemptions* from and *limitations* of liability. See also *Stag Line Ltd v Foscolo Mango & Co* [1932] A.C. 328, esp. 340 (relating to the effect of deviation on "exceptions" under the Hague Rules): in *The Kapitan Petko Voivoda*, the Hague Rules had been incorporated *by contract*.

[79] Arts III(6) and IV(5)(a).

[80] *Kenya Railways v Antares Co. Pte Ltd (The Antares (No.2)* [1987] 1 Lloyd's Rep. 424.

or unit limitation[81] applicable even in cases of unauthorized carriage on deck. The decisions to this effect were not concerned with containerised cargo and in American cases concerning such cargo there is a conflict of opinion on the point. According to one view, the "package or unit" limitation applies, notwithstanding deviation[82]; but other cases[83] hold that deviation (including on-deck carriage of a container)[84] deprives the carrier of the benefit of the limitation.

21–092 **Effect of the breach under the Hague-Visby Rules.** The second question concerns the effect of unauthorised deviation under the Hague-Visby Rules. The legal nature of these Rules differs from that of the Hague Rules in that the Hague Rules take effect by virtue of contract (*i.e.* by virtue of their incorporation in the contract of carriage), while the Hague-Visby Rules have "the force of law",[85] so that the provision of these Rules which protect the carrier operate, not as contractual terms,[86] but as directly enacted limitations and exceptions. They can therefore override common law principles which govern the construction of contracts; the question whether they protect the carrier in cases of carriage on deck turns on the construction, not of the contract, but of the Rules. In *The Antares*[87] it was accordingly held that unauthorised carriage on deck did not deprive the carrier of the protection of the time limit on claims provided by Art. III(6) of the Rules: the court relied in particular on the emphatic statement in the Hague-Visby Rules that after one year the carrier was to be discharged from all liability "whatsoever".[88] This word does not occur in Art. IV(5)(a). which lays down the package or unit limitation, but in *The Kapitan Petko Voivoda*[89] the Court of Appeal held that this limitation protected a carrier who had wrongfully carried goods on deck because it was expressed to apply "in any event".[90] That case was concerned with the interpretation of the Hague Rules (which had there been incorporated by contract); but there seems to be no reason to suppose that the words "in any event"

[81] *The Kapitan Petko Voivoda*, above n.78, overruling *Wibau Maschinenfabrik Hartman SA v Mackinnon Mackenzie & Co. (The Chanda)* [1989] 2 Lloyd's Rep. 494 and by implication disapproving *Nelson Pine Industries v Seatrans New Zealand Ltd (The Pembroke)* [1995] 2 Lloyd's Rep 290 (New Zealand High Court): and see *Carver on Bills of Lading*, 2nd ed. (2005) para.9–058.

[82] *Atlantic Mutual Insurance v Poseidon Schiffahrt*, 313 F.2d 872 (1963).

[83] *Jones v The Flying Clipper*, 116 F.Supp. 386 (1963); *Encyclopedia Britannica v The Hong Kong Producer*, 422 F. 2d 7 (1969); [1969] 2 Lloyd's Rep. 536.

[84] *Encyclopedia Britannica v The Hong Kong Producer*, above; *cf.* (as to the effect of on deck carriage) *St. John's Shipping Corp. v SA Comparhia Geral do Rio De Janeiro* 263 U.S. 119 (1923).

[85] Carriage of Goods by Sea Act 1971, s.1(2).

[86] Except where they are incorporated by agreement into a contract to which they would not otherwise apply: see *Browner International Ltd v Monarch Shipping Co. Ltd (The European Enterprise)* [1989] 2 Lloyd's Rep. 185; below para.21–105, n.91.

[87] *Kenya Railways v Antares Co. Pte Ltd (The Antares)(No. 2)* [1987] 1 Lloyd's Rep. 424.

[88] In Art. III(6) of the Hague-Visby Rules. The word "whatsoever" does not occur in Art. III(6) of the Hague Rules.

[89] Above, para.21–090. n.78.

[90] These words occur also in Art. III(6), but the decision in *The Antares*, above n.87 was not based on them.

would not have the same meaning in the Hague-Visby Rules, where Art. IV(5)(a) lays down the package or unit or weight limitation. At first instance in *The Kapitan Petko Voivoda* Langley J. had, however, further held that the exemptions from liability contained in Art. 1V(2)(and in particular those which protected the carrier from liability in respect of perils of the sea and insufficiency of packing) were "properly construed to apply only to carriage under deck"[91] and there was no appeal on this point.[92] The question whether any, and if so which, of the other exceptions listed in Art. IV(2) protect a carrier in cases of unauthorised carriage on deck remains an open one. Since these exceptions are neither stated to apply "in any event", nor to discharge the carrier from all liability "whatsoever", it is arguable that they may be displaced by unauthorised on-deck carriage even where the time limit or the package or unit (or weight) limitation would not be so displaced. The point is one of considerable practical importance even where the bill is worded so as to make the container "the" package[93]; for, as already noted, the alternative "weight" limitation under the Hague-Visby Rules may, even in such a case, make a carrier who is deprived of the "exceptions" liable for very substantial amounts.[94]

Special factors affecting on deck carriage of containerised cargo. 21–093
Neither The *Antares* nor *The Kapitan Petko Voivoda* concerned containerised cargo; and this fact, as well as the continuing doubt on the point whether any, and if so which, of the Art. IV(2) exemptions apply to unauthorised carriage on deck,[95] raise the question whether the traditional approach[96] to such is appropriate at all in cases of container transport. A negative answer to this question was given by Kerr J. when he said that "It would be quite wrong to apply to this form of contract the old law originally evolved in relation to bill of lading contracts, so as to hold, that the mere fact of this container having been . . . carried on deck during this part of the transit involved the defendants in a fundamental breach of the whole contract."[97] The reason why it is wrong to apply the "old law" to this form of transport is that the physical risks of on-deck carriage are much reduced by containerisation. Whether the traditional rule applies depends, it is submitted, on a three-fold distinction. First, there are cases in which the carrier (or a multi-modal transport operator who is not himself the carrier by sea) makes an express contractual promise that the goods will be carried under deck. It has been held by the Court of Appeal that, if the goods are nevertheless carried on deck, the person who made the promise is in breach of a fundamental term and is not protected by exemption clauses in the contract of carriage.[98] Secondly, the container may be carried on the deck

---

[91] [2002] EWCH 1306 (Comm). [2002] 2 All E.R. (Comm) 56 at [27].
[92] See [2003] EWCA Civ 451, [2003] 1 All E.R. (Comm) 801 at [9].
[93] Art. IV(5)(c), above, para.21–087.
[94] Art. IV.5(a), above, para.21–085.
[95] See above, para.21–092 after n.92.
[96] See above, para.21–090 at n.76 and para.21–091 at n.83.
[97] *J Evans & Sons (Portsmouth) Ltd v Andrea Merzario Ltd* [1975] 1 Lloyd's Rep. 162 at 168; revsd. on another ground [1976] 1 W.L.R. 1078: see next note.
[98] *J Evans & Sons (Portsmouth) Ltd v Andrea Merzario Ltd*, above. The promise in that case was made by a forwarding agent or multimodal transport operator. The actual sea carrier had successfully excluded liability; *See* above, para.21–089, at n.75.

of a ship that is not a container ship. An American case holds that in this situation, too, carriage on deck amounts to deviation, so that the carrier is liable in full for any resulting loss[99]; though it is possible for this rule to be excluded by proof of a custom of the port of loading, permitting the carriage of containers on deck.[1] The third, and now the most common, type of case is that in which the container is carried on the deck of a ship specifically built (or adapted) for the purpose of carrying containers. In an American case of this kind, it was held that carriage on deck was not a breach,[2] amounting, at most, to a "reasonable deviation" permitted by the Hague (and Hague-Visby) Rules,[3] so that the carrier was entitled to the benefit of the limitation of liability provided by the Rules. It follows from this reasoning that the carrier would also be entitled to the protection of other provisions of the Rules; so that his liability for on-deck carriage in a container ship is no greater than that for under-deck carriage in a traditional cargo ship.

(d) *Sale Terms and Container Transport*

21–094 **Application of common sale terms in cases of combined container transport.** Sales of goods to be carried by multimodal container transport may be made on c.i.f., f.o.b.[4] and other similar terms. Many of the ordinary incidents attached to these terms will apply without any (or with very little) modification to such cases. For example, there is no reason why, if the sale is on c.i.f. terms, the buyer should not be obliged to pay against documents even though the goods have been lost; nor why, if the sale is on f.o.b. terms, he should not be obliged to give effective instructions as to the transportation of the goods; nor why the price should not be fixed on a c.i.f. basis (to include the cost of transport and insurance) or on an f.o.b. basis (not to include these items); nor why, if the sale is on terms analogous to an ex-ship contract, the seller should not be bound to deliver the actual goods at an agreed destination; nor why the passing of property should not depend on dealings with the documents, as under c.i.f. and frequently under f.o.b. contracts;[5] nor why there should not be separate rights of rejection of

---

[99] *Encyclopaedia Britannica v The Hong Kong Producer* 422 F. 2d 7 (1969), [1969] 2 Lloyd's Rep. 536.

[1] This is assumed in the *Encyclopaedia Britannica* case above, and in *DuPont de Nemours v SS Mormacvega*, 493 F.2d. 97 (1974); [1974] 1 Lloyd's Rep. 296; though in the former case the attempt to prove a custom failed, while in the latter the carrier was held entitled to limit his liability on another ground: see next note.

[2] *DuPont de Nemours v SS Mormacvega*, above; *cf. Mitsui & Co. Ltd v American Export Lines Inc.* 636 F.2d. 807 (1981), where the carrier's liability was in part limited under the Hague Rules by reference to the number of "packages" within containers carried on deck.

[3] Art. IV.4.

[4] *e.g. Frebold and Sturznickel (Trading as Panda OHG) v Circle Products Ltd* [1970] 1 Lloyd's Rep. 499; *PS Chellaram & Co. Ltd v China Ocean Shipping Co. (The Zhi Jiang Kou)* [1991] 1 Lloyd's Rep. 493.

[5] If the multimodal transport document were not a document to which the Carriage of Goods by Sea Act 1992 applied (see s.l(l) and above, para.21–076) nor a

the documents and the goods, as under c.i.f. and, in certain cases, under f.o.b. contracts.[6] But obviously certain other rules relating to the common terms of sale would require modification where the goods are to be sent by multimodal container transport, in that the consignor generally has little or no control over the goods after they are put in charge of the multimodal transport operator; while the consignee (or other person who may have acquired rights under the contract of carriage contained in or evidenced by the multimodal transport document[7]) usually does not acquire such control until the goods are delivered to him at the inland place of delivery. It would therefore seem appropriate for these points to be given the significance traditionally attached to the points at which the goods are loaded on, and discharged from, the carrying ship.[8] It is impossible at this stage of the development of the law relating to multimodal container transport to predict to what extent the courts will adopt this view, or to foresee more than a few of the problems which may arise. Some of these are discussed in the following paragraphs.

Shipping documents. The question whether a c.i.f. seller can perform his obligations by tendering a multimodal transport document is in some respects analogous to the question whether such a document is a document of title[9]; but the two questions are not identical. No doubt the prima facie rule, under which a c.i.f. seller must tender a shipped bill of lading[10] is partly based on the fact that only such a bill has the characteristics of a document of title at common law[11]; and the fact that a multimodal transport document will often at most be a received bill and so lack these characteristics[12] is one objection to the tender of such a document under a c.i.f. contract. Other objections to it are that it may not be issued by or on behalf of a carrier (but by a forwarding agent, acting on behalf of the shipper or as an independent contractor); that it may not be issued "on" 21–095

document of title in the traditional common law sense (above, para.21–081), then its transfer to the consignee (the buyer) could not (like the transfer of a bearer or an order bill of lading) transfer contractual rights or constructive possession to him. But this would not preclude the passing of property at this stage: this depends on the intention of the seller, who may intend property to pass on transfer of the document against payment even though that transfer does not produce the other consequences that would result from the transfer of a bill of lading.

[6] Though if the combined transport document does not contain a date of "shipment" (below, para.21–096) it is less likely that two separate rights to reject will arise: for example the situation in *Kwei Tek Chao v British Traders and Shippers* [1954] 2 Q.B. 459 (above, para.19–191) could not arise in relation to a document not containing that date.

[7] *e.g.* by assignment (above, para.18–147) or under the Contracts (Rights of Third Parties) Act 1999 (above, para.21–077). It is here assumed that the Carriage of Goods by Sea Act 1992 does not apply to multimodal transport documents (see above, para.21–076).

[8] Even before the advent of containerisation, c.i.f. contracts sometimes provided for despatch from, or delivery to, inland points: *e.g. Burstall v Grimsdale* (1906) 11 Com.Cas. 280; *Johnson v Taylor Bros & Co. Ltd* [1920] A.C. 144.

[9] Above, para.21–081.

[10] Above, para.19–030.

[11] Above, paras 18–063, 18–079.

[12] Above, para.21–079.

shipment[13] in the English sense,[14] referring to the placing of the goods on board ship; and that it will often not be in transferable form but be a "non-negotiable" or "straight" document.[15] One way in which a c.i.f. seller can avoid these difficulties is by procuring separate carriage documents for each stage of the multimodal transport[16] and tendering either the bill of lading alone or all those documents; though this would give rise to the problem whether he had provided "continuous documentary cover"[17] if (in the cases of multimodal transport) it were held that such cover was required between the inland points at which the goods were respectively put into and taken out of the container. Alternatively, the seller can rely on the possibility of relaxing the prima facie requirements as to tender of documents by the terms of the contract of sale. Just as a c.i.f. contract can expressly permit the seller to tender a delivery order instead of a bill of lading,[18] so it can expressly permit him to tender a multimodal transport document. The normal requirements as to tender of documents may similarly be relaxed by custom.[19] It is submitted that the seller's duty to tender a shipped bill should be relaxed in this way where the contract of sale envisages, or provides for, container transport. In such a case, tender of multimodal transport documents, if issued by, or on behalf of, *a sea carrier*, should be sufficient, for their now common use has probably made them "usual" documents[20] and thus enables them to satisfy the requirements of a c.i.f. contract. Alternatively, the fact that the contract of sale provided for container transport might give rise to an implied term permitting tender of such a document. Tender of a multimodal carriage document issued by *a forwarding agent* would probably not suffice[21] unless the contract of sale expressly gave the seller the right to tender a document of this kind, or unless the agent had acted, not only as such, but also as carrier,[22] or had signed the document on behalf of the carrier.[23]

---

[13] Above, para.19–034.
[14] Above, para.18–268.
[15] Above, paras 18–018, 18–067 *et seq*.
[16] This appears to have been done in *P. S. Chellaram & Co. Ltd v China Ocean Shipping Co. (The Zhi Jiang Kou)* [1991] 1 Lloyd's Rep. 493 (f.o.b. contract).
[17] Above, para.19–027; *cf.* above, para.21–080.
[18] Above, para.19–024.
[19] Above, para.19–024.
[20] Above, para.21–081 esp. at n.6. The fact that multimodal transport documents are acceptable to banks under UCP 500 Art. 26 supports the view that they are "usual" documents, even though it may *not* give them the characteristics of documents of title (see above, para 21–081). In *Burstall v Grimsdale* (1906) 11 Com.Cas. 280 no objection was taken to a combined transport document on the ground that it was not issued by a carrier by sea, but by an American rail carrier; and other objections to it were dismissed on the ground that it was a "usual" document: above, para.19–024. It should be recalled that in the United States a carriage document issued by a rail carrier is known as a bill of lading and recognised as a document of title: above, paras 18–012, n.95, 21–081, n.98.
[21] Above, para.21–081.
[22] Above, para.21–073; *cf.* UCP 500 Art. 30(i).
[23] Above, paras 21–073, 21–081; *cf.* UCP 500 Art. 30(ii).

Date of shipment. Under c.i.f. and f.o.b. contracts, stipulations as to the time of shipment refer (in English law) to the time at which the goods are put on board the carrying ship[24]; and such stipulations must be strictly complied with. For example, a c.i.f. seller must ensure that the goods are put on board within the shipment period specified in the contract[25]; while an f.o.b. buyer must give shipping instructions which enable the seller to put the goods on board by the end of that period,[26] and the seller must then load within that period.[27] Where multimodal container transport is used, the time at which the goods are put on board is, however, wholly outside the control of buyer and seller. Hence it would seem more appropriate to have regard, for these purposes[28] to the times at which the goods are placed into the container and put in charge of the multimodal transport operator. In *Customs & Excise Commissioners v ApS Samex*[29] goods were sold on c.i.f. terms and packed into a container which was taken by lorry to the loading port, there taken off the lorry and eventually put on board ship. Bingham J. said: "It may be that, where goods are consigned inland in a container, where there will be no transhipment, no unpacking and no breaking bulk, goods may be shipped at that earlier moment, but that, as I understand the facts, is not this case since in any event the goods were unloaded from the lorries at the docks and awaiting loading in the vessel."[30] As such unloading would normally take place, except where the sea transit was short, Bingham J.'s dictum might seem to suggest that in the normal case, where containers are unloaded from a lorry or train before being placed on board ship, they would not be "shipped" until they were actually loaded on the ship. But in the *Samex* case the learned judge was concerned with the interpretation of the word "shipped" in an EEC regulation (and in an import licence issued under it) requiring goods to be "shipped" by the end of 1979.[31] In this context, "shipped" was no doubt intended to indicate that the movement of the goods out of the country of origin was imminent. Where the word is used in a contract of sale, its meaning must depend on the intention of the parties, to whom the question whether the goods were unloaded from the lorry or train at the port might not be decisive, particularly if the process of multimodal transport was regarded as a single operation in a commercial sense. For this purpose, the fact that a contracting party has done all that 21–096

---

[24] Above, para.18–268; for a possible qualification see above, para.20–090. Contrast the American position stated in UCC, s.2–320, Comment 13, under which "shipment by rail . . . within the contract period" is good. Under the proposed (2003) amendments to Art. 2 of the UCC s.2–320 is to be deleted.

[25] Above, paras 19–012, 19–013.

[26] Above, paras 20–029 *et seq.*, 20–040 *et seq.*

[27] Above, para.20–029.

[28] Though not for the purpose of specifying the date of shipment in a bill of lading issued by a sea carrier: see *United City Merchants (Investments) Ltd v Royal Bank of Canada (The American Accord)* [1983] 1 A.C. 168; *cf. Customs Commissioners v ApS Samex* [1983] 1 All E.R. 1042, where two "bills of lading" were issued—one by the initial land carrier and one by the sea carrier.

[29] [1983] 1 All E.R. 1043; above, para.18–268.

[30] At p.1051.

[31] The goods had been sold on c.i.f. tenns under a contract which required them to be shipped by January 1980 and they were in fact put on board the carrying ship on January 15.

he can normally be expected to do in the performance of his obligation in relation to "shipment" may be of more significance than the fact that the container was unloaded from the lorry or train before being placed on board ship.

21–097 **Shipping instructions, etc.** The duty of an f.o.b. buyer to nominate an effective ship[32] appears to be inapposite where the goods are to be conveyed by multimodal container transport; it can at most be a duty to nominate a multimodal transport operator who is ready and willing to take charge of the goods from the seller. It is submitted that the seller would discharge his duty of delivery under an f.o.b. contract by transferring possession to the multimodal transport operator and that, as between buyer and seller, any expenses payable before or at the moment of such transfer would fall on the seller. On the other hand if the sale was on f.a.s.[33] terms any expenses payable at the moment of transfer of possession would, as between buyer and seller, fall on the buyer, the seller being responsible only for those payable before transfer. Thus if (for example) duty was payable on delivery to the multimodal transport operator, it would be payable by the seller under an f.o.b. contract and by the buyer under an f.a.s. contract. The above submissions assume that the multimodal transport operator is himself a carrier. If he is not a carrier but rather in the position of a forwarding agent, and if he does not obtain possession of the goods,[34] delivery would take place on the transfer of possession of the goods to the first carrier engaged by such a multimodal transport operator.

21–098 **Passing of property.** Under an f.o.b. contract property is sometimes said to pass on shipment, though it is probably more accurate to say that it does not normally pass before shipment.[35] In cases of multimodal container transport, the more appropriate rule would, it is submitted, be that property does not normally pass before the goods are delivered to the multimodal transport operator, or, if he is a forwarding agent, before they are delivered to the first carrier engaged by him.[36] Unless the seller retains a right of disposal or there is other evidence of contrary intention, property will pass at this point under section 18, rule 5(2) of the Sale of Goods Act 1979, *i.e.* by virtue of the delivery of the goods "to a carrier or other bailee . . . for the purpose of transmission to the buyer", without any reservation of a right of disposal.

Section 19(2), which provides that a seller who takes a bill of lading to his own order is prima facie taken to reserve a right of disposal, is not easy to

---

[32] Above, paras 20–042, 20–043.
[33] Above, para.20–010.
[34] *Jones v European and General Express Co. Ltd* (1920) 25 Com.Cas. 296; *Marston Excelsior Ltd v Arbuckle and Smith & Co. Ltd* [1971] 2 Lloyd's Rep. 306. *Cf. Upman v Elkan* (1871) L.R. 12 Eq. 140; but it is far from clear in what sense the expression "forwarding agent" is used in that case. A forwarding agent may also be a carrier (above, para.21–073) or some other kind of bailee: *Norwich Pharmacal Co. v Commissioners of Customs* [1974] A.C. 133 at 140.
[35] Above, para.20–071.
[36] Above, para.21–097.

apply to the situation under discussion since the subsection begins with the words "Where the goods are shipped". But it is submitted that, quite apart from the subsection, property would not pass on delivery to the multimodal transport operator where a seller took a multimodal transport document from a carrier making the goods deliverable to his own order; or indeed where he took such a document making the goods deliverable to the buyer or his order and did not transfer the document to him. For a multimodal transport document in such a form would appear to have this much in common with a bill of lading, that delivery of the goods could not be demanded from the combined transport operator without producing the document[37]; and its retention by the seller would therefore be evidence of his intention to reserve the right of disposal. The position is less clear where (as appears to be commonly the case) the document was expressed to be "not negotiable" or made the goods deliverable simply to a named consignee, without adding words importing transferability; or where it was issued by a forwarding agent and was not such that any holder of it could claim delivery of the goods, but was one entitling the consignee named in it to claim delivery without producing it[38] (or one of its copies or parts, where it was issued as one of a set). In such cases the document would certainly not be a document of title in the traditional common law sense.[39] This fact would weaken the seller's control over the goods at the destination and would consequently, at least if he knew that this was the position, also weaken the inference that, by retaining the document, he intended to reserve the right of disposal. Where goods are carried under such a document, the seller might, indeed, have power to redirect the goods to another consignee (as under a sea waybill[40]) and so retain some degree of control over the goods. Since this power to redirect the goods does not seem to depend on the seller's being in possession of the document, its retention by him would not of itself be evidence of his intention to reserve the right of disposal. It could, however, be a ground for invoking the presumption that, in overseas sales, a seller does not intend to relinquish property until he has been paid in full.[41] A stipulation for payment against the document could be a ground for giving effect to that presumption even though possession of the document was not, as a matter of law, necessary to give the seller control over the goods.

Delivery. Under section 32(1) of the Sale of Goods Act 1979 "delivery of the goods to a carrier" is in certain circumstances deemed to be delivery to the buyer. It is submitted that the carrier in question would be the multimodal transport operator, or, where that person was a forwarding agent,[42] **21–099**

[37] *cf.* above, para.21–082. Contrast the position in cases of international carriage by air, road and rail (above, paras 21–052, 21–060, 21–066, 21–067).
[38] As in *The Maheno* [1977] 1 Lloyd's Rep. 81, above, para.21–081.
[39] *cf.* above, paras 18–075, 18–076 and 21–081.
[40] Above, para.18–025; a multimodal carriage document would not be a sea waybill within Carriage of Goods by Sea Act 1992, s.1(3) see above, para.21–076; hence s.2(5) of that Act (which preserves the shipper's right to redirect the goods) would not in terms apply to it.
[41] See above, paras 18–209, 19–103, 20–082.
[42] Above, paras 21–073, 21–097.

the first actual carrier engaged by him.[43] It is further submitted that the traditional view that "shipment" in an English contract means the loading of the goods on a ship (as opposed to some vehicle for inland transport)[44] should not apply where the contract of sale allowed for, or envisaged, multimodal container transport.[45]

Where the buyer deals as consumer[46] section 32(1) "must be ignored"; and even "if in pursuance of the contract of sale the seller is authorised or required to send the goods to the buyer, delivery of the goods to the carrier is not delivery of the goods to the buyer".[47] It might seem to follow that delivery to the consumer did not occur until the goods were taken out of the container and transferred into his actual possession. But this would not, it is submitted, necessarily be the position. In particular, where all the arrangements for carriage were made by the buyer, the situation might be regarded as one, or as analogous to one, in which the buyer had sent his own transport to collect the good.[48] In that case, delivery might be taken to have occurred when the goods were handed over to the multimodal transport operator.

21–100 **Risk.** Under the usual terms of overseas sales, risk often passes on shipment (as in c.i.f.[49] or f.o.b. contracts) or when the goods are unloaded from the ship (as in ex ship contracts). Where the stage of land transit precedes or follows that of sea transit, it is common for the goods to be at the risk of one party at one of these stages, and at the risk of the other during the following stage. These rules could without great difficulty be applied to multimodal container transport where the container was lost or wholly destroyed at a particular, identifiable, stage of the transit; or where it was clearly established that loss by theft of all or part of the contents of the container had taken place at one such stage: *e.g.* before the container was put on board.[50] But they would be inappropriate where goods within a container deteriorate or are damaged, for in such a case it may be

---

[43] *cf.* Vienna Convention on Contracts for the International Sale of Goods (above, para.1–024), Art. 31(a).

[44] *Mowbray Robinson & Co. v Rosser* (1922) 91 L.J.K.B. 524; above, para.18–268.

[45] *cf.* above, para.21–095.

[46] See (in cases of overseas sales) above, para.18–259. A consumer is highly unlikely to be the buyer of the entire contents of a container, but there is a somewhat greater possibility of his having bought an item or items in a container filled with goods intended for several consignees (see above, para.21–072).

[47] Sale of Goods Act 1979, s.32(4). discussed in relation to overseas sales in para.18–260 above.

[48] See above, paras 21–011 n.35, 18–262.

[49] Under c.i.f. contracts, risk may also pass "as from" shipment: above, paras 19–110, 19–112.

[50] As in *NSW Leather Co. Pty Ltd v Vanguard Insurance Co. Ltd* (1991) 25 N.S.W.L.R. 699, where goods which had been sold on f.o.b. terms were packed into containers by agents of (apparently) the sellers and were then taken by thieves out of the containers before these had been put on board. It was said by a majority of the Supreme Court of New South Wales (Kirby P. *dubitante*) that, at the time of the theft, the risk had not yet passed to the buyer. The actual decision was that the buyer was nevertheless entitled to recover the value of the goods from his insurers by virtue of a "lost or not lost" clause in the policy.

impossible to tell at what stage of the transit the damage had occurred. It is accordingly submitted that the risk of deterioration or damage should pass at the point at which possession of the goods is given to,[51] or (as the case may be) relinquished by, the multimodal transport operator.[52]

Where the buyer deals as consumer,[53] section 20(4) of the Sale of Goods Act 1979 provides that "the goods remain at the seller's risk until they are delivered to the consumer".[54] The difficulties which arise in applying this provision to overseas sales on c.i.f. and f.o.b. terms have been discussed earlier in this book.[55] They relate, in particular, to the questions when "delivery" takes place under such contracts and whether section 20(4) can be excluded by express or implied agreement. Those discussions apply *mutatis mutandis* where the carriage operation is a multimodal one: and it should not, therefore, be assumed that there can be no "delivery" until the goods are taken out of the container and handed over to the buyer. It is, however, clear that some parts of those discussions cannot be applied without modification where the carriage operation is a multimodal one. For example, since a multimodal transport document is not a document of title in the traditional common law sense,[56] the transfer of such a document could not be the "symbolical delivery" which forms one of the "three stages of delivery"[57] in a c.i.f. contract.

Seller's duty to give notice enabling the buyer to insure. One particular difficulty as to risk in sales involving multimodal container transport arises from section 32(3) of the Sale of Goods Act 1979 under which goods remain at the seller's risk if he fails to perform his duty to give notice to the 21–101

[51] The Vienna Convention on Contracts for the International Sale of Goods (above, para.1–024), Art. 67(1) lays down two rules which apply where "the contract of sale involves carriage". The first applies "where the seller is not bound to hand [the goods] over at a particular place" and provides that risk passes when the goods are handed over to the first carrier for transmission to the buyer: this would typically apply to a c.i.f. contract. The second applies "where the seller is bound to hand the goods over to a carrier at a particular place" and provides that risk does not pass until the goods are handed over to the carrier at that place: this could apply to an f.o.b. contract, at least if the circumstances were such that the contract was one which "involves carriage" (*cf.* above, para.20–088, n.94). Where the contract does not involve carriage, Art. 69(1) provides that risk passes "when [the buyer] takes over the goods". None of these provisions refers to "shipment"; it seems that, where the goods were carried by combined transport in a container they would lead to the same results as those suggested (as a matter of common law) in the text above.

[52] Such a view would not, as was suggested in the *NSW Leather* case, above n.50, at p.705, give rise to unacceptable uncertainty: the concept of goods being in the possession of the multimodal transport operator is no more uncertain than that of "shipment": *cf.* above paras 18–268, 20–089, 20–090. The uncertainty in the *NSW Leather* case arose because the buyer also argued that risk might pass at one of a number of *other* stages in the performance of the contract, and it was not clear how the choice between these stages was to be made.

[53] See above, paras 18–259 and 21–099, n.40.

[54] Discussed, in relation to overseas sales in paras 18–259 to 18–264 above.

[55] See above, paras 18–261, 18–262, 18–229F. 19–123 and 20–094.

[56] See above, para.21–081.

[57] See above, para.19–072.

buyer enabling him to insure.[58] This subsection generally does not apply to c.i.f. contracts, but it may apply to some f.o.b. contracts.[59] The subsection is hard to apply to cases of multimodal container transport as it refers three times to "sea transit": it applies where the goods are sent by a route involving sea transit; it imposes on the seller a duty to give notice enabling the buyer to insure during sea transit; and if the seller fails to give such notice the goods are at his risk during sea transit. This constant emphasis on sea transit makes it very difficult to argue that the duty to give notice applies in relation to land transit which precedes, or follows, the sea transit in cases of multimodal container transport: and yet, if the duty exists at all in such cases, it clearly should relate to the whole of the transit. Perhaps such a duty to give notice enabling the buyer to insure during the whole transit could be said to arise at common law or by analogous extension of section 32(3).[60]

21–102 **Place of examination and damages.** A buyer may lose the right to reject goods by "acceptance" and the question whether he has accepted the goods may depend on whether he has had a reasonable opportunity of examining the goods.[61] In the case of a c.i.f. contract this opportunity usually arises at the stage of "complete delivery",[62] that is, delivery of the goods at the agreed destination. In the case of an f.o.b. contract, "delivery" takes place when the goods are put on board, but it is impossible to lay down any general rule for determining whether the point of inspection is that point or the point at which the goods actually get into the possession of the buyer.[63] Where the goods are sent by container, the nature of the packing will generally make the place where the goods are put on board ship inappropriate as the place of examination.[64] Where the point of inspection would normally be on complete delivery to the buyer, the same rule will

[58] Above, para.18–246.
[59] Above, paras 18–246, 18–247, 19–117, 20–091. Where the buyer deals as consumer, s.32(3) "must be ignored" (s.32(4)). For the difficulties arising from this provision, see above, paras 18–261, 18–264, 19–123. For the possibility of the buyer's dealing as consumer, see above, paras 18–259, 21–099; n.46. *Cf.* Vienna Convention on Contracts for the International Sale of Goods (above, para.1–024), Art. 32(3) (which is not expressed in terms of risk).
[60] The objection that s.32(3) is based on Scots and not on English law (see *Wimble Sons & Co. v Rosenberg & Sons* [1913] 3 K.B. 743 at 761) should no longer be decisive now that the principle has been a part of English law for over 100 years.
[61] Sale of Goods Act 1979, s.35.
[62] Above, para.19–072. *Cf.* The Vienna Convention on Contracts for the International Sale of Goods (above, para.1–024) likewise makes the destination of the goods the point of examination: Art. 38(2).
[63] Above, paras 20–108 to 20–110. Under the Vienna Convention on Contracts for the International Sale of Goods (above, para.1–024), the question would be whether an f.o.b. contract would be one which "involves carriage of the goods" within Art. 38(2); *cf.* above, n.51. If so, the destination would be the point of examination. If not, the buyer would have to examine the goods "within as short a period as is practicable in the circumstances": Art. 38(1). In the case of an f.o.b. contract, the point of examination might under this rule be either the place of shipment or the destination, depending on where the buyer had facilities for examination.
[64] *cf. Molling & Co. v Dean & Son Ltd* (1901) 18 T.L.R. 217; *Van den Hurk v R Martens & Co Ltd* [1920] 1 K.B. 850 (above, para.20–109).

apply in cases of multimodal container transport, though that point will be, not the place where the container is discharged from the ship, but the inland point at which the goods are delivered to the buyer. Where on the other hand the point of inspection would normally be the point at which the goods are put on board ship it is submitted that, in cases of container transport, it will be the place at which the goods are put into the hands of the multimodal transport operator.[65] The rules relating to the time and place for assessing damages[66] would, it is submitted, be modified in the same way where the goods were to be conveyed by multimodal container transport: *i.e.* the point of "shipment" would become the point at which the goods were to be put into the hands of the combined transport operator,[67] and the destination would be the inland point at which the goods are delivered to the buyer.

Where the buyer deals as consumer.[68] further difficulties arise from the fact that the buyer has certain "additional rights" under Part 5A of the Sale of Goods Act 1979 if "the goods do not conform to the contract at the time of delivery".[69] One of these rights is the right, in specified circumstances,[70] to "rescind" the contract."[71] Exercise of this right can produce practical results similar to those of rejection; and the right to "rescind" under Part 5A is not barred by acceptance. But its exercise does depend on non-conformity of the goods "at the time of delivery"; and the difficulties that arise from determining when this time occurs in c.i.f. and f.o.b. contracts have already been discussed.[72] Those discussions apply *mutatis mutandis* where the carriage operation is a multimodal one.

Stoppage in transit.[73] For the purpose of the right of stoppage, transit may begin when the goods are handed to the combined transport operator, whether he is a "carrier" or not; for section 45(1) of the Sale of Goods Act 1979 provides that "goods are deemed to be in the course of transit from the time when they are delivered to a carrier *or other bailee* . . ." Section 45(5), which provides for the case of delivery of the goods "to a ship chartered by the buyer", is in practice unlikely to apply to cases of multimodal container transport; though under this subsection it is theoretically possible (in the event of the buyer's chartering a container ship) for the transit to end when the container is put on board. 21–103

[65] Or, if the multimodal transport operator is a forwarding agent who does not himself take possession of the goods, the time when the goods are put into the hands of the first actual carrier engaged by him: *cf.* above, para.21–073.

[66] Above, paras 19–177, 19–186, 19–201, 19–216 (c.i.f.); paras 20–115—20–116, 20–133 *et seq.*, (f.o.b.); para.21–031 (ex ship).

[67] Subject to the qualification stated in n.65, above.

[68] See above, paras 18–259, 21–099, n.40.

[69] Sale of Goods Act 1979, s.48A(l)(b).

[70] *ibid.*, s.48C(2).

[71] *ibid.*, ss.48A(2)(b)(i).48C(l)(b).

[72] Above, paras 19–123, 20–113.

[73] For an analogous right, see Vienna Convention on Contracts for the International Sale of Goods (above, para.1–024), Art. 71(2).

(e) *Provisions for Mixed Carriage*

21–104 **Container transport governed by existing conventions.** Under the Hague or Hague-Visby Rules,[74] the expression "contract of carriage" "applies only to contracts of carriage covered by a bill of lading or any similar document of title, *in so far as such document relates to the carriage of goods by sea*."[75] It is true that the Rules envisage the issue of a "received" bill of lading[76] and that the exact point at which "carriage . . . by sea" begins to some extent depends on the agreement of the parties, so that, for example, the process of loading may be part of the carriage by sea.[77] But the words italicised above make it plain that if a shipowner issued a multimodal transport document (which would at most be a "received" bill) showing receipt of the goods at an inland point and carried the goods by road or rail to a seaport, then the land part of the carriage would not be governed by the Hague or Hague-Visby Rules.[78] The position is similar under the 1955 amended (Warsaw) Convention, the MP4 Convention and the 1999 Montreal Convention[79] which provide[80] that, in cases of combined carriage, performed partly by air and partly by some other mode of carriage, the Convention shall apply only to the air part of the carriage; and then only if that part is "international carriage" as defined by the Conventions.[81] Of course it may be possible to apply the Hague and Hague-Visby Rules and the above air carriage Conventions to part of the carriage to which they do not, of their own force, apply by expressly so providing in the contract of carriage; though such an express term may be invalid if it purports to reduce the liability of the carrier under some other Convention which has the force of law and applies to the part of the carriage in question. For example, an attempt by contract to apply the Hague-Visby Rules to road carriage preceding carriage by sea might be ineffective on the ground that it contravened the CMR Convention and the Carriage of Goods by Road Act 1965,[82] since the CMR Convention imposes higher standards of liability than the Hague-Visby Rules.[83] The financial limit of the carrier's liability (in the absence of a special agreement raising it) is also different under the two Conventions.[84]

---

[74] Above, para.21–047.
[75] Carriage of Goods by Sea Act 1971, Sch., Art. I(b).
[76] *ibid.*, art. III, r. (3), (7); *cf.* above, para.18–027.
[77] *Pyrene Co. Ltd v Scindia Navigation Co. Ltd* [1954] 2 Q.B. 402, the reasoning of which was approved in *Jindal Iron & Steel Co. Ltd v Islamic Solidarity Shipping Co. Jordan Inc. (The Jordan II)* [2004] UKHL 49, [2005] 1 W.L.R. 363.
[78] *Mayhew Foods Ltd v Overseas Containers Ltd* [1984] 1 Lloyd's Rep. 317 at 320; *Bhatia Shipping and Agencies PVT Ltd v Alcobex Metals Ltd* [2004] EWHC 2323 (Comm.), [2005] 2 Lloyd's Rep. 336 at [21].
[79] For these three Conventions, see above, para.21–047.
[80] Art. 31 of the 1955 amended and MP4 Conventions; Art. 38 of the 1999 Montreal Convention.
[81] Above, para.21–051.
[82] Above, paras 21–058 *et seq.*
[83] See, for example, *Michael Galley Footwear Ltd v Iaboni* [1982] 2 All E.R. 200.
[84] Contrast Carriage of Goods by Road Act 1965, Sch., Art. 23(3), as amended by Carriage by Air and Road Act 1979, s.4(2), with Carriage of Goods by Sea Act 1971,

The CMR Convention on international carriage by road may apply (unlike the Hague or Hague-Visby Rules and the 1955 amended (Warsaw) Convention, the MP4 Convention and the 1999 Montreal Convention[85]) to the *whole* carriage in cases of multimodal carriage.[86] It would, for example, apply where, for part of the journey, the vehicle containing the goods is carried by sea and the goods are not unloaded from the vehicle[87]: this commonly happens when containers are carried by what is known as the "roll-on/roll-off" method. Similarly, certain contracts for the international carriage of goods by rail may be wholly governed by the CIM Uniform Rules even though the goods are carried for part of the journey by sea.[88] It is also possible for one of the Conventions to apply to part of the carriage since a contract can be one "for the carriage of goods by road" within the CMR Convention, if it provides for or permits part of the carriage operation to be so carried out, even though a larger part of it is carried out by some other means of transport and so is governed during that part by one of the other Conventions.[89] Moreover, even where the whole carriage is governed by the CMR Convention or the CIM Uniform Rules, the Hague-Visby Rules do not for that reason alone become wholly irrelevant. They may to some extent govern even the relations between the sender (or consignor) and the road or rail carrier[90]; and, even where this is not the case, they may still govern the relations between that carrier and the sea carrier: for example, where the sea carrier issues to the road carrier a bill of lading which provides that the Hague-Visby Rules are to govern the contract of carriage, or a non-negotiable receipt if the contract contained in or evidenced by it is a contract for the carriage of goods by sea which expressly provides that the Rules are to govern the contract as if the receipt were a bill of lading.[91] 21–105

Sch., Art. IV(5). In the American case of *The OOCL Bravery* [2000] 1 Lloyd's Rep. 394, the entire carriage by sea and road was expressed to be subject to the United States Carriage of Goods by Sea Act 1936 and the limitations of liability under that Act, which were *higher* than those of the CMR Convention, were held to apply to loss occurring during the final stage of transport from Antwerp to an inland destination in the Netherlands. See also above, para.21–074, n.44 for this case and the contrasting American case of *Norfolk Southern Railway Co. v James N. Kirby Pty Ltd* 125 S.Ct.385 (2004).

[85] See the provisions of these three Conventions referred to in para.21–104 n.80.

[86] Above, paras 21–058, 21–059.

[87] "Vehicle" includes trailer: Carriage of Goods by Road Act 1965, Sch., Art. 1(2).

[88] Above, paras 21–058, 21–065.

[89] *Quantum Corp. Inc. v Plane Trucking Ltd* [2002] EWCA Civ 350. [2002] 1 W.L.R. 2678, above para.21–076 n.60.

[90] Above, paras 21–059 (CMR Convention); where the CIM Uniform Rules govern the whole carriage, the sea carrier's liability is broadly similar to that to which he would be subject under the Hague or Hague-Visby Rules: above, para.21–065.

[91] Carriage of Goods by Sea Act 1971, s.1(6)(b); *McCarren & Co. Ltd v Humber International Transport Ltd (The Vechscroon)* [1982] 1 Lloyd's Rep. 301; above, paras 21–058, 21–065. There is a conflict between this case and *Browner International Ltd v Monarch Shipping Co. Ltd (The European Enterprise)* [1989] 2 Lloyd's Rep. 185 as to the meaning of the formal requirements for such incorporation set out in Carriage of Goods by Sea Act 1971, s.1(6)(b), and as to the possibility of so incorporating a part only of the Rules.

21–106 There is a further difference between the various Conventions on international carriage which is relevant for the present purpose. The air carriage Conventions, the CMR Convention and the CIM Uniform Rules apply as a matter of law to all carriage which is "international carriage" within the Conventions. The Hague or Hague-Visby Rules, however, are in this sense facultative, that they only apply where the contract of carriage is "covered by a bill of lading or any similar document of title"[92] or, under the Carriage of Goods by Sea Act 1971, if the contract is contained in or evidenced by a non-negotiable receipt which expressly provides that the Hague-Visby Rules are to govern the contract as if it were a bill of lading .[93] The parties may therefore be able to exclude the Rules by agreeing that their relations are to be governed by a charterparty[94] or by some other agreement made before shipment, not superseded by a bill of lading[95] and having contractual force[96]; they can also do so by special agreement "in regard to particular goods" provided that no bill of lading is issued and provided that the goods are not an ordinary commercial shipment made in the ordinary course of trade.[97] But once the statutory conditions for the applicability of the Hague-Visby Rules are satisfied, they have "the force of law" in the United Kingdom and cannot be excluded to the prejudice of the shipper.[98] The position is further complicated by the fact that a multimodal transport document may expressly provide that the air, road or rail part of the carriage shall be governed by air carriage Conventions, by the CMR Convention or by the CIM Uniform Rules, as the case may be[99]; and that, if it cannot be proved where damage to the goods occurred, liability for such damage shall be governed by the Hague or Hague-Visby Rules. If however the whole carriage is actually governed by a different Convention, which has the force of law, such provisions might well be attempts to exclude or vary the terms of the applicable Convention and therefore be void in law. This would be the case, for example, if the whole carriage was within the CMR Convention or the CIM Uniform Rules and the carrier attempted to define his liability by reference to the (in the circumstances) more lenient Hague or Hague-Visby Rules. Of course the converse possibility would cause no such difficulty as it is open to the carrier under any of the

---

[92] Carriage of Goods by Sea Act 1971, s.1(2) and (3) and Sch., Art. I(b); the Rules can also apply to a bill of lading not within these provisions if it expressly incorporates the Rules: *ibid.*, s.1(6)(a).

[93] *ibid.*, s.1(6)(b) (as to which see n.91 above).

[94] *e.g. Exercise Shipping Co. Ltd v Bay Maritime Lines Ltd (The Fantasy)* [1991] 2 Lloyd's Rep. 391 (affirmed [1992] 1 Lloyds Rep. 235).

[95] Above, para.18–047 at n.75.

[96] *cf.* above, para.18–047.

[97] Carriage of Goods by Sea Act 1971, Sch., Art. VI; see *Harland & Wolff Ltd v Burns & Laird Lines* 1931 S.C. 722; *McCarren & Co. Ltd v Humber International Transport Ltd (The Vechscroon)* [1982] 1 Lloyd's Rep. 301; *Re Welsh Irish Ferries Ltd* [1985] 2 Lloyd's Rep. 372.

[98] Carriage of Goods by Sea Act 1971, s.1(2) and Sch., Art. III(8); *The Hollandia* [1983] 1 A.C. 565. *Cf.* above, para.21–089.

[99] The relevant Convention may then by force of contract apply even to cases where the carriage would not under the rules stated in paras 21–051, 21–058, 21–059 or 21–065 fall within its scope as a matter of law: *Princes Buitoni Ltd v Hapag-Lloyd AG* [1991] 2 Lloyd's Rep. 383.

Conventions to increase his liability. Even in such a case, however, difficulties might arise in that the documents relating to the carriage would have to be those required by the Convention as a matter of law actually applicable, and certain other rights, such as the rights of disposition or disposal or to modify the contract of carriage and to demand delivery of the documents and the goods[1] would likewise be governed by that Convention.

[1] See the air carriage Conventions (above, para.21–047), Art. 12, CMR Convention Arts 12(1), 13, CIM Uniform Rules, Arts 17, 18, 19.

Chapter 22

NEGOTIABLE INSTRUMENTS IN OVERSEAS SALES

	PARA.
1. Introduction	22–001
2. Direct payment by banker	22–006
(a) Payment on open account	22–006
(b) Payment by bankers' draft	22–018
3. Payment by use of bill of exchange	22–031
(a) Nature of negotiable instruments	22–031
(b) Nature of bills of exchange	22–038
4. Discount and collection of bills of exchange	22–067
(a) Engagement of banker	22–067
(b) The Uniform Rules for Collections	22–076
(c) Liabilities and responsibilities of bankers	22–087
(d) Presentment for acceptance and payment	22–097
(e) Procedure on dishonour	22–120
5. The banker's lien	22–139

1. Introduction

Role of banks in overseas sales. The trading and merchant banks of the United Kingdom play an important role in overseas sales. In the first place, a substantial part of all overseas sales is financed by the banks. Credit may be extended either to the seller or to the buyer. Secondly, most payments for goods imported to the United Kingdom as well as payments for goods exported by United Kingdom merchants are made through banking channels. As from the end of the Second World War this traditional role of the banks gained momentum from the exchange control legislation, which remained in force until the end of 1979. Under this legislation, payments in transactions involving owners of external accounts or persons residing outside the Scheduled Territories had to be effected by "authorised banks".[1] All substantial trading and merchant banks held such an authorisation. **22–001**

Method of effecting payment. Payment of the price of goods supplied under an overseas sale may be effected either by direct payment made by a banker, at the buyer's instruction, to the seller or by the use of a bill of exchange drawn by the seller on the buyer.[2] Direct payment by a banker may be effected by a transfer of funds (which is referred to as "payment on **22–002**

[1] For a detailed account of the Exchange Control Act 1947 and regulations and orders made thereunder, see Benjamin's *Sale of Goods* (1974 ed.), Ch.25. The 1947 Act was repealed *in toto* by the Finance Act 1987, s.68(1).

[2] But note that in certain cases the seller's bill is drawn on a third party, such as a banker who has opened a documentary credit.

open account") or by means of a banker's draft. Where the seller draws a bill of exchange for the price on the buyer, the seller usually requests his bankers to discount it and to present it through their correspondents to the buyer for his acceptance and, subsequently, for payment. This method is used in many c.i.f. and f.o.b. contracts. Thus, negotiable instruments (which include the seller's bill on the buyer as well as some bankers' drafts) play an important role in overseas sales.

22–003 **Methods of financing overseas sales.** Bankers finance overseas sales by extending credit either to the buyer or to the seller. Finance may be granted to the seller at his own request (*e.g.* where he is granted a bank facility covered by an export credit guarantee) or where amounts due to the seller [receivables] are assigned to the bank or factored) or at the instruction of the buyer (*e.g.* where the seller is furnished with an irrevocable credit). An extension of credit to the buyer is usually arranged at his own request (as is the case where documents of title are hypothecated, pledged or released to the buyer under a trust receipt by the banker who finances the transaction).[3] But in some cases finance is made available to the buyer at the seller's request (*e.g.* in the case of a "line of credit"[4]).

22–004 **Loan and overdraft; security.** The underlying relationship between the banker and the customer, at whose request finance is made available, is that of creditor and debtor. This is the position regardless of the actual scheme or method used for financing a specific transaction. Credit may be extended either by means of a specific loan or by means of an overdraft. In the case of a loan, a special account is opened and the amount advanced is debited to it and credited to the customer's general account. In the case of an overdraft, the customer is granted a ceiling up to which he may draw at any one time. The debt is incurred as the cheques are drawn under the overdraft. The main difference between the two types of arrangement relates to the charging of interest. Interest on an overdraft is charged on the daily debit balance; in the case of a loan, it is charged on the debit balance in the loan account. In most overseas sales, the banker obtains as a security for the overdraft or loan granted to the customer a pledge over, or other right in, documents of title or similar documents. This type of security is discussed in Chapter 18. In addition, the banker has a lien over the documents and all other property of the customer which is in the banker's actual or constructive possession.

22–005 **Scope of chapter.** The present chapter is mainly concerned with the methods used for making payment of the price in overseas sales. Apart from the discussion of payment on open account and payment by bankers' drafts, it includes a discussion of payment by the use of a bill of exchange drawn by the seller on the buyer. Certain aspects of bills of exchange, including their legal nature, acceptance and payment, the duties of the

[3] As regards a pledge of documents see above, para.18–209; as regards hypothecation see above, para.18–234; as regards trust receipts see above, paras 18–235 *et seq.*
[4] See below, paras 24–034 *et seq.*

drawer (the seller) and of the holder and discount and collection, are of relevance. But a discussion of all the legal aspects of bills of exchange is outside the scope of this book. However, it has been thought advisable to include references to the discussion in other works of aspects of bills of exchange which are not directly relevant to overseas sales.[5] The last section of this chapter concerns the banker's lien.

2. Direct Payment by Banker

(a) *Payment on Open Account*

Advantage of method. Where payment is made by a mail transfer (M/T), by a telegraphic or telecommunicated transfer (T/T) or by a SWIFT[6] transfer the buyer's banker remits the price to his correspondent in the seller's locality.[7] The correspondent notifies the seller and pays the amount to the seller or to the credit of his banking account. The main advantage of this system is that it avoids the risk of loss in the post. As the amount is transferred by means of an authority to the correspondent to debit the account of the buyer's banker against payment to the seller, the loss of the letter of transfer merely makes it necessary to dispatch a further letter, telegram or telex confirming the original instruction. 22–006

Spot and forward transfers: Object. One risk that is not eliminated by the remittance of the price due under a contract of sale by a direct transfer on open account is that of a fluctuation in the currency of account. This, in most cases, is the currency in which the parties have expressed the price. A devaluation is disadvantageous from the seller's point of view; a revaluation enures to his benefit.[8] Conversely, the buyer gains if the currency of account is devalued and loses if it is revalued. The risk occurs in most overseas sales and affects a party even if the currency of account is that of his own country (local currency). However, the risk borne by a party to a contract of sale is accentuated where the currency of account is that of a foreign country. The reason for this is that a fluctuation in the rate of the local currency has a direct effect on the economy of the country; the general shift in prices assists a merchant to absorb a loss incurred from a specific contract as the result of the fluctuation of the local currency. It is more difficult to absorb a 22–007

---

[5] In particular to *Chitty on Contracts* (29th ed.), Vol. 2, Ch.34; Chalmers and Guest, *Bills of Exchange* (16th ed.).

[6] An independent network run by the Society for World Wide International Financial Communications. See, generally, Ellinger, Lomnicka and Hooley, *Modern Banking Law* (4th ed., 2006), pp. 521 *et seq.*

[7] As regards information to be provided where the remittance is to a payee in a EEA state, see the Cross Border Credit Transfer Regulations 1999, SI 1999/1876.

[8] This is the case where the currency of account is also the currency of payment. Where these differ, the seller sustains a loss from a devaluation of the currency of account *vis-à-vis* the currency of payment; he gains from a devaluation of the currency of payment which, from his point of view, is similar to a revaluation of the currency of account.

loss resulting from fluctuation in a foreign currency, especially if the relevant contract forms an isolated transaction. In effect, the gravest risk from the seller's point of view is the devaluation of a foreign "currency of account" whilst the buyer stands to lose most severely where the foreign currency of account is revalued.

The legal problems relating to the method of determining the rate of exchange and the currency of account and of payment are discussed elsewhere in this book.[9] However, the risk of fluctuation in a foreign currency can be covered under two special types of contracts developed by the banking world and known as "spot" and "forward" contracts. In both types of agreement the banker assumes the risk of fluctuation in the relevant currency. As bankers deal in currencies, they are in a better position to assume such a risk than most traders.

22–008 **Defined.** A spot transaction consists of the purchase or sale by a bank of one currency against another for prompt settlement which, on the London market, is two working days ahead. In a forward contract a rate of exchange is fixed at once for the purchase or sale of one currency against another at that rate at a stipulated future date. The main difference between the two types of transaction is that in a spot contract there is a prompt exchange of currencies whilst in a forward contract the actual exchange takes effect at an agreed future date. Thus, where a contract of sale is expressed in a currency other than that of the buyer's country, the buyer can cover himself by a spot or by a forward contract. If the seller agrees to take payment in a foreign currency, he can cover himself by selling it to his bankers under a forward contract.[10]

22–009 **Risks.** Most spot and forward contracts include a clause under which "any currency held by [the bank or its] correspondents as the result of the . . . spot purchase or as the result of the matured forward contract, will be at [the customer's] risk". The main object of this clause is to protect the banker where the currency is transferred under a spot or forward contract made with a buyer of goods for the purpose of rendering payment to the seller at a future date. The clause exempts the banker from responsibility for a loss that may result from an unexpected development such as the freezing of the funds by a government directive. The apprehension of Orders precluding the remittance of funds from the country, such as the imposition of fresh exchange control regulations, has led to the introduction of yet a further clause, under which this type of risk and any loss resulting therefrom are borne by the customer. Usually, such a clause provides that the making of an Order of this type suspends the bank's duty

[9] See below, para.25–193.

[10] Alternatively, he may be granted a loan in foreign currency of the amount due and this is exchanged on spot terms. Generally, on issues arising in respect of settlements of foreign currency remittances see Geva, *Bank Collections and Payment Transactions* (OUP, 2001), Pt E.

to make payment or confers on it the right to discharge the contract in a currency other than the designated currency of payment.[11]

China Mutual: facts. An interesting case concerning the effect of a freezing order was *China Mutual Trading Co. v Banque Belge Pour L'Etranger (Extreme Orient) SA.*[12] The claimants, a firm of importers of Hong Kong, entered into forward exchange contracts with the defendants, a Belgian bank operating in Hong Kong, under which the defendants agreed to sell to the plaintiffs US dollars. The US dollars covered by these forward contracts were transferred by the defendants to their correspondents in the United States and formed part of the balance standing to the credit of the defendants' account. Subsequently, the United States Treasury froze the defendants' account with their correspondents, a measure that was probably connected with the American boycott of companies trading with the People's Republic of China. After the freezing of their account, the defendants obtained the permission of the Treasury to pay the sum held for the claimants into a special frozen account opened in the claimants' name. Refusing to pay the amounts involved, the defendants argued that the forward exchange contracts had been performed or, alternatively, that they were excused from performing them on the ground of supervening illegality. 22–010

Decision. Reynolds J. held that by paying the amounts due to the claimants into a blocked account in the United States, the defendants did not discharge their debt, and that the plaintiffs were entitled to be repaid in Hong Kong. He thought that even if the debt was not reclaimable in Hong Kong, the claimants should succeed and held, in this connection, that the proper law of the contracts was the law of Hong Kong. He then added that it was common ground that the performance of the forward exchange contracts became impossible in view of the currency regulations in the United States and that, therefore, the money would be reclaimable under section 3 of the Law Reform (Frustrated Contracts) Ordinance of Hong Kong, which was similar to the corresponding English Act.[13] Since the defendants did not deliver any US dollars to the claimants or to their order, the forward exchange contracts were not completely performed and the sums were, therefore, reclaimable. 22–011

Review of case. In the *China Mutual* case the forward exchange contracts did not include an exemption clause of the type mentioned earlier. If they had, it is possible that the decision would have been different. Under any 22–012

---

[11] This type of clause has become common in the wake of the Exchange Control Measures imposed in Malaysia on September 1, 1998. The effect of these ECMs, under which the remittance of Malaysian Ringgit was abrogated to a substantial extent, was the sudden discontinuation of trade in this currency on international currency markets and, in consequence, problems in the settlement of contracts denominated in it. See Choo Han Teck J.C.'s instructive judgment in *Shenyin Wangou-Aps Management Pte Ltd v Commerzbank (South East Asia) Ltd* [2001] 4 S.L.R. 275 (affirmed by CA on February 19, 2002).

[12] (1954) 39 Hong Kong L.R. 144.

[13] Law Reform (Frustrated Contracts) Act 1943, s.1.

such a clause, the US dollars would have been held by the defendants' correspondents at the claimants' risk. Presumably, this would include the risk of the freezing of the account (or a confiscation of the currency) by an Act of State. However, as, in the instant case, the defendants arranged for the payment of the currency into a separate current account, they had, in any event, exceeded their authority and had also failed to "hold" the currency in the manner envisaged by the parties. Whether they could under these circumstances rely on the type of clause under discussion is questionable.[14]

22–013 **Further cases.** Further conclusions can be drawn from later decisions respecting fixed deposits. In two of the cases in question, *Libyan Arab Foreign Bank v Bankers Trust Co.*[15] and *Libyan Arab Foreign Bank v Manufacturers Hanover Trust Co. (No.2)*[16] the High Court applied the general principle,[17] under which a deposit placed with a bank is governed by the law applicable at the place of the branch with which the respective account is maintained. In *Bankers Trust Co.'s* case the L Bank maintained two accounts denominated in US dollars with BT. The first, which was predominantly a trading account, was kept with the New York office whilst the second, which was an investment account, was maintained with the London office. There was an arrangement under which the balance of the New York account was to be kept at an optimal level. If it fell beneath it, BT had the authority to transfer funds to New York from the London account. If the level was exceeded, an appropriate sum was automatically remitted to the credit of the London account. When President Reagan issued an order freezing all assets maintained by the L Bank with any branch of an American bank, BT refused to pay the amount of approximately US $140m standing to the credit of the London account, arguing that such payment was prohibited by the law of New York which governed the contract between itself and the L Bank. Staughton J. held that although only one contractual relationship existed between the L Bank and BT, it was, nevertheless, governed by two proper law systems. The London account, he concluded, was governed by English law, which did not recognise the effect of President Reagan's order. His Lordship emphasised, at the same time, that an English court would not order a bank to perform an act that would be illegal in the place at which it had to be carried out. Consequently, payment would not be ordered if it had to be effected through clearing channels situated in the United States, in which President Reagan's order prohibited the transfer involved. But in the instant case, payment could be effected in London either by the inconvenient method of

---

[14] The answer depends on the interpretation of the exemption clause. See, generally, above, paras 13–020.

[15] [1988] 1 Lloyd's Rep. 259.

[16] [1989] 1 Lloyd's Rep. 608; and see earlier proceedings in [1988] 2 Lloyd's Rep. 494, concerning the application for summary judgment, denied by Hirst J.

[17] *Hamlyn v Talisker Distillery* [1894] A.C. 202; *Kahler v Midland Bank* [1950] A.C. 24; *Arab Bank Ltd v Barclays Bank (D.C.O.)* [1954] A.C. 495; *X, Y & Z v B* [1983] 2 Lloyd's Rep. 535; *Mackinnon v Donaldson, Lufkin & Jenrette Securities Corp.* [1986] Ch. 482; *Attock Cement Co. Ltd v Romanian Bank for Foreign Trade* [1989] 1 W.L.R. 1147.

payment of cash or by the payment of an appropriate amount in pounds sterling. Payment was, likewise, ordered by Hirst J. in the *Manufacturers Hanover Trust* case, in which the facts were similar in most regards. Hirst J., however, took the view that each of the two accounts was the subject of a separate contract between the parties. The contract respecting the London account was, in his judgment, governed by English law. A particular fact emphasised by Hirst J. was that in the case before him the deposit receipts, issued by MHT periodically, stated that the deposits were governed by English law. His Lordship was unimpressed by the argument that this clause was inserted in the deposit receipts mainly for certain fiscal considerations concerning MHT's reserves.

ECM of Malaysia. Issues relating to the risk of government intervention surfaced again in the wake of the Exchange Control Measures, introduced by BNM (the central bank) on September 1, 1998. Effectively, these new ECM rendered the payment of all undertakings expressed in the local currency—the MYR—out of or into accounts maintained by non-residents, defined as "external accounts", subject to BNM's approval. When, in consequence, the trading in MYR on international foreign exchange markets ceased forthwith, banks in Singapore and elsewhere accelerated the maturity of all contracts expressed in that currency and settled the amounts involved by remittances in US dollars at a rate determined on the basis of a recommendation of the Singapore Foreign Exchange Market Committee. Moreover, they did so even in cases in which the depositor refused to accept such payment and demanded settlement in MYR. In *Shenyin Wanguou-Aps Management Pte Ltd v Commerzbank (South East Asia) Ltd*[18] Choo Han Teck J.C. upheld the banks' right to discharge their contracts in US dollars, basing his decision on both an express term in the General Terms and Conditions considered by him in the relevant case and on the doctrine of frustration. 22–014

In respect of the second point, Choo Han Teck J.C. relied on expert evidence which established that a deposit in foreign currency, made on the Forex money market in Singapore, had to be settled by means of a remittance of funds through the international money market. As that market had collapsed upon the introduction of the new ECM, the contracts considered by him were frustrated by a supervening event, that had taken effect in the offshore Forex money market. In reaching this conclusion, His Honour took into account an express condition under which the deposits were governed by the law of Singapore, which, in any event, was also the place at which payment was due. As the export of MYR from Malaysia was also proscribed by the ECM, the bank was not ordered to make payment by tendering MYR banknotes.

American doctrine. The underlying common law doctrine involved has been modified in the United States. Basically, American law, too, recognises the principle under which a deposit is governed by the law prevailing at the place of the branch where the account is kept.[19] Moreover, under the 22–015

[18] [2001] 4 S.L.R. 275 (affirmed by CA on February 19, 2002).

[19] *Sokoloff v National City Bank* (1927) 224 N.Y.S. 102, affirmed 227 N.Y.S. 907, affirmed (1928) 164 N.E. 745.

"act of state doctrine", American courts usually recognise the validity of a confiscation order made by a foreign government in respect of funds deposited with a branch or office within its jurisdiction.[20] Nevertheless, some modern cases have recognised a customer's right to recover from a bank's head office in the United States funds deposited by him with an overseas office.

Thus, in *Vishipco Line v Chase Manhattan Bank*[21] Vietnamese nationals were allowed to recover from the bank's head office in New York amounts deposited with its Saigon office. The Second Circuit's decision was largely based on the fact that the bank had closed its Saigon office prior to the fall of South Vietnam and before the making of the confiscation order published shortly thereafter by the new government.[22] The debts were, accordingly, treated as having reverted to New York prior to their confiscation. On this basis, the same decision would, probably, have been reached by an English court. Doubts can, however, be raised as regards the soundness of the Second Circuit's additional ground, which was that, by operating abroad through branches rather than through subsidiaries, American banks assured Vietnamese customers that their deposits would be safer with them than with a locally incorporated bank.[23] The suggestion that, on this basis, the debt was repayable at the place of the head office overlooks the very nature of branch banking, under which a deposit is deemed to be situated where placed.

22–016 **Later cases.** The principle of *Vishipco Line's* case was extended in *Garcia v Chase Manhattan Bank*,[24] in which the bank was ordered to repay in New York an amount deposited with its office in Cuba. This decision was reached although the office in question had remained operative until its nationalisation by the revolutionary government in Cuba. The Second Circuit based its decision on the fact that the bank's officers had given the customers verbal assurances that the money was safe when deposited with the branch in question and, in addition, had asserted that payment was guaranteed by the head office. Yet a further extension of the principle is manifest in *Wells Fargo Asia Ltd v Citibank NA*,[25] in which the customers were allowed to recover in the United States a deposit placed with the bank's Manila office and, effectively, frozen by an order made by the Philippine government in 1983. In reaching its decision, the Second Circuit emphasised that, in the ultimate, a parent bank was liable for obligations assumed by its foreign branches and, further, that, in the absence of the parties' agreement to the contrary, a creditor was entitled to claim a debt at

---

[20] *Underhill v Fernandez* (1876) 92 U.S. 510; *Banco Nacional de Cuba v Sabbationo* (1964) 376 U.S. 398; *Allied Bank International v Banco Credito Agricola* (1985) 757 F. 2d 516.
[21] (1981) 66 F. 2d 854.
[22] *ibid.*, at pp.862–863. His Honour relied on *Manas y Pineiro v Chase Manhattan Bank* (1980) 433 N.Y.S. 2d 868 for the proposition that for the purposes of the act of state doctrine the situs of a debt depended on whether the parties and the *res* were in the foreign country at the time of confiscation.
[23] 660 F. 2d at p.863.
[24] (1984) 735 F. 2d 645.
[25] (1991) 936 F. 2d 723 (2nd Cir.).

the place at which it was made payable. As the parties had not ruled out payment in New York, the Second Circuit, somewhat surprisingly, concluded that the deposit was recoverable in New York.

Critique. It is clear that, at the present state of the authorities, English courts are unlikely to follow the American decisions just discussed. *Wells Fargo*, in particular, is at variance with English law which, in the absence of an agreement to the contrary, regards a deposit as payable at the branch with which it is placed and as being subject to the law there applicable. However, in order to avoid any doubts as regards issues of the type under consideration, banks should be advised to take two precautionary steps. The first is neatly set out by the Second Circuit in *Vishipco*[26]: "A bank which accepts deposits at a foreign branch becomes a debtor, not a bailee, with respect to its depositors. In the event that unsettled local conditions require it to cease operations, it should inform its depositors of the date when its branch will close and give them the opportunity to withdraw their deposits or, if conditions prevent such steps, enable them to obtain payment at an alternative location." This advice ought to be observed once a branch has to close down or to cease operations. 22–017

The second precautionary step ought to be taken so as to avoid the type of litigation encountered in the case of freezing orders, such as the Philippine Government's order in *Wells Fargo*. Banks should be advised to incorporate in the deposit receipt (or deposit confirmation) a clause making payment available solely at the respective branch. The effectiveness of such a clause was demonstrated in *Libyan Arab Foreign Bank v Manufacturers Hanover Trust Co. (No.2)*.[27]

(b) *Payment by Bankers' Draft*

Danger of loss. The main danger when payment is effected by a bankers' draft is that it may be lost in the post. The lost draft may fall into the hands of an unscrupulous person who forges the payee's indorsement, presents the draft to the drawee and obtains payment. If it is impossible to recover payment from the forger, the question arises as to which of the innocent persons involved must bear the loss. The problem may arise in regard to the relationship (a) between the buyer who procures the bankers' draft (and who will be referred to as the customer) and the seller (who is the payee of the draft); (b) between the banker who draws the draft and the payee (seller); and (c) between the bank that is the drawee and a collecting banker. The legal nature of the bankers' draft is relevant in all these situations. 22–018

Legal nature of bankers' draft. A bankers' draft is usually drawn to the order of a specified person and is payable on demand.[28] If it is drawn by one banker on another, it is a cheque as defined in section 73 of the Bills of 22–019

---

[26] Above, at p.864.
[27] [1989] 1 Lloyd's Rep. 608, above.
[28] Bankers' drafts payable to bearer have been treated as banknotes since the enactment of s.11 of the Stamp Act 1854. The issue of banknotes is today a monopoly of the Bank of England in respect of England and Wales: the Currency and Bank Notes Act 1928.

Exchange Act 1882.[29] But where a draft is drawn by one branch of a bank on its head office or on another branch of the same bank, it is not "drawn by one person on another" and therefore does not constitute a bill of exchange or a cheque.[30] However, according to section 5(2) of the Bills of Exchange Act 1882, the holder may treat such a document, at his option, either as a bill of exchange or as a promissory note.[31] This section places the holder of such a draft in as favourable a position as if he were the holder of a negotiable instrument. But the section does not enable a party to the draft, who is not a holder, to treat it as a negotiable instrument.[32] This leads to a strange result. While the holder can enforce the draft against the acceptor, the latter cannot assert against a person who sues as "true owner" that the draft is negotiable.

22–020 **Effect of loss on relationship of customer and payee.** A bankers' draft may be dispatched to the payee (the seller in overseas sales) either by the customer (the buyer) or, at the customer's instruction, by the banker who draws it.[33] As between the customer and the payee, the risk of loss is borne by the customer.[34] But if the payee has specifically requested that payment be effected by a bankers' draft to be dispatched by post, the risk of its loss is borne by himself.[35] However, if the lost draft is of the negotiable type, that is, drawn by one banker on another, the payee is entitled to demand a replacement from the drawer. The reason for this is that, as the post office handles the draft on behalf of the payee, he has the constructive possession of the draft and is a "holder" within the meaning of this term in section 2.[36] Under section 69 of the Bills of Exchange Act 1882, a person who was at any time the "holder" of a lost bill is entitled to demand from the drawer a bill of similar tenor. But the payee must furnish the banker, or drawer, with an indemnity against claims by third parties. It is noteworthy that the position is similar if the payee loses the draft after it is delivered to him by post.[37]

---

[29] According to which "a cheque is a bill of exchange payable on demand." But note that some bankers' drafts are currently crossed and available for collection to "A/c payee only." Such drafts are not negotiable instrument: *Chitty on Contracts* (29th ed.), paras 34–168 *et seq.*

[30] *Capital and Counties Bank Ltd v Gordon* [1903] A.C. 240 at 250; *contrast*: *Ross v London County Westminster and Parr's Bank Ltd* [1919] 1 K.B. 678 at 687 doubted in *Slingsby v Westminster Bank (No.1)* [1931] 1 K.B. 173 at 187. And see *Thomas Cook (NZ) Ltd v Inland Revenue Commissioner* [2004] UKPC 53 (PC: Lord Bingham) as to when a draft is payable.

[31] In *Commercial Banking Co. of Sydney Ltd v Mann* [1961] A.C. 1 at 7, a bankers' draft drawn by a branch on the head office was described as being equivalent to a promissory note of the bank.

[32] *Capital and Counties Bank Ltd v Gordon*, above, at p.250.

[33] As regards the position where delivery is obtained by a trick, see *Citibank NA v Brown Shipley & Co.* [1991] 1 Lloyd's Rep. 576.

[34] *Charles v Blackwell* (1877) 2 C.P.D. 151 at 157–158.

[35] *ibid.* This is the case also where the payee loses the cheque: *Charles v Blackwell*, above, 158.

[36] As to definition of "holder" see below, para.22–059.

[37] He may as holder sue on the lost bill and the county court may enjoin the bank from setting up the loss: s.70 of the Bills of Exchange Act 1882, discussed in *Chitty on Contracts* (29th ed.), Vol. 2, paras 34–147—34–148.

Relationship of customer (buyer) and banker. As between the banker and the customer, the customer appears to bear the risk of the loss of the draft. Where the draft is dispatched by the customer, the banker can hardly be held responsible for its loss. Where the banker dispatches it, he is not responsible for loss as long as he follows his instructions. In the absence of specific instructions, the dispatch of the draft by registered mail is sufficient and the banker need not effect insurance against loss.[38] 22–021

As a matter of practice, bankers replace a lost draft provided the customer agrees to furnish an indemnity. However, it appears that the customer cannot compel the banker to replace the lost draft. This is the position both where the lost draft is of the negotiable type and where it is drawn by the banker on himself. The reason for this is that, as the customer is neither the payee nor an indorsee of the lost bankers' draft, he cannot be regarded as a person who was at any time its "holder".[39] It follows that section 69 does not apply even if the lost draft is of the negotiable type. *A fortiori*, the customer is not entitled to demand a replacement of a draft drawn by the banker on himself; as such an instrument is not a bill of exchange or cheque it is altogether outside the scope of section 69.[40]

Effect of indemnity. Even if a lost draft of the negotiable type, which is a cheque, is replaced by the banker who drew it, the customer continues to bear the risk of a financial loss that may accrue if the draft falls into the hands of a rogue. When the drawer replaces the draft, he usually insists on obtaining from the customer the type of indemnity mentioned in section 69, that is, an indemnity against claims "by all persons whatever" in case the draft is found again. This type of indemnity is wide enough to cover the drawer where the draft is paid by the drawee to a person who holds it under a forged indorsement. It is true that, in English law, a person cannot enforce payment of a cheque which he holds under a forged indorsement.[41] But the drawee, who in the ordinary course of business pays the cheque to such a person, is entitled to debit the account of the drawer.[42] Presumably, the indemnity would entitle the drawer (or banker) to debit the customer's account with a similar amount. However, in most cases the drawer would be able to notify the drawee in time; the drawee would then dishonour the draft. The process of notification is simplified where a draft is drawn by a banker on himself. In point of fact, cases of lost drafts have not been the subject of much litigation. 22–022

It should be added that if a draft is destroyed or is lost and does not turn up again, the customer can recover the amount paid for it, less the charges for its issue, in an action in restitution based on total failure of consideration.[43]

---

[38] *Ose Gesellschaft v Jewish Colonial Trust* (1927) 43 T.L.R. 398.

[39] See definition of holder, below, para.22–059.

[40] As regards the title to a draft, see *Midland Bank v Brown Shipley & Co.*, above.

[41] *Bobbett v Pinkett* (1876) 1 Ex.D. 368 at 374; *Lacave & Co. v Crédit Lyonnais* [1897] 1 Q.B. 148 at 152–153. But the position may differ where the bill is governed by foreign law: *Embiricos v Anglo-Austrian Bank* [1905] 1 K.B. 677. See, generally, *Chitty on Contracts* (29th ed.), Vol. 2, paras 34–055—34–056; 34–207 *et seq*.

[42] s.60 of the Bills of Exchange Act 1882. See, generally, Chitty, *op. cit.*, paras 34–327 *et seq*.

[43] *cf. Fibrosa Spolka Akcyjna v Fairbairn Lawson Combe Barbour Ltd* [1943] A.C. 32 at 62–63.

22–023 **Position of drawee.** Is the drawee banker liable if he has paid the bankers' draft to a person other than the payee or a person holding the draft under the payee's genuine indorsement?[44] The question arises both where the lost bankers' draft is of the negotiable type, that is where it is drawn by one bank on another, and in the case of a draft drawn by a banker on himself. In the case of a negotiable draft, which constitutes a cheque, the action may be brought either by the banker who has drawn it and who contests the drawee's right to debit his account with the amount of the draft or by the "true owner" in conversion.[45] The true owner is the person who has the property in the draft[46] and who is entitled to its immediate possession.[47] Whether in a specific case the true owner is the customer or the payee depends on the facts.[48]

The position is somewhat different where a draft is drawn by the banker on himself, because the banker acts both as drawer and as drawee. The liability of such a banker as drawer has been discussed above. But such a banker may be sued in conversion by the "true owner", if he pays the draft to a person who holds it under a forged indorsement.[49] The fact that the draft is not a negotiable instrument does not preclude an action of this type.[50]

22–024 **Drawee's defence.** In most cases the drawee banker has an adequate defence. In the case of a negotiable draft, which is a cheque, he has the protection of section 60 of the Bills of Exchange Act 1882, provided he has

---

[44] And note that, where the draft constitutes a cheque or—in other words—is of the negotiable type, it is covered by the Deregulation (Bills of Exchange) Order, SI 1996/2993, which makes provisions for the truncation of cheques.

[45] That a banker who pays a draft to an unauthorised person may be sued in conversion, see *Smith v Union Bank of London* (1875) L.R. 10 Q.B. 291 at 293, 295, affirmed (1875) 1 Q.B.D. 31 at 35. The damages equal the face value of the bill: *Morison v London County and Westminster Bank Ltd* [1914] 3 K.B. 356 at 365; *Bavins Jnr. and Sims v London and South Western Bank Ltd* [1900] 1 Q.B. 270 at 275; *Macbeth v North and South Wales Bank* [1908] 1 K.B. 13 at 22, affirmed [1908] A.C. 137. As regards an alternative action in money had and received see Ellinger, Lomnicka and Hooley, *Modern Banking Law*, (4th ed.), pp.466 *et seq.*

[46] *Great Western Ry Co. v London and County Banking Co.* [1901] A.C. 414 at 419–420; *Morison v London County and Westminster Bank Ltd*, above, 364, 375; *Lloyds Bank Ltd v Savory & Co.* [1933] A.C. 201. But if the bill comes into the hands of a holder in due course, he becomes the true owner: *Smith v Union Bank of London* (1875) 1 Q.B.D. 31 at 35–36. See also *Edelstein v Schuler & Co.* [1902] 2 K.B. 144 at 156–157.

[47] *Bute (Marquess of) v Barclays Bank Ltd* [1955] 1 Q.B. 202.

[48] But in certain cases the property may vest in the rogue, as is the case where an agent fraudulently draws a cheque on his principal's account and obtains a bankers' draft against it. Moreover, if the principal ratifies the agent's act, the principal may acquire the property in the draft but is then precluded from suing the bank: *Union Bank of Australia Ltd v McClintock* [1922] 1 A.C. 240; *Commercial Banking Co. of Sydney Ltd v Mann* [1961] A.C. 1. *Cf. Lipkin Gorman v Karpnale Ltd* [1991] 2 A.C. 548.

[49] See above, n.41.

[50] *Fine Art Society Ltd v Union Bank of London Ltd* (1886) 17 Q.B.D. 705 at 709–710, 711–712; *Bavins Jnr. and Sims v London and South Western Bank Ltd* [1900] 1 Q.B. 270 at 275–277. *Cf. Clegg v Baretta* (1887) 56 L.T. 775, doubting the amount of damages for the conversion of a non-negotiable instrument.

paid the draft in good faith and in the ordinary course of business.[51] Although section 60 does not apply where a draft is drawn by a banker on himself, the banker who issues such a draft can plead the defence of section 19 of the Stamp Act 1853.[52] Under this section, "any draft or order drawn upon a banker for a sum of money payable to order on demand which shall, when presented for payment, purport to be indorsed by the person to whom the same shall be drawn payable, shall be sufficient authority to such banker to pay the amount of such draft to the bearer thereof; and it shall not be incumbent on such banker to prove that such indorsement . . . was made by or under the direction or authority of the person to whom the said draft or order was, or is, made payable . . ." Since the enactment of section 60 of the Bills of Exchange Act 1882, section 19 has no application in the case of bills of exchange and cheques.[53] Moreover, it is arguable that the section applies only where the instrument is an "order" given by the customer to his banker and not a draft or "order" drawn by the banker upon himself. But authorities have extended the application of the section to cases in which a banker pays a draft drawn on himself to a person who holds it under a forged indorsement of the payee.[54]

Foreign drafts. A question of some difficulty is whether section 19 applies only in the case of inland drafts or also in the case of foreign drafts, *e.g.* a draft drawn by an overseas branch on the bank's head office in London. In *Capital and Counties Bank Ltd v Gordon*[55] Lord Lindley had some doubts on this point. Presumably, these were based on the fact that under the Stamp Act 1853 foreign bills and "orders" were not made subject to stamp duty and it was thought that the Act applied only to instruments that it rendered subject to duty. But in *Brown, Brough & Co. v National Bank of India Ltd*[56] Bigham J. was of the view that section 19 was applicable where a draft drawn by the Madras branch of a bank on its head office in London was paid against a forged indorsement. At the same time, Bigham J. felt bound to follow the decision of the Court of Appeal in the *Gordon* case,[57] which he thought decided that section 19 was inapplicable where the instrument paid was not negotiable. But, in point of fact, section 19 was not cited to the Court of Appeal in the *Gordon* case and the decision was confined to the question of the application to non-negotiable drafts of section 60 of the Bills of Exchange Act 1882. The House of Lords, in the *Gordon* case, held that section 19 was applicable in the case of drafts drawn by a bank on one of its branches or on its head office, that is, to non-negotiable drafts. Admittedly, the drafts in the *Gordon* case were inland 22–025

---

[51] See, generally, *Chitty on Contracts* (29th ed.), Vol. 2, paras 34–339—34–341.
[52] Most of the sections of the Stamp Act 1853 were repealed by the Inland Revenue Repeal Act 1870, s.2, and the Inland Revenue Regulation Act 1890, s.40.
[53] *Carpenters' Co. v British Mutual Banking Co.* [1938] 1 K.B. 511 at 531–532.
[54] *Capital and Counties Bank Ltd v Gordon* [1903] A.C. 240 at 251–252. See also *Charles v Blackwell* (1877) 2 C.P.D. 151 at 159 *et seq. Cf. Halifax Union v Wheelwright* (1875) L.R. 10 Ex. 183 at 193–194.
[55] [1903] A.C. 240 at 251. For a definition of inland and foreign bills, see below, para.22–040.
[56] (1902) 18 T.L.R. 669.
[57] [1902] 1 K.B. 242 at 272–274.

drafts; but section 19 does not draw any distinction between inland and foreign drafts.

It is submitted that the key to the interpretation of the section is to be found in its object. Although section 19 was included in the Stamp Act 1853, its object is to give the drawee of bills and of non-negotiable orders and drafts a defence against actions based on the forgery of the payee's indorsement. The drawee is just as unfamiliar with the payee's signature in the case of a foreign draft as he is in the case of an inland draft. As the section does not specifically exclude foreign drafts and bills and as foreign instruments are excluded in other provisions of this Act, it is arguable that the section applies to foreign drafts.[58]

It is noteworthy that the proposed construction leads to similarity between section 19 of the Stamp Act 1853 and section 60 of the Bills of Exchange Act 1882. There is no hint in the latter Act that its provisions are inapplicable to foreign bills. The classification of bills in section 4 into foreign bills and inland bills shows that the generic term "bill" applies to both types. There is no reason to presume that section 60 is an exception.[59]

22–026 **Missing or irregular indorsement.** What is the position of the drawee banker if he pays a bankers' draft to an unauthorised person and the draft either bears an indorsement of the payee which is both forged and irregular in form[60] or does not bear an indorsement at all? In the case of negotiable drafts, which are cheques, section 60 protects the drawee only where the forged indorsement is regular on its face.[61] But section 1(1) of the Cheques Act 1957 protects a banker who in the ordinary course of business[62] and in good faith pays a cheque which is not indorsed or which is irregularly indorsed: a banker who pays such a cheque is deemed to have paid it in due course within the meaning of section 59 of the Bills of Exchange Act 1882 and does not incur any liability by reason only of the absence of or irregularity in indorsement. However, the Committee of London Clearing Bankers has taken the view that the public interest would best be served by retaining the need for indorsement in certain circumstances. These circumstances are set out in a circular of September 23, 1957,[63] forwarded by the Committee to clearing bank managers. Under the circular, which continues to be reflected in current banking practice despite the passage of time, a cheque requires a regular indorsement of the payee when the cheque is cashed over the counter. If a cheque (or a negotiable bankers' draft) is paid over the counter against a forged and irregular indorsement of the payee,

---

[58] See also Paget, *Law of Banking* (12th ed.), p.255; Ellinger, Lomnicka and Hooley, *Modern Banking Law* (4th ed.), pp.454 *et seq.*

[59] As regards questions of conflicts arising in connection with foreign bills, see *Chitty on Contracts* (29th ed.), Vol. 2, paras 34–198 *et seq.*

[60] An indorsement is irregular where the indorser signs in a name materially different from that by which he is described in the bill: *Arab Bank Ltd v Ross* [1952] 2 Q.B. 216.

[61] *Charles v Blackwell* (1877) 2 C.P.D. 151 at 159–160; *Slingsby v District Bank* [1931] 2 K.B. 588, affirmed [1932] 1 K.B. 544.

[62] The language of the section indicates that, for its purposes, the irregularity of the indorsement does not render payment outside the ordinary course of business.

[63] See further Chitty, *op. cit.*, Vol. 2, para.34–342.

the banker is acting in disregard of standard banking practice. He therefore does not act in the ordinary course of business and stands to lose the protection of section 1(1).

Stamp Act 1853, section 19. The position is similar in the case of non-negotiable drafts. Originally, section 19 of the Stamp Act 1853 protected a banker only where the draft appeared to be indorsed in the payee's name. The section did not apply where a draft was unindorsed when it was paid. But under section 1(2)(b) of the Cheques Act 1957, a banker who pays such a draft in good faith and in the ordinary course of business does not, in doing so, incur any liability by reason only of the missing indorsement. It may perhaps be argued that where the banker pays a draft drawn on himself to the wrong person, his liability arises not by reason of the missing indorsement, but because payment has not been effected in accordance with the instruction of the customer. But if this were the position, a banker who paid an unindorsed draft to a person other than the payee or his transferee would never be able to rely on the defence of section 19 of the Stamp Act 1853. Section 1(2)(b) would then be without any effect. It is submitted that section 1(2)(b) must be read together with section 19 and that, accordingly, section 19 now applies even where a draft drawn by a banker on himself is unindorsed when paid. The point is of importance because in the light of section 4(2)(d) of the Cheques Act 1957 collecting bankers do not require the payee to indorse a bankers' draft.[64] It should be added that the circular of the Committee of Clearing Bankers and the modern Clearing Rules based on it apply the provisions relating to cheques to non-negotiable bankers' drafts. 22–027

Position of collecting banker. Bankers' drafts are frequently collected on behalf of the payee (or a subsequent holder) by a collecting banker. If the holder does not have a title to the draft, *e.g.* when he holds it under a forged indorsement of the payee, the collecting banker may be sued in conversion by the true owner. This is the position both in the case of a negotiable draft and of a non-negotiable draft.[65] In the case of a negotiable draft, which is a cheque, the banker is entitled to the protection of section 4(1) of the Cheques Act 1957. Under section 4(2)(d) the collecting banker is entitled to the same defence where he collects a non-negotiable draft.[66] In the case of a negotiable draft, the collecting banker would further be able to rely on his position as a holder in due course, provided he gave the customer value for the draft before clearance and provided further that he took it in good faith and that the draft was at that time complete and regular on its face.[67] 22–028

Draft issued by mistake. In certain cases a bankers' draft may be made payable to the order of the bank with whom the payee intends to deposit the funds. Where such a draft is of the negotiable type, the property in it 22–029

---

[64] *ibid.*, para.34–342.

[65] See above, para.22–023.

[66] On the nature of this defence, generally, see Chitty, *op. cit.* Vol. 2, para.34–342. Note that s.19 of the Stamp Act 1853 does not apply to protect a collecting banker but is confined to protecting the drawee banker: *Ogden v Benas* (1874) L.R. 9 C.P. 513.

[67] *ibid.*, para.34–348.

vests in the nominated payee bank upon its delivery. In *Midland Bank v Brown Shipley & Co. Ltd*[68] fraudsters, who managed to get access to an account maintained with the claimant bank, induced this bank to issue certain bankers' drafts payable to the defendant bank. On obtaining the claimant bank's assurances about the regularity of the drafts, the instruments were presented by the defendant bank for payment and the amount received was placed to the credit of the fraudsters' account. Dismissing the claimant bank's action in conversion, Waller J. held that, as the drafts in question were delivered to the defendant bank by a person authorised to do so by the claimant bank, title in them had passed to the defendant bank. His Lordship further found, on the facts, that the representations made by the claimant bank in reply to the defendant bank's enquiries would preclude the defendant bank from denying the valid transfer and delivery of the instruments. It is to be noted that, as the funds had been paid out by the defendant bank to the fraudsters, an action in money had and received would have failed due to the change in that bank's position.[69]

22–030 **Effect of crossing.** Where a draft is negotiable, that is, drawn by one banker on another, the effect of a crossing is similar to that which a crossing has on any other type of cheque.[70] Moreover, section 5 of the Cheques Act 1957 applies the provisions of the Bills of Exchange Act 1882 relating to crossed cheques to drafts drawn by a banker on himself. The position was similar before the passing of the Act.[71]

3. PAYMENT BY USE OF BILL OF EXCHANGE

(a) *Nature of Negotiable Instruments*

22–031 **The meaning of negotiability.** A negotiable instrument has three essential features. First, any "holder", that is, the payee or indorsee who is in possession of it or the bearer,[72] can bring an action to enforce it.[73] Secondly, a negotiable instrument may be transferred from person to person. Where the instrument is payable to the order of a specified person, it may be transferred by the payee's indorsement completed by the delivery of the instrument to the transferee; where the instrument is payable to bearer, it is transferable by mere delivery.[74] Thirdly, a bona fide transferee who takes for value an instrument that is complete and regular on its face becomes a "holder in due course" and is entitled to enforce payment of the instrument despite any defects in the title of the transferor.[75]

---

[68] [1991] 2 Lloyd's Rep. 576.
[69] *Gowers v Lloyds and National Provincial Foreign Bank Ltd* [1938] 1 All E.R. 766; *Lipkin Gorman v Karpnale Ltd* [1991] 2 A.C. 548.
[70] Chitty, *op. cit.* Vol. 2, para.34–161.
[71] See the Revenue Act 1883, s.17, and the Bills of Exchange Act (1882) and Amendment Act 1932, s.1, repealed by the Cheques Act 1957, s.6(3).
[72] Bills of Exchange Act 1882, s.2.
[73] See below, para.22–062.
[74] See below, para.22–055.
[75] See below, para.22–062. For a comparison of negotiable instruments with simple contracts, see Chitty, *op cit.*, Vol. 2, paras 34–001—34–002.

Types of negotiable instrument. When a person wants to create a negotiable instrument, he must choose one of the forms recognised by law. Persons cannot, at will, create novel types of negotiable instruments. The negotiability of an instrument can only be established by statute or by a mercantile usage.[76] The most widely used types of negotiable instrument are bills of exchange (including cheques)[77] and promissory notes. 22–032

The Bills of Exchange Act 1882. The most important source of the law of negotiable instruments in England is the Bills of Exchange Act 1882. But the Act is not exhaustive and, by section 97(2), the rules of common law, including the law merchant, continue to apply to bills of exchange, cheques and promissory notes, save in so far as these rules are inconsistent with the Act. Cases decided before the Act are, therefore, not without importance. However, in *Bank of England v Vagliano Bros*[78] the House of Lords indicated that such decisions may be used as a source of construction only when the sections of the Act are ambiguous or their language technical. When the language of the Act is clear, there is, indeed, no need to refer to decisions predating it. 22–033

Uniform Law of the Geneva Convention. Statutes based on the Bills of Exchange Act 1882 are in force in most Commonwealth countries.[79] Article 3 of the Uniform Commercial Code of the United States is, in certain respects, based on similar principles.[80] In other countries, including the civilian based EU members, the law of negotiable instruments is based on the Uniform Law on Bills of Exchange and Promissory Notes promulgated by the Geneva Convention of 1930.[81] A detailed comparison of the 22–034

---

[76] *ibid.*, para.34–006.

[77] Cheques are a category of bills of exchange: the Bills of Exchange Act 1882, s.73.

[78] [1891] A.C. 107 at 120, 127, 144–145.

[79] See, *e.g.* the Bills of Exchange Act 1908 (N.Z.); the Bills of Exchange Act 1909–73 (Australia).

[80] The article covers bills of exchange, cheques and promissory notes. Negotiable securities are covered in Art. 8.

[81] Signed at Geneva on June 7, 1930, League of Nations Treaty Series, Vol. CXLIII, p.259, No.3313 (it has not been ratified by Ireland, Spain and the United Kingdom). For decisions concerning the construction of this law, see E. von Caemmerer, *Internationale Rechtsprechung zum Genfer Einheitlichen Wechsel-und Scheckrecht*, Berlin, Vol. I, 1954; Vol. II, 1967; Vol.III, 1976; R. Roblot, *Les Effets de Commerce* (Paris, 1975). For its background and history see E.P. Ellinger, "Negotiable Instruments" being Ch.4 in Vol. IX of the *International Encyclopedia of Comparative Law* (Hamburg, 2001), pp.29 *et seq*. All the members of the EEC, except the United Kingdom, Spain and Ireland, have also ratified or accepted the Convention providing a Uniform Law for Cheques, signed at Geneva on March 19, 1931, League of Nations Treaty Series, Vol. CXLIII, p.357, No.3316; the Convention for the Settlement of Certain Conflicts of Laws in Connection with Bills of Exchange and Promissory Notes, signed at Geneva on June 7, 1930, League of Nations Treaty Series, Vol. CXLIII, p.319, No.3314; the Convention for the Settlement of Certain Conflicts of Laws in Connection with Cheques, signed at Geneva on March 19, 1931, League of Nations Treaty Series, Vol. CXLIII, p.409, No.3317. All the members of the E.U. (including the United Kingdom and Ireland, but excluding Greece and Spain) have ratified or accepted the Convention on the Stamp Laws in

Uniform Law with the Bills of Exchange Act 1882 is outside the scope of this study. But reference to provisions of the Uniform Act, which are of particular importance in regard to overseas sales, are included in the footnotes of this chapter.

22–035 **The United Nations Convention.** The United Nations Convention on International Bills of Exchange and International Promissory Notes was adopted by the United Nations Commission on International Trade Law (UNCITRAL) on August 14, 1987 and by the General Assembly on December 9, 1988. By and large, the Working Group in charge of the project sought to provide a law that would strike a balance between the common law systems, as expressed in the Bills of Exchange Act 1882 and in Article 3 of the Uniform Commercial Code (USA), and the civilian systems based on the Uniform Law of the Geneva Convention.

The Convention does not seek to replace the existing systems. Instead, it provides an alternative regime available only in respect of certain "international" instruments. Thus, under Article 1 the Convention applies to an "international bill of exchange" only if it includes the heading "International Bill of Exchange (UNCITRAL Convention)". A comparable provision is made as regards international promissory notes. Under Article 2, a bill or note is "international" if two of the incidents related to the drawing and payment thereof are shown as taking place in different States. The application of the Convention is, thus, at the option of the issuer of a given international bill or note. As, at the time of going to press, the Convention has not been adopted in the United Kingdom it is unnecessary to deal with its provisions here.[82]

22–036 **Electronically produced bills.** Traditionally, a negotiable instrument is executed in writing on a paper signed by the issuer and by any subsequent parties wishing to incur liability thereon. Transfer is effected by indorsement and delivery, or in the case of a bearer instrument, by the mere delivery of the document. This concept of negotiable instruments is manifest in the Bills of Exchange Act 1882, under which an instrument has to be in writing and requires the issuer's signature which, at present, does not encompass an electronic signature.[83] An instrument recorded merely as

Connection with Bills of Exchange and Promissory Notes, signed at Geneva on June 7, 1930, League of Nations Treaty Series, Vol. CXLIII, p.339, No.3315 and the Convention on the Stamp Laws in Connection with Cheques, signed at Geneva on March 19, 1931, League of Nations Treaty Series, Vol. CXLIII, p.9, No.3301 (this last convention has been ratified by Greece but not by Spain). The laws in regard to bills of exchange, promissory notes and cheques of all nations are set out in W. Schettler and H. Büeler, *Das Wechsel-und Scheckrecht aller Länder*, (Deutscher Wirtschaftsdienst).

[82] The text was set out in full in an Appendix to Chalmers and Guest, *Bills of Exchange* (15th ed.). For an excellent brief account of the Convention, see Hermann, "International Bills of Exchange and Promissory Notes: Legal Problems and Disparities Overcome by the New United Nations Convention" in Horn (ed.) *Law of International Trade Finance* (Dventer Boston, 1988), pp.259 *et seq.*; Hermann, "Saliant Features of U.N. Convention on International Bills of Exchange" (1988) 10 U.P.J.I.B.L. 167.

[83] Bills of Exchange Act 1882, s.3(1). But see Pt II of the Electronic Communications Act 2000. The Electronic Signatures Regulations 2002, SI 2002/318 do not affect the issue.

an entry in an electronic data base or central depository and transferred by means of screen-based book entries is outside the scope of the definition. It is true that "writing" includes print[84] as well as typing, lithography, photography and other modes of reproducing words in visible form.[85] It is, on this basis, arguable that a negotiable instrument that can be reproduced in its traditional form on a video screen may satisfy the requirement of writing. But a pure book entry, recorded solely in terms of amount, maturity period and the name of the parties is not encompassed by the definition. Furthermore, such an entry, even if reproducible on a screen, could not be regarded as signed, as a "signature" implies an identifiable record, executed in one manner or another by the person to whom it is attributed.

The need for negotiable instruments to be electronically recorded with a central depositary and to be transferred by book entries, was, however, recognised by the Review Committee on Banking Services Law and Practice (the "Jack Committee").[86] Their recommendation was to introduce changes in the existing law so as to apply the law of negotiable instruments also to such electronically created instruments. This approach obtained the support of the Government, which has expressed its intention to "legislate when other pressures on the parliamentary time table permit, to give transactions in dematerialised instruments the same status as transactions in negotiable instruments generally."[87] To date, however, no such legislation has been introduced. In 1990, the Bank of England commenced the provision, through its Central Moneymarkets Office (CMO), of screen-based transfers for money market instruments held in paper form. But in 2003, non-material equivalents of certain money market instruments began to be issued into CREST[88] and the CMO system was shut down. These are governed by regulations made under s.207 of the Companies Act 1989.[89]

Scope of discussion. The negotiable instrument which is used most widely in overseas sales is the bill of exchange. In many c.i.f., f.o.b. and similar types of contract, the seller draws a bill of exchange for the price on the buyer, who is expected to accept it. Promissory notes are used occasionally, *e.g.* where the transaction is financed by an export credit guarantee.[90] In certain transactions payment is made by a bankers' draft and, on rare occasions, payment may be by the buyer's cheque. The discussion of bills of exchange in this chapter concentrates on the aspects relevant to sale of goods, including the discount and collection of trading bills. But for the sake of clarity it is necessary to cover some of the 22–037

84 Bills of Exchange Act 1882, s.2.
85 Interpretation Act 1978, s.5 Sch.1.
86 (1989) Cm. 622, paras 8.33—8.40.
87 White Paper on *Banking Services: Law and Practice* (1990) Cm. 1026, Annex 6, para.6.10. And see Chalmers and Guest, *Bills of Exchange* (16th ed.), pp.25, 304–305.
88 *www.crestco.co.uk.*
89 SI 2001/3755, SI 2003/1633.
90 See below, paras 24–032 *et seq*. For a discussion of promissory notes, see *Chitty on Contracts* (29th ed.), Vol. 2, paras 34–186 *et seq.*

fundamental general principles of the law of negotiable instruments. A detailed discussion of bills of exchange is to be found elsewhere.[91]

(b) *Nature of Bills of Exchange*

22–038 **Definition.** Under section 3(1) of the Bills of Exchange Act 1882, a bill of exchange is an unconditional order in writing, addressed by one person to another, signed by the person giving it, requiring the person to whom it is addressed to pay on demand or at a fixed or determinable future time a sum certain in money to, or to the order of, a specified person or to bearer. According to section 3(2), an instrument which does not comply with these conditions, or which requires an additional act to be done, is not a bill of exchange. Section 3(4) provides that a bill is not invalid if it is not dated, or fails to specify the value given for it or the place at which it has been drawn or is to be payable. The definition of a bill requires some further discussion. But it will be convenient at first to discuss the role assumed, as regards the bill, by the parties to overseas sales.

22–039 **Parties to a bill.** The person who draws the bill is known as the drawer. In an overseas sale, this role is assumed by the seller. The person on whom the bill is drawn and who is ordered to pay the amount specified in it is known as the "drawee". If the drawee agrees to comply with the order, he signifies his assent by "accepting the bill". By doing so he promises to honour the bill and becomes an "acceptor". The acceptor frequently specifies a place at which the bill must be presented for payment, *e.g.* at the premises of his bankers. The bill is then "domiciled" at this place. In most overseas sales the bill is drawn on the buyer. But where a documentary credit is opened in favour of the seller, the bill is usually drawn on the issuing banker or on the confirming banker.[92] The person to whose order the bill is made payable is the "payee". In overseas sales the bill is usually made payable either to the seller's own order or to the order of the banker who finances the transaction or who collects the bill. The payee and any subsequent transferee may sign his name on the back of the bill; by doing so he warrants that the bill will be duly honoured by the drawee. Such a signature is known as an "indorsement" and the person so signing is an "indorser". In overseas sales the seller is usually required to indorse a bill, which is payable to himself and drawn on the buyer, when he arranges for its discount or collection. The payee or any other person who validly obtains the physical possession of the bill is known as the "holder". When the bill is payable to the order of a specified person, the holder obtains the valid possession only through the payee's indorsement completed by the delivery of the bill.[93] Where the bill is payable to bearer, mere delivery is adequate. The rights of the holder depend on whether he is a "mere

[91] For general works on the subject, see Chitty, *op. cit.*, Vol. 2, Ch.34; Chalmers and Guest, *Bills of Exchange* (16th ed.).
[92] See below, para.23–003.
[93] See below, paras 22–055, 22–059.

holder", a "holder for value" or a "holder in due course".[94] These terms are discussed subsequently.[95]

Foreign and inland bills. According to section 4, "an inland bill is a bill which is or on the face of it purports to be (a) both drawn and payable within the British Islands, or (b) drawn within the British Islands upon some person resident therein. Any other bill is a foreign bill." It follows that a foreign bill is one which is either (a) drawn by a person who is not resident in the British Islands, or (b) drawn by a person resident in the British Islands on a person residing abroad and payable abroad.[96] It should be noted that, if a bill is drawn and payable in the British Islands, it is not a foreign bill, even if the payee resides abroad. Moreover, an inland bill does not become a foreign bill because of any subsequent contract embodied in it, as for instance by indorsements or by the signature of a surety executed in foreign countries. The most important difference between an inland bill and a foreign bill is that a foreign bill must be protested if dishonoured, whilst protest is not, usually, required in the case of an inland bill.[97] In most other regards the provisions of the Bills of Exchange Act 1882 do not draw any distinction between an inland bill and a foreign bill. 22–040

Unconditional order. It will now be convenient to discuss in further detail the definition of a bill of exchange and its basic features. Under section 3(1) of the Bills of Exchange Act 1882, the drawer's order to the drawee must be unconditional. The order is not unconditional if the instruction to pay the bill is subject to any qualification, such as an instruction to pay only if the payee signs a receipt form written on the back of the bill.[98] However, if such an instruction or request is directed to the payee and not to the drawee, it does not render the bill conditional.[99] A problem that may arise in some overseas sales is whether a bill is conditional if the drawee is requested to pay the bill out of a specific fund. It has been held that such an order renders the instrument conditional.[1] But under section 3(3), an order which is in itself unqualified is unconditional although it is coupled with (a) an indication of a particular fund out of 22–041

---

[94] As regards the position of the drawer, see below, para.22–048, as regards the position of the drawee, see below, para.22–047; as regards the payee, see below, para.22–046; as regards the indorser, see below, para.22–049.

[95] See below, paras 22–059 *et seq*.

[96] See further Chitty, *op. cit.*, Vol. 2, paras 34–201—34–206, and authorities there cited. For an interesting authority involving a draft drawn by a bank's office in one country on an overseas branch, see *Canada Life Assurance Co. v Canadian Imperial Bank of Commerce* (1979) 98 D.L.R. (3d) 670.

[97] s.51; but this is inapplicable in the case of promissory notes: s.89(4).

[98] *Bavins Jnr and Sims v London and South Western Bank Ltd* [1900] 1 Q.B. 270.

[99] *Nathan v Ogdens Ltd* (1905) 93 L.T. 553, affirmed (1905) 94 L.T. 126; *Roberts & Co. v Marsh* [1915] 1 K.B. 42; *cf. Thairlwall v Great Northern Railway* [1910] 2 K.B. 509 at 510.

[1] *Jenney v Herle* (1723) 2 Ld.Raym. 1361; *Dawkes v Lord De Lorane* (1771) 3 Wils.K.B. 207; *Fisher v Calvert* (1879) 27 W.R. 301; *cf. Griffin v Weatherby* (1868) L.R. 3 Q.B. 753 at 759. For cases decided after the coming into effect of the Act, see *Peacocke Co. v Williams* (1909) 28 N.Z.L.R. 354; *Wood v Jackson* (1910) 12 G.L.R. 413 (N.Z.).

which the drawee is to reimburse himself or a particular account to be debited with the amount, or (b) a statement of the transaction which gives rise to the bill. Thus, a statement in the bill, that it is drawn under a documentary credit or under a bank facility covered by an export credit guarantee, does not render the bill conditional.

22–042 **Claused bills.** Section 3(3)(b) is of particular importance as regards a "claused bill", in which the drawer includes words indicating the nature of the underlying transaction, *e.g.* "drawn against cotton" or "drawn against shipment of 160 bales of wool from Sydney to U.K. per M.v Gloria". In most cases such a reference appears after the words "for value given" or at the top of the bill, next to the date of drawing. In *Guaranty Trust Co. of New York v Hannay & Co.*[2] the Court of Appeal held that such a phrase does not necessarily render the bill conditional. Warrington L.J. said that "such an expression is used by lawyers simply to denote the fact that the draft is drawn as part of a mercantile transaction, and not to indicate that the fund produced by the goods referred to is the only fund from which the amount of the draft is to be paid".[3] But a clause referring to the nature of the transaction would render a bill conditional if it qualified the order given to the drawee. In an Australian case, *Lister v Schulte*,[4] the maker of a promissory note added after the undertaking to pay: "One hundred and fifty one pound shares in [D Ltd] attached." The Supreme Court of Victoria held that these words, and the attachment of the shares, indicated that the note would be paid only if accompanied by the shares. The promise to pay was, therefore, not unconditional. The same reasoning could be applied to a bill of exchange in which the drawer instructed the drawee to accept the bill only against the tender of certain documents. There is no direct authority in point.[5]

22–043 **When payable.** According to section 3(1) a bill of exchange may be payable on demand or at a fixed or determinable future time. Under section 10(1), a bill is payable on demand if it is expressed to be so payable (or payable at presentation or at sight) as well as where no time for payment is mentioned in it. Under section 10(2), where a bill is accepted or indorsed when it is overdue it is, as regards the acceptor and indorsers, deemed to be payable on demand. A bill of exchange drawn under an overseas sale is usually payable not on demand but at some other "usance"; in most cases it is payable either at a fixed period after the date of drawing or at a fixed date after "sight", that is, its presentation for acceptance. Under section 11(1), such a bill is deemed to be payable at a determinable future time. However, a bill is invalid if there is an ambiguity respecting the time at which it is to fall due. In *Korea Exchange Bank v Debenhams*

[2] [1918] 2 K.B. 623.
[3] *ibid.*, at p.656; and see also *ibid.*, pp.630, 666. *Cf. Brown, Shipley & Co. v Kough* (1885) 29 Ch.D. 848.
[4] [1915] V.L.R. 374 at 379–380.
[5] In *Rosenhain v Commonwealth Bank of Australia* (1922) 31 C.L.R. 46 at 52–53, the Australian High Court refrained from deciding whether the words "documents against acceptance" rendered a bill conditional.

(Central Buying) Ltd,[6] a bill was payable "at 90 days D/A of this first bill of exchange". It was held by the Court of Appeal that it was not clear whether this instrument was payable at 90 days after its presentation for acceptance, after its actual acceptance or after its date. It was, therefore, not a bill of exchange.

Under section 11(2), a bill may be payable on or at a fixed period after the occurrence of a specified event which is certain to happen, though the time of its happening may be uncertain. But an instrument expressed to be payable on a contingency is not a bill and the happening of the event does not cure the defect. Whether a specific event is certain to happen or contingent is a delicate question.[7] It is noteworthy that an instrument that was payable at "30 days after the arrival of the ship P" was held not to be a bill as the arrival of the ship could not be regarded as a certainty.[8]

Due date of usance bill. Under section 14(1), as amended by section 3(2) **22–044**
of the Banking and Financial Dealings Act 1971, a bill which is not payable on demand is due on the last day of the time of payment as fixed by the bill or, if that is a non-business day, on the succeeding business day.[9] According to section 92 of the Bills of Exchange Act 1882, as amended by the Banking and Financial Dealings Act,[10] "non-business days" mean Sundays, Saturdays, Good Friday, Christmas Day and bank holidays.[11]

Under section 14(2) of the Bills of Exchange Act 1882, where a bill is payable at a fixed period after date, after sight, or after the happening of a specified event, the time of payment is determined by excluding the day from which the time is to begin to run and by including the day of payment. Under section 14(3), where a bill is payable at a fixed period after sight, the time begins to run from the date of its acceptance, or, if acceptance is refused, from the date of noting or of protest.

Under section 14(4), the term "month" in a bill means calendar month. Thus, bills dated, for example, respectively November 28, 29 and 30, payable at three months after date, all fall due on February 28 in an ordinary year, but in a leap-year the first falls due on the 28th and the second and third on the 29th. It is assumed that none of these due dates is a non-business day.

---

[6] [1979] 1 Lloyd's Rep. 548, reversing [1979] 1 Lloyd's Rep. 100. But note that, if at all possible, the courts will uphold the negotiability of a bill: *HKSB Banking Corp. Ltd v GD Trade Co. Ltd* [1998] C.L.C. 238; *Novaknit Hellas SA v Kumar Bros Int. Ltd* [1998] Lloyd's Rep. Bank 287.

[7] See *Chitty on Contracts* (29th ed.), Vol. 2, paras 34–015—34–016.

[8] *Palmer v Pratt* (1824) 2 Bing. 185. See also *Baker v Efford* (1873) 4 A.J.R. 161 (Aust.). A bill payable "on or before" a specific date is invalid because the option concerning the date of payment creates an uncertainty: *Williamson v Rider* [1963] 1 Q.B. 89 at 98, 101, 102–105 followed in *Salot v Naidoo* [1981] 3 S.A.L.R. 959. Contrast: *John Burrows Ltd v Subsurface Surveys Ltd* [1968] S.C.R. 607 (Canada); *Creative Press Ltd v Harman* [1973] I.R. 313. The same rule applies where the bill is payable "by" a given date: *Claydon v Bradley* [1987] 1 All E.R. 522.

[9] The Act was passed on December 16, 1971, but s.3 came into effect one month thereafter.

[10] s.3(1).

[11] See s.92(b), which should be read together with s.1 of the 1971 Act. Under s.2 of the 1971 Act, as amended by the Finance Act 1981, s.136(2), the Treasury has the power to suspend financial dealings on certain days.

22–045 **Sum certain in money.** According to section 3(1) of the Act, a bill of exchange must be for a sum certain in money. Under section 9(1), a sum is certain within the meaning of the Act, although it is required to be paid (a) with interest[12] at a given rate[13] (b) by stated instalments with or without provision that upon default in payment of any instalment the whole shall become due[14] and (c) according to an indicated rate of exchange to be ascertained as directed in the bill.[15] Under section 9(2), when a bill is payable with interest, the interest runs, in the absence of stipulation to the contrary, from the date of the bill or, if it is undated, from the date of issue. A bill drawn for a given amount "plus bank charges" has been held to be for an uncertain amount.[16]

22–046 **The payee.** According to section 8(2) of the Act, a bill of exchange may be payable either to the order of a specified person or to bearer. Under section 5(1), a bill may be payable to the order of the drawer or of the drawee.[17] In most overseas sales the bill of exchange is made payable either to the seller's own order or to the order of the banker who finances the transaction.

Under section 8(3), a bill is payable to bearer either if it is expressed to be so payable or if the last indorsement is in blank. Under section 8(4), it is payable to order either if it is expressed to be so payable or if it is expressed to be payable to a particular person and does not contain words prohibiting its transfer. Under section 7(1), where the bill is payable to order it must specify with reasonable certainty the identity of the payee. Under section 7(2), a bill may be made payable to two or more payees jointly or to one or more out of several payees in the alternative. It may also be made payable to the holder of an office for the time being. Where there is difficulty in establishing the identity of the payee because of some ambiguity in his description in the bill, resort must be had to the intention of the drawer.[18] Extrinsic evidence is probably admissible to identify a misnamed payee or one designated by description only.[19] However, if it is impossible to ascertain the identity of the payee, *e.g.* due to the lack of evidence regarding the drawer's intention, the bill is invalid, unless it may be treated as payable to a fictitious or non-existing person.[20]

---

[12] But the sum is uncertain if the period for which interest is payable depends on a contingency: *Rosenhain v Commonwealth Bank of Australia* (1922) 31 C.L.R. 46; *McLeod Savings and Credit Union Ltd v Perrett* [1978] 6 W.W.R. 178 (where interest was to run from date of advance).

[13] Interest at the rate "applied to most credit-worthy customers" has been held uncertain: *Bank of Montreal v Dezcan Industries Ltd* (1983) 5 W.W.R. 83.

[14] For a recent example see *Canada Permanent Trust Co. v Kowal* (1981) 32 O.R. (2d) 37.

[15] As regards problems of rate of exchange, see below, para.25–160 and Chitty, *op. cit.*, paras 34–015, 34–022 which includes also a discussion of discrepancies between the amount stated in words and in figures (at para.34–021).

[16] *Dalgety Ltd v John J Hilton Pty Ltd* [1981] 2 N.S.W.L.R. 169.

[17] As regards an instrument which is made payable for a specific purpose, such as "cash or order", see Chitty, *op. cit.*, para.34–016.

[18] *Bird & Co. v Thomas Cook & Son Ltd* [1937] 2 All E.R. 227 at 230–231.

[19] *Willis v Barrett* (1816) 2 Stark. 29; *cf. Soares v Glyn* (1845) 8 Q.B. 24.

[20] The problem of fictitious and non-existing payees does not usually arise in overseas sales; but see Chitty, *op. cit.*, para.34–025.

The drawee. Under section 53(1), a bill of exchange does not constitute an assignment of funds which the drawer has in the hands of the drawee, and a drawee who does not accept a bill is, therefore, not liable on it.[21] But under section 17(1), the drawee may show his assent[22] to the drawer's order by accepting the bill. According to section 54(1), when the drawee accepts the bill he undertakes to pay it according to the tenor of the acceptance. Under section 54(2), the acceptor is estopped from denying: (a) the existence of the drawer, the genuineness of the drawer's signature and his capacity and authority to draw the bill, (b) if the bill is payable to the drawer's order, the capacity of the drawer to indorse, but not the genuineness and validity of his indorsement, (c) if the bill is payable to the order of a third party, the existence of the payee and his capacity to indorse the bill, but not the genuineness and validity of his indorsement. It should be stressed that these estoppels operate only in favour of a holder in due course, and a mere holder is not entitled to plead them.[23] As the provisions of the Act are not exhaustive, a holder may in certain cases be able to rely on a common law estoppel to preclude the acceptor from raising certain defences. Thus, if before discounting a bill, the holder was assured by the acceptor that a certain indorsement was genuine, the acceptor could not subsequently allege that it was a forgery.[24] When in an overseas sale the buyer accepts the seller's draft, he adds currency to the draft and facilitates its discount. 22–047

The drawer. Under section 55(1)(a), by drawing the bill, the drawer engages that it will be honoured by the drawee when duly presented and that if it is dishonoured he will compensate the holder, or any indorser who is compelled to pay it, provided the required proceedings on dishonour are taken.[25] Under section 55(1)(b), the drawer is precluded from denying to a holder in due course the existence of the payee and his capacity to indorse the bill, but not the genuineness of his indorsement. The drawer is, therefore, able to resist an action by a person who holds the bill under a forged indorsement of the payee.[26] 22–048

The indorser. An engagement similar to that of the drawer is undertaken by each indorser towards all subsequent indorsers and the holder.[27] Under section 55(2)(b), the indorser is estopped from denying to a holder 22–049

---

[21] *Hopkinson v Forster* (1874) L.R. 19 Eq. 74; *Schroeder v Central Bank* (1876) 34 L.T. 735. That the drawing of the bill does not constitute an equitable assignment follows from *Shand v du Buisson* (1874) L.R. 18 Eq. 283 at 288–289. The position is different in Scotland: s.53(2) and the new s.75A inserted by the Law Reform (Miscellaneous Provisions) (Scotland) Act 1985, s.11.

[22] As regards the requisites of form of an acceptance, see below, para.22–103; as regards the time for acceptance, see below, para.22–098; as regards consideration, see Chitty, *op. cit.*, paras 34–062 *et seq.*; as regards general and qualified acceptance, see below, para.22–104.

[23] *cf. Ayres v Moore* [1940] 1 K.B. 278 at 286–287.

[24] See Chitty, *op. cit.*, para.34–045.

[25] As to which, see below, paras 22–120 *et seq.*

[26] That such a holder is not a holder in due course, see below, para.22–059.

[27] This follows from s.55(2)(a).

in due course the genuineness and regularity in all respects of the drawer's signature and of all previous indorsements. Under section 55(2)(c), as against an immediate or subsequent indorsee, the indorser is precluded from denying that, at the time of his indorsement, the bill was valid and subsisting and that he had a good title to it. In effect, both the drawer and the indorser undertake that the bill will be honoured by the drawee and are, for most purposes, in a position similar to that of joint guarantors of a debt. Thus, when the bill is dishonoured, the holder is entitled to sue the acceptor, the drawer or the indorser, or all of them together. The drawer and indorser are entitled to the equities of a surety.[28]

22–050 **Importance of signature.** According to section 23 of the Act, a person is liable as drawer, acceptor or indorser of a bill only if he has signed it in such a capacity. The Act does not specify what amounts to a sufficient signature, but it has been held that a signature written by pencil,[29] a lithographed signature or one attached by a rubber stamp is sufficient.[30] The signature need not be in the person's own name. Section 23(1) provides that, where a person signs a bill in a trade name or in an assumed name, he is liable thereon as if he had signed it in his true name.[31] The signature need not be executed by the person's own hand. Under section 91 of the Act, the signature may be written by some other person who acts under the authority of the drawer, the acceptor or the indorser. But in such a case the signature must be in the name of the principal and not in that of the agent.[32]

22–051 **Security indorsement.** Under section 56, "where a person signs a bill otherwise than as drawer or acceptor, he thereby incurs the liabilities of an indorser to a holder in due course". It has been observed that this section does not have the effect of restricting such a signer's liability to a claimant who is able to establish that he is a holder in due course but, rather, defines the signer's liability by equating it with that incurred by an ordinary indorser to a holder in due course.[33] Usually, this type of "security

---

[28] *Duncan Fox & Co. v North and South Wales Bank* (1880) 6 App.Cas. 1 at 19–20 (an indorser who pays a bill is entitled to the benefit of securities given by the acceptor to the holder). See also *Rouquette v Overmann* (1875) L.R. 10 Q.B. 525 at 537; but *cf. Scholefield Goodman & Sons Ltd v Zyngier* [1984] V.R. 445, affirmed [1985] 3 All E.R. 105, PC which shows that the drawer who has been called upon to pay the bill does not have an automatic right to securities deposited with the payee by a surety of the defaulting acceptor. It all depends on the position of the surety. See also as regards subrogation: *State Savings Bank of Victoria v Patrick Intermarine Acceptances Ltd (In Liqu.)* [1981] 1 N.S.W.L.R. 175 (Aust.).

[29] *Geary v Physic* (1826) 5 B. & C. 234.

[30] *Re London and Mediterranean Bank, Ex p. Birmingham Banking Co.* (1868) L.R. 3 Ch.App. 651 at 653–654; *cf. Bird & Co. v Thomas Cook & Son Ltd* [1937] 2 All E.R. 227 at 230–231. See also definition of writing in s.2 of the Act.

[31] As regards signatures by partnerships, see s.23(2) and *Geo. Thompson (Aust.) Pty Ltd v Vittadello* [1978] V.R. 199.

[32] As regards the liability of an agent, see *Chitty on Contracts* (29th ed.), Vol. 2, para.31–057 (*re* Companies), para.31–083.

[33] *per* Saville J. in *G & H Montage GmbH v Irvani* [1988] 1 W.L.R. 1285; [1988] 1 Lloyd's Rep. 460.

indorsement" is executed in order to give currency to the bill. It is enforceable only by parties who acquire the bill after its execution.[34] By contrast, an orthodox guarantee would be enforceable by any party except the main obligor, who is the acceptor. A further distinction between a security indorsement and a guarantee, which when executed on a negotiable instrument is known as an *aval*, is that the indorser's liability is subject to the performance by the holder of the formalities prescribed by the Act in respect of dishonoured bills.

Availability *aval*. The validity of an *aval* is recognised in all countries which have adopted the Uniform Law on Bills of the Geneva Convention as well as in the United States.[35] By contrast, the prevailing view is that an *aval* executed on a bill of exchange issued in England has the effect of a security indorsement. Further light has, however, been shed on this question in *G & H Montage GmbH v Irvani*.[36] A German contractor, who had undertaken to erect certain buildings in Iran, drew bills of exchange for the price on the employers, IDS. Initially, these bills, drawn by the contractor in Germany and accepted by IDS in Iran, were indorsed on their back by IR, who was one of IDS' main shareholders. Subsequently, though, by an agreement between the parties, the words "*bon pour aval pour les tiŕes*" were inscribed above IR's signature. In the event, IDS dishonoured the bills and the contractor brought an action in London to enforce IR's *avals*. As the contractor had not protested the bills and, further, had failed to give notice of dishonour, the question of the validity of the *avals* became the central issue. Obviously, if IR's signature constituted a mere security indorsement as opposed to a guarantee, he would be discharged from liability provided the contractor's duties upon the dishonour of the bill were governed by English law. 22–052

Mustill L.J. concluded that under section 72(3) of the Bills of Exchange Act 1882 the holder's duties were, indeed, governed by English law, which was the law of the place at which the acts in question, *viz.* the giving of notice of dishonour and of protest, had to be done. However, the nature and the validity of IR's undertaking were governed by the place at which his undertaking was given. As the instant *avals* were governed either by German or by Iranian law, both of which recognised the validity of an *aval*, the *avals* in question would also be treated as effective by an English court. Consequently, IR was held liable.

Recognition of aval in English law. *Irvani's* case was, thus, decided on the basis of the applicable principles of the conflict of laws. However, the case suggests that the prevailing view respecting the unavailability of an 22–053

---

[34] *Stagg, Mantle & Co. Brodrick* (1895) 12 T.L.R. 12.

[35] U.L.B., Arts 30–32; Uniform Commercial Code (USA), s.3–419 (Revised Version), under which the *aval* (recognised in s.3–416 of the original version) is treated as a specie of accommodation signature and binding as such; Ellinger, "Negogiable Instruments", being Ch.4 of the *Encyclopedia of Comparative Law* (Hamburg 2001), Vol. IX, para.389.

[36] [1990] 1 Lloyd's Rep. 14, affg. [1989] 1 W.L.R. 1285 (Saville J.). See, further, as regards the jurisdiction of English courts in respect of *avals* executed in other countries: *Banco Atlantico SA v British Bank of the Middle East* [1990] 2 Lloyd's Rep. 504.

aval in English law may be open to argument. Traditionally, the main argument used to deny the validity of an *aval* was the absence of a memorandum in writing complying with the provisions of the Statute of Frauds.[37] In *Irvani's* case, their Lordships disposed of this question by holding that it did not arise in the case of a bill issued abroad. They added, however, that even if the Statute had applied, the bills of exchange and the words used to express the *avals* could well satisfy the requirements of section 4. Notably, this dictum casts doubts on one of the traditional objections to the recognition of the validity of an *aval* in English law.

22–054 **Acceptance by third party.** There are cases in which a person other than the drawee purports to accept the bill in his own name. As the bill is drawn on a specific drawee, a signature by any other person who wishes to accept it is not an acceptance,[38] and will in all probability be construed as a security indorsement.[39]

22–055 **Negotiation of bill.** According to section 31(1), a bill is negotiated when it is transferred from one person to another in such a manner as to constitute the transferee the holder of the bill. In practice, negotiation takes place only if a bill is discounted or acquired by a third party.[40] Under section 31(3), a bill payable to the order of a specified payee is negotiated by the indorsement of the payee, or the holder to whom the bill has been specially indorsed, and by its delivery. Under section 31(2), a bill payable to bearer is negotiated by mere delivery. It should in this context be noted that when the last indorsement on a bill is in blank, the bill is payable to bearer.[41] Section 31(4) provides that where the holder of a bill payable to his order transfers it for value without indorsing it, the transfer gives the transferee such title as the transferor had in the bill, and the transferee, in addition, acquires the right to demand the indorsement of the transferor.[42] However, until this has been obtained the transferee is in the position of an assignee of a chose in action, and has no better title than the assignor.[43] He does not have a right to indorse the bill in the transferor's name. Moreover, cases decided before the passing of the Act indicate that he may not be able to sue on the bill without joining the transferor as a party to the action.[44] The position appears to be unchanged by the Act. As such a transferee is

---

[37] *Jackson v Hudson* (1810) 2 Camp. 447 at 448; *Steele v M'Kinlay* (1880) 5 App.Cas. 754 at 772. *Cf. McCall Bros v Hargreaves* [1932] 2 K.B. 423.
[38] *Jackson v Hudson* (1810) 2 Camp. 447 at 448; *Davis v Clarke* (1844) 6 Q.B. 16; *Steele v M'Kinlay* (1880) 5 App.Cas. 754 at 772.
[39] s.56. As to acceptance for honour, see Chitty, *op. cit.*, para.34–144.
[40] But note that the acquisition of the bill by a third party may be for security purposes; below, paras 22–073, 22–075.
[41] As to when a bill is payable to order and when to bearer, see above, para.22–046.
[42] *Walters v Neary* (1904) 21 T.L.R. 146.
[43] *Whistler v Forster* (1863) 14 C.B.(N.S.) 248. As regards the validity of an assignment of the chose in action conferred by a bill, see *Geo. Thompson (Aust.) Ltd v Vittadello* [1978] V.R. 199 at 208–212.
[44] *Cunliffe v Whitehead* (1837) 3 Bing.N.C. 828 at 830–831; *Harrop v Fisher* (1861) 10 C.B.(N.S.) 196. As to when an indorsement is valid to effect a transfer, see s.32, discussed in Chitty, *op. cit.*, para.34–089. Where a bill is indorsed conditionally the drawee may ignore the condition and pay it to the indorsee: s.33.

not a holder within the definition of section 2, he cannot enforce the bill in his own name.

Indorsement in blank and special indorsement. An indorsement in blank specifies no indorsee, and a bill so indorsed becomes payable to bearer. A special indorsement specifies the person to whom, or to whose order, the bill is to be payable. The provisions of the Act relating to the payee of the bill apply with the necessary modifications to an indorsee who holds the bill under a special indorsement.[45] Under section 34(4), when a bill has been indorsed in blank, any holder may convert the blank indorsement into a special indorsement by writing above the indorser's signature a direction to pay the bill to or to the order of himself or some other person. A holder is, further, entitled to strike out an indorsement of a previous party. The indorser whose indorsement has been struck out and all subsequent indorsers are then discharged.[46] An indorser often strikes out his own indorsement and those of subsequent parties when he pays the bill after it has been dishonoured by the acceptor or drawer; the object is to avoid liability if the bill is lost. By striking out these indorsements, the indorser who pays the bill does not lose his right of recourse against all prior parties.[47] 22–056

Delivery. The delivery of a bill is essential where it is negotiated. According to section 2 of the Act, delivery means the transfer of possession, whether actual or constructive, from one person to another.[48] In most cases possession is transferred by the physical delivery of the bill. Constructive delivery takes place when a person who originally holds the bill in one capacity subsequently holds it in some other capacity.[49] Thus, if a collecting banker originally holds the bill on behalf of the seller who drew it, but subsequently makes an advance against it and holds it for himself, there is a constructive transfer of the possession of the bill.[50] 22–057

Delivery and completion. Delivery is important not only as regards the negotiation of the bill but also as regards the contractual relationships evidenced by it. Under section 21(1) of the Act, every contract on a bill, whether it is the drawer's, the acceptor's or the indorser's, is incomplete and revocable until the delivery of the bill.[51] But where an acceptance is 22–058

---

45 s.34(1)–(3).

46 As to an indorsement struck out by mistake, see *Wilkinson v Johnson* (1824) 3 B. & C. 428.

47 s.59(2)(b); *cf. Hadley & Co. v Henry* (1896) 22 V.L.R. 230 (Aust.). As regards restrictive indorsements and destruction of negotiability, see Chitty, *op. cit.*, paras 34–092, 34–027; as regards indorsements of overdue bills, see *ibid.*, para.34–093; as regards negotiation of a bill to a party already liable on it, see *ibid.*, para.34–094.

48 As regards the position where delivery is obtained by a trick, see *Citibank NA v Brown Shipley & Co.* [1991] 1 Lloyd's Rep. 576.

49 See, *e.g. Bosanquet v Forster* (1841) 9 C. & P. 659; *cf. Belcher v Campbell* (1845) 8 Q.B. 1; *Barclays Bank v Bank of England* [1985] 1 All E.R. 385.

50 As regards the authority to effect delivery, see Chitty, *op. cit.*, para.34–033.

51 As regards the effect of conditional delivery, see *Clifford Chance v Silver* [1992] N.P.C. 103. But see as regards a holder in due course, below, para.22–062.

written on the bill and the drawee gives notice that he has accepted it, the acceptance becomes complete. Delivery of the bill by the acceptor is therefore not necessary. But the delivery of the accepted bill constitutes notice of the acceptance.[52]

22–059 **Types of holder.** In most disputes the person who seeks to enforce the bill is the holder.[53] The rights of the holder depend on whether he is a "holder" (or "mere holder"), a "holder for value" or a "holder in due course". But it is important to bear in mind that not every person who obtains the possession of the bill is a holder. The word "holder" is defined in section 2 of the Act as the "payee or indorsee of a bill . . . who is in possession of it, or the bearer thereof." It follows that in the case of a bill to bearer, the physical possession of the bill constitutes the possessor a holder. But where a bill is payable to the order of a specified payee, a person who obtains the bill under a forged indorsement of the payee is not the "payee", an "indorsee" or the bearer; it follows that he is not a holder.[54]

22–060 **Holder for value.** The term "holder for value" is not defined in the Act. But "value" is defined and means "consideration".[55] Thus, a holder for value is a holder who has given consideration for the bill. The consideration need not be given to the acceptor or to any specific party who is sued on the bill.[56] If the holder of a bill negotiates it without value to a donee, and the latter transfers it for value to a third party, the third party is a holder for value.[57] Section 27(2) of the Act augments this rule by providing that, where value has at any time been given for a bill, the holder is deemed to be a holder for value as regards the acceptor and all persons who became parties to the bill prior to such time. He can sue all prior parties to the bill including those who did not obtain value. Thus, a banker who gives value for a bill to a transferor becomes a holder for value and can sue the acceptor or the drawer even if they have not obtained any consideration for it.[58] Under section 27(3), where the holder of a bill has a lien on it, arising either from a contract or by implication of law, he is deemed to be a holder for value to the extent of the sum for which he has a lien.[59] This is

---

[52] As to cancellation of an acceptance before its communication or the delivery of the bill, see *Cox v Troy* (1822) 5 B. & A. 474; *Bank of Van Diemen's Land v Bank of Victoria* (1871) L.R. 3 P.C. 526.
[53] As to whether a holder's nominee is a holder, see *Emmett v Tottenham* (1853) 8 Exch. 884; *Arcona v Marks* (1862) 31 L.J.Ex. 163.
[54] *Smith v Union Bank* (1875) L.R. 10 Q.B. 291 at 295–296, affirmed (1875) 1 Q.B.D. 31; *Lacave & Co. v Crédit Lyonnais* [1897] 1 Q.B. 148. See also Chitty, *op. cit.*, para.34–056. Contrast the position under Art. 16 of the Uniform Law of the Geneva Convention, mentioned, above, para.22–034.
[55] As to what constitutes consideration for this purpose, see Chitty, *op. cit.*, para.34–062. And see *MK International Development Co. Ltd v Housing Bank* [1991] 1 Bank L.R. 74, CA, noted in [1991] J.B.L. 279 *et seq.*; *AEG (UK) Ltd v Lewis* (1993) 137 S.J.L.B. 24; *Wheeler v Roberts*, decision of July 11, 1994, (CA unreported).
[56] *ibid.*
[57] *Scott v Lifford* (1808) 1 Camp. 246.
[58] *Barber v Richards* (1851) 6 Exch. 63 at 65; and see *Banque Nationale de Paris Plc v International Bulk Commodities* (unreported, February 7, 1992) (Hobhouse J.); Chitty, *op. cit.*, para.34–056.
[59] But apparently not if the holder takes the bill when it is overdue or with knowledge of defects in the transferor's title: *Redfern v Rosenthal* (1902) 18 T.L.R. 718.

important in cases where a banker advances money to the seller in connection with an overseas sale. Even if the amount is not advanced against the seller's bill on the buyer, the banker obtains a lien over the bill if it is given to him for collection.[60] He is therefore a holder for value of the bill. However, if he brings an action to enforce the bill, he becomes a resulting trustee in favour of the transferor, or seller, as regards the balance between the amount of the bill and the amount for which he has a lien over it.[61]

Holder in due course. According to section 29(1), four requirements must be fulfilled before a person may be considered a holder in due course. First, he must take the bill when it is complete and regular on its face. A bill is not complete on its face if any material detail, such as the amount payable or a necessary indorsement, is missing.[62] A bill is considered irregular whenever anything on its face or back can give rise to doubts or is out of the ordinary.[63] Secondly, a holder in due course must take the bill before it is overdue[64] and without notice that it was previously dishonoured, if such was the fact. Thirdly, he must take it in good faith and without having notice, either on his own or through an executive in his employment,[65] of any defect in the title of the person who negotiates the bill to him.[66] In particular the title of the person who negotiates the bill is defective when he obtained the bill or its acceptance by fraud, duress or other unlawful means, or for an illegal consideration, or when he negotiates it in breach of faith or under circumstances amounting to fraud.[67] The list, though, is not exhaustive. Thus, a modern Canadian authority suggests that a transferee, who is aware that the transferor holds the bill under an 22–061

---

[60] *Re Keever* [1967] Ch. 182 (lien arising from general indebtedness of customer to banker); *Barclays Bank Ltd v Astley Industrial Trust Ltd* [1970] 2 Q.B. 527.

[61] *Reid v Furnival* (1833) 1 Cr. & M. 538. A stay of proceedings may in such a case be granted if, in an action on the bill, it turns out that the plaintiff is trustee of part of the sum and the defendant has a claim which he could plead by way of set-off against the beneficiary of the trust: *Barclays Bank Ltd v Aschaffenburger Zellstoffwerke AG* [1967] 1 Lloyd's Rep. 387.

[62] *Whistler v Forster* (1863) 14 C.B.(N.S.) 248 at 258; *Slingsby v District Bank* [1931] 2 K.B. 588, affirmed [1932] 1 K.B. 544; *Arab Bank Ltd v Ross* [1952] 2 Q.B. 216 at 226. But a bill is not incomplete merely because it has not been accepted: *National Park Bank of New York v Berggren & Co.* (1914) 110 L.T. 907. As regards inchoate bills and the right to complete missing details, see *Chitty on Contracts* (29th ed.), Vol. 2, paras 34–036, 34–039.

[63] *Arab Bank Ltd v Ross* [1952] 2 Q.B. 216 (indorsement in name different from payee's description on face of bill); *cf. Heller Factors Pty Ltd v Toy Corporation Pty Ltd* [1984] 1 N.S.W.L.R. 121 (Aust.), showing that an indorsement of a director is not irregular merely because he fails to add the company's name after the addition of the words showing that he acts in a representative capacity. And see, generally, Chitty, *op. cit.*, paras 34–076—34–077.

[64] As to when a bill payable on demand is overdue, see s.36(3).

[65] *Bank of Credit and Commerce International SA v Dawson and Wright* [1987] F.L.R. 342.

[66] As to good faith, see Chitty, *op. cit.*, paras 34–078—34–080. And see *Bank of Cyprus (London) Ltd v Jones* (1984) 134 N.L.J. 522; *Bank of Credit and Commerce International SA v Dawson and Wright* [1987] F.L.R. 342.

[67] s.29(2). For a recent case concerning a negotiable instrument issued for an illegal consideration, see *Ladup Ltd v Shaikh* [1983] Q.B. 225.

indorsement that was meant to be restrictive, is not a holder in due course.[68] Lastly, a holder in due course must take the bill for value, *i.e.* consideration. But under section 30(1), every party whose signature appears on the bill is prima facie deemed to have given value for it. Moreover, under section 30(2) of the Act, every holder is presumed to be a holder in due course. But the burden of proof is shifted if, in an action on a bill, it is admitted or proved that the acceptance, issue or subsequent negotiation of the bill has been effected with fraud, duress, force and fear, or illegality. In such a case the holder has to prove that subsequent to the alleged event, value has in good faith been given for the bill.[69] It should be added that it follows from the language of section 29 that a holder in due course must be a "holder who has taken a bill . . .". It has been held that these words refer to a holder to whom the bill has been *negotiated* and that the original payee of a bill cannot, therefore, be a holder in due course.[70]

22–062 **Rights of mere holder and holder in due course.** The rights of a mere holder may be contrasted with those of a holder in due course. Under section 38(1), a mere holder has the right to sue on the bill in his own name. But the defendant can raise against the holder all the defences which he has against any party to the bill, except a partial failure of the consideration that cannot be ascertained as a liquidated amount.[71] Under section 38(2), a holder in due course holds the bill free from any defects in the title[72] of previous parties as well as from any equities available to prior parties among themselves and may enforce payment against all parties liable on the bill. The position of the holder in due course is safeguarded by other provisions of the Act.[73] The effect of section 38(2) is that the rights of a holder in due course of the bill are unqualified by, and independent of, the rights of the parties to an underlying transaction that has led to the drawing of the bill. By way of illustration consider the case where the buyer accepts the seller's bill of exchange, which is accompanied by a forged bill

---

[68] *Williams and Glyn's Bank Ltd v Belkin Packaging Ltd* [1981] 123 D.L.R. (3d) 612. As regards the materiality of the date on which the bill is issued and its date of maturity, see *Heller Factors Pty Ltd v Toy Corporation Pty Ltd* [1984] 1 N.S.W.L.R. 121.

[69] *Jones v Gordon* (1877) 2 App.Cas. 616; *Barclays Bank Ltd v Astley Industrial Trust Ltd* [1970] 2 Q.B. 527 at 536–537. See also *Bank für Gemeinwirtschaft AG v City of London Garages Ltd* [1971] 1 W.L.R. 149.

[70] *Jones (RE) Ltd v Waring and Gillow Ltd* [1926] A.C. 670; *Williams v Williams* 1980 S.L.T. 25 (Sheriff's Ct.).

[71] *Day v Nix* (1824) 9 Moore C.P. 159; 2 L.J.(O.S.) C.P. 133; *Sully v Frean* (1854) 10 Exch. 535; *Warwick v Nairn* (1855) 10 Exch. 762 (alleged inferior quality of goods); *Nova (Jersey) Knit Ltd v Kammgarn Spinnerei GmbH* [1977] 1 W.L.R. 713 (claim for unliquidated damages under a contract of sale). See also *Williams and Glyn's Bank Ltd v Belkin Packaging Ltd* [1981] 123 D.L.R. (3d) 612. Similarly, a defence based on an innocent misrepresentation pertaining to the underlying transaction is not a defence to an action on a bill: *Re A Company No. 005070 of 1994 (Mitrebrook Ltd)* (unreported, decision of October 18, 1994) (Harman J.).

[72] As to what constitutes a defect in title, see s.29(2) discussed above; see generally Chitty, *op. cit.*, para.33–071.

[73] ss.12 and 20(2) relating to completion of blank instruments; s.21(2) under which delivery is conclusively presumed; ss.54(2) and 55(2) as to which, see above, paras 22–047—22–049; s.64 relating to alterations on bill.

of lading, and the seller indorses the bill of exchange to a holder in due course. The forgery of the bill of lading, which may result in a total failure of the consideration provided by the seller for the buyer's acceptance, is not a defence to an action brought against the buyer by a holder in due course of the bill.[74]

Of particular advantage to the seller, and this applies regardless of whether he is a mere holder or a holder in due course, is that, where the price is covered by a bill of exchange, the seller should be able to obtain summary judgment under Part 24 of the CPR. In such proceedings, save in exceptional circumstances or upon strong grounds, the defendant will not be allowed to set up a counterclaim or set-off for unliquidated damages for breach of the underlying or some other contract.[75]

Rights of holder for value. The rights of a holder for value, who is not a holder in due course, are not defined in the Act. The position of such a holder may be relevant in an overseas sale where a discounting banker is not a holder in due course of the seller's bill on the buyer, *e.g.* where the banker gives value for a bill that is irregularly indorsed. Basically, the position of a holder for value is similar to that of a mere holder.[76] Thus, his action on the bill would be defeated if the bill was obtained by means of fraud or of duress or where the consideration was illegal. This proposition derives support from the language of the Act. Section 29(2) specifically mentions fraud, duress, force and fear, and an illegal consideration as factors that render the transferor's title defective. Section 38(2) grants the holder in due course a right to enforce the bill despite such defects in the transferor's title. It follows that if a holder is not a holder in due course, but a mere holder or a holder for value, his rights are defeated by such defects in the transferor's title. 22–063

Where consideration fails. Can the holder for value enforce the bill where there has been a total or partial failure of the consideration furnished to the person who is sued on the bill or where no consideration has been furnished to him? As the holder for value has furnished consideration to the transferor, the absence of consideration between prior parties to the bill does not constitute a valid defence against him.[77] Moreover, when a person signs a bill without obtaining a consideration for 22–064

---

[74] *Robinson v Reynolds* (1841) 2 Q.B. 196; *Guaranty Trust Co. of New York v Hannay & Co.* [1918] 2 K.B. 623 at 652. As regards the position of a person who derives his title from a holder in due course, see Chitty, *op. cit.*, para.34–081. Note also the position of a drawer who regains the possession of the bill by paying it to a holder in due course: *Jade International Steel Stahl und Eisen GmbH & Co. KG v Robert Nicholas (Steels) Ltd* [1978] Q.B. 917.

[75] Previously RSC, Ord.14, r.1 and see the Supreme Court Practice 1999, paras 14/3—14/4/16; 14/4/20; *Chalmers and Guest on Bills of Exchange* (16th ed.), pp.233 *et seq.*; *Chitty on Contracts* (29th ed.), Vol. 2, para.34–097, n.16, and authorities there cited. See also *Paclantic Financing Co. Inc. v Moscow Narodny Bank* [1984] 1 W.L.R. 930.

[76] *Whistler v Forster* (1863) 14 C.B.(N.S.) 248, esp. 258.

[77] *Mills v Barber* (1836) 1 M. & W. 425 at 430–431; and see s.27(2). *Cf. Forman v Wright* (1851) 11 C.B. 481 at 492.

it, he usually acts as an accommodation party.[78] Under section 28(2), such a party is liable to a holder *for value* who takes the bill with knowledge of this specific fact.

In the case of partial failure of consideration it is necessary to draw a distinction between an action brought against an immediate party to the bill, *e.g.* an action by a seller (or drawer) who sues the buyer on his acceptance, and a dispute between remote parties, *e.g.* an action by a banker, who has discounted the bill, against the buyer (acceptor). As between immediate parties, partial failure of consideration may be pleaded if it involves an ascertained and liquidated amount. Thus, if the seller supplies only one half of the goods, he cannot recover more than half the amount of the bill drawn for the price and accepted by the buyer.[79] But if goods, which turn out to be of an inferior quality, are not rejected by the buyer, a loss resulting from the defective condition cannot be raised as a defence to the seller's action on the bill.[80] Thus, in *Thoni GmbH v RTP Equipment Ltd*[81] the defendants, who had received a shipment of hoses from the claimant, accepted a bill of exchange and undertook to make specified periodic payments. When a subsequent shipment comprised defective hoses, the claimants claimed a refund. They ceased to make the outstanding periodic payments and dishonoured the bill of exchange. Granting leave to defend an action on the bill and, thus, refusing to grant summary judgment, Buckley L.J. stressed that there was a prima facie defence in respect of a substantial and defined part of the amount involved. His Lordship based his conclusion on the finding that it was established on the facts that the defendants' indebtedness was limited to a specified and hence liquidated amount. There was therefore a defence in respect of the balance as the consideration furnished for this amount had failed. As against a remote party to the bill, partial failure of the consideration does not afford a defence even if the deficiency or loss resulting from the partial failure of consideration is liquidated.[82]

---

[78] As to accommodation bills, see *Chitty on Contracts* (29th ed.), Vol. 2, para.34–074.

[79] *Agra and Masterman's Bank v Leighton* (1866) L.R. 2 Ex. 56 at 64, 65. And see n.69 above as to position in case of mere holder. See also *Forman v Wright* (1851) 11 C.B. 481 at 492.

[80] *Glennie v Imri* (1839) 3 Y. & C. Ex. 436 at 442–443; *Agra and Masterman's Bank v Leighton*, above; *cf. Hitchings and Coulthurst Co. v Northern Leather Co.* [1914] 3 K.B. 907; *Montebianco Industrie Tessali SpA v Carlyle Mills (London) Ltd* [1981] 1 Lloyd's Rep. 509. See also *Fielding and Platt Ltd v Najjar* [1969] 1 W.L.R. 357 where the seller had performed part of the bargain before the buyer dishonoured the bill. But note that the buyer may counterclaim. As to whether a stay of proceedings would be granted pending the counterclaim see: *James Lamont & Co. Ltd v Hyland Ltd (No.2)* [1950] 1 All E.R. 929; *All Trades Distributors Ltd v Agencies Kaufman Ltd* (1969) 113 S.J. 995; *Nova (Jersey) Knit Ltd v Kammgarn Spinnerei GmbH* [1977] 1 W.L.R. 713; *Montecchi v Shimco Ltd* [1979] 1 W.L.R. 1180. And see, as regards a counterclaim based on an unliquidated loss of profits: *Cebora SNC v SIP (Industrial Products) Ltd* [1976] 1 Lloyd's Rep. 271. But note that the amount of a dishonoured bill can be set off against an amount of damages recoverable under the underlying contract: *Handley Page Ltd v Rockwell Machine Tool Co. Ltd* [1970] 2 Lloyd's Rep. 459 at 465, affirmed [1971] 2 Lloyd's Rep. 298. As regards a stay based on a right of set-off related to a liquidated demand, see above, n.61.

[81] [1979] 2 Lloyd's Rep. 282.

[82] *Archer v Bamford* (1822) 3 Stark. 175; *cf. Harris Oscar & Co. v Vallarman & Co.* [1940] 1 All E.R. 185.

Whether total failure of consideration is a defence against an action by a holder for value who is a "remote party" has not been the subject of decision. As section 38(2) perfects the right of action only where the person who seeks to enforce the bill is a holder in due course, it is arguable that a total failure of consideration can be raised against other types of holder, including a holder for value. But it may be argued, against this view, that as the holder for value provides a consideration for the bill, the failure of a consideration provided by a prior party is of no relevance.[83]

Commercial object. These principles throw light on one of the objects of obtaining the buyer's acceptance of a bill of exchange for the price. It is clear that in certain cases the seller, or a discounter, may be able to enforce the buyer's acceptance although the buyer has a good defence to an action on the contract of sale. By way of illustration take a case in which the buyer has accepted a bill of exchange for the price of goods supplied under a contract of sale. If on arrival the goods turn out to be defective, the buyer may have a good defence to an action for the price.[84] But he may, nevertheless, be liable on his acceptance.[85] It is true that the buyer may have an adequate defence to such an action, provided it is brought by the seller, who is an immediate party, and provided further that the goods are in such a defective condition as to justify their rejection. In such a case the buyer may be able to plead that there has been a total failure of the consideration provided by the seller.[86] But, as pointed out above, the buyer may not be able to plead such total failure of consideration as a defence to an action brought by a "remote party" such as a banker who has discounted or purchased the bill. **22–065**

Bills in a set. In some overseas sales the seller attaches one of a set of bills of exchange to each set of documents. The different parts of the set of bills are usually numbered[87] and refer to each other. One part is retained by the seller and the others are sent, each under separate cover, to the buyer. The object is to minimise the danger of loss by mail. According to section 71, such parts constitute one bill and the position is as follows: where the holder of a set indorses two or more parts to different persons, he is liable on every such part, and every indorser subsequent to him is liable on the part he has himself indorsed, as if the different parts were separate bills. **22–066**

[83] For some support of this view, see *Watson v Russell* (1864) 5 B. & S. 968. But as between immediate parties, total failure of the underlying consideration is a good defence to an action on the bill: *Fielding and Platt Ltd v Najjar*, above. As to whether the court may grant an injunction to restrain negotiation where there has been a total failure of consideration, see *Patrick v Harrison* (1792) 3 Bro.C.C. 476; *Glennie v Imri* (1839) 3 Y. & C. Ex. 436; *Bainbrigge v Hemingway* (1865) 12 L.T. 74. See also Chitty, *op. cit.*, para.34–099.

[84] But note that this is no longer so in respect of contracts c.i.f.: above, paras 19–187 *et seq*.

[85] For an illustration relating to a contract c.i.f., see *Barry v Slade* (1920) 20 S.R.(N.S.W.) 121.

[86] *James Lamont & Co. Ltd v Hyland Ltd* (*No.2*) [1950] 1 All E.R. 929 at 932.

[87] The parts are usually expressed to be "First", "Second", etc. "of Exchange". A bill not in a set is known as a *sola*.

Where two or more parts of a set are negotiated to different holders in due course, the holder whose title first accrues is, as between such holders, deemed the true owner of the bill; but this does not, in itself, affect the rights of a person who in due course accepts or pays the part first presented to him. The acceptance may be written on any part, and it must be written on one part only. If the drawee accepts more than one part, and such accepted parts get into the hands of different holders in due course, he is liable on every such part as if it were a separate bill. When the acceptor of a bill drawn in a set pays it without requiring the part bearing his acceptance to be delivered up to him, and that part is at maturity outstanding in the hands of a holder in due course, the acceptor is liable to this holder. Subject to the preceding rules, where any one part of a bill drawn in a set is discharged, the entire bill is discharged.

4. DISCOUNT AND COLLECTION OF BILLS OF EXCHANGE

(a) *Engagement of Banker*

22–067 **Function of bank.** The seller's bill of exchange for the price is usually presented to the buyer for acceptance and for payment by the seller's banker or by this banker's correspondents. The role assumed by the seller's banker when he is asked to present a draft to the buyer varies from case to case. The view prevailing in the banking community is that the seller's banker may assume one of the following three roles. First, the banker may agree to "negotiate" the seller's bill. When the bill is delivered to him, the "negotiating banker" credits the seller's account with the full amount of the bill (less the banking charges)[88]; it is said that the negotiating banker usually becomes a holder in due course of the bill. Secondly, the banker may agree to advance the seller a percentage of the face value of the bill. In such a case the seller's account is immediately credited with the amount advanced against the bill but it is not credited with the balance until the bill is paid by the buyer. It is said that such an advance gives the banker a lien over the bill and that under section 27(3) of the Bills of Exchange Act 1882 he becomes a holder for value of the bill to the extent of the amount that he advances.[89] Thirdly, the banker may not be prepared to grant the seller any credit against the bill before it is paid by the buyer. In such a case the banker presents the bill to the buyer on behalf of the seller and acts as a "collecting banker". The seller's account is credited with the amount of the bill (less the banking charges) after payment.

From a legal point of view, however, the distinction between these three roles is not always clear cut. It will be convenient to discuss, in the first place, the distinction between a negotiating banker and a banker who makes an advance against a bill. The question of the banker's right of

---

[88] These charges constitute a "discount", as to the nature of which see *Ditchfield (Inspector of Taxes) v Sharp* [1983] 3 All E.R. 681.

[89] As regards s.27(3), see above, para.22–060, as regards the banker's lien, see below, paras 22–139 *et seq*.

recourse against the customer arises in both types of transaction. The consideration of this problem is followed by a discussion of the distinction between the role assumed by a banker who either negotiates or makes an advance against a bill ("discounting banker") and the role of a collecting banker.[90]

Advance and negotiation distinguished. It is inaccurate to describe the banker who negotiates the bill as a holder in due course and the banker who advances a percentage of its amount as a holder for value. Under section 27(1)(a), valuable consideration for a bill may be constituted by any consideration sufficient to support a simple contract. It follows that the consideration for a bill need not be equal to its face value and that a banker may become a holder in due course of a bill even if he advances a relatively small amount against it.[91] Moreover, the payment to the seller of the full amount of the bill does not, by itself, constitute the banker a holder in due course. He must, in addition, be able to show that he has obtained the bill in circumstances complying with the requirements laid down in section 29(1) of the Act. Two of these requirements are of particular importance as regards the position of the seller's banker. First, he can be a holder in due course only if the bill is complete and regular on its face.[92] If he has paid the seller the full amount of an irregular bill, he cannot be a holder in due course. Secondly, the banker must be a person who "has taken" or obtained the transfer of the bill. Thus, if the bill is payable to the seller's own order and transferred to the banker, the latter "has taken" the bill and may become a holder in due course even if he has advanced only part of the amount of the bill. But if the bill is payable to the banker's order and delivered to him by the seller, the banker is not a person who "has taken" the bill within the meaning of section 29(1) and hence not a holder in due course.[93] While the delivery of such a bill constitutes the banker a "holder", he can, at best, be a holder for value; this is the position even if he advances the full amount of the bill. 22–068

Discounting banker. It follows that the distinction between the negotiation of a bill against payment of its face value and the making of an advance of a percentage is of limited importance from a legal point of view. The term "discounting banker" will be used to describe a banker who is a holder of a bill, regardless of whether the transaction involves negotiation or an advance of a percentage. But the distinction is of importance where a discounting banker brings an action based on the bill, and the buyer (or acceptor) raises defences which he has against the seller (the drawer). In 22–069

---

[90] See, generally, Craigie, "The Collection of Bills in International Trade", *Current Problems of International Trade Financing* (2nd ed., Singapore, 1990), pp.58 *et seq.*
[91] *cf. Re Firth* (1879) 12 Ch.D. 337, esp. 347; *Re Bunyard* (1880) 16 Ch.D. 330 concerning bills negotiated by a customer who is adjudicated a bankrupt. See, generally, *Chitty on Contracts* (29th ed.), Vol. 2, para.34–062.
[92] See above, para.22–061.
[93] *Jones (R E) Ltd v Waring and Gillow Ltd* [1926] A.C. 670.

Barclays Bank Ltd v Aschaffenburger Zellstoffwerke AG[94] an English exporter drew bills of exchange covering the price of goods supplied to a German buyer. The bills, which were payable to the seller's own order, were indorsed by him to the bank against an advance of 73 per cent of their face value. The buyer accepted the bills but subsequently dishonoured them by non-payment. When the bank brought an action to enforce the bills, the buyer applied for leave to defend on the ground that he was entitled to damages from the seller for delays and for the defective condition of the goods. It was held that as the bank was a holder in due course it was entitled to judgment for the full amount of the bills. But as the bank was a trustee of the seller as to 27 per cent of the amount of the bills, a stay of execution pending decision in an action brought by the buyer against the seller was granted in respect of this percentage. The basis of the decision was that the bank should not recover from the buyer an amount which it was, in effect, claiming as a trustee of the seller. If the bank had purchased (or acquired the full property in) the bills for 73 per cent of their face value, a stay of execution would probably have been refused as the bank would then have claimed the whole amount for its own account. Whether the bank was a "holder in due course" or a "holder for value" was, in this specific situation, of limited importance.[95]

22–070 **"Without recourse" transactions.** In most discount transactions the banker retains a right of recourse against the customer. This is the case regardless of whether the transaction involves an advance against the bill or its negotiation. Thus, if the drawee of the bill dishonours it by non-acceptance or by non-payment the banker can recover the amount of the bill from the customer.[96] The banker's right of recourse is usually based on the customer's indorsement[97] and, in addition, may be derived from a specific clause contained in a "collection order" signed by the customer.[98] But in certain transactions involving the finance of overseas sales, the discounting banker may be prepared to assume the risk of a financial loss

---

[94] [1967] 1 Lloyd's Rep. 387. For a similar approach, see *Thornton v Maynard* (1875) L.R. 10 C.P. 695; *Re Firth* (1879) 12 Ch.D. 337; *Re Bunyard* (1880) 16 Ch.D. 330. *Cf.* as regards the question of a stay of proceedings generally, *Nova (Jersey) Knit Ltd v Kammgarn Spinnerei GmbH* [1977] 1 W.L.R. 713. See also *Banque Nationale de Paris Plc v International Bulk Commodities* (unreported, February 7, 1992) (Hobhouse J.).

[95] The bank is described in parts of the judgment as a holder in due course and in others as a holder for value. The case can also be explained on the basis that the bank was in a position similar to that of a pledgee; *cf.* Chalmers and Guest, *Bills of Exchange* (16th ed.), p.259.

[96] As to what constitutes dishonour by non-acceptance and by non-payment, see below, paras 22–105, 22–117. Note that if the banker makes an advance of a fraction of the amount of the bill and agrees to credit the customer's account with the balance after receiving the proceeds, he cannot recover more than the amount advanced.

[97] As to the liability of an indorser, see above, para.22–049. If the bill is payable to the bankers' order, the seller is liable as drawer (above, para.22–048).

[98] As to the nature of such a document, see below, para.22–081. A collection order is not signed in transactions involving the discount of accepted trading bills.

resulting from the dishonour of a bill of exchange for the price.[99] This occurs where an irrevocable credit stipulates for negotiation "without recourse" of a bill drawn by the seller on the buyer and in certain "bank facilities" covered by export credit guarantees.[1]

When the customer transfers to the banker a bill drawn in connection with a "without recourse" transaction, he inserts in the bill words excluding his liability on it. This is authorised by section 16(1) of the Act, under which the drawer of a bill and any indorser may insert therein an express stipulation negativing or limiting his own liability to the holder. As between remote parties, the exclusion of a right of recourse is effective only in so far as words such as "Pay to the order of X *sans recours*"[2] appear in the relevant part of the bill. But as between immediate parties, such as the drawer and his transferee, the right of recourse may be excluded by the terms of an underlying agreement and, in the absence of express words excluding liability, may be inferred from the circumstances of the transaction.[3] It should be noted that the seller who draws a bill of exchange under a contract of sale, and the banker who discounts it, are in most cases immediate parties.

Liability in cases of "without recourse". A drawer or indorser who excludes a right of recourse is not necessarily exonerated from all liability. An American authority which has been reported in England suggests that his position is similar to that of a transferor by delivery,[4] *i.e.* a person who negotiates a bill of exchange payable to bearer without indorsing it. Under section 58(2), a transferor by delivery is not liable on the bill. But under subsection (3), the transferor by delivery warrants to his immediate transferee being a holder for value that the bill is what it purports to be, that he has a right to transfer it and that at the time of the transfer he is not aware of any fact which renders the bill valueless. On this basis it is arguable that a seller who transfers an unaccepted bill to a discounting banker "without recourse" is liable if he is aware that the bill is accompanied by forged shipping documents and is, therefore, worthless. 22–071

Forfaiting.[5] A modern type of "without recourse" financing is forfaiting. The system enables the seller to raise medium-term finance for the export of his goods without incurring the risk of a recourse action in the event of 22–072

[99] To a certain extent his position may be similar to that of a factor who discounts the book debts or accounts receivable of a dealer. But factoring does not, usually, involve the drawing of negotiable instruments covering the amount advanced against the book debts. See, generally, on factoring, Biscoe, *Law and Practice of Credit Factoring* (London, 1975); Salinger, *Factoring: a Guide to Factoring Practice and Law* (3rd ed., 1999); T. G. Huston [1965] *Journal of the Institute of Bankers* 69; below, para.23–311.

[1] As regards documentary credits, see below, para.23–003, as regards export credit guarantees, see below, paras 24–040 *et seq*.

[2] *Wakefield v Alexander & Co.* (1901) 17 T.L.R. 217.

[3] *Castrique v Buttigieg* (1855) 10 Moore P.C. 94; *cf. Montefiore v O'Connor* (1878) 1 S.C.R. (N.S.W.)(N.S.) 227 at 233 (Aust.).

[4] *Dumont v Williamson* (1867) 17 L.T. 71 at 72 (the case is a decision of the Superior Court of Cincinnati). As to the position of a transferor by delivery, see *Chitty on Contracts* (29th ed.), Vol. 2, para.34–124.

[5] See, generally, Guild and Harris, *Forfaiting* (Universe Books, N.Y.); Chalmers and Guest, *Bills of Exchange* (16th ed.), pp.84–86.

the buyer's default. Its operation is as follows. The seller draws on the buyer bills payable to his own order at an agreed usance and inserts words excluding recourse to himself. The bills are accepted by the buyer. They are backed by a bank in the buyer's country which either executed an *aval*[6] on the bills or, alternatively, provides a separate guarantee. The seller then indorses the bills "without recourse" and discounts them through his own bank on the *á forfait* market. The transaction can also be carried out by means of promissory notes, made by the buyer in favour of the seller. These are, again, backed by a bank and indorsed by the seller without recourse.[7]

At maturity, each instrument is presented for payment to the buyer. In the case of its dishonour, payment is demanded from the bank that issued the *aval* or guarantee. The effect of the transaction is that the seller obtains unconditional payment of the price of the goods (less the usual charges and discount fee). But although a remote holder of the bill does not have a right of recourse against the seller, an immediate transferee may very well be in a position to exercise the rights considered in the previous paragraph.[8] In practical terms, a seller, who discounts a "without recourse" instrument on the *á forfait* market, is in a position similar to that of a beneficiary who has obtained payment under a documentary credit.

22–073 **Discount and collection distinguished.** From a theoretical point of view, there is a clear distinction between a collecting banker and a discounting banker. The discounting banker advances money or gives the seller some other value for the bill and thereupon becomes a holder. When he presents it to the buyer for acceptance and later on for payment he acts for himself. The collecting banker does not make an advance against the bill and does not become its holder; he is an agent of the seller and handles the bill on his behalf. Although the distinction between the collecting banker and the discounting banker has been worked out mainly in cases concerning cheques[9] it is relevant also in the case of transactions involving other types of bills of exchange.[10]

Whether in a specific transaction the banker acts as a collecting banker or as a discounting banker depends mainly on the facts. It is important to bear in mind that the decisions relating to the collection of cheques are not necessarily conclusive where the instrument involved is a bill of exchange drawn by the seller on the buyer. Thus, the crediting of a customer's account with the proceeds of a cheque before its clearance does not, by

---

[6] As to which see above, paras 22–052—22–053.

[7] Chalmers and Guest, *loc. cit.* point out that the use of notes instead of bills is occasioned by Art. 9 U.L.B., under which the drawer of a bill cannot exclude his liability to the holder. And see Ellinger, "Negotiable Instruments" being Ch.4 of the *International Encyclopedia of Comparative Law* (Hamburg, 2001), Vol. IX, paras 372 *et seq.*

[8] And see Chalmers and Guest, *loc. cit.*

[9] *Capital and Counties Bank Ltd v Gordon* [1903] A.C. 240; *Re Farrow's Bank Ltd* [1923] 1 Ch. 41; *Underwood (A L) Ltd v Barclays Bank Ltd* [1924] 1 K.B. 775. See Chitty, *op. cit.*, para.34–337.

[10] See, *e.g. Giles v Perkins* (1807) 9 East 12; *Thompson v Giles* (1824) 2 B. & C. 422 at 433.

itself, constitute the banker a holder of the cheque.[11] The reason for this is that the crediting of the customer's account with the proceeds of uncleared cheques is a matter of convenience and the customer is not entitled to draw against the amount so credited until the cheque is honoured. But if the banker credits the customer's account with the amount of an unmatured bill of exchange, he is likely to be considered a discounting banker.[12] The reason for this is that in the case of bills of exchange which are not payable on demand, the customer's account is usually credited with the cash proceeds only after the payment of the bills at maturity.[13] If the account is credited before that time, the customer is in effect granted an overdraft. It is noteworthy that the indorsement of a bill of exchange by the drawer (or seller) does not by itself show that the banker is a holder or a discounting banker. Thus, an indorsement is required for collection purposes if the bill is payable to the seller's own order, or it may be executed where a bill is handed to a creditor as a security. The presumption is that an indorsement indicates transfer[14]; but evidence may be called to explain the object of the indorsement.

Practical significance. The distinction between a discounting banker and a collecting banker is in certain cases important from a practical point of view. First, the collecting banker, who acts as an agent, is concerned only with the instructions given to him by the customer. These are usually set out in a "collection order" signed by the customer.[15] If the banker adheres to the instructions, he incurs no liability to the customer. The discounting banker, on the other hand, becomes a holder of the bill. If it is dishonoured by the drawee—the buyer in most overseas sales—the discounting banker obtains an immediate right of recourse against the drawer (the seller). But the banker stands to lose this right if he fails to comply with the relevant procedure laid down by the Bills of Exchange Act 1882.[16] Secondly, it is important to bear in mind that a collecting banker, who is not a holder of the bill, cannot bring an action to enforce it. The discounting banker, on the other hand, has the usual rights of a holder. 22–074

---

[11] *Akrokerii (Atlantic) Mines Ltd v Economic Bank* [1904] 2 K.B. 465; *Bevan v National Bank Ltd* (1906) 23 T.L.R. 65; *Re Farrow's Bank Ltd*, above, at p.48; *Underwood (A L) Ltd v Barclays Bank Ltd*, above, at p.804; *Westminster Bank Ltd v Zang* [1966] A.C. 182. The decision to the contrary on this point, in *Capital and Counties Bank Ltd v Gordon*, above, can no longer be regarded good law. *Cf.* the Cheques Act 1957, s.4(1)(b) and see *Barclays Bank Plc v Tackport Ltd* (CA, unreported, decision of April 25, 1991).

[12] *Giles v Perkins* (1807) 9 East 12 (provided customer's account is overdrawn); *Thompson v Giles* (1824) 2 B. & C. 422 at 430–432 (provided bill is entered as "cash" with customer's consent); *Re Harrison* (1858) 2 De G. & J. 194. But see *Re Carew's Estate Act (No.2)* (1862) 31 Beav. 39. *Cf. Re Firth* (1879) 12 Ch.D. 337; *Dawson v Isle* [1906] 1 Ch. 633.

[13] Such bills used to be entered in a specific column of the pass book or ledger with the amounts short of the cash column; they are therefore called "short bills".

[14] *Ex p. Twogood* (1812) 19 Ves.Jun. 229; *Re Firth*, above, at p.347. As regards an indorsement where a bill constitutes a collateral, see *Lloyd v Howard* (1850) 15 Q.B. 995 at 999.

[15] But a collection order may be signed also in certain cases involving discount, below, para.22–075.

[16] Discussed in detail, below, paras 22–119 *et seq.*

22–075 **Borderline cases.** In certain situations it may not be easy to determine whether a banker has acted as a discounting banker or as a collecting banker. First, if the customer's account is overdrawn, the banker obtains a lien over all the securities of the customer which are in the banker's possession, including negotiable instruments handed to the banker for collection.[17] Under section 27(3) of the Act the banker is, in such a case, deemed to be a holder for value of these negotiable instruments to the extent of the lien. As the banker is deemed a holder of these instruments, he is in a position similar to that of a discounting banker, despite the fact that the instruments are given to him for collection.[18] Secondly, even if the banker negotiates a bill or grants the customer an advance against it, he usually requests the customer to sign a collection order which includes instructions concerning the procedure to be adopted if the bill is dishonoured. It follows that most "discounting" transactions involve an element of agency. Presumably, the banker can recover the amount advanced to the customer only if he follows these instructions and his merely adhering to the procedure laid down in the Bills of Exchange Act 1882 is, in such a case, inadequate. Thus, the roles of a collecting banker and of a discounting banker are not mutually exclusive. This has been recognised in *Barclays Bank Ltd v Astley Industrial Trust Ltd*,[19] where Milmo J. observed: "A banker who permits his customer to draw £5 against an uncleared cheque for £100 has given value for it but is it to be said that in consequence he is no longer the customer's agent for the collection of that cheque?"

(b) *The Uniform Rules for Collections*

22–076 **Object.** The collection and discount[20] of negotiable instruments drawn under an overseas sale are usually governed by the Uniform Rules for Collections promulgated by the International Chamber of Commerce (the "I.C.C."). The first version of these Rules was published in 1956[21] but gained little recognition. Revised versions appeared in 1967 and in 1978.[22] The latter version became so popular that in *Harlow and Jones Ltd v American Express Bank Ltd*[23] Gatehouse J. held that it governed a

---

[17] On the banker's lien generally, see below, paras 22–139 *et seq.* That a collecting banker can be a holder within the meaning of s.27(3) is supported by *Akrokerri (Atlantic) Mines Ltd v Economic Bank* [1904] 2 K.B. 465 at 472; *Sutters v Briggs* [1922] 1 A.C. 1 at 16, 18. See also *Midland Bank Ltd v Reckitt* [1933] A.C. 1 at 18.
[18] *Barclays Bank Ltd v Astley Industrial Trust Ltd* [1970] 2 Q.B. 527 at 538–539; *Barclays Bank Plc v Tackport Ltd* (CA unreported, decision of April 25, 1991).
[19] Above, at p.538.
[20] As regards the application of the Uniform Rules to discounts, see below, para.22–084.
[21] I.C.C. Brochure No.156.
[22] I.C.C. Brochures Nos 254 and 322 respectively.
[23] [1990] 2 Lloyd's Rep. 343; but *cf. AA Valibhoy & Sons (1907) Pte Ltd v Bank Nationale de Paris* [1994] 2 S.L.R. 772, in which Goh Joon Seng J. held that unless the Uniform Rules are incorporated in the collection instruction they do not bind parties other than banks.

collection although the Rules were not incorporated in the collection instruction. The latest, 1995, version[24] came into effect on January 1, 1996.

The object of the Uniform Rules is to regulate the rights and obligations of the parties in transactions involving the collection and discount of negotiable instruments. Their aim, in other words, is to standardise the rights of the parties where a bank is instructed to present documents to the drawee and to collect from him the amount due against them. Basically, the Rules govern the rights of banks collecting documents tendered under c.i.f., f.o.b and similar contracts when payment is not facilitated by a documentary credit. They apply also where the beneficiary of a documentary credit is unable to tender regular documents and, accordingly, asks his bank to handle the documents on a collection basis. By contrast, the Uniform Rules do not apply where a bank negotiates documents under a documentary credit.[25] Although the Uniform Rules apply only in the absence of intention to the contrary by the parties, they are departed from in very few cases.

Structure. The 1995 version is neatly divided into seven parts[26] and is considerably more detailed than its predecessors. This is manifest even in Part A, which comprises the "General Provisions and Definitions". Thus, Art. 1(a)[27] provides that the Uniform Rules apply only if they are incorporated in the collection instruction. Notably, Gatehouse J.'s decision in *Harlow & Jones'* case, discussed above, is not echoed in this provision. It is important to add that, under the same clause, any specific provision of the Uniform Rules can be excluded by express stipulation and, in any event, is without effect if proved to be contrary to any imperative provision of the governing domestic law. 22–077

Banks need not handle. Clause (b) of Article 1 declares that banks are not obliged to handle collections or "subsequent related instructions". However, under clause (c), a bank has to communicate without delay its refusal to handle a collection received by it. 22–078

Terminology. Under Article 1(a), the Uniform Rules apply to all "collections" as defined in Article 2. According to clause (a) of the latter provision, collection means the handling by banks, on instructions received, 22–079

---

[24] I.C.C. Brochure No.522. The text of the Uniform Rules and a list of the countries the bankers of which adhere to them, is obtainable from the I.C.C. British National Committee, Centre Point, 103 New Oxford Street, London WC1A 1QB and the I.C.C. website: *www.iccbooks.com*.

[25] The negotiating bank's position is then primarily governed by the Uniform Customs and Practice for Documentary Credits, 1993 Version (I.C.C. Brochure No.500), Art. 10.

[26] Pt A, comprising Arts 1–3, is entitled "General provisions and Definitions"; Pt B, comprising Art. 4, defines the "Form and Structure of Collections"; Pt C, encompassing Arts 6–8, determines the "Form of Presentation"; Pt D, comprising Arts 9–15, prescribes the "Liabilities and Responsibilities" of the parties; Pt E (Arts 16–19) is entitled "Payment"; Pt F (Arts 20–22), deals with the incidental matter of "Interest, Charges and Expenses" whilst Pt G, which is appropriately entitled "Other Provisions" and which encompasses Arts 22–25, covers acceptances, promissory notes and other instruments, protest, case of need and the service of notices.

[27] A considerably more detailed provision than General Provision A of the 1978 Version.

of "documents" in order to (a) obtain acceptance or payment, or (b) to deliver documents against acceptance or payment, or (c) to deliver documents on other terms and conditions. Documents are divided in clause (b) into two classes. "Financial documents" means bills of exchange, promissory notes, cheques, or other similar documents used for obtaining the payment of money. "Commercial documents" means invoices, transport documents, documents of title, or other similar documents or any other documents whatever, not being financial documents. Article 2 further distinguishes between a "clean collection" and a "documentary collection". Under clause (c), the former means the collection of "financial documents" not accompanied by "commercial documents". The latter, according to clause (d), means the collection of financial documents accompanied by commercial documents or of commercial documents not accompanied by financial documents. Obviously, the collection of a "documentary bill", *i.e.* a bill of exchange accompanied by the documents used in overseas sales, constitutes a "documentary collection".[28] Usually, such a documentary bill includes a bill of lading or some other document of transport, an insurance policy or certificate and an invoice.

22–080 **Parties.** Article 3(a) defines the parties to the transaction. The customer, who instructs his banker to collect the documents is called "the principal". In an overseas sale this will usually be the seller, who in most cases draws a documentary bill of exchange on the buyer. The principal's banker is the "remitting banker". Any bank involved in processing the collection, other than the remitting banker, is called a "collecting banker". Usually a collecting banker is a correspondent engaged by the remitting banker. In certain cases the original collecting banker, engaged by the remitting banker, is unable to present the documents and therefore engages the services of yet a further bank. Article 3(a)(iv) defines a collecting banker, who presents the documents to the drawee, as "the presenting bank". Under Article 3(b) the party to whom the documents are to be presented is the "drawee". The word "drawee" as defined in the Uniform Rules does not necessarily refer to the drawee of the financial document itself. Thus, in a documentary credit the issuing banker may undertake to negotiate without recourse a bill of exchange (a "financial document") drawn by the seller on the buyer.[29] If the seller instructs his own banker to collect the bill and to present it to the issuing banker, the latter is the drawee within the meaning of the Uniform Rules, although the buyer is the drawee of the bill.

22–081 **Collection instruction.** Under Article 4(a)(i) all documents sent for collection must be accompanied by a "collection instruction" incorporating the Uniform Rules and giving complete and precise instructions. Banks are only permitted to act upon instructions given in such collection instructions and "in accordance with these Rules". The validity of the proviso is, however, questionable. The Uniform Rules cannot abrogate the general freedom of banks to incorporate in their correspondent banks agreements

[28] See also above, paras 18–221 *et seq.*
[29] See below, para.22–131.

any provision for the giving of mutual instructions that they consider fit. In consequence, Article 4(a)(i) is to be treated as a guideline rather than a normative rule. A more significant provision is to be found in clause 4(a)(ii), under which banks "will not examine documents in order to obtain instructions". Obviously, their mandate must be set out, fairly and squarely, in the collection instruction. Another important provision, clause 4(a)(iii), confers on banks the authority to disregard any instruction given by a party other than the one from whom they receive the collection.

Contents of instruction. A list of the details that need be included in every collection instruction is set out in Article 4(b). It provides that the instructions must identify the principal, the drawee, the remitting bank and the presenting bank. The instruction must, further, spell out the amount to be collected, a list of the documents enclosed, the terms of the delivery of the documents, details respecting interest and other charges, the method of payment and details of any steps to be taken upon dishonour. Clause (c) reiterates the need of giving full details identifying the drawee and frees banks from liability for losses caused by delays resulting from their endeavour to ascertain the drawee's proper address. 22–082

Scope: application to all parties. It will be recalled that, under Article 1(a), the Uniform Rules are binding on all parties to a transaction, unless it is otherwise expressly agreed or in so far as the Uniform Rules conflict with any national, State or local law which may not be departed from. But it is to be doubted whether the Uniform Rules achieve this wide scope of application. Undoubtedly, they govern the contract between the remitting banker and the principal; a clause incorporating the Uniform Rules is usually included in the written agreement between these two parties. The Uniform Rules also govern the contract between the remitting banker and the collecting banker. Usually, their application to the contract between these parties is provided for in a clause set out in the collection order. But it has been held that, in view of the general adherence to the Uniform Rules in international banking, they govern this contract even in the absence of such an express clause.[30] On the same basis the Uniform Rules ought to be binding also on the "presenting bank", regardless of whether or not they are incorporated in the collection order. But it is difficult to see why the "drawee" should be considered bound by the Uniform Rules. Usually, neither a "commercial document" nor a "financial document" incorporate the Uniform Rules and they are most unlikely to be included in the underlying agreement between the principal and the drawee. Moreover, the Uniform Rules do not constitute an independent source of law, and—at this stage—can hardly have the standing of a trade usage.[31] 22–083

[30] *Harlow and Jones Ltd v American Express Bank Ltd* [1990] 2 Lloyd's Rep. 343 at 349, *per* Gatehouse J. relying on evidence establishing the general adherence to the Uniform Rules by London banks.

[31] And note that in *AA Valibhoy & Sons (1907) Pte Ltd v Bank Nationale de Paris* [1994] 2 S.L.R. 772, Goh Joon Seng J. held that the Uniform Rules bind parties other than banks only to the extent of their incorporation in the collection instruction.

22–084 **Scope: application to discounts.** Article 1(a) refers to the collection of documents but does not mention discount. It may appear to follow that while the Uniform Rules govern the agreements between parties to a transaction involving collection they do not apply where the remitting banker discounts the documents. But it is submitted that the Uniform Rules apply in both types of transaction. First, the term "collection" is defined to mean "the handling by banks of documents as defined . . . in accordance with instructions received". This phraseology indicates that the term "collection" is not used in the strict legal sense discussed earlier in this chapter. It would appear that a transaction involves collection within the meaning of the Uniform Rules whenever the customer is asked to sign a collection order, setting out instructions concerning the handling of the documents and incorporating the Uniform Rules. Secondly, it has been shown that a transaction may involve elements both of discount and of collection.[32] If the Uniform Rules were intended to apply solely to transactions involving collection, a clear provision to this effect would probably have been included.

22–085 **The Uniform Rules and the Bills of Exchange Act 1882.** The Uniform Rules define the duties of the remitting banker, of the collecting banker and of a presenting banker and also concern such matters as the presentment of the documents for payment and the steps to be taken if they are dishonoured by non-acceptance or by non-payment. The Uniform Rules do not state what is the effect of the banker's failure to follow the prescribed procedure. But an answer is provided by the law relating to agency contracts. A banker who fails to take a prescribed step is in the position of an agent who has failed to comply with his instructions and who is therefore unable to claim his remuneration or to seek reimbursement from the principal.[33]

22–086 **Possible conflicts.** The Bills of Exchange Act 1882 prescribes certain steps that must be taken by the holder of a bill upon its dishonour and also includes provisions concerning the presentation of a bill for acceptance and for payment. If the holder fails to comply with these requirements, and if this failure is not excused under the Act, the holder loses the right of recourse against the drawer and the indorsers which is conferred on him upon the dishonour of the bill. A discounting banker, as has been pointed out, is a holder. If he wishes to retain the right of recourse conferred on him under the Act, must he follow the procedure laid down in the Act itself or is he primarily concerned with the provisions of the Uniform Rules incorporated in the relevant collection order? While the Act and the Uniform Rules frequently make similar provisions, they are not always consistent. It is submitted that if the customer has signed a collection instruction incorporating the Uniform Rules, the discounting banker must

---

[32] Above, para.22–075.

[33] *Midland Bank Ltd v Seymour* [1955] 2 Lloyd's Rep. 147 at 168; *European Asian Bank Ltd v Punjab and Sind Bank (No.2)* [1983] 1 W.L.R. 642 noted in [1984] J.B.L. 379 and, generally, *Chitty on Contracts* (29th ed.), Vol. 2, para.31–111.

adopt the course prescribed in them rather than the procedure laid down in the Act. This view is supported by two arguments. First, under section 16(2) the drawer of a bill and any indorser may insert therein an express stipulation waiving as regards himself some or all of the holder's duties.[34] Moreover, as between immediate parties such a waiver is operative even if it is not mentioned in the bill but is included in a separate contractual document, such as the collection instruction. As the incorporation of the Uniform Rules in a collection instruction determines the procedure to be followed by the discounting banker, it involves—by implication—a waiver of the need to take alternative steps prescribed by the Act. Secondly, most discounts of bills relating to overseas sales involve elements of collection; as has been pointed out above, the discount and the collection of bills are not mutually exclusive. Thus, in most discount transactions the collecting banker assumes, at least for certain purposes, the role of an agent of the transferor of the bill. The banker's main concern is, therefore, to adhere to his instructions. The same arguments apply, it is submitted, as regards the duties of a presenting bank, which is primarily concerned to follow the instruction given to it in the collection instruction.

(c) *Liabilities and Responsibilities of Bankers*

Position of remitting banker. The remitting banker is the customer's—the principal's—agent. He must adhere strictly to his instructions and should not deviate from them without the customer's consent.[35] This principle is emphasised in Article 4(a)(i) of the Uniform Rules, under which "All documents sent for collection must be accompanied by a collection instruction . . . giving complete and precise instructions.[36] Banks are only permitted to act upon the instructions given in such collection instructions, and in accordance with these Rules." The remitting banker must also be diligent and is under a duty to exercise due care and skill. In particular, he must be careful to carry out his instructions within any time limit prescribed for the performance of a relevant act, *e.g.* the time prescribed for presenting the bill for acceptance or the time for the sending of notice of dishonour.[37] 22–087

Right to employ correspondent. While the remitting banker may collect the bill through his own branch in the seller's place of business, he frequently uses the services of a correspondent. At common law, the remitting banker is liable to the customer for the acts of such a collecting 22–088

---

[34] The same point arises as regards the exclusion of the right of recourse under s.16(1) (above, para.22–070).

[35] *Bank of Scotland v Dominion Bank* [1891] A.C. 592.

[36] As regards ambiguous instructions, see the position in the case of documentary credits, below, para.23–117. And note that, where the collection is effected for the credit of a payee in an EEA state the information needs to spell out the details prescribed in the Cross Border Credit Transfers Regulation 1999, SI 1999/1876.

[37] *Bank of Van Diemen's Land v Bank of Victoria* (1871) L.R. 3 P.C. 526 at 542.

banker. In *Mackersy v Ramsays, Bonars & Co.*[38] a merchant instructed his bank in Edinburgh to arrange for the collection of a bill which he drew on an Indian merchant. The bank engaged its correspondents in London, who remitted the bill to their agent in India. The drawee paid the bill but the Indian agent failed before remitting the proceeds to London. It was held that the customer was entitled to recover the amount of the bill from his bank in Edinburgh as that bank was liable for any negligence as well as for the default of the collecting banker.

22–089 **Exemption clause.** However, modern banking forms include a clause which exonerates the remitting banker from liability for any act or default of the collecting banker. In *Calico Printers' Association v Barclays Bank*[39] it was held that a clause, under which the collecting banker was appointed at the customer's risk, exempted the remitting banker from liability for the collecting banker's negligence in failing to insure the goods covered by the documents attached to the bill. It was further held that the clause did not run counter to the main object of the transaction. Such a clause is at present included in most collection instructions by virtue of Article 11(a) of the Uniform Rules. In addition Article 5(c) provides that, for the purpose of giving effect to the customer's (the principal's) instructions, the remitting banker is expected to employ as a collecting bank either the bank nominated for this purpose in the collection instruction or, in the absence of such nomination, "any bank of its own, or another bank's choice, in the country of payment or acceptance or in the country where other terms and conditions have to be complied with".

22–090 **Remitting banker's failure.** In the situations discussed above, it is irrelevant whether the remitting banker has discounted the bill or has merely agreed to arrange for its collection without making an advance against it. But this point is of vital importance where the remitting banker becomes insolvent. If the banker has discounted a bill he becomes its holder and obtains the property in it. It follows that the bill constitutes an asset of the estate of the insolvent banker; the customer has to prove for the amount covered, even if the bill has been honoured by the drawee after the banker's failure.[40] But where the remitting banker has acted merely as an agent or collecting banker, he does not obtain the property in the bill; if he

[38] (1843) 9 Cl. & Fin. 846–851 considered in *Lewis & Peat (Produce) Ltd v Alamatu Properties Ltd, The Times*, May 14, 1992, CA. See also *Equitable Trust Co. of New York v Dawson Partners Ltd* (1927) 27 Ll.L.R. 49; and see generally, *Trading and General Investment Corp. v Gault, Armstrong & Kemble Ltd* [1986] 1 Lloyd's Rep. 195; and the Singapore case of *AA Valibhoy & Sons Pte Ltd v Bank Nationale de Paris* [1994] 2 S.L.R. 772.

[39] (1931) 145 L.T. 51. It seems unlikely that this type of clause could be challenged under the Unfair Contract Terms Act 1977 as it would appear to meet the reasonableness test laid down in s.11. And see above, paras 13–052 *et seq.*, especially para.13–059.

[40] *Re Sikes & Co.* (1829) Mont. & M. 263 (but here discount was motivated by the customer's request that the banker meet some acceptances; as the banker's failure led to his dishonouring the acceptances, the customer was entitled to redeem the bills). See also *Re Dilworth* (1828) Mont. & M. 102.

fails before the bill has been honoured by the drawee, the customer is entitled—as between the remitting banker and himself—to demand the return of the bill.[41] The remitting banker may also be considered the customer's trustee of the proceeds of a bill which is paid after the commencement of the bankruptcy; the customer is then entitled to obtain payment of the amount in full.[42] However, if the bill is honoured by payment before the remitting banker's failure, the proceeds will usually form part of the balance standing to the credit of the customer's current account. In such a case the customer is in the position of a general creditor.

Position of collecting banker. The collecting banker is the remitting banker's agent, regardless of whether the latter acts as discounter or merely as the customer's agent. The collecting banker is liable to compensate the remitting banker for any loss resulting directly from a failure to observe the instructions. In *Bank of Scotland v Dominion Bank*[43] the acceptor of a bill of exchange dishonoured it by non-payment. Subsequently, he offered to pay it, provided he was released from his obligation to pay interest and certain expenses. The collecting banker accepted payment on these terms without obtaining the approval of the remitting banker; he stamped the word "paid" on the bill and permitted the acceptor to cancel his signature. The remitting banker, who had discounted the bill, declined to accept the amount paid by the acceptor. The collecting banker thereupon returned the bill together with a memorandum showing that it had been cancelled by mistake. Due to the apparent cancellation of the bill, summary judgment could not be obtained against the acceptor and he was adjudicated a bankrupt before judgment was given against him in the ordinary action brought by the remitting banker. It was accepted that the remitting banker would have been entitled to summary judgment if the acceptor had not been permitted to cancel his signature and that such judgment would have been obtained before the acceptor's adjudication. It was held that the collecting banker was liable for the amount of the bill plus interest and expenses. 22–091

---

[41] *Giles v Perkins* (1807) 9 East 12; *Thompson v Giles* (1824) 2 B. & C. 422; *Tennant v Strachan* (1829) 4 C. & P. 31; *Re Dilworth* (1832) 1 Deac. & Ch. 435; *Re Forster* (1840) 1 Mont.D. & De G. 10; 4 Jur. 224; *Re Wise* (1842) 3 Mont.D. & De G. 103; 7 Jur. 95; *Re Harrison* (1858) 2 De G. & J. 194. *Cf. Re Burrough* (1810) 1 Rose 153; *Re Burrough* (1811) 18 Ves.Jun. 229; *Re Dilworth* (1828) Mont. & M. 102 (in which it was said that the position would differ if the bills were treated as cash).

[42] *Re Wise*, above; *Re Dilworth* (1828) 2 Gl. & J. 371; *Re Forster*, above; *Re Burrough* (1811) 18 Ves.Jun. 229. As regards tracing, which may be of relevance to the customer and, in certain instances, to his remitting bank, see generally, *Re Hallett's Estate, Knatchbull v Hallet* (1879) 13 Ch.D. 696; *Banque Belge pau L'Etranges v Hambrouck* [1921] 1 K.B. 321; and the modern cases of *Agip (Africa) Ltd v Jackson* [1991] Ch. 547, affd [1990] Ch. 265 (Millett J.); *Polly Peck International Plc v Nadir (No.2)* [1992] 4 All E.R. 769; *El Ajou v Dollar Land Holdings Plc* [1993] 3 All E.R. 717 (Millett J.), varied: [1994] 2 All E.R. 685 (tracing point left unturned); note that *Chase Manhattan Bank NA v Israel British Bank (London) Ltd* [1981] Ch. 105 has been doubted by the House of Lords in *Westdeutsche Landesbank Girozentrale v London Islington BC* [1996] A.C. 669. See also the Singapore authority of *Re Untalan, Hong Kong and Shanghai Banking Corp. v United Overseas Bank Ltd* [1992] 2 S.L.R. 195.

[43] [1891] A.C. 592.

22–092 **Relationship with principal.** As the collecting banker is the agent of the remitting banker, there is no privity of contract between him and the customer.[44] This is based on the principle that there is normally no privity of contract between a principal and his agent's sub-agent. Even if the remitting banker engages a collecting banker who is specifically nominated by the customer, and who is not one of the remitting banker's usual correspondents, there is no privity between this collecting banker and the customer.[45] In practice, the customer is in a disadvantageous position. First, if the remitting banker fails, the collecting banker has a lien over the bills remitted to him to the extent of the remitting banker's indebtedness,[46] although the bills remain the customer's property.[47] Secondly, as the remitting banker usually absolves himself from liability for the acts of the collecting banker, the customer may remain without any effective remedy. Apart from the remote possibility of suing the collecting banker in tort, the customer's only redress is to request the remitting banker to bring an action against the collecting banker. The remitting banker usually agrees to such a demand only if the customer executes an indemnity, covering expenses to be incurred; the effect is that the customer has to bear the hazards of an action to be brought overseas.

22–093 **Specific exemptions under the Uniform Rules.** Under Article 12(a), banks must determine that the documents received appear to be as listed in the collection instruction and must advise by telecommunication, or if that is not possible, by other expeditious means, without delay, the party from whom the collection instruction was received of any documents missing or found to be other than listed.[48] But the banks do not have any further obligation in this respect. The extent of their duty is defined in Article 9,

---

[44] *Prince v Oriental Bank Corp.* (1878) 3 App.Cas. 325 at 335, following *Mackersy v Ramsays, Bonars & Co.* (1843) 9 Cl. & Fin. 818.

[45] *Calico Printers' Association v Barclays Bank* (1931) 145 L.T. 51 at 56. Applied in *Henderson v Merrett Syndicates Ltd* [1995] A.C. 145; *Bastone & Firminger Ltd v Nasima Enterprises (Nigeria) Ltd* [1996] C.L.C. 1902, QBD. But note that, in the latter case, Rix J. took the view that this principle may have been modified in respect of collections governed by the Uniform Rules for Collection. His Lordship referred to the definition of "parties" and to provisions in the Code rendering the "principal" liable to the "banks" in the transaction and then observed: "It seems to me to be fully arguable . . . that the Rules have affected a change in this regard . . . In that context there is in my judgment sufficient force in the concept, that a Code which provides for the rights and liabilities for what are described as 'parties' to a collection contemplates that those rights and liabilities are to be vindicated contractually, to entitle me to say that there is a good arguable case of privity of contract between a principal and a collecting bank within the Rules" (transcript p.6).

[46] *Johnson v Robarts* (1875) L.R. 10 Ch.App. 505. If the collecting banker fails while the remitting banker's account is in credit, the remitting banker is entitled to the return of the bills: *Ex p. Rowton* (1810) 17 Ves.Jun. 426; *Re Boldero & Co.* (1812) 19 Ves.Jun. 25.

[47] *Re Parker* (1843) 3 Mont.D. & De G. 332; 7 Jur. 910.

[48] Under Art. 12(b), if the documents do not appear to be listed, the remitting bank is precluded from disputing the type and number of documents received by the collecting bank. Under clause (c) the documents may, in all other regards, be presented as received.

under which banks "will act in good faith and exercise reasonable care". Obviously, neither the remitting banker nor the collecting banker is expected to verify the genuineness or examine the regularity of the documents. Moreover, the Uniform Rules give effect to the principle under which a holder who presents a documentary bill for acceptance, for negotiation or for payment does not warrant the genuineness and regularity of the documents.[49] It is noteworthy that the notification about any missing document is to be given to the party from whom they were received. The Rules do not require that the drawee be acquainted with this fact. In reality, the effect of Articles 9 and 12 is to define the collecting banker's liability towards the remitting banker and to protect the collecting banker against claims by the drawee.[50]

Articles 14(a) and 15 protect both bankers, in certain cases, against liability towards the person who remits the documents. Under Article 14(a), "banks assume no liability or responsibility for the consequences arising out of delay and/or loss in transit of any message(s), letter(s) or document(s), or for delay, mutilation or other error(s) arising in the transmission of any telecommunication or for error(s) in translation and/or interpretation of technical terms". Article 15 exempts banks concerned with the collection of documents from liability or responsibility for loss resulting from causes beyond their control, such as strikes, riots, wars or an Act of God.

Responsibility for goods. When a customer dispatches goods to the drawee on D/A or D/P terms[51] he may arrange that the documents of title attached to the draft be made out to the order of the remitting banker or of the collecting banker. According to Article 10(a), the goods themselves should not be dispatched direct or consigned to a bank without its prior consent. Moreover, the article expressly exempts a banker from liability or responsibility for the goods, where these are addressed to him without prior arrangement. It provides that the banker has no obligation to take delivery of the goods and that these remain at the consignor's risk. Another relevant provision is Article 10(b)–(c). Bankers need not take any action in respect of goods represented by a documentary collection. "Nevertheless in the case that banks take action for the protection of the goods, whether instructed or not, they assume no liability or responsibility with regard to the fate and/or condition of the goods and/or for any acts and/or omissions on the part of any third parties entrusted with the custody and/or protection of the goods. However, the collecting bank must advise without delay the bank from which the collection instruction was received of any such action taken." All expenses incurred are under Article 10(d), to be borne by the "principal", *i.e.* the customer. 22–094

[49] Art. 13; and see, at common law, *Guaranty Trust Co. of New York v Hannay & Co.* [1918] 2 K.B. 623. These clauses are unlikely to be affected by the Unfair Contract Terms Act 1977; see above, n.39, and see *Linklaters v HKSB* [2003] 2 Lloyd's Rep. 545 at 556–557, where Gross J. took the view that Art.13(1) of the URC did not affect the common law position.

[50] But it is doubtful whether the Uniform Rules govern the relationship between the bankers and the drawee, above, para.22–083. However, Art. 13 will preclude any attempt by the collecting banker to render the remitting banker liable for the genuineness of the bill and documents.

[51] See below, para.22–096.

22–095 **Case of need.** To protect his interest in the goods, a consignor or seller frequently appoints a representative in the buyer's country who should act as a "case of need" in the event of the dishonour of the documentary draft. Usually, this representative is given instructions concerning the storage and the disposal of the goods. Problems concerning the "case of need" are discussed subsequently.[52]

22–096 **Liability for method of handling documents.** Under Article 5(c) of the Uniform Rules, the documents must be presented to the drawee *in the form in which they are received*, except that the banks are authorised to affix any necessary stamp, execute any required indorsement, and "place any rubber stamps or other identifying marks or symbols customary to or required for the collection operation". This provision suggests that a documentary collection must be presented to the drawee together with the documents attached to it. It seems to follow that, if a drawee, to whom a bill has been so presented, wrongfully retains the shipping documents while dishonouring the bill of exchange by non-payment or by non-acceptance, the collecting banker is not liable to its principal for any resulting loss.[53] But Article 5(c) appears to conflict in this regard with Article 7. Under clause (b) of this provision if "a collection contains a bill of exchange payable at a future date,[54] the collection instruction should state whether the commercial documents are to be released to the drawee against acceptance (D/A) or against payment (D/P).[55] In the absence of such statement commercial documents will be released only against payment and the collecting bank will not be responsible for any consequences arising out of any delay in the delivery of the documents." Clause (c) augments: "If a collection contains a bill of exchange payable at a future date and the collection instruction indicates that commercial documents are to be released against payment, documents will be released only against such payment and the collecting bank will not be responsible for any consequences arising out of any delay in the delivery of documents." This article prohibits the release of the documents, which accompany the usual type of documentary bill, except in accordance with the terms of the collection order. Thus, while Article 5(c) requires the presentation of the bill with the documents attached to it, Article 7 prohibits the release of the documents without obtaining the required acceptance or payment.[56]

In practice, bankers present the bill of exchange, without the attached documents, to the drawee and indicate that the commercial documents may be perused at their premises. By doing so, they do not really present the

---

[52] Below, para.22–138.

[53] Although the drawee does not obtain the property in the bill of lading if he dishonours the bill of exchange (above, paras 18–221 *et seq.*), he may be able to obtain the goods by presenting the bill of lading and may further be able to confer a good title on a third party (above, para.18–222).

[54] In the case of a bill payable at sight (*viz.* on demand) presentment for acceptance is not required; below, para.22–097.

[55] But note that Art. 7(a) discourages the use of a D/P instruction where the bill of exchange is payable at a future date (*i.e.* is a usance bill).

[56] See, as regards Art. 7, *Harlow and Jones Ltd v American Express Bank Ltd* [1990] 2 Lloyds Rep. 343.

documents in the form in which they receive them and a punctillious drawee may refuse to accept the bill unless it is presented to him together with the commercial documents. But it is submitted that, as the object of the established banking practice is to comply with Article 7, it is acceptable. As Article 7 is specifically concerned with documentary collections it should, in so far as the presentation of commercial documents is concerned, prevail over Article 5(c). Thus, the banker's main concern is to refrain from releasing the commercial documents until he obtains the acceptance or the payment of the bill, as the case may be. It is noteworthy that the position is similar at common law.[57] Moreover, if the drawee relies on the banker's failure to present the commercial documents for perusal as a ground for the non-acceptance or for the non-payment of the bill, the collecting banker will usually present the bill again—accompanied by the commercial documents—with a view to noting the bill for dishonour. Such a second presentment appears to be valid.[58]

(d) *Presentment for Acceptance and Payment*

When presentment for acceptance required. When the drawer accepts a bill he undertakes to honour it by payment according to its tenor.[59] The Act specifies the situations in which a holder must present a bill for acceptance; if he fails to discharge this duty, the drawer and indorsers are usually discharged from their liability on the bill.[60] Presentment for acceptance is required in the case of three types of bill. First, according to section 39(1) it is required in order to determine the maturity of a bill payable at a fixed date after sight. Most bills drawn in connection with overseas sales fall into this category. Secondly, under section 39(2), presentment for acceptance is required when the bill stipulates that it must be so presented. While bills of this type are not common, a requirement that a bill be presented for acceptance is in certain cases included in a collection order. In such a case Article 9 of the Uniform Rules makes it incumbent on the "presenting" banker to present the bill for acceptance. Thirdly, under section 39(2), a bill which is drawn payable elsewhere than at the place of business of the drawee must be presented for acceptance before it may be presented for payment[61]; the object is to enable the drawee to arrange for funds at the relevant place. One result of this provision is that a bill which is payable on demand but at a place other than the place of business of the drawee must be presented for acceptance. It appears to follow that such a bill cannot be presented simultaneously for acceptance and for payment. Under section 39(3), presentment for acceptance is not necessary, in any other case, in 22–097

---

[57] For observations to this effect, see Wright J. in *Calico Printers' Association v Barclays Bank* (1931) 145 L.T. 51 at 54.

[58] For a discussion of this problem in regard to presentment of drafts drawn under documentary credits, see below, para.23–204.

[59] See above, para.22–047.

[60] *Infra*. As regards the effect of the holder's failure duly to present the bill on a party's liability on the underlying contract, see below, paras 22–114, 22–134.

[61] See subs.(4), which excuses a delay resulting from the need to present such a bill for acceptance at a place other than the place of payment.

order to render liable any party to the bill. But it should be noted that a drawee who has not accepted a bill is not a party to it and that the bill cannot be enforced against him. In practice, it is quite usual to present bills for acceptance even where this is not required under the Act. The reason for this is that the drawee's acceptance gives additional currency to the bill. Moreover, under section 43(2), if the drawee dishonours the bill by non-acceptance, the holder obtains an immediate right of recourse against the indorsers and the drawer.

22–098 **Time for presentment for acceptance.** The Act lays down a requisite of time only in the case of bills payable after sight. Under section 40(1), the holder must either present such a bill or negotiate it within a reasonable time. Under section 40(2), if the holder fails to do so, the drawer and indorsers are discharged. According to subsection (3), in determining what is a reasonable time regard is to be had to the nature of the bill, any relevant usage of trade and the facts of the particular case.[62] Other types of bill in which presentment for acceptance is obligatory must be presented by the holder before they are overdue.[63] The duties of a collecting banker are more stringent. Under Article 6 of the Uniform Rules, any documents which require to be accepted must be presented "without delay".

22–099 **Rules as to presentment for acceptance.** These are laid down in section 41(1) of the Act. Under rule (a), the bill must be presented by or on behalf of the holder to the drawee or to some person authorised to accept or refuse acceptance on the drawee's behalf at a reasonable hour and on a business day.[64] The emphasis is on the presentment of the bill to the drawee or to his agent; the place at which presentment for acceptance is effected appears to be immaterial. It is said that even if a bill is drawn payable at the drawee's bank, it must be presented for acceptance to the drawee and that presentment to the bank is insufficient.[65] But it is arguable that, in such a case, the holder may be entitled to assume that the bank has the authority to act on the drawee's behalf. In the case of a collecting banker, the position is governed by the Uniform Rules. Basically such a banker discharges his duties if he follows the instructions given in the collection order. Under Article 4(c)(i), a collection instruction should bear the

---

[62] *Fry v Hill* (1817) 7 Taunt. 397 (four days held reasonable); *Shute v Robins* (1828) 3 C. & P. 80 (do.); *Mellish v Rawdon* (1832) 9 Bing. 416 (four months held reasonable); *Straker v Graham* (1839) 4 M. & W. 721 (three months considered unreasonable); *Ramchurn Mullick v Luchmeechund Radakissen* (1854) 9 Moore P.C. 46 (five months and nine days held unreasonable); *Godfray v Coulman* (1859) 13 Moore P.C. 11 (37 days held unreasonable). But a court may be guided by business practice rather than by nineteenth-century decisions.

[63] s.41(1), r. (a).

[64] Reasonable hour in the case of merchants means business hours (*cf. Barclay v Bailey* (1810) 2 Camp. 527) or, in the case of a drawee who is a banker, "banking hours": *Parker v Gordon* (1806) 7 East 385; *Elford v Teed* (1813) 1 M. & S. 28; *Baines v National Provincial Bank* (1927) 96 L.J.K.B. 801. In other cases presentment before retirement at night is valid: *Wilkins v Jadis* (1831) 2 B. & Ad. 188. For the meaning of "business day", see above, para.22–044.

[65] *Chitty on Bills* (11th ed.), p.196, *cf.* Chalmers and Guest, *Bills of Exchange* (16th ed.), p.376.

complete address of the drawee or the domicile at which presentation is to be made.[66] If the address is incomplete or incorrect, the collecting banker may, without any liability and responsibility on his part, endeavour to ascertain the proper address. Under subclause (c)(ii), the collecting bank is not liable for any delay resulting from the incomplete or incorrect address provided.

Under rule (b) of section 41(1), where a bill is addressed to two or more drawees, who are not partners, presentment must be made to all of them, unless one has authority to accept it for all.[67] Under rule (c), where the drawee is dead the bill may be presented to his personal representative and, under rule (d), where the drawee is a bankrupt the bill may be presented to the trustee in bankruptcy. In both cases presentment is optional; it is, in fact, excused under section 41(2). Under rule (e) of section 41(1), presentment through the post office is sufficient where it is authorised by agreement or by usage. The practice is recognised in the United Kingdom, although it has not been the subject of decision.

Method of presentment: usual procedure. Neither the Act nor the Uniform Rules prescribe the actual manner in which the bill is to be presented for acceptance. The usual procedure is to deliver the bill to the drawee, either by messenger or through the post office, and to leave it with him[68] for a period of 24 hours.[69] In computing the 24 hours, non-business days are excluded.[70] If it is thought unsafe to leave the bill with the drawee, the holder may exhibit it and leave a formal notice that the bill is retained for acceptance at a specified address.[71] In the case of a documentary bill, the presenting banker usually retains the documents even if the bill is left with the drawee for acceptance; the drawee is invited to peruse the documents at the premises of the bank.[72] 22–100

Position under the Uniform Rules. The Uniform Rules do not include express provisions introducing a different procedure. But they confer on the principal the power to depart from the ordinary time limits. Under Article 5(a) "presentation", for the purpose of the Rules, is defined as "the procedure whereby the presenting bank makes the documents available to 22–101

---

[66] See also Art. 4(a)(iii) as regards the inclusion in the collection instruction of other details respecting the drawee; and see above, para.22–080, defining "drawee".

[67] Note that if one of the drawees dishonours the bills by non-acceptance, the acceptance is qualified: below, para.22–104.

[68] The practice appears well established: *Jeune v Ward* (1818) 1 B. & A. 653 at 659; *Bank of Van Diemen's Land v Bank of Victoria* (1871) L.R. 3 P.C. 526 at 542–543. The language of s.42, which states the position where a bill "is not accepted within the customary time", indicates that a bill may be left in the drawee's hand for acceptance within this time.

[69] *Bank of Van Diemen's Land v Bank of Victoria*, above, at pp.542–543.

[70] *ibid.*, at pp.546–547. As to which days constitute business days, see above, para.22–044.

[71] Chalmers and Guest, *Bills of Exchange* (16th ed.), p.362. As to the effect of a short day, see *Bank of Van Diemen's Land v Bank of Victoria*, above, at p.546.

[72] And see above, para.22–096. Presentment for acceptance under the Uniform Law on Bills of Exchange and Promissory Notes of the Geneva Convention (above, para.22–034) is governed by Arts 21–25.

the drawee as instructed". Obviously, presentment by means not sanctioned in the collection instruction does not constitute "presentation". Under clause (b), the "collection instruction should state the exact period of time within which any action is to be taken by the drawee. Expressions such as 'first', 'prompt', 'immediate' and the like should not be used in connection with presentation or with reference to any period of time within which documents have to be taken up or for any other action that is to be taken by the drawee. If such terms are used, banks will disregard them." Effectively, these provisions sanction the prescription of a period longer or shorter than that sanctioned by common banking practice. Notably, the provisions are silent as regards the actual physical steps to be taken for the presentment of documents.

22–102 **When presentment for acceptance is excused.** According to section 41(2) of the Act, presentment for acceptance is excused and the bill may be treated as dishonoured by non-acceptance in the following cases: (a) where the drawee is dead or bankrupt or is a fictitious or non-existing person or a person not having capacity to contract; (b) where after the exercise of reasonable diligence presentment cannot be effected; and (c) where although presentment has been irregular, acceptance has been refused on some other ground. Under section 41(3), the fact that the holder has reason to believe that the bill, on presentment, will be dishonoured does not excuse presentment. In the case of a collecting banker, the position is governed by Article 8 of the Uniform Rules, which has been discussed above; if the collection order does not give a complete and correct address at which presentment is to be effected, the collecting banker is not responsible for a failure to present it. This provision, in effect, falls within the scope of the second branch of section 41(2).

22–103 **Requisites of an acceptance.** According to section 17(2) an acceptance is invalid unless it complies with the following conditions: First, it must be written on the bill. It is usual to write the acceptance on the face of the bill, but an acceptance written on its back is probably valid.[73] Secondly, the acceptance must be signed by the drawee; his mere signature without additional words is sufficient.[74] Thirdly, the acceptance may not state that the drawee will perform his promise by any other means than by payment of money. Thus, if the drawee accepts a bill as "payable in bills"[75] or as "payable in goods", the bill must be treated as dishonoured by non-acceptance. Under section 18(1), a bill may be accepted before it has been signed by the drawer or while it is otherwise incomplete. Under section 18(2), a bill may be accepted when it is overdue[76] or when it has been

[73] *Young v Glover* (1857) 3 Jur.(N.S.) 637, *per* Lord Campbell C.J.
[74] The signature may be executed by an agent: s.91.
[75] *Russell v Phillips* (1850) 14 Q.B. 891 at 901; as regards an acceptance in a currency other than that in which the bill is drawn, see *Boehm v Garcias* (1808) 1 Camp. 425 (n.2). Note that an acceptance, in which the drawee undertakes to pay out of funds standing to the credit of a specified account, is a promise to pay money and constitutes an acceptance: *Banca Popolare di Novara v John Livanos & Sons Ltd* [1965] 2 Lloyd's Rep. 149.
[76] In such a case it becomes payable on demand: s.10(2).

previously dishonoured by non-acceptance. Under section 18(3), when a bill payable after sight is dishonoured by non-acceptance and the drawee subsequently accepts it, the holder, in the absence of different agreement, is usually entitled to have it accepted as of the date of the first presentment.[77]

General and qualified acceptance. Under section 19(2), a general acceptance is one in which the drawee assents without qualification to the drawee's order. A qualified acceptance is one which varies in express terms the effect of the bill as drawn. In particular, an acceptance is qualified if it is conditional, partial, local, or qualified as to time or an acceptance by some of the drawees only. A conditional acceptance is one which makes payment by the acceptor subject to the fulfilment of a condition.[78] Thus, an acceptance was held conditional where the drawee accepted the bill as "payable on giving up of bills of lading for . . . clover per [ship] Amazon."[79] But such an acceptance is quite common where a documentary bill is presented without the attached documents; it has been suggested that an authority to take such an acceptance may, therefore, be implied.[80] A partial acceptance is one in which the acceptor undertakes to pay a smaller amount than that for which the bill is drawn.[81] An acceptance that makes the bill payable at a specific place is not always qualified. It is qualified if it expressly renders the bill payable solely at the specified place, *e.g.* if it makes the bill "payable at the X Bank and not elsewhere" or "payable at the X Bank only".[82] But the mere designation of a place of payment does not have such an effect. The reason for this is that in such a case the failure to present the bill at the place at which it is domiciled does not discharge the acceptor.[83] An acceptance is qualified as to time, if it alters the date on which the bill falls due; *e.g.* if a bill drawn payable two months after date is accepted as payable six months after date or after sight.[84] 22–104

[77] As regards an undated acceptance, see s.12, discussed in *Chitty on Contracts* (29th ed.), Vol. 2, para.34–031.

[78] The acceptance, though, need be qualified or conditional on its face. An arrangement between the drawer and the acceptor, which is unknown to the holder, does not impinge on the general nature of the acceptance: *Heller Factors Pty Ltd v Toy Corp. Pty Ltd* [1984] 1 N.S.W.L.R. 121 (Aust.).

[79] *Smith v Vertue* (1860) 30 L.J.C.P. 56 at 60; *cf. Smith and Palmer v Scarffe and Abbott* (1741) 7 Mod. 426. See now s.19(2)(a). But words purporting to restrict the negotiability of the bill are not necessarily a qualification: *Meyer (H) & Co. v Decroix (J), Verley et Cie* [1891] A.C. 520; *cf. Hibernian Bank Ltd v Gysin and Hanson* [1939] 1 K.B. 483.

[80] Chalmers, *Bills of Exchange* (13th ed.), p.143; the view is, however, not advocated in the current, 16th ed., at p.364; for the form of such an acceptance, see *Ex p. Brett Re Howe* (1871) L.R. 6 Ch.App. 838, in which it was treated as conditional.

[81] s.19(2)(b).

[82] s.19(2)(c); *Halstead v Skelton* (1843) 5 Q.B. 86. As to what constitutes a particular place, see *Eimco Corp. v Tutt Bryant Ltd* [1970] 2 N.S.W.R. 249; *cf. Day v Bate* (1979) 41 F.L.R. 222 (Aust.). As regards the acceptance by one partner only, who was acting in his personal capacity, of a bill drawn on the partnership, see *Geo. Thompson (Aust.) Pty Ltd v Vittadello* [1978] V.R. 199 at 207.

[83] *Ex p. Hayward* (1887) 3 T.L.R. 687; *Bank Polski v Mulder (KJ) & Co.* [1941] 2 K.B. 266, affirmed [1942] 1 K.B. 497 and see below, para.22–114.

[84] s.19(2)(d); *Russell v Phillips* (1850) 14 Q.B. 891 at 900; *cf. Fanshaw v Peet* (1857) 26 L.J.Ex. 314.

22–105 **Effect of non-acceptance.** Under section 42, when a bill is presented for acceptance and is not accepted within the usual time,[85] the person presenting it, *i.e.* the holder, must treat it as dishonoured by non-acceptance. If the holder does not treat it as such he stands to lose his right of recourse against the drawer and the indorsers. According to section 43(1) a bill is dishonoured by non-acceptance if it is duly presented and acceptance is refused or cannot be obtained or when presentment is excused and the bill is not accepted. Under subsection (2), the effect of non-acceptance is to confer an immediate right of recourse on the holder against the drawer and the indorsers. Presentment for payment is then not required but the holder has to comply with the procedure applicable in cases of dishonour.[86] The steps that need to be taken by a collecting banker upon the dishonour of the bill by non-acceptance are usually set out in detail in the collection order; certain aspects are covered by provisions of the Uniform Rules.[87]

22–106 **Effect of qualified acceptance.** Under section 44(1), a holder who fails to obtain an unqualified acceptance may treat the bill as dishonoured by non-acceptance; it follows that he is entitled to refuse to take a qualified acceptance. It is clear from subsection (2) that the holder should be advised to adopt this course. If he takes a qualified acceptance without obtaining the assent of the drawer and of the indorsers, they are discharged from their liability on the bill.[88] But under subsection (3), a drawer or indorser who receives notice of a qualified acceptance and does not within a reasonable time express his dissent, is deemed to have assented to it. The Uniform Rules do not make any specific provisions relating to qualified acceptances. As a qualified acceptance is, in law, a refusal by the drawee to give a general acceptance, it is arguable that a presenting banker should refuse to take it; the holder's instruction to present the bill for acceptance must be regarded as an instruction to seek the drawee's undertaking to pay the bill according to its tenor. This argument derives support from Article 15, under which the presenting banker is responsible "for seeing that the form of the acceptance of a bill of exchange appears to be complete and correct . . .". A qualified acceptance may, perhaps, be regarded as either incomplete or as incorrect in form within the meaning of this provision.

22–107 **Regularity of acceptance.** It is clear from the language of sections 43(1)(a) and 19(2) of the Act that, usually, the holder can treat the bill as accepted only if he obtains an unqualified assent of *the drawee* to the

---

[85] *Bank of Van Diemen's Land v Bank of Victoria* (1871) L.R. 3 P.C. 526 at 542, 546 which suggests that the customary time used to be 24 hours. And see *Jeune v Ward* (1818) 1 B. & A. 653 at 659 which shows that it used to be customary to deliver the bill by messenger and call for it after 24 hours. Presentment by post is the common method at present: there is no authority indicating what amounts at present to the "usual time."

[86] Sending notice of dishonour and, in certain cases, protesting the bill. See *infra*.

[87] *ibid.* As regards the scope of the application of the Uniform Rules, see above, paras 22–083—22–085.

[88] But a proviso authorises the taking of a partial acceptance. Note also that, according to this section, where a foreign bill is accepted as to part, the holder has to protest it for the balance.

drawer's order; the acceptance must also comply with the prescribed requisites of form.[89] Thus, the holder can treat an acceptance as valid only if it is both regular and is a genuine acceptance of the drawee. If the acceptance is forged, it is a nullity[90] and does not constitute an assent of the drawee. If the holder treats it as valid the drawer and the indorsers are probably discharged. The position of a presenting banker is governed by Article 15 of the Uniform Rules. According to it, the presenting banker is responsible for seeing that the form of the acceptance appears to be complete and correct, but is not responsible for the genuineness of any signature or for the authority of any signatory to sign the acceptance. It should be recalled that the Uniform Rules apply whenever they are incorporated in a collection order and that they may thus apply also in transactions involving a discount or an advance.

Presentment for payment: when required. As a general rule every bill of exchange must be presented for payment. This rule, as well as the rules concerning the manner in which a bill must be presented for payment, is set out in section 45 of the Act.[91] Rule 3 of this section prescribes the basic procedure that needs to be followed: "Presentment must be made by the holder or by some person authorised to receive payment on his behalf [*e.g.* a collecting banker] at a reasonable hour on a business day,[92] at the proper place as hereinafter defined, either to the person designated by the bill as payer, or to some person authorised to pay or refuse payment on his behalf if with the exercise of reasonable diligence such person can be found." This rule is augmented by section 52(4); the holder must exhibit the bill to the person from whom he demands payment and must deliver it to him when it is honoured.[93] In some cases the bill is presented for payment to the drawee. But in most cases the bill is accepted by the drawee as payable at a specific bank or branch. In such cases the bill is "domiciled" at that bank or branch and presentment must be made there. 22–108

A bill need not be presented by the holder in person or through a messenger. Under rule 8 of section 45, presentment through the post office[94] is sufficient where it is authorised by agreement or by usage. At present there is probably a general usage permitting such presentment.

The remaining rules of section 45 prescribe the place at which presentment should be effected, the time for presentment and other specific principles. These rules are discussed in the following paragraphs.

---

89 See above.

90 s.24 of the Act, discussed in *Chitty on Contracts* (29th ed.), Vol. 2, paras 34–053 *et seq*.

91 A similar duty exists under the Uniform Law on Bills of Exchange and Promissory Notes of the Geneva Convention (above, para.22–034), Art. 38.

92 As to what constitutes a reasonable hour see above, para.22–099; as to what constitutes a "business day" see above, para.22–044.

93 For the origin and basis of this rule see *Hansard v Robinson* (1827) 7 B. & C. 90 at 94; *Griffin v Weatherby* (1868) L.R. 3 Q.B. 753 at 760–761. As regards a lien over bills for costs see *Woodward v Pell* (1868) L.R. 4 Q.B. 55. And see the Deregulation (Bills of Exchange) Order, SI 1996/2993, which facilitates the truncation of cheques (including bankers' drafts encompassed in the definition of a negotiable instrument). Up to now, truncation has not been introduced in practice.

94 And note that, under the Postal Service Act 2000 (Consequential Modifications) No.1 order 2001, SI 2001/1149, "post" is to be read as a reference to a postal operator.

22–109 **Time for presentment for payment.** Under rule 1 of section 45, a bill which is not payable on demand must be presented for payment on the day on which it falls due.[95] Article 9 of the Uniform Rules includes a similar provision.

Under rule 2 of section 45, a bill which is payable on demand must be presented for payment within a reasonable time after its issue in order to render the drawer liable and within a reasonable time after its indorsement in order to render the indorser liable. The factors taken into account in determining what is a reasonable time are similar to those used for determining what constitutes a reasonable time for presentment for acceptance of a bill payable after sight.[96] The nature of the transaction is of major importance in this regard. Thus, a bill payable on demand which is drawn in connection with a sale involving carriage by air may have to be presented for payment more promptly than a bill drawn under a contract involving carriage of goods by sea. The Uniform Rules prescribe a more definite rule: Under Article 9, documents payable at sight must be presented for payment without delay.

22–110 **Place of presentment for payment.** Rule 4 of section 45 covers most of the possible situations. It distinguishes between bills that specify a place of payment ("domiciled bills") and bills in which such a place is not designated. Bills of the former type must be presented for payment at the designated place. Thus, a bill domiciled at a specified branch of a bank may be presented to a clerk on the premises.[97] If the designated premises are shut although the holder attempts to present the bill during ordinary working hours, the holder may treat the bill as dishonoured and he is not obliged to seek out the acceptor or drawee.[98] This principle applies even if the acceptor of a domiciled bill dies before the date on which it falls due; presentment at the designated place is sufficient and there is no need to present it to the executors.[99] Where a bill specifies a place of payment, it is insufficient to present it personally to the acceptor at some other place.[1] Moreover, a domiciled bill must be presented at the designated place even if the acceptor informs the holder that there are no funds for meeting the bill at this place. In *Yeoman Credit Ltd v Gregory*[2] a bill was accepted payable at the Piccadilly Branch of the National Provincial Bank. The

---

[95] As regards the computation of the date at which the bill falls due, see above, para.22–044.

[96] See above, para.22–098. In the case of *Chartered Mercantile Bank of India, London and China v Dickson* (1871) L.R. 3 P.C. 574 at 579, it was held that the retention of a promissory note that was given as a "continuing security" for a period of about nine months did not constitute an unreasonable delay in presentment for payment.

[97] *Reynolds v Chettle* (1811) 2 Camp. 596 (presentment to drawee's clerk at clearing house sufficient); *Harris v Packer* (1833) 6 Tyr. 370n.

[98] *Hine v Allely* (1833) 4 B. & Ad. 624; *cf. Crosse v Smith* (1813) 1 M. & S. 545 at 554 (concerning notice); *Buxton v Jones* (1840) 1 Man. & G. 83.

[99] *Philpott v Bryant* (1827) 3 C. & P. 244.

[1] *Gibb v Mather* (1832) 2 Cr. & J. 254; *Saul v Jones* (1858) 28 L.J.Q.B. 37. *Cf. Bailey v Porter* (1845) 14 M. & W. 44, in which the bill was made payable at the premises of the holder, who was a banker.

[2] [1963] 1 W.L.R. 343.

acceptor advised the holder that no funds had been made available for meeting the bill at that branch and asked that it be presented to the Golden Square branch of the Midland Bank. The bill was presented at the latter branch on the date of its maturity but was dishonoured. On the following day it was presented for payment at the Piccadilly Branch, where it was again dishonoured. It was held that the bill should have been presented for payment at the Piccadilly Branch on the date it was due and that it was insufficient to present it there on the subsequent day. The indorser was therefore discharged.

The place at which a bill is made payable may be inserted either by the drawer[3] or by the acceptor.[4] If the bill is made payable at two places, presentment in either place is probably sufficient.[5]

Where bill not domiciled. The drawer may insert the drawee's address in the bill, without making it payable at this place. When the drawee accepts such a bill, he may make it payable ("domiciled") at some other place, such as a branch of a bank. But if the drawee does not make a bill which mentions his address payable elsewhere, the holder must present it for payment at this address. Where a bill specifies neither a place for payment nor the drawee's address, the holder must present it for payment at the drawee's place of business, and if it is unknown, at the drawee's usual residence. If this is also unknown, the bill may be presented to the drawee wherever he can be found or at his last known place of business or residence.[6] 22–111

Under rule 5 of section 45, where a bill is presented for payment at the proper place and, after the exercise of reasonable diligence, no person authorised to pay or to refuse the bill is found, no further presentment to the drawee or acceptor is required. This rule applies both in the case of domiciled bills and as regards bills which are not made payable at a specified place.

Collecting bank. The position of a collecting banker, who is asked to present a bill for payment (a "presenting banker"), is primarily governed by Article 5(c) of the Uniform Rules.[7] His duty is to adhere to the instructions given to him in the collection order. In most cases the presenting banker is asked to act in a manner that aims at preserving the right of recourse of the customer, who is the holder of the bill, against the drawer and any indorser. But if the bill is drawn by a customer, who is an exporter, on a purchaser, there are usually no indorsers. In effect, the question of recourse arises in overseas sales mainly where the bill has been discounted by the customer's banker (the remitting banker) and forwarded by the latter to a collecting banker. 22–112

---

[3] See, *e.g. Gibb v Mather* (1832) 2 Cr. & J. 254; *Bank Polski v Mulder (KJ) & Co.* [1941] 2 K.B. 266, affirmed [1942] 1 K.B. 497.

[4] This is the more usual form (*e.g.* "payable at Branch X of the A.B. Bank"); for an early example see *Saul v Jones* (1858) 28 L.J.Q.B. 37.

[5] *Beeching v Gower* (1816) Holt 313.

[6] s.45, r.4(b)–(d).

[7] As regards the release of the documents, see above, para.22–099; as regards Art. 4(c)(i), respecting the contents of the collection instruction, see above, para.22–099.

22–113 **Other aspects of proper presentment for payment.** Under rule 6 of section 45, where a bill is drawn upon or accepted by two or more persons who are not partners and no place of payment is specified, the bill must be presented to all of them. But there is, of course, no need to present the bill to all the drawees if one of them pays it. Similarly, if one drawee, who is the agent of the others, dishonours the bill by non-payment on behalf of all the drawees, no further presentment is required. Under rule 7, where the drawee or acceptor is dead, and no place of payment is specified, the bill must be presented to a personal representative, provided such a person can be found.

22–114 **Effect of failure to present bill for payment.** Under section 45, if a bill is not presented for payment, the drawer and the indorsers are discharged. But are they discharged also from liability arising from the underlying contract or on the consideration? In a case decided before the passing of the Act it was held that they were so discharged.[8] But it was suggested in one edition of a standard work[9] that the discharge of the drawer and of the indorsers from such liability might cause an injustice, especially where the holder's failure to present the bill did not by itself result in any loss. There is considerable force in this argument. The acceptor is not discharged by the holder's failure to present the bill. In the case of a bill, that has been generally accepted, this is expressly stated in section 52(1).[10] Moreover, even in the case of a qualified acceptance, section 52(2) provides that the failure to present the bill for payment discharges the acceptor only if this has been expressly stipulated in the bill. In so far as the acceptor remains liable to pay the bill, it is difficult to see why the failure to present it for payment should automatically discharge the drawer and the indorser from liability based on an underlying contract. It is noteworthy that the failure to present a *cheque* for payment, discharges the drawer only to the extent of the loss that he has sustained.[11]

22–115 **Effect on position of collecting banker.** It will be recalled that the position of the collecting banker is governed by the Uniform Rules and by the principles of the law of agency. It is established that if the collecting banker fails to present the bill for payment he is liable to his principal, who may be either an individual customer or a remitting banker.[12] Moreover,

---

8 *Peacock v Purssell* (1863) 32 L.J.C.P. 266; 8 L.T. 636. See also *Soward v Palmer* (1818) 8 Taunt. 277; *Crowe v Clay* (1854) 9 Exch. 604 (aspect relating to lost bill now governed by s.70). The holder's failure to present the bill constitutes laches: *Turner v Hayden* (1825) 4 B. & C. 1 at 2; *Peacock v Purssell*, above.

9 Chalmers, *Bills of Exchange* (11th ed.), p.113 (the editor, Judge Batt, referred to *United Australia Ltd v Barclays Bank Ltd* [1941] A.C. 1 the view is not advocated in the current edition).

10 Although if the holder sued without presenting the bill he would probably not be awarded interest or costs; see s.57(3) and *Macintosh v Hayden* (1826) Ry. & M. 362 at 363.

11 s.74(1). And see the special provisions made to facilitate the truncation of cheques: The Deregulation (Bills of Exchange) Order, SI 1996/2993.

12 *Lubbock v Tribe* (1838) 3 M. & W. 607 at 612; *Lysaght v Bryant* (1850) 19 L.J.C.P. 160. See also Paget, *Law of Banking* (11th ed.), pp.408–410. The same rule applies where a bill is in the hands of a pledgee or indorsed for security purposes: *Peacock v Purssell* (1863) 32 L.J.C.P. 266.

the collecting banker is likewise unable to seek reimbursement.[13] But the principal is probably unable to recover from the collecting banker any amount exceeding the actual loss caused by the non-presentment of the bill.[14] Thus, if the acceptor pays the bill despite the collecting banker's failure to present it, the principal is under a duty to reimburse to the collecting banker any advance made against the bill. However, if the acceptor fails to pay the amount due from him, the non-presentment of the bill may preclude the principal, who is the holder of the bill, from exercising his right of recourse against the indorsers or the drawer. In such a case, the principal is able to claim his loss from the collecting banker.[15]

When presentment for payment excused. Section 46 applies different standards for excuses for delay in presentment for payment than those applied under section 41 for failure to present the bill for acceptance. Under section 46(1), delay in making presentment for payment is excused when it is caused by circumstances beyond the control of the holder and not imputable to his default, misconduct or negligence. When the cause of the delay ceases to operate presentment must be made with reasonable diligence. If presentment is delayed at the request of the drawer or the indorser, it is probably excused *vis-à-vis* the party that has requested it.[16] Under subsection (2), presentment for payment is altogether dispensed with in five cases. The first is where after the exercise of reasonable diligence due presentment cannot be effected.[17] Thus, where a bill is made payable at a specified town but the acceptor does not reside there, it is sufficient if the holder presents the bill to two banks in this town. If they dishonour it, he is not obliged to present it to every other bank in town.[18] Similarly, presentment for payment is excused if at the date of maturity the place at which the bill is domiciled is under enemy occupation.[19] But it is provided that the fact that the holder has reasons to believe that the bill will be dishonoured does not dispense with the need to present it for payment. Thus, presentment is not excused by the acceptor's bankruptcy,[20] by the holder's knowledge that the drawer has instructed the acceptor or drawee to dishonour the bill,[21] or where the acceptor has notified the holder that he will dishonour the bill when presented.[22] 22–116

The second case in which presentment for payment is excused is where the drawee is a fictitious person. But unlike in the case of presentment for

[13] *cf. Midland Bank Ltd v Seymour* [1955] 2 Lloyd's Rep. 147 at 168.
[14] *cf. Deverill v Burnell* (1873) L.R. 8 C.P. 475.
[15] The Uniform Rules do not include a provision defining the collecting banker's liability for his failure to perform his duties.
[16] *Ward v Oxford Ry Co.* (1852) 2 De G.M. & G. 750.
[17] For a case in which cheques were drawn on a fictitious bank, see *Aziz v Knightsbridge Gaming and Catering Services and Supplies* (1982) 79 L.S.Gaz. 1412.
[18] *Hardy v Woodroofe* (1818) 2 Stark. 319; and see *Day v Bate* (1979) 41 F.L.R. 222 (Aust.). But a bill accepted by an agent must be presented to him if the acceptor is abroad at the date of maturity of the bill: *Phillips v Astling* (1809) 2 Taunt. 206.
[19] *Cornelius v Banque Franco-Serbe* [1942] 1 K.B. 29.
[20] *Esdaile v Sowerby* (1809) 11 East 114 at 117; *Bowes v Howe* (1813) 5 Taunt. 30; *Sands v Clarke* (1849) 19 L.J.C.P. 84. Contrast, as regards presentment for acceptance, s.41(2) (above, para.22–102).
[21] *Hill v Heap* (1823) Dowl. & Ry.N.P. 57.
[22] *Baker v Birch* (1811) 3 Camp. 107; *Ex p. Bignold, re Brereton* (1836) 1 Deac. 712.

acceptance,[23] presentment for payment is not excused where the drawee or acceptor is a person who does not have capacity to contract. The third case, which applies only as regards the drawer, is where the drawee or acceptor is not bound, as between himself and the drawer, to accept or pay a bill and the drawer has no reason to believe that the bill would be paid if presented. Thus, if the drawer draws a cheque on a bank with which he does not have any funds and which is not bound to meet it, presentment is excused as regards the drawer.[24] A similar case is that in which a beneficiary draws a bill under a documentary credit but fails to attach the required documents. A discounter of the bill would probably have recourse against the beneficiary, or drawer, even if he failed to present the bill to the drawee, or issuing banker. The fourth case in which presentment for payment is excused applies only as regards the indorser; it concerns a bill accepted or made for the accommodation of the indorser and provided he has no reason to believe that it would not be met when presented for payment.[25] Finally, presentment is not necessary where it has been waived expressly or by implication. The waiver may occur either before or after the date of maturity of the bill.

22–117 **Dishonour by non-payment.** Under section 47(1), a bill is to be treated as dishonoured in two cases. The first is where it is duly presented for payment and payment is refused or cannot be obtained; the second case is where presentment is excused and the bill is overdue and unpaid. Under section 47(2), when a bill is dishonoured by non-payment an immediate right of recourse against the drawer and the indorser accrues to the holder. But this right is perfected only when the holder takes certain steps which are discussed subsequently.

22–118 **What constitutes payment.** The word "payment" is not defined in the Act. With the holder's consent the bill may be paid by any mode of payment that discharges an ordinary debt.[26] A bill is discharged by payment of the amount due under it in currency that constitutes legal tender, even if the bill is expressed in a foreign currency.[27] The holder is entitled to demand payment in cash, which is complete when the money is handed to him, *e.g.* across the counter of a bank,[28] and he is entitled to refuse any

---

[23] As to which see above, para.22–102.

[24] *Wirth v Austin* (1875) L.R. 10 C.P. 689; *cf. Re Bethell* (1887) 34 Ch.D. 561 at 566–567. For a recent analysis see, *Fiorentino Comm Giuseppe SRL* v *Farnesi* [2005] EWHC 160; [2005] 2 All E.R. 737.

[25] As regards accommodation bills, see *Chitty on Contracts* (28th ed.), Vol. 2, para.34–074.

[26] *Sibree v Tripp* (1846) 15 M. & W. 23 as explained in *D & C Builders Ltd v Rees* [1966] 2 Q.B. 617 (by bill for lesser amount); *Belshaw v Bush* (1851) 11 C.B. 191 at 207 (by acceptance of a bill drawn by the payee on a third party; as to whether this amounts to absolute or conditional payment see above, paras 9–030—9–031). As regards accord and satisfaction, see *Cook v Lister* (1863) 32 L.J.C.P. 121 at 126; *Abrey v Crux* (1869) L.R. 5 C.P. 37 at 44. Note that discharge of the underlying contract, *e.g.* by providing fresh security, does not necessarily discharge the instrument: *Glasscock v Balls* (1889) 24 Q.B.D. 13 at 16.

[27] See below, para.25–167.

[28] *Chambers v Miller* (1862) 32 L.J.C.P. 30 and see *Balmoral Supermarket Ltd v Bank of New Zealand* [1974] 2 N.Z.L.R. 155. *Cf. London Banking Corp. Ltd v Horsnail* (1898) 14 T.L.R. 266.

other method of payment. He is, for example, under no obligation to accept, in payment of a bill, a cheque drawn by the drawee or even a bankers' draft.[29] But the holder may in certain cases be prepared to accept payment by means other than cash. Thus, in *Meyer & Co. Ltd v Sze Hai Tong Banking and Insurance Co. Ltd*[30] a banker paid a crossed cheque across the counter by giving the holder a bankers' draft. It was held that, as the holder did not insist on demanding cash, the draft constituted payment of the cheque.[31] If the holder is a customer of the drawee bank, payment can be effected by crediting his account with the amount of the cheque or bill.[32] This method is used extensively where a bill is drawn on a banker and presented by a holder, who is also a banker, through the clearing house.[33] But an advice by a banker, who is the drawee of the bill, that it would be paid if presented does not constitute payment.

Provisions of Uniform Rules. The definition of payment at common law does not take into account problems that arise due to exchange control legislation. A foreign exporter who draws a bill on an importer in the United Kingdom may not be satisfied by the payment of sterling in London, unless the amount so paid qualifies for transfer overseas. While there are no longer any restrictions on the transfer of funds from the United Kingdom, there are exchange control restrictions on transfers of funds in other trading countries. The Uniform Rules attempt to safeguard the rights of an exporter by imposing on a presenting banker a duty not to release the documents unless the amount paid is transferable to the exporter's country. Under Article 17, in the case of documents expressed to be payable in the currency of the country of payment (local currency) "the presenting bank must, unless otherwise instructed in the collection instruction, release the documents to the drawee against payment in local currency only if such currency is immediately available for disposal in the manner specified in the collection instruction". Usually the instruction requires the transfer of the price to the exporter's banker in his country. Under Article 18, where documents are expressed to be payable in a currency other than that of the country of payment (foreign currency), "the presenting bank must, unless otherwise instructed in the collection instruction, release the documents to 22–119

[29] This follows from the language of s.3(1); and see as to the general rule, above, para.9–028.

[30] [1913] A.C. 847.

[31] As to whether a cheque would constitute absolute or conditional payment see above, para.9–032; and see para.9–034 as to payment by a cheque backed by a cheque card.

[32] *Bissell & Co. v Fox* (1885) 53 L.T. 193.

[33] As to when payment is complete when effected through a clearing house see *Warwick v Rogers* (1843) 5 Man. & G. 340. See also *Pollard v Bank of England* (1871) L.R. 6 Q.B. 623 (no clearing house involved). As to when payment by mail or telegraphic transfer is complete see *Rekstin v Severo Sibirsko Gosudarstvennoe Akcionernoe* [1933] 1 K.B. 47; *Momm v Barclays Bank International Ltd* [1977] 1 Q.B. 790. See also *Astro Amo Compania Naviera SA v Elf Union SA* (*The "Zographia M"*) [1976] 2 Lloyd's Rep. 382 at 390. *Cf. Mardorf Peach & Co. Ltd v Attica Sea Carriers Corp. of Liberia* [1976] 1 Q.B. 835 at 847, 850, reversed [1977] A.C. 850 at 879–880, 884–885; and see *Agip (Africa) Ltd v Jackson* [1991] Ch. 547. And see *Chitty on Contracts* (29th ed.), Vol. 2, paras 34–398 *et seq.*

the drawee against payment in the relative foreign currency only if such currency can immediately be remitted in accordance with the instructions given in the collection instruction".

Two further practical problems are neatly covered by the Uniform Rules. In the first place, according to Article 16(a) any amounts collected (less the appropriate charges, etc.) must be made available without delay to the bank from which the collection instruction was received.[34] Secondly, Article 19 deals with the difficult question of partial payments. In respect of a "clean collection", *i.e.* a set which does not include shipping documents or other documents of title, partial payments may be accepted to the extent to which and on the condition on which partial payments are authorised by the law in force in the place of payment. The "financial documents" (*e.g.* the bill of exchange) will only be released to the drawee when full payment of the total due has been made.[35] In respect of a documentary collection, such as a documentary bill, partial payments may be accepted only if specifically authorised in the collection instruction. Even then, in the absence of an instruction to the contrary, the documents may be released only after full payment has been received. The provisions of Articles 17 and 18, concerning transfers of amounts paid, and of Article 16, mentioned above, apply *mutatis mutandis* to partial payments.

(e) *Procedure on Dishonour*

22–120 **Condition precedent.** The Bills of Exchange Act 1882 prescribes certain steps that must be taken by the holder when a bill is dishonoured by non-acceptance or by non-payment.[36] If the holder fails to comply with the duties imposed on him, the drawer and indorsers are usually discharged from liability on the bill.[37] Thus, the holder's compliance with these duties is a condition precedent to the liability of the drawer and of the indorsers. But the drawer and the indorser may dispense with the need to take these steps and this can be done when the bill is drawn or even after its dishonour.[38] The acceptor, who is the primary debtor, remains liable on the bill even if the holder does not take the required steps.[39]

The position of a collecting banker and of a presenting banker is governed by the collection instruction and by the Uniform Rules. In most cases the collection instruction prescribes the steps to be taken if the bill is dishonoured. If the collecting banker complies with these instructions he discharges his duty as agent and the principal is liable to reimburse him.[40]

---

[34] And note that, under Art. 14(b), the amount is to be so remitted even if the funds were, unexpectedly, received following a refusal to handle the collection.

[35] In English law, the presenting bank's right to accept partial payment would depend on its having a mandate to do so; see above, para.22–091.

[36] As regards the procedure prevailing under Arts 43–46 of the Uniform Law on Bills of Exchange and Promissory Notes (above, para.22–034) see Ellinger, "Negotiable Instruments" being Ch.4 of *International Encyclopedia of Comparative Law* (Hamburg, 2001), Vol. IX, paras 436 *et seq*.

[37] As regards liability on the consideration see above, paras 22–070, 22–073.

[38] See below, para.22–084.

[39] s.52(3).

[40] See above, paras 22–084—22–086.

The Uniform Rules prescribe a procedure that is to be followed when the collection instruction does not specify the steps that need to be taken upon dishonour. It should be borne in mind that the Uniform Rules apply also in certain transactions involving discounts.[41]

Notice of dishonour. According to the Bills of Exchange Act 1882 the first step that must be taken by the holder when a bill is dishonoured by non-acceptance or by non-payment is the sending of a notice of dishonour. "Notice of dishonour" means a notification that the bill has been dishonoured.[42] In the case of inland bills, the requirement of sending a notice of dishonour is in effect a substitute for the need of protest.[43] In the case of foreign bills, it is an additional requirement to protesting the bill.[44] Under section 48, notice of dishonour must be given to the drawer and to each indorser and any such party, to whom notice is not given, is discharged. But the section includes two provisos. First, if a bill is dishonoured by non-acceptance and is subsequently transferred to a holder in due course, his rights are not prejudiced by the omission. But a transferee of a bill is a holder in due course only if he is unaware, when he takes it, that it has been dishonoured. Secondly, when a bill is dishonoured by non-acceptance and notice is thereupon given, it is not necessary to give notice of dishonour if the bill is subsequently dishonoured by non-payment, unless the bill has been accepted in the meantime. 22–121

Rules as to notice of dishonour: by whom to be given. Section 49 sets out 15 rules concerning notice of dishonour. A notice is valid only if it complies with all of them. Rules 1 and 2 prescribe who must give such notice. Under rule 1, it must be given by or on behalf of the holder or an indorser who is himself liable on the bill at the time the notice is given. An indorser is usually liable on the bill only if a valid notice of dishonour has been given to him. Thus, an indorser can give notice to previous indorsers and to the drawer only if he has himself received valid notice of dishonour. If the holder gives notice to an indorser one day too late—whereupon the indorser is discharged—a notice given by this indorser to previous parties is ineffective.[45] Under rule 2, notice of dishonour may be given by an agent, either in his own name or in the name of a party that is entitled to give notice, regardless of whether this party is his principal. Thus, an agent of the holder may give the drawer notice in the name of an indorser who is liable on the bill.[46] But the agent must be acting under the authority of one of the parties to the bill; if his authority has been terminated then any notice given by him is invalid.[47] 22–122

---

41 See above, para.22–084.

42 *Burgh v Legge* (1839) 5 M. & W. 418 at 422; *Carter v Flower* (1847) 16 M. & W. 743 at 749; *cf. Re Fenwick, Stobart & Co. Ltd* [1902] 1 Ch. 507 at 511. The notice must state that the bill has been dishonoured; a mere statement demanding payment from the indorser is inadequate: *Solarte v Palmer* (1831) 7 Bing. 530, affirmed (1834) 1 Bing.N.C. 194.

43 *Solarte v Palmer*, above, 533.

44 The notice need not mention that the foreign bill has been protested and it is adequate to refer to the dishonour: *Ex p. Lowenthal* (1874) L.R. 9 Ch.App. 591.

45 *Turner v Leech* (1821) 4 B. & A. 451.

46 See, *e.g. Harrison v Ruscoe* (1846) 15 M. & W. 231.

47 *Stewart v Kennett* (1809) 2 Camp. 177; *East v Smith* (1847) 16 L.J.Q.B. 292 at 295.

22–123 **To whose benefit notice enures.** This aspect is governed by rules 3 and 4 of section 49. Under rule 3, a notice given by or on behalf of the holder enures for the benefit of all subsequent holders and of all prior indorsers who have a right of recourse against the party to whom notice is given. Under rule 4, notice given by an indorser enures for the benefit of the holder and all indorsers subsequent to the party to whom notice is given. The effect of rule 4 is similar to that of rule 3. Notice enures in favour of all parties who have a right of recourse against the recipient. Thus, if the holder sends notice of dishonour to an indorser and the latter sends notice to the drawer, the holder is entitled to sue not only the indorser but also the drawer. In practice, a party to a bill usually sends notice of dishonour only to the immediate party preceding him, that is, the transferor, and expects the latter to give notice to prior parties.

22–124 **Manner of giving notice.** Under rule 5, notice may be given either in writing or by personal communication; the notice must identify the bill and must intimate that it has been dishonoured by non-acceptance or by non-payment, as the case may be. It follows that the notice need not be in writing[48] and can, probably, be given over the telephone.[49] There is no need to mention in the notice whether the bill has been protested after its dishonour.[50] Under rule 6, the return of a dishonoured bill to the drawer or the indorsers is, in point of form, deemed a sufficient notice. Under rule 7, a written notice need not be signed and an insufficient written notice may be supplemented and validated by oral communication. A misdescription of the bill invalidates the notice only if it misleads the party to whom it is given. Thus, a notice that does not give the correct name of the acceptor is valid and effective if the party to whom it is given is not misled and recognises the bill.[51]

22–125 **To whom notice may be delivered.** The position is governed by rules 8 to 11 of section 49. Under rule 8, notice may be given either to the party concerned in person or to his agent in that behalf. Thus, where a bill is presented through banking channels, the collecting banker may send notice of dishonour either to the remitting banker or directly to the customer, who is usually the drawer. The drawer and indorsers of a bill are under a duty to

[48] This was the accepted view before the Act; see, *e.g. Metcalfe v Richardson* (1852) 11 C.B. 1011.

[49] *Quaere* whether such a message may be considered a "personal" communication. *Cf. Lombard Banking Ltd v Central Garage and Engineering Co. Ltd* [1963] 1 Q.B. 220 at 233.

[50] *Ex p. Lowenthal* (1874) L.R. 9 Ch.App. 591. For versions that have been regarded as adequate see: *King v Bickley* (1842) 2 Q.B. 419; *Bailey v Porter* (1845) 14 M. & W. 44; *Armstrong v Christiani* (1848) 5 C.B. 687; *Everard v Watson* (1853) 1 El. & Bl. 801; *Paul v Joel* (1858) 27 L.J.Ex. 380, affirmed (1859) 28 L.J.Ex. 143; *Maxwell v Brain* (1864) 10 L.T. 301; *Bain v Gregory* (1866) 14 L.T. 601.

[51] *Harpham v Child* (1859) 1 F. & F. 652. See also *Stockman v Parr* (1843) 11 M. & W. 809 (bill described as note); *Bromage v Vaughan* (1846) 16 L.J.Q.B. 10 (misdescription of bank at which bill was domiciled); *Mellersh v Rippen* (1852) 7 Exch. 578 (name of drawer and drawee confused in notice); *Bain v Gregory*, above (bill described as note).

see that someone is entitled to receive notice on their behalf, if they are absent from their premises or place of business.[52] Notice can be delivered to a person who is on the premises and who can be regarded as usually having the authority to act on behalf of the person to whom notice is given. The recipient's wife[53] or, where he is a trader, his clerk[54] come within this category. However, it is insufficient to deliver the notice to a "referee in case of need" mentioned in the bill.[55] Under rule 9, notice of dishonour must be given to the personal representatives of a deceased drawer or indorser, provided they can be found. In the case of a bankrupt, rule 10 provides that notice may be delivered either to him or to the trustee in bankruptcy. Under rule 11, where there are two or more drawers or indorsers who are not partners, notice must be given to each of them, unless one of them has the authority to receive notice for the others.[56]

Time for giving notice. The position is governed by rule 12 of section 49, 22–126
according to which notice may be given as soon as the bill is dishonoured and must be given within a reasonable time thereafter. It is clear from the language of this rule, that a notice *given* before the bill has been dishonoured is invalid. But it has been held that notice is effectively given not when it is posted but at the time it is received by the addressee. A notice may therefore be valid although it has been posted before the dishonour of the bill, provided it is delivered thereafter. If the dishonour of the bill and the delivery of the notice take place on the same day, and it is impossible to prove which event preceded the other, the court will assume that the acts took place in the order in which they ought to have been done. On this basis the dishonour of the bill will be regarded as having occurred before the giving of the notice.[57]

What constitutes "reasonable time" within the meaning of rule 12 is primarily a mixed question of fact and law.[58] But the rule provides two principles which assist in determining what constitutes such reasonable time. The first principle applies where the person who gives the notice and the person to whom it must be given reside in the same place; the notice must then be given or sent off in time to reach the recipient on the day after the dishonour of the bill. The word "place" is not defined in the Act, but its meaning was determined in *Hamilton Finance Co. v Coverley Westray*

---

[52] *Allen v Edmundson* (1848) 2 Exch. 719 at 723 (if the holder does not find an authorised person on the premises, notice is excused).
[53] *Housego v Cowne* (1837) 2 M. & W. 348; *Wharton v Wright* (1844) 1 Car. & K. 585.
[54] *Viale v Michael* (1874) 30 L.T. 463; *cf. Allen v Edmundson*, above, at p.724.
[55] *Re Leeds Banking Co.* (1865) L.R. 1 Eq. 1 at 5, where it was held that a referee in case of need nominated by an indorser was an agent for payment but not for receiving notice.
[56] As regards the position where a partnership is dissolved, see *Goldfarb v Bartlett and Kremer* [1920] 1 K.B. 639.
[57] *Eaglehill Ltd v J Needham Builders Ltd* [1973] A.C. 992.
[58] *Gladwell v Turner* (1870) L.R. 5 Ex. 59 at 61; *cf. Hirschfeld v Smith* (1866) L.R. 1 C.P. 340 at 351.

Walbaum and Tosetti Ltd.[59] It was held that two postal districts of London were "in the same place" for the purposes of rule 12, because it "would in all circumstances be reasonable to send the notice by hand rather than rely upon the general post." The second principle applies where the giver of the notice and the recipient reside in different places: in such a case notice must be sent off on the day after the dishonour of the bill, if there is a post at a convenient hour on that day: if there is no such post on that day, notice must be sent by the next post thereafter.[60] The two principles of section 12 apply only in the absence of special circumstances. There is no definition of the term "special circumstances", but they exist when it is difficult to locate the drawer or the indorser,[61] or when the bill is dishonoured on a festival observed by a religious group of which the holder is a member.[62] It has also been held that, where a bill is presented through a banker, the holder is entitled to wait to get the bill back into his hands before giving notice of dishonour.[63] Rule 12 applies not only where one party, such as the holder, gives notice to all prior parties but also where there is a chain of notices. This follows from rule 14: "Where a party to a bill receives due notice of dishonour, he has after the receipt of such notice the same period of time for giving notice to antecedent parties that the holder has after the dishonour."

22–127 **Loss by post office.** Under rule 15, where a notice of dishonour is duly addressed and posted, the sender is deemed to have given notice notwithstanding any miscarriage by the post office. But the sender must prove that the letter was correctly addressed and posted.[64] If the sender has made a mistake in addressing the letter, he may rectify this by giving notice of dishonour by telegram before the due time for giving notice has expired.[65]

22–128 **Position of agent.** Rule 13 makes special provisions applicable where the bill is handled by an agent. This rule is important as regards a collecting banker. Article 26 of the Uniform Rules must also be discussed in this context. Under rule 13 of section 49, where a bill is dishonoured in the hands of an agent, he may give notice either to the party liable on the bill or to his principal. If the agent gives notice to the principal, he must do so within the same time as if he were the holder; when the principal receives this notice, he has the same time for giving notice to prior parties as if the agent had been an independent holder. Although the rule does not extend

---

59 [1969] 1 Lloyd's Rep. 53 at 72–73. Before this decision it was doubted whether "place" meant postal district or town: Chalmers and Guest, *Bills of Exchange* (16th ed.), pp.436–437.

60 But note that, under s.92, non-business days are excluded where an act need be done in less than three days; and see above, para.22–044.

61 *The Elmville* [1904] P. 319 (bill drawn by master of ship, the position of which was unknown).

62 *Lindo v Unsworth* (1811) 2 Camp. 602.

63 *Lombard Banking Ltd v Central Garage and Engineering Co. Ltd* [1963] 1 Q.B. 220 at 231; *Yeoman Credit Ltd v Gregory* [1963] 1 W.L.R. 343 at 355.

64 *Hawkes v Salter* (1828) 4 Bing. 715. As to what constitutes evidence of posting see *Skilbeck v Garbett* (1845) 7 Q.B. 846.

65 *Fielding & Co. v Corry* [1898] 1 Q.B. 268.

the time within which the principal must give notice,[66] it has the effect of treating each agent as an independent party to the bill. By way of illustration take a case in which a bill is forwarded by the holder's bank to a correspondent banker, who in turn forwards it to an agent operating in the place at which the bill is to be presented. If the bill is dishonoured, each of these agents must give notice either to his principal or to the party liable on the bill (*e.g.* the drawer) within the time specified in rule 12.

For the purpose of rule 13, each branch of a bank is treated as a separate entity. Thus, in *Clode v Bayley*[67] the holder asked the Portmadoc Branch of the National Provincial Bank to collect a bill. This branch forwarded it to the Pwllheli Branch, which in turn forwarded it to the Head Office in London. When the bill was dishonoured, the Head Office gave notice to the Pwllheli Branch, which gave notice to the Portmadoc Branch, which notified the holder. It was held that each branch had the usual time for giving such notice. Moreover, if each agent sends the notice within the prescribed time, it is irrelevant that a few days elapse between the time of dishonour and the time at which notice is delivered to the drawer.[68]

Uniform Rules. The principal and agent, or customer and banker, may by their contract abrogate the duty imposed on the agent by rule 13. Thus, the need to send notice of dishonour may be excluded by the provisions of the collection instruction. In point of fact, it is quite common to include in the collection instruction specific provisions concerning the steps to be taken by the collecting banker if the bill is dishonoured. 22–129

In the absence of such provision, the position is governed by Article 26 of the Uniform Rules which imposes on the banks involved with the collection the duty "to advise fate" in accordance with a number of rules. First, under clause (a), any advice or information dispatched by a collecting bank must bear appropriate details including the "reference" of the bank from which the documents were received "as stated in the collection instruction". Secondly, under clause (b), the remitting bank is required to specify the method by which the advice is to be given. In the absence of such an instruction, the choice of method is left to the collecting bank and the expense is to be borne by the bank from which the collection instruction was received. Clause (c) spells out the specific requirements respecting the three types of advice, which are: advice of payment, advice of acceptance and advice of dishonour.[69] Under subclause (i), "the collecting bank must send without delay advice of payment to the bank from which the collection instruction was received, detailing the amount or amounts collected, charges and/or disbursement and/or expenses deducted, where appropriate, and method of disposal of the funds". According to subclause (ii), the collecting bank must send "without delay" advice of acceptance to the bank

---

[66] *Yeoman Credit Ltd v Gregory* [1963] 1 W.L.R. 343; the fact that the agent sends notice to the principal before the expiry of the time given to him, does not extend the time given to the principal.

[67] (1843) 12 M. & W. 51. See also *Prince v Oriental Bank Corp.* (1878) 3 App.Cas. 325 at 332. *Cf. Fielding & Co. v Corry* [1898] 1 Q.B. 268.

[68] *Goodall v Polhill* (1845) 14 L.J.C.P. 146.

[69] Somewhat clumsily entitled "Advice of non-payment and/or acceptance".

from which the collection instruction was received.[70] Considerably more complex rules apply, under subclause (iii), in cases of dishonour. The basic rule pertains to the bank whose demand for payment or for acceptance is not met by the drawee, that is, the "presenting bank". This bank is obliged to "endeavour to ascertain the reason for the non-payment and/or non-acceptance and advise, accordingly, the bank from which it received the collection instruction". The presenting bank's next duty is to "send without delay advice of non-payment and/or advice of non-acceptance to the bank from which it received the collection instruction". The steps to be taken by the latter bank are spelt out in the last paragraph of sub-clause (iii). "On receipt of such advice the remitting bank must give appropriate instructions as to the further handling of the documents. If such instructions are not received by the presenting bank within 60 days after its advice of non-payment and/or non-acceptance, the documents may be returned to the bank from which the collection instruction was received without any further responsibility on the part of the presenting bank."

22–130 **Excuse for delay in giving notice.** Delay in giving notice of dishonour is excused in the same circumstances that excuse a delay in making presentment for payment.[71] In *The Elmville*[72] a bill drawn by the master of a ship was dishonoured by the acceptor on a Saturday. The holder's banker, who had presented the bill, informed the holder on the following Monday. The holder spent five days in an attempt to discover the exact location of the drawer's ship and finally sent a notice, addressed to the drawer as master of the vessel at Newcastle-on-Tyne, on the fifth day, which was a Thursday. It was held that the holder had discharged his duty and that the delay occasioned by the inquiries was excused. Similarly, a delay, which is caused because the indorser gives a wrong address in the bill, is excused[73] as is a delay which occurs because the indorser's address is not given in the bill and the holder has to make inquiries in order to discover it.[74] However, in such a case the party who has caused the delay, *e.g.* by failing to give his correct address in the bill, is probably out of time and cannot give valid notice to prior parties.[75]

22–131 **When notice of dishonour is dispensed with.** The position is similar, though not identical, with the position applicable in the case of presentment for payment. Under section 50(2)(a), notice is dispensed with when, after the exercise of reasonable diligence, notice cannot be given or does not reach the drawer or indorser sought to be charged. This rule is similar

---

[70] Note that, accordingly, the new version departs from the earlier practice, considered by Longmore J. in *Minories Finance Ltd v Afribank Nigeria Ltd* [1995] 1 Lloyd's Rep. 130 at 140.
[71] s.50(1), which is similar to s.46(1) discussed in para.22–116, above.
[72] [1904] P. 319. See also *Gladwell v Turner* (1870) L.R. 5 Ex. 59.
[73] *Hewitt v Thomson* (1836) 1 M. & Rob. 543; *cf. Berridge v Fitzgerald* (1869) L.R. 4 Q.B. 639.
[74] *Baldwin v Richardson* (1823) 1 B. & C. 245; *Firth v Thrush* (1828) 8 B. & C. 387; *Gladwell v Turner* (1870) L.R. 5 Ex. 59.
[75] *cf. Shelton v Braithwaite* (1841) 8 M. & W. 252.

to that of section 46(2) concerning presentment for payment.[76] The holder's duty to send notice is not excused merely because the drawer and indorser, who are sought to be charged, had reason to believe that the bill would be dishonoured on presentation.[77] If the holder of a dishonoured bill is unable to find somebody at the drawer's or indorser's place of business to whom notice may be given, the need to give notice is excused.[78] But the holder should make inquiries in order to ascertain the address.[79] Under section 50(2)(b), notice is dispensed with by waiver, express or implied; it may be waived both before the time for giving notice has arrived or afterwards. Waiver of notice of dishonour in favour of the holder enures for the benefit of all other parties to the bill.[80] The courts tend to infer waiver even if the evidence in its support is limited.[81] In *Phipson v Kneller*[82] the drawer suggested, before the bill fell due, that he would call in order to be advised whether it was paid. It was held that he waived the need to send notice. Notice is also waived if the drawer or indorser promises to pay the dishonoured bill although no notice has been given.[83] Similarly, notice is waived if an indorser, to whom notice has not been given, fails to raise this matter as a defence to an action to enforce the bill.[84] But if an indorser, who has not been given notice, pays an amount on account of the bill in the mistaken belief that he is a joint acceptor, the failure to give notice is not waived.[85]

As regards drawer. Section 50(2)(c) prescribes when notice is dispensed with as regards the drawer. The first case is where the drawer and the drawee are the same person. The second case is where the drawee is a fictitious person or a person not having capacity to contract; obviously, in such a case the drawer cannot really expect the bill to be honoured. The third case is where the drawer is the person to whom the bill is presented for payment; this situation arises mainly when the bill is accepted to accommodate the drawer.[86] The fourth case is where the drawee or 22–132

[76] See above, para.22–116.
[77] *Carew v Duckworth* (1869) L.R. 4 Ex. 313 at 319.
[78] *Allen v Edmundson* (1848) 2 Exch. 719 at 723; *Studdy v Beesty* (1889) 60 L.T. 647 at 649.
[79] *Beveridge v Burgis* (1812) 3 Camp. 262; *Allen v Edmundson*, above; *Berridge v Fitzgerald* (1869) L.R. 4 Q.B. 639; *Studdy v Beesty*, above.
[80] *Rabey v Gilbert* (1861) 30 L.J.Ex. 170 at 172.
[81] *Lombard Banking Ltd v Central Garage and Engineering Co. Ltd* [1963] 1 Q.B. 220 at 233.
[82] (1815) 4 Camp. 285. See also *Burgh v Legge* (1839) 5 M. & W. 418.
[83] *North Staffordshire Loan and Discount Co. v Wythies* (1861) 2 F. & F. 563; *Woods v Dean* (1862) 32 L.J.Q.B. 1; *Cordery v Collville* (1863) 32 L.J.C.P. 210; *Killby v Rochussen* (1865) 18 C.B.(N.S.) 357. *Cf. Pickin v Graham* (1833) 1 Cr. & M. 725 (where indorser's promise to pay, given before actual notification, was not considered waiver); *Lecaan v Kirkman* (1859) 6 Jur.(N.S.) 17. As to position where one person is employed by both drawer and acceptor and has knowledge of dishonour, see *Re Fenwick Stobart & Co. Ltd* [1902] 1 Ch. 507.
[84] *Lombard Banking Ltd v Central Garage and Engineering Co. Ltd* [1963] 1 Q.B. 220 at 232–233.
[85] *Mactavish's Judicial Factor v Michael's Trustees*, 1912 S.C. 425.
[86] *Sharp v Bailey* (1829) 9 B. & C. 44 (where bill was drawn payable at drawer's premises). But if the drawer signs the bill to accommodate the drawee, he is entitled to notice: *Sleigh v Sleigh* (1850) 5 Exch. 514; *cf. Carter v Flower* (1847) 16 M. & W. 743.

acceptor is not bound as between the drawer and himself to accept the bill. This provision is similar to that of section 46(2)(c) which concerns excuses for non-presentment for payment.[87] It applies where the drawer does not have any funds in the hands of the drawee or has not arranged for the honour of the bill.[88] Thus, if an exporter draws a bill on the buyer, which falls due at a date earlier than the date agreed for the payment of the price, the exporter is not entitled to notice of dishonour from the indorsee.[89] The last case in which notice is dispensed with as regards the drawer, is where the drawer has countermanded payment. This occurs mainly in the case of cheques. Section 50(2)(d) dispenses with notice as regards indorsers in the following three cases: (a) where the drawee is a fictitious person or a person not having capacity to contract and the indorser was aware of this fact when he indorsed the bill; (b) where the indorser is the person to whom the bill is presented for payment; (c) where the bill is made or accepted for the indorser's accommodation. The second type of case arises, for example, where the indorser of a bill becomes the acceptor's executor and the bill is therefore presented to him for payment.[90]

22–133 **Position of guarantors.** A person who guarantees the payment of the bill by the *acceptor* is not entitled to notice of dishonour. This is hardly surprising because the acceptor is, likewise, not entitled to notice.[91] The principle applies not only where the guarantee refers specifically to the acceptor's undertaking on the bill, but also where it constitutes a collateral of the underlying contract which leads to the acceptance of the bill.[92] Thus, a person who guarantees an importer's undertaking to pay the price, is not entitled to notice of dishonour if the importer who has accepted a bill for the price, dishonours it by non-payment.[93] Furthermore, the principle applies where an indorser gives a bond securing payment of the bill; the indorser can be sued on the bond even if notice of the dishonour of the bill is not given to him.[94] However, a person who guarantees the undertaking of the *drawer* is entitled to notice of dishonour if the bill is not accepted or not paid by the drawee.[95] This principle is important in certain types of overseas sales. If the seller draws a bill on the buyer and a third party guarantees the seller's obligation, that third party is entitled to notice if the bill is dishonoured by the buyer.

---

[87] See above, para.22–116, but s.46 is of a more limited nature as it applies only if the drawer has no reason to believe that the bill would be paid.
[88] The rule is based on *Bickerdike v Bollman* (1786) 1 T.R. 405. For applications of the rule see *Laffitte v Slatter* (1830) 6 Bing. 623; *Turner v Samson* (1876) 2 Q.B.D. 23; *Foster v Parker* (1876) 2 C.P.D. 18; *Maltass v Siddle* (1859) 28 L.J.C.P. 257.
[89] *Claridge v Dalton* (1815) 4 M. & S. 226.
[90] *Gaunt v Thompson* (1849) 18 L.J.C.P. 125.
[91] s.52(3).
[92] *Holbrow v Wilkins* (1822) 1 B. & C. 10. See also *Murray v King* (1821) 5 B. & A. 165; *Walton v Mascall* (1844) 13 M. & W. 452; *Mallough v Dick* [1927] 2 D.L.R. 370; and see *G & H Montage GmbH v Irvani* [1990] 1 Lloyd's Rep. 14.
[93] *cf. Carter v White* (1883) 25 Ch.D. 666 at 670.
[94] *Murray v King*, above.
[95] *Philips v Astling* (1809) 2 Taunt. 206; *Hitchcock v Humfrey* (1843) 5 Man. & Gr. 559 at 564.

Position of persons liable on the consideration. A question on which there is some doubt is whether a person, who is liable on the consideration for which the bill has been accepted, is entitled to notice of dishonour. In *Smith v Mercer*[96] a buyer agreed to pay for goods by "cash or by approved banker's bills". The buyer's broker, to whom the buyer had remitted the amount due, obtained a banker's bill, that is, a bill drawn by one banker on another. It was payable on the broker's order and was indorsed by him to the seller. The bill was presented to the drawee for acceptance after a considerable delay and in the meantime the banker, who was the drawer, failed. The drawee dishonoured the bill by non-acceptance. It was held that the buyer was not liable to pay the price as he was not, *inter alia*, given notice of the dishonour of the bill. But it is important to bear in mind that, in this case, the failure to present the bill in time resulted in its dishonour by non-acceptance. Moreover, the buyer stood to lose if he had to pay the price over again. The case may therefore be based on the principle that a person who takes a bill in payment of a debt, takes it as a conditional discharge and that the debt is not revived upon the dishonour of the bill, unless the bill is handled expeditiously.[97] In effect, by failing to present the bill in time the seller destroyed the value of an instrument that could be regarded as a security given to him; this would have discharged the buyer, or debtor, under the principle of *Polak v Everett*.[98] 22–134

Protest. The protest of a bill is carried out after its dishonour by procuring its presentment to the drawee or acceptor by a notary public. If the bill is dishonoured when it is presented by the notary, he makes a copy of it in his register and "notes" on the original bill the date of presentment and a mark or number referring to his register. He then attaches to the bill a ticket or label in which he sets out the answer given by the drawee, *e.g.* "not arranged for". After completing this procedure of "noting", the notary sends a formal notice of protest to the drawer and to the indorsers.[99] When it is impossible to obtain the services of a notary public or some other person authorised to act in this capacity, a householder or substantial resident of the place may, in the presence of two witnesses, give a certificate attesting the dishonour of the bill.[1] The legal aspects of protest are governed by sections 51, 93 and 94 of the Bills of Exchange Act 1882; in the case of a collecting banker, Article 24 of the Uniform Rules is also of importance. 22–135

---

[96] (1867) L.R. 3 Ex. 51. See also *Bridges v Berry* (1810) 3 Taunt. 130. Contrast *Swinyard v Bowes* (1816) 5 M. & S. 62, in which it was held that only a party to the bill was entitled to notice. Where the bill is payable to bearer and the seller was at any time its holder, he is entitled to notice: *Camidge v Allenby* (1827) 6 B. & C. 373 at 381. See also above, para.22–114.

[97] See above, para.9–030.

[98] (1876) 1 Q.B.D. 669 at 675–676.

[99] Brooke's *Notary* (12th ed.), pp.103–105.

[1] s.94. Solicitors may be authorised to act as notaries outside London: The Public Notaries Act 1833, s.2. As regards Wales, see the Welsh Church Act 1914, s.37.

22–136 **When required.** Under section 51(1) protest is optional when an inland bill[2] is dishonoured.[3] Under subsection (2), it is required where a bill which both is, and on its face appears to be, a foreign bill is dishonoured by non-acceptance or by non-payment. But it follows from subsection (3) that, where a foreign bill has been protested for non-acceptance, protest for subsequent dishonour by non-payment is optional. Failure to protest a foreign bill discharges the drawer and the indorsers. Under section 52(3), protest is not necessary to charge the acceptor of the bill.[4]

The need to protest the bill can be waived.[5] Thus, protest is waived as regards the drawer where a bill is drawn "without protest"; protest may also be waived in the underlying contract between the drawer and the holder.[6] Where a bill is presented to the drawee through banking channels, the collection order should include instructions concerning the steps to be taken by the collecting banker upon the dishonour of the bill. According to Article 24 of the Uniform Rules, in the absence of specific instructions the banks concerned with collection are not obliged to protest the bill for non-acceptance or for non-payment.

22–137 **Requisites.** Under section 51(4),[7] a bill must be noted either on the day of its dishonour or on the next succeeding business day. When the bill has been duly noted, the protest may be extended "at any time thereafter"[8] as of the day of noting. But, presumably, the quoted words must be understood as referring to a "reasonable time" after the noting of the bill. Under subsection (6), the bill must be protested at the place[9] at which it was dishonoured. But this is subject to two provisos. First, where the bill is presented and returned dishonoured through the post office, it *may* be protested at the place to which it has been returned on the date it is received back, or if it is received after business hours, on the next business day. The result of this rule is that if a bill is sent to the drawee through the post office and returned through it to the holder after dishonour, the bill can be protested at the premises of the holder. The object of such a protest

[2] As regards the distinction between inland and foreign bills, see above, para.22–040. But an inland bill requires noting and protest in cases of acceptance for honour supra protest. See ss.65, 67 discussed in *Chitty on Contracts* (29th ed.), Vol. 2, paras 34–144—34–145.

[3] When the drawee or acceptor becomes insolvent the bill may be protested for better security against the drawer and indorsers: s.51(5); Brooke's *Notary* (12th ed.), pp.115 *et seq.*

[4] It is doubtful whether protest carried out in the UK proves due presentment: *Chesmer v Noyes* (1815) 4 Camp. 129; *cf. Poole v Dicas* (1835) 1 Bing.(N.C.) 649. As regards the standing of a notarial act made in a country in which it constitutes a judicial act, see: *Brain v Preece* (1843) 11 M. & W. 773 at 775.

[5] As in the case of notice of dishonour, as to which see above, para.22–131. And see s.16(2).

[6] *e.g.* in the case of an export credit guarantee: see generally below, para.24–044.

[7] As amended by s.1 of the Bills of Exchange (Time of Noting) Act 1917.

[8] s.93.

[9] It has been suggested that "place" in the context of s.51 means the town or city where the bill is dishonoured. See Chalmers and Guest, *Bills of Exchange* (16th ed.), pp.436–437. The meaning may differ from that given to the word "place" in s.49(12).

is obscure. Secondly, where a bill which is drawn payable at the residence or place of business of a person other than the drawee (*e.g.* branch of a bank), is dishonoured by *non-acceptance* it must be protested for *non-payment* at the place where it is domiciled, and no further presentment for payment to the drawee is then necessary. It is difficult to comprehend the object of this rule. As the drawee refuses to accept the bill, it seems pointless to present it for payment at the business premises of a third party. Such a third party would inevitably refuse to pay the bill, even if funds of the drawee were available, unless he had instructions of the drawee. It should be emphasised that this proviso applies only where the place of payment is stipulated by the drawer. It does not apply to bills domiciled at the premises of a third party, such as a bank, by the drawee. Subsection (7) lays down requisites of form relating to the notice of protest sent to the drawer and to the indorsers. The form must be signed by the notary who makes the protest and must specify the person at whose request the bill is protested, the place and date of protest, the cause or reason for protesting the bill, the demand made, the answer given, if any, or the fact that the drawee or acceptor could not be found.[10] The protest may be made in duplicate or in triplicate.[11]

Case of need. In some overseas transactions the vendor appoints a business associate, known as a "referee in case of need" or a "case of need", who is expected to safeguard the vendor's rights if the buyer commits a breach of the contract of sale. It is advisable, though not imperative, to appoint as case of need a person who resides in the same place as the buyer. But in certain cases the vendor may decide to nominate a referee in case of need who carries on business in London although the buyer resides elsewhere in the United Kingdom. The name of the "case of need" may be inserted in the bill of exchange by the drawer or by any indorser. Under section 15 of the Act, the holder has the option of resorting to the case of need if the bill is dishonoured by the drawee. If it is dishonoured by non-acceptance, the referee in case of need is entitled to accept the bill supra protest.[12] But it is clear from the language of section 65 of the Act, that the holder must protest the bill before it can be accepted by the case of need. The holder may also present the bill to the case of need for payment but, before doing so, he must protest the bill for non-payment.[13] 22–138

A referee in case of need may be nominated in a collection order given by the holder to the bankers who are asked to collect the bill. Under Article 25 of the Uniform Rules the collection instruction must clearly and fully indicate the powers of such a case of need. "In the absence of such indication banks will not accept any instructions from the case of need." Surprisingly, even if a case of need is nominated in the collection order, the

---

[10] See Brooke's *Notary* (12th ed.), p.107 and forms.
[11] As to the evidentiary value of a duplicate see *Geralopulo v Wieler* (1851) 20 L.J.C.P. 105.
[12] As regards payment or acceptance supra protest, see *Chitty on Contracts* (29th ed.), Vol. 2, paras 34–145—34–146.
[13] s.67.

article does not expressly require the collecting or presenting banker to resort to the case of need if the bill is dishonoured. But the customer's instruction to resort to the case of need may be inferred from his nomination in the collection order. Moreover, section 15 of the Act, which confers on a holder an option as to whether or not to resort to the case of need, may not apply as between a banker charged with the collection and his customer. The reason for this is that their relationship is in most cases governed by the collection order, even if the transaction involves an element of discount.[14]

5. THE BANKER'S LIEN[15]

22–139 **Nature of lien.** Bankers and brokers[16] have a lien over securities deposited with them by customers. As such securities frequently relate to advances made in connection with overseas sales, it is important to discuss the nature of the lien. The general rule concerning the nature of such a lien has been stated by Lord Kenyon in *Davis v Bowsher*[17] "by the general law of the land a banker has a general lien upon all the securities in his hands belonging to any particular person for his general balance, unless there be evidence to shew that he received any particular security under special circumstances, which would take it out of the common rule". Similarly, in *Brandao v Barnett*[18] Lord Lyndhurst said that "by the law-merchant, a banker has a lien for his general balance on securities deposited with him." However, there is a difference between the banker's lien and other types of lien. This has been explained by Lord Denning M.R., in *Halesowen Presswork and Assemblies Ltd v Westminster Bank Ltd*[19]: "The lien which we call a 'banker's lien' has no resemblance to any other kind of lien. In the ordinary way a lien gives a creditor a right to retain possession of a thing until his account is paid. If the creditor lets it out of his possession he loses his lien. The creditor has no right to sell the thing or dispose of it. He is only entitled to retain possession. But when a banker has a lien over a cheque belonging to a customer or its proceeds, it means that the banker can retain the cheque or its proceeds until the customer has paid the banker the amount of his overdraft; and the banker can realise the cheque and apply the proceeds in discharge *pro tanto* of the overdraft. The banker does not lose the lien by allowing the customer to draw against the proceeds. That only means that he has released his lien to that extent."

---

[14] See above, para.22–084.

[15] See, generally, Paget, *Law of Banking* (12th ed.), pp.593 *et seq.*; Ellinger, Lomnicka and Hooley, *Modern Banking Law* (4th ed.), pp.803 *et seq.*

[16] *Jones v Peppercorne* (1858) Johns. 430; *Re London and Globe Finance Corp.* [1902] 2 Ch. 416.

[17] (1794) 5 Term Rep. 488 at 491.

[18] (1846) 12 Cl. & Fin. 786 at 810.

[19] [1971] 1 Q.B. 1 at 33–34; the decision was reversed by the House of Lords on another point ([1972] A.C. 785), but the words cited do not appear to have been questioned.

Extent of lien. The lien covers all the "paper securities"[20] of the customer which are in the banker's possession. "Paper securities" include negotiable instruments, such as bills of exchange discounted or collected by the banker[21] and share certificates[22]; non-negotiable securities, such as an order to pay money to a particular person[23]; and also other instruments used to secure a debt, such as a life assurance policy.[24] It is doubtful whether "paper securities" include a deed for the conveyance of land. In *Wylde v Radford*[25] a customer deposited with his bankers a deed of conveyance relating to two separate properties and gave the bankers, at the same time, a memorandum under which he pledged one of the properties to secure a specific advance and the general balance. Kindersley V.C. held that as the deposit of the deed was for the purpose of giving a security in regard to one property the banker did not have a general lien over the deed in regard to the other property. But he also expressed the view that the term "securities" was confined to "such securities as promissory notes, bills of exchange, exchequer bills, coupons, bonds of foreign governments, etc".[26] But this dictum was questioned by Buckley L.J. in *Re London and Globe Finance Corporation*[27] where documents relating to shares in mining companies were held to be subject to the banker's general lien. 22–140

Deposit to secure specific debt or for specific purpose. Is a security subject to the banker's general lien if it is deposited by the customer to secure a specific debt or for some other specific purpose? In *Jones v Peppercorne*[28] Wood V.C. said that "the general lien is not excluded by a special contract unless the special contract be inconsistent with it". The most common type of contract which is inconsistent with the general lien is one in which a deposited security is expressed to cover an advance made for a specific purpose.[29] In *Re Bowes, Strathmore v Vane*[30] a customer deposited with his bankers a life assurance policy accompanied by a memorandum which stated that the object of the deposit was to secure an overdraft not exceeding a limit of £4,000. North J. held that it would be inconsistent with the memorandum to permit the banker to treat the policy as a security for any amount exceeding this limit; the general lien was displaced by the terms of the memorandum. The lien is also excluded if a security, such as a bill of exchange or share certificate, is deposited for a specific object, *e.g.* its sale 22–141

---

[20] *Davis v Bowsher*, above, p.491. The words used in *Brandao v Barnett*, above, p.806 were: "all securities".
[21] *Davis v Bowsher*, above; *Brandao v Barnett*, above; *Jones v Peppercorne* (1858) Johns. 430; *Bank of New South Wales v Ross, Stuckey and Morawa* [1974] 2 Lloyd's Rep. 110 at 112 (Sup.Ct., West Aust.).
[22] *Re United Service Co.* (1870) L.R. 6 Ch.App. 212 at 217.
[23] *Misa v Currie* (1876) 1 App.Cas. 554 at 565, 567.
[24] *Re Bowes* (1886) 33 Ch.D. 586.
[25] (1863) 33 L.J.Ch. 51.
[26] *ibid.*, at p.53.
[27] [1902] 2 Ch. 416 at 420.
[28] (1858) Johns. 430 at 442.
[29] See, *e.g. Wilkinson v London and County Banking Co.* (1884) 1 T.L.R. 63; *Cuthbert v Robarts, Lubbock & Co.* [1909] 2 Ch. 226.
[30] (1886) 33 Ch.D. 586.

in the ordinary course of the banker's business.[31] But a security deposited for such a specific purpose may be rendered subject to the general lien by the conduct of the parties. In *Re London and Globe Finance Corp.*[32] a customer deposited with his broker some documents relating to shares as security for a specific advance of £15,000. When the advance was repaid, the documents were left in the broker's possession and the customer was granted credit from time to time. It was held that the documents became subject to the broker's general lien.

22–142 **Deposit for safe custody.** Does the banker's lien extend to securities handed to him for safe custody? The answer, basically, depends on the intention of the parties. In *Brandao v Barnett*[33] a customer gave the banker for safe keeping a locked box containing exchequer bills. Periodically, the customer removed bills from the box and gave them to the bankers for the purpose of collecting interest accrued thereon. It was held that the bills were deposited for a special purpose which was inconsistent with the existence of a lien. But securities held by the banker for safe keeping may be subject to the general lien, if the deposit is not made solely for this purpose.[34] In *Re United Service Co.*[35] documents relating to shares were deposited with a firm of bankers for safe keeping and also for the purpose of collecting interest accrued thereon. James L.J. observed that the documents "came into [the bankers'] custody in the ordinary course of their business as bankers, that they were deposited with the bank by a customer of the bank, and that such deposit was made under such circumstances as would have entitled the bank to a lien upon them for their general banking account." It should be emphasised that in the last case, unlike in the case of *Brandao v Barnett*, the documents were delivered to the bankers and were not kept separately in a locked box.[36]

22–143 **Bills remitted for collection.** The banker has a lien over instruments remitted to him by the customer for collection.[37] This is of importance where the banker collects a documentary bill which the customer has not indorsed over to him. It is clear that the bill is subject to the banker's general lien for advances made to the customer. Some authorities suggest that the banker's lien extends also to the proceeds of the bill.[38] But as these

---

[31] *Symons v Mulkern* (1882) 46 L.T. 763.

[32] [1902] 2 Ch. 416. *Cf. London and County Banking Co. v Ratcliffe* (1881) 6 App.Cas. 722.

[33] (1846) 12 Cl. & Fin. 787.

[34] *Jones v Peppercorne* (1858) Johns. 430 at 439–440.

[35] (1871) L.R. 6 Ch.App. 212 at 217. *Cf.* Paget, *Law of Banking* (11th ed.), pp.523–525; Ellinger, Lomnicka and Hooley, *Modern Banking Law* (4th ed.), p.804.

[36] See also *Smorgon v Australia and New Zealand Banking Group Ltd* (1976) 134 C.L.R. 475; *Commissioner of Taxation v Australia and New Zealand Banking Group Ltd* (1979) 53 A.L.J.R. 336.

[37] *Misa v Currie* (1876) 1 App.Cas. 554 at 565, 569, 573. See also *Giles v Perkins* (1807) 9 East 12 at 14; *Re Firth* (1879) 12 Ch.D. 337 at 340; *Dawson v Isle* [1906] Ch. 633 at 637–638.

[38] *Re Keever* [1967] Ch. 182; *Bank of New South Wales v Ross, Stuckey and Morawa* [1974] 2 Lloyd's Rep. 110 at 112 (Sup.Ct., West Aust.).

are usually credited to the customer's account, the better explanation is that they become subject to the bank's right of set-off.[39]

Application to bank balances. There is authority for the view that the banker's lien extends to a balance standing to the credit of the customer's account with the banker. Thus, in *Misa v Currie*[40] Lord Hatherley explained this principle on the basis that "all moneys paid into a bank are subject to a lien". But money paid to the credit of a customer's account is not held by the banker in specie; it is co-mingled with the general funds of the bank and constitutes a debt due to the customer from the banker.[41] Such a debt is a chose in action and it is, therefore, difficult to see how it can be subject to a lien.[42] Moreover, the banker cannot have a lien over the funds, because these are the banker's own property.[43] The better explanation is that the banker's lien over funds standing to the credit of the customer's account constitutes a right to set off against such a credit balance a debt incurred by the customer on any other account or in connection with some specific transaction. This view is supported by the authorities including Millett J.'s classic decision in *Re Charge Card Services Ltd*.[44] 22–144

Third party rights. In *Cuthbert v Robarts, Lubbock & Co.*[45] Cozens-Hardy M.R. said that "bankers cannot claim a general bankers' lien except upon the customers' own property."[46] But this rule applies only if the banker knows that the security deposited with him is not the property of the customer.[47] However, it is to be presumed that if the security is not a negotiable instrument and is made out to a person other than the customer, the banker is put on inquiry. 22–145

---

[39] See below, para.22–144.
[40] (1876) 1 App.Cas. 554 at 569; *Sutters v Briggs* [1922] 1 A.C. 1 at 20.
[41] *Foley v Hill* (1848) 2 H.L.C. 28; *Joachimson v Swiss Bank Corp.* [1921] 3 K.B.110.
[42] See Paget, *Law of Banking* (12th ed.), p.596; Ellinger, Lomnicka and Hooley, *Modern Banking Law* (4th ed.), pp.804–805.
[43] *Halesowen Presswork and Assemblies Ltd v Westminster Bank Ltd* [1971] 1 Q.B. 1 at 34, 36. This part of the decision is supported by the judgments of the House of Lords: [1972] A.C. 785 at 802, 810.
[44] [1987] Ch. 150, affirmed [1989] Ch. 497; and see *Re Morris* [1922] 1 I.R. 81; *Halesowen's* case, above. But see *Welsh Development Agency v Export Finance Co.* [1991] B.C.L.C. 936, varied on another point: [1992] B.C.L.C. 149 at 166. The right to combine accounts is closely linked with this problem: *Chitty on Contracts* (29th ed.), Vol. 2, para.34–313. *Cf.*, *Bank of Credit and Commerce International SA (No. 8)* [1998] A.C. 214 (charge in favour of bank of debt owed by customer to bank).
[45] [1909] 2 Ch. 226.
[46] *ibid.*, at p.233. See also *Watts v Christie* (1849) 11 Beav. 546 at 555 (where it was held that a banker does not have a lien over a customer's private account to secure debts incurred by a firm of which the customer is a partner); *Kerrison v Glyn, Mills, Currie & Co.* (1912) 81 L.J.K.B. 465 (which shows that the banker does not have a lien over money paid into the customer's account by a third party acting under a mistake of fact). And see *Jeffreyes v Agra and Masterman's Bank* (1866) L.R. 2 Eq. 674; *Siebe Gorman & Co. Ltd v Barclays Bank Ltd* [1979] 2 Lloyd's Rep. 142.
[47] *Brandao v Barnett* (1846) 12 Cl. & Fin. 787 at 805–806; *Jones v Peppercorne* (1858) Johns. 430 at 446; *Union Bank of Australia Ltd v Murray-Aynsley* [1898] A.C. 693.

CHAPTER 23

DOCUMENTARY CREDITS AND FINANCE BY MERCANTILE HOUSES

PARA.

1. Practice and classification 23–001
   (a) Introductory 23–001
   (b) The UCP and eUCP 23–009
   (c) Classification of documentary credits 23–049
   (d) Transfer of documentary credits 23–068
2. Contract of buyer and seller 23–083
   (a) Buyer's duty to furnish credit 23–083
   (b) Effect of opening of credit and its realisation 23–097
3. Contract of issuing banker and buyer 23–113
   (a) Opening of credit 23–113
   (b) Realisation of documentary credit 23–126
   (c) Banker's security for his advances 23–132
4. Contract of issuing banker and seller 23–134
   (a) Legal effect of documentary credit 23–134
   (b) Banker's right of recourse against seller 23–162
   (c) Seller's remedies 23–171
5. The correspondent banker 23–173
   (a) Contract of issuing banker and correspondent banker 23–173
   (b) Correspondent banker's contract with seller and buyer 23–181
6. Position of holders of seller's draft 23–186
   (a) Holder's relationship with issuing banker 23–186
   (b) Holder's rights against seller and buyer 23–194
7. The tender of documents 23–196
   (a) Strict compliance generally 23–196
   (b) Specific aspects of strict compliance 23–205
   (c) Documents of carriage 23–217
   (d) Insurance documents 23–229
   (e) Other documents 23–234
8. Standby credits and performance bonds 23–237
   (a) Introduction 23–237
   (b) Standby credits 23–239
   (c) Performance bonds and first demand guarantees 23–270
9. Confirming houses and financing by merchants 23–307
   (a) Functions of confirming houses 23–307
   (b) Liabilities of parties 23–310
   (c) Other methods used by mercantile firms 23–316

1. PRACTICE AND CLASSIFICATION

(a) *Introductory*

Object of documentary credits.[1] The documentary letter of credit is a commercial instrument which has been used in the last 175 years as a **23–001**

[1] For specific works on the subject see E. P. Ellinger, *Documentary Letters of Credit—A Comparative Study* (Singapore, 1970); H. C. Gutteridge and M. Megrah,

means of financing international business transactions.[2] Its main object is to solve two problems that arise in most sales involving a substantial period of shipment: the problem of furnishing security and that of raising credit. The first problem arises because the contract of sale does not, by itself, provide a security for either party. If the seller parts with the possession and property of the goods and ships them solely on the basis of the buyer's promise in the contract of sale, the seller has no effective security against the buyer's insolvency.[3] But if the buyer pays the price before the shipment of the goods, he may not have an adequate protection against default in performance by the seller or against his insolvency. The second problem—that of raising credit—arises because both parties are usually reluctant or unable to tie up capital while the goods are on board the ship.

23–002 **The D/A system.** A partial solution to both problems is to be found in the D/A (or "documents on acceptance") system. Its basis is the principle of treating documents of title as representing the goods to which they relate; the transfer of a document of title confers on the transferee both the property in and the right to the possession of the goods.[4] The operation of the D/A system is as follows: after shipping the goods, the seller draws on the buyer a bill of exchange (or draft) for the price and attaches it to the document of title (usually a bill of lading), an invoice and, if the contract is on c.i.f. terms, an insurance policy. He then discounts the bill with his bankers.[5] In this manner the seller obtains an amount similar to the price shortly after shipping the goods. The bankers present the bill of exchange to the buyer and release the documents to him against his acceptance.[6] In this way the buyer obtains the documents of title and, through them, the property in the goods upon his accepting a bill of exchange for the price.

But the system has two shortcomings. First, the seller does not obtain an effective security. If the buyer accepts the bill but dishonours it subsequently by non-payment, the bankers will seek recourse against the seller.[7] In point of fact, the buyer's acceptance of a bill of exchange is no more effective as a security than his promise in the contract of sale.[8] Secondly,

---

Law of Bankers' Commercial Credits (8th ed., 2001); B. Kozolchyck, *Commercial Letters of Credit in the Americas* (Albany, 1966); B. Kozolchyk, "Letters of Credit", in *International Encyclopedia of Comparative Law*, Vol. 9, Ch.5; J. F. Dolan, *Letters of Credit*, Boston (Looseleaf); R. Jack and Malik *Documentary Credits* (3rd ed., 2001); L. Sarna, *Letters of Credit* (Looseleaf).

[2] The terms "documentary letter of credit" (or "documentary credit") and "commercial letter of credit" are synonymous.

[3] Although in certain circumstances the seller may be able to exercise a right of stoppage in transit (as to which see above, paras 15–061 *et seq.*). But this right is of limited value; the seller may not obtain information of the buyer's bankruptcy in time.

[4] See further below, para.23–132 and above, paras 18–006 *et seq.*, 18–062.

[5] As to "discount" and "sale" of bills of exchange see above, paras 22–068 *et seq.*

[6] For a discussion of the D/A system, see *Guaranty Trust Co. of New York v Hannay & Co.* [1918] 2 K.B. 623 at 659–660; as regards the meaning of the abbreviations D/A and D/P, see *Korea Exchange Bank v Debenhams (Central Buying) Ltd* [1979] 1 Lloyd's Rep. 100 at 102, reversed on another point: [1979] 1 Lloyd's Rep. 548.

[7] As regards this right of recourse, see above, para.22–070.

[8] But the holder (seller) is usually entitled to summary judgment. Defences based on defects in the goods cannot be raised by the buyer against the seller in such an action (above, paras 22–061—22–063).

the D/A system does not always enable the seller to obtain credit or finance. If the buyer's name is not well known in the country of export, the seller may find it difficult to induce his bankers to discount the bill (or to grant him credit against it) before it is accepted by the buyer.[9] Thus the D/A system does not provide a perfect solution to the problems of furnishing security and of raising credit. The best solution to these problems is achieved if a third party, whose creditworthiness and commercial integrity are beyond doubt, agrees to be the drawee of the seller's draft and promises to honour it provided the seller discharges his duties under the contract of sale. This type of solution forms the basis of the documentary credit system.[10]

Nature of documentary credit. The definition of documentary credit which is currently accepted by the banking world is that of Article 2 of the Uniform Customs and Practice for Documentary Credits.[11] According to this definition a documentary credit is "any arrangement . . . whereby a bank (the issuing bank), acting at the request and in accordance with the instructions of a customer (the Applicant) or on its own behalf, (i) is to make payment to or to the order of a third party (the Beneficiary),[12] or is to accept and pay bills of exchange (Drafts) drawn by the Beneficiary, or (ii) authorises another bank to effect such payment, or to accept and pay such bills of exchange (Drafts), or authorises another bank to negotiate against stipulated document(s), provided that the terms and conditions of the Credit are complied with."[13] 23–003

This definition requires explanation. Basically, at the request of the buyer, the issuing banker promises to pay the price of the goods to the seller against the tender of the relevant documents. The nature of the banker's undertaking varies: it may be an irrevocable promise or one subject to revocation.[14] Moreover, the method of payment promised by the banker may assume three different forms. First, he may agree to pay cash when the documents are presented or at a deferred date, such as 90 days after presentment.[15] Secondly, he may undertake to accept a bill of

---

[9] This problem is less pronounced in the D/P (or "documents on payment") system, which provides for the release of the documents to the buyer against honour by payment of the seller's bill of exchange (see further above, paras 22–094, 22–096). But even in this type of arrangement, it may be difficult to discount or negotiate a bill drawn on a relatively unestablished buyer. Moreover, the buyer may not be able to honour a draft before the realisation of the goods.

[10] But note that the seller's right to claim payment under the documentary credit is not subject to his performing all his duties under the contract of sale; below, paras 23–061 *et seq.*

[11] UCP 500 (the 1993 Revision). As to history and relevance of the Uniform Customs see below, paras 23–009 *et seq.*

[12] Note that the applicant is usually the buyer; the beneficiary is the seller.

[13] The need to comply with the term of the credit constitutes a condition precedent to the bank's duty to pay both in cases falling within (i) and (ii). Note that this definition is now applicable, under the same article, to standby credits, as to which see below, paras 23–237 *et seq.*

[14] See the classification into revocable and irrevocable credits (below, para.23–003) and confirmed and unconfirmed credits (below, para.23–055).

[15] As regards credits in which cash is payable at a "deferred time", see below, para.23–062.

exchange for the price drawn on him by the seller. Thirdly, he may agree to negotiate without recourse a bill of exchange drawn by the seller on the buyer. In the last two cases the documents must be attached to the seller's bill. In certain cases the seller may not be interested in a promise of a banker operating in the buyer's locality; in such cases the buyer may request his bankers to arrange that a credit be opened by their correspondents in the seller's country.[16]

23–004 **Mechanism of documentary credits.** While the detailed procedure of opening documentary credits varies from bank to bank there is a fair degree of uniformity as regards the general practice. The transaction is carried out in four stages and usually involves four parties: the buyer, the issuing banker, the correspondent banker and the seller. The first stage in the transaction relates to the contract of sale. The buyer and the seller agree that payment of the price shall be effected by a banker's documentary credit to be procured by the buyer. In some contracts the parties nominate the issuing banker, but usually the contract of sale stipulates for a credit to be opened by a "first class banker".

23–005 **Application form.** In the second stage of the transaction the buyer requests the issuing banker to open a documentary credit in favour of the seller. The banker usually asks the buyer to complete an "application form".[17] This is a standard form of the banker and includes the general terms on which he is prepared to open documentary credits. It also includes blank spaces. The buyer completes these by inserting his instructions as to the documents to be tendered by the seller, the description of the goods in these documents and the type of credit to be opened. If the banker agrees to open the required credit he notifies the buyer in writing; the application form will then constitute the basis of the contract between the buyer and the issuing banker.

23–006 **Opening of credit.** In the third stage the issuing banker notifies the seller of the opening of the documentary credit in his favour. On occasions the banker dispatches the documentary credit directly to the seller. But in most cases the issuing banker employs the services of a second banker, who operates in the country of the seller. This "correspondent banker" advises the seller of the opening of the documentary credit by the issuing banker and, if required to do so by the issuing banker, adds his "confirmation". In the last type of case the correspondent banker gives the seller an undertaking of his own in terms similar to that of the issuing banker.[18] If the correspondent bank is not prepared to confirm the documentary credit, it

---

[16] See below, para.23–173.

[17] An application form is executed even if the parties had previously agreed upon a general line of credit entitling the buyer to apply for letters of credit up to an agreed ceiling.

[18] But note that if the issuing banker promises to accept a bill of exchange drawn on him by the seller, the confirming banker will undertake to negotiate this draft without recourse or promises that the drafts drawn on the issuing bank will be accepted and paid.

must inform the issuing bank without delay.[19] One of the advantages of the employment of a correspondent banker is that the terms of the documentary credit can be dispatched to him by telex, by cable or by a SWIFT message.[20] SWIFT, in particular, provides a speedy and relatively inexpensive method of notification. The documentary credit constitutes the contract between the issuing banker and the seller; if the correspondent banker confirms the credit, a contract is established between himself and the seller.[21]

Realisation of credit. The fourth stage in the transaction is the realisation of the credit. The seller ships the goods[22] and acquires the documents specified in the documentary credit. The documents are usually tendered by the seller to the correspondent banker but in certain cases the seller asks his own bankers to handle the documents and to present them on his behalf to the issuing banker.[23] If the documents comply with the terms of the documentary credit,[24] the correspondent or issuing banker is obliged to accept the tender and to perform his promise to pay the specified amount or to accept or to negotiate the seller's draft.[25] A set containing faulty documents will be rejected by the correspondent banker or by the issuing banker unless the buyer authorises its acceptance. 23–007

When a banker accepts a set of complying documents tendered under a documentary credit, he is entitled to claim reimbursement of the amount paid to the seller from the party who has instructed him. The correspondent banker presents the documents to the issuing banker and usually debits the issuing banker's account with the amount of the documentary credit; the latter presents the documents to the buyer. If the buyer is unable to reimburse the issuing banker before the delivery of the goods or their realisation, the banker may release the documents to the buyer under a "trust receipt". This system enables the issuing banker to retain his security rights in the documents of title and in the goods.[26]

Other uses of documentary credits. Although documentary credits continue to be used predominantly for the financing of international sales of goods, they figure also in other transactions, such as project financing and contracts for the supply of technology. The basic principle in the trans- 23–008

---

[19] This was an innovation of the 1983 Revision of the UCP: (Art. 10(c)); see now the UCP 500, Art. 7(a).

[20] SWIFT (or the Society for Interbank Financial Telecommunications) is an international independent network run by banks. To use it, both the sender and the recipient of the message must have access to terminals linked to SWIFT.

[21] See further below, para.23–055.

[22] But in certain cases he may not ship the goods before obtaining payment; see, *e.g.* below, para.23–066.

[23] This is loosely called a negotiation of the documents and the seller's bank is described as a negotiating bank. The negotiating banker usually discounts or purchases the seller's draft.

[24] As to the doctrine of strict compliance see below, paras 23–196 *et seq.*

[25] The correspondent banker is bound *vis-à-vis* the seller to accept the tender only if he has confirmed the credit; see below, para.23–052.

[26] As to the banker's security or pledge over the documents of title and the goods see above, para.18–062.

action, though, remains the same. The issuing and confirming bank's undertaking to pay cash or to accept or to negotiate drafts is conditional upon the tender of specified documents.

(b) *The UCP and eUCP*

23–009 **Background of UCP** The wide use of documentary credits in international transactions has led to a need for uniformity. The first genuine drive for international standardisation was initiated by the 1929 Congress of the International Chamber of Commerce—the ICC—held in Amsterdam.[27] But the ensuing set of regulations was adopted only in Belgium and in France. A fully revised version of this text was adopted by the ICC's 7th Congress held in Vienna in 1933. This version of the UCP was adopted by the bankers in a number of European countries and, on an individual basis, by some banks in the United States.[28] As might be expected, there were no developmnents of any significance during the Second World War. In 1951, the Code was subjected to a thorough revision which was adopted by the ICC's 13th Congress held in Lisbon.[29] It was adhered to by the bankers in a substantial number of countries in Asia, in Africa, in Europe and in America including, this time, the United States. The 1951 version was, however, rejected, partly for political reasons, by the banks in the United Kingdom and in most Commonwealth countries.

23–010 **The 1962 Revision: Britain joins.** The Uniform Customs were revised for the second time in 1962 and this new version was adopted by all previous participants as well as by the bankers in the United Kingdom and the Commonwealth of Nations.[30] This Revision, which came into effect in 1963, may therefore be described as a breakthrough. Its main merits were the achievement of a general clarification of the practice pertaining to documentary credits and the comprehensive nature of the new provisions. Thus, the 1962 Revision included six General Provisions which gave effect to the basic principles of documentary credits. In particular, clauses (c) and (f) removed any doubts regarding the independence of the documentary credit from any underlying contractual relationship of the transaction.

23–011 **The 1974 Revision.** The Code was revised again in 1974.[31] On this occasion the ICC was assisted by the United Nations Commission on International Trade Law (UNCITRAL). Banking organisations in socialist countries, which were not members of the ICC, made contributions through an *ad hoc* Working Party. The ensuing new Revision had deservedly

---

[27] Stoufflet, *Le Crédit Documentaire* (Paris, 1959), p.102; Bontoux, *Le Crédit Documentaire* (Paris, 1970), p.22.

[28] ICC Brochure No.82. And see Jirad (1976) 8 U.C.C.L.J. 109; Wiele, *Das Dokumentenakkreditiv und der Anglo-Amerikansiche Documentary Letter of Credit* (1955), p.22. For its mention by European courts see Swiss BG 22.1.1952, ZR, Vol. 51, No.116 at pp.173–174.

[29] Brochure No.151.

[30] Brochure No.222. By 1973 the Revision had been adopted in 178 countries.

[31] ICC Brochure 290.

attained worldwide acclaim. Its main improvements over the 1962 Revision may be summarised as follows. First, the 1974 Revision abolished many of the "options" which were conferred on banks in the 1951 and in the 1962 Revisions by means of provisions which stated that "banks may" do certain acts or "may" accept certain types of document. In contrast, the 1974 Revision used the imperative "will" or "must". This has remained the position in both the 1983 and 1993 Revisions.

Secondly, many provisions of the 1962 Revision were redrafted in 1974 so as to achieve added clarity and certainty. Thus, Article 3, which defined the nature of the banks' undertakings in irrevocable and confirmed credits, was rephrased so as to affirm beyond any doubt that the bank's undertaking to negotiate a bill drawn under an irrevocable credit involved an exclusion of the right of recourse.[32] The very nature of the issuing and confirming banks' undertakings was, likewise, more clearly expressed in this provision.

Finally, the 1974 Revision included three important innovations. Article 23 regulated the tender of combined transport documents. It was changed into a generic provision in the 1983 Revision[33] but reintroduced in a modified form in Article 26 of the current UCP Article 47 of the 1974 Revision—which was of declaratory nature—clarified that the assignment of the beneficiary's right to obtain payment under the letter of credit was governed by the "applicable law", meaning the law of the place at which the credit was payable. This important provision is currently to be found in Article 49 of the current UCP The last provision to be mentioned—Article 13—provided that a paying or negotiating bank, authorised to claim reimbursement from a third bank nominated by the issuer, need not confirm to that third bank that payment or negotiation has been effected in accordance with the terms of the credit. This provision is, currently, set out in Article 19(b) of the current UCP.

The 1983 Revision. The fourth Revision of the UCP—published in 1983—came into effect on October 1, 1984.[34] Its promulgation was prompted by technological developments that took place in the late seventies and early eighties, by the general wish to keep the Code up to date by periodic revisions and by the need of clarifying controversial points that arose under the 1974 Revision. 23–012

The 1983 Revision introduced five major improvements. First, the 1983 Revision changed the structure of the Code in that it ceased to include the definitions and fundamental principles in a separate part comprising "General Provisions". Instead, the provisions in point were placed in the first part of the Code. To underscore the cardinal importance of the

---

[32] Which would otherwise apply under the law of negotiable instruments. See the Bills of Exchange Act 1882, ss.43(2), 47(2); the Uniform Commercial Code, s.3–503(1)—(2)(Rev.); and the Uniform Law on Bills of the Geneva Convention, Art. 43. Another controversy settled by the 1974 Revision was the definition in Art. 41 (Art. 43(a) of UCP 500) of stale documents (as to which see below, para.23–203).

[33] Art. 25, which covered documents other than a marine bill of lading (covered in Art. 26) and a postal receipt (covered in Art. 30).

[34] ICC Brochure No.400. For its comparison with the 1974 Revision, see *Documentary Credits: UCP 1974/83 Revisions Compared and Explained*, ICC Brochure No.411 (prepared by BS Wheble); Ellinger [1984] L.M.C.L.Q. 578.

principle that, in documentary credit transactions all parties deal in documents and not in goods, this rule was included in this part.

Secondly, the 1983 revision made provision for two forms of documentary credit which were not expressly covered in the earlier version. One was the standby letter of credit the popularity of which had increased during the preceding decade.[35] The other facility encompassed (in Article 10(a)(ii)) was the deferred-payment-credit, in which a bank undertakes to pay cash at a given period after the tender of the documents.

Thirdly, the 1983 Revision took into account the developments in telecommunications affecting letter of credit transactions. Instead of referring to "telegrams" or "telex messages", as did the earlier versions, the 1983 Revision referred consistently to "teletransmission". The phrase was, obviously, wide enough to encompass a SWIFT communication.

Fourthly, the 1983 Revision sought to provide an exhaustive definition and classification of the four forms of a bank's undertaking in a documentary credit: (i) the cash credit, (ii) the deferred payment credit, (iii) the acceptance credit, in which the issuing bank undertook to pay and to accept a bill of exchange drawn on it by the beneficiary, and (iv) the credit available by negotiation, in which, usually, the issuing bank undertook to negotiate without recourse a bill of exchange drawn by the beneficiary on the applicant for the credit.

Finally, the 1983 Revision provided a thorough, though perhaps not a particularly effective, revision of the provisions respecting transport documents. The earlier division into marine bills of lading and combined transport documents was replaced by a classification of transport documents into marine bills of lading (Art. 26), postal receipts (Art. 30) and "other transport documents", which were meant to cover, *inter alia*, combined transport documents (Art. 25).

23–013 **The 1993 Revision: UCP 500.** The ten years following the promulgation of the 1983 Revision were marked by a rise in the volume of letters of credit issued all over the world and also by a substantial increase in disputes and ensuing litigation. Many of the inadequacies of the 1983 Revision (especially of the provisions respecting transport documents) surfaced in this process. Others became the subject of specific points of controversy referred to the ICC's banking commission. The 1993 Revision currently in force (to be referred to as "UCP 500" or simply as "the UCP"), which came into effect on January 1, 1994,[36] sought to cure these defects. There has also been an attempt to improve the draftsmanship. All the same, UCP 500 is, basically, an updated and improved version of the 1983 Revision.

23–014 **UCP 500: definition of "bank".** The provisions of the UCP 500 are discussed in detail where relevant. It will, however, be useful to outline the main innovations introduced in 1993. To start with, Article 2 states that

[35] As to which see below, paras 23–237 *et seq*.

[36] ICC Brochure No.500. And see, *Documentary Credits—UCP 500 & 400 Compared* (Busto, Ed.); ICC Brochure No.511, p.III; Ellinger, "The Uniform Customs and Practice for Documentary Credits—the 1993 Revision" [1994] L.M.C.L.Q. 377. The text of the UCP and a list of the countries the bankers of which adhere to the Code is obtainable from the ICC, United Kingdom, 14/15 Belgrave Square, London, SW1X 8PS.

"for the purposes of these Articles, branches of a bank in different countries are considered another bank". This new provision sanctions the confirmation and the negotiation of a documentary credit, opened in one country, by the issuing bank's branch in another country. In practical terms, this provision gives effect to a practice that has prevailed for at least twenty-five years.

Nature of bank's payment undertaking. UCP 500 has sought to clarify the classification of documentary credits. Although Article 9 adheres to the previous division of documentary credits into cash credits, deferred payment credits, credits available by acceptance and credits available by negotiation, much has been done to avoid the confusion that resulted from overlaps in the definitions of the last two types in Article 10(a)(iii) and (iv) of the 1983 Revision. It is now clear, under Article 9(a), that a credit is available by acceptance if the issuing bank either undertakes to accept and pay a draft drawn on itself or warrants such acceptance and payment if the draft is to be drawn on some other designated drawee bank. A credit available by negotiation is one in which the issuer undertakes to pay without recourse a draft negotiated under the credit. Notably, Article 9(a)(iv) discourages the use of drafts drawn on the applicant.[37] 23–015

"Nominated bank"; negotiation. Another clarification of the position of the parties to a letter of credit transaction, effected in UCP 500, concerns the question of the availability of the credit and the meaning of negotiation. Under Article 10(b), which superseded Article 11 of the 1983 Revision, in a freely negotiable credit, any bank is a "nominated bank", which term defines the bank authorised to make payment or to accept or negotiate a draft drawn under the credit. In addition, "negotiation" is defined, in the new Article 10(b)(ii), as the giving of value for drafts or documents by a bank authorised to negotiate.[38] Mere examination of the documents without giving value does not constitute negotiation.[39] 23–016

Duties of banks. Important amendments were introduced in the provisions determining the liabilities and responsibilities of banks. Article 13(a) of UCP 500, which replaced Article 15 of the 1983 Revision, provides 23–017

[37] But note that the practice is not proscribed. And note further that the confirming bank's undertaking is defined, in similar terms, in Art. 9(b); as in the old Art. 10(b) it mirrors the issuing bank's undertaking. A revision of this breakdown is expected for the next session of the UCP.

[38] As to whether negotiation has to be "without recourse", see below, para.23–192.

[39] This provision gives effect to a view held by the banking commission: *Documentary Credits—UCP 1974/1983 Revisions Compared and Explained* (ICC Brochure No.411), para.3 at p.23; *Cases Studies on Documentary Credits* (ICC Brochure No.459 by Dekker), Case 14, which reaffirmed an earlier determination by the Banking Commission, of October 21, 1977, which treated "negotiation" as purchase—*Decisions (1975–1979) of the ICC Banking Commission*, ICC Brochure No.371, Case R.7, pp.18–19; Case 182 of *More Case Studies on Documentary Credits*, Brochure 489, at p.27. And see *European Asian Bank AG v Punjab & Sind Bank (No.2)* [1983] 1 W.L.R. 642 at 656; *Amixco Asia (Pte) Ltd v Bank Bumiputra Malaysia Brhd* [1992] 2 S.L.R. 943 (Sup.Ct. S'pore, Selvam J.C.) and *Indian Bank v Union Bank of Switzerland* [1994] 2 S.L.R. 121, CA. The decision to the contrary in *Flagship Cruises Ltd v New England Merchants National Bank* 569 F. 2d 699 (1st Cir. 1978) must be considered as wrongly decided.

that the compliance of the stipulated documents is to be determined "by international standard banking practice as reflected in these articles". An additional clause, comprising the second paragraph of Article 13(a), provides that "documents not stipulated in the credit will not be examined by banks. If they receive such documents, they shall return them to the presenter or pass them on without responsibility." Whilst both provisions reflect current banking practice and legal opinion, it is useful to have the principles involved enshrined in the Code.[40] Another important provision is Article 13(c): if a credit contains conditions without stating the documents to be presented in compliance therewith, banks will deem such conditions as not stated and will disregard them. The effect of this innovative clause is to enable banks to ignore "non-documentary conditions" occasionally inserted in a letter of credit by inexperienced banks.

23–018 **Time for rejection of documents.** The principle respecting the time available to banks for the rejection of a discrepant set of documents has been clarified in UCP 500. Under Article 16(c) of the 1983 Revision, the issuing bank was granted a "reasonable time"—a vague provision which led to costly litigation.[41] The current Article 13(b) provides for a "reasonable time not to exceed seven banking days following the day of the receipt of the documents". Such time is granted to the issuing bank, to the confirming bank and to a "nominated bank" acting on their behalf. A related point is covered in Article 14(c), under which the issuing bank may "in its sole judgment approach the applicant for a waiver" of discrepancies discovered in the documents. However, the time spent on such an approach does not extend the period for rejection set out in Article 13(b).[42]

23–019 **Documents generally.** The most extensive revision in UCP 500 is to be found in Part D, comprising the provisions respecting documents. Augmenting the somewhat scanty Article 22(c) of the 1983 Revision, the current Article 20(b) defines as an "original" any document produced by reprographic, automated or computerised systems as well as a carbon copy, provided it is marked as an original and, where necessary, appears to be signed.[43] A document may be signed by handwriting, by facsimile signature, by perforated signature, by stamp, by symbol or by any other mechanical or electronic method of authentication.[44] Under Article 22(d) any such signature satisfies a requirement that a document be authenticated. Article

---

[40] See, *e.g. Kydon Compania Naviera SA v National Westminster Bank Ltd (The "Lena")* [1981] 1 Lloyd's Rep. 68; the principle can, basically, be traced back to *Equitable Trust Co. of New York v Dawson Partners* (1927) 27 Ll.L.R. 49.

[41] *Sumitomo Bank v Co-operative Centrale Raiffeisen-Boerenleenbank (The "Royan")* [1988] 2 Lloyd's Rep. 250, affg. in part [1987] 1 Lloyd's Rep. 345; *Bankers Trust Co. v State Bank of India* [1991] 1 Lloyd's Rep. 587, affirmed [1991] 2 Lloyd's Rep. 443, CA.

[42] The principle is, actually, in accord with the decision reached by the majority of the Court of Appeal in *Bankers Trust Co. v State Bank of India*, above.

[43] Rather than "authenticated" as generically stated in the old provision. And see further below, paras 23–208 *et seq*.

[44] As regards the electronic transmission of documents, see below, paras 23–031 *et seq*.

22(c)(i) defines a copy as a document which is either labelled as a copy or not marked an original. Under clause (ii), the requirement for the tender of multiple copies, such as "duplicate", "two fold" or "two copies", is satisfied by the tender of an original and the remaining number in copies.

Transport documents. In addition to the revision of these general provisions respecting documents, UCP 500 includes a fully revised set of provisions concerning transport documents. Whilst the current Article 23, respecting marine bills of lading, adheres, generally, to Article 26 of the 1983 Revision, the remaining provisions in this group are new. Thus, Article 24 makes specific provisions respecting non-negotiable sea waybills and Article 25 makes provisions respecting charterparty bills of lading, *i.e.* bills of lading issued subject to a charterparty. The next provision, Article 26, covers multi-modal transport documents. Whilst there was a provision of this type in the 1974 Revision (Art. 23), the 1983 Revision covered them in a generic provision, Article 25, which applied generally where the letter of credit called for a transport document other than a marine bill of lading or a postal receipt. The current provision, which takes into account the specific problems arising in respect of multi-modal transport documents, is—as could be expected—a considerable improvement. Three other provisions in this group deal, respectively, with air transport documents (Art. 27), with road, rail and inland waterway transport documents (Art. 28) and with courier and post receipts (Art. 29).[45] 23–020

The remaining provisions concerning transport documents, Articles 30–33, adhere, with minor modifications, to the provisions of the 1983 Revision (Arts 26(c)(iv), 28, 31–34). The subjects covered include "on deck stowage" (Art. 31), the meaning of a "clean transport document" (Art. 32) and the provisions respecting "freight prepaid" clauses (Art. 33).

Insurance documents. Only two innovations were introduced in the provisions respecting insurance documents—Articles 34–36 (incorporating the provisions of Arts 35–40 of the 1983 Revision). First, the new Article 34(b) stipulates that, unless otherwise provided, if the insurance document indicates that it has been issued in more than one original, all the originals must be presented. Secondly, Article 34(d) sanctions the tender of an "insurance certificate or a declaration under an open cover pre-signed by insurance companies or underwriters or their agents". However, the credit may, of course, stipulate otherwise, which means that, where a policy is specifically called for, such a certificate or declaration remains unacceptable. 23–021

Invoice. Radical departures were, likewise, absent in Article 37 (replacing Art. 41 of the 1983 Revision) concerning the invoice. The only innovation is to be found in the new clause (a)(iii), under which the invoice need not be signed. The clause gives effect to a generally recognised norm. 23–022

[45] Note that, by contrast, Art. 30 of the 1983 Revision covered only postal receipts. The current provision is far more detailed.

23–023 **Miscellaneous provisions.** A general adherence to the provisions of the 1983 revision is also manifest in the next Part of the new Revision, Part E, comprising the "miscellaneous provisions"—Articles 39–47 (replacing Arts 43–53 of the 1983 Revision).[46]

23–024 **Transfer of credit.** By contrast, certain important changes were introduced in Article 48, regulating transferable credits and replacing the old Article 54. Basically, two important modifications have been introduced in the new provision. First, Article 48(a) introduced a new term, or concept, namely the "transferring bank". The transferring bank is the bank which the original beneficiary of the transferable credit (defined as the "first beneficiary") may request to transfer the credit. The provision further defines the "transferring bank" as the bank authorised to pay, to incur a deferred payment undertaking, to accept or to negotiate under the credit or, in the case of a freely negotiable credit, the bank specifically authorised in the credit as a transferring bank. The strange practice, under which certain banks asserted the right to transfer any "freely negotiable" transferable credit which they were prepared to negotiate, was brought to a timely end by this clear provision.

The second innovation respecting transferable credits, introduced in Article 48(d), concerns the advice of amendments. When the first beneficiary makes a request for the transfer of the credit, he must instruct the transferring bank whether or not he retains the right to refuse the communication of amendments to the second beneficiary. The second beneficiary has to be advised of the first beneficiary's instruction where the amendments are to be withheld. Thirdly, under clause (e), if a credit is transferred to more than one second beneficiary, the rejection of an amendment by one or more of them does not invalidate the acceptance of the amendment by the remaining second beneficiaries. With respect to the second beneficiary who has rejected the amendment, the credit remains unamended.

23–025 **Assignment of proceeds.** The last innovation of UCP 500 to be mentioned relates to Article 49 (replacing Article 55 of the 1983 revision), which concerns the assignment of proceeds. To avoid confusion, it is provided that this provision "relates only to the assignment of proceeds and not the assignment of the right to perform under the credit itself".

23–026 **Effect of UCP** The current UCP, UCP 500, does not modify the general effect of the Code. Under Article 1 it applies to all documentary credits and is binding on all parties thereto unless otherwise expressly agreed. But the UCP has not been given the force of law by the legislature of the United Kingdom or of any Commonwealth country.[47] The application of the Code

---

[46] But note the current Art. 39(c), with its detailed provisions of tolerances in drawings.

[47] In *M Golodetz & Co. Inc. v Czarnikow-Rionda Co. Inc.* [1980] 1 W.L.R. 495 at 509, 517, 519, Donaldson J. observed that the UCP did not, in itself, have the force of law. Note that in the United States the law of letters of credit is regulated in Art. 5

depends, therefore, on its adoption by the individual banks or by the bankers' associations in specific countries. This point has been recognised by the ICC Article 1 of the UCP stipulates that documentary credits should include words rendering the transaction subject to the provisions of the Code. The ICC would not have insisted on the inclusion of such a stipulation in documentary credits if it thought that the Code had achieved the standing of an independent source of law.

To give effect to Article 1, application forms and documentary credits issued in countries in which the UCP prevails include a clause incorporating the provisions of the Code. Thus, the UCP regulates most of the matters concerning the contract between the issuing banker and the buyer and the contract between the issuing banker and the seller as well as the rights and obligations of a correspondent banker. But in most cases the UCP does not govern the contract between the seller and the buyer, as this contract does not usually incorporate the Code.

Traditionally, it was thought that the fact that the UCP constituted a set of rules promulgated by the business community ought to affect the Code's construction. This view was well summarised in an American authority, which suggested that the Code should not be interpreted in as strict a manner as a statute but rather as a contractual document drafted by businessmen.[48] Some sympathy for this view was evident in the mode of construction employed in one modern decision of the Court of Appeal.[49] But in another, somewhat later, decision, the Court of Appeal construed the same provision of the UCP as if it were a section in an Act of Parliament.[50]

Failure to incorporate UCP In the present era the UCP is incorporated in the standard forms of virtually all banks engaged in the business of issuing letters of credit. But it happens, occasionally, that a letter of credit issued by means of tested telex or telegram fails to include a reference to the Code.[51] Would the UCP, nevertheless, govern the transaction? In some cases the answer may depend on previous dealings between the parties concerned. It may be presumed that if the UCP governed a number of 23–027

of the Uniform Commercial Code (Revised Version); but under s.5–103(c) the provisions may be varied by adherence to terms such as the UCP: Uniform Laws Annotated: U.C.C., Vol. 2B, p.169. For the position under the older version of the Article as adopted in New York, see *Shanghai Commercial Bank Ltd v Bank of Boston International*, 53 A.D. 2d 830; 385 N.Y.S. 2d 548 (1976).

[48] *Marine Midland Grace Trust Co. v Banco del Pais SA*, 261 F.Supp. 884 (1966); and see *Forestal Minosa Ltd v Oriental Credit Ltd* [1986] 1 W.L.R. 631 at 638 *et seq.* and, to the same effect, Mustill J. in *Royal Bank of Scotland v Cassa di Risparmio Belle Province Lombard* [1992] 1 Bank L.R. 251 at 256.

[49] *Sumitomo Bank v Co-operative Centrale Raiffeisen-Boerenleenbank BA* [1988] 2 Lloyd's Rep. 250.

[50] *Bankers Trust Co. v State Bank of India* [1991] 2 Lloyd's Rep. 443, affg. [1991] 1 Lloyd's Rep. 587 (Hirst J.).

[51] No reference to the UCP is incorporated in letters of credit communicated by SWIFT. It is, however, generally accepted that, as the message is conveyed by an inter-bank network, the incorporation of the UCP is to be implied. The reason for this is that the UCP have been adopted by banks on a worldwide basis. Banks are, accordingly, presumed to issue credits governed by the Code.

transactions between the parties, they had the intention of incorporating the Code in subsequent deals.[52] But in the absence of evidence of this type, or of evidence showing that the failure to incorporate the Code was occasioned by a technical error, it is uncertain whether the UCP applies to a transaction which does not expressly incorporate the Code.

The main argument in support of the application of the UCP in such a case is that the Code has been used extensively by banks in the United Kingdom and elsewhere since 1962 and a knowledge of its existence and of its general implications can be attributed also to most firms active in the import and export of goods. Indeed, the UCP is, undoubtedly, better known and more widely used than the Uniform Rules for Collection, which have been held to apply even in transactions in which they are not expressly incorporated in the relevant documentation.[53] As against the conclusion supported by this analogy it has to be pointed out that the UCP comprises a far more detailed set of rules than the Uniform Rules and it is, therefore, not absolutely certain that the Code, with all its technicalities, has gained the notoriety required for the establishment of a trade usage.[54] American authorities are of limited assistance as regards this question. Judgments delivered in cases concerning letters of credit which failed to incorporate the Code do not suggest that the UCP was, nevertheless, applicable.[55] However, it has been argued that the Code should apply in such cases as it reflects current trade practices.[56]

In one respect, the problem under consideration has been exacerbated, even in cases involving the incorporation of the UCP in earlier transactions between given parties, because the Code is revised from time to time. What, for instance, is the position if the first transaction incorporated the 1974 Revision but the second one took place in 1989, when the 1983 Revision ought to have been included or in 1996 when the new UCP 500 was already in force? On the one hand, it is arguable that the parties enter into their dealings on the basis of contractual terms known to them from earlier transactions. On the other hand, it is well understood that common terms, promulgated by agencies active in the volatile field of modern commercial law, are subject to periodic revisions. It is believed that, on

---

[52] As to a term implied by reason of previous dealings between the parties, see, generally, *Chitty on Contracts* (29th ed.), Vol. 1, para.12–011.

[53] *Harlow and Jones Ltd v American Express Bank Ltd* [1990] 2 Lloyd's Rep. 343 at 349; above, para.22–083.

[54] As regards the requirement of certainty and of notoriety for the establishment of a trade usage see *Sewell v Corp.* (1824) 1 Car. & P. 392 at 393; *Tucker v Linger* (1883) 8 App.Cas. 508; *Devonald v Rosser & Sons* [1906] 2 K.B. 728 at 743; *Strathlorne SS Co. Ltd v Hugh Baird & Sons Ltd*, 1916 S.C.(H.L.) 134 at 136; *Oricon Waren-Handels GmbH v Intergraan NV* [1967] 2 Lloyd's Rep. 82 at 96; R. W. Aske, *Law Relating to Custom and the Usages of Trade* (1909), pp.167–168.

[55] *West Virginia Housing Development Fund v Sroka*, 415 F.Supp. 1107 (1976); *United Bank Ltd v Cambridge Sporting Goods Corp.*, 360 N.E. 2d 943 (1976). *Cf. Oriental Pacific (USA) Inc. v Toronto Dominion Bank*, 357 N.Y.S. 2d 957 (1974); *Talbot v Bank of Hendersonville*, 495 S.W. 2d 548 at 553–554 (Tenn. 1972).

[56] Dolan, *Letters of Credit*, Boston (2nd ed.), pp.4–23—4–25. And see *AMF Head Sports Wear Inc. v Ray Scott's All American Sports Club*, 448 F.Supp. 222 (1978); *Fertico Belg. SA v Phosphate Chemicals Export Assoc.*, 100 A.D. 2d 165, 473 N.Y.S. 2d 403 (1984).

balance, the latter argument is the more forceful one. Parties who manifest the intention of adhering to standard terms used by the banking community may be regarded as ready to adopt the provisions applicable from time to time. The same arguments would apply if the issue were to be raised in respect of a choice between the 1983 Revision and UCP 500.

Conflicts between UCP and decisions. Certain aspects of documentary credits were the subject of judicial decision before the adoption of the UCP by the bankers of the United Kingdom. What is the position if a provision of the UCP conflicts with the *ratio* of such a decision? An illustration may be found in the problems relating to the description of the goods in the documents of title. At one time it was held that the goods must be described fully and accurately in each document tendered under a documentary credit.[57] But under Article 37(c) of the UCP it is sufficient if the goods are described in an accurate manner in the invoice; the remaining documents may describe them in general terms. It is submitted that where such a conflict occurs, the provisions of the UCP should usually prevail. The reason for this is that in most decisions relating to documentary credits the courts purported to give effect either to the intention of the parties or to prevailing banking practice. But there is nothing to prevent the parties to a documentary credit transaction from agreeing on any lawful terms. In effect, this is done when the parties agree that their contractual relationship is to be governed by the UCP[58] This express term is of greater significance than the intention attributed to other parties in earlier decided cases, especially as the judgments in some of these cases are based on a practice now obsolete. At the same time, the provisions of the UCP cannot prevail over a mandatory rule of English law, which is not based on the intention attributed to the parties of a contract.[59] 23–028

Conflict between Code and express terms. A related thorny question concerning the construction of the UCP is whether the provisions of the Code are to have effect only where a given letter of credit fails to include an express stipulation on a given point or are to be read together with such stipulations throughout. In *Forestall Mimosa Ltd v Oriental Credit Ltd*[60] a 23–029

---

[57] *Rayner (J H) & Co. Ltd v Hambro's Bank Ltd* [1943] 1 K.B. 37. But see below, para.23–213.

[58] This view derives support from an observation of McNair J. in *Soproma SpA v Marine and Animal By-Products Corp.* [1966] 1 Lloyd's Rep. 367 at 389. See also *Gian Singh & Co. Ltd v Banque de L'Indochine* [1974] 1 Lloyd's Rep. 56 at 59, 61, affirmed [1974] 2 Lloyd's Rep. 1.

[59] Note that even an established trade usage, however extensive, may not prevail if it is contrary to positive law: *Crouch v Crédit Foncier of England* (1873) L.R. 8 Q.B. 374 at 386; *Goodwin v Robarts* (1875) L.R. 10 Ex. 337 at 357, affirmed (1876) 1 App.Cas. 476. See, generally, Halsbury, *Laws of England* (4th ed.), Vol. 12, pp.35–36; Ellinger, *Documentary Letters of Credit—A Comparative Study* (1970), pp.110 *et seq*.

[60] [1986] 1 W.L.R. 631, but see *Royal Bank of Scotland v Cassa di Ricparmio delle Provinci Lombard* [1992] 1 Bank L.R. 251 esp. at 256 (Mustill J.). And note that in *Kumgai-Zenecon Construction Pte Ltd v Arab Bank Ltd* [1997] 3 S.L.R. 770, the Singapore Court of Appeal held that, where there is an irreconcilable clash between the express terms of the letter of credit and the UCP, the express term prevails.

documentary credit included an oddly phrased undertaking to the effect that drafts drawn on the account party and duly accepted by him would be honoured by the confirming bank at maturity. The UCP were incorporated by means of a marginal note, under which they were to apply "except so far as otherwise expressly stated." Initially the confirming bank rejected the documents tendered by the beneficiary by alleging that the documents were discrepant. Subsequently, though, the bank pleaded, as one of the grounds on which it sought leave to defend an action brought under RSC, Order 14, that its undertaking in the documentary credit was confined to the payment of drafts which had been accepted by the account party.

Bingham J., who accepted this argument and granted the bank unconditional leave to defend, concluded that under its express terms, the letter of credit was to become operative only in the event that the account party accepted drafts drawn on it under the credit. The Court of Appeal reversed this decision. Sir John Megaw took the view that although Bingham J.'s construction of the credit was unexceptional if the credit was construed as a self-contained document, the position differed if its terms were read together with the provision of the UCP He explained that, under Article 10(b)(iii) of the 1983 Revision (currently Art. 9(b)(iii)), where a credit provided for acceptance of a draft drawn on the account party, the confirming bank agreed to be responsible for both its acceptance and payment on maturity. His Lordship refused to regard this provision as excluded by reason of its being at variance with the words of the express undertaking set out in the credit. Article 10 of the 1983 Revision—and indeed the UCP as a whole—were brought in as terms of the contract and, in effect, the Court of Appeal read the bank's undertaking conjointly with, or perhaps even as subordinate to, the undertaking set out in clause (b)(iii).

23–030 **Principles derived.** Two principles are to be derived from this decision. First, when the UCP are incorporated in a letter of credit they become express terms of the facility. They are to be read together with, and be given the same prominence as, the express terms set out in the document. Secondly, a departure from, or any contracting out of, the provisions of the UCP ought to be stated in unequivocal terms.[61] A current example of a provision in which banks set out to achieve such an effect is a clause, inserted in the application form, in which the issuer bargains for the right to debit the account party's account notwithstanding discrepancies in the documents overlooked by his own staff and regardless of their negligence. Where the bank seeks to make such an objectionable provision airtight, it is well advised to exclude the duty to examine the documents imposed on it under Article 13(a).

23–031 **The eUCP.** Despite the developments that have taken place since the promulgation of UCP 500 in 1993 there is—at the time of writing—no indication that a new revision is forthcoming. However, to facilitate the electronic transmission of documents tendered under letters of credit, the ICC has promulgated a new set of guidelines entitled "the eUCP", which

---

[61] And see, in support, UCP, Art. 1.

makes provision for the dematerialisation of documents for the purpose of their being transmitted and tendered electronically.[62] According to Article e1(a), they accommodate the presentation of electronic records alone or in combination with paper documents.

A supplement. The eUCP do not replace the UCP but constitute a supplement. To avoid confusion, the letter "e" precedes the number of each article thereof. When the eUCP are incorporated in a letter of credit, it is not necessary also to incorporate the UCP because, under Articles e1(b) and e2(a), the supplement incorporates the UCP in any facility subject to it. However, under Article e2(b), where the eUCP applies, its provisions prevail "to the extent that they would produce a result different from the application of the U.C.P". At the same time, the eUCP remains subordinate to the UCP if the letter of credit confers on the beneficiary the option of choosing between the presentation of paper documents and electronic records. If, in such a case, he "chooses to present only paper documents, the UCP alone shall apply to that presentation. If only paper documents are permitted under an eUCP Credit, the UCP alone shall apply". It is likely that, in the case of letters of credit available by acceptance, banks and businessmen will continue to opt for the presentation of paper documents because under the negotiable instruments laws prevailing in most countries a bill of exchange is issued, accepted and transferred by means of a "signature" in the traditional sense. 23–032

Important definitions. To blend the eUCP with the UCP where both apply to a letter of credit, Article e3(a) redefines certain terms for the purpose of applying the UCP to an electronic record presented under the eUCP. "Appears on their face"—used in Art. 13(a) of the UCP—is applied to the examination of data content of an electronic record. The generic term "document" includes an "electronic record" and "place of presentation" of electronic records means an "electronic address". Of particular importance is that "'sign' and the like shall include an electronic signature". Where a letter of credit is subject to the eUCP, this definition would, accordingly, apply to "signature" of a document, for instance a marine bill of lading.[63] It would not, however, apply outside the ambit of the UCP, so that, under the provisions of the applicable local law[64] a negotiable instrument, such as a bill of exchange, will still require a manual or facsimile signature. 23–033

Definitions of terms in eUCP. Further definitions, respecting the eUCP itself, are spelt out in Article e3(b). An "electronic record" means data created, generated, sent, communicated or stored by electronic means, 23–034

[62] The eUCP (1st Version) constitute a supplement to the UCP and have come into force on April 1, 2002. Their adoption by the ICC signals the end of the *Bolero* scheme (as to which see "Bolero.net") which had been developed for the same purpose but which met with no success.
[63] UCP, Art. 23(a)(i). As regards "superimposed", "notation" and "stamped", see Art. e3(i)(v).
[64] As to which see above, para.22–050.

provided its sender and data source can be authenticated and provided further that it is capable of being examined for compliance with the terms and conditions of the eUCP credit. An "electronic signature" means a data process attached to or logically associated with an electronic record and executed to identify the person executing it and to signify his authentication of the electronic record. "Received" means the time when an electronic record enters the information system of the applicable recipient in a form capable of being accepted by that system. An acknowledgement of receipt does not imply an acceptance or refusal of the electronic record under an eUCP credit. A document in the traditional form is called a "paper document".

23–035 **Format.** Under Article e4, a credit must specify the formats in which electronic records are to be presented. If no format is specified, any format would do. In Article e3(b)(iii), "format" is defined as the data organisation in which the electronic record is expressed. A word processing system, for instance, constitutes a "format".

23–036 **Presentation.** Article 5(a) requires that a place be stated for the presentation of the electronic record and of paper documents. Under Article 5(b) electronic records may be presented separately and need not be presented at the same time. If the eUCP credit allows for the presentation of one or more electronic records, the beneficiary must give notice to signify that the presentation is complete. Such notice may be given as an electronic record or as a paper document and has to identify the credit to which it relates. Presentation is deemed not to have been made if the beneficiary's notice is not received. Article e5(d) restates this last provision, as a general rule, in respect of all presentations made under an eUCP credit. In effect, this means that the beneficiary has to ensure that his communications have been received by the bank. In addition, Article e5(f) provides that an electronic record that "cannot be authenticated" is deemed not to have been presented.

23–037 **Bank's inability to receive.** Article e5(e) deals with cases in which a bank is open but its system is unable to receive a transmitted electronic record on the stipulated expiry date or on the designated last day of a designated period. In such a case, the bank is deemed to be closed on the relevant date, which is then postponed (or extended) to "the first following banking day on which such Bank is able to receive an electronic record". However, if the only electronic record remaining to be presented is the notice of completeness, it may be given by telecommunication or by a paper document and is deemed timely as long as it is sent before the bank is able to receive an electronic record.

23–038 **Examination.** Article e6 augments the provisions of Article 13(a) of the UCP Under clause e6(a), an electronic record at an external system or hyperlink to which reference is made constitutes the electronic record to be examined. The failure of a stipulated system to provide the required access to the applicable electronic record constitutes a discrepancy. Under sub-clause (b), the forwarding of electronic records by the nominated bank[65]

[65] For the definition of "nominated bank" see below, para.23–183.

signifies that the bank has checked the apparent authenticity of the electronic record. Under sub-clause (c), the inability of the issuing bank or of the confirming bank to examine an electronic record in a format required by the eUCP or, if no format is required, to examine it in the format presented is not a basis for the refusal of the documents.

Time for examination of documents. Article e7(a) adapts the provisions of Articles 13(b) and 14 of the UCP to documents presented electronically. Under Article e7(a)(i), the time for the examination of the documents commences on the banking day following the banking day on which the beneficiary's notice of completeness was received. The reasonable time period not exceeding seven days, prescribed in Article 13(b), is not—in itself—varied. Under Article e7(a)(ii), if the time for the presentation of documents or of the notice of completeness is extended, the time for the examination of the documents commences on the banking day following the day on which the bank to which presentation is to be made is able to receive the notice of completeness. 23–039

Notice of refusal. Article e7(b) does not modify the contents of the notice of refusal—spelt out in Article 14(d) of the UCP—which are to be served by a bank that decides to reject documents tendered to it. However, the clause provides that, if the rejected presentation includes electronic records and the bank that rejects the tender does not receive, within 30 days, instructions from the "presenter" as regards the disposition of the electronic records, "the Bank shall return any paper documents not previously returned to the presenter but may dispose of the electronic records in any manner deemed appropriate without any responsibility". Obviously, the electronic record may be shredded. Its return to the presenter would not serve any commercial purpose. 23–040

Originals and copies. Under Article e8, any requirement of the UCP or an eUCP credit for the presentation of one or more originals or copies of an electronic record is satisfied by the presentation of one electronic record. In respect of paper documents, the position remains governed by Article 20(b) of the UCP[66] 23–041

Issuance. According to Article e9, unless an electronic record contains a specific date of issuance, it is deemed to have been issued on the day on which it appears to have been sent by the issuer. The date of receipt is deemed to be the date on which it was sent if no other date is apparent. 23–042

Transport. If an electronic record evidencing transport does not specify a date of shipment or of dispatch, Article e10 provides that the date of the issuance of the record is to be treated as the relevant date. This presumption does not apply, however, if the record includes a notation setting out the date of shipment or of transport. Such a notation need not be separately signed or authenticated. 23–043

---

[66] See below, para.23–206.

23–044 **Corruption of record.** Under Article e11(a), if upon its receipt an electronic record "appears to have been corrupted", the recipient—be it the issuing bank, the confirming bank or another nominated bank—may request the presenter that the record be re-presented. Under sub-clause (b)(ii) if the nominated bank, to which notice is given, is not the confirming bank, it must communicate the request to the issuing bank and any confirming bank. Under sub-clause (b)(i), the time for examination is thereupon suspended and resumes when the electronic record is re-presented. Under sub-clause (b)(iii)–(iv), if the electronic record is not presented again within thirty calendar days, the bank may treat the electronic record as not presented and "any deadlines are not extended".

23–045 **Additional disclaimer.** The general disclaimer available to banks under the articles of the UCP are discussed elsewhere in this chapter.[67] Article e12 includes additional disclaimers available where documents are tendered electronically. It provides that by checking the apparent authenticity of an electronic record, banks assume no liability for the identity of the sender, the source of information or its complete and unaltered character other than that which is apparent in the electronic record received by the use of a commercially acceptable data process for the receipt, authentication and identification of electronic records. A bank is, accordingly, not entitled to ignore a red flag which is staring in its face in consequence of a patent irregularity in the electronic record received.

23–046 **Assessment.** The eUCP were adopted by the vote of an overwhelming majority of the Banking Commission.[68] To date, they have not gained popularity. Two practical problems, that are not easily overcome, may continue to quench any enthusiasm for their use. One is that the electronic transmission of documents is bound to facilitate the recirculation of documents transmitted in this manner. Where a fraudster and his negotiating bank are in league, the eUCP is bound to play into their hands. The other problem arises where the documentary credit transaction involves the use of negotiable instruments drawn at a usance other than at sight. As negotiation and transfer require the indorsement of the instrument (by means of a physically executed signature) completed by its delivery, dematerialisation thereof is ruled out. As the remaining documents are, invariably, tendered together with the bill of exchange, their electronic transmission without the bill is of no practical benefit.

23–047 **New Revision.** At the time of writing, the ICC'S Banking Commission is revising the UCP 500. A draft of a new revision—probably to be entitled the UCP 600—is currently under consideration by the banking committees of Member States.

23–048 **The ISPB.** Many disputes respecting letters of credit concern the regularity of the documents tendered to the issuing bank. Under Article 13(a) of the UCP 500, the "compliance of the stipulated documents on their face

---

[67] See below, para.23–130.
[68] By 63 to 3 votes: of November 7, 2001; see *Documentary Credit World*, Vol. 6, issue 2 (February 2001), p.28.

with the terms and conditions of the Credit, shall be determine by **international standard banking practice as reflected in these Articles**". In an attempt to shed light on the meaning of the emphasised words, the ICC's Banking Commission promulgated the *International Standard Banking Practice* (the ISPB).[69] This document does not seek to amend the UCP 500. "It explains how the practices articulated in the UCP are to be applied by documentary practitioners. It is, of course, recognised that the law in some countries may compel a different practice than that stated here."[70] It follows that issues respecting banking practice remain issues of fact. Whilst the provisions of the ISPB are bound to have a bearing when an issue respecting banking practice is litigated, the opinions of experts remain of paramount importance.

(c) *Classification of Documentary Credits*

Documentary and open credits. Documentary credits constitute only one type of letter of credit. Another category is that of "clean credits" or "open credits", which are also known as "travellers' letters of credit".[71] Although this type of letter of credit is becoming rare it is still made available by some of the smaller bankers to customers who wish to raise funds when travelling abroad. In an open credit a banker makes an unconditional promise to honour bills of exchange drawn on himself by the customer and negotiated by discounters; details of each bill drawn must be indorsed on the back of the open credit and the total amount drawn may not exceed a specified limit. An open credit may be special (or specially advised) or general. In the former type, the banker's promise to honour the customer's drafts is addressed to a specified correspondent, who, according to cases decided in the United States, is the only person entitled to enforce it.[72] In the second type, the banker's promise is addressed to the mercantile community generally (or "to whom it may concern"). Any financial institution may negotiate the customer's bill of exchange and is entitled to enforce the banker's promise.[73] The open credit is not an instrument of international trade and authorities relating to its legal aspects are not necessarily applicable to documentary credits. It does not fall within the definition of "documentary credit" or "credit" in Article 2 of the UCP. 23–049

Standby credits. A type of letter of credit which has become established during the last three decades is the standby credit, which may be either "clean" or "documentary". Its function, though, differs from both that of an 23–050

---

[69] ICC Brochure No.645, published in January 2003.

[70] ISPB, p.8.

[71] The name "open credit" stems from the fact that the customer's draft in such a credit is not accompanied by documents of title. For the classic definition of open credits, see Story, *Commentaries on the Law of Bills of Exchange* (2nd ed.), para.459. Another contract which is somewhat similar to a documentary credit is that of a confirming house. See below, paras 23–302 *et seq*.

[72] *Birckhead and Carlisle v Brown*, 5 Hill (N.Y.) 634 at 642–643 (1843), affirmed 2 Den.(N.Y.) 375 (1845); *Evansville National Bank v Kaufman*, 93 N.Y. 273 at 280 (1883).

[73] *Northumberland County Bank v Eyer*, 58 Pa.St. 97 at 103 (1868).

ordinary documentary credit and an ordinary open credit. In the latter types the bank's obligation matures when the beneficiary performs his contract with the purchaser, who is also known as the "account party" or "the applicant for the credit". In a standby credit the bank is obliged to perform when the beneficiary, or a designated third party, confirms that the account party has failed duly to perform his contract with the beneficiary. By way of illustration, payment may be due under the standby credit when the beneficiary draws a bill of exchange accompanied by a certificate attesting that the account party, a construction firm, has failed to complete the erection of a building on time. When the bill of exchange drawn under the standby credit has to be accompanied by such a certificate of default, the credit is of the documentary type. If the issuing bank undertakes to accept a bill of exchange, which need not be accompanied by a certificate of any sort, the standby credit is of the open or clean type.

It is clear that the function of a standby credit resembles that of a first demand guarantee and a performance bond. All three types of document are discussed in section 8 of this chapter, which also considers the application to standby credits of the UCP and the new guidelines known as the ISP98.[74]

23–051 **Revocable and irrevocable credits.** A fundamental classification of documentary credits is their division into revocable and irrevocable credits. This classification is recognised in Article 6 of the UCP, which also requires that all credits should clearly indicate whether they are revocable or irrevocable. In the absence of such indication the credit is deemed to be irrevocable.[75] Whether a documentary credit is revocable or irrevocable depends on the terms of the promise given by the issuing banker to the seller.[76]

23–052 **Nature of revocable credit.** Under Article 8(a) of the UCP a revocable credit does not constitute a legally binding undertaking between the issuing banker and the seller, and such a credit may be modified or cancelled at any moment without notice to the seller. A similar rule applied in England before the UCP was adopted by its bankers.[77] But Article 8(b) safeguards the interests of a correspondent banker, be he a branch of the issuing banker or another banker, who has been instructed to transmit the revocable credit to the seller and to take up documents presented thereunder. If the correspondent banker accepts documents tendered under the credit and pays, accepts or negotiates a draft before obtaining notice of its

---

[74] The "International Standby Practices", developed by the Institute of International Banking Law and Practice and approved by the ICC; now available as ICC Brochure No.1516: in force since January 1, 1999.

[75] Reversing the presumption spelt out in Art. 7(c) of the 1983 Revision and its predecessors.

[76] If in a credit in which the UCP is not incorporated the promise is definite, the letter of credit is treated as irrevocable, even if it is not specifically so designated: *West Virginia Housing Development Fund v Sroka*, 415 F.Supp. 1107 (1976). Contrast *Beathard v Chicago Football Club Inc.*, 419 F.Supp. 1133 (1976) where the opposite conclusion was reached under Art. 1(c) of the 1974 Revision, *viz.* Art. 7(c) of 1983, in respect of a letter of credit which incorporated the UCP.

[77] *Cape Asbestos Co. Ltd v Lloyds Bank Ltd* [1921] W.N. 274.

revocation or cancellation, he is entitled to be reimbursed by the issuing banker. This principle applies also to deferred payment credits. An issuing bank is obliged to reimburse the correspondent bank for such a payment if notice of the revocation of the credit or of its amendment reaches the correspondent bank after it has accepted the documents tendered under the credit.

Nature of irrevocable credit. According to Article 9(a) of the UCP an irrevocable credit constitutes a definite undertaking on the part of an issuing banker that the provisions for payment contained in the credit will be duly fulfilled, provided that all terms and conditions of the credit are complied with. The provision for payment may assume one of four forms. First, under clause (a)(i) it may assume the form of a promise to pay in cash when the documents are tendered. Secondly, under clause a(ii) it may assume the form of a promise to make payment in cash at some deferred date, determinable in accordance with the provisions of the credit. A third type of undertaking, defined in clause (a)(iii), is given by the bank where the beneficiary is asked to draw a bill of exchange covering the amount of the credit. If the draft is to be drawn on the issuing bank, that bank undertakes to accept and pay the draft on maturity. If the draft is to be drawn not on the issuing bank but on "another drawee bank", the issuing bank's duty is "to accept and pay on maturity draft(s) drawn by the beneficiary in the event the drawee bank stipulated in the credit does not accept drafts(s) drawn on it, or to pay draft(s) accepted but not paid by such drawee bank at maturity". Presumably, the draft to be drawn by the beneficiary on the issuing bank, following the designated drawee's non-acceptance of the original draft drawn under the credit, can be presented after the expiry date of the credit. The fourth type of undertaking is used in credits available by negotiation. In such a credit the issuing bank undertakes to "negotiate" a bill of exchange drawn by the beneficiary. According to clause (a)(iv) the issuing bank is, then, deemed to have undertaken "to pay without recourse to drawers and/or bona fide holders, draft(s) drawn by the beneficiary and/or document(s) presented under the credit". No hint is given as to who is to be the drawee of such a draft.[78] The only point clarified in the second and third sentences of the clause is that a "credit should not be issued available by draft(s) on the applicant. If the credit nevertheless calls for draft(s) on the applicant, banks will consider such draft(s) as an additional document."[79] Under Article 9(d)(i) an irrevocable credit can neither be amended nor cancelled without the agreement of the issuing bank,[80] the confirming bank (if any) and the beneficiary. 23–053

---

[78] A credit in which a bank undertakes that a draft will be paid if accepted by the buyer is considered irrevocable: *Forestal Mimosa Ltd v Oriental Credit Ltd* [1986] 1 W.L.R. 631.

[79] Art. 9(a)(iv) has not brought an end to the use of credits calling for drafts to be drawn on the applicant. The legal effect of the provision remains shrouded in mystery.

[80] This means that the bank, too, may reject a proposed amendment: *AMF Head Sports Wear Inc. v Ray Scott's All-American Sports Club Inc.*, 4487. Supp 222 (1978). And note also, that under the same provision of the UCP, a "partial acceptance of amendments is not effective without the agreement of all parties thereto."

23–054 **Time.** While it is accepted that an irrevocable credit constitutes a contract between the issuing banker and the seller,[81] it is not certain at what point of time this contract is established and when the undertaking becomes irrevocable. The UCP does not solve this problem. In *Urquhart Lindsay & Co. Ltd v Eastern Bank Ltd*[82] Rowlatt J. said that an irrevocable credit may not be revoked once the seller has acted on it, *e.g.* by commencing performance of his contract with the buyer. But the decision of Greer J. in *Dexters Ltd v Schenker & Co.*[83] supports the view that the engagement of the issuing banker becomes irrevocable as soon as the documentary credit reaches the hands of the seller. The latter view prevails in the United States[84] and appears preferable. First, it coincides with and gives effect to the intention of the parties. Secondly, it puts forward a simple test for determining the time of the commencement of the irrevocability of the credit. There is support for the view that a documentary credit is not established until it reaches the seller's hands.[85]

23–055 **Confirmed and unconfirmed credits.** Whether a documentary credit is confirmed or unconfirmed depends on the role assumed by the correspondent banker.[86] If the correspondent banker is merely instructed by the issuing banker to notify the seller about the opening of the documentary credit by the issuing banker, the correspondent banker acts as an agent of the issuing

---

[81] *Urquhart, Lindsay & Co. Ltd v Eastern Bank Ltd* [1922] 1 K.B. 318 at 321–322; *Donald H. Scott & Co. Ltd v Barclays Bank Ltd* [1923] 2 K.B. 1 at 14; *Trans Trust SPRL v Danubian Trading Co. Ltd* [1952] 2 Q.B. 297 at 304–305; *Midland Bank Ltd v Seymour* [1955] 2 Lloyd's Rep. 147 at 166; *Malas (Hamzeh) & Sons v British Imex Industries Ltd* [1958] 2 Q.B. 127 at 129; *Commercial Banking Co. of Sydney Ltd v Jalsard Pty Ltd* [1973] A.C. 279 at 286; *McInerny v Lloyds Bank Ltd* [1973] 2 Lloyd's Rep. 389, affirmed [1974] 1 Lloyd's Rep. 246; *United City Merchants (Investments) Ltd v Royal Bank of Canada* [1983] A.C. 168; *Westpac Banking Corp. v South Carolina National Bank* [1986] 1 Lloyd's Rep. 311 at 315. In the USA, see: *American Steel Co. v Irving National Bank*, 266 F.41, 43 (1920); *Lamborn v National Park of New York*, 148 N.E. 664 at 665–666 (1925); *Asbury Park and Ocean Grove Bank v National City Bank of New York*, 35 N.Y.S. 2d 985 at 988 (1942); *Harvey Estates Construction Co. v Dry Dock Savings Bank*, 381 F.Supp. 271 (1974); *Courtaulds North America v North Carolina National Bank*, 528 F. 2d 802 (1975); *Brown v United States National Bank*, 371 N.W. 2d 692 (Neb. 1985). And see Uniform Commercial Code (USA), s.5–114.

[82] Above, at pp.321–322. See also *Midland Bank Ltd v Seymour*, above, at p.166; *Bank of New South Wales v Commonwealth Steel Co. Ltd* [1983] 1 N.S.W.L.R. 69 and *Westpac Banking Corp. v Commonwealth Steel Co. Ltd, ibid.*, 735 (Aust.).

[83] (1923) 14 Ll.L.R. 586 at 588, discussed further below, para.23–137. This view leads to some theoretical problems.

[84] *American Bank and Trust Co. v National City Bank of New York*, 6 F. 762 at 769 (1925); *Bril v Suomen Pankki Finlands Bank*, 97 N.Y.S. 2d 22 at 32 (1950); *Distribuidora del Pacifico SA v Gonzales*, 88 F.Supp. 538 at 541 (1950) where it was said that the buyer could instruct the banker to modify the terms of the credit before its notification to the seller; *Savatin Corp. v National Bank of Pakistan*, 447 F.2d 727 (2nd Circ 1971); the principle is now enshrined in s.5–106 of the Uniform Commercial Code (USA).

[85] *Bunge Corp. v Vegetable Vitamin Foods (Pte.) Ltd* (1984) 134 N.L.J. 125. But note that the time from which an amendment is binding is defined in Art. 9(d); see below, para.23–136.

[86] That the issuing bank's branch or office in another country may be a confirming bank follows from Art. 2, as to which see above, para.23–014.

banker. In such cases the correspondent banker assumes the role of an "advising banker" and the commercial credit is unconfirmed on his part, although it may contain an irrevocable undertaking of the issuing banker. If the correspondent banker accepts from the seller documents tendered under such an unconfirmed credit, he does so on behalf of the issuing banker. But in certain transactions the seller may insist on obtaining a binding undertaking of a banker operating in his locality. In such cases the issuing banker may ask the correspondent banker to confirm the documentary credit.[87] The correspondent banker then adds his own promise to that of the issuing banker and the credit becomes a confirmed credit. Under Article 9(b) of the UCP such a confirmation constitutes a definite undertaking by the confirming banker, given to the beneficiary in addition to that of the issuing banker, and falling due provided the terms and conditions of the credit are complied with. The form which the confirming banker's engagement may assume is similar to that of the issuing banker's: he may promise to pay cash on presentment or at a deferred date; he may undertake to accept and pay a documentary bill drawn on himself or to accept and pay such a bill if a nominated third bank dishonours a bill drawn under the credit; or he may promise to negotiate or purchase without recourse a documentary bill drawn on a third party other than the applicant.[88] It is essential that the confirming banker's undertaking be definite and unconditional. Thus, if the confirming banker reserves to himself a right of recourse against the seller, his undertaking does not constitute a confirmation.[89] In practice, the correspondent banker is asked to confirm a credit only if it is irrevocable.[90]

Correspondent bank's refusal to confirm. The 1974 Revision assumed that a correspondent or intermediary bank that was asked to confirm a documentary credit would be prepared to do so. Experience has shown that this is not always the case. To regularise the position, Article 10(c) of the 1983 Revision stipulated that if a bank authorised or requested to confirm a credit refused to do so, it had to inform the issuing bank without delay. This rule is, currently, spelt out in Article 9(c)(i) of UCP 500. Subclause (ii) provides that, in the absence of a stipulation to the contrary, the correspondent bank will in such a case advise the credit to the beneficiary without 23–056

---

[87] Before the adoption of the UCP in the United Kingdom there was some confusion as regards the meaning of the term "confirmed credit". Thus, in *Panoutsos v Raymond Hadley Corp.* [1917] 2 K.B. 473 and in *Sassoon (MA) & Sons Ltd v International Banking Corp.* [1927] A.C. 711 at 724 it was treated as synonymous with "irrevocable credit".

[88] See below, paras 23–162, 23–178.

[89] *Wahbe Tamari & Sons Ltd v "Colprogeca" Sociedade Geral de Fibras, Cafes e Produtos Coloniais Lda.* [1969] 2 Lloyd's Rep. 18.

[90] In theory a correspondent banker may be asked to confirm a revocable credit. In such a credit the seller would be informed that the credit was revocable by the issuing banker but "confirmed" or "irrevocable" on the part of the correspondent. In practice, if the seller does not require an irrevocable undertaking of the issuing banker, the correspondent banker is instructed to *issue* the documentary credit. In such a case the seller's contract is solely with the correspondent, who issues an irrevocable credit. See below, para.23–182.

adding its confirmation. It is clear that even if the correspondent bank fails to advise the issuing bank of its refusal to confirm, it does not become bound towards the beneficiary. There is, further, no suggestion that the correspondent bank becomes bound to confirm the credit as against the issuing bank. Presumably, the correspondent bank is liable to compensate the issuing bank for any loss sustained by it as a result of the correspondent bank's failure to advise promptly its refusal to confirm. This argument is based on the supposition that the UCP constitutes a master agreement between the banks adhering to it. The problem, though, is to establish any loss sustained by the issuing bank. It will be shown that the engagement of the correspondent is at the buyer's expense and risk.[91] How, then, can the correspondent bank's failure to comply with the provision of Article 10(c) cause loss to the issuer?

23–057 **Silent confirmation.** A problem that arises in modern practice is that of a confirmation solicited by the beneficiary where the letter of credit is issued as irrevocable but unconfirmed. Occasionally, the beneficiary, who receives such a letter of credit, requires the correspondent bank to confirm it and agrees to pay the usual confirmation fees. It is clear that such a "silent confirmation" is not encompassed by the accepted definition of a confirmed credit.[92] According to Article 9(b) of the UCP a confirmation is given "upon the authorisation or request of the issuing bank." When the correspondent bank agrees to do so, it carries out the issuer's instructions and acquires a right of reimbursement when payment is effected in compliance with the terms of the credit. In a silent confirmation, by contrast, the correspondent bank acts at another party's request and, it is arguable, departs from the mandate conferred on it. Consequently, the correspondent bank may have to account to its principal—the issuing bank—for any profit made.[93] The correspondent bank's position is further complicated by the fact that the confirmation is issued at the request of the beneficiary, whose interest may be in conflict with the issuing bank's.

23–058 **Hybrid cases.** In some letters of credit, issued in South East Asia, the issuing bank's advice to the correspondent includes the following instruction: "You may confirm this letter of credit at the beneficiary's request and expense" or words to a similar effect. If the correspondent bank enters into such an arrangement with the beneficiary, is it adding a "confirmation" as defined in the UCP and is the facility thereupon rightly described as a confirmed credit? Conceptually, the correspondent bank is in such a case "authorised" by the issuing bank to confirm the letter of credit. On this basis, it would appear that the undertaking issued by the correspondent constitutes a "confirmation" within the meaning of Article 9(b). Consequently, the rights conferred on the correspondent bank against the issuing

[91] See below, para.23–119.

[92] And note that in *Dibrell Bros Int. SA v Banca Nazionale de Livoro*, 38 F. 3rd 1571 (11th Cir. 1994) it was held that a silent confirmation is not encompassed by Art. 5 of the Uniform Commercial Code (USA); Ellinger, (2001) 5 *Documentary Credit World* 19 (May issue).

[93] See, generally, *Chitty on Contracts* (29th ed.), Vol. 2, para.31–118.

bank when the correspondent takes up a regular set of documents are those of a confirming bank. The fact that the correspondent's remuneration is paid by the beneficiary does not, in itself, militate against this conclusion. But what is the correspondent bank's position if it decides not to confirm a facility of the type under consideration? Does it still have to follow the procedure prescribed in Article 9(c), under which, it will be recalled, the correspondent must notify the issuing bank without delay if it is not prepared to confirm the letter of credit? On the one hand, Article 9(c) applies whenever the correspondent bank is "authorised or requested by the issuing bank to add its confirmation". On this basis it is arguable that the procedure is applicable. On the other hand, when the correspondent bank receives a letter of credit including the instruction set out above, it is not required to reach a decision about the confirmation of the facility unless and until it receives the beneficiary's request. Moreover, as the issuing bank does not authorise the correspondent to act on its own behalf, why should the correspondent bank be expected to convey its decision to the issuing bank? There may, perhaps, be room for the argument that, in the context of Articles 9(b) and 9(c), the word "authorise" should be understood as referring to the correspondent bank's authority to issue a confirmation on the issuing bank's behalf. Under this construction, the instant type of facility would not constitute a confirmed credit as defined in the UCP and Article 9(c) would be inapplicable.

Effect of irrevocable and confirmed credits. Article 9(d) defines the effect of irrevocable credits and of confirmed credits. Under sub-clause (i) an irrevocable credit can be neither amended nor cancelled without the agreement of the issuing bank, the confirming bank, if any, and the beneficiary. Obviously, either bank is entitled to withhold its approval of a proposed amendment even if all other parties want it. Under sub-clause (ii) the issuing bank is "irrevocably bound by an amendment(s) issued by it from the time of the issuance of such amendment(s). A Confirming Bank may extend its confirmation to an amendment and shall be irrevocably bound by it as of the time of its advice of the amendment. A Confirming Bank may, however, choose to advise an amendment to the Beneficiary without extending its confirmation and, if so, must inform the Issuing Bank and the Beneficiary without delay." The rights of the beneficiary are safeguarded by sub-clause (iii). "The terms of the original Credit (or a Credit incorporating previously accepted amendment(s)) will remain in force for the Beneficiary until the Beneficiary communicates his acceptance of the amendment to the bank that advised such amendment. The Beneficiary should give notification of acceptance or rejection of amendment(s). If the Beneficiary fails to give such notification, the tender of documents to the Nominated Bank or Issuing Bank, that conform to the credit and to not yet accepted amendment(s), will be deemed to be notification of acceptance by the Beneficiary of such amendment(s) and as of that moment the Credit will be amended." 23–059

Partial acceptance. Article 9(d)(iv) proscribes partial acceptances of amendments contained in one and the same advice. It provides that such a partial acceptance "will not be given any effect". In consequence, the letter of credit remains effective in its unamended version. 23–060

23–061 **Straight and negotiation credits.** In some documentary credits issued in the United Kingdom, the issuing banker's promise is directed solely to the seller. Such credits are known as "straight credits" and are enforceable only by the seller. In this regard, the straight documentary credit resembles the "specially advised" open or travellers' letter of credit.[94] But in other documentary credits, known as "negotiation credits", the issuing banker's promise is not confined to the seller but extends to any bona fide holders of a bill of exchange drawn by the seller under the documentary credit, provided it is accompanied by the stipulated documents.[95] This type of promise gives additional currency to the documentary credit because a bank or financial house which discounts a draft drawn under such a credit is entitled to enforce the issuing banker's promise in its own name.[96] In this regard, a negotiation credit is similar to a "general" open letter of credit.[97]

23–062 **Deferred negotiation credit.** Can a deferred payment credit[98] constitute a negotiation credit? A plain reading of Article 9(a) of the UCP might lead to the conclusion that the word "negotiation credit" refers only to credits available by negotiation as described in sub-clause (a)(iv). Article 10 of the UCP, however, refers to "negotiation" in a different sense, *i.e.* to an arrangement under which a bank, or third party, is invited to "negotiate" drafts or documents drawn under any documentary credit. A decision of the Singapore Court of Appeal[99] supports the view that the divisions of credits into negotiation and straight credits is, indeed, separate from their classification on the basis of the method stipulated for the issuing bank's performance undertaking. The case of *Banco Santander SA v Banque Paribas*[1] goes in the same direction. Here a fraud was discovered after the date on which the documents were tendered under a deferred payment credit but before payment was due. As the intermediary bank, which brought an action to enforce the credit, relied on its position as an assignee of the proceeds, the Court of Appeal held that the fraud could be raised against it. But their Lordships accepted that, if the bank had brought its

---

[94] As to which, see above, para.23–024. As to whether the amount of a straight credit is assignable, see below, para.23–024.
[95] For a different view see Dolan Negotiation Letters of Credit [2003] *Annual Survey of Letter of Credit Law and Practice* 21.
[96] *Sassoon (M A) & Sons Ltd v International Banking Corp.* [1927] A.C. 711 at 722, 724 where it was, however, held on the facts that the documentary credit in question was of the straight type. In the USA, see: *Banco Nacional Ultramarino v First National Bank of Boston*, 289 F. 169 at 173–174 (1923); *Courteen Seed Co. v Hong Kong and Shanghai Banking Corp.*, 215 N.Y.S. 525 at 529 (1926), affirmed 157 N.E. 272 (1927). (The rule is adopted in s.5–114 of the Uniform Commercial Code.) See further below, para.23–188.
[97] Whilst the straight credit used to be the norm, the trend has been changing for the past fifteen years or so. Currently, the negotiation credit is more common in British Banking than the straight credit.
[98] Above, para.23–052.
[99] *Banque Nationale de Paris v Credit Agricole* [2001] 2 S.L.R. 1.
[1] [1999] 2 All E.R. 18, affirmed [2000] Lloyd's Rep. Bank 165; see also *Czarnikow Rionda Sugar Trading Inc. v Standard Bank of London Ltd* [1999] 2 Lloyd's Rep. 187. *Cf.* the decision of the High Court of Korea in *Industrial Bank of Korea v BNP Paribas* reported in [2004] *Annual Survey of Letter of Credit Law and Practice* 372.

action on the basis of rights acquired by it as a negotiating bank, the position would have differed.

Borderline cases. In some cases a documentary credit may not indicate clearly whether it is a straight credit or a negotiation credit. For example, some credits state specifically that "negotiation is permitted" and the undertaking reads: "We hereby undertake to honour all drafts drawn under and in conformity with the terms of this credit." It is difficult to say categorically whether this engagement is directed only to the seller or extends also to third parties who rely on the "permission to negotiate" and discount the seller's drafts. The tendency of the courts in cases of such ambiguity is to regard the instrument as a straight credit.[2] This approach derives support from two arguments. First, all documentary credits are specifically addressed to the seller. It is therefore to be presumed that, in the absence of clear language to the contrary, the promise is meant to be confined to this promisee. Secondly, the main object of a documentary credit is to enable the seller to obtain payment of the price from the issuing or confirming banker. It is, of course, true that a documentary credit has the additional object of assisting the seller to raise credit. But the banker's undertaking in a straight credit is adequate for this purpose as it enables the seller to obtain discount facilities from his own bankers. There is therefore not much room for implying a promise by the issuing banker to reimburse any third party who provides bridging or temporary finance by negotiating the seller's drafts. It may be added that a similar type of ambiguity arises occasionally in open or travellers' letters of credit. The courts have treated such instruments as general letters of credit.[3] But these authorities are not applicable to cases of comparable ambiguities in documentary credits. The object of open letters of credit is to enable the customer to raise credit against his drafts on the issuing banker. It is therefore reasonable to assume that the issuing banker undertakes to reimburse holders or discounters of such drafts. But, as has been pointed out, documentary credits serve a different object. 23–063

Conflict in provisions. The problem of whether a documentary credit is of the straight or of the negotiation type is exacerbated if there is an inconsistency in the letter of credit itself. In *European Asian Bank AG v Punjab and Sind Bank (No.2)*[4] the defendant bank in New Delhi issued a documentary credit and asked its correspondent in Singapore, the A.B.N. Bank, both to advise the credit and to confirm it to the beneficiary through the claimant bank. Clause 6 of the letter of credit stipulated that the credit 23–064

---

[2] *Sassoon (M A) & Sons Ltd v International Banking Corp.*, above, at p.722 and see *Banque Nationale de Paris v Credit Agricole* [2001] 2 S.L.R. 1 (S'pore CA). In the USA, see: *Banco Nacional Ultramarino v First National Bank of Boston*, above, at pp.173–174.

[3] *Re Agra and Masterman's Bank, Ex p. Asiatic Banking Corp.* (1867) L.R. 2 Ch.App. 391; *Maitland v Chartered Mercantile Bank* (1869) 38 L.J.Ch. 363. In the USA, see: *Smith and Ferguson v Ledyard Goldwaithe & Co.*, 49 Ala. 279 at 282 (1873); *Lyon v Van Raden*, 85 N.W. 727 (1901).

[4] [1983] 1 W.L.R. 642, discussed in [1984] J.B.L. 379.

was "divisionable and unrestricted for negotiation". Clause 9, however, appeared to conflict with this provision. Although it included an undertaking addressed to the drawers, indorsers and bona fide holders of bills drawn under the documentary credit, it stipulated that "negotiations under this credit [were] restricted to the A.B.N. Bank". Eventually documents were tendered by the beneficiary directly to the claimant bank. When disputes arose about the regularity of the documents, that bank sued the defendant bank, relying, *inter alia*, on its position as negotiation bank. One of the defences raised by the defendant bank was that negotiation had been restricted to the A.B.N. Bank so that the claimant bank could not assume the role of a negotiation bank. The Court of Appeal concluded that the credit restricted negotiation to the A.B.N. Bank. It reconciled the two conflicting provisions by pointing out that the word "negotiation" had been used in an inconsistent manner. In clause 6 it referred to the general transferability of the credit, making provision for it. In clause 9, it was used to define the issuing bank's undertaking. Here it required that the documents be negotiated through the A.B.N. Bank, which meant that it prohibited negotiation by other banks. The documentary credit was, thus, treated as a straight credit.

23–065 **Relation to Article 10, UCP** One unsatisfactory result of this decision is that it gives effect to a practice which, far from seeking to protect the interests of the commercial parties to the transaction, attempts to give a specified bank, usually the issuer's correspondent, a monopoly on the negotiation of commercial paper advised through it. Unfortunately, Article 10(b)(i) of the UCP sanctions the practice. It calls for the nomination of a negotiation bank, unless the credit allows negotiation by any bank.

23–066 **"Red clause" credits.** This type of letter of credit, which is also known as "anticipatory credit" or "packing credit", originated in the South African trade in hides. Its object is to enable the seller to obtain the price, or an advance against it, before the shipment of the goods. Usually, the advance authorised by the "red clause" is conditional upon the tender by the seller of provisional documents, such as a receipt from a forwarding agent or from a warehouse in his locality. In most cases the provisional documents must relate to the goods stipulated in the letter of credit but in some cases they may relate to the raw materials from which goods are ultimately to be manufactured. In "red clause" credits the buyer takes the risk involved in advancing money without adequate security. He is liable to reimburse the issuing banker even if the seller absconds with the amount advanced or fails to ship the goods and becomes insolvent.[5]

23–067 **Revolving ("evergreen") credits.** Where the contract of sale contemplates delivery of goods by instalments, recourse may be had to the revolving credit, commonly found in the petroleum industry and of

---

[5] *Oelbermann v National City Bank of New York*, 79 F. 2d 534 at 537 (1935). See generally on "red clause" credits *South African Reserve Bank v Samuel & Co.* (1931) 40 Ll.L.R. 291.

increasing international popularity. Such facilities are also known as letters of credit with an evergreen clause.[6] The term "revolving credit" is loosely applied to a credit which is renewable but should be confined to those which are automatically replenished to the original amount as bills drawn thereunder are run off and paid. The term is sometimes used to describe long-term credits where regular drawings are anticipated and limits are imposed as to the maximum amount to be drawn in any given period.[7]

(d) *Transfer of Documentary Credits and Assignment of Proceeds*

Assignment and transfer distinguished. It is important to distinguish between the assignment by the seller of his right to claim the amount of the credit and a transfer of the credit itself. Under Article 49 of the UCP "the fact that a credit is not stated to be transferable shall not affect the Beneficiary's rights to assign any proceeds to which he may be, or may become, entitled under such credit, in accordance with the provisions of the applicable law". Where the credit is governed by English law there is, it is submitted, nothing to prevent a seller from assigning to a third party his rights to the amount of the credit. The seller has a contingent right to claim a liquidated amount and such a demand or claim can be assigned in equity and by way of statutory assignment. In equity it is even possible to assign part of the proceeds of the documentary credit.[8] To perfect his rights, the assignee ought to give notice to the issuing or confirming bank, which is the debtor. 23–068

Object and effect of assignment. The assignment of the proceeds of a documentary credit may be effected both before and after the tender of the documents. In the latter case, there is a need for an assignment only if payment under the letter of credit is due not at sight but at a given time after the tender of the documents, which is the case either where the credit stipulates for deferred payment in cash or for the acceptance of an after sight draft. The object of the assignment of the proceeds of the documentary credit is to furnish security to a discounter of the beneficiary's draft or deferred payment claim, or, where the assignment is effected before the 23–069

---

[6] See, *e.g. Axa Assurances Inc. v Chase Manhattan Bank* (2001) 339 N.J. Super. 22.

[7] *cf.* the opinion of the expert witness in *Nordskog v National Bank* (1922) 10 Ll.L.R. 652 with that of Witheridge, *The Finance of Overseas Trade* (Spring Lectures of the Institute of Bankers, 1950), p.37. That the ceiling continues to revolve even if there has been no reimbursement of drawings down, see *Nisho Iwai Europe v Korea First National Bank*, 752 N.Y.S. 2d 259 (2003).

[8] See, generally, *Chitty on Contracts* (29th ed.), Vol. 1, paras 19–020 *et seq.* The undertaking to pay money is usually not considered a personal contract which may not be assigned: *ibid.* para.19–020; *Fitzroy v Cave* [1905] 2 K.B. 364. An assignment of the amount of a credit is valid in the USA: Uniform Commercial Code, s.5–114 (Rev.), and see the prior s.5–116(2) discussed in *Pastor v National Republic Bank of Chicago*, 56 Ill.App. 421, 371 N.E. 2d 1127 (1978); *Shaffer v Brooklyn Park Garden Apartments*, 250 N.W. 2d 172 (Minn. 1977); the position was similar under pre-Code law: H. Harfield, *Bank Credits and Acceptances* (6th ed., 1974), 191–192; *Old Colony Trust Co. v Continental Bank*, 288 F. 979 at 981 (1921); *Eriksson v Refiners Export Co.*, 35 N.Y.S. 2d 829 (1942).

tender of the documents, to a bank that finances the transaction. The assignee becomes entitled to be paid the proceeds of the credit when the beneficiary's claim against the issuing or confirming bank matures.[9] The assignee does not become a party to the commercial venture in the sense of his being expected to procure the documents or to ship the goods.[10] This role remains to be performed by the beneficiary, although the documents may be delivered by him to the assignee who will then tender them to the bank. An Austrian court has held that, even in such a case, the assignee ought to tender the documents on behalf of the beneficiary, although the assignee acquires the right to the proceeds.[11] This view is subject to the criticism that it is artificial to expect the assignee to tender the documents on behalf of the beneficiary but to claim the proceeds for himself! Such legal niceties are not readily understood by bankers and businessmen.[12] Moreover, if the documentary credit is of the negotiation type, an assignee of the proceeds, who has given value for the documents, may in any event be entitled to tender them in his own name because he is a promisee.[13]

23–070 **Nature and mechanism of transfer.** The transfer of a documentary credit serves a commercial object different from that of an assignment of the proceeds. When a credit is transferred, a third party—known as "second beneficiary"—steps for most purposes into the shoes of the seller. Usually, a transfer of the documentary credit occurs when the seller is not the manufacturer of the goods but procures them from a supplier who will ship the goods and procure the bulk of the documents called for in the letter of credit. The transfer is arranged in a manner that prevents any direct contact between the buyer and the supplier. The object is to prevent the buyer from ordering a subsequent consignment directly from the supplier.

23–071 **Article 48, UCP** The transferability of a documentary credit is governed by Article 48 of the UCP Paragraph (a) defines a transferable credit as one under which the beneficiary (the "First Beneficiary") may request the "transferring bank"[14] to make the credit available in whole or in part to one or more transferees ("Second Beneficiary"). According to paragraph (b), a documentary credit can be transferred only if it is expressly designated as transferable by the issuing banker.[15] Moreover, under paragraph (g) of

---

[9] But note that the assignee takes the debt—the proceeds—subject to the equities available against the assignor (beneficiary) by the debtor (issuing bank), *e.g.* a plea based on fraud: *Banco Santander SA v Bank Paribas* [1999] 2 All E.R. 18, affirmed [2000] Lloyd's Rep. Bank. 165.

[10] The point is now emphasised in the last sentence of Art. 49.

[11] *Singer & Friedlander v Creditanstalt-Bankverein* [1981] Com.L.R. 69 (Com.Ct. of Vienna).

[12] For a full analysis see Eberth and Ellinger, "Assignment and Presentation of Documents in Commercial Credit Transactions," 24 Arizona L.Rev. 277 (1982) (abbreviated version in 1 I.B.L. 107 (1983)).

[13] Above, para.23–061.

[14] For the definition of a "transferring bank", see above, para.23–024.

[15] The law was similar in the USA before the adoption of the UCP: *Eriksson v Refiners Export Co.*, 35 N.Y.S. 2d 829 (1942). *Cf. Old Colony Trust Co. v Continental Bank*, 288 F. 979 (1921).

Article 48 and in the absence of stipulation to the contrary, a transferable credit may be transferred only once.[16]

The initiative for the transfer must come from the seller. When he informs the transferring bank of the identity of the transferee, a new credit is issued in favour of this second beneficiary. It states that it is opened at the instruction of the seller[17]; in this way the buyer's identity remains unknown to the second beneficiary. Under paragraph (h) the credit can be transferred only on the terms and conditions specified in the original credit, but with the following three exceptions. First, the amount of the original credit or any unit price stated therein may be reduced in the new credit. In practice, the amount of the new credit will equal the price promised by the seller to the second beneficiary. Secondly, the expiry date of the fresh credit and the last day for the presentation of the documents may be earlier than that of the original credit and the shipping period may be curtailed. The object is to allow for a few days between the date on which performance is due from the second beneficiary and that on which the seller must tender the remaining documents. Thirdly, the percentage for which insurance cover must be effected may be increased so as to provide for the amount of cover required under the original credit.

Tender of documents. The second beneficiary obtains payment by tendering the required documents, including his own invoice. Under paragraph(h) of Article 48, the documents tendered by the second beneficiary may be made out in the seller's name; but if the original credit specifically requires that some documents (other than the invoice) be made out in the buyer's name, such requirement must be fulfilled.[18] Under paragraph (i) the seller has the right to substitute for the invoice of the second beneficiary his own invoice and, where required, drafts for a sum not in excess of the original amount stipulated in the main credit and of the original unit prices stipulated therein. Usually, the difference in time between the expiry date of the original credit and of the new credit leaves the seller ample time for this step. Moreover, under paragraph (j) of Article 48, the seller has the right to request that payment or negotiation be effected to the second beneficiary, at the place to which the credit has been transferred, up to and including the expiry date of the original credit and without prejudice to the seller's right subsequently to substitute his own invoice and drafts for those of the second beneficiary and to claim any difference due to him. This provision, which applies only in the absence of stipulation on the contrary, appears to have the effect of permitting the seller to tender his own invoice after the expiry date of the original credit. In practice, some sellers lodge their invoice with the banker ahead of time. This enables the banker to substitute it for that of the second beneficiary as soon as the latter tenders the documents. 23–072

[16] But note that Art. 49(f) sanctions a retransfer to the first beneficiary.
[17] This is specifically authorised by para.(e) of Art. 54.
[18] In certain transactions the bills of lading may have to be made out in the buyer's name. But usually, when a credit is transferable, exporters oppose such a requirement, so as not to disclose the buyer's name.

23–073 **Rights of first beneficiary.** Under the second passage of Article 48(i), when the seller's invoice is substituted for that of the second beneficiary, the seller is entitled to draw for the difference between the amounts of the two invoices. When a credit has been transferred and the first beneficiary is to supply his own invoice in exchange for the second beneficiary's invoice but fails to do so on demand, the transferring bank has the right to deliver to the issuing banker the documents received under the credit, including the second beneficiary's invoice and draft, without further responsibility to the seller, *viz.*, the first beneficiary. Surprisingly, Article 48 does not make a similar provision to enable the issuing banker to claim reimbursement from the buyer against the second beneficiary's invoice. Presumably, such a right may be implied from the buyer's instruction for the opening of a transferable credit.

23–074 **Transfer of fraction.** Under the second passage of Article 48(g), fractions of a transferable credit (not exceeding in the aggregate the amount of the credit) can be transferred separately, provided partial shipments or drawings are not prohibited by the credit. The aggregate of such transfers is considered as constituting only one transfer of the credit.[19] In practice, the banker will issue a new credit as regards each fraction. It is clear from the language of Article 48 that the seller may transfer different fractions or portions of the credit to different transferees and may retain a fraction for performance by himself.[20] Article 48 does not provide that when there is a multiple transfer each fraction must relate to a specific shipment. But this is the position in practice.

23–075 **Amendments.** An innovative provision, regulates the problems arising as regards the communication of amendments agreed upon after transfer has been effected. Under Article 48(d), "at the time of making a request for transfer and prior to the transfer of the Credit, the First Beneficiary must irrevocably instruct the Transferring Bank whether or not he retains the right to refuse to allow the Transferring Bank to advise amendments to the Second Beneficiary(ies). If the Transferring Bank consents to the transfer under these conditions, it must, at the time of transfer, advise the Second Beneficiary(ies) of the First Beneficiary's instructions regarding amendments."

23–076 **Liability of bank.** The new credit opened by the issuing or by the correspondent banker in favour of the second beneficiary is similar to the original credit. Thus, if the original credit is irrevocable and confirmed, the

---

[19] Note that a credit may be transferred once only; above. Note that the transfer fee, of up to one-quarter per cent of the amount of the credit, may be quite substantial in transactions involving large amounts. Under Art. 48(f) the charges are to be borne by the first beneficiary and the transferring bank is not obliged to effect transfer until they have been paid.
[20] Credits transferable to more than one beneficiary used to be known as "divisible" or "fractionable". But under Art. 49(b), terms such as "divisible", "fractionable", "assignable" and "transmissible" do not render the credit transferable and, if used, are to be disregarded.

new credit will be of the same type. Under the 1974 Revision it was not clear whether the issuing or confirming bank was invariably obliged to transfer a transferable credit. On the one hand, paragraph (a) of Article 46 of that Revision defined a transferable credit as one under which the beneficiary had the right to instruct that it be transferred. On the other hand, paragraph (b) of the same provision provided that the bank was not under an obligation to transfer a documentary credit except to the extent that it consented to the instruction. In *Bank Negara Indonesia v Lariza (Singapore) Pte Ltd*[21] the Singapore Court of Appeal held that paragraph (b) was subject to paragraph (a). Thean J. took the view that any other construction would mean that, even where a credit was designated as transferable, its transferability would remain subject to the bank's discretion. The Privy Council reversed this decision.[22] On the construction given to Article 46 by Lord Brandon, the right conferred on the beneficiary in paragraph (a) was effectively taken away by the express stipulation in paragraph (b).

Current position. Article 54 of the 1983 Revision amended the language of the relevant paragraphs, taken from Article 46, so as to ensure that the final decision be left to the bank. So does Article 48 of the current revision. Paragraph (a) defines a transferable credit as one under which "the Beneficiary may request the . . . Transferring Bank . . . to make the credit available in whole or in part to one or more other Beneficiary(ies). . .". It is clear that a "request" issued by the beneficiary under this provision is less binding on the bank than the "instruction" he was entitled to give under Article 46(a) of the 1974 Revision. The bank's position is further safeguarded by paragraph (c). Adopting the spirit of Article 46(b) of the 1974 revision, it emphasises that the "Transferring Bank shall be under no obligation to effect such transfer except to the extent and in the manner expressly consented to by such bank." The transferring bank's position is further protected by Article 48(f). Bank charges arising in respect of transfers are payable by the seller and the transferring bank is under no obligation to effect transfer until they have been settled. 23–077

Policy. It may be asked whether the transferring bank is entitled to withhold its consent to the transfer of the credit at will even where the seller is prepared to pay the charges and there appears to be no good reason for a refusal of his request. The language of paragraph (c) supports a positive answer. But such a construction runs counter to the spirit of Article 48, which provides, in paragraph (b), that credits are transferable if expressly so designated. If the bank has manifested its consent to such a transaction by issuing or confirming a transferable credit, should it be allowed to escape its bargain without cause? It is submitted that the bank may refuse a request to transfer a transferable credit only on reasonable grounds.[23] A provision which is frequently used in practice is to grant the 23–078

[21] [1986] 1 M.L.J. 287.

[22] [1988] A.C. 583.

[23] An analogy may perhaps be drawn from decisions relating to a refusal by a landlord to grant his consent to the transfer of a lease: Woodfall, *Landlord and Tenant* (Looseleaf ed.), Vol. 1, paras 11.138—11.145. But the cases are based on s.19(1) of the Landlord and Tenant Act 1927.

bank a right to restrict transfer to an "approved" second beneficiary or transferee. Such a clause in the transferable credit enables the issuing bank, or the buyer whose advice is then sought, to investigate the standing of the person concerned.

23–079 **Legal effect of transfer.** Article 48 does not throw light on the legal nature of the transfer of a documentary credit and the question has not been the subject of decision in the United Kingdom. There are two views concerning the nature of a transfer. One regards the transfer as an equitable assignment of the benefit of the documentary credit.[24] In the other view—supported mainly in the United States[25]—the transfer operates as a novation; the seller drops out of the transaction and the second beneficiary steps into his shoes. Both views have shortcomings. The first view fails to take into account that the second beneficiary is entitled to the amount transferred to him only if he performs some of the conditions precedent to the banker's duty to pay the amount of the credit. Usually, the second beneficiary has to tender most of the documents listed in the credit. The second view ignores the fact that the seller remains a party to the transaction and that the balance of the amount of the documentary credit is paid to him against the tender of his own invoice. In view of the comprehensive provisions of Article 48, an attempt to analyse the exact legal nature of a transfer may be superfluous. However, the transfer of a documentary credit may be described as an assignment of some of the seller's rights to the second beneficiary, who can enforce them only against the tender of certain documents. The seller remains a party to the transaction.

23–080 **Back-to-back credits.** In certain cases the seller may prefer to disguise the fact that the goods are not manufactured by himself but are ordered from an ultimate supplier. In such cases he prefers not to request a transferable credit. The "back-to-back credit" or "subsidiary credit" enables the seller to use a non-transferable credit as the basis for procuring a new credit in favour of the supplier. In point of fact, the practice involved is similar to that of a transfer. The seller lodges the documentary credit opened in his favour with the correspondent bankers or with his own bankers and instructs them to open a new documentary credit in favour of the supplier. Its terms will be similar to those of the original credit, except that the amount will be smaller and the date of expiry earlier than that of the original credit. The main practical difference between the furnishing of a "back-to-back credit" and the transfer of a transferable credit is that in the case of the back-to-back credit it is essential to obtain the seller's invoice. The correspondent banker and the issuing banker cannot claim reimbursement against an invoice of the supplier, even in cases where

[24] Gutteridge and Megrah, *Law of Bankers' Commercial Credits* (8th ed.), pp.125–126, which is less definite on this point than the 7th ed., pp.103–105; Jack, R., *Documentary Credits*, (3rd ed.), paras 10.18 *et seq.*, who conclude in para.10.25 that this is not the correct solution.

[25] Kozolchyk, *Commercial Letters of Credit in the Americas*, p.498; *cf. Meb Export Co. Inc. v National City Bank of New York*, 131 N.Y.L.J. 4 (1954).

unforeseen circumstances prevent the seller from tendering his own invoice.[26] To safeguard against such an event, the seller will usually be asked to furnish a *pro forma* invoice before the back-to-back credit is opened.[27]

Compared to transfer. But there is a difference between the legal effect of the transfer of a credit and that of the opening of a back-to-back credit. Although the issuing or correspondent banker agrees to transfer the credit at the request of the seller, the banker nevertheless consents to this transfer on the basis of the authority conferred on him by the buyer. The transfer therefore is not the result of a new contract between the banker and the seller. In the case of the back-to-back credit, the buyer makes no provision for the opening of a secondary credit. The seller gives his own instructions for the opening of this new credit to the issuing banker or to the correspondent banker, and has to sign an "application form". Thus, the opening of a back-to-back credit is the result of a new contract between the seller and the correspondent or issuing banker. This is of importance, because an issuing or correspondent banker who opens a back-to-back credit undertakes towards the seller some obligations that he usually owes only to the buyer.[28] 23–081

By correspondent. It seems clear that there is nothing to prevent the seller's own bankers from opening a back-to-back credit based on the original credit. They perform a specific service for their customer and regard the original credit as a security. But it is not altogether certain whether a correspondent banker, who is instructed by the issuing banker to confirm a non-transferable credit or merely to advise it to the seller, exceeds his authority if he opens a back-to-back credit based on it. Similarly, it is not certain whether an issuing banker instructed by the buyer to open a non-transferable credit exceeds his mandate if he opens a back-to-back credit. In both cases the instruction is for the furnishing of a credit that, by its nature, is non-transferable.[29] If the issuing or correspondent banker were to transfer such a credit, he would commit a breach of his contract and exceed his mandate.[30] As the opening of a back-to-back credit has the same practical effect as a transfer, it is perhaps arguable that opening it is forbidden by the prohibition of a transfer. It may be further argued that the buyer expects to have goods supplied by the seller and that the issuing and correspondent bankers should not facilitate the supply of these goods from any other source. The problem has not been the subject of decision in the United Kingdom.[31] American decisions give effect to the 23–082

[26] This follows from the doctrine of strict compliance: below, para.23–205; *Laudisi v American Exchange National Bank*, 146 N.E. 347 at 349 (1924).

[27] If the documents tendered under the back-to-back credit are the ones required under the original credit, the seller's invoice will replace that of the supplier. The set as a whole then complies with the requirements of the original credit.

[28] For an interesting analysis of the position see *Meb Export Co. Inc. v National City Bank of New York* 131 N.Y.L.J. 4 (1954).

[29] Only a transferable credit may be transferred; see above.

[30] *Eriksson v Refiners Export Co.*, 35 N.Y.S. 2d 829 (1942).

[31] The system is discussed in *Ian Stach Ltd v Baker Bosley Ltd* [1958] 2 Q.B. 130, where no objection was raised against its use.

system.[32] It may be that the opening of a back-to-back credit should be regarded as an independent transaction. To a certain extent, the buyer's position is protected because the amount of the original credit is payable only against documents tendered by the seller, including his invoice. If the documents, as a set, confer on the buyer the rights for which he has bargained in the application for the original credit, it is probably irrelevant that some of the documents (such as the bills of lading) are procured by a third party. It is to be hoped that the approach of the American decisions in point will be adopted by the English courts; this would give effect to the prevailing business practice.

2. CONTRACT OF BUYER AND SELLER

(a) *Buyer's Duty to Furnish Credit*

23–083 **Condition precedent.** The documentary credit transaction commences when a buyer and a seller agree in their contract of sale that payment should be effected by the furnishing of a documentary credit. This clause is known as the "documentary credit clause" and its inclusion in the contract of sale puts the buyer under an obligation to have a documentary credit opened in favour of the seller. This obligation is usually a condition precedent to the seller's duty to deliver the goods,[33] but it is not necessarily a condition precedent to the performance of all the seller's duties. The contract of sale may impose on the seller a duty, the performance of which constitutes a condition precedent to the buyer's duty to furnish a credit. Thus, in *Knotz v Fairclough, Dodds and Jones Ltd*[34] the defendants agreed to purchase copra from the plaintiff. Payment was to be by a confirmed credit, which was to cover 97 per cent of the amount of a provisional invoice of the plaintiff. Sellers J. held that the plaintiff's duty to furnish the defendants with a provisional invoice was a condition precedent to the defendant's duty to cause the opening of a confirmed credit.

23–084 **Type of credit to be opened.** The buyer must furnish the seller with the type of credit that has been agreed upon in the contract of sale.[35] Thus, if the contract provides for the opening of a confirmed credit, the furnishing

---

[32] *Kingdom of Sweden v New York Trust Co.*, 96 N.Y.S. 2d 779 at 789–791 (1949); *Meb Export Co. Inc. v National City Bank of New York*, 131 N.Y.L.J. 4 (1954); Kozolchyk, *Commercial Letters of Credit in the Americas*, p.488; Dolan, *Letters of Credit* (revised ed., Looseleaf), para.1–108.

[33] *Dix v Grainger* (1922) 10 Ll.L.R. 496 at 497; *Garcia v Page & Co. Ltd* (1936) 55 Ll.L.R. 391 at 392; *Trans Trust SPRL v Danubian Trading Co. Ltd* [1952] 2 Q.B. 297 at 304; *Lindsay (A E) & Co. Ltd v Cook* [1953] 1 Lloyd's Rep. 328 at 335; *Soproma SpA v Marine and Animal By-Products Corp.* [1966] 1 Lloyd's Rep. 367.

[34] [1952] 1 Lloyd's Rep. 226.

[35] An attempt to modify the contract of sale by inserting onerous, unagreed, requirements in the documentary credit, constitutes a breach of contract on the buyer's part: *H & JM Bennett Europe Ltd v Angrexco Co. Ltd*, unreported, decision of April 6, 1990.

of a revocable credit[36] or of an irrevocable but unconfirmed credit[37] is insufficient. Similarly, if the contract of sale calls for an irrevocable credit to be opened in London, the buyer does not perform his duty by furnishing an irrevocable credit available in another place.[38] The credit furnished by the buyer must conform not only in form but also in substance to the type specified in the contract of sale. In *Wahbe Tamari & Sons Ltd v Colprogeca Sociedade Geral de Fibras, Cafes e Produtos Coloniais Lda,*[39] the contract of sale called for a confirmed credit. The correspondent banker purported to confirm the credit but reserved a right of recourse against the seller in regard to all bills drawn and negotiated under the documentary credit. It was held that this undertaking did not constitute a confirmation and that the buyer had failed to furnish the type of credit required by the contract of sale.

Where contract silent. Difficulties arise if the contract of sale does not specify what type of documentary credit is to be opened. As a revocable credit does not constitute good security, it may be presumed that the seller and the buyer agree that an irrevocable credit must be furnished. In *Giddens v Anglo-African Produce Co. Ltd*[40] the contract of sale provided that a credit was to be "established" with a certain bank. The buyers furnished the sellers with a revocable credit of that bank, whereupon the sellers declined to ship the goods. An action by the buyers was dismissed. Bailhache J. read the word "established" as describing the word "credit", and explained that the revocable credit furnished by the buyers could not be considered an "established credit". In effect, his Lordship treated the term "established credit" as synonymous with "irrevocable credit". The case indicates that if the contract of sale does not specify what type of credit should be opened, the courts tend to construe the contract as stipulating for an irrevocable credit.[41] However, one authority suggests that if the parties fail to reach an agreement as to the nature of the credit to be furnished, or the documents against which payment is to be made, the contract of sale is incomplete.[42] 23–085

Time when credit is to be available. If the contract of sale provides a date for the opening of the credit, the buyer must furnish it by that date.[43] If the contract of sale requires that a credit be opened immediately, the buyer must have such time as is needed by a person of reasonable diligence to get 23–086

---

[36] *Panoutsos v Raymond Hadley Corp.* [1917] 2 K.B. 473.
[37] *Soproma SpA v Marine and Animal By-Products Corp.* [1966] 1 Lloyd's Rep. 367 at 386.
[38] *Furst (E) & Co. v W E Fischer Ltd* [1960] 2 Lloyd's Rep. 340.
[39] [1969] 2 Lloyd's Rep. 18 at 21.
[40] (1923) 14 Ll.L.R. 230. A provision to this effect is found in s.2–325 of the Uniform Commercial Code (USA).
[41] *cf.* UCP, Art. 6(c), under which a credit is assumed to be irrevocable if not stated to be revocable.
[42] *Schijveschuurder v Canon (Export) Ltd* [1952] 2 Lloyd's Rep. 196.
[43] An extension of date does not preclude the seller from insisting that the furnishing of a credit by that date is of essence: *Nichimen Corp. v Gatoil Overseas Inc.* [1987] 2 Lloyd's Rep. 46.

such a credit established.[44] A provision that a credit be furnished within a few weeks, means that it must be opened within a reasonable time; what constitutes a reasonable time depends on the facts of each case.[45]

23–087 **Ambiguous clauses.** Problems arise if the clause, which stipulates the time for the opening of the letter of credit, is unclear. Thus, in *Sohio Supply Co. v Gatoil (USA) Inc,*[46] the contract of sale required the buyer to furnish a documentary credit "10 days prior to estimated load date". The seller argued that he was, accordingly, entitled to receive the letter of credit ten days prior to the commencement of the stipulated shipping period. The buyer argued that the ten days involved were to be calculated as from either the last day of the shipping period or from the day on which the buyer "would properly estimate that the ship would arrive". Although the Court of Appeal found it unnecessary to decide this point, Staughton L.J. indicated that he preferred the construction proposed by the sellers.[47]

A considerably more complex clause was used in *Transpetrol Ltd v Transöl Olieprodukten Nederland BV.*[48] Here the contract required that the buyer furnish the letter of credit within one day following his receipt of the seller's nomination of a vessel; but it was provided that the seller should, in addition, give the buyer three days' notice of his intention to nominate. In the event, the seller nominated a given vessel, without sending a prior notice of intention. The buyer claimed that the seller's failure to comply with this aspect of the stipulated procedure excused the delay in the actual furnishing of a letter of credit. Rejecting this argument, Phillips J. held that the "concept of [the seller] being required to give a minimum of three days' notice of intention to nominate [was] nonsensical".[49] Such notice would be of no use to the buyer. His Lordship concluded that the true effect of the clause was to impose on the seller a duty to nominate a vessel which would deliver the oil at least three days before the vessel's e.t.a. at the designated port of delivery. The only stipulation respecting the credit was that it be furnished within one day of the date of nomination. As the buyer had failed to comply therewith, the seller acquired the right to repudiate the contract of sale.

23–088 **Where no time stipulated; c.i.f. contracts.** In most cases a contract of sale does not stipulate a time for the furnishing of the credit, but specifies a date or period for the shipment of the goods. Where the contract provides a period of shipment, it is not certain whether the documentary credit must be furnished, at the latest, on the first day on which shipment may take place or at a reasonable time before this date. In *Pavia & Co. SpA v Thurmann-Nielsen,*[50] where a contract for the sale of groundnuts called for shipments during February to April 1949, the buyers did not open the

[44] *Garcia v Page & Co. Ltd* (1936) 55 Ll.L.R. 391 at 392.
[45] *Etablissements Chainbaux SARL v Harbormaster Ltd* [1955] 1 Lloyd's Rep. 303.
[46] [1989] 1 Lloyd's Rep. 588.
[47] *ibid.*, at p.591.
[48] [1989] 1 Lloyd's Rep. 309.
[49] *ibid.*, at pp.310–313.
[50] [1952] 2 Q.B. 84.

required documentary credit until April 22. Holding that the buyers had failed to furnish the documentary credit on time, Denning L.J. said: "In the absence of express stipulation . . . the credit must be made available to the seller at the beginning of the shipment period. The reason is because the seller is entitled, before he ships the goods, to be assured that, on shipment, he will be paid. The seller is not bound to tell the buyer the precise date when he is going to ship; and whenever he does ship the goods, he must be able to draw on the credit. He may ship on the very first day of the shipment period. If, therefore, the buyer is to fulfil his obligations he must make the credit available to the seller at the very first date when the goods may be lawfully shipped in compliance with the contract."[51] On its face, this dictum supports the view that a documentary credit must be furnished at the very latest on the first day of the shipment period. But Lord Denning's suggestion that the seller is entitled to be assured of payment before he ships the goods, supports the view that the documentary credit must be opened at the very latest at a reasonable time before the first date on which shipment may take place.

Lord Denning's view. This second view is expressly supported in Lord Denning's judgment in *Sinason-Teicher Inter-American Grain Corp. v Oilcakes and Oilseeds Trading Co. Ltd.*[52] A contract for the sale of barley provided for shipments during October to November 1952. When the buyers, who had agreed to provide a bank guarantee, failed to furnish it by September 10, the sellers cancelled the contract. The Court of Appeal held that the buyers had not been in default. Lord Denning said that *Pavia & Co.'s* case "does not decide that the buyer can delay right up to the first date for shipment. It only decides that he must provide the letter of credit at latest by that date. The correct view is that, if nothing is said about time in the contract, the buyer must provide the letter of credit within a reasonable time before the first date for shipment. The same applies to a bank guarantee."[53] This dictum shows preference for the view that the documentary credit must be furnished at a reasonable time before the commencement of the shipping period. But as the sellers, in *Sinason-Teicher's* case, cancelled the contract long before the beginning of the shipping period, the guarantee was not due at the date of cancellation even under the view expressed in this case. 23–089

Application to f.o.b. contracts. The two views were discussed again in *Ian Stach Ltd v Baker Bosley Ltd*,[54] which concerned a sale of steel plates on f.o.b. terms. It was argued that, as an f.o.b. buyer had the right to determine the date of shipment, the documentary credit had to be opened at a reasonable time before the date nominated by the buyer in the shipping instructions. Diplock J. thought that such a rule would lead to uncertainties; the buyer could not know how long it would take the seller to bring the 23–090

---

[51] *ibid.*, at pp.88–89.
[52] [1954] 1 W.L.R. 1394.
[53] *ibid.*, at p.1400.
[54] [1958] 2 Q.B. 130.

goods from the place at which they were situated to the port or how long it would take to turn them into a deliverable state. He concluded that the prima facie rule is that the credit must be opened, at the latest, on the first day of the shipping period. Thus, Diplock J. applied to a case concerning a sale on terms f.o.b., a rule similar to that originally proposed in *Pavia & Co.'s* case in regard to contracts c.i.f.

23–091 **Conclusion.** It follows that the cases do not lay down a conclusive rule either in the case of contracts f.o.b. or in the case of contracts c.i.f. It is clear that, from the seller's point of view, the rule expressed in *Sinason-Teicher's* case is to be preferred. A documentary credit furnished at a reasonable time before the commencement of the shipping period enables him to prepare the goods for punctual shipment. He can also use the credit in order to furnish, right at the beginning of the shipping period, a back-to-back credit in favour of an ultimate supplier of the goods.

23–092 **Position where no period of shipment is specified.** If the contract of sale specifies an actual date and not a period of shipment, the buyer must furnish the documentary credit at a reasonable time before this date.[55] The reason for this is that the seller is entitled to have the credit before he actually prepares the goods for shipment. But in certain cases the contract of sale makes different provisions concerning the time for opening the credit. It may, for example, render the buyer's duty to furnish a credit dependent upon the prior receipt of explicit instructions from the seller. In such a case the buyer is not obliged to furnish, in the meantime, a letter from the issuing bankers indicating that the credit will be established as soon as these instructions are received.[56]

23–093 **Absolute nature of duty to furnish credit.** The buyer's duty to furnish the documentary credit in time is not excused by a delay caused by factors beyond his control. In *Lindsay (A E) & Co. Ltd v Cook*[57] the buyer made punctual arrangements for the opening of the documentary credit. But due to a delay in the inter-bank communication the credit reached the hands of the seller at a very late date. The seller was held entitled to repudiate the contract of sale.

23–094 **Remedying defects.** If, initially, the documentary credit furnished by the buyer deviates in any manner from the requirements laid down in the contract of sale, the buyer may cure the defect before the time at which the credit is required. If this is done, the seller has no cause for complaint.[58]

23–095 **Waiver.** In certain cases the seller may decide to ship the goods despite the buyer's failure to open the credit either on the due date or in its appropriate form. In such a case it is important to consider whether the

---

[55] *Plasticmoda Societa per Azioni v Davidsons (Manchester) Ltd* [1952] 1 Lloyd's Rep. 527 at 538.

[56] *Nicolene Ltd v Simmonds* [1952] 2 Lloyd's Rep. 419, affirmed [1953] 1 Q.B. 543.

[57] [1953] 1 Lloyd's Rep. 328 at 335. But see *"Baltimex" Baltic Import and Export Co. Ltd v Metallo Chemical Refining Co. Ltd* [1955] 2 Lloyd's Rep. 438, where the parties contemplated a delay.

[58] *Kronman & Co. v Steinberger* (1922) 10 Ll.L.R. 39.

seller has waived the breach or has agreed to a variation of the contract. The distinction is of practical importance, in particular where a contract involves a number of shipments. If the seller waives an objection concerning a documentary credit furnished in regard to one shipment, he may nevertheless give notice that he insists on strict compliance as regards the remaining shipments. But if the acceptance of a non-conforming credit involves a variation of the contract of sale, it may affect the entire transaction. In most cases in point the courts regarded the seller's acceptance of a non-conforming credit as waiver.

Thus, in *Panoutsos v Raymond Hadley Corp.*[59] the buyer furnished a revocable credit instead of the confirmed credit stipulated in the contract of sale. Despite this fact, the seller made certain shipments and applied to the buyer for an extension of time for the remaining ones. Before that time had elapsed, the seller suddenly purported to cancel the contract of sale on the ground that the credit furnished was not of the specified type. The Court of Appeal concluded that, as the buyer had been led to believe that the breach of the condition precedent had been waived, he was entitled to reasonable notice to enable him to comply with the condition in regard to the remaining shipments. The purported cancellation was therefore unjustified.

El Nasr. A similar attitude was taken by the Court of Appeal in *Plasticmoda Societa Per Azioni v Davidsons (Manchester) Ltd*[60] but a difference of opinion occurred in *W J Alan & Co. Ltd v El Nasr Export and Import Co.*[61] The buyers undertook to furnish a confirmed credit covering the sale on f.o.b. terms of two shipments of coffee at a price of Kenyan shs. 262 per ton. The sellers did not raise any objection when the buyers furnished a confirmed credit expressed in sterling and, in point of fact, began to operate the credit and asked for an extension of the shipping time. After the second shipment but before the presentment of the documents, the pound sterling was devalued; the value of the Kenyan currency remained unaltered. The sellers obtained payment under the confirmed credit and then sued the buyers for the difference between the amount paid and the amount in Kenyan currency for which the credit ought to have been opened. The Court of Appeal held that the sellers were not entitled to recover. Lord Denning M.R. said: "the sellers, by their conduct, waived the right to have payment by means of a letter of credit in Kenyan currency and accepted instead a letter of credit in sterling".[62] Megaw L.J. based his concurring judgment on the ground that the acceptance of the sterling credit by the sellers was "that the original term of the contract of sale as to 23–096

[59] [1917] 2 K.B. 473 at 477–478.

[60] [1952] 1 Lloyd's Rep. 527 at 538. See also *Ian Stach Ltd v Baker Bosley Ltd* [1958] 2 Q.B. 130 at 144; *Furst (E) & Co. v W E Fischer Ltd* [1960] 2 Lloyd's Rep. 340; *Soproma SpA v Marine and Animal By-Products Corp.* [1966] 1 Lloyd's Rep. 367.

[61] [1972] 2 Q.B. 189.

[62] *ibid.*, at p.214. But waiver would not be too readily implied from circumstances such as a single extension of time: *Nichimen Corp. v Gatoil Overseas Inc.* [1987] 2 Lloyd's Rep. 46; and see *Glencore Grain Rotterdam NV v Lebanese Organisation for International Commerce* [1997] 2 Lloyd's Rep. 386 where the Court of Appeal held that the evidence of waiver must be unequivocal.

the money of account was varied from Kenyan currency to sterling".[63] He conceded that if there were no variation of the contract, the buyers would still be entitled to succeed on the ground of waiver. A similar view was expressed by Stephenson L.J., who doubted whether the waiver doctrine would apply in cases where the buyer had not altered his position to his detriment.

It should be added that whether, in a specific case, the seller's conduct is indicative of waiver or evidences a variation of the contract depends on the circumstances. A variation of a contract is, of course, invalid unless it is supported by consideration.[64]

(b) *Effect of Opening of Credit and its Realisation*

23–097 **Seller's duty to claim payment from bank.** As it is agreed in the contract of sale that payment should be made by the furnishing of a documentary credit, the seller has to claim payment from the banker in the first instance and only on the banker's default from the buyer.[65] If the seller fails to present the documents to the banker and, as a consequence, is unable to claim payment under the documentary credit, he is guilty of laches in enforcing his security and the buyer is thereupon discharged.[66] A question that has not been the subject of decision relates to the position of the seller where documents tendered by him under a confirmed credit are rejected by the confirming banker. Is the seller thereupon entitled to claim payment from the buyer or must he first tender the documents to the issuing banker? It is submitted that as the confirming banker is, for certain purposes, the issuing banker's agent,[67] the seller is entitled to regard a rejection of the documents by the confirming banker as constituting a rejection by both banks. It follows that, in such a case, the seller's right to claim payment from the buyer is not conditional upon his first presenting the documents rejected by the confirming banker to the issuing banker.

23–098 **Opening of credit does not discharge buyers.** Authorities indicate that the buyer's obligation to pay the price of the goods is not absolutely discharged by the opening of the credit, and that upon the banker's default the seller can claim payment from the buyer.[68] In *Saffron v Société Minière Cafrika*[69] the High Court of Australia suggested that while this principle

---

[63] *ibid.*, at p.217.
[64] See *Chitty on Contracts* (29th ed.), Vol. 1, para.22–035.
[65] *Hindley & Co. v Tothill, Watson & Co.* (1894) 13 N.Z.L.R. 13 at 23. See also *Saffron v Société Minière Cafrika* (1958) 100 C.L.R. 231 at 244–245; *Soproma SpA v Marine and Animal By- Products Corp.* [1966] 1 Lloyd's Rep. 367 at 386.
[66] *W J Alan & Co. v El Nasr Export and Import Co.* [1972] 2 Q.B. 189 at 211. See also *Peacock v Pursell* (1863) 14 C.B.(N.S.) 728; *Polak v Everett* (1876) 1 Q.B.D. 669 at 675–676.
[67] See below, para.23–072.
[68] *Newman Industries Ltd v Indo-British Industries Ltd* [1956] 2 Lloyd's Rep. 219 at 236, rvsd. on a different point: [1957] 1 Lloyd's Rep. 211; *Soproma SpA v Marine and Animal By-Products Corp.*, above. In the USA see: *Lamborn v Allen Kirkpatrick*, 135 A. 541 at 542–543 (1927); *Greenough v Munroe*, 53 F. 2d 362 (1931).
[69] (1958) 100 C.L.R. 231 at 243–244.

applies in the case of revocable and "irrevocable but unconfirmed" credits, the opposite is true in the case of confirmed credits. It is, however, difficult to see why the furnishing of a confirmed credit should discharge the buyer. The only difference between a "confirmed" and an "irrevocable but unconfirmed" credit is that in the former the seller obtains promises from both the issuing banker and the correspondent banker whilst in the latter he obtains only the issuing banker's promise. An attempt to resolve the problem was made in *W J Alan & Co. v El Nasr Export and Import Co.* by Lord Denning M.R., who expressed the view that, in the ordinary way and in the absence of agreement to the contrary by the parties, "when the contract of sale stipulates for payment to be made by confirmed irrevocable letter of credit, then, when the letter of credit is issued and accepted by the seller, it operates as a conditional payment of the price. It does not operate as absolute payment".[70] He added: "If the letter of credit is honoured by the bank when documents are presented to it, the debt is discharged. If it is not honoured the debt is not discharged."[71] But the other judges refrained from determining this point and it must be conceded that the case was decided on a different ground.[72]

Acceptance of draft by banker. In some documentary credits the banker does not promise to pay cash or to honour a sight draft (that is, a bill of exchange payable on demand) but undertakes to accept a draft payable at a fixed period after sight. It has been held that the acceptance of such a draft by the banker does not discharge the buyer. If the banker dishonours the draft by non-payment, the seller is entitled to claim the price of the goods from the buyer.[73] In such a case the buyer may have to pay twice: once to the seller and once, in pursuance of an undertaking given by the buyer in the application form or in a trust receipt, to the issuing banker. 23–099

But the court may release the buyer from any obligation assumed by him towards the defaulting issuing banker. Thus, in *Sale Continuation Ltd v Austin Taylor & Co. Ltd*[74] the defendants, as selling agents, contracted in London for the sale of timber by Malaysian principals to a Belgian buyer. The defendants, who for all practical purposes assumed the position of a buyer *vis-à-vis* the Malaysian sellers, instructed the claimants, a firm of merchant bankers, to furnish the sellers with an irrevocable credit to be confirmed by a correspondent banker in Malaysia. In the application form the defendants promised to provide funds as soon as the claimants should receive advice about the negotiation of the sellers' draft by the correspondent banker in Malaysia. A draft drawn by the sellers under the credit and accompanied by the required document was, in due course, negotiated in

---

[70] [1972] 2 Q.B. 189 at 212. See also *Maran Road Saw Mill v Austin Taylor & Co. Ltd* [1975] 1 Lloyd's Rep. 156 at 159 noted in 40 M.L.R. 91 (1977); *E D & F Man Ltd v Nigerian Sweets and Confectionery Co.* [1977] 2 Lloyd's Rep. 50.
[71] *ibid*.
[72] See *ibid*., at pp.218, 220.
[73] *Hindley & Co. v Tothill, Watson & Co.* (1894) 13 N.Z.L.R. 13 at 23. In the USA see: *Greenough v Munroe*, 53 F. 2d 362 at 364–365 (1931); *Bank of United States v Seltzer*, 251 N.Y.S. 637 at 644 (1931); *Re Canal Bank and Trust Co.'s Liquidation*, 152 So. 297 at 300 (1933). *Cf.* the Uniform Commercial Code, ss.3–310.
[74] [1968] 2 Q.B. 849, following *Bank of United States v Seltzer*, above.

Malaysia and accepted by the claimants in London. Subsequently, but before the payment of the draft, the documents were released by the claimants to the defendants under a trust receipt. In this document the defendants agreed to hold the documents and the proceeds as trustees of the claimants. Shortly afterwards the claimants stopped payment and it was clear that they would dishonour the draft of the Malaysian sellers. The defendants thereupon refused to remit the price of the goods, paid to them by the Belgian buyer, to the claimants, paying the amount due directly to the Malaysian sellers. An action brought by the receiver of the claimants was dismissed. Paull J. held that the claimants were under an obligation to honour by payment the draft drawn by the Malaysian sellers under the documentary credit. By entering into a voluntary liquidation, the claimants had evinced an intention not to fulfil this obligation and the defendants were, thereupon, discharged from their obligation to provide funds for meeting the claimants' acceptance of the draft of the Malaysian sellers. Thus the defendants became entitled to be released from their obligations under the trust receipt and were entitled to pay the price directly to the Malaysian sellers.

23–100 **Critique.** Austin Taylor & Co.'s case has been criticised on two grounds.[75] First, it is suggested that the case runs counter to *Re Agra Bank, Ex p. Tondeur*[76] and to *Re Barber & Co., Ex p. Agra Bank*.[77] But these cases are not directly in point. The second argument raised against *Austin Taylor & Co.'s* case[78] is that by accepting a bill drawn under a documentary credit the banker performs some of his duties under the contract with the buyer and that there is, therefore, no total failure of the consideration furnished for this contract when the bill is subsequently dishonoured by non-payment. It is argued that for this reason, and also because the property in the goods passes when the bill is accepted, the buyer is obliged to perform his contract with the banker. But the main object of the contract between the banker and the buyer is to arrange for the payment of the amount of the credit to the seller. The object of arranging for a bill of exchange payable at a fixed period after sight and not for payment by cash against the documents is to grant the buyer short-term credit. It is unrealistic to regard the acceptance by the banker of the seller's bill as performance of the banker's duties towards the buyer. It is submitted that Paull J.'s decision, that the dishonour of the draft by non-payment amounts to total failure of the consideration furnished by the banker to the buyer, is unexceptional. But the buyer should be advised to pay the price directly to the seller only if the bill has been presented to the banker and dishonoured.[79]

23–101 **Banker's failure after payment by buyer.** In certain cases the buyer places the issuing banker in funds before the latter pays the seller the amount of the credit or honours a draft drawn under it. If the issuing

[75] Gutteridge and Megrah, *Law of Bankers' Commercial Credits* (8th ed.), pp.48–49.
[76] (1867) L.R. 5 Eq. 160.
[77] (1870) L.R. 9 Eq. 725.
[78] Gutteridge and Megrah, *op. cit.*, pp.48–49.
[79] And note that the holder of the bill has to prove in the bank's winding-up; the acceptance of the bill of exchange does not confer on him any right over the goods: *Re Barned's Banking Co.* (1871) L.R. 5 H.L. 157.

banker fails before making payment, should the buyer be liable to pay the relevant amount to the seller? An affirmative answer to this question was given in *Maran Road Saw Mill v Austin Taylor & Co. Ltd*,[80] where it was held that, in such a case, the buyer is not entitled to claim that he has performed his entire bargain by furnishing the letter of credit and by remitting to the banker the funds necessary for making payment. He is not discharged from his duty to pay the price to the seller, because he promises "to *pay* by letter of credit; not to provide by letter of credit a source of payment which [*does*] *not* pay".[81]

Position where issuer nominated by seller. Ackner J.'s decision is based on the fact that the issuing bank is engaged by the buyer, who should therefore bear any loss resulting from his bank's failure. This premise is not necessarily displaced where the issuing bank is nominated in the underlying contract.[82] In such a case the parties have, simply, agreed on the identity of the bank to be utilised by the buyer. But should the general presumption hold even if the bank is specifically designated by the beneficiary, possibly against the initial objections of the buyer, who would prefer to use his ordinary bank? An older American decision suggests that in such a case the account party should be regarded as having performed all that could be expected of him by procuring that nominated bank's services.[83] 23–102

Re Charge Card Services Ltd. Although this view runs counter to the prevailing trend of the English authorities, it may be applied in appropriate cases. The English decisions are based on imputing to the parties to the underlying, commercial, transaction an intention to treat the furnishing of the credit and the subsequent acceptance of drafts thereunder as conditional rather than as absolute payment. *Re Charge Card Services Ltd*[84] demonstrates that in certain circumstances this presumption can be rebutted. In that case a company engaged in the issuing of credit cards went into liquidation. One of the questions to be decided was whether dealers, who had supplied goods or services to card-holders upon their executing a sales docket on which the details of their respective card were imprinted by the use of the dealer's machine, had the right to fall back on such holders when the company suspended payment. Cases respecting the buyer's position following his furnishing of negotiable instruments as well as the leading cases respecting the effect of the furnishing of documentary credits were cited in support of the proposition that the execution of a docket constituted conditional and not absolute payment. 23–103

Millett J.'s decision. Millett J. drew a distinction between a transaction involving the furnishing of a documentary credit and a credit card transaction. Even where the identity of the bank that is expected to issue 23–104

---

[80] [1975] 1 Lloyd's Rep. 156, noted in 40 M.L.R. 91 (1977).

[81] *ibid.*, at p.159. For a critique see Millett J. in *Re Charge Services Ltd* [1987] Ch. 150 at 167–168. See also *E D & F Man Ltd v Nigerian Sweets and Confectionery Co.* [1977] 2 Lloyd's Rep. 50.

[82] *ED & F Man Ltd v Nigerian Sweets and Confectionery Co.*, above.

[83] *Vivacqua Irmaos SA v Hickerson* 190 So. 657 at 659 (1939), applied also in *Ornstein v Hickerson* 40 F. Supp. 305 at 308–309 (1941), where it was not clear at whose request the bank in question had been nominated.

[84] [1987] Ch. 150, affirmed [1989] Ch. 497.

the letter of credit is specified in the underlying contract, the "sole purpose of the letter of credit is to provide security to the seller to replace that represented by the shipping documents which he gives up in exchange of the credit . . . By contrast, credit and charge cards are used mainly to facilitate payment of small consumer debts arising out of transactions between parties who may well not be known to each other, and the terms of which are not usually the subject of negotiation."[85] His Lordship added: "The essence of the [credit card] transaction, which in my view has no close analogy, is that the supplier and the customer have for their mutual convenience each previously arranged to open an account with the same company, and agree that any account between themselves may, if the customer wishes, be settled by crediting the supplier's and debiting the customer's account with that company."[86]

23–105 **Ratio and Appeal.** Millett J. concluded that the circumstances of this type of transaction were "sufficient not only to displace any presumption that payment by such means [was] conditional payment only, but to support a presumption to the contrary".[87] His reasoning was adopted by the Court of Appeal. Referring to the decisions respecting documentary credits, Browne-Wilkinson V. C. pointed out that Lord Denning did not purport to lay down a general principle in *El Nasr's* case but treated the matter as "one of construction to be determined in the light of the consequences."[88] Pointing out that, usually, the furnishing of the documentary credit constitutes conditional payment, his Lordship added: "if, unusually, the seller does select the bank, this factor may rebut the presumption of conditional payment by letter of credit".[89]

23–106 **Conclusion.** *Re Charge Card Services Ltd* thus shows that the presumption that a documentary credit constitutes conditional rather than absolute payment is rebuttable.[90] It is significant that Browne-Wilkinson V. C. mentioned that one such instance might very well occur where the selection of the issuing bank was effected by the beneficiary. In such a case, there is much to be said for the conclusion that the account party performs all the duties undertaken by him when he procures the letter of credit from the designated bank and remits to it the funds required for the making of payment thereunder. Commercially, such a conclusion is sound as a buyer who is specifically required to utilise a bank other than his usual bankers may have to remit to that bank the required funds in advance or, at the very

85 *ibid.*, at p.168.
86 *ibid.*, at p.169.
87 *ibid.*, and note that on this issue the decision is not affected by *Re Bank of Credit and Commerce Int. SA (No.8)* [1998] A.C. 214.
88 [1989] Ch. at 512.
89 *ibid.*, at p.516.
90 Note that even in the case of negotiable instruments, it can be shown that the parties have agreed that the acceptance or negotiation of a bill of exchange is to constitute absolute payment. Usually, this occurs in transactions in which the debtor furnishes to the creditor a third party's instrument. See the analysis in *Gunn v Bolkow, Vaughan & Co.* (1875) L.R. 10 Ch.App. 491 at 501 and, generally, above, para.9–030 and authorities there cited.

least, to furnish to it a security, such as a back-to-back credit, of his own bank.

Damages. The damages that may be recoverable by the seller from the buyer in the event of the banker's default are similar to those recoverable for non-payment of money. If, which has been doubted,[91] the law rigidly limits those damages to the amount of money due, together with such interest as the court may award,[92] the limitation will apply, provided that the credit has been opened. Damages for the failure of the buyer to furnish the credit are wider in extent, and embrace any loss to the exporter that was at the time of the contract reasonably foreseeable by both parties as the probable consequence of the breach.[93] 23–107

Buyer's remedies after realisation of credit. In the majority of cases the discharge of the credit by the bank brings the transaction to its conclusion. But the principle of the autonomy of the different contractual relationships of the documentary credit transaction, which is discussed subsequently,[94] means that the payment effected by the bank does not necessarily discharge the mutual rights and duties of the parties to the contract of sale. Thus, if the documents tendered by the seller to the bank turn out to be false, the buyer may have an action against him in deceit[95] or for a breach of contract. If the documents are waste paper, the buyer may, further, have against the seller a quasi-contractual action based on total failure of consideration. 23–108

Buyer's position when bank rejects discrepant documents. What is the seller's position if the bank rejects the documents by reason of their non-compliance with the terms of the documentary credit? It is clear that if, despite the bank's rejection of the documents, the buyer accepts the goods, he is under a duty to pay.[96] The buyer cannot possibly accept the goods but claim that the bank's rejection of the documents discharges him from his duty to pay the price. The acceptance of the goods by the buyer has to be regarded as his waiver of any rights based on the discrepancies in the documents. 23–109

Buyer's right to repudiate. But does the beneficiary's failure to furnish the required documents entitle the buyer to repudiate the underlying contract and to reject the goods? This was, actually, the issue in *Shamsher Jute Mills v Sehtia (London)*.[97] An exporter of goods sold on terms f.o.b. 23–110

---

[91] *Trans Trust SPRL v Danubian Trading Co. Ltd* [1952] 2 Q.B. 297 at 306–307. See also above, para.16–028, and see *Wadsworth v Lydall* [1981] 1 W.L.R 598; *President of India v La Pintada Compania Navegacion SA* [1985] A.C. 104 at 124–127; *Chitty on Contracts* (29th ed.), Vol. I, para.26–089.
[92] In pursuance of the Law Reform (Miscellaneous Provisions) Act 1934, s.3; and see the Supreme Court Act 1981, s.35A; the County Courts Act 1984, s.69A.
[93] On the basis of *Hadley v Baxendale* (1854) 9 Exch. 341; see *Trans Trust SPRL v Danubian Trading Co. Ltd*, above; *Ian Stach Ltd v Baker Bosley Ltd* [1958] 2 Q.B. 130.
[94] Below, paras 23–139 *et seq*.
[95] See, *e.g. Famouri v Dialcord Ltd* (1983) 133 N.L.J. 153.
[96] *cf. Saffron v Société Minière Cafrika* (1958) 100 C.L.R. 231.
[97] [1987] 1 Lloyd's Rep. 388, following *Ficom SA v Sociedad Cadex Ltda* [1980] 2 Lloyd's Rep. 118; and see *Darg Offshore Ltd v Emerald Field Contracting Ltd* [1992] 2 Lloyd's Rep. 142 at 155.

failed to present to the issuing bank a set of documents complying with the terms of the irrevocable credit opened at the importer's request. Bingham J. held that, as the exporter's inability to obtain payment under the irrevocable credit was occasioned by his own failure to tender the required documents, he was also in breach of the underlying contract of sale. Consequently, he was unable to recover the price from the buyer, notwithstanding that there was no evidence to suggest that the goods were unmerchantable or defective.

23–111 **Possible conflict with autonomy principle.** One point to be raised as regards this decision is that the documentary credit and the underlying contract are independent transactions which are not qualified by one another.[98] It is true that the underlying contract, which stipulates that payment is to be made by the furnishing of an irrevocable credit, sets up an agreed machinery for the discharge of the buyer's duty to pay for the goods. But it has been shown that, usually, the documentary credit itself constitutes a conditional rather than an absolute source of payment. Why then should the bank's rejection of the documents, which may well be justified under the letter of credit, necessarily discharge the account party from all his duties under the underlying contract? After all, the buyer would not necessarily be discharged from his obligations under the contract of sale by reason only of technical defects in the goods themselves. Why then should he be discharged by reason of a technical discrepancy in the documents? It is arguable that the buyer's failure to instruct the bank to waive technical discrepancies in the documents constitutes a breach of his contract to purchase the goods. In *Shamsher*, Bingham J. effectively read the contract of sale as incorporating the terms of the documentary credit and the doctrine of strict compliance applicable to it. It is, with respect, submitted that this conclusion militates against the doctrine of the autonomy of the separate contracts of the documentary credit transaction.

23–112 **Remedy where buyer seeks to frustrate transaction.** In some cases the buyer attempts to safeguard his interests by including in the list of documents to be tendered under a letter of credit a document to be completed by himself, such as a certificate attesting the conformity of the goods or their shipment, or, alternatively, stipulates that a given document be valid only if countersigned by himself.[99] If the buyer attempts to repudiate the commercial object of the transaction by wrongfully refusing to issue or to countersign such a document, the court has the power, under section 39 of the Supreme Court Act 1981, to issue an order compelling him to do so. The court can further order that, if the buyer fails to comply by a given date, the certificate be issued, or the necessary countersignature be executed, by a designated third party, such as an officer of the court.[1] It is, however, uncertain whether the validity of a document so issued or

---

[98] Below, para.23–136.
[99] See, *e.g. Gian Singh & Co. v Banque de l'Indochine* [1974] 1 W.L.R. 1234, affg. [1974] 1 Lloyd's Rep. 56.
[1] *Astro Exito Navegacion SA v Southland Enterprise Co. (No.2)* [1983] 2 A.C. 787; and see Jack, *Documentary Credits* (3rd ed.), para.9.70.

executed would be recognised in another jurisdiction. It follows that a confirming bank that is compelled to pay against such a document may not be able to obtain reimbursement from the issuing bank which operates in another country.

3. CONTRACT OF ISSUING BANKER AND BUYER

(a) *Opening of Credit*

The application form. Pursuant to the contract of sale the buyer requests his own bankers to open a documentary credit in favour of the seller. The buyer completes an "application form" provided by the banker. The buyer should specify whether the credit is to be opened by air mail or by some teletransmission such as a cable; the type of credit to be opened and its expiry date; details of the manner in which shipment and insurance is to be effected; an accurate description of the goods; a list of the documents against which the banker is to make payment and to whose order the bill of lading should be addressed. If the seller has nominated a correspondent banker, this should be mentioned in the application form; otherwise the issuing banker may dispatch the documentary credit directly to the seller or may employ the services of a correspondent banker who is not acceptable to the seller. If the issuing banker is prepared to open the documentary credit, he will usually notify the buyer in writing. The application form then becomes the basis of the contract between the issuing banker and the buyer. **23–113**

Autonomy of agreement. The legal relationship between the issuing banker and the buyer depends solely on the terms of the contract between them and is not affected by other contractual relationships of the documentary credit transaction. Thus, if the issuing banker, at the instruction of the buyer, issues an irrevocable credit, then despite any dispute that the buyer may thereafter have with the seller under the contract of sale, the buyer cannot compel the issuing banker to revoke this credit,[2] once it has been opened.[3] **23–114**

Strict adherence to application form. If the banker agrees to open the documentary credit, he must adhere strictly to the buyer's instructions as set out in the application form. Thus, if the buyer has stipulated the form of any document against which payment is to be made, the banker must at his peril insist upon complete compliance. "There is no room for documents **23–115**

---

[2] *Sovereign Bank of Canada v Bellhouse, Dillon & Co.* (1911) 23 Que.K.B. 413. In the USA see: *Moss v Old Colony Trust Co.*, 140 N.E. 803 at 808 (1923); *Kingdom of Sweden v New York Trust Co.*, 96 N.Y.S. 2d 779 at 791 (1949); *Liberty National Bank and Trust Co. v Bank of America*, 116 F.Supp. 233 at 236–237 (1953), affirmed 218 F. 2d 831 (1955); Uniform Commercial Code, s.5–106. English authorities, discussed in below, para.23–136, relate to the autonomy of the documentary credit itself.

[3] See, *Bunge Corp. v Vegetable Vitamin Foods (Pte.) Ltd* (1984) 134 N.L.J. 125, which supports the view that the letter of credit is not open until it reaches the beneficiary's hands.

which are almost the same, or which will do just as well. Business could not proceed securely on any other lines."[4] In *Midland Bank Ltd v Seymour*[5] the buyer instructed the issuing banker to open in favour of the seller a documentary credit to be available in Hong Kong. The banker opened a documentary credit which provided for the acceptance of drafts in London instead of Hong Kong. Devlin J. held that if the banker was authorised to pay only in Hong Kong, then although the place of payment might be commercially immaterial the banker had exceeded his mandate and could not recover.[6] Similarly, in *Rayner (J H) & Co. Ltd v Hambro's Bank Ltd*[7] Goddard L.J. said that the banker should not attempt to exercise a discretion with a view to giving the best protection to the buyer; the banker's only concern is to carry out the orders given to him.

23–116 **Waiver or ratification.** In *Midland Bank Ltd v Seymour*[8] Devlin J. thought that if the buyer, after having come to know of a breach of authority by the issuing banker, adopts his act, he may be considered to have ratified and is obliged to reimburse the issuing banker. But it is arguable that the principle is to be based on the doctrine of waiver rather than on ratification. While the doctrine of ratification is not necessarily confined to agency contracts, its main application is in situations where an agent exceeds his authority when he enters into a contract on behalf of his principal.[9] But in a documentary credit transaction, the issuing banker does not contract on the buyer's behalf. Usually, at the buyer's request, the issuing banker enters into an independent contractual relationship with the seller.[10] Thus, he does not purport to act as an agent.[11] For this reason, it may be more accurate to regard the buyer who accepts documents although the issuing banker has deviated from his instructions as waiving the breach.[12] But it is to be doubted whether this distinction between waiver and ratification has any practical implications.

23–117 **Ambiguous instructions.** Under Article 5 of the UCP the instructions for the opening of the credit, the credit itself and any instruction for amendments thereto must be complete and precise. In order to guard against

---

[4] *Equitable Trust Co. of New York v Dawson Partners Ltd* (1927) 27 Ll.L.R. 49 at 52. See also *South African Reserve Bank v Samuel & Co.* (1931) 40 Ll.L.R. 291.
[5] [1955] 2 Lloyd's Rep. 147.
[6] *ibid.*, at p.168. But it is inaccurate to describe the issuing banker as an agent; *infra*.
[7] [1943] K.B. 37 at 43.
[8] [1955] 2 Lloyd's Rep. 147 at 168–169.
[9] See *Chitty on Contracts* (28th ed.), Vol. 2, paras 32–026 *et seq*.
[10] See above, para.23–051, and below, para.23–136.
[11] For the rule that a person is not liable towards third parties when he acts as an agent: see *Jenkins v Hutchinson* (1849) 13 Q.B. 743; *Lewis v Nicholson* (1852) 18 Q.B. 503. But note that an agent can accept personal liability together with his principal: *International Ry. Co. v Niagara Parks Commission* [1941] A.C. 328; *Anglo-African Shipping Co. of New York v J Mortner Ltd* [1962] 1 Lloyd's Rep. 610.
[12] For some interesting American cases see *Courtaulds North America v North Carolina National Bank*, 528 F. 2d 802 (1975); *Far Eastern Textile Ltd v City National Bank and Trust Co.*, 430 F.Supp. 193 (1977) in both of which it was inferred that waiver could arise from a course of dealings. *Cf. Beckman Cotton Co. v First National Bank* 34 U.C.C. Rep.Ser. 986 (1982).

confusion and misunderstanding, banks should discourage any attempt to include excessive detail in the application form in the credit or in any amendment thereto. This provision is augmented by Article 12: if the instructions are incomplete or unclear, the banker who is asked to act on them may give the seller preliminary notification for information only and without responsibility.[13] In this case the credit is issued, confirmed, or advised only when the necessary information has been received.

It has been held that if the buyer's instructions are ambiguous, the issuing banker is entitled to be reimbursed as long as he gives the instructions a reasonable construction and acts accordingly.[14] This principle, which applies although the relationship is not one of pure agency,[15] is inapplicable if the ambiguity is patent. In such a case the bank cannot make its own decision as to the buyer's intention and is required to refer back to him for further instructions or clarifications. In the words of Goff L.J. in *European Asian Bank AG v Punjab and Sind Bank (No.2)*[16]: "Obviously it cannot be open to every contracting party to act upon a bona fide, but mistaken, interpretation of a contractual document prepared by the other, and to hold that other party to that interpretation . . . Furthermore, even in the context of agency and other analogous transactions, the principle [under discussion] presupposes . . . that a party relying on his own interpretation of the relevant document must have acted reasonably in all the circumstances in doing so. If instructions are given to an agent, it is understandable that he should act on these instructions without more; but if, for example, the ambiguity is patent on the face of the document it may well be right (especially with the facilities of modern communications available to him) to have his instructions clarified by the principal, if time permits, before acting upon them." This ratio is applicable in all the contractual relationships of a documentary credit transaction. Thus, a bank instructed to confirm a documentary credit, which is patently ambiguous in parts, ought to seek clarifications from the issuer.

Dispatch of credit to seller. Frequently the documentary credit is not dispatched to the seller directly by the issuing banker but through a correspondent, and many bankers reserve the right to employ a correspondent in a standard clause of the application form. This right is now laid down in Article 7(a) of the UCP But in some cases it is not sufficient if the correspondent banker notifies the seller of the opening of the credit by the issuing banker. Under Article 11(a)(ii) of the UCP, when an issuing bank instructs the advising bank by any teletransmission to advise a credit or an 23–118

---

[13] The bank from whom the unclear or incomplete instructions were received has to be notified of the act taken. It must supply the missing details without delay.

[14] *Midland Bank Ltd v Seymour* [1955] 2 Lloyd's Rep. 147 at 153, 168, applying, in effect, the principle in *Ireland v Livingston* (1872) L.R. 5 H.L. 395. See also *Commercial Banking Co. of Sydney Ltd v Jalsard Pty Ltd* [1973] A.C. 279 at 285–286; *Patel v Standard Chartered Bank* [2001] All E.R. (D.) 66. An application form may in certain cases be construed by referring to earlier dealings between the parties: but this approach is discouraged by Art. 5(a)(ii) of the UCP if the earlier credit has been subject to amendments.

[15] *Credit Agricole Indosuez v Muslim Commercial Bank* [2000] 1 Lloyd's Rep. 275.

[16] [1983] 1 W.L.R. 642 at 656.

amendment thereto, and intends the mail confirmation to be the operative credit instrument or amendment it must state "full details to follow" (or words to a similar effect), or that the mail confirmation will be the operative amendment. Article 11(b) provides that an amendment must be sent through the advising bank that was utilised for the dispatch of the letter of credit. The issuing bank must forward the operative credit instrument or amendment to the advising bank without delay. Under Article 11(a)(i) the relevant teletransmission is deemed to constitute the effective credit or amendment unless it includes the required formula or words to the same effect. Under Article 11(c), where the bank has given a preliminary advice of the issuance of a credit or of an amendment, it is irrevocably bound to issue the same without delay "in terms not inconsistent with the pre-advice". However, the issuing bank's failure duly to dispatch a required mail confirmation does not render the teletransmission the operative document by default.

23–119 **Responsibility for acts of correspondent.** The engagements of a correspondent banker for the opening of a documentary credit involves certain risks. Article 16 of the UCP protects the issuing banker against liability for consequences arising from the delay or loss in transit of messages as well as from loss arising out of errors in translations and decoding of messages. Under Article 18, if the issuing banker utilises the services of a correspondent banker, he does so at the buyer's risk and account and assumes no liability if the correspondent banker does not carry out instructions transmitted to him.[17] This provision appears wide enough to protect the issuing banker against responsibility for the negligence of the correspondent banker and applies even if the issuing bank has taken the initiative in selecting the correspondent. Under the last paragraph of Article 18, the buyer is bound by and liable to indemnify the issuing banker and the correspondent banker against all obligations and responsibilities imposed by foreign law and by usages. At the same time, Article 18 does not preclude the applicant from contesting in a dispute with the issuer the regularity of documents accepted by the correspondent as a regular tender.[18]

23–120 **Issuing bank's duty of care.** The complexity of modern trade has given rise to the question of whether the issuing bank owes its customer a duty of care which, basically, requires him to caution the customer as regards such matters as the documents to be tendered by the seller or the desirability of obtaining a report on a new trading partner. The problems arise because merchants do not always comprehend that the documentary credit transaction is of a formal nature and that all that it secures is that payment is made against documents that are regular on their face.

23–121 **Existing case law.** There is no doubt that banks are usually more familiar with the documentary credit transaction and with its implications than their customers. Some banks tend to give advice to their customers but deny any

---

[17] As regards the position where the UCP does not apply, see *Equitable Trust Co. of New York v Dawson Partners Ltd* (1927) 27 Ll.L.R. 49.
[18] *Credit Agricole Indosuez v Generale Bank* [2000] 1 Lloyd's Rep. 123.

legal duty to do so. The case law in point is inconclusive. In *Midland Bank Ltd v Seymour*[19] the customer, who had instructed his bank to open a documentary credit, pleaded that the bank had failed to convey to him some adverse information received about the exporter. Devlin J. found on the facts that no request for information had been made by the customer and that the bank had not been negligent. He thought that, generally, a bank's duty was confined to its not supplying misleading information and doubted that the bank was under a duty "to prosecute enquiries with due diligence". In *Commercial Banking Co. of Sydney Ltd v Jalsard Pty Ltd*[20] a consignment of Christmas lights turned out to be defective although a certificate of inspection attested that the lights appeared to be in good condition. The importer refused to reimburse his bank, claiming that it should have advised him to stipulate for a certificate attesting that the goods had passed a suitable electrical test. The Privy Council found on the facts that the bank had not broken a duty of care, as the importer had expressly instructed the bank to stipulate for a certificate of inspection issued by a designated surveyor.

Conclusion. The above two cases are of limited assistance. However, they show that the existence of such a duty of care may not be dismissed lightly. The answer probably depends on the facts. On the one hand, it would appear unwarranted to impose on an issuing bank a general duty of care to advise its clients about their documentary credit transactions. An experienced importer is familiar with the transaction. On the other hand, a bank may owe a duty of care to a new customer, whom it advises to start using documentary credits as a means for facilitating exports and for securing payment. The answer may possibly depend on the reliance that, to the bank's knowledge, is placed on its advice by a given customer. 23–122

Terms in forms. The conclusion just reached is based on the analysis of the existing common law authorities. Standard terms incorporated in modern banking forms seek to exclude liability on the bankers' part and, in addition, confer on banks wide discretion in matters such as the determination of the regularity of the documents. The validity of such clauses awaits decision. 23–123

The banker's commission. Both the issuing banker and the confirming banker are entitled to a commission or fee for the service rendered to the buyer. Most bankers in the United Kingdom make one charge at the time the credit is established and another at the time it is utilised. In these cases it is clear that the first amount relates to the opening of the credit and is, in all probability, not repayable if the credit is not realised. But problems may arise if the banker charges a single fee or commission in respect of the entire transaction. Is this commission or part of it repayable to the buyer if the seller does not utilise the documentary credit? Some guidance is to be 23–124

---

[19] [1955] 2 Lloyd's Rep. 147 at 155 *et seq.*; and see Ellinger [1981] J.B.L. 258 at 267–269.

[20] [1973] A.C. 279.

found in an American decision, *Baring v Lyman*,[21] in which the court had to decide when the commission, which a banker charged for issuing an *open* letter of credit, became due. Story J. said that when a draft is drawn under the open credit and negotiated, the banker is bound to accept it. He therefore held that even though, subsequently, the draft may not be presented to the banker, his commission is not reclaimable. This decision can be adapted to irrevocable credits. As the banker is bound as soon as the credit reaches the hands of the seller,[22] the commission should fall due at that time.

23–125 **Deposit of funds or securities.** The issuing banker may require funds or securities to be deposited by the buyer before any drafts drawn under the credit fall due. Provided there is sufficient evidence of appropriation, funds[23] or securities[24] so deposited will not go in satisfaction of the general creditors of the banker in the event of his failure prior to payment but are recoverable in full by the buyer. But such appropriation is not easy to prove,[25] and in most cases the buyer will be in the position of a general creditor.[26]

(b) *Realisation of Documentary Credit*

23–126 **Banker's duty to take up documents.** When the issuing banker agrees to open a documentary credit, he undertakes towards the buyer a duty to accept from the seller a draft accompanied by the required documents. If the banker fails to accept or to pay a draft which complies with the terms of the application form, he is in breach of his contract with the buyer.[27] The buyer, on his part, undertakes to take up conforming documents tendered by the seller to the banker and agrees to reimburse the banker for his advances to the seller. But the banker's right of reimbursement depends on his taking up a faultless tender. "There is really no question here of . . . diligence or of negligence or of breach of contract of employment to use reasonable care and skill."[28] Thus, the banker must adhere as strictly to his instructions at the time of the realisation of the credit as at the time he opens it.[29]

---

[21] 1 Story 396; 2 Fed.Cas. 794 (1841).
[22] See above, para.23–052.
[23] *Farley v Turner* (1857) 26 L.J.Ch. 710.
[24] *Jombart v Woollett* (1837) 2 My. & C. 390.
[25] *Re Barned's Banking Co. Ltd, Massey's Case* (1870) 39 L.J.Ch. 635.
[26] See also above, para.23–101.
[27] *Sale Continuation Ltd v Austin Taylor & Co. Ltd* [1968] 2 Q.B. 849 at 860–861. In the United States see: *Leslie v Bassett*, 29 N.E. 834 at 835 (1892); *Bank of United States v Seltzer*, 251 N.Y.S. 637 at 641 (1931); *Greenough v Munroe*, 53 F. 2d 362 at 365 (1931).
[28] *Equitable Trust Co. of New York v Dawson Partners Ltd* (1927) 27 Ll.L.R. 49 at 52. See also *Midland Bank Ltd v Seymour* [1955] 2 Lloyd's Rep. 147 at 168; *Gian Singh & Co. Ltd v Banque de L'Indochine* [1974] 1 Lloyd's Rep. 56, affirmed [1974] 2 Lloyd's Rep. 1.
[29] As to which see above, para.23–115. For an argument for the relaxation of this duty see J.F. Dolan., "Letter of Credit Disputes between Issuer and Customer" 105 Banking L.J. 380 (1988). But see *Guaranty Trust Co. of New York v Van den Berghs Ltd* (1925) 22 Ll.L.R. 447 at 454, implying an exception in respect of provisions inserted solely in the bank's own interest.

Banker's duty to examine the documents. Under Article 13(a) of the UCP banks must examine all documents with reasonable care to ascertain that they appear on their face to be in accordance with the terms and conditions of the credit. The article provides that "compliance of the stipulated documents on their face with the terms and conditions of the credit, shall be determined by international banking practice as reflected in these articles." It is further provided that documents which appear on their face to be inconsistent with one another are to be treated as irregular on their face.[30] 23–127

The language of Article 13(a) indicates that the issuing banker is not responsible if he fails to notice a defect that a prudent inspection is unlikely to disclose. Basically, the examination concerns the description of the goods and the regularity of each document. It is not the duty of the banker to consider the legal effect of each clause in a document or to look at it under a fine microscope.[31] But the banker must undertake a more thorough examination if documents, which appear to comply with the provisions of the application form, contain any unusual feature. According to an American authority, such a "red flag" puts the banker under an obligation to scrutinise the documents for any clues which may aid in determining whether the terms of the documentary credit and the application form have been met.[32] However, even in these cases a prolonged scrutiny is prohibited by Article 13(b) of the UCP according to which the examination must be conducted within a "reasonable time" not exceeding seven banking days following the receipt of the documents.[33] Under Article 14(e), a prolonged retention of the documents, without giving notice that they are held at the issuing banker's disposal,[34] precludes the issuing banker from alleging that they are non-conforming.[35]

Genuineness of documents. The principle of Article 13 is augmented by paragraph (b) of Article 14 and by Article 15. As long as the documents, on their face, comply with the application form and with the documentary 23–128

---

[30] And see cases cited in below, n.30, particularly *Gian Singh & Co. Ltd v Banque de L'Indochine* [1974] 1 Lloyd's Rep. 56 at 60–61, affirmed [1974] 2 Lloyd's Rep. 1.

[31] This is the position at common law: *National Bank of Egypt v Hannevig's Bank Ltd* (1919) 1 Ll.L.R. 69; 3 *Legal Decisions Affecting Bankers* 211 at 213; *British Imex Industries Ltd v Midland Bank Ltd* [1958] 1 Q.B. 542 at 552; *Gian Singh & Co. Ltd v Banque de L'Indochine* [1974] 1 Lloyd's Rep. 56, affirmed [1974] 2 Lloyd's Rep. 1 at 11. See also Art. 17. *Cf. Commercial Banking Co. of Sydney Ltd v Jalsard Pty Ltd* [1973] A.C. 279 at 286, *cf. Westpac Banking Corp. v South Carolina National Bank* [1986] 1 Lloyd's Rep. 311 at 315, showing also that the bank should not speculate about the facts behind the documents.

[32] *Liberty National Bank and Trust Co. v Bank of America*, 116 F.Supp. 233 at 240 (1953), affirmed 218 F. 2d 831 (1955).

[33] Note that under Art. 13(b) a similar period of time is applied to the examination of the documents by the confirming bank and by a nominated bank.

[34] Note that in *Marine Midland Grace Trust Co. v Banco del Pais SA*, 261 F.Supp. 884 (1966) it was decided that a cable asking for instructions indicated that the documents were being held at the remitting bank's disposal.

[35] In *Marine Midland Grace Trust Co. v Banco del Pais SA*, above, it was held that the retention of the documents for 10 days was too long to be reasonable; see further below, para.23–157.

credit, the banker is not responsible for their genuineness, accuracy or legal effect. These provisions protect the issuing banker not only in cases where the documents are forgeries but also in cases where they include untrue statements concerning the goods. The position is similar at common law.[36] However, both at common law and under the UCP the banker must exercise in his examination of the documents a reasonable degree of care and skill. If he fails to discharge this onus and as a result overlooks points indicating that a given document is a forgery, the bank has to bear the loss.[37]

23–129 **Condition of goods.** The banker's duty of strict compliance relates solely to the documents. Under Article 4 of the UCP, in documentary credit operations all parties concerned deal in documents and not in goods services or other performances to which the documentary credit may relate. Under Article 14(a), if a bank so authorised effects payment, or incurs a deferred payment undertaking, or accepts or negotiates against documents which appear on their face to be in accordance with the terms and conditions of a credit, the issuing bank or the confirming bank which has given the authorisation is bound to take up the documents and to reimburse the bank which has effected the payment, given the deferred payment undertaking or effected the acceptance or negotiation. The principle that the banker is not concerned with the goods derives support from decided cases[38] and has two effects. First, if the documents constitute a good tender, the condition of the goods is irrel evant. Secondly, if the documents are faulty, the issuing banker cannot justify a claim for reimbursement by proving that the goods are those stipulated in the contract of sale.[39]

23–130 **Exemption clauses.** Most application forms include clauses exempting the banker from responsibility for matters which are not in his control. At present most of these are set out in the UCP[40] The articles excluding responsibility for acts of the correspondent and for delays in messages have

---

[36] *Woods v Thiedemann* (1862) 1 H. & C. 478; *Ulster Bank v Synnott* (1871) 5 I.R.Eq. 595; *Basse and Selve v Bank of Australasia* (1904) 90 L.T. 618; *Guaranty Trust Co. of New York v Hannay & Co.* [1918] 2 K.B. 623. In the USA see: *Brown v C Rosenstein Co.*, 200 N.Y.S. 491 (1923), affirmed 203 N.Y.S. 922 (1924); *Philip A Feinberg Inc. v Varig SA*, 363 N.Y.S. 2d 195 (1974), affirmed 370 N.Y.S. 2d 499 (1975).

[37] *Gian Singh & Co. Ltd v Banque de L'Indochine*, above.

[38] *Basse and Selve v Bank of Australasia*, above. In the United States see: *Benecke v Haebler*, 58 N.Y.S. 16 (1899), affirmed 60 N.E. 1107 (1901); *Banco Espan ol de Credito v State Street Bank and Trust Co.*, 226 F.Supp. 106 (1967) reversed on another point: 385 F. 2d 230 (1967); *United Bank Ltd v Cambridge Sporting Goods Corp.*, 360 N.E. 2d 943 (1976). See also *Talbot v Bank of Hendersonville*, 495 S.W. 2d 548 (Tenn. 1972), which emphasises that the bank is under no duty to investigate.

[39] See authorities relating to the independence between the documentary credit and the contract of sale; below, para.23–136.

[40] The bankers in some countries use the Standard Forms for Issuing Documentary Credits, published as ICC Brochure No.516. These forms do not include specific exemption clauses but the incorporation of the UCP, in these standard forms, leads to the result attained by the specific inclusion of exemption clauses.

been discussed above.[41] Article 17 exonerates bankers from liability for consequences arising out of the interruption of their business by Acts of God, riots, civil commotions, insurrections, wars or any other causes beyond their control or by any strikes or lock-outs. The article further provides that, unless specifically authorised, banks will not effect payment acceptance or negotiation when business is resumed if the credit has expired during the period of the interruption.

Wider clauses. Some application forms include wide-ranging exemption clauses and certain bankers purport to exempt themselves even from responsibility for acts or omissions of their own clerks. But it would seem that such a clause runs counter to the main object of the agreement between the issuing banker and the buyer.[42] This object may, for this purpose, be summarised as the making of payment to the seller against a strictly conforming set of documents. If the banker can claim reimbursement, even if an error of his clerk results in the acceptance of a non-conforming tender, this object is frustrated. It is submitted that, as a matter of construction, exemption clauses of the application form should be regarded as subordinate to and qualified by the banker's duty of strict compliance.[43] This argument is supported by the Court of Appeal's decision in *Forestall Mimosa Ltd v Oriental Credit Ltd*,[44] which shows that such a wide exemption clause would be read together with rather than as overriding Article 13(a) of the UCP, unless the duty imposed on the bank under Article 13(a) was expressly excluded. Exclusion of liability for the consequences of events which are beyond the banker's control is of course justifiable from a commercial point of view and, further, does not militate against any provision of the UCP. 23–131

(c) *Banker's Security for his Advances*

Documents of title as security. In most cases the banker does not expect to be reimbursed by the buyer until after he has paid the amount of the credit to the seller or until after the arrival of the goods. As a security for the amount paid to the seller, the banker retains the documents of title. It is usually stated in the application form that these are pledged to the banker. In most cases involving imports of goods from overseas, the documents include a bill of lading which is made out either to the banker's 23–132

---

[41] See above, para.23–119.

[42] Contrast *Netherlands Trading Society v Wayne and Haylitt Co.* (1952) 36 Hong Kong L.R. 109. *Cf. Royal Bank of Scotland v Cassa di Risparnio delle Provincie Lombard* [1992] 1 Bank L.R. 251.

[43] This argument derives support from *Frenkel v MacAndrews & Co. Ltd* [1929] A.C. 545 at 562; *Suisse Atlantique Société d'Armement Maritime SA v NV Rotterdamsche Kolen Centrale* [1967] A.C. 361. See, generally, *Chitty on Contracts* (29th ed.), Vol. 1, paras 14–020 *et seq.*, showing that later decisions, such as *Photo Production Ltd v Securicor Transport Ltd* [1980] A.C. 827 and *George Mitchell (Chesterfield) Ltd v Finney Lock Seeds Ltd* [1983] 2 A.C. 803, indicate that a clearly worded clause will be given effect to even if it conflicts with the commercial object of the transaction.

[44] [1986] 1 W.L.R. 631, above, para.23–029.

order or to the seller's order[45] and indorsed by him in blank. The bill of lading represents the goods while these are on board the ship and confers on the banker, as holder, the constructive possession of the goods[46] as well as a security title in them as a pledgee.[47] Moreover, the pledge effected in this way gives the banker a right to sell the goods in the event of the buyer's default.[48]

23–133 **Nature of trust receipt.** If the buyer is able to reimburse the issuing banker on the arrival of the goods, the documents of title are surrendered to him. This enables the buyer to collect the goods from the ship and to deal with them in the ordinary course of his business. Frequently, however, the buyer has to rely on the proceeds of the sale of goods in order to reimburse the issuing banker. In such a case the banker may agree to release the documents to the buyer under a trust receipt. This type of transaction is discussed in Chapter 18.[49]

4. CONTRACT OF ISSUING BANKER AND SELLER

(a) *Legal Effect of Documentary Credit*

23–134 **Form.** According to American decisions, a documentary credit, whether revocable or irrevocable, need not be in any specified form and any letter[50] or cable[51] is usually sufficient. But most current forms follow a fairly uniform pattern. When the credit is issued on a standard form, this form is usually both dated and numbered, and clearly sets out its duration and the amount of cover provided. It is addressed to the seller and states that, on the instructions of the buyer, the banker authorises the seller to draw bills of exchange up to the stated amount.[52] There then follows the list of the documents which are to accompany the draft and which are to be surrendered upon its acceptance or payment. The letter of credit specifies

---

[45] Or to the order of an original shipper, such as to an ultimate supplier. And note that the bank cannot obtain a pledge from a c. & f., or c.i.f., buyer, as the seller invariably reserves a title to the goods pending payment: *The "Future Express"* [1993] 2 Lloyd's Rep. 542.

[46] *Glyn, Mills, Currie & Co. v East and West India Dock Co.* (1882) 7 App.Cas. 591 at 606; *Sanders Bros v Maclean & Co.* (1883) 11 Q.B.D. 327 at 341; *Guaranty Trust Co. of New York v Van Den Berghs Ltd* (1925) 22 Ll.L.R. 447 at 452.

[47] *Sewell v Burdick* (1884) 10 App.Cas. 74 at 86; *Brandt v Liverpool, Brazil and River Plate Steam Navigation Co.* [1924] 1 K.B. 575. The pledgee can sue in conversion: *Bristol and West of England Bank v Midland Ry Co.* [1891] 2 Q.B. 653 at 663. As regards combined transport documents, see below, para.23–225.

[48] *Rosenberg v International Banking Corp.* (1923) 14 Ll.L.R. 344 at 347.

[49] See above, paras 18–208—18–210.

[50] *Second National Bank of Hoboken v Columbia Trust Co.*, 288 F. 17 at 20–21 (1923); *Drinc-OMatic Inc. v Frank*, 141 F. 2d 177 at 179 (1944).

[51] *Border National Bank v American National Bank*, 282 F. 73 at 79 (1922); *Moss v Old Colony Trust Co.*, 140 N.E. 803 (1923).

[52] Alternatively payment in cash, deferred payment or the negotiation of a bill drawn on the buyer may be promised (above, para.23–003).

the manner in which the documents are to be made out and "nominates" the bank to which they must be tendered. It concludes with the banker's undertaking to pay the amount of the credit, or honour all bills of exchange drawn in compliance with its terms,[53] provided that they bear on their face the number and date of the credit to enable identification.[54] The same details, except the issuing bank's express undertaking, are included in an abbreviated manner where the documentary credit is opened by means of a tested telex or a SWIFT message. At present, most letters of credit are issued by such telecommunications.

Legal effect. In the case of a revocable credit the seller does not obtain a binding promise of the issuing banker or of the correspondent banker and the credit may be revoked at any time prior to the acceptance of documents by the issuing banker or to their being negotiated by a correspondent or by a negotiating banker.[55] An irrevocable credit, in contrast, creates a legally binding contract between the issuing banker and the seller.[56] It can be enforced by the seller even if the issuer is a foreign central bank. Thus, in *Trendtex Trading Corporation v Central Bank of Nigeria*,[57] the Court of Appeal rejected the plea of sovereign immunity which was raised by the issuing bank as a defence to the seller's action on the letter of credit. But a letter of credit will not be enforceable if its opening is tainted with illegality. In *United City Merchants (Investments) Ltd v Royal Bank of Canada*[58] a letter of credit, issued at the instruction of a Peruvian purchaser, was opened for an amount far exceeding the price of the goods on the understanding that the extra sum would be transferred by the seller to the purchaser's Swiss bank account in violation of the Peruvian exchange control laws. As both Peru and the United Kingdom had ratified the I.M.F. treaties, the arrangement was therefore unenforceable in the United Kingdom under the Bretton-Woods Agreements Order in Council 1946.[59] 23–135

---

[53] In a revocable credit the issuing banker states that he is not bound to honour the draft or to make payment.

[54] Some banks utilise the *Standard Forms for Issuing Documentary Credits*, ICC Brochures No.516.

[55] See above, para.23–051; and see *Beathard v Chicago Football Club Inc.*, 419 F.Supp. 1133 (1976) which describes a revocable credit as constituting a contractual undertaking subject to revocation.

[56] See above, para.23–052. It has been traditionally enforceable by summary procedure under RSC Ord. 14, r. 1. As to when leave to defend will be granted, see *Forestal Mimosa Ltd v Oriental Credit Ltd* [1986] 1 W.L.R. 631.

[57] [1978] Q.B. 529. See also *Hispano Americana Mercantil SA v Central Bank of Nigeria* [1979] 2 Lloyd's Rep. 277 and the State Immunity Act 1978, s.3(3)(b) of which would appear to reinforce the decisions in these two cases as a commercial credit would constitute a commercial transaction; accordingly a State, that entered into it, would not be allowed to claim immunity. For the American view, see *Dekor by Nikkei International Inc. v Federal Republic of Nigeria*, 647 F. 2d. 300 (1981). And see as regards implied waiver: *Sperry International Trade Inc. v Government of Israel*, 532 F.Supp. 901 (1982).

[58] [1983] A.C. 168, affg. on this point [1981] 2 Lloyd's Rep. 604 (case also known as "the *American Accord*").

[59] Schedule, Part I Art. VIII. As regards the effect of orders invalidating facilities at their place of issue, see *Shanning International Ltd v Lloyds TSB Bank Plc*, *The Times*, January 19, 2000.

The House of Lords held that the letter of credit was enforceable to the extent that it covered the amount genuinely due to the seller but not in respect of the balance. This conclusion was based on the fact that the offending part of the bank's undertaking could be severed from the valid commercial promise, and, undoubtedly, on that the confirming bank had been unaware of the arrangement between the buyer and the seller.

23–136 **Amendments.** Once the irrevocable credit is established it can be revoked or amended only with the consent of all the parties.[60] This means that the issuing and the confirming bank, both of whom are parties to the letter of credit, may reject a proposed amendment although both the buyer and the seller demand it.[61] In practice, the banks will resort to this right only if they fear that the proposed amendment may jeopardise their position, as is the case where the other parties seek to exclude a stipulation for a certificate of inspection in a situation in which the banks already suspect some collusion between buyer and seller. Where an amendment is required by the purchaser, the beneficiary's consent thereto is not readily deduced from his failing to raise an objection to it: and this may be the case even if the credit's expiry date is extended after the communication of the purported amendment to the beneficiary.[62]

If the credit is both irrevocable and confirmed, the correspondent banker is jointly and severally bound with the issuing banker towards the seller and in most regards the two bankers have similar rights and obligations. However, certain specific matters concerning the relationship between the seller and a confirming banker, as well as the position of a correspondent banker who does not confirm the credit, are discussed subsequently.[63]

23–137 **Theoretical analysis.** The prevailing view is that the contract between the issuing banker and the seller is established as soon as the irrevocable credit reaches the hands of the seller.[64] But this view leads to theoretical difficulties, because no consideration appears to move from the seller at the time he receives the documentary credit.[65] There are two possible explanations. First, it has been argued that the seller provides consideration at the time he receives the letter of credit. Reliance is placed for this proposition

---

[60] *Stein v Hambro's Bank of Northern Commerce* (1921) 9 Ll.L.R. 433 at 507, rvsd. on a different ground: (1922) 10 Ll.L.R. 529; *Malas (Hamzeh) & Sons v British Imex Industries Ltd* [1958] 2 Q.B. 127 at 129. See also *Sovereign Bank of Canada v Bellhouse, Dillon & Co.* (1911) 23 Que.K.B. 413. In the USA see: *Decker Steel Co. v Exchange National Bank*, 330 F. 2d. 82 at 86 (1964). As to whether an irrevocable credit may be amended before its notification to the seller, see *Distribuidora Del Pacifco SA v Gonzales*, 88 F.Supp. 538 at 541 (1950). Note that an amendment may be introduced by an informal contract: *Floating Dock Ltd v Hong Kong and Shanghai Banking Corp.* [1986] 1 Lloyd's Rep. 65.

[61] *AMF Head Sports Wear Inc. v Ray Scott's All-American Sports Club Inc.*, 4487 Supp. 222 (1978).

[62] *The "American Accord"* [1979] 1 Lloyd's Rep. 267, which on this point remains unaffected by the decisions of the House of Lords and Court of Appeal, above.

[63] See below, paras 23–181 *et seq.*

[64] See above, para.23–052.

[65] For a full analysis of these problems see Ellinger, *Documentary Letters of Credit—A Comparative Study*, Chs III–V.

on *Dexters Ltd v Schenker & Co.*[66] The claimants sold goods to A. & Co. Payment was to be made by a banker's confirmed credit but, instead of such a credit, A. & Co. furnished an irrevocable credit opened by the defendants, a Dutch mercantile firm. The claimants thereupon shipped the goods but the defendants rejected the documents tendered to them and refused payment. The defence of lack of consideration was pleaded by the defendants but was abandoned in court. Nevertheless Greer J. observed that in his view this plea was without merit and said: "Now it is clear that, until they got a form of banker's credit which would comply with the terms of the contract, [claimants] were not bound to send the goods forward at all; and therefore, not having got the banker's credit until there was a substituted arrangement for some other credit elsewhere, they were under no obligation to anybody to send forward the goods. Therefore, it is quite clear there was full and ample consideration for this undertaking."[67] This dictum could be applied in most documentary credit transactions. It will be recollected that the seller becomes bound to ship the goods only when the irrevocable credit reaches his hands.[68] Moreover, the seller is bound to claim payment, in the first place, from the issuing banker.[69] He can claim payment from the buyer only if the banker defaults. It has been argued that, from a practical point of view, the seller forbears, on the basis of the irrevocable credit, from demanding direct payment from the buyer.[70] Such forbearance, if established, constitutes good consideration.[71] However, it must be conceded that, primarily, the seller becomes bound to ship the goods at the time at which he receives the irrevocable credit because of the stipulations in the contract of sale.

Mercantile usage. The second explanation of the legal nature of an irrevocable credit is based on regarding it as established by a mercantile usage recognised all over the world. This explanation derives support from an observation of Jenkins L.J. in *Malas (Hamzeh) & Sons v British Imex Industries Ltd*[72]: "[T]he opening of a confirmed letter of credit constitutes a bargain between the banker and the vendor of the goods, which imposes upon the banker an absolute obligation to pay . . . An elaborate commercial system has been built up on the footing that bankers' confirmed credits are of that character, and, in my judgment, it would be wrong for this court in the present case to interfere with that established practice." This decision further intimates that arguments assailing the validity of irrevocable credits 23–138

---

66 (1923) 14 Ll.L.R. 586; *cf. Bank of New South Wales v Commonwealth Steel Co.* [1983] 1 N.S.W.L.R. 69 and *Westpac Banking Corp. v Commonwealth Steel Co., ibid.*, 735 (Aust.).
67 (1923) 14 Lloyd's Rep. 588.
68 See above, para.23–083.
69 See above, para.23–097.
70 Treitel, *Law of Contract* (11th ed.), pp.152–153.
71 As regards "actual forbearance" see *Pullin v Stokes* (1794) 2 H.Bl. 312; *Oldershaw v King* (1857) 2 H. & N. 517; *Alliance Bank Ltd v Broom* (1864) 2 Dr. & Sm. 289; *Miles v New Zealand Alford Estate Co.* (1886) 32 Ch.D. 266 at 291; *Crears v Hunter* (1887) 19 Q.B.D. 341.
72 [1958] 2 Q.B. 127 at 129. See also *International Banking Corp. v Barclays Bank Ltd* (1925) 5 *Legal Decisions Affecting Bankers* 1 at 4.

will meet with little sympathy from the courts. Support for this view is to be found in Kerr J.'s description of bankers' irrevocable undertakings as the lifeblood of international commerce.[73] It is inconceivable that such vital facilities would be rendered ineffective on the strength of a technical argument based on difficulties arising from the doctrine of consideration, even if the absence thereof were pleaded by the liquidator of an insolvent issuing bank.

23–139 **The autonomy of irrevocable credits.** An irrevocable credit constitutes an independent contract between the issuing banker and the seller. In *Urquhart, Lindsay & Co. v Eastern Bank Ltd*[74] Rowlatt J. held that an irrevocable credit is not qualified by or subject to the terms of the contract of sale made between the buyer and the seller. Moreover, in the United States it has been held that an irrevocable credit is independent also of the contract between the issuing banker and the buyer.[75] This principle of the autonomy of the irrevocable credit is at present clearly expressed in and reinforced by Articles 3 and 6 of the UCP Its effect is illustrated by the decision of the Court of Appeal in *Malas (Hamzeh) & Sons v British Imex Industries Ltd*.[76] The claimants, a Jordanian firm, agreed to purchase two shipments of reinforced steel rods from the defendants. The Midland Bank opened two confirmed credits in favour of the defendants, who thereupon sent the first shipment and realised the first confirmed credit. The claimants alleged that the goods were defective and applied for an injunction to restrain the defendants from drawing on the second letter of credit. Refusing to grant the injunction, Jenkins L.J. held that the confirmed credit constituted an absolute obligation of the bankers to pay "irrespective of any dispute there may be between the parties as to whether the goods are up to contract or not". He added that the system of financing sales of goods by irrevocable credits "would break down completely if a dispute as between the vendor and the purchaser was to have the effect of 'freezing'. . . the sum in respect of which the letter of credit was opened".[77]

---

[73] In *Harbottle (R D) (Mercantile) Ltd v National Westminster Bank* [1978] 1 Q.B. 146 at 155–156: *Centri Force Engineering v Bank of Scotland* 1993 S.L.T. 190.

[74] [1922] 1 K.B. 318 at 322–323. The American authorities in point are too numerous to be cited but most of the early cases are referred to in *Dulien Steel Products Inc. v Bankers Trust Co.*, 189 F.Supp. 922 (1960), affirmed 298 F. 2d 836 (1962). For more recent cases see *AMF Head Sports Wear Inc. v Ray Scott's All-American Sports Club Inc.*, 448 F. 2d 222 (1978) (where the modification of the underlying contract was held not to affect the letter of credit); *Professional Modular Surface v Uniroyal* 440 N.E. 2d 177 at 179 (Ct.App.Ill. 1982); *Eljay Jrs. Inc. v Rhada Exports* 470 N.Y.S 2d 12 (App.Div. 1984); *Andy Marine Inc. v Ziddell Inc.* 812 F. 2d 534 (9th Cir., 1987); *Crompton Corp. v Kellog* 831 F. 2d 586 (5th Cir., 1988) *Eakin v Continental Illinois National Bank*, 875 F. 2d 114 (7th Cir., 1989); *All Service Exportacao SA v Banco Bamerindus do. Brazil SA* 921 F. 2d 32 (2nd Cir., 1990); *Mid-America Tire Inc. v Ptz Trading Ltd*, 745 N.E. 2d 438 (Ohio, 2001). See also s.5–109 of the Uniform Commercial Code (Rev.).

[75] *North American Manufacturers Export Associates Inc. v Chase National Bank of City of New York*, 77 F.Supp. 55 (1948); *Kingdom of Sweden v New York Trust Co.*, 96 N.Y.S. 2d 779 at 791, (1949); *Consolidated Sales Co. Inc. v Bank of Hampton Roads*, 68 S.E. 2d 658 (1952); *Savage v First National Bank and Trust Co.*, 413 F.Supp. 447 (1976).

[76] [1958] 2 Q.B. 127.

[77] *ibid.*, at p.129. See also *Davies O'Brien Lumber Co. Ltd v Bank of Montreal* [1951] 3 D.L.R. 536 at 550.

Clash with foreign court orders. The cardinal importance of the principle of the autonomy of documentary credits is demonstrated by the fact that an English court may enforce payment despite an injunction issued by a foreign court. Thus, in *Power Curber International Ltd v National Bank of Kuwait*[78] the Court of Appeal of Kuwait issued an injunction precluding payment of a letter of credit opened by the defendant bank in Kuwait in favour of a beneficiary in North Carolina. Although the order prohibited payment in Kuwait and elsewhere and despite the fact that the only nexus of the facility with the United Kingdom was that negotiation was effected in London, the English Court of Appeal ordered the bank to pay. Lord Denning M.R., who delivered one of the majority judgments, observed that the rules of comity of nations did not bind an English court to stay proceedings in order to avoid a clash with the order made in Kuwait. A similar approach was taken in *European Asian Bank AG v Punjab and Sind Bank (No.1)*,[79] where an Indian bank was ordered to make payment in London under a documentary credit opened in India, despite an injunction issued in India and although the letter of credit was not available in England. Another manifestation of the autonomy of documentary credits is the courts' reluctance to grant a freezing injunction to prevent the escape of the amount paid from the United Kingdom.[80] 23–140

It follows that if the seller tenders documents which conform with the requirements of the irrevocable credit, the banker is under a duty to pay the amount covered by it; the banker should not concern himself with disputes between the buyer and the seller arising from the contract of sale. This principle is closely linked with the rule expressed in Article 4 of the UCP, according to which all parties to the documentary credit transaction deal in documents and not in goods and according to which the banker must determine, on the basis of the documents alone, whether the seller is entitled to the amount of the credit.

The fraud rule. The only exception to the principle of the autonomy of the irrevocable credit occurs in the case of fraud.[81] It applies where the seller has committed a fraud, such as the tender of forged documents or documents which, to the seller's knowledge, contain a false and fraudulent 23–141

---

[78] [1981] 2 Lloyd's Rep. 395 at 399. Note that the proper law of the contract was that of North Carolina, *i.e.* the place of payment. See also *Offshore International SA v Banco Central SA* [1977] 1 W.L.R. 399. An absence of a clear nexus with London might, presently, lead a court to the conclusion that London constituted a forum non-conveniens. See *Bank of Baroda v Vysya Bank Ltd* [1994] 2 Lloyd's Rep. 87; *Bank of Credit and Commerce Hong Kong Ltd v Sonali Bank* [1995] 1 Lloyd's Rep. 227.

[79] [1981] 2 Lloyd's Rep. 651. For a certain softening in the approach of the courts, see *Esal (Commodities) Ltd v Oriental Credit Ltd* [1985] 2 Lloyd's Rep. 546 at 550.

[80] *Intraco Ltd v Notis Shipping Corp. of Liberia (The Bhoja Trader)* [1981] 2 Lloyd's Rep. 256. And see *Z. Ltd v A–Z and AA–LL* [1982] Q.B. 558 at 574, stating that the effect of such an injunction is not to preclude payment but to attach the proceeds in order to preclude their escape from the jurisdiction.

[81] To date there are no authorities considering the effect of illegality on the issuer's duty to accept the tender. But note that, in *Mahonia Ltd v JP Morgan Chase Bank* [2003] 2 Lloyd's Rep. 911, Colman J. refused to strike out a defence based on illegality as being bad in law.

description of the goods. In an American case, *Sztejn v J Henry Schroder Banking Corp.*[82] the issuing banker opened an irrevocable credit covering a shipment of bristles. The seller shipped crates containing rubbish but succeeded in obtaining documents, which complied on their face with the requirements of the documentary credit and which described the goods as bristles. When the buyers discovered the fraud, they applied for an injunction to restrain the issuing banker from accepting these documents. It was held that in "such a situation, where the seller's fraud has been called to the bank's attention before the drafts and documents have been presented for payment, the principle of the independence of the bank's obligation under the letter of credit should not be extended to protect the unscrupulous seller."[83] This principle has been approved in modern English decisions.

23–142 **United City Merchants.** Thus, in *United City Merchants (Investments) Ltd v Royal Bank of Canada*,[84] a bill of lading issued on December 16 was fraudulently dated December 15 so as to convey the impression that the goods had been shipped before the end of the shipping period specified in the letter of credit. This fraud was committed by the shipping agents and without the sellers' knowledge.

The House of Lords held that, in the circumstances, the fraud exception did not apply. Lord Diplock emphasised two points. The first was the lack of any rational ground for drawing a distinction between a case in which the documents contained an inaccurate detail inserted inadvertently by the maker of the document and "the like documents where the same inaccuracy had been inserted by the maker of the document with intent to deceive, among others, the seller/beneficiary himself."[85] His Lordship's second point concerned the nature of the fact misrepresented in the instant case. Counsel for the bank urged that as a bill of lading showing the true loading date of October 16, would have been a bad tender, the misstatement related to a material fact. Lord Diplock held this to be too wide a construction of materiality. The bill of lading here tendered was in no way a

---

[82] 31 N.Y.S. 2d 631 (1941).

[83] *ibid.*, at p.634. See also *Old Colony Trust Co. v Lawyers' Title and Trust Co.*, 297 F. 152 at 158 (1924). The modern American case law in point is substantial. See, *e.g. Marine Midland Grace Trust Co. v Banco del Pais SA*, 261 F.Supp. 884 (1966); *Banco Espan ol de Credito v State Street Bank and Trust Co.*, 409 F. 2d 711 (1969); *United Bank Ltd v Cambridge Sporting Goods Corp.*, 360 N.E. 2d 943 (N.Y. 1976) (where the description of old mildewed gloves as new boxing gloves was held a fraud) and cases concerning standby credits, below, para.23–242. *Cf. Maurice O'Meara Co. v National Park Bank of New York*, 146 N.E. 636 at 639 (1925).

[84] [1983] A.C. 168 rvsg., on this point, [1981] 1 Lloyd's Rep. 604 and restoring [1979] 1 Lloyd's Rep. 267. For earlier dicta, see *Société Metallurgique D'Aubrives & Villerupt v British Bank for Foreign Trade* (1922) 11 Ll.L.R. 168 at 170; *Malas (Hamzeh) & Sons v British Imex Industries Ltd* [1958] 2 Q.B. 127 at 130. See also cases concerning performance bonds, below, paras 23–275 *et seq.*

[85] [1983] A.C. 168 at 187. Under U.C.C. s.5–109(b) (Rev.) an injunction may be granted to enjoin payment if the documents are forged or fraudulent or if the beneficiary perpetrated a fraud on the issuer or applicant: *Cromwell v Commerce and Energy Bank*, 464 So. 2d 721 (La. 1985); and see *WorldLink Inc. v HSBC Bank, No.604118/1999* (NY Sup. Ct, May 23, 2000).

nullity. The goods shipped were those contracted for and there was, accordingly, no misrepresentation concerning their nature or value. His Lordship indicated that the beneficiary might possibly be able to enforce the letter of credit even if the documents were rendered valueless by a third party's fraud, but appears to have left the point open.[86]

Critique. It is clear that in *United City Merchants'* case the document was valid and that the fraud was of a technical nature. In terms of commercial reality, the House of Lord's decision may be regarded with sympathy. But, conceptually, why should the beneficiary of the letter of credit be exonerated from liability for fraudulent statements contained in a document tendered by him to the bank? The beneficiary is promised payment against a set of documents described in the documentary credit. Can it be seriously argued that the promise is meant to cover false documents? Even if the fraudulent document cannot be described as waste paper, the misrepresentation may have been inserted with the intention of giving the appearance that the document is a good tender under the documentary credit. *United City Merchants* illustrates this point. It is disturbing that whilst a document stating the true loading date could have been rejected by the bank in the light of the doctrine of strict compliance, a document in which the loading date was fraudulently misrepresented by its maker constituted a valid tender in the beneficiary's hands. 23–143

Etablissement Esefka. Support for the view that a forged or fraudulent document constitutes a bad tender is to be found in *Etablissement Esefka International Anstalt v Central Bank of Nigeria*.[87] The bank had paid out most of the amount of the credit against a set of documents including a bill of lading and a certificate of origin, the former of which was alleged to have been a forgery and the latter to include fraudulent misstatements. In respect of some interim applications made in respect of the seller's action for the balance of the credit, Lord Denning observed that the "documents ought to be correct and valid in respect of each parcel. If that condition is broken by forged or fraudulent documents being presented—in respect of any one parcel—the defendants [the bankers] have a defence in point of law against being liable in respect of that parcel."[88] His Lordship thought that the bankers would further have a counterclaim in respect of money already paid against the documents in question. Notably, the beneficiary's misstatement which induces the negotiating bank to believe that an irregular set of documents is regular, involves fraud or deceit.[89] 23–144

---

[86] *ibid.*, at pp.186–188. And note that the law does not recognise a separate or complementary doctrine of "nullity" under which a false document could be rejected even if it was not tainted with fraud: *Montrod Ltd v Grundkotter Fleischvertriebs GmbH* [2001] 1 All E.R. (Comm) 368; rev. in part [2002] 1 W.L.R. 1975 (CA).
[87] [1979] 1 Lloyd's Rep. 445.
[88] *ibid.*, at p.447. But see further, para.23–143 concerning the fact that the forgery in the *Esefka* case was committed by the transferee of the letter of credit.
[89] *KBC Bank v Industrial Steels (UK) Ltd* [2001] 1 All E.R. (Comm) 409. For misstatements in documents tendered under an international sale of goods, see *Shinhan Bank Ltd v Sea Containers Ltd* [2000] 2 Lloyd's Rep. 406.

23–145 **Limitations of fraud principle.** The fraud principle must, however, be applied with care.[90] First, it is not always easy to determine whether an alleged discrepancy between the description of the goods in the documents and their actual nature is indicative of a fraud. Unless there is a blatant fraud, the banker cannot assert the deficiency of the goods against the seller.[91] There must, in other words, be fraud as defined at common law, *viz*., deceit.[92] Mere suspicions of frauds or base allegations raised by the applicant for the credit are inadequate.[93] Secondly, fraud is difficult to prove.[94] However, in *United Trading Corp. v Allied Arab Bank Ltd*,[95] which concerned an allegedly fraudulent call made under a performance bond, Ackner L.J., who delivered the Court of Appeal's judgment, thought the onus of proof, borne by the account party who asserted the beneficiary's fraud, ought not to be overstated. To establish fraud it was not necessary to rule out any other, innocent, explanation for the beneficiary's demand. It was important not to impose such an unrealistic requisite. His Lordship observed: "We would expect the Court to require strong corroborative evidence of the allegation, usually in the form of contemporary documents, particularly those emanating from the [beneficiary]. In general, for the evidence of fraud to be clear, we would expect the [beneficiary] to have been given an opportunity to answer the allegation and to have failed to provide any, or any adequate answer in circumstances where one could properly be expected. If the Court considers that on the material before it the only realistic inference to draw is that of fraud, then the seller would have made out a sufficient case of fraud."[96] Ackner L.J. added that it was contrary to the interests of international commerce or of the banking community as a whole that the important machinery furnished by bankers' irrevocable undertakings be misused for the purposes of fraud. Support for this view is echoed in other modern cases.[97]

23–146 **Not against third parties.** The third restriction to the fraud rule is that, on the present state of the authorities, it is available only against the beneficiary and, even in this case, subject to the principle of *United City*

[90] For an interesting comparison of the English and Chinese law in point, see [2004] J.B.L. 155.
[91] *Discount Records Ltd v Barclays Bank Ltd* [1975] 1 W.L.R. 315.
[92] *G K N Contractors Ltd v Lloyds Bank Plc* (1985) 30 Build L.R. 48; *Korea Industry Co. v Andoll* [1990] 2 Lloyd's Rep. 183 (CA S'pore).
[93] *Society of Lloyds v Canadian Imperial Bank of Commerce* [1993] 2 Lloyd's Rep. 579; and see further cases dealing with performance bonds, below, paras 23–270 *et seq.* For a recent definition of fraud see *Standard Chartered Bank v Bank of Pakistan* [2000] 1 Lloyd's Rep. 218.
[94] But prima facie evidence, or strong evidence that a fraud had taken place, may induce the court to refuse to grant summary judgment: *Solo Industries (UK) Ltd v Camara Bank* [2001] 1 W.L.R. 1800 (CA).
[95] [1985] 2 Lloyd's Rep. 554; and see [1985] J.B.L. 232.
[96] *ibid.*, at p.561. That a mere suspicion of fraud does not justify rejection of a tender, see *Society of Lloyd's v Canadian Imperial Bank of Commerce*, above; *Inflatable Toy Co. Pty Ltd v State Bank of NSW* (1994) 34 N.S.W.L.R. 243.
[97] *Tukan Timber Ltd v Barclays Bank Plc* [1987] 1 F.T.L.R. 154 and the Australian authorities of *Contronic Distributors Pty Ltd v Bank of NSW* [1984] 3 N.S.W.R. 110; *Hortico (Australia) Pty Ltd v Energy Equipment Co. (Aust) Pty Ltd* [1985] 1 N.S.W.R. 545.

Merchants' case.[98] Moreover, in *Discount Records Ltd v Barclays Bank Ltd*[99] Megarry J. held that a holder in due course of a bill drawn under the documentary credit should not be enjoined from enforcing it by reason of the seller's fraud and, on the same reasoning, the fraud should not constitute a defence to that holder's action to enforce the credit. Equally, questions can arise if the fraud is committed by the transferee of the documentary credit. Could the fraud, *e.g.* the forgery of a bill of lading, be raised against the original beneficiary when he tenders the documents? Is it arguable that he warrants the genuineness of the bill of lading proferred by the transferee?[1]

Enjoining beneficiary alone. Where the party seeking to enforce the letter of credit is the beneficiary, it is occasionally sought to obtain an injunction precluding him from making a call but without joining the issuing bank or the confirming bank as a defendant.[2] The argument is that the order granted in such a case would not overtly preclude the bank from performing its irrevocable undertaking. The injunction, the argument proceeds, would accordingly not interfere with the operations of international trade. In consequence, a mere allegation of fraud on the beneficiary's part ought to be an adequate ground for the exercise of the court's discretion. Although the argument has found favour in one recent authority,[3] it has been rejected by Phillips J. in *Deutsche Rückversicherung AG v Walbrook Insurance Co. Ltd.*[4] His Lordship held that an injunction restraining the beneficiary from making a call under the credit would be granted only to the extent that the facts of the case justified the granting of an order precluding the bank from making payment. 23–147

Summary. It would appear to follow that, in English law, the fraud doctrine has remained subject to telling restrictions. The best advice that can be given to a banker, when a buyer demands that he reject a set of documents on the ground of the seller's alleged fraud, is to request the 23–148

---

[98] [1983] A.C. 168.

[99] Above. This point was already emphasised in the *Sztejn* case and is now established in s.5–109(a) of the Uniform Commercial Code (Rev.). The point, though, was left open by the House of Lords in *United City Merchants'* case, above. As regards the position of an assignee of a deferred payment credit if fraud is discovered after the acceptance of the documents tendered but prior to the maturity of the payment obligation, see *Banco Santander SA v Bank Paribas* [1999] 2 All E.R. 18, affirmed [2001] All E.R. (Comm) 776.

[1] Such a fraud was alleged to have occurred in *Etablissement Esefka International Anstalt v Central Bank of Nigeria*, above, but the question was not resolved in the case. Neither was it conclusively answered in *United City Merchants*, above, see above, para.23–142.

[2] And see *Agasha Mugasha* [2004] J.B.L. 515.

[3] *Themehelp Ltd v West* [1996] Q.B. 84, CA (in which, however, there was evidence of fraud); and see below, para.23–280.

[4] [1996] 1 Lloyd's Rep. 345; but contrast, as regards performance bonds *Themehelp Ltd v West* [1996] Q.B. 84.

buyer to apply for an injunction restraining the seller from utilising the credit and precluding payment on the bank's part.[5]

23–149 **Relaxation of rule in the United States.** In what appeared a novel approach at the time, American courts granted temporary restraining orders on the basis of a strong suspicion of fraud respecting demands made under standby credits opened in favour of Iranian beneficiaries just before the revolution.[6] Principally, such interim injunctions were granted where the account party brought strong evidence that the demand was unjustified and that the enforcement of the facility would cause him irreparable harm because an amount paid would be practically irrecoverable by proceedings in Iran.[7] A brief analysis of the American doctrine is warranted.

23–150 **Nature of American doctrine.** The modern American doctrine is governed by section 5–109(a)(Rev.) of the Uniform Commercial Code. According to it, if "a required document is forged or fraudulent or honour of the presentation would facilitate a material fraud by the beneficiary on the issuer or applicant" the bank must nevertheless make payment to an innocent third party, such as a negotiating bank or even an assignee. In other—appropriate—cases payment may be enjoined. This provision is, in effect, traceable to the classic case of *Sztejn v J Henry Schroder Banking Corporation*, discussed earlier.[8] That this doctrine could not be invoked where there was a mere variation in quality or a defect in the goods was, originally, established in *Maurice O'Meara Co. v National Park Bank of New York*.[9] A later decision of the Circuit Court of Appeals reinforces this proposition, by showing that to be pleaded successfully a fraud has to go to the very root of the matter and, further, that mere suspicions based on allegations are not to be confused with proof.[10] The case of *Paris Savings and Loan Association v Walden*[11] shows that this basic concept has not changed. At the same time, a fundamental departure in the documents from the true facts, such as the description of old, padded ripped and

---

[5] For the feasibility of this advice, see the observation of Sellers L.J. in *Malas (Hamzeh) & Sons v British Imex Industries Ltd* [1958] 2 Q.B. 127 at 130. But note that, even if evidence of fraud is available, an injunction will be granted only if on the "balance of convenience" it ought to be approved: *Czarnikow-Rionda Sugar Trading Inc. v Standard Bank London Ltd* [1999] 2 Lloyd's Rep. 187.

[6] *Dynamics Corp. of America v Citizens and Southern National Bank*, 356 F.Supp. 991 (1973); *Harris Corp. v National Iranian Radio and Television*, 691 F. 2d 1344 (1982); *Itek Corp. v First National Bank of Boston*, 566 F.Supp. 1210 (1983). But the strict rule has not been universally abandoned in the United States; see: *KMW International v Chase Manhattan Bank*, 609 F. 2d 10 (1979); *American Bell International Inc. v Islamic Republic of Iran*, 474 F.Supp. 420 (1979); *Werner Lehara International Inc. v Harris Trust and Savings Bank*, 484 F.Supp. 65 (1980).

[7] *Touche, Ross & Co. v Manufacturers Hanover Trust Co.*, 434 N.Y.S. 2d 575 (1980); *Harris Corp. v National Iranian Radio and Television*, 691 F. 2d 1344 (1982); *Rockwell International v Citibank*, 719 F. 2d 583 (1983).

[8] 31 N.Y.S. 2d 631 (1941), above, para.23–138.

[9] 146 N.E. 636 (1925), affirmed 148 N.E. 725 (1925).

[10] *Dulien Steel Products Inc. v Bankers Trust Co.* 298 F. 2d 836 (1962).

[11] 730 S.W. 2d 355 (Ct.App. Tex. 1987).

mildewed gloves as new boxing gloves, constitutes a fraud within section 5-109(a).[12]

Recent analysis: the main points. The American courts have widened the scope of the doctrine in recent years, showing a readiness to grant temporary restraining orders pending trial where such a course is dictated by considerations of justice. This important development took place during the Iranian crisis, when unfounded calls were made under performance bonds issued in favour of Iranian companies. In *Warner v Central Trust Co.*, the Sixth Circuit Court of Appeals summarised the new doctrine respecting the grant of such orders in the following words: "the factors to be considered by a district court in exercising its discretion to grant a preliminary injunction are: (1) Whether the claimant (*viz*., the buyer) has shown a strong or substantial likelihood or probability of success on the merits; (2) Whether the claimant has shown irreparable injuries; (3) Whether the issuance of a preliminary injunction would cause substantial harm to others; (4) Whether the public interest would be served by issuing a preliminary injunction."[13] The third factor in question was described in *Friendship Materials v Michigan Brick Inc.*[14] as the "balance of hardship" principle. Under it, a court is required to assess whether the granting of the injunction would cause greater harm to the beneficiary than what its refusal would cause to the buyer. 23–151

Irreparable harm: *Itek*. Many of the American cases concerning the new doctrine concentrated on the issue respecting the irreparable harm that might be caused by a refusal to grant a restraining order. This point, as well as the modern definition of fraud, are analysed in *Itek Corp. v First National Bank of Boston*.[15] Prior to the outbreak of the Islamic revolution, Itek—the account party—agreed to sell certain optical equipment to the Iranian Ministry of War. To cover the Ministry in respect of down payments made under the contract of sale and also as against the supply of defective goods, Itek instructed FNBB to issue its own standby credits in favour of Bank Melli Iran, which in turn issued first demand guarantees in favour of the Ministry. The contract of sale included a *force majeure* clause, entitling either party to withdraw from the contract if an export licence was cancelled in the United States. Following the outbreak of the revolution which led to cancellation of the licences, Itek eventually invoked the *force majeure* clause and served notice cancelling the contract. The Ministry then made a demand on Bank Melli, which had by then been nationalised, and Bank Melli in turn made a demand on FNBB. 23–152

---

[12] *United Bank Ltd v Cambridge Sporting Goods Corp.,* 392 N.Y.S. 2d 265 at 267 (N.Y.C.A. 1976); and see *United Technologies Corp. v Citibank NA*, 469 F. Supp. 473 at 478 (1979); *Prutscher v Fidelity International Bank* 502 F. Supp. 535 (1980); *Siderius Inc. v Wallace Co.* 583 S.W. 2d 852 (1981). As regards the meaning of fraud in calls made under standby credits, see below, para.23–240.

[13] 715 F. 2d 1121 at 1123 (1983). See also *Mason County Medical Association v Knebel,* 563 F. 2d 256 at 261 (6th Cir. 1977); *Martin-Marietta Corp. v Bendix Corp.,* 690 F. 2d. 558 at 564–65 (6th Cir. 1982).

[14] 679 F. 2d 100 at 102 (6th Cir. 1982).

[15] 730 F. 2d 19 (1984).

Upholding the District Court's injunction, the First Circuit Court of Appeals held that the call was fraudulent and that the refusal of an injunction would cause irreparable harm to Itek. If FNBB had to pay, Itek's only course would be to institute proceedings in Iran according to the law of that country. The Court held: "The recent history of relations between Iran and the United States indicates that this remedy is inadequate. Itek's efforts to recover money that Itek is legally owed through the Iranian courts would be futile."[16] A discharge of the injunction would thus mean that Itek could not recover the loss sustained by it.

23–153 **Irreparable harm: further cases.** Itek suggests that the account party stands to sustain irreparable harm from the court's refusal to grant an injunction if he does not have any realistic alternative remedy in the event of payment. Thus, in *Itek* and in the slightly later Iranian case of *Rockwell International Systems Inc. v Citibank*[17] an action in Iran was, obviously, deemed an unrealistic alternative. Another instance is where the account party is insolvent or faces bankruptcy.[18] If payment were ordered, there would be no viable way to recover the money. But not every financial injury that might be incurred by the account party as a consequence of the court's refusal to grant a temporary restraining order constitutes irreparable harm. Thus, the mere fact that the refusal to grant the injunction would force the account party to make payment he can ill afford, does not constitute such harm.[19] Another important principle is that, if the account party has a viable alternative remedy such as arbitration in accordance with a term of the underlying contract, the refusal of an injunction is not seen as causing him irreparable harm.[20] It is accepted that where the account party is unable to establish irreparable harm, an injunction is refused.[21]

23–154 **Unauthorised letters of credit: Bank of China's case.** Different problems arise if a letter of credit is issued by one of the issuing bank's employees without authority as a result of collusion between him and the applicant for the credit or if the applicant himself uses a blank form supplied by such an employee in order to execute the facility. The type of problem arising in such a case was considered in two modern cases, one of which dealt with a forged form and the other with tested telexes issued by fraudsters. In the first case, *Bank of China v Standard Chartered Bank of Australia Ltd*,[22] the claimants agreed to grant a facility to D Ltd, provided they were furnished with a standby credit for the amount involved. Such a

[16] *ibid.*, at p.22.
[17] 719 F. 2d 583, 587 (2nd Cir. 1983).
[18] *Paccar International Inc. v Commercial Bank of Kuwait,* 587 F. 2d 783 at 787–788 (C.D. Cal. 1984); *Alamo Savings Association v Forward Construction Corp.*, 746 S.W. 2d 897 at 901 (CA Tex 1988).
[19] *Sperry International Trade Inc. v Government of Israel,* 670 F. 2d 8 at 11 (2nd Cir. 1982); but contrast *Philip Bros Inc. v Oil Country Specialists*, 709 S.W. 2d 262 (CA Tex. 1986).
[20] *Foxboro Co. v Arabian American Oil Co.,* 805 F. 2d 34 at 37 (1st Cir. 1986).
[21] *Würtembergische Fire Insurance Co. v Pan Atlantic Underwriters Ltd,* 519 N.Y.S. 2d 57 at 58 (App. Div. 1987).
[22] Unreported, decision of July 16, 1991; rvsg. Giles J. (1991) 23 N.S.W.L.R. 164.

document, executed on the letterhead of the defendants' Hong Kong office and signed by two individuals above the words "authorised signatures", was in due course handed by an officer of D Ltd to the claimants. At the request of the claimants' Sydney branch, which did not have a correspondent banks relationship with the defendants' Hong Kong office and accordingly did not have a record of the defendants' authorised signatures, two of the officers of the defendants' Sydney office examined the letter of credit and appended their signatures beneath a rubber stamp reading "signatures verified". It subsequently turned out that the signatures on the letter of credit were forgeries.

The Court of Appeal of New South Wales decided that the defendants were not estopped from pleading the forgeries. What the defendants' officers at the Sydney branch had been asked to do was to verify the apparent correspondence of the signatures on the letter of credit with those set out in the Hong Kong office's authorised signatures book. The defendants' officers did not verify that signatures were, in addition, genuine.

The conclusion to be drawn from the decision of the New South Wales Court of Appeal is that the only verification to be relied upon with safety by a bank, which finds itself in the position of the claimants in the instant case, is a representation emanating from the very office that is supposed to have issued the letters of credit. Bearing in mind the danger that an enquiry directed to that office might be answered by the very person who had perpetrated the fraud, the beneficiary bank is in an unenviable position.

***Bank of Tokyo* case: unauthorised telex.** A different principle applies where a documentary credit is opened by an unauthorised tested telex. In *Standard Bank London Ltd v Bank of Tokyo Ltd*[23] one X asked the S Bank in London to finance certain transactions on the security of standby credits to be issued by the Kuala Lumpur office of BOT, a Japanese bank. Over a period of some eighteen months, X delivered to the S Bank three letters of credit which, on their face, appeared to have been issued by BOT. In reality, all three were skillfully perpetrated forgeries. Any suspicions which the S Bank may have had were, however, allayed when it received in respect of each letter of credit a tested telex in which BOT confirmed the authenticity of the facility. In reality, though, these tested telexes were also issued by the fraudsters, who got access to BOT's terminal and code. When called upon to pay, BOT denied liability. Its main argument was that the circumstances of each transaction were such as to put the S Bank on enquiry. In failing to investigate, the S Bank had committed a breach of a duty of care owed to BOT and, in consequence, was not entitled to enforce the letters of credit. 23–155

Waller J. gave judgment for the S Bank. Having cited the evidence of an expert witness, who described a "tested telex" as "the electronic signature of the bank sending the message", his Lordship emphasised that it was unchallenged that banks all over the world relied with complete confidence on tested telexes. "The tested telex system" he added "is meant to avoid

[23] [1995] 2 Lloyd's Rep. 169.

arguments in relation to authority".[24] Rejecting an argument to the effect that, in the instant case, the S Bank was put on enquiry, his Lordship said that "the duty to inquire will depend on the circumstances of each and every case, and what should, or may, put someone on enquiry, will also depend on the circumstances of any individual case. Thus, the more usual the circumstances and the clearer a representation appears to be, the less the duty to inquire should be, and the less likely there will be to be circumstances which will put anyone on enquiry."[25] It may be safely concluded that, when a documentary credit bears an appropriate test, the recipient of the message is put on enquiry only in the most unusual circumstances.

23–156 **Acceptance of tender.** Under Article 16(c) of the 1983 Revision, the issuing banker had a "reasonable time" for the examination of the documents tendered under the documentary credit. This time honoured rule[26] was modified in the new UCP Under Article 13(b) the issuing banker has to complete the examination of the documents within a "reasonable time not to exceed seven banking days following the day of receipt of the documents". A confirming bank and any nominated bank are granted the same length of time.

The phrase "reasonable time", used in the earlier versions of the Code without amplification, was too vague for comfort. Generally, it was believed that the length of the period involved varied, depending primarily on the number of the documents tendered, on their language and complexity, on the amount involved and on other circumstances such as the time left between the tender of the documents and the arrival of the goods at their destination. A survey conducted on the subject suggested that, by and large, banks regarded documents as rejected out of time if the issuing banker retained them for more than five or six days, although a period of seven to eight days might be acceptable in special circumstances. However, the practice in point varied to a considerable extent in different parts of the world. What might have been considered unreasonable in Zürich could very well be considered acceptable in a less developed centre.[27] The object of the new Article 13(b) is to define the maximum period allowed in precise terms. But the "reasonable time" element is not excised. Whilst the maximum period of seven days would now be available in the case of unusually bulky and complex sets of documents a shorter "reasonable time" remains applicable in the case of run of the mill sets.

---

24 *ibid.*, at p.173.

25 *ibid.*, at p.176.

26 1974 Revision, Art. 8(d); 1963 Revision, Art. 8; 1951 Revision, Art. 10. As regards rejection of electronically presented documents, see above, para.23–040.

27 Thus, in *Marine Midland Grace Trust Co. v Banco del Pais SA*, 261 F.Supp. 884 at 889 (1966) ten days were held to be on the long side but the matter was left to the jury; in *Morgan Guarantee Trust Co. v Vend Technologies*, 100 A.D. 2d 782 (N.Y. 1984) a period of six calendar days was considered reasonable; but the German *Bundesgerichtshof*, in its judgment of July 2, 1984, *Wertpapier Mitteilungen* 1984, p.1214, regarded eight calendar days unreasonable for the rejection of a run of the mill set. See further Ellinger [1985] J.B.L. 406; *cf.* "UCP 1974/1983 Compared", ICC Brochure No. 411, p.33; "UCP 500/400 compared", ICC Brochure No.511, pp.40–43. As regards the nature of the bank's examination, see above, para.23–126.

Bankers Trust case. The problems that arise from the use of the phrase "reasonable time" are illustrated by *Bankers Trust Co. v State Bank of India*.[28] In this case the set, comprising over 900 documents, was released by the issuing bank to the buyer, so as to enable him to examine the documents for the purpose of deciding whether to reject them or to waive the discrepancies discovered in them. The buyer took approximately three days for the examination of the set, which was a period comparable to that spent by the issuing bank's own staff on their examination. Relying on expert evidence and disagreeing with a view expressed by Gatehouse J. in an earlier decision,[29] Hirst J. held that the documents should not be released to the buyer for a prolonged examination but only for a short period required to enable the buyer to consider the points referred to him by the bank. He held that the release of the documents to the buyer for a period of three days was excessive. His Lordship also indicated that a period of eight days was an unreasonable time for the bank's own examination of the documents. In reaching this second conclusion, Hirst J. relied principally on evidence respecting the practice of the London clearing banks whose aim it was to reach a decision on any set within three working days. **23–157**

Hirst J.'s decision was affirmed by the Court of Appeal.[30] On the question of reasonable time, their Lordships held that despite the complexity of the documents tendered under the documentary credit, a major bank operating in London ought not to have taken eight days for their examination.[31] There was, however, a disagreement on the related issue, of whether the issuing bank was entitled to release the documents to the buyer for his own examination. This issue has since been settled in Article 14(c) of the new UCP "If the issuing bank determines that the documents appear on their face not to be in accordance with the terms and conditions of the Credit, it may in its sole judgment approach the Applicant for a waiver of the discrepancy(ies). This does not, however, extend the period mentioned in sub-Article 13(b)." It follows that the "reasonable time not exceeding seven banking days", determined in Article 13(b), comprises the time spent by the issuing bank on its consultation with the applicant. Notably, Article 14(c) does not sanction the submission of the documents to the applicant for approval where the issuing bank concludes that they constitute a valid tender. In the same spirit, Article 14(b) states that banks must determine, "on the basis of the documents alone whether they appear on their face to be in accordance with the terms and conditions of the Credit".[32]

---

[28] [1991] 1 Lloyd's Rep. 587, noted in [1991] J.B.L. at 170.
[29] *Co-operative Centrale Raiffaisen-Boerenleen-Bank BA v Sumitomo Bank (The Royan)* [1987] 1 Lloyd's Rep. 345 at 348, revd. on another point and affirmed in part: [1988] 2 Lloyd's Rep. 250.
[30] [1991] 2 Lloyd's Rep. 443.
[31] The flexibility of "reasonable time" has been emphasised in other commercial centres. See, *e.g. United Bank Ltd v Banque Nationale de Paris* [1992] 2 S.L.R. 64 (Chao Hick Tin J., S'pore Sup. Ct.).
[32] But note that the general practice of consulting the applicant was recognised by Farquharson L.J. and by Sir John Megaw in *Bankers Trust Co. v State Bank of India,* above; and see to the same effect *Bhojwani v Chung Khiaw Bank Ltd* [1990] 3 M.L.J.

23–158 **Notification to beneficiary.** Article 13(b) of the new UCP is augmented by Article 14(d). If the banker decides that the documents do not comply with the requirements of the credit, he must give notice—stating that the documents are rejected[33]—without delay (but no later than the close of the seventh banking day following the receipt of the documents) by telecommunication or, if that is not possible, by other expeditious means to the bank from which he received the documents or to the beneficiary. Such notice, which may also be given by telephone or *inter partes*,[34] must state all the discrepancies in respect of which the documents are being rejected.[35] The formulation of this provision, taken with but minor amendments from Article 16(d) of the 1983 Revision, differs from that of earlier versions—such as Article 8(e) of the 1974 Revision—under which the banker's duty was confined to stating "reasons" for the rejection. The object of the current formulation is to discourage vague reasons such as "documents rejected for various non-conformities".

23–159 **Rejection formula.** Under the new Article 14(d), identical to Article 16(d) of the 1983 Revision, the notice of rejection must state whether the issuing bank is holding the documents at the tenderor's order or is returning them to him. Two decisions of the Court of Appeal shed light on the meaning of these words. In *Co-operative Centrale Raiffeisen-Boerenleenbank BA v Sumitomo Bank Ltd (The Royan)*[36] the confirming bank raised objections to the documents tendered by the negotiating bank and advised the negotiating bank: "Please consider these documents at your disposal until we receive our Principal's instructions concerning the discrepancies mentioned". . . . Gatehouse J. held that these words did not comply with the procedure for rejection. The reason for this was that the words used in *The Royan* did not bring the matter to an end by a conclusive rejection of the documents. Instead, they manifested the confirming bank's intention to await the negotiating bank's instructions. Reversing his decision, the Court of Appeal held that the formula involved indicated in clear terms that the documents had not been accepted. Lloyd L.J. said that "it was not necessary for [the confirming bank] to say, in so many words, that they were holding the documents at [the negotiating bank's] disposal".[37] Article 14(d) did not go so far as to require the use of a precise formula. It was sufficient for the confirming bank to indicate, in unambiguous language, that it was not accepting the documents.

If, however, the confirming or issuing bank uses words that do not manifest a clear intention to release the documents, it fails to comply with

---

260 (S'pore, CA). For a more recent consideration of "reasonable time" see *Seaconsar Far East Ltd v Bank Markazi Jomhouri Islami Iran* [1997] 2 Lloyd's Rep. 89, affirmed [1999] 1 Lloyd's Rep. 36, CA.

33 *Voest-Alpine Trading USA Corp. v Bank of China*, 288 F. 3rd. 262 (5th Cir. 2000). A mere listing of the discrepancies is inadequate.

34 *Seaconsar Far East Ltd v Bank Markazi Jomhouri Islami Iran*, above.

35 But note that failure to state such reasons does not necessarily preclude the bank from relying on them, if their disclosure could not have aided the seller to remedy the defects: *Wing on Bank Ltd v American National Bank and Trust Co.*, 457 F. 2d 328 (1972).

36 [1988] 2 Lloyd's Rep. 250, affg. and rev. in pt [1987] 1 Lloyd's Rep. 345.

37 [1988] 2 Lloyd's Rep. 250 at 254.

the procedure in question. In *Bankers Trust Co. v State Bank of India*[38] the issuing bank advised that it would hold the documents at the negotiating bank's disposal only after that bank had reimbursed the amount drawn by it under the letter of credit. Their Lordships held, unanimously, that these words implied that the issuing bank was retaining the documents for the time being. The formula used was, accordingly, incompatible with Article 14(d). More recently, David Steel J. considered a telex in which the issuing bank stated: "should the [goods] be accepted by the applicant, we shall release the docs to them without further notice to you unless yr instructions to the contrary received prior to our payment". His Lordship held that, as this notice did not manifest the tenderee's unequivocal intention to part with the documents, the prescribed rejection procedure had not been compiled with. A similarly strict construction was given to Article 14(d) by the Supreme Court of Singapore in *United Bank Ltd v Banque Nationale de Paris.*[39] Chao Hick Tin J. held that the issuing bank's notice, in which it listed certain discrepancies and stated that it was holding the documents on a "collection basis", did not constitute a valid rejection in terms of this provision. The position is the same under the current Article 14(d).

Effect of failure to comply. If the issuing bank rejects a faulty set of documents in a manner which complies with the procedure laid down in Article 14 of the new UCP, it is entitled to claim from the remitting bank the refund of any amounts already paid in respect of the transaction. Under paragraph (e) of Article 14, an issuing bank which fails to comply with the foregoing provisions or which fails to return the documents is precluded from asserting their non-conformity.[40] It is, however, important to recall that Article 14 applies only where the issuing bank, the confirming bank or a nominated bank wish to reject a set of documents discovered to be discrepant. There are, of course, situations in which the decision to refuse a tender is based on grounds other than "discrepancies" in the documents, for instance, on fraud in the transaction or on the fact that a third party bank, that claims payment, did not "negotiate" the document by furnishing value. It has been held that Article 14(e) does not bar the issuing bank from raising such "non-documentary objections" despite its non-compliance with the prescribed rejection procedure.[41] 23–160

Need to verify payee's identity. Apart from satisfying itself that the documents are regular, the bank must also ensure that it makes payment to the right party. Thus, the bank should not assume that an agent, who is 23–161

[38] [1991] 2 Lloyd's Rep. 443.

[39] [1992] 2 S.L.R. 64; and see *Hing Yip Fat Co. Ltd v Daiwa Bank Ltd* [1991] 2 H.K.L.R. 35; and the leading American case of *Kerr-McGee Chemical Corp. v Federal Deposit Insurance Corp.*, 872 F. 2d 971 (1989). For an interesting analysis, see *Hamilton Bank NA v Kookmin Bank*, 245 F. 3d 82 (2001).

[40] As regards the position where the UCP does not apply, *cf. Hansson v Hamel and Horley Ltd* [1922] 2 A.C. 36 at 46 with *Bank Melli Iran v Barclays Bank D.C.O.* [1951] 2 Lloyd's Rep. 367 at 377–378. *Cf. Commercial Banking Co. of Sydney Ltd v Jalsard Pty Ltd* [1973] A.C. 279 at 286, which indicates that a prolonged retention of the documents by the bank may constitute a breach of its contracts with the buyer and seller.

[41] *Amixco Asia (Pte) Ltd v Bank Bumiputra Malaysia Brhd* [1992] 2 S.L.R. 943 (Selvam J., Sup. Ct. S'pore).

asked by the seller to prepare the documents and to arrange for their tender, is also authorised to receive payment. If the bank pays the amount of the credit to the agent, it may have to pay it over again to the seller.[42]

(b) *Banker's Right of Recourse Against Seller and of Set-Off*

23–162 **Problem of recourse.** In certain cases the issuing banker may wish to claim repayment of the amount paid to the seller under a documentary credit. A typical situation in which this problem may arise is where the issuing banker accepts a faulty tender of documents and has it rejected by the buyer. But it is dubious whether the issuing banker has such a right of recourse. The question must be considered both from the point of view of the law of negotiable instruments and of the general principles of the law of contract. The provisions of the UCP must likewise be examined.

23–163 **Position under law of negotiable instruments.** As regards the law of negotiable instruments, it should be borne in mind that the undertaking of the banker may assume one of three forms. First, he may promise to pay cash against the tender of the required documents or to make such payment at a stated deferred time. Secondly, he may promise to accept a draft drawn on him and accompanied by the documents. Thirdly, he may promise to negotiate a draft drawn by the seller on the buyer and accompanied by the documents. In the first case the law of negotiable instruments will, obviously, not apply. In the second case, where the banker is the acceptor of the draft and the seller the drawer, the law of negotiable instruments does not confer on the former a right of recourse against the latter.

The third case, however, gives rise to problems. The seller here is the drawer and the banker an indorser or holder. Thus, if the draft is dishonoured by the drawee (the buyer), the issuing banker may claim to have a right of recourse against the seller under section 43(2) or 47(2) of the Bills of Exchange Act 1882. Moreover, the case of *Sassoon (MA) & Sons Ltd v International Banking Corp.*[43] lays down that the fact that a draft is stated to be drawn under a documentary credit does not necessarily exclude a right of recourse. However, this was a case in which a discounting banker sought to claim recourse against the seller after the dishonour of a draft by the buyer. As regards the relationship of seller and issuing banker, an American authority suggests that the "general provision . . . which permits the holder or any subsequent indorser of a negotiable instrument dishonoured to maintain an action thereon against the drawer is not applicable . . . because the drafts here involved specifically state that they are drawn under the irrevocable letter of credit, and by that the bank was required to pay when a draft and other documents specified were presented."[44] Thus, the Supreme Court of Washington treated the statement,

---

[42] *Cleveland Manufacturing Co. Ltd v Muslim Commercial Bank Ltd* [1981] 2 Lloyd's Rep. 646.
[43] [1927] A.C. 711 at 731.
[44] *Bank of East Asia Ltd v Pang*, 249 P. 1060 at 1063 (1926).

that a draft was drawn under a documentary credit, as tantamount to an exclusion of a right of recourse.[45] From a mercantile point of view this appears to be a satisfactory conclusion, as the parties do not intend to confer on the banker a right of recourse against the seller if the buyer dishonours the draft. In fact, if the banker were granted such a right of recourse, the main object of the transaction would be destroyed.

Position at common law.[46] In considering whether, in certain circumstances, the general principles of the common law may confer on the banker a right of recourse against the seller, a distinction must be drawn between three types of cases. First, the banker might wish to recover an amount paid to the seller, if the tender was affected with fraud. In this type of case the banker should be entitled to claim against the seller in deceit.[47] Secondly, the banker may wish to reclaim payment from the seller if the buyer fails. It is, however, difficult to see on what principle the issuing banker may establish such a claim, especially as a documentary credit constitutes a security given by the banker to the seller. Thirdly, the banker may wish to seek recourse to the seller if he has accepted, by mistake, a faulty set of documents tendered by the seller.[48] It is, however, to be doubted whether the banker should be allowed to claim the amount back as money paid under a mistake. In most cases the seller would change his position by parting with the documents against the banker's acceptance or payment. The decision of the House of Lords in *Lipkin Gorman v Karpnale Ltd*[49] shows that the bank would, thereupon, lose its action in restitution. In addition, it might, perhaps, be argued that the banker should be estopped from claiming that the money was paid under a mistake. Moreover, the banker is under a duty to examine the documents tendered to him and the seller is, thus, entitled to presume that, if the banker accepts the documents tendered, the set is regular.[50] In this situation, the seller might perhaps be entitled to claim that the banker had waived inquiry and that he should, therefore, be precluded from claiming that he had paid the amount of the credit under a mistake.[51] American authorities support the view that if the banker accepts a tender of documents he is not entitled to reclaim payment 23–164

---

[45] As to which exclusion, in England, see s.16(1) of the Bills of Exchange Act 1882. But the section applies only if the drawer inserts an express stipulation excluding a right of recourse.

[46] For a different view see D. Sheehan "Right of Recourse in Documentary Credit Transactions" [2005] J.B.L. 326.

[47] The money could in such a case be reclaimable in a quasi-contractual action: *Edward Owen Engineering Ltd v Barclays Bank International Ltd* [1978] Q.B. 159 at 170 citing with approval the unreported decision in *Bank Russo-Iran v Gordon, Woodroffe & Co. Ltd*, 1972. As regards the feasibility of a recourse action based on a misrepresentation in the invoice as to the nature of the goods see *Bank Leumi Le Israel BM v Cablefast Ltd*, decision of October 19, 1988 (CA unreported).

[48] And not that a defence based on a change in the payee's position when a nominated bank receives payment in the belief it is entitled to the funds: *Niru Baltery Manufacturing Co. v Milestone Trading* (No.1) [2004] All E.R. (Comm) 193, (CA).

[49] [1991] A.C. 548.

[50] *cf. Burke v Utah National Bank*, 66 N.W. 295 at 297 (1896).

[51] *cf. Beevor v Marler* (1898) 14 T.L.R. 259.

from the seller, even if the banker, due to a mistake, overlooked the irregularity of the documents.[52]

23–165 **Application of UCP** The argument, that the issuing banker does not have a right of recourse against the seller after the acceptance of documents tendered, is supported in respect of documentary credits incorporating the UCP by Articles 9(a) and 14(e). Under Article 9(a) the banker's undertaking to accept is definite and, where it assumes the form of a promise to negotiate a draft drawn on the buyer, it is defined as being an undertaking to negotiate without recourse. This language suggests that the draftsman meant to exclude the right of recourse in the only situation in which he thought it might arise. Under Article 14(e) if the issuing bank fails to comply with the procedure prescribed for the rejection of non-conforming documents, it is precluded from claiming that the documents are not in accordance with the terms and conditions of the credit. This, too, suggests that the Code rules out litigation, involving the regularity of the documents or the seller's right to the amount of the credit, once a tender has been accepted by the issuing banker. This principle would be defeated if the issuing banker could claim a right of recourse against the seller after the acceptance of documents tendered under the credit. There may, however, be room in certain cases for an action in deceit.

23–166 **Recourse where documents accepted under reserve.** Where the issuing or confirming banker disputes the regularity of the documents it may nevertheless agree to take them up and pay against a reserve or an indemnity. Unless the seller executes an indemnity, which defines the terms upon which the bank is entitled to claim repayment, the practice can lead to disputes. Thus, in *Banque de L'Indochine et de Suez SA v J H Rayner (Mincing Lane) Ltd*[53] the claimant bank, which had confirmed a letter of credit, agreed to accept under reserve documents tendered by the beneficiary. The bank, which did not obtain a formal indemnity from the beneficiary, set out in a letter details of the discrepancies which induced it to refuse to make unconditional payment. When the issuing bank, at the buyer's instruction, rejected the documents, the claimant bank demanded repayment from the beneficiary. The latter claimed that as the documents were regular he was entitled to retain the amount paid. Parker J. held that payment could be reclaimed only if the documents were faulty. But he gave judgment for the bank as he held that the documents were a bad tender. On the second point, his judgment was affirmed. But the Court of Appeal disagreed with his construction of the arrangement for payment under reserve. Kerr L.J. observed: "payment was to be made under reserve in the sense that the beneficiary would be bound to repay the money on demand if the issuing bank should reject the documents, whether on its own initiative

[52] *National City Bank of New York v Partola Manufacturing Co.*, 181 N.Y.S. 464 at 465 (1920); *Hibernia Bank and Trust Co. v J Aron & Co. Inc.*, 233 N.Y.S. 486 (1928). But under s.5–111 of the Uniform Commercial Code the banker may have an action for breach of warranty relating to the genuineness and regularity of the documents. No such warranty is recognised in English law: above, para.23–127.

[53] [1983] 1 Lloyd's Rep. 228, affg. [1982] 2 Lloyd's Rep. 476.

or on the buyer's instruction".[54] This duty was based on the reserve arrangement, which constituted a binding agreement between the parties. The bank would not have been prepared to pay under a reserve if its right of recourse would have been subject to its being able to prove that the documents were faulty.

Conclusions. Two conclusions can be drawn from this case. First, to avoid subsequent disputes, a bank that makes payment under reserve ought to spell out the conditions upon which it agrees to do so and, in particular, has to clarify that repayment is due quite regardless of the reasons given by the issuing bank or by the buyer for the rejection of the documents. Ideally, the bank should obtain an indemnity from the beneficiary. Secondly, the beneficiary ought to consider carefully whether to accept payment under reserve or to insist that the funds be paid unconditionally. If he believes that the documents are regular, his best course may be to insist on his rights rather than to accept conditional payment with the hope that matters will be sorted out. **23–167**

Finally, it should be pointed out that the arrangement for payment under reserve is strictly one between the bank and the beneficiary. This point is settled by Article 14(f) of the UCP, which is discussed subsequently.[55]

Issuing bank's right of set-off. Is the issuing bank entitled to set off against the amount, payable to the beneficiary under the letter of credit, an amount due to the bank from the beneficiary? In *Hong Kong and Shanghai Banking Corp. v Kloeckner & Co. AG*,[56] Hirst J. rejected the argument that such a set-off was incompatible with the doctrine of the autonomy of the letter for credit. Undoubtedly, the doctrine in question precluded the granting of an injunction to prevent payment and, further, implied that pleas related to the underlying transaction could not be raised as defences to the beneficiary's claim under the letter of credit. A set-off, however, involved the setting up of a cross-claim against the amount due to the beneficiary under the letter of credit. The independence of the letter of credit was not abrogated thereby. Allowing the set-off, Hirst J. emphasised that, in the instant case, the claim, the subject of the set-off, was closely linked with the demand made under the letter of credit. It was also a liquidated demand. His Lordship concluded: ". . . it would seem to me anomalous that such a set off should be unavailable in letter of credit cases, but available against bills of exchange which . . . are closely analogous in that a bill of exchange is also virtually equivalent to cash".[57] **23–168**

Position where proceeds assigned. Hirst J.'s decision suggests that problems may arise in cases in which the issuing bank, which seeks to exercise a right of set-off, is advised that the beneficiary has assigned the **23–169**

---

[54] *ibid.*, at p.234.
[55] Below, para.23–181.
[56] [1990] 2 Q.B. 514.
[57] *ibid.*, at p.526. Notably, Hirst J. held in respect of another issue arising in this case that a clause, excluding a right of set-off, was valid. As regards the tracing of money paid under a documentary credit issued on the basis of a fraudulent statement, see *Bank Tejarat v Hong Kong and Shanghai Banking Corp.* [1995] 1 Lloyd's Rep. 239.

proceeds of the documentary credit to his own bank.[58] Which of such two claims has priority, the issuing bank's right of set-off or the claim of the beneficiary's bank as assignee?

It will be recalled that the object of an assignment of the proceeds of a letter of credit is to enable the beneficiary to obtain credit against the security of the payment obligation undertaken by the issuing bank. Ordinarily, the assignment takes place before the beneficiary is ready to procure the documents to be tendered under the credit. In practice, the proceeds are assigned after the tender of the documents only where the facility involved is a deferred payment credit,[59] which does not provide for the drawing of a bill of change. Where the credit is available by the drawing of bills of exchange payable at a designated usage (such as 90 or 180 days sight) on the issuing or on the confirming bank, the beneficiary is able to raise credit after the tender of the documents but before the maturity of the bills by arranging for their negotiation or discount. The beneficiary's bank, which then becomes the negotiating bank, acquires an excellent security by obtaining the issuing or confirming bank's acceptances.

23–170 **Ranking.** The beneficiary's bank obtains an equally effective security where it obtains an assignment of the proceeds of the credit prior to the tender of the documents to the issuing or confirming bank. In such a case, the beneficiary's bank serves notice of the assignment on the issuing or confirming bank and, naturally, will tender the documents under the credit at a later stage. The notice served on the issuing or confirming bank gives the beneficiary's bank priority as from that time except as regards claims accrued to that other bank before it received notice of the assignment, even if these claims had not matured by the date of the notice but provided they matured by the time the assigned debt fell due.[60] As the word "accrued" means, in all probability, "ascertained" or "quantified", the end result is that usually the notice of assignment gives the beneficiary's bank priority as from the date of is communication to the issuing or confirming bank. In practice, if the issuing or confirming bank has claims that it seeks to set up in priority to the assignment, it advises the beneficiary's bank of their existence. The beneficiary's bank, in turn, is able to retain the bargaining power conferred on it by the possession of the shipping documents.

The beneficiary's bank acquires a considerably poorer security by an assignment executed after the tender of documents effected under a deferred payment credit. If, in such a case, the issuing or confirming bank, to whom the documents were tendered, sought to exercise a right of set-off which it had against the beneficiary, the beneficiary's bank might find that its claim was ranked below rights accrued to the other bank prior to the date of the notice of the assignment in question.[61] Consequently, the

[58] As regards assignment of proceeds, see above, paras 23–067 *et seq.*

[59] As defined in UCP, Art. 9(a)(ii), above, para.23–052.

[60] *Jeffryes v Agra and Masterman's Bank* (1886) L.R. 2 Eq. 674; *Re Pinto Leite, Ex p. Olivaes* [1929] 1 Ch. 221 at 236; see also *Business Computers Ltd v Anglo-African Leasing Ltd* [1977] 1 W.L.R. 578 at 585; Ellinger, Lomnicka and Hooley, *Modern Banking Law* (4th ed.), pp.812 *et seq.*

[61] As regards an assignee's position generally in letter of credit cases, see *Banco Santande SA v Banque Paribas* [2000] Lloyd's Rep. Bank 165, discussed above, para.23–062.

beneficiary's bank could very well lose out if the beneficiary had, in one way or another, managed to obtain credit also from that other bank.

(c) *Seller's Remedies*

Measure of damages. If the banker wrongfully refuses to accept a draft accompanied by the required documents, the seller is entitled to bring an action for the amount of the documentary credit and, where appropriate, for interest.[62] At the same time, some authorities indicate that the seller may opt to accept a breach of the banker's contract and sue for damages similar to those awarded for a breach of the buyer's obligation to accept delivery under a contract of sale. In *Urquhart, Lindsay & Co. Ltd v Eastern Bank Ltd*[63] the issuing banker opened an irrevocable credit covering several shipments of machinery. He wrongfully dishonoured one draft of the seller on the ground that, although the draft and documents conformed to the terms of the documentary credit, their amount exceeded the sum agreed upon in the contract of sale. The seller treated the dishonour of the draft as a repudiation by the banker of the entire documentary credit. The seller was allowed to recover the difference between, on the one hand, the value of the materials left on his hands plus the cost of such as he would have further provided, and, on the other hand, what the seller would have been entitled to receive for the manufactured goods from the buyers.[64] 23–171

Damages for delay in payment. It has been held that a bank is liable for loss directly resulting from an inexcusable delay in the performance of its undertaking in the letter of credit. In *Ozalid Group Export Ltd v African Continental Bank Ltd*[65] a letter of credit for US $125,939.22 was opened in favour of a British exporter. Although the exporter tendered the required documents before the expiry of the credit, the bank delayed payment for approximately two months. During this period the US dollar lost in parity as against the pound sterling and, as a result, the exporter obtained £2,987.17 less for the amount eventually paid in US dollars than he would have got if conversion had been effected at the time at which payment had been due. Giving judgment for the exporter for this amount plus interest 23–172

---

[62] *Belgian Grain and Produce Co. Ltd v Cox & Co. (France) Ltd* (1919) 1 Ll.L.R. 256; *Stein v Hambro's Bank of Northern Commerce* (1921) 9 Ll.L.R. 433 at 507, rvsd. on a different point: (1922) 10 Ll.L.R. 529; *Dexters Ltd v Schenker & Co.* (1923) 14 Ll.L.R. 586; *British Imex Industries Ltd v Midland Bank Ltd* [1958] 1 Q.B. 542.
[63] [1922] 1 K.B. 318 at 324. For an interesting American authority concerning anticipatory breach, see *Zeevi & Sons Ltd v Grindlays Bank (Uganda) Ltd*, 371 N.Y.S. 2d 892 (1975).
[64] As to the bank's duty to mitigate its loss where it claims back an amount paid out on the basis of documents including false statements, see *Standard Chartered Bank v Pakistan National Shipping Corp.* [2000] All E.R. (D.) 1085 and [2001] All E.R. (D.) 186. *Cf.* the American approach as expressed in s.5–111 (Rev.) of the Uniform Commercial Code, under which the damages may be up to the full amount recoverable for an anticipatory breach by a buyer of a contract of sale. And see *Second National Bank of Hoboken v Columbia Trust Co.*, 288 F.17 (1923); *Maurice O'Meara Co. v National Park Bank of New York*, 146 N.E. 636 at 640 (1925).
[65] [1979] 2 Lloyd's Rep. 231.

and disbursements, Donaldson J. observed that the bank ought to have realised that the British exporter intended to convert promptly any amount paid in US dollars into pounds sterling. His Lordship held that the exporter, the beneficiary of the credit, had the option of claiming judgment in US dollars or in pounds sterling. "Notwithstanding that in the present case the price of the goods was agreed to be paid in US dollars, it is clear that the [exporter's] loss was incurred in sterling and that this was foreseeable by the [issuing bank]."[66]

5. THE CORRESPONDENT BANKER

(a) *Contract of Issuing Banker and Correspondent Banker*

23–173 **Roles of correspondent.** In most documentary credit transactions the issuing banker engages a correspondent who operates in the seller's locality. The correspondent is usually asked to assume one of the following three roles. First, the issuing banker may instruct the correspondent banker to open the documentary credit in his own name. The only undertaking which the seller obtains in this type of case is that of the correspondent banker, who assumes the role of a "correspondent issuer".[67] Secondly, the issuing banker may instruct the correspondent banker to confirm the credit; the latter then adds his own undertaking to that of the issuing banker and assumes the role of a "confirming banker".[68] Thirdly, the seller may not insist on obtaining an undertaking of a banker operating in his own locality. In such cases the correspondent banker is asked to notify the seller of the opening of the documentary credit by the issuing banker and may further be asked to accept on behalf of the issuing banker a set of conforming documents tendered by the seller. To safeguard his position, the correspondent banker, who in such cases is known as an "advising banker", expressly states that the credit does not include an undertaking on his part. As between himself and the issuing banker, the advising banker may, however, be authorised to accept a tender and to make payment.

23–174 **Legal position of correspondent.** The legal effect of the engagement of a correspondent banker depends on the terms of his employment. Where he assumes the role of a correspondent issuer, his contract with the issuing banker is similar to that usually made between the issuing banker and the buyer. The correspondent issuer is entitled to a banking commission or to a fee and to reimbursement for his advances to the seller in consideration of the opening of the credit and the acceptance of a conforming tender.[69] The relationship between the issuing banker and the advising banker is that of

---

[66] *ibid.*, at p.234. His Lordship analysed in this context the principle of *Miliangos v George Frank (Textile) Ltd* [1976] A.C. 443.

[67] For cases of this type see *National Bank of Egypt v Hannevig's Bank Ltd* (1919) 1 Ll.L.R. 69; *Skandinaviska Kreditaktiebolaget v Barclays Bank* (1925) 22 Ll.L.R. 523.

[68] See also above, para.23–055.

[69] *Pan-American Bank and Trust Co. v National City Bank of New York*, 6 F. 2d 762 at 766 (1925).

principal and agent.[70] It has been said that the confirming banker is, likewise, the agent of the issuing banker.[71] But, in effect, the confirming banker combines the roles of the correspondent issuer and of the advising banker. When he transmits the letter of credit to the seller, he informs him, *inter alia*, of the opening of the credit by the issuing banker and to this extent he acts as an agent. But by confirming the credit, he assumes *vis-à-vis* the seller the role of a principal.[72] However, as the contract includes elements of agency, some principles, such as ratification, are probably applicable.[73]

Independence of contract. The contract of the issuing banker and the correspondent banker is independent of any other contractual relationship of the documentary credit transaction. This principle is now based on Article 3(b) of the UCP and is also supported by American authorities.[74] One result of this principle is that the communications between the two bankers do not by themselves create any obligation which is enforceable by the seller.[75] Similarly, the buyer is not a party to the inter-bank communication and cannot rely on it.[76] This fundamental principle applies irrespective of the role assumed by the correspondent banker, because in all three cases the correspondent banker is employed by the issuing banker and it is from him alone that the correspondent banker takes his instructions. But to these instructions the correspondent banker must adhere with the same degree of strictness as that applicable in the other contractual relationships occurring in the transaction. 23–175

Fraudulent documents. If the documents tendered by the correspondent banker to the issuing banker are regular on their face, the correspondent banker is entitled to reimbursement even if the documents turn out to be false or forged. First, this follows from paragraph (a) of Article 14 and from Article 15 of the UCP Secondly, in this regard the position of the correspondent banker should be similar to that of the issuing banker, who can claim reimbursement from the buyer against forged or false documents 23–176

---

[70] *Kronman (Samuel) & Co. Inc. v Public National Bank of New York*, 218 N.Y.S. 616 at 622 (1926).

[71] *Equitable Trust Co. of New York v Dawson Partners Ltd* (1927) 27 Ll.L.R. 49 at 52, 57, but the point was obiter and not supported in the other speeches. The dictum was followed by McNair J. in *Bank Melli Iran v Barclays Bank D.C.O.* [1951] 2 Lloyd's Rep. 367 at 376, who referred to *Rayner (J H) & Co. Ltd v Hambro's Bank Ltd* [1943] 1 K.B. 37 (although this case does not appear to be in point).

[72] This view derives support from older American authorities. See *Pan-American Bank and Trust Co. v National City Bank of New York*, 6 F. 2d 762 at 771 (1925); *Kingdom of Sweden v New York Trust Co.*, 96 N.Y.S. 2d 779 at 791 (1949).

[73] *Bank Melli Iran v Barclays Bank D.C.O.*, above; this part of McNair J.'s decision is, it is submitted, good law.

[74] *Asbury Park and Ocean Grove Bank v National City Bank of New York*, 35 N.Y.S. 2d 985 at 989 (1942), affirmed 52 N.Y.S. 2d 583 (1944); *Tuet v Rodriguez*, 176 So.2d 550 at 552 (1965). See also UCP, Art. 14(f) discussed below, para.23–179.

[75] *Bril v Suomen Pankki Finlands Bank*, 97 N.Y.S. 2d 22 at 32 (1950), affd. 101 N.Y.S. 2d 256 (1950).

[76] *Kunglig Jarnvagsstyrelsen v National City Bank of New York*, 20 F. 2d 307 at 309 (1927).

provided these are regular on their face.[77] In the case of the correspondent issuer and of the confirming banker this argument derives support from the general similarlity between their respective contracts with the issuing banker and the latter's contract with the buyer. In the case of the advising banker this view can be based on the principle that an agent, who carries out his instructions with care and skill, is not responsible for defects he cannot reasonably be expected to discover.[78]

23–177 **Need of correspondent to adhere to his mandate.** What is the position if the correspondent banker deviates from his instructions when he notifies the seller of the opening of the credit, *e.g.* if the correspondent banker fails to stipulate for a required certificate of origin or calls for a single bill of lading instead of a full set? It is clear that unless the correspondent banker is protected by a provision of the UCP,[79] the issuing banker is entitled to claim any resulting loss in an action for breach of contract.[80] But it is submitted that where an advising banker or a confirming banker makes an error of this sort, his act binds the issuing banker towards the seller. The reason for this is that as regards the notification of the issuing banker's credit to the seller, both the advising banker and the confirming banker assume the role of an agent[81] and convey the terms to the seller while acting within the scope of their apparent authority.[82] However, in most cases the issuing banker is unlikely to bear the loss as, according to Article 18(a) of the UCP, the correspondent banker is engaged at the buyer's risk. Moreover, under Article 18(b) "banks assume no liability or responsibility should the instructions they transmit not be carried out . . ." The issuing banker, therefore, can pass the loss on to the buyer and is in difficulties only if the buyer becomes insolvent.

23–178 **Right of recourse.** Does the issuing banker have a right of recourse against the correspondent banker if the buyer rejects the tender? The law of negotiable instruments may lead to a right of recourse only where the draft is drawn on the buyer. The position in such a case will, however, depend on the principles governing the issuing banker's right of recourse against the seller.[83] The reason for this is that as regards rights of recourse, the correspondent banker, who acts as an indorser, is in the same position as the seller, who draws the draft.[84]

---

[77] See above, para.23–126.
[78] *Lamert v Heath* (1846) 15 M. & W. 486; *Beal v South Devon Ry* (1864) 3 H. & C. 337 at 342; *Commonwealth Portland Cement Co. Ltd v Weber, Lohmann & Co. Ltd* [1905] A.C. 66 at 70. For an interesting American authority in point, see *Investitions-und Handels-Bank AG v United California Bank International*, 277 F.Supp. 1006 (1968).
[79] *e.g.* if the deviation resulted from an error in translation or decoding: Art. 16. Note also that if the issuer decides to reject a tender he has to follow the procedure prescribed by Article 14; above, para.23–158 and below, para.23–203.
[80] For a case in which the correspondent notified the credit himself instead of using another designated bank see *Investitions-und Handels-Bank AG v United California Bank International*, 227 F.Supp. 1006 (1968).
[81] See above, para.23–173.
[82] See *Chitty on Contracts* (29th ed.), Vol. 2, paras 32–057 *et seq.*
[83] See above, para.23–161.
[84] ss.43(2) and 47(2) of the Bills of Exchange Act 1882.

Common law position. As regards the position under the general law of contract, it is necessary to recall the three situations discussed in connection with the issuing banker's right of recourse against the seller.[85] In the first situation—that of the buyer's insolvency or default—it is difficult to envisage any argument that would justify an issuing banker's claim to receive repayment from the correspondent banker. In the second situation—where the documents turn out to be false or forged—the correspondent banker is, as has been pointed out above, absolved from liability. But it is difficult to give a definite answer in the third type of case, where the issuing banker takes up a faulty set of documents tendered by the correspondent banker and these are subsequently rejected by the buyer. On the one hand, all three types of correspondent banker may be able to plead the estoppel discussed in connection with the issuing banker's recourse to the seller. The argument is reinforced if the issuing banker proposes to exercise his right of recourse after the end of the reasonable period available for the examination of the documents. If the lapse of time were to preclude the issuing banker from rejecting a set which he had not accepted, how could he possibly be in a stronger position if he sought to reject the documents after he had taken them up? Moreover, quite apart from the last point, the advising banker, who is employed as an agent, may be able to invoke the doctrine of waiver, which may also apply in the case of a confirmed credit.[86] On the other hand, the issuing banker may, perhaps, argue that, by accepting the documents from the seller and by tendering them under the credit, the correspondent banker tacitly states that they comply with the terms of the credit. As the correspondent banker is expected to examine the documents with care and skill he may, perhaps, be liable for a negligent misrepresentation.[87] But this argument has been weakened by the wording of Article 19(b) of the UCP, which implies that the correspondent bank is not expected to warrant the conformity of documents taken up by it.[88] In the absence of direct authority on this complex problem, the point has to be regarded as open. 23–179

Accounting for profits as agent. If a draft drawn under a documentary credit is payable at a fixed time after sight or at a specified future date, the seller may wish to have it discounted. Is the correspondent banker entitled to discount such a draft? It seems clear that there is nothing to preclude the correspondent issuer or the confirming banker, both of whom act as parties to the transaction in their own name, from discounting the seller's draft. 23–180

---

[85] See above, para.23–162 *et seq.*
[86] That in certain respects the contract of an issuing banker and a confirming banker resembles an agency agreement, see above, paras 23–116, 23–117, 23–173.
[87] Under the doctrine of *Hedley, Byrne & Co. Ltd v Heller and Partners Ltd* [1964] A.C. 465. As to the scope of this doctrine, which is rather limited, see *Chitty on Contracts* (28th ed.), Vol. 1, paras 6–081 *et seq.* In certain cases the correspondent banker takes up the documents subject to their being accepted by the issuing banker. In such a case he is able to reject them, following a rejection by the issuing banker.
[88] See below, para.23–197. Note that Art. 19 is expressly made applicable to any paying, accepting or negotiating bank and is therefore applicable to a correspondent bank.

This is the position even if the draft is drawn on the correspondent issuer or on the confirming banker. A drawee may discount a draft which falls due at a future date.[89] But problems may arise if a draft drawn by the seller under the documentary credit is discounted by an advising banker. It may be that under orthodox agency theory the advising banker, as agent, is bound to account to the issuing banker, who is his principal, for any profit which he gains from the transaction in excess of the usual commission.[90] However, it is perhaps arguable that a commercial usage permits the advising banker to engage in such discount transactions and that a term to that effect is to be implied into the contract between the issuing banker and the advising banker. Moreover, the agency relationship between the issuing banker and the advising banker may be terminated when the advising banker notifies the seller of the opening of the credit.[91] But the last argument is inapplicable in cases where the advising banker is asked not only to transmit the credit but also to accept on behalf of the issuing banker regular documents tendered by the seller.

(b) *Correspondent Banker's Contract with Seller and Buyer*

23–181 **Relationship with seller.** The relationship between the correspondent banker and the seller depends on the role assumed by the former. Where the correspondent banker opens the credit in his own name, or confirms a credit opened by the issuing banker, he enters into a contract with the seller. But such a contractual relationship is not established where the correspondent banker acts as an advising banker.

23–182 **Seller's contract with correspondent issuer or confirming banker.** The seller's contract with the correspondent issuer or with the confirming banker does not give rise to any special difficulties. When the correspondent banker opens the documentary credit, he is in the very same position as an issuing banker. The position of the confirming banker is similar. It is true that he is not the only party who promises payment to the seller; the issuing banker, too, gives such a promise. But the existence of more than one promise does not change the nature of any of them. Each of the undertakings is a separate and distinct contract between the banker issuing the new undertaking and the seller.[92] Article 9(b) of the UCP[93] supports

[89] See, generally above, paras 22–099 *et seq*.

[90] Note that the problem may also arise in the case of a silent confirmation, given by a correspondent bank at the beneficiary's request. Here the correspondent makes an extra profit by charging the beneficiary a "confirmation fee". See, generally, *Chitty on Contracts* (29th ed.), Vol. 2, para.32–073.

[91] *cf. Carter v Palmer* (1841) 8 Cl. & F. 657. This view is widely accepted in banking circles. An American authority, *Courteen Seed Co. v Hong Kong and Shanghai Banking Corp.*, 157 N.E. 272 (1927) is sometimes cited as showing that the courts will not compel the advising banker to disgorge a profit made in connection with such a discount. But the case concerned the rights of a negotiation banker, who was expressly invited in the documentary credit to discount drafts drawn under it.

[92] But the issuing banker's and the confirming banker's liability is probably joint and severable. See, generally, on the liability on a confirmed credit, *Courteen Seed Co. v Hong Kong and Shanghai Banking Corp.*, 215 N.Y.S. 525 at 529 (1926), affirmed 157 N.E. 272 (1927).

[93] See above, paras 23–052, 23–054.

this conclusion. Thus, the principles relating to the seller's contract with the issuing banker[94] also govern his contract with the correspondent issuer or with the confirming banker. In particular under Article 9(b)(iv), an undertaking by the confirming banker to negotiate drafts drawn under the credit is deemed to be without recourse to the drawer, the seller.

Position of advising banker. The advising banker notifies the seller of the opening of the documentary credit by the issuing banker and in most cases specifically states that he is not a party to the resulting contractual relationship. But the acts of the advising banker can lead to two problems. First, what is the position if the advising banker gives the seller misleading information about the terms of the credit opened by the issuing banker? If the seller, as a result, obtains the wrong type of documents, his tender may be rejected by the issuing banker.[95] As it is clear that the seller must rely on the information supplied by the advising banker, it is perhaps arguable that the advising banker owes the seller a duty of care and that its breach justifies an action in negligence under the rule in *Hedley, Byrne & Co. Ltd v Heller and Partners Ltd.*[96] Article 7(a) of the UCP, under which the advising banker has to take reasonable care to check the apparent authenticity of a credit which he advises, fails to clarify the point. On the one hand, the article may be construed as imposing on the advising banker a duty confined to verifying the authenticity of a credit. On the other hand, Article 8 may be based on a tacit recognition that there is a general relationship of proximity between this bank and the beneficiary. 23–183

Secondly, what is the position if the advising banker accepts from the seller a set of faulty documents which are, in turn, rejected by the issuing banker? If the advising banker takes up the documents under a discount arrangement with the seller, he retains the usual right of recourse of a holder.[97] But does he have such a right of recourse if he has accepted the documents and paid the amount of the documentary credit for the account of the issuing banker? There is no direct authority in point. The principle of waiver or estoppel, discussed in connection with the issuing banker's right of recourse against the seller,[98] can hardly apply. As the advising banker does not have a contractual relationship with the seller, he cannot be said to waive a term or to be estopped from enforcing it. Similarly, as the advising banker is not obliged *vis-à-vis* the seller to take up the documents, his acceptance of a tender cannot be regarded as a tacit assertion that the documents comply with the terms of the credit. It is therefore arguable that

---

[94] See above, paras 23–138 *et seq*.

[95] It is likely that the issuing banker is bound (see above, para.23–161). But the seller may prefer an action against the advising banker, who operates in the same locality, to the hazards of an action to be brought overseas.

[96] [1964] A.C. 465; *cf. Scanlon v First National Bank of Mexico*, 162 N.E. 567 at 568 (1928); *Associacion de Azucareros de Guatamala v United States National Bank*, 423 F. 2d 638 (1970); *National American Corp. v Federal Republic of Nigeria*, 425 F.Supp. 1365 (1977); and see below, n.1.

[97] See above, paras 22–070—22–071. As to whether such a discount is permitted see above.

[98] See above, para.23–163. But it may be difficult for the advising banker to establish the mistake of fact.

the advising banker may recover the amount paid to the seller against faulty documents in an action for money paid under a mistake. Notably, the UCP does not provide a clear answer. It is true that Article 14 treats the acceptance of a tender as a final step. As already mentioned,[99] under paragraph (d), the issuing bank, the confirming bank (if any) and a "nominated bank" have to adhere to the prescribed rejection procedure. Moreover, under Article 10(b) any bank authorised to accept the documents or, in other words, the bank at whose premises the credit is available is a "nominated bank".[1] It follows that the procedure outlined in Article 14(d) has to be observed by an advising bank with whom the credit has been made available.[2] However, the estoppel, based on Article 14(e) and arising from a failure to observe the prescribed rejection procedure, applies only as against an issuing bank and a confirming bank. This, in turn, leads to the conclusion that an advising bank, even if "nominated", is not precluded under the UCP from claiming recourse against the party from whom it accepted the documents. If these are rejected by the issuing bank or by the confirming bank, the advising bank's position remains to be determined on the basis of common law principles.[3]

23–184 **Acceptance of documents under reserve.** In certain cases an advising bank may agree to accept a faulty tender of documents "under reserve" or subject to an indemnity furnished by the seller. The rights of the issuing bank in cases of this type are governed by Article 14(f) of the UCP: "If the remitting bankdraws the attention of the Issuing Bank and/or Confirming Bank, if any, to any discrepancy(ies) in the document(s) or advises such banks that it has paid, incurred a deferred payment undertaking, accepted Draft(s) or negotiated under reserve or against an indemnity in respect of such discrepancy (ies), the Issuing Bank and/or Confirming Bank, if any, shall not be thereby relieved from any of their obligations under any provision of this Article. Such reserve or indemnity concerns only the relations between the remitting bank and the party towards whom the reserve was made, or from whom, or on whose behalf, the indemnity was obtained." The effect of this provision is two-fold. First, it emphasises that the contract between the advising bank and the seller is independent of the contract between the issuing bank and the seller. Secondly, it emphasises that, even if the issuing bank is notified that the correspondent has informed the seller about the discrepancies in the documents, the issuing bank must still perform its duties under the letter of credit. In particular, it has to reach its own decision as to whether or not to assert that the documents are non-conforming. If it does so, it must then take the steps

[99] See above, para.23–165.
[1] But note that, if the credit is available for negotiation generally, any bank that negotiates the documents becomes a nominated bank.
[2] And see *Seaconsar Far East Ltd v Bank Markazi Jomhouri Islami Iran* [1993] 1 Lloyd's Rep. 236 at 241, revd. on another point: [1994] 1 A.C. 438. For further proceedings in the case, see: [1999] 1 Lloyd's Rep. 36.
[3] It is unclear whether or not, under Art. 14(e), the issuing bank is precluded from relying on discrepancies not raised by an advising bank charged with the examination of the documents.

prescribed in Article 14 in respect of the procedure to be followed upon rejection.[4] This is so even if the correspondent indicates that, due to the discrepancies, the documents are forwarded on a collection basis.[5]

Correspondent banker's relationship with buyer. As the correspondent banker is engaged by the issuing banker, he has no privity of contract with the buyer. This principle applies regardless of whether the correspondent banker is engaged as an advising banker,[6] as a confirming banker,[7] or as a correspondent issuer.[8] A question of some difficulty is whether the buyer may in certain cases be entitled to sue the correspondent banker in negligence. This problem may arise where the correspondent banker asks for instructions concerning a specific tender and gives misleading information about the documents. On the one hand, the correspondent banker must be aware that information supplied to the issuing banker will be conveyed to the buyer. There may, therefore, be a relationship of proximity. Moreover, the information relates to a business transaction. On the other hand, it is doubtful whether the correspondent banker intends to assume responsibility. This applies particularly in the case of an advising banker; the buyer is aware of the fact that the advising banker is not a party to the transaction and that he may not be in full command of the facts. The application of the doctrine of *Hedley, Byrne & Co. Ltd v Heller and Partners Ltd*[9] may be regarded as questionable. 23–185

6. POSITION OF HOLDERS OF SELLER'S DRAFT

(a) *Holder's Relationship with Issuing Banker*

Practice. In the case of an irrevocable but unconfirmed credit, the seller may not be in a position to tender the documents in person to the issuing banker. Moreover, even in the case of a confirmed credit, some sellers prefer to tender the documents through their own bankers. One of the main reasons for this is that where a seller has a large volume of transactions, he may find it convenient to use the services of one bank for the handling of all his documents. In addition, the seller's own bankers may 23–186

---

[4] See above, para.23–156 *et seq*.

[5] *Harlow and Jones Ltd v American Express Bank Ltd* [1990] 2 Lloyd's Rep. 343 at 348; *Minories Finance Ltd v Afribank Nigeria Ltd* [1995] 1 Lloyd's Rep. 134 at 137.

[6] *Calico Printers' Association Ltd v Barclays Bank Ltd* (1930) 36 Com.Cas. 71, affirmed *ibid.*, 197. In the USA see: *Kronman (Samuel) & Co. Inc. v Public National Bank of New York*, 218 N.Y.S. 616 at 622 (1926).

[7] *Equitable Trust Co. of New York v Dawson Partners Ltd* (1927) 27 Ll.L.R. 49. In the USA see: *Distribuidora Del Pacifico SA v Gonzales*, 88 F.Supp. 538 at 541 (1950); *Linden v National City Bank of New York*, 208 N.Y.S. 2d 182 at 184 (1960).

[8] *Kunglig Jarnvagsstyrelsen v National City Bank of New York*, 20 F. 2d. 307 at 309 (1927).

[9] [1964] A.C. 465. See also *Ministry of Housing v Sharp* [1970] 2 Q.B. 223; *Mutual Life and Citizens' Assurance Co. Ltd v Evatt* [1971] A.C. 793 and more recently *Caparo Industries Plc v Dickman* [1990] 2 A.C. 605. For the general scope of the doctrine, see *Chitty on Contracts* (29th ed.), Vol. 1, paras 6–081 *et seq*.

offer him particularly favourable credit terms; as many drafts drawn under documentary credits fall due at 90 or even at 180 days after sight, the seller may require bridging finance for such periods. He may, further, require financial accommodation for the period in which he manufactures the goods or prepares them for shipment.

Where the seller remits the draft and the documents to his own banker, the latter may assume one of two roles. First, where the seller does not require an advance he simply instructs his banker to present the draft and the documents to the issuing banker or to the confirming banker. In such a case the seller's banker is an agent for collection and usually has no rights of his own under the documentary credit. His rights against the seller as well as his position as a "remitting banker" are discussed elsewhere.[10] Secondly, the banker may agree to make an advance to the seller against the draft. In such a case the banker "negotiates" or "purchases" the seller's draft and becomes a "holder".[11]

23–187 **"Mere holder" or "negotiation banker".** The holder's rights against the issuing banker[12] depend on whether the draft is drawn under a "straight credit" or under a "negotiation credit".[13] As the undertaking in a straight credit is directed solely to the seller, the holder of a draft drawn under it does not acquire rights of his own against the issuing banker.[14] A banker who purchases a draft drawn under a straight credit is therefore a "mere holder". In a negotiation credit, on the other hand, the issuing banker's promise to honour drafts accompanied by the required documents is addressed not only to the seller but also to bona fide holders, purchasers and discounters of the seller's drafts. A banker who negotiates or purchases a draft drawn under such a credit will be referred to as a "negotiation banker".

23–188 **Rights of negotiation banker: common law position.** When the negotiation banker purchases a draft drawn under the negotiation credit, he accepts the issuing banker's promise. A contract is thereupon established between the two banks and the negotiation banker becomes entitled to enforce the documentary credit.[15] But the negotiation banker must pur-

---

[10] See above, paras 22–073—22–074, 22–080.

[11] See above, paras 22–069—22–070 and note the meaning of "purchase", "negotiation" and "discount".

[12] If the credit is confirmed, the holder usually has similar rights against the issuing banker and the confirming banker. As negotiation is more common in the case of unconfirmed credits, the following discussion refers to the issuing banker only.

[13] See above, para.23–061; and note that Art. 10(b)(i) of the UCP sanctions the restriction of negotiation by nominating a designated bank for this purpose.

[14] *Sassoon (M A) & Sons Ltd v International Banking Corp.* [1927] A.C. 711 at 722. In the USA see: *Banco Nacional Ultramarino v First National Bank of Boston*, 289 F. 169 at 174 (1923).

[15] *Sassoon (M A) & Sons Ltd v International Banking Corp.*, above, 722, 724, where it was however held on the facts that the credit was of the straight type. See also *European Asian Bank AG v Punjab and Sind Bank (No. 2)* [1983] 1 W.L.R. 642, discussed above, para.23–140. In the USA see: *Second National Bank of Toledo v M Samuel & Sons Inc.*, 12 F. 2d 963 at 965, 967 (1926); *Courteen Seed Co. v Hong Kong and Shanghai Banking Corp.*, 215 N.Y.S. 525 at 529 (1926), affirmed 157 N.E. 272 at 273 (1927); *Scanlon v First National Bank of Mexico*, 162 N.E. 567 at 568 (1928).

chase the draft in reliance on the documentary credit. Obviously, a bank cannot enforce a letter of credit which restricts negotiation to some other bank.[16] Moreover, even if negotiation is permitted generally, a bank cannot enforce a credit if it has discounted bills drawn thereunder solely on the basis of an arrangement with the seller. Thus, in an American case, *Banco Nacional Ultramarino v First National Bank of Boston*[17] a banker purchased a draft drawn under a negotiation credit. The draft was not, at that time, accompanied by the required documents, but the seller supplied these documents before the expiration of the credit. It was held that the negotiation banker could not enforce the documentary credit. As at the time of the purchase the draft did not comply with the terms of the credit, the negotiation banker relied on the credit of the seller and not on the issuing banker's undertaking. The case further indicates that the negotiation banker can enforce the documentary credit only in so far as he purchases a draft accompanied by strictly conforming documents.[18]

Effect of UCP The general effect of Article 10 of the UCP on the position of a negotiation bank was discussed earlier.[19] Three points require to be reiterated at this stage. First, paragraph (b)(ii) affirms that negotiation means the giving of value for the documents by the bank authorised to negotiate and, further, that the mere handling of the documents does not constitute negotiation. There is, however, no basis for saying that "negotiation" is valid only if effected without recourse.[20] The existence of a right of recourse does not render the consideration furnished at the time of the discount nugatory.[21] Secondly, Article 10(c) confirms that the negotiation bank's receipt and examination of the documents does not, in itself, render it liable to effect payment. In practice, the negotiation bank incurs such a duty only when it assumes the role of a confirming bank. Thirdly, Article 10(d) states that by "nominating another bank, or by allowing for negotiation by any bank", the issuing bank authorises such bank to pay against a regular set of documents and undertakes to reimburse it. On this point, paragraph (d) complements articles 9(a) and 14(a). 23–189

Need to follow rejection procedure. The principle, applying the doctrine of strict compliance to a negotiation banker, is well entrenched.[22] The corollary is that the issuing bank loses its right to reject the documents if it 23–190

[16] As sanctioned by Art. 10(b), (d) of the UCP.
[17] 289 F. 169 at 175–176 (1923). See also *Scanlon v First National Bank of Mexico*, above, at pp.568–569.
[18] See also *Courteen Seed Co. v Hong Kong and Shanghai Banking Corp.*, above, 215 N.Y.S. 529; *Second National Bank of Toledo v M Samuel & Sons Inc.*, above, at p.965; *Flagship Cruises Ltd v New England Merchants National Bank of Boston*, 569 F. 2d 699 (1978).
[19] Above, para.23–016.
[20] Rosenblit, "To Negotiate or not to Negotiate" (2000) 11 IFSA (issue 9). And see, generally, Dolan, Negotiation Letters of Credit, 119 *Banking L.J.* 409 (2002).
[21] Ellinger, "Silent Confirmations and À Forfait Financing" [2002] *Annual Survey of Letters of Credit Law* 63.
[22] See cases discussed in paras 23–188 *et seq.*; for a particularly neat summary of all authorities in point, see *United Bank Ltd v Banque Nationale de Paris* [1992] 2 S.L.R. 64 (Sup. Ct. S'pore, Chao Hick Tin J.).

fails to comply with the requirements of, and with the procedure laid down in, Article 14 of the UCP[23] Notably, the issuing bank has to comply with the provisions of this article even if the negotiation banker advises that, due to discrepancies discovered in the documents, he has negotiated them "under reserve" or taken them up on a collection basis. In *Harlow and Jones Ltd v American Express Bank Ltd*[24] the beneficiaries of a documentary credit delivered to the negotiating bank a set of discrepant documents after the expiry of the letter of credit. Consequently, the documents were forwarded to the issuing bank under cover of a letter suggesting that they be handled on a collection basis. The account party accepted the draft accompanying the documents, and thereupon obtained delivery of the documents, but eventually dishonoured the draft by non-payment. Allowing the beneficiary's action to recover the amount of the documentary credit from the issuing bank, Gatehouse J. relied, initially, on the evidence given by experts on the effect of the release of discrepant documents to the issuing bank on a collection basis. Summing up the experts' views his Lordship said: ". . . the expert witnesses for all parties were agreed that the words 'on a collection basis' or 'for collection' are equivocal and must take their meaning from their context. The experts were also agreed that it is common practice that documents which are discrepant, including documents presented after the expiry date of a letter of credit, are sent to the issuing bank for collection or on a collection basis under the letter of credit which will be expressly or impliedly extended if, after inspection, the opener and his bank decide to accept the documents and thus waive the discrepancies. In this event, in the strict analysis, it is probably a re-negotiation of the credit in which the opener may, but will not necessarily, require allowances."[25]

Gatehouse J. concluded on this basis that discrepant documents, dispatched to the issuing bank on a collection basis, were still tendered under the documentary credit. Consequently, a decision to accept them invoked the banks' duty to make payment under the documentary credit. Notably, Article 14(f) of the UCP provides that, if "the remitting bank draws the attention of the Issuing Bank and/or Confirming Bank, if any, to any discrepancy(ies) in the document(s) or advises such banks that it has paid . . . or negotiated under reserve or against an indemnity . . . the Issuing Bank and/or Confirming Bank, if any, shall not be thereby relieved from any of their obligations under any provision of this Article." Thus, the issuing bank's duties under Article 14 remain intact even if it is advised that the negotiation banker has obtained an indemnity or has acted under a reserve. Gatehouse J.'s decision extends this principle to cases involving the handling of discrepant documents on a collection basis.

23–191 **Fraudulent documents or claims.** Is the negotiation banker entitled to claim the amount of the credit where he has taken from the seller in good faith a draft accompanied by documents which are regular on their face but

[23] Above, para.23–157; below, paras 23–203.
[24] [1990] 2 Lloyd's Rep. 343. See also *Minories Finance Ltd v Afribank Nigeria Ltd* [1995] 1 Lloyd's Rep. 134.
[25] *ibid.*, at p.348.

which turn out to be false or forged? While the issuing banker is entitled to reject such documents when tendered by the seller,[26] he is obliged to take them up when tendered by a negotiation banker. First, when the negotiation banker purchases a draft accompanied by regular documents, he acts on the promise of the issuing banker. The negotiation banker is not asked to verify the genuineness of the documents and, as a holder, does not warrant it by presenting them with the draft.[27] Secondly, under Article 14(a), if a bank, which is authorised to do so, negotiates "against documents which appear on their face to be in compliance with the terms and conditions of the credit", the party giving such authority is bound to take up the documents and to effect reimbursement. The negotiation credit authorises the banker to purchase a draft accompanied by documents which are regular on their face.[28] The negotiating bank is, at the same time, liable if statements made by it as regards the documents are untrue. Thus, if the negotiating bank states that documents were presented to it before the expiry date when, in reality, presentation took place thereafter, it is liable in deceit.[29]

Right of recourse. Can the issuing banker claim a right of recourse against the negotiation banker if the buyer rejects the documents? Where the issuing banker has had a chance to examine the documents, there is no room for such a right. The negotiation banker is a promisee of the negotiation credit. The position should therefore be governed by the principles discussed above as regards the issuing banker's recourse against the seller.[30] The same principles should apply where a draft is negotiated under a straight credit. While the "mere holder" is not entitled to claim payment of the amount of the credit in his own name, he is probably entitled to assume that the issuing banker's acceptance of a tender is a conclusive step. The mere holder may therefore be able to invoke the relevant principles of waiver and of estoppel. 23–192

Right of reimbursement. The issuer's correspondent or a negotiation bank can be reimbursed in different ways for the payment made to the beneficiary. Such bank may, for instance, be asked to debit the issuing banker's account with itself. In other cases, the correspondent or the negotiation bank is asked to draw on the issuing banker or on some other designated bank. Article 19 of the UCP attempts to regulate this last type of arrangement. To start with the provision defines two terms. The paying, 23–193

[26] See above, para.23–141.

[27] *Guaranty Trust Co. of New York v Hannay & Co.* [1918] 2 K.B. 623 at 631–632. See also *Sztejn v J Henry Schroder Banking Corp.*, 31 N.Y.S. 2d 631 at 635 (1941). *Cf.* the Uniform Commercial Code, s.5–110 (Rev).

[28] See also *Discount Records Ltd v Barclays Bank Ltd* [1975] 1 W.L.R. 315. But note that Megarry J. would apply the same principle whenever the draft was presented by a holder in due course and regardless of whether the credit was of the straight or of the negotiation type. As the holder of a draft drawn under a straight credit is not a promisee of the letter of credit, the point is debatable.

[29] *Standard Chartered Bank v Pakistan National Shipping Corp.* [2000] 1 Lloyd's Rep. 218 at 224–225.

[30] See above, paras 23–162—23–165.

accepting or negotiation bank which claims reimbursement is called the "Claiming Bank". The bank authorised to effect reimbursement is the "Reimbursing Bank".[31] Under paragraph (a), the issuing bank is under a duty to "provide the Reimbursing Bank in good time with proper instructions or authorisation to honour such reimbursement claim". Under paragraph (b), the issuing bank "shall not require a Claiming Bank to supply a certificate of compliance with the terms and conditions of the Credit to the Reimbursing Bank". This provision reinforces the principle that a party who presents a documentary draft does not warrant the genuineness of the documents attached.[32] Notably, though, Article 19 does not invalidate an instruction requiring the reimbursing bank to demand the delivery or communication of such a certificate as a condition precedent to its making payment. Such instructions have remained common in modern practice.

Under paragraph (c) the issuing banker is not relieved from his obligations to the correspondent or to the negotiation bank if the reimbursing bank fails to meet a claim. It follows that the issuing banker is not freed from his duty to reimburse the correspondent or the negotiation bank if the reimbursing bank becomes insolvent after it has received the funds required to meet a demand based on the letter of credit. Furthermore, under paragraph (d), the issuing banker is liable to compensate the correspondent or negotiation bank for loss resulting from the reimbursing bank's default.[33]

(b) *Holder's Rights against Seller and Buyer*

23–194 **Contract with seller.** According to an American case, when a banker agrees to purchase a draft drawn by the seller under a documentary credit, the banker "buys commercial paper relying on the credit of the drawer [*viz.* the seller] and the security that is offered".[34] The relationship between the banker and the seller is therefore that of a holder of a draft and its drawer. Moreover, in most cases the seller signs a "collection order" in which he sets out his instructions to the banker. Usually these include an order to present the draft to the issuing banker and to release the documents to him against his acceptance. This is the position irrespective of whether the draft is drawn under a straight credit or under a negotiation credit. In effect, the banker who purchases the seller's draft combines the roles of a discounting banker and of a collecting banker. His contract with the seller is therefore governed by the principles applying to the discount and collection of negotiable instruments, which are discussed elsewhere.[35] But two points need to be mentioned. First, the fact that the seller's draft is drawn under a

---

[31] As regards the recovery of amounts paid out by the reimbursing bank due to its overlooking the paying bank's cancellation of its mandate, see *Gulf International Bank BSC v Albaraka Islamic Bank* [2003] All E.R.(D) 460.

[32] See above, para.22–093.

[33] As regards charges, see Art. 19(e).

[34] *Courteen Steel Co. v Hong Kong and Shanghai Banking Corp.*, 157 N.E. 272 at 273 (1927).

[35] See above, paras 22–067 *et seq.*

documentary credit does not, by itself, preclude the holder from seeking recourse against the seller—the drawer—if the draft is dishonoured by the drawee.[36] Secondly, the banker's right of recourse against the seller is conditional upon his presenting the documents to the issuing banker with due diligence and before the expiry of the credit.[37] This principle follows from the rule in *Polak v Everett*[38] under which a creditor must account to the debtor not only for money he has actually made out of a security, but also for amounts which he failed to obtain due to laches or to negligence in the handling of a security. The documentary credit is a security within the meaning of this rule.[39]

Relationship with buyer. There is no contractual relationship between the buyer and the negotiation banker.[40] As the latter is engaged by the seller and not by the issuing banker, the buyer's relationship with the negotiation banker is even more remote than his relationship with the correspondent banker.[41] It is therefore to be doubted whether the buyer can succeed against the negotiation banker in cases involving negligent statements. The negotiation banker can hardly be regarded as assuming responsibility for the accuracy of information supplied by him. This applies *a fortiori* as regards a mere holder of a draft drawn under a straight credit, who does not purport to act under the documentary credit. 23–195

An American authority suggests[42] that if the buyer wrongfully instructs the issuing banker to reject regular documents, the negotiation banker can sue the buyer in *quasi contract*. An English court is unlikely to take such a view but the negotiation banker may, in certain cases of this type, be able to succeed against the buyer in tort.[43]

---

[36] *Sassoon (M A) & Sons Ltd v International Banking Corp.* [1927] A.C. 711 at 731. In the USA see: *Courteen Seed Co. v Hong Kong and Shanghai Banking Corp.*, 215 N.Y.S. 525 at 529 (1926), affirmed 157 N.E. 272 (1927).

[37] *Sassoon (M A) & Sons Ltd v International Banking Corp.*, above, at pp.714, 730. But in this case the negotiation banker was absolved from this duty as the seller gave ambiguous instructions in the remittance letter.

[38] (1876) 1 Q.B.D. 669 at 675–676.

[39] For a discussion as to whether the seller may in certain cases be able to sue the negotiation banker for negligence in transmitting information, see *Scanlon v First National Bank of Mexico*, 162 N.E. 567 (1928). It is dubious whether the principle in *Hedley, Byrne & Co. Ltd v Heller and Partners Ltd* [1964] A.C. 465 applies: see above, paras 23–179, 23–185.

[40] *Courteen Seed Co. v Hong Kong and Shanghai Banking Corp.*, 157 N.E. 272 at 274 (1927).

[41] As to which see above, para.23–191.

[42] *Second National Bank of Toledo v M Samuel & Sons Inc.*, 12 F. 2d 963 at 968 (1926).

[43] For inducing breach of contract, see generally, *Clerk and Lindsell on Torts* (18th ed.), paras 24–15 *et seq.*

7. THE TENDER OF DOCUMENTS

(a) *Strict Compliance Generally*

23–196 **Construction of terms of credit.** The insistence upon strict compliance is continually reiterated. In *English, Scottish and Australian Bank v Bank of South Africa*, Bailhache J. remarked[44]: "It is elementary to say that a person who ships in reliance on a letter of credit must do so in exact compliance with its terms. It is also elementary to say that a bank is not bound or indeed entitled to honour drafts presented to it under a letter of credit unless those drafts with the accompanying documents are in strict accord with the credit as opened." Thus, if a certificate signed by *experts* is required, a certificate signed by a single expert is a bad tender.[45] Similarly, a set is non-conforming if the bill of exchange is drawn on the issuing bank instead of the buyer.[46] The duty of strict compliance prevails in all the contracts which occur in a documentary credit transaction, that is, the contract between the buyer and the banker, the contract of banker and seller and in the relationship of issuing and correspondent banker.[47] The doctrine is best illustrated by the fact that the rule *de minimis non curat lex* does not apply in documentary credit transactions.[48] However, some

---

[44] (1922) 13 Ll.L.R. 21 at 24. See also *Belgian Grain and Produce Co. Ltd v Cox & Co. (France) Ltd* (1919) 1 Ll.L.R. 256 at 257; *Donald H Scott & Co. Ltd v Barclays Bank Ltd* [1923] 2 K.B. 1 at 11; *Bank Melli Iran v Barclays Bank D.C.O.* [1951] 2 Lloyd's Rep. 367 at 374; *Midland Bank Ltd v Seymour* [1955] 2 Lloyd's Rep. 147 at 154; *Kydon Compañia Naviera SA v National Westminster Bank Ltd* (*The* "*Lena*") [1981] 1 Lloyd's Rep. 68 at 74–75; *Glencore International AG v Bank of China* [1996] 1 Lloyd's Rep. 135. In the USA see: *Venizelos SA v Chase Manhattan Bank*, 425 F. 2d 461 (1970); *Oriental Pacific* (*USA*) *Inc. v Toronto Dominion Bank*, 357 N.Y.S. 2d 957 (1974); *Flagship Cruises Ltd v New England Merchants National Bank of Boston*, 569 F. 2d 699 (1978); *Re Coral Petroleum*, 878 F.2d 830 (5th Cir., 1989); *Trifinery v Banque Paribas*, 762 F. Supp. 1119 (S.D. N.Y., 1991); *Ocean Rig ASA v Safra National Bank of New York* 72 F. Supp 2d 193. *Cf. Banco Español de Credito v State Street Bank and Trust Co.*, 385 F. 2d. 230 (1967) (which suggests that the standard of strict compliance may be relaxed when a discrepancy does not relate to the description of goods). In Canada, see *Davis O'Brien Lumber Co. Ltd v Bank of Montreal* [1951] 3 D.L.R. 536 at 550.

[45] *Equitable Trust Co. of New York v Dawson Partners Ltd* (1927) 27 Ll.L.R. 49.

[46] *Kydon Compañia Naviera SA v National Westminster Bank Ltd* (*The* "*Lena*") [1981] 1 Lloyd's Rep. 68.

[47] Thus, *Equitable Trust Co. of New York v Dawson Partners Ltd*, above (which was an action between a banker and a buyer) has been cited in *Rayner* (*J. H.*) *& Co. Ltd v Hambro's Bank Ltd* [1943] 1 K.B. 37 (an action by a seller against a banker). The general application of the doctrine is emphasised in *Camp v Corn Exchange National Bank*, 132 A. 189 at 191 (1926). Contrast *Far Eastern Textile Ltd v City National Bank and Trust Co.*, 430 F.Supp. 193 (1977), which supports strict compliance in respect of the contract of banker and seller but postulates substantial compliance in respect of the contract of banker and buyer. For a forceful argument in support of this view, see Dolan, "Letter of Credit Disputes Between Issuer and Customer" 105 Banking L.J. 380 (1989).

[48] *Moralice* (*London*) *Ltd v E D and F Man* [1954] 2 Lloyd's Rep. 526; *Soproma SpA v Marine and Animal By-Products Corp.* [1966] 1 Lloyd's Rep. 367 at 390; *Astro Exito Navegacion SA v Chase Manhattan Bank* (*The* " *Messiniaki Tolmi*") [1986] 1 Lloyd's

mitigation of the harshness of the doctrine is to be found in the principle that the credit should be interpreted as a whole.[49] Thus, an isolated technical phrase may occasionally be construed in the light of other terms or conditions of the credit.[50] Apart from this, the interpretation of certain technical terms is provided for by the UCP, Article 13(a) of which emphasises the importance of banking practice, and other matters have been the subject of judicial decision.[51]

Meaning of discrepancy. Whilst the doctrine of strict compliance is, in itself, well entrenched and understood, there is little authority to explain the exact nature of a "discrepancy" or "irregularity". Undoubtedly, the exclusion of the principle that *de minimis non curat lex* suggests that any meaningful deviation in the documents from the requirements set out in the letter of credit constitutes a discrepancy and vitiates the tender. But would it be correct to conclude that even a minor typographical error or a patent omission or slip constitutes a discrepancy? The problem was considered in two modern American cases. In the first case, *Beyene v Irving Trust Co.*[52] a documentary credit called for a bill of lading including a notation stating "notify *Mohammed Sofan*". The bill of lading tendered by the beneficiary referred instead to *Mohammed Soran*. The Second Circuit Court of Appeals concluded that the issuing bank could not be certain that *Mohammed Sofan* and *Mohammed Soran* were one and the same person or that the difference in name was a pure misnomer or typographical error. The documents were, therefore, considered discrepant. In the second case, *Bank of Montreal v Federal National Bank*[53] a group of companies known as the "Blow Out Companies" needed an advance from the claimant bank. To secure this loan, the group instructed the defendant bank to open a standby credit in favour of the claimant bank. Payment under the facility so issued was due against the claimant bank's bill of exchange accompanied by a default certificate, that had, *inter alia*, to attest that the amount of the bill would be set off against the liabilities of one of the members of the group described as "Blow Out *Prevention* Ltd". In reality, the group did not encompass a company by this name, the correct style of the member 23–197

Rep. 455, affirmed [1988] 2 Lloyd's Rep. 217; *Seaconsar Far East Ltd v Bank Markzi Jomhouri Islami Iran* [1993] 1 Lloyd's Rep. 236, where Lloyd L.J. at 240 said: "I cannot regard as trivial something which, whatever may be the reason, the credit specifically requires"; note reversal on other grounds: [1994] 1 A.C. 438.

[49] *Elder Dempster Lines Ltd v Ionic Shipping Agency Inc.* [1968] 1 Lloyd's Rep. 529 at 535–536. Some American cases construe the credit so as to uphold the transaction: *Venizelos SA v Chase Manhattan Bank*, 425 F. 2d 461 (1970); *CNA Mortgage Investors Ltd v Hamilton National Bank*, 540 S.W. 2d 238 (Tenn. 1975); *West Virginia Housing Development Fund v Sroka*, 415 F.Supp. 1107 (1976) (which also emphasises that the credit needs to be construed *contra proferentem*); *Bank of North Carolina v Rock Island Bank*, 570 F. 2d 202 (1978).

[50] But note that a court will imply a term into a bank's irrevocable undertaking only in exceptional circumstances: *Cauxell Ltd v Lloyds Bank Plc, The Times*, December 26, 1995.

[51] In certain cases an analogy can be drawn from cases concerning contracts c.i.f.; see below, para.23–217.

[52] 762 F. 2d 4 (1985).

[53] 622 F.Supp. 6 (1986).

involved being "Blow Out *Products* Ltd". Upon the group's default the claimant bank drew a bill of exchange, in which it described the relevant company under its correct style, attaching a memorandum explaining that the style as set out in the letter of credit involved a misnomer. Russell J., in the United States District Court, rested his decision for the claimant bank on the finding that the substitution of names was occasioned by a draftsman's error. A construction of the letter of credit, which treated the error as such, was, in his opinion, fair and gave effect to the intention of the parties as it was, of course, clear that the company to whose affairs the standby credit related was "Blow Out Products Ltd". Treating the documents as discrepant would have frustrated the object of the transaction.

23–198 **Rationale.** It is believed that Russell J.'s decision is correct. Where it can be shown that the supposed discrepancy results from a patent error, it is unrealistic to treat the entire tender as invalid by reason only of a technical slip or mistake. Undoubtedly, where it is not clear that the departure from the details set out in the letter of credit constitutes a mistake, even a minor discrepancy justifies the rejection of the documents. *Beyene's* case illustrates the point. But to treat any typographical error or patent mistake as a discrepancy would convert the commercial transaction covered by the letter of credit into a proof reading exercise. A wish to preclude the transaction from being so treated is, actually, evident in the decision respecting one of the discrepancies pleaded in the classic case of *Equitable Trust Co. of New York v Dawsons Partners Ltd.*[54] The respective objection was that a certificate of quality had been countersigned by the "Handelsvereeniging te Batavia" and not, as stipulated, by the "Chamber of Commerce" of Batavia. Relying on the evidence, Bateson J. held that the two bodies were known to be the same. His decision that the departure was, therefore, not a discrepancy was affirmed by the Court of Appeal[55] and, although the House of Lords reversed judgment on other grounds, it left this specific finding undisturbed.[56] To hold that the certificate was defective as it described the certifying body in its Dutch rather than in an English style would have frustrated the transaction on the ground of a meaningless technicality.

23–199 **Elucidation of principle.** Further light on the distinction between a slip, error or meaningless departure and a discrepancy is thrown by the decision of the Supreme Court of Singapore in *United Bank Ltd v Banque Nationale de Paris*.[57] In this case the beneficiary, whose correct style was "P. S. (*Pte*) Ltd", was described in the letter of credit as "P. S. Ltd". The issuing bank claimed that, as the invoice was issued in the beneficiary's full name, the documents were discrepant. Although evidence was called to show that in

---

[54] (1927) 27 Ll.L.R. 49. For another American authority treating a patent error as irrelevant, see *New Braunfels National Bank v Okorne*, 780 S.W. 2d. 313 (Tex.App., 1989). See also *Voest-Alpine Trading USA Corp. v Bank of China*, 288 F. 3rd. 262 (5th Cir. 2000).

[55] (1925) 25 Ll.L.R. 90, affg. (1924) 24 Ll.L.R. 261.

[56] See, in particular, (1927) 27 Ll.L.R. at 51 (Viscount Cave, L.C.) and at 54 (Viscount Sumner).

[57] [1992] 2 S.L.R. 64.

Singapore the Registrar of Companies would usually refuse to register a company by a name which so nearly resembled that of another as to cause confusion, Chao Hick Tin J. concluded, though not without some hesitation, that the documents were rendered defective by the addition of "Pte" to the invoice. On the facts and evidence, the issuing bank could not be certain that the issuer of the invoice was the very same person as the beneficiary named in the letter of credit.

In *United Bank Ltd's* case it was, thus, not clearly established on the record that the omission of "Pte" in the letter of credit was a pure error. That a mere typographical error does not constitute a discrepancy was decided by the Supreme Court of Hong Kong. In *Hing Yip Fat Co. Ltd v Daiwa Bank Ltd*[58] the applicant for the credit was described as "Cheergoal *Industries* Ltd" but the drawing described him as "Cheergoal *Industrial* Ltd". Kaplan J. concluded that the variation in the name constituted a patent typographical error. His Lordship was influenced by the fact that the error was minor and was "the sort of mistake that could easily occur in a society where English is not the first language of 98 per cent. of the population." He was, further, influenced by the fact that the issuing bank was aware that the error was a slip and also by the repetition of the error in some of the communications emanating from the issuing bank itself.

Kredietbank Antwerp. The doctrine of strict compliance has been fine tuned in *Kredietbank Antwerp v Midland Bank Plc*.[59] One of the documents called for in the letter of credit issued in this case was a "draft survey report issued by Griffith Inspectorate". The document eventually tendered was executed on the letterhead of a firm described as "Daniel C. Griffith (Holland) BV" and signed for that company. However, at the foot of the document was a logo stating "Inspectorate" and underneath it appeared the words: "Member of the Worldwide Inspectorate—dedicated to the elimination of risk". Affirming Diamond Q.C.'s finding that the document was regular, Evans L.J., in the Court of Appeal, noted that banks were concerned with the form of the documents presented to it and not with the underlying facts. At the same time, his Lordship accepted that mere trivialities or misprints had to be ignored because " . . . the requirement of strict compliance is not equivalent to a test of exact literal compliance in all circumstances and as regards all documents. To some extent, therefore, the banker must exercise his own judgment whether the requirement is satisfied by the documents presented to him".[60] His Lordship added[61]: "the requirement of a Report . . . issued by 'Griffith Inspectorate' is amply met by the documents issued by the Dutch company named which declares itself a member of the Inspectorate Group. If there is a literal requirement that the name 'Griffith Inspectorate' shall appear in the documents, then it does so, assuming only that there is a worldwide Inspectorate group and that the company bearing the name Daniel Griffith (Holland) is a member of it. 23–200

[58] [1991] 2 H.K.L.R. 35.
[59] [1998] 2 Lloyd's Rep. 173, affd. [1999] 1 All E.R. (Comm) 801.
[60] [1999] 1 All E.R. at 806.
[61] *ibid.*, at p.816.

That is an assumption which, as the [trial] judge held, an experienced banker can be expected to assume." *Kredietbank Antwerp* thus defeats any attempt to rely on a discrepancy based on asserting a "mirror image" test as the yardstick of strict compliance. At the same time, the Court of Appeal did not seek to modify the strict compliance doctrine. This fundamental doctrine of the law of letters of credit remains intact but has to be given a reasonable and not a literal robotic construction.

23–201 **Technical defences.** One result of the doctrine of strict compliance, which is unaffected by *Kredietbank Antwerp*, is that the person to whom the documents are tendered may raise any lawful objections against the documents, even if in fact his objection is purely technical and the true motive for his rejection of the tender is to be found in a falling market or in some other extraneous circumstances.[62] Thus, if a banker suspects that the buyer is unable to take up the documents, he may raise against the seller minute discrepancies in the documents in order to justify their rejection.

23–202 **Good faith.** As the law stands at present, the bank can reject documents tendered under a documentary credit in reliance on the most trivial and insignificant technicalities. In modern commerce, this principle is frequently utilised by the applicant for the credit—the buyer—as a weapon in his dealings with the beneficiary. A well known strategy is the insertion in the application form of requisites that cannot easily be complied with. When, in consequence, the documents tendered by the beneficiary are technically discrepant, the applicant demands a reduction of the price of the goods as a condition to this waiving the discrepancy. Whilst English law is on his side, other legal systems will, in appropriate circumstances, defeat the applicant's tactics by applying principles demanding good faith in the exercise of contractual rights. This, indeed, is the position in Swiss law,[63] which has been given effect to in the United Kingdom in a case respecting a letter of credit governed by the law of Switzerland.[64] Although English law has not, to date, developed a similar doctrine, it may, perhaps, reach the same result in extreme cases on the basis of Phillips J.'s decision in *Transpetrol Ltd v Transöl Olieprodukten Nederland BV*[65] It will be recalled that, in that case, his Lordship refused to give effect to a contractual term as he concluded that the requirement involved was nonsensical. It is true that the term in question was not a term of the letter of credit itself but one of the requisites spelt out in the documentary credit clause of the contract of sale, which, of

[62] *Guaranty Trust Co. of New York v Van Den Berghs Ltd* (1925) 22 Ll.L.R. 447 at 455. As regards the position in the USA, see *Liberty National Bank and Trust Co. v Bank of America*, 116 F.Supp. 233 at 237, 243 (1953), affirmed 218 F. 2d 831 (1955); *Courtaulds North America v North Carolina National Bank*, 387 F.Supp. 92 (1975), rvsd. 528 F. 2d 802 (1975); *Far Eastern Textile Ltd v City National Bank and Trust Co.*, 430 F.Supp. 193 (1977); *AMF Head Sports Wear Inc. v Ray Scott's All-American Sports Club Inc.*, 448 F.Supp 222 (1978); *cf. Exotic Transfers Far East Buying Office v Exotic Trading USA Inc.*, 717 F.Supp. 14 (Mo. 1991).

[63] *Société de Banque Suisse v Société Generale Alsacienne de Banque* [1989] J.T. 1342.

[64] *Mannesman Handel AG v Kaunlaran Shipping Corp.* [1993] 1 Lloyd's Rep. 89.

[65] [1989] 1 Lloyd's Rep. 309 at 310–313.

course, is not governed by the strict compliance doctrine. However, it is difficult to see why Phillips J.'s robust common sense approach should not be equally applied to the commercial facility—the letter of credit—the opening of which is bargained for in the documentary credit clause of the contract of sale.

Time for raising objections; waiver.[66] Some American authorities take the view that the person to whom the documents are tendered must raise all his objections to the documents at the time of their rejection and that he is usually precluded from raising further defences at a later stage.[67] Traditionally, English courts took to the opposite view, allowing the pursuit of all available defences, including those raised for the first time at the trial.[68] The position was clarified by Article 16(d) of the 1983 revision, which adopted the American doctrine. Under this provision, currently reproduced in Article 14(d) of the UCP 1993, the banker to whom the documents are tendered has to state the discrepancies in respect of which the documents are rejected. If that banker fails to do so, he is precluded, under Article 14(e), from disputing the regularity of the documents. In *Bankers Trust Co. v State Bank of India*[69] the Court of Appeal gave effect to this provision and distinguished the earlier cases. Moreover, their Lordships emphasised that, under Article 16(d), the notice had to be dispatched as soon as the bank in question had reached its decision to reject. Conceptually, the bank's failure to refer to given discrepancies may be considered waiver.[70] This, indeed was the view taken by Kaplan J. in *Hing Yip Fat Co.* 23–203

[66] As regards the procedure for rejection, see above, para.23–087.

[67] *Bank of Taiwan Ltd v Union National Bank*, 1 F. 2d 65 at 66 (1924); *Second National Bank of Allegheny v Lash Corp.*, 299 F. 371 at 373–374 (1924); *North Valley Bank v National Bank of Austin*, 437 F.Supp. 70 (1977); *Pringle-Associated Mortgage Corp. v Southern National Bank*, 571 F. 2d 871 (1978). But the rule applies only to objections which are known at the time of rejection: *Old Colony Trust Co. v Lawyers' Title and Trust Co.*, 297 F. 152 at 156 (1924).

[68] *Skandinaviska Kreditaktiebolaget v Barclays Bank* (1925) 22 Ll.L.R. 523 at 525; *Westminster Bank v Banca Nazionale Di Credito* (1928) 31 Ll.L.R. 306 at 311; *Soproma SpA v Marine and Animal By-Products Corp.* [1966] 1 Lloyd's Rep. 367 at 387. *Cf. Kydon Compañia Naviera SA v National Westminster Bank Ltd* (*The "Lena"*) [1981] 1 Lloyd's Rep. 68 at 78–80 which suggested that Art. 8(e) of the 1974 Revision had not changed the position. The wording of the new Art. 14(d), though, is clearer. And note that it would be too late to raise a point for the first time at the stage of an appeal: *Gian Singh & Co. Ltd v Banque de L'Indochine* [1974] 2 Lloyd's Rep. 1 at 12.

[69] [1991] 1 Lloyd's Rep. 587, affirmed [1991] 2 Lloyd's Rep. 443, CA, followed recently in *Bayerische Vereinsbank AG v National Bank of Pakistan* [1997] 1 Lloyd's Rep. 59 (Mance J.). But note that, in *Amixco Asia (Pte) Ltd v Bank Bumiputra Malaysia Brhd* [1992] 2 S.L.R. 943, Selvam J.C., in the Sup. Ct. of Singapore, held that Art. 14 did not preclude the bank in question from raising non-documentary objections, such as the tendering bank's failure to "negotiate". As such a point cannot be discerned from an examination of the documents, the decision is supportable.

[70] See *Wing On Bank Ltd v American National Bank and Trust Co.*, 457 F. 2d 328 (1972), which suggests, however, that a failure to raise an objection might not result in an estoppel if the tender was beyond correction. See also *Flagship Cruises Ltd v New England Merchants National Bank of Boston*, 569 F. 2d 699 (1978).

Ltd v Daiwa Bank Ltd.[71] In certain cases waiver may also be inferred from the bank's conduct.[72]

23–204 **Subsequent tenders.** One of the objects of requiring the person to whom the documents are tendered to raise all objections at the time he rejects the tender is to enable the tenderor to cure all defects and to retender the documents before the expiration of the documentary credit. The right to retender is recognised in the United States.[73] In the United Kingdom it derives support from *Basse and Selve v Bank of Australasia*[74] in which the documents were originally rejected by the banker due to a defect in a certificate of analysis but were held to comply with the requirements of the credit when retendered by the seller after the correction of the certificate.

(b) *Specific Aspects of Strict Compliance*

23–205 **All documents need to be tendered.** If a tender does not include all the documents specified in the documentary credit, it should be rejected. Thus, where a full set of bills of lading is called for, the tender of two bills out of a set of three is unacceptable.[75] Similarly, American authorities indicate that all the certificates required in the credit must be tendered.[76] A more difficult problem is whether a tender may include one document which comprises, or performs the function of, two documents stipulated in the documentary cred it. In an American case, *Richard v Royal Bank of Canada*,[77] the documentary credit called for an invoice and for a certificate of weight. The tender did not include a separate certificate of weight but the weight was certified by a qualified person on the invoice. It was held that the documents complied with the requirements of the documentary credit. But this decision can be doubted. A buyer may require a separate certificate of weight (or any other specific document) in order to tender it to a sub-purchaser. A different question is whether fractional certificates, which cover a whole shipment, may be tendered instead of a single

71 Above; see also *Kerr-McGee Chemical Corp. v Federal Deposit Insurance Corp.* 872 F. 2d 971 (11th Cir. 1989); *Paramount Export Co. v Asia Trust Bank* 238 Cal. Rep. 920 (App. 1987).

72 *Floating Dock Ltd v Hong Kong and Shanghai Banking Corp.* [1986] 1 Lloyd's Rep. 65.

73 *Kingdom of Sweden v New York Trust Co.*, 96 N.Y.S. 2d 779 at 790–791 (1949).

74 (1904) 90 L.T. 618. See also *United City Merchants (Investments) Ltd v Royal Bank of Canada* [1979] 1 Lloyd's Rep. 267 at 275 unaffected on this point by the decision of the House of Lords: [1983] A.C. 168.

75 *Donald H Scott & Co. Ltd v Barclays Bank Ltd* [1923] 2 K.B. 1.

76 *Anglo-South American Trust Co. v Uhe*, 184 N.E. 741 (1933). *Cf. Bank of New York and Trust Co. v Atterbury Bros Inc.*, 234 N.Y.S. 442 at 447 (1929), affirmed 171 N.E. 786 (1930). See also *Bounty Trading Corp. v SEK Sportswear Ltd*, 370 N.Y.S. 2d 4 (1975) which indicates that the tender of documents without the stipulated draft constitutes non-compliance. *Cf. Titanium Metals Corp. of America v Space Metals Inc.*, 529 P. 2d 431 (Utah 1974).

77 23 F. 2d 430 (1928). See also *Overseas Union Bank Ltd v Chua* (1964) 30 M.L.J. 165. As regards attestation of weight in a transaction involving transport other than by sea, see Art. 38 of the UCP.

certificate. As the fractional certificates perform the function of the required single certificate, it is arguable that they constitute a good tender.[78]

Regularity of documents. Apart from having to comply strictly with the requirements of the credit, each document must also be regular on its face. This means that it must, in the first place, be effective and legal. Thus, a bill of lading which became void due to the outbreak of war was considered irregular.[79] Secondly, the document must be of the type current in trade generally and one on which questions cannot be raised.[80] But this principle must be applied with care. The banker is not expected to obtain a knowledge of the specific requirements in each trade and is not concerned with particular trade usages.[81] The point is borne out by Article 13(a) of the UCP, under which the compliance of documents is to be determined "by international standard banking practice as reflected in these Articles". Thirdly, a document must not be "stale", that is, be presented after an unduly long delay from the date on which it was issued. Under Article 43(a) of the UCP, a letter of credit which calls for a transport document, should, in addition to its expiry date, "also stipulate a specified period of time after the date of shipment during which presentation must be made in compliance with the terms and conditions of the Credit. If no such period of time is stipulated, banks will not accept documents presented to them later than 21 days after the day of shipment. In any event, documents must be presented not later than the expiry date of the Credit".[82] In addition the set, as a whole, must be regular. Under Article 13(a) of the UCP the documents are deemed to be a bad tender if they "appear on their face to be inconsistent with one another".[83] This principle, however, applies only to documents called for in documentary credit. Under a proviso to Article 13(a), "documents not stipulated in the Credit will not be examined by 23–206

---

[78] *Netherlands Trading Society v Wayne and Haylitt Co.* (1952) 36 Hong Kong L.R. 109.

[79] *Karberg (Arnhold) & Co. v Blythe, Green, Jourdain & Co.* [1916] 1 K.B. 495. A similar view was taken in an American decision of a warehouse receipt which was illegal on its face: *Old Colony Trust Co. v Lawyers' Title and Trust Co.*, 297 F. 152 at 157 (1924). Contrast *Grob v Manufacturers Trust Co.*, 29 N.Y.S. 2d 916 (1941).

[80] *National Bank of South Africa v Banca Italiana De Sconto* (1922) 10 Ll.L.R. 531 at 536; *Skandinaviska Kreditaktiebolaget v Barclays Bank* (1925) 22 Ll.L.R. 523 at 525; *Midland Bank Ltd v Seymour* [1955] 2 Lloyd's Rep. 147 at 152, 155. It would appear that some banks regard a document bearing an obvious typed-over alteration of a material detail as irregular: *United City Merchants (Investments) Ltd v Royal Bank of Canada* [1979] 1 Lloyd's Rep. 267 at 272. The point was not decided in that case and was not considered by the House of Lords [1983] A.C. 168; but see *Talbot v Bank of Hendersonville*, 495 S.W. 2d 548 (Tenn. 1972) which regarded the presence of such a correction as irrelevant.

[81] *Rayner (J H) & Co. Ltd v Hambro's Bank Ltd* [1943] 1 K.B. 37 at 41. See also *Old Colony Trust Co. v Lawyers' Title and Trust Co.*, 297 F. 152 at 156–157 (1924); *Marine Midland Grace Trust Co. v Banco del Pais SA*, 261 F.Supp. 884 (1966).

[82] And see *M. Golodetz & Co. Inc. v Czarnikow-Rionda Co. Inc.* [1980] 1 W.L.R. 495 in which it was held that a delay of 13 days between the shipment of the goods and the issuing of the bill of lading did not render it stale.

[83] And see *Banque de L'Indochine et de Suez SA v J. H. Rayner (Mincing Lane) Ltd* [1983] Q.B. 711 and, in the US, *Voest-Alpine International Corp. v Chase Manhattan Bank N.A.*, 545 F.Supp. 301 (1982), varied: 707 F. 2d 680 (1983).

banks". Instead, they may be either returned to the "presenter" or be passed on without responsibility on the bank's part.[84] Obviously, the irregularity of such a superfluous document, as well as its inconsistency with one of the prescribed documents, is immaterial.

23–207 **Original document defined.** An innovative provision, included in the UCP in order to accommodate needs arising primarily from technological developments, is to be found in Article 20(b). Unless otherwise stipulated the credit banks will accept as originals documents produced: (i) by a reprographic system (such as a photocopying machine); (ii) by means of an automated or computerised system (such as SWIFT); or (iii) as a carbon copy. In all three cases the document has to be marked as an original and, where necessary, appear to be signed. In *Glencore International AG v Bank of China*[85] it was held that the two requisites were cumulative. Accordingly, where it was sought to give the status of an original to a document produced, or appearing to have been produced, by one of the three methods specified, it had to be marked as an original. Its being signed by hand did not, in itself, convert it into an original. But where the appearance of a document demonstrates, in itself, that it is an original, there is no need to mark it as such.[86]

In the majority of cases, Article 20(b) gives effect to recognised banking practice. But the article may also lead to problems. For instance, is a stipulation for a full set of bills of lading met by the tender of two bills of lading issued as originals plus a carbon copy authenticated by the carrier? On the one hand, it is arguable that as a set usually comprises three originals, the tender of two signed bills of lading plus an authenticated copy, which is deemed an original, is a good tender. On the other hand, it may be asserted that a "full set" means all the bills of lading initially issued by the carrier in respect of the shipment involved.

23–208 **Meaning of "signature" and "authentication".** For the sake of clarity, Article 20(b) provides that a "document may be signed by handwriting, by facsimile signature, by perforated signature, by stamp, by symbol, or by any other mechanical or electronic method of authentication".[87] An attempt to avoid confusion and ambiguity is made in Article 20(d). "Unless otherwise stipulated in the Credit, a condition under a Credit calling for a document to be authenticated, validated, legalised, visaed, certified or indicating a similar requirement, will be satisfied by a signature, mark, stamp or label on such document that on its face appears to satisfy the above condition." Obviously, even if a document need be validated by a notarial act, the banks only concern is to satisfy itself that, on the face of it, the document

[84] As to whether a document listed in a "special condition" constitutes a stipulated document, see *Credit Apricole Indosuez v Muslim Commercial Bank Ltd* [2000] 1 Lloyd's Rep. 275.
[85] [1996] 1 Lloyd's Rep. 135.
[86] *Kredietbank Antwerp v Midland Bank Plc* [1999] 1 All E.R. (Comm) 801 and see also *Credit Industriel et Commerciale v China Merchant Bank* [2002] 2 All E.R. (Comm) 427 (David Steel J.).
[87] But note meaning of signature where eUCP is incorporated, above, para.23–034.

appears to be so validated. The bank is not expected to verify the genuineness of the signature or that the person whose signature and stamp have been placed on the document is a legally qualified notary authorised to act in that capacity.

Meaning of copy. The basic provision is spelt out in Article 20(c)(i). Unless otherwise stipulated in the credit, a copy is a document so labelled or a document not marked as an original. Under subparagraph (ii), a call for multiple documents, such as "duplicate", "two fold" or "two copies" and the like is satisfied by the tender of "one original and the remaining number in copies except where the document itself indicates otherwise". 23–209

Compliance with time. According to Article 42(a) of the UCP all credits "must stipulate an expiry date and a place for the presentation of documents for payment, for acceptance, or, with the exception of freely negotiable Credits, a place for the presentation of documents for negotiation. An expiry date stipulated for payment, acceptance or negotiation will be construed to express an expiry date for presentation of documents". The date so stipulated is additional to any period or to a latest date specified for shipment.[88] 23–210

It is well established that the documents must be presented to the banker before the expiry of the credit.[89] Moreover, if the documentary credit specifies a date or a period of shipment, the banker must reject a tender which shows that the goods have not been shipped on time.[90] Under Article 44(b) "if no such latest date for shipment is stipulated in the credit or amendments thereto, banks will not accept transport documents indicating a date of issuance later than the expiry date stipulated in the Credit or amendments thereto". The need strictly to comply with the date set for shipment is of particular importance where a credit covers partial shipments. According to Article 41 of the UCP, if any instalment is not shipped within the period stipulated for it, the credit ceases to be available for that or for any subsequent instalment.[91]

---

[88] American authorities indicate that if an irrevocable credit does not include an expiry date, it remains open for a reasonable time, the length of which depends largely on the shipment period: *Lamborn v National Park Bank of New York*, 208 N.Y.S. 428 at 434 (1925), affirmed 148 N.E. 664 at 666 (1925). *Cf. Second National Bank of Hoboken v Columbia Trust Co.*, 288 F. 17 at 21–22 (1923).

[89] UCP, Art. 42(b) and, under Art. 45, during banking hours; and see *Midland Bank Ltd v Seymour* [1955] 2 Lloyd's Rep. 147 at 166 *et seq.* In the USA see: *Liberty National Bank and Trust Co. v Bank of America*, 116 F.Supp. 233 at 244 (1953), affirmed 218 F. 2d 831 (1955); *Banco Tornquist SA v American Bank and Trust Co.*, 337 N.Y.S. 2d 489 (1972); *W. Pat Crow Forgings v Mooring Aero Industries Inc.*, 403 N.Y.S. 2d 399 (1978); *Flagship Cruises Ltd v New England Merchants National Bank of Boston*, 569 F. 2d 699 (1978). As to accidental delay of tender by mail see *Second National Bank of Toledo v M Samuel & Sons Inc.*, 12 F. 2d 963 (1926).

[90] *Stein v Hambro's Bank of Northern Commerce* (1922) 10 Ll.L.R. 529. See also *Davis O'Brien Lumber Co. Ltd v Bank of Montreal* [1951] 3 D.L.R. 536; *Liberty National Bank and Trust Co. v Bank of America*, above, at p.243; *Voest-Alpine Corp. v Chase Manhattan Bank*, 546 F.Supp. 301 (1982), varied: 707 F. 2d 680 (1983).

[91] Partial shipments are allowed unless expressly prohibited: Art. 40(a).

Article 44(b) of the UCP deals also with problems concerning extensions of time. It provides that the latest date for shipment is not extended by reason of the extension of the expiry date of the credit in accordance with this article.[92] This reference is to paragraph (a), under which a stipulated expiry date, which falls on a day on which the banks are closed for a reason other than the interruption of their business,[93] is extended to the first succeeding business day.[94] In order to avoid misunderstandings, the UCP defines certain terms relating to dates and times.[95]

23–211 **Quantity and weight.** Article 39(b) of the UCP permits, in the absence of stipulation to the contrary, a discrepancy of up to 5 per cent of the stipulated weight or quantity, provided the total amount of the drawings does not exceed the amount of the credit. Moreover, the stipulated tolerance does not apply when the credit specifies quantity in terms of a stated number of packaging units or individual items.[96] Under Article 39(a) the words "about" "circa" or other similar expressions permit a tolerance of up to 10 per cent. The quantity or weight of the goods must be stated in the documents either in the words of the documentary credit or in such manner as to make it possible to calculate it.[97]

23–212 **Tolerance in amount.** The new Article 39(c) of the UCP allows a certain tolerance in the amount drawn under a documentary credit which prohibits partial shipments. Except where such a credit stipulates otherwise, or precludes any tolerance in the quantity of the goods, "a tolerance of 5 per cent less in the amount of the drawing will be permissible, always provided that if the Credit stipulates the quantity of the goods, such quantity of

---

[92] And note that the agreement to accept documents "as tendered" does not, in itself, extend a period stipulated in the credit, such as 21 days from the date of shipment: *Credit Apricole Indosuez v Credit Suisse* [2001] All E.R. (D.) 161.

[93] Where the bank is closed due to such reasons as strikes or other causes beyond the bank's control, the expiry date of a credit, falling due during the interruption, is not extended: Art. 17. But note that the nomination of a ship may tacitly extend the expiry date of the credit: *English, Scottish and Australian Bank Ltd v Bank of South Africa* (1922) 13 Ll.L.R. 13 at 24.

[94] For a construction of this provision see *Bayerische Vereinshank AG v National Bank of Pakistan* [1997] 1 Lloyd's Rep. 59 (Mance J.). Article 44(a) further extends in such cases the period during which the set may under Art. 43(a) be tendered without being considered stale. And note that, under Art. 44(c), the bank to whom such delayed presentment is made on the first succeeding business day must provide a statement that the documents were so presented. It has been held that the confirming bank's failure to provide such a statement entitled the issuing bank to a claim in damages: *Bayerische Vereinsbank AG v National Bank of Pakistan* [1997] 1 Lloyd's Rep. 59. His Lordship did not decide whether or not Art. 14(d)–(e) would be applicable.

[95] Arts 42(c), 46 and 47, construing and discouraging the use of terms such "for one month". As to ambiguities in matters of time, generally, see *Midland Bank Ltd v Seymour* [1955] 2 Lloyd's Rep. 147 at 164–167. The latest shipment date on any of the transport documents presented is deemed the date of shipping: Art. 43(b).

[96] But see *Kydon Compañia Naviera SA v National Westminster Bank Ltd* (*The "Lena"*) [1981] 1 Lloyd's Rep. 68 at 76 which shows that the provision in point is applicable only to weight and quantity *strictu sensu*.

[97] *London and Foreign Trading Corp. v British and North European Bank* (1921) 9 Ll.L.R. 116.

goods is shipped in full, and if the Credit stipulates a unit price, such price is not reduced." It is provided that this article does not apply where the letter of credit uses phrases such as "approximately" or "circa", in which case the position is governed by Article 39(a).

The description of the goods. At one time it was thought that each document should contain a full and accurate description of the goods in the words of the documentary credit.[98] More recent authorities show that it is, in fact, sufficient if all the documents, when read together, give a full description of the goods.[99] A similar solution is adopted by Article 37(c) of the UCP, according to which the description of the goods in the commercial invoice must correspond with the description in the credit. In the remaining documents the goods may be described in general terms not inconsistent with the description of the goods in credit. The decision of the Court of Appeal in *Glencore International AG v Bank of China*[1] confirms that, accordingly, a packing list need not include a detailed description of the goods. Their Lordships further held that, even in the commercial invoice, the description of the goods need not follow the words used in the letter of credit literally. In that case the documentary credit provided, *inter alia*: "Origin: Any Western Brand". The invoice tendered in due course described the origin of the goods shipped as "Any Western Brand—Indonesia (Inalum Brand)". The argument for the issuing bank was that, as the words used in invoice departed from the plain language of the letter of credit, the invoice was a bad tender. Reversing Rix J.'s decision on this specific point, the Court of Appeal rejected this argument. In the words of Bingham M.R.: "It seems to us quite plain on the face of the document that the additional words were to indicate the precise brand of the goods, it being implicit that the brand fell within the broad generic description that was all that was required. The additional words could not, on any possible reading of the documents, have been intended to indicate that the goods did not fall within the description 'Any Western Brand'."[2] 23–213

Contradictory documents. However, a set of documents which include any contradictory statements constitutes a bad tender. Thus, in *Bank Melli Iran v Barclays Bank DCO*[3] the letter of credit called for documents evidencing the shipment of "100 new Chevrolet trucks". The documents tendered included an invoice which described the trucks as being "in new 23–214

---

[98] See, *e.g. London and Foreign Corp. v British and North European Bank*, above; *cf. Rayner (J H) & Co. Ltd v Hambro's Bank Ltd* [1943] 1 K.B. 37.

[99] *Midland Bank Ltd v Seymour* [1955] 2 Lloyd's Rep. 147 at 152; *Soproma SpA v Marine and Animal By-Products Corp.* [1966] 1 Lloyd's Rep. 367.

[1] [1996] 1 Lloyd's Rep. 135; and see *Kydon Compañia Naviera SA v National Westminster Bank Ltd* (*The "Lena"*) [1981] 1 Lloyd's Rep. 68 at 75–77. As to what constitutes part of the description, see *Astro Exito Navegacion SA v Chase Manhattan Bank* [1986] 1 Lloyd's Rep. 455, affirmed [1988] 2 Lloyds Rep. 217. See as regards an earlier article in point, in the 1962 version: *Courtaulds North America v North Carolina National Bank*, 528 F. 2d 802 (1975).

[2] [1996] 1 Lloyd's Rep. at 154.

[3] [1951] 2 Lloyd's Rep. 367 esp. at 375. And see also Art. 13(a) of the UCP, discussed above, para.23–206.

condition", a certificate which described them as "100, new, good Chevrolet . . . trucks", and a delivery order describing them as "new (hyphen) good . . ." McNair J. held that these descriptions were inconsistent with each other and that the tender was therefore faulty. Similarly, in *Soproma SpA v Marine and Animal By-Products Corp.*[4] the letter of credit called for documents evidencing the shipment of "Chilean Fish Full meal, steam-dried, minimum 70 per cent protein". The seller's invoice described the goods as "Chilean Fish Full Meal, 70 per cent protein", the bill of lading as "Chilean Fishmeal" and an invoice of the ultimate supplier, which was by mistake attached to the documents tendered, as "Chilean Fishmeal minimum 67 per cent protein". Certificates of analysis and of quality certified a protein content of slightly less than 70 per cent. McNair J. held that the certificates vitiated the documents. But he thought that the bill of lading by itself, described the goods in sufficient detail and constituted a good tender. He also expressed the view that the description of the goods in the ultimate supplier's invoice was irrelevant as the tender of this document was not required under the documentary credit. But McNair J. thought that this document would entitle the person to whom it was tendered to doubt the truthfulness of the description of the goods in the seller's invoice. Whether the documents were vitiated by the omission of the word "steamdried" from the description of the goods in the invoice, was not decided.

23–215 **Identification of goods.** A tender is considered "inconsistent" within the scope of this doctrine if the goods are not properly identified in each document. In *Banque de l'Indochine et de Suez SA v J H Rayner (Mincing Lane) Ltd*[5] Donaldson M.R. said that Article 32(c) of the 1974 Revision—the predecessor of Article 37(c) of the current version—relaxed the requirement of the inclusion of full details in each document only in respect of the description of the goods. "But however general the description, the identification . . . must be unequivocal. Linkage between the documents is not, as such, necessary, provided that each directly or indirectly refers unequivocally to the goods."[6]

23–216 **Expert evidence.** Issues respecting the conformity of documents tendered under documentary credits are frequently determined on the basis of prevailing banking practice. The point is highlighted by Article 13(a) of the UCP, under which the compliance of documents is to be determined "by international standard banking practice as reflected in these Articles". It is, accordingly, quite common to adduce expert evidence when one of the issues in a documentary credit dispute concerns the regularity of documents or the validity of the steps taken for their rejection. *Davis v Tenco*[7] suggests

[4] [1966] 1 Lloyd's Rep. 367.
[5] [1983] 1 Lloyd's Rep. 228.
[6] *ibid.*, at p.233.
[7] Unreported, February 25, 1992, decision of Simpson J. in the City Court of London: [1992] C.L. 2064. For cases in which expert witnesses were called see, for instance, *Sumitomo Bank v Co-operative Centrale Raiffeisen-Boerenleenbank (The "Royan")* [1988] 2 Lloyd's Rep. 250, affg. in part [1987] 1 Lloyd's Rep. 345; *Bankers Trust Co. v State Bank of India* [1991] 1 Lloyd's Rep. 587, affirmed [1991] 2 Lloyd's Rep. 443, CA; *Glencore International AG v Bank of China* [1996] 1 Lloyd's Rep. 135.

that experts called on such occasions should be bankers and not a bank's legal advisers.

(c) *Documents of Carriage*

Documents of carriage and contracts c.i.f. The documents of carriage which are most commonly required in documentary credit transactions are the bill of lading and the combined transport document. These are also the documents which are required under most sales on c.i.f. terms. When a documentary credit is opened for the finance of a contract c.i.f., it stipulates for the type of transport document required in such contracts. There is therefore much similarity between the type of bill of lading or combined transport document required under a contract c.i.f. and documents tendered under a documentary credit. The aspects of compliance which are connected with the general requirements of contracts c.i.f. are discussed elsewhere in this book[8]; the aspects related to documentary credits are discussed in this part. 23–217

The 1974 Revision of the UCP had special provisions for bills of lading and one provision—Article 23—which purported to deal comprehensively with combined transport documents. The 1983 Revision departed from this structure dividing documents of carriage into bills of lading (covered in Art. 26), postal receipts (Art. 30) and other documents, including combined transport documents (Art. 25). The new, 1993 Revision, has far more elaborate provisions. Whilst the new Article 23, respecting marine bills of lading, adheres, generally, to Article 26 of the 1983 Revision, the remaining provisions in this group are new. Thus, Article 24 makes specific provisions respecting non-negotiable sea waybills and Article 25 deals with charter-party bills of lading. The next provision, which bears certain similarities to Article 23 of the 1974 Revision, regulates multimodal or "combined" transport documents. Three other provisions in this group deal, respectively, with air transport documents (Art. 27), with road, rail and inland waterway transport documents (Art. 28) and with courier and post receipts (Art. 29).

Requirements of bill of lading. The transport document used most widely in documentary credit transactions is the marine bill of lading. The provisions concerning it have by now become well defined. To start with, if a bill of lading of a certain type is required, the tender of a bill of a different type is unacceptable. Thus, if a straight bill of lading in the buyer's name is called for, a bill of lading made out to the seller's order and blank indorsed is a bad tender.[9] Similarly, a straight bill of lading cannot be tendered in lieu of a bill made out to order and indorsed in blank.[10] Several rules defining the type of bill of lading to be tendered in the absence of 23–218

---

[8] See above, paras 19–023 *et seq*.

[9] *Williams Ice Cream Co. Inc. v Chase National Bank*, 199 N.Y.S. 314 (1923), rvsd. on a different point: 205 N.Y.S. 446 (1924).

[10] *Soproma SpA v Marine and Animal By-Products Corp.* [1966] 1 Lloyd's Rep. 367 at 388.

stipulation to the contrary in the documentary credit are spelt out in the UCP Thus, Article 30 prohibits the tender of bills of lading issued by a freight forwarder unless he issues the bill either whilst acting as a carrier or as the agent of the named carrier. Bills of lading which are subject to a charterparty and bills of lading which indicate that the vessel is propelled by sail only are deemed a bad tender by Article 23(a)(vi). Under Article 23(a)(iii)(b), a bill of lading must further be rejected if it contains the indication "intended" in relation to either the port of loading or the port of discharge unless the document "also states the port of loading and/or discharge stipulated in the Credit". In addition, Article 23(a) lists two types of documents which, in the absence of stipulation to the contrary, are to be accepted. The first is a "short form bill of lading", that is, a bill which incorporates all or some of the conditions of the contract of carriage by reference to some other source (Art. 23(a)(v)). Secondly, a bill of lading, which indicates the designated ports of loading and of discharge, is not to be rejected merely because it indicates a place of taking in charge different from the port of loading and a place of final destination different from the port of discharge (Art. 23(a)(iii)(a)). It is clear that this rule, known from the 1983 Revision, has been introduced in order to accommodate the needs of containerised cargo. A further principle, based the opening words of Article 23(a), is that banks will accept a document as a valid marine bill of lading regardless of how it is named, provided it meets the requirements spelt out in the UCP It follows that a document entitled, for instance, "combined transport document" is to be accepted as a good bill of lading if it meets the substantive requirements applicable.

23–219 **Basic principle.** Article 23 has not modified the basic principle concerning bills of lading. This is now set out in paragraph (a), under which, in the absence of stipulation to the contrary, banks have to accept as a valid bill of lading a document which is dated[11] appears on its face to have been issued by a named carrier or his agent,[12] which indicates that the goods have been loaded on board or shipped on a named vessel and which meets all other stipulations of the credit.[13] Where the bill of lading is issued in more than one original, banks have to accept a full set. It will be recalled that problems arise as to whether certain types of copies can be treated as originals for this purpose. Article 23 is augmented by Article 31, under which bankers have to reject a bill of lading showing stowage on deck, except where specifically authorised in the credit. However, "banks will accept a transport document which contains a provision that the goods may be carried on deck, provided it does not specifically state that they are or will be loaded on deck". This provision is drafted so as to apply also to the sea carriage portion of a multimodal transport document.

[11] An undated bill of lading is unacceptable even if the words "a presented" are included in the l/c: *Credit Apricole Indosuez v Credit Suisse First Boston* [2001] 1 All E.R. (Comm) 1088.

[12] And note that under Art. 23(a)(i) the agent must also indicate the name and capacity of the party on whose behalf he is signing.

[13] A bill of lading dated after the last date of shipment is irregular: *Credit Apricole Indosuez v Credit Suisse* [2001] All E.R. (D.) 161 (construing also the provisions of Art. 28).

The principles of the UCP are, effectively, similar to rulings in decided cases. It has been held that at common law, quite apart from insisting on a bill of lading of the required type, the banker must also insist on obtaining the required number of bills. Thus, where a full set of bills of lading is required, the tender of two bills out of a set of three is insufficient.[14] But in certain places a trade usage may permit the substitution of a bank indemnity for one bill of lading of the set.[15]

"Shipped" and "received for shipment". The UCP here draws a distinction between bills of lading and multimodal transport documents. In the absence of stipulation to the contrary in the credit, a bill of lading is a good tender only if it evidences shipment.[16] Multimodal transport documents are acceptable even if they merely indicate that the goods were taken in charge or received for shipment.[17] Under Article 23(a)(ii), loading on board or shipment on a named vessel "may be indicated by pre-printed wording on the bill of lading that the goods have been loaded on board a named vessel or shipped on a named vessel, in which case the date of the bill of lading will be deemed to be the date of loading on board and the date of shipment. In all other cases loading on board a named vessel must be evidenced by a notation on the bill of lading which gives the date on which the goods have been loaded on board, in which case the date of the notation will be deemed the date of shipment." **23–220**

Clean bill of lading. Under Article 32(b) of the UCP, a bill of lading or other transport document which is not clean is a bad tender. This article adopts the English view.[18] It further stipulates, in paragraph (a), that a clean document is one which bears no superimposed clause or notation which expressly declares a defective condition of the goods or of the packaging. Thus, if the words "shipped in good order and condition" are deleted and replaced by a notation that "ship not responsible for kind and condition of merchandise"[19] or by a specific exclusion of liability for **23–221**

---

[14] *Donald H Scott & Co. Ltd v Barclays Bank Ltd* [1923] 2 K.B. 1; *Westminster Bank v Banca Nazionale Di Credito* (1928) 31 Ll.L.R. 306, 310.

[15] *Dixon, Irmaos & Cia Ltda. v Chase National Bank*, 144 F. 2d 759 (1944). As regards problems arising in connection with the bills of lading where goods are shipped in containers, see above, paras 21–072 *et seq*.

[16] Art. 23(a)(ii). This is also the position at common law: *Diamond Alkali Export Corp. v Bourgeois* [1921] 3 K.B. 443; *Yelo v SM Machado & Co. Ltd* [1952] 1 Lloyd's Rep. 183 at 192 (time of loading to be acknowledged). As regards contracts c.i.f. generally, see above, para.19–030, as regards stowage on deck of containers, see above, paras 21–088 *et seq*. The same requirement applies to charterparty bills of lading: Art. 25(a)(iv).

[17] UCP, Art. 26(a)(ii), validating documents indicating that "the goods have been dispatched, taken in charge or loaded on board."

[18] *British Imex Industries Ltd v Midland Bank Ltd* [1958] 1 Q.B. 542 at 551–552. Contrast *Camp v Corn Exchange National Bank*, 132 A. 189 at 191–192 (1926). As regards c.i.f. contracts, see above, paras 19–038 *et seq*.

[19] *Westminster Bank v Banca Nazionale Di Credito* (1928) 31 Ll.L.R. 306 at 311. See also *Liberty National Bank and Trust Co. v Bank of America*, 116 F.Supp. 233 at 238 (1953); affirmed 218 F. 2d 831 at 838 (1955); *Camp v Corn Exchange National Bank*, above.

weight,[20] the bill is unclean. But a bill of lading is not unclean merely because it includes a specific clause excluding liability for the condition of the goods or a clause exempting liability for goods not marked in a specific manner.[21] Moreover, under Article 31(ii), in the absence of stipulation to the contrary, banks will accept a document which bears on its face a clause such as "shipper's load and count" or "said by shipper to contain."

During the ten years that followed the promulgation of the 1974 Revision, some banks persistently maintained that a transport document had to be accepted as "clean" only if it was so described in its heading. To combat this practice, Article 34(c) of the 1983 Revision provided that the requirement for a "clean on board" document was met if the document was "clean" as defined. This provision is reproduced with minor modifications in the current Article 32(c). Another innovative provision originating in the 1983 Revision is the current Article 31(iii), which, in the absence of stipulation to the contrary, sanctions the tender of a document of carriage which names a party other than the beneficiary as consignor of the goods. This provision is essential where the beneficiary is in effect a middleman and the goods are shipped by the ultimate supplier. It seems clear that in the light of this provision such a transport document is "clean", within the meaning of the UCP, although it is provided by a party other than the beneficiary.

23–222 **Voyage and destination.** According to Article 23(c), the entire voyage must be covered by one document of carriage.[22] It has been held that if a bill of lading in effect covers the entire voyage, then it is not rendered invalid by a clause in small print limiting the carrier's liability to the part of the voyage performed by vessels under his own management.[23] Article 23(b) provides that, in the absence of stipulation to the contrary, a document of carriage showing that the goods will be transhipped *en route* is a good tender. But, under Article 23(d)(ii), even where transhipment is prohibited, a document is a good tender notwithstanding that it includes a small-print clause reserving a right to tranship.[24] However, in such case a bill is a bad tender if it indicates that the goods will actually be transhipped.[25] Another requirement, originally laid down in a decision of the United States

[20] *Bailey v United Chinese Bank Ltd* (1953) 37 Hong Kong L.R. 102 at 107–108.
[21] *British Imex Industries Ltd v Midland Bank Ltd*, above, at p.551. See also *M Golodetz & Co. Inc. v Czarnikow-Rionda Co. Inc.* [1980] 1 W.L.R. 495 in which it was held that a clause which indicated that, subsequent to loading the goods had to be discharged due to a fire, did not render the bill of lading unclean. Neither was the bill rendered unclean or stale by its having been issued 13 days after the date of shipment. A received for shipment bill of lading is, of course, not rendered unclean by a notation certifying loading: *Westpac Banking Corp. v South Carolina National Bank* [1986] 1 Lloyd's Rep. 31, PC.
[22] This is also a requirement in contracts.
[23] *Bailey v United Chinese Bank Ltd* (1953) 37 Hong Kong L.R. 102 at 108–110.
[24] *Soproma SpA v Marine and Animal By-Products Corp.* [1966] 1 Lloyd's Rep. 367 at 388.
[25] Art. 23(d)(i) makes further provisions concerning transhipment in the case of carriage in containers. For the definition of transhipment for the purposes of the UCP, see Art. 23(b).

Supreme Court,[26] is that the bill of lading must indicate the correct destination.[27]

23–223 **Freight.** According to Article 33(a) bankers may, in the absence of stipulation to the contrary, honour documents stating that freight or delivery charges have still to be paid.[28] But the paragraph emphasises that this statement must not be inconsistent with any other document. The object of this safeguard is to invalidate a bill of lading which is marked "freight collect" if the accompanying invoice does not deduct the freight from the c.i.f. price. According to Article 33(b) if any words indicating that freight has been paid by the seller appear by a stamp or by other means in the carriage documents they are to be accepted as evidence of such prepayment. Under Article 31(c) the words "freight pre-payable" or "freight to be pre-paid" do not constitute evidence that payment has taken place.[29]

23–224 **Other transport documents of carriage of goods by sea.** The provisions governing marine bills of lading are applied, subject to certain modifications, to other transport documents used in sea transport. The new Article 24 of the UCP deals with non-negotiable sea waybills, which differ from marine bills of lading mainly in that they are non-negotiable.[30] Article 25 governs charterparty bills of lading, which are bills of lading issued subject to a charterparty. Again, the provisions of Article 23 are applied with the necessary modifications.[31] A provision of particular importance is to be found in paragraph (b). "Even if the Credit requires the presentation of a

---

[26] *Lamborn v National Bank of Commerce*, 276 U.S. 469 at 48 S.Ct. 378 (1928). But it was held that in f.o.b. contracts it was adequate that the ship in effect proceeded to the port after being so diverted at sea.

[27] As regards terms indicating shipment, see Art. 46(a); as regards partial shipments, see Art. 40.

[28] Such bills of lading were not favoured by English bankers before the adoption of the UCP Even at present many customers are advised to insist on a "freight prepaid" clause where the contract is in terms c.i.f. In the United States such bills have always been acceptable: *Dixon, Irmaos & Cia Ltda. v Chase National Bank*, 144 F. 2d 759 at 763 (1944). Whether such a bill of lading is valid at common law as a tender under a c.i.f. or c. & f. contract, see *Soproma SpA v Marine and Animal By-Products Corp.* [1966] 1 Lloyd's Rep. 367 at 390 (above, para.19–009).

[29] As regards references in the transport document to additional charges, see Art. 33(d), construed in *Banque de l'Indochine et de Suez SA v J H Rayner (Mincing Lane) Ltd* [1983] 1 Lloyd's Rep. 228 at 231; as regards courier charges, see Art. 33(b).

[30] It is not altogether clear from the wording of Art. 24(a), whether or not a mate's receipt is a good tender where a non-negotiable sea waybill is called for in the credit. It is true that, under paragraph (a), the title inscribed on the documents is immaterial. However, the waybill must be signed by the carrier or his agent and, further, must appear to contain all the terms and conditions of carriage either expressly or by reference to some other source document. In practice, many mate's receipts do not meet with these requirements. See, generally, above, para.18–163. Delivery orders and delivery warrants, as to which see above, paras 18–169 *et seq.*; esp. para.18–193, are not documents of transport and hence cannot be regarded sea waybills anymore than they constitute bills of lading.

[31] But note that the provisions respecting transshipment, set out in Art. 23(b)–(d), are not applied.

charterparty contract in connection with a charterparty bill of lading, banks will not examine such charterparty contract, but will pass it without responsibility on their part."

23–225 **Multimodal transport document.** Article 26(a) defines a multimodal transport document as a "transport document covering at least two different modes of transport (multimodal transport)". Although, conceptually, a document is encompassed by the definition where it covers transport by truck and airfreight, one of the modes of transport covered by such a document is, in the ordinary course, carriage by sea. In consequence, it is not surprising that, once again, most of the principles applied to multimodal transport documents are based on Article 23, which deals with marine bills of lading. Three main modifications are, however, introduced in respect of multimodal transport documents. First, under Article 26(a)(i), the document may refer to, or be signed by, a multimodal operator (or his agent) instead of a carrier. Secondly, under subparagraph (ii), the document need not evidence shipping or loading. It is sufficient if it indicates that the goods have been dispatched or taken in charge. Thirdly, under paragraph (b), even if the documentary credit prohibits transshipment, "banks will accept a multimodal transport document which indicates that transshipment may or will take place, provided that the entire carriage is covered by one and the same multi-modal transport document". This provision is wider than Article 23(d)(i), which applies a comparable rule where cargo is shipped in containers, trailers or "Lash" barges.

23–226 **Air transport documents.** The innovative Article 27 takes account of the lack of uniformity and standardisation in documents covering air transport. Paragraph (a), accordingly, states that if a credit calls for an "air transport document" banks will, in the absence of stipulation to the contrary, accept "a document, however named" provided certain basic requirements are satisfied. First, under subparagraph (i), the document has to be signed by the carrier or by a named agent acting on his behalf. Secondly, under subparagraph (ii), the document must indicate that the goods have been accepted for carriage. Thirdly, if the documentary credit calls for an actual date of dispatch, the document must, under subparagraph (iii), have a specific notation of such date. As in the case of a bill of lading, the date of dispatch is deemed to be also the date of shipment.[32] Four further requirements, set out in subparagraphs (iv)–(vi), are that the document must indicate the airport of departure and of dispatch, must appear to be "the original for consignor/shipper even if the Credit stipulates a full set of originals", must "appear to contain all the terms and conditions of the credit, or some of such terms and conditions, by reference to a source document other than the air transport document; and must in all other respects meet the stipulations of the letter of credit.[33]

[32] Note that, in the ordinary case, the date of the issuance of the air transport document is deemed to be the date of shipment. However, for the purposes of Art. 27, the flight number and date appearing in the box in the document, marked "For Carrier Use" or similar expression, are not to be considered a specific notation of dispatch.

[33] And note provisions respecting transshipment in Art. 27(b)–(c).

Road, rail or inland waterway transport documents. Provisions similar to those applicable to air transport documents are applied in Article 28 to transport documents used in the carriage of goods by road, by rail and by inland waterways. The main difference respects the number of documents tendered. Under paragraph (b), "in the absence of any indication on the transport document as to the numbers issued, banks will accept the transport document(s) presented as constituting a full set. Banks will accept as original(s) the transport document(s) whether marked as original(s) or not". 23–227

Post receipts and courier receipts. Under Article 29(a), a "post receipt" or "certificate of posting" must comply with two basic requirements. First, it must appear on its face to have been stamped or otherwise authenticated and dated "in the place from which the Credit stipulated the goods are to be dispatched". The date so specified is, then, deemed to be the date of dispatch. Secondly, the document must, in all other respects, meet the stipulations of the credit. Similar provisions are applied, under Article 29(b), to documents issued by a courier or by an expedited delivery service. An important addition, spelt out in subparagraph (ii), is that the document must indicate "a date of pick-up or of receipt or wording to this effect". The date in question is deemed to be the date of shipment or dispatch. 23–228

(d) *Insurance Documents*

Type. According to Article 35(a) of the UCP, the credit must stipulate the type of insurance required and any additional risks to be covered. Imprecise terms, such as "usual risks" or "customary risks" are to be avoided. If used, "banks will accept insurance documents as presented, without responsibility for any risks not being covered". Under paragraph (b), where the letter of credit fails to include specific stipulations as regards the insurance document, bank will, likewise, accept the document as tendered and without responsibility on their part.[34] Under Article 34(b), if the insurance document indicates that it has been issued in more than one original, all the originals must be presented unless otherwise authorised in the credit. 23–229

Basic requirements. The insurance document must be of a type current in trade and one to which no reasonable objections may be taken.[35] Under Article 34(a), insurance documents must appear on their face to be issued and signed by insurance companies or underwriters or by their agents. Cover notes issued by brokers are, under paragraph (c), acceptable only if their tender is specifically authorised in the credit. Paragraph (d) grapples 23–230

---

[34] But note that one authority suggests that the policy ought to cover the risks contemplated by the parties and that, in this context, regard may be had to trade usage: *Borthwick v Bank of New Zealand* (1900) 6 Com.Cas. 1; 17 T.L.R. 2; and see above, para.19–042.

[35] *Borthwick v Bank of New Zealand* (1900) 6 Com.Cas. 1 at 4; *Donald H Scott & Co. Ltd v Barclays Bank Ltd*, above, at pp.14, 17. And see UCP, Art. 13(a).

with the well known problem arising where the document tendered to the bank is a certificate of insurance issued under a global policy. At common law, such a certificate is a bad tender where the documentary credit calls for an insurance policy.[36] The rationale is that such a certificate differs fundamentally from a policy because it does not incorporate all the terms of the insurance contract involved. Consistently, some American certificates, in which the terms are fully spelt out, are acceptable.[37] Under the new paragraph (d), "banks will accept an insurance certificate or a declaration under an open cover pre-signed by insurance companies or underwriters or their agents". This provision applies, however, only in the absence of stipulation to the contrary. Accordingly, it is arguable that an express stipulation for an "insurance policy" excludes a certificate or a declaration under open cover. Support for this argument, which effectively preserves the common law position, is to be found in the concluding sentence of paragraph (d). According to it, if "a credit specifically calls for an insurance certificate or a declaration under an open cover, banks will accept, in lieu thereof, an insurance policy". The imperative language of this rule recognises the clear difference between policies and certificates. Furthermore, the wording is at variance with the dispositive phraseology of the first sentence.

23–231 **Date, voyage and description.** Under Article 34(e), the insurance document must either bear a date not later than the loading on board, the dispatch or the taking in charge of the goods or must indicate that cover is effective from that date. The document should cover the entire voyage.[38] It need not describe the goods in detail.[39]

23–232 **Currency and amount.** Under Article 34(b)(i) of the UCP the policy must be expressed in the same currency as the documentary credit.[40] Under paragraph (f)(ii), the minimum amount for which insurance must be effected is the c.i.f. or c.i.p. value of the goods plus 10 per cent. However, when the c.i.f. or c.i.p. value of the goods cannot be determined from the face of the documents, the amount covered must be equal to that of the

---

36 See, before the UCP, *Diamond Alkali Export Corp. v Bourgeois* [1921] 3 K.B. 443; *Donald H Scott & Co. Ltd v Barclays Bank Ltd* [1923] 2 K.B. 1 at 12, 15. As regards brokers' certificates, see *Wilson, Holgate & Co. Ltd v Belgian Grain and Produce Co. Ltd* [1920] 2 K.B. 1 at 8.

37 *Wilson, Holgate & Co. Ltd v Belgian Grain and Produce Co. Ltd*, above, at p.7; *Malmberg v H J Evans & Co.* (1924) 41 T.L.R. 38 at 39–40; *Donald H Scott & Co. Ltd v Barclays Bank Ltd*, above, at pp.12–13, 15–16.

38 *Landauer & Co. v Craven & Speeding Bros* [1912] 2 K.B. 94 at 105–106, relating to contracts c.i.f. Where the bill of lading permits transshipment, it is adequate that the policy states "all liberties as per contract of affreightment": *Belgian Grain and Produce Co. Ltd v Cox & Co. (France) Ltd* (1919) 1 Ll.l.R. 256.

39 Art. 37(c) of the UCP See also *Crocker First National Bank v De Sousa*, 27 F. 2d 462 at 463 (1928). As regards the requirements of an insurance document tendered under a c.i.f. contract, see above, paras 19–042 *et seq*.

40 Where the UCP does not apply, the position is dubious: *Donald H Scott & Co. Ltd v Barclays Bank Ltd*, above, at p.16. *Cf. Pan-American Bank and Trust Co. v National City Bank of New York*, 6 F 2d 762 at 767 (1925).

draft or the commercial invoice, whichever is greater.[41] Under Article 35(c), a policy which indicates that cover is subject to a franchise or an excess (deductible), is in the absence of stipulation to the contrary a good tender.

All risks cover. An important point is settled in Article 36 of the UCP When a documentary credit stipulates for an "all risks" cover, any insurance document which contains an "all risks" notation or clause is a good tender and the banker is not responsible if a specific risk is, in effect, not covered. This is so even if the policy does not have an "all risks" heading or indicates that certain risks are excluded. 23–233

(e) *Other Documents*

Invoice. The invoice must be made out by the seller and should usually be in the form described in *Ireland v Livingston*.[42] It should debit the consignee with the agreed amount and should give him credit for the amount of freight he may have to pay on delivery. Under the first paragraph of Article 37 of the UCP, the invoice must appear on its face to be issued by the beneficiary and made out in the buyer's name. It need not be signed. Under the second paragraph, the invoice may not be for an amount exceeding that of the credit.[43] Under the last paragraph, the description of the goods in the invoice must correspond with the description in the credit.[44] This is a sensible provision: a deviation in the description of the goods in the invoice may indicate that the seller recognises that they are not the ones called for in the credit.[45] 23–234

In the absence of specific stipulation, the seller is under no obligation to furnish an invoice from his suppliers, even if the credit describes the goods by reference to their foreign origin.[46]

Certificates. To avoid complete dependence on the seller's honesty, documentary credits frequently demand the tender of certificates relating to the goods and supplied by qualified persons or firms, such as the Société 23–235

---

[41] See also *Bank Melli Iran v Barclays Bank D.C.O.* [1951] 2 Lloyd's Rep. 367 at 376. See also above, para.19–051.

[42] (1872) L.R. 5 H.L. 395 at 406. That this is the proper form of an invoice, see *Biddell Bros v Clemens (E.) Horst Co.* [1911] 1 K.B. 214 at 220 revsd. *ibid.*, at p.934 but restored [1912] A.C. 18. In the United States see: *Laudisi v American Exchange National Bank*, 146 N.E. 347 at 349 (1924). An invoice showing that part of the goods do not belong to the seller is a bad tender: *Wells Fargo Nevada National Bank v Corn Exchange National Bank*, 23 F. 2d 1 at 2 (1927). The fact that the invoice bears an obvious correction, does not render it irregular: *Talbot v Bank of Hendersonville*, 495 S.W. 2d 548 (Tenn. 1972).

[43] But note that banks have the option of paying against the excessive invoice the amount for which the credit has been issued.

[44] For a discussion of an earlier version of this provision, see *Oriental Pacific (USA) Inc. v Toronto Dominion Bank*, 357 N.Y.S. 2d 957 (1974).

[45] See also *International Banking Corp. v Irving National Bank*, 283 F. 103 (1922); *Crocker First National Bank v De Sousa*, 27 F. 2d 462 at 463 (1928).

[46] *Société Metallurgique D'Aubrives & Villerupt v British Bank for Foreign Trade* (1922) 11 Ll.L.R. 168.

Generalle de Surveillance. It is, however, important to emphasise that the tender of a certificate does not necessarily rule out sharp practices by the seller. In the first place, the certificate may bear a forged signature of the certifying agency.[47] Secondly, some surveyors tend to take a very casual attitude to the completion of a certificate or even supply blank signed forms to the seller.[48] The value of the certificates is, thus, marginal.[49]

There are various types of certificate, such as certificates of inspection, of origin, of weight, of analysis and of quality. A special type of certificate is a consular invoice, on which the origin of the goods is certified by a designated consular department located in the country of export. The principles governing the requirements applicable to certificates are now stated in Article 21 of the UCP, which applies to all documents other than documents of carriage, insurance documents and invoices.[50] Under this article the credit should specify by whom a certificate or other generic document is to be issued and its wording or data content.[51] "If the Credit does not so stipulate, banks will accept such documents as presented, provided that their data content is not inconsistent with any other stipulated document presented."[52]

This provision gives effect to common law principles which demand compliance with some basic requirements even in the case of such documents. In the case of certificates, the first aspect of compliance is that the document must confirm and certify that for which it is issued. Thus, a certificate of inspection must certify that the goods have been inspected and are in apparent good order and condition. But if it is intended that a particular method of inspection be adopted or that particular information as to the result of the inspection be recorded, this would need to be expressly stated in the documentary credit and application form.[53] Moreover, a certificate need not confirm details which are not within its usual scope. Thus, a certificate of weight need not describe the quality of the goods.[54] Secondly, the certificate must be made out by the person designated in the credit or, if the credit does not name a specific firm, by the

[47] See, *e.g. Gian Singh & Co. Ltd v Banque de L'Indochine* [1974] 1 Lloyd's Rep. 56, affirmed [1974] 2 Lloyd's Rep. 1.

[48] See, *e.g. Etablissement Esefka International Anstalt v Central Bank of Nigeria* [1979] 1 Lloyd's Rep. 445.

[49] As regards problems arising where the execution of a certificate requires the buyer's co-operation, see above, para.23–112.

[50] Note that Art. 33 of the 1974 Revision specifically referred to warehouse receipts and delivery orders. These would appear to fall within the ambit of the new Art. 21 (just as they were encompassed by Art. 23 of the 1983 Revision).

[51] As to the need to conform in this regard, see *Astro Exito Navégacion SA v Chase Manhattan Bank* [1986] 1 Lloyd's Rep. 455, affirmed [1988] 2 Lloyd's Rep. 217.

[52] Note that Art. 23 of the 1983 Revision required that the certificate identify the goods in the sense of relating them to those covered in the invoice.

[53] *Commercial Banking Co. of Sydney Ltd v Jalsard Pty Ltd* [1973] A.C. 279 at 285. See also *Bank Melli Iran v Barclays Bank DCO* [1951] 2 Lloyd's Rep. 367 at 375 (a certificate must identify the goods); *Overseas Union Bank Ltd v Chua* (1964) 30 M.L.J. 165.

[54] *Société Metallurgique D'Aubrives & Villerupt v British Bank for Foreign Trade* (1922) 11 Ll.L.R. 168 at 169. Similarly, a packing list need not describe the goods in detail and need not confirm details such as their origin; above, para.23–205.

type of firm envisaged.[55] The bank, however, is not obliged to verify the genuineness of the signature of the person in whose name the certificate is purported to be made out.[56] Thirdly, the certificate must identify the goods.[57] Usually this is done by referring in the certificate to the identifying marks of the parcels. However, there is no need to test the whole consignment and it is sufficient if a sample, taken from the goods to be shipped, is properly tested and certified.[58] Finally, the documents must include all the required certificates, but a tender of fractional certificates instead of a global one may in certain cases be permissible.[59]

Draft. In *Kydon Compania Naviera SA v National Westminster Bank Ltd (The "Lena")*[60] Parker J. held that, even although a sight draft might have no legal effect and served no useful commercial object, it had to be tendered if called for in the letter of credit. Moreover, it had to be drawn on the designated drawee and not on some other party. American decisions go in the same direction. It is true that, as the drawing of the draft is essentially a method of, or procedure employed for, obtaining payment, it was, at one stage, held that the tender of a draft could be excused even where it was specifically required in the documentary credit.[61] But in view of the general principles of strict compliance, the opposite view, expressed in recent cases, is to be preferred.[62] Moreover, the draft is an efficient 23–236

---

[55] *Equitable Trust Co. of New York v Dawson Partners Ltd* (1927) 27 Ll.L.R. 49. As to whether the certificate may be made out by an agent of the designated person, see *Dynamics Corp. of America v Citizens and Southern National Bank*, 356 F.Supp. 991 (1973); *Far Eastern Textile Ltd v City National Bank and Trust Co.*, 430 F.Supp. 193 (1977).

[56] *Gian Singh & Co. Ltd v Banque de L'Indochine*, above. For an interesting American case in point, see *Marino Industries Corp. v Chase Manhattan Bank*, 686 F. 2d 112 (1982). And see, as regards false certificates presented with knowledge by the tenderor of a related fraud: *Montrod Ltd v Grundkotter Fleischvertriebs GmbH* [2002] 1 W.L.R. 1975 affg. on this point [2001] 1 All E.R. (Comm) 368 (importance of innocence of issuer of certificate).

[57] *Re an Arbitration between Reinhold & Co. and Hansloh* (1896) 12 T.L.R. 422; *Basse and Selve v Bank of Australasia* (1904) 90 L.T. 618 (first tender rejected as goods not identified); *Bank Melli Iran v Barclays Bank D.C.O.* [1951] 2 Lloyd's Rep. 367 at 375.

[58] *Basse and Selve v Bank of Australasia*, above, at p.620; *Chairmasters Inc. v Public National Bank and Trust Co.*, 127 N.Y.S. 2d 806 (1954); *Banco Español de Credito v State Street Bank and Trust Co.*, 385 F. 2d 230 (1967); and see further proceedings in case: 409 F. 2d 711 (1969).

[59] See on these points and on whether a combined multi-purpose certificate is permissible, above, para.23–205. And note that the bank cannot demand additional documents in order to verify the certificate: *Bank of Canton v Republic National Bank*, 509 F.Supp. 1310 (1980), affd. 636 F. 2d 30 (1980).

[60] [1981] 1 Lloyd's Rep. 68 at 74–75. And note that Art. 9(a)(iv) and 9(b)(iv), which treats drafts drawn on the applicant as "additional documents", lends general support to this decision.

[61] *Richard v Royal Bank of Canada*, 23 F. 2d 430 at 433 (1928).

[62] *Bounty Trading Corp. v SEK Sportswear Ltd*, 370 N.Y.S. 2d 4 (1975); *Dovenmuehle Inc. v East Bank of Colorado Springs*, 563 P. 2d 24 (Col. 1977). *Cf. Titanium Metals Corp. of America v Space Metals Inc.*, 529 P. 2d 431 (Utah, 1974) and *Crist v J Henry Schroder Bank and Trust Co.*, 693 F. Supp. 1429 (S.D. N.Y. 1988) (holding that a draft complied though drawn as payable to the designated payee's receiver). Note

method for determining the date of payment and it has been held that where a draft payable at a specific usance is required (*e.g.* one payable at 60 days after sight) a draft of a different usance (*e.g.* one payable at 90 days after sight) is a bad tender.[63] The draft must be for the correct amount,[64] be expressed in the currency of the credit[65] and be payable at the designated place.[66] There are only two mitigations of the requirement of strict compliance in respect of drafts. First, if the intention of the parties is clear, a documentary credit calling for one draft may be treated as covering several drafts drawn for the specified amount.[67] Secondly, it is sufficient if the draft identifies the letter of credit under which it is drawn in general terms.[68]

However, the imposition of stamp duty on bills of exchange has led to a tendency to avoid the use of sight drafts.[69] In many countries it has become customary to provide for payment in cash against the documents and to obtain the payee's receipt.

8. STANDBY CREDITS AND PERFORMANCE BONDS[70]

(a) *Introduction*

23–237 **Background.** From a practical point of view, standby credits, performance bonds and first demand guarantees serve one and the same purpose. In all three types of document the issuing bank, at the request of the "account party", undertakes to pay a certain amount of money to the "beneficiary" provided a certain event takes place. The event in question is usually the non-performance of an obligation undertaken by the account party towards the beneficiary. Payment, or the acceptance of the beneficiary's bill of exchange on the issuer, is, however, due against a demand to be made in a prescribed form. In a standby credit it usually assumes the form of a bill of exchange accompanied by a certificate attesting the account party's default. In the case of a first demand guarantee or of a performance bond payment is usually due against the beneficiary's "written demand".

---

that under American law a telex may constitute a draft: *Chase Manhattan Bank v Equibank*, 394 F.Supp. 352 at 356 (1975) reversed on a different point: 550 F. 2d 882 (1977). It is unlikely that this view will be adopted by an English court.

[63] *Birckhead and Carlisle v Brown*, 5 Hill (N.Y.) 634 (1843), affirmed 2 Den. (N.Y.) 375 (1845); *Lockwood and Manning v Brownson*, 53 Tex. 523 (1880).

[64] *Lamborn v Lake Shore Banking and Trust Co.*, 188 N.Y.S. 162 (1921). *Cf. Huston v Newgass*, 84 N.E. 910 (1908).

[65] *Grouf v State National Bank of St. Louis*, 40 F. 2d 2 at 7 (1930).

[66] *Edmondston v Drake & Mitchel*, 5 Pet. (30 U.S.) 624 at 638–639 (1825); *Lindley v First National Bank of Waterloo*, 41 N.W. 381 (1889). The cases concern open credits but appear applicable to documentary credits.

[67] *Union Bank of Medina v Shea*, 58 N.W. 985 at 986 (1894); and see above, para.23–205.

[68] *Flagship Cruises Ltd v New England Merchants National Bank of Boston*, 569 F. 2d 699 (1978).

[69] Some South American countries have introduced particularly high rates.

[70] Wunnicke and Wunnicke, *Standby Letters of Credit* (N.Y. 1989).

The similarity is obvious. The point to be emphasised is that in all three types of document, just as in the case of documentary letters of credit, payment is due when the beneficiary complies with a prescribed procedure. The policy involved is to separate the letter of credit, the performance bond or the first demand guarantee from the underlying transaction between the beneficiary and the account party.[71]

Practice. The development of standby credits took place in the United States where, traditionally the banks did not have the power to issue performance bonds and first demand guarantees.[72] Banks in other countries tend to use standby credits mainly in transactions in which one of the parties is an American bank. When British banks act as sureties for their clients in international transactions they usually use a first demand guarantee or a performance bond. **23–238**

It will be convenient to discuss separately the principles applying to standby credits and those applying to first demand guarantees and to performance bonds. Most of the authorities concerning standby credits were decided by American courts.

(b) *Standby Credits*

Transactions used in. The versatility of standby credits is demonstrated by the remarkable variety of legal transactions in which they have been used in the United States. In transactions concerning real property, standby credits have been used to secure the payment to a lender of a penalty accruing if the developer failed to take up the loan[73]; to cover loss incurred by the landowner where the builder failed to complete the construction of the building[74]; and to secure repayment of a loan covered by a mortgage.[75] Standby credits have also been used in connection with business loans.[76] In transactions involving the manufacturing or the sale of goods, standby credits have been used to secure the payment of the price[77]; the payment of **23–239**

---

[71] As regards the distinction in function between standby credits and documentary credits see above, para.23–050.

[72] See 12 U.S.C., para.24, 7th Power. The provision applied already in the 1875 version—Rev.Stat. para.5136. See Harfield, 61 Harv.L.Rev. 782 at 789 (1948).

[73] *Fidelity Bank v Lutheran Mutual Life Insurance Co.*, 465 F. 2d 211 (1972); *Harvey Estes Construction Co. v Dry Dock Savings Bank*, 381 F.Supp. 271 (1974); *Chase Manhattan Bank v Equibank*, 394 F.Supp. 352 (1975), revsd. 550 F. 2d 882 (1977); and see *Connecticut General Life Insurance Co. v Chicago Title and Trust Co.*, 714 F.2d 48 (1983) (in lieu of commitment fee).

[74] *Wichita Eagle and Beacon Publishing Co. Inc. v Pacific National Bank*, 343 F.Supp. 332 (1971), revsd. 493 F. 2d 1285 (1974).

[75] *Barclays Bank DCO v Mercantile National Bank*, 339 F.Supp. 457 (1972), affd. 481 F. 2d 1224 (1973), [1973] 2 Lloyd's Rep. 541; *Lindy v Lynn*, 395 F.Supp. 769 (1974), affd. (no opinion) 515 F. 2d 507 (1975); *Baker v National Boulevard Bank*, 399 F.Supp. 1021 (1975) (where the credit secured portion of the amount due only, the balance being more than adequately covered by a mortgage).

[76] *Banco Tornquist SA v American Bank and Trust Co.*, 71 Misc. 2d 874, 337 N.Y.S. 2d 489 (1972).

[77] *Key Appliance Inc. v First National City Bank*, 46 A.D. 2d 622, 359 N.Y.S. 2d 886 (1974); *J & K Plumbing and Heating Co. Inc. v International Telephone and Telegraph Corp.*, 51 A.D. 2d 638, 378 N.Y.S. 2d 828 (1976).

liquidated damages for faulty performance[78]; and to cover a deposit repayable in the event of the non-performance of the underlying contract.[79] Losses which could be incurred in a take-over of a company and arising from the non-payment of a promissory note,[80] the payment of a rental[81] and the payment of an amount contested in an admiralty action brought against a ship[82] have been, likewise, secured by standby credits. The instrument has also been used to secure the payment of wages of a football player[83] and to facilitate the payment of a ransom.[84]

23–240 **Form of undertaking.** A perusal of standard instruments discloses that, usually, the issuing bank's engagement in a standby credit effected in the United Kingdom, assumed the form of an undertaking to pay a sight draft, drawn under the letter of credit and accompanied by two documents: (a) a matured bill of exchange for a given amount drawn by the beneficiary on the account party and (b) a certificate, signed either by the beneficiary or by a third party, attesting the dishonour of the bill. In some cases, though, the standby credit stipulated for the tender of a notarial protest of the bill drawn on the account party instead of the default certificate.

23–241 **Legal nature of standby credit.** In the English authorities which consider standby credits, including the decision in *Society of Lloyd's v Canadian Imperial Bank of Commerce*,[85] no distinction was drawn between standby credits and other types of documentary credit. Indeed, in *Kvaerner John Brown Ltd v Midland Bank Plc*,[86] Cresswell J. referred to standby credit as facilities sometimes used in lieu of first demand guarantees. In the circumstances, it is best to concentrate on the topical American authorities which may be of persuasive value in future cases.

Whilst a standby credit need not be in any specified form,[87] it has to include a clear undertaking by the issuer to make payment. Thus, in *Johnston v State Bank*, the Supreme Court of Iowa observed: "The essential

---

[78] *Savage v First National Bank and Trust Co.*, 413 F.Supp. 447 (1976); *cf. Victory Carriers Inc. v United States*, 467 F. 2d 1334 (1972) where it was issued in lieu of a performance bond.

[79] *Dynamics Corp. of America v Citizens and Southern National Bank*, 356 F.Supp. 991 at 996 (1973). See also *Offshore International SA v Banco Central SA* [1977] 2 Lloyd's Rep. 402; *King v Texacally Joint Venture*, 690 S.W. 2d 618 (Tex Ct. App.).

[80] *Steinmeyer v Warner Consolidated Corp.*, 42 Cal.App. 3d 515, 116 Cal.Reptr. 57 (1974).

[81] *Intraworld Industries Inc. v Girard Trust Bank*, 336 A.2d 316 (Pa. 1975).

[82] *National Surety Corp. v Midland Bank and Trust Co.*, 408 F.Supp. 684 (1976).

[83] *Beathard v Chicago Football Club Inc.*, 419 F.Supp. 1133 (1976).

[84] Verkuil, 25 Stan.L.Rev. 716 at 717. The possibility of using a standby credit to secure an issue of commercial paper is explored by Harfield, *op. cit.*, 252.

[85] [1993] 2 Lloyd's Rep. 579. Other English cases in which the letter of credit under consideration was of the standby type are: *Offshore International SA v Banco Central SA* [1977] 1 W.L.R. 239 (case on conflict of laws) and *Hong Kong and Shanghai Banking Corp. v Klockner & Co. AG* [1989] 2 Lloyd's Rep. 332 (concerned set-off).

[86] [1998] C.L.C. 446.

[87] *Wichita Eagle and Beacon Publishing Co. Inc. v Pacific National Bank*, 343 F.Supp. 322 at 338 (1971) revsd. on a different point: 493 F. 2d 1285 (1974).

element of a letter of credit . . . is a direct promise by the bank to pay the addressee of the letter."[88]

From the bank's point of view, its undertaking in a standby credit is just as binding as that in any other form of letter of credit. Moreover, just as a documentary credit, a standby credit constitutes an independent and autonomous undertaking of the issuing bank. Thus, in *Barclays Bank DCO v Mercantile National Bank*, the Circuit Court of Appeals observed that the contract between the issuing bank and the beneficiary "is independent of the underlying contract between the customer and the beneficiary."[89] It follows that the bank is under a duty to perform its undertaking in a standby credit even if the contract between the beneficiary and the account party is void.[90]

Frequency of sharp practices. The autonomy of a standby credit leads to certain problems. As the bank's undertaking frequently assumes the form of a promise to accept a bill of exchange accompanied by a default certificate, the beneficiary, who executes the two documents, is in a position to abuse the rights conferred on him. *Dynamics Corporation of America v Citizens and Southern National Bank*[91] furnishes a good illustration in point. An American firm entered into a contract for the sale to the Government of India of defence orientated equipment, to be manufactured over a given period of time and to be delivered at the firm's premises. The price was payable in instalments against periodic invoices. To safeguard India in respect of amounts so paid, the firm undertook to furnish a bank's standby credit for amounts roughly corresponding to those of the invoices. The standby credit, opened at the firm's instruction by the bank, provided for payment against a sight draft accompanied by a certificate, signed by the President of India, attesting that the firm had failed to carry out certain obligations imposed on it under the contract of sale. A number of invoices were duly paid but problems arose when India intervened in the war between Pakistan and Bangladesh. An embargo imposed by President Nixon precluded India from arranging for the export of the equipment purchased from the firm although the latter was in a position to deliver it. As India lost interest in the equipment, it presented the documents stipulated in the standby credit to the issuing bank and claimed payment. The firm brought an action for an injunction, pleading, *inter alia*, that India's demand for payment was tainted with fraud. The United States District Court granted a preliminary injunction, which precluded payment 23–242

---

[88] 195 N.W. 2d 126 at 130 (1972).

[89] 481 F. 2d 1224 at 1239 (1973), affming. 339 F.Supp. 457 (1972). See also *Fidelity Bank v Lutheran Mutual Life Insurance Co.*, 465 F. 2d 211 (1972); *Intraworld Industries Inc. v Girard Trust Bank*, 336 A.2d 316 (Pa. 1975); *J & K Plumbing and Heating Co. Inc. v International Telephone and Telegraph Corp.*, 51 A.D. 2d 638; 378 N.Y.S. 2d 822 (1976); *American Bell International Inc. v Islamic Republic of Iran*, 474 F.Supp. 420 (1979). *Cf. Touche Ross & Co. v Manufacturers Hanover Trust Co.*, 434 N.Y.S. 2d 575 (1980).

[90] See, *e.g. Savage v First National Bank and Trust Co.*, 413 F.Supp. 447 (1976); *Braun v Intercontinental Bank*, 466 So. 2d 1130 (1985).

[91] 356 F.Supp. 991 (1973). See also *Intra World Industries Inc. v Girard Trust Bank* 336 A. 2d 316 (Pa. 1975).

pending the determination of the fraud issue. The court, however, emphasised that the issuing bank was concerned solely with the contract between itself and the Government of India as expressed in the standby credit. Issues related to the contract between India and the firm were considered irrelevant.

23–243 **Scope of fraud rule.** The *Dynamics Corporation of America* case demonstrates, also, that the fraud rule is applied in standby credit transactions subject to the same restrictions as in the case of documentary credits.[92] It will be recalled that the default certificate issued in that case by the Government of India attested a fact which, allegedly, did not correspond with the actual state of affairs. Although a preliminary injunction was granted to the account party, the court indicated that difficulties would arise in respect of the award of a permanent injunction. Such remedy was going to be granted only if India's demand was proved to be both unconscientious and without any basis of fact.

23–244 **Underlying transaction.** In a subsequent case, *Bossier Bank & Trust Co. v Union Planters National Bank*,[93] the Circuit Court of Appeals emphasised that an injunction could be granted only if the alleged fraud related to the relationship between the issuer of the credit and the beneficiary and not to the underlying contract between the beneficiary and the account party. However, the rule has been somewhat relaxed in some of the Iranian cases.[94] Thus, in *Itek Corp. v First National Bank of Boston*[95] the First Circuit Court of Appeals stated the applicable principle as follows: "if [the beneficiary] has no plausible or colorable basis under the contract to call for payment of the letters [of credit], [his] effort to obtain the money is fraudulent and payment can be enjoined".[96] On the facts of that case, the beneficiary, was aware that the underlying contract of sale had been legitimately cancelled by the account party before he made his call. The call, which implied liability on the account party's part, was therefore fraudulent.

23–245 **Strict compliance.** Just as in the case of commercial credits, the payment of a standby credit is subject to the tender of a fully complying set of documents by the beneficiary.[97] At first glance, one may doubt the relevance

[92] As regards the development of the fraud rule in respect of documentary credits, see above, para.23–140.
[93] 550 F. 2d 1077 (1977). See also *Foreign Venture Limited Partnership v Chemical Bank*, 399 N.Y.S. 2d 714 (1977); *Travellers' Indemnity Co. v Flushing National Bank*, 396 N.Y.S. 2d 754 (1977); *Werner v A L Grootemaat & Sons Inc.*, 259 N.W. 2d 310 (1977).
[94] Above, para.23–148.
[95] 730 F. 2d 19 (1984), discussed above, para.23–149.
[96] *ibid.*, at p.25. See also *American Bell International Inc. v Islamic Republic of Iran* 474 F.Supp. 420 (1979); *American National Bank and Trust Co. v Hamilton Industries Inc.* 583 F.Supp. 1148 (1983).
[97] See, *e.g. Kelly v First Westroads Bank*, 840 F. 2d 554 (8th Cir. 1988); *Wood v R R Donnelley & Sons Co.*, 888 F. 2d 313 (3rd Cir. 1989); *Tuthill v Union Savings Bank*, 561 N.Y.S. 2d 286 (App. Dir. 1990).

of this doctrine to standby credits. As the documents to be tendered are frequently prepared by the beneficiary, he should have no difficulty in attaining strict compliance with the terms set out in the credit. Indeed, neither the drafting of the default certificate nor the execution of the bill of exchange requires any specific skill. The text of the former may, in any event, be gleaned from the letter of credit even if specific detailed statements are required to be made. Compliance, therefore, becomes more of a pure formality even than in the case of documentary credits. There are, however, cases in which the beneficiary fails to present one of the required documents, such as the bill of exchange[98] or tenders the entire set out of time. In such a case the beneficiary stands to lose out, although his position may, in certain cases, be saved by two exceptions to the strict compliance doctrine.

Fair construction rule. The first exception to the strict compliance doctrine in regard to standby credits may be described as the "fair construction rule". In essence it means that the courts construe the terms of the credit so as to give the instruments business efficacy.[99] Thus, in the *Dynamics Corporation of America* case,[1] where the letter of credit called for a certificate to be executed by the President of India, it was left open whether or not a document, prepared and signed on his behalf by a government official, constituted a good tender. The court observed that if the words of a letter of credit are susceptible of two constructions, "one which makes the letter fair, customary, and reasonable for prudent men to naturally undertake and another which makes it inequitable—the former interpretation must be preferred to the latter".[2] In another case, *Fair Pavilions Inc. v First National City Bank,*[3] a standby credit included a clause under which the issuing bank was required to cancel the letter of credit if it received the account party's notification that any one of a number of specified events had taken place. The account party served a notice in which he did not disclose which of the relevant events had occurred but simply stated that one of them had eventuated. The Court of Appeals of New York decided that, as one of the objects of the cancellation clause was 23–246

---

[98] *Bounty Trading Corp. v SEK Sportswear Ltd*, 48 A.D. 2d 811, 370 N.Y.S. 2d 4 (1975). See also *Key Appliance Inc. v First National City Bank*, 46 A.D. 2d 622; 359 N.Y.S. 2d 886 (1974), where the beneficiary failed to present an invoice countersigned by a designated third party; *Mercantile Safe Deposits and Trust Co. v Baltimore County* 562 A 2d 591 (Md. 1987) (inadequate certification); *Colorado National Bank v County Commissioners*, 634 P. 2d 32 (1981), in which a sight draft was held to constitute a bad tender under a credit calling for a usance draft; contrast *Colonial Cedar Co. v Royal Wood Products Inc.* 448 So 2d 1218 (1984); *Temple-Eastex Inc. v Addison Bank*, 672 S.W. 2d 793 (1984), in both of which a letter of demand satisfied or could replace a draft called for in the letter of credit; *Armanac Industries Ltd v Citytrust*, 525 A. 2d 77 (Conn. 1987).

[99] Note, in respect of documentary credits, the comparable rule according to which the instrument has to be construed as a whole; above, para.23–196.

[1] 356 F.Supp. 991 (1973).

[2] *ibid.*, at p.999. And note that, under American law, a telex may constitute a bill of exchange; above, para.23–216.

[3] 24 A.D. 2d 109; 264 N.Y.S. 2d 255 (1965); revsd. 19 N.Y. 2d 512; 227 N.E. 2d 839, esp. 841 (1967).

to give the beneficiary an opportunity to tender again, it was necessary to disclose to him the ground for the account party's demand that the credit be cancelled.[4]

23–247 **Waiver or estoppel.** The second doctrine which may, on occasions, support a claim made by a beneficiary who has failed to comply strictly with the terms of a letter of credit is based on waiver or on estoppel. In essence, it is based on the assertion that the issuing bank should not be allowed to raise at the trial a defence based on deficiencies which the bank did not bring to the beneficiary's attention when the documents were rejected. This doctrine is established in the United States in respect of commercial credits and is favoured by the UCP[5] It has been applied in American cases concerning standby credits.[6]

23–248 **Application of UCP** It is clear that the UCP applies to a standby credit only in so far as the Code is expressly incorporated in the instrument.[7] A study of forms used in the United States, in the United Kingdom and on the Continent suggests that there is no uniformity of practice. By and large, it would appear that the UCP are incorporated in approximately one-half of existing standby credits, although in standby credits issued by American banks they are often replaced by the ISP98.[8] Where a standby credit issued by a bank incorporates the UCP, there is no reason to doubt the validity of the clause, provided payment is due against the presentation of specified documents such as a certificate attesting the account party's default. Such a facility falls fairly and squarely within the definition of a "letter of credit" in Article 2 of the UCP and Article 1 contemplates that the Code will be incorporated in it.[9] By way of contrast, a standby credit under which payment is due upon the occurrence of a given event, such as the nonperformance of the underlying contract between the account party and the beneficiary or upon the mere presentation of a non-documentary bill of exchange, is not governed by the UCP even if the Code is purported to be incorporated in the document. First, Article 2 excludes clean credits from the ambit of the Code. Secondly, clean standby credits have been held, in American authorities, to constitute guarantees. As such they are, of course, not meant to be covered by the UCP[10]

---

[4] And see UCP, Art. 14(d).
[5] See above, paras 23–155, 23–203.
[6] *Barclays Bank DCO v Mercantile National Bank*, 339 F.Supp. 457 at 460 (1972), affirmed 481 F. 2d 1224 at 1236–7 (1972); [1973] 2 Lloyd's Rep. 541; *Chase Manhattan Bank v Equibank*, 394 F.Supp. 352 at 357 (1975), revsd. on a different point: 550 F. 2d 882 (1977).
[7] Above, paras 23–029 *et seq*.
[8] Discussed below, para.23–251 *et seq*.
[9] As to which see above, paras 23–003, 23–052. The Uniform Customs were applied, *inter alia*, in the decision concerning the standby credits issued in *Intraworld Industries Inc. v Girard Trust Bank*, 336 A.2d 316 (Pa. 1975); *Offshore International SA v Banco Central SA* [1976] 2 Lloyd's Rep. 402.
[10] See, *e.g. Wichita Eagle and Beacon Publishing Co. Inc. v Pacific National Bank*, 493 F. 2d 1285 (1974); *Steinmeyer v Warner Consolidated Corp.*, 116 Cal.Reptr. 57 (1974).

23–249 **Non-bank facilities.** A problem which poses some difficulty concerns the application of the UCP to standby credits of the documentary type which are issued by financial institutions other than banks. Article 2 defines a documentary credit as well as a standby credit as an instrument issued by a bank. Moreover, the word "bank" is used throughout the Code when reference is made to an institution that issues, confirms or advises a letter of credit. A literal interpretation of this definition, and of the UCP as a whole, suggests that the Code does not apply to letters of credit issued by non-banks and that its incorporation in such credits is ineffective.[11] This, however, is an undesirable proposition. First, the word "bank" does not have a uniform meaning throughout the world. Indeed, in some jurisdictions, including the United Kingdom, it is debatable whether or not a merchant bank, which does not maintain current accounts and which does not collect cheques for its clients, engages in banking business.[12] It would be lamentable if the Code was held to be inapplicable to letters of credit issued by such a merchant bank by reason of the technical interpretation of the definition. Secondly, the proposed, restrictive, construction defeats the intention of the parties to the contract, who rely on the UCP in order to augment the short text of the standby credit. Thirdly, it is submitted that the UCP, which constitutes a code representing the commercial practice developed by banks and by merchants, ought not to be subjected to the same rigorous mode of construction as an Act of Parliament drafted by lawyers.[13]

23–250 **Practical effect of application of UCP** Although the application of the UCP to a standby credit may, on occasions, assist in determining such practical questions as whether the instrument is revocable or irrevocable,[14] there are many provisions in the Code which have no application to standby credits. Thus, the provisions concerning transport documents, the provisions respecting insurance policies and the provisions concerning invoices are clearly of no relevance in standby credit transactions. As the only documents usually called for under a standby credit are a bill of exchange and a certificate of default, the two main provisions concerning documents, which are pertinent to such credits, are Article 21,[15] concerning documents other than documents of carriage and insurance and invoices, and Articles 42 and 44 which are relevant as regards the expiry date. Other articles

---

[11] So argued by Peden, 52 Tex.L.Rev. 578 at 580 n.9.

[12] Ellinger, Lomnicka and Hooley, *Modern Banking Law* (14th ed.), pp.68 *et seq*.

[13] And see above, para.23–026 concerning the non-technical construction of the UCP in general. See also *Barclays Bank DCO v Mercantile National Bank*, 481 F. 2d 1224; [1973] 2 Lloyd's Rep. 541, in which an equally technical or literal construction was rejected in respect of s.5–103(1)(f) (now s.5–102(a)(4)) of the Uniform Commercial Code, concerning the confirmation of a letter of credit opened by a non-bank.

[14] Compare *West Virginia Housing Development Fund v Sroka*, 415 F.Supp. 1107 (1976), in which the letter of credit was not subject to the UCP, with *Beathard v Chicago Football Club Inc.*, 419 F.Supp. 1133 (1976), in which the instrument incorporated the Code. But note that under the current Art. 6(c) of the 1993 Revision the position would differ.

[15] Discussed above, para.23–235.

which may, in certain cases, be of relevance are the general provisions defining the liabilities and the responsibilities of the parties.[16] In particular, it is important to bear in mind that under Article 4 of the UCP, all parties to a letter of credit transaction deal in documents and not in goods. Of similar importance is Article 13(a), which defines the bank's duty to examine the documents.[17]

23–251 **The ISP98.** A detailed regulation of standby credits is provided by the International Standby Practices, known as the ISP98.[18] These guidelines, drafted by an American team, aim to deal specifically with the problems arising in respect of standby credits, performance bonds and first demand guarantees. At the time of writing, they are being incorporated mainly in facilities of American banks, or issued in finance deals involving such institutions; but their use is increasing.

23–252 **Scope and application.** Under rule 1.01(a), the ISP98 are intended to be applied to standby letters of credit however named and, under rule 1.01(b) any such facility, however named, may be made subject to them. The undertaking is then to be referred to as a "standby" (rule 1.01(d)).[19] Under rule 1.01(c), an undertaking subject to the Rules may expressly modify or exclude their application and, presumably, the application of any specific rule thereof. Where incorporated, the ISP98 rule 1.02(b) provides that they supersede any conflicting provision in other "rules of practice" to which a standby letter of credit is also made subject. The object is, obviously, to give them priority where the UCP are also incorporated in a facility and their provisions clash with a rule of the ISP98. Under rule 1.02(a), the ISP98 supplement the applicable law "to the extent not prohibited by that law". Obviously, there is no attempt to subject the imperative provisions of a governing law system to the provisions promulgated by the new Rules. To avoid doubt, rule 1.05 declares that the Rules do not seek to define or otherwise provide for "power or authority to issue a standby" (*i.e.* capacity), matters respecting formal requirements and "defences to honour based on fraud, abuse or similar matters". These matters are to be determined by the applicable law.

23–253 **Mercantile usages.** Under rule 1.03, the ISP98 are to be construed as mercantile usages. Rule 1.04 augments this provision, by stating that, as a general rule, the ISP98 "apply as terms and conditions incorporated into a standy". Rule 1.11 adds that "these Rules are to be interpreted in the context of applicable banking practice".

23–254 **Autonomy.** Rule 1.06 asserts the independence of a standby. The issuer's duty to perform is absolute and does not depend on the validity of any extraneous relationship. Rule 1.07 emphasises its independence from the

---

[16] Discussed above, paras 23–115 *et seq.*

[17] Discussed above, para.23–126.

[18] Originally promulgated by the Institute of International Banking Law and Practice Inc. The ISP98 came into force on January 1, 1999; for a detailed review see Byrne *et al., Official Commentary on the ISP98* (MD 1998); Byrne, *ISP 98 & UCP500 Compared* (MD 2000).

[19] And see, further, r.1.11(b) refining the definition of "standby" and "standby letter of credit".

contract between the issuer and the applicant. Rule 1.06(d) provides that the standby cannot be amended or revoked without the consent of the parties thereto. Most importantly, rule 1.06(d) states that neither a standby nor an amendment thereof "is binding when issued". The "documentary principle" is stated in rule 1.06(d): an issuer's obligations depend on the presentation of documents and an examination of the required documents on their face.[20] Notably, even if the standby does not say so expressly, rule 4.08 prescribes that a demand made thereunder must be documentary.

Obligations. Rule 2.01(a) imposes on both the issuer and the confirmer a duty to the beneficiary to honour a "presentation" which complies on its face with the terms and conditions of the standby. The four methods of "honour"—akin to those defined in Article 9 of the UCP—are set out, in respect of the issuer, in rule 2.01(b). Rule 2.01(c) provides that payment is timely as long as it takes place within the time provided for the examination of the documents. Rule 2.01(d)(i) enables the confirmer to perform its undertaking "in a manner of honour consistent with the issuer's undertaking". Under subparagraph (ii), if the confirmation permits presentation to the issuer, the confirmer "undertakes also to honour upon the issuer's wrongful dishonour by performing as if presentation had been made to the confirmer". A comparable provision, defining the issuer's undertaking, is made in subparagraph (ii) where the standby also sanctions presentation to the confirmer. It follows that, if the beneficiary has the option of presenting the documents either to the issuer or to the confirmer, the dishonour by one of them entitles him to proceed against either or both of them. In any case, rule 2.01(e) stipulates that payment must be made "in immediately available funds". For the purposes of the ISP98, any branch or office of a bank acting in a capacity other than as issuer, is obligated in that capacity only and is to be treated as a different person. This formulation differs from, and is superior to that, of Article 2 of the UCP. **23–255**

Nomination. A standby may nominate a "person" (usually a bank) to advise, negotiate or perform any other obligation pertaining to a standby. Such a nomination does not, in itself, oblige the nominee to act and, further, he is not authorised to bind the person making the nomination. **23–256**

Amendments and cancellation. Rule 2.06 recognises provisions for "automatic amendments". In the absence of such arrangement, the amendment binds the issuer and the confirmer from the respective date on which it leaves their terminals. It is not binding unless the beneficiary consents to it. Under rule 2.07 all amendments must be routed through one advising bank. Moreover, an amendment does not affect the issuer's undertaking to a nominated person. Provisions respecting requests for cancellation are to be found in rules 7.01 and 7.02. **23–257**

Presentation. Under rule 3.01, the standby has to set out the requirements applicable to presentation, including the place, the time, the person to whom presentation is to be effected and the medium thereof. According **23–258**

---

[20] And note that, to remove any doubt, r.1.08 exempts the issuer from liability for any matters outside his engagement as well as for the genuineness, effect and accuracy of documents.

to rule 3.02, receipt of the documents constitutes presentation even if some are missing. Under rule 3.03, the presentation has to identify the respective standby. Where and to whom the documents have to be presented when the standby does not cover a point is provided in rule 3.04 and the requisites of time and medium are spelt out in rules 3.05 and 3.06 respectively. Rule 3.07 sanctions successive presentations and rule 3.08 approves partial drawings and multiple presentations.[21] Under rule 3.10, the issuer is not required to notify the applicant of the receipt of the presentation.

23–259 **Extend or pay.** The troublesome issue, under which a beneficiary requires the issuer to extend the facility or make payment, is dealt with in rule 3.09. Under rule 3.09(a), such a demand is treated as a presentation; under rule 3.09(b) it signifies the beneficiary's consent to the extension and consequential amendments.[22]

23–260 **Examination.** The examination of the documents tendered under a standby is governed by rule 4. Under rule 4.02, documents not required by the standby need not be examined and may be returned, without responsibility to the presenter. According to rule 4.03 examination for inconsistency is required only if prescribed in the facility. Under rule 4.04 the documents need be in the language of the standby and, under rule 4.05, are to be issued by the beneficiary unless the standby calls for a third party document. Matters respecting the signature are settled in rule 4.07. A document need be signed only if the standby so requires or if it is of a document of a type usually signed. The signature may be made in any manner that corresponds with the medium in which the standby is presented.[23] Under rule 4.11, any non-documentary requirement or condition in a standby is to be disregarded. Issues pertaining to "originals", "copies", and "multiple documents" are settled in rule 4.15.

23–261 **Standby document types.** The remaining clauses of rule 4 make special provisions affecting the documents usually presented under standbys. Rule 4.16(a) provides that a demand for payment need not be separate from the beneficiary's statement or other required document. If a separate demand is required, it must—under rule 4.16(b)—contain the beneficiary's demand directed to the issuer or nominated person, the date on which the demand is issued, the amount demanded and the beneficiary's signature. Sub-clause (c), provides that the demand may assume the form of a draft, bill of exchange or other instruction.[24] Under rule 4.17, a certificate of default

---

[21] "Circa", "about" and "approximately" are defined in r.3.08(f), allowing a tolerance of up to 10 per cent.

[22] Certain issues of "waiver" are covered in r.3.11. Loss of standby is covered in r.3.12, extensions resulting from expiration on a non-business day in r.3.13 and issues arising from closure of issuer bank in r.3.14.

[23] As regards the degree of exact correspondence of words, see r.4.09; as regards issues of formality, see r.4.12; the issue of the identification of the beneficiary is dealt with in r.4.13 and that of "merged names" in r.4.14.

[24] As regards indorsements of negotiable instruments, see r.4.18; as regards court orders and legal documents, see r.4.19; and see r.4.21 as to requests to issue separate undertakings.

must—in the absence of other stipulation—spell out that payment is due because the anticipated event had occurred, the date of issue of the demand and the beneficiary's signature. According to clause 4.20(a), any other documents comply if they appear to be "appropriately titled or to serve the function of that document under standard standby practice". Under clause (b), a document presented under a standby is to be examined in the context of this type of practice even if it is a document (such as an invoice) for which the UCP make detailed provisions.

Notice of rejection. The procedure applicable for dishonour prevailing under the ISP98 is by and large similar to that of Articles 13 and 14 of the UCP Under rule 5.01, the "reasonable time" is not less than three but not more than seven days and begins to run on the business day following presentation. Notice has to be given to the presenter by telecommunication or, if this is unavailable, by other means which allow prompt notice. Any notice received within the prescribed time is given by prompt means. Under clause 5.02, the notice of dishonour must state all the discrepancies upon which the dishonour is based.[25] Under rule 5.03, failure to give an appropriate notice precludes the assertion of the discrepancy left out. Under clause 5.07, dishonoured documents must be returned, held or disposed of as reasonably instructed by the presenter. However, failure to give notice of the disposition in the notice of dishonour does not invalidate the rejection. An innovative provision is to be found in rule 5.09. An applicant who objects to the honour of complying documents by the issuer must raise a timely objection by prompt means. Under clause (c), the applicant's failure to give such notice precludes him from asserting the discrepant nature of the documents.[26] 23–262

Transfer. The provisions for transfer of the ISP98 are superior to Article 49 of the UCP Under rule 6.01 a transfer constitutes a request by the beneficiary that the issuer or nominated person "honour a drawing from another person as if that person were the beneficiary". Under rule 6.02(a) a standby is not transferable unless it so states. Under clause (b), a transferable standby may be transferred more than once but only in its entirety and only if the issuer, confirmer or nominated person "agrees to and effects the transfer requested by the beneficiary".[27] However, according to rule 6.04, once the standby has been transferred the draft or demand must be signed by the transferee, whose name is then to figure in all the required documents instead of the beneficiary's. An issuer or nominated person paying under a transfer is, under rule 6.05, entitled to reimbursement as if payment had been made to the beneficiary. 23–263

Assignment of proceeds. As under Article 49 of the UCP, rule 6.06 sanctions an assignment of proceeds—in whole or in part—as long as it is not proscribed by the law of the land. However, under rule 6.07(a), an 23–264

[25] As regards waiver of discrepancies, see rr.5.05 and 5.06.
[26] As regards cover instructions and transmittal letters, see r.5.08.
[27] As to conditions to be satisfied as a prerequisite to the issuer's or nominated person's consent, see r.6.03.

issuer or nominated person is not obligated to effect an assignment of proceeds which he has not acknowledged and, in addition, is not obliged to acknowledge the assignment.[28] Moreover, even if the assignment is acknowledged it remains, under rule 6.07(b), subject to the equities and, it would appear, subject to the issuer's (or nominated person's) right of set-off. In the event of conflicting claims to the proceeds, rule 6.09 provides that "payment to an acknowledged assignee may be suspended pending resolution of the conflict". Where payment is made, rule 6.10 provides that the payee is entitled to the same rights of reimbursement as if he had made payment to the beneficiary.[29]

23–265 **Reimbursement.** Under rule 8.01(a), payment against a complying presentation gives rise to a reimbursement claim. Accordingly, the applicant must reimburse the issuer and the issuer has to reimburse a nominated person. In addition, clause (b) entitles the issuer to be indemnified by the applicant against all claims, obligations and responsibilities arising (i) from the imposition of law and practice other than that chosen in the standby, (ii) out of fraud, forgery or illegal actions of others, and (iii) from the issuer's performance of the obligations of a confirmer who had wrongfully dishonoured. According to clause (c), rule 8.01 applies in addition to specific indemnity provisions expressly agreed upon by the parties.[30] Where reimbursement is obtained by the nominated person before the timely honour of the presentation, he must, under rule 8.03, refund the reimbursement with interest to the issuer.[31]

23–266 **Timing.** Under rule 9.01 a standby must include an expiry date or a provision for termination upon reasonable prior notice or payment. But, under rule 9.02, the rights of a nominated person who acts within the scope of his nomination are not affected by the subsequent expiry of the standby.[32] According to rule 9.04, expiry occurs at the close of the business day at the place of presentation. The retention of the standby does not—under rule 9.05—preserve any rights.[33]

23–267 **The standby credit and assignment.** There is no reason to doubt that, regardless of the Code incorporated in it, a standby credit may be transferred or assigned. Where it is governed by the UCP, this emerges from Articles 48 and 49.[34] Where it is governed by the ISP98, the position is governed by rule 6. In reality, though, the assignment or the transfer of a standby credit is of questionable practical value. The reason for this is to be found in an important difference between a commercial credit and a

---

[28] As regards conditions the issuer may impose to his consent to the assignment, see r.6.08.
[29] For transfer by operation of law, see rr.6.11–6.14.
[30] As regards charges, see r.8.02.
[31] Inter bank reimbursement is subject to the ICC's standard rules for bank to bank reimbursement: r.8.04.
[32] For the calculation of time, see r.9.03.
[33] For syndications and participations, see r.10.
[34] Discussed above, paras 23–068 *et seq.*

standby credit. In a commercial credit, the bank expects to perform its obligation when the seller ships the goods. This is an event which is contemplated by the parties as likely to take place. In a standby credit, the bank is bound to perform its obligation when the account party, who is in a position similar to that of the buyer of a commercial credit, fails to discharge his obligations. This is an event which the parties wish to indemnify against but which they do not consider as a likely eventuality.[35]

Allocation of risk. The discussion in the foregoing paragraphs concentrated on the legal aspects of standby credits. It seems, further, important to discuss the practical allocation of risks when parties enter into transactions involving such instruments. It is clear that in the majority of cases the beneficiary is in the most advantageous position. As long as he tenders strictly complying documents to the issuing bank, he is assured of obtaining payment. The fraud rule is highly unlikely to constitute a handicap to his freedom of drawing. The main risk is assumed by the account party, who is almost entirely at the mercy of the beneficiary. There are, however, two devices which the account party may use in order to protect himself. One is a cancellation clause, which entitles the account party to demand the revocation of the instrument by submitting a certificate attesting that the underlying contract has been discharged.[36] In the majority of cases, though, the beneficiary will resist such a clause as its inclusion leaves him in just as disadvantageous a position as that of the beneficiary in a standby credit without the cancellation clause. **23–268**

Third-party document. The only other device which can be used to protect the interests of the account party is to insist that the certificate of default, against which payment is to be made by the issuing banker, be furnished by an independent third party. Thus, where a standby credit covers liquidated damages due under a building contract, payment should be made subject to the tender of a suitable certificate by an engineer or by an architect. Where the standby credit is issued to secure a loan granted by the beneficiary to the account party, payment should be made against the tender of a certificate signed by auditors or by a firm of accountants. Where the standby credit covers damages payable if goods supplied under a contract of sale turn out to be defective, the certificate could be provided by an independent firm of surveyors. It is true that even this type of provision does not eliminate the risk in its entirety. In certain cases the beneficiary may be able to acquire and tender a false certificate signed by the designated third party. However, such an untruthful certificate would usually confer on the account party a right of action in deceit or in negligence against the issuer of the certificate. Naturally, there may be extreme cases in which the beneficiary may simply forge the third party's **23–269**

---

[35] For issues respecting an equitable assignment of, and of the subrogation to, rights acquired under a standby credit, see *Commercial Banking Co. of Sydney Ltd v Patrick Intermarine Acceptances Ltd* (1978) 19 A.L.R. 563.

[36] Note that a type of cancellation clause was included in the standby credit effected in *Wichita Eagle and Beacon Publishing Co. Inc. v Pacific National Bank*, 493 F. 2d 1285 (1974).

certificate. If he obtains payment from the bank against this forgery, the account party stands to sustain the loss as the bank is not liable for the genuineness of the certificate.[37] Against cases of this type there simply is no iron-clad safeguard.

(c) *Performance Bonds and First Demand Guarantees*[38]

23–270 **Terminology.** In practice there is no distinction between a first demand guarantee and a performance bond: the two terms are used interchangeably and a performance bond is, usually, just as payable upon the beneficiary's first demand as the very first demand guarantee itself. In point of fact, the essence of both facilities is that they include an undertaking by the issuer to pay a certain amount of money, or to accept a bill of exchange, when a demand to that effect is made by the beneficiary. In both facilities, the parties seek to furnish the beneficiary with an autonomous and independent undertaking of a bank or a first class financial institution.

23–271 **Practice.** First demand guarantees and performance bonds serve the same function as standby credits. All three facilities are usually opened in order to indemnify the beneficiary against a loss incurred as the result of the non-performance of a contract made between the beneficiary and the account party or a faulty performance of the same contract. In sale of goods transactions, a performance bond (or a first demand guarantee) is normally issued by the bank at the request of the seller for the benefit of the buyer. It may cover an amount of liquidated damages due from the seller if the goods are defective or supplied out of time, or it may cover the repayment of a deposit paid by the buyer at the initial stages.

23–272 **Legal nature.** In view of the special features of performance bonds and first demand guarantees they are treated by the courts as being closer to letters of credit than to traditional guarantees.[39] In *Howe Richardson Scale Co. Ltd v Polimex-Cekop*,[40] a contract for the supply of valuable equipment, made between English manufacturers and Polish importers, stipulated for a bank guarantee assuring the importers of the repayment of a deposit, paid on account of the price, if the manufacturers failed to dispatch the goods. After supplying a portion of the goods, the manufacturers refused to send the balance as the Polish importers had failed to furnish an irrevocable credit agreed upon in the contract of sale. The importers reacted by claiming payment under the first demand guarantee. The manufacturers applied for an injunction to restrain the importers from making this claim. Refusing to grant such an injunction, Roskill L.J. in the Court of Appeal,

---

[37] See above, para.23–127.

[38] For the current use of performance bonds, see Siptro Report on the use of Demand Guarantees in the UK [2004] *Annual Survey of Letters of Credit Law and Practice* 216.

[39] An interesting application of this principle is to be found in *Cauxell Ltd v Lloyds Bank Plc*, *The Times*, December 26, 1995, in which the court refused to imply a term into a performance bond, treating it as a bank's irrevocable undertaking.

[40] [1978] 1 Lloyd's Rep. 161.

said: "The bank, in principle, is in a position not identical with but very similar to the position of a bank which has opened a confirmed irrevocable letter of credit. Whether the obligation arises under a letter of credit or under a guarantee, the obligation of the bank is to perform that which it is required to perform by that particular contract, and that obligation does not in the ordinary way depend on the correct resolution of a dispute as to the sufficiency of performance by the seller to the buyer or by the buyer to the seller as the case may be under the sale and purchase contract; the bank here is simply concerned to see whether the event has happened upon which its obligation to pay has arisen. The bank takes the view that that time has come and that it is compelled to pay."[41]

Distinguished from conditional bonds and guarantees. The authorities just cited do not, however, apply to every document which is styled a performance bond or a first demand guarantee. A facility is considered a bankers' irrevocable undertakings only if the issuer's undertaking is to pay unconditionally when he receives the beneficiary's demand.[42] A facility under which payment is due upon the happening of a specified event, such as proof of the account party's default, constitutes a promise to answer for another's default and is governed by the ordinary principles of the law of guarantees. Problems as to whether a given facility falls into the one group or the other arise mainly in two cases. The first is where the facility sets out the issuer's undertaking to pay on demand but, at the same time, includes detailed references to aspects of the underlying transaction. The second is where the issuer's undertaking to pay on demand is subject to his being furnished a specific document, such as a third party's report attesting the account party's default. In all cases of this type the answer depends on whether the ultimate object of the facility is to arrange for payment against a formal demand, in which case it constitutes a first demand guarantee, or upon the occurrence of a given event, in which case it is an ancillary undertaking or guarantee.[43] 23–273

Facilities reciting the underlying transaction. Authorities suggest that, as long as the issuer promises unconditionally to pay on demand, the recital of details of the underlying transaction does not affect the nature of the facility. In *Australian Conference Association Ltd v Mainline Construction Pty Ltd*[44] a facility, furnished by a contractor in lieu of retention money, recited certain aspects of the underlying construction contract and then set 23–274

---

[41] *ibid.*, at p.165. See also *Edward Owen Engineering Ltd v Barclays Bank International Ltd* [1978] 1 Lloyd's Rep. 166; *Intraco Ltd v Notis, Shipping Corp. (the "Bhoja Trader")* [1981] 2 Lloyd's Rep. 256 at 257; *Bolivinter Oil SA v Chase Manhattan Bank N.A.* [1984] 1 W.L.R. 392, *Banque Saudi Fransi v Lear Siegler Services Inc.* [2006] 1 Lloyd's Rep. 222, *cf. Potton Homes Ltd v Coleman Contractors Ltd* (1984) 28 Build L.R. 19, suggesting certain distinctions between performance bonds and standby credits.

[42] See as regards "conditional bonds" used in the construction industry *Trafalgar House Ltd v General Surety Co.* [1996] A.C. 199.

[43] That a performance bond may be construed as autonomous despite cumbersome draftsmanship, see *Siporex Trade SA v Banque Indosuez* [1986] 2 Lloyd's Rep. 146.

[44] (1978) 53 A.L.J.R. 63.

out the bank's unconditional promise to meet a demand made by the beneficiary, the employer. Gibbs A.C.J., in the High Court of Australia, observed that, although in substance the guarantee was meant to cover an amount due upon the account party's, namely the contractor's, default, it was in substance unconditional.[45]

The rationale was explained by the High Court in *Wood Hall Ltd v Pipeline Authority*.[46] Here the issue was whether the bank, which had issued the very type of retention money guarantee encountered in the previous case, was obligated to pay against the landowner's demand or had to satisfy itself that the contractor's default had really taken place. Gibbs J. explained the position as follows: "By each of the bank guarantees, the Bank 'unconditionally' undertakes 'to pay on demand' the sum demanded up to the limit specified in the bank guarantee. To hold that the bank guarantees are conditional upon the making of a demand that conforms to the requirements of the contract between the Authority [*viz*., the landowner and beneficiary] and the contractor [account party] would of course be quite inconsistent with the express statement in the bank guarantees that the undertaking of the Bank is unconditional. To hold that the Bank should not pay upon receiving a demand, but should be bound to inquire into the rights of the Authority and the contractor under a contract to which the Bank was not a party would be to depart from the ordinary meaning of the undertaking that the Bank was to pay on demand."[47]

23–275 **Autonomy and the fraud rule.** That the courts regard an unconditional first demand guarantee or performance bond as an autonomous undertaking of the banker, which is not qualified by the underlying contract between the beneficiary and the account party, is clear from *Howe Richardson's* case. Moreover, the courts are reluctant to enjoin the bank from meeting a demand made by the beneficiary even if the account party alleges that it is tainted with fraud. The point is demonstrated by *Harbottle (R. D.) (Mercantile) Ltd v National Westminster Bank*,[48] which was another case in which a seller refused to ship the goods on the ground, *inter alia*, of the buyers' failure to open an agreed letter of credit. The buyer, in turn, called for payment under a first demand guarantee. The seller applied for an injunction to restrain the bank from honouring its guarantee on the basis that the buyer's demand was tainted with fraud. Refusing to grant this remedy, Kerr J. said: ". . . this is not a case of an established fraud at all. The [seller] may well be right in contending that the buyers have no contractual right to payment of any part, let alone the whole, of the guarantee . . . But all these issues turn on contractual disputes. They are a long way from fraud, let alone established fraud."[49] His Lordship further observed: "It is only in exceptional cases that the courts will interfere with

[45] (1978) 53 A.L.J.R. 63 at 71. Similar views were expressed by Stephen and Aickin JJ. *ibid.*, at pp.74, 80 respectively.
[46] (1979) 53 A.L.J.R. 487 esp. at 492.
[47] *ibid.*, at p.490; and see Barwick C.J. at pp.487–488. See also *Hortico (Australia) Pty Ltd v Energy Equipment Co. (Australia) Ltd* [1985] 1 N.S.W.R. 545 at 549–551.
[48] [1978] 1 Q.B. 146.
[49] *ibid.*, at p.155.

the machinery of irrevocable obligations assumed by banks. They are the lifeblood of international commerce. Such obligations are regarded as collateral to the underlying rights and obligations between the merchants at either end of the banking chain. Except possibly in clear cases of fraud of which the banks have notice, the courts will leave the merchants to settle their disputes under the contracts by litigation or arbitration as available to them or stipulated in the contracts."[50]

Edward Owen. This reasoning was adopted by the Court of Appeal in *Edward Owen Engineering Ltd v Barclays Bank International Ltd*,[51] in which the facts were similar to those of *Harbottle's* case. Refusing to grant an injunction sought by the seller to restrain the bank from making payment under the first demand guarantee, Lord Denning observed that "as one takes instance after instance, these performance guarantees are virtually promissory notes payable on demand. So long as the [beneficiaries] make an honest demand, the banks are bound to pay: and the banks will rarely, if ever, be in a position to know whether the demand is honest or not. At any rate they will not be able to prove it to be dishonest. So they will have to pay."[52] It follows that, in practice, the fraud rule is an inefficient means of combatting unjustified demands made under first demand guarantees and performance bonds. Whilst it is, of course, arguable that the account party may be able to recover the amount of such an improper drawing from the beneficiary by a direct action, it is important to bear in mind that this advice is of limited use where the beneficiary resides in a country which is not renowned for the efficacy of its legal system.[53] 23–276

Invoked successfully. One instance in which the fraud rule was successfully invoked in the United Kingdom related to a demand made by the beneficiary, which involved a sharp practice affecting the contract between the issuer and himself. In *Elian and Rabbath v Matsas and Matsas*,[54] shipowners claimed a lien based on demurrage over certain goods. In order to release the goods, the owners furnished the shipowners with a banker's first demand guarantee, covering the payment of an amount that might be agreed upon between the shipowners and the charterers in respect of the demurrage involved. Although the shipowners lifted the original lien upon receiving the guarantee, they immediately claimed a second lien in respect 23–277

---

[50] *ibid.*, at pp.155–156.

[51] [1978] 1 Lloyd's Rep. 166; and see *Consolidated Oil Ltd, v American Express Bank Ltd* [2002] C.L.C. 488, *Banque Saudi Fransi v Lear Siegler Services Inc*. [2006] 1 Lloyd's Rep. 272.

[52] *ibid.*, at p.171. See also Browne L.J. at pp.172–173. And see *State Trading Corp. v Mar (Sugar) Ltd* [1981] Com.L.R. 235; *Bolivinter Oil SA v Chase Manhattan Bank NA* [1984] 1 W.L.R. 392; *Esal (Commodities) Ltd v Oriental Credit Ltd* [1985] 2 Lloyd's Rep. 546 at 549; *GKN Contractors Ltd v Lloyds Bank Plc* (1985) 30 Build. L.R. 48, restricting the principle to instances of "common law" fraud.

[53] But note that, although such bonds are treated as the equivalent of cash, summary judgment would be refused if the bond itself was issued in consequence of fraud or collusion involving the beneficiary and the applicant: *Solo Industries UK Ltd v Canara Bank* [2001] All E.R. (D.) 34.

[54] [1966] 2 Lloyd's Rep. 495.

of another claim. The Court of Appeal granted an injunction to restrain the shipowners from drawing on the guarantee. Lord Denning observed: "The guarantee was given [to the shipowners] on the understanding that the lien was raised and that no further lien [would be] imposed: and that when the shipowners, in breach of that understanding, imposed a further lien, they were disabled from acting on the guarantee."[55] The case may, however, be regarded as being based on its special facts and it was distinguished in *Howe Richardson's* case.[56] The case could, furthermore, be based on a plea of total failure of consideration. In view of the fact that the merchandise remained subject to the shipowner's lien, it was arguable that the consideration furnished by the beneficiary, the promisee, had totally failed.

It is, thus, clear that the fraud rule has a narrow scope of application. It is true that there is an indication that a more liberal approach may be adopted by the courts in the future. The decision of the Court of Appeal in *United Trading Corp. SA v Allied Arab Bank Ltd*[57] suggests that the onus of proof borne by the account party may be lightened to a certain extent.[58] But many performance bonds and first demand guarantees contain a conclusive evidence clause, which adds strength to the beneficiary's position. The difficulty in all these cases is to convince a court, first, that the beneficiary's claim is made without any cause whatsoever and without his having any belief in his right to the amount involved and, secondly, that the irreparable harm done to the account party by the refusal of an injunction outweighs the disruption caused to the banking system when payment is enjoined. To date, account parties have had little success in discharging this onus.

23–278 **Conclusive evidence.** Some first demand guarantees and performance bonds include a clause according to which the default notice, submitted by the beneficiary, is to be considered conclusive evidence that liability under the instrument has accrued in respect of the amount claimed. In view of the decisions discussed in the foregoing paragraphs, such a clause adds little to the value of a guarantee or bond which is payable on first demand. It is, nevertheless, worthwhile noting that the validity of the conclusive evidence clause has been upheld by the Court of Appeal. In *Bache & Co. (London) Ltd v Banque Vernes et Commerciale de Paris SA*[59] a French bank, at the request of French importers, issued a guarantee securing English commodity brokers in respect of orders placed by them with vendors at the importers' request. One of the terms of this instrument was a conclusive evidence clause. Before the expiry of the guarantee, the commodity brokers served notice of demand on the bank. The latter refused to pay, arguing that the French importers were not in default. It assailed the validity of the

[55] *ibid.*, at p.497.
[56] Above, at p.165.
[57] [1985] 2 Lloyd's Rep. 554; [1984] T.L.R. 475, noted in [1985] J.B.L. 232; and see *Tukan Timber Ltd v Barclays Bank Plc* [1987] 1 F.T.L.R. 154; and the Australian cases of *Contronic Distributors Pty Ltd v Bank of N.S.W.* [1984] 3 N.S.W.R. 110; *Hortico (Aust). Pty Ltd v Energy Equipment Co. (Aust) Pty Ltd* [1985] 1 N.S.W.R. 545.
[58] And see above, para.23–145.
[59] [1973] 2 Lloyd's Rep. 437.

conclusive evidence clause on the ground of its being contrary to public policy. Holding the commodity brokers entitled to enforce the guarantee, Lord Denning said: "It seems to me that notice of default given by the English brokers is perfectly good. There is no public policy against it. On the contrary, public policy is in favour of enforcing it."[60] His Lordship relied, in reaching this conclusion, on expert evidence which showed that clauses of this type were normal in contracts in which an agent assumed liability together with his foreign principal.

Enjoining the beneficiary. In the fraud cases discussed up to now, the seller, or account party, sought an injunction to preclude payment by the bank. The difficulty of obtaining such an order has, in recent years, led to the lodging of applications for injunctions precluding the beneficiary from making a call on the facility. The main argument raised in cases of this type is that an order, which enjoins the beneficiary from making a demand, cannot affect the bank's reputation and, further, does not disrupt the international practice pertaining to bankers' irrevocable undertaking. In *Deutsche Rückversicherung AG v Walbrook Insurance Co. Ltd*[61] Phillips J. rejected this argument. His Lordship held that an injunction restraining the beneficiary from making a call under a banker's irrevocable undertaking would be made only to the extent that it could be granted to preclude the bank from making payment. The case, however, concerned a letter of credit. 23–279

Themehelp. A very different view was later taken by the majority of the Court of Appeal in *Themehelp Ltd v West*,[62] which concerned a first demand guarantee. The case arose out of a contract for the sale of a business, in pursuance of which the buyer had furnished a third party's first-demand guarantee to secure the outstanding balance of the price. Subsequently, the buyer discovered that the seller had made certain misrepresentations concerning the business. He thereupon refused to complete the purchase and applied for an injunction to restrain the seller from making a call on the first-demand guarantee. The trial judge granted an injunction and his decision was affirmed by the Court of Appeal. Delivering the leading majority judgment, Waite L.J. concluded that the autonomy of a first-demand guarantee was not threatened if the beneficiary was placed under a temporary restraint from enforcing it. His Lordship said: "In a case where fraud is raised as between the parties to the main transaction at an early stage, before any question of the enforcement of the guarantee, as between the beneficiary and the guarantor, has yet arisen at all, it does not seem to me that the slightest threat is involved to the autonomy of the performance guarantee if the beneficiary is injuncted from enforcing it in proceedings to which the guarantor is not a party."[63] Waite L.J. added that in such proceedings there was "no risk to the integrity of the performance 23–280

[60] *ibid.*, at p.440. See also *Dobbs v National Bank of Australasia* (1935) 53 C.L.R. 643.
[61] [1994] 4 All E.R. 181.
[62] [1996] Q.B. 84, CA.
[63] *ibid.*, at pp.98–99.

guarantee and therefore no occasion for involving the guarantor at that stage in any question as to whether or not fraud [was] established".[64] His Lordship further concluded that, on the evidence presented, the trial judge was entitled to conclude that the buyer had established a seriously arguable case to the effect that fraud was the only realistic inference in the instant case. He also gave weight to the consideration that, if the injunction was refused and the money was paid out under the guarantee, the buyer had poor prospects of recovering it even if he was wholly successful in the trial of the commercial cause.

It remains to be seen whether this reasonsing would be accepted by the House of Lords. One thorny problem is that, in some cases of this type, the injunction so granted may result in the expiry of the guarantee without the beneficiary having the chance of making his demand prior to the prescribed deadline. As the guarantor, or bank, is not a party to the proceedings, it is difficult to see how the court may make the injunction subject to an appropriate extension of the relevant expiry date. In all other respects, the decision is believed to be unexceptional.[65]

23–281 **Unconscionability.** The trend of authority[66] is in support of the strict approach taken in the *Deutsche Ruckversicherungs* case. In reality, though, *Themehelp* applies a test of unconscionability. If the beneficiary of the first-demand guarantee demands an amount which, in view of the circumstances of the case, is not due to him, he exercises the technical right conferred on him in the facility in an unconscionable manner. A commercially objectionable demand, such as the importer's demand in *Edward Owen*, ought to be enjoined.

23–282 **Singapore doctrinal analysis.** A number of recent cases, decided in Singapore, postulate an unconscionability exception.[67] It is treated as a separate doctrine, recognised as an alternative to the fraud exception.[68] The principle is applicable only in respect of a party that exercises its rights under the on-demanded-guarantee in an unfair and commercially

---

[64] *ibid.*, at p.99.

[65] As regards the account party's right to reclaim from the beneficiary an amount paid out under an improper call, see *General International SA v Bangladesh Sugar and Food Industries Corp.* [1996] 2 Lloyd's Rep. 524. And note that where the beneficiary acts unconscionably in making his demand, a court in Singapore will issue an injunction against him even if no fraud *stricto sensu* is established: *Bocotra Construction v AG (No.2)* [1995] 2 S.L.R. 733; *GHL Pte Ltd v Unitrack Building Construction Pte Ltd* [1999] 4 S.L.R. 604.

[66] For a critique of *Themehelp* see, in particular, *Group Josi v Walbrook Insurance Co.* [1996] 1 W.L.R. 1152. See also *Czarnikow Rionda Sugar Trading Inc. v Standard Bank of London Ltd* [1999] 1 All E.R. (Comm) 890; *Britten Norman Ltd v State Ownership Fund of Romania* [2000] All E.R. (D) 935.

[67] Proclaimed in *Boctra Construction Pte Ltd v AG (No.2)* [1995] 2 S.L.R 733, not following the reasoning of *Royal Design Studio Pte Ltd v Cang Development Pte Ltd* [1991] 2 M.L.J. 229 and *Kvaerner Singapore Pte Ltd v Shipbuilding (S) Pte Ltd* [1993] 3 S.L.R. 350, similar to the reasoning in *Themehelp*.

[68] See, *e.g. Min Thai Holdings Pte Ltd* [1999] 2 S.L.R. 368; *GHL Pte Ltd v Unitrack Building Construction Pte Ltd* [1999] 4 S.L.R. 604, CA; *New Civilbuild Pte Ltd v Guobena* [1999] 1 S.L.R. 374, affirmed [2000] 2 S.L.R. 378, CA.

objectionable manner. An injunction based on unconscionability would, accordingly, not be granted against a bank that seeks to carry out its undertaking. But injunctions have been granted against a commercial party that demands payment without a sound commercial basis. It is to be hoped that this well-defined doctrine will be adopted in other jurisdictions.[68a]

Strict compliance. The mechanism of first-demand guarantees and performance bonds is straightforward. Consequently, it is uncommon to encounter in their operations the problem of strict compliance, which arises regularly in documentary credits and in standby credits. Undoubtedly, if the performance bonds stipulates that the beneficiary's letter of demand be accompanied by a specified document, such as a third party's certificate, the document in question has to be tendered together with the letter of demand and prior to the expiry of the facility. In most cases, though, payment is due against the beneficiary's written demand; provided this is made prior to the expiry of the credit, the issuer has to pay. 23–283

Form of demand. Problems can, however, arise where the facility refers to the event upon which the beneficiary is expected to make a demand or describes the object of the facility. In such a case, is the beneficiary's bare demand adequate or must he, in addition, assert that the demand is compatible with the details set out in the facility? The basic principle is to be found in *Siporex Trade SA v Banque Indosuez*.[69] In this case Hirst J. said that the doctrine of strict compliance did not apply in its full severity, as known from the law of letters of credit, to demands made under performance bonds. In his Lordship's view a demand was, fundamentally, acceptable if there was no ambiguity in it and provided there was no risk of the bank being misled or prejudiced by it. However, in the slightly earlier case of *Esal (Commodities) Ltd v Oriental Credit Ltd*[70] the Court of Appeal was divided on whether, in addition to making a bare demand, the beneficiary was also obliged to inform the bank of the basis of his call on the facility. In that case Ackner L.J. took the view that the beneficiary had to inform the bank that he was exercising his rights on the basis provided in the performance bond.[71] By contrast, Neill L.J. wished to leave open the question of whether it was "necessary for the beneficiary to give express notice to the bank that the qualifying event has occurred".[72] Their Lordship's difference of opinion related, however, to the construction of the relevant facility and did not arise from a disagreement on a point of principle. 23–284

[68a] But see *Banque Saudi Fransi v Lear Siegler Services Inc.* [2006] 1 Lloyd's Rep. 272.

[69] [1986] 2 Lloyd's Rep. 146 esp. at 159. And see below, paras 23–293 *et seq.* as regards the position under the Uniform Rules for Demand Guarantees.

[70] [1985] 2 Lloyd's Rep. 546. See also *Frans Maas (UK) Ltd v Habib Bank* [2001] 1 Lloyd's Rep Bank 14.

[71] For a similar opinion in the USA, see *Avery Dennison Corp. v Home Trust & Savings Bank* [2003] US Dist. Lexis 204/3.

[72] *ibid.*, at p.550. Glidewell L.J. concurred.

23–285 **IE Contractors.** The issue arose again in *IE Contractors Ltd v Lloyds Bank Plc.*[73] Here the terms of a construction contract required the contractor to furnish to the Iraqi employer a performance bond issued by the R Bank in Iraq. Such a bond was in due course furnished by the R Bank against three counter indemnities executed at the contractor's request by Lloyds Bank. The performance bond issued by the R Bank was expressed to cover "damages which you [*viz*., the employers] claim are duly and properly owing to your organisation by [the contractor] under the terms" of the respective construction contract. The R Bank undertook "to pay you, unconditionally, the said amount on demand, being your claim for damages brought about by [the contractor]". In two counter-indemnities Lloyds Bank undertook to pay on their receipt of a demand; only under the third facility was the R Bank obliged to state in its demand that it had been required to make payment under the performance bond. The demand under the performance bond, eventually made by the employer, merely stated that the contractor had not "fulfilled the contractual obligations in respect of" the project involved. No reference was, apparently, made to the demand being a claim for damages. The R Bank's claim under all the counter-indemnities read: "At beneficiaries demand please credit full guarantee amount equivalent to . . . due to shortages not yet finished."[74] No statement was made about the R Bank's liability to make payment under the performance bond.

Concluding that, in the ultimate, the validity and sufficiency of a demand depended on the wording of the performance bond involved, Leggatt J. held that the demands were defective. The reason for this was that each demand had failed to show unequivocally that payment was being demanded on the basis provided in the respective facility. The demand served on R Bank did not specify that it was for damages; the demand served on Lloyds Bank failed to specify that the R Bank was obliged to make payment to the employers. The Court of Appeal reversed this decision. Agreeing with Hirst J.'s view in *Siporex*, Staughton L.J. said that in the instant case all except the R Bank's last demand indicated that they were made on the basis provided in the respective facility. The beneficiary's demand stated that the account party had failed to perform its contractual obligation. This implied, further, that the demand involved a claim for damages. As regards the first two counter-indemnities, their wording indicated that a bare demand was adequate. Such a demand was, however, inadequate under the third facility furnished by Lloyds Bank. Here, again, the difference between Leggatt J.'s view and the Court of Appeal's rests on a disagreement concerning the construction of relevant documents. There is no division on the fundamental principle, which is that a demand can be met only if it purports to be made on the basis provided in the facility.

23–286 **Place of payment.** In most cases the first-demand guarantee is made available at a designated place, which is thereby rendered the place for the lodging of a demand as well as the place of payment. The difficulties that

---

[73] [1989] 2 Lloyd's Rep. 205, vard. [1990] 2 Lloyd's Rep. 496. For another instance see *Bangkok Bank Ltd v Cheng* [1990] 2 M.L.J. 5 (CA Singapore). And see *Avery Dennison Corp. v Home Trust & Savings Bank* [2003] US Dist. Lexis 204/3.

[74] Some difficulties arose as a result of the translation of the demand, made in Arabic, into English.

arise when no such place is specified are illustrated by *Turkiye Is Bankasi AS v Bank of China*.[75] At the instruction of BOC in Beijing, which, in turn, had been instructed by a Chinese construction company, CSC, the TI Bank in Turkey issued three performance bonds in favour of CSC's employers, another Chinese company, ETA. The security obtained by the TI Bank for the issuing of the performance bond was BOC's undertaking, spelt out in each instruction for the opening of the performance bonds, which read: "In consideration of your issuing the said guarantee we hereby undertake that we shall pay you at your first written demand stating that you have been called upon to make payment under your guarantee. . ." A call having been made under the performance bonds, the TI Bank made a demand under the counter-guarantee. It was resisted by BOC. A preliminary issue respecting the resulting action was whether the governing law was that of Turkey or some other system.

As the counter-guarantee did not include an express choice of law clause, the matter had to be determined on the basis of common law principles. One factor relevant in this context was the place at which payment was due. The arguments for BOC was that, as a matter of general principle, a bank that gives a counter-guarantee in an international banking transaction was contractually obliged and entitled to honour its undertaking at its own place of business. In the instant case, this pointed to Beijing, where the counter-guarantee had been issued. Rejecting this argument, Phillips J. said: "In practice, in international banking transactions of this nature, the place of payment will either be expressly agreed or the creditor bank will specify the place at which it wishes to have an account credited with the monies due and the debtor will normally comply with such request . . . Any attempt to formulate some general rule as to the contractual place of performance is unrealistic."[76] His Lordship emphasised the close link between the counter-guarantee and the performance bonds and noted that the TI Bank did not have any account in Beijing. Phillips J. concluded that there was, accordingly, no sound base for treating Beijing as the place of payment.

Subrogation. The question of subrogation may arise in the context of first-demand guarantees and performance bonds where a bank makes payment under the instrument to a beneficiary who holds additional security furnished by the account party. There appears to be no direct authority in point. Usually, a guarantor is entitled to be subrogated to the creditor's (beneficiary's) rights against the debtor (account party).[77] It remains to be seen whether, for the purposes of this specific question, the courts will treat first-demand guarantees as "secondary undertakings" or as "primary undertakings", which may not be subject to the application of the doctrine of subrogation. 23–287

Right to surplus. A question that arises occasionally, especially in respect of performance bonds issued in the context of building contracts, is the right to a surplus, or balance, left after the beneficiary has utilised the 23–288

[75] [1993] 1 Lloyd's Rep. 132; see also *Wahda Bank v Arab Bank Plc* [1994] 2 Lloyd's Rep. 411.
[76] [1993] 1 Lloyd's Rep. 132 at 136. Phillips J. concluded, on the facts, that the governing law was that of Turkey.
[77] *Chitty on Contracts* (29th ed.), Vol. 1, para.30–176.

funds to recoup his loss. Is the amount involved to be paid back to the issuing bank or to the account party? The question is of considerable importance where the account party becomes insolvent. Effectively, the competing claims for the surplus are then those of the liquidator or trustee in bankruptcy and the bank's. As the making of an excessive demand is, basically, a breach of the beneficiary's underlying contract, the amount ought to be regarded as received in breach of that contract and, hence, as repayable to the account party rather than to the bank.

23–289 **Australian cases.** Support for the view just expressed is to be found in a decision of the High Court of Australia, which is based on the principle that the amount paid by the issuing bank has to be utilised for the purpose stipulated in the underlying transaction. In *Australian Conference Association Ltd v Mainline Construction Pty Ltd (in Liq.)*,[78] which concerned a dispute arising in respect of a construction contract, the employer was the beneficiary of a first-demand retention money guarantee furnished by the bank at the contractor's instruction. When the contractor became insolvent, the employer, in pursuance of clause 22, terminated the construction contract and arranged for the completion of the the project by the sub-contractors. He made a call under the guarantee, with the object of using the funds so received in order to settle debts due to the sub-contractors. The utilisation of the funds for this purpose was challenged by the liquidators, appointed in the contractor's winding-up. The High Court (by a majority) held that the use of the funds for the making of payments to the sub-contractors was sanctioned by clause 22(c)(ii) of the construction contract. Gibbs J. said: "It seems right to conclude that the parties to the guarantee mutually contemplated and agreed that the money provided by the Bank would be dealt with as the building contract required."[79] His Honour added: "In my opinion under the contract it is [the contractor] that is entitled to any surplus remaining of the money provided under the security [*viz.*, the guarantee] once the obligations of [the contractor] have been discharged."[80]

Further support for this view is to be found in *Wood Hall Ltd v The Pipe Line Authority*,[81] another case concerning a performance bonds issued in respect of a construction contract. Here, too, the High Court took the view that, as between the employer (beneficiary) and the contractor (account party), a call on the guarantee or performance bond could be rightly made only for the purposes specified in the underlying building agreement. Consequently, the employer was not entitled to retain an excess left in his hands once his justified claims were satisfied. This decision reinforces the conclusion that such an excess would be payable to the account party.[82]

---

[78] (1979) 53 A.L.J.R. 66.

[79] *ibid.*, at p.72, cln. 1.

[80] *ibid.*, at p.73, cln. 1. Stephen and Aickin JJ. dissented as, in their view, payment to the subcontractors was not an object contemplated in the facility. This led them also to the conclusion that, on technical grounds, the surplus was due to the bank rather than to the account party, *viz*. the contractor.

[81] (1979) 53 A.L.J.R. 487.

[82] As regards the account party's right to recover an amount improperly claimed by the beneficiary, see *Cargill International SA v Bangladesh Super and Food Industries Corp.* [1998] 1 W.L.R. 461.

Attempt to incorporate the UCP It is clear from Articles 1 and 2 of the UCP that the Code applies only to documentary credits and standby credits. The Code is, thus, not meant to apply to performance bonds and first-demand guarantees.[83] There are, however, instances in which such a facility includes a clause purporting to incorporate the UCP It is believed that the object of such a clause is to indicate that the facility is meant to be an autonomous undertaking akin to an irrevocable credit. Consequently, the inclusion of such a clause in a performance bond or first-demand guarantee ought to constitute an important factor in determining whether the issuer's undertaking is autonomous or ancillary. 23–290

Suitability of ISP98. Unlike the UCP, which were not originally drafted with a view to their being applied to first-demand guarantees and performance bonds, the draftsmen of the ISP98 set out to prepare a set of guidelines suitable for incorporation also in facilities of this sort. To this end, the definition of "standby"[84] has been phrased so as to apply to any facilities used for the purposes served by standby credits, performance bonds and first-demand guarantees. However, at the time of writing, the ISP98 are used primarily in facilities granted by American banks or in the context of transactions financed by such houses. For performance bonds and first-demand guarantees issued by other financial institutions the Uniform Rules for Demand Guarantees provide a more suitable model. This set of guidelines requires a detailed discussion. 23–291

The Uniform Rules for Contract Guarantees. An attempt to settle the problems arising in the issuing of first-demand guarantees and performance bonds was made by the International Chamber of Commerce in 1978. The Uniform Rules for Contract Guarantees,[85] promulgated in collaboration with UNCITRAL, made detailed provisions for three types of guarantee, namely "tender guarantees", "performance guarantees" and "repayment guarantees". The main shortcoming of these Rules was that, as a precondition to payment, the beneficiary had to submit either a court decision or an arbitral award substantiating his claim. A direct consequence of this cumbersome regime was that the Rules gained no momentum and, though still available, are practically obsolete. 23–292

The Uniform Rules for Demand Guarantees. A new set of rules was promulgated by the ICC in 1992. Known as the Uniform Rules for Demand Guarantees,[86] they reflect more closely the prevailing international practice in point. At the same time, they make a new attempt to balance the interests of the different parties to the transaction and seek to curb common abuses. However, despite the considerable effort that has gone into the preparation of these new Rules they have not, to date, gained 23–293

---

[83] And see *Esal (Commodities) Ltd v Oriental Credit Ltd* [1985] 2 Lloyd's Rep. 546 at 550.

[84] Above, para.23–252.

[85] Brochure No.325.

[86] Brochure No.458; and see Goode, "Abstract Payment Undertakings and the Rules of the ICC", 39 St Louis U.L.J. 725 (1995).

popularity and their incorporation in current forms remains sporadic. Whilst a detailed discussion of the Rules is therefore outside the scope of this book, a brief review is appropriate.

23–294 **Basic object.** The type of guarantee covered by the new Rules is described in the official introduction: "It is characteristic of all guarantees subject to these Rules that they are payable on presentation of one or more documents. The documentary requirements specified in demand guarantees vary widely. At one end is the guarantee which is payable on simple written demand, without a statement of default or other documentary requirements. At the other end is the guarantee which requires presentation of a judgment or arbitral award." It follows that the type of facility that was, originally, meant to be covered under the old 1978 Rules could, currently, be covered under the new Rules. However, a guarantee or suretyship contract under which payment is subject to a non documentary requirement, such as an actual event of default, is not meant to be covered by these Rules. The Rules, in other words, do not apply to conditional bonds, conditional guarantees or other accessory or ancillary undertakings.

23–295 **Structure.** The Uniform Rules are divided into six parts. Part A, comprising Article 1 alone, is entitled Scope and Application of Rules. Part B, entitled Definitions and General Provisions (and comprising Arts 2–8) lays down the policy of the Code. Part C, on "Liabilities and Responsibilities", comprises Articles 9–16, which define the risks borne by the parties. Part D encompasses five articles (17–21) which spell out the principles to be observed in the making of calls on guarantees and counter-guarantees. Part E (comprising Arts 22–26) includes the Expiry Provisions and the two provision in Part F (27–28) deal with Governing Law and Jurisdiction.

23–296 **Terminology.** Under Article 2(a), the person in whose favour the first-demand guarantee is issued is known as the "beneficiary". The party that orders the furnishing of the facility, and whose position is similar to that of the applicant of a documentary credit, is defined in paragraph (a)(i) as the "principal". The person that furnishes the guarantee, and who may be "a bank, insurance company or other body or person" is the "guarantor" (Art. 2(a)). The instruction to furnish the facility may be given to him either directly by the principal or by an intermediary, defined in Article 2(a)(ii) as the "instructing party", engaged for this purpose by the principal. The reimbursement undertaking or indemnity given by an instructing party to the guarantor is known as a "counter-guarantee" (Art. 2(b)).

23–297 **Incorporation and autonomy.** According to Article 1, the Uniform Rules apply to any demand guarantee (and amendments thereto) provided they have been incorporated. Guarantees in which the Uniform Rules are so incorporated are deemed, under Article 2(b), to be "separate transactions from" the underlying contract. The same principle of autonomy is applied, under paragraph (c), to a counter-guarantee, which is deemed separate not only from the underlying commercial contract, but also from the demand guarantee to which it relates. The autonomy principle is, further, reflected in the definition, in Article 2(b), of the guarantor's undertaking. His duty is to pay the sum covered on presentation of a written[87] demand for payment accompanied by any other documents specified in the guarantee "which appear on their face to be in accordance with the terms of the Guarantee".

General provisions. The general or basic provisions applied to first-demand guarantees show a clear influence of the principles enshrined in the UCP Thus, under Article 3 of the Uniform Rules all instructions for the issuing of guarantees and amendments thereto should be clear and precise and should avoid excessive detail. The article further lists eight details which have to appear in every facility, including, *inter alia*, the maximum amount payable, the currency of payment and the expiry date or an "expiry event". According to Article 4, the beneficiary's right to make a demand is not assignable but this prohibition does not affect his right to assign the proceeds. Articles 5 and 6 deal with the issue of irrevocability. Under the former provision, all guarantees and counter-guarantees are "irrevocable unless otherwise indicated". Under the latter provision, a guarantee enters into effect from the date of its issue, except where the facility provides that it is to come into effect as from a later date or subject to a condition precedent "specified in the Guarantee and determinable by the Guarantor on the basis of documents therein specified". It is to be noted that, in harmony with the basic doctrinal approach of the Uniform Rules, Article 6 gives effect to the "documentary principle". Article 7(b) preserves the guarantor's right not to issue the guarantee unless he has agreed to do so. Notably, paragraph (a) imposes on him a duty to inform the instructing party without delay if the law prevailing in his place poses obstacles to the issuing of, or to the performance of, the duties imposed by the guarantee. 23–298

Reduction of amount. A principle which has no counterpart in the UCP is to be found in Article 8 of the Uniform Rules. It sanctions the inclusion in the guarantee of an express provision "for reduction by a specified or determinable amount or amounts on a specified date or dates or upon presentation to the Guarantor of the Document(s) specified for this purpose in the Guarantee". Clauses of this type are common in performance bonds issued in respect of certain building and engineering contracts. Their inclusion in the Uniform Rules gives effect to the practice in point. 23–299

Liabilities and responsibilities. The articles defining the liabilities and responsibilities of the parties, set out in Articles 9–14, are, again, largely based on the UCP Articles 9 and 10 of the Uniform Rules are based, respectively and subject to certain modification, on Articles 13 and 14 of the UCP Article 9 imposes on guarantors the duty to examine the documents whilst Article 10 lays down a simplified rejection procedure. Notably, Article 10(a) provides for a reasonable time for the examination of the documents but does not impose a seven day limit. The exemption 23–300

---

[87] "Written" is defined in Art. 2(d) so as to include an authenticated teletransmission or tested telex.

clauses, spelt out in Articles 11–14, free the guarantor and the instructing party from liability for the genuineness and authenticity of the documents tendered, from loss resulting from delays or loss in communications or errors in translation, from the effect of *force majeure* and from liability for the acts or omissions of correspondents.

A principle not encountered in the UCP is to be found in Article 15 of the Uniform Rules. Under it, guarantors and instructing parties are "not to be excluded from liability or responsibility under the terms of Articles 11, 12 and 14 above for their failure to act in good faith and with reasonable care". This useful provision underscores the importance of fair dealings and diligence in transactions involving first demand guarantees. Another original provision is Article 16, under which the guarantor is liable to the beneficiary "only in accordance with the terms specified in the Guarantee . . . and in these Rules, and up to an amount not exceeding" that provided in the facility.

23–301 **Demands.** The Uniform Rules seek to obviate the problems that, as shown earlier on, arise occasionally in respect of the beneficiary's demand. To this end, the Code introduces a detailed regime. Thus, Article 17 requires the guarantor to inform the principal or, where applicable, the instructing party that a demand has been made. The instructing party, in turn, has to advise the principal. According to Article 21, the "demand" itself (which comprises the formal letter of demand and the accompanying documents) has to be transmitted to the principal without delay. The amount available is defined in Article 18. According to it, the original amount for which the facility is issued has to be reduced by any amount paid thereunder or by a "reduction" applicable under Article 8. When the full amount covered has been paid out, the guarantee terminates. The actual return or cancellation of the document is not a precondition to such expiry. Under Article 19, the "demand" must be presented at the place at which the guarantee is issued and before its expiry. The demand has to be "made in accordance with the terms of the guarantee" and, in particular, all the specified documents and any statement (as defined in Art. 20) must be presented.

23–302 **Form of demand.** The formal requirements of a demand are set out in Article 20. Under paragraphs (a), a demand made under a guarantee has to be in writing and, in addition to other documents specified in the facility, must be "supported by a written statement (whether in the demand itself or in a separate document or documents accompanying the demand and referred to in it) stating: (i) that the Principal is in breach of his obligation(s) under the underlying contract(s) or, in the case of a tender guarantee, the tender conditions; and (ii) the respect in which the Principal is in breach." Under paragraph (b), any demand made under a counter-guarantee has to be supported by a written statement confirming that the guarantor "has received a demand for payment under the Guarantee in accordance with its terms and with this Article". The object of this detailed provision is to discourage the furnishing of facilities providing for payment against a bare demand. However, under Article 20(c) both paragraphs (a) and (b) may be excluded by an express term to that effect.

Expiry provisions. Article 22 distinguishes between an "expiry date" and an "expiry event", which occurs "upon presentation to the Guarantor of the document(s) specified for the purpose of expiry". If the facility specifies both an expiry date and an expiry event, the guarantee expires on whichever "occurs first, whether or not the Guarantee and any amendment(s) thereto are returned". Article 23 provides that, regardless of any expiry provision set out in the facility, the guarantee is cancelled on presentation to the guarantor of the guarantee itself or of the beneficiary's written "statement of release from liability under the Guarantee". In the latter case, the statement releases the guarantor even if the guarantee and the amendments thereto are not surrendered. This last principle is given further emphasis in Article 24, under which "where a Guarantee has terminated by payment, expiry, cancellation or otherwise, retention of the Guarantee or of any amendments thereto shall not preserve any rights of the Beneficiary under the Guarantee".[88] 23–303

Extension as alternative to demand. Article 26 makes provisions applicable in cases in which the beneficiary resorts to the well-known strategy of requesting an extension of the validity of the guarantee as an alternative to his making an outright demand for payment. The guarantor's first duty in such a case is to inform without delay the party who ordered the furnishing of the facility. "The Guarantor shall then suspend payment of the demand for such time as is reasonable to permit the Principal and the Beneficiary to reach agreement on the granting of such extension and for the Principal to arrange for such extension to be issued." If no such extension is arranged within the time provided, the guarantor "is obliged to pay the Beneficiary's conforming demand without requiring any further action on the Beneficiary's part". It is, in this context, important to note that the demand is conforming only insofar as it complies with the terms of the facility, including its expiry date. 23–304

Article 26 includes two provisos. The first clarifies that the guarantor is not liable for any loss sustained by the beneficiary in consequence of a delay resulting from the prescribed procedure. Under the second proviso, the extension, even if sanctioned by the principal, can be granted only with the consent of the guarantor and any instructing party.

Governing law and jurisdiction. Under Article 27 the governing law of a guarantee and of a counter-guarantee is that of the place of business of the guarantor or of the instructing party. If the party in question has more than one place of business, the applicable law is that of the branch that issued the facility. Exclusive jurisdiction is, under Article 28, conferred on the competent court in that place. Both provisions apply only in the absence of a term to the contrary in the facility. 23–305

The UN Convention. A development respecting both standby credits and first-demand guarantees is the United Nations Convention on Independent Guarantees and Standby Letters of Credit, adopted by the General 23–306

[88] And note Art. 25, which applies the notification requirement, applicable under Arts 17 and 21 in respect of a demand, to cases in which the guarantee terminates or where its amount has been subject to a reduction.

Assembly on December 11, 1995.[89] Its detailed provisions are, generally, in harmony with both the common law principles and the Uniform Rules for Demand Guarantees. The Convention is still open for signature but has not been adopted by any major commercial nation.[90] A discussion of its provisions has, accordingly, remained premature.

9. CONFIRMING HOUSES AND FINANCING BY MERCHANTS

(a) *Functions of Confirming Houses*

23–307 **Background and practice.** Many overseas sales, involving parties who reside in countries within the Commonwealth, are financed by confirming houses. The function of this type of firm, which developed from the commission merchants or commission agents of the nineteenth century,[91] is to confirm to an exporter an order placed by an overseas buyer. The usual practice is that the confirming house obtains an order or "indent" from the buyer and transmits it, together with its "confirmation", to the seller. The confirming house may execute such a confirmation on the indent signed by the buyer; but in certain cases the confirming house retains the document signed by the buyer and places its own order for the goods with the seller. The object of the confirmation is to arrange for the payment of the price of exported goods by a house of first class standing operating in the seller's country. Moreover, some confirming houses undertake to perform the duties of a forwarding agent, and, in effect, arrange for the export of the goods.[92] The confirming house finances transactions confirmed by it by granting credit facilities to the buyer. The latter is required to reimburse the confirming house upon the arrival of the goods or at the expiration of an agreed prior thereafter. The confirming house can safeguard its own interest under an export credit policy or guarantee.[93]

Obviously, the function of a confirming house is in some respects similar to that of a banker who confirms an irrevocable credit. The main difference between the undertaking given to the seller by a confirming house and a

[89] Fifth Session, Resolution No.50/48. For its background and final text see, A/CN.9/330, 342, 345, 358, 361, 372, 374, 388, 391, 405 and 408, reproduced in UNCITRAL Yearbooks vol. XXI: 1990 to XXVI: 1995. For a detailed commentary, see A/CN.9/431 of July 4, 1996.

[90] The Convention has been signed and ratified by six Member States (Belarus, Ecuador, El Salvador, Kuwait, Panama and Tunisia) and signed but not ratified by the United States (information gratefully received from UNCITRAL); and see Herrmann, *2000 Annual Survey of Letters of Credit Law and Practice*, p.234.

[91] For a discussion of the role of a commission agent see *Ireland v Livingston* (1872) L.R. 5 H.L. 395 at 406–409; *Cassaboglou v Gibb* (1883) 11 Q.B.D. 797. See, generally, on confirming houses: Schmitthoff [1957] J.B.L. 17 at 19–21; Schmitthoff, *The Export Trade* (10th ed.), pp.601 *et seq*; Hill, 3 *Journal of Maritime Law and Commerce* 307 (1972).

[92] Facilities similar to those of confirming houses, known as "non-recourse finance" are offered by other types of finance houses. But these do not undertake any duties except the making of payment: Schmitthoff, *The Export Trade* (10th ed.), pp.238–239.

[93] Discussed in Ch.24.

banker's confirmed credit is that, whilst the banker's only obligation is to pay the amount of the credit against the tender of the required documents, the confirming house becomes a party to the main contract established between the buyer and the seller or simply steps into the buyer's shoes. The principle of the autonomy of the confirmed credit[94] does not apply to contracts made by confirming houses.

Legal nature and classification. The legal nature of the contracts created by the confirming house depends on the specific role assumed by it in each case. Basically, its engagement may assume one of the following four forms[95]: First, the buyer may simply order the goods from the confirming house. In such a transaction the confirming house enters in its own name into a contract for the purchase of the goods from the seller and resells them to the buyer. The confirming house acts as principal in both contracts and does not have the authority to create a contract between the buyer and the seller.[96] The only similarity between this type of transaction, which is sometimes described as "merchanting", and a transaction involving an agency contract is that the confirming house's profit is based on an agreed percentage of the price paid to the seller; the confirming house's remuneration therefore resembles an agent's commission. In the second type of transaction the buyer instructs the confirming house to purchase the goods from the seller in its own name and undertakes to reimburse the confirming house and to pay its commission upon the delivery of the goods; the confirming house is not authorised to create a contract between the buyer and the seller.[97] As regards the contract between the seller and the confirming house, there is, in effect, no difference between transactions of this type and of the first type. But whilst in transactions of the first type the contract between the buyer and the confirming house is one of buyer and seller, in transactions of the second type it is a contract of principal and agent. That a commission agent or confirming house may combine the roles of a principal (or seller) and of an agent has been well established for about 100 years.[98] 23–308

In the third type of transaction the confirming house is instructed to order the goods on behalf of the buyer and to confirm this order to the seller. The contracts of the confirming house and seller and of the buyer and the confirming house are in such a case similar to the contracts

---

[94] See above, para.23–138.

[95] See *Bolus & Co. Ltd v Inglis Bros Ltd* [1924] N.Z.L.R. 164 at 174–176; *Witt & Scott Ltd v Blumenreich* [1949] N.Z.L.R. 806 at 809–811.

[96] See *Anglo-African Shipping Co. of New York v J Mortner Ltd* [1962] 1 Lloyd's Rep. 81, affirmed *ibid.*, at p.610, where Diplock L.J., in a dissenting judgment, thought the transaction was of this type. For a transaction of this type see *Brown and Gracie Ltd v F W Green & Co. Ltd* [1960] 1 Lloyd's Rep. 289 where a firm of mercantile agents of Melbourne agreed to sell beans produced by an Australian firm to importers in London.

[97] See, *e.g. Witt & Scott Ltd v Blumenreich* [1949] N.Z.L.R. 806; *Rusholme and Bolton and Roberts Hadfield Ltd v S G Read & Co. (London) Ltd* [1955] 1 W.L.R. 146.

[98] *Ireland v Livingston* (1872) L.R. 5 H.L. 395; *Cassaboglou v Gibb* (1883) 11 Q.B.D. 797. See also *Sobell Industries Ltd v Cory Bros & Co. Ltd* [1955] 2 Lloyd's Rep. 82 at 90–91; *Teheran-Europe Co. Ltd v Belton (Tractors) Ltd* [1968] 2 Q.B. 545 at 558–559.

established in the second type of transaction. But there is a direct contract between the buyer and the seller.[99] Whether a specific transaction falls into the second or third class depends on all the surrounding circumstances. The mere fact that the buyer's name is not disclosed to the seller is inconclusive; the buyer may in certain cases be in the position of an undisclosed principal who has privity of contract with the third party or seller.[1] In the fourth type of transaction the confirming house is instructed to order the goods from the seller on behalf of the buyer without adding its confirmation to the order. In such a case the confirming house assumes the role of a mere agent, who creates a contract between his principal, the buyer, and the third party, who is the seller, without entering into a contract in his own name with the third party.

23–309 **Practical implication and scope.** The role assumed by a confirming house in a specific transaction determines its duties towards the seller and the buyer. In effect, transactions of the first and fourth types discussed above are not within the scope of this chapter. In the first type the confirming house assumes the role of an exporter whilst in transactions of the fourth type it acts as a mere agent and without financing the transaction. The discussion is therefore confined to the legal relationships established in the second and third type of transaction. It should be added that in certain cases the confirming house may agree to perform services not directly connected with its ordinary business. Thus it may, in addition to confirming the order, act as a forwarding agent.[2] But the main business of a confirming house has become well defined and is distinguishable from the business of a factor[3] and of a *del credere agent*, who guarantees the third party's solvency to the principal.[4]

(b) *Liabilities of Parties*

23–310 **Contract of seller and confirming house.** This contract is established when the seller accepts the order for the supply of the goods (the "indent") to which the confirming house has added its confirmation. The liability of the confirming house is not confined to making payment against the delivery of the goods, but is similar to that of a buyer. In *Rusholme and Bolton and Roberts Hadfield Ltd v S G Read & Co. (London) Ltd*[5] an order of an Australian firm for the supply of textiles was confirmed to the English supplier by a confirming house. Due to a trade recession the Australian

---

[99] See, *e.g. Bolus & Co. Ltd v Inglis Bros Ltd* [1924] N.Z.L.R. 164; *Sobell Industries Ltd v Cory Bros & Co. Ltd*, above.

[1] *Teheran-Europe Co. Ltd v Belton (Tractors) Ltd* [1968] 2 Q.B. 53 at 59–61, affirmed on this point: *ibid.*, at pp.545, 557–559. See also *Bow (R and J) Ltd v Hill* (1930) 37 Ll.L.R. 46.

[2] See, *e.g. Anglo-African Shipping Co. of New York v J Mortner Ltd* [1962] 1 Lloyd's Rep. 81, affirmed *ibid.* at p.610.

[3] *Tellrite Ltd v London Confirmers Ltd* [1962] 1 Lloyd's Rep. 236.

[4] *Rusholme and Bolton and Roberts Hadfield Ltd v S G Read & Co. (London) Ltd* [1955] 1 W.L.R. 146 at 151.

[5] [1955] 1 W.L.R. 146.

firm cancelled the order and the confirming house informed the supplier that it would refuse to take delivery. Pearce J. held that the confirming house was liable in damages to the supplier and added: "I see no reason why 'payment' should be restricted to payment on delivery and should exclude other payments such as payments due for breach of contract. Such a restriction would make the [confirming house's] functions less onerous, but also far less valuable. It would leave the English merchant completely unprotected against cancellation at the last moment."[6] In *Sobell Industries Ltd v Cory Bros & Co. Ltd*[7] McNair J. mentioned that in certain situations the confirming house may be under a duty to give the seller the relevant shipping instructions. Defining the nature of the "confirmation", he said: "using the word in its ordinary sense, 'to confirm' means that the party confirming guarantees that the order will be carried out by the purchaser".[8] McNair J. added that it was immaterial whether the contract was solely between the seller and the confirming house or whether an additional contract was established between the seller and the overseas buyer.[9] Moreover, the confirmation binds the confirming house towards the seller even if, in granting it, the confirming house has exceeded the authority conferred on it by the buyer.[10]

Contract of confirming house and buyer. The role assumed by the confirming house in a specific transaction determines its liability towards the buyer. Obviously, in transactions of the first type the confirming house assumes the role and duties of a seller.[11] In transactions of the second and third types the confirming house's obligations to the buyer are determined by the law of principal and agent. Thus, the confirming house is under a duty to exercise the care and skill required of an agent in the execution of the order given to it. But if the confirming house is unable to procure the goods specified in the buyer's order, it is not liable for non-delivery.[12] A question of some difficulty is whether the confirming house is liable for the non-conformity of or any defects in the goods. In a New Zealand case, *Downie Bros v Henry Oakley & Sons*,[13] a buyer in New Zealand instructed a confirming house in London to order some hollow ware from British manufacturers. The confirming house ordered the goods in its own name and did not establish a direct contract between the buyer and the manufacturers. It arranged for the shipment of the goods and, in due course, paid the price to the manufacturers. But the buyer rejected the goods and refused to reimburse the confirming house, alleging *inter alia* that the goods did not comply with their description. Dismissing the confirming house's action, Adams J. said that its liability to the buyer was that of an agent who was bound to exercise "that due diligence which is 23–311

[6] *ibid.*, at p.152.
[7] [1955] 2 Lloyd's Rep. 82 at 89.
[8] *ibid.*, at p.89.
[9] *ibid.*, at p.90.
[10] *Robertson (J S) (Aust.) Pty Ltd v Martin* (1956) 94 C.L.R. 30 at 69.
[11] See, *e.g. Brown and Gracie Ltd v F W Green & Co. Ltd* [1960] 1 Lloyd's Rep. 289.
[12] *Cassaboglou v Gibb* (1883) 11 Q.B.D. 797.
[13] [1923] N.Z.L.R. 734.

required of all persons who take upon themselves to act for others, to satisfy themselves before payment and shipment that the goods tendered were in accordance with the contract as reasonably understood."[14]

23–312 **Anglo-African.** A similar conclusion about the nature of the confirming house's liability was reached by the majority of the Court of Appeal in *Anglo-African Shipping Co. of New York v J Mortner Ltd.*[15] But Diplock L.J., in a dissenting judgment, emphasised that it remained an open question "whether the confirming house warrants to the client that the seller will perform his obligations under the contract of sale between him and the confirming house so as to render the confirming house liable to the client for damages for any breach of contract by the seller". He added: "There is much to be said for the view that it does; for otherwise, in the absence of privity of contract between the seller and the client, the latter would be without remedy against anyone although the confirming house would itself have a remedy over against the seller."[16] It should be noted that Diplock L.J. thought that the transaction was of the first type, *i.e.* that the confirming house had acted as a seller *vis-à-vis* the buyer. However, from a practical point of view, the same argument applies to transactions of the second type, where there is, likewise, no privity of contract between the seller and the buyer.

23–313 **No cancellation.** Where the confirming house carries out the instructions given to it in the indent, it is entitled to reimbursement for the amount paid to the seller plus its commission.[17] The buyer is not entitled to instruct the confirming house to cancel an order which it has confirmed to the seller.[18] Unlike a factor, the confirming house does not have a lien over documents of title or goods shipped to the buyer as a security for a general indebtedness incurred by him.[19]

23–314 **Contract of buyer and seller.** Such a contract is established only in the third and fourth type of transaction. In the first and second type the parties to the contract for the purchase of the goods are the seller and the confirming house. Unfortunately, it is not always easy to determine the exact nature of a specific transaction. In particular, it may be difficult to decide whether a transaction is of the second or of the third type or, in other words, whether the confirming house, acting as the buyer's agent, has or has not established a contract between the buyer and the seller. In

[14] *ibid.*, at p.736.
[15] [1962] 1 Lloyd's Rep. 610.
[16] *ibid.*, at p.622.
[17] *Anglo-African Shipping Co. of New York v J Mortner Ltd,* above; *Bolus & Co. Ltd v Inglis Bros Ltd* [1924] N.Z.L.R. 164.
[18] *Anglo-African Shipping Co. of New York v J Mortner Ltd*, above; but the trial judge, Megaw J., thought that it was the confirming house's duty towards the buyers to raise any objection available against the seller and, if necessary, to reject non-conforming goods: [1962] 1 Lloyd's Rep. 81 at 93.
[19] *Tellrite Ltd v London Confirmers Ltd* [1962] 1 Lloyd's Rep. 236.

Teheran-Europe Co. Ltd v Belton (Tractors) Ltd[20] Persian buyers instructed a London confirming house to order 12 air compressors from English suppliers. The compressors were duly shipped and paid for by the confirming house but the buyers alleged that they were not up to contract and brought an action against the suppliers for breach of contract. It was raised as a preliminary issue that the Persian buyers were undisclosed foreign principals and had no privity of contract with the suppliers. The documents concerning the transaction showed that, in its correspondence with the suppliers, the confirming house stated that it was instructed to place the order on behalf of "clients", although the clients' name was not disclosed. It was held that there was a contract between the buyers and the supplier. Lord Denning M.R. said: "It is a well-established rule of English law that an undisclosed principal can sue and be sued upon a contract, even though his name and even his existence is undisclosed, save in those cases when the terms of the contract expressly or impliedly confine it to the parties to it."[21] It was further held that this rule applied although the principals, or buyers, were carrying on business in a foreign country. This decision clarifies that, in the absence of indications of an intention to the contrary, a transaction, in which the confirming house acts as an agent, is likely to be regarded as a transaction of the third type.

Defect in goods. If goods, delivered in a transaction of the third type, turn out to be defective, the buyer may have an option of suing either the seller or the confirming house. An action against the seller would be for the breach of the contract of sale; the confirming house would be sued for a failure to perform its duties as an agent. The seller can, likewise, benefit from his being a party to the two contracts. If the goods are rejected by the confirming house or if payment is refused, the seller can bring an action either against the confirming house or against the buyer.[22] But the seller is obliged to demand payment in the first place from the confirming house and only upon its default from the buyer. However, if the confirming house has purported to cancel the order or has denied its duty to pay, the seller is not obliged to claim payment from it and may tender the shipping documents and demand payment directly from the buyer.[23] 23–315

(c) *Other Methods used by Mercantile Firms*

Factoring services. Some bankers and mercantile firms arrange for the financing of overseas sales by providing factoring services. Under such an arrangement the firm, or "factor", takes over the book debts of the exporter on a non-recourse basis. It pays the exporter the price of goods shipped overseas against a duplicate of his invoice and collects the price 23–316

---

[20] [1968] 2 Q.B. 53, affirmed on the agency issue: *ibid.*, 545. See also *Witt and Scott Ltd v Blumenreich* [1949] N.Z.L.R. 806; *The "Santa Carina"* [1977] 1 Lloyd's Rep. 478.

[21] [1968] 2 Q.B. at 552.

[22] But note that the seller cannot sue both the buyer and the confirming house but has to elect: *Chitty on Contracts* (29th ed.), Vol. 2, para.32–071.

[23] *Stunzi Sons Ltd v House of Youth Pty Ltd* (1960) 60 S.R. (N.S.W.) 220.

from the buyer through correspondents operating in his country. The factor takes over the risk of bad debts. In certain cases the factor may also be prepared to advance to the exporter up to 90 per cent of the price of goods before shipment. A specific advantage from the exporter's point of view is that upon the engagement of a factor he is able to dispense with the need of having his own sales collections and accounting departments.

The use of factoring services is not confined to overseas sales; they are used widely for the finance of inland transactions. A detailed discussion of the system is outside the scope of this work.[24]

---

[24] See, generally, Schmitthoff, *The Export Trade* (10th ed.), pp.226–232 and see pp.232–235 as regards forfaiting; T. G. Huston [1965] *Journal of the Institute of Bankers* 69. For a historical account see Steffen and Danziger, 36 Columbia L.Rev. 745 (1936). As regards the International Factoring Convention adopted by the Diplomatic Conference of Ottawa in 1988, see, Goode [1988] J.B.L. 347 at 510; Schmitthoff, *op. cit*, 458 *et seq.* For general works on the subject, see Biscoe, *Law and Practice of Credit Factoring* (London, 1976); Salinger, *Factoring: A Guide to Factoring Practice and Law* (1984).

CHAPTER 24

EXPORT CREDIT GUARANTEES

	PARA.
1. Introduction	24–001
2. Export and Investment Guarantees Act 1991	24–007
3. Supplier's credit policies	24–011
(a) General principles	24–011
(b) Policies available	24–016
(c) Common provisions in comprehensive policies	24–018
(d) Assignment of credit insurance policies	24–025
4. Guarantees	24–031
(a) Guarantees for supplier's credit financing	24–031
(b) Guarantees for buyer's credit financing	24–035
(c) Lines of credit	24–044
5. Other ECGD facilities	24–045
6. Overseas investment insurance	24–047
7. International aspects	24–050

1. INTRODUCTION

Objects. Exporting goods to overseas markets on deferred payment terms brings with it two types of credit risk for the exporter: commercial or buyer risk (for example, the buyer becoming insolvent or failing to pay for some other reason) and political or non-buyer risk (for example, actions of overseas governments or other events such as war or civil unrest or natural disasters which prevent the buyer from paying). Depending on the length of time for which credit is extended, export credits are traditionally divided into "short-term" (under two years), "medium-term" (two to five years) and "long-term" (over five year) credits. **24–001**

Arrangements are available which enable an exporter to limit these "export credit" risks. The arrangements take a number of forms, but legally they are in essence either contracts of insurance or guarantees—although they are often loosely referred to as "export credit guarantees" irrespective of their actual legal form.[1] In a so-called "buyer credit" arrangement, the exporter arranges for a financial institution to make a loan to the overseas buyer to enable him to purchase the exports and for that loan to be guaranteed or insured against non-payment. In so-called "supplier credit", the exporter (or supplier) extends credit to the buyer himself and then arranges for insurance or a guarantee against non-payment.

In effect, the export credit guarantee serves a purpose similar to that of a confirmed credit.[2] But there are two important differences between the

[1] Thus the ECGD's insurance policy for short-term credit was (before that part of its activities were privatised, see below, para.24–004) termed the "Comprehensive Short Term Guarantee", see below, para.24–012.

[2] In which the seller obtains a binding promise from a banker in his own country (above, para.23–052).

instruments. First, while a confirmed credit is furnished by the buyer and at his expense, the export credit guarantee is effected by the seller and the premium is paid by him.[3] Secondly, a confirmed credit enables the seller to obtain the price of the goods against the tender of the required documents irrespective of a dispute relating to the goods.[4] In contrast, the export credit guarantee does not always cover the seller where the buyer's rejection of the goods is based on a defect in the goods, such as their failure to comply with a sample.[5]

24–002 **Raising finance.** A further, subsidiary, object of export credit guarantees may be to assist the seller to raise finance. While the export credit guarantee does not by itself provide finance, it enables the seller to obtain the necessary finance from his bankers, whose interests can be safeguarded either by an assignment to them of the insurance policy or by the furnishing of an independent guarantee of the credit guarantor. This aspect points to a further similarity between the export credit guarantee and a confirmed credit. The latter gives added currency to bills of exchange drawn by the seller on the buyer and in this way enables the seller to obtain discount facilities. But while in the documentary credit system finance is to be arranged by the buyer, the export credit guarantee system involves, in effect, an extension of credit by the seller to the buyer. The seller's ability to provide such finance is frequently an advantage as the availability of attractive credit terms may assist him to secure export contracts.

24–003 **Insurance and guarantee providers.** Governments of countries that wish to encourage exports—including the United Kingdom—have established "Export Credit Agencies" (ECAs), which provide the requisite insurance and guarantees as well as other forms of aid such as direct loans.[6] The Export Credits Guarantee Department (the ECGD) is the United Kingdom's ECA. As will be seen below, the ECGD is a government department but ECAs in other countries can take the form of commercial institutions, which administer support for export credits on behalf of the government which underwrites the risks.

In addition, private sector insurers,[7] operating on their own account, also provide export credit insurance but mainly for "short-term" credit. The ECAs generally complement this private sector provision by providing cover for risks, which the private sector is not prepared to undertake.

---

[3] But the seller will take the premium so payable into account when he calculates the price.

[4] See above, para.23–143.

[5] This depends on the form of the "guarantee". If it is an insurance policy, then it does not cover the seller when in default. If it is a true guarantee, then the seller's default does not absolve the guarantor from paying under the guarantee.

[6] The ECAs also provide (i) "investment insurance" covering investment overseas against political risks and (ii) "project finance" (or "limited recourse finance") financing major projects on the basis of the income they are expected to generate. These will be noted below (see paras 24–047 and 24–046), although this chapter will focus on support for the export of goods.

[7] The ECGD website lists the following, which operate in the UK: (a) Atradius (formerly Gerling NCM) website *www.atradius.com*; (b) Euler Hermes; (c) Coface UK.

The ECGD.[8] The ECGD is a separate government department reporting to the Secretary of State for Trade and Industry. It was established in 1911—the world's first government export credit insurer—and now derives its powers from the Export and Investment Guarantees Act 1991. This is considered in more detail below. 24–004

Before 1991, the ECGD comprised two divisions. The Insurance Services Group, based in Cardiff and comprising a network of nine regional offices, granted cover for short-term transactions, although this Group was also responsible for covering certain longer terms contracts for the sale of products. The Project Group, based in London, provided cover for "one off" medium and longer term contracts, which unlike the shorter term types of export transactions were underwritten individually. The Project Group also helped UK companies to insure new investments overseas against risks such as restrictions on transfer of profits, war and nationalisation. A structural change took place in 1991. Whilst the business of the Project Group continues to be transacted by the ECGD, which has remained a government body,[9] the Insurance Services Group was acquired by Nederlandsche Credietverzekering Maatschappij ("NCM") of the Netherlands. The sale and transfer in question were sanctioned by sections 8–12 of the Export and Investment Guarantees Act 1991. NCM was renamed Atradius in 2004, following a shareholder restructuring.

Role of ECGD. Following a major review of the "Mission and Status" of the ECGD in July 2000, the ECGD issued a new "Mission Statement". This confirms the ECGD's trade facilitation role as its "core purpose", but now requires the ECGD also to "underpin" the Government's wider international policies to promote sustainable development, human rights and good governance throughout the world. The ECGD's management board now has two non-executive directors, and the role of the Export Guarantees Advisory Council (the EGAC) has changed from advising on individual risks to advising the ECGD on its underlying policies and principles. In addition, the EGAC was active in devising the ECGD's new "Business Principles" which were adopted to guide it in putting its "Mission Statement" into practice. 24–005

The ECGD complements—and does not compete with—private sector provision, in particular by backing those large-scale, long-term projects in non-OECD or developing countries for which private sector insurance is not available. The 2000 Review considered whether its current portfolio of medium- to long-term export guarantee business should also be privatised, but came to the firm conclusion that this was not desirable as such backing was not available from the private sector and UK exporters would therefore be at a disadvantage in competition with overseas buyers having the benefit of official export credit support. However, the ECGD operates on a break-even basis and it seeks full recovery from the defaulting buyer—although some debts are later written off, for example as a result of the Heavily Indebted Poor Country (HIPCs) Debt and Development initiative.

---

8 Its website is: *www.ecgd.gov.uk*

9 The Export and Investment Guarantees Act 1991, s.13(1), under which the ECGD is to remain a Department of the Secretary of State.

The ECGD has negotiated a number of "One Stop Shop" co-operation agreements with ECAs in other countries,[10] to allow joint export projects involving exporters from both countries to be supported by export credit packages involving both ECAs. The ECA in the country whose exporter has the largest share of the deal becomes the "lead ECA", providing export credit support on its usual terms for the whole deal. The other ECA generally provides re-insurance.

24–006 **Types of export credit "guarantees".** As noted above, legally export credit "guarantees" take the form either of insurance policies or true guarantees. Both are arranged and paid for by the exporter—although the premium is reflected in the price the overseas buyer pays. Insurance policies covering the exporter against the risk of non-payment by the overseas buyer ("supplier's credit policies") are available both from the private sector and, to the extent that they are not available in the circumstances from that sector, the ECGD. As noted above, the availability of private sector provision is generally limited to short-term credit risks and the ECGD steps in to provide cover in other circumstances. The relevant policies are considered in more detail below.[11]

There is a notable degree of uniformity in the actual terms granted by the ECGD and by the private sector to the different holders of each type of policy. The importance of the practice that has been established necessitates a departure from the usual pattern of the discussion given in this study to commercial documents and instruments. In addition to the ordinary analysis of the purely legal aspects of export credit guarantees, it is necessary to consider in some detail the main clauses used in the standard forms of the policies as well as some of the financial terms, such as the extent of cover granted and the length of credit periods approved. Naturally, a discussion of each variant of every type of facility available would be outside the scope of this analysis. It is necessary to concentrate on the main types of policies and on the salient principles emerging from the contractual clauses contained therein.

In addition to insurance policies, the ECGD provides guarantees to those financing institutions that extend credit either to the buyer or to the supplier. Thus as part of its "Supplier Credit Finance Facility" (SCF) the ECGD gives a guarantee to a bank in respect of finance it provides (usually by the purchase of negotiable instruments accepted by the overseas buyer) to the exporter. And as part of its "buyer credit" financing package, the ECGD provides a guarantee to a lending institution providing the buyer with credit. Again, these packages will be considered in more detail below.[12]

Before considering the law and practice in relation to these policies and guarantees, it is necessary to discuss the general powers of the ECGD—as conferred by the Export and Investment Guarantees Act 1991—as it continues to play a major role in the field.

---

[10] At the time of writing, with those in 25 countries. These are listed on the ECGD website, see above, n.8.
[11] See below, paras 24–011. *et seq*.
[12] See below, paras 24–031 and 24–035.

2. EXPORT AND INVESTMENT GUARANTEES ACT 1991

The Act. The powers of the ECGD are defined in the Export and Investment Guarantees Act 1991, which repealed and replaced the Export Guarantees and Overseas Investment Act 1978, which, in turn had, consolidated earlier enactments.[13] The 1991 Act defines the ECGD's functions as regards the issue of both export credit guarantees and of policies insuring investments overseas.[14] 24–007

Powers of ECGD. The ECGD's principal powers[15] are defined in sections 1 and 2 of the Export and Investment Guarantees Act 1991. Section 1(4) defines the "arrangements" that may be made by the ECGD under section 1. These cover arrangements for providing financial facilities or assistance for, or for the benefit of, persons carrying on business; and the facilities or assistance may be provided in any form, including guarantees (which, under s.4(3)(b), include indemnities), insurance, grants or loans. Under subsection (1) the ECGD may make such arrangements with a view to facilitating, directly or indirectly, supplies by persons carrying on business in the United Kingdom of goods or services to persons carrying on business outside that United Kingdom. Under subsection (2) the ECGD may make arrangements, as defined, for the purpose of rendering economic assistance to countries outside the United Kingdom. The powers so defined are augmented by subsection (3) under which the ECGD may make such arrangements with a view to facilitating the performance of obligations created or arising, directly or indirectly, in connection with matters under which powers have been exercised under sections 1 or 2 of the Act. They can further be made to facilitate the reduction or avoidance of losses arising in connection with any failure to perform such obligations. An important complementary provision is to be found in section 11(2). It empowers the ECGD to reinsure persons providing insurance for the risks defined in section 1. The ECGD is also granted the power to determine in respect of which of such risks to provide reinsurance; but may exercise this power only if it considers it expedient to do so in the national interest. 24–008

The ECGD's powers as regards the granting of insurance for overseas investment are defined in section 2. Under subsection (1) such a policy may

---

[13] The Export Guarantees Act 1975 and the Overseas Investment and Export Guarantees Act 1972, ss.1, 2. These Acts were preceded by the Export Guarantees Act 1968 as amended by the Export Guarantees and Payments Act 1970. As regards earlier Acts see the Export Guarantees Acts 1949–67 as amended by s.10(4)(a) and (5) of the National Loans Act 1968 and, before then, the Overseas Trade Acts 1920–34, which were repealed and replaced by the Export Guarantees Act 1937, which was in turn repealed by the Export Guarantees Acts 1939–48.

[14] The Act came into effect on October 23, 1991: the Export and Investment Guarantees Act 1991 (Commencement) Order 1991, SI 1991/2430, made under s.15(6) of the Act.

[15] The sections confer the powers defined in them on the "Secretary of State", meaning one of the principal Secretaries of State (the Interpretation Act 1978, s.5, Sch.I). The relevant Secretary is the Secretary of State for Trade and Industry. Note that under s.13(1) of the 1991 Act most of the powers of this Secretary of State are to be exercised through the ECGD, which remains a Department of the Secretary of State.

be granted to "any person carrying on business in the United Kingdom" against losses arising either in connection with any investment of resources by the insured in enterprises carried on outside the United Kingdom or in connection with guarantees given by the insured in respect of any investment of resources by others in such enterprises, "being enterprises in which the insured has an interest". The risks covered are losses resulting directly or indirectly from war, expropriation, restrictions on remittances and "other similar events". Subsection (2) empowers the ECGD to make arrangements for insuring persons providing such insurance. Subsection (3) provides that a person carrying on business in the United Kingdom includes any company controlled directly or indirectly by him. Notably, the Act does not define the meaning of the word "control". Presumably the words "controlled company" mean, contextually, a company in which one person has the majority of votes.[16]

24–009 **Financial management.** Section 3(1) confers on the ECGD special powers to make any arrangements which are in the interests of the proper financial management of the ECGD portfolio or any part thereof. Obviously, the word "arrangement" as used in this section is wider than in section 1 where, it will be recalled, its scope is narrowed by the definition of subsection (4). Under section 3(6), the term "ECGD portfolio" means the rights and liabilities to which the ECGD is entitled or subject by virtue of the exercise of its powers under the present Act or the 1978 Act "or in consequence of arrangements made in the exercise of those powers". The scope of the powers conferred under section 3 is clarified in subsection (2), which provides that, in pursuance of any arrangements so made, the ECGD may enter into any form of transaction, including lending and the providing and taking out of insurance and guarantees. To a certain extent, the ECGD's powers are restricted under subsection (3), under which it is precluded from entering, in pursuance of such arrangements, into any transaction for the purpose of borrowing money; but the mere fact that a given transaction involves borrowing does not, in itself, preclude the ECGD from entering into it. Under subsection (7), the ECGD's certification that any transaction has been entered into in the exercise of the powers conferred under section 3 constitutes conclusive evidence of the matters stated therein. One effect of this provision is that the ECGD's power to enter into a specific transaction would be hard to dispute in civil litigation.

[16] See *British American Tobacco Co. v IRC* [1943] A.C. 339 at 340, *per* Simon L.C. (on meaning of "control" and "controlling interest" in Finance Act 1937, Sch.IV). Cases considering the meaning of "control" in the taxation context are likely to be helpful (see, for example, *IRC v Bibby & Sons Ltd* [1945] 1 All E.R. 667 at 670 (on Finance (No.2) Act 1939, s.13(3), (9)), *IRC v Harton Coal Co.* [1960] Ch. 563 (on Finance Act 1922, s.21(6)), *Barclays Bank Ltd v IRC* [1961] A.C. 509 at 523 (on Finance Act 1940, s.55)). "Control" is defined in the Income and Corporation Taxes Act 1988, ss.416(2) and 840. Contrast the definition of "controller of body corporate" in the Enterprise Act 2002, s.222(4). Note also the meaning of "control", in the company law definitions of a "subsidiary" company in Companies Act 1985, ss.258–260 and 736 and see *Lonhro Ltd v Shell Petroleum Co. Ltd* [1980] 1 W.L.R. 627, HL; *Re Technicon Investments Ltd* [1985] B.C.L.C. 434.

Other provisions. The Act also enables the ECGD to provide—and charge for—information and ancillary services[17] and requires it to produce an annual report and annual return (showing separately the aggregate amounts of the ECGD commitments in sterling and foreign currency) which must be laid before Parliament.[18] **24–010**

Special provision is made in section 6 as to the maximum commitments the ECGD may undertake under arrangements it makes under the Act. These limits may be—and have been—increased by Order made by the Secretary of State.[19]

3. SUPPLIER'S CREDIT POLICIES

(a) *General Principles*

Introductory. As already mentioned, the ECGD's short-term export credit insurance provision was privatised in 1991 and taken over by NCM, now re-named Atradius. In consequence, most short-term credit cover for export contracts—generally effected by the issuing of a supplier's credit policy—is currently provided by the private sector. In view of Atradius's leading role in this type of business, the references to the various policies of this type in the following discussion are to those issued by Atradius. **24–011**

Legal nature. In a "supplier's credit policy", the insurer undertakes to indemnify the seller against loss accruing either from the buyer's insolvency or from the buyer's failure to pay the price within six months from its due date or the non-receipt of the price due to political reasons, such as economic legislation.[20] When the seller approaches the insurer in order to effect such cover he is asked to complete a proposal form. A minimum premium[21] is to be paid when the policy is granted to him. From a legal point of view the supplier's credit policy constitutes an insurance policy and not a guarantee. In *Re Miller, Gibb & Co. Ltd*,[22] the ECGD granted a Liverpool company a "Comprehensive Guarantee (Shipments)" covering the company's exports to certain markets including Brazil. Due to exchange control legislation a Brazilian buyer was unable to accept the company's bill of exchange, expressed in sterling, for the price. The documents of title were eventually released to the buyer against payment of an amount in local currency, equal to the price of the goods, into an account opened with **24–012**

---

[17] s.5.

[18] s.7.

[19] See, most recently, the Export and Investment Guarantees (Limit on Foreign Currency Commitments) Order 2000, SI 2000/2087 (exhausting the statutory power to increase the foreign currency limits by increasing it to £30,000 million special drawing rights).

[20] For a detailed discussion of the risks covered see below, paras 24–020 *et seq*.

[21] See below, para.24–016.

[22] [1957] 1 Lloyd's Rep. 258 at 262, 264, favourably referred to by Lord Templeman in *Napier and Ettrick (Lord) v R. F. Kershaw* [1993] A.C. 713 at 734 and followed in *Re Casey (a Bankrupt)* (unreported, HC Ireland, March 1, 1992).

a Brazilian bank in the name of the company's bankers. The ECGD thereupon paid 90 per cent of the price to the company and it was specifically agreed that any amount, remitted thereafter by the Brazilian bank to the company's bankers in the United Kingdom, should be paid by the bankers to the ECGD. Subsequently, the company was ordered to be wound up and a liquidator was appointed. When the full price of the goods supplied to the Brazilian buyer was remitted by the Brazilian bank to the bankers of the company, the ECGD demanded the payment to it of 90 per cent of this amount. The liquidator took the view that the ECGD was not entitled to payment in full of such an amount, but had to prove in respect of it. Allowing the ECGD's claim, Wynn-Parry J. held that the "guarantee" constituted an insurance policy and that the doctrine of subrogation applied as a matter of law.[23] The ECGD was therefore entitled to the payment of 90 per cent of the amount remitted by the Brazilian bank.

24–013 **Uberrimae fidei.** As the supplier's credit policy constitutes an insurance contract, the seller is under a duty to disclose any matters that are material to the risk.[24] Apart from specific clauses in the policy requiring such disclosure, this duty is established at law in regard to insurance policies.[25] Moreover, the policy incorporates the seller's proposal form and is based on it. Thus, the statements made by the seller in the proposal form constitute warranties of the policy; an incorrect statement entitles the insurer to avoid the policy even if the statement has been made in good faith.[26] The insurer, too, is subject to a duty of disclosure. In *Culford Metal Industries v Export Credits Guarantee Department*,[27] Neill J. held the ECGD (which, at that time, issued such policies) liable where it gave the policy-holder negligent advice concerning the insurance effected. His Lordship based his decision on the duty of care established in *Hedley, Byrne & Co. Ltd v Heller and Partners Ltd.*[28] In appropriate cases a similar decision could be based on a breach of the *uberrimae fidei* duty, which is imposed on both parties to an insurance contract.

24–014 **The comprehensive principle.** The traditional policy of the ECGD was to spread the risks covered by it as widely as possible. This led to the establishment of the "comprehensive principle". By offering attractive premium rates for comprehensive policies, the ECGD encouraged expor-

[23] See also *L Lucas Ltd v Exports Credits Guarantee Department* [1974] 1 W.L.R. 909 at 921 and *Lonrho Exports Ltd v Export Credits Guarantee Department* [1999] Ch. 158. Note that in those cases the supplier's credit policy included a clause entitling the ECGD to be subrogated to the seller's rights against a defaulting buyer.

[24] And note that the duty is of a continuing nature remaining intact throughout the relationship involved: *Formica Ltd v Export Credits Guarantee Department* [1995] 1 Lloyd's Rep. 692 at 701–703 (concerning also the issue of the discovery of documents in proceedings against the ECGD).

[25] See, generally, *Chitty on Contracts* (29th ed.) Vol.2, paras 41–029 *et seq.* Moreover, a clause making full disclosure a condition precedent to the insurer's liability is included in most standard supplier's credit policies.

[26] *ibid.*, para.41–035 and especially *Dawsons v Bonnin* [1922] 2 A.C. 413.

[27] (QB, Commercial Court) March 16, 1981; *The Times*, March 25, 1981.

[28] [1964] A.C. 465.

ters to insure the highest proportion of their business. Moreover, in most cases the ECGD declined to cover part only of the seller's export business and this avoided a situation in which a seller insured only his dubious contracts. This policy has been adopted by private credit insurers, including Atradius. However, the comprehensive principle is applied mainly as regards policies covering consumer goods and to engineering goods, where sales are of a continuous and repetitive nature. The principle is not applied in the case of contracts for the supply of capital goods or for major projects (such as a contract for railway electrification), which are usually covered under specific policies some of which are still provided by the ECGD. Moreover, even where the principle applies, the seller may exclude sales to certain markets, provided the remaining business offers a reasonable proportion of his total exports and is not confined to bad markets. The different types of comprehensive policies are discussed subsequently.

Subrogation and debt recovery. Where the insurer meets a claim made by the seller under the policy, he is subrogated to the seller's rights against the buyer.[29] Ordinarily a clause in the policy entitles the insurer to demand a written assignment of such rights. The same clause requires the seller to take all necessary steps in order to effect recovery of the debt from the buyer or from his guarantors. Any amounts obtained by the seller are shared between the seller and the insurer in the same proportion as the loss.[30] On occasions this principle enables the insurer to recover a higher amount than that paid to the seller. All depends on the wording of the clause. Thus in the case of *L Lucas Ltd v Export Credits Guarantee Department*,[31] a contract for the sale of flour by an English seller to a buyer in the United Arab Republic was covered by an ECGD policy. Exchange control restrictions, imposed in the United Arab Republic in 1966, precluded the buyer from remitting the price in US Dollars to the seller, whereupon the ECGD paid the seller 90 per cent of the seller's loss in sterling, based on the rate of exchange when the payment was due. When the currency restrictions of the United Arab Republic ceased to operate, the buyer remitted the original price due in US Dollars, but meanwhile sterling had been devalued and so the seller in fact received a greater amount in sterling than he would have received originally. The relevant clause in the policy required the amount recovered in respect of a claim paid out to be divided between insurer and insured on the same basis as the "loss" itself. The House of Lords[32] construed "loss" as meaning the original sum due in sterling and therefore the ECGD was only to able to recover an amount equal to 90 per cent of that original sum and not 90 per cent of the sterling equivalent actually recovered. 24–015

---

[29] See above, para.24–012.

[30] Note that usually a supplier's credit policy covers only up to 95 per cent of any loss.

[31] [1974] 1 W.L.R. 909, reversing [1973] 1 W.L.R. 914. As regards the question of a set-off between claims arising under a policy and amounts due in respect of subrogation on reimbursement claims, see *Export Credits Guarantee Department v Davenport (Shoes) Ltd* (CA, unreported, February 3, 1983).

[32] Reversing the Court of Appeal and restoring Cooke J.'s judgment (see [1973] 1 W.L.R. 914).

As a result of this decision, the wording of the relevant clause was altered to make it clear that the ECGD is entitled to the benefit of any currency exchange rate fluctuations by providing that amounts recovered are to be shared on the same basis as the amount of the loss "whether or not such division [resulted] in the retention by the insurer of a greater or lesser sum than the amount paid by the insurer under this guarantee".[33] Most current policies follow this later version.[34]

(b) *Policies available*

24–016 **The ECGD's policies.** The ECGD issues two types of insurance policy, the "Export Insurance Policy" (the EXIP) and the "Bond Insurance Policy" (the BIP).

The EXIP is an individual contract insuring individual export contracts, with the premium[35] being determined on a case-by-case basis. The risks covered are negotiable, but generally exporters obtain cover for both commercial and political risk.[36]

Such an insurance policy is either used on its own (especially if the overseas buyer does not require extended credit) or as additional cover in the case of financial facilities. Under the terms of the policy, liability may be declined if an exporter's non-performance leads to buyer default on payment and consideration of the claim may be suspended whilst any dispute between exporter and overseas buyer is resolved. The EXIP covers two types of loss, with most exporters usually insuring against both. The first is loss arising in relation to costs incurred before the right to payment arises, for example, manufacturing costs that arise before the contract is finally concluded or delivery effected. In this way, as discussed below, it may supplement financing packages—which only cover risks once payment is due. The second type of loss which may be covered is non-payment of amounts owing. The EXIP may also (for an additional premium) extend to plant used to perform the contract overseas, which may be lost through events such as confiscation or destroyed in hostilities. In general, 95 per cent of the value of any loss is reimbursed—although a lower percentage may be negotiated for a lower premium. The EGCD requires the exporter to retain his beneficial interest in the "uninsured percentage" and so this cannot be laid off on a third party.

As well as operating as a stand-alone insurance facility, the EXIP can also be used in conjunction with ECGD guarantees.[37] Thus it may provide

---

33 Such a clause was at issue in *Lonrho Exports Ltd v Export Credits Guarantee Department* [1999] Ch. 158. Note that most current policies include a clause prescribing the method for converting amounts expressed in foreign currency into sterling.

34 As regards issues of jurisdiction and a plea of *forum non conveniens* in the context of export credit guarantees, see *Norbrook Laboratories Ltd v Export Credits Guarantee Department* (CA of N.I., unreported, October 10, 1992).

35 This is in sterling, whatever the currency of the contract.

36 The risks covered are similar to those under the private sector policies, considered further below.

37 See s.4, below.

insurance against risks before payment is due. It may also cover any elements of the contract that are not backed by ECGD guarantees or any payments made directly to the supplier by the buyer ("direct payment risks"). Thus, in the case of a Supplier Credit Finance Facility,[38] or a "simple" Buyer Credit (that is, one which only provides for payment instalments from the financed loan) [39] on a disbursement basis, EXIP cover may be obtained for both the financed elements and any un-financed elements (such as termination settlements or arbitral awards). In the case of a "complex" disbursement Buyer Credit (which does permit the financing of termination settlements and arbitral awards),[40] EXIP cover cannot be provided for the financed elements of the contract, but is available to insure any un-financed elements. Finally, if the buyer is to pay the supplier directly, the buyer obtaining reimbursement from the ECGD-backed finance, EXIP cover may be obtained for the "direct payment risk".

It is an explicit condition of the EXIP that the exporter notifies the ECGD of any event likely to cause loss within 30 days of the exporter becoming aware of it. Thus failure to comply with this obligation renders any subsequent claim invalid. Moreover, the policy usually requires the exporter to take recovery action and reimburses a percentage of the costs incurred. If this has not proved fruitful, it may require the exporter to assign his rights under the contract to the ECGD so it can continue the action itself.

Unlike the EXIP (which can be taken out either as stand-alone policy or as a supplement to other ECGD facilities), the Bond Insurance Policy (the "BIP") is only available as a supplement to basic ECGD cover for the underlying contract. It covers either advance payment guarantees (where the buyer makes an advance payment and obtains a guarantee of its repayment should the contract not be performed) and performance bonds (guarantees given in respect of construction projects). The BIP provides insurance against calls which are either "unfair" in the sense of not being commercially justified (because performance in accordance with the contract has, in fact, occurred) or made where failure to perform is due to specified political causes (similar to those identified as giving rise to "political risk").

Atradius Policies. Since acquiring the ECGD's short-term export credit insurance facilities, Atradius has developed a number of policies—especially "comprehensive" policies to cover export credit risk geared at specific segments of the market. There are policies designed for UK companies with large turnovers who wish to insure both their exports and domestic trade debts, policies for smaller UK businesses and policies for multinational companies whose head office may not be in United Kingdom.[41-42] The policies cover either all the seller's exports for a period of one 24–017

---

[38] See paras 24–032 *et seq.*, below.
[39] See para.24–035, below.
[40] *ibid.*
[41–42] Atradius also offers policies that cover UK domestic trade only and policies that do not cover political risks, but only "buyer risks".

year or his turnover in certain markets only for such period.[43] The seller is charged a non-refundable "annual charge" or administration fee at the commencement of each year of insurance. Apart from that, the seller pays a—usually monthly—premium, based on a standard premium rate fixed for each policy and calculated on the amount of exports declared by him. In addition, for exports to certain higher risk countries, the premium is varied by means of a Market Rate Additon.

(c) *Common Provisions in Comprehensive Policies*

24–018 **General.** The Atradius "comprehensive" policies are typical of those offered by the private sector for short-term export credits. They generally have the following terms.

24–019 **Credit limit.** It follows from the nature of the comprehensive policy that the seller is not required to obtain the insurer's approval of each transaction covered by the agreement. But the seller is required to have "credit limit" which restricts the amount of the cover that the seller may have in respect of his dealings with any single buyer. Normally, the insurer will issue a "credit limit" at the seller's request but the amount of the "credit limit" will depend to a large extent on the insurer's perception of the risk as well as on the volume of previous dealings between the seller and the buyer. However, once a credit limit has been fixed in respect of dealings with a given buyer, it remains in force unless it is varied or withdrawn by the insurer. The credit limit is of a revolving nature; as payments are made which reduce the buyer's outstandings, further transactions with him up to the agreed limit may be covered by the policy. Apart from these limits per buyer, the policy sets out an additional figure which limits the total liability of the insurer under the policy.

24–020 **Risks covered.** Most comprehensive policies cover risks that may be broadly classified as follows: first, there are the risks related to the buyer's default. These are the buyer's insolvency and his failure to pay the price within six months from the date on which it is due. Secondly, the policy covers risks of an economic or of a political nature. These include a general moratorium on external debts decreed by the government of the buyer's country; political events, economic difficulties, currency shortages or legislative or administrative measures in the buyer's country which prevent or delay the transfer of amounts deposited by the buyer; the legal discharge of a debt deposited in a foreign currency, which results in a shortage at the date of transfer; war[44] and natural disasters; measures taken by the government of the buyer's or another foreign country which in whole or in

---

[43] The policies cover not only sales, but also certain contracts for services (such as consultancy, refitting, conversion and repair services for overseas customers), sales through overseas subsidiaries, goods sold from stocks held overseas, goods manufactured or traded outside the UK and exports invoiced in foreign currencies.

[44] But see para.24–023: loss resulting from war between the five great powers is usually excluded.

part prevent performance of the contract; and the cancellation of an export licence. Thirdly, where the buyer is stated to be a "public buyer" in the credit limit, loss resulting from any failure by such a buyer to fulfil any of the terms of the contract is covered.

The policy only covers contracts with all buyers in the countries that are listed in a Schedule to the policy. For the cover of economic or political risks, the currency of the contracts must also fall within a predetermined list.

Extent of cover. Most credit insurers expect the seller to bear part of the loss. The highest cover under a policy, which is, for instance, applicable in certain cases involving "political risks", is 95 per cent of the loss. Where a loss is incurred as a result of the buyer's default, however, cover is often restricted to 90 per cent. **24–021**

The amount that the seller may claim in respect of a specific loss is also dependent on the credit limit stipulated in the policy in respect of transactions with the relevant buyer. The seller's claim is restricted to the appropriate percentage of the applicable credit limit; no claim can be made in regard to amounts due from the buyer in excess of this limit. This principle is illustrated by a New Zealand case, *Hill and Lichtenstein Ltd v Export Guarantee General Manager*,[45] based on a policy similar in all relevant respects to the type of comprehensive policy issued in the United Kingdom. The claimants, a New Zealand firm, sustained a loss of NZ $116,250 as the result of the insolvency of a Tanzanian importer to whom they had sold tallow. These transactions were covered by a policy issued by the defendant under which the credit limit, stipulated in respect of the Tanzanian importer, was $90,000; the policy covered 85 per cent of any loss arising from an importer's insolvency. The claimants argued that they were entitled to claim either 85 per cent of their total loss (*i.e.* $112,312) or, alternatively, up to the full amount of the credit limit of $90,000. But the Court of Appeal held that they were entitled only to $76,500, *i.e.* 85 per cent of the agreed credit limit.[46]

Ascertainment of loss. A comprehensive policy includes detailed provisions concerning the manner and the time at which a loss is to be ascertained. Basically, the seller is entitled to payment either immediately after the loss has been so ascertained or, in certain cases, within a specified period thereafter. An important provision is that, where the buyer claims "for any reason whatsoever that he is justified" in withholding payment or not performing any of his obligations, the insurer will not ascertain loss until the claim is settled or withdrawn.[47] **24–022**

---

[45] [1972] N.Z.L.R. 802, SC, affirmed [1973] 2 N.Z.L.R. 730, CA.

[46] A particularly useful provision concerning the appropriation of payments is spelt out in the Atradius policies. According to it, all amounts received in connection with any contract (whether or not covered under the policy) are, as between the insurer and the assured, to be applied to amounts owing under all contracts with the same buyer in chronological order of due dates.

[47] And note below, para.24–023: liability for a loss sustained where there has been a failure by the seller (assured) or a person acting on his behalf "to fulfil any of the terms and conditions of the [underlying] contract" or a non-compliance with the provisions of any applicable law, excluded.

24–023 **Risks excluded.** Certain risks are specifically excluded under a comprehensive policy. First, loss resulting from failure by the seller to perform the contract or comply with any relevant law is not covered. Secondly, the insurer is not liable for loss resulting from a failure to obtain any import or export licence (or other authorisation) or where performance would contravene any exchange control regulation, unless these requirements arise after the insurer's liability commences. Thirdly, policies do not usually cover loss arising "directly or indirectly" from war between any of the five great powers: China, France, the United Kingdom, the Russian Federation and the United States. In addition, policies usually exclude liability for loss resulting from radioactive contamination and loss arising in connection with a country other than the buyer's country where the goods are to be despatched to or payment is to be made from such a country.

24–024 **Seller's obligations when loss suffered.** The policies impose the usual obligations on the seller-insured to notify immediately of any event likely to cause loss or to report any payment overdue for more than 60 days and to use due care and diligence to prevent and minimise loss. The seller is also obliged to take all steps—including legal proceedings—required by the insurer in connection with the loss. The insurer may also require the seller to assign all relevant rights to it or to appoint the insurer as his agent or attorney with power to act in his name in litigation or to collect amounts due.

(d) *Assignment of Credit Insurance Policies*

24–025 **Introductory.** A credit insurance policy may assist the seller to obtain from his bankers finance for his export transactions. Moreover, when a transaction is covered by such a policy the bankers in the United Kingdom are frequently prepared to provide credit at a reduced rate of interest. The banker can safeguard his position when a transaction is covered by such a policy either by obtaining its assignment to himself or by requiring the seller to furnish a direct guarantee in the banker's favour.[48]

24–026 **Method of assignment.** An assignment of a supplier's credit insurance policy to his banker may assume one of three forms. First, the seller may assign to the banker any amount that may become payable by the insurer in respect of a specific transaction covered by the policy. Secondly, the seller may assign to the banker the amounts due under all the claims relating to the transactions in a designated market or markets. These types of assignment are used where the banker finances only specific export transactions of the seller. Thirdly, the seller may assign all amounts payable under the policy. This type of assignment is used where the seller obtains his entire finance from one source.

24–027 **Effect.** To effect an assignment, the seller completes a standard form[49] in which he gives the insurer an irrevocable authority to pay to the banker all amounts due under claims arising in connection with the relevant trans-

[48] See below, para.24–031.

[49] The assignment is described in banking circles as an hypothecation. The phraseology of the standard form is, however, that usually used in an assignment.

actions. The form is signed by the seller and countersigned by the banker, who forwards it to the insurer. The latter acknowledges the assignment on a duplicate copy, which is returned to the banker. In *Paul and Frank Ltd v Discount Bank (Overseas) Ltd*,[50] Pennycuick J. observed that such an arrangement constitutes an assignment by way of charge and not an absolute assignment.

Disadvantage of assignment. From the banker's point of view, the assignment of a credit insurance policy has a significant disadvantage. The insurer, as debtor, can plead against the banker, who assumes the role of the assignee, any defences or equities that it has against the seller, the assignor. Apart from being well established by authority,[51] this right is usually reserved by the insurer when he acknowledges the assignment.[52] Thus, where the policy has been obtained by the seller by means of a fraud or of a misrepresentation in the proposal form, the insurer can avoid the policy and, in this way, defeat any claims raised by the banker under the assignment. Moreover, the banker can make a claim only in so far as it arises from a loss that is covered under the policy and only to the extent of the cover given to the seller.[53] 24–028

Registration. An assignment of a policy does not constitute a charge on "book debts" and therefore does not require registration in accordance with section 396(1)(e) of the Companies Act 1985. In *Paul and Frank Ltd v Discount Bank (Overseas) Ltd*,[54] an English company, which had effected a comprehensive policy of the ECGD,[55] drew a bill of exchange on Belgian purchasers for the price of furs. The Belgian purchasers accepted the bill and took delivery of the furs. The English company discounted the bill with the Discount Bank. As a security for the amount advanced on the bill, the English company furnished a letter of authority directing the ECGD to pay sums due under the comprehensive policy to the Discount Bank. The Belgian purchasers became insolvent and dishonoured the bill. The ECGD, in due course, paid to the Discount Bank the amount that was due under the comprehensive policy. Shortly afterwards the English company was wound up and its liquidator took the view that the letter of authority (or assignment) constituted a charge over book debts and was void for non-registration. He brought an action for the amount paid by the ECGD to the Discount Bank. Dismissing this action, Pennycuick J. held that the rights of the company under the ECGD policy, at the time the company furnished the letter of authority, were not "book debts". The company merely had 24–029

[50] [1967] Ch. 348 at 364. Contrast *Re Miller, Gibb & Co. Ltd* [1957] 1 Lloyd's Rep. 258 at 266, where Wynn-Parry J. held that the assignment was absolute. But in this case the court considered a document executed after the ECGD had paid a claim of the exporter (above, para.24–017).

[51] See, generally, *Chitty on Contracts* (29th ed.), Vol.1, para.19–069.

[52] The clause appears in the standard form of assignment and in the copy addressed to the banker.

[53] In most cases 90 or maximum 95 per cent of the loss (above, para.24–021).

[54] [1967] Ch. 348.

[55] In fact, the policy was issued after the transaction relating to the furs, but with retrospective effect. The court did not attach any importance to this fact.

rights "under a contingency contract" and such rights, before the contingency occurred, would not have been entered in the company's books. This decision has been the subject of criticism in the light of well established case-law[56] (distinguished by Pennycuick J.) that certain "future" debts may be "book debts".[57] However, it appears to be authority for the proposition that as the amounts due under an insurance policy (or guarantee) only arise on a contingency—rather than automatically in the ordinary course of business—such "contingency debts" are not book debts.

24–030 **Not a bill of sale.** *Paul and Frank Ltd v Discount Bank (Overseas) Ltd*[58] does not decide whether an assignment of an ECGD policy constitutes a bill of sale. It is submitted that an instrument assigning an ECGD policy does not constitute a bill of sale. Section 4 of the Bills of Sale Act 1878 confines the definition of a "bill of sale" to "assurances of personal chattels". An assignment of an ECGD policy does not involve an assurance of chattels; it is an assignment of a chose in action, or—putting it more accurately—of an amount of money payable upon a contingency. It follows that an instrument assigning an ECGD policy does not fall within the definition of a bill of sale and does not require registration either under the 1878 Act.

4. GUARANTEES

(a) *Guarantees for Supplier's Credit Financing*

24–031 **Background.** If the supplier decides to extend credit to the buyer himself by means of finance from his bank, the ECGD has traditionally offered direct guarantees to the supplier's bank, undertaking to indemnify the banker in full against any loss resulting from the buyer's failure to pay any amount due from him under his contract with the supplier regardless of the cause of this default. On the basis of such a guarantee bankers are prepared to grant to the supplier the required finance usually by the purchase of negotiable instruments accepted by the overseas buyer. Although, in the past, the ECGD offered a number of "comprehensive" guarantees, presently it only offers two. First, specific guarantees as part of its "supplier Credit Finance Facility" ("SCF"), which is considered in more detail below. Secondly, guarantees under the so-called "Sovereign Star Facility", also considered below.

24–032 **Supplier Credit Finance Facility (SCF).** This facility—the central feature of which is a guarantee given by the ECGD to the exporter's (supplier's) bank—is often used where the supplier extends short-term

[56] *Independent Automatic Sales Ltd v Knowles & Foster* [1962] 1 W.L.R. 974, Buckley J. (a charge on existing hire-purchase contracts).

[57] See *Contemporary Cottages (N.Z.) Ltd v Margin Traders Ltd* [1981] 2 N.Z.L.R. 114 (High Court of New Zealand), Thorp J. and Australian cases cited therein. See also *Re Brush Aggregates Ltd* [1983] B.C.L.C. 320, Wright Q.C.

[58] [1967] Ch. 348.

credit to his overseas buyer himself. Otherwise, the "buyer's credit guarantee", considered further below,[59] is generally used to cover more complex, longer-term risks.

Usually the supplier takes bills of exchange or promissory notes accepted by the buyer and sells these negotiable instruments to his bank under a letter of facility issued to him by the bank. To cover the risks of non-payment undertaken by the bank in buying these instruments, the ECGD offers a an SCF whereby it provides a 100 per cent guarantee to cover any payment defaults. In practice, banks enter into Master Guarantee Agreements (MGAs) with the ECGD that provide the framework for guarantees issued in relation to individual export contracts.[60] A supplier wishing to take advantage of an SCF in relation to a particular export contract will therefore approach such a bank, completing a proposal form. The bank then adds details of the support to be provided and forwards the proposal to the ECGD. The ECGD makes a formal offer of a guarantee to the bank under the terms of its MGA. If the supplier and the bank are satisfied with the terms of the offer, the bank obtains the premium from the supplier and sends the acceptance to the ECGD. The premiums are determined case-by-case depending on risk and are charged on the value of the instruments to be purchased.

The ECGD usually insists that a private sector overseas buyer provides instruments that are unconditionally guaranteed by an acceptable third party (the surety). In providing an unconditional guarantee, the surety becomes liable when the instrument is not paid, irrespective of any dispute over contract performance. This guarantee may take many forms: a bank *aval* or an indorsement on the instrument or even a standby letter of credit. An SCF is usually "without recourse" and disputes over performance do not affect the buyer's liability to pay under the instrument or the surety's liability under his unconditional guarantee.

The supplier may also enter into a supplementary Export Insurance Policy (an EXIP)[61] to protect himself against risks which are not covered by the SCF arrangements—in particular the risk of costs incurred in the pre-finance period, before the instruments are bought under the SCF.

Legal nature. The "direct guarantee" given by the ECGD to the supplier's banker constitutes a guarantee[62] and not an insurance policy. This conclusion is supported by two arguments. First, the guarantee is given to the banker in order to induce him to make an advance to the supplier. In effect, the ECGD guarantees the payment of a debt incurred by the buyer which, under the agreement between the banker and the supplier, becomes **24–033**

---

[59] See paras 24–035 *et seq*.

[60] For a list of banks that have MGAs with the ECGD, see the EGCD website: *www.ecgd.gov.uk*

[61] See above, para.24–016.

[62] As such guarantees are invariably reduced into writing, it seems unnecessary to consider whether they constitute guarantees *strictu sensu* or indemnities. Contrast *Chitty on Contracts* (29th ed.), Vol.2, para.44–012. Moreover, questions of the main debtor's capacity and the validity of his contract, in relation to which it is important to determine whether an instrument is a guarantee or an indemnity, are not likely to arise in the case of transactions covered by the ECGD.

payable to the banker. Secondly, the banker does not submit a proposal form or an application for the direct guarantee; it is given to him at the request and at the expense of the supplier. It is therefore wrong to regard the banker as a person who effects insurance against a credit risk.[63] As the contract between the banker and the ECGD is not an insurance policy, the banker does not owe the ECGD a duty of full disclosure. Longmore J.'s decision in *Credit Lyonnais Bank Nederland v Export Credits Guarantee Department*[64] illustrates the point. In this case one C, who had moved to London from Singapore, induced an employee of the ECGD to grant the claimant bank a direct guarantee covering the payment of bills of exchange to be drawn by him under contracts purported to be made with Nigerian importers. In reality, there were no such importers in existence. The transactions were shams and the importers' purported acceptances of the bills were forgeries executed thereon by C. One of the defences raised by the ECGD to the bank's action to enforce the guarantee was that certain aspects of C's transactions should have raised the bank's suspicions and, further, that the bank ought to have disclosed certain irregularities when it lodged the application for the ECGD's cover. Rejecting this argument, Longmore J. said[65]: "I do not accept that there is any such general duty on a banker in making applications for guarantees to ECGD. To so hold would be to apply the duties of an insured to a creditor and, for that, there is no authority. It may be that, in general, there is an implied representation that unusual matters, material to the guarantee, do not exist but the scope for any such general implication must be limited where explicit questions are asked and answers given." His Lordship concluded, however, that, on the facts, the ECGD was entitled to rescind the guarantee because the bank had given incomplete and hence incorrect answers to certain questions raised in the relevant standard documents. Thus, although concealment is not, in itself, a cause for the rescission of a direct guarantee, it can, on occasions, constitute a misrepresentation. This is particularly so where an answer to a given question conceals certain facts and, accordingly, conveys the wrong impression.

24–034 **Sovereign Star Facility.** The ECGD has entered into a "Master Financing Agreement" (similar to the MGAs in the context of the SCF) with Sovereign Star Trade Finance Ltd (SSTF)—a subsidiary of a number of major banks—whereby it guarantees credit provided by SSTF to overseas buyers under relatively small-value (up to £2 million) and medium-term (two to five years) export contracts. Whilst technically "buyer credit" in the sense that it provides credit to buyers, rather than suppliers, commercially the facility operates in a similar manner to, and in similar circumstances as, an SCF. The credit facility, which is negotiated by the supplier, is available for up to 85 per cent of the contract value and there is no ECGD recourse to the UK supplier.

---

[63] For the definition of an insurance policy, see Chitty, *op. cit.*, para.41–001. See also *ibid.*, para.44–001 as regards the definition of a guarantee.
[64] [1996] 1 Lloyd's Rep. 200. The decision was upheld on appeal, but without reference to this issue: [2000] A.C. 486.
[65] *ibid.*, at p.216. That a contract of suretyship is not an *uberrimae fidei* contract, see Chitty, *op. cit.*, para.6–154.

(b) *Guarantees for Buyer's Credit Financing*

Practice. In the case of export or construction contracts for large amounts,[66] the ECGD is prepared to give a guarantee to bankers who make finance available to the overseas buyer. This is the so-called Buyer Credit (BC) guarantee. It is available for contracts involving £5 million and more and made between an overseas buyer and a specific exporter or supplier in the United Kingdom. The repayment term must be at least two years. The ECGD calls guarantees in respect of a loan which only covers instalments due "simple cover", whilst guarantees in respect of loans that cover other payments (such as termination settlements and arbitral awards) are termed "complex cover". Under both variants the lender is left free to negotiate the loan without any direct ECGD involvement. **24–035**

Contracts established in buyer credit guarantees. This scheme leads to the establishment of four contractual relationships. The first is the contract made between the supplier in the United Kingdom and the overseas buyer.[67] In practice the ECGD requires the overseas buyer to pay a minimum deposit of 15 per cent of the contract price when the contract is concluded, so that in fact a maximum of 85 per cent of the contract value is financed by the buyer credit. The second contract is between the overseas buyer and the banker in the United Kingdom[68] who finances the balance of the transaction. The third contract is between this banker and the ECGD ("the support agreement") and the fourth is the "premium agreement" between the ECGD and the supplier. **24–036**

There are many variations to this basic structure and the ECGD states that it is also willing to discuss "special" financing arrangements tailored to innovative financing techniques. An exporter often takes out supplementary credit insurance under an EXIP.[69] For example, if the exporter only has "simple cover", he is exposed to the risk of not getting paid for sums not financed by the loan, such as arbitral awards and termination payments. Even if he has "complex cover", the loan may not be enough to finance all such sums due, in which case the exporter might also take out an EXIP to cover the risks of these payments not being made. Recently the ECGD has begun to offer a "local currency financing scheme" which seeks to remove the buyer's foreign currency exchange risk by guaranteeing a loan made by local financial institutions in the local currency. The scheme is particularly appropriate to projects that will generate local income (such as infrastructure projects) which will repay the loan.

Contract of buyer and banker (the Loan Agreement). In this contract the banker agrees to lend to the buyer the balance of the amount payable to the supplier. The loan is usually operated on a disbursement basis. The **24–037**

---

[66] For simple, short-term credit where the supplier himself is prepared to extend credit to the buyer, the SCF (Supplier Credit Finance Facility) is usually used, see above, para.24–032. Alternatively, the Sovereign Star Facility may be use, see above, para.24–034.

[67] This is either an agreement to sell goods or a contract for the supply of skilled services. It does not require specific discussion in this part of the book.

[68] The banker must carry on business in the UK and be authorised to do so under the Financial Services and Markets Act 2000.

[69] See above, para.24–016.

buyer makes promissory notes which are payable to the banker and each of which relates to a specific shipment or is for an amount equal to that of any specific instalment payable under the contract of sale. The date on which each note falls due depends on the period of credit granted to the buyer in this agreement. The notes are given to the banker when the agreement between him and the buyer is signed and, originally, are held by the banker under a letter of trust. When the seller becomes entitled to be paid for goods shipped to the buyer, the banker "purchases" the promissory note relating to the relevant shipment and pays its face value to the seller. To safeguard his position, the banker's agreement to purchase the notes is usually subject to the buyer's compliance with certain formalities such as exchange control regulations in his own country. Moreover, in most cases supervisors and consultants are appointed, and the supplier must tender their certificates as well as the usual documents of title when he makes a claim for an amount due under the contract of sale. Interest on the promissory notes begins to run from the date of their purchase by the banker. The buyer is entitled to retire his notes before the date of maturity by paying the amount of principal due under them together with interest to the date of payment. If the buyer dishonours any promissory note, all the outstanding notes become due.

In the case of "simple cover", the loan only covers the payments due for the goods or services supplied whilst in the case of "complex cover" it also covers other payments due from the buyer, for example arbitral awards or termination payments. Moreover, the loan may either be at a fixed or floating rate and the ECGD offers schemes which reduce the risk to banks offering credit at such rates. If a fixed rate of interest is attractive to the buyer, the ECGD offers a "Fixed Rate Export Finance" (FREF)[70] scheme, which provides an interest equalisation mechanism known as "Interest Make Up" (IMU) under which the ECGD makes up any shortfall between the "Agreed Rate" (the actual interest the bank has to pay on the money markets plus a margin) and the fixed rate paid by the borrower. If the fixed rate is higher than the Agreed Rate, the bank pays the difference to the ECGD.

Payment to the supplier may be made on a reimbursement rather than a disbursement basis if the buyer pays the instalments directly to the supplier. Then the buyer needs to present a Reimbursement Certificate, supported by a receipt of payment from the supplier, to the bank. Again, if the bank is satisfied that all is in order it will allow the buyer to draw down the relevant part of the loan.

24–038 **Contract of banker and ECGD (the Support Agreement).** The guarantee given by the ECGD to the banker in connection with a Buyer Credit Guarantee is similar in all regards to the ECGD's guarantee for supplier's credit financing.[71] The banker is granted full cover[72] against any loss

[70] The minimum is determined by the OECD Arrangement, see further, below, para.24–052.
[71] Discussed above, paras 24–031 *et seq*.
[72] *i.e.*, the ECGD offers guarantees for 100 per cent of the loan, although lower percentages are negotiable (and, of course, result in a lower premium).

resulting from the buyer's failure to honour any promissory note or notes. If the buyer dishonours any one note, the ECGD is entitled to purchase those remaining in the banker's hands against payment of their face value together with interest up to the date of such acquisition. The banker agrees to act in accordance with the directions of the ECGD in regard to the payment of amounts due to the seller.

Premium Agreement. The fourth contract is the "Premium Agreement" between the ECGD and the supplier whereby the supplier agrees to pay the premium for the facility given by the ECGD, usually on signature of the agreement or as a first drawing from the loan. The amount of the premium is based on the percentage of the loan value and the risks involved. As the ECGD is liable under the guarantee regardless of any non-performance by the supplier, the ECGD includes "recourse" provisions in its agreement with the supplier so that if the buyer refuses to pay due to the supplier's default under the contract, the ECGD has the right to claim the money it pays over back from the supplier. Where the supplier is a member of a group of companies, other companies in its group are usually asked to join in the recourse arrangements and occasionally the supplier may be asked to secure its recourse liability by other means such as bank guarantees. Where recourse is available against others in addition to the supplier it is taken on a "joint and several" basis so all parties have a primary obligation to meet any recourse demand in full, although, of course, as between themselves they may decide how to distribute the liability. The ECGD sets limits on the amount of recourse, the amount being set by the underwriter according to the risk and is based on a percentage—from 10 per cent upwards—of the ECGD's maximum liability under the guarantee. A Lloyds Recourse Indemnity Policy is available to suppliers who would otherwise be unable to meet the ECGD's recourse requirements. 24–039

Rights of supplier. Although the ECGD undertakes in the "Premium Agreement" to "procure the Bankers to . . . continue to buy Notes and to pay the proceeds thereof to the" supplier, the latter does not have a legal right to demand payment from the bankers. Moreover, the scheme does not, by itself, provide a credit policy in the supplier's favour.[73] It follows that the supplier does not obtain cover, in his own right, against the default or the insolvency of the buyer or of the banker. Thus, if the buyer defaults and the banker refuses to purchase any of his remaining notes,[74] the supplier does not appear to have an effective remedy; he depends on the willingness of the ECGD to compel the banker to perform the duties undertaken in the Support Agreement. If the banker becomes insolvent, it is to be doubted whether the supplier can demand actual payment of amounts accruing on any notes relating to his shipments. Admittedly, a court may allow the buyer to retrieve the promissory notes given to the banker and to make payment to the seller.[75] But if the buyer refuses to adopt such a course, the 24–040

[73] The supplier may effect, separately, a specific ECGD policy, but this involves an additional premium.
[74] Such a right is reserved by the bankers in most financial agreements.
[75] This is based on the fact that the notes are held under a letter of trust; see on this point, above paras 23–098 *et seq*. The supplier may have an action for the price against the buyer. See on the question of discharge, above, para.23–099; the giving of the promissory notes does not discharge the buyer (above, para.9–030).

supplier may have to prove as a general creditor in the banker's bankruptcy. Undoubtedly, such events are unlikely to occur. But the fact remains that, from all the parties to the Buyer Credit Guarantee transaction, the supplier is in the least secure position.

24–041 **Advantages.** At the same time, some exporters in the United Kingdom prefer the guarantees for buyer's credit financing to guarantees for supplier's credit financing. There are two reasons for this. First, progress payments are available under the Buyer Credit Guarantee scheme but not under supplier's credit guarantees. Secondly, under the Buyer Credit Guarantee the ECGD's right of recourse against the supplier is restricted. This right, which is conferred on the ECGD in the premium agreement, applies only in cases where the buyer dishonours his promissory notes on the ground of a breach of the contract of sale by the supplier. In all other cases the supplier obtains, in fact if not at law, full cover for that part of the price of the goods covered by the Buyer Credit Guarantee and regardless of the cause of any loss.

24–042 **Extent of recourse.** The right of recourse exercisable by the ECGD against the supplier under the Premium Agreement is, however, wider than may be expected. In *Export Credits Guarantee Department v Universal Oil Products Co.*,[76] a group of Canadian oil refining companies (the "N.F. Cos") engaged a British group of companies (the "Procon Cos") to build a refinery. To finance the transaction, a consortium of British banks agreed to advance the required amounts to the N.F. Cos against a series of promissory notes made out by one of them. In pursuance of a contract made with the Procon Cos (the "premium contract"), the ECGD guaranteed to the consortium the payment of these notes. Clause 7 of the premium agreement stipulated that the guarantee in question did not cover payments made by the ECGD in respect of notes dishonoured by reason of any default by the Procon Cos or made at a time at which they were in default of the performance of their contract with the N.F. Cos The Procon Cos were, accordingly, made liable to reimburse any amount paid by the ECGD in respect of notes dishonoured in such situations.

The refinery was completed in due course but the N.F. Cos went into liquidation whilst some payments remained outstanding. As a result they dishonoured promissory notes totalling at about £39 million. The ECGD paid the amounts involved to the consortium and sought reimbursement from the Procon Cos, claiming that they were in default in the performance of certain obligations owed to the N.F. Cos The Procon Cos resisted this claim, *inter alia*, on the ground that clause 7 was a penalty and hence unenforceable. Deciding this matter as a preliminary issue, Staughton J. held that the clause did not provide for a penalty, and his decision was affirmed by the Court of Appeal and by the House of Lords.

24–043 **Decision.** The main argument against the validity of the clause was that it imposed on the Procon Cos a liability that could require the payment of amounts disproportionate to the nature of their default. Staughton J. did

[76] [1983] 1 Lloyd's Rep. 449, affirmed [1983] 2 Lloyd's Rep. 152.

not think that the separation between the premium agreement and the contract involving the default, *i.e.* the agreement between the N.F. Cos and the Procon Cos, necessarily ruled out the application of the doctrine vitiating a penalty clause. He further thought that clause 7 could constitute a penalty although the duty, the breach of which invoked the clause, was owed to a third party. But he concluded that the clause was not a penalty as it did not provide for payment of an amount of money upon the occurrence of a specified event which constituted a breach of contract. In the instant case, there was a demand for reimbursement rather than a direct call for the payment of a sum due upon the breach of a contract. In the Court of Appeal, Waller L. J. reached the same conclusion on the basis that, far from constituting a penalty, clause 7 had the object of apportioning the risk of a loss, resulting from the dishonour of the N.F. Cos notes, between the Procon Cos. and the ECGD. In a concurring judgment, Slade L.J. observed[77]: "the Court would *not* have regarded 'the penalty area' as extending to a case where there is no question of the agreed stipulated sum taking the place of an award of damages. . ." In the House of Lords, Lord Roskill pointed out that the main object of the doctrine against penalties was to prevent a party from making a windfall as a result of the other party's default. In the present case, the ECGD was "only seeking to recover [its] actual loss, namely, the sum which [it] became legally obliged to pay and [has] paid to [the consortium]. I am afraid I find it impossible to see how on these facts there can be any room for the invocation of the law relating to penalty clauses."[78]

(c) *Lines of Credit*

Lines of Credit (LOCs). These are arrangements between a UK bank and an overseas bank (or other borrower) to finance a series of export contracts, the UK suppliers being paid by the UK bank on shipment whilst the overseas buyer is provided with credit. They are often established where the overseas buyer wishes to acquire goods or services from the United Kingdom without committing himself to purchase from specific suppliers. The UK bank undertakes to provide credit up to a specified amount in respect of contracts of a type stipulated in the credit. As explained below, the ECGD issues a guarantee to the UK bank that it will be paid if the borrower defaults, by providing either an SFC[79] or a BC Guarantee.[80] The ECGD requires the buyer to pay a deposit of at least 15 per cent of the contract value and the credit is usually provided for between two and five years, although longer periods are sometimes negotiable. 24–044

There are two categories of ECGD-backed LOCs available. The first is the General Purpose Line of Credit (GPLOC), which may be used to finance a number of contracts with a range of buyers. The ECGD provides either an SFC or a BC Guarantee and cover is only committed on a

77 *ibid.*, at p.459.
78 [1983] 2 Lloyd's Rep. at 155.
79 See paras 24–032 *et seq.*
80 See paras 24–035 *et seq.*

contract-by-contract basis. SCF-GPLOCs are only available to those UK banks that have MGAs with the ECGD. The supplier provides such a bank with a completed SCF proposal form in respect of each contract for approval by the ECGD, the premium being paid by the bank (although recouped from the supplier).

The second category of ECGD-backed LOCs is the Project Line of Credit (PLOC), which is used for a specific project such as an electrification scheme, or for a wider purpose such as farm mechanisation or the development of one or more industries. The ECGD only provides BC Guarantees in relation to PLOCs. For BC-GPLOCs and PLOCs, the contract must be nominated for approval by the buyer/borrower, the nomination being submitted via the UK bank to the ECGD for approval.

As in the cases of an SCF or BC, a supplier may take out a supplementary EXIP so as to insure against risks not covered by the LOC, for example costs incurred in performing the contract before payment is due or so-called "un-financed costs" such as local costs or direct payments.

5. OTHER ECGD FACILITIES

24–045 **New facilities.** Changes in trade patterns have led to the introduction of new types of ECGD facilities. Amongst these have been the project financing scheme, the cost escalation cover policy, policies covering participants in consortia and in joint ventures, exchange risk cover and guarantees related to the issuing of performance bonds. However, with the emphasis now on the ECGD acting in a complementary manner to the private sector,[81–82] those facilities which that sector is best placed to provide have been withdrawn. Only the "Project Financing Scheme" has survived and will now briefly be considered.

24–046 **Project financing scheme.** This type of scheme, which is a variant of the buyer's credit financing scheme,[83] is used to facilitate the financing of major projects, such as major building contracts, in which the lenders rely primarily on the revenues from the project to repay their loans. The scheme is usually only available for projects with an ECGD guaranteed loan of at least £20 million. In this type of scheme, the project sponsors are usually responsible for ensuring that the project is properly launched and operated successfully. Although the ECGD emphasises that it is very flexible in its approach to such projects, it does impose a number of requirements. Thus, in certain clearly defined circumstances the sponsors must take the responsibility for making up any shortfall in the earnings produced by the project. Moreover, the ECGD adopts a "risk sharing" policy with a number of features. Thus it expects that part of the project will be financed (without its support) by other acceptable financiers and that at least 25 per cent of the project capital will be financed in the form of equity and/or subordi-

[81-82] See above, para.24–005.
[83] See above, paras 24–035. *et seq.*

nated debt. Its participation is usually restricted to guaranteeing loans representing no more than 40 per cent of the project capital—with all lending covered by ECAs[84] not normally exceeding 60 per cent of the total project capital costs.

The ECGD has also started providing, on a case-by-case basis in relation to certain countries, support for foreign exchange earning projects where the sovereign repayment risk is great. In order to attract ECGD support, the projects must have majority private sector ownership and professional management.

6. Overseas Investment Insurance

The Act. Overseas investment insurance (OII) was first made available under the Overseas Investment and Export Guarantees Act 1972. It is now governed by section 2 of the 1991 Act, discussed earlier on.[85] In essence, it is political risk insurance which the ECGD provides to UK enterprises investing overseas (especially in "HIPCs", see below) through equity or loans. One advantage of OII cover from the ECGD is that UK Government intervention may resolve problems caused to UK investors by political events overseas, without the matter giving rise to a claim on the policy. 24–047

Type of policy. Under section 2 of the 1991 Act, an overseas investment policy is available only to persons who carry on business in the United Kingdom and to companies controlled by such persons.[86] In practice, United Kingdom subsidiaries of foreign countries are excluded where they serve as a conduit for overseas investments of the parent company. While section 2 authorises the insurance of investments in enterprises carried on in any country except the United Kingdom, the main aim is to provide cover for, and in this way to encourage, investments in developing countries or HIPCs ("heavily indebted poor countries"). It is clear from the language of the subsection that the Act does not restrict the type of investment that qualifies for cover as long as it constitutes an "investment of resources" in an enterprise. Thus, in principle, it is irrelevant whether the investment involves a contribution of capital, the furnishing of plant or of know-how or the granting of loans. But in practice the scheme caters primarily for equity or loan investments involving a management or a trade interest, although in certain circumstances it is extended to portfolio investments. In order to qualify for cover an investment must involve a contribution to an enterprise in which the mean repayment period is not less than three years. Cover is usually available only if it is in the national interest to encourage the project involved. It will be denied or restricted if the risk appears exceptional.[87] 24–048

OII can provide cover for three types of transaction. First, "foreign direct investment" cover is available in respect of equity or loan investment.

---

[84] See below, para.24–003.

[85] Above, para.24–007. For further details see the ECGD website: *www.ecgd.gov.uk*.

[86] As to the meaning of "controlled company" see above, para.24–008.

[87] The ECGD website (see n.8, above) lists the types of risk and the types of policy available in relation to each country.

Secondly, "support loans" cover is available to banks providing loans to an overseas enterprise in support of a project with a UK sponsor (so-called "complementary investment loans") or loans to an overseas enterprise to help pay for UK exports (so-called "export loans"). Thirdly, "bank portfolio loans" cover is available to banks lending to certain overseas projects where there is no UK sponsor or UK export.

24–049 **Risks covered.** Usually the policy covers three categories of political risk. The first, which is "expropriation", includes not only direct nationalisation or confiscation, but also indirect forms of expropriation (so-called "creeping expropriation") employed by a government with the intention of discriminating against the UK investor or the overseas enterprise. The second risk, which is war, covers loss to the enterprise resulting from war, revolution or insurrection. Insurance is provided not only against damage to property, but also against the inability of the overseas enterprise to operate the project. The third risk—restrictions on remittances—includes loss due to the inability to convert into sterling or dollars and remit any profits, earnings or capital repayments. The risk of currency conversion at a rate of exchange which discriminates against the UK investor, is also included. Cover may be considered for other forms of political risks by special arrangement. Moreover, where the investment is in the context of project financing, insurance for breach, for political reasons, of undertakings given to the UK investor or the overseas enterprise by the host government may also be available from the ECGD on a case-by-case basis. The commitment in respect of these risks is normally for a period of 15 years, with the UK investor having the sole option to renew on an annual basis (although, as noted above, the investor must intend to invest for at least three years).

7. INTERNATIONAL ASPECTS

24–050 **General.**[88] Export credit guarantee schemes are in operation in most industrial countries. As the result of the keen competition for exports, credit insurers are frequently under pressure brought by exporters and their organisations for the extension of longer and more favourable terms of cover. The need to avoid unrestrained competition in the field of credit insurance was one of the major reasons for the establishment in 1934 of the Berne Union, considered below. By the early 1970s, a "credit race" began to develop whereby governments effectively subsidised their exporters by supporting favourable financing terms. Consequently, the OECD countries began co-ordinating their policies on export credit in order to encourage competition on the basis of which exporters provided the best services at a competitive price rather than on the basis of which government provided the most favourable financing terms. As will be noted below, in April 1978

[88] See, generally, P. Dorscheid, "Export Credit Insurance and its International Co-ordination" in Horn (ed.), *Law of International Trade Finance* (Dventer, 1988), pp.587–588.

this resulted in the so-called "OECD Consensus" (now called the "OECD Arrangement", see below) which has been incorporated into EC law by a Decision. Meanwhile, in 1960 the EC established a Policy Co-ordination Group for Credit Insurance, Credit Guarantees and Financial Credits[89] and has issued a series of legislative instruments dealing with this area.

The Berne Union. The International Union of Credit and Investment Insurers—the Berne Union—was established in 1934,[90] with four export credit insurers members from the United Kingdom, France, Italy and Spain. It is now a worldwide association of credit insurers (both ECAs and private companies) with 52 members from 43 countries. Just over one-third of the members come from non-OECD countries. In 1993, the Berne Union and the EBRD (European Bank for Reconstruction and Development) founded the "Prague Club", an information exchange network for new agencies in Central and Eastern Europe, with a view to helping them towards satisfying the entrance requirements for the Berne Union. Later, certain Asian and African agencies joined and presently membership stands at 30. The Prague Club shares a Secretariat with and enjoys close links with the Berne Union. 24–051

The main object of the Union is to encourage cross-border trade by the acceptance of sound principles of export credit insurance and the maintenance of disciplined competition in credit terms made available for international trade. This is achieved by meetings between members and by the circulation, through the secretariat, of information about claims experiences and about defaulting buyers. The development of day-to-day exchange of information concerning the terms being proposed in regard to specific transactions has assisted in restraining competition. Moreover, the exchange of information on contracts which are in the stage of negotiations enables credit insurers to check the credit rating of firms figuring in prospective deals. The Union also constitutes a centre for consultation on overseas investment insurance.

The OECD Arrangement. In order to discourage the distortion of competition by government subsidy of export credit guarantees—an "export credit race"—the OECD produced an "Arrangement on Guidelines for Officially Supported Export Credits", then known as the OECD Consensus, in April 1978.[91] This provides an institutional framework for an orderly market for officially supported export credit with repayment terms of two years or more and is regularly revised, the last version being dated December 2005. Annexed to it are four "Sector Understandings" which set out special guidelines for certain sectors such as ships, nuclear power plants, aircraft and renewable energies and water projects. However, the Arrangement does not apply to other sectors such as military equipment and agricultural products. The Arrangement is not an OECD Act (although 24–052

---

[89] EEC Council Decision ([1960] O.J. Spec. Ed. 66), see further, below, para.24–053.
[90] As an association under the Swiss Civil Code. Its secretariat is in London and its website is: *www.berneunion.org.uk*
[91] See generally, the OECD website: *www.oecd.org*

it receives the administrative support of the OECD Secretariat) but is a "Gentlemen's Agreement" among its "Participants" whereby "Participants" agree to be bound by it. The EU is a "Participant",[92] and the Arrangement been incorporated into EC law by a Council Decision.[93]

The Arrangement applies to export credits that benefit from any form of official support, whether in the form of "pure cover" (*i.e.* insurance or guarantees given to exporters or lending institutions without financing support) and "financing support" (*i.e.* direct credits to the overseas buyer, refinancing, and all forms of interest rate support). It also applies to tied aid. It does not cover the conditions or terms of the insurance, guarantees, or direct lending itself; it covers the conditions or terms of the export credits that benefit from such official support. First, it requires a minimum cash down-payment by the "starting point of credit" for each transaction of 15 per cent of the export contract value and therefore credit may only be made available for 85 per cent of the contract value. The "starting point of credit" is defined by the Arrangement as the date on which the buyer has to start to repay the credit. Secondly, the Arrangement sets out the maximum credit periods, which depend on the buyer's country. Countries are classified into two categories, the maximum repayment period being five years (or in certain circumstances 8.5 years) for the first category and 10 years for the second. Thirdly, it limits repayment terms. Finally, the Arrangement also regulates the minimum fixed interest rates—the CIRRs (Commercial Interest Reference Rates)—that can be made available with the support of exporter governments. Thus the ECGD's FREF scheme[94] must comply with the CIRRs—which are calculated on the 15th of each month for most of the OECD Agreement Participants currencies. The rates reflect commercial market rates for long-term, fixed-rate export finance for a first class corporate borrower. Premium rates are also controlled by the "Guiding Principle of Setting Premia and Related Conditions".

The Arrangement was devised and is kept under review by the OECD's Export Credit Division (ECD). Within the ECD there is the "Working Party on Export Credits and Credit Guarantees" which deals *inter alia* with issues such as the environment, bribery and "unproductive expenditure". Thus it has issued a Statement of Principles designed to discourage the provision of officially supported export credits for "unproductive" expenditures in HIPCs (Heavily Indebted Poor Countries).

24–053 **EU harmonising measures.** As noted above, the EU has been concerned with official export credit support since its inception[95] and has issued a series of legislative instruments in this area, aimed primarily at eliminating distortions in competition resulting from differences between official guarantee and insurance systems in different member states of the EU The most significant harmonising measure is the Directive on medium-and long-

[92] Others include Australia, Canada, Japan and the USA.
[93] See below, para.24–053, n.97.
[94] See above, para.24–037.
[95] The Council, by a Decision, created a Policy Co-ordination Group for Credit Insurance, Credit Guarantees and Financial Credits in 1960: [1960] O.J. Spec. Ed. 66.

term export credit insurance.[96] In the area of short-term export credit insurance, an (amended[97]) Communication[98] has been issued by the Competition Directorate which defines "marketable risks" and precludes these being covered with official support. In addition, Decisions have incorporated the OECD Arrangement[99] and have made specific provision in various areas such as officially supported project finance.[1]

---

[96] Directive 1998/29/EC of May 7, 1998 ([1998] O.J. L148/22). The Annex sets out the common principles for export credit support. It repeals and replaces Directives 1970/509/EEC ([1970] O.J. L254/1) and 1970/510/EEC ([1970] O.J. L254/26).

[97] By 2001/C217/02. It alters the definition of "marketable risk".

[98] 97/C281/03. Its duration was extended by 2001/C217/02 and 2004/C307/04.

[99] See above, para.24–053. The most recent Decision is 2001/76/EC ([2001] O.J. L32/1), containing the 1998 Consensus test. Previous Decisions incorporated previous versions (and amendments to) the Consensus.

[1] See 2001/77/EC ([2000] O.J. L32/55). The full list, which is constantly being amended, is available on the EU website: *www.europa.eu.int*

term export credit insurance.[6] In the area of short-term export credit insurance, an ("amended") Communication[7] has been issued by the Competition Directorate which defines "marketable risks"[8] and precludes these being covered with official support. In addition, Decisions have incorporated the OECD Arrangement[9] and have made specific provision in various areas such as officially supported project finance.[1]

[6] Directive 1998/29/EC of May 7, 1998 [1998] O.J. L148/22. The Annex sets out the common principles for export credit support. It repeals and replaces Directives 1970/509/EEC ([1970] O.J. L254/1) and 1970/510/EEC ([1970] O.J. L254/26).
[7] 2001/C217/02. It alters the definition of "marketable risk".
[8] 97/C 281/03. Its duration was extended by 2001/C217/02 and 2004/C 307/04.
[9] See above, para.24-053. The most recent Decision is 2001/76/EC ([2001] O.J. L32/1), containing the 1998 Consensus text. Previous Decisions incorporated previous versions (and amendments to) the Consensus.
[1] See 2001/77/EC ([2001] O.J. L32/55). The full list which is constantly being amended is available on the EU website: www.europa.eu.int.

Part Eight
CONFLICT OF LAWS

Chapter 25

CONFLICT OF LAWS

	PARA.
1. Preliminary considerations	25–001
2. Common law: The proper law doctrine	25–005
3. The Rome Convention	25–015
(a) General considerations	25–015
(b) Choice of law by the parties	25–029
(c) Applicable law in absence of choice	25–057
4. Contracts ancillary to contract of sale	25–069
5. Formation and validity of the contract of sale	25–078
6. Property	25–121
(a) General issues	25–121
(b) Validity of a transfer of title to goods	25–127
(c) The passing of title: the general rules	25–128
(i) Goods not in transit: no documents issued	25–129
(ii) Goods not in transit: documents issued	25–134
(iii) Goods in transit: no documents issued	25–138
(iv) Goods in transit: documents issued	25–139
(d) Retention of title	25–141
7. Risk	25–154
8. Performance of the contract of sale	25–156
(a) Delivery	25–157
(b) Duty to pass title	25–159
(c) Payment of the price	25–161
(d) Licences and permits	25–168
(e) Quality and compliance with description	25–169
9. Discharge of obligations under a contract of sale	25–173
10. Remedies of the seller	25–178
(a) Remedies affecting the goods	25–178
(i) Lien and withholding of delivery	25–180
(ii) Stoppage in transit and rescission of the transfer	25–183
(iii) Right of resale	25–189
(b) Personal remedies of the seller	25–190
11. Remedies of the buyer	25–196
12. Procedure	25–203

1. Preliminary Considerations

Scope and arrangement of this chapter. This chapter is concerned with the rules of choice of law[1] in sale of goods cases. Very broadly speaking, **25–001**

[1] For an exhaustive account of choice of law in relation to commercial, as opposed to consumer sales, see Fawcett, Harris and Bridge, *International Sale of Goods in the Conflict of Laws* (2005), Chs 12–21. The distinct topic of the jurisdiction of English courts in sale of goods cases is governed by the general principles of English jurisdiction *in personam,* as to which see Fawcett, Harris and Bridge, *op. cit.*, Chs 2–10 and generally, Dicey and Morris, *The Conflict of Laws* (13th ed.), Chs 11 and 12;

these choice of law rules fall into two groups which reflect the dual aspect of a sale as both a contractual and proprietary transaction.[2] As to the first group therefore the chapter examines contractual choice of law rules in the light of their relevance to a contract of sale. Originally these choice of law rules were developed by the common law and, essentially, contractual issues thereunder are referred to the "proper law" of the relevant contract. These common law rules are substantially reformulated as a result of the implementation in the United Kingdom of the Rome (EEC) Convention on the Law Applicable to Contractual Obligations 1980 ("the Rome Convention") in the Contracts (Applicable Law) Act 1990.[3] The rules of that Convention, as implemented in the Act of 1990, will apply to determine the law applicable to a contract of sale which is entered into after April 1, 1991.[4] The effluxion of time means that primary importance must now attach to the Rome Convention rather than to the principles of the common law.[5] Section 2 nonetheless provides a relatively brief account of the common law,[6] by way of background to the Convention and because some cases on the application of the Convention have revealed, perhaps, a judicial tendency to reach the same or similar positions under the Convention as had been reached in the common law,[7] although it has also been stressed in the cases that when considering the meaning of the Convention it is necessary to pay regard to its international character and to adopt an approach which will tend to produce uniformity of interpretation.[8] Section

---

Cheshire and North, *Private International Law* (13th ed.), Chs 10–14. Other topics omitted from this chapter, include the recognition and enforcement of foreign judgments as to sales (see Fawcett, Harris and Bridge, *op. cit.*, Ch.11 and generally, Dicey and Morris, *op. cit.*, Chs 14 and 15; Cheshire and North, *op. cit.*, Chs 15–16) and the conflicts aspects of arbitration of disputes arising out of sales contracts (see Dicey and Morris, *op. cit.*, Ch.16; Cheshire and North, *op. cit.*, Ch.17).

[2] For choice of law in tort and restitutionary claims which may arise in connection with sales, see Fawcett, Harris and Bridge, *op. cit.*, Chs 17 and 19. For choice of law in the context of concurrent claims, see *ibid.*, Ch.20.

[3] Throughout this chapter, the Convention is referred to as the Rome Convention: see below, para.25–002. The Convention appears as Sch.1 to the Contracts (Applicable Law) Act 1990: see below, para.25–015.

[4] The date on which the Act entered into force: see Rome Convention, Art. 17; below, para.25–015.

[5] Though see *Zebrarise Ltd v De Nieffe* [2005] 1 Lloyd's Rep. 154; *King v Brandywine Reinsurance Co.* [2005] EWCA Civ. 235; [2005] 1 Lloyd's Rep. 655.

[6] See below, paras 25–005—25–014. For a more detailed discussion, see the 4th edition of this work, paras 25–005—25–019. See also, Dicey and Morris, *The Conflict of Laws* (11th ed.), Ch.32.

[7] See, *e.g. Bank of Baroda v Vysya Bank Ltd* [1994] 2 Lloyd's Rep. 87 (below, para.25–076); *Egon Oldendorff v Libera Corp.* [1995] 2 Lloyd's Rep. 64; *Egon Oldendorff v Libera Corp. (No.2)* [1996] 1 Lloyd's Rep. 381 (below, para.25–031).

[8] See, *e.g. Crédit Lyonnais v New Hampshire Insurance Co.* [1997] 2 Lloyd's Rep. 1; *Raiffeisen Zentralbank Osterreich AG v Five Star General Trading LLC* [2001] 2 W.L.R. 1344; *Definitely Maybe (Touring) Ltd v Marek Lieberberg Konzertagentur GmbH* [2001] 1 W.L.R. 1745; *Samcrete Egypt Engineers and Contractors SAE v Land Rover Exports Ltd* [2001] EWCA Civ. 2019; [2002] C.L.C. 533; *Kenburn Waste Management Ltd v Bergmann* [2002] EWCA Civ. 98; [2002] F.S.R. 711; *Ennstone Building Products Ltd v Stanger Ltd* [2002] EWCA Civ. 916; [2002] 1 W.L.R. 3059; *American Motorists Insurance Co. v Cellstar Corp.* [2003] EWCA Civ. 206; [2003] I.L.Pr. 370. See below, para.25–019.

3 contains a detailed account of the Rome Convention as it affects contracts for the sale of goods.[9] Section 4 gives an outline account of the application of the Convention and, where relevant, the common law, to the contracts most customarily ancillary to the contract of sale.[10] Sections 5 and 7–11 of the chapter deal with the various major issues arising in relation to a contract for the sale of goods which involve choice of law from the perspective of the Rome Convention and, where relevant, the common law.[11] Section 6 discusses the proprietary aspects of sale.[12] At common law, proprietary issues are generally referred to the law of the country[13] where the goods are situated at the relevant time (*lex situs*). The proprietary aspects of sale are generally untouched by the Rome Convention.[14] The chapter concludes in Section 12 with a discussion of procedure as it affects contracts for the sale of goods.[15]

Terminology. It will be convenient to identify certain terminology used in this chapter. Throughout, the phrase "Rome Convention" refers to the EEC Convention on the Law Applicable to Contractual Obligations 1980 as implemented in the United Kingdom by the Contracts (Applicable Law) Act 1990. The Convention does not adopt the term "proper law of a contract" as used in the common law, but this term is used in the discussion of the common law in Section 2. After that section, the term proper law is dropped in favour of the Convention usage, *viz*, variously "applicable law", "law applicable to the contract" and "governing law" or "law governing the contract". No substantive change is implied in this change of language. 25–002

Role of choice of law in sale. At common law issues of conflict of laws are not often considered in cases involving sale of goods. One reason for this may be that, in many respects, the law and practice in this area amongst individual countries have become standardised to a high degree.[16] A second reason is that if foreign law is to be applied in an English court, it must 25–003

[9] Below, paras 25–015—25–068.
[10] Below, paras 25–069—25–077.
[11] Below, paras 25–078—25–120, 25–154—25–202.
[12] Below, paras 25–121—25–153.
[13] Here and generally in this chapter, "country" has its conflict of laws' meaning of "the whole of a territory subject under one sovereign to one body of law" (Dicey and Morris, *The Conflict of Laws* (13th ed.), para.1–060). Thus, in relation to a federal nation, it generally means a state or province, not the nation as a whole: *ibid.*, para.1–061. For the meaning of "country" for the purposes of the Rome Convention (which is essentially identical) see below, para.25–021.
[14] See below, para.25–121.
[15] See below, paras 25–203—25–206.
[16] See, *e.g.* Schmitthoff, *The Export Trade* (10th ed.), Ch.3; Sundstrom [1966] J.B.L. 122 at 245. For attempts to unify international sales law, see above, para.1–024. This chapter does not discuss the Uniform Laws on International Sales Act 1967 which implemented in the UK the Uniform Law on International Sale of Goods 1964 (ULIS) and the Uniform Law on the Formation of Contracts for the International Sale of Goods 1964 (ULFIS). ULIS only applies to the contract of sale if it has been chosen by the parties (1967 Act, s.1(3)) and in practice such a choice is rarely, if ever, made. For a discussion, see Graveson, Cohn and Graveson, *The Uniform Law on International Sales Act 1967* (1968).

usually be pleaded and proved as a question of fact: otherwise English law is applied.[17] There are indeed, innumerable cases on sale of goods where the facts presented issues of conflict of laws, but they were never brought before the court because neither party saw fit to plead foreign law.[18] There is no real evidence that implementation of the Rome Convention has increased the problems of conflict of laws engendered by sales of goods, though the position may change as resort to electronic commerce becomes more common.[19] Nonetheless, the application of the Rome Convention to sales of goods inevitably involves a degree of speculation, not least because the Convention is not a complete code of the applicable rules, so that reference has still to be made to the common law on which authority is often lacking. Accordingly, it is often necessary to rely on arguments derived from academic writings, foreign authorities and general principle in what follows.

25–004 **The characterisation of "goods" in conflict of laws.** One final preliminary point remains, namely, to indicate how the English domestic law concept of "goods"[20] is treated in conflict of laws. In general, "goods" in this sense are characterised as "tangible movables" and are accordingly regulated by the choice of law principles applicable to this type of property, which are the principles discussed in this chapter. Some exceptional types of goods may, however, be differently characterised; for instance, a growing crop before harvest[21] could be considered to be immovable property, and commodities such as gas and electricity[22] could be considered to be intangible movables. In such doubtful cases, the law which resolves the issue of characterisation is the *lex situs* of the goods at the time at which the characterisation is relevant.[23] In the unlikely event that this law should

---

[17] See generally, Dicey and Morris, *op. cit.*, Ch.9; Cheshire and North, *op. cit.*, Ch.7. The position seems to be the same under the Rome Convention: see below, para.25–029.

[18] See, *e.g. Aluminium Industrie Vaassen BV v Romalpa Aluminium Ltd* [1976] 1 W.L.R. 676, above, paras 5–131—5–170 and below, paras 25–141—25–153. This phenomenon can be explained on several grounds: *e.g.* that neither party saw any advantage in pleading foreign law, or that the uncertainties and complexities involved in determining the relevant English choice of law rule and the relevant rule of foreign law were a sufficient deterrent, or simply that the parties' legal advisers wholly overlooked the matter of conflict of laws.

[19] See below, paras 25–049—25–053.

[20] This concept of "goods" (discussed above, Ch.1) marks the limits of the type of property dealt with in this chapter, as in the rest of the book. It is not thought that the concept as described in Ch.1 is affected by the implementation of the Rome Convention so that the principle of this paragraph will continue to apply to cases falling within the Convention.

[21] This is within the English concept of "goods": Sale of Goods Act 1979, s.61(1).

[22] These may be "goods" (above, paras 1–085, 1–087).

[23] See *Turner v Barclay* (1854) 9 Moo.P.C. 264; *Freke v Carbery* (1873) L.R. 16 Eq. 461; *Re Hoyles* [1911] 1 Ch. 179; *Re Berchtold* [1923] 1 Ch. 192; Dicey and Morris, *op. cit.*, Ch.22. Where the goods are, in a conflicts sense, "in transit" at this time (see below, para.25–123), it is submitted that the law of the forum (*lex fori*) should determine this question of characterisation. Such an approach may also be justified in relation to certain types of computer software, where it may be unrealistic to try to ascribe a particular *situs*: see above, para.1–086. And see Fawcett, Harris and Bridge, *op. cit.*, paras 21–211—21–238.

prescribe a characterisation other than "tangible movables", choice of law principles different from those set out in this chapter would be applicable.[24] The *situs* of goods is ascertained by reference to English law as *lex fori*, by virtue of which goods are, in general, situated in the country where they are at the relevant time.[25]

2. COMMON LAW BACKGROUND: THE PROPER LAW DOCTRINE

The proper law doctrine.[26] At common law, a contract was governed by its "proper law". The expression "proper law" meant "the system of law by which the parties intended the contract to be governed, or, where their intention is neither expressed nor to be inferred from the circumstances, the system of law with which the transaction has its closest and most real connection."[27] Broadly speaking, the proper law of a contract for the sale of goods was determined in accordance with this general proper law doctrine and there were no principles which were specifically directed towards contracts for the sale of goods.[28] The proper law doctrine applied to determine the law applicable to contracts for the sale of goods which were entered into on or before April 1, 1991.[29] 25–005

Power to choose. At common law, the parties to the contract were permitted, if they so wished, to nominate the law of a particular country as the proper law of the contract and if they did this their choice was normally conclusive.[30] That power to choose could, of course, be restricted by statute.[31] Further it was said, judicially (and somewhat obscurely), that the 25–006

---

[24] If they are characterised as immovables, the choice of law principles applicable are those set out in Dicey and Morris, *op. cit.*, Ch.23 and paras 33–212—33–237. If they are characterised as intangible movables, the choice of law principles are those set out *ibid.*, paras 24–046—24–071.

[25] Dicey and Morris, *op. cit.*, paras 22–023, 22–025, 22–053.

[26] See Dicey and Morris, *The Conflict of Laws* (11th ed.), Chs 32 and 33.

[27] *ibid.*, pp.1161–1162, Rule 180. For authoritative statements by the HL, see especially *James Miller and Partners Ltd v Whitworth Street Estates (Manchester) Ltd* [1970] A.C. 583; *Compagnie d'Armement Maritime SA v Compagnie Tunisienne de Navigation SA* [1971] A.C. 572; *Amin Rasheed Shipping Corp. v Kuwait Insurance Co.* [1984] A.C. 50.

[28] See below, paras 25–011—25–013. For detailed discussion of the application of the general principle in the specific context of contracts for the sale of goods, see the 4th edition of this work, paras 25–005—25–019. See also Dicey and Morris, *The Conflict of Laws* (11th ed.), pp.1260 *et seq*; Rabel, *The Conflict of Laws* (2nd ed.), Vol. 3, Ch.36.

[29] The date on which the Rome Convention entered into force: see above, para.25–001 and below, para.25–015.

[30] The leading case is *Vita Food Products Inc. v Unus Shipping Co. Ltd* [1939] A.C. 277. See also *R. v International Trustee* [1937] A.C. 500 at 529; *Perry v Equitable Life Insurance Society of the United States of America* (1929) 45 T.L.R. 468 at 470; and see the cases cited in n.27, above.

[31] See generally, *The Hollandia* [1982] Q.B. 872, CA, affirmed [1983] 1 A.C. 565. Further restrictions in the specific context of sale of goods were found and are still to be found in connection with essential validity of contracts of sale and implied

choice of law had to be "bona fide and legal".[32] And, clearly, "there must be no reason for avoiding [the choice] on the ground of public policy".[33] Subject to these restrictions, there appeared to be no requirement that the law chosen had to have some connection with the particular transaction in question.[34]

25–007 **Implied choice of proper law.** Where there was no valid express choice of a proper law,[35] the court would consider whether the parties had, by implication, come to an agreement[36] as to what should be the proper

---

undertakings. These are discussed in detail, below, paras 25–090—25–100, 25–159—25–160.

[32] *Vita Food Products Inc. v Unus Shipping Co. Ltd* [1939] A.C. 277 at 290. The meaning of this formula has never been determined in a reported case in England. It was contended in Cheshire and North, *Private International Law* (11th ed.), p.454 that its possible effect was that "the parties cannot pretend to contract under one law in order to validate an agreement that clearly has its closest connection with another law. If, after having discovered that one particular provision was void under the proper law, they were to try to evade its consequences by claiming that the provision was subject to another legal system, their claim should not be considered as a *bona fide* expression of their intention." The formula has never been applied by an English court to strike down a choice of law. For judicial consideration of the formula in Australia, see *Kay's Leasing Corp. Pty Ltd v Fletcher* (1964) 116 C.L.R. 124 at 143–144; *Golden Acres Ltd v Queensland Estates Ltd* [1969] St. R. Qd. 378 (affirmed on different grounds *sub nom. Freehold Land Investments Ltd v Queensland Estates Ltd* (1970) 123 C.L.R. 418).

[33] *Vita Food Products Inc. v Unus Shipping Co. Ltd*, above, at p.290. This is merely an example of the general principle that a foreign law will not be enforced if it offends English public policy: see below, para.25–043.

[34] *Vita Food Products Inc. v Unus Shipping Co. Ltd*, above; *British Controlled Oilfields v Stagg* [1921] W.N. 31; *W.J. Alan & Co. Ltd v El Nasr Export and Import Co.* [1972] 2 Q.B. 189. *Cf. Boissevain v Weil* [1949] 1 K.B. 482 (affirmed on other grounds [1950] A.C. 327); *Re Helbert Wagg & Co. Ltd* [1956] Ch. 323 at 341. The absence of a connection between the contract and the chosen law may be evidence that the choice of law is not "bona fide and legal": see Cheshire and North, *op. cit.*, p.454. But it was (and still is) common for a contract of sale to have no connection with the law chosen, particularly where the parties deal on a standard form issued by a London commodity association. A choice of law clause must be distinguished from a clause which seeks to incorporate into a contract, as part of its terms and conditions, the provisions of a particular system of law regarding a particular aspect of sale. On this "incorporation by reference", see below, para.25–028. At common law a choice of law clause had to be capable of identifying the proper law at the time the contract was made. A "floating" choice of law clause was not permitted: *Dubai Electricity Co. v Islamic Republic of Iran Shipping Lines (The Iran Vojdan)* [1984] 2 Lloyd's Rep. 380 at 385. See *Armar Shipping Co. Ltd v Caisse Algerienne D'Assurance et de Reassurance (The Armar)* [1981] 1 W.L.R. 207; *The Mariannina* [1983] 1 Lloyd's Rep. 12; *Cantieri Navali Riuniti SpA v NV Omne Justitia (The Stolt Marmaro)* [1985] 2 Lloyd's Rep. 428.

[35] This included situations where the parties attempted to make an express choice but failed to do so with sufficient clarity: *Compagnnie d'Armement Maritime SA v Compagnie Tunisienne de Navigation SA* [1971] A.C. 572. As to what law determines whether a choice of law is valid, see below, para.25–034.

[36] It was said that there had to be actual agreement on the point: *James Miller and Partners Ltd v Whitworth Street Estates (Manchester) Ltd* [1970] A.C. 583 at 603.

law.[37] Probably the clearest instance[38] of such an "implied" choice of law occurred when the contract contained a clause naming a particular court, country, city or town[39] as the place where settlement of disputes arising out of the contract was to take place by litigation or arbitration.[40] This type of clause (much used in standard form contracts of sale)[41] was a strong indicator that the law of the country where litigation or arbitration was to occur had been chosen by the parties as the proper law.[42] The implication to be drawn from such a clause was not, however, conclusive[43] and could be outweighed by the presence of other factors.[44] A clause of this type could not, therefore, be regarded as a substitute for an express choice of law.[45]

---

[37] See in addition to the two cases last cited, *R. v International Trustee* [1937] A.C. 500 at 529–531; *Re United Railways of the Havana and Regla Warehouses Ltd* [1960] Ch. 52 (rvsd. in part on other grounds, *sub nom. Tomkinson v First Pennsylvania Banking and Trust Co.* [1961] A.C. 1007); *Amin Rasheed Shipping Corp. v Kuwait Insurance Co.* [1984] A.C. 50.
[38] For other instances see below, paras 25–030—25–032.
[39] The reference had to be sufficient to indicate a system of law. Thus there was no implication as to the proper law where the clause provided, *e.g.* for submission of disputes to the Court of Arbitration of the International Chamber of Commerce or to an arbitrator nominated by a specified person such as the president of a trade association (see *James Miller and Partners v Whitworth Street Estates (Manchester) Ltd*, above). A clause specifying arbitration under I.C.C. Rules in a *particular country* could, of course, raise the implication that the law of that country was the proper law: *Atlantic Underwriting Agencies Ltd v Compagnia di Assicurazione di Milano SpA* [1979] 2 Lloyd's Rep. 240.
[40] *Hamlyn & Co. v Talisker Distillery* [1894] A.C. 202; *Spurrier v La Cloche* [1902] A.C. 446; *NV Kwik Hoo Tong Handel Maatschappij v James Finlay & Co.* [1927] A.C. 604; *Compagnie d'Armement Maritime SA v Compagnie Tunisienne de Navigation SA* [1971] A.C. 572.
[41] See, *e.g. WJ Alan & Co. Ltd v El Nasr Export and Import Co.* [1972] 2 Q.B. 189 (London Cotton Trade Association's standard f.o.b. contract).
[42] See cases cited in n.40, above.
[43] *Compagnie d'Armement Maritime SA v Compagnie Tunisienne de Navigation SA*, above, at p.609, disapproving *Tzortsis v Monark Line A/B* [1968] 1 W.L.R. 406, where such a clause was treated as creating a virtually conclusive presumption. The law governing the arbitration proceedings will be conclusively indicated by such a clause: *Compagnie d'Armement Maritime SA v Compagnie Tunisienne de Navigation SA, ibid.*
[44] See below, paras 25–009—25–010.
[45] *cf. Tzortsis v Monark Line A/B*, above. In *Steel Authority of India Ltd v Hind Metals Inc.* [1984] 1 Lloyd's Rep. 405 at 409, it was held that a clause stipulating for arbitration in England (which was not otherwise connected with the contract) constituted an implied choice of English law since it indicated the parties intended a "neutral" law to govern. See also *WJ Alan & Co. Ltd v El Nasr Export and Import Co.* [1972] 2 Q.B. 189.

25–008 **Absence of express or implied choice.** Where the proper law was not expressly or impliedly chosen, the proper law was to be taken to be the law of the country or the system of law[46] with which the transaction[47] had the "closest and most real connection".[48]

25–009 **Examination of all relevant factors.** In deciding in accordance with these rules whether the parties to a contract for the sale of goods had impliedly chosen a proper law, or what should be the proper law where no choice at all had been made,[49] the court was required to make a close examination of the terms of the contract and of all relevant circumstances surrounding its making.[50] No single aspect of the contract was decisive; instead, a wide range of different factors had to be taken into account, and their importance varied according to the type of sale in question and the individual circumstances of the case.[51] Thus, where the parties to the contract of sale had their place of business in the same country, that country's law had a strong claim to be the proper law of the contract by way of implied choice of the parties.[52] If there was no single country where the parties both carried on business or if there was some good reason for

---

[46] It has been said that whether it was the "system of law" of the "law of the country" that must be considered depended on the circumstances: *James Miller and Partners Ltd v Whitworth Street Estates (Manchester) Ltd* [1970] A.C. 583 at 603–604. However, most versions of the test refer to "system of law": see, *e.g. James Miller and Partners Ltd v Whitworth Street Estates (Manchester) Ltd*, above, at pp.610–611, 615; *Compagnie d'Armement Maritime SA v Compagnie Tunisienne de Navigation SA* [1971] A.C. 572 at 587, 603; *Rossano v Manufacturers Life Insurance Co.* [1963] 2 Q.B. 352 at 360–362; *Sayers v International Drilling Co. NV* [1971] 1 W.L.R. 1176 at 1180–1181, 1183; *Coast Lines Ltd v Hudig and Veder Chartering NV* [1972] 2 Q.B. 34 at 44, 46; *Amin Rasheed Shipping Corp. v Kuwait Insurance Co.* [1984] A.C. 50 at 61, 69. As to the position under the Rome Convention, see below, para.25–021.

[47] The use of the word "transaction" instead of "contract" may be significant: *Coast Lines Ltd v Hudig and Veder Chartering NV*, above, at pp.46, 50. *Cf.* the Rome Convention, below, para.25–065.

[48] *Bonython v Commonwealth of Australia* [1951] A.C. 201 at 219; *Tomkinson v First Pennsylvania Banking and Trust Co.* [1961] A.C. 1007 at 1068, 1081–1082; *James Miller and Partners Ltd v Whitworth Street Estates (Manchester) Ltd*, above, at pp.603, 605–606, 610–611; *Compagnie d'Armement Maritime SA v Compagnie Tunisienne de Navigation SA*, above, at pp.583, 587, 603; *Amin Rasheed Shipping Corp. v Kuwait Insurance Co.* [1984] A.C. 50. Reference to the intention of the parties in these circumstances was to be avoided: *Amin Rasheed Shipping Corp. v Kuwait Insurance Co.*, above, though opinions could differ, however, as to whether a case presented an example of implied choice or no choice. Compare the views of Lord Diplock, *ibid.* at pp.62–65 with those of Lord Wilberforce at p.69. In practice, the line was hard to draw. As to the position under the Rome Convention see below, para.25–031.

[49] Although these were strictly two distinct steps in the process of selecting the proper law, they are for reasons of convenience treated together in the ensuing discussion. The clearest instance of an implied choice has already been discussed (above, para.25–007).

[50] *Jacobs v Crédit Lyonnais* (1884) 12 Q.B.D. 589 at 601–603.

[51] See generally Dicey and Morris, *The Conflict of Laws* (11th ed.), pp.1182 *et seq*; Cheshire and North, *Private International Law* (11th ed.), pp.457 *et seq.*

[52] *Jacobs v Crédit Lyonnais*, above, at pp.601–602; *Mann, George & Co. v James and Alexander Brown* (1921) 10 L.L.R. 221; *cf. AV Pound & Co. Ltd v MW Hardy & Co. Inc.* [1956] A.C. 588.

thinking that the law of such a country was not impliedly intended to be the proper law, the law of any country where all, or a significant portion, of the obligations imposed by the contract, were to be performed had a claim to be the proper law.[53] If the various obligations were to be performed in different countries, it might not have been possible to say that any one country was of particular importance,[54] though there was a tendency to treat the country in which the act of physical delivery[55] by the seller took place as being particularly significant,[56] especially where it coincided with the place where the seller or buyer carried on business or the country of payment.[57]

Other relevant factors included the form,[58] language[59] and terminology[60] of the contract, the currency in which the price or any other money obligation was expressed or was to be paid or discharged,[61] the existence of 25–010

[53] *Jacobs v Crédit Lyonnais*, above; *Chatenay v Brazilian Submarine Telegraph Co.* [1891] 1 Q.B. 79; *Benaim & Co. v Debono* [1924] A.C. 514; *NV Handel Maatschappij J Smits v English Exporters (London) Ltd* [1955] 2 Lloyd's Rep. 317 at 322.

[54] See *H Glynn (Covent Garden) Ltd v Wittleder* [1959] 2 Lloyd's Rep. 409 at 420.

[55] *e.g.* the act whereby in accordance with the contract, the seller or his agent places the goods at the disposition of the buyer, or of a carrier who is to transport them to the buyer or of some agent or bailee acting on behalf of the buyer. *Cf.* Sale of Goods Act 1979, s.32(1), above, para.8–014; American Law Institute, Restatement of the Law, Second, Conflict of Laws (1971) (hereafter referred to as "Restatement"), para.191d. As to the various possibilities of the meaning of "delivery" see above, paras 8–002, 8–007—8–015.

[56] *Benaim & Co. v Debono*, above; *NV Handel Maatschappij J. Smits v English Exporters (London) Ltd*, above, at p.320; Dicey and Morris, *op. cit.*, pp.1260–1261; *cf. Mendelson-Zeller Co. Inc. v T & C Providores Pty Ltd* [1981] 1 N.S.W.L.R. 366 at 371. The law of the country of delivery had no significance at all where the contract did not impose any obligations on the seller as regards physical delivery *e.g.* a sale of goods afloat) or where the seller had the right to nominate the country of delivery since it could not reasonably be argued that he should thereby have the right to choose the proper law as well.

[57] See *Sanitary Packing Co. Ltd v Nicholson and Bain* (1916) 33 W.L.R. 594 at 599 (Supreme Court of Manitoba); *cf. Mendelson-Zeller Co. Inc. v T & C Providores Pty Ltd*, above.

[58] *James Miller and Partners Ltd v Whitworth Street Estates (Manchester) Ltd* [1970] A.C. 583; *Amin Rasheed Shipping Corp. v Kuwait Insurance Co.* [1984] A.C. 50.

[59] *Chatenay v Brazilian Submarine Telegraph Co.* [1891] 1 Q.B. 79 at 82; *NV Handel Maatschappij J Smits v English Exporters (London) Ltd*, above, at p.323; *H Glynn (Covent Garden) Ltd v Wittleder* [1959] 2 Lloyd's Rep. 409 at 421; *Wahbe Tamare and Sons Co. v Bernhard Rothfos* [1980] 2 Lloyd's Rep. 553 at 555; *cf. Re Helbert Wagg & Co. Ltd* [1956] Ch. 323. But in commercial contracts, particularly in the maritime field, the use of the English language was and is of little significance because it was and is so commonly used; *The Metamorphosis* [1953] 1 W.L.R. 543 at 549; *Amin Rasheed Shipping Corp. v Kuwait Insurance Co.*, above.; *The Komninos S* [1990] 1 Lloyd's Rep. 541; Dicey and Morris, *op. cit.*, p.1185.

[60] *The Industrie* [1894] P. 58; *Spurrier v La Cloche* [1902] A.C. 446 at 450.

[61] *The Assunzione* [1954] P. 150; *Rossano v Manufacturers Life Insurance Co.* [1963] 2 Q.B. 352 at 369; *cf. Re Helbert Wagg & Co. Ltd*, above; *NV Handel Maatschappij J Smits v English Exporters (London) Ltd*, above, at p.323. But this was less significant if the currency was an international one such as sterling: *Sayers v International Drilling Co. NV* [1971] 1 W.L.R. 1176 at 1183, 1186.

other related agreements between the same parties[62] or involving the same subject-matter,[63] the general course of dealing and conduct of the parties up to the time of the contract, though not subsequent thereto,[64] considerations of business efficacy and convenience,[65] including the fact that the contract concerned a commodity dealt with internationally, in a particular market,[66] and the nationality[67] of each party. In borderline cases, all these matters may have had to be considered, and the list here given is not exhaustive as to all relevant considerations.[68]

---

[62] *Re United Railways of the Havana and Regla Warehouses Ltd* [1960] Ch. 52 (rvsd. in part on other grounds *sub nom. Tomkinson v First Pennsylvania Banking and Trust Co.* [1961] A.C. 1007); *The Njegos* [1936] P. 90; *The Broken Hill Pty Co. Ltd v Theodore Xenakis* [1982] 2 Lloyd's Rep. 304; *Illyssia Compania Naviera SA v Ahmed Abdul-Qawi Bamaodah (The Elli 2)* [1985] 1 Lloyd's Rep. 107; *cf. The Metamorphosis*, above, at p.548; *Forsikringsaktieselskapet Vesta v Butcher* [1989] A.C. 852. In the case of "string" contracts, *i.e.* successive contracts relating to the same goods, it is desirable to achieve uniformity as to the governing law by appropriately worded choice of law clauses in all the relevant contracts or through arbitration clauses: see *Compagnie d'Armement Maritime SA v Compagnie Tunisienne de Navigation SA* [1971] A.C. 572 at 609; below, para.25–068. If the various contracts are all concluded subject to the rules of the same commodity association, the same choice of law clause or arbitration clause is, in fact, likely to appear in all of them.

[63] See below, para.25–068.

[64] *James Miller and Partners Ltd v Whitworth Street Estates (Manchester) Ltd* [1970] A.C. 583.

[65] *Lloyd v Guibert* (1865) L.R. 1 Q.B. 115 at 129; *The Adriatic* [1931] P. 241; *The Njegos*, above.

[66] *Wahbe Tamare & Sons Co. v Bernhard Rothfos* [1980] 2 Lloyd's Rep. 553 (Robusta coffee dealt with on London Coffee Exchange, pointed to English law as the proper law).

[67] *Cood v Cood* (1863) 33 Beav. 314 at 322; *P and O Steam Navigation Co v Shand* (1865) 3 Moo.P.C. (N.S.) 272 at 290–291.

[68] The fact that one of the parties to the contract was a government or governmental agency of a particular country could be a factor suggesting (though not very strongly) that the law of that country should be the proper law: *R. v International Trustee* [1973] A.C. 500 at 557; *Bonython v Commonwealth of Australia* [1951] A.C. 501; *The Assunzione* [1954] P. 150. The *situs* of the goods and the place where property in them passed were not of particular relevance as such: *Mendelson-Zeller Co. Inc. v T & C Providores Pty Inc.* [1981] 1 N.S.W.L.R. 366. If, to the knowledge of the parties, one or more terms of the contract would be valid under one of two possible governing laws but invalid (though not illegal) under the other, some authorities supported the view that the former law, rendering the term valid, was to be preferred as the proper law: *P and O Steam Navigation Co. v Shand* (1865) 3 Moo.P.C. (N.S.) 272; *Re Missouri Steamship Co. Ltd* (1889) 42 Ch.D. 321; *Hamlyn & Co. v Talisker Distillery* [1894] A.C. 202 at 208, 215; *South African Breweries v King* [1900] 1 Ch. 273; *NV Handel Maatschappij J Smits v English Exporters (London) Ltd* [1955] 2 Lloyd's Rep. 317; *Sayers v International Drilling Co. NV* [1971] 1 W.L.R. 1176 at 1184 (a pointer towards a validating law, but one the importance of which should not be exaggerated); *Coast Lines Ltd v Hudig and Veder Chartering NV* [1972] 2 Q.B. 34; *S.C.F. Finance Co. Ltd v Masri* [1986] 1 Lloyd's Rep. 293 at 304. For the contrary view, see *British South Africa Co. v De Beers Consolidated Mines Ltd* [1910] 2 Ch. 502 (rvsd. on other grounds [1912] A.C. 52); *Monterosso Shipping Co. v International Transport Workers Federation* [1982] 3 All E.R. 841 at 848.

F.o.b. contracts.[69] Although, in general, the proper law of a contract of sale f.o.b. was to be found in the application of general principles,[70] there was an observable tendency in the relatively few authorities to treat the country of shipment[71] as the place of performance by delivery on board the ship and to regard the contract as governed by the law of that place in the absence of any countervailing considerations.[72] Implicit in the view was the idea that shipment at the stipulated port was the most importance act of performance of an f.o.b. contract.[73] Countervailing considerations could, of course, exist.[74] **25–011**

C.i.f. contracts.[75] In general, the proper law of a c.i.f. contract had to be identified in accordance with the general rules regarding ascertainment of the proper law,[76] without any special rules or factors being applicable merely by virtue of its being a c.i.f. contract.[77] However, there was slender **25–012**

---

[69] This discussion is applicable to "classic" f.o.b. contracts and to f.o.b. contracts "with additional duties", as described above, paras 20–002—20–007. On the other hand, any contract not imposing an obligation on the seller to consign the goods to the buyer from a specified place is excluded, even if it bears the label "f.o.b." For the position under the Rome Convention, see below, para.25–066.
[70] *The Nile Co. for the Export of Agricultural Crops v H & JM Bennett (Commodities) Ltd* [1987] 1 Lloyd's Rep. 555. For the Rome Convention see below, para.25–066.
[71] This might have been subject to an exception in the case of a "multi-port" f.o.b. contract (*e.g.* "f.o.b. UK port") giving the seller the right to choose a port of shipment out of a number of ports in different countries, since there was no identifiable country of shipment at the time the contract was concluded.
[72] *Benaim & Co. v Debono* [1924] A.C. 514; *Re Viscount Supply Co. Ltd* (1963) 40 D.L.R. (2d) 501 at 506–508; Restatement, para.191d. The conclusion if fortified by the fact that in an f.o.b. contract, the country of delivery may well coincide with the country of payment, as was the case in *Benaim & Co. v Debono*, above, though the point is not mentioned in the judgments. *Cf. Re Columbia Shirt Co.* (1922) 3 C.B.R. 268; *Re Hudson Fashion Shoppe Ltd* [1926] 1 D.L.R. 199; *Clarke v Harper and Robinson* [1938] N.I. 162.
[73] *Benaim & Co. v Debono*, above, at p.520.
[74] See *NV Handel Maatschappij J Smits v English Exporters (London) Ltd* [1955] 2 Lloyd's Rep. 317.
[75] For the position under the Rome Convention see below, para.25–066.
[76] Above, paras 25–005—25–010. The paucity of authorities on c.i.f. contracts is probably, to a large extent, due to the existence of relatively uniform standard commercial practices in relation to them. For the Rome Convention, see below, para.25–066.
[77] *H Glynn (Covent Garden) Ltd v Wittleder* [1959] 2 Lloyd's Rep. 409 at 420 (negotiations prior to contract included an interview in England, contract expressed in English language pointed to English law in case where principal duties or seller under the contract were split between different countries); *NV Kwik Hoo Tong Handel Maatschappij v James Finlay & Co. Ltd* [1927] A.C. 604 (English arbitration clause pointed to English law as proper law, though *cf.* Lord Phillimore at p.609 and Bankes L.J. in the CA (Appendix to HL printed Case (1927) and *Compagnie d'Armement Maritime SA v Compagnie Tunisienne de Navigation SA* [1971] A.C. 572 at 589, 597, 606 where the CA judgments are discussed). In the latter case, the HL judgments in the former case were interpreted as referring to the "curial law", *i.e.* the law governing the arbitration proceedings between the parties rather than the proper law itself: see [1971] A.C. 572 at 606, 607.

judicial authority,[78] and some academic authority,[79] to the effect that where the parties carried on business in different countries, the law of the country of shipment of the goods should prima facie be the proper law. The view was, however, open to the objection that a c.i.f. seller may prima facie have the right to tender documents in respect of goods sold afloat.[80] In any event, the principal duties of a c.i.f. seller, unlike those of a f.o.b. seller, are not clearly concentrated upon the country of shipment. The contract is quite likely to require performance of his duty to tender appropriate documents (a duty of prime importance) in the buyer's country, or elsewhere outside the country of shipment.[81] The most that might be said is that in a situation where the seller has no right to tender goods afloat *e.g.* where he is bound to manufacture and ship the goods c.i.f. in a specified country)[82] there could be a strong pointer towards that country's law as the proper law.

25–013 **Other types of overseas sale.** There were very few authorities specifically dealing with ascertainment of the proper law in the case of other recognised types of overseas sale contract,[83] but the principles already set out give some measure of guidance. It is submitted, for instance, that "f.a.s.",[84] "f.o.r." and "f.o.t." contracts could be dealt with in a similar fashion to f.o.b. contracts, because, like f.o.b. contracts, they usually impose a primary obligation on the seller to consign the goods to the buyer at a specified place or to bring them to a specified place for the purposes of consignment to the buyer. "C. & f."[85] contracts could for present purposes be assimilated to c.i.f. contracts. As to "ex-works" or "ex-store" contracts, the law of the country in which the buyer collects the goods from the seller or a bailee on his behalf had some claim to be the proper law. By contrast, in an "ex-ship" or "arrival" contract, the country where the seller has agreed to have the goods brought for receipt by the buyer should probably have received the chief emphasis.

25–014 **No renvoi.** Speaking for a majority of the House of Lords, Lord Diplock stated that where parties expressly or impliedly chose a law to govern a contract it was the substantive law of that country to which reference was made "but excluding any renvoi, whether of remission or transmission, that

[78] See *Lewis Construction Co. Ltd v Tichauer SA* [1966] V.R. 341 at 345–346; and note that in a number of cases under what became RSC, Ord.11, r.1(1)(e), (now CPR, r.6.20(6)) a failure to deliver goods, or the delivery of defective goods, under c.i.f. contracts has been treated as a breach of contract occurring at the port of shipment, not at the port of receipt by the buyer (see, *e.g. Johnson v Taylor Bros & Co. Ltd* [1920] A.C. 144; Dicey and Morris, *op. cit.*, pp.323–324).

[79] Dicey and Morris, *op. cit.*, pp.1260–1261; Rabel, *op. cit.*, Vol. 3, p.62; Restatement, para.191d.

[80] See above, para.19–011. Alternatively the contract may be a "multi-port" one; *cf.* above, para.25–011, n.71, where the same possibility in regard to f.o.b. contracts is considered.

[81] As in *H Glynn (Covent Garden) Ltd v Wittleder*, above.

[82] Above, para.19–011.

[83] See generally above, Chs 18, 21.

[84] *Gill and Duffus Landauer Ltd v London Export Corp. GmbH* [1982] 2 Lloyd's Rep. 627.

[85] *cf. Mendelson-Zeller Co. Inc. v T & C Prividores Pty Ltd* [1981] 1 N.S.W.L.R. 366.

the courts of that country might themselves apply if the matter was litigated before them".[86] And there is no reason to doubt that renvoi was also excluded where the proper law was reached by identification of the system of law with which the contract has the closest and most real connection.[87] Accordingly, only the domestic rules of the proper law of the contract of sale or, indeed, of any other contract were applied in determining the parties' rights under that contract, and the conflicts rules of the proper law were ignored.

3. THE ROME CONVENTION

(a) *General Considerations*

Historical Background. In 1980 the then Member States of the European Economic Community concluded a Convention on the Law Applicable to Contractual Obligations. Known as the Rome Convention[88] (because it was opened for signature in Rome) this Convention was ratified by the United Kingdom in 1991 and was implemented in UK law in the Contracts (Applicable Law) Act 1990.[89] The provisions of the 1990 Act which give the force of law to the Rome Convention entered into force on April 1, 1991,[90] and the rules of the Convention will apply to determine the law applicable to contracts falling within its scope which are entered into 25–015

[86] *Amin Rasheed Shipping Corp. v Kuwait Insurance Co.* [1984] A.C. 50 at 62. Lord Wilberforce who reached the same decision as the majority by different reasoning did not express disagreement with this view. In the Court of Appeal it had also been said that "the principle of renvoi finds no place in the field of contract": *Re United Railways of the Havana and Regla Warehouses Ltd* [1960] Ch. 52 at 97 (rvsd. in part on other grounds *sub nom. Tomkinson v First Pennsylvania Banking and Trust Co.* [1961] A.C. 1007); see also *ibid.* at p.115. There is a somewhat discredited dictum to the contrary in *Vita Food Products Inc. v Unus Shipping Co.* [1939] A.C. 277 at 292 and an ambiguous remark by Lord Diplock in *The Hollandia* [1983] 1 A.C. 565 at 573. For comment see F.A. Mann, 33 I.C.L.Q. 193 at 195 (1984); Spiro, 33 I.C.L.Q. 201 (1984). The same principle prevails under the Rome Convention: see below, para.25–026.

[87] Mann, *ibid. Re United Railways of the Havana Regla Warehouses Ltd*, above, was such a case.

[88] There is an extensive body of literature on the Convention. The following are among the more significant contributions in English: Fawcett, Harris and Bridge, *International Sale of Goods in the Conflict of Laws* (2005), Chs 13 and 14; Plender, *The European Contracts Convention* (2nd ed.); Kaye, *The New Private International Law of Contract of the European Community* (1993); Lasok and Stone, *Conflict of Laws in the European Community* (1987), Ch.9; North (ed.), *Contract Conflicts* (1982): Dicey and Morris, *The Conflict of Laws* (13th ed.), Chs 32 and 33; Cheshire and North, *Private International Law* (13th ed.), Ch.18; Anton, *Private International Law* (2nd ed.), Ch.11; North, 220 *Hague Recueil*, I, 3, pp.176–205 (1990); Diamond, 216 *Hague Recueil*, IV, 233 (1986); Williams, 35 I.C.L.Q. 1 (1986); Nadelmann, 33 Am.J.Comp.L. 297 (1985); Jaffey, 33 I.C.L.Q. 531 (1984); Morse, 2 Ybk.Eur.L. 107 (1982); North (1980) J.B.L. 382.

[89] Contracts (Applicable Law) Act 1990, s.2(1). The text of the Convention appears as Sch.1 to the Act. References to the Rome Convention hereafter are references to the articles set out in that schedule.

[90] SI 1991/707.

after that date.[91] Schedule 3 of the Act contains the text of the Brussels Protocol which provides for the reference of questions of interpretation of the Rome Convention to the European Court of Justice.[92] Belgium finally ratified the Protocol on May 5, 2004 and it entered into force internationally on August 1, 2004.[93]

25–016 **Purpose of the Convention.** The purpose of the Convention is to create uniform choice of law rules in relation to contracts which fall within its scope with a view to achieving two principal aims. First, such uniformity was perceived as necessary for achieving free movement of goods, services and capital amongst the Member States.[94] Secondly, such uniformity was regarded as a necessary corollary of the Brussels Convention on Jurisdiction and the Enforcement of Judgments in Civil and Commercial Matters 1968,[95] which purported to establish uniform rules for the international jurisdiction of courts within the European Community.[96] That Convention, in particular, "enables the parties in many matters to reach agreements assigning jurisdiction and to choose among several courts". The outcome may be that preference is given to the court of a state whose law seems to offer a better solution to the proceedings. To prevent this "'forum shopping', increase legal certainty and anticipate more easily the law which will be applied, it would be advisable for the rules of conflict to be unified in fields of particular economic importance so that the same law is applied

---

[91] Rome Convention, Art. 17 (providing that the Convention has no retrospective effect). Sch.2 to the Act contains the text of the Luxembourg Convention providing for accession to the Rome Convention by Greece. An Accession Convention providing for the accession of Spain and Portugal to the Rome Convention (the Funchal Convention) was signed on May 18, 1992 and entered into force on September 1, 1993. The Funchal Convention is scheduled to the Act as Sch.3A (SI 1994/1900). A Convention providing for the accession of Austria, Finland and Sweden was signed on November 29, 1996 and entered into force on January 1, 2001. The text of this Convention is scheduled to the Act as Sch.3B (SI 2000/1825). A Convention on the accession of the Czech Republic, Estonia, Cyprus, Latvia, Lithuania, Hungary, Malta, Poland, Slovenia and the Slovak Republic was signed on April 14, 2005, but is not yet in force.

[92] See below, para.25–018. The text of the Protocol (hereafter referred to as the Brussels Protocol) is set out as Sch.3 to the Contracts (Applicable Law) Act 1990.

[93] The Protocol is brought into force in UK law by SI 2004/3448 as from March 1, 2005. The Accession Convention for the new Member States referred to in the preceding note also provides for their accession to the Protocol. A consolidated version of the Convention and the Protocol is printed in [2005] O.J. C334/1.

[94] See the speech of the Director-General for the Internal Market and Approximation of Legislation at the European Commission at the opening meeting of the Committee of governmental experts (formed to draft the Convention) in 1969. This speech is extracted in the Report on the Convention by Professor Giuliano of Italy and Professor Lagarde of France, [1980] O.J. C282/1, at pp.4–5, hereafter referred to as Giuliano-Lagarde Report. On the role of the Report in interpreting the Convention see below, para.25–019.

[95] Giuliano-Lagarde Report, p.5.

[96] The Brussels Convention has been replaced, with respect to all Member States except Denmark, with effect from March 1, 2002, by Council Regulation 44/2001/EC of December 22, 2001 on jurisdiction and the recognition and enforcement of judgments in civil and commercial matters ([2001] O.J. L12/1). For implementation of the Regulation in the UK, see SI 2001/3929.

irrespective of the State in which the decision is given".[97] The need for harmonisation or unification based on these considerations has not gone unquestioned[98]: nor has the Rome Convention as a whole been received with universal acclaim in the United Kingdom.[99] Nonetheless, the uniform rules contained in the Convention will, to the extent indicated in that instrument, replace the common law rules for determining the law applicable to a contract, and thus will be of the utmost significance in an important sector of commercial law in the United Kingdom. This significance is no less considerable in the particular context of sales of goods.

Revision of the Rome Convention.[1] The provisions inserted into the EC Treaty by the Treaty of Amsterdam[2] which are concerned with the introduction of "measures in the field of judicial co-operation in civil matters" envisage revisions of the Rome Convention in due course.[3] In an Action Plan announced in December 1998, the Council and the Commission indicated an intention to "begin revision, where necessary, of certain provisions of the Convention on the Law Applicable to Contractual Obligations, taking into account special provisions on conflict of law rules in other Community instruments".[4] In January 2003, the Commission issued a Green Paper "on the conversion of the Rome Convention of 1980 on the law applicable to contractual obligations into a Community instrument and its modernisation"[5] as part of a process of consultation on a wide variety of issues concerning the Convention. Such consultation was followed in December 2005 by a Commission Proposal for a Regulation of the European Parliament and the Council on the law applicable to contractual obligations (Rome I).[6] Apart from converting the Convention into a 25–017

---

[97] *ibid*.

[98] Collins, 25 I.C.L.Q. 35 (1976); Lipstein, in Lipstein (ed.), *Harmonisation of Private International Law by the EEC* (1978), p.1; Morse, 2 Ybk.Eur.L. 107 at 108–110 (1982).

[99] Its most notable, persistent and vociferous critic has been the late Dr F A Mann: see 32 I.C.L.Q. 265 (1983); 107 L.Q.R. 353 (1991). See also his letter to *The Times*, December 4, 1989. *Cf.* the reply by Dr P M North (who participated in the negotiation of the Convention), *The Times*, December 19, 1989. In the debate on the Contracts (Applicable Law) Bill in the House of Lords, the Convention was criticised by Lord Wilberforce (*Hansard*, HL Vol. 515, Cols 1476–1478) and by Lord Goff of Chieveley. According to the latter "there has been no real criticism of that part of the common law which lays down a test for choice of a governing law of a contract. So far as I know, it is accepted throughout the whole common law world under which between a quarter and a third of the world's population live. All this is set out in the work of Dicey and Morris, *The Conflict of Laws*, which is the prince of legal textbooks and is used throughout the common law world": *Hansard*, HL Vol. 515, Col.1482.

[1] See Meeusen, Pertegas and Straetmans (eds), *Enforcement of International Contracts in the European Union* (2004); Plender, *op. cit.*, Ch.14.

[2] Art. 65. See [1997] O.J. C340/1.

[3] See, in particular, Art. 65(b).

[4] [1999] O.J. C19/1.

[5] COM(2002) 654 final.

[6] COM(2005) 650 final.

Regulation[7], the Proposal seeks to make significant changes to the Convention, though whether the Proposal will prove acceptable in its present form remains to be seen.[8]

25–018 **Interpretation.**[9] In practice, most of the problems posed by the Rome Convention will be problems of interpretation of the meaning of its provisions. Some general observations on interpretation are therefore appropriate. The existence of the Brussels Protocol providing for the jurisdiction of the European Court to give preliminary rulings on questions of interpretation referred to it by national courts has already been noted.[10] In the United Kingdom context, the House of Lords and other courts from which no further appeal is possible[11] and any other United Kingdom court when acting as an appeal court[12] may request a preliminary ruling from the European Court on a question of interpretation if any of those courts consider that a decision on the question is necessary to enable it to give judgment in a case.[13] It is important to note that no national court is *bound* to make such a reference.[14] Interpretative guidance to United Kingdom courts is provided in section 3 of the Contracts (Applicable Law) Act 1990.

[7] Harmonisation of private international law rules through Regulations is now a feature of the Community's legislative process, as illustrated by Council Regulation 44/2001/EC of December 22, 2000 on jurisdiction and the recognition and enforcement of judgments in civil and commercial matters ([2001] O.J. L12/1). In the field of obligations, the Commission presented a Proposal for a Regulation of the European Parliament and the Council on the law applicable to non-contractual obligations ("Rome II") in July 2003, covering tort and some aspects of restitution (COM(2003) 427 final). See on this proposal House of Lords, European Union Committee, *The Rome II Regulation: Report with Evidence*, HL Paper 66 (2004). Responding to a European Parliament legislative resolution on the proposal for a regulation of the European Parliament and of the Council on the law applicable to non-contractual obligations ("Rome II") (P6-TTA-PROV (2005) 284, July 6, 2005), the Commission issued an Amended Proposal for a European Parliament and Council Regulation on the law applicable to non-contractual obligations ("Rome II") in February 2006 (see COM(2006) 83 final).

[8] Information from the Department of Constitutional Affairs indicates that the UK will not, at least at present, participate in the adoption and application of the proposed Regulation: and see Recital 18 of the Proposal. Denmark is not participating: *ibid.*, Recital 19.

[9] Plender, *op. cit.*, Ch.2; Kaye, *op. cit.*, pp.77–83; Dicey and Morris, *op. cit.*, paras 32–013—32–019; Cheshire and North, *op. cit.*, pp.538–542.

[10] See above, para.25–015.

[11] Brussels Protocol, Art. 2(a).

[12] *ibid.* Art. 2(b).

[13] Art. 2, preamble.

[14] Compare the situation under the Protocol to the Brussels Convention on Jurisdiction and the Enforcement of Judgments in Civil and Commercial Matters 1968 providing for the European Court's jurisdiction to give preliminary rulings on questions of interpretation arising in relation to that Convention. By Art. 2(2) of that Protocol an appellate court from which no further appeal is possible is *required* to make a reference to the European Court. Under Regulation 44/2001/EC references to the European Court will no longer be under a separate Protocol, but will be under Art. 234 (ex Art. 177) of the Treaty establishing the European Community: references to the European Court under such a regulation can only be made by a court or tribunal of a Member State against whose decisions there is no judicial remedy under national law: see Arts 65 and 68.

This makes it clear that any question as to the meaning or effect of any provision of the Rome Convention shall, if not referred to the European Court in accordance with the Brussels Protocol, be determined in accordance with the principles laid down by, and any relevant decision of, the European Court.[15] The likely approach of the European Court in this context is, thus, of first importance. One principle which will be influential is the need to have regard to the objectives and scheme of the Convention. This principle has often been referred to by the European Court in interpreting the provisions of the Brussels Convention on Jurisdiction and the Enforcement of Judgments in Civil and Commercial Matters of 1968.[16] Application of that principle has led the European Court more often than not to adopt a uniform, or convention, or autonomous meaning for terms and concepts used in that Convention.[17] Since the purpose of the Rome Convention is to introduce uniform choice of law rules into the law of states which are parties to it, it would seem likely that the European Court will seek, so far as possible, to provide autonomous meanings for terms used in the Rome Convention as well.[18]

"Relevant decisions" of the European Court are binding on United Kingdom courts and judicial notice must be taken on any decision of, or expression of opinion by, that court on any question as to the meaning or effect of the Rome Convention that is referred to it.[19] One issue here is what amounts to a "relevant decision". Is it confined to decisions concerning the Rome Convention itself or are decisions in other contexts *e.g.* expressing general principles of community law or interpreting terminology appearing elsewhere which also appears in the Rome Convention) also included? In principle, it is suggested that binding force is confined to decisions on the Rome Convention itself, though this, of course, does not mean that the United Kingdom courts are prevented from referring to decisions of the European Court in other contexts as persuasive analogies where relevant.

Uniform interpretation. Since there is no compulsion on national courts to refer questions to the European Court for a preliminary ruling, the chances of uniformity in interpretation are considerably reduced. However, account of the need for uniform interpretation in national courts is taken in the Convention itself, Article 18 providing that in the interpretation and application of its uniform rules, regard shall be had to their international character and to the desirability of achieving uniformity in their interpretation and application.[20] Further, if judgments given by the courts of a Contracting State *i.e.* a state party to the Convention) conflict with the interpretation given either by the European Court or in a judgment given in 25–019

[15] *cf.* Civil Jurisdiriction and Judgments Act 1982, s.3(3).
[16] See, *e.g.* *LTU v Eurocontrol* (29/76) [1976] E.C.R. 1541.
[17] See, *e.g.* Dicey and Morris, *op. cit.*, para.11–049; Giuliano-Lagarde Report, p.38.
[18] The European Court has perceived a link between the Brussels Convention of 1968 and the Rome Convention: see *Ivenel v Schwab* (133/81) [1982] E.C.R. 1891.
[19] Contracts (Applicable Law) Act 1990, s.3(2).
[20] This formula is derived from the United Nations Convention on the International Sale of Goods.

a court of another Contracting State, the Brussels Protocol empowers the competent authority of the former Contracting State to request the European Court to give a ruling on the conflict of interpretation.[21] This also suggests that decisions of courts of other Contracting States as to the interpretation of the Convention are at least of persuasive authority in the United Kingdom courts which, as such, should have regard to them.[22] United Kingdom courts have frequently referred to the need for uniform interpretation of the Rome Convention,[23] and have on occasion referred to decisions on the Convention rendered in other Contracting States.[24] Finally, section 3(3)(a) of the Contracts (Applicable Law) Act 1990, states that the Report on the Convention by Professors Giuliano and Lagarde may be considered in ascertaining the meaning or effect of any provision of the Convention.[25] The Giuliano-Lagarde Report plays an important role in interpretation and in achieving uniformity therein, not least because it is a text which the negotiators representing the Member States were able to revise (and into which, incidentally, the United Kingdom negotiators put revisions).[26] United Kingdom courts frequently refer to the Giuliano-Lagarde Report in interpreting the provisions of the Convention.[27]

---

[21] Brussels Protocol, Art. 3. In the UK competent authorities will presumably be the Attorney-General, for England and Wales, and the Lord Advocate, for Scotland: Plender, *op. cit.*, para.2–22.

[22] Dicey and Morris, *op. cit.*, para.32–018. In order to make available information about decisions of national courts, Contracting States added a joint declaration to the Brussels Protocol (which does not appear in Sch.3 to the Contracts (Applicable Law) Act 1990) whereby they placed themselves ready to organise co-operation with the European Court to exchange information on national decisions concerning the Rome Convention. National authorities agreed to forward national court decisions to the European Court which would, in turn, communicate the material to the national authorities of the other Contracting States and to the Commission and Council. For the latest text of the declaration see [2005] O.J. C334/1, at 19.

[23] See, *e.g. Raiffeisen Zentralbank Osterreich AG v Five Star General Trading LLC* [2001] 2 W.L.R. 1344; *Samcrete Egypt Engineers and Contractors SAE v Land Rover Exports Ltd* [2001] EWCA Civ. 2019; [2002] C.L.C. 533; *Bergmann v Kenburn Waste Management Ltd* [2002] EWCA Civ. 98; [2002] F.S.R. 711; *Ennstone Building Products Ltd v Stanger Ltd* [2002] EWCA Civ. 916; [2002] 1 W.L.R. 359; *Iran Continental Shelf Oil Co. v IRI International Corp.* [2002] EWCA Civ. 1024; [2004] 2 C.L.C. 696, *Caledonia Subsea Ltd v Microperi SRL*, 2002 S.L.T. 1022.

[24] See *Raiffeisen Zentralbank Osterreich AG v Five Star General Trading LLC*, above; *Definitely Maybe (Touring) Ltd v Marek Lieberberg Konzertagentur GmbH* [2001] 1 W.L.R. 1745; *Samcrete Egypt Engineers and Contractors SAE v Land Rover Exports Ltd*, above; *Iran Continental Shelf Oil Co. v IRI International Corp.*, above; *Caledonia Subsea Ltd v Microperi SRL*, above.

[25] This is without prejudice to any other material the court is permitted to look at: see opening words to s.3(3).

[26] *Hansard*, HL Vol. 513, Col.1259.

[27] See, *e.g. Raiffeisen Zentralbank Osterreich AG v Five Star General Trading LLC*, above; *Print Concept GmbH v GEW (EC) Ltd* [2001] EWCA Civ. 352; [2002] C.L.C. 382; *Mirchandani v Somaia* (February 23, 2001, Morritt V.-C.); *Definitely Maybe (Touring) Ltd v Marek Lieberberg Konzertagentur GmbH*, above; *Aeolian Shipping SA v ISS Machinery Services Ltd* [2001] EWCA Civ. 1162; [2001] 2 Lloyd's Rep. 641; *Samcrete Egypt Engineers and Contractors SAE v Land Rover Exports Ltd*, above; *Bergmann v Kenburn Waste Management Ltd*, above; *Ennstone Building Products Ltd v Stanger Ltd, above; European Bank for Reconstruction & Development v Tekoglu*

Sphere of application. Article 1(1) of the Rome Convention provides that the rules contained in the Convention "shall apply to contractual obligations in any situation involving a choice between the laws of different countries".[28] Article 2 of the Convention goes on to stipulate that "any law specified by" the Convention "shall be applied whether or not it is the law of a Contracting State". In combination, these articles first mean that there is no requirement that the different countries whose laws are concerned in the problem have to be either states which are parties to the Convention or Member States of the European Community and, secondly, that the rules of the Convention must be applied by a United Kingdom court even if the law the application of which they dictate is neither the law of a Contracting State nor the law of a Member State of the European Community. The Convention will thus apply if the choice of law is between the law of England and the law of India,[29] or between the law of India and the law of Japan, as it will if the choice is between the law of England and the law of Germany,[30] or between the law of France and the law of Germany. 25–020

It should also be stressed that the application of the Convention is not dependent on the facts of the situation having a link (other than the fact that the forum is in the United Kingdom) with a Contracting State or with a Member State of the European Community. Essentially, therefore, the rules of the Convention will apply to all cases brought in United Kingdom

---

[2004] EWHC 846 (Comm); *Apple Corps Ltd v Apple Computer Inc.* [2004] EWHC 768 (Ch); [2004] I.L.Pr. 597; *Base Metal Trading Ltd v Shamurin* [2004] EWCA Civ. 1316; [2005] 1 W.L.R. 1157; *Opthalmic Innovations (United Kingdom) Ltd v Opthalmic Innovations International Inc.* [2004] EWHC 2948 (Ch); [2005] I.L.Pr. 109; *Caledonia Subsea Ltd v Microperi SRL*, above; *Atlantic Telecom GmbH, Noter*, 2004 S.L.T. 1031.

[28] For discussion of this formulation see below, para.25–023.

[29] *e.g. Bank of Baroda v Vysya Bank Ltd* [1994] 2 Lloyd's Rep. 87; *Egon Oldendorff v Libera Corp.* [1996] 1 Lloyd's Rep. 380 (law of England and law of Japan); *Gan Insurance Co. Ltd v Tai Ping Insurance Co. Ltd* [1999] 2 All E.R. (Comm) 54 (law of England and law of Taiwan); *Tiernan v Magen Insurance Co. Ltd* [2000] I.L.Pr. 517 (law of England and law of Israel); *Aeolian Shipping SA v ISS Machinery Services Ltd* [2001] EWCA Civ. 1162; [2001]2 Lloyd's Rep. 641 (law of England and law of Japan); *Samcrete Egypt Engineers and Contractors SAE v Land Rover Exports Ltd* [2001] EWCA Civ. 2019; [2002] C.L.C. 533 (law of England and law of Egypt).

[30] *e.g. Definitely Maybe (Touring) Ltd v Marek Lieberberg Konzertagentur GmbH* [2001] 1 W.L.R. 1745; *Bergmann v Kenburn Waste Management Ltd* [2002] EWCA Civ. 98; [2002] 2 F.S.R. 711. See also *Raiffeisen Zentralbank Osterreich AG v Five Star General Trading LLC* [2001] 2 W.L.R. 1344 (law of England and law of France).

courts[31] provided the dispute falls within the scope of the Convention itself.[32]

25–021 **Meaning of "law of a country".** In discussing Article 1(1) of the Convention, the Giuliano-Lagarde Report[33] makes it clear that the rules of the Convention are to apply in all cases where the dispute would give rise to a conflict between two or more *legal systems* despite the fact that the wording of the article refers to the laws of *different countries*, which may not necessarily be the same thing.[34] This is confirmed by Article 19(1) of the Convention in which it is provided that where a state comprises territorial units, each of which has its own rules of law in respect of contractual obligations, each territorial unit shall be considered as a country for the purposes of identifying the law applicable under the Convention. Accordingly, the rules of the Convention will apply to determine whether a contract is governed, say, by the law of England or by the law of New York,[35] or, say, by the law of Texas or by the law of California, whether a contract is governed, say, by the law of England or the law of Italy, or whether a contract is, say, governed by the law of France or the law of Belgium.

---

[31] The rules of the Convention will apply in cases where it is necessary to determine whether a contract "is governed by English law" for the purposes of CPR, r.6.20(5)(a), whereby the court may, in its discretion, give permission for a claim form to be served out of the jurisdiction: see *Bank of Baroda v Vysya Bank Ltd*, above; *Egon Oldendorff v Libera Corp.*, above, decided under the slightly different wording of RSC Ord.11, r.1(1)(d)(iii); *Burrows v Jamaica Private Power Co. Ltd* [2002] 2 All E.R. (Comm) 374; *Marubeni Hong Kong and South China Ltd v Mongolian Government* [2002] 2 All E.R. (Comm) 873; *Apple Corps Ltd v Apple Computer Inc.* [2004] EWHC 768 (Ch); [2004] I.L.Pr. 597; *Opthalmic Innovations International (United Kingdom) Ltd v Opthalmic Innovations International Inc.* [2004] EWHC 2948 (Ch); [2005] I.L.Pr. 109; *Cadre SA v Astra Asigurari* [2005] EWHC 2504 (Comm). The court will not give permission for such service "unless satisfied that England and Wales is the proper place in which to bring the claim": CPR, r.6.21(2A). The rules of the Convention will also apply to determine the law applicable to the contract in the context of deciding where the "place of performance" of the obligation in question is for the purposes of Art. 5(1) of Council Regulation 44/2001/EC on jurisdiction and the recognition and enforcement of judgments in civil and commercial matters: *Definitely Maybe (Touring) Ltd v Marek Lieberberg Konzertagentur GmbH*, above; *Bergmann v Kenburn Waste Management Ltd*, above; *Tavoulareas v Tsavliris* [2005] EWHC 2140 (Comm); [2006] 1 All E.R. (Comm) 109.

[32] Giuliano-Lagarde Report, p.13. This result was criticised by Lords Wilberforce and Goff (*Hansard*, HL Vol. 515, Cols 1476–1482, Vol. 517, Cols 1537–1541) on the ground that application of a "European" test to contracts between parties who come from outside Europe would deter such parties from litigating in the English Commercial Court.

[33] Giuliano-Lagarde Report, p.10.

[34] *cf.* the controversy at common law which emerged in *James Miller & Partners v Whitworth Street Estates (Manchester) Ltd* [1970] A.C. 583, above, para.25–008, n.46.

[35] *Centrax Ltd v Citibank NA* [1999] 1 All E.R. (Comm) 557; *Iran Continental Shelf Oil Co. v IRI International Corp.*, above (law of England or law of Texas); *Apple Corps Ltd v Apple Computer Inc.*, above; *Opthalmic Innovations International (United Kingdom) Ltd v Opthalmic Innovations International Inc.*, above (law of England or law of California).

Intra-United Kingdom conflicts. Article 19(2) of the Convention provides that a state within which different territorial units have their own rules of law in respect of contractual obligations shall not be bound to apply the Convention to conflicts solely between the laws of such units. But application of the Convention rules to such conflicts is not prohibited and the United Kingdom decided to apply those rules to intra-United Kingdom cases in section 2(3) of the Contracts (Applicable Law) Act 1990. The rules of the Convention will thus apply to situations involving a choice between the laws of England, Scotland[36] and Northern Ireland, as the case may be, as well as to situations involving a choice between the laws of England and France.[37] 25–022

Situations to which the Convention applies. The Convention rules will apply to contractual obligations "in any situation involving a choice between the laws of different countries". The question arises as to when such situations are presented. The Giuliano-Lagarde Report ventures the view that these are "situations which involve one or more elements foreign to the internal social system of a country (for example, the fact that one or all of the parties to the contract are foreign nationals or persons habitually resident abroad, the fact that one or more of the obligations of the parties are to be performed in a foreign country, etc.), thereby giving the legal systems of several countries claims to apply".[38] From this it would appear that the foreign element in the transaction must possess some legal relevance in the context of the connections which the transaction has with foreign countries in the normal usage of private international law. Such a foreign element would seem to exist even if the only such element in the transaction is the choice of a foreign law to govern a contract which is otherwise purely domestic in nature.[39] 25–023

Specific exclusions. Although it is clear that, in general, contracts for the sale of goods fall within the Convention so that the law applicable to such a contract will be determined by the rules contained therein, certain issues which might arise in the context of a sale and certain types of contract which might be ancillary to a sale are specifically excluded from the scope of the Convention.[40] Thus, questions involving the status or legal capacity of 25–024

---

[36] See *Ennstone Building Products Ltd v Stanger Ltd* [2002] EWCA Civ; [2002] 1 W.L.R. 3059.

[37] It may still be an open question whether the European Court of Justice will have jurisdiction to interpret the Convention under the Brussels Protocol above, paras 25–015, 25–018 when a request for a preliminary ruling is made in a dispute arising in the intra-UK context despite the ruling in *Kleinwort Benson Ltd v City of Glasgow DC* (E346/93) [1995] E.C.R. I–615, where the Court held that it lacked jurisdiction to interpret the modified version of the Brussels Convention on Jurisdiction and the Enforcement of Judgments in Civil and Commercial Matters 1968 which applies within the UK: see Plender, *op. cit.*, paras 2–28—2–32.

[38] Giuliano-Lagarde Report, p.10.

[39] This conclusion is also implicit in Art. 3(3) of the Convention, as to which see below, paras 25–037—25–041.

[40] The excluded matters which are unlikely to arise directly in relation to sale are

natural persons are, subject to one limited exception,[41] not governed by the rules of the Convention[42] with the consequence that such issues will continue to be determined by common law principles.[43] Likewise excluded are questions concerning the legal capacity of companies and "other bodies corporate or unincorporate",[44] to which questions common law choice of law rules will continue to apply.[45] Similarly, the question (which may arise in the general context of sales) whether an agent is able to bind a principal cannot be determined by reference to the choice of law rules contained in the Convention[46] and will remain subject to common law principles.[47] Finally, subject to one exception, the Convention does not seek to control the law applicable to evidence and procedure[48] which will also remain in the province of the common law.[49] As to obligations which may be related to contracts for the sale of goods, the choice of law rules in the Convention do not apply to "obligations arising under bills of exchange, cheques and promissory notes and other negotiable instruments to the extent that obligations under such other negotiable instruments arise out of their negotiable character".[50] The law applicable to such obligations will continue to be determined according to traditional English law.[51] Nor will the law applicable to arbitration agreements and agreements on the choice of court

---

contractual obligations relating to wills and succession, rights in property arising out of a matrimonial relationship and rights and duties arising out of a family relationship, parentage, marriage or affinity, including maintenance obligations in respect of children who are not legitimate: Art. 1(2)(b). For general discussion of the matters excluded from the Convention, see Plender, *op. cit.*, Ch.4; Kaye, *op. cit.*, Ch.6; Lasok and Stone, *op. cit.*, pp.348–356; Dicey and Morris, *op. cit.*, paras 32–030—32–055; Cheshire and North, *op. cit.*, pp.546–551; Anton, *op. cit.*, pp.319–325.

41 See Art. 11, discussed below, para.25–084.

42 Art. 1(2)(a). Legal capacity (essentially capacity to contract) was excluded because of disagreement between common law and civil law negotiators as to the proper classification of this issue. The common lawyer usually, regards the contractual capacity of an individual as a contractual issue: see below, para.25–084. To a civil lawyer, however, this issue belongs to the law of status: see North in *Contract Conflicts, op. cit.*, p.10.

43 Below, para.25–084.

44 Art. 1(2)(e). See *Continental Enterprises Ltd v Shandong Zhucheng Foreign Trade Group Co.* [2005] EWHC 92 (Comm). Essentially this provision is designed to exclude all matters of company law, because separate work is being carried out by the Community in this area: Giuliano-Lagarde Report, p.12. On this work see, generally, Dine, *European Company Law* (1991); Edwards *EC Company Law* (1999). On the meaning of "company law" for the purposes of this provision, see *Base Metal Trading Ltd v Shamurin* [2004] EWCA Civ. 1316; [2005] 1 W.L.R. 1157; *Atlantic Telecom GmbH, Noter*, 2004 S.L.T. 1031. See also Benedetelli in Meeusen, Pertegas and Straetmans (eds), *op. cit.*, pp.225–254.

45 Below, para.25–085.

46 Art. 1(2)(f).

47 Below, paras 25–073, 25–081—25–082.

48 Art. 1(2)(h).

49 Below, paras 25–203—25–206.

50 Art. 1(2)(c).

51 Below, para.25–077. See *Zebrarise Ltd v De Nieffe* [2005] 1 Lloyd's Rep. 154.

be determined according to the Convention rules.[52] This exclusion is particularly problematic since international contracts for the sale of goods often contain an arbitration clause or a choice of court clause.[53] Although the law applicable to the "sale aspect" of the transaction will have to be determined by reference to the rules of the Rome Convention, the law applicable to the arbitration or choice of court clause will have to be determined according to common law choice of law rules.[54] Further, the Convention rules are inapplicable to the constitution of trusts and the relationship between settlors, trustees and beneficiaries.[55] Finally, although the Convention rules will apply to determine the law applicable to contracts of re-insurance,[56] they do not apply to determine the law applicable to contracts of insurance which cover risks situated in the territories of the Member States of the European Economic Community.[57] Where the insurance contract covers risks situated outside such territories,[58] the law applicable to the contract will be determined by the choice of law rules contained in the Convention.

Relationship with other conventions. According to Article 21 of the Rome Convention, the Convention is not "to prejudice the application of international conventions to which a Contracting State is, or becomes, a party."[59] This means that existing and future conventions entered into by Contracting States will apply despite the existence of the Rome Convention. At present this provision is unlikely to be of specific effect in the United Kingdom in the context of sale of goods,[60] although it is worth noting that some Contracting States are parties to the Hague Convention on the Law Applicable to International Sale of Goods of June 15, 1955[61] 25–025

[52] Art. 1(2)(d). For the reasons for this see Giuliano-Lagarde Report, p.11; Morse in Meeusen, Pertegas and Straetmans (eds), *op. cit.*, pp.191–209. See also below, para.25–030.

[53] See, *e.g. NV Kwik Hoo Tong v Finlay* [1927] A.C. 604 (arbitration clause); *J. Braconnot et Cie v Compagnie des Messageries Maritime* [1975] 1 Lloyd's Rep. 372. See above, para.25–007.

[54] See *Halpern v Halpern* [2006] EWHC 603 (Comm) at [52]; Dicey and Morris, *op. cit.*, paras 12–077, 16–013. See also *XL Insurance v Owens Corning* [2000] 2 Lloyd's Rep. 500 ("severability" of arbitration clause).

[55] Art. 1(2)(g).

[56] Art. 1(4).

[57] Art. 1(3). See below, paras 25–074—25–075.

[58] In determining whether a risk is situated within or without such territories, the court shall apply its internal law: Art. 1(3). See below, para.25–075.

[59] See also Arts 23, 24 and 25. Art. 20 seeks to avoid conflicts between the rules of the Convention and choice of law provisions contained in acts of the institutions of the European Communities or in national law harmonised in accordance with such acts by providing that the latter provisions shall take precedence over the rules contained in the Convention.

[60] Though the parties will remain free to select the provisions of ULIS: contracts which may be ancillary to a sale will continue to be governed by international conventions where relevant: see for example, Carriage of Goods by Sea Act 1971 implementing in the UK the Hague-Visby Rules: see below, paras 25–071—25–072.

[61] Denmark, Finland, France, Italy and Sweden. Belgium has denounced the Convention. For comment on the Convention, see Fawcett, Harris and Bridge, *op. cit.*, paras 15–10—15–64. See also Hague Convention on the Law Applicable to

and that all Contracting States except Malta, Portugal, the Republic of Ireland and the United Kingdom are parties to the Vienna Convention on the International Sale of Goods 1980.

25–026 **No renvoi.** In accordance with the position at common law,[62] Article 15 excludes the doctrine of renvoi by providing that application of the law of any country specified by the Convention means "the application of the rules of law in force in that country other than its rules of private international law". Since the provision refers to the exclusion of the private international law rules of the country of the applicable law, it would seem that if that particular country is a party to an international convention containing rules of substantive (as opposed to rules of private international) law, then such rules may be applied to the contract if the applicable law would regard them as being applicable. It is therefore possible that a United Kingdom court may have to apply the Vienna Convention on the International Sale of Goods 1980,[63] if the law applicable under the Rome Convention is found to be the law of a country which is a party to that Convention and that country would regard that Convention as applicable.[64] This conclusion cannot be reached with any certainty, however, since the position is complicated by Article 21, preserving the application of existing, and future international conventions to which Contracting States are or become, parties. It is possible to construe that provision as rendering international conventions applicable only as between Contracting States which are parties thereto, with the consequence that since the United Kingdom is not a party to the United Nations Convention, the law applicable to the contract of sale, if that of a foreign country which is a party to that Convention, will be the contract law of that country excluding the Convention rules.[65]

25–027 **Mandatory nature of Convention.** It has been suggested by a distinguished critic of the Rome Convention that parties to a contract may be able to exclude the application of the uniform rules contained therein by making a choice, in the contract, of "English law excluding the Act of 1990", *i.e.* the Contracts (Applicable Law) Act 1990, or of "English law as in force on March 31, 1991".[66] It is difficult to accept this conclusion for a number of reasons. First, it is necessary to identify the legal authority which would permit such a choice. This cannot be located in the Convention or the implementing United Kingdom legislation. The former provides, quite explicitly, that the Convention "*shall* apply in a Contracting State to contracts made after the date on which this Convention has entered into

---

International Sale of Goods 1986 (not in force), discussed *ibid.*, paras 15–65—15–129; McLachlan, 102 L.Q.R. 591 (1986). See generally, Plender, *op. cit.*, paras 1–09—1–24.

[62] Above, para.25–014.

[63] Above, para.1–024.

[64] The same reasoning would not apply if the country of the applicable law is a party to ULIS, since when ULIS applies is determined by statute as a matter of English law: above, para.25–003.

[65] *cf.* Fawcett, Harris and Bridge, *op. cit.*, paras 13–70—13–94.

[66] F A Mann, 107 L.Q.R. 353 (1991). *Cf.* Hogan, 108 L.Q.R. 12 (1992); Dicey and Morris, *op. cit.*, para.32–043.

force with respect to that State."[67] The mandatory tone of this language is reflected in section 2(1) of the Contracts (Applicable Law) Act 1990 which states that subject to subsections (2) and (3) the Convention "*shall have the force of law* in the United Kingdom."[68] Identical language in legislation implementing other international conventions designed to introduce uniform rules of law has been treated in English decisions as indicating that those rules are mandatory.[69] Secondly, it is difficult to see that the requisite legal authority resides in the common law, since the applicability of a United Kingdom statute and an international convention implemented therein must depend on the construction of the statute. And it seems tolerably clear that the purpose of the Contracts (Applicable Law) Act 1990 is to replace the rules of the common law with the rules of the Rome Convention to the extent indicated in the statute and the Convention.[70] Thirdly, it is hardly likely that Parliament intended that legislation, the express purpose of which was to introduce uniform choice of law rules, can be avoided in a manner that would produce an opposite result to that intended or that the European Court of Justice, would attribute such an intent to the draftsman of the Convention. It is therefore submitted that the rules of the Rome Convention are mandatory and cannot be avoided by adoption of this suggested device.[71]

Incorporation by reference. The rules of the Rome Convention do not appear to affect the power of the parties to the contract to incorporate, as part of the contract's terms and conditions, the provisions of substantive law of a specified[72] legal system regarding a particular aspect of the contract of sale[73] (for example, implied terms as to the quality of the goods).[74] Here there is no choice of the specified law as the applicable law[75]; the clause is merely a "shorthand device" for adding terms to the contract.[76] Further- 25–028

[67] Art. 17, italics added.
[68] Italics added.
[69] *The Hollandia* [1993] A.C. 565. See also [1982] Q.B. 872, CA.
[70] This is supported by s.5 and Sch. 4 to the 1990 Act expunging the term "proper law" of a contract from legislation where that term appears and replacing it with the terminology of the Convention.
[71] See *Halpern v Halpern* [2006] EWHC 603 (Comm) at [49]. Mann's criticism is theoretically distinct from the problem raised by the doctrine of renvoi since it goes to the threshold question of what body of choice of law rules should be used to determine the governing law rather than to the question of what is meant by the governing law when so determined, which is the renvoi problem.
[72] The parties must have sufficiently indicated the provisions of a foreign law or an international convention which are apt to be incorporated as terms of the contract. Thus, *e.g.* a broad reference to principles of Sharia law is insufficient to incorporate such principles (*Shamil Bank of Bahrain v Beximco Pharmaceuticals Ltd* [2004] EWCA Civ. 19:, [2004] 1 W.L.R. 1784). See, to the same effect, *Halpern v Halpern* [2006] EWHC 603 (Comm) (reference to Jewish law).
[73] Above, para.25–006, n.034.
[74] See generally below, para.25–160.
[75] *Shamil Bank of Bahrain v Beximco Pharmaceuticals Ltd*, above; Dicey and Morris, *op. cit.*, paras 32–086—32–088; *cf. Re Helbert Wagg & Co. Ltd* [1956] Ch. 323 at 340.
[76] *Shamil Bank of Bahrain v Beximco Pharmaceuticals Ltd*, above; *Halpern v Halpern*, above; *Dobell & Co. v Steamship Rossmore Co.* [1895] 1 Q.B. 408. See also *Amin Rasheed Shipping Corp. v Kuwait Insurance Co.* [1984] A.C. 50 at 69–70; Dicey and Morris, *op. cit.*, para.32–086.

more, the relevant provisions remain in the contract even though they are subsequently repealed or amended in the system of law from which they were derived.[77] In contrast, a subsequent alteration in the content of the applicable law of a contract will in general alter the parties' rights to the extent that it purports to bear thereon.[78]

(b) *Choice of Law by the Parties*

25–029 **The general principle.** The first sentence of Article 3(1) of the Rome Convention provides that "a contract shall be governed by the law chosen by the parties", so that, where a contract for the sale of goods contains a choice of law satisfying Article 3(1),[79] the chosen law will apply except to the extent that freedom of choice of law is restricted by other provisions of the Convention.[80] The initial issue which arises is whether this rule requires the court, in the case of a contract containing a choice of foreign law, to apply that foreign law where it is neither pleaded nor proved by either contracting party, a situation which, as has been seen,[81] is not uncommon in the case of contracts of sale where English law has been applied despite an express choice of foreign law in the contract. Although use of the word "shall" in the sentence carries a mandatory connotation, it is submitted that the practice of the common law remains unchanged. This is because the English rule that foreign law must be pleaded and proved, failing which English law will be applied,[82] is a rule of evidence,[83] or procedure[84] and as such a matter which is excluded from the control of the rules of the Rome Convention by Article 1(2)(h).[85] Further, the law chosen by the parties must be the law of a country,[86] in the sense of a recognised and definable body of national law rules.[87] Thus if the parties stipulate in the contract that it shall be governed by Sharia law[88] or by "general principles of law"[89] or by "its own terms" or by "the *lex mercatoria*",[90] there will be no choice of law

[77] See, *e.g. Vita Food Products Inc. v Unus Shipping Co. Ltd* [1939] A.C. 277.
[78] *Re Helbert Wagg & Co. Ltd*, above, at p.341; *Empresa Exportadora de Azucar v Industria Azucazero National SA (The Playa Larga)* [1983] 2 Lloyd's Rep. 171 at 189–190 and para.25–175, below, in relation to the discharge of a contract of sale by supervening changes in the applicable law.
[79] See below, para.25–030.
[80] See below, paras 25–36—25–043.
[81] Above, para.25–003.
[82] Fentiman, *Foreign Law in English Courts* (1998); Dicey and Morris, *op. cit.*, Ch.9; Fentiman, 108 L.Q.R. 142 (1992); Hartley, 45 I.C.L.Q. 271 (1996).
[83] *ibid.*
[84] See Giuliano-Lagarde Report, p.18.
[85] Subject to Art. 14 (below, paras 25–205—25–206) which, it is submitted, does not affect the point.
[86] As to which see above, para.25–021.
[87] *Shamil Bank of Bahrain v Beximco Pharmaceuticals Ltd*, above; *Halpern v Halpern*, above.
[88] *Shamil Bank of Bahrain v Beximco Pharmaceuticals Ltd*, above. See also *Halpern v Halpern*, above (Jewish law).
[89] See *Shamil Bank of Bahrain v Beximco Pharmaceuticals Ltd*, above, at [43]; *Halpern v Halpern*, above, at [48], [50].
[90] *ibid.*

satisfying the Convention.[91] In such situations, it is submitted, the court will have to determine the applicable law by reference to Article 4 of the Convention (dealing with identification of the applicable law in the absence of choice[92]) and it will then be for the law so applicable to determine whether such a clause is effective.[93]

Making the choice of law. A choice of law by the parties "must be express or demonstrated with reasonable certainty by the terms of the contract or the circumstances of the case".[94] Permitting a choice of law to be made expressly is a reproduction of common law principles[95] and creates no difficulties.[96] But more difficulty arises with the notion that a choice may be "demonstrated with reasonable certainty" by reference to the factors indicated in Article 3(1).[97] At common law it was recognised that the parties may impliedly choose the governing law and that such an intention could be inferred from the terms and nature of the contract and from the general circumstances of the case.[98] But use of the word "demonstrated" in the Convention might connote a stronger display of evidence of the parties' intention than is required in the common law test, where an intention is merely inferred.[99] Be that as it may, the Giuliano-Lagarde Report suggests that the Convention envisages a test which is very similar to that of the common law. After pointing out that the relevant words require a demonstration that the parties have made a real choice of law in the sense that there must be a clear intention to choose,[1] the Giuliano-Lagarde 25–030

---

[91] See Dicey and Morris, *op. cit.*, paras 32–079—32–080. *Cf.* Commission Proposal for a Regulation of the European Parliament and the Council on the law applicable to contractual obligations (Rome I), COM(2005) 650 final (hereafter Commission Proposal), Art. 3(2): "The parties may also choose as the applicable law the principles and rules of the substantive law of contract recognised internationally or in the Community. However, questions relating to matters governed by such principles or rules which are not expressly settled by them shall be governed by the general principles underlying them or, failing such principles, in accordance with the law applicable in the absence of choice under this Regulation." According to the Explanatory Memorandum, this formulation excludes the *lex mercatoria* which is not precise enough.

[92] Below, paras 25–057—25–068.

[93] See *Halpern v Halpern* [2006] EWHC 603 (Comm). And see Plender, *op. cit.*, paras 3–19—3–20.

[94] Art. 3(1).

[95] See above, para.25–006.

[96] The parties may make an express oral agreement as to the applicable law (*Oakley v Ultra Vehicle Design Ltd* [2005] EWHC 872 (Ch); [2005] I.L.Pr. 747).

[97] Morse, 2 Ybk.Eur.L. 107 at 116–117 (1982); Hill, 53 I.C.L.Q. 325 (2004). And see the difference between the English and French versions of the text referred to in Anton, *op. cit.*, p.325. *Cf.* Plender, *op. cit.*, paras 5–07—5–16.

[98] Above, para.25–007.

[99] See Morse, *op. cit.*, p.117. *Cf.* Plender, *op. cit.*, paras 5–07—5–08. The provision may, therefore, lead to divergent practice in the courts of the different Contracting States in the application of Art. 3(1): see Plender, *op. cit.*, para.5–11.

[1] Giuliano-Lagarde Report, p.17. See *Egon Oldendorff v Libera Corp. (No.2)* [1996] 1 Lloyd's Rep. 381; *Aeolian Shipping SA v ISS Machinery Services Ltd* [2001] EWCA Civ. 1162 [2001] 2 Lloyds Rep. 641; *Samcrete Egypt Engineers and Contractors S.A.E. v Land Rover Exports Ltd* [2001] EWCA Civ. 2019; [2002] C.L.C. 533; *Marubeni Hong Kong and South China Ltd v Mongolian Government* [2002] 2 All E.R. (Comm) 873; *American Motorists Insurance Co. v Cellstar Corp.* [2003] EWCA Civ. 206; [2003] I.L.Pr. 370.

Report goes on to identify factors which might indicate that such a choice might have been made: "For example, the contract may be in a standard form which is known to be governed by a particular system of law, even though there is no express statement to this effect such as a Lloyd's policy[2] of marine insurance.[3] In other cases a previous course of dealing between the parties under contracts containing an express choice of law may leave the court in no doubt that the contract in question is to be governed by the law previously chosen where the choice of law clause has been omitted in circumstances which do not indicate a deliberate change of policy by the parties.[4] In some cases, the choice of a particular forum may show in no uncertain manner that the parties intend the contract to be governed by the law of that forum[5], but this must always be subject to the other terms of the contract and all the circumstances of the case.[6] Similarly references in a contract to specific articles of the French Civil Code may leave the court in no doubt that the parties have chosen French law, although there is no expressly stated choice of law. Other matters that may impel the court to the conclusion that a real choice of law has been made might include an express choice of law in related transactions between the same parties,[7] or the choice of a place where disputes are to be settled by arbitration in circumstances indicating that the arbitrator should apply the law of that place."[8]

---

[2] As was held in *Tiernan v Magen Insurance Co. Ltd* [2000] I.L.Pr. 517, in relation to a reinsurance contract which was placed on the Lloyd's market in the usual way, was on a Lloyd's standard form and contained London market clauses. See also *Munchener Ruckversicherungs Gesellschaft v Commonwealth Insurance Co.* [2004] EWHC 914 (Comm); [2004] 2 C.L.C. 665; *Tryg Baltica International (UK) Ltd v Boston Compania De Seguros SA* [2004] EWHC 1186 (Comm); [2005] Lloyd's Rep. I.R. 40. *Cf. American Motorists Insurance Co. v Cellstar Corp.*, above; *Evialis SA v SIAT* [2003] EWHC 863; [2003] 2 Lloyd's Rep. 377.

[3] *cf. Amin Rasheed Shipping Corp. v Kuwait Insurance Co.* [1984] A.C. 50, decided after the Giuliano-Lagarde report was written, in which it was held that the use of a Lloyd's standard form *and* the absence of any indigenous code of marine insurance in Kuwait, together indicated an implied choice of English law.

[4] See *Aeolian Shipping SA v ISS Machinery Services Ltd* [2001] EWCA Civ. 1162; [2001] 2 Lloyd's Rep. 641

[5] *Marubeni Hong Kong and South China Ltd v Mongolian Government* [2002] 2 All E.R. (Comm) 873.

[6] *Marubeni Hong Kong and South China Ltd v Mongolian Government*, above. See Morse in Meeusen, Pertegas and Straetmans (eds), *op. cit.*, p.191, at pp.197–201. *Cf.* Commission Proposal, Art. 3(1) (where parties agree to confer jurisdiction on the court of a Member State, they shall also be presumed to have chosen the law of that Member State). *Cf. Burrows v Jamaica Private Power Co. Ltd* [2002] 1 All E.R. (Comm) 374.

[7] See *Samcrete Egypt Engineers and Contractors SAE v Land Rover Exports Ltd* [2001] EWCA Civ. 2019; [2002] C.L.C. 533; *European Bank for Reconstruction and Development v Tekoglu* [2004] EWHC 846 (Comm). Contrast *Gan Insurance Co. Ltd v Tai Ping Insurance Co. Ltd* [1999] 2 All E.R. (Comm) 54. And see *Raiffeisen Zentralbank Osterreich Aktiengesellschaft v National Bank of Greece SA* [1999] 1 Lloyd's Rep. 408.

[8] Note, however, that no reference is made to choice of law in *favorem negotii* as being a potentially relevant factor: see Plender, *op. cit.*, para.5–16; *cf.* above, para.25–010, n.68.

25–031 Virtually all the factors mentioned in this passage could be present in the case of a contract for the sale of goods and are thus, in principle, capable by such presence of demonstrating with reasonable certainty that the parties to the contract have made a choice of law.[9] In the case of arbitration clauses, however, it seems that the application of Article 3(1) involves a shift of emphasis[10] from that which was found in the common law.[11] This is because, as stated in the extract from the Giuliano-Lagarde Report quoted in the previous paragraph, the circumstances surrounding the arbitration clause must indicate that it is the intention of the parties that the arbitrator should apply the law of the country in which arbitration is to take place.[12] This is, perhaps, not quite the same test as prevailed at common law,[13] but there is probably, in practice, little difference between the two regimes.[14] Nonetheless, just as difficulty existed at common law in determining whether a case fell within the implied choice or "no choice" category,[15] difficulty will remain in determining whether a case falling within the Convention is a case governed by Article 3 since there is a choice of law by the parties or is a case falling within Article 4[16] because there is no such choice.[17] This is because the notion that a choice of law may be "demonstrated with reasonable certainty by the terms of the contract or the circumstances of the case" is sufficiently imprecise to permit disagreement as to whether a true choice of law has in fact been made. The advantages inherent in making an express choice of law are therefore obvious.

---

[9] *cf.* above, paras 25–007, 25–009—25–010.
[10] Dicey and Morris, *op. cit.*, paras 32–093—32–095, approved in *Egon Oldendorff v Libera Corp. (No.2)* [1996] 1 Lloyd's Rep. 381 (Clarke J.). See also *Egon Oldendorff v Libera Corp. (No.1)* [1995] 2 Lloyd's Rep. 64 (Mance J.).
[11] *Egon Oldendorff v Libera Corp. (No.2)*, above, at pp. 389–390.
[12] Common law decisions did not always stress this additional indication, but there are also dicta which support it: see, *e.g. Compagnie d'Armement Maritime SA v Compagnie Tunisienne de Navigation SA* [1971] A.C. 572 at 599, 600, 605, 609.
[13] See preceding note. The Commission Proposal, Art. 3(1) contains no proposal in respect of arbitration clauses, in contrast to the position in relation to jurisdiction clauses: see above, para.25–030, n.6.
[14] *Egon Oldendorff v Libera Corp. (No.2)*, above, at p. 390. In this case the parties had agreed to English arbitration, by arbitrators conversant with shipping matters, of disputes arising out of a well-known English form of charterparty containing standard clauses with well-known meanings in English law. From all of this it was held that the parties had intended English law to be the applicable law for the purposes of Art. 3(1). See also, *Egon Oldendorff v Libera Corp. (No.1)*, above. No implication can be drawn, however, if the clause provides for arbitration in alternative countries: *cf. The Star Texas* [1993] 2 Lloyd's Rep. 445.
[15] Compare the views of Lords Diplock and Wilberforce in *Amin Rasheed Shipping Corp. v Kuwait Insurance Co.* [1984] A.C. 50. See above, para.25–008, n.48.
[16] See below, paras 25–057—25–068.
[17] See, *e.g. Tiernan v Magen Insurance Co. Ltd* [2000] I.L.Pr. 517 (reinsurance contract); *American Motorists Insurance Co. v Cellstar Corp.* [2003] EWCA Civ. 206; [2003] I.L.Pr. 370 (insurance contract); *Tryg Baltica International (UK) Ltd v Boston Compania De Seguros SA* [2004] EWHC 1186 (Comm); [2005] Lloyd's Rep. I.R. 40 (reinsurance contract); *Cadre SA v Astra Asigurari* [2005] EWHC 2504 (Comm); (insurance contract).

25–032 **Subsequent conduct.** It is also submitted that, contrary to the position taken in the common law,[18] it is possible to take account of the conduct of the parties subsequent to the making of the contract in determining whether a choice of law has been demonstrated with reasonable certainty, at least where such conduct is indicative of the intention of the parties at the time the contract was made.[19] The English common law view is not adopted in other countries[20] and, accordingly, it would not accord with the aim of uniformity to apply it so as to defeat the intentions of the parties.

25–033 **Severability.** Article 3(1) envisages that "by their choice the parties can select the law applicable to the whole or a part only of the contract",[21] thus introducing into the Convention the notion of severability or *dépeçage*, which was probably recognised in the common law.[22] Permitting parties, in this way, to choose different laws to govern different parts of a contract is justified as the logical conclusion of the principle of party autonomy in choice of law.[23] For the provision to operate it appears that a contract must consist of several parts "which are separable and independent of each other from the legal and economic point of view".[24] Further, when the contract is severable in this sense "the choice must be logically consistent, *i.e.* it must relate to elements which can be governed by different laws without giving rise to contradictions. For example, an 'index-linking clause' may be made subject to a different law; on the other hand it is unlikely that repudiation of the contract for non-performance would be subjected to two different laws, one for the vendor and one for the purchaser."[25] If the chosen laws cannot be reconciled as a matter of logic, then neither choice of law is effective and the law applicable to the contract will have to be determined

---

[18] *James Miller and Partners Ltd v Whitworth Street Estates (Manchester) Ltd* [1970] A.C. 583 at 603; *Amin Rasheed Shipping Corp. v Kuwait Insurance Co.* [1984] A.C. 50 at 69. See above, para.25–010.
[19] Plender, *op. cit.*, para.5–15; Dicey and Morris, *op. cit.*, para.32–058. The question is not considered in the Giuliano-Lagarde Report.
[20] F.A. Mann, 89 L.Q.R. 464 (1973). See, *e.g.* Italian Civil Code, para.1362.
[21] For discussion of this provision see Plender, *op. cit.*, paras 5–17—5–18; Morse, *op. cit.*, pp.117– 118. See also Maclachlan, 61 B.Y.I.L. 311 (1990); Dicey and Morris, *op. cit.*, paras 32–048—32–052; Cheshire and North, *op. cit.*, pp.553–554.
[22] See *Kahler v Midland Bank Ltd* [1950] A.C. 24 at 42; *Re United Railways of the Havana and Regla Warehouses Ltd* [1960] Ch. 52 at 92; Dicey and Morris, *op. cit.*, paras 32–046—32–052.
[23] Giuliano-Lagarde Report, p.17.
[24] *ibid*.
[25] *ibid.* See *CGU International Insurance Plc v Szabo* [2002] 1 All E.R. (Comm) 83 (no logical or commercially sensible basis on which words of an insurance policy defining the insured can be "severed" so as to be interpreted by different laws and given possibly different meanings); *American Motorists Insurance Co. v Cellstar Corp.* [2003] EWCA Civ. 206; [2003] I.L.Pr. 370 at [20] ("neither the parties nor the Rome Convention could sensibly be taken to have intended to scissor up" a composite but single and probably multipartite insurance policy and to subject different aspects of it to different governing laws). See also *Travelers Casualty & Surety Co. v Sun Life Assurance Co. of Canada (UK) Ltd* [2004] EWHC 1704 (Comm); [2004] I.L.Pr. 793 at [46]. For a sceptical view of *depeçage*, see the majority view of the Court of Appeal in *Centrax Ltd v Citibank NA* [1999] 1 All E.R. (Comm) 557 and contrast the dissenting judgment of Waller L.J. *Cf. XL Insurance Ltd v Owens Corning* [2000] 2 Lloyd's Rep. 500.

according to Article 4 as if the parties had made no choice of law at all.[26] Further where parties make a choice of law in relation to one severable part of a contract, but no choice of law in relation to the other part or parts, the law applicable to the latter will also have to be determined according to Article 4.[27]

Validity of choice of law. At common law it was unclear what law determined whether a valid choice of law by the parties had been made.[28] The Convention provides that the validity of the choice of law is to be determined by the law chosen, the so-called "bootstrap rule".[29] It should be noted, however, that this rule is not apt to yield a solution in a case involving a so-called "battle of the forms",[30] in which there are conflicting standard forms, emanating, respectively, from the seller and the buyer and which either contain conflicting choice of law clauses, or where one contains a choice of law clause and the other does not. In such circumstances, it does not seem possible to conclude that a choice of law has been expressed or demonstrated with reasonable certainty for the purposes of Article 3(1) of the Convention, so that, accordingly, the applicable law will have to be determined according to Article 4,[31] as a case where there is an absence of a choice of law satisfying Article 3(1).[32] **25–034**

Varying the choice of law. Further uncertainty existed in the common law as to what law determined whether the parties might change the law which governed the contract to a new and different governing law.[33] Article 3(2) of the Rome Convention provides a specific rule on this question in the following terms. "The parties may at any time agree to subject the contract to a law other than that which previously governed it, whether as a result of an earlier choice under this Article or of other provisions of this Convention. Any variation by the parties of the law to be applied made after the conclusion of the contract shall not prejudice its formal validity **25–035**

[26] *ibid.* See below, paras 25–057—25–068.
[27] *ibid.* See below, paras 25–057—25–068.
[28] Dicey and Morris, *op. cit.*, paras 32–098—32–101.
[29] Arts 3(4), 8(1) and 9(4). See *Seapremium Shipping Ltd v Seaconsortium Ltd* (April 11, 2001, Steel J.); Plender, *op. cit.*, paras 10–02—10–03. The same rule is expressed in the Hague Convention on the Law Applicable to International Sale of Goods 1955, Art. 2(3) and in the Hague Convention on the Law Applicable to Contracts for the International Sale of Goods 1986, Art. 10 (not in force). See above, para.25–025.
[30] See Dannemann in Rose (ed.), *Lex Mercatoria: Essays in Honour of Francis Reynolds* (2000), p.199.
[31] Dicey and Morris, *op. cit.*, para.32–01. And see *Ferguson Shipbuilders Ltd v Voith Hydro GmbH*, 2000 S.L.T. 229.
[32] See Fawcett, Harris and Bridge, *op. cit.*, paras 13–107—13–111; See below, paras 25–057—25–068.
[33] See Fawcett, Harris and Bridge, *op. cit.*, paras 13–107—13–111; Dicey and Morris, *op. cit.*, paras 32–082—32–083; Cheshire and North, *op. cit.*, pp.554–556; Plender, *op. cit.*, paras 5–19—5–24; Hill, *op. cit.*, pp.332–333; Morse, *op. cit.*, pp.119–122; Diamond, *op. cit.*, at pp.261–264; F. A. Mann, 31 B.Y.B.I.L. 216 at 222 (1954); North in *Multum non Multa, Festschrift für Kurt Lipstein* (1980), p.205, reprinted in North, *Essays in Private International Law* (1993), p.51.

under Article 9 or adversely affect the rights of third parties." Subject to the proviso as to formal validity,[34] and the need to preserve the rights of third parties which might be adversely affected by a change in the governing law,[35] the parties are left with maximum freedom as to the time when the ultimate choice of law is made because of this wide freedom to change the applicable law.[36] The freedom extends to changing the applicable law when the law was expressly chosen by the parties or applicable because of the absence of a choice of law according to the provisions of Article 4.[37] To be effective, however, the choice of law which purports to vary or change the original governing law must itself satisfy the requirements of Article 3(1).[38]

25–036 **Limitations on choice of law by the parties.** Very few limitations are imposed on the freedom of the parties to choose the law governing a contract for the sale of goods. Such restrictions that exist emanate from general rules of the Convention[39] and from a special provision thereof[40] concerned with "certain consumer contracts" which may include, but is not confined to, certain contracts for the sale of goods. These various restrictions will be considered in the following paragraphs.

25–037 **Mandatory rules: Article 3(3).** This provision of the Convention is likely to have relatively little practical effect in the context of typical international sale transactions.[41] It stipulates that "[t]he fact that the parties have chosen

---

[34] See below, para.25–086.

[35] "In certain legal systems, a third party may have acquired rights in consequence of a contract concluded between two other persons. These rights cannot be affected by a subsequent change in the choice of the applicable law.": Giuliano-Lagarde Report, p.18.

[36] *ibid.* This power to vary the applicable law is distinct from and in addition to any power which may exist as a matter of procedure, in national law (such as English law) to make, or change, a choice of law in the course of legal proceedings: *ibid.* Further it must be stressed that the provision is only concerned with *changing* the applicable law and does not affect the principle of the common law, which is equally a principle of the Convention, that there must be a law governing the contract at the outset of the contract so that the applicable law cannot "float": see above, para.25–006, n.34.

[37] *ibid.*

[38] *ibid.*; *Aeolian Shipping SA v ISS Machinery Services Ltd* [2001] EWCA Civ. 1162; [2001] 2 Lloyd's Rep. 641.

[39] Directive 2000/31EC of the European Parliament and of the Council of June 8, 2000 on certain legal aspects of information society services, in particular electronic commerce ("Directive on electronic commerce") ([2000] O.J. L178/1), implemented in the UK in the Electronic Commerce (EC Directive) Regulations 2002 (SI 2002/2013), is generally thought to introduce a "country of origin" principle (reg.4) for regulating the liability of a service provider established in a Member State. This principle cannot, however, affect the power of parties to choose the law to govern a contract of sale which is concluded "online" because the Directive and the Regulations are explicitly expressed not to apply to the freedom of the parties to choose the law applicable to their contract (see Directive, Art. 3(3) and Annex; Regulations, reg.4(4) and Schedule). As to consumer contracts concluded online, see below, paras 25-049–25-053).

[40] Art. 5, below, paras 25–044—25–056.

[41] North, 220 *Recueil des Cours*, I, 13 at 184 (1990). For general discussions of Art. 3(3) see Plender, *op. cit.*, paras 5–25—5–27; Morse, *op. cit.*, pp.122–124; Philip, in *Contract Conflicts, op. cit.*, pp.81, 95–97; Dicey and Morris, *op. cit.*, paras 32–129—32–134; Cheshire and North, *op. cit.*, pp.557–559.

a foreign law, whether or not accompanied by the choice of a foreign tribunal, shall not, where all the other elements relevant to the situation at the time of the choice are connected with one country only, prejudice the application of rules of the law of that country which cannot be derogated from by contract, hereinafter called mandatory rules". The purpose of this provision would appear to be the prevention of the evasion of mandatory rules as defined therein in relation to a contract which, but for a choice of foreign law, would be essentially a domestic contract, by the simple device of including in the contract, such a choice of foreign law.[42] So narrow a situation does not appear to have been considered by the English courts in application of the common law rules.[43] A number of difficulties arise. First, it may not be clear whether "all the other elements relevant to the situation are connected with one country only", though it is clear that the judgment as to relevance must be made in the light of circumstances prevailing at the time the choice of law is made. Use of the word "situation" might be thought to indicate that although all the elements relevant to the *contract* of sale are connected with one country only, Article 3(3) will nevertheless *not* apply if the "situation" involves connections with another country in a relevant way. Here it seems clear that the reference to elements "relevant to the situation" is wider than "elements relevant to the contract".[44] For example, goods may be manufactured abroad by a seller and subsequently exported to England where they are the subject of a commercial (as opposed to a "consumer" sale). The sale contract itself may be exclusively connected with England but contain a choice of foreign law, say, the law of the country where the goods are manufactured. The fact that the goods are manufactured abroad, and/or the fact (if such be the case) that the seller/manufacturer is foreign should be regarded as a relevant element, so that it is possible to say that all the elements relevant to the situation (apart from the choice of foreign law) are not connected with England only so that Article 3(3) does not apply.[45]

Conversely, it is likely that Article 3(3) will apply if an English buyer enters into a contract with an English seller through the seller's website on the internet and the only foreign element (apart from a choice of foreign law) is the fact that the website is hosted by a third party in a foreign country, since the physical location of the server would not seem to be an element relevant to the situation.[46]

---

[42] *Caterpillar Financial Services Corp. v SNC Passion* [2004] EWHC 569 (Comm); [2004] 2 Lloyd's Rep. 99 at [17]–[18]; Giuliano-Lagarde Report, p.18.

[43] The common law principle (above, para.25–006) that the choice of law must be "bona fide and legal" was capable of a much broader application.

[44] *Caterpillar Financial Services Corp. v SNC Passion* cited above, at [17]–[18], where it is also pointed out that whether factors are relevant or irrelevant depends on the proper construction of Art. 3(3) and not on factors which the allegedly applicable mandatory rules would regard as relevant or irrelevant.

[45] *Caterpillar Financial Services Corp. v SNC Passion*, above. See Lasok and Stone, *op. cit.*, pp.377–378.

[46] *cf.* Directive 2000/31/EC of the European Parliament and Council of June 8, 2000 on certain legal aspects of information society services, in particular electronic commerce in the Internal Market ("Directive on electronic commerce") ([2000] O.J.

25–038 A second difficulty is presented by the concept of "mandatory rules". The wording of Article 3(3) suggests that the definition of mandatory rules there given ("rules which cannot be derogated from by contract") applies wherever these rules are referred to elsewhere in the Convention ("hereinafter referred to as mandatory rules"). Reference to such rules appears in Article 5 (dealing with consumer contracts[47]), Article 6 (dealing with employment contracts[48]) and Article 7(1), which is of more general application. Article 7(1) does not have the force of law in the United Kingdom[49] and therefore it is unnecessary to discuss it in detail; but a comparison of Article 3(3) and Article 7(1) suggests that the Convention contemplates two kinds of mandatory rules.[50] Article 7(1) gives the courts of a country which applies the provision a discretion, when applying, under the Convention, the law of one country, to give effect to "the mandatory rules of the law of another country with which the situation has a close connection, if and in so far as, under the law of the latter country, those rules must be applied whatever law is applicable to the contract." Thus to be capable of being applied under Article 7(1) a rule must not only be mandatory in the sense of Article 3(3), but must also be one which must be applied whatever the law applicable to the contract. This comparison indicates that Article 3(3) is concerned with preserving the application of mandatory rules which are domestic in character, *i.e.* rules which cannot be derogated from in a purely domestic contract even by a choice of foreign law in the contract, but which can be derogated from in a contract possessing an international character.[51] In contrast, Article 7(1) preserves the possibility, for the courts of states which utilise it, of applying mandatory rules of a higher order: these rules are rules which apply whatever law is applicable to the contract, *i.e.* rules which apply even if the contract is of an international character.[52]

L178/1), Recital 19 and the Electronic Commerce (EC Directive) Regulations 2002, reg.2(1) (SI 2002/2013, which implements the Directive in the UK). See also *Menashe Business Mercantile Ltd v William Hill Organization Ltd* [2002] EWCA Civ; 1702; [2003] 1 W.L.R. 1462; Fawcett, Harris and Bridge, *op. cit.*, paras 21–40—21–45. And see below, para.25–053.

[47] See below, para.25–054.

[48] Which are not discussed in this chapter.

[49] Contracts (Applicable Law) Act 1990, s.2(2). The Convention permits Contracting States to make a reservation to the application of this provision: Art. 22. The UK entered such a reservation on signing the Convention.

[50] See generally, Plender, *op. cit.*, paras 5–25—5–27, 7–21, 9–01—9–22; Philip in *Contract Conflicts, op. cit.*, Ch.5; Jackson, *ibid.*, Ch.4; Diamond, *op. cit.*, pp.288–298; North, 220 *Recueil des Cours*, I, 13 at 191–194 (1990); Morse, *op. cit.*, pp.121–124, 142–147; Dicey and Morris, *op. cit.*, paras 32–129—32–148; Cheshire and North, *op. cit.*, pp.557–558, 575–584.

[51] See *Caterpillar Financial Services Corp. v SNC Passion* [2004] EWHC 569 (Comm); [2004] 2 Lloyd's Rep. 99.

[52] This interpretation is supported by reference to the French text of the Convention. Mandatory rules in Art. 3(3) are described in translation as "*dispositions imperatives*". The collective description in the heading to Art. 7 is, however, in translation, "*Lois de Police*". The change in terminology reflects a distinction drawn in some Continental legal systems between the former class of laws from which derogation may be permitted in international contracts, and the latter class from which no derogation is permitted even in such contracts: Plender, *op. cit.*, para.5–26.

25–039 Even if the general distinction referred to above is accepted, a further difficulty arises from the actual wording of Article 3(3).[53] That wording opens with the statement that "[t]he fact that the parties have chosen a foreign law", etc., and continues "shall not . . . prejudice" application of the relevant mandatory rules. The wording might be thought to indicate that rules are mandatory for this purpose if they cannot be contracted out of in a contract containing no choice of foreign law even if the legal system of which they form part *would* permit such contracting out through choice of a foreign law. If this is correct, a court applying Article 3(3) would be required to apply, as a mandatory rule, a rule of a country which would not regard that rule as applicable in relation to a contract containing a choice of foreign law. It is submitted, however, that this interpretation cannot be correct. In principle, it must be for the legal system of which a rule forms part to determine whether that rule should apply to a particular transaction: it cannot be the purpose of the Convention to give greater effect to these rules than the legal system of which they form part would give them. This principle can just be fitted in to the wording of Article 3(3) by laying emphasis on the words "shall not prejudice" the application of relevant mandatory rules.[54] These words do not *require* application of such rules, but might be thought to indicate that the court must consider whether their application will be materially impeded by application of inconsistent rules contained in the chosen law. If the legal system in which the alleged mandatory rules are contained would not seek to apply them to a contract containing a choice of foreign law there will be no such impediment so that the chosen law will prevail.

25–040 Article 3(3) may require English courts to consider the potential application both of foreign and English mandatory rules. For example, if all the other elements relevant to the situation are connected with France, but the contract contains a choice of English law, the court will have to apply any French mandatory rules.[55] Equally, if all the other elements relevant to the situation are connected with England, but the contract contains a choice of French law, the court will have to apply any relevant English mandatory rules.[56] Considerable difficulty exists, however, in deciding whether any particular rule of English law, including the law relating to sale of goods, is mandatory in this context. If a statute, for example, gives an express indication of its spatial reach,[57] then the difficulty is alleviated, but this is not always the case and further problems arise if the alleged mandatory rule is contained in a rule of common law. An obvious general category which suggests itself in the context of sale is that of rules relating

---

53 Plender, *op. cit.*, para.5–27; Morse, *op. cit.*, pp.123–124; Philip in *Contract Conflicts, op. cit.*, pp.95–97.

54 Plender, *op. cit.*, para.5–27; Philip, above, p.96; Fawcett, Harris and Bridge, *op. cit.*, para.13–100.

55 See *Caterpillar Financial Services Corp. v SNC Passion*, above.

56 Though see the discussion of Art. 7(2), below, para.25–042.

57 See Unfair Contract Terms Act 1977, s.27(2) (below, paras 25–094—25–100) though it is not clear whether this provision is an example of a mandatory rule in the sense of Art. 3(3) or in the sense of Art. 7(2).

to consumer protection.[58] All that can be said with any confidence is that whether any given rule possesses the necessary character will depend, in the absence of express indications, on the proper construction of the rule.[59]

25–041 Finally, it must be emphasised that Article 3(3) only restricts the application of the chosen law to the extent that the chosen law conflicts with relevant mandatory rules. To the extent that application of these rules is not prejudiced, the chosen law holds sway.[60]

25–042 **Mandatory rules of English law.** Article 7(2) provides that nothing in the Convention restricts the application of the rules of the forum in a situation where they are mandatory irrespective of the law which would otherwise apply to the contract.[61] The provision thus preserves the application of any English rules possessing this character, the English court being empowered to give effect to those rules so as to override the law chosen by the parties. Rules envisaged as applicable through the provision are, notably, rules on cartels, competition and restrictive practices, consumer protection[62] and certain rules concerning carriage.[63] Mandatory rules in this sense are rules which cannot be derogated from even in an international transaction, as opposed to mandatory rules which are the subject of Article 3(3) where what are relevant are rules which are domestically, but not internationally, mandatory.[64] In the context of sale, the principal subject-matter of this category of mandatory rules is likely to be rules providing for consumer protection.[65] Thus, for example, provisions of the Unfair Contract Terms Act 1977 may be mandatory to the extent indicated by the statute[66] even in an international transaction. Further, in the Unfair Terms in Consumer Contracts Regulations 1999,[67] it is specifically provided that the Regulations apply notwithstanding any contract term which applies or purports to apply the law of a non-Member State,[68] if the

---

[58] Unless applicable by virtue of the special provision in Art. 5.
[59] See *Ingmar GB Ltd v Eaton Leonard Technologies Inc.* (C–39/98) [2000] E.C.R. I–9305. *cf. The Hollandia* [1983] 1 A.C. 565.
[60] But presumably contracting parties could avoid the application of mandatory rules by not pleading or proving them in the event of litigation. See above, para.25–029.
[61] A similar power exists under traditional English law: see, *e.g. The Hollandia*, above, para.25–006. For discussion of Art. 7(2), see Knofel [1999] J.B.L. 239.
[62] See below, paras 25–094—25–118.
[63] Giuliano-Lagarde Report, p.28. The UK entered a reservation to Art. 7(1) which provides for the application (in the discretion of the court) of the mandatory rules of a country with which situation has a close connection even if that country is neither the country of the applicable law or the law of the forum: see Contracts (Applicable Law) Act 1990, s.2(2); Rome Convention, Art. 22(1)(a), above, para.25–038.
[64] Above, paras 25–038—25–040.
[65] Giuliano-Lagarde Report, p.38. Other examples given are rules on cartels, competition and restrictive practices.
[66] Above, para.13–101. Below, paras 25–094—25–100.
[67] SI 1999/2083, revoking and replacing Unfair Terms in Consumer Contracts Regulations 1994, SI 1994/3159, which originally implemented Council Directive 1993/13/EEC of April 5, 1993 on unfair terms in consumer contracts ([1993] O.J. L95/29). For detailed discussion of the Regulations, see above, paras 13–103, 14–030—14–040.
[68] *i.e.* a State which is not a contracting party to the EEA agreement: reg.3(1).

contract has a close connection with the territories of the Member States.[69] A virtually identical anti-avoidance formula is to be found in the Consumer Protection (Distance Selling) Regulations 2000.[70] In contrast, the Sale and Supply of Goods to Consumers Regulations 2002 make no specific provision for anti-avoidance,[71] the view having been taken that the issue could be dealt with through the relevant provisions of the Unfair Contract Terms Act 1977, a view which gives rise to no little difficulty as discussed later in this chapter.[72]

Public policy. A further general restriction on the effect of a choice of law is to be found in Article 16 according to which the application of a rule of the law of any country specified by the Convention "may be refused only if such application is manifestly incompatible with the public policy ('ordre public') of the forum." Public policy in this context is said by the Giuliano-Lagarde Report to include "community public policy".[73] In the context of the Brussels Convention on Jurisdiction and the Enforcement of Judgments in Civil and Commercial Matters, the European Court of Justice has held that, although it is for national law to define the content of the public policy of a Contracting State, the limits of the concept are a matter of interpretation of the Convention, which limits, therefore, are subject to review by the European Court of Justice.[74] It is likely that the European Court of Justice will adopt the same general approach to the concept of public policy as it appears in the Rome Convention.[75] Insertion of the word "manifestly" is designed to indicate that there must be special grounds, of an exceptional nature for the public policy exclusion to apply.[76] Further, the concept cannot be applied to a foreign law in the abstract. It may only be resorted to when a provision of foreign law, if applied to an actual case, would offend English public policy.[77] Although the Convention would not seem to 25–043

[69] Reg.9. For more detailed discussion of this provision see below, paras 25–101—25–106.
[70] SI 2000/2334, as amended by SI 2004/2095 and SI 2005/1689 implementing Directive 1997/7/EC of the European Parliament and of the Council of May 20, 1997 on the protection of consumers in respect of distance contracts ([1997] O.J. L144/19). For discussion of the formula, see below, paras 25–107—25–110.
[71] SI 2002/3045, implementing Directive 1999/44/EC of the European Parliament and of the Council of May 25, 1999 on certain aspects of the sale of consumer goods and associated guarantees ([1999] O.J. L171/12). The Directive did contain a specific anti-avoidance provision in Art. 7(2). See below, para.25–112.
[72] See below, paras 25–111—25–118.
[73] Giuliano-Lagarde Report, p.38.
[74] *Krombach v Bamberski* (C–7/98) [2000] E.C.R. I–1935; [2001] Q.B. 709; *Regie National des Usines Renault SA v Maxicar SA* (C–38/98) [2000] E.C.R. I–2973. These cases establish that fundamental principles of human rights, as contained in the European Convention on Human Rights, may inform the content of community public policy, a view which has been accepted in England (see *Maronier v Larmer* [2002] EWCA Civ. 603; [2003] Q.B. 603). *Cf. Oppenheimer v Cattermole* [1976] A.C. 249; *Kuwait Airways Corp. v Iraqi Airways Co. (Nos 4 and 5)* [2002] UKHL 19; [2002] 2 A.C. 883 at [15]–[29], [111]–[118], [135]–[149]. See generally Peruzzetto in Meeusen, Pertegas and Straetmans (eds), *op. cit.*, pp.343–361; Medianis, 30 E.L.Rev. 95 (2005). And see below, para.25–119.
[75] See Plender, *op. cit.*, paras 9–24.
[76] Giuliano-Lagarde Report, p.38.
[77] *ibid.*

affect the content of English public policy as developed by the common law in any specific way,[78] the terms of Article 16 require abstention from an over-zealous application of the concept.[79]

25–044 **"Certain consumer contracts".** Article 5 of the Rome Convention makes special provision for consumer contracts as defined therein, which may include, but is not limited to, certain contracts for the sale of goods.[80] The philosophy of the Article is that application of the general rules of the Convention to this type of contract could fail to give effect to considerations of social policy which might be thought to be relevant in this field, and which involve, very broadly, the need to protect the consumer from the consequences of the latter's unequal bargaining power even at an international level.[81] The ensuing discussion focuses, first, on general questions raised by Article 5 and on the application of the provision in the context of traditional mechanisms for concluding contracts[82] and, secondly, on the specific application of the Article to contracts concluded "on-line".[83]

25–045 **Contracts subject to Article 5.** A contract falls within Article 5 if it is "a contract the object of which is the supply of goods or services to a person ("the consumer") for a purpose which can be regarded as being outside his trade or profession, or a contract for the provision of credit for that object."[84] The imprecision of this definition (which was deliberate[85]) gives rise to a number of difficulties even in relation to its application to a contract of sale of goods, though it is designed to include both cash and credit sales.[86] It is most likely that the European Court of Justice will try to

---

[78] Below, para.25–119. See Dicey and Morris, *op. cit.*, paras 32–227—32–238.
[79] Giuliano-Lagarde Report, p.38. See also *Re COLT Telecom Group Plc* [2002] EWHC 2815 (Ch); [2003] B.P.I.R. 324; *Tekron Resources Ltd v Guinea Investment Co. Ltd* [2003] EWHC 2577 (Comm); [2004] 2 Lloyd's Rep. 26. For the relationship between public policy and illegality see below, para.25–119.
[80] See Dicey and Morris, *op. cit.*, paras 33–001—33–046; Plender, *op. cit.*, Ch.7; Anton, *op. cit.*, pp.344–347; Lasok and Stone, *op. cit.*, pp.380–384; Hartley in *Contract Conflicts, op. cit.*, Ch.6; Morse, 41 I.C.L.Q. 1–11 (1992); Morse, 2 Ybk.Eur. Law 107 at 134–138 (1982). For the application of Art. 5 to consumer contracts concluded "online", see below, paras 25–049—25–053. *Cf.* Commission Proposal, Art. 5.
[81] Giuliano-Lagarde Report, p.23. As to formal validity of such contracts see Art. 9(5) discussed below, para.25–086.
[82] Below, paras 25–045—25–048.
[83] Below, paras 25–049—25–053.
[84] Art. 5(1).
[85] Giuliano-Lagarde Report, p.23. A more precise definition was avoided so as not to introduce conflict with the various definitions of such contracts given in national legislation: *ibid. Cf.* Unfair Contract Terms Act 1977, s.12(1), above, paras 13–071—13–079. See also Unfair Terms in Consumer Contracts Regulations 1999 (above, para.14–030), regs 3(1), 4, 5 and Sch.2; Consumer Protection (Distance Selling) Regulations 2000 (above, paras 15–054—15–059), regs 2–6; Sale and Supply of Goods to Consumers Regulations 2002 (above, paras 14–008—14–028), reg.2. See below, paras 25–090—25–118).
[86] Giuliano-Lagarde Report, p.23. Sales of "securities" are excluded, *ibid.* The provision applies to a contract for the supply of services unless (Art. 5(4)(b)) the services are to be supplied to the consumer exclusively in a country other than that in which he has his habitual residence. A contract of carriage is excluded from Art. 5

resolve such definitional problems by reference to an autonomous interpretation of the terminology[87] and in so doing may well have regard to the observation in the Giuliano-Lagarde Report that the scope of the Article "should be interpreted in the light of its purpose which is to protect the weaker party and in accordance with other international instruments with the same purpose such as the Judgments Convention".[88]

First, the text indicates that a sale of goods to a consumer must be for a purpose which can be regarded as being outside the consumer's trade or profession. Thus Article 5 will not "apply to contracts made by traders, manufacturers or persons in the exercise of a profession (doctors, for example) who buy equipment . . . for that trade or profession".[89] But what if such a person acts partly within and partly outside his trade or profession? Here it is suggested that the contract falls within Article 5 only if the buyer acts primarily outside his trade or profession.[90] Secondly, what happens if a buyer of goods acted outside his trade or profession, but the seller did not know of this? The suggestion is made that in such circumstances the situation falls outside Article 5 if, taking into account all the circumstances, the seller should not reasonably have known it.[91] Thus if 25–046

(Art. 5(4)(a)), but the Article *does* apply to a contract which for an inclusive price provides for a combination of travel and accommodation (Art. 5(5)). See Giuliano-Lagarde Report, pp.24–25; Plender, *op. cit.*, paras 7–26—7–27.

[87] Above, para.25–018; Dicey and Morris, *op. cit.*, para.33–04; Plender, *op. cit.*, paras 7–11—7–12. See following note.

[88] Giuliano-Lagarde Report, p.23. "Judgments Convention" refers to the Brussels Convention on Jurisdiction and the Enforcement of Judgments in Civil and Commercial Matters 1968, as amended (above, paras 25–016, 25–018), Art. 13 of which contains a specific rule about jurisdiction in relation to consumer contracts. For interpretation of Art. 13, see *Société Bertrande v Paul Ott K.G.* (C–150/77) [1978] E.C.R. 1431; *Shearson Lehman Hutton Inc. v TVB Treuhandgesellschaft för Vermögensverwaltung und Beteiligungen mbH* (C–89/91) [1993] E.C.R. 1–139; *Brenner v Dean Witter Reynolds Inc.* (C–318/93) [1994] E.C.R. 1–4275; *Benincasa v Dentalkit Srl* (C–269/95) [1997] E.C.R. I–3767; *Mietz v Intership Yachting Sneek BV* [1999] E.C.R. I–2277; *Gabriel v Schlank & Schick GmbH* (C–96/00) [2002] E.C.R. I–6367; *Engler v Janus Versand GmbH* (C–27/02) [2005] E.C.R. I–481; *Gruber v Bay Wa AG* (C–464/01) [2005] E.C.R. I–439; [2006] 2 Q.B. 204. See also *Standard Bank London Ltd v Apostolakis (No.1)* [2000] I.L.Pr. 766; *Standard Bank London Ltd v Apostolakis (No.2)* [2001] Lloyd's Rep. Bank 240 (contract held to be consumer contract); *cf. Standard Bank of London Ltd v Apostolakis* [2003] I.L.Pr. 499 (on same facts Greek court holds contract *not* to be a consumer contract); Dicey and Morris, *op. cit.*, paras 11–319—11–326. Special rules, formulated somewhat differently to the provisions of the Brussels Convention, are also to be found in Arts 15–17 of Council Regulation 44/2001/EC of December 22, 2001 on jurisdiction and the recognition and enforcement of judgments in civil and commercial matters ([2001] O.J. L12/1): see above, para.25–016 and below, para.25–051. *Cf.* Commission Proposal, Art. 5(2).

[89] Giuliano-Lagarde Report, *ibid.*

[90] *ibid. Gruber v Bay Wa AG* (C–464/01) [2005] E.C.R. I–439; [2006] Q.B. 204 (person who concluded a contract for the sale of goods intended for purposes which were in part within and in part outside his trade or profession could not rely on the special rules applicable to consumers in Arts 13–15 of the Brussels Convention (above, n.88) unless the trade or professional purpose is so limited as to be negligible in the overall context of the sale, the fact that the private element is predominant being irrelevant in that respect).

[91] Giuliano-Lagarde Report, *ibid.*

the buyer "holds himself out as a professional, *e.g.* by ordering goods which might well be used in his trade or profession on his professional paper the good faith of the other party is protected and the case will not be governed by Article 5".[92] Thirdly, the wording of the provision contains no positive (or indeed any) indication that the seller must be acting in the course of his trade or profession in relation to a transaction with a buyer. No definite conclusion can be reached on this point. According to a majority of delegations participating in the drafting of the Convention, Article 5 will "*normally*"[93] only apply if the seller acts in the course of his trade or profession. Subject to the qualification of "normally" which begs, to say the least, several questions, this majority view accords with common sense. But even if it is correct, it may need to be refined to enable Article 5 to apply to a situation where although, for example, the seller acted outside his trade or profession, the buyer was unaware of that fact and could not have been reasonably expected to have been aware of it and/or the seller led the buyer to believe (perhaps by "holding out") that he was acting in the course of his trade or profession.

25–047 **Effect of choice of law by parties.** The effect of a choice of law by the parties which satisfies Article 3 of the Convention is limited when the contract falls within the definition contained in Article 5. Such a choice of law shall not have the result of depriving the consumer (buyer) of the protection afforded to him by the mandatory rules of the law of the country in which he has his habitual residence if any *one* of the three conditions set out in the indents to Article 5(2) are satisfied.

25–048 **The three conditions.** The first condition is where, in the country of the consumer's (buyer's) habitual residence,[94] the conclusion of the contract was preceded by a specific invitation or by advertising and the consumer had taken in that country all the steps necessary on his part for the conclusion of the contract. "Specific invitation" appears to connote an invitation which is specific to the buyer bringing the claim and it would be relatively easy, where the contract is concluded by a traditional method,[95] to determine whether that invitation has been addressed to a buyer in the country where the buyer is habitually resident. The reference to "advertising"[96] is more problematic, since it is unclear whether the seller must have

---

[92] *ibid*. *Cf. Gruber v Bay Wa AG*, above, where it was held that Arts 13–15 of the Brussels Convention were not applicable even if the contract did serve a negligible trade or professional purpose if the party claiming to be a consumer had given the impression to the other party that he was acting for trade or professional purposes.
[93] *ibid*., italics added.
[94] As to the meaning of which see below, paras 25–056, 25–062. For the role of these conditions when the parties have not chosen the governing law, see below, para.25–067.
[95] As to contracts concluded "online", see below, paras 25–049—25–053.
[96] *cf.* The similar phraseology in Art. 13(3) of the Brussels Convention (above, n.88): see *Rayner v Davies* [2002] EWCA Civ. 1880; [2003] 1 All E.R. (Comm) 394; *Standard Bank London v Apostolakis (No.2)* [2001] Lloyd's Rep Bank. 240. Contrast the different and more broadly worded provision contained in Art. 15(1)(c) of the Council Regulation (*ibid.*) and that of the Commission Proposal, Art. 5(2). And see below, para.25–051, n.20.

intended to advertise to the buyer in the latter's country of habitual residence. The Giuliano-Lagarde Report suggests that such an intention is necessary,[97] a view which, if correct, places a quite stringent limitation in the scope of the provision. Doubt also surrounds the requirement that the buyer must have taken in the country of his habitual residence "all the steps necessary on his part for the conclusion of the contract".[98] These words were adopted to "avoid the classical problem of determining the place where the contract was concluded."[99] But it is not clear from this whether the words refer to legal or factual steps. The Giuliano-Lagarde Report states that "'steps'—includes *inter alia* writing or any action taken in consequence of an offer or advertisement",[1] which seems to indicate that only the necessary factual steps are referred to so that it matters not that such factual steps are deemed, as a matter of law, to occur in a country other than that in which the buyer habitually resides.[2] The second condition is where the other party (seller) or his agent received the consumer's (buyer's) order in the country where the buyer is habitually resident. For this purpose "agent" "is intended to cover all persons acting on behalf of the trader"[3] so that it does not seem necessary that a strict legal relationship of principal and agent need exist. Further, although there is considerable overlap between this condition and the first condition discussed above the overlap is not complete since the former "applies in situations where the consumer has addressed himself to the stand of a foreign firm at a fair or exhibition taking place in the consumer's country or to a permanent branch or agency of a foreign firm established in the consumer's country even though the foreign firm has not advertised in the consumer's country in a way covered"[4] by the latter consideration. The third condition is expressly limited to contracts for the sale of goods: if the consumer (buyer) travelled from the country of his habitual residence to another country and there gave his order the limitations on the effect of an express choice of law imposed by Article 5(2) will apply provided the consumer's journey was arranged by the seller for the purpose of inducing the consumer to buy. This condition is intended to deal with the problem of "cross-border excursion selling", for example, a situation where a store owner in country X arranges one-day bus trips for consumers in neighbouring country Y with the main purpose of inducing consumers to buy in his store.[5] Such practices are, it is thought, more common on the European continent than in the United Kingdom.[6]

Application to contract concluded "on-line". Article 5 was drafted at a time when the impact of the internet on the conclusion of contracts was not known.[7] It is now common practice for a consumer (buyer) to contract with 25–049

---

97 Giuliano-Lagarde Report, p.24, criticised in Lasok and Stone, *op. cit.*, p.383.
98 *cf.* the language of Unfair Contract Terms Act 1977, s.27(2)(b), below, para.25–098.
99 Giuliano-Lagarde Report, p.24.
1 *ibid.*
2 As might be the case in relation to offer and acceptance; see below, para.25–079.
3 Giuliano-Lagarde Report, p.24.
4 *ibid.*
5 *ibid.*
6 *ibid.*; Plender, *op. cit.*, para.7–20.
7 See North, 50 I.C.L.Q. 477 at 503 (2001).

a seller over the internet so that it is necessary, assuming the contract so concluded is within the definition contained in Article 5, to consider, albeit somewhat speculatively, how Article 5 might apply to such transactions.[8] Principally, the discussion revolves around the question as to how the first two conditions described above[9] apply in this context.[10] The assumption is made that the eventual contract between seller and buyer is on the seller's standard terms which contain an express choice of the law of a country other than that in which the buyer is habitually resident.[11]

25–050 As to the first condition, it would seem uncontroversial that a specific invitation can be addressed by the seller to the consumer by electronic mail. However, the provision requires the specific invitation to precede the contract in the country of the consumer's habitual residence which appears to suggest that the consumer must receive the specific invitation in the country of his habitual residence, and raises, in turn, the question of when and where a communication by electronic mail is received for these purposes. It is suggested that such a communication is received when it is accessed by the consumer and that it is irrelevant that the communication is earlier received and stored on a server, prior to being accessed by the consumer.[12] Where the consumer accesses his electronic mail in the country where he has his habitual residence, then it will be clear that he has received the specific invitation in that country. Difficulty arises, however, when the consumer accesses his electronic mail, as he might well do, for example, when travelling, from a country other than that in which he habitually resides. Common sense suggests that the first indent to Article 5(2) should continue to be applicable, since it is hard to justify relieving the seller of the legal risk otherwise placed upon him by this chance happen-

---

[8] See Plender, *op. cit.*, para.7–19; Dicey and Morris, *op. cit.*, paras 33–011—33–014; Murray, in Edwards and Waelde (eds), *Law & the Internet* (2000), p.17; Niemann, 5 Communications Law 99 (2000); Kronke in Boele-Woelki and Kessedjian (eds) *Internet: Which Court Decides? Which Law Applies?* (1998), p.65; Schu, 5 *International Journal of Law and Information Technology* 192 (1997). On jurisdiction in respect of online consumer contracts, see Øren, *International Jurisdiction and Consumer Contracts* (2004); Øren, 52 I.C.L.Q. 665 (2003).

[9] Above, para.25–048.

[10] The terms of the third condition appear to make it clear that it cannot apply to an internet contract: see above, para.25–048.

[11] In practice standard terms are likely to be subject to the law of the country in which the customer is likely to reside, and therefore, at least for major commercial operators, the chosen law will differ, depending upon which country or state this is. See, *e.g.* standard terms of amazon.com, containing an express choice of the law of the State of Washington, excluding its rules of the conflict of laws (*www.amazon.com/exec/obidos/tg/browse/*); the standard terms of amazon.co.uk, containing an express choice of English law (*www.amazon.co.uk/ exec/obidos/tg/browse/*); the standard terms of amazon.fr, containing an express choice of French law (*www.amazon.fr/exec/obidos/tg/browse/*).

[12] Schu, *op. cit.*, pp.210–211. *Cf.* Directive 2000/31/EC of the European Parliament and Council of June 8, 2000 on certain legal aspects of information society services, in particular electronic commerce ("Directive on electronic commerce") ([2000] O.J. L178/1), Art. 11(1) and (3) and the UK implementing legislation, the Electronic Commerce (EC Directive) Regulations 2002 (SI 2002/2013), reg. 11(2)(a). See below, para.25–051, n.16.

stance. Such an outcome is, however, impossible to reconcile with the actual wording of the indent. The most that can be said is that a bold interpretation of it might enable the court to conclude that if the consumer did not act immediately on the invitation, retained the communication and then re-accessed it in the country of his habitual residence that circumstance could constitute receipt for the purposes of the provision under discussion.[13] It could also be argued that the provision creates an evidential presumption that the buyer did receive the specific invitation in the country of his habitual residence which presumption it is incumbent on the seller to rebut.[14]

A second major difficulty with the first condition in Article 5(2) in this context relates to advertisements and websites. There can be little doubt that a website which seeks to ply the seller's wares can constitute advertising for the purposes of the provision.[15] The problem is that such an advertisement can be accessed from most, if not all, parts of the world, thus opening up the seller to potential liability under a wide variety of foreign laws. On one view, it can be argued that the seller should bear the risk of a choice of law in the contract being overridden by the mandatory rules of the consumer's habitual residence, since the seller must be aware of the potential reach of his website and because bearing this risk is part of the cost of doing business on the internet, which must be balanced against the commercial benefits of doing business in this manner.[16] A somewhat narrower interpretation of the provision is, however, possible. This involves drawing an analogy with an example suggested in the Giuliano-Lagarde 25–051

---

[13] *ibid.*
[14] *ibid.*
[15] Plender, *op. cit.*, para.7–18; Dicey and Morris, *op. cit.*, para.33–011.
[16] See Dicey and Morris, *op. cit.*, para.33–011. *Cf. King v Lewis* [2004] EWCA Civ. 1329; [2005] I.L.Pr. 185; *Dow Jones & Co. Inc. v Gutnick* [2002] HCA 56; (2003) 210 C.L.R. 575. Directive 2000/31/EC of the European Parliament and Council of June 8, 2000 on certain legal aspects of information society services, in particular electronic commerce ("Directive on electronic commerce") ([2000] O.J. L178/1), and the UK implementing legislation, the Electronic Commerce (EC Directive) Regulations 2002 (SI 2002/2013) are generally thought to support a "country of origin" principle for regulating electronic commerce, a principle which might be thought to be inconsistent with interpreting Art. 5(2) in favour of the consumer. However, it is submitted that this Directive has no bearing on the matter under discussion. This is because (a) the Directive specifically states that it does not establish additional rules on private international law (Art. 1(4) and Recital 23); (b) its provisions are explicitly expressed not to apply to the freedom of the parties to choose the law applicable to their contract and to consumer contracts (Art. 3(3) and Annex); (c) Recital 55 states that "this Directive cannot have the result of depriving the consumer of the protection afforded to him by the mandatory rules relating to contractual obligations of the law of the Member State in which he has his habitual residence". Although the 2002 Regulations do not reproduce Art. 1(4) and Recital 23 of the Directive they do reproduce Art. 3(3) of, and the Annex to, the Directive (see reg. 4(4) and Schedule). Accordingly, the Regulations do not bear on the matter under discussion. The effect of the Regulations on the rules of the English conflict of laws more generally is controversial (see Fawcett, Harris and Bridge, *op. cit.*, paras 21–15—21–34). On the country of origin principle, see Thunken, 51 I.C.L.Q. 909 (2002); Hornle, 12 International Journal of Law and Information Technology 333 (2004); 54 I.C.L.Q. 89 (2005).

Report of a consumer who responds to an advertisement appearing in an American publication which has been sold in Germany. The Report states that this situation would not fall within Article 5 unless the advertisement had appeared in special editions of the publication intended for distribution in European countries.[17] This remark may be construed to indicate that the condition under discussion is only applicable if the consumer, either individually or more generally as a consumer, has been "targeted" in the country of his habitual residence by the seller.[18] It cannot be said that this interpretation will be particularly easy to apply in the context of sales through websites which are, in principle, accessible throughout the world. If, however, the seller specifies that the site is only addressed to a particular country or countries, the conclusion can perhaps be drawn that consumers habitually resident in those countries are covered by Article 5, whereas consumers habitually resident elsewhere are not.[19] The same conclusion could be drawn if the material on the website is expressed in a language which is readily understood in relatively few countries. If there is no country based limitation stated on the website or if the material on it is expressed in a language which is readily understood in many countries (for example, English) then it will be hard to conclude that the seller was targeting any particular consumer or group of consumers, but, rather, was directing his activities towards consumers worldwide. In such a case, it seems appropriate to regard the seller rather than the consumer as bearing the legal risk and to conclude that the situation falls within Article 5.[20] It is tentatively suggested that this interpretation should be adopted, not least because it attempts to achieve an appropriate balance between the competing interests of consumers and sellers.

25–052 The last requirement of this condition is that the consumer takes in the country of his habitual residence all the steps necessary on his part for the conclusion of the contract. In relation to a contract concluded by electronic mail, this will involve the consumer sending relevant communications from

---

[17] Giuliano-Lagarde Report, p.24.

[18] Plender, *op. cit.*, para.7–18—7–19. *Cf. King v Lewis* [2004] EWCA Civ. 1329; [2005] I.L.Pr. 185.

[19] The seller may take technical steps to block access from particular countries or structure the transaction in such a way as to ascertain the consumer's habitual residence before any contract is concluded: see Gringras, *Laws of the Internet* (2nd ed.), pp.66–68.

[20] Such an interpretation would produce consistency with Art. 15(3) of the Council Regulation 44/2001/EC of December 22, 2001 on jurisdiction and the recognition and enforcement of judgments in civil and commercial matters, above, para.25–016 ([2001] O.J. L12/1), which provides that the rules of the Regulation concerned with consumers apply, *inter alia*, if "the contract has been concluded with a person who pursues commercial or professional activities in the Member State of the consumer's domicile or, by any means, directs such activities to that Member State or to several States including that Member State, and the contract falls within the scope of those activities". See Commission Proposal, Art. 5(2) which would allow Art. 5 to apply where a professional directs its activities to the Member State where the consumer is habitually resident or to several States including that Member State. And see Basedow in Meeusen, Pertegas and Straetmans (eds), *op. cit.*, pp.286–288. *Cf. King v Lewis* [2004] EWCA Civ. 1329; [2005] I.L.Pr. 185. And see Plender, *op. cit.*, para.7–19.

the country of his habitual residence to the seller.[21] In relation to a response by the consumer to an advertisement on the seller's website, this, normally, will involve the consumer indicating his agreement to the terms and conditions by "clicking" on an appropriate icon on the relevant site which action must take place in the country of his habitual residence.[22]

The second condition in Article 5(2) also causes considerable difficulty in the case of contracts for the sale of goods concluded by electronic methods, since it requires that the other party or his agent receive the consumer's order in the country in which the consumer is habitually resident and doubts may arise, first, as to the meaning of "agent" in this context and, secondly, as to where the order is "received". As to the first issue, it is submitted that neither a web server nor a passive third party service provider can be regarded as an agent of the seller for these purposes.[23] A server can be located anywhere and is a communications medium, the location of which is not necessarily related in any way to the seller's business. A passive third party service provider merely provides a technical mechanism by which the seller can pass information, etc. to potential customers. If, however, the third party service provider took action on behalf of the seller, such as processing orders, it might be possible to say that the provider was a "person acting on behalf of the trader"[24] and to conclude, in these circumstances, that the provider was an agent.[25] As to the second issue, it appears, at least technically, that an order by electronic mail is "received" by the seller or his agent at the server where the mail is stored and that an order addressed to a website is "received" by the seller or his agent at the server on which the website is established.[26] If this is the meaning of "received" for the purposes of the provision under discussion, the order will be received in the country of the consumer's habitual residence only if the relevant server is located in that country. This could produce unfortunate consequences, for example, in a case in which a consumer, habitually resident in England, approaches an English agent of a seller based, *e.g.* in Germany, and places his order on a website hosted for the agent by a third party in Peru. If it is concluded that the order is received in Peru, then the consumer could not rely on the mandatory rules of English law to the extent that they are more favourable to him than the rules of the foreign law expressly applicable to the contract.[27] To avoid such a result, it is suggested, though unsupported by any relevant authority, that the country in which the order is "received" in relation to this condition should be construed to mean the country in which the physical place of 25–053

---

[21] See Schu, *op. cit.*, p.215.
[22] Niemann, *op. cit.*, p.100; Schu, *ibid.*
[23] Chissick and Kelman, *Electronic Commerce: Law and Practice* (3rd ed.), para.4–35; Niemann, *ibid.* Nor, it is submitted should so-called "electronic agents" be treated as agents for these purposes: *cf.* Weitzenboeck, 9 *International Journal of Law and Information Technology* 204 (2001); Øren, 9 *International Journal of Law and Information Technology* 249 (2001).
[24] Giuliano-Lagarde Report, p.24.
[25] Chissick and Kelman, *op. cit.*, para.4–34.
[26] Schu, *op. cit.*, p.216.
[27] The example assumes that the first condition in Art. 5(2) is inapplicable.

business of the seller or his agent from which the relevant server is accessed by the seller or his agent, as the case may be, is situated, and that if one of those places is in the country where the consumer is habitually resident, then the requirements of the provision should be regarded as being satisfied, irrespective of whether the relevant server is also located in the same country.[28]

25–054 **Mandatory rules.** Assuming the contract falls within the definition contained in Article 5 and assuming one of the conditions discussed in the previous paragraphs exists, a choice of law by the parties shall not have the result of "depriving" the consumer (buyer) of the protection afforded to him by the mandatory rules of the law of the country of his habitual residence. "Mandatory rules" in this context are used in the definitional sense of Article 3(3),[29] *i.e.* are rules of the law of that country which "cannot be derogated from by contract", and it would not seem to be necessary that the rules are also rules which apply "whatever the law applicable to the contract."[30] Further, it would seem that the nature of these mandatory rules must be further delimited by reference to the context of Article 5 in that they should be concerned with consumer protection.[31] However, the relationship between the chosen law and these mandatory rules is not entirely clear. If, for example, the rules of the chosen law are less protective of the buyer than the mandatory rules of the law of the buyer's habitual residence, it seems fair to say that the buyer would be deprived, by application of the chosen law, of the protection of these mandatory rules. But what if the chosen law is more protective of the buyer than the law of his habitual residence?[32] If the chosen law is applied it is hard to say that the buyer is "deprived" of the protection of the mandatory rules of the law of his habitual residence, since he is better off than he would have been had these rules been applied. It is therefore submitted that the proper interpretation of Article 5(2) is that it enables a buyer to rely on the mandatory rules of the law of his habitual residence if they are more favourable to him than the chosen law or on the chosen law if it is more favourable to him than are the mandatory rules of the law of his habitual residence.[33] The law of the habitual residence thus defines the minimum protection available, but it does not necessarily define the maximum. The submission does not necessarily resolve the difficulties in ascertaining, in any particular case, which set of rules is most favourable to the buyer but is, it is suggested, preferable to allowing the buyer to rely, cumulatively, on the chosen law and on the mandatory rules of his habitual residence.[34] The policy of Article 5(2) would appear to be that the

---

[28] *cf.* Directive on electronic commerce, above, para.25–051, n.16, Recital 19 and Art. 11(1); Electronic Commerce (EC Directive) Regulations 2002, reg.11(2)(a); *Menashe Business Mercantile Ltd v William Hill Organization Ltd* [2002] EWCA Civ. 1702; [2003] 1 W.L.R. 1462.
[29] Above, para.25–038.
[30] *cf.* Art. 7(1) which does not have the force of law in the UK: Contracts (Applicable Law) Act 1990, s.2(2), above, para.25–038.
[31] Morse, 2 Ybk.Eur. Law 107 at 136 (1982).
[32] *ibid.*, at pp.136–137; Plender, *op. cit.*, para.7–21.
[33] See preceding note.
[34] *cf.* Philip in *Contract Conflicts, op. cit.*, pp.81 and 99.

consumer (buyer) should not be deprived of the minimum protection of the law of his habitual residence. If the chosen law gives him greater protection so be it, but there seems to be no justification for giving him double protection.

Lastly it should be noted that, independently of Article 5, Article 7(2) enables the court to restrict the scope of the law chosen to govern a consumer contract through the application of mandatory rules of English law in a situation where these rules apply irrespective of the law applicable to the contract.[35] In contrast to the mandatory rules applicable through Article 5(2), these mandatory rules need not relate to consumer protection.[36] **25–055**

Habitual residence. This concept is not defined in the Convention[37] and in due course the European Court may have to provide an autonomous meaning of the term so as to avoid the lack of uniformity which may result **25–056**

---

[35] *cf.* Lasok and Stone, *op. cit.*, p.385 who suggest that the exhaustive character of Art. 5 impliedly excludes application of Art. 7, including Art. 7(2). Art. 7(1) does not have the force of law in the UK: above, para.25–038.

[36] For examples of consumer protection legislation which might be mandatory for the purposes of Art. 7(2), see Consumer Protection (Cancellation of Contracts Concluded away from Business Premises) Regulations 1987, SI 1987/2117, as amended by SI 1988/958 (above para.14–045) implementing Council Directive 1985/577/EEC of December 20, 1985 to protect the consumer in respect of contracts negotiated away from business premises ([1985] O.J. L372/31, see also *Travel Vac SL v Sanchis* (C–423/97) [1999] E.C.R. I–2195); Unfair Terms in Consumer Contracts Regulations 1999, SI 1999/2083, as amended by SI 2001/1186 (above, paras 14–030—14–040 and below, paras 25–101—25–106) implementing Council Directive 1993/ 13/EEC of April 5, 1993 on unfair terms in consumer contracts ([1993] O.J. L95/29, see also *Oceano Grupo Editorial SA v Rocio Muriano Quintero* (C–240–244/98) [2000] E.C.R. I–4941); and *Commission v Spain* (C–70/03) [2004] E.C.R. I–7999; Consumer Protection (Distance Selling) Regulations 2000, SI 2000/2334, as amended by SI 2004/2095 and SI 2005/689 (above paras 14–053—14–008–059 and below paras 25–107—25–110) implementing Directive 1997/7/EC of the European Parliament and Council of May 20, 1997 on the protection of consumers in respect of distance contracts ([1997] O.J. L144/19); Sale and Supply of Goods to Consumers Regulations 2002 (SI 2002/3045, above, paras 14–028 and below, paras 25–111—25–118) implementing Directive 1999/44/E.C. of the European Parliament and Council of May 25, 1999 on certain aspects of the sale of consumer goods and associated guarantees ([1999] O.J. L171/12); see also Enterprise Act 2002, Pt. 8 repealing and replacing Stop Now Orders (EC Directive) Regulations 2001 (SI 2001/1422) (above, paras 14–040—14–059) implementing Directive 1998/27/EC of the European Parliament and Council of May 19, 1998 on injunctions for the protection of consumers' interests ([1998] O.J. L166/51); Regulation 2006/2004 of the European Parliament and of the Council of October 27, 2004 on co-operation between national authorities responsible for the enforcement of consumer protection laws (the regulation on consumer protection cooperation) [2004] O.J. L364/1, above, para.14–136); Directive 2005/29/EC of the European Parliament and of the Council of May 11, 2005 concerning unfair business-to-consumer commercial practices in the internal market and amending Council Directive 84/450/EEC, Directives 97/7/EC, 98/27/EC and 2002/65/EC of the European Parliament and of the Council and Regulation 2006/2004 of the European Parliament and of the Council ("Unfair Commercial Practices Directive") ([2005] O.J. L149/22, para. 14–134) not yet implemented in the UK. See also *Office of Fair Trading v Lloyds TSB Bank Plc* [2006] EWCA Civ. 268; [2006] 1 All E.R. (Comm) 629. See Plender, *op. cit.*, paras 7–28—7–33, 9–14—9–21.

[37] Nor it is discussed in the Giuliano-Lagarde Report.

from divergent national law interpretations.[38] English case-law has not given the concept a consistent definition.[39] It has been stated (in a non-commercial context) that habitual residence refers to a person's abode in a particular country which he has adopted voluntarily and for settled purposes as part of the regular order of his life for the time being whether of short or long duration.[40] Depending on how the concept is interpreted, it may be possible for a consumer (buyer) to be habitually resident in more than one country, a fact which could give rise to further difficulties in the application of Article 5.[41] It has been suggested that in such a case only the law of one habitual residence should apply and that this should be the law of the place having the closest relationship to the contract and its performance, having regard to the circumstances known to or contemplated by the parties at any time before or at the conclusion of the contract.[42] Lastly, it is possible that a person may be without any habitual residence.[43] It is thus conceivable, if, in practice unlikely, that a consumer may have no habitual residence at the time the contract is concluded and so, presumably, in such a situation, the only mandatory rules on which he can rely will be those which might be applicable under Article 7(2) of the Convention.

(c) *Applicable Law in Absence of Choice*

25–057 **The general principle.** Article 4(1) of the Rome Convention provides that "[t]o the extent that the law applicable to the contract has not been chosen in accordance with Article 3, the contract shall be governed by the law of the country with which it is most closely connected".[44] This general

---

[38] *cf. Swaddling v Administration Officer* (C–90/97) [1999] E.C.R. I–1075 (consideration of habitual residence in the context of Council Regulation 1408/71/EEC of June 14, 1971 on the application of social security schemes to employed persons, to self-employed persons and to members of their families moving within the Community ([1971] O.J. L149/366), as amended).

[39] Dicey and Morris, *op. cit.*, paras 6–123—6–126.

[40] *Kapur v Kapur* [1984] F.L.R. 920; *R. v Barnet LBC, ex p. Nilish Shah* [1984] 2 A.C. 309; *Re J (A Minor) (Abduction)* [1990] A.C. 562; *Re M (Minors) (Residence Order: Jurisdiction)* [1993] 1 F.L.R. 495; *Re A (Minors) (Abduction: Habitual Residence)* [1996] 1 All E.R. 24; *Re S. (A Minor) (Custody: Habitual Residence)* [1998] A.C. 750; *Nessa v Chief Adjudication Officer* [1999] 1 W.L.R. 1937; *Mark v Mark* [2005] UKHL 42; [2006] 1 A.C. 98. See also below, para.25–062.

[41] See *Ikimi v Ikimi* [2002] Fam. 72 (where spouses had consistently maintained two matrimonial homes in different countries, they could be habitually resident in both jurisdictions at the same time for the purposes of jurisdiction to grant a divorce under Domicile and Matrimonial Proceedings Act 1973, s.5(2)). See also *Leyvand v Barasch, The Times*, March 23, 2000 (possibility of ordinary residence in two countries at the same time in the context of security for costs).

[42] Plender, *op. cit.*, para.7–24, who relies on Art. 10(a) of the United Nations Convention on the International Sale of Goods, 1980.

[43] See *Hack v Hack* (1976) Fam. Law 177; *Re J. (A Minor)(Abduction)* [1990] 2 A.C. 562; Dicey and Morris, *op. cit.*, para.6–126; Cheshire and North, *op. cit.*, pp.168–169.

[44] See Hill, 53 I.C.L.Q. 325 (2004); Atrill, 53 I.C.L.Q. 549 (2004). The law applicable under Art. 4 must be the law of a country and cannot be a non-national body of rules; (*Halpern v Halpern* [2006] EWHC 603 (Comm). Note the special rule for certain consumer contracts (below, para.25–067) and employment contracts (not discussed in this chapter).

principle is strikingly similar to that which was established in the common law.[45] It should be initially noticed that the above text includes the possibility of *dépéçage*.[46] Allowing Article 4 to operate "to the extent that" a law has not been chosen means that if the parties have made a choice of law in relation to certain aspects of the contract only and have made no choice in regard to other aspects, Article 4 will apply to determine the law applicable to the latter aspects, but the chosen law will govern the former aspects.[47] The second sentence of Article 4(1) extends the concept of *dépéçage* by conceding the possibility that a severable part of the contract which has a closer connection with another country may "by way of exception" be governed by the law of that country though the remaining part or parts of the contract will be governed by the law of the country with which they are most closely connected. According to the Giuliano-Lagarde Report "the words 'by way of exception' . . . are to be interpreted in the sense that the courts must have regard to severance as seldom as possible".[48] In practice, therefore, it would seem that the second sentence of Article 4(1) will be of limited relevance.[49]

Presumptions. Although this general principle is familiar enough to English lawyers, the way in which it is applied is significantly different to that which ultimately prevailed in the common law. This is because Article 4(2)–(4) sets out a series of presumptions which are to be used to determine the law of the country with which the contract is most closely connected.[50] Specific presumptions are established for certain contracts concerning immovables[51] and contracts for the carriage of goods.[52] Article 4(2) establishes a somewhat controversial presumption which will be relevant in sale of goods cases: this is examined in detail below.[53] At the outset, however, it must be noted that the presumptions are, according to Article 4(5), to be disregarded if it appears from the circumstances as a whole that the contract is more closely connected with another country than it is with the country whose law is indicated as applicable pursuant to the presumption. In such circumstances the more closely connected country will supply the applicable law. This provision is also examined in more detail below.[54] 25–058

---

[45] See above, para.25–008.
[46] *cf.* above, para.25–033.
[47] Giuliano-Lagarde Report, p.20. See *Centrax Ltd v Citibank NA* [1999] 1 All E.R. (Comm.) 557; *XL Insurance Ltd v Owens Corning* [2000] 2 Lloyd's Rep. 500; *American Motorists Insurance Co. v Cellstar Corp.* [2003] EWCA Civ. 206; [2003] I.L.Pr. 370; *Travelers Casualty and Surety Co. of Europe Ltd v Sun Life Assurance Co. of Canada (UK) Ltd* [2004] EWHC 1704 (Comm); [2004] I.L.Pr. 793; *CGU International Insurance Plc v Astrazeneca Insurance Co. Ltd* [2005] EWHC 2755 (Comm).
[48] Giuliano-Lagarde Report, p.23. See *Governor & Company of Bank of Scotland of the Mound v Butcher* (July 28, 1998, CA); *CGU International Insurance Plc v Szabo* [2002] 1 All E.R. (Comm) 83.
[49] See cases cited in preceding note.
[50] Presumptions were eventually abandoned in the common law in *Coast Lines Ltd v Hudig & Veder Chartering NV* [1972] Q.B. 34.
[51] Art. 4(3).
[52] Art. 4(4). See below, para.25–071.
[53] Below, paras 25–059—25–064.
[54] Below, paras 25–065—25–066.

25–059 **The general presumption.** Article 4(2) contains the text of the general presumption which will apply, *inter alia*, to contracts for the sale of goods.[55] Its importance jutifies quotation in full. "Subject to the provisions of paragraph 5 of this Article, it shall be presumed that the contract is most closely connected with the country where the party who is to effect the performance which is characteristic of the contract has, at the time of the conclusion of the contract, his habitual residence, or, in the case of a body corporate or unincorporate, its central administration. However, if the contract is entered into in the course of that party's trade or profession, that country shall be the country in which the principal place of business is situated or, where under the terms of the contract the performance is to be effected through a place of business other than the principal place of business, the country in which that other place of business is situated." Generally, in outline, applying this presumption involves the following process. First the characteristic performance of the relevant contract (sale of goods, insurance, etc.) must be identified. The applicable law will then, presumptively, be the law of the habitual residence or central administration, as the case may be, of the party who is to effect this characteristic performance unless the contract is entered into in the course of the characteristic performer's trade or profession in which case the applicable law will, presumptively, be the law of that party's principal place of business, though where under the terms of the contract performance is to be affected through a place of business other than that principal place the applicable law will, presumptively, be the law of the country in which the other place of business is situated. The various elements of this presumption are examined, in relation to a contract of sale, in the following paragraphs.[56]

25–060 **Characteristic performance.** The concept of the "characteristic performance" of a contract is novel in the law of the Member States of the Community and is probably Swiss in origin.[57] It is based on the notion that when the general concept of contract is broken down into *types* of contract *e.g.* sale, insurance, etc.), the performance of one of the parties will be revealed as the performance which characterises or typifies the relevant contract.[58] The notion of characteristic performance has been much

---

[55] Unless the sale of a consumer contract within the meaning of Art. 5. See below, para.25–067.

[56] For general discussions, see Dicey and Morris, *op. cit.*, paras 32–106—32–125, 33–088—33–114; Cheshire and North, *op. cit.*, pp.564–574; Kaye, *op. cit.*, Ch.9; Plender, *op. cit.*, paras 6–09—6–21; Schultsz, in *Contract Conflicts, op. cit.*, pp.185, 187; Diamond, 216 *Recueil des Cours*, iv, 233 at 273–276 (1986); Lasok and Stone, *op. cit.*, pp.361–364; Morse, 2 Ybk.Eur.L. 107 at 126–131 (1982); Lipstein, 3 Northwestern Journal Int'l L. & Bus. 402 (1981); Jessurun d'Oliveira, 25 Am.J.Comp.L. 303 (1977).

[57] See Lipstein, above, n.56. For present Swiss law see Swiss Private International Law Act 1987 (text in Karrer and Arnold, *Switzerland's Private International Law Act 1987* (1989)), Art. 117. Switzerland it should be noted is also a party to the Hague Convention on the Law Applicable to International Sale of Goods, 1955.

[58] See Lipstein, above, n.56, at p.404.

criticised,[59] but equally extravagant praise has been heaped upon it.[60] This is not the place to discuss the various arguments for or against the concept, but rather the place to determine how a concept which, for better or worse, has become part of English law applies in relation to a contract of sale. The Giuliano-Lagarde Report in analysing the characteristic performance of reciprocal or bilateral contracts in which each party has to perform obligations points out that the performance of "one of the parties in a modern economy usually takes the form of the payment of money. This is not, of course, the characteristic performance of the contract. It is the performance for which payment is due, *i.e.* depending on the type of contract, the delivery of goods, the granting of the right to make use of an item of property, the provision of a service, transport, insurance, banking operations, security, etc., which usually constitutes the centre of gravity and the socio-economic function of the contractual transaction".[61] Thus put, it is tolerably clear that characteristic performance of a contract is a somewhat abstract notion in the sense that it is not the payment of money but the performance for which such payment is due. In the particular context of sale,[62] the passage means that the characteristic performance in a contract of sale is that of the seller since he provides the performance for which the buyer is required to pay the price. This view has been accepted in English decisions.[63] Such a conclusion seems to follow irrespective of the kind of

---

[59] See the references to Lasok and Stone, Morse and Jessurun d'Oliveria in n.56, above. According to the latter, at p.326, the concept is "a reflection of the prejudices of Helvetian hotel-keepers and cuckoo-clock makers, prejudices that will not be shared in countries that export tourists and import cuckoo-clocks . . . ."

[60] See, *e.g.* the Giuliano-Lagarde Report, p.20 (concept "defines connecting factor of the contract from the inside, and not from the outside by elements unrelated to the substance of the obligation such as the nationality of the parties or the place where the contract was concluded . . ." and "refers to the function which the legal relationship involved fulfils in the social life of any country. The concept of characteristic performance essentially links the contract to the social and economic environment of which it will form part").

[61] *ibid*. As to unilateral contracts, see *Waldwiese Stiftung v Lewis* [2004] EWHC 2589 (gift); *Opthalmic Innovations International (United Kingdom) Ltd v Opthalmic Innovations International Inc.* [2004] EWHC 2948 (Ch); [2005] I.L.Pr. 109 (indemnification agreement); *Ark Therapeutics Plc v True North Capital Ltd* [2005] EWHC 1585 (Comm); [2006] 1 All E.R. (Comm) 138 (letter of intent); Maher, Jur. Rev. 317 (2002).

[62] See Fawcett, Harris and Bridge, *op. cit*, para.13–115; Plender, *op. cit.*, para.6–15; Dicey and Morris, *op. cit.*, paras 32–114—32–094; North, 220 *Recueil des Cours*, I, 13 at 186 (1990); Feltham [1991] J.B.L. 413; Lipstein, above, n.56.

[63] See *WH Martin Ltd v Feldbinder Spezialfahrzeugwerke GmbH* (April 8, 1998, CA); *Print Concept GmbH v GEW (EC) Ltd* [2001] EWCA Civ. 352; [2002] C.L.C. 352; *ISS Machinery Services Ltd v Aeolian Shipping SA* [2001] EWCA Civ. 1162; [2001] 2 Lloyd's Rep. 641; *Iran Continental Shelf Oil Co. v IRI International Oil Corp.* [2002] EWCA Civ. 1162; [2004] 2 C.L.C. 696. For Scotland, see *William Grant & Sons International Ltd v Marie Brizard Espana SA*, 1998 S.C. 536; *Ferguson Shipbuilders Ltd v Voith Hydro GmbH & Co. KG*, 2000 S.L.T. 229. See also the decision of the Dutch Supreme Court to the same effect in *Société Nouvelle des Papeteries de l'Aa v BV Machinefabriek BOA* , 1992 N.J. 750, discussed by Struycken [1996] L.M.C.L.Q. 18 and Plender, *op. cit.*, para.6–17. English courts have also held that in a contract to supply services the characteristic performance is that of the supplier: *see Definitely Maybe (Touring) Ltd v Marek Lieberberg Konzertagentur* GmbH [2001] 1 W.L.R.

sale (c.i.f., f.o.b., etc.) and irrespective of the fact that the buyer may be under obligations additional to the obligation to pay the price and further irrespective of the fact that the seller may be under obligations additional to that of delivery of the goods (in whatever form, depending on the type of sale involved, such "delivery" must take place).[64]

25–061 It would therefore seem that the law applicable to a sale will, as a matter of presumption, be the "seller's law". According to the other terms of Article 4(2) this law will be the law of the country in which the seller (if an individual) is *habitually resident* or the law of the seller's *central administration* (in the case of a body corporate or unincorporate). If the sale is in the course of the seller's trade or profession the applicable law will be that of the country of the seller's *principal place of business* unless performance is to be effected through another *place of business* in which case it will be the law of the country in which the other *place of business* is situated. Each of the italicised phrases in this paragraph needs further explanation.[65]

25–062 **Habitual residence.** This concept has been discussed earlier in this chapter.[66] Here, it may be added, however, that it is possible, as pointed out earlier, that a person may have a habitual residence in more than one place.[67] Here the relevant habitual residence may be the one (if any), to which the characteristic performance is linked, or, alternatively, such circumstances may result in the presumption being disregarded according to Article 4(5).[68] It has also been suggested that it is conceivable, if unlikely, that a person may be without any habitual residence,[69] in which case it would seem that the applicable law will have to be determined without reference to the presumption in Article 4(2). The relevant time for determining the seller's habitual residence and whether such exists is the time at which the contract is concluded.[70]

25–063 **Central administration.** In the case where the seller is a body corporate or unincorporate, the law of the country where the seller's central administration is located may apply. "Central administration" is not defined in the Convention.[71] It is likely, however, that the relevant analogy is with the

---

1745; *Ennstone Building Products Ltd v Stanger Ltd* [2002] EWCA Civ. 916; [2002] 1 W.L.R. 3059. The same view has been taken in Scotland: see *Caledonia Subsea Ltd v Microperi SRL*, 2002 S.L.T. 1022.

[64] See *Iran Continental Shelf Oil Co. v IRI International Corp.* [2002] EWCA Civ. 1024; [2004] 2 C.L.C. 696. This seems to be the effect of the Swiss case-law: see reference at n.57, above. See also Swiss Private International Law Act 1987, Art. 117(3)(a) (in contracts to pass title, characteristic performance is that of transferor). Switzerland is a party to the Hague Sales Convention 1955 (above, n.57), but this places main emphasis on the seller's law also.

[65] See generally Fawcett, Harris and Bridge, *op. cit.*, paras 13–117—13–123.

[66] Above, para.25–056.

[67] *ibid*.

[68] Below, paras 25–065—25–066.

[69] Above, para.25–056.

[70] According to the Giuliano-Lagarde Report, p.12, this view was adopted "to counter the possibility of changes in the connecting factor (*conflit mobiles*)" in the application of Art. 4(2).

[71] Little, if any, assistance is to be found in the Giuliano-Lagarde Report.

concept of "central management and control" of a corporation or association as used in the Civil Jurisdiction and Judgments Act 1982,[72] but this Act gives no definition of that concept.[73] Case-law suggests that the question is one of fact which is answered by scrutiny of the course of business and trading, the place where the principal office is, the place where the directors and shareholders reside, the place where the directors meet (where relevant) and where control over business operations and major policy decisions is exercised.[74] Further, it appears that one must have regard to the place where management and control is actually exercised and not, for example, the place where it might be exercised according to the memorandum and articles of association of the corporation.[75] English courts have decided that applying the central management and control test to determine residence of a corporation, for the purposes of taxation, can, in exceptional cases, mean that where the controlling authority over a corporation is divided or peripatetic, a corporation may have dual residence and thus may be resident in each country where "some portion of controlling power and authority can be identified".[76] If this conclusion were adopted in the context of Article 4(2) some difficulty in the application of the presumption would result. However, it is submitted that if emphasis is given to the term "central", there will be few situations in which the places of exercise of authority will be equally split, and if such a rare case were to arise, Article 4(5) might, in any event, become relevant. Further, a sale by a body corporate or unincorporate will normally be entered into in the course of that body's trade or profession and thus either the law of the body's principal place of business will be applicable, or, if performance is to be effected through a place of business other than the principal place, the law of the country in which the other place of business is situated will apply. Lastly, the relevant time for determining the place of central administration is the time at which the contract is concluded.[77]

Principal place of business and place of business. The second sentence of Article 4(2) will place a qualification on the application of the seller's habitual residence or, as the case may be, central administration if the contract is entered into in the course of the seller's trade or profession. Such a situation is most commonly likely to exist in sales which are the 25–064

[72] Which implemented the Brussels Convention on jurisdiction and the enforcement of judgments in civil and commercial matters 1968 and provided this concept as one of the definitions of domicile for the purposes of the Convention (see s.42). The same concept is adopted as one of the definitions of domicile in Council Regulation 44/2001/EC of December 22, 2001 on jurisdiction and the recognition and enforcement of judgments in civil and commercial matters (above, para.25–016), Art. 60(1)(b). The European Court of Justice might seek to formulate an autonomous definition of central administration for the purposes of Art. 4(2), but the propositions in this paragraph may well provide the contours for such an interpretation.

[73] See Dicey and Morris, *op. cit.*, paras 30–005–30–007. Nor is the concept defined in the Council Regulation, *ibid*.

[74] *The Rewia* [1991] 1 Lloyd's Rep. 69; see also, *The Deichland* [1990] Q.B. 361.

[75] Dicey and Morris, *op. cit.*, para.30–005.

[76] *Unit Construction Co. v Bullock* [1960] A.C. 351 at 367; Dicey and Morris, *op. cit.*, para.30–006.

[77] See above, n.70.

principal subject of this book. In such cases the applicable law will either be the law of the principal place of business of the seller at the time of the conclusion of the contract,[78] or if the seller's performance is to be effected through a place of business other than the principal place of business the applicable law will be that of the country in which the relevant place of business is situated.[79] "Principal place of business" and "place of business" are not defined in the Convention. It is suggested, however, that some guidance as to the meaning of "place of business" may be drawn from English cases concerned with whether a corporation is present in England for the purposes of the *in personam* jurisdiction of English courts.[80] These cases established that a place of business constitutes a place which is fixed and definite[81] and that the activity carried on at that place must have been carried on for a sufficient period of time for it to be characterised as a business.[82] The question of which of two or more places of business will be considered the principal place of business, will, it is submitted, be a question of fact and degree.

25–065 **Displacing the presumption.** Article 4(2) cannot apply at all if the characteristic performance of the contract cannot be determined. This is expressly stated in Article 4(5) and in such situations the law of the country with which the contract is most closely connected will have to be determined without the assistance of any presumption. However, it would appear that a contract of sale is not a contract which falls into this category.[83] Accordingly, Article 4(5) is relevant in the context of sale to the extent that the provision stipulates that the law indicated by Article 4(2) (the seller's law) "shall be disregarded if it appears from the circumstances as a whole

---

[78] *ibid*.

[79] See *Ennstone Building Products Ltd v Stanger Ltd* [2002] EWCA Civ. 916; [2002] 1 W.L.R. 3059; *Iran Continental Oil Co. v IRI International Corp.* [2002] EWCA Civ. 1024; [2004] 2 C.L.C. 696; Briggs, 73 B.Y.B.I.L. 453 (2002); Hill, 53 I.C.L.Q. 325 (2004).

[80] See, generally, Dicey and Morris, *op. cit.*, paras 11–094—11–102; see in particular, *Adams v Cape Industries Plc* [1990] Ch. 433 at 512–550. An autonomous interpretation by the European Court of Justice might well follow the broad principles of this paragraph.

[81] *e.g. The Theodohos* [1977] 2 Lloyd's Rep. 428.

[82] *Dunlop Pneumatic Tyre Co. v AG Cudell & Co.* [1902] 1 K.B. 342. In relation to a contract concluded "on-line", the country in which the seller's server is located cannot, on the basis of that connection alone, be regarded as a place of business of the seller: see Directive on electronic commerce (above, para.25–053), Recital 19; Chissick and Kelman, *Electronic Commerce: Law and Practice* (3rd ed.), paras 4–09—4–12.

[83] Unlike a contract of barter (above, paras 1–034—1–038) which is. For a description and analysis of more sophisticated forms of counter-trade, see Schmitthoff, *The Export Trade* (10th ed.), Ch.10. In *Governor & Company of Bank of Scotland of the Mound v Butcher* (July 28, 1998, CA), it was held, in relation to a contract of guarantee, that Art. 4(2) could not be applied where there were two guarantors habitually resident in different countries. In *Apple Corps Ltd v Apple Computer Inc.* [2004] EWHC 768 (Ch); [2004] I.L.Pr. 597, it was similarly held that the characteristic performance of a contract between two companies regulating the use of their respective trade marks could not be determined. And see Plender, *op. cit.*, para.6–15.

that the contract is more closely connected with another country". While it is thus clear that the presumption in Article 4(2) can be rebutted, it is not clear what the strength of the presumption is to be. Since the purpose of introducing presumptions into the Convention was to produce some certainty in the search for the applicable law,[84] it can be argued that the circumstances as a whole must be particularly compelling before it should be held that the presumption is rebutted. But as is pointed out in the Giuliano-Lagarde Report, "Article 4(5) obviously leaves the judge a margin of discretion as to whether a set of circumstances exists in each specific case justifying the non-application of the"[85] presumption, a proposition that does not suggest a particularly compelling standard. The correct approach to this question has been considered in English case-law.[86] It has been said, *obiter*, that Article 4(5) means that the presumption is "displaced if the court concludes that it is not appropriate in the circumstances of any given case. This, formally, makes the presumption very weak . .".[87] However, the more widely held and, it is submitted, the better, view is that the presumption in Article 4(2) must be given "due weight"[88] and that "unless Article 4(2) is regarded as a rule of thumb which requires a preponderance of contrary connecting factors to be established before the presumption can be disregarded, the intention of the Convention is likely to be subverted".[89] It is thus possible to state that the court will apply the presumptively applicable law unless satisfied on a balance of probabilities that the contract, having regard to the circumstances as a whole, is clearly more closely connected with another country.[90] What circumstances will be

---

[84] Giuliano-Lagarde Report, p.20.

[85] *ibid.*, at p.22.

[86] *Bank of Baroda v Vysya Bank Ltd* [1994] 2 Lloyd's Rep. 87; *Crédit Lyonnais v New Hampshire Insurance Co.* [1997] 2 Lloyd's Rep. 1; *Definitely Maybe (Touring) Ltd v Marek Lieberberg Konzertagentur GmbH* [2001] 1 W.L.R. 1745; *Samcrete Engineers and Contractors SAE v. Land Rover Exports Ltd* [2001] EWCA Civ. 2019; [2002] C.L.C. 533; *Bergmann v Kenburn Waste Management Ltd* [2002] EWCA Civ. 98; [2002] F.S.R. 45; *Ennstone Building Products Ltd v Stanger Ltd* [2002] EWCA Civ. 916; [2002] 1 W.L.R. 3059; *Iran Continental Shelf Oil Co. v IRI International Corp.* [2002] EWCA Civ. 1024; [2004] 2 C.L.C. 696. For Scotland, see *Ferguson Shipbuilders v Voith Hydro GmbH*, 2000 S.L.T. 229; *Caledonia Subsea Ltd v Microperi SRL*, 2002 S.L.T. 1022.

[87] *Crédit Lyonnais v New Hampshire Insurance Co.*, above, at p.5.

[88] *Definitely Maybe (Touring) Ltd v Marek Lieberberg Konzertagentur GmbH*, above, at p.1750. See also, *Caledonia Subsea Ltd v Microperi SRL*, above.

[89] *Samcrete Egypt Engineers and Contractors SAE v Land Rover Exports Ltd*, above, at [41]. See also *Bergmann v Kenburn Waste Management Ltd*, above; *Ennstone Building Products Ltd v Stanger Ltd*, above; *Iran Contintal Shelf Oil Co. v IRI International Corp.*, above. In *Société Nouvelle des Papeteries de L'Aa v BV Machinenfabriek BOA* , 1992 N.J. 750, the Dutch Hoge Raad decided that Art. 4(5) should be applied restrictively. The presumption in Art. 4(2) was the "main rule", which rule should only be disregarded if in the special circumstances of the case the place of business of the party who is to effect the characteristic performance has "no real significance as a connecting factor". See Struycken [1996] L.M.C.L.Q. 18. In England and in Scotland the Dutch approach was explicitly rejected in the cases cited in this and the preceding note. And see Plender, *op. cit.*, paras 6–17—6–21.

[90] *Samcrete Egypt Engineers and Contractors SAE v Land Rover Exports Ltd*, above; *Iran Continental Shelf Oil Co. v IRI International Corp.*, above. See Dicey and

relevant for these purposes? First, at a general level, it is suggested in the Giuliano-Lagarde Report that, contrary to the position at common law,[91] it will be possible, in determining the most closely connected law, to take account of factors which supervene after the conclusion of the contract.[92] Secondly, any circumstance which might be regarded as relevant at common law as indicating a connection between a country and the contract will be equally relevant under Article 4(5).[93] Thirdly, in general terms, there may be a tendency to regard the presumption as most easily rebutted in a case where the characteristic performance is to be effected in a country other than the country whose law is indicated by the presumption.[94] Essentially, however, the application of the Article will very much be conditioned by the circumstances of individual cases and general statements are of limited value.[95] The following paragraph, however, offers some examples as to how the relationship between Article 4(2) and (5) might work in practice in relation to contracts for the sale of goods.

25–066 **Particular examples.** Where in the case of an f.o.b. sale, the seller's place of business and the place of delivery of the goods are situated in the same country,[96] it is unlikely that any question as to the displacement of the presumption will arise. This is also likely to be the case in such circumstances in f.a.s., f.o.r. and f.o.t. contracts. It is also submitted that this result is likely to ensue even if the place of contracting and buyer's place of business is in another country under the law of which the contract is valid although the contract is invalid under the law of the seller's place of business and the place of delivery.[97] A presumption in *favorem negotii*[98] cannot, it is submitted, be resorted to under Article 4. Such a presumption is a presumption as to the governing law which the parties intended to choose. It is not a presumption which can operate where, *ex hypothesi*, there is no choice of law.[99] If, in an f.o.b. contract, the seller's place of business

Morris, *op. cit.*, para.32–123. The burden of proving this lies on the party who asserts it: *Definitely Maybe (Touring) Ltd v Marek Lieberberg Konzertagentur GmbH*, above; *Samcrete Egypt Engineers and Contractors SAE v Land Rover Exports Ltd*, above.

[91] *James Miller and Partners Ltd v Whitworth Street Estates (Manchester) Ltd* [1970] A.C. 583 at 603; *Compagnie d'Armement Maritime SA v Compagnie Tunisienne de Navigation SA* [1971] A.C. 572 at 593, 603; *Amin Rasheed Shipping Corp. v Kuwait Insurance Co.* [1984] A.C. 50 at 69; Dicey and Morris, *op. cit.*, paras 32–057—32–058, 32–110.

[92] At p.20. See also, Dicey and Morris, *ibid*.

[93] See above, paras 25–009—25–010.

[94] *Bank of Baroda v Vysya Bank Ltd*, above; *Definitely Maybe (Touring) Ltd v Marek Lieberberg Konzertagentur GmbH*, above; *Samcrete Egypt Engineers and Contractors S.A.E. v Land Rover Exports Ltd*, above; *Bergmann v Kenburn Waste Management Ltd, above; Caledonia Subsea Ltd v Microperi SRL*, above. *Cf. Iran Continental Shelf Oil Co. v IRI International Corp.*, above.

[95] See cases cited in preceding note. This was also the case with the common law. above, paras 25–009—25–010.

[96] *cf. Benaim & Co. v Debono* [1924] A.C. 514, above, para.25–011.

[97] *cf. NV Handel Maatschappij J. Smits & Co. v English Exporters* (*London*) *Ltd* [1955] 2 Lloyd's Rep. 317.

[98] Above, paras 25–010, n.68, 25–030, n.8.

[99] *cf. Sayers v International Drilling Co. NV* [1976] 1 W.L.R. 1113. above, para.25–010, n.68.

and place of delivery (shipment) do not coincide a potential clash between the presumption and Article 4(5) is raised. The common law tended to favour the place of shipment as the governing law.[1] Where performance by the seller is effected through his place of business in the country of shipment the law of that country will apply by virtue of the presumption. But if the seller has no such place of business there, will the presumption in favour of the law of his principal place of business be displaced in favour of the law of the place of shipment? It is tentatively submitted that the presumption should prevail since the law of the *place* of characteristic performance (which will be the place of shipment in f.o.b. and analogous contracts) should not *per se*, be allowed to prevail over the presumption,[2] despite the tendency, earlier referred to, which might regard the presumption as most easily rebuttable in a case where the characteristic performance is to be effected in a country other than that whose law would be applicable pursuant to the presumption.[3] This might be qualified if the place of shipment is in the buyer's country but in such a case there will usually be other connections with that country, *e.g.* possession by the seller of a warehouse there or of an agent who will have secured the sale.[4] In principle the foregoing propositions are capable of being applied to c.i.f. contracts, to which, for these purposes, c. & f. contracts may be assimilated. Account may, however, have to be taken of the fact that in a c.i.f. contract the seller may be under a duty to tender appropriate documents in the buyer's country, or elsewhere outside the country of shipment, or the seller may have the right to tender documents relating to goods afloat. In the first and second of these situations, it is possible that the presumption could be displaced,[5] though in the third situation it would appear that the presumption should prevail. Likewise it is conceivable that in the case of ex-works or ex-store contracts, in the absence of the seller having a place of business in the country in which the buyer collects the goods from the seller or a bailee on his behalf, the law of the latter country could prevail over the law indicated by the presumption, *viz.* the law of the seller's principal place of business. More generally, if goods sold have to be manufactured and delivered in the country of the buyer's place of business, the law of the buyer should prevail over that of the seller.[6] But in such a case the seller is likely to have a place of business in the buyer's country so that the laws of the two parties will coincide. If the seller's agent holds stocks of goods

---

[1] *e.g. Benaim & Co. v Debono*, above.

[2] *cf. Gill and Duffus Landauer Ltd v London Export Corp. GmbH* [1982] 2 Lloyd's Rep. 627; Restatement, para.191e. This is probably so if the contract is a "multi-port" f.o.b. contract giving the seller the right to choose a port of shipment out of a number of ports in different countries: *cf.* above, para.25–011, n.71; para.25–012, n.80. The position may be different in relation to other contracts where it might be easier to rebut the presumption in a case where the place of performance differs from the place of business of the characteristic performer: see *Bank of Baroda v Vysya Bank Ltd* [1994] 2 Lloyd's Rep. 87 (letter of credit) discussed below, para.25–076; Dicey and Morris, *op. cit.*, para.33–100.

[3] Above, para.25–065.

[4] See Lando, in *International Encyclopedia of Comparative Law* (Lipstein ed.), Ch.III, Vol. 24, pp.132–133.

[5] *cf.* Lando, *ibid.*

[6] *ibid.*

belonging to the seller in the buyer's country (the agent's place of business not constituting a place of business of the seller) and the agent is to deliver those goods to the buyer in that country, then a good case would seem to exist for displacing the presumption.[7] No such case would appear to exist where the seller is obliged merely to deliver the goods from his country to that of the buyer.

25–066A **Application to sale concluded "on-line".** In the absence of a choice of law in the contract, Article 4(2) will point to the country of the habitual residence, central administration, principal place of business or place of business, as the case may be, of the seller. It is suggested that, in the context of an online sale, circumstances in which this presumptively applicable law will be displaced are likely to be rare.[8]

25–067 **"Certain consumer contracts".** The provisions of Article 4 do not apply to contracts falling within the scope of Article 5. This definition was discussed in paragraphs 25–045—25–046 of this chapter. Article 5(3) provides that in the absence of a choice of law in accordance with Article 3 of the Convention, such contracts shall be governed by the law of the country in which the consumer has his habitual residence[9] if it is entered into in any one of the three circumstances set out in Article 5(2). These circumstances were discussed in paragraphs 25–048—25–053.

25–068 **Successive contracts of sale relating to the same goods.** Since, presumptively, Article 4(2) of Convention points towards the law of the seller's place of business as the governing law, it is the likely result that a variety of applicable laws may be relevant in the case of successive contracts of sale of the same goods. To ensure uniformity as to the governing law in relation to such "string" contracts,[10] it will be necessary, as far as possible, to insert appropriate choice of law clauses or suitably worded arbitration clauses into each contract or for the parties to the successive sales to deal on the same, or at least consistent, standard forms.[11]

---

[7] *ibid.*
[8] See Fawcett, Harris and Bridge, *op. cit.*, paras 21–49—21–90. It is also submitted that these choice of law principles are also unaffected by the Electronic Commerce Directive and the implementing UK Regulations (above, para.050). The Directive specifically states (Art. 1(4) and Recital 23) that it does not establish additional rules on private international law. This provision is not implemented in the Regulations and the outcome of this is that the position is obscure and uncertain (see Fawcett, Harris and Bridge, *op. cit.*, paras 21–10—21–34). There would, however, seem to be no intelligible policy reason justifying application of the country of origin principle to the exclusion of Art. 4 just because the parties have not chosen a law to govern the contract. See above, para.25–051.
[9] Above, paras 25–056, 25–062.
[10] Above, para.25–010, n.62.
[11] *ibid.* It has been suggested, but without reaching a decision on the point, that an express choice of law in a related contract is not a connecting factor for the purposes of Art. 4 which can be looked to in determining the law applicable to the accompanying contract: *Samcrete Egypt Engineers and Contractors SAE v Land Rover Exports Ltd* [2001] EWCA Civ. 2019; [2002] C.L.C. 533. See also *Crédit Lyonnais v New Hampshire Insurance Co.* [1997] 2 Lloyd's Rep. 1.

4. CONTRACTS ANCILLARY TO CONTRACT OF SALE

Generally. In virtually all international sales[12] and a sizeable proportion of domestic sales, the contract of sale is not the only contract entered into. Ancillary contracts are made as well: they are usually essential to the implementation of the whole transaction and often of considerable importance as regards the remedies of one or other party if the sale breaks down.[13] Each such contract has its own applicable law, which may or may not be the same as that of the contract of sale itself, and very generally, both at common law and under the Rome Convention, such applicable law is found by application of the general principles, discussed in the preceding two sections.[14] Space does not permit a detailed discussion of these ancillary contracts, but, as regards the most important of them, a few general points may usefully be made. 25–069

Contracts for the carriage of goods.[15] At common law, there were no special factors indicating what the law applicable to a contract for the carriage of goods should be. In the absence of an express or implied selection of the governing law by the parties,[16] it was necessary to weigh up a variety of factors, notably the place of business of the parties, the form of the contract, the language[17] and the technical terminology used in the contract and the country from which the goods were dispatched in order to ascertain the country or system of law with which the transaction was most closely connected.[18] 25–070

---

[12] See above, Ch.18.

[13] *e.g.* if goods shipped under a c.i.f. contract governed by English law are lost at sea, the buyer, being still bound to pay the price against tender of documents (above, para.19–080), will look to the carrier or insurer for recompense.

[14] Above, paras 25–005—25–068. Conflict of laws' problems can of course, be minimised if the various auxiliary contracts in a sale transaction are governed by the same law as the contract of sale, this being made clear by an appropriate choice of law clause. But this may not be possible to achieve in practice. In relation to the Rome Convention it should be noted that adoption of the presumptions in Art. 4(2) (above, paras 25–057—25–066) and Art. 4(4) (below, paras 25–076—25–072) is likely to increase the possibility that some contracts ancillary to the contract of sale may be governed by laws which are different to the law governing the latter contract, and, indeed, where several ancillary contracts are involved in one sale, different laws may apply to each such contract. The importance of making, so far as possible, a choice of law in the contracts cannot therefore be overstressed.

[15] See generally, Fawcett, Harris and Bridge, *International Sale of Goods in the Conflict of Laws* (2005), Ch.14; Plender, *The European Contracts Convention* (2nd ed.), paras 6–28—6–32; Dicey and Morris, *The Conflict of Laws* (13th ed.), paras 33–256—33–284; Kaye, *The New Private International Law of Contract of the European Community* (1993), pp.197–202; Schultsz in North (ed.) *Contract Conflicts* (1982), 185, pp.187–201. For a discussion of the possible conflict of laws' implications of the Carriage of Goods by Sea Act 1992, see Toh Kian Sing [1994] L.M.C.L.Q. 280. These contributions are primarily concerned with contracts for the carriage of goods by sea.

[16] Above, paras 25–006—25–007.

[17] The use of English was not particularly significant.

[18] See *e.g. Moore v Harris* (1876) 9 App.Cas. 318; *Chartered Mercantile Bank of India v Netherlands India Steam Navigation Co.* (1883) 10 Q.B.D. 521; *The Industrie* [1894] P. 58; *Akt. August Freuchen v Steen Hanzen* (1919) 1 Ll.L.R. 393; *The Adriatic* [1931] P. 241; *Anselme Dewavrin v Wilsons and N.E. Ry Shipping Co. Ltd* (1931) 39 Ll.L.R. 289; *The Assunzione* [1954] P. 150.

25–071 Where the Rome Convention applies, to the extent that the law applicable to a contract for carriage of goods (by whatever mode of transport) has not been chosen by the parties, that contract will be governed by the law of the country with which it is most closely connected.[19] In determining which law this is resort is to be had, initially, not to the presumption in Article 4(2),[20] but rather to a special presumption contained in Article 4(4). According to this "[i]n such a contract if the country in which, at the time the contract is concluded, the carrier has his principal place of business is also the country in which the place of loading or place of discharge or the principal place of business of the consignor is situated, it shall be presumed that the contract is most closely connected with that country".[21] Since Article 4(4) also states expressly that Article 4(2) is not to apply to a contract for the carriage of goods, where the factors mentioned in Article 4(4) are not present in relation to a particular contract, the law of the country with which the contract is most closely connected will have to be determined without the aid of any presumption. And, of course, pursuant to Article 4(5), the presumption itself is to be disregarded if it appears from the circumstances as a whole that the contract is more closely connected with another country. Although it is by no means clear what is comprised in the term "contract for the carriage of goods" for the purposes of Article 4(4), the provision stipulates that "single voyage charter-parties and other contracts the main purpose of which is the carriage of goods shall be treated as contracts for the carriage of goods." On one view, in the context of carriage by water, this wording might suggest that consecutive voyage charterparties are not within the presumption,[22] but it is suggested that such charterparties can be regarded as having as their substantial purpose, the carriage of goods and thus should be treated as falling within the provision.[23] Furthermore, identification of the law applicable to a

[19] Rome Convention, Art. 4(1).

[20] See above, paras 25–057—25–066. Apparently it was thought inappropriate to submit contracts for the carriage of goods to Art. 4(2) "having regard to the peculiarities of this type of transport": Giuliano-Lagarde Report, p.21. *Cf.* Commission Proposal, Art. 4(1)(c).

[21] Where a party who contracts to carry goods for another does not carry them himself but arranges for a third party to do so, Art. 4(4) will, apparently, still apply since the term "carrier" means the party "who undertakes to carry the goods whether or not he performs the carriage himself": Giuliano-Lagarde Report, p.22. According to that Report (p. 21) the term "consignor" refers "in general to any person who consigns goods to the carrier", and (p. 22) "the places of loading and unloading are those agreed at the time the contract is concluded". *Cf.* Commission Proposal, Art. 4(1)(c).

[22] See Schultsz, above, n.15, at p.22.

[23] See Kaye, *op. cit.*, p.200; Plender, *op. cit.*, para.6–32; Dicey and Morris, *op. cit.*, para.33–258; The Giuliano-Lagarde Report suggests that the reference to single voyage charterparties, etc. was introduced to make it clear that charterparties may be considered to be contracts for the carriage of goods in so far as that is their substance (see p.22). A demise charter does not have this character: see the description in Scrutton, *Chaterparties and Bills of Lading* (20th ed.), pp.14, n.6, 39. Such a charterparty is outside Art. 4(4). See Plender, *ibid.*: Dicey and Morris, *ibid.* Schultsz, above, n.15. Whether a time charter falls within the provision is controversial, but it is tentatively suggested that it does: see Dicey and Morris, *ibid.*; Kaye, *ibid.*; and see the description in Scrutton, above, Art. 27. For a different view see Plender, *ibid.*; Schultsz, *ibid.*

contract evidenced in a bill of lading should similarly be subject to the presumption.[24]

The increasing volume of international carriage of goods has brought about a range of international conventions which attempt to regulate carriage by particular modes of transport or a combination thereof.[25] Where a matter was regulated by the provisions of one of these conventions could render it unnecessary to determine the law applicable to the contract at common law.[26] The Rome Convention does not prejudice the application of international conventions (including transport conventions)[27] to which a Contracting State is, or becomes a party,[28] so that the importance of the law applicable to the contract will continue to be reduced where such conventions are relevant.[29]

Rules contained in international conventions concerning carriage may be construed as having such importance that it is not possible to contract out of them by choosing, as the applicable law, the law of a country which is not a party to the relevant convention. Thus it was held, at common law, that the parties could not contract out of the Hague-Visby Rules, as implemented in the Carriage of Goods by Sea Act 1971 by choosing, as the governing law, the law of a country which has not enacted the Rules[30] or by 25–072

---

[24] Dicey and Morris, *op. cit.*, para.33–259.

[25] For a brief account, see Dicey and Morris, *op. cit.*, paras 33–239—32–253.

[26] The most important example is, perhaps, to be found in the availability of the Hague or Hague-Visby Rules (see above, para.21–047), relating to sea carriage, as forms of maritime code amongst most countries. Where it was necessary to identify the applicable law of a contract for carriage by sea despite the existence of these conventions, the following factors (additional to those mentioned in paras 25–009—25–010) were regarded as relevant in determining the law with which the contract was most closely connected: the country where the goods were to be delivered (*The Assunzione*, above); the country and currency in which the freight was payable (*ibid.*); the law referred to in any "clause paramount" adopting the Hague Rules (*The Stensby* [1974] 2 All E.R. 786; *Karel Chajkin v Mitchell Cotts & Co. (Middle East) Ltd* (1948) 64 T.L.R. 88); the law applicable to the charterparty when the clause was contained in a bill of lading issued pursuant to the charterparty and incorporating the terms thereof (*The Njegos* [1936] P. 90; *Pacific Molasses Co. v Entre Rios Compania Naviera SA, The San Nicholas* [1976] 1 Lloyd's Rep. 8; *Mineracoas Brasilievas Reunidas v EF Marine SA, The Freights Queen* [1977] 2 Lloyd's Rep. 140; *The Broken Hill Pty Co. Ltd v Theodore Xenakis* [1982] 2 Lloyd's Rep. 304; *Illyssia Compania Naviera SA v Ahmed Abdul-Qawi Bamoadah (The Elli 2)* [1985] 1 Lloyd's Rep. 107; *The Paros* [1987] 2 Lloyd's Rep. 269 at 272; *The Delfini* [1988] 2 Lloyd's Rep. 599; *cf. The Metamorphosis* [1953] 1 W.L.R. 543); in the last resort the law of the flag of the carrying ship might be applicable (*Lloyd v Guibert* [1865] L.R. 1 Q.B. 115 as confined and explained in *The Assunzione*, above, at pp.178, 194; *Coast Lines Ltd v Hudig and Veder Chartering NV* [1972] 2 Q.B. 34 at 44, 47–48; *cf. Bangladesh Chemical Industries Corp. v Henry Stephens Shipping Co. Ltd* (*The SLS Everest*) [1981] 2 Lloyd's Rep. 389; *Dubai Electricity Co. v Islamic Republic of Iran Shipping Lines (The Iran Vojan)* [1984] 2 Lloyd's Rep. 380).

[27] See Dicey and Morris, *op. cit.*, paras 33–239—33–253.

[28] Art. 21; Giuliano-Lagarde Report, p.22.

[29] See above, para.21–047.

[30] *The Hollandia* [1983] 1 A.C. 565, in which the view of Morris, 95 L.Q.R. 57 at 64–67 (1979) was preferred to that of F.A. Mann who contended that the 1971 Act and the Rules scheduled thereto could not apply even to an outward shipment from the

conferring exclusive jurisdiction on the courts of such a country in the contract itself.[31] Furthermore, Article 7(2) of the Rome Convention will enable a court to apply such conventions to which the United Kingdom is a party, if the legislation implementing them and the rules they contain are construed as rules of the forum which are mandatory irrespective of the law applicable to the contract and thus are rules the application of which is not restricted by the Convention.[32]

25–073 **Contracts of agency.**[33] In the course of a sale, a wide variety of agents (using the term in a loose commercial sense) may be employed by the parties to the sale: for example, freight forwarders, loading brokers, commission merchants, confirming houses and so on. Such agents may in turn employ sub-agents. At common law, the law governing such contracts was determined by applying general choice of law principles.[34] The law applicable to the contract only governed the relationship between the principal and the agent.[35] It did not generally govern the rights and liabilities of principal and agent *vis-à-vis* third parties with whom the agent had dealings in the course of his duties.[36] Similarly, Article 1(2)(f) of the

---

UK, unless it had first been decided that the law applicable to the contract was the law of some part of the UK: see 46 B.Y.B.I.L. 117 at 125–126; 99 L.Q.R. 376 at 393–406 (1983). See also *The Antares (Nos. 1 and 2)* [1987] 1 Lloyd's Rep. 424; *The Amazonia* [1990] 1 Lloyd's Rep. 236; *cf. The Amazonia and Yayamaria* [1989] 2 Lloyd's Rep. 130; *The Komninos S* [1990] 1 Lloyd's Rep. 541; *The Happy Ranger* [2001] 2 Lloyd's Rep. 530.

[31] *The Hollandia*, above. *Cf. The Benarty* [1985] Q.B. 325. This is subject to the operation of the Civil Jurisdiction and Judgments Act 1982, Schs 1 and 3C, Art. 17 and to Council Regulation 44/2001/EC of December 22, 2001, Art. 23 (above, para.25–018): see Dicey and Morris, *op. cit.*, para.12–116.

[32] See above, para.25–042. *The Hollandia*, above, would thus be decided in the same way under the Convention. *Cf. Primetrade AG v Ythan Ltd* [2005] EWHC 2399 (Comm); [2006] 1 All E.R. 367, at [14]–[15], where it is suggested that the Carriage of Goods by Sea Act 1992 is not mandatory and only applies if English law is the applicable law. See Fawcett, Harris and Bridge, *op. cit.* , paras 14–46—14–48, 14–97—14–100; Toh Kian Sing, *op. cit*.

[33] See Dicey and Morris, *op. cit.*, paras 33–395—33–413; Rabel, *Conflict of Laws: A Comparative Study* (2nd ed.), Vol. 3, pp.125–186, 200–203; Verhagen, *Agency in Private International Law* (1995); Rigaux, in Lipstein (ed.), *International Encyclopedia of Comparative Law*, Vol. III, Ch.29; Breslauer, 50 Jur.Rev. 282 (1938); Reese and Flesch, 60 Col.L.Rev. 764 (1960).

[34] See above, paras 25–005—25–010. There were no clear or specific guidelines as to how these general principles applied. In the absence of positive indications, the applicable law was likely to be the law of the country where both parties carried on business if such existed; or the law of the country where the agent was to perform his duties (see *Albeko Schuhmaschinen AG v Kamborian Shoe Machine Co. Ltd* (1961) 111 L.J. 519; *SCF Finance Co. Ltd v Masri* [1986] 1 Lloyd's Rep. 293), but this was of little assistance where there was more than one such country (see *Mauroux v Soc. Com. Abel Pereira da Fonseca* [1972] 1 W.L.R. 962 at 968), or the law of the country where the agency relationship was created and where either the principal or agent carried on business (*Atlantic Underwriting Agencies Ltd v Compagnia di Assicurazione di Milano SpA* [1979] 2 Lloyd's Rep. 240; *Albeko Schuhmaschinen AG v Kamborian Shoe Machine Co. Ltd*, above; *Re Anglo Austrian Bank* [1920] 1 Ch. 69; *Arnott v Redfern* (1826) 3 Bing. 353).

[35] *Arnott v Redfern*, above.

[36] As to this question see below, para.25–081.

Rome Convention excludes from the scope of the Convention the question whether an agent is able to bind a principal, or an organ to bind a company or body corporate or unincorporate, to a third party.[37] This question will, therefore, continue to be governed by common law rules.[38] However it is important to emphasise that the exclusion only applies to the relationship between the principal, etc. and the third party. The Convention does apply to the relationship between principal and agent and to that between agent and third party.[39] As far as the former relationship is concerned, in the absence of a choice of law in the contract,[40] the applicable law will be determined by initial reference to the presumption in Article 4(2),[41] subject to the possibility of rebuttal under Article 4(5).[42] The characteristic performance in an agency contract is that of the agent,[43] so that, presumptively, the applicable law will be the law of the agent's habitual residence or central administration, as the case may be, unless (as is likely to be the case) the contract is made in the course of the agent's trade or profession in which case that law will be that of the agent's principal place of business unless performance by the agent is to be effected through a place of business other than his principal place of business, in which case it will be the law of the country in which the other place of business is situated which will, presumptively, constitute the applicable law. As regards the relationship between agent and third party, to the extent that the relationship arises out of a contract, the applicable law will be that chosen

---

[37] The exclusion is justified on the ground that it is "difficult to justify" application of the wide freedom of choice of law, permitted by the Convention, to this issue. For criticism, see Dicey and Morris, *op. cit.*, para.33–418; Lasok and Stone, *op cit.*, p.354. See also Plender, *op. cit.*, paras 4–36—4–39.

[38] Below, paras 25–081—25–082.

[39] See *Marubeni Hong Kong and South China Ltd v Mongolian Government* [2002] 2 All E.R. (Comm) 873; Giuliano-Lagarde Report, p.13.

[40] *Marubeni Hong Kong and South China Ltd v Mongolian Government*, above. Note the potential applicability of Council Directive 86/653 EEC of December 18, 1986 on the co-ordination of the laws of the Member States relating to self-employed commercial agents ([1986] O.J. L382/17), implemented in the UK by the Commercial Agents (Council Directive) Regulations 1993 (SI 1993/3053, as amended by SI 1993/3173 and SI 1998/2868 and in Northern Ireland SI 1993/483(N.I.)). In *Ingmar GB Ltd v Eaton Leonard Technologies Inc.* (C–381/98) [2000] E.C.R. I–9305, the European Court of Justice held that Arts 17 and 18 of the Directive (implemented in regs 17 and 18 of the Regulations), which guarantee certain rights to commercial agents after termination of the agency contract, must be applied, as mandatory rules, where the commercial agent carries out his activity in a Member State even though the principal is established in a non-Member State and a clause in the contract stipulates that it is to be governed by the law of that non-Member State: see Plender, *op. cit.*, paras 9–20—9–21; Dicey and Morris, *op. cit.*, paras 33–405–33–413; *Bowstead and Reynolds on Agency* (17th ed.), paras 11–006—11–010; Verhagen, 51 I.C.L.Q. 135 (2002).

[41] Above, paras 25–057—25–065.

[42] Above, paras 25–066—25–068. *Cf.* Commission Proposal, Art. 7.

[43] *Bank of Baroda v Vysya Bank Ltd* [1994] 2 Lloyd's Rep. 87; *PT Pan Indonesia Bank Ltd TBK v Marconi Communications International Ltd* [2005] EWCA Civ. 422; [2005] 2 All E.R. (Comm) 325; Plender, *op. cit.*, para.6–14; Dicey and Morris, *op. cit.*, paras 33–400—33–401. *Cf. Print Concept GmbH v GEW (EC) Ltd* [2001] EWCA Civ. 352; [2001] E.C.C. 36 (characteristic performance of distributorship agreement intended to be fulfilled by individual contracts of sale and purchase is that of the vendor).

by the parties, if any, failing which the relevant presumption in Article 4[44] will initially apply and will be subject to displacement under Article 4(5).[45] What will be the characteristic performance of this contract if Article 4(2) is applicable will depend on the type of contract which has been concluded between agent and third party.

25–074 **Contracts of insurance.**[46] At common law, the law applicable to a contract of insurance was determined by reference to general principles.[47] In the absence of an express or implied choice of law[48] in the contract itself, the contract was governed by the system of law with which the transaction had the closest and most real connection and, in the most recent decisions, there was an observable tendency to regard the latter law as that of the country of the market by reference to which the insurance contract was made.[49] Insurance contracts fall within the Rome Convention only if the risks which they cover are situated outside the territories of a Member State of the European Economic Community.[50] In such cases, the applicable law will be that (if any) chosen by the parties, failing which resort will be had, initially, to the presumption in Article 4(2)[51] which will be subject to rebuttal under Article 4(5).[52] It is suggested that the characteristic performance of an insurance contract is that of the insurer[53] so that, presumptively, since the insurance contract will inevitably be made in the course of the insurer's trade or profession, the applicable law will be that of the insurer's principal place of business unless the insurance is effected

---

[44] Above, paras 25–058—25–064, 25–071, and Art. 4(3). Below, paras 25–074—25–076.

[45] Above, paras 25–065—25–066.

[46] See Dicey and Morris, *op. cit.*, *Fourth Cumulative Supplement* (2004), paras S33R–116—S33–196 Seatzu, *Insurance in Private International Law* (2003); Colinvaux and Merkin, *Insurance Contract Law* (2002-), Ch.D, paras D–0750 *et seq.*.

[47] See Dicey and Morris, *op. cit.*, *Fourth Cumulative Supplement* (2004), paras S33–121—S33–123.

[48] Such an implied choice may be indicated by the use of a standard form associated with a particular insurance market: *cf. Amin Rasheed Shipping Corp. v Kuwait Insurance Co.* [1984] A.C. 50. See also *King v Brandywine Reinsurance Co.* [2005] EWCA Civ. 235; [2005] 1 Lloyd's Rep. 655.

[49] *Cantieri Navali Riuniti SpA v NV Omne Justitia* [1985] 2 Lloyd's Rep. 428; *E.I. du Pont de Nemours v Agnew* [1987] 2 Lloyd's Rep. 585. Earlier practice favoured the head office of the insurer: see *Greer v Poole* (1880) 5 Q.B.D. 572; *Atlantic Underwriting Agencies Ltd v Compagnia di Assicurazione di Milano SpA* [1979] 2 Lloyd's Rep. 240 at 245.

[50] Art. 1(3). The rules of the Convention are now inapplicable to contracts covering risks situated in an EEA Member State: see Financial Services and Markets Act 2000 (Law Applicable to Contracts of Insurance) Regulations 2001, SI 2001/2635, as amended by SI 2001/3542, made under Financial Services and Markets Act 2000; EEA Agreement; European Economic Area Act 1993. See below, para.25–075. The rules of the Rome Convention apply fully to re-insurance contracts wherever the risk is situated: Art. 1(4). See Dicey and Morris, *op. cit.*, paras 33–199—33–209. Contrast Commission Proposal, Arts 3, 4, 22 and Annex 1.

[51] Above; *cf.*, paras 25–058—25–064.

[52] Above, paras 25–065—25–066.

[53] *Credit Lyonnais v New Hampshire Insurance Co.* [1997] 2 Lloyd's Rep. 1; *American Motorists Insurance Co. v Cellstar Corp.* [2003] EWCA Civ. 206; [2003] I.L.Pr. 370; Giuliano-Lagarde Report, p.20.

through another place of business possessed by the insurer, in which case the applicable law will be the law of the country in which that place of business is situated. It should be noted that an insurance contract may fall within the definition of a consumer contract subject to Article 5, in which case that provision will apply to determine the applicable law rather than the rules in Articles 3 and 4.[54]

Exclusion of insurance contracts covering risks situated within the territories of the Member States of the European Economic Community which now extends to insurance contracts covering risks situated in a Member State of the European Economic Area,[55] is justified by the fact that work on harmonisation of insurance law is taking place in the Community.[56] This work has produced two Directives on Non-Life Insurance and one Directive on Life Insurance containing choice of law rules which have been implemented in the United Kingdom.[57] The implementing legislation also contains rules for determining where a risk is situated.[58] The Rome Convention provides that in order to determine where a risk is situated, the court shall apply its internal law,[59] but since the concept of the *situs* of a risk played no role in English insurance law,[60] no such internal law rules, existed, so that specific rules[61] had to be adopted. Space forbids the discussion of these new choice of law rules and the reader is referred to an appropriate source.[62] **25–075**

---

[54] *ibid.*, at p.13. See above, paras 25–044—25–053, 25–067.
[55] See n.49, above.
[56] *ibid.*
[57] See Second Council Directive 88/357, June 22, 1988, on the co-ordination of laws, regulations and administrative provisions relating to direct insurance other than life assurance ([1988] O.J. L172/1); Third Council Directive 1992/49/EEC of June 18, 1992 on the co-ordination of laws, regulations and administrative provisions relating to direct insurance other than life insurance ([1992] O.J. L228/1); Second Council Directive 1990/619/EEC on the co-ordination of laws, regulations and administrative provisions relating to direct life assurance ([1990] O.J. L330/50). The choice of law rules contained in these Directives are now implemented in the UK by Financial Services and Markets Act 2000 (Law Applicable to Contracts of Insurance) Regulations 2001, SI 2001/2635, as amended by SI 2001/3542, made under Financial Services and Markets Act 2000. A further Directive 202/83/EC of the European Parliament and of the Council of November 5, 2002 concerning life assurance ([2002] O.J. L345/1) was promulgated primarily to "recast" the earlier life insurance Directives in the "interests of clarity" (see Recital 1). The choice of law rules contained in this Directive (Art. 32) are, apart from minor verbal differences, the same as those contained in the Second Life Directive and the 2001 Regulations. Since references to Directives repealed by this Directive shall be construed as references to the new Directive and must be read in accordance with a correlation table set out in Annex VI (Art. 72) further implementing legislation will not be necessary in order to comply with Art. 32. For the history of the implementation of the Directives, see Dicey and Morris, *op. cit.*, *Fourth Cumulative Supplement* (2004), paras S33–117—S33–120.
[58] Financial Services and Markets Act 2000 (Law Applicable to Contracts of Insurance) Regulations 2001, reg.2(2).
[59] Art. 1(3).
[60] Dicey and Morris, *op. cit.*, para.S33–125.
[61] Contracts (Applicable Law) Act 1990, s.2(1A)(a), inserted by Financial Services and Markets Act 2000 (Consequential Amendments and Repeals) Order 2001, SI 2001/3649, art. 320.
[62] Dicey and Morris, *op. cit.*, paras S33–139—S33–196.

25–076 **Banking contracts.**[63] At common law, the law applicable to a contract between banker and customer, in general, was, in the absence of an express or implied choice of law, normally the law of the country in which the branch at which the account was held was situated.[64] In cases falling within the Rome Convention, in the absence of a choice of law by the parties,[65] the applicable law will be determined, presumptively, by reference to the presumption in Article 4(2),[66] which law, of course, may be displaced in accordance with the principle in Article 4(5) of the Convention.[67] The characteristic performance of a banking contract is that of the bank,[68] with the consequence that the law of the place of business of the bank through which the transaction is effected will be the presumptively applicable law.[69] Although these general principles are clear, their application to a common method of payment agreed between buyer and seller, *i.e.* a letter of credit requires more detailed analysis,[70] and involves separating the various contracts and relationships which may be involved in a letter of credit transaction. Initially, however, it is necessary to emphasise that because of the autonomous nature of a letter of credit,[71] its applicable law is in no sense dependent on the law applicable to the underlying sale transaction.[72] Of the various contracts and relationships involved in a letter of credit, the

---

[63] Brindle and Cox (eds), *Law of Bank Payments* (3rd ed.), pp.749–756; Dicey and Morris, *op. cit.*, paras 33–290—33–312; Cresswell *et al.*, *Encyclopaedia of Banking Law*, Division F, paras 401 *et seq.*, 751 *et seq.*; Jack, Malek and Quest, *Documentary Credits* (3rd ed.), Ch.13.

[64] *X.A.G. v A Bank* [1983] 2 All E.R. 464; *Libyan Arab Foreign Bank v Bankers Trust Co.* [1989] Q.B. 728; *Libyan Arab Foreign Bank v Manufacturers Hanover Trust Co.* [1988] 2 Lloyd's Rep. 494; *Libyan Arab Foreign Bank v Manufacturers Hanover Trust Co. (No.2)* [1989] 1 Lloyd's Rep. 608; *Attock Cement Co. Ltd v Romanian Bank for Foreign Trade* [1989] 1 W.L.R. 1147; *Stewart v Royal Bank of Scotland Plc*, 1994 S.L.T. 27.

[65] Which must be the choice of the law of a country (*Shamil Bank of Bahrain v Beximco Pharmaceuticals Ltd* [2004] EWCA Civ. 19; [2004] 1 W.L.R. 1784). See on the principle of choice by the parties *Caterpillar Financial Services Corp. v SNC Passion* [2004] EWHC 569 (Comm); [2004] 2 Lloyd's Rep. 99; *European Bank for Reconstruction and Development v Tekoglu* [2004] EWHC 846 (Comm); *Shamil Bank of Bahrain v Beximco Pharmaceuticals Ltd*, above; *Centrax Ltd v Citibank NA* [1999] 1 All E.R. (Comm) 557; *cf. Raiffeisen Zentralbank Osterreich AG v National Bank of Greece S.A.* [1999] 1 Lloyd's Rep. 408; *Atlantic Telecom GmbH, Noter,* 2004 S.L.T. 1031.

[66] Above, paras 25–058—25–064.

[67] Above, paras 25–065—25–066.

[68] *PT Pan Indonesia Bank Ltd TBK v Marconi Communications International Ltd* [2005] EWCA Civ. 422; [2005] 2 All E.R. (Comm) 325; *Sierra Leone Telecommunications Co. Ltd v Barclays Bank Plc* [1998] 2 All E.R. 821; *Bank of Baroda v Vysya Bank Ltd* [1994] 2 Lloyd's Rep. 87 at 92; Giuliano-Lagarde Report, p.20.

[69] *Sierra Leone Telecommunications Co. Ltd v Barclays Bank Plc*, above.

[70] Dicey and Morris, *op. cit.*, paras 33–301—33–305; See Morse [1994] L.M.C.L.Q. 560; Davenport and Smith, *Butterworths Journal of International Banking and Financial Law* 3 (1994). This particular problem is not discussed in the Giuliano-Lagarde Report.

[71] See above, para.23–139.

[72] *Offshore International SA v Banco Central SA* [1976] 2 Lloyd's Rep. 402; *Attock Cement Co. Ltd v Romanian Bank for Foreign Trade* [1989] 1 W.L.R. 1147 (performance bond). *Cf. Wahda Bank v Arab Bank Plc* [1996] 1 Lloyd's Rep. 470 (counter-guarantee governed by same law as governed guarantee).

first which arises is that between the buyer and the issuing bank when the former instructs the latter to open the credit. The law applicable to this contract is the law of the country in which the place of business of the bank through which the credit is opened is situated[73] both at common law[74] and under the Rome Convention (the characteristic performance being that of the bank in providing this banking facility).[75] A contract will then arise between the issuing bank and any correspondent bank engaged to make payments. General conditions of business or a previous course of dealing may point to a choice of law by the parties, but where this conclusion could not be drawn, the position at common law was that the contract was normally regarded as having the closest and most real connection with the country where the branch of the bank at which payment was to be made was situated.[76] The same result has been reached under the Rome Convention in a case involving a confirmed letter of credit.[77] For the purposes of Article 4(2) of the Convention, the characteristic performance of the contract, a contract of agency,[78] was that of the confirming (correspondent) bank in adding its confirmation to the credit and its honouring of the obligations accepted thereby in relation to the beneficiary (seller). Article 4(2) would then lead to the application of the "place of business" through which performance (payment) was to be affected and to the country in which that place was situated as the governing law.[79] The same conclusion is likely to follow if the correspondent bank does not add its confirmation to the credit since the contract between the two banks is one of agency[80] and the characteristic performance of such a contract is that of the agent who is the correspondent bank in this situation.[81] Where the correspondent bank adds it confirmation to the credit, an independent

[73] Assuming there is no choice of law by the parties. Standard forms of letters of credit do not normally state a choice of law. It has been suggested that practice is changing to make an express choice of law (Brindle and Cox (eds), *op. cit.*, p.756).
[74] This because the contract involves the relationship of banker and customer which was normally governed by that law: see cases cited at n.64, above.
[75] See Morse, *op. cit.*, at p.570. See also *Sierra Leone Telecommunications Co. Ltd v Barclays Bank Plc* [1998] 2 All E.R. 821; *Bank of Baroda v Vysya Bank Ltd* [1994] 2 Lloyd's Rep. 87 at 92.
[76] *Bank of Credit and Commerce Hong Kong Ltd v Sonali Bank* [1995] 1 Lloyd's Rep. 223. See also *European Asian Bank AG v Punjab and Sind Bank* [1981] 2 Lloyd's Rep. 651.
[77] *Bank of Baroda v Vysya Bank Ltd* [1994] 2 Lloyd's Rep. 87. *Cf. PT Pan Indonesia Bank Ltd TBK v Marconi Communications International Ltd*, above, in which the confirming bank had no place of business in England where payment was to be made through an advising bank. As issuing and confirming bank were both situated in Indonesia, it is likely (see at [67]) that the contract between the two banks, which was not an issue in the case, would have been governed by Indonesian law as a result of Art. 4(2). See also *Arab Banking Corp. BSC v First Union National Bank* (March 3, 2001, David Steel J.).
[78] *Bank of Baroda v Vysya Bank Ltd*, above, at p.92. See also Giuliano-Lagarde Report, p.20.
[79] *ibid. Cf. PT Pan Indonesia Bank Ltd TBK v Marconi Communications International Ltd*, above, at [67]. See also *Bank of Credit and Commerce Hong Kong Ltd v Sonali Bank*, above,
[80] *Bank of Baroda v Vysya Bank Ltd*, above, at p.93.
[81] Giuliano-Lagarde Report, p.20.

contract arises between that bank and the seller (beneficiary).[82] Again at common law this contract was regarded as having the closest connection with the country where the branch of the bank at which payment was to be made to the seller was situated.[83] It has also been concluded, *obiter*, that this continues to be the position under the Rome Convention.[84] This is because the characteristic performance is still that of the bank either because the bank provides a banking service[85] or because it is of the essence of a letter of credit that the confirming bank undertakes to pay the seller (beneficiary) on presentation of conforming documents.[86] The presumption in Article 4(2) would therefore point to the law of the country in which the branch (as place of business) of the bank where payment is to be made is situated.[87] In each of the foregoing situations it would, in relation to the Rome Convention, be unlikely that circumstances will be present justifying rebuttal of the presumption in Article 4(2) by reference to Article 4(5).[88] The remaining contract is that which arises between the seller (beneficiary) and the issuing bank. At common law, this contract was regarded as being most closely connected with the law of the country where payment was to be made against presentation of documents.[89] In relation to the Rome Convention, in this context, the characteristic performance of the contract would appear to be that of the bank so that the presumption in Article 4(2) would point to the law of the country in which the principal place of business or the place of business of the bank, as the case may be, is situated.[90] It has, however, been suggested, *obiter*, in an English decision that such a result would lead to confusion and a lack of clarity and simplicity in the issue and operation of international letters of credit.[91] In the light of these factors, it was possible to avoid the undesirable results of applying Article 4(2) by invoking Article 4(5) and deciding that the presumption in Article 4(2) should be displaced in favour of the law of the

---

[82] Above, para.23–181.
[83] *European Asian Bank AG v Punjab and Sind Bank* [1981] 2 Lloyd's Rep. 651.
[84] *Bank of Baroda v Vysya Bank Ltd*, above.
[85] Giuliano-Lagarde Report, p.20.
[86] *Bank of Baroda v Vysya Bank Ltd*, above, at p.92. See also *Bank of Credit and Commerce Hong Kong Ltd v Sonali Bank*, above.
[87] *Bank of Baroda v Vysya Bank Ltd*, above. Where a credit is subject to the eUCP (International Chamber of Commerce, Supplement to UCP 500 for electronic presentation (eUCP)-Version 1.0), above, paras 23–031—23–048, the place for presentation of any electronic record means an electronic address (Art. e3), but this does not in any way appear to affect the point made in the text which focuses not on the place of presentation but on the place of payment.
[88] *Bank of Baroda v Vysya Bank Ltd*, above, at p.92. *Cf.* the unusual case where confirming bank and issuing bank are located in the same foreign country, but payment is to be made through an advising bank in England. In such circumstances the presumption would be displaced in favour of English law as a result of Art. 4(5) (see *PT Pan Indonesia Bank Ltd TBK v Marconi Communications International Ltd*, above).
[89] *Offshore International SA v Banco Central SA* [1977] 1 W.L.R. 399.
[90] *Bank of Baroda v Vysya Bank Ltd*, above, at p.93; *PT Pan Indonesia Bank Ltd TBK v Marconi Communications International Ltd*, above.
[91] *ibid*.

country where payment was to be made against presentation of documents.[92]

Negotiable instruments. By virtue of the Bills of Exchange Act 1882 and various general rules of law, any bill of exchange involved in a sale transaction may be governed by a number of different laws. The reader is referred to appropriate sources.[93] The uniform rules contained in the Rome Convention do not apply to bills of exchange, cheques and promissory notes which will, therefore, continue to be governed by traditional English law.[94] More problematic, in the present context, is the exclusion of "other negotiable instruments to the extent that the obligations arising under such other negotiable instruments arise out of their negotiable character".[95] According to the Giuliano-Lagarde Report, the effect of this is that such documents as, *inter alia*, bills of lading and similar documents issued in connection with transport contracts may be excluded from the Convention if they can be regarded as negotiable instruments and the issue in the case concerns an obligation which arises out of their negotiable character.[96] Whether a document is to be regarded as a negotiable instrument is, according to the Report, a matter for the law of the forum including its rules of private international law, and is not governed by the Convention,[97] though it has also been suggested that the European Court of Justice might attempt to create an autonomous notion[98] of negotiable instrument for the purposes of the Convention.[99] Whether or not this suggestion will be implemented by the European Court remains, however, to be seen.[1] As far as English law is concerned, a bill of lading is not a true negotiable instrument since the holder of it cannot acquire a better title than his predecessor possessed.[2] For the purposes of private international law, an instrument must also possess this character to be negotiable,[3] but whether any particular instrument is negotiable in this sense is a question to be determined by the law of the country where the alleged transfer by way of 25–077

[92] *Bank of Baroda v Vysya Bank Ltd*, above, at p.93, where Mance J. relied on a passage now to be found in Dicey and Morris, *op. cit.*, para.33–124 to the effect that "the presumption may be most easily rebutted where the place of performance differs from the place of business of the party whose performance is characteristic of the contract". See to the same effect *PT Pan Indonesia Bank Ltd TBK v Marconi Communications International Ltd*, above. *Cf.* above. para.25–066.
[93] See Dicey and Morris, *op. cit.*, paras 33–315—33–369; *Chitty on Contracts* (29th ed.), Vol. 2, paras 34–198—34–218; *Byles on Bills of Exchange and Cheques* (27th ed.), Ch.25; Crawford and Falconbridge, *Banking and Bills of Exchange* (8th ed.), Ch.60; Chalmers and Guest, *On Bills of Exchange, Cheques and Promissory Notes* (16th ed.), paras 12–001—12–043. Some specific aspects of foreign bills are considered in Ch.22, above.
[94] Art. 1(2)(c). See *Zebrarise Ltd v De Nieffe* [2005] 1 Lloyd's Rep. 154 at [36].
[95] Art. 1(2)(c).
[96] P.11. Also mentioned are bonds, debentures, guarantees, letters of indemnity, certificates of deposit, warrants and warehouse receipts.
[97] *ibid*.
[98] Above, para.25–018.
[99] See Schultsz in *Contract Conflicts, op. cit.*, p.185 at p.188.
[1] See Plender, *op. cit.*, paras 4–16—4–17.
[2] See above, para.18–084.
[3] Dicey and Morris, *op. cit.*, paras 33–315—33–316.

negotiation takes place, *i.e.* the country in which the instrument is situated at the time of delivery.[4] Thus, a bill of lading transferred in England can never be a negotiable instrument and thus will always fall within the Convention. But a bill of lading transferred abroad in a country whose law attributes to it the character of a negotiable instrument as defined by English law may be negotiable and thus may fall outside the Convention to the extent that the obligation in issue arises out of its negotiable character.

5. FORMATION AND VALIDITY OF THE CONTRACT OF SALE

25–078 **Scope of this section.** The general question to be discussed in this section is what laws determine whether a contract of sale is duly formed and free from any defect rendering it invalid or unenforceable in whole or in part. The section accordingly covers such issues as contractual consent and capacity, and the formalities, essential validity and legality of the contract. Some of these issues arise also in the context of the proprietary aspects of a sale; thus, for example, the capacity of the parties to acquire or transfer title to goods must be considered in determining whether the title to the goods can pass under the sale. These issues in their proprietary aspect are, however, distinct from the contractual issues about to be dealt with, and are reserved for a later section dealing with proprietary matters in general.[5] The common law developed rules to deal with the various questions that arise on a case-by-case basis, though the general principle which emerged is that such questions were determined by the law applicable to the contract. This general principle is reflected in the Rome Convention which provides in Article 8(1) as follows. "The existence and validity of a contract, or of any term of a contract, shall be determined by the law which would govern it under this Convention if the contract or term were valid." Exceptionally, however, both at common law and under the Convention, other laws may impinge on the law which is generally applicable to the contract.

25–079 **Acts required to form the contract.**[6] Leaving aside formalities,[7] the question as to what minimum acts must be performed to constitute any contract, including a contract of sale, was, at common law, determined by the "putative proper law" of the contract, *i.e.* the law which would be the

---

[4] *ibid.*, at paras 32–318—33–320. *Cf. Macmillan Inc. v Bishopsgate Investment Trust Plc. (No.3)* [1996] 1 W.L.R. 387 at 400, *per* Staughton L.J.

[5] Below, paras 25–121 *et seq.*

[6] See generally Fawcett, Harris and Bridge, *International Sale of Goods in the Conflict of Laws* (2005), Ch.13; Plender, *The European Contracts Convention* (2nd ed.), paras 10–03—10–08; Dicey and Morris, *The Conflict of Laws* (13th ed.), paras 32–154—32–165; Cheshire and North, *Private International Law* (13th ed.), pp.587–589; Kaye, *The New Private International Law of Contract of the European Community* (1993), Ch.13; Lagarde in *Contract Conflicts* (North ed.) (1982), pp.49–51; Jaffey, 24 I.C.L.Q. 603 (1975); Libling, 42 M.L.R. 169 (1979); Thomson, 43 M.L.R. 650 (1980).

[7] See below, paras 25–086—25–088.

governing law if the transaction were in fact found to constitute a contract.[8] This rule was specifically laid down in relation to offer and acceptance,[9] and consideration.[10] The same solution to the problem is to be found in Article 8(1)[11] of the Rome Convention, which submits these matters to the "putative" applicable law.[12] Article 8(2), however, creates an exception to this general rule. "Nevertheless a party may rely upon the law of the country in which he has his habitual residence to establish that he did not consent if it appears from the circumstances that it would not be reasonable to determine the effect of his conduct in accordance with the law specified in" Article 8(1). The purpose of this rule is to "solve the problem of the implications of silence by one party as to the formation of the contract",[13] but the rule is not confined to that issue since the "word 'conduct' must be taken to cover both action and failure to act by the party[14] in question."[15] In deciding whether it would not be reasonable to determine the effect of the relevant party's conduct in accordance with the putative applicable law regard must be had to all the circumstances of the case and not only to the circumstances in which the party who is claiming not to have consented to the contract has acted. A court may, thus, apparently give particular consideration to the practices followed by the parties *inter se* as well as their previous business relationship.[16] This suggests that the exception may be relied upon by both natural and legal persons although it is likely that it will be applied more liberally to protect the former than the latter. If legal

---

[8] *Compania Naviera Micro SA v Shipley International Inc.* (*The Parouth*) [1982] 2 Lloyd's Rep. 351, where, it seems, the point did not in fact arise; *Astro Venturoso Compania Naviera v Hellenic Shipyards SA* (*The Mariannina*) [1983] 1 Lloyd's Rep. 12; *Chevron International Oil Co. Ltd v A/S Sea Team* (*The TS Havprins*) [1983] 2 Lloyd's Rep. 356; *Dubai Electricity Co. v Islamic Republic of Iran Shipping Lines* (*The Iran Vojdan*) [1984] 2 Lloyd's Rep. 380; see also *Wahbe Tamari and Sons Co. v Bernhard Rothfos* [1980] 2 Lloyd's Rep. 553; *Marc Rich & Co. AG v Soc. Italiana Impianti PA* (*The Atlantic Emperor*) [1989] 1 Lloyd's Rep. 548; *Union Transport Plc v Continental Lines SA* [1992] 1 W.L.R. 15 at 23; *Dimskal Shipping Co. SA v International Transport Workers Federation* [1992] 2 A.C. 152 (duress); contrast *Oceanic Sun Line Special Shipping Co. Inc. v Fay* (1988) 165 C.L.R. 197; *The Heidberg* [1994] 2 Lloyd's Rep. 287 (*lex fori*); Briggs [1989] L.M.C.L.Q. 192.

[9] *Albeko Schuhmaschinen AG v Kamborian Shoe Machine Co. Ltd* (1961) 111 L.J. 519 (though the point was only dealt with *obiter*).

[10] *Re Bonacina* [1912] 2 Ch. 394.

[11] Above, para.25–078.

[12] See *Egon Oldendorff v Libera Corp. (No.1)* [1995] 2 Lloyd's Rep. 64; *The Epsilon Rosa (No.2)* [2002] EWHC 2033 (Comm); [2002] 2 Lloyd's Rep. 701, affirmed on other grounds [2003] EWCA Civ. 938; [2003] 2 Lloyd's Rep. 509; *Horn Linie GmbH & Co. v Panamericana Formas E Impresos SA* [2006] EWHC 373 (Comm). This law also applies to the issue of consent to a choice of law in the contract itself. See above, para.25–034.

[13] Giuliano-Lagarde Report, p.28. See also discussion of Art. 9(4), below, para.25–086. Such a rule has support in Wolff, *Private International Law* (2nd ed.), p.349; Dicey and Morris, *op. cit.*, para.32–158. See *Egon Oldendorff v Libera Corp. (No.2)* [1996] 1 Lloyd's Rep. 380. For discussion of German case law applying Art. 8(2), see Plender, *op. cit.*, paras 10–06—10–08.

[14] The term can relate either to the offeror or the offeree: Giuliano-Lagarde Report, *ibid*.

[15] *ibid*.

[16] *ibid*.

persons can rely on the exception, however, further amplification will have to be given to the concept of habitual residence,[17] which may, perhaps, be construed in the case of a commercial contract entered into by such persons as the principal place of business thereof or where appropriate the place of business through which the contract is alleged to have been concluded.[18] Some brief consideration was given to the operation of Article 8(2) in *Egon Oldendorff v Libera Corp. (No.1)*,[19] where it was assumed, without argument that the provision could be relied upon by a legal person, and that the "habitual residence" of a Japanese corporation was in Japan. Mance J. held that English law should apply to determine whether a clause providing for arbitration in London was incorporated into that contract because the contract was governed by English law.[20] The defendants sought, pursuant to Article 8(2),[21] to rely on Japanese law, as the law of their habitual residence, claiming that it would not be reasonable to determine the effects of their conduct in accordance with English law. Mance J. held, however, that it would be unreasonable *not* to apply English law and to apply Japanese law. If Japanese law was applied, this would, in effect, be to ignore the arbitration clause, a result which would be contrary to normal commercial expectations. It may be thought that this case suggests that legal persons engaging in commercial transactions will receive little protection from Article 8(2) of the Convention, at least in typical, as opposed to unusual, commercial situations.[22]

It must be stressed that Article 8(2) can only have the effect of releasing a party from a contract to which he would be otherwise bound under Article 8(1). It cannot bind a party to a contract to which he would not be bound under the applicable law.[23]

25–080 At common law it was sometimes maintained that the putative proper law should be determined without regard to any choice of law made by the parties.[24] The better view, and that which is supported by the bulk of authority,[25] is that both an express and an implied choice of law can

[17] As to the meaning of which see above, paras 25–056, 25–062.
[18] See Lasok and Stone, *Conflict of Laws in the European Community* (1987), p.368. The analogy is drawn with Art. 4(2) of the Convention, above, paras 25–063—25–064.
[19] [1995] 2 Lloyd's Rep. 64. See also *The Epsilon Rosa (No.2)*, above; *Horne Linie GmbH & Co. v Panamericana Formas E Impresos SA*, above.
[20] See above, para.25–031.
[21] The onus of establishing that Art. 8(2) applies lies on the party who asserts its application: *Egon Oldendorff v Libera Corp. (No.1)*, above, at p.71.
[22] See *Horn Linie GmbH & Co. v Panamericana Formas E Impresos SA* [2006] EWHC 373 (Comm).
[23] Giuliano-Lagarde Report, p.28.
[24] *e.g.* Cheshire and North, *Private International Law* (11th ed.), pp.471–477. It is possible that this view rests on a confusion between the distinct concepts of "the putative proper law" and the "objective proper law".
[25] *The Parouth*, above; *The Iran Vojdan*, above; *Union Transport Plc. v Continental Lines SA* [1992] 1 W.L.R. 15 at 23; *Dimskal Shipping Co. SA v International Transport Workers Federation* [1992] 2 A.C. 152; *The Heidberg* [1994] 2 Lloyd's Rep. 287. *Cf. Mackender v Feldia* [1967] Q.B. 590, discussed in Dicey and Morris, *op. cit.*, para.32–163.

constitute the putative proper law and that it is not necessary to determine this law purely by reference to the law with which the contract has the closest and most real connection on objective grounds[26] unless, of course, the contract does not contain an express or implied choice of law. The wording of Article 8(1) of the Rome Convention clearly demonstrates that the same result is reached in cases falling within that Convention. There is nothing to suggest that the putative applicable law is to be determined through adoption of any rules other than the general rules.[27]

Third parties and agency. At common law the law applicable to the contract determined also who could sue or be sued upon the contract.[28] It followed that, where an agent, such as a commission merchant, had entered into a contract of sale for the account of the seller or the buyer, the question whether the agent alone,[29] or the principal alone,[30] or both principal and agent[31] could sue the other party to the contract or be sued by him was regulated by the law governing the contract.[32] This was, however, subject to a possible proviso to the effect that the principal would not be bound, whatever the law applicable to the contract of sale might say, if according to the law applicable to the contract between the principal and the agent, the agent had no authority at all to bind the principal in any contract,[33] or to act in the country in question.[34] 25–081

In determining the effect of the Rome Convention on these questions, it is first necessary to bear in mind that the rules of the Convention shall not apply to the question of whether an agent is able to bind a principal, or an 25–082

---

[26] Above, paras 25–008—25–010.

[27] Above, paras 25–029—25–068.

[28] *Scott v Pilkington* (1862) 2 B. & S. 11 at 43; *Maspons v Mildred* (1882) 9 Q.B.D. 530 at 539 (affirmed on other grounds *sub nom. Mildred v Maspons* (1883) 8 App.Cas. 874); *Anspach & Co. Ltd v CNR* [1950] 3 D.L.R. 26. By contrast, the question of joinder of parties, being a matter of procedure, is governed by the *lex fori*: *General Steam Navigation Co. v Guillou* (1843) 11 M. & W. 877.

[29] As is a common result in civil law systems, where the commission merchant contracting in his own name is recognised as a person of a distinct status, operating independently of the principal employing him.

[30] This is the more likely result under English law, even where the existence or the name of the principal is not disclosed to the other party: see *Bowstead & Reynolds on Agency* (17th ed.), Art. 78, paras 8–070 *et seq.*

[31] As in the case of "agents with special responsibility", such as confirming houses. The use of a confirming house may serve to avoid conflicts issues, *e.g.* where a seller in country X has an order from a buyer in country Y confirmed by a confirming house in country X: see Schmitthoff, 21 *Law and Contemporary Problems* 429 at 448–450 (1956).

[32] *Armstrong v Stokes* (1872) L.R. 7 Q.B. 598 at 605; *Maspons v Mildred* (1882) 9 Q.B.D. 530 (affirmed on other grounds *sub nom. Mildred v Maspons* (1883) 8 App.Cas. 874); *Chatenay v Brazilian Submarine Telegraph Co.* [1891] 1 Q.B. 79; *Kahler v Midland Bank Ltd* [1950] A.C. 24; *Girvin, Roper & Co. v Monteith* (1895) 23 R. 129; see too Dicey and Morris, *op. cit.*, paras 33–417—33–430.

[33] See *Sinfra AG v Sinfra Ltd* [1939] 2 All E.R. 675; *Ruby SS Corp. v Commercial Union Assurance Co. Ltd* (1933) 39 Com.Cas. 48; Schmitthoff, *Hague Recueil*, 1, 109, pp.174–179 (1970); Dicey and Morris, *op. cit.*, paras 33–420—33–426. The law applicable to the contract between principal and agent is discussed above, para.25–073.

[34] Dicey and Morris, *op. cit.*, para.33–428.

organ to bind a company or body corporate or unincorporate to a third party.[35] Such matters will continue to be governed by the common law rules discussed above. However, these questions must be distinguished from the more general question of the extent to which rights and obligations of the parties to a contract of sale are capable of affecting third parties. Strictly speaking this issue would not seem to fall within Article 8(1) which is intended to cover all aspects of "*formation* of the contract other than *general validity*".[36] Whether a contract is capable of affecting a third party seems to be a matter of general validity in the sense that it concerns the effects[37] of a contract which has, admittedly, been formed. Accordingly we are not dealing with the putative applicable law, but rather with the applicable law itself. The scope of the applicable law is set out in Article 10(1) of the Convention, which contains a list of issues which will be governed by the applicable law. Although the issue under discussion is not mentioned in that list, the list is not exhaustive[38] and other contractual issues are capable of being governed by the applicable law.[39] It is submitted that the extent to which third parties are affected by the contract is such an issue[40] which should as a matter of principle be referred to the applicable law.[41] However, if the question arises as to whether a person has become *a party* to a contract of sale, such question might properly be the subject of Article 8(1) and demand application of the putative applicable law.[42]

25–083 **Elements vitiating consent.**[43] At common law, the question whether an otherwise valid contract of sale was voidable on the ground of misrepresentation,[44] duress,[45] non-disclosure[46] or operative mistake or some other

---

[35] Art. 1(2)(f). See *Marubeni Hong Kong and South China Ltd v Mongolian Government* [2002] 2 All E.R. (Comm) 873, above, paras 25–024, 25–073. Note also that a change in the applicable law cannot affect the rights of third parties: see Art. 3(2), above, para.25–035.

[36] Giuliano-Lagarde Report, p.28, emphasis added.

[37] Dicey and Morris, *op. cit.*, para.32–187.

[38] "The law applicable to a contract, by virtue of . . . this Convention shall govern in particular."

[39] Giuliano-Lagarde Report, p.23.

[40] *cf. Atlas Shipping Agency (UK) Ltd v Suisse Atlantique Sociéte D'Armement Maritime SA* [1995] 2 Lloyd's Rep. 188 (where A contracts with B to pay a sum of money to C, an action brought to enforce the obligation by C involves "matters relating to a contract" for the purposes of Art. 5(1) of the Lugano Convention on Jurisdiction and the Enforcement of Judgments in Civil and Commercial matters 1988 (Civil Jurisdiction and Judgments Act 1982, Sch.3C)).

[41] Subject to the exceptions set out in Arts 1(2)(f) and 3(2). It is also submitted that the Contracts (Rights of Third Parties) Act 1999 (see *Chitty on Contracts* (29th ed.), paras 18–084—18–112) only applies if the contract is governed by English law: see *Prime Trade AG v Ythan Ltd* [2005] EWHC 2399; [2006] 1 All E.R. (Comm) 367 at [14]–[15].

[42] *Laemthong International Lines Co. v Artis (No.3)* [2005] EWHC 1595 (Comm).

[43] See generally Dicey and Morris, *op. cit.*, paras 32–163—32–165; Cheshire and North, *op. cit.*, pp.587–589; Jaffey, 24 I.C.L.Q. 603 (1975); Libling, 42 M.L.R. 169 (1979); Thomson, 43 M.L.R. 650 (1980).

[44] *British Controlled Oilfields Ltd v Stagg* [1921] W.N. 31.

[45] *Dimskal Shipping SA v International Transport Workers Federation* [1992] 2 A.C. 152; *cf. Kaufman v Gerson* [1904] 1 K.B. 591.

[46] *Mackender v Feldia AG* [1967] 2 Q.B. 590.

similar element vitiating consent was also, it seems, a matter for the law governing the contract.[47] Under the Rome Convention, the existence and effect of these vitiating elements would, pursuant to Article 8(1),[48] be determined by the law which would apply to the contract if the contract were valid.[49] But the rule set out in Article 8(2)[50] does not apply where it is alleged that consent is vitiated by the existence of such factors: that rule is limited to factors which concern the *existence* of consent and does not extend to factors which affect the *validity* of consent.[51]

Capacity of natural persons.[52] Despite contrary suggestions[53] (which are largely antiquated), it is submitted that, at common law, the contractual capacity of a natural person was governed by the law applicable to the contract.[54] It was also likely, though there was no authority approving the point, that the governing law, in this context, meant that law objectively determined without taking account of any choice of law in the contract itself.[55] Subject to one special rule, the uniform rules of the Rome Convention do not apply to questions involving the status or legal capacity of natural persons.[56] In general terms, therefore, the common law rule, will continue to apply on this issue even if, in other respects, the contract falls 25–084

[47] Note, however, the suggestion in *Mackender v Feldia AG*, above, at pp.598, 602–603, that if according to the *lex fori* a contract is totally void for mistake, this is enough to vitiate it irrespective of the applicable law. It has been maintained that this suggestion is to be confined to the separate issue of whether a contract exists for the sake of service out of the jurisdiction: see Cheshire and North, *Private International Law* (11th ed.), pp.476–477. This suggestion is inconsistent with that of the House of Lords in *Dimskal Shipping Co. SA v International Transport Workers Federation*, above: see Dicey and Morris, *op. cit.*, paras 32–163–32–164.
[48] Above, para.25–078.
[49] Giuliano-Lagarde Report, p.28; Lagarde in *Contract Conflicts, op. cit.*, pp.49–50; Lasok and Stone, *op. cit.*, pp.367–368. See *Halpern v Halpern* [2006] EWHC 603 (Comm); *cf. Credit Suisse First Boston (Europe) Ltd v Seagate Trading Co. Ltd* [1999] 1 Lloyd's Rep. 784.
[50] Above, para.25–079.
[51] Giuliano-Lagarde Report, p.28; Lagarde, above, at p.50.
[52] See generally Dicey and Morris, *op. cit.*, paras 32–214—32–224; Cheshire and North, *op. cit.*, pp.592–595; Blaikie [1984] S.L.T. 161.
[53] The *lex domicilii* is favoured in *Sottomayor v de Barros (No.1)* (1877) 3 P.D. 1, 5; *Re Cooke's Trusts* (1887) 56 L.J.Ch. 637 at 639; *Cooper v Cooper* (1888) 13 App.Cas. 88 at 89, 100; *Viditz v O'Hagan* [1900] 2 Ch. 87. The *lex loci contractus* is favoured in *Simonin v Mallac* (1860) 2 Sw. & Tr. 67 at 77; *Sottomayor v de Barros (No.2)* (1879) 5 P.D. 94 at 100–101; *Baindail v Baindail* [1946] P. 122 at 128; *McFeetridge v Stewarts and Lloyds Ltd*, 1913 S.C. 773; *Bondholders Securities Corp. v Manville* [1933] 4 D.L.R. 699; *Kent v Salomon* [1910] T.P.D. 637 (a sale of goods case); *cf. Male v Roberts* (1800) 3 Esp. 163 (a sale of goods case, but not free from ambiguity).
[54] *Charron v Montreal Trust Co.* (1958) 15 D.L.R. (2d) 240; *cf. The Bodley Head Ltd v Flegon* [1972] 1 W.L.R. 680; and see the authorities cited above, n.52. It is possible that the *lex domicilii* may be applied if it would give capacity but the objective proper law would not. See Dicey and Morris, *op. cit.*, para.32–222.
[55] It has been said that a party to a contract should not be permitted to confer capacity on himself through the express choice of a proper law: *Cooper v Cooper*, above, at p.108.
[56] Art. 1(2)(a). The matter is excluded because although common lawyers regard it as a contractual matter, civil lawyers tend to view it as a matter of status: see North in *Contract Conflicts, op. cit.*, p.3, at p.10.

within the provisions of the Convention. The special rule relating to capacity is contained in Article 11 of the Convention which provides as follows. "In a contract concluded between persons who are in the same country, a natural person who would have capacity under the law of that country may invoke his incapacity resulting from another law only if the other party to the contract was aware of this incapacity at the time of the conclusion of the contract or was not aware thereof as a result of negligence."[57] The limited scope of this rule is evident: it only applies to contracts which are concluded between persons who are in the same country, at least one of whom is a natural person who would have capacity under that country's law, but who invokes an incapacity imposed on him by the law of another country. That incapacity is rendered nugatory unless the other contracting party was aware of it or was unaware of it as a result of negligence.[58] In relation to a contract concluded "online", assuming that the parties are in the same country, the seller is even less likely to be aware of an incapacity imposed on a natural person by another law than he would be in the more traditional contractual situations envisaged in the Rome Convention. However, it is possible that a seller could be regarded as negligent in not being aware of such an incapacity, if, say, he took no steps at all to determine whether the other party was of full age by the law of the country where the parties were and the goods in which the seller dealt were likely to attract the attention of minors.[59]

25–085 **Corporate capacity.** In so far as the capacity of a corporation to enter into a contract for the sale of goods depends upon its powers under its constitution, the law of its country of incorporation is the governing law[60] and must be taken into account in addition to the law governing the contract on objective grounds.[61] Thus, a corporation must be taken to lack the capacity to enter into such a contract if the law of its country of incorporation so provides by virtue of matters pertaining to its powers under its constitution (for example, under the doctrine of *ultra vires*),[62] or if the law applicable to the contract on objective grounds so provides under a rule of capacity not specifically bearing upon the corporation's powers under its own constitution.[63] The Rome Convention excludes from its scope

---

57 Such a rule is not uncommon in civil law countries which regard contractual capacity as a matter of status to be governed by the personal law: see Giuliano-Lagarde Report, p.34; Wolff, *op. cit.*, pp.281–282.

58 "This wording implies that the burden of proof lies on the incapacitated party. It is he who must establish that the other party knew of his incapacity or should have known of it." Giuliano-Lagarde Report, *ibid*.

59 *cf.* amazon.co.uk, Marketplace, Auctions and Shops Participation Agreement, cl.1.1.1, which provides that "Use of the Services is limited to parties that can lawfully enter into and form contracts under English law (for example minors are not permitted to use the Services)": see *www.amazon.co.uk/exec/obidos/tg/browse/*.

60 *Risdon Iron and Locomotive Works Ltd v Furness* [1906] 1 K.B. 49; *Carl Zeiss Stiftung v Rayner and Keeler Ltd* (*No.2*) [1967] 1 A.C. 853.

61 Dicey and Morris, *op. cit.*, paras 30R–020—30–023; *cf. Carse v Coppen*, 1951 S.C. 233.

62 *cf. Janred Properties Ltd v Ente Nazionale Italiano per il Turismo* [1989] 2 All E.R. 444.

63 This is unlikely to happen in practice; the nearest English analogy is probably the now-repealed law of mortmain.

"questions governed by the law of companies and other bodies corporate or unincorporate"—such as "legal capacity".[64] According to the Giuliano-Lagarde Report this reference is to limitations which may be imposed by law on companies or firms.[65] It does not extend to *ultra vires* acts by organs of the company or firm[66]: these fall under Article 1(2)(f) which provides, *inter alia*, that the Convention does not apply to the question whether an organ can bind a company or body corporate or unincorporate to a third party. Although the wording of each of these provisions is not free from difficulty,[67] their combined intent would seem to be to exclude, generally, the issue of the contractual capacity of a corporation, however arising, from the scope of the Covention so that the common law rules, referred to above[68] will continue to apply to this issue.

Formalities.[69] It was generally accepted at common law that in general any contract, including a contract of sale, was valid in point of form if it complied with the formal requirements[70] of either the law applicable to the contract[71] or the *lex loci contractus*.[72] Similar principles are expressed in Article 9 of the Rome Convention, though the rules therein are of a more detailed character. Where a contract is concluded between persons who are in the same country, the contract will be formally valid if it satisfies the formal requirements of the law which governs the contract under the Convention or the formal requirements of the law of the country where it is concluded.[73] Where the contract is concluded between persons who are in different countries, the contract will be formally valid if it satisfies the formal requirements either of the law applicable to it under the Convention or the law of one of those different countries.[74] If the contract is concluded by an agent the relevant country for the purposes of the preceding rules is 25–086

---

[64] Art. 1(2)(e). See above, para.25–024.

[65] Giuliano-Lagarde Report, p.12. The example given is a limitation on power to acquire immovable property.

[66] *ibid.*, at p.13.

[67] Dicey and Morris, *op. cit.*, paras 30–025—30–028; Lasok and Stone, *op. cit.*, p.353.

[68] Above, paras 25–024, 25–073, 25–081—25–082.

[69] See generally Plender, *op. cit.*, paras 10–009—10–012; Dicey and Morris, *op. cit.*, paras 32–173—32–183; Cheshire and North, *op. cit.*, pp.589–592; Kaye, *op. cit.*, pp.251–295; Lagarde in *Contract Conflicts, op. cit.*, p.49, at pp.51–54.

[70] If an apparently formal requirement under a foreign law is on a proper characterisation procedural only, it must be ignored for the purpose of this rule. For an instance, see n.87, below.

[71] *Van Grutten v Digby* (1862) 31 Beav. 561; *NV Handel Maatschappij J Smits v English Exporters (London) Ltd* [1955] 2 Lloyd's Rep. 317 (and see *Re Bankes* [1902] 2 Ch. 333; *Viditz v O'Hagan* [1899] 2 Ch. 569 (rvsd. on other grounds [1900] 2 Ch. 87)).

[72] *Guépratte v Young* (1851) 4 De G. & Sm. 217; *Green v Lewis* (1867) 26 U.C.Q.B. 618 (a sale of goods case); *cf.* the contrary implication in *NV Handel Maatschappij J Smits v English Exporters (London) Ltd*, above. In a few early cases, dealing with stamp duty laws for the most part, compliance with the *lex loci contractus* was said to be essential, but in each of them this law seems also to have been the law applicable to the contract: see *Alves v Hodgson* (1797) 7 T.R. 241; *Clegg v Levy* (1812) 3 Camp. 166; *Trimbey v Vignier* (1834) 1 Bing.N.C. 1; *Bristow v Sequeville* (1850) 5 Exch. 275.

[73] Art. 9(1).

[74] Art. 9(2).

the country where the agent acts.[75] By way of exception to these rules, the formal validity of a contract of sale which is a consumer contract within the meaning of Article 5 of the Convention and which is concluded in the circumstances set out in Article 5(2) thereof[76] is governed by the law of the country in which the consumer is habitually resident.[77] Article 9 also deals with the formal validity of an act intended to have legal effect in relation to an existing or contemplated contract, *e.g.* notice of termination[78] or an offer expressed to be open for a specified time.[79] Such an act is formally valid if it satisfies the formal requirements of the law which applies, or would apply, to the contract or the law of the country where the act was done.[80] Article 3(2) enables the parties to the contract to change the law which governs it.[81] However, the change in the applicable law shall not prejudice the formal validity of the contract: this means that the contract is valid, in this respect, if it complies with the formalities required by either the original or the new governing law or the laws of the country or countries where the parties were when they concluded the contract.[82] If a contract is subject to several governing laws (either because the parties have selected the law applicable to a part of the contract under Article 3(1)[83] or the court has, exceptionally, severed the contract under Article 4(1)),[84] it is suggested that "it would seem reasonable to apply the law applicable to the part of the contract most closely connected with the disputed condition on which its formal validity depends".[85]

25–087 A difficulty which exists both under the common law and under the Rome Convention is as to what requirements are properly characterised as formalities. The issue of formal validity has not been prominent in the common law because "English courts have a strong tendency to characterise as matters of procedure, especially as questions of evidence, many issues which abroad are characterised as matters of form".[86] If such a characterisation is placed upon an English rule which renders a contract invalid or unenforceable, then the rule will apply as part of the *lex fori* even if, were the requirement to be characterised as formal, the relevant applicable law or laws would regard it as valid.[87] The Rome Convention

[75] Art. 9(3).
[76] Above, paras 25–045, 25–048.
[77] Art. 9(5). For the meaning of habitual residence see above, paras 25–056, 25–062. There is also a special rule for contracts the subject-matter of which is a right in or a right to use immovable property: see Art. 9(6).
[78] Giuliano-Lagarde Report, p.29.
[79] Lasok and Stone, *op. cit.*, p.305.
[80] Art. 9(4).
[81] Above, para.25–038.
[82] Giuliano-Lagarde Report, p.30; Lagarde in *Contract Conflicts, op. cit.*, p.49 at pp.52–53.
[83] Above, para.25–033.
[84] Above, para.25–057.
[85] Giuliano-Lagarde Report, p.30.
[86] Dicey and Morris, *op. cit.*, para.32–176. See *Leroux v Brown* (1852) 12 C.B. 801; *G & H Montage GmbH v Irvani* [1990] 1 W.L.R. 667.
[87] *Leroux v Brown*, above (classifying s.4 of the Statute of Frauds 1677 in this

eschews any definition of formal validity or formal requirements,[88] but it has been suggested that it "is nevertheless permissible to consider form, for the purpose of Article 9, as including every external manifestation required on the part of a person expressing the will to be legally bound, and in the absence of which such expression of will would not be regarded as fully effective".[89] It may be that this approach to the definition of form will intrude on the scope of the category of procedure in English law, so that under the Convention the category of formal requirements should be enlarged at the expense of the category of procedure.[90]

A further difficulty arises with requirements of the law of the forum which are imposed with the aim of protecting a party presumed to be in a weak bargaining position.[91] It would seem that, at common law, such requirements were not procedural, but that their application depended on the true construction of the scope of the relevant (usually statutory) requirements.[92] Under the Rome Convention, it is submitted, such requirements if not applicable as part of the governing law, ought to be applicable if they are construed to be mandatory rules of the law of the forum whose application is required by Article 7(2).[93] **25–088**

---

manner). This decision has been much criticised: see, *e.g. Williams v Wheeler* (1860) 8 C.B.(N.S.) 299 at 316; *Gibson v Holland* (1865) L.R. 1.C.P. 1 at 8; *Monterosso Shipping Co. Ltd v International Transport Workers Federation* [1982] 3 All E.R. 841 at 845–846, 847–848; Dicey and Morris, *op. cit.*, paras 7–018—7–019. But it was approved in *G & H Montage GmbH v Irvani*, above. For consideration of issues relating to formalities in the context of commercial transactions and electronic commerce in English domestic law, see Law Commission, *Electronic Commerce: Formal Requirements in Commercial Transactions, Advice from the Law Commission* (December 2001). And see above, para.2–021.

[88] According to the Giuliano-Lagarde Report, p.29, it "seemed realistic to leave open this difficult problem of definition".

[89] *ibid.*

[90] Though, of course, the rules in the Rome Convention do not apply to evidence and procedure (subject to Art. 14): see Art. 1(2)(h). If the proposition in the text is correct this might require a reversal of *Leroux v Brown*, above, since s.4 of the Statute of Frauds 1677 could be treated as a question of form, the applicability of which would be determined by Art. 9. Alternatively, s.4 could be regarded as subject to Art. 14(2) which permits any act intended to have legal effect to be proved in any manner permitted by the law of the forum or in any manner permitted by the law which renders the contract or act formally valid under Art. 9, provided that the relevant mode of proof can be administered by the forum. If s.4 falls within this provision (as maintained by Lasok and Stone, *op. cit.*, pp.366–367, see too Dicey and Morris, *op. cit.*, paras 7–019, 32–176), *Leroux v Brown* would be reversed since the contract could have been proved by oral testimony under the (French) law which governed it. And see below, para.25–206.

[91] *e.g.* Consumer Credit 1974, ss.60–65. See Dicey and Morris, *op. cit.*, paras 33–031—33–037.

[92] See *English v Donnelly*, 1958 S.C. 494, not followed in *Hong Kong Shipping Ltd v The Cavalry* [1987] Hong Kong L. Rep. 287. *Cf. Kay's Leasing Corp. Pty Ltd v Fletcher* (1964) 116 L.L.R. 124. See also above, para.25–006, n.31.

[93] Above, para.25–042.

25–089 **Essential validity.**[94] Where there is no question of illegality,[95] the essential validity of each of the various terms of a contract of sale was, on general common law principles, governed by the law applicable to the contract.[96] Under the Rome Convention this question would appear to be properly characterised as one relating to the material validity of a term of the contract which, pursuant to Article 8(1), will be governed by the law which would be applicable to the contract, or if relevant, the term thereof, if the contract or term were valid. Thus, under both régimes, the law governing the contract will determine whether a clause purporting to vary normal f.o.b. terms is valid,[97] and whether or not, subject to the statutory provisions discussed in paragraphs 25–090—25–105, a term which purports to exclude or restrict liability is effective.[98] Since the uniform rules of the Convention do not apply to arbitration agreements or to agreements on the choice of court,[99] the validity of an arbitration clause or a jurisdiction clause in a contract of sale will continue to be determined by the law which governs the contract according to common law rules.[1]

25–089A **Effect of statutes.** The effect of the governing law may be specifically limited by the provisions of a statute.[2] Such provisions may be construed to apply to a contract governed by a foreign law[3] or may be applicable by virtue of a specific provision in the statute itself. An important example of the latter technique is to be found in the Unfair Contract Terms Act 1977, discussed in the following paragraphs.

25–090 **Unfair Contract Terms Act.** As regards the statutory controls imposed by the Unfair Contract Terms Act 1977 on contractual terms which purport to exclude or restrict liability,[4] the general principle that the law applicable to the contract[5] determines the validity of such a term has been substan-

[94] See generally Dicey and Morris, *op. cit.*, paras 32–166—32–170; Cheshire and North, *op. cit.*, pp.587–589.
[95] See below, para.25–119.
[96] *R. v International Trustee* [1937] A.C. 500; *Vita Food Products Inc. v Unus Shipping Co. Ltd* [1939] A.C. 277; *Amin Rasheed Shipping Corp. v Kuwait Insurance Co.* [1984] A.C. 50.
[97] *cf. NV Handel Maatschappij J Smits v English Exporters (London) Ltd* [1955] 2 Lloyd's Rep. 317.
[98] *P and O Steam Navigation Co. v Shand* (1865) 3 Moo.P.C. (N.S.) 272; *Re Missouri Steamship Co. Ltd* (1889) 42 Ch.D. 321; *Jones v Oceanic Steam Navigation Co.* [1924] 2 K.B. 730; *Drew Brown Ltd v The "Orient Trader"* (1972) 34 D.L.R (3d) 339.
[99] Art. 1(2)(d).
[1] *Hamlyn & Co. v Talisker Distillery* [1894] A.C. 202; *Spurrier v La Cloche* [1902] A.C. 446. (arbitration clause); *OT Africa Line Ltd v Magic Sportswear Corp.* [2005] EWCA Civ. 710; [2005] 2 Lloyd's Rep. 170; *Horn Linie GmbH & Co. v Panamericana Formas E Impresos SA* [2006] EWHC 373 (Comm) (jurisdiction clause).
[2] Rome Convention, Art. 7(2).
[3] See *Office of Fair Trading v Lloyds TSB Bank Plc* [2006] EWCA Civ. 268; [2006] 1 All E.R (Comm) 629 ("connected lender" liability of credit card issuer to a customer under Consumer Credit Act 1974, s.75(1) extended to transactions effected abroad). See also *Jarrett v Barclays Bank* [1999] Q.B. 1.
[4] The details of these statutory controls are discussed above, paras 13–062 *et seq*, 18–280.
[5] The following discussion applies to cases subject to the common law and to those falling within the Rome Convention.

tially modified by section 27 of the Act. Subsection (1) of this section (discussed in paragraphs 25–091—25–093) deals with cases where the law applicable to the relevant contract is "the law of some part of the United Kingdom" (hereafter abbreviated to "United Kingdom law").[6] Subsection (2), discussed in paragraphs 25–094—25–100, deals with cases where the law applicable is "the law of some country outside the United Kingdom" (hereafter abbreviated to "a foreign law").[7]

A specific preliminary limitation on the operation of section 27 should be noted, since numerous sales contracts which would otherwise fall within the section are excluded from it by virtue of section 26. This section provides in effect, that the Act's major provisions do not apply to "international supply contracts", as defined in section 26(3).[8] Accordingly, where, for example, a contract for the sale of high explosive detonators, made between an English manufacturer and a French buyer, provides for delivery from England to France and contains an exemption clause restricting liability for personal injury caused by negligent manufacture, the question whether section 2 of the 1977 Act, under which such a clause would be void, is applicable may be resolved by simply saying that this is an international supply contract under section 26, so that there is no need to invoke section 27. This leaves for regulation under section 27 sales contracts which do have a foreign element, so as to attract choice of law rules, but are not "international" in the sense laid down in section 26. Examples are (i) a contract of sale involving English parties and taking place wholly within England, but containing a choice of law clause selecting French law and (ii) the converse, *i.e.* a contract wholly French but for the choice of English law as the governing law. In the case of contracts not for the sale of goods and not otherwise involving the passing of ownership or possession of goods, section 27 is potentially relevant so long as there is a foreign element, because the contract cannot be an "international supply contract".

---

[6] As originally enacted, s.27(1) used the term "proper law" of the contract. This terminology is substituted by "law applicable to" as a result of Contracts (Applicable Law) Act 1990, s.5 and Sch.4. See above, para.25–002.

[7] In s.27(3), a separate version of s.27(2)(b) is set out for Scotland. For commentary on s.27, see Fawcett, Harris and Bridge, *op. cit.*, paras 13–301—13–320; Plender, *op. cit.*, paras 7–02—7–04; Dicey and Morris, *op. cit.*, paras 1–054, 1–058—1–059, 33–028—33–030, 33–106—33–108; Cheshire and North, *op. cit.*, pp.579–581; Thompson, *Unfair Contract Terms Act 1977* (1978), Ch.8; Mann, 26 I.C.L.Q. 903 (1977); 27 I.C.L.Q. 661 (1978). As to the application of s.27 in relation to the Sale and Supply of Goods to Consumers Regulations 2002, see below, paras 25–111 *et seq.* For proposals to reform ss.26 and 27, see Law Commission, *Unfair Terms in Contracts*, Law Com. No.292 (2005), paras 7.1–7.64 and Draft Bill, cl. 18–20.

[8] This definition is set out and discussed above, para.18–281; too Thompson, *op. cit.*, paras 96–101. It is submitted that s.26 applies to contracts with a foreign governing law as well as to contracts governed by UK law: the contrary view leads to glaring anomalies when s.27(2) is taken into account. See, on the interpretation of s.26(3), *Ocean Chemical Transport Inc. v Exnor Craggs Ltd* [2000] 1 Lloyd's Rep. 446; *Amiri Flight Authority v BAE Systems Plc* [2003] EWCA Civ. 1447; [2003] 2 Lloyd's Rep. 767.

25–091 **Choice of law by the parties: United Kingdom law.** Subsection (1) of section 27 of the Unfair Contract Terms Act 1977 provides as follows: "Where the law applicable to[9] a contract is the law of any part of the United Kingdom only by choice of the parties (and apart from that choice would be the law of some country outside the United Kingdom) sections 2 to 7[10] . . . of this Act do not operate as part of the law applicable to the contract."[11] The statutory provisions thus excised from United Kingdom law in its role as the applicable law deal with exclusion or restriction of certain specified categories of liability, as follows: negligence liability (section 2), liabilities arising in contract where one party deals as consumer or on the other's written standard terms of business (section 3) and liability for breach of a seller's implied undertakings as to title, etc., as to conformity of the goods with a description or sample, or as to their quality or fitness for a particular purpose (section 6). In addition, the provisions in question invalidate contractual terms purporting to impose an unreasonable indemnity upon a person dealing as a consumer (section 4) and terms or notices purporting to exclude or restrict liability in specified categories of case where the term or notice is contained in or operates by reference to a "guarantee" of goods in consumer use, but the parties are not the seller and buyer of such goods (section 5). With relation to other miscellaneous contracts, apart from contracts for sale or hire purchase, under which possession or ownership of goods passes, exclusion and restriction of various specified forms of liability are also covered (section 7).

25–092 Ascertainment of the precise scope and effect of section 27(1) is difficult in several respects. First, it is clear that the phrase "only by choice of the parties" includes an express choice of law, but does it also include a choice of law which is demonstrated with reasonable certainty by the terms of the contract or the circumstances of the case according to Article 3(1) of the Rome Convention?[12] It is submitted that the phrase is apt to cover such a choice of law since it contemplates circumstances where the parties have manifested an intention to have their contractual relations governed by a particular law even if they have not designated it as such expressly.[13] It is suggested that section 27(1) is thus attempting to draw a distinction between the law chosen by the parties, expressly or impliedly, and the law which would apply in the absence of such a choice, as a result of the rules contained in Article 4 of the Rome Convention,[14] a distinction which, it is submitted, is implicit in the amendments to section 27(1) introduced by the Contracts (Applicable Law) Act 1990[15] where no opportunity is taken to

---

[9] Language substituting the words "proper law of" the contract contained in the original version of s.27(1): Contracts (Applicable Law) Act 1990, s.5 and Sch.4.
[10] As regards Scotland, the relevant provisions are ss.16–21.
[11] Language substituting the words "of the proper law" contained in the original version of s.27(1): Contracts (Applicable Law) Act 1990, s.5 and Sch.4. *Cf.* Late Payment of Commercial Debts (Interest) Act 1998, s.12(1), below, para.25–162.
[12] Above, paras 25–030—25–032. For analysis of s.27(1) in the context of the common law choice of law rules, see the 5th ed. of this work paras 25–086—25–087.
[13] See *Surzur Overseas Ltd v Ocean Reliance Shipping Co. Ltd* [1997] C.L.Y. 906; Giuliano-Lagarde Report, p.17; Plender, *op. cit.*, para.7–03.
[14] Above, paras 25–057—25–067.
[15] s.5 and Sch.4, above, nn. 9, 11.

limit the meaning of the phrase to an express choice of law, it being preferred instead, it would appear, to include any choice of law which satisfies Article 3. This distinction, however, may not be particularly easy to draw in practice in the sense that it may not be obvious in a particular case whether a choice satisfying Article 3(1) has in fact been made.[16] However, it would seem that if there is such a choice of United Kingdom law, the applicable law "apart from that choice would be the law of some country outside the United Kingdom" if application of the rule in Article 4 of the Rome Convention would point to that being the case. If, therefore, United Kingdom law is not only the chosen law but also the law which is applicable by virtue of Article 4, then the controls in the Act will operate as part of the applicable law. It would also seem that objective factors (*e.g.* an arbitration clause selecting arbitration in the United Kingdom) can be referred to in determining the law, applicable under Article 4 even if that factor is also regarded as relevant in deciding whether the parties have chosen United Kingdom law as the applicable law.[17]

A further problem arising out of section 27(1) relates to the phrase "do not operate as part of the law applicable to the contract." Its apparent effect is that where a contract falls within the subsection, any term excluding or restricting liability is free from the controls imposed by sections 2 to 7 of the Act, but is still subject to other subsisting statutory controls imposed by United Kingdom law—for example, section 8 of the Act, which deals with terms purporting to exclude or restrict liability for misrepresentation—and to such common law principles for the control of such clauses as may exist.[18] But if the parties, believing that the controls imposed by sections 2 to 7 of the Unfair Contract Terms Act were indeed fair, desired that they should apply to the contract, would section 27(1) render this impossible? The wording is "*do* not operate *as part of the law applicable to the contract*", not "may not apply to the contract". It would seem to follow, though this submission is inevitably tentative, that the parties could invoke the principle of "incorporation by reference", discussed earlier,[19] because this is not the same as choosing a governing law. They could accordingly both choose United Kingdom law as the governing law and stipulate that, notwithstanding section 27(1), the provisions of sections 2 to 7 were incorporated by reference into the contract. A final problem with section 27(1) concerns its relationship with Articles 3(3) and 5 of the Rome Convention. The former provision stipulates that if the parties have chosen a foreign law to govern the contract, but all the other elements relevant to the situation at the time of the choice are connected with one country only, then the choice of law shall not prejudice the application of the mandatory rules of that one country.[20] Assume that a **25–093**

---

[16] *cf. Amin Rasheed Shipping Corp. v Kuwait Insurance Co. Ltd* [1984] A.C. 50.
[17] Under Art. 4, this fact could be used to rebut the presumption under Art. 4(2) if that presumption prima facie indicated that the law of some country outside the UK was applicable.
[18] Above, para.13–006.
[19] Above, paras 25–006, n.34, 25–028.
[20] Above, paras 25–037—25–041.

contract of sale, otherwise entirely connected with France, contains an express choice of English law. Section 27(1) would indicate that the controls in sections 2 to 7 of the Unfair Contract Terms Act 1977 will not apply. Nonetheless, the English court would seem to be obliged, according to Article 3(3), to apply any French mandatory rules which might be more stringent than sections 2 to 7 or less stringent than those sections but more stringent than those English rules which will still apply to the contract.[21] A similar problem arises, in relation to Article 5,[22] if the consumer is habitually resident abroad but there is a choice of English law which would not, according to section 27(1), attract the controls of sections 2 to 7. If the circumstances stipulated in Article 5 exist, the consumer cannot be deprived of the protection afforded to him by the mandatory rules of the law of his habitual residence.[23] In English proceedings, therefore, the court will have to apply these mandatory rules if they are more stringent than the relevant English rules which are applicable (excluding, of course, sections 2 to 7).

25–094 **Choice of law by the parties: a foreign law.** Subject to the important limitations of scope described in paragraph 25–090 above, subsection 2 of section 27 of the Unfair Contract Terms Act 1977 renders the Act applicable to certain contracts even though they have or purport to have a foreign governing law. The wording of the subsection is as follows:

> "(2) This Act has effect notwithstanding any contract term which applies or purports to apply the law of some country outside the United Kingdom, where (either or both)—
>
> (a) the term appears to the court, or arbitrator or arbiter to have been imposed wholly or mainly for the purpose of enabling the party imposing it to evade the operation of this Act; or
>
> (b) in the making of the contract one of the parties dealt as consumer, and he was then habitually resident in the United Kingdom, and the essential steps necessary for the making of the contract were taken there, whether by him or by others on his behalf."

This subsection is fraught with problems.[24] The following questions call particularly for consideration.

25–095 First, the subsection speaks of a "contract term" which applies, or purports to apply the law of a country outside the United Kingdom. This clearly covers an express choice of law clause. But is this apt to exclude a choice which though not express is demonstrated with reasonable certainty under Article 3(1) of the Rome Convention? It is submitted that in,

---

[21] Above, para.25–040.
[22] Above, paras 25–044—25–056.
[23] Above, paras 25–047—25–056.
[24] For analysis of these problems in the context of the common law choice of law rules, see the 5th ed. of this work, paras 25–089—25–094. *Cf.* Late Payment of Commercial Debts (Interest) Act 1998, s.12(2), below, paras 25–162—25–163.

principle, such a choice of law is covered, since otherwise the obvious policy of the subsection—that of ensuring that the Act applies in cases of attempted "evasion" and to consumer sales having specified links with the United Kingdom—could be frustrated by the simple device of avoiding an express choice of law while including, say, a foreign jurisdiction clause which by demonstration with reasonable certainty, may constitute an effective choice of law. This general submission does not resolve, however, all the difficulties. The subsection speaks of a "*contract term*" which applies, or purports to apply the law of a country outside the United Kingdom. While an arbitration clause or a jurisdiction clause is such a term which purports to apply a foreign law, a choice which is demonstrated with reasonable certainty may also be derived from factors other than contract terms.[25] Article 3(1) of the Rome Convention, indeed, refers to a choice being demonstrated with reasonable certainty by the circumstances of the case as an explicit alternative to such[26] demonstration by the terms of the contract. Although the submission relies on a comparatively liberal interpretation of the phraseology under discussion, it is submitted that the subsection should be read as applying whenever a foreign law is the applicable law because it is demonstrated with reasonable certainty from the terms of the contract or the circumstances of the case. To interpret the subsection otherwise would be to strike at its policy as described above. To support this argument further, one might argue that when a choice of law is found to have been made by way of demonstration with reasonable certainty, then that choice of law becomes a term (perhaps implied) of the contract so that minimum violence is done to the language of the subsection.

Secondly, a choice of foreign law by the parties which is ineffective under **25–096**
the Rome Convention[27] (*e.g.* because valid consent was not given[28]) might nonetheless be thought to fall within the subsection because it "purports to apply" a foreign law. In such a case, the correct approach is seemingly (i) to determine whether the choice of law clause is effective according to Article 3; (ii) if it is not, to ascertain the objective governing law by applying the test contained in Article 4 of the Rome Convention; and (iii) if such law is *not* United Kingdom law, then and only then to determine whether the criteria in either paragraph (a) or paragraph (b) of section 27(2) are satisfied. If at step (iii) in the above analysis the law applicable to the contract under Article 4 of the Rome Convention, is United Kingdom law, there is no need to consider section 27(2) because the Unfair Contract Terms Act will be applicable on general choice of law principles.

Thirdly, the key concepts in paragraph (a) of the subsection need further **25–097**
elucidation. The paragraph speaks of one party to the contract "imposing" a choice of foreign law upon the other(s) with the "purpose" of "evading"

[25] Above, paras 25–030—25–032.
[26] Above, para.25–030.
[27] Above, paras 25–036—25–043.
[28] Above, para.25–034.

the Act's operation. The correct approach to the interpretation of the paragraph, it is submitted, entails construing "evade" in the light of "impose" and "purpose". If a party having dominant bargaining power expressly insists or insidiously ensures[29] that the other party or parties agree to the selection of a foreign law and he does so "wholly or mainly" with a view to ensuring that one or more exemption clauses operating in his favour should not be struck down by the Unfair Contract Terms Act, there is, it is submitted, an "imposition" of the foreign law with the "purpose" of "evading" the Act. According to this interpretation, it is not essential that apart from the selection of the foreign law the contract would have been subject, following Article 4 of the Rome Convention, to United Kingdom law. It is sufficient that the party "imposing" the choice of foreign law believes, however mistakenly, that if he did not do this, the Unfair Contract Terms Act would be applicable and that his purpose, wholly or mainly, was to evade the Act. In extreme situations, this may produce the result, perhaps anomalous, that a court in the United Kingdom applies the Act to a contract having virtually no objective links with the United Kingdom, simply because a dominant party, misled by an erroneous view of the law, acted in the manner and with the motives just described.

25–098 Fourthly, several phrases in paragraph (b) require consideration. The words "dealt as consumer" have a statutory definition in section 12 of the Act which is discussed elsewhere in this book.[30] "Habitually resident" is not defined in the Act itself, but it is a concept now employed in a number of United Kingdom statutes and is also discussed elsewhere in this book.[31] Paragraph (b) also speaks of "the essential steps necessary for the making of the contract" being taken in the United Kingdom, whether by the party dealing as consumer or others on his behalf. This does not, it is submitted, mean that *all* the steps required to constitute the contract in accordance (*semble*) with its "putative applicable law"[32] need to be taken in the United Kingdom, but only those incumbent upon the party dealing as consumer who, by hypothesis, habitually resides in the United Kingdom.[33] In cases of sale of goods, however, the choice between these two interpretations is unlikely to matter very much, because when the steps necessary to form the contract are taken partly in the United Kingdom and partly abroad, the contract will most likely, though not inevitably, be an "international supply contract" exempted from the operation of the Act by section 26. Having regard to section 26, the paradigm for a sale of goods case falling within

---

[29] As, for example, where a choice of foreign law is introduced into a standard form contract with an evasive purpose in mind.
[30] Above, paras 13–071 *et seq.*
[31] Above, paras 25–056, 25–062.
[32] This is the law determining whether the steps necessary to form a contract have been performed: above, para.25–079. Although s.27(2) curtails the operation of a foreign applicable law to the extent deemed necessary to give due scope to the rest of the Act, a contract falling within it is still governed in other respects by the applicable law, ascertained according to the relevant principles of the Rome Convention.
[33] See also the discussion of the similar terminology adopted in the first indent to Art. 5(2) of the Rome Convention, above, para.25–048.

section 27(2)(b) is a purchase of consumer goods by a person habitually resident in England from the English branch of a New York firm, where the goods are in England at all material times and the contract is wholly made in England, but it contains a clause nominating New York law as the governing law. This is not an "international supply contract" under section 26 and while it may fall within section 27(2)(a), the purchaser would face difficult problems in proving this. The natural way for him to establish that any exemption clause in the contract is subject to the Act despite the choice of a foreign law is to invoke section 27(2)(b).

A fifth difficulty concerns the relationship between section 27(2) of the Act and Article 5 of the Rome Convention. Section 27(2)(a) is of wider import than Article 5 and can apply to contracts of sale which do not fall within the definition of consumer contract[34] for the purposes of the latter provision. It is also likely that section 27(2)(a) constitutes a mandatory rule of English law which the court is free to apply, for that reason, as a result of Article 7(2) of the Convention.[35] As far as section 27(2)(b) is concerned, it would seem that the definition of consumer contract is in Article 5 wider than that given to the phrase "deals as consumer" in section 27(2)(b).[36] It is conceivable, therefore, that where the requirements of section 27(2)(b) cannot be established, but the requirements of Article 5 can be established, the consumer, if habitually resident in the United Kingdom, can rely on United Kingdom mandatory rules. But these rules would not appear to include the provisions of the Unfair Contract Terms Act because section 27(2)(b) includes the circumstances in which those controls are mandatory and such circumstances do not exist.[37] Where circumstances satisfying section 27(2)(b) do exist, then the controls may constitute mandatory rules of English law applicable under Article 7(2) of the Convention.[38] 25–099

Finally, it may be asked whether the parties to a sale taking place wholly within the United Kingdom would avoid the operation of the Act if they invoked ULIS as the governing law. Although probably unintended by the legislature, this seems to be the inevitable result because the phrase "law of some country outside the United Kingdom" in section 27(2) cannot on any view be interpreted to include ULIS. For reasons indicated below,[39] however, this expedient would not oust the operation of sections 12 to 15 of the Sale of Goods Act 1979, whereby undertakings as to title, compliance with description or sample, quality and fitness for purpose are implied into contracts of sale. To this extent the policy underlying the Unfair Contract Terms Act 1977 would still be implemented. 25–100

---

[34] Above, paras 25–045—25–046, 25–048.
[35] Above, para.25–042.
[36] See Hartley, in *Contract Conflicts*, *op. cit.*, at p.125. For the definition of "deals as consumer" see s.12(1), Unfair Contract Terms Act 1977, above, paras 13–071 *et seq.*
[37] But ss.12–15 of the Sale of Goods Act 1979 will apply, see below, para.25–160.
[38] Above, para.25–042.
[39] Below, paras 25–160, 25–169—25–171. As to ULIS itself, see above, para.25–003.

25–100A **EC consumer protection legislation.** The European Community has legislated significantly in the field of consumer protection in a fashion which attempts to take account of cross-border situations.[40] The following paragraphs identify and discuss some of the principal measures affecting sale of goods.

25–101 **Unfair Terms in Consumer Contracts Regulations 1999.** These Regulations[41] implement in the United Kingdom the EEC Council Directive of April 5, 1993 on unfair terms in consumer contracts.[42] The purpose of the Directive and the implementing Regulations (which are discussed in detail elsewhere in this work)[43] is to protect consumers against unfair contract terms in "contracts concluded between a seller or a supplier[44] and a" consumer[45] which protection obviously extends to contracts for the sale or supply of goods.[46] The Directive requires that Member States shall take the necessary measures to ensure that the consumer does not lose the protection of the Directive by virtue of a choice of the law of a non-Member country as the law applicable to the contract if the contract has a

---

[40] See generally Regulation (EC) 2006/2004 of the European Parliament and of the Council of October 27, 2004 on co-operation between national authorities responsible for the enforcement of consumer protection laws (the Regulation on consumer protection co-operation) ([2004] O.J. L364/1), Chs I, IV and V, applicable from December 29, 2005, Chs II and III applicable from December 29, 2006. See also Directive 2005/29/EC of the European Parliament and of the Council of May 11, 2005 concerning unfair business-to-consumer commercial practices and amending Council Directive 84/450/EEC, Directives 97/7/EC, 98/27EC and 2002/65/EC of the European Parliament and of the Council and Regulation (EC) 2006/2004 of the European Parliament and of the Council (Unfair Commercial Practices Directive) ([2005] O.J. L149/22), which must be implemented by June 12, 2007.

[41] SI 1999/2083, as amended by SI 2001/1186, revoking and replacing Unfair Terms in Consumer Contract Regulations 1994, SI 1994/3159.

[42] Council Directive 1993/13/EEC of April 5, 1993 on unfair terms in consumer contracts ([1993] O.J. L95/29).

[43] See above, paras 13–103, 14–030 *et seq.*

[44] Defined as "any natural or legal person who, in contracts covered by these Regulations, is acting for purposes relating to his trade, business or profession, whether publicly owned or privately owned": reg.3(1).

[45] reg.4(1). "Consumer" is defined as "any natural person who, in contracts covered by these Regulations, is acting for purposes outside his trade, business or profession": *ibid*.

[46] The 1994 Regulations, above, n.41, explicitly excluded contracts of employment, contracts relating to succession rights, contracts relating to rights under family law and contracts relating to the incorporation and organisation of companies or partnership (reg.3(1)) and Sch.1. There is no such explicit exclusion in the 1999 Regulations, but it would nonetheless appear that such contracts are not covered by the Regulations since they do not fall within the definition contained in reg.4(1) (above, n.45) and are also explicitly excluded from the scope of the Directive by Recital 10: see *Chitty on Contracts* (29th ed.) Vol. 1, paras 15–019—15–028 and above, para.14–031. It will be noted that many "consumer" contracts which might be ancillary to a contract of sale (*e.g.* insurance and certain banking contracts, above, paras 25–074—25–076) may be covered by the Regulations. The 1999 Regulations are expressed not to apply to contractual terms which reflect (a) mandatory statutory or regulatory provisions (including such provisions under the law of any Member State or in Community legislation having effect in the UK without further enactment); and (b) the provisions or principles of international conventions to which the Member States or the Community are party (reg.3(2)).

close connection with the territories of the Member States.[47] This obligation is implemented in the Regulations by a provision which stipulates that the "Regulations shall apply notwithstanding any contract term which applies or purports to apply the law of a non-Member State, if the contract has a close connection with the territory of the Member States".[48] Although the purpose of the provision—the prevention of the evasion of the Regulations by the choice of the law of a non-Member State—is clear, the provision is not free of interpretative difficulties, and further problems also arise in relation to the operation of the Regulations in the context of the conflict of laws.

It seems implicit in Regulation 9 that the Regulations will not apply when the law chosen in the contract is the law of a *Member State* other than the United Kingdom. This is presumably because the Directive will be part of the law of that State and, accordingly, the choice of that State's law will include the Directive as implemented in that State. However, the somewhat imprecise language[49] of the Directive may be interpreted differently in different Member States. Additionally, the indicative and non-exhaustive list of terms which may be regarded as unfair, contained in the Directive[50] (and in the Regulations)[51] may be supplemented by the addition of terms in the law of some Member States which are not added in the law of other Member States. It is conceivable, therefore, that a consumer could gain greater protection in an English court than would be received under the Regulations if the contract contains a choice of the law of a Member State where the Directive is interpreted more liberally than in England, or less protection if the choice of law is that of a Member State in which the Directive is interpreted less liberally than it is in England. Further, if the contract contains a choice of the law of another Member State and that law has expanded the non-exhaustive list of terms beyond that which is adopted in England, the consumer might again obtain greater protection than would be received under the Regulations. The consumer cannot obtain less protection than would be received under the non-exhaustive list contained in the Regulations by a choice of the law of another Member State since that list, taken from the Directive, would seem to constitute an irreducible minimum list of terms. **25–102**

Regulation 9 initially provides that the "Regulations shall apply notwithstanding any *contract term which applies or purports to apply* the law of a non-Member State". The italicised words in this statement reflect the **25–103**

[47] Art. 6(2).

[48] Reg.9. "Member State" is defined as "a State which is a contracting party to the EEA Agreement" (reg.3(1)) and EEA Agreement means the Agreement on the European Economic Area signed at Oporto on May 2, 1992 as adjusted by the Protocol signed at Brussels on March 17, 1993 (*ibid.*).

[49] See above, para.14–034. A choice of law clause in a contract between a seller or a supplier and a consumer is normally a "contractual term which has not been individually negotiated" (reg.5(1)), but since such clauses are specifically catered for in reg. 9, they would not appear to be subject to the general provisions of the Regulations. *Cf. Oceano Grupo Editorial SA v Rocio Murciano Quintero* (C–241/98–C–244/98) [2000] E.C.R. I–4941 (choice of jurisdiction clause). See also *Standard Bank London Ltd v Apostolakis* [2002] C.L.C. 939.

[50] Art. 3(3) and Annex.

[51] Reg.4(4) and Sch.3.

language of section 27(2) of the Unfair Contract Terms Act 1977 and were discussed earlier in this section.[52] It is submitted that the same conclusions should be reached as to the meaning of these words in the context of Regulation 9 as were there reached in relation to section 27(2) of the 1977 Act.[53] According to Regulation 9, however, the Regulations will only apply in this situation "if the contract has a close connection with the territory of the Member States". First, it would seem that, in an English court, the Regulations will be applied if the contract has no, or no close, connection with England or the United Kingdom provided that the contract has a close connection with the territory of another Member State.[54] Secondly, the Regulations will apply in litigation in the United Kingdom if there is a choice of the law of a non-Member State, but the contract has a close connection with the United Kingdom. Thirdly, there is no indication in the provision of what factors will point to a "close connection" between the contract and the territory of the Member States. Drawing on an analogy with section 27(2)(b) of the Unfair Contract Terms Act 1977, a close connection might be found to exist between the contract and a particular Member State if the consumer was habitually resident in that country and the essential steps necessary for the making of the contract were taken there whether by him or by others on his behalf.[55] Further such a connection might be thought to exist if a consumer purchases goods over the counter from the seller at the seller's place of business in a Member State even if the consumer was not habitually resident in that State. Equally, such a connection might be established if a seller solicits business from consumers in other countries (which, perhaps, need not not be Member States) from the seller's place of business in a Member State by mail shots or advertising, or electronic means.[56] And, doubtless, other factors may give rise to the required connection in particular cases. It seems fairly clear that in requiring a *close* connection with the territory of the Member States, it is not necessary, for the purposes of Regulation 9, that the contract has its *closest* connection with the territory of the Member States, *i.e.* it is not necessary to establish that the law of a particular Member State would have been the applicable law in the absence of the choice of the law of a non-Member State.[57] Thus the Regulations should apply if there is the choice of the law of a non-Member State in the contract even if that law is not the law that would be applicable to the contract on objective grounds, provided there is a connection between the contract and the territory of the Member States which can be concluded to be a close connection. What is less clear is whether a close connection must be established between the contract and the territory of one Member State or whether it is enough that there be a close connection between the

[52] Above, paras 25–095—25–096.
[53] *ibid.*
[54] *cf.* Unfair Contract Terms Act 1977, s.27(1).
[55] Above, para.25–098.
[56] *cf.* above, paras 25–049—25–053.
[57] *cf.* Rome Convention, Art. 3(3) (above, paras 25–037—25–041 and Art. 7(1) (which does not have the force of law in the UK, Contracts (Applicable Law) Act 1990, s.2(2)), above, para.25–038.

contract and the territories of two or more Member States when the circumstances of the connections are analysed cumulatively, even though, if the circumstances were to be analysed by reference to connections between the contract and each particular Member State it would not be possible to establish a close connection with any one particular State. It is not possible to answer this question with any degree of confidence.[58] However, it is suggested that it will certainly be enough to establish a close connection between the contract and the territory of one Member State, and that, probably, it will be enough to establish, collectively, a close connection with the territory of the Member States even though individual connections with particular Member States may not be close. This suggestion is made, first, because Regulation 9 and Article 6(2) of the Directive use the expression "territory of the Member States", *i.e.* the plural, and secondly, because the Directive is a Community wide measure designed to protect consumers who engage in transactions within the internal market that the Community has created.[59] If this observation is correct, it should also follow that the general scope of the Directive (and the Regulations) should be limited to transactions effected within the internal market, so that the provisions should not extend to transactions taking place in a non-Member State.

The 1999 Regulations are silent upon other conflict of laws' questions which may arise. It may be noted, first, however, that there is no provision equivalent to section 26 of the Unfair Contract Terms Act 1977, excluding "international supply contracts" from the scope of the Regulations.[60] Secondly, there is no provision equivalent to section 27(1) of the 1977 Act excluding the operation of the Regulations where, but for the choice of law by the parties, the law applicable to the contract would be the law of a non-Member State.[61] The relationship between the Regulations and the Unfair Contract Terms Act 1977 is, in many respects, unclear, though it is fairly obvious that the provisions of the former are somewhat wider than the provisions of the latter. Whether, for the purposes of choice of law, in so far as each piece of legislation covers the same contract term, Regulation 9 will be construed to operate co-extensively with section 27(2) of the 1977 Act remains to be seen in the Community context. **25–104**

Where there is no choice of law in the contract, the applicability of the Regulations (and the Directive) will depend on general choice of law principles, *i.e.* on Article 5 of the Rome Convention if it is applicable[62] or on Article 4 of the Rome Convention in cases where Article 5 is inapplicable.[63] **25–105**

---

58 *cf.* the wording of Consumer Protection (Distance Selling) Regulations 2000, SI 2000/2334, reg.25(5), discussed below, paras 25–107—25–110.
59 See Preamble to the Directive, para.1.
60 Above, para.25–090.
61 Above, paras 25–091—25–092.
62 Above, para.25–067.
63 Above, paras 25–057—25–066.

25–106 The 1999 Regulations impose a duty upon the Office of Fair Trading to consider complaints[64] made to it that any contract term drawn up for general use is unfair.[65] If having considered a complaint about any such term, the Office of Fair Trading considers the term unfair, it may, if it considers it appropriate, bring proceedings for an injunction against any person appearing to it to be using or recommending use of such a term in contracts concluded with consumers.[66] Similar powers and duties are imposed on certain "qualifying bodies" specified in the Regulations.[67] The powers and duties of the Office of Fair Trading or any relevant "qualifying body", in these respects belong to what one might call the public or regulatory law of consumer protection which appear to involve no choice of law questions. Presumably, however, such powers may only be exercised within the United Kingdom and then only against persons who are subject to the jurisdiction of the United Kingdom courts.[68]

25–107 **Consumer Protection (Distance Selling) Regulations 2000.** Although these Regulations[69] are not, strictly speaking, concerned with the validity of a contract or term thereof, they may be conveniently treated alongside the Unfair Terms in Consumer Contracts Regulations 1999[70] since, like the latter, they form part of the European Union's consumer protection programme and also contain an anti-avoidance provision which is similar, but not identical to, that contained in the latter Regulations.[71] The 2000 Regulations implement in the United Kingdom the European Parliament and Council Directive of May 20, 1997 on the protection of consumers in respect of distance contracts.[72] Very broadly, the Regulations seek to protect consumers who enter into "distance contracts",[73] which include, but are not limited to, contracts for the sale or supply of goods,[74] by providing

---

[64] See above, para.14–040 for more detailed consideration of these questions.
[65] Reg.10(1); Enterprise Act 2002, s.2(3).
[66] Reg. 12(1).
[67] Regs 10(1), 11, 12 and Sch.1; SI 2003/1374; SI 2003/1593.
[68] *cf.* Enterprise Act 2002, Pt 8, repealing and replacing Stop Now Orders (E.C. Directive) Regulations 2001 (SI 2001/1422), implementing Directive 1998/27/EC of the European Parliament and Council of May 19, 1998 on injunctions for the protection of consumers' interests ([1998] O.J. L166/51). See above, para.14–040.
[69] SI 2000/2334, as amended by SI 2004/2095 and SI 2005/689, implementing Directive 1997/7/EC of the European Parliament and Council of May 20, 1997 on the protection of consumers in respect of distance contracts ([1997] O.J. L144/19). The Regulations are discussed in detail, above, paras 14–053 *et seq.*
[70] Above, paras 25–101—25–106.
[71] Above, para.25–103.
[72] Above, n.69.
[73] Defined as "any contract concerning goods or services concluded between a supplier and a consumer under an organised distance sales or service provision scheme run by the supplier who, for the purpose of the contract, makes exclusive use of one or more means of distance communication up to and including the moment at which the contract is concluded": Reg.3(1). Consumer "means any natural person who, in contracts to which these Regulations apply, is acting for purposes which are outside his business": *ibid.* Supplier "means any person who, in contracts to which these Regulations apply, is acting in his commercial or professional capacity": *ibid.*
[74] For contracts to which the Regulations do not apply, or apply only in part, see Regs 5 and 6.

consumers, with, *inter alia*, the right to certain information,[75] the right to cancel the contract within a certain period of time[76] and the right to recover sums paid by the consumer on cancellation.[77] A distance contract may be concluded by a variety of "means of distance communication",[78] an indicative, but non-exhaustive, list of which is set out in the Regulations[79] and in the Directive.[80] The Directive provides that "Member States shall take the measures needed to ensure that the consumer does not lose the protection granted by this Directive by virtue of the choice of the law of a non-member country as the law applicable to the contract if the latter has close connection with the territory of one or more Member States."[81] This obligation is implemented in Regulation 25(5) which provides that the "Regulations shall apply notwithstanding any contract term which applies or purports to apply the law of a non-Member State if the contract has a close connection with the territory of a Member State."[82] Each of these provisions has the same purpose as their equivalents in the Directive and Regulations concerning unfair terms in consumer contracts already discussed,[83] but there are some differences of terminology to which attention must be drawn and consideration must also be given to the difference between the wording of the provision of the Directive and the wording of the implementing provision found in Regulation 25(5). Before examining these issues attention can be briefly given to other questions of conflict of laws generated by this legislation.

It is implicit in Regulation 25(5) that the Regulations will not apply if the law chosen in the contract is the law of a *Member State* other than the United Kingdom, and that if such a law is chosen the Directive, as implemented in that State, will apply as part of the law of that State. The Directive may be interpreted differently in different Member States, 25–108

[75] Regs 6 and 7.
[76] Regs 10–13.
[77] Reg.14.
[78] Defined as "any means which, without the simultaneous physical presence of the supplier and the consumer, may be used for the conclusion of a contract between those parties": Reg.3(1).
[79] Sch.1, which lists: unaddressed printed matter; addressed printed matter; letter; press advertising with order form; catalogue; telephone with human intervention; telephone without human intervention (automatic calling machine, audiotext); radio; videophone (telephone with screen); videotext (microcomputer and television screen) with keyboard or touch screen; electronic mail; facsimile machine (fax); television (teleshopping). While websites are not explicitly mentioned, it would seem inevitable that the list will be extended to include them.
[80] Annex 1, which contains the same list as that set out in the preceding note.
[81] Art. 10(2). Member State means a State which is a contracting party to the EEA Agreement and EEA Agreement means the Agreement on the European Economic Area signed at Oporto on May 2, 1992 as adjusted by the Protocol signed at Brussels on March 17, 1993.
[82] See also Financial Services (Distance Marketing) Regulations 2004 (SI 2004/2095), Art. 16(3), implementing Directive 2002/65/EC of the European Parliament and of the Council of September 23, 2002 concerning the distance marketing of consumer financial services and amending Council Directive 90/619/EEC and Directives 97/7/EC and 98/27/EC ([2002] O.J. L271/16).
[83] Above, para.25–101.

thereby raising the possibility that, say, an English resident consumer, party to such a contract, might receive more, or, less, protection, under the law of the other Member State than would be available under the Regulations.[84] Further, since the list of means of distance communication is only indicative, and not exhaustive, it is conceivable that some Member States may extend the list of means beyond that adopted in England so that a consumer who is party to a contract governed by the law of one of these Member States will receive the protection of the Directive when he would not be protected by the Regulations.[85]

25–109 In relation to Regulation 25(5), the phrase "any contract term which applies or purports to apply the law of a non-Member State" must be interpreted in the same manner as the identical phrase used in Regulation 9 of the Unfair Terms in Consumer Contract Regulations 1999.[86] However, whereas the latter Regulation stipulated that in a contract governed by the law of a non-Member State, the 1999 Regulations apply if the contract has a *close connection with the territory of the Member States*; Regulation 25(5) provides that in relation to a contract containing such a choice of law clause, the 2000 Regulations apply if the contract has a *close connection with the territory of a Member State*. These different formulations raise the question of whether the 2000 Regulations will only apply in the situation under discussion if the close connection is with one Member State only, whereas it is possible that the 1999 Regulations apply if there is no close connection with any one Member State, though there is cumulatively a close connection with the territory of the Member *States* because of less than close connections with several of them.[87] It is hard to believe that the difference of treatment referred to was intended by the draftsman, not least because the terminology of the provision of the Directive which is implemented in Regulation 25(5) speaks of a "close connection with the territory of *one or more Member States*."[88] It is therefore tentatively suggested that Regulation 25(5) should be interpreted in a manner consistent with the Directive[89] and that the choice of the law of a non-Member State should not prejudice application of the Regulations if there is a close cumulative connection with the territory of the Member States though no particularly close connection with any one of them.[90]

25–110 While it is not possible to state exhaustively the circumstances in which a sufficiently close connection will be found to exist, it seems likely that the fact that the consumer is habitually resident in a Member State would be

[84] *cf.* above, para.25–102.
[85] *cf.* above, para.25–102.
[86] *cf.* above, para.25–103.
[87] *cf.* above para.25–103. See also the terminology in the Directive on consumer sales and associated guarantees, below, para.25–112.
[88] Art. 10(2).
[89] See *Litster v Forth Dry Dock and Engineering Co. Ltd* [1990] 1 A.C. 546; *Marleasing v La Comercial Internacional de Alimentacion SA* (C–106/89) [1990] E.C.R. I-3313.
[90] If this conclusion is unacceptable the wording of the Regulations will have to be changed to bring the provision into line with the Directive.

one such circumstance[91] and it is also possible that the same conclusion could be reached where the seller directs his activities towards a Member State or States with a view to inducing consumers to buy.[92] The fact that the seller has a business establishment in a Member State or States from which any means of distance communication are conducted is also likely to be regarded as sufficient.

Sale and Supply of Goods to Consumers Regulations 2002. These Regulations[93] implement in the United Kingdom the Directive of the European Parliament and of the Council of May 25, 1999 on certain aspects of the sale of consumer goods and associated guarantees.[94] Implementation in the Regulations largely takes the form of amendments to the Sale of Goods Act 1979[95] to increase the protection afforded to a buyer who "deals as consumer".[96] A free-standing provision applicable independently of the 1979 Act is concerned with consumer guarantees.[97] 25–111

Article 7(2) of the Directive contains an anti-avoidance provision to the effect that "Member States shall take the necessary measures to ensure that consumers are not deprived of the protection afforded by this Directive as a result of opting for the law of a non-Member State as the law applicable to the contract where the contract has a close connection with the territory of the Member States".[98] Article 7(2) has not, however, been specifically transposed into the 2002 Regulations,[99] it being thought, apparently, that the obligation to transpose the provision was discharged in existing legislation, namely section 27 of the Unfair Contract Terms Act 1977.[1] This assumption is almost certainly incorrect. 25–112

The anti-avoidance provision in section 27 of the Unfair Contract Terms Act 1977 is found in section 27(2), discussed in detail earlier in this section,[2] but the terms of which it is necessary to repeat at this point. 25–113

---

[91] *cf.* above, para.25–103.
[92] *cf.* above, para.25–103.
[93] SI 2002/3045.
[94] Directive 1999/44/EC of the European Parliament and of the Council of May 25, 1999 on certain aspects of the sale of consumer goods and associated guarantees ([1999] O.J. L171/12).
[95] See, in particular, Sale of Goods Act 1979, s.14 and regs 3–5. For full discussion, see above, paras 11–033 *et seq.*, 12–071 *et seq.*, 14–008 *et seq.*
[96] Sale of Goods Act 1979, s.61(5A); Unfair Contract Terms Act 1977, s.12(1). See above, para.13–071 *et seq.*
[97] Reg.15. See above, para.14–066 *et seq.*
[98] This formula is slightly different to that used in the Directive on Unfair Terms in Consumer Contracts (above, para.25–101) and to that used in the Directive on Distance Selling (above, para.25–109).
[99] In contrast to the position taken in the Unfair Terms in Consumer Contract Regulations 1999, reg.9 (above, para.25–101) and in the Consumer Protection (Distance Selling) Regulations 2000, reg.25(2) (above, para.25–109).
[1] *See Department of Trade and Industry, Consumer and Competition Policy Directorate*, Directive 1999/44/EC of the European Parliament and of the Council of May 25, 1999 on certain aspects of the sale of consumer goods and associated guarantees, Transposition Note.
[2] Above, paras 25–094—25–099.

"This Act has effect notwithstanding any contract term which applies or purports to apply the law of some country outside the United Kingdom, where (either or both)—

(a) the term appears to the court or arbitrator or arbiter to have been imposed wholly or mainly for the purpose of enabling the party imposing it to evade the operation of this Act; or
(b) in the making of the contract one of the parties dealt as consumer and he was then habitually resident in the United Kingdom, and the essential steps necessary for the making of the contract were taken there, whether by him or others on his behalf."

The following paragraphs draw attention to specific points affecting the application of this subsection in the context of the 2002 Regulations.

25–114 The principal difficulty in implementing Article 7(2) of the Directive through the Unfair Contract Terms Act 1977 lies in the fact that that Act does not apply at all where the contract is an "international supply contract", as defined in section 26 of the 1977 Act, and a contract may be an international supply contract for these purposes even if it is concluded by a buyer who deals as consumer.[3] It is highly likely that a cross-border consumer contract concluded by a buyer who deals as consumer will be excluded from the 1977 Act by section 26, as for example, in a case where a consumer habitually resident in England orders goods from a seller whose place of business is in France, it being agreed that the goods will be carried from France to England.[4] If this is correct then if the contract is expressed to be governed by French law and contains a term which purports to exclude section 14 of the Sale of Goods Act 1979, as amended by the present Regulations, then the effect of that term will be determined by French law, including the Directive as implemented in France and the controls in the 1977 Act will not apply. If the contract is expressed to be governed by English law then the validity of the exclusionary term would also have to be determined, as a result of section 26, without regard to the controls contained in the 1977 Act. And if the contract is expressed to be governed by the law of a non-Member State, say the law of New York, and the exclusion of the seller's liability was effective under that law, section 26 would again seem to indicate that the controls in the 1977 Act will not apply. The outcomes in the Second and third examples hardly seem consistent with proper implementation of the Directive and the outcome in the third example seems to be in direct contravention of Article 7(2) of the Directive, so that in consequence the Directive will not, in this respect, have been properly implemented in the United Kingdom.[5]

---

[3] For detailed discussion of s.26, see above, para.18–281.
[4] See Unfair Contract Terms Act 1977, s.26(3) and (4); above, para.18–281.
[5] See Law Commission, *Unfair Terms in Contracts*, Law Com. No.292 (2005), para.7.4. This conclusion may be reinforced by the fact that the free-standing provision concerned with consumer guarantees (reg.15, above, para.14–066 *et seq.*) which is unconnected with the amendments to the Sale of Goods Act 1979 does not,

Where the contract is excluded from the Unfair Contract Terms Act 1977 by section 26, it is unlikely that section 14 of the Sale of Goods Act 1979, as amended, or other relevant provisions of the 2002 Regulations can be construed as mandatory rules of the law of the forum applicable by virtue of Article 7(2) of the Rome Convention[6] or, for the same reason, as mandatory rules of the law of the consumer's habitual residence applicable under Article 5 of the Rome Convention.[7] It is, however, possible that a term excluding relevant provisions of the Regulations in a contract expressed to be governed by the law of a non-Member State which would regard the exclusion as effective will fall foul of the Unfair Terms in Consumer Contracts Regulations 1999.[8] Those Regulations do not contain any provision equivalent to section 26 of the Unfair Contract Terms Act 1977. Accordingly, those Regulations will apply notwithstanding the choice of the law of a non-Member State if the contract has a close connection with the territory of the Member States.[9] Thus, in the example given above, where the contract between the consumer and the seller contains a choice of New York law, the 1999 Regulations could, in an appropriate case, be invoked to strike down the exclusionary term. And where the contract is governed by English law, the 1999 Regulations, as part of the applicable law, may also be applied to strike down any offending term.

Even if it can be established that the relevant contract is not excluded from the Unfair Contract Terms Act 1977 by section 26 of the Act, that does not resolve the difficulties that arise, since the application of the anti-avoidance provision in section 27(2) of the 1977 Act referred to above also presents problems.

First, the opening words of the subsection stipulate that the controls in the 1977 Act apply notwithstanding any contract term which applies or purports to apply *the law of some country outside the United Kingdom*. The italicised words clearly include the laws of countries which are not Member States, as envisaged by Article 7(2) of the Directive. Thus, for example, it will not be possible, as against a buyer who deals as consumer, to exclude the provisions of section 14 of the Sale of Goods Act 1979, as amended by the Regulations, by the choice of the law of a non-Member State which has provisions less protective of the consumer than those which are contained **25–115**

on the face of it, seem subject to any anti-avoidance provision. It has also been argued that s.26 of the 1977 Act is in breach of EC Treaty, Art. 12, in that it discriminates against purchasers who are nationals of Member States (see Burbidge [2002] N.L.J. 1544), but this conclusion is debateable: (see Law Commission, *ibid.*, paras 7.44–7.51). The section may, further, be in breach of Arts 28 and 29 of the Treaty as constituting a restriction on the free movement of goods and of Art. 49 as constituting a restriction on the free movement of services (*cf. Phillip Alexander Securities and Futures Ltd v Bamberger* [1997] I.L.Pr. 73). The Law Commission recommends that s.26 should not be replicated for consumer contracts (Law Commission, *ibid.*, paras 7.5–7.6).

[6] Above, paras 25–042, 25–055.

[7] Above, para.25–055.

[8] See Unfair Terms in Consumer Contracts Regulations 1999, regs 5–8, above, paras 14–031 *et seq.*

[9] *ibid.*, reg.9, above, para.25–101.

in section 14, if the circumstances required by section 27(2) are present. Further, it would not, it is suggested, be possible to exclude the new remedies established by the Regulations.[10] These provisions would thus apply in relation to a purchase of goods by a buyer dealing as consumer who is habitually resident in England from the English branch of a New York firm where the goods are in England at all material times and the contract is wholly made in England, but the contract is expressed to be governed by the law of New York.[11]

It will, however, be noticed that the italicised words set out above are also apt to include the laws of countries which are Member States. A literal reading of the words appears to envisage the application of the controls in the 1977 Act even where the chosen law is the law of another Member State and even where the chosen law is more favourable to the consumer[12] than are the provisions of the 1977 Act. On this basis, where a buyer dealing as consumer who is habitually resident in England purchases goods from an English branch of a French firm, where the goods are in England at all material times and the contract is wholly made in England, but the contract is expressed to be governed by French law, then the controls in the 1977 Act must be applied even if the buyer would receive greater protection under French law than he would receive under the 1977 Act. It is, however, arguable that the clear implication to be derived from Article 7(2) of the Directive is that where the contract is governed by the law of another Member State, by reason of a choice by the parties, then that State's law will be the governing law.[13] Accordingly, it may be that the Directive envisages that the Directive, as implemented in the other Member State, should apply in such a case.

25–116 Secondly, section 27(2) of the 1977 Act can only apply if its terms are satisfied. It is possible, however, that a contract containing the choice of the law of a non-Member State may have a close connection with England for the purposes of Article 7(2) of the Directive even though the precise requirements of section 27(2) do not exist in the particular case. Such a situation may exist where a buyer dealing as consumer is habitually resident in, for example, Germany and purchases goods from the English branch of a New York firm, where the goods are in England at all material times and the contract is wholly made in England, but the contract is expressed to be governed by New York law. Section 27(2)(b) cannot apply since the consumer is not habitually resident in England and it may not be possible to prove that the requirements of section 27(2)(a) are satisfied[14] so that section 27(2) as a whole is inapplicable.

---

[10] It may be possible to exclude the provisions concerned with consumer guarantees (see above, para.25–114). As to the new s.20(4) concerned with risk, see above, paras 6–013 *et seq.*

[11] *cf.* Unfair Contract Terms Act 1977, ss.5, 6(2)(a) and 13(1)(b). See above, para.25–114 and below, para.25–171.

[12] This is clearly possible since the Directive only establishes a minimum standard of protection for the consumer: see above, para.14–008.

[13] See the discussion of Unfair Terms in Consumer Contracts Regulations 1999, reg.9 and Consumer Protection (Distance Selling) Regulations 2000, reg.25(2), above, paras 25–102—25–103, 25–107, 25–110.

[14] See above, para.25–095.

It is highly unlikely that in such circumstances relevant provisions of the Regulations may be applicable as mandatory rules of the law of the forum pursuant to Article 7(2) of the Rome Convention.[15] This is because section 27(2) determines the circumstances in which those provisions will be regarded as mandatory. For the same reason it is highly unlikely that Article 5 of the Rome Convention may have the effect of making relevant provisions of the Regulations applicable.[16] It may, however, be possible to resort to the Unfair Terms in Consumer Contracts Regulations 1999, which is not subject to the restrictions found in section 27(2) in an appropriate case.[17]

Thirdly, even if the terms of section 27(2) are satisfied, that subsection can only be used to ensure the application of English law. It is possible, however, that a contract containing the choice of the law of a non-Member State will have a close connection with the territory of a Member State other than the United Kingdom, though the case is brought before an English court because the seller is subject to English jurisdiction. In such a case, Article 7(2) of the Directive would seem to envisage application of the law of the Member State (including the Directive as implemented in that State) with which the contract has a close connection, but section 27(2) cannot be used to reach this conclusion. 25–117

Fourthly, reference to "section 27" of the Unfair Contract Terms Act 1977 in the Transposition Note referred to above[18] suggests that the applicability of the controls in the 1977 Act may also depend on section 27(1) of that Act. That subsection provides that "Where the law applicable to a contract is the law of any part of the United Kingdom only by choice of the parties (and apart from that choice would be the law of some country outside the United Kingdom) sections 2 to 7 . . . of this Act do not operate as part of the law applicable to the contract."[19]. Section 27(1) is not an anti-avoidance provision in the sense of Article 7(2) of the Directive and there is no other provision of the Directive equivalent to it. It would, therefore, not seem necessary to apply section 27(1) of the 1977 Act in order to comply with the Directive. Indeed, it can be said that in some circumstances application of section 27(1) can be positively inimical to the purposes of the Directive. If the provision is applicable in the present context, the effect will be that if English law is applicable only by choice of the parties, that will not prevent exclusion of, say, section 14 of the Sale of Goods Act 1979, as amended by the Regulations, even if the contract would, apart from the choice of law, be governed by the law of another Member State. This outcome hardly seems consistent with the overall policy of minimum consumer protection which informs the Directive, particularly when it is recalled that the policy of section 27(1) was to avoid discouraging "foreign businessmen from agreeing to arbitrate their disputes in England or Scotland",[20] a policy which has little, if any, relevance to consumer 25–118

---

[15] See above, paras 25–042, 25–055.
[16] See above, para.25–055.
[17] See above, para.25–104.
[18] Above, para.25–112, n.1.
[19] For detailed discussion, see above, para.25–091-25–054.
[20] Law Com. No.69 (1975), para.232.

protection. It would be most consistent with the policy of the Directive not to apply section 27(1) at all where the applicable law in the absence of choice is the law of a Member State.[21]

25–119 **Legality.**[22] In order to determine whether any contract, including a contract of sale, is wholly or partly unenforceable on account of illegality, it is necessary to refer to a number of different principles. In the first place, a contract is unenforceable for illegality to the extent that it is illegal under its governing law,[23] at common law, or, under the Rome Convention, illegal by the law which would be applicable to the contract if the contract was valid.[24] Secondly, if any party in making or performing the contract commits or assists another to commit in England a criminal offence under English law,[25] or commits abroad an act which is a criminal offence under English law by virtue of a statutory provision which has sufficient extra-territorial operation to apply to the act,[26] then, even though the governing law is not English law, the contract is unenforceable in England by the party in question.[27] In cases to which the Rome Convention applies, this principle seems to continue in effect since the rules applicable by virtue of it would appear to be mandatory rules of the law of the English forum which apply irrespective of the law applicable to the contract so that Article 7(2)[28] may be invoked to secure their application. This principle does not, however, apply if the relevant rule of English law is not intended to affect the validity of contracts.[29] Thirdly, a

---

[21] If it is not possible to do this, further problems will arise concerning the relationship between the subsection and Arts 3(3) and 5 of the Rome Convention, as discussed above, para.25–054.

[22] See generally Dicey and Morris, *op. cit.*, paras 32–137—32–148, 32–166—32–170; Cheshire and North, *op. cit.*, pp.600–603; Jaffey, 23 I.C.L.Q. 1 (1974); Wyatt, 37 M.L.R. 399 (1974).

[23] *Kahler v Midland Bank Ltd* [1950] A.C. 24; *Zivnostenska Banka v Frankman* [1950] A.C. 57 (exchange control legislation). See below, para.25–102. But the rule will not apply if the relevant provision of a foreign governing law, through being, for instance, a grave infringement of, or offence against, human rights, is not recognised in England on grounds of public policy: see *Empresa Exportadora de Azucar v Industria Azucazeio National SA* (*The Playa Larga*) [1983] 2 Lloyd's Rep. 171 at 189–190. See also *Re Helbert Wagg Ltd* [1956] Ch. 323 at 345–346, 351–352; *Oppenheimer v Cattermole* [1976] A.C. 249; *Royal Boskalis Westminster NV v Mountain* [1999] Q.B. 674; *Kuwait Airways Corp. v Iraqi Airways Co. (Nos 4 and 5)* [2002] UKHL 19; [2002] 2 A.C. 883 at [15]–[29], [111]–[118], [135]–[149]. See above para.25–043.

[24] Rome Convention, Art. 8(1). See Lagarde in *Contract Conflicts, op. cit.*, p.49; Lasok and Stone, *op. cit.*, p.368; Plender, *op. cit.*, para.10–02. This is of course, subject to the foreign law complying with public policy under Art. 16.

[25] Examples in the context of sale of goods are: (a) where a statutory provision as to the minimum deposit in a credit sale has been violated; and (b) where a foreign seller dispatching goods to a buyer in England has packed them so as to assist the buyer to smuggle them into England (*Clugas v Penaluna* (1791) 4 T.R. 466; *Waymell v Reed* (1794) 5 T.R. 599; *Vandyke v Hewitt* (1800) 1 East 96; *cf. Pellecat v Angell* (1835) 2 Cr.M. & R. 311; and see *Holman v Johnson* (1775) 1 Cowp. 341).

[26] *Boissevain v Weil* [1950] A.C. 327; *Martovana v Morley* [1958] C.L.Y. 2943; *Al-Kishtaini v Shansal* [2001] EWCA Civ. 264 [2001] 2 All E.R. (Comm) 601.

[27] *cf.* the somewhat wider dictum of Diplock L.J. in *Mackender v Feldia AG* [1967] 2 Q.B. 590 at 601.

[28] See above, para.25–042.

[29] As to this aspect of English domestic law, see *Chitty on Contracts*, (29th ed.), Vol. 1, paras 16–014 *et seq.*

contract, whatever its governing law, is unenforceable in England in so far as its enforcement would offend English public policy, both at common law and under the Rome Convention.[30] The specific principles deriving from public policy in this context are numerous and diverse.[31] Earlier case-law is likely, however, to influence the attitude of the courts to the application of Article 16 of the Rome Convention, though the requirement that any applicable law must be *manifestly* incompatible with English public policy[32] should lead the courts to proceed with caution. In the particular context of sale of goods, the most significant principles of public policy are (a) that a contract involving trading with an alien enemy is illegal and unenforceable[33]; (b) that a contract or contractual term which is in unreasonable restraint of trade is unenforceable in England at least so far as it affects trade in England[34]; (c) that where the parties make the contract[35] with the intention[36] that its performance should involve the commission in a foreign and friendly country[37] of an act which would violate that country's laws, neither party[38] can enforce the contract in England[39]; and (d) where a contract governed by English law involves a transaction to be performed abroad which is contrary to a head of English public policy based on general principles of morality, the same public

---

[30] Art. 16. And see above, para.25–043.

[31] They are not co-extensive with the rules of public policy in the purely domestic sphere, but are somewhat narrower: see, *e.g. Addison v Brown* [1954] 1 W.L.R. 779.

[32] Which must be understood to include "Community public policy" (see above, para.25–043).

[33] *Dynamit AG v Rio Tinto Co. Ltd* [1918] A.C. 260 (a sale of goods case).

[34] *cf. Rousillon v Rousillon* (1880) 14 Ch.D. 351. Strictly speaking, this is not a question of illegality, but it is most conveniently dealt with in the context thereof.

[35] This principle clearly applies where the applicable law is English law, and probably where it is a foreign law: see Dicey and Morris, *op. cit.*, paras 32–236—32–238; Mann, 18 B.Y.B.I.L. 97 at 109 (1937); but *cf. Regazzoni v K C Sethia (1944) Ltd* [1958] A.C. 301 at 323.

[36] Such intention need not, it seems, form part of the contract: *Regazzoni v K C Sethia (1944) Ltd*, above; *contra Fielding and Platt Ltd v Najjar* [1969] 1 W.L.R. 357. Where one party does not have the necessary illicit intention he cannot be affected by this principle (see *ibid.*; *Continental Lines SA v W H Holt & Sons (Chorlton-cum-Hardy) Ltd* (1932) 43 Ll.L.R. 392; *Pye Ltd v BG Transport Service Ltd* [1966] 2 Lloyd's Rep. 300); *quaere* whether the other party can be so affected. The four authorities cited in this note are all sale of goods cases.

[37] The principle does not apply if the act is committed outside the foreign country and is only illegal under its law by virtue of the extra-territorial operation thereof: *British Nylon Spinners Ltd v Imperial Chemical Industries Ltd* [1953] Ch. 19; *Sharif v Azad* [1967] 1 Q.B. 605 at 617.

[38] Except, perhaps, a party who "repents" and performs the contract in a legal manner: *Fielding and Platt Ltd v Najjar*, above, at p.362.

[39] See, in addition to the authorities already cited, *De Wütz v Hendricks* (1824) 2 Bing. 314; *Foster v Driscoll* [1929] 1 K.B. 470; *Mahonia Ltd v JP Morgan Chase Bank* [2003] EWHC 1927 (Comm); [2003] 2 Lloyd's Rep. 911; *Tekron Resources Ltd v Guinea Investment Co. Ltd* [2003] EWHC 2577 (Comm); [2004] 2 Lloyd's Rep. 26; *Mahonia Ltd v JP Morgan Chase Bank, West LB AG* [2004] EWHC 1938 (Comm); *JSC Zestafoni G Nikoladze Ferroalloy Plant v Ronly Holdings Ltd* [2004] EWHC 245 (Comm); [2004] 2 Lloyd's Rep. 335; *Barros Mattos Junior v MacDaniels Ltd* [2004] EWHC 1188 (Ch); [2005] 1 W.L.R. 247; *Royal Trust Co. Ltd v Campeau Corp.* (1981) 118 D.L.R. (3d) 207. A contract between nationals of two countries which are friendly to England but at war with each other will, however, be enforced: *Dalmia Dairy Industries Ltd v National Bank of Pakistan* [1978] 2 Lloyd's Rep. 223.

policy applying in the country of performance so that the contract would not be enforceable under the law of that country.[40] Finally, the case of *Ralli Bros v Compania Naviera Sota y Aznar*[41] laid down a common law rule that where an act required by a contract to be performed in a foreign country becomes illegal under a provision of that country's law,[42] the contractual obligation to perform that act is *pro tanto* discharged.[43] The exact scope of this principle is controversial. It has been suggested that it applies whether or not the contract is governed by English law,[44] but the better view is that the governing law must be English law[45] and that the effect of illegality by the *lex loci solutionis* on a contract governed by a foreign law is a matter for that foreign law.[46] The principle of the *Ralli Bros* case[47] presumably covers cases of initial illegality[48] as well as supervening illegality, though this point has been doubted.[49] It has been applied in a number of sale of goods cases where under the *lex loci solutionis* an export or import licence had to be obtained[50]

---

[40] *Lemenda Trading Co. Ltd v African Middle East Petroleum Co. Ltd* [1988] Q.B. 448.

[41] [1920] 2 K.B. 287; see also *The Playa Larga* [1983] 2 Lloyds Rep. 171 at 190–191; *The Nile Co. for the Export of Agricultural Crops v H & J M Bennett* (*Commodities*) *Ltd* [1986] 1 Lloyd's Rep. 555; *Euro-Diam Ltd v Bathurst* [1990] 1 Q.B. 1; *Libyan Arab Foreign Bank v Banker's Trust Co.* [1989] Q.B. 728; *Society of Lloyd's v Fraser* [1998] C.L.C. 1630 at 1653; *Ispahani v Bank Melli Iran* [1998] Lloyd's Rep. Bank. 133; *Royal Boskalis Westminster NV v Mountain* [1999] Q.B. 674; *Fox v Henderson Investment Fund Ltd* [1999] 2 Lloyd's Rep. 303; *Tekron Resources Ltd v Guinea Investment Co. Ltd* [2003] EWHC 2577 (Comm); [2004] 2 Lloyd's Rep. 26; *Barros Mattos Junior v MacDaniels Ltd* [2004] EWHC 1188 (Ch); [2005] 1 W.L.R. 247; *Continental Enterprises Ltd v Shandong Zhucheng Foreign Trade Group Co.* [2005] EWHC 92 (Comm); and above, para.18–339.

[42] Except, perhaps, a provision of revenue law: *Mackender v Feldia AG* [1967] 2 Q.B. 590 at 601.

[43] Though there may be an action based on a collateral warranty that the contract is legal under the foreign law: see *Peter Cassidy Seed Co. Ltd v Osuustukkukappa I.L.* [1957] 1 W.L.R. 273; *Walton* (*Grain and Shipping*) *Ltd v British Italian Trading Co.* [1959] 1 Lloyd's Rep. 223 at 236; *The Playa Larga*, above; see above, paras 18–342—18–345.

[44] *Zivnostenska Banka v Frankman* [1950] A.C. 57 at 78; *Mackender v Feldia AG*, above, at p.601; and see *Cantiere* Navale Triestina v Russian Soviet Naphtha Agency [1925] 2 K.B. 172 at 208–209; *De Bèeche v South American Stores* (*Gath & Chaves*) *Ltd* [1935] A.C. 148 at 156; *R. v International Trustee* [1937] A.C. 500 at 519; *Kleinwort Sons & Co. v Ungarische Baumvolle Industrie AG* [1939] 2 K.B. 678 at 697–698.

[45] *Kahler v Midland Bank Ltd* [1950] A.C. 24 at 48; *Société Co-opérative Suisse des Céréales, etc. v La Plata Cereal Co. SA* (1949) 80 Ll.L.R. 530 at 543–544; *Walton* (*Grain and Shipping*) *Ltd v British Italian Trading Co.*, above, at p.236; *Ispahani v Bank Melli Iran* [1998] Lloyd's Rep. Bank 133; *Royal Boskalis Westminster NV v Mountain* [1999] Q.B. 674 at 733–734; and see, the further authorities mentioned in Dicey and Morris, *op. cit.*, paras 32–141—32–148. See also *Prodexport State Company for Foreign Trade v E D & F Man Ltd* [1973] Q.B. 389.

[46] Subject to the third instance of public policy just described; though see n.35, above.

[47] [1920] 2 K.B. 287.

[48] See *ibid.*, at p.303; *Cunningham v Dunn* (1878) 3 C.P.D. 443; *Walton* (*Grain and Shipping*) *Ltd v British Italian Trading Co.* [1959] 1 Lloyd's Rep. 223 at 236.

[49] *Partabmull Rameshar v K C Sethia (1944) Ltd* [1951] 2 Lloyd's Rep. 89 at 96.

[50] See, *e.g. Partabmull Rameshar v K C Sethia (1944) Ltd*, above; *A V Pound & Co. Ltd v M W Hardy & Co. Inc.* [1956] A.C. 568; *Walton* (*Grain and Shipping*) *Ltd v British Italian Trading Co.*, above; above, paras 18–339—18–341.

or export or import of the relevant goods was prohibited[51] or price control was in operation.[52] Since the United Kingdom has made a reservation to Article 7(1) of the Rome Convention, the *Ralli Bros* principle cannot be applied in cases falling within the Convention by reference to that provision.[53] If the principle only applies, as suggested above, where the contract is governed by English law, then it will operate where relevant, if the law applicable under the Convention is the law of England.[54] But if the principle is of wider import so that it applies irrespective of the law applicable to the contract, then it can only operate as a principle of English public policy under Article 16,[55] or, possibly, but very doubtfully, as a mandatory rule of English law under Article 7(2) of the Convention.

Illegality under any other foreign law—for example, the law of one party's nationality or place of business or residence,[56] or of a country where performance may but need not take place, or, it is submitted, of the place of contracting[57]—did not *per se* affect the contract's enforceability in England at common law, nor because of the United Kingdom's reservation to Article 7(1) of the Rome Convention[58] would there appear to be any place for the argument that illegality under these laws has any effect, as such, on a contract which falls within the provisions of the Convention.

Exchange control. Although a detailed examination of problems of exchange control in the conflict of laws must be sought in specialist works, some brief points may nevertheless be usefully made here.[59] First, a contract may be invalidated if it infringes the exchange control legislation of the governing law both at common law[60] and under the Rome Convention, in relation to the latter, either because the violation affects the material validity of the contract[61] or because the applicable law governs the performance of **25–120**

[51] See, *e.g. Kursell v Timber Operators & Contractors Ltd* [1927] 1 K.B. 299; *Société Co-opérative Suisse des Céréales etc. v La Plata Cereal Co. SA* (1949) 80 Ll.L.R. 530; *cf. Congimex Companhia Geral de Commercio Importadora & Exportadora SARL v Tradax Export SA* [1983] 1 Lloyd's Rep. 250; see above, paras 18–342—18–342.

[52] See, *e.g. Harrison Sons & Co. Ltd v Jules Cavroy* (1922) 12 Ll.L.R. 390; *cf. Mann, George & Co. v James and Alexander Brown* (1921) 10 Ll.L.R. 221.

[53] Contracts (Applicable Law) Act 1990, s.2(2), Sch.1, Art. 22. See Plender, *op. cit.*, paras 9–05—9–06.

[54] See Dicey and Morris, *op. cit.*, paras 32–145—32–148; Reynolds, 108 L.Q.R. 553 (1992).

[55] Lasok and Stone, *op. cit.*, p.373.

[56] *Trinidad Shipping Co. v Alston* [1920] A.C. 888; *Kleinwort Sons & Co. v Ungarische Baumvolle Industrie AG* [1939] 2 K.B. 678; *Toprak Mahsulleri Ofisi v Finagrain Compagnie Commerciale Agricole et Financie're SA* [1979] 2 Lloyd's Rep. 98.

[57] *Contra The Torni* [1932] P. 78 and a dictum in *Re Missouri Steamship Co. Ltd* (1889) 42 Ch.D. 321 at 336; but see the comments on these in *Vita Food Products Inc. v Unus Shipping Co. Ltd* [1939] A.C. 277 at 297–300; Dicey and Morris, *op. cit.*, paras 32–143—32–144.

[58] Contracts (Applicable Law) Act 1990, s.2(2) and Sch.1, Art. 22. Note, however, Art. 9(6) which applies to contracts the subject-matter of which is a right in, or right to use, immovable property.

[59] Dicey and Morris, *op. cit.*, paras 36–081—36–097; Proctor (ed.) *Mann, The Legal Aspect of Money* (6th ed.).

[60] See, *e.g. Kahler v Midland Bank Ltd* [1950] A.C. 24.

[61] Art. 8(1).

the contract.[62] Secondly, the same result might have ensued at common law if the contract infringed the exchange control legislation of the place where it was to be performed,[63] though under the Rome Convention it would seem that if the law applicable to the contract is foreign and that law does not recognise the effect of the legislation, it will have to be established that to the extent that it does not do so, application of the foreign applicable law would be manifestly contrary to public policy.[64] Each of these situations is an illustration of the effect of principles already discussed.[65] Finally, whatever its governing law and whatever the place of performance, an "exchange contract" involving the currency of any state which is a member of the International Monetary Fund and which is contrary to the exchange control regulations of any member maintained or imposed consistently with the International Monetary Fund Agreement—the Bretton Woods Agreement—is unenforceable in England.[66] It has been held that an "exchange contract" is a contract to exchange the currency of one country for the currency of another[67] rather than "any contract which in any way affects the country's exchange resources".[68] By such a definition a contract for the sale of goods would not be struck down by the Bretton Woods Agreement. However, it has also been held that a contract for the sale of goods may be an "exchange contract" if it is a monetary transaction in disguise, as, for example, where the price is increased so as to enable a foreign buyer to obtain foreign currency in breach of the exchange control legislation of his country.[69] Whether the sale is a monetary transaction in disguise is not a question of the construction of the contract but of the substance of the transaction to which enforcement of the contract would give effect.[70] Accordingly, an

---

[62] Art. 10(1)(b).

[63] *Ralli Bros v Companiera Naviera Sota y Aznar* [1920] K.B. 287; above, para.25–119 (noting the controversy surrounding the general principle).

[64] Art. 16. See *Ispahani v Bank Melli Iran* [1998] Lloyd's Rep. Bank. 133. above, para.25–043.

[65] Above, paras 25–043, 25–119. These rules are subject to the proviso that the exchange control legislation does not infringe public policy. A state's exchange control legislation will not affect proprietary rights situated outside its jurisdiction. Such rights are subject to the *lex situs*: see Dicey and Morris, *op. cit.*, para.36–087.

[66] International Monetary Fund Agreement, Art. VIII 2(b). The Agreement, usually known as the Bretton Woods Agreement, became part of English law by the Bretton Woods Agreements Order in Council, S.R. & O. 1946 No. 36, Art. 3, made under the Bretton Woods Agreements Act 1945. The Agreement will apply to cases falling within the Rome Convention since it is an international convention, the application of which is preserved by Art. 21. See above, para.25–025.

[67] *Wilson Smithett and Cope Ltd v Terruzzi* [1976] Q.B. 703. The English judgment was, however, refused enforcement in Italy on the ground that as the contract which it sought to uphold violated Italian exchange control legislation, it was contrary to Italian public policy: see Abbatescianni, 135 N.L.J. 179 (1985). The meaning of "exchange contract" adopted in *Terruzzi's* case was approved by the House of Lords in *United City Merchants (Investments) Ltd v Royal Bank of Canada* [1983] 1 A.C. 168 at 189. For criticism of *Terruzzi* see Gold, 33 I.C.L.Q. 777 (1984). See, also, on the *United City Merchants* case, Mann, 98 L.Q.R. 526 (1982).

[68] *Sharif v Azad* [1967] 1 Q.B. 605.

[69] *United City Merchants (Investments) Ltd v Royal Bank of Canada*, above. See also *Mansouri v Singh* [1986] 1 W.L.R. 1393.

[70] *United City Merchants (Investments) Ltd v Royal Bank of Canada*, above.

apparent sale which is, in effect, a disguised monetary transaction will be unenforceable.[71]

6. PROPERTY

(a) *General Issues*

The *lex situs* principle.[72] It is established in modern conflicts law[73] that from the point of view of proprietary rights the law governing particular transfers of title to goods, whether by sale or otherwise, is in general the *lex situs*.[74] "I do not think", said Maugham J. in *Re Anziani*,[75] "that anyone can 25–121

---

[71] But not illegal. It "is unenforceable by the courts and nothing more": *United City Merchants (Investments) Ltd v Royal Bank of Canada*, above, at p.184, *per* Lord Diplock. See also *Mahonia Ltd v JP Morgan Chase Bank* [2003] EWHC 1927 (Comm), [2003] 2 Lloyd's Rep. 911.

[72] See generally Fawcett, Harris and Bridge, *International Sale of Goods in the Conflict of Laws* (2005), Ch.18; Carruthers, *The Transfer of Property in the Conflict of Laws* (2005), Chs 1, 3, 8 and 9; Dicey and Morris, *The Conflict of Laws* (13th ed.), Ch.24; Cheshire and North, *Private International Law* (13th ed.), Chs 30 *et seq.*; Collier, *Conflict of Laws* (3rd ed.) Ch.14; Zaphiriou, *The Transfer of Chattels in Private International Law* (1956); Lalive, *The Transfer of Chattels in the Conflict of Laws* (1956); Bridge in Bridge and Stevens (eds), *Cross-Border Security and Insolvency* (2001), Ch.7; Stevens, *ibid.*, Ch.11; Morris, 22 B.Y.B.I.L. 232 (1945). On the treatment of cultural property, see Carruthers, *op. cit.*, Ch.5. And see below, para.25–131, n.22.

[73] An earlier view favoured the law of the domicile (*lex domicilii*) of the owner (*e.g. Sill v Worswick* (1791) 1 H.Bl. 665 at 690; *North Western Bank v Poynter* [1895] A.C. 56 at 66, 75; *Liverpool Marine Credit Co. v Hunter* (1868) 3 Ch.App. 479 at 483), but as a general governing law in regard to tangible movables this law is now confined to succession on death: *Provincial Treasurer for Alberta v Kerr* [1933] A.C. 710 at 721. There are also dicta favouring the law of the place of transfer (*lex loci actus*) (*e.g. City Bank v Barrow* (1880) 5 App.Cas. 664 at 667; *Alcock v Smith* [1892] 1 Ch. 238 at 267; *Embiricos v Anglo-Austrian Bank* [1905] 1 K.B. 677 at 683–684), but as a general governing law this is only applicable to the transfer of negotiable instruments by indorsement, where the *lex loci actus* and the *lex situs* at the time of transfer inevitably coincide: Dicey and Morris, *op. cit.*, para.24–002. See generally, Fawcett, Harris and Bridge, *op. cit.*, paras 18–18—18–33; Carruthers, *op. cit.*, paras 3–02—3–10.

[74] The leading authority is *Cammell v Sewell* (1860) 5 H. & N. 728, discussed below, para.25–130; see too *Castrique v Imrie* (1870) L.R. 4 HL 414 at 429; *Inglis v Robertson* [1898] A.C. 616; *Re Korvine's Trust* [1921] 1 Ch. 343; *Re Anziani* [1930] 1 Ch. 407 at 420; *Bank voor Handel en Scheepvart NV v Slatford* [1953] 1 Q.B. 248 at 257; *Hardwick Game Farm v Suffolk Agricultural Poultry Producers Association* [1966] 1 W.L.R. 287 at 330 (affirmed *sub nom. Henry Kendall & Sons v William Lillico & Sons Ltd* [1969] 2 A.C. 31); *Winkworth v Christie Manson and Woods Ltd* [1980] Ch. 496; *City of Gotha v Sotheby's, The Times*, October 8, 1998; *Glencore International AG v Metro Trading International Inc.* [2001] 1 Lloyd's Rep. 284; *Air Foyle Ltd v Center Capital Ltd* [2002] EWHC 2535 (Comm); [2003] 2 Lloyd's Rep. 753; see also *Peer International Corp. v Termidor Music Publishers Ltd* [2003] EWCA Civ. 1156; [2004] Ch. 212; *R. Griggs Group Ltd v Evans* [2004] EWHC 1088 (Ch); [2005] Ch.153 (copyright); Dicey and Morris, *op. cit.*, paras 24–002 *et seq.*; Cheshire and North, *op. cit.*, Ch.30. General adherence to the *lex situs* is criticised in Fawcett, Harris and Bridge, *op. cit.* paras 18–39—18–54; Carruthers, *op. cit.*, Chs 8 and 9. As to the meaning of *situs* see above, para.25–004.

[75] [1930] 1 Ch. 407 at 420. For a lucid analysis of the policy justifying the *lex situs* rule, see *Glencore International AG v Metro Trading International Inc.* [2001] 1 Lloyd's Rep. 284 at 294–295 (Moore-Bick J.).

doubt that, with regard to the transfer of goods, the law applicable must be the *lex situs*. Business could not be carried on if that were not so." This general principle is unaffected by the existence of the Rome Convention since, generally, proprietary questions do not fall within its remit.[76]

25–122 ***Renvoi.***[77] One of the various justifications put forward for the *lex situs* principle is that uniformity with the court sitting at the *situs* and having control of the goods is desirable. This consideration has induced several writers to recommend that where the *lex situs* is applicable not only its domestic rules but also its conflicts rules should be consulted,[78] *i.e.* that the "foreign court" or "total *renvoi*" theory should be applied.

25–123 **Goods in transit.** The *lex situs* principle is subject to an important limitation: it does not apply when at the relevant time the goods are "in transit."[79] The phrase "in transit" in this particular context within the conflict of laws has not been authoritatively defined, though it seems clear that the "transit" in question has a different point of commencement,[80] and a different endpoint,[81] from the "transit" during which the English remedy of stoppage in transit[82] can be invoked by a seller. It is submitted that, for the purpose of conflict of laws, goods are "in transit" when, while being

---

[76] Giuliano-Lagarde Report, p.10.

[77] For general discussions of this question, see Dicey and Morris, *op. cit.*, Ch.4; Cheshire and North, *op. cit.*, Ch.5.

[78] Dicey and Morris, *op. cit.*, paras 4–023, 24–004; Cheshire and North, *op. cit.*, pp.948–950; Morris, 22 B.Y.B.I.L. 232 at 237–238 (1945); *cf. Dulaney v Merry & Sons* [1901] 1 Q.B. 536; *Green v Van Buskirk*, 7 Wall. 139 (1868). See also *Winkworth v Christie Manson and Woods Ltd*, above, where the preliminary question which was put to the court was in the form of whether the issue of title was to be determined by English or Italian *domestic* law. However Slade J. heard no evidence as to the content of Italian law, [the *lex situs*] but observed (at p.514) that "it is theoretically possible that the evidence as to Italian law would show that the Italian court would itself apply English law on the particular facts of the present case . . . In this event I suppose it would be open to the [claimant] to argue that English law should, in the final result be applied by the English court by virtue of the doctrine of renvoi." In *Glencore International AG v Metro Trading International Inc.* [2001] 1 Lloyd's Rep. 284 at 297, it was held that it was unnecessary to reach any final conclusion on whether, according to English conflict of laws' rules, *renvoi* applied in this context. Contrast *Macmillan Inc. v Bishopsgate Investment Trust Plc (No.3)* [1995] 1 W.L.R. 987 at 1008 Millett J.) affirmed on other grounds, [1996] 1 W.L.R. 387, see Staughton. J. at p.405 (*renvoi* does not apply when applying *lex situs* to the question of title to shares). And see Carter, 52 B.Y.B.I.L. 329 (1982). Restatement, para.222e, suggests that the answer to this question "varies from situation to situation". And see Fawcett, Harris and Bridge, *op. cit.*, paras 18–68—18–70; Carruthers, *op. cit.*, paras 1–43—1–45.

[79] See Fawcett, Harris and Bridge, *op. cit.*, paras 18–55, 18–59; Carruthers, *op. cit.*, paras 3–31—3–35.

[80] Thus, for example, in *Inglis v Usherwood* (1801) 1 East 515, the goods were not treated as "in transit", and (on one view at least) were subjected to the *lex situs*, even though according to the relevant position of English domestic law regarding stoppage in transit (Sale of Goods Act 1979, s.45(1)), transit would have commenced but for the fact that the carrying ship had been chartered by the buyer.

[81] Compare, for example, s.45(4) and (6) of the Sale of Goods Act 1979 with the description of "transit" given in this paragraph.

[82] As to the scope of this remedy, see generally Ch.15, above.

carried from one country, X, to another, Z, they are for a time not situated in any country at all (being, for example, in a ship on the high seas[83]), or are only casually and fortuitously in an intermediate country, Y (being, for example, on a train which on its way from X to Z passes through Y), or are pursuing an uninterrupted journey from their point of departure in X to the border of X, or from the border of Z to their destination in Z.[84] In such circumstances, the *lex situs* principle is inapplicable; even if the goods can be said to have a legal *situs* at all, the fortuitous nature of such *situs* and the fact that it may not be known to the relevant parties make the principle inappropriate. If, however, the journey is interrupted to the extent that the goods come to rest in any country for a reasonable period of time,[85] the principle will be applicable, even though the interruption was not intended or foreseen by any of the relevant parties.[86] Similarly, if the relevant journey begins and ends within a single country, it is submitted that the goods should never be considered "in transit" but should be subject throughout to the *lex situs* principle on the basis that they have a *situs* in that country.

The proper law of the transfer. Where goods are in transit, the role normally played by the *lex situs* is taken over by other laws; this matter is discussed in detail below.[87] However, one of these laws which may act as a "substitute" for the *lex situs* requires preliminary explanation. This is the "proper law of the transfer"[88]; it means, broadly speaking, the law having the "closest and most real connection" with the transfer of property rights which takes place by virtue of the sale. The proper law of the transfer is ascertained by a process similar to that employed in ascertaining the law governing the contract of sale, according to common law rules,[89] though without (it is submitted) taking account of any purported choice by the parties in the contract of sale itself.[90] In many cases, it will be the same law as the law governing the contract of sale itself. 25–124

---

[83] It is surely unsatisfactory in such a case that the goods should be subject to the law of the ship's flag as a form of *lex situs*, yet see Cheshire and North, *op. cit.*, p.952.

[84] *cf.* the definition of "transit", in the conflicts sense, in Hellendall, 17 Can.Bar Rev. 7 and 105, 25 *et seq.* (1939).

[85] Wolff, *Private International Law* (2nd ed.), para.494.

[86] *Cammell v Sewell* (1860) 5 H. & N. 728, discussed below, para.25–130; Dicey and Morris, *op. cit.*, paras 24–016—24–017; Cheshire and North, *op. cit.*, pp.951–952.

[87] Below, paras 25–138—25–140.

[88] Below, para.25–138. It has at times been suggested (*e.g.* in the 7th edition of Cheshire, *Private International Law*, pp.409–411; Schmitthoff, *English Conflict of Laws* (3rd ed.), p.198) that the proper law of the transfer should have the wider function of determining all proprietary questions as between the parties to a transfer, whilst the *lex situs* should only operate when third parties are involved. But this view cannot now be supported; it is inconsistent with the leading authorities on the scope of the *lex situs* (see n.74, above) and has been abandoned by its leading exponent: Cheshire and North, *op. cit.* (13th ed.), p.941. In any event, in cases of sale, it is usually in situations involving third parties that property questions are important: see above, paras 5–003—5–004; Dicey and Morris, *op. cit.*, para.24–006.

[89] Above, paras 25–008—25–110.

[90] *cf.* the concept of "objective proper law", discussed above, paras 25–079—25–080, 25–083—25–084.

25–125 **Retention of title.** There is a dearth of authority as to the relevant conflict of laws rules in cases where the seller purports to reserve his title in the goods pending the occurrence of some future event such as the payment of the price. This question is discussed in paragraphs 25–141—25–153, where it will be seen that not all issues raised by such clauses are necessarily governed by the *lex situs*.

25–126 **"Documents representing goods" and "documents of title".** If documents are issued to "represent" the goods, this is a further factor which may curtail the operation of the *lex situs* principle. The phrase "documents representing goods" means here any documents which are prepared in the course of a sale of goods and which purport to confer upon the holder thereof any proprietary or possessory right in relation to the goods being sold. The narrower phrase "documents of title" will be taken to mean any documents representing goods, the transfer of which may, under the appropriate law, operate as a transfer of title to the goods. This definition resembles the common law definition of a document of title,[91] with the significant difference that it makes no stipulation that the transfer of the document should constitute constructive delivery of the goods. The laws which determine whether a document representing goods is in fact a true document of title and whether a purported transfer of a document of title is actually effective to transfer title to the goods are discussed below.[92]

(b) *Validity of a Transfer of Title to Goods*

25–127 **Operation of the *lex situs*.** When the title to goods is purportedly transferred in pursuance of a contract of sale, it is submitted that the *lex situs* at the time of such a transfer[93] should in general[94] determine whether the transfer is void or voidable on any of the following grounds,[95] *viz.* that the seller lacks capacity to transfer title[96] or the buyer lacks capacity to acquire title[97] or there is some element vitiating consent,[98] or the transfer is

---

[91] As to which, see above, para.18–007.

[92] Below, paras 25–134—25–137, 25–139, 25–140. A bill of lading, the commonest instance of a document of title, may have the separate function of providing evidence of the contract of carriage; in this aspect, it is governed by the law governing the contract of carriage and not by any of the laws relevant to its operation as a document of title: see above, paras 25–070—25–072, 25–077.

[93] As to the time of transfer, see below, paras 25–132, 25–134, 25–136, 25–140.

[94] As to goods in transit and retention of title clauses see below, paras 25–138—25–140, 25–141—25–156.

[95] The related grounds of the seller lacking power to pass title or the proper formalities not being carried out are considered below, paras 25–128 *et seq.*

[96] *Farmers and Mechanics' National Bank v Loftus*, 19 A. 347 (1890); *Campbell v Bagley*, 276 F. 2d 28 at 32 (1960); Dicey and Morris, *op. cit.*, para.24–005, Rabel, *The Conflict of Laws* (2nd ed.), Vol. 4, p.45; *contra* Restatement, para.244h. Where a corporation is involved, the law of its country of incorporation is also relevant to the extent indicated above, para.25–085.

[97] See n.96, above.

[98] See three US cases dealing with fraud on the part of a buyer: *Keegan v Lenzie*, 135 P. 2d 717 (1943); *Dobbins v Martin Buick Co.*, 227 S.W. 2d 620 (1950); *McRae v Bandy*, 115 So. 2d 479 (1959). See too Rabel, *op. cit.*, Vol. 3, p.83, and the comment in n.96, above, regarding corporations.

illegal in some respect, or lacks essential validity.[99] As has already been indicated[1] these proprietary issues are distinct from their contractual equivalents and are properly submitted to a separate law. It follows that a contract of sale may be void for some such defect as is discussed here, whilst the transfer of title is in no way defective under the *lex situs*; it is suggested that in such a case title may nonetheless pass as if by way of gift.[2] Conversely, if the contract is valid in all respects but the transfer is void under the *lex situs*, title cannot pass,[3] but the contract, if not discharged,[4] may confer remedies[5] on one or other party.

(c) *The Passing of Title: The General Rules*[6]

Sub-division of the topic. So far as property rights are concerned, it is further necessary to consider what laws govern two specific issues: whether the seller has the power to pass a good title to the goods and what acts and events must occur to cause title, *i.e.* property, to pass. As already indicated, the *lex situs* of the goods is the primary governing law,[7] but it is liable to be displaced if the goods are in transit[8] or if documents representing them have been issued.[9] It is accordingly convenient to divide the discussion into four separate sections, so as to reflect the various combinations possible according as to whether the goods are or are not in transit at the time when the property is alleged to pass, and whether documents[10] have or have not been issued at this time. It will be assumed throughout that the transfer of title is not defective on the ground of incapacity, illegality, essential invalidity or any element vitiating consent.[11] 25–128

---

[99] *Republica de Guatemala v Nunez* [1927] 1 K.B. 669 at 696; *Campbell v Bagley*, above, at p.32; Dicey and Morris, *op. cit.*, para.24–005; *cf.* Restatement, para.244j. In *River Stave Co. v Sill* (1886) 12 O.R. 557 and *Royal Baking Powder Co. v Hessey*, 76 F. 2d 645 (1935) (cert. denied *sub nom. Lowendahl v Hessey* 296 U.S. 595 (1935)), the *lex situs* was applied to strike down transfers of goods as being in fraud of creditors.

[1] Above, para.25–001.

[2] A dictum in *Lee v Abdy* (1886) 17 Q.B.D. 309 at 313 suggests otherwise, but see the remark in *Stocks v Wilson* [1913] 2 K.B. 235 at 246 that where an infant's contract was void under the now repealed s.1 of the Infants Relief Act 1874, property might nonetheless pass on delivery, and see also the rule of English law that under an illegal contract of sale property may likewise pass on delivery (above, para.3–030; *Chitty on Contracts*, (29th ed.), Vol. 1, para.16–172). No doubt the requirements of the *lex situs* as to transfer of title by gift must be satisfied.

[3] See Falconbridge, *Conflict of Laws* (2nd ed.), pp.467–468.

[4] Discharge is in general governed by the law applicable to the contract: below, para.25–173.

[5] As to remedies under the contract of sale, see below, paras 25–178 *et seq*.

[6] The particular problems presented by retention of title clauses are discussed in the next section: see, below, paras 25–141—25–156.

[7] Above, para.25–121.

[8] Above, para.25–123.

[9] Above, para.25–126.

[10] See generally on dealings in documents, Fawcett, Harris and Bridge, *op. cit.,* paras 18–78—18–92.

[11] These matters are dealt with in the preceding paragraph.

(i) *Goods not in Transit: no Documents issued*

25–129 **The seller's power to pass title.** The question whether a seller is the true owner of the goods, or, though not the true owner, is to be taken to have the power to pass a good title to the buyer, is determined in general by the *lex situs* of the goods at the time when the alleged transfer of title takes place.[12]

25–130 **The seller as owner.** In so far as the seller's alleged title depends upon any earlier transaction concerning the goods, the validity of the title acquired by the seller or his predecessor through such earlier transaction is governed by the *lex situs* at the time thereof.[13] The chief authority for this proposition is the leading case of *Cammell v Sewell*.[14] Here a Prussian ship carrying a cargo of deals from Russia to England was wrecked on the coast of Norway. Without authority from their owner, the deals were sold by the captain by public auction in Norway. At this sale the purchaser acquired a good title to them under Norwegian law, though not under English law. The purchaser consigned them to England under a bill of lading indorsed to the defendants, whereupon the claimants, who were underwriters to whom the original owner had abandoned the deals, sued the defendants in conversion. It was held in the Exchequer Chamber that the defendants had acquired a good title because according to Norwegian law, the *lex situs* at the time of the auction, their predecessor had acquired a good title at the auction, and the subsequent change of *situs* was on this point irrelevant.[15] The following remark of Pollock C.B. during argument in the Court of Exchequer[16] was cited with approval in the majority judgment of the Exchequer Chamber.[17] "If personal property is disposed of in a manner binding according to the law of the country where it is, that disposition is binding everywhere."

25–131 **The seller as non-owner.** Where the seller is not the true owner in accordance with the *lex situs* at the time of the alleged transfer of title, this law may nonetheless consider him to have the power to confer good title

[12] *Cammell v Sewell* (1860) 5 H. & N. 728; and see further authorities cited in the ensuing footnotes.
[13] It is submitted, however, that if a court at the *situs* at the time of the alleged transfer of title from seller to buyer would apply a different choice of law rule, this rule should be followed: *cf.* above, para.25–122; *Fuller v Webster*, 95 A. 335 (1915).
[14] (1860) 5 H. & N. 728, disapproving *Freeman v East India Co.* (1822) 5 B. & A. 617; see too *Castrique v Imrie* (1870) L.R. 4 HL 414 at 439; *Liverpool Marine Credit Co. v Hunter* (1868) 3 Ch.App. 479; *Glencore International AG v Metro Trading International Inc.* [2001] 1 Lloyd's Rep. 284; *Air Foyle Ltd v Center Capital Ltd* [2002] EWHC 2535 (Comm), [2003] 2 Lloyd's Rep. 753; and *cf.* *Simpson v Fogo* (1863) 1 H. & M. 195 at 222.
[15] (1860) 5 H. & N. 728 at 741, 743–744; and see *Todd v Armour* (1882) 9 R. 901 and *Winkworth v Christie Manson and Woods Ltd* [1980] Ch. 496, discussed in the next paragraph; *Glencore International AG v Metro Trading International Inc.*, above; *Air Foyle Ltd v Center Capital Ltd*, above.
[16] (1858) 3 H. & N. 617 at 638.
[17] (1860) 5 H. & N. 728 at 744–745.

upon the buyer. This may be the case because he is considered to have the true owner's actual authority to sell, though here the effect of such authority in creating contractual relations between the buyer and the true owner should, on general principles,[18] be determined by the law applicable to the contract of sale. Alternatively, the circumstances may be such that, according to the *lex situs*, the seller (because he is the apparent owner, for instance, or has apparent authority to sell on behalf of the true owner) can pass good title notwithstanding that he has no title and no actual authority to sell.[19]

The applicability of the *lex situs* in the latter situation is established by *Cammell v Sewell*[20] and by subsequent English and Scottish authorities. In *Winkworth v Christie Manson and Woods Ltd*[21] works of art were stolen from the claimant, an English resident, and taken to Italy, where they were sold to the second defendant, an Italian citizen, who purchased in ignorance of the theft and of the claimant's claim to ownership. The second defendant sent them back to England to the first defendants, with instructions that they be put up for sale by auction. The claimant sued the first and second defendants for detinue and conversion respectively, but later abandoned the claim against the first defendants. It was held by way of preliminary ruling that Italian domestic law, being the *lex situs* at the time of the sale to the second defendant, was the law determining whether the second defendant obtained a good title pursuant to this sale. Slade J. rejected arguments to the effect that a foreign *lex situs* should not be applicable where it might do injustice to an English citizen, or where the goods in question had been stolen in England, or where the goods had been returned to England, or where there were several factors connecting the case with England.[22] In

---

[18] Above, paras 25–081—25–082.

[19] For examples in English domestic law, see the Sale of Goods Act 1979, ss.21–26 (above, paras 7–008—7–030, 7–055—7–068) and the Hire-Purchase Act 1964, Pt III, as re-enacted in the Consumer Credit Act 1974, Sch.4 (above, paras 7–087—7–068). A sale falling within the Factors Act 1889, s.2 (above, paras 7–031—7–054) may likewise be dealt with as a case of apparent ownership.

[20] (1860) 5 H. & N. 728 (discussed in the preceding paragraph); see too *City Bank v Barrow* (1880) 5 App.Cas. 664; *Alcock v Smith* [1892] 1 Ch. 238 at 267; *Janesich v George Attenborough & Son* (1910) 102 L.T. 605; *cf. Mehta v Sutton* (1913) 108 L.T. 214. Where the relevant rule of the *lex situs* refers to subsidiary concepts such as the good faith of the buyer, these must also, it seems, be interpreted in accordance with the *lex situs*: *Embiricos v Anglo-Austrian Bank* [1904] 2 K.B. 870 at 876 (affirmed [1905] 1 K.B. 677); *Mehta v Sutton*, above; *cf. Hooper v Gumm* (1867) 2 Ch.App. 282; *contra Todd v Armour* (1882) 9 R. 901 at 905. In *Winkworth v Christie Manson and Woods Ltd*, below, Slade J., *obiter*, appeared to accept the view that there was an exception to the *lex situs* where the purchaser claiming title had not acted bona fide. The better view is that lack of bona fides is relevant only to the extent that it affects title under the *lex situs*: See *Glencore International AG v Metro Trading International Inc.* [2001] 1 Lloyd's Rep. 284 at 295; and see Carter, 52 B.Y.B.I.L. 329 (1982).

[21] [1980] Ch. 496. See Carter, 52 B.Y.B.I.L. 329 (1982).

[22] *cf.* SI 1994/501, as amended by SI 1997/1719 and SI 2001/3972, which provides that where a "cultural object" found in the United Kingdom has (on or after January 1, 1993) been unlawfully removed from a Member State of the European Community, the Member State in question may bring proceedings, for its return. Compensation must be paid to a possessor of the object who exercised due care in acquiring it. See generally, Carruthers, *op. cit.*, Ch.5.

Todd v Armour,[23] the Court of Session held that where a horse was stolen and sold in market overt in Ireland, then brought to Scotland and resold there, both purchasers acquired a good title against the original owner, as this was the position under Irish law, the *lex situs* at the time of the first sale, though not under Scottish law. In Canada[24] and the United States,[25] sales by non-owners have been held to confer good title on a purchaser in good faith, when according to the *lex situs* the true owner was estopped from denying the seller's authority, or the seller had power to pass good title by virtue of a statutory provision corresponding to section 24 or section 25 of the Sale of Goods Act 1979.[26]

As a matter of general principle, of course, an English court could refuse to recognise the title conferred on the purchaser if the law under which such title was acquired conflicts with English public policy, but such cases are likely to be rare indeed, and it has been said that public policy in such situations should be limited to circumstances "where the content of the particular foreign law on which [the person claiming title] relied was so outrageous that this court regarded it as wholly contrary to justice and morality".[27]

25–132 **Passing of property between seller and buyer.** Assuming that the seller has power to confer good title upon the buyer, it remains to consider what law determines the steps, formal[28] or otherwise, that are sufficient to cause property to pass[29] to the buyer.[30] It is submitted that this law should be "the law of the country where the goods are situate at the time when the acts relied upon as passing the property have taken place."[31] Thus, if goods in

---

[23] (1882) 9 R. 901. This decision has been approved in England: see *Alcock v Smith*, above, at p.267; *Embiricos v Anglo-Austrian Bank* [1904] 2 K.B. 870 at 874 (affirmed [1905] 1 K.B. 677).

[24] *Century Credit Corp. v Richard* (1962) 34 D.L.R. (2d) 291; *Re Fuhrmann and Miller* (1977) 78 D.L.R. (3d) 284; *cf. Traders Finance Corp. v Dawson Implements Ltd* (1959) 15 D.L.R. (2d) 515.

[25] See, *e.g. Zendman v Harry Winston Inc.*, 111 N.E. 2d 871 (1953).

[26] Above, paras 7–055—7–068. Any preconditions which must be satisfied before title is acquired pursuant to such corresponding provisions should also be a matter for the *lex situs*. *Cf.* cases cited at n.20, above.

[27] *Winkworth v Christie Manson and Woods Ltd* [1980] Ch.496 at 510, *per* Slade J. See also *Glencore International AG v Metro Trading International Inc.* [2001] 1 Lloyd's Rep. 284 at 295; *Peer International Corp. v Termidor Music Publishers Ltd* [2003] EWCA Civ. 1156; [2004] Ch. 212.

[28] In this sense, the topic "passing of property" comprehends the question of formalities of the transfer of property. It may also involve acts such as appropriating the goods to the contract, putting them in a deliverable state, or even actually delivering them to the buyer, depending on the provisions of the relevant *lex situs*.

[29] An English lawyer speaks here of passing of "property", although the term "title" might be considered more appropriate in the context of conflict of laws.

[30] These vary considerably amongst different legal systems. Some, for instance, require actual delivery to the buyer as a general rule (*e.g.* the German Civil Code, para.929), while others generally allow for property to pass at an earlier stage, or leave the matter to the intention of the parties (*e.g.* the French Civil Code, para.1583; and English law, discussed above, Ch.5).

[31] *Luttges & Co. v Ormiston and Glass Ltd*, Reports of the Decisions of the Mixed Arbitral Tribunals, Vol. 6, 564, 569 (1926); and see *Hardwick Game Farm v Suffolk*

country X are sold and are sent to the buyer in country Y in accordance with the contract, property should be taken to have passed at the time of dispatch from X if according to the law of X enough has already been done or occurred to bring about this result[32]; the fact that according to the law of Y or any other law property has not passed and, indeed, never passes is irrelevant.[33] On the other hand, if, according to the law of X, property is still in the seller at the time of dispatch, then, assuming no material change occurs during transit, property should not be taken to pass to the buyer until the goods have arrived in Y and some act or event has then occurred which under the law of Y is sufficient to cause property to pass.[34]

Impact of the law applicable to the contract. It is noteworthy that several authorities recommend applying the law governing the contract of sale to determine what acts are sufficient to cause property to pass[35]; the advantage of so doing is that the parties' own expectations are thereby most likely to be borne out.[36] This is no doubt the reason why, in a number of English cases[37] involving contracts of sale governed by English law, the terms of a foreign *lex situs* were not pleaded by either party, with the result that the Sale of Goods Act 1979 (as it now is) was applied to determine the passing of property in goods situated abroad.[38] In principle, a direct 25–133

Agricultural Poultry Producers Association [1966] 1 W.L.R. 287 at 330; *ibid. sub nom. Henry Kendall & Sons v William Lillico & Sons Ltd* [1969] 2 A.C. 31 at 101; *Glencore International AG v Metro Trading International Inc.* [2001] 1 Lloyd's Rep. 284 at 292–295, specifically rejecting the applicability of the law applicable to the contract where the issue of title arises as between buyer and seller and holding that the *lex situs* applies in such situations in the same way as it does when third parties are involved; *District of Columbia v Upjohn Co.*, 185 F. 2d 992 (1950); *Rayn v McCalley*, 228 S.W. 2d 61 (1950); Dicey and Morris, *op. cit.*, para.33–109; Cheshire and North, *op. cit*, p.798; Wolff, *op. cit.*, para.498; Rabel, *op. cit.*, Vol. 3, pp.84–85; Morris, 22 B.Y.B.I.L. 232 at 235–237 (1945); Hellendall, 17 Can.Bar Rev. 7 and 105, 8 *et seq.* (1939). Contrast Bridge, *op. cit.*, pp.126–138; Fawcett, Harris and Bridge, *op. cit.*, paras 18–51—18–54; Carruthers, *op. cit.*, paras 3–61—3–67, 4–22.

[32] *Luttges & Co. v Ormiston and Glass Ltd*, above, at p.569.

[33] "Once title has passed, it has passed": *District of Columbia v Upjohn Co.*, above, at p.994. See too the authorities cited above, n.20.

[34] *Luttges & Co. Ltd v Ormiston and Glass Ltd, above; Busse v British Manufacturing Stationery Co.*, Reports of the Decision of the Mixed Arbitral Tribunals, Vol. 7, 345 (1927); *cf. Re Deveze* (1873) 9 Ch.App. 27 at 31.

[35] See *Re Central Bank* (1892) 21 O.R. 515 at 520 (though this should perhaps be treated as a case on goods in transit); *Gross v Jordan*, 22 A. 250 (1891); *cf. Mehta v Sutton* (1913) 108 L.T. 214 (formalities of pledge); *The Byzantion* (1922) 38 T.L.R. 744 (formalities of chattel mortgage). In *Re Hudson Fashion Shoppe Ltd* [1926] 1 D.L.R. 199 at 203–204 and *Re Viscount Supply Co. Ltd* (1963) 40 D.L.R. (2d) 501 at 506, the *lex loci contractus* was held to be applicable, but, in the latter case at least, this law coincided with the law generally applicable (*ibid.*, at p.508).

[36] *cf.* the suggestion that the proper law of the transfer should govern all property issues as between the parties alone (above, para.25–124, n.88). See Bridge, *op. cit.*, pp.126–138. *Cf. Glencore International AG v Metro Trading International Inc.*[2001] 1 Lloyd's Rep. 284 at 292–295.

[37] See, *e.g. Badische Anilin und Soda Fabrik v Basle Chemical Works Bindschedler* [1898] A.C. 200 at 204; *Kursell v Timber Operators & Contractors Ltd* [1927] 1 K.B. 299 at 312.

[38] *cf.* above, para.25–003.

application of the law applicable to the contract is incorrect,[39] though there is a roundabout way in which the rules of that law may become applicable. Where the *lex situs* allows the passing of property to depend upon the intention of the parties (as is generally the case under the Sale of Goods Act 1979[40]) and the parties have chosen a law other than the *lex situs* to be the governing law, a court may infer from such choice (though it should not do so automatically) that they intended the rules of that law as to the passing of property to apply to their transaction.[41]

(ii) *Goods not in Transit: Documents issued*

25–134 **Dealings not involving the documents.** It is submitted that the principles just outlined for goods not in transit which are not represented by documents should apply equally where such goods are represented by documents, so long as the relevant issue (*i.e.* the seller's power to pass title or the time when property passes) arises out of a sale in which the goods themselves were dealt with directly and no attention was paid to the documents.[42] By way of example, if A's goods are represented by documents for the sake of a sale to B, but he proceeds to sell and deliver them to C in a transaction in which the documents play no part, his power to confer a good title upon C (being an issue on which his prior arrangement with B is likely to have some effect) and the passing of property to C should both be governed by the *lex situs* of the goods at the time when the property is alleged to pass.

25–135 **Dealings involving the documents: power to pass title to the goods.** Where the acts relied upon as causing property to pass are or include a dealing or dealings with documents representing the goods, it is submitted that once more the *lex situs* of the goods at the time when property is alleged to pass determines whether the seller has power to confer a good title.[43] There may, however, be an exception in cases where the seller is alleged to be able to confer a better title than he himself has by virtue of the relevant document being "negotiable", in the full sense of the word.[44] It

---

[39] *Glencore International AG v Metro Trading International Inc.* [2001] 1 Lloyd's Rep. 284.

[40] See ss.16–19 and s.20A, discussed above, Ch.5.

[41] *Glencore International AG v Metro Trading International Inc.*, above, at p.297; *The Parchim* [1918] A.C. 157 at 161; *cf. Re Satisfaction Stores* [1929] 2 D.L.R. 435. If the *lex situs* coincides with the law applicable to the contract then, of course, no problem arises.

[42] 58 Col.L.Rev. 212 at 228 (1958); *cf.* Schmitthoff, *English Conflict of Laws* (3rd ed.), pp.263–264; Rabel, *op. cit.*, Vol. 4, pp.56–58.

[43] This view is consistent with the treatment of the Factors Act 1889 in *Inglis v Robertson* [1898] A.C. 616 (below, para.25–136). It is accordingly submitted that so far as they deal with sales of "documents of title", ss.24 and 25 of the Sale of Goods Act 1979 (above, paras 7–055—7–061) are operative only when the goods are situated in England at the time of the relevant transfer of the document.

[44] Compare the definition of "negotiable" given above, para.18–084. Under English domestic law, documents representing goods are scarcely ever negotiable in the full sense, though an instance is afforded by statutory dock warrants under the Port of London Act 1968, s.146(4) (above, para.18–198).

has been suggested that the question whether a document gives its holder this power as regards the goods is determined by the *lex situs* of the goods at the time when the document is issued.[45] It would seem to follow that the quality of negotiability must be taken to inhere in the document even though at the time of the actual sale the goods have acquired a new *situs* under whose law the document would not be negotiable. In the reverse situation, *i.e.* where the document is not negotiable according to the *lex situs* at the time of its issue, but is negotiable according to the *lex situs* of the goods at the time of the sale, it is submitted that, in accordance with the normal rule, the latter law should apply and the seller should have power to confer a good title through dealing with the document in accordance with such law.

Dealings involving the documents: passing of property in the goods. 25–136
There is some controversy as to the law or laws applicable to this question.[46] It is submitted in the first place that if *either* the *lex situs* of the goods at the time of issue of the documents *or* the *lex situs* thereof at the time when the property is alleged to pass would treat the document as a document of title,[47] it should be so treated.[48] On the other hand, the adequacy of the particular mode of transfer of the document should be a matter for the law of the *situs* of the document (*lex situs cartae*) at the time of the act, or the last of the acts,[49] alleged to constitute the transfer,[50] subject to the proviso that if according to the *lex situs* of the goods themselves at such time some additional mandatory formality is essential for property to pass, the *lex situs* of the goods should to this extent prevail.[51] The first of these propositions is directly supported by *Inglis v Robertson*,[52]

---

[45] Rabel, *op. cit.*, Vol. 4, pp.56–58; and see the next paragraph. In *Selliger v Kentucky*, 213 U.S. 200 (1909), preference for the *lex situs* of the goods over that of the documents (*lex situs cartae*) was made clear, but the time factor was not in issue. The *lex situs cartae* is probably applicable, however, if the goods are in transit at the time of issue of the documents.

[46] For academic discussion, providing support in varying degrees for the views expressed here, see Fawcett, Harris and Bridge, *op. cit.,* para.18–92; Schmitthoff, *English Conflict of Laws* (3rd ed.), pp.263–264; Graveson, *Conflict of Laws* (7th ed.), pp.466–467; Rabel, *op. cit.*, Vol. 4, pp.56–58; Hellendall, 17 Can.Bar Rev. 7 and 105, at pp.19–24 (1939); and a note in 58 Col.L.Rev. 212 at 225 *et seq.* (1958).

[47] *i.e.* as a document whose transfer may effect a transfer of title to the goods: see above, para.25–126.

[48] *Inglis v Robertson* [1898] A.C. 616; *Barrett v Bank of the Manhattan Co.*, 218 F. 2d 263 (1954); *Craig v Columbia Compress and Warehouse Co.*, 210 So. 2d 645 at 649 (1968); *cf. Selliger v Kentucky*, 213 U.S. 200 (1909). If the goods are in transit at this time, the *lex situs cartae* should apply instead. See *North Western Bank v Poynter* [1895] A.C. 56, below, para.25–140.

[49] This takes account of the possibility that the relevant acts of transfer may take place in different countries: *e.g.* indorsement in one country, delivery in another.

[50] *Barrett v Bank of the Manhattan Co.*, above.

[51] *Inglis v Robertson*, above, at pp.625–626; *Henry Kendall & Sons v William Lillico & Sons Ltd* [1969] 2 A.C. 31 at 101 (but contrast *ibid.*, at p.120); *Hallgarten v Oldham*, 45 Am.Rep. 433 (1893); *cf. Lynn Storage Warehouse Co. v Senator*, 3 F. 2d 558 (1925); *Barrett v Bank of the Manhattan Co.*, above, at p.768. *Cf.* Fawcett, Harris and Bridge, *op. cit.,* paras 18–88—18–90.

[52] [1898] A.C. 616.

the leading authority in this field, and the proviso to the second is suggested in dicta therein.[53] In this case, whisky stored in a warehouse in Scotland was purportedly pledged by the indorsement in England of delivery-warrants relating thereto, which had been issued by the warehouse-keeper. It was held by the House of Lords that the pledge, although valid under English law, was ineffective as against execution creditors of the pledgor who arrested the whisky in Scotland. This was because under Scottish law, the *lex situs* of the whisky, indorsement of the delivery-warrants was not sufficient to transfer a proprietary interest in the goods in the absence of notice to the warehouse-keeper.

25–137 **Impact of the law applicable to the contract.** If the *lex situs* of the goods at the time of the alleged passing of property refers the question of passing of property to the intention of the parties, it is submitted that, in accordance with principles already suggested,[54] the rules of the law governing the contract of sale as regards passing of property in documentary sales may be applicable because they represent such intention. Thus, for example, if the *lex situs* contained a provision of this nature and under the governing law property would pass on an appropriate transfer[55] of (say) a bill of lading because this was a "symbolical delivery" of the goods,[56] this rule of that law should be applicable. On the other hand, the fact that under that law this transfer constituted a symbolical delivery[57] would not be sufficient to cause property to pass if the *lex situs* at the time of the transfer insisted upon actual receipt of the goods by the buyer.

(iii) *Goods in Transit: no Documents issued*

25–138 **The proper law of the transfer.** In these somewhat rare cases, the seller's power to confer a good title and the requirements to be satisfied for property to pass have been variously referred by different writers to the proper law of the transfer,[58] the law of the flag of the carrying ship,[59] the law of the country from which the goods were dispatched (*lex loci*

---

[53] *ibid.*, at pp.625–626.
[54] Above, para.25–133.
[55] The form of the transfer must still, it is submitted, be governed generally by the *lex situs cartae*: see the preceding paragraph.
[56] As, for example, under a c.i.f. contract governed by English law (above, paras 19–102, 19–157).
[57] It is submitted below, para.25–157, that the question whether the shipment of the goods and the transfer of a document, as under a c.i.f. contract, fulfil the seller's duty of delivery of the goods is determined by the law applicable to the contract of sale. It is only, however, by virtue of the reasoning in the present paragraph that the relevant rule of that law can affect the question of property.
[58] Dicey and Morris, *op. cit.*, para.24–016 (though the rule suggested there says no more than that transfers valid under the proper law should be treated as valid); Cheshire and North, *op. cit.*, pp.951–952; and see *Winkworth v Christie Manson and Woods Ltd* [1980] Ch.496 at 501; *cf. Re Central Bank* (1892) 21 O.R. 515. The meaning of the phrase, "proper law of the transfer", is discussed above, para.25–124.
[59] Cheshire and North, *op. cit.*, p.952, restricting its application to the case of a single transfer occurring while the goods are on board.

expeditionis),[60] the law of the country of their intended destination (*lex loci destinationis*)[61] or the last two of these together.[62] None of these alternatives is wholly satisfactory, but it is submitted that both issues under discussion are best referred to the proper law of the transfer.[63] This rule makes for comparative simplicity when the proper laws of the transfer and of the contract are the same.

(iv) *Goods in Transit: Documents issued*

Power to pass title. It is submitted that the question whether a seller has power (whether as owner or non-owner) to transfer title to goods in transit by transferring a document representing them should be a matter for the *lex situs cartae* at the time of the final act necessary to effect the transfer.[64] If however the goods are not in transit at the time of issue of the document, and under the law of their *situs* at this time the document has full "negotiability" in the sense that the holder thereof can give a better title to the goods than he himself has, such negotiability should be taken to persist until the time of the sale itself.[65] 25–139

Passing of property. It is submitted that the question whether a document representing goods is a document of title is a matter for the *lex situs* of the goods at the time of issue of the document,[66] but that the *lex situs cartae* at the time of the final act necessary to effect the transfer should say whether the acts relied on as transferring the document are sufficient to do so.[67] It will be noted that this analysis to some extent parallels that set out 25–140

---

[60] See, *e.g.* Hellendall, 17 Can.Bar Rev. 7 and 105, 32–35 (1939).

[61] See, *e.g.* Rabel, *op. cit.*, Vol. 4, pp.101–102.

[62] Wolff, *op. cit.*, para.494, suggests that if the requirements of either the *lex loci expeditionis* or the *lex loci destinationis* are satisfied as to the passing of property, property should be taken to have passed. On the other hand, he refers the question of a non-owner's power to pass title to the *lex situs* in all cases; this appears to imply that in cases of goods in transit an unauthorised non-owner can never pass title.

[63] This is more or less by a process of elimination. At the time of sale, the *lex loci expeditionis* no longer has any real link with the goods (it is merely a former *lex situs*) and the *lex loci destinationis* is uncertain in so far as the destination may change or the goods may never arrive. The law of the flag will usually be fortuitous and in no way related to the goods or to the expectations of the parties as to the law governing their dealings. The control of the proper law in this situation, by way of exception to the *lex situs*, was approved, *obiter*, in *Winkworth v Christie Manson and Woods Ltd* [1980] Ch. 496 at 501 where Slade J. relied upon what is now Dicey and Morris, *op. cit.*, para.24–016 to the same effect.

[64] *Roland M. Baker Co. v Brown*, 100 N.E. 1025 (1913).

[65] *cf.* above, para.25–077.

[66] See authorities cited above, n.48; also Rabel, *op. cit.*, Vol. 4, p.56; Hellendall, 17 Can.Bar Rev. 7 and 105, 19 (1939); 58 Col.L.Rev. 212 at 225–228 (1958); Restatement, para.248(1). If the goods are in transit at this time (*e.g.* in the case of a sale of goods afloat), the *lex situs cartae* should apply instead.

[67] *Hardwick Game Farm v Suffolk Agricultural Poultry Producers Association* [1966] 1 W.L.R. 287 at 301; *ibid. sub nom. Henry Kendall & Sons v William Lillico & Sons Ltd* [1969] 2 A.C. 31 at 101, 119; Rabel, *op. cit.*, Vol. 4, p.101; 58 Col.L.Rev. 212 at 229–232 (1958). *Cf. North Western Bank v Poynter* [1895] A.C. 56 at 66, 75, 76, where the

above[68] in relation to the transfer of goods represented by documents where the goods are not in transit, except that the overriding control of the *lex situs* of the goods is absent; this seems a desirable result. In any event, uniformity of international practice with regard to documentary sales of goods in transit (notably c.i.f. sales) means that the above rules are not likely to be called on frequently.

(d) *Retention of Title*

25–141 **Generally.** In an international sale contract a seller may attempt to retain his title in the goods until the occurrence of a future event, *e.g.* payment of the price in full. Clauses which purport to do this ("Romalpa" clauses[69]) may take a variety of forms but the basic function of such clauses is to provide the seller with security in the event of the price not being paid or in the event of the buyer's receivership or insolvency. The complex problems of private international law which may be generated by such clauses have never been directly considered by the English courts[70] and are treated somewhat cursorily in a handful of Irish[71] and Scottish[72] decisions.

---

question whether a pledgee of the documents of title to goods in transit could redeliver them to the pledgor for a limited purpose without losing his security was said to be governed by the *lex loci actus* and the *lex domicilii* of the parties; this was also the *lex situs cartae. Cf.* too *Inglis v Robertson* [1898] A.C. 616 at 626–627, where the *lex loci destinationis* was explicitly rejected in favour of the *lex loci actus* (coinciding again with the *lex situs cartae*).

[68] Above, paras 25–134—25–137.

[69] See above, paras 5–131—5–170.

[70] Canadian cases deal with the issue of passing of title where goods have been the subject of a prior security transaction, such as a conditional sale or chattel mortgage, and the position has become complicated by one or more changes of *situs* since the prior transaction and by the presence of provisions for registration of security transactions in one or more of the relevant *leges situs*: for discussion of some of these cases see Dicey and Morris, *op. cit.*, paras 24–020— 24–038; Falconbridge, *op. cit.*, pp.452 *et seq*; Goode and Ziegel, *Hire-Purchase and Conditional Sale* (1967), pp.209 *et seq.*; Morris, 22 B.Y.B.I.L. 232 (1945); Davies, 13 I.C.L.Q. 53 (1964); Ziegel, 45 Can.Bar Rev. 284 (1967). These authorities may be of some assistance in determining whether title has passed by virtue of a sale-on by the buyer under the original contract, but they by no means address the further problems to which "Romalpa" clauses may give rise. *Glencore International AG v Metro Trading International Inc.* [2001] 1 Lloyd's Rep. 284 sheds some light on the latter question but the case did not appear to be concerned with a "Romalpa" clause. In the United States the matter is governed almost exclusively by the UCC: see Scoles, Hay, Borchers and Symeonides, *Conflict of Laws* (4th ed.), pp.1081 *et seq.*; Mooney in Bridge and Stevens (eds), *Cross-Border Security and Insolvency* (2001), Ch.10. For retention of title in cases falling within the European Union Regulation on insolvency proceedings (Regulation 1346/2000/EC of May 29, 2000 ([2000] O.J. L160/1)), see below, paras 25–150—25–152. For retention of title in relation to Directive 2000/35/EC of the European Parliament and Council of June 29, 2000 on combating late payment in commercial transactions ([2000] O.J. 2000 L200/35), see below, para.25–153.

[71] *Re Interview Ltd* [1975] I.R. 382; *Kruppstahl AG v Quittmann Products Ltd*, [1982] I.L.R.M. 551. See Binchy, *Irish Conflicts of Law* (1988), pp.496–499.

[72] *Emerald Stainless Steel Ltd v South Side Distribution Ltd* 1983 S.L.T. 162; *Deutz Engines Ltd v Terex Ltd*, 1984 S.L.T. 273; *Hammer and Sohne v HWT Realisations*

Accordingly, therefore, any conclusions[73] on the law relating to the issue must be tentative.[74] In approaching the question, it is, at the outset, appropriate to bear in mind that the basic problem in these situations stems from a commingling of issues of a proprietary and contractual nature and of the additional considerations of priority in insolvency law which become involved in the paradigm "Romalpa" case, *i.e.* when the buyer is potentially or actually insolvent.

It is suggested that the most useful method of analysing these complex issues is to examine the typical elements of a "Romalpa" clause[75] and to consider the repercussions which they may have in the context of private international law.

Retention of title. In its simplest form, a retention of title clause reserves title in the seller until the price is paid. According to the principles discussed in the preceding section, the question whether such a reservation is valid, as between buyer and seller, should be governed by the *lex situs* of the goods at the time they are despatched to the buyer.[76] However, the issue arises whether the clause must also be valid by the law applicable to the contract. In the case where the goods are situated, at the time of despatch, in the country of that governing law (which will usually be the country where the seller carries on business) there will normally be no problem, since the reservation will be valid or invalid by that law as the case 25–142

Ltd, 1985 S.L.T. (Sh. Ct.) 21; *Zahnrad Fabrik Passau GmbH v Terex Ltd,* 1986 S.L.T. 94. These cases held that a retention of title clause was an attempt to create a non-possessory security interest which was void under Scots law. However, in *Armour v Thyssen Edelstahlwerke AG* [1991] 2 A.C. 339, the House of Lords held that the clause did not, as a matter of Scots law, have that effect and expressly overruled the first two cases cited above, it being implicit also that the remaining cases are no longer authoritative on that point. However, because the House of Lords does not even refer to the conflict of laws' issues since the courts below (1989 S.L.T. 183, see also 1986 S.L.T. 94) had held that German law, the law governing the contract, had not been relevantly pleaded and proved, that decision does not, in principle, affect the issues of conflict of laws discussed in the earlier cases and in the courts below in *Armour*. Accordingly use is made of these decisions in what follows. For discussion of Scots law see Anton, *Private International Law* (2nd ed.), pp.618–620; Stewart, 1985 S.L.T. 149; Sellar, 1985 S.L.T. 313; Patrick, 1986 S.L.T. 265, 277; North, 220 *Recueil des Cours*, 1, 3, 267–271 (1990).

[73] See generally Fawcett, Harris and Bridge, *op. cit.*, paras 18–93—18–125; Dicey and Morris, *op. cit.*, paras 33–111—33–113; Cheshire and North, *op. cit.*, pp.947–948; Anton, above, n.72; North, above, n.72; Binchy, above, n.71. Morse [1993] J.B.L. 168; For comparative studies see Verheuil in Voskuil and Wade (eds) *Hague-Zagreb Essays on the Law of International Trade*, Vol. 5 (1985), pp.54 *et seq.*; Schilling, 34 I.C.L.Q. 87 (1985); Kreuzer (1995) Rev. Crit. d.i.p. 465. For discussion of German conflict of laws rules, see Drobnig in Bridge and Stevens (eds), *Cross-Border Security and Insolvency* (2001), Ch.8. For discussion of French conflict of laws rules, see Kessedjian, *ibid.*, Ch.9. For a survey of retention of title provisions in the domestic law of European jurisdictions see Pennington, 27 I.C.L.Q. 277 (1978).

[74] Potentially relevant foreign law is often not pleaded (see *Aluminium Industrie Vaasen BV v Romalpa Aluminium Ltd* [1976] 1 W.L.R. 676, above, para.25–003) or, correctly or incorrectly, is thought not to be different from English law (*Pfeiffer Weinkellerie Weinenkauf GmbH v Arbuthnot Factors Ltd* [1988] 1 W.L.R. 150).

[75] Above, paras 5–131—5–170.

[76] Above, paras 25–129—25–133.

may be. But what if the governing law and *lex situs* do not coincide in this way? It would seem that if the law governing the contract regards the reservation of title as valid but the *lex situs* would not, the latter law should prevail. Conversely, if the reservation was invalid by the governing law but valid by the *lex situs* the same result should ensue.[77] Accordingly, the law applicable to the contract is relevant only to the extent that the *lex situs* takes account of it in determining whether title has or has not passed.[78]

25–143 **Extent of reservation.** In principle, the extent of the clause should be governed by the foregoing principle. Thus, whether the clause vests in the seller title in products manufactured by the buyer with materials supplied by the former would depend on the efficacy under the *lex situs* of a clause which purported to have this effect. In this context, however, the relevant *lex situs* will, it is suggested, be that of the country where the manufactured product is produced[79] rather than the law of the place where the goods were situated at the time of despatch if these countries are different.

25–144 **Reservation constituting a charge.** In English domestic law one of the main grounds of attack on a "Romalpa" clause is that it gives rise to a charge created by the buyer company within section 396(1) of the Companies Act 1985 and so requires to be registered under section 395(1) of that Act.[80] For the purposes of English proceedings, the question whether a charge has been so created by the buyer is, it is submitted, determined according to English law,[81] though it is also submitted that the court must

---

[77] In the Irish cases cited in n.71, above, the goods seem to have been situated in Germany (which was also the country of the proper law) at the time of the original contract. In *Hammer and Sohne v HWT Realisations Ltd*, above, the relevant *lex situs* was said to be Scotland, the place of delivery of the goods. The security created by the German retention of title clause was, as a non-possessory security, held to be opposed to a fundamental principle of Scots law and therefore ineffective (though see now *Armour v Thyssen Edelstahlwerke AG*, above). But it would appear that the jewels were in Germany at the time of the contract and the case could just as easily have been decided on the ground that although a valid security had been created by German law as the *lex situs* at the time of the contract, it would not be recognised in Scotland on the grounds of public policy, a concept which is also referred to in the judgment: see 1985 S.L.T. 21 at 23. *Cf.* Anton, *op. cit.*, p.620.

[78] See *Glencore International AG v Metro Trading International Inc.* [2001] 1 Lloyd's Rep. 284 at 293, 297–298. *Cf. Zahnrad Fabrik Passau GmbH v Terex Ltd*, above, pp.88–89. See North, 220 *Recueil des Cours*, 1, 23, 268 (1990).

[79] *Glencore International AG v Metro Trading International Inc.*, above, at p.296; Dicey and Morris, *op. cit.*, para.24–010. *Cf. Kruppstahl AG v Quittmann Products Ltd* [1982] I.R.L.M. 551; *Zahnrad Fabrik Passau GmbH v Terex Ltd*, 1986 S.L.T. 845; *Armour v Thyssen Edelstahlwerke AG,* 1986 S.L.T. 94 *ibid.*, 453, revd. without reference to the point [1991] 2 A.C. 339.

[80] See above, paras 5–142—5–144, 5–149—5–150, 5–153—5–154, 5–156, 5–160.

[81] *Re Interview Ltd* [1975] I.R. 382 at 395–396; *Kruppstahl AG v Quittmann Products Ltd*, above, at p.560. The goods or proceeds will normally be in England at the time of the proceedings. If the charge created by the buyer is a floating charge, it may however extend to goods or proceeds situated abroad: see *Re Anchor Line (Henderson Brothers) Ltd* [1937] Ch.483. But the charge may fail to gain recognition in the foreign country as in *Luckins v Highway Motel (Caernarvon) Pty Ltd* (1975) 133 C.L.R. 164 on the ground of non-registration there and in such a case an

look to the terms of that contract and their effect under the law governing it to ascertain whether the elements which are alleged to constitute the charge in English law are in fact present.[82] In this situation, the clause must, of course, be valid by the *lex situs* at the time of despatch if the case involves the original goods and by the law of the place where the manufactured products are produced in the case of products. Whether the charge requires registration is also a matter for English law.[83]

Proceeds of sale. Where the retention of title clause is effective under the rules set out above, the buyer may nevertheless, expressly or impliedly, have the right to resell the goods.[84] Two problems may then arise. First, what law determines whether the buyer is under an obligation to account to the seller for the proceeds of sale? Secondly, which system of law governs the precise remedy by which any obligation to account, as is found to exist under the appropriate law, is to be enforced? The following discussion suggests possible solutions to each of these problems, though in the absence of any direct authorities, the submissions made are very tentative indeed.[85] As to the first problem, to render the buyer accountable to the seller and in an attempt to confer upon the seller a proprietary interest in the proceeds of sale (usually to the exclusion of other creditors of the buyer) a "Romalpa" clause may expressly provide that the buyer shall hold the proceeds of sale on trust, or in some other fiduciary capacity for the seller.[86] In the context of determining the law applicable to such a clause an initial question which arises is as to the proper characterisation to be placed on it. Although the clause is contained in a contract between buyer and seller, it purports to give the seller proprietary rights which suggests a proprietary, rather than a contractual, characterisation.[87] If this submission is correct, it must then be borne in mind that the relevant property is money, as opposed to goods, so that the *lex situs* has little claim, in principle, to apply since the policy underlying the *lex situs* is posited on security of title and commercial convenience neither of which has any particular impact in a claim to money arising between parties in a contractual nexus. Accordingly, it is suggested 25–145

English court will not, at the suit of debenture holders, restrain a creditor from bringing proceedings to recover his debt in the foreign country out of assets situated there: see *Re Maudslay, Sons & Field* [1900] Ch.602. On the recognition of English floating charges in France, see Kessedjian, *op. cit.*, pp.173–174; Dahan, 1996 *Clunet* 381.

[82] *Re Weldtech Equipment Ltd* [1991] B.C.C. 16. *Cf. Hammer and Sohne v HWT Realisations Ltd,* 1985 S.L.T. 21; *Kruppstahl AG v Quittmann Products Ltd* [1982] I.L.R.M. 551 at 559.

[83] *Re Weldtech Equipment Ltd* [1991] B.C.C. 16; *Re Interview Ltd* [1975] I.R. 382; *Kruppstahl AG v Quittmann Products Ltd*, above. As to registration requirements imposed on oversea companies see Companies Act 1985, s.409.

[84] See above, para.5–144.

[85] See Fawcett, Harris and Bridge, *op. cit.,* paras 19–81—19–97.

[86] In English law, the result seems to be that legal title to the proceeds of sale vests in the buyer, but the beneficial ownership of them is in the seller so that the latter has the right to trace them: See above, para.5–152. Such a claim may however give rise to a charge which requires registration: see above, para.5–153. *Cf. Kruppstahl AG v Quittmann Products Ltd* [1982] 1 L.R.M. 551.

[87] *cf. Kruppstahl AG v Quittmann Products Ltd*, above.

that the correct approach is to treat the obligation to account, however arising, as an independent proprietary obligation which is to be submitted to its own governing law.[88] Thus, if the trust concept is used to impose the obligation on the buyer, the validity of the clause will be determined by the choice of law rules applicable to trusts.[89] It may well be the case that the application of these rules will mean that the law applicable to the trust will be the same as that applicable to the original contract, of sale, particularly if there is an express choice of law in that contract.[90] However, if the law applicable to the contract of sale does not recognise the concept of a trust and thus would not regard the obligation to account for the proceeds of sale as subsisting, it is possible, by assuming that the parties must have intended to create a valid obligation to account, to ignore the law applicable to the contract and to ascertain, by applying the choice of law rules for trusts, whether the trust obligation is governed by a different system of law by which the obligation to account is enforceable.[91] A similar kind of analysis may be applied to a clause which purports to impose a fiduciary obligation on the buyer otherwise than through the mechanism of a trust.[92] So far it has been assumed that the "Romalpa" clause deals in terms with the obligation to account for the proceeds of sale. Where there is no such express provision, then, in general, the question of whether the buyer is nevertheless under an obligation to account should be determined by the law applicable to the sale contract since this law will normally be the

---

[88] See *United States Surgical Corporation v Hospital Products International Pty Ltd* [1983] 2 N.S.W.L.R. 157 at 192 which provides implicit support for this view (reversed without reference to the question of choice of law, (1984–85) 156 C.L.R. 41).

[89] See Dicey and Morris, *op. cit.*, Ch.29. These rules will include those contained in the Recognition of Trusts Act 1987, discussed in Dicey and Morris, *op. cit.*, *ibid*.

[90] The Rome Convention does not apply to trusts: Art. 1(2)(g), above, para.25–024. But according to the Recognition of Trusts Act 1987 the settlor (seller) may choose the law to govern a trust (Art. 6) which might therefore result in a coincidence of applicable laws. The Rome Convention cannot prejudice the application of the Recognition of Trusts Act 1987 since the latter implements an international convention (the Hague Convention on the Law Applicable to Trusts and their Recognition 1986) to which the United Kingdom is a party: Rome Convention, Art. 21. A seller who includes an express choice of law in a contract of sale containing a trust obligation would be prudent to ensure that the chosen law recognises the trust or to segregate the trust obligation and submit it to a law which recognises it if the law chosen to govern the contract would not recognise it. *Cf.* Rome Convention, Arts 3(1), 4(1) on "severability", above, paras 25–032, 25–057.

[91] That the trust obligation may be subject to a law different to that applicable to the contract is implicitly recognised in the exclusion of trusts from the Rome Convention (above, n.90) and in the existence of particular choice of law rules for trusts. A court could conclude that the express choice of law in the contract was not intended to apply to the trust obligation, the law applicable to that obligation being determined as if there was no choice of law. In such circumstances, the trust is governed by the law of the country with which it is most closely connected (Recognition of Trusts Act 1987, Sch., Art. 7) which law may well be that of the buyer's place of business.

[92] See *United States Surgical Corporation v Hospital Products International Pty Ltd*, above, where it was implicitly recognised in the New South Wales Court of Appeal (the High Court making no observation on the point) that the law applicable to a fiduciary obligation need not necessarily be the same as that applicable to the contract, if any, with which it is connected.

law applicable to the obligation to account. But if that law would not regard the obligation to account as subsisting, treatment of the obligation to account as an independent obligation, subject to its own choice of law rules might result in the ascertainment of a different governing law which could regard the obligation to account as enforceable.[93]

As to the second problem, very difficult questions may arise as to the law which ought to govern the precise remedy by which the obligation to account is to be enforced. The difficulties become acute indeed if, for example, the law applicable to the obligation to account would give effect to the seller's remedy by means of a tracing remedy but no such remedy exists in English law, or, conversely, a right to trace exists in English law but no such right exists under the law governing the obligation, and the difficulties may be further exacerbated if the proceeds of sale are situated in a country which would not recognise a tracing remedy whether or not such a remedy existed under English law or the law governing the obligation (if that law is a foreign law).[94] Nevertheless it is tentatively suggested that, in principle, the court should supply the remedy by which the obligation to account would be enforced under the law applicable to that obligation.[95] In the situation under discussion, the matter of the existence of the seller's right and the manner in which it is to be enforced are inextricably linked, and, "save in very special circumstances, it is as idle to ask whether the court vindicates the suitor's substantive right or gives the suitor a procedural remedy as to ask whether thought is a mental or cerebral process."[96] Such special circumstances could, however, exist if recognition of the remedy by which the foreign right is enforced would cause the English court undue inconvenience, as, for example, where there is no appropriate procedural machinery for giving effect to it.[97] In such circumstances, the English court might be justified in classifying the foreign remedy as procedural rather than substantive and in applying the corresponding English remedy instead. 25–146

Sub-sale by buyer. The proprietary effect of a sub-sale by the buyer to a third party is, according to the general principles governing the passing of title which were discussed in the previous section, governed by the *lex situs* 25–147

---

[93] Thus the seller's claim could be characterised as sounding in unjust enrichment and so governed by the proper law of the obligation to restore the benefit obtained by the buyer at the seller's expense: see Dicey and Morris, *op. cit.*, Rule 200(1). It must be admitted, however, that it is possible that where the obligation to restore the benefit arises in connection with a contract, the proper law of the restitutionary obligation will normally be the law applicable to the contract: Dicey and Morris, *op. cit.*, Rule 200(1)(a).

[94] See Panagopoulos, *Restitution in Private International Law* (2000), pp.94–103; Panagopoulos, R.L.R. 73 (1998); Harris, 73 B.Y.B.I.L. 65 (2002).

[95] *cf. Chase Manhattan Bank NA v Israel British Bank (London) Ltd* [1981] Ch. 105; *El Ajou v Dollar Land Holdings Plc* [1993] 3 All E.R. 717 (reversed without reference to the conflict of laws issues [1994] 2 All E.R. 685). See also, *Thahir v Pertamina* [1994] 3 Sing. L.R. 257 (Singapore CA) (constructive trust a substantive concept); Dicey and Morris, *op. cit.*, paras 34–039—34–041.

[96] *ibid.*, at p.124, *per* Goulding J.

[97] *cf. Phrantzes v Argenti* [1960] 2 Q.B. 19; Rome Convention, Art. 10(1)(c); Dicey and Morris, *op. cit.*, para.7–007.

of the goods (or products made thereof) at the time of the sub-sale.[98] It is that law which should determine whether the buyer has passed a good title to the sub-purchaser[99] unencumbered by the title which the seller purported to retain.[1] As this situation involves third parties the law governing the contract is irrelevant[2] except in so far as the *lex situs* regards it as in some way affecting the passing of title to the sub-purchaser.[3]

25–148 **Claims by original seller against sub-purchaser.** If the sub-purchaser does not acquire a good title from the buyer under the *lex situs*, the original seller may have an action for wrongful interference against the sub-purchaser provided that the seller can establish that he has validly retained title to the goods according to the foregoing principles. If the alleged act of interference has been committed abroad, the question of whether the original seller may maintain an action will be governed by the English rules for the choice of law in tort.[4] These rules have been largely placed on a statutory basis by Part III of the Private International Law (Miscellaneous Provisions) Act 1995.[5] As a general rule, the 1995 Act requires application of the law of the country in which the events which constitute the tort occur.[6]

If all the relevant acts of interference occur in one country and the goods are situated in the same country at the time when those acts take place, then it is highly likely that the law of that country will be determined to be the applicable law.[7] The general rule may be displaced in favour of the law of another country if it appears, in all the circumstances, from a comparison of (a) the significance of the factors which connect the tort with the country whose law would be applicable under the general rule and (b) the significance of any factors which connect the tort with another country that it is substantially more appropriate for the applicable law to be the law of that other country.[8] The fact that the sub-sale contract is governed by the law of a country other than the country in which the acts of interference occurred (and in which the goods are situated at the time of those acts) will be insufficient, under this provision, to displace the general rule.[9]

---

98 Above, paras 25–129—25–133, 25–143. See *Century Credit Corporation v Richard* (1962) 34 D.L.R. (2d) 291.

99 As for example under the Factors Act 1889, s.9 or the Sale of Goods Act 1979, s.25(2) or the foreign equivalents thereto.

1 *Re Interview Ltd* [1975] I.R. 382 at 392–394.

2 Above, paras 25–129—25–132.

3 Above, para.25–133.

4 *Glencore International AG v Metro Trading International Inc.* [2001] 1 Lloyd's Rep. 284.

5 In force from May 1, 1996: SI 1996/995. See Fawcett, Harris and Bridge, *op. cit.*, Ch.17, esp. at paras 17–53—17–87; Dicey and Morris, *op. cit.*, Ch.35; Cheshire and North, *op. cit.*, Ch.19; Briggs [1995] L.M.C.L.Q. 519; Morse, 45 I.C.L.Q. 888 (1996).

6 S.11(1). See also, ss.11(2)(c), and 12.

7 *Glencore International AG v Metro Trading International Inc.*, above, at p.298. *cf. ibid.* at p.296.

8 Private International Law (Miscellaneous Provisions) Act 1995, s.12(1).

9 *Glencore International AG v Metro Trading International Inc.*, above, at p.298. Such displacement can occur if a claim for wrongful interference is brought by the

25–149 "Romalpa" clauses sometimes attempt to enable the seller to maintain a direct action against sub-purchasers for the sub-sale price of the goods by stipulating that where the goods are sold by the buyer to sub-purchasers before payment has been received by the seller, any claim against sub-purchasers for the purchase price of the goods under the sub-sale is to vest in or to be transferred to the seller.[10] The validity and effect of such a provision would seem to involve those principles of private international law relating to the assignment of debts. Although it is not possible to state the English common law[11] on this topic with confidence, it is suggested that whether the buyer could assign to the seller the debt which was owed to him by the sub-purchaser was a matter governed by the law applicable to the sub-sale, that being the law which created the debt. If that law regarded the debt as capable of assignment it was then for the law governing the assignment (in this case the original contract of sale) to determine whether, as between the buyer (assignor) and seller (assignee), the debt had been validly assigned.[12] The same principle would appear to apply in cases which fall within the Rome Convention, Article 12 of which draws a distinction between the assignability of a right (governed by the law applicable to the right to which the assignment relates,[13] in this context, again, the law applicable to the sub-sale) and the mutual obligations arising between assignor and assignee (governed by the law applicable to the contract between them,[14] in this context, again, the law applicable to the original contract of sale). Should the buyer also effect an assignment of the proceeds of sale to a person other than the seller, a question of priority as between competing assignments may arise if each assignment is valid by its governing law.[15] At common law, the better view was that priority was governed by the law which creates the debt (the law applicable to the sub-sale).[16] The same position, it is submitted, obtains under Article 12 of the

---

original seller against the original purchaser and the contract between them is governed by a law other than that of the country in which the acts of interference occurred (and in which the goods are situated at the time of those acts). Here it might be substantially more appropriate to apply the law governing the contract to the claims in tort since they arise out of the relationship created by the contract and are closely related to the contractual claims: see *Glencore International AG v Metro Trading International Inc.*, above, at p.296.

[10] Above, para.5–160. Such a provision may, however, give rise to a charge: see, above, para.5–160.

[11] See Moshinsky, 109 L.Q.R. 591 (1992).

[12] See Dicey and Morris, *op. cit.*, para.24–050; Cheshire and North, *op. cit.*, pp.958–965. Application of the *lex situs* of the debt was rejected in *Raiffeisen Zentralbank Osterreich AG v Five Star General Trading LLC* [2001] Q.B. 825.

[13] Art. 12(2). On the scope of Art. 12, see *Raiffeisen Zentralbank Osterreich AG v Five Star General Trading LLC*, above; Stevens and Struycken, 118 L.Q.R. 15 (2002). See also Struycken [1998] L.M.C.L.Q. 345; Stevens in Bridge and Stevens (eds), *Cross-Border Security and Insolvency* (2001), pp.213–216; Plender, *op. cit.*, paras 11–19—11–25.

[14] Art. 12(1).

[15] See Dicey and Morris, *op. cit.*, para.25–040.

[16] Dicey and Morris, *op. cit.*, para.25–040; Cheshire and North, *op. cit.*, pp.960–961; Stevens, *op. cit.*, pp.214–215.

Rome Convention, since the question of priorities relates to "the conditions under which the assignment can be invoked against the debtor".[17]

25–150 **Council Regulation on insolvency proceedings.** This Regulation[18] purports to establish uniform rules of jurisdiction, choice of law and recognition of judgments in relation to insolvency proceedings which fall within its remit.[19] Very broadly, the Regulation permits the opening of "main" insolvency proceedings in the Member State in which a debtor's centre of main interests is situated[20] and proceedings can only be opened in another Member State if the debtor has an establishment in that State.[21] The latter proceedings are "secondary"[22] or "territorial"[23] proceedings and their effects are limited to assets of the debtor which are situated in that Member State.[24] The general choice of law rule applicable under the Regulation is that a court having jurisdiction shall apply the *lex fori*.[25] However, certain specific issues are subject to special and different choice of law rules and one such special issue is reservation of title.[26] Where, therefore, the issue of retention of title arises in the course of insolvency proceedings subject to the Regulation, this special rule will be applied and brief consideration is here given to its content.[27]

25–151 According to Article 7(1) of the Regulation the "opening of insolvency proceedings against the purchaser of an asset shall not affect the seller's rights based on reservation of title where at the time of the opening of proceedings the asset is situated within the territory of a Member State other than the State of opening of proceedings". This would seem to mean that where the reservation of title clause is struck down by the *lex fori*, such

---

[17] Art. 12(2). In *Raiffeisen Zentralbank Osterreich AG v Five Star General Trading LLC*, above, it was held that whether notice of the assignment must be given to the debtor is a matter for the law applicable to the debt pursuant to Art. 12(2). While the case does not deal with the issue of priorities, it is submitted that the general tenor of the decision supports application of Art. 12(2) to priorities as well. And see Dicey and Morris, *op. cit.*, para.25–057; Cheshire and North, *op. cit.*, pp.961–962; Stevens, *op. cit.*, pp.214–215. Contrast Bridge in Bridge and Stevens (eds), *Cross-Border Security and Insolvency* (2001), pp.140–143.

[18] Council Regulation 1346/2000/EC of May 29, 2000 on insolvency proceedings ([2000] O.J. L160/1). The Regulation entered into force on May 31, 2002. For implementation in the UK, see SI 2002/1240. For discussion, see Fletcher, *Insolvency in Private International Law* (2nd ed.), Ch.7; Virgos and Garcimartin, *The European Insolvency Regulation: Law and Practice* (2004); Dicey and Morris, *op. cit. Fourth Cumulative Supplement,* paras S30R–137—S30–322; Moss, Fletcher and Isaacs (eds), *The EC Regulation on Insolvency Proceedings* (2002).

[19] See Art. 1 of the Regulation.

[20] Art. 3(1).

[21] Art. 3(2).

[22] Arts 3(3), 27.

[23] Art. 3(2), (4).

[24] Art. 3(2).

[25] Art. 4.

[26] Art. 7. See also Art. 5, concerned with third parties rights *in rem*.

[27] For more detail, see Fletcher, *op. cit.*, paras 7–104—7–107; Fawcett, Harris and Bridge, *op. cit.,* paras 18–122—18–125; Dicey and Morris, *op. cit. Fourth Cumulative Supplement*, paras S30R–219—S30–227; Moss, Fletcher and Isaacs (eds), *op. cit.*, paras 8–105—8–108.

a provision should not be given effect.[28] Article 7(1) is noticeably obscure on what constitutes a valid reservation of title for these purposes. It does not state that such validity is determined by the law of the *situs* of the asset and it may well be that the provision contemplates that it is enough if the clause is valid under the law applicable to the contract in which it is contained.[29] Another possibility is that the forum should apply its rules of private international law to determine whether the clause is effective, though this could produce inconsistency with the policy of the provision which would seem to seek to uphold the reservation of title against provisions of the law of the forum (including provisions of private international law) which would render the reservation of title ineffective. It is therefore suggested, with great hesitation, that the provision should be construed to establish a *lex situs* rule whereby a reservation of title effective under the law of the Member State in which an asset is located at the time of the opening of the proceedings (which State is not the State in which proceedings have been opened) will normally be effective to preserve the seller's rights in the face of provisions of the *lex fori* which would not give effect to those rights.[30]

Article 7(2) provides that the "opening of insolvency proceedings against the seller of an asset, after delivery of the asset, shall not constitute grounds for rescinding or terminating the sale and shall not prevent the purchaser from acquiring title where at the time of the opening of the proceedings the asset sold is situated within the territory of a Member State other than the State of opening of the proceedings." Where, therefore, the seller effectively retains title in an asset situated in a Member State other than the State in which the proceedings are opened that asset does not fall into his estate upon insolvency and the buyer is not prevented from acquiring title.[31] This rule is not, in truth, a choice of law rule but a uniform rule of substantive law.[32] **25–152**

Directive on combating late payment in commercial transactions. This Directive seeks to deal with the problem of late payment in commercial transactions in the internal market[33] and is implemented, generally, in the United Kingdom by Regulations which amend[34] the Late Payment of **25–153**

[28] See *e.g.* Companies Act 1985, ss.395, 396. See above, para.25–144.
[29] See Fletcher, *op. cit.*, para.7–105.
[30] It would seem to be irrelevant that the asset has been moved to another Member State subsequently to the opening of the proceedings. It is unclear whether Art. 7(1) is applicable in a retention of title arrangement which gives the seller rights to the proceeds of sale of an asset or whether it is limited to arrangements affecting tangible movable assets.
[31] *e.g.* by continuing to make payments throughout the period set out in the contract: see Dicey and Morris, *op. cit. Fourth Cumulative Supplement*, para.30–224.
[32] See Fletcher, *op. cit.*, para.7–106. According to Art. 7(3), Art. 7(1) and Art. 7(2) shall not preclude actions for voidness, voidability or unenforceability as referred to in Art. 4(2)(m) under which the rules of the law of the forum are to be applied if they relate to voidness, voidability or unenforceability of legal acts detrimental to all the creditors.
[33] Directive 2000/35/EC of the European Parliament and Council of June 29, 2000 on combating late payment in commercial transactions ([2000] O.J. L200/35).
[34] Late Payment of Commercial Debts Regulations 2002, SI 2002/1674.

Commercial Debts (Interest) Act 1998.[35] Retention of title clauses are seen as one aspect of combating this problem and an obligation is placed on Member States in relation to such clauses in Article 4 of the Directive. The principal provision, in this respect, in Article 4(1) of the Directive provides that "Member States shall provide in conformity with the applicable national provisions designated by private international law that the seller retains title to goods until they are fully paid for if a retention of title clause has been expressly agreed between the buyer and the seller before the delivery of the goods."[36] Curiously, this provision has not been transposed into the implementing Regulations and its precise meaning is unclear.[37] Reference to Recital 21 to the Directive indicates that it "is desirable to ensure that creditors are in a position to exercise a retention of title on a non-discriminatory basis throughout the Community, if the retention of title clause is valid under the applicable national provisions designated by private international law." This explanation suggests that where the seller and the buyer have expressly agreed on a retention of title clause before delivery of the goods and that clause is valid under the law or laws declared applicable under the private international law rules of the Member State forum, then that Member State shall ensure that effect is given to the clause and that the clause is not declared unenforceable by reference to a rule of the law of the forum. It is possible, though, that the matter is far from clear[38], that it was thought that this was already the position in United Kingdom law (or at least, perhaps, in English law) so that specific further implementation was unnecessary.

7. RISK

25–154 **Risk governed by the proper law.** It is generally agreed among academic writers that the question as to what must occur to make the risk of accidental loss of, or deterioration in, goods pass from seller to buyer[39] should be characterised as a contractual question and allocated to the control of the law applicable to the contract.[40] It is submitted that this was

---

[35] See below, paras 25–162—25–164.

[36] Art. 4(2) provides that "Member States may adopt or retain provisions dealing with down payments already made by the debtor."

[37] See Fawcett, Harris and Bridge, *op. cit.*, paras 18–104—18–107.

[38] *ibid*.

[39] In the legal systems of the world one finds rules prescribing at least four different times at which, prima facie, the risk should pass: (a) when the contract is concluded (*e.g.* the Swiss Code of Obligations, para.185); (b) when property passes (*e.g.* the French Civil Code, para.1138; English law, discussed above, Ch.6); (c) when the seller has done everything required of him by the contract (*e.g.* the Uniform Commercial Code, paras 2–503, 2–509); and (d) when the goods are received by the buyer (*e.g.* the German Civil Code, para.446). In international sales, such as c.i.f. and f.o.b., these rules are commonly displaced by the contrary intention of the parties: see above, paras 19–110, 20–088.

[40] See, *e.g.* Fawcett, Harris and Bridge, *International Sale of Goods in the Conflict of Laws* (2005), paras 13–196—13–200, 18–132—18–134; Rabel, *The Conflict of Laws*

not only the position at common law, but is also the case under the Rome Convention. Although Article 10(1) of the Convention does not specifically mention risk as one of the matters governed by the applicable law, the list of matters specified therein is not exhaustive so that, accordingly, risk can be submitted to the governing law[41] as one of the "effects of a contract", a category of issues which on principle should fall within the control of the applicable law.[42] Being a question which concerns the seller and the buyer only, it should be relegated to the law to which they have in most cases expressly or impliedly submitted their legal relations.[43] The fact that, in a commercial transaction[44], under section 20(1) of the Sale of Goods Act 1979 the risk is presumed, unless otherwise agreed, to pass simultaneously with the property[45] does not prevent an English court from treating risk as a contractual question. Likewise, where the buyer deals as consumer, the fact that under section 20(4) of the Sale of Goods Act 1979 the risk passes only on the delivery of the goods to the buyer[46] does not make risk anything other than a contractual question.

Connection with passing of property. When a contract of sale is governed by English law but the goods are situated abroad at all relevant times, the attitude to be adopted to section 20(1) calls for further comment. Parties contracting under English law may be assumed, in the absence of contrary indications, to expect that property will pass in accordance with the relevant provisions (sections 16–19) of the Sale of Goods Act 1979[47] and that, by virtue of section 20(1), risk will pass at the same time as property. Accordingly, if, under a foreign *lex situs*, property passes at a different time to that prescribed by sections 16 to 19, the application of section 20(1) as part of the governing law may well produce a result contrary to the parties' expectations regarding risk. It is therefore possible that in such a case the court would hold that the parties may properly be taken to have displaced section 20(1) by an implicit contrary agreement, this being to the effect that risk should pass at the time when the property 25–155

(2nd ed.), Vol. 3, pp.91–94; Zaphiriou, *The Transfer of Chattels in Private International Law* (1956), Ch.10; Goode and Ziegel, *Hire-Purchase and Conditional Sale* (1967), p.229. This view is also implicit in Dicey and Morris, *The Conflict of Laws* (13th ed.), para.33–109, n.92, and in *Busse v British Manufacturing Stationery Co.*, Reports of the Decisions of the Mixed Arbitral Tribunals, Vol. 7, 345 (1927).

[41] *cf.* Hague Convention on the Law Applicable to the International Sale of Goods 1985 (not yet in force) which provides in Art. 12(d) that the applicable law shall determine "the time from which the buyer bears the risk with respect to the goods".

[42] Plender, *The European Contracts Convention* (2nd ed.), para.11–02 .

[43] This consideration makes it important to ensure that where the goods are lost the issue between the parties is treated as one of risk, not property; see, *e.g. Kursell v Timber Operators and Contractors Ltd* [1927] 1 K.B. 299 at 312.

[44] Subject to s.20(4) where the buyer deals as consumer (see above, paras 6–013—0-016).

[45] Above, para.6–002.

[46] Above, paras 6–013—6–016.

[47] These sections and s.20A, which gives rise to greater difficulty, are dealt with above, Ch.5.

would have passed if its passing had been regulated by sections 16 to 19, instead of by the foreign *lex situs*.[48]

8. PERFORMANCE OF THE CONTRACT OF SALE

25–156 **General principles.**[49] By virtue of basic common law choice of law principles regarding performance of any contract, including a contract of sale, the substance of the obligations to be performed thereunder were determined by the terms of the contract as interpreted in accordance with the governing law,[50] and supplemented where necessary by that law.[51] The general principle of the Rome Convention is the same since it is explicitly provided in Article 10(1) that the law applicable to the contract under the Convention shall govern the "interpretation"[52] and "performance"[53] of the contract. On the other hand, the *mode* of performance of each such obligation was, at common law, determined by the terms of the contract, interpreted as aforesaid, but supplemented by the law of the place where the obligation was to be performed (*lex loci solutionis*).[54] Article 10(2) of the Rome Convention reflects a similar idea when it provides that "in relation to the manner of performance and the steps to be taken in the

---

[48] This approach could have been taken in *Kursell v Timber Operators and Contractors Ltd*, above, and it is consistent with the decision therein. See also *Glencore International AG v Metro Trading International Inc.* [2001] 1 Lloyd's Rep. 284 at 297–298. *Cf.* Fawcett, Harris and Bridge, *op. cit.*, paras 13–198—13–200. On s.20A, see preceding note.

[49] See Fawcett, Harris and Bridge, *International Sale of Goods in the Conflict of Laws* (2005), paras 13–159—13–185; Dicey and Morris, *The Conflict of Laws* (13th ed.), paras 32–191—32–197; Cheshire and North, *Private International Law* (13th ed.), pp.596–597; Plender, *The European Contracts Convention* (2nd ed.), paras 11–08—11–10.

[50] *Rowett, Leakey & Co. v Scottish Provident Institution* [1927] 1 Ch. 55 (though note the possible qualification, asserted *ibid.*, at pp.64–65, but denied *ibid.*, at p.69, that where interpretation in accordance with the proper law produces meaningless results, some other law, based upon the parties' presumed intention, may have to be applied); *St. Pierre v South American Stores (Gath and Chaves) Ltd* [1937] 3 All E.R. 349.

[51] *Jacobs v Crédit Lyonnais* (1884) 12 Q.B.D. 589; *Bonython v Commonwealth of Australia* [1951] A.C. 201; *Mount Albert Borough Council v Australasian etc. Life Assurance Society Ltd* [1938] A.C. 224.

[52] Art. 10(1)(a). See *CGU International Reinsurance Plc v Astrazeneca Insurance Co. Ltd* [2005] EWHC 2755 (Comm); [2006] 1 C.L.C. 162. And see *The Ikariada* [1999] 2 Lloyd's Rep. 365, 373; *OT Africa Line v Magic Sportswear Group* [2005] EWCA Civ. 710; [2005] 2 Lloyd's Rep. 170.

[53] Art. 10(1)(b).

[54] *Mount Albert Borough Council v Australasian etc. Life Assurance Society Ltd*, above, at pp.240–241; see too the other cases cited in n.51. It is however suggested in *Compagnie d'Armement Maritime SA v Compagnie Tunisienne de Navigation SA* [1971] A.C. 572 at 603 that the *lex loci solutionis* is only to be consulted here if the applicable law is English law; presumably in other cases the foreign governing law itself indicates which law governs the mode of performance. *Cf. Amin Rasheed Shipping Corp. v Kuwait Insurance Co.* [1984] A.C. 50 at 60, where it is said that the applicable law governs the mode of performance, a *dictum* which is, it is submitted, to be taken to refer to the substance of the obligation.

event of defective performance regard shall be had to the law of the country in which performance takes place." The broad distinction (which is to be drawn according to the *lex fori*[55]) under each régime is that between the substance of the obligation, governed by the applicable law, and matters of detail which affect the mode or manner or performance but which do not impinge on the substance of what must be done under the contract.[56] One distinction may, however, need to be drawn between Article 10(2) and its common law counterpart. As to the latter, it would seem to be a choice of law rule, the application of which did not depend on any discretionary element. The former rule requires, in contrast, that "regard shall be had" to the law of the place of performance. According to the Giuliano-Lagarde Report the court "may consider whether such law has any relevance to the manner in which the contract should be performed and has a discretion whether to apply it in whole or in part so as to do justice between the parties."[57] If this interpretation is correct the potential role of Article 10(2) becomes, to say the least, uncertain.

By virtue of these general principles, the rights and duties implied by law in a contract of sale[58] and the extent of any power of the parties to exclude or vary such rights and duties[59] are determined in general by the law applicable to the contract. As already indicated,[60] however, an exception to this proposition is created by subsection (2) of section 27 of the Unfair Contract Terms Act 1977. The impact of this exception upon the seller's duties with regard to title, compliance with sample or description, and quality or fitness for purpose is discussed below.[61]

Some specific instances of performance of a contract of sale are dealt with in the ensuing paragraphs.

(a) *Delivery*

Making delivery. The substance of the acts constituting and surrounding the delivery of the goods is regulated by the applicable law in the light of the terms of the contract both at common law and under the Rome **25–157**

---

[55] Giuliano-Lagarde Report, p.33. *Cf.* Dicey and Morris, *op. cit.*, para.32–194.

[56] *East West Corp. v DKBS 1912 A/S* [2002] EWHC (Comm); [2002] 2 Lloyd's Rep. 182, affirmed without argument on the point [2003] EWCA Civ. 83; [2003] Q.B. 1309; *Import Export Metro Ltd v Compania Sud Americana De Vapores SA* [2003] EWHC 11 (Comm); [2003] 1 Lloyd's Rep. 405. Thus if waiver of any particular obligation is alleged, its validity and effect is a matter for the applicable law, whereas if a contract governed by, say, English law, provides for delivery of goods in Paris during "usual business hours", French law will determine what hours those are. See, generally, Dicey and Morris, *op. cit.*, para.32–196; Cheshire and North, *op. cit.*, pp.596–597. *Cf.* Fawcett, Harris and Bridge, *op. cit.*, para.13–163. Plender, *op. cit.*, para.11–10. According to the Giuliano-Lagarde Report, p.33, "manner of performance" includes rules governing public holidays, the manner in which goods are to be examined and the steps to be taken if they are refused.

[57] *ibid.*

[58] *Henry Kendall & Sons v Williams Lillico & Sons Ltd* [1969] 2 A.C. 31; below, para.25–170.

[59] See authorities cited above, para.25–089, n.96.

[60] See generally above, paras 25–089, 25–090, 25–094—25–100.

[61] Below, para.25–160 (title); para.25–171 (quality and compliance with description); As to sales where the buyer deals as consumer, see above, paras 25–111 *et seq.*

Convention. Accordingly, in the absence of any express or implied stipulation, the applicable law will determine such matters as the persons other than the buyer (if any) to whom delivery may be made, the identity and quantity of the goods to be delivered,[62] the permissible place or places,[63] and time or times,[64] of delivery, the nature of any accompanying duties of the seller in respect of the goods,[65] and the documents, if any, that must be prepared and tendered by the seller.[66] On the other hand, questions relating to the mode of delivery, such as the usages governing the unloading of goods at a particular port,[67] are regulated by the *lex loci solutionis*.[68] The precise borderline between the "substance" and the "mode" of delivery may often be obscure and it has scarcely been considered in the case law.

25–158 **Taking delivery.** It is submitted that by virtue of the foregoing principles the applicable law, in the absence of any stipulation in the contract, should determine the existence and content of any duty on the part of the buyer to do any act with regard to taking delivery,[69] both at common law and under the Rome Convention.

(b) *Duty to pass title*

25–159 **Duty to pass title governed by applicable law and statutory provisions.** Although, as already indicated,[70] the power of the seller to pass a good title and the acts required to cause property to pass are determined,

[62] This includes the question as to how far, if at all, the seller may depart from the terms of the contract by delivering insufficient or excessive or mixed goods. Defective goods are considered more fully below, paras 25–169 *et seq*.

[63] *cf.* the authorities on the ascertainment of the place of delivery for the purposes of the former RSC, Ord.11, r.1(1)(*e*), discussed by Dicey and Morris, *op. cit.*, para.11–175. RSC, Ord.11, r.1(1)(e) has been replaced by CPR, r.6.20(6) which provides that the court may give permission for the claim form to be served out of the jurisdiction if "a claim is made in respect of a breach of contract committed within the jurisdiction". *Cf.* also below, para.25–161, regarding the place of payment of the price.

[64] This includes the question whether the seller may deliver by instalments and how far, if at all, he may depart from the terms of the contract by delivering early or late.

[65] *e.g.* his duties, if any, as regards measuring, packing and insuring the goods, finding shipping space for them, making a contract for their carriage to the buyer and paying the expenses of delivery.

[66] Rabel, *The Conflict of Laws* (2nd ed.), Vol. 3, pp.100–101. Linked with this, and also regulated by the applicable law, are two further issues: the question whether tender of documents constitutes a "symbolic delivery" of the goods and the significance of such a concept.

[67] See *Robertson v Jackson* (1845) 2 C.B. 412; *Norden SS Co. v Dempsey* (1876) 1 C.P.D. 654; Rome Convention, Art. 10(2) and *cf. Trent Valley Woollen Manufacturing Co. v Oelrichs* (1894) 23 S.C.R. 682.

[68] See *Import Export Metro Ltd v Compania Sud Americana De Vapores SA* [2003] EWHC 11 (Comm); [2003] 1 Lloyd's Rep. 405 at [20]. In addition, the custom or usage of the *locus solutionis* may have to be referred to in regard to aspects of performance which are governed by the applicable law. That law may, for example, prescribe that delivery must be made "at a reasonable hour" (see, *e.g.* the Sale of Goods Act 1979, s.29(5)), but in such a case it would be the business custom of the place of delivery that would indicate what hours are "reasonable".

[69] *e.g.* notifying the seller of the time and place for delivery, finding shipping space for the goods, giving effective shipping instructions in regard to their carriage, paying the expenses of delivery, and accepting a proper tender of documents.

[70] Above, paras 25–127 *et seq*.

subject to exceptions, by the *lex situs*, the extent to which a seller is under a duty to confer title upon the buyer, and the nature of the title to be conferred, are matters governed by the law applicable to the contract save in so far as the contract, interpreted in accordance with that law, does not make provision for these issues.[71]

These propositions are subject to the provisions of the Unfair Contract Terms Act 1977,[72] the operation of which is not without difficulty. As indicated in a lengthy discussion earlier in this chapter,[73] the controls imposed by the Unfair Contract Terms Act 1977 on contractual terms purporting to exclude or restrict liability are expressly made inapplicable to "international supply contracts"[74] and to contracts whose governing law is a law of some part of the United Kingdom "only by choice of the parties".[75] On the other hand, they are applicable "notwithstanding any contract term which applies or purports to apply the law of some country outside the United Kingdom", where this term seems to have been imposed in order to evade the Act or where the place of habitual residence of a party dealing as consumer, is in the United Kingdom and the essential steps necessary for the making of the contract were taken there whether by the consumer or others acting on his behalf.[76] The controls in the Act include a provision in subsection (1)(a) of section 6 that the seller's implied undertakings as to title, etc., in section 12 of the Sale of Goods Act 1979 "cannot be excluded or restricted by reference to any contract term".[77] **25–160**

In consequence of the interaction of these provisions with the underlying general principle that the law applicable to a contract determines both the nature of any implied terms and the extent to which they may be excluded or restricted, the extent to which section 12 of the 1979 Act is applicable (to a contract for the sale of goods) in English litigation may be resolved in any one of three ways:

(i) Section 12 is applicable and cannot be excluded by a contractual term. This is the position with any contract governed by the law of any part of the United Kingdom unless it is an "international supply contract" or this law exists as the governing law "only by choice of the parties".[78] The evident intent of the 1977 Act is that this should also be the position with contracts, other than international supply contracts, which are governed by a foreign law, when it is found that this law has been chosen to evade the Act or that the habitual residence of a party dealing as consumer is in the United Kingdom and the essential steps necessary for the making of the contract were taken there whether by the consumer or others acting on his behalf. It

---

[71] Above, para.25–135.

[72] Above, paras 25–090 *et seq.*

[73] Above, paras 25–091—25–106.

[74] Unfair Contract Terms Act 1977, s.26; see above, paras 18–281, 25–090.

[75] *ibid.*, s.27(1), as amended by Contracts (Applicable Law) Act 1990, s.5 and Sch.4.

[76] *ibid.*, s.27(2) as amended, *ibid*.

[77] For Scotland, the equivalent provision is s.20(1). In addition, s.12 remains a mandatory provision for the purposes of ULIS: Uniform Laws on International Sales Act 1967, s.1(4)(c), as amended by Sale of Goods Act 1979, Sch.2, para.15.

[78] It is also the position, where the contract, whether or not it is an international supply contract, is governed by ULIS.

can be argued, however, that it does not achieve this result, because while the prohibition in section 6 of the 1977 Act against excluding or restricting the implied undertakings as to title, etc. in section 12 of the 1979 Act is made applicable to such contracts, there is nothing in either Act to say that, contrary to normal principles of choice of law, the undertakings contained in United Kingdom law should form part of a contract governed by a foreign law. It is submitted however, that this technical defect, which was not present in the comparable legislation affecting contracts made between May 18, 1973, and January 31, 1978, would most likely be passed over by a court interpreting the 1977 Act, on the ground that the Act clearly intended the relevant undertakings both to apply to the type of contract being discussed and to be incapable of exclusion or restriction. Further, it can be argued that where the habitual residence of the party dealing as consumer is in the United Kingdom and the essential steps necessary for the making of the contract were taken there by the consumer or others acting on his behalf, section 12 may be construed to apply to the contract by virtue of Article 5 of the Rome Convention[79] as a mandatory rule of the law of the consumer's habitual residence, provided the relevant contract of sale otherwise falls within the provisions of that article. Lastly, it is likely, also, that section 12 may be construed as a mandatory rule of English law which applies irrespective of the law otherwise governing the contract so that its application may be secured by reference to Article 7(2) of the Rome Convention,[80] at least in those circumstances where the requirements of the 1977 Act are satisfied.

(ii) Section 12 is applicable, but can be excluded or restricted by an appropriate contractual term. This is the position with contracts governed by the law of any part of the United Kingdom if they are "international supply contracts" or if such a law applies to the contract "only by choice of the parties".

(iii) Section 12 is inapplicable to the contract. This is the position with contracts, including "international supply contracts", which are governed by the law of some country outside the United Kingdom,[81] subject to the exception outlined under heading (i) above.

It has been submitted elsewhere in this work that where the seller is acting for purposes relating to his business and the buyer is a consumer within the meaning of the Unfair Terms in Consumer Contracts Regulations 1999, any attempt to exclude the undertakings implied in section 12 of the Sale of Goods Act 1979 would be regarded as unfair within the meaning of the Regulations and thus not binding on the consumer.[82] This will be so if the contract is governed by the law of a non-Member State[83] which would regard such an exclusion as effective, provided the other conditions contained in regulation 9, the anti-avoidance provision, discussed earlier in this chapter, are present.[84]

[79] Above, paras 25–044—25–056.
[80] Above, para.25–042.
[81] Though not by ULIS.
[82] Above, para.14–038.
[83] Unfair Terms in Consumer Contracts Regulations 1999, reg. 9. Above, paras 25–101.*et. seg*.
[84] See above, paras 25–101—25–103. There is no provision in the 1999 Regulations equivalent to s.26 of the Unfair Contract Terms Act 1977 (see above, para.25–104).

(c) *Payment of the Price*

Time and place of payment and ascertainment of amount. It is submitted that, as with delivery, the place or alternative places of payment of the purchase-price,[85] the time or times at which payment should be made[86] and the method or methods of payment available to the buyer[87] are determined by the law applicable to the contract of sale, in so far as this contract, interpreted in accordance with that law, does not deal with such matters.[88] Equally, when the contract does not name a specific price or rate of payment in money terms, the amount payable must be determined by construction of the contract in accordance with the applicable law, or by a substantive provision of that law,[89] which may take the form of a trade usage.[90] The question whether interest on late payment is chargeable and, if so, at what rate, is also governed by the law applicable to the contract,[91] subject to an important exception discussed below.[92] These propositions are as equally applicable under the Rome Convention as at common law, the position under the Convention being reached because questions of inter- 25–161

---

[85] *cf.* the following authorities interpreting an earlier equivalent of the former RSC, Ord.11, r.1(1)(*e*): *Malik v Narodni Banka Ceskoslovenska* [1946] 2 All E.R. 663; *Korner v Vitkowitzer* [1950] 2 K.B. 128 at 159–161; *ibid. sub nom. Vitkovice Horni a Hutni Tezirstvo v Korner* [1951] A.C. 869. See too Dicey and Morris, *op. cit.*, para.11–175 and *cf.* n.4, above. RSC, Ord.11, r.1(1)(e) has been replaced by CPR, r. 6.20(6): see above, para.25–157.

[86] Including the existence and length of any period of credit.

[87] *e.g.* whether he may or must supply cash, or tender a cheque, or accept a bill of exchange tendered by the seller, or pay by way of banker's commercial credit. The validity and effect of any cheque or other bill of exchange tendered or accepted will, however, be determined by its own governing laws (above, para.25–077). Similarly, the right of a seller to sue an issuing banker on a credit issued on the instructions of the buyer depends upon the law applicable to the letter of credit, which is not necessarily the same as the law governing the contract of sale: *Offshore International SA v Banco Central SA* [1977] 1 W.L.R. 399; *Power Curber International v National Bank of Kuwait* [1981] 1 W.L.R. 1233; *European Asian Bank AG v Punjab and Sind Bank* [1982] 2 Lloyd's Rep. 356; *Bank of Baroda v Vysya Bank Ltd* [1994] 2 Lloyd's Rep. 87; *Bank of Credit and Commerce Hong Kong Ltd v Sonali Bank* [1995] 1 Lloyd's Rep. 227; *PT Pan Indonesia Bank Ltd TBK v Marconi Communications International Ltd* [2005] EWCA Civ. 422; [2005] 2 All E.R. (Comm) 325; and see *Attock Cement Co. Ltd v Romanian Bank for Foreign Trade* [1989] 1 W.L.R. 1147 (performance bond); contrast *Wahda Bank v Arab Bank Plc* [1996] 1 Lloyd's Rep. 470 (counter-guarantee). See above, para.25–076.

[88] Above, para.25–156.

[89] Though note Unfair Terms in Consumer Contract Regulations 1999, reg. 5(5) and Sch.2, para.1(l) which lists amongst terms which may be regarded as unfair, terms providing for the price of goods to be determined at the time of delivery or allowing a seller of goods or supplier of services to increase their price without in both cases giving the consumer the corresponding right to cancel the contract if the final price is too high in relation to the price agreed when the contract was concluded. The application of these Regulations may be mandatory: see above, para.25–103.

[90] *Sanitary Packing Co. Ltd v Nicholson and Bain* (1916) 33 W.L.R. 594 (Supreme Court of Manitoba), where the phrase "opening prices" in a contract of sale governed by the law of Ontario was interpreted in the light of Ontario usages.

[91] *Sociètè des Hôtels le Touquet Paris-Plage v Cummings* [1922] 1 K.B. 451; *Mount Albert Borough Council v Australasian, etc. Life Assurance Society Ltd* [1938] A.C. 224; Dicey and Morris, *op. cit.*, paras 33–372—33–375.

[92] See below, para.25–162.

pretation of the contract[93] and performance[94] are to be referred to the governing law, because, in any event, the list of issues covered by Article 10(1) is not exhaustive and because it would seem that matters traditionally referred to the governing law at common law would be so referred under the Convention in the absence of strong contrary indications in the Convention itself.

25–162 **Late Payment of Commercial Debts (Interest) Act 1998.** The scope of the applicable law in relation to the matters referred to in the preceding paragraph may, of course, be limited or modified by particular statutory provisions. One such provision to which it is worth drawing attention at this point is found in section 12 of the Late Payment of Commercial Debts (Interest) Act 1998.[95] The purpose of the 1998 Act is to make provision with respect to the late payment of certain debts.[96] According to Part I of the Act, it is an implied term in a contract for the supply of goods or services where the purchaser and supplier are each acting in the course of business[97] that any "qualifying debt"[98] created by the contract carries simple interest, referred to as "statutory interest"[99] subject to and in accordance with Part I of the Act.[1] Part II of the Act details the circumstances in which contract terms are permissible to oust or vary this right to statutory interest.[2] Section 12(1) of the Act stipulates that the provisions of the Act do not have effect in relation to a contract governed by the law of a part of the United Kingdom by choice of the parties if: (a) there is no significant connection between the contract and that part of the United Kingdom; and (b) but for that choice, the applicable law would be a foreign law, defined as the law of a country outside the United Kingdom.[3] The effect of this subsection is, first, that if the parties to a contract of sale choose English law to govern the contract in accordance with Article 3(1) of the Rome Convention,[4] but there is no significant connection between the contract and England, and, were it not for that choice of law, the contract would be governed by, *e.g.* German law, pursuant to Article 4 of the Rome Convention,[5] the provisions of the 1998 Act will not apply.[6] Secondly, this

[93] Art. 10(1)(a). See *CGU International Insurance Plc v Astrazeneca Insurance Co. Ltd* [2005] EWHC 2755 (Comm); [2006] 1 C.L.C. 162.
[94] Art. 10(1)(b).
[95] For detailed discussion, see Dicey and Morris, *op. cit.*, paras 33–376—33–383; *Chitty on Contracts* (29th ed.), Vol. 1, paras 30–154—30–157.
[96] For discussion of the substantive provisions of the 1998 Act, see above, paras 16–010—16–013.
[97] Late Payment of Commercial Debts (Interest) Act 1998, ss.1(1), 2(1), (2), (3), (7), 12(3). Certain contracts are "excepted" from the requirements of the Act: see s.2(5) and (7).
[98] ss.1(1), 3(1).
[99] s.1(2).
[1] s.1(1).
[2] ss.7–10.
[3] s.12(3).
[4] Above, paras 25–029 *et seq.*
[5] Above, paras 25–057 *et seq.*
[6] *cf.* Unfair Contract Terms Act 1977, s.27(1), above, paras 25–091—25–093. See also *Surzur Overseas Ltd v Ocean Reliance Shipping Co. Ltd* [1997] C.L.Y. 906.

conclusion would also seem to follow even if the contract has a significant connection with a part of the United Kingdom other than the part whose law has been chosen in the contract, since section 12(1), by its specific terms, requires the absence of a significant connection with the part whose law has been chosen. Thirdly, however, the Act will apply if there is a choice of English law in the contract but, apart from that choice, the contract would be governed by the law of a country outside the United Kingdom, if there is, nonetheless, a significant connection between the contract and England. It follows from this that section 12(1) of the Act envisages that a contract may have a significant connection with the part of the United Kingdom whose law has been chosen, even though, by virtue of Article 4 of the Rome Convention,[7] it is most closely connected with a country outside the United Kingdom. Fourthly, it appears that the factors which will give rise to a significant connection and whether such a connection exists or not will depend on the circumstances of the particular case, but in relation to a contract of sale the relevant connection might exist if English law is chosen and England is the place of business of the purchaser or the place where the price is to be paid or the place where the goods are to be delivered, but apart from the choice of law, the contract would be governed by the law of Germany, pursuant to Article 4(2),[8] because Germany is the country in which the seller's place of business is situated. Lastly, the Act appears to apply if the law of one part of the United Kingdom is chosen in the contract but, were it not for that choice, the contract would be governed by the law of another part of the United Kingdom. This will be so irrespective of whether there is a significant connection between the contract and the law of the part of the United Kingdom chosen in it because section 12(1) only comes into effect if, in the absence of a choice of law, the contract would be governed by a foreign law[9] and foreign law is defined as the law of a country outside the United Kingdom.[10]

Section 12(2) of the 1998 Act contains an anti-avoidance provision.[11] It provides that the Act has effect in relation to a contract governed by a foreign law by choice of the parties if: (a) but for that choice, the applicable law would be the law of a part of the United Kingdom; and (b) there is no significant connection between the contract and any country other than that part of the United Kingdom. Thus, first, if a contract of sale contains a choice of, *e.g.* German law in accordance with Article 3 of the Rome Convention,[12] but were it not for that choice, the applicable law under 25–163

[7] Above, paras 25–057 *et seq*.
[8] *ibid*.
[9] Late Payment of Commercial Debts (Interest) Act 1998, s.12(1)(b).
[10] s.12(3).
[11] *cf.* Unfair Contract Terms Act 1977, s.27(2), above, paras 25–094—25–100. There is no explicit anti-avoidance provision in Directive 2000/35/EC of the European Parliament and Council of June 29, 2000 on combating late payment in commercial transactions ([2000] O.J. L200/35), implemented in the UK in the Late Payment of Commercial Debts Regulations 2002, SI 2002/1674, which amend the 1998 Act. S.12 (2) would therefore seem to apply to control attempts to evade the provisions of the Directive implemented in the amending Regulations. And see above, para.25–153.
[12] Above, paras 25–029 *et seq*.

Article 4 of the Rome Convention[13] would be English law, the Act will apply unless the contract has a significant connection with a country other than England. Secondly, that significant connection may be with the country whose law has been chosen, German law in the above example, or with a different foreign country, say Belgium, or with a part of the United Kingdom other than England, say, Scotland. For although the expression "country" is not defined in the Act, it seems clear that it includes the different parts of the United Kingdom in section 12(2) because that provision expressly refers to any country "other than *that part of the United Kingdom*"[14] whose law has been chosen and these words, in relation to the above example, are apt to include Scotland. Thirdly, what will be found to constitute a significant connection will depend on the circumstances of the particular case,[15] but it is, fourthly, clear that although the contract may be most closely connected[16] with the law of a particular part of the United Kingdom, it can, nonetheless, have a significant connection with a country other than that part of the United Kingdom.[17]

25–164 Section 12(2) only controls the prevention of avoidance of the 1998 Act by a choice of foreign law, *i.e.* the law of a country outside the United Kingdom.[18] Should, however, an issue arise in English proceedings involving a contract of sale which contains a choice of the law of a different part of the United Kingdom, the Act appears to apply on general principles,[19] subject, of course, to the proviso that section 12(1) is inapplicable.[20] The Act further appears to apply if a contract of sale contains no choice of law but, because of Article 4 of the Rome Convention,[21] the applicable law is the law of a part of the United Kingdom.[22]

25–165 **Money of account.** Where the price or rate of payment is fixed by the contract in money terms, determination of the currency in which payment should be made, and the amount thereof, raises a number of choice of law questions, which can only be briefly dealt with here.[23] In the first place, the "money of account",[24] which is the currency in which the amount of the

---

[13] Above, paras 25–057 *et seq*.
[14] Emphasis added. See also s.12(3), defining foreign law as the law of a country outside *the United Kingdom.*
[15] *cf.* s.12(1), above, para.25–162.
[16] Above, para.25–162.
[17] *cf.* s.12(1), above, para.25–162.
[18] s.12(3).
[19] Rome Convention, Art. 3(1), above, paras 25–029 *et seq*.
[20] Above, para.25–162.
[21] Above, paras 25–057 *et seq*.
[22] The Act applies in England and Wales and in Scotland and is expressly stated to extend to Northern Ireland: s.17(5).
[23] See generally Dicey and Morris, *op. cit.*, paras 36R–031—36–045; Morris, 6 Vanderbilt L.Rev. 505 (1953); Baxter, 35 Can.Bar Rev. 697 at 714–716 (1957). Further authorities are cited in Dicey and Morris, *op. cit.*, para.36R–031, n.44. As to "spot" and "forward" transfers of currency, see above, paras 22–007—22–013.
[24] Also referred to as "the money of measurement", or the "money of contract". It is not necessarily the same currency as that in which the price is to be paid (see below, para.25–167) and there may be more than one money of account for a single contract: *cf. Tota Societa Italiana per Azioni v Liberian Trans-Ocean Navigation Corp.* [1971] 2 Lloyd's Rep. 469 at 474 (affirmed [1972] 1 Lloyd's Rep. 399).

price is to be measured, must be identified. This is done by construing the contract in order to determine the parties' intention in the matter,[25] the canons of construction being supplied by the governing law.[26] If English law is the governing law, then in the absence of any clear intention emerging from the contract when construed according to English law,[27] the parties will be presumed to have intended the currency of the country with which the contract is most closely connected[28], *i.e.* the money of account will be identified in a manner similar to, though not identical with,[29] that in which the applicable law itself is identified.[30] Moreover, where the parties have expressly or impliedly specified a single country where payment is to take place, there is in English domestic law a prima facie presumption that the currency of that country is the money of account.[31] This presumption may be rebutted by the terms of the contract,[32] or by a countervailing factor,[33] and where several places of payment (whether alternative or otherwise) are named in the contract, the presumption virtually disappears.[34]

---

[25] Rome Convention, Art. 10(1)(a); *King Line Ltd v Westralian Farmers Ltd* (1932) 48 T.L.R. 398; *Adelaide Electricity Supply Co. Ltd v Prudential Assurance Co. Ltd* [1934] A.C. 122; *Auckland Corporation v Alliance Assurance Co. Ltd* [1937] A.C. 587; *De Bueger v Ballantyne & Co.* [1938] A.C. 452; *Bonython v Commonwealth of Australia* [1951] A.C. 201; *National Bank of Australasia Ltd v Scottish Union and National Insurance Co. Ltd* [1952] A.C. 493; *National Mutual Life Association of Australasia Ltd v Att-Gen for New Zealand* [1956] A.C. 369.

[26] *Bonython v Commonwealth of Australia*, above, at p.217; *WJ Alan & Co. Ltd v El Nasr Export and Import Co.* [1972] 2 Q.B. 189 at 206; Dicey and Morris, *op. cit.*, paras 32–188—32–190; *contra Adelaide Electric Supply Co. Ltd v Prudential Assurance Co. Ltd* [1934] A.C. 122 at 156, advocating the *lex loci solutionis*.

[27] The use of a recognised currency abbreviation often sufficiently indicates the parties' intention: *e.g.* in *WJ Alan & Co. Ltd v El Nasr Export and Import Co.*, above, a contractual provision that the price of goods being sold was "Shs. 262/- per cwt." pointed to the currency of Kenya (a country with which the sale was closely connected), even though English law was the law governing the contract.

[28] *Bonython v Commonwealth of Australia*, above; *National Bank of Australasia Ltd v Scottish Union and National Insurance Co. Ltd*, above; *WJ Alan & Co. Ltd v El Nasr Export and Import Co.*, above.

[29] *National Mutual Life Association of Australasia Ltd v Att-Gen for New Zealand*, above, at p.387; Dicey and Morris, *op. cit.*, para.36–037.

[30] This, it is submitted, is the case both at common law and under the Rome Convention.

[31] *Adelaide Electric Supply Co. Ltd v Prudential Assurance Co. Ltd*, above; *Mount Albert Borough Council v Australasian, etc. Life Assurance Society Ltd* [1938] A.C. 224 at 241; *National Mutual Life Association of Australasia Ltd v Att-Gen for New Zealand* [1956] A.C. 369 at 387; *WJ Alan & Co. Ltd v El Nasr Export and Import Co.* [1971] 1 Lloyd's Rep. 401 at 412, 415 (reversed on other grounds [1972] 2 Q.B. 189).

[32] See, *e.g. Bain v Field & Co. Fruit Merchants Ltd* (1920) 5 Ll.L.R. 16 (discussed below, para.25–193); *De Bueger v Ballantyne & Co.* [1938] A.C. 452.

[33] The identity of the applicable law is a relevant factor, particularly when it is chosen by the parties expressly: *WJ Alan & Co. Ltd v El Nasr Export and Import Co.* [1971] 1 Lloyd's Rep. 401 at 412, 414–415 (reversed on other grounds [1972] 2 Q.B. 189). If the government or a governmental authority of a particular country is a party to the contract, this is a pointer towards the currency of that particular country: *Bonython v Commonwealth of Australia* [1951] A.C. 201 at 221–222.

[34] *ibid.*, at p.221; *National Bank of Australasia Ltd v Scottish Union and National Insurance Co. Ltd* [1952] A.C. 493 at 511–512.

25–166 **The principle of nominalism.** The money of account being established, the principle of nominalism is applicable.[35] The effect of this is that the quantum of the price payable by the buyer is its nominal amount, as expressed in the contract, in the currency of the money of account, irrespective of any fluctuation in exchange rates affecting that currency.[36] Any difficulty as to what is legal tender in the money of account is resolved in accordance with the law governing the money of account (*lex pecuniae*) as at the time when payment falls due.[37] In the event of devaluation of the money of account between the date of the contract and the date when payment falls due, any provision of the applicable law that the price should be "revalorised"—*i.e.* that the buyer should pay more than the nominal amount to compensate for the devaluation—will be effective,[38] but it is irrelevant that the *lex pecuniae* itself, or indeed any other law, may have so provided.[39]

25–167 **Money of payment.** The actual currency in which the price is payable (the "money of payment") is not necessarily the money of account; indeed, the contract may expressly or impliedly stipulate, or the seller may give the buyer an option to elect, that the money of account and the money of payment should be different.[40] Where there is no stipulation as to the money of payment, it is at common law determined by the law of the country in which payment is made[41] since the question what money tokens the buyer must tender to the seller is one concerning the mode of

[35] Strictly, this principle only applies if it forms part of the proper law, but in fact nominalism is adopted by the law of virtually every "civilised" country: see Dicey and Morris, *op. cit.*, para.36–005.

[36] See, *e.g. Gilbert v Brett* (1604) Davis 18; *Re Chesterman's Trusts* [1923] 2 Ch. 466; *Ottoman Bank of Nicosia v Chakarian* (*No.2*) [1938] A.C. 260; *Pyrmont Ltd v Schott* [1939] A.C. 145; *Marrache v Ashton* [1943] A.C. 311. See too *Sociètè des Hôtels le Touquet Paris-Plage v Cummings* [1922] 1 K.B. 451; para.25–187, n.23. This does not necessarily mean that the seller will be unable to recover for exchange losses suffered by him because of late payment by the buyer: see below, para.25–192.

[37] *Pyrmont Ltd v Schott*, above; (with which *cf. Marrache v Ashton*, above, as to the facts); and see *British Bank for Foreign Trade Ltd v Russian Commercial and Industrial Bank* (*No.2*) (1921) 38 T.L.R. 65; *Re Chesterman's Trusts*, above; *Anderson v Equitable Life Assurance Society of the US* (1929) 45 T.L.R. 468; *Campos v Kentucky and Indiana Terminal Railroad Co.* [1962] 2 Lloyd's Rep. 459. For discussion of the implications of a single European currency, see Dicey and Morris, *op. cit.*, paras 36–008—36–010. See also *Virani Ltd v Manuel Rivert Y Cia SA* [2003] EWCA Civ. 1651; [2004] 2 Lloyd's Rep. 14.

[38] See *Re Schnapper* [1936] 1 All E.R. 322; *Kornatzki v Oppenheimer* [1937] 4 All E.R. 133.

[39] *Anderson v Equitable Life Assurance Society of the US*, above. Alternatively, the parties may seek to provide against fluctuation in exchange rates, *e.g.* by inserting a "gold-value" clause in the contract. Such methods of protection are dealt with in Dicey and Morris, *op. cit.*, paras 36–021—36–029.

[40] For a sale of goods instance arising out of the devaluation of sterling in 1967, see *Woodhouse AC Israel Cocoa Ltd SA v Nigerian Produce Marketing Co. Ltd* [1972] A.C. 741. Here the money of account was Nigerian currency, but the buyers were given an option to choose between paying in Nigerian currency or in sterling.

[41] *Adelaide Electric Supply Co. Ltd v Prudential Assurance Co. Ltd* [1934] A.C. 122; *Auckland Corporation v Alliance Assurance Co. Ltd* [1937] A.C. 587; *Mount Albert Borough Council v Australasian etc. Life Assurance Society Ltd* [1938] A.C. 224.

performance and thus is referrable to the law of the place of performance.[42] Whether this rule survives in cases falling within the Rome Convention depends upon the correct interpretation of Article 10(2), which, it will be recalled says, *inter alia*, that in relation to the "manner of performance" "regard shall be had" to that law of the country in which performance takes place.[43] If "manner of performance" can be equated with "mode of performance" in common law cases, then the rule will survive (albeit, perhaps, as a matter for the discretion of the English court[44]). Nonetheless, the position must remain speculative because the Giuliano-Lagarde Report does not include the money of payment among the examples of issues covered by Article 10(2) but suggests, in contrast, that "where performance consists of the payment of a sum of money, the conditions relating to the discharge of the debtor who has made the payment"[45] are governed by Article 10(1)(b). It is submitted, however, that the better view is that this observation should be confined to the determination, in this context, of the money of account. Determination of the money of payment according to the *lex loci solutionis* has much to commend it on obvious practical grounds, and it is therefore suggested that the English courts should interpret Article 10(2) of the Convention to include this issue.[46]

Where the law of the country of payment is English law there is a presumption that the money of payment is the same as the money of account.[47] If it differs from the money of account, the exchange rate between the two is, it seems, determined by the law applicable to the contract.[48] A price paid in England under a contract governed by English law may be paid in units of the money of account or in sterling[49]; in the latter case the rate of exchange is the rate at which, on the day payment falls due, units of the money of account can be bought in London at a recognised and accessible market, irrespective of the official rate of exchange.[50]

---

[42] Dicey and Morris, *op. cit.*, para.36–052.
[43] Above, para.25–156.
[44] Above, para.25–156.
[45] pp. 42–43.
[46] And see Plender, *op. cit.*, para.11–07.
[47] *Auckland Corporation v Alliance Assurance Co. Ltd*, above; *Parsons & Co. v Electricity Trust* (1976) 16 S.A.S.R. 93.
[48] Dicey and Morris, *op. cit.*, paras 36–051—36–058; but note the comment at para.36–054 to the effect that in the cases where English law has determined the rate of exchange, this may have been *qua* law of the country of payment and not *qua* applicable law.
[49] *Marrache v Ashton* [1943] A.C. 311; *Syndic for Khoury v Khayat* [1943] A.C. 507 at 514; Dicey and Morris, *op. cit.*, para.30–054, but *cf. National Bank of Australasia Ltd v Scottish Union and National Insurance Co. Ltd* [1952] A.C. 493; *National Mutual Life Association of Australasia Ltd v Att.-Gen. for New Zealand* [1956] A.C. 369. If payment in the foreign currency is impossible, the buyer must pay in sterling: he cannot choose to pay in the foreign currency and then claim that his obligation is discharged or suspended by reason of the impossibility: *Libyan Arab Foreign Bank v Bankers Trust Co.* [1989] Q.B. 728.
[50] *Marrache v Ashton*, above; *Syndic for Khoury v Khayat*, above; *Barclays Bank International Ltd v Levin Brothers (Bradford) Ltd* [1977] Q.B. 270; *George Veflings Rederi A/S v President of India* [1978] 1 W.L.R. 982 *affirmed* [1979] 1 W.L.R. 59; but *cf. Graumann v Treitel* (1940) 112 L.T. 383; and see *Re Parana Plantations Ltd* [1946] 2 All E.R. 214, where there was no commercial rate of exchange for the money of account.

(d) *Licences and Permits*

25–168 **Governing law and *lex loci solutionis*.** It is implicit from the decision of the House of Lords in *A V Pound & Co. Ltd v M W Hardy & Co. Inc.*[51] that the law applicable to the contract of sale determined, at common law, whether it was the seller or the buyer who had to obtain any necessary export licence for the goods and whether, on the licence not being obtained, the party responsible for obtaining it was excused for his failure in this regard or must be deemed in breach of contract. The law of the country in which the licence is to be obtained was only relevant to the question of export licences in so far as it determined the extent, if any, to which it was necessary and/or possible for a licence to be obtained.[52] It is submitted that the obtaining of an import licence or any other licence or permit required for due performance of the contract was regulated in the same way. It is also submitted that the principle of this case is accurately reflected in the Rome Convention, the distinction between the two sets of issues described above corresponding to matters relating to the substance of the performance which according to Article 10(1) are determined by the applicable law and to matters relating to the manner of performance where, according to Article 10(2), reference may be made to the law of the country of performance, *i.e.* the law of the country in which the relevant licence or permit is to be obtained.[53]

(e) *Quality and Compliance with Description*

25–169 **Express terms.** The question whether goods delivered under a contract of sale are in conformity with the appropriate description, sample, quality or fitness for a purpose may depend, in part at least, upon the express terms of the contract. Those terms must, on general principles,[54] be interpreted in accordance with the law applicable to the contract. An alternative way of expressly providing for these matters is to "incorporate by reference" the provisions of a law other than the governing law.[55] Whichever method is

[51] [1956] A.C. 588 at 601; see too the Court of Appeal judgment, *sub nom. MW Hardy & Co. Inc. v AV Pound & Co. Ltd* [1955] 1 Q.B. 499, and several cases involving international sales, where the governing law was assumed without argument to be English law and it was also assumed that one or other or both of these questions should be governed by English law: *e.g. Partabmull Rameshwar v K C Sethia (1944) Ltd* [1951] 2 Lloyd's Rep. 89; *Brauer & Co. (Great Britain) Ltd v James Clark (Brush Materials) Ltd* [1952] 2 All E.R. 497; *Beves & Co. Ltd v Farkas* [1953] 1 Lloyd's Rep. 103; *Peter Cassidy Seed Co. Ltd v Osuustukkukappa I.L.* [1957] 1 W.L.R. 273. As to the rules of English domestic law in regard to these questions, see above, paras 18–308—18–332.

[52] *AV Pound & Co. Ltd v MW Hardy & Co. Inc.*, above, at p.601; *ibid.*, *sub nom. M W Hardy & Co. Inc. v AV Pound & Co. Ltd*, above, at pp.510, 512; *Société d'Avances Commerciales (London) Ltd v A Besse & Co. (London) Ltd* [1952] 1 T.L.R. 645 at 647–648. *Cf.* the principle in *Ralli Bros v Companiera Naviera Sota y Aznar* [1920] 2 K.B. 287 as to illegality of contracts, discussed above, para.25–119.

[53] See Dicey and Morris, *op. cit.*, para.32–196; Plender, *op. cit.*, para.11–10.

[54] Above, para.25–156, and see *Markey v Brunson*, 286 F. 893 (1923); *Miles v Vermont Fruit Co.*, 124 A. 559 (1924); Rabel, *op. cit.*, Vol. 3, pp.94–97.

[55] See above, paras 25–006, n.32, 25–028.

used, the extent to which express terms may supersede undertakings implied by law is a matter which must be taken into account; it is discussed below.[56]

Where a term in the contract purports to exclude or restrict the seller's liability for breach of an express clause regarding quality or description, its validity and effect are determined by the applicable law, subject to the important exceptions introduced, with regard to certain categories of contract, by the Unfair Contract Terms Act 1977.[57] and the Unfair Terms in Consumer Contracts Regulations 1999.[58]

Implied undertakings governed generally by applicable law. According to general principles of choice of law, both at common law and under the Rome Convention, the nature and the extent of any implied terms as to the description or quality of the goods are referable to the law applicable to the contract. In *Henry Kendall & Sons v William Lillico & Sons Ltd*,[59] the House of Lords held, with relatively little discussion, that the implied conditions as to fitness and merchantability laid down in the then version of section 14 of the Sale of Goods Act 1979 were applicable to a contract of sale governed by English law, irrespective of other foreign elements.[60] No doubt this ruling covers as well the implied undertakings laid down in sections 13 and 15 of the same Act.[61] In addition, the extent to which a contractual term may exclude or restrict the operation of implied undertakings as to description or quality is, on general principles, a matter for the governing law.[62] These general propositions are, however, significantly modified by the statutory rules discussed in the next section. 25–170

Statutory provisions as to implied undertakings. An earlier section dealing with the seller's duty to pass title (para.25–160) endeavoured to explain the effect of the provisions of the Unfair Contract Terms Act 1977, in extending or purporting to extend the operation of section 12 of the Act of 1979 (containing implied undertakings as to title, etc.) to certain contracts of sale not governed by the law of any part of the United Kingdom, and prohibiting exclusion or restriction of the operation of section 12 in certain circumstances. *Mutatis mutandis*, this same pattern of provisions applies to sections 13, 14 and 15 of the Act of 1979. Only one specific difference calls for comment. Whereas the prohibition on excluding or restricting section 12 is absolute in the circumstances in which it 25–171

---

[56] Below, paras 25–169, 25–170.
[57] See para.25–089, above.
[58] Above, paras 25–101 *et seq*.
[59] [1969] 2 A.C. 31.
[60] See *ibid*., at pp.120, 129; see too *Teheran (Europe) Co. v Belton (ST) Tractors* [1968] 2 Q.B. 545 (though the point was not specifically taken); *Mendelson-Zeller Co. Inc. v T & C Providores Pty Ltd* [1981] 1 N.S.W.L.R. 366. S.14 is discussed above, Ch.11.
[61] Dicey and Morris, *op. cit*., para.33–105; *cf. Shohfi v Rice*, 135 N.E. 141 (1922). ss.13 and 15 are discussed above, Ch.11.
[62] See sources cited above, para.25–089, n.98.

applies,[63] the equivalent prohibition with regard to sections 13, 14 and 15 is absolute only as regards consumer sales; in other cases, its operation depends on considerations of fairness and reasonableness.[64] Subject to this difference, the relevant passage in paragraph 25–160 should be treated as bearing also upon the scope of operation of the implied undertakings as to description and quality in sections 13, 14 and 15 of the Sale of Goods Act 1979 and the extent to which these undertakings may be excluded or restricted.

The case of *Henry Kendall & Sons v William Lillico & Sons Ltd*[65] provides a further instance of an English statutory provision as to the quality of goods comprised in a sale being applied irrespective of the law applicable to the contract. In that case, the House of Lords considered the range of application of subsection (2) of section 2 of the Fertilisers and Feeding Stuffs Act 1926,[66] which arises "on the sale" of any of the products specified in the Act and cannot be excluded or modified by the parties to the sale. The case concerned a number of c.i.f. contracts of sale where the parties were English business organisations trading in England, the governing law was English law and the subject-matter was groundnut meal, which was shipped under the contracts from Brazil to England. By a majority of three to two,[67] the warranty was held to apply to each of these transactions on two distinct grounds: (a) that the governing law was English law[68] (though this might not have been enough *per se*[69]); and (b) that the "place of sale", *i.e.* the place where the documents of title were transferred from seller to buyer so as to transfer title to the goods, was in England.[70] Their Lordships did not make it clear whether these grounds were cumulative or alternative or, if the latter, which was preferable.[71] However, their decision shows that, in the case of sales having foreign elements, the applicability of an English statutory provision which lays down an implied term as to the quality of the

63 See Unfair Contract Terms Act 1977, s.6(1)(a) (for Scotland, s.20(1)(a)).

64 See Unfair Contract Terms Act 1977, s.6(2)(a) (for Scotland, s.20(2)(a)). Note also Unfair Terms in Consumer Contracts Regulations 1999, regs 5(5), 9 and Sch.2, para.1(m), above, paras 25–101—25–105 and the discussion of Sale and Supply of Goods to Consumers Regulations 2002, above, paras 25–111—25–118.

65 [1969] 2 A.C. 31. The principle of this case would be applicable to cases falling within the Rome Convention by virtue of Art. 7(2).

66 See now the Agriculture Act 1970, s.72.

67 By Lord Morris, Lord Pearce and Lord Wilberforce, Lord Reid and Lord Guest dissenting.

68 [1969] 2 A.C. 31 at 101, 121, 129–130.

69 Lord Pearce thought it relevant that virtually all the other elements of the transaction were linked with England (*ibid.*, at p.121) and Lord Wilberforce that the place of actual delivery to the buyer was in England (*ibid.*, at pp.129–130).

70 *ibid.*, at pp.101, 120, 128. In ruling that the "place of sale" under a c.i.f. contract governed by English law was the place where the documents of title were transferred to the buyer, not the actual *situs* of the goods at the time of such transfer, the HL overruled the decision of the CA in *CEB Draper & Son Ltd v Edward Turner & Son Ltd* [1965] 1 Q.B. 424. Where the transfer of title is not effected by means of documents, the "place of sale" would, however, presumably be the *situs* of the goods at the time of transfer.

71 Except for Lord Wilberforce, who expressed a preference for the former ground ([1969] 2 A.C. 31 at 129).

goods is in the last resort a question of construction of the provision, involving consideration of (*inter alia*) its wording, the existence or non-existence of a power to exclude it and the policy underlying its enactment,[72] considerations which, it is also submitted, are relevant to determining whether a rule is mandatory for the purposes of Article 7(2) of the Rome Convention.[73] It does not follow, however, that similar provisions of a foreign law would be dealt with in the same way; indeed, it is submitted despite the *Henry Kendall* case[74] that, as the question of implied terms is in general a contractual one to be dealt with by the law applicable to the contract,[75] such foreign statutory provisions should only be applied by an English court if they form part of the law applicable to the particular contract of sale before the court and on a proper construction are intended to apply to such contract. This general principle is, however, qualified in two respects where the particular contract of sale is one to which the Rome Convention applies. First, where there is a choice of English law but all the other elements relevant to the situation at the time of the choice are connected with one country only (other than England), the application of English law shall not prejudice the application of the mandatory rules[76] of the only connected country.[77] If the mandatory rules of the only connected country include implied terms of the kind being discussed here, then it would seem that those rules must be applied if they are more favourable to the buyer than the corresponding English rules.[78] Secondly, if the contract of sale falls within the definition of consumer contract in Article 5[79] and is concluded in one of the three circumstances set out in that provision then the English court will, even if the law applicable to the contract as a matter of choice by the parties is English law, have to apply any rules as to implied terms of the law of the consumer's habitual residence if that country regards those rules as mandatory and they are more favourable to the consumer than the corresponding rules of English law.[80]

Other matters. Remedies in respect of defective goods, and certain other subsidiary matters connected therewith, are considered later in this chapter.[81] 25–172

[72] See *ibid.*, at p.121, *per* Lord Pearce. *Cf.* the rules as to illegality under an English statute (above, para.25–119).
[73] See Plender, *op. cit.*, paras 9–12—9–13.
[74] [1969] 2 A.C. 31.
[75] Rabel, *op. cit.*, Vol. 3, pp.95–96. If however, a term imposed by a foreign law other than the proper law is mandatory, and its breach constitutes a criminal offence, the choice of law rules relating to illegality (above, para.25–119) must be consulted too.
[76] Above, paras 25–037—25–041.
[77] Rome Convention, Art. 3(3).
[78] Above, para.25–036.
[79] Above, paras 25–044—25–056.
[80] Above, para.25–54.
[81] Below, paras 25–196 *et seq.*

9. DISCHARGE OF OBLIGATIONS UNDER A CONTRACT OF SALE

25–173 **General principles.**[82] Subject to a few exceptions, some of which are noted below, the law determining whether a contract of sale has been discharged is the law applicable to the contract, both at common law and under the Rome Convention.[83]

25–174 **Discharge by performance.** The question whether an obligation arising under a contract of sale is discharged by performance is in general determined by the applicable law.[84]

25–175 **Discharge by virtue of frustration or other similar principles.** The question whether an obligation has been discharged by virtue of frustration[85] or some similar legal principle is also determined by the applicable law.[86] In *Jacobs v Crédit Lyonnais*,[87] a contract for the sale of a quantity of esparto provided for delivery from Algeria to England. Due to a rebellion in Algeria, the seller failed to deliver part of the quantity contracted for, but, when sued by the buyer for damages, he raised the defence of *force majeure*. It was held in the Court of Appeal that this defence failed because, although available on these facts under Algerian law, the *lex loci solutionis*, it was not available under English law, the applicable law.

25–176 It would appear that when, according to the law applicable to it, a contract of sale is discharged through frustration or some similar cause, the question whether, and to what extent, either or both of the parties must restore benefits which have accrued to them under the contract, or make any other form of restitution, is determined by the English choice of law rules relating to restitution.[88] This is also the case under the Rome

---

[82] See generally Dicey and Morris, *The Conflict of Laws* (13th ed.), paras 32–201—32–206

[83] Art. 10(1)(d); Plender, *The European Contracts Convention* (2nd ed.), para.11–14.

[84] Rome Convention, Art. 10(1)(b),(d); *The Baarn* (*No.1*) [1933] P. 251; (*No.2*) [1934] P. 171; *Mount Albert Borough Council v Australasian, etc. Life Assurance Society Ltd* [1938] A.C. 224; *Bonythor v Commonwealth of Australia* [1951] A.C. 201. Thus the applicable law determines, for example, whether payment of the price by tendering a bill of exchange or arranging a documentary credit, discharges the obligation to pay: see, *e.g. WJ Alan & Co. Ltd v El Nasr Export and Import Co.* [1972] 2 Q.B. 189.

[85] This includes frustration by virtue of illegality, but in cases of illegality laws other than the proper law may also be relevant: see above, para.25–119.

[86] Rome Convention, Art. 10(1)(d); *Jacobs v Crédit Lyonnais*, below.

[87] (1884) 12 Q.B.D. 589; and, for other instances in the field of sale of goods, see *Mann, George & Co. v James and Alexander Brown* (1921) 10 Ll.L.R. 221; *Dalmia Dairy Industries Ltd v National Bank of Pakistan* [1978] 2 Lloyd's Rep. 223.

[88] Fawcett, Harris and Bridge, *International Sale of Goods in the Conflict of Laws* (2005), Ch.19; Dicey and Morris, *op. cit.*, Ch.34, esp. paras 34–019—34–027; Cheshire and North, *Private International Law* (13th ed.), Ch.20; Panagopoulos, *Restitution in Private International Law* (2000); Rose (ed.), *Restitution and the Conflict of Laws* (1995), Chs 3, 4 and 5; Dickenson [1996] L.M.C.L.Q. 566; *cf. Fibrosa Spolka Akcyjna v Fairbairn Lawson Combe Barbour Ltd* [1943] A.C. 52; *Arab Bank Ltd v Barclays Bank* (*Dominion, Colonial and Overseas*) [1953] 2 Q.B. 527 at 572; *Etler v Kertesz* (1960) 26 D.L.R. (2d) 209.

Convention. For although Article 10(1)(e) provides that the law applicable under the Convention governs "the consequences of nullity of the contract", the United Kingdom has entered a reservation to this provision, as permitted by the Convention,[89] so that it does not have the force of law in the United Kingdom.[90] Having said that, however, it is thought that the obligation to make restitution is governed by the "proper law" of the obligation[91] and if that obligation arises in connection with a contract, the "proper law" will normally, but not invariably,[92] be the law applicable to the contract.[93] And indeed by its express terms, the Law Reform (Frustrated Contracts) Act 1943 can only be applied to resolve these issues where the contract is governed by English law.[94]

Other forms of discharge. The question whether a contractual obligation imposed on a party to a contract is wholly or partly discharged through breach by the other party,[95] or accord and satisfaction,[96] or novation,[97] or some legislative or executive act directed at such obligation,[98] must be referred to the law applicable to the contract under common law rules. Each of these methods of discharge should, equally, be submitted to the applicable law where the contract is one to which the Rome Convention 25–177

---

[89] Art. 22(1)(b).

[90] Contracts (Applicable Law) Act 1990, s.2(2). In *Kleinwort Benson Ltd v Glasgow City Council* [1999] A.C. 153, a majority of the House of Lords held that a claim for money paid under a void contract was not a matter "relating to a contract" for the purposes of Art. 5(1) of the modified version of the Brussels Convention on Jurisdiction and the Enforcement of Judgments in Civil and Commercial Matters 1968 (Civil Jurisdiction and Judgments Act 1982, Sch.4) which used to be applicable as between the component parts of the United Kingdom. See also, above para.25–016.

[91] Dicey and Morris, *op. cit.*, Rule 200(1).

[92] See Dicey and Morris, *op. cit.*, Rule 200(2)(a) and paras 34–019—34–027; Plender, *op. cit.*, paras 11–15—11–18; North in North (ed.) *Contract Conflicts* (1982), p.3, at p.17. *Cf. Baring Bros & Co. v Cunninghame District Council* [1997] C.L.C. 108.

[93] Dicey and Morris, *op. cit.*, Rule 200(2)(a).

[94] See s.1(1) of the Act; *BP Exploration Co. v Hunt* [1976] 1 W.L.R. 788 at 795; Dicey and Morris, *op. cit.*, para.34–020. It is submitted that this does *not* mean where English law, *qua lex loci solutionis*, governs the incidents of performance only.

[95] *cf. AV Pound & Co. Ltd v MW Hardy & Co. Inc.* [1956] A.C. 566; considered above, para.25–161.

[96] *Ralli v Denistoun* (1851) 6 Exch.483.

[97] *Re United Railways of the Havana and Regla Warehouses Ltd* [1960] Ch.52 (reversed in part on other grounds *sub nom. Tomkinson v First Pennsylvania Banking and Trust Co.* [1961] A.C. 1007); see *Raiffeisen Zentralbank Osterreich AG v Five Star General Trading LLC* [2001] Q.B. 825 at 842; *Wight v Eckhardt Marine GmbH* [2003] UKPC 37; [2004] 1 A.C. 147.

[98] *Tomkinson v First Pennsylvania Banking and Trust Co.*, above; *Re Helbert Wagg & Co. Ltd* [1956] Ch. 323 at 340; *National Bank of Greece and Athens SA v Metliss* [1958] A.C. 509; *Adams v National Bank of Greece SA* [1961] A.C. 255; *Wight v Eckhardt Marine GmbH*, above. The relevant legislative or executive act, if foreign, may however be refused recognition in England on grounds of public policy: *cf.* para.25–119, n.23, above. An important instance of this form of discharge is discharge under foreign exchange control legislation: see above, para.25–120.

applies since they would all seem to be ways of "extinguishing obligations" within the meaning of Article 10(1)(d).[99]

10. REMEDIES OF THE SELLER

(a) *Remedies affecting the Goods*

25–178 **Issues of principle.** In considering the various ways in which an unpaid seller can assert rights against the goods, in particular after property has passed to the buyer, an initial difficulty is encountered, *viz.* to decide whether the particular right being asserted should be treated as contractual or proprietary in nature. It is submitted that the law governing this issue should in general be the *lex fori*; characterisation according to the *lex situs*[1] is likely to present problems as to time, and possibly even circularity, if the goods change *situs*. The alleged right having thus been characterised, it should then be referred to the law applicable to the contract in so far as it is found to be contractual, and to the *lex situs* at the time when the alleged right is asserted in so far as it is proprietary. As a general proposition, it is preferable, partly on grounds of convenience, for rights as between seller and buyer only to be characterised as contractual. But where third parties, such as the carrier or a sub-buyer, intervene the clash between competing claims raises a proprietary issue.

25–179 **Effect of Rome Convention.** This effect of the Rome Convention on the foregoing principles is by no means clear.[2] Article 10(1)(c) provides that the law applicable to the contract shall govern, within the limits of the powers conferred on the court by its procedural law, the consequences of breach, including the assessment of damages in so far as it is governed by rules of law. In general terms, this provision would submit the remedies of the seller to the applicable law and it would also seem that remedies in this context will include contractual remedies. What is not clear, however, is whether proprietary remedies are excluded from the scope of the applicable law and whether, when the issue arises as between seller and buyer, the matter of remedy should continue to be characterised, according to the *lex fori*, as contractual, proprietary characterisation being reserved for situations where third parties intervene. As to the first of these points, it is submitted that

---

[99] Plender, *op. cit.*, para.11–14. As to discharge by bankruptcy, see Dicey and Morris, *op. cit.*, paras 31–081—31–090. *Cf. Wight v Eckhardt Marine GmbH*, above. It is probable that Art. 10(1)(d) does not cover discharge by bankruptcy: see Lasok and Stone, *Conflict of Laws in the European Community* (1987), p.371.

[1] This is recommended (with reservations) by Rabel, *The Conflict of Laws* (2nd ed.), Vol. 4, pp.64–66; Falconbridge, 15 Can.Bar Rev. 215 at 237–238 (1937); Hellendall, 17 Can.Bar Rev. 7 and 105, 106–109 (1939). Characterisation generally is dealt with in Dicey and Morris, *The Conflict of Laws* (13th ed.), paras 2–001—2–043; Cheshire and North, *Private International Law* (13th ed.), Ch.3.

[2] See Fawcett, Harris and Bridge, *International Sale of Goods in the Conflict of Laws* (2005), paras 13–205—13–239.

since the Convention does not apply to property rights[3] it is legitimate, also, to infer that proprietary remedies are excluded and that the availability of these will continue to be a matter for the *lex situs*. As to the second, in the absence of any guidance in the Giuliano-Lagarde Report, it is tentatively submitted that characterisation should be carried out according to the *lex fori* and that thus, in general, issues arising between seller and buyer should be treated as contractual, though when rights of third parties are involved the issue should be properly characterised as proprietary.[4]

It is now proposed to discuss the specific remedies affecting the goods which an unpaid seller may have, basing the discussion on the characterisations which English law, as *lex fori*, should adopt.[5]

(i) *Lien and Withholding of Delivery*

Seller and buyer. In the absence of clear English authority,[6] it is submitted that any right of a seller as against a buyer to retain possession of the goods beyond the time fixed for delivery, by virtue of having not received payment, or for any other such reason, is a contractual right,[7] being at this stage a matter between these two parties only.[8] For this reason the appropriate law to determine the availability and duration of such right is the law applicable to the contract both at common law[9] and under the Rome Convention.[10] 25–180

Third parties claiming rights against the goods. The buyer may seek to defeat the seller's lien; *e.g.* where documents have been issued in respect of the goods, he may transfer the documents to a sub-buyer or pledgee. In 25–181

---

[3] Giuliano-Lagarde Report, p.10.

[4] *cf. Glencore International AG v Metro Trading International Inc.* [2001] 1 Lloyd's Rep. 284 disapproving the distinction between cases involving buyer and seller and cases involving third parties but only in the (different) context of the passing of title. See also McKendrick (ed.), *The Sale of Goods* (2001), para.15–098.

[5] See generally Chesterman, 22 I.C.L.Q. 213 (1973). *Cf.* the discussion of retention of title above, paras 25–141—25–149.

[6] A possessory lien of a repairer of goods in a foreign country was considered in *London and Provincial Leather Processes Ltd v Hudson* [1939] 2 K.B. 274, but on the issue of the governing law, no choice was made between the *lex situs* and the law applicable to the contract for repairs.

[7] If what the seller alleges is that property in the goods has revested in him, he is, it is submitted, going further than asserting a mere lien, and the right he claims is more properly termed "rescission of the transfer", or "revendication". This right is dealt with in the next paragraph.

[8] This characterisation harmonises with the rule in English domestic law that an unpaid vendor's lien may arise from the express or implied terms of the contract of sale, as well as under the Sale of Goods Act 1979: see above, para.15–031. It also reflects the consideration that time of delivery and time of payment are matters of performance falling under the applicable law: see above, paras 25–157, 25–161.

[9] *Livesley v Clemens Horst Co.* [1925] 1 D.L.R. 159 at 160–161; Falconbridge, *Conflict of Laws* (2nd ed.), pp.469–470. *Cf.* Rabel, *op. cit.*, Vol. 4, pp.64–66; and contrast *Willis v Glenwood Cotton Mills*, 200 F. 301 at 305 (1912), where a clear preference for the *lex situs* is expressed.

[10] Art. 10(1)(c).

such event, by virtue of principles set out earlier in this chapter,[11] the *lex situs*, the *lex situs cartae*, the proper law of the transfer or a combination of the first two of these will in general determine whether the buyer has the power to confer upon the transferee a title unencumbered by the lien.[12] In examining the provisions of any of these laws[13] on this point, due account should however be taken of the fact that under the law applicable to the original contract of sale, which is the law governing the contractual relationship between seller and buyer, a valid lien has arisen. It follows that only a provision giving clear paramountcy to the transferee should be considered sufficient to defeat the lien. In the reverse situation, *i.e.* where under the law applicable to the contract the seller's lien is extinguished upon a sub-sale,[14] it is arguable that such a provision should be effective in the transferee's favour whatever the *lex situs*, the *lex situs cartae* or the proper law of the transfer may say. The basis of this contention is that the law under which a seller's right to retain possession arises also controls the termination of that right as against the buyer, and that if this right has come to an end a transferee can take advantage of the fact. It will thus be seen that while the *lex situs*, the *lex situs cartae* and the proper law of the transfer have in theoretical terms an overriding control over questions of property and right to possession as between the seller and the transferee, it is only in rare cases that they will have any real impact; the more common determining factor will be the relevant rule of the law governing the original contract of sale.

25–182 It is submitted that where the seller claims a lien against another category of third party who acquires rights in respect of the goods, such as a trustee in bankruptcy or execution creditor of the buyer, the validity of his claim as against the buyer is still determined by the law governing the original contract of sale, but the *lex situs* at the time of the bankruptcy or execution should determine whether a lien, being treated as valid under the law applicable to the contract, prevails against the third party.[15] The question whether someone other than the seller himself (*e.g.* an agent or consignor who has paid the price to the seller[16]) may step into the seller's shoes and assert such lien as he has should be a matter for the law applicable to the contract.[17]

---

[11] Above, paras 25–121 *et seq*.
[12] See too *Willis v Glenwood Cotton Mills*, above.
[13] Including the conflicts rules thereof: see above, para.25–122.
[14] As is the case under the Sale of Goods Act 1979, s.47(2) (above, para.15–047).
[15] *cf. Re Sykes* (1932) 101 L.J.Ch.298 (bankruptcy); *Liverpool Marine Credit Co. v Hunter* (1867) 3 Ch.App. 479 (execution creditor as against mortgagee).
[16] See, *e.g.* the Sale of Goods Act 1979, s.38(2) (above, para.15–013).
[17] The third party must of course have taken a valid assignment of the seller's contractual rights. The validity of such assignment should be determined in general by the law applicable to the assignment itself, not the law governing the contract of sale which merely operates to determine whether the right is assignable: Rome Convention, Art. 12; Dicey and Morris, *op. cit.*, paras 24–047—24–057; Cheshire and North, *op. cit.*, pp.958–963.

(ii) *Stoppage in Transit and Rescission of the Transfer*[18]

Introduction. Here the position is speculative both at common law and under the Rome Convention. As to the former, in the leading decision the law applied to the question of the availability of the right of stoppage in transit was both the *lex situs* and the law applicable to the contract of sale and the judgment does not indicate the precise basis on which the relevant law was applied.[19] As to the latter, there is, as yet, no guidance as to the proper principles to be applied. 25–183

The position is thus very much at large, but submissions as to the appropriate governing laws may be tentatively put forward. These depend upon the parties as between whom the right of stoppage or rescission is in issue.

Seller and buyer. It is submitted that the existence of a right of stoppage or rescission as between seller and buyer alone, and the mode of its exercise, should be regulated by the law governing the contract of sale.[20] It is true that, in accordance with the general principle that the *lex situs* governs proprietary issues,[21] any right of rescission of the transfer (*i.e.* a right to say that property has revested in him, by virtue, for example, of the buyer's insolvency) should be available to the seller if the *lex situs* so provides.[22] But it is at least arguable that this does not of itself entitle him to reacquire possession. 25–184

---

[18] "In transit" here is a general phrase whose scope will depend in each case on the appropriate rules of domestic law; as already indicated (above, para.25–123), it is distinct from the equivalent concept in conflict of laws. The meaning of "rescission" in the present context is indicated in n.7, above.

[19] *Inglis v Usherwood* (1801) East 515 (which might have raised an issue of rescission as well as stoppage in transit, but the former issue is not referred to in the judgments). See also *Bohtlink v Inglis* (1803) East 381. Several Canadian cases dealing with the right to rescission conferred by Quebec law show a preference for the law governing the contract or *lex loci contractus* rather than the *lex situs*. See *Rhode Island Locomotive Works v South Eastern Ry Co.* (1886) 31 L.C.J. 86; *Re Columbia Shirt Co.* (1922) 3 C.B.R. 268; *Re Hudson Fashion Shoppe Ltd* [1926] 1 D.L.R. 199; *Re Hollinger* (1927) 2 C.B.R. 174; *Re Viscount Supply Co. Ltd* (1963) 40 D.L.R. (2d) 501; *Re Modern Fashions Ltd* (1969) 8 D.L.R. (3d) 590. A few cases, however, favour the *lex situs* of the goods at the time of rescission which also has academic support. See *Re Satisfaction Stores* [1929] 2 D.L.R. 435; *Re Meredith* (1930) C.B.R. 405; *Re Farley and Grant* [1936] 1 D.LR. 57; Fawcett, Harris and Bridge, *op. cit.*, paras 13–227—13–229, 18–46, 19–57—19–61; Dicey and Morris, *op. cit.*, para.33–114; Wolff, *Private International Law* (2nd ed.), para.492; Rabel, *op. cit.*, Vol. 4, pp.40–42; *cf.* Falconbridge, *op. cit.*, pp.462–467; Hellendall, 17 Can.Bar Rev. 7 and 105, 105–106 (1939).

[20] *cf. Rhode Island Locomotive Works v South Eastern Ry Co.* (1886) 31 L.C.J. 86. There are at least two disadvantages in applying the *lex situs*: (a) that it does not so easily allow for the right of stoppage to be varied by agreement of the parties; and (b) that it leads to difficulties where the goods acquire a new *situs* in the course of the sale or are at the relevant time in transit. See also Vienna Convention, Art. 71(2).

[21] Above, para.25–121.

[22] This raises the issue of characterisation of the relevant rule of the *lex situs*: see above, paras 25–178—25–179.

25–185 **Third parties claiming rights against the goods.** It is submitted that the position as between a seller claiming a right of stoppage and a sub-buyer or pledgee should be determined according to the same laws as have already been suggested with regard to a seller claiming a lien against a sub-buyer,[23] *i.e.* the *lex situs*, the *lex situs cartae*, the proper law of the transfer to the sub-buyer or pledgee and the law governing the original contract of sale, or one or more of them. A similar position should obtain when the seller asserts a right of rescission, except that, as already indicated, the seller's right may itself arise out of the *lex situs* at the time when he asserts such right,[24] instead of the law applicable to the contract of sale.[25]

25–186 Further, it is submitted that[26] the prevalence of a valid right of stoppage against an execution creditor should be referred to the *lex situs*, and that the position of any third party claiming a right of stoppage or rescission as assignee of the seller should be regulated as in the case of a seller's lien.[27]

25–187 **The position of the carrier.** Difficult three-cornered situations may arise when the law governing the contract of sale and the law governing the contract of carriage,[28] being different laws, contain conflicting provisions as to the duty of the carrier[29] in the event of a purported stoppage. It is submitted that in general the carrier's duty to redeliver the goods on the exercise of such a right by the seller should be treated as regulated by the law governing the contract of sale.[30] If this law does not confer a right of stoppage, it should accordingly not be open to the seller to demand redelivery from the carrier and, in the event of non-compliance, to sue him for damages,[31] merely because according to the law governing the contract

[23] Above, para.25–181.

[24] This is not necessarily the same *situs* as that of the goods at the time of the sub-sale, though a change of *situs* would be infrequent.

[25] The seller may also be defeated if, according to the *lex situs*, the original sale is a conditional sale by virtue of the right of rescission being conferred by the applicable law, and failure to register a conditional sale under the *lex situs* makes the seller's right subject to those of bona fide sub-buyers: *Re Satisfaction Stores* [1929] 2 D.L.R. 435; *Re Meredith* (1930) 11 C.B.R. 405.

[26] *Inglis v Usherwood* (1801) 1 East 515; *cf. Rogers v Mississippi and Dominion Steamship Co.* (1888) 14 Q.L.R. 99, dealing with goods in transit.

[27] Above, para.25–182.

[28] As to the ascertainment of this law, see above, paras 25–070—25–072. The right to sue the carrier on the contract of carriage may at the time of stoppage be vested either in the seller, as the original party thereto, or in the buyer, as the original party or by virtue of an assignment of the seller's rights, or in both: see further para.25–195, below.

[29] For the purposes of this discussion, "carrier" includes any other bailee of the goods during their transit.

[30] This view is implicit in *Inglis v Usherwood* (1801) 1 East 515.

[31] If the seller sues in conversion, the carrier can defend the action by pleading that, by virtue of the law governing the contract of sale, the seller does not have the immediate right to possession of the goods: *cf. Kahler v Midland Bank Ltd* [1950] A.C. 24. If the seller, being the party entitled to sue on the contract of carriage (see n.28, above), claims damages for breach of contract, the carrier's defence is in essence that the provisions of the law applicable to this contract regarding stoppage are not relevant because stoppage is an aspect of sale, not carriage.

of carriage the seller would, in the given situation, have a right of stoppage. Conversely, if the law governing the contract of sale does confer a right of stoppage and the carrier redelivers to the seller on the exercise thereof, the buyer should not have an action for damages[32] against the carrier merely because according to the law governing the contract of carriage no right of stoppage would have arisen. The most difficult conflict to reconcile is, however, where the law governing the contract of sale confers a right of stoppage on the seller, but the law governing the contract of carriage contains a mandatory provision[33] whereby, in the given situation, the carrier is bound to deliver to the buyer.[34] It is submitted that, since as between seller and buyer the right to possession has become vested in the seller, the proper course for the carrier here is to redeliver to the seller. It is difficult to see, however, what defence the carrier can raise if the buyer brings proceedings for damages against him, invoking the law governing the contract of carriage. If he can show that according to the law governing the contract of sale the right to possession would have remained with the seller even if the goods had been delivered to the buyer, he might argue that the buyer's damages are nominal only. Otherwise, there is no clear line of defence, so that the carrier's only protection may be to require an indemnity from the seller on redelivery.

Further problems may arise when, after the valid exercise of a right of stoppage by the seller, the carrier claims a lien on the goods for unpaid freight due from the buyer and accordingly refuses to redeliver the goods to the seller. It is submitted that the existence and duration of such a lien as against the buyer should be determined by the law applicable to the contract of carriage,[35] and that, if this law coincides with the law applicable to the contract of sale, it should determine also whether or not the lien prevails over the seller's right of stoppage. Where there is no such coincidence, this issue of priority should instead be referred to the *lex situs* at the time when the lien is asserted, or, if the goods are then in transit, to the *lex fori*.[36] 25–188

[32] The buyer's claims in tort and contract can be defended by the carrier along lines similar to those explained in the preceding footnote.
[33] As may be the case under the law of a country in which the provisions of the COTIF Convention have the force of law: see above, paras 21–069—21–071. The buyer may become entitled under these provisions (Arts 30, 31) to give a "notice modifying the contract," whereupon, irrespective of the position as regards stoppage as between himself and the seller, he has a positive right as against the carrier to require that the goods be delivered to him. *Cf.* CMR, Arts 12, 13, whereby the buyer, as consignee, may acquire a similar right to demand delivery of the goods, or a "right of disposal" thereof.
[34] The reverse situation is possible, but unlikely.
[35] *cf.* the position as regards the exercise of an unpaid seller's lien against the buyer, discussed above, para.25–180.
[36] *cf.* Dicey and Morris, *op. cit.*, para.7–032; *Norton v Florence Land and Public Works Co.* (1877) 7 Ch.D. 332 (*lex situs* applied in a case dealing with land); *The Zigurds* [1932] P. 113 (*lex fori* applied in Admiralty proceedings). If the issue of priorities arises in English bankruptcy proceedings, it is probable that English law, *qua lex fori*, will be applied anyway: *Ex parte Melbourn* (1870) 6 Ch.App. 64; Dicey and Morris, *op. cit.*, paras 31–040—31–041.

(iii) *Right of Resale*

25–189 *Lex situs* and law applicable to contract. It is submitted that, in accordance with general principles discussed earlier,[37] the power of an unpaid seller to confer a good title upon any person to whom he resells the goods in the purported exercise of a right of resale must depend upon the *lex situs* of the goods, or, as the case may be, the *lex situs cartae* or proper law of the transfer. On the other hand, the existence of a right[38] of resale as against the original buyer, and the right to sue the buyer for any deficiency on resale, should be determined by the law applicable to the contract of sale.[39]

(b) *Personal Remedies of the Seller*

25–190 **Remedies against the buyer.** The personal remedies of the seller against the buyer, such as an action for the price or for damages for failure to take delivery, arise in general[40] out of the contract, and as has been shown[41] the question whether the buyer has in fact broken the contract by failing to perform it properly depends primarily upon the law applicable to that contract. It is submitted that the law applicable to the contract also determines what personal remedy or remedies the seller can assert in the event of a breach by the buyer and that this is the correct position both at common law[42] and under the Rome Convention.[43] As far as the common law was concerned, it is true that a number of English authorities[44] contain general statements to the effect that the availability of remedies is a procedural matter and accordingly governed by the *lex fori*, but the width of

[37] Above, paras 25–127 *et seq*.

[38] This distinction between a power and a right of resale is also relevant in English domestic law, and is discussed in that context in paras 15–102—15–105, above. The question whether there is a right of resale under the law applicable to the contract may be relevant in determining whether there is a power of resale under the *lex situs*; it depends on what a court at the *situs* would decide on this point: *cf.* above, para.25–122.

[39] *Livesley v Clemens Horst Co.* [1925] 1 D.L.R. 159 at 160–161; see too Goode and Ziegel, *Hire-Purchase and Conditional Sale* (1967), pp.232–234. But in some cases the availability of an action for the deficiency has been characterised as procedural and referred to the *lex fori*: see *Industrial Acceptance Corp. Ltd v Jordan* (1969) 6 D.L.R. (3d) 625; *United Securities Corp. v Tomlin*, 198 A. 2d 179 (1964); and the next paragraph.

[40] The right to sue for a deficiency on resale has just been dealt with. For restitutionary remedies resulting from frustration of the contract, see above, para.25–176, and for choice of law rules in tort actions, see Private International Law (Miscellaneous Provisions) Act 1995, Part III; Dicey and Morris, *op. cit.*, Ch.35.

[41] Above, para.25–156.

[42] *Livesley v Clemens Horst Co.*, above, at pp.160–161; *Drew Brown Ltd v The "Orient Trader"* (1972) 34 D.L.R. (3d) 339; and see Dicey and Morris, *op. cit.*, paras 32–198—32–200; Cheshire and North, *op. cit.*, pp.598–599.

[43] Art. 10(1)(c).

[44] *Baschet v London Illustrated Standard Co.* [1900] 1 Ch. 73 at 78; *Chaplin v Boys* [1971] A.C. 356 at 394; Dicey and Morris, *op. cit.*, paras 7–006—7–009.

such a proposition is open to question.[45] In the first place, it should not in any event bear upon a seller's right to rescind the contract, as this is a remedy for which he need not invoke the aid of a court.[46] Secondly, even when confined to judicial remedies, the proposition creates serious anomalies.[47] At common law, the correct rule it is submitted, was that, whilst the law applicable to the contract determined the available remedy, it would not be granted unless such remedy, or a reasonably close equivalent, is to be found within the procedural law of the forum and was accordingly one which the forum has adequate machinery to grant and to enforce.[48] This view is virtually explicitly recognised in Article 10(1)(c) of the Rome Convention which submits, within the limits of the powers conferred on the court by its procedural law, the consequences of breach including the assessment of damages in so far as it is governed by rules of law, to the law which governs the contract under the Convention.

Specific aspects of the remedies available. The applicable law also bears upon the seller's personal remedies against the buyer in a number of more specific ways. In actions for the price, that law determines whether interest to the date of judgment may be recovered.[49] Where damages for breach of contract[50] are awarded, the applicable law determines the issue of remoteness of damage,[51] the heads under which damages can be claimed,[52] the 25–191

---

45 See *Amin Rasheed Shipping Corp. v Kuwait Insurance Co.* [1984] A.C. 50 at 60 (applicable law determines "consequences of breach of the contract"); *cf. Monterosso Shipping Co. Ltd v International Transport Workers Federation* [1982] 3 All E.R. 841 at 846, *per* Lord Denning M.R. ("remedies for breach" of a contract, "procedural law"). *Cf. Harding v Wealands* [2004] EWCA Civ. 1735; [2005] 1 W.L.R. 1539; *John Pfeiffer Pty Ltd v Rogerson* (2000) 203 C.L.R. 503.

46 See the discussion of the buyer's right to rescind in para.25–196, below. Rescission for nondisclosure or misrepresentation is also governed by the applicable law (above, para.25–083).

47 If one accepts the proposition as correct, one reaches the following result in a case where a seller sues a buyer in England for damages for failure to take delivery: the applicable law determines whether the buyer's conduct constitutes a breach of contract (above, para.25–156); then English law *qua lex fori* determines whether the proper remedy is damages or the price (*cf.* the Sale of Goods Act 1979, s.49); then, if damages are awarded, the applicable law has to be called on again to determine a number of subsidiary issues such as remoteness and mitigation (below, para.25–199). The interposition of the *lex fori* here has no reasonable justification.

48 *Phrantzes v Argenti* [1960] 2 Q.B. 19.

49 Above, para.25–161.

50 Damages for deceit and, it would seem, other forms of misrepresentation should be dealt with as a claim in tort: *Bank Russo-Iran v Gordon Woodroffe & Co. Ltd* (1972) 116 S.J. 921; and see authorities cited above, n.40.

51 *J D'Almeida Araujo Lda. v Sir Frederick Becker & Co. Ltd* [1953] 2 Q.B. 329 (a claim for damages for non-acceptance); *Livesley v Clemens Horst Co.* [1925] 1 D.L.R. 159. See also *Amin Rasheed Shipping Corp. v Kuwait Insurance Co.*, above; Dicey and Morris, *op. cit.*, paras 7–034—7–039, 32–198—32–200; Cheshire and North, *op. cit.*, pp.598–599. That the issue of remoteness of damage falls within Art. 10(1)(c) of the Rome Convention would seem incontrovertible: see Morse, 2 Ybk.Eur.L. 107 at 154 (1982).

52 See *Chaplin v Boys* [1971] A.C. 356; *Coupland v Arabian Gulf Oil Co.* [1983] 1 W.L.R. 1136; *Edmunds v Simmonds* [2001] 1 W.L.R. 1003; *Hulse v Chambers* [2001] 1 W.L.R. 2386; *Roerig v Valiant Trawlers Ltd* [2002] 1 All E.R. 961; *Harding v*

existence and nature of any duty to mitigate damage,[53] the effect of any "agreed damages" clause,[54] the issue of limitation of damages,[55] the question whether interest is payable by way of damages[56] and probably also the question whether a deposit or advance payment received from the buyer can be retained. On the other hand, the actual quantification of damages is carried out according to the *lex fori*, both at common law[57] and under the Rome Convention unless such quantification is governed by rules of law contained in the applicable law in which case such rules of the applicable law must be resorted to under the Convention as required by

---

Wealands, above; *contra Kremezi v Ridgway* [1949] 1 All E.R. 662. The issue would doubtless fall within Art. 10(1)(c). At common law this rule has been chiefly developed in the context of tort law, and its application to contracts is by no means easy to determine. It is submitted that an instance of an issue of "heads of damage" both at common law and under Art. 10(1)(c) is whether damages could be claimed by a seller for deterioration in his business where this loss was caused by a buyer's failure to take delivery of and pay for goods and was not too remote under the relevant remoteness rule. See too n.57, below.

[53] *J D'Almeida Araujo Lda. v Sir Frederick Becker & Co. Ltd*, above, at p.340; Rabel, *op. cit.*, Vol. 3, p.102. The position is the same under Art. 10(1)(c) of the Rome Convention.

[54] *Livesley v Clemens Horst Co.*, above, at p.163; and see Dicey and Morris, *op. cit.*, paras 7–034—7–035. The position is the same under Art. 10(1)(c) of the Rome Convention: see Giuliano- Lagarde Report, p.33.

[55] This is a substantive rather than a procedural question: *Cope v Doherty* (1858) 4 K. & J. 367 at 384–385; 2 De G. & J. 614 at 623; *Allan J Panozza Pty Ltd v Allied Interstate (Queensland) Pty Ltd* [1976] 2 N.S.W.L.R. 192; see also *Harding v Wealands* [2004] EWCA Civ. 1735; [2005] 1 W.L.R.1539; Dicey and Morris, *op. cit.*, para.7–038. Such an issue would fall within Art. 10(1)(c) of the Rome Convention: see Giuliano-Lagarde Report, p.33.

[56] *Miliangos v George Frank (Textiles) Ltd (No.2)* [1977] Q.B. 489; *Helmsing Schiffarts GmbH v Malta Drydocks Corp.* [1977] 2 Lloyd's Rep. 444; *Manners v Pearson & Son* [1898] 1 Ch. 581 at 588; *Livesley v Clemens Horst Co.*, above, at p.162; The contrary view was taken in *Midland International Trade Services Ltd v Sudairy, Financial Times*, May 2, 1990, and in *Kuwait Oil Tanker Co. SAK v Al Bader, The Independent*, January 11, 1999, but on appeal in the latter case the Court of Appeal ([2000] 2 All E.R. (Comm) 271) in allowing the appeal found it unnecessary to pronounce upon the question (in a case of tort to which the common law applied) of whether the right to claim interest by way of damages was procedural or substantive. The point was left open by the Court of Appeal in *Lesotho Highlands Development Authority v Impregilo SpA* [2003] EWCA Civ. 1159; [2003] 2 Lloyd's Rep. 497 and, on appeal, no view was expressed on it by the House of Lords since the Lords held that an arbitrator's power to award interest under s.49(3) of the Arbitration Act 1969 had not been expressly excluded by the parties ([2005] UKHL 43; [2006] 1 A.C. 221). A further inconclusive authority is *Zebrarise Ltd v De Nieffe* [2005] 1 Lloyd's Rep. 154. The better view, it is submitted, is that the right is not procedural but substantive and should also be so treated for the purposes of Art. 10(1)(c): see Dicey and Morris, *op. cit.*, para.33–385; contrast Guest in Rose (ed.), *Lex Mercatoria: Essays in Honour of Francis Reynolds* (2000), p.271. As to claims to interest under the Late Payment of Commercial Debts (Interest) Act 1998, see above, paras 25–162—25–164.

[57] *J D'Almeida Araujo Lda. v Sir Frederick Becker & Co. Ltd*, above, at p.338; and see *Hansen v Dixon* (1906) 96 L.T. 32; *Kremezi v Ridgway* [1949] 1 All E.R. 662; *Kohnke v Karger* [1951] 2 K.B. 670; *Chaplin v Boys* [1971] A.C. 356; *Coupland v Arabian Gulf Oil Co.* [1983] 1 W.L.R. 1136; *Edmunds v Simmonds* [2001] 1 W.L.R. 1003; *Hulse v Chambers* [2001] 1 W.L.R. 2386; *Roerig v Valiant Trawlers Ltd* [2002] 1 All E.R. 961; *cf. Harding v Wealands*, above. And see *John Pfeiffer Pty Ltd v Rogerson* (2000) 203 C.L.R. 503.

Article 10(1)(c).[58] The *lex fori* will determine whether a claim can be raised by way of counterclaim since this is a matter of procedure[59] and should be so treated at common law and under the Rome Convention. Whether a set-off amounting to an equity attaching to the claimant's claim and which may operate in partial or total extinction thereof, exists, is a matter of substance,[60] which should be referred to the applicable law, both at common law and under the Convention.

The rate of such interest as the applicable law may award by way of damages is, it is submitted, governed by the *lex fori*, both at common law[61] and under the Rome Convention. Accordingly, the rate of interest which will be awarded by an English court is governed by section 35A of the Supreme Court Act 1981[62] which confers a general judicial discretion as to simple interest. Prima facie, if the currency of payment is stipulated in the contract itself, the rate of interest will be that applicable to that currency and to the ensuing judgment if judgment is also in that currency.[63] However, if, for example, the creditor is unable to borrow in the currency of account and is thus compelled, reasonably and foreseeably, to borrow in his own currency in his own country the prima facie rule is displaced and the rate applicable is that at which a loan is normally obtainable in that country.[64] In the exercise of this flexible statutory discretion the English

---

[58] It is submitted that a rule whereby the seller's damages are to be assessed by reference to the price of goods at an available market (see, *e.g.* the Sale of Goods Act 1979, s.50(3), discussed, above, paras 16–062—16–076) is a rule of this kind. Assessment is carried out according to the *lex fori* only when such assessment depends on purely factual considerations: see Giuliano-Lagarde Report, p.33.

[59] *South African Republic v Compagnie Franco-Belge du Chemin de Fer du Nord* [1897] Ch. 487; Dicey and Morris, *op. cit.*, para.7–031.

[60] *MacFarlane v Norris* (1862) 2 B. & S. 783; *Meridien BIAO Bank GmbH v Bank of New York* [1997] 1 Lloyd's Rep. 437; Dicey and Morris, *op. cit.*, para.7–031. A set-off which is merely a claim of a certain kind which the defendant has against the claimant and which can be conveniently tried together with the claimant's claim against the defendant is procedural and thus a matter for the *lex fori* both at common law and under the Convention: see *Meher v Dresser* (1864) 16 C.B.(N.S.) 646. As to insolvency set-off (Insolvency Rules 1986, r. 4.90), see *Re Bank of Credit and Commerce International SA (No.10)* [1997] Ch. 213; Council Regulation (EC) No.1346/2000 of May 29, 2000 on insolvency proceedings, Art. 6.

[61] *Miliangos v George Frank (Textiles) Ltd (No.2)* [1977] Q.B. 489; *Midland International Trade Services Ltd v Sudairy, Financial Times*, May 2, 1990; *Kuwait Oil Tanker Co. SAK v Al Bader, The Independent*, January 11, 1999, appeal allowed in part without expressing a view on the point, [2000] 2 All E.R. (Comm) 271; *Lesotho Highlands Development Authority v Impregilo SpA* [2003] EWCA Civ. 1159; [2003] 2 Lloyd's Rep. 497, reversed, without reference to the point [2005] UKHL 43; [2006] 1 A.C. 221 (above, n.56); *Rogers v Markel Corp.* [2004] EWHC 1375 (QB); [2004] EWHC 2046 (QB); Law Com. No.124 (1888) paras 2.32, 3.55; Dicey and Morris, *op. cit.*, paras 33–387—33–391; Guest, *op. cit.* See also *Shell Tankers (UK) Ltd v Astro Comino Armadora SA (The Pacific Colocotronis)* [1981] 2 Lloyd's Rep. 40. For the *obiter* view that the rate of interest is determined by the applicable law see *Helmsing Schiffahrts GmbH v Malta Drydocks Corp.* [1977] 2 Lloyd's Rep. 444 at 449–450.

[62] See also County Courts Act 1984, s.69; Arbitration Act 1996, s.49.

[63] *Miliangos v George Frank (Textiles) Ltd (No.2)* [1977] Q.B. 489; *The Pacific Colocotronis*, above, at pp.45–47, where emphasis was laid on the prima facie character of the principle; *Rogers v Markel Corp.*, above. See also Law Com. No.124 (1983), para.2.33.

[64] *Helmsing Schiffahrts GmbH v Malta Drydocks Corp.* [1977] 2 Lloyd's Rep. 444; *The Pacific Colocotronis*, above.

court should be able to arrive at an appropriate rate of interest whether English or foreign.[65] The rate of interest on the judgment itself, is a matter for the *lex fori*,[66] even when the judgment is expressed in a foreign currency.[67]

25–192 Finally, it would also appear that the law governing the contract determines whether a buyer who has paid for goods after the due date is liable for exchange losses if the currency in which payment is expressed to be made depreciates in value relative to the currency in which the seller operates.[68] Where English law is the proper law of the contract, recovery of such losses will depend on whether they were foreseeable by the buyer,[69] that is, "if the criterion ordinarily applied in damages cases in contract were satisfied."[70]

---

[65] *Miliangos v George Frank (Textiles) Ltd (No.2)*, above (Swiss law the applicable law, sum payable in Swiss francs, rate applied is that at which Swiss francs could be borrowed in Switzerland, the seller's country); *Helmsing Schiffahrts GmbH v Malta Drydocks Corp.*, above (English law the applicable law, sum payable in Maltese pounds which cannot be borrowed in Germany, the creditor's country, so creditor has to borrow Deutschmarks: rate applied is German rate); *The Pacific Colocotronis*, above (English law the applicable law, contract in US dollars, with judgment in US dollars: rate applied is US dollar rate and not sterling rate); *BP Exploration Co. (Libya) Ltd v Hunt (No.2)* [1979] 1 W.L.R. 783, affirmed [1981] 1 W.L.R. 232, CA, [1983] 2 A.C. 352 (English law the applicable law: restitutionary award under Law Reform (Frustrated Contracts) Act 1943 in US dollars, rate calculated by reference to London Eurodollar Market); *Empresa Cubana Importadora De Alimentos v Octavia Shipping Co. SA (The Kefalonia Wind)* [1986] 1 Lloyd's Rep. 273 at 292 (judgment in Cuban pesos, Cuban plaintiff awarded interest at Cuban rate); *Rogers v Markel Corp.*, above (Virginian law applicable law, rate of interest that applicable to US dollars in so far as award is in that currency); see also, *CIA Barca de Panama SA v George Wimpey & Co. Ltd* [1980] 1 Lloyd's Rep. 598 at 615–617; Dicey and Morris, *op. cit.*, paras 33–391—33–393.

[66] Dicey and Morris, *op. cit.*, para.33–390.

[67] Judgments Act 1838, s.17(1); above, para.16–013; Dicey and Morris, *op. cit.*, para.33–390; Administration of Justice Act 1970, s.44A, inserted by Private International Law (Miscellaneous Provisions) Act 1995, s.1(1). For judgments in the county court, see County Courts Act 1984, s.74(5A), inserted by Private International Law (Miscellaneous Provisions) Act 1995, s.2. For arbitral awards, see Arbitration Act 1996, s.49; *Lesotho Highlands Development Authority v Impregilo SpA* [2005] UKHL 43; [2006] 1 A.C. 221 (above, para.25–191, n.56). See above, para.16–012.

[68] *President of India v Lips Maritime Corp.* [1988] A.C. 395; *Ozalid Group (Export) Ltd v African Continental Bank Ltd* [1979] 2 Lloyd's Rep. 231; *Isaac Naylor & Sons Ltd v New Zealand Co-operative Wool Marketing Association Ltd* [1981] 1 N.Z.L.R. 361; *Rogers v Markel Corp.* [2004] EWHC 2046 (QB). Although the point was not explicitly made in these cases it would seem to follow from the fact that the matter was treated as one of remoteness of damage, the rules applicable to which are derived from the law governing the contract: see cases cited, above, n.51.

[69] *President of India v Lips Maritime Corp.*, above; *Ozalid Group (Export) Ltd v African Continental Bank Ltd*, above; *Isaac Naylor & Sons Ltd v New Zealand Co-operative Wool Marketing Association Ltd*, above; and see *Rogers v Markel Corp*, above where Virginian law seems to be the same as English law on this point. For a full discussion of English remoteness rules in the context of sales, see above, paras 16–043—16–051.

[70] *Isaac Naylor & Sons Ltd v New Zealand Co-operative Wool Marketing Association Ltd*, above, at p.365.

Currency questions.[71] In addition to the foregoing, the currency in which damages for non-acceptance are calculated is, it seems, determined in accordance with the law applicable to the contract.[72] There is no reason to doubt that this remains the case under Article 10(1)(c) of the Rome Convention. Where English law is the governing law, the approach to be adopted was laid down by Lord Wilberforce as follows[73] : "[T]he first step must be to see whether, expressly or by implication, the contract provides an answer to the currency question. This may lead to selection of the 'currency of the contract'. If from the terms of the contract it appears that the parties have accepted a currency as the currency of account and payment[74] in respect of all transactions arising under the contract, then it would be proper to give a judgment for damages in that currency . . . But there may be cases in which, although obligations under the contract are to be met in a specified currency, or currencies, the right conclusion may be that there is no intention shown that damages for breach of the contract should be given in that currency or currencies . . . If then the contract fails to provide a decisive interpretation, the damage should be calculated in the currency in which the loss was felt by the claimant or 'which most truly expresses his loss'. This is not limited to that in which it first and immediately arose. In ascertaining which this currency is, the court must ask what is the currency, payment in which will as nearly as possible compensate the claimant in accordance with the principle of restitution, and whether the parties must be taken reasonably to have had this in contemplation." This is compatible with the decision in *Bain v Field & Co. Fruit Merchants Ltd*,[75] where, in the course of negotiating to sell a quantity of condensed milk to a London buyer, a seller in Winnipeg quoted the price in "dollars". The Court of Appeal held that Canadian currency was both the money of account and the currency in which damages payable by the buyer for failure to accept should be calculated, even though the milk was to be shipped f.o.b. New York and the freight was calculated in US dollars. 25–193

---

[71] See generally Dicey and Morris, *op. cit.*, paras 36–002—36–013, 36–032—36–076; Law Com. No.124 (1983); Law Commission Working Paper No.80 (1981) and *cf.* above, paras 25–165—25–167.

[72] *Services Europe Atlantique Sud (SEAS) v Stockholms Rederiaktebolag SVEA, The Folias* [1979] A.C. 685 at 700, *per* Lord Wilberforce; *cf. Jean Kraut AG v Albany Fabrics Ltd* [1977] Q.B. 182.

[73] *Services Europe Atlantique Sud (SEAS) v. Stockholms Rederiaktebolag SVEA, The Folias*, above, at pp.700–701, approving *Jean Kraut AG v Albany Fabrics Ltd*, above, and *Federal Commerce and Navigation Co. Ltd v Tradax Export SA* [1977] Q.B. 324 (reversed on other grounds [1978] A.C. 1); *The Texaco Melbourne* [1994] 1 Lloyd's Rep. 473, HL; *Virani Ltd v Manuel Revert Y Cia SA* [2003] EWCA Civ. 1651; [2004] 2 Lloyd's Rep. 14. See further Bowles and Whelan, 42 M.L.R. 452 (1979).

[74] As to the meanings of "currency of account" and "currency of payment", see above, paras 25–165, 25–167.

[75] (1920) 5 I.L.R. 16 (discussed by Baxter, 35 Can.Bar Rev. 697 at 714–716 (1957)). For another example see *Metaalhandel JA Magnus BV v Ardfields Transport Ltd* [1988] 1 Lloyd's Rep. 197 and see *Ottoman Bank of Nicosia v Chakarian (No.1)* [1930] A.C. 277.

25–194 **Currency of judgment.** An English court may give judgment for a debt or an award of damages expressed in a foreign currency.[76] Where a judgment is so framed, conversion into a sterling amount takes place on the date of payment,[77] which, in cases where execution is levied on the judgment, is generally[78] taken to be the date when the court authorises enforcement.[79] These principles, replacing earlier rules to the effect that an English court could only frame money judgments in sterling and that the date for conversion was the date when the relevant debt became due or the breach giving rise to damages occurred,[80] flow chiefly from the judgment of the House of Lords in *Miliangos v George Frank (Textiles) Ltd (No. 1)*.[81] The claimant, a Swiss citizen, sold a quantity of polyester yarn to the defendants, an English company, under a contract which stipulated a price in Swiss francs, provided for payment in Switzerland and was governed by Swiss law. The yarn was delivered, but the defendants defaulted in payment, whereupon the claimant instituted proceedings for the price in England. Subsequently, the statement of claim was amended so as to seek judgment in Swiss francs. Between the date when payment was due and the date of the hearing, some three years later, the Swiss franc increased in value

---

[76] See *Miliangos v George Frank (Textiles) Ltd (No.1)* [1976] A.C. 443; *Schorsch Meier GmbH v Hennin* [1975] Q.B. 416; *The Halcyon the Great* [1975] 1 W.L.R. 515; *Virani Ltd v Manuel Revert Y Cia SA* [2003] EWCA Civ. 1651; [2004] 2 Lloyd's Rep. 14; *Carnegie v Giessen* [2005] EWCA Civ. 191; [2005] 1 C.L.C. 259 (charging order may be expressed in foreign currency); *Commerzbank A/G v Large*, 1977 S.L.T. 219; and cases cited below, n.84. See also Law Com. No.124 (1983); Law Commission Working Paper No.80 (1981). For academic commentary, see Dicey and Morris, *op. cit.*, paras 36–061—36–076; Cheshire and North, *op. cit.*, pp.90–98; Lipstein [1975] C.L.J. 215; Bowles and Phillips, 39 M.L.R. 196 (1976); Mann, 92 L.Q.R. 165 (1976); Libling, 93 L.Q.R. 212 (1977); Marshall [1977] J.B.L. 225; Isaacs [1977] L.M.C.L.Q. 356; Morris, *Law and Contemporary Problems* (1977) Vol. 41, No.2, p.44; Becker, 25 Amer.J.Comp.Law 303 (1977); Powles [1979] L.M.C.L.Q. 485; Maher, 44 I.C.L.Q. 72 (1995); Stern [1995] L.M.C.L.Q. 494. As to procedure, see CPR, Pt. 16, Practice Direction, para.9; *ibid.* Pt. 40, Practice Direction 40B, para.10.

[77] This date for conversion is repeated in some specific statutory provisions (*e.g.* Carriage of Goods by Road Act 1965, Sch., Art. 27(2)), but varied in others (*e.g.* Carriage by Air Act 1961, Sch.1, Art. 22(5)). The sums in the latter provisions expressed in gold francs are replaced by special drawing rights as defined by the International Monetary Fund but this does not affect the date for conversion: Carriage by Air and Road Act 1979, s.4. See also Railways (Convention on International Carriage by Rail) Regulations 2005, SI 2005/2092, reg. 7 (not yet in force). Where the debtor is an insolvent company in liquidation, the date chosen is that of the winding-up order: *Re Dynamics Corporation of America (No.2)* [1976] 1 W.L.R. 757; *cf.* [1976] A.C. 443 at 469, 498. In the case of a creditor's voluntary liquidation the date for conversion is the date of the winding-up resolution: *Re Lines Bros Ltd* [1983] Ch.1.

[78] The precise date may depend on the nature of the enforcement procedure involved (see *Carnegie v Giessen*, above (charging order)).

[79] *Miliangos v George Frank (Textiles) Ltd (No.1)*, above, at p.468. The relevant date for these purposes is that on which the judgment creditor sets a process of execution in motion: *ibid.* For counterclaims, see *The Transoceanica Franceska* and *Nicos V* [1987] 2 Lloyd's Rep. 155. As to charging orders, see *Carnegie v Giessen*, above.

[80] The leading authority for the earlier rules was the HL decision in *Tomkinson v First Pennsylvania Banking and Trust Co.* [1961] A.C. 1007. This decision was explicitly overruled in the *Miliangos* case.

[81] [1976] A.C. 443.

against sterling, to the extent that at the former date the contract price was worth about £42,000 but at the date of the hearing it was worth about £60,000. The House of Lords held (Lord Simon of Glaisdale dissenting) that judgment for the claimant could be entered in Swiss francs "or the sterling equivalent at the time of payment." It would seem that if sterling had risen against the Swiss franc over the relevant period, the defendants would have been held entitled to insist that judgment be entered in Swiss francs.[82]

The speeches in the *Miliangos* case confine the decision to claims for a liquidated debt (such as the price of goods) where the debt is expressed in a foreign currency, the money of account and the money of payment are foreign and the law applicable to the contract is foreign.[83] In later decisions, however, judgments for damages have been expressed in a foreign currency even when the damages are for breach of a contract governed by English law.[84] There seems to be little doubt that where the price of goods is payable in a foreign currency, judgment may be given in that currency notwithstanding that the contract is governed by English law.

The *Miliangos* principle applies to arbitrators' awards[85] and to actions brought on bills of exchange.[86] It does not, however, affect pre-existing rules to the effect that a rate of exchange fixed by contract will be applied by the court[87] and that a buyer may defeat an action for the price by tendering or paying to the seller the appropriate amount in the appropriate foreign currency, or paying this amount into court after the claim form is issued.[88]

The rule established in *Miliangos v George Frank (Textiles) Ltd*[89] is a rule of procedure.[90] Its status, therefore, is unaffected by the implementation of the Rome Convention.[91]

---

[82] *cf. ibid.*, at p.466; *Barclays Bank International Ltd v Levin Brothers (Bradford) Ltd* [1977] Q.B. 270 at 278.
[83] [1976] A.C. 443 at 467–468, 497–498, 503.
[84] *Jean Kraut AG v Albany Fabrics Ltd* [1977] Q.B. 182; *Barclays Bank International Ltd v Levin Brothers (Bradford) Ltd*, above; *Federal Commerce and Navigation Co. Ltd v Tradax Export SA* [1977] Q.B. 324 (reversed on other grounds [1978] A.C. 1); *George Veflings Rederi A/S v President of India* [1978] 1 W.L.R. 982; *Services Europe Atlantique Sud. (SEAS) v. Stockholm Rederiaktebolag SVEA, The Folias* [1979] A.C. 685. Further implications of these decisions are discussed above, para.25–193.
[85] *Jugoslavenska Oceanska Plovidba v Castle Investment Co. Inc.* [1974] Q.B. 292, as modified by dicta in *Miliangos v George Frank (Textiles) Ltd (No.1)*, above, at p.469.
[86] Administration of Justice Act 1977, s.4, repealing provisions to the contrary effect in the Bills of Exchange Act 1882, ss.57(2), 72(4). See too *Barclays Bank Ltd v Levin Bros Ltd*, above.
[87] *Boissevain v Weil* [1950] A.C. 327.
[88] *Société des Hôtels Le Touquet Paris-Plage v Cummings* [1922] 1 K.B. 451; CPR, Practice Direction 36, para.9.
[89] [1976] A.C. 443.
[90] [1976] A.C. 443 at 465. And see *Services Europe Atlantique Sud (SEAS) v. Stockholm Rederiaktebolag SVEA, The Folias* [1979] A.C. 685 at 704.
[91] See Art. 1(2)(h).

25–195 **Remedies against the carrier.**[92] Where the contract of carriage is made between the seller and the carrier, the law applicable to this contract governs generally[93] any contractual remedies which the seller may assert against the carrier in the event of the goods being lost or damaged or allegedly misdelivered.[94]

11. REMEDIES OF THE BUYER

25–196 **Rejection of the goods and rescission of the contract.** It is submitted that, when the seller is in breach of the contract (*e.g.* through failing to pass a good title or delivering defective goods), the question whether the buyer is entitled thereby to reject the goods and/or treat the contract as repudiated should in general[95] be determined in accordance with the law applicable to the contract both at common law and under the Rome Convention.[96] This submission derives support from arguments already put forward in relation to the personal remedies of a seller,[97] and also from the existence of a principle that is relatively well established, *viz.* that the applicable law determines what acts or omissions on the part of the buyer constitute sufficient "acceptance" of the goods to debar him from exercising a right to reject them.[98] Further, the existence of any duty to return

---

[92] See too above, para.25–187, regarding the position of the carrier when the seller exercises remedies against the goods.

[93] See, *e.g. Anselme Dewavrin Fils et Cie v Wilsons and NE Ry Shipping Co. Ltd* (1931) 39 Ll.L.R. 289; Rome Convention, Art. 10(1)(c). Note however that conventions such as CMR and COTIF may be applicable (above, paras 21–047—21–071) and, in cases of carriage by sea, the impact of the Carriage of Goods by Sea Act 1971 will be to make the Hague-Visby Rules applicable in an English court even though they do not form part of the governing law: *The Hollandia* [1983] 1 A.C. 565; Rome Convention, Arts 7(2) and 21. See above, para.25–070—25–072. See too authorities cited above, n.52, regarding claims in tort.

[94] Although the applicable law determines what constitutes a misdelivery, the provisions of Art. 10(2) of the Rome Convention may require reference to be made to the law of the place of delivery to determine the steps which may have to be taken in the event of misdelivery: see Giuliano-Lagarde Report, p.33.

[95] It is submitted that where the provisions of ss.12 to 15 of the Sale of Goods Act 1979 are applicable to the contract only by virtue of statutory provisions already discussed (see above, paras 25–160, 25–171), the law of the relevant part of the UK should determine whether a breach of any such provision by the seller gives the buyer a right to rescind or reject, even though the contract is in other respects governed by a foreign law. The same principle seems to apply to the remedies in the Sale of Goods Act 1979, ss.48A–48F where the buyer deals as consumer: see above, paras 25–111 *et. seq*.

[96] Art. 10(1)(c). Thus, the applicable law determines whether any agreement between the parties barring the right of rejection is valid and effective and whether, in the event of the seller delaying in making delivery (there being no time fixed therefor), the buyer must give notice requiring delivery and allow a reasonable time to elapse before he can treat the contract as repudiated (see, *e.g.* the German Civil Code, para.326; there is no corresponding rule in English domestic law): see Giuliano-Lagarde Report, p.33. It also determines whether the buyer can rescind for misrepresentation or non-disclosure on the part of the seller (*cf.* above, para.25–083).

[97] Above, para.25–190.

[98] *Benaim & Co. v Debono* [1924] A.C. 514; *H Glynn* (*Covent Garden*) *Ltd v Wittleder* [1959] 2 Lloyd's Rep. 409 at 422; *Linderne Machine Works Co. v Kuntz Brewery Ltd* (1921) 21 O.W.N. 551; Giuliano-Lagarde Report, p.33.

rejected goods or notify the seller of defects in them, the time within which such duty must be carried out and the effect of failure to carry out the duty within the proper time upon the buyer's right of rejection[99] are all matters to be determined by the law applicable to the contract.[1] On the other hand, the mode of inspection of the goods and the general issue of custody of rejected goods, being analogous to incidents of performance,[2] are governed by the law of the country where inspection and rejection occurs.[3]

The effect of a rejection of the goods by the buyer upon the property in the goods is, it would appear, a matter for the *lex situs* of the goods at the time of the rejection,[4] but again no clear authority is available. 25–197

Rejection of documents. It is submitted that the existence of any right of the buyer to reject documents tendered to him by the seller in purported discharge of his obligations under the contract of sale, and the extent to which the continuance of such right may depend upon the continued existence of a right to reject the goods[5] (or vice versa), are matters to be governed by the law applicable to the contract of sale. 25–198

Damages. Just as the law applicable to the contract determines whether a right to reject is lost through "acceptance", so too it determines whether an act of acceptance or waiver by the buyer, or a delay by the buyer in asserting his rights by notice to the seller or otherwise,[6] is sufficient to debar the buyer from suing for damages in respect of a breach by the seller.[7] By virtue of this rule, and of arguments already set forth,[8] it is submitted that the question whether damages and/or any payment on account of the price can be recovered at all from the seller should also depend in general[9] upon the law applicable to the contract. 25–199

---

99 While some legal systems (*e.g.* the English—see above, para.12–055) require notice of defects to be given "within a reasonable time", others insist on notice "within a short time" (*e.g.* the French Civil Code, para.1648) or within a specified period (*e.g.* the Italian Civil Code, para.1495, which generally stipulates eight days).

1 *Linderne Machine Works Co. v Kuntz Brewery Ltd*, above; Rome Convention, Art. 10(1)(c); Giuliano-Lagarde Report, p.33. *Cf.* Rabel, *The Conflict of Laws* (2nd ed.), Vol. 3, pp.97–100.

2 See above, para.25–156.

3 Rome Convention, Art. 10(2); Giuliano-Lagarde Report, p.33; Rabel, *op. cit.*, Vol. 3, pp.98–99.

4 *cf.* above, paras 25–121, 25–128, *et seq*. It is conceivable, though not likely, that the goods might be in transit at this time, in which case this proposition would have to be varied appropriately (see above, paras 25–123, 25–138—25–140).

5 In English domestic law, the right to reject the documents may be lost if the goods are accepted or if the right to reject the goods is in some other way barred (above, paras 19–144 *et seq.*).

6 See, *e.g.* the German Civil Code, para.477, which requires notice of defects to be given within six months, save in exceptional cases.

7 *H Glynn (Covent Garden) Ltd v Wittleder* [1959] 2 Lloyd's Rep. 409 at 422; Rome Convention, Art. 10(1)(c); Giuliano-Lagarde Report, p.33.

8 Above, para.25–190.

9 *Mutatis mutandis*, the point made in n.95, above, applies here also.

25–200 Other aspects of a buyer's remedies in damages (*e.g.* remoteness, mitigation, heads of damage[10] and limitation of damages) are governed by the same laws as will apply when damages are awarded to a seller.[11] So, for example, the currency of an award of damages for non-delivery or for breach of an express or implied undertaking regarding title or the quality of the goods will be determined by the applicable law. If this is English law, the currency of the contract will be selected unless this seems contrary to the parties' intention, in which event the court will fix upon the currency which "most truly expresses" the buyer's loss.[12] In the situation mentioned, this is likely to be the currency in which he is compelled to buy goods in substitution for those promised in the contract or to arrange for defects to be put right in the goods which the seller has delivered.

25–201 **Other remedies against the seller.** It has been suggested that, at common law, the availability of specific performance or any other remedy whereby the goods are to be delivered to the buyer *in specie* was a matter of procedure to be governed by the *lex fori.*[13] In view of arguments already set forth,[14] it may be argued that this view is much too broad and that the nature of the remedy available to the buyer should, in general, be governed by the law applicable to the contract of sale. This would seem to be the clear meaning of Article 10(1)(c) of the Rome Convention.[15] Nonetheless, that provision requires regard to be had to the limits on the powers conferred on the court by its procedural law. Such limits may affect the powers of the court to grant a decree of specific performance, *e.g.* if the decree would require constant supervision by the court.[16] Subject to these limits, which, it is submitted, should be narrowly construed, the availability of specific performance or analogous remedies should depend on the applicable law.[17]

---

[10] A clear issue of heads of damage in the case of an action by the buyer is whether he can claim on the contract for personal injuries which result from a defect in the goods and are not too remote.
[11] Above, paras 25–191—25–194. Thus damages for misrepresentation would apparently be dealt with as a claim in tort. As to this and other tort claims, see authorities cited above, para.25–190, n.40, para.25–191, n.52.
[12] See *Services Europe Atlantique Sud (SEAS) v Stockholms Rederiaktebolag SVEA, The Folias* [1979] A.C. 685 at 700–701; *The Texaco Melbourne* [1994] 1 Lloyd's Rep. 473, HL; *Virani Ltd v Manuel Revert Y Cia SA* [2003] EWCA Civ. 1651; [2004] 2 Lloyd's Rep. 14; above, para.25–193.
[13] Dicey and Morris, *The Conflict of Laws* (13th ed.), paras 7–006, 7–009, 32–200.
[14] Above, para.25–190.
[15] *cf.* Dicey and Morris, *op. cit.*, para.32–200 where this view is only "suggested, with some hesitation".
[16] Dicey and Morris, *ibid.*; Lasok and Stone, *Conflict of Laws in the European Community* (1987), p.370.
[17] If the goods are situated elsewhere than in the country of the forum, a decree of specific performance should provide that any formal requirements of the *lex situs* regarding transfer of title should be observed.

Remedies against the carrier. The buyer's contractual remedies[18] against the carrier, like those of the seller,[19] depend primarily[20] upon the law applicable to the contract of carriage. This law will determine generally the nature and extent of any liability of the carrier if the goods are lost, or misdelivered,[21] or delivered in a damaged condition,[22] or delivered late due to a deviation from the contractual voyage. However, the buyer must in such a case establish that he is a person entitled to sue upon the contract of carriage, and this may raise problems if the contract was made in the first instance with the seller.[23] It is clear that the question whether the seller's rights under such contract are assignable at all and the extent of the rights assigned is a matter for the law applicable to the contract itself.[24] On the other hand, the question whether such an assignment[25] has been validly effected should be referred to the law applicable to the assignment itself.[26] If the buyer claims contractual rights against the carrier, not on the basis of an assignment, but on the ground that between himself and the carrier a new implied contract has arisen (*e.g.* on tender of documents and receipt of the goods[27]), this new contract has its own governing law, which is not necessarily that of the original contract of carriage.[28] 25–202

[18] As to alternative remedies in tort, see *The Stensby* [1947] 2 All E.R. 786; and authorities cited above, para.25–190, n.40.

[19] Above, para.25–195.

[20] Conventions such as CMR and COTIF may be applicable (above, paras 21–047—21–071 and in cases of carriage by sea the Hague or Hague-Visby Rules may apply even though they do not form part of the governing law: see above, n.93.

[21] See however n.94, above, as to the law determining what constitutes a misdelivery.

[22] See, *e.g. Vincentelli & Co. v John Rowlett & Co.* (1911) 16 Com.Cas. 310 at 321–322.

[23] *cf. The Tilly Russ* C—71/83, [1985] Q.B. 931; *Reunion Européene v Spliethoff's Bevrachtingskantoor BV* C–51/97 [1998] E.C.R. I–6511; *Coreck Maritime GmbH v Handelsveem BV* C–387/98 [2000] E.C.R. I–9337; see also *Nisshin Shipping Co. Ltd v Cleaves & Co. Ltd* [2003] EWHC 2602 (Comm); [2004] 1 Lloyd's Rep. 38. See Takahashi [2001] L.M.C.L.Q. 107. The converse situation may also arise in the case of "through" carriage: *i.e.* the carrier being sued may not be the one with whom the original contract was made. In *Anspach & Co. Ltd v CNR* [1950] 3 D.L.R. 26, the question whether such a carrier could be made liable on the original contract was referred to the law applicable to that contract. *Cf.* CMR, Ch.6; COTIF, Art. 55.

[24] Rome Convention, Art. 12(2), *Moore v Harris* (1876) 1 App.Cas. 318; *The Torni* [1932] P. 78; *The Njegos* [1936] P. 90; *Anspach & Co. Ltd v CNR*, above; *Trendtex Trading Corp. v Credit Suisse* [1980] Q.B. 629, affirmed on other grounds [1982] A.C. 679; *Campbell Connelly & Co. Ltd v Noble* [1963] 1 W.L.R. 255; Dicey and Morris, *op. cit.*, paras 24–047—24–060; Cheshire and North, *Private International Law* (13th ed.), pp.958–962. *Cf.* Takahashi, *op. cit.*, p.115.

[25] See above, paras 3–043—3–044.

[26] Rome Convention, Art. 12(1). See the authorities cited in n.23, above. *Cf.* CMR, Art. 13; COTIF, Arts 28, 54. *Cf.* Takahashi, *op. cit.*, p.115.

[27] As in the English common law (above, para.18–098.

[28] See *The Torni* [1932] P. 27 at 42 (affirmed [1932] P. 78); *The St. Joseph* [1933] P. 119; *Illyssia Compania Naviera SA v Ahmed Abdul-Qawi Bamaodah* (*The Elli 2*) [1985] 1 Lloyd's Rep. 107.

12. PROCEDURE

25–203 **Procedure governed by the *lex fori*.** There is a general rule at common law that matters of procedure are referred to the *lex fori*.[29] This general rule continues to apply in cases which fall within the Rome Convention since Article 1(2)(h) thereof excludes "evidence and procedure" from the scope of the uniform choice of law rules, subject to the operation of Article 14 which is discussed below.[30] The impact of the general rule has been referred to in a number of contexts earlier in this chapter.[31] But it is also to be borne in mind that in some of those contexts the Rome Convention has had the effect of narrowing the category of procedure as understood in the common law so that some matters which were thought of as procedural in the common law are, under the Convention, regarded as governed by the applicable law rather than by the *lex fori*.[32] This tendency is particularly noticeable in the area of remedies.[33] Although full discussion of matters which should, or should not, be characterised as relating to evidence and procedure must be sought in specialist works,[34] the following paragraphs discuss some issues of particular importance which have not been discussed elsewhere in this chapter.

25–204 **Limitation of actions.** It should be noted that an important inroad on matters which have been generally classified as procedural at common law was made in the Foreign Limitation Periods Act 1984.[35] Broadly speaking, and subject to an exception based on public policy,[36] that statute requires that the rules for the limitation of actions of the *lex causae*[37] are to be applied, which means, in the case of contract, the limitation rules of the governing law,[38] and not, as was the usual position at common law, the limitation rules of the *lex fori*. In the context of contracts, the 1984 Act anticipated Article 10(1)(d) of the Rome Convention which provides, *inter alia*, that the law applicable to the contract according to the Convention governs "prescription and limitation of actions". When the Rome Convention is applicable the questions of prescription and limitation of actions

[29] See generally Dicey and Morris, *The Conflict of Laws* (13th ed.), Ch.7; Cheshire and North, *Private International Law* (13th ed.), Ch.6.
[30] Below, para.25–205.
[31] Above, paras 25–081—25–082 (joinder of parties); paras 25–086—25–088 (formalities); para.25–188 (priorities); para.25–190 (availability of remedies); paras 25–191—25–200 (quantification of damages, set-off and counter-claim); paras 25–194, 25–200 (currency in which payment of a debt or damages is ordered by English courts).
[32] Above, paras 25–087, 25–190—25–191, 25–194, 25–201—25–202.
[33] Above, paras 25–190 *et seq.*, 25–196 *et seq.*
[34] See the authorities cited above, n.29.
[35] The Act is based on the recommendations of the Law Commission: Law Com. No.114 (1982). For comment see Dicey and Morris, *op. cit.*, paras 7–043—7–045, Cheshire and North, *op. cit.*, pp.73–74; Carter, 101 L.Q.R. 68 (1985); Stone [1985] L.M.C.L.Q. 497.
[36] s.2(1), (2).
[37] s.1(1).
[38] For discussion of the common law position see Dicey and Morris, *op. cit.*, para.7–042.

would seem to be governed by the law governing the contract as a result of Article 10(1)(d) rather than by the 1984 Act.[39]

Burden of proof and presumptions. Article 14(1) of the Rome Convention provides that the law governing the contract pursuant to the rules of the Convention "applies to the extent that it contains, in the law of contract, rules which raise presumptions of law or determine the burden of proof."[40] As far as the burden of proof is concerned, the tendency at common law was to characterise the issue as procedural and thus a matter for the *lex fori*,[41] though this tendency had been cogently criticised.[42] The effect of Article 14(1), however, is that the applicable law will determine the location of the burden of proof provided that the rules for identifying its location are contained "in the law of contract". This qualification gives rise to no little difficulty. The Giuliano-Lagarde Report seems to suggest that a rule relating to the burden of proof is contained in the law of contract to the extent that the rule is, in effect, a rule of substance, as opposed to a rule which is part of procedural law.[43] The example given is Article 1147 of the French Civil Code which provides that a debtor who has failed to fulfil his obligation shall be liable for damages "unless he shows that this failure is due to an extraneous cause outside his control".[44] As far as presumptions of law are concerned, the common law regards such presumptions which are irrebuttable as substantive[45] and probably attributes the same characterisation to those presumptions which are rebuttable.[46] Article 14(1) would seem to refer both irrebuttable and rebuttable presumptions to the applicable law provided they are contained in the law of 25–205

[39] Dicey and Morris, *op. cit.*, para.32–206. The 1984 Act is not intended to apply to periods of limitation referred to in the contract itself: see Law Com. No.114 (1982), para.4.52: Dicey and Morris, *op. cit.*, paras 7–047—7–048. At common law such periods were probably substantive and thus referable to the law governing the contract: Dicey and Morris, *ibid.; cf. Allan J Panozza & Co. Pty Ltd v Allied Interstate (Queensland) Pty Ltd* [1976] 2 N.S.W.L.R. 192. It is unclear whether such a clause would be regarded as affecting limitation of actions within Art. 10(1)(d) of the Rome Convention. But if not such a clause can be regarded as a way of extinguishing an obligation which is also governed by the applicable law according to Art. 10(1)(d). As to restitutionary claims and the 1984 Act, see *Barros Mattos Junior v MacDaniels Ltd* [2005] EWHC 1323 (Ch); [2005] I.L.Pr. 45.

[40] See Morse, 2 Ybk Eur. L. 107 at 156–157 (1982).

[41] *e.g. The Roberta* (1937) 58 LL.L.R. 159.

[42] Dicey and Morris, *op. cit.*, para.7–026.

[43] p. 36. *Cf.* Lasok and Stone, *Conflict of Laws in the European Community* (1987), p.355 who express the hope that the qualification will be ignored. See also Dicey and Morris, *op. cit.*, para.32–054.

[44] Giuliano-Lagarde Report, *ibid.* For possible examples in English law see above, para.6–029 (burden of proving loss not caused by failure to take reasonable care rests on bailee); para.13–082 (Unfair Contract Terms Act 1977, s.12(3)); paras 8–091, 13–086 (Unfair Contract Terms Act, 1977, s.11(5)); paras 18–346—18–352 (party seeking to rely on "prohibition of export clause" must prove facts required to bring clause into operation). See also *Joseph Constantine Steamship Line Ltd v Imperial Smelting Corp. Ltd* [1942] A.C. 154 (plaintiff has legal burden or proving fault when frustration pleaded as defence to action on contract). *Cf.* Misrepresentation Act 1967, s.2(1), above, para.12–014.

[45] Dicey and Morris, *op. cit.*, para.7–028.

[46] Dicey and Morris, *op. cit.*, paras 7–028—7–029.

contract. As to irrebuttable presumptions, it is not easy to think of examples in English law which can be said to arise in the law of contract.[47] Examples of rebuttable presumptions are more obvious and might include, in English law, the presumption of undue influence in relation to contracts between people in a special relationship with each other (*e.g.* parent and child).[48] Although this presumption can arise in other areas of the law, such as the law of trusts there seems no obvious reason why it should not also be regarded as "contained in the law of contract" for the purposes of the Convention.[49]

25–206 **Contract or act intended to have legal effect.** According to Article 14(2) of the Rome Convention, a "contract or an act intended to have legal effect may be proved by any mode of proof recognised by the law of the forum or by any of the laws referred to in Article 9 under which that contract or act is formally valid, provided that such mode of proof can be administered by the forum." Thus, in an English court, a contract of sale or the terms thereof may be proved by any method of proof available by English law. If a law applicable by virtue of Article 9 would render the contract formally valid, the English court can allow any method of proof permitted by that law[50] to the extent that the method of proof can be administered by the forum. According to the Giuliano-Lagarde Report, this proviso enables the court to disregard modes of proof which its law of procedure cannot generally allow, such as an affidavit, the testimony of a party or common knowledge.[51]

---

[47] This is because, in effect, an irrebuttable presumption is a rule of substantive law and what might be formulated as a presumption is almost invariably formulated as a rule of substantive law. Even a "deeming provision" is perhaps more accurately regarded as a rule of substantive law: see, *e.g.* Unfair Contract Terms Act 1977, s.12(2), above, para.13–071. For an example in French Law, which is not relevant to sale, see Giuliano-Lagarde Report, p.36.

[48] See above, para.3–010; *Chitty on Contracts*, (29th ed.), Vol. 1, paras 7–058—7–078.

[49] There might be a point at which a presumption is of such general scope that it ceases to be "contained in the law of contract" because of that generality. But such a presumption may nevertheless be regarded as substantive and referable to the applicable law on general principles: see Dicey and Morris, *op. cit.*, paras 7–028—7–029. The Giuliano-Lagarde Report mentions, as procedural presumptions (p.36), "the rule whereby the claim of a party who appears is deemed to be substantiated if the other party fails to appear, or the rule making silence on the part of a party to an action with regard to facts alleged by the other party equivalent to an admission of these facts." But neither of these rules involves any "presumption" as far as English law is concerned.

[50] See Lasok and Stone, *op. cit.*, pp.366–367.

[51] See Giuliano-Lagarde Report, pp.36–37.

Appendix

SALE OF GOODS ACT 1979

(1979 C. 54)

An Act to consolidate the law relating to the sale of goods. [6th December 1979] A–001

Part I

Contracts to Which Act Applies

Contracts to which Act applies A–002

1.—(1) This Act applies to contracts of sale of goods made on or after (but not to those made before) 1 January 1894.

(2) In relation to contracts made on certain dates, this Act applies subject to the modification of certain of its sections as mentioned in Schedule 1 below.

(3) Any such modification is indicated in the section concerned by a reference to Schedule 1 below.

(4) Accordingly, where a section does not contain such a reference, this Act applies in relation to the contract concerned without such modification of the section.

Part II

Formation of the Contract

Contract of Sale

Contract of sale A–003

2.—(1) A contract of sale of goods is a contract by which the seller transfers or agrees to transfer the property in goods to the buyer for a money consideration, called the price.

(2) There may be a contract of sale between one part owner and another.

(3) A contract of sale may be absolute or conditional.

(4) Where under a contract of sale the property in the goods is transferred from the seller to the buyer the contract is called a sale.

(5) Where under a contract of sale the transfer of the property in the goods is to take place at a future time or subject to some condition later to be fulfilled the contract is called an agreement to sell.

(6) An agreement to sell becomes a sale when the time elapses or the conditions are fulfilled subject to which the property in the goods is to be transferred.

Capacity to buy and sell

3.—(1) Capacity to buy and sell is regulated by the general law concerning capacity to contract and to transfer and acquire property.

(2) Where necessaries are sold and delivered to a minor or to a person who by reason of [*mental incapacity or*] drunkenness is incompetent to contract, he must pay a reasonable price for them.

(3) In subsection (2) above "necessaries" means goods suitable to the condition in life of the minor or other person concerned and to his actual requirements at the time of the sale and delivery.[1]

Formalities of Contract

A–004 **How contract of sale is made**

4.—(1) Subject to this and any other Act, a contract of sale may be made in writing (either with or without seal), or by word of mouth, or partly in writing and partly by word of mouth, or may be implied from the conduct of the parties.

(2) Nothing in this section affects the law relating to corporations.

Subject-Matter of Contract

A–005 **Existing or future goods**

5.—(1) The goods which form the subject of a contract of sale may be either existing goods, owned or possessed by the seller, or goods to be manufactured or acquired by him after the making of the contract of sale, in this Act called future goods.

(2) There may be a contract for the sale of goods the acquisition of which by the seller depends on a contingency which may or may not happen.

(3) Whereby a contract of sale the seller purports to effect a present sale of future goods, the contract operates as an agreement to sell the goods.

---

[1] In subs. (2) the words "to a minor or" and in subs. (3) the words "minor or other" were repealed, in Scotland only, by the Age of Legal Capacity (Scotland) Act 1991, s.10 and Sch.2. In subs. (2), by the Mental Capacity Act 2005, Sch.6, para.24, the words "mental incapacity or" cease to have an effect in England and Wales.

Goods which have perished

6.—Where there is a contract for the sale of specific goods, and the goods without the knowledge of the seller have perished at the time when the contract is made, the contract is void.

Goods perishing before the sale but after agreement to sell

7.—Where there is an agreement to sell specific goods and subsequently the goods, without any fault on the part of the seller or buyer, perish before the risk passes to the buyer, the agreement is avoided.

The Price

Ascertainment of price **A–006**

8.—(1) The price in a contract of sale may be fixed by the contract, or may be left to be fixed in a manner agreed by the contract, or may be determined by the course of dealing between the parties.

(2) Where the price is not determined as mentioned in subsection (1) above the buyer must pay a reasonable price.

(3) What is a reasonable price is a question of fact dependent on the circumstances of each particular case.

Agreement to sell at valuation

9.—(1) Where there is an agreement to sell goods on the terms that the price is to be fixed by the valuation of a third party, and he cannot or does not make the valuation, the agreement is avoided; but if the goods or any part of them have been delivered to and appropriated by the buyer he must pay a reasonable price for them.

(2) Where the third party is prevented from making the valuation by the fault of the seller or buyer, the party not at fault may maintain an action for damages against the party at fault.

[*Implied terms etc.*][2]

Stipulations about time

10.—(1) Unless a different intention appears from the terms of the contract, stipulations as to time of payment are not of the essence of a contract of sale. **A–007**

---

[2] This heading was substituted for the previous heading " *Conditions and Warranties*" by the Sale and Supply of Goods Act 1994, Sch.2, para. 10 (operative January 3, 1995).

(2) Whether any other stipulation as to time is or is not of the essence of the contract depends on the terms of the contract.

(3) In a contract of sale "month" prima facie means calendar month.

When condition to be treated as warranty

11.—(1) [This section does not apply to Scotland.]

(2) Where a contract of sale is subject to a condition to be fulfilled by the seller, the buyer may waive the condition, or may elect to treat the breach of the condition as a breach of warranty and not as a ground for treating the contract as repudiated.

(3) Whether a stipulation in a contract of sale is a condition, the breach of which may give rise to a right to treat the contract as repudiated, or a warranty, the breach of which may give rise to a claim for damages but not to a right to reject the goods and treat the contract as repudiated, depends in each case on the construction of the contract; and a stipulation may be a condition, though called a warranty in the contract.

(4) [Subject to s.35A below,] where a contract of sale is not severable and the buyer has accepted the goods or part of them, the breach of a condition to be fulfilled by the seller can only be treated as a breach of warranty, and not as a ground for rejecting the goods and treating the contract as repudiated, unless there is an express or implied term of the contract to that effect.

(5) [*Repealed*]

(6) Nothing in this section affects a condition or warranty whose fulfilment is excused by law by reason of impossibility or otherwise.

(7) Paragraph 2 of Schedule 1 below applies in relation to a contract made before 22 April 1967 or (in the application of this Act to Northern Ireland) 28 July 1967.[3]

A–008 **Implied terms about title, etc.**

12.—(1) In a contract of sale, other than one to which subsection (3) below applies, there is an implied [term] on the part of the seller that in the case of a sale he has a right to sell the goods, and in the case of an agreement to sell he will have such a right at the time when the property is to pass.

(2) In a contract of sale, other than one to which subsection (3) below applies, there is also an implied [term] that—

(a) the goods are free, and will remain free until the time when the property is to pass, from any charge or encumbrance not disclosed or known to the buyer before the contract is made, and

---

[3] s.11 was amended by the Sale and Supply of Goods Act 1994 (operative January 3, 1995) in the following respects: (i) by Sch.2, para. 5(2), subs. (1) was substituted for the words "Subsections (2) to (4) and (7) below do not apply to Scotland and subsection (5) below applies only to Scotland"; (ii) by s.3(2), the words in square brackets were inserted in subs. (4); and (iii) by Sch.3, subs. (5) was repealed.

(b) the buyer will enjoy quiet possession of the goods except so far as it may be disturbed by the owner or other person entitled to the benefit of any charge or encumbrance so disclosed or known.

(3) This subsection applies to a contract of sale in the case of which there appears from the contract or is to be inferred from its circumstances an intention that the seller should transfer only such title as he or a third person may have.

(4) In a contract to which subsection (3) above applies there is an implied [term] that all charges or encumbrances known to the seller and not known to the buyer have been disclosed to the buyer before the contract is made.

(5) In a contract to which subsection (3) above applies there is also an implied [term] that none of the following will disturb the buyer's quiet possession of the goods, namely—

(a) the seller;

(b) in a case where the parties to the contract intend that the seller should transfer only such title as a third person may have, that person;

(c) anyone claiming through or under the seller or that third person otherwise than under a charge or encumbrance disclosed or known to the buyer before the contract is made.

[(5A) As regards England and Wales and Northern Ireland, the term implied by subsection (1) above is a condition and the terms implied by subsections (2), (4) and (5) above are warranties.]

(6) Paragraph 3 of Schedule 1 below applies in relation to a contract made before 18 May 1973.[4]

Sale by description A–009

13.—(1) Where there is a contract for the sale of goods by description, there is an implied [term] that the goods will correspond with the description.

[(1A) As regards England and Wales and Northern Ireland, the term implied by subsection (1) above is a condition.]

(2) If the sale is by sample as well as by description it is not sufficient that the bulk of the goods corresponds with the sample if the goods do not also correspond with the description.

(3) A sale of goods is not prevented from being a sale by description by reason only that, being exposed for sale or hire, they are selected by the buyer.

---

[4] s.12 was amended by the Sale and Supply of Goods Act 1994 (operative January 3, 1995) as follows: (i) by Sch.2, para. 5(3), there was substituted "term" for "condition" in subs. (1) and "warranty" in subs. (2)(4) and (5); and (ii) by Sch.2, para. 5(3)(b), subs. (5A) was inserted.

(4) Paragraph 4 of Schedule 1 below applies in relation to a contract made before 18 May 1973.[5]

Implied terms about quality or fitness

14.—(1) Except as provided by this section and section 15 below and subject to any other enactment, there is no implied [term] about the quality or fitness for any particular purpose of goods supplied under a contract of sale.

[(2) Where the seller sells goods in the course of a business, there is an implied term that the goods supplied under the contract are of satisfactory quality.

(2A) For the purposes of this Act, goods are of satisfactory quality if they meet the standard that a reasonable person would regard as satisfactory, taking account of any description of the goods, the price (if relevant) and all the other relevant circumstances.

(2B) For the purposes of this Act, the quality of goods includes their state and condition and the following (among others) are in appropriate cases aspects of the quality of goods—

(a) fitness for all the purposes for which goods of the kind in question are commonly supplied,

(b) appearance and finish,

(c) freedom from minor defects,

(d) safety, and

(e) durability.

(2C) The term implied by subsection (2) above does not extend to any matter making the quality of goods unsatisfactory—

(a) which is specifically drawn to the buyer's attention before the contract is made,

(b) where the buyer examines the goods before the contract is made, which that examination ought to reveal, or

(c) in the case of a contract for sale by sample, which would have been apparent on a reasonable examination of the sample.]

(2D) If the buyer deals as consumer or, in Scotland, if a contract of sale is a consumer contract, the relevant circumstances mentioned in subsection (2A) above include any public statements on the specific characteristics of the goods made about them by the seller, the producer or his representative, particularly in advertising or on labelling.

---

[5] s.13 was amended by the Sale and Supply of Goods Act 1994 (operative January 3, 1995) as follows: (i) by Sch.2, para 5(4)(a), there was substituted "term" for "condition" in subs. (1); and (ii) by Sch.2, para 5(4)(b), subs. (1A) was inserted.

(2E) A public statement is not by virtue of subsection (2D) above a relevant circumstance for the purposes of subsection (2A) above in the case of a contract of sale, if the seller shows that—

(a) at the time the contract was made, he was not, and could not reasonably have been, aware of the statement,

(b) before the contract was made, the statement had been withdrawn in public or, to the extent that it contained anything which was incorrect or misleading, it had been corrected in public, or

(c) the decision to buy the goods could not have been influenced by the statement.

(2F) Subsections (2D) and (2E) above do not prevent any public statement from being a relevant circumstance for the purposes of subsection (2A) above (whether or not the buyer deals as consumer or, in Scotland, whether or not the contract of sale is a consumer contract) if the statement would have been such a circumstance apart from those subsections.]

(3) Where the seller sells goods in the course of a business and the buyer, expressly or by implication, makes known—

(a) to the seller, or

(b) where the purchase price or part of it is payable by instalments and the goods were previously sold by a credit-broker to the seller, to that credit-broker.

any particular purpose for which the goods are being bought, there is an implied [term] that the goods supplied under the contract are reasonably fit for that purpose, whether or not that is a purpose for which such goods are commonly supplied, except where the circumstances show that the buyer does not rely, or that it is unreasonable for him to rely, on the skill or judgment of the seller or credit-broker.

(4) An implied [term] about quality or fitness for a particular purpose may be annexed to a contract of sale by usage.

(5) The preceding provisions of this section apply to a sale by a person who in the course of a business is acting as agent for another as they apply to a sale by a principal in the course of a business, except where that other is not selling in the course of a business and either the buyer knows that fact or reasonable steps are taken to bring it to the notice of the buyer before the contract is made.

[(6) As regards England and Wales and Northern Ireland, the terms implied by subsections (2) and (3) above are conditions.]

(7) Paragraph 5 of Schedule 1 below applies in relation to a contract made on or after 18 May 1973 and before the appointed day,[6] and paragraph 6 in relation to one made before 18 May 1973.

---

[6] SI 1983/1572 appointed May 19, 1985, for the purposes of subs. (7).

(8) In subsection (7) above and paragraph 5 of Schedule 1 below references to the appointed day are to the day appointed for the purposes of those provisions by an order of the Secretary of State made by statutory instrument.[7]

Sale by Sample

A–010 **Sale by sample**

15.—(1) A contract of sale is a contract for sale by sample where there is an express or implied term to that effect in the contract.

(2) In the case of a contract for sale by sample there is an implied [term]—

(a) that the bulk will correspond with the sample in quality;

(b) [*Repealed*];

(c) that the goods will be free from any defect, [making their quality unsatisfactory], which would not be apparent on reasonable examination of the sample.

[(3) As regards England and Wales and Northern Ireland, the term implied by subsection (2) above is a condition.]

(4) Paragraph 7 of Schedule 1 below applies in relation to a contract made before 18 May 1973.[8]

---

[7] s.14 was amended by the Sale and Supply of Goods Act 1994 (operative January 3, 1995) in the following respects: (i) by Sch.2, para. 5(5)(a), there was substituted the word "term" for "condition or warranty" in subs. (1) and (4) and for "condition" in subs. (3); (ii) by s.1(1), new subs. (2)(2A)(2B) and (2C) were inserted in place of the previous subs. (2) which read—

"(2) Where the seller sells goods in the course of a business, there is an implied condition that the goods supplied under the contract are of merchantable quality, except that there is no such condition—

(a) as regards defects specifically drawn to the buyer's attention before the contract is made; or

(b) if the buyer examines the goods before the contract is made, as regards defects which that examination ought to reveal."

(iii) by Sch.2, para. 5(5)(b), the present subs. (6) was substituted in place of the previous subs. (6) which read—

"(6) Goods of any kind are of merchantable quality within the meaning of subsection (2) above if they are as fit for the purpose or purposes for which goods of that kind are commonly bought as it is reasonable to expect having regard to any description applied to them, the price (if relevant) and all the other relevant circumstances."

The section was further amended by reg. 3 of the Sale and Supply of Goods to Consumers Regulations 2002, SI 2002/3045 (operative March 31, 2003) by the insertion of subs. (2D) (2E) (2F).

[8] s.15 was amended by the Sale and Supply of Goods Act 1994 (operative January 3, 1995) in the following respects: (i) by Sch.2, para. 5(6)(a), there was substituted the word "term" for "condition" in subs. (2); (ii) by Sch.3, subs. (2)(b) was repealed; (iii) by s.1(2), the words in square brackets in subs. (2)(c) were substituted for "rendering them unmerchantable"; and (iv) by Sch.2, para. 5(6)(b), the present subs. (3) was substituted for "In subsection 2(c) above 'unmerchantable' is to be construed in accordance with section 14(6) above."

Modification of remedies for breach of condition in non-consumer cases

[**15A.**—(1) Where in the case of a contract of sale—

(a) the buyer would, apart from this subsection, have the right to reject goods by reason of a breach on the part of the seller of a term implied by section 13, 14 or 15 above, but

(b) the breach is so slight that it would be unreasonable for him to reject them,

then, if the buyer does not deal as consumer, the breach is not to be treated as a breach of condition but may be treated as a breach of warranty.

(2) This section applies unless a contrary intention appears in, or is to be implied from, the contract.

(3) It is for the seller to show that a breach fell within subsection (1)(b) above.

(4) This section does not apply to Scotland.][9]

Remedies for breach of contract as respects Scotland

[**15B.**—(1) Where in a contract of sale the seller is in breach of any term of the contract (express or implied), the buyer shall be entitled—

(a) to claim damages, and

(b) if the breach is material, to reject any goods delivered under the contract and treat it as repudiated.

(2) Where a contract of sale is a consumer contract, then, for the purposes of subsection (1)(b) above, breach by the seller of any term (express or implied)—

(a) as to the quality of the goods or their fitness for a purpose,

(b) if the goods are, or are to be, sold by description, that the goods will correspond with the description,

(c) if the goods are, or are to be, sold by reference to a sample, that the bulk will correspond with the sample in quality,

shall be deemed to be a material breach.

(3) This section applies to Scotland only.][10]

---

[9] s.15A was inserted by s.4(2) of the Sale and Supply of Goods Act 1994 (operative January 3, 1995).

[10] s.15B was inserted by s.5(1) of the Sale and Supply of Goods Act 1994 (operative January 3, 1995).

PART III

EFFECTS OF THE CONTRACT

Transfer of Property as between Seller and Buyer

A–011 **Goods must be ascertained**

16. [Subject to section 20A below] where there is a contract for the sale of unascertained goods no property in the goods is transferred to the buyer unless and until the goods are ascertained.[11]

Property passes when intended to pass

17.—(1) Where there is a contract for the sale of specific or ascertained goods the property in them is transferred to the buyer at such time as the parties to the contract intend it to be transferred.

(2) For the purpose of ascertaining the intention of the parties regard shall be had to the terms of the contract, the conduct of the parties and the circumstances of the case.

Rules for ascertaining intention

18. Unless a different intention appears, the following are rules for ascertaining the intention of the parties as to the time at which the property in the goods is to pass to the buyer.

Rule 1.—Where there is an unconditional contract for the sale of specific goods in a deliverable state the property in the goods passes to the buyer when the contract is made, and it is immaterial whether the time of payment or the time of delivery, or both, be postponed.

Rule 2.—Where there is a contract for the sale of specific goods and the seller is bound to do something to the goods for the purpose of putting them into a deliverable state, the property does not pass until the thing is done and the buyer has notice that it has been done.

Rule 3.—Where there is a contract for the sale of specific goods in a deliverable state but the seller is bound to weigh, measure, test, or do some other act or thing with reference to the goods for the purpose of ascertaining the price, the property does not pass until the act or thing is done and the buyer has notice that it has been done.

Rule 4.—When goods are delivered to the buyer on approval or on sale or return or other similar terms the property in the goods passes to the buyer:—

---

[11] In s.16, the words in square brackets were inserted by the Sale of Goods (Amendment) Act 1995, s.1(1) (operative September 19, 1995).

(a) when he signifies his approval or acceptance to the seller or does any other act adopting the transaction;

(b) if he does not signify his approval or acceptance to the seller but retains the goods without giving notice of rejection, then, if a time has been fixed for the return of the goods, on the expiration of that time, and, if no time has been fixed, on the expiration of a reasonable time.

Rule 5.—(1) Where there is a contract for the sale of unascertained or future goods by description, and goods of that description and in a deliverable state are unconditionally appropriated to the contract, either by the seller with the assent of the buyer or by the buyer with the assent of the seller, the property in the goods then passes to the buyer; and the assent may be express or implied, and may be given either before or after the appropriation is made.

(2) Where, in pursuance of the contract, the seller delivers the goods to the buyer or to a carrier or other bailee or custodier (whether named by the buyer or not) for the purpose of transmission to the buyer, and does not reserve the right of disposal, he is to be taken to have unconditionally appropriated the goods to the contract.

[(3) Where there is a contract for the sale of a specified quantity of unascertained goods in a deliverable state forming part of a bulk which is identified either in the contract or by subsequent agreement between the parties and the bulk is reduced to (or to less than) that quantity, then if the buyer under that contract is the only buyer to whom goods are then due out of the bulk—

(a) the remaining goods are to be taken as appropriated to that contract at the time when the bulk is so reduced; and

(b) the property in those goods then passes to that buyer.

(4) Paragraph (3) above applies also (with the necessary modifications) where a bulk is reduced to (or to less than) the aggregate of the quantities due to a single buyer under separate contracts relating to that bulk and he is the only buyer to whom goods are then due out of that bulk.][12]

Reservation of right of disposal

19.—(1) Where there is a contract for the sale of specific goods or where goods are subsequently appropriated to the contract, the seller may, by the terms of the contract or appropriation, reserve the right of disposal of the goods until certain conditions are fulfilled; and in such a case, notwithstanding the delivery of the goods to the buyer, or to a carrier or other bailee or custodier for the purpose of transmission to the buyer, the property in the goods does not pass to the buyer until the conditions imposed by the seller are fulfilled.

---

[12] Paragraphs (3) and (4) of Rule 5 were inserted by s.1(2) of the Sale of Goods (Amendment) Act 1995 (operative September 19, 1995).

(2) Where goods are shipped, and by the bill of lading the goods are deliverable to the order of the seller or his agent, the seller is prima facie to be taken to reserve the right of disposal.

(3) Where the seller of goods draws on the buyer for the price, and transmits the bill of exchange and bill of lading to the buyer together to secure acceptance or payment of the bill of exchange, the buyer is bound to return the bill of lading if he does not honour the bill of exchange, and if he wrongfully retains the bill of lading the property in the goods does not pass to him.

A–012 **Passing of risk**

20.—(1) Unless otherwise agreed, the goods remain at the seller's risk until the property in them is transferred to the buyer, but when the property in them is transferred to the buyer the goods are at the buyer's risk whether delivery has been made or not.

(2) But where delivery has been delayed through the fault of either buyer or seller the goods are at the risk of the party at fault as regards any loss which might not have occurred but for such fault.

(3) Nothing in this section affects the duties or liabilities of either seller or buyer as a bailee or custodier of the goods of the other party.

[(4) In a case where the buyer deals as consumer or, in Scotland, where there is a consumer contract in which the buyer is a consumer, subsections (1) to (3) above must be ignored and the goods remain at the seller's risk until they are delivered to the consumer.][13]

Undivided shares in goods forming part of a bulk

[**20A.**—(1) This section applies to a contract for the sale of a specified quantity of unascertained goods if the following conditions are met—

(a) the goods or some of them form part of a bulk which is identified either in the contract or by subsequent agreement between the parties; and

(b) the buyer has paid the price for some or all of the goods which are the subject of the contract and which form part of the bulk.

(2) Where this section applies, then (unless the parties agree otherwise), as soon as the conditions specified in paragraphs (a) and (b) of subsection (1) above are met or at such later time as the parties may agree—

(a) property in an undivided share in the bulk is transferred to the buyer, and

(b) the buyer becomes an owner in common of the bulk.

[13] Subs. (4) was inserted and the marginal note to this section was amended by reg. 4 of the Sale and Supply of Goods to Consumers Regulations 2002, SI 2002/3045 (operative March 31, 2003).

(3) Subject to subsection (4) below, for the purposes of this section, the undivided share of a buyer in a bulk at any time shall be such share as the quantity of goods paid for and due to the buyer out of the bulk bears to the quantity of goods in the bulk at that time.

(4) Where the aggregate of the undivided shares of buyers in a bulk determined under subsection (3) above would at any time exceed the whole of the bulk at that time, the undivided share in the bulk of each buyer shall be reduced proportionately so that the aggregate of the undivided shares is equal to the whole bulk.

(5) Where a buyer has paid the price for only some of the goods due to him out of a bulk, any delivery to the buyer out of the bulk shall, for the purposes of this section, be ascribed in the first place to the goods in respect of which payment has been made.

(6) For the purposes of this section payment of part of the price for any goods shall be treated as payment for a corresponding part of the goods.

Deemed consent by co-owner to dealings in bulk goods

20B.—(1) A person who has become an owner in common of a bulk by virtue of section 20A above shall be deemed to have consented to—

(a) any delivery of goods out of the bulk to any other owner in common of the bulk, being goods which are due to him under his contract;

(b) any dealing with or removal, delivery or disposal of goods in the bulk by any other person who is an owner in common of the bulk in so far as the goods fall within that co-owner's undivided share in the bulk at the time of the dealing, removal, delivery or disposal.

(2) No cause of action shall accrue to anyone against a person by reason of that person having acted in accordance with paragraph (a) or (b) of subsection (1) above in reliance on any consent deemed to have been given under that subsection.

(3) Nothing in this section or section 20A above shall—

(a) impose an obligation on a buyer of goods out of a bulk to compensate any other buyer of goods out of that bulk for any shortfall in the goods received by that other buyer;

(b) affect any contractual arrangement between buyers of goods out of a bulk for adjustments between themselves; or

(c) affect the rights of any buyer under his contract.][14]

Transfer of Title

Sale by person not the owner **A–013**

21.—(1) Subject to this Act, where goods are sold by a person who is not their owner, and who does not sell them under the authority or with the

[14] Sections 20A and 20B were inserted by s.1(3) of the Sale of Goods (Amendment) Act 1995 (operative September 19, 1995).

consent of the owner, the buyer acquires no better title to the goods than the seller had, unless the owner of the goods is by his conduct precluded from denying the seller's authority to sell.

(2) Nothing in this Act affects—

(a) the provisions of the Factors Acts or any enactment enabling the apparent owner of goods to dispose of them as if he were their true owner;

(b) the validity of any contract of sale under any special common law or statutory power of sale or under the order of a court of competent jurisdiction.

Market overt

22.—(1) [*Repealed*][15]

(2) This section does not apply to Scotland.

(3) Paragraph 8 of Schedule 1 below applies in relation to a contract under which goods were sold before 1 January 1968 or (in the application of this Act to Northern Ireland) 29 August 1967.

Sale under voidable title

23. When the seller of goods has a voidable title to them, but his title has not been avoided at the time of the sale, the buyer acquires a good title to the goods, provided he buys them in good faith and without notice of the seller's defect of title.

Seller in possession after sale

24. Where a person having sold goods continues or is in possession of the goods, or of the documents of title to the goods, the delivery or transfer by that person, or by a mercantile agent acting for him, of the goods or documents of title under any sale, pledge, or other disposition thereof, to any person receiving the same in good faith and without notice of the previous sale, has the same effect as if the person making the delivery or transfer were expressly authorised by the owner of the goods to make the same.

Buyer in possession after sale

25.—(1) Where a person having bought or agreed to buy goods obtains, with the consent of the seller, possession of the goods or the documents of title to the goods, the delivery or transfer by that person, or by a mercantile

---

[15] s.22(1) was repealed, from January 3, 1995, by s.1 of the Sale of Goods (Amendment) Act 1994. The repeal is not retrospective (s.3(2)) and extends to Northern Ireland.

agent acting for him, of the goods or documents of title, under any sale, pledge, or other disposition thereof, to any person receiving the same in good faith and without notice of any lien or other right of the original seller in respect of the goods, has the same effect as if the person making the delivery or transfer were a mercantile agent in possession of the goods or documents of title with the consent of the owner.

(2) For the purposes of subsection (1) above—

(a) the buyer under a conditional sale agreement is to be taken not to be a person who has bought or agreed to buy goods, and

(b) "conditional sale agreement" means an agreement for the sale of goods which is a consumer credit agreement within the meaning of the Consumer Credit Act 1974 under which the purchase price or part of it is payable by instalments, and the property in the goods is to remain in the seller (notwithstanding that the buyer is to be in possession of the goods) until such conditions as to the payment of instalments or otherwise as may be specified in the agreement are fulfilled.

(3) Paragraph 9 of Schedule 1 below applies in relation to a contract under which a person buys or agrees to buy goods and which is made before the appointed day.[16]

(4) In subsection (3) above and paragraph 9 of Schedule 1 below references to the appointed day are to the day appointed for the purposes of those provisions by an order of the Secretary of State made by statutory instrument.

Supplementary to sections 24 and 25

26. In sections 24 and 25 above "mercantile agent" means a mercantile agent having in the customary course of his business as such agent authority either—

(a) to sell goods, or

(b) to consign goods for the purpose of sale, or

(c) to buy goods, or

(d) to raise money on the security of goods.

PART VI

PERFORMANCE OF THE CONTRACT

Duties of seller and buyer A–014

27. It is the duty of the seller to deliver the goods, and of the buyer to accept and pay for them, in accordance with the terms of the contract of sale.

---

[16] SI 1983/1572 appointed May 19, 1985, for the purposes of subs. (3).

Payment and delivery are concurrent conditions

28. Unless otherwise agreed, delivery of the goods and payment of the price are concurrent conditions, that is to say, the seller must be ready and willing to give possession of the goods to the buyer in exchange for the price and the buyer must be ready and willing to pay the price in exchange for possession of the goods.

Rules about delivery

29.—(1) Whether it is for the buyer to take possession of the goods or for the seller to send them to the buyer is a question depending in each case on the contract, express or implied, between the parties.

(2) Apart from any such contract, express or implied, the place of delivery is the seller's place of business if he has one, and if not, his residence; except that, if the contract is for the sale of specific goods, which to the knowledge of the parties when the contract is made are in some other place, then that place is the place of delivery.

(3) Where under the contract of sale the seller is bound to send the goods to the buyer, but no time for sending them is fixed, the seller is bound to send them within a reasonable time.

(4) Where the goods at the time of sale are in the possession of a third person, there is no delivery by seller to buyer unless and until the third person acknowledges to the buyer that he holds the goods on his behalf; but nothing in this section affects the operation of the issue or transfer of any document of title to goods.

(5) Demand or tender of delivery may be treated as ineffectual unless made at a reasonable hour; and what is a reasonable hour is a question of fact.

(6) Unless otherwise agreed, the expenses of and incidental to putting the goods into a deliverable state must be borne by the seller.

Delivery of wrong quantity

30.—(1) Where the seller delivers to the buyer a quantity of goods less than he contracted to sell, the buyer may reject them, but if the buyer accepts the goods so delivered he must pay for them at the contract rate.

(2) Where the seller delivers to the buyer a quantity of goods larger than he contracted to sell, the buyer may accept the goods included in the contract and reject the rest, or he may reject the whole.

[(2A) A buyer who does not deal as consumer may not—

(a) where the seller delivers a quantity of goods less than he contracted to sell, reject the goods under subsection (1) above, or

(b) where the seller delivers a quantity of goods larger than he contracted to sell, reject the whole under subsection (2) above,

if the shortfall or, as the case may be, excess is so slight that it would be unreasonable for him to do so.

(2B) It is for the seller to show that a shortfall or excess fell within subsection (2A) above.

(2C) Subsections (2A) and (2B) above do not apply to Scotland.

(2D) Where the seller delivers a quantity of goods—

(a) less than he contracted to sell, the buyer shall not be entitled to reject the goods under subsection (1) above,

(b) larger than he contracted to sell, the buyer shall not be entitled to reject the whole under subsection (2) above,

unless the shortfall or excess is material.

(2E) Subsection (2D) above applies to Scotland only.]

(3) Where the seller delivers to the buyer a quantity of goods larger than he contracted to sell and the buyer accepts the whole of the goods so delivered he must pay for them at the contract rate.

(4) [*Repealed*]

(5) This section is subject to any usage of trade, special agreement, or course of dealing between the parties.[17]

Instalment deliveries

31.—(1) Unless otherwise agreed, the buyer of goods is not bound to accept delivery of them by instalments.

(2) Where there is a contract for the sale of goods to be delivered by stated instalments, which are to be separately paid for, and the seller makes defective deliveries in respect of one or more instalments, or the buyer neglects or refuses to take delivery of or pay for one or more instalments, it is a question in each case depending on the terms of the contract and the circumstances of the case whether the breach of contract is a repudiation of the whole contract or whether it is a severable breach giving rise to a claim for compensation but not to a right to treat the whole contract as repudiated.

Delivery to carrier

32.—(1) Where, in pursuance of a contract of sale, the seller is authorised or required to send the goods to the buyer, delivery of the goods to a carrier (whether named by the buyer or not) for the purpose of transmission to the buyer is prima facie deemed to be a delivery of the goods to the buyer.

(2) Unless otherwise authorised by the buyer, the seller must make such contract with the carrier on behalf of the buyer as may be reasonable having regard to the nature of the goods and the other circumstances of the

[17] s.30 was amended by the Sale and Supply of Goods Act 1994 (operative January 3, 1995) in the following respects: (i) by s.4(2), new subsections (2A) (2B) and (2C) were inserted; (ii) by s.5(2), new subsections (2D) and (2E) were inserted; and (iii) by Sch.3, subs. 30(4) was repealed.

case; and if the seller omits to do so, and the goods are lost or damaged in course of transit, the buyer may decline to treat the delivery to the carrier as a delivery to himself or may hold the seller responsible in damages.

(3) Unless otherwise agreed, where goods are sent by the seller to the buyer by a route involving sea transit, under circumstances in which it is usual to insure, the seller must give such notice to the buyer as may enable him to insure them during their sea transit; and if the seller fails to do so, the goods are at his risk during such sea transit.

[(4) In a case where the buyer deals as consumer or, in Scotland, where there is a consumer contract in which the buyer is a consumer, subsections (1) to (3) above must be ignored, but if in pursuance of a contract of sale the seller is authorised or required to send the goods to the buyer, delivery of the goods to the carrier is not delivery of the goods to the buyer.][18]

Risk where goods are delivered at distant place

33. Where the seller of goods agrees to deliver them at his own risk at a place other than that where they are when sold, the buyer must nevertheless (unless otherwise agreed) take any risk of deterioration in the goods necessarily incident to the course of transit.

A–015 **Buyer's right of examining the goods**

34.—[*Repealed*]

Unless otherwise agreed, when the seller tenders delivery of goods to the buyer, he is bound on request to afford the buyer a reasonable opportunity of examining the goods for the purpose of ascertaining whether they are in conformity with the contract [and, in the case of a contract for sale by sample, of comparing the bulk with the sample.][19]

Acceptance

35.—(1) The buyer is deemed to have accepted the goods[subject to subsection (2) below—

(a) when he intimates to the seller that he has accepted them, or

(b) when the goods have been delivered to him and he does any act in relation to them which is inconsistent with the ownership of the seller.

(2) Where goods are delivered to the buyer, and he has not previously examined them, he is not deemed to have accepted them under subsection

[18] Subs. (4) was inserted by reg. 4 of the Sale and Supply of Goods to Consumers Regulations 2002, SI 2002/3045 (operative March 31, 2003).

[19] s.34 was amended by the Sale and Supply of Goods Act 1994 (operative January 3, 1995) in the following respects: (i) by s.2(2)(a), subs. (1) was repealed; and (ii) by s.2(2)(b) the words in square brackets were added to the section.

(1) above until he has had a reasonable opportunity of examining them for the purpose—

(a) of ascertaining whether they are in conformity with the contract, and

(b) in the case of a contract for sale by sample, of comparing the bulk with the sample.

(3) Where the buyer deals as consumer or (in Scotland) the contract of sale is a consumer contract, the buyer cannot lose his right to rely on subsection (2) above by agreement, waiver or otherwise.

(4) The buyer is also deemed to have accepted the goods when after the lapse of a reasonable time he retains the goods without intimating to the seller that he has rejected them.

(5) The questions that are material in determining for the purposes of subsection (4) above whether a reasonable time has elapsed include whether the buyer has had a reasonable opportunity of examining the goods for the purpose mentioned in subsection (2) above.

(6) The buyer is not by virtue of this section deemed to have accepted the goods merely because—

(a) he asks for, or agrees to, their repair by or under an arrangement with the seller, or

(b) the goods are delivered to another under a sub-sale or other disposition.

(7) Where the contract is for the sale of goods making one or more commercial units, a buyer accepting any goods included in a unit is deemed to have accepted all the goods making the unit; and in this subsection "commercial unit" means a unit division of which would materially impair the value of the goods or the character of the unit.

(8)] Paragraph 10 of Schedule 1 below applies in relation to a contract made before 22 April 1967 or (in the application of this Act to Northern Ireland) 28 July 1967.[20]

Right of partial rejection

[**35A.**—(1) If the buyer—

---

[20] s.35 was amended by s.2(1) of the Sale and Supply of Goods Act 1994 (operative January 3, 1995) in the following respects:

(i) the present wording of s.35(1) was substituted for the previous subs. (1) which read:
"The buyer is deemed to have accepted the goods when he intimates to the seller that he has accepted them, or (except where section 34 above otherwise provides) when the goods have been delivered to him and he does any act in relation to them which is inconsistent with the ownership of the seller, or when after the lapse of a reasonable time he retains the goods without intimating to the seller, that he has rejected them".

(ii) subs. (2) to (7) were inserted; and (iii) subs. (2) was re-numbered as subs. (8).

(a) has the right to reject the goods by reason of a breach on the part of the seller that affects some or all of them, but

(b) accepts some of the goods, including, where there are any goods unaffected by the breach, all such goods,

he does not by accepting them lose his right to reject the rest.

(2) in the case of a buyer having the right to reject an instalment of goods, subsection (1) above applies as if references to the goods were references to the goods comprised in the instalment.

(3) For the purposes of subsection (1) above, goods are affected by a breach if by reason of the breach they are not in conformity with the contract.

(4) This section applies unless a contrary intention appears in, or is to be implied from, the contract.][21]

Buyer not bound to return rejected goods

36. Unless otherwise agreed, where goods are delivered to the buyer, and he refuses to accept them, having the right to do so, he is not bound to return them to the seller, but it is sufficient if he intimates to the seller that he refuses to accept them.

A–016 **Buyer's liability for not taking delivery of goods**

37.—(1) When the seller is ready and willing to deliver the goods, and requests the buyer to take delivery, and the buyer does not within a reasonable time after such request take delivery of the goods, he is liable to the seller for any loss occasioned by his neglect or refusal to take delivery, and also for a reasonable charge for the care and custody of the goods.

(2) Nothing in this section affects the rights of the seller where the neglect or refusal of the buyer to take delivery amounts to a repudiation of the contract.

PART V

RIGHTS OF UNPAID SELLER AGAINST THE GOODS

Preliminary

A–017 **Unpaid seller defined**

38.—(1) The seller of goods is an unpaid seller within the meaning of this Act—

---

[21] s.35A was inserted by the Sale and Supply of Goods Act 1994, s.3(1) (operative January 3, 1995).

(a) when the whole of the price has not been paid or tendered;

(b) when a bill of exchange or other negotiable instrument has been received as conditional payment, and the condition on which it was received has not been fulfilled by reason of the dishonour of the instrument or otherwise.

(2) In this Part of this Act "seller" includes any person who is in the position of a seller, as, for instance, an agent of the seller to whom the bill of lading has been indorsed, or a consignor or agent who has himself paid (or is directly responsible for) the price.

Unpaid seller's rights

39.—(1) Subject to this and any other Act, notwithstanding that the property in the goods may have passed to the buyer, the unpaid seller of goods, as such, has by implication of law—

(a) a lien on the goods or right to retain them for the price while he is in possession of them;

(b) in case of the insolvency of the buyer, a right of stopping the goods in transit after he has parted with the possession of them;

(c) a right of re-sale as limited by this Act.

(2) Where the property in goods has not passed to the buyer, the unpaid seller has (in addition to his other remedies) a right of withholding delivery similar to and co-extensive with his rights of lien or retention and stoppage in transit where the property has passed to the buyer.

Attachment by seller in Scotland

40. [*Repealed.*][22]

Unpaid Seller's Lien

Seller's lien A–018

41.—(1) Subject to this Act, the unpaid seller of goods who is in possession of them is entitled to retain possession of them until payment or tender of the price in the following cases:—

(a) where the goods have been sold without any stipulation as to credit;

(b) where the goods have been sold on credit but the term of credit has expired;

(c) where the buyer becomes insolvent.

---

[22] This section was repealed by the Debtors (Scotland) Act 1987, s.108 and Sch.8.

(2) The seller may exercise his lien or right of retention notwithstanding that he is in possession of the goods as agent or bailee or custodier for the buyer.

Part delivery

42. Where an unpaid seller has made part delivery of the goods, he may exercise his lien or right of retention on the remainder, unless such part delivery has been made under such circumstances as to show an agreement to waive the lien or right of retention.

Termination of lien

43.—(1) The unpaid seller of goods loses his lien or right of retention in respect of them

(a) when he delivers the goods to a carrier or other bailee or custodier for the purpose of transmission to the buyer without reserving the right of disposal of the goods;

(b) when the buyer or his agent lawfully obtains possession of the goods;

(c) by waiver of the lien or right of retention.

(2) An unpaid seller of goods who has a lien or right of retention in respect of them does not lose his lien or right of retention by reason only that he has obtained judgment or decree for the price of the goods.

Stoppage in Transit

A–019 **Right of stoppage in transit**

44. Subject to this Act, when the buyer of goods becomes insolvent the unpaid seller who has parted with the possession of the goods has the right of stopping them in transit, that is to say, he may resume possession of the goods as long as they are in course of transit, and may retain them until payment or tender of the price.

Duration of transit

45.—(1) Goods are deemed to be in course of transit from the time when they are delivered to a carrier or other bailee or custodier for the purpose of transmission to the buyer, until the buyer or his agent in that behalf takes delivery of them from the carrier or other bailee or custodier.

(2) If the buyer or his agent in that behalf obtains delivery of the goods before their arrival at the appointed destination, the transit is at an end.

(3) If, after the arrival of the goods at the appointed destination, the carrier or other bailee or custodier acknowledges to the buyer or his agent

that he holds the goods on his behalf and continues in possession of them as bailee or custodier for the buyer or his agent, the transit is at an end, and it is immaterial that a further destination for the goods may have been indicated by the buyer.

(4) If the goods are rejected by the buyer, and the carrier or other bailee or custodier continues in possession of them, the transit is not deemed to be at an end, even if the seller has refused to receive them back.

(5) When goods are delivered to a ship chartered by the buyer it is a question depending on the circumstances of the particular case whether they are in the possession of the master as a carrier or as agent to the buyer.

(6) Where the carrier or other bailee or custodier wrongfully refuses to deliver the goods to the buyer or his agent in that behalf, the transit is deemed to be at an end.

(7) Where part delivery of the goods has been made to the buyer or his agent in that behalf, the remainder of the goods may be stopped in transit, unless such part delivery has been made under such circumstances as to show an agreement to give up possession of the whole of the goods.

How stoppage in transit is effected

46.—(1) The unpaid seller may exercise his right of stoppage in transit either by taking actual possession of the goods or by giving notice of his claim to the carrier or other bailee or custodier in whose possession the goods are.

(2) The notice may be given either to the person in actual possession of the goods or to his principal.

(3) If given to the principal, the notice is ineffective unless given at such time and under such circumstances that the principal, by the exercise of reasonable diligence, may communicate it to his servant or agent in time to prevent a delivery to the buyer.

(4) When notice of stoppage in transit is given by the seller to the carrier or other bailee or custodier in possession of the goods, he must re-deliver the goods to, or according to the directions of, the seller; and the expenses of the re-delivery must be borne by the seller.

Re-sale, etc., by Buyer

Effect of sub-sale, etc. by buyer A–020

47.—(1) Subject to this Act, the unpaid seller's right of lien or retention or stoppage in transit is not affected by any sale or other disposition of the goods which the buyer may have made, unless the seller has assented to it.

(2) Where a document of title to goods has been lawfully transferred to any person as buyer or owner of the goods, and that person transfers the document to a person who takes it in good faith and for valuable consideration, then—

(a) if the last-mentioned transfer was by way of sale the unpaid seller's right of lien or retention or stoppage in transit is defeated; and

(b) if the last-mentioned transfer was made by way of pledge or other disposition for value, the unpaid seller's right of lien or retention or stoppage in transit can only be exercised subject to the rights of the transferee.

Rescission: and Re-sale by Seller

Rescission: and re-sale by seller

48.—(1) Subject to this section, a contract of sale is not rescinded by the mere exercise by an unpaid seller of his right of lien or retention or stoppage in transit.

(2) Where an unpaid seller who has exercised his right of lien or retention or stoppage in transit re-sells the goods, the buyer acquires a good title to them as against the original buyer.

(3) Where the goods are of a perishable nature, or where the unpaid seller gives notice to the buyer of his intention to re-sell, and the buyer does not within a reasonable time pay or tender the price, the unpaid seller may re-sell the goods and recover from the original buyer damages for any loss occasioned by his breach of contract.

(4) Where the seller expressly reserves the right of re-sale in case the buyer should make default, and on the buyer making default re-sells the goods, the original contract of sale is rescinded but without prejudice to any claim the seller may have for damages.

[PART 5A

ADDITIONAL RIGHTS OF BUYER IN CONSUMER CASES

A–021 **48A Introductory**

(1) This section applies if—

(a) the buyer deals as consumer or, in Scotland, there is a consumer contract in which the buyer is a consumer, and

(b) the goods do not conform to the contract of sale at the time of delivery.

(2) If this section applies, the buyer has the right—

(a) under and in accordance with section 48B below, to require the seller to repair or replace the goods, or

(b) under and in accordance with section 48C below—
  (i) to require the seller to reduce the purchase price of the goods to the buyer by an appropriate amount, or
  (ii) to rescind the contract with regard to the goods in question.

(3) For the purposes of subsection (1)(b) above goods which do not conform to the contract of sale at any time within the period of six months starting with the date on which the goods were delivered to the buyer must be taken not to have so conformed at that date.

(4) Subsection (3) above does not apply if—

(a) it is established that the goods did so conform at that date;

(b) its application is incompatible with the nature of the goods or the nature of the lack of conformity.

48B Repair or replacement of the goods A–022

(1) If section 48A above applies, the buyer may require the seller—

(a) to repair the goods, or

(b) to replace the goods.

(2) If the buyer requires the seller to repair or replace the goods, the seller must—

(a) repair or, as the case may be, replace the goods within a reasonable time but without causing significant inconvenience to the buyer;

(b) bear any necessary costs incurred in doing so (including in particular the cost of any labour, materials or postage).

(3) The buyer must not require the seller to repair or, as the case may be, replace the goods if that remedy is—

(a) impossible, or

(b) disproportionate in comparison to the other of those remedies, or

(c) disproportionate in comparison to an appropriate reduction in the purchase price under paragraph (a), or rescission under paragraph (b), of section 48C(1) below.

(4) One remedy is disproportionate in comparison to the other if the one imposes costs on the seller which, in comparison to those imposed on him by the other, are unreasonable, taking into account—

(a) the value which the goods would have if they conformed to the contract of sale,

(b) the significance of the lack of conformity, and

(c) whether the other remedy could be effected without significant inconvenience to the buyer.

(5) Any question as to what is a reasonable time or significant inconvenience is to be determined by reference to—

(a) the nature of the goods, and

(b) the purpose for which the goods were acquired.

48C Reduction of purchase price or rescission of contract

(1) If section 48A above applies, the buyer may—

(a) require the seller to reduce the purchase price of the goods in question to the buyer by an appropriate amount, or

(b) rescind the contract with regard to those goods,

if the condition in subsection (2) below is satisfied.

(2) The condition is that—

(a) by virtue of section 48B(3) above the buyer may require neither repair nor replacement of the goods; or

(b) the buyer has required the seller to repair or replace the goods, but the seller is in breach of the requirement of section 48B(2)(a) above to do so within a reasonable time and without significant inconvenience to the buyer.

(3) For the purposes of this Part, if the buyer rescinds the contract, any reimbursement to the buyer may be reduced to take account of the use he has had of the goods since they were delivered to him.

48D Relation to other remedies etc.

(1) If the buyer requires the seller to repair or replace the goods the buyer must not act under subsection (2) until he has given the seller a reasonable time in which to repair or replace (as the case may be) the goods.

(2) The buyer acts under this subsection if—

(a) in England and Wales or Northern Ireland he rejects the goods and terminates the contract for breach of condition;

(b) in Scotland he rejects any goods delivered under the contract and treats it as repudiated;

(c) he requires the goods to be replaced or repaired (as the case may be).

A–023 **48E Powers of the court**

(1) In any proceedings in which a remedy is sought by virtue of this Part the court, in addition to any other power it has, may act under this section.

(2) On the application of the buyer the court may make an order requiring specific performance or, in Scotland, specific implement by the seller of any obligation imposed on him by virtue of section 48B above.

(3) Subsection (4) applies if—

(a) the buyer requires the seller to give effect to a remedy under section 48B or 48C above or has claims to rescind under section 48C, but

(b) the court decides that another remedy under section 48B or 48C is appropriate.

(4) The court may proceed—

(a) as if the buyer had required the seller to give effect to the other remedy, or if the other remedy is rescission under section 48C

(b) as if the buyer had claimed to rescind the contract under that section.

(5) If the buyer has claimed to rescind the contract the court may order that any reimbursement to the buyer is reduced to take account of the use he has had of the goods since they were delivered to him.

(6) The court may make an order under this section unconditionally or on such terms and conditions as to damages, payment of the price and otherwise as it thinks just..

48F Conformity with the contract

For the purposes of this Part, goods do not conform to a contract of sale if there is, in relation to the goods, a breach of an express term of the contract or a term implied by section 13, 14 or 15 above.][23]

PART VI

ACTIONS FOR BREACH OF THE CONTRACT

Seller's Remedies

Action for price A–024

49.—(1) Where, under a contract of sale, the property in the goods has passed to the buyer and he wrongfully neglects or refuses to pay for the goods according to the terms of the contract, the seller may maintain an action against him for the price of the goods.

(2) Where, under a contract of sale, the price is payable on a day certain irrespective of delivery and the buyer wrongfully neglects or refuses to pay such price, the seller may maintain an action for the price, although the property in the goods has not passed and the goods have not been appropriated to the contract.

---

[23] Part 5A (ss 48A–48F) was inserted by reg. 5 of the Sale and Supply of Goods to Consumers Regulations 2002, SI 2002/3045 (operative March 31, 2003).

(3) Nothing in this section prejudices the right of the seller in Scotland to recover interest on the price from the date of tender of the goods, or from the date on which the price was payable, as the case may be.

Damages for non-acceptance

50.—(1) Where the buyer wrongfully neglects or refuses to accept and pay for the goods, the seller may maintain an action against him for damages for non-acceptance.

(2) The measure of damages is the estimated loss directly and naturally resulting, in the ordinary course of events, from the buyer's breach of contract.

(3) Where there is an available market for the goods in question the measure of damages is prima facie to be ascertained by the difference between the contract price and the market or current price at the time or times when the goods ought to have been accepted or (if no time was fixed for acceptance) at the time of the refusal to accept.

Buyer's Remedies

A–025 **Damages for non-delivery**

51.—(1) Where the seller wrongfully neglects or refuses to deliver the goods to the buyer, the buyer may maintain an action against the seller for damages for non-delivery.

(2) The measure of damages is the estimated loss directly and naturally resulting, in the ordinary course of events, from the seller's breach of contract.

(3) Where there is an available market for the goods in question the measure of damages is prima facie to be ascertained by the difference between the contract price and the market or current price of the goods at the time or times when they ought to have been delivered or (if no time was fixed) at the time of the refusal to deliver.

Specific performance

52.—(1) In any action for breach of contract to deliver specific or ascertained goods the court may, if it thinks fit, on the plaintiff's application, by its judgment or decree direct that the contract shall be performed specifically, without giving the defendant the option of retaining the goods on payment of damages.

(2) The plaintiff's application may be made at any time before judgment or decree.

(3) The judgment or decree may be unconditional, or on such terms and conditions as to damages, payment of the price and otherwise as seem just to the court.

(4) The provisions of this section shall be deemed to be supplementary to, and not in derogation of, the right of specific implement in Scotland.

Remedy for breach of warranty

53.—(1) Where there is a breach of warranty by the seller, or where the buyer elects (or is compelled) to treat any breach of a condition on the part of the seller as a breach of warranty, the buyer is not by reason only of such breach of warranty entitled to reject the goods; but he may—

(a) set up against the seller the breach of warranty in diminution or extinction of the price, or

(b) maintain an action against the seller for damages for the breach of warranty.

(2) The measure of damages for breach of warranty is the estimated loss directly and naturally resulting, in the ordinary course of events, from the breach of warranty.

(3) In the case of breach of warranty of quality such loss is prima facie the difference between the value of the goods at the time of delivery to the buyer and the value they would have had if they had fulfilled the warranty.

(4) The fact that the buyer has set up the breach of warranty in diminution or extinction of the price does not prevent him from maintaining an action for the same breach of warranty if he has suffered further damage.

[(5) This section does not apply to Scotland.][24]

Measure of damages as respects Scotland

[**53A.**—(1) The measure of damages for the seller's breach of contract is the estimated loss directly and naturally resulting, in the ordinary course of events, from the breach.

(2) Where the seller's breach consists of the delivery of goods which are not of the quality required by the contract and the buyer retains the goods, such loss as aforesaid is prima facie the difference between the value of the goods at the time of delivery to the buyer and the value they would have had if they had fulfilled the contract.

(3) This section applies to Scotland only.][25]

Interest, etc. A–026

54. Nothing in this Act affects the right of the buyer or the seller to recover interest or special damages in any case where by law interest or special damages may be recoverable, or to recover money paid where the consideration for the payment of it has failed.

---

[24] Subs. (5) was substituted by the Sale and Supply of Goods Act 1994, Sch.2, para. 5(7) (operative January 3, 1995) in place of the previous wording, which read "Nothing in this section prejudices or affects the buyer's right of rejection in Scotland as declared by this Act".

[25] s.53A was inserted by the Sale and Supply of Goods Act 1994, s.5(3) (operative January 3, 1995).

PART VII

SUPPLEMENTARY

A–027 **Exclusion of implied terms**

55.—(1) Where a right, duty or liability would arise under a contract of sale of goods by implication of law, it may (subject to the Unfair Contract Terms Act 1977) be negatived or varied by express agreement, or by the course of dealing between the parties, or by such usage as binds both parties to the contract.

(2) An express [term] does not negative a [term] implied by this Act unless inconsistent with it.

(3) Paragraph 11 of Schedule 1 below applies in relation to a contract made on or after 18 May 1973 and before 1 February 1978, and paragraph 12 in relation to one made before 18 May 1973.[26]

Conflict of laws

56. Paragraph 13 of Schedule 1 below applies in relation to a contract made on or after 18 May 1973 and before 1 February 1978, so as to make provision about conflict of laws in relation to such a contract.

A–028 **Auction sales**

57.—(1) Where goods are put up for sale by auction in lots, each lot is prima facie deemed to be the subject of a separate contract of sale.

(2) A sale by auction is complete when the auctioneer announces its completion by the fall of the hammer, or in other customary manner; and until the announcement is made any bidder may retract his bid.

(3) A sale by auction may be notified to be subject to a reserve or upset price, and a right to bid may also be reserved expressly by or on behalf of the seller.

(4) Where a sale by auction is not notified to be subject to a right to bid by or on behalf of the seller, it is not lawful for the seller to bid himself or to employ any person to bid at the sale, or for the auctioneer knowingly to take any bid from the seller or any such person.

(5) A sale contravening subsection (4) above may be treated as fraudulent by the buyer.

(6) Where, in respect of a sale by auction, a right to bid is expressly reserved (but not otherwise) the seller or any one person on his behalf may bid at the auction.

A–029 **Payment into court in Scotland**

58. In Scotland where a buyer has elected to accept goods which he might have rejected, and to treat a breach of contract as only giving rise to

[26] In s.55(2), the word "term" was substituted for "condition or warranty", where this twice occurred, by the Sale and Supply of Goods Act 1994, Sch.2, para 5(8) (operative January 3, 1995).

a claim for damages, he may, in an action by the seller for the price, be required, in the discretion of the court before which the action depends, to consign or pay into court the price of the goods, or part of the price, or to give other reasonable security for its due payment.

Reasonable time a question of fact

59. Where a reference is made in this Act to a reasonable time the question what is a reasonable time is a question of fact.

Rights, etc., enforceable by action

60. Where a right, duty or liability is declared by this Act, it may (unless otherwise provided by this Act) be enforced by action.

Interpretation A–030

61.—(1) In this Act, unless the context or subject matter otherwise requires,—

"action" includes counterclaim and set-off, and in Scotland condescendence and claim and compensation;

["bulk" means a mass or collection of goods of the same kind which—

(a) is contained in a defined space or area; and
(b) is such that any goods in the bulk are interchangeable with any other goods therein of the same number or quantity;][27]

"business" includes a profession and the activities of any government department (including a Northern Ireland department) or local or public authority;

"buyer" means a person who buys or agrees to buy goods;

["consumer contract" has the same meaning as in section 25(1) of the Unfair Contract Terms Act 1977; and for the purposes of this Act the onus of proving that a contract is not to be regarded as a consumer contract shall lie on the seller;][28]

"contract of sale" includes an agreement to sell as well as a sale;

"credit-broker" means a person acting in the course of a business of credit brokerage carried on by him, that is a business of effecting introductions of individuals desiring to obtain credit—

(a) to persons carrying on any business so far as it relates to the provision of credit, or
(b) to other persons engaged in credit brokerage;

"defendant" includes in Scotland defender, respondent, and claimant in a multiplepoinding;

---

[27] The definition of "bulk" was inserted by s.2(a) of the Sale of Goods (Amendment) Act 1995 (operative September 19, 1995).
[28] The definition of "consumer contract" was inserted by Sch.2, para. 5(9)(a)(i) of the Sale and Supply of Goods Act 1994 (operative January 3, 1995).

"delivery" means voluntary transfer of possession from one person to another [except that in relation to sections 20A and 20B above it includes such appropriation of goods to the contract as results in property in the goods being transferred to the buyer.][29]

"document of title to goods" has the same meaning as it has in the Factors Acts;

"Factors Acts" means the Factors Act 1889, the Factors (Scotland) Act 1890, and any enactment amending or substituted for the same;

"fault" means wrongful act or default;

"future goods" means goods to be manufactured or acquired by the seller after the making of the contract of sale;

"goods" includes all personal chattels other than things in action and money, and in Scotland all corporeal moveables except money; and in particular "goods" includes emblements, industrial growing crops, and things attached to or forming part of the land which are agreed to be severed before sale or under the contract of sale [and includes an undivided share in goods;][30]

"plaintiff " includes pursuer, complainer, claimant in a multiplepoinding and defendant or defender counter-claiming;

["producer" means the manufacturer of goods, the importer of goods into the European Economic Area or any person purporting to be a producer by placing his name, trade mark or other distinctive sign on the goods;][31]

"property" means the general property in goods, and not merely a special property;

["*quality"—repealed*;][32]

["repair" means, in cases where there is a lack of conformity in goods for the purposes of section 48F of this Act, to bring the goods into conformity with the contract;][33]

"sale" includes a bargain and sale as well as a sale and delivery;

"seller" means a person who sells or agrees to sell goods;

"specific goods" means goods identified and agreed on at the time a contract of sale is made [and includes an undivided share, specified as a fraction or percentage, of goods identified and agreed on as aforesaid;][34]

"warranty" (as regards England and Wales and Northern Ireland) means an agreement with reference to goods which are the subject of a contract of sale, but collateral to the main purpose of such

---

[29] The words in square brackets were added by s.2(b) of the Sale of Goods (Amendment) Act 1995 (operative September 19, 1995).

[30] The words in square brackets were added by s.2(c) of the Sale of Goods (Amendment) Act 1995 (operative September 19, 1995).

[31] The definition of "producer" was inserted by reg. 6 of the Sale and Supply of Goods to Consumers Regulations 2002, SI 2002/3045 (operative March 31, 2003).

[32] The definition of "quality was repealed by Sch.3 of the Sale and Supply of Goods Act 1994 (operative January 3, 1995).

[33] The definition of "repair" was inserted by reg. 6 of the Sale and Supply of Goods to Consumers Regulations 2002, SI 2002/3045 (operative March 31, 2003).

[34] The words in square brackets were added by s.2(d) of the Sale of Goods (Amendment) Act 1995 (operative September 19, 1995).

contract, the breach of which gives rise to a claim for damages, but not to a right to reject the goods and treat the contract as repudiated.

(2) [*Repealed.*][35]

(3) A thing is deemed to be done in good faith within the meaning of this Act when it is in fact done honestly, whether it is done negligently or not.

(4) A person is deemed to be insolvent within the meaning of this Act if he has either ceased to pay his debts in the ordinary course of business or he cannot pay his debts as they become due, [...][36]

(5) Goods are in a deliverable state within the meaning of this Act when they are in such a state that the buyer would under the contract be bound to take delivery of them.

[(5A) References in this Act to dealing as consumer are to be construed in accordance with Part I of the Unfair Contract Terms Act 1977; and, for the purposes of this Act, it is for a seller claiming that the buyer does not deal as consumer to show that he does not.][37]

(6) As regards the definition of "business" in subsection (1) above, paragraph 14 of Schedule 1 below applies in relation to a contract made on or after 18 May 1973 and before 1 February 1978, and paragraph 15 in relation to one made before 18 May 1973.

Savings: rules of law, etc. A–031

62.—(1) The rules in bankruptcy relating to contracts of sale apply to those contracts, notwithstanding anything in this Act.

(2) The rules of the common law, including the law merchant, except in so far as they are inconsistent with the provisions of this Act, and in particular the rules relating to the law of principal and agent and the effect of fraud, misrepresentation, duress or coercion, mistake, or other invalidating cause, apply to contracts for the sale of goods.

(3) Nothing in this Act or the Sale of Goods Act 1893 affects the enactments relating to bills of sale, or any enactment relating to the sale of goods which is not expressly repealed or amended by this Act or that.

(4) The provisions of this Act about contracts of sale do not apply to a transaction in the form of a contract of sale which is intended to operate by way of mortgage, pledge, charge, or other security.

(5) Nothing in this Act prejudices or affects the landlord's right of hypothec or sequestration for rent in Scotland.

---

[35] Subs. (2) was repealed by Sch.3 of the Sale and Supply of Goods Act 1994 (operative January 3, 1995).

[36] The final words "whether he has committed an act of bankruptcy or not, and whether he has become a notour bankrupt or not" in s.61(4) were repealed (in England and Wales) by s.235 of, and Sch.10, Part III, to, the Insolvency Act 1985. The words "and whether he has become a notour bankrupt or not" in s.61(4) were repealed (in Scotland) by s.75(2) of, and Sch.8 to, the Bankruptcy (Scotland) Act 1985. Neither of these repeals extends to Northern Ireland.

[37] Subs. (5A) was inserted by Sch.2, para. 5 (9)(c), of the Sale and Supply of Goods Act 1994 (operative January 3, 1995).

Consequential amendments, repeals and savings

63.—(1) Without prejudice to section 17 of the Interpretation Act 1978 (repeal and re-enactment), the enactments mentioned in Schedule 2 below have effect subject to the amendments there specified (being amendments consequential on this Act).

(2) The enactments mentioned in Schedule 3 below are repealed to the extent specified in column 3, but subject to the savings in Schedule 4 below.

(3) The savings in Schedule 4 below have effect.

A–032 **Short title and commencement**

64.—(1) This Act may be cited as the Sale of Goods Act 1979.

(2) This Act comes into force on 1 January 1980.

SCHEDULES

A–033 **Section 1** SCHEDULE 1

MODIFICATION OF ACT FOR CERTAIN CONTRACTS

Preliminary

1.—(1) This Schedule modifies this Act as it applies to contracts of sale of goods made on certain dates.

(2) In this Schedule references to sections are to those of this Act and references to contracts are to contracts of sale of goods.

(3) Nothing in this Schedule affects a contract made before 1 January 1894.

Section 11: *Condition Treated as Warranty*

2. In relation to a contract made before 22 April 1967 or (in the application of this Act to Northern Ireland) 28 July 1967, in section 11(4) after "or part of them," insert "or where the contract is for specific goods, the property in which has passed to the buyer,".

Section 12: *Implied Terms about Title, etc.*

3. In relation to a contract made before 18 May 1973 substitute the following for section 12:—

Implied terms about title, etc.

12. In a contract of sale, unless the circumstances of the contract are such as to show a different intention, there is—

(a) an implied condition on the part of the seller that in the case of a sale he has a right to sell the goods, and in the case of an agreement to sell he will have such a right at the time when the property is to pass;

(b) an implied warranty that the buyer will have and enjoy quiet possession of the goods;

(c) an implied warranty that the goods will be free from any charge or encumbrance in favour of any third party, not declared or known to the buyer before or at the time when the contract is made.

Section 13: *Sale by Description*

4. In relation to a contract made before 18 May 1973, omit section 13(3).

Section 14: *Quality or Fitness (i)*

5. In relation to a contract made on or after 18 May 1973 and before the appointed day, substitute the following for section 14:—

Implied terms about quality or fitness

14.—(1) Except as provided by this section and section 15 below and subject to any other enactment, there is no implied condition or warranty about the quality or fitness for any particular purpose of goods supplied under a contract of sale.

(2) Where the seller sells goods in the course of a business, there is an implied condition that the goods supplied under the contract are of merchantable quality, except that there is no such condition—

(a) as regards defects specifically drawn to the buyer's attention before the contract is made; or

(b) if the buyer examines the goods before the contract is made, as regards defects which that examination ought to reveal.

(3) Where the seller sells goods in the course of a business and the buyer, expressly or by implication, makes known to the seller any particular purpose for which the goods are being bought, there is an implied condition that the goods supplied under the contract are reasonably fit for that purpose, whether or not that is a purpose for which such goods are commonly supplied, except where the circumstances show that the buyer does not rely, or that it is unreasonable for him to rely, on the seller's skill or judgment.

(4) An implied condition or warranty about quality or fitness for a particular purpose may be annexed to a contract of sale by usage.

(5) The preceding provisions of this section apply to a sale by a person who in the course of a business is acting as agent for another as they apply to a sale by a principal in the course of a business, except where that other is not selling in the course of a business and either the buyer knows that fact or reasonable steps are taken to bring it to the notice of the buyer before the contract is made.

(6) Goods of any kind are of merchantable quality within the meaning of subsection (2) above if they are as fit for the purpose or purposes for which goods of that kind are commonly bought as it is reasonable to expect having regard to any description applied to them, the price (if relevant) and all the other relevant circumstances.

(7) In the application of subsection (3) above to an agreement for the sale of goods under which the purchase price or part of it is payable by instalments any reference to the seller includes a reference to the person by whom any antecedent negotiations are conducted; and section 58(3) and (5) of the Hire-Purchase Act 1965, section 54(3) and (5) of the Hire-Purchase (Scotland) Act 1965 and section 65(3) and (5) of the Hire-Purchase Act (Northern Ireland) 1966 (meaning of antecedent negotiations and related expressions) apply in relation to this subsection as in relation to each of those Acts, but as if a reference to any such agreement were included in the references in subsection (3) of each of those sections to the agreements there mentioned.

Section 14: *Quality or Fitness (ii)*

6. In relation to a contract made before 18 May 1973 substitute the following for section 14:—

Implied terms about quality or fitness

14.—(1) Subject to this and any other Act, there is no implied condition or warranty about the quality or fitness for any particular purpose of goods supplied under a contract of sale.

(2) Where the buyer, expressly or by implication, makes known to the seller the particular purpose for which the goods are required, so as to show that the buyer relies on the seller's skill or judgment, and the goods are of a description which it is in the course of the seller's business to supply (whether he is the manufacturer or not), there is an implied condition that the goods will be reasonably fit for such purpose, except that in the case of a contract for the sale of a specified article under its patent or other trade name there is no implied condition as to its fitness for any particular purpose.

(3) Where goods are bought by description from a seller who deals in goods of that description (whether he is the manufacturer or not), there is an implied condition that the goods will be of merchantable quality; but if the buyer has examined the goods, there is no implied condition as regards defects which such examination ought to have revealed.

(4) An implied condition or warranty about quality or fitness for a particular purpose may be annexed by the usage of trade.

(5) An express condition or warranty does not negative a condition or warranty implied by this Act unless inconsistent with it.

Section 15: *Sale by Sample*

7. In relation to a contract made before 18 May 1973, omit section 15(3).

Section 22: *Market Overt*

8. In relation to a contract under which goods were sold before 1 January 1968 or (in the application of this Act to Northern Ireland) 29 August 1967, add the following paragraph at the end of section 22(1):—

"Nothing in this subsection affects the law relating to the sale of horses."

Section 25: *Buyer in Possession*

9. In relation to a contract under which a person buys or agrees to buy goods and which is made before the appointed day, omit section 25(2).

Section 35: *Acceptance*

10. In relation to a contract made before 22 April 1967 or (in the application of this Act to Northern Ireland) 28 July 1967, in section 35(1) omit "(except where section 34 above otherwise provides)".

Section 55: *Exclusion of Implied Terms (i)*

11. In relation to a contract made on or after 18 May 1973 and before 1 February 1978 substitute the following for section 55:—

Exclusion of implied terms

55.—(1) Where a right, duty or liability would arise under a contract of sale of goods by implication of law, it may be negatived or varied by express agreement, or by the course of dealing between the parties, or by such usage as binds both parties to the contract, but the preceding provision has effect subject to the following provisions of this section.

(2) An express condition or warranty does not negative a condition or warranty implied by this Act unless inconsistent with it.

(3) In the case of a contract of sale of goods, any term of that or any other contract exempting from all or any of the provisions of section 12 above is void.

(4) In the case of a contract of sale of goods, any term of that or any other contract exempting from all or any of the provisions of section 13, 14 or 15 above is void in the case of a consumer sale and is, in any other case, not enforceable to the extent that it is shown that it would not be fair or reasonable to allow reliance on the term.

(5) In determining for the purposes of subsection (4) above whether or not reliance on any such term would be fair or reasonable regard shall be had to all the circumstances of the case and in particular to the following matters—

(a) the strength of the bargaining positions of the seller and buyer relative to each other, taking into account, among other things, the availability of suitable alternative products and sources of supply;

(b) whether the buyer received an inducement to agree to the term or in accepting it had an opportunity of buying the goods or suitable alternatives without it from any source of supply;

(c) whether the buyer knew or ought reasonably to have known of the existence and extent of the term (having regard, among other things, to any custom of the trade and any previous course of dealing between the parties);

(d) where the term exempts from all or any of the provisions of section 13, 14 or 15 above if some condition is not complied with, whether it was reasonable at the time of the contract to expect that compliance with that condition would be practicable;

(e) whether the goods were manufactured, processed, or adapted to the special order of the buyer.

(6) Subsection (5) above does not prevent the court from holding, in accordance with any rule of law, that a term which purports to exclude or restrict any of the provisions of section 13, 14 or 15 above is not a term of the contract.

(7) In this section "consumer sale" means a sale of goods (other than a sale by auction or by competitive tender) by a seller in the course of a business where the goods—

(a) are of a type ordinarily bought for private use or consumption; and

(b) are sold to a person who does not buy or hold himself out as buying them in the course of a business.

(8) The onus of proving that a sale falls to be treated for the purposes of this section as not being a consumer sale lies on the party so contending.

(9) Any reference in this section to a term exempting from all or any of the provisions of any section of this Act is a reference to a term which purports to exclude or restrict, or has the effect of excluding or restricting, the operation of all or any of the provisions of that section, or the exercise of a right conferred by any provision of that section, or any liability of the seller for breach of a condition or warranty implied by any provision of that section.

(10) It is hereby declared that any reference in this section to a term of a contract includes a reference to a term which although not contained in a contract is incorporated in the contract by another term of the contract.

(11) Nothing in this section prevents the parties to a contract for the international sale of goods from negativing or varying any right, duty or liability which would otherwise arise by implication of law under sections 12 to 15 above.

(12) In subsection (11) above "contract for the international sale of goods" means a contract for sale of goods made by parties whose places of business (or if they have none, habitual residences) are in the territories of different States (the Channel Islands and the Isle of Man being treated for this purpose as different States from the United Kingdom) and in the case of which one of the following conditions is satisfied:—

(a) the contract involves the sale of goods which are at the time of the conclusion of the contract in the course of carriage or will be carried from the territory of one State to the territory of another; or

(b) the acts constituting the offer and acceptance have been effected in the territories of different States; or

(c) delivery of the goods is to be made in the territory of a State other than that within whose territory the acts constituting the offer and the acceptance have been effected.

Section 55: *Exclusion of Implied Terms (ii)*

12. In relation to a contract made before 18 May 1973 substitute the following for section 55:—

Exclusion of implied terms

55. Where a right, duty or liability would arise under a contract of sale by implication of law, it may be negatived or varied by express agreement, or by the course of dealing between the parties, or by such usage as binds both parties to the contract.

Section 56: *Conflict of Laws*

13.—(1) In relation to a contract made on or after 18 May 1973 and before 1 February 1978 substitute for section 56 the section set out in sub-paragraph (3) below.

(2) In relation to a contract made otherwise than as mentioned in subparagraph (1) above, ignore section 56 and this paragraph.

(3) The section mentioned in sub-paragraph (1) above is as follows:—

Conflict of laws

56.—(1) Where the proper law of a contract for the sale of goods would, apart from a term that it should be the law of some other country or a term to the like effect, be the law of any part of the United Kingdom, or where any such contract contains a term which purports to substitute, or has the effect of substituting, provisions of the law of some other country for all or any of the provisions of sections 12 to 15 and 55 above, those sections shall, notwithstanding that term but subject to subsection (2) below, apply to the contract.

(2) Nothing in subsection (1) above prevents the parties to a contract for the international sale of goods from negativing or varying any right, duty or liability which would otherwise arise by implication of law under sections 12 to 15 above.

(3) In subsection (2) above "contract for the international sale of goods" means a contract of sale of goods made by parties whose places of business (or, if they have none, habitual residences) are in the territories of different States (the Channel Islands and the Isle of Man being treated for this purpose as different States from the United Kingdom) and in the case of which one of the following conditions is satisfied:—

(a) the contract involves the sale of goods which are at the time of the conclusion of the contract in the course of carriage or will be carried from the territory of one State to the territory of another; or

(b) the acts constituting the offer and acceptance have been effected in the territories of different States; or

(c) delivery of the goods is to be made in the territory of a State other than that within whose territory the acts constituting the offer and the acceptance have been effected.

Section 61(1): *Definition of "Business" (i)*

14. In relation to a contract made on or after 18 May 1973 and before 1 February 1978, in the definition of "business" in section 61(1) for "or local or public authority," substitute "local authority or statutory undertaker".

Section 61(1): *Definition of "Business" (ii)*

15. In relation to a contract made before 18 May 1973 omit the definition of "business" in section 61(1).

A–034 **Section 63**

SCHEDULE 2

CONSEQUENTIAL AMENDMENTS

1. [*Repealed.*][38]

Law Reform (Frustrated Contracts) Act 1943 (6 & 7 Geo. 6 c. 40)

2. In section 2(5)(c) of the Law Reform (Frustrated Contracts) Act 1943 for "section seven of the Sale of Goods Act 1893" substitute "section 7 of the Sale of Goods Act 1979".

Frustrated Contracts Act (Northern Ireland) 1947 (c. 2)

3. In section 2(5)(c) of the Frustrated Contracts Act (Northern Ireland) 1947 for "section seven of the Sale of Goods Act 1893" substitute "section 7 of the Sale of Goods Act 1979".

Hire-Purchase Act 1964 (c. 53)

4. In section 27(5) of the Hire-Purchase Act 1964 (as originally enacted and as substituted by Schedule 4 to the Consumer Credit Act 1974)—

(a) in paragraph (a) for "section 21 of the Sale of Goods Act 1893" substitute "section 21 of the Sale of Goods Act 1979;"

(b) in paragraph (b) for "section 62(1) of the said Act of 1893" substitute "section 61(1) of the said Act of 1979".

Hire-Purchase Act 1965 (c. 66)

5. In section 20 of the Hire-Purchase Act 1965—

[38] This entry relating to the War Risks Insurance Act 1939 was repealed by the Statute Law (Repeals) Act 1981, S.1(1) and Sch.1, Part XI.

(a) in subsection (1) for "Sections 11(1)(c) of the Sale of Goods Act 1893" substitute "section 11(4) of the Sale of Goods Act 1979";

(b) in subsection (3) for "sections 12 to 15 of the Sale of Goods Act 1893" substitute "sections 12 to 15 of the Sale of Goods Act 1979".

6. In section 54 of the Hire-Purchase Act 1965 for "section 25(2) of the Sale of Goods Act 1893" substitute "section 25(1) of the Sale of Goods Act 1979".

7. In section 58(1) of the Hire-Purchase Act 1965 for "the Sale of Goods Act 1893" substitute "the Sale of Goods Act 1979".

Hire-Purchase (Scotland) Act 1965 (c. 67)

8. In section 20 of the Hire-Purchase (Scotland) Act 1965 for "1893" substitute "1979".

9. In section 50 of the Hire-Purchase (Scotland) Act 1965 for "section 25(2) of the Sale of Goods Act 1893" substitute "section 25(1) of the Sale of Goods Act 1979".

10. In section 54(1) of the Hire-Purchase (Scotland) Act 1965 for "the Sale of Goods Act 1893" substitute "the Sale of Goods Act 1979".

Hire-Purchase Act (Northern Ireland) 1966 (c. 42)

11. In section 20 of the Hire-Purchase Act (Northern Ireland) 1966—

(a) in subsection (1) for "Section 11(1)(c) of the Sale of Goods Act 1893" substitute "Section 11(4) of the Sale of Goods Act 1979";

(b) in subsection (3) for "1893" substitute "1979".

12. In section 54 of the Hire-Purchase Act (Northern Ireland) 1966 for "section 25(2) of the Sale of Goods Act 1893" substitute "section 25(1) of the Sale of Goods Act 1979".

13. In section 62(5) of the Hire-Purchase Act (Northern Ireland) 1966 (as originally enacted and as substituted by Schedule 4 to the Consumer Credit Act 1974)—

(a) in paragraph (a) for "1893" substitute "1979";

(b) in paragraph (b) for "section 62(1) of the said Act of 1893" substitute "section 61(1) of the said Act of 1979".

14. In section 65(1) of the Hire-Purchase Act (Northern Ireland) 1966 for "the Sale of Goods Act 1893" substitute "the Sale of Goods Act 1979".

Uniform Laws on International Sales Act 1967 (c. 45)

15. For section 1(4) of the Uniform Laws on International Sales Act 1967 substitute the following:—

"(4) In determining the extent of the application of the Uniform Law on Sales by virtue of Article 4 thereof (choice of parties)—

(a) in relation to a contract made before 18 May 1973, no provision of the law of any part of the United Kingdom shall be regarded as a mandatory provision within the meaning of that Article;

(b) in relation to a contract made on or after 18 May 1973 and before 1 February 1978, no provision of that law shall be so regarded except sections 12 to 15, 55 and 56 of the Sale of Goods Act 1979;

(c) in relation to a contract made on or after 1 February 1978, no provision of that law shall be so regarded except sections 12 to 15 of the Sale of Goods Act 1979".

Supply of Goods (Implied Terms) Act 1973 (c. 13)

16. In section 14(1) of the Supply of Goods (Implied Terms) Act 1973 (as originally enacted and as substituted by Schedule 4 to the Consumer Credit Act 1974) for "Section 11(1)(c) of the principal Act" substitute "Section 11(4) of the Sale of Goods Act 1979".

17. For the definition of "consumer sale" in section 15(1) of the Supply of Goods (Implied Terms) Act 1973 substitute—

"consumer sale" has the same meaning as in section 55 of the Sale of Goods Act 1979 (as set out in paragraph 11 of Schedule 1 to that Act).

Consumer Credit Act 1974 (c. 39)

18. In section 189(1) of the Consumer Credit Act 1974, in the definition of "goods", for "section 62(1) of the Sale of Goods Act 1893" substitute "section 61(1) of the Sale of Goods Act 1979".

Unfair Contract Terms Act 1977 (c. 50)

19. In section 6 of the Unfair Contract Terms Act 1977—

(a) in subsection (1)(a) for "section 12 of the Sale of Goods Act 1893" substitute "section 12 of the Sale of Goods Act 1979";

(b) in subsection (2)(a) for "section 13, 14 or 15 of the 1893 Act" substitute "section 13, 14 or 15 of the 1979 Act".

20. In section 14 of the Unfair Contract Terms Act 1977, in the definition of "goods", for "the Sale of Goods Act 1893" substitute "the Sale of Goods Act 1979".

21. In section 20(1)(a) and (2)(a) of the Unfair Contract Terms Act 1977 for "1893" substitute (in each case) "1979".

22. In section 25(1) of the Unfair Contract Terms Act 1977, in the definition of "goods", for "the Sale of Goods Act 1893" substitute "the Sale of Goods Act 1979".

SCHEDULE 3 A–035

REPEALS

Chapter	Short title	Extent of repeal
56 & 57 Vict. c.71.	Sale of Goods Act 1893.	The whole Act except section 26.
1967 c. 7	Misrepresentation Act 1967.	Section 4. In section 6(3) the words ", except section 4(2),".
1967 c. 14 (N.I.)	Misrepresentation Act (Northern Ireland) 1967.	Section 4.
1973 c. 13	Supply of Goods (Implied Terms) Act 1973.	Sections 1 to 7. Section 18 (2).
1974 c. 39.	Consumer Credit Act 1974.	In Schedule 4, paragraphs 3 and 4.
1977 c. 50.	Unfair Contract Terms Act 1977.	In Schedule 3, the entries relating to the Sale of Goods Act 1893.

Section 63

SCHEDULE 4 A–036

SAVINGS

Preliminary

1. In this Schedule references to the 1893 Act are to the Sale of Goods Act 1893.

Orders

2. An order under section 14(8) or 25(4) above may make provision that it is to have effect only as provided by the order (being provision corresponding to that which could, apart from this Act, have been made by an order under section 192(4) of the Consumer Credit Act 1974 bringing into operation an amendment or repeal making a change corresponding to that made by the order under section 14(8) or 25(4) above).

Offences

3. Where an offence was committed in relation to goods before 1 January 1969 or (in the application of this Act to Northern Ireland) 1 August 1969, the effect of a conviction in respect of the offence is not affected by the repeal by this Act of section 24 of the 1893 Act.

1893 Act, section 26

4. The repeal by this Act of provisions of the 1893 Act does not extend to the following provisions of that Act in so far as they are needed to give

effect to or interpret section 26 of that Act, namely, the definitions of "goods" and "property" in section 62(1), section 62(2) and section 63 (which was repealed subject to savings by the Statute Law Revision Act 1908).

Things Done before 1 January 1894

5. The repeal by this Act of section 60 of and the Schedule to the 1893 Act (which effected repeals and which were themselves repealed subject to savings by the Statute Law Revision Act 1908) does not affect those savings, and accordingly does not affect things done or acquired before 1 January 1894.

6. In so far as the 1893 Act applied (immediately before the operation of the repeals made by this Act) to contracts made before 1 January 1894 (when the 1893 Act came into operation), the 1893 Act shall continue so to apply notwithstanding this Act.

INDEX

Acceptance
acceptance of part, 12–060, 12–061
anticipatory breach, 9–013, 9–015
anticipatory refusal, 9–016
breach of term
defective goods, 12–038
express affirmation, 12–038, 12–045
implied affirmation, 12–038, 12–047
right of rejection, 12–038
statutory provisions, 12–037, 12–038
and see **Breach of term**
buyer's duty, 9–001
"click-wrap" contracts, 2–012, 2–015, 14–053
and see **"Click-wrap" contracts**
commercial units, 12–062
contract
communication, of, 2–011
contractual terms, 12–063
requirement, as to, 2–011
unqualified acceptance, 2–011
see also **Formation of contract**
damages
anticipatory breach, for, 9–013, 9–015
non-acceptance, for, 9–011, 9–013
quantum of damages, 9–014, 9–020
delivery
goods, 19–157
sub-buyers, to, 19–154
documents
acceptance, of, 19–155
examination, of, 19–156
effect, 19–153
examination of goods, 12–048—12–050, 19–156, 19–157
and see **Examination of goods**
express acceptance, 12–063
goods
acceptance, of, 19–153, 19–155
delivery, 19–157
examination, of, 12–048—12–050, 19–156, 19–157
insurance, of, 19–154
sale or return, 5–040, 5–047
unsolicited goods, 2–014
and see **Goods**
instalment contracts, 12–060
intimation, of, 12–045
meaning, 9–002, 12–044, 19–153
ownership, and, 12–046, 12–047, 12–050, 12–051

Acceptance—*cont.*
passing of property, and, 12–046, 12–058, 12–064
and see **Passing of property**
policy, as to, 12–047
reasonable time, 12–056
repudiation
charterparties, 9–015
expiration of time, 9–013
grounds, for, 9–002, 9–010
principles, governing, 9–016
seller's acceptance, 9–017, 9–020
seller's non-acceptance, 9–018, 9–019
substituted performance, 9–019
unjustifiable, 9–012—9–015
and see **Repudiation**
resale, and, 19–154
revocation, 14–022
Sale of Goods Act (1979), A-015
and see **Sale of Goods Act (1979)**
sellers
acceptance, 9–017, 9–020
fundamental breach, 9–015
inability to perform, 9–011, 9–012, 9–016
non-acceptance, 9–018, 9–019
repudiation, 9–017—9–020
"shrink-wrap" contracts, 2–012
and see **"Shrink-wrap" contracts**
statutory provisions, 9–002, 12–044
taking delivery
delayed delivery, 9–008
distinguished, 9–003
failure after request, 9–009
hour, of, 9–007
place, of, 9–004
postponement, 9–006
refusal, 9–010
repudiation, 9–009, 9–010
risk, 9–008
sub-buyers, 19–154
timing, 9–004, 9–006
waiver, 9–006
waiver, and, 9–006, 19–150, 19–153
and see **Waiver**
Administration orders
administrators, 5–162
disposal of goods, 5–163
see also **Right of disposal**
effect, of, 5–162
retention of title, and, 5–162, 5–163
and see **Retention of title**

Administrative protection
see also **Consumer protection**
codes of practice, 14–137
Community infringements, 14–129, 14–130, 14–133, 14–136
Consumer Protection Advisory Committee, 14–126
delegated legislation, 14–126, 14–128
enforcement, 14–128
Enterprise Act (2002), 14–125—14–127
and see **Enterprise Act (2002)**
Fair Trading Act (1973), 14–125, 14–126, 14–137
Injunctions Directive (1998/27/EC), 14–129, 14–136
Office of Fair Trading (OFT), 14–125, 14–127, 14–128
*and see*Office of Fair Trading (OFT)
Stop Now Orders (EC Directive) Regulations (2001), 14–129, 14–130. 14–156
Affirmation (election)
acceptance, and, 12–037, 12–038
and see **Acceptance**
breach of term, and, 12–037, 12–038
effect, of, 12–036
estoppel by conduct, 12–037
and see **Estoppel**
express, 12–038, 12–045
implied, 12–038, 12–047
intention to affirm, 12–047
misrepresentation, and, 12–006
and see **Misrepresentation**
rejection of contract, and, 12–037, 12–047
reliance, and, 12–037, 12–047
retraction, 12–037
statutory affirmation, 12–037, 12–047
Agency
see also **Agent**
agency contracts
choice of law, 25–073
contract applicable law, 25–073
governing law, 25–073
see also **Conflict of laws (contract)**
agency sales
fitness for purpose, 11–053
quality of goods, 11–026
authority
actual, 15–008
express, 7–031
implied, 7–031
ostensible, 15–008
common law rules, 3–002, 7–031
dealers, 3–005
del credere commission, 1–048
estoppel, and, 7–008, 7–010
and see **Estoppel**
general principles, 3–002
Agency—*cont.*
good title, passing of, 7–031
instalment credit transactions, 3–005
married women, 3–007
mercantile agents, 3–002, 3–004, 7–031, 7–032
and see **Mercantile agents**
nature of transaction, 1–049
necessity, of, 3–006
payment provisions, 9–043, 9–044
see also **Payment**
sale, distinguished, 1–048
and see **Sale**
sale or return, and, 5–045
and see **Sale or return**
scope, of, 3–003
Agent
see also **Agency**
authority
actual, 3–003
apparent, 3–003
description, 1–049
mercantile agents, 3–002, 3–004, 7–031, 7–032
and see **Mercantile agents**
passing of property
agency relationships, 18–232, 18–233
buyers/sellers, 18–232
disposal of goods, 18–230
shipment, and, 18–229, 18–231
status, 18–232
transfer of title, 18–233
and see **Passing of property (overseas sales)**
payment provisions, 9–043, 9–044
see also **Payment**
reliance, on, 11–063
remuneration, 1–049
representations, by, 7–010
types
auctioneers, 3–004
brokers, 3–004
commercial agent, 3–004
commission agent, 3–004
dealers, 3–005
del credere agent, 1–049, 3–004, 5–045
factors, 3–004
mercantile agents, 3–002, 3–004
Agreement to sell
buyer in possession, 7–070
and see **Buyer in possession**
frustration of contract, 6–035
and see **Frustration of contract**
sale, distinguished, 1–028
and see **Sale**
seller in possession, 7–056
and see **Seller in possession**

Agreement to sell—*cont.*
statutory definition, 1–025, 1–026
voidable title, and, 7–022, 7–027
and see **Voidable title**
Air waybills
contents, of, 21–052
document of title, 21–053, 21–054
and see **Document of title**
Appropriation
assent
agent, of, 5–083
buyer, of, 5–075, 5–078, 5–079
implied, 5–076, 5–079
inferred, 5–077
parties, of, 5–074, 5–088
previous assent, 5–078
seller, of, 5–082
statutory provisions, 5–068
subsequent assent, 5–075
bulk goods, 5–103—5–108
and see **Bulk goods**
conditional, 5–072
contract
attached to goods, 5–070, 5–081, 5–086, 5–099
conformity, with, 5–085, 5–086
delivery, and, 5–099, 5–100
and see **Delivery**
ex works contract, 5–089
and see **Ex works contract**
final completion, 5–079, 5–080
future goods, 5–090—5–095
and see **Future goods**
goods
delivery, of, 5–081
identification, of, 5–069
unascertained goods, 5–067—5–069
meaning, 5–069, 5–070
mistake, by, 5–087
passing of property, 5–067, 5–069, 5–070, 18–210, 18–287
and see **Passing of property**
place of sale, 5–088
risk, 5–084
unascertained goods, 5–067—5–069
and see **Unascertained goods**
unconditional, 5–068, 5–071, 5–073, 5–099
Approval
see **Goods on approval**
Assignment
competing assignments, 5–161
contract of sale, 3–043
and see **Contract of sale**
deed, by, 2–025
documentary credits, 23–068, 23–069
and see **Documentary credits**
equitable principles, 1–107, 1–108
Assignment—*cont.*
export credit guarantees, 24–025—24–030
and see **Export credit guarantees**
future goods, 1–107, 1–108
insurance policy, 19–042, 19–052
land, of, 5–028
personal rights, 3–044
rights, of, 3–043, 3–044
Romalpa clauses, 25–149
and see ***Romalpa* clauses**
standby credits, 23–267
and see **Standby credits**
Auction sales
completion, 2–004
fixed bidding, distinguished, 2–004
fraud, 3–009
nature, of, 2–004
reserve price, 2–006
Sale of Goods Act (1979), A-028
and see **Sale of Goods Act (1979)**
without reserve, 2–005

Bailment
bailees
buyer's duties, 6–026
consumer sales, 6–032
liability, as, 6–026, 6–027, 6–030, 6–031
remedies, 6–028
seller's duties, 6–026, 6–027
vicarious liability, 6–030
goods on approval, and, 5–044
and see **Goods on approval**
incidental, 1–062
intermixing, and, 1–058
manufactured goods, 1–060
manufacturing components, 1–060
mixed goods, 1–059
nature, of, 1–057
ownership of goods
construction materials, 1–060
containers, 1–061
sacks, 1–061
passing of property, and, 5–010
and see **Passing of property**
pledge, and, 1–063
and see **Pledge**
risk, and, 6–026—6–032
and see **Risk**
sale, distinguished, 1–057, 1–059
and see **Sale**
sale or return, and, 5–044
and see **Sale or return**
substituted goods, 1–059
Banker's commercial credit
payment
failure of, 16–019
f.o.b. contracts, 20–024

Banker's draft
see **Direct payment**
Banker's lien
see also **Lien**
bank balances, and, 22–144
bills for collection, 22–143
extent, of, 22–140
nature, of, 22–139
paper securities, and, 22–140
security
deposit, of, 22–141
safe custody, 22–142
specific debt, for, 22–141
specific purpose, for, 22–141
third party rights, 22–145
Bankruptcy
see also **Insolvency**
effect, of, 3–046
preferences given, 3–047
rules, 3–045
statutory provisions, 3–045
undervalue transactions, 3–047
Barter
nature, of, 1–037
remedies, 1–035, 1–036
and see **Remedies**
sale, distinguished, 1–034—1–036
and see **Sale**
Bills of exchange
acceptance, of, 22–065, 22–067
aval, 22–052
bank
advances, 22–068
agency principles, and, 22–092
collecting banker, 22–073—22–075, 22–091, 22–092
correspondent, use of, 22–088
discounting banker, 22–069, 22–073—22–075
forfeiting, 22–072
function, of, 22–067, 22–068
holder, as, 22–068, 22–090
insolvency, 22–090
liability, 22–087—22–090
privity of contract, 22–092
remitting banker, 22–087—22–090
responsibilities, 22–093—22–096
right of recourse, 22–070
"without recourse" transactions, 22–070—22–072
Bills of Exchange Act (1882), 22–033, 22–085, 22–086
claused bills, 22–042
collection
collection instruction, 22–081, 22–082, 22–120
dishonour, and, 22–120
refusal to handle, 22–078
Bills of exchange—*cont.*
collection—*cont.*
Uniform Rules for Collections, 22–076
see also **Uniform Rules for Collections**
consideration, failure of, 22–064, 22–065
contractual relationships, 22–058
definition, 22–038, 22–041
delivery, 22–057, 22–058
dishonour
agency, and, 22–128, 22–129
case of need, 22–095, 22–138
collection instruction, and, 22–120
condition precedent, 22–120
non-payment, 22–117
notice provisions, 22–121—22–127
procedure, 22–120
protest of bill, 22–135—22–137
Uniform Rules, 22–129
drawees, 22–047
drawers, 22–048
electronic bills, 22–036
see also **Electronic commerce**
foreign bills, 22–040
Geneva Convention (1930), 22–034
holders
bank, as, 22–068, 22–090
failure of consideration, 22–064, 22–065
holder for value, 22–060, 22–063, 22–064
holder in due course, 22–061, 22–062
mere holders, 22–059, 22–062
rights, of, 22–062, 22–063
types, of, 22–059
indorsement
blank, in, 22–056
indorsers, 22–049
security indorsement, 22–051
special indorsement, 22–056
inland bills, 22–040
liability
collecting banker, 22–091, 22–092
documentation, for, 22–095, 22–096
remitting banker, 22–087—22–090
nature, of, 22–038
negotiation, of, 22–055
notice of dishonour
agency, and, 22–128, 22–129
benefit, of, 22–123
delay, 22–130
delivery, 22–125
dispensed with, 22–131, 22–132
entitlement, 22–134
excusal, 22–131, 22–132
guarantors, 22–133
loss, of, 22–127
meaning, 22–121

Bills of exchange—*cont.*
notice of dishonour—*cont.*
procedure, 22–124
rules, as to, 22–122
timing, 22–126
parties, 22–039
payees, 22–046
payment, 22–043, 22–044, 22–067, 22–118, 22–119
and see **Payment**
presentment for acceptance
conditional acceptance, 22–104
excusal, 22–102
general acceptance, 22–104
invalid acceptance, 22–103
method, 22–100
non-acceptance, 22–105
procedure, 22–100, 22–101
qualified acceptance, 22–104, 22–106
requirement, as to, 22–097
rules, 22–099
timing, 22–098
Uniform Rules, 22–101
valid acceptance, 22–107
presentment for payment
bill not domiciled, 22–111
collecting bank, 22–112, 22–115
exchange controls, 22–119
excusal, 22–116, 22–117
failure to present, 22–114, 22–115
payment refused, 22–117
place, 22–110, 22–111
requirements, as to, 22–108, 22–113
timing, 22–109
Uniform Rules, 22–119
recognition, 22–053
responsibility
documentation, 22–093, 22–095, 22–096
goods, 22–094
set of bills, 22–066
signature, 22–050
sum certain, for, 22–045
third party acceptance, 22–054
UNCITRAL Convention, 22–035
unconditional order, 22–041
use, of, 22–037
validity, 22–052
Bills of lading
bearer bills
document of title, 18–063
presentation, of, 18–017
transfer, of, 18–016
bulk shipments, 18–303
and see **Bulk shipments**
charterparty terms
conflict, with, 18–050—18–053
incorporation, of, 18–050
collateral contracts, 18–146
Bills of lading—*cont.*
contractual document
affirmation of fact, 18–049
charterparties, 18–050—18–054
contract of carriage, 18–048
contractual terms, 18–049
evidence of contract, 18–047
third parties, 18–055—18–057
contractual rights
see **Bills of lading (contractual rights)**
delivery of goods, 18–082, 18–093, 18–139
destroyed goods
"cannot be identified", 18–137
Carriage of Goods by Sea Act (1992), 18–135
"cease to exist", 18–136
deviation
effects, of, 18–060, 18–061, 18–109
meaning, of, 18–059
waiver, and, 1–109
discharge of bill
agreement, 18–082
frustration, 18–082
performance, 18–082
repudiatory breach, 18–082
disposal of goods, 5–137, 5–139, 5–140
see also **Right of disposal**
documentary credits, and, 23–218—23–223
and see **Documentary credits**
document of title
attornment, 18–066
bailment, and, 18–065
bearer bills, 18–063
common law sense, 18–062, 18–067, 18–074, 18–083
delivery of goods, 18–063, 18–064
function, as, 18–012, 18–074
order bills, 18–063, 18–068
received bills, 18–079
spent bills, 18–080
statutory sense, 18–062, 18–083
straight (non-negotiable) bills, 18–067
and see **Document of title**
electronic bills, 18–202, 18–203, 18–205, 18–206
false statements
Carriage of Goods by Sea act (1992), 18–039, 18–043
delivery orders, 18–041
effects, of, 18–030
estoppel, and, 18–108
fraudulent statements, 18–046
Hague-Visby Rules, 18–034
liability, for, 18–046
quantity, as to, 18–031, 18–039, 18–043
shipment, as to, 18–030, 18–043

Bills of lading—*cont.*
false statements—*cont.*
statutory provisions, 18–033, 18–036, 18–039
f.o.b. contracts
see **F.O.B. contracts**
function
contractual document, 18–012
conveyancing function, 18–074
document of title, 18–012, 18–074
receipt, as, 18–012
Hague-Visby Rules, 18–013, 18–034, 18–035
and see **Hague-Visby Rules**
hypothecation, of, 19–205
liabilities
see **Bills of lading (liabilities)**
meaning, 18–103
nature, of, 18–012
negotiability, 18–074, 18–076—18–078, 18–084
order bills
document of title, 18–063, 18–068
effect, of, 18–068
presentation, of, 18–017
transfer, 18–016, 18–068
part-delivery, 18–093
passing of property, and, 5–008
and see **Passing of property**
receipt
Carriage of Goods by Sea Act (1992), 18–036, 18–037, 18–042, 18–044
evidence of facts, 18–028
false statements, 18–030, 18–031
received bills, 18–038
signature on bill, 18–033, 18–036, 18–037, 18–045
unauthorised statements, 18–029
received bills
Carriage of Goods by Sea Act (1992), 18–038
document of title, 18–079
meaning, 18–103
nature, of, 18–038
receipt for shipment, 18–038
redirection of goods, 18–021—18–025
sea waybills, distinguished, 18–018, 18–020
and see **Sea waybills**
sets of bills
competing pledges, 18–091
delivery by carrier, 18–092
issue, of, 18–090—18–092, 18–095, 20–023
multiple sets, 18–095
tender to buyer, 18–094
shipping instructions, and, 20–063—20–066

Bills of lading—*cont.*
signature
authority, 18–045
liability, for, 18–045, 18–046
receipt, and, 18–033, 18–036, 18–037, 18–045
spent bills
carrier's liability, 18–081
constructive possession, and, 18–080
contractual rights, 18–080, 18–081, 18–113, 18–131
delivery of goods, 18–082
discharge of bill, 18–082
document of title, 18–080
meaning, 18–080
negotiability, 18–081
purposes, of, 18–080
statements
Carriage of Goods by Sea Act (1992), 18–039, 18–043
common law rule, 18–029, 18–032
delivery orders, 18–041
estoppel, and, 18–108
false statements, 18–030, 18–031, 18–033, 18–034
fraudulent statements, 18–046
legislative provisions, 18–033, 18–036, 18–039
liability, for, 18–046
quantity, as to, 18–031, 18–036, 18–039, 18–043
received goods, as to, 18–043
representations, 18–036
shipment, as to, 18–030, 18–043
unauthorised, 18–029
straight (non-negotiable) bills
consignees, 18–018
delivery of goods, 18–018, 18–069—18–071, 18–073
document of title, 18–067, 18–074, 18–078
nature, of, 18–018
negotiability, 18–074, 18–078
production, of, 18–069—18–074
redirection of goods, 18–025, 18–070
sea waybills, distinguished, 18–020
transferability, 18–018, 18–069, 18–074, 18–077
third parties
charterparties, 18–056, 18–057
Contracts (Rights of Third Parties) Act (1999), 18–024, 18–055, 18–117
contractual rights, 18–112, 18–117, 18–145
delivery, to, 18–096
limitation clauses, 18–058
privity of contract, 18–096

Bills of lading—*cont.*
transfer
agency, and, 18–097
assignment, and, 18–097, 18–147
bailment, and, 18–115
Bills of Lading Act (1855), 18–100
Carriage of Goods by Sea Act (1992), 18–101, 18–102
charterers, and, 18–110, 18–111, 18–116
common law rules, 18–098, 18–099
consideration, 18–088
contractual effect, 18–096
contractual liability, 18–099
contractual rights, 18–102
indorsement, 18–084, 18–085
intermediate transferees, 18–118
loss of rights, 18–115
loss suffered, 18–119
privity of contract, 18–096, 18–097
property, of, 18–089
right to sue, 18–099
risk, 18–120
shipper's rights, 18–115
statutory provisions, 18–087
stoppage in transit, 18–086, 18–088
third parties, delivery to, 18–096
transferor's title, defects in, 18–085
transferability
bearer bills, 18–016
indications, as to, 18–015
order bills, 18–016
types
bearer bills, 18–014
borderline cases, 18–019
distinctions, 18–013, 18–062
electronic bills, 18–202, 18–203, 18–205, 18–206
order bills, 18–015
received bills, 18–027, 18–038
shipped bills, 18–07
straight (non-negotiable) bills, 18–018
Bills of lading (contractual rights)
see also **Bills of lading**
acquisition, of, 18–102, 18–104
charterer's rights, 18–116
collateral contracts, 18–146
consideration, 18–141
delivery
agent, as, 18–144
goods, of, 18–139
entitlement, 18–122
extent, of, 18–121
good faith, 18–105
implied contract, 18–038—18–041
intention, as to, 18–142, 18–143
interest in goods, 18–120
intermediate transferees, 18–118
Bills of lading (contractual rights)—*cont.*
lawful holders, 18–104, 18–105
liability, and, 18–125
loss
loss of rights, 18–115
loss suffered, 18–119
presentation of documents, 18–140
scope, of, 18–14
shipper's rights, 18–107, 18–109, 18–114, 18–115
spent bills, 18–113, 18–131
statutory provisions, 18–102, 18–103
third parties, 18–112, 18–117, 18–145
transfer, of, 18–102
transferred rights, 18–106, 18–107
Bills of lading (liabilities)
see also **Bills of lading**
Bills of lading Act (1855), 18–123
Carriage of Goods by Sea Act (1992), 18–123—18–125
carriers
delivery, from, 18–127
liability, of, 18–129
charterparties, 18–129
contract
consideration, 18–141
contracting parties, 18–134
contract of carriage, 18–129
contractual intent, 18–142, 18–143
contractual rights, 18–125
implied contract, 18–138—18–141
delivery
agent, as, 18–144
carrier, from, 18–127
delivered goods, 18–128
implied contract, 18–139
part delivery, 18–128
persons taking delivery, 18–126, 18–127
extent of liability, 18–133
formal claims, 18–129, 18–130
imposition, of, 18–123, 18–129
intermediate transferee, 18–132
presentation of documents, 18–10
shippers, 18–134
tortious liability
buyer's interest, 18–149
carriers, 18–148, 18–149
concurrent liability, 18–151
contractual relationships, and, 18–151
negligence, 18–148, 18–149
proprietary interests, 18–149, 18–150
third party interest, 18–150
and see **Tortious liability**
Bills of sale
see also **Bills of Sale Acts (1878–1891)**
Romalpa clauses, and, 5–167, 5–168
and see ***Romalpa* clauses**

Bills of Sale Acts (1878–1891)
application, 1–016, 1–017
commercial transactions, 1–017
company law, 1–016
documentary requirements, 1–016, 1–017
effect, 1–017
fraudulent transactions, 1–016
objective, 1–016
transfer of ownership, 1–016
Breach of term
acceptance
implied affirmation, 12–038
statutory provisions, 12–037, 12–038
and see **Acceptance**
affirmation, 12–034, 12–037
see also **Affirmation (election)**
anticipatory breach, 12–021, 12–027
breach of condition
condition precedent, 12–056
contrary intention, 12–025
description of goods, 12–025
discharge of contract, 10–027—10–030, 12–025, 12–028
express terms, 12–025
failure of performance, 12–022
fitness for purpose, and, 12–022
implied terms, 12–025
implied title, 12–025
non-consumer sales, 12–024, 12–025
rejection of contract, 12–025—12–028
repudiation, and, 10–027, 10–028
satisfactory quality, and, 12–022
statutory limits, 12–024
statutory modification, 10–038
technical breaches, 12–024
see also **Conditions**
buyer's rights, 12–027
commercial units
definition, of, 12–062
rejection of contract, 12–062
condition precedent, 12–056
consumer sales, 12–071
and see **Consumer sales**
damages, entitlement to, 12–017, 12–021
defective goods, 12–054
and see **Defective goods**
discharge of contract
breach of condition, 10–027—10–030, 12–025, 12–028
breach of term, 12–018—12–024
rejection, distinguished, 12–028
documentary sales
delivery of goods, 12–052
difficulties, with, 12–052
disposition of documents, 12–052
overseas sales, 12–052
examination of goods
see **Examination of goods**
Breach of term—*cont.*
instalment contracts, 12–019
misrepresentation
see **Misrepresentation**
passing of property, 12–058, 12–064
and see **Passing of property**
performance
failure, of, 12–019, 12–022, 12–023
impossibility, 12–020
refusal, as to, 12–019
quantity of goods
de minimis rule, 12–030
excessive delivery, 12–029, 12–030
repudiation, and, 12–029
short delivery, 12–029, 12–030
slight shortfall, 12–030
see also **Quantity of goods (delivery)**
rejection of contract
see **Rejection of contract**
renunciation, 12–019
repudiation, and, 12–021, 12–029
and see **Repudiation**
restitutio in integrum, and, 12–047, 12–057
re-tender, right to, 12–031
return of goods, 12–051, 12–059
seller
failure to perform, 12–019
refusal to perform, 12–019
renunciation, by, 12–019
re-tender, by, 12–031
return of goods, 12–051
sub-buyer, delivery to, 12–047, 12–051
waiver, 12–034—12–036
and see **Waiver**
Buildings
contracts for work, 1–096
land, and, 1–090, 1–096
and see **Land**
removal, 1–096
sale, of, 1–096
Bulk goods
aggregate quantities, 5–107
appropriation, 5–103—5–108
and see **Appropriation**
bulk, meaning of, 5–105, 5–113
delivery
co-owner's consent, 8–017
deliverable state, 5–106
statutory provisions, 8–017
and see **Delivery**
frustration of contract, 6–036
and see **Frustration of contract**
future goods, 5–094
and see **Future goods**
identifiable part, 5–103, 5–104
identification of bulk, 5–114

Bulk goods—*cont.*
intention of parties, 5–108
passing of property
aggregate shares, 5–118
compensation provisions, 5–127
conditions, governing, 5–061, 5–062, 5–103, 5–104, 5–113
co-ownership, 5–109, 5–124—5–126, 5–130, 8–017
deemed consent, 5–124, 5–126
f.o.b. contracts, 20–086
fungible goods, 5–113
identified part, 5–109
overselling, 5–121—5–123
part payments, 5–120
price, payment of, 5–115, 5–130
proportionate share, 5–118—5–120
quantity unknown, 5–119
specified quantity, 5–111
statutory provisions, 5–109, 5–110
unascertained goods, 5–112
undivided share, 5–109, 5–116
and see **Passing of property**
reduction, in, 5–107
risk, 6–004—6–008
and see **Risk**
sale by sample, 11–078, 11–079, 11–086
and see **Sale by sample**
Sale of Goods Act (1979), A-012
and see **Sale of Goods Act (1979)**
seller in possession, 7–067
and see **Seller in possession**
separate contracts, for, 5–107
shipment
see **Bulk shipments**
specified quantity, within, 5–060—5–062, 5–103, 5–111
statutory provisions, 5–103, 5–107
sub-sales, 7–085
unascertained goods, 5–061, 5–062, 5–103, 5–104, 5–112, 7–085
and see **Unascertained goods**
undivided share, 5–109, 7–085, 8–017
and see **Undivided share**
Bulk shipments
see also **Bulk goods**
bulk
characteristics, 18–295
identification, of, 18–295
meaning, of, 18–295
commodity trading, 18–307
loss/deterioration of goods
destruction of goods, 18–306
deterioration, 18–06
risk, and, 18–300—18–302
and see **Loss/deterioration of goods**

Bulk shipments—*cont.*
passing of property
appropriation, 18–287
ascertainment, and, 18–287, 18–288, 18–292
competing interests, 18–299
consolidation, 18–288
contract, effect of, 18–296
contrary agreement, 18–298
exhaustion, 18–288, 18–290
fractions of bulk, 18–290, 18–294
legal consequences, 18–292
part payments, 18–297
payment of price, 18–287
policy issues, 18–297
specific goods, 18–290, 18–294
specified quantities, 18–291, 18–292
statutory provisions, 18–287, 18–293—18–295
undivided parts, 18–289, 18–290
and see **Passing of property**
payment of price, 18–287, 18–295
problems, associated with, 18–285
risk
bills of lading, 18–303
c.i.f. contracts, 18–301, 18–302, 18–304
contractual remedies, and, 18–302
dealing as consumer, 18–307
delivery orders, 18–303, 18–304
f.o.b. contracts, 18–301, 18–303
intention of parties, 18–305
loss/deterioration of goods, 18–300—18–302
and see **Risk**
shipping documents
bills of lading, 18–286
delivery orders, 18–286
ship's delivery order, 18–286
tender of documents, 18–286, 18–292, 18–307
unascertained goods, 18–285
Buyer
delivery, to, 5–097, 5–101
and see **Delivery**
possession
see **Buyer in possession**
remedies
acceptance of goods, 4–009
acquisition of title, 4–013
consequential losses, 4–029
damages, 4–006, 4–009, 4–012, 4–013, 4–017, 4–029
exclusion, of, 4–020
exemption clauses, 4–018, 4–020
freedom from encumbrance, 4–024
hire-purchase agreements, 4–013, 4–107
improvements, allowance for, 4–007

Buyer—*cont.*
remedies—*cont.*
legal costs, 4–029
purchase price, recovery of, 4–006—4–008, 4–010
repudiation, 4–006, 4–009, 4–010, 4–029
restitution, 4–008
settlement with owner, 4–012
see also **Buyer's remedies**
Buyer in possession
agreement to sell, 7–070
bulk goods, 7–085
and see **Bulk goods**
conditional sale, 7–070, 7–071
delivery of goods
actual delivery, 7–077
constructive delivery, 7–077
effect, 7–081—7–084
meaning, 7–077
passing title, 7–077
pledge, under, 7–079, 7–083, 7–084
sale, under, 7–079, 7–084
sub-purchasers, 7–078
voluntary surrender, 7–078
disposition, 7–079, 7–080, 7–084
good faith, 7–086
notice requirement, 7–086
passing title
seller's consent, 7–074
statutory provisions, 7–069—7–071
transfer of goods, 7–077, 7–081, 7–082
possession
bailees, 7–073, 7–077
actual, 7–072
constructive, 7–072
continuation, of, 7–076
documents of title, 7–069, 7–072, 7–073, 7–075
goods, 7–069, 7–072, 7–073
physical possession, 7–077
post-agreement, 7–073
seller
consent, of, 7–074, 7–076
continuing right, 7–071
unpaid seller, 7–071
statutory provisions
agreement to purchase, 7–070
protection, 7–069, 7–070
purchase of goods, 7–070, 7–071
sub-purchasers, 7–078
transfer of property, 7–070, 7–071
vehicle registration documents, 7–075
Buyer's remedies
see also **Remedies**
acceptance of goods, 4–009
acquisition of title, 4–013
breach of contract, 12–001, 12–017

Buyer's remedies—*cont.*
carrier, against, 25–202
c.i.f. contracts
see **Buyer's remedies (c.i.f. contracts)**
conflict of laws
carrier, against, 25–202
contract applicable law, 25–199, 25–200
damages, 25–198, 25–200
governing law, 25–196, 25–198
lex fori, 25–201
lex situs, 25–197
rejection of documents, 25–198
rejection of goods, 25–196, 25–197
rescission, 25–196
Rome Convention, 25–196, 25–201
specific performance, 25–201
and see **Conflict of laws**
consequential losses, 4–029
consumer sales, 12–001, 17–097
and see **Consumer sales**
criminal sanctions, 17–107
damages
see **Buyer's remedies (damages)**
declaration, 17–104
defective goods, 12–001
and see **Defective goods**
EC legislation, 12–001
exclusion, of, 4–020
exemption clauses, 4–018, 4–020
and see **Exemption clauses**
false representation, 12–001
f.o.b. contracts
see **Buyer's remedies (f.o.b. contracts)**
freedom from encumbrance, 4–024
hire-purchase agreements, 4–013, 4–017
improvements, allowance for, 4–007
indemnity, 12–003
injunctions, 17–102, 17–103
invalidating causes
frustration, 17–095
illegality, 17–095
misrepresentation, 17–095
mistake, 17–095
legal costs, 4–029
misrepresentation, 12–001—12–003
proprietary claims
claims for possession, 17–105
conversion, for, 17–105, 17–106
retaking by seller, 17–106
wrongful resale, 17–106
purchase price, recovery of, 4–006—4–008, 4–010
quiet possession, 4–029
and see **Quiet possession**

Buyer's remedies—*cont.*
rejection
documents, 25–198
goods, 17–093, 25–196, 25–197
repudiation, 4–006, 4–009, 4–010, 4–029
rescission, 17–094, 25–196
and see **Rescission**
restitution
advance payments, 17–092
divisible contracts, 17–091
failure of consideration, 4–008
failure to deliver, 17–090
repayment of price, 17–090
and see **Restitution**
Sale of Goods Act (1979), A-025
and see **Sale of Goods Act (1979)**
settlement with owner, 4–012
specific performance
see **Specific performance**
termination of contract, 17–093
Buyer's remedies (c.i.f. contracts)
see also **C.I.F contracts**
consumer sales, 19–144, 19–203
and see **Consumer sales**
damages
actions, for, 19–216—19–219
defective delivery, 19–187
non-delivery, 19–175
and see **Damages**
dealing as consumer, 19–144, 19–203
injunctions, 19–204
non-conforming documents, 19–144, 19–147
non-conforming goods, 19–144, 19–146
reduction in price, 19–203
rejection of goods 19–144, 19–145, 19–149
and see **Rejection of goods**
rescission, 19–144, 19–203
and see **Rescission**
specific performance, 19–204
and see **Specific performance**
Buyer's remedies (damages)
anticipatory repudiation
acceptance, of, 17–013—17–015
mitigation rules, 17–015
non-acceptance, 17–016
seller, by, 17–013, 17–014, 17–016
assessment of damages
available market, 17–004, 17–021
basis, for, 17–002, 17–023
market price, 17–001, 17–004, 17–007, 17–008, 17–015
market value, 17–007
mitigation, and, 17–023, 17–026
available market
absence, of, 17–021, 17–022, 17–037
availability, 17–005
"black" market, 17–006
consequential loss, 17–037
Buyer's remedies (damages)—*cont.*
available market—*cont.*
equivalent goods, 17–023—17–025
immediate access, 17–005
meaning, of, 17–005
measure of damages, 17–004, 17–021
mitigation of damage, 17–004, 17–005, 17–023
relevant market, 17–005
resale, 17–022, 17–029
specially manufactured goods, 17–006, 17–021
substitute goods, 17–004—17–006, 17–023
breach of condition, 4–006
breach of warranty, 4–009
conflict of laws, 25–198, 25–200
and see **Conflict of laws**
consumer sales, 17–003
and see **Consumer sales**
conversion, for, 4–012
deceit, and, 17–089
defective quality
see **Defective quality**
delayed delivery, 17–038—17–046
and see **Delayed delivery**
delivery of goods
anticipatory repudiation, 17–013
delayed delivery, 17–038—17–046
instalment deliveries, 17–008
no fixed time, 17–010
postponed, 17–011
refused, 17–010
waiver, and, 17–011
diminution in value
see **Diminution in value**
equivalent goods, purchase of, 17–023—17–025
expenditure
defence costs, 17–065
expenses, 17–062, 17–070
fines, 17–065
pre-contract, 17–064
reliance on contract, 17–063
sub-sales, involving, 17–068
wasted expenditure, 17–062, 17–070
hire-purchase goods, 4–017
implied warranties, 17–086
market price assessment
damages, and 17–001, 17–004, 17–007, 17–008, 17–015
delivery postponed , 17–011, 17–012
delivery refused, 17–010
evidence required, 17–018
instalment deliveries, 17–008
payment in advance, 17–009
relevant price, 17–015, 17–017
resale, 17–029

Buyer's remedies (damages)—*cont.*
market price assessment—*cont.*
substitute goods, 17–019, 17–020
timing 17–008, 17–010
misrepresentation, and, 17–089, 17–095
mitigation
assessment of damages, 17–023, 17–026
available market, and, 17–004, 17–005, 17–023
buyer's duty, 17–027
seller's offer, 17–026
non-conforming goods, 17–026
negligence, and, 17–089
non-delivery
assessment of damages, 17–002
Hadley v Baxendale, 17–001, 17–007
loss of profits, 17–037
passing of property, 17–002
refusal to deliver, 17–002
statutory provisions, 17–001, 17–002
wrongful neglect, 17–002
resale, 17–022, 17–029
and see **Resale**
right of rejection, and, 17–087
Sale of Goods Act (1979), A-025
and see **Sale of Goods Act (1979)**
statutory obligations, and, 17–088
substitute goods
mitigation of damage, 17–023
purchase, of, 17–004, 17–005, 17–006, 17–023, 17–037
resale, 17–024
wrongful interference, 4–012, 4–013
Buyer's remedies (f.o.b. contracts)
see also **F.O.B. contracts**
action for damages
anticipatory breach, 20–116
assessment of damages, 20–114, 20–116, 20–117
consequential loss, 20–119
defective delivery, 20–118
market price, and, 20–116
mitigation, 20–116
non-delivery, 20–115
refusal to deliver, 20–116
dealing as consumer, 20–113, 20–120, 20–122
defective delivery, for, 20–122
reduction in price, 20–120
rejection of goods
acts inconsistent with ownership, 20–111
dealing as consumer, 20–113, 20–120, 20–122
inspection of goods, 20–108, 20–109
insurance, and, 20–110
loss of rights, 20–107
non-conforming goods, 20–113, 20–120
Buyer's remedies (f.o.b. contracts)—*cont.*
rejection of goods—*cont.*
non-rejection clauses, 20–110, 20–112, 20–113
rejection of documents, 20–106
right of rejection, 20–105, 20–109, 20–110, 20–112
wrong reason, 20–112
and see **Rejection of goods**
rescission, 20–113
and see **Rescission**
specific performance, 20–121
and see **Specific performance**

C&F contracts (cost & freight)
duties, relating to, 21–012
nature, of, 21–012
passing of property, 21–103
and see **Passing of property**
risk, 21–103
and see **Risk**
Cargo
cargo receipts, 18–199, 21–053, 21–054
sale of cargo
see **Sale of cargo**
Carriage by air
air waybills, 21–052—21–054
and see **Air waybills**
cargo receipts, 21–052—21–054
Montreal Convention (1999), 21–051, 21–052
right of disposal, 21–052, 21–055, 1–056
and see **Right of disposal**
statutory provisions, 21–051
stoppage in transit, 21–057
and see **Stoppage in transit**
Warsaw Convention, 21–052, 21–055
Carriage by rail
CIM Uniform Rules, 21–065
and see **CIM Uniform Rules**
consignment note, 21–066—21–068
COTIF, 21–065
documentary credits, and, 23–227
and see **Documentary credits**
document of title, and, 21–068
and see **Document of title**
modification of contract, 21–069, 21–070
right of disposal, 21–067
and see **Right of disposal**
stoppage in transit, 21–071
and see **Stoppage in transit**
Carriage by road
CMR Convention, 21–058, 21–059
and see **CMR Convention**
consignment note, 21–060, 21–061
documentary credits, and, 23–227
and see **Documentary credits**
Hague-Visby Rules, 21–059
and see **Hague-Visby Rules**

Carriage by road—*cont.*
right of disposal, 21–062
and see **Right of disposal**
statutory provisions, 21–058
stoppage in transit, 21–064
and see **Stoppage in transit**
Carriage by sea
Carriage of Goods by Sea Act (1992)
bills of lading, 18–123—18–125, 18–135—18–139, 18–042—18–044
delivery orders, 18–175
multimodal transport documents, 18–175
paperless transactions, 18–202
sea waybills, 18–040, 18–153, 18–154
ship's delivery order, 18–189, 18–195
see also **Bills of lading**
c.i.f. contracts
see **C.I.F. contracts**
documentary credits, and, 23–224
and see **Documentary credits**
f.o.b. contracts
see **F.O.B. contracts**
Carriage of goods
carriers
contract of carriage, 8–015, 8–016
delivery, to, 8–014, 8–015
conflict of laws (contract)
choice of law, 25–072
closest country connection, 25–071
contract applicable law, 25–070, 25–071
place of business, 25–071
Rome Convention, 25–071
and see **Conflict of laws (contract)**
disposal of goods, 5–136
see also **Right of disposal**
frustration of contract
c.i.f. contracts, 6–043, 6–049
f.o.b. contracts, 6–049
lack of transport, 6–049
route closures, 6–049
and see **Frustration of contract**
international conventions
see **International conventions**
passing of property, and, 5–009
and see **Passing of property**
risk
c.i.f. contracts, 6–018
condition of goods, 6–019
delivery to carrier, 6–017, 6–019
f.o.b. contracts, 6–018
loss in transit, 6–020
notification of shipment, 6–021
overseas sales, 6–018
payment on arrival, 6–020
seller's responsibilities, 6–019
seller's risk, 6–022
and see **Risk**
Carriage of goods—*cont.*
sellers
responsibilities, 6–019
risk, 6–022
Carriers
acknowledgement to buyer, 15–077
attornment, by, 15–075
consent, of, 15–078
container transport
carriage on deck, 21–088—21–093
liability, 21–085—21–087, 21–091
and see **Container transport**
duties, of, 15–088
liability
carriage on deck, 21–088—21–093
damage in transit, 21–084
Hague Rules, 21–085, 21–086, 21–091
Hague-Visby Rules, 21–085, 21–087, 21–089, 21–092
loss in transit, 21–084
lien, 15–079, 15–089
and see **Lien**
part delivery, 15–084
refusal to deliver, 15–074, 15–083
stoppage in transit, 15–074, 15–083, 15–084
and see **Stoppage in transit**
Cash
payment, by, 9–028
and see **Payment**
Chain transactions
damages, recovery of, 4–015
effect, of, 4–014
seller's liability, 4–016
true owner, and, 4–014, 4–015
wrongful interference, 4–014
Chattels
contract for sale, and, 1–042, 1–043, 1–080
and see **Contract for sale**
personal chattels, 1–080
sale, distinguished, 1–042, 1–043
and see **Sale**
Cheque
payment, by, 9–034
and see **Payment**
Choice of law
see also **Conflict of laws (contract)**
agency contracts, 25–073
arbitration clauses, 25–030, 25–031
banking contracts, 25–076
consumer contracts, 25–044—25–047
contractual transactions, 25–001
express choice, 25–030
general principle, 25–029
habitual residence, and, 25–048, 25–052, 25–056
insurance contracts, 25–074, 25–075

Choice of law—*cont.*
limitations, 25–036
mandatory rules, 25–037—25–042
negotiable instruments, 25–077
proper law, 25–001, 25–005
proprietary transactions, 25–001
public policy, 25–043
retention of title, and, 25–145
and see **Retention of title**
Rome Convention
see **Rome Convention**
rules, as to, 25–001
sale of goods, 25–001, 25–003, 25–044, 25–046
subsequent conduct, 25–032
validity, 25–034
variation, 25–035
C.I.F contracts
acceptance, 19–153—19–157
and see **Acceptance**
appropriation of goods
appropriation to contract, 19–011, 19–015
notice, 19–017—19–023
payment of price, 19–082—19–084
timing, 19–016
bill of lading
alterations, 19–040
charterparties, 19–041
clean bills, 19–038
continuous documentary cover, 19–027—19–029
contract of affreightment, 19–025
destination provisions, 19–031
deviation clauses, 19–033
erasures, 19–040
freight prepaid, 19–039
genuine bill, 19–035
issued on shipment, 19–034
quantity of goods, 19–036
received bills, 19–030
rejection, of, 19–094
requirements, for, 19–026
seller's duty, as to, 19–025
shipment route, 19–032, 19–033
shipped bills, 19–030
transhipment, 19–028
valid and effective, 19–037
see also **Bills of lading**
bulk shipments, 18–301, 18–302, 18–304
and see **Bulk shipments**
buyers
choice of destination, 19–089
contractual duties, 19–089
dealing as consumer, 19–065, 19–071
payment of price, 19–075—19–089
see also **Buyer's remedies (c.i.f. contracts)**

C.I.F contracts —*cont.*
contract
antecedent contract, 19–097
conforming goods, 19–012, 19–065
non-conforming goods, 19–071
subject to shipment, 19–014
contractual relationships
antecedent contract, 19–097
bill of lading , and, 19–094—19–096
buyer as shipper, 19–093
carriers, 19–090, 19–095
continuous documentary cover, 19–094
contract variations, 19–095
original relationship, 19–090, 19–092, 19–097
seller as shipper, 19–091, 19–094
third parties, 19–092, 19–096
damages
actions, for, 19 -216—19–219
defective delivery, 19–187
market loss damages, 19–188, 19–190—19–196, 19–201—19–203
non-delivery, 19–175
and see **Damages**
delivery
complete, 19–072—19–074
duty, as to, 19–073
illegality, and, 19–072
impossibility, 19–072
provisional, 19–072
stages, of, 19–072
symbolic, 19–072
and see **Delivery**
demurrage, 19–088, 19–089
features
delivery of goods, 18–261, 19–002
delivery order, 19–003
destination provisions, 19–004, 19–031
essential features, 19–01
passing of property, 19–007
payment of price, 19–001, 19–006
tender of documents, 19–001, 19–002, 19–059
frustration of contract, 19–124—190–138
and see **Frustration of contract**
import duty, 19–088
insurance policy
affirmation, 19–042
"all risks" policy, 19–045
alternative documents, 19–048
amount of insurance, 19–051
assignment, 19–042, 19–052
bulk shipments, 19–048
carrier's breach, 19–050
certificate of insurance, 19–047, 19–048
continuous cover, 19–042, 19–043
contract of sale, and, 19–045

C.I.F contracts *—cont.*
insurance policy*—cont.*
deviation, effect of, 19–049, 19–050
duration of cover, 19–045
excluded risks, 19–046
extent of cover, 19–045
foreign policy, 19–044
requirement, for, 18–264
seller's obligations, 19–042
specified policy, 19–045
specified risks, 19–045
supplementary insurance, 19–052
tender of policy, 19–042, 19–043, 19–048
transhipment, 19–049
usual policy, 19–043
see also **Insurance**
invoice
contents, 19–054
form, of, 19–053
misstatements, 19–056
provisional invoice, 19–057
loss/deterioration of goods, 18–261
and see **Loss/deterioration of goods**
passing of property
appropriation, on, 19–100
ascertained goods, 19–098
contract, on, 19–098
dealings after shipment, 19–106
destroyed goods, 19–108
equitable title, 19–101
intention of parties, 19–098, 19–103
lost goods, 19–108
payment of price, 19–098, 19–103
performance of condition, 19–105
retention of property, 19–104
revesting of property, 19–109
shipment, and, 19–099, 19–107
transfer of documents, 19–102, 19–105, 19–106
unascertained goods, 19–098
and see **Passing of property**
payment of price
additional payments, 19–088
appropriation of goods, 19–082—19–084
conforming documents, 19–077—19–079
deterioration of goods, 19–084
examination of goods, and, 19–076
fraud, 19–078
fundamentally different goods, 19–078
loss in transit, 19–080
loss of goods, 19–080—19–082
method, 19–087
non-conforming goods, 19–077, 19–078
place of payment, 19–086
tender of documents, on, 19–075
timing, 19–085

C.I.F contracts *—cont.*
provisions
destination, 19–004
freight, 19–009
insurance, 19–009
payment of price, 19–001, 19–006
performance guarantee, 19–005
risk, as to, 19–006
rejection of goods
see **Rejection of goods**
repair of goods, 19–071
replacement of goods, 19–071
risk
bailment, and, 19–122
bulk shipments, 18–301, 18–302, 18–304
contractual provisions, 19–119
dealing as consumer, 19–123
delayed delivery, 19–121
deterioration, and, 19–111, 19–112, 19–118, 19–123
freight, payment of, 19–120
non-conforming goods, 19–111
notice to insure, 19–117
prior to shipment, 19–114
provisions, as to, 19–006
quality of goods, 19–111
reasonable contract, requirement for, 19–116, 19–123
shipment of goods, 19–110
subsequent deterioration, 19–111
total loss, 19–113
transit, in, 19–115—19–118, 19–123
unascertained goods, 19–113
and see **Risk**
sale
documents, of, 19–008
goods, of, 19–008
seller's duties
delivery of goods, 19–010
documentation, as to, 19–010, 19–024
shipment of goods, 19–010, 19–011
tender of document, 19–010
seller's remedies
see **Seller's remedies (c.i.f. contracts)**
shipment of goods
actual shipment, 19–011
buying goods afloat, 19–011
conforming goods, 19–012, 19–065
deviation, and, 19–035, 19–049, 19–050
passing of property, 19–099, 19–107
risk, and, 19–110
shipment period, 19–013
shipment route, 19–032, 19–033
transhipment, 19–028, 19–049
shipping documents
bill of lading, 19–024, 19–025
certificate of origin, 19–058

C.I.F contracts —*cont.*
shipping documents—*cont.*
inspection certificates, 19–024, 1–058
insurance policy, 19–024, 19–042
invoice, 19–024, 19–053
licences, 19–058
meaning, 19–058
performance guarantees, 19–024, 19–058
variations, in, 19–024
tender of documents
dealing as consumer, 19–065, 19–071
defective tender, 19–071
delivery, on, 19–072
duty, as to, 19–059
failure to tender, 19–06
payment of price, and, 19–075
place of tender, 19–069
recipients, 19–070
repudiation, and, 19–071
re-tender, 19–071
"string" of contracts, 19–067
timing, 19–060—19–064, 19–066, 19–068
waiver, and, 19–150—19–153
and see **Waiver**
CIM Uniform Rules
see also **Carriage by rail**
application, 21–065
consignment note, 21–066—21–068
container transport, 21–106
and see **Container transport**
modification of contract, 21–069, 21–070
"Click-wrap" contracts
acceptance, 2–012, 2–015
and see **Acceptance**
consumer protection, 14–053
and see **Consumer protection**
distance selling, and, 14–053
and see **Distance selling**
formation, 2–012, 2–015
see also **Formation of contract**
offer, 2–012, 2–015
and see **Offer**
terms, 2–012
CMR Convention
see also **Carriage by road**
application, 21–058
consignment note, 21–060, 21–061
container transport, 21–105
and see **Container transport**
right of disposal, 21–062, 21–063
and see **Right of disposal**
scope, 21–058, 21–059
Collateral contracts
breach, of, 10–013, 10–014
collateral warranty, 10–012, 10–013
consumer protection, and, 14–042
and see **Consumer contracts**

Collateral contracts—*cont.*
damages, 10–013
and see **Damages**
exemption clauses, 10–013, 13–016, 13–017
and see **Exemption clauses**
intermediate distributors, 14–063
and see **Intermediate distributors**
liability, for, 10–012, 10–013
manufacturers, 14–062
and see **Manufacturers**
misrepresentation, 10–013, 10–014, 12–002, 12–011
and see **Misrepresentation**
nature, of, 10–012
non-consensual transactions, 1–071
parties, to, 2–027
use, of, 10–013
Common law
agency, and, 3–002, 7–031
and see **Agency**
conditional sale agreements, 1–052
and see **Conditional sale agreements**
contract of sale, and, 1–031
and see **Contract of sale**
formation of contract, 2–021
and see **Formation of contract**
fraud, and, 3–008
and see **Fraud**
frustration of contract, 6–034
and see **Frustration of contract**
hire-purchase agreements, 1–019, 1–052
and see **Hire-purchase agreements**
implied terms, 1–031
and see **Implied terms**
misrepresentation, 3–008, 12–002
and see **Misrepresentation**
mistake, 3–011
and see **Mistake**
passing of property, 5–001, 5–030
and see **Passing of property**
resale price maintenance, 3–037
and see **Resale price maintenance**
sale by sample, 11–073
and see **Sale by sample**
transfer of title, 7–001
see also **Transfer of title (non-owners)**
Companies
administration orders
see **Administration orders**
company charges, 5–143, 5–144
contractual capacity, 2–043
disposal of goods
see **Right of disposal**
floating charges, 5–161, 5–162
insolvency, 3–049, 5–165
and see **Insolvency**

Companies—*cont.*
receivership, 5–165
retention of title, 5–162—5–165
and see **Retention of title**
Romalpa clauses
see ***Romalpa* clauses**
ultra vires doctrine, 2–043
voluntary liquidation, 3–049, 5–164
winding up, 3–049
Compensation payments
defect, knowledge of, 17–079
defence costs, 17–077
settlement out of court, 17–078
strangers, to, 17–075
"string" contracts, 17–081—17–085
sub-buyers, and, 17–076—17–078, 17–080—17–082, 17–084, 17–085
Competition law (European Union)
block exemptions, 3–041
direct application, 3–041
dominant position, abuse of, 3–041
effect, of, 3–041
free movement, 3–042
market share, 3–041
penalties, 3–041
scope, of, 3–041
undertakings, subject to, 3–041
vertical agreements, 3–041
Computer software
composite transactions, 1–086
implied terms
fitness for purpose, 1–086
quality, 1–086
licences, 1–086
"shrink-wrap" contracts, 2–012
and see **"Shrink-wrap" contracts**
supply of services, 1–086
Conditional sale agreements
common law, 1–052
consumer credit transactions, 14–147
and see **Consumer credit transactions**
hire-purchase agreements, 1–052
and see **Hire-purchase agreements**
instalment payments, 1–052
motor vehicles, 7–088—7–090, 7–100
and see **Motor vehicles**
nature, of, 1–052
quality, 1–052
statutory provisions, 1–052
title, 1–052
voidable title, and, 7–022
and see **Voidable title**
Conditions
breach of condition
condition precedent, 12–056
discharge, by, 10–027—10–030
failure of performance, 12–022
Conditions—*cont.*
breach of condition—*cont.*
fitness for purpose, and, 12–022
repudiation, and, 10–027, 10–028
satisfactory quality, and, 12–022
statutory limits, 12–024
statutory modification, 10–038
charterparties, 10–030
contracts for carriage, 10–031
see also **Carriage of goods**
conveyancing terminology, and, 10–026
examples, 10–037
intermediate terms, distinguished, 10–033, 10–035
and see **Intermediate terms**
meaning, 10–024, 10–026
modern practice, relating to, 10–027—10–028
performance, of, 10–025
promises, relating to, 10–025
role, of, 10–032
usage, 10–024, 10–026, 10–027, 10–037
warranty, distinguished, 10–029, 10–030
see also **Warranties**
Confirming houses
confirmed orders
no cancellation, 23–313
reimbursement, 23–313
contracts
buyer/confirming house, 23–311
buyer/seller, 23–314
classification, 23–308
defective goods, 23–315
legal nature, 23–308
remuneration, 23–308
seller/confirming house, 23–310
duties, 23–09
functions, 23–307—23–309
liabilities, 23–310—23–315
"merchanting", 23–308
Conflict of laws (contract)
ancillary contracts
agency contracts, 25–073
banking contracts, 25–076
carriage of goods, 25–070—25–072
contract applicable law, 25–069
insurance contracts, 25–074, 25–075
negotiable instruments, 25–077
remedies, 25–069
significance, of, 25–069
buyer's remedies
see **Buyer's remedies**
choice of law
arbitration clauses, 25–030, 25–031
consumer contracts, 25–044—25–047
contractual transactions, 25–001
express choice, 25–030

Conflict of laws (contract)—*cont.*
choice of law—*cont.*
habitual residence, 25–048, 25–052, 25–056
limitations, 25–036
mandatory rules, 25–037—25–042
proper law, 25–001, 25–005
proprietary transactions, 25–001
public policy, 25–043
rules, as to, 25–001
sale of goods, 25–001, 25–003, 25–044, 25–046
severability, 25–033
subsequent conduct, 25–032
validity, 25–034
variation, 25–035
see also **Rome Convention**
common law, and, 25–001, 25–005
consumer contracts
see **Unfair Terms in Consumer Contracts Regulations (2002)**
consumer protection
see **Consumer Protection (Distance Selling) Regulations (2000)**
contract of sale
see **Contract of sale (conflict of laws)**
contractual transactions
choice of law, 25–001
Contracts (Applicable Law) Act (1990), 25–001
proper law, 25–001, 25–005
goods, characterisation of, 25–004
procedure
see **Procedure**
proper law doctrine
see **Proper law doctrine**
proprietary issues
see **Conflict of laws (property)**
Rome Convention
see **Rome Convention**
seller's remedies
see **Seller's remedies**
terminology, 25–002
unfair contract terms
see **Unfair Contract Terms Act (1977)**
Conflict of laws (property)
choice of law, 25–001
goods in transit
documents issued, 25–139
documents not issued, 25–138
passing of title, 25–138, 25–139
goods not in transit
documents issued, 25–134—25–137
documents not issued, 25–129—25–133
lex situs, 25–129—25–131, 25–135
passing of title, 25–129

Conflict of laws (property)—*cont.*
goods not in transit—*cont.*
seller as non-owner, 25–131
seller as owner, 25–130
seller's powers, 25–129
insolvency
see **Insolvency**
lex situs
documents of title, 25–126
documents representing goods, 25–126
goods in transit, 25–123, 25–124
renvoi, 25–122
retention of title, 25–125
significance, 25–001, 25–121
transfer of title, 25–127
licences
see **Licences**
passing of property
buyer/seller, 25–132
documents issued, 25–136
goods in transit, 25–140
goods not in transit, 25–132, 25–133, 25–136, 25–137
governing law, 25–132, 25–133, 25–137
intention of parties, 25–133
lex situs, 25–133, 25–136, 25–140
and see **Passing of property**
passing of title
general rules, 25–128
goods in transit, 25–138, 25–139
goods not in transit, 25–129, 25–134
lex situs, 25–128—25–131, 25–135
procedure
see **Procedure**
retention of title
charge, creation of, 25–144
choice of law, 25–145
EC Directive (2000/35/EC), 25–153
effect, 25–142
extent of reservation, 25–143
governing law, 25–142
insolvency, and, 25–141
late payments, 25–153
lex situs, 25–142, 25–145, 25–147
proceeds of sale, 25–146, 25–147
remedies, 25–146
Romalpa clauses, 25–141, 25–144
seller's claims, 25–148
sub-purchasers, 25–148, 25–149
sub-sales, 25–147, 25–148
tracing, 25–146
validity, 25–142
and see **Retention of title**
risk, 25–154, 25–155
and see **Risk**
transfer of title
closest/real connection, 25–124
lex situs, and, 25–127

Conflict of laws (property)—*cont.*
transfer of title—*cont.*
proper law, 25–124
Consequential loss
f.o.b. contracts, 20–119, 20–138
and see **F.O.B. contracts**
price claims, and, 16–030
and see **Price claims**
resale, and, 17–037
and see **Resale**
seller's claim, 16–086
Consumer Credit Act (1974)
advertising controls, 14–155
application, 1–019
conditional sale agreements, 1–021, 14–147
and see **Conditional sale agreements**
contractual formalities, 2–023
see also **Formation of contract**
control provisions, 14–143—14–145
"cooling-off" period, 14–145
credit, meaning of, 1–022
credit sale agreements, 1–055
enforcement, 14–156
financial limits, 1–021, 14–144
hire-purchase, 14–147
individuals, 14–144
licensing, 14–146
partnerships, 14–144
restrictions, 14–145
scope, 1–021
Consumer credit transactions
see also **Consumer Credit Act (1974)**
advertising controls, 14–155
conditional sale agreements, 14–147
and see **Conditional sale agreements**
credit cards, 14–149
creditor's liability, 14–153, 14–154
credit sales, 14–148
foreign contracts, 14–155
four-party transactions, 14–155
hire-purchase, 14–147
implied terms, 14–152
and see **Implied terms**
unfair relationships, 14–151
Consumer protection
administrative protection
see **Administrative protection**
breach of statutory duty
Consumer Protection Act (1987), 14–095
illegality, and, 14–097
rights directly conferred, 14–094
rights indirectly conferred, 14–096
buyer's rights
conformity with description, 14–009, 14–012
Consumer protection—*cont.*
buyer's rights—*cont.*
intermediate distributor, against, 14–061, 14–063
late delivery, 14–006
manufacturers, against, 14–061
non-delivery, 14–005
quality of goods, 14–008, 14–010
title, 14–007
unordered goods, 14–004
cancellation of contract, 2–020
civil law, and, 14–003, 14–004
codes of practice, 14–137
collateral contracts, 14–042
conformity with contract
awareness, of, 14–014
labelling, 14–014
packaging, 14–014
presumption, as to, 14–012—14–015
satisfactory quality, 14–014
strict liability, 14–017
time limits, 14–015, 14–016
consumer
definition of, 14–001
rights, of, 14–003, 14–004
consumer credit transactions
see **Consumer credit transactions**
Consumer Protection Act (1987), 14–080—14–095
and see **Consumer Protection Act (1987)**
Consumer Sales Directive (1999/44/EC), 14–008, 14–011, 14–013—14–015, 14–070
and see **Consumer Sales Directive (1999/44/EC)**
contract law, and, 14–002, 14–018, 14–019
"cooling-off" period, 14–045, 14–057
criminal law, and, 14–003, 14–108—14–118
and see **Criminal law**
dealing as consumer, 14–008, 14–010, 14–011
defective goods, 12–127, 14–020—14–022
and see **Defective goods**
description of goods
conformity, with, 14–009, 14–012
strict liability, 14–017
development, of, 14–001
distance selling, 1–023, 2–014, 14–053—14–055
and see **Distance selling**
door-step sales, 14–045
economic interests, 13–105
electronic commerce, 1–023, 14–060
Electronic Commerce Directive (2000/37/EC), 14–060
and see **Electronic Commerce Directive (2000/37/EC)**
enforcement, 14–003

Consumer protection—*cont.*
exemption clauses, and, 4–019, 13–003, 14–029
and see **Exemption clauses**
extended warranties, 14–042, 14–043
fitness for purpose
reasonable fitness, 14–010, 14–013
strict liability, 14–017
goods
conformity with contract, 14–012—14–016
consumer goods, 13–078
defective goods, 12–127, 14–020
description of goods, 14–009, 14–012
express warranties, as to, 14–014
fitness for purpose, 14–010, 14–012, 14–013
public statements, as to, 14–012, 14–014
supply of goods, 14–046, 14–047
hire-purchase transactions, 14–044
improvements, allowances for, 14–007
indirect protection
advertising control, 14–140
labelling regulations, 14–140
packing regulations, 14–140
statutory provisions, 14–140—14–142
trading practices, 14–141
inertia selling, 14–004
intermediate distributors
see **Intermediate distributors**
internet payments, 9–036
see also **Internet**
late payments, 1–023
manufacturers
see **Manufacturers**
minimum requirements, 14–008
non-buyer's rights
contractual remedies, 14–077
defective products, 14–076, 14–079
implied warranty, 14–078
product liability, 14–078
tortious remedies, 14–076
USA position, 14–078
privity of contract, 14–018, 14–019
product liability, 1–023
quality of goods
appearance and finish, 14–010
brand names, 14–010
Consumer Sales Directive (1999/44/EC), 14–008
durability, 14–010
fitness for purpose, and, 14–010
implied obligations, 14–008
minor defects, 14–010
safety, and, 14–010
Sale and Supply of Goods to Consumers Regulations (2002), 14–008
satisfactory quality, 14–010

Consumer protection—*cont.*
quality of goods—*cont.*
strict liability, 14–017
and see **Quality of goods**
remedies
Consumer Sales Directive (1999/44/EC), 14–023
damages, 14–020, 14–023
price reduction, 14–024
rejection of goods, 14–020—14–023
remedial action, 14–022, 14–023
repair of goods, 14–021, 14–023—14–025
replacement of goods, 14–022—14–025
rescission, 14–024
statutory provisions, 13–077, 13–078
see also **Consumer remedies**
representations
effect, of, 14–041
fraudulent, 14–041
negligence, and, 14–041
statutory provisions, 14–041
seller's guarantees, 14–042
statutory protection, 14–001
supply of goods
contracts, for, 14–046
implied conditions, 14–047
quality of goods, 14–047
unfair contract terms, 14–047
supply of services
care and skill, 14–051
contracts, for, 14–050
delays, 14–052A
express terms, 14–051
implied terms, 14–051
installation of goods, 14–051
package holidays, 14–050
professional services, 14–050
reasonable charge, 14–052A
unfair contract terms, 14–052A
third parties, 14–019
title
breach of condition, 14–007
nemo dat quod non habet, 14–007
passing of property, 14–007
tort law, and, 14–002
see also **Tortious liability**
trade practices
see **Trade practices**
unfair contract terms, 1–23, 14–036—14–038
Unfair Contract Terms Act (1977), 14–029, 25–090
and see **Unfair Contract Terms Act (1977)**
Unfair Terms in Consumer Contract Regulations (1999), 14–030—14–032, 14–037
and see **Unfair Terms in Consumer Contract Regulations (1999)**

Consumer Protection Act (1987)
background, 14–080
causation, 14–091
damage, covered by, 14–087
defect
meaning of, 14–084, 14–085
nature, of, 14–086
defences, 14–088—14–090
development risk, 14–089
EC Directive (1985/374/EC), 14–080, 14–081
effect, of, 14–093
exemption clauses, 13–104
and see **Exemption clauses**
liability, under, 14–083
limitation period, 14–092
loss, covered by, 14–087
products, covered by, 14–082
remoteness of damage, 14–091
right of action, 14–095
strict liability, 14–088, 14–091
subsequent products, 14–090
Consumer Protection (Distance Selling) Regulations (2000)
see also **Distance selling**
choice of law
closest country connection, 25–109, 25–110
EU Member States, 25–108
non-Member States, 25–109
and see **Choice of law**
consumer protection, 25–107
and see **Consumer Protection**
purpose, 25–107
Consumer remedies
see also **Consumer protection**
advice, 14–099, 14–137
arbitration, 14–100
civil litigation, 14–102
Civil Procedure Rules (CPR), 14–104
class actions, 14–103
compensation agreements, 14–106, 14–107
complaints, 14–099
conditional fee agreements, 14–105
damages, 17–003
see also **Buyer's remedies (damages)**
group actions, 14–103, 14–104
importance, of, 14–098
small claims proceedings, 14–101
Consumer sales
acceptance, effect of, 12–112
advertising, 25–048, 25–051
bailment, and, 6–032
and see **Bailment**
Consumer Sales Directive (1999/44/EC), 12–071, 14–008, 14–011
and see **Consumer Sales Directive (1999/44/EC)**

Consumer sales—*cont.*
contracts
applicable law, 25–067
choice of law, 25–044—25–047
consumer protection, 25–044—25–047
mandatory rules, affecting, 25–054, 25–055
supply of goods, 25–045
supply of services, 25–045
damages, 12–071, 12–086, 17–003
see also **Buyer's remedies (damages)**
dealing as consumer
agency, and, 13–080
burden of proof, 13–082
businesses, 13–072—13–074, 13–081
buyer's remedies, 19–144, 19–203
course of business, 13–075, 13–076, 13–080
definition, 13–072, 13–077, 13–079
goods, restrictions as to, 13–081
overseas sales, 18–259
provisions, relating to, 12–072, 12–073, 13–071
rejection of goods, 19–145, 19–150
remedies, 13–071, 13–077—13–079, 13–081
sale of goods provisions, 13–083, 13–084
defective installation, 12–116
defective quality, 17–048, 17–050
and see **Defective quality**
disconformity, presumption as to, 12–075, 12–087, 12–117, 13–064
exemption clauses, and, 4–019, 13–003, 14–029
and see **Exemption clauses**
force majeure, and, 8–105
and see Force majeure
freedom of contract, 1–014
and see **Freedom of contract**
goods
conformity with contract, 12–071, 12–115, 12–118, 12–071
conformity with description, 11–001
defective goods, 12–001, 12–071
delivery, 5–098, 6–025, 8–014, 19–206
examination of goods, 12–043
loss/deterioration of goods, 18–260—18–264
loss of use, 12–086
non-conforming goods, 12–072, 12–074, 12–080, 12–115, 12–118, 19–206
non-delivery, 12–071
reduction in price, 12–077, 19–203
rejection, of, 12–077, 12–078, 12–090
repair, of, 12–076—12–079, 12–081, 19–150, 19–203, 19–206

Consumer sales—*cont.*
goods—*cont.*
replacement, of, 12–076—12–079, 19–150, 19–203, 19–206
instalment sales, 12–099, 12–118
intermediate terms, 10–036
and see **Intermediate terms**
internet
on-line contracts, 25–049—25–052
payments, 9–036
sales, 25–049—25–052
see also **Internet**
loss/deterioration of goods
c.i.f. contracts, 18–261
consumer fault, 18–263
contrary agreements, 18–264
dealing as consumer, 18–259
delayed delivery, 18–263
delivery of goods, 18–260—18–263
f.o.b. contracts, 18–262
seller's risk, 18–260—18–264
and see **Loss/deterioration of goods**
market loss, and, 19–203
passing of property, 6–013, 6–014, 6–016
and see **Passing of property**
payment, 9–026
and see **Payment**
price claims, and, 16–002
and see **Price claims**
quality of goods
public statements, 11–033, 11–034, 12–071
satisfactory quality, 11–033
and see **Quality of goods**
reasonableness, 13–079, 13–084
reduction in price
amount, of, 12–093
comparative legal systems, 12–091
damages, 12–094
defective goods, 12–091, 12–092
defective quality, 12–091
excess payment, 12–092
remedy, as, 12–089, 12–090
statutory provisions, 12–088, 12–091
rejection of contract, 12–071
and see **Rejection of contract**
remedies
buyer's remedies, 17–094, 19–203
common law, 12–071
criteria, for, 12–073
dealing as consumer, 12–073, 13–071, 13–077—13–079, 13–081
defective goods, 12–071
reduction in price, 12–089, 12–090
repair of goods, 12–076—12–081
replacement of goods, 12–076—12–081

Consumer sales—*cont.*
remedies—*cont.*
Sale of Goods Act (1979), 13.064, 13–071, 13–083
scope, of, 12–071
specialised remedies, 12–071
specific performance, 17–101, 17–103
statutory provisions, 12–001, 12–071, 12–072, 12–075
summary, of, 12–072
and see **Remedies**
repair of goods
buyer's cooperation, 12–083
duty, as to, 12–081, 12–087
enforcement, and, 12–084
loss of use, 12–086
meaning, 12–081
provisions, relating to, 12–076—12–079
reasonable time, for, 12–110, 12–118
risk, and, 12–085
replacement of goods
buyer's cooperation, 12–083
damages, 12–086
duty, as to, 12–087
enforcement, 12–084
loss of use, 12–086
meaning, 12–082
provisions, relating to, 12–076—12–079
reasonable time, for, 12–110, 12–118
risk, 12–085
rescission. 12–077, 12–089, 12–090, 12–118, 19–203
and see **Rescission**
Sale of Goods Act (1979)
buyer's rights, A-021
court's powers, A-023
implied terms, A-009
performance of contract, A-014
rescission of contract, A-022
reduction of price, A-022
repair of goods, A-022
replacement of goods, A-022
and see **Sale of Goods Act (1979)**
specific performance, and, 12–071, 17–101, 17–103
and see **Specific performance**
statutory provisions, 1–001, 1–006, 12–088, 12–095, 12–097
Vienna Convention, and, 12–071, 12–077, 12–093, 12–100, 12–101

Consumer Sales Directive (1999/44/EC)
see also **Consumer sales**
binding nature, 14–028
business activity, under, 14–011
buyer's inactivity, 12–109
buyer's rights, 12–071, 12–077
choice of law clauses, 14–028
compliance, with, 14–011

Consumer Sales Directive (1999/44/EC)—*cont.*
consumers, under, 13–077, 14–008, 14–011, 14–071
contracting-out, 12–117
defective installation, 12–116
effect, of, 12–071
goods
conformity with contract, 12–071, 12–074, 14–013—14–015
consumer goods, 13–078, 14–011
defective goods, 12–071
public statements, 12–071
quality of goods, 14–008
repair, of, 12–077, 12–111
replacement, of, 12–077, 12–111
implementation, 14–070
manufacturers' guarantees, 14–066, 14–070, 14–073—14–075
see also **Manufacturers**
minimum requirements, 14–008
protection, 13–078
rescission, and, 14–024, 14–06
and see **Rescission**
sellers, under, 14–011
time limits, 12–107
Container transport
carriage on deck
fundamental terms, 21–090
Hague Rules, 21–091
Hague-Visby Rules, 21–089, 21–092
legal consequences, 21–088
special factors, affecting, 21–093
unauthorised carriage, 21–092, 21–093
carrier's liability
carriage on deck, 21–088—21–093
damage in transit, 21–084
Hague Rules, 21–085, 21–086, 21–091
Hague-Visby Rules, 21–085, 21–087, 21–089, 21–092
loss in transit, 21–084
package limitation, 21–085—21–087, 21–091
unit limitation, 21–085—21–087, 21–091
forms, of, 21–072
liabilities, 21–073, 21–074
mixed terms
CIM Uniform Rules, 21–106
CMR Convention, 21–105
Hague Rules, 21–104, 21–106
Hague-Visby Rules, 21–104, 21–106
provisions, for, 21–104—21 -106
multimodal transport document
see **Multimodal transport document**
problems, associated with, 21–073
sale terms
common sale terms, 21–094
dealing as consumer, 21–099, 21–100, 21–102
Container transport—*cont.*
sale terms—*cont.*
delivery, 21–099, 21–100, 21–102
examination of goods, 21–102
notice to insure, 21–101
passing of property, 21–098
rescission, 21–102
risk, 21–100, 21–101
shipping date, 21–096
shipping documents, 21–095
shipping instructions, 21–097
stoppage in transit, 21–103
Contract
see **Contract of sale**
Contract for services
sale, distinguished, 1–041, 1–046
and see **Sale**
Contract for work
sale, distinguished, 1–041—1–043, 1–046, 1–047
and see **Sale**
Contract of sale
see also **Formation of contract**
absolute contracts, 1–109
agreement to sell, and, 1–026
analogous transactions, 1–030, 1–031
assignment of rights, 3–043
and see **Assignment**
bankruptcy, and, 3–045, 3–046
and see **Bankruptcy**
bargaining power, 14–001
caveat emptor, 14–001
chattels, and, 1–042, 1–043, 1–080
and see **Chattels**
choice of law, 25–162, 25–164, 25–165
see also **Contract of sale (conflict of laws)**
common law rules, 1–031
components
skill component, 1–047
work component, 1–047
conditional contracts, 1–051, 1–109
see also **Conditional sale agreements**
conditional purchase, 1–052
conflict of laws
see **Contract of sale (conflict of laws)**
contractual principles, 3–001
crops, 1–093
and see **Crops**
definition, 4–001
discharge of contract
applicable law, 25–173—25–177
frustration of contract, 25–175, 25–176
general principles, 25–173
performance, by, 25–174
restitution, and, 25–176

Contract of sale—*cont.*
distinctions
agency contracts, 1–048
barter, 1–034—1–036
components, 1–047
contract for services, 1–041, 1–046
contract for work, 1–041—1–043, 1–046, 1–047
exchange, 1–034—1–036
free offers, 1–033
gifts, 1–032
independent services, 1–046
option to buy, 1–050
supply of materials, 1–041, 1–043—1–045
trading-in, 1–039
duress, 3–010
EC legislation, effect of. 1–023
elements, of, 1–030
fraud, 3–008
and see **Fraud**
goods
see **Goods**
governing law, 25–161
illegality, 3–027—3–042, 17–095
and see **Illegality**
implied undertakings, 25–171
insolvency, and, 3–046, 3–048
and see **Insolvency**
intellectual property rights, 1–077
intention of parties, 14–001
invalidating causes
frustration, 17–095
illegality, 17–095
misrepresentation, 17–095
mistake, 17–095
late payment, 25–162—25–164
misrepresentation, 3–008, 17–095
and see **Misrepresentation**
mistake, 3–011, 17–095
and see **Mistake**
money of account, 25–165
money of payment, 25–167
nature, of, 1–025, 1–030, 1–042
nominalism, 25–166
non-consensual transactions, 1–067—1–076
and see **Non-consensual transactions**
ownership
see **Ownership**
parties
death, of, 3–050
passing of property
see **Passing of property**
payment of price
ascertainment of amount, 25–161
contract applicable law, 25–161, 25–162
late payment, 25–162—25–164

Contract of sale—*cont.*
payment of price—*cont.*
place, 25–161
timing, 25–161
protection, under, 14–001
see also **Consumer protection**
sale, meaning of, 1–025, 1–027
and see **Sale**
statutory definition, 1–025
statutory rules, 1–031
subject matter
chattels, 1–080
goods, 1–078, 1–079
substance, 1–030, 1–042
undue influence, 3–010
Contract of sale (conflict of laws)
see also **Contract of sale**
choice of law, 25–156, 25–162, 25–164, 25–165
and see **Choice of law**
contract applicable law, 25–156—25–159, 25–161—25–162, 25–168, 25–169
delivery, 25–157—25–158
description of goods, 25–169
discharge of contract, 25–173—25–177
exchange controls
Bretton Woods Agreement, 25–120
contract applicable law, 25–120
governing law, 25–120
place of performance, 25–120
Rome Convention, 25–120
express terms, 25–169
formation
agency, and, 25–081, 25–082
capacity, 25–084, 25–085
contractual imbalance, 25–088
corporate capacity, 25–085
determining laws, 25–078
formalities, 25–086, 25–087
lex fori, 25–087, 25–088
lex loci contractus, 25–086
minimum acts, 25–079
putative proper law, 25–079, 25–080
Rome Convention, 25–078, 25–079, 25–082, 25–087
third parties, 25–081, 25–082
vitiating elements, 25–083
see also **Formation of contract**
governing law, 25–156, 25–161
Guiliano—Lagarde Report, 25–156
implied undertakings, 25–170, 25–171
legality
common law, 25–119
contract applicable law, 25–119
criminal offences, 25–119
governing law, 25–119
public policy, 25–119
Ralli Bros Case, 25–119

Contract of sale (conflict of laws)—*cont.*
legality—*cont.*
Rome Convention, 25–119
lex fori, 25–156
lex loci solutionis, 25–156, 25–157
lex pecuniae, 25–166
licences, 25–168
and see **Licences**
money of account, 25–165, 25–166
nominalism, 25–166
passing of title, 25–159—25–160
payment
late payments, 25–162—25–164
money of payment, 25–167
price, 25–161—25–167
quality of goods, 25–169
remedies, 25–172
Rome Convention, 25–078, 25–079, 25–082, 25–087, 25–119, 25–156
and see **Rome Convention**
Unfair Contract Terms Act (1977), 25–160
and see **Unfair Contract Terms Act (1977)**
validity
determining laws, 25–078
essential validity, 25–089
Rome Convention, 25–078
statutory effect, 25–089
Correspondent banker
see also **Documentary credits**
acceptance of documents
faulty tender, 23–184
indemnities, 23–184
reserve, under, 23–184
accounting for profits, 23–180
adherence to mandate, 23–177
contractual position
advising banker, 23–183, 23–184
buyer, 23–185
issuing banker, 23–174, 23–175
seller, 23–181, 23–182
fraudulent documents, 23–176
legal position, 23–174
right of recourse, 23–178, 23–179
role, of, 23–173, 23–181
Course of business
customary, 7–032, 7–043
ordinary, 7–041, 7–043, 7–044
sale, during, 11–027, 11–029, 11–070
Credit
bills/notes, relating to, 9–063
conditional, 9–063
credit periods, 9–062, 9–063
credit sales, 9–061—9–063, 14–148
entitlement, 9–063
instalment payments, 9–065
meaning, of, 1–022
no credit allowed, 9–067
revolving credit, 9–066
Credit card
payment, by, 9–033
and see **Payment**
protection, 14–150
transactions, 23–103—23–105
Credit sale agreements
definition, 1–055
instalment payments, 1–055
statutory controls, 1–055
Criminal law
consumer protection
Consumer Protection Act (1987), 14–108, 14–109, 14–114—14–117, 14–124
Food Safety Act (1990), 14–110
misleading prices, 14–124
safety provisions, 14–115, 14–116
Trade Descriptions Act (1968), 14–112, 14–113
Weights and Measures Act (1985), 14–111
and see **Consumer protection**
enforcement, by, 14–108
forfeiture of goods, 14–118
notices
prohibition, 14–117
suspension, 14–118
warning, 14–117
passing of property, and, 5–013
and see **Passing of property**
safety
product safety, 14–119, 14–123
regulations, 14–115
requirements, 14–115, 14–116
see also **General Product Safety Regulations (2005)**
statutory regulation, 14–108, 14–109
strict liability, 14–108
Crops
chattels, as, 1–093
and see **Chattels**
contract of sale, 1–093, 1–094
and see **Contract of sale**
emblements, 1–093
fructus industriales, 1–093, 1–094
fructus naturales, 1–093
goods, as, 1–093
and see **Goods**
Statute of Frauds (1677), 1–093
transfer of land, 1–094

Damages
acceptance of goods
delivery time, and, 16–073
no time fixed, 16–072
see also **Acceptance**
actions
anticipatory breach, 19–217, 20–116, 20–140

Damages—*cont.*
actions—*cont.*
consequential loss, 20–119
defective delivery, 19–021, 20–118
market rule, 19–216, 20–116, 20–123
mitigation, 20–116
non-acceptance, for, 19–216, 19–218, 20–123, 20–137, 20–138
refusal of delivery, 19–219, 20–116, 20–139
shipment of goods, 20–134, 20–135
amenity, loss of, 16–048
anticipatory breach, for, 9–013, 9–015, 16–080, 19–179, 20–116
anticipatory repudiation, 16–081, 16–082
assessment of damages
available market, and, 16–062
defective delivery, 19–201
f.o.b. contracts, 20–114, 20–116, 20–117, 20–123, 20–136
market price, and, 16–062, 16–071, 16–072, 19–175
non-acceptance, for, 16–061
non-delivery, 17–002, 19–177, 19–180—19–183
available market
absence, of, 16–077—16–079
availability, 16–066, 16–067
"black" market, 16–069
fixed retail price, 16–064, 16–065
loss of profits, 16–079
market area, 16–068
market price, 16–062, 16–071
market size, 16–069
meaning, of, 16–066, 16–068
measure of damages, 16–062
price indicators, 16–069
relevant market, 16–070
resale, and, 16–075, 16–078, 16–079
test, for, 6–063
breach of contract
breach of term, 12–017, 12–021
forfeiture of payments, 16–038, 16–039
invoicing back clauses, 16–037
limitation clauses, 16–036
liquidated damages, 16–032
loss of chance, 16–050
multiple breach, 16–034
pre-estimate of damage, 16–032, 16–033
single sum payable, 16–034
unfair terms, 16–041
buyer's claim
breach of condition, 4–006
breach of warranty, 4–009
conversion, for, 4–012
hire-purchase goods, 4–017
wrongful interference, 4–012, 4–013

Damages—*cont.*
see also **Buyer's remedies (damages)**
causation, 16–049
collateral contracts, relating to, 10–013
and see **Collateral contracts**
consequential loss, 20–119, 20–138
consumer sales, 12–071
and see **Consumer sales**
contributory negligence, 16–051
conversion, for, 16–089
credit agreements, 16–042
defective delivery
assessment of damages, 19–201
breach of contract, 19–199
breach of intermediate term, 19–187
breach of warranty, 19–187, 19–194
deceit, and, 19–200
defective documents, 19–187, 19–190, 19–191, 19–193, 19–197, 19–198
defective goods, 19–187, 19–189, 19–190, 19–193, 19–197
f.o.b. contracts, 20–118
market loss, 19–188, 19–190—19–192, 19–194—19–196, 19–201, 19–202
market movements, and, 19–199
market value, 19–188, 19–189, 19–198
misrepresentation, and, 19–200
quality of goods, 19–187
freight charges, and, 20–138
insurance charges, and, 20–138
limitation clauses, 16–036
loss of chance, 16–050
market loss, 19–188, 19–190—19–196, 19–201—19–023
market price
assessment of damages, 16–062, 16–071, 16–072
available market, and, 16–062, 16–071
buying price, 16–074
non-delivery, and, 19–175
proof, of, 16–074
resale, and, 16–075, 16–076
selling price, 16–074
misrepresentation, for, 12–002, 12–004, 12–010, 12–011, 12–015
and see **Misrepresentation**
mitigation
anticipatory repudiation, 16–081
avoidable loss, 16–052, 16–056
avoided losses, 16–056
debt claims, 16–059
expenses incurred, 16–058
impecunious claimant, 16–054, 16–055
losses incurred, 16–058
market price, and, 16–062
mitigating action, 16–053
redeployment of resources, 16–057

Damages—*cont.*
mitigation—*cont.*
timing, 16–053
non-acceptance, for, 9–011, 9–013, 16–060, 16–061
non-delivery
anticipatory breach, 19–179
appropriation to contract, 19–180
assessment, 19–177, 19–180—19–183
contract price, 19–175
delivery period, 19–182
market price, 19–175
market rule, 19–175—19–177
market value, 1–177
relevant market, 19–186
similar goods, purchase of, 19–184
statutory provisions, 17–001, 17–002, 19–175
tender of documents, 19–178, 19–180, 19–185
timing considerations, 19–177, 19–178, 19–180—19–183
non-pecuniary losses, 16–047
penalties
breach of contract, 16–032
legal scope, 16–035
quantum of damages, 9–014, 9–020
remoteness of damage
see **Remoteness of damage**
resale price, and, 20–137
seller's claim
anticipatory breach, 16–080—16–082
assessment of damages, 16–031
available market, and, 16–063—16–068
breach of contract, 16–031, 16–032
compensatory nature, 16–031
consequential loss, 16–086
conversion, for, 16–089
expenses, for, 16–086, 16–087
fixed retail price, 16–064, 16–065
incidental losses, 16–086
loss of profits, 16–085
market price, and, 16–062, 16–071, 16–072
non-acceptance, 16–060, 16–061, 16–071
reselling expenses, 16–087
storage charges, 16–088
see also **Seller's remedies**
special cases
bills of exchange, 16–084
contracts of carriage, 16–084
documentary credits, 16–084
statutory resale, 16–083
statements, relating to, 10–010
and see **Statements**
tortious liability, 12–012, 12–015
and see **Tortious liability**

Damages—*cont.*
unfair contract terms, and, 16–041
see also **Unfair Contract Terms Act (1977)**
warranty, breach of, 10–023
see also **Warranties**
Deceit
defective delivery, 19–200
liability, for, 12–012, 12–016
Defective goods
acceptance of goods, 14–021, 14–027
breach of contract, 12–001
consumer protection, 14–020—14–022
and see **Consumer protection**
consumer sales, 12–001, 12–071, 12–091, 12–092
and see **Consumer sales**
damages, for, 14–020
delivery, and, 14–024, 17–043
see also **Delivery**
description, conformity with, 11–003
and see **Description**
EC legislation, 12–001
fitness for purpose
see **Fitness for purpose**
known defects, 11–041
latent defects, 11–080, 13–089
liability, for, 14–061
misrepresentation, 12–001
and see **Misrepresentation**
mitigation of damages, 14–022
quality
see **Defective quality**
rectification, 12–054
reduction in price, 12–091, 12–092
rejection of contract, 12–059, 12–067
rejection of goods, 14–020—14–022
remedial action, 14–022
remedies, 12–001, 12–071, 14–020, 14–021
and see **Remedies**
repair of goods, 12–054, 14–021
replacement of goods, 14–022
re-tender, 14–022
risk, 12–059
and see **Risk**
subsequent deterioration, 12–075
tortious liability, 12–001, 12–121, 12–124, 12–127
and see **Tortious liability**
waiver, and, 12–034, 12–035
and see **Waiver**
Defective quality
see also **Quality of goods**
action for price, 17–049
breach of warranty, 17–049
buyer's remedies
see **Buyer's remedies (damages)**

Defective quality—*cont.*
compensation payments, 17–075—17–081
and see **Compensation payments**
consumer sales, 17–048, 17–050
and see **Consumer sales**
damage
goods, to, 17–073
property, to, 17–074
diminution in value, 17–051—17–058
discovery
discovery on use, 17–061
examination of goods, 17–060
failure to discover, 17–060
expenditure
defence costs, 17–077
expenses, 17–062, 17–070
fines, 17–065
recovery, of, 17–062—17–064
wasted expenditure, 17–062—17–064, 17–070
Hadley v Baxendale, 17–047
knowledge
actual knowledge, 17–059, 17–060
imputed knowledge, 17–060
loss
amenity, 17–071
custom, 17–069
profits, 17–066—17–070
non-conforming goods, 17–048, 17–050
physical injury, and, 17–072
price reduction, 17–050
profit-earning warranty, 17–067
remedial costs, 17–055
remedies, 17–048, 17–050
and see **Remedies**
repeat orders, 17–069
settlement out of court, 17–078
statutory provisions, 17–047, 17–048
sub-contract, performance of, 17–057, 17–058
substitute goods, 17–056

Delayed delivery
see also **Delivery**
acceptance of goods, 17–038
consumer sales, 6–025, 18–263
and see **Consumer sales**
damages, for, 17–038
defective goods, 17–043
effect, of, 6–023
expenditure
extra expense, 17–046
wasted expense, 17–046
limited liability, 17–042
loss
loss/deterioration of goods, 18–258
loss of custom, 17–043
profits, 17–040—17–042
resulting loss, 6–023, 6–024

Delayed delivery—*cont.*
machine parts, 17–041
market
market price, 17–039
market value, 17–038, 17–039
no available market, 17–038
repeat orders, 17–043
resale, and, 17–044, 17–045
and see **Resale**
risk
c.i.f. contracts, 19–121
transfer of risk, 6–024
and see **Risk**

Delivery
acceptance, and, 9–003—9–010
and see **Acceptance**
appropriation, and, 5–099, 5–100
and see **Appropriation**
bailee, to, 5–098
see also **Bailment**
bulk goods
co-owner's consent, 8–017
statutory provisions, 8–017
undivided share, 8–017
and see **Bulk goods**
buyer, to, 5–097, 5–101
carrier, to, 5–098, 5–100, 5–101, 8–014, 8–015
consumer sales, 5–098, 6–025, 8–014
and see **Consumer sales**
contract of carriage, 8–015, 8–016
see also **Carriage of goods**
defective delivery
assessment of damages, 19–201
breach of contract, 19–199
breach of intermediate term, 19–187
breach of warranty, 19–187, 19–194
deceit, and, 19–200
defective documents, 19–187, 19–190, 19–191, 19–193, 19–197, 19–198
defective goods, 19–187, 19–189, 19–190, 19–193, 19–197
market loss, 19–188, 19–190—19–192, 19–194—19–196, 19–201, 19–202
market movements, and, 19–199
market value, 19–188, 19–189, 19–198
misrepresentation, and, 19–200
quality of goods, 19–187
delay
consumer sales, 6–025
effect, of, 6–023
loss, resulting from, 6–023, 6–024
transfer of risk, 6–024
see also **Delayed delivery**
document of title
issue, of, 8–013
transfer, of, 8–013
and see **Document of title**

Delivery—*cont.*
early delivery, 8–043
exemption clauses, 8–063, 8–088, 8–101
and see **Exemption clauses**
expenses, 8–005
force majeure, 8–088
and see Force majeure
goods
contract description, 8–003
identification, 5–099
mixed goods, 12–060
possession, of, 8–004
similar goods, 8–003
specific goods, 8–003
unascertained goods, 8–003
and see **Goods**
instalments
see **Instalment deliveries**
insurance, and, 8–016
intention of parties, 5–101
late delivery, 8–028, 8–042
meaning, 8–002, 8–017
methods
agreement, as to, 8–007
carrier, to, 8–014, 8–015
contract of carriage, 8–015, 8–016
buyer in possession, 8–011
document of title, issue of, 8–013
licence to remove, 8–010
seller as bailee, 8–009
symbolic delivery, 8–008
third party in possession, 8–012
non-delivery, 17–001
see also **Buyer's remedies (damages)**
passing of property, 5–097—5–102
and see **Passing of property**
payment
possession, and, 8–004
timing, 8–004
place of delivery
agreement, as to, 8–018, 8–019
common law presumption, 8–018
licence to enter, 8–022
licence to remove, 8–022
option, as to, 8–020
overseas transactions, 8–021
place of business, 8–019, 8–023
residence, 8–019
specific goods, 8–019
unascertained goods, 8–019
wrong place, 8–024
quantity of goods
de minimis rule, 12–030
excessive quantity, 8–049, 8–051, 12–029, 12–030
insufficient delivery, 8–046—8–048, 8–052, 12–029, 12–030

Delivery—*cont.*
quantity of goods—*cont.*
repudiation, and, 12–029
slight shortfall, 12–030
see also **Quantity of goods (delivery)**
request, on, 8–039
risk, and, 6–023—6–025
and see **Risk**
Sale of Goods Act (1979), A-014, A-016
and see **Sale of Goods Act (1979)**
seller's breach
breach of condition, 8–006
repudiation, 8–006
seller's duty
contract terms, 8–001
delivery of goods, 8–001
short delivery, 12–069
special terms, 5–102
statutory provisions, 5–096
timing
see **Timing of delivery**
unascertained goods, 5–099
and see **Unascertained goods**
Delivery orders
see also **Document of title**
attornment, and, 18–174, 18–194
bulk cargoes, 18–169, 18–194, 18–303, 18–304
contractual effects
attornment, 18–174
estoppel, 18–174
intention of parties, 18–173
nature of agreement, 18–173
remedies, 18–173
contractual rights
Carriage of Goods by Sea Act (1992), 18–175
ship's delivery orders, 18–175
transfer, of, 18–175
definition, 18–170
dock warrants, 18–198
document of title
common law sense, 18–193
mercantile custom, 18–193, 18–201
statutory sense, 18–196, 18–197, 18–201
and see **Document of title**
identified deliveree, 18–182
legal problems, 18–169
passing of property, 18–194
and see **Passing of property**
risk, 18–303, 18–304
and see **Risk**
ship's delivery order
see **Ship's delivery order**
use, of, 18–169
warehouse warrants, 18–193, 18–198

Description
absence, of, 11–011
breach of condition, 11–001, 13–051
and see **Conditions**
conformity
absolute compliance, 11–005
admixtures, 11–020
commercial transactions, 11–001
considerable discrepancies, 11–019
consumer transactions, 11–001, 11–019
failure to conform, 11–018
future goods, 11–018
historical background, 11–002
implied terms, 11–001, 11–002
overseas sales, 11–018, 18–266
small discrepancies, 11–018
statutory provisions, 11–001
toxic substances, 11–020
unascertained goods, 11–018
unfair contract terms, 11–005
descriptive words
identification of goods, 11–014
interpretation, 11–014
meaning, of, 11–012
misrepresentations, 11–012
use, of, 11–012, 11–013
warranties, 11–013
discrepancies, 11–018, 11–019
exemption clauses, 11–005
and see **Exemption clauses**
form of contract, 11–015
goods
future goods, 11–007, 11–008, 11–018
identity, of, 11–014, 11–015
mixed goods, 12–060
purpose, of, 11–017
quality, of, 11–016
selection by buyer, 11–010
self-service shopping, 11–010
specific goods, 11–007, 11–008
unascertained goods, 11–007, 11–008, 11–014, 11–018
implied terms, 12–071
and see **Implied terms**
modification, of, 13–066
quality
satisfactory quality, 11–032, 11–070
statements as to, 11–016
see also **Quality of goods**
reliance, on, 11–007—11–009
sale by description, 11–001—11–006, 18–266
and see **Sale by description**
sale by sample, 11–022
and see **Sale by sample**
statutory provisions, 11–023
trade custom, 11–021
unfair contract terms, 11–005

Diminution in value
damages, for, 17–051
market
market price, 17–054
market value, 17–051, 17–052, 17–055
no available market, 17–052, 17–055
price
ascertaining value, 17–052—17–054
contract price, 17–052
resale price, 17–053
remedial costs, 17–055
substitute goods, 17–056
Direct payment
see also **Payment**
banker's draft
collecting banker, 22–028
crossing, effect of, 22–030
drawees, 22–023, 22–024, 22–026
foreign drafts, 22–025
indemnity, effect of, 22–022
irregular indorsement, 22–026—22–028
legal nature, 22–019
loss of draft, 22–018, 22–020—22–023
missing indorsement, 22–026, 22–027
mistaken issue, 22–029
risk allocation, 22–020, 22–021
Stamp Act (1853), 22–027
payment on account
advantages, 22–006
case law, 22–010—22–013, 22–016, 22–017
China Mutual Case, 22–010—22–012
currency fluctuations, 22–007
Exchange Control Measures (Malaysia), 22–014
"forward" contracts, 2–007, 22–009
freezing orders, 22–009, 22–010, 22–013, 22–017
risk, 22–009
"spot" contracts, 22–007, 22–008
USA experience, 22–015
Disposal of goods
see **Right of disposal**
Distance selling
"click wrap" contracts, 14–053
"cold calling", 14–055
consumer protection, 1–023, 2–014
and see **Consumer protection**
Consumer Protection (Distance Selling) Regulations (2000)
choice of law, 25–108, 25–109
closest country connection, 25–109, 25–1120
provisions, 14–054, 25–107
purpose, 25–107
contract
cancellation rights, 14–057
delayed performance, 14–056

Distance selling—*cont.*
contract—*cont.*
distance contracts, 14–054
duration, 14–055
excluded contracts, 14–054
performance, of, 14–056
Distance Selling Directive (1997/7/EC), 14–054, 14–060
enforcement measures, 14–059
force majeure, and, 8–106
and see Force majeure
growth, in, 14–053
goods
delivery, 8–038
restoration, 14–058
information requirements, 14–055
internet
payments, 9–036
sales, 14–053, 14–054
and see **Internet**
premium rate calls, 14–055
telephone sales, 14–053, 14–055
Documentary bills
discount, of, 5–140
disposal of goods, 5–138—5–140
see also **Right of disposal**
nature, of, 5–138
passing of property, 18–221—18–225
see also **Passing of property (overseas sales)**
use, of, 5–138
Documentary credits
acceptance, 23–060
amendments, 23–059
assignment
effect, 23–069
object, 23–069
transfer, distinguished, 23–068
buyer and seller
see **Documentary credits (buyer and seller)**
classification
borderline cases, 23–063
confirmed credits, 23–055
conflicting provisions, 23–064, 23–065
irrevocable credits, 23–051, 23–053
negotiation credits, 23–061—23–064
open credits, 23–049
"red clause" credits, 23–066
revocable credits, 23–051, 23–052
revolving credits, 23–007
standby credits, 23–050
straight credits, 23–061, 23–063, 23–064
unconfirmed credits, 23–055
confirmation
confirmed credits, 23–055
hybrid cases, 23–058
Documentary credits—*cont.*
confirmation—*cont.*
refusal to confirm, 23–056
silent confirmation, 23–057
confirmed credits, 23–055, 23–059
correspondent banker
see **Correspondent banker**
deferred payment credit, 23–062
documents on acceptance (D/A) system, 23–002
first demand guarantees, 23–237
and see **First demand guarantees**
irrevocable credits
effect, 23–059
nature, of, 23–051, 23–052
timing, 23–053
issuing banker/buyer
see **Documentary credits (issuing banker/buyer)**
issuing banker/seller
see **Documentary credits (issuing banker/seller)**
nature, of, 23–003
negotiation bank, 23–065
objects
credit, 23–001
security, 23–001
performance bonds
see **Performance bonds**
procedure
agreement on use, 23–004
application form, 23–005
opening of credit, 23–006
realisation of credit, 23–007
revocable credits, 23–051, 23–052
seller's draft
buyer, rights against, 23–195
confirmed credit, 23–186
discrepant documents, 23–190
fraudulent documents, 23–191
irrevocable credit, 23–186
issuing banker, and, 23–186, 23–187
mere holders, 23–187
negotiation banker, 23–187—23–190
negotiation credit, 23–187
reimbursement, 23–193
rejection procedure, 23–190
right of recourse, 23–192
seller, rights against, 23–194
straight credit, 23–187
unconfirmed credit, 23–186
UCP, effect of, 23–189, 23–190
standby credits
see **Standby credits**
tender of documents
see **Documentary credits (tender of documents)**

Documentary credits—*cont.*
transfer
amendments, 23–075
assignment, distinguished, 23–068
back-to-back credits, 23–080—23–082
bank liability, 23–076, 23–077
first beneficiary, rights of, 23–073
fraction, transfer of, 23–074
initiative, for, 23–071
legal effect, 23–079, 23–081
nature, of, 23–070
object, 23–070
procedure, 23–070
subsidiary credit, 23–080
tender of documents, 23–072
transferable credit, 23–077, 23–078
UCP provisions, 23–071
Uniform Customs and Practice for Documentary Credits (UCP)
see **Uniform Customs and Practice for Documentary Credits (UCP)**
use, of, 23–008
Documentary credits (buyer and seller)
acceptance of goods, 23–109
agreement, between, 23–083
ambiguous clauses, 23–087
buyer's duty
conformity of credit, 23–084, 23–085
provision of credit, 23–083, 23–084, 23–093
c.i.f. contracts, 23–088
and see **C.I.F. contracts**
credit
conformity, 23–084, 23–085
timing, 23–086—23–089
credit card transactions, 23–103—23–105
damages, 23–107
delivery of goods, 23–083
documentary credit clause, 23–083
documents
discrepant, 23–108—23–110
non-compliant, 23–109, 23–111
f.o.b. contracts, 23–090, 23–091
and see **F.O.B. contracts**
issuing bank
failure, of, 23–101
nomination, of, 23–102
opening of credit
acceptance of draft, 23–099, 23–103
effect, 23–097, 23–098
non-payment, and, 23–099, 23–100
payment from bank, 23–097
payment of price, 23–098
payment
absolute payment, 23–103, 23–106, 23–111
bank, from, 23–097
claim, for, 23–097, 23–099

Documentary credits (buyer and seller)—*cont.*
payment—*cont.*
conditional payment, 23–103, 23–105, 23–106, 23–111
non-payment, 23–099, 23–100
price, 23–097, 23–098
realisation of credit
buyer's remedies, 23–108
non-compliant documents, 23–109, 23–111
remedial action, 23–094
remedies, 23–108, 23–111
repudiation, 23–110, 23–112
shipment period, 23–088, 23–092
time not stipulated, 23–088
variation of contract, 23–095, 23–096
waiver, 23–095, 23–096
and see **Waiver**
Documentary credits (issuing banker/buyer)
see also **Documentary credits (buyer and seller)**
banker's security
documents of title, 23–132, 23–133
trust receipts, 23–133
opening of credit
ambiguous instructions, 23–117
application form, 23–113, 23–115
autonomous agreement, 23–114
banker's commission, 23–124
case decisions, 23–121, 23–122
correspondent banker, 23–119
deposit of funds, 23–125
deposit of securities, 23–125
dispatch of credit, 23–118
duty of care, 23–120
ratification, 23–116
standard terms, 23–123
waiver, 23–116
realisation of credit
banker's duty, 23–126, 23–127
condition of goods, 23–129
conforming documents, 23–126, 23–128
examination of documents, 23–127
exemption clauses, 23–130
reimbursement, 23–126
tender of documents, 23–126
wider clauses, 23–131
Documentary credits (issuing banker/seller)
see also **Documentary credits (buyer and seller)**
acceptance of tender
examination of documents, 23–156
non-conforming documents, 23–158
notice to beneficiary, 23–158
payee's identity, 23–161
timing, 23–156, 23–157
amendments, 23–136

Documentary credits (issuing banker/seller)—*cont.*
contract
consideration, 23–137
formation, of, 23–137
theoretical analysis, 23–137
foreign court orders, 23–140
form, of, 23–134
fraud rule
beneficiaries, and, 23–147
case decisions, 23–142—23–144
effect, 23–141
injunctions, 23–149, 23–151—23–153
irreparable harm, 23–152
limitations, 23–145, 23–148
third parties, 23–146
USA experience, 23–149—23–152
irreparable harm
case decisions, 23–152, 23–153
restraining orders, 23–151—23–153
irrevocable credit
autonomy, 23–139—23–141
legal effect, 23–134, 23–135
legal effect
irrevocable credit, 23–134, 23–135
revocable credit, 23–134, 23–135
standard form, 23–134
mercantile usage, 23–138
nominated bank, 23–134
rejection of documents
fraud, 23–160
non-conforming documents, 23–158, 23–160
non-documentary objections, 23–160
notice to beneficiary, 23–158
refunds, 23–160
rejection formula, 23–159
right of recourse
banker's claim, 23–162—23–167
common law principles, 23–164
faulty tender, 23–162
negotiable instruments, and, 23–163
payment against reserve, 23–166, 23–167
UCP, and, 23–165
seller's remedies
damages, 23–171, 23–172
delayed payment, 23–172
set-off
entitlement, 23–168
problems, associated with, 23–169
ranking, 23–170
unauthorised letters of credit, 23–154
unauthorised telex, 23–155
Documentary credits (tender of documents)
see also **Documentary credits**
bills of lading
"clean bills", 23–221
destination, covering, 23–222
freight, and, 23–223

Documentary credits (tender of documents)—*cont.*
bills of lading—*cont.*
multimodal transport documents, distinguished, 23–220
requirements, as to, 23–218
shipment, evidence of, 23–220
transhipment, and, 23–222
UCP, and, 23–218—23–220
voyage, covering, 23–222
and see **Bills of lading**
certificates, 23–235
discrepancies
documents, 23–197—23–199, 23–203
quantity, 23–211, 23–212
weight, 23–211
documents
acceptance, 23–210
all documents tendered, 23–205
authentication, 23–208
contradictory documents, 23–214
copies, 23–209
description of goods, 23–213
discrepant documents, 23–197—23–199, 23–203
expert evidence, as to, 23–216
expiry date, 23–210
irregularity, 23–197
non-conforming documents, 23–196—23–199
original document, 23–207
presentation, 23–210
regularity, 23–206
signature, 23–208
documents of carriage
air transport documents, 23–226
bills of lading, 23–217, 23–218
carriage by rail, 23–227
carriage by road, 23–227
carriage by sea, 23–224
charterparties, 23–224
c.i.f. contracts, 23–217
combined transport documents, 23–217
courier receipts, 23–228
destination, as to, 23–222
freight, covering, 23–223
inland waterways, 23–227
multimodal transport documents, 23–220, 23–225
post receipts, 23–228
sea waybills, 23–224
UCP, and, 23–217, 23–218
voyage, covering, 23–222
drafts, 23–236
insurance documents
basic requirements, 23–230
cover date, 23–231
currency provisions, 23–234
description of goods, 23–231
risks covered, 23–229, 23–233

Documentary credits (tender of documents)—*cont.*
insurance documents—*cont.*
type, of, 23–229
voyage, covered by, 23–231
and see **Insurance**
invoice, 23–234
strict compliance
all documents tendered, 23–205
description of goods, 23–213
discrepant documents, 23–197—23–199, 23–203
good faith, 23–202
identification of goods, 23–215
importance, of, 23–196, 23–197, 23–200
non-conforming documents, 23–196—23–199
objections, 23–203, 23–204
presentation of documents, 23–210
quantity, as to, 23–211, 23–212
subsequent tenders, 23–204
technical defences, 23–201
terms of credit, 23–196
time considerations, 23–210
tolerance levels, 23–212
UCP, and, 23–196
waiver, 23–203
weight, as to, 23–211
Document of title
air waybills, 18–199, 21–053, 21–054
bills of lading
see **Bills of lading**
cargo receipts, 18–199, 21–053, 21–054
consignment notes, 18–199
delivery of goods, and, 18–008
delivery orders
see **Delivery orders**
mate's receipt, 18–163
and see **Mate's receipt**
meaning
common law, 18–006, 18–007, 18–009
negotiability, 18–007, 18–008, 18–010
statutory meaning, 18–006, 18–009, 18–010
transferability, 18–007, 18–008, 18–010
multimodal transport documents, 18–200
paperless transactions
see **Paperless transactions**
production, of, 18–201
rules, governing, 18–011
sea waybills
see **Sea waybills**
self-styled, 18–201
Duress
contract of sale, and, 3–010
and see **Contract of sale**
Electronic commerce
consumer protection, 1–023, 1–053, 14–054
and see **Consumer protection**
EC legislation, 1–023
and see **EC legislation**
electronic bill of lading, 18–202, 18–203, 18–05, 18–206
see also **Bills of lading**
Electronic Commerce Directive (2000/37/EC), 14–060
and see **Electronic Commerce Directive (2000/37/EC)**
internet
payments, 9–036, 9–037
sales, 14–053, 14–054
and see **Internet**
sea waybills, 18–206, 18–207
and see **Sea waybills**
ship's delivery orders, 18–206
and see **Ship's delivery orders**
UK legislation, 1–024
UNCITRAL (Model law), 1–024
E.contracts
"click-wrap" contracts, 2–012
and see **"Click-wrap" contracts**
formation, 2–012, 2–015
see also **Formation of contract**
internet payments, 9–036, 9–037
see also **Internet**
web-page advertisements, 2–002
EC legislation
competition law, 3–041
and see **Competition law (European Union)**
consumer protection, 1–023
and see **Consumer protection**
Consumer Sales Directive (1999/44/EC), 12–071, 14–008, 14–011
and see **Consumer Sales Directive (1999/44/EC)**
Distance Selling Directive (1997/7/EC), 14–054, 14–060
effect, of, 1–023
Electronic Commerce Directive (2000/37/EC), 14–060
and see **Electronic Commerce Directive (2000/37/EC)**
passing of property, 6–014
and see **Passing of property**
Unfair Commercial Practices Directive (2005/29/EC), 14–139
unfair contract terms, 1–014, 6–013, 6–014
see also **Unfair Contract Terms Act (1977)**

Electronic Commerce Directive (2000/37/EC)
contractual process, 14–060
information requirements, 14–060
objective, 14–060
scope, of, 14–060
Enterprise Act (2002)
see also **Administrative protection**
Community infringements, 14–133, 14–136, 14–140, 14–156
consumer codes, 14–137
consumer, definition of, 14–131
consumer protection, 14–125—14–127
and see **Consumer protection**
domestic infringements, 14–131, 14–132, 14–136, 14–140, 14–156
enforcement
enforcers, 14–134, 14–135
orders, 14–135
provisions, 14–130, 14–134—14–136
Entire agreement clause
collateral warranties, 13–056
effect, of, 13–056
exemption clauses, and, 13–056
and see **Exemption clauses**
Estoppel
affirmation, and, 12–037
see also **Affirmation (election)**
agency, and, 7–008, 7–010
and see **Agency**
conduct, by, 12–037
conversion actions, 7–011
judgment (*per rem judicatam*), 7–019
negligence, and, 7–015—7–017
passing of property, and, 16–024
and see **Passing of property**
promissory estoppel, 19–150
rejection of goods, and, 19–150
and see **Rejection of goods**
transfer of title
bulk goods, and, 7–014
documents of title, 7–013
representation, by, 7–009—7–012
see also **Transfer of title (non-owners)**
waiver, and, 19–150, 19–151
and see **Waiver**
European Court of Justice (ECJ)
decisions, 25–018
preliminary rulings, 25–018
referrals, to, 25–019
Examination of goods
see also **Breach of term**
acceptance of goods, 12–039, 12–041, 12–048—12–050
see also **Acceptance**
buyer's right, 12–039
conformity with contract, 12–039
Examination of goods—*cont.*
consumer sales, 12–043
and see **Consumer sales**
contrary agreement, 12–039, 12–042
fitting of goods, 12–040
insufficient delivery, 8–047
place, 12–043, 12–049, 12–051
quality of goods, 11–041, 11–042, 11–072, 11–080, 11–081
and see **Quality of goods**
reasonable time, 12–053, 12–055, 12–056
request, for, 12–039
right of rejection, 12–039, 12–048
sale by sample, 12–039
and see **Sale by sample**
testing of goods, 12–040, 12–041
timing, 12–041
Exchange
sale, distinguished, 1–034—1–036
and see **Sale**
Exemption clauses
applicable law, 4–018, 13–100
arbitration clauses, and, 13–069, 14–041
authorised terms
competent authority, by, 13–098
consumer codes, 13–098
international agreement, by, 13–098
statute, by, 13–098
certification clauses, 13–040
choice of law
English law, 13–100
foreign law, 13–101
collateral contracts, 10–013
and see **Collateral contracts**
common law rules, 11–005, 13–006—13–008, 13–010
complete protection, 13–031
consumer protection, and, 4–019, 13–003, 13–021
and see **Consumer protection**
contracting parties, 13–060
contractual principles, and, 13–006, 13–010
contra proferentem rule, 13–006, 13–020, 13–036
control, of, 13–012
defective goods, 13–089
and see **Defective e goods**
definitional problems, 13–065
delivery of goods
clauses, relating to, 8–063, 8–088
conditions precedent, 8–101
quantity of goods, 8–063
rejection of goods, 8–063
description
conformity, with, 13–083
definition, of, 13–033
errors, in, 13–029

Exemption clauses—*cont.*
description—*cont.*
interpretation, 13–033
effect, of, 13–001
enforcement, 13–105
entire agreement clause
see **Entire agreement clause**
examination of goods, 13–102
exclusion(s)
cancelling clauses, 13–035
consequential loss, 13–037
death, 13–092, 13–106
errors of description, 13–029
exclusion of liability, 4–018, 4–020
express condition, 13–031
express terms, and, 13–031
implied conditions, 13–026, 13–031
indirect loss, 13–037
negligence, 13–008, 13–021, 13–022, 13–093
particular duties, 13–023
personal injury, 13–092, 13–106
recovery of damages, 13–036
right of rejection, 13–032, 13–033
right to damages, 13–034
set-off clauses, 13–039
warranties, 13–031, 13–025, 13–026
formation of contract
basic principles, 13–012
collateral contracts, 13–016, 13–017
course of dealing, 13–014, 13–015
incorporation, 13–013, 13–016
misrepresentation, 13–013, 13–016
non est factum, 13–013
privity of contract, 13–017
third parties, 13–017, 13–018
and see **Formation of contract**
freedom from encumbrance, 4–031
and see **Freedom from encumbrance**
freedom of contract, 1–014, 1–015
and see **Freedom of contract**
fundamental breach, 13–04, 13–042
and see **Fundamental breach**
indemnity clauses, 13–001, 13–097
inoperative, 13–016
interpretation
acknowledgement of fact, 13–030
contra proferentem rule, 13–020
intermediate terms, 13–027
non-reliance clauses, 13–030
"no warranty given", 13–024
strict interpretation, 13–020, 13–021
Unfair Contract Terms Act (1977), 13–021
"with all faults", 13–028
legislation
Consumer Protection Directive, 13–009
Misrepresentation Act (1967), 13–008, 13–010, 13–053

Exemption clauses—*cont.*
legislation—*cont.*
Unfair Contract Terms Act (1977), 13–008, 13–010, 13–021
liability
death, for, 13–092, 13–106
exclusion, of, 13–054, 13–055, 13–059, 13–064, 13–084
limits, on, 13–091, 13–096
negligence, 13–008, 13–021, 13–022, 13–093
personal injury, 13–092, 13–106
restriction, of, 13–054, 13–055, 13–084
specified sums, 13–091
limited title, and, 4–034
see also **Seller's title**
manufacturer's guarantees, 13–097
and see **Manufacturers**
modification clauses, 13–066
negligence
death, caused by, 13–092, 13–106
negligence clauses, 13–093
personal injury, 13–092, 13–106
non-conforming goods, 13–033
objections, to, 13–002, 13–003
quiet possession, and, 4–031
and see **Quiet possession**
reasonableness
bargaining position, 13–088, 13–090
burden of proof, 13–086
case law, 13–090
guidelines, 13–088—13–090, 13–096
indemnities, 13–097
manufacturer's guarantees, 13–097
meaning, 13–086
partial, 13–087
unfair terms, and, 13–060
reform, proposals for, 13–011
rejection of contract, 13–102
and see **Rejection of contract**
risk
balance, of, 13–004
distribution, 13–002
limitation, 13–004
and see **Risk**
sale by description, 11–005
and see **Sale by description**
sample, conformity with, 13–029, 13–083
see also **Sale by sample**
standard terms
burden of proof, 13–095
requirements, for, 13–095
use, of, 13–095
statements of opinion, 13–057
statutory control
Consumer Protection Act (1987), 13–104
intervention, 13–007, 13–008

Exemption clauses—*cont.*
statutory control—*cont.*
provisions, 4–018, 13–008—13–010, 13–053, 13–054
Supply of Goods (Implied Terms) Act (1973), 13–053, 13–061
testing clauses, 13–040
third parties
actions, against, 13–017, 13–018
consumer protection, 13–019
legislative provisions, 13–018
negligence actions, 13–017
privity of contract, 13–017
separate contract, with, 13–017
time limits, 13–038
unfair contract terms, 4–018, 4–019, 4–034, 13–003, 13–054, 13–055, 13–064—13–066
see also **Unfair Contract Terms Act (1977)**
use, of, 13–001
validity, 13–005
Export Credit Guarantee Department (ECGD)
see also **Export credit guarantees**
ancillary services, 24–010
credit financing
buyers, 24–035, 24–036
lines of credit (LOCs), 24–044
new facilities, 24–045
Sovereign Star Facility, 24–034
Supplier Credit Finance Facility (SCF), 24–006, 24–032
suppliers, 24–031
facilities
business, 24–008
financial, 24–008, 24–009
information services, 24–010
maximum commitments, 24–010
financial management, 24–009
insurance, provision of, 24–008
joint export projects, 24–005
policies
Atradius policies, 24–017, 24–018
Bond Insurance Policy (BIP), 24–016
Export Insurance Policy (EXIP), 24–016
powers, 24–007, 24–008, 24–009
project financing scheme, 24–045
right of recourse, 24–042
role, 24–005—24–007
status, 24–004
statutory provisions, 24–007
structure, 24–004
terms offered, 24–006
Export credit guarantees
assignment of policies
bill of sale, as, 24–030
disadvantage, 24–028
effect, 24–027
Export credit guarantees—*cont.*
assignment of policies—*cont.*
method, 24–026
registration, 24–029
buyer's credit financing
advantages, 24–041
banker/ECGD contract, 24–038
buyer/banker contract, 24–037
buyer's credit guarantees, 24–036
practice, relating to, 24–035
premium agreement, 24–039, 24–040, 24–042
right of recourse, 24–042, 24–043
supplier's rights, 24–040
comprehensive policies
ascertainment of loss, 24–022
credit limit, 24–019
excluded risks, 24–023
extent o cover, 24–021
risks covered, 24–020
seller's obligations, 24–024
terms, 24–018
confirmed credit, distinguished, 24–001
credit risk, 24–001
Export & Investment Guarantees Act (1991), 24–007
Export Credit Guarantee Department (ECGD), 24–003
and see **Export Credit Guarantee Department (ECGD)**
financing, by, 24–002
guarantees
buyer's credit financing, 24–035—24–044
buyer's credit guarantees, 24–036
legal nature, 24–033
Sovereign Star Facility, 24–034
supplier's credit financing, 24–031—24–034
international aspects
Berne Union, 24–051, 24–052
EU harmonisation, 24–054
government subsidies, 24–051, 24–053
OECD arrangement, 24–053, 24–054
subsidised exports, 24–051
lines of credit (LOCs)
general purpose line of credit (GPLOC), 24–044
nature, of, 24–044
project line of credit (PLOC), 24–044
overseas investment insurance (OII)
bank portfolio loans, 24–049
developing countries, and, 24–049
foreign direct investment, 24–049
investment type, 24–049
risks covered, 24–050
scope, 24–049
statutory provisions, 24–048
support loans, 24–049

Export credit guarantees—*cont.*
policies
Atradius policies, 24–017, 24–018
Bond Insurance Policy (BIP), 24–016
buyer credit, 24–001
comprehensive policies, 24–018—24–024
Export Insurance Policy (EXIP), 24–016
supplier credit, 24–001, 24–011, 24–012
providers
Export Credit Agencies (ECAs), 24–003
Export Credit Guarantee Department (ECGD), 24–003
private sector insurers, 24–003, 24–006
purpose, 24–001, 24–002
Supplier Credit Finance Facility (SCF), 24–006, 24–032
supplier credit policies
assignment, 24–025—24–030
Atradius, role of, 24–011
comprehensive principle, 24–014, 24–017
debt recovery, 24–015
disclosure, 24–013
subrogation, 24–015
uberrimae fidei, 24–013
types, 24–006
Export/import clauses
burden of proof, 18–346—18–352
construction, of, 18–344
effects, of, 18–342—18–345
frustration of contract, 18–342
partial prevention
allocation of supplies, 18–353, 18–354
seller's liability, 18–355
prohibition, of, 18–342—18–345
scope, of, 18–343
"string" of contracts, 18–350
supervening events
defective notice, 18–357, 18–358
notice, of, 18–356—18–358
Export/import licences
see also **Overseas sales**
claims, relating to, 18–329, 18–330
contract
construction, of, 18–317
frustration of contract, 18–326, 18–331, 18–332
performance, of, 18–331
subject to licence, 18–318, 18–328, 18–331
licensing requirements, 18–308, 18–309
obtaining
absolute duty, 18–319, 18–325
content of duty, 18–319—18–322
duties, as to, 18–309—18–311, 18–319, 18–320, 18–325
failure to obtain, 18–312, 18–323—18–326, 18–328
Export/import licences—*cont.*
obtaining—*cont.*
reasonable steps, 18–320, 18–321
standard of duty, 18–313—18–317
revocation of licence, 18–322, 18–332
standard of duty
best endeavours, 18–313
construction of terms, 18–317
contractual terms, as to, 18–315
due diligence, 18–314
duty of diligence, 18–314, 18–327
extraneous factors, affecting, 18–316
reasonable diligence, 18–313
reasonable efforts, 18–314, 18–327, 18–328
Export/import prohibitions
see also **Overseas sales**
effect, of, 18–333
embargo
absolute, 18–347, 18–349
availability of goods, 18–349
partial, 18–348, 18–349, 18–353, 18–355
post-sale, 18–343
un-appropriated goods, 18–349
frustration of contract, 18–333, 18–334, 18–341, 18–342
and see **Frustration of contract**
performance of contract
illegal, 18–335
prevented, 18–335, 18–349, 18–352
temporary interference, 18–336
prohibition
antecedent, 18–340
foreign, 18–339
partial, 18–338
qualified, 18–337
supervening prohibition, 18–334, 18–337, 18–340
Ex ship contracts
arrival
approximate date, 21–030
arrival terms, 21–022—21–044
expected arrival, 21–030
timing, 21–029
c.i.f. contracts, distinguished, 21–10521–106
damages, 21–031
definition, 21–104
failure to ship, 21–026, 21–027
frustration of contract, 21–028
and see **Frustration of contract**
landing charges, 21–109
nominated ship, 21–025, 21–027
passing of property, 21–020
and see **Passing of property**

Ex ship contracts—*cont.*
payment
documents, against, 21–107
timing, 21–018
risk, 21–020, 21–021
and see **Risk**
Ex store contracts
see **Ex works contracts**
Ex works contracts
bulk goods, 21–007
delivery
delivery orders, 21–008
place of delivery, 21–002
seller's duty, 21–002
seller's works, from, 21–002
third party warehouse, 21–007
nature, of, 21–002
passing of property, 21–003—21–005, 21–007
and see **Passing of property**
risk, 21–003, 21–006
and see **Risk**
specific goods, 21–005
unascertained goods, 21–007
warehouseman, liability of, 21–009

Factoring services
overseas sales, 23–316
Factors Act (1889)
application, 1–018
F.A.S. contracts (free alongside ship)
appropriation, and, 21–011
consumer sales, 21–011
and see **Consumer sales**
dealing as consumer, 21–011
duties, relating to, 21–010
nature, of, 21–010
passing of property, 21–011
and see **Passing of property**
risk, 21–011
and see **Risk**
unascertained goods, 21–011
First demand guarantees
see also **Performance bonds**
autonomous undertaking, 23–275, 23–280
beneficiaries, and, 23–27
compliance, 23–283
demand, form of, 23–284, 23–285
fraud rule, 23–275—23–277, 23–279, 23–280
function, 23–271
liability, evidence of, 23–278
nature, 23–272
payment, 23–270, 23–286
recital of details, 23–274
subrogation, 23–287
unconscionability, 23–281, 23–282

Fitness for purpose
see also **Quality of goods**
agency sales, 11–053
see also **Agency**
course of business, 11–052
deterioration in transit, 11–067
durability, 11–066
express provisions
conditions, 11–068
warranties, 11–068
implied condition, 11–024, 11–030
legislative background, 11–025
manufactured products, 11–031
misuse, and, 11–057
purpose
knowledge, of, 11–059
particular purpose, 11–055, 11–059
reliance
agents, 11–063
claims, as to, 11–059
compound goods, 11–060
dealers, 11–061
examination of goods, 11–062
partial reliance, 11–060
particular purpose, 11–059
satisfactory quality, 11–060
skill/judgment, 11–059, 11–072
special requirements, 11–060
requirement, as to, 11–024
safety, and, 11–039
sale
agency sales, 11–053
course of business, 11–052, 11–070
credit-brokers, 11–056
related contracts, 11–069
supply under contract, 11–054
trade name, by, 11–065
Sale of Goods Act (1979), 11–051, 11–071
second-hand goods, 11–058
seller's duty, 11–057, 11–064
standard
absolute suitability, 11–057
particular suitability, 11–057
reasonably fit, 11–057
statutory provisions, 11–024—11–026, 11–031, 11–051
strict liability, 14–017
time element, 11–066
warranty, as to, 11–024, 11–025, 11–030, 11–068
see also **Warranties**
Fixtures
goods, as, 1–090, 1–095
and see **Goods**
meaning, 1–095
sale, of, 1–095
severance, 1–095
tenant's fixtures, 1–095

F.O.B. contracts
agency, and, 20–008
and see **Agency**
bills of lading
buyer's order, to, 20–083
form, of, 20–021
goods deleted, from, 20–066
goods not shipped, 20–064, 20–065
issue, of, 20–063—20–065, 20–076
passing of property, 20–077—20–083
responsibility, for, 20–020, 20–025
seller's order, to, 20–026, 20–077—20–080
sets, of, 20–023
subsequent non-payment, 20–085
tender, of, 20–022—20–025
and see **Bills of lading**
bulk shipments, 18–301, 18–303
and see **Bulk shipments**
buyer's duties
payment of price, 20–055—20–058
shipping instructions, 20–041—20–045
buyer's remedies
see **Buyer's remedies (f.o.b. contracts)**
carriers
contractual relationships, 20–003—20–005, 20–059
failure to load, 20–013
carrying charges
action, for, 20–131, 20–132
nature, of, 20–131
wrongful repudiation, 20–132
c.i.f. contracts, distinguished, 20–008, 20–009
and see **C.I.F. contracts**
conformity of goods
contract description, 20–038
duty, as to, 20–038
fitness for purpose, 20–038
quality of goods, 20–038
quantity of goods, 20–038
right of rejection, 20–038
contractual relationships
agency, 20–069
carriers, 20–003—20–005, 20–059
"classic" f.o.b. contract, 20–003—20–005
implied contract, 20–069
privity of contract, 20–069
shipping arrangements, and, 20–061, 20–067
shipping space, and, 20–060—20–062
third parties, 20–059, 20–068
definition, 20–001
delivery
delivery alongside, 20–010
delivery at dock, 20–010

F.O.B. contracts—*cont.*
delivery—*cont.*
free on board, 20–012, 20–015
provisions, as to, 18–262, 18–263, 20–037
delivery free on board
delivery on board, 20–012, 20–015
demurrage, 20–018
designated ship, 20–012, 20–014, 20–020
duty, as to, 20–012, 20–015
expenses, 20–018
failure to load, 20–013
place of delivery, 20–014
safety of goods, 20–017
special provisions, 20–016
statutory provisions, 20–012
demurrage, 20–018, 20–019
duties
additional duties, 20–007, 20–040
buyer's duties, 20–002, 20–041, 20–055
conformity of goods, 20–038
delivery, 20–012, 20–015
insurance, as to, 20–039
relative duties, 20–002
seller's duties, 20–002, 20–011
shipping instructions, 20–041, 20–042
essential features, 20–002, 20–006
expenses, payment of, 20–012, 20–018
frustration of contract, 20–095—20–104
and see **Frustration of contract**
insurance
amount, of, 20–39
destruction of goods, 20–039
duty, as to, 20–039
nature, of, 20–039
and see **Insurance**
loading
failure to load, 20–029, 20–033
method, 20–031
notice, as to, 20–031, 20–032
rate, of, 20–031—20–033
timing, 20–031, 20–033
loss/deterioration of goods, 18–262, 18–263
and see **Loss/deterioration of goods**
passing of property
appropriation to contract, 20–070
bills of lading, 20–077—20–083
bulk goods, 20–086
goods afloat, 20–070
intention of parties, 20–070
mate's receipts, and, 20–076
owners in common, 20–086
right of disposal, and, 20–071, 20–075—20–077
risk, and, 20–071

F.O.B. contracts—*cont.*
passing of property—*cont.*
shipment, 20–071—20–074
shipment of part, 20–074
shipping documents, 20–075
specific goods, 20–070
subsequent dealing, 20–084, 20–085
unascertained goods, 20–070, 20–086
undivided share, 20–086
and see **Passing of property**
payment of price
bills of lading, against, 20–055
buyer's duty, 20–055
compliance, 20–057
place, 20–056
seller's breach, 20–058
statutory provisions, 20–055
timing, 20–056
risk
bulk shipments, 18–301, 18–303
contractual terms,. covering, 20–093
contrary agreement, 20–094
dealing as consumer, 20–087, 20–094
loading of goods, 20–089, 20–090
shipment, and, 20–088, 20–090—20–092, 20–094
and see **Risk**
seller's duties
additional duties, 20–040
collaborative activity, 20–011
conformity of goods, 20–038
delivery, as to, 20–012
demurrage, payment of, 20–018
expenses, payment of, 20–012, 20–018
insurance, 20–039
safety of goods, 20–017
shipping documents, 20–020
shipping space, 20–028
time of shipment, 20–029
variations, in, 20–011
shipment
buyer's option, 20–030, 20–034, 20–047, 20–051
control, over, 20–034
delivery of goods, and, 20–037
divided option, 20–036, 20–049, 20–050
expenses, 20–054
failure to load, 20–029
nominated ship, 20–051—20–053
place, of, 20–045
seller's option, 20–035, 20–048
shipping space, 20–028, 20–060—20–062
third parties, and, 20–034
timing, 20–029, 20–030, 20–034—20–036, 20–046—20–049
shipping documents
banker's commercial credits, 20–024
bills of lading, 20–020—20–022

F.O.B. contracts—*cont.*
shipping documents—*cont.*
inspection certificate, 20–027
responsibility, for, 20–020
subsequent dealing, with, 20–084
tender, of, 20–022—20–024
trade custom, 20–027
weight certificate, 20–027
shipping instructions
bills of lading, and, 20–063—20–065
buyer, and, 20–067, 20–076
contractual terms, 20–044
duty, as to, 20–041, 20–042
effective, 20–043
goods not shipped, 20–064, 20–065
place of shipment, 20–045
received bill issued, 20–064
seller, and, 20–061, 20–067
third parties, and, 20–067
time of shipment, 20–046—20–049
shipping space
provision, of, 20–028, 20–060—20–062
responsibility, for, 20–028
Force majeure
certainty of contract, and, 2–016
consumer contracts, 8–015
delivery of goods, 8–102
and see **Delivery**
force majeure clauses
burden of proof, 8–091
distance selling, 8–106
effect, 8–088
interpretation, 8–089
mitigation, 8–091
nature, of, 8–088
specified events, 8–089, 8–097
wording, of, 8–089—8–096
foreseeability, 8–100
frustration of contract, 19–138, 19–141, 19–142
and see **Frustration of contract**
meaning, 8–098, 8–099
performance of contract
delayed, 8–095, 8–099
hindered, 8–094, 8–099
insufficient delivery, 8–102, 8–103
prevented, 8–092, 8–093, 8–099, 8–102
pro-rating, 8–103
unfair contract terms, 8–014
F.O.R contracts (free on rail)
see also **F.O.T. contracts**
appropriation, 21–044
damages, 21–046
duties, relating to, 21–042
inspection of goods, 21–045
nature, of, 21–042
passing of property, 21–043
and see **Passing of property**

F.O.R contracts (free on rail)—*cont.*
right of disposal, 21–044
and see **Right of disposal**
risk, 21–043
and see **Risk**
unascertained goods, 21–044
Formation of contract
acceptance, 2–011
and see **Acceptance**
agreement
contractual principles, 2–001
intention to create, 2–019
auction sales, 2–004
and see **Auction sales**
cancellation
cooling-off period, 2–020
right, of, 2–020
capacity
corporate bodies, 2–043
drunkenness, 2–041
married women, 2–042
mental incapacity, 2–041
minors, 2–029—2–039
requirements, 2–028
see also **Minors' contracts**
certainty
commercial agreements, 2–017
force majeure, and, 2–016
importance, of, 2–016
"lock-out" agreements, 2–016
price, as to, 2–046
commercial agreements
certainty, 2–017
previous course of dealing, 2–017
trade custom, 2–017
e.mail contracts, 2–015
exemption clauses
see **Exemption clauses**
formalities
assignment by deed, 2–025
common law, 2–021
Consumer Credit Act (1974), 2–023
evidential rules, 2–024
Merchant Shipping Act (1995), 2–023
Sale of Goods Act (1893), 2–022
Sale of Goods Act (1979), 2–021
Statute of Frauds (1677), 2–022
statutory provisions, 2–021
written contracts, 1–092, 2–024
intention of parties, 14–001
invitation to treat, 2–002, 2–012
non-existent contract
belief, in, 2–018
goods supplied, 2–018
offer
see **Offer**
Formation of contract—*cont.*
parties
bilateral contracts, 2–026
capacity, 2–028
collateral contracts, 2–027
contractual relationship, 2–019
intention, of, 2–019
minors, 2–029, 2–040
multipartite transactions, 2–026
number, 2–026
place, 2–015
price
agreement, as to, 2–046
alternative, 2–048
certainty, as to, 2–046
fixing, of, 2–045
money requirement, 2–044
reasonable price, 2–046, 2–047
third party valuation, 2–049—2–052
variation, 2–048
Sale of Goods Act (1979)
formalities, A-004
price, A-006
subject matter, A-005
and see **Sale of Goods Act (1979)**
tenders, 2–003
terms
battle of forms, 2–013
certainty, 2–016
"click-wrap" contracts, 2–012, 2–015
incorporation, 2–012
notice requirement, 2–012
printed terms, 2–012
standard form terms, 2–012, 2–013
unsolicited goods, 2–014
timing, 2–015
unsolicited goods, 2–014
F.O.T contracts
see also **F.O.R contracts (free on rail)**
duties, relating to, 21–042
nature, of, 21–042
passing of property, 21–043
and see **Passing of property**
risk, 21–043
and see **Risk**
Fraud
auction sales, 3–009
and see **Auction sales**
common law rules, 3–008
goods on approval, 5–046
and see **Goods on approval**
liability, for, 12–012, 12–016
Free offers
sale, distinguished, 1–033
and see **Sale**

Freedom from encumbrance
see also **Seller's title**
buyer's remedies, 4–024
see also **Remedies**
damages, entitlement to, 4–024
exceptions
disclosed encumbrances, 4–028
known encumbrances, 4–028
exemption clauses, and, 4–031
and see **Exemption clauses**
implied term, as, 4–023
see also **Implied terms**
limited title, and, 4–033
see also **Seller's title**
right to sell, and, 4–023
Sale of Goods Act (1979), 4–023
unascertained goods, 4–023
and see **Unascertained goods**
warranty, as to, 4–024, 4–030
Freedom of contract
consumer sales, 1–014
exemption clauses, 1–014, 1–015
and see **Exemption clauses**
restrictions, 1–014
statutory provisions, 1–013
unfair terms, 1–014
see also **Unfair contract terms**
Frustration of contract
benefit obtained
"just sum", award of, 6–061, 6–065
nature of benefit, 6–062
obligations, relating to, 6–064
payment, for, 6–061
valuation, 6–063
buying afloat, 19–141
carriage of goods
c.i.f. contracts, 6–043, 6–049, 19–124—19–138
f.o.b. contracts, 6–049, 20–095—20–104
lack of transport, 6–049
route closures, 6–049
and see **Carriage of goods**
causes, of, 19–124—19–138
change in circumstances, 6–055
commercial relations, and, 19–135
common law rules, 6–034
consequences
benefit obtained, 6–061
contrary contractual provisions, 6–071
cross-claims, 6–066
expenses incurred, 6–060
insurance money, 6–070
interest payments, 6–067
prior breach, 6–068
provisions, governing, 6–058, 6–059
repayment provisions, 6–060, 6–061, 6–068
severability, 6–069
Frustration of contract—*cont.*
consequences—*cont.*
sums paid, 6–060
sums payable, 6–060
contrary contractual provisions, 6–071
delay, provision for, 19–138
diplomatic relations, and, 19–135
doctrine, of, 3–050
effect, of, 6–001, 6–034, 19–143
exclusion, provision for, 19–42
export/import restrictions
effect, of, 19–137
foreign governments, 6–048
insufficient goods, 6–052
licences, 6–047
statutory embargo, 6–046, 6–047
express clauses
contrary contractual provisions, 6–071
effect, of, 6–056, 6–057
overseas sales, 6–057
use, of, 6–056, 6–057
f.o.b. contracts
delay, provision for, 20–103
destruction of goods, 20–096, 20–097
effects, 20–104
export/import licences, 20–095
export/import prohibitions, 20–095, 20–098, 20–102
illegality, 20–101
inability to ship, 20–100
performance method, and, 20–098, 20–099
and see **F.O.B. contracts**
force majeure, and, 6–052, 19–138, 19–141, 19–142
and see Force majeure
goods
destruction, of, 6–051, 19–124, 19–125
insufficient, 6–052
part-delivery, 19–143
prorating, 6–053
shipment, 19–124, 19–125, 19–130—19–133
unavailable, 19–130
illegality
effect, of, 19–136, 19–137
foreign law, 6–045
legislative provisions, 6–045
supervening, 6–045, 19–142
and see **Illegality**
insurance, lack of, 19–134
legislation
export prohibitions, 6–046, 6–047
import prohibitions, 6–046, 6–047
supervening illegality, 6–045
payment, and, 19–143
performance
alternative, 19–129
impossibility, 19–126—19–129

Frustration of contract—*cont.*
performance—*cont.*
non-performance, 19–139
requisitioning, and, 6–050
risk, distinguished, 6–001
and see **Risk**
shipping space, lack of, 19–132, 19–133
specific goods
agreement avoided, 6–039
agreement to sell, 6–035
apportionment of loss, 6–039
bulk goods, 6–036
definition, 6–036
expenses, recovery of, 6–039
Howell v Coupland, 6–038
part delivery, 6–040
perished goods, 6–035, 6–040
price, recovery of, 6–039, 6–040
requisitioning, 6–050
right of disposal, 6–037
statutory provisions, 6–035, 6–037—6–039, 6–041
undivided share, 6–036
and see **Specific goods**
supervening events, 6–045, 19–138—19–142
trading with the enemy, 19–136
unascertained goods, 6–041, 6–050, 6–051
and see **Unascertained goods**
unprofitable contracts, 6–054
war, effect of, 6–042—6–044
Fundamental breach
see also **Exemption clauses**
deliberate breach, 13–052
doctrine
application, 13–042
basis, 13–043
case law, 13–045—13–050
doubts, as to, 13–043
effect, 13–042
interpretation, 13–043, 13–044, 13–047
rule of law, as, 14–044—13–046
Securicor Case, 13–047
separate entity, as, 13–048, 13–049
Suisse Atlantique Case, 13–045, 13–046
goods
description, 13–051
qualitative defects, 13–051
specification, 13–051
intention of parties, 13–043
wrong thing supplied, 13–050
Future goods
see also **Goods**
absolute contracts, 1–109, 1–110, 1–112
appropriation, and, 5–090—5–095
and see **Appropriation**
assignment, and, 1–107, 1–108
and see **Assignment**

Future goods—*cont.*
bulk goods, 5–094
and see **Bulk goods**
chance, sale of, 1–112
conditional contracts, 1–109, 1–111
construction materials, 5–093
definition, 5–090
delivery, and, 1–104
and see **Delivery**
difference(s) in price, 1–104
equitable rules, 5–094
gaming contracts, 1–104
goods to be acquired, 5–094
inspection, 5–092
instalment payments, 5–092
intention of parties, as to, 5–092
manufactured goods, 5–091, 5–093
meaning, 1–102
passing of property, 5–092
and see **Passing of property**
potential property, 1–106, 5–095
purported sale, 1–105
sale by description, 11–007, 11–008
and see **Sale by description**
sale, of, 1–103, 1–105
Sale of Goods Act (1979), A-005
and see **Sale of Goods Act (1979)**
specific goods, as, 1–114
and see **Specific goods**

Gift
sale, distinguished, 1–032
and see **Sale**
Goods
aircraft, 1–082
animals, 1–088
approval
see **Goods on approval**
ascertained goods, 1–101, 1–116, 6–004
assignment
equitable principles, 1–107, 1–108
future property, 1–107, 1–108
banknotes, 1–084
body parts, 1–089
brand goods, 11–089
chattels, 1–080
and see **Chattels**
cheques, 1–084
classification
ascertained goods, 1–101, 1–116
existing goods, 1–101, 1–102
fungible goods, 1–101, 1–120
future goods, 1–101—1–103
non-existent goods, 1–122
specific goods, 1–101, 1–113
statutory classifications, 1–101
unascertained goods, 1–101, 1–113
coins, 1–084
commodities, 1–085

Goods—*cont.*
compound goods, 11–047, 11–060
conformity with contract, 14–012—14–017
credit cards, 1–084
crops, 1–090, 1–093
and see **Crops**
damaged goods, 12–057, 12–059
defective goods, 11–003, 11–041, 11–080
and see **Defective goods**
delivery
see **Delivery**
description, 11–007, 11–008, 11–014, 11–018
and see **Description**
destruction, of, 6–051, 12–057, 12–059
disposal
see **Right of disposal**
electricity, 1–085
equitable assignment, 1–107, 1–108
examination of goods
see **Examination of goods**
existence, of, 1–135
fitness for purpose, 11–024—11–026, 11–030, 11–031
and see **Fitness for purpose**
fitting, of, 12–040
foreign currency, 1–084
free movement, 3–042
frustration of contract,6–051, 6–052, 6–053
and see **Frustration of contract**
fungible goods, 1–101, 1–120
future goods, 1–101—1–103
and see **Future goods**
gaming chips, 1–084
gas, 1–087
human remains, 1–089
identification, of, 5–099
insufficient goods, 6–052
land
see **Land**
latent defects, 11–080
loss/deterioration of goods
see **Loss/deterioration of goods**
meaning, 1–078, 1–079
mixed goods, 12–060
money, 1–084
motor vehicles, 1–083
and see **Motor vehicles**
non-conforming goods, 12–060, 12–061, 12–066, 12–072, 12–074, 12–080
non-existent goods
agreements, as to, 1–122
buyer's liability, 1–134
effect on contract, 1–123
fault, 1–131
knowledge, as to, 1–131
liability, 1–132—1–134

Goods—*cont.*
non-existent goods—*cont.*
perished goods, 1–124—1–128
sale, of, 1–122
seller's liability, 1–132, 1–133
undivided share, 1–129, 1–130
warranty of existence, 1–133
oil, 1–087
perishable goods, 6–014
perished goods
damage, 1–128
deterioration, 1–128
fault, 1–131
frustration, and, 6–035, 6–040
knowledge, as to, 1–131
liability, 1–128
meaning, 1–125, 1–126
merchantable character, 1–128
part of goods, 1–127
physical destruction, 1–128
specific goods, 1–124, 1–125
undivided share, 1–129
potential property, 1–106
quality
caveat emptor, 11–024
implied condition, 11–024, 11–030
statements, as to, 11–016
statutory provisions, 11–024—11–026
warranty, as to, 11–024, 11–030
see also **Quality of goods**
rejected goods, 12–060—12–062, 12–065
repair, of, 12–076—12–079, 12–081
replacement, of, 12–076—12–079
risk
ascertained goods, 6–004
bulk goods, 6–004—6–008
identifiable goods, 6–004
loss, responsibility for, 6–001, 6–015
partly destroyed, 6–008
rejected goods, 6–011
and see **Risk**
sale by description, 11–007, 11–008, 11–014, 11–018
and see **Sale by description**
Sale of Goods Act (1979)
existing goods, A-005
future goods, A-005
perished goods, A-005
and see **Sale of Goods Act (1979)**
satisfactory quality, 11–080, 11–081, 11–085, 11–086
see also **Quality of goods**
second-hands goods, 11–048, 11–058
ships, 1–082
specific goods, 1–101, 1–113, 1–114
and see **Specific goods**
statutory terms, 1–079
testing, of, 12–040, 12–041

Goods—*cont.*
unascertained goods, 1–101, 1–113
and see **Unascertained goods**
undivided interest, 1–081
undivided share
see **Undivided share**
water, 1–087
wrongful interference
conversion, 4–012
detention, 4–012
Goods on approval
approval, 5–040, 5–047
bailment, and, 5–044
and see **Bailment**
conditions
condition precedent, 5–042
condition subsequent, 5–043
damaged goods, 5–056
delivery, 5–041, 5–048, 5–049
destruction of goods, 5–055, 5–057
fraud, and, 5–046
loss of goods, 5–055, 5–057
passing of property
adopting the transaction, 5–047—5–049, 5–051
condition precedent, 5–042
condition subsequent, 5–043
delivery on trial, 5–049
expiration of time, 5–040, 5–050
statutory rules, 5–040
and see **Passing of property**
pledge of goods, 5–047
price, notification of, 5–041
rejection notice, 5–052, 5–053
retention of goods, 5–040, 5–041
risk, 5–058, 6–009
and see **Risk**
stock financing schemes, 5–051
third party, delivery to, 5–048

Hague-Visby Rules
bills of lading, and, 18–013, 18–034, 18–035
and see **Bills of lading**
carriage by road, 21–059
and see **Carriage by road**
carriage on deck, 21–089, 21–092
container transport, 21–085, 21–087, 21–089, 21–092, 21–104, 21–106
and see **Container transport**
sea waybills, 18–035, 18–040, 18–044
and see **Sea waybills**
Hire Purchase Acts (1964–1965)
application, 1–019, 1–020
financial limits, 1–021
scope, 1–020

Hire-purchase agreements
block discounting, 1–054
common law, 1–019, 1–052
conditional sale agreements, and, 1–052
and see **Conditional sale agreements**
consumer credit transactions, 14–147
and see **Consumer credit transactions**
definition, 1–052
direct collection, 1–054
financing, 1–054
motor vehicles, 7–088—7–090
and see **Motor vehicles**
seller's title, and, 4–035
and see **Seller's title**
statutory controls, 1–109, 1–053
see also **Hire Purchase Acts (1964–1965)**
voidable title, and, 7–022
and see **Voidable title**

Illegality
conditions, for, 3–028
contractual principles, 3–027, 3–028
effect, of, 3–029, 3–030, 3–031
enforceability, and, 3–029, 3–030
frustration of contract, 6–045
and see **Frustration of contract**
illegal element
nature, of, 3–028
performance, 3–028
purpose, 3–028
terms, 3–038
parties *in pari delicto*, 3–032
passing of property, 3–030
and see **Passing of property**
public policy, and, 3–028
repudiation, 3–033
and see **Repudiation**
restitution, 3–031
and see **Restitution**
restraint of trade, 3–034—3–037
and see **Restraint of trade**
supervening, 6–045
Implied terms
brand goods, 11–089
common law, and, 1–031
description of goods, 11–001, 11–002, 12–071
and see **Description**
fitness for purpose, 11–024, 11–030
and see **Fitness for purpose**
freedom from encumbrance, 4–023, 4–024
and see **Freedom from encumbrance**
limited title, and, 4–033
overseas sales
see **Implied terms (overseas sales)**

Implied terms—*cont.*
quality of goods, 11–024, 11–030, 12–071, 18–255
and see **Quality of goods**
quiet possession, 4–025, 4–026
and see **Quiet possession**
sale by sample, 11–073
and see **Sale by sample**
Sale of Goods Act (1979)
consumer sales, A-009
fitness for purpose, A-009, A-033
payment, A-007
provisions, 11–089, A-007, A-008
quality of goods, A-009, A-033
title, A-008, A-033
warranties, A-007
and see **Sale of Goods Act (1979)**
trade usage, 11–088
Implied terms (overseas sales)
see also **Implied terms**
description
goods, corresponding to, 18–266
physical characteristics, 18–273
place of shipment, 18–267, 18–284
specifications, 18–273
time of shipment, 18–267, 18–268, 18–284
and see **Description**
fitness for purpose
market conditions, 18–274
particular purpose, 18–274
seller's skill/judgment, 18–274
and see **Fitness for purpose**
rejection of goods
Sale of Goods Act (1979), 18–284
statutory restrictions, 18–284
shipment
arrival of ship, 18–269
goods "afloat", 18–271
goods "under deck", 18–272
method, of, 18–272
place, of, 18–267, 18–284
"shipped", meaning of, 18–268
statements, relating to, 18–270, 18–271
time, of, 18–267, 18–268, 18–284
statutory provisions, 18–265
Insolvency
buyer's insolvency, 15–019, 15–024—15–026, 15–036, 15–037, 15–108
companies, 3–049
and see **Companies**
conflict of laws
choice of law, 25–150
Council Regulation (1346/2000/EC), 25–150
jurisdiction, 25–150
lex fori, 25–150, 25–151
lex situs, 25–151
Insolvency—*cont.*
conflict of laws—*cont.*
opening of proceedings, 25–150—25–152
recognition of judgments, 25–150
and see **Conflict of laws**
definition, 15–024
effect, of, 3–046, 3–048, 15–025
meaning, 3–048
passing of property, and, 5–005
and see **Passing of property**
timing, 15–026
Instalment deliveries
see also **Delivery**
acceptance, 8–064
agreement, as to, 8–065
amount not specified, 8–067
average instalments, 8–068
discharge
breach, by, 8–077
compensation, 8–077
defective deliveries, 8–077
payment default, 8–077
repudiation, 8–077
right of, 8–071
severable breach, 8–077
entire contract
breach, of, 8–072
complete delivery, 8–072
payment provisions, 8–072
performance, of, 8–072
rejection, under, 8–072
entitlement, 8–064
insolvency, effect of, 8–086
market price assessment, 17–008
payment
default, 8–077, 8–085
entire contract, under, 8–072
performance
failure, 8–080
inability, 8–079
postponement, 8–069, 8–070
remedies
damages, 8–087
repudiation, 8–077, 8–081
repudiation
breach of contract, 8–077, 8–081
buyer's insolvency, 8–086
effect, 8–082
non-repudiatory breach, 8–083, 8–084
performance, and, 8–079, 8–080
payment default, 8–085
renunciation, by, 8–078
and see **Repudiation**
seller's election, 8–066
separate contracts
individual deliveries, 8–076
severable contracts, distinguished, 8–075

Instalment deliveries—*cont.*
severable contracts
definition, 8–074
performance, 8–074
separate contracts, distinguished, 8–075
Instalment payments
forfeiture of payments, 16–038, 16–039
pre-payments, 16–038
price payable, 16–029
recovery, of, 16–040
Insurance
cargo, 21–041
see also **Sale of cargo**
c.i.f. contracts
see **C.I.F. contracts**
delivery of goods, 8–016
see also **Delivery**
f.o.b. contracts
see **F.O.B. contracts**
insurable interest, 6–012, 21–041
insurance charges, 20–138
loss/deterioration of goods, 18–246—18–248
and see **Loss/deterioration of goods**
passing of property, and, 5–012, 5–027
and see **Passing of property**
rejection of goods, 20–110
and see **Rejection of goods**
stoppage in transit, 15–090
and see **Stoppage in transit**
Intellectual property rights
sale, and, 1–077
and see **Sale**
Interest payments
see also **Price claims**
arbitration awards, 16–012, 16–013
basis, for, 16–008
commercial debts, 16–010
commercial rates, 16–008
contractual terms, 16–009
entitlement, 16–009
interest period, 16–011
judgment debts, 16–013
powers, relating to, 16–007, 16–008
statutory provisions, 16–007
Intermediate distributors
collateral contracts, 14–063
and see **Collateral contracts**
dangerous goods, 14–063
indemnity, 14–064
negligence, 14–063
Part 20 proceedings, 14–064
representations, 14–063
strict liability, 14–063
Intermediate terms
commercial disputes, 10–034
Intermediate terms—*cont.*
conditions, distinguished, 10–033, 10–035, 10–037
and see **Conditions**
consumer transactions, 10–036
discharge by breach, 10–033, 10–034
effect, of, 10–033
innominate terms, 10–033
nature, of, 10–033
repudiatory breach, 10–033
warranties, distinguished, 10–033
and see **Warranties**
Intermixing
bailment, and, 1–058
and see **Bailment**
ownership of goods, 1–058
International conventions
carriage by air
see **Carriage by air**
carriage by rail
see **Carriage by rail**
carriage by road
see **Carriage by road**
common terms, 21–049
purpose, 21–048
rights, under, 21–050
scope, 21–047
third parties, 21–050
International sale of goods
International Sales Act (1967), 1–024
UNCITRAL, 1–024
Uniform Law on Formation of Contracts (ULFIS), 1–024
Uniform Law on International Sale of Goods (ULIS), 1–024
Vienna Convention, 1–024
International Standard Banking Practice (ISBP)
documentary credits, and, 23–048
and see **Documentary credits**
International Standby Practices (ISP 98)
see also **Standby credits**
amendments, 23–257
cancellations, 23–257
examination of documents, 23–260
extension of facility, 23–259
mercantile usage, and, 23–253
nomination, under, 23–256
notice of rejection, 23–262
obligations, under, 23–255
payment, 23–259
presentation, 23–258, 23–259
regulation, by, 23–251
scope, 23–252, 23–253
standby documents, 23–261
transfer, 23–263

International supply contracts
conditions, governing, 18–281
definition, 18–281
governing law, 18–281
non-rejection clauses, 18–281
place of business, 18–281
statutory provisions, 25–114
unfair contract terms, 25–090, 25–160
see also **Unfair Contract Terms Act (1977)**
Internet
e.mail contracts, 2–015
internet payments
advance of delivery, 9–036
conflict of laws, 9–036
consumer protection, 9–036, 14–053, 14–054
consumer transactions, 9–036
defective performance, 9–036
distance selling, 9–036
encryption, 9–037
risk, 9–036, 9–037
security concerns, 9–036, 9–037
site verification service, 9–036
internet sales, 14–053, 14–054
web-page advertisements, 2–002

Land
assignment, of, 5–028
buildings, 1–090, 1–096
crops, and, 1–090, 1–093
and see **Crops**
fixtures, 1–090, 1–095
and see **Fixtures**
goods, distinguished, 1–090—1–092
and see **Goods**
gravel, 1–097
minerals, 1–090, 1–097
passing of property, 1–100
and see **Passing of property**
profits à prendre, 1–090, 1–097
sale, of, 1–090—1–093, 5–028
Sale of Goods Act (1893), 1–092
Sale of Goods Act (1979), 1–090, 1–093
and see **Sale of Goods Act (1979)**
severance, 1–099, 1–100
soil, 1–097
Statute of Frauds (1677), 1–091, 1–092
transfer, 1–094
trees, 1–090, 1–093, 1–098
written contracts, 1–092
Letter of credit
documentary credits
see **Documentary credits**
payment, by, 9–053
and see **Payment**
Licences
see also **Export/import licences**
conflict of laws
governing law, 25–168
lex loci solutionis, 25–168
Rome Convention, 25–168
and see **Conflict of laws**
Lien
see also **Seller's remedies**
advantages, of, 15–028
analogous rights, 15–053
banker's lien
see **Banker's lien**
bills of exchange, and, 15–036
and see **Bills of exchange**
buyer's insolvency, 15–036, 15–037
conditions
attornment to buyer, 15–040
credit expired, 15–035
credit sales, 15–033, 15–034
express agreement, 15–030
non-credit sales, 15–032
possession of goods, 15–038—15–040
unpaid seller, 15–030, 15–032
definition, 15–028
effect, of, 15–043
extent, of, 15–044
instalment contracts, 15–042
judgment for price, 15–059
nature, of, 15–028
negotiable instruments, and, 15–036
and see **Negotiable instruments**
part delivery, and, 15–041, 15–051
possession
meaning, 15–038
possession of goods, 1–064, 15–028, 15–029, 15–038—15–040
seller's rights, 15–028
rescission, and, 15–101
and see **Rescission**
sale, distinguished, 1–064
and see **Sale**
security, nature of, 1–064
termination
attornment, 55–052, 15–060
delivery orders, 15–052
delivery to carrier, 15–046
disposal of goods, 15–060
inconsistent arrangements, 15–058
inconsistent dealing, 15–057
part delivery, 15–051
possession by buyer, 15–049, 15–050, 15–053—15–055
right of disposal, and, 15–047
statutory provisions, 15–045
stoppage in transit, 15–048
sub-sales, 15–060
waiver, 15–056

Lien—*cont.*
termination—*cont.*
wrongful possession, 15–055
unpaid seller's lien
creation, of, 15–030
credit expired, 15–035
credit sales, 15–033, 15–034
disposal of goods, 15–060
nature, of, 15–028
non-credit sales, 15–032
part delivery, 15–041
possession of goods, 15–038—15–040
quasi-lien, 15–029
retaining possession, 15–029
Sale of Goods Act (1979), A-018
sub-sales, 15–060
termination, 15–045
waiver, 15–036
withholding delivery, 15–029
waiver, 15–036, 15–056
and see **Waiver**
Loss/deterioration of goods
bulk shipments, 18–00—18–302
and see **Bulk shipments**
commercial sales, 18–244—18–258
consumer sales, 18–259—18–264
and see **Consumer sales**
contract of carriage, 18–245
deterioration
causes, of, 18–256
defective packing, 18–258
delayed delivery, 18–258
deterioration in transit, 18–243
extraordinary, 18–251
necessary, 18–251—18–253
seller's breach, and, 18–254, 18–258
implied terms
condition of goods, 18–255, 18–256
quality, as to, 18–255
insurance, 18–246—18–248
loss in transit, 18–243, 18–250
risk, 18–224, 18–249, 18–251, 18–252, 18–300—18–302
and see **Risk**
seller's duty, 18–245, 18–246
transit
excluded categories, 18–257
meaning, of, 18–250
normal, 18–255
sea transit, 18–246—18–248

Manufacturers
collateral contracts, 14–062
and see **Collateral contracts**
defective goods, 14–061
direct sales, 14–061
duty of care, 14–062
false representations, 14–062
Manufacturers—*cont.*
guarantees
benefit, of, 14–071, 14–072
common law, 14–066
Consumer Protection Act (1987), 14–069
Consumer Sales Directive (1999/44/EC), 14–066, 14–070, 14–073—14–075
consumer use, and, 14–069
content, 14–067, 14–073
damages, relating to, 14–074
effect, of, 14–065, 14–066, 14–068
failure to honour, 14–074
goods. linked to, 14–071, 14–072
interpretation, 14–067
negligence, and, 14–069
non-transferable, 14–072
reliance, on, 14–074
removal of rights, 14–068
statutory provisions, 14–066
statutory rights, 14–065, 14–075
surrender of rights, 14–069
transparency, of, 14–073
Unfair Contract Terms Act (1977), 14–069
use, of, 14–062, 14–065
wording, of, 14–073
indemnity, from, 14–064
intermediate distributors, 14–061
liability
strict liability, 14–061, 14–062
tortious liability, 14–061, 14–062
negligence, 14–061, 14–069
Part 20 proceedings, 14–064
Married women
agency, and, 3–007
and see **Agency**
necessaries, and, 3–007
and see **Necessaries**
Materials
relative value, 1–044
supply, of, 1–041, 1–043—1–045
Mate's receipt
custom, proof of, 18–166
document of title
common law sense, 18–166
statutory sense, 18–167
and see **Document of title**
false statements, 18–164
f.o.b. contracts, 20–076
and see **F.O.B. contracts**
function, of, 18–164, 18–165, 18–168
nature, of, 18–163
passing of property, and, 18–228
see also **Passing of property (overseas sales)**
security for payment, 18–168

Mercantile agents
agency, and, 7–031, 7–032
and see **Agency**
authority, 7–032, 7–043, 7–045, 7–054
consignees, 7–053
definition, 7–032
first receipts, 7–033
good faith
meaning, 7–046
negligence, and, 7–046
requirement, 7–045
notice
meaning, 7–047
objective approach, 7–047
requirement, 7–045
owners
consignment, by, 7–053
rights preserved, 7–054
pledge, and, 7–042, 7–050
and see **Pledge**
possession of goods, 7–035, 7–037, 7–039
sale
effect, of, 7–048
price, recovery of, 7–048
transfer of title, 7–048
statutory provisions, governing, 7–032, 7–034
transfer of title
course of business, 7–032, 7–034
disposition, by, 7–034, 7–035, 7–041, 7–042
documents of title, 7–035, 7–036, 7–039
good title, 7–032, 7–055
owner's consent, 7–037—7–039, 7–044
sale, by, 7–048
see also **Transfer of title (non-owners)**
Minerals
extraction, of, 1–097
licences, 1–097
sale, of, 1–097, 1–098
Minors
see also Minors' contracts
contractual capacity, 2–028, 2–029
tortious liability, 2–040
and see **Tortious liability**
Minors' contracts
capacity, 2–029
enforceability, 2–037, 2–039
mixed goods, 2–034
necessaries, 2–030, 2–033
and see **Necessaries**
overall benefit, 2–033
ratification, 2–037
restitution, 2–038
and see **Restitution**
sale of goods, 2–039
Minors' contracts—*cont.*
trading contracts, 2–037
warranties, 2–037
Misrepresentation
affirmation, and, 12–006
see also **Affirmation (election)**
collateral contracts, 10–013, 10–014
and see **Collateral contracts**
common law rules, 3–008
equitable principles, 12–119
fraudulent, 12–014, 12–015
identification, of, 12–003
inducement to contract, 10–040
Misrepresentation Act (1967), 12–004, 12–005, 12–010, 12–014, 12–119
negligent, 12–013
remedies
collateral contracts, 12–002, 12–011
common law, 12–002
damages, 12–002, 12–004, 12–010, 12–011, 12–015
entitlement, 12–004
equitable remedies, 12–002, 12–003
rescission, 12–002, 12–003, 12–005, 12–008—12–010
restitutio in integrum, 12–005, 12–007, 12–008
and see **Remedies**
rescission, and, 12–119, 12–120
and see **Rescission**
statements, amounting to, 10–008
and see **Statements**
subsequent incorporation, 10–040, 12–119, 12–120
tortious liability
see **Tortious liability**
Mistake
attributes, as to, 3–013, 3–015
common law rules, 3–011
common mistake
allocation of risk, 3–021
conditions, governing, 3–021
effect, 3–018, 3–021
fundamental mistake, 3–018, 3–020
mistaken belief, 3–017, 3–021
quality, as to, 3–020, 3–021
res extincta, 3–019, 3–021
res sua, 3–019
documents
non est factum, 3–024
rectification, 3–024
signature, 3–024
equity
equitable principles, 3–011
mistake, in, 3–021, 3–024, 3–026
fundamental assumptions, 3–022
fundamental mistake, 3–018, 3–020

Mistake—*cont.*
identity, as to, 3–011, 3–012, 3–013, 3–015
inter praesentes, 3–014
non est factum, 3–011, 3–024
quality, as to, 3–017, 3–020
quantity, as to, 3–023
rescission, 3–026
and see **Rescission**
subject matter, as to, 3–011, 3–019, 12–128
terms
interpretation, 3–016
latent ambiguity, 3–016
negligence, as to, 3–016
quality, as to, 3–017, 3–020
Montreal Convention (1999)
see also **Carriage by air**
application, of, 21–051, 21–052
provisions, of, 21–051, 21–052
Motor vehicles
conditional sale agreements
creditor's title, 7–094, 7–095
debtors, 7–089
meaning, 7–088
sale, under, 7–088, 7–100
void/voidable, 7–090
and see **Conditional sale agreements**
creditor's title, 7–094, 7–095
disposition
admissions, 7–104
anomalies, 7–097, 7–098
conditional sale agreement, 7–088
debtor, by, 7–101—7–103
good faith, 7–094—7–096, 7–099
good title, 7–094—7–096
hire-purchase agreements, 7–087
meaning, 7–091
notice requirement, 7–094—7–096, 7–099
presumptions, 7–100, 7–101
protection, extent of, 7–105, 7–106
statutory provisions, 7–087, 7–108
third party, to, 7–092, 7–094
hire-purchase agreements
bailment, under, 7–088, 7–089, 7–100
creditor's title, 7–094, 7–095
debtors, 7–089
meaning, 7–088
statutory provisions, 7–088
void/voidable, 7–090
and see **Hire-purchase agreements**
purchasers
private purchasers, 7–092—7–094, 7–096, -097, 7–100
trade/finance purchasers, 7–092, 7–093, 7–095
Motor vehicles—*cont.*
title
acquisition, of, 7–107
creditor's title, 7–094, 7–095
good title, 7–094—7–096
nature, of, 7–107
Multimodal transport document
see also **Container transport**
bills of lading, and, 21–076
and see **Bills of lading**
Carriage of Goods by Sea Act (1992), 21–076
contractual effects, 21–076
document of title, 21–079—21–081, 21–083
and see **Document of title**
form
negotiable, 21–082
non-negotiable, 21–082
function, 21–075
implied contract, 21–078
legal nature, 21–075
sea waybills, and, 21–076
and see **Sea waybills**
third parties, 21–077
Tokyo Rules, 21–082
UNCTAD/ICC Rules, 21–082

Necessaries
see also **Minors' contracts**
examples, 2–031
executory contracts, 2–032
loans, for, 2–035
married women, and, 3–007
meaning, 2–030
mixed goods, 2–034
proof, as to, 2–030
seller's liability, 2–036
Negotiable instruments
banks, role, of, 22–001
bills of exchange, and, 22–002, 22–005
and see **Bills of exchange**
cash, equivalent to, 9–032
Civil Procedure Rules (CPR), 9–032
consideration, need for, 9–032
enforcement, 22–031
financing, and, 22–003
nature, of, 22–031
negotiability, 22–031
payment, by, 9–030—9–032, 16–018, 22–002, 22–005
and see **Payment**
types, of, 22–032
Nemo dat quod non habet
see also **Transfer of title (non-owners)**
bulk goods, and, 7–085
and see **Bulk goods**
buyer in possession, 7–069
and see **Buyer in possession**

Nemo dat quod non habet—cont.
consumer protection, 14–007
and see **Consumer protection**
effect, of, 7–001
estoppel, and, 7–008
and see **Estoppel**
hire-purchase agreements, 7–087
and see **Hire-purchase agreements**
meaning, of, 7–001
motor vehicles, 7–087, 7–108
and see **Motor vehicles**
seller in possession, 7–055
and see **Seller in possession**
Non-consensual transactions
arbitration awards, 1–068
collateral contracts, 1–071
compulsory acquisition, 1–070
implied contracts, 1–067
incapacitated persons, 1–076
indemnity payments, 1–069
judgment in tort, 1–072
minor's contracts, 1–076
and see **Minor's contracts**
public duty, and, 1–071
quasi-contracts, 1–067
statutory obligation, and, 1–071
transfer by non-owner, 1–075
waiver in tort, 1–073, 1–074
Non-owners
see **Transfer of title (non-owners)**
Non-rejection clauses
applicable law, 18–283
common law, 18–276—18–279
effect, of, 18–276—18–279
fundamental breach, 18–276, 18–277
international supply contracts, 18–281
and see **International supply contracts**
non-conforming goods, 18–275, 18–279
restrictions, on, 18–280
specification clauses, 18–279
Unfair Contract Terms Act (1977), 18–280
and see **Unfair Contract Terms Act (1977)**
Unfair Terms in Consumer Contracts Regulations (1999), 18–282, 18–283
and see **Unfair Terms in Consumer Contracts Regulations (1999)**

Offer
acceptance, 2–001
and see **Acceptance**
advertisements, 2–002
"click-wrap" contracts, 2–012, 2–015
and see **"Click-wrap" contracts**
conditional offers, 2–007
inferred from conduct, 2–008
invitation to treat, distinguished, 2–002
preliminary inquiries, 2–002

Offer—*cont.*
revocation, 2–010
standing offer, 2–009
Office of Fair Trading (OFT)
codes of practice, and, 14–137
complaints, to, 14–127, 14–128
enforcement, and, 14–128, 14–134, 14–136, 14–138
role, of, 14–040, 14–125, 14–138
trade practices, and, 14–138, 14–139
Option to buy
conditional sale, and, 1–051
contract for sale, distinguished, 1–050
and see **Contract for sale**
sale or return, 1–056
and see **Sale or return**
Overseas sales
banks, role of, 22–001
bills of exchange, and, 22–002, 22–005
and see **Bills of exchange**
bulk shipments
see **Bulk shipments**
delivery points, 21–001
direct payment
see **Direct payment**
document of title
see **Document of title**
export/import clauses
see **Export/import clauses**
export/import licences
see **Export/import licences**
export/import prohibitions
see **Export/import prohibitions**
financing methods, 22–003
INCOTERMS (2000), 18–002
loans, 22–004
loss/deterioration of goods
see **Loss/deterioration of goods**
negotiable instruments
see **Negotiable instruments**
non-rejection clauses
see **Non-rejection clauses**
overdraft facilities, 22–004
passing of property
see **Passing of property (overseas sales)**
payment methods, 22–002, 22–005
problems, associated with, 18–001
risk
allocation, 18–001
financial, 18–001
loss/deterioration of goods, 18–244, 18–249, 18–251, 18–252
passing of property, 18–244
physical, 18–001
and see **Risk**

Overseas sales—*cont.*
third parties
common law, 18–005
Contracts (Rights of Third Parties) Act (1999), 18–005
privity of contract, 18–005
Uniform Law on International Sale of Goods (ULIS), 18–003
and see **Uniform Law on International Sale of Goods (ULIS)**
Vienna Convention, 18–004
and see **Vienna Convention**
Ownership
co-ownership, 5–109, 5–124—5–126, 5–130
disposal of goods, 5–149, 5–150
see also **Right of disposal**
owners
consent, of, 7–001, 7–037—7–039, 7–044
consignment, by, 7–053
non est factum, 7–018
part-owners, 1–121
recovery of possession, 7–002
remedies, available to, 7–002—7–004
rights preserved, 7–054
tracing, by, 7–003
transfer of title
see **Transfer of title (non-owners)**

Paperless transactions
see also **Documents of title**
bills of lading
electronic bill of lading, 18–202, 18–203, 18–205, 18–206
straight (non-negotiable) bills, 18–207
and see **Bills of lading**
Carriage of Goods by Sea Act (1992), 18–202
contract
contractual rights, 18–206, 18–207
contractual solutions, 18–204
delivery, and, 18–202
document of title
common law sense, 18–207
statutory sense, 18–205
and see **Document of title**
holders, 18–202
indorsement, 18–02
sea waybills, 18–206, 18–207
and see **Sea waybills**
ship's delivery orders, 18–206
and see **Ship's delivery orders**
transfer of possession, 18–04
use, of, 18–202, 18–203
Passing of property
bailment, and, 5–010
and see **Bailment**
bills of lading, and, 5–008
and see **Bills of lading**

Passing of property—*cont.*
bulk goods
aggregate shares, 5–118
compensation provisions, 5–127
conditions, governing, 5–061, 5–062, 5–103, 5–104, 5–113
co-ownership, 5–109, 5–124—5–126, 5–130
deemed consent, 5–124, 5–126
identified part, 5–109
overselling, 5–121—5–123
part payments, 5–120
price, payment of, 5–115, 5–130
proportionate share, 5–118—5–120
quantity unknown, 5–119
specified quantity, 5–11
statutory provisions, 5–109, 5–110
unascertained goods, 5–112
undivided share, 5–109, 5–116
and see **Bulk goods**
carriage of goods, and, 5–009
and see **Carriage of goods**
consumer sales, 6–013, 6–014, 6–016, 14–007
and see **Consumer sales**
criminal offences, and, 5–013
delivery of goods, and, 5–002, 5–097—5–102
see also **Delivery**
disposal of goods
see **Right of disposal**
ex works contracts, 5–089
and see **Ex works contracts**
f.o.b. contracts
see **F.O.B. contracts**
illegality, and, 3–030
and see **Illegality**
importance, of, 5–002
insolvency, and, 5–005
insurance, and, 5–012, 5–027
intention, as to, 5–001
legal process, and, 5–014
overseas sales
see **Passing of property (overseas sales)**
possession, and, 5–002, 5–010
presumptions
common law, 5–001
Sale of Goods Act (1979), 5–001
prize goods, and, 5–015
rejected goods, 6–011
risk
ascertained goods, 6–004
bulk goods, 6–004—6–008
condition subsequent, 6–010
consumer sales, 6–013, 6–014, 6–016
delivery of goods, 6–013, 6–015
EC legislation, 6–014

Passing of property—*cont.*
risk—*cont.*
f.o.b. contracts, 6–004
goods on approval, 6–009
identifiable goods, 6–004
perishable goods, 6–014
provisions, governing, 5–002, 5–007, 5–009, 5–027, 6–002—6–006
rejected goods, 6–011
sale or return, 6–009
undivided share, 6–005—6–008
unfair contract terms, 6–013, 6–014
and see **Risk**
Sale of Goods Act (1979), A-011
and see **Sale of Goods Act (1979)**
sale or return, 1–056
and see **Sale or return**
seller's remedies, 5–006
specific goods (deliverable state)
see **Specific goods (deliverable state)**
specific goods (non-deliverable state)
see **Specific goods (non-deliverable state)**
specific goods (weighing/measuring/testing)
see **Specific goods (weighing/measuring/testing)**
third parties
negligence, 5–010, 5–011
title, 5–004
timing, 5–001
title
buyer's title, 5–003
third party, 5–004
title documents, 5–002
unascertained goods
see **Unascertained goods**
undivided share, 5–109, 5–110
and see **Undivided share**
voidable title, and, 7–021, 7–022
and see **Voidable title**
wrongful interference, and, 5–010
Passing of property (overseas sales)
agents
agency relationships, 18–232, 18–233
buyers/sellers, as, 18–232
disposal of goods, 18–230
shipment, and, 18–229, 18–231
status, 18–232
transfer of title, 18–233
and see **Agents**
appropriation, 18–210
bills of exchange, 18–221—18–223, 18–241
and see **Bills of exchange**
bill of lading
form, of, 18–214
fraud, obtained by,18–227
hypothecation, of, 18–234
Passing of property (overseas sales)—*cont.*
bill of lading—*cont.*
indorsement, of, 18–126
registration, 18–238
return, of, 18–223
security for advance, 18–126, 18–235
transmission, of, 18–126
trust receipts, and, 18–235, 18–236
wrongful retention, 18–222
see also **Bills of lading**
documentary bills, 18–21—18–225
lien, and, 18–209, 18–233
and see **Lien**
mate's receipts, 18–228
and see **Mate's receipts**
payment
documentary credit, by, 18–128
effect, of, 18–226
payment of price, 18–209
prior to payment, 18–220
prize cases, 18–242
right of disposal
contract terms, 18–212
reservation, of, 18–211, 18–212, 1–218
surrender, of, 18–129
risk
ascertained goods, 6–004
bulk goods, 6–004—6–008
condition subsequent, 6–010
consumer sales, 6–013, 6–014, 6–016
delivery of goods, 6–013, 6–015
EC legislation, 6–014
f.o.b. contracts, 6–004, 20–071
goods on approval, 6–009
identifiable goods, 6–004
overseas sales, 18–244
provisions, governing, 6–002—6–006
rejected goods, 6–011
sale or return, 6–009
undivided share, 6–005—6–008
unfair contract terms, 6–013, 6–014
and see **Risk**
Romalpa clauses, 18–240
and see ***Romalpa* clauses**
rules, as to, 18–208, 18–209
security for payment, 18–209, 18–127
shipping documents, and, 18–125
specific goods, 18–209
stoppage in transit, 18–209, 18–233
and see **Stoppage in transit**
subsequent dealings, 18–219
trust receipts, and, 18–235—18–239
unascertained goods, 18–209, 18–210
variation of agreement, 18–213
Payment
agency, and, 9–043, 9–044
and see **Agency**

Payment—*cont.*
amount
adjustment, 9–023
discount, 9–023
full contract price, 9–023
lesser sums, 9–024
"no set-off" clauses, 9–026
part payment, 9–025
unfair contract terms, 9–026
appropriation, and, 9–046
and see **Appropriation**
buyer's duty, 9–021
consumer contracts, 9–026
see also **Consumer sales**
consumer credit agreements, 9–065
credit
credit periods, 9–062, 9–063
credit sales, 9–061—9–063
letters of credit, 9–053
and see **Credit**
currency, use of, 9–045
default, 8–077, 8–085, 9–027
deposit, payment of, 9–052
direct payment
see **Direct payment**
goods
buyer's risk, 9–056
delivery, 9–021
lost/destroyed, 9–056
possession, 9–021
instalment payments, 9–065
interest payments, 9–068
internet payments, 9–036, 9–037
see also **Internet**
late payments, 1–023
letters of credit, 9–053
methods
accounts sated, 9–041
banker's commercial credits, 9–040
banking system, 9–038
cash, 9–028
charge card, 9–033
cheque, 9–034
cheque card, 9–034
credit card, 9–033
digital cash card, 9–035
direct debits, 9–09
future arrangements, 9–029
negotiable instrument, 9–030—9–032
post, by, 9–042
stored value card, 9–035
place of payment
agreement, as to, 9–047
commercial transactions
contracts of carriage, 9–049
intention of parties, 9–047
overseas sales, 9–048
place of business, 9–047

Payment—*cont.*
place of payment—*cont.*
place of residence, 9–047
unspecified, 9–047
waiver, 9–050
right to sue, 9–021
sub-sales, 15–100
third party, by, 9–044
timing
condition precedent, 9–059
credit sales, 9–061—9–063
deposit, payment of, 9–052
letters of credit, 9–053
notice requirement, 9–059, 9–060
overseas sales, 9–058
payment on demand, 9–059
specified time, 9–051
terms, as to, 9–054
unspecified time, 9–057
waiver, 9–055
trading accounts, 9–064

Performance bonds
see also **Documentary credits**
Australian cases, 23–289
autonomous undertaking, 23–275
beneficiaries, and, 23–279
conditional bonds, distinguished, 23–273
default notice, 23–278
demand
form, 23–284, 23–285
sufficiency, 23–285
validity, 23–285
fraud rule
Edward Owen Engineering, 23–076
effect, of, 23–275—23–277, 23–279, 23–280
Harbottle's Case, 23–275
Themehelp Case, 23–280
function, 23–271
guarantees, distinguished, 23–273
ISP 98, and, 23–291
and see **International Standby Practices (ISP 98)**
liability, evidence of, 23–278
nature, of, 23–237, 23–272
non-performance, and, 23–237
payment, 23–270, 23–286
purpose, 23–237
recital of details, 23–274
strict compliance, 23–283
subrogation, 23–287
surplus, right to, 23–288
terminology, 23–270
UCP, incorporation of, 23–290
and see **Uniform Customs and Practice for Documentary Credits (UCP)**
unconscionability, 23–281, 23–82

Performance bonds—*cont.*
Uniform Rules for Contract Guarantees (1978), 23–292
Uniform Rules for Demand Guarantees (1992), 23–293
and see **Uniform Rules for Demand Guarantees (1992)**
Pledge
bailment, and, 1–063
and see **Bailment**
definition, 7–049
disposition, by, 7–042
effect, 7–049—7–052
lack of authority, 7–050
nature, of, 1–06, 1–064
possession of goods, 1–064
redemption, right of, 7–050
sale, distinguished, 1–063
and see **Sale**
security, and, 1–064, 7–051, 7–052
Possession
actual, 7–072
bailee, as, 7–073
see also **Bailment**
buyer in possession
see **Buyer in possession**
constructive, 7–072
continuation, of, 7–076
documents of title, 7–069, 7–072, 7–073, 7–075
lien, and, 1–064
and see **Lien**
meaning, 7–057—7–060
mercantile agents, 7–035, 7–037, 7–039
and see **Mercantile agents**
mere possession, 7–022
passing of property, 5–002, 5–010
and see **Passing of property**
post-agreement, 7–073
quiet possession
see **Quiet possession**
recovery, of, 7–002
seller in possession
see **Seller in possession**
Price claims
see also **Seller's remedies**
consequential loss, 16–030
consumer sales, 16–002
and see **Consumer sales**
contract in force, 16–001
contractual terms, and, 16–001, 16–003
damages claims, distinguished, 16–004, 16–005
delivery of goods, 16–001
deposit, allowance for, 16–014
entitlement to sue
action for price, 16–021, 16–022, 16–025, 16–028
Price claims—*cont.*
entitlement to sue—*cont.*
contractual terms, 16–028
instalment payments, 16–029
passing of property, 16–021—16–023, 16–028
failure of payment
banker's commercial credit, 16–019
deposit, allowance for, 16–014
negotiable instrument, 16–018
passing of property, 16–015
refusal to pay, 16–016
seller's previous breach, 16–020
tender of payment, 16–017
termination of contract, 16–015
wrongful neglect, 16–016
foreign currency, 16–006
instalment payments, 16–005, 16–029
interest payments, 16–007—16–013
and see **Interest payments**
passing of property
action for price, 16–021—16–023
estoppel, 16–024
price payable, 16–028
waiver, 16–024
wrongful prevention, 16–023
and see **Passing of property**
personal remedy, 16–001
price
definition, of, 16–014
price reduction, 16–002
price payable
contingent event, on, 16–026
"day certain", on, 16–025, 16–027
instalment payments, 16–029
passing of property, 16–028
timing, 16–028
property with buyer
action for price, 16–021
f.o.b. contracts, 16–022
statutory provisions, 16–021
statutory provisions, 16–001, 16–003
tender of payment, 16–017
Procedure
asset recovery, 7–117
burden of proof, 25–205
civil litigation, 14–102
Civil Procedure Rules (CPR), 7–122, 14–104, 17–096
class actions, 14–103
conflict of laws
governing law, 25–203
Guiliano-Lagarde Report, 25–205
lex fori, 25–203, 25–205
Rome Convention, 25–203, 25–205, 25–206
and see **Conflict of laws**
execution debtors, 7–113

Procedure—*cont.*
group actions, 14–103, 14–104
legal presumptions, 25–0205
limitation of actions, 25–204
method of proof, 25–206
Rome Convention, and, 25–203, 25–205, 25–206
and see **Rome Convention**
small claims, 14–101
warrant of execution, 7–114
writ of execution, 7–113
Product liability
consumer protection, and, 14–078
and see **Consumer protection**
Product Safety Regulations (2005)
see also **Consumer protection**
Community Rapid Information System (RAPAX), 14–123
distributors, 14–121
enforcement provisions, 14–122, 14–123
European Commission, and, 14–123
forfeiture of goods, 14–122
notification requirement, 14–123
producers, under, 14–120, 14–121
provisions, of, 14–119, 14–120
safe products, 14–120
serious risks, 14–123
suspension notices, 14–122
withdrawal notices, 14–122
Profits à prendre
meaning, of, 1–090, 1–097
nature, of, 1–090, 1–097
Proper law doctrine
see also **Conflict of laws (contract)**
choice, and, 25–006—25–009
c.i.f. contracts, 25–012
and see **C.I.F. contracts**
close/real connection
law of country, 25–008
legal system, 25–008
contracts, governed by, 25–005
f.o.b. contracts, 25–011
and see **F.O.B. contracts**
overseas sales, 25–013
place of business, and, 25–009
relevant factors, 25–009, 25–010
renvoi, exclusion of, 25–014
Rome Convention
see **Rome Convention**
Public statements
see also **Quality of goods**
advertising, 11–034
consumer protection, 14–012, 14–014
and see **Consumer protection**
consumer sales, regarding, 11–033, 11–034, 12–071
and see **Consumer sales**
contractual promises, 11–034

Public statements—*cont.*
existing laws, 11–037
labelling, 11–034
misrepresentation, 11–034
and see **Misrepresentation**
producers, by, 11–035
representatives, by, 11–035
sellers, by, 11–034, 11–035
withdrawal, of, 11–036

Quality of goods
business
course of business, 11–027, 11–029
meaning, 11–028
caveat emptor, 11–024
consumer protection, 14–010
and see **Consumer protection**
defective quality
see **Defective quality**
fitness for purpose, 11–025, 11–026, 11–030, 11–038, 14–010
and see **Fitness for purpose**
goods
examination, of, 11–042, 11–080, 11–081, 11–086
known defects, 11–041
latent defects, 11–080
supplied under contract, 11–030
guidelines
appearance and finish, 11–038
durability, 11–040
fitness for purpose, 11–038, 11–070, 11–071
minor defects, 11–038
safety, 11–039
state of goods, 11–038
implied condition, 11–024, 11–030
implied terms, 12–071
and see **Implied terms**
legislative background, 11–025
merchantable quality, 11–025, 11–031, 11–041, 11–044
public statements, 11–033, 11–034
and see **Public statements**
sale
agency sales, 11–029
course of business, 11–027, 11–029, 11–070
description, by, 11–032, 11–070
related contracts, 11–050
sale by sample
examination of goods, 11–080, 11–081
free from defect, 11–080
satisfactory quality, 11–080, 11–081, 11–085, 11–086
and see **Sale by sample**
satisfactory quality
advertising, 11–034
agency sales, 11–026

Quality of goods—*cont.*
satisfactory quality—*cont.*
compound goods, 11–047
consumer sales, 11–033
definition, 11–070
description of goods, 11–032, 11–070
durability, 11–040
duty, as to, 11–043
examination of goods, 11–041, 11–072
examples, of, 11–044
interpretation, of, 11–044
known defects, 11–041, 11–072
labelling, 11–034
manufactured products, 11–031
price indicators, 11–032
public statements, 11–033, 11–034
reliance, on, 11–060
sale by sample, 11–080, 11–081, 11–085, 11–086
Sale of Goods Act (1979), 11–024, 11–026, 11–031, 11–070, 11–071
second-hand goods, 11–048
standard, for, 11–031
subsequent knowledge, 11–045, 11–046
time of sale, 11–045, 11–049
statutory provisions, 11–024—11–026
strict liability, 14–017
warranty, as to, 11–024, 11–030
see also **Warranties**
Quantity of goods (delivery)
see also **Delivery**
adjustments, 8–055
approximate quantities, 8–054
buyers
exclusive dealing agreements, 8–061
liability, 8–059
requirements, 8–059, 8–060, 8–061
cargo, sale of, 8–057
correct quantity, 8–045
course of dealing, 8–053
derogation, 8–053, 8–054, 8–063
estimated quantities, 8–056
excessive delivery
acceptance, 8–049
breach of term, 12–029, 12–030
corrective action, 8–052
payment, 8–049
rejection, 8–049, 8–051
statutory provisions, 8–049
exemption clauses, 8–063
and see **Exemption clauses**
goods "as required", 8–058, 8–059
insufficient delivery
acceptance, and, 8–046, 8–047
breach of term, 12–029, 12–030
corrective action, 8–052
examination of goods, 8–047
force majeure, 8–102
Quantity of goods (delivery)—*cont.*
insufficient delivery—*cont.*
recovery of payment, 8–046
rejection, 8–046—8–048
slight shortfall, 12–030
statutory provisions, 8–046
undelivered balance, 8–046
rejection
consumer contracts, 8–063
delivery by instalments, 8–048
de minimis rule, 8–050, 8–051
excessive delivery, 8–049, 8–051
exemption clauses, 8–063
insufficient goods, 8–046
restrictions, on, 8–050, 8–051
repudiation, and, 12–029
and see **Repudiation**
seller's duty, 8–045
special agreement, 8–053, 8–054, 8–063
trade usage, 8–053, 8–062
Quiet possession
buyer's remedies
consequential losses, 4–029
damages, 4–029
legal costs, 4–029
repudiation, 4–029
see also **Remedies**
disturbance, affecting, 4–026, 4–027, 4–030
exemption clauses, and, 4–031
and see **Exemption clauses**
extent, of, 4–025, 4–026
implied term, 4–025, 4–026
see also **Implied terms**
limited title, and, 4–033
see also **Seller's title**
warranty, as to, 4–029, 4–030

Rejection of contract
affirmation (election), and, 12–037, 12–047
and see **Affirmation (election)**
breach of condition, 12–025—12–027
buyer's duties, 12–065
commercial units, 12–062
conditions, for, 12–032
consumer sales, 12–071
and see **Consumer sales**
contractual terms, as to, 12–063
damaged goods, 12–057, 12–059
damages, and, 12–067
and see **Damages**
destroyed goods, 12–057, 12–059
discharge, distinguished, 12–028
examination of goods, 12–039, 12–048, 12–050, 12–053, 12–055
and see **Examination of goods**
exemption clauses, 12–063
and see **Exemption clauses**

Rejection of contract—*cont.*
failure of consideration, 12–067
instalment contracts, 12–070
insufficient grounds, 12–033
non-conforming goods, 12–060, 12–061, 12–066
ownership, and, 12–047, 12–050
reasonable time, 12–053, 12–055, 12–056
rejection of part, 12–060—12–062
restitution, 12–067
and see **Restitution**
right of rejection, 12–034, 12–037, 12–039, 12–048
risk, and, 12–065
and see **Risk**
seller's duties, 12–065
short delivery, 12–069
trade usage, 12–056
waiver, and, 12–034, 12–037
and see **Waiver**
whole delivery, 12–061

Rejection of goods
breach of contract
absence, of, 19–168
non-repudiatory breach, 19–169
simultaneous breaches, 19–162
buyer's conduct, 19–171
dealing as consumer, 19–145, 19–150
documents
defective, 19–147, 19–148
examination, 19–156
missing, 19–148
non-conforming, 19–144, 19–147, 19–155
rejection, of, 20–106
tender, of, 19–144, 19–145, 19–149, 19–168
estoppel
operation, of, 19–160
promissory estoppel, 19–150
examination
documents, 19–156
goods, 19–145, 19–156, 19–157
force majeure, and, 19–150
and see Force majeure
goods
delayed delivery, 19–161
delivery to sub-buyer, 19–154
examination, 19–145, 19–156, 19–157, 20–108, 20–109
non-arrival, 19–145
non-conforming, 19–144, 19–146, 19–149, 19–154, 19–155, 19–163—19–165
passing of property, 19–174
qualitative defects, 19–145
repair of goods, 19–150
replacement of goods, 19–150
resale, 19–154

Rejection of goods—*cont.*
goods—*cont.*
right to reject, 19–144, 19–145, 19–149, 20–105, 20–109, 20–110, 20–112
shipment, and, 19–144
loss of rights, 19–150, 19–154, 19–157, 20–107
non-rejection clauses, 19–172, 20–110, 20–112, 20–113
partial rejection, 19–158
repudiation, and, 19–161, 19–163, 19–164, 19–170
rescission, and, 19–145, 19–165, 19–166
and see **Rescission**
Sale of Goods Act (1979), A-015
and see **Sale of Goods Act (1979)**
statutory restriction, 19–173, 19–174
timing, 19–149
valid grounds, 19–160, 19–161
waiver, and, 19–160
and see **Waiver**
wrong reason, 19–159—19–161, 19–165—19–167, 20–112

Remedies
breach of term, 12–017
and see **Breach of term**
buyer's remedies
see **Buyer's remedies**
c.i.f. contracts
see **Buyer's remedies (c.i.f. contracts), Seller's remedies (c.i.f. contracts)**
collateral contracts, 12–002, 12–011
consumer remedies
alternative remedies, 12–110
Consumer Sales Directive (1999/44/EC), 14–023
damages, 14–020, 14–023
price reduction, 14–024
rejection of goods, 14–020—14–023, 14–027
remedial action, 14–022, 14–023
repair of goods, 14–021, 14–023—14–025, 14–027
replacement of goods, 14–022—14–025, 14–027
rescission, 14–024, 1–026
specific performance, 14–025
and see **Consumer remedies**
consumer sales
acceptance, effect of, 12–112
alternative remedies, 12–110
buyer's inactivity, 12–109
buyer's rights, 12–072, 12–075
choice, as to, 12–102, 12–118
common law, 12–090, 12–097, 12–118
contracting-out, 12–117
court's powers, 12–113, 12–114

Remedies—*cont.*
consumer sales—*cont.*
damages, 12–104, 12–105, 12–094, 12–114, 17–003
defective goods, 12–075, 12–087
defective installation, 12–116
disproportionate, 12–080
enforcement, 12–114
entitlement, 12–114
estoppel, 12–108, 12–109
inconsistent remedies, 12–103
interaction of remedies, 12–118
mitigation, 12–105
priority, 12–106
reduction in price, 12–077, 12–089, 12–090
rejection of goods, 12–096, 12–111, 12–118
repair of goods, 12–076—12–079, 12–081, 12–118
replacement of goods, 12–076—12–079, 12–118
rescission, 12–077, 12–089, 12–090, 12–095—12–101, 12–118
specific performance, 12–114, 17–101, 17–103
statutory provisions, 12–001, 12–072, 12–075, 12–076
time limits, 12–107
waiver, 12–108
and see **Consumer sales**
damages, 12–002, 12–004, 12–010, 12–011, 12–015
and see **Damages**
defective goods, 12–071, 14–020, 14–021
and see **Defective goods**
defective quality, 17–048, 17–050
and see **Defective quality**
f.o.b. contracts
see **Buyer's remedies (f.o.b. contracts), Seller's remedies (f.o.b. contracts)**
misrepresentation
collateral contracts, 12–002, 12–011
common law, 12–002
damages, 12–002, 12–004, 12–010, 12–011, 12–015
entitlement, 12–004
equitable remedies, 12–002, 12–003
rescission, 12–002, 12–003
restitutio in integrum, 12–005, 12–007, 12–008
and see **Misrepresentation**
reduction in price, 12–089, 12–090, 12–094
rejection of goods, 14–020—14–023, 14–027

Remedies—*cont.*
rescission, 12–077, 12–089, 12–090, 12–095—12–101, 12–118
and see **Rescission**
restitutio in integrum, 12–005, 12–007, 12–008
seller's remedies
see **Seller's remedies**
specific performance, 12–071
tortious liability
and see **Tortious liability**
transfer of title
confiscation orders, 7–007
damages, 7–002, 7–004
police powers, 7–006, 7–007
restitutionary claims, 7–003
restitution orders, 7–006
seizure orders, 7–006, 7–007
tracing, 7–003
see also **Transfer of title (non-owners)**
Vienna Convention
see **Vienna Convention**

Remoteness of damage
actual knowledge, 16–046, 16–061
foreseeability, 16–043, 16–044
Hadley v Baxendale, 16–043, 16–046, 16–061
imputed knowledge, 16–045
principles, relating to, 16–043
probability, 16–044
special circumstances, 16–046, 16–061
statutory provisions, 16–043

Repudiation
acceptance of goods, and, 4–009, 9–002, 9–010
see also **Acceptance**
breach of condition, 10–027, 10–028
see also **Conditions**
breach of contract, 8–077, 8–081, 12–021, 12–029
buyers
buyer's insolvency, 8–086
buyer's remedy, 4–006, 4–009, 4–010
effect, 8–082
expiration of time, 9–013
feeding title, 4–010, 4–013
grounds, for, 9–002, 9–010
illegality, and, 3–033
and see **Illegality**
non-repudiatory breach, 8–083, 8–084
payment default, 8–085
renunciation, by, 8–078
sellers
acceptance, by, 9–017, 9–020
non-acceptance, by, 9–018, 9–019
unjustifiable, 9–012—9–015

Resale
agency of necessity, 15–106
buyer
fundamental breach, 15–109, 15–110
possession, with, 15–114, 15–115, 15–117
property, with, 15–117
repudiation, 15–107—15–110
case decisions
Hall v Pim, 17–030—17–033, 17–036
Williams v Agius, 17–032, 17–033
damages
buyer's entitlement, 17–036
sub-buyer, to, 17–036
see also **Buyer's remedies (damages)**
defective goods
loss of custom, 17–034
repeat orders, 17–034
delayed delivery, 17–044, 17–045
and see **Delayed delivery**
express right
common law remedies, 15–130
conditions, for, 15–129
express reservation, 15–128
forfeiture
deposit, 15–132, 15–133
prepayments, 15–134
good title, and, 15–102, 15–112
knowledge
actual knowledge, 17–030
imputed knowledge, 17–030
loss
consequential loss, 17–037
custom, 17–034
profits, 17–029—17–031, 17–034—17–036, 17–044
market
market price, 17–029
no available market, 17–035
method, of, 15–131
notice to resell, 15–119, 15–121, 15–123
perishable goods
good title, 15–126
meaning, 15–120
notice to resell, 15–121, 15–123
payment, for, 15–121—15–123
possession of goods, 15–124—15–126
statutory rights, 15–119, 15–120
termination of contract, 15–127
rescission, and, 15–101, 15–107, 15–110
and see **Rescission**
revesting of property, 15–101, 15–113, 15–118
Sale of Goods Act (1979), A-020
and see **Sale of Goods Act (1979)**

Resale—*cont.*
sellers
property, with, 15–114, 15–115
remedies, 15–117
retaking goods, 15–116
rights, 15–105, 15–112, 15–113
statutory powers, 15–103
statutory right, 15–119, 15–120
sub-contracts, 17–028
termination of contract
affirmation of contract, and, 15–111
alternative remedies, 15–110
buyer's repudiation, 15–107—15–110
conditions, 15–101
damages, 15–110
entitlement, 15–101
fundamental breach, 15–109, 15–110
insolvency, 15–108
perishable goods, 15–127
resale, following, 15–112, 15–113
rescission, and, 15–101, 15–107, 15–110
revesting of property, 15–101, 15–113, 15–118
terms, 17–031
wrongful resale, 15–104
Resale price maintenance
see also **Restraint of trade**
common law, 3–037
competition law, 3–037
and see **Competition law (European Union)**
legislative provisions, 3–037
privity of contract, 3–037
Rescission
affirmation, and, 12–006
see also **Affirmation (election)**
buyer's remedy, 17–094, 19–144, 19–203
see also **Buyer's remedies**
conditions, governing, 10–009
consumer sales
damaged goods, 12–098
instalment sales, 12–099
meaning, 12–095
partial rejection, 12–100
quantitative shortages, 12–101
rejection of goods, 12–096, 12–111, 12–118
remedy, as, 12–077, 12–089, 12–090, 12–118
statutory rescission, 12–097
and see **Consumer sales**
court's powers, 12–004, 12–010
damages in lieu, 12–120
entire contract, 12–003
entitlement, 12–003
f.o.b. contracts, 20–113, 20–123—20–125
and see **F.O.B. contracts**

Rescission—*cont.*
lapse of time, 12–009
lien, and, 15–101
and see **Lien**
loss of right, 12–005, 12–010
misrepresentation, and, 12–002—12–005, 12–010, 12–119, 12–120
and see **Misrepresentation**
mistake, and, 3–026
and see **Mistake**
notification, and, 12–003
payment
payment stipulations, 20–123
refusal to pay, 20–124
rejection of goods, and, 19–145, 19–165, 19–166
and see **Rejection of goods**
Romalpa clauses, and, 5–146
and see ***Romalpa* clauses**
resale, and, 15–101, 15–107, 15–110
and see **Resale**
Sale of Goods Act (1979), A-020
and see **Sale of Goods Act (1979)**
scope, 12–003
seller's remedies, 19–207—19–210
see also **Seller's remedies (c.i.f. contracts)**
shipping instruction, and, 20–125
statutory provisions, 10–009
stoppage in transit, and, 15–101
and see **Stoppage in transit**
third party rights, 12–008
voidable title, and, 7–024
and see **Voidable title**
Restitution
advance payments, 17–092
buyer's remedy, 4–008, 17–090
see also **Buyer's remedies**
change of position, and, 4–008
choice of law rules, 25–176
see also **Choice of law**
divisible contracts, 17–091
failure to deliver, 17–090
illegality, and, 3–031
and see **Illegality**
minors' contracts, 2–038
and see **Minors' contracts**
rejection of contract, and, 12–067
and see **Rejection of contract**
repayment of price, 17–090
statutory provisions, 12–067
transfer of title
restitutionay claims, 7–003
restitution orders, 7–006
Restraint of trade
Restraint of trade—*cont.*
competition law, 3–040, 3–041, 3–034, 3–037
see also **Competition law (European Union)**
contracts, in, 3–034
distribution controls, 3–034
exceptions, 3–035
exclusive dealing, 3–038
goods sold, 3–036
illegality, and, 3–034—3–037
and see **Illegality**
price fixing, 3–034
resale price maintenance, 3–037
and see **Resale price maintenance**
trade agreements
legislative control, 3–040, 3–041
restrictive, 3–039, 3–040
Retention of title
administration orders, 5–162, 5–163
and see **Administration orders**
building contracts, 5–157, 5–158
choice of law, 25–145
and see **Choice of law**
disposal of goods, 5–144—5–148, 5–151
see also **Right of disposal**
receivership, and, 5–165
remedies, 25–146
Romalpa clauses, 5–144—5–148, 5–151
and see ***Romalpa* clauses**
sub-sales
buyers, 25–147, 25–148
seller's claims, 25–148
sub-purchasers, 5–156, 25–148, 25–149
tracing, 25–146
voluntary arrangements, 5–164
Right of disposal
bills of lading, 5–137, 5–139, 5–140
and see **Bills of lading**
building contracts, 5–157, 5–158
carriage by sea, 5–136
conditions, governing, 5–131, 5–133, 5–137
contractual terms, 5–132
delivery, and, 5–135
and see **Delivery**
documentary bills, 5–138—5–140
and see **Documentary bills**
f.o.b. contracts, 20–128
and see **F.O.B. contracts**
frustration of contract, 6–037
and see **Frustration of contract**
payment, and, 5–135
products
incorporation, of, 5–149, 5–167
loss of identity, 5–149
manufacturing processes, 5–149
ownership, 5–149, 5–150

Right of disposal—*cont.*
products—*cont.*
retention of title, 5–149
reservation
express, 5–132
implied, 5–132
retention of title, 5–134, 5–135, 5–144—5–149, 5–151
and see **Retention of title**
Romalpa clauses, 5–141
and see ***Romalpa* clauses**
Sale of Goods Act (1979), A-011
and see **Sale of Goods Act (1979)**
sub-purchasers
claims, against, 5–160
title, 5–156

Risk
accrued benefits, entitlement to, 6–033
allocation, of, 6–001, 6–006, 6–012
bailment, and, 6–026—6–032, 19–122
and see **Bailment**
buyer's risk, 6–001
carriage of goods, 6–017—6–022
and see **Carriage of goods**
c.i.f. contracts, 19–110—19–123
and see **C.I.F. contracts**
conflict of laws
applicable law, 25–154
dealing as consumer, 25–154
governing law, 25–154
Rome Convention, 25–154
lex situs, 25–155
passing of property, 25–155
and see **Conflict of laws**
consumer sales, 6–013, 6–014, 6–016, 6–032
and see **Consumer sales**
delivery of goods
delay, 6–023—6–025
passing of property, 6–013, 6–015
refused, 6–015
see also **Delivery**
EC legislation, 6–014
f.o.b. contracts
see **F.O.B. contracts**
frustration, distinguished, 6–001
see also **Frustration of contract**
goods
ascertained goods, 6–004
bulk goods, 6–004—6–008
delivery, of, 6–015
goods on approval, 6–009
identifiable goods, 6–004
loss/deterioration, 18–244, 18–249, 18–251, 18–252
partly destroyed, 6–008
perishable goods, 6–014
rejected goods, 6–011

Risk—*cont.*
goods—*cont.*
repaired goods, 6–016
replacement goods, 6–016
sale or return, 6–009
and see **Goods**
insurable interest, 6–012
loss/deterioration
overseas sales, 18–244, 18–249, 18–251, 18–252
responsibility for, 6–001, 6–015
see also **Loss/deterioration of goods**
overseas sales, 18–244, 18–249, 18–251, 18–252
and see **Overseas sales**
passing of property
ascertained goods, 6–004
bulk goods, 6–004—6–008
condition subsequent, 6–010
consumer sales, 6–013, 6–014, 6–016
delivery of goods, 6–013, 6–015
EC legislation, 6–014
f.o.b. contracts, 6–004
goods on approval, 6–009
identifiable goods, 6–004
overseas sales, 18–244
provisions, governing, 6–002—6–006
rejected goods, 6–011
sale or return, 6–009
undivided share, 6–005—6–008
unfair contract terms, 6–013, 6–014
and see **Passing of property**
Sale of Goods Act (1979), A-012
and see **Sale of Goods Act (1979)**
seller's risk, 6–001, 6–002

***Romalpa* clauses**
see also **Right of disposal**
administration orders, 5–162
and see **Administration orders**
assignment
competing assignments, 25–149
debts, 25–149
governing law, 25–149
Rome Convention, 25–149
bailment, and, 5–147
and see **Bailment**
bills of sale, 5–167, 5–168
building contracts, 5–157, 5–158
charge, created by, 25–144
companies
company charges, 5–143, 5–144
floating charges, 5–161, 5–162
and see **Companies**
competing assignments, 5–161
disadvantages, 5–170
effect, of, 5–141, 5–142
fixtures, 5–159

Romalpa **clauses**—*cont.*
non-corporate buyer, 5–166
operation, of, 5–141, 5–142
outstanding debts, 5–146
passing of property, and, 18–240
see also **Passing of property (overseas sales)**
payment provisions, 5–146, 5–147
priorities, 5–161
proceeds of sale, 5–151—5–154, 25–145, 25–146, 25–149
products
incorporation, of, 5–148
manufactured products, 5–150, 5–167
manufacturing processes, 5–149, 5–167
rescission, and, 5–146
and see **Rescission**
retention of title, and, 5–144—5–148
and see **Retention of title**
sub-purchasers, 5–156, 5–160, 25–149
unfair clauses, 5–169
unpaid goods, 5–146
unpaid seller, 15–001
Rome Convention
see also **Conflict of laws (contract)**
applicable law
absence of choice, 25–057
central administration (companies), 25–063
characteristic performance, 25–059, 25–060, 25–066
closest country connection, 25–058, 25–059
consumer contracts, 25–067
general principle, 25–057
habitual residence, 25–061, 25–062
on-line sales, 25–066
particular contracts, 25–066
place of business, 25–059, 25–064, 25–066, 25–068
place of shipment, 25–066
presumptions, 25–058, 25–059, 25–065, 25–066
severability, 25–057
successive contracts, 25–068
application, of, 25–020, 25–023
Brussels Protocol, 25–018, 25–019
carriage of goods, 25–071
and see **Carriage of goods**
choice of law
absence of choice, 25–057
arbitration clauses, 25–030, 25–031
consumer contracts, 25–044—25–047
express choice, 25–030
general principle, 25–029
Guiliano-Lagarde Report, 25–030, 25–031, 25–045
Rome Convention—*cont.*
choice of law—*cont.*
habitual residence, 25–048, 25–052, 25–056
limitations, 25–036
mandatory rules, 25–037—25–041
mandatory rules (English law), 25–042
parties, by, 25–029, 25–030, 25–045
public policy, 25–043
sale of goods, 25–044, 25–046
severability, and, 25–033
subsequent conduct, 25–032
validity, 25–034
variation, 25–035
and see **Choice of law**
closest country connection, 25–058, 25–059
conflicts
intra-UK, 25–022
legal systems, 25–021
consumer contracts
advertising, 25–048, 25–051
choice of law, 25–044, 25–047
conditions, governing, 25–048
consumer protection, 25–044—25–047
habitual residence, 25–048, 25–052
internet sales, 25–049—25–052
mandatory rules, 25–054, 25–055
on-line contracts, 25–049—25–053
specific invitations, 25–048, 25–050
supply of goods, 25–045
supply of services, 25–045
contract of sale, 25–078, 25–079, 25–082, 25–087, 25–119, 25–156
see also **Contract of sale (conflict of laws)**
contractual formalities, 25–087
European Commission proposals, 25–017
European Court of Justice (ECJ)
decisions, of, 25–018
preliminary rulings, 25–018
referrals, to, 25–019
exchange controls, 25–120
exclusions, 25–024
historical background, 25–015
incorporation by reference, 25–028, 25–093
international conventions, and, 25–025
interpretation, 25–018, 25–019
law of country
meaning of, 25–021
territorial units, 25–021
licences, 25–168
mandatory nature, 25–027
procedural law, 25–203, 25–205, 25–206
see also **Procedure**
purpose, 25–016
renvoi, exclusion of, 25–026
revision, of, 25–017

Rome Convention—*cont.*
risk, 25–154
and see **Risk**
seller' remedies, 25–179
and see **Seller's remedies**
unfair contract terms, 25–093, 25–095—25–097
see also **Unfair Contract Terms Act (1977)**

Sale
see also **Contract of sale**
actual sale, 1–027
agency, distinguished, 1–048
and see **Agency**
agreement to sell, distinguished, 1–028
bailment, distinguished, 1–057, 1–059
and see **Bailment**
bargain, and, 1–029
chattels, and, 1–042, 1–043
and see **Chattels**
composite arrangements, 1–066
construction materials, 1–060
containers, ownership of, 1–061
contract for services, and, 1–041, 1–046
contract for work, and, 1–041—1–043, 1–046, 1–047
definition, 1–063
delivery, and, 1–029
and see **Delivery**
distinctions
barter, 1–034–1–036
exchange, 1–034—1–036
free offers, 1–033
gift, 1–032
lien, 1–064
non-consensual transactions, 1–067
pledge, 1–063
executed sale, 1–027
intellectual property rights, 1–077
intention of parties, 1–066
manufacturing components, 1–060
non-consensual transactions, 1–067
and see **Non-consensual transactions**
options, exercise of, 1–038
pledge, distinguished, 1–063
and see **Pledge**
security transactions
apparent sale, 1–0656
composite arrangements, 1–066
distinguishing factors, 1–064, 1–065
statutory definition, 1–025, 1–027
trading-in, and, 1–039
trading stamps, 1–040

Sale and Supply of Goods to Consumers Regulations (2002)
anti-avoidance provisions, 25–113
choice of law
closest country connection, 25–112
English law, 25–117
EU Member States, 25–115
non-Member States, 25–112, 25–115—25–117
UK law, 25–118
Unfair Contract Terms Act (1977), 25–113—25–118
and see **Choice of law**
consumer protection, 25–112
dealing as consumer, 25–111, 25–115
EC Directive (1999/44/EC), 25–111, 25–112
international supply contracts, 25–114
Sale by description
see also **Description**
buyer, selection by, 11–010
condition of contract, 11–001, 11–002
see also **Conditions**
contractual duty, 11–002, 11–003
defective goods, 11–003
exemption clauses, 11–005
and see **Exemption clauses**
express terms, 11–002
failure to conform, 11–004
failure to perform, 11–004
future goods, 11–007, 11–008
interpretation, 11–002
modern practice, 11–007
overseas sales, 18–266
see also **Implied terms (overseas sales)**
quality of goods, 11–032, 11–070
and see **Quality of goods**
reliance on description, 11–007—11–009
rules, governing, 11–003
Sale of Goods Act (1979), A-009
and see **Sale of Goods Act (1979)**
selection by buyer, 11–010
self-service shopping, 11–010
specific goods, 11–003, 11–007, 11–008
unascertained goods, 11–007, 11–008, 11–014
and see **Unascertained goods**
Sale by sample
bulk goods, 11–078, 11–079, 11–086
and see **Bulk goods**
common law, 11–073
contract
prior to tender, 11–077
written contracts, 11–076
definition, 11–074
description
conformity, with, 11–086
sale, by, 11–086

Sale by sample—*cont.*
examination of goods
practicable, 11–081
quality, for, 11–080, 11–081, 11–086
reasonable, 11–081, 11–083, 11–085
quality of goods
examination of goods, 11–080, 11–081, 11–086
free from defect, 11–080
latent defects, 11–080
satisfactory quality, 11–080, 11–081, 11–085, 11–086
and see **Quality of goods**
sale
business sales, 11–082
consumer sales, 11–082
related contracts, 11–087
sale by description, 11–086
Sale of Goods Act (1979), 11–073, 11–083, A-010
and see **Sale of Goods Act (1979)**
sample
bulk goods, 11–079, 11–086
conformity, with, 11–079, 11–086
examination, of, 11–080, 11–081, 11–083, 11–085, 11–086
exhibition, of, 11–075, 11–086
tender, of, 11–077
specific goods, 11–078
and see **Specific goods**
statutory provisions, 11–073
time element, 11–084
trade usage, 11–079
unascertained goods, 11–078
and see **Unascertained goods**
Sale of cargo
damages, 21–040
destruction of cargo, 21–041
insurable interest, 21–041
meaning, 21–032, 21–034
quantity
contracted quantity, 21–040
discrepancy, 21–033
estimated, 21–033, 21–035
limit, on, 21–036
remainder of cargo, 21–038
whole cargo, 21–034, 21–037—21–039
risk, 21–041
and see **Risk**
shipment, and, 21–039, 21–041
Sale of Goods Act (1893)
application, 1–003
codification, 1–002
construction, 1–002
contractual formalities, 2–022
see also **Formation of contract**
effect, 1–001, 1–002
enactment, 1–001
Sale of Goods Act (1893)—*cont.*
influence, 1–001
land, and, 1–092
and see **Land**
scope, 1–006
Sale of Goods Act (1979)
acceptance, A-015
amendments
consequential amendments, A-034
consumer sales, 1–001, A-009
subsequent, 1–001. 1–005
application, 1–001, 1–030, A-002
auction sales, A-028
bills of sale, 1–012
breach of contract
action for price, A-024
breach of warranty, A-025
buyer's remedies, A-025
damages, A-024, A-025
interest payments, A-026
seller's remedies, A-024
specific performance, A-025
conflict of laws, A-033
and see **Conflict of laws**
consolidation, 1–004, 1–006
construction, 1–004, 1–005
consumer sales
buyer's rights, A-021
court's powers, A-023
dealing as consumer, 13–071, 13–077—13–079, 13–081
provisions, covering, 1–001, 1–006, A-009, A-014
reduction of price, A-022
repair of goods, A-022
replacement of goods, A-022
rescission of contract, A-022
special remedies (Part 5A), 13–064, 13–071, 13–083
and see **Consumer sales**
contractual formalities, 2–021, A-004
see also **Formation of contract**
definitions
agreement to sell, 1–025
contract of sale, 1–025
sale, 1–025
effect, 1–001, 1–004, 1–006
equitable rules
application, 1–008, 1–009, 1–010
compatibility, 1–010
displacement, 1–010
equitable remedies, 1–009, 1–011
incorporation, 1–009
exemption clauses, 1–014, 1–015
and see **Exemption clauses**
fitness for purpose, 11–051, 11–071, A-009, A-033
and see **Fitness for purpose**

Sale of Goods Act (1979)—*cont.*
formation of contract
contract of sale, A-003
existing goods, A-005
formalities, A-004
future goods, A-005
perished goods, A-005
subject matter, A-005
and see **Formation of contract**
freedom from encumbrance, 4–023
and see **Freedom from encumbrance**
freedom of contract, 1–013—1–015
and see **Freedom of contract**
implied terms
consumer sales, A-009
exclusion, of, A-027, A-033
fitness for purpose, A-009, A-033
payment, A-007
provisions, as to, 11–089, A-007, A-008
quality of goods, A-009, A-033
title, A-008, A-033
warranties, A-007
and see **Implied terms**
interpretation, A-030
land, and, 1–090, 1–093
and see **Land**
liability, under, 1–006
modifications, A-033
passing of property, 18–293—18–295
and see **Passing of property**
performance of contract
acceptance, A-015
consumer sales, A-014
delivery, A-014, A-016
duties, A-014
price
ascertainment, A-006
valuation, A-006
procedural rules, 1–006
and see **Procedure**
property rights, 1–007, 1–008
provisions, of, 1–001
quality of goods, 11–024, 11–026, 11–031, 11–070, 11–071, A-009, A-033
and see **Quality of goods**
reasonable time, provisions for, A-029
rejection of goods, 18–284, A-015
and see **Rejection of goods**
related statutes, 1–016—1–024
remedies, 1–009, 1–011, 12–067
and see **Remedies**
repeals, A-035
resale, A-020
and see **Resale**
rescission, A-020
and see **Rescission**
restitution, under, 12–067
and see **Restitution**

Sale of Goods Act (1979)—*cont.*
risk, A-012
and see **Risk**
sale by description, A-009
and see **Sale by description**
sale by sample, 11–073, 11–083, A-010
and see **Sale by sample**
savings
bankruptcy, 1–012, A-031
bills of sale, 1–012
common law, 1–007, A-031
equitable rules, 1–008—1–011
factors, 1–012, 1–018
security transactions, 1–012
scope, 1–006
Scotland
buyer's remedies, A-025
payment into court, A-029
seller
unpaid seller, A-017
unpaid seller's lien, A-018
stoppage in transit, A-019
and see **Stoppage in transit**
transfer of property
ascertainment of goods, A-011
bulk goods, A-012
intention of parties, A-011
passing of property, A-011
right of disposal, A-011
undivided shares, A-012
transfer of title, A-013
unfair terms, 1–006, 1–013, 1–014
see also **Unfair Contract Terms Act (1977)**

Sale or return
acceptance of goods, 5–040, 5–047
agency, and, 5–045
and see **Agency**
bailment, and, 5–044
and see **Bailment**
conditions
condition precedent, 5–042
condition subsequent, 1–056, 5–043
damaged goods, 5–056
delivery, and, 1–056, 5–048, 5–049
destruction of goods, 5–055, 5–057
expiration of time, 5–040, 5–041, 5–050
fraud, 5–046
inability to return, 5–054, 5–055
intention of parties, 1–056
loss of goods, 5–055, 5–057
meaning, 5–041
option to buy, 1–056
and see **Option to buy**
passing of property
adopting the transaction, 5–047—5–049, 5–051
condition precedent, 5–042

Sale or return—*cont.*
passing of property—*cont.*
condition subsequent, 1–056, 5–043
delivery on trial, 5–049
different intention, 5–041
provisions, governing, 1–056, 5–040
risk, and, 6–009
and see **Passing of property**
pledge of goods, 5–047
rejection notice, 5–052, 5–053
retention of goods, 5–040, 5–045
risk, 5–058, 6–009
and see **Risk**
stock financing schemes, 5–051
third party, delivery to, 5–048
voidable title, and, 7–022
and see **Voidable title**
Sample
see **Sale by sample**
Sea waybills
bills of lading, distinguished,
and see **Bills of lading**
Carriage of Goods by Sea Act (1992), 18–040, 18–153, 18–154
carriers, and, 18–158
consignees, 18–161
contract
contractual liabilities, 18–162
contractual rights, 18–153, 18–154
evidence, of, 18–157
definition, 18–083, 18–154—18–156
document of title, 18–067
and see **Document of title**
Hague-Visby Rules, 18–035, 18–040, 18–044
and see **Hague-Visby Rules**
nature, of, 18–152
receipt for goods, 18–156
redirection of goods, 18–025
shipper's rights, 18–160
"spent" documents, 18–159
status, 18–083
straight (non-negotiable) bills, distinguished, 18–020, 18–083
third parties, 18–026
Seller in possession
see also **Transfer of title (non-owners)**
agreement to sell, 7–056
and see **Agreement to sell**
bailee, as, 7–058, 7–059
bulk goods, 7–067
and see **Bulk goods**
buyer's consent, 7–061
delivery of goods
effect, 7–065
passing title, 7–062, 7–063
disposition, 7–064
good faith, 7–068
Seller in possession—*cont.*
hire-purchase agreements, 7–057, 7–058
and see **Hire-purchase agreements**
notice requirement, 7–068
passing of property, 7–056
and see **Passing of property**
passing of title
documents of title, 7–057, 7–062
statutory provisions, 7–055
transfer of goods, 7–062, 7–063
possession
continuing, in, 7–055, 7–058—7–060
meaning, 7–057—7–060
separate agreement, under, 7–058
statutory provisions, 7–055
unascertained goods, 7–067
and see **Unascertained goods**
undivided share, 7–067
and see **Undivided share**
Seller's remedies
see also **Remedies**
buyers
bankruptcy, 15–027, 15–072
insolvency, 15–019, 15–024—15–026, 15–036, 15–037, 15–108
sub-sales, 15–092
carriers, against, 25–195
c.i.f. contracts
see **Seller's remedies (c.i.f. contracts)**
conflict of laws
currency issues, 25–193
governing law, 25–178
Guiliano-Lagarde Report, 25–179
lex fori, 25–178, 25–179
lex situs, 25–178, 25–179, 25–183, 25–189
lien, 25–180—25–182, 25–188
personal remedies, 25–190—25–192
resale, 25–189
rescission, 25–183, 25–184
Rome Convention, 25–179
stoppage in transit, 25–183—25–186
third party rights, 25–181, 25–182
withholding delivery, 25–180
and see **Conflict of laws**
conversion, for, 16–089
damages
see **Damages**
declarations, 16–092
documentary credits
damages, 23–171, 23–172
delayed payment, 23–172
and see **Documentary credits**
document of title
meaning, 15–097
mortgage, 15–099
pledge, 15–089

Seller's remedies—*cont.*
document of title—*cont.*
transfer, of, 15–097, 15–098
and see **Document of title**
forfeiture
deposits, 16–091
pre-payments, 16–091
goods
restitution, 15–116
retaking, 15–115, 15–117
injunctions, 16–093
insolvency
buyers, 15–019, 15–024—15–026, 15–036, 15–037, 15–108
definition, 15–024
effect, 15–025
timing, 15–026
and see **Insolvency**
lien, 15–002, 15–028, 15–029, 25–180—25–182, 25–188
and see **Lien**
misrepresentation, and, 16–090
mistake, relating to, 16–090
payment of price
banker's commercial credit, 15–021
bills of exchange, 15–019, 15–020, 15–036
buyer's insolvency, 15–019
interpretation, 15–017
negotiable instrument, 15–108, 15–036
partial payment, 15–017
tender of price, 15–022, 15–023
personal remedies
buyer, against, 25–190—25–192
currency of account, 25–193
currency of contract, 25–193
currency of judgment, 25–194
price claims
see **Price claims**
recovery of possession, 16–089, 16–090
resale
see **Resale**
rescission, 25–183, 25–184
and see **Rescission**
Sale of Goods Act (1979)
action for price, A-024
damages, A-024
and see **Sale of Goods Act (1979)**
seller
agency arrangements, and, 15–013
commission agents, and, 15–013
definition, 15–013
rejection of goods, 15–015
surety, as, 15–014
special remedies, 16–094
specific performance, 16–093
and see **Specific performance**

Seller's remedies—*cont.*
stoppage in transit, 15–061, 25–183—25–186
and see **Stoppage in transit**
sub-sales
attornment, 15–096
buyer, by, 15–092
payment of price, 15–100
seller's assent,15–093—15–095
statutory provisions, 15–092
stoppage in transit, 15–100
termination of contract, 15–117
unpaid seller
action for price, 15–001, 15–006
agency, and, 15–008
bills of exchange, 15–019, 15–020, 15–036
common law, 15–007
damages, 15–001
definition, 15–016
extra-judicial remedies, 15–001
goods unallocated, 15–012
instalment contracts, 15–010, 15–011
law merchant, and, 15–001
lien, 15–002, 15–028, 15–029, 15–030
payment of price, 15–017
personal remedies, 15–001
power to act, 15–004
real remedies, 15–001
resale, 15–003
retention of property, 15–010, 15–011
right to act, 15–004
Romalpa clauses, 15–001
statutory provisions, 15–001, 15–009
stoppage in transit, 15–002, 15–017, 15–019
tender of price, 15–022, 15–023
third parties, and, 15–005
Seller's remedies (c.i.f. contracts)
see also **C.I.F. contracts**
actions
damages, for, 19–216—19–219
price, for, 19–211—19–215
instalment payments, 19–208
payment provisions, 19–207
rescission, 19–207—19–210
and see **Rescission**
rights against goods, 19–220
Seller's remedies (f.o.b. contracts)
see also **F.O.B. contracts**
action for damages
absence of market, 20–137
anticipatory breach, 20–140
assessment of damages, 20–123, 20–136
consequential loss, 20–138
freight charges, 20–138
insurance charges, 20–138
market rule, 20–123

Seller's remedies (f.o.b. contracts)—*cont.*
action for damages—*cont.*
non-acceptance, 20–123, 20–137, 20–138
refusal of delivery, 0–139
resale price, 20–137
shipment of goods, 20–134, 20–135
action for the price
limits, on, 20–130
part shipment, 20–127
passing of property, and, 20–126, 20–129
right of disposal, 20–128
shipment, and, 20–126
carrying charges, 20–131
rescission
payment stipulations, and, 20–123
refusal to accept, 20–124
refusal to pay, 20–124
shipping instructions, and, 20–125
and see **Rescission**
rights against goods, 20–141
Seller's title
absence of title, 4–003, 4–005, 4–012
chain transactions, 4–014, 4–015, 4–016
and see **Chain transactions**
encumbrance
see **Freedom from Encumbrance**
exemption clauses, 4–018—4–020
and see **Exemption clauses**
express undertaking
breach, of, 4–021
consumer remedies, 4–021
effect, of, 4–021
hire-purchase agreements, 4–013, 4–017, 4–035
and see **Hire-purchase agreements**
liability
damages, for, 4–022
fraud, 4–022
misrepresentation, 4–022
limited title
caveat emptor, 4–032
exemption clauses, and, 4–034
express term, as to, 4–032
freedom from encumbrance, 4–033
implied terms, as to, 4–033
inferred intention, 4–032
quiet possession, 4–033
sale, of, 4–032
statutory provisions, 4–032
quiet possession
see **Quiet possession**
right to sell
breach of condition, 4–006, 4–009
buyer's remedies, 4–006—4–008
caveat emptor, 4–001
conditions, 4–001, 4–030
extent, of, 4–003, 4–004
Seller's title—*cont.*
right to sell—*cont.*
feeding title, 4–010, 4–013
implied undertaking, 4–001—4–003
improvements, allowances for, 4–007
purchase price, recovery of, 4–006—4–008, 4–010
statutory provisions, 4–001, 4–002
strict liability, 4–002
subsequent acquisition, 4–011
time of contract, 4–005
trade usage, 4–001
title
feeding title, 4–010
subsequent acquisition, 4–011
wrongful interference, 4–012
transfer of property, 4–036
true owner
chain transactions, 4–014, 4–015
damages, claimed by, 4–102, 4–013
extinguishment of title, 4–012, 4–013
settlement, with, 4–012
validity, 4–001
Severable contracts
breach of condition, 8–084
damages, 8–087
definition, 8–074
non-repudiatory breach, 8–084
performance, 8–074
separate contracts, distinguished, 8–075
Ship's delivery order
see also **Delivery orders**
bills of lading
distinguished, 18–177
holders, 18–186
and see **Bills of lading**
Carriage of Goods by Sea Act (1992), 18–189, 18–195
carrier's undertaking, 18–178, 18–181, 18–182
consignees, 18–187
contract
contract of carriage, and, 18–179, 18–184
contractual liabilities, 18–189, 18–191, 18–192
contractual rights, 18–175, 18–184, 18–186
countersignature, 18–171, 18–172
delivery of goods, 18–171, 18–182
effect, of, 18–171
goods, relating to, 18–180
identification, of, 18–183
meaning, 18–171, 18–176
sea waybills, distinguished, 18–177
and see **Sea waybills**

Ship's delivery order—*cont.*
shipment
carriage by sea, 18–179
part, of, 18–185, 18–190, 18–192
shipper's liability, 18–191
shipper's rights, 18–186
ship's release, 18–171, 18–174
third parties, 18–188
"Shrink-wrap" contracts
see also **Formation of contract**
contractual terms, 2–012
effect, of, 2–012
Specific goods
see also **Goods**
deliverable state
see **Specific goods (deliverable state)**
existence, of, 1–132
frustration of contract
agreement avoided, 6–039
agreement to sell, 6–035
apportionment of loss, 6–039
bulk goods, 6–036
definition, 6–036
expenses, recovery of, 6–039
Howell v Coupland, 6–038
part delivery, 6–040
perished goods, 6–035, 6–040
price, recovery of, 6–039, 6–040
requisitioning, 6–050
right of disposal, 6–037
statutory provisions, 6–035, 6–037—6–039, 6–041
undivided share, 6–036
and see **Frustration of contract**
future goods, as, 1–114
and see **Future goods**
meaning, 1–113, 1–115, 1–116, 1–118, 1–129, 5–022
nature, of, 1–114
non-deliverable state
see **Specific goods (non-deliverable state)**
sale by description, 11–003, 11–007, 11–008
and see **Sale by description**
sale by sample, 11–078
and see **Sale by sample**
unascertained goods, distinguished, 1–119
and see **Unascertained goods**
undivided share, 1–116, 1–118, 1–129
and see **Undivided share**
Specific goods (deliverable state)
conditional contract, 5–021
deliverable state, meaning of, 5–023, 5–024
Specific goods (deliverable state)—*cont.*
land
assignment, of, 5–028
sale, of, 5–028
passing of property
insurance provisions, 5–027
intention of parties, 5–016, 5–026
risk provisions, 5–027
statutory rules, 5–016, 5–107, 5–019, 5–022, 5–026
timing, 5–016—5–019, 5–022, 5–026
undivided share, 5–025
and see **Passing of property**
postponement
delivery, 5–018
payment, 5–018
sale by description, 5–020
special terms sales, 5–029
unconditional contract, 5–019
Specific goods (non-deliverable state)
deliverable state, converting to, 5–031—5–033
obligation
buyer's obligation, 5–033
seller's obligation, 5–032, 5–033
passing of property
carriage of goods, 5–031
common law, 5–030
intention of parties, 5–030, 5–031
notice to buyer, 5–034
statutory rules, 5–030
and see **Passing of property**
Specific goods (weighing/measuring/testing)
passing of property
differing intention, 5–039
statutory rules, 5–035
and see **Passing of property**
price, ascertainment of, 5–035, 5–037, 5–038
quality, ascertainment of, 5–035
seller's obligation, 5–035—5–037
Specific performance
see also **Remedies**
Civil Procedure Rules (CPR), 17–096
consumer sales, 12–071, 12–114, 14–025, 17–101, 17–103
and see **Consumer sales**
discretion, as to, 17–099, 17–100
equitable remedy, 17–096, 17–099
f.o.b. contracts, 20–121
and see **F.O.B. contracts**
goods
defective delivery, 19–206
eligible goods, 17–099
non-conforming goods, 17–101, 17–103
repair, of, 17–101, 17–103
replacement, of, 17–101, 17–103

Specific performance—*cont.*
goods—*cont.*
"specific or ascertained" goods, 17–097, 17–098, 19–204
passing of property, and, 17–098
statutory provisions, 17–096, 19–204
Standby credits
see also **Documentary credits**
assignment, 23–264, 23–267
autonomy, of, 23–242, 23–254
bills of exchange, and, 23–237
and see **Bills of exchange**
development, of, 23–238
expiry date, 23–266
form of undertaking, 23–240
fraud, 23–242—23–244
International Standby Practices (ISP 98), 23–251—23–253
and see **International Standby Practices (ISP 98)**
mercantile usage, 23–253
nature, of, 23–237, 23–241, 23–242, 23–254
non-bank facilities, 23–249
non-performance, and, 23–237
payment, 23–237
and see **Payment**
proceeds, assignment of, 23–264
purpose, 23–237
reimbursement, 23–265
risk allocation, 23–268
sharp practices, 23–24
strict compliance
estoppel, 23–247
fair construction rule, 23–246
requirement, for, 23–246
waiver, 23–247
termination provisions, 23–266
third party document, 23–269
transfer, 23–263, 23–267
UCP, and, 23–248—23–250
and see **Uniform Customs and Practice for Documentary Credits (UCP)**
underlying transaction, 23–244
use, of, 23–239
Statements
belief, 10–006
buyers, by, 10–002
classification, 10–001, 10–003, 10–039, 10–040
collateral contracts, 10–012—10–014
and see **Collateral contracts**
common law, 10–008
and see **Common law**
conditions, 10–024—10–032
and see **Conditions**
damages, 10–010
and see **Damages**
Statements—*cont.*
effect, of, 10–008
equitable relief, 10–008, 10–009
express statements, 10–001
fact, of, 10–003
inducement to contract, 10–008, 10–011
intention, as to, 10–007
intermediate terms, 10–033—10–038
and see **Intermediate terms**
interpretation, 10–003
law, of, 10–003
legal development, 10–004
legal liability, 10–001, 10–005, 10–006, 10–039
mere puffs, 10–005
mere representations, 10–008
misrepresentation, 10–008
and see **Misrepresentation**
negligence, 10–010
non-promissory conditions, 10–039
opinion, 10–006
public statements, 11–033, 11–034, 12–071
and see **Public statements**
rescission, and, 10–008, 10–009
and see **Rescission**
sellers, by, 10–002
significance, of, 10–011
special knowledge, 10–006
third parties, 10–002
value, as to, 10–006
warranties, 10–015—10–023
and see **Warranties**
Statute of Frauds (1677)
contractual formalities, 2–022
see also **Formation of contract**
crops, and, 1–093
and see **Crops**
land, and, 1–091, 1–092
and see **Land**
Stoppage in transit
see also **Seller's remedies**
carriers
see **Carriers**
conflict of laws
carriers, position of, 25–187
buyer/seller, involving, 25–184
third party rights, 25–185
and see **Conflict of laws**
destination
"appointed", 15–074, 15–080
"further", 15–080
duration of transit
acknowledgement to buyer, 15–077
agents, delivery to, 15–071, 15–076
assent of parties, 15–078
attornment, 15–075, 15–078
bills of lading, and, 15–067
buyer's bankruptcy, 15–072

Stoppage in transit—*cont.*
duration of transit—*cont.*
buyer takes delivery, 15–068, 15–070, 15–074
carrier's lien, 15–079
contractual terms, 15–069
early delivery, 15–074, 15–076
incorrect delivery, 15–074
part delivery, 15–084
possession, and, 15–066
refusal to deliver, 15–083
rejection of goods, 15–081
rules, as to, 15–066
ship, delivery to, 15–073, 15–082
entitlement
agents, 15–065
seller's right, 15–065
exercise of right
carrier's lien, 15–089
contract of carriage, 15–087
duties, relating to, 15–088
effect, of, 15–091
insurance money, 15–090
methods, 15–085
notice requirements, 15–085, 15–086
justification, 15–064
lien, and, 15–062
and see **Lien**
passing of property, and, 15–063
and see **Passing of property**
purpose, 15–062
rescission, and, 15–101
and see **Rescission**
right of stoppage, 15–061—15–063, 15–065, 15–085
Sale of Goods Act (1979), A-019
and see **Sale of Goods Act (1979)**
statutory provisions, 15–061
transit, meaning of, 15–066
Supply of Goods and Services Act (1982)
excepted contracts, 1–031
implied terms, and, 1–031
and see **Implied terms**
transfer of goods, 1–031

Timing of delivery
see also **Delivery**
abandonment, 8–031
acceptance, 8–028
affirmation, 8–028
commercial contracts, 8–025
computation of time, 8–032—8–035
condition precedent, 8–040
delayed delivery, 6–023—6–025, 8–042
delivery on request, 8–039
distance selling, 8–038
and see **Distance selling**
early delivery, 8–043

Timing of delivery—*cont.*
estoppel, 8–030
and see **Estoppel**
express stipulations, 8–025
hour, of, 8–041
late delivery, 8–028, 8–042
new time-limit, 8–030
no time fixed, 8–037
overseas transactions, 8–044
payment, 8–004
postponement, 8–030
presumptions, as to, 8–025
termination, and, 8–027
time of the essence, 8–026—8–028, 8–030
variation, 8–029
waiver, 8–030
words/phrases, 8–036
Title
consumer protection
breach of condition, 14–007
nemo dat quod non habet, 14–007
passing of property, 14–007
and see **Consumer protection**
limited title
caveat emptor, 4–032
exemption clauses, and, 4–034
express term, as to, 4–032
freedom from encumbrance, 4–033
implied terms, as to, 4–033
inferred intention, 4–032
quiet possession, 4–033
sale, of, 4–032
statutory provisions, 4–032
motor vehicles
see **Motor vehicles**
transfer of title (non-owners)
see **Transfer of title (non-owners)**
seller
see **Seller's title**
Tortious liability
actions
burden of proof, 12–121
distributors, against, 12–122
jurisdictional differences, 12–121
manufacturers, against, 12–122
negligence, 12–121
sellers, against, 12–121
causation, 12–012
consumer protection, 12–127
and see **Consumer protection**
damages, 12–012, 12–015, 12–121
and see **Damages**
deceit, 12–012, 12–016
defective goods, 12–121, 12–124, 12–127
duty of care, 12–123, 13–106, 13–107
duty to warn, 12–124
economic loss, 12–126, 13–107

Tortious liability—*cont.*
exclusion, of, 13–106
exemption clauses, 13–106, 13–107
and see **Exemption clauses**
fraud, 12–012, 12–016
and see **Fraud**
fraudulent misrepresentation, 12–014, 12–015
manufacturers, 14–061, 14–062
and see **Manufacturers**
misrepresentation, 12–125
and see **Misrepresentation**
remoteness of damage, 12–012
and see **Remoteness of damage**
Trade practices
competition, contrary to, 14–138
control, of, 14–138, 14–139, 14–141
licensing, and, 14–138
Unfair Commercial Practices Directive (2005/29/EC), 14–139
Transfer of title (non-owners)
see also Nemo dat quod non habet
assets, recovery of, 7–117
buyer in possession
see **Buyer in possession**
common law powers, 7–109, 7–110
consent
owner's consent, 7–001, 7–037—7–039, 7–044
withdrawal, 7–040
course of business
customary, 7–032, 7–043
ordinary, 7–041, 7–043, 7–044
document of title, 7–013
and see **Document of title**
duty of care, 7–016, 7–017
estoppel, and, 7–008—7–019
and see **Estoppel**
improvements, allowances for, 7–005
market overt, 7–001, 7–020
mercantile agents, 7–031, 7–032
and see **Mercantile agents**
motor vehicles
see **Motor vehicles**
negligence
duty of care, 7–016, 7–017
estoppel, and, 7–015
owners
consent, of, 7–001, 7–037—7–039, 7–044
non est factum, 7–018
recovery of possession, 7–002
remedies, available to, 7–002—7–004
representations, by, 7–009—7–012
tracing, by, 7–003
Transfer of title (non-owners)—*cont.*
procedural matters
asset recovery, 7–117
Civil Procedure Rules (CPR), 7–122
execution debtors, 7–113
limitation period, 7–115—7–117
warrant of execution, 7–114
writ of execution, 7–113
and see **Procedure**
proceeds of crime, 7–007, 7–117
protection
commercial transactions, 7–001
common law, 7–001
property, of, 7–001
remedies
confiscation orders, 7–007
damages, 7–002, 7–004
police powers, 7–006, 7–007
restitutionary claims, 7–003
restitution orders, 7–006
seizure orders, 7–006, 7–007
tracing, 7–003
and see **Remedies**
representations
agents, by, 7–010
owners, by, 7–009—7–012
seller in possession
see **Seller in possession**
statutory provisions, 7–001, 7–109, 7–110
unlawful conduct, an, 7–117
voidable title
see **Voidable title**
Trees (timber)
goods, as, 1–090, 1–093, 1–098
and see **Goods**

Unascertained goods
see also **Goods**
agreement to sell, 5–060
appropriation, 5–067
and see **Appropriation**
ascertainment
ascertained goods, change to, 1–118
exhaustion, by, 5–062, 5–063
requirement, for, 5–059, 5–066
bulk goods, 5–061, 5–062, 5–103, 5–104, 5–112, 7–085
and see **Bulk goods**
categories, 1–116
delivery, and, 5–099
and see **Delivery**
equitable interests, 5–064
estoppel, and, 5–065
and see **Estoppel**
freedom from encumbrance, 4–023
and see **Freedom from encumbrance**
frustration of contract, 6–041, 6–050, 6–051
and see **Frustration of contract**

Unascertained goods—*cont.*
future goods, 5–060
generic goods, 5–060
meaning, 1–113, 5–060
nature, of, 1–113, 1–116
passing of property
appropriation, 5–067
ascertainment, requirement for, 5–059, 5–066
bulk goods, 5–061, 5–062, 5–103, 5–104
intention of parties, 5–066
provisions, governing, 1–119, 1–121, 5–059
and see **Passing of property**
sale by description, 11–007, 11–008, 11–014, 11–018
and see **Sale by description**
sale by sample, 11–078
and see **Sale by sample**
seller in possession, 7–067
and see **Seller in possession**
separation, of, 5–061, 5–062
specific goods, distinguished, 1–119
and see **Specific goods**
specified quantity, within, 5–060—5–062, 5–111

UNCITRAL
electronic commerce, 1–024
and see **electronic commerce**
international sale of goods, 1–024

Undivided share
extent, of, 5–117
frustration of contract, 6–036
and see **Frustration of contract**
non-existent goods, 1–129, 1–130
passing of property
acquisition, of, 5–116
aggregate shares, 5–118
bulk goods, and, 5–109, 5–113, 5–114, 7–085
proportionate share, 5–118—5–120
statutory provisions, 5–109, 5–110
unascertained goods, 5–112
and see **Passing of property**
perished goods, 1–129
specific goods, and, 1–116, 1–118, 1–129, 5–025, 5–129, 6–036
and see **Specific goods**
seller in possession, 7–067
and see **Seller in possession**
trading, in, 5–128

Undue influence
contract of sale, and, 3–010
and see **Contract of sale**

Unfair contract terms
see also **Unfair Contract Terms Act (1977)**
EC Directive (93/13/EC), 1–014
effect, of, 14–036
examples, 14–036
exemption clauses, and, 4–018, 4–019, 4–034, 13–008, 13–010, 13–021
and see **Exemption clauses**
force majeure, and, 8–104
and see Force majeure
freedom of contract, 1–014
and see **Freedom of contract**
risk, and, 6–013, 6–014
and see **Risk**
scope, of, 14–037, 14–038
supply of services, 14–052A

Unfair Contract Terms Act (1977)
see also **Unfair contract terms**
authorised terms
competent authority, by, 13–098
international agreement, by, 13–098
statute, by, 13–098
avoidance, 25–100
business liability, 13–094
choice of law
English law, 13–100
foreign law, 13–101, 25–090, 25–094—25–099
provision, as to, 25–160
UK law, 25–090—25–093
and see **Choice of law**
contract applicable law, 13–100, 25–090, 25–160
dealing as consumer, 13–094, 14–029, 14–037
see also **Consumer sales**
examination of goods, 13–102
excluded contracts, 25–090
exemption clauses
business liability, 13–070
clauses covered, by, 13–064—13–069
contracting parties, 13–059
dealing as consumer, 13–071—13–075, 13–083
entire agreement clauses, 13–056
excluded clauses, 13–054, 13–055, 13–064—13–066
exclusion of liability, 13–083
hire-purchase provisions, 13–083
limitation of duty, 13–057
methods used, 13–063
misrepresentation, 13–054, 13–058
pure contractual terms, 13–058
reasonableness, 13–060
related transactions, 13–085
sale of goods provisions, 13–083, 13–084

Unfair Contract Terms Act (1977)—*cont.*
exemption clauses—*cont.*
scope, of, 13–062
statements of opinion, 13–057
and see **Exemption clauses**
guidelines, 14–034
international supply contracts, 13–099, 25–090, 25–160
manufacturers guarantees, 14–069
non-rejection clauses, 18–280
and see **Non-rejection clauses**
reasonableness requirement, 13–088—13–090, 13–094, 13–096, 14–029
Rome Convention, and, 25–093, 25–095—25–097
and see **Rome Convention**
tortious liability, 13–106, 13–107
and see **Tortious liability**
validity of terms, 25–090
Unfair Terms in Consumer Contract Regulations (1999)
choice of law
EU Member States, 25–102
non-Member States, 25–103
and see **Choice of law**
complaints procedure, 25–106
consideration, adequacy of, 14–032
consumer protection, 25–101, 25–102
consumers, under, 14–031, 14–037
EC Directive (1993/13/EC), 25–101, 25–102
effect, of, 13–103, 14–030
enforcement provisions, 14–040
excluded terms, 14–031
exemption clauses, 13–103
and see **Exemption clauses**
fairness, 14–033—14–035
general principles, reliance on, 25–105
non-rejection clauses, 18–282, 18–283
and see **Non-rejection clauses**
scope, of, 14–031, 25–104
subject matter, definition of, 14–032
unfairness, 14–034, 14–035
unfair terms
consumer sales, 14–037, 14–038
effect, of, 14–036, 14–039
"entire agreement" clauses, 14–039
examples, of, 14–036, 14–039
"grey" list, 14–036
Uniform Customs and Practice for Documentary Credits (UCP)
see also **Documentary credits**
background, 23–009
bills of lading, 23–218—23–220
and see **Bills of lading**
case decisions, conflicting with, 23–028
documents of carriage, 23–217, 23–218
effect, 23–026
Uniform Customs and Practice for Documentary eUCP
copies of documents, 23–041
corruption of record, 23–044
definition of terms, 23–033
disclaimers, 23–045
electronic documents, 23–038, 23–039
electronic transmission, 23–031
format, 23–035
fraud, 23–046
inability to receive, 23–037
indorsement, 23–046
issuance date, 23–042
notice of refusal, 23–040
original documents, 23–041
presentation, 23–036
receipt date, 23–042
role, of, 23–032
transport details, 23–043
express terms, conflict with, 23–029, 23–030
failure to incorporate, 23–027
revisions, 23–010, 23–011, 23–012
right of recourse, 23–165
seller's draft, and, 23–189, 23–190
standby credits, and, 23–248—23–250
and see **Standby credits**
tender of documents, 23–196, 23–218—23–220
see also **Documentary credits (tender of documents)**
transfer, and, 23–071
UCP 500
assignment of proceeds, 23–025
bank, definition under, 23–014
bank's payment undertaking, 23–015
classification issues, 23–015
credit, availability of, 23–016
documents, dealing with, 23–019, 23–020
duties of banks, 23–017
effect, 23–026
insurance documents, 23–021
International Standard Banking Practice (ISBP), 23–048
invoices, 23–022
miscellaneous provisions, 23–023
negotiation, meaning of, 23–016
nominated bank, 23–016
rejection of documents, 23–018
revision, of, 23–047
transfer of credit, 23–024
transport documents, 23–020
UNCITRAL, and, 23–011
Uniform Law on International Sale of Goods (ULIS)
effect, of, 18–003

Uniform Rules for Collections
see also **Bills of exchange**
collection instruction, 22–081, 22–082
dishonour, 22–129
object, 22–076
parties, 22–080, 22–083
presentment
acceptance, 22–101
payment, 22–119
refusal to handle, 22–078
scope, 22–083, 22–084
structure, 22–077
terminology, 22–079
Uniform Rules for Demand Guarantees (1992)
see also **Performance bonds**
application, 23–297
autonomy principle, 23–297
basic object, 23–294
demands, 23–301, 23–302
documentary requirements, 23–294
expiry provisions, 23–303
extensions, 23–304
general provisions, 23–298
governing law, 23–305
incorporation, 23–297
jurisdiction, 23–305
liabilities, 23–300
reduction of amount, 23–299
responsibilities, 23–300
scope, 23–294
structure, 23–295
terminology, 23–296
UN Convention, and, 23–306

Valuation
failure, 2–051
third party, 2–049—2–051
Valuer
appointment, 2–050
referral, to, 2–052
Vienna Convention
avoiding the contract, 12–129
disadvantages, 18–004
effect, of, 18–004
non-delivery of goods, 12–129
performance of contract, 12–129
reduction of price, 12–129
remedies, under, 12–129
repair of goods, 12–129
scope, of, 18–004
significance, of, 12–129
Voidable title
absence of title, 7–023
agreement to sell, and, 7–022, 7–027
avoidance, 7–024—7–026
buyer
buyer's title, 7–021, 7–023, 7–027, 7–029
sale, to, 7–027

Voidable title—*cont.*
conditional sale, 7–022
see also **Conditional sale agreements**
good faith, requirement for, 7–021, 7–029, 7–030
hire-purchase agreements, 7–022
and see **Hire-purchase agreements**
mere possession, 7–022
notice, requirement for, 7–021, 7–029, 7–030
passing of property, 7–021, 7–022
and see **Passing of property**
pledge, and, 7–028
and see **Pledge**
rescission, and, 7–024
and see **Rescission**
sale or return, 7–022
and see **Sale or return**
sale, under, 7–021
seller, with, 7–021, 7–027
transfer of title, 7–022
see also **Transfer of title (non-owners)**
void title, distinguished, 7–023

Waiver
acceptance, and, 9–006, 19–150, 19–153
and see **Acceptance**
affirmation of contract, 19–150, 19–151
breach of term, 12–034—12–036
and see **Breach of term**
damages, right to, 19–150, 19–151
defective goods, 12–034
and see **Defective goods**
defective performance, 12–035
delivery, timing of, 8–030
and see **Delivery**
discharge of contract, 12–034—12–036
estoppel, and, 19–150, 19–151
and see **Estoppel**
lien, and, 15–036, 15–056
and see **Lien**
loss of rights, 19–150
non-conforming documents, 19–151
non-conforming goods, 19–150, 19–151
partial waiver, 19–152
payment
place, as to, 9–050
timing, as to, 9–055
and see **Payment**
performance, right to, 19–150
rejection of contract, 12–034, 12–037
reservation of rights, 19–151
retraction, of, 12–035
tort, in, 1–073, 1–074
"without prejudice", use of, 19–151
Warranties
collateral, as, 10–022

Warranties—*cont.*
collateral warranty, 10–012, 10–013
see also **Collateral contracts**
contractual liability, 10–015, 10–017, 10–019
damages, relating to, 10–023
and see **Damages**
defects, as to, 10–019
examples, 10–018
extended warranties, 14–042, 14–043
future events, 10–021
legal basis, 10–017
legal development, 10–015
less important term, as, 10–023
nature, of, 10–015—10–017
parties
conduct, 10–017
intention, 10–016, 10–017
statements, amounting to, 10–016
and see **Statements**

Warranties—*cont.*
timing, 10–020
Warrants
see also **Delivery orders**
definition, 18–170
delivery warrant
attornment, 18–174, 18–193
documents of title, 18–193
dock warrant, 18–198
warehouse warrant, 18–193, 18–198
Warsaw Convention
see also **Carriage by air**
provisions, of, 21–052, 21–055
Wrongful interference
see also **Goods**
conversion, 4–012
detention of goods, 4–012
passing of property, and, 5–010
and see **Passing of property**